Subject Collections

Subject Collections

A guide to special book collections
and subject emphases as reported by
university, college, public, and
special libraries and museums
in the United States and Canada

Sixth Edition
Revised and Enlarged

Compiled by
Lee Ash
Library Consultant, Bethany, Connecticut
and
William G. Miller
Watertown Public Library, Connecticut

With the collaboration of Barbara J. McQuitty

Volume 1
A – L

R.R. Bowker Company
New York & London, 1985

Published by R. R. Bowker Company
205 East Forty-second Street, New York, NY 10017

Printed and bound in the United States of America.
International Standard Book Numbers:
Set 0-8352-1917-8, Vol. 1 0-8352-1967-4, Vol. 2 0-8352-1968-2

To My Wife
Marian Neal Ash
of whom I am so proud
and continue to owe so much
– from the First to the
Sixth Edition and Beyond

and

To My Mother
Elsie Ann Eklund
for whose love, support,
and understanding I am
forever indebted.

– WGM

Preface

The Sixth Edition of *Subject Collections* has been a pleasure to compile because, after several problems were confronted and then solved, the computers really did their work. The problems were major ones, and one of my rewards has been the publisher's faith in the book that encouraged them to underwrite it at much greater cost than had been planned.

Once again we followed the same questionnaire system used for the Fifth Edition, although in a somewhat different format: printouts were sent to libraries covering all entries submitted for the Fifth Edition or described from my notes accumulated between editions. Libraries were asked to return the forms with revisions, deletions, and new additions. We believe that nearly (but not quite!) 100 percent of these changes have been noted, with some subject headings altered to conform to the Library of Congress or to our own authority lists; notes have been revised to correct ambiguities and the like. Some subject headings have been changed for clarity or modernization, and we have, I hope, cross-referenced all of the old forms to the new and added many more *see* references; as usual, we have not used *see also* references.

This Sixth Edition continues our practice of including from the previous edition all entries formerly sent by libraries that did not respond to the current questionnaire. These and entries I have made from my between-edition notes, without reconfirmation from the institution, are marked with a dagger (†).

We have not attempted to guess at the number of entries other than to recognize that there are certainly at least 6,500 new ones and that over the years, every week we have discovered new and unusual collections that enhance opportunities for reference or research in additional subject fields. One observation that seems interesting is the continuing increase in collections of materials by or about individual persons.

Many more libraries have reported to us, and some of the larger ones have literally hundreds of additional entries. As noted in the Fifth Edition, very few libraries eliminated entries, a few small libraries (mostly industrial or commercial) were dissolved, and a few – mainly small ones – asked not to be included. A number of collections were transferred to other libraries, which we noted when made aware of the transfer. Once again, in spite of repeated requests by mail or telephone, a few libraries, including some large ones, did not respond at all to our efforts or, for one reason or another, did not report fully.

The growing number of antiquarian booksellers who made use of *Subject Collections* is well known to us. It is for this reason (they quote materials for possible sale to libraries) that we continue to list smaller as well as large special collections. To repeat for emphasis – as from edition to edition – librarians should read the Preface to the Third Edition before criticizing the qualitative differences between collections. Similarly, to those who want an index to an expanded *American Library Directory,* the description of the genesis of *Subject Collections* recorded in the First Edition (1958) must suffice.

ACKNOWLEDGMENTS

My enjoyment in undertaking this compilation since 1958 is appreciated on two levels: first, as a professional contribution in which I take pride through the frequent use of the book in libraries around the world; second, and even more pleasurable, is the recognition of the friendly sacrifice of time and effort that literally thousands of librarians have put into the book. I have said this before and it continues as the greater reward.

I am especially proud to have had Bill Miller as my associate in editing the Sixth Edition. He has helped me on different editorial projects and with other work since he was thirteen. During his last year in high school, Bill took charge of all cross-references in the Fourth Edition and he did the same for the Fifth Edition in his last year of college. Then he went to library school at the University of North Carolina, and here he is now as a colleague of whom I am very proud! I look forward to many years of working with him on this and other projects.

This edition of *Subject Collections* could not have been made into a book without the careful and accurate attention of Barbara J. McQuitty and her staff at the Jaques Cattell Press in Tempe, Arizona. Our continual interfacing by mail and telephone and her expert solutions of difficult computer and editorial problems (compounded by my dreadful handwritten entries) are only partial recognition of what she had to face. My debt to her and her co-workers is immeasurable.

My "Sharon workshop" at our summer base has grown up. All of the teenaged boys who helped with other editions have gone away, except Bill Miller, but my indebtedness, acknowledged by name in previous editions, continues. My reliance upon them and their assistance in manipulating cards – sorting, alphabetizing, and other things, some done now by computer – were always an encouraging factor leading to another edition because I knew they would be there to help. They all remain close friends and the friendliest computer cannot replace them.

Louis A. Rachow of the Edwin Booth/Walter Hampden Memorial Library, The Players, New York City, continues to be a major contributor to references about new collections not reported directly to me or noted in the library press. Similarly, Philip Weimerskirch at The Burndy Library, Norwalk, Connecticut, has given me lists of libraries with new or unrecorded collections. Additional help has come from assistance by Michael Cahill (formerly of Sharon), Bruce Hescock, and Lee Brockett, who have taken special interest in their assignments over the past two years.

Gary Ink, at the Bowker Company, has been my special connection and supervised *Subject Collections* as a project for the publisher. He has been very easy to work with and to enjoy as a new friend. I am gratified by his support and interest in the book. Everyone at Bowker and at the Jaques Cattell Press has been remarkably patient with me and ever so helpful, for which I am humbly appreciative.

Most of all, the continuing devotion and advice of my wife, Marian Neal Ash, must be recognized. Her tolerance level for the mess of notes, cards, printouts, and correspondence that flows over from my study to the library, porch, and dining room have tested her, and she has always been patient. More than that, her work as a senior university press editor always helps me to solve problems. Dedication of all editions of *Subject Collections* to her is only a partial expression of appreciation and love.

Six editions of *Subject Collections* in twenty-six years is an encouraging record that prompts plans for the Seventh Edition. As I have written before, however, the compiler of any standard reference work has a responsibility to do the best for those who use the book. I hope that our errors are few and I apologize for them. I am anxious that we may know what to correct in the future. Therefore, I welcome any suggestions that could make the book a better one and more inclusive, so that future scholars, librarians, antiquarian booksellers, and others may know more about the collections that have been preserved for them.

Lee Ash

Bethany, Connecticut
September 1984

Introduction

INCLUSIVENESS

What we said in the Fifth Edition remains true for the Sixth: "Virtually all libraries included in this book are listed in the *American Library Directory;* however, not all libraries listed there are included in *Subject Collections,* either because the libraries did not return their questionnaires, or because their replies were unusable."

Once again *museums* were questionnaired, and returns for this edition were better in number and quality than the previous edition. We must continue to urge these institutions to report their holdings more explicitly, however, because they are often unique or extensive and should be a part of the corpus of research materials available to scholars or students. We hope to continue to improve our efforts among them. United States government libraries still report poorly, except for the careful coverage at the Library of Congress. It seems that we must again "emphasize that we have expended our best efforts to include all the material that has been submitted but have no legal responsibility for accidental omissions or errors in any listing."

EXCLUSIONS

Generally, in this edition, as in the previous ones, local history collections have not been listed. The public library and/or historical society in any town are usually prime sources for these materials, as well as for genealogical reference work; however, we have not been quite as exclusive of these collections as in the past. In future editions, as descriptive notes concerning these local history collections become more explicit, it is likely that more collections of this type will be listed.

I have not tried to complete listings of college and university departmental libraries when these were not reported; neither are listings of medical, nursing school, or law libraries complete. (These are available on Bowker mailing lists or in other directories.) For law, I have arbitrarily excluded the smaller county libraries, too. Unspecialized U.S. Department of Agriculture field libraries and teachers' college professional libraries also are not all listed.

OTHER SOURCES

There has been no effort to duplicate material in the *National Union Catalogue of Manuscript Collections* or in similar directories at the state or regional level, but it must be remembered that *Subject Collections* and *NUCMC* are complementary to one another. *Subject Collections* stands, similarly, in relation to other standard guides such as Downs' *American Library Sources: A Bibliographical Guide* and its supplements; the Special Libraries Association's *Directory of Special Libraries,* as well as local guides compiled from time to time by the Association's various state and regional chapters; Hamer's *Guide to Archives and Manuscripts in the United States* (still useful and greatly in need of its planned updating). Many new local and regional guides have been published since the previous edition of *Subject Collections.* All, though they vary in character, can be helpful to the researcher who is careful enough to search them out. New special collections are frequently described in library, book trade, and historical publications such as *College and Research Libraries News, AB Bookman's Weekly, Publishers Weekly, Library Journal,* and publications of "Friends" of libraries groups, the scholarly press, and the daily newspapers.

ARRANGEMENT

Subject headings are alphabetized and based, with some adaptation, on the most recent edition of the Library of Congress list and its supplements. Following each subject heading, entries are arranged alphabetically by state name abbreviated and designated in boldface type. The abbreviated state names, including the District of Columbia (D.C.), are listed first, followed by Puerto Rico and other U.S. territories, then Canada. Within each of these *geographical divisions,* the arrangement is alphabetical by *city,* then alphabetical by the *name of the library.*

Abbreviations and Symbols. Where reported, I have indicated that a collection is cataloged (Cat.), that manuscripts are included in the collection (Mss.), and that there are pictures (Pix). Other abbreviations used are self-evident. **Parentheses.** If parentheses enclose the number of volumes or budget dollars, this indicates that the enclosed figure represents the total for the library or collections, *not* the amount for the specific subject. **Parallel Lines** (//) following the number of volumes indicate that the collection is no longer being enlarged. Sometimes the double virgule appears alone, signifying that the number of volumes was not reported and that additions are not being made. **The Dagger** (†). The dagger symbol has been explained above, as it relates to the compiler's notes about unreported collections.

LOAN AND PHOTOGRAPHING FACILITIES

Most libraries permit interlibrary loans or have institutional or local facilities for photographic reproduction – photocopying or microform; therefore, I have not cited such facilities. Instead, I noted exceptions imposed by resource libraries which limit these commonly accepted privileges. Users of interlibrary loans should be aware of the new copyright restrictions which are in force everywhere.

Abbreviations

The names of the subject collections in the text are preceded by the two-letter abbreviations used by the U.S. Post Office for the various states. A list of such abbreviations follows for anyone who may be unfamiliar with them.

AMERICAN STATES AND TERRITORIES

AK Alaska
AL Alabama
AR Arkansas
AZ Arizona
CA California
CO Colorado
CT Connecticut
CZ Canal Zone
DC District of Columbia
DE Delaware
FL Florida
GA Georgia
HI Hawaii
IA Iowa
ID Idaho
IL Illinois
IN Indiana
KS Kansas
KY Kentucky
LA Louisiana
MA Massachusetts
MD Maryland
ME Maine
MI Michigan
MN Minnesota
MO Missouri
MS Mississippi
MT Montana
NC North Carolina
ND North Dakota
NE Nebraska
NH New Hampshire
NJ New Jersey
NM New Mexico
NV Nevada
NY New York
OH Ohio
OK Oklahoma
OR Oregon
PA Pennsylvania
PI Pacific Islands (Incl Guam, Western Samoa, Samoa, Mariana Islands, Wake Island)
PR Puerto Rico
RI Rhode Island
SC South Carolina
SD South Dakota
TN Tennessee
TX Texas
UT Utah
VA Virginia
VI Virgin Islands
VT Vermont
WA Washington
WI Wisconsin
WV West Virginia
WY Wyoming

CANADIAN PROVINCES

AB Alberta
BC British Columbia
MB Manitoba
NB New Brunswick
NF Newfoundland
NS Nova Scotia
NT Northwest Territories
ON Ontario
PE Prince Edward Island
PQ Quebec
SK Saskatchewan
YT Yukon Territory

Subject Collections

A

A.E.

GA —EMORY UNIVERSITY, Robert W Woodruff Library, Special Collections Dept, Atlanta, 30322. Linda M Matthews, Head Special Collections; Virginia J H Cain, Processing Archivist; Richard H F Lindemann, Reference Archivist
Holdings: Mss Cat
Notes: 10 linear feet mss. Papers of Sir William Henry Gregory, of his wife, Lady Augusta Gregory, and of their son, Robert Gregory. Incl are correspondence with John Masefield, George Russell (A E), and William Butler Yeats, as well as material about the Abbey Theatre and political conditions in Ireland and Ceylon.

IL —NORTHERN ILLINOIS UNIVERSITY, Founders Memorial Library, Rare Books and Special Collections Dept, De Kalb, 60115. William R DuBois, Dept Head
Holdings: Vols 30 // Cat Mss
Notes: The Alan Denson Collection. Emphasis on George Russell, "A.E." Includes Denson's correspondence with many mid-20th century literary figures. Mss indexed but not cataloged.

IN —INDIANA UNIVERSITY, Lilly Library, Seventh St, Bloomington, 47405. William R Cagle, Librn
Holdings: Vols 100 Cat Mss
Notes: Many of the vols are from the library of A E. Mss incl both his correspondence and writings and the papers of his biographer, Alan Denson.

KY —UNIVERSITY OF LOUISVILLE, Ekstrom Library, Rare Books & Special Collections, 2301 S Third St, Louisville, 40208. George T McWhorter, Cur; Delinda Stephens Buie, Asst Cur
Holdings: Vols 3000 Cat
Budget: $1000
Notes: The Richard M Kain Collection. Literary first editions of Joyce, Yeats, A E, Lady Gregory and others; cultural and political documents; mss; periodical runs; clippings and related materials. Catalog in progress.

PA —BUCKNELL UNIVERSITY, Ellen Clarke Bertrand Library, Lewisburg, 17837. Ann de Klerk, Librn
Holdings: Cat Mss
Notes: Includes books and letters.

BC —UNIVERSITY OF VICTORIA, McPherson Library, Victoria, V8W 3H5, Can.
Notes: Incl letters to W K Magee, Charles Weekes, Daniel N Dunlop; 3 pages, 1925, to Robert Graves.

ON —UNIVERSITY OF TORONTO, Thomas Fisher Rare Book Library, 120 Saint George St, Toronto, M5S 1A5, Can. Richard G Landon, Head
Holdings: Vols 5200 Cat
Notes: DeLury Collection named for original donor, Alfred DeLury, Dean of Arts, University of Toronto. Centered on works of W B Yeats and his circle. Especially good holdings of the Yeats family. A E, Lady Gregory, and J M Synge. Incl extensive holdings of many of the minor writers.

AAKJAER, JEPPE

MN —UNIVERSITY OF MINNESOTA, O Meredith Wilson Library, 309 19 Ave S, Minneapolis, 55455. Austin J McLean, Chief, Special Collections
Holdings: Vols 119 Cat Mss
Notes: First editions, original manuscripts and some correspondence.

ABANDONED CHILDREN see Child Welfare

ABBE, CLEVELAND

NY —CITY UNIVERSITY OF NEW YORK, City College, Morris R Cohen Library, North Academic Center, Convent Ave & 137th St, New York, 10031. Barbara J Dunlap, Archivist
Holdings: Cat Mss Pix
Notes: Incl personal papers.

ABBE, GEORGE WALDO, 1811-1879

MA —BOSTON UNIVERSITY, Mugar Memorial Library, Special Collections Dept, 771 Commonwealth Ave, Boston, 02215. Howard B Gotlieb, Dir
Holdings: Cat Mss

NY —CORNELL UNIVERSITY LIBRARIES, Collection of Regional History, Dept of Manuscripts and Univ Archives, Ithaca, 14853.
Notes: Family papers, 1840-83, of George and Charlotte Colgate Abbe; 37 items. Merchant.

ABBEY THEATRE

CA —CLAREMONT COLLEGES, Honnold Library, Ninth & Dartmouth, Claremont, 91711. Tania Rizzo, Special Collections Dept Head
Holdings: Vols (250) // Uncat Mss Doc Pix Scrapbooks
Notes: Papers of Elbert A Wickes, 1884-1975, theatrical and lecture tour manager. Among his clients were Winston Churchill, William Butler Yeats, Houdini, Lowell Thomas, Vilhjalmur Stefansson, and Roy Chapman Andrews. He managed three American tours for the Abbey Players during the 1930s, was partner and producer of Fritz Leiber Shakespeare plays, the Water Follies of 1937, and the Affiliated Lyceum and Chautauquas Association. The collection is rich in autograph and photographic materials. There are 750 items relative to the Abbey Players. Card file and inventory available. Restricted use.

GA —EMORY UNIVERSITY, Robert W Woodruff Library, Special Collections Dept, Atlanta, 30322. Linda M Matthews, Head Special Collections; Virginia J H Cain, Processing Archivist; Richard H F Lindemann, Reference Archivist
Holdings: Mss Cat
Notes: 10 linear feet mss. Papers of Sir William Henry Gregory, of his wife, Lady Augusta Gregory, and of their son, Robert Gregory. Incl are correspondence with John Masefield, George Russell (A E), and William Butler Yeats, as well as material about the Abbey Theatre and political conditions in Ireland and Ceylon.

IL —SOUTHERN ILLINOIS UNIVERSITY, CARBONDALE, Delyte W Morris Library, Special Collections Dept, Carbondale, 62901. David V Koch, Cur of Special Collections; Louisa Bowen, Cur of Manuscripts
Holdings: Vols 2200 Cat Mss Pix Audiotapes
Notes: The papers of Lennox Robinson, Irish playwright and producer, incl in addition to his own mss, letters from William Butler Yeats, Lady Augusta Gregory, George Bernard Shaw, Sean O'Casey, Sara Allgood, and others associated with the Abbey Theatre. The Irish collection also has extensive correspondence between philosopher-author, Arland Ussher, and Yeats' biographer Joseph Hone, covering some 30 years, and correspondence relating to the affairs of the Abbey from the files of Abbey Director, Gabriel Fallon. Tape recordings of Eoin O'Mahony give background and identify figures in the Irish Renaissance. (*The Irish Collection, Rare Book Room, Morris Library, Southern Illinois University at Carbondale*, 1970; Donald Peake, *The Big House Themes in Plays of Lennox Robinson*, 1972.)

BC —UNIVERSITY OF VICTORIA, McPherson Library, Victoria, V8W 3H5, Can.
Notes: (Frank O'Connor) Incl Michael O'Donnovan, author, librn, director of Abbey Theatre, Dublin. Mss, "Scholar and artist," "The beauty," "Fish for Friday," "The others," "The weeping children," "Modern Irish literature," "The lament for Art O'Leary," and "Oration at W B Yeats' graveside by Frank O'Connor."

ABBOT, CHARLES GREELEY

IA —HERBERT HOOVER PRESIDENTIAL LIBRARY, West Branch, 52358. Dale C Mayer, Archivist
Notes: Papers.

ABBOTT, BERENICE

NY —MUSEUM OF THE CITY OF NEW YORK, Photo Archives, Fifth Ave & 103 St, New York, 10029. Esther Brumberg, Librn
Holdings: Mss Maps Pix
Notes: All aspects of New York City--history, costume, social life and customs, etc. Also, Byron Collection--about 10,000 prints, 1880-1930, of views of New York, commercial interiors, interiors and exteriors of private residences, social events, shipping, immigration; Wurts Collection--15,000 glass negatives, 1890-1940, mostly architectural; 100,000 Wurts Architectural Photographs, to be cataloged. Underhill Collection--about 900 glass negatives, mostly architectural, 1896-1936; McKim, Mead & White Collection--1000 glass negatives of the work of the firm, 1880-1915; and Berenice Abbott Collection, Changing New York--about 350 negatives taken by Miss Abbott for the Federal Arts Project, 1930s. Other FAP photographs incl a series on Coney Island, one on Harlem, Sewing Project, and Sabbath Studies.

ABBOTT, JACOB, 1803-1879

DC —LIBRARY OF CONGRESS, Children's Literature Center, Washington, 20540.

ABBOTT, JACOB, 1803-1879 (cont.)

Sybille Jagusch, Chief
Notes: Extensive holdings of works by Jacob Abbott, Oliver Optic (Adams, William T), Alden (Pansy), Samuel G Goodrich (Peter Parley), many in Rare Book and Special Collections Division.

ME —BOWDOIN COLLEGE, Library, Brunswick, 04011. Dianne M Gutscher, Cur of Special Collections
Holdings: Vols Mss
Notes: The Abbott Memorial Collection contains almost every first edition, as well as later ones, of Jacob Abbott's Rollo series and many other children's stories.

ME —PORTLAND PUBLIC LIBRARY, 5 Monument Sq, Portland, 04101. Edward V Chenevert, Library Dir
Holdings: Vols 159 // Cat Pix
Notes: This collection contains mostly fiction and some history written by a Congregational clergyman, educator and Maine author of children's books. Of the 28 titles in the Rollo series, Portland Public Library has 22.

OH —OHIO UNIVERSITY, Vernon R Alden Library, Department of Archives and Special Collections, Athens, 45701. Gary A Hunt, Head
Holdings: Vols (1400) Uncat
Notes: A miscellaneous collection of children's books by American and English authors, with most imprint dates in the period 1870-1930; numerous series books. Authors incl Jacob Abbott (196 v), "Oliver Optic" (84 v), Horatio Alger (89 v), J H Ewing (53 v), Martha Finley (47 v), G A Henty (46 v), Frank V Webster (38 v), and many others.

ABBOTT, LYMAN

DC —LIBRARY OF CONGRESS, Rare Book & Special Collections Div, Washington, 20540. William Matheson, Chief
Notes: The Juvenile Collection covers the early 18th century to the present and is particularly strong in fiction. Authors extensively represented are: Alcott, Alger, Abbott, Goodrich, Fosdick, Lothrop and McGuffey.

ABBOTT FAMILY

ME —BOWDOIN COLLEGE, Library, Brunswick, 04011. Dianne M Gutscher, Cur of Special Collections
Holdings: Vols Mss Pix
Notes: The Abbott Memorial Collection contains both printed and manuscript materials relating to Jacob Abbott, John S C Abbott, Edward Abbott and Lyman Abbott, as well as other members of the family. It consists of approximately 25,000 items, including correspondence, sermons, diaries and journals, addresses, the archives of both the *Literary World* and *Outlook* magazines, and the Lyman Abbott autograph collection. First and subsequent editions of almost all of the family's published writings are also present.

ABDULLAH, ACHMED

VA —UNIVERSITY OF VIRGINIA, Alderman Library, Manuscripts Dept, Charlottesville, 22901. Edmund Berkeley Jr, Cur
Holdings: Cat Mss
Notes: First editions, mss, papers, etc.

ABDURAHMAN, ABDULLAH

IL —NORTHWESTERN UNIVERSITY, Melville J Herskovits Library of African Studies, Evanston, 60201. Hans E Panofsky, Cur
Holdings: Vols (85,000) Mss
Budget: ($70,000)
Notes: Papers, etc. Mostly southern Africa. *See also* entry under Africa

ABE MARTIN

IN —INDIANA UNIVERSITY, Lilly Library, Seventh St, Bloomington, 47405. William R Cagle, Librn
Notes: First and early editions, many signed. Mss incl pen and ink drawings and scrapbooks of Abe Martin cartoons, photographs, and correspondence. 112 items.

IN —BUTLER UNIVERSITY, Irwin Library, Hugh Thomas Miller Rare Book Room, 4600 Sunset Ave, Indianapolis, 46208. Gisela Terrell, Rare Books Librn
Holdings: Cat Mss Pix
Notes: *Gaar Williams/Kin Hubbard* Collection. This collection was presented to the library by Blanche Stillson in 1964. It contains original cartoons and other drawings, books (many of them inscribed), magazines, letters and other manuscripts, photographs, and memorabilia by both Hoosier cartoonists and humorists. A catalogue of the Gaar Williams ("Abe Martin") items was printed in 1981. It is available upon request.

ABEL, ELIE

MA —BOSTON UNIVERSITY, Mugar Memorial Library, Special Collections Dept, 771 Commonwealth Ave, Boston, 02215. Howard B Gotlieb, Dir
Holdings: Cat Mss
Notes: Mss, correspondence, etc collected in depth; incl publications by or about.

ABEL, WALTER

NY —NEW YORK PUBLIC LIBRARY, Performing Arts Research Center, Billy Rose Theatre Collection, 111 Amsterdam Ave, New York, 10023. Dorothy L Swerdlove, Cur
Holdings: Cat Mss Pix
Notes: Papers, scrapbooks, mss, photographs, memorabilia, etc.

ABERCROMBIE, LASCELLES

MA —AMHERST COLLEGE, Library, Amherst, 01002. John Lancaster, Special Collections Librn
Holdings: Vols (500) Uncat Mss
Notes: Concentration on the Georgian poets Lascelles Abercrombie, Edmund Blunden, W H Davies, John Drinkwater, Wilfrid Gibson, Harold Monro, Edward Thomas.

NY —HOFSTRA UNIVERSITY, Library, 1000 Fulton Ave, Hempstead, 11550. Charles R Andrews, Dean of Library Services

ABERNETHY, BYRON R.

TX —NORTH TEXAS STATE UNIVERSITY, Archives, NT Station Box 5188, Denton, 76203. Robert LaForte, University Archivist
Notes: 24 linear feet. Papers of arbitrators Byron R Abernethy, J D Dunn, and Elvis Stephens. These arbitration papers cover the years 1960-1980 and emphasize cases in the southwestern United States and Puerto Rico. Published Description: J D Dunn and Elvis Stephens Collections, *The National Union Catalog of Manuscript Collections: Catalog* 1979 Washington: Library of Congress, 1980.

ABERRATION, CHROMATIC AND SPHERICAL see Optical Instruments

ABILITY—TESTING

OH —UNIVERSITY OF AKRON, Archives of the History of American Psychology, Akron, 44325. John A Popplestone, Dir
Holdings: Cat Mss Pix Slides Films
Notes: Nearly 1200 ft of psychologists' personal papers and documents, as well as organizational records, and over 600 items of historic laboratory apparatus. Also, photographs, films, intelligence and aptitude tests, etc from the 19th century to date.

ABIOGENESIS see Life—Origin

ABNORMAL CHILDREN see Exceptional Children; Handicapped Children

ABNORMALITIES see Deformities; Monsters

ABOLITIONISTS

CA —LOS ANGELES PUBLIC LIBRARY, Social Sciences Dept, 630 W Fifth St, Los Angeles, 90071. Marilyn C Wherley, Principal Librn
Holdings: Vols 5000 Cat Microforms
Budget: ($150,000)
Notes: Black Studies Collection. Pamphlets, bibliographies, indexes, periodicals, with some historical runs on microfilm, strong collection on slavery and anti-slavery, abolition, civil rights movements, with emphasis on the black experience in the United States. No separate catalog.

CA —UNIVERSITY OF CALIFORNIA, SANTA BARBARA, Library, Dept of Special Collections, Santa Barbara, 93106. Christian F Brun, Head
Holdings: Vols 24,500 Cat Mss Maps Pix Microforms
Budget: $7000
Notes: The William Wyles Collection of Americana. Incl American Civil War, Abraham Lincoln, Westward Movement, Americans for the Orient, slavery, abolition movement etc.

DC —HOWARD UNIVERSITY, Moorland-Spingarn Research Center, 500 Howard Place NW, Washington, 20059. Clifford L Muse, Jr, Acting Dir

DC —LIBRARY OF CONGRESS, Rare Book & Special Collections Div, Washington, 20540. William Matheson, Chief
Notes: Daniel Murray Pamphlet Collection on Afro-American history, 1850-1920, pertains chiefly to slavery and the abolitionist movement.

DC —LIBRARY OF CONGRESS, Manuscript Division, Washington, 20540. John C Broderick, Chief
Holdings: Cat Mss
Notes: More than 5000 Frederick Douglass items, principally letters addressed to him; mss by Douglass, etc. Transferred from the National Park Service collections.

IL —NEWBERRY LIBRARY, 60 W Walton St, Chicago, 60610. Diana Haskell, Cur of Modern Mss
Holdings: Cat
Notes: Very strong collection.

IL —WHEATON COLLEGE, Buswell Memorial Library, Wheaton, 60187. Paul Snezek, Library Dir
Holdings: Mss Pix
Notes: Blanchard's papers, correspondence, books and photographs. Also a complete set of the periodical Christian Cynosure. *Related Topics:* Anti-slavery, Abolitionists, Secret Societies, Wheaton College.

IN —WILLARD LIBRARY, 21 First Ave, Evansville, 47710. Joan Elliott, Special Collections Librn
Holdings: Vols (500) Cat Mss
Budget: ($4000)
Notes: Incl books and pamphlets (slave narratives, works by and about abolitionists, accounts of underground railroad activity), some abolitionist newspapers. Incl some reprints, but mostly original 19th century imprints.

KS —WICHITA STATE UNIVERSITY, Ablah Library, Box 68, Wichita, 67208. Michael T Kelly, Cur of Special Collections
Notes: The Eunice McIntosh Merrill Memorial Collection of letters and papers of the abolitionist William Lloyd Garrison.

KY —BEREA COLLEGE, Hutchins Library, Berea, 40404. Gerald F Roberts, Librn Special Collections
Holdings: Vols 500 Cat Mss Maps Pix Microforms Phonorecords
Notes: Private papers and library of John G Fee, abolitionist and founder of Berea College. Incl papers of other 19th-century abolitionists and liberals as pertain to Berea College or interests of John Fee.

MD —UNIVERSITY OF MARYLAND, Library, Rare Book Collection, College Park, 20742. Donald Farren, Assoc Dir for Special Collections
Holdings: Vols (10,000) Cat
Notes: Ranging from incunabula to modern first editions, the Rare Book Collection is particularly strong in materials relating to the history of France and in *exempla* of interest to students of bibliography. Related collections include sizable groups of books and other items relating to the Savoy, to *Expressionismus,* and to Pompeii. Pamphlet

ABOLITIONISTS (cont.)

collections include many Mazarinades, many pamphlets relating to slavery and abolition, numerous French plays, and press books.

MA —UNIVERSITY OF MASSACHUSETTS AT AMHERST, Library, Amherst, 01003. Siegfried Feller, Assoc Dir for Collection Development
Holdings: Cat
Notes: Incl 375 pamphlets, mainly abolitionist and oriented to the US publications of antislavery societies, etc, 1725-1911. Indexed calendar.

MA —BOSTON PUBLIC LIBRARY, Rare Books and Manuscripts, Copley Square, Boston, 02117. Laura V Monti, Keeper of Rare Books
Notes: Significant material, in volume, is devoted to economic and political relationships between New England and the Maritime Provinces in the 18th Century; much on Abolitionists and the antisalvery movement. Described in *Canadian Manuscripts in the Boston Public Library* (Boston: G K Hall), 1 vol. Incl about 17,000 items.

MA —PEABODY INSTITUTE LIBRARY, Danvers Archival Center, 15 Sylvan St, Danvers, 01923. Richard B Trask, Archivist, Rare Books & Special Collections
Holdings: Vols 200 Cat
Notes: The Parker Pillsbury Collection is made up primarily of 19th century antislavery tracts and books owned by abolitionist Parker Pillsbury, 1809-1898.
See also entry Slavery and Antislavery

NY —NEW YORK HISTORICAL SOCIETY, Library, 170 Central Park W, New York, 10024. James Gregory, Librn
Holdings: Mss
Notes: Incl original mss, illustrative materials, etc.

NY —NEW YORK PUBLIC LIBRARY, Research Libraries, General Research Division, Fifth Ave & 42 St, New York, 10018. Rodney Phillips, Chief
Holdings: Vols (2,225,000) Cat Maps Pix Microforms
Budget: ($775,718)
Notes: Also microforms; strong collection incl files of early abolitionist periodicals.

NY —UNIVERSITY OF ROCHESTER, Rush Rhees Library, Department of Rare Books and Special Collections, Rochester, 14627. Peter Dzwonkoski, Librn
Holdings: Mss Cat
Notes: Autograph letters of Frederick Douglass, William C Nell, Gerritt Smith, and other mss incl in the Isaac and Amy Post family papers, and the William Henry Seward Papers.

NY —SYRACUSE UNIVERSITY LIBRARIES, Ernest S Bird Library, George Arents Research Library for Special Collections, Syracuse, 13210. Carolyn A Davis, Manuscripts Librn; Amy S Doherty, University Archivist; Mark F Weimer, Rare Book Librn
Notes: Mss of abolitionist editor Theodore Tilton; 4 letters.

OH —HUDSON LIBRARY & HISTORICAL SOCIETY, Library, 22 Aurora St, Hudson, 44236. Thomas L Vince, Dir
Holdings: Vols 78 Cat Mss Maps Pix Slides
Notes: The John Brown Collection was acquired mainly from the collection of Dr Clarence S Gee of Lockport, New York, formerly of Hudson, who began collecting John Brown material in 1924, when he learned that Brown (a one-time resident of Hudson) had been baptized in his church in 1816. Incl four original John Brown letters, 12 boxes of mss, the standard genealogy of the Brown family as drawn up by Dr Gee and much collateral family correspondence and documents. No catalog as yet. Inquiries, students, scholars are welcome.

OH —KENT STATE UNIVERSITY, University Archives, Kent, 44242. Stephen C Morton, University Archivist
Holdings: Uncat Mss
Notes: One cubic foot of manuscripts and printed materials of Betsy Mix Cowles, abolitionist, educator and women's rights advocate. Ms Cowles chaired the Women's Rights Convention at Salem, Ohio in 1850. The collection contains correspondence dating from 1832, diaries, financial records, anti-slavery tracts, addresses, poems, pamphlets, and materials about Ms Cowles.

OH —WILMINGTON COLLEGE, Watson Library, Quaker Collection, Pyle Center, Box #1227, Wilmington, 45177. Audrey Haines, Cur
Holdings: Vols (6000) Cat Mss Maps Pix Microforms
Notes: Collection houses Wilmington College archives, 1870-present, and serves as repository for the records of the Wilmington and Ohio Valley Yearly Meetings of the Religious Society of Friends (Quakers), ca 1800-present. Also incl 120 Quaker periodical and newsletter titles, ca 1828-present; several hundred pamphlets, tracts, and epistles; 220 genealogical works, primarily Quaker families; and 3900 vols on Quaker history, philosophy, thought, and practice, particularly peace, war, slavery, education, and biography, ca 1750-present. Incl some fiction, poetry and children's books. Rare or fragile materials, reference works, pamphlets, and genealogies do not circulate. Please notify prior to visiting.

PA —HISTORICAL SOCIETY OF PENNSYLVANIA, Library, 1300 Locust St, Philadelphia, 19107. David Fraser, Librn
Holdings: Vols (230,000) Mss Maps Pix Microforms
Notes: Incl over 14,000,000 ms pieces. The Library Company of Philadelphia mss are on deposit with the Historical Society of Pennsylvania. Many of the Society's rare books are on deposit with the Library Company. The Society maintains the collections of the Genealogical Society of Pennsylvania, incl some 20,000 printed genealogies, original mss, family, church, and civil records.

PA —LIBRARY COMPANY OF PHILADELPHIA, 1314 Locust St, Philadelphia, 19107. Edwin Wolf II, Librn; Kenneth Finkel, Cur of Prints
Holdings: Vols (400,000) Cat Mss Maps Pix
Budget: ($25,000)
Notes: With the collection of The Historical Society of Pennsylvania, one of the richest collections of mss, books and other materials on the slave trade, the abolition movement and other chapters of Blacks in the New World. Incl printed material on the history of Blacks in the US, the West Indies, and Africa, to 1906.

PA —FRIENDS HISTORICAL LIBRARY OF SWARTHMORE COLLEGE, Swarthmore, 19081. J William Frost, Dir
Holdings: Vols (35,000) Cat Mss Pix Microforms
Notes: Library's collections contain information on the history and doctrine of the Society of Friends, Quaker contributions to literature, science, business, education, and government, plus their reform efforts in peace, Indian rights, women's rights, and abolition of slavery. Among the more than 250 mss collections are papers of several Quaker abolitionists, incl Lucretia Mott and John Greenleaf Whittier. Library also has several antislavery newspapers.

RI —BROWN UNIVERSITY, John Hay Library, 20 Prospect St, Providence, 02912. Mark N Brown, Cur Mss
Holdings: / / Mss
Notes: Samuel Sullivan Cox, lawyer, diplomat, and Congressman from Ohio and New York. About 1200 letters to Cox dealing chiefly with his role in politics. They cover the period 1852 to 1887 but are concentrated during 1861-1863 and 1883-1886. Correspondents incl his constituents, journalists, members of the Democratic Party. There are references to Salmon P Chase, General Hugh McClellan, C L Vallandigham, national elections, and abolitionists.

RI —BROWN UNIVERSITY, John Carter Brown Library, Providence, 02912. Norman Fiering, Librn; Everett C Wilkie Jr, Bibliographer; Susan Danforth, Cur Maps & Prints
Notes: Works documenting slavery and slave trade in European possessions in the New World until 1833. Particular strengths are British and French abolition movements in the early nineteenth century. (Little material on slavery in what became the United States).

RI —PROVIDENCE PUBLIC LIBRARY, 150 Empire St, Providence, 02903. Lance J Bauer, Special Collections Librn
Holdings: Vols 5000 Cat Mss Maps Pix
Notes: The Harris Collection on the American Civil War and Slavery. Incl 18th and 19th century books, rare pamphlets, and periodicals concerning slavery and the slave trade, and origins, progress and results of the Civil Civil War; also regimental histories; military and naval tactics; personal narratives; women's accounts of the Civil War; works on abolition; sheet music; Union and Confederate broadside ballads; Confederate imprints; *The Liberator* from 1843 through the Civil War; and over 85 editions of *Uncle Tom's Cabin* in 14 languages. Excellent primary and secondary sources for the study of the Civil War and slavery. Material must be used in-house. Photocopying when condition of material allows.

TX —UNIVERSITY OF TEXAS LIBRARIES, General Libraries, PO Box P, Austin, 78713. Carolyn Bucknell, Asst Dir for Collection Development
Holdings: Vols Cat Microforms
Notes: The Littlefield Collection of research materials, incl many rare items, on the history of the Old South.

ON —CHATHAM PUBLIC LIBRARY, 120 Queen St, Chatham, N7M 2G6, Can. Arlene Mason, Head of Reference
Holdings: Vols 20 Cat
Notes: Books, pamphlets, and articles on Henry Bibb, William King, Martin Delaney, and John Brown and their work in the Chatham, Ont region.

ABORIGINES see Ethnology

ABORTION

CA —LOS ANGELES PUBLIC LIBRARY, Social Sciences Dept, 630 W Fifth St, Los Angeles, 90071. Marilyn C Wherley, Principal Librn
Holdings: Vols 3000 Cat
Budget: ($150,000)
Notes: Books, clippings, pamphlets, periodicals, government publications, bibliogrpahies, popular and scholarly works on homosexuality, husband-wife relations, abortion, rape, and sex education.

DC —CENTER FOR BIOETHICS, Library, Kennedy Institute, Georgetown University, 3520 Prospect St NW, Washington, 20057. Doris Goldstein, Dir; Judith Mistichelli, Senior Librn
Holdings: Vols 8200
Notes: Largest library of its kind. Incl 31, 000 journal articles. Collects in the following subject areas: applied ethics; medical ethics; philosophy of medicine; science, technology and society; sociology of medicine; patient-physician care; sexuality; contraception; abortion; population policy; reproductive technologies; in vitro fertilization; genetic counseling and screening; genetic engineering; mental organ transplantation; death and dying; "baby doe" issues; euthanasia; suicide; use of chemical and biological weapons. Produces computer database *Bioethicsline,* available through MEDLARS; and the printed annual *Bibliography of Bioethics.* Other library publications are: *New Titles in Bioethics* (monthly); *Scope Notes* series on current topics.

MA —RADCLIFFE COLLEGE, Arthur & Elizabeth Schlesinger Library on the History of Women in America, 3 James St, Cambridge, 02138. Patricia Miller King, Dir; Eva Moseley, Cur of Mss
Holdings: Uncat Mss Pix Phonorecords Audiotapes Videotapes
Notes: Books, pamphlets, newsletters, clippings; also oral history interviews in the Family Planning Oral History Project, and information in several manuscript

ABORTION (cont.)

collections, especially in the records of the Society for Humane Abortion/Association to Repeal Abortion Laws and the National Abortion Rights Action League (restricted). Also newsletters and some papers of anti-abortion movement.

NY —PLANNED PARENTHOOD FEDERATION OF AMERICA, Katharine Dexter McCormick Library, 810 Seventh Ave, New York, 10019. Gloria A Roberts, Head Librn
Holdings: Vols (4000) Cat
Notes: Birth control, teenagers, contraception and contraceptive research, family planning, religion and birth control.

NC —CAROLINA POPULATION CENTER, Library, University Sq E, Chapel Hill, 27514. Patricia Shipman, Head Librn
Notes: Collection of reprints, photocopied articles, reports, unpublished papers on abortion, maintained as a separate file because of the great demand for materials on this subject.

ABRAHAM LINCOLN BRIGADE

MA —BRANDEIS UNIVERSITY, Goldfarb Library, 415 South St, Waltham, 02154. Bessie Hahn, Dir
Holdings: Vols 6500 Cat Mss Pix Slides 16mm Films
Notes: Spanish Civil War Collection. Comprising 7000 books and pamphlets in all languages relating to the armed conflict in Spain from 1936-1939. This is a multi-media collection consisting of not only books and pamphlets, but photographs, documentary film footage, newspapers, propaganda leaflets, wall posters, taped interviews, personal memoirs, memorabilia, recordings and some original art work. The collection also includes the archives of American volunteers who served with the Republican forces. There is an author-title card catalog in the Special Collections Card Catalog for the books and pamphlets. There are some finding lists for the other material such as newspapers and periodicals, photographs and wall posters. Some material is restricted from use.

ABRAHAMSEN, DAVID

†NY —COLUMBIA UNIVERSITY LIBRARIES, Butler Library, Rare Book and Manuscript Library, 535 W 114 St, New York, 10027.
Notes: The Papers of Dr David Abrahamsen, incl letters and mss. Contains letters from and interviews with family and friends of Richard M Nixon and 167 typed and handwritten letters sent by David Berkowitz to Dr Abrahamsen from Attica Prison during 1979-81.

ABRAMOV, GEN. FEDOR F.

CA —HOOVER INSTITUTION ON WAR, REVOLUTION & PEACE, Stanford University, Stanford, 94305. Milorad M Drachkovitch, Archivist
Holdings: / / Mss
Notes: Correspondence of White Russian military leaders with Bulgarian administrative officials concerning Russian military contingents in Bulgaria; together with correspondence and files of the military coroner at the general headquarters of the White Russian mission. 6 ft.

ABRAMOVITZ, MAX

NY —SYRACUSE UNIVERSITY LIBRARIES, Ernest S Bird Library, George Arents Research Library for Special Collections, Syracuse, 13210. Carolyn A Davis, Manuscripts Librn; Amy S Doherty, University Archivist; Mark F Weimer, Rare Book Librn
Notes: The George Arents Research Library for Special Collections at Syracuse University contains the papers of Harley James McKee, Lorimer Rich, Frederick Lear, Max Abramovitz, James I Arnold, Pietro Bulluschi, Claude Bragdon, Marcel Breuer, William Lescaze, Skidmore Owings & Merrill, Ralph Walker, Eric Fisher Wood, Minoru Yamasaki, Joseph Louis Young, and Archimedes Russell.

ABRASIVES

MA —NORTON COMPANY, Library, 1 New Bond St, Worcester, 01606. Joan K Chaffey, Librn
Holdings: Cat
Notes: Abrasive industry collection.

ABSAHROKEE INDIANS see Crow Indians

ABSAROKA INDIANS see Crow Indians

ABSENT TREATMENT see Mental Healing

ABSORPTION, ATMOSPHERIC see Solar Radiation

ABSTINENCE see Temperance

ABYSSINIA see Ethiopia

ABYSSINIAN EXPEDITION, 1867-1868

CA —UNIVERSITY OF CALIFORNIA, LOS ANGELES, Research Library, Dept of Special Collections, 405 Hilgard Ave, Los Angeles, 90024. Edward Shreeves, Chairman, Bibliographers Group; David S Zeidberg, Head
Holdings: Pix
Notes: 73 photographs of the British Expeditionary Force under General Sir Robert Napier.

ABYSSINIAN MANUSCRIPTS see Manuscripts, Ethiopic

ACADEMY PUBLICATIONS see Society and Academy Publications

ACADIA AND ACADIANS

LA —UNIVERSITY OF SOUTHERN LOUISIANA, Dupre Library, Jefferson Caffery Louisiana Room, 302 East St Mary Blvd, Lafayette, 70504. Cynthia J Rice, Louisiana Room Ref Librn

LA —SAINT MARTIN PARISH LIBRARY, 105 S New Market St, PO Box 79, Saint Martinville, 70582. Dorothy R Selby, Dir
Holdings: Cat Maps Pix Slides Microforms
Notes: Emphasis on south Louisiana. Incl Louisiana history and genealogy. Some Acadian-Canadian history and genealogy.

NH —ASSOCIATION CANADO-AMERICAIN (FRATERNAL LIFE INSURANCE SOCIETY), Institute Canado-Americain, 52 Concord St, Manchester, 03101. Robert A Beaudoin, Librn
Holdings: Vols (40,000) Cat Mss Maps Pix Slides Phonorecords Audiotapes Microforms
Budget: ($2000)
Notes: Contains books, pamphlets, mss, university dissertations, newspapers, manuscripts, periodicals, and archives of various other societies (active of defunct). Subjects covered incl art, music, literature, folklore, religion, politics, sociology, history, etc of the French in France, Canada, and US (especially New England's Franco-Americans, Louisiana's Cajuns, and Quebec's French-Canadians). There is also an extensive collection of genealogical works dealing with Quebec Acadia, and New England Francophones. Articles dealing with the library are: "The Library of the Association Canado-Americaine" by Edward B Ham in *Modern Language Notes*, vol LII, no 7, November 1937 and a bilingual article "Appel d'un jeune aux jeunes en faveur de al Bibliotheque ACA" by Robert B Perreault in *Le Canado-Americain*, nouvelle serie, vol 1, no 5, julliet-aout-septembre 1975, pp 18-19.

NB —MOUNT ALLISON UNIVERSITY, Ralph Pickard Bell Library, Sackville, E0A 3C0, Can. M Fancy, Librn
Holdings: Vols 6600 Cat Maps Microforms Slides VF
Notes: The Winthrop P Bell Collection on Acadian history concentrates on foreign Protestant settlements in, and history of, the area once known as Acadia. Also contains material on the French Acadians.

NS —UNIVERSITE SAINTE-ANNE, Library Louis R Comeau, PO Box 40, Church Point, B0W 1M0, Can. Neil Boucher, Director
Holdings: Vols (600) Cat Mss Maps Pix Slides 16mm Films
Notes: Material by and about Acadians. Incl 800 pictures, 3500 slides and over 300 films.

ACADIAN AUTHORS see Authors, Acadian

ACAROLOGY

HI —BERNICE P BISHOP MUSEUM, Library, PO Box 19000-A, Honolulu, 96819. Cynthia Timberlake, Librn
Holdings: Vols (90,000) Cat Mss Maps Pix Slides Microforms
Budget: ($30,000)
Notes: Only American library devoted exclusively to the Pacific region. Collection reflects historical and contemporary research emphases of Bishop Museum; ie the natural and cultural history of the Pacific. Areas of concentration incl archaeology, ethnology, linguistics, voyages and explorations, history, vertebrate and invertebrate zoology, botany and museology. Strong special collections incl photographs, mss and archives, maps and art. Publications: Quarterly "Additions to the Catalog," *Dictionary Catalog of the* Library (9 vols and 2 suppl; Boston: G K Hall, 1964-69).

ACCELERATORS, ELECTRON see Particle Accelerators

ACCELERATORS, LINEAR see Linear Accelerators

ACCENT (MAGAZINE)

IL —UNIVERSITY OF ILLINOIS, URBANA/CHAMPAIGN, Library, University Archives, 19 Library, 1408 W Gregory Drive, Urbana, 61801. Maynard Brichford, University Archivist
Holdings: Cat Mss Maps Pix Slides Microforms
Notes: Papers, archival records, etc.

ACCESSORIES (DRESS) see Dress Accessories

ACCIDENT INSURANCE see Insurance, Accident

ACCIDENT INVESTIGATION

MI —UNIVERSITY OF MICHIGAN, Transportation Research Institute, Library, 2901 Baxter Rd, Ann Arbor, 48109. Ann C Grimm, Librn
Holdings: Vols (57,000) Cat Mss Maps
Budget: ($25,000)
Notes: Special emphasis on accident investigation and data analysis, vehicle dynamics, biomechanical aspects of trauma, vision and visibility, alcohol and driving.

ACCIDENT PREVENTION see Accidents—Prevention

ACCIDENTS—PREVENTION

IL —NATIONAL SAFETY COUNCIL, Library, 444 N Michigan Ave, Chicago, 60611. Ruth K Hammersmith, Mgr, Library
Holdings: Cat Microforms
Budget: ($22,000)
Notes: NSC Library has a comprehensive collection of accident prevention, occupational and industrial safety and health material. The Safety Research Information Section (SRIS) begun in 1968 has a collection of over 12,000 indexed and

ACCIDENTS—PREVENTION (cont.)

cataloged research documents. The Library also has a collection of over 5000 safety-related books, 12,000 Research Reports, 60, 000 general information items, a collection of historically valuable safety-related information. The Library data is part of an inhouse computer system.

MI —UNIVERSITY OF MICHIGAN, Transportation Research Information Institute, Public Information Materials Center, 2901 Baxter Rd, Ann Arbor, 48109. Ann Grimm, Librn
Holdings: Vols (5000) Cat Print Materials Slides Phonorecords Audiotapes 16mm Films
Budget: ($200)
Notes: Collection of materials (mostly available free from originators) produced for public information campaigns on alcohol and highway safety, and adult and child restraint systems. Book catalogs to collection available (mailing list): *Alcohol/Safety Public Information Materials Catalog*, no 7. A C Grimm (UMTRI, June 1983); and *Restraint System Public Information Materials Catalog*, no 5, A C Grimm (UMTRI, June 1983).

ACCIDENTS—PREVENTION—STUDY AND TEACHING see Safety Education

ACCIDENTS, MARINE see Marine Accidents

ACCIDENTS, TRAFFIC see Traffic Accidents

ACCOUNTING

AL —UNIVERSITY OF ALABAMA, Business Library, Box 2937, University, 35486. Dorothy Eady Brown, Librn; Linda Suttle Harris, Ref Librn and Data Base Searcher
Holdings: Vols (105,000) Cat Microforms
Budget: ($60,000)
Notes: Incl 90,000 corporation reports and 38,500 microforms.

CA —COOPERS & LYBRAND, Library, 1000 W Sixth St, Los Angeles, 90017. Joan Schlimgen, Librn; Paula Edwalds, Technical Library Asst
Holdings: Vols 1500 Cat
Notes: Incl 200 periodicals.

CA —UNIVERSITY OF CALIFORNIA, LOS ANGELES, Graduate School of Management Library, UCLA Campus, Los Angeles, 90024. Robert Bellanti, Head Librn
Holdings: Vols (128,000) Cat Mss Microforms
Notes: The UCLA Graduate School of Management Library serves the instructional and research needs of students and faculty in the Graduate School of Management. The collection is broad in scope covering all aspects of business and management; emphasis is placed on in-depth collecting in the Graduate School of Management's core curriculum areas: accounting, behavioral and organizational science, business economics, computers and information science, production and operations management, public/not-for-profit management and urban land economics. The Library receives 2500 current periodical and serial titles and has strong retrospective holdings. The collection of uncataloged hard-copy annual reports of U.S. and foreign corporations numbers over 80,000. The library also holds over 160,000 microforms of annual and 10K reports of U.S. corporations, journals and newspapers. Special collections include the Robert E. Gross collection of Rare Books in Business and Economics (2,500 imprints prior to 1800), the microfilm of the University of London Goldsmiths' Library of Economic Literature and the Harvard Kress Library of Business and Economics of Printed books through 1850, a corporate history collection of over 3000 volumes, and the microfilm Business History Collection (primary source material representing the American economy during the 20th century).

CA —UNIVERSITY OF SOUTHERN CALIFORNIA, Crocker Business Library, Hoffman Hall, University Park, Los Angeles, 90007. Judith A Truelson, Head Librn
Holdings: Vols (100,000) Cat Microforms
Notes: The Roy P Crocker Library of Business Administration, located in Hoffman Hall, houses more than 100,000 volumes and regularly receives approximately 1500 trade, financial, economics, labor, and general business periodicals and newspapers. The areas of subject concentration include business economics, finance and investments, general management/management theory, international business, finance and management, marketing/food marketing, and quantitative business analysis.

DC —BENJAMIN FRANKLIN UNIVERSITY, Library, 1100 16th St NW, Washington, 20036. Robert Lewis, Librn
Holdings: Vols (4000) Cat
Budget: ($5000)

DC —EDISON ELECTRIC INSTITUTE, Library-8th Floor, 1111 19th St NW, Washington, 20036. Ethel Tiberg, Mgr, Library Services
Holdings: Vols (13,321) Cat Maps Pix Microforms

HI —HAWAII PACIFIC COLLEGE, Meader Library, 1060 Bishop St, Honolulu, 96813. Barbara Burton Hoefler, Head Librn
Holdings: Vols 450 Cat
Notes: The Hawaii Society of Certified Public Accountants has given us a collection of approximately 450 items. This collection has been cataloged and added to the regular collection, but we maintain a separate card catalog drawer with author cards and analytics for the collection. It is a growing collection.

IL —NORTHERN TRUST COMPANY LIBRARY, 50 S LaSalle St, Chicago, 60675. Marianne Lee, Head Librn
Holdings: Vols (2500) Cat Audiotapes Microforms

IN —PURDUE UNIVERSITY LIBRARIES, Graduate School of Management, Krannert Library, West Lafayette, 47907. Gordon Law, Librn
Holdings: Vols (142,727) Cat Microforms
Budget: ($69,700)
Notes: There is an extensive collection of corporate reports and labor information material (some 115,000 items). Over 2500 periodicals are currently received.

†LA —TULANE UNIVERSITY, Graduate School of Business Administration, New Orleans, 70118.

MA —HARVARD UNIVERSITY, Graduate School of Business Administration, Baker Library, Soldiers Field, Boston, 02163. Mary V Chatfield, Librn; Florence Bartoshesky, Cur of Manuscripts and Archives

MI —UNIVERSITY OF MICHIGAN, Graduate School of Business Administration, Business Administration Library, Institute for International Commerce Reading Rm, Ann Arbor, 48109. Carol Holbrook, Dir
Holdings: Vols Cat Microforms
Notes: Incl periodicals.

NH —NEW HAMPSHIRE COLLEGE, Harry A B and Gertrude C Shapiro Library, 2500 N River Rd, Manchester, 03104. Richard Pantano, Dir
Holdings: Vols (66,000) Cat Maps Slides Audiotapes Videotapes 16mm Films Filmstrips Microforms
Notes: Library is a selective US Government Documents depository, and New Hampshire State Documents depository. Subscribe to microfiche SEC 10K reports to AMEX and NYSE (1975-), as well as AMEX and NYSE company annual reports (1977-); AICPA publications and cassettes. Strong collections in accounting; business; business education; computers; hotel and restaurant management; and social service.

NY —BROOKLYN PUBLIC LIBRARY, Business Library, 280 Cadman Plaza W, Brooklyn, 11201. Sylvia Mechanic, Business Librn
Holdings: Vols (107,000) Cat
Notes: Library received about 1800 periodicals, 3000 serials, 2700 directories, 1600 telephone books from all over the world with a complete back file on microfilm for greater New York. Library is a selective US Government Documents depository. Subscribes to microfiche SEC 10K reports for AMEX, NYSE and OTC from 1976 to date; annual reports for earlier years. Transnational annual reports, on fiche from 1982-to date. 78 vertical file trays; Sanborn maps for Brooklyn, special collection of corporation histories. Publish monthly newsletter, *Service to Business and Industry* with our Science Division.

NY —CORNELL UNIVERSITY LIBRARIES, Graduate School of Management, Malott Hall, Ithaca, 14853. Betsy Ann Olive, Librn
Holdings: Vols (135,000) Cat Microforms
Budget: ($130,000)

NY —BERNARD M BARUCH COLLEGE (CUNY), Library, 156 E 25 St, New York, 10010. Alan Weiner, Head of Reference

NY —COLUMBIA UNIVERSITY LIBRARIES, Rare Book & Manuscript Library, 801 Butler Library, 535 W 114 St, New York, 10027. Kenneth A Lohf, Librn
Holdings: Vols 2000 Cat
Notes: The Montgomery Library of Accountancy, formed by Robert Hiester Montgomery. Restricted use.

NY —NEW YORK PUBLIC LIBRARY, Research Libraries, Economic & Public Affairs Div, Fifth Ave & 42 St, New York, 10018. Edward DiRoma, Chief
Holdings: Vols (1,500,000) Cat Microforms

NC —GREENSBORO PUBLIC LIBRARY, Business Library, 201 Greene St, Drawer X-4, Greensboro, 27402. Lebby B Lamb, Business Librn
Holdings: Vols (6000) Cat Microforms
Budget: ($12,000)

NC —TECHNICAL INSTITUTE OF ALAMANCE, Learning Resources Center, Jimmy Kerr Rd, PO Box 623, Haw River, 27258. Ron Plummer, Coordr
Holdings: Vols (1025) Cat Pix Audiotapes Filmstrips Microforms
Notes: Accounting, banking & finance, business administration.

OH —CLEVELAND PUBLIC LIBRARY, Business, Economics and Labor Department, 325 Superior Ave, Cleveland, 44114. Joan Sorger, Head
Holdings: Cat
Notes: Currently receiving over 1700 periodicals and 1300 serial titles; 1000 individual trade, industrial and professional directories, worldwide; 324 file drawers annual reports of old companies, many local; 24 drawers historical information on Cleveland companies. Annual reports, 10-K's, Proxy Statements (disclosure SEC filings on fiche); over 200 loose-leaf services; 1700 current telephone and city directories. Emphasis on current material. Areas of special strength are banking, investments, marketing and management. Also strong insurance, accounting, real estate and transportation collections. Computerized sources available incl Dow Jones News Service and a variety of Dialog business-related databases.

OH —ERNST & WHINNEY, National Office Library, 2000 National City Ctr, Cleveland, 44114. Naomi Clifford, Librn
Holdings: Vols (5000) Cat Periodicals
Notes: The collection consists of books, periodicals (350), and VF materials related to (1) technical accounting and auditing and (2) general business management. The emphasis is on current matters, not historical

ACCOUNTING (cont.)

developments. AICPA and FASB publications are collected *in toto.*

PA —DREXEL UNIVERSITY LIBRARIES, W W Hagerty Library, 32 & Chestnut Sts, Philadelphia, 19104. R L Snyder, Dir
Holdings: Vols (66,500) Cat Microforms
Budget: ($2900)
Notes: Incl 25,000 microforms of annual reports of companies traded on the NYSE and the ASE.

RI —BRYANT COLLEGE, Edith M Hodgson Memorial Library, Rte 7, Douglas Pike, Smithfield, 02917. John P Hannon, Dir
Holdings: Vols (103,000) Cat Phonorecords Audiotapes Videotapes 16mm Films Filmstrips Microforms
Budget: ($175,000)
Notes: Incl 6000 bound periodical vols, 250 phonorecords, 220 audiotapes, 120 videotapes, 30 16mm films, 150 filmstrips and 7500 microforms.

TX —UNIVERSITY OF TEXAS LIBRARIES, General Libraries, PO Box P, Austin, 78713. Carolyn Bucknell, Asst Dir for Collection Development
Holdings: Cat Microforms

TX —ECTOR COUNTY LIBRARY, Department of Business and Technology, 321 W 5th St, Odessa, 79760. Pat Jones, Dept Head
Holdings: Vols 2000 Cat
Notes: 25,000 Corporate Annual Reports microfilmed reports are complete from 1978-1983. 200 vertical files, 30 periodicals. Collection includes the subjects of Business, Management, Real Estate Accounting, Land Economics, Labor Economics, Finance, Personal Finance and Environmental Economics. Also included are stock and dividend reports, commodities and bond reports as well as business rankings. All items are referenced and cataloged.

WY —US AIR FORCE INSTITUTE OF TECHNOLOGY, Library, Dept 9 Bldg 831, FE, Warren AFB, 82001. Patricia A Johnson, Librn
Holdings: Vols (7000) Cat Microforms
Budget: ($9000)
Notes: The Library supports graduate programs for students (Air Force Missile-Combat Crewman) seeking a Master of Business Administration Degree. Civilian students and other military personnel are also admitted.

MB —UNIVERSITY OF MANITOBA, Faculty of Administrative Studies, Administrative Studies Library, Winnipeg, R3T 2N2, Can. Judith Head, Librn
Holdings: Vols (15,000) Cat Microforms
Notes: Public policy. 15,000 volumes cat, 11, 000 microfiche cat.

ON —INSTITUTE OF CHARTERED ACCOUNTANTS OF ONTARIO, The Merrilees Library, 69 Bloor St E, Toronto, M4W 1B3, Can. Theresa Wolak, Librn
Holdings: Vols 503 Cat

ACCOUNTING—HISTORY

IN —PURDUE UNIVERSITY LIBRARIES, Graduate School of Management, Krannert Library, West Lafayette, 47907. Gordon Law, Librn
Holdings: Vols (7000) Cat Mss Maps Pix Microforms
Notes: The collection consists of books, journals and pamphlets dating from the early 16th to late 19th century, covering to a large degree the early literature in economic thought and business practices both here and abroad. No photocopying.

NY —SAINT JOHN'S UNIVERSITY, Special Collections Dept, Grand Central & Utopia Pkwys, Jamaica, 11439. Szilvia E Szmuk, Librn
Holdings: Vols 160 // Cat
Notes: The Joseph C Myer Collection consists of books, issues of journals, and ledgers from the early 16th through the early 20th century. A very large part of the collection is 17th and 18th century French, English, and German titles on methods of bookkeeping and business practices. Many of these volumes are in fine and unusual bindings which have been recently restored. No photocopying.

ACCOUNTING MACHINES

DE —HAGLEY MUSEUM AND LIBRARY, Eleutherian Mills-Hagley Foundation Inc, PO Box 3630, Greenville, 19807. Richmond D Williams, Dir; Heddy A Richter, Imprints Librn
Notes: Sperry Univac has deposited a large amount of historical records. Approximately 2000 cubic feet of records, files and photographs that document the invention and development of computers and the rapid growth of the industry were officially released by Sperry Corporation to the Library. The collection includes technical and legal documents relating to the ENIAC and UNIVAC computers as well as records of the founding of the E Remington Typewriter Company and other predecessor companies of the Sperry organization, such as The Library Bureau, Kardex, Rodic Rubber and the Powers Accounting Machinery Company. Thus our knowledge of the Sperry predecessors dates back in this collection to 1902.

ACHIEVEMENT TESTS see Examinations

ACID RAIN

MO —US FISH & WILDLIFE SERVICE, Columbia National Fisheries Research Laboratory, Rte One, Columbia, 65201. Axie Hindman, Librn
Holdings: Vols (2000) Cat Microforms
Budget: ($7000)
Notes: Pesticides in aquatic biota; fisheries research; fresh-water ecology. Also incl collection in water pollution, acid rain, aquatic invertebrets, environment and 10,000 reprints.

ACIDS, FATTY

OH —EMERY INDUSTRIES, Research Library, 4900 Este Ave, Cincinnati, 45232. B A Bernard, Librn
Holdings: Cat
Notes: Special subjects: fatty acids and organic chemical derivatives, ozone, plasticizers, polymer, synthetic lubricants.

ACKERMAN, DIANE

MA —BOSTON UNIVERSITY, Mugar Memorial Library, Special Collections Dept, 771 Commonwealth Ave, Boston, 02215. Howard B Gotlieb, Dir
Holdings: Cat Mss

ACKERMAN, FORREST J.

NM —EASTERN NEW MEXICO UNIVERSITY, Golden Library, Special Collections, Portales, 88130. Mary Jo Walker, Special Collections Librn
Holdings: Vols 11,940 Cat Mss Pix Audiotapes
Notes: Incl 700 magazine titles (10,318 issues), 11,940 vols, mss and correspondences of the following science fiction writers: Jack Williamson, Edmond Hamilton, Leigh Brackett, Forrest J Ackerman and Piers Anthony (Jacob), plus *Astounding/Analog* ms files (1954-1975). Also serves as a depository for Science Fiction Writers of America. Incl separate catalog for published books and unpublished registers to personal papers. The Williamson Register is being prepared for publication. Collection is described in *Anatomy of* Wonder, by Neil Barron (NY: Bowker, 1981); and *Special Collections, II* (winter, 1982), pp 49-57.

ACMEISM

IL —UNIVERSITY OF ILLINOIS, URBANA/CHAMPAIGN, Slavic and East European Library, Urbana, 61801. Marianna Tax Choldin, Head
Holdings: Cat Microforms
Notes: IDC microfiche collection of 959 titles of symbolism, futurism, constructivism, acmeism, imagism, and zemstvo publications.

ACORN, MILTON

BC —SIMON FRASER UNIVERSITY, Library, Burnaby, V5A 1S6, Can. Percilla Groves, Special Collections Librn
Holdings: Cat Mss
Notes: Mss of 20 finished poems and many pages of preliminary drafts; 10 pp prose mss, 4 letters.

ACOUSTICS

CA —CALIFORNIA STATE UNIVERSITY, LONG BEACH, Library, Dept of Special Collections & Archives, 1250 Bellflower Blvd, Long Beach, 90840. John Ahouse, Special Collections Librn
Holdings: Mss Phonorecords Audiotapes
Notes: Almost all of the papers, recordings, etc, published and unpublished, of Gerald V Strang.

CA —UNIVERSITY OF CALIFORNIA, LOS ANGELES, Physics Library, 213 Kinsey Hall, Los Angeles, 90024. J Wally Pegram, Librn
Holdings: Vols (37,000) Cat
See also entry under Physics

PA —FRANKLIN INSTITUTE LIBRARY, 20 & The Parkway, Philadelphia, 19103. Miriam Padusis, Dir; Charles Wilt, Readers Servs Librn
Holdings: Vols (300,000) Cat Maps Pix Microforms

ACOUSTICS—HISTORY

DC —LIBRARY OF CONGRESS, Motion Pictures, Broadcasting and Recorded Sound Div, Washington, 20540.
Notes: Recordings, photographs, correspondence, scrapbooks and other memorabilia concerning the invention of the lateral cut disc gramophone record, basis of the modern recording industry, Emile Berliner (1851-1929). Devised word "Gramophone," and invented acoustic tiling.

ACROGENS see Cryptogams; Ferns; Mosses

ACRONYMS

MI —GALE RESEARCH CO, Book Tower, Detroit, 48226. Annie Brewer, Librn
Holdings: Vols (65,000) Cat
Notes: Large collection of reference materials, incl computerized files used in the preparation of familiar contemporary reference books and guides to special fields.

ACTING—COSTUME see Costume

ACTION

DC —ACTION, Photo Library, 806 Connecticut Ave NW, Washington, 20525.
Holdings: Pix Slides
Notes: Volunteer photos for ACTION, VISTA, and older Americans programs. 15, 000 photographs.

ACTIVATED CARBON see Carbon, Activated

ACTIVATED CHARCOAL see Carbon, Activated

ACTON, HAROLD

DC —GEORGETOWN UNIVERSITY, Library, Special Collections Div, 37 & O Sts NW, Washington, 20057. George M Barringer, Special Collections Librn; Nicholas B Sheetz, Mss Librn
Holdings: Mss Pix
Notes: The papers of Christopher Sykes, biographer, journalist, and novelist; containing mss, letters, photographs, and drawings. With extensive correspondence

ACTON, HAROLD (cont.)

from Harold Acton; Angela, Countess of Antrim; Sir John Betjeman; Ivy Compton-Burnett; Alick Dru; T S Eliot; Max Beerbohm; Graham Greene; John Hayward; Lord Patrick Kinross; Compton Mackenzie; Nancy Mitford; Anthony Powell; Dame Flora Robson; Cecil Roth; Sir John Russell; Osbert Sitwell; John Sparrow; Freya Stark; James Stern; and Evelyn Waugh, among others. Also, considerable research material about Evelyn Waugh, Adam von Trott, Robert Byron, Lady Nancy Astor; and the foundation of the state of Israel.

ACTORS—BIOGRAPHY see Actors and Actresses

ACTORS AND ACTRESSES

CA —ACADEMY OF MOTION PICTURE ARTS & SCIENCES, Margaret Herrick Library, 8949 Wilshire Blvd, Beverly Hills, 90211. Linda Harris Mehr, Library Administrator
Holdings: Vols (16,000) Cat Mss Pix Slides
Budget: ($250,000)
Notes: Also posters, scrapbooks, clippings and press books. Collection emphases are the moving picture industry, moving picture history, biographical material on actors, actresses and industry personnel. Files on specific films, reviews, cast and credits, production data, etc, on more than 65,000 moving pictures. (Over 5000 films, incl early 28mm films in Film Archive). Over 5 million pictures. Special collections: papers of Mary Pickford, Mack Sennett, Adolph Zukor, Lewis Milestone, George Stevens, George Cukor, John Huston, Edith Head; Paramount scripts and stills archive, MGM stills archive, RKO stills archive, Thomas H Ince stills collection, Cecil B DeMille stills collection.

CA —UNIVERSITY OF CALIFORNIA, DAVIS, Shields Library, Dept of Special Collections, Davis, 95616. Donald Kunitz, Head; C Danial Elliott, Asst Head
Holdings: Uncat Mss Pix
Notes: Photographs, clippings, and correspondence of personalities of American and British theatre in the 19th and 20th centuries, such as Edwin Booth, Joseph Jefferson, Julia Marlowe, E H Sothern, Ellen Terry, Henry Irving, McKee Rankin, Fanny Davenport, and Zero Mostel.

CA —AMERICAN FILM INSTITUTE, Louis B Mayer Library, 2021 N Western Ave, PO Box 27999, Los Angeles, 90027. Anne G Schlosser, Dir
Holdings: Vols (3500) Cat
Notes: Collection contains 2500 American film scripts and 1000 television scripts; oral histories conducted in the American Film Institute Louis B Mayer Oral History Program; the MGM Script Collection of 400 MGM scripts from the silent period up to the mid-1950's; Columbia Stills Collection covering the period 1930-1950; special mss collections of Henry Hathaway (director), Harry Horner, Buster Keaton, George Byron Sage and Stewart Stern (writer). Also clipping files on motion pictures, personalities, television shows, production organizations and technical topics; film festival file of all US and foreign festivals. Rare periodical holdings incl *Film Daily* newspaper (1923-1969); *Radio-TV Daily* newspaper (1939-1964); *RKO Radio Flash,* house organ of RKO (1932-1955); *TV Guide* (1948 to date).

CA —INSTITUTE OF THE AMERICAN MUSICAL, Library, 121 N Detroit St, Los Angeles, 90036. Miles Kreuger, Cur
Holdings: Cat Mss Maps Pix Slides Phonorecords
Notes: Reference materials on the American musical theatre and motion pictures incl 40, 000 phonograph records, sound tapes, and cylinders dating back to the 1890s; record catalogs to 1900; thousands of theatre and film programs, periodicals, sheet music and vocal scores as early as 1830; thousands of motion picture press books and over 200,000 stills from 1914 to the present; every musical comedy script published in America and dozens in ms form, original or photocopy materials from the archives of movie palaces, films and record companies, incl discographies of many major Broadway and Hollywood stars; and thousands of books on theatre, film, broadcasting, world's fairs and other allied areas of showmanship.

CA —LOS ANGELES PUBLIC LIBRARY, Frances Howard Goldwyn Hollywood Regional Library, 1623 Ivar Ave, Los Angeles, 90028. Sally Dumaux, Librn
Holdings: Vols (100,000) Cat Mss Pix VF
Budget: ($60,000)
Notes: A general and a research collection covering motion pictures, radio broadcasting, and television. Over 2000 motion picture and television scripts. Biographical information on actors and actresses. Casts, credits, and other production information on over 1500 motion pictures from the 1920s to the present. Collections also include posters, lobby cards, souvenir programs, scrapbooks, vertical files, and over 3000 publicity stills. Including the following Special Collections: Fred Archer Collection, photographs, including the Hunchback of Notre Dame (1923), and personalities of the stage and screen, 1907-1930; Gilbert A Adrian, designer, sketches and photographs; Hazel Flynn, publicist, correspondence and photographs.

CA —UNIVERSITY OF CALIFORNIA, LOS ANGELES, Research Library, Dept of Special Collections, 405 Hilgard Ave, Los Angeles, 90024. Edward Shreeves, Chairman, Bibliographers Group; David S Zeidberg, Head
Holdings: Cat Pix
Notes: 2000 turn-of-the-century cabinet cards of American and foreign theatre, opera, and vaudeville personalities; 80 linear feet of theatrical ephemera.

CA —UNIVERSITY OF CALIFORNIA, LOS ANGELES, Theater Arts Library, Los Angeles, 90024. Edward Shreeves, Chairman, Bibliographers Group; Audree Malkin, Head, Theater Arts Library
Holdings: Vols (12,500) Cat Mss Pix Films
Notes: Over 15,000 moving picture stills; over 32,636 screenplays and scripts from American and British films. Incl radio (1740) scripts, television script collection (3000). Extensive poster collection (over 7,000, 1915 to date); many for Polish and Czech productions. Script Collection, Screenplays: a collection of more than 32,636 unpublished scripts for American, British and some foreign language films. An important part of the collection is the Metro Goldwyn Mayer Screenplay Collection which covers the period 1924-1947. Incl are the *Andy Hardy, Dr Kildare,* and *Maisie* film series which are virtually complete, and a number of short features, such as *Robert Benchley Series, Pete Smith Specialties,* and *Our Gang* Comedies Walt Disney Collection. A small but rare collection ofcartoon continuities and shooting scripts dated 1937-1939. Television Scripts: approximately 3500 scripts incl such television series as *Mission Impossible,* all episodes for the years 1966-1970; *The Real* McCoys, 78 episodes, 1959-1961; *My Friend Irma,* 1965-1966; *The George Burns Show,* 232 episodes, 1958-1959; *My Mother the* Car, 30 episodes, 1965-1966. Radio Scripts: A collection of more than 1000 scripts which include the complete *Amos 'n Andy* radio series, 354 episodes, 1943-1953; *Our Miss* Brooks, 222 scripts, 1948-1954; *The Bob Hope Show,* 29 scripts, 1949-1950; *Philco Radio Time,* starring Bing Crosby, 7 scripts and 6 comedy sketches, 1946-1947.

CA —UNIVERSITY OF CALIFORNIA, LOS ANGELES, Theater Arts Library, Los Angeles, 90024. Edward Shreeves, Chairman, Bibliographers Group; Audree Malkin, Head, Theater Arts Library
Notes: The Charlton Heston Archives, incl correspondence, scripts, movie posters, still photographs, scrapbooks, interviews, awards, etc, covering his forty-year acting career in fifty-four films. He served six terms as President of the Screen Actors Guild, longer than anyone else.

CA —UNIVERSITY OF SOUTHERN CALIFORNIA, Edward L Doheny Memorial Library, Archives of Performing Arts, University Park, Los Angeles, 90089. Robert Knutson, Librn
Holdings: Mss
Notes: Approx 15,000 vols of books and serials about film, incl a large collection of foreign language books and periodicals. Current subscriptions to over 200 serials. Large collection of clippings about motion pictures and television. Warner Brothers Films Collection (1920-1968) incl 700,000 stills and negatives; 3,000 titles of feature, short subject and television screenplays, script materials, set designs, engineering drawings, production records, patent records, music and legal files. Over 1000 bound vols describing the inventory and 100 bound vols of index to the inventory. Universal Pictures Corporation Collection incl 600 boxes of production and publicity department records, incl 1,500 screenplays. Metro-Goldwyn-Mayer Collection incl screenplays from 1919-1958. Twentieth Century-Fox Collection incl screenplays and story department notes from 1919-1967.Hal Roach Studio Collection contains studio records from 1916-mid fifties. More than 150 personal collections from actors, directors, producers, writers, etc. Also have 2,000 additional screenplays; 1,000 posters, 110,000 photographs; 750 recorded soundtracks; 1,500 interview tapes; 400 David Wolper videotapes. A collection of feature films on videotape is being created. There is also a historical collection of motion picture cameras, projectors and other equipment from the earliest times to present.

CA —SAN DIEGO PUBLIC LIBRARY, Art, Music & Recreation Sect, 820 E St, San Diego, 92101. Barbara A Tuhill, Supvr
Holdings: Vols 500 Cat
Notes: The gift of Elwyn B Gould, the collection consists of many first editions of biographies of famous actors and actresses and histories of the American, London and European stages. Theatre program scrapbooks dating from 1890 to 1928, some of local events. For reference use only.

CA —UNIVERSITY OF CALIFORNIA, SANTA CRUZ, University Library, Special Collections, Santa Cruz, 95064. Rita Bottoms, Special Collections Librn; Margaret Felts, South Pacific Collection Bibliographer
Holdings: Cat Mss Pix
Notes: The Robert McNulty Collection of books by Sir Henry Irving also photographs, hand-written letters, biographies, prompt books and programs.

CT —YALE UNIVERSITY, Box 1603A, Yale Station, New Haven, 06520.
Holdings: Cat Mss Pix
Notes: Incl American Musical Theater and complete archives of the Theater Guild; also the Crawford Theatre Collection, and memorabilia.

DC —HOWARD UNIVERSITY, Founders Library, Channing Pollock Theatre Collection, 500 Howard Place NW, Washington, 20059. Marilyn Mahanand, Librn
Holdings: Vols (16,440) Cat Mss Pix Slides Microforms
Notes: Much on the Black Theatre.

DC —LIBRARY OF CONGRESS, Music Division, Washington, 20540.
Notes: The Geraldine Farrar Collection incl correspondence, scripts, contracts, programs, playbills, scrapbooks, posters, and photographs. Also in the Motion Picture, Broadcasting, and Recorded Sound Division are 50 disc recordings of radio broadcast transcriptions and special pressings made by the Gramophone and Typewriter Company, Ltd.

DC —LIBRARY OF CONGRESS, Motion Pictures, Broadcasting and Recorded Sound Div, Washington, 20540.
Notes: Films of Mary Pickford.

GA —GEORGIA STATE UNIVERSITY, William R Pullen Library, Atlanta, 30303. Leslie S Hough, Dir
Notes: Large collection of the papers of songwriter, singer, composer, and publisher Johnny Mercer. Incl correspondence, music

ACTORS AND ACTRESSES (cont.)

scores, an unpublished autobiography, phono discs, water colors, etc.

IL —CHICAGO HISTORICAL SOCIETY, Library, Clark St at North Ave, Chicago, 60614. Robert L Brubaker, Librn
Holdings: Vols (150,000) Cat Mss Pix
Notes: Chicago theatre programs (5000); scrapbooks containing reviews and other clippings; a few letters, reminiscences, account books, and other records of theatres, actors and actresses, and managers; theatre posters; Thomas Conolly Collection of Theatrical Portraits; other photographs of theatres, productions, and casts.

IL —CHICAGO PUBLIC LIBRARY, Art Section, Fine Arts Division, 78 E Washington St, Chicago, 60602. Rosalinda I Hack, Fine Arts Division Chief; Yvonne S Brown, Head, Art Section
Holdings: Vols 8000
Notes: Reference and circulating collection of books, periodicals, pamphlets, pictures, and microform. Special emphasis on general theatre history, theatre of the United States, biographies of actors and actresses, and acting techniques. Collection is supplemented by Chicago stagebills and reviews of area theater productions, a pamphlet and curio file on Chicago theater. Much additional materials can be found in our Special Collections Department.

IL —ILLINOIS STATE UNIVERSITY, Milner Library, Dept of Special Collections, Normal, 61761. Robert Sokan, Librn
Holdings: Vols (6200) Cat Mss Pix Slides
Notes: Circus and related arts collection consists of approx 6200 book items and approx 250,000 nonbook items. The books date from the 16th century to the present, and incl vols specifically concerned with the circus past and present, vaudeville, music halls and variety theaters, theatrical and animal history, biographies, autobiographies and memoirs, novels, poetry, drama, juvenalia and other subjects relating to the circus. Many of the books are limited editions, presentation copies or autographed copies. Incl archives of the Dobritch International Circus (20,000 items).

KY —UNIVERSITY OF LOUISVILLE, Ekstrom Library, Photographic Archives, Louisville, 40292. J C Anderson, Cur; David G Horvath, Asst Cur
Holdings: Vols (750,000) Cat Pix Slides
Budget: ($60,000)
Notes: Photographs of actors and actresses and of Louisville's Macauley Theatre. Print duplication service.

ME —BOOTHBAY THEATRE MUSEUM, Library, Corey Lane, Boothbay, 04537. Franklyn Lenthall, Cur
Holdings: Vols 6000 Cat Mss Pix Slides Phonorecords Audiotapes
Notes: The only Theatre Museum, as such, in America. Very extensive photo collection.

†MD —MARYLAND HISTORICAL SOCIETY, Library, 201 W Monument St, Baltimore, 21201.
Notes: Eubie Blake's personal and professional archive. Incl the Baltimore-born pianist, composer, and songwriter's collection of songs and instrumental pieces in mss, extensive documentation of his collaboration with Noble Sissle, Flournog Miller, Milton Reddie, and others. The Broadway musical comedy, Shuffle Along, is represented in box office records, programs, scores and parts, photographs, and sheet music. Blake's involvement with other productions is similarly documented.

MA —BOSTON UNIVERSITY, Mugar Memorial Library, Special Collections Dept, 771 Commonwealth Ave, Boston, 02215. Howard B Gotlieb, Dir
Holdings: Cat Mss Pix
Notes: Incl personal papers and literary productions of numerous modern actors, actresses, musicians (composers and performers) of all kinds. A complete list is available. See personal name entries.

MA —HARVARD UNIVERSITY LIBRARY, Theatre Collection, Cambridge, 02138. Jeanne T Newlin, Cur
Holdings: Cat Mss Pix Slides Microforms
Notes: One of the largest existing collections of playbills, programs, prints, photographs, promptbooks, and other materials relating to the performing arts, the scope is worldwide; resources on the English-speaking stage of the 18th and 19th centuries are unequalled. Incl materials on ballet and modern dance, the circus, magic, minstrel shows, cinema, and pantomime. For description, see *Harvard Library Bulletin,* VI (1925): pp 281-301.

MA —LENOX LIBRARY ASSOCIATION, Main St, Lenox, 01240. Denis J Lesieur, Dir
Holdings: Mss Pix
Notes: Frances Anne "Fanny" Kemble (Mrs Pierce M Butler), the English actress who lived in Lenox. Some of her books.

MI —UNIVERSITY OF MICHIGAN, Library, Dept of Rare Books & Special Collections, Ann Arbor, 48109. Robert J Starring, Head
Holdings: Cat Mss Pix
Notes: Extensive holdings of books on the theatre. Also, in the Charles Sanders Collection, about 14,000 British and American playbills and programs mostly of the 19th century, as well as scrapbooks, posters, and about 750 photographs and prints of actors and actresses. In the Ellen Van Volkenburg--Maurice Browne Collection, about 4000 photographs of stage productions and friends and associates, as well as programs, posters, scrapbooks of mounted clippings, about 200 original stage and costume designs, promptbooks, and play manuscripts, representing the American and British careers of this husband-wife team from 1912 to about 1940. The Chicago Little Theatre, 1912-1917, is well represented. Also contains more than 6000 items of correspondence with theatrical and literary figures. Another collection contains 143 Alfred Lunt letters, mainly from 1909-1915.

MI —DETROIT PUBLIC LIBRARY, Music & Performing Arts Dept, 5201 Woodward, Detroit, 48202. Jean Currie Church, Cur
Holdings: Vols (1375) Cat Mss Pix
Notes: The E Azalia Hackley Collections document achievements of Blacks in the fields of music, dance, theatre, motion pictures, and broadcasting. World-wide in scope. Extensive clipping files arranged by personal names, titles and subjects. Incl musical scores (1500), recordings, and plays. No taping or other copying of recordings permitted.

NJ —PRINCETON UNIVERSITY, Library, William Seymour Theatre Collection, Princeton, 08544. Mary Ann Jensen, Cur
Holdings: Vols (8000) Cat
Budget: ($10,000)
Notes: Plus scrapbooks, playbills, posters.

NJ —MONMOUTH COLLEGE, Murry & Leonie Guggenheim Memorial Library, New Jersey Collection, West Long Branch, 07764. Audrey K Wilson, Librn
Holdings: Vols (3025) Cat Maps Pix Microforms
Budget: ($1000)
Notes: Espec Monmouth County region. Incl periodicals, pamphlets, clippings. New Jersey Documents Depository. Picture collection, incl pictures of theatre personalities who came to this popular summer resort. Weather records kept by William Martin and his father at Long Branch, 1909-1963. Collection noncirculating.

NY —STATE UNIVERSITY OF NEW YORK, BINGHAMTON, Glenn G Bartle Library, Binghamton, 13901. Marion Hanscom, Special Collections Librn
Holdings: Cat
Budget: ($8000)
Notes: Max Reinhardt Archive. Library has extensive (approx 250,000 items) archival material relating to Max Reinhardt, as well as his personal library. This personal library is not a subject collection per se, but contains much information about German theater in the 20th century. The archival material contains letters, prompt books, photographs, playbills, etc.

†NY —COLUMBIA UNIVERSITY LIBRARIES, Butler Library, Rare Book and Manuscript Library, 535 W 114 St, New York, 10027.
Notes: The papers, etc, of Ira A Hards, American theatre producer and his actress wife Ina Hammer Hards.

NY —HAMPDEN-BOOTH THEATRE LIBRARY AT THE PLAYERS, 16 Gramercy Park, New York, 10003. Louis A Rachow, Librn/Cur
Holdings: Vols 15,000 Cat Mss Pix Slides Phonotapes
Notes: A strong collection on theatre history, with special emphasis on 19th and 20th century English and American stage. Large collection of English playbills of the 18th and 19th centuries; important collection of prompt books (mainly 19th century); Edwin Booth, incl memorabilia, rare books, association items, his 2nd, 3rd, and 4th Shakespeare Folios, etc. Large collection of English and American biographies and pictures of actors and acresses; the Chuck Callahan Burlesque Collection (qv Burlesque); and other specialties described elsewhere in this volume. The library is open to all qualified researchers upon application. Also, the British Actors Orphanage Fund Collection. The Fund was incorporated in Los Angeles, California, in July 1940 "to promote and effect the transfer of male and female minor orphans of deceased British actors and actresses from their present home or homesin Great Britain to America...and to provide and pay for their complete maintenance, housing and schooling therein, during the pendency of the present war between Great Britain and Germany, to the end that these orphans may be removed from the horrors and perils of such war." The duties and activities of the Fund came to a successful conclusion in 1946. The collection consists of copies of the charter and by-laws, minutes, journals and ledgers, children's travel arrangements, working files and preliminary and general correspondence for the years 1940-1946 featuring such luminaries as Noel Coward, Dame May Whitty, Boris Karloff, Maurice Evans, Cole Porter, Peggy Wood and Margaret Webster. Described in *Theatre & Performing Arts* Collections (New York: Haworth Press, 1981).

NY —NEW YORK PUBLIC LIBRARY, Performing Arts Research Center, Billy Rose Theatre Collection, 111 Amsterdam Ave, New York, 10023. Dorothy L Swerdlove, Cur
Holdings: Cat Pix
Notes: The larger part of the collection is nonbook materials: clippings, programs, iconography, autographs, letters, scrapbooks, etc., about theatre production. The archives of David Belasco, R. H. Burnside, Theodore Liebler, Winthrop Ames; the memorabilia of such performing artists as Katharine Cornell, Helen Hayes, Maurice Evans, Burl Ives, Paul Muni, Sophie Tucker. In addition to the records of producing offices listed above, the Theatre Collection has the archives of John Golden, Alexander H. Cohen, Leland Hayward, the Chamberlain and Lyman Brown Theatrical Agency, as well as the papers of various press agents e.g., Karl Bernstein, Bill Doll, and Richard Maney, also the Robinson Locke Collection of the 18th-19th centuries. British Theatre; the Henin Collection of the 19th century French theatre; the working papers memorabilia of Jerome Lawrence and Robert E. Lee; typescripts and promptbooks, mainly American theatre 1875-date; Shakespeare production, American and British, 19th-20th century; Becks Collection—19th century English and American theatre; working scripts of Edward Albee. The Theatre Collection currently clips, catalogs and files new material about stage production—universally. We add typescripts and promptbooks of new plays, programs and photographs of productions, etc. A collection of scrapbooks of the New York reviews of all productions done in the New York theatre (by season) from the season of 1917/18-date; earlier reviews are also available.

ACTORS AND ACTRESSES (cont.)

NY —NEW YORK PUBLIC LIBRARY, Performing Arts Research Center, Dance Collection, 111 Amsterdam Ave, New York, 10023. Genevieve Oswald, Cur
Holdings: Vols (36,752) Cat
Notes: Oral

†NY —SHUBERT ARCHIVE, Lyceum Theatre, 149 W 45th St, New York, 10036. Brigitte Kueppers, Archivist
Notes: The vast Shubert Archive, mostly unexplored is the largest collection in the world representative of the "business" of the theatre. It includes almost all of the Shubert empire's correspondence from the turn of the century to the 1950s, road company records, thousands of playscripts (American and European), set and costume designs, music scores for Shubert productions, business, financial, and legal records, actors' contracts, etc.

NY —THEATRE COLLECTION OF THE INTERNATIONAL THEATRE INSTITUTE OF THE UNITED STATES, INC, Library, Suite 1510, 1860 Broadway, New York, 10023. Elizabeth B Burdick, Dir
Holdings: Vols (4525) Cat Mss Pix
Budget: ($35,000)
Notes: The International Theatre Institute was founded by UNESCO to "promote the exchange of knowledge and practice in the theatre arts." In 1948, eleven nations, incl the United States, became charter members of the international organization, which today has national centers or affiliates in 64 countries. The American center is the International Theatre Institute of the United States (ITI/US). In 1970, as one of its programs to strengthen communication among theatre people, ITI/US opened a library devoted to international theatre since World War II. The Collection's main holdings have been amassed over the 35-year operation of ITI/US through its world-wide exchange of information, publications, and people. Holdings document theatre activity in 140 countries. The 4525 vols on American and foreign theatre(covering history, management, design, stagecraft, theory, criticism, biography, playscripts) represent only a small part of the total collection. Focus is on foreign theatre companies, directors, playwrights, designers, managers, actors. The emphasis is on the acquisition of material which is generally unavailable in this country: foreign yearbooks, house organs, newsletters, programs, press releases, production schedules, brochures, periodicals, monographs, articles, newspaper clippings. While these fugitive items have never been counted, they have been cataloged by country, then indexed by title, subject, or name of theatre. The library receives regularly 250 periodicals on the performing arts (cataloged by country, then indexed by title). It now owns 6417 foreign plays from 80 countries in ms or publishedmss or published editions, in collections and anthologies, and in periodicals. Each play is cataloged by author, title, and country of origin. The section on American theatre incl books, programs, reviews, over 60 periodicals, 2061 American plays. The activities of approx 700 theatres across the country are documented by annual files containing production schedules, press releases, programs, brochures for each theatrical season.

NY —STATE UNIVERSITY OF NEW YORK, COLLEGE AT PURCHASE, Library, Lincoln Ave, Purchase, 10577. Robert W Evans, Dir
Holdings: Vols (1400) Mss Pix Slides
Notes: The Gerald D McDonald Collection. Over 1400 books on moving pictures and all aspects of the industry: production, directing, acting. Thousands of pictures of actors and actresses, directors, etc. Also about 2000 slides picturing movie personalities, etc; stereopticon pictures, buttons, bottle caps, playing cards, etc.

NY —UNIVERSITY OF ROCHESTER, Rush Rhees Library, Department of Rare Books and Special Collections, Rochester, 14627. Peter Dzwonkoski, Librn
Holdings: Cat Mss Pix
Notes: Lillian Russell's papers, etc.

NC —DUKE UNIVERSITY, William R Perkins Library, Durham, 27706. Elvin E Strowd, University Librn
Holdings: Cat Mss Pix
Notes: Montrose J Moses' collection of books, mss, and papers, mostly concerned with men and women of the theatre, and creative writers of the first third of the century. 3000 books; 22,000 mss.

NC —NORTH CAROLINA SCHOOL OF THE ARTS, Semans Library, PO Box 12189, Winston-Salem, 27107. William D VanHoven, Head Librn
Holdings: Vols (98,000) Cat Slides Microforms Phonorecords Films
Budget: ($105,000)
Notes: Incl clippings, pictures and programs.

†OH —HEBREW UNION COLLEGE, American Jewish Archives, 3101 Clifton Ave, Cincinnati, 45220.
Notes: Papers and correspondence of Sophie Tucker (1884-1966).

OH —CLEVELAND PUBLIC LIBRARY, Literature Dept, 325 Superior Ave, Cleveland, 44114. Evelyn Ward, Head
Holdings: Cat Mss Pix Phonorecords Microforms VF
Notes: Comprehensive collection of works on stage, cinema, radio, and television, incl history, production, staging, acting, biographies of actors. Non-book materials: theatrical memorabilia such as programs, playbills, pictures; play reviews, clippings from newspapers and magazines. Recordings: plays, sound effects. Reference aids and indexes, incl indexes to plays, theaters, and actors in Cleveland. File of *Film Daily* reviews from the late 1920s and other clippings from 1961. Large collection of stills and photographs from cinema and television. *Variety*: 1905-date. Also, the W Ward Marsh Cinema Archives: The personal library and other collections of W Ward Marsh, critic for the Cleveland *Plain Dealer*. Collection incl production stills, actor/actress file folders for personalities containing studio and agent biographies, pressbooks, areview file clipped from *Boxoffice, Variety* and misc trade journals, specially bound copy of the shooting script for Cecil B deMille's remake of *The Ten Commandments*, and a collection of more than 700 46g x 56g glass slides used by theatre owners to promote their upcoming attractions.

OK —UNIVERSITY OF OKLAHOMA, Drama Library, 550 Parrington Oval, Norman, 73019. Jan Seifert, Dir
Holdings: Vols (6683) Mss Pix Phonorecords
Notes: Incl VF material, newspaper clippings and magazine cut-outs covering the theatre and dance. Material dates from 1900. Collection of nearly 6000 plays.

OK —UNIVERSITY OF OKLAHOMA, Bizzell Memorial Library, Western History Collections, 401 W Brooks, Norman, 73069. John Ezell, Cur
Notes: Papers of Helen Gahagan Douglas, stage actress and US Representative. Guide available.

PA —FRANKLIN & MARSHALL COLLEGE, Library, Lancaster, 17604. Kathleen J Moretto, Library Dir
Holdings: Vols Uncat Mss Pix
Notes: The Alexander Corbett Collection of Theatre Memorabilia consists of 650 letters and photographs of actors and actresses during the Victorian era in America.

PA —FREE LIBRARY OF PHILADELPHIA, Theatre Collection, Logan Sq, Philadelphia, 19103. Geraldine Duclow, Librn-in-Charge
Holdings: Vols (1,250,000) Uncat Pix
Notes: The Theatre Collection contains books, magazines, playbills, broadsides, posters, photographs, and other memorabilia covering theatre, motion pictures, minstrels, vaudeville, circus, radio and television. The Library's Philadelphia Theatre Index lists the major productions here since 1855, and partially indexes the collection of local playbills which date back to 1803. There are also programs from many other cities, incl New York; some from London date back to 1800. Early film companies as well as the present movie industry are represented by advertising materials and over 30,000 film stills. The Lubin Film Co (1910-1916) Archive has been established with over 600 photographs and related items. Circus programs and route books date back to 1900. There are minstrel programs as early as 1865. Most significant are the mss from Philadelphia's Dumont Minstrels. Variousfiles contain autographs, photographs, newspaper articles and reviews in all pertinent subject areas. Noncirculating.

PA —UNIVERSITY OF PITTSBURGH, Special Collections Dept, Curtis Theatre Collection, 363 Hillman Library, Pittsburgh, 15260. Jeanette Blanco, Cur
Holdings: Vols (4000) Cat Mss Pix Slides Microforms VF
Notes: The legitimate theatre of plays, musicals and vaudeville, chiefly of New York City and Pittsburgh, from 1865, and other US, community, summer, college and foreign theatre. Incl 500,000 programs, 12, 000 pictures, 300 posters, the Oliver P Merriman Scrapbooks and 300 other scrapbooks, clippings and other ephemera. Vols incl over 3000 acting editions and playscripts. Separate collections: Ralph G Allen Burlesque Skits Collection; Michael Ellis Papers; William P Halstead Theatre Collection; Kenyon Family Papers; Philip Dunning Playscripts Collection; Pittsburgh Playhouse Records; Pittsburgh Savoyards Records. Noncirculating.

TN —MEMPHIS STATE UNIVERSITY, John Willard Brister Library, Memphis, 38152. John Terreo, Special Collections Librn
Notes: Theatre Collection, 1789-1972. Correspondence, scripts, programs, handbills, musical scores, clippings, drawings, sketches, and photographs, documenting careers of artists, production of plays, ballett and theatre companies, and theaters and opera houses centering in New York and London, England. Incl drawings, prints, publications, and other personal papers of British producer and designer Edward Gordon Craig (1872-1966), relating to his career, radio talks (1951-1961) for the BBC, acting school in Florence, Italy, and his mother, actress Ellen Terry; and correspondence, scripts, programs, reviews, scrapbooks, photos, and other materials, of American producer Jed Harris (?)-1979, relating to his stage productions (1926-1945).

TN —PUBLIC LIBRARY OF NASHVILLE & DAVIDSON COUNTY, Nashville Room, Eighth Ave N & Union, Nashville, 37203. David Marshall Stewart, Chief Librn
Holdings: Vols Cat Mss Pix
Notes: The Naff Collection of programs, autographed photographs, posters, etc tells the story of professional theatre in Nashville between 1900 and 1960. All materials noncirculating.

†TX —UNIVERSITY OF TEXAS LIBRARIES, Hoblitzelle Theatre Arts Library, Austin, 78712.
Notes: A 100,000-item collection of correspondence and documents related to the career and personal life of Gloria Swanson, one of the largest archives from 1913 to 1983. Correspondence with Mary Pickford, William Faulkner, and the Kennedy Family, the latter to remain sealed until the year 2000.

TX —DALLAS PUBLIC LIBRARY, Fine Arts Div, 1515 Young St, Dallas, 75201. Richard L Waters, Acting Dir; Jane Holahan, Manager
Holdings: / / Uncat Mss Pix
Notes: *The Margo Jones Theatre Collection*

ACTORS AND ACTRESSES (cont.)

(75 linear ft) contains the office papers of this theatre: financial, business, legal records, scripts, programs, photos of productions, reviews and clippings, personal correspondence; organizational records. Gift of Dallas Civic Theatre, Inc, 1962 after theatre ceased operation. Described in LC card catalog MS 66-1622. Also *The W E Hill Theatre Collection,* 18th- 20th centuries, ca 75,000 items. Contains letters, portraits, and photos of leading American, British, and European dramatists, actors, managers, and other persons associated with the stage or the performing arts, particularly music; playbills, posters of stage plays, minstrel shows, and circuses; and newspaper and magazine clippings. The bulk of the collection consists of 19th and 20th century items. Described in LC card catalog MS 66-1621. Partiallydescribed in the "Fine Arts Department of the Dallas Public Library presents an exhibit of selected material from the W E Hill theatre collection on the occasion of the opening of the collection..." (1966). Gift of estate of William Ely Hill, 1963. Also *The John Rosenfield Collection* consisting of ca 2000 playbills assembled by this Amusements Critic of the *Dallas Morning News,* from both his travels and local productions. Also correspondence with various important artists in the theatre. There are also photographs, telegrams etc of these people. *The Dallas Little Theatre* Collection: consists of printed programs of this group which won the Belasco Cup three consecutive years in New York City; many clippings, photographs and other related newspaper articles. Oral histories are being assembled from persons connected with the theatre during its lifetimefrom 1922-1944.

TX —SOUTHERN METHODIST UNIVERSITY, Fondren Library, McCord Theater Collection, Room 301, Dallas, 75275. Edyth Renshaw, Cur; Linda Sellers, Pub Serv
Holdings: Vols (2000) Uncat Mss Pix Slides Phonorecords
Notes: See *Theatre Collections in Libraries and Museums*, Gilder and Freedley (Theatre Arts, 1936). The McCord Theatre Collection encompasses the entire spectrum of the performing arts. The central purpose is to gather records of our regional theater before such ephemeral material is lost. Records of over two hundred early Texas theaters, some fragmentary and some relatively complete, are in the files. These records incl photographs of buildings, stagehands, orchestras, and performers. Local theatre history incl the once famous Dallas Little Theatre and the Margo Jones Theatre. The national theatre, opera, ballet, and circus archives incl pictures (some autographed), programs, posters, throw-aways, tear sheets, clippings, and letters. Our international archives are small, but we have some excellent material, eg, artifacts from Max Reinhardt's production of"The Miracle" which happened to go bankrupt in Dallas. After a few years the items were given to us. There are posters, tear sheets, souvenir programs, and other colorful items from Morris Gest and the Artef Collection. We have about 200 19th century English playbills and a few from the 18th century. There is a collection of modern English, French, and other European programs, many of them illustrated souvenir programs. Also, magazines on theater, cinema, and television (1800). Scrapbooks covering both southwest and Dallas theater, 1890s-1950s. Special Collections: artifacts and documents on puppets; masks; costume design; circus; and ballet and dance. The Harriet Bacon MacDonald Collection of over 200 photographs of musicians appearing in Dallas during the first three decades of the 20th century. Many autographed. Affiliated with Meadow Theatre of the Arts.

TX —FORT WORTH PUBLIC LIBRARY, Arts Division, 300 Taylor St, Fort Worth, 76102. Heather Gobel, Head
Holdings: Pix
Notes: Photographs of concert artists appearing on Fort Worth stages (many are autographed). Nucleus collection from the estate of the late Mrs John F Lyons. Additions are made as performing artists make their appearances in this area.

VA —GEORGE MASON UNIVERSITY, Fenwick Library, Special Collections Dept, 4400 University Drive, Fairfax, 22030. Ruth Kerns, Public Services Librn
Notes: Some 275,000 items (incl administrative, play service and research, library and production records) pertaining to the WPA Federal Theatre Project, on permanent loan from the Library of Congress.

†WA —WASHINGTON STATE UNIVERSITY, Library, Manuscripts, Archives & Special Collections, Pullman, 99164. John F Guido, Head
Notes: The Robert Cushman Butler Collection of Theatrical Illustrations contains: approx 1600 illustrations, sheet music covers, programs and playbills; approx 100 mss of actors, actresses and playwrights; and approx 200 volumes of theatrical history and reminiscences, several extra-illustrated, concentrating on 18th-19th century British and American drama. A guide to the collection is in preparation.

WA —UNIVERSITY OF WASHINGTON LIBRARIES, Drama Library, BH-20, Seattle, 98195. Liz Fugate, Drama Librn
Holdings: Vols
Budget: ($13,182)
Notes: Collection incl history; criticism; costume; make-up; scene design; lighting; creative dramatics; children's theatre; directing; playwriting; acting. Special Collections include 19th century acting editions, contemporary acting editions and local theatre posters. 17,731 items cataloged, 24,255 uncataloged.

WA —GONZAGA UNIVERSITY, Crosby Library, East 502 Boone Ave, Spokane, 99258. Robert Burr, Dir
Notes: Books, records, memorabilia and papers, incl Jack Benny Radio Show scripts.

†WI —STATE HISTORICAL SOCIETY OF WISCONSIN, Library, 816 State St, Madison, 53706.
Notes: Papers, correspondence, production records, radio programs, columns, and other writings. Also films and other documentation of the Ed Sullivan Show.

ON —MCMASTER UNIVERSITY, Mills Memorial Library, Div of Archives & Research Collections, Hamilton, L8S 4L6, Can. G R Hill, Univ Librn
Holdings: Mss
Notes: Extensive correspondence with theatrical figures, such as Tyrone Guthrie and Jean Grascon, authors' scripts for stage plays, television, and radio work, prose works, and research notes on creative interests, and also on Artists Brief to Turgeon Committee which led to Canada Council. Collection described in *Library Research News*, vol 6, no 2, Fall 1982; vol 7, no 1, Spring 1983.

ON —NATIONAL FILM, TELEVISION AND SOUND ARCHIVES, Documentation & Public Service, 395 Wellington St, Ottawa, K1A 0N3, Can. Jana Vosikovska, Chief; Gloria Grant, Librn; Sylvie Robitaille, Stills and Posters Librn
Holdings: Vols (7000) Pix
Budget: ($35,000)
Notes: Several collections supporting the documentation on film, television and recorded sound: 1060 periodical titles (450 current), some on microfilm. Picture-stills, 265,000; moving picture posters, 6000; cataloged microfiche, 33,000 (vertical file material put on microfilm, then into a fiche format). Index cards (periodical references, credits): 334,000 cards (Film Title Index: 250,000 cards; Personalities Index: 84,000 cards).

ON —METROPOLITAN TORONTO LIBRARY, Theatre Dept, 789 Yonge St, Toronto, M4W 2G8, Can. Heather McCallum, Head
Holdings: Vols (30,500) Mss Pix Slides Phonorecords Microforms
Notes: Book

ACTORS AND ACTRESSES—PICTURES, ILLUSTRATIONS, ETC.

IN —INDIANA UNIVERSITY, Lilly Library, Seventh St, Bloomington, 47405. William R Cagle, Librn
Holdings: // Mss Pix
Notes: Photographs, etc, of actors and actresses are located in 5 ms collections: (1) Johnson, William Spencer, 1813-1897, printer. Correspondence and photographs from actors and actresses, 1846-1894. 129 items; (2) Stock, Keith Lievesley, 1911-, professor. Autographs, etc of people associated with 19th-early 20th century theatre in England. 279 items; (3) Woodward, Sidney C, journalist. Correspondence, autographs, and pictures, 1769-1961, of actors, actresses, and other theatre people, mostly American and British. 1235 items. (4) Ford, John, 1906-1976, motion picture director. Includes stills for most of the movies directed by Ford. (5) Welles, Orson, 1915- , actor, etc. Papers include photographs of theatre and radio personalities as well as movie stills. 2164 items. Also inPrinted Books Division: small pictures (largely engravings excerpted from books of Shakespearean actors and actresses, 18th into 20th century).

†WA —WASHINGTON STATE UNIVERSITY, Library, Manuscripts, Archives & Special Collections, Pullman, 99164. John F Guido, Head
Holdings: // Cat Mss Pix
Notes: The Robert Cushman Butler Collection of Theatrical Illustrations contains: approx 1600 illustrations, sheet music covers, programs and playbills; approx 100 mss of actors, actresses and playwrights; and approx 200 volumes of theatrical history and reminiscences, several extra-illustrated, concentrating on 18th-19th century British and American drama. A guide to the collection is in preparation.

ACTORS' REPERTORY THEATRE, SAN FRANCISCO

NY —NEW YORK PUBLIC LIBRARY, Performing Arts Research Center, Billy Rose Theatre Collection, 111 Amsterdam Ave, New York, 10023. Dorothy L Swerdlove, Cur
Holdings: Cat Mss Pix
Notes: Incl scripts, photographs, posters, scrapbooks, office files, other papers, and memorabilia relating to this company under the management of Herbert Blau and Jules Irving.

ACTRESSES—BIOGRAPHY see Actors and Actresses

ACTUARIAL SCIENCE

MA —MASSACHUSETTS MUTUAL LIFE INSURANCE CO, Library, 1295 State St, Springfield, 01111. Yvette Jensen, Librn
Holdings: Vols 1000 Cat

MI —UNIVERSITY OF MICHIGAN, Mathematics Library, 3027 Angell Hall, Ann Arbor, 48109. John W Weigel II, Physical Sciences Librn
Holdings: Vols 2000 Cat
Budget: $1300

RI —BRYANT COLLEGE, Edith M Hodgson Memorial Library, Rte 7, Douglas Pike, Smithfield, 02917. John P Hannon, Dir
Holdings: Vols (103,000) Cat Phonorecords Audiotapes Videotapes 16mm Films Filmstrips Microforms
Budget: ($175,000)
Notes: Incl 6000 bound periodical vols, 250 phonorecords, 220 audiotapes, 120 videotapes, 30 16mm films, 150 filmstrips and 7500 microforms.

MB —UNIVERSITY OF MANITOBA, Faculty of Administrative Studies, Administrative Studies Library, Winnipeg, R3T 2N2, Can. Judith Head, Librn
Holdings: Vols (15,000) Cat Microfiche
Notes: Actuarian science and management sciences; accounting; finance; public policy. Incl 11,000 microfiche, cataloged; annual reports of 800 companies.

ACULEATA see Ants; Bees and Beekeeping; Wasps

ACUPUNCTURE

NJ —PRINCETON UNIVERSITY, Library, Gest Oriental Library & East Asian

ACUPUNCTURE (cont.)

Collections, 317 Palmer Hall, Princeton, 08544. D E Perushek, Cur
Holdings: Vols (1700) Cat Mss Pix
Notes: All in Chinese. Collection emphasis is on pre-20th century works on traditional medicine in all areas. Contemporary works on acupuncture and materia medica are also acquired.

ADAGES see Aphorisms, Apothegms, Epigrams, Maxims, and Proverbs

ADAM, PAUL

MN —CARLETON COLLEGE LIBRARY, Northfield, 55057.
Holdings: Vols 7000 Cat
Notes: Books and periodicals relating to French literature of the second half of the 19th century, incl the French symbolist and decadent writers and critical works about them. Major writers are well represented as are some of the relatively minor figures, such as Paul Adam, Rene Boylesve, Abel Hermant, Pierre Louys, and others. The collection incl 69 plays written and produced in the period.

ADAMIC, LOUIS, 1899-1951

NJ —PRINCETON UNIVERSITY, Library, Manuscript Collection, Nassau St, Princeton, 08540. Jean F Preston, Cur
Holdings: Vols 800 Mss
Notes: The book collection incl the author's library; the author's papers fill 70 archival cartons.

ADAMS, ANSEL E., 1902-1984

AZ —UNIVERSITY OF ARIZONA, Center for Creative Photography, 843 E University Blvd, Tucson, 85721. James Enyeart, Dir; Terence Pitts, Cur and Librn
Notes: The archives, incl photographs, correspondence and mss of the famous American photographer, Ansel E Adams. The bequest announced on public radio, April 24, 1984, the day after his death.

CA —CALIFORNIA STATE UNIVERSITY, LONG BEACH, Library, Dept of Special Collections & Archives, 1250 Bellflower Blvd, Long Beach, 90840. John Ahouse, Special Collections Librn
Holdings: Vols 600
Notes: Libraries of Dr Fred Modern and photojournalist Richard Cross, and incl signed books and photographs of photographer Ansel Adams.

CA —UNIVERSITY OF CALIFORNIA, LOS ANGELES, Research Library, Dept of Special Collections, 405 Hilgard Ave, Los Angeles, 90024. Edward Shreeves, Chairman, Bibliographers Group; David S Zeidberg, Head
Holdings: Vols 40 Pix
Notes: Collection contains 40 books and 200 photographs, incl 170 photographs taken at US Relocation Camp, Manzanar, California, by Ansel Adams for the book, *Born Free and Equal.*

ADAMS, ARTHUR STANTON

DC —LIBRARY OF CONGRESS, Manuscript Division, Washington, 20540. John C Broderick, Chief
Holdings: 11,000 Items
Notes: Papers.

ADAMS, AUSTIN, AND FAMILY

IA —IOWA STATE UNIVERSITY, Library, Dept of Special Collections, Ames, 50011. Stanley M Yates, Head
Holdings: // Mss
Notes: Austin Adams Family Papers. Collection contains correspondence, diaries (1872-1874, 1900) notes, and lectures and essays of Mary Newbury Adams (1837-1901) and her husband, Austin Adams (1827-1890), lawyer and Iowa Supreme Court Justice, of Dubuque, Iowa. Contains references to Ralph Waldo Emerson and A Bronson Alcott (including letters from him). 2 linear feet. Finding aid available.

ADAMS, BROCK

WA —UNIVERSITY OF WASHINGTON LIBRARIES, Suzzallo Library, Manuscripts Section, FM-25, Seattle, 98195. Karyl Winn, Librn
Notes: Incl 350 linear feet, circa 1965-1976.

ADAMS, BROOKS

MA —HARVARD UNIVERSITY LIBRARY, Houghton Library, Cambridge, 02138. Rodney G Dennis, Cur of Manuscripts
Holdings: Cat Mss
Notes: Personal papers.

ADAMS, CYRUS HALL, III

IL —CHICAGO HISTORICAL SOCIETY, Library, Clark St at North Ave, Chicago, 60614. Archie Motley, Manuscript Librn
Notes: Papers.
See also entry under education-illinois.

ADAMS, EPHRAIM

IA —STATE HISTORICAL SOCIETY OF IOWA LIBRARY, 402 Iowa Ave, Iowa City, 52240. Darold J Brown, Librn
Holdings: Cat
Notes: Thousands of individual items and smaller collections. Two hundred larger collections incl the papers of Cyrus C Carpenter, Jonathan P Dolliver, Gilbert Haugen, W W Waymack, Ephraim Adams, A C Dodge, Dorothy Houghton, Jesse Macy, Agnes Samuelson, Donald Johnson, Jack Miller, Ruth Sayre, Samuel Kirkwood, Thomas McKnight, Robert Lucas, Dwight McCarty, William Larrabee. Includes church, school, company and organization records, Civil War materials.

ADAMS, FRANKLIN P. (FPA)

NY —HAMPDEN-BOOTH THEATRE LIBRARY AT THE PLAYERS, 16 Gramercy Park, New York, 10003. Louis A Rachow, Librn/Cur
Holdings: Uncat Mss
Notes: The Newman Levy Collection, incl his correspondence, research notes, 100 typescripts of short stories, plays, and poems, with holograph corrections and additions; original typescript of an unpublished biography of Franklin P Adams by Levy with extensive holograph corrections and additions. Three feet of indexed material. Described in *Theatre & Performing Arts Collections* (New York: Haworth Press, 1981).

ADAMS, HARRIET CHALMERS

CA —STOCKTON-SAN JOAQUIN COUNTY PUBLIC LIBRARY, California Reference Room, 605 N El Dorado St, Stockton, 95202.
Holdings: Vols 650 // Cat
Notes: Collection consists of personal library of Harriet Chalmers Adams, approx 600 titles, interfiled in the general collection. Incl are fiction, languages, literature, history, science. Particularly valuable are the travel and geography materials, with emphasis on the areas Adams explored. Most important are the scrapbooks which Adams compiled on her life, and copies of her books and periodical articles, which are in the California Reference Rm.

ADAMS, HENRY

MA —HARVARD UNIVERSITY LIBRARY, Houghton Library, Cambridge, 02138. Rodney G Dennis, Cur of Manuscripts
Holdings: Cat Mss

VA —UNIVERSITY OF VIRGINIA, Alderman Library, Clifton Waller Barrett Collection, Charlottesville, 22901. Joan St C Crane, Cur of American Literature Collections
Notes: Papers.

ADAMS, HERBERT BAXTER

MD —JOHNS HOPKINS UNIVERSITY, Milton S Eisenhower Library, Charles & 34 Sts, Baltimore, 21218. Ann S Gwyn, Assistant Dir for Special Collections
Holdings: Cat Mss
Notes: Ms autobiography, lectures, articles, and letters. Some 6000 pieces.

ADAMS, JOEY

MA —BOSTON UNIVERSITY, Mugar Memorial Library, Special Collections Dept, 771 Commonwealth Ave, Boston, 02215. Howard B Gotlieb, Dir
Holdings: Cat Mss Pix
Notes: Mss, correspondence, etc collected in depth; incl publications by or about.

ADAMS, JOHN

MI —NORTHERN MICHIGAN UNIVERSITY, Lydia M Olson Library, Elizabeth L Harden Drive, Marquette, 49855. Stephen H Peters, Cataloger
Notes: A major section of the personal library of Moses Coit Tyler. Strong in the Colonial and Early National periods. Includes biographies and published letters and writings of such figures as Benjamin Franklin, John Adams, John Jay, Thomas Jefferson, Charles Sumner.

ADAMS, JOHN QUINCY

NY —NEW YORK HISTORICAL SOCIETY, Library, 170 Central Park W, New York, 10024. James Gregory, Librn
Notes: Miscellaneous papers, correspondence, etc.

RI —BROWN UNIVERSITY, John Hay Library, 20 Prospect St, Providence, 02912. Mark N Brown, Cur Mss
Holdings: // Mss
Notes: Within the Jonathan Russell Manuscript Collection are found about 120 letters exchanged with Jonathan Russell for the period 1798-1823. See entry for Jonathan Russell for fuller description.

ADAMS, ROGER

IL —UNIVERSITY OF ILLINOIS, URBANA/CHAMPAIGN, Library, University Archives, 19 Library, 1408 W Gregory Drive, Urbana, 61801. Maynard Brichford, University Archivist
Holdings: Cat Mss Maps Pix Slides Microforms
Notes: Papers, archival records, etc.

ADAMS, SAMUEL

NY —NEW YORK PUBLIC LIBRARY, Rare Books and Manuscripts Div, Fifth Ave & 42 St, New York, 10018. William L Joyce, Asst Dir; Susan E Davis, Cur of Mss
Holdings: Mss
Budget: ($7161)
Notes: Incl personal mss, papers etc.

ADAMS, SHERMAN

NH —DARTMOUTH COLLEGE, Baker Memorial Library, Hanover, 03755.
Holdings: Cat Mss
Notes: His papers.

ADAMS, WILLIAM TAYLOR

MA —BRANDEIS UNIVERSITY, Goldfarb Library, 415 South St, Waltham, 02154. Bessie Hahn, Dir
Notes: Dime Novel and Juvenile Literature Collection. Over 1000 dime novels, an extensive collection of the works of Horatio Alger, Harry Castlemon, Oliver Optic and other boys and girls literature of the 19th and early 20th century. Access to this collection is through the card catalog in Special Collections.

ADAMS FAMILY

CA —AZUSA PACIFIC COLLEGE, Marshburn Memorial Library, Citrus &

ADAMS FAMILY (cont.)

Alosta, Azusa, 91702. Edward Peterman, Librn
Holdings: Vols (331) // Uncat
Notes: The Irving Stone Collection of Lincolniana. Books used by Irving Stone in the prepartion of his bestselling novel *Love is Eternal* (Lincoln). The books are signed by Stone; many contain his editorial comments. Also, his collection for *Those Who Love* (John and Abigail Adams). No photocopying.

CT —UNIVERSITY OF CONNECTICUT, Library, Storrs, 06268. R H Schimmelpfeng, Dir of Special Collections
Holdings: Vols 4600 // Uncat Mss Maps
Notes: The library of Pierce Welch Gaines of Federalist material, chiefly contempory books and mss. Emphasis on Washington, Jefferson and Adams.

MA —MASSACHUSETTS HISTORICAL SOCIETY LIBRARY, 1154 Boylston St, Boston, 02215. John D Cushing, Librn
Holdings: Mss Maps Microforms
Notes: One of more than 5000 individual collections in the Library, this collection incl the Adams Family papers and materials relating to Massachusetts and New England. The Library's collection of mss has been cataloged and issued in nine folio vols by G K Hall & Co of Boston. It is widely distributed throughout the United States and Europe.

ADANSON, MICHEL, 1727-1806

PA —HUNT INSTITUTE FOR BOTANICAL DOCUMENTATION, Hunt Botanical Library, Michel Adanson Library, Carnegie-Mellon University, Pittsburgh, 15213. Bernadette G Callery, Librn
Holdings: Vols 390 // Cat Mss Pix
Notes: Extensively annotated personal library including manuscripts and corrected copies of his own works. Also his collection of more than 10,000 illustrations clipped from publications of his day and bearing his identifications and notes. 260 holographic letters. Collection described in *Adanson, the Bicentennial of Michel Adanson's Famille des Plantes* (Pittsburgh: Hunt Botanical Library, 1963).

ADDAMS, JANE

CO —UNIVERSITY OF COLORADO, Libraries, Western Historical Collections, Boulder, 80309.
Holdings: Cat Mss
Notes: The Women's International League for Peace and Freedom Papers consist mostly of correspondence and reports between its Geneva headquarters and its national affiliates in Europe and the Americas. While the letters in this collection come from many countries, most are written in English. The WILPF, an activist women's group founded in 1915 by America's Jane Addams and European leaders, is concerned with modifying public policy and attitudes toward war and other conditions which are detrimental to human welfare. 115 boxes. A printed guide is available.

MA —RADCLIFFE COLLEGE, Arthur & Elizabeth Schlesinger Library on the History of Women in America, 3 James St, Cambridge, 02138. Patricia Miller King, Dir; Eva Moseley, Cur of Mss
Holdings: Cat Mss Microforms
Notes: A few personal papers and mss, many in microform. (Main Jane Addams collections at University of Illinois at Chicago Circle and at Swarthmore College).

PA —SWARTHMORE COLLEGE, Peace Collection, Swarthmore, 19081. Jean R Soderlund, Cur of Peace Collection
Holdings: Vols (10,000) Cat Mss Pix Microforms
Notes: The Peace Collection originated in 1930 when Jane Addams (1860-1935), social worker, feminist, and Nobel laureate in peace gave her papers and some 500 books to Swarthmore College. Supplementary accessions have been received since that time. The bulk of the collections of correspondence (1873-1935), Rockford Seminary notebooks, diary calendars, and manuscripts and published materials by and about Jane Addams.
See also entry under Pacifism - History.

ADDICTION, DRUG see Drug Habit

ADDING MACHINES see Calculating Machines

ADE, GEORGE

IL —NEWBERRY LIBRARY, 60 W Walton St, Chicago, 60610. Diana Haskell, Cur of Modern Mss
Holdings: Cat Mss Pix
Notes: Incl books, mss, clippings by and about him. About 1600 items.

IN —PURDUE UNIVERSITY LIBRARIES, Special Collections Dept, West Lafayette, 47907. Keith Dowden, Asst Dir, Special Collections
Holdings: Vols 1140 // Cat Mss Pix
Notes: His collection of 20th century English and American literature.

KY —UNIVERSITY OF LOUISVILLE, Ekstrom Library, Rare Books & Special Collections, 2301 S Third St, Louisville, 40208. George T McWhorter, Cur; Delinda Stephens Buie, Asst Cur

†MA —WILLIAMS COLLEGE, Chapin Library of Rare Books, PO Box 426, Williamstown, 01267. Robert L Volz, Custodian
Holdings: Vols 53 Cat
Notes: The Sprague Collection, Editions, inscribed copies, ephemerra, etc. No ILL.

ADHESIVES AND ADHESION

CA —AVERY INTERNATIONAL CORP, Information Center, 325 N Altadena Dr, Pasadena, 91107. Louanne A Kalvinskas, Information Specialist
Holdings: Vols 800 Cat
Notes: Also many reports.

CA —UNIVERSITY OF CALIFORNIA, RICHMOND, Forest Products Library, 1301 S 46th St, Richmond, 94804. Peter A Evans, Librn
Holdings: Vols (8000) Cat Maps Audiotapes Microforms
Notes: Areas of strength are pulp and paper, physical properties of wood, seasoning, wood preservation, wood extractives chemistry, adhesion and adhesives.

SC —SONOCO PRODUCTS CO, Research Laboratory, Technical Information Center, One N Second St, Hartsville, 29550. Ken Chavis, Dir
Holdings: Vols (4000) Cat Mss Slides Microforms
Notes: Restricted to Sonoco employees. No photocopying.

ADIASPIROMYCOSIS

OH —MIAMI UNIVERSITY, Science Library, Oxford, 45056.
Notes: Zoonoses and related diseases. Collection partially transferred from Parker-Davis Memorial Library, Hamilton, Mont.

ADIRONDACK MOUNTAINS

NY —ADIRONDACK HISTORICAL ASSOCIATION, Museum Library, Blue Mountain Lake, 12812. Jerold Pepper, Librn
Holdings: Vols (7500) Cat Mss Maps Pix Phonorecords Audiotapes 16mm Films Microforms
Notes: Anything about the Adirondacks--history, people, economics, places, things. Strong in Adirondack art, outdoor recreation, logging, small boats. Resources incl more than 1000 maps, 40,000 pictures, 1600 microfilm reels, 576 linear ft of ms material, and 12 cabinets of VF ephemera, etc.

NY —SAINT LAWRENCE UNIVERSITY, Owen D Young Library, Canton, 13617. Mahlon Peterson, Librn
Holdings: Cat Mss Pix
Notes: Northern New York and the Adirondacks. 900 items, incl books.

NY —STATE UNIVERSITY OF NEW YORK, COLLEGE AT PLATTSBURGH, Feinberg Library, Special Collections, 153 Hawkins Hall, Plattsburgh, 12901. Joseph G Swinyer, Librn
Holdings: Vols (1000) Cat Mss Maps Pix Phonorecords Microforms
See also entry under New York (State) - History

†NY —UNION COLLEGE, Adirondack Research Center, Schenectady, 12308.
Notes: Books, periodicals, maps, and historical and political records of the Adirondack Park area.

ADLER, ALFRED, 1870-1937

DC —LIBRARY OF CONGRESS, Manuscript Division, Washington, 20540. John C Broderick, Chief
Holdings: Cat Mss Pix
Notes: The papers of Alfred Adler, incl a number of professional studies; a selection of letters by him (1891-1937); documents, photographs, etc.

ADLER, ELMER, 1884-1962

NJ —PRINCETON UNIVERSITY, Library, Manuscript Collection, Nassau St, Princeton, 08540. Jean F Preston, Cur
Holdings: Vols Mss
Notes: The mss, consisting largely of the working papers of Pynson Printers, are housed in over 150 archival cartons.

ADLER, FELIX, 1851-1933

†NY —COLUMBIA UNIVERSITY LIBRARIES, Butler Library, Rare Book and Manuscript Library, 535 W 114 St, New York, 10027.
Notes: Papers, correspondence, etc.

SC —COLLEGE OF CHARLESTON LIBRARY, Special Collections Dept, Charleston, 29401.
Notes: Correspondence within the Lancelot Minor Harris Papers.

ADMINISTRATION see Civil Service; Management; Political Science

ADMINISTRATION, PUBLIC see Public Administration

ADOLESCENCE

CA —LOS ANGELES PUBLIC LIBRARY, Social Sciences Dept, 630 W Fifth St, Los Angeles, 90071. Marilyn C Wherley, Principal Librn
Holdings: Vols (3000) Cat Microforms
Budget: ($150,000)
Notes: Over 500 bound periodicals. Collection also incl government publicatons, agency reports, statistics, yearbooks, directories, pamphlets, bibliographies, child and adolescent psychology theories and history, college catalogs on microfiche, and nearly complete collection of California catalogs.

IL —JACKSONVILLE STATE HOSPITAL, Training & Research Library, 1201 S Main St, Jacksonville, 62650. Lois E Wells, Librn
Notes: Concerned particularly with developmental disabilities.

KS —JOHNSON COUNTY MENTAL HEALTH CENTER, John R Keach Memorial Library, 6000 Lamar Ave, Mission, 66202. Krista Hilton-Ross, Librn
Holdings: Vols (10,000) Cat Mss

NY —BANK STREET COLLEGE OF EDUCATION LIBRARY, 610 W 112 St, New York, 10025. Eleanor Kule Seid, Library Dir
Holdings: Vols (90,000) Cat Microforms
Notes: Education, guidance, psychology, educational psychology, curricula, textbooks, Black Studies, etc. All subjects are integrated in one professional collection; in addition there are two separately cataloged and shelved collections: Children's and Elementary Curriculum Materials.

TN —GEORGE PEABODY COLLEGE FOR TEACHERS, Education Library, Science

ADOLESCENCE (cont.)

Library, Peabody College, Box 325, Nashville, 32703. Mary Beth Blalock, Librn
Holdings: Vols (25,148) Cat Slides Audiotapes
Budget: ($7000)
Notes: Incl collection of adolescent and children's literature. There are separate catalogs for this collection and the library science collection.

ADOPTION

NJ —NEW JERSEY HISTORICAL SOCIETY, Library and Museum, 230 Broadway, Newark, 07104. Joan C Hull, Exec Dir; Barbara S Irwin, Library Dir; Alan R Fraser, Cur
Budget: ($100,000)
Notes: Records of eight Newark orphanages and child service organizations dating back to 1847. Incl records, casebooks, registers, adoption contracts, minutes of meetings, financial and administrative records, case studies by student interns in social work, and related printed materials.

ADRIAN, (GILBERT A.)

CA —LOS ANGELES PUBLIC LIBRARY, Frances Howard Goldwyn Hollywood Regional Library, 1623 Ivar Ave, Los Angeles, 90028. Sally Dumaux, Librn
Holdings: Vols (100,000) Cat Mss Pix VF
Budget: ($60,000)
Notes: A general and a research collection covering motion pictures, radio broadcasting, and television. Over 2000 motion picture and television scripts. Biographical information on actors and actresses. Casts, credits, and other production information on over 1500 motion pictures from the 1920s to the present. Collections also include posters, lobby cards, souvenir programs, scrapbooks, vertical files, and over 3000 publicity stills. Including the following Special Collections: Fred Archer Collection, photographs, including the Hunchback of Notre Dame (1923), and personalities of the stage and screen, 1907-1930; Gilbert A Adrian, designer, sketches and photographs; Hazel Flynn, publicist, correspondence and photographs.

ADSORBENTS

NJ —WITCO CHEMICAL CORP, Corporate Research Center Library, 100 Bauer Dr, Oakland, 07436. Jo Therese Smith, Mgr, Information Services
Holdings: Vols (18,000) Cat
Budget: ($60,000)

ADULT EDUCATION

MA —MOUNT AUBURN HOSPITAL, Health Sciences Library, 330 Mount Auburn St, Cambridge, 02138. Cherie Haitz, Librn
Holdings: Vols (3000) Cat Audiotapes Videotapes
Notes: Incl 300 periodical subscriptions.

NY —GIRL SCOUTS OF THE USA, Library Archives, 830 Third Ave, New York, 10022.
Holdings: Vols (3000)
Budget: ($2000)
Notes: Emphasis on adult education. No photocopying.

NY —NEW YORK PUBLIC LIBRARY, Research Libraries, General Research Division, Fifth Ave & 42 St, New York, 10018. Rodney Phillips, Chief
Holdings: Vols (2,225,000) Cat Maps Pix Microforms
Budget: ($775,718)

NY —SYRACUSE UNIVERSITY LIBRARIES, Ernest S Bird Library, George Arents Research Library for Special Collections, Syracuse, 13210. Carolyn A Davis, Manuscripts Librn; Amy S Doherty, University Archivist; Mark F Weimer, Rare Book Librn
Notes: Records of the National Association of Public School Adult Educators. Papers 1934-64 (3 linear feet).

PA —CARLOW COLLEGE, Grace Library, Fifth Ave, Pittsburgh, 15213. Joan M Mitchell, Dir of Library Services
Holdings: Vols (252) Cat
Budget: ($300)
Notes: The Career Resources Center consists of career and counseling materials for college students with special emphasis on the career guidance needs of the Continuing Education Student.

VT —FLETCHER FREE LIBRARY, 235 College St, Burlington, 05401. Maxie Ewins, Librn
Holdings: Vols 1200 Cat Maps Pix
Notes: Concentration on Burlington, Vermont. Complete run of Burlington City Reports, from 1860. Limited genealogies.

BC —VANCOUVER COMMUNITY COLLEGE, King Edward Campus Library, 1155 E Broadway, PO Box 24620, Station C, Vancouver, V6B 4H2, Can. Paul Cook, Campus Librn
Holdings: Vols (25,000) Cat Maps Slides Audiotapes 16mm Films Filmstrips
Notes: Teaching English as a second language. Curriculum development.

ON —CANADA, DEPT OF EMPLOYMENT & IMMIGRATION LIBRARY, Ottawa, K1A 0J9, Can. P E Sunder-Raj, Dir Library Services
Holdings: Vols (35,000) Cat Microforms
Notes: In addition to cataloged material, library has approximately 1800 current journals and serials. We have holdings of selected ERIC documents on microfiche.

ADVANCED MATERIALS see Materials, Advanced

ADVENT

MI —ANDREWS UNIVERSITY, James White Library, Berrien Springs, 49104. Marley H Soper, Dir
Holdings: Cat Mss Pix
Notes: Advent Source Collection. Deals with prophecy of the Bible and the Advent hope in historical context. About 3700 items. Materials gathered by Dr L R Froom in the preparation of his four-volume set entitled *Prophetic Faith of Our Fathers*, ca 1946-1954. Not available by interlibrary loan, but may be used at this library.

ADVENT CHRISTIAN CHURCH AND ADVENTIST MOVEMENT

IL —AURORA COLLEGE, Library, 347 Gladstone Ave, Aurora, 60506. Mary M Howrey, Library Dir
Holdings: Vols 2260 Cat Mss Pix Microforms
Notes: The Orrin Roe Jenks Memorial Collection of Adventual Materials. The Millerite Movement is incl in the cataloged materials of the Jenks Memorial Collection of Adventual Materials. The papers of William Miller, 1782-1849, correspondence, sermon notes, date books, personal affidavits are housed as a unit. Also, Dr Jenks assembled a collection of writings relating to the history and theology of the Adventist Christian Church. There is a separate card catalog for the books; some archival materials, reports, and minutes of organizations are in files. Also have Prophetic Charts.

ADVENT MUSIC

MI —ANDREWS UNIVERSITY, James White Library, Berrien Springs, 49104. Marley H Soper, Dir
Holdings: Vols 110 // Cat
Notes: Hymns of the Seventh-Day Adventist faith. The collection begins with the 1840 edition of the hymnal and continues to the present. Not available by interlibrary loan, but may be used at this library.

ADVENTURE AND ADVENTURERS

†MD —UNIVERSITY OF MARYLAND, BALTIMORE COUNTY, Library, Baltimore, 21228. Maureen Dwyer-Hirten, Librn
Notes: 4000 detective and adventure pulps and 500 TV scripts.

MN —UNIVERSITY OF MINNESOTA, James Ford Bell Library, 309 19th Ave S, Minneapolis, 55455. John Parker, Cur
Notes: Collection of original materials relating to European expansion, 1400-1800.

NY —AMERICAN MUSEUM OF NATURAL HISTORY, Library Services Dept, Central Park W & 79th St, New York, 10024. Nina J Root, Chairwoman; Mary Genett, Asst Librn for Reference Services
Holdings: Vols (385,000) Cat Mss Maps Pix Slides Microforms
Notes: Nearly all collections are outstanding for depth of coverage and international range. Early and historic works, rare books, colored illustrations, and relevant serial publications supplement to the modern scientific publications necessary to the researches of the scientific staff and the work of the educational division. Open to the public.

NY —EXPLORERS CLUB, James B Ford Memorial Library, 46 E 70 St, New York, 10021. Janet Baldwin, Librn
Holdings: Vols (24,000) Cat Maps
Notes: Additions to the collection depend upon gifts. Access by appointment only.

TX —TEXAS A&M UNIVERSITY, Sterling C Evans Library, Special Collections Div, College Station, 77843. Donald H Dyal, Librn
Holdings: Vols (16,000) Mss Pix
Notes: Jeff Dykes Range Livestock Collection (incl a 600-item collection of J Frank Dobie works). Part of the Dobie Collection is described in Dykes, Jeff C *My Dobie Collection* (College Station, Tex: Friends of the Texas A&M University Library).

ADVERTISING

IL —BURSON-MARSTELLER LIBRARY, Information Services, One E Wacker Dr, Chicago, 60601. Ellen Steininger, Librn
Holdings: Vols 5000
Notes: Incl 10,000 pictures, 1200 serial titles.

IL —J WALTER THOMPSON CO, Information Center, 875 N Michigan Ave, Chicago, 60611. Edward G Strable, Dir
Holdings: Vols 500 Cat Microforms
Notes: Books are not an important part of this collection. Data files of ephemeral material-clippings, studies, reports, releases-of approx 25 drawers are what make this a special collection. In addition, collection of print advertisements from past 18 years (1, 000,000 items) but some as early as 1902, with emphasis on consumer products. Indexing and organization make for immediate access.

IL —UNIVERSITY OF ILLINOIS, URBANA/CHAMPAIGN, Library, Communications Library, 122 Gregory Hall, Urbana, 61801. Nancy Allen, Librn
Holdings: Vols (18,000) Cat
Budget: ($27,000)
Notes: Advertising history theory and skills. Also recently acquired D'Arcy, MacManus, and Masius Collection of Advertisements, 1890-1960.

MI —D'ARCY, MACMANUS, MASIUS, Library Information Center, 1725 N Woodward, PO Box 811, Bloomfield Hills, 48303. Lois W Collet, Dir, Library Information Services; Harriet Siden, Art Librn
Holdings: Vols 5000 Cat Mss Pix Microforms

MI —CAMPBELL-EWALD CO, Reference Center, 30400 Van Dyke, Warren, 48093. Susan Stepek, Mgr
Holdings: Vols 825 Cat Pix
Notes: Bound advertising trade publications, books and yearbooks. 70 vertical file drawers of clippings and pamphlets, most categories from 1924. Incl pictorials and visuals, sales promotion. Current advertising and marketing periodicals.

NY —BROOKLYN PUBLIC LIBRARY, Business Library, 280 Cadman Plaza W,

ADVERTISING (cont.)

Brooklyn, 11201. Sylvia Mechanic, Business Librn
Holdings: Vols (107,000) Cat
Notes: Library received about 1800 periodicals, 3000 serials, 2700 directories, 1600 telephone books from all over the world with a complete back file on microfilm for greater New York. Library is a selective US Government Documents depository. Subscribes to microfiche SEC 10K reports for AMEX, NYSE and OTC from 1976 to date; annual reports for earlier years. Transnational annual reports, on fiche from 1982-to date. 78 vertical file trays; Sanborn maps for Brooklyn, special collection of corporation histories. Publish monthly newsletter, *Service to Business and Industry* with our Science Division.

NY —ADVERTISING RESEARCH FOUNDATION, Information Center, 3 E 54 St, New York, 10022. Elizabeth R Proudfit, Mgr
Holdings: Vols (3000) Cat

NY —ASSOCIATION OF NATIONAL ADVERTISERS, Information Center, 155 E 44 St, New York, 10017. Rosemary Collins, Librn
Holdings: Vols 1500 Cat
Notes: Main collection is vertical files of clippings and speeches--250 drawers.

NY —BERNARD M BARUCH COLLEGE (CUNY), Library, 156 E 25 St, New York, 10010. Alan Weiner, Head of Reference

NY —NEW YORK PUBLIC LIBRARY, Research Libraries, Economic & Public Affairs Div, Fifth Ave & 42 St, New York, 10018. Edward DiRoma, Chief
Holdings: Vols (1,500,000) Cat Microforms
Notes: Strong in history of advertising, advertising periodicals.

NY —NEW YORK PUBLIC LIBRARY, Research Libraries, General Research Div, Fifth Ave & 42 St, New York, 10018. Keith McKinney, Assistant Div Chief
Holdings: Cat
Notes: Current periodicals. Subjects incl advertising, business and professional periodicals, international affairs, labor and trade unions, political and social sciences, humanities in general. Division holds 10,000 titles. Incl little magazines.

NC —GREENSBORO PUBLIC LIBRARY, Business Library, 201 Greene St, Drawer X-4, Greensboro, 27402. Lebby B Lamb, Business Librn
Holdings: Vols (6000) Cat Microforms
Budget: ($12,000)

OH —OHIO STATE UNIVERSITY, Library for Communication and Graphic Arts, 242 W 18th St, Columbus, 43210. Lucy S Caswell, Curator
Notes: Library will receive collection of materials on this subject at a future date.

OR —BASSIST COLLEGE LIBRARY, 2000 SW Fifth Ave, Portland, 97201. Norma Bassist, Librn
Holdings: Vols 350 Cat Mss Pix Slides
Notes: Incl general texts, but specializes in fashion and interiors-oriented material.

VA —AMERICAN NEWSPAPER PUBLISHERS ASSOCIATION, ANPA, Library, 11600 Sunrise Valley Dr, Reston, (Mailing add: PO Box 17407, Dulles Intl AP, Washington, DC, 20041). Yvonne Egertson, Librn

WI —STATE HISTORICAL SOCIETY OF WISCONSIN, Archives, 816 State St, Madison, 53706. Harold L Miller, Reference Archivist
Holdings: Mss Pix Films Microforms
Notes: Areas represented in collection incl radio, television, the press, public relations and advertising. Emphasis is on development of media in the 20th century; materials are mainly professional papers of individuals or organization or organizational records of firms or associations in the media. Collections are described in *Sources for Mass Communications, Film and Theater Research: A Guide,* (1982) and in current accession notes in the *Wisconsin Magazine of History.* Major collections are also listed in Hamer, *Guide to Manuscripts and Archives in the United States,* (1961) and in the *National Union Catalog of Manuscripts Collections,* (1959-date). Also incl, disc recordings and tape recordings.

WI —UNIVERSITY OF WISCONSIN, MADISON, Journalism Reading Room (Nieman-Grant), (formerly Bleyer Memorial Reading Room, School of Journalism), Vilas Communication Hall, Rm 2130, Madison, 53706. Arthur Cran, Librn; Mary Nagel, Asst Librn
Holdings: Vols 750 Cat
Budget: ($500)

AB —SOUTHERN ALBERTA INSTITUTE OF TECHNOLOGY, Learning Resources Centre, 1301 16 Ave NW, Calgary, T2M 0L4, Can. Tom Skinner, Historian
Holdings: Vols (7000) Cat Pix Slides Films Audiotapes Filmstrips Videotapes
Notes: Serves Alberta College of Art (4-year professional course).

ADVERTISING—DRUG TRADE

IN —MILES LABORATORIES, Library Resources and Services, 1127 Myrtle St, PO Box 40, Elkhart, 46515. Allam Hagopian, Mgr
Holdings: Vols (16,500) Cat Audiotapes Microforms
Notes: Incl files of pharmaceutical product advertising pieces, extensive literature files on company related drugs; domestic and international marketing files. 32,000 bound periodicals.

ADVERTISING—HISTORY

IL —J WALTER THOMPSON CO, Information Center, 875 N Michigan Ave, Chicago, 60611. Edward G Strable, Dir
Holdings: Vols 50 Cat Microforms
Notes: Books are not an important part of this collection. Data files of ephemeral material-clippings, studies, reports, releases-of approx 25 drawers are what make this a special collection. In addition, collection of print advertisements from past 18 years (1, 000,000 items) but some as early as 1902, with emphasis on consumer products. Indexing and organization make for immediate access.

IN —INDIANA UNIVERSITY, Lilly Library, Seventh St, Bloomington, 47405. William R Cagle, Librn
Holdings: Vols 335 / / Cat Mss Pix
Notes: Street cries, chiefly from the Virginia Warren Collection. Limited photocopying.

NC —DUKE UNIVERSITY, William R Perkins Library, Manuscript Dept, Durham, 27706. Ellen Gartrell, Cur of Mss
Notes: Incl 6000 printed items (trade cards, pamphlets, leaflets, broadsides, etc), mainly from US 19th-20th centuries. Also hundreds of tobacco premiums and advertising devices, 1880s.

WI —STATE HISTORICAL SOCIETY OF WISCONSIN, Archives, 816 State St, Madison, 53706. Harold L Miller, Reference Archivist
Holdings: Cat Mss Pix Microforms
Notes: Areas represented in collection incl radio, television, the press, public relations, advertising, motion pictures, theatre; emphasis on development of media in 20th century; materials are mainly professional papers of individuals or organizational records of firms, or associations in the media. Also incl disc recordings, tape recordings, newsfilms.

ADVERTISING—PHARMACEUTICALS

IN —MILES LABORATORIES, Library Resources and Services, 1127 Myrtle St, PO Box 40, Elkhart, 46515. Allam Hagopian, Mgr
Holdings: Vols (16,500) Cat Audiotapes Microforms
Notes: Incl files of pharmaceutical product advertising pieces, extensive literature files on company related drugs; domestic and international marketing files. 32,000 bound periodicals.

ADVERTISING—RETAIL TRADE see Advertising

ADVERTISING, ART IN see Commercial Art

ADVERTISING, CONSUMER see Advertising

ADVERTISING, DIRECT MAIL

NY —DIRECT MAIL/MARKETING ASSOCIATION, Information Central, 6 E 43 St, New York, 10017. Glenda Sasho, Dir of Information Central & Research
Holdings: Vols (350) Cat Slides Audiotapes
Notes: Slide/tape presentations of award-winning advertising direct marketing advertising campaigns. Incl 3000 award portfolios of direct marketing campaigns. Restricted use.

ADVERTISING, OUTDOOR

NJ —FAIRLEIGH DICKINSON UNIVERSITY, Friendship Library, 285 Madison Ave, Madison, 07940. James Fraser, Library Dir; Renee Weber, Cur
Holdings: Vols 1200 Cat Mss Pix Slides Phonorecords 16mm Films
Notes: Official depository for the Outdoor Advertising industry. Collection initiated in August 1972. About 100,000 items. It is the concern of the Outdoor Advertising Association of America that this collection become the definitive collection on the industry in this country. Incl 20,000 mss, 10, 000 pictures, 30,000 slides. 15 original billboards.

ADVERTISING, PICTORIAL see Commercial Art; Posters—Collections

ADVERTISING, RADIO see Radio Advertising

ADVERTISING, RETAIL see Advertising

ADVERTISING, TELEVISION see Television Advertising

ADVERTISING, TRANSPORTATION see Advertising Cards

ADVERTISING ART see Commercial Art

ADVERTISING CARDS

CT —YALE UNIVERSITY, Box 1603A, Yale Station, New Haven, 06520.
Holdings: Cat Mss Pix
Notes: Graphic arts. A collection of 19th century advertising art, incl trade cards, cards of special interest, books and miscellaneous maps; also vols on the history of 18th and 19th century trade cards and scrapbooks filled with mounted cards.

IL —CHICAGO HISTORICAL SOCIETY, Library, Clark St at North Ave, Chicago, 60614. Robert L Brubaker, Librn
Holdings: Cat Pix
Notes: 6000 advertising cards.

MA —AMERICAN ANTIQUARIAN SOCIETY LIBRARY, 185 Salisbury St, Worcester, 01609. Marcus A McCorison, Dir & Librn
Holdings: Cat Maps Pix
Notes: Over 6000 American prints, arranged by lithographer. Incl political caricatures and cartoons, maps, sheet music. Also advertising cards, Valentines, etc.

ADVERTISING CATALOGS see Catalogs, Commercial

AEBERSOLD, PAUL C.

TX —TEXAS A&M UNIVERSITY, Sterling C Evans Library, University Archives, College Station, 77843. Charles R Schultz, University Archivist
Notes: The Archives of Southwestern Technology: Papers of nuclear physicist Paul C Aebersold, 1933-1965.

AEGEAN ARCHAEOLOGY

PA —BRYN MAWR COLLEGE, Canaday Library, Bryn Mawr, 19010. James Tanis, Dir
Notes: Classical and Near Eastern archaeology, Greek architecture and sculpture; Anatolian and Aegean Archaeology. In Art and Archaeology Library.

AEGEAN AREA

†MA —UNIVERSITY OF MASSACHUSETTS AT AMHERST,

AEGEAN AREA (cont.)

Library, Amherst, 01003.
Notes: Classical art and archaeology. Special emphasis: Aegean area.

AERIAL LAW see Aeronautics—Laws and Legislation

AERIAL PHOTOGRAPHY see Photography, Aerial

AERIAL ROCKETS see Rockets and Rocketry—History

AERO CLUB OF ILLINOIS

IL —CHICAGO HISTORICAL SOCIETY, Library, Clark St at North Ave, Chicago, 60614. Archie Motley, Manuscript Librn
Notes: Papers of aviation promoters.

AERODROMES see Airports

AERODYNAMICS

FL —EMBRY-RIDDLE AERONAUTICAL UNIVERSITY, Regional Airport, Daytona Beach, 32014. M Judy Luther, Dir of Learning Resources

OH —PREFORMED LINE PRODUCTS CO, Research & Engineering Library, 660 Beta Drive, Mayfield Village, (Mailing add: PO Box 91129, Cleveland, 44101). Edwina T Barron, Librn
Holdings: Vols (11,500) Cat Mss Pix Microfiche VF
Budget: ($30,500)
Notes: Library covering research and engineering fields emphasizing this subject. Aerodynamic characteristics and electrical characteristics of power cables, communication cables (including fiber optics), cable support systems, as well as associated fittings and hardware; in service behavior of manufactured products and materials as it relates to its static and dynamic forces and environmental conditions; oceanographic cable fittings and terminations.

PA —FRANKLIN INSTITUTE LIBRARY, 20 & The Parkway, Philadelphia, 19103. Miriam Padusis, Dir; Charles Wilt, Readers Servs Librn
Holdings: Vols (300,000) Cat Maps Pix Microforms

TN —UNIVERSITY OF TENNESSEE, Space Institute Library, Tullahoma, 37388. Helen B Mason, Librn
Holdings: Vols (14,000) Cat Microforms
Budget: ($50,000)
Notes: Incl NASA and other series of technical reports.

TX —GENERAL DYNAMICS/FORT WORTH DIV, Technical Library & Information Services, PO Box 748, Mail Zone 2246, Fort Worth, 76101. P Rogers de Tonnancour, Dir
Holdings: Vols 36,000 Cat Maps Slides Microforms
Budget: $100,000
Notes: Incl 500,000 microforms. Catalogs for books and documents are separate. Collection is strong in mathematics, nuclear physics, materials and aerodynamics. Emphasis on the mission of the division--the development and production of manned aircraft. Division also involved in electronic manufacturing (avionic components), so collection strength in this area is growing very rapidly.

AERODYNAMICS—HISTORY

CA —CALIFORNIA INSTITUTE OF TECHNOLOGY, Robert A Millikan Memorial Library, Archives, 1201 E California Blvd, Pasadena, 91125. Judith R Goodstein, Archivist
Notes: 145,000 pages of letters, documents, scientific manuscripts, unpublished speeches, lecture notes, medals, photographs, and pictorial material, the papers of Theodore von Karman, aerodynamicist. A microfiche copy of the collection is at the Smithsonian Institution's National Air and Space Museum.

AERODYNAMICS, SUBSONIC see Aerodynamics

AEROLITES see Meteorites

AEROLOGY see Meteorology

AERONAUTICAL CHARTS

DC —LIBRARY OF CONGRESS, Geography and Map Division, Washington, 20540. John A Wolter, Chief
Holdings: Cat Mss Maps Pix Slides Microforms
See also entry under Maps and Atlases - Collections

AERONAUTICAL ENGINEERING

CA —UNIVERSITY OF CALIFORNIA, DAVIS, Physical Sciences Library, Davis, 95616. Scott Kennedy, Head
Holdings: Vols (170,000) Cat VF
Notes: Collection covers aeronautical, agricultural, chemical, civil, electrical, mechanical, water science, hydrology, nuclear reactor, extensive cold regions collection in vertical file drawers, and computer science engineering academic programs. Good strength in journal runs.

FL —EMBRY-RIDDLE AERONAUTICAL UNIVERSITY, Regional Airport, Daytona Beach, 32014. M Judy Luther, Dir of Learning Resources

NJ —PRINCETON UNIVERSITY, Library, Rare Books Dept, Princeton, 08544. Stephen Ferguson, Cur

NY —AMERICAN INSTITUTE OF AERONAUTICS & ASTRONAUTICS, Technical Information Service, 555 West 57th St, New York, 10019. Patricia Marshall, Dir, Library Resources
Holdings: Vols (57,000) Cat Microforms
See also entry under Aeronautics

AB —SOUTHERN ALBERTA INSTITUTE OF TECHNOLOGY, Learning Resources Centre, 1301 16 Ave NW, Calgary, T2M 0L4, Can. Tom Skinner, Historian
Holdings: Vols (40,000) Cat Maps Pix Slides Films Videotapes Microforms
Budget: ($50,000)
Notes: Wide range of current technical information about electronics and engineering (mechanical, electrical, chemical); emphasis on vocational-technical material. Incl (50,000) slides, (300) videotapes, and (500) films.

ON —NATIONAL RESEARCH COUNCIL OF CANADA, Aeronautical/Mechanical Engineering Branch Library, Montreal Rd, Ottawa, K1A 0R6, Can. Louise Fletcher, Head
Notes: This branch library of the Canada Institute for Scientific and Technical Information (CISTI) of the National Research Council of Canada, Ottawa, has a collection strong in aeronautical engineering, automatic control, CAD/CAM, robotics, ocean, wind, and solar energy power, hydraulic and coastal engineering, icing, low temperature research, naval engineering, metals and metallurgy, incl composites, tribology, and air, railroad, marine transportation. Library supported the Council contribution to the development of the remote manipular Canadarm for NASA's Space Shuttle Orbiters and more recently, the Canadian Astronaut Program which will contribute payload specialists to NASA's Space Shuttle Program in 1984. 35, 000 monographs, 1200 serials. Report collection: over 500,000 items.

AERONAUTICS

CA —NORTHROP CORPORATION, Aircraft Group, Library Services Dept, 3360/82, One Northrop Ave, Hawthorne, 90250. J E Reynolds, Manager
Holdings: Vols (15,000) Cat Microforms
Notes: Incl file of military specifications and standards, Air Force Technical Orders, and other military manuals, handbooks, regulations, instructions, etc. Also 400,000 microfiche; 60,000 reports. Library use restricted to employees; others by interlibrary loan.

CA —MCDONNELL DOUGLAS CORP, Douglas Aircraft Company, Technical Library, 3855 Lakewood Blvd, PO Box 200, Long Beach, 90846. Pat Ackerman, Librn
Notes: Incl 20,000 NASA and RAE reports; 100,000 microforms.

CA —UNIVERSITY OF CALIFORNIA, LOS ANGELES, Law Library, Los Angeles, 90024.
Notes: The David Bernard Memorial Aviation Law Library.

CA —UPDATA PUBLICATIONS INC, Library, 1756 Westwood Blvd, Los Angeles, 90024. Sara Ferguson, Dir; Judith Harrington, Librn
Holdings: Vols (300) Uncat Maps microforms
Notes: Incl 800,000 microforms, 35 periodicals.

CA —NASA, Ames Research Center, Libraries, Library Br 202-3, Moffett Field, 94035. Sarah Dueker, Chief, Library Branch
Holdings: Cat Audiotapes Microforms
Notes: Main library collections cover physical sciences, engineering and mathematical fields related to research programs in aeronautics-space research. Life sciences library collections cover medical, physiological, behavioral and biological sciences related to research programs. Also emphases on remote sensing of earth resources and the search for extraterrestrial life. 950 journal titles and 85,000 monographs. Reports collection includes 60, 000 hard copy reports and 900,000 microfiche.

CA —CALIFORNIA INSTITUTE OF TECHNOLOGY, Aeronautics Library, Pasadena, 91125. Virginia Anderson, Librn
Holdings: Vols 7500 Cat
Notes: Collection contains 6000 journals, 175,000 reports, 300,000 microfiche, and 210 current subscriptions.

CA —SAN DIEGO PUBLIC LIBRARY, Science & Industry Section, 820 E St, San Diego, 92101. Joanne Anderson, Senior Librn
Budget: ($33,000)

CA —UNITED AIRLINES, Engineering Dept, Library, San Francisco International Airport, San Francisco, 94128. J J Whitney, Technical Librn
Holdings: Vols 4500 Cat
Budget: $4000
Notes: Mostly current books on technical aspects; some history books.

CO —US AIR FORCE ACADEMY, Library, USAF Academy, Colorado Springs, 80840. Reiner H Schaeffer, Dir
Holdings: Vols 6400 Cat Maps Pix Microfilm

DC —AIR TRANSPORT ASSOCIATION OF AMERICA, Library, 1709 New York Ave NW, Washington, 20006. Nellis Gysin, Adm Asst
Holdings: Vols 14,000 Cat Maps Pix Microfilm
Budget: $6000
Notes: Emphasis of collection is air transport, its history and economics. Incl standard transportation texts, official administrative and statistical reports of the regulatory agencies, Congressional documents, annual reports of US scheduled airlines, and a limited number of technical reports.

IL —UNIVERSITY OF ILLINOIS, URBANA/CHAMPAIGN, Library, 221 Engineering Hall, Urbana, 61801. William Mischo, Librn
Holdings: Vols (175,000) Cat Slides Microforms
Notes: Incl 3500 periodicals. Collection designed to serve teaching and research programs. Supports instructional faculty research. Also, 470 microfilm reels and 6000 microfiche sheets.

IN —PURDUE UNIVERSITY LIBRARIES, Engineering Library, A A Potter Engineering Center, West Lafayette, 47907. Edwin D Posey, Engineering Librn
Holdings: Vols (225,178) Cat Maps Audiotapes Microforms
Budget: ($300,000)

AERONAUTICS (cont.)

MA —UNIVERSITY OF MASSACHUSETTS AT AMHERST, Physical Sciences Library, Amherst, 01003. Siegfried Feller, Assoc Dir for Collection Development
Holdings: Vols Cat Microforms
Notes: Incl extensive holdings of journals, NACA and NASA publications, and AEC documents (microfiche).

MA —MASSACHUSETTS INSTITUTE OF TECHNOLOGY, Institute Archives, Special Collections, Cambridge, 02139.
Notes: Vail collection incl many early works on telecommunications, electricity, ballooning, aeronautics, and animal magnetism.

MO —FEDERAL AVIATION ADMINSTRATION, Central Region Library, Federal Bldg, Rm 1556, 601 E 12 St, Kansas City, 64106. Judy Shifrin, Librn
Holdings: Vols (7000) Maps Microforms

NY —POLYTECHNIC INSTITUTE OF NEW YORK, Long Island Center Library, Route 110, Farmingdale, 11735. Lorraine Schein, Branch Librn
Holdings: Vols 2000 Cat
Notes: Wood Memorial Collection (reference); NACA/NASA documents.

NY —AMERICAN INSTITUTE OF AERONAUTICS & ASTRONAUTICS, Technical Information Service, 555 West 57th St, New York, 10019. Patricia Marshall, Dir, Library Resources
Holdings: Vols (57,000) Cat Microforms
Notes: Basis of published literature input to NASA Information System; Special index--Semimonthly issues of *International Aerospace Abstracts* with cumulated annual indexes.

NY —COLUMBIA UNIVERSITY LIBRARIES, Engineering Library, 422 Mudd Bldg, New York, 10027.
Holdings: Vols (177,000) Cat
Notes: All aspects of engineering--aeronautical, industrial mining, civil, chemical, mechanical, electrical, nuclear. Incl applied mathematics and applied physical sciences. Over (1,000,000) technical reports.

NY —NEW YORK PUBLIC LIBRARY, Research Libraries, Science and Technology Research Center, Fifth Ave & 42 St, New York, 10018.
Holdings: Vols (1,100,000) Cat Microforms
Budget: ($647,259)

NY —PAN AMERICAN WORLD AIRWAYS, Corporate Library, 200 Park Ave, Rm 904, New York, 10166. Liwa Chiu, Librn
Holdings: Vols 450 Uncat 16mm Films Microforms
Budget: $2500
Notes: No photocopying.

NY —DOWLING COLLEGE, Library, Idle Hour Blvd, Oakdale, 11769. Wendell A Guy, Dir
Holdings: Vols 500 Cat
Budget: $700

NY —ROCHESTER MUSEUM & SCIENCE CENTER, Strasenburgh Planetarium, Todd Library, 663 East Ave, Rochester, 14607. Donald Hall, Dir
Holdings: Vols 500 Cat Maps Slides
Notes: Also, 10,000 slides of astronomical and aeronautical subjects; 400 recordings; 150 celestial charts.

OH —AKRON-SUMMIT COUNTY PUBLIC LIBRARY, Science & Technology Div, 55 S Main St, Akron, 44326. Joyce McKnight, Head
Holdings: Vols 820 Cat Pix
Notes: The Lighter-Than-Air Society book collection is in the Akron Public Library. Incl foreign language books.

OH —OHIO STATE UNIVERSITY, Engineering Library, 2024 Neil Ave, Columbus, 43210. Mary Jo V Arnold, Librn
Holdings: Vols (132,000) Cat Microforms
Budget: ($110,000)

PA —ALLIANCE COLLEGE, Washington Hall Library, Fullerton Ave, Cambridge Springs, 16403. Stanley J Kozaczka, Head Librn
Holdings: Vols (8687)
Notes: A NASA depository of declassified documents since May, 1969.

PA —FRANKLIN INSTITUTE LIBRARY, 20 & The Parkway, Philadelphia, 19103. Miriam Padusis, Dir; Charles Wilt, Readers Servs Librn
Holdings: Vols (300,000) Cat Maps Pix Microforms

PA —UNIVERSITY OF PENNSYLVANIA, Towne Scientific Library, 220 S 33 St, Philadelphia, 19104. Charles Meyers, Librn
Holdings: Vols (65,000) Cat

†SD —SOUTH DAKOTA SCHOOL OF MINES & TECHNOLOGY, Devereaux Library, Rapid City, 57701.
Holdings: Vols (3000) Uncat Maps Pix Slides Audiotapes 16mm Films Filmstrips
Notes: A somewhat limited Aviation Resource Center to an area approx 90,000 sq miles in breadth and width, covering western South Dakota; western North Dakota; western Nebraska; eastern Montana; eastern Wyoming; and northeast corner of Colorado. Materials incl are books, periodicals, posters, pictures, etc from NASA, FAA and various aviation and aeronautics-related companies in the US.

WA —BOEING COMPANY, Boeing Technical Libraries, PO Box 3707, Seattle, 98124. Corrine Campbell, Mgr Technical Library
Holdings: Vols (75,000) Cat Microforms
Notes: Books are distributed between 3 libraries, Kent, Renton, and Bellevue. Also contains many periodicals and Boeing Documents Library restricted to Boeing Personnel.

WA —SEATTLE PUBLIC LIBRARY, 1000 Fourth Ave, Seattle, 98104. Ronald A Dubberly, City Librn
Holdings: Vols 20,000 Cat Microforms

WV —SALEM COLLEGE, Library, Salem, 26426. Myron J Smith, Jr, Librn

WI —EAA AVIATION MUSEUM, Whittman Airfield, Oshkosh, 54903. Ralph Bufano, Dir
Holdings: Vols (3000) Cat Maps Pix Slides Films Microforms
Notes: 2000 bound periodicals, engineering reports, aircraft construction designs, and other nonbook materials; also about 1500 books, mostly textbooks and historical works. Aeronautical ephemera and aircraft plans.

ON —NATIONAL MUSEUMS OF CANADA, Library Services Directorate, Ottawa, K1A 0M8, Can. Valerie Monkhouse, Director
Holdings: Vols 15,500
Budget: $25,000
Notes: History and technology of agriculture, astronomy, aviation, chemistry, communications, computers, electrical engineering, exploration and surveying, fire prevention, forestry, industrial technology, mathematics, medicine, mining, photography, physics, printing, space and transportation. research collection, interlibrary loans available, public may use on the premises.

ON —NATIONAL RESEARCH COUNCIL OF CANADA, Aeronautical/Mechanical Engineering Branch Library, Montreal Rd, Ottawa, K1A 0R6, Can. Louise Fletcher, Head
Holdings: Microforms
Notes: This branch library of the Canada Institute for Scientific and Technical Information (CISTI) of the National Research Council of Canada, Ottawa, has a collection strong in aeronautical engineering, automatic control, CAD/CAM, robotics, ocean, wind, and solar energy power, hydraulic and coastal engineering, icing, low temperature research, naval engineering, metals and metallurgy, incl composites, tribology, and air, railroad, marine transportation. Library supported the Council contribution to the development of the remote manipular Canadarm for NASA's Space Shuttle Orbiters and more recently, the Canadian Astronaut Program which will contribute payload specialists to NASA's Space Shuttle Program in 1984. 35, 000 monographs, 1200 serials. Report collection: over 500,000 items.

AERONAUTICS—BIOGRAPHY

DC —SMITHSONIAN INSTITUTION LIBRARIES, National Air & Space Museum Branch, NASM Bldg, Sixth & Independence Ave SW, Washington, 20560. Frank A Pietropaoli, Branch Chief
Holdings: Vols (39,000) Cat Mss Maps Pix Slides Microforms
Notes: History of flight and aerospace development, incl biographical material on aviation pioneers, balloons and ballooning. Extensive photographic collection (600,000 pictures). Incl the Sherman Fairchild Collection of aeronautical photographs (transferred from the American Institute of Aeronautics and Astronautics). Also incl the Bella Landauer Aeronautical Sheet Music Collection (1500 pieces). 2000 films; 800,000 microforms; 9000 volumes bound.

AERONAUTICS—DICTIONARIES

†ON —UNIVERSITY OF WESTERN ONTARIO, School of Library and Information Science, Special Collections Room, London, N6A 5B9, Can.
Notes: Archive of lexicographical materials of the Committee on Lexicography of the Modern Language Association. Incl lexicographical slips for *The United States Air Force Dictionary* and The *Second Aerospace Glossary,* by Woodford Heflin. 13 cartons of slips.

AERONAUTICS—HISTORY

CA —CLAREMONT COLLEGES, Norman F Sprague Memorial Library, 12 & Dartmouth, Claremont, 91711. David Kuhner, Librn
Holdings: Vols 4000 Cat Mss Maps Pix Phonorecords
Notes: Gift of Rev and Mrs John F B Carruthers of Pasadena, 1950. Emphasis on history of ballooning, early aviation. World War I and World War II military aviation, pioneer flyers and flights, women in aviation, cartoons, songs, memorabilia, some diaries and journals. Restricted use. Collection transferred here from Honnold Library.

CA —OCCIDENTAL COLLEGE, Library, 1600 Campus Rd, Los Angeles, 90041. Michael C Sutherland, Special Collections Librn
Holdings: Vols 1200 / / Cat Pix
Notes: Northrup-Millar Aviation Collection: history of aviation and aviation industry to the 1950's.

CA —UNIVERSITY OF CALIFORNIA, LOS ANGELES, Research Library, Dept of Special Collections, 405 Hilgard Ave, Los Angeles, 90024. Edward Shreeves, Chairman, Bibliographers Group; David S Zeidberg, Head
Holdings: Cat Mss Maps Pix
Notes: Various sources, incl the collection of Elizabeth Hiatt Gregory, aviation journalist and lecturer, and papers of Alexander Klemin, aeronautical engineer and teacher.

CA —CALIFORNIA INSTITUTE OF TECHNOLOGY, Robert A Millikan Memorial Library, Archives, 1201 E California Blvd, Pasadena, 91125. Judith R Goodstein, Archivist
Holdings: Vols (3000) Uncat Mss Maps Pix Slides
Notes: Over 70 collections (1830s-present) relating to history of 19th-20th centuries science and technology and the history of the Institute. Included are personal and professional papers of Caltech scientists and administrative officers; divisional records and faculty committees; over 5000 photographs of American and European scientists. Mss collections documents more than a century of American political, social, and intellectual history; the development of the physical sciences, aeronautics, molecular biology, and seismology in the US and abroad; and social and political conditions in Europe between the two World Wars. There are also family letters relating to 19th century American life before and during the Civil War (the Morley and A G Throop papers); to 19th century social conditions in Russia and Hungary (the Paul Epstein papers and Theodore von Karman papers); andto the development of 20th century Italian mathematics.

CA —SAN DIEGO AERO-SPACE MUSEUM, N Paul Whittier Historical

AERONAUTICS—HISTORY (cont.)

Aviation Library, 2001 Pan American Plaza, Balboa Park, San Diego, 92101. B C Reynolds, Archivist
Holdings: // Uncat Microforms
Notes: 98 percent of this aeronautics and aerospace collection was destroyed by fire in early 1978. The only item saved was a large scrapbook of newspaper clippings (1913-14) compiled by Hillery Beachey.

CA —UNITED AIRLINES, Engineering Dept, Library, San Francisco International Airport, San Francisco, 94128. J J Whitney, Technical Librn
Holdings: Vols 4500 Cat
Budget: $53,500
Notes: Mostly current books on technical aspects; some history books.

CA —HOOVER INSTITUTION ON WAR, REVOLUTION & PEACE, Stanford University, Stanford, 94305. Milorad M Drachkovitch, Archivist
Holdings: Mss Pix
Notes: Papers of Radu Irimescu, Rumanian Minister of Air and Navy, 1932-40, and Rumanian Ambassador to the United States, 1938-40, incl correspondence, reports, dispatches, memoranda, clippings, photos, and other material, 1918-40, relating to his service in the Rumanian government and to the development of aviation in Rumania. Primarily in Rumanian. 5 ms boxes. Also, papers of Charles E Weakley, Vice Admiral, US Navy, commander, Antisubmarine Warfare Force, Atlantic Fleet, 1963-67, and assistant administrator for management development, National Aeronautics and Space Administration, 1968-72, incl correspondence, orders, drafts of speeches, printed matter, photographs, and sound recordings, 1945-72, relating to post-World War II US antisubmarine force operations and to NASA activities. 4 ms boxes.

CO —US AIR FORCE ACADEMY, Library, USAF Academy, Colorado Springs, 80840. Reiner H Schaeffer, Dir
Holdings: Vols 6000 Cat Mss Maps Pix
Notes: The Colonel Richard Gimbel Aeronautical History Collection. Incl material from ancient myth to 1903 on manned flight: early scientific works on physical properties of the atmosphere, and imaginative literature on moon voyages. Collection is most complete in manned pioneer balloon ascents (1783ff). Also the Richard Upjohn Light Collection formerly at Culver Military Academy. Separate catalog, index to be published. 250 mss, 100 maps, 2000 pictures, 5000 prints, 7000 clippings.

CO —DENVER PUBLIC LIBRARY, 1357 Broadway, Denver, 80203.
Holdings: Vols 9000 Cat Pix
Notes: The Ross-Barrett Historical Aeronautics Collection. Aeronautics from the early myths through present space flight. The picture collection is heavily weighted with photos of planes used on the Western Front in the First World War though it does incl other material. Do not purchase current technical material on airplane construction with the exception of homebuilts, but do purchase such materials up to about 1930. Many aeronautical periodicals are incl in the collection.

CT —YALE UNIVERSITY, Box 1603A, Yale Station, New Haven, 06520.

CT —CONNECTICUT AERONAUTICAL HISTORICAL ASSOCIATION, Bradley Air Museum Library, Bradley International Airport, Windsor Locks, 06095. Robert Stepanek, Archivist; John W Ramsay, Librn
Holdings: Mss Maps Pix Slides Phonorecords 16mm Films Filmstrips
Budget: $2000

DE —HAGLEY MUSEUM AND LIBRARY, Eleutherian Mills-Hagley Foundation Inc, PO Box 3630, Greenville, 19807. Richmond D Williams, Dir; Heddy A Richter, Imprints Librn
Notes: A very large collection of about 3000 vols, incl name rows rarities.

DC —AIR TRANSPORT ASSOCIATION OF AMERICA, Library, 1709 New York Ave NW, Washington, 20006. Nellis Gysin, Adm Asst
Holdings: Vols 14,000 Cat Maps Pix Microfilm
Budget: $6000
Notes: Emphasis of collection is air transport, its history and economics. Incl standard transportation texts, official administrative and statistical reports of the regulatory agencies, Congressional documents, annual reports of US scheduled airlines, and a limited number of technical reports.

DC —GEORGETOWN UNIVERSITY, Library, Special Collections Div, 37 & O Sts NW, Washington, 20057. George M Barringer, Special Collections Librn; Nicholas B Sheetz, Mss Librn
Holdings: Cat
Notes: The Ernest Larue Jones Collection consists of seven large volumes of photographs which document the development of American aeronautics from 1863-1917. The majority of the pictures are of the period 1907-1915 when Jones was publisher of the pioneer technical journal "Aeronautics".

DC —LIBRARY OF CONGRESS, Manuscript Division, Washington, 20540. John C Broderick, Chief
Notes: The American Institute of Aeronautics and Astronautics Archives incorporates primary source material documenting the history of aeronautics. Incl clippings, articles, questionnaires, printed matter, and original mss pertaining to individual aeronauts, the personal papers of balloonist Thaddeus S C Lowe, and a corporate file consisting entirely of printed information on aircraft companies. Incl 30, 000 items.

DC —LIBRARY OF CONGRESS, Prints & Photographs Div, Washington, 20540.
Notes: Incl the great French collection of Albert and Gaston Tissandier, and the aeronautical biography files compiled by Jules Francois Dupuis-Delcourt. Ms materials are in the Manuscript Division.

DC —SMITHSONIAN INSTITUTION, Archives Div, Washington, 20560. William W Moss, Archivist
Holdings: Cat Mss Pix
Notes: The Archives holds records of the Office of the Secretary and of third Smithsonian Secretary Samuel Pierpont Langley, documenting his construction of a flying machine. Other Secretaries' records incl material on the Langley-Wright Brothers controversy, and the National Advisory Committee for Aeronautics. The Archives also has records of the National Air and Space Museum.

DC —SMITHSONIAN INSTITUTION LIBRARIES, National Air & Space Museum Branch, NASM Bldg, Sixth & Independence Ave SW, Washington, 20560. Frank A Pietropaoli, Branch Chief
Holdings: Vols (39,000) Cat Mss Maps Pix Microforms
Notes: History of flight and aerospace development, incl biographical material on aviation pioneers, balloons and balloonists. Extensive photographic collection (600,000 pictures). Incl the Sherman Fairchild Collection of aeronautical photographs (transferred from the American Institute of Aeronautics and Astronautics). Also incl the Bella Landauer Aeronautical Sheet Music Collection (1500 pieces). 2000 films; 800,000 microforms; 9000 volumes bound.

FL —EMBRY-RIDDLE AERONAUTICAL UNIVERSITY, Regional Airport, Daytona Beach, 32014. M Judy Luther, Dir of Learning Resources

KS —WICHITA STATE UNIVERSITY, Ablah Library, Box 68, Wichita, 67208. Michael T Kelly, Cur of Special Collections
Holdings: Vols Cat Mss

MD —US NAVAL ACADEMY, Nimitz Library, Annapolis, 21402. Alice S Creighton, Assistant Librn for Special Collections
Holdings: Mss
Notes: The William Adger Moffett Papers are a collection of official and personal letters, speeches, news releases, communications, memoranda, notes, news clippings, etc, by and about Rear Admiral William Adger Moffett, first Chief of the Bureau of Aeronautics, US Navy. The collection is a primary source for any research regarding the early history of naval aviation. Papers relate to numerous topics, including the London Naval Treaty and its ramifications, military airships, United Air Service controversy, coastal defense, carriers, etc. Index available in Special Collections Department.

MD —JOHNS HOPKINS UNIVERSITY, Milton S Eisenhower Library, Charles & 34 Sts, Baltimore, 21218. Ann S Gwyn, Assistant Dir for Special Collections
Holdings: Cat Mss Pix Audiotapes
Notes: Almost entirely a ms collection. Personal papers, etc. 144 linear ft.

NJ —PRINCETON UNIVERSITY, Library, Rare Books Dept, Princeton, 08544. Stephen Ferguson, Cur
Holdings: Vols 60 Cat Pix
Notes: The Harold McCormick Collection of early aeronautics.

NY —STATE UNIVERSITY OF NEW YORK, BINGHAMTON, Glenn G Bartle Library, Binghamton, 13901. Marion Hanscom, Special Collections Librn
Notes: A portion of the personal library of Edwin A Link, pioneer in aeronautics, with his invention of the Link Trainer. This is a small collection of some 75 books dealing with aviation. The books augment an extensive collection of Link's papers.

NY —GLENN H CURTISS MUSEUM OF LOCAL HISTORY, Lake & Main Sts, Hammondsport, 14840. Merrill Stickler, Cur
Holdings: Vols 500 Uncat Mss Maps Pix Slides Audiotapes 16mm Films Microforms
Budget: $1000
Notes: The library may only be used by appointment by serious researchers. Some copying is allowed under special circumstances. Collection is basically concerned with Glenn H Curtiss and his accomplishments in early aviation. Also collecting material about his contemporaries.

NY —NEW YORK PUBLIC LIBRARY, Research Libraries, Science and Technology Research Center, Fifth Ave & 42 St, New York, 10018.
Holdings: Vols (1,100,000) Cat Microforms
Budget: ($647,259)
Notes: Strong collection.

NY —DOWLING COLLEGE, Library, Idle Hour Blvd, Oakdale, 11769. Wendell A Guy, Dir
Holdings: Vols 500 Cat
Budget: $700

OH —CLEVELAND PUBLIC LIBRARY, Science & Technology Dept, 325 Superior Ave, Cleveland, 44114. Jean Z Piety, Head
Holdings: Cat
Notes: Notable segments in aeronautics, automobile engineering, and most other branches of engineering.

OH —WRIGHT STATE UNIVERSITY, Greater Miami Valley Research Center, University Library, Dayton, 45431. Patrick B Nolan, Head of Archives
Holdings: Vols 2000 Mss Pix
Notes: Books, private papers and business records of aviation pioneers, companies, etc. Incl 100 linear ft of mss, and 5000 photographs.

OK —NINETY-NINES, Library, PO Box 59964, Will Rogers World Airport, Oklahoma City, 73159. Lorretta Craig, Librn
Holdings: Vols 350 Cat Pix
Notes: 10,000 books, periodicals, catalogs on history of aviation. Women's aviation resource center. Collection from the first women aviatrix, Harriet Quinley, 1905-, Matilda Morant, 1925-. 7000 bound periodicals from 1929, 10 issues a year, from the magazine first called "Airwomen" to the "Ninety-Nines". Members of the "Ninety-Nines" incl 7 women astronauts (Betty Smith).

PA —PENNSYLVANIA STATE UNIVERSITY, Fred Lewis Pattee Library, Special Collections Dept, University Park, 16802. Charles Mann, Chief, Special Collections
Holdings: Vols (122,533) Cat Mss Maps Pix Slides Phonorecords Audiotapes Videotapes

AERONAUTICS—HISTORY (cont.)

16mm Films Microforms
Budget: ($37,000)
Notes: Special Collections and Rare Books includes several collections described separately. The holdings are particularly strong in aeronautics.

TX —SOUTHERN METHODIST UNIVERSITY, DeGolyer Library, Box 396, SMU, Dallas, 75275. Clifton H Jones, Dir
Holdings: Vols (80,000) Cat Mss Maps Pix Slides Microforms

TX —RICE UNIVERSITY, Fondren Library, 6100 S Main St, PO Box 1892, Houston, 77251. Dr Samuel M Carrington, Jr, University Librn
Notes: The Johnson Space Center History Archive, a manned flight collection transferred from NASA, originally housed at the Lyndon B Johnson Space Center. Contains documentation on the Mercury, Gemini, and Skylab programs; Soyuz Test Project. Incl 500 linear ft.

†WA —WASHINGTON STATE UNIVERSITY, Library, Manuscripts, Archives & Special Collections, Pullman, 99164. John F Guido, Head
Holdings: Cat Mss Maps Pix
Notes: The ms collection incl personal and professional papers of aviators. Described in *Selected Manuscript Resources in the Washington State University Library* (Pullman,1974); also about 1500 books, mostly textbooks and historical works.

WI —EAA AVIATION MUSEUM, Whittman Airfield, Oshkosh, 54903. Ralph Bufano, Dir
Holdings: Vols (3000) Cat Maps Pix Slides Films Microforms
Notes: 2000 bound periodicals, engineering reports, aircraft construction designs, and other nonbook materials; also about 1500 books, mostly textbooks and historical works. Aeronautical ephemera and aircraft plans.

WY —UNIVERSITY OF WYOMING, William Robertson Coe Library, 13 & Ivinson, Laramie, 82071.
Notes: The papers of Octave Chanute (1832-1910), pioneer railroad engineer and prominent aeronautic pioneer. Incl several hundred aviation photographs, letters, articles, pamphlets, speeches, and clippings, particularly on early-day gliders, with which Chanute was greatly involved.

AB —CENTENNIAL PLANETARIUM, Library, PO Box 2100, 701 Eleventh St, Calgary, T2P 2M5, Can. Sig Wieser, Librn
Holdings: Vols (400) Uncat Pix Audiotapes 16mm Films
Notes: Also western Canadian aviation history with bias towards technology; and history of space technology.

ON —NATIONAL MUSEUMS OF CANADA, Library Services Directorate, Ottawa, K1A 0M8, Can. Valerie Monkhouse, Director
Holdings: Vols 7000 Cat Pix
Budget: $25,000
Notes: Historical aviation, stressing Canadian contributions. The 10,000 pictures, with negatives, are not part of the library; photos under supervision of curator of National Museum of Science and Technology. Prints may be ordered and used in publication with credit to the National Museum of Science and Technology. Incl National Aviation Museum and aircraft manuals.

AERONAUTICS—LAWS AND LEGISLATION

CA —UNIVERSITY OF CALIFORNIA, LOS ANGELES, Law Library, Los Angeles, 90024.
Notes: The David Bernard Memorial Aviation Law Library.

DC —AIR TRANSPORT ASSOCIATION OF AMERICA, Library, 1709 New York Ave NW, Washington, 20006. Nellis Gysin, Adm Asst
Holdings: Vols 14,000 Cat Maps Pix Microfilm
Budget: $6000
Notes: Emphasis of collection is air transport, its history and economics. Incl standard transportation texts, official administrative and statistical reports of the regulatory agencies, Congressiional documents, annual reports of US scheduled airlines, and a limited number of technical reports.

AERONAUTICS—MAPS

AL —UNITED STATES AIR FORCE, Air University Library, Cartographic Information Division, Maxwell Air Force Base, 36112. Donald Flournoy, Cartographer
Notes: Approx 500,000 maps.

AERONAUTICS—MEDICAL ASPECTS see Aviation Medicine

AERONAUTICS—PHOTOGRAPHY see Photography, Aerial

AERONAUTICS—PICTURES, ILLUSTRATIONS, ETC.

DC —LIBRARY OF CONGRESS, Prints & Photographs Div, Washington, 20540.
Holdings: 1400 Items
Notes: A collection of pictorial aeronautics assembled by Bella C Landauer (1874-1960). Incl aeronautical prints, drawings, posters, photographs, clippings, and printed ephemera dating from the 1780s to 1945, as well as portraits of early aeronauts and depictions of balloon ascents.

WY —UNIVERSITY OF WYOMING, William Robertson Coe Library, 13 & Ivinson, Laramie, 82071.
Notes: The papers of Octave Chanute (1832-1910), pioneer railroad engineer and prominent aeronautic pioneer. Incl several hundred aviation photographs, letters, articles, pamphlets, speeches, and clippings, particularly on early-day gliders, with which Chanute was greatly involved.

AERONAUTICS, COMMERCIAL

CA —STANFORD UNIVERSITY LIBRARIES, Cecil H Green Library, Stanford, 94305. Michael T Ryan, Cur
Holdings: Vols (1700) // Cat Mss Maps Pix
Notes: The Timothy Hopkins Transportation Collection. Some materials on aviation.

DC —AIR TRANSPORT ASSOCIATION OF AMERICA, Library, 1709 New York Ave NW, Washington, 20006. Nellis Gysin, Adm Asst
Holdings: Vols 14,000 Cat Maps Pix Microfilm
Budget: $6000
Notes: Emphasis of collection is air transport, its history and economics. Incl standard transportation texts, official administrative and statistical reports of the regulatory agencies, Congressional documents, annual reports of US scheduled airlines, and a limited number of technical reports.

IL —NORTHWESTERN UNIVERSITY, Transportation Center Library, Evanston, 60201. Mary Roy, Librn
Holdings: Vols (116,000)
Notes: The emphasis in this collection is on current developments in transportation operations and socioeconomics--management, planning, impact and regulation. All modes of transportation and containerization are incl; the geographic scope covers domestic and foreign activity at the urban, intercity and international levels. Publications on new systems developments and the application of analytic techniques to operations are well represented. Incl 19,000 pamphlets; 9000 company reports. *Services are offered on research conducted outside Northwestern. A fee schedule is available on request.* Publications: *Current Literature in Traffic and Transportation* (bi-monthly accessions bulletin citing 625 books, reports and periodical articles per issue).

NY —PAN AMERICAN WORLD AIRWAYS, Corporate Library, 200 Park Ave, Rm 904, New York, 10166. Liwa Chiu, Librn
Holdings: Vols 450 Uncat 16mm Films Microforms
Budget: $2500
Notes: No photocopying.

AERONAUTICS, MILITARY

CA —CLAREMONT COLLEGES, Norman F Sprague Memorial Library, 12 & Dartmouth, Claremont, 91711. David Kuhner, Librn
Holdings: Vols 4000 Cat Mss Maps Pix Phonorecords
Notes: Gift of Rev and Mrs John F B Carruthers of Pasadena, 1950. Emphasis on history of ballooning, early aviation, World War I and World War II military aviation, pioneer flyers and flights, women in aviation, cartoons, songs, memorabilia, some diaries and journals. Restricted use. Collection transferred here from Honnold Library.

CA —NORTHROP CORPORATION, Aircraft Group, Library Services Dept, 3360/82, One Northrop Ave, Hawthorne, 90250. J E Reynolds, Manager
Holdings: Vols (15,000) Cat Microforms
Notes: Incl file of military specifications and standards, Air Force Technical Orders, and other military manuals, handbooks, regulations, instructions, etc. Also 400,000 microfiche; 60,000 reports. Library use restricted to employees; others by interlibrary loan.

CO —US AIR FORCE ACADEMY, Library, USAF Academy, Colorado Springs, 80840. Reiner H Schaeffer, Dir
Holdings: Vols 3100 Cat Mss Microforms

MD —US NAVAL ACADEMY, Nimitz Library, Annapolis, 21402. Alice S Creighton, Assistant Librn for Special Collections
Holdings: Mss
Notes: The William Adger Moffett Papers are a collection of official and personal letters, speeches, news releases, communications, memoranda, notes, news clippings, etc, by and about Rear Admiral William Adger Moffett, first Chief of the Bureau of Aeronautics, US Navy. The collection is a primary source for any research regarding the early history of naval aviation. Papers relate to numerous topics, including the London Naval Treaty and its ramifications, military airships, United Air Service controversy, coastal defense, carriers, etc. Index available in Special Collections Department.

ON —NATIONAL MUSEUMS OF CANADA, Library Services Directorate, Ottawa, K1A 0M8, Can. Valerie Monkhouse, Director
Holdings: Vols 12,000 Cat
Budget: ($60,000)
Notes: Collection includes; arms and armour, military aeronautics, military and naval arts and sciences, military and naval equipment, general military and naval history, military and naval history of Canada. Research collection, interlibrary loans available, public may use on the premises.

AERONAUTICS, NAVAL see Aeronautics, Military

AERONAUTICS, WOMEN IN see Women in Aeronautics

AEROSPACE—DICTIONARIES

†ON —UNIVERSITY OF WESTERN ONTARIO, School of Library and Information Science, Special Collections Room, London, N6A 5B9, Can.
Notes: Archive of lexicographical materials of the Committee on Lexicography of the Modern Language Association. Incl lexicographical slips for *The United States Air Force Dictionary* and The *Second Aerospace Glossary,* by Woodford Heflin. 13 cartons of slips.

AEROSPACE ENGINEERING

CA —ROCKWELL INTERNATIONAL, Space Div, Technical Information Center, 12214 Lakewood Blvd, Downey, 90241. Nan H Paik, Librn
Holdings: Vols 76,000 Cat Microforms
Notes: Primarily for use by company

AEROSPACE ENGINEERING (cont.)

employees. Incl journals and technical reports in the aerospace sciences and engineering; also 600,000 microforms.

CA —UNIVERSITY OF CALIFORNIA, LOS ANGELES, Engineering & Mathematical Sciences Library, 405 Hilgard, Los Angeles, 90024. Rosalee I Wright, Librn
Holdings: Vols (180,000) Cat Microforms
Notes: NASA depository; SAE Aerospace Standards; AIAA journals and papers.
See also entry under Engineering

CA —NASA, Ames Research Center, Libraries, Library Br 202-3, Moffett Field, 94035. Sarah Dueker, Chief, Library Branch
Holdings: Cat Audiotapes Microforms
Notes: Main library collections cover physical sciences, engineering and mathematical fields related to research programs in aeronautics-space research. Life sciences library collections cover medical, physiological, behavioral and biological sciences related to research programs. Also emphases on remote sensing of earth resources and the search for extraterrestrial life. 950 journal titles and 85,000 monographs. Reports collection includes 60, 000 hard copy reports and 900,000 microfiche.

CA —CALIFORNIA STATE POLYTECHNIC UNIVERSITY, POMONA, University Library, 3801 W Temple Ave, Pomona, 91768. Harold Schleiser, Actg Dir
Notes: General reference materials on aerospace, chemical, civil, electrical, electronics, industrial, mechanical and manufacturing engineering.

GA —GEORGIA INSTITUTE OF TECHNOLOGY, Price Gilbert Memorial Library, 225 North Ave, Atlanta, 30332. Edward Graham Roberts, Dir
Holdings: Vols (1,661,559) Cat Maps Slides Microforms
Budget: ($1,383,302)

IA —IOWA STATE UNIVERSITY, Library, Ames, 50011. Warren B Kuhn, Dean of Library Services
Holdings: Cat Microforms
Notes: Extensive serial holdings.

KY —UNIVERSITY OF KENTUCKY, Robert E Shaver Library of Engineering, 355 Anderson Hall, Lexington, 40506. Russell H Powell, Engineering Librn
Holdings: Vols (48,000) Cat Microforms

MA —BOSTON UNIVERSITY, Mugar Memorial Library, Special Collections Dept, 771 Commonwealth Ave, Boston, 02215. Howard B Gotlieb, Dir
Notes: Over 10,000 papers and reports from NASA, the Jet Propulsion Laboratory (California Institute of Technology), the armed services, etc. Gift of Allied Research Corp, Concord, Mass.

MI —UNIVERSITY OF MICHIGAN, Engineering-Transportation Library, 312 Undergraduate Library, Ann Arbor, 48109. Maurita Holland, Librn
Holdings: Vols (400,000) Cat Microforms
Budget: ($225,000)

NY —GRUMMAN AEROSPACE CORP, Technical Information Center, Plant 35, Bethpage, 11714. Harold Smith, Mgr of Library & Info Services
Holdings: Vols (15,000) Cat Microforms
Notes: Aerospace science and technology. Incl 650,000 microforms.

NY —AMERICAN INSTITUTE OF AERONAUTICS & ASTRONAUTICS, Technical Information Service, 555 West 57th St, New York, 10019. Patricia Marshall, Dir, Library Resources
Holdings: Vols (57,000) Cat Microforms
See also entry under Aeronautics

NC —SCHIELE MUSEUM OF NATURAL HISTORY, Library, 1500 E Garrison Blvd, Gastonia, 28052. Dot Gray, Librn; Margaret Summerill, Librn
Holdings: Vols (3800) Cat Maps Pix Slides Phonorecords Audiotapes 16mm Films Filmstrips Microforms
Budget: ($2800)
Notes: Listed on RECON computer with Library of Congress as Reference Center in Southeast in subject areas of natural sciences, aerospace and planetarium technology, and anthropology.

NC —NORTH CAROLINA STATE UNIVERSITY, D H Hill Library, Box 7111, Raleigh, 27695. I T Littleton, Dir
Holdings: Vols 6560 Cat
Budget: $8000
See also entry under Transportation - History.

OH —UNIVERSITY OF CINCINNATI, Engineering Library, 880 Baldwin Hall, Cincinnati, 45221. Dorothy Furber Byers, Head
Holdings: Vols (50,000) Cat Videotapes Microforms
Budget: ($100,000)

PA —FRANKLIN INSTITUTE LIBRARY, 20 & The Parkway, Philadelphia, 19103. Miriam Padusis, Dir; Charles Wilt, Readers Servs Librn
Holdings: Vols (300,000) Cat Maps Pix Microforms

PA —PENNSYLVANIA STATE UNIVERSITY, Engineering Library, 325 Hammond St, University Park, 16802. Tom Conkling, Librn
Holdings: Vols (60,000) Microforms
Notes: This collection includes substantial microform holdings and extensive runs of periodicals.

TN —UNIVERSITY OF TENNESSEE, Space Institute Library, Tullahoma, 37388. Helen B Mason, Librn
Holdings: Vols (14,000) Cat Microforms
Budget: ($50,000)
Notes: Incl NASA and other series of technical reports.

TX —UNIVERSITY OF TEXAS LIBRARIES, Richard W McKinney Engineering Library, 1.3 ECJ, Austin, 78712. Susan B Ardis, Librn
Holdings: Vols (103,000) Cat Microforms
Notes: Incl 400,000 uncataloged microfiche.

TX —GENERAL DYNAMICS/FORT WORTH DIV, Technical Library & Information Services, PO Box 748, Mail Zone 2246, Fort Worth, 76101. P Rogers de Tonnancour, Dir
Holdings: Vols 36,000 Cat Maps Slides Microforms
Budget: $100,000
Notes: Incl 500,000 microforms. Catalogs for books and documents are separate. Collection is strong in mathematics, nuclear physics, materials and aerodynamics. Emphasis on the mission of the division--the development and production of manned aircraft. Division also involved in electronic manufacturing (avionic components), so collection strength in this area is growing very rapidly.

VA —NASA-LANGLEY RESEARCH CENTER, Technical Library, MS-185, Hampton, 23665. Jane S Hess, Head, Tech Library Branch
Holdings: Vols (102,000) Microforms
Notes: 70,000 titles, 102,000 volumes, 1,000, 000 documents (hard copy and microfiche). Open to the public. No photocopying.

AEROSPACE ENGINEERING—HISTORY

DC —SMITHSONIAN INSTITUTION LIBRARIES, National Air & Space Museum Branch, NASM Bldg, Sixth & Independence Ave SW, Washington, 20560. Frank A Pietropaoli, Branch Chief
Holdings: Vols (39,000) Cat Mss Maps Pix Slides Microforms
Notes: History of flight and aerospace development, incl biographical material on aviation pioneers, balloons and ballooning. Extensive photographic collection (600,000 pictures). Incl the Sherman Fairchild Collection of aeronautical photographs (transferred from the American Institute of Aeronautics and Astronautics). Also incl the Bella Landauer Aeronautical Sheet Music Collection (1500 pieces). 2000 films; 800,000 microforms; 9000 volumes bound.

AEROSPACE MEDICINE

AL —UNITED STATES ARMY, Aeromedical Research Laboratory, USAARL Scientific Information Center, PO Box 577, Fort Rucker, 36362. Sybil H Bullock, Librn
Holdings: Vols (35,000) Cat Microforms
Notes: Aeronautical and aerospace medicine.

CA —NASA, Ames Research Center, Libraries, Library Br 202-3, Moffett Field, 94035. Sarah Dueker, Chief, Library Branch
Holdings: Cat Audiotapes Microforms
Notes: Main library collections cover physical sciences, engineering and mathematical fields related to research programs in aeronautics-space research. Life sciences library collections cover medical, physiological, behavioral and biological sciences related to research programs. Also emphases on remote sensing of earth resources and the search for extraterrestrial life. 950 journal titles and 85,000 monographs. Reports collection includes 60, 000 hard copy reports and 900,000 microfiche.

OK —CIVIL AERO MEDICAL INSTITUTE LIBRARY (CAMI), PO Box 25082, AAC 64D1, Oklahoma City, 73125. Darrell R Goulden, Medical Librn
Holdings: Vols 8500 Cat Mss
Budget: $28,000
Notes: Aviation and aerospace medicine. About 175 current periodicals.

TX —US AIR FORCE, School of Aerospace Medicine, Strughold Aeromedical Library, Brooks AFB, 78235. Fred W Todd, Chief Librn
Holdings: Vols (119,188) Cat Mss Maps Pix Microforms
Budget: ($499,000)
Notes: Aviation and space medicine and physiology, including the physiological effects of altitude and decompression. Biomedical and human engineering. Military medicine, including chemical and biological warfare. Emergency medicine in both professional and technical areas. Radiobiology, including atomic medicine, nuclear medicine, and space radiation. Material not oriented to the School of Aerospace Medicine are excluded. Incl also 45,787 microforms and 142,371 technical documents.

AEROSPACE SCIENCES—HISTORY

DC —SMITHSONIAN INSTITUTION LIBRARIES, National Air & Space Museum Branch, NASM Bldg, Sixth & Independence Ave SW, Washington, 20560. Frank A Pietropaoli, Branch Chief
Holdings: Vols (39,000) Cat Mss Maps Pix Slides Microforms
Notes: History of flight and aerospace development, incl biographical material on aviation pioneers, balloons and ballooning. Extensive photographic collection (600,000 pictures). Incl the Sherman Fairchild Collection of aeronautical photographs (transferred from the American Institute of Aeronautics and Astronautics). Also incl the Bella Landauer Aeronautical Sheet Music Collection (1500 pieces). 2000 films; 800,000 microforms; 9000 volumes bound.

AEROSTATION see Aeronautics

AESCHYLUS

NC —DUKE UNIVERSITY, William R Perkins Library, Durham, 27706. Elvin E Strowd, University Librn
Notes: The Spranger Collection of classical studies contains 2500 items. The principal dramatists, Euripides, Aeschylus, Aristophanes and Sophocles are fairly comprehensively covered by way of critical texts and studies up to 1968. Practically all the texts are represented by Loeb and Bude translations, and also Didot's 19th century series. Reference books includes a complete Pauly-Wissowa, Briquet, long runs of the Classical Review and Quarterly, the O E D and some 30 to 40 volumes of codex facsimiles of Euripides and others.

AESOP'S FABLES AND IMITATIONS

CA —CLAREMONT COLLEGES, Ella Strong Denison Library, Scripps College,

AESOP'S FABLES AND IMITATIONS (cont.)

Claremont, 91711. Judy Harvey Sahak, Librn
Holdings: Vols 63 Cat
Notes: Incl 36 vols of Aesop's fables (earliest, 1554), 9 vols of Gay's fables (earliest, 1729), and 8 vols of LaFontaine (earliest, 1734).

MA —HARVARD UNIVERSITY LIBRARY, Widener Library, Cambridge, 02138.
Holdings: Cat
Notes: See *Harvard Library Index Notes,* (1923), pp 242-248.

MS —UNIVERSITY OF SOUTHERN MISSISSIPPI, William David McCain Graduate Library, Box 5148, Southern Sta, Hattiesburg, 39406.
Holdings: Vols Cat
Notes: In the Lena Y de Grummond Collection of Children's Literature. The earliest volume was published by Froben in Basel, 1530. Over 150 editions, incl 30 pre-1750 imprints.

NY —METROPOLITAN MUSEUM OF ART, Dept of Prints & Photographs, 82 St & Fifth Ave, New York, 10028. Colta Ives, Cur

NY —PIERPONT MORGAN LIBRARY, 29 E 36 St, New York, 10016. Paul Needham, Cur
Notes: One of the largest collections, with many rarities, unique works and mss.

OH —CLEVELAND PUBLIC LIBRARY, Fine Arts and Special Collections Department, 325 Superior Ave, Cleveland, 44114. Alice N Loranth, Head
Holdings: Vols (700) Cat Mss
Notes: Part of the Fables Collection, which is strong in Medieval European and Oriental works. Numerous rare and early editions of Reynard the Fox (200 vols), Panchatantra, Bidpai, Hitopadesa, etc, are incl. Aesop and the modern fabulists are incl only by representative editions.
See also entry under Fables

AESTHETICS

MA —HARVARD UNIVERSITY LIBRARY, Cambridge, 02138.
Holdings: Cat

PA —UNIVERSITY OF PITTSBURGH, Hillman Library, Pittsburgh, 15260. Glenora E Rossell, Head
Holdings: Vols 15,565 Cat Microforms
Notes: The collection covers all periods and philosophical disciplines. Its strength is in modern and contemporary philosophy. The rare books, as part of the British philosophy to 1900, are located in Special Collections.

WA —UNIVERSITY OF WASHINGTON LIBRARIES, Philosophy Library, 331 Savery, DK-50, Seattle, 98195. Carolyn Mateer, Acting Selector
Holdings: Vols (18,302) Cat
Budget: ($27,516)
Notes: Collection includes materials in philosophy of language, law, mind, ethics, logic, mataphysics, religion, science, epistemology, social and political philosophy and the history of philosophy.

AETHIOPIC LANGUAGE AND LITERATURE see Ethiopic Language and Literature

AFFIRMATIVE ACTION PROGRAMS

MA —RADCLIFFE COLLEGE, Arthur & Elizabeth Schlesinger Library on the History of Women in America, 3 James St, Cambridge, 02138. Patricia Miller King, Dir; Eva Moseley, Cur of Mss
Notes: The papers of the 1974 class action suit against *The New York Times* that charged the newspaper with "a pattern and practice of discrimination in employment on the basis of sex." The *Times* agreed to an affirmative action plan, and the suit was resolved in 1978.

AFFLECK, RAYMOND T.

AB —UNIVERSITY OF CALGARY, Libraries, Special Collections Div, 2500 University Dr, Calgary, T2N 1N4, Can.
Holdings: Cat Pix
Notes: Collection consists of 1379 original architectural drawings & sketches some 115 smaller, private projects of Raymond T Affleck, from 1956 onwards; mostly alterations and additions to residences. A project list is on hand.

AFGHAN LANGUAGE AND LITERATURE

NY —NEW YORK PUBLIC LIBRARY, Oriental Div, Fifth Ave & 42 St, New York, 10018. E Christian Filstrup, Chief
Holdings: Cat Mss Microforms
Budget: ($56,455)
Notes: Published catalog of holdings.

AFGHANISTAN

CA —HOOVER INSTITUTION ON WAR, REVOLUTION & PEACE, Stanford University, Stanford, 94305. Peter Duignan, Cur; Karen Fung, Deputy Cur
Holdings: Vols (100,000)
Notes: For full description of collection, see Hoover Institution entry under Near East.

MA —HARVARD UNIVERSITY LIBRARY, Cambridge, 02138.
Holdings: Cat

MI —UNIVERSITY OF MICHIGAN, Graduate Library, South Asian Dept, Ann Arbor, 48109. Om P Sharma, Librn
Holdings: Vols (365,000) Cat Maps Slides Microforms
Notes: The major emphasis is on social sciences and humanities. Besides materials in classical languages, South Asian vernaculars being retained are Hindi, Bengali, Urdu, Marathi and Tamil; Strong in classical languages, especially Sanskrit, Pali, and Prakrit.

NE —UNIVERSITY OF NEBRASKA, OMAHA, Library, 60 & Dodge Sts, Omaha, 68132. Mel Bohn, Librn
Notes: Afghanistan Area Collection: Incl 1000 vols cataloged; 1000 vols uncataloged. Monographs and serials in English, Dari, Pashto, and other languages. Oral History Collection on cassette tape. Resistance newspapers and transcriptions of radio broadcasts on microfiche. Post-Soviet invasion periodicals.

NY —NEW YORK PUBLIC LIBRARY, Oriental Div, Fifth Ave & 42 St, New York, 10018. E Christian Filstrup, Chief
Holdings: Cat Mss Microforms
Budget: ($56,455)
Notes: Described in *Dictionary Catalog of the Oriental Collection.* The Research Libraries of the New York Public Library, 1960, 16 vols, and *First Supplement,* 1976, 8 vols (144,000 cards). This catalog incl 318, 000 entries for works in about 100 languages of the East, and all the works in Western languages on Oriental subjects. The Oriental Collection numbers about 120,000 vols; its Arabic and Indic holdings and those on ancient Egypt and the ancient Near East are among the largest in the US. Other outstanding features incl a unique collection of linguistic works, grammars, and dictionaries; and unusually good coverage of the field of Oriental religions and philosophies, as well as subject references to periodical articles in all languages. All entries are arranged alphabetically according to the Roman alphabet.

AFRICA

CA —UNIVERSITY OF CALIFORNIA, BERKELEY, University Library, Afro-American Studies, Berkeley, 94720. Phyllis Bischof, Librn
Notes: Extensive

CT —YALE UNIVERSITY, Box 1603A, Yale Station, New Haven, 06520.
Holdings: Cat Mss

DC —HOWARD UNIVERSITY, Moorland-Spingarn Research Center, 500 Howard Place NW, Washington, 20059. Clifford L Muse, Jr, Acting Dir
Holdings: Vols (106,086) Cat Mss Maps Pix Slides Phonorecords Audiotapes 16mm Films Filmstrips Microforms
Budget: $854,753
Notes: *The Glenn Carrington Collection: A Guide to the Books, Manuscripts, Music and Recordings* (DC MSRC, 1977). *Dictionary Catalog of the Jesse E Moorland Collection of Negro Life and History,* 9 vols and Supplement, 3 vols (Boston: G K Hall, 1970, 1977). *Dictionary Catalog of the Arthur Spingarn Collection of Negro Authors,* 2 vols (Boston: G K Hall, 1970). Guide to Processed Collections in the Manuscript Division of the Moorland-Spingarn Research Center (DC, MSRC, 1983). The Moorland-Spingran Research Center is recognized as one of the largest and most comprehensive repositories in the world for the collection, preservation and dissemination of historical materials documenting from antiquity to the present the history and culture of Black people in Africa, Europe, the Caribbean and the US. Since 1973, the Research Center has greatly expanded its facilitiesand resources and currently provides research services in all aspects of library and archival research, including manuscripts, oral history, music, prints and photographs and general library materials. The Research Center also maintains professional zerographic, micrographic, photographic and similar reproduction laboratories.

DC —LIBRARY OF CONGRESS, General Reference & Bibliography Div, African Section, Washington, 20540. Julian W Witherell, Head
Holdings: Vols (33,000)
Notes: Library of Congress collections of Africana (material issued in or relating to Africa) are among the best in the world, encompassing every major field of study except technical agriculture and clinical medicine. Most of the publications, including especially strong holdings in economics, history, linguistics, and literature, are dispersed in the Library's general book and periodical collections. The largest single block of material on Africa is the collection of surveys, yearbooks, histories, and general descriptive works (the DT classification). In the Library's shelflist, this is represented by about 32,000 titles. The shelflist also indicates, for example, that the number of bibliographic guides on Africa totals about 1100. An additional wealth of Africana may be found in special collections of legal material, manuscripts, maps, microforms, music, newspapers,photographs and films in various custodial divisions of the Library. In the Africa Section, researchers may consult card indexes to Africa monographs and periodical articles and collections of published bibliographies, yearbooks, pamphlets, and current issues of major periodicals. The section's reference collection also includes unpublished research papers prepared for academic congresses and sample issues of works in African languages and literature. Additional information can be found in *The African Section in the Library of Congress,* a five-page brochure available free on request from the section, Room 1040-C. Thomas Jefferson Building, Library of Congress, Washington, DC 20540.

IL —CENTER FOR RESEARCH LIBRARIES, 6050 S Kenwood Ave, Chicago, 60637. Donald B Simpson, Dir; Esther Smith, Collection Development Librn
Holdings: Microforms
Budget: $18,000
Notes: 10,934 reels of film, 5822 fiches. Cooperative Africana microform Project. Borrowing restricted to members of project, but anyone may purchase copies from CAMP-owned negatives. Material cataloged to date listed in *CAMP Catalog 1977,* Cumulative Edition (Cooperative Africana Microform Project and the Center for Research Libraries.) Also have supplements to the catalog.

IL —CHICAGO PUBLIC LIBRARY, G Woodson Regional Library, George C Hall Branch, 9525 S Halsted, Chicago, 60628. Steven C Newsome, Cur; Hattie L Power, Regional Library Dir
Holdings: Vols 8000 Cat Mss Audiotapes

AFRICA (cont.)

Microforms
Notes: The Vivian G Harsh Collection on Afro-American History and Literature, in the George Cleveland Hall Branch of the Chicago Public Library, contains books, in print and on microfilm, periodicals, recordings, tapes, pamphlets and mss. Specializes in Afro-Americana, but contains a sizeable number of books on Africa. Also contains these noteworthy items: *The Negro in Illinois: the Illinois Writers Project Files; The Chicago Afro-American Union Analytic Catalog; Big Boy Leaves Home*, by Richard Wright (an original typewritten ms); *The Big Sea*, by Langston Hughes (3 original typewritten mss of this work). 7800 vols on microfilm.

IL —NORTHWESTERN UNIVERSITY, Melville J Herskovits Library of African Studies, Evanston, 60201. Hans E Panofsky, Cur
Holdings: Vols (85,000) Mss
Budget: ($70,000)
Notes: Although the collection incl the papers of Melville J Herskovits, the last ten years of this archive is closed until 1988. Also have papers of the African Studies Association, Carter/Karis, Abdullah Abdurahman, Alex Hepple, Leo Kuper, Dennis Brutus; further, on West Africa--John Paden, Umar Falke, Liberian economic survey. Supplements for 1972-1977 for our book catalog (8 vols) was published by G K Hall in 1978; unlike 1972, the supplement to the *Joint Acqusitions List of Africana* will be published in seperate vols from the Northwestern Catalog supplement. There are, in 1978, 16,000 additional vols.

IN —UNIVERSITY OF NOTRE DAME, University Libraries, Notre Dame, 46556.
Holdings: Vols 3000
Notes: Collection, mostly in English and French, originally assembled in Africa by priests of the Society of Missionaries of Africa (known as the White Fathers) and brought to the US in 1966.

MA —HARVARD UNIVERSITY LIBRARY, Widener Library, Cambridge, 02138.
Holdings: Cat
Notes: *Widener Library Shelflist* No 34 (Africa) lists 22,001 vols. There are good collections of Afrikaans, but other vernacular-language materials are not well represented.

MA —BOSTON COLLEGE LIBRARIES, Thomas P O'Neill Library, Nicholas M Williams Ethnological Collection, Chestnut Hill, 02167. Frank J Seegraber, Special Collections Librn
Holdings: Vols 10,000 // Cat Mss Maps
Notes: Collection emphasizes Caribbeana, especially Jamaica, to 1940. Incl discovery, exploration and natural history of the British, French and Spanish settlements; the slave question; piracy. There are over 6000 mss, 5000 of which are Anansi folk tales recorded by native school children. Also small ancillary sections of Africana and Judaica. For reference use only, by arrangement with librarian.

MI —UNIVERSITY OF MICHIGAN, Center for Research on Economic Development, Library, 240 Lorch Hall, Ann Arbor, 48109. Carol Wilson, Information/Resources Coordinator
Holdings: Vols (21,000) Cat 16mm Films Microforms Periodicals
Budget: ($7000)
Notes: Publications that list library and its collection: *National Reference Center* Directory 1983 (NRC), *World Guide to* Libraries 1983 (Seur Verlag), *Research Centers Directory* 1984 (Gale Research Co), *Third World Studies in the US* (African Studies Assn, 1981); and *A Directory of Information Resources in the US* (Library of Congress, 1978). Collection's focus is Third World's economic development. Other areas of interest are economic planning, developing countries, Africa (specifically francophone Africa), the Sahel, African agricultural economics, commodities production, financial statistics, development plans from less developed countries (LDC), and international development. Each part of the library's collection (working papers/reports, periodicals and government documents) has its own catalog and cataloging systems.

MI —MICHIGAN STATE UNIVERSITY, International Library, Africana Collection, East Lansing, 48824. Eugene de Benko, Librn; Onuma Ezera, Bibliographer for Africana
Holdings: Vols (82,700) Cat Mss Maps Pix Slides Phonorecords Audiotapes Videotapes Filmstrips Microforms
Budget: ($78,000)
Notes: Research collection covering all aspects of Africa with emphasis on the continent South of the Sahara. For North Africa, the concentration is in European languages. Anthropology, sociology, history, economics, political science & government, health sciences, education, languages & literature, agriculture and rural development are collected in depth. Significant library and archival holdings on Nigeria, Ghana, Kenya, Tanzania, Rhodesia, South Africa and Zaire. The Maurice M deRijck collection on Zaire, Rwanda and Burundi, 1890-1960. Retrospective files of newspapers on microfilm: *Rand Daily Mail* (1902-); *Rhodesia Herald* (1892-); *East African* Standard (1902-) and many shorter runs. Africana Area File contains over 23,000 items of pamphlets and ephemera. Extensive holdings of Kenyan, Tanzanian archival records and British Colonial Office and Foreign Officerecords on microfilm including the 1200-plus reels FO-84 class "Slave Trade: Original Correspondence." Description of collection in *Research Sources for African Studies...at MSU* (1969, 384 pp); *Africana in Microform in the MSU* Library (1975, 51 pp); *Swahili Ephemera in the MSU Libraries* (1971, 22 pp); *Africana-Select Recent Acquisitions* (1965, bimonthly); and Sahel: *Bibliographic Bulletin/ Bulletin Bibliographique* (1977-, quarterly, bilingual).

NH —PLYMOUTH STATE COLLEGE, Lamson Library, Plymouth, 03264. Phillip Wei, Dir of Library Services
Holdings: Vols 5000// Cat Slides
Budget: ($30,000)
Notes: Collection emphasis is on the humanities and social sciences, incl education. Science and technology incl only when relevant. Basic bibliography and supplements prepared annually available upon request. Incl A-V materials; textbooks.

NY —STATE UNIVERSITY OF NEW YORK, COLLEGE AT NEW PALTZ, Sojourner Truth Library, World Study Center, New Paltz, 12561. Corinne Nyquist, Librn
Holdings: Vols (36,294) Cat Maps Pix
Notes: 36,294 volumes on Africa, Asia and the Near East, not incl reference books or pamphlets which have been integrated into the general collection.

NY —AFRICAN-AMERICAN INSTITUTE, Educational Materials Center Library, 833 United Nation Plaza, New York, 10017.
Holdings: Vols 1300 Cat Maps Pix
Notes: The collection is general but does incl all the major reference materials in the field; also 300 journals. There is a special section on African published books for children plus one on African literature.

NY —AMERICAN MUSEUM OF NATURAL HISTORY, Library Services Dept, Central Park W & 79th St, New York, 10024. Nina J Root, Chairwoman; Mary Genett, Asst Librn for Reference Services
Holdings: Cat Mss Maps Pix Slides

NY —COLUMBIA UNIVERSITY LIBRARIES, Rare Book & Manuscript Library, 801 Butler Library, 535 W 114 St, New York, 10027. Kenneth A Lohf, Librn
Notes: General and special collections on Africa, incl African architecture, music, papyrus mss, geology, maps, law and political science.

NY —NEW YORK PUBLIC LIBRARY, Research Libraries, General Research Division, Fifth Ave & 42 St, New York, 10018. Rodney Phillips, Chief
Holdings: Vols (2,225,000) Cat Maps Pix Microforms
Budget: ($775,718)

NY —NEW YORK PUBLIC LIBRARY, Donnell Foreign Language Library, 20 W 53 St, New York, 10019. Bosiljka Stevanovic, Supvr Librn
Notes: A circulating collection of books written in about 80 languages. The collections are general and popular in character - current topics, travel, histories, biography, etc, emphasizing the literature of the country - fiction, drama, poetry, literary criticism. The collections are primarily intended for use of readers whose first language is other than English. Separate catalogs for each language. Collections containing less than 100 volumes are not listed. Translations are moderately included.

OH —OHIO UNIVERSITY, Vernon R Alden Library, Athens, 45701. Kent Mulliner, Africana Specialist
Holdings: Vols (30,000) Cat Maps Microforms
Notes: Major emphasis on South Africa, East Africa, and Nigeria. Incl extensive collection of government reports and newspapers on microfilm.

OH —CLEVELAND PUBLIC LIBRARY, Fine Arts and Special Collections Department, 325 Superior Ave, Cleveland, 44114. Alice N Loranth, Head
Holdings: Vols 13,000 Cat Mss
Notes: Part of the research and reference collection on Orientalia. Contains scholarly materials in Western and in the vernacular languages of of Africa. African languages and philology, folklore, native cultures, ethnology, early travels, archaeology, and African history prior to the impact of Western influence are emphasized. The folklore collection incl archival materials pertaining to Africa and Black American folklore. Publication: Puckett, Newbell N: *Black Names in America: Origins and* Usage, collected by Newbell Niles Puckett, ed by Murray Heller. (Boston: G K Hall, 1975).
See also entries under Arabic Language and Literature; Egyptology; Folklore; Oriental Languages and Literatures.

OK —LANGSTON UNIVERSITY, M B Tolson Black Heritage Library, Langston, 73050. Rosaland Savage, Cur
Holdings: Vols (4000) Cat Mss Maps Pix Slides Microforms Filmstrips Records
Budget: ($1000)
Notes: Main objective is to fill a large gap in the Afro-American academic community and to serve as a depository of Afro-Americana for research scholars in the Southwest.

PA —DUQUESNE UNIVERSITY, Library, 600 Forbes Ave, Pittsburgh, 15219.
Holdings: Vols (7407) Cat Maps Slides Microforms
Notes: Mostly concerned with Africa south of the Sahara. CIDESA file (Centre International de Documentation Economique et Social Africaine) contains material dealing with economic and social problems of the African continent. Collection strong in materials on economics and Hausa and Swahili languages.

TX —TEXAS STATE LIBRARY, Archives Div, 1201 Brazos, PO Box 12927, Capitol Sta, Austin, 78711. David B Gracy II, State Archivist

TX —SOUTHERN METHODIST UNIVERSITY, DeGolyer Library, Box 396, SMU, Dallas, 75275. Clifton H Jones, Dir
Holdings: Vols (80,000) Cat Mss Maps Pix Slides Microforms
Notes: Small collection of first editions of prominent authors.

TX —FORT WORTH PUBLIC LIBRARY, Southeast Branch, 4300 E Berry, Fort Worth, 76105. Michael Roseborough, Special Collections Librn
Holdings: Vols 2500 Cat Mss Pix Phonorecords Audiotapes Filmstrips Microforms
Budget: ($6000)
Notes: Studies Collection incl most titles by and about Blacks published since 1972, plus many older titles on Afro-American history. Library also maintains up-to-date index to more than 20 Black periodicals.

TX —TEXAS TECH UNIVERSITY, Library, Lubbock, 79409. David J Murrah, Assoc Dir for Special Collections

AFRICA (cont.)

WI —UNIVERSITY OF WISCONSIN, MADISON, Memorial Library, 728 State St, Madison, 53706. David Henige, Librn
Holdings: // Cat Mss Maps Microforms
Notes: 5 microfilm reels of archival materials relating to the career of Maurice Martin de Ryck, who served as Governor of Equateur Province, Belgian Congo, as well as other miscellaneous data relating to Equateur Province. In addition to the microforms, the originals of these microforms are housed in the Rare Book Department of the Memorial Library.

AFRICA—COLONIZATION

DC —HOWARD UNIVERSITY, Moorland-Spingarn Research Center, 500 Howard Place NW, Washington, 20059. Clifford L Muse, Jr, Acting Dir
Holdings: Vols (106,086) Mss Maps Pix Slides Phonorecords Audiotapes 16mm Films Filmstrips Microforms
Budget: ($854,753)
See also entry under Blacks

NY —STATE UNIVERSITY OF NEW YORK, COLLEGE AT NEW PALTZ, Sojourner Truth Library, World Study Center, William J Haggerty Collection of French Colonial History, New Paltz, 12561. Corinne Nyquist, Librn
Holdings: Vols (19,153) // Uncat Mss Maps Pix
Notes: French colonial history. In 1966 this college acquired the research Library of the Comite Francais pour l'outre-mer. This library served the needs of a society in Paris whose membership incl French colonial administrators, scholars, and students. The more than 19,000 books and pamphlets and 135 sets of periodicals date from 1830, and cover the administration and development of the former colonies of France. Much of the material is economic, statistical, or agricultural, reflecting the interests of the collectors. British colonial history is well represented. Described in *Africana Library* Journal, Winter 1971.

WI —UNIVERSITY OF WISCONSIN, MADISON, Memorial Library, 728 State St, Madison, 53706. David Henige, Librn
Holdings: Cat Microforms
Notes: Collection consists of 90 microfilm reels of extant records of the Royal African Company (T70 series in the Public Record Office, London) together with several smaller collections of materials relating to the English presence on the Gold Coast in the 17th and 18th centuries. It is the most complete collection of its kind in the US. Various parts are described in David Henige, "Some Materials on the Early Guinea Coast in the United Kingdom," *African Research and Documentation,* no 11 (1976), pp 25-28. Also incl economics and social documents relating to the Belgian Congo particularly Katanga Province.

AFRICA—DESCRIPTION AND TRAVEL

DC —HOWARD UNIVERSITY, Moorland-Spingarn Research Center, 500 Howard Place NW, Washington, 20059. Clifford L Muse, Jr, Acting Dir

DC —SMITHSONIAN INSTITUTION, Archives Div, Washington, 20560. William W Moss, Archivist
Holdings: Mss Maps Pix
Notes: The Archives holds correspondence and records of a number of scientific expeditions with which the Smithsonian was connected, incl the Western Union Telegraph Expedition, the Smithsonian Roosevelt African Expedition, and the United States Exploring Expedition.

MN —UNIVERSITY OF MINNESOTA, James Ford Bell Library, 309 19th Ave S, Minneapolis, 55455. John Parker, Cur
Holdings: Vols (11,000) Cat Mss Maps
Notes: Collection of original materials relating to European expansion, 1400-1800.

NY —EXPLORERS CLUB, James B Ford Memorial Library, 46 E 70 St, New York, 10021. Janet Baldwin, Librn
Holdings: Vols (24,000) Cat Maps
Notes: Additions to the collection depend upon gifts. Access by appointment only. Collections incl the Ted Banks Collection; begun by Prof Harley H Bartlett, bequeathed to American Institute for Exploration, with additions by Prof Ted Bank II, and subsequently acquired by the Explorers Club. Incl field notes, diaries, and photographs of Bank, who led more than 30 scientific expeditions to the Arctic, Aleutians, Sea of Okhotsk, Japan, Taiwan, Southeast Asia and Africa.

AFRICA—ECONOMIC CONDITIONS

DC —HOWARD UNIVERSITY, Moorland-Spingarn Research Center, 500 Howard Place NW, Washington, 20059. Clifford L Muse, Jr, Acting Dir

MI —MICHIGAN STATE UNIVERSITY, International Library, Africana Collection, East Lansing, 48824. Eugene de Benko, Librn; Onuma Ezera, Bibliographer for Africana
Holdings: Vols (82,700) Cat Mss Maps Pix Slides Phonorecords Audiotapes Videotapes Filmstrips Microforms
Budget: ($78,000)
See also entry under Africa for full description.

PA —DUQUESNE UNIVERSITY, Library, 600 Forbes Ave, Pittsburgh, 15219.
Holdings: Vols (7407) Cat Maps Slides Microforms
Notes: Mostly concerned with Africa south of the Sahara. CIDESA file (Centre International de Documentation Economique et Social Africaine) contains material dealing with economic and social problems of the African continent. Collection strong in materials on economics and Hausa and Swahili languages.

AFRICA—GOVERNMENT PUBLICATIONS

CA —UNIVERSITY OF CALIFORNIA, LOS ANGELES, Research Library, Public Affairs Service, 405 Hilgard Ave, Los Angeles, 90024. Edward Shreeves, Chairman, Bibliographers Group; Eugenia Eaton, Head, Public Affairs Service
Holdings: Microforms
Notes: Selected publications of foreign governments (with emphasis on major world powers, Africa, Latin America and the Near and Middle East) and intergovernmental organizations.

DC —HOWARD UNIVERSITY, Moorland-Spingarn Research Center, 500 Howard Place NW, Washington, 20059. Clifford L Muse, Jr, Acting Dir

IL —NORTHWESTERN UNIVERSITY, Melville J Herskovits Library of African Studies, Evanston, 60201. Hans E Panofsky, Cur
Notes: The bulk of these are uncataloged and arranged in vertical files according to issuing agency.

NY —NEW YORK PUBLIC LIBRARY, Research Libraries, Economic & Public Affairs Div, Fifth Ave & 42 St, New York, 10018. Edward DiRoma, Chief
Holdings: Vols (1,500,000) Cat Microforms
Notes: Strong in government gazettes and statistical publications.

AFRICA—HISTORY

CA —UNIVERSITY OF CALIFORNIA, LOS ANGELES, Research Library, African Studies Collection, 405 Hilgard Ave, Los Angeles, 90024. Edward Shreeves, Chairman, Bibliographers Group; Joseph J Lauer, African Studies Bibliographer
Holdings: Vols (80,000) Maps Pix Slides Phonorecords Audiotapes Microforms
Notes: General collection mainly in the humanities and social sciences, covering prehistoric times to the present. Particular strengths include: early travel and exploration, mission field, literature, vernacular languages and literatures, Portuguese Africa, slavery (have the British Foreign Office's *General Correspondence. Slave Trade* on microfilm). Extensive holdings of journals, newspapers and government publications. The collection was described in the *Handbook of American Resources for African Studies* (1967).

CA —HOOVER INSTITUTION ON WAR, REVOLUTION & PEACE, Stanford University, Stanford, 94305. Peter Duignan, Cur; Karen Fung, Deputy Cur
Holdings: Vols (60,000) Cat Mss Maps Pix Slides Microforms
Notes: Politics, economics, and history from 1870 to the present. About 500 current periodicals titles, about 90 current newspaper titles. Legislative debates, political ephemera. Have microfilm of Portuguese African nationalist material, confidential prints of Great Britian's foreign and colonial offices 1870 through 1922. Nigerian pamphlets (market literature, political and historical tracts), collection of the correspondence pamphlets and ephemera of Alfred B Xuma, collections on Zaire (1955-1963), South African nationalist publications on microfilm. Descriptions of the Collection: *African and Middle East Collections* pub by Hoover Institute, *Handbook of American Resources for African Studies* pub by Hoover. Holdings of the Collection in *Hoover Institute on War, Revolution, and Peace Library Catalog* pub by G K Hall,*Emerging Nationalism in Portuguese Africa: A Bibliography* pub by Hoover, *German Africa* pub by Hoover. *The Treason Trail in South Africa: A Guide to the Microfilm Record of the Trial* pub by Hoover. *History of the Library and Archives of the Hoover Institution on War, Revolution and Peace,* edited by Peter Duignan (Hoover Institution Press), *Guide to Non-federal Archives and Manuscripts in the United States Relating to Africa,* compiled Aloha P Smith (East Ardsley, Eng, Microform Ltd).

CT —YALE UNIVERSITY, Box 1603A, Yale Station, New Haven, 06520.

DC —HOWARD UNIVERSITY, Moorland-Spingarn Research Center, 500 Howard Place NW, Washington, 20059. Clifford L Muse, Jr, Acting Dir

DC —LIBRARY OF CONGRESS, Washington, 20540.
Notes: Project of a consortium to microfilm about 200,000 pp of material on Great Britain, France, Russia and Prussia, for the period 1848-1918 in the ms and documentary collections of the Austrian State Archives. The collection will incl among others, documents on the Congo Conference in Berlin, 1884-1887 and the British-Portuguese conflict in East Africa, 1889-1891.

FL —BETHUNE-COOKMAN COLLEGE LIBRARY, Daytona Beach, 32015. Albert M Bethune, Jr, College Archivist
Notes: Papers and private library of the historian, Joseph Henry Taylor.

IL —NORTHWESTERN UNIVERSITY, Melville J Herskovits Library of African Studies, Evanston, 60201. Hans E Panofsky, Cur
Notes: Primary and secondary sources; collected in depth.

MA —BRANDEIS UNIVERSITY, Goldfarb Library, 415 South St, Waltham, 02154. Bessie Hahn, Dir
Notes: Albert Schweitzer Collection. This collection consists of 255 letters of correspondence to and from Dr Albert Schweitzer and other staff members of the Lambarene Hospital, Gabon, Africa. Also included in the collection are some artifacts, memorabilia and two commemorative Albert Schweitzer volumes. A guide to the collection was published in *Guide to Albert Schweitzer Collections in the United States,* New York, 1981.

MI —MICHIGAN STATE UNIVERSITY, International Library, Africana Collection, East Lansing, 48824. Eugene de Benko, Librn; Onuma Ezera, Bibliographer for Africana
Holdings: Vols (82,700) Cat Mss Maps Pix Slides Phonorecords Audiotapes Videotapes Filmstrips Microforms
Budget: ($78,000)
See also entry under Africa for full description.

AFRICA—HISTORY (cont.)

NY —NEW YORK PUBLIC LIBRARY, Research Libraries, General Research Division, Fifth Ave & 42 St, New York, 10018. Rodney Phillips, Chief
Holdings: Vols 20,000 Cat Maps Pix Microforms

NY —NEW YORK PUBLIC LIBRARY, Schomburg Center for Research in Black Culture, 515 Lenox Ave, New York, 10037. Catherine J Lenix Hooker, Interim Administrator
Holdings: Vols (85,000) Cat Mss Maps Pix Slides
Notes: Materials in all formats about Black peoples throughout the world. Extensive archival holdings, vertical files, Afro-American and African art. Collections incl 182 groups of mss, 100,000 photographs, 6500 slides, 5600 phonorecords, 2300 audiotapes, and over 30,000 microforms. Described in *The Dictionary Catalog of the Schomburg Collection,* 9 vols, and supplements to 1974, 7 vols (Boston: G K Hall, 1962-1975); and *Bibliographic Guide to Black Studies* (Boston: G K Hall). Since 1972, the Center's holdings have been incl in the *Dictionary Catalog of the Research Libraries, New York Public Library.*

AFRICA—MAPS

†CA —STANFORD UNIVERSITY LIBRARIES, General Reference Dept, Central Map Collection, Stanford, 94305.

OR —UNIVERSITY OF OREGON, Map Library, Eugene, 97403. Peter L Stark, Map Librarian
Holdings: Cat Maps Pix
Budget: ($4000)
Notes: Incl 50 atlases, 12,000 maps. Former British colonies of Nigeria and Ghana are emphasized.

AFRICA—NATURAL RESOURCES

OH —ANTIOCH COLLEGE, Olive Kettering Library, Livermore St, Yellow Springs, 45387. Nina Myatt, Cur
Notes: Personal papers and correspondence (1920-1975) of Arthur E Morgan former President of Antioch (1920-1936), first director of Ohio's Miami Valley Conservancy District, and first Chairman of the Tennessee Valley Authority (TVA). Mss, film, out-takes, much on the engineering of over 50 water-control projects in this country, Africa, and India. Materials on Edward Bellamy (Morgan wrote biography of Bellamy). Incl family papers. About 175 file boxes.

AFRICA—POLITICS AND GOVERNMENT

CA —HOOVER INSTITUTION ON WAR, REVOLUTION & PEACE, Stanford University, Stanford, 94305. Milorad M Drachkovitch, Archivist
Holdings: Mss
Notes: Papers of Ernest W Lefever, 1956-1969, incl ms, drafts, correspondence, reports, interviews, notes, pamphlets, newspaper clippings, and printed matter, relating to modern politics in Zaire (Republic of the Congo). Ethopia, and other African nations. 3 ms boxes. Also, a collection of sound recordings of interviews with British, Portuguese and South African diplomats, politicians, economic advisors, journalist, and businessmen, 1970-1976, relating to political events in Portugal and South Africa, collected by Keith Middlemas, Professor at the University of Sussex, England. Also incl are documents and correspondence pertaining to British, Portuguese and South African relations and various political events. 1966-1973. 7 ms boxes.

CA —HOOVER INSTITUTION ON WAR, REVOLUTION & PEACE, Stanford University, Stanford, 94305. Peter Duignan, Cur; Karen Fung, Deputy Cur
Holdings: Vols (60,000) Cat Mss Maps Pix Slides Microforms
Notes: Politics, economics, and history from 1870 to the present. About 500 current periodicals titles, about 90 current newspaper titles. Legislative debates, political ephemera. Have microfilm of Portuguese African nationalist material, confidential prints of Great Britian's foreign and colonial offices 1870 through 1922. Nigerian pamphlets (market literature, political and historical tracts), collection of the correspondence pamphlets and ephemera of Alfred B Xuma, collections on Zaire (1955-1963), South African nationalist publications on microfilm. Descriptions of the Collection: *African and Middle East Collections* pub by Hoover Institute, *Handbook of American Resources for African Studies* pub by Hoover. Holdings of the Collection in *Hoover Institute on War, Revolution, and Peace Library Catalog* pub by G K Hall, *Emerging Nationalism in Portuguese Africa: A Bibliography* pub by Hoover, *German Africa* pub by Hoover. *The Treason Trail in South Africa: A Guide to the Microfilm Record of the Trial* pub by Hoover. *History of the Library and Archives of the Hoover Institution on War, Revolution and Peace,* edited by Peter Duignan (Hoover Institution Press), *Guide to Non-federal Archives and Manuscripts in the United States Relating to Africa,* compiled Aloha P Smith (East Ardsley, Eng, Microform Ltd).

DC —HOWARD UNIVERSITY, Moorland-Spingarn Research Center, 500 Howard Place NW, Washington, 20059. Clifford L Muse, Jr, Acting Dir

IL —NORTHWESTERN UNIVERSITY, Melville J Herskovits Library of African Studies, Evanston, 60201. Hans E Panofsky, Cur
Notes: Records of African legislative assemblies and some of the quantitative data found in Morrison, Donald G and others, *Black Africa* (Irvington Publishers, 1984).

MI —MICHIGAN STATE UNIVERSITY, International Library, Africana Collection, East Lansing, 48824. Eugene de Benko, Librn; Onuma Ezera, Bibliographer for Africana
Holdings: Vols (82,700) Cat Mss Maps Pix Slides Phonorecords Audiotapes Videotapes Filmstrips Microforms
Budget: ($78,000)
See also entry under Africa for full description.

AFRICA—POPULATION

DC —HOWARD UNIVERSITY, Moorland-Spingarn Research Center, 500 Howard Place NW, Washington, 20059. Clifford L Muse, Jr, Acting Dir

NC —CAROLINA POPULATION CENTER, Library, University Sq E, Chapel Hill, 27514. Patricia Shipman, Head Librn
Holdings: Vols (20,000) Cat
Notes: Try to acquire everything published in English on population, with particular emphasis on the US and developing countries. Also acquire conference proceedings, seminar papers. These and journal articles are indexed and the analytics are incl in the catalog. Incl 13,000 reprints and other pieces of ephemera. Most extensive area files are on India, Africa, Thailand, Iran, Korea, and Latin America. Holdings are recorded on an automated data base. A microfiche catalog is available for use in the Library and for purchase. Access by subject & geographic area are available through the Library's own thesaurus-based indexing systems.

AFRICA—RELIGION

DC —HOWARD UNIVERSITY, Moorland-Spingarn Research Center, 500 Howard Place NW, Washington, 20059. Clifford L Muse, Jr, Acting Dir

GA —EMORY UNIVERSITY, Candler School of Theology, Pitts Theology Library, Atlanta, 30322. Channing Jeschke, Librn; Anita K Delaries, Curator
Notes: 9.5 linear feet of mss and printed materials documenting the history of the independent African Orthodox Church (1880-1974), and the role of Archbishop Daniel William Alexander (1882-1970), sent to the Library for fear of its possible destruction if kept in South Africa. Finding aid available.

MA —COLLEGE OF THE HOLY CROSS, Dinand Library, College St, Worcester, 01610. James M Mahoney, Cur of Special Collection
Holdings: / / Mss
Notes: The Joseph J Williams, SJ Collection contains 107 mss and 865 letters concerning religious practices of tribes in Africa. Collection is indexed, restricted use.

AFRICA—SOUTH OF THE SAHARA
see Africa South of the Sahara

AFRICA, EAST

DC —HOWARD UNIVERSITY, Moorland-Spingarn Research Center, 500 Howard Place NW, Washington, 20059. Clifford L Muse, Jr, Acting Dir
Holdings: Vols (106,086) Mss Maps Pix Slides Phonorecords Audiotapes 16mm Films Filmstrips Microforms
Budget: ($854,753)
See also entry under Blacks

IL —NORTHWESTERN UNIVERSITY, Melville J Herskovits Library of African Studies, Evanston, 60201. Hans E Panofsky, Cur
Notes: Virtually all scholarly publications on and from East Africa.

MI —MICHIGAN STATE UNIVERSITY, International Library, Africana Collection, East Lansing, 48824. Eugene de Benko, Librn; Onuma Ezera, Bibliographer for Africana
Holdings: Vols (82,700) Cat Mss Maps Pix Slides Phonorecords Audiotapes Videotapes Filmstrips Microforms
Budget: ($78,000)
See also entry under Africa for full description.

OH —OHIO UNIVERSITY, Vernon R Alden Library, Athens, 45701. Kent Mulliner, Africana Specialist
Holdings: Vols (30,000) Cat Maps Microforms
Notes: Major emphasis on South Africa, East Africa, and Nigeria. Incl extensive collection of government reports and newspapers on microfilm.

AFRICA, NORTH

CA —HOOVER INSTITUTION ON WAR, REVOLUTION & PEACE, Stanford University, Stanford, 94305. Peter Duignan, Cur; Karen Fung, Deputy Cur
Holdings: Vols (100,000)
Notes: For full description of collection, see Hoover Institution entry under Near East.

DC —HOWARD UNIVERSITY, Moorland-Spingarn Research Center, 500 Howard Place NW, Washington, 20059. Clifford L Muse, Jr, Acting Dir
Holdings: Vols (106,086) Mss Maps Pix Slides Phonorecords Audiotapes 16mm Films Filmstrips Microforms
Budget: ($854,753)
See also entry under Blacks

IL —NORTHWESTERN UNIVERSITY, Melville J Herskovits Library of African Studies, Evanston, 60201. Hans E Panofsky, Cur
Notes: The concentration is on publications in European languages.

MI —MICHIGAN STATE UNIVERSITY, International Library, Africana Collection, East Lansing, 48824. Eugene de Benko, Librn; Onuma Ezera, Bibliographer for Africana
Holdings: Vols (82,700) Cat Mss Maps Pix Slides Phonorecords Audiotapes Videotapes Filmstrips Microforms
Budget: ($78,000)
See also entry under Africa for full description.

AFRICA, SOUTH

CA —LOS ANGELES STATE & COUNTY ARBORETUM, Plant Science Library, 301

AFRICA, SOUTH (cont.)

N Baldwin Ave, Arcadia, 91006. Joan DeFato, Librn
Holdings: Vols (24,000) Cat 16mm Films
Budget: ($6000)
Notes: Emphasis on woody plants, particularly of Australia and South Africa. Botany is weighted toward taxonomy rather than plant physiology.

CA —CALIFORNIA INSTITUTE OF TECHNOLOGY, Munger Africana Library, 115B Baxter Hall, Pasadena, 91125. Mary Ellen Perez, Librn
Holdings: Vols 30,000 Cat Mss Maps Pix Phonorecords Audiotapes
Notes: All aspects of sub-Saharan Africa, with special emphasis on South Africa, politics and history. Strong on rare books, early accounts of European exploration and missionary accounts, folklore and linguistics, political ephemera, art. Separate catalog.

CA —HOOVER INSTITUTION ON WAR, REVOLUTION & PEACE, Stanford University, Stanford, 94305. Milorad M Drachkovitch, Archivist
Notes: Collection of sound recordings of interviews with British, Portuguese and South African diplomats, politicians, economic advisors, journalists, and businessmen, 1970-76, relating to political events in Portugal and Southern Africa, collected by Keith Middlemas, Professor at the University of Sussex, England. Also incl are documents and correspondence pertaining to British, Portuguese and South African relations and various political events, 1966-1973. 7 ms boxes. Collection of leaflets, newsletters, pamphlets, and other ephemera of various political action groups and other organizations, 1969-1974, relating to political and economic developments in southern African countries, incl Angola, Mozambique, Rhodesia (Zimbabwe), Union of South Africa, and South West Africa (Namibia). 5 ms boxes. In addition, papers of W H Vatcher, Jr, 1939-65, incl correspndence,mss, pamphlets, leaflets, slides, photographs, etc, relating to South African political parties; Afrikaner and African nationalism; Afrikaner Broederbond. 18 ms boxes.

DC —HOWARD UNIVERSITY, Moorland-Spingarn Research Center, 500 Howard Place NW, Washington, 20059. Clifford L Muse, Jr, Acting Dir
Holdings: Vols (106,086) Mss Maps Pix Slides Phonorecords Audiotapes 16mm Films Filmstrips Microforms
Budget: ($854,753)
See also entry under Blacks

GA —EMORY UNIVERSITY, Candler School of Theology, Pitts Theology Library, Atlanta, 30322. Channing Jeschke, Librn; Anita K Delaries, Curator
Notes: 9.5 linear feet of mss and printed materials documenting the history of the independent African Orthodox Church (1880-1974), and the role of Archbishop Daniel William Alexander (1882-1970), sent to the Library for fear of its possible destruction if kept in South Africa. Finding aid available.

IL —NORTHWESTERN UNIVERSITY, Melville J Herskovits Library of African Studies, Evanston, 60201. Hans E Panofsky, Cur
Notes: Historical material and race relations interpreted very broadly. Also, the collections of papers assembled by Dennis Brutus and Gwendolen M Carter.

MI —MICHIGAN STATE UNIVERSITY, International Library, Africana Collection, East Lansing, 48824. Eugene de Benko, Librn; Onuma Ezera, Bibliographer for Africana
Holdings: Vols (82,700) Cat Mss Maps Pix Slides Phonorecords Audiotapes Videotapes Filmstrips Microforms
Budget: ($78,000)
See also entry under Africa for full description.

MI —WESTERN MICHIGAN UNIVERSITY, Dwight B Waldo Library, Kalamazoo, 49008. Jacqueline Driscoll, Social Science Ref Librn
Holdings: Vols (18,000) Cat Maps Phonorecords Microforms
Budget: $1000
Notes: The Ann Kercher Memorial Collection of Africa. No separate catalog or index to the collection. Collection covers sub-Saharan Africa and emphasizes anthropology, history, economics, education, geography, travel, sociology, politcal science, languages and linguistics, literature. Some government documents, African newspapers, pamphlet collection dating back to mid-1950's. Incl 300 African journals described in *Serials in African Studies Held by Western Michigan University Library* rev, ed, comp by D Kercher (Kalamazoo: Western Michigan Univ Library, 1976), 63 pp. Also incl 1000 maps, 20 phonorecords, and 400 microforms.

NY —AMERICAN MUSEUM OF NATURAL HISTORY, Library Services Dept, Central Park W & 79th St, New York, 10024. Nina J Root, Chairwoman; Mary Genett, Asst Librn for Reference Services
Holdings: Cat Mss Maps Pix Slides

OH —OHIO UNIVERSITY, Vernon R Alden Library, Athens, 45701. Kent Mulliner, Africana Specialist
Holdings: Vols (30,000) Cat Maps Microforms
Notes: Major emphasis on South Africa, East Africa, and Nigeria. Incl extensive collection of government reports and newspapers on microfilm.

AFRICA, SOUTH-WEST see Namibia

AFRICA, WEST

DC —HOWARD UNIVERSITY, Moorland-Spingarn Research Center, 500 Howard Place NW, Washington, 20059. Clifford L Muse, Jr, Acting Dir
Holdings: Vols (106,086) Mss Maps Pix Slides Phonorecords Audiotapes 16mm Films Filmstrips Microforms
Budget: ($854,753)
See also entry under Blacks

IL —NORTHWESTERN UNIVERSITY, Melville J Herskovits Library of African Studies, Evanston, 60201. Hans E Panofsky, Cur
Holdings: Vols (85,000) Mss
Budget: ($70,000)
Notes: Although the collection incl the papers of Melville J Herskovits, the last ten years of this archive is closed until 1988. Also have papers of the African Studies Association, Carter/Karis, Abdullah Abdurahman, Alex Hepple, Leo Kuper, Dennis Brutus; further, on West Africa--John Paden, Umar Falke, Liberian economic survey. Supplements for 1972-1977 for our book catalog (8 vols) was published by G K Hall in 1978; unlike 1972, the supplement to the *Joint Acqusitions List of Africana* will be published in seperate vols from the Northwestern Catalog supplement. There are, in 1978, 16,000 additional vols.

MI —MICHIGAN STATE UNIVERSITY, International Library, Sahel Documentation Center, East Lansing, 48824. Eugene deBenko, Librn; Learthen Dorsey, Librn
Holdings: Vols (5100) Cat Mss Maps Pix Slides Phonorecords Audiotapes Videotapes Microforms
Budget: ($8000)
Notes: Sahel Documentation Center was established in September 1976 in support of research on the development of the drought-stricken Sahelian countries (Chad, Niger, Senegal, Mauritania, Mali, Upper Volta, The Gambia and Cape Verde). Emphasis on the socio-economic conditions and rural development of the area. Collection contains primary and secondary sources: books, mss, maps, reports, journals and microforms. Description of the collection: *Sahel-Bibliographic Bulletin/Bulletin* Bibliographique, a bilingual quarterly (v 1 nos 1-4, 1977); and *Documentation for Development in the Sahel* (1977, 3 pp).

AFRICA SOUTH OF THE SAHARA

CA —UNIVERSITY OF CALIFORNIA, LOS ANGELES, Research Library, African Studies Collection, 405 Hilgard Ave, Los Angeles, 90024. Edward Shreeves, Chairman, Bibliographers Group; Joseph J Lauer, African Studies Bibliographer
Holdings: Maps Pix Slides Phonorecords Audiotapes Microforms
Notes: General collection mainly in the humanities and social sciences, covering prehistoric times to the present. Particular strengths include: early travel and exploration, mission field, literature, vernacular languages and literatures, Portuguese Africa, slavery (have the British Foreign Office's *General Correspondence. Slave Trade* on microfilm). Extensive holdings of journals, newspapers and government publications. The collection was described in the *Handbook of American Resources for African Studies* (1967).

CA —CALIFORNIA INSTITUTE OF TECHNOLOGY, Munger Africana Library, 115B Baxter Hall, Pasadena, 91125. Mary Ellen Perez, Librn
Holdings: Vols 30,000 Cat Mss Maps Pix Phonorecords Audiotapes
Notes: All aspects of sub-Saharan Africa, with special emphasis on South African politics and history. Strong on rare books, early accounts of European exploration and missionary accounts, folklore and linguistics, political ephemera, art. Separate catalog.

CA —HOOVER INSTITUTION ON WAR, REVOLUTION & PEACE, Stanford University, Stanford, 94305. Peter Duignan, Cur; Karen Fung, Deputy Cur
Holdings: Vols (60,000) Cat Mss Maps Pix Slides Microforms
Notes: Politics, economics, and history from 1870 to the present. About 500 current periodicals titles, about 90 current newspaper titles. Legislative debates, political ephemera. Have microfilm of Portuguese African nationalist material, confidential prints of Great Britian's foreign and colonial offices 1870 through 1922. Nigerian pamphlets (market literature, political and historical tracts), collection of the correspondence pamphlets and ephemera of Alfred B Xuma, collections on Zaire (1955-1963), South African nationalist publications on microfilm. Descriptions of the Collection: *African and Middle East Collections* pub by Hoover Institute, *Handbook of American Resources for African Studies* pub by Hoover. Holdings of the Collection in *Hoover Institute on War, Revolution, and Peace Library Catalog* pub by G K Hall,*Emerging Nationalism in Portuguese Africa: A Bibliography* pub by Hoover, *German Africa* pub by Hoover. *The Treason Trail in South Africa: A Guide to the Microfilm Record of the Trial* pub by Hoover. *History of the Library and Archives of the Hoover Institution on War, Revolution and Peace*, edited by Peter Duignan (Hoover Institution Press), *Guide to Non-federal Archives and Manuscripts in the United States Relating to Africa*, compiled Aloha P Smith (East Ardsley, Eng, Microform Ltd).

CT —YALE UNIVERSITY, Box 1603A, Yale Station, New Haven, 06520.
Holdings: Cat

DC —HOWARD UNIVERSITY, Moorland-Spingarn Research Center, 500 Howard Place NW, Washington, 20059. Clifford L Muse, Jr, Acting Dir
Holdings: Vols (106,086) Cat Mss Maps Pix Slides Phonorecords Audiotapes 16mm Films Filmstrips Microforms
Budget: ($854,753)
Notes: *The Glenn Carrington Collection: A Guide to the Books, Manuscripts, Music and Recordings* (DC MSRC, 1977). *Dictionary Catalog of the Jesse E Moorland Collection of Negro Life and History*, 9 vols and Supplement, 3 vols (Boston: G K Hall, 1970, 1977). *Dictionary Catalog of the Arthur Spingarn Collection of Negro Authors*, 2 vols (Boston: G K Hall, 1970). Guide to Processed Collections in the Manuscript Division of the Moorland-Spingarn Research Center (DC, MSRC, 1983). The Moorland-Spingran Research Center is recognized as one of the largest and most comprehensive repositories in the world for the collection, preservation and dissemination of historical

AFRICA SOUTH OF THE SAHARA (cont.)

materials documenting from antiquity to the present the history and culture of Black people in Africa, Europe, the Caribbean and the US. Since 1973, the Research Center has greatly expanded its facilitiesand resources and currently provides research services in all aspects of library and archival research, including manuscripts, oral history, music, prints and photographs and general library materials. The Research Center also maintains professional zerographic, micrographic, photographic and similar reproduction laboratories.

IL —NORTHWESTERN UNIVERSITY, Melville J Herskovits Library of African Studies, Evanston, 60201. Hans E Panofsky, Cur
Holdings: Vols (85,000) Mss
Budget: ($70,000)
Notes: Although the collection incl the papers of Melville J Herskovits, the last ten years of this archive is closed until 1988. Also have papers of the African Studies Association, Carter/Karis, Abdullah Abdurahman, Alex Hepple, Leo Kuper, Dennis Brutus; further, on West Africa--John Paden, Umar Falke, Liberian economic survey. Supplements for 1972-1977 for our book catalog (8 vols) was published by G K Hall in 1978; unlike 1972, the supplement to the *Joint Acqusitions List of Africana* will be published in seperate vols from the Northwestern Catalog supplement. There are, in 1978, 16,000 additional vols.

MI —MICHIGAN STATE UNIVERSITY, International Library, Africana Collection, East Lansing, 48824. Eugene de Benko, Librn; Onuma Ezera, Bibliographer for Africana
Holdings: Vols (82,700) Cat Mss Maps Pix Slides Phonorecords Audiotapes Videotapes Filmstrips Microforms
Budget: ($78,000)
See also entry under Africa for full description.

MI —WESTERN MICHIGAN UNIVERSITY, Dwight B Waldo Library, Kalamazoo, 49008. Jacqueline Driscoll, Social Science Ref Librn
Holdings: Vols (18,000) Cat Maps Phonorecords Microforms
Budget: $1000
Notes: The Ann Kercher Memorial Collection of Africa. No separate catalog or index to the collection. Collection covers sub-Saharan Africa and emphasizes anthropology, history, economics, education, geography, travel, sociology, politcal science, languages and linguistics, literature. Some government documents, African newspapers, pamphlet collection dating back to mid-1950's. Incl 300 African journals described in *Serials in African Studies Held by Western Michigan University Library* rev, ed, comp by D Kercher (Kalamazoo: Western Michigan Univ Library, 1976), 63 pp. Also incl 1000 maps, 20 phonorecords, and 400 microforms.

NY —AMERICAN MUSEUM OF NATURAL HISTORY, Library Services Dept, Central Park W & 79th St, New York, 10024. Nina J Root, Chairwoman; Mary Genett, Asst Librn for Reference Services
Holdings: Cat Mss Maps Pix Slides

NY —NEW YORK PUBLIC LIBRARY, Research Libraries, General Research Division, Fifth Ave & 42 St, New York, 10018. Rodney Phillips, Chief
Holdings: Vols (2,225,000) Cat Maps Pix Microforms
Budget: ($775,718)

NY —NEW YORK PUBLIC LIBRARY, Schomburg Center for Research in Black Culture, 515 Lenox Ave, New York, 10037. Catherine J Lenix Hooker, Interim Administrator
Holdings: Vols (85,000) Cat Mss Maps Pix Slides Phonorecords Audiotapes Videotapes 16mm Films Filmstrips Microforms
See also entry under Black Studies.

PA —DUQUESNE UNIVERSITY, Library, 600 Forbes Ave, Pittsburgh, 15219.
Holdings: Vols (7407) Cat Maps Slides Microforms
Notes: Mostly concerned with Africa south of the Sahara. CIDESA file (Centre International de Documentation Economique et Social Africaine) contains material dealing with economic and social problems of the African continent. Collection strong in materials on economics and Hausa and Swahili languages.

PA —UNIVERSITY OF PITTSBURGH, Hillman Library, Pittsburgh, 15260.
Holdings: Vols (5279) Cat Microforms
Notes: Special emphasis of the Afro-American Collection is on the blacks in the United States; incl materials on Africa south of the Sahara and Caribbean areas of the world.

BC —SIMON FRASER UNIVERSITY, Library, Burnaby, V5A 1S6, Can. Percilla Groves, Special Collections Librn
Holdings: Vols 9000 Cat Maps Microforms
Notes: Emphasis on history and government documents. Over 3000 maps; 1250 microforms.

AFRICAN ART see Art, African and Afro-American

AFRICAN CHILDREN'S LITERATURE see Children'S Literature, African

AFRICAN COMPANY, ROYAL see Royal African Company

AFRICAN DIAMOND RUSH see Diamond Rush, African

AFRICAN DIASPORA

DC —HOWARD UNIVERSITY, Moorland-Spingarn Research Center, 500 Howard Place NW, Washington, 20059. Clifford L Muse, Jr, Acting Dir

AFRICAN DRAMA

DC —HOWARD UNIVERSITY, Moorland-Spingarn Research Center, 500 Howard Place NW, Washington, 20059. Clifford L Muse, Jr, Acting Dir

PA —PENNSYLVANIA STATE UNIVERSITY, Fred Lewis Pattee Library, University Park, 16802. Stuart Forth, Dean of Libraries
Holdings: Vols (4000) Cat Phonorecords Microforms
Budget: ($2,300,000)
Notes: Strong in Austsralian Literature, lesser holdings in Canadian, Caribbean, New Zealand, Indian and West Africa. Special collections of African Plays, Australian Literature.

AFRICAN FOLK SONGS see Folk Songs, African

AFRICAN FOLKLORE see Folklore, African

AFRICAN GOLD COAST see Ghana

AFRICAN GOLD RUSH see Gold Rush, African

AFRICAN LANGUAGES AND LITERATURES

CA —UNIVERSITY OF CALIFORNIA, LOS ANGELES, Research Library, African Studies Collection, 405 Hilgard Ave, Los Angeles, 90024. Edward Shreeves, Chairman, Bibliographers Group; Joseph J Lauer, African Studies Bibliographer
Holdings: Maps Pix Slides Phonorecords Audiotapes Microforms
Notes: General collection mainly in the humanities and social sciences, covering prehistoric times to the present. Particular strengths include: early travel and exploration, mission field, literature, vernacular languages and literatures, Portuguese Africa, slavery (have the British Foreign Office's *General Correspondence. Slave Trade* on microfilm). Extensive holdings of journals, newspapers and government publications. The collection was described in the *Handbook of American Resources for African Studies* (1967).

DC —HOWARD UNIVERSITY, Moorland-Spingarn Research Center, 500 Howard Place NW, Washington, 20059. Clifford L Muse, Jr, Acting Dir
Holdings: Vols (106,086) Mss Maps Pix Slides Phonorecords Audiotapes 16mm Films Filmstrips Microforms
Budget: ($854,753)
See also entry under Blacks

DC —LIBRARY OF CONGRESS, General Reference & Bibliography Div, African Section, Washington, 20540. Julian W Witherell, Head
Holdings: Vols (33,000)
Notes: Libray of Congress collections of Africana (material issued in or relating to Africa) are among the best in the world, encompassing every major field of study except technical agriculture and clinical medicine. Most of the publications, including especially strong holdings in economics, history, linguistics, and literature, are dispersed in the Library's general book and periodical collections. The largest single block of material on Africa is the collection of surveys, yearbooks, histories, and general descriptive works (the DT classification). In the Library's shelflist, this is represented by about 32,000 titles. The shelflist also indicates, for example, that the number of bibliographic guides on Africa totals about 1100. An additional wealth of African may be found in special collections of legal material, manuscripts, maps, microform, music, newspapers,photographs and films in various custodial divisions of the Library. In the African Section, researchers may consult card indexes to Africana monographs and periodical articles and collections of published bibliographies, yearbooks, pamphlets, and current issues of major periodicals. The section's reference collection also includes unpublished research papers prepared for academic congresses and sample issues of works in African languages and literature. Additional information can be found in *The African Section in the Library of Congress*, a five-page brochure available free on request from the section, Room 1040-C, Thomas Jefferson Bulding, Library of Congress, Washington, D C 20540

IL —NORTHWESTERN UNIVERSITY, Melville J Herskovits Library of African Studies, Evanston, 60201. Hans E Panofsky, Cur
Notes: Collected in depth. Incl a complete set of the recordings by and on African authors assembled by the Transcription Centre, London. Also about 3000 books and pamphlets on African languages.

MA —HARVARD UNIVERSITY LIBRARY, Cambridge, 02138.
Holdings: Cat

NY —AFRICAN-AMERICAN INSTITUTE, Educational Materials Center Library, 833 United Nation Plaza, New York, 10017.
Holdings: Vols 1300 Cat Maps Pix
Notes: The collection is general but does incl all the major reference materials in the field; also 300 journals,. There is a special section on African published books for children plus one on African literature.

NY —NEW YORK PUBLIC LIBRARY, Research Libraries, General Research Division, Fifth Ave & 42 St, New York, 10018. Rodney Phillips, Chief
Holdings: Vols (2,225,000) Cat Maps Pix Microforms
Budget: ($775,718)
Notes: Over 300 languages represented.

NY —NEW YORK PUBLIC LIBRARY, Donnell Foreign Language Library, 20 W 53 St, New York, 10019. Bosiljka Stevanovic, Supvr Librn
Notes: African writings in French language incl in the French collection. No separate catalog.

PA —DUQUESNE UNIVERSITY, Library, 600 Forbes Ave, Pittsburgh, 15219.
Holdings: Vols (7407) Cat Maps Slides Microforms
Notes: Mostly concerned with Africa south

AFRICAN LANGUAGES AND LITERATURES (cont.)

of the Sahara. CIDESA file (Centre International de Documentation Economique et Social Africaine) contains material dealing with economic and social problems of the African continent. Collection strong in materials on economics and Hausa and Swahili languages.

PA —PENNSYLVANIA STATE UNIVERSITY, Fred Lewis Pattee Library, University Park, 16802. Stuart Forth, Dean of Libraries
Holdings: Vols (4000) Cat Phonorecords Microforms
Budget: ($2,300,000)
Notes: Strong in Australian Literature, lesser holdings in Canadian, Caribbean, New Zealand, Indian and West African. Special collections of African Plays, Australian Literature.

AFRICAN MUSIC see Music, African

AFRICAN NATIONALISM see Nationalism—Africa

AFRICAN NEWSPAPERS see Newspapers, African

AFRICAN ORTHODOX CHURCH

GA —EMORY UNIVERSITY, Candler School of Theology, Pitts Theology Library, Atlanta, 30322. Channing Jeschke, Librn; Anita K Delaries, Curator
Notes: 9.5 linear feet of mss and printed materials documenting the history of the independent African Orthodox Church (1880-1974), and the role of Archbishop Daniel William Alexander (1882-1970), sent to the Library for fear of its possible destruction if kept in South Africa. Finding aid available.

AFRICAN PERIODICALS see Periodicals, African

AFRICAN STUDIES ASSOCIATION

DC —HOWARD UNIVERSITY, Moorland-Spingarn Research Center, 500 Howard Place NW, Washington, 20059. Clifford L Muse, Jr, Acting Dir
Notes: Papers (1960-).

IL —NORTHWESTERN UNIVERSITY, Melville J Herskovits Library of African Studies, Evanston, 60201. Hans E Panofsky, Cur
Holdings: Vols (85,000) Mss
Budget: ($70,000)
See also entry under Africa

AFRICAN SWINE FEVER

NY —US DEPT OF AGRICULTURE, Agriculture Research Service, Plum Island Animal Disease Laboratory, PO Box 848, Greenport, 11944. Stephen Perlman, Librn
Holdings: Vols (15,000) Cat Pix Slides Microforms
Budget: ($37,000)

AFRICANA

MI —CENTRAL MICHIGAN UNIVERSITY, Clarke Historical Library, Mount Pleasant, 48859. William H Mulligan, Jr, Dir; William Miles, Biography Collections Librn
Holdings: Vols 900
Notes: Wilbert Wright Collection of Africana and Afro-Americana.

AFRICANS IN FOREIGN COUNTRIES

DC —HOWARD UNIVERSITY, Moorland-Spingarn Research Center, 500 Howard Place NW, Washington, 20059. Clifford L Muse, Jr, Acting Dir
Holdings: Vols (106,086) Mss Maps Pix Slides Phonorecords Audiotapes 16mm Films Filmstrips Microforms
Budget: ($854,753)
See also entry under Blacks

AFRIKAANS-ARABIC DIALECT see Arabic-Afrikaans Dialect

AFRIKANER LANGUAGE see Afrikaans Language and Literature

AFRIKANERS

CA —HOOVER INSTITUTION ON WAR, REVOLUTION & PEACE, Stanford University, Stanford, 94305. Milorad M Drachkovitch, Archivist
Holdings: Mss Pix Slides
Notes: Papers of W H Vatcher, Jr, 1939-65, incl correspondence, mss, pamphlets, leaflets, slides, photographs, and other material, relating to South African political parties; Afrikaner and African nationalism; Afrikaner Broederbond; US Japanese and North Korean propaganda and psychological warfare methods during World War II and the Korean war. Incl "Siberian Sketchbook," a ms with photos by W H Vatcher. 18 ms boxes, 1 box, 4 envelopes.

AFRO-AMERICAN ART see Art, African and Afro-American

AFRO-AMERICAN FAMILY AND COMMUNITY SERVICES

IL —CHICAGO HISTORICAL SOCIETY, Library, Clark St at North Ave, Chicago, 60614. Archie Motley, Manuscript Librn
Notes: Working records of organization, working in Cabrini-Green area, 1968-1982. 40 linear ft.

AFRO-AMERICAN LITERATURE

AR —UNIVERSITY OF ARKANSAS, John Brown Watson Memorial Library, Pine Bluff, 71601. Vitory Davis, Librn
Holdings: Vols 3044 Cat Pix Microforms
Notes: Collection is comprised mainly of books and materials of a sociological nature, with history and literature being the next two areas respectively containing the most materials. The entire collection deals mainly with materials by and about Black Americans.

DC —HOWARD UNIVERSITY, Moorland-Spingarn Research Center, 500 Howard Place NW, Washington, 20059. Clifford L Muse, Jr, Acting Dir
Holdings: Vols (106,086) Mss Maps Pix Slides Phonorecords Audiotapes 16mm Films Filmstrips Microforms
Budget: ($854,753)
See also entry under Blacks

IL —JOHNSON PUBLISHING CO, Library, 820 S Michigan Ave, Chicago, 60605. Pamela J Cash, Librn
Holdings: Vols 8000 Cat Maps Microforms
Notes: Incl all publications of Johnson Publishing Company and many more Black publications.

PA —BALCH INSTITUTE FOR ETHNIC STUDIES, Library, 18 S Seventh St, Philadelphia, 19106. R Joseph Anderson, Library Dir
Holdings: 100 Vols Cat

PA —TEMPLE UNIVERSITY LIBRARIES, Special Collections Dept, Rare Books & Mss Section, Philadelphia, 19122. Thomas M Whitehead, Cur
Holdings: Vols (10,000) Mss Pix
Notes: "The Charles Blockson Afro-American Historical Collection". Curated by Charles Blockson. The Private Library of Charles Blockson established as a collection at Temple University. Approximately 25,000 items of Afro-American literature, history of slavery and African and Caribbean history and culture. Selective catalog (exhibition) available. The Contemporary Culture Collection also has Afro American literature. See US - Social Life and Customs for full entry for that collection.

TX —UNIVERSITY OF TEXAS LIBRARIES, General Libraries, PO Box P, Austin, 78713. Carolyn Bucknell, Asst Dir for Collection Development
Holdings: Cat Microforms

AFRO-AMERICAN MUSIC see Music, Afro-American

AFRO-AMERICAN POLICE LEAGUE

IL —CHICAGO HISTORICAL SOCIETY, Library, Clark St at North Ave, Chicago, 60614. Archie Motley, Manuscript Librn
Notes: Papers of Black policemen's organization.

AFRO-AMERICAN STUDIES

CA —UNIVERSITY OF CALIFORNIA, BERKELEY, University Library, Afro-American Studies, Berkeley, 94720. Phyllis Bischof, Librn
Notes: Extensive holdings of books, manuscripts, newspapers, serials, dissertations, documents, oral histories, music, recordings, microforms. Research level collection, with Afro-American materials collected by more than twenty campus libraries. Mss collections incl the papers of the NAACP Western Regional Office, 1944-1980, the records of the Brotherhood of Sleepinng Car Porters, and some mss and letters of Langston Hughes. The Afro-American Writers Collection of The Bancroft Library incl first editions, correspondence, and mss of black writers, particularly those working or living in the western United States.

DC —DISTRICT OF COLUMBIA PUBLIC LIBRARY, Martin Luther King Memorial Library, Black Studies Div, 901 G St NW, Washington, 20001. Alice Robinson, Chief
Holdings: Vols (12,000) Cat Phonorecords Microforms
Budget: ($14,000)
Notes: The Black Studies Division was established with the opening of the Martin Luther King Memorial Library in 1972. The collection consists of books and other materials in all subject areas by and about Black Americans and other people of African descent throughout the world. The collection provides primary resource information to a broad range of patrons, from the general reader to the scholarly researcher. A separate catalog for the collection is located in the division. All materials are non-circulating.

DC —HOWARD UNIVERSITY, Moorland-Spingarn Research Center, 500 Howard Place NW, Washington, 20059. Clifford L Muse, Jr, Acting Dir
Holdings: Vols (106,086) Mss Maps Pix Slides Phonorecords Audiotapes 16mm Films Filmstrips Microforms
Budget: ($854,753)
See also entry under Blacks

DC —LIBRARY OF CONGRESS, Rare Book & Special Collections Div, Washington, 20540. William Matheson, Chief
Notes: Daniel Murray Pamphlet Collection on Afro-American history, 1850-1920, pertains chiefly to slavery and the abolitionist movement.

DC —UNIVERSITY OF THE DISTRICT OF COLUMBIA, Mount Vernon Campus, Library & Media Services Div, 800 Mount Vernon Pl, NW, Washington, 20001. Lottie Wright, Librn
Holdings: Vols (4000) Uncat Pix Phonorecords Audiotapes Videotapes 16mm Films Microforms
Notes: The collection consists of limited print and nonprint materials related to the rise and development of Black culture in America. Collecting emphasis is being placed on first editions, works of major Black authors and significant minor ones, rare books, mss, and memorabilia. In keeping with the policy of acquiring books by and about Afro-Americans, the collection also contains 462 dissertations by Black PhD candidates at universities throughout the US.

GA —ATLANTA UNIVERSITY CENTER, Woodruff Library, 111 Chestnut St SW, Atlanta, 30314. Minnie H Clayton, Division Director
Holdings: Vols (25,000) Cat Mss Photographs VF Microforms
Notes: Incl 25,000 books and rare books,

AFRO-AMERICAN STUDIES (cont.)

mss, 7,500 linear feet of institutional/ organizational records, individual papers, photographs, verticle file of ephemera, microforms, artifacts and memorabilia. Card catalog; preliminary inventories, guide to archival holdings.

GA —MARTIN LUTHER KING, JR, CENTER FOR NONVIOLENT SOCIAL CHANGE, INC, King Library and Archives, 449 Auburn Ave, Atlanta, 30312. D Louise Cook, Dir of Library and Archives
Holdings: Vols 4000 Cat Mss Audiotapes Microforms
Notes: The philosophy of Martin Luther King and the movement he led. Emphasis on obscure information and ephemeral pieces. Oral history project has over 500 tapes. Incl collection of mss of various civil rights organizations of the 1950s and 1960s. All materials are noncirculating.

KS —BAKER UNIVERSITY, Library, Eighth St, Baldwin City, 66006. Ray Firestone, Dir of Libraries
Notes: Collection now integrated into general library.

KS —UNIVERSITY OF KANSAS, Kenneth Spencer Research Library, Kansas Collection, Lawrence, 66045. Sheryl K Williams, Cur
Holdings: Vols (92,000) Mss Pix
Notes: Collection incl personal papers, organizational and religious records relating to Afro-American life in Kansas and the Plains region. Incl are literary manuscripts of Langston Hughes; records of the Greater Kansas City Area Council on Race and Religion, the Kansas Advisory Council on Civil Rights; and photographs documenting black military life at Fort Riley.

LA —AMISTAD RESEARCH CENTER, 400 Esplanade Ave, New Orleans, 70116. Clifton H Johnson, Exec Dir; Florence E Borders, Senior Archivist
Holdings: Vols (10,000) Cat Mss Pix Audiotapes Microforms
Budget: ($315,000)
Notes: In addition, 8,000,000 ms pieces, 10, 000 pictures, 3500 microforms, and 500 audiotapes. Amistad Research Center is an historical research library devoted to the collection and use of primary source materials on the history of America's ethnic minorities, with particular emphasis on Afro-Americans, American Indians, and immigrant groups. Among the larger institutional collections held are the archives and records of the American Missionary Association, the American Home Missionary Society, the Race Relations Dept of the Anti-Defamation League, the Catholic Committee of the South, and the National Association of Human Rights Workers, (formerly NAIRO). Also, private papers of the Harlem Renaissance poet, Countee Cullen; educator and civil rights leader, Mary McLeod Bethune;20th century civil rights lawyer, Alexander P Tureaud; 19th century Black attorney and judge, George Ruffin; founder and director of Operation Crossroads Africa, Dr James H Robinson; and over 70 others.

MD —UNIVERSITY OF MARYLAND, BALTIMORE COUNTY, Albin O Kuhn Library and Gallery, 5401 Wilkens Ave, Baltimore, 21228. Larry Wilt, Collection Management Librn
Holdings: Cat Microforms
Notes: The collection incl: Series I and II of the Schomburg Collection on microfilm, from the Research Libraries of the New York Public Library; *Afro-American Rare Book Collection* (microfiche of 152 items from the holdings of the Western States Black Research Center) of works primarily from the nineteenth and twentieth centuries; *Papers of the NAACP, 1909-1950*; *Black Culture Collection: African and Afro-American Publications*, containing 1431 microfilmed titles on African Culture and History; *Black Abolitionist Papers*, 1830-1865 which incl 14,000 documents on microfilm; and many other works on African and Afro-American literature, history, politics and culture.

MA —UNIVERSITY OF MASSACHUSETTS AT AMHERST, Library, Archives and Manuscripts, Amherst, 01003. Siegfried Feller, Assoc Dir for Collection Development
Holdings: Mss
Notes: In the Archives are the papers, personal and professional, of Horace Mann Bond, 1926-1972; administrative and teaching records pertaining to his career, especially his presidencies of Fort Valley State College (1939-45) and Lincoln University (1945-57), and later career at Atlanta University (1957-1971); research data; manuscripts of published and unpublished speeches, articles, and books; Bond family papers. Incl correspondence of James Bond (1863-1929) detailing social and race conditions in Kentucky. *The Horace Mann Bond Papers, 1830 (1926-72) 1979; a* Guide, by Barbara S Meloni, Rita Norton, and Katherine Emerson, 1982. Special Collections and Rare Books has nearly complete collection of imprints of Broadside Press, Detroit, Mich.
See also entries under DuBois, W E B; Bond, Horace Mann

MA —HARVARD UNIVERSITY LIBRARY, Widener Library, Cambridge, 02138.
Holdings: Mss Microforms
Notes: A *Guide* was published by the library in 1976. Resources incl numerous mss, notably those of Higginson, Sumner, Vallard, and Booker T Washington.

MO —UNIVERSITY OF MISSOURI-SAINT LOUIS, Thomas Jefferson Library, Manuscript and Historical Society Collection, 8001 Natural Bridge Rd, Saint Louis, 63121.
Holdings: Mss Pix Tapes
Notes: ca

NJ —PRINCETON UNIVERSITY, Firestone Library, Afro-American Studies Collection, Princeton, 08540. William Wellburn, Cur
Holdings: Vols (2000) Cat Pix Phonorecords Audiotapes Microforms
Notes: Our emphasis is primarily Afro-American: catalogs of other collections, biographical and vertical files, reference materials, indexes, bibliographies and serials.

NY —NEW YORK CITY TECHNICAL COLLEGE, Library, 300 Jay St, Brooklyn, 11201. Catherine T Brody, Chief Librn
Holdings: Vols 2700 Cat Maps Pix Films Phonorecords Audiotapes Microforms
Notes: Three bibliographies of the collection *available--Black Perspectives.* (Community College Press of the Faculty-Student Association for NYCCC, Inc, 1971). *A Guide to the Afro-American Resources at the Library of the New York City Community College* introduces students to the collection and annotates important reference materials. Afro-American Studies--A Guide to Resources in the Namm Library.

NC —DUKE UNIVERSITY, William R Perkins Library, Durham, 27706. Elvin E Strowd, University Librn

OK —LANGSTON UNIVERSITY, M B Tolson Black Heritage Library, Langston, 73050. Rosaland Savage, Cur
Holdings: Vols (4000) Cat Mss Maps Pix Slides Phonorecords Filmstrips Microforms
Budget: ($1000)
Notes: Main objective is to fill a large gap in the Afro-American academic community and to serve as a depository of Afro-Americana for research scholars in the Southwest.

SC —SOUTH CAROLINA STATE COLLEGE, Miller F Whittaker Library, College Ave, PO Box 1991, Orangeburg, 29117. Barbara Williams Jenkins, Dir
Holdings: Vols 5910 Cat Maps Pix Microforms
Notes: Afro-American historical background.

TN —FISK UNIVERSITY, Library, Special Collections, 17 & Jackson St, Nashville, 37203. Ann Allen Shockley, Assoc Librn
Holdings: Vols 45,000 Cat Mss Pix Slides Phonorecords Audiotapes Videotapes Filmstrips Microforms
Notes: There is an author catalog in the Special Collections Room. A published catalog has been done, *Dictionary Catalog of* the Negro Collection, 5 vols, Greenwood Press, 1974. The collection includes all aspects of the Negro in America, Africa, and the Caribbean. Oral history tapes, archival and ms collections, newspapers, magazines and journals.

TX —FORT WORTH PUBLIC LIBRARY, Southeast Branch, 4300 E Berry, Fort Worth, 76105. Michael Roseborough, Special Collections Librn
Holdings: Vols Cat Mss Pix Phonorecords Audiotapes Filmstrips Microforms
Budget: ($6000)
Notes: Studies Collection incl most titles by and about Blacks published since 1972, plus many older titles on Afro-American history. Library also maintains up-to-date index to more than 20 Black periodicals.

WA —SEATTLE PUBLIC LIBRARY, Douglass-Truth Branch, 23 & E Yesler Way, Seattle, 98104. Marcia Myers, Branch Librn
Holdings: Vols 5500 Cat Pix Phonorecords
Notes: Focus is on the Afro-American experience in the US, with emphasis on the Pacific Northwest, incl works of local Black authors. Incl 5500 cataloged volumes, 2200 pamphlets and pictures, 300 recordings, 32 periodical subscriptions.

AFRO-AMERICANA

MI —CENTRAL MICHIGAN UNIVERSITY, Clarke Historical Library, Mount Pleasant, 48859. William H Mulligan, Jr, Dir; William Miles, Biography Collections Librn
Holdings: Vols 900
Notes: Wilbert Wright Collection of Africana and Afro-Americana.

VI —COLLEGE OF THE VIRGIN ISLANDS, Ralph M Paiewonsky Library, Saint Thomas, 00802. Ernest C Wagner, Dir
Holdings: Vols 5000 Cat
Notes: West Indies: history, literature, economics and social conditions. Incl copies of materials published in journals and pamphlets from the late 19th century to the present.

AFRO-ASIAN POLITICS

DC —HOWARD UNIVERSITY, Moorland-Spingarn Research Center, 500 Howard Place NW, Washington, 20059. Clifford L Muse, Jr, Acting Dir
Holdings: Vols (106,086) Mss Maps Pix Slides Phonorecords Audiotapes 16mm Films Filmstrips Microforms
Budget: ($854,753)
See also entry under Blacks

AFSCME see American Federation of State, County and Municipal Employees (Afscme)

AGASSIZ, LOUIS

MA —HARVARD UNIVERSITY, Museum of Comparative Zoology, Library, 26 Oxford St, Cambridge, 02138. Eva S Jonas, Librn
Holdings: Cat Mss Microforms
Notes: Incl personal papers and archives.

MA —MASSACHUSETTS INSTITUTE OF TECHNOLOGY, Institute Archives, Special Collections, Cambridge, 02139.
Notes: Papers of William Barton Rogers, geologist, founder and first President of the Massachusetts Institute of Technology (1862-1870, 1878-1881). Major correspondents incl Louis Agassiz, Joseph Henry, Thomas Sterry Hunt, and Ellen Swallow Richards. Unpublished finding aid, incl correspondent index, available in Archives.

AGE OF ROCKS see Geological Time

AGED see Aging and Aged

AGEE, JAMES

NV —UNIVERSITY OF NEVADA, RENO, University Library, Special Collections Dept, Reno, 89557. Robert E Blesse, Head
Holdings: Vols (33) Cat
Notes: Includes individual works by author

AGEE, JAMES (cont.)

in all editions including translations; also prefaces, introductions, published correspondence, appearances in anthologies, periodicals, etc. Bibliographical research collection, part of Modern Authors Collection. Other appearances 130 cataloged.

AGENCIES, THEATRICAL see Theatrical Agencies

AGETON, ARTHUR AINSLIE

MA —BOSTON UNIVERSITY, Mugar Memorial Library, Special Collections Dept, 771 Commonwealth Ave, Boston, 02215. Howard B Gotlieb, Dir
Holdings: // Cat Mss Pix
Notes: Mss correspondence, etc collected in depth; incl publications by or about.

AGGLUTINANTS see Adhesives and Adhesion

AGILITY see Motor Ability

AGING AND AGED see Geriatrics and Gerontology

AGNEW, CORNELIUS REA

NY —COLUMBIA UNIVERSITY LIBRARIES, Rare Book & Manuscript Library, 801 Butler Library, 535 W 114 St, New York, 10027. Kenneth A Lohf, Librn
Holdings: Mss
Notes: Nearly 6000 letters, notes and mss relating to Cornelius Rea Agnew, professor of deseases of the eye and ear at Columbia's College of Physicians and Surgeons, and a founder of the Manhattan Eye and Ear Hospital. Much of the material relates to the treatment of eye diseases during the latter half of the 19th century. Restricted use.

AGNICH, FRED

TX —NORTH TEXAS STATE UNIVERSITY, Archives, NT Station Box 5188, Denton, 76203. Robert LaForte, University Archivist
Notes: Part of Oral History Collection. Interviews 1972-77 with businessman and member of Texas legislature.

AGNON, SHMUEL YOSEF HALEVI (S. Y.), 1888-1970

OH —HEBREW UNION COLLEGE-JEWISH INSTITUTE OF RELIGION, Klau Library, 3101 Clifton Ave, Cincinnati, 45220. David J Gilner, Reference Librn
Holdings: Cat Mss
Notes: Major collection of Hebrew literature; incl some Agnon manuscripts and Agnon works in many languages.

AGNOSTICISM

CA —ATHEIST ASSOCIATION, Atheist Library, 3024 Fifth Ave, PO Box 2832, San Diego, 92112. James Hervey Johnson, Librn
Notes: The Atheist Library and the building at 3024 Fifth Ave were completely destroyed by fire in October of 1981. There is no library at this time.

MA —HARVARD UNIVERSITY LIBRARY, Cambridge, 02138.
Holdings: Cat

TX —SOCIETY OF SEPARATIONISTS, Library, 2210 Hancock Dr, PO Box 2117, Austin, 78756. R Murray-O'Hair, Dir
Holdings: Vols (50,000)
Notes: Atheism, separation of church and state, biographical archives on Atheists, agnostics, humanists, and iconoclasts.

AGONEASEAH INDIANS see Iroquois Indians

AGRARIAN QUESTION see Agriculture—Economic Aspects; Land Tenure

AGRARIAN WRITERS

TN —VANDERBILT UNIVERSITY, Library, Nashville, 37240. Marice Wolfe, Special Collections Librn
Holdings: Vols 1000 Cat Mss Pix
Notes: Collection relating to the Fugitive poets of the 1920s, the Agrarian writers of the 1930s and their subsequent careers, as a complement to extensive mss collections in this field. Chief figures incl Allen Tate, John Crowe Ransom, Robert Penn Warren, Andrew Lytle, Donald Davidson, Merrill Moore, Laura Riding, et al.

AGRIBUSINESS see Agriculture—Economic Aspects

AGRIBUSINESS ACCOUNTABILITY PROJECT

IA —IOWA STATE UNIVERSITY, Library, Dept of Special Collections, Ames, 50011. Stanley M Yates, Head
Holdings: // Mss
Notes: Founded in 1970, the Agribusiness Accountability Project was a non-profit, non-partisan, public-interest research organization which investigated various aspects of agribusiness. 15 linear ft, finding aid available.

AGRICOLA, GEORG, 1494-1555

CA —CLAREMONT COLLEGES, Norman F Sprague Memorial Library, 12 & Dartmouth, Claremont, 91711. David Kuhner, Librn
Notes: President Herbert Hoover's personal collection of rare mining books-about 1000 vols of the 15th-17th centuries.

IL —UNIVERSITY OF ILLINOIS, URBANA/CHAMPAIGN, Library, Rare Book Room, 346 Library, Urbana, 61801. Norman B Brown, Asst Dir for Special Collections; N Frederick Nash, Librn
Holdings: Cat Mss Maps
Notes: Extensive collection, described in: *Catalog of the Rare Book Room,* (Boston: G K Hall, 1972). Supplement (1978).

AGRICULTURAL ASSOCIATIONS see Agricultural Societies

AGRICULTURAL BACTERIOLOGY see Bacteriology, Agricultural

AGRICULTURAL BANKS see Agricultural Credit; Banks and Banking

AGRICULTURAL BOTANY see Botany, Economic

AGRICULTURAL CATALOGS

OK —MUSEUM OF THE GREAT PLAINS, Research Center, 601 Ferris, PO Box 68, Lawton, 73502. Steve Wilson, Dir; Paula Williams, Special Collections
Notes: Large holdings of hardware and agricultural catalogs and trade periodicals dating 1869 to 1926. Collection incl over 2000 photographs of wagons and carriages from various manufacturer's catalogs and trade periodicals. Catalogs and periodicals are indexed. Collections are described in Vol 17 (1978) Great Plains Journal published by the Museum.

AGRICULTURAL CENSUSES see Agriculture—Statistics

AGRICULTURAL CHEMISTRY

CA —UNIVERSITY OF CALIFORNIA, DAVIS, Environmental Toxicology Library, Davis, 95616. Ming-yu Li, Documentation Specialist
Holdings: Vols (5000) Cat
Notes: Library is open to the public for reference only. In addition to the cataloged holdings, the library also maintains a pamphlet collection of 50 file drawers on agricultural chemicals, environmental pollution, heavy metals, food toxicants, toxicology, pesticides and trace elements.

IA —IOWA STATE UNIVERSITY, Library, Ames, 50011. Warren B Kuhn, Dean of Library Services
Holdings: Cat

OH —PPG INDUSTRIES, Chemical Div, Research Library, PO Box 31, Barberton, 44203. Diane Danko, Chemical Information Specialist
Holdings: Vols (20,000) Cat Microforms
Notes: Organic, inorganic, analytical and agricultural chemistry, with special emphasis on applied and chemical engineering.

OH —SDS BIOTECH CORP, PO Box 348, Painesville, 44077. Violet Forgach, Business Librn
Holdings: Cat Pix Microforms

PA —FRANKLIN INSTITUTE LIBRARY, 20 & The Parkway, Philadelphia, 19103. Miriam Padusis, Dir; Charles Wilt, Readers Servs Librn
Holdings: Vols (300,000) Cat Maps Pix Microforms

AGRICULTURAL CLIMATOLOGY see Crops and Climate; Meteorology, Agricultural

AGRICULTURAL CLUBS see Agricultural Societies

AGRICULTURAL COLONIES

WI —UNIVERSITY OF WISCONSIN, MADISON, Land Tenure Center Library, 434 Steenbock Memorial Library, 550 Babcock Dr, Madison, 53706. Teresa J Anderson, Librn
Holdings: Vols (60,000) Cat Mss Maps Microforms
Budget: ($65,000)
Notes: Socio-economic aspects of agricultural development in the Third World. All materials in the collection are cataloged and classified. The library has its own catalog.

AGRICULTURAL COOPERATION see Agriculture, Cooperative

AGRICULTURAL COOPERATION, INTERNATIONAL see International Agricultural Cooperation

AGRICULTURAL CREDIT

IL —NORTHERN ILLINOIS REGIONAL HISTORY CENTER, Sven Parson Hall, Northern Illinois University, De Kalb, 60115. Glen Gildemeister, Dir
Holdings: Cat Mss Maps Pix Slides Phonorecords Audiotapes 16mm Films Microforms
Notes: "A research center for advanced research in the humanities. This northern area of Illinois (excluding Cook County) has been virtually untouched by collecting agencies and we hope to fill that void. We will be strong in agribusiness, agricultural implement business, and hybrid farming mechanics....Will be primarily a ms repository, but [have] already taken responsibility for many artifacts and books, some rare."

IA —IOWA STATE UNIVERSITY, Library, Ames, 50011. Warren B Kuhn, Dean of Library Services
Holdings: Cat Mss
Notes: Incl agriculture finance and policy, agricultural marketing, farm management, land valuation, and rural development. Extensive serial holdings.

OH —OHIO STATE UNIVERSITY, Agriculture Library, 2120 Fyffe Rd, Agricultural Administration Bldg, Columbus, 43210. Mary P Key, Head
Holdings: Vols (12,000) Cat Mss Maps Pix
Notes: The Arnold Agricultural Credit Collection. There is a special catalog which is not being kept up-to-date. Much of the material is in a pamphlet file arranged by country or other geographical unit. All interlibrary loan requests are handled through the interlibrary loan department of our main library, Ohio State University, 1858 Neil Ave, Columbus, Ohio 43210.

AGRICULTURAL ECONOMICS see Agriculture—Economic Aspects

AGRICULTURAL ENGINEERING

CA —UNIVERSITY OF CALIFORNIA, DAVIS, Physical Sciences Library, Davis,

AGRICULTURAL ENGINEERING (cont.)

95616. Scott Kennedy, Head
Holdings: Vols (170,000) Cat VF
Notes: Collection covers aeronautical, agricultural, chemical, civil, electrical, mechanical, water science, hydrology, nuclear reactor, extensive cold regions collection in vertical file drawers, and computer science engineering academic programs. Good strength in journal runs.

CA —CALIFORNIA STATE POLYTECHNIC UNIVERSITY, POMONA, University Library, 3801 W Temple Ave, Pomona, 91768. Harold Schleiser, Actg Dir
Notes: General reference materials on agricultural business management, agricultural engineering, animal science, horticulture and plant and soil science.

DE —UNIVERSITY OF DELAWARE, Agriculture Library, 2 Townsend Hall, Newark, 19717. Frederick Getze, Assoc Librn
Holdings: Vols (32,500)
Notes: Strong in entomology and ornamental horticulture. Extensive collection of state agriculture documents for each US state and Puerto Rico. Library subscribes to 600 serials (English and foreign).

GA —UNIVERSITY OF GEORGIA, College of Agriculture, Coastal Plain Experiment Station Library, Moore Hwy, Tifton, 31793. Emory Cheek, Library Specialist
Holdings: Vols (13,500) Cat

IL —NORTHERN ILLINOIS REGIONAL HISTORY CENTER, Sven Parson Hall, Northern Illinois University, De Kalb, 60115. Glen Gildemeister, Dir
Holdings: Cat Mss Maps Pix Slides Phonorecords Audiotapes 16mm Films Microforms
Notes: "A research center for advanced research in the humanities. This northern area of Illinois (excluding Cook County) has been virtually untouched by collecting agencies and we hope to fill that void. We will be strong in agribusiness, agricultural implement business, and hybrid farming mechanics....Will be primarily a ms repository, but [have] already taken responsibility for many artifacts and books, some rare."

†IL —UNIVERSITY OF ILLINOIS, URBANA/CHAMPAIGN, Agricultural Library, 226 Mumford Hall, 1301 W Gregory Dr, Urbana, 61801.

IN —PURDUE UNIVERSITY LIBRARIES, Life Sciences Library, Lilly Hall of Life Sciences, West Lafayette, 47907. Martha J Bailey, Librn
Notes: Incl materials in agronomy, animal sciences, botany, entomology, forestry, horticulture, biological sciences and agricultural engineering.

IA —IOWA STATE UNIVERSITY, Library, Dept of Special Collections, Ames, 50011. Stanley M Yates, Head
Holdings: / / Mss Pix
Notes: Agricultural engineering materials in the general library. Special Collections incl papers of J B Davidson (1880-1957), one of the organizers and first president of the American Society of Agricultural Engineers. 13 linear feet, finding aid available.

KY —UNIVERSITY OF KENTUCKY, Agricultural Library, Agricultural Science Center North, Lexington, 40506. Antoinette Paris Powell, Librn
Holdings: Vols (90,000) Cat Microforms
Budget: ($110,385)

NY —NEW YORK STATE OFFICE OF PARKS & RECREATION, TACONIC REGION, Clermont State Historic Park, Library, RR 1, Box 215, Germantown, 12526. Bruce E Naramore, Historic Site Manager
Holdings: Vols (5000) Cat Mss Maps
Notes: Period editions of pre - and post-American Revolutionary War agricultural technology. Many belonged to the Chancellor Robert R Livingston (1746-1813). Incl land drainage, hybrids, fertilizers, and the introduction of Merino sheep.

NY —ENGINEERING SOCIETIES LIBRARY, 345 E 47 St, New York, 10017. S Kirk Cabeen, Dir
Holdings: Vols 250,000 Cat Maps 16mm Films Microforms
Notes: One of the largest, most comprehensive engineering libraries in the world. Covers all engineering disciplines; particularly strong in electrical and electronic, mechanical, mining and metallurgical, petroleum, chemical, industrial, air conditioning and refrigeration engineering. Incl Wheeler Collection of early materials on magnetisn and electricity. 125, 000 bound periodical volumes; 10,000 maps; 5000 serial subscriptions (many foreign-language). Virtually all materials abstracted in *Engineering Index* (1884-date) are incl in Library. Noncirculating, except to members of professional engineering societies which support the Library. See *Engineering Societies Library, New York, Classed Subject Catalog and Index* (Boston: G K Hall, 1963); and *Supplements*, 1-10, 1964-1973.

OH —OHIO STATE UNIVERSITY, Engineering Library, 2024 Neil Ave, Columbus, 43210. Mary Jo V Arnold, Librn
Holdings: Vols (132,000) Cat Microforms
Budget: ($110,000)

PA —FRANKLIN INSTITUTE LIBRARY, 20 & The Parkway, Philadelphia, 19103. Miriam Padusis, Dir; Charles Wilt, Readers Servs Librn
Holdings: Vols (300,000) Cat Maps Pix Microforms

SC —HORRY GEORGETOWN TECHNICAL COLLEGE, Library, Hwy 501, Box 1966, Conway, 29526. Barbara Brittain, Librn
Holdings: Vols (20,000) Cat Maps Slides Microforms

WI —UNIVERSITY OF WISCONSIN, MADISON, College of Agricultural & Life Sciences, Steenbock Memorial Library, 550 Babcock Dr, Madison, 53706. Jan Kennedy, Dir
Holdings: Vols (186,312) Cat Docs Slides

MB —UNIVERSITY OF MANITOBA, Engineering Library, Winnipeg, R3T 2N2, Can. Y Cho, Head
Holdings: Vols (28,000) Cat Videotapes Microforms
Notes: The Engineering Library serves four academic departments: Agricultural, Civil, Electrical and Mechanical Engineering.

AGRICULTURAL ENGINEERING—HISTORY

CA —UNIVERSITY OF CALIFORNIA, DAVIS, Shields Library, Dept of Special Collections, Davis, 95616. Donald Kunitz, Head; C Danial Elliott, Asst Head
Notes: 13,000 VF cataloged; mss and pictures uncataloged. Manufacturer's catalogs, manuals, parts lists, ephemera, and literature pertaining to historical as well as current data on such items as tractors, engines, combines, hay equipment, etc. Described in "The Higgins Library: A Source for the Study of Agricultural History," Don Kunitz, *Agricultural History,* vol 49, 1975, pp 89-91.

AGRICULTURAL LABORERS

CA —UNIVERSITY OF CALIFORNIA, BERKELEY, Giannini Foundation of Agricultural Economics, Library, 248 Giannini Hall, Berkeley, 94720. Grace Dote, Librn
Holdings: Cat Microforms Mss
Notes: Particularly as applying to California.

CA —CALIFORNIA STATE UNIVERSITY, FULLERTON, Library, Box 4150, Fullerton, 92634. Alfredo H Zuniga, Coord
Notes: Some materials on the subject; not maintained as a separate collection.

CA —UNIVERSITY OF CALIFORNIA, LOS ANGELES, Research Library, Dept of Special Collections, 405 Hilgard Ave, Los Angeles, 90024. Edward Shreeves, Chairman, Bibliographers Group; David S Zeidberg, Head
Holdings: / / Uncat Mss
Notes: Personal papers, clippings, and reports relating to migrant farm labor are incl in the Carey McWilliams Collection.

CA —CALIFORNIA STATE UNIVERSITY, NORTHRIDGE, Delmar T Oviatt & South Libraries, 1811 Nordhoff St, Northridge, 91330. Donald L Read, Special Collections Dept
Notes: Three newspaper boxes. Some runs incomplete. Between 1935 and 1939, the US Government maintained camps to assist the migrant farm laborers of the Great Depression. This small collection records the activities of those camps.

DC —HOWARD UNIVERSITY, Moorland-Spingarn Research Center, 500 Howard Place NW, Washington, 20059. Clifford L Muse, Jr, Acting Dir
Holdings: Vols (94,000) Mss Maps Pix Slides Phonorecords Audiotapes 16mm Films Filmstrips Microforms
Budget: ($854,753)
See also entry under Blacks

FL —FLORIDA DEPT OF COMMERCE, Research Library, 408 Fletcher Bldg, Tallahassee, 32301. Dennis Hitchens, Librn
Holdings: Vols (3000) Cat Mss Maps VF
Budget: ($6000)
Notes: Collect materials related to the 2 divisions of the Florida Dept of Commerce: Economic Development and Tourism, incl titles on Florida (historical and current), international trade, transportation, education, employment, management, industrial development and business. The Florida and US documents collection covers population, manufacturing, employment, agriculture, retail trade, wholesale trade and labor. VF incl files on every city and county, especially local economic data, SIC coded material, out-of-state information, county files, Florida specific material and general subject material. 100 VF drawers.

IL —NORTHERN ILLINOIS REGIONAL HISTORY CENTER, Sven Parson Hall, Northern Illinois University, De Kalb, 60115. Glen Gildemeister, Dir
Holdings: Cat Mss Maps Pix Slides Phonorecords Audiotapes 16mm Films Microforms
Notes: "A research center for advanced research in the humanities. This northern area of Illinois (excluding Cook County) has been virtually untouched by collecting agencies and we hope to fill that void. We will be strong in agribusiness, agricultural implement business, and hybrid farming mechanics....Will be primarily a ms repository, but [have] already taken responsibility for many artifacts and books, some rare."

IA —UNIVERSITY OF IOWA, University Libraries, Iowa City, 52242. Robert A McCown, Mss Librn
Holdings: Mss
Notes: Speeches, correspondence, news clippings, and other papers of the farm leader (Milo Reno) relating to the Iowa Division of the Farmers' Educational and Co-operative Union of America and the National Farmers' Holiday Association. 3 ft of mss.

NY —CORNELL UNIVERSITY LIBRARIES, Collection of Regional History, Dept of Manuscripts and Univ Archives, Ithaca, 14853.
Notes: Oral history interviews, 1968; 1 vol., 3 tape recordings.

AGRICULTURAL MACHINERY

AL —US DEPT OF AGRICULTURE, SCIENCE & EDUCATION ADMINISTRATION, National Tillage Machinery Laboratory, Library, PO Box 792, Auburn, 36830. William A Gill, Collaborator
Holdings: Vols (39,000) Cat Mss Maps Pix Slides 16mm Films Microforms
Budget: ($20,000)
Notes: The National Tillage Machinery Laboratory (NTML) has a special technical library comprised of highly selective engineering and physical science materials pertinent to soil-machine relations, such as tillage, earthmoving, mining, soil trafficability, and vehicle mobility. A high

AGRICULTURAL MACHINERY (cont.)

percentage of the library material comes from sources outside the US and outside agriculture. Particularly strong in Russian-language literature.

CA —UNIVERSITY OF CALIFORNIA, DAVIS, Shields Library, Dept of Special Collections, Davis, 95616. Donald Kunitz, Head; C Danial Elliott, Asst Head
Holdings: Vols 6000 Cat Mss Pix VF
Notes: 13,000 VF cataloged; mss and pictures uncataloged. Manufacturer's catalogs, manuals, parts lists, ephemera, and literature pertaining to historical as well as current data on such items as tractors, engines, combines, hay equipment, etc. Described in "The Higgins Library: A Source for the Study of Agricultural History," Don Kunitz, *Agricultural History,* vol 49, 1975, pp 89-91.

CA —THE HAGGIN MUSEUM, Petzinger Library of Californiana, 1201 N Pershing Ave, Stockton, 95203. Diane Freggiaro, Librn/Archivist
Holdings: Vols (7000) Cat Mss Maps Pix Slides Audiotapes 16mm Films
Notes: The Petzinger Library is open by appointment only. Special emphasis on Stockton and San Joaquin County and Valley area, local biography, agriculture, agricultural history, industrial history, farm machinery (especially Holt Manufacturing Co, Stockton). There is a photograph collection of 8500 pictures, and extensive manuscript holdings (about 17,000 pieces).

GA —UNIVERSITY OF GEORGIA, College of Agriculture, Coastal Plain Experiment Station Library, Moore Hwy, Tifton, 31793. Emory Cheek, Library Specialist
Holdings: Vols (13,500) Cat

IL —NORTHERN ILLINOIS REGIONAL HISTORY CENTER, Sven Parson Hall, Northern Illinois University, De Kalb, 60115. Glen Gildemeister, Dir
Holdings: Cat Mss Maps Pix Slides Phonorecords Audiotapes 16mm Films Microforms
Notes: "A research center for advanced research in the humanities. This northern area of Illinois (excluding Cook County) has been virtually untouched by collecting agencies and we hope to fill that void. We will be strong in agribusiness, agricultural implement business, and hybrid farming mechanics....Will be primarily a ms repository, but [have] already taken responsibility for many artifacts and books, some rare."

IL —DEERE & CO LIBRARY, John Deere Rd, Moline, 61265. Betty S Hagberg, Mgr, Library Services
Holdings: Vols 35,000 Cat Mss Maps Pix Slides Microforms
Notes: Serves all specialists and management personnel in the corporation.

NC —WILSON COUNTY TECHNICAL INSTITUTE, Library, 902 Herring Ave, PO Box 4305, Wilson, 27893. Shirley Gregory, Librn
Holdings: Vols (150) Cat Slides Phonorecords Audiotapes 16mm Films Filmstrips
Notes: Emphasis on operation, maintenance, and safety for operators of earthmoving equipment and cranes. Incl 50 operator's manuals and 80 audiovisual programs.

OH —WRIGHT STATE UNIVERSITY, Greater Miami Valley Research Center, University Library, Dayton, 45431. Patrick B Nolan, Head of Archives
Holdings: Mss
Notes: Records of OS Kelly Company of Springfield, Ohio--early manufacturer of farm machinery. Incl 100 linear ft of archives and manuscript collections.

PA —FRANKLIN INSTITUTE LIBRARY, 20 & The Parkway, Philadelphia, 19103. Miriam Padusis, Dir; Charles Wilt, Readers Servs Librn
Holdings: Vols (300,000) Cat Maps Pix Microforms

SK —WESTERN DEVELOPMENT MUSEUM, George Shepherd Library, 2935 Melville St, PO Box 1910, Saskatoon, S7K 3S5, Can. Warren Clubb, Research Coordr
Holdings: Vols (13,000) Documents Maps Pix Slides Audiotapes
Budget: $3500
Notes: Staff reference library. Open to the public although not a lending library. Extensive holdings of agricultural machinery catalogs, from Canadian and American manufacturers and distributors. Other holdings incl automobiles, aviation, museology and Western Canadian history. Partially cataloged.

AGRICULTURAL MACHINERY—CATALOGS

OK —MUSEUM OF THE GREAT PLAINS, Research Center, 601 Ferris, PO Box 68, Lawton, 73502. Steve Wilson, Dir; Paula Williams, Special Collections
Notes: Large holdings of hardware and agricultural catalogs and trade periodicals dating 1869 to 1926. Collection incl over 2000 photographs of wagons and carriages from various manufacturer's catalogs and trade periodicals. Catalogs and periodicals are indexed. Collections are described in Vol 17 (1978) Great Plains Journal published by the Museum.

AGRICULTURAL MACHINERY—HISTORY

IN —INDIANA UNIVERSITY, Lilly Library, Seventh St, Bloomington, 47405. William R Cagle, Librn
Holdings: // Mss Pix
Notes: Champ, George W, 1830-1905, Indiana physician and businessman: Papers relating to Dublin (Indiana) agriculture company, manufacturers of agricultural machinery, 1880-1905. Incl assignments of patents for agricultural machinery, 1860-1886; 134 items. Oliver Corporation papers, 1860-1952; Incl correspondence and printed material, scrapbooks, and annual reports (Oliver manufactured agricultural machinery in Chicago, Illinois); 27 items. Rumely, Edward Aloysius, 1882-1964, physician and educator, etc; Incl papers relating to the family agricultural implement business and to his development of the Rumely Oil Pull Farm Tractor; 95,355 items. Scott, Emmet Hoyt, 1842-1924, railroadman and manufacturer. Papers on Niles & Scott, manufacturers of wheels for agricultural implements and vehicles, 1876-1902; 65,166 items.

AGRICULTURAL METEOROLOGY see Crops and Climate; Meteorology, Agricultural

AGRICULTURAL NEWSPAPERS see Newspapers, Agricultural

AGRICULTURAL PERIODICALS see Periodicals, Agricultural

AGRICULTURAL SOCIETIES

IL —ILLINOIS FARM BUREAU LIBRARY, 1701 Towanda Ave, PO Box 1901, Bloomington, 61701. Rue E Olson, Librn
Holdings: Vols (24,000) Cat Microforms
Budget: ($25,000)

IA —IOWA STATE UNIVERSITY, Library, Dept of Special Collections, Ames, 50011. Stanley M Yates, Head
Holdings: // Mss
Notes: Mss of the Iowa Farm Bureau Federation and the Iowa Farmers Union.

SC —CLEMSON UNIVERSITY, Libraries, Clemson, 29631. Michael F Kohl, Head of Special Collections
Holdings: // Cat Mss
Notes: Ms collections and books of the Pendleton Farmers' Association; the South Carolina Farmers' Alliance; the South Carolina State Grange, 1872-1895 (Patrons of Husbandry). Clemson University Archives, 1890-present.

AGRICULTURAL STATISTICS see Agriculture—Statistics

AGRICULTURAL WORKERS see Agricultural Laborers

AGRICULTURE

AL —NATIONAL FERTILIZER DEVELOPMENT CENTER, Tennessee Valley Authority Technical Library, TVA National Fertilizer Development Center, Muscle Shoals, 35660. Shirley G Nichols, Librn
Holdings: Vols (32,000) Cat Mss Maps Pix Slides Microforms
Notes: One of the most complete collections of material on fertilizer as it relates to agriculture, agro-economics, chemistry, chemical engineering, etc, in the country.

CA —UNIVERSITY OF CALIFORNIA, BERKELEY, Science Libraries, Natural Resources Library, 40 Giannini Hall, Berkeley, 94720. Norma Kobzina, Head Librn
Holdings: Vols (100,000) Cat Maps Microforms
Budget: ($40,000)
Notes: Subject emphasis is on basic agricultural and pest management research, particularly in the areas of tropical and subtropical agriculture and plantation crops, ie, cotton, rice, tobacco, and sugar. Materials in agricultural engineering, farm Machinery, and veterinary medicine are not acquired for the Berkeley campus. Serials, especially the extensive holdings of foreign titles, constitute the collection's major strength. Over 5700 serials are being received currently.

CA —UNIVERSITY OF CALIFORNIA, DAVIS, General Library, Davis, 95616. Bernard Kreissman, University Librn; C Danial Elliott, Asst Head, Dept Special Collections
Holdings: Vols 79,031

CA —LOS ANGELES PUBLIC LIBRARY, Science & Technology Dept, 630 W Fifth St, Los Angeles, 90071. Billie M Connor, Dept Head
Holdings: Vols (14,000) Cat Maps
Notes: Includes agricultural publications of the US Department of Agriculture, California and other state experiment station publications on all aspects of plant and animal husbandry, soil science and analysis, including Soil Surveys. Emphasis is on the Western states and semi-tropical areas.

CA —UPDATA PUBLICATIONS INC, Library, 1756 Westwood Blvd, Los Angeles, 90024. Sara Ferguson, Dir; Judith Harrington, Librn
Holdings: Vols (300) Uncat Maps Microforms
Notes: Incl 800,000 microforms, 35 periodicals.

CA —CALIFORNIA STATE POLYTECHNIC UNIVERSITY, POMONA, University Library, 3801 W Temple Ave, Pomona, 91768. Harold Schleiser, Actg Dir
Notes: General reference materials on agricultural business management, agricultural engineering, animal science, horticulture and plant and soil science.

CA —UNIVERSITY OF CALIFORNIA, RIVERSIDE, University Library, Bio-Agricultural Library, Batchelor Hall, Riverside, 92521. Barbara Montanary, Head
Holdings: Vols (130,000) Cat Mss Maps Pix Microforms
Notes: The Bio-Agricultural Library (formerly the Library of Citrus Experiment Station of the University of California) is well known for its complete collections in the fields of the agriculture sciences. It is especially known for its emphasis on entomology, incl bio-control; botany, citriculture, plant sciences, nematology and plant pathology; arid and semi-arid lands research and subtropical agriculture. Specific areas of interest are avocados, dates, desert flora, jojoba, guayule and carob.

CA —THE HAGGIN MUSEUM, Petzinger Library of Californiana, 1201 N Pershing Ave, Stockton, 95203. Diane Freggiaro, Librn/Archivist
Holdings: Vols (7000) Cat Mss Maps Pix Slides Audiotapes 16mm Films
Notes: The Petzinger Library is open by appointment only. Special emphasis on Stockton and San Joaquin County and Valley area, local biography, agriculture, agricultural history, industrial history, farm machinery (especially Holt Manufacturing Co, Stockton). There is a photograph collection of 8500 pictures, and extensive manuscript holdings (about 17,000 pieces).

AGRICULTURE (cont.)

CO —COLORADO STATE UNIVERSITY, Libraries, Fort Collins, 80523. Curtis L Gifford, Forestry & Agricultural Sciences Librn
Holdings: Vols 95,810 Cat Maps
Budget: $9000

DE —UNIVERSITY OF DELAWARE, Agriculture Library, 2 Townsend Hall, Newark, 19717. Frederick Getze, Assoc Librn
Holdings: Vols (32,500) Cat Pix Microforms
Notes: Strong in entomology and ornamental horticulture. Extensive collection of state agriculture documents for each US state and Puerto Rico. Library subscribes to 600 serials (English and foreign).

FL —UNIVERSITY OF FLORIDA, Institute of Food & Agricultural Sciences, Hume Library, Gainesville, 32611. Albert C Strickland, Librn
Holdings: Vols (135,000) Cat Mss Microforms
Notes: Including journals and monographs, this collection is a general agricultural one. The emphasis is on tropical agriculture, especially Latin America. Entomology is very strong. The library offers on-line information retrieval using Lockheed and SDC data bases.

GA —UNIVERSITY OF GEORGIA, College of Agriculture, Coastal Plain Experiment Station Library, Moore Hwy, Tifton, 31793. Emory Cheek, Library Specialist
Holdings: Vols (13,500) Cat

HI —BERNICE P BISHOP MUSEUM, Library, PO Box 19000-A, Honolulu, 96819. Cynthia Timberlake, Librn
Holdings: Vols (90,000) Cat Mss Maps Pix Slides Microforms
Budget: ($30,000)
Notes: Only American library devoted exclusively to the Pacific region. Collection reflects historical and contemporary research emphases of Bishop Museum; ie the natural and cultural history of the Pacific. Areas of concentration incl archaeology, ethnology, linguistics, voyages and explorations, history, vertebrate and invertebrate zoology, botany and museology. Strong special collections incl photographs, mss and archives, maps and art. Publications: Quarterly "Additions to the Catalog," *Dictionary Catalog of the* Library (9 vols and 2 suppl; Boston: G K Hall, 1964-69).

IL —ILLINOIS FARM BUREAU LIBRARY, 1701 Towanda Ave, PO Box 1901, Bloomington, 61701. Rue E Olson, Librn
Holdings: Vols (24,000) Cat Microforms
Budget: ($25,000)
Notes: Emphasis on Illinois.

IL —NORTHERN ILLINOIS REGIONAL HISTORY CENTER, Sven Parson Hall, Northern Illinois University, De Kalb, 60115. Glen Gildemeister, Dir
Holdings: Cat Mss Maps Pix Slides Phonorecords Audiotapes 16mm Films Microforms
Notes: "A research center for advanced research in the humanities. This northern area of Illinois (excluding Cook County) has been virtually untouched by collecting agencies and we hope to fill that void. We will be strong in agribusiness, agricultural implement business, and hybrid farming mechanics....Will be primarily a ms repository, but [have] already taken responsibility for many artifacts and books, some rare."

IL —DEERE & CO LIBRARY, John Deere Rd, Moline, 61265. Betty S Hagberg, Mgr, Library Services
Holdings: Vols 35,000 Cat Mss Maps Pix Slides Microforms
Notes: Serves all specialists and management personnel in the corporation.

†IL —UNIVERSITY OF ILLINOIS, URBANA/CHAMPAIGN, Agricultural Library, 226 Mumford Hall, 1301 W Gregory Dr, Urbana, 61801.

IN —INTERNATIONAL MINERALS & CHEMICAL CORP, R & D Library, 1331 S First St, PO Box 207, Terre Haute, 47808. Ruth Smedlund, Librn
Holdings: Vols (114,574) Cat Microforms
Notes: Incl materials in agronomy, animal sciences, botany, entomology, forestry, horticulture, and biological sciences.

IN —PURDUE UNIVERSITY LIBRARIES, Life Sciences Library, Lilly Hall of Life Sciences, West Lafayette, 47907. Martha J Bailey, Librn
Holdings: Vols (73,404) Cat Microforms
Budget: ($223,445)
Notes: Incl materials in agronomy, animal sciences, botany, entomology, forestry, horticulture, biological sciences and agricultural engineering.

IA —IOWA STATE UNIVERSITY, Library, Ames, 50011. Warren B Kuhn, Dean of Library Services
Holdings: Cat
Notes: Areas of particular emphasis: Agronomy, agricultural economics, animal science, crop science, farm operations, and soil science. Extensive serial holdings.

IA —IOWA STATE UNIVERSITY, Library, Dept of Special Collections, Ames, 50011. Stanley M Yates, Head
Holdings: // Mss
Notes: Incl papers of Roswell Garst, Iowa's most famous farmer, initiator of experimental feeding of corncobs to produce beef, use of hybrid seedcorn, and commercial fertilizers, credited with opening of agricultural sales and exchanges with Russia in the 1950s. Also, papers of Agribusiness Accountability Project, non-partisan, non-profit, public-interest research organization which investigated various aspects of agribusiness founded in 1970. 15 linear ft, finding aid available.

KY —UNIVERSITY OF KENTUCKY, Agricultural Library, Agricultural Science Center North, Lexington, 40506. Antoinette Paris Powell, Librn
Holdings: Vols (90,000) Cat Microforms
Budget: ($110,385)

LA —LOUISIANA STATE UNIVERSITY, Middleton Library, Dept of Archives & Manuscripts, Room 202, Baton Rouge, 70803. M Stone Miller Jr, Head
Holdings: Cat Mss Maps Pix Microforms
Notes: History of Louisiana and lower Mississippi Valley, colonial through 20th century. Scope: political, social and literary history; economic history, incl forestry, banking, agriculture, transportation and trade; national, regional, and Louisiana history; military history. About 4,500,000 items. The Louisiana Room has large subject collection on Louisiana, sugar culture and technology, Southern history, petroleum engineering, plant pathology, micropaleontology, ornithology, and various aspects of crawfish life, biology and culture. LSU theses and dissertations from 1900-date. LSU Faculty Collection.

LA —UNIVERSITY OF SOUTHERN LOUISIANA, Dupre Library, Jefferson Caffery Louisiana Room, 302 East St Mary Blvd, Lafayette, 70504. Cynthia J Rice, Louisiana Room Ref Librn
Holdings: Vols (20,000) Cat Doc Maps Microforms VF
Budget: ($3800)
Notes: Emphasis is on state, regional, and local history, genealogy, and culture; also politics and government, industry, agriculture, geology, language and literature. Collection is closed-stack and non-circulating, and is open to the public for on-site use only. Copying services are available.

MD —US DEPT OF AGRICULTURE, National Agricultural Library, 10301 Baltimore Blvd, Beltsville, 20705. Joseph H Howard, Director
Holdings: Vols (2,000,000) Cat Mss Maps Pix Slides Microforms
Notes: Worldwide coverage of all aspects of agriculture and related fields. Crop ecology, agro-climatic analogs; air pollution effects. Agronomy: agricultural and tropical and desert agriculture. For use by the staff of the USDA. Incl in the former collections of American Institute of Crop Ecology.

MA —UNIVERSITY OF MASSACHUSETTS AT AMHERST, Library, Amherst, 01003. Siegfried Feller, Assoc Dir for Collection Development
Holdings: Cat Maps Microforms
Notes: Extensive holdings of state and foreign agricultural experiment publications. In addition to cataloged materials, 40,000 US and 2500 other governmental publications on agriculture are housed in the Documents Collection.

MA —HARVARD UNIVERSITY, Baker Library of the Graduate School of Business Administration, Kress Library of Business and Economics, Soldiers Field, Boston, 02163. Ruth E Rogers, Cur
Holdings: Cat Microforms
Notes: Covers the progress of economic thought and the evolution of economic institutions and business life, with special strength in agriculture, banking, commerce, finance, industry, money, railroads, socialism, tariff. Restricted use: noncirculating. Collection available on microfilm: *Goldsmiths'-Kress Library of Economic Literature,* published by Research Publications, Inc. Downs 1477, 2704, 2712, 2719, 2727, Supplement 962, 963.

MI —EDISON INSTITUTE, Greenfield Village and Henry Ford Museum, Archives & Research Library, PO Box 1970, Dearborn, 48121. Steve Hamp, Dir; Joan W Gartland, Librn
Holdings: Vols 400,000 Cat Mss Maps Mircoforms
Notes: 400,000 vols incl pamphlets. The Archives and research library supports the program of Greenfield Village and the Henry Ford Museum. Special collections incl: automotive literature, ephemera, McGuffey Readers, trade catalogs, photographs and graphics.

MN —MINNESOTA HISTORICAL SOCIETY LIBRARY, 690 Cedar St, Saint Paul, 55101. Patricia C Harpole, Chief of Reference Library; Bonnie G Wilson, Head of Special Libraries

MO —DOANE PUBLISHING, Information Center, 11701 Borman Dr, Saint Louis, 63146. Gloria D Lyles, Librn
Holdings: Vols 1800 Cat Mss Maps Pix
Notes: One of the largest agri-business libraries in area. Subscribes to all State Agricultural Extension publications, which are cataloged and entered into the computerized Doane Information Center Indexing System (DICIS).

NE —NEBRASKA STATE HISTORICAL SOCIETY, Archives, 1500 R St, Box 82554, Lincoln, 68501. James E Potter, State Archivist
Holdings: Cat Mss Microforms
Budget: ($290,000)
Notes: Strong emphasis in areas of agriculture, irrigation, 19th century agrarian political movements, and settlement of the Great Plains.

NE —NEBRASKA STATE HISTORICAL SOCIETY, Library, 1500 R St, Box 82554, Lincoln, 68501. M Ann Reinert, Library Dept Head
Holdings: Vols (100,000) Cat Maps Pix Microforms
Budget: ($200,000)
Notes: Extensive collection of Nebraska and Western Americana publications, especially Nebraska local historical and biographical materials, but also a strong emphasis in the subject areas of Indians of North America, archeology of the Great Plains, and Trans-Missouri history. A special collection of Nebraska authors, particularly Willa Cather and John G. Neihardt. Repository since 1905 of publications of state government. Approximately 30,000 vols. of genealogical materials, especially for the colonial and migration west to Nebraska period including most major genealogical and historical society periodicals. Collection of 400 atlases and 3000 separate maps

AGRICULTURE (cont.)

primarily relating to Nebraska 1854-present including county maps; landowners maps and atlases; plans of cities and 563 sets of Sanborn Fire Insurance Maps dating back to 1883 for 135 towns in Nebraska. Repository for State Department of Roads printed maps. See Hermon Dunlap Smith Center for the history of Cartography–Newberry Library, CHECKLIST OF PRINTED MAPS OF THE MIDDLE WEST TO 1900, vol. 12 (Boston: G. K. Hall, 1981) for description of pre-1900 Nebraska separate maps. Approximately 120,000 photographs of Nebraska and Nebraskans including the 2500 photographs of sod houses in the Solomon D. Butcher Collection, the 465 photographs in the John A. Anderson collection of Brule Sioux.

NE —UNIVERSITY OF NEBRASKA-LINCOLN, C Y Thompson Library, East Campus, Lincoln, 68583. Lyle Schreiner, Librn
Holdings: Vols (220,000) Cat
Notes: Agriculture, with major strength in entomology, agromony, and animal science; medicine; veterinary medicine; and home economics.

†NH —UNIVERSITY OF NEW HAMPSHIRE, Biological Science Library, Kendall Hall, Durham, 03824. Lloyd Heldgard, Librn
Holdings: Vols (45,000)

NH —DARTMOUTH COLLEGE, Dartmouth-Hitchcock Medical Center, Dana Biomedical Library, Hanover, 03756. Shirley J Grainger, Librn
Holdings: Vols (143,611) Cat Mss Phonorecords Audiotapes Videotapes Microforms
Budget: ($280,000)

NY —NEW YORK BOTANICAL GARDEN LIBRARY, Bronx, 10458. Charles R Long, Asst Vice Pres & Dir
Holdings: Vols (385,000) Cat Mss Pix Slides Microforms VF
Budget: ($356,000)
Notes: One of the largest botanical collections in the world. Over 900,000 items. Covers botany (150,000 vols), botanists (3000), horticulture (45,000) plant diseases (25,000), plant physiology (15,000), history of botany (1500), conservation of natural resources (15,000), gardening (13,000), paleobotany (7000), ecology (20,000), forestry (5000) medical botany (3000), agriculture (9000) and biology (20,000). Reference library; materials do not circulate, except for member circulating collection (1200) and standard inter-library loan. About 5000 vols uncataloged. Incl art, books, serials, pamphlets, archives and manuscripts, vertical files, microfiche and microfilm, nursery and seed catalogs, photographs, paintings, prints, drawings and engravings. Covers all areas of botanical sciences. This is an OCLC library with fullresource services incl photocopying and photography.

NY —CORNELL UNIVERSITY LIBRARIES, Albert R Mann Library, Ithaca, 14853. Henry T Murphy, Librn
Holdings: Vols (300,000) Cat Maps Microforms
Notes: Especially strong in plant sciences.

NY —CORNELL UNIVERSITY LIBRARIES, Collection of Regional History, Dept of Manuscripts and Univ Archives, Ithaca, 14853.
Notes: The noncurrent records, letters, records of meetings and other historic data dating back to Dec 4, 1867, the date of organization of the National Grange. Also the papers of Louis I Taber, National Master of the Grange from 1923 to 1941.

NY —NEW YORK PUBLIC LIBRARY, Research Libraries, Economic & Public Affairs Div, Fifth Ave & 42 St, New York, 10018. Edward DiRoma, Chief
Holdings: Vols (1,500,000) Cat Microforms

NY —NEW YORK PUBLIC LIBRARY, Mid-Manhattan Library, Science & Business Dept, 455 Fifth Ave, New York, 10016. Frederick E Dusold, Sr Principal Librn
Holdings: Vols (110,000) Cat Microforms
Budget: ($134,000)
Notes: All works are in English. Material is current; policy precludes archival collecting. Collection is geared toward the undergraduate college student, with consideration given to the professional, the lay reader and the beginning graduate student. Collection incl monographs, texts, treatises, standard reference works and periodicals in agriculture, horticulture, home economics, crafts, engineering, industrial chemistry, construction and other technologies. Books are available for circulation in addition to an extensive reference collection.

NY —SYRACUSE UNIVERSITY LIBRARIES, Ernest S Bird Library, George Arents Research Library for Special Collections, Syracuse, 13210. Carolyn A Davis, Manuscripts Librn; Amy S Doherty, University Archivist; Mark F Weimer, Rare Book Librn
Notes: Papers of Paul H Appleby. He was Undersecretary of Agriculture under Pres Franklin D Roosevelt, Asst Dir of the US Bureau of the Budget under Roosevelt and Truman, and Dean of the Maxwell School at Syracuse University from 1947-1954.

NC —NORTH CAROLINA STATE UNIVERSITY, D H Hill Library, Box 7111, Raleigh, 27695. I T Littleton, Dir
Holdings: Vols 32,600 Cat Microforms
Budget: $40,000
Notes: Incl almost complete collection of all publications issued by Agriculture Experiment stations in the 50 states. New England states, southeastern states, midwestern states on microfilm. Monographs.

NC —R J REYNOLDS TOBACCO CO, Scientific Information Services Library, Bowman Gray Technical Center, BGTC 611-12/205, Winston-Salem, 27102. Nellie W Sizemore, Librn
Holdings: Vols 1000 Cat

ND —NORTH DAKOTA STATE UNIVERSITY, Library, Fargo, 58105. John E Bye, Archivist
Holdings: Vols (2500) Cat Mss Maps Pix
Budget: ($14,000)
Notes: The Collection is administered by the North Dakota Institute for Regional Studies. It contains materials on North Dakota history, especially the Red River Valley, with emphasis on bonanza farming, pioneer life, agriculture, local history, literary figures, business, Fargo, ND, and some political collections, particularly of the Nonpartisan League. Also, there is an extensive photographic collection covering the pioneer to post-World War I period and includes the "Hultstrand 'History in Pictures' Collection" of sod houses, pioneer life and farming. For the small collections, there has been published, *Guide to the Small Collection Manuscripts of the North Dakota Institute for Regional Studies,* by John E Bye, 1977.

OH —AKRON-SUMMIT COUNTY PUBLIC LIBRARY, Business, Labor & Government Div, 55 S Main St, Akron, 44326. William G Johnson, Head
Holdings: Vols (10,000) Cat Microforms
Budget: ($20,000)

OH —LLOYD LIBRARY & MUSEUM, 917 Plum St, Cincinnati, 45202. John B Griggs, Librn
Holdings: //
Notes: Large collection incl publications of state experimental stations. No longer adding to the collection.

OK —MUSEUM OF THE GREAT PLAINS, Research Center, 601 Ferris, PO Box 68, Lawton, 73502. Steve Wilson, Dir; Paula Williams, Special Collections
Notes: Large holdings of hardware and agricultural catalogs and trade periodicals dating 1869 to 1926. Collection incl over 2000 photographs of wagons and carriages from various manufacturer's catalogs and trade periodicals. Catalogs and periodicals are indexed. Collections are described in Vol 17 (1978) Great Plains Journal published by the Museum.

OK —OKLAHOMA STATE UNIVERSITY, Library, Stillwater, 74708. Roscoe Rouse, Dir
Holdings: Vols (820,000) Cat
Notes: Incl 7800 serial publications received currently in science, technology, and agriculture.

PA —TEMPLE UNIVERSITY, Ambler Campus Library, Meetinghouse Road, Ambler, 19002. Esther G Bloomsburgh, Librn
Notes: Rare herbals are housed in Special Collections, Paley Library, Temple University (Thomas Whitehead, Curator). Incl 2500 items.

PA —PENNSYLVANIA STATE UNIVERSITY, Fred Lewis Pattee Library, Life Sciences Library, University Park, 16802. Keith Roe, Head
Holdings: Vols
Notes: This collection is strong in periodical runs, particularly European learned societies and agriculture. It contains extensive collections of Experiment Station publications and has developed specialties in Mycology and Fusaria. There is also a special collection of 1105 glass slides on early Pennsylvania lumbering.

RI —UNIVERSITY OF RHODE ISLAND, Library, Special Collections, Kingston, 02881. David Maslyn, Head
Notes: Extensive collections.

SC —SUMTER TECHNICAL COLLEGE, Library, 506 Guignard Dr, Sumter, 29150. Fanny M Davis
Holdings: Vols (20,000) Cat Mss Maps Pix Slides Microforms
Budget: ($50,000)
Notes: Incl 53 books on agriculture.

TN —TENNESSEE VALLEY AUTHORITY (TVA), Technical Library, 400 W Summit Hill Dr, E2 B7, Knoxville, 37902. Jesse C Mills, Chief Librn
Holdings: Vols (106,900) Cat Mss Maps Pix Audiotapes Microforms
Budget: ($2,025,000)
Notes: The Technical Library Headquarters Staff (order, cataloging, information, and administration) is located in Knoxville, Tenn. In addition there are branch libraries in Knoxville, Norris, and Chattanooga, Tennessee, and Muscle Shoals, Alabama.

TN —UNIVERSITY OF TENNESSEE, KNOXVILLE, Agriculture-Veterinary Medicine Library, A113 Vet Teach Hospital, Knoxville, 37916. Don W Jett, Librn
Holdings: Vols (100,000) Cat Microforms
Budget: ($50,500)
Notes: The Agriculture Library serves the Tennessee Agriculture Experiment Station, the Agriculture Extension Service and the Colleges of Agriculture and Veterinary Medicine. Incl 2000 microforms. Separate catalog; holdings also listed in public catalog in Main Library and in the union list of serials of the technical libraries in the Oak Ridge/Knoxville area.

TN —W R GRACE & CO, Planning Services Library, 100 N Main, PO Box 277, Memphis, 38103. Carolyn A Wilhite, Librn
Holdings: Vols (6000) Cat Mss Maps Microforms
Budget: ($85,000)
Notes: Animal nutrition production; fertilizers; weather; and agricultural statistics.

TX —ABILENE CHRISTIAN UNIVERSITY, Margaret & Herman Brown Library, ACU Sta, Abilene, 79601. Callie Faye Milliken, Assoc Dir

TX —AMARILLO PUBLIC LIBRARY, 413 E Fourth, Amarillo, 79101. Mary Kay Snell, Librn
Holdings: Vols Cat Mss Maps Pix
Notes: The southwest collections incl materials on the history of Texas, Louisiana, New Mexico, Arkansas, Missouri and Kansas. General subjects covered incl overland journeys, early narratives, early biographies, Indian captivities, outlaws, US government reports, Mississippi and Ohio Rivers, the Mexican War, reports of Catholic missionaries, Niles Register, early publications, fur trade, western trails, Texas Rangers, sheriffs and Texas as a sovereign

AGRICULTURE (cont.)

state, buffalo hunting, Indian wars, cowboys, the arrival of farmers, fences, and towns. Over 1600 items which incl books, documents, maps, mss, pamphlets, unpublished theses, interviews and photographs. The three major collections are the William Henry Bush Collection, the Laurence J Fitzsimon Collection and the Calendar of John L McCarty.

TX —TEXAS A&M UNIVERSITY, Sterling C Evans Library, University Archives, College Station, 77843. Charles R Schultz, University Archivist
Holdings: Vols 3000 Mss Pix
Notes: The Archives of Texas Agriculture: publications (bulletins, miscellaneous publications, progress reports, leaflets, circulars, and annual reports) of the Texas Agricultural Experiment Station and the Texas Agricultural Extension Service; detailed ms annual reports of substations of the Texas Agricultural Experiment Station; and photographs of experimental agricultural activities as well as Extension Service work. All of these date from 1890 to the present. Also incl are records of the screwworm eradication program in Texas, ca 1962 to 1974; small collections of records of several farm mutual insurance companies in Texas; and transcripts of oral interviews with agricultural scientists in Texas. Uncataloged.

TX —TEXAS TECH UNIVERSITY, Library, Lubbock, 79409. David J Murrah, Assoc Dir for Special Collections

TX —SLOVANSKA PODPORUJICI JEDNOTA STATU TEXAS, Slavonic Benevolent Order of the State of Texas, SPJST Library, Archives, Museum, 520 N Main St, Temple, 76501. Otto Hanus, Cur-Librn; Thelma Bartosh, Asst Cur-Librn
Holdings: Vols (400) Cat
Notes: Our agricultural section contains US Dept of Agriculture books plus many bound magazines dealing with agriculture, gardening and flower growing.

VT —VERMONT TECHNICAL COLLEGE, Hartness Library, Randolph Center, 05061. Dewey Patterson, Library Dir
Holdings: Vols 4820 Cat

WI —BLACKHAWK TECHNICAL INSTITUTE, PO Box 5009, 6004 Prairie Rd, Janesville, 53547. Grace M Sweeney, Libn
Holdings: Vols 2500 Cat
Budget: $2500

WI —STATE HISTORICAL SOCIETY OF WISCONSIN, Archives, 816 State St, Madison, 53706. Harold L Miller, Reference Archivist
Holdings: Cat Mss Pix Microforms
Notes: About 22 million pieces. Major ms emphasis is American, with special collections in the history of anti-Vietnam War, agriculture, civil rights, industry, labor, mass communications, motion pictures and theatre, and Wisconsin. There is a separate card catalog to mss. Collections are described in the *Guide to Manuscripts of the State Historical Society of Wisconsin* (3 vols, 1944, 1957, 1966), *Guide to the Wisconsin State Archives* (1966), in current accession notes in the *Wisconsin Magazine of History*, and in other special Society publications. Major collections are also listed in Hamer, *Guide to Manuscripts and Archives in the United States* (1961) and in the *National Union Catalog of Manuscript Collections* (1959-date).

WI —UNIVERSITY OF WISCONSIN, MADISON, College of Agricultural & Life Sciences, Steenbock Memorial Library, 550 Babcock Dr, Madison, 53706. Jan Kennedy, Dir
Holdings: Vols (186,312) Cat Docs Maps Microforms Slides
Notes: Extensive general agricultural collection supporting the College of Agricultural and Life Sciences in agronomy, dairy science, agricultural engineering, entomology, botany, natural resources, nutrition, forestry, genetics, veterinary science, meat and animal science, poultry science, and soils. Collection includes USDA, USDI, experiment station and state documents.

WI —UNIVERSITY OF WISCONSIN, MILWAUKEE, Library, Box 604, Milwaukee, 53201. William C Roselle, Dir
Holdings: Cat Microforms
Notes: Wisconsin Legislative Referencee Bureau Clippings File. Special strength in a collection mostly of Wisconsin emphasis. 440 reels of 16mm microfilm. A subject-chronological arrangement (approximately 1200 subjects covering the years from the 1890s through 1970) of pamphlets and a variety of fugitive materials and of clippings from national and Wisconsin newspapers, popular magazines and scholarly journals, and federal, state, and local government documents.

BC —UNIVERSITY OF BRITISH COLUMBIA, Macmillan Library, 2357 Main Mall, Vancouver, V6T 2A2, Can. Mary W Macaree, Head
Holdings: Vols (50,000) Cat Maps Slides Microforms
Budget: ($200,000)

MB —AGRICULTURE CANADA, Research Station Library, 195 Dafoe Rd, Winnipeg, R3T 2M9, Can. Mike Malyk, Librn
Holdings: Vols (8000) Cat
Notes: Incl the Buller Botanical Library. 5000 bound jounals, 5000 unbound journals, 200 periodicals, 12,000 government publications, 30,000 reprints. Founded 1926.

MB —UNIVERSITY OF MANITOBA, Agriculture Library, Dafoe Rd, Winnipeg, R3T 2N2, Can. Judy Harper, Head
Holdings: Vols 16,000 Cat

NB —AGRICULTURE CANADA, Research Station Library, Box 20280, Fredericton, E3B 4Z7, Can. Donald B Gammon, Area Coord (Atlantic)
Holdings: Vols 5000 Cat
Budget: $30,000
Notes: Also 20,000 reprints, etc. Branch library of Agriculture Canada, Ottawa.

ON —UNIVERSITY OF GUELPH, McLaughlin Library, Guelph, N1G 2W1, Can. Margaret Beckman, Head Librn; David Hull, Sciences Librn
Holdings: Vols 250,000 Cat Mss Maps Pix Slides Phonorecords Audiotapes Videotapes 16mm Films Microforms
Notes: British and North American emphasis. Special catalogues can be produced for any part of the collections from automated library records. (All records for all formats are in machine readable form.)

ON —UNIVERSITY OF GUELPH, Library, Guelph, N1G 2W1, Can. Margaret Beckman, Chief Librn; Ellen Pearson, Ref Librn
Notes: 15,000 monographs, 350 periodical subscriptions, 5000 documents, also maps, mss, audio/videotapes, 16mm films. Supports research activities related to planning theory, public administration, rural sociology, rural planning and development, rural and urban community studies, regional analysis, rural environment and resource use, policy design.

ON —NATIONAL MUSEUMS OF CANADA, Library Services Directorate, Ottawa, K1A 0M8, Can. Valerie Monkhouse, Director
Holdings: Vols 15,500
Budget: $25,000
Notes: History and technology of agriculture, astronomy, aviation, chemistry, communications, computers, electrical engineering, exploration and surveying, fire prevention, forestry, industrial technology, mathematics, medicine, mining, photography, physics, printing, space and transportation. research collection, interlibrary loans available, public may use on the premises.

PE —AGRICULTURE CANADA, Research Station Library, PO Box 1210, Charlottetown, C1A 7M8, Can. Barrie Stanfield, Librn
Holdings: Vols (2300) Cat
Budget: ($5000)

PQ —UNIVERSITY OF MONTREAL, Veterinary Medical Library, CP 5000, Saint-Hyacinthe, J2S 7C6, Can. Jean-Paul Jette, Librn
Holdings: Vols (11,000) Cat Microforms

SK —CANADA PRAIRIE FARM REHABILITATION ADMINISTRATION LIBRARY, Motherwell Bldg, Regina, S4P 0R5, Can. C Kosack, Head
Holdings: Vols (10,000) Cat
Budget: ($33,000)
Notes: PFRA is a Canadian federal government agency initiated to alleviate the effects of drought and water shortages on the prairies. The collection covers engineering (dams), agricultural economics, hydrology, irrigation, community pastures, and soil and water conservation.

AGRICULTURE—BIOGRAPHY see Farmers

AGRICULTURE—CANADA

SK —AGRICULTURE CANADA, Research Station Library, Box 440, Regina, S4P 3A2, Can. Susan Yanasik, Librn Tech
Holdings: Vols 1000
Notes: Holdings are listed with the Canada Agriculture Library, Sir John Carling Building, in Ottawa. Also a copy of the shelf-list card is sent to the Saskatchewan Provincial Library, Regina.

AGRICULTURE—CHINA

NY —ROCKEFELLER UNIVERSITY, Rockefeller Archive Center, Hillcrest, Pocantico Hills, North Tarrytown, 10591. Joseph W Ernst, Dir; J William Hess, Assoc Dir
Notes: Papers relative to the Rockefeller Family, Foundations, University, and other specific enterprises and contributions to particular areas of social, physical, educational, and historic reform, preservation, conservation, or development. Extensive records of administrative, financial, physical, or intellectual relationships.

AGRICULTURE—DESERT see Desert Agriculture

AGRICULTURE—ECONOMIC ASPECTS

AL —NATIONAL FERTILIZER DEVELOPMENT CENTER, Tennessee Valley Authority Technical Library, TVA National Fertilizer Development Center, Muscle Shoals, 35660. Shirley G Nichols, Librn
Holdings: Vols (32,000) Cat Mss Maps Pix Slides Microforms
Notes: One of the mnost complete collections of material on fertilizer as it relates to agriculture, agro-economics, chemistry, chemical engineering, etc, in the country.

CA —UNIVERSITY OF CALIFORNIA, BERKELEY, Giannini Foundation of Agricultural Economics, Library, 248 Giannini Hall, Berkeley, 94720. Grace Dote, Librn
Holdings: Vols (18,000) Cat Mss Maps Pix Microforms
Notes: Open to graduate students, faculty and research personnel of universities and colleges and to general public. Noncirculating collection. No interlibrary loans. Agricultural economics and related fields. Incl about 124,000 pamphlets. See *Dictionary Catalog of the Giannini Foundation of Agricultural Economics Library, University of California* (Boston: G K Hall, 1971), 12 vols.

CA —UNIVERSITY OF CALIFORNIA, DAVIS, General Library, Davis, 95616. Bernard Kreissman, University Librn; C Danial Elliott, Asst Head, Dept Special Collections
Holdings: Vols 12,500 Cat
Notes: Incl the holdings of both the Shields Library and Agricultural Economics Library. Literature concerning the marketing and pricing of agricultural commodities and land use is emphasized.

CA —CALIFORNIA STATE POLYTECHNIC UNIVERSITY, POMONA, University

AGRICULTURE—ECONOMIC ASPECTS (cont.)

Library, 3801 W Temple Ave, Pomona, 91768. Harold Schleiser, Actg Dir
Notes: General reference materials on agricultural business management, agricultural engineering, animal science, horticulture and plant and soil science.

CA —STANFORD UNIVERSITY, Food Research Institute Library, Stanford, 94305. Charles C Milford, Librn
Holdings: Vols (13,565) Cat Map Pix Microforms
Budget: ($31,565)
Notes: The economic aspects of the production, trade, disposition, and and prices of food, feed, and fiber commodities throughout the world. Incl 25,000 pamphlets.

DE —UNIVERSITY OF DELAWARE, Agriculture Library, 2 Townsend Hall, Newark, 19717. Frederick Getze, Assoc Librn
Holdings: Vols (32,500) Cat Pix Microforms
Notes: Strong in entomology and ornamental horticulture. Extensive collection of state agriculture documents for each US state and Puerto Rico. Library subscribes to 600 serials (English and foreign).

DC —INTERNATIONAL MONETARY FUND AND WORLD BANK, Joint Bank-Fund Library, Washington, 20431. Maureen M Moore, Librn
Holdings: Vols Cat Films Microforms
Notes: Incl foreign trade and statistical bulletins and yearbooks, central bank reports and bulletins, budget papers, security yearbooks, economic development plans and reports on economic conditions from the 132 member countries. An index of periodical material compiled by the Library staff has been published as: *Economics and Finance; Index to Periodical Articles, 1947-1971;* First Supplement, 1972, 1973, 1974 (Second Supplement, 1975, 1976, 1977, in preparation), 5 vols. (Boston: G K Hall, 1972, 1975). Also, The Developing Areas: *A Classed Bibliography of the Joint Bank-Fund Library,* Vol 1: *Latin America and the* Caribbean; Vol 2: *Africa and the Middle* East; Vol 3: *Asia and Oceania* (Boston: G K Hall, 1976).

IL —ILLINOIS FARM BUREAU LIBRARY, 1701 Towanda Ave, PO Box 1901, Bloomington, 61701. Rue E Olson, Librn
Holdings: Vols (24,000) Cat Microforms
Budget: ($25,000)
Notes: Emphasis on Illinois.

IL —CHICAGO BOARD OF TRADE, Library, 141 W Jackson Blvd, Chicago, 60604. Darlene Appleman, Librn
Holdings: Vols (4000) Cat Microforms
Notes: Incl materials on commodity exchanges, commodities that are traded on futures exchanges, finance, and agricultural economics. *Commodity Futures Trading, A* Bibliography is published annually. The archives of the Chicago Board of Trade are located in the Manuscript Collection at the University of Illinois at Chicago Circle Campus. A published catalog, *The Archives of the Chicago Board of Trade, 1859-1925,* is available from the Chicago Board of Trade.

IL —FEDERAL RESERVE BANK OF CHICAGO, Library, 230 S La Salle St, PO Box 834, Chicago, 60690. Dorothy Phillips, Librn
Holdings: Vols (19,000) Cat
Notes: Restricted use: noncirculating. No photocopying.

†IL —UNIVERSITY OF ILLINOIS, URBANA/CHAMPAIGN, Agricultural Library, 226 Mumford Hall, 1301 W Gregory Dr, Urbana, 61801.

IN —PURDUE UNIVERSITY LIBRARIES, Graduate School of Management, Krannert Library, West Lafayette, 47907. Gordon Law, Librn
Holdings: Vols (142,727) Cat Microforms
Budget: ($69,700)
Notes: There is an extensive collection of publications from the US Department of Agriculture's Economic Research Service.

IA —IOWA STATE UNIVERSITY, Library, Ames, 50011. Warren B Kuhn, Dean of Library Services
Holdings: Cat Mss
Notes: Incl agriculture finance and policy, agricultural marketing, farm management, land valuation, and rural development. Extensive serial holdings.

KY —UNIVERSITY OF KENTUCKY, Agricultural Library, Agricultural Science Center North, Lexington, 40506. Antoinette Paris Powell, Librn
Holdings: Vols (90,000) Cat Microforms
Budget: ($110,385)

MO —DOANE PUBLISHING, Information Center, 11701 Borman Dr, Saint Louis, 63146. Gloria D Lyles, Librn
Holdings: Vols 1800 Cat Mss Maps Pix
Notes: One of the largest agri-business libraries in area. Subscribes to all State Agricultural Extension publications, which are cataloged and entered into the computerized Doane Information Center Indexing System (DICIS).

NY —CORNELL UNIVERSITY LIBRARIES, Collection of Regional History, Dept of Manuscripts and Univ Archives, Ithaca, 14853.
Notes: Incl records, 1919-51; marketing and price information, reports, by-laws, financial statements and some correspondence pertaining to cooperative organizations.

NC —UNIVERSITY OF NORTH CAROLINA, CHAPEL HILL, Wilson Library, Rare Book Collection, Chapel Hill, 27514. Paul S Koda, Cur of Rare Books
Holdings: Cat Mss
Notes: 160 letterfile boxes of the extensive correspondence of Eugene Cunningham Branson, Professor of Rural Economics at the University of North Carolina from 1914 to 1933.

NC —NORTH CAROLINA STATE UNIVERSITY, D H Hill Library, Box 7111, Raleigh, 27695. I T Littleton, Dir
Holdings: Vols 36,500 Cat
Budget: $40,000
Notes: Incl agriculture and life sciences. Monographs.

WI —UNIVERSITY OF WISCONSIN, MADISON, College of Agricultural & Life Sciences, Steenbock Memorial Library, 550 Babcock Dr, Madison, 53706. Jan Kennedy, Dir
Holdings: Vols (186,312) Cat Docs Microforms
Notes: Includes agricultural commodities, agricultural marketing, rural development. USDA, experiment station and state publications.

MB —UNIVERSITY OF MANITOBA, Agriculture Library, Dafoe Rd, Winnipeg, R3T 2N2, Can. Judy Harper, Head
Holdings: Vols (16,000) Cat

ON —DEPT OF REGIONAL INDUSTRIAL EXPANSION, Ottawa Library, 235 Queen St, Ottawa, K1A 0H5, Can. Steven Rush, Librn
Holdings: Vols (100,000) Cat Maps Microforms
Notes: Contains 1500 reports of ARDA projects (Agricultural Rehabilitation and Development Agency); also NEWSTART project reports. There is a published book catalog and two supplements. 15,000 documents; 3000 periodical subscriptions.

AGRICULTURE—HISTORY

AL —TROY STATE UNIVERSITY, Library, Troy, 36081. Kenneth Croslin, Dir of University Libraries
Holdings: // Mss
Notes: Incl the John Horry Dent Papers, 1851-1892, 25 vols, mss, farm journals, account books, letters, legal documents, clippings and miscellaneous memorabilia of a planter, plantation owner, investor, who lived in Barbour County, Alabama from 1837 to 1867 and in Floyd County, Georgia from 1867 to 1892. Typescript from tape "Sharecropping farming in Pike County, Alabama in early 1900's" (56p). Typescript of tapes of "Source material extracted from Troy, Alabama newspapers, 1871-1935" indexed under 9 subjects by color code.

CA —THE HAGGIN MUSEUM, Petzinger Library of Californiana, 1201 N Pershing Ave, Stockton, 95203. Diane Freggiaro, Librn/Archivist
Holdings: Vols (7000) Cat Mss Maps Pix Slides Audiotapes 16mm Films
Notes: The Petzinger Library is open by appointment only. Special emphasis on Stockton and San Joaquin County and Valley area, local biography, agriculture, agricultural history, industrial history, farm machinery (especially Holt Manufacturing Co, Stockton). There is a photograph collection of 8500 pictures, and extensive manuscript holdings (about 17,000 pieces).

†CT —UNIVERSITY OF CONNECTICUT LIBRARY, Special Collections Dept, Storrs, 06268. Richard H Schimmelpfeng, Dir of Special Collections

†IL —UNIVERSITY OF ILLINOIS, URBANA/CHAMPAIGN, Agricultural Library, 226 Mumford Hall, 1301 W Gregory Dr, Urbana, 61801.

IN —PURDUE UNIVERSITY LIBRARIES, Graduate School of Management, Krannert Library, West Lafayette, 47907. Gordon Law, Librn
Holdings: Vols (7000) Cat Mss Maps Pix Microforms
Notes: The collection consists of books, journals and pamphlets dating from the early 16th to late 19th century, covering to a large degree the early literature in economic thought and business practices both here and abroad.

IN —PURDUE UNIVERSITY LIBRARIES, Special Collections Dept, West Lafayette, 47907. Keith Dowden, Asst Dir, Special Collections
Notes: Papers of Earl L Butz relating to his service as Secretary of Agriculture under Presidents Nixon and Ford (1971-76).

IA —IOWA STATE UNIVERSITY, Library, Dept of Special Collections, Ames, 50011. Stanley M Yates, Head
Notes: Iowa State General Library has extensive holdings of serial backfiles. Also papers of Earle D Ross, an early researcher in agricultural history; mss of the National Farmers Process Tax Recovery Association.

KS —UNIVERSITY OF KANSAS, Kenneth Spencer Research Library, Kansas Collection, Lawrence, 66045. Sheryl K Williams, Cur
Holdings: Vols (92,000) Cat Mss Maps Pix
Notes: All aspects of the American West and trans-Mississippi history, especially Kansas and the Plains region. Overland diaries, cartographic history, Indians, emigration and immigration, printing history, cattle industry, agriculture and farm life, conservation are some special interests, in addition to the usual political, economic, military and social interests. The collection incl the business records of the J B Watkins Land Mortgage Co, one of the largest farm mortgage businesses in the central US, incorporated in 1883. The collection (622 ln ft) incl correspondence and records from the Lawrence, KS office (1873-1939), the New York office (1876-94), the London office (1878-1921), the Dallas office (1881-95) and the Lake Charles, LA office (1883-1929). 4000 linear feet.

KS —HARVEY COUNTY HISTORICAL SOCIETY, Historical Library & Museum, 203 Main St, Newton, 67114. Mike Smurr, Dir
Holdings: Maps Pix
Notes: Our Library-Museum is limited to literature, pictures and artifacts of interest to the locality, Harvey County, KS. Newton has been a RR point since the Santa Fe built here in 1871, so we have an unusually good collection of railroad items. Hundreds of pictures, many timetables, passes, and items small enough to be housed in our building. Attention is also given to early-day agriculture in mid-Kansas, especially wheat-raising by early settlers in central Kansas.

MD —US DEPT OF AGRICULTURE, National Agricultural Library, 10301 Baltimore Blvd, Beltsville, 20705. Joseph H Howard, Director
Holdings: Vols (2,000,000) Cat Mss Maps Pix Slides Microforms
Notes: Worldwide coverage of all aspects of

AGRICULTURE—HISTORY (cont.)

agriculture and related fields. Crop ecology, agro-climatic analogs; air pollution effects. Agronomy: agricultural and tropical and desert agriculture. For use by the staff of the USDA. Incl in the former collections of American Institute of Crop Ecology.

MA —HARVARD UNIVERSITY, Baker Library of the Graduate School of Business Administration, Kress Library of Business and Economics, Soldiers Field, Boston, 02163. Ruth E Rogers, Cur
Holdings: Cat Mss
Notes: See *Agricultural History,* XXXVI (1962): PP 171-173.

MA —HISTORIC DEERFIELD-POCUMTUCK VALLEY MEMORIAL ASSOCIATION, Libraries, Memorial St, Box 53, Deerfield, 01342. David R Proper, Librn
Holdings: Vols (17,000) Cat Mss Maps Pix Microforms
Notes: Local and regional history, especially western Massachusetts. Extensive collection of photographs of the people and buildings of Deerfield and its environs. Houses the Connecticut Valley Bibliography, a comprehensive card file on the history and culture of the Connecticut Valley of Massachusetts.

MA —OLD STURBRIDGE VILLAGE, Research Library, Sturbridge, 01566. Theresa Rini Percy, Librn
Holdings: Cat Mss
Notes: Northeastern US, some English, to 1850. Incl botany, horticulture, fruit culture, animal husbandry.

MA —WENHAM HISTORICAL ASSOCIATION AND MUSEUM, Timothy Pickering Library, 132 Main St, Wenham, 01984. Eleanor E Thompson, Dir
Holdings: Vols (1000) Cat Mss Pix
Notes: Incl books and broadsides on agriculture from 1800s.

MT —MONTANA STATE UNIVERSITY, Library, Bozeman, 59717. Minnie Ellen Paugh, Special Collections Librn
Holdings: Vols 2000 //
Notes: Private library of M L Wilson, Asst Sectreary of Agriculture in FDS's Cabinet and later head of the National Extension Service.

NE —NEBRASKA STATE HISTORICAL SOCIETY, Archives, 1500 R St, Box 82554, Lincoln, 68501. James E Potter, State Archivist
Holdings: // Uncat Mss Maps Pix
Notes: Agriculture, reclamation, and irrigation on the Great Plains from 1910 to 1957. Collection of Val Kuska, agricultural development for CB&O Railroad.

NJ —RUTGERS, THE STATE UNIVERSITY OF NEW JERSEY, Alexander Library, Special Collections and Archives, College Ave & Huntington St, New Brunswick, 08903. Ronald L Becker, Cur of Manuscripts and Rare Books
Holdings: Cat
Notes: Several hundred early publications, 15th-19th century.

NY —NEW YORK STATE HISTORICAL ASSOCIATION, Library, Lake Rd, Cooperstown, 13326. Amy Barnum, Librn
Holdings: Vols (60,000) Cat Mss Maps Pix Slides Audiotapes
Notes: Emphasis on New York State to 1860, but northeastern US and later 19th century incl. Noncirculating. Also incl bound periodicals.

NY —NEW YORK STATE OFFICE OF PARKS & RECREATION, TACONIC REGION, Clermont State Historic Park, Library, RR 1, Box 215, Germantown, 12526. Bruce E Naramore, Historic Site Manager
Holdings: Vols (5000) Cat Mss Maps
Notes: Period editions of pre - and post-American Revolutionary War agricultural technology. Many belonged to the Chancellor Robert R Livingston (1746-1813). Incl land drainage, hybrids, fertilizers, and the introduction of Merino sheep.

NY —STATE UNIVERSITY OF NEW YORK, COLLEGE AT NEW PALTZ, Sojourner Truth Library, World Study Center, William J Haggerty Collection of French Colonial History, New Paltz, 12561. Corinne Nyquist, Librn
Holdings: Vols (19,153) // Uncat Mss Maps Pix
Notes: French colonial history. In 1966 this college acquired the research Library of the Comite Francais pour l'outre-mer. This library served the needs of a society in Paris whose membership incl French colonial administrators, scholars, and students. The more than 19,000 books and pamphlets and 135 sets of periodicals date from 1830, and cover the administration and development of the former colonies of France. Much of the material is economic, statistical, or agricultural, reflecting the interests of the collectors. British colonial history is well represented. Described in *Africana Library* Journal, Winter 1971.

NY —COLUMBIA UNIVERSITY LIBRARIES, Rare Book & Manuscript Library, 801 Butler Library, 535 W 114 St, New York, 10027. Kenneth A Lohf, Librn
Holdings: Mss
Notes: The papers of Professor Frank Tannenbaum, approx 28,000 items of correspondence and mss relating to Latin American and Mexican history, also the US Farm Security Program, 1934-1937. Professor Tannenbaum also bequeathed his research library of more than 3000 vols on all phases of Latin American history and literature to Columbia. Restricted use.

NY —NEW YORK HISTORICAL SOCIETY, Library, 170 Central Park W, New York, 10024. James Gregory, Librn
Holdings: Mss
Notes: Incl original mss, illustrative materials, etc.

NC —DUKE UNIVERSITY, William R Perkins Library, Manuscript Dept, Durham, 27706. Ellen Gartrell, Cur of Mss
Holdings: Cat Mss
Notes: Especially US South. Plantation records; US Census of Agriculture, 1850-1880, for Georgia, Kentucky, Louisiana, Tennessee. Many collections relate to agricultural labor, particular crops, and marketing.

ND —UNIVERSITY OF NORTH DAKOTA, Chester Fritz Library, Dept of Special Collections, Grand Forks, 58202. Daniel F Rylance, Special Collections Coordr
Holdings: Vols (5500) Uncat Mss Maps Pix Microforms
Budget: ($2500)
Notes: Also the Orin G Libby Manuscript Collection (900 collections), and the Aandahl Collection of Western History on North Dakota and the Northern Great Plains. Emphasis on agriculture, politics, pioneering, Germans from Russia, etc. Guides to the collections available from the Coordinator of Special Collections.

OH —CLEVELAND PUBLIC LIBRARY, Science & Technology Dept, 325 Superior Ave, Cleveland, 44114. Jean Z Piety, Head
Holdings: Cat
Notes: Collection from 18th century to present incl books, journals, and files of federal government publication. Also incl some early and rare vols.

PA —PENNSYLVANIA DIV OF ARCHIVES & MANUSCRIPTS, State Archives, PO Box 1026, Harris, 17108. Roland M Baumann, Chief, History & Museums
Holdings: Vols (3000) // Uncat Mss Maps Pix
Budget: ($40,000)
Notes: The Harmony Society (1785-1905), a German communistic and spiritual community, which immigrated to the US in 1805 and established their community in Harmony, Pennsylvania, moved to New Harmony, Indiana, and returned to Pennsylvania to set up the town of Economy, 20 miles north of Pittsburgh on the Ohio River. The Harmonists had a vast impact on the economy of the areas in which they lived. They were involved in agriculture, manufacturing and investing. 300,000 cu ft.

PA —LIBRARY COMPANY OF PHILADELPHIA, 1314 Locust St, Philadelphia, 19107. Edwin Wolf II, Librn; Kenneth Finkel, Cur of Prints
Holdings: Vols 685 Cat Mss
Notes: Incl 18th and early 19th century English and American texts and periodicals on agriculture and animal husbandry; with mss vols of contemporary correspondence of the Philadelphia Society for Promoting Agriculture.

PA —UNIVERSITY OF PENNSYLVANIA, Van Pelt Library, Rare Books Collection, 34 & Walnut Sts, Philadelphia, 19104. Daniel Traister, Special Collections Librn
Holdings: Vols 685 Cat Mss
Notes: Incl 18th and early 19th century English and American texts and periodicals on agriculture and animal husbandry; with mss vols of contemporary correspondence of the Philadelphia Society for Promoting Agriculture.

PA —FRIENDS HISTORICAL LIBRARY OF SWARTHMORE COLLEGE, Swarthmore, 19081. J William Frost, Dir
Holdings: Vols (35,000) Cat Mss Pix Microforms
Notes: Library's collection contain information on the history and doctrine of the Society of Friends, Quaker contributions to literature, science, business, education, and government, plus their reform efforts in peace, Indian rights, women's rights, and abolition of slavery. Incl in the more than 250 mss collections are farm journals, account books, and correspondence of several rural families, mostly from the 19th century.

TX —SOUTHERN METHODIST UNIVERSITY, DeGolyer Library, Box 396, SMU, Dallas, 75275. Clifton H Jones, Dir
Holdings: Vols (80,000) Cat Mss Maps Pix Slides Microforms
Notes: First editions of prominent authors; also of books in subject emphasis collections. All subjects listed in this vol are strong. Numerous collections of personal papers relating to subjects also.

VA —VIRGINIA POLYTECHNIC INSTITUTE AND STATE UNIVERSITY LIBRARY, Blacksburg, 24061. Glenn L McMullen, Special Collections Librn
Holdings: Vols (1500)
Notes: Collection of primarily nineteenth century imprints on transportation, communications, and agricultural technology; technological encyclopedias and compendia; books on inventions and inventors; and travel accounts dealing with industrial and technological change.

VA —UNIVERSITY OF VIRGINIA, Alderman Library, Manuscripts Dept, Charlottesville, 22901. Edmund Berkeley Jr, Cur
Holdings: Vols 23 Cat Mss
Notes: The Atcheson Laughlin Hench Memorial Collection of Richard Doddridge Blackmore manuscripts consists of ca 1035 items, 1812-1973, by, about, and relating to the English poet, novelist, and agricultural experimenter. The collection chiefly contains correspondence but also includes bills; exercises; examination questions and answers from Exeter College, Oxford; proofs for the novels *Cradock Nowell* and *Perlycross*; a patent; and some printed materials. Another part of the collection consists of miscellanea from the files of Atcheson L Hench, longtime Univ of Virginia professor of English, who acquired the major portion of this collection and presented it to the Library. The most significant part of the collection is the correspondence which illuminates the most important facets of Blackmore's life; his strong family ties; his fruit growing and gardening; his novels andpoetry, and his negotiations with editors, illustrators, and publishers. An unpublished register is available in the repository. In addition 19th century Virginia Family Papers Collections enable a researcher to obtain an excellent picture of the economic and social interactions on large plantations in Virginia during the 19th century. They are invaluable as research sources in the study of slavery, women's history, economic history, agrarian and political history. Among the more notable collections are the papers of John

AGRICULTURE—HISTORY (cont.)

Hartwell Cocke and the Cocke family, Berkeley family, Joseph Carrington Cabell, Carter family, Watson family, Carter-Smith family, Pocket Plantation, Bruce family, Hubard family, and many others. 100 linear ft of mss.

VA —COLONIAL WILLIAMSBURG FOUNDATION, Research Center Library, PO Drawer C, Williamsburg, 23187. John E Ingram, Research Archivist
Holdings: Vols (30,000) Cat Mss Maps Pix Microforms
Budget: ($20,000)
Notes: Virginia and the Chesapeake in the 17th-18th centuries. Particular strengths include social, economic, agricultural and architectural history. The collection encompasses over 6000 rare books, 18th Century music scores and 12,000 manuscripts, as well as a complete set of Virginia Colonial Records Project microfilm (1000 reels).

†WA —WASHINGTON STATE UNIVERSITY, Library, Manuscripts, Archives & Special Collections, Pullman, 99164. John F Guido, Head
Holdings: Cat Mss Maps Pix
Notes: The ms collection incl business and financial records of banks, breweries, insurance, land, lumber and livestock companies, trade and commodity associations; as well as the personal and professional papers of authors, aviators, educators, engineers, farmers, historians, pioneers, politicians and scientists; especially rich in documents relating to the exploration, settlement and development of the Palouse Country, in Inland Empire, the Columbia Basin and the Pacific Northwest. Described in *Selected Manuscript resources in the Washington State University Library* (Pullman, 1974); and other published and unpublished inventories and registers.

ON —UNIVERSITY OF TORONTO, Thomas Fisher Rare Book Library, 120 Saint George St, Toronto, M5S 1A5, Can. Richard G Landon, Head
Holdings: Vols 4000
Notes: The Science Collection is especially rich in works on Renaissance astronomy, physics and mechanics and has noteworthy holdings of works of English experimental scientists in the 17th and 18th centuries with excellent collections of the works of Robert Boyle, Robert Hooke, and Sir Isaac Newton. Includes virtually all important early editions of Euclid; alchemical works of the 16th and 17th centuries together with the works of 18th century chemists like Lavoisier and Priestly; works on agriculture with special emphasis on British agriculture in the 18th century; and a variety of other works important in the history of science in all its branches. In addition the Fisher Library has many other specialized scientific collections which are listed separately.

AGRICULTURE—MAPS

MD —US DEPT OF AGRICULTURE, National Agricultural Library, 10301 Baltimore Blvd, Beltsville, 20705. Joseph H Howard, Director

AGRICULTURE—NORTH CAROLINA

NC —DUKE UNIVERSITY, William R Perkins Library, Durham, 27706. Elvin E Strowd, University Librn
Notes: The Weldon N Edwards and Marmaduke Hawkins collection consists of 2500 volumes. It includes many rare North Carolina state documents and materials on history and agriculture.

AGRICULTURE—MEXICO

AZ —UNIVERSITY OF ARIZONA, Library, Tucson, 85721. W David Laird, Librn
Notes: Incl the collection of Professor L Fourton who taught at the National School of Agriculture in Chipingo, near Mexico City, for 57 years prior to his death in 1964. In Rare Books Dept.

†WA —WASHINGTON STATE UNIVERSITY, Library, Manuscripts, Archives & Special Collections, Pullman, 99164. John F Guido, Head
Holdings: // Cat Mss Maps
Notes: Regla, Counts of: The papers of the Romero de Terreros family, to whom were granted the titles of Regla, San Cristoval, and San Francisco, include wills, deeds, titles, property maps, litigation over such things as sheep walks, water rights, and the titles themselves. Incl also is much detailed correspondence between hacienda administrators and the family concerning weather, crops, and commodity prices. Several large vols, bound in 1783, document the history of land acquisitions by the Jesuit Colegio Maximo de San Pedro y San Pablo of Mexico City, especially the hacienda of Santa Lucia, from 1576 to the time of the Expulsion. Other early papers deal with the holdings and genealogy of the Marquisates of Salinas, Salvatierra, and Santiago. Described by J Horace Nunemaker in the *Hispanic American Historical Review* (August 1945) 25:409; andby Jacquelyn M Gaines in *Three Centuries of Mexican* Documents: A *Partial Calendar of the Regla* Papers (Pullman, Washington, 1963).

AGRICULTURE—OREGON

OR —BAKER COUNTY PUBLIC LIBRARY, 2400 Resort St, Baker, 97814. Paul C Crouthamal, Librn
Holdings: Vols (1700) Cat Mss Maps Pix Mircoforms
Budget: ($2000)
Notes: Baker County, Oregon materials, historical and current, emphasizing genealogy, mining, agriculture and the people. Incl any fiction with Oregon as the locale. Local newspapers on microfilm, 1870-date, but incomplete for early years. 50 files on local plants, Incl 1953-date, with separate catalog. Incl 300 maps.

AGRICULTURE—SOUTHERN STATES

NC —DUKE UNIVERSITY, William R Perkins Library, Manuscript Dept, Durham, 27706. Ellen Gartrell, Cur of Mss
Holdings: Cat Mss
Notes: Plantation records; US Census of Agriculture, 1850-1880, for Georgia, Kentucky, Louisiana, Tennesee. Many collections relate to agricultural labor, particular crops and marketing.

AGRICULTURE—STATISTICS

DC —US BUREAU OF THE CENSUS, Library, Federal Office Bldg 3, Rm 2451, Washington, 20233. Betty Baxtresser, Chief, ASD Library Branch
Holdings: Vols (200,863) Cat Microforms
Notes: Emphases on statistics of agriculture, business, construction, economics, foreign trade, governments, housing, industry, population, transportation, statistical methodology, and data processing. Library holdings are largely current materials covering the Bureau's programs. Outdated materials are withdrawn regularly.

GA —UNIVERSITY OF GEORGIA, Libraries, Special Collections Division, Athens, 30602. Vesta Lee Gordon, Asst Dir for Special Collections
Notes: The Arbitron Collection of television and radio program ratings, 1949-date (except past year). In-depth, statistical analyses of the listening public by age, sex, county, some ethnic groups, farm population, listening preferences, etc. 26,302 bound vols. 2 reports, 1949-81. To be added to annually.

AGRICULTURE—TEXAS

†TX —TEXAS A&M UNIVERSITY, Library, University Archives, College Station, 77843.
Notes: Papers of Reagan Brown, former Texas Agriculture Commissioner.

TX —NORTH TEXAS STATE UNIVERSITY, Archives, NT Station Box 5188, Denton, 76203. Robert LaForte, University Archivist
Notes: FortWorth Stockyards Company Collection. A B Jolley Collection, Morrison Milling Company Collection, Tom Harpool Seed Company Collection. The development of agriculture and businesses dependent on agriculture in the North Texas area is a collecting strength at the NTSU Archives. The Fort Worth Stockyards Company Collection includes correspondence, reports, and business ledgers of a major Texas stockyards from 1893-1956. The A B Jolley Collection contains extensive information on the development of Dallas County agriculture from the perspective of the County Agricultural Agent from 1929-1953. The Morrison Milling Company Collection and the Tom Harpool Seed Company Collection focus on agricultural businesses in the city of Denton from the 1930's to the early 1980's. Published Description: A B Jolley Collection,*The National Union Catalog of Manuscript Collections: Catalog* 1979 Washington: Library of Congress, 1980.

AGRICULTURE—TROPICS

FL —UNIVERSITY OF FLORIDA, Institute of Food & Agricultural Sciences, Hume Library, Gainesville, 32611. Albert C Strickland, Librn
Holdings: Vols (135,000) Cat Mss Microforms
Notes: Including journals and monographs, this collection is a general agricultural one. The emphasis is on tropical agriculture, especially Latin America. Entomology is very strong. The library offers on-line information retrieval using Lockheed and SDC data bases.

AGRICULTURE—U.S.

†PA —LIBRARY COMPANY OF PHILADELPHIA, 1314 Locust St, Philadelphia, 19107. Edwin Wolf II, Librn
Holdings: Vols (450,000)

AGRICULTURE, COOPERATIVE

IL —ILLINOIS FARM BUREAU LIBRARY, 1701 Towanda Ave, PO Box 1901, Bloomington, 61701. Rue E Olson, Librn
Holdings: Vols (24,000) Cat Microforms
Budget: ($25,000)

WI —UNIVERSITY OF WISCONSIN, MADISON, Land Tenure Center Library, 434 Steenbock Memorial Library, 550 Babcock Dr, Madison, 53706. Teresa J Anderson, Librn
Holdings: Vols (60,000) Cat Mss Maps Microforms
Budget: ($65,000)
Notes: Socio-economic aspects of agricultural development in the Third World. All materials in the collection are cataloged and classified. The library has its own catalog.

AGRICULTURE, DESERT see Desert Agriculture

AGRICULTURE, TROPICAL see Agriculture—Tropics

AGROMETEOROLOGY see Crops and Climate; Meteorology, Agricultural

AGRONOMY see Agriculture

AGROSTOLOGY see Grasses

AGUE see Malarial Fever

AHASUERUS

RI —BROWN UNIVERSITY, John Hay Library, 20 Prospect St, Providence, 02912. Mark N Brown, Cur Mss
Holdings: Vols 1500 Cat // Mss
Notes: A virtually complete collection of the literature dealing with the Legend of the Wandering Jew printed from the 17th century to date. In addition to historical discussion of the legend there are sections devoted to the appearance of Ahasuerus in

AHASUERUS (cont.)

drama, fiction, illustrations, poetry, song, and music.

AID REFUGEE CHINESE INTELLECTUALS (ARCI)

CA —HOOVER INSTITUTION ON WAR, REVOLUTION & PEACE, Stanford University, Stanford, 94305. Milorad M Drachkovitch, Archivist
Holdings: Mss
Notes: Records of Air Refugee Chinese Intellectuals (ARCI), a private US relief organization, incl correspondence, reports, minutes of meetings, financial records and photographs, 1952-1970, relating to ARCI relief work for Chinese refugees. 44 ms boxes, 3 albums.

AID THE ALLIES COMMITTEE see Committee to Defend America by Aiding the Allies

AID TO UNDERDEVELOPED AREAS see Technical Assistance

AIDS TO NAVIGATION

CT —YALE UNIVERSITY, Box 1603A, Yale Station, New Haven, 06520.
Holdings: Cat Maps
Notes: "The best collection of printed rutters in America is that of Henry C Taylor at Yale University Library," S E Morison, *The European Discovery of America*, 1971, p 150.

AIKEN, CONRAD POTTER, 1889-1973

CA —HUNTINGTON LIBRARY, Art Gallery & Botanical Gardens, 1151 Oxford Rd, San Marino, 91108. Robert L Middlekauff, Dir; Daniel H Woodward, Librn
Holdings: Vols 400 Cat Mss Pix
Notes: His literary archive, incl 390 mss, 900 letters, 80 photographs and ephemera. Refer to David Mike Hamilton, "The Conrad Potter Aiken Collection of the Henry E Huntington Library," *Studies in the Literary Imagination* (Fall, 1980, vol 13, no 2), 137-142.

GA —GEORGIA SOUTHERN COLLEGE, Library, Statesboro, 30458. Edna Earle Brown, Acting Dir
Holdings: Cat

MA —HARVARD UNIVERSITY LIBRARY, Houghton Library, Cambridge, 02138. Rodney G Dennis, Cur of Manuscripts
Holdings: Cat Mss

MO —WASHINGTON UNIVERSITY, John M Olin Library, Campus Box 1061, St Louis, 63130.
Notes: A major collection, incl mss, correspondence, literary papers, photographs, etc. Described in *Special Collections: an Annotated Guide to the Holdings of the Manuscript Division and the University Archives and Research Collection.*

NV —UNIVERSITY OF NEVADA, RENO, University Library, Special Collections Dept, Reno, 89557. Robert E Blesse, Head
Holdings: // Vols (92) Cat
Notes: Includes individual works by author in all editions including translations; also prefaces, introductions, published correspondence, appearances in anthologies, periodicals, etc. Bibliographical research collection, part of Modern Authors Collection. Other appearances 820 cataloged.

NY —STATE UNIVERSITY OF NEW YORK, STONY BROOK, Melville Library, Dept of Special Collections, Stony Brook, 11794. Evert Volkersz, Head
Holdings: Vols 110 Cat Mss

SK —UNIVERSITY OF SASKATCHEWAN, Library, Saskatoon, S7N 0W0, Can. S Perkins, Librn
Holdings: Vols 250// Cat Mss Phonorecords Audiotapes
Notes: Bibliographies of original writings and critical articles. Collection includes books and articles by Aiken, and 14 volumes of critical articles on Aiken works.

AIKEN, SEN. GEORGE D.

VT —UNIVERSITY OF VERMONT, Guy W Bailey/David W Howe Library, Burlington, 05405. John Buehler, Asst Dir for Special Collections

AIKEN, GOV. WILLIAM

SC —CHARLESTON MUSEUM LIBRARY, 360 Meeting St, Charleston, 29403. K Sharon Bennett, Librn
Holdings: Vols (500) // Cat
Notes: The Governor William Aiken Collection. Housed at the Aiken House on Elizabeth Street, includes 400-500 volumes as well as numerous magazines and over 5000 pieces of sheet music, 1820-1880. Its value lies in its reflection of the habits and tastes of the upper class during this time.

SC —COLLEGE OF CHARLESTON LIBRARY, Special Collections Dept, Charleston, 29401.
Notes: William Martin Aiken Collection. Incl notebook, sketchbooks composed in Europe and the US, architectural designs, correspondence, miscellaneous printed material, and a photograph of Aiken; contains also collections of other architectural designs and building adornments.

AINO LANGUAGE see Ainu Language

AINSWORTH, WILLIAM HARRISON, 1805-1882

CA —UNIVERSITY OF CALIFORNIA, LOS ANGELES, Research Library, Dept of Special Collections, 405 Hilgard Ave, Los Angeles, 90024. Edward Shreeves, Chairman, Bibliographers Group; David S Zeidberg, Head
Holdings: Vols 100 Cat Mss
Notes: 100 first and other editions of Ainsworth's books; 900 letters and mss.

NJ —PRINCETON UNIVERSITY, Library, Morris L Parrish Collection, Princeton, 08540. Alexander D Wainwright, Cur
Holdings: Vols 54 Cat Mss
Notes: There are over 54 vols found within the Morris L Parrish Collection. Details about Cruikshank's illustrations for William Harrison Ainsworth can be found in the *Chronicle* XXV, 1 & 2 (autumn and winter, 1973-74) pp 15, 17-19, 24, 83, 108 ff, 144-1465, 183 and 221.

NY —NEW YORK PUBLIC LIBRARY, Rare Books and Manuscripts Div, Fifth Ave & 42 St, New York, 10018. William L Joyce, Asst Dir; Bernard McTigue, Cur, Arents Collection
Holdings: Cat Mss Pix
Budget: $7161

AINU LANGUAGE

NY —NEW YORK PUBLIC LIBRARY, Oriental Div, Fifth Ave & 42 St, New York, 10018. E Christian Filstrup, Chief
Holdings: Cat Mss Microforms
Budget: ($56,455)
Notes: Published catalog of holdings.

AIR—POLLUTION AND CONTROL

CA —LOS ANGELES PUBLIC LIBRARY, Science & Technology Dept, 630 W Fifth St, Los Angeles, 90071. Billie M Connor, Dept Head
Holdings: Vols 8000 Cat Microforms
Notes: Shop manuals for American and foreign made cars, trucks, motorcycles, and tractors. Specialized manuals on transmissions, air conditioning, air pollution control devices, electrical components, restoration prices, etc. Parts Lists Directories including flat rate and parts price manuals. Indexes include car and other motor vehicles repair manuals by make and model, road tests for specific models appearing in popular automotive periodicals, and an automobile illustration index.

CA —UNIVERSITY OF CALIFORNIA, LOS ANGELES, Engineering & Mathematical Sciences Library, 405 Hilgard, Los Angeles, 90024. Rosalee I Wright, Librn
Notes: Partial depository for NTIS (pollution, environment, meteorology, and bioengineering) since 1970.

CA —CALIFORNIA DEPT OF TRANSPORTATION, Transportation Library, 5900 Folsom Blvd, PO Box 19128, Sacramento, 95819. Eva Caro, Librn
Holdings: Vols (10,000) Cat Mss Maps Pix Slides Phonorecords Audiotapes 16mm Films Filmstrips Microforms

CO —COLORADO STATE UNIVERSITY, Libraries, Fort Collins, 80523. K Suzanne Johnson, Biomedical Sciences, Librn
Holdings: Vols (4000) Cat Maps Microforms
Notes: Atmospheric Sciences: climatotogy, Weather modification, air-pollution, cloud physics, etc.

KY —UNIVERSITY OF KENTUCKY, Robert E Shaver Library of Engineering, 355 Anderson Hall, Lexington, 40506. Russell H Powell, Engineering Librn
Holdings: Vols (48,000) Cat Microforms

MD —US DEPT OF AGRICULTURE, National Agricultural Library, 10301 Baltimore Blvd, Beltsville, 20705. Joseph H Howard, Director
Holdings: Vols (2,000,000) Cat Mss Maps Pix Slides Microforms
Notes: Crop ecology, agro-climatic analogs; air pollution effects. Agronomy: agriculture and tropical and desert agriculture. For use by the staff of the Institute. Incl 5000 pamphlet items. Former collection of American Institute of Crop Ecology.

MA —CAMP, DRESSER & MCKEE, Herman G Dresser Library, One Center Plaza, Boston, 02108. Virginia L Carroll, Librn
Holdings: Vols (15,000) Cat Maps Slides Microforms
Notes: Air, land, and water pollution; environmental engineering; hazardous wastes; water resources; solid wastes; resource recycling.

MA —ABCOR, INC, Library, 850 Main St, Wilmington, 01887. Eileen Smith, Librn
Holdings: Vols (2000) Cat
Budget: ($10,000)
Notes: Environmental technology; ultrafiltration; waste treatment processes. Incl technical reports. Extensive microfiche collection on air pollution.

MI —US ENVIRONMENTAL PROTECTION AGENCY, Motor Vehicle Emission Laboratory Library, 2565 Plymouth Rd, Ann Arbor, 48105. Debra Talsma, Librn
Holdings: // Uncat Microforms
Notes: No separate catalog. Collection described in: US EPA, Library System Branch, *Guide to EPA Libraries*, July, 1977. Collection includes 9500 technical reports on air pollution from mobile sources (especially automobiles); air pollution legislation (350 vols); fuel economy and conservation (800 technical reports); automobile engineering (300 vols); emission control technology for mobile source (8000 reports and papers); use of methanol and other alternative fuels in motor vehicles (600 technical reports).

NY —NASSAU COUNTY DEPARTMENT OF HEALTH, Division of Laboratories & Research, 209 Main St, Hempstead, 11550. Madeline Burston, Librn; Beatrice R Sewald, Asst Librn
Holdings: Vols 1200

NY —BOYCE THOMPSON INSTITUTE FOR PLANT RESEARCH, Library, Cornell University, Tower Rd, Ithaca, 14853. Greta Colavito, Librn
Holdings: Vols (5300) Cat
Budget: ($46,000)
Notes: Mainly plant physiology, biochemistry, entomology, air and water pollution, pesticides, and plant pathology.

NY —NEW YORK PUBLIC LIBRARY, Research Libraries, Science and Technology Research Center, Fifth Ave & 42 St, New York, 10018.
Holdings: Vols (1,100,000)
Budget: ($647,259)

NY —US ENVIRONMENTAL PROTECTION AGENCY, Region II, Technical Library, 26 Federal Plaza, New York, 10278. Audrey Thomas, Regional

AIR—POLLUTION AND CONTROL (cont.)

Librn
Holdings: Vols 4200 Cat
Notes: Incl 16,000 reports, 225,000 microfiche, 100 current subscriptions.

NY —UNIVERSITY OF ROCHESTER, Engineering Library, Gavett Hall, River Campus, Rochester, 14627. Isabel Kaplan, Librn
Holdings: Vols (22,465) Cat
Notes: Strong collection in the field and related areas.

OH —CASE WESTERN RESERVE UNIVERSITY LIBRARIES, Cleveland, 44106. Susie Hanson, Special Collections Librn
Holdings: Vols 1000 Cat
Notes: The collection was previously titled thee Lake Erie Study Collection. As its scope has increased, it has been renamed the Environmental Sciences Collection and has been fully incorporated into the collection of the Sears Library, which serves the University in the areas of sciece and technology, econonomics and management. The Environmental Science Collection incl government and nongovernment reports, monographs and serials.

OH —CLEVELAND PUBLIC LIBRARY, Science & Technology Dept, 325 Superior Ave, Cleveland, 44114. Jean Z Piety, Head
Holdings: Cat Pix
Notes: Special collection covers the environmental sciences concerned with the Great Lakes-St Lawrence drainage basins. Emphasis is on limnology, ecology, meteorology, hydraulics, biology, pollution of air and water, natural history and general research. Most of the material indexed has been donated by numerous agencies around the Great Lakes.

PA —PENNSYLVANIA DEPT OF ENVIRONMENTAL RESOURCES, Office of Environmental Protection, Technical Reference Library, Fulton Bldg, 17th Floor, Box 2063, Harrisburg, 17120. Wanda R Bell, Librn
Holdings: Vols (2000) Cat Slides Microfilm Microfiche
Budget: 5
Notes: 10,000 technical reports; water and wastewater feasibility plans; PA Bulletin, 1970-Present; water pollution; solid waste; mining and reclamation; air quality; acid mine drainage.

PA —DREXEL UNIVERSITY LIBRARIES, Engineering Library, 32 & Chestnut Sts, Philadelphia, 19104. Charlotte T Duvally, Librn
Holdings: Vols 18,545 Uncat Microforms
Notes: The only library in Philadelphia area holding the Bay Area (San Francisto) air pollution control microfilm library. Access via uniterm subject cards (manual retrieval system) index, accession card file index, author card file indes.

PA —FRANKLIN INSTITUTE LIBRARY, 20 & The Parkway, Philadelphia, 19103. Miriam Padusis, Dir; Charles Wilt, Readers Servs Librn
Holdings: Vols (300,000) Cat Maps Pix Microforms

UT —NORTH AMERICAN WEATHER CONSULTANTS, Technical Library, 1141 E 3900 South, Suite A130, Salt Lake City, 84124. Eleanor Furnival, Librn
Holdings: Vols (7000) Maps 16mm Films Microforms
Budget: ($5000)
Notes: Incl 500 maps and 3000 microforms.

WI —COLT INDUSTRIES, FM Engine Div, Library, 701 Lawton Ave, Beloit, 53511. Westley A Brill, Library Admin
Holdings: Vols 100 Cat Mss

AB —ALBERTA DEPT OF THE ENVIRONMENT, Library, Oxbridge Place, 9820 106th St, Edmonton, T5K 2J6, Can. Marilyn Corbett, Head, Library Services Branch
Holdings: Vols (20,000) Cat Microforms

AIR CARRIERS see Airlines—History

AIR CONDITIONING

CA —LOS ANGELES PUBLIC LIBRARY, Science & Technology Dept, 630 W Fifth St, Los Angeles, 90071. Billie M Connor, Dept Head
Holdings: Vols 8000 Cat Microforms
Notes: Shop manuals for American and foreign made cars, trucks, motorcycles, and tractors. Specialized manuals on transmissions, air conditioning, air pollution control devices, electrical components, restoration prices, etc. Parts Lists Directories including flat rate and parts price manuals. Indexes include car and other motor vehicles repair manuals by make and model, road tests for specific models appearing in popular automotive periodicals, and an automobile illustration index.

KY —UNIVERSITY OF KENTUCKY, Robert E Shaver Library of Engineering, 355 Anderson Hall, Lexington, 40506. Russell H Powell, Engineering Librn
Holdings: Vols (48,000) Cat Microforms

NY —ENGINEERING SOCIETIES LIBRARY, 345 E 47 St, New York, 10017. S Kirk Cabeen, Dir
Holdings: Vols 250,000 Cat Maps 16mm Films Microforms
Notes: One of the largest, most comprehensive engineering libraries in the world. Covers all engineering disciplines; particularly strong in electrical and electronic, mechanical, mining and metallurgical, petroleum, chemical, industrial, air conditioning and refrigeration engineering. Incl Wheeler Collection of early materials on magnetism and electricity. 125, 000 bound periodical volumes; 10,000 maps; 5000 serial subscriptions (many foreign-language). Virtually all materials abstracted in *Engineering Index* (1884-date) are incl in Library. Noncirculating, except to members of professional engineering societies which support the Library. See *Engineering Societies Library, New York, Classed Subject Catalog and Index* (Boston: G K Hall, 1963); and *Supplements*, 1-10, 1964-1973.

†NY —TECHNICAL CAREER INSTITUTE LIBRARY, 320 W 31st Street, New York, 10001. Michael Brent, Librn
Holdings: Vols (3500)

NY —CARRIER CORPORATION, Logan Lewis Library, Research Division, Carrier Parkway, Syracuse, 13221. Christine Greene, Librn
Holdings: Vols (5000)
Notes: Emphasis on technical and research and development aspects of the air conditioning, heating and refrigeration industry. Incl 4000 documents.

NC —TECHNICAL INSTITUTE OF ALAMANCE, Learning Resources Center, Jimmy Kerr Rd, PO Box 623, Haw River, 27258. Ron Plummer, Coordr
Holdings: Vols (265) Cat Pix Phonorecords Audiotapes 16mm Films Filmstrips Microforms

PA —FRANKLIN INSTITUTE LIBRARY, 20 & The Parkway, Philadelphia, 19103. Miriam Padusis, Dir; Charles Wilt, Readers Servs Librn
Holdings: Vols (300,000) Cat Maps Pix Microforms

PA —CARNEGIE LIBRARY OF PITTSBURGH, Science & Technology Dept, 4400 Forbes Ave, Pittsburgh, 15213. Catherine M Brosky, Dept Head
Notes: Collection incl material on general construction, carpentry, masonry, plumbing, heating, air conditioning, corrosion and painting and numerous other building trades.

AIR LAW see Aeronautics—Laws and Legislation

AIR LINES see Airlines—History

AIR MAIL SERVICE AND AIR LETTER SHEETS

CA —SAN DIEGO AERO-SPACE MUSEUM, N Paul Whittier Historical Aviation Library, 2001 Pan American Plaza, Balboa Park, San Diego, 92101. B C Reynolds, Archivist
Holdings: / / Uncat Microforms

CO —US AIR FORCE ACADEMY, Library, USAF Academy, Colorado Springs, 80840. Reiner H Schaeffer, Dir
Notes: Air letter sheets issued by all countries throughout the world, and the United Nations, from 1941 to 1974. Incl are sheets used by Germany and given to captive prisoners of war during World War II.

AIR NAVIGATION see Aeronautics

AIR POLLUTION see Air—Pollution and Control

AIR TRANSPORT see Aeronautics, Commercial

AIR TRAVEL

NJ —NEW JERSEY DEPT OF TRANSPORTATION, Library, 1035 Parkway Ave, Trenton, 08625. Margaret L Webb, Librn
Holdings: Vols 2000 Cat Mss Maps Microforms
Notes: Emphasis is on highway, bus, rail, and air transportation. There is a finding-list-index to the department archives, over 1800 items.

AIRCRAFT ENGINES see Airplanes—Motors

AIRCRAFT GAS TURBINES

PQ —PRATT & WHITNEY AIRCRAFT OF CANADA, Library, PO Box 10, Longueuil, J4K 4X9, Can. Joyce Chalevois, Librn
Holdings: Cat Slides 16mm Films Microforms
Notes: Gas turbine engines.

AIRFRAMES see Airplanes

AIRLINE PILOTS ASSOCIATION

MI —WAYNE STATE UNIVERSITY, Walter P Reuther Library, Archives of Labor & Urban Affairs, Detroit, 48202. Philip Mason, Dir
Notes: The Archives of Labor History and Urban Affairs of Wayne State University has long been known for its large and extensive ms collections related to the labor movement and to the city in 20th century America. As the official deposity for the United Automobile, Aerospace and Agriculture Implement Workers, Congress of Industrial Organizations, United Farm Workers Organizing Committee, American Newspaper Guild, Air Line Pilots Association, and Industrial Workers of the World, the Archives has established itself as a distinguished research institution.

AIRLINES—HISTORY

CA —SAN DIEGO AERO-SPACE MUSEUM, N Paul Whittier Historical Aviation Library, 2001 Pan American Plaza, Balboa Park, San Diego, 92101. B C Reynolds, Archivist
Holdings: / / Uncat Microforms

AIRPLANES

MA —MASSACHUSETTS INSTITUTE OF TECHNOLOGY, Institute Archives, Special Collections, Cambridge, 02139.
Notes: Correspondence, newsletters, fact-sheets, newspaper and magazine articles, books and reports of the Citizens' League Against the Sonic Boom, established in 1967 by William Shurcliff to oppose the sonic boom, stop commercial supersonic transport production, and influence public opinion and policy decisions on the SST. Major correspondents incl Bo Lundberg, Richard Wiggs, several US congressmen, and CLASB members.

PA —FRANKLIN INSTITUTE LIBRARY, 20 & The Parkway, Philadelphia, 19103. Miriam Padusis, Dir; Charles Wilt, Readers Servs Librn
Holdings: Vols (300,00) Cat Maps Pix Microforms

AIRPLANES—DESIGN AND CONSTRUCTION

CA —MCDONNELL DOUGLAS CORP, Douglas Aircraft Company, Technical Library, 3855 Lakewood Blvd, PO Box 200, Long Beach, 90846. Pat Ackerman, Librn
Notes: Incl 175,000 technical reports; 500, 000 microforms; 300,000 government/ industry standard and specifications.

WA —BOEING COMPANY, Boeing Technical Libraries, PO Box 3707, Seattle, 98124. Corrine Campbell, Mgr Technical Library
Holdings: Vols (75,000) Cat Microforms
Notes: Books are distributed between 3 libraries, Kent, Renton, and Bellevue. Also contains many periodicals and Boeing Documents Library restricted to Boeing Personnel.

AIRPLANES—ENGINES see Airplanes—Motors

AIRPLANES—HISTORY

CA —SAN DIEGO AERO-SPACE MUSEUM, N Paul Whittier Historical Aviation Library, 2001 Pan American Plaza, Balboa Park, San Diego, 92101. B C Reynolds, Archivist
Holdings: // Uncat Microforms

DC —SMITHSONIAN INSTITUTION LIBRARIES, National Air & Space Museum Branch, NASM Bldg, Sixth & Independence Ave SW, Washington, 20560. Frank A Pietropaoli, Branch Chief
Holdings: Vols (39,000) Cat Mss Maps Pix Slides Microforms
Notes: History of flight and aerospace development, incl biographical material on aviation pioneers, balloons and ballooning. Extensive photographic collection (600,000 pictures). Incl the Sherman Fairchild Collection of aeronautical photographs (transferred from the American Institute of Aeronautics and Astronautics). Also incl the Bella Landauer Aeronautical Sheet Music Collection (1500 pieces). 2000 films; 800,000 microforms; 9000 volumes bound.

IN —PURDUE UNIVERSITY LIBRARIES, Aviation Technology Library, Aviation Technology Bldg, West Lafayette, 47907. Edwin Posey, Engineering Librn
Holdings: Vols (4000) Cat Pix Slides Audiotapes Filmstrips Microform
Notes: Emphasis on piloting, aircraft, and power plant maintenance, and histories of individual aircraft. Also have an aerospace education collection recognized by General Aviation Manufacturers' Association. Incl 135 serial titles.

MO —NATIONAL MUSEUM OF TRANSPORT, Reference Library, 3105 Barrett Station Rd, Saint Louis, 63122. John P Roberts, Secretary
Holdings: Vols (10,000) Cat Mss Maps Pix Slides

AIRPLANES—MAINTENANCE AND REPAIR

IN —PURDUE UNIVERSITY LIBRARIES, Aviation Technology Library, Aviation Technology Bldg, West Lafayette, 47907. Edwin Posey, Engineering Librn
Holdings: Vols (4000) Cat Pix Slides Audiotapes Filmstrips Microforms
Notes: Emphasis on piloting, aircraft, and power plant maintenance, and histories of individual aircraft. Also have an aerospace education collection recognized by General Aviation Manufacturers' Association. Incl 135 serial titles.

AIRPLANES—MOTORS

IN —PURDUE UNIVERSITY LIBRARIES, Aviation Technology Library, Aviation Technology Bldg, West Lafayette, 47907. Edwin Posey, Engineering Librn
Holdings: Vols (4000) Cat Pix Slides Audiotapes Filmstrips Microforms
Notes: Emphasis on piloting, aircraft, and power plant maintenance, and histories of individual aircraft. Also have an aerospace education collection recognized by General Aviation Manufacturers' Association. Incl 135 serial titles.

AIRPLANES—OPERATION see Airplanes—Piloting

AIRPLANES—PILOTING

IN —PURDUE UNIVERSITY LIBRARIES, Aviation Technology Library, Aviation Technology Bldg, West Lafayette, 47907. Edwin Posey, Engineering Librn
Holdings: Vols (4000) Cat Pix Slides Audiotapes Filmstrips Microforms
Notes: Emphasis on piloting, aircraft, and power plant maintenance, and histories of individual aircraft. Also have an aerospace education collection, incl pilot training, recognized by General Aviation Manufacturers's Association. Incl 135 serial titles.

AIRPLANES, PILOTLESS see Guided Missiles

AIRPORTS

CA —UNIVERSITY OF CALIFORNIA, BERKELEY, Institute of Transportation Studies Library, Library, 412 McLaughlin Hall, Berkeley, 94720.
Holdings: Vols (82,000)
Budget: ($215,000)
Notes: US Department of Transportation depository through NTIS.

FL —EMBRY-RIDDLE AERONAUTICAL UNIVERSITY, Regional Airport, Daytona Beach, 32014. M Judy Luther, Dir of Learning Resources

MA —MASSACHUSETTS INSTITUTE OF TECHNOLOGY, Institute Archives, Special Collections, Cambridge, 02139.
Notes: Correspondence, newsletters, fact-sheets, newspaper and magazine articles, books and reports of the Citizens' League Against the Sonic Boom, established in 1967 by William Shurcliff to oppose the sonic boom, stop commercial supersonic transport production, and influence public opinion and policy decisions on the SST. Major correspondents incl Bo Lundberg, Richard Wiggs, several US congressmen, and CLASB members.

AIRSHIPS

DC —SMITHSONIAN INSTITUTION LIBRARIES, National Air & Space Museum Branch, NASM Bldg, Sixth & Independence Ave SW, Washington, 20560. Frank A Pietropaoli, Branch Chief
Holdings: Vols (39,000) Cat Mss Maps Pix Slides Microforms
Notes: History of flight and aerospace development, incl biographical material on aviation pioneers, balloons and ballooning. Extensive photographic collection (600,000 pictures). Incl the Sherman Fairchild Collection of aeronautical photographs (transferred from the American Institute of Aeronautics and Astronautics). Also incl the Bella Landauer Aeronautical Sheet Music Collection (1500 pieces). 2000 films; 800,000 microforms; 9000 volumes bound.

MD —US NAVAL ACADEMY, Nimitz Library, Annapolis, 21402. Alice S Creighton, Assistant Librn for Special Collections
Holdings: Mss
Notes: The William Adger Moffett Papers are a collection of official and personal letters, speeches, news releases, communications, memoranda, notes, news clippings, etc, by and about Rear Admiral William Adger Moffett, first Chief of the Bureau of Aeronautics, US Navy. The collection is a primary source for any research regarding the early history of naval aviation. Papers relate to numerous topics, including the London Naval Treaty and its ramifications, military airships, United Air Service controversy, coastal defense, carriers, etc. Index available in Special Collections Department.

MD —MARYLAND HISTORICAL SOCIETY, Library, 201 W Monument St, Baltimore, 21201. William B Keller, Head Librn
Holdings: Cat Mss Pix
Notes: The Hammond Duggan Collection; papers of the only Maryland native among US Navy officers in the American dirigible program. Incl scrapbooks, mss, pictures, memorabilia.

OH —AKRON-SUMMIT COUNTY PUBLIC LIBRARY, Science & Technology Div, 55 S Main St, Akron, 44326. Joyce McKnight, Head
Holdings: Vols 820 Cat Pix
Notes: The Lighter-Than-Air Society book collection is in the Akron Public Library. Incl foreign language books.

OR —UNIVERSITY OF OREGON LIBRARY, Special Collections Div, Eugene, 97403. Kenneth W Duckett, Curator
Holdings: Vols 250 // Uncat Pix
Notes: The Hallett Cole Collection also incl newspaper clippings and memorabilia, 1920s-1950s.

AKADEMIIA NAUK, SSSR

IL —CENTER FOR RESEARCH LIBRARIES, 6050 S Kenwood Ave, Chicago, 60637. Donald B Simpson, Dir; Esther Smith, Collection Development Librn
Notes: Receive about 1200 current serials in science and technology, and all monographs published by Akademiia Nauk SSSR. Have extensive backfiles of Akademiia Nauk SSSR monographic and serial publications.

AKELEY, CARL ETHAN, 1864-1926

NY —AMERICAN MUSEUM OF NATURAL HISTORY, Library Services Dept, Central Park W & 79th St, New York, 10024. Nina J Root, Chairwoman; Mary Genett, Asst Librn for Reference Services
Holdings: Cat Mss Maps Pix Slides 16mm Films
Notes: Manuscripts, diaries, correspondence, artifacts, some art work, and collected materials. Not all cataloged as of 1983.

NY —UNIVERSITY OF ROCHESTER, Rush Rhees Library, Department of Rare Books and Special Collections, Rochester, 14627. Peter Dzwonkoski, Librn
Notes: Papers, correspondence, mss, ephemera, etc.

AKELEY, MARY L. JOBE

NY —AMERICAN MUSEUM OF NATURAL HISTORY, Library Services Dept, Central Park W & 79th St, New York, 10024. Nina J Root, Chairwoman; Mary Genett, Asst Librn for Reference Services
Holdings: Cat Mss Maps Pix Slides 16mm Films
Notes: Manuscripts, diaries, correspondence, artifacts, some art work, and collected materials. Not all cataloged as of 1983.

AKINS, ZOE

MO —SAINT LOUIS PUBLIC LIBRARY, Gardner Rare Book Room, 1301 Olive St, Saint Louis, 63103. Julanne M Good, Supervisor; Martha Riley, Rare Books Librn
Holdings: Vols (2300) Cat
Budget: ($5573)
Notes: First editions of authors having some association with William Marion Reedy and *Reedy's Mirror*, such as Sara Teasdale, Zoe Akins, Fannie Hurst, Edgar Lee Masters, Babette Deutsch, Richard LeGallienne, etc. Also first editions of selected St Louis and/or Missouri authors such as T S Eliot, Samuel L Clemens, Theodore Dreiser and Tennessee Williams. Noncirculating.

AKKADIAN (EAST SEMITIC) LANGUAGE AND LITERATURE

NY —NEW YORK PUBLIC LIBRARY, Oriental Div, Fifth Ave & 42 St, New York,

AKKADIAN (EAST SEMITIC) LANGUAGE AND LITERATURE (cont.)

10018. E Christian Filstrup, Chief
Holdings: Cat Mss Microforms
Budget: ($56,455)
Notes: Published catalog of holdings.

ALABAMA

AL —AUBURN UNIVERSITY, Ralph Brown Draughon Library, Mell St, Auburn, 36830. Gene Geiger, Special Collections Librn
Holdings: Vols 10,000 Cat
Budget: $7500

AL —JACKSONVILLE STATE UNIVERSITY, University Library, Jacksonville, 36265. Thomas Freeman, Dir, Print Media
Holdings: Vols 2500 Cat Maps
Notes: Books and materials about Alabama and about or by Alabamians.

AL —ALABAMA PUBLIC LIBRARY SERVICE, 6030 Monticello Drive, Montgomery, 36130. Anthony W Miele, Dir
Holdings: Vols 2500 Cat 16mm Films Microforms
Notes: Alabamiana collection contains books about Alabama and by Alabama authors. Incl major Alabama newspapers on microfilm.

NC —DUKE UNIVERSITY, William R Perkins Library, Durham, 27706. Elvin E Strowd, University Librn
Notes: The Flowers Collection of Southern Americana currently consists of 4,300,500 items. Additions are ongoing. Included in this collection are several types of materials, which are housed in appropriate sections of the library. The various types of materials are: manuscripts, books, pamphlets, maps, music, broadsides, newspapers, photographs, engravings, prints and memorabilia.

ALABAMA—CENSUSES

†AL —UNIVERSITY OF ALABAMA, Amelia Gayle Gorgas Library, PO Box S, University, 35486.
Notes: This collection of 159 reels covers the US Census for years 1830-1880. Incl lists of persons interviewed by the census taker.

ALABAMA—DESCRIPTION AND TRAVEL—VIEWS

AL —BIRMINGHAM PUBLIC LIBRARY, Dept of Archives & Mss, 2020 Seventh Ave N, Birmingham, 35203. Marvin Y Whiting, Archivist & Cur
Holdings: Mss Pix Slides Audiotapes Microforms
Notes: Especially Birmingham history. Largest available collections are the Robert Jemison, Jr. Papers (ca 1.2 million items) and the Donald Comer Papers (ca 390,000 items). Photographs incl ca one million negatives from the collection of Birmingham photographer Charles Preston.

ALABAMA—GENEALOGY

AL —BIRMINGHAM PUBLIC LIBRARY, Dept of Archives & Mss, 2020 Seventh Ave N, Birmingham, 35203. Marvin Y Whiting, Archivist & Cur
Holdings: Cat Docs Mss Photos //
Notes: Collections concentrate on the history of Birmingham and Jefferson County, Alabama, and to a lesser extent, the state of Alabama, 1819-1960. Records of real estate companies, coal, steel, and iron industries, city government, and selected prominent individuals. Extensive photograph collections showing general views of the city, photographic portraits of prominent individuals, major buildings and streets, and development of mass transit. Also incl articles, brochures, correspondence, family genealogies, maps, newspaper clippings, pamphlets, and programs concerning significant families, individuals, organizations, and events.

AL —SAMFORD UNIVERSITY, Special Collections Library, 800 Lakeshore Dr, Birmingham, 35229. Annie Ford Wheeler, Acting Head Librn
Holdings: Vols 2500 Cat Mss Microforms
Budget: $4500
Notes: Chiefly southeast US and Ireland. Incl abstracts, printed genealogies, and census indexes (microfilm). Substantial amounts of material in the Bledsoe-Kelly mss.

AL —WHEELER BASIN REGIONAL LIBRARY, 504 Cherry St NE, PO Box 1766, Decatur, 35602. Margarete Lange, Reference Librn
Holdings: Vols 300 Cat Mss Microforms
Notes: Primary emphasis on Alabama and Southern genealogy, although other areas are incl.

AL —ENTERPRISE STATE JUNIOR COLLEGE, Learning Resources Center, PO Box 1300, Enterprise, 36330. Jean Southwall, Ref Librn
Holdings: Vols 447 Cat Microforms

AL —MOBILE PUBLIC LIBRARY, Special Collections Div, 701 Government St, Mobile, 36602.
Holdings: Mss Maps Pix Microfilm
Notes: Alabama and local history; about 4500 vols, 100,000 clippings; 1750 microfilm rolls of newspapers, etc. Approx 8000 vols of genealogy, 1000 periodicals, 2000 clippings, etc. Census on 1800 microfilm rolls.

†AL —UNIVERSITY OF ALABAMA, Amelia Gayle Gorgas Library, PO Box S, University, 35486.
Notes: The Alabama Genealogy Collection incl 236 vols of Pauline Gandrud's *Alabama* Records for the following counties: Autauga, Benton, Bibb, Blount, Calhoun, Chambers, Cherokee, Clarke, Colbert, Coosa, Dallas, De Kalb, Fayette, Franklin Greene, Jackson, Jefferson, Lauderdale, Lawrence, Limestone, Lowndes, Madison, Marengo, Marion, Marshall, Mobile, Montgomery, Morgan, Perry, Pickens, Shelby, Sumter, Talladega, Tallapoosa, Tuscaloosa, Wilcox.

FL —ORLANDO PUBLIC LIBRARY, Local History & Genealogy Dept, 100 Block of Central Ave, Orlando, 32806. Eileen B Willis, Librn
Holdings: Vols 11,000 Cat Maps Microforms
Budget: $8000
Notes: Genealogy collection on Md, Del, W Va, NC, SC, Ala, Miss, La, Texas, Ark, Ky, Ohio, Ill, Ind, and Mich are well represented. Most other states are covered by smaller collections.
See also entry under Genealogy - Collections.

ALABAMA—HISTORY

AL —BIRMINGHAM PUBLIC LIBRARY, Dept of Archives & Mss, 2020 Seventh Ave N, Birmingham, 35203. Marvin Y Whiting, Archivist & Cur
Holdings: Mss Pix Slides Audiotapes Microforms
Notes: Collections concentrate on the history of Birmingham and Jefferson County, Alabama, and to a lesser extent, the state of Alabama, 1819-1960. Records of real estate companies, coal, steel, and iron industries, city government, and selected prominent individuals. Extensive photograph collections showing general views of the city, photographic portraits of prominent individuals, major buildings and streets, and development of mass transit. Also incl articles, brochures, correspondence, family genealogies, maps, newspaper clippings, pamphlets, and programs concerning significant families, individuals, organizations, and events.

AL —SAMFORD UNIVERSITY, Special Collections Library, 800 Lakeshore Dr, Birmingham, 35229. Annie Ford Wheeler, Acting Head Librn
Holdings: Vols 4000 Cat Mss Maps Pix
Notes: Alabama literature and history; ms collection exceeds 200,000 pieces, chiefly of Joseph J Willett papers and Bledsoe-Kelly Collection. Representative collection of maps, some pictures.
See also entry under Baptists - History

AL —UNIVERSITY OF ALABAMA, BIRMINGHAM, Lister Hill Library of the Health Sciences, University Sta, Birmingham, 35294. Richard B Fredericksen, Dir
Holdings: Vols 45,000 Cat Mss Maps Pix Slides Phonorecords Audiotapes Videotapes 16mm Films Filmstrips
Notes: Alabama medical, dental, nursing and optometry history. Incl museum items, such as furniture and instruments.

AL —WHEELER BASIN REGIONAL LIBRARY, 504 Cherry St NE, PO Box 1766, Decatur, 35602. Margarete Lange, Reference Librn
Holdings: Vols (600) Cat Maps Pix Microforms
Notes: Alabama history, politics, folklore, economy, archaeology, and books by Alabama authors.

AL —GADSDEN PUBLIC LIBRARY, 254 College St, Gadsden, 35999. Margaret C Rouse, Reference Librn
Holdings: // Cat Mss Pix
Notes: Lay Collection, the papers of William Patrick Lay, founder of the Alabama Power Company. Mr Lay was a Cherokee County native and Gadsden resident, 1853-1940. Separate card index to collection of 221 items, which incl clippings, pamphlets and scrapbooks.

AL —MOBILE PUBLIC LIBRARY, Special Collections Div, 701 Government St, Mobile, 36602.
Holdings: Mss Maps Pix Microfilm
Notes: Alabama and local history; about 4500 vols, 100,000 clippings; 1750 microfilm rolls of newspapers, etc. Approx 8000 vols of genealogy, 1000 periodicals, 2000 clippings, etc. Census on 1800 microfilm rolls.

AL —SPRING HILL COLLEGE, Thomas Byrne Memorial Library, Mobile, 36608. Benjamin F Shearer, Librn
Holdings: Vols (1350) Cat Mss Maps Pix
Budget: ($225,000)
Notes: Mobiliana. Incl pamphlets.

AL —MONTGOMERY CITY-COUNTY PUBLIC LIBRARY, 445 S Lawrence St, Montgomery, 36104. Julia Rutledge, Ref Librn
Holdings: Vols 1400 // Cat
Notes: Separate index.

AL —TROY STATE UNIVERSITY, Library, Troy, 36081. Kenneth Croslin, Dir of University Libraries
Holdings: // Mss
Notes: Incl the John Horry Dent Papers, 1851-1892, 25 vols, mss, farm journals, account books, letters, legal documents, clippings and miscellaneous memorabilia of a planter, plantation owner, investor, who lived in Barbour County, Alabama from 1837 to 1867 and in Floyd County, Georgia from 1867 to 1892. Typescript from tape "Sharecropping farming in Pike County, Alabama in early 1900's" (56p). Typescript of tapes of "Source material extracted from Troy, Alabama newspapers, 1871-1935" indexed under 9 subjects by color code.

†AL —UNIVERSITY OF ALABAMA, Amelia Gayle Gorgas Library, PO Box S, University, 35486.
Holdings: Vols 6325 Cat Mss Maps Pix Slides Microforms
Notes: The Alabama Collection contains books about Alabama; by Alabama authors; scrapbooks, pamphlets, newspapers. Such ms collections as the Manly Family, Papers, 1819-1930; Samuel Townsend, Estate papers, 1827- 90; Harry Mell Ayers, 1885-1964; and the Gorgas Family, papers 1821- 1920.

NC —DUKE UNIVERSITY, William R Perkins Library, Manuscript Dept, Durham, 27706. Ellen Gartrell, Cur of Mss
Holdings: Cat Mss
Notes: Especially strong for North Carolina, South Carolina, Virginia, Georgia, and Alabama. 18th-20th centuries. See *Guide to the Cataloged Collections of the Manuscript Department of the William R Perkins* Library (1980, ed by Richard C Davis and Linda A Miller).

TX —UNIVERSITY OF TEXAS LIBRARIES, General Libraries, PO Box P, Austin, 78713. Carolyn Bucknell, Asst Dir for Collection Development
Holdings: Vols Cat Microforms
Notes: The Littlefield Collection of research

ALABAMA—HISTORY (cont.)

materials, incl many rare items, on the history of the Old South.

ALABAMA—IMPRINTS

AL —SAMFORD UNIVERSITY, Special Collections Library, 800 Lakeshore Dr, Birmingham, 35229. Annie Ford Wheeler, Acting Head Librn
Holdings: Uncat Mss Maps Pix Microforms
Notes: The William H Brantley Collection is in superb condition, consisting of early works on travels, Indians, and law in the southeast, plus scarce imprints of Alabama.

ALABAMA—MAPS

†AL —AUBURN UNIVERSITY LIBRARY, Special Collections Dept, Auburn, 36830.
Notes: Incl Alabama and environs; historical maps of Alabama; aerial photographs.

AL —SAMFORD UNIVERSITY, Special Collections Library, 800 Lakeshore Dr, Birmingham, 35229. Annie Ford Wheeler, Acting Head Librn
Notes: Emphases: early maps of Alabama and the Southeast; local maps of Ireland which support Irish history and genealogy collection; some early atlases and bibliographies; basic works on cartography and map bibliography. Incl about 3000 maps. Published catalog of the collection.

†AL —MOBILE PUBLIC LIBRARY, Gallalee Cartographic Collection, 704 Government St, Mobile, 36602.
Notes: A collection of maps of the Mobile Bay and Gulf Coast area of Alabama, 80 percent of which are pre-1900.

AL —UNIVERSITY OF ALABAMA, W S Hoole Special Collections Library, Amelia Gayle Goorgas Library, PO Box S, University, 35486. Joyce H Lamont, Cur
Notes: 3500 maps, primarily early maps of Alabama and the Southeast, but also rare 16th and 17th century maps of Europe. Also 6000 Sanborn Fire Insurance Maps for every Alabama county (1888-1925).

ALABAMA—POLITICS AND GOVERNMENT

AL —BIRMINGHAM PUBLIC LIBRARY, Dept of Archives & Mss, 2020 Seventh Ave N, Birmingham, 35203. Marvin Y Whiting, Archivist & Cur
Holdings: Mss
Notes: The main features of this collection are the Birmingham City Commission Papers, 1940-1963; the Albert Boutwell Mayoral Papers, 1963-1967; and the Birmingham City Council Papers, 1963-1976. 718,000 ms pieces.

AL —BIRMINGHAM PUBLIC LIBRARY, Southern Women's Archives, 2020 Park Place, Birmingham, 35203. Theresa A Ceravolo, Archivist
Holdings: Docs Mss Photos Microforms
Notes: Collections concentrate on the history of women in Birmingham and Jefferson County, Alabama, but do incl some material on women and politics in the state. Collections show contributions of women in social, cultural, and family spheres, politics, and volunteer activities from ca 1862-1983. Monthly legislative reports, 1981-1983, which discuss Alabama legislative and, to some extent, US Congress activities regarding abortion, domestic violence, child support, and other related issues.

ALABAMA AUTHORS see Authors, Alabama

ALABAMA CLAIMS

MD —JOHNS HOPKINS UNIVERSITY, Milton S Eisenhower Library, Charles & 34 Sts, Baltimore, 21218. Ann S Gwyn, Assistant Dir for Special Collections
Holdings: Vols 67 // Cat
Notes: Perhaps the most complete collection of written and printed material on this arbitration case.

ALABAMA FEDERATION OF BUSINESS AND PROFESSIONAL WOMEN'S CLUBS

AL —BIRMINGHAM PUBLIC LIBRARY, Southern Women's Archives, 2020 Park Place, Birmingham, 35203. Theresa A Ceravolo, Archivist
Holdings: Cat Docs Mss
Notes: Collected records, 1919-1969. Bylaws, constitution, convention files, minutes of meeting, and presidents' correspondence files, 1919-1969; lists of new clubs and members, 1923-1969; and the following publications: *Can Happen, The Alabama Businesswoman, B. P. W. Bulletin, The Pepper Pot, The Independent Woman,* and *The National Businesswoman.*

ALARODIAN LANGUAGE see Vannic Language

ALASKA

AK —Z J LOUSSAC PUBLIC LIBRARY, 524 W 6th Ave, Anchorage, 99501. Michael Catoggio, Alaskana Supervisor
Holdings: Vols 6000 Cat Mss Microforms
Budget: $30,000
Notes: Incl prints by Alaskan artists.

AK —UNIVERSITY OF ALASKA, Elmer E Rasmuson Library, Fairbanks, 99701. Robert H Geiman, Dir
Holdings: Vols Cat Mss Maps Pix Slides Phonorecords Audiotapes Films Microforms
Notes: The Alaska Collection is strong in all disciplines concerning Alaska. Main strengths are exploration and travel, pioneer memoirs, and materials on Alaska natives. Bulk of collection is in English with significant holdings in Russian, Native American, and European languages. Archival holdings incl 6000 cu ft of mss, 110,000 historic photographs, 2319 tape recordings, 727 films and videotapes, 200 rare maps and 1273 microfilms. Ms collection strongest in political and economic areas. A Guide to the Collections is available in hard copy and microfiche. About 1000 special collections, some 300 quite significant.

AK —ALASKA STATE LIBRARY, Alaska Historical Library Collection, Pouch G, Juneau, 99811. Phyllis Demuth, Readers Services Librn
Holdings: Vols (24,000) Cat Mss Maps Pix Slides Phonorecords Audiotapes Videotapes 16mm Films Microforms

CA —LOS ANGELES PUBLIC LIBRARY, Science & Technology Dept, 630 W Fifth St, Los Angeles, 90071. Billie M Connor, Dept Head
Holdings: Vols 18,000 Maps Microforms
Notes: Extensive holdings of state geology department publications and maps of the Western states including Alaska and Hawaii, US Geological Survey, US Bureau of Mines, and the geology departments of major universities. Complete sets of publications and indexes of major geological societies including the Geological Society of American and the American Association of Petroleum Geologists. Partially cataloged.

WA —WASHINGTON STATE LIBRARY, Washington/Northwest Rm, State Library Bldg, Olympia, 98504. Nancy B Pryor, Research Consultant
Holdings: Vols 8000 Cat Mss Maps Pix Microforms
Notes: Mss, photographs and microfilm largely limited to Washington territorial and state materials as is the file of pamphlets and newspaper clippings, which includes both historical and current material. The book collection incl works on the four Pacific Northwest States, Alaska, and British Columbia, and books by Washington authors.

WA —UNIVERSITY OF WASHINGTON LIBRARIES, Pacific Northwest Collection, Seattle, 98195. Andrew F Johnson, Librn
Holdings: Vols (50,000) Cat Mss Maps Pix
Budget: ($12,000)
Notes: The Pacific Northwest Collection contains printed materials documenting the historic and contemporary life and culture of the region in a broad range of subject areas. The Pacific Northwest is defined as the geographic region including Washington, Oregon, Idaho, Montana, British Columbia, Yukon Territory, and Alaska. Printed materials including books, periodicals, government documents, maps, weekly and local regional newspapers, theses and dissertations, as well as photographs and architectural drawings are included in the Pacific Northwest Collection. Photographic works of over 200 photographers active in the Pacific Northwest, Alaska, and the Yukon Territory (Canada) during the period 1860-1930, including Asahel and Edward S Curtis, Eric Hegg, and Clark Kinsey, are represented in a print collection of more than 300,000 images. The architecturaldrawings collection includes over 19,000 original plans, drawings, sketches, renderings and blue prints pertaining to the history of architecture and urban planning and landscape gardening in the Pacific Northwest ca 1880-1940. Areas of particular strength are the holdings of over 1100 published journals of Pacific Northwest exploration expeditions, photographs of Northwest Coast Native Americans and of historic Seattle, newspapers issued within the Japanese-American relocation camps, 1942-1945, materials relating to the 1980 eruption of Mt St Helens, and Sanborne fire insurance maps for Washington. A unique feature of the Collection is the subject index to regional periodicals and local newspapers maintained by the PNW Collection staff; over 100 titles are currently indexed. G K Hall Company published a books catalog of the Pacific Northwest Collectionin 1973.

ALASKA—DESCRIPTION AND TRAVEL—VIEWS

WA —UNIVERSITY OF WASHINGTON LIBRARIES, Pacific Northwest Collection, Seattle, 98195. Andrew F Johnson, Librn
Holdings: Vols (50,000) Cat Maps Pix
Budget: ($12,000)
Notes: The Pacific Northwest Collection contains printed materials documenting the historic and contemporary life and culture of the region in a broad range of subject areas. The Pacific Northwest is defined as the geographic region including Washington, Oregon, Idaho, Montana, British Columbia, Yukon Territory, and Alaska. Printed materials including books, periodicals, government documents, maps, weekly and local regional newspapers, theses and dissertations, as well as photographs and architectural drawings are included in the Pacific Northwest Collection. Photographic works of over 200 photographers active in the Pacific Northwest, Alaska, and the Yukon Territory (Canada) during the period 1860-1930, including Asahel and Edward S Curtis, Eric Hegg, and Clark Kinsey, are represented in a print collection of more than 300,000 images. The architecturaldrawings collection includes over 19,000 original plans, drawings, sketches, renderings and blue prints pertaining to the history of architecture and urban planning and landscape gardening in the Pacific Northwest ca 1880-1940. Areas of particular strength are the holdings of over 1100 published journals of Pacific Northwest exploration expeditions, photographs of Northwest Coast Native Americans and of historic Seattle, newspapers issued within the Japanese-American relocation camps, 1942-1945, materials relating to the 1980 eruption of Mt St Helens, and Sanborne fire insurance maps for Washington. A unique feature of the Collection is the subject index to regional periodicals and local newspapers maintained by the PNW Collection staff; over 100 titles are currently indexed. G K Hall Company published a books catalog of the Pacific Northwest Collectionin 1973.

ALASKA—ECONOMIC CONDITIONS

OR —UNIVERSITY OF OREGON, Library, Eugene, 97403. Kenneth W Duckett,

ALASKA—ECONOMIC CONDITIONS (cont.)

Curator
Notes: Papers of James C Rettie, Senior Economist of the Department of the Interior.

ALASKA—GOVERNMENT PUBLICATIONS

WA —WASHINGTON STATE LIBRARY, Olympia, 98504. Ann Bregent, Librn
Holdings: 100,000 Documents
Notes: Regional deposetory for US documents. Incl documents from the Western States and Washington State.

ALASKA—HISTORY

AK —UNIVERSITY OF ALASKA, Elmer E Rasmuson Library, Fairbanks, 99701. Robert H Geiman, Dir
Holdings: Vols Cat Mss Maps Pix Slides Phonorecords Audiotapes Films Microforms
Notes: The Alaska Collection is strong in all disciplines concerning Alaska. Main strengths are exploration and travel, pioneer memoirs, and materials on Alaska natives. Bulk of collection is in English with significant holdings in Russian, Native American, and European languages. Archival holdings incl 6000 cu ft of mss, 110,000 historic photographs, 2319 tape recordings, 727 films and videotapes, 200 rare maps and 1273 microfilms. Ms collection strongest in political and economic areas. A Guide to the Collections is available in hard copy and microfiche. About 1000 special collections, some 300 quite significant.

AK —ALASKA STATE LIBRARY, Alaska Historical Library Collection, Pouch G, Juneau, 99811. Phyllis Demuth, Readers Services Librn
Holdings: Vols (24,000) Cat Mss Maps Pix Slides Phonorecords Audiotapes Videotapes 16mm Films Micorforms

AK —TONGASS HISTORICAL SOCIETY, Library, 629 Dock St, Ketchikan, 99901. Marjorie Anne Voss, Librn
Holdings: Vols 400 Cat Pix
Notes: Alaskan and regional history and art, as well as Northwest Coast Indian history and art. Extensive photograph collection.

CA —UNIVERSITY OF CALIFORNIA, BERKELEY, Bancroft Library, Manuscripts Division, Berkeley, 94720. James D Hart, Dir
Holdings: Vols Mss Maps Pix Slides Microforms
Notes: Approxi. twelve million pieces, with primary emphasis on California, with a lesser emphasis on the other Pacific States, incl. Alaska and the Province of British Columbia. In general, the Bancroft Library seeks to acquire historical and biographical works and primary source materials, documenting: the development of a geographic area or political unit; man and his activities, and his impact on the land and on his institutions. Methodological and theoretical work and texts in the physical and biological sciences are not collected, as a rule; exceptions here are publications essential to the study of an area's historical development and those providing general background information. Hubert Howe Bancroft's own distinguished holdings, assembled 1860-1880, constitute the core of the collection. The Bancroft Library's collections are noncirculating. A. G. K. Hall catalog has been published. The Bolton Collection (146,000 pages of archival material) contains ms. materials for the history of the Pacific Coast and the Southwest, gathered by Herbert Eugene Bolton. There is a comprehensive key to the arrangement of the collection.

DC —GEORGETOWN UNIVERSITY, Library, Special Collections Div, 37 & O Sts NW, Washington, 20057. George M Barringer, Special Collections Librn; Nicholas B Sheetz, Mss Librn
Holdings: Vols (100) Cat Mss Maps Pix
Notes: A number of early Alaskan mission imprints are included in the papers (1867-1920) of Rev Francis A Barnum, SJ, who served in Alaska ca 1890 and wrote an "Innuit" grammar.

NY —STATE UNIVERSITY OF NEW YORK, COLLEGE OF ARTS & SCIENCE AT GENESEO, Milne Library, Geneseo, 14454. William T Lane, Head of Information Services & Archivist
Holdings: / / Pix Slides
Notes: The Martha Blow Wadsworth Collection. Photographs taken or collected by Mrs Wadsworth from the 1890s to around 1910. There are 33 albums containing 4561 mounted photographs, and 3 boxes containing 345 hand-tinted lantern slides. Subjects include horseback rides from Washington, DC to Avon, NY. (1905-1909); US Army packtrain trips in the Southwestern US (1907-1910); Hopi, Navajo, and Zuni Indians (1910); motor trip through France and England (1909); Panama Canal Construction; Alaskan boundary survey trip; and the Wadsworth family of Livingston County, NY. There are no negatives. Inventory in repository. Open to qualified investigators with permission of archivist. Gift of Michael Moukhanoff, Ashantee, NY, 1976.

TX —SOUTHERN METHODIST UNIVERSITY, DeGolyer Library, Box 396, SMU, Dallas, 75275. Clifton H Jones, Dir
Holdings: Vols (80,000) Cat Mss Maps Pix Slides Microforms
Notes: First editions of prominent authors; also of books in subject emphasis collections. All subjects listed in this vol are strong. Numerous collections of personal papers relating to subjects also.

WA —WESTERN WASHINGTON UNIVERSITY, Center for Pacific Northwest Studies, High St, Bellingham, 98225. James W Scott, Dir
Holdings: / / Cat Mss Maps Pix
Notes: The Archie W Shiels Collection. Archie W Shiels, who died in 95th year in 1974, was formerly Managing Dir of Pacific American Fisheries and an author of some note on Alaskan topics. A few papers of his company are incl in the collection, which is primarily focused on Alaska, particularly its history and its seal and other fisheries. See also entry for Galen A Biery.

WA —UNIVERSITY OF WASHINGTON LIBRARIES, Pacific Northwest Collection, Seattle, 98195. Andrew F Johnson, Librn
Holdings: Vols (50,000) Cat Maps Pix
Budget: ($12,000)
Notes: The Pacific Northwest Collection contains printed materials documenting the historic and contemporary life and culture of the region in a broad range of subject areas. The Pacific Northwest is defined as the geographic region including Washington, Oregon, Idaho, Montana, British Columbia, Yukon Territory, and Alaska. Printed materials including books, periodicals, government documents, maps, weekly and local regional newspapers, theses and dissertations, as well as photographs and architectural drawings are included in the Pacific Northwest Collection. Photographic works of over 200 photographers active in the Pacific Northwest, Alaska, and the Yukon Territory (Canada) during the period 1860-1930, including Asahel and Edward S Curtis, Eric Hegg, and Clark Kinsey, are represented in a print collection of more than 300,000 images. The architecturaldrawings collection includes over 19,000 original plans, drawings, sketches, renderings and blue prints pertaining to the history of architecture and urban planning and landscape gardening in the Pacific Northwest ca 1880-1940. Areas of particular strength are the holdings of over 1100 published journals of Pacific Northwest exploration expeditions, photographs of Northwest Coast Native Americans and of historic Seattle, newspapers issued within the Japanese-American relocation camps, 1942-1945, materials relating to the 1980 eruption of Mt St Helens, and Sanborne fire insurance maps for Washington. A unique feature of the Collection is the subject index to regional periodicals and local newspapers maintained by the PNW Collection staff; over 100 titles are currently indexed. G K Hall Company published a books catalog of the Pacific Northwest Collectionin 1973.

AB —GLENBOW-ALBERTA INSTITUTE, Historical Library & Archives, 130 9th Avenue SE, Calgary, T2G 0P3, Can. Leonard J Gottseleg, Chief Librn
Holdings: Vols (60,000) Cat Mss Maps Pix Microforms
Notes: Main emphasis is on Western Canadian history. Equally important emphasis is placed on the Canadian Arctic and Alaska, Northwest Coast explorations, Aboriginal peoples of the North and Canadian West, and the fur trade in the US Northwest.

BC —PRINCE RUPERT LIBRARY, 101 W Sixth Ave, Prince Rupert, V8J 1Y9, Can. Denise St Arnaud, City Librn
Holdings: Vols 270 Cat Mss Audiotapes 16mm Films
Notes: This collection of Northwest History deals chiefly with this area but extends to parts of Alaska and the Queen Charlotte Islands and BC inland and north. Noncirculating.

ALASKA—MAPS

AK —UNIVERSITY OF ALASKA, Elmer E Rasmuson Library, Fairbanks, 99701. Robert H Geiman, Dir
Notes: The Alaska Collection is strong in all disciplines concerning Alaska. Main strengths are exploration and travel, pioneer memoirs, and materials on Alaska natives. Bulk of collection is in English with significant holdings in Russian, Native American, and European languages. Archival holdings incl 6000 cu ft of mss, 110,000 historic photographs, 2319 tape recordings, 727 films and videotapes, 200 rare maps and 1273 microfilms. Ms collection strongest in political and economic areas. There is a guide published by the University of Alaska to these collections and is available in hard copy and microfiche.

CA —LOS ANGELES PUBLIC LIBRARY, Science & Technology Dept, 630 W Fifth St, Los Angeles, 90071. Billie M Connor, Dept Head
Notes: Extensive holdings of state geology department publications and maps of the Western states including Alaska and Hawaii, US Geological Survey, US Bureau of Mines, and the geology departments of major universities. Complete sets of publications and indexes of major geological societies including the Geological Society of American and the American Association of Petroleum Geologists. Partially cataloged.

ALASKA, RUSSIAN see Russian Alaska

ALASKA GOLD RUSH see Gold Rush, Klondike

ALASKA INDIANS see Indians of North America and Mexico—Alaska

ALASKA PACKERS ASSOCIATION

AK —ALASKA STATE LIBRARY, Alaska Historical Library Collection, Pouch G, Juneau, 99811. Phyllis Demuth, Readers Services Librn
Holdings: Vols (24,000) Cat Mss Maps Pix Slides Phonorecords Audiotapes Videotapes 16mm Films Microforms

ALASKAN RUSSIAN CHURCH RECORDS

DC —LIBRARY OF CONGRESS, Manuscript Division, Washington, 20540. John C Broderick, Chief
Holdings: Cat Mss Pix
Notes: Mss, papers, records, etc.

ALBANIA

MA —HARVARD UNIVERSITY LIBRARY, Widener Library, Cambridge, 02138. Ellen H Brow, Specialist in Book Selection
Holdings: Cat
Notes: Small collection of several thousand volumes. No separate listing.

ALBANIAN LANGUAGE AND LITERATURE

NY —NEW YORK PUBLIC LIBRARY, Donnell Foreign Language Library, 20 W 53 St, New York, 10019. Bosiljka Stevanovic, Supvr Librn
Holdings: Vols 163 Cat
Notes: Albanian collection incl Albanian authors of Albanian expression. No separate catalog.

ALBANIAN ORTHODOX CHURCH

†MA —ST GEORGE ALBANIAN ORTHODOX CATHEDRAL, Fan S Noli Library, South Boston, 02127.

ALBANIANS IN THE U.S.

MN —UNIVERSITY OF MINNESOTA, Immigration History Research Center, 826 Berry St, Saint Paul, 55114. Susan Griegs, Cur
Holdings: Vols (35,000) Mss Maps Pix Phonorecords Audiotapes 16mm Films Microforms
See also entry under US - Emigration and Immigration

PA —BALCH INSTITUTE FOR ETHNIC STUDIES, Library, 18 S Seventh St, Philadelphia, 19106. R Joseph Anderson, Library Dir
Holdings: Cat Microforms

ALBANY, N.Y.—HISTORY

NY —ALBANY INSTITUTE OF HISTORY & ART, McKinney Library, 125 Washington Ave, Albany, 12210. Daryl Severson, Actg Librn; Suzanne Roberson, Photographic Librn
Holdings: Vols 4000 Cat Mss Maps Pix
Notes: Local history of the Albany, New York area and arts related to it.

ALBEE, EDWARD

CT —TRINITY COLLEGE LIBRARY, Watkinson Library, 300 Summit St, Hartford, 06106. Jeffrey Kaimowitz, Cur
Holdings: Cat
Notes: First editions, etc.

NY —NEW YORK PUBLIC LIBRARY, Performing Arts Research Center, Billy Rose Theatre Collection, 111 Amsterdam Ave, New York, 10023. Dorothy L Swerdlove, Cur
Holdings: Cat Mss Pix
Notes: Papers, scrapbooks, mss, photographs, memorabilia, etc.

RI —BROWN UNIVERSITY, John Hay Library, Harris Collection, Prospect St, Providence, 02912. Rosemary L Cullen, Cur
Holdings: Vols (200,000) Cat Mss Pix Phonorecords Microforms
Budget: ($15,000)
Notes: The Harris Collection of American Poetry and Plays is principally composed of American and Canadian poetry and plays, 17th century-date. Extensive holdings in songsters, gift books and annuals, hymnals, pageants, broadside verse, carriers' addresses, women poets, juvenile poetry, (incl Mother Goose and *The Night Before* Christmas), sheet music with lyrics, small press publications, fine printing, black poets, "little magazines," Yiddish-American literature. All movements or schools of American poetry are represented. Incl first editions of most American poets and playwrights, notably Whitman, Poe, Wallace Stevens, Eugene O'Neill, Edward Albee, Ezra Pound, T S Eliot, William Carlos Williams, Amy Lowell, Phyllis Wheatley, Robert Frost, Allen Ginsberg, Bliss Carman, and Stephen Foster sheet music. Also incl the Saunders Walt Whitman Collection (1300 vols); the LangdonCollection of Pageants (250 vols); the Asa Cushman Collection of plays in ms and prompt copies; the MacDougall Collection of Psalters and Hymnals; 4000 plays issued by Walter H Baker Co, Boston (1890-1957); the Vaxer Collection of Yiddish Poetry, Plays and Music (1700 vols). Collections incl 200,000 vols, 30,000 broadsides, 55,000 mss, 170,000 pieces of sheet music, 450 phonorecords, and 375 microfilm reels. See *Dictionary Catalog of the Harris Collection of American Poetry and Plays* (Boston: G K Hall, 1972), 13 vols; *Supplement* (1977), 3 vols. See also, *American Poetry,* 1609-1900, *A Collection on Microfilm, Segment I* (1609-1820); *Segment II* (1821-1850); *Segment III* (1851-1870) (Woodbridge, Conn: Research Publications). Separate catalog.

ALBEE, EDWARD FRANKLIN, 1857-1930

IA —UNIVERSITY OF IOWA, University Libraries, Iowa City, 52242. Robert A McCown, Mss Librn
Holdings: Mss
Notes: Keith/Albee Vaudeville Collection. Records of a vaudeville, theatre, and moving-pictures business established by Benjamin Franklin Keith, 1846-1914, and Edward Franklin Albee, 1857-1930. The collection includes clipping books, report books, cash books, subject files, signs and posters. Theatres in the following cities are represented in the collection: Providence, RI, Pawtucket, RI, Woonsocket, RI, and Webster, Mass. The business was later part of RKO Pictures, Inc. Unpublished register in the library. 50 ft of mss.

ALBERT, CARL

OK —UNIVERSITY OF OKLAHOMA, Bizzell Memorial Library, Western History Collections, 401 W Brooks, Norman, 73069. John Ezell, Cur
Holdings: Vols Mss Pix Microforms Audiotapes Maps
Notes: US Representative; Speaker of the House. His papers.

ALBERTA—HISTORY

AB —GLENBOW-ALBERTA INSTITUTE, Historical Library & Archives, 130 9th Avenue SE, Calgary, T2G 0P3, Can. Leonard J Gottseleg, Chief Librn
Holdings: Vols (60,000) Cat Mss Maps Pix Microforms
Notes: Main emphasis is on Western Canadian history. Equally important emphasis is placed on the Canadian Arctic and Alaska, Northwest Coast explorations, Aboriginal peoples of the North and Canadian West, and the fur trade in the US Northwest.

ALBERTA ASSOCIATION OF ARCHITECTS

AB —UNIVERSITY OF CALGARY, Libraries, Special Collections Div, 2500 University Dr, Calgary, T2N 1N4, Can.
Holdings: Mss
Notes: Files of the Alberta Association of Architects from its foundation in 1906 onwards: Acts and By-Laws; Correspondence Membership and Temporary Licence Applications; Ledgers, Minutes; Yearbooks and Newsletters. Also contains files of correspondence with the Royal Architectural Institute of Canada and provincial Architectural Associations. An inventory is on hand. 16.1 m document boxes.

ALBERTA OIL SANDS

AB —ALBERTA OIL SANDS INFORMATION CENTRE, 6th Floor, Highfield Place, 10010-106 St, Edmonton, T5J 3L8, Can. Helga Radvanyi, Mgr
Notes: "Major activity of the Centre has been preparation of the Alberta Oil Sands Index. However...scope has broadened to include the Heavy Oil/Enhanced Recovery Index," and other informative literature.

ALBERTSON FAMILY

DE —UNIVERSITY OF DELAWARE, Hugh M Morris Library, S College Ave, Newark, 19711. T Stuart Dick, Special Collections
Holdings: / / Mss
Notes: Personal and business letters and receipts, of the Albertson family, Quaker lumber and lime merchants (1782-1862) residing in Plymouth, Montgomery Co, Pa. Included are many letters concerning the Plymouth RR and rules and regulations for its administration.

ALBORUTHENICA see Byelorussia—History; Byelorussian Language and Literature

ALBRAND, MARTHA

MA —BOSTON UNIVERSITY, Mugar Memorial Library, Special Collections Dept, 771 Commonwealth Ave, Boston, 02215. Howard B Gotlieb, Dir
Holdings: Cat Mss
Notes: Mss, correspondence, etc collected in depth; incl publications by or about.

ALBRECHT-CARRIE, RENE

†NY —COLUMBIA UNIVERSITY LIBRARIES, Butler Library, Rare Book and Manuscript Library, 535 W 114 St, New York, 10027.
Notes: Papers, mss, correspondence, etc.

ALBRIGHT, HORACE MARDEN, 1890-

CA —UNIVERSITY OF CALIFORNIA, LOS ANGELES, Research Library, Dept of Special Collections, 405 Hilgard Ave, Los Angeles, 90024. Edward Shreeves, Chairman, Bibliographers Group; David S Zeidberg, Head
Notes: 80 linear feet of correspondence and ephemera recording his activity as a conservationist and his directorship of the US National Park Service.

ALCHEMY

AZ —WORLD UNIVERSITY, Library, 711 E Blacklidge Dr, Tucson, 85719. Howard John Zitko, Cur
Holdings: Vols (15,000) Cat Mss Maps Audiotapes
Notes: Collection concerns what are generally called the "frontier sciences." No interlibrary loan.

CA —CLAREMONT COLLEGES, Norman F Sprague Memorial Library, 12 & Dartmouth, Claremont, 91711. David Kuhner, Librn
Holdings: Vols (1000) Cat Mss Pix VF
Notes: President Herbert Hoover's personal collection of rare technical books of the 15th-19th centuries. *Bibliotheca De Re Metallica: The Herbert Clark Hoover Collection of Mining and Metallurgy* (Claremont, 1980). Restricted use.

CT —YALE UNIVERSITY, Box 1603A, Yale Station, New Haven, 06520.
Holdings: Cat Mss Maps Pix
Notes: See *Alchemy and the Occult: A Catalogue of Books and Manuscripts from the Collection of Paul and Mary Mellon, Given to Yale University Library* (New Haven: Yale University Library, 1968-1977), 4 vols.

DE —UNIVERSITY OF DELAWARE, Hugh M Morris Library, S College Ave, Newark,

ALCHEMY (cont.)

19711. T Stuart Dick, Special Collections
Holdings: Cat Mss
Notes: The Unidel History of Chemistry Collection. 60 percent of the collection deals with chemistry prior to 1780. Particularly strong in alchemical works incl some 6 alchemical mss. Also works on mining, medicine and pharmacy. Notable chemical pioneers of the 1780-1860 period are well represented by such men as Lavoisier, Avogardo, Chaptal, Davy, Faraday, Fourcroy, Liebig and Volta. Majority of the collection in French and Itaian.

†DC —LIBRARY OF CONGRESS, Rare Book Division, Washington, 20540.
Notes: A collection of considerable strength.

IA —GRAND LODGE OF IOWA, AF & AM Iowa Masonic Library, 813 First Ave SE, Cedar Rapids, 52406. Tom Eggleston, Librn
Holdings: Vols 135 // Cat
Notes: The Arthur E Waite Collection of Mysticism, Freemasonry, Alchemy. No photocopying.

MA —FRANCIS A COUNTWAY LIBRARY OF MEDICINE, Boston Medical Library/ Harvard Medical Library, 10 Shattuck St, Boston, 02115. C Robin LeSueur, Librn; Richard J Wolfe, Cur, Rare Books & Manuscripts
Holdings: Vols (500,000) Cat Mss Maps Pix Microforms
Notes: Combines resources of the Harvard Medical School and the Boston Medical Library. Strong in serials and medical history in all fields of medicine, incl incunabula, non-medical books by doctors, travel books by doctors. 500,000 medical dissertations and theses. Special strength in all medical subjects listed in this volume.

MA —HARVARD UNIVERSITY LIBRARY, Widener Library, Cambridge, 02138.
Holdings: Cat
Notes: Particularly strong in French materials.

NY —COLUMBIA UNIVERSITY LIBRARIES, Rare Book & Manuscript Library, 801 Butler Library, 535 W 114 St, New York, 10027. Kenneth A Lohf, Librn
Holdings: Mss Pix
Notes: Restricted use.

†NY —COLUMBIA UNIVERSITY LIBRARIES, Butler Library, Rare Book and Manuscript Library, 535 W 114 St, New York, 10027.
Notes: 76 vols of diaries of Lynn Thorndike, 1902-63. A record of his daily reading, progress in research and writing, European travels, relations with scholars and librarians, and other personal matters.

NY —NEW YORK SOCIETY LIBRARY, 53 E 79 St, New York, 10021. Mark Piel, Librn
Notes: Incl Governor John Winthrop's Collection on chemistry and alchemy (part of which is at the New York Academy of Medicine Library).

PA —UNIVERSITY OF PENNSYLVANIA, Van Pelt Library, Edgar Fahs Smith Memorial Collection in the History of Chemistry, 3420 Walnut St, Philadelphia, 19104. Arnold W Thackray, Cur
Holdings: Vols (15,000) Cat Mss Pix
Notes: The Smith Collection, 15,000 vols, is one of the most comprehensive collections on the history of chemistry in North America, covering chemistry and its allied disciplines, from the Renaissance to the early 20th century. The Collection's traditional strengths lie in classical history of chemistry, ie pre-1800. However, acquisitions over the past 15 years have substantially built up the post-1800 holdings, especially in areas of chemical technology. News of the Collection may be found in the Center's twice yearly newsletter *CHOC News* which is available free of charge to interested persons. A convenient description is provided in Herbert S Klickstein, "Edgar Fahs Smith-His Contributions to the History of Chemistry," *Chymia,* 5 (1959), 11-30. A published catalog of our holdings now needs considerable revision,due to continued acquisitions: *Catalog of the Edgar Fahs Smith Memorial Collection* (Boston: G K Hall and Co, 1960). Portions of our manuscript collection have been described in Norman P Zacour and Rudolf Hirsch, *Catalogue of the Manuscripts in the Libraries of the University of Pennsylvania to 1800* (Philadelphia: University of Pennsylvania Press, 1965), 231-243; and R Hirsch, "Catalogue of Manuscripts... Supplement A(5)," *Library Chronicle,* 37 (1971), 91-115.

RI —BROWN UNIVERSITY, John Hay Library, 20 Prospect St, Providence, 02912. Mark N Brown, Cur Mss
Holdings: Vols (900) // Mss
Notes: John William Graham Collection of Literature of Psychic Science; 350 predominantly late 19th and early 20th century books dealing with alchemy, black magic, dreams, demonology, church history, mysticism, mediumship, physical and somatic types of psychic experience. Collection described in *Index to Psychic* Science compiled by S R Morgan (Swarthmore, 1950). Also, the Damon Collection of Occult and Visionary Literature; 550 vols devoted to the development of western mysticism with particular emphasis on American and British thought, incl texts on alchemy, black magic, esoteric church history, dream interpretations, mysticism, witchcraft, the Kabbalah, and visionary testaments and manifestations of all types printed during the 16th to 20th centuries; and the Samuel Wyllys Papers; 125 mss, transcripts, and photocopies of legal and government papers relating to Indianaffairs, colonial wars, civil and criminal cases, and the witchcraft trials of 1692-1693. Partially cataloged.

WI —UNIVERSITY OF WISCONSIN, MADISON, Memorial Library, History of Science Collection, 728 State St, Madison, 53706. John Neu, Bibliographer
Holdings: Cat
Notes: Major research collection of primary and secondary materials in the history of chemistry and alchemy. See Dennis I Duveen, *Bibliotheca Alchemica et Chemica: An Annotated Catalogue of Printed Books on Alchemy, Chemistry and Cognate Subjects in the Library of Dennis I Duveen* (London: Dawsons of Pall Mall, 1965). Restricted use: Rare Book Department.

ALCOHOL

IL —ILLINOIS FARM BUREAU LIBRARY, 1701 Towanda Ave, PO Box 1901, Bloomington, 61701. Rue E Olson, Librn
Holdings: Vols (24,000) Cat Microforms
Budget: ($25,000)
Notes: Emphasis on Illinois.

NJ —RUTGERS, THE STATE UNIVERSITY OF NEW JERSEY, Center of Alcohol Studies Library, Smithers Hall, New Brunswick, 08903. Penny Page, Librn
Holdings: Vols (8075) Cat Mss Microforms
Budget: ($110,000)
Notes: Alcohol and alcohol problems. Special holdings within collection: Master Catalog of the Alcohol Literature (over 125, 000 references in all major languages); Classified Abstract Archive of the Alcohol Literature-CAAAL (English-language abstracts on edge-notched cards, covering approximately 20,000 documents); McCarthy Memorial Collection of full-text originals matching the CAAAL abstracts; *Journal of Studies on Alcohol* and other scholarly publications specializing in alcohol-related research; Connor Alcohol Research Reference File (CARRF) of approximately 500 questionnaires, interview schedules and survey forms used in research on alcohol and alcoholism, archives and mss of public and private agencies, Temperance groups, treatment centers, etc, dealing with alcohol problems. The collection is comprehensive for all scientific and scholarly aspectsof alcohol and alcohol problems. It excludes technical and industrial use materials on alcohol but incl selective popular publications on alcohol problems.

VT —FLETCHER FREE LIBRARY, 235 College St, Burlington, 05401. Maxie Ewins, Librn
Holdings: Vols 1200 Cat Maps Pix
Notes: Concentration on Burlington, Vermont. Complete run of Burlington City Reports, from 1860. Limited genealogies.

ALCOHOL—PHYSIOLOGICAL EFFECTS

MI —UNIVERSITY OF MICHIGAN, Transportation Research Institute, Library, 2901 Baxter Rd, Ann Arbor, 48109. Ann C Grimm, Librn
Holdings: Vols (57,000) Cat Mss Maps Pix Slides Microforms
Budget: ($25,000)

ALCOHOLISM

CA —UNIVERSITY OF SOUTHERN CALIFORNIA, School of Medicine, Norris Medical Library, 2025 Zonal Ave, Los Angeles, 90033. Nelson J Gilman, Librn
Holdings: Vols 1700 Cat AV
Budget: $8000
Notes: Substance abuse collection.

CT —CONNECTICUT ALCOHOL AND DRUG ABUSE COMMISSION, Library, 999 Asylum Ave, Hartford, 06105. Patti Camera, Librn
Notes: Collection of classified abstracts covering many publications on the uses and effects of alcohol.

CT —YALE MEDICAL LIBRARY, 333 Cedar St, New Haven, 06510.
Notes: A special subject emphasis.

IL —JACKSONVILLE STATE HOSPITAL, Training & Research Library, 1201 S Main St, Jacksonville, 62650. Lois E Wells, Librn
Notes: Concerned particularly with developmental disabilities.

IN —CENTRAL STATE HOSPITAL, Medical Library, 3000 W Washington St, Indianapolis, 46222. Aurella S Baker, Librn
Holdings: Vols (10,400) Cat Audiotapes
Budget: ($41,000)

†MA —UNIVERSITY OF MASSACHUSETTS AT AMHERST, Library, Amherst, 01003.
Notes: The development of the temperance and prohibition movements in the US during the 19th and early 20th centuries.

MA —MCLEAN HOSPITAL MEDICAL LIBRARY, 115 Mill St, Belmont, 02178. Hector Bossange, Dir
Holdings: Vols 25,611 Cat
Notes: Extensive collection.

MO —SAINT LOUIS POLICE LIBRARY, 315 S Tucker Blvd, Saint Louis, 63102. Cathy Reilly, Librn
Holdings: Vols (21,000) Cat Mss Pix Microforms
Budget: ($18,400)
Notes: Library on all subjects of police work is open to the public for general reference use.

NH —NEW HAMPSHIRE TECHNICAL INSTITUTE, Paul E Farnum Library, 5 Fan Rd, Concord, 03301. Wm John Hare, Librn
Notes: Collection incl mental health, alcoholism and counseling.

NJ —RUTGERS, THE STATE UNIVERSITY OF NEW JERSEY, Center of Alcohol Studies Library, Smithers Hall, New Brunswick, 08903. Penny Page, Librn
Holdings: Vols (8075) Cat Mss Microforms
Budget: ($110,000)
Notes: Alcohol and alcohol problems. Special holdings within collection: Master Catalog of the Alcohol Literature (over 125, 000 references in all major languages); Classified Abstract Archive of the Alcohol Literature-CAAAL (English-language abstracts on edge-notched cards, covering approximately 20,000 documents); McCarthy Memorial Collection of full-text originals matching the CAAAL abstracts; *Journal of Studies on Alcohol* and other scholarly publications specializing in alcohol-related research; Connor Alcohol Research Reference File (CARRF) of approximately 500 questionnaires, interview schedules and survey forms used in research on alcohol and alcoholism, archives and mss of public and private agencies, Temperance groups, treatment centers, etc, dealing with alcohol problems. The collection is comprehensive for all scientific and scholarly aspectsof

ALCOHOLISM (cont.)

alcohol and alcohol problems. It excludes technical and industrial use materials on alcohol but incl selective popular publications on alcohol problems.

NY —NEW YORK PUBLIC LIBRARY, Research Libraries, General Research Division, Fifth Ave & 42 St, New York, 10018. Rodney Phillips, Chief
Holdings: Vols (2,225,000) Cat Maps Pix Microforms
Budget: ($775,718)
Notes: Incl James Black Temperance Collection.

TX —TEXAS DEPT OF MENTAL HEALTH & MENTAL RETARDATION, Central Office Library, 909 W 45, Box 12668, Austin, 78711. Becky Renfro, Librn
Holdings: Vols (4600) Cat

TX —SOUTHWEST FOUNDATION FOR RESEARCH AND EDUCATION LIBRARY, Preston C Northrup Memorial Library, Baboon Information Center, W Loop 410 at Military Dr, PO Box 28147, San Antonio, 78284. Dorothy M Brooks, Baboon
Notes: Principle field of research: Birth defects, atherosclerosis, reproductive physiology, cancer, genetics, organic chemistry, parasitology, primatology and behavioral sciences and their application to problems of drug abuse, alcoholism and ecology. Maintains the largest baboon colony in the world.

ON —ONTARIO MINISTRY OF CORRECTIONAL SERVICES, Library, 2001 Eglinton Ave E, Scarborough, M1L 4P1, Can. T J B Anderson, Chief Librn
Holdings: Vols (3676) Cat VF
Notes: Approx 135 periodicals received. Library services also provided in approx 50 jails and adult institutions.

ON —ALCOHOLISM & DRUG ADDICTION RESEARCH FOUNDATION, Library, 33 Russell St, Toronto, M5S 2S1, Can. D Fridenberg, Manager, Library Services
Holdings: Vols 8000 Cat
Notes: All aspects of the use and misuse of psychotropic drugs. Incl temperance material.

ALCOHOLISM AND TRAFFIC ACCIDENTS see Drinking and Traffic Accidents

ALCORAN see Koran

ALCOTT, ABIGAIL MAY

MA —CONCORD FREE PUBLIC LIBRARY, 129 Main St, Concord, 01742. Rose Marie Mitten, Dir
Notes: Alcott Collection, primarily material on Amos Bronson Alcott and Louisa May Alcott, incl some representation of Abigail May Alcott and May Alcott Nieriker material (for example, May Alcott's *Concord Sketches*).

ALCOTT, AMOS BRONSON

MA —HARVARD UNIVERSITY LIBRARY, Houghton Library, Cambridge, 02138. Rodney G Dennis, Cur of Manuscripts
Holdings: Cat Mss

MA —CONCORD FREE PUBLIC LIBRARY, 129 Main St, Concord, 01742. Rose Marie Mitten, Dir
Holdings: Cat Mss Pix
Notes: Extensive collections.

ALCOTT, LOUISA MAY

DC —LIBRARY OF CONGRESS, Rare Book & Special Collections Div, Washington, 20540. William Matheson, Chief
Notes: The Juvenile Collection covers the early 18th century to the present and is particularly strong in fiction. Authors extensively represented are: Alcott, Alger, Abbott, Goodrich, Fosdick, Lothrop and McGuffey.

MA —HARVARD UNIVERSITY LIBRARY, Houghton Library, Cambridge, 02138. Rodney G Dennis, Cur of Manuscripts
Holdings: Cat Mss

MA —CONCORD FREE PUBLIC LIBRARY, 129 Main St, Concord, 01742. Rose Marie Mitten, Dir
Holdings: Cat Mss Maps Pix Slides
Notes: Extensive collection.

VA —UNIVERSITY OF VIRGINIA, Alderman Library, Clifton Waller Barrett Collection, Charlottesville, 22901. Joan St C Crane, Cur of American Literature Collections
Notes: Papers.

WI —UNIVERSITY OF WISCONSIN, MADISON, Memorial Library, British & American Language & Literature Collection, 728 State St, Madison, 53706. Yvonne Schofer, Bibliographer
Holdings: Vols 2200 Mss Microforms Documents Periodicals
Notes: A collection of primary and secondary materials for nine major American women writers: Anne Bradstreet; Louisa May Alcott, Emily Dickinson, Kate Chopin, Mary Williams Freeman, Margaret Fuller, Sarah Orne Jewett, Charlotte Perkins Gilman, Harriet Beecher Stowe. Primary materials also collected for a list of less well known authors together with manuscripts and archives of letters of special research interest. Variety of holdings: fiction, poetry, drama, biography and autobiography, letters, memoirs, diaries, travel, domestic economy and other kinds of writings by women mostly of the 19th century. Held in Dept of Rare Books and Special Collections.

ALDEN, HENRY MILLS

NY —UNIVERSITY OF ROCHESTER, Rush Rhees Library, Department of Rare Books and Special Collections, Rochester, 14627. Peter Dzwonkoski, Librn
Holdings: Cat Mss
Notes: Correspondents include Robert Underwood Johnson, Will Carlton, Henry Mills Alden, Richard Watson Gilder; Howell's proof of article on Henrik Ibsen (1906).

ALDEN, ROBERT ROSS

MO —WASHINGTON UNIVERSITY, Libraries, Special Collections Dept, Campus Box 1061, St Louis, 63130.
Notes: The Ira Adler Collection (of the noted bookman), incl his collection of mss, autographs, and correspondence of 19th and 20th century literary and historical figures.

†NY —COLUMBIA UNIVERSITY LIBRARIES, Butler Library, Rare Book and Manuscript Library, 535 W 114 St, New York, 10027.
Notes: Papers of Robert Ross Alden, incl correspondence.

ALDINGTON, HILDA

MA —HARVARD UNIVERSITY LIBRARY, Cambridge, 02138.
Holdings: Cat Mss

NV —UNIVERSITY OF NEVADA, RENO, University Library, Special Collections Dept, Reno, 89557. Robert E Blesse, Head
Holdings: // Vols (54) Cat Other appearances 525 Cat
Notes: Includes individual works by author in all editions including translations; also prefaces, introductions, published correspondence, appearances in anthologies, periodicals, etc. Bibliographical research collection, part of Modern Authors Collection.

ALDINGTON, RICHARD, 1892-1962

CA —UNIVERSITY OF CALIFORNIA, LOS ANGELES, Research Library, Dept of Special Collections, 405 Hilgard Ave, Los Angeles, 90024. Edward Shreeves, Chairman, Bibliographers Group; David S Zeidberg, Head
Holdings: Vols 100 Cat Mss
Notes: 100 first and other editions of Richard Aldington's books; 900 letters and mss.

CT —YALE UNIVERSITY, Box 1603A, Yale Station, New Haven, 06520.
Holdings: Cat

IL —SOUTHERN ILLINOIS UNIVERSITY, CARBONDALE, Delyte W Morris Library, Special Collections Dept, Carbondale, 62901. David V Koch, Cur of Special Collections; Louisa Bowen, Cur of Manuscripts
Holdings: Vols 239 Cat Mss Pix
Notes: Personal papers, 1920-1962, acquired from his daughter, other members of the family, friends and his literary executor. 18 linear feet. Inventory and name index avaiable at library.

†NC —WAKE FOREST UNIVERSITY, Z Smith Reynolds Library, Box 7777, Reynold Sta, Winston-Salem, 27109. Richard J Murdoch, Rare Book Librn
Holdings: Vols 78 Cat

PA —TEMPLE UNIVERSITY LIBRARIES, Special Collections Dept, Rare Books & Mss Section, Philadelphia, 19122. Thomas M Whitehead, Cur
Holdings: Vols 350 Cat Mss Pix
Notes: First, limited and signed editions; proof and presentation copies; letters and mss; photographs. Printed catalog of basic collection available free.

ON —UNIVERSITY OF TORONTO, Thomas Fisher Rare Book Library, 120 Saint George St, Toronto, M5S 1A5, Can. Richard G Landon, Head
Holdings: Vols 5400 Cat Mss
Notes: Three collections. Duncan Collection is named for donor, Douglas Duncan, art dealer and collector,, Toronto. Contains first and subsequent important editions of Richard Aldington, Max Beerbohm, Norman Douglas, Aldoux Huxley, and D H Lawrence. Manuscripts by Beerbohm, Aldington, Lawrence, William Sharp. Endicott Collection named in honor of Norman J Endicott, Professor of English, University of Toronto, contains first and significant later editions of over fifty British writers whose major work falls into the period from 1880 to 1930. Fisher Collection named for donor, Charles B Fisher, contains first and significant editions of Kipling, Norman Douglas, and Lord Dunsany.

ALDISS, BRIAN

TX —DALLAS PUBLIC LIBRARY, Central Library, Humanities Division, 1515 Young St, Dallas, 75201. Richard L Waters, Acting Dir; Ron Boyd, Fiction Librn
Holdings: Vols Cat Microforms
Notes: Cited in Tymn, Marshall, Roger C Schlobin, and L W Currey. *A Research Guide to Science Fiction* New York: Garland, 1977. The science fiction collection now exceeds 8000 circulating vols. In addition, the Library purchased in 1983 the personal library and archives of Brian Aldiss (which will be for reference use only). This collection consists of 350 books by Aldiss, 1900 other books by other science fiction writers, 800 issues of science fiction and fantasy periodicals, 100 vols concerning astronautics and space travel, over 1000 typescript pages of mss(incl 6 corrected mss), several sound recordings (incl BBC tapes), and a considerable amount of correspondence.

ALDREDGE, ROBERT C.

SC —COLLEGE OF CHARLESTON LIBRARY, Special Collections Dept, Charleston, 29401.
Notes: Collection of Christmas and New Year's greeting cards cleverly designed by Robert C Aldredge, who was a high official in the US Weather Bureau in Washington, DC.

ALDRICH, THOMAS BAILEY, 1836-1907

MA —HARVARD UNIVERSITY LIBRARY, Widener Library, Cambridge, 02138.
Holdings: Cat Mss
Notes: See *Harvard Alumni Bulletin,* XXII (1920): pp 852-854.

ALDRICH, THOMAS BAILEY, 1836-1907 (cont.)

NJ —PRINCETON UNIVERSITY, Library, Rare Books Dept, Princeton, 08544. Stephen Ferguson, Cur
Holdings: Vols 100 Cat Mss
Notes: Mss incl a few letters and poems.

NY —SAINT JOHN'S UNIVERSITY, Special Collections Dept, Grand Central & Utopia Pkwys, Jamaica, 11439. Szilvia E Szmuk, Librn
Holdings: / / Cat
Notes: No photocopying.

VA —UNIVERSITY OF VIRGINIA, Alderman Library, Clifton Waller Barrett Collection, Charlottesville, 22901. Joan St C Crane, Cur of American Literature Collections
Notes: Papers.

ALDRICH, WINTHROP W.

MA —HARVARD UNIVERSITY, Graduate School of Business Administration, Baker Library, Soldiers Field, Boston, 02163. Mary V Chatfield, Librn; Florence Bartoshesky, Cur of Manuscripts and Archives
Holdings: Mss
Notes: Business papers.

ALE see Brewing

ALE HOUSES see Hotels, Taverns, Etc.

ALEATORY MUSIC see Chance Composition (Music)

ALEKSINSKII, GRIGORII ALEKSEVICH

MA —HARVARD UNIVERSITY LIBRARY, Houghton Library, Cambridge, 02138. Rodney G Dennis, Cur of Manuscripts
Holdings: Mss
Notes: Archives dealing with the Zemstvo and Russian Social Democratic Worker's party.

ALEUTIAN ISLANDS

AK —ALASKA STATE LIBRARY, Alaska Historical Library Collection, Pouch G, Juneau, 99811. Phyllis Demuth, Readers Services Librn
Holdings: Vols (24,000) Cat Mss Maps Pix Slides Phonorecords Audiotapes Videotapes 16mm Films Microforms

NY —EXPLORERS CLUB, James B Ford Memorial Library, 46 E 70 St, New York, 10021. Janet Baldwin, Librn
Notes: Ted Banks Collection was begun by Prof Harley H Bartlett, bequeathed to American Institute for Exploration, with additions by Prof Ted Bank II, and subsequently acquired by the Explorers Club. Incl field notes, diaries, and photographs of Bank, who led more than 30 scientific expeditions to the Arctic, Aleutians, Sea of Okhotsk, Japan, Taiwan, Southeast Asia and Africa.

OR —UNIVERSITY OF OREGON LIBRARY, Special Collections Div, Eugene, 97403. Kenneth W Duckett, Curator
Holdings: Cat and Uncat Mss Pix
Notes: Research material, incl correspondence, documents, and tapes of oral interviews, and ms of *The Thousand-Mile War: World War II in Alaska and the* Aleutians (1969) by Brian Garfield. Also, correspondence, reminiscences, documents, published articles, and photographs relating to the Aleutian campaign, compiled by Lawrence Reineke.

ALEXANDER, CHARLES P.

DC —SMITHSONIAN INSTITUTION, Archives Div, Washington, 20560. William W Moss, Archivist
Holdings: Cat Mss Pix
Notes: The Archives holds the records of the National Museum of Natural History's Division of Insects and the Department of Entomology, 1850-1974, as well as some papers of entomologists, incl Charles P Alexander.

NY —CORNELL UNIVERSITY LIBRARIES, Collection of Regional History, Dept of Manuscripts and Univ Archives, Ithaca, 14853.
Notes: Entomologist. Incl miscellanea, ca 1915; official forms, announcements, photos and other ephemera.

ALEXANDER, ABP. DANIEL WILLIAM, 1882-1970

GA —EMORY UNIVERSITY, Candler School of Theology, Pitts Theology Library, Atlanta, 30322. Channing Jeschke, Librn; Anita K Delaries, Curator
Notes: 9.5 linear feet of mss and printed materials documenting the history of the independent African Orthodox Church (1880-1974), and the role of Archbishop Daniel William Alexander (1882-1970), sent to the Library for fear of its possible destruction if kept in South Africa. Finding aid available.

ALEXANDER, FREDERICK DOUGLAS

NC —UNIVERSITY OF NORTH CAROLINA, CHARLOTTE, J Murrey Atkins Library, UNCC Station, Charlotte, 28223. Robert F Brabham Jr, Special Collections Librn
Holdings: Cat Mss
Notes: Papers of Frederick Douglas Alexander, first black city councilman in Charlotte, NC in the 20th century.

ALEXANDER, GEORGE

NY —UNIVERSITY OF ROCHESTER, Rush Rhees Library, Department of Rare Books and Special Collections, Rochester, 14627. Peter Dzwonkoski, Librn
Holdings: Vols (300) Cat Mss Pix
Notes: 19th century English and American plays and works on theatre. Also includes manuscript collections on theatre, and papers of Clement William Scott, John Lawrence Toole, Arthur Wing Pinero, George Alexander, Henry Irving, Charles Kean, Lillian Russell and Leon Marks Lion, collection of 130 lithographic theatre posters, and collection of programs and playbills, chiefly Rochester, NY, and New York City, 1870-1950. Unpublished guides to ms collections available in repository.

ALEXANDER, ROBERT EVANS, 1907-

NJ —RUTGERS, THE STATE UNIVERSITY OF NEW JERSEY, Alexander Library, Special Collections and Archives, College Ave & Huntington St, New Brunswick, 08903. Ronald L Becker, Cur of Manuscripts and Rare Books
Notes: Papers of the Inter-American Association for Democracy and Freedom, the Pan American Women's Association, and their director, Frances Grant (1930-). Also papers of Robert Alexander, incl transcripts of several thousand interviews with Latin American political leaders, students, etc (1950-).

NY —CORNELL UNIVERSITY LIBRARIES, Collection of Regional History, Dept of Manuscripts and Univ Archives, Ithaca, 14853.
Notes: Architect. Papers, 1942-67; 18 in.

ALEXANDER THE GREAT

OH —CLEVELAND PUBLIC LIBRARY, Fine Arts and Special Collections Department, 325 Superior Ave, Cleveland, 44114. Alice N Loranth, Head
Holdings: Vols (3000) Cat Mss
Notes: Part of the Romances Collection, which incl critical studies, and early printed editions. The Arthurian and Charlemagne cycles, the Nibelungenlied and other Germanic titles, Amadis de Gaula and his numerous progeny, Alexander the Great, Barlaam and Joasaph, and the Seven Wise Masters of Rome are some of the strengths of the collection. Material in the Dewey/Brett Collection is classified by related cycles and their versions in various languages.
See also entry under Romances.

TX —AUSTIN COLLEGE, Arthur Hopkins Library, 900 N Grand Ave, Sherman, 75090. Gene Gibson, College Librn
Holdings: Vols 883 / / Cat Maps Pix
Notes: Collection of Professor Julio Berzunza, acquired by Austin College in 1958. Restricted use: Noncirculating; not available on interlibrary loan.

ALEXANDERSON, ERNST FREDRICK WERNER

NY —UNION COLLEGE, Schaffer Library, Archives of Science and Technology, Schenectady, 12308. Ellen Fladger, Archivist
Notes: Papers etc.

ALFONSO X, SPAIN

WI —UNIVERSITY OF WISCONSIN, MADISON, Seminary of Medieval Spanish Studies, 1130 Van Hise Hall, Madison, 53706. Lloyd A Kasten, Emeritus Prof of Spanish
Holdings: Vols (7500) / / Cat Mss Pix Slides Microforms
Notes: Medieval materials and subjects. 100 reels of microfilm, 2500 pamphlets and reprints. Incl a 300-volume collection on 13th century Spanish law. Other emphases: language studies (incl 616,247 vocabulary cards), dictionaries, bibliographies, periodicals. The nucleus of the collection is photostats of the mss of unpublished works of Alfonso X. Restricted circulation.

ALGAE

CA —UNIVERSITY OF CALIFORNIA, DAVIS, Shields Library, Dept of Special Collections, Davis, 95616. Donald Kunitz, Head; C Danial Elliott, Asst Head
Notes: Food technology files, 1943-1959, involving the research of Leonard Born on the irradiation of foods, cold sterilization, and algae production. Also, mss, correspondence, photographs, and clippings on various aspects of growing and processing fruit and vegetables, with an emphasis on canning. 3800 items.

CA —STANFORD UNIVERSITY, Hopkins Marine Station Library, Cabrillo Point, Pacific Grove, 93950. Alan Baldridge, Librn
Holdings: / / Cat
Notes: The G M Smith Algae Reprint Collection; 300 items.

DC —SMITHSONIAN INSTITUTION LIBRARIES, Botany Branch, Washington, 20560. Ruth Schallert, Branch Librn
Holdings: Vols (21,000) Cat Maps Pix Microforms
Notes: Taxonomic botany; with the J D Smith Collection of general botany, the Dawson Collection on algae, and the Hitchcock-Chase Collection on grasses.

ME —BIGELOW LABORATORY FOR OCEAN SCIENCES & MAINE DEPT OF MARINE RESOURCES, Library, McKown Point, West Boothbay Harbor, 04575. Pamela Shephard-Lupo, Librn
Holdings: Vols Cat Periodicals
Budget: ($55,000)
Notes: This library presently serves two institutions. The Maine Dept of Marine Resources has maintained the library since 1957 and thus the majority of our holdings are geared to their needs, ie fish biology and stock assessment on a local, national and international level. In 1973 Bigelow Laboratory for Ocean Sciences came to West Boothbay Harbor and began to contribute to the library with a very specialized collection on the Gulf of Maine marine chemistry, phytoplankton and nutrient cycles.

MA —HARVARD UNIVERSITY LIBRARY, Farlow Reference Library, 20 Divinity Ave, Cambridge, 02138. Geraldine C Kaye, Librn
Holdings: Vols (60,000) Cat Mss Serials Pix Microforms
Notes: The Farlow Reference Library provides complete coverage of the systematic literature on algae, bryophytes,

ALGAE (cont.)

fungi, and lichens. Established by bequest of Professor William G Farlow, it is one of the most extensive cryptogamic botany libraries in the US. Books do not circulate.

MI —UNIVERSITY OF MICHIGAN, Herbarium Library, University Herbarium, 2003 N University Bldg, Ann Arbor, 48109. Robert L Shaffer, Dir, Herbarium
Holdings: Vols (22,000) Cat Mss Maps Microforms
Notes: Systematic Botany including floristics, revisions and monographs in all groups of plants. Collection incl maps, mss (fieldbooks, correspondence, etc), photographs, microfiches, and approx 100, 000 reprints that are not officially part of the University Library. These are indexed and are available to qualified scholars. Incl botanical libraries of Parke, Davis & Co, Harley H Bartlett, Bruce Fink (lichens), Howard A Kelly (mycology).

†NH —UNIVERSITY OF NEW HAMPSHIRE, Biological Science Library, Kendall Hall, Durham, 03824. Lloyd Heldgard, Librn
Holdings: Vols (45,000)

OR —OREGON STATE UNIVERSITY, Marine Science Center, Library, Newport, 97365. Marilyn Guin, Librn
Holdings: Vols (8000) Cat Maps Microforms
Budget: ($15,000)
Notes: Collection emphasizes marine ecology, invertebrate zoology and marine algae. The portion of the collection concerned with fisheries emphasizes aquaculture. Collection is divided between the Marine Science Library and the Main OSU Library.

ON —LAURENTIAN UNIVERSITY LIBRARY, Ramsey Lake Rd, Sudbury, P3E 2C6, Can. Suzanne Brunette, Special Collection Librn; Sue Vongpeisal, Head Librn
Notes: Materials on northern Canada, incl 2200 books and pamphlets, 60,000 press clippings on northern topics 75 series of periodicals and over 1500 maps, plus photographs and thousands of samples of arctic and subarctic plants incl mosses, lichens, algae and wood sections. Much of the material is in French.

ALGER, HORATIO

DC —LIBRARY OF CONGRESS, Rare Book & Special Collections Div, Washington, 20540. William Matheson, Chief
Notes: The Juvenile Collection covers the early 18th century to the present and is particularly strong in fiction. Authors extensively represented are: Alcott, Alger, Abbott, Goodrich, Fosdick, Lothrop and McGuffey.

IL —NORTHERN ILLINOIS UNIVERSITY, Founders Memorial Library, Rare Books and Special Collections Dept, De Kalb, 60115. William R DuBois, Dept Head
Holdings: Vols (1000)
Budget: ($5000)
Notes: Mass-appeal publications, ca 1865-1920. Includes Horatio Alger, "Oliver Optic" and other popular writers.

MA —HARVARD UNIVERSITY LIBRARY, Cambridge, 02138.
Holdings: Cat Mss

MA —REVERE PUBLIC LIBRARY, 179 Beach St, Revere, 02151. Walter Punch, Dir
Holdings: Vols 123 Cat
Notes: Horatio Alger's birthplace is across the street.

MA —BRANDEIS UNIVERSITY, Goldfarb Library, 415 South St, Waltham, 02154. Bessie Hahn, Dir
Notes: Dime Novel and Juvenile Literature Collection. Over 1000 dime novels, an extensive collection of the works of Horatio Alger, Harry Castlemon, Oliver Optic and other boys and girls literature of the 19th and early 20th century. Access to this collection is through the card catalog in Special Collections.

MS —UNIVERSITY OF SOUTHERN MISSISSIPPI, William David McCain Graduate Library, Box 5148, Southern Sta, Hattiesburg, 39406.
Holdings: Vols 181
Notes: The Lena Y de Grummond Collection of Children's Literature. Incl the Robert L Dartt Collection of over 1800 books for boys from the late 19th and early 20th centuries. Extensive Henty (over 550 vols), Alger, Brereton, Castlemon, Fenn, Kingston, Optic, and Stratemeyer holdings. Catalog in progress.

OH —OHIO UNIVERSITY, Vernon R Alden Library, Department of Archives and Special Collections, Athens, 45701. Gary A Hunt, Head
Holdings: Vols (1400) Uncat
Notes: A miscellaneous collection of children's books by American and English authors, with most imprint dates in the period 1870-1930; numerous series books. Authors incl Jacob Abbott (196v), "Oliver Optic" (84 v), Horatio Alger (89 v), J H Ewing (53 v), Martha Finley (47 v), G A Henty (46 v), Frank V Webster (38 v), and many others.

ALGER, PHILIP L.

NY —UNION COLLEGE, Schaffer Library, Archives of Science and Technology, Schenectady, 12308. Ellen Fladger, Archivist
Notes: Papers etc.

ALGERIA

CA —HOOVER INSTITUTION ON WAR, REVOLUTION & PEACE, Stanford University, Stanford, 94305. Peter Duignan, Cur; Karen Fung, Deputy Cur
Holdings: Vols (100,000)
Notes: For full description of collection, see Hoover Institution entry under Near East.

DC —HOWARD UNIVERSITY, Moorland-Spingarn Research Center, 500 Howard Place NW, Washington, 20059. Clifford L Muse, Jr, Acting Dir

ALGERIA—HISTORY

CA —HOOVER INSTITUTION ON WAR, REVOLUTION & PEACE, Stanford University, Stanford, 94305. Milorad M Drachkovitch, Archivist
Notes: Papers of Yves Godard, officer, French Army, 1932-1961; director of police in Algeria, 1958-60; and organizer of the Organisation de l'Armee Secrete (OAS) 1961-62; incl correspondence, messages, reports, dossiers, maps, photos, news clippings, speeches and writings, and other material, 1929-74, related to military and resistance operations during World War II; to military operations during Indochinese War; and to military, police, and terrorist activities during the Algerian independence struggle. Incl records of the Armee Secrete de Haute-Savoie (Secret Army of Resistance Fighters of Haute-Savoie). 13 ms boxes; 1 oversize volume; 1 envelope.

ALGIN

CA —KELCO DIV OF MERCK, Library, 8355 Aero Dr, San Diego, 92123. Ann A Jenkins, Librn
Holdings: Cat Mss Maps Pix Slides Microforms
Notes: Kelco, as the largest producer of algin and xanthan gum in the world, supports a library specialized in the subject of natural gums and polysaccharides, incl all aspects of the subject; chemistry, biology, microbiology, applications (food, industrial, petroleum), etc.

ALGOLOGY

†NC —UNIVERSITY OF NORTH CAROLINA, CHAPEL HILL, Department of Botany Library, 301 Coker Hall 010-A, Chapel Hill, 27514. William R Burk, Botany Librn
Notes: The mycology collection incl some 6000 pamphlets. It contains papers of the following scientists: William C Coker, John N Couch, Lindsay F Olive, mycologists; also, Victor A Greulach, plant pathologist. The mycology catalog is in preparation (1983), and will provide author, title, and subject access.

ALGREN, NELSON, 1909-1981

NV —UNIVERSITY OF NEVADA, RENO, University Library, Special Collections Dept, Reno, 89557. Robert E Blesse, Head
Holdings: Vols (40) Cat Other appearances 160 Cat
Notes: Includes individual works by author in all editions including translations; also prefaces, introductions, published correspondence, appearances in anthologies, periodicals, etc. Bibliographical research collection, part of Modern Authors Collection.

OH —OHIO STATE UNIVERSITY, William Oxley Thompson Memorial Library, 1858 Neil Ave Mall, Columbus, 43210. Robert A Tibbetts, Cur of Special Collections
Holdings: Vols 835 Cat Mss
Notes: Incl the original gift of his papers (donated in the 1960s), with 9000 more pages of history mss, 1400 pages of correspondence, and 1400 books from Algren's personal library. Also, some 340 letters from Simone de Beauvoir written between the late 1940s and mid 1950s, incl their joint Mexican diary of 1948.

ALI, MUHAMMED see Muhammed Ali

ALIMENTATION see Nutrition

ALKALIES

OH —SDS BIOTECH CORP, PO Box 348, Painesville, 44077. Violet Forgach, Business Librn
Holdings: Cat Pix Microforms

ALKORAN see Koran

ALLAIRE PAPERS (HOWELL WORKS)

NJ —MONMOUTH COUNTY HISTORICAL ASSOCIATION, Library, 70 Court St, Freehold, 07728. Loretta M Zwolak, Archivist & Librn
Notes: Especially Monmouth County area. See *Monmouth County Historical Association Bulletin,* vol 1, no 2 July 1948, p 23-48. Allaire Papers (Howell Works); Battle of Monmouth; Mott Family Papers; North American Phalanx; Philip Freneau; Steamship Coll.

ALLBEURY, TED

MA —BOSTON UNIVERSITY, Mugar Memorial Library, Special Collections Dept, 771 Commonwealth Ave, Boston, 02215. Howard B Gotlieb, Dir
Holdings: Cat Mss
Notes: Mss, correspondence, etc, collected in depth; incl publications by or about.

ALLDERDICE, NORMAN

AZ —NORTHERN ARIZONA UNIVERSITY, Special Collection Library, CU Box 6022, Flagstaff, 86011. Peter M Whiteley, Coordr/Archivist; William Mullane, Librn
Holdings: Vols Cat
Notes: Collection of Norman Allderdice, Tucson, Ariz, political conservative. The large collection incl thousands of books, pamphlets, periodicals, and organizational files and reflects the conservative, communist, socialist, facist, anarchist, and other viewpoints, etc, during the 20th century. Also incl correspondence, subject and title files.

ALLEGHENY, PENNSYLVANIA

PA —UNIVERSITY OF PITTSBURGH, Hillman Library, Archives of Industrial Society, 363 Hillman Library, Pittsburgh, 15260. Frank A Zabrosky, Cur
Holdings: Mss Maps Pix Microforms
Notes: Unique collections: Allegheny,

ALLEGHENY, PENNSYLVANIA (cont.)

Pennsylvania, city records, 3000 vols, incl tax assessment records (1840-1907).

ALLEN, A. H.

IL —NEWBERRY LIBRARY, 60 W Walton St, Chicago, 60610. Diana Haskell, Cur of Modern Mss

ALLEN, AGNES M.

AZ —NORTHERN ARIZONA UNIVERSITY, Special Collection Library, CU Box 6022, Flagstaff, 86011. Peter M Whiteley, Coordr/Archivist; William Mullane, Librn
Notes: Dr Agnes Allen was formerly a science professor at NAU. Collection contains her papers.

ALLEN, DONALD

CA —UNIVERSITY OF CALIFORNIA, SAN DIEGO, Central University Library, Mandeville Dept of Special Collections, La Jolla, 92093. Lynda Corey Claassen, Head; Michael Davidson, Cur, Archive for New Poetry
Notes: The collection of papers belonging to editor and publisher Donald Allen represents the work of one of the first publishers to make innovative poetry available through his landmark anthology, *The New American Poetry, 1945-1960,* and through his two presses, The Four Seasons Foundation and Grey Fox Press.

ALLEN, ETHAN

MA —HARVARD UNIVERSITY LIBRARY, Cambridge, 02138.
Holdings: Cat Mss

VT —UNIVERSITY OF VERMONT, Guy W Bailey/David W Howe Library, Burlington, 05405. John Buehler, Asst Dir for Special Collections

ALLEN, FRED

DC —GEORGETOWN UNIVERSITY, Library, Special Collections Div, 37 & O Sts NW, Washington, 20057. George M Barringer, Special Collections Librn; Nicholas B Sheetz, Mss Librn
Holdings: Mss Pix
Notes: Correspondence, clippings, photographs, and memorabilia incl items relating to Mr Dolan's activities in the Democratic Party in and around Chicago, his friendships with James A Farley, John W McCormack, and Fred Allen, and his student days at Georgetown University.

ALLEN, HERVEY

CT —LEE ASH, (personal collection), 66 Humiston Dr, Bethany, 06525.
Notes: First editions, mss, ephemera, memorabilia.

MA —HARVARD UNIVERSITY LIBRARY, Cambridge, 02138.
Holdings: Cat Mss

PA —UNIVERSITY OF PITTSBURGH, Hillman Library, Special Collections Dept, Hervey Allen Collection, Pittsburgh, 15260. Charles E Aston, Jr, Coordr
Holdings: Vols (2747) Cat Mss Memorabilia Pix
Notes: Substantially all of the author's mss, from first draft to published first edition, of his major works. Incl author's entire personal library. Mss incl correspondence from contemporary writers and poets. Occasional additions to this collection, of lacunae.

ALLEN, IRA

VT —UNIVERSITY OF VERMONT, Guy W Bailey/David W Howe Library, Burlington, 05405. John Buehler, Asst Dir for Special Collections

ALLEN, IRWIN

CA —UNIVERSITY OF CALIFORNIA, LOS ANGELES, Theater Arts Library, Los Angeles, 90024. Edward Shreeves, Chairman, Bibliographers Group; Audree Malkin, Head, Theater Arts Library
Notes: Irwin Allen (producer) Television Collection: scripts, production and original sketches relating to the television series: *Land of the Giants, Voyage to the Bottom of the Sea, Swiss Family Robinson, Lost in Space, Time Tunnel,* and *Animal World.*

ALLEN, JAMES LANE

KY —UNIVERSITY OF KENTUCKY, Margaret I King Library, Dept of Special Collections, Lexington, 40506. William Marshall, Head
Holdings: Vols 77 Cat Mss Pix
Notes: 331 ms items plus 3 boxes contain letters and ms of Allen's works.

ALLEN, MARILYN R.

AZ —NORTHERN ARIZONA UNIVERSITY, Special Collection Library, CU Box 6022, Flagstaff, 86011. Peter M Whiteley, Coordr/Archivist; William Mullane, Librn
Notes: Marilyn R. Allen was a political conservative, anticommunist, isolationist, anti-ethnic, minorities author, Salt Lake City, Utah. Incl correspondence, mss, 1947-1967. Inventory available.

ALLEN, NATHANIEL S.

LA —LOUISIANA STATE UNIVERSITY, SHREVEPORT, Library-Archives, 8515 Youree Dr, Shreveport, 71129. Patricia L Meador, Archivist & Asst Librn
Notes: Theatre and music is documented in the John Wray and Margaret Mary Young Theatre Collection, (5 linear ft), (1929-1981), the Joe Gifford Papers (1946-1960) (3 linear ft), the Shreveport Little Theatre Records (6 linear ft), the Nathaniel S Allen Papers (1860-1930), the records of the Shreveport Symphony (1948-1978) and oral history interviews on the topics. The archives collection also incl 60 linear ft of records (1949-1981) of Holiday-In-Dixie, Shreveport-Bossier's spring-time festival.

ALLEN, STEVE

CA —UNIVERSITY OF SOUTHERN CALIFORNIA, Edward L Doheny Memorial Library, Archives of Performing Arts, University Park, Los Angeles, 90089. Robert Knutson, Librn
Holdings: Mss Pix
Notes: Personal collection of papers, pictures, etc.

ALLEN, W. H.

IL —NEWBERRY LIBRARY, 60 W Walton St, Chicago, 60610. Diana Haskell, Cur of Modern Mss

BC —UNIVERSITY OF VICTORIA, McPherson Library, Victoria, V8W 3H5, Can.

ALLERGIES see Asthma; Hay Fever; Ragweed

ALLIANCE FOR THE GUIDANCE OF RURAL YOUTH

NC —DUKE UNIVERSITY, William R Perkins Library, Manuscript Dept, Durham, 27706. Ellen Gartrell, Cur of Mss
Holdings: Cat Mss
Notes: Especially strong for Southern states, 19th-20th centuries. Education of women and blacks, regional and national organizations, public and private schools. Papers of black educator Charles N Hunter; Alliance for the Guidance of Rural Youth; NEA official Belmont Farley, and much more.

ALLIANCE TO END REPRESSION

IL —CHICAGO HISTORICAL SOCIETY, Library, Clark St at North Ave, Chicago, 60614. Archie Motley, Manuscript Librn
Notes: Papers.
See also entry under Civil Rights.

ALLIED HEALTH PERSONNEL

CA —LOS ANGELES PUBLIC LIBRARY, Science & Technology Dept, 630 W Fifth St, Los Angeles, 90071. Billie M Connor, Dept Head
Holdings: Vols (7500)
Notes: A well-rounded collection of materials related to consumer health, medicine and drugs as well as materials for the allied health and medical professions. Includes a sound representative selection of basic texts covering various aspects of medical treatment, drugs, diseases and syndromes. Indexes are collected as well as a basic collection of journals. The directories collection is strong. The broadest possible collection of books oriented toward consumer health, medicine, diets and nutrition is maintained, both traditional and alternative. Texts and examination study books are collected for nurses, laboratory technicians, physcial therapists, speech therapists, paramedics and other allied health professions.

IL —LIBRARY OF THE AMERICAN HOSPITAL ASSOCIATION, Asa S Bacon Memorial, 840 N Lake Shore Dr, Chicago, 60611. Eloise C Foster, Dir
Holdings: Vols (39,000) Cat
Budget: ($95,000)
Notes: Literature on non-clinical aspects of health care administration, planning and financing of hospitals and related health care institutions; administrative aspects of the medical, paramedical, and prepayment fields. Special Collection: Ray E Brown Management Collection. *Hospital Literature* Index prepared by the Library of the American Hospital Association in cooperation with the National Library of Medicine; *Catalog of the Library of the American Hospital Association,* published by G K Hall, Boston.

MA —BERKSHIRE MEDICAL CENTER, Medical Library, 725 North St, Pittsfield, 01201. Jutta Luhde, Medical Librn
Holdings: Vols (15,000) Cat
Notes: Medicine and allied health sciences.

NC —WAKE TECHNICAL COLLEGE, Library, Audio-Visual Dept, 9101 Fayetteville Road, Raleigh, 27603. James Gray, Librn; Horst Garloff, Audio-Visual Specialist
Holdings: Vols (32,332) Cat Maps Slides Phonorecords Audiotapes Videotapes 16mm Films Filmstrips Microforms

OH —CLEVELAND MEDICAL LIBRARY ASSOCIATION/CASE WESTERN RESERVE UNIVERSITY, Cleveland Health Sciences Library, Historical Division, Allen Memorial Medical Library, 11000 Euclid Ave, Cleveland, 44106. Glen Jenkins, Rare Book Librarian & Archivist
Holdings: Cat
Notes: Biographies of health science professionals, Sigmund Frued, and naturalists.

OH —KETTERING COLLEGE OF MEDICAL ARTS, Learning Resources Center, 3737 Southern Blvd, Kettering, 45429. Edward Collins, Librn
Holdings: Vols 53,513 Cat Audiotapes Videotapes 16mm Films

PA —SAINT JOSEPH HOSPITAL, Hospital Library, 250 College Ave, PO Box 3509, Lancaster, 17604. Eileen B Doudna, Librn
Holdings: Vols (3000) Cat Journals Videocassettes Filmstrips Slides

PA —TEMPLE UNIVERSITY, Health Sciences Center Library, Broad & Tioga Sts, Philadelphia, 19140. Ruth Diamond, Dir
Holdings: Vols (87,480) Cat Slides Microforms
Budget: ($340,950)

ALLIED HEALTH SCIENCES see Health Sciences

ALLISON, ALEXANDER

LA —NEW ORLEANS PUBLIC LIBRARY, Louisiana Div, 219 Loyola Ave, New

ALLISON, ALEXANDER (cont.)

Orleans, 70140. Collin B Hamer Jr, Head; Brenda M Osbey, Library Associate
Holdings: Cat Maps Pix
Notes: Louisiana and New Orleans Picture File Collection ranges from the late 19th century-date and incl the following separate collections: Alexander Allison (ca 1898-1951, 337 pieces); Charles Franck (ca 1920-50, 170 pieces); Leda Plauche (ca 1935-53, 220 pieces); C Milo Williams (ca 1910, 85 pieces); Wilson S Howell (ca 1890, 49 pieces); Grauman Marks (ca 1960, 268 pieces); Robert Tallant (ca 1940-50, 70 pieces); Robert E Tracy (1959, 87 pieces); Anthony J Flaherty (ca 1970-84, 83 pieces); George F Mugnier (1880-1920, 186 pieces); Color Slides (ca 1945-date, 500 pieces); 30, 000 photographs incl 500 color slides and 104 negatives. Use of the material is restricted to on-site research. Publication must be accompanied by credit cut line.

ALLISON, FRED, 1882-1974

AL —AUBURN UNIVERSITY, Ralph Brown Draughon Library, Mell St, Auburn, 36830. Gene Geiger, Special Collections Librn
Notes: His papers are housed in the University Archives (10 boxes).

IL —UNIVERSITY OF CHICAGO LIBRARY, Dept of Special Collections, 1100 E 57 St, Chicago, 60637.
Notes: Papers.

ALLISON, YOUNG EWING

KY —UNIVERSITY OF KENTUCKY, Margaret I King Library, Dept of Special Collections, Lexington, 40506. William Marshall, Head
Holdings: Vols 15 Cat Mss Pix
Notes: 74 pieces of ms, 7 vols, majority of material is contained in scrapbooks of letters, mss and ephemera.

ALLOCATION OF TIME see Time Allocation

ALLOYS

IL —ARGONNE NATIONAL LABORATORY, Materials Sciences Branch Library, 9700 S Cass Ave, Argonne, 60439. Veronica E Johnson, Librn
Notes: Properties of alloys. Incl 8000 vols monographs, 130 current journals, some scientific and technical reports. Materials may be used by the public in the library by prior arrangement. Photocopies may be supplied for interlibrary loan, for which a processing and handling charge is made.

IA —IOWA STATE UNIVERSITY, Library, Ames, 50011. Warren B Kuhn, Dean of Library Services
Holdings: Cat
Notes: Specific strength: rare-earth metals and alloys.

KY —UNIVERSITY OF KENTUCKY, Robert E Shaver Library of Engineering, 355 Anderson Hall, Lexington, 40506. Russell H Powell, Engineering Librn
Holdings: Vols (48,000) Cat Microforms

OH —BRUSH WELLMAN, Technical Library, 17876 Saint Clair Ave, Cleveland, 44110. Nancie Skonezny, Tech Librn
Holdings: Vols 1000 Cat
Notes: Beryllium technology--its metals, alloys and ceramics. Incl approx 5000 uncat government documents and international technical reports.

†OH —GENERAL MOTORS CORP, Inland Manufacturing Div, Engineering Library, PO Box 1224, Dayton, 45401.

PA —ENSANIAN PHYSICOCHEMICAL INSTITUTE, Electrotopography Library, PO Box 98, Eldred, 16731. Elisabeth Anahid Ensanian, Chief Librn
Holdings: Cat Maps Slides
Budget: ($45,000)
Notes: Electrotopography is a new science (the Institute has pioneered the field and has coined the terms "electrotopograph" and "electrotopography") concerned with the mapping of electrical fields associated with metals, alloys, semiconductors, and living organisms. These fields may be natural and/ or induced, and are converted into mappings which exhibit certain systems characteristics for both normal and stress states.

PA —FRANKLIN INSTITUTE LIBRARY, 20 & The Parkway, Philadelphia, 19103. Miriam Padusis, Dir; Charles Wilt, Readers Servs Librn
Holdings: Vols (300,000) Cat Maps Pix Microforms

PA —COLT INDUSTRIES, Crucible Research Center Library, Box 88, Pittsburgh, 15230. Patricia J Aducci, Technical Librn

PA —CABOT CORPORATION, Reading Technology Library, PO Box 1296, Reading, 19603. Pamela L Hehr, Librn
Holdings: Vols (3800) Cat Mss Slides Microforms
Notes: Copper-beryllium and special metals and alloys. Incl 2100 patents, 9000 reports and articles.

ALLRED, GOV. JAMES V.

TX —NORTH TEXAS STATE UNIVERSITY, Archives, NT Station Box 5188, Denton, 76203. Robert LaForte, University Archivist
Notes: Part of Oral History Collection. Incl interviews with Mrs Allred about the political career of the Texas governor. Also, interviews with David Allred, journalist, Texas legislator, and son of the governor. Restricted.

TX —UNIVERSITY OF HOUSTON, M D Anderson Memorial Library, University Park, Houston, 77004. David Farmer, Cur, Special Collections; Jean Jackson, Assistant Cur
Holdings: Cat Mss Pix Audiotapes
Notes: This collection consists of 360 document boxes of the personal and public papers of Gov James V Allred, 1920-1960, and family material from 1960 to present date. Some material restricted.

ALMAN, DAVID AND EMILY

MA —BOSTON UNIVERSITY, Mugar Memorial Library, Special Collections Dept, 771 Commonwealth Ave, Boston, 02215. Howard B Gotlieb, Dir
Holdings: Cat Mss Pix
Notes: Mss, correspondence, etc collected in depth; incl publications by or about David or Emily Alman.

ALMANACS

CT —YALE UNIVERSITY, Box 1603A, Yale Station, New Haven, 06520.

IL —UKRAINIAN NATIONAL MUSEUM, Library, 2453 W Chicago Ave, Chicago, 60622. Emil Basiuk, Librn
Notes: Department has been organized in collaboration with the Ukrainian Librarians of America Association, Ukrainian Bibliographic-Reference Center. Interlibrary loans. Collection of books and pamphlets incl material in Ukrainian and other languages on Ukrainian history, geography, literature, language, art, social sciences, religion and Ukrainian fiction. Large collection of Ukrainian calendars and almanacs. Around 100 current periodicals. Collection of serials and monographs of the Ukrainian scholarly institutions, collection of publications of the Institute for the Study of the USSR. There is a large collection of Ukrainian postcards showing all aspects of Ukrainian civilization and culture.

MI —MICHIGAN STATE UNIVERSITY, Libraries, Special Collections Div, East Lansing, 48824. Jannette Fiore, Librn
Notes: The Russel B Nye Popular Culture Collection in the Michigan State Univ Libraries incl over (45,000) items. Most of the collection is organized into 4 categories: comic art, popular fiction, popular information materials and materials relating to the popular performing arts. About 3900 items. Almanacs, Blue Books, and works popularizing knowledge or offering self-help and how-to advice. There are ca 350 issues of 100 19th and 20th century almanacs. The Blue Books incl ca 2000 Little Blue Books, over 600 Big Blue Books and a good number of issues of the various Haldeman-Julius magazines. In addition to almanacs and Blue Books, Popular Information incl books of advice on etiquette, life and love, how-to-succeed books, popular history, science and biography, and several hundred public schooltextbooks from the 19th and early 20th centuries.

MI —APPLE TREE PRESS, Library, Box 1012, Flint, 48501. W D Chase, Editor/ Librn
Holdings: Vols (1200) Uncat Mss Maps Pix Microforms

NY —UNIVERSITY OF ROCHESTER, Rush Rhees Library, Department of Rare Books and Special Collections, Rochester, 14627. Peter Dzwonkoski, Librn
Holdings: Vols 400
Notes: Mainly nineteenth century American.

RI —BROWN UNIVERSITY, John Carter Brown Library, Providence, 02912. Norman Fiering, Librn; Everett C Wilkie Jr, Bibliographer; Susan Danforth, Cur Maps & Prints
Notes: Almanacs published in America or European almanacs with American content before 1800. Incl nautical almanacs.

WI —UNIVERSITY OF WISCONSIN, MADISON, Memorial Library, 728 State St, Madison, 53706. Erwin K Welsch, Social Studies Bibliographer
Notes: An extensive collection of English almanacs of the 17th century. Rare Books Dept.

NS —DALHOUSIE UNIVERSITY LIBRARY, Halifax, B3H 4H8, Can.
Holdings: 600 Cat
Notes: Canadian almanacs. Strongest holdings are for Nova Scotia as collection spans 1772 to 1927. New Brunswick, Prince Edward Island, Newfoundland, and general Canadian almanacs for the 19th century are represented. A number of the early 19th century Nova Scotia almanacs contain mss notes; earliest almanacs are examples of some of the first printing done in Canada.

†ON —METROPOLITAN TORONTO LIBRARY, Social Sciences Dept, 789 Yonge St, Toronto, M4W 2G8, Can. Abdus Salam, Head
Holdings: Vols Cat Maps Phonorecords Audiotapes 16mm Films Microforms
Notes: Current and backfiles of Canadian, British and American almanacs. "Canadian Almanac" from 1848, "Whitaker's Almanac" from 1867, "World Almanac" from 1886.

ALMANACS, AMERICAN

CA —UNIVERSITY OF CALIFORNIA, LOS ANGELES, Research Library, Dept of Special Collections, 405 Hilgard Ave, Los Angeles, 90024. Edward Shreeves, Chairman, Bibliographers Group; David S Zeidberg, Head
Holdings: Vols 5000 Cat
Notes: 5000 separate issues of 1000 titles; chiefly 18th and 19th century publications.

CT —YALE UNIVERSITY, Box 1603A, Yale Station, New Haven, 06520.
Holdings: Cat

DC —LIBRARY OF CONGRESS, Rare Book & Special Collections Div, Washington, 20540. William Matheson, Chief
Holdings: Vols 3895 Cat
Notes: Some late 17th century, but chiefly 18th and 19th century, American almanacs constitute the bulk of this collection, some with ms annotations. Contains all the issues of *Poor Richard's Almanac* after 1735. Incl many unique items such as the first book printed in Wisconsin. Holdings incl Milton Drake's *Almanacs of the US* (New York: 1962), 2 vols.

IN —INDIANA UNIVERSITY, Lilly Library, Seventh St, Bloomington, 47405. William R Cagle, Librn
Holdings: Vols 6000 // Cat
Notes: Almanacs published in what is now continental US. Largely 19th century with some 18th and 20th century materials.

MA —NEW ENGLAND HISTORIC GENEALOGICAL SOCIETY, Library, 101

ALMANACS, AMERICAN (cont.)

Newbury St, Boston, 02116. Ralph J Crandell, Dir
Holdings: Vols (250,000) Mss Maps Microforms Pix
Notes: New England genealogy. Especially strong Massachusetts, Maine, and New Hampshire, although all states are well represented, as are the relevancies of each subject listed in this volume with regard to British antecedent and contemporary history. Special strengths in local history and biography, obituaries, etc, incl parish registers, censuses, British and American, 3125 linear ft of mss.

MA —AMERICAN ANTIQUARIAN SOCIETY LIBRARY, 185 Salisbury St, Worcester, 01609. Marcus A McCorison, Dir & Librn
Holdings: Vols 18,000 Cat
Notes: Strongest for New York, Pennsylvania, Massachusetts and Connecticut. Incl Canada, Hawaii, Mexico, the West Indies; also Pennsylvania German. About 18,000 or 90 percent of the almanacs and yearbooks known to have been printed in the United States before 1850; the Latin American and Canadian collections are the most complete in this country.

NJ —GLASSBORO STATE COLLEGE, Savitz Library, Stewart Room, Glassboro, 08028. Clara Kirner, Special Collection Librn
Holdings: Vols 48 Cat
Notes: These almanacs stress early New Jersey and Philadelphia. Several unique.

NJ —RUTGERS, THE STATE UNIVERSITY OF NEW JERSEY, Alexander Library, Special Collections and Archives, College Ave & Huntington St, New Brunswick, 08903. Ronald L Becker, Cur of Manuscripts and Rare Books
Holdings: Vols 5500
Notes: Primarily American, 18th-19th century. Partially cataloged.

NY —NEW YORK STATE LIBRARY, State Education Bldg Annex, Washington Ave, Albany, 12224.
Holdings: Cat
Notes: Over 5000 early American almanacs, from all of the original 13 states but mostly from New York and New England.

NY —BUFFALO & ERIE COUNTY PUBLIC LIBRARY, Rare Book Room, Lafayette Sq, Buffalo, 14203. William H Loos, Cur

NY —NEW YORK HISTORICAL SOCIETY, Library, 170 Central Park W, New York, 10024. James Gregory, Librn
Holdings: Mss
Notes: Incl original mss, illustrative materials, etc.

NY —NEW YORK PUBLIC LIBRARY, Research Libraries, General Research Division, Fifth Ave & 42 St, New York, 10018. Rodney Phillips, Chief
Holdings: Vols (2,225,000) Cat Maps Pix Microforms
Budget: ($775,718)

NC —DUKE UNIVERSITY, William R Perkins Library, Rare Book Room, Durham, 27706. John L Sharpe, III, Cur
Notes: American almanac collection of more than 500 almanacs. These almanacs range in date from1788 to 1977.

OH —OHIO UNIVERSITY, Vernon R Alden Library, Department of Archives and Special Collections, Athens, 45701. Gary A Hunt, Head
Holdings: Vols (200) Uncat
Notes: A small collection of American almanacs, 1818-1960, incl a few early German-American almanacs.

OH —PUBLIC LIBRARY OF CINCINNATI & HAMILTON COUNTY, Dept of Rare Books & Special Collections, 800 Vine St, Library Square, Cincinnati, 45202. Yeatman Anderson III, Cur
Holdings: Cat

ALMANACS, GERMAN

CA —STANFORD UNIVERSITY LIBRARIES, Cecil H Green Library, Stanford, 94305. Peter R Frank, Cur, CDP-Germanic Collection
Notes: Library of Prof Rudolf Hildebran, Leipzig, the first large collection acquired by Stanford in 1895/1896, laid the foundation for an extensive German collection. Hildebrand's library is especially strong in German and Austrian philology (rare dictionaries, etc.), but also in literary works. The collection is now especially strong for the period of the Reformation and Baroque, up to the present, with many rare editions, journals, almanacs, and the like. Sizable collections of women's working class and popular literature, dissertations and Schulschriften. Rare and valuable items in the Stanford Collection of German, Austrian and Swiss Culture, Special Collections. Catalog: *Katalog der Bibliothek des Herrn Prof Dr Rudolf Hildebrand.* Description: *The German Area Collection: A Stanford Tradition* by Peter R Frank.

IL —UNIVERSITY OF CHICAGO LIBRARY, Dept of Special Collections, 1100 E 57 St, Chicago, 60637.
Notes: 1600 Almanache and Tauschenbuecher.

IL —NORTHWESTERN UNIVERSITY, Library, Special Collections Dept, 1937 Sheridan Rd, Evanston, 60201. R Russell Maylone, Cur
Holdings: Vols 1200 Cat
Notes: Literary almanacs ("Taschenbucher") published 1780-1850.

OH —OHIO UNIVERSITY, Vernon R Alden Library, Department of Archives and Special Collections, Athens, 45701. Gary A Hunt, Head
Holdings: Vols (200) Uncat
Notes: A small collection of American almanacs, 1818-1960, incl a few early German-American almanacs.

ALMANACS, PORTUGUESE

CA —UNIVERSITY OF CALIFORNIA, LOS ANGELES, Research Library, Dept of Special Collections, 405 Hilgard Ave, Los Angeles, 90024. Edward Shreeves, Chairman, Bibliographers Group; David S Zeidberg, Head
Notes: 176 volumes, 1850-1920.

ALMAND, CLAUDE MARION, 1915-1957

KY —UNIVERSITY OF LOUISVILLE, School of Music, Dwight Anderson Memorial Music Library, 2301 S Third St, Louisville, 40292. Marion Korda, Librn
Notes: Composer, Musician and former Dean School of Music. Holographs of all his compositions (30).

ALMOND, EDWARD

PA —US ARMY MILITARY HISTORY INSTITUTE, Carlisle Barracks, 17013. Richard J Sommers, Chief Archivist-Historian
Holdings: Mss Cat
Notes: TheKorean War collection, personal correspondence, daily logs, recollections, and official papers of US officers and soldiers serving in the Korean War, incl Generals Edward Almond, George Barth Bruce Clarke, Matthew Ridgway, and Arthur Trudeau.

ALMONDS, CALIFORNIA

CA —UNIVERSITY OF CALIFORNIA, DAVIS, Shields Library, Dept of Special Collections, Davis, 95616. Donald Kunitz, Head; C Danial Elliott, Asst Head
Holdings: Cat Mss Pix
Notes: The California Promotional Collection incl material relating to the California Almond Growers' Exchange.

ALPHABETS

VA —UNIVERSITY OF VIRGINIA, Alderman Library, Rare Book Dept, Charlottesville, 22901. Julius P Barclay, Cur
Holdings: Vols (6500) // Mss
Notes: The Oscar Ogg Collection of Book Arts covers calligraphy, letterforms, typography, printing, and graphic arts. Contains early writing books and printed works, as well as modern manuals and other works on printing, publishing, and promotion through graphic arts. The Dept also has the Edward L Stone Collection of Printing Specimens, 3000 items. Contains materials tracing the history of printing, inks, binding styles and materials, types. Also the Tompkins Collection (2000 vols), and the Stevens Watts collection (900 vols).

ALPINE CLUB, AMERICAN

WA —MOUNTAINEERS INC, Library, 300 3rd Ave West, Seattle, 98119. Verna M Ness, Library Cur
Holdings: Vols (3000) Cat
Notes: Collection incl some 19th century vols of Alpine information, incl the first issue of *The Alpine Journal* (1863). Bound serials of many important American climbing publications. Small sub-collections for American Alpine Club members and for The Mountaineer Foundation, the latter on conservation and ecology. In the main collection backpacking, skiing and natural history are also represented.

ALPINE CLUB OF CANADA

AB —ALPINE CLUB OF CANADA LIBRARY, Archives of the Canadian Rockies, Box 160, Banff, T0L 0C0, Can. E J Hart, Head Archivist
Holdings: Vols (2429) Cat Mss Maps Pix Slides Audiotapes
Budget: ($1000)
Notes: The Archives of the Canadian Rockies is the custodian of the library and archival collection of the Alpine Club of Canada. The materials cover mountaineering technique and attempts worldwide, incl the Alps, Rockies, Himalayas, Andes, etc. Subject areas incl history, personal records, mountain rescue and medicine, alpine flora and fauna, guide books, manuals and handbooks. A large part of the archival collection is concentrated on the Canadian Rocky Mountains, as the headquarters of The Alpine Club of Canada is in Banff, Alberta.

ALSCHULER, SAMUEL

IL —ILLINOIS STATE HISTORICAL SOCIETY, Library, Old State Capitol, Springfield, 62706. Roger D Bridges, Head Librn
Notes: His papers; about 3000 items.

ALSOP, JOSEPH

DC —LIBRARY OF CONGRESS, Manuscript Division, Washington, 20540. John C Broderick, Chief
Notes: Papers of the journalist, Joseph Alsop.

ALSOP, STEWART

MA —BOSTON UNIVERSITY, Mugar Memorial Library, Special Collections Dept, 771 Commonwealth Ave, Boston, 02215. Howard B Gotlieb, Dir
Holdings: Cat Mss
Notes: Mss, correspondence, etc collected in depth; incl publications by or about.

ALSTON, THEODOSIA BURR

NJ —AARON BURR ASSOCIATION LIBRARY, RD 1, RT 33, Box 429, Hightstown-Freehold Rd, Hightstown, 08520. Samuel E Burr, Jr, Librn
Holdings: Vols 100 Cat Pix Microforms
Notes: Materials concerning Col Aaron Burr, his life, his career and members of his immediate family. Incl some materials on his daughter, Mrs Theodosia Burr Alston, Jefferson Davis and Mrs Jefferson Davis (Varina Howell Davis). Open to the public by appointment only.

ALTERNATE ENERGY SOURCES see Renewable Energy Sources

ALTERNATIVE ENERGY SOURCES see Renewable Energy Sources

ALTERNATE FUELS

MI —US ENVIRONMENTAL PROTECTION AGENCY, Motor Vehicle

ALTERNATE FUELS (cont.)

Emission Laboratory Library, 2565 Plymouth Rd, Ann Arbor, 48105. Debra Talsma, Librn
Holdings: // Uncat Microforms
Notes: No separate catalog. Collection described in: US EPA, Library System Branch, *Guide to EPA Libraries,* July, 1977. Collection includes 9500 technical reports on air pollution from mobile sources (especially automobiles); air pollution legislation (350 vols); fuel economy and conservation (800 technical reports); automobile engineering (300 vols); emission control technology for mobile source (8000 reports and papers); use of methanol and other alternative fuels in motor vehicles (600 technical reports).

ALTERNATIVE LIFESTYLES

CT —UNIVERSITY OF CONNECTICUT, Library, Storrs, 06268. Ellen Embardo, Cur Special Collections
Holdings: Cat
Notes: Alternative Press Collection. Primarily periodicals and newspapers from the 1960s to today of an alternative or underground nature. Books and pamphlets are incl, representing both the left and the right-wing viewpoints. A catalog is available. Also have archives of the First Casualty Press, which was deeply involved with Vietnam veterans' experiences in Vietnam.

ALTERNATIVE PRESS

CA —UNIVERSITY OF CALIFORNIA, LOS ANGELES, Research Library, Public Affairs Service, 405 Hilgard Ave, Los Angeles, 90024. Edward Shreeves, Chairman, Bibliographers Group; Eugenia Eaton, Head, Public Affairs Service
Holdings: Uncat
Notes: Current non-governmental English-language pamphlets (192,819), broadsides, leaflets and other ephemera on public affairs, from 1960, representing a wide spectrum of political and social opinions. Social welfare and industrial relations are strong fields. Legal loose-leaf labor services, such as the *Daily Labor Report,* the *Government Employee Relations Report* and the *Labor Relations Reporter,* as well as labor pamphlets from the mid-1940s, reflect a long-standing responsibility to the University's Institute of Industrial Relations.

CA —UNIVERSITY OF CALIFORNIA, LOS ANGELES, Research Library, Social Sciences Collection, 405 Hilgard Ave, Los Angeles, 90024. Edward Shreeves, Chairman, Bibliographers Group; Oscar L Sims, Social Sciences Bibliographer
Notes: A collection of over 200 underground newspapers on 26 reels of microfilm. Among the titles included are: *The Tribe, The Berkeley Barb, New York Roach, Rat,* and *Win.*

CT —UNIVERSITY OF CONNECTICUT, Library, Storrs, 06268. Ellen Embardo, Cur Special Collections
Holdings: Cat
Notes: Alternative Press Collection. Primarily periodicals and newspapers from the 1960s to today of an alternative or underground nature. Books and pamphlets are incl, representing both the left and the right-wing viewpoints. A catalog is available. Also have archives of the First Casualty Press, which was deeply involved with Vietnam veterans' experiences in Vietnam, as well as the Fat Liberation Movement.

DC —LIBRARY OF CONGRESS, Serial and Government Publications Division, Washington, 20540.
Notes: The Alternative Press Collection contains American newspaper-format publications issued outside the publishing mainstream since the mid-1960s. Approx 350 titles from 26 states.

IL —NORTHWESTERN UNIVERSITY, Library, Special Collections Dept, 1937 Sheridan Rd, Evanston, 60201. R Russell Maylone, Cur
Holdings: Vols 1000 Cat
Notes: Very large collection of original journals from the 1960s and 1970s, mostly American and Canadian, but also several English and French. Also high school papers. Subjects incl left-wing politics, American Indian ecology, drug culture, anti-war and environmental issues. Women's collection of serial holdings largest in country. All hard copy with exception of some of the Women's collection.

MI —MICHIGAN STATE UNIVERSITY, Libraries, Special Collections Div, East Lansing, 48824. Jannette Fiore, Librn
Holdings: Cat
Notes: Approximately 80 current subscriptions, and a sample collection of 1200 titles, 1965 to present.

MI —OAKLAND UNIVERSITY, Kresge Library, Rochester, 48063. Suzanne O Frankie, Dean; Elizabeth Titus, Special Collections Librn
Holdings: Uncat Microforms
Notes: Underground newspapers predominantly of Michigan and the Midwest; 750 titles. Some indexed in *Underground Newspaper Microfilm* Collection, by Bell and Howell or the *Alternative Press Index.*

NY —GRADUATE CENTER OF THE CITY UNIVERSITY OF NEW YORK, William H and Gwynne K Crouse Library for Publishing Arts, 33 W 42 St, New York, 10036. Alfred H Lane, Dir
Notes: Recently established and still growing, but intended to become the authoritative source of materials in the field, of particular value in research about the publishing industry. Open to staff members of publishing houses, students, scholars, authors, printers, and booksellers. Primarily 20th century materials, and particularly useful for research on technical, financial, and historical matters. Much on the history of individual houses, economics of authorship; marketing and distribution of books; etc.

PA —TEMPLE UNIVERSITY LIBRARIES, Special Collections Dept, Contemporary Culture Collection, Philadelphia, 19122. Patricia J Case, Cur
Notes: The Contemporary Culture Collection. See full entry under US-Social Life and Customs.

RI —BROWN UNIVERSITY, John Hay Library, Harris Collection, Prospect St, Providence, 02912. Rosemary L Cullen, Cur
Holdings: Vols (200,000) Cat Mss Pix Phonorecords Microforms
Budget: ($15,000)
Notes: The Harris Collection of American Poetry and Plays is principally composed of American and Canadian poetry and plays, 17th century-date. Extensive holdings in songsters, gift books and annuals, hymnals, pageants, broadside verse, carriers' addresses, women poets, juvenile poetry, (incl Mother Goose and *The Night Before* Christmas), sheet music with lyrics, small press publications, fine printing, black poets, "little magazines," Yiddish-American literature. All movements or schools of American poetry are represented. Incl first editions of most American poets and playwrights, notably Whitman, Poe, Wallace Stevens, Eugene O'Neill, Edward Albee, Ezra Pound, T S Eliot, William Carlos Williams, Amy Lowell, Phyllis Wheatley, Robert Frost, Allen Ginsberg, Bliss Carman, and Stephen Foster sheet music. Also incl the Saunders Walt Whitman Collection (1300 vols); the LangdonCollection of Pageants (250 vols); the Asa Cushman Collection of plays in ms and prompt copies; the MacDougall Collection of Psalters and Hymnals; 4000 plays issued by Walter H Baker Co, Boston (1890-1957); the Vaxer Collection of Yiddish Poetry, Plays and Music (1700 vols). Collections incl 200,000 vols, 30,000 broadsides, 55,000 mss, 170,000 pieces of sheet music, 450 phonorecords, and 375 microfilm reels. See *Dictionary Catalog of the Harris Collection of American Poetry and Plays* (Boston: G K Hall, 1972), 13 vols; *Supplement* (1977), 3 vols. See also, *American Poetry,* 1609-1900, *A Collection on Microfilm, Segment I* (1609-1820); *Segment II* (1821-1850); *Segment III* (1851-1870) (Woodbridge, Conn: Research Publications). Separate catalog.

WI —STATE HISTORICAL SOCIETY OF WISCONSIN, Library, Newspaper and Periodicals Section, 816 State St, Madison, 53706. James P Danky, Librn
Holdings: Cat Microforms
Notes: Incl largest collection (over 4000) of US and Canadian underground or alternative publications in North America. Only postive microfilm circulates on ILL. Holdings described in James Danky's *Undergrounds: A Union List of Alternative Periodicals in Libraries of the United States and Canada* (1974).

WI —UNIVERSITY OF WISCONSIN, MADISON, Cooperative Children's Book Center, Helen C White Hall, Rm 4290, 600 N Park St, Madison, 537G6. Ginny Moore Kruse, Dir
Holdings: Vols (25,000) Cat
Notes: Cooperative Children's Book Center collections incl most US trade books published for children in last 24 months; first editions of recommended US children's trade books published since 1965; over 400 alternative press books published for children in US and Canada since 1970; children's books about Wisconsin and by Wisconsin authors and illustrators; representative 19th and early 20th century American children's books; 19th century children's periodicals; first and significant editions of Newbury and Caldecott Medal books; historical and contemporary toybooks; 75 vols of Mother Goose published since 1828; 160 vols of Thorton Burgess books, many first editions; ms and original artwork for Ellen Raskin's *The Westing Game* and *The Mysterious Disappearance of Leon (I Mean Noel);* juvenile mass market and traderomance fiction.

BC —SIMON FRASER UNIVERSITY, Library, Burnaby, V5A 1S6, Can. Percilla Groves, Special Collections Librn
Holdings: Vols (12,000) Cat Mss Tapes
Notes: This collection concentrates on avant-garde American poetry since World War II. Incl some Canadian poetry (particularly West Coast poets), some British and certain of the International Concrete school. It particularly features the Black Mountain and San Francisco schools and those American and Canadian poets influenced by them. There is a relatively complete collection of works by Ezra Pound (qv), William Carlos Williams, Charles Olson, Gertrude Stein and Louis Zukofsky together with considerable criticism on these authors. Also incl certain underground newspapers and 1600 periodical titles.

NS —DALHOUSIE UNIVERSITY LIBRARY, Halifax, B3H 4H8, Can.
Holdings: Vols 10,000 Cat
Notes: Extensive collection of Canadian small press publications with special strengths in poetry, drama, little magazines, poetry broadsides, and Atlantic Canada creative writing. Good holdings in various early Canadian literary periodicals and early Canadian small publishers, but main focus from 1970 to present.

ALTERNATIVE THEATRE

CA —UNIVERSITY OF CALIFORNIA, DAVIS, Shields Library, Dept of Special Collections, Davis, 95616. Donald Kunitz, Head; C Danial Elliott, Asst Head
Holdings: Vols (28,000) Mss Pix Slides Audiotapes Videotapes 16mm Films
Notes: Production records of American and foreign alternative theatre groups incl mss, financial and legal records, photographs, films, programs and correspondence. Incl are the Living Theatre, Bread and Puppet Theatre, San Francisco Mime Troupe, Firehouse Theatre, Open Theatre, Le Theatre Euh, Theatre Laboratoire Vicinal, etc. Files of the Universal Movement Theatre Repertory, a booking agency in New York, provide breadth to these holdings. 28, 000 items. Described in: Whalon, Marion K, "Avant-Garde and Radical Theater Holdings," *Broadside,* vol 3, no 3 (winter 1976).

ALUCONIDAE see Owls

ALUMINUM

PA —FRANKLIN INSTITUTE LIBRARY, 20 & The Parkway, Philadelphia, 19103. Miriam Padusis, Dir; Charles Wilt, Readers Servs Librn
Holdings: Vols (300,000) Cat Maps Pix Microforms

ON —ALCAN INTERNATIONAL LIMITED, Research Centre, PO Box 8400, Kingston, K7L 4Z4, Can. E M Vanags, Tech Information Centre
Holdings: Vols 20,000 Cat Mss Maps Pix Slides Microforms Films
Notes: Plus 250,000 documents.

ALUMINUM INDUSTRY AND TRADE

OH —ALCAN ALUMINUM CORP, Library, 100 Erieview Plaza, Cleveland, 44114. Winifred B Bowes, Librn
Holdings: Vols 3000 Cat

VA —REYNOLDS METALS COMPANY, Executive Office Library, 6601 W Broad St, Richmond, 23261. Kathie P Anderson, Corporate Librn
Holdings: Vols 10,000 Cat
Notes: Covers US and international aluminum industry and trade.

ALUMNI RELATIONS

DC —COUNCIL FOR ADVANCEMENT & SUPPORT OF EDUCATION, Reference Center, Eleven Dupont Circle NW, Suite 400, Washington, 20036. Cynthia Snyder, Dir
Holdings: Vols (600) Cat Mss Audiotapes Microforms
Notes: A membership service containing information in educational fund raising, institutional relations, government relations, alumni administration, publications, and management techniques for higher education and independent schools. Collection, in addition, contains mss, microfiches, and tapes. Succeeds the American Alumni Council, dissolved in 1974.

NY —CORNELL UNIVERSITY LIBRARIES, Collection of Regional History, Dept of Manuscripts and Univ Archives, Ithaca, 14853.
Notes: Incl papers, 1882-1921; Associate Alumni Papers (1882-1912), and Eastern New York Alumni Association Record Books (1884-1921).

ALVERSON, CHARLES

MA —BOSTON UNIVERSITY, Mugar Memorial Library, Special Collections Dept, 771 Commonwealth Ave, Boston, 02215. Howard B Gotlieb, Dir
Holdings: Cat Mss

ALZHEIMER'S DISEASE see Presenile Dementia

AMADIS OF GAUL

OH —CLEVELAND PUBLIC LIBRARY, Fine Arts and Special Collections Department, 325 Superior Ave, Cleveland, 44114. Alice N Loranth, Head
Holdings: Vols (3000) Cat Mss
Notes: Part of the Romances Collection, which incl critical studies, and early printed editions. The Arthurian and Charlemagne cycles, the Nibelungenlied and other Germanic titles, Amadis de Gaula and his numerous progeny, Alexander the Great, Barlaam and Joasaph, and the Seven Wise Masters of Rome are some of the strengths of the collection. Material in the Dewey/Brett Collection is classified by related cycles and their versions in various languages.

AMARDIC LANGUAGE see Elamite Language

AMALGAMATED CLOTHING AND TEXTILE WORKERS UNION

NY —AMALGAMATED CLOTHING & TEXTILE WORKERS UNION, Research Dept Library, 15 Union Sq, New York, 10003. Mohammad Homayon Pour, Librn
Notes: Papers and other material by or about Sidney Hillman, President of the Amalgamated Clothing Workers of America. Incl ms collection.

AMATEUR HOUR (RADIO PROGRAM)

DC —LIBRARY OF CONGRESS, Motion Pictures, Broadcasting and Recorded Sound Div, Washington, 20540.
Notes: The *Amateur Hour* Collection consists of original radio recordings of the Major Bowes series (1935-1944) and disc, tape, and television coverage of the Ted Mack series (1948-1968). Incl applications to appear on the program and accompanying correspondence and news clippings.

AMATEUR HOUR (TELEVISION PROGRAM)

DC —LIBRARY OF CONGRESS, Motion Pictures, Broadcasting and Recorded Sound Div, Washington, 20540.
Notes: The *Amateur Hour* Collection consists of original radio recordings of the Major Bowes series (1935-1944) and disc, tape, and television coverage of the Ted Mack series (1948-1968). Incl applications to appear on the program and accompanying correspondence and news clippings.

AMATEUR NEWSPAPERS see Newspapers, Amateur

AMATEUR SPORTS

CA —UNIVERSITY OF THE PACIFIC, Holt-Atherton Pacific Center for Western Studies, Stockton, 95211. Hiram L Davis, Dir of Libraries
Holdings: Cat Mss
Notes: Primarily correspondence and newspaper clippings from the papers of Amos Alonzo Stagg, football coach and athletic director at the University of Chicago and later at the College of the Pacific. 1 linear ft (2 document boxes).

IL —UNIVERSITY OF ILLINOIS, URBANA/CHAMPAIGN, Library, University Archives, 19 Library, 1408 W Gregory Drive, Urbana, 61801. Maynard Brichford, University Archivist
Holdings: Vols (1663) // Cat Mss Pix
Notes: The Avery Brundage Collection. Incl his papers and material on amateur athletics. Olympic games, and sports. Published guide is available: *Avery Brundage Collection*, 1908-1975 (Cologne: Karl Hofmann Schorndorf, 1977). 517,000 ms pieces. There is also a collection on Olympic sports and other aspects of sports kept in the Brundage Room.

AMAUROSIS see Blindness

AMAZING (MAGAZINE)

CA —CALIFORNIA STATE UNIVERSITY, FULLERTON, Library, Box 4150, Fullerton, 92634. Linda Herman, Special Collections Librn
Notes: A major collection of science fiction magazines dating from the 1930s. Incl a complete run from 1926 to 1940 of *Amazing*, the first major science fiction magazine. Also incl are short-span publications and runs of British s/f publications.

AMBLER, ERIC

MA —BOSTON UNIVERSITY, Mugar Memorial Library, Special Collections Dept, 771 Commonwealth Ave, Boston, 02215. Howard B Gotlieb, Dir
Holdings: Cat Mss

AMBROTYPES

KY —UNIVERSITY OF LOUISVILLE, Ekstrom Library, Photographic Archives, Louisville, 40292. J C Anderson, Cur; David G Horvath, Asst Cur
Holdings: Vols (750,000) Cat Pix Slides
Budget: ($60,000)
Notes: Photographs in three broad areas: works of outstanding photographers; examples of major developments in the art and technology of photography; photographs important as sociological, historical, or behavioral documents. Other collections described in unpublished brochure. Print duplication service.

AMBULANCE DRILL see First Aid

AMBULANCES

VA —US ARMY TRANSPORTATION MUSEUM, Library, Bldg 300, Fort Eustis, 23604. Dennis P Mroczkowski, Museum Cur
Holdings: Vols (1254) Uncat Maps Pix 16mm Films
Budget: ($150)
Notes: Mainly US Army transportation from WW II on.

AMBULATORY CARE see Hospitals—Outpatient Services

AMERICA (MAGAZINE)

DC —GEORGETOWN UNIVERSITY, Library, Special Collections Div, 37 & O Sts NW, Washington, 20057. George M Barringer, Special Collections Librn; Nicholas B Sheetz, Mss Librn
Holdings: Vols (500) Cat Mss Maps Pix Slides
Notes: Includes the archives of Woodstock College (1866-); seminary of the Maryland Province, on deposit; the archives (1640-) of the Maryland Province of the Society of Jesus, on deposit; personal papers of Revs John LaFarge, SJ, Wilfrid Parsons, SJ, Edmund A Walsh, SJ, among others. In the Woodstock archives are included papers of Revs John Courtney Murray, SJ, and Gustave Weigel, SJ. Also present are editorial files (1900-1920, incomplete later) of *America* magazine.

AMERICA—DISCOVERY AND EXPLORATION

CT —YALE UNIVERSITY, Box 1603A, Yale Station, New Haven, 06520.
Holdings: Cat Mss Maps

DC —LIBRARY OF CONGRESS, Rare Book & Special Collections Div, Washington, 20540. William Matheson, Chief
Notes: John Boyd Thacher Collection of Books, Pamphlets, Broadsides, and Manuscripts, which incl Early Americana and works regarding Christopher Columbus. The Henry Harrisse Collection of 213 volumes, cataloged, comprises works and bibliographies relating to Americana, incl the author's own interleaved and profusely annotated copies of his writings on the Columbus period, together with volumes containing his correspondence with bibliographers and collectors of the latter part of the 19th century.
See also entry under Incunabula

IL —NEWBERRY LIBRARY, 60 W Walton St, Chicago, 60610. Diana Haskell, Cur of Modern Mss
Holdings: Cat Mss Maps
Notes: The Ayer Collection.

KS —UNIVERSITY OF KANSAS, Kenneth Spencer Research Library, Special Collections Dept, Lawrence, 66045. Alexandra Mason, Librn
Holdings: Vols 400 Cat Maps
Notes: Largely 17th-18th century. Noncirculating.

MD —JOHNS HOPKINS UNIVERSITY, Milton S Eisenhower Library, Charles & 34 Sts, Baltimore, 21218. Ann S Gwyn, Assistant Dir for Special Collections
Holdings: Vols Cat
Notes: Specially strong in the works of Henry Harrisse. 83 titles, some rare, belonged to the author.

MI —UNIVERSITY OF MICHIGAN, William L Clements Library, Ann Arbor, 48109.

AMERICA—DISCOVERY AND EXPLORATION (cont.)

John C Dann, Dir
Notes: The William L. Clements Library of Americana is a non-circulating rare book library of original source material, printed and manuscript, dealing with America, from the discovery period into the late nineteenth century. The collection includes approximately 55,000 books and pamphlets, 550 linear feet of manuscripts, 4,100 volumes of newspapers, 36,000 maps, 40,000 pieces of sheet music, and 1,000 prints. The collection is strongest for the period of the American Revolution, and includes the papers of Thomas Gage, Sir Henry Clinton, and the Earl of Shelburne. Other areas of strength include antislavery, cartography and geography, discovery and exploration, American Indians, The Civil War, tune-books, sermons and orations, and the War of 1812. There are selective research collections dealing with Christopher Columbus, Thomas Paine, Benjamin Franklin, George Washington, Thomas Jefferson, and the Federalist Papers. Publications describing the collections of the library are: Author/Title catalog of Americana 1493-1860 in the William L. Clements Library... 7 volumes, Boston, G. K. Hall, 1970; Guide to the manuscript collections of the William L. Clements Library, by Arlene P. Shy 3d edition, Boston, G. K. Hall, 1978; Guide to the manuscript maps in the William L. Clements Library, compiled by Christian Burn, Ann Arbor, U. of Michigan, 1959; and Research catalog of maps of America, to 1860 in the William L. Clements Library...,edited by Douglas W. Marshall, 4 volumes, Boston, G. K. Hall, 1972.

MN —MINNEAPOLIS PUBLIC LIBRARY & INFORMATION CENTER, 300 Nicollet Mall, Minneapolis, 55401. Richard J Hofstad, Athenaeum Librn
Holdings: Vols (600) Cat Maps
Notes: Incl "travel." Pre-Civil War.

MN —UNIVERSITY OF MINNESOTA, James Ford Bell Library, 309 19th Ave S, Minneapolis, 55455. John Parker, Cur
Holdings: Vols (11,000) Cat Mss Maps
Notes: Collection of original materials relating to European expansion, 1400-1800.

NY —NEW YORK STATE LIBRARY, State Education Bldg Annex, Washington Ave, Albany, 12224.
Holdings: Cat Maps
Notes: Important collection of printed and manuscript material on the early explorations in the Western hemisphere. Incl maps.

NY —CORNELL UNIVERSITY LIBRARIES, John M Olin Library, Fiske Icelandic Collection, Ithaca, 14853. Louis A Pitschmann, Librn
Holdings: Vols (34,000) Cat Mss Maps Pix Microforms
Budget: ($3000)
Notes: Collection aims at comprehensive coverage of Iceland in all aspects with major emphasis on the literature and language (both old and modern). Such subjects as runology, Scandinavian and Germanic mythology, early Norwegian history and history of the Viking period and of the Norse explorations of Greenland and North America are also well represented. For printed catalogs of the Collection's holdings see Downs 3608, 3609. Records for approximately 40 percent of the collection have been entered into OCLC and RLIN.

NY —EXPLORERS CLUB, James B Ford Memorial Library, 46 E 70 St, New York, 10021. Janet Baldwin, Librn
Holdings: Vols (24,000) Cat Maps
Notes: Additions to the collection depend upon gifts. Access by appointment only.

NY —NEW YORK PUBLIC LIBRARY, Research Libraries, General Research Division, Fifth Ave & 42 St, New York, 10018. Rodney Phillips, Chief
Holdings: Vols (2,225,000) Cat Maps Pix Microforms
Budget: ($775,718)

PA —FREE LIBRARY OF PHILADELPHIA, Rare Book Dept, Logan Sq, Philadelphia, 19103. Marie E Korey, Rare Book Librn
Holdings: Vols (281) Cat
Notes: The William M Elkins Collection, with 150 additions, of rare and early printed books relating to the voyages of discovery of America.

PA —UNIVERSITY OF PITTSBURGH, Darlington Memorial Library, Special Collections, 601 Cathedral of Learning, Pittsburgh, 15260. Dennis Lambert, Darlington Librn
Holdings: Vols (17,000) Cat Mss Maps Pix
Notes: The Darlington Collection is especially rich in American history of the colonial period, the French and Indian War, the Revolution, and the War of 1812 with geographical emphasis on Western Pennsylvania and Ohio Valley history to 1870 and on Pittsburgh history to 1900. Indian treaties, captivity accounts, US and Pennsylvania travel and description, and early American fiction and prose are represented. A partial guide to the Darlington Manuscript Collections is available by writing for *Darlington Memorial Library: A Descriptive Checklist of its Manuscript Collections,* University of Pittsburgh Bibliographic Series 5, 1969. Noncirculating.

RI —BROWN UNIVERSITY, John Carter Brown Library, Providence, 02912. Norman Fiering, Librn; Everett C Wilkie Jr, Bibliographer; Susan Danforth, Cur Maps & Prints
Holdings: Vols 40,000 Cat Mss Maps Pix
Notes: History of the Americas during the Colonial Period. See also *The John Carter Brown Library Catalogues; Opportunities for Research in the John Carter Brown Library; Reprint of the John Carter Brown Library Annual Reports and Index-1901-1966.*

TX —HARDIN-SIMMONS UNIVERSITY, Richardson Library, Abilene, 79601. Joe F Dahlstrom, Dir
Holdings: Vols (10,000) Cat Mss Maps Pix Microforms
Notes: Special collection name is Richardson Research Center, named in honor of Dr Rupert N Richardson. Collect in the areas of his own research interests, especially that portion of the US that was once a part of Mexico. Emphases on the history of ranching, railroads, discovery and exploration, Texas county histories, etc. Incl 350 items printed and/or designed by El Paso printer Cart Hertzog; the Judge R C Crane collection of Texana and a similar collection of Louise Kelley's; and the Research Publication's Western Americana collection (microfilm).

TX —UNIVERSITY OF TEXAS, ARLINGTON, Library, PO Box 19497, Arlington, 76019. Chas Colley, Dir Special Collections
Holdings: Uncat Maps Slides
Notes: The collection focuses on the history of cartography in general, specializing in the discovery and exploration of North America, with special emphasis on Texas and the American West. The collection consists of thousands of rare maps and atlases dating from 1493, coupled with an extensive collection of related reference works and primary works on exploration and discovery.

TX —UNIVERSITY OF TEXAS LIBRARIES, Nettie Lee Benson Latin American Collection, Sid Richardson Hall 1.109, Austin, 78712. Laura Gutierrez-Witt, Head Librn
Holdings: Vols (450,000) Cat Mss Maps Pix Phonorecords Filmstrips Microforms
See also entry under Latin America.

ON —UNIVERSITY OF GUELPH, McLaughlin Library, Guelph, N1G 2W1, Can. Margaret Beckman, Head Librn; David Hull, Sciences Librn
Holdings: Vols 2000 Cat Maps Phonorecords Audiotapes Videotapes 16mm Films Microforms
Notes: Monographs. Early travel and exploration, emphasis on North America. *See also* entry under Canada - Description and Travel; Canada - History

ON —METROPOLITAN TORONTO LIBRARY, History Dept, 789 Yonge St, Toronto, M4W 2G8, Can. Michael Pearson, Head
Holdings: Vols (2500) Cat
Notes: The collection includes reports, diaries and personal narratives of travels and voyages of exploration and discovery from the Renaissance to the present day. Areas of emphasis are the exploration of the interior of North America, early oceanic voyages of discovery and accounts of travellers to Russia. The collection also includes a number of early editions, standard collected works such as the publications of the Hakluyt Society, accounts of shipwrecks as well as a representative collection of guide books from the 18th century to the present.

AMERICA FIRST COMMITTEE

CA —HOOVER INSTITUTION ON WAR, REVOLUTION & PEACE, Stanford University, Stanford, 94305. Milorad M Drachkovitch, Archivist
Holdings: Mss
Notes: Records of the America First Committee, 1940-1941. Correspondence of General Robert F Wood, chairman, and R Douglas Stuart, Jr, national director, contributors' correspondence, letters of criticism, research files, State chapter records, speakers bureau files, financial ledgers, and newspaper clippings, relating to the work of the America First Committee to influence US foreign policy. 205 ft. Unpublished register is available in repository.

AMERICAN ALMANACS see Almanacs, American

AMERICAN ALPINE CLUB see Alpine Club, American

AMERICAN AND FOREIGN ANTISLAVERY SOCIETY

LA —AMISTAD RESEARCH CENTER, 400 Esplanade Ave, New Orleans, 70116. Clifton H Johnson, Exec Dir; Florence E Borders, Senior Archivist
Budget: ($315,000)
Notes: Originally established at Fisk University, in Nashville, by the American Missionary Association (AMA), this research center on Black American History consists of mss, photographs, clippings, books, pamphlets, taped speeches and interviews; also, the papers of such leaders as W E B DuBois, Countee Cullen, and Mary McLeod Bethune. Also materials on other American minorities, such as Native Americans, Asian Americans, Hispanics, etc.

AMERICAN ARBITRATION ASSOCIATION

IA —UNIVERSITY OF IOWA, University Libraries, Iowa City, 52242. Robert A McCown, Mss Librn
Holdings: Mss
Notes: Arbitration awards, 1963-1971. 50 ft.

AMERICAN ARCHIVES OF THE FACTUAL FILM

IA —IOWA STATE UNIVERSITY, Library, Dept of Special Collections, Ames, 50011.

AMERICAN ARCHIVES OF THE FACTUAL FILM (cont.)

Stanley M Yates, Head
Holdings: Mss Audiotapes 16mm Films Filmstrips
Notes: Contains over 7000 films and papers and records of individuals and organizations active in the field of the nontheatrical film. This is the first serious attempt by a major institution to collect materials relating to the factual film in the US and abroad.

AMERICAN ART see Art, American

AMERICAN ART THERAPY ASSOCIATION

KS —MENNINGER FOUNDATION, Archives, 5600 W Sixth St, Box 829, Topeka, 66601. Alice Brand, Librn; Mark West, Archivist
Notes: 9 boxes, 1968-date. Incl committee minutes, correspondence, annual reports, newsletters and miscellaneous materials.

AMERICAN ARTISTS see Artists, American

AMERICAN ASSOCIATION FOR HEALTH, PHYSICAL EDUCATION AND RECREATION

NY —NEW YORK PUBLIC LIBRARY, Performing Arts Research Center, Dance Collection, 111 Amsterdam Ave, New York, 10023. Genevieve Oswald, Cur
Budget: ($9,280)
Notes: Records of the American Association for Health, Physical Education and Recreation, 1931-1968. Primarily financial and administrative files and reports.

AMERICAN ASSOCIATION FOR LABOR LEGISLATION

MI —MICHIGAN STATE UNIVERSITY, Labor and Industrial Relations Library, East Lansing, 48824. Martha Jane Soltow, Librn
Holdings: Cat Microforms
Notes: This material is composed primarily of special collections of papers on microfilm or microfiche.

AMERICAN ASSOCIATION FOR THE HISTORY OF NURSING

MA —BOSTON UNIVERSITY, Mugar Memorial Library, Special Collections Dept, 771 Commonwealth Ave, Boston, 02215. Howard B Gotlieb, Dir
Holdings: Cat Mss Records

AMERICAN ASSOCIATION OF PHYSICS TEACHERS

NY —AMERICAN INSTITUTE OF PHYSICS, Center for the History of Physics, Niels Bohr Library, 335 E 45 St, New York, 10017. John Aubry, Librn
Notes: Papers and records.

AMERICAN ASSOCIATION OF UNIVERSITY PROFESSORS (AAUP)

IA —IOWA STATE UNIVERSITY, Library, Dept of Special Collections, Ames, 50011. Stanley M Yates, Head
Notes: The L H Pammel papers. An extensive and important file of personal correspondence and other documents. He was instrumental in conservation movements, founder of the American Association of University Professors. Best known as the father of Iowa State Park System.

NY —CORNELL UNIVERSITY LIBRARIES, Collection of Regional History, Dept of Manuscripts and Univ Archives, Ithaca, 14853.
Notes: Incl records, 1913-18; 3 reels, microfilm, correspondence, pamphlets, clippings, and other printed matter.

AMERICAN ASSOCIATION OF UNIVERSITY WOMEN

AZ —NORTHERN ARIZONA UNIVERSITY, Special Collection Library, CU Box 6022, Flagstaff, 86011. Peter M Whiteley, Coordr/Archivist; William Mullane, Librn
Notes: Collection of the Flagstaff, Ariz, branch of AAUW, incl correspondence, subject files, membership lists, 1938-1963.

TX —TEXAS WOMAN'S UNIVERSITY, Bralley Memorial Library, Box 23715, TWU Sta, Denton, 76204. Metta Nicewarner, Spec Collections Libn
Holdings: Uncat Mss Pix
Notes: TWU is the official repository of AAUW archives for the state of Texas. Includes correspondenc, legal documents, yearbooks, financial documents, minutes and reports.

AMERICAN ASTRONOMICAL SOCIETY

NY —AMERICAN INSTITUTE OF PHYSICS, Center for the History of Physics, Niels Bohr Library, 335 E 45 St, New York, 10017. John Aubry, Librn
Notes: Papers and records.

AMERICAN AUTHORS see Authors, American

AMERICAN BALLADS AND SONGS

CT —YALE UNIVERSITY, Beincke Rare Book & Manuscript Library, Western Americana Collection, Wall & High St, New Haven, 06520. George Miles, Cur
Holdings: Cat
Notes: Incl California broadside ballads of the 19th century.

PA —UNIVERSITY OF PITTSBURGH, Stephen Foster Memorial, Foster Hall Collection, Pittsburgh, 15260. Deane L Root, Cur
Holdings: Vols (1000) Cat Mss Pix Phonorecords VF //
Budget: ($50,000)
Notes: More than 10,000 separate items: original mss and letters; first editions, and early modern editions of Foster's music; personal possessions of the composer; books; magazine and newspaper articles; pictures and portraits; phonograph records; broadsides; and other material.

RI —BROWN UNIVERSITY, John Hay Library, Harris Collection, Prospect St, Providence, 02912. Rosemary L Cullen, Cur
Holdings: Vols (200,000) Cat Mss Phonorecords Microforms
Budget: ($15,000)
Notes: The Harris Collection of American Poetry and Plays is principally composed of American and Canadian poetry and plays, 17th century-date. Extensive holdings in songsters, gift books and annuals, hymnals, pageants, broadside verse, carriers' addresses, women poets, juvenile poetry, (incl Mother Goose and *The Night Before* Christmas), sheet music with lyrics, small press publications, fine printing, black poets, "little magazines," Yiddish-American literature. All movements or schools of American poetry are represented. Incl first editions of most American poets and playwrights, notably Whitman, Poe, Wallace Stevens, Eugene O'Neill, Edward Albee, Ezra Pound, T S Eliot, William Carlos Williams, Amy Lowell, Phyllis Wheatley, Robert Frost, Allen Ginsberg, Bliss Carman, and Stephen Foster sheet music. Also incl the Saunders Walt Whitman Collection (1300 vols); the LangdonCollection of Pageants (250 vols); the Asa Cushman Collection of plays in ms and prompt copies; the MacDougall Collection of Psalters and Hymnals; 4000 plays issued by Walter H Baker Co, Boston (1890-1957); the Vaxer Collection of Yiddish Poetry, Plays and Music (1700 vols). Collections incl 200,000 vols, 30,000 broadsides, 55,000 mss, 170,000 pieces of sheet music, 450 phonorecords, and 375 microfilm reels. See *Dictionary Catalog of the Harris Collection of American Poetry and Plays* (Boston: G K Hall, 1972), 13 vols; *Supplement* (1977), 3 vols. See also, *American Poetry,* 1609-1900, *A Collection on Microfilm, Segment I* (1609-1820); *Segment II* (1821-1850); *Segment III* (1851-1870) (Woodbridge, Conn: Research Publications). Separate catalog.

RI —BROWN UNIVERSITY, John Hay Library, 20 Prospect St, Providence, 02912. Mary T Russo, Cur of Broadsides
Notes: Within this collection of poetry broadsides are numerous examples of early American ballads. Another collection of 5000 separate and 2000 bound slip sheets or slip ballads published from 1830 to 1870, record all aspects of everyday life and illustrate the manner in which people responded to political, military, social and economic events. Civil War ballads are included. Retrospective pieces are added annually. Partial catalog.

AMERICAN BALLET THEATRE

NY —NEW YORK PUBLIC LIBRARY, Performing Arts Research Center, Dance Collection, 111 Amsterdam Ave, New York, 10023. Genevieve Oswald, Cur
Holdings: Mss Pix Audiotapes Videotapes 16mm Films
Budget: ($9,280)
Notes: Extensive material on this major company founded in 1939 as Ballet Theatre and since 1957 called American Ballet Theatre, and on the dancers, choreographers, designers, and productions of the company. Collection includes manuscripts, correspondence, programs, souvenir booklets, clippings, scrapbooks, photographs, stage and costume designs for various productions, tape-recorded interviews with company members, motion pictures and videotapes of productions.

AMERICAN BANDMASTERS' ASSOCIATION

†MD —UNIVERSITY OF MARYLAND, Library, American Bandmasters Association Research Center, College Park, 20742. Pearl Z Tubiash, Supvr
Holdings: Cat Pix Phonorecords Audiotapes
Notes: Materials on bands and band music; organizational and personal papers, with sizable collections relating to the careers of distinguished bandmasters, notably Edwin Franko Goldman.

AMERICAN BANKERS ASSOCIATION

MA —HARVARD UNIVERSITY, Graduate School of Business Administration, Baker Library, Soldiers Field, Boston, 02163. Mary V Chatfield, Librn; Florence Bartoshesky, Cur of Manuscripts and Archives
Holdings: Cat
Notes: Theses from Stonier Graduate School of Banking, American Bankers Association.

AMERICAN BAR ASSOCIATION

IL —AMERICAN BAR FOUNDATION, Cromwell Library, 1155 E 60 St, Chicago, 60637. Olavi Maru, Librn
Notes: Research library emphasizing social/scientific literature. Also includes Bar Association publications and continuing legal education materials.

AMERICAN BEEKEEPING FEDERATION

CA —UNIVERSITY OF CALIFORNIA, DAVIS, Shields Library, Dept of Special Collections, Davis, 95616. Donald Kunitz, Head; C Danial Elliott, Asst Head
Holdings: Vols 5600 Cat Mss Pix Slides
Notes: Records of the American Beekeeping Federation (1940-69). Described in: USDA Agricultural Research Service, *Beekeeping in the United States* (Agricultural Handbook no 335, rev ed 1977); and Johansson, Tag Sigvard Kjell, *Apicultural Literature*

AMERICAN BEEKEEPING FEDERATION (cont.)

Published in Canada and the United States (New York, 1972).

AMERICAN BISON see Bison, American

AMERICAN BOARD OF COMMISSIONERS FOR FOREIGN MISSIONS

HI —HAWAIIAN MISSION CHILDREN'S SOCIETY LIBRARY, 553 S King St, Honolulu, 96813. Mary Jane Knight, Librn
Holdings: Vols 15,000 Cat Mss Pix
Notes: Missionary period of Hawaiian history, 1819-1880, incl a general collection of Hawaiian history and travel, an outstanding collection of early voyages to the Pacific, and an almost complete collection of early Hawaiian imprints, ie, publications in the Hawaiian language during the 19th century. Ms material incl letters, journals and reports of the Protestant missionaries who came to Hawaii (the Sandwich Islands) under the auspices of the American Board of Commissioners for Foreign Missions. The material is for research only; the stacks are closed. Unpublished papers may be examined by qualified researchers on application to the librarian. Published material is cataloged. Hawaiian imprints are cataloged, except for the Dewey classification 300's which are mainly government documents. Ms collections are cataloged or in the process of being completely arranged and cataloged.

MA —HARVARD UNIVERSITY LIBRARY, Houghton Library, Cambridge, 02138. Rodney G Dennis, Cur of Manuscripts
Holdings: Mss
Notes: For account of the board's archives, see *Harvard Library Bulletin,* VI (1952): pp 52-68.

AMERICAN BOTANISTS see Botanists, American

AMERICAN BUREAU FOR MEDICAL AID TO CHINA

†NY —COLUMBIA UNIVERSITY LIBRARIES, Butler Library, Rare Book and Manuscript Library, 535 W 114 St, New York, 10027.
Notes: Papers of the American Bureau for Medical Aid to China, incl correspondence, memoranda, reports, minutes, membership and financial records, photographs, posters and printed material. Approx 45,000 pieces. Also, some 6000 photographs of Chinese medical colleges, hospitals, laboratories, and personnel.

AMERICAN-CHINESE RELATIONS

MA —HARVARD UNIVERSITY LIBRARY, Widener Library, Cambridge, 02138.
Holdings: Cat
Notes: Surveys of collections by Robert L Irick and Valentin H Rabe published by Harvard University Press, 1960 (*Research Aids for American Far Eastern Policy* Studies, 1 and 3).

†NY —COLUMBIA UNIVERSITY LIBRARIES, Butler Library, Rare Book and Manuscript Library, 535 W 114 St, New York, 10027.
Notes: Papers of the American Bureau for Medical Aid to China, incl correspondence, memoranda, reports, minutes, membership and financial records, photographs, posters and printed material. Approx 45,000 pieces. Also, some 6000 photographs of Chinese medical colleges, hospitals, laboratories, and personnel.

AMERICAN CATHOLIC HISTORICAL SOCIETY OF PHILADELPHIA

PA —SAINT JOSEPH'S UNIVERSITY, Drexel Library, 5600 City Ave, Philadelphia, 19131. Josephine Savaro, Dir of Library
Notes: The collection of Martin I J Griffin (1842-1911), leading figure in Catholic historiography, and founder of the American Catholic Historical Society of Philadelphia. Correspondence, scrapbooks, and pamphlets.

AMERICAN CHORAL FOUNDATION

PA —FREE LIBRARY OF PHILADELPHIA, Music Dept, Drinker Library of Choral Music, Logan Sq, Philadelphia, 19103. Frederick James Kent, Head
Holdings: VOLS 348,000 Cat
Notes: The Drinker Library is primarily sacred choral works of the 16th-19th centuries in multiple copies, incl the Bach cantatas in English translation, many with orchestral parts. Loaned to subscribers of the Drinker Library. The Library of the American Choral Foundation was given to the Drinker Library in 1970 and contains many short 20th century works.

AMERICAN CIVIL LIBERTIES UNION (ACLU)

CA —UNIVERSITY OF CALIFORNIA, LOS ANGELES, Research Library, Dept of Special Collections, 405 Hilgard Ave, Los Angeles, 90024. Edward Shreeves, Chairman, Bibliographers Group; David S Zeidberg, Head
Holdings: Cat Mss Pix
Notes: 127 linear feet of legal, organizational, and education files relating to the work of the ACLU of Southern California. Incl correspondence, scrapbooks, and ephemera. Additional material in the papers of Ed Cray, Stanley Fleishman, Nathan L Schoichet, etc.

IL —SOUTHERN ILLINOIS UNIVERSITY, CARBONDALE, Delyte W Morris Library, Special Collections Dept, Carbondale, 62901. David V Koch, Cur of Special Collections; Louisa Bowen, Cur of Manuscripts
Holdings: Cat Mss
Notes: Papers and correspondence of Theodore A Schroeder, constitutional lawyer and founder, with Lincoln Steffens, of the Free Speech League, a forerunner of the American Civil Liberties Union. Contains extensive correspondence with Comstock, Gompers, Debs, H Ellis, Sanger, Sinclair, John Dewey, Darrow, Mencken, A G Hays, Emma Goldman, W E B Dubois, etc. Incl several thousand letters; notes and mss, records of legal cases and extensive files relating to the early history of psychiatry.

MS —UNIVERSITY OF SOUTHERN MISSISSIPPI, William David McCain Graduate Library, Box 5148, Southern Sta, Hattiesburg, 39406.
Holdings: Cat Mss
Notes: 1 cubic feet holdings. Southern Regional Office. Legal briefs and trial transcripts of noteworthy civil liberties cases, 1964-70. Incl those of Muhammed Ali, Robert L Barbe, the Democratic Party of Alabama, Cleveland L Sellers, Julious Sullivan, the UFO Coffee House, and John D Wallace. Also incl is an October 1969 "Five Year Report of the Southern Regional Office of the ACLU" and a report to the Democratic National Committee concerning the filling of the Alabama vacancy on the committee.

NJ —PRINCETON UNIVERSITY, Library, Manuscript Collection, Nassau St, Princeton, 08540. Jean F Preston, Cur
Holdings: Cat Mss
Notes: ACLU Archives and other papers; 1861 albums; as of 1983, 935 cartons. The Archives cover the period 1912 to date. Indexes for 1917 to date are available.

VA —UNIVERSITY OF VIRGINIA, Alderman Library, Manuscripts Dept, Charlottesville, 22901. Edmund Berkeley Jr, Cur
Holdings: Cat Mss
Notes: Papers of the American Civil Liberties Union (ACLU) of Virginia (partially restricted) and the Virginia Council of Human Relations focus chiefly on desegregation but contain material on the civil liberties of a variety of minority groups, incl students, prisoners, and the mentally ill, and causes such as fair housing, fair employment, gun control, capitol punishment, draft resistance and personal liberty.

AMERICAN CIVIL WAR see U.S. —History—Civil War

AMERICAN CIVILIZATION see U.S. —Social Life and Customs

AMERICAN COLLEGE OF NURSE MIDWIVES

MD —NATIONAL LIBRARY OF MEDICINE, History of Medicine Division, 8600 Rockville Pike, Bethesda, 20014.
Notes: Books and journals related to nursing and the nursing profession, both early and current items. A manuscripts collection incl the archives of the American College of Nurse Midwives (1946-1976) and the National League for Nursing (1894-1952). Photographs in the Prints and Photographs Collection document the history of nursing from the Middle Ages to the 1960s.

AMERICAN COLLEGE PERSONNEL ASSOCIATION (ACPA)

OH —BOWLING GREEN STATE UNIVERSITY, Jerome Library, Center for Archival Collections, Bowling Green, 43403. Paul D Yon, Dir; Elaine R Ezell, Reference Archivist; Nancy Steen, Rare Books Librn
Notes: Incl pamphlets. The archives of four national professional associations have been donated to the CAC, creating a special collecting area concerning student affairs in higher education. The National Association for Women Deans, Counselors and Administrators (NAWDAC), the National Association of Student Personnel Administrators (NASPA), the American College Personnel Association (ACPA), and the Association of Fraternity Advisors (AFA), to date, have designated the CAC as the repository for their archives. These collections document the issues, professional education and activities of those employed within the student affairs area in colleges and universities in the US.

AMERICAN COLONIZATION SOCIETY

DC —LIBRARY OF CONGRESS, Manuscript Division, Washington, 20540. John C Broderick, Chief
Holdings: Cat Mss Pix
Notes: Mss, papers, records, etc.

AMERICAN COMMITTEE FOR THE PROTECTION OF FOREIGN BORN

MI —UNIVERSITY OF MICHIGAN, Dept of Rare Books & Special Collections, Ann Arbor, 48109. Edward C Weber, Head, Labadie Collection
Notes: The Labadie Collection of radical materials, containing papers, tracts, handbills, and publications of minority political and social reform organizations from the mid-1800s to the present, incl 8000 serial titles and 20,000 uncataloged pamphlets. Also ms collections of the papers of the American Committee for the Protection of Foreign Born.

AMERICAN COMMITTEE ON AFRICA

LA —AMISTAD RESEARCH CENTER, 400 Esplanade Ave, New Orleans, 70116. Clifton H Johnson, Exec Dir; Florence E Borders, Senior Archivist
Notes: In addition, 8,000,000 ms pieces, 10, 000 pictures, 3500 microforms, and 500 audiotapes. Amistad Research Center is an historical research library devoted to the collection and use of primary source materials on the history of America's ethnic minorities, with particular emphasis on Afro-Americans, American Indians, and immigrant groups. Among the larger

AMERICAN COMMITTEE ON AFRICA (cont.)

institutional collections held are the archives and records of the American Missionary Association, the American Home Missionary Society, the Race Relations Dept of the Anti-Defamation League, the Catholic Committee of the South, and the National Association of Human Rights Workers, (formerly NAIRO). Also, private papers of the Harlem Renaissance poet, Countee Cullen; educator and civil rights leader, Mary McLeod Bethune;20th century civil rights lawyer, Alexander P. Tureaud; 19th century Black attorney and judge, George Ruffin; founder and director of Operation Crossroads Africa, Dr James H Robinson; and over 70 others.

AMERICAN COUNCIL FOR EMIGRES IN THE PROFESSIONS

NY —STATE UNIVERSITY OF NEW YORK AT ALBANY, Library, Special Collections Dept, 1400 Washington Ave, Albany, 12222. Marion P Munzer, Coordr
Notes: Photocopies of histories, reports, and correspondence file (11 linear feet). Incl biographical sketches of individual emigres, 1941-73. Part of the Library's German Exile Collection.
See also entry under Exiles, Political

AMERICAN COUNCIL OF LEARNED SOCIETIES' BRITISH MANUSCRIPT PROJECT

DC —LIBRARY OF CONGRESS, General Reading Rooms Division, Microform Reading Room, Washington, 20540.
Holdings: Cat Mss Maps Pix Microforms
Notes: Microform materials only in this LC Division. Works of individual authors; holdings of collections; archival records, etc, press releases and translations, etc.

AMERICAN COUNCIL ON EDUCATION

†DC —AMERICAN COUNCIL ON EDUCATION, Library & Information Service, One Dupont Circle, Suite 640, Washington, 20036. Judith Pfeiffer, Librn
Holdings: Vols 5000 Cat
Notes: The collection reflects the need and interests of the building tenants. All tenants are nonprofit, nongovernmental associations in the field of post-secondary education. The collection is particularly strong in the areas of the economics, finance, history, management, and teaching in higher education. The library is a depository library for the Carnegie Commission on Higher Education and the Carnegie Council on Policy Studies in Higher Education. In addition, the library maintains an archival collection of the publications of the American Council on Education.

AMERICAN DANCE SYMPOSIA

KS —WICHITA PUBLIC LIBRARY, Art & Music Division, 223 S Main, Wichita, 67202. Leonard Messineo, Jr, Head, Art & Music Division; Deborah Hamilton, Special Collections Librn
Holdings: Uncat Audiotapes Videotape Pix
Notes: Alice Bauman Dance Symposia Collection. Contains 300 hours of audio tapes, 1 hour-long video tape, several hundred photographs, and fugitive material of the American Dance Symposia held in Wichita from 1968-1972. The symposia covered all dance idioms-ballet, modern, jazz, folk, ethnic, dance education and therapy-and featured such notable figures such as Leonide Massine, Martha Hill, William Christensen, Alfonso Cimber, Toni Intravaia, James Clouser, Eleo Pomare, Juana de Laban, and many others. Characterized by the *Kansas City Star* as the "most distinguished faculties of fine artists ever assembled in the contemporary world of dance."

AMERICAN DRAMA

CA —CALIFORNIA STATE UNIVERSITY, LONG BEACH, Library, Dept of Special Collections & Archives, 1250 Bellflower Blvd, Long Beach, 90840. John Ahouse, Special Collections Librn
Holdings: Vols (5000) Cat Pix
Notes: Incl, playbills, scripts, scrapbooks from the former Pasadena Playhouse, together with former Hildebrand Collection of English and American Drama before 1830.

†CA —UNIVERSITY OF SAN FRANCISCO, Richard A Gleeson Library, The Countess Bernardine Murphy Donohue Rare Book Room, San Francisco, 94117. D Steven Corey, Special Collections Librn
Notes: Some highly specialized materials.

DC —LIBRARY OF CONGRESS, Rare Book & Special Collections Div, Washington, 20540. William Matheson, Chief
Holdings: Vols 3062 Cat
Notes: Separate collection (over 3000 items), cataloged, of mss and plays consists of typescript (chiefly) and handwritten copies of plays submitted to the Copyright Office. Most of the titles date from 1880 to 1920, though occasional items are as early as 1870 or as late as 1954. Authors represented from the later years are Eugene O'Neill, Arthur Miller, et al. Also, the Theatre Playbill Collection consists of 7500 playbills relating to performances in Washington (largely), New York, Boston, Philadelphia, Cincinnati, Buffalo, Charlestown, etc, between 1823 and 1930, with a concentration in late 19th and early 20th century performances.

FL —UNIVERSITY OF SOUTH FLORIDA, Library, Tampa, 33620. J B Dobkin, Special Collections Librn
Holdings: Vols 1000 Cat
Budget: ($7500)
Notes: 19th Century Play Collection. Consists of acting editions of British and American plays only (pamphlet format). Although concentration is in the area of 19th century plays, some items of 18th and early 20th century origin are also present in the collection. Some of the playscripts incl contemporary manuscript copies of published plays. Emphasis in the collection is given to American playscripts.

IL —UNIVERSITY OF CHICAGO LIBRARY, Dept of Special Collections, 1100 E 57 St, Chicago, 60637.
Notes: Atkinson and Morton Collection.

IL —LAKE FOREST COLLEGE, Donnelley Library, Lake Forest, 60045. Arthur H Miller Jr, College Librn
Holdings: Cat Mss
Notes: Coverage from 17th century to the present, about 5000 pieces, particularly American and English. Garrett Leverton Memorial Theatre Library emphasizes the American drama renaissance of the early 20th century. It includes, though, more than 1000 published playscripts, of which a significant number are 19th century.

IN —MORRISSON-REEVES LIBRARY, 80 N Sixth St, Richmond, 47374. Harriet E Bard, Librn
Holdings: Vols 1250 Cat
Notes: 1000 titles are individual plays or plays-in-collections, largely American and British; 250 titles are history and criticism, stories, plots, etc.

MA —AMHERST COLLEGE, Library, Amherst, 01002. John Lancaster, Special Collections Librn
Holdings: Vols (20,000) Uncat Mss
Notes: Contains a comprehensive collection of paperbound Samuel French acting editions (15,000) and many from other publishers; also Augustin Daly manuscripts, David Warfield acting scripts, and the library of Clyde Fitch. 200 mss.

MA —BOSTON PUBLIC LIBRARY, Boston, 20117.
Holdings: Uncat Microforms
Notes: Microform Publications by Readex Microprint Corp. Three Centuries of English and American Plays, 1500-1800; English and American Plays of the 19th Century.

MA —HARVARD UNIVERSITY LIBRARY, Cambridge, 02138.
Holdings: Cat Mss

MI —UNIVERSITY OF MICHIGAN, Library, Dept of Rare Books & Special Collections, Ann Arbor, 48109. Robert J Starring, Head
Holdings: Cat
Notes: Plays of minor, as well as major, dramatists, chiefly 19th century.

MO —UNIVERSITY OF MISSOURI-COLUMBIA, Ellis Library, Language and Literature Dept, Columbia, 65201. Jeaneice Brewer, Librn
Holdings: Vols Cat
Notes: Comprehensive collection of acting editions of plays of individual playwrights. Retrospective and current publications are added regularly.

NY —BUFFALO & ERIE COUNTY PUBLIC LIBRARY, Rare Book Room, Lafayette Sq, Buffalo, 14203. William H Loos, Cur
Holdings: Vols 80 Cat
Notes: All listed in F P Hill's *American Plays Printed 1714-1830* (Stanford, 1934).

NY —AMERICAN ACADEMY & INSTITUTE OF ARTS & LETTERS, Library, 633 W 155 St, New York, 10032. Casindania P Eaton, Librn; Nancy Johnson, Researcher
Notes: Works of members of the Academy only. Incl mss, letters, memorabilia, etc.

NY —COLUMBIA UNIVERSITY LIBRARIES, Rare Book & Manuscript Library, 801 Butler Library, 535 W 114 St, New York, 10027. Kenneth A Lohf, Librn
Holdings: Vols (5000) Cat Mss
Notes: First editions of plays, autograph letters and mss, most of which relate to Brander Matthews. Incl 18,000 mss items. Restricted use.

NY —NEW YORK PUBLIC LIBRARY, Performing Arts Research Center, Billy Rose Theatre Collection, 111 Amsterdam Ave, New York, 10023. Dorothy L Swerdlove, Cur
Holdings: Cat
Notes: Described in *Catalog of the Theatre and Drama Collections,* The Research libraries of The New York Public Library, 1967. To be supplemented. Part I, *Drama Collection: Listing by Cultural Origin,* 6 vols (120,000 cards), $585; Part II, *Drama Collection: Author Listing,* 6 vols (115,000 cards), $790. This catalog represents the major portion of the Research Libraries' Drama Collection. Incl are more than 120, 000 plays written in western languages. Translations of plays published in the Cyrillic, Hebrew and Oriental alphabets are also listed. Excluded are children's plays, Christmas plays, and moralities. The catalog is in two parts: a listing by author (or title, in the case of anonymous plays); and a listing by cultural origin. An analysis of this latter section reveals the Research Libraries' interest in collecting widely from the literatures of theworld; American, 20,000; Spanish, 16,000; German, 14,000; and a strong representation of plays written in minor languages.

NY —NEW YORK PUBLIC LIBRARY, Research Libraries, General Research Division, Fifth Ave & 42 St, New York, 10018. Rodney Phillips, Chief
Holdings: Vols (2,225,000) Cat Maps Pix Microforms
Budget: ($775,718)

NY —THEATRE COLLECTION OF THE INTERNATIONAL THEATRE INSTITUTE OF THE UNITED STATES, INC, Library, Suite 1510, 1860 Broadway, New York, 10023. Elizabeth B Burdick, Dir
Holdings: Vols (4525) Cat Mss Pix
Budget: ($35,000)
Notes: The International Theatre Institute was founded by UNESCO to "promote the exchange of knowledge and practice in the theatre arts." In 1948, eleven nations, incl the United States, became charter members of the international organization, which today has national centers or affiliates in 64 countries. The American center is the International Theatre Institute of the United States (ITI/US). In 1970, as one of its programs to strengthen communication among theatre people, ITI/US opened a library devoted to international theatre since World War II. The Collection's main holdings have been amassed over the 35-year

AMERICAN DRAMA (cont.)

operation of ITI/US through its world-wide exchange of information, publications, and people. Holdings document theatre activity in 140 countries. The 4525 vols on American and foreign theatre(covering history, management, design, stagecraft, theory, criticism, biography, playscripts) represent only a small part of the total collection. Focus is on foreign theatre companies, directors, playwrights, designers, managers, actors. The emphasis is on the acquisition of material which is generally unavailable in this country: foreign yearbooks, house organs, newsletters, programs, press releases, production schedules, brochures, periodicals, monographs, articles, newspaper clippings. While these fugitive items have never been counted, they have been cataloged by country, then indexed by title, subject, or name of theatre. The library receives regularly 250 periodicals on the performing arts (cataloged by country, then indexed by title). It now owns 6417 foreign plays from 80 countries in ms or publishedmss or published editions, in collections and anthologies, and in periodicals. Each play is cataloged by author, title, and country of origin. The section on American theatre incl books, programs, reviews, over 60 periodicals, 2061 American plays. The activities of approx 700 theatres across the country are documented by annual files containing production schedules, press releases, programs, brochures for each theatrical season.

NY —UNIVERSITY OF ROCHESTER, Rush Rhees Library, Department of Rare Books and Special Collections, Rochester, 14627. Peter Dzwonkoski, Librn
Holdings: Vols (300) Cat Mss Pix
Notes: 19th century English and American plays and works on theatre. Also includes manuscript collections on theatre, and papers of Clement William Scott, John Lawrence Toole, Arthur Wing Pinero, George Alexander, Henry Irving, Charles Kean, Lillian Russell and Leon Marks Lion, collection of 130 lithographic theatre posters, and collection of programs and playbills, chiefly Rochester, NY, and New York City, 1870-1950. Unpublished guides to ms collections available in repository.

NC —DUKE UNIVERSITY, William R Perkins Library, Durham, 27706. Elvin E Strowd, University Librn

NC —DUKE UNIVERSITY, William R Perkins Library, Jay B Hubbell Center for American Literary Historiography, Durham, 27706. Erma Whittington, Librn
Notes: 77,312 items, including manuscripts, pictures, clippings, and correspondence. "The objective of the Center is to gather the papers and materials of significant scholars and critics in American literary history." The Center is a part of the Perkins Library Manuscripts Department.

OH —CLEVELAND PUBLIC LIBRARY, Literature Dept, 325 Superior Ave, Cleveland, 44114. Evelyn Ward, Head
Holdings: Vols Cat Microforms Phonorecords
Notes: Comprehensive collection of literary texts, with a large body of literary history, criticism and biography. Strong in drama and poetry. Many first editions, books from special presses, and rarities. Microprint. Reference aids.

OH —OHIO STATE UNIVERSITY, William Oxley Thompson Memorial Library, 1858 Neil Ave Mall, Columbus, 43210. Robert A Tibbetts, Cur of Special Collections
Holdings: Uncat Mss
Notes: American Playwrights' Theatre papers, incl business records and scripts of plays produced or considered for production.

PA —UNIVERSITY OF PENNSYLVANIA, Van Pelt Library, Rare Books Collection, 34 & Walnut Sts, Philadelphia, 19104. Daniel Traister, Special Collections Librn
Holdings: Vols 700 Cat Mss Pix
Notes: Before 1865, incl playbills and mss. See Downs (Supplement), 1652-3. Also, first editions of modern drama.

RI —BROWN UNIVERSITY, John Hay Library, Harris Collection, Prospect St, Providence, 02912. Rosemary L Cullen, Cur
Holdings: Vols (200,000) Cat Mss Pix Phonorecords Microforms
Budget: ($15,000)
Notes: The Harris Collection of American Poetry and Plays is principally composed of American and Canadian poetry and plays, 17th century-date. Extensive holdings in songsters, gift books and annuals, hymnals, pageants, broadside verse, carriers' addresses, women poets, juvenile poetry, (incl Mother Goose and *The Night Before* Christmas), sheet music with lyrics, small press publications, fine printing, black poets, "little magazines," Yiddish-American literature. All movements or schools of American poetry are represented. Incl first editions of most American poets and playwrights, notably Whitman, Poe, Wallace Stevens, Eugene O'Neill, Edward Albee, Ezra Pound, T S Eliot, William Carlos Williams, Amy Lowell, Phyllis Wheatley, Robert Frost, Allen Ginsberg, Bliss Carman, and Stephen Foster sheet music. Also incl the Saunders Walt Whitman Collection (1300 vols); the LangdonCollection of Pageants (250 vols); the Asa Cushman Collection of plays in ms and prompt copies; the MacDougall Collection of Psalters and Hymnals; 4000 plays issued by Walter H Baker Co, Boston (1890-1957); the Vaxer Collection of Yiddish Poetry, Plays and Music (1700 vols). Collections incl 200,000 vols, 30,000 broadsides, 55,000 mss, 170,000 pieces of sheet music, 450 phonorecords, and 375 microfilm reels. See *Dictionary Catalog of the Harris Collection of American Poetry and Plays* (Boston: G K Hall, 1972), 13 vols; *Supplement* (1977), 3 vols. See also, *American Poetry,* 1609-1900, *A Collection on Microfilm, Segment I* (1609-1820); *Segment II* (1821-1850); *Segment III* (1851-1870) (Woodbridge, Conn: Research Publications). Separate catalog.

†TX —FORT WORTH PUBLIC LIBRARY, Fort Worth, 76102.
Notes: Collection of works of individual playwrights.

VA —UNIVERSITY OF VIRGINIA, Alderman Library, Clifton Waller Barrett Collection, Charlottesville, 22901. Joan St C Crane, Cur of American Literature Collections
Holdings: Vols (300,000) Cat Mss Pix
Notes: The Library takes as its province 175 years of American literature, from 1775 to 1980. It contains, insofar as it has been possible to assemble them, all fiction, poetry, drama, and essays published by an American in book form up to 1875; for the years since, it contains a very nearly complete collection of the works of every major American writer, as well as of those whose achievements were not of the first rank, but who, nevertheless, occupy a place in the literary history of the Republic. With the first editions are important later editions, many translations and periodical appearances, and a vast amount of biographical and critical material. Mss and letters of quality have been brought together in such quantity that few similar collections can approach it in size and scholarly importance. Publications: *A Brief Account of the Clifton Waller Barrett Library,*Herbert Cahoon (Charlottesville: University of Virginia, 1960); "The Mighty Manuscripts of Mr C Waller Barrett," C Brian Kelly, *The Commonwealth: The Magazine of Virginia,* vol 38, no 8, Aug 1971, pp 21-28. To determine the manuscript holdings in the Library for particular American authors, consult the second edition of *American Literary Manuscripts.*

VA —GEORGE MASON UNIVERSITY, Fenwick Library, Special Collections Dept, 4400 University Drive, Fairfax, 22030. Ruth Kerns, Public Services Librn
Notes: Some 275,000 items (incl administrative, play service and research, library and production records) pertaining to the WPA Federal Theatre Project, on permanent loan from the Library of Congress.

†WA —WASHINGTON STATE UNIVERSITY, Library, Manuscripts, Archives & Special Collections, Pullman, 99164. John F Guido, Head
Holdings: // Cat Mss Pix
Notes: The Robert Cushman Butler Collection of Theatrical Illustrations contains; approx 1600 illustrations, sheet music covers, programs and playbills; approx 100 mss of actors, actresses and playwrights; and approx 200 volumes of theatrical history and reminiscences, several extra-illustrated, concentrating on 18th-19th century British and American drama. A guide to the collection is in preparation.

AMERICAN DRAMATISTS see Playwrights, American

AMERICAN EMERGENCY COMMITTEE FOR TIBETAN REFUGEES

CA —HOOVER INSTITUTION ON WAR, REVOLUTION & PEACE, Stanford University, Stanford, 94305. Milorad M Drachkovitch, Archivist
Holdings: Mss Pix
Notes: Records of the American Emergency Committeee for Tibetan Refugees, incl correspondence, reports, minutes of meetings and photographs, 1959-1970, relating to relief work for Tibetan refugees in Napal and India. 17 ms boxes.

AMERICAN EXPLORERS see Explorers, American

AMERICAN FEDERATION OF LABOR

AZ —NORTHERN ARIZONA UNIVERSITY, Special Collection Library, CU Box 6022, Flagstaff, 86011. Peter M Whiteley, Coordr/Archivist; William Mullane, Librn
Notes: All records of the central office of the Arizona AFL-CIO; ca 100 linear feet.

WI —STATE HISTORICAL SOCIETY OF WISCONSIN, Archives, 816 State St, Madison, 53706. Harold L Miller, Reference Archivist
Holdings: Mss Pix Microforms
Notes: Records and papers documenting the history of the labor and Socialist movements in the United States from 1850s to the present. Incl are records of labor and socialist organizations incl American Federation of Labor and the Socialist Labor Party, and papers of individual labor and socialist leaders such as Morris Hillquit and John L Lewis. Collections are described in *A Guide to Labor Papers in the State Historical Society of Wisconsin* (1978) and in current accession notes in the *Wisconsin Magazine of History.* Major collections are also listed in Hamer, *Guide to Manuscripts and Archives in the United States,* (1961) and in the *National Union Catalog of Manuscript Collections,* (1959-date).

AMERICAN FEDERATION OF STATE, COUNTY AND MUNICIPAL EMPLOYEES (AFSCME)

MI —WAYNE STATE UNIVERSITY, Walter P Reuther Library, Archives of Labor & Urban Affairs, Detroit, 48202. Philip Mason, Dir
Notes: The inactive historical files of AFSCME's national officers and departments for the period 1935-1975 have been transferred to the Archives. Those records over ten years old are available to qualified scholars for research. In addition to these files, the Archives is engaged in a concerted effort to collect the files of various AFSCME locals and councils, as well as papers held by individuals active in the union. The Archives is also conducting an "AFSCME Oral History Project," interviewing a selected group of both retired and active AFSCME's development which goes beyond what traditional historical documents contain.

AMERICAN FEDERATION OF TEACHERS

CO —UNIVERSITY OF COLORADO, Libraries, Western Historical Collections, Boulder, 80309.
Holdings: Mss
Notes: Papers of Herrick Roth (b 1916), who was one of the founders in 1946 of the American Federation of Teachers local in Denver. In 1951 he left teaching to devote himself full-time to the labor movement. From 1962 until his ouster by George Meany in 1973 he served as President of the Colorado Labor Council. Since then he has taught at Denver University, run unsuccessfully for the US Senate and served as head of the State Employment Service. The collection contains correspondence, pamphlets, clippings and other material on Roth's labor union, political and social interests. The largest portion of the material deals with the Colorado Labor Council and the American Federation of Teachers. 25 boxes, 1950s-1970s. Typescript inventory is available.

MI —WAYNE STATE UNIVERSITY, Walter P Reuther Library, Archives of Labor & Urban Affairs, Detroit, 48202. Philip Mason, Dir
Notes: The records of the American Federation of Teachers, as well as the files of the Detroit, Toledo, East Detroit, and other Federations of Teachers, are now preserved in the Archives. The personal papers of several teacher union leaders, incl Arthur Elder, Selma M Borchardt, Henry R Linville, Mary Herrick, and others are important supplements to the national union's file.

AMERICAN FICTION

CA —LOS ANGELES PUBLIC LIBRARY, Fiction Dept, 630 W 5th St, Los Angeles, 90071. Helene G Mochedlover, Dept Librn
Holdings: Uncat Microforms
Notes: American fiction on microfilm (1381 reels). Based on the Lyle H Wright bibliography, vols I, II, III: 1774-1900, etc.

CA —CALIFORNIA STATE UNIVERSITY, NORTHRIDGE, Delmar T Oviatt & South Libraries, 1811 Nordhoff St, Northridge, 91330. Donald L Read, Special Collections Dept
Holdings: Vols 2500 Cat
Notes: McDermott collection of contemporary writers of American fiction and poetry, signed, first editions. Emphasis is upon both established and new contemporary writers. Collection fully cataloged.

CT —YALE UNIVERSITY, Box 1603A, Yale Station, New Haven, 06520.
Holdings: Cat Mss

IL —NEWBERRY LIBRARY, 60 W Walton St, Chicago, 60610. Diana Haskell, Cur of Modern Mss
Holdings: Cat
Notes: Holdings recorded in Wright bibliographies.

IL —NORTHERN ILLINOIS UNIVERSITY, Founders Memorial Library, Rare Books and Special Collections Dept, De Kalb, 60115. William R DuBois, Dept Head
Holdings: Vols (1000)
Budget: ($5000)
Notes: Mass-appeal publications, ca 1865-1920. Includes Horatio Alger. "Oliver Optic" and other popular writers.

IA —UNIVERSITY OF NORTHERN IOWA, Library, Cedar Falls, 50613. Gerald L Peterson, Special Collections Librn
Holdings: Vols (3500) Audiotapes
Budget: ($2000)
Notes: This is a collection of work done by American novelists who began their work after 1960. First editions only. We add as these novelists continue to publish. Include galley and page proofs when possible--also movie scripts and typescripts. Cataloged.

KY —UNIVERSITY OF KENTUCKY COMMUNITY COLLEGES, Southeast Community College, Library, Learning Resource Center, Cumberland, 40823. Parker Boggs, Dir
Holdings: Vols (700) Cat Mss Maps Pix Slides Phonorecords Audiotapes Videotapes 16mm Films Filmstrips Microforms
Notes: Literature of southern Appalachia; fiction and non-fiction.

MA —BOSTON UNIVERSITY, Mugar Memorial Library, Special Collections Dept, 771 Commonwealth Ave, Boston, 02215. Howard B Gotlieb, Dir
Holdings: Cat Mss
Notes: See names of individual writers.

MA —HARVARD UNIVERSITY LIBRARY, Cambridge, 02138.
Holdings: Cat Mss

MA —AMERICAN ANTIQUARIAN SOCIETY LIBRARY, 185 Salisbury St, Worcester, 01609. Marcus A McCorison, Dir & Librn
Holdings: Vols 5000 Cat
Notes: An outstanding collection to 1876.

MI —MICHIGAN STATE UNIVERSITY, Libraries, Special Collections Div, East Lansing, 48824. Jannette Fiore, Librn
Holdings: Vols (30,000) Cat
Notes: Collection of 19th/20th century authors, including selected expatriate authors. Popular Culture Collections have four principal categories of materials: Comic Art, ca 23,500 items (comics, aprox 21,000 cataloged issues, big-little books, reprints and anthologies, etc); Popular Fiction, ca 24,000 items (dime novels, story magazines and pulps, juvenile series, detective, science fiction, western and romantic novels); Popular Information, ca 5000 items (over 2000 public school text books, along with almanacs, big and little blue books, "self-education" materials, etc); Popular Performing Arts, ca 2300 items (tent-show materials, including 250 scripts, photographs, handbills, records and correspondence; plays and entertainments for home and popular performance and print materials relating to radio-TV-film). Partially cataloged.

MS —UNIVERSITY OF SOUTHERN MISSISSIPPI, William David McCain Graduate Library, Box 5148, Southern Sta, Hattiesburg, 39406.
Holdings: Cat Mss
Notes: 4.3 cubic feet holdings. Literary mss and related correspondence of Con Sellers, a best selling author of popular novels and historical novels. Sellers writes under numerous pseudonyms and has written such best sellers as *Dallas* and *Night Shadows.*

NY —NEW YORK PUBLIC LIBRARY, Research Libraries, General Research Division, Fifth Ave & 42 St, New York, 10018. Rodney Phillips, Chief
Holdings: Vols (2,225,000) Cat Maps Pix Microforms
Budget: ($775,718)

NY —NEW YORK SOCIETY LIBRARY, 53 E 79 St, New York, 10021. Mark Piel, Librn
Notes: James Hammond Library (circulating library of Newport, RI) of fiction published 1750-1830 incl 920 titles.

NY —NEW YORK UNIVERSITY, Elmer Holmes Bobst Library, Div of Special Collections, Washington Sq S, New York, 10012. Frank Walker, Librn; Patrick McGuire, Asst Librn
Holdings: Vols (100,000) Cat Mss Pix
Notes: The Fales Collection of first (and other) editions of English and American novels from about 1750 to date (about 70, 000 titles). Mss (30,000) pieces. 8000 examples of 19th century Dime Novels.

NY —STATE UNIVERSITY OF NEW YORK, COLLEGE AT ONEONTA, James M Milne Library, Oneonta, 13820. Richard D Johnson, Librn
Holdings: Vols (427,646) Cat Mss Maps Pix Slides Phonorecords Audiotapes 16mm Films Filmstrips Microforms
Budget: ($338,299)
Notes: New York State Collection; 19th & early 20th century popular fiction; New York State Verse Collection; Early Textbook & Early Educational Theory Collection.

NC —DUKE UNIVERSITY, William R Perkins Library, Durham, 27706. Elvin E Strowd, University Librn

NC —DUKE UNIVERSITY, William R Perkins Library, Jay B Hubbell Center for American Literary Historiography, Durham, 27706. Erma Whittington, Librn
Notes: 77,312 items, including manuscripts, pictures, clippings, and correspondence. "The objective of the Center is to gather the papers and materials of significant scholars and critics in American literary history." The Center is a part of the Perkins Library Manuscripts Department.

OH —PUBLIC LIBRARY OF CINCINNATI & HAMILTON COUNTY, Dept of Rare Books & Special Collections, 800 Vine St, Library Square, Cincinnati, 45202. Yeatman Anderson III, Cur
Holdings: Cat
Notes: Emphasis on Cincinnati and Ohio authors. American Nobel Literature Prize Winners.

OH —PUBLIC LIBRARY OF CINCINNATI & HAMILTON COUNTY, Fiction Dept, 800 Vine St, Cincinnati, 45202. Janet C Wiehe, Head
Holdings: Vols 110,000 Cat
Notes: Circulating collection of approx 58, 000 titles; classic and contemporary fiction with emphasis on 19th and 20th century American novels and short stories, and incl a widely representative selection of fiction translated from foreign languages.

OH —OHIO STATE UNIVERSITY, William Oxley Thompson Memorial Library, 1858 Neil Ave Mall, Columbus, 43210. Robert A Tibbetts, Cur of Special Collections
Holdings: Vols 6750 Cat
Notes: Espec American fiction through the 19th century, incl but not limited to the scope of Wright's bibliographies. The Charvat Collection of American Fiction, extended by a 1982 grant to incl works published during the first quarter of the 20th century.

OH —RUTHERFORD B HAYES LIBRARY, 1337 Hayes Ave, Fremont, 43420. Watt P Marchman, Dir
Holdings: Vols 700 Cat
Notes: 19th century.

PA —ATHENAEUM OF PHILADELPHIA, 219 S Sixth St, Philadelphia, 19106. Roger W Moss Jr, Librn
Holdings: Vols (20,000)
Notes: American fiction, 1774-1900. Separate catalog by date.

PA —UNIVERSITY OF PENNSYLVANIA, Van Pelt Library, Rare Books Collection, 34 & Walnut Sts, Philadelphia, 19104. Daniel Traister, Special Collections Librn
Holdings: Vols 2000 Cat
Notes: American fiction, first editions, 1774-1875.

PA —UNIVERSITY OF PITTSBURGH, Hillman Library, Special Collections Dept, Hervey Allen Collection, Pittsburgh, 15260. Charles E Aston, Jr, Coordr
Holdings: Vols (2747) Cat Memorabilia Pix
Notes: Emphasis on American historical fiction.

RI —PROVIDENCE ATHENAEUM, 251 Benefit St, Providence, 02903. Sally Duplaix, Dir
Holdings: Vols 25,000 Cat
Budget: $5000
Notes: Classic and contemporary fiction with emphasis on 19th and 20th century American fiction and incl large selection translated from foreign languages.

SC —WOFFORD COLLEGE, Sandor Teszler Library, N Church St, Spartanburg, 29301. Frank J Anderson, Librn
Holdings: Vols (11,500)
Notes: American novels, 1920s-1970s, incl about 1500 mystery novels.

TN —UNIVERSITY OF TENNESSEE, KNOXVILLE, Library, Knoxville, 37996. John Dobson, Special Collections Librn
Holdings: Vols (20,000) Cat Mss Maps Pix
Notes: Tennesseana; 19th century American fiction; southern Indians; early imprints. Separate catalog; holdings also listed in comprehensive public catalog in main library. Rare books card catalog with special headings calling attention to unusual features of the books; unpublished registers and calendars to ms collection.

TX —UNIVERSITY OF TEXAS, ARLINGTON, Library, PO Box 19497, Arlington, 76019. Chas Colley, Dir Special

AMERICAN FICTION (cont.)

Collections
Notes: The Library of American Fiction includes works of American authors whose professional reputations rest primarily upon the production of fictitious prose narratives, or novels and whose literary careers flourished during the period from 1870-1910. Writing forms other than novels are included only to the extent that they relate to the author's fiction. Reference works and studies directly supporting research in the literature of these authors are also included.

TX —UNIVERSITY OF TEXAS LIBRARIES, General Libraries, PO Box P, Austin, 78713. Carolyn Bucknell, Asst Dir for Collection Development
Holdings: Cat Microforms
Notes: 19th century fiction.

TX —TRINITY UNIVERSITY, Elizabeth Coates Maddux Library, 715 Stadium Dr, San Antonio, 78284. Richard Hume Werking, Library Dir; Craig Likness, Head Bibliographer
Notes: General reference.

VA —UNIVERSITY OF VIRGINIA, Alderman Library, Clifton Waller Barrett Collection, Charlottesville, 22901. Joan St C Crane, Cur of American Literature Collections
Holdings: Vols (300,000) Cat Mss Pix
Notes: The Library takes as its province 175 years of American literature, from 1775 to 1950. It contains, insofar as it has been possible to assemble them, all fiction, poetry, drama, and essays published by an American in book form up to 1875; for the years since, it contains a very nearly complete collection of the works of every major American writer, as well as of those whose achievements were not of the first rank, but who, nevertheless, occupy a place in the literary history of the Republic. With the first editions are important later editions, many translations and periodical appearances, and a vast amount of biographical and critical material. Mss and letters of quality have been brought together in such quantity that few similar collections can approach it in size and scholarly importance. Publications:*A Brief Account of the Clifton Waller Barrett Library,* Herbert Cahoon (Charlottesville: University of Virginia, 1960); "The Mighty Manuscripts of Mr C Waller Barrett," C Brian Kelly, *The Commonwealth: The Magazine of Virginia,* vol 38, no 8, Aug 1971, pp 21-28. To determine the manuscript holdings in the Library for particular American authors, consult the second edition of *American Literary Manuscripts.*

VA —UNIVERSITY OF VIRGINIA, Alderman Library, Rare Book Dept, Charlottesville, 22901. Julius P Barclay, Cur
Holdings: Vols (6500) Cat
Notes: (1) Marvin Tatum Collection of Contemporary Prose and Poetry contains some extremely rare items (mostly paperback) of American and British poetry and prose in the 1960s and 1970s. Some of Lawrence Ferlinghetti's earliest publications in mimeograph form are here. Poster, portfolios. (2) Mrs Robert Coleman Taylor Collection of First Editions of American Best Sellers (Fiction). Almost without exception, these books are in mint and fine condition. Scope: 1752-1949. Incl very rare early American fiction.

WI —MILWAUKEE PUBLIC LIBRARY, 814 W Wisconsin Ave, Milwaukee, 53233. Donald J Sager, City Librn
Holdings: Vols (2700) Cat
Notes: Collection of definitive editions of collected works of British and American authors; incl most of the significant editions of Shakespeare starting with Rowe.

AMERICAN FILM FESTIVAL

NY —EDUCATIONAL FILM LIBRARY ASSOCIATION, Film Reference Library, 45 John St, New York, 10038. Nadine Covert, Exec Dir
Holdings: Vols (2600) Cat Pix 16mm Films Filmstrips
Budget: (1500)
Notes: Primarily a print collection emphasizing the documentary and educational film areas, but also film as art, animation and independent film in general. Maintain film title file of over 60,000 cards (primarily educational film titles), incl credit information, running time, release date, summary, and distributor. File is a mixture of EFLA evaluations, LC cards, etc. Subject file also separates film flyers by subject or topic. Maintain festivals file (film festivals, educational film festivals, etc); a film library administration file; a filmmakers file (with bio, credits, clippings, program notes); and a vertical file (incl information on grants, distribution, showcases, film activities in the metropolitan area and in major film centers around the country). Membership organization providing telephone, mail and in-person reference. Open to the generalpublic. Do not publish a catalog, but publish annual Film Library Administration bibliography of current or noteworthy reference books for $2.00.

AMERICAN FILM INSTITUTE

CA —AMERICAN FILM INSTITUTE, Louis B Mayer Library, 2021 N Western Ave, PO Box 27999, Los Angeles, 90027. Anne G Schlosser, Dir
Holdings: Vols (3500) Cat
Notes: Collection contains 2500 American film scripts and 1000 television scripts; oral histories conducted in the American Film Institute Louis B Mayer Oral History Program; the MGM Script Collection of 400 MGM scripts from the silent period up to the mid-1950's; Columbia Stills Collection covering the period 1930-1950; special mss collections of Henry Hathaway (director), Harry Horner, Buster Keaton, George Byron Sage and Stewart Stern (writer). Also clipping files on motion pictures, personalities, television shows, production organizations and technical topics; film festival file of all US and foreign festivals. Rare periodical holdings incl *Film Daily* newspaper (1923-1969); *Radio-TV Daily* newspaper (1939-1964); *RKO Radio Flash,* house organ of RKO (1932-1955); *TV Guide* (1948 to date).

AMERICAN FOLK SONGS see Folk Songs, American

AMERICAN FORCES RADIO AND TELEVISION SERIES

DC —LIBRARY OF CONGRESS, Motion Pictures, Broadcasting and Recorded Sound Div, Washington, 20540.
Notes: The American Forces Radio and Television service (AFRTS) Collection contains disc recordings transferred to the Library as early as 1945 as well as selected early wartime broadcasts. Since 1967 the Library has received AFRTS's complete radio program package.

AMERICAN FOREIGN LANGUAGE NEWSPAPERS see Newspapers, American Foreign Language

AMERICAN FOREST INSTITUTE

CA —FOREST HISTORY SOCIETY INC, Library, 109 Coral St, Santa Cruz, 95060. Mary E Johnson, Librn
Notes: Incl archives of the Society of American Foresters, the American Forestry Association, the National Lumber Manufacturers Association, National Forest Products Association, and the American Forest Institute.

AMERICAN FORESTRY ASSOCIATION

CA —FOREST HISTORY SOCIETY INC, Library, 109 Coral St, Santa Cruz, 95060. Mary E Johnson, Librn
Notes: Incl archives of the Society of American Foresters, the American Forestry Association, the National Lumber Manufacturers Association, National Forest Products Association, and the American Forest Institute.

AMERICAN FRIENDS OF IRISH NEUTRALITY

NY —SAINT JOHN'S UNIVERSITY, Special Collections Dept, Grand Central & Utopia Pkwys, Jamaica, 11439. Szilvia E Szmuk, Librn
Holdings: // Uncat Mss
Notes: O'Dwyer Collections: papers dealing with Northern Ireland. 1973-1977; American Friends of Irish Neutrality, World War II. a) The Paul O'Dwyer Papers deal with conditions in Northern Ireland, incl correspondence, speeches, press releases, and periodical articles contain in 18 labeled manila envelopes and roughly indexed. b) American Friends of Irish Neutrality collection consist of 109 letters, membership and donation cards, minutes, press clippings, post cards, speechs, pamphlets, in 6 manila envelopes. No photocopying.

AMERICAN FRIENDS OF VIETNAM

MI —MICHIGAN STATE UNIVERSITY, International Library, South and Southeast Asia Collection, East Lansing, 48824. Clinton Lockert, Bibliographer
Holdings: Vols (3500) Cat Mss Maps Pix Audiotapes Microforms
Notes: Emphasis is on South Vietnam (1955-1962). The University had a Vietnam Advisory Group headquartered in Saigon during this period. Have complete holdings for years 1955-1962 of *Reports & Documents Series of* the MSU Vietnam, and of the International Rescue Committee. Very extensive clippings, correspondence, documents, and photographs from the Gilbert Jonas Collection, and the Wesley Fishel Collection. Significant unique items. Representative selection of Vietnamese literature.

AMERICAN FRIENDS SERVICE COMMITTEE

†PA —FRIENDS HISTORICAL LIBRARY OF SWARTHMORE COLLEGE, Swarthmore, 19081.
Notes: Works on prison conditions, capital punishment, and works by and about Quaker prison reformers, Elizabeth Fry, John Howard, Richard Vaux, Robert Vaux, American Friends Service Committee, and others.

AMERICAN GEOGRAPHICAL SOCIETY

MD —JOHNS HOPKINS UNIVERSITY, Milton S Eisenhower Library, Charles & 34 Sts, Baltimore, 21218. Ann S Gwyn, Assistant Dir for Special Collections
Holdings: Cat Mss
Notes: Collected papers, 1904-1948. Correspondence incl council on Foreign Relations, 1931-1949, and American Geographical Society, 1915-1950. Together, about 10,000 ms pieces. Restricted access; apply in advance.

AMERICAN GREEK DEMOCRATIC ASSOCIATION

†PA —BALCH INSTITUTE FOR ETHNIC STUDIES, Library, 18 S Seventh St, Philadelphia, 19106.
Notes: Papers of Nicholas Vagionis, president of the American Greek Democratic Association.

AMERICAN HISTORIC BUILDINGS SURVEY see Historic American Buildings Survey

AMERICAN HOME ECONOMICS ASSOCIATION CHILD DEVELOPMENT PROJECT

NY —ROCKEFELLER UNIVERSITY, Rockefeller Archive Center, Hillcrest,

AMERICAN HOME ECONOMICS ASSOCIATION CHILD DEVELOPMENT PROJECT (cont.)

Pocantico Hills, North Tarrytown, 10591. Joseph W Ernst, Dir; J William Hess, Assoc Dir
Notes: Papers relative to the Rockefeller Family, Foundations, University, and other specific enterprises and contributions to particular areas of social, physical, educational, and historic reform, preservation, conservation, or development. Extensive records of administrative, financial, physical, or intellectual relationships.

AMERICAN HOME MISSIONARY SOCIETY

LA —AMISTAD RESEARCH CENTER, 400 Esplanade Ave, New Orleans, 70116. Clifton H Johnson, Exec Dir; Florence E Borders, Senior Archivist
Holdings: Vols (10,000) Cat Mss Pix Audiotapes Microforms
Budget: ($315,000)
Notes: 8,000,000 ms pieces, 10,000 pictures, 3500 microforms, and 500 audiotapes. Amistad Research Center is an historical research library devoted to the collection and use of primary source materials on the history of America's ethnic minorities, with particular emphasis on Afro-Americans, American Indians, and immigrant groups. Among the larger institutional collections held are the archives and records of the American Missionary Association and the American Home Missionary Society.

AMERICAN HUMOR see American Wit and Humor

AMERICAN IMPRINTS INVENTORY

IL —NEWBERRY LIBRARY, 60 W Walton St, Chicago, 60610. Diana Haskell, Cur of Modern Mss

AMERICAN IMPRINTS—PRE-1850

DC —GEORGETOWN UNIVERSITY, Library, Special Collections Div, 37 & O Sts NW, Washington, 20057. George M Barringer, Special Collections Librn; Nicholas B Sheetz, Mss Librn
Holdings: Cat

IL —NEWBERRY LIBRARY, 60 W Walton St, Chicago, 60610. Diana Haskell, Cur of Modern Mss
Holdings: Cat
Notes: Strong collection.

IN —INDIANA UNIVERSITY, Lilly Library, Seventh St, Bloomington, 47405. William R Cagle, Librn
Holdings: Vols 4600 Cat

MD —JOHNS HOPKINS UNIVERSITY, Milton S Eisenhower Library, Charles & 34 Sts, Baltimore, 21218. Ann S Gwyn, Assistant Dir for Special Collections
Holdings: Vols 30,000 Cat Microforms
Notes: *Evans American Bibliography* 1639-1800 on microfilm.

MD —NATIONAL LIBRARY OF MEDICINE, 8600 Rockville Pike, Bethesda, 20209. Harold M Schoolinam, Actg Dir
Holdings: Vols (3,150,000) Cat Mss Audiotapes Videotapes 16mm Films Filmstrips Microforms
Budget: ($46,400)
Notes: The world's largest medical library. Materials are collected exhaustively in some 40 biomedical areas and, to a lesser degree, in related subject areas such as general chemistry, physics, zoology, botany, and instrumentation. Holdings include 82,000 monographic volumes, pre-1871; 438,000 monographic volumes, 1871-present; 714,000 bound serial volumes; 281,000 theses; 172, 000 pamphlets; 1,207,000 manuscripts; 156, 000 microforms; 12,000 audiovisuals; and 75, 000 prints and photographs. Pre-1871 material is in a separate historical collection. Approximately 24,000 serial titles are currenlty received.

†MA —BOSTON PUBLIC LIBRARY, Copley Sq, Boston, 02117.
Holdings: Cat Microforms
Notes: Microforms Publication by Readex Microprint Corp. Early American Imprints, 1639-1800 1st series (Evans); 1801-1819 2nd series (Shaw-Shoemaker).

MA —AMERICAN ANTIQUARIAN SOCIETY LIBRARY, 185 Salisbury St, Worcester, 01609. Marcus A McCorison, Dir & Librn
Holdings: Vols 60,000 Cat
Notes: Sixty percent of the total of books and pamphlets known to have been printed in the United States before 1821. Source of Readex Microprint Corp project called *Early American Imprints, 1639-1800*, a Microprint edition of every extant book, pamphlet, and broadside printed in what is now the United States. Keyed to Evans *American* Bibliography it reprints in full the texts of nearly 50,000 titles and includes all of Shipton's revision of Evans. A second series, keyed to Shaw and Shoemaker's *American* Bibliography will bring these Microprint reproductions up to 1820. One of the great strengths of the collection is its broadsides and American newspapers--the best anywhere. From it emerged Clarence Bringham's monumental *History and Bibliography of American Newspapers.* 1690-1820, which locates every surviving copy of every newspaper printed in the United States before 1821. ReadexMicroprint Corp is also reproducing this collection. The Society's collections extend beyond 1820, in special strengths, to the turn of the century. The collection incl unusual strengths in Amateur Newspaper (about 50,000 issues), and Bolivian, Chilean, and West Indian newspapers.

NY —NEW YORK STATE LIBRARY, State Education Bldg Annex, Washington Ave, Albany, 12224.
Holdings: Microforms
Notes: Extensive collection; imprints before 1800; New York State Imprints to 1850. Not indexed for complete retrieval. Also Readex microprint edition of Early American imprints, 1639-1800 (indexed by Evans) and Second Series 1801-1819 (indexed by Shaw-Shoemaker).

NY —BUFFALO & ERIE COUNTY PUBLIC LIBRARY, Rare Book Room, Lafayette Sq, Buffalo, 14203. William H Loos, Cur
Holdings: Vols 5000 Cat
Notes: Collection of imprints (1000) before 1801 described in *A Check List of Evans Titles in the Rare Book Room of the Buffalo and Erie County Public Library* (Buffalo, 1969).

NY —HOFSTRA UNIVERSITY, Library, 1000 Fulton Ave, Hempstead, 11550. Charles R Andrews, Dean of Library Services
Notes: Strong collection. Incl some mss.

NY —STATE UNIVERSITY OF NEW YORK, COLLEGE AT NEW PALTZ, Sojourner Truth Library, New Paltz, 12561. W E Connors, Dir
Holdings: Cat Microforms
Notes: Microform publications by Readex Microprint Corp. Early American imprints, 1639-1800 (first series), 1801-1805 (second series).

NY —NEW YORK PUBLIC LIBRARY, Research Libraries, General Research Division, Fifth Ave & 42 St, New York, 10018. Rodney Phillips, Chief
Holdings: Vols (2,225,000) Cat Maps Pix Microforms
Budget: ($775,718)

NC —SOUTHEASTERN BAPTIST THEOLOGICAL SEMINARY LIBRARY, PO Box 752, Wake Forest, 27587. H Eugene McLeod, Librn
Holdings: Microforms
Notes: Readex Microprint edition of materials listed in Evans' *American* Bibliography and in Shaw and Shoemaker's *American Bibliography: a Preliminary* Checklist.

PA —AMERICAN PHILOSOPHICAL SOCIETY, Library, 105 S Fifth St, Philadelphia, 19106. Edward C Carter II, Librn
Holdings: Cat Mss Maps Pix Microforms
Notes: 18th and 19th century Americana. General guide printed.

PA —FRIENDS HISTORICAL LIBRARY OF SWARTHMORE COLLEGE, Swarthmore, 19081. J William Frost, Dir
Holdings: Vols (35,000)
Notes: The Library's collection of 17th and 18th century books and pamphlets comprises the writings of early Friends in England and America, plus numerous pamphlets and tracts describing religious controversies between Quakers and their opponents. Much of the important early 19th century serial and tract literature in the Library emerged from the Quaker schisms in 1827 and later in the 1840s. For a detailed description of the Library's holdings, see *Catalog of the Book and Serials Collections of the Friends Historical Library* (Boston: G K Hall, 1982).

TX —UNIVERSITY OF TEXAS LIBRARIES, Nettie Lee Benson Latin American Collection, Sid Richardson Hall 1.109, Austin, 78712. Laura Gutierrez-Witt, Head Librn
Holdings: Vols (450,000) Cat Mss Maps Pix Phonorecords Filmstrips Microforms
See also entry under Latin America.

TX —FORT WORTH PUBLIC LIBRARY, Humanities Division, 300 Taylor St, Fort Worth, 76102. Linda Bostic, Manager
Holdings: Microforms
Notes: Early American Imprints (in microprint form)--Series 1: 1639-1800; Series 2: 1801-1819.

TX —ROSENBERG LIBRARY, Fox Rare Book Room, 2310 Sealy Ave, Galveston, 77550. Fernando Basilza, Rare Book Librn
Holdings: Vols (2000) Cat Mss Pix
Notes: The Col Milo Pitcher Fox and Agnes Peel Fox Rare Book Room contains 2000 vols incunabula, first printings, and modern fine printing. Incl clay tablets, horn books, parchment material, illuminated books and mss fine printing (principally 15th-18th centuries), fine binding, fore-edge paintings, etc.

VA —UNIVERSITY OF VIRGINIA, Alderman Library, Clifton Waller Barrett Collection, Charlottesville, 22901. Joan St C Crane, Cur of American Literature Collections
Holdings: Vols (300,000) Cat Mss Pix
See also entry under American Language and Literature

VA —UNIVERSITY OF VIRGINIA, Alderman Library, Rare Book Dept, Charlottesville, 22901. Julius P Barclay, Cur
Holdings: Vols (1200) // Cat
Notes: The Mrs Robert Coleman Taylor Collection of First Editions of American Best Sellers (Fiction). Almost without exception, these books are in mint and fine condition. Scope: 1752-1949. Incl very rare early American fiction.

AMERICAN INSTITUTE OF AERONAUTICS AND ASTRONAUTICS

DC —LIBRARY OF CONGRESS, Manuscript Division, Washington, 20540. John C Broderick, Chief
Notes: The American Institute of Aeronautics and Astronautics Archives incorporates primary source material documenting the history of aeronautics. Incl clippings, articles, questionnaires, printed matter, and original mss pertaining to individual aeronauts, the personal papers of balloonist Thaddeus S C Lowe, and a corporate file consisting entirely of printed information on aircraft companies. Incl 30, 000 items.

AMERICAN INSTITUTE OF COOPERATION

NY —CORNELL UNIVERSITY LIBRARIES, Collection of Regional History, Dept of Manuscripts and Univ Archives, Ithaca, 14853.
Notes: Records, ca 1945-66; 16.3 ft.

AMERICAN INSTITUTE OF GRAPHIC ARTS

NY —COLUMBIA UNIVERSITY LIBRARIES, Rare Book & Manuscript

AMERICAN INSTITUTE OF GRAPHIC ARTS (cont.)

Library, 801 Butler Library, 535 W 114 St, New York, 10027. Kenneth A Lohf, Librn
Holdings: Vols (3500) Uncat
Notes: The annual selections. Restricted use.

AMERICAN INSTITUTE OF NUTRITION

TN —VANDERBILT UNIVERSITY, Medical Center Library, Nashville, 37232. Mary H Teloh, Special Collections Librn
Holdings: Uncat Mss Pix Videotapes
Notes: The nucleus of the developing nutrition collection at Vanderbilt is the papers of medical researcher Joseph Goldberger, MD, and his associate W Henry Sebrell, Jr, MD. The collection consists of first editions and translations of classic books on pellagra, and the letters, mss, and notebooks compiled by Dr Goldberger and Dr Sebrell during their years of research on pellagra. See *Nutrition Reviews,* 33(10):310-312, Oct 1975. 10 linear ft of mss. Library also has the archives of the American Institute of Nutrition and manuscripts representing the work of Karl Mason, PhD, Helen S Mitchell, PhD, Lydia J Roberts, PhD, and John B Youmans, MD.

AMERICAN INSTITUTE OF PHYSICS

NY —AMERICAN INSTITUTE OF PHYSICS, Center for the History of Physics, Niels Bohr Library, 335 E 45 St, New York, 10017. John Aubry, Librn
Notes: Papers and records.

AMERICAN INSTITUTE OF PLANNERS

NY —CORNELL UNIVERSITY LIBRARIES, Collection of Regional History, Dept of Manuscripts and Univ Archives, Ithaca, 14853.
Notes: Records, 1934-78; 56 ft.

AMERICAN JEWISH COMMITTEE

†PA —BALCH INSTITUTE FOR ETHNIC STUDIES, Library, 18 S Seventh St, Philadelphia, 19106.
Notes: Papers of Edwin Lukas, head of the civil rights and social action department of the American Jewish Committee.

AMERICAN JEWS see Jews, American

AMERICAN JOURNAL OF NURSING COMPANY, INC.

MA —BOSTON UNIVERSITY, Mugar Memorial Library, Special Collections Dept, 771 Commonwealth Ave, Boston, 02215. Howard B Gotlieb, Dir
Holdings: Mss
Notes: Incl the Sophia F Palmer Historical Collection of the American Journal of Nursing Co and papers of editor Mary M Roberts.

AMERICAN JOURNAL OF PSYCHOLOGY

NY —CORNELL UNIVERSITY LIBRARIES, Collection of Regional History, Dept of Manuscripts and Univ Archives, Ithaca, 14853.
Notes: Records, 1948-65; 31 ft.

AMERICAN LABOR PARTY OF NEW YORK

DC —GEORGE WASHINGTON UNIVERSITY, Gelman Library, 2130 H St NW, Washington, 20052.
Holdings: Cat Mss Pix
Notes: The Eli L. Oliver labor papers cover the period 1930-1952 and particularly concern labor's involvement in politics. The correspondence contains letters from union officials nationwide. Organizational papers of Labor's Non-Partisan League incl financial records, memos, campaign pamphlets, press releases, etc. Oliver's papers also include reports discussing primary and general election strategies for 1938-1940; similar material is present for the American Labor Party of New York relating to the 1940 campaign and for the Labor Committee's backing of the Truman-Barkley and the Stevenson-Sparkman campaigns of 1948-1952, respectively. The collection also contains some of Oliver's speeches, addresses, etc and some personal files including photos, financial records, clippings, etc. Cataloged as a collection with unpublished inventory for access.

NJ —RUTGERS, THE STATE UNIVERSITY OF NEW JERSEY, Alexander Library, Special Collections and Archives, College Ave & Huntington St, New Brunswick, 08903. Ronald L Becker, Cur of Manuscripts and Rare Books
Holdings: //
Notes: Papers, etc (72 linear feet).

AMERICAN LANGUAGE AND LITERATURE

AZ —UNIVERSITY OF ARIZONA, University Library, Special Collections, Tucson, 85721. Louis A Hieb, Head
Holdings: Vols 7000 Cat Mss Microforms
Budget: ($30,000)
Notes: In the area of American literature, the major authors collected are Twain, Garland, Hart, Irving, Melville and James. In the 20th century, the major emphasis is Bukowski, Wakoski, Wilder, Reznikoff, Ginzberg, Ferlinghetti, Snyder, Whalen, Everson, Joyce Carol Oates, and Kurt Vonnegut. Another aspect of the collection is the belle lettres of the American Southwest. The collection covers the complete scope of works by Southwest authors and those works which are set in the Southwest. The major authors are Edward Abbey, Coolidge, Eastlake, Fergusson, Garfield, Horgan, King, McMurtry, Nichols and Rhodes.

CA —CONTRA COSTA COUNTY LIBRARY, 1750 Oak Park Blvd, Pleasant Hill, 94523. Barbara Potter, Librn

CA —HUNTINGTON LIBRARY, Art Gallery & Botanical Gardens, 1151 Oxford Rd, San Marino, 91108. Robert L Middlekauff, Dir; Daniel H Woodward, Librn
Notes: Approx 350,000 rare books, 250,000 reference books, manuscript collection of nearly 2,500,000 pieces and between 200, 000 and 300,000 prints, rare photographs and other related materials. The fullest available survey is now *Guide to Literary Manuscripts in the Huntington Library,* a 539-page handlist published by the Library in 1979. Also, *Guide to American Historical Manuscripts in the Huntington Library* (1979).

CA —COLLEGE OF SAN MATEO, Library, 1700 W Hillsdale Blvd, San Mateo, 94402. Gregg T Atkins, Coordinator of Library Services
Holdings: Vols (14,000) Cat Microforms
Notes: Library of American Civilization (beginnings to 1915) produced by Encyclopedia Britannica. The entire collection is on microfiche. The fiche as well as portable readers are availabe to students.

CA —STANFORD UNIVERSITY LIBRARIES, Cecil H Green Library, Stanford, 94305. Michael T Ryan, Cur
Holdings: Vols (23,000) Cat Mss Pix
Notes: The Charlotte Ashley Felton Memorial Library. English and American literature; the American component begins with the period of Hawthorne and his contemporaries and incl first editions of 20th century authors such as William Faulkner and John Steinbeck. Ms collections incl papers of Ambrose Bierce, Bruce Bliven, Bernard Devoto, Mary Hallock Foote, Janet Lewis, Jack London, Wallace Stegner, John Steinbeck, and Yvor Winters.

CO —COLORADO STATE UNIVERSITY, Libraries, Fort Collins, 80523. John Newman, Special Collections Librn
Holdings: Vols (11,000) Cat Mss Pix
Notes: The Western American Literature Collection incl fiction, poetry, pictures, art, and other works of the imagination set in the American Frontier West and modern rural West, especially the Rocky Mountain Area.

CT —YALE UNIVERSITY, Box 1603A, Yale Station, New Haven, 06520.

DC —LIBRARY OF CONGRESS, Motion Pictures, Broadcasting and Recorded Sound Div, Washington, 20540.
Notes: The Archive of Recorded Poetry and Literature contains discs and tapes of readings of American literary figures from the 1940s to the present.

DC —UNIVERSITY OF THE DISTRICT OF COLUMBIA, Mount Vernon Campus, Library & Media Services Div, 800 Mount Vernon Pl, NW, Washington, 20001. Lottie Wright, Librn
Holdings: Vols (2500) // Uncat
Notes: American history, incl literature, education, politics, and government.

FL —UNIVERSITY OF MIAMI, Otto G Richter Library, PO Box 248214, Coral Gables, 33124. Frank Rodgers, Dir of Libraries
Notes: 3500 items. Nineteenth century well represented by Longfellow and Thoreau collections organized by Thomas DeValcourt at Longfellow House. Additional Thoreau items were purchased later. Innovative and experimental writing of 1960s and 1970s, incl press books from Black Sparrow, Unicorn, Kayak and other small presses, as well as privately published works and many small magazines. Format ranges from postcard and poster to fine limited editions of codex form.

FL —UNIVERSITY OF SOUTH FLORIDA, Library, Tampa, 33620. J B Dobkin, Special Collections Librn
Holdings: Vols 20,000 Cat Mss Pix
Budget: ($7500)
Notes: 19th Century American Literature Collection. First and other significant editions of literary works (including fiction, poetry, drama, etc) by American writers written before 1900. Incl are both adult and juvenile literature. In cases of special authors, an attempt is made to collect all publications, incl items appearing after 1900. These are exceptional cases, however, and in general post-1900 works of writers whose careers extend into the 20th century are not collected. Supporting material (literary manuscripts, contemporary photographs of authors, etc) is incl in the collection although critical and scholarly works relating to 19th century literature are not within the collection parameters. Incl in the materials comprising the holdings are juvenile works of all types and formats with many miniatures, chapbooks and toybooks.

GA —EMORY UNIVERSITY, Robert W Woodruff Library, Special Collections Dept, Atlanta, 30322. Linda M Matthews, Head Special Collections; Virginia J H Cain, Processing Archivist; Richard H F Lindemann, Reference Archivist
Holdings: Vols (16,000) Cat Mss Maps Pix Microforms

IL —NEWBERRY LIBRARY, 60 W Walton St, Chicago, 60610. Diana Haskell, Cur of Modern Mss
Holdings: Cat
Notes: American literature to 1930.

IL —NORTHWESTERN UNIVERSITY, Library, Special Collections Dept, 1937 Sheridan Rd, Evanston, 60201. R Russell Maylone, Cur
Holdings: Vols 11,000 Cat Mss Pix
Notes: First, limited, special editions, letters, ephemera of Walt Whitman and Mark Twain; also of major 20th century writers

AMERICAN LANGUAGE AND LITERATURE (cont.)

such as Faulkner, Hemingway, Hughes, Cullen, Moore, O'Neill. Incl the D R Wagner archive and a large number of avant garde writers such as Eigner, Levy, Bukowski, Brautigan and Dorn. 15,000 "little magazine" titles (exclusive of runs in the general library collection). A portion of the personal library of Margerite Wilkinson containing presentation copies and works inscribed by authors incl in her anthologies.

IL —AUGUSTANA COLLEGE, Library, Rock Island, 61201. Marjorie M Miller, Special Collections Librn
Holdings: Vols (5000) Cat

IL —SKOKIE PUBLIC LIBRARY, 5215 Oakton St, Skokie, 60077. Mary Radmacher, Chief Librn
Holdings: Vols (20,000) Cat Phonorecords
Budget: ($346,500)
Notes: Maintained as American and English literature and criticism subject center under the North Suburban Library System's Coordinated Acquisitions Program.

IN —INDIANA UNIVERSITY, Lilly Library, Seventh St, Bloomington, 47405. William R Cagle, Librn
Holdings: Cat Mss Pix
Notes: Extensive collections for all periods. Strong collection of portraits of authors.

KS —UNIVERSITY OF KANSAS, Kenneth Spencer Research Library, Special Collections Dept, Lawrence, 66045. Alexandra Mason, Librn
Holdings: Cat Mss
Notes: Whitman, Mencken, Mark Twain, nonacademic poetry after 1960, science fiction, miscellaneous 19th and 20th century authors, 19th and 20th children's literature. Noncirculating.

KY —UNIVERSITY OF KENTUCKY, Margaret I King Library, Dept of Special Collections, Lexington, 40506. William Marshall, Head
Holdings: Vols (8000) Cat Mss
Notes: W Hugh Peal Collection of mss and books chiefly relating to British and American literature. Particularly strong in Lamb, Wordsworth, Coleridge and Southey. Incl 4 cubic feet of mss. Incl 16th-20th centuries.

LA —R W NORTON ART GALLERY, Library, 4747 Creswell Ave, Shreveport, 71106. Jerry M Bloomer, Librn
Holdings: // Cat

†MA —BOSTON PUBLIC LIBRARY, Copley Sq, Boston, 02117.
Holdings: Microforms
Notes: Microform Publication by Readex Microprint Corp. Based on Jacob Blank's *Bibliography of American Literature.*

MA —BOSTON UNIVERSITY, Mugar Memorial Library, Special Collections Dept, 771 Commonwealth Ave, Boston, 02215. Howard B Gotlieb, Dir
Holdings: Cat Mss

MA —HARVARD UNIVERSITY LIBRARY, Widener Library, American History Collection, Cambridge, 02138. F Nathaniel Bunker, Bibliographer; Charles Warren, Bibliographer
Holdings: Cat Mss Microforms
Notes: *Widener Library Shelflist* Nos 26-27 (1970) lists 62,217 vols on American literature; there are also great rare book and manuscript collections in this subject.

MA —WHEATON COLLEGE, Library, Norton, 02766. Sherrie S Bergman, College Librn
Holdings: Vols (2100) Cat
Notes: The Cole Collection. English and American literature and poetry based on the personal library of Dr Samuel Valentine Cole.

MA —BRANDEIS UNIVERSITY, Goldfarb Library, 415 South St, Waltham, 02154. Bessie Hahn, Dir
Notes: Collections of John Cheever; Leo Rosten; Ludwig Lewisohn; Joseph Heller; Henry James; Walt Whitman. American Best Sellers Collection, top ten annual best sellers of popular literature from 1900-1975.

MI —UNIVERSITY OF MICHIGAN, Library, Dept of Rare Books & Special Collections, Ann Arbor, 48109. Robert J Starring, Head
Holdings: Cat Mss Pix
Notes: 8500 manuscript items. The collection comprises chiefly the correspondence with noted writers and critics concerning participation as judges in the annual University of Michigan Hopwood Awards contests in dramatic writing, fiction, poetry, and the essay, or as lecturers at the annual award ceremony. It also includes 32 book manuscripts of former award winners, manuscripts of 16 of the lectures, and correspondence with several award winners about publication of their later work, as well as the papers of Broadway playwright Avery Hopwood whose bequest has funded the Avery Hopwood and Jule Hopwood Awards since their inception in 1931.

MI —NORTHERN MICHIGAN UNIVERSITY, Lydia M Olson Library, Elizabeth L Harden Drive, Marquette, 49855. Stephen H Peters, Cataloger
Notes: A major section of the personal library of Moses Coit Tyler, strong in the forms he held significant: novels, essays, journals, and almanacs. Includes works by British, French, Dutch, West Indian, and other writers.

MO —UNIVERSITY OF MISSOURI-KANSAS CITY, General Library, 5100 Rockhill Road, Kansas City, 64110. Kenneth J LaBudde, Dir; Gordon Hendrickson, Assoc Dir; Marilyn Carbonell, Ref Librn
Holdings: Vols 108,000 Cat
Notes: (4121 current serial subscriptions) includes an emphasis on drama and includes Thomas and Mila Baker Collection of Twentieth-Century British and American Literature.

MO —UNIVERSITY OF MISSOURI-SAINT LOUIS, Thomas Jefferson Library, 8001 Natural Bridge Rd, Saint Louis, 63121.
Notes: American and British Utopian Literature: Approximately 1000 vols of Literary Utopias. Collection is partially described and listed in Sargent, Lyman Tower *British and American Utopian Literature, 1516-1975: An Annotated* Bibliography, (G K Hall, 1979); note: a second edition is in preparation. Collection also includes galley proofs of some of the titles.

MO —WASHINGTON UNIVERSITY, John M Olin Library, Campus Box 1061, St Louis, 63130.
Holdings: Cat Mss
Notes: Incl material from the George N Meissner and the William K Bixby Collections. Particular strength in 19th and 20th century original editions. Also autographs and mss of prominent literary figures, entered under personal names elsewhere in this volume.

NJ —PRINCETON UNIVERSITY, Library, Rare Books Dept, Princeton, 08544. Stephen Ferguson, Cur
Holdings: Cat Mss Microforms

NJ —WILLIAM PATERSON COLLEGE OF NEW JERSEY, Sarah Byrd Askew Library, 300 Pompton Rd, Wayne, 07470. Robert Lopresti, Librn
Holdings: Vols (500) Cat
Notes: First editions of US and English authors. Bibliography available.

NY —ALFRED UNIVERSITY, Herrick Memorial Library, Alfred, 14802. June E Brown, Head Librn
Notes: The Howells/Frechette Collection. Family documents, 7000 letters of William Cooper Howells (American consul to Quebec, later to Toronto), William Dean Howells, his sister Annie Frechette, Achille Frechette (official translator, Canadian House of Commons), and Louis Frechette (poet laureate of Canada).

NY —SAINT JOHN'S UNIVERSITY, Special Collections Dept, Grand Central & Utopia Pkwys, Jamaica, 11439. Szilvia E Szmuk, Librn
Holdings: Cat
Notes: The John E Baxter Collection includes the works of four American authors: Thomas Bailey Aldrich, William Dean Howells, Henry Van Dyke, and Edith Wharton. Many of the volumes are first or limited editions, some are autographed. No photocopying.

NY —AMERICAN ACADEMY & INSTITUTE OF ARTS & LETTERS, Library, 633 W 155 St, New York, 10032. Casindania P Eaton, Librn; Nancy Johnson, Researcher
Notes: Works of members of the Academy only. Incl mss, letters, memorabilia, etc.

NY —NEW YORK PUBLIC LIBRARY, Research Libraries, General Research Division, Fifth Ave & 42 St, New York, 10018. Rodney Phillips, Chief
Holdings: Vols (2,225,000) Cat Maps Pix Microforms
Budget: ($775,718)

NY —NEW YORK PUBLIC LIBRARY, Mid-Manhattan Library, Literature and Language Dept, 455 Fifth Ave, New York, 10016. Eric Steele, Sr Principal Librn
Holdings: Vols (160,000) Cat Phonorecords Microforms Audiotapes
Budget: ($92,000)
Notes: Extensive collection of works, criticism and biographies of major and minor American writers for undergraduate study; special attention directed towards Black American literature. Collection includes material on the teaching of literature, the techniques of creative writing, and the history of the theater when relevant to the study of dramatic literature. Substantial or complete runs of the major journals. Representative collection of literary magazines. Recordings of prose, poetry and drama.

NY —NEW YORK PUBLIC LIBRARY, Berg Collection of English & American Literature, Fifth Ave & 42 St, New York, 10018. Lola L Szladits, Cur
Holdings: Vols 20,000 Cat Mss
Notes: The preface to the Collection's G K Hall catalog, 1969, (5 vols), prints an outline of history and guide to the catalog: "The Berg Collection of English and American Literature is one of America's most celebrated collections of first editions, rare books, autograph letters, and mss. Among the 20,000 printed items and 50,000 mss, covering the entire range of English and American literature, there can be found rarities considered museum pieces by the book world. Irving, Hawthorne, Emerson, Thoreau, Whitman are represented in first editions as well as in mss. Mark Twain can be studied in depth by scholars who have not only correspondence but also the original mss of *A Connecticut Yankee in King Arthur's Court* and *Following the Equator,* besides many others, to consult. The policy of the Collection has been to acquire work of contemporaries. James RussellLowell's mss are next to ms poems by Robert Lowell. Gertrude Stein's printed works are followed by those of John Steinbeck. For the following 20th-century authors, the Collection is justly famous: Arnold Bennett, Joseph Conrad, George Gissing, Thomas Hardy, John Masefield, Bernard Shaw, Virginia Woolf, Lewis Carroll, Rudyard Kipling, and Robert Browning. The Irish Literary Renaissance survives in the papers of Lady Gregory."

NY —NEW YORK UNIVERSITY, Elmer Holmes Bobst Library, Div of Special Collections, Washington Sq S, New York, 10012. Frank Walker, Librn; Patrick McGuire, Asst Librn
Holdings: Vols (100,000) Cat Mss Pix
Notes: The Fales Collection of first (and other) editions of English and American novels from about 1750 to date (about 70, 000 titles). Mss (30,000) pieces.

NC —BELMONT ABBEY COLLEGE, Abbot Vincent Taylor Library, Belmont, 28012. Marjorie McDermott, Dir
Holdings: Vols (10,000) Cat Mss Pix
Notes: Patristics (incl Migne's *Patrologie*), Roman Catholic Church history, philosophy, literature (American and British), and both US and North Carolina history. A substantial number of the books date from the 15th, 16th, and 17th centuries. Most of the source material in Catholic studies particularly could not be obtained elsewhere in the Southeast.

NC —UNIVERSITY OF NORTH CAROLINA, CHARLOTTE, J Murrey

AMERICAN LANGUAGE AND LITERATURE (cont.)

Atkins Library, UNCC Station, Charlotte, 28223. Robert F Brabham Jr, Special Collections Librn
Holdings: Vols 2000 Cat
Notes: First and other significant editions of American writers, 1800-1950. Also have children's books.

NC —DUKE UNIVERSITY, William R Perkins Library, Manuscript Dept, Durham, 27706. Ellen Gartrell, Cur of Mss
Holdings: Cat Mss
Notes: Emphasis on US South. Incl papers of Paul Hamilton Hayne, T N Page, E D E N Southworth, Thomas Chivers, Carson McCullers, William Styron, Fred Chappell, Frank G Slaughter, Ovid W Pierce, Anne Tyler. Study and teaching of American literature is represented in papers of William Blackburn, Jay Hubbell, "American Literature" (periodical), and others.

NC —DUKE UNIVERSITY, William R Perkins Library, Rare Book Room, Durham, 27706. John L Sharpe, III, Cur
Notes: Paul Hamilton Hayne collection of American poets and poetry (1800 books, pamphlets and periodicals).

NC —DUKE UNIVERSITY, William R Perkins Library, Jay B Hubbell Center for American Literary Historiography, Durham, 27706. Erma Whittington, Librn
Notes: 77,312 items, including manuscripts, pictures, clippings, and correspondence. "The objective of the Center is to gather the papers and materials of significant scholars and critics in American literary history." The Center is a part of the Perkins Library Manuscripts Department.

†NC —WAKE FOREST UNIVERSITY, Z Smith Reynolds Library, Box 7777, Reynold Sta, Winston-Salem, 27109. Richard J Murdoch, Rare Book Librn
Holdings: Cat
Notes: Literature collections with emphasis on a select list of English, Irish and American authors total 13,000 vols. Incl are first and significant editions, works about the authors and some ephemera. Noncirculating.

OH —CLEVELAND PUBLIC LIBRARY, Literature Dept, 325 Superior Ave, Cleveland, 44114. Evelyn Ward, Head
Holdings: Vols Cat Microforms Phonorecords
Notes: Comprehensive collection of literary texts, with a large body of literary history, criticism and biography. Strong in drama and poetry. Many first editions, books from special presses, and rarities. Microprint. Reference aids.

PA —PHILIP H & A S W ROSENBACH FOUNDATION LIBRARY, 2010 DeLancey Pl, Philadelphia, 19103. Clive E Driver, Dir
Holdings: Cat Mss Pix

PA —TEMPLE UNIVERSITY LIBRARIES, Special Collections Dept, Rare Books & Mss Section, Philadelphia, 19122. Thomas M Whitehead, Cur
Holdings: Vols (3000) Cat Mss
Notes: Extensive holdings of modern English and American literature, late 19th, 20th centuries. First and limited editions, association copies, supported by mss holdings. Special sub-collections of Walter de la Mare, Joseph Conrad, Robert Louis Stevenson, Joel Chandler Harris, E H W Meyerstein, Thackeray, George MacDonald, W W Gibson, John Masefield, Tennyson, Sir Walter Scott.

PA —UNIVERSITY OF PENNSYLVANIA, Van Pelt Library, Rare Books Collection, 34 & Walnut Sts, Philadelphia, 19104. Daniel Traister, Special Collections Librn
Notes: Primarily papers of modern American authors. Approx 2000 linear feet.

RI —BROWN UNIVERSITY, John Hay Library, Harris Collection, Prospect St, Providence, 02912. Rosemary L Cullen, Cur
Holdings: Vols (200,000) Cat Mss Pix Phonorecords Microforms
Budget: ($15,000)
Notes: The Harris Collection of American Poetry and Plays is principally composed of American and Canadian poetry and plays, 17th century-date. Extensive holdings in songsters, gift books and annuals, hymnals, pageants, broadside verse, carriers' addresses, women poets, juvenile poetry, (incl Mother Goose and *The Night Before* Christmas), sheet music with lyrics, small press publications, fine printing, black poets, "little magazines," Yiddish-American literature. All movements or schools of American poetry are represented. Incl first editions of most American poets and playwrights, notably Whitman, Poe, Wallace Stevens, Eugene O'Neill, Edward Albee, Ezra Pound, T S Eliot, William Carlos Williams, Amy Lowell, Phyllis Wheatley, Robert Frost, Allen Ginsberg, Bliss Carman, and Stephen Foster sheet music. Also incl the Saunders Walt Whitman Collection (1300 vols); the LangdonCollection of Pageants (250 vols); the Asa Cushman Collection of plays in ms and prompt copies; the MacDougall Collection of Psalters and Hymnals; 4000 plays issued by Walter H Baker Co, Boston (1890-1957); the Vaxer Collection of Yiddish Poetry, Plays and Music (1700 vols). Collections incl 200,000 vols, 30,000 broadsides, 55,000 mss, 170,000 pieces of sheet music, 450 phonorecords, and 375 microfilm reels. See *Dictionary Catalog of the Harris Collection of American Poetry and Plays* (Boston: G K Hall, 1972), 13 vols; *Supplement* (1977), 3 vols. See also, *American Poetry,* 1609-1900, *A Collection on Microfilm, Segment I* (1609-1820); *Segment II* (1821-1850); *Segment III* (1851-1870) (Woodbridge, Conn: Research Publications). Separate catalog.

SC —UNIVERSITY OF SOUTH CAROLINA, Thomas Cooper Library, Columbia, 29208. Kenneth E Toombs, Dir of Libraries; Roger Mortimer, Rare Book Librn
Holdings: Vols 3000 Cat
Notes: Very strong in the 18th, 19th and 20th centuries for American literature. First editions.
See also entries under Frost, Robert; Literary Annuals and Giftbooks; Wharton, Edith; Whitman, Walt.

TX —UNIVERSITY OF TEXAS LIBRARIES, General Libraries, PO Box P, Austin, 78713. Carolyn Bucknell, Asst Dir for Collection Development
Holdings: Cat Microforms
Notes: 19th century fiction.

TX —TEXAS CHRISTIAN UNIVERSITY, Mary Couts Burnett Library, Fort Worth, 76129.
Holdings: Vols 1500 Cat Mss
Notes: Incl the William Luther Lewis Collection. See Kendall, Lyle H *A Descriptive Catalogue of the W L Lewis Collection: Part I Manuscripts, Inscriptions,* Art. (Fort Worth: TCU Press, 1979).

TX —TRINITY UNIVERSITY, Elizabeth Coates Maddux Library, 715 Stadium Dr, San Antonio, 78284. Richard Hume Werking, Library Dir; Craig Likness, Head Bibliographer
Notes: General reference.

UT —BRIGHAM YOUNG UNIVERSITY, Harold B Lee Library, Unversity Hill, Provo, 84602. Sterling Albrecht, Dir
Holdings: Vols 119,766 Cat Mss Maps Pix Microforms

VT —MIDDLEBURY COLLEGE, Abernethy Library of American Literature, Middlebury, 05753. Robert Buckeye, Librn
Holdings: Vols 14,500 Cat Mss Audiotapes
Budget: $16,500
Notes: 19th and 20th century American literature.

VA —UNIVERSITY OF VIRGINIA, Alderman Library, Clifton Waller Barrett Collection, Charlottesville, 22901. Joan St C Crane, Cur of American Literature Collections
Holdings: Vols (300,000) Cat Mss Pix
Notes: The Library takes as its province 175 years of American literature, from 1775 to 1980. It contains, insofar as it has been possible to assemble them, all fiction, poetry, drama, and essays published by an American in book form up to 1875; for the years since, it contains a very nearly complete collection of the works of every major American writer, as well as of those whose achievements were not of the first rank, but who, nevertheless, occupy a place in the literary history of the Republic. With the first editions are important later editions, many translations and periodical appearances, and a vast amount of biographical and critical material. Mss and letters of quality have been brought together in such quantity that few similar collections can approach it in size and scholarly importance. Publications: *A Brief Account of the Clifton Waller Barrett Library,*Herbert Cahoon (Charlottesville: University of Virginia, 1960); "The Mighty Manuscripts of Mr C Waller Barrett," C Brian Kelly, *The Commonwealth: The Magazine of Virginia,* vol 38, no 8, Aug 1971, pp 21-28. To determine the manuscript holdings in the Library for particular American authors, consult the second edition of *American Literary Manuscripts.*

VA —VIRGINIA COMMONWEALTH UNIVERSITY, James Branch Cabell Library, Richmond, 23284. Daniel Yanchisin, Special Collections Librn
Holdings: Vols (3600)
Notes: A collection of approximately 3600 volumes by post 1945 American poets including some bibliography and criticism. 2000 books are cataloged and the remainder are accessible by author. The collection includes the library and archival holdings of two literary support organizations, New Virginia Review, Inc and the Poetry Society of Virginia.

WA —SEATTLE PUBLIC LIBRARY, 1000 Fourth Ave, Seattle, 98104. Ronald A Dubberly, City Librn
Holdings: Cat

WA —UNIVERSITY OF WASHINGTON LIBRARIES, Suzzallo Library, Special Collections Division, Rare Book Collection, FM-25, Seattle, 98195. Gary Menges, Coordinator for Special Collections
Holdings: Vols
Notes: Printing history, including early printed books and modern fine printing; book arts, including papermaking, decorated papers, bookbinding, book design, and artist's books; American literature, 19th century includes: Stephen Crane, Ralph Waldo Emerson, Nathaniel Hawthorne, Henry James, Henry Wadsworth Longfellow, Herman Melville, Frank Norris, Harriet Beecher Stowe and Walt Whitman and 20th century includes: Theodore Roethke; illustrated books, including emblem books, historical children's illustration, books illustrated with prints, and artist's books; costume history; voyages and travels; preservation of library materials.

WI —UNIVERSITY OF WISCONSIN, MADISON, Memorial Library, 728 State St, Madison, 53706. Erwin K Welsch, Social Studies Bibliographer
Notes: Incl the Miles L Hanley Collection of English and American Linguistics; the Edna Ferber Collection, 1300 vols; the O Henry Collection, ca 20 first editions; the Pitman Library; the Jesse Stuart Collection; the Mark Twain collection; the Twentieth Century Literary Collection; the Underground Press; and others.

WI —MILWAUKEE PUBLIC LIBRARY, 814 W Wisconsin Ave, Milwaukee, 53233. Donald J Sager, City Librn
Holdings: Vols (2700) Cat
Notes: Collection of definitive editions of collected works of British and American authors; incl most of the significant editions of Shakespeare starting with Rowe.

WI —UNIVERSITY OF WISCONSIN, MILWAUKEE, Library, Box 604, Milwaukee, 53201. William C Roselle, Dir
Holdings: Vols (68,000) Cat Mss Phonorecords Audiotapes
Notes: Special strengths of the literature collection include Shakespeare Research Collection (1800 volumes), 17th Century Collection (600 volumes), William Blake, James Joyce, Howard Fast (English-language editions and unique collection of foreign-language translations), contemporary small press poetry publications, etc.

BC —VANCOUVER PUBLIC LIBRARY, Language & Literature Div, 750 Burrard St,

AMERICAN LANGUAGE AND LITERATURE (cont.)

Vancouver, V6Z 1X5, Can. B Kinnear, Head
Notes: General collection of poetry, drama criticism, novels, pamphlets. Index files of author biographies, poetry in periodicals, criticism in periodicals; also poetry index, both compiled by the staff to books and unindexed periodicals. Partially cataloged. Also incl audiotapes.

NS —MOUNT SAINT VINCENT UNIVERSITY, Library, 166 Bedford Hwy, Halifax, B3M 2J6, Can. Lucian Bianchini, University Librn
Holdings: Vols 7000 Cat
Budget: ($125,000)
Notes: The MacDonald Collection consists of 19th and 20th century English and American literature, fine bindings, a few examples of fore-edge painting, limited editions, first editions, and autographed copies.

ON —NATIONAL LIBRARY OF CANADA, 395 Wellington St, Ottawa, K1A 0N4, Can. Andre Preibish, Dir
Holdings: Vols 34,000
Notes: Includes 350 serial titles. The Library has been receiving on legal deposit all current literary works in English and French published in Canada since 1950. Intensive acquisition of earlier works and those published abroad. The collection aims to be comprehensive. In addition, the collection is supported by representative resources for English, American, French and Commonwealth Literature.

AMERICAN LAW see Law, American

AMERICAN LIBRARY ASSOCIATION

IL —UNIVERSITY OF ILLINOIS, URBANA/CHAMPAIGN, Library, University Archives, 19 Library, 1408 W Gregory Drive, Urbana, 61801. Maynard Brichford, University Archivist
Holdings: Cat Mss Pix
Notes: Ms archives of the American Library Association. Subjects incl librarians, library science, library associations. Controls cards, ADP, and supplementary finding aids for intellectual control of the archives.

†NY —COLUMBIA UNIVERSITY LIBRARIES, Butler Library, Rare Book and Manuscript Library, 535 W 114 St, New York, 10027.
Notes: Files relating to the American Library Association's Special Committee to Aid Italian Libraries' assistance to Italian libraries to help restore books, mss and other library materials after the 1966 floods in Florence.

AMERICAN LITERARY MANUSCRIPT PROJECT

NC —DUKE UNIVERSITY, William R Perkins Library, Jay B Hubbell Center for American Literary Historiography, Durham, 27706. Erma Whittington, Librn
Notes: 77,312 items, including manuscripts, pictures, clippings, and correspondence. "The objective of the Center is to gather the papers and materials of significant scholars and critics in American literary history." The Center is a part of the Perkins Library Manuscripts Department.

AMERICAN LITERATURE (PERIODICAL)

NC —DUKE UNIVERSITY, William R Perkins Library, Manuscript Dept, Durham, 27706. Ellen Gartrell, Cur of Mss
Notes: Emphasis on US South. Incl papers of Paul Hamilton Hayne, T N Page, E D E N Southworth, Thomas Chivers, Carson McCullers, William Styron, Fred Chappell, Frank G Slaughter, Ovid W Pierce, Anne Tyler. Study and teaching of American literature is represented in papers of William Blackburn, Jay Hubbell, "American Literature" (periodical), and others.

AMERICAN LOYALISTS

OH —OHIO HISTORICAL SOCIETY, Archives Library Division, 1982 Velma Ave, Columbus, 43211. Dennis East, Division Chief
Holdings: Vols 400 // Cat Mss
Notes: Based on the collection of Wilbur H Siebert; incl manuscripts and notes.

AMERICAN MATHEMATICAL SOCIETY

GA —UNIVERSITY OF GEORGIA, Libraries, Athens, 30602. Arlene E Luchsinger, Asst Dir Branch Libraries
Holdings: Vols 19,500 Cat
Notes: The collection incl the bulk of the collection originally held by the American Mathematical Society, and purchased by the University of Georgia from Columbia University several years ago. It is strong in foreign dissertations in mathematics.

AMERICAN MEDICAL ASSOCIATION

IL —AMERICAN MEDICAL ASSOCIATION, Div of Library & Archival Services, 535 N Dearborn St, Chicago, 60610. Arthur W Hafner, Dir
Holdings: Vols (130,000) Cat Mss Pix Microforms
Notes: "One of world's most comprehensive collections in sociology and economics of medicine," some 150,000 items, 1964 to date. Archival collection of materials relating to history of AMA and its constituent societies. Incl historical biographical resource file on American physicians, incl obituary data and genealogy.

AMERICAN MEDICAL WOMEN'S ASSOCIATION

PA —MEDICAL COLLEGE OF PENNSYLVANIA, Florence A Moore Library of Medicine, Archives & Special Collections on Women in Medicine, 3300 Henry Ave, Philadelphia, 19129. Sandra L Chaff, Archivist
Holdings: Vols 700 Cat Mss Pix Slides Phonorecords Audiotapes 16mm Films
Notes: "One of the most comprehensive US collections of historical material on women physicians." Incl personal papers of women physicians; audiotapes and transcripts of interviews conducted by the Oral History Project on Women Physicians; the American Medical Women's Association historical collection; the American Women's Hospitals Service collection; the Kate Campbell Hurd-Mead collection; a file of 10,000 photos relating to women physicians; and 5100 reprints of which 4000 citations appear in *Women in Medicine: A Bibliography of the Literature on Women Physicians,* by Sandra L Chaff et al. (Metuchen, NJ: Scarecrow Press, 1977).

AMERICAN MISSIONARY ASSOCIATION

LA —AMISTAD RESEARCH CENTER, 400 Esplanade Ave, New Orleans, 70116. Clifton H Johnson, Exec Dir; Florence E Borders, Senior Archivist
Holdings: Vols (10,000) Cat Mss Pix Audiotapes Microforms
Budget: ($315,000)
Notes: 8,000,000 ms pieces, 10,000 pictures, 3500 microforms, and 500 audiotapes. Originally established at Fisk University, in Nashville, by the American Missionary Association (AMA), this research center on Black American History consists of mss, photographs, clippings, books, pamphlets, taped speeches, and interviews; also the papers of such leaders as W E B DuBois, Countee Cullen, and Mary McLeod Bethune. Also materials on other American minorities, such as Native Americans, Asian Americans, Hispanics, etc.

ME —BOWDOIN COLLEGE, Library, Brunswick, 04011. Dianne M Gutscher, Cur of Special Collections
Holdings: Mss
Notes: The Charles Henry Howard Papers contain more than 400 pieces of correspondence, articles, and addresses, 1852-1907, of this Civil War officer and Secretary of the American Missionary Association. The papers complement those of his brother, Oliver Otis Howard.

SC —COLLEGE OF CHARLESTON LIBRARY, Special Collections Dept, Charleston, 29401.
Notes: The Avery Institute Collection consists mostly of photocopied materials (correspondence, annual reports, financial records, etc) housed at the Amistad Research Center of Dillard University. Established and maintained through much of its history by the American Missionary Assn, this material reflects the organization's work in South Carolina beginning in the Reconstruction era. Incl also oral histories of graduates of Avery Institute.

AMERICAN MUSEUM OF NATURAL HISTORY

NY —AMERICAN MUSEUM OF NATURAL HISTORY, Library Services Dept, Central Park W & 79th St, New York, 10024. Nina J Root, Chairwoman; Mary Genett, Asst Librn for Reference Services
Notes: The Photographic Collection consist of over 500,000 black-and-white prints and almost 50,000 color transparencies and slides in this and many other subjects. Many from Museum expeditions and fieldwork. Examples of human beings, scenery, animals, plants and minerals from all over the world, as well as visual documentation of scientific phenomena. Subject areas covered incl anthropology, archeology, astronomy, some botany, ecology, geography and travel, geology, the history of natural history, mineralogy, gemstones, paleontology, fossils, primitive art, scientists, and zoology.

AMERICAN MUSIC see Music, American

AMERICAN MUSICAL THEATRE

CT —YALE UNIVERSITY, Box 1603A, Yale Station, New Haven, 06520.
Holdings: Cat Mss Pix
Notes: Incl American Musical Theater and complete archives of the Theater Guide; also memorabilia.

CT —YALE UNIVERSITY, Sterling Memorial Library, Yale Collection of Historical Sound Recordings, 120 High St, New Haven, 06520. Richard Warren Jr, Cur
Holdings: Vols Mss Pix Phonorecords Audiotapes
Notes: Incl "classical music" ("concert music") of all types from Western culture, jazz, the American Musical Theatre, spoken material (literary, dramatic, documentary). The aim of the Collection is to document performance practice in the fields collected. See the article by Karol Berger in the *Journal of the Association for Recorded Sound Collections,* vol VI, no 1, pp 13-25. Partically cataloged.

KY —HOPKINSVILLE COMMUNITY COLLEGE, Library, North Dr, Hopkinsville, 42240. Marjanna J Frising, Librn
Holdings: Vols (500) Cat Phonorecords Audiotapes Filmstrips
Notes: Incl most notable Broadway plays, both musical and non-musical, with sound-tracks available for most. Also a large collection of children's and one-act plays as well as non-musical but best known 3-act plays, incl comedy and mystery plays.

NY —NEW YORK PUBLIC LIBRARY, Performing Arts Research Center, Rodgers & Hammerstein Archives of Recorded Sound, 111 Amsterdam Ave, New York, 10023.
Holdings: Cat Phonorecords Audiotapes
Notes: Comprehensive collection of commercial recordings of American musicals. Part of this collection consists of aircheck recordings from the broadcast *Railroad Hour* series produced by Jerome Lawrence and Robert E Lee between 1948 and 1954, comprising in abridged form productions of American operetta and musical comedy from the Victor Herbert era

AMERICAN MUSICAL THEATRE (cont.)

to the post-World War II period, and featuring leading stars in the lead roles. Virtually the entire history of the American musical theatre from the turn of the century is covered. Many of the productions represented have never appeared on commercial discs. Important collection of early vaudeville and music hall performers on tape.

AMERICAN NEWSPAPER GUILD

MI —WAYNE STATE UNIVERSITY, Walter P Reuther Library, Archives of Labor & Urban Affairs, Detroit, 48202. Philip Mason, Dir
Notes: The most recent national labor union to place its records in the Archives is the American Newspaper Guild. The collection contains many personal papers and writings of Heywood Broun. The records of local Guild offices are being collected and those from the Detroit Newspaper Guild have already been obtained.

AMERICAN NEWSPAPERS see Newspapers, American

AMERICAN NURSES ASSOCIATION

MA —BOSTON UNIVERSITY, Mugar Memorial Library, Special Collections Dept, 771 Commonwealth Ave, Boston, 02215. Howard B Gotlieb, Dir
Holdings: Cat Mss Pix
Notes: Mss, correspondence, etc collected in depth.

AMERICAN NURSES' FOUNDATION, INC.

MA —BOSTON UNIVERSITY, Mugar Memorial Library, Special Collections Dept, 771 Commonwealth Ave, Boston, 02215. Howard B Gotlieb, Dir
Holdings: Cat Mss Records

AMERICAN ORATIONS

IL —NEWBERRY LIBRARY, 60 W Walton St, Chicago, 60610. Diana Haskell, Cur of Modern Mss
Holdings: Cat
Notes: Fourth of July orations.

MA —NEW ENGLAND HISTORIC GENEALOGICAL SOCIETY, Library, 101 Newbury St, Boston, 02116. Ralph J Crandell, Dir
Holdings: Vols (250,000) Mss Maps Microforms Pix
Notes: New England genealogy. Especially strong Massachusetts, Maine, and New Hampshire, although all states are well represented, as are the relevancies of each subject listed in this volume with regard to British antecedent and contemporary history. Special strengths in local history biography, obituaries, etc, incl parish registers, censuses, British and American. 3125 linear ft of mss.

MA —AMERICAN ANTIQUARIAN SOCIETY LIBRARY, 185 Salisbury St, Worcester, 01609. Marcus A McCorison, Dir & Librn
Holdings: Vols 5000 Cat
Notes: An outstanding collection to 1876.

NY —NEW YORK HISTORICAL SOCIETY, Library, 170 Central Park W, New York, 10024. James Gregory, Librn
Holdings: Mss
Notes: Incl original mss, illustrative materials, etc.

AMERICAN ORIENTAL SOCIETY

CT —YALE UNIVERSITY, American Oriental Society Library, 120 High St, New Haven, 06520. Rutherford B Rogers, Librarian
Holdings: Vols 22,000 Cat Mss
Notes: On deposit.

AMERICAN PATRIOTIC POETRY see Patriotic Poetry, American

AMERICAN PARTY

SC —COLLEGE OF CHARLESTON LIBRARY, Special Collections Dept, Charleston, 29401.
Notes: Papers and newsclippings regarding the Know-Nothings.

AMERICAN PEACE SOCIETY, 1828-1947

ME —BOWDOIN COLLEGE, Library, Brunswick, 04011. Dianne M Gutscher, Cur of Special Collections
Holdings: Mss
Notes: The Rowland Bailey Howard Papers contain about 250 letters, as well as diaries, newsclippings, and ephemera, primarily for the period 1848-1891, of this clergyman and Secretary of the American Peace Society. The collection contains almost exclusively family letters and complements those of Rowland's brothers, Oliver Otis Howard and Charles Henry Howard.

PA —SWARTHMORE COLLEGE, Peace Collection, Swarthmore, 19081. Jean R Soderlund, Cur of Peace Collection
Holdings: / / Mss Pix
Notes: Personal papers and correspondence of American Peace Society's secretary Benjamin Franklin Trueblood, minutes, reports, as well as printed publications which include addresses, books, pamphlets, leaflets; files of the periodicals, *Harbinger of Peace* (1828-1831), *Calumet* (1831-1835), *American Advocate of Peace* (1834-1836), *Advocate of Peace* (with title variations, 1837-1932), and *World Affairs* (1932 to date). 10 linear feet for APS may be found in Swarthmore College Peace Collection among the personal papers of individual leaders (eg, William I Hull, William Ladd, Joshua Blanchard, Elihu Burritt, Henry Wadsworth Longfellow Dana, etc) and among the papers of local peace groups that maintained some affiliation with APS. The Peace Collection has been described in Downs 972, 978, 4633, and in Downs 1950-1961 Supplement 507 and 916. Fordecriptions of major document groups, see the *Guide to the Swarthmore College Peace Collection,* 2nd ed (1981).
See also entry under Pacifism - History.

AMERICAN PERIODICALS see Periodicals, American

AMERICAN PHILOSOPHICAL SOCIETY

PA —AMERICAN PHILOSOPHICAL SOCIETY, Library, 105 S Fifth St, Philadelphia, 19106. Edward C Carter II, Librn
Holdings: Vols (162,430) Cat Mss Maps
Notes: Collection (as it was in 1970) is incl in *Catalog of Books in the American Philosophical Society Library* (Westport, Conn: Greenwood Publishing Corp, 1970) and *Catalog of Manuscripts in the American Philosphical Society Library* (Westport, Conn: Greenwood Publishing Corp, 1970). Both of these are reproductions of APS Library catalog cards, incl author, subject, and title entries.

AMERICAN PHILOSOPHICAL SOCIETY (WESTERN DIVISION)

IL —UNIVERSITY OF ILLINOIS, URBANA/CHAMPAIGN, Library, University Archives, 19 Library, 1408 W Gregory Drive, Urbana, 61801. Maynard Brichford, University Archivist
Holdings: Cat Mss Maps Pix Slides Microforms
Notes: Papers, archival records, etc.

AMERICAN PHYSICAL SOCIETY

NY —AMERICAN INSTITUTE OF PHYSICS, Center for the History of Physics, Niels Bohr Library, 335 E 45 St, New York, 10017. John Aubry, Librn
Notes: Paper and records of the American Physical Society. Also papers of physicist Karl Kelchner Darrow's professional correspondence (1928-73), diaries (1911-75), and early undergraduate notes, as well as materials on lectures, speeches, offprints, and family correspondence. Most of Dr Darrow's career was with the Bell Telephone Laboratories, and he was Secretary of the American Physical Society for 25 years.

AMERICAN PLAYWRIGHTS see Playwrights, American

AMERICAN PLAYWRIGHTS' THEATRE

OH —OHIO STATE UNIVERSITY, William Oxley Thompson Memorial Library, 1858 Neil Ave Mall, Columbus, 43210. Robert A Tibbetts, Cur of Special Collections
Holdings: Uncat Mss
Notes: American Playwrights' Theatre papers, incl business records and scripts of plays produced or considered for production.

AMERICAN POETRY

CA —UNIVERSITY OF CALIFORNIA, DAVIS, Shields Library, Dept of Special Collections, Davis, 95616. Donald Kunitz, Head; C Danial Elliott, Asst Head
Holdings: Vols 7500 Cat
Notes: Ephemeral and rare post-1946 titles which are experimental or innovative in nature. Incl Bukowski, Dorn, Everson, Ferlinghetti, Ashbery, DiPrima, Snyder, etc.

CA —UNIVERSITY OF CALIFORNIA, SAN DIEGO, Central University Library, Mandeville Dept of Special Collections, La Jolla, 92093. Lynda Corey Claassen, Head; Michael Davidson, Cur, Archive for New Poetry
Holdings: Vols (28,000) Audiotapes Phonorecords
Notes: An extensive collection of modern English-language poetry published since World War II, the Archive contains over 28, 000 books, over 1000 magazine titles, and some 900 tapes and records. The Archive maintains substantial collections of papers from Paul Blackburn, Charles Reznikoff, Lew Welch, Jerome Rothenberg, Louis Zukofsky, and other major contemporary American poets. The collection of papers belonging to editor and publisher Donald Allen represents the work of one of the first publishers to make innovative poetry available through his anthology, *The New American Poetry, 1945-1960,* and through his two presses, The Four Seasons Foundation and Grey Fox Press.

CA —SAN DIEGO PUBLIC LIBRARY, Literature & Language Sect, 820 E St, San Diego, 92101. Alyce Archuleta, Senior Librn
Holdings: Cat
Notes: Collection of both well-known and lesser known American contemporary poets.

CT —YALE UNIVERSITY, Box 1603A, Yale Station, New Haven, 06520.

DC —GEORGETOWN UNIVERSITY, Library, Special Collections Div, 37 & O Sts NW, Washington, 20057. George M Barringer, Special Collections Librn; Nicholas B Sheetz, Mss Librn
Holdings: Vols (3000) Uncat Mss
Notes: The Murray L Marshall Collection, including several thousand issues of American poetry magazines; a complete run of *Sonnet Sequences,* 1929-58; and Mr Marshall's editorial files for *Sonnet Sequences.*

DC —LIBRARY OF CONGRESS, Motion Pictures, Broadcasting and Recorded Sound Div, Washington, 20540.
Notes: The Archive of Recorded Poetry and Literature contains discs and tapes of readings of American literary figures from the 1940s to the present.

IL —NEWBERRY LIBRARY, 60 W Walton St, Chicago, 60610. Diana Haskell, Cur of Modern Mss
Notes: Strong on 19th century figures; 20th century to 1950.

IN —INDIANA UNIVERSITY, Lilly Library, Seventh St, Bloomington, 47405. William R Cagle, Librn
Holdings: Cat Mss Pix
Notes: Extensive collection. Incl libraries of Louis Untermeyer and Oscar Williams. Mss incl many 19th and 20th century poets.

AMERICAN POETRY (cont.)

IN —BUTLER UNIVERSITY, Irwin Library, Hugh Thomas Miller Rare Book Room, 4600 Sunset Ave, Indianapolis, 46208. Gisela Terrell, Rare Books Librn
Holdings: Vols Cat Periodicals Mss
Notes: Wesenberg Collection of 20th-century American poetry (mostly pre-1950). It includes first editions, poetry magazines, author's photographs, and manuscripts from the library of Alice Bidwell Wesenberg, poet. Mss include the Irwin Library by Dr Allegra Stewart, in 1981.

KS —UNIVERSITY OF KANSAS, Kenneth Spencer Research Library, Special Collections Dept, Lawrence, 66045. Alexandra Mason, Librn
Holdings: Vols 2235 Cat Mss
Notes: Modern American poetry, 1960 to date. Nonacademic, especially fugitive and ephemeral. Noncirculating.

MA —BOSTON UNIVERSITY, Mugar Memorial Library, Special Collections Dept, 771 Commonwealth Ave, Boston, 02215. Howard B Gotlieb, Dir
Holdings: Cat Mss
Notes: See names of individual poets.

MA —CARY MEMORIAL LIBRARY, 1874 Massachusetts Ave, Lexington, 02173. Robert C Hilton, Dir
Holdings: Cat
Notes: Strong in modern American poetry, the collection also incl ancient, foreign, and English poetry.

MA —AMERICAN ANTIQUARIAN SOCIETY LIBRARY, 185 Salisbury St, Worcester, 01609. Marcus A McCorison, Dir & Librn
Holdings: Vols 5000 Cat
Notes: An outstanding collection to 1876.

MI —WAYNE STATE UNIVERSITY, Kresge Library (Education), Detroit, 48202. Theodore Manheim, Librn
Holdings: Vols (65,000) Cat Mss Microforms
Budget: ($2000)
Notes: The Eloise Ramsey Collection (10, 000 vols). See, *The Eloise Ramsey Collection of Literature for Young People: A Catalogue;* compiled by Joan Cusenza (Detroit: Wayne State University Libraries, 1967). Besides the Ramsey Collection, which is housed separately and does not circulate, the Education Library has approx 55,000 volumes of children's and young adults' literature, with a very large picture-book collection, a large poetry collection; all with special emphasis on urban and ethnic materials.

NY —NEW YORK STATE LIBRARY, State Education Bldg Annex, Washington Ave, Albany, 12224.
Holdings: Vols 10,000 Cat
Notes: American poetry of more than 10,000 vols. Strong in minor poetry, extensive to 1900. Over 1300 broadside ballads.

†NY —SARAH LAWRENCE COLLEGE, Esther Raushenbush Library, 1 Meadway, Bronxville, 10708. Rose Ann Burstein, Librn
Notes: Emily Dickinson Collection and contemporary poetry.

NY —AMERICAN ACADEMY & INSTITUTE OF ARTS & LETTERS, Library, 633 W 155 St, New York, 10032. Casindania P Eaton, Librn; Nancy Johnson, Researcher
Notes: Works of members of the Academy only. Incl mss, letters, memorabilia, etc.

NY —NEW YORK PUBLIC LIBRARY, Research Libraries, General Research Division, Fifth Ave & 42 St, New York, 10018. Rodney Phillips, Chief
Holdings: Vols (2,225,000) Cat Maps Pix Microforms
Budget: ($775,718)

NY —POETRY SOCIETY OF AMERICA, Van Voorhis Library, 15 Gramercy Park, New York, 10003. Jason Shinder, Dir
Holdings: Vols 5000 Cat Mss
Notes: The American poetry ranges from the turn of the century to contemporary poets. There is a separate catalog for American poetry. American and other poetry anthologies, biography, criticism, essays, and poetics. A large holograph collection and memorabilia of the Poetry Society of America are included in the Rare Book Division of the NY Public Library.

NY —STATE UNIVERSITY OF NEW YORK, COLLEGE AT ONEONTA, James M Milne Library, Oneonta, 13820. Richard D Johnson, Librn
Holdings: Vols (427,646) Cat Mss Maps Pix Slides Phonorecords Audiotapes 16mm Films Filmstrips Microforms
Budget: ($338,299)
Notes: New York State Collection; 19th and early 20th century popular fiction; New York State Verse Collection; Early Textbook & Early Educational Theory Collection.

NC —DUKE UNIVERSITY, William R Perkins Library, Durham, 27706. Elvin E Strowd, University Librn

NC —DUKE UNIVERSITY, William R Perkins Library, Rare Book Room, Durham, 27706. John L Sharpe, III, Cur
Notes: Paul Hamilton Hayne collection of American poets and poetry (1800 books, pamphlets and periodicals).

NC —DUKE UNIVERSITY, William R Perkins Library, Jay B Hubbell Center for American Literary Historiography, Durham, 27706. Erma Whittington, Librn
Notes: 77,312 items, including manuscripts, pictures, clippings, and correspondence. "The objective of the Center is to gather the papers and materials of significant scholars and critics in American literary history." The Center is a part of the Perkins Library Manuscripts Department.

OH —CLEVELAND PUBLIC LIBRARY, Literature Dept, 325 Superior Ave, Cleveland, 44114. Evelyn Ward, Head
Holdings: Vols Cat Microforms Phonorecords
Notes: Comprehensive collection of literary texts, with a large body of literary history, criticism and biography. Strong in drama and poetry. Many first editions, books from special presses, and rarities. Microprint. Reference aids.

PA —ATHENAEUM OF PHILADELPHIA, 219 S Sixth St, Philadelphia, 19106. Roger W Moss Jr, Librn
Holdings: Vols 2000 Uncat Mss Pix
Notes: The Charles Wharton Stork Collection of 20th Century Poetry. Charles Wharton Stork (d 1972) was editor of the all poetry journal, *Contemporary Verse.* His entire library of first editions and inscribed works by American poets, in addition to correspondence files for the journal, were presented to the Athenaeum in 1972. In the process of being cataloged. Mss and correspondence, approx 30 large Hollinger cases. The Athenaeum will add to this collection in the area of American poets, c 1900-1925. No photocopying until cataloged.

PA —UNIVERSITY OF PITTSBURGH, Hillman Library, Special Collections Dept, 363 Hillman Library, Pittsburgh, 15260. Charles E Aston Jr, Coordinator
Holdings: Vols 1000 Cat
Notes: Emphasis on American poetry of the 20th century with special focus on the period 1950-date. Largely small press publications.

RI —BROWN UNIVERSITY, John Hay Library, Harris Collection, Prospect St, Providence, 02912. Rosemary L Cullen, Cur
Holdings: Vols (200,000) Cat Mss Phonorecords Microforms
Budget: ($15,000)
Notes: The Harris Collection of American Poetry and Plays is principally composed of American and Canadian poetry and plays, 17th century-date. Extensive holdings in songsters, gift books and annuals, hymnals, pageants, broadside verse, carriers' addresses, women poets, juvenile poetry, (incl Mother Goose and *The Night Before* Christmas), sheet music with lyrics, small press publications, fine printing, black poets, "little magazines," Yiddish-American literature. All movements or schools of American poetry are represented. Incl first editions of most American poets and playwrights, notably Whitman, Poe, Wallace Stevens, Eugene O'Neill, Edward Albee, Ezra Pound, T S Eliot, William Carlos Williams, Amy Lowell, Phyllis Wheatley, Robert Frost, Allen Ginsberg, Bliss Carman, and Stephen Foster sheet music. Also incl the Saunders Walt Whitman Collection (1300 vols); the LangdonCollection of Pageants (250 vols); the Asa Cushman Collection of plays in ms and prompt copies; the MacDougall Collection of Psalters and Hymnals; 4000 plays issued by Walter H Baker Co, Boston (1890-1957); the Vaxer Collection of Yiddish Poetry, Plays and Music (1700 vols). Collections incl 200,000 vols, 30,000 broadsides, 55,000 mss, 170,000 pieces of sheet music, 450 phonorecords, and 375 microfilm reels. See *Dictionary Catalog of the Harris Collection of American Poetry and Plays* (Boston: G K Hall, 1972), 13 vols; *Supplement* (1977), 3 vols. See also, *American Poetry,* 1609-1900, *A Collection on Microfilm, Segment I* (1609-1820); *Segment II* (1821-1850); *Segment III* (1851-1870) (Woodbridge, Conn: Research Publications). Separate catalog.

RI —BROWN UNIVERSITY, John Hay Library, 20 Prospect St, Providence, 02912. Mary T Russo, Cur of Broadsides
Holdings: Vols (30,000)
Notes: A major collection of 30,000 pieces of American verse in broadside form dating from the 18th through the 20th century. Ephemeral in nature and all inclusive, it covers a broad spectrum of American life. Numerous examples of early American poetry, admonishing, proclaiming, celebrating, advertising and mourning are represented. Poets range from the anonymous to major figures, incl Cummings, Eliot, Emerson, Frost, Pound and Whitman as well as contemporary authors. The Beat Movement, Black Mountain School, Concrete Poetry and Poetry of the Harlem Renaissance are represented as well as that of the young black poets published by the Detroit Broadside Press and a good selection of poetry by women. Retrospective and current pieces are added annually. Partial catalog.

TN —VANDERBILT UNIVERSITY, Library, Nashville, 37240. Marice Wolfe, Special Collections Librn
Holdings: Vols 1000 Cat Mss Pix
Notes: Collection relating to the Fugitive poets of the 1920s, the Agrarian writers of the 1930s and their subsequent careers, as a complement to extensive mss collections in this field. Chief figures incl Allen Tate, John Crowe Ransom, Robert Penn Warren, Andrew Lytle, Donald Davidson, Merrill Moore, Laura Riding, et al.

†TX —UNIVERSITY OF TEXAS LIBRARIES, General Libraries, Humanities Research Center, PO Box 7219, Austin, 78712. John Chalmers, Librn
Notes: Complete archives of the Pulitzer Prize poet, Anne Sexton (1928-1974). Includes some of her suicide notes; also correspondence with Maxine Kumin, another Pulitzer winner.

TX —UNIVERSITY OF HOUSTON-CLEAR LAKE CITY, Neumann Library, 2700 Bay Area Blvd, Houston, 77058.
Notes: The Dee Walker Poetry Collection. A collection of poetry books by mostly American and English authors, many autographed. Collected and subsequently donated to the College by the one-time alternate poet laureate of Texas.

VA —UNIVERSITY OF VIRGINIA, Alderman Library, Clifton Waller Barrett Collection, Charlottesville, 22901. Joan St C Crane, Cur of American Literature Collections
Holdings: Vols (300,000) Cat Mss Pix
Notes: The Library takes as its province 175 years of American literature, from 1775 to 1950. It contains, insofar as it has been possible to assemble them, all fiction, poetry, drama, and essays published by an American in book form up to 1875; for the years since, it contains a very nearly complete collection of the works of every major American writer, as well as of those whose achievements were not of the first rank, but who, nevertheless, occupy a place in the literary history of the Republic. With the first editions are important later editions, many translations and periodical appearances, and a vast amount of

AMERICAN POETRY (cont.)

biographical and critical material. Mss and letters of quality have been brought together in such quantity that few similar collections can approach it in size and scholarly importance. Publications: *A Brief Account of the Clifton Waller Barrett Library,* Herbert Cahoon(Charlottesville: University of Virginia, 1960); "The Mighty Manuscripts of Mr C Waller Barrett," C Brian Kelly, *The Commonwealth: The Magazine of Virginia,* vol 38, no 8, Aug 1971, pp 21-28. To determine the manuscript holdings in the Library for particular American authors, consult the second edition of *American Literary Manuscripts.*

VA —VIRGINIA COMMONWEALTH UNIVERSITY, James Branch Cabell Library, Richmond, 23284. Daniel Yanchisin, Special Collections Librn
Holdings: Vols (3600)
Notes: A collection of approximately 3600 volumes by post 1945 American poets including some bibliography and criticism. 2000 books are cataloged and the remainder are accessible by author. The collection includes the library and archival holdings of two literary support organizations, New Virginia Review, Inc and the Poetry Society of Virginia.

WI —BELOIT COLLEGE LIBRARIES, Beloit, 53511. Dennis W Dickinson, Dir
Holdings: Vols 3000 Cat
Budget: $500
Notes: This is a collection of contemporary American poetry. Format of material varies from very slim to regular book-size vols; also backfiles of numerous poetry magazines. Kept together as a "special collection" for those interested in studying the tenor of contemporary American poetry (good and bad). Incl the *Beloit Poetry Journal* Collection.

AMERICAN POETS see Poets, American

AMERICAN POLITICAL SCIENCE ASSOCIATION

DC —GEORGETOWN UNIVERSITY, Library, Special Collections Div, 37 & O Sts NW, Washington, 20057. George M Barringer, Special Collections Librn; Nicholas B Sheetz, Mss Librn
Holdings: Cat Mss Maps Pix Slides Phonorecords Audiotapes
Notes: Includes the papers (1912-49) of Sen Robert F Wagner; the archives (1903-) of the American Political Science Association and of its local Washington chapter; the archives of the Center for Public Financing of Elections; a collection of several hundred political cartoons by Eric Smith; and other smaller collections.

AMERICAN PORTRAITS see Portraits, American

AMERICAN PROPAGANDA see Propaganda, American

AMERICAN PUBLIC HEALTH ASSOCIATION

MA —BOSTON UNIVERSITY, Mugar Memorial Library, Special Collections Dept, 771 Commonwealth Ave, Boston, 02215. Howard B Gotlieb, Dir
Holdings: Cat Records
Notes: Public Health Nursing Section

AMERICAN RED CROSS

DC —AMERICAN NATIONAL RED CROSS, National Headquarters Library, 17th & D St NW, Washington, 20006. Roberta F Biles, Library Director
Holdings: Vols 1500 Cat
Notes: National and International Red Cross.

DC —LIBRARY OF CONGRESS, Prints & Photographs Div, Washington, 20540.
Holdings: Cat Pix
Notes: Incl 62,000 captioned photoprints and a smaller number of glass plate negatives documenting the history and relief work of the American Red Cross during the early decades of the 20th century. The collection is comprised largely of photographs taken by Red Cross staff members during and following World War I. These depict living conditions, medical facilities, refugees, US military personnel, buildings, and topography in over 16 European and Asian countries. Paul Ramey and Lewis Hine are among the World War I photographers represented.

DC —NATIONAL ARCHIVES AND RECORDS SERVICE, National Archives Library, Pennsylvania Ave & Eighth St NW, Washington, 20408.
Notes: American National Red Cross has transferred its archives, 1881-1946, to NARS. 900 linear ft.

†NY —COLUMBIA UNIVERSITY LIBRARIES, Butler Library, Rare Book and Manuscript Library, 535 W 114 St, New York, 10027.
Notes: Papers of the US Solicitor General, 1930-33, relating to the American Red Cross Mission to Russia, 1917-18.

AMERICAN RELIEF ADMINISTRATION

CA —HOOVER INSTITUTION ON WAR, REVOLUTION & PEACE, Stanford University, Stanford, 94305. Milorad M Drachkovitch, Archivist
Holdings: // Mss
Notes: Records of the American Relief Administration, 1919-1923. Correspondence, reports, memoranda, lists, minutes of meetings, and other material relating to the work of the American Relief Administration in Europe and Russia. 550 ft. Unpublished finding aid is available in repository.

AMERICAN REPUBLICS see Pan-Americanism

AMERICAN RESTORATION MOVEMENT

NE —YORK COLLEGE, Levitt Library, York, 67467. Charles Van Baucom, Dir
Holdings: Vols (1430) Cat Mss Pix Audiotapes
Notes: In the Levitt Library, The American Restoration Movement Collection currently focuses on titles related to the Churches of Christ, although titles on the Christian Churches (Independents) and the Disciples of Christ make up a fair percentage of the collection. To promote the development and the use of the Restoration History Collection, York College participates in the Christian College Librarians Conference with sister colleges David Lipscomb, Nashville, TN; Abilene Christian University, Abilene, TX; Oklahoma Christian College, Oklahoma City, OK; Harding College, Searcy, AR; Pepperdine University, Malibu, CA, and others; also, with the Disciples of Christ Historical Society, 1101 19th Ave S, Nashville, TN 37212.

AMERICAN REVOLUTION see U.s.—History_Revolution

AMERICAN SCHOOL OF WILDLIFE PROTECTION

IA —IOWA STATE UNIVERSITY, Library, Dept of Special Collections, Ames, 50011. Stanley M Yates, Head
Holdings: // Mss
Notes: School existed from 1919-1941. One box, finding aid available

AMERICAN SCIENCE see Science—History

AMERICAN SCULPTURE see Sculpture, American

AMERICAN SOCIALIST PARTY see Socialist Party (U.s.)

AMERICAN SOCIETY FOR MICROBIOLOGY

DC —AMERICAN SOCIETY FOR MICROBIOLOGY, Archives, 1913 I Street NW, Washington, 20006. Donald Shay, Archivist
Notes: Collection of American and foreign books (texts, monographs, laboratory manuals, etc) on microbiology. 10,000 reprints are mostly old or connected to a past officer or award recipient. 150 theses incl American and foreign. Reprint collection incl Pratt collection on antibiotics, and C W Dodge collection on medical mycology. Ownership of all titles resides with the Society; Special Collections of University of Maryland Baltimore County serves as repository. The Society address is in Washington.

AMERICAN SOCIETY FOR QUALITY CONTROL

IL —UNIVERSITY OF ILLINOIS, URBANA/CHAMPAIGN, Library, University Archives, 19 Library, 1408 W Gregory Drive, Urbana, 61801. Maynard Brichford, University Archivist
Holdings: Cat Mss Maps Pix Slides Microforms
Notes: Papers, archival records, etc.

AMERICAN SOCIETY OF CIVIL ENGINEERS

TX —TEXAS A&M UNIVERSITY, Sterling C Evans Library, University Archives, College Station, 77843. Charles R Schultz, University Archivist
Notes: The Archives of Southwestern Technology: Records of the Texas Section of the American Society of Civil Engineers, ca 1914-1980.

AMERICAN SOCIETY OF PLANNING OFFICIALS

NY —CORNELL UNIVERSITY LIBRARIES, Collection of Regional History, Dept of Manuscripts and Univ Archives, Ithaca, 14853.
Notes: Incl records, 1935-71; 9 ft.

AMERICAN SONGS see Songs, American

AMERICAN-SPANISH WAR, 1898 see U.s.—History_War of 1898

AMERICAN SUNDAY-SCHOOL UNION

PA —FREE LIBRARY OF PHILADELPHIA, Rare Book Dept, Logan Sq, Philadelphia, 19103. Marie E Korey, Rare Book Librn
Holdings: Vols (10,000) Cat
Notes: The American Sunday-School Union Collection of its publication issued from 1824 until about 1900.

AMERICAN SWEDISH HISTORICAL MUSEUM

PA —BALCH INSTITUTE FOR ETHNIC STUDIES, Library, 18 S Seventh St, Philadelphia, 19106. R Joseph Anderson, Library Dir
Notes: The Amandus Johnson Collection of his papers, incl biographical material on 20th century Swedish-Americans, records from the American Swedish Historical Museum in South Philadelphia, and source documents on the early Swedish settlement of the Delaware Valley, and historical writings based on these documents.

AMERICAN TELEPHONE AND TELEGRAPH COMPANY

DC —GEORGE WASHINGTON UNIVERSITY, Gelman Library, Telecommunications Information Center, Washington, 20052. Cathy Haworth, Librn
Holdings: Vols (1500) Periodicals
Notes: Incl

AMERICAN TELEVISION SOCIETY

NY —NEW YORK PUBLIC LIBRARY, Performing Arts Research Center, Billy Rose

AMERICAN TELEVISION SOCIETY (cont.)

Theatre Collection, 111 Amsterdam Ave, New York, 10023. Dorothy L Swerdlove, Cur
Holdings: Cat
Notes: See entry under Television.
See also entry under Television

AMERICAN THEATRE ASSOCIATION

NY —NEW YORK PUBLIC LIBRARY, Performing Arts Research Center, Billy Rose Theatre Collection, 111 Amsterdam Ave, New York, 10023. Dorothy L Swerdlove, Cur
Holdings: Cat
Notes: Considerable correspondence, clippings, and other material.

AMERICAN TINWARE see Tinware, American

AMERICAN TUNG OIL INSTITUTE

MS —UNIVERSITY OF SOUTHERN MISSISSIPPI, William David McCain Graduate Library, Box 5148, Southern Sta, Hattiesburg, 39406.
Holdings: Uncat Mss
Notes: 18 cubic feet holdings. Research notes, progress reports, formula specifications, patent records, organization by-laws, minute books, legal reocrds and correspondence (1939-1971) of the institute and its predecessor organizations which sought to promote the use of tung oil.

AMERICAN VOLUNTEER GROUP (FLYING TIGERS)

CA —HOOVER INSTITUTION ON WAR, REVOLUTION & PEACE, Stanford University, Stanford, 94305. Milorad M Drachkovitch, Archivist
Holdings: // Mss
Notes: Papers, 1941-1954, of Claire Lee Chennault, civilian flyer and Army Air Force officer in China. Correspondence, diaries, mss of writings, articles, combat reports, group field orders, flight material, radiograms, memoranda, press comments and clippings, and other papers relating to the American Volunteer Group ("Flying Tigers"), China Air Task Force, US 14th Air Force, Civil Air Transports, incl, "Plan for the Modernization of Chinese Air Force" and Freedom Cause. Correspondents incl Allied and Chinese authorities. Ca 5 ft (ca 7800 items). Detailed inventory in the respository. Also, papers of Paul W Frillmann, chaplain of the American Volunteer Group ("Flying Tigers"), 1941-45, and US consular official in China and Hong Kong, 1946-50, incl correspondence, memoranda, orders, notes and photos, 1941-69, relating to activitiesof the American Volunteer Group in China during World War II, US foreign relations with China, 1946-50, and conditions in China during the civil war. 3 ms boxes, 3 framed certificates.

AMERICAN WIT AND HUMOR

CA —UNIVERSITY OF CALIFORNIA, LOS ANGELES, Research Library, Dept of Special Collections, 405 Hilgard Ave, Los Angeles, 90024. Edward Shreeves, Chairman, Bibliographers Group; David S Zeidberg, Head
Holdings: Vols 800 Cat
Notes: 800 books by American humorists, primarily 19th century writers.

DC —LIBRARY OF CONGRESS, Prints & Photographs Div, Washington, 20540.
Notes: Incl the Caroline and Erwin Swann Collection of caricatures and cartoons. Strong in the work of modern artists from the middle of the 19th century. *The New Yorker* Collection contains original cartoons and cover illustrations from the magazine, mid-20th century.

IL —UNIVERSITY OF ILLINOIS, URBANA/CHAMPAIGN, Library, Rare Book Room, 346 Library, Urbana, 61801. Norman B Brown, Asst Dir for Special Collections; N Frederick Nash, Librn
Holdings: Cat Mss Maps
Notes: Meine Collection. Extensive collection, described in: *Catalog of the Rare Book Room,* (Boston: G K Hall, 1972). Supplement (1978).

IN —BUTLER UNIVERSITY, Irwin Library, Hugh Thomas Miller Rare Book Room, 4600 Sunset Ave, Indianapolis, 46208. Gisela Terrell, Rare Books Librn
Holdings: Cat Mss Pix
Notes: *Gaar Williams/Kin Hubbard* Collection. This collection was presented to the library by Blanche Stillson in 1964. It contains original cartoons and other drawings, books (many of them inscribed), magazines, letters and other manuscripts, photographs, and memorabilia by both Hoosier cartoonists and humorists. A catalogue of the Gaar Williams ("Abe Martin") items was printed in 1981. It is available upon request.

KY —UNIVERSITY OF LOUISVILLE, Ekstrom Library, Rare Books & Special Collections, 2301 S Third St, Louisville, 40208. George T McWhorter, Cur; Delinda Stephens Buie, Asst Cur
Holdings: Vols 1200 Cat
Budget: ($1500)
Notes: Over 1200 works of 19th and 20th century American humorists: sketches, short stories, novels, poetry and graphics.

MA —BOSTON PUBLIC LIBRARY, Print Collection, Dartmouth St at Copley Sq, Boston, 02117. Sinclair H Hitchings, Keeper of Prints
Holdings: Cat
Notes: The caricature collection incl 300 American prints (colonial period to 1900), 65 of these are by Thomas Nast; 400 English prints (mostly 18th century) many by Thomas Rowlandson and James Gillray; and several thousand 19th century French items, large numbers of them by Daumier. Items are cataloged by artist when known; or else by publisher or country. In addition, the American caricatures are arranged chronologically.

MA —AMERICAN ANTIQUARIAN SOCIETY LIBRARY, 185 Salisbury St, Worcester, 01609. Marcus A McCorison, Dir & Librn
Holdings: Vols 5000 Cat
Notes: An outstanding collection to 1876.

NY —HAMPDEN-BOOTH THEATRE LIBRARY AT THE PLAYERS, 16 Gramercy Park, New York, 10003. Louis A Rachow, Librn/Cur
Holdings: Mss Pix
Notes: Nearly 300 burlesque scripts and vaudeville skits, music in ms, 25 photographs in character, two song books of the period, a notebook of stage gags and repartee, typescript of biography of Chuck Callahan (30 pages), and a number of ephemeral pieces, stage money, programs, etc. 4 boxes of indexed material. Described in *The Players Bulletin*, Spring 1966, pp 20-21; and *Performing Arts Resources* vol 3 (New York: Theatre Library Association, 1976), pp 143-150. Described in *Theatre & Performing Arts Collections* (New York: Haworth Press, 1981).

NY —UNION COLLEGE, Schaffer Library, Schenectady, 12308. Ann Seemann, Librn; Ellen Fladger, Archivist
Holdings: Vols 2200 Cat
Notes: The Bailey Collection of 19th century North American Wit and Humor.

TX —SOUTHERN METHODIST UNIVERSITY, DeGolyer Library, Box 396, SMU, Dallas, 75275. Clifton H Jones, Dir
Holdings: Vols (80,000) Cat Mss Maps Pix Slides Microforms
Notes: First editions of prominent authors; also of books in subject emphasis collections. All subjects listed in this vol are strong. Numerous collections of personal papers relating to subjects also.

WY —UNIVERSITY OF WYOMING, William Robertson Coe Library, 13 & Ivinson, Laramie, 82071.
Notes: 2000 volumes of popular humor, incl books of cartoons, humorous novels, and the like.

AMERICAN WOMEN see Women, American

AMERICANA

CA —AZUSA PACIFIC COLLEGE, Marshburn Memorial Library, Citrus & Alosta, Azusa, 91702. Edward Peterman, Librn
Holdings: Vols 25,280 Cat
Notes: Incl the *Library of American* Civilzation in ultra-microfiche.

CA —COPLEY NEWSPAPERS, James S Copley Library, 1134 Kline St, PO Box 1530, La Jolla, 92038. Richard Reilly, Cur; Suzanne Carnes, Librn
Holdings: Vols (10,000) Cat
Notes: Collection incl materials on American Revolutionary period, Benito Juarez correspondence, California and western Americana. Library open to graduate students who obtain reading privileges from curator or librarian.

CA —HUNTINGTON LIBRARY, Art Gallery & Botanical Gardens, 1151 Oxford Rd, San Marino, 91108. Robert L Middlekauff, Dir; Daniel H Woodward, Librn
Notes: Approx 350,000 rare books, 250,000 reference books, manuscript collection of nearly 2,500,000 pieces and between 200, 000 and 300,000 prints, rare photographs and other related materials. The fullest available survey is now *Guide to Literary Manuscripts in the Huntington Library,* a 539-page handlist published by the Library in 1979. Also, *Guide to American Historical Manuscripts in the Huntington Library* (1979).

CA —COLLEGE OF SAN MATEO, Library, 1700 W Hillsdale Blvd, San Mateo, 94402. Gregg T Atkins, Coordinator of Library Services
Holdings: Vols 14,000 Cat Microforms
Notes: This is the Library of American Civilization (beginnings to 1915) produced by Encyclopeadia Britannica. The entire collection is on microfiche. The fiche as well as portable readers are available to students and all "serious" interested adults, student or not.

CT —TRINITY COLLEGE LIBRARY, Watkinson Library, 300 Summit St, Hartford, 06106. Jeffrey Kaimowitz, Cur
Holdings: Cat Mss Maps Microforms
Notes: Incl George Brinley Jr Collection.

CT —YALE UNIVERSITY, Box 1603A, Yale Station, New Haven, 06520.
Holdings: Cat Mss Maps Pix

DC —LIBRARY OF CONGRESS, Rare Book & Special Collections Div, Washington, 20540. William Matheson, Chief
Notes: John Boyd Thacher Collection of Books, Pamphlets, Broadsides, and Manuscripts, which incl Early Americana and works regarding Christopher Columbus. The Henry Harrisse Collection of 213 volumes, cataloged, comprises works and bibliographies relating to Americana, incl the author's own interleaved and profusely annotated copies of his writings on the Columbus period, together with volumes containing his correspondence with bibliographers and collectors of the latter part of the 19th century.

DC —SMITHSONIAN INSTITUTION LIBRARIES, National Museum of American History Branch, Washington, 20560. Rhoda S Ratner, Branch Librn
Holdings: Vols (369,650) Cat Mss Maps Pix Slides Microforms

FL —FLORIDA STATE UNIVERSITY, Robert Manning Strozier Library, Special Collections Dept, Tallahassee, 32306. Opal M Free, Head, Special Collections
Holdings: Vols 337 // Cat
Notes: McGregor Collection of Early Americana. Noncirculating. No photocopying.

GA —WESLEYAN COLLEGE, Willet Memorial Library, 4760 Forsyth Rd, Macon, 31201. Hasseltine Roberts, Librn
Holdings: Vols 4000 Cat Mss Maps Pix
Notes: The Orville A Park and Tracy McGregor Collections.

AMERICANA (cont.)

ID —UNIVERSITY OF IDAHO, Library, Dept of Special Collections & Archives, Moscow, 83843.
Holdings: Vols (11,200) Cat Mss Maps Pix Slides Microforms
Budget: ($4000)
Notes: Emphasis on Idaho and the Pacific Northwest. Incl 20,000 pictures and 700 slides. Charles A Webbert, *Check List of Western Americana in the Day-NW Collection, University of Idaho Library, July 1, 1969* (University of Idaho Publication No 8, June 1970).

IL —J WALTER THOMPSON CO, Information Center, 875 N Michigan Ave, Chicago, 60611. Edward G Strable, Dir
Holdings: Vols 150 Cat Microforms Data Files
Notes: Emphasis is on nostalgia as reflected by movies, radio, TV, art, social customs, lifestyle change.

IL —NEWBERRY LIBRARY, 60 W Walton St, Chicago, 60610. Diana Haskell, Cur of Modern Mss
Holdings: Cat Mss Maps Pix
Notes: Americana, incl trans-Mississippi West.

IN —INDIANA UNIVERSITY, Lilly Library, Seventh St, Bloomington, 47405. William R Cagle, Librn
Holdings: Cat Mss Maps Pix
Notes: Some strength in all periods of Americana. Special emphasis on contemporary works in the following areas: War of ideas leading to the Americana Revolution; US Constitution; War of 1812; Lincoln; Indiana History; US--Plains and Rockies. Strong collection of authors' portraits.

IN —SAINT MARY-OF-THE-WOODS COLLEGE, College Library, Saint Mary-of-the-Woods, 47876. Sister Emily Walsh, SP, Administrator
Holdings: Vols 2500 Cat
Notes: Catholic Americana. Principally notable books of the last century no longer used today.

KS —SAINT MARY COLLEGE, Library, Leavenworth, 66048. Therese Deplazes, Special Collections Librn
Notes: Holographs of American personalities, mostly of Colonial, Revolutionary, Confederacy periods, and 19th Century. Incl ms letters, deeds, petitions, wills, slave papers. Holographs of Col Philip Marsteller (one of George Washington's pall bearers), family papers of Richard, Mary and Edward Cutts; love letters to Mary "Polly" Carter, Frank Ellery (grandson of William Ellery, signer of the Declaration of Independence), letters of Connie Mack and Babe Ruth, of some American authors.

ME —PORTLAND PUBLIC LIBRARY, 5 Monument Sq, Portland, 04101. Edward V Chenevert, Library Dir
Holdings: Vols 2600 // Cat
Notes: Library of William Willis, 1794-1870, a noted Portland historian. The library, with the addition of a number of titles added by his immediate heirs, has been kept intact. Contains books, pamphlets and periodicals printed in the 18th and 19th centuries, many autographed by the authors. Its subject matter is general in scope though it is strong in Maine material.

MD —UNIVERSITY OF BALTIMORE, Langsdale Library, 1420 Maryland Ave, Baltimore, 21201. Gerry Watkins, Head of Special Collections Dept
Holdings: Cat Mss Maps
Notes: Incl the entire stock (10,000 vols) of Peter Decker, New York antiquarian bookdealer (acquired in 1970); incl Peter Decker's mss of his published works and his records as a dealer in Americana.

MD —MOUNT SAINT MARY'S COLLEGE, Hugh J Phillips Library, Emmitsburg, 21727. Stephen Rockwood, Librn
Holdings: Vols (140,000) Cat Mss Maps Pix
Notes: Early Catholic Americana, especially for western Maryland.

MA —BOSTON PUBLIC LIBRARY, Print Collection, Dartmouth St at Copley Sq, Boston, 02117. Sinclair H Hitchings, Keeper of Prints
Holdings: Cat
Notes: The Americana collection is especially strong in the 19th century. Incl 250 prints of American views, tradesmen's calling cards, illustrated diplomas and advertisements. Also in it is the McGreevey Baseball Collection of 225 photos, photoreproductions and paintings from the period 1870 to 1914. The American portrait collection contains 300 engravings, etchings and lithographs of prominent figures of the 18th and 19th century. In addition there are 200 portraits of Benjamin Franklin. Items cataloged by subject. Prints also by artist/publisher.

MA —BOSTON UNIVERSITY, Mugar Memorial Library, Special Collections Dept, 771 Commonwealth Ave, Boston, 02215. Howard B Gotlieb, Dir
Holdings: Cat Mss Pix

MA —CHILDREN'S MUSEUM, Resource Center, Museum Wharf, 300 Congress St, Boston, 02210. Marie Ariel, Librn; Maria Russell, Resource Services Mgr
Holdings: Vols (400) Cat Mss Slides Audiotapes Phonorecords Filmstrips
Notes: Focus is on changes in US life over the past 100 years. Curriculum materials and materials for children and adults. Available for reference use by the public; borrowing privileges for Museum members; activity and curriculum kits available to public, schools and community groups for rental fee. Subject-related programs and services offered by Museum staff.

MA —GORDON COLLEGE, Winn Library, Vining Collection, 255 Grapevine Rd, Wenham, 01984. John Beauregard, Dir
Holdings: Vols 2600 Cat Maps
Notes: The Vining Collection (of rare books).

†MA —WILLIAMS COLLEGE, Chapin Library of Rare Books, PO Box 426, Williamstown, 01267. Robert L Volz, Custodian
Holdings: Vols 1800 Cat Mss Maps
Notes: No material available on interlibrary loan.

MA —AMERICAN ANTIQUARIAN SOCIETY LIBRARY, 185 Salisbury St, Worcester, 01609. Marcus A McCorison, Dir & Librn
Holdings: Cat Mss Maps Pix Slides Microforms
Notes: Over half a million manuscript pieces; extensive collection of contemporary imprints before 1850 (with supplementary supporting studies); over 10,000 maps (weak for 15th-17th centuries; excellent for 18th, strongest in 19th century, especially maps of local nature). Strongest collection of American newspapers before 1821 (see entry under Newspapers, American). Also a good collection of portraits of early New Englanders; paintings, engravings, and miniatures. Further, the largest collection of regional, state, county, and local histories. Also, extensive bibliographic notes concerning Thomas W Streeter's collection of Americana.

MA —COLLEGE OF THE HOLY CROSS, Dinand Library, College St, Worcester, 01610. James M Mahoney, Cur of Special Collection
Holdings: Vols 580 Cat
Notes: Books printed in US up to 1830. Restricted use and noncirculating.

MI —UNIVERSITY OF MICHIGAN, William L Clements Library, Ann Arbor, 48109. John C Dann, Dir
Notes: The William L. Clements Library of Americana is a non-circulating rare book library of original source material, printed and manuscript, dealing with America, from the discovery period into the late nineteenth century. The collection includes approximately 55,000 books and pamphlets, 550 linear feet of manuscripts, 4,100 volumes of newspapers, 36,000 maps, 40,000 pieces of sheet music, and 1,000 prints. The collection is strongest for the period of the American Revolution, and includes the papers of Thomas Gage, Sir Henry Clinton, and the Earl of Shelburne. Other areas of strength include antislavery, cartography and geography, discovery and exploration, American Indians, The Civil War, tune-books, sermons and orations, and the War of 1812. There are selective research collections dealing with Christopher Columbus, Thomas Paine, Benjamin Franklin, George Washington, Thomas Jefferson, and the Federalist Papers. Publications describing the collections of the library are: Author/Title catalog of Americana 1493-1860 in the William L. Clements Library... 7 volumes, Boston, G. K. Hall, 1970; Guide to the manuscript collections of the William L. Clements Library, by Arlene P. Shy 3d edition, Boston, G. K. Hall, 1978; Guide to the manuscript maps in the William L. Clements Library, compiled by Christian Burn, Ann Arbor, U. of Michigan, 1959; and Research catalog of maps of America, to 1860 in the William L. Clements Library...,edited by Douglas W. Marshall, 4 volumes, Boston, G. K. Hall, 1972.

MI —EDISON INSTITUTE, Greenfield Village and Henry Ford Museum, Archives & Research Library, PO Box 1970, Dearborn, 48121. Steve Hamp, Dir; Joan W Gartland, Librn
Holdings: Vols 400,000 Cat Mss Maps Microforms
Notes: 400,000 vols incl pamphlets. The Archives and research library supports the program of Greenfield Village and the Henry Ford Museum. Special collections incl: automotive literature, ephemera, McGuffey Readers, trade catalogs, photographs and graphics.

MO —CULVER-STOCKTON COLLEGE, Carl Johann Memorial Library, Canton, 63435. Robert Lin, Librn
Holdings: Vols 1500 Cat
Budget: $1000
Notes: The Johann Collection covers all aspects of Midwest Americana, with special emphasis on Missouri and Mark Twain.

MO —UNIVERSITY OF MISSOURI-KANSAS CITY, General Library, Snyder Collection of Americana, 5100 Rockhill Road, Kansas City, 64110. Kenneth J LaBudde, Dir; Robert Paustian, Asst Dir
Holdings: Vols 25,000 Cat
Notes: Nucleus was Robert M Snyder, Jr Americana Collection of some 14,000 items. Contains printed materials on 19th-century American history, especially the Trans-Mississippi West. Strengths include the history of Kansas City and Jackson County, Missouri, Kansas and Missouri county and state histories, American frontier religion (esp the Mormons and Alexander Campbell's Disciples of Christ), the history of railroads and transportation, the cattle trade, 19th-Century biography and autobiography, North American Indians and early Kansas and Missouri imprints.

MO —WASHINGTON UNIVERSITY, John M Olin Library, Campus Box 1061, St Louis, 63130.
Holdings: Vols (1800) Cat Mss
Notes: Incl material from the Arthur C Hoskins, Richard S Hawes, Ernst C Krohn, George N Meissner, Stratford Lee Morton, and Edgar M Queeny collections; strong in early travel literature of the U S and Latin America; accounts of exploration in the Mississippi Valley and Trans-Mississippi West; miscellaneous accounts of history,

AMERICANA (cont.)

pioneer life, and travel in the Ohio Valley, Old Southwest, and California; material on the American Indian; 18th century American music; early American imprints. Also incl the Isador Mendle Collection on the History of Printing; the Richard S Hawes and Stratford Lee Morton Collection on Western Americana; etc.

NJ —PRINCETON UNIVERSITY, Library, Rare Books Dept, Princeton, 08544. Stephen Ferguson, Cur
Holdings: Cat Mss Microforms

NY —WELLS COLLEGE LIBRARY, Aurora, 13026. Marie G Delaney, Head Librn
Holdings: Vols 500 Cat
Notes: Noncirculating.

NY —BUFFALO & ERIE COUNTY PUBLIC LIBRARY, Rare Book Room, Lafayette Sq, Buffalo, 14203. William H Loos, Cur
Holdings: Vols 8000 Cat Mss Maps Pix

NY —ADELPHI UNIVERSITY, Library, Garden City, 11530. Jerome Yavarkovsky, Dean of Libraries
Holdings: Vols 2100 Cat Mss Maps Pix Slides
Notes: Source materials illustrative of life in the US from the Revolution to the end of the late 19th century.

NY —STATE UNIVERSITY OF NEW YORK, COLLEGE AT NEW PALTZ, Sojourner Truth Library, New Paltz, 12561. W E Connors, Dir
Holdings: Cat Microforms
Notes: Microform publications by Readex Microprint Corp. Early American imprints, 1639-1800 (first series), 1801-1805 (second series).

NY —NEW YORK ACADEMY OF MEDICINE, Library, 2 E 103 St, New York, 10029. Brett A Kirkpatrick, Librn
Holdings: Vols Cat Mss
Notes: One of the largest collections of medical Americana - incl books, pamphlets, serials publications and ephemera.

NY —NEW YORK PUBLIC LIBRARY, Research Libraries, General Research Division, Fifth Ave & 42 St, New York, 10018. Rodney Phillips, Chief
Holdings: Vols (2,225,000) Cat Maps Pix Microforms
Budget: ($775,718)

NY —NEW YORK PUBLIC LIBRARY, Rare Books and Manuscripts Div, Fifth Ave & 42 St, New York, 10018. William L Joyce, Asst Dir; Francis O Mattson, Curator
Holdings: Vols 110,000 Cat
Budget: ($7161)
Notes: The chief strength is Americana, especially before 1801. The collection is particularly rich in the earliest period, 1493-1550; in English Americana before 1641; and in the period of the American Revolution. Other strengths incl: voyages and travels to all parts of the world, incl one of the most extensive collections of De Bry and Hulsius and one of the finest sets of Canadian Jesuit Relations; 18th century American newspapers and periodicals; American literary first editions.

NY —NEW YORK SOCIETY LIBRARY, 53 E 79 St, New York, 10021. Mark Piel, Librn
Holdings: Vols 275
Notes: Incl Governor John Winthrop's Collection on chemistry and alchemy (part of which is at the New York Academy of Medicine Library).

NY —MARGARET WOODBURY STRONG MUSEUM, 1 Manhattan Square, Rochester, 14607.
Holdings: Vols (20,000) Periodicals
Notes: The Margaret Woodbury Strong Museum Library contains a collection of approx 20,000 books, periodicals and ephemera of and concerning the 19th and early 20th centuries. A large part of the library's holdings reflect the interests of Margaret Strong and her family: domestic life and literature of the 19th century and world travel, with particular emphasis on the Orient. The library's resources are available to all visitors for research. Book stacks and rare book storage are not open for browsing and do not circulate, but facilities are provided in reading room for study.

NC —UNIVERSITY OF NORTH CAROLINA, CHAPEL HILL, Wilson Library, Rare Book Collection, Chapel Hill, 27514. Paul S Koda, Cur of Rare Books
Holdings: Vols 50 // Cat
Notes: The Preston Davie Collection consists of works relating to the Americas, published in the 16th century or later.

OH —HEBREW UNION COLLEGE-JEWISH INSTITUTE OF RELIGION, Klau Library, 3101 Clifton Ave, Cincinnati, 45220. David J Gilner, Reference Librn
Holdings: Cat
Notes: Incl the first Hebrew Bible printed in the US. (Philadelphia, 1814); first printed Jewish Prayerbook; first Jewish periodical in the US (*The Jew*).

OH —RUTHERFORD B HAYES LIBRARY, 1337 Hayes Ave, Fremont, 43420. Watt P Marchman, Dir
Holdings: Vols 10,000 Cat Mss Maps Pix
Notes: The Rutherford B Hayes personal library collection (10,000 vols) incl the Robert Clarke Collection of Americana which Hayes purchased in 1874, and also part of the library of James Hall. Also have about 1800 vols from the personal libraries of the Hayes children. Further, correspondence, letterbooks, diaries, speeches, account books, financial and real estate records, law cases, memorabilia and ephemera of or relating to President Hayes. Much on U S political activities of friends and opponents of the period (search individual names).

OH —OTTERBEIN COLLEGE, Courtright Memorial Library, Main & Grove Sts, Westerville, 43081. John Becker, Librn
Holdings: Vols 1820 Cat
Budget: $400

OK —THOMAS GILCREASE INSTITUTE OF AMERICAN HISTORY & ART LIBRARY, 1400 North 25th West Ave, Tulsa, 74127. Sarah Hirsch, Librn
Holdings: Vols Cat Mss Maps Pix
Notes: Trans-Mississippi West, US, Indian and Hispanic history. The Gilcrease Library contains a total of about 40,000 mss; 10,000 imprints; 5000 photographs; 600 maps and 50,000 vols.

PA —AMERICAN PHILOSOPHICAL SOCIETY, Library, 105 S Fifth St, Philadelphia, 19106. Edward C Carter II, Librn
Holdings: Cat Mss Maps Pix Microforms
Notes: 18th and 19th century Americana. General guide printed.

PA —FREE LIBRARY OF PHILADELPHIA, Rare Book Dept, Logan Sq, Philadelphia, 19103. Marie E Korey, Rare Book Librn
Holdings: Vols (281) Cat
Notes: The William M Elkins Collection, with 150 additions, of rare and early printed books relating to the voyages of discovery of America.

PA —HISTORICAL SOCIETY OF PENNSYLVANIA, Library, 1300 Locust St, Philadelphia, 19107. David Fraser, Librn
Holdings: Vols (230,000) Mss Maps Pix Microforms
Notes: Incl over 14,000,000 ms pieces. The Library Company of Philadelphia mss are on deposit with the Historical Society of Pennsylvania. Many of the Society's rare books are on deposit with the Library Company. The Society maintains the collection of the Genealogical Society of Pennsylvania, incl some 20,000 printed genealogies, orginal mss, family, church, and civil records.

PA —LIBRARY COMPANY OF PHILADELPHIA, 1314 Locust St, Philadelphia, 19107. Edwin Wolf II, Librn; Kenneth Finkel, Cur of Prints
Holdings: Vols (450,000) Cat Mss Maps Pix
Notes: Extensive collections of American imprints before 1860. Special categories incl Afro-Americana, American science, technology, architecture, agriculture, natural history, education and philanthropy, the woman's rights movement, and prints, maps and photographs of Philadelphia, all chiefly of the 18th and 19th centuries.

PA —PHILIP H & A S W ROSENBACH FOUNDATION LIBRARY, 2010 DeLancey Pl, Philadelphia, 19103. Clive E Driver, Dir
Holdings: Cat Mss Maps Pix

PA —UNIVERSITY OF PENNSYLVANIA, Van Pelt Library, Rare Books Collection, 34 & Walnut Sts, Philadelphia, 19104. Daniel Traister, Special Collections Librn
Holdings: Vols 2500 //
Notes: Robert Dechert Collection: Early exploration, 17th and 18th centuries; western Americana, 19th century; Canadiana, incl Jesuit relations.

PA —UNIVERSITY OF PITTSBURGH, Hillman Library, Pittsburgh, 15260.
Holdings: Vols (10,000)
Notes: The entire contents of the oldest used book shop in Pittsburgh, the John C Daub Book Store. The collection deals mainly in the areas of military history; works dealing with the Civil War, the World Wars and other military topics; and local history: county histories, city, state or regional histories. Also incl are military works containing colored plates; a large group of Americana; and many framed, colored prints on military subjects.

PA —UNIVERSITY OF PITTSBURGH, Darlington Memorial Library, Special Collections, 601 Cathedral of Learning, Pittsburgh, 15260. Dennis Lambert, Darlington Librn
Holdings: Vols (17,000) Cat Mss Maps Pix
Notes: The Darlington Collection is especially rich in American history of the colonial period, the French and Indian War, the Revolution, and the War of 1812 with geographical emphasis on Western Pennsylvania and Ohio Valley history to 1870 and on Pittsburgh history to 1900. Indian treaties, captivity accounts, US and Pennsylvania travel and description, and early American fiction and prose are represented. A partial guide to the Darlington Manuscript Collections is available by writing for *Darlington Memorial Library: A Descriptive Checklist of its Manuscript Collections,* University of Pittsburgh Bibliographic Series 5, 1969. Noncirculating.

PA —WEST CHESTER UNIVERSITY, Francis Harvey Green Library, West Chester, 19380. R Gerald Schoelkopf, Special Collections Librn
Holdings: Uncat Mss Pix
Notes: Historical Treasures Collection contains: all four Shakespeare Folios, *Biographies of the Signers of the Declaration of Independence* by John Sanderson, illustrated by Thomas Addis Emmet. Inset in the volumes are actual autographs of the signers. Also, Anthony Wayne Letters--15 original letters comprising correspondence between General Anthony Wayne and Generals Washington, Arnold, Gates, Putnam and Schuyler, as well as others.

RI —BROWN UNIVERSITY, John Hay Library, Harris Collection, Prospect St, Providence, 02912. Rosemary L Cullen, Cur
Holdings: Vols (200,000) Cat Mss Pix Phonorecords Microforms
Budget: ($15,000)
Notes: The Harris Collection of American Poetry and Plays is principally composed of American and Canadian poetry and plays, 17th century-date. Extensive holdings in songsters, gift books and annuals, hymnals, pageants, broadside verse, carriers' addresses, women poets, juvenile poetry, (incl Mother Goose and *The Night Before* Christmas), sheet music with lyrics, small press publications, fine printing, black poets, "little magazines," Yiddish-American literature. All movements or schools of American poetry are represented. Incl first editions of most American poets and playwrights, notably Whitman, Poe, Wallace Stevens, Eugene O'Neill, Edward Albee, Ezra Pound, T S Eliot, William Carlos Williams, Amy Lowell, Phyllis Wheatley, Robert Frost, Allen Ginsberg, Bliss Carman, and Stephen Foster sheet music. Also incl the Saunders Walt Whitman Collection (1300 vols); the LangdonCollection of Pageants (250 vols); the Asa Cushman Collection of plays in ms and prompt copies; the MacDougall Collection of Psalters and Hymnals; 4000 plays issued by Walter H Baker Co, Boston (1890-1957); the Vaxer Collection of Yiddish Poetry, Plays and

AMERICANA (cont.)

Music (1700 vols). Collections incl 200,000 vols, 30,000 broadsides, 55,000 mss, 170,000 pieces of sheet music, 450 phonorecords, and 375 microfilm reels. See *Dictionary Catalog of the Harris Collection of American Poetry and Plays* (Boston: G K Hall, 1972), 13 vols; *Supplement* (1977), 3 vols. See also, *American Poetry, 1609-1900, A Collection on Microfilm, Segment I* (1609-1820); *Segment II* (1821-1850); *Segment III* (1851-1870) (Woodbridge, Conn: Research Publications). Separate catalog.

RI —BROWN UNIVERSITY, John Carter Brown Library, Providence, 02912. Norman Fiering, Librn; Everett C Wilkie Jr, Bibliographer; Susan Danforth, Cur Maps & Prints
Holdings: Vols 40,000 Cat Mss Maps Pix
Notes: History of the Americas during the Colonial Period. See also *The John Carter Brown Libray Catalogues; Opportunities for Research in the John Carter Brown Library; Reprint of the John Carter Brown Library Annual Reports and Index-1901-1966.*

SC —GREENVILLE COUNTY LIBRARY, 300 College St, Greenville, 29601. Joan Sorensen, Asst Dir of Public Servs
Holdings: Vols 19,000 // Cat Microforms
Notes: This is the microbook *Library of American Civilization* distributed by Library Resources, Inc. Americana to 1914. No photocopying.

TX —UNIVERSITY OF TEXAS LIBRARIES, General Libraries, Barker Texas History Center, PO Box P, Austin, 78712. Don Carleton, Dir
Holdings: Vols (132,000) Cat Mss Maps Pix Slides Phonorecords Audiotapes Microforms
Notes: Materials pertaining to the historical, social, economic, scientific, humanistic and literary development of Texas and the American Southwest. Rich in early state imprints, as well as the period of the Republic. Archival and ms holdings measure over 22,000 linear feet. Texas history prior to the Republic is covered by the Bexar Archives.

TX —WEST TEXAS STATE UNIVERSITY, Cornette Library, PO Box 748 WT Sta, Canyon, 79016. Faye Hendrickson, Special Collections Asst
Holdings: Vols (451,253) Uncat Microforms
Notes: Includes microform collections.

TX —AMON CARTER MUSEUM, Library, 3510 Camp Bowie Blvd, PO Box 2365, Fort Worth, 76113. Nancy G Wynne, Librn
Holdings: Vols (25,000) Cat Mss Pix
Notes: The book collection, microfilm and photo archives have been built toward the goal of the interpretation of American history through art. At present, the greatest strengths are in Americana, Western Canadiana, bibliography, American exhibition catalogs and history of photography. Substantial books and files on American artists of the 19th and early 20th century, and particularly of Charles M Russell and Frederic Remington. Incl 25,000 pictures; 13,000 slides.
See also entries under Newspapers, American; Pictures - Collections.

VA —CENTRAL VIRGINIA COMMUNITY COLLEGE, Library, 3506 Wards Rd, Lynchburg, 24502. John B St Leger, Dir of Library Servs
Holdings: Vols (6000)

WY —UNIVERSITY OF WYOMING, William Robertson Coe Library, Div of Rare Books & Special Collections, Laramie, 82071. Gene M Gressley, Dir, Asst to Pres
Holdings: Vols (10,000) Cat Mss Maps Pix Slides Microforms
Notes: Main efforts have been in the area of ms collecting in several subject areas, most of which can be grouped under Western Economic History.

AMERICANISM

CA —UNIVERSITY OF CALIFORNIA, LOS ANGELES, Research Library, Dept of Special Collections, 405 Hilgard Ave, Los Angeles, 90024. Edward Shreeves, Chairman, Bibliographers Group; David S Zeidberg, Head
Holdings: Cat Mss Audiotapes
Notes: 11 cartons of materials, recordings, etc relating to the John Birch Society, with runs of relevant periodicals, government documents, etc; 6.5 linear feet on Loyalty Oaths incl in other collections; 6 transcribed Oral History interviews.

TX —ABILENE CHRISTIAN UNIVERSITY, Margaret & Herman Brown Library, ACU Sta, Abilene, 79601. Callie Faye Milliken, Assoc Dir
Holdings: Vols 5000 // Cat
Notes: Donner Library of Americanism. Books, pamphlets, documents, and periodical materials dealing with American politics of the far right collected by Robert Donner during and after World War II. Also incl materials on Jews and Freemasonry.

AMERICANS FOR DEMOCRATIC ACTION (ADA)

IL —CHICAGO HISTORICAL SOCIETY, Library, Clark St at North Ave, Chicago, 60614. Archie Motley, Manuscript Librn
Notes: Records 1944-1964 of Independent Voters of Illinois, an affiliate of Americans for Democratic Action.

AMERICANS IN CANADA

PA —BALCH INSTITUTE FOR ETHNIC STUDIES, Library, 18 S Seventh St, Philadelphia, 19106. R Joseph Anderson, Library Dir
Notes: Ethnic Heritage Collection.

AMES, EDWARD SCRIBNER

IL —SOUTHERN ILLINOIS UNIVERSITY, CARBONDALE, Delyte W Morris Library, Special Collections Dept, Carbondale, 62901. David V Koch, Cur of Special Collections; Louisa Bowen, Cur of Manuscripts
Holdings: Cat Mss
Notes: Twenty Collections related to 20th century American Philosophy, incl the papers of John Dewey, Henry Nelson Wieman, Stephen C Pepper and Toyohiko Kagawa; the archives of the *Library of Living Philosophers* and the Open Court Publishing Company; and small collections James H Tufts, Edward Scribner Ames and Sidney Hook.

AMES, WINTHROP

NY —NEW YORK PUBLIC LIBRARY, Performing Arts Research Center, Billy Rose Theatre Collection, 111 Amsterdam Ave, New York, 10023. Dorothy L Swerdlove, Cur
Holdings: Cat Mss Pix
Notes: Papers, scrapbooks, mss, photographs, memorabilia, etc.

AMES FAMILY

MA —STONEHILL COLLEGE, Donahue Hall, Washington St, North Easton, 02356. Louise M Kenneally, Archivist & Special Collections Librn
Holdings: //
Notes: The Arnold B Tofias Industrial Archives; 2000 linear feet of records and correspondence of the Ames Shovel Company of North Easton, Mass. About 800 shovels and other artifacts. Covers the period 1774-1956.

AMHARIC LANGUAGE AND LITERATURE

MN —SAINT JOHN'S ABBEY & UNIVERSITY, Hill Monastic Manuscript Library, Collegeville, 56321. Julian G Plante, Dir
Holdings: Vols 100 Uncat Mss Slides Microforms
Notes: Microforms of 7500 Amharic and Geez mss, mostly from Ethiopia. A systematic program of microfilming mss in the monasteries and churches of Ethiopia was established in 1973. To complement this body of primary source material, a larger collection of secondary source materials published in the field of Ethiopic studies is available and being added to.

NY —NEW YORK PUBLIC LIBRARY, Oriental Div, Fifth Ave & 42 St, New York, 10018. E Christian Filstrup, Chief
Holdings: Cat Mss Microforms
Budget: ($56,455)
Notes: Published catalog of holdings.

AMHERST, MASSACHUSETTS—HISTORY

MA —JONES LIBRARY, 43 Amity St, Amherst, 01002. Daniel J Lombardo, Cur of Special Collections
Holdings: Vols 2768 Cat
Notes: Books by people born in Amherst or resident for more than 3 years; excluding publications by faculty members of the University of Massachusetts, Amherst College and Hampshire unless they come under the preceding clause. Incl a collection of Amherst imprints to the mid-20th century. Materials do not circulate.

NJ —PRINCETON UNIVERSITY, Library, Rare Books Dept, Princeton, 08544. Stephen Ferguson, Cur
Holdings: Cat Pix
Notes: Books by and about Emily Dickinson, incl works inspired by her poetry; material by or about "The Dickinson Circle," etc, as well as on the Amherst community. Gift of Mrs John Pershing.

NC —UNIVERSITY OF NORTH CAROLINA, GREENSBORO, Walter Clinton Jackson Library, Special Collections Dept, 1000 Spring Garden St, Greensboro, 27412. Emilie W Mills, Librn
Holdings: Vols 100 Cat
Notes: First, variant and other editions of the poems of Emily Dickinson. Early critical works, biographies. Dickinson poems set to music and related Amherst, Mass items. Three letters from Mabel Loomis Todd and Millicent Todd Bingham.

AMHERST, MASSACHUSETTS—IMPRINTS

MA —AMHERST COLLEGE, Library, Amherst, 01002. John Lancaster, Special Collections Librn
Holdings: Vols 550 Cat
Notes: Amherst imprints.

AMIS, KINGSLEY

NV —UNIVERSITY OF NEVADA, RENO, University Library, Special Collections Dept, Reno, 89557. Robert E Blesse, Head
Holdings: Vols (105) Cat
Notes: Includes individual works by author in all editions including translations; also prefaces, introductions, published correspondence, appearances in anthologies, periodicals, etc. Bibliographical research collection, part of Modern Authors Collection. Other appearances 450 cataloged.

AMISH

OH —BLUFFTON COLLEGE, Mennonite Historical Library, Bluffton, 45817. Delbert Gratz, Librn
Holdings: Vols (15,000) Cat Mss Maps Pix Slides Phonorecords 16mm Films Microforms
Budget: $1500
Notes: Collection incl all materials available relating to Mennonites, Anabaptists, Amish, Hutterian Brethren and related religious bodies, as well as the topic of peace. The library has a special collection and index of Mennonite and Amish family histories and genealogies; also a special index to periodical articles in non-Mennonite periodicals that relate to Mennonites, Amish, and Anabaptists. Library is a depository for the Central District of the General Conference Mennonite Church and the Africa Inter-Mennonite Mission. Incl archives of the Africa Inter-Mennonite Mission.

AMISH (cont.)

PA —LANCASTER MENNONITE CONFERENCE HISTORICAL SOCIETY LIBRARY, 2215 Millstream Rd, Lancaster, 17602. Lloyd Zeager, Librn; David J Smucker, Genealogist
Holdings: Vols (55,000) Cat Mss Maps Pix Slides Phonorecords Microforms
Budget: ($3186)
Notes: Depository for the Lancaster Mennonite Conference. Large collection of Mennonite and Amish history books, current Mennonite titles, Mennonite periodicals and newspapers, and archival collection. Publish quarterly journal *Pennsylvania Mennonite* Heritage. Membership organization of 1700.

AMMONS, A. R.

NV —UNIVERSITY OF NEVADA, RENO, University Library, Special Collections Dept, Reno, 89557. Robert E Blesse, Head
Holdings: Vols (26) Cat
Notes: Includes individual works by author in all editions including translations; also prefaces, introductions, published correspondence, appearances in anthologies, periodicals, etc. Bibliographical research collection, part of Modern Authors Collection. Other appearances 225 cataloged.

AMMUNITION

OK —US ARMY FIELD ARTILLERY SCHOOL LIBRARY, Morris Swett Library, Snow Hall, Fort Sill, 73503. Lester L Miller Jr, Chief Librn
Holdings: Vols (265,958) Documents Pix Maps Slides Microforms
Notes: Field artillery; artillery; ordnance; military history; military science; weapons and weapons systems; ammunition; ballistics; missiles; Field Artillery unit histories; military periodicals analytical index file (VF). Incl US and foreign artillery; survey data; photographs on army subjects.

†WA —WASHINGTON STATE UNIVERSITY, Library, Manuscripts, Archives & Special Collections, Pullman, 99164. John F Guido, Head
Holdings: Cat Mss Maps Pix
Notes: The Carl Parcher Russell papers, a vast resource (24,916 items; 45 linear feet) on American Indian and Western pioneer activities and artifacts. Much on the fur trade; pioneer life; mountain men and trapping; wildlife; primitive life in detail. Also the National Park Service, parks, monuments, etc. Described in *Carl Parcher Russell: An Indexed Register of His Scholarly and Professional Papers, 1920-1967, in the Washington State University* Library (Pullman,1970), 149 pp.

AMNESTY INTERNATIONAL

†NY —COLUMBIA UNIVERSITY LIBRARIES, Butler Library, Rare Book and Manuscript Library, 535 W 114 St, New York, 10027.
Notes: Papers of Dr Ivan Morris, American Section chairman of Amnesty International, his researches into Japanese literature and culture, and his books on puzzles.

AMOS N ANDY

CA —UNIVERSITY OF CALIFORNIA, LOS ANGELES, Theater Arts Library, Los Angeles, 90024. Edward Shreeves, Chairman, Bibliographers Group; Audree Malkin, Head, Theater Arts Library
Holdings: Cat Mss Pix
Notes: Incl the complete *Amos 'n Andy* radio series, 354 episodes, 1943-1953.

AMOSKEAG MANUFACTURING COMPANY (1831-1936)

NH —MANCHESTER HISTORIC ASSOCIATION, Library, 129 Amherst St, Manchester, 03104. Elizabeth Lessard, Librn
Notes: Business and production records; real estate holdings; personnel name index (70,000 pieces; biographies of employees); insurance surveys, etc. Photographs, glass negatives (1414 pieces), cynotypes, reproductions of glass negatives (3 volumes), prints (3 volumes and 500 items).

AMPELOGRAPHY

CA —UNIVERSITY OF CALIFORNIA, DAVIS, General Library, Davis, 95616. Bernard Kreissman, University Librn; C Danial Elliott, Asst Head, Dept Special Collections
Holdings: Vols 3000
Notes: Viticulture collection incl classic treatises and recent texts on grapes and grape growing of worldwide scope, eg, US, Europe, South Africa, South America, Australia, etc. Holdings of ampelographic works (grape variety classification) are especially significant.

AMPHIBIA see Reptiles and Amphibians

AMPHIBIOUS WARFARE

FL —US NAVAL COASTAL SYSTEMS CENTER, Technical Information Service Branch, Panama City, 32407. Myrtle J Rhodes, Librn
Holdings: Vols (30,000) Cat
Notes: Coastal and ocean technology, inshore undersea warfare, mine countermeasures, torpedo defense, underwater sound.

AMPHIMIXIS see Reproduction

AMRAM, DAVID

MA —BOSTON UNIVERSITY, Mugar Memorial Library, Special Collections Dept, 771 Commonwealth Ave, Boston, 02215. Howard B Gotlieb, Dir
Holdings: Cat Mss Pix
Notes: Scores, mss, correspondence, etc collected in depth; incl publications by or about.

AMRINE, MICHAEL

DC —GEORGETOWN UNIVERSITY, Library, Special Collections Div, 37 & O Sts NW, Washington, 20057. George M Barringer, Special Collections Librn; Nicholas B Sheetz, Mss Librn
Notes: The papers incl a large quantity of Amrine's literary mss, together with correspondence, print and near print material relating to a number of subjects, most importantly, atomic energy research and development. Michael Amrine (1918-1974) began his career in journalism in 1934, working for a number of years with the Federation of Atomic Scientists while editing the *Bulletin* of Atomic Scientists. Amrine is the author of a number of books, incl *This Awesome Challenge* (1964). Correspondents incl: Albert Einstein, Hans Bethe, Harold Urey, Thomas Hart Benton and William Allen White. Other materials incl a collection of black and white still photographs relating to Amrine's research interests and tape recorded interviews, used as background for a number of his books.

AMULETS

OH —CLEVELAND PUBLIC LIBRARY, Fine Arts and Special Collections Department, 325 Superior Ave, Cleveland, 44114. Alice N Loranth, Head
Holdings: Vols (1600) Cat
Notes: Part of the Witchcraft Collection, which incl witchcraft, magic, sorcery, magical manuals, devil worship, incantations, charms, talismans, amulets and spells. Contemporary urban practices are almost entirely omitted.
See also entry under Folklore; Witchcraft

AMUSEMENT PARKS

IL —CHICAGO HISTORICAL SOCIETY, Library, Clark St at North Ave, Chicago, 60614. Archie Motley, Manuscript Librn
Notes: Papers of White City Construction Co (Chicago amusement park operators).

NY —NEW YORK PUBLIC LIBRARY, Performing Arts Research Center, Billy Rose Theatre Collection, 111 Amsterdam Ave, New York, 10023. Dorothy L Swerdlove, Cur
Holdings: Cat Pix
Notes: Clippings, photographs, reviews of acts, etc, periodicals devoted to news of activity in the field.

AMYOTROPHY see Atrophy, Muscular

ANA see Aphorisms, Apothegms, Epigrams, Maxims, and Proverbs

ANABAPTISTS

KS —CENTER FOR MENNONITE BRETHREN STUDIES, Tabor College Library, 401 S Jefferson, Hillsboro, 67063. Wesley J Prieb, Dir
Holdings: Uncat Mss Maps Pix Slides Phonorecords Audiotapes 16mm Films Filmstrips Microforms
Budget: ($25,000)
Notes: Historical materials relating to Mennonite Brethern Conference of churches and its activities. Focus on US Conference of Mennonites, incl minutes and correspondence. Keeps all data for districts, except the Pacific. Collects all data on birth of Mennonites incl local church histories, family records, and genealogy. Anabaptists classics and picture collection. Periodicals and papers incl; collection partly cataloged.

†KS —BETHEL COLLEGE, Mennonite Library and Archives, North Newton, 67117.
Notes: Anabaptists, Mennonites in Europe, America, Latin America and Asia.

OH —BLUFFTON COLLEGE, Mennonite Historical Library, Bluffton, 45817. Delbert Gratz, Librn
Holdings: Vols (15,000) Cat Mss Maps Pix Slides
Budget: $1500
Notes: Collection incl all materials available relating to Mennonites, Anabaptists, Amish, Hutterian Brethren and related religious bodies, as well as the topic of peace. The library has a special collection and index of Mennonite and Amish family histories and genealogies; also a special index to periodical articles in non-Mennonite periodicals that relate to Mennonites, Amish, and Anabaptists. Library is a depository for the Central District of the General Conference Mennonite Church and the Africa Inter-Mennonite Mission. Incl archives of the Africa Inter-Mennonite Mission.

PA —JUNIATA COLLEGE LIBRARY, Huntingdon, 16652. David Eyman, Dir
Holdings: Vols 5000 // Cat Mss
Notes: Early Pennsylvania imprints, many in German. Large collection of imprints from Christopher Sauer's press. Early Brethren and other German sectarian (Schwenkfelders, Anabaptists) tracts from Pennsylvania and Europe. Several of the collections have been described in *American German Review* (1941), *Pennsylvania* History (1940, 1959), and *Pennsylvania* Magazine (1943).

VA —EASTERN MENNONITE COLLEGE, Menno Simons Historical Library & Archives, Harrisonburg, 22801. Grace Showalter, Librn
Holdings: Vols (15,318) Cat Maps Microforms
Budget: ($30,500)
Notes: Anabaptist, Mennonite, and local history and genealogy. Incl art reproductions and prints.

ANALOG COMPUTERS see Computers, Electronic

ANALYSIS (CHEMISTRY) see Chemistry, Analytic

ANALYSIS, CHROMATOGRAPHIC see Chromatographic Analysis

ANALYSIS, MICROSCOPIC see Metallography; Microscopes and Microscopy

ANALYSIS, SPECTRUM see Spectrum Analysis and Spectroscopy

ANALYSIS OF FOOD see Food—Analysis

ANALYTICAL CHEMISTRY see Chemistry, Analytic

ANANSI FOLKLORE

MA —BOSTON COLLEGE LIBRARIES, Thomas P O'Neill Library, Nicholas M

ANANSI FOLKLORE (cont.)

Williams Ethnological Collection, Chestnut Hill, 02167. Frank J Seegraber, Special Collections Librn
Holdings: Vols 10,000 // Cat Mss Maps
Notes: Collection emphasizes Caribbeana, especially Jamaica, to 1940. Incl discovery, exploration and natural history of the British, French and Spanish settlements; the slave question; piracy. There are over 6000 mss, 5000 of which are Anansi folk tales recorded by native school children. Also small ancillary sections of Africana and Judaica. For reference use only, by arrangement with librarian.

ANARCHISM AND ANARCHISTS

AZ —NORTHERN ARIZONA UNIVERSITY, Special Collection Library, CU Box 6022, Flagstaff, 86011. Peter M Whiteley, Coordr/Archivist; William Mullane, Librn
Holdings: Vols 9000 Cat Mss Phonorecords Microforms
Notes: The large Allderdice Collection of thousands of books, pamphlets, periodicals, and organizational files reflects the conservative, communist, socialist, facist, anarchist, and other viewpoints, etc, during the 20th century.
See also entry under Hennacy, Ammon.

DC —LIBRARY OF CONGRESS, Rare Book & Special Collections Div, Washington, 20540. William Matheson, Chief
Notes: Incl 800 items. Largely in languages other than English, these pamphlets, broadsides, and posters date from 1895-1972, deal with European anarchism, and were aimed at the Italian, German, and Russian immigrant communities in the US.

IL —NORTHWESTERN UNIVERSITY, Library, Special Collections Dept, 1937 Sheridan Rd, Evanston, 60201. R Russell Maylone, Cur
Holdings: Vols (14,000) Cat
Notes: Periodicals and pamphlets concerning many social and political movements in the 20th century, with emphasis on anarchism, struggles of the working class, women's rights, and student protest of the 1960s. Foreign material incl. An additional 10,000 pieces arranged by subject.

IN —INDIANA STATE UNIVERSITY, Cunningham Memorial Library, Dept of Rare Books & Special Collections, Terre Haute, 47809. Lawrence J McCrank, Head
Holdings: Uncat Mss Pix
Budget: ($1350)
Notes: The Debs Collection consists of aprox 7000 pieces of correspondence between Theodore Debs (brother of E V) and other persons, such as Sinclair Lewis, Upton Sinclair, Ethel Barrymore, Emma Goldman, Robert G Ingersoll, Carl Sandburg, Norman Thomas, Sacco and Vanzetti and many others. Many of the letters are from E V Debs to his brother; a good portion of these are from the federal penitentiary at Atlanta. Entire correspondence file has been microfilmed. 750 pamphlets cover all aspects of the labor movement, socialism and radical thought from the 19th century to appprox 1950. A collection ca 200 related books is also housed in the collection. See: J Robert Constantine and Gail Malmgreen, eds, *The Papers of Eugene V Debs, 1834-1945. A Guide to the Microfilm Edition.* NY: Microfilming Corp of America, 1983 (University Microfilms is the new distributer).

KS —WICHITA STATE UNIVERSITY, Ablah Library, Box 68, Wichita, 67208. Michael T Kelly, Cur of Special Collections
Holdings: Vols Cat

MA —HARVARD UNIVERSITY LIBRARY, Cambridge, 02138.
Holdings: Cat

MA —HARVARD UNIVERSITY LIBRARY, Law School Library, Langdell Hall, Cambridge, 02138. Erika S Chadbourn, Cur of Mss
Notes: Legal documents, pictorial material, microfilms. Incl holograph letters of Sacco and Vanzetti, 1920-1928. Typed chronological list in repository.

MA —BRANDEIS UNIVERSITY, Goldfarb Library, 415 South St, Waltham, 02154. Bessie Hahn, Dir
Notes: Sacco and Vanzetti Case Collection. Incl 23 linear feet of material collected by both Tom O'Connor and Francis Russell relating to this celebrated American trial. This collection is unprocessed, spring 1984.

MI —UNIVERSITY OF MICHIGAN, Dept of Rare Books & Special Collections, Ann Arbor, 48109. Edward C Weber, Head, Labadie Collection
Holdings: Vols (40,000) Cat Mss Pix Microforms
Notes: International coverage, with particular strengths in the U S, Great Britian, France, Italy and Spain.

PA —BALCH INSTITUTE FOR ETHNIC STUDIES, Library, 18 S Seventh St, Philadelphia, 19106. R Joseph Anderson, Library Dir
Notes: American anarchism.

WI —UNIVERSITY OF WISCONSIN, GREEN BAY, Library/Learning Center, Green Bay, 54301. Marian A Gould, Acting Dir, Special Collections/University Archives
Holdings: Vols 700 // Cat
Notes: This represents the collection Leon Kramer, "idealist, philosophical anarchist and bookseller." Much of the material concerns radical literature and small socialist and communist parties in the US, although there is a considerable amount of books, booklets, and pamphlets published in Germany, Italy, and other parts of Europe. Incl uncounted pamphlets.

WI —UNIVERSITY OF WISCONSIN, MADISON, Memorial Library, Slavic Studies Collection, 728 State St, Madison, 53706. Aleksander Rolich, Bibliographer for Slavic Studies; Robert P Gakovich, Slavic Cataloger; Valdis J Zeps, Baltic Studies Center
Holdings: Vols (1000) Cat
Notes: The Komadinich Collection in Serbian and Yogoslav social and political history embraces publications and pamphlets of peasant, socialist and other radical movements of the last half of the nineteenth century up to World War II. It consists of some 1000 items mostly in Serbo-Croatian, and represents only part of the private library acquired from the survivors of Milan Komadinic (1882-1944).

ANASAZI CULTURE see Pueblo Indians

ANATOLIA

PA —BRYN MAWR COLLEGE, Canaday Library, Bryn Mawr, 19010. James Tanis, Dir
Notes: Classical and Near Eastern archaeology, Greek architecture and sculpture; Anatolian and Aegean Archaeology. In Art and Archaeology Library.

ANATOMICAL ATLASES

CT —YALE MEDICAL LIBRARY, 333 Cedar St, New Haven, 06510.

ANATOMY

AL —UNIVERSITY OF ALABAMA, BIRMINGHAM, Lister Hill Library of the Health Sciences, University Sta, Birmingham, 35294. Richard B Fredericksen, Dir

CT —YALE MEDICAL LIBRARY, 333 Cedar St, New Haven, 06510.
Holdings: Vols (334,215) Cat Mss Pix Slides Microforms
Budget: ($361,650)
Notes: Incl films, audiotapes, artifacts, etc.

IL —UNIVERSITY OF ILLINOIS, URBANA/CHAMPAIGN, Library, Biology Library, 101 Burrill Hall, 407 S Goodwin, Urbana, 61801. Elisabeth B Davis, Librn
Holdings: Vols (115,000) Cat Microforms
Budget: ($200,000)
Notes: The Biology Library incl books, periodicals, and reference works that cover the fields of anatomy, biophysics, botany, ecology, entomology, genetics, immunology, microbiology, physiology and zoology. About three-quarters of the total collection is made up of journals and other serials representing 2000 distinctive titles. The serial list is comprehensive for the biological sciences, contains most of the major international titles and consists of complete runs for almost all titles. Additional materials (approx 90,000 vols) in the biological sciences are available in the Natural History Survey Library and the bookstacks at the Main Library on the Urbana campus. Professional assistance is available for reference service, online searching, and library instruction. Interlibrary loan service is provided. Photocopying.

IA —IOWA STATE UNIVERSITY, College of Veterinary Medicine, Veterinary Medical Library, Ames, 50011. Sara R Peterson, Librn
Holdings: Vols (17,000) Cat Microforms
Notes: Incl comparative and veterinary medicine with emphasis in the fields of mammalian anatomy and physiology, laboratory animal medicine, pathology, toxicology, biomedical engineering and clinical veterinary medicine. Incl 2000 uncataloged German theses.

MA —FRANCIS A COUNTWAY LIBRARY OF MEDICINE, Boston Medical Library/ Harvard Medical Library, 10 Shattuck St, Boston, 02115. C Robin LeSueur, Librn; Richard J Wolfe, Cur, Rare Books & Manuscripts
Holdings: Vols (500,000) Cat Mss Maps Pix Microforms
Notes: Combines resources of the Harvard Medical School and the Boston Medical Library. Strong in serials and medical history in all fields of medicine, incl incunabula, non-medical books by doctors, travel books by doctors. 500,000 medical dissertations and theses. Special strength in all medical subjects listed in this volume.

MA —NEW ENGLAND COLLEGE OF OPTOMETRY, Library, 420 Beacon St, Boston, 02115. F Eleanor Warner, Librn
Holdings: Vols (7750) Cat Mss Slides Phonorecords Audiotapes Videotapes 16mm Films Microforms
Budget: ($30,000)
Notes: Acquisitions in optometry and ophthalmology are comprehensive; they are selective in areas of surgery and the therapeutic use of drugs. Collection incl 75 slide/tape programs; 75 videotapes; 11 VF drawers of pamphlets and reprints; 16 units of realia; 275 periodical subscriptions. Publishes periodicals holdings list, audiovisual holdings list and an acquisitions list. Open to the public for reference use.

MI —UNIVERSITY OF MICHIGAN, Transportation Research Institute, Library, 2901 Baxter Rd, Ann Arbor, 48109. Ann C Grimm, Librn
Holdings: Vols (57,000) Cat Mss Maps Pix Slides Microforms
Budget: ($25,000)

NY —UNIVERSITY OF ROCHESTER, School of Medicine and Dentistry, Edward G Miner Library, 601 Elmwood Ave, Rochester, 14642. Lucretia McClure, Medical Librn; Janet Brady Berk, History of Medicine Librn
Notes: Strong in yellow fever, cholera, orthopaedics, anatomy and original historic medical photographs.

ND —UNIVERSITY OF NORTH DAKOTA, Harley E French Medical Library, Grand Forks, 58202. David W Boilard, Dir; Lila Pedersen, Asst Dir
Holdings: Vols (56,000) Cat
Budget: ($206,000)
Notes: 1075 current periodical subscriptions.

PA —COLLEGE OF PHYSICIANS OF PHILADELPHIA, Library, 19 S 22 St, Philadelphia, 19103. Christine Ruggere, Cur, Historical Collections
Holdings: Vols (316,223) Cat Mss
Budget: ($1,096,557)
Notes: Very strong collection.
See also entry under Medicine

ANATOMY (cont.)

TX —UNIVERSITY OF TEXAS HEALTH SCIENCE CENTER, SAN ANTONIO, 7703 Floyd Curl Dr, San Antonio, 78284. Joyce M Ray, Archivist/Special Collections Librn; JoAnn Glisson, Library Asst

ANATOMY—HISTORY

CA —UNIVERSITY OF CALIFORNIA, SAN FRANCISCO, Library, Special Collections, San Francisco, 94143. Nancy Witten Zinn, Librn
Holdings: Vols (23,000) Cat Mss Pix
Budget: ($8500)

GA —MEDICAL COLLEGE OF GEORGIA, Library, Laney Walker Blvd, Augusta, 30902. Dorothy H Mims, Librn for Special Collections
Holdings: Vols (2500) // Cat
Notes: Special collection of late 18th and early 19th century medical works, incl classic texts and atlases in anatomy. A number of hand-colored atlases from France are in the collection.

IA —UNIVERSITY OF IOWA, Health Sciences Library, John Martin Rare Book Room, Iowa City, 52242. Richard Eimas, Librn
Holdings: Vols (2200) Cat Slides
Notes: Catalog: Iowa, University, Health Sciences Library. *Heirs of Hippocrates* (Iowa City, IA, Friends of the University of Iowa Libraries, 1980). Collection is particularly strong in areas of anatomy and surgery. It also contains 300 books and reprints by and about Sir William Osler as well as over 80 letters written by Osler.

MD —UNIVERSITY OF MARYLAND, BALTIMORE, Health Sciences Library, 111 S Greene St, Baltimore, 21201. Cyril C H Feng, Dir
Holdings: Vols 225 // Cat Pix

MN —UNIVERSITY OF MINNESOTA, Owen H Wangensteen Historical Library of Biology & Medicine, Diehl Hall, Minneapolis, 55455. Judith Overmier, Cur
Holdings: Vols (35,000) Cat
Budget: ($80,000)
Notes: Incl historic materials.

NY —CORNELL UNIVERSITY LIBRARIES, John M Olin Library, History of Science Collections, Ithaca, 14853. Lillian A Clark, Administrative Supervisor; David W Corson, History of Science Librn
Holdings: Vols (33,000) Cat
Notes: Howard B Adelmann Collection of early printed source materials in embryology, human and comparative anatomy (6,000 vols). Emphasis on 16th, 17th, and early 18th centuries in general, Malpighi and Italian anatomists in particular. Noncirculating.
See also entry under Science - History

NY —COLUMBIA UNIVERSITY LIBRARIES, Health Sciences Library, 701 W 168 St, New York, 10032. Rachael K Goldstein, Librn
Holdings: Vols 1100 Cat
Notes: Landmark works, incl the George S Huntington Collection. Restricted.

NY —NEW YORK ACADEMY OF MEDICINE, Library, 2 E 103 St, New York, 10029. Brett A Kirkpatrick, Librn
Holdings: Vols Cat
Notes: Samuel W Lambert, Jr. Collection on anatomy, surgery and history of medicine.

OH —CLEVELAND MEDICAL LIBRARY ASSOCIATION/CASE WESTERN RESERVE UNIVERSITY, Cleveland Health Sciences Library, Historical Division, Allen Memorial Medical Library, 11000 Euclid Ave, Cleveland, 44106. Glen Jenkins, Rare Book Librarian & Archivist
Notes: Incl 15,000 historical vols, 6000 in the supporting collection. Incl about 1000 16th-18th century titles. Strength of collection: diseases, epidemiology, anatomy, surgery, medicine, obstetrics, gynecology, pediatrics and yellow fever. Incl also medical Americana, listed in Robert B Austin *Early American Medical Imprints,* 1668-1820 (Washington, DC, HEW, Public Health Service, 1961) and ca 7000 19th century works. Our total medical Americana collection also incl journals (not counted), mss and archives (900 linear ft) and 5000 pictures, especially of the Western Reserve. Anatomical works discussed in I Ebner and G Jenkins *Skeletons in Our Closet* (Cleveland, Cleveland Health Sciences Library, 1983)

ANATOMY, COMPARATIVE

IN —PURDUE UNIVERSITY LIBRARIES, Veterinary Medical Library, C J Lynn Hall of Veterinary Medicine, West Lafayette, 47907. Gretchen Stephens, Librn
Holdings: Vols (31,022) Cat
Budget: ($106,281)
Notes: The collection contains the outstanding books and serials in English that are germane to comparative and veterinary medicine. Foreign language materials are added selectively. Subjects of particular strength are laboratory animal medicine, pathology, comparative anatomy, animal behavior and clinical veterinary medicine.

PA —CARNEGIE LIBRARY OF PITTSBURGH, Science & Technology Dept, 4400 Forbes Ave, Pittsburgh, 15213. Catherine M Brosky, Dept Head
Notes: Except for certain special areas, such as entomology and ornithology and a few others that are emphasized, this general subject is of secondary interest. Incl both modern and classic works. Kept up to date in cooperation with the Library in Carnegie Museum of Natural History. Materials available on the various phyla, classes, orders and species. Abstracts, indexes, bibliographies, taxonomic manuals and standard reference books. Many journals and society publications complete from the beginning.

ANATOMY, MICROSCOPIC see Histology

ANCESTRY see Heredity

ANCIENT ART see Art, Ancient

ANCIENT HISTORY see History, Ancient

ANDALUSIA, SPAIN

CA —UNIVERSITY OF CALIFORNIA, SAN DIEGO, Central University Library, Mandeville Dept of Special Collections, La Jolla, 92093. Lynda Corey Claassen, Head
Notes: Hispanic Collection: Approx 6000 vols describe cultures of Spain, Portugal, Mexico, Latin America, and South America. Works of literature, history, philosophy and art date from the 15th to the mid-19th century. Highlights of the collection include rare 18th century Spanish provincial dramas and works on the history of Seville and Andalusia.

ANDEAN REGION

MO —WASHINGTON UNIVERSITY, John M Olin Library, Campus Box 1061, St Louis, 63130.
Holdings: Vols (50,000) Cat
Notes: Strong collection. Much unusual material.

TX —UNIVERSITY OF TEXAS LIBRARIES, Nettie Lee Benson Latin American Collection, Sid Richardson Hall 1.109, Austin, 78712. Laura Gutierrez-Witt, Head Librn
Holdings: Vols (450,000) Cat Mss Maps Pix Phonorecords Filmstrips Microforms
See also entry under Latin America

ANDERSEN, HANS CHRISTIAN

DC —LIBRARY OF CONGRESS, Rare Book & Special Collections Div, Washington, 20540. William Matheson, Chief
Holdings: Vols 567 Cat Mss Pix
Notes: An extensive collection of the author's first editions, original letters, ms, texts and presentation copies of Hans Christian Andersen, assembled by the late Danish-born actor, Jean Hersholt. The collection is the largest outside Denmark. A description of the collection is found in the *Quarterly Journal of the Library of* Congress, vol 4, (May 1952): no 3. A catalog was published by the Library of Congress in 1954: *Catalog of the Jean Hersholt Collection of Hans Christian Andersen* (Washington, D C).

IN —INDIANA UNIVERSITY, Lilly Library, Seventh St, Bloomington, 47405. William R Cagle, Librn
Holdings: // Cat Mss
Notes: Collections incl papers of folklorists Richard M Dorson, 1916-, and Stith Thompson, 1885-1976. Also a small collection (76 items) of Andrew Lang letters and writings, 1886-1913. Incl first and early editions of Andrew Lang and Hans Christian Andersen.

MS —UNIVERSITY OF SOUTHERN MISSISSIPPI, William David McCain Graduate Library, Box 5148, Southern Sta, Hattiesburg, 39406.
Holdings: Vols
Notes: Small but significant selection of Andersen's works, primarily in Danish, incl *Samlede Digte* (1833), *Nye Eventyr* (1847-48), *H C Andersen's Eventyr* (1850), *I* Sverrig (1851), *Historier* (1852-53), and *Nye Eventyr og Historier* (1858).

WA —UNIVERSITY OF WASHINGTON LIBRARIES, Suzzallo Library, Scandinavian Collections, FM-25, Seattle, 98195. A Gerald Anderson, Librn
Holdings: Vols (800)
Budget: ($15,546)
Notes: Research collection with emphasis on Andersen's works, biography, translations, history and criticism.

ANDERSON, CARL

CA —CALIFORNIA INSTITUTE OF TECHNOLOGY, Robert A Millikan Memorial Library, Archives, 1201 E California Blvd, Pasadena, 91125. Judith R Goodstein, Archivist
Notes: Interviewed for the Oral History Program of the Archives.

ANDERSON, FREDERICK L.

CA —HOOVER INSTITUTION ON WAR, REVOLUTION & PEACE, Stanford University, Stanford, 94305. Milorad M Drachkovitch, Archivist
Holdings: Mss
Notes: Papers, correspondence, etc.

ANDERSON, ISABEL WELD (PERKINS)

MA —BOSTON UNIVERSITY, Mugar Memorial Library, Special Collections Dept, 771 Commonwealth Ave, Boston, 02215. Howard B Gotlieb, Dir
Holdings: // Mss

ANDERSON, JAMES

KY —UNIVERSITY OF KENTUCKY, Margaret I King Library, Dept of Special Collections, Lexington, 40506. William Marshall, Head
Holdings: Cat Mss Pix Slides Microforms
Notes: Comprehensive collection of books on typography and history of printing; fine press books (incl Lexington imprints); ms books and illumination, paleography; mss of W A Dwiggins (gift of C H Griffith); James Anderson papers; bookbinding; 2 hand-presses and working collection for summer seminars in hand-press printing; bookplates, bookmarks, book jackets, etc.

ANDERSON, DAME JUDITH

CA —UNIVERSITY OF CALIFORNIA, SANTA BARBARA, Library, Dept of Special Collections, Santa Barbara, 93106. Christian F Brun, Head
Holdings: Mss Pix Ephemera
Notes: Papers of Dame Judith Anderson.

ANDERSON, LEE, 1896-1974

MO —WASHINGTON UNIVERSITY, Libraries, Special Collections Dept, Campus

ANDERSON, LEE, 1896-1974 (cont.)

Box 1061, St Louis, 63130.
Notes: A major collection, incl mss, correspondence, literary papers, photographs, etc. Described in *Special Collections: an Annotated Guide to the Holdings of the Manuscript Division and the University Archives and Research Collection.*

ANDERSON, MARIAN

PA —UNIVERSITY OF PENNSYLVANIA, Van Pelt Library, Rare Books Collection, 34 & Walnut Sts, Philadelphia, 19104. Daniel Traister, Special Collections Librn
Holdings: Mss Pix
Notes: Mss, scores, scrapbooks, correspondence and photographs of the American contralto. 1960 linear feet.
Catalog: *Marian Anderson, a Catalog of the Collection at the University of Pennsylvania,* eds Neda M Westlake and Otto E Albrecht, University of Pennsylvania Press, 1981.

ANDERSON, PATRICK

MA —BOSTON UNIVERSITY, Mugar Memorial Library, Special Collections Dept, 771 Commonwealth Ave, Boston, 02215. Howard B Gotlieb, Dir
Holdings: Cat Mss

ANDERSON, SHERWOOD

IL —NEWBERRY LIBRARY, 60 W Walton St, Chicago, 60610. Diana Haskell, Cur of Modern Mss
Holdings: Cat Mss Pix
Notes: Primary ms repository; about 17,000 pieces. First editions; many translations and reprints. See "Special Sherwood Anderson Number," *The Newberry Library Bulletin,* vol VI, no 8.

NV —UNIVERSITY OF NEVADA, RENO, University Library, Special Collections Dept, Reno, 89557. Robert E Blesse, Head
Holdings: // Vols (89) Cat Other appearances 320 Cat
Notes: Includes individual works by author in all editions including translations; also prefaces, introductions, published correspondence, appearances in anthologies, periodicals, etc. Bibliographical research collection, part of Modern Authors Collection.

VA —VIRGINIA POLYTECHNIC INSTITUTE AND STATE UNIVERSITY LIBRARY, Blacksburg, 24061. Glenn L McMullen, Special Collections Librn
Holdings: Vols 450
Notes: First and other editions of Anderson's works printed during his lifetime; many printings within each edition; numerous translations; periodical issues incl Anderson's contributions; two of Anderson's books containing ms revisions by him.

VA —UNIVERSITY OF VIRGINIA, Alderman Library, Manuscripts Dept, Charlottesville, 22901. Edmund Berkeley Jr, Cur
Holdings: Cat Mss Pix
Notes: Extensive collection of mss and printed materials.

VA —UNIVERSITY OF VIRGINIA, Alderman Library, Clifton Waller Barrett Collection, Charlottesville, 22901. Joan St C Crane, Cur of American Literature Collections

ANDHRA LANGUAGE see Telugu Language and Literature

ANDRE, MAJ. JOHN

NY —HISTORICAL SOCIETY OF THE TARRYTOWNS, Library, One Grove St, Tarrytown, 10591. Adelaide R Smith, Cur
Holdings: Vols 45 Cat Mss Maps Pix VF
Notes: Since the capture of Major Andre occurred in the Tarrytown area, 23 Sept 1780, we have comprehensive documentation and a variety of artifacts relating to this event. Our files cover the lives of the 3 captors, John Paulding, Isaac Van Wart and David Williams, as well as Major Andre. Limited material on Benedict Arnold.

ANDREAS-SALOME, LOU, 1861-1937

MA —BRANDEIS UNIVERSITY, Goldfarb Library, 415 South St, Waltham, 02154. Bessie Hahn, Dir
Notes: Lou Andreas-Salome Collection. 6 linear ft of mss material and books by and about Lou Andreas-Salome, novelist and poet, who took an active interest in psychoanalysis in the early part of the 20th century. There is a finding list to the collection in Special Collections.

ANDREWS, CHARLES THOMAS, 1842-1931

NY —CORNELL UNIVERSITY LIBRARIES, Collection of Regional History, Dept of Manuscripts and Univ Archives, Ithaca, 14853.
Holdings: Mss
Notes: Educator, journalist, public official. Papers, essays, 1854-1922. Incl annotated scrapbooks containing correspondence, broadsides, pamphlets, historical sketches, commemorative addresses, newspaper clippings, editorials, letters to editors, and other printed items. Also, one mss volume and Andrews and Clark family genealogical and biographical data and reminiscences concerning Andrews' teaching career, appointments, and other positions.

ANDREWS, JOHN WILLIAMS

CT —YALE UNIVERSITY, Box 1603A, Yale Station, New Haven, 06520.
Notes: Papers.

MA —BOSTON UNIVERSITY, Mugar Memorial Library, Special Collections Dept, 771 Commonwealth Ave, Boston, 02215. Howard B Gotlieb, Dir
Holdings: Cat Mss

ANDREWS, ROBERT HARDY

MA —BOSTON UNIVERSITY, Mugar Memorial Library, Special Collections Dept, 771 Commonwealth Ave, Boston, 02215. Howard B Gotlieb, Dir
Holdings: Cat Mss Pix
Notes: Mss, correspondence, etc collected in depth; incl publications by or about.

ANDREWS, ROY CHAPMAN

CA —CLAREMONT COLLEGES, Honnold Library, Ninth & Dartmouth, Claremont, 91711. Tania Rizzo, Special Collections Dept Head
Holdings: Vols 250// Uncat Mss
Notes: Papers of Elbert A Wickes, 1884-1975, theatrical and lecture tour manager. Among his clients were Winston Churchill, William Butler Yeats, Houdini, Lowell Thomas, Vilhjalmur Stefansson, and Roy Chapman Andrews.

NY —AMERICAN MUSEUM OF NATURAL HISTORY, Library Services Dept, Central Park W & 79th St, New York, 10024. Nina J Root, Chairwoman; Mary Genett, Asst Librn for Reference Services
Holdings: Cat Mss Maps Pix 16mm Films
Notes: Incl mss, monographs, diaries, correspondence, artifacts, art work. Extensive archive.

ANDREWS FAMILY

MA —NEW ENGLAND HISTORIC GENEALOGICAL SOCIETY, Library, 101 Newbury St, Boston, 02116. Ralph J Crandell, Dir
Notes: Family papers, likely to incl personal correspondence, diaries, business records, etc.

ANECDOTES see Wit and Humor

ANESTHESIA AND ANESTHETICS

CA —FITZ HUGH LUDLOW MEMORIAL LIBRARY, PO Box 99346, San Francisco, 94109. Michael R Aldrich, Exec Cur
Holdings: Vols (300) Cat Pix Slides Phonorecords Videotapes
Notes: Collection stored. Important mail inquiries only. No interlibrary loan or telephone queries. We collect many old pharmacopoeias, dispensatories, formularies, medical history books and records, old pharmaceutical bottles and labels, etc valuable for researching the history of psychoactive drug use. Incl a small but valuable collection of works on anesthesia and toxicology.

CT —YALE MEDICAL LIBRARY, 333 Cedar St, New Haven, 06510.
Holdings: Vols (334,215) Cat Mss Pix Slides Microforms
Budget: ($361,650)
Notes: Incl films, audiotapes, artifacts, etc.

IL —NORTHWESTERN UNIVERSITY, Dental School Library, 311 E Chicago Ave, Chicago, 60611. Minnie Orfanos, Dir
Holdings: Vols 67,987 Cat Mss Pix Slides Microforms
Notes: Special collections: G V Black mss and artifacts; George Teuscher mss and artifacts; NUDS archives: anesthesia, old prints, rare books, dental proceedings. Incl 16,000 pamphlets.

ANESTHESIA AND ANESTHETICS—HISTORY

CA —UNIVERSITY OF CALIFORNIA, SAN FRANCISCO, Library, Special Collections, San Francisco, 94143. Nancy Witten Zinn, Librn
Holdings: Vols 370 Cat Mss Pix
Notes: 19 Boxes of mss and pictures.

CT —YALE UNIVERSITY, Medical Historical Library, 333 Cedar St, New Haven, 06510. Ferenc A Gyorgyey, Librn
Holdings: Cat
Notes: 600 items. Collection described in John F Fulton and Madeline E Stanton, *The Centennial of Surgical Anesthesia: An Annotated Catalogue.* New York: H Schuman, 1946.

IL —AMERICAN SOCIETY OF ANESTHESIOLOGISTS, Wood Library-Museum of Anesthesiology, 515 Busse Hwy, Park Ridge, 60068. Patrick Sim, Librn
Holdings: Vols 7000 Cat Mss Pix Slides Audiotapes
Notes: History of anesthesiology.

KY —UNIVERSITY OF LOUISVILLE, Kornhauser Health Sciences Library, 520 S Preston St, PO Box 35260, Louisville, 40292. Leonard M Eddy, Dir; Sherrill R McConnell, Archivist
Holdings: Vols 400 Cat Mss
Notes: The Emmett F Horine Collection.

MD —UNIVERSITY OF MARYLAND, BALTIMORE, Health Sciences Library, 111 S Greene St, Baltimore, 21201. Cyril C H Feng, Dir
Holdings: Vols (1000) Cat Mss Pix VF
Notes: The Clarence J Grieves Dental Historical Collection is one of the strongest collections of its kind in the United States. It includes some of the most significant early dental imprints; early records of the Maryland State Dental Association; and an excellent collection of prints on early dentistry and St Apollonia.

MN —MAYO MEDICAL LIBRARY, History of Medicine Collection, Rochester, 55905. Nancy R Hensel, Librn
Holdings: Vols (18,000) Cat Mss Maps Pix Slides
Notes: The collection consists of over 18,000 vols, 6500 of which are considered source material (rare or reprint editions of classics). 4308 items from Garrison-Morton are available in the collection. Appropriate bibliographies, biographies and histories of medicine are a part of the collection. Fields of collecting interest are anesthesiology, dermatology, cardiology, neurology, immunology and radiology. Eight medical incunabula.

NY —COLUMBIA UNIVERSITY LIBRARIES, Health Sciences Library, 701 W 168 St, New York, 10032. Rachael K Goldstein, Librn
Holdings: Vols 350
Notes: Landmark works, incl the Lena and

ANESTHESIA AND ANESTHETICS—HISTORY (cont.)

Louis Hyman collection in the history of anesthesia. Restricted.

PA —UNIVERSITY OF PITTSBURGH, Falk Library of the Health Professions, History of Medicine Collection, Scaife Hall, Pittsburgh, 15261. Jonathon Erlen, Cur
Holdings: Vols (13,500) Cat Pix
Budget: ($425,269)
Notes: Medicine, dentistry, nursing, pharmacy, public health, psychiatry materials, incl some rare books and 300 pamphlets on anesthesia.

ANGELA, COUNTESS OF ANTRIM

DC —GEORGETOWN UNIVERSITY, Library, Special Collections Div, 37 & O Sts NW, Washington, 20057. George M Barringer, Special Collections Librn; Nicholas B Sheetz, Mss Librn
Holdings: Mss Pix
Notes: The papers of Christopher Sykes, biographer, journalist, and novelist; containing mss, letters, photographs, and drawings. With extensive correspondence from Harold Acton; Angela, Countess of Antrim; Sir John Betjeman; Ivy Compton-Burnett; Alick Dru; T S Eliot; Max Beerbohm; Graham Greene; John Hayward; Lord Patrick Kinross; Compton Mackenzie; Nancy Mitford; Anthony Powell; Dame Flora Robson; Cecil Roth; Sir John Russell; Osbert Sitwell; John Sparrow; Freya Stark; James Stern; and Evelyn Waugh, among others. Also, considerable research material about Evelyn Waugh, Adam von Trott, Robert Byron, Lady Nancy Astor; and the foundation of the state of Israel.

ANGELI, PIETRO (C.F. BARGEO)

IL —NEWBERRY LIBRARY, 60 W Walton St, Chicago, 60610. Diana Haskell, Cur of Modern Mss
Holdings: Vols 50 Cat Mss
Notes: His papers and annotated books.

ANGELIQUE

IN —INDIANA UNIVERSITY, Lilly Library, Seventh St, Bloomington, 47405. William R Cagle, Librn
Holdings: Cat Mss Pix //
Notes: Letters of Jean Giono, 1895-1970; and manuscript of his *Angelique* (1028 items).

ANGELL, SIR NORMAN

IN —BALL STATE UNIVERSITY, University Libraries, Special Collections Dept, University Ave, Muncie, 47306. David C Tambo, Head of Special Collections
Holdings: // Mss
Notes: Incl 200 linear feet of mss, correspondence, research files, literary mss, as well as Angell's personal library. Many books annotated.

ANGERT, EUGENE

MO —WASHINGTON UNIVERSITY, Libraries, Special Collections Dept, Campus Box 1061, St Louis, 63130.
Notes: Family and business correspondence.

ANGLE, H. H.

BC —UNIVERSITY OF VICTORIA, McPherson Library, Victoria, V8W 3H5, Can.
Notes: Okanagan, BC; Army officer (British Columbia Dragoons). Transcripts: 61 pages; 1945; Personal diary, 1945.

ANGLICAN CHURCH see Church of England

ANGLICAN COMMUNION

NY —GENERAL THEOLOGICAL SEMINARY, Saint Marks Library, 175 Ninth Ave, New York, 10011. David Green, Dir
Holdings: Vols (200,000) Cat
Notes: Extensive collection.

†NY —COLGATE ROCHESTER DIVINITY SCHOOL, Ambrose Swasey Library, 1100 S Goodman St, Rochester, 14620.
Notes: Incl general works about worship, its history and practice and contains manuals of worship, liturgies of primarily Protestant denomination, a sizable collection of hymn books, with particular emphasis upon the Anglican tradition.

NY —UNIVERSITY OF ROCHESTER, Rush Rhees Library, Department of Rare Books and Special Collections, Rochester, 14627. Peter Dzwonkoski, Librn

MB —UNIVERSITY OF MANITOBA, Saint John's College, Library, 400 Dysart Rd, Winnipeg, R3T 2M5, Can. Patrick D Wright, Head
Holdings: Vols (45,600) Cat

ON —HURON COLLEGE, Silcox Memorial Library, 1349 Western Rd, London, N6G 1H3, Can. Pamela MacKay, Chief Librn
Holdings: Uncat Mss Maps Pix
Notes: This collection is in the Charles Addington Archives. Archives of the Anglican Diose of Huron. Records date back to before the creation of the diocese including parish registers, account books, synod reports. Records from 1840 to the present. Collection open by appointment for Scholarly research only.

ON —ANGLICAN CHURCH OF CANADA, Chancellor R V Harris Memorial Library, 600 Jarvis St, Toronto, M4Y 2J6, Can. Alice Marie Hedderick, Librn
Holdings: Vols (2000) Cat Maps Pix
Notes: Reference Library for the National headquarters of the Anglican Church of Canada. Most significant part of the collection is in reference, periodicals and VF materials.

ON —TORONTO SCHOOL OF THEOLOGY, Consortium of Libraries, University of Toronto, Toronto, M5S 1A5, Can. R Grane Bracewell, Library Coordr
Holdings: Cat
Notes: A consortium of 7 theological college and faculty libraries at the University of Toronto.

ON —WYCLIFFE COLLEGE, Leonard Library, 5 Hoskin Ave, Toronto, M5S 1H7, Can. Adrienne Taylor, Librn; Gayle Ford, Library Technician
Holdings: Vols (47,000) Cat Microforms
Budget: ($11,000)
Notes: Collection of early and rare books of prayer books, sermons, Bibles. Basic reference collection of standard theological dictionaries, encyclopedias, commentaries. Homiletics collection including 19th century works. Strong in church history, Evangelical Anglicanism, English Reformation, Wycliffe studies.

PQ —BISHOP'S UNIVERSITY, John Bassett Memorial Library, Laurie Allison Room for Special Collections, Lennoxville, J1M 1Z7, Can. Germain Belisle, Chief Librn
Holdings: Vols 10,000
Notes: Partially cataloged. Relates to ecclesiastical subjects, dating from as early as the 16th century, largely concerned with the history of the Church of England in Canada and elsewhere.

ANGLING see Fishing and Angling

ANGLO-AMERICAN FOLK SONGS see Folk Songs, Anglo-American

ANGLO-AMERICAN LAW see Law, American

ANGLO-CATHOLICISM

NY —GENERAL THEOLOGICAL SEMINARY, Saint Marks Library, 175 Ninth Ave, New York, 10011. David Green, Dir
Holdings: Vols (200,000) Cat
Notes: Extensive collection.

ANGLO-INDIAN DIALECT see Hobson-Jobson

ANGLO-IRISH AUTHORS see Authors, Anglo-Irish

ANGLO-IRISH LANGUAGE AND LITERATURE

IL —NORTHERN ILLINOIS UNIVERSITY, Founders Memorial Library, Rare Books and Special Collections Dept, De Kalb, 60115. William R DuBois, Dept Head
Holdings: Vols 30 // Cat Mss
Notes: The Alan Denson Collection. Emphasis on George Russell, "A.E." Includes Denson's correspondence with many mid-20th century literary figures. Mss indexed but not cataloged.

KS —UNIVERSITY OF KANSAS, Kenneth Spencer Research Library, Special Collections Dept, Lawrence, 66045. Alexandra Mason, Librn
Holdings: Vols 2000 Cat Mss
Notes: Joyce Collection (950 vols), Yeats Collection (525 vols), and parts of the P S O'Hegarty Collection of some 25,000 vols. Noncirculating.

MA —BOSTON COLLEGE LIBRARIES, Thomas P O'Neill Library, Irish Collection, Chestnut Hill, 02167. Ralph Coffman, Cur
Holdings: Vols (10,000) Cat Mss Maps Pix
Notes: Nearly every aspect of Irish history and literature are covered in this collection. Items of special interest are the many papers of Patrick Andrew Collins, president of the Irish Land League, and letters of Jeremiah O'Donovan Rossa, poet, editor and leader in the Fenian and related organizations. Holdings also incl a facsimile of the famous illuminated ms of the Gospels, the *Book of Kells*; a complete vol of *Malton's Views of Dublin, 1799; The Ordinance Surveys;* a complete set of the *Irish Bulletin;* and Colgan's *Acta Sanctorum Hiberniae* describing the lives of the Irish saints.

BC —UNIVERSITY OF BRITISH COLUMBIA, Library, Special Collections Div, 1956 Main Mall, Vancouver, V6T 1Y3, Can. Anne Yandle, Head
Holdings: Vols Cat
Notes: Colbeck Collection.

ON —MCMASTER UNIVERSITY, Mills Memorial Library, Div of Archives & Research Collections, Hamilton, L8S 4L6, Can. G R Hill, Univ Librn
Holdings: Cat Mss
Notes: The main part of this collection consists of works from the Anglo-Irish renaissance, 1890 to 1939. There is also a small archival collection, as well as extensive runs of some Irish periodicals.

ON —QUEEN'S UNIVERSITY, Douglas Library, Kingston, K7L 5C4, Can. William F E Morley, Cur, Special Collections
Holdings: Vols (3250) Cat
Notes: Collection incl all the original volumes in the Cuala Press series and a facsimile reprint of each plus about 170 other works by and about W B Yeats, 200 by and about James Joyce, 240 by and about G B Shaw, 100 by "A E," George W Russell.

ON —UNIVERSITY OF TORONTO, Thomas Fisher Rare Book Library, 120 Saint George St, Toronto, M5S 1A5, Can. Richard G Landon, Head
Holdings: Vols 5200 Cat
Notes: DeLury Collection named for original donor, Alfred DeLury, Dean of Arts, University of Toronto. Centered on works of W B Yeats and his circle. Especially good holdings of the Yeats family. A E, Lady Gregory, and J M Synge. Incl extensive holdings of many of the minor writers.

ANGLO-NORMAN LANGUAGE AND LITERATURE

GA —EMORY UNIVERSITY, Robert W Woodruff Library, Atlanta, 30322. Herbert Johnson, Dir
Holdings: Vols (650,000) Cat Mss Microforms
Notes: Strong in 18th and 19th century literature, especially 19th century prose fiction, incl first editions and "yellow backs." Also incl the Kemp Malone collection of Old English, Middle English, Anglo-Norman and supporting materials.

ANGLO-SAXON LANGUAGE AND LITERATURE

CT —YALE UNIVERSITY, Beinecke Rare Book & Manuscript Library, Osborn Collection, New Haven, 06520. Stephen R Parks, Cur
Holdings: Mss

ANGLO-SAXON LANGUAGE AND LITERATURE (cont.)

GA —EMORY UNIVERSITY, Robert W Woodruff Library, Atlanta, 30322. Herbert Johnson, Dir
Holdings: Cat Mss
Notes: The extensive personal library of Kemp Malone (1889-1971), a leading authority on Old English; incl 66 editions of Beowulf.

KS —UNIVERSITY OF KANSAS, Kenneth Spencer Research Library, Special Collections Dept, Lawrence, 66045. Alexandra Mason, Librn
Holdings: Vols 225 Cat Mss
Notes: Collection name: The Clubb Collection. Anglo-Saxon texts printed in the special typefaces designed for that language; largely 16th-18th centuries. Works of the septentrional antiquaries. Anglo-Saxon mss.

NY —NEW YORK PUBLIC LIBRARY, Mid-Manhattan Library, Literature and Language Dept, 455 Fifth Ave, New York, 10016. Eric Steele, Sr Principal Librn
Holdings: Vols (160,000) Cat Phonorecords Microforms Audiotapes
Budget: ($92,000)
Notes: Large number of bibliographic tools for undergraduate study of all aspects of literature. Important journals in the field with significant or complete runs of the major serials. Representative selection of American and English little magazines. Extensive collection of works, criticism and biographies of major and minor American and English writers; special attention directed towards Black American literature. Strong in works in translation and criticism of Spanish and French literature, representative in other foreign literatures. Considerable collection of criticism in Spanish and French. Department includes material on the teaching of literature, the techniques of creative writing, and the history of the theater when important to the study of dramatic literature. Collection has many facsimile and microfiche editions of primary and secondary sources with emphasis on English literature, from the Old English period to 1784. Substantial collection of recordings of prose, poetry and drama.

ANGLO-SAXON MANUSCRIPTS see Manuscripts, Anglo-Saxon

ANGOFF, CHARLES

MA —BOSTON UNIVERSITY, Mugar Memorial Library, Special Collections Dept, 771 Commonwealth Ave, Boston, 02215. Howard B Gotlieb, Dir
Holdings: Cat Mss

ANGOLA

CA —HOOVER INSTITUTION ON WAR, REVOLUTION & PEACE, Stanford University, Stanford, 94305. Milorad M Drachkovitch, Archivist
Notes: Collection of leaflets, newsletters, pamphlets, and other ephemera of various political action groups and other organizations, 1969-1974, relating to political and economic developments in southern African countries, incl Angola, Mozambique, Rhodesia (Zimbabwe), Union of South Africa, and South West Africa (Namibia). 5 ms boxes.

DC —HOWARD UNIVERSITY, Moorland-Spingarn Research Center, 500 Howard Place NW, Washington, 20059. Clifford L Muse, Jr, Acting Dir

ANGUILLA

CT —LEE ASH, (personal collection), 66 Humiston Dr, Bethany, 06525.
Holdings: Cat Mss Maps Pix Slides

ANGULO, JAIME DE, 1887-1950

CA —UNIVERSITY OF CALIFORNIA, LOS ANGELES, Research Library, Dept of Special Collections, 405 Hilgard Ave, Los Angeles, 90024. Edward Shreeves, Chairman, Bibliographers Group; David S Zeidberg, Head
Notes: Ten books, 25 mss, 50 letters and 20 photographs of this folklorist who spent many years with the Pit River Indians of Northern California.

ANHALONIUM see Peyote

ANIMAL BEHAVIOR see Animals, Habits and Behavior of

ANIMAL DISEASES, FOREIGN see Veterinary Medicine

ANIMAL ECOLOGY

NV —FORESTA INSTITUTE FOR OCEAN AND MOUNTAIN STUDIES, Library, 6205 Franktown Rd, Carson City, 89701. Shannon Porter, Librn
Holdings: Vols (3000) Cat Mss Maps Pix Slides
Notes: Material on plant, animal, and human ecology with special emphasis on far western US and Nevada ecology and environmental problems. Also hold about 2000 reprints, pamphlets, reports, etc.

ANIMAL HUSBANDRY see Domestic Animals

ANIMAL INTELLIGENCE

PA —CARNEGIE LIBRARY OF PITTSBURGH, Science & Technology Dept, 4400 Forbes Ave, Pittsburgh, 15213. Catherine M Brosky, Dept Head
Notes: Except for certain special areas, such as entomology and ornithology and a few others that are emphasized, this general subject is of secondary interest. Incl both modern and classic works. Kept up to date in cooperation with the Library in Carnegie Museum of Natural History. Materials available on the various phyla, orders and species. Abstracts, indexes, bibliographies, taxonomic manuals and standard reference books. Many journals and society publications complete from the beginning.

ANIMAL KINGDOM see Zoology

ANIMAL LORE

NY —AMERICAN MUSEUM OF NATURAL HISTORY, Library Services Dept, Central Park W & 79th St, New York, 10024. Nina J Root, Chairwoman; Mary Genett, Asst Librn for Reference Services
Holdings: Vols (385,000) Cat Mss Maps Pix Slides Microforms
Notes: Nearly all collections are outstanding for depth of coverage and international range. Early and historic works, rare books, colored illustrations, and relevant serial publications supplement the modern scientific publications necessary to the researches of the scientific staff and the work of the educational division. Open to the public.

ANIMAL MAGNETISM see Hypnotism

ANIMAL NUTRITION see Feeding; Nutrition

ANIMAL OILS see Oils and Fats

ANIMAL PARASITES see Parasitology

ANIMAL PHYSIOLOGY

WI —UNIVERSITY OF WISCONSIN, MADISON, College of Agricultural & Life Sciences, Steenbock Memorial Library, 550 Babcock Dr, Madison, 53706. Jan Kennedy, Dir
Holdings: Vols (186,312) Cat Docs Maps Microforms Slides
Notes: Extensive general agricultural collection supporting the College of Agricultural and Life Sciences in agronomy, dairy science, agricultural engineering, entomology, botany, natural resources, nutrition, forestry, genetics, veterinary science, meat and animal science, poultry science, and soils. Collection includes USDA, USDI, experiment station and state documents.

ANIMAL POPULATIONS

IA —IOWA STATE UNIVERSITY, Library, Ames, 50011. Warren B Kuhn, Dean of Library Services
Holdings: Cat
Notes: Incl: ecology, fresh water fisheries biology, wildlife biology and management, and wildlife conservation. Extensive serial holdings.

IA —IOWA STATE UNIVERSITY, Library, Dept of Special Collections, Ames, 50011. Stanley M Yates, Head
Holdings: // Mss Pix
Notes: The Paul Errington (1902-1962) Papers. Professor of zoology at ISU (1932-1962) and a leading authority on vertebrate ecology and animal population dynamics. Collection incl correspondence, mss and articles. Collection is 15 linear feet.

NY —UNIVERSITY OF ROCHESTER, Carlson Library, Hutchison Hall, River Campus, Rochester, 14627. Michael W Poulin, Librn
Holdings: Vols (48,720) Cat Microforms
Notes: Strong collection in the field and related areas.

ANIMAL TRAINING see Animals, Training of

ANIMALS

CA —UNIVERSITY OF CALIFORNIA, DAVIS, General Library, Davis, 95616. Bernard Kreissman, University Librn; C Danial Elliott, Asst Head, Dept Special Collections
Holdings: Vols 20,566

DE —UNIVERSITY OF DELAWARE, Agriculture Library, 2 Townsend Hall, Newark, 19717. Frederick Getze, Assoc Librn
Holdings: Vols (32,500)
Notes: Strong in entomology and ornamental horticulture. Extensive collection of state agriculture documents for each US state and Puerto Rico. Library subscribes to 500 serials (English and foreign).

FL —UNIVERSITY OF FLORIDA, Institute of Food & Agricultural Sciences, Hume Library, Gainesville, 32611. Albert C Strickland, Librn
Holdings: Vols (135,000) Cat Mss Microforms
Notes: Including journals and monographs, this collection is a general agricultural one. The emphasis is on tropical agriculture, especially Latin America. Entomology is very strong. The library offers on-line information retrieval using Lockheed and SDC data bases.

IN —PURDUE UNIVERSITY LIBRARIES, Life Sciences Library, Lilly Hall of Life Sciences, West Lafayette, 47907. Martha J Bailey, Librn
Holdings: Vols (73,404) Cat Microforms
Budget: ($223,445)
Notes: Incl materials in agronomy, animal sciences, botany, entomology, forestry, horticulture, biological sciences and agricultural engineering.

KS —TOPEKA ZOOLOGICAL PARK, Topeka Zoo Library, 635 Gage Blvd, Topeka, 66606. Ron Kaufman, Education Coordinator
Holdings: Vols (800) Cat Mss Maps Pix Slides Audiotapes 16mm Films Filmstrips Microforms
Budget: ($500)

ANIMALS (cont.)

KY —UNIVERSITY OF KENTUCKY, Agricultural Library, Agricultural Science Center North, Lexington, 40506. Antoinette Paris Powell, Librn
Holdings: Vols (90,000) Cat Microforms
Budget: ($110,385)

MA —UNIVERSITY OF MASSACHUSETTS AT AMHERST, Library, Amherst, 01003. Siegfried Feller, Assoc Dir for Collection Development
Holdings: Cat
Notes: Veterinary medicine and animal sciences. Special emphases: reproductive physiology, poultry genetics, animal nutrition.

NE —UNIVERSITY OF NEBRASKA-LINCOLN, C Y Thompson Library, East Campus, Lincoln, 68583. Lyle Schreiner, Librn
Holdings: Vols (220,000) Cat
Notes: Agriculture, with major strength in entomology, agronomy, and animal science; medicine; veterinary medicine; and home economics.

NY —AMERICAN MUSEUM OF NATURAL HISTORY, Library Services Dept, Central Park W & 79th St, New York, 10024. Nina J Root, Chairwoman; Mary Genett, Asst Librn for Reference Services

MB —UNIVERSITY OF MANITOBA, Agriculture Library, Dafoe Rd, Winnipeg, R3T 2N2, Can. Judy Harper, Head
Holdings: Vols (9000) Cat

ANIMALS—CAPTIVE MANAGEMENT see Wild Animals, Captive

ANIMALS, AQUATIC see Marine Fauna

ANIMALS, CAPTIVE see Wild Animals, Captive

ANIMALS, CRUELTY TO see Animals, Treatment of

ANIMALS, DISEASES OF see Veterinary Medicine

ANIMALS, DOMESTIC see Domestic Animals

ANIMALS, EXPERIMENTAL see Laboratory Animals

ANIMALS, FOSSIL see Paleontology

ANIMALS, GEOGRAPHIC DISTRIBUTION OF see Zoogeography

ANIMALS, HABITS AND BEHAVIOR OF

DC —SMITHSONIAN INSTITUTION, Smithsonian Tropical Research Institute, Washington, 20560. Carol Jopling, Chief Librn
Holdings: Vols (22,000) Cat Mss Maps Pix Slides 16mm Films Microforms
Budget: ($70,000)
Notes: Smithsonian Institution, Smithsonian Tropical Research Institute is located in Balboa, Panama.

DC —SMITHSONIAN INSTITUTION LIBRARIES, National Zoological Park Branch, Washington, 20008. Kay Kenyon, Chief Librn
Holdings: Vols (5500) Cat
Notes: Collection incl animal nutrition, capture and care of animals in captivity, conservation and endangered species, pathology, veterinary medicine, zoology.

FL —ARCHBOLD BIOLOGICAL STATION, Library, Rt 2, Box 180, Lake Placid, 33852. Fred E Lohrer, Librn
Holdings: Vols (2000) Cat Periodicals

FL —RINGLING MUSEUM OF THE CIRCUS, Library, PO Box 1838, Sarasota, 33578. Nan Fisher, Visitor Services Specialist
Holdings: Vols (350) Cat
Notes: Collection also incl long runs (and indexes) of circus periodicals.

IN —PURDUE UNIVERSITY LIBRARIES, Veterinary Medical Library, C J Lynn Hall of Veterinary Medicine, West Lafayette, 47907. Gretchen Stephens, Librn
Holdings: Vols (31,022) Cat
Budget: ($106,281)
Notes: The collection contains the outstanding books and serials in English that are germane to comparative and veterinary medicine. Foreign language materials are added selectively. Subjects of particular strength are laboratory animal medicine, pathology, comparative anatomy, animal behavior and clinical veterinary medicine.

KS —TOPEKA ZOOLOGICAL PARK, Topeka Zoo Library, 635 Gage Blvd, Topeka, 66606. Ron Kaufman, Education Coordinator
Holdings: Vols (800) Cat Mss Maps Pix Slides Audiotapes 16mm Films Filmstrips Microforms
Budget: ($500)

MA —MASSACHUSETTS AUDUBON SOCIETY, Hathaway Environmental Education Institute, Lincoln, 01773. Louise C Maglione, Librn
Holdings: Cat Maps Pix Slides Phonorecords Audiotapes 16mm Films Filmstrips
Notes: Largest and most comprehensive collection in the field of environmental education; especially good in the curriculum area. Extensive sections on animal, behavioral and environmental issues, and quality of environment.

NY —AMERICAN MUSEUM OF NATURAL HISTORY, Library Services Dept, Central Park W & 79th St, New York, 10024. Nina J Root, Chairwoman; Mary Genett, Asst Librn for Reference Services
Holdings: Vols (385,000) Cat Mss Maps Pix Slides Microforms
Notes: Nearly all collections are outstanding for depth of coverage and international range. Early and historic works, rare books, colored illustrations, and relevant serial publications supplement the modern scientific publications necessary to the researches of the scientific staff and the work of the educational division. Open to the public.

NY —UNIVERSITY OF ROCHESTER, Carlson Library, Hutchison Hall, River Campus, Rochester, 14627. Michael W Poulin, Librn
Holdings: Vols (48,720) Cat Microforms
Notes: Strong collection in the field and related areas.

NC —UNIVERSITY OF NORTH CAROLINA, CHAPEL HILL, Zoology Dept Library, Wilson Hall 046A, Chapel Hill, 27514. John B Darling, Librn
Holdings: Vols (31,000) Cat
Notes: Collection incl theses and dissertations.

PA —CARNEGIE LIBRARY OF PITTSBURGH, Science & Technology Dept, 4400 Forbes Ave, Pittsburgh, 15213. Catherine M Brosky, Dept Head
Notes: Except for certain special areas, such as entomology and ornithology and a few others that are emphasized, this general subject is of secondary interest. Incl both modern and classic works. Kept up to date in cooperation with the Library in Carnegie Museum of Natural History. Materials available on the various phyla, classes, orders and species. Abstracts, indexes, bibliographies, taxonomic manuals and standard reference books. Many journals and society publications complete from the beginning.

†WA —WASHINGTON STATE UNIVERSITY, Library, Manuscripts, Archives & Special Collections, Pullman, 99164. John F Guido, Head
Holdings: Cat Mss Maps Pix
Notes: The Carl Parcher Russell papers, a vast resource (24,916 items; 45 linear feet) on American Indian and Western pioneer activities and artifacts. Much on the fur trade; pioneer life; mountain men and trapping; wildlife; primitive life in detail. Also the National Park Service, parks, monuments, etc. Described in *Carl Parcher Russell: An Indexed Register of His Scholarly and Professional Papers, 1920-1967, in the Washington State University Library* (Pullman, 1970), 149 pp.

ANIMALS, PROTECTION OF see Animals, Treatment of

ANIMALS, RESTRAINT OF see Animals, Treatment of

ANIMALS, SEA see Marine Fauna

ANIMALS, SYMBOLIC see Symbolism

ANIMALS, TRAINING OF

FL —RINGLING MUSEUM OF THE CIRCUS, Library, PO Box 1838, Sarasota, 33578. Nan Fisher, Visitor Services Specialist
Holdings: Vols (350) Cat
Notes: Collection also incl long runs (and indexes) of circus periodicals.

IL —ILLINOIS STATE UNIVERSITY, Milner Library, Dept of Special Collections, Normal, 61761. Robert Sokan, Librn
Holdings: Vols 6200 Cat Mss Pix Slides
Notes: Circus and related arts collection consists of approx 6200 book items and approx 250,000 nonbook items. The books date from the 16th century to the present, and incl vols specifically concerned with the circus past and present, vaudeville, music halls and variety theaters, theatrical and animal history, biographies, autobiographies and memoirs, novels, poetry, drama, juvenalia and other subjects relating to the circus. Many of the books are limited editions, presentation copies or autographed copies. Incl archives of the Dobritch International Circus (20,000 items).

ANIMALS, TREATMENT OF

CO —AMERICAN HUMANE ASSOCIATION, Denver, 80231.
Notes: The American Humane Association no longer maintains a library.

DC —SMITHSONIAN INSTITUTION LIBRARIES, National Zoological Park Branch, Washington, 20008. Kay Kenyon, Chief Librn
Holdings: Vols (5500) Cat
Notes: Collection incl animal nutrition, capture and care of animals in captivity, conservation and endangered species, pathology, veterinary medicine, zoology.

KS —TOPEKA ZOOLOGICAL PARK, Topeka Zoo Library, 635 Gage Blvd, Topeka, 66606. Ron Kaufman, Education Coordinator
Holdings: Vols (800) Cat Mss Maps Pix Slides Audiotapes 16mm Films Filmstrips Microforms
Budget: ($500)

NY —NEW YORK ZOOLOGICAL SOCIETY LIBRARY, Bronx Zoo, Bronx, 10460. Steven P Johnson, Archivist and Librn
Holdings: Vols (6000) Cat Mss
Budget: ($50,000)
Notes: Collection consists primarily of journals in captive management of animals, vertebrate zoology, and veterinary medicine. Primarily intended for the scientific staff, the collection is open to the public on a noncirculating basis, by appointment, (212) 220-6874.

ANIMALS IN CAPTIVITY see Wild Animals, Captive

ANIMATED CARTOONS see Moving Picture Cartoons

ANIMATION (CINEMATOGRAPHY)

CA —CALIFORNIA INSTITUTE OF THE ARTS, Library, 24700 McBean Pkwy, Valencia, 91355. James Elrod, Dir
Holdings: Vols Cat Videotapes 16mm Films Cat
Budget: ($7500)
Notes: Incl 320 videotapes and 320 16mm films.

IN —INDIANA UNIVERSITY, Lilly Library, Seventh St, Bloomington, 47405. William R

ANIMATION (CINEMATOGRAPHY) (cont.)

Cagle, Librn
Holdings: Cat Mss
Notes: 1500 issues of Marvel Comics. Mss incl illustrations for "Toonerville Trolley" and "Brenda Starr;" also a growing collection of individual pieces representative of comic strip art and animation.

NY —EDUCATIONAL FILM LIBRARY ASSOCIATION, Film Reference Library, 45 John St, New York, 10038. Nadine Covert, Exec Dir
Holdings: Vols (2600) Cat Pix 16mm Films Filmstrips
Budget: ($1500)
Notes: Primarily a print collection emphasizing the documentary and educational film areas, but also film as art, animation and independent film in general. Maintain film title file of over 60,000 cards (primarily educational film titles), incl credit information, running time, release date, summary, and distributor. File is a mixture of EFLA evaluations, LC cards, etc. Subject file also separates film flyers by subject or topic. Maintain festivals file (film festivals, educational film festivals, etc); a film library administration file; a filmmakers file (with bio, credits, clippings, program notes); and a vertical file (incl information on grants, distribution, showcases, film activities in the metropolitan area and in major film centers around the country). Membership organization providing telephone, mail and in-person reference. Open to the generalpublic. Do not publish a catalog, but publish annual Film Library Administration bibliography of current or noteworthy reference books for $2.00.

ANNALS see History

ANNAMITIC LANGUAGE AND LITERATURE

NY —NEW YORK PUBLIC LIBRARY, Oriental Div, Fifth Ave & 42 St, New York, 10018. E Christian Filstrup, Chief
Holdings: // Cat Mss Microforms
Budget: ($56,455)
Notes: Published catalog of holdings. Currently collected in Western language materials only.

ANNE OF BRITTANY

NE —UNIVERSITY OF NEBRASKA-LINCOLN, Don L Love Library, University Archives and Special Collections, Lincoln, 68588. Joseph G Svoboda, University Archivist
Holdings: // Cat

ANNIVERSARY VOLUMES see Festschriften

ANNUAL EVENTS

MI —APPLE TREE PRESS, Library, Box 1012, Flint, 48501. W D Chase, Editor/Librn
Holdings: Vols (1200) Uncat Mss Maps Pix Microforms

ANNUALS see Almanacs; Calendars; Literary Annuals and Giftbooks; Giftbooks (Annuals, Etc.)

ANONYMA AND PSEUDONYMA

CT —LEE ASH, (personal collection), 66 Humiston Dr, Bethany, 06525.

ANSELL, JACK

MA —BOSTON UNIVERSITY, Mugar Memorial Library, Special Collections Dept, 771 Commonwealth Ave, Boston, 02215. Howard B Gotlieb, Dir
Holdings: Cat Mss Maps
Notes: Mss, correspondence, etc collected in depth; incl publications by or about.

ANSHEN, RUTH NANDA, 1900-

NY —COLUMBIA UNIVERSITY LIBRARIES, Rare Book & Manuscript Library, 801 Butler Library, 535 W 114 St, New York, 10027. Kenneth A Lohf, Librn
Holdings: Mss
Notes: Her papers (1938-1982). 12,000 items. Restricted use.

†NY —COLUMBIA UNIVERSITY LIBRARIES, Butler Library, Rare Book and Manuscript Library, 535 W 114 St, New York, 10027.
Notes: Her literary papers and correspondence.

ANSLINGER, HARRY

PA —PENNSYLVANIA STATE UNIVERSITY, Fred Lewis Pattee Library, Special Collections Dept, University Park, 16802. Charles Mann, Chief, Special Collections
Holdings: // Mss
Budget: ($37,000)
Notes: The papers of Harry Anslinger, formerly US Commissioner of Narcotics. No photocopying.

ANSPACHER, LOUIS KAUFMAN

NY —COLUMBIA UNIVERSITY LIBRARIES, Rare Book & Manuscript Library, 801 Butler Library, 535 W 114 St, New York, 10027. Kenneth A Lohf, Librn
Holdings: Mss
Notes: Mss, poems, plays, stories, lectures, family correspondence. About 2000 items. Restricted use.

ANT see Ants

ANTARCTIC EXPEDITIONS see Antarctic Regions

ANTARCTIC REGIONS

AK —UNIVERSITY OF ALASKA, Elmer E Rasmuson Library, Fairbanks, 99701. Robert H Geiman, Dir
Holdings: Vols Cat Mss Maps Pix Slides Phonorecords Audiotapes Films Microforms
Notes: The Alaska Collection is strong in all disciplines concerning Alaska. Main strengths are exploration and travel, pioneer memoirs, and materials on Alaska natives. Bulk of collection is in English with significant holdings in Russian, Native American, and European languages. Archival holdings incl 6000 cu ft of mss, 110,000 historic photographs, 2319 tape recordings, 727 films and videotapes, 200 rare maps and 1273 microfilms. Ms collection strongest in political and economic areas. A Guide to the Collections is available in hard copy and microfiche. About 1000 special collections, some 300 quite significant.

CO —WORLD DATA CENTER A: GLACIOLOGY (SNOW AND ICE), CIRES, University of Colorado, Boulder, 80309. Ann M Brennan, Librn
Holdings: Vols 10,000 Maps Pix Microforms
Budget: $2000
Notes: Glaciology, all forms of snow and ice. Bibliographic information will be contained in a data file which will be fully searchable. Partially cataloged (UDC).

CT —YALE UNIVERSITY, Box 1603A, Yale Station, New Haven, 06520.

DC —NATIONAL ARCHIVES AND RECORDS SERVICE, Civil Archives Division, Washington, 20408.
Holdings: Vols (1500) Uncat
Notes: Repository for records created by federal government agencies engaged in Arctic and Antarctic activities, and for gifts of private papers relating to the regions. Collection maintained for reference use by staff and researchers only.

DC —NATIONAL GEOGRAPHIC SOCIETY, Library, 1146 16th St NW, Washington, 20036. Susan Fifer Canby, Dir
Holdings: Vols (63,000) Cat Mss Maps Pix
Notes: Material concerning land, sea, and space exploration--past and present. All fields of anthropology, natural history, geography, etc.

HI —PACIFIC SUBMARINE MUSEUM, Library, Naval Submarine Base, Pearl Harbor, 96860. Ray W de Yarmin, Cur
Holdings: Vols (1500) Cat Mss Maps Pix Slides Phonorecords 16mm Films
Budget: ($600)
Notes: Incl 3000 pictures. Extensive missile and torpedo collection; submarine models; salvage/deep-sea diver exhibit; Arctic exploration by submarines Worl War II submarine components. Research program for students, authors, lecturers, etc.

MA —HARVARD UNIVERSITY LIBRARY, Cambridge, 02138.
Holdings: Cat

MA —BOSTON COLLEGE LIBRARIES, Catherine B O'Connor Geophysics Library, Weston Observatory, Weston, 02193. F Clifford McElroy, Science Librn
Holdings: Vols (7813) Cat Maps Pix Microforms
Notes: This collection is being absorbed into the general collection.

MI —UNIVERSITY OF MICHIGAN, Library, Dept of Rare Books & Special Collections, Ann Arbor, 48109. Robert J Starring, Head
Holdings: Cat Mss Maps Pix
Notes: Includes over 100 books, mostly autographed presentation copies from polar explorers to donor William H Hobbs, and 62 scrapbooks, notebooks, albums, and made-up volumes of pamphlets, documents and correspondence, 11 relating to Admiral Peary. Also there are such primary records from Professor Hobbs' own expeditions as his journals, radio logs, purchase requisitions, pilot balloon ascension reports and graphs, and anemoscope records. In addition there are an estimated 3500 items of correspondence with explorers and other notables, 800 photographs, and maps.

MI —OLIVET COLLEGE, Burrage Library, Olivet, 49076. Chris Miko, Dir
Holdings: Vols (2000) Cat
Notes: The collection consists primarily of early printed voyages of the arctic and antarctic from the earliest times to the mid-20th century.

NV —FORESTA INSTITUTE FOR OCEAN AND MOUNTAIN STUDIES, Library, 6205 Franktown Rd, Carson City, 89701. Shannon Porter, Librn
Holdings: Vols 500 Cat Mss Maps Pix Slides
Notes: Collection incl historical and contemporary accounts of Antarctic voyages; special emphasis on ecology, plant and animal life, fish, and whales. Also about 1500 pamphlets, etc. Bibliography of whales and whaling materials in library published in 1977.

NV —UNIVERSITY OF NEVADA, RENO, Desert Research Institute, PO Box 60220, Reno, 89557. Roberta Kiefer Orcutt, Librn
Holdings: Vols (10,480) Cat Maps Microforms
Notes: Incl materials in atmospheric physics, meteorology, climatology, weather modification, antarctic studies and related materials in basic sciences. Over 3000 microforms; also 1300 technical reports and 18,000 government publications.

NH —DARTMOUTH COLLEGE, Baker Memorial Library, Hanover, 03755.
Holdings: Cat Mss Maps
Notes: 1200 atlases and 90,000 maps. Areas of special interest: historical cartography, polar regions.

NY —COLUMBIA UNIVERSITY LIBRARIES, Rare Book & Manuscript Library, 801 Butler Library, 535 W 114 St, New York, 10027. Kenneth A Lohf, Librn
Holdings: 700 Cat
Notes: First editions, mss, letters and memorabilia relating to the exploration of the North and South Poles. 700 vols, 500 ms items. Restricted use.

NY —EXPLORERS CLUB, James B Ford Memorial Library, 46 E 70 St, New York, 10021. Janet Baldwin, Librn
Holdings: Vols (24,000) Cat Maps
Notes: Additions to the collection depend upon gifts. Access by appointment only.

NY —NEW YORK PUBLIC LIBRARY, Research Libraries, General Research

ANTARCTIC REGIONS (cont.)

Division, Fifth Ave & 42 St, New York, 10018. Rodney Phillips, Chief
Holdings: Vols (2,225,000) Cat Maps Pix Microforms
Budget: ($775,718)

OH —CLEVELAND PUBLIC LIBRARY, History and Geography Department, 325 Superior Ave, Cleveland, 44114. JoAnn Petrello, Head
Holdings: Cat Maps
Notes: Collection incl rare books.

RI —BROWN UNIVERSITY, John Carter Brown Library, Providence, 02912. Norman Fiering, Librn; Everett C Wilkie Jr, Bibliographer; Susan Danforth, Cur Maps & Prints
Holdings: Vols (40,000)
Notes: Exploration and discovery until the establishment of permanent stations on the continent (ca 1950).
See also entries under Arctic Regions; Spanish America - History

VA —UNIVERSITY OF VIRGINIA, Alderman Library, Manuscripts Dept, Charlottesville, 22901. Edmund Berkeley Jr, Cur
Holdings: Cat Mss Pix
Notes: Papers of Edwin Swift Balch, author of *The North Pole* and *Bradley Land*, and *Antarctica*, and authority on the Cook-Peary controversy incl scrapbooks and correspondence.

WI —UNIVERSITY OF WISCONSIN, MADISON, Geophysical & Polar Research Center Library, Weeks Hall, 1215 W Dayton St, Madison, 53706. Alison N Mares, Librn
Holdings: Vols (1000) Cat Mss Maps Microforms
Notes: Collection incl large bibliography of Arctic and Antarctic subjects available. Library has some 1500 pamphlets; 500 maps, mostly bathymetric and geological; reprint collection from Cold Regions Research & Engineering Lab (CRREL); collection of Russian materials, dealing with the Antarctic.

ANTEDILUVIAN ANIMALS see Paleontology

ANTERIOR SPINAL PARALYSIS see Poliomyelitis

ANTHEIL, GEORGE, 1900-1959

CA —UNIVERSITY OF CALIFORNIA, LOS ANGELES, Music Library, Schonberg Hall, Los Angeles, 90024. Stephen M Fry, Music Librn
Notes: Manuscripts, performing parts, and copies of the film music of composer George Antheil (1900-1959).

DC —LIBRARY OF CONGRESS, Music Division, Washington, 20540.
Notes: Music mss, papers, and recordings of composer George Antheil.

ANTHEMS

CA —OAKLAND PUBLIC LIBRARY, Art, Music and Recreation Section, 125 14 St, Oakland, 94612. Richard Colvig, Senior Librn
Holdings: Vols (5000) Cat Phonorecords Audiotapes
Budget: ($6700)
Notes: 10,000 scores, incl chamber music, instrumental music (piano and organ collections especially strong), miniature scores, opera scores, songs and song collections; 30,000 octavos (anthems and choral music of all kinds); 5000 books about music; 8000 phonorecords; and audiocassettes.

LA —NEW ORLEANS BAPTIST THEOLOGICAL SEMINARY, Martin Music Library, 4110 Seminary Place, New Orleans, 70126. Douglas G Broomoe, Music Librn
Holdings: Vols 38,000 Cat Mss Microforms
Budget: ($10,000)
Notes: Martin Music Library serves the Division of Church Music Ministries of the New Orleans Baptist Theological Seminary. As such, its holdings lean toward church music: books (7500); scores (11,000); anthems (15,000); records (4500). Martin Music Library is maintained as a separate division of the Seminary's library and is housed in the main library. Separate catalog.

ANTHOENSEN PRESS

ME —PORTLAND PUBLIC LIBRARY, 5 Monument Sq, Portland, 04101. Edward V Chenevert, Library Dir
Holdings: Vols 448 Cat
Notes: Originated as the Southworth Printing Company and was concerned with producing religious tracts. The scope of the press broadened under the later ownership (ca 1923) of Fred Anthoensen; it is still publishing.

ME —UNIVERSITY OF MAINE AT PORTLAND-GORHAM, Portland Campus Library, 96 Falmouth St, Portland, 04103. Albert A Howard, Special Collections Librn
Holdings: Vols 900 Cat
Notes: Collection incl broadsides, prospectuses and other printed ephemera (not cataloged). Also some imprints of Southworth-Anthoensen. Collection is comprehensive. Collection is the main catalog and there is a separate shelf list.

ANTHONY (JACOB), PIERS

NM —EASTERN NEW MEXICO UNIVERSITY, Golden Library, Special Collections, Portales, 88130. Mary Jo Walker, Special Collections Librn
Holdings: Vols 11,940 Cat Mss Pix Audiotapes
Notes: Incl 700 magazine titles (10,318 issues), 11,940 vols, mss and correspondences of the following science fiction writers: Jack Williamson, Edmond Hamilton, Leigh Brackett, Forrest J Ackerman and Piers Anthony (Jacob), plus *Astounding/Analog* ms files (1954-1975). Also serves as a depository for Science Fiction Writers of America. Incl separate catalog for published books and unpublished registers to personal papers. The Williamson Register is being prepared for publication. Collection is described in *Anatomy of* Wonder, by Neil Barron (NY: Bowker, 1981); and *Special Collections, II* (winter, 1982), pp 49-57.

ANTHONY, SUSAN BROWNELL, 1820-1906

DC —LIBRARY OF CONGRESS, Rare Book & Special Collections Div, Washington, 20540. William Matheson, Chief
Holdings: Vols 272 Cat
Notes: The Susan B Anthony Collection represents her personal library, presented to the Library in 1903. Incl, apart from Miss Anthony's own books, are a large number of inscribed copies given to the reformer by authors and friends, nearly all of which are relevant to the rights of women, enfranchisement, etc. Supplementary are files of such materials as official reports of the National Suffrage Conventions, addresses made at Congressional hearings, scrapbooks containing clippings from newspapers and periodicals, handbills, and other memorabilia.

DC —LIBRARY OF CONGRESS, Manuscript Division, Washington, 20540. John C Broderick, Chief
Notes: Susan B Anthony's papers in the Manuscript Division incl scrapbooks, correspondence, speeches, and related material. Diaries from the years 1865-1906 contain brief comments regarding her lecture tours on behalf of woman suffrage and referrences to such associates as Amelia Bloomer, Lucretia Mott, and Lucy Stone.

MA —RADCLIFFE COLLEGE, Arthur & Elizabeth Schlesinger Library on the History of Women in America, 3 James St, Cambridge, 02138. Patricia Miller King, Dir; Eva Moseley, Cur of Mss
Holdings: Cat Mss
Notes: Diaries, correspondence, speeches, photographs, etc. Anthony was an abolitionist and women's rights leader. Papers available only on microfilm. Inventory published by G K Hall, 1984.

MO —MISSOURI HISTORICAL SOCIETY, Library, Jefferson Memorial Bldg, Saint Louis, 63112. Stephanie Klein, Librn-Archivist; Peter Michel, Cur of Manuscripts
Notes: A collection of material on 119 women who lived or worked in St Louis and Missouri as educators, artists, and homemakers, or played significant roles in US politics and social reform. Incl Sacajawea, Susan B Anthony, Fannie Hurst, Carry Nation, Patience Worth, etc.

NY —UNIVERSITY OF ROCHESTER, Rush Rhees Library, Department of Rare Books and Special Collections, Rochester, 14627. Peter Dzwonkoski, Librn
Holdings: Cat Mss Pix
Notes: Approximately 300 letters including correspondence with Rachel Foster Avery (178 letters); Harriet Taylor Upton, Amy Post, Elizabeth Cady Stanton, and others. Also includes photographs, printed ephemera, and museum pieces.

OH —RUTHERFORD B HAYES LIBRARY, 1337 Hayes Ave, Fremont, 43420. Watt P Marchman, Dir
Notes: Correspondence in the Lyman-Lincoln Collection.

†PA —FRIENDS HISTORICAL LIBRARY OF SWARTHMORE COLLEGE, Swarthmore, 19081.
Notes: Works from 1654 to the present, with emphasis on the Quaker leaders in women's rights, Susan B Anthony, Sarah M Grimke, Lucretia Mott, and some non-Quakers.

ANTHRACITE COAL see Coal, Anthracite

ANTHROPOLOGICAL PERIODICALS see Periodicals, Anthropological

ANTHROPOLOGISTS

DC —LIBRARY OF CONGRESS, Manuscript Division, Washington, 20540. John C Broderick, Chief
Notes: Margaret Mead's papers. Access to parts of the collection restricted. Additional papers at the American Museum of Natural History, New York, NY.

MA —AMHERST COLLEGE, Library, Amherst, 01002. John Lancaster, Special Collections Librn
Notes: Personal "working library" of Margaret Mead, donated by Mary Catherine Bateson, Dr Mead's daughter. Other collections of Margaret Mead's papers, books, mss, etc are at the Library of Congress, the American Museum of Natural History, etc. Dr Bateson has also given her mother's film collection to the Five College collection housed at Hampshire College.

BC —UNIVERSITY OF VICTORIA, McPherson Library, Victoria, V8W 3H5, Can.
Notes: Anthropologist Franz. Incl types mss *Indian Legends of the North Pacific Coast of America*, a translation by Dietrich Bertz of anthropologist Franz Boas' *Indianische Sagen von der Nord-Pacifischen Ku06ste* Amerikas.

ANTHROPOLOGY

AZ —NORTHERN ARIZONA UNIVERSITY, Special Collection Library, CU Box 6022, Flagstaff, 86011. Peter M Whiteley, Coordr/Archivist; William Mullane, Librn
Notes: David P Seaman Collection of mss on the Hopi language. Incl books on anthropology collected by H C Diehl, an amateur anthropologist who was especially interested in the Hopi Indians. Most of the books contain handwritten notes written in the margin by Diehl, 1950's-1970's. Also incl a photocopy of H R Voth's mss, "Hopi-English Vocabulary," 1902, and "Hopi Field Notes," 1890's. (5 feet).

AZ —HEARD MUSEUM, Library, 22 E Monte Vista Rd, Phoenix, 85004. Mary

ANTHROPOLOGY (cont.)

Graham, Librn
Holdings: Vols (40,000) Cat
Notes: Anthropology and primitive art. Incl 124 periodical titles and contemporary Native American Art.

AZ —NAVAJO COMMUNITY COLLEGE, Naaltsoos Ba' Hoogan, Library, Tsaile, 86556. Marvin E Pollard Jr, Dir, Library Services
Holdings: Vols (10,000) Cat Mss Maps Pix Slides Phonorecords Audiotapes Videotapes 16mm Films Filmstrips Microforms
Budget: ($15,000)
Notes: The Moses/Donner Collection emphasizes Navajos and other tribes of the Southwest; also, all Indians of North America and Mexico. All aspects of the geology, geography, sociology, archaeology, anthropology, etc, of the Four Corners region. The Collection includes a comprehensive collection of Doctoral dissertations dealing with Indians of North America and Mexico.

AZ —ARIZONA STATE MUSEUM, Library, University of Arizona, Tucson, 85721. Hans R Bart, Museum Librn
Holdings: Vols (35,000) Cat Mss Maps Pix Slides Phonorecords Microforms

CA —UNIVERSITY OF CALIFORNIA, BERKELEY, Humanities-Social Sciences Libraries, Anthropology Library, 230 Kroeber Hall, Berkeley, 94720. Dorothy A Koenig, Librn
Holdings: Vols (55,000) Cat Microforms
Notes: The library maintains general research collections covering all aspects of social and physical anthropology, anthropological linguistics and archaeology (excluding classical archaeology). Serials constitute the collection's special strength.

CA —UNIVERSITY OF CALIFORNIA, SAN DIEGO, Central University Library, Mandeville Dept of Special Collections, La Jolla, 92093. Lynda Corey Claassen, Head
Notes: Hill Collection: One of the most distinguished collections on early voyages to all parts of the Pacific Ocean, these materials include more than 2000 accounts of and commentaries on important voyages from the 16th to the mid 19th century, plus extensive anthropological, botanical, and zoological reports made by scientists who accompanied the explorers.

CA —LOS ANGELES PUBLIC LIBRARY, History Dept, 630 W Fifth St, Los Angeles, 90071. Leah Simon Kornbluth, Librn
Holdings: Vols (6000) Cat Maps Phonorecords Microforms
Budget: ($85,000)
Notes: See entry under Indians of North America and Mexico for full description of collection.

CA —SAN DIEGO MUSEUM OF MAN, Scientific Library, 1350 El Prado, Balboa Park, San Diego, 92101. Jane Bentley, Librn
Holdings: Vols 5500 Cat Mss
Notes: Incl 300 serial titles and 75 mss.

CA —CALIFORNIA ACADEMY OF SCIENCES, J W Mailliard Jr Library, Golden Gate Park, San Francisco, 94118. Ray Brian, Librn
Notes: Downs No 2160.

CA —UNIVERSITY OF CALIFORNIA, SANTA CRUZ, University Library, Special Collections, Santa Cruz, 95064. Rita Bottoms, Special Collections Librn; Margaret Felts, South Pacific Collection Bibliographer
Holdings: Vols (10,000) Cat
Notes: South Pacific Collection. Monographs, rare books, serials, documents and atlases which treat of the Pacific areas of Polynesia, Melanesia, Micronesia, Australia and New Zealand, but excluding western New Guinea (Irian Jaya), the Philippines and Southeast Asia. Approximately 10 percent of the titles are multi-volume documents such as parliamentary papers, legislative journals, official yearbooks, statistical sourcebooks, laws and statutes. The collection includes an exhaustive selection of current journals and monographic series from and about the Pacific: early serials, South Pacific Commission publications, US Government and US Trust Territory publications, serials from museums, universities and scholarly societies. Chief emphasis has been placed on acquisition of the literature of history, description and travel, ethnology andanthropology, literature and literary criticism, political and constitutional histories. Other extensive holdings are in the fields of geography and maps, voyages, mission histories, mythology and folklore, art, linguistics, and science fields of natural history, environmental studies, biology, zoology, botany, geology and astronomy. Printed catalog is available. This is an on-going, growing collection.

CO —COLORADO SPRINGS FINE ARTS CENTER LIBRARY, 30 W Dale St, Colorado Springs, 80903. Roderick Dew, Librn
Holdings: Vols (20,000) Cat
Budget: ($4000)
Notes: Specialize in fine arts and anthropology of the Southwest. Incl auction and exhibition catalogs.

CT —YALE UNIVERSITY, Anthropology Library, Peabody Museum of Natural History, C-8 KBT, New Haven, 06511.
Holdings: Vols (12,400) Cat Maps

†CT —PHILIPPINE-AMERICAN RESEARCH CENTER, Library, PO Box507, Sharoni, 06069. John Silva, Dir
Holdings: Vols 200 Maps Pix
Notes: Philippine history and culture from pre-colonial times to the present, as well as under Spanish, Japanese, and American regimes, and post-independence. Mostly rare works of the late 19th and early 20th century; history and anthropology. Over 2, 500 photographs. Incl maps, posters, memorabilia. Limited copying. Visits by appointment.

DC —HOWARD UNIVERSITY, Moorland-Spingarn Research Center, 500 Howard Place NW, Washington, 20059. Clifford L Muse, Jr, Acting Dir
Holdings: Vols (106,086) Mss Maps Pix Slides Phonorecords Audiotapes 16mm Films Filmstrips Microforms
Budget: ($854,753)
See also entry under Blacks

DC —LIBRARY OF CONGRESS, Manuscript Division, Washington, 20540. John C Broderick, Chief
Notes: Papers of Margaret Mead (1901-1978). Approx 370,000 items, incl general correspondence files, correspondence with organizations, and correspondence about attendance at and participation in meetings and conferences. Also, items reflecting teaching and lecturing activities, and an extensive subject file. Drafts, galley proofs, research materials, notes, memoranda and correspondence representing her publication of books and articles, in addition to a comprehensive file of the published versions of her works. Other materials at American Museum of Natural History, New York, NY, and Columbia University Departments of Anthropology.

DC —NATIONAL GEOGRAPHIC SOCIETY, Library, 1146 16th St NW, Washington, 20036. Susan Fifer Canby, Dir
Holdings: Vols (63,000) Cat Mss Maps Pix
Notes: Material concerning land, sea, and space exploration--past and present. All fields of anthropology, natural history, geography, etc.

DC —SMITHSONIAN INSTITUTION, Smithsonian Tropical Research Institute, Washington, 20560. Carol Jopling, Chief Librn
Holdings: Vols (22,000) Cat Mss Maps Pix Slides 16mm Films Microforms
Budget: ($70,000)
Notes: Smithsonian Institution, Smithsonian Tropical Research Institute is located in Balboa, Panama.

DC —SMITHSONIAN INSTITUTION LIBRARIES, Anthropology Branch, Washington, 20560. Jean C Smith, Asst Dir for Bureau Services
Holdings: Vols (54,000) Cat Mss Maps Pix Slides Microforms
Budget: ($7041)
Notes: Physical anthropology, archaeology, ethnology, language and languages; Indians of both continents.

FL —HISTORICAL ASSOCIATION OF SOUTHERN FLORIDA, Charlton W Tebeau Library of Florida History, 101 W Flager St, Miami, 33130. Rebecca A Smith, Cur of Research Materials
Holdings: Vols (3000) Cat Mss Maps Pix Slides Audiotapes 16mm Films Microforms
Notes: History of Florida, with emphasis on southern area. Less extensively, history of the Caribbean area, especially as related to Florida. Florida materials incl anthropology, archaeology, Indians of south Florida, incl Seminole Indians, Dade County history, and a complete run of the newspaper *The American Eagle* (1906-date), printed by Koreshan Unity, Estero, Florida. Incl 300 feet of mss, 1500 maps, 75,000 pictures, 2000 slides, 125 audiotapes, 25 16mm films, 200 microforms, 50 feet of vertical files, and 7000 postcards. Work in progress on guide to ms collection and on indexing of photographs. Also incl books and journals on museum science: conservation and preservation of museum materials.

HI —BERNICE P BISHOP MUSEUM, Library, PO Box 19000-A, Honolulu, 96819. Cynthia Timberlake, Librn
Holdings: Vols (90,000) Cat Mss Maps Pix Slides Microforms
Budget: ($30,000)
Notes: Only American library devoted exclusively to the Pacific region. Collection reflects historical and contemporary research emphases of Bishop Museum; ie the natural and cultural history of the Pacific. Areas of concentration incl archaeology, ethnology, linguistics, voyages and explorations, history, vertebrate and invertebrate zoology, botany and museology. Strong special collections incl photographs, mss and archives, maps and art. Publications: Quarterly "Additions to the Catalog," *Dictionary Catalog of the* Library (9 vols and 2 suppl; Boston: G K Hall, 1964-69).

ID —IDAHO MUSEUM OF NATURAL HISTORY, Research Library, Campus Box 8096, Pocatello, 83209. Michael L Perry, Dir
Holdings: Vols 2500 Mss Maps Pix Slides

IL —FIELD MUSEUM OF NATURAL HISTORY, Library, Roosevelt Rd & Lake Shore Dr, Chicago, 60605. W Peyton Fawcett, Librn; Benjamin W Williams, Assoc Librn
Holdings: Vols (210,000) Cat
Budget: ($100,000)
Notes: Extensive collections--publications of learned societies and institutions and monographic works--in all fields of natural history, with emphasis on taxonomy and evolutionary biology; and on museum publications, American and foreign: anthropology, especially archaeology and ethnology of the Americas, Africa, East Asia, and Oceania; botany, particularly strong for the Americas; geology, chiefly paleontology and meteoritic studies; and zoology, worldwide (birds, fishes, insects, mammals, mollusks, reptiles and amphibians).

IL —NORTHWESTERN UNIVERSITY, Melville J Herskovits Library of African Studies, Evanston, 60201. Hans E Panofsky, Cur
Holdings: Vols (85,000) Mss
Budget: ($70,000)
Notes: Although the collection incl the papers of Melville J Herskovits, the last ten years of this archive is closed until 1988. Also have papers of the African Studies Association, Carter/Karis, Abdullah Abdurahman, Alex Hepple, Leo Kuper, Dennis Brutus; further, on West Africa--John Paden, Umar Falke, Liberian economic survey. Supplements for 1972-1977 for our book catalog (8 vols) was published by G K Hall in 1978; unlike 1972, the supplement to the *Joint Acqusitions List of Africana* will be published in seperate vols from the Northwestern Catalog supplement. There are, in 1978, 16,000 additional vols.

IL —UNIVERSITY OF ILLINOIS, URBANA/CHAMPAIGN, Library, University Archives, 1408 W Gregory Drive,

ANTHROPOLOGY (cont.)

Urbana, 61801. Maynard Brichford, Univ Archivist
Holdings: Cat Mss Pix
Notes: Original mss and 91 tapes of interviews for anthropological work, the gift of Oscar Lewis, largely concerning his studies of the culture of poverty.

LA —LOUISIANA STATE UNIVERSITY, Troy H Middleton Library, Louisiana Room, Baton Rouge, 70803. Evangeline Mills Lynch, Head Librn; Ruth Murray, Associate Librn
Holdings: Vols (33,500) Cat Maps VF
Notes: Louisiana Collection of history, description and travel, biography, agriculture, literature, politics and government, folklore, anthropology, geography, geology, education, language, music and natural history. Especially large subject collections may be found on Louisiana, the history of the lower Mississippi Valley, Abraham Lincoln, Romance languages and literatures, sugar culture and technology, Southern history, petroleum engineering, plant pathology, micropaleontology, ornithology, and various aspects of crawfish life, biology and culture. Complete depository of Louisiana State Documents; extensive newspapers clipping files; separate card catalog; items listed in Louisiana Union Catalog; restricted use (research and reference). Incl both materials about Louisiana and by Louisianians without regard to subject. LSU Press Collection(preservation copy of each title kept for exhibit purposes only). LSU theses and dissertations from 1900-date. LSU Faculty Collection. Also, 1300 maps, 104 VF drawers, 250 boxes of uncataloged pamphlets.

LA —TULANE UNIVERSITY, Howard-Tilton Memorial Library, Latin American Library, New Orleans, 70118. Thomas Niehaus, Dir
Holdings: Vols (150,000) Cat Mss Maps Pix Microforms VF
Budget: ($67,000)
Notes: *Catalog of the Latin American* Library (Boston: G K Hall, 1970, suppl. 1973,1975,1978); Downs 5338-41; suppl (1961), 2727, 2737. The Latin American Library is a general collection, but specializes in Central American, Mexican, and Brazilian materials. The disciplines which are most strongly represented are history, anthropology, and archaeology. The Viceregal Ecclesiastical Mexican Collection contains manuscripts from the colonial period. The France V Scholes Collection contains a large number of photoprints and microfilm of colonial documents from the archives of Spain and Mexico. The Merle Greene Robertson Rubbings Collection contains nearly five hundred rubbings of relief sculpture from Mayan archaeological sites in Mexico and Guatemala. The Photographic Collection contains photos of archaeological sites inMeso-America, of pre-Columbian Peruvian architecture, and a general group of historic photos from Latin America.

MA —HARVARD UNIVERSITY LIBRARY, Tozzer Library, 21 Divinity Ave, Cambridge, 02138. Nancy J Schmidt, Librn
Holdings: Vols (152,000) Cat Microforms
Budget: ($337,000)
Notes: (Formerly Peabody Museum Library). Believed to have the strongest collection in the United States for prehistoric archaeology generally, anthropology, and ethnology. Does not collect classical archaeology. Catalog, in 54 volumes, published in 1963, with 12-volume supplement in 1970, 5-volume supplement in 1971, 7-volume supplement in 1975, and 7-volume supplement in 1979, analyzes contents of serial publications. Quarterly journal, *Anthropological Literature, 1979-*. Described in *Harvard Library Bulletin,* III (1949): pp 94-101; J O Brew, *People and Projects of the Peabody Museum, 1866-1966* (Cambridge, Mass: The Museum, 1966), pp 57-59; and Nancy J Schmidt, Tozzer Library, Harvard University: *Special* Libraries Association Boston Chapter News Bulletin, 48, 2 (1982), pp 167-169.

MA —HARVARD UNIVERSITY LIBRARY, Botanical Museum Library, Cambridge, 02138.
Holdings: Vols (2400) Mss Pix
Notes: The Tina and Gordon Wisson Ethnomycological Collection, one of the most important modern collections, acquired as an adjunct to the Museum's Economic Botany Library of Oakes Ames. From 15th to 20th century, it deals with hallucinogenic mushrooms in art, religion, and folklore; chemistry, pharmacology, linguistics, archaeological artifacts of Mexico, Guatemala, India, Japan, China, etc. Personal papers, etc.

MI —UNIVERSITY OF MICHIGAN, Museums Library, Ann Arbor, 48109. Patricia B Yocum, Librn
Holdings: Vols 15,000 Cat
Notes: Especially Indians and archaeology of the Americas.

MI —MICHIGAN STATE UNIVERSITY, International Library, Africana Collection, East Lansing, 48824. Eugene de Benko, Librn; Onuma Ezera, Bibliographer for Africana
Holdings: Vols (82,700) Cat Mss Maps Pix Slides Phonorecords Audiotapes Videotapes Filmstrips Microforms
Budget: ($78,000)
See also entry under Africa for full description.

MI —MICHIGAN STATE UNIVERSITY, International Library, South and Southeast Asia Collection, East Lansing, 48824. Clinton Lockert, Bibliographer
Holdings: Vols (58,000) Cat Mss Maps Audiotapes Microforms
Notes: Serials and monographs of South Asia received on PL 480 for India, Pakistan, Sri Lanka, and Nepal since 1968. Emphasis is upon Social Sciences, Humanities, and Science. Areas of strength are Anthropology and rural development. Only selected holdings were received.

MI —WESTERN MICHIGAN UNIVERSITY, Dwight B Waldo Library, Kalamazoo, 49008. Jacqueline Driscoll, Social Science Ref Librn
Holdings: Vols (18,000) Cat Maps Phonorecords Microforms
Budget: $1000
Notes: The Ann Kercher Memorial Collection of Africa. No separate catalog or index to the collection. Collection covers sub-Saharan Africa and emphasizes anthropology, history, economics, education, geography, travel, sociology, politcal science, languages and linguistics, literature. Some government documents, African newspapers, pamphlet collection dating back to mid-1950's. Incl 300 African journals described in *Serials in African Studies Held by Western Michigan University Library* rev, ed, comp by D Kercher (Kalamazoo: Western Michigan Univ Library, 1976), 63 pp. Also incl 1000 maps, 20 phonorecords, and 400 microforms.

MN —MINNEAPOLIS PUBLIC LIBRARY & INFORMATION CENTER, Sociology Dept, 300 Nicollet Mall, Minneapolis, 55401. Eileen Scwartzbauer, Dept Head
Holdings: Vols (90,000) Cat Phonorecords Audiotapes Microforms
Budget: ($69,890)
Notes: Special collections: Foundation Center Regional Collection; college catalogs on fiche; adult basic education collection. Separate department catalog.

MO —UNIVERSITY OF MISSOURI-COLUMBIA, Museum of Anthropology Archives, 104 Swallow Hall, Columbia, 65201. Lawrence H Feldman, Museum Dir
Holdings: Vols (30) Cat Mss Maps Slides Microforms
Notes: Copies of Latin American and colonial mss. Many of the ms copies are of census, or census-like, documents of late colonial Verapaz; a few are from Sonsonate, El Salvador or Chiapas, Mexico. Additional material in the archives incl an original Eskimo manuscript (ca 1930) and an origianl Diegueno Yuman card vocabulary (ca 1964) and the Museum archives (papers on old accession systems, etc). Uncataloged microfilm copies of colonial Otomi and other vocabularies are also part of the collection. A catalog of material in this collection will appear in the Annual Report of the Museum of Anthropology, beginning with the 1976-77 volume.

MO —UNIVERSITY OF MISSOURI-COLUMBIA, Ellis Library, Art, Archaeology and Music Dept, Columbia, 65201. Bonnie MacEwan, Librn
Holdings: Vols Cat
Notes: Outstanding collection in Oriental and classical prehistory.

NM —MUSEUM OF NEW MEXICO, Laboratory of Anthropology Library, PO Box 2087, Santa Fe, 87503. Laura Holt, Librn
Holdings: Vols (16,000) Cat Mss Maps
Notes: Southwestern archaeology, anthropology, ethnology. Noncirculating. Also incl the personal Library (2000 vols) of Sylvanus Morley, Meso-American archaeologist and historian. Some materials on Indians of Middle America.

NY —MUSEUM OF THE AMERICAN INDIAN, Library, 9 Westchester Square, Bronx, 10401. Mary B Davis, Librn
Holdings: Vols Cat
Notes: Incl information in Indians of North, Central, and South America; archaeology of North, Central, and South America; American Indian ethnology; anthropology, history.

NY —BUFFALO MUSEUM OF SCIENCE, Buffalo Society of Natural Sciences, Research Library, Humboldt Park, Buffalo, 14211. Marcia T Morrison, Chief Librn
Holdings: Vols 37,000 Cat Mss Pix
Notes: Natural sciences, anthropology, archaeology.

NY —HOFSTRA UNIVERSITY, Library, 1000 Fulton Ave, Hempstead, 11550. Charles R Andrews, Dean of Library Services
Notes: The personal library of Paul Radin. See description of the American Philosophical Society Library's collection of his anthropological papers under this entry (Pa).

NY —AMERICAN MUSEUM OF NATURAL HISTORY, Library Services Dept, Central Park W & 79th St, New York, 10024. Nina J Root, Chairwoman; Mary Genett, Asst Librn for Reference Services
Holdings: Vols (385,000) Cat Mss Maps Pix Slides Microforms
Notes: Nearly all collections are outstanding for depth of coverage and international range. Early and historic works, rare books, colored illustrations, and relevant serial publications supplement the modern scientific publications necessary to the researches of the scientific staff and the work of the educational division. Open to the public.

NY —AMERICAN SOCIETY FOR PSYCHICAL RESEARCH LIBRARY, 5 W 73 St, New York, 10023. Rhea A White, Consultant to the Library
Holdings: Vols (7000) Cat Mss Pix
Budget: ($1500)
Notes: Incl books on spiritualism, as well as works in psychology, religion, philosophy, physics, anthropology, etc which have a possible bearing on parapsychology. An attempt is made to obtain all serious books on parapsychology in English.

NY —EXPLORERS CLUB, James B Ford Memorial Library, 46 E 70 St, New York, 10021. Janet Baldwin, Librn
Holdings: Vols (24,000) Cat Maps
Notes: Additions to the collection depend upon gifts. Access by appointment only.

NY —NEW YORK PUBLIC LIBRARY, Research Libraries, General Research Division, Fifth Ave & 42 St, New York, 10018. Rodney Phillips, Chief
Holdings: Vols (2,225,000) Cat Maps Pix Microforms
Budget: ($775,718)
Notes: The collections are strongest for Black Africans, the American Indian, the Gypsies, Australian aborigines and those of Oceania.

NY —NEW YORK PUBLIC LIBRARY, Mid-Manhattan Library, History and Social

ANTHROPOLOGY (cont.)

Sciences Dept, 455 Fifth Ave, New York, 10016. Robert Sheehan, Sr Principal Librn
Holdings: Vols (60,000) Cat Phonorecords Audiotapes Microforms
Budget: $15,000
Notes: Duplicate reference and circulating copies.

NY —RESEARCH INSTITUTE FOR THE STUDY OF MAN, Library, 162 E 78 St, New York, 10021. Judith Selakoff, Librn
Holdings: Vols (14,500) Cat Mss Maps VF
Notes: The non-Hispanic Caribbean. Incl material on all aspects of life in non-Hispanic Caribbean, with primary emphasis on anthropology and the social sciences.

NY —WENNER-GREN FOUNDATION FOR ANTHROPOLOGICAL RESEARCH LIBRARY, 1865 Broadway, New York, 10023. Renata Rose, Librn
Holdings: Vols 3000 Cat
Budget: $5000
Notes: 95 periodicals, journals and newsletters. Not open to public.

NY —UNIVERSITY OF ROCHESTER, Rush Rhees Library, Rochester, 14627. Datta S Kharbas, Head
Holdings: Vols 100,000 Cat Maps Microforms
Notes: Area studies collection on East Asia and South Asia. Major emphasis is on social sciences and humanities. Over 57,000 volumes on East Asia, out of which 29,000 volumes are in Chinese and 15,000 in Japanese. Extensive holdings on Chinese and Japanese histories. Catalog of East Asian collection consisting of Chinese and Japanese language holdings published in 1968, with two subsequent supplements. Over 33,000 volumes on South Asia. Considerable depth in social sciences, history, politics and anthropology. Extensive holdings in Sanskrit, Hindi, and Marathi.

NC —GEO-TECH INTERNATIONAL LTD, Paleontological Research Laboratory, Library, 3616 Garden Club Lane, Charlotte, 28210. Elizabeth Carson, Librn
Holdings: Maps Pix Slides
Notes: Special emphasis on paleontological collection devoted to reprints, source materials, and all current publications and journals on paleoanthropology and evolution. Prior collections of oceanography and Mollusca turned over to University of North Carolina Library. Partially cataloged.

NC —SCHIELE MUSEUM OF NATURAL HISTORY, Library, 1500 E Garrison Blvd, Gastonia, 28052. Dot Gray, Librn; Margaret Summerill, Librn
Holdings: Vols (3800) Cat Maps Pix Slides Phonorecords Audiotapes 16mm Films Filmstrips Microforms
Budget: ($2800)
Notes: Listed on RECON computer with Library of Congress as Reference Center in Southeast in subject areas of natural sciences, aerospace and planetarium technology, and anthropology.

OK —MUSEUM OF THE GREAT PLAINS, Research Center, 601 Ferris, PO Box 68, Lawton, 73502. Steve Wilson, Dir; Paula Williams, Special Collections
Notes: Anthropology; archaeology; ecology and history of Trans-Mississippi West, especially Great Plains.

PA —AMERICAN PHILOSOPHICAL SOCIETY, Library, 105 S Fifth St, Philadelphia, 19106. Edward C Carter II, Librn
Notes: The anthropological papers of Paul Radin in fields of ethnology, social organization, primitive religion, linguistics, and mythology. He worked mostly among the Winnebago, Ojibwa, Fox, Zapotec, Wappo, Wintun, and Huave Indian tribes; also Italian and other ethnic minorities of San Francisco. Also, the Boas Family Papers, incl 60,000 pieces of correspondence of Franz Boas'. Also 600 groups of items in honor of Dr Boas. Chiefly field notes, lexical files, dictionaries, texts, etc concerning the American Indian and especially, Indian linguistics. Numerous papers of other anthropologists are also in the APS Library: Sylvanus G Morley, Frans M Olbrechts, Ely S Parker, Elsie Clews Parsons, Paul Radin, Frank G Speck, etc. See *A Guide to Manuscripts Relating to the American Indian in the Library of American Philosophical Society*, by John F Freeman and Murphy DSmith (1966).

PA —UNIVERSITY OF PENNSYLVANIA, Annenberg School of Communications Library, 3620 Walnut St, Philadelphia, 19104. Sandra B Grilikhes, Head
Holdings: Vols 20,000 Cat Microforms
Notes: Theory and research in communication, incl visual communication, via social psychology, anthropology, ethnography, and sociology. All aspects of mass media with emphasis on methodology in research. Utilizes content analysis and computer operations. Special collections: film catalogs; collection of Annenberg Faculty Publications.

PA —UNIVERSITY OF PENNSYLVANIA, University Museum Library, 33 & Spruce Sts, Philadelphia, 19104. Jean S Adelman, Librn
Holdings: Vols (80,000) Cat Microforms
Notes: Incl (5000) pamphlets, fully cataloged. Mss (primarily American Indian word lists) in Brinton collection.

PA —CARNEGIE LIBRARY OF PITTSBURGH, Science & Technology Dept, 4400 Forbes Ave, Pittsburgh, 15213. Catherine M Brosky, Dept Head
Notes: Of secondary interest in acquisitions because of the department's role in cooperating with Pittsburgh institutions and others across the Commonwealth in sharing resources, the cooperative acquisition of materials, and the provision of services and information. However, some aspects of the subject are emphasized. There are separate entries for each of these specialties in the vol.

PA —UNIVERSITY OF PITTSBURGH, Hillman Library, Pittsburgh, 15260. Glenora E Rossell, Head
Holdings: Vols (10,059) Cat
Notes: Emphasis is on cultural anthropology and archaeology.

RI —UNIVERSITY OF RHODE ISLAND, International Center for Marine Resource Development, Library, Main Library Building, Kingston, 02881.
Holdings: Vols (13,000) Periodicals
Notes: Devoted to the development of marine resources in third world countries. Small-scale fisheries, anthropology of fishing peoples, coastal fisheries, aquaculture program planning. Approx 13,000 documents, 200 periodicals.

SC —CHARLESTON MUSEUM LIBRARY, 360 Meeting St, Charleston, 29403. John Brumgardt, Museum Dir
Holdings: Vols 30,000 Cat Mss Maps Pix

SC —UNIVERSITY OF SOUTH CAROLINA, Institute of Archaeology and Anthropology, Robert L Stephenson Research Library, Macxy College, Columbia, 29208. Robert L Stephenson, Dir & State Archaeologist
Holdings: Vols 6500 Uncat
Notes: Anthropology, with special emphasis on American archaeology. Private collection of Robert L Stephenson, Director of the Institute and State Archeologist of South Carolina. Incl most national, regional and state archaeological journals and complete Bureau of American Ethnology publications.

TX —TEXAS STATE LIBRARY, Archives Div, 1201 Brazos, PO Box 12927, Capitol Sta, Austin, 78711. David B Gracy II, State Archivist

TX —SOUTHERN METHODIST UNIVERSITY, DeGolyer Library, Box 396, SMU, Dallas, 75275. Clifton H Jones, Dir
Holdings: Vols (80,000) Cat Mss Maps Pix Slides Microforms
Notes: First editions of prominent authors; also of books in subject emphasis collections. All subjects listed in this vol are strong. Numerous collections of personal papers relating to subjects also.

†WA —UNIVERSITY OF WASHINGTON LIBRARIES, Seattle, 98195.

WI —BELOIT COLLEGE LIBRARIES, Beloit, 53511. Dennis W Dickinson, Dir
Holdings: Vols 20,000 Cat Maps
Budget: $3500
Notes: Members of the anthropology department faculty have been vigorous in keeping anthropology holdings growing and developing. Many items not normally purchased by small college libraries have been acquired over the past hundred years.

WI —MILWAUKEE PUBLIC MUSEUM, Reference Library, 800 W Wells St, Milwaukee, 53233. Judith Campbell Turner, Museum Librn
Holdings: Vols (90,000) Cat Maps Microforms

BC —VANCOUVER PUBLIC LIBRARY, Sociology Div, 750 Burrard St, Vancouver, V6Z 1X5, Can.
Holdings: Cat
Notes: Incl special files of pamphlets, clippings, etc.

MB —UNIVERSITY OF MANITOBA, Elizabeth Dafoe Library, Archives and Special Collections Dept, Winnipeg, R3T 2N2, Can. Richard E Bennett, Dept Head; Corrado A Santoro, Reference Archivist
Notes: Correspondence, reports and various papers of Dr Bruce H Chown. Haemolitic diseases of the newborn, especially erthroblastosis fetalis and the maternal Rh-factor. Incl correspondence with Dr Louis Diamond of Boston. Also incl are human anthropological blood group studies of Eskimo, Indian and Canadian-Japanese communities.

ON —NATIONAL LIBRARY OF CANADA, 395 Wellington St, Ottawa, K1A 0N4, Can. Andre Preibish, Dir
Holdings: Vols 10,000
Notes: Includes 130 serial titles, theses, pamphlets, government publications relating to family and marriage. The following disciplines covered: anthropology, psychology and psychiatry, law, economics, religion, sociology, demography, education, political science and biology. Earliest title 1630.

†ON —METROPOLITAN TORONTO LIBRARY, Social Sciences Dept, 789 Yonge St, Toronto, M4W 2G8, Can. Abdus Salam, Head
Holdings: Vols Cat Maps Phonorecords Audiotapes 16mm Films Microforms
Notes: Strong collection on folklore, education, religion, anthropology. Also includes bibles in Canadian Indian languages.

ON —ROYAL ONTARIO MUSEUM, Main Library and Archives, 100 Queen's Park, Toronto, M5S 2C6, Can. Julia Matthews, Head Librn
Holdings: Vols (85,000) Cat
Notes: Since January 1977, acquisitions have been entered in UTLAS.

ANTHROPOLOGY, PHYSICAL

CA —UNIVERSITY OF CALIFORNIA, BERKELEY, Humanities-Social Sciences Libraries, Anthropology Library, 230 Kroeber Hall, Berkeley, 94720. Dorothy A Koenig, Librn
Holdings: Vols (55,000) Cat Microforms
Notes: The library maintains general research collections covering all aspects of social and physical anthropology, anthropological linguistics and archaeology (excluding classical archaeology). Serials constitute the collection's special strength.

CT —YALE UNIVERSITY, Anthropology Library, Peabody Museum of Natural History, C-8 KBT, New Haven, 06511.
Holdings: Vols (16,000) Cat
Budget: ($11,000)

DC —SMITHSONIAN INSTITUTION LIBRARIES, Anthropology Branch, Washington, 20560. Jean C Smith, Asst Dir for Bureau Services
Holdings: Vols (54,000) Cat Mss Maps Pix Slides Microforms
Budget: ($7041)
Notes: Physical anthropology, archaeology, ethnology, language and languages; Indians of both continents.

ANTIBIOTICS

DC —AMERICAN SOCIETY FOR MICROBIOLOGY, Archives, 1913 I Street NW, Washington, 20006. Donald Shay, Archivist
Notes: Collection of American and foreign

ANTIBIOTICS (cont.)

books (texts, monographs, laboratory manuals, etc) on microbiology. 10,000 reprints are mostly old or connected to a past officer or award recipient. 150 theses incl American and foreign. Reprint collection incl Pratt collection on antibiotics, and C W Dodge collection on medical mycology. Ownership of all titles resides with the Society; Special Collections of University of Maryland Baltimore County serves as repository. The Society address is in Washington.

IN —ELI LILLY AND COMPANY, Scientific Library, 307 E McCarty St, Indianapolis, 46285. Adele Hoskin, Chief Librn
Holdings: Vols (35,000) Cat Microforms
Notes: Drug product information (1.7 million cards); drug encyclopedias, foreign and domestic; foreign pharmacopoeias. Restricted use: company employees and approved outsiders.

MI —WARNER-LAMBERT/PARKE-DAVIS, Research Library, 2800 Plymouth Rd, Ann Arbor, 48106. Katherine C Owen, Mgr, Library Services
Holdings: Vols (27,977) Cat

MI —THE UPJOHN COMPANY, Corporate Technical Library, 301 Henrietta St, Kalamazoo, 49001. Lorraine Schulte, Manager
Holdings: Cat Microforms Books Journals

NJ —RUTGERS, THE STATE UNIVERSITY OF NEW JERSEY, Waksman Institute of Microbiology, Library, PO Box 759, Piscataway, 08854. Helen Hoffman, Librn
Holdings: Vols (17,000) Cat
Budget: ($40,000)
Notes: Primarily concerned with basic research and applied microbiology. Little emphasis on clinical microbiology.

ANTICATHOLICISM

MI —MICHIGAN STATE UNIVERSITY, Libraries, Special Collections Div, East Lansing, 48824. Jannette Fiore, Librn
Notes: Ku Klux Klan pamphlets, magazines, and ephemera dating from the late 1920s and early 1930s. Incl issues of the *Kourier,* the official monthly magazine of the Klan; a Klan newspaper published in Alma, Mich; position pamphlets and leaflets; advertisements for Klan merchandise; and Michigan Klan ephemera; other Nationalist and Anti-Catholic materials.

MO —SAINT LOUIS UNIVERSITY, Pius XII Memorial Library, 3655 W Pine Blvd, Saint Louis, 63108. William Cole, Dir
Holdings: Vols (1503) Microfiche Uncat //
Notes: Pamphlets drawn from all periods of United States history, with concentration between the years 1820-1970. There is a printed bibliographic guide to the collection.

PA —BALCH INSTITUTE FOR ETHNIC STUDIES, Library, 18 S Seventh St, Philadelphia, 19106. R Joseph Anderson, Library Dir
Holdings: Vols 115 Cat

ANTICORROSIVE PAINT see Corrosion and Anticorrosives

ANTI-DEFAMATION LEAGUE

LA —AMISTAD RESEARCH CENTER, 400 Esplanade Ave, New Orleans, 70116. Clifton H Johnson, Exec Dir; Florence E Borders, Senior Archivist
Holdings: Vols (10,000) Cat Mss Pix Audiotapes Microforms
Budget: ($315,000)
Notes: 8,000,000 ms pieces, 10,000 pictures, 3500 microforms, and 500 audiotapes. Amistad Research Center is an historical research library devoted to the collection and use of primary source materials on the history of America's ethnic minorities, with particular emphasis on Afro-Americans, American Indians, and immigrant groups. Among the larger institutional collections held are the archives and records of the American Missionary Association, the American Home Missionary Society, the Race Relations Dept of the Anti-Defamation League, the Catholic Committee of the South, and the National Association of Human Rights Workers, (formerly NAIRO).

ANTIDISCRIMINATION LAWS see Race Discrimination

ANTIDOTES see Poisons

ANTI-NUCLEAR MOVEMENT

AZ —NORTHERN ARIZONA UNIVERSITY, Special Collection Library, CU Box 6022, Flagstaff, 86011. Peter M Whiteley, Coordr/Archivist; William Mullane, Librn
Notes: Arizonans for Safe Energy (anti-nuclear organization), Flagstaff Chapter, Collection; records, clippings, 1973-1976.

CT —UNIVERSITY OF CONNECTICUT, Library, Storrs, 06268. Ellen Embardo, Cur Special Collections
Notes: Alternative Press Collection. Primarily periodicals and newspapers from the 1960s to today of an alternative or underground nature. Books and and pamphlets are incl, representing both the left and the right-wing viewpoints. A catalog is available. Also have archives of the First Casualty Press, which was deeply involved with Vietnam veterans' experiences in Vietnam, as well as the Fat Liberation Movement.

ANTIOCH COLLEGE

OH —ANTIOCH COLLEGE, Olive Kettering Library, Livermore St, Yellow Springs, 45387. Nina Myatt, Cur
Holdings: Cat Mss Pix
Notes: Personal papers, correspondence, of Arthur E Morgan, 1920-1975 Mss, film out-takes, diaries, materials from Tennessee Valley Authority (Morgan was first chairman), Antioch College (Morgan was president 1920-1936), materials on Edward Bellamy (Morgan wrote biography of Bellamy). About 175 file boxes.

ANTIOCHIAN ORTHODOX CHRISTIAN ARCHDIOCESE

†NJ —ANTIOCHIAN ORTHODOX CHRISTIAN ARCHDIOCESE OF NORTH AMERICA, Library, 358 Mountain Rd, Englewood, 07631.
Notes: History of Arab Orthodox Christians in North America.

ANTI-PAPACY see Anticatholicism; Papacy and Anti-Papacy

ANTIQUARIAN BOOKSELLERS ASSOCIATION OF AMERICA (ABAA), SOUTHERN CALIFORNIA CHAPTER

CA —UNIVERSITY OF CALIFORNIA, LOS ANGELES, Research Library, Dept of Special Collections, 405 Hilgard Ave, Los Angeles, 90024. Edward Shreeves, Chairman, Bibliographers Group; David S Zeidberg, Head
Notes: 8 linear feet of the Antiquarian Booksellers Association of America (ABAA), Southern California Chapter, archives; related papers, posters, etc, that refer to various aspects of international antiquarian bookselling.

ANTIQUE AUTOMOBILES see Vintage Cars

ANTIQUES

IL —CHICAGO PUBLIC LIBRARY, Art Section, Fine Arts Division, 78 E Washington St, Chicago, 60602. Rosalinda I Hack, Fine Arts Division Chief; Yvonne S Brown, Head, Art Section
Holdings: Vols 42,000
Notes: Reference and circulating collection of books, periodicals, exhibition catalogs, dissertations, picture collections, and microforms on all aspects of the visual arts. Major concentration of art history, especially European, with concentration on 19th and 20th century art movements and artists. We attempt to represent the works of recognized artists past and present. The Decorative Arts are well represented especially in the areas of antiques, interior decoration, and handicrafts. The collection is supplemented by a strong periodical collection, consisting of 330 current English and Foreign subscriptions, the majority of these titles we bind, as well as strong bound retrospective collections. The visual arts is supported by a clipping File on Chicago Artists, a current exhibition catalogs collection, as well as by the microfilm collections of the*Chicago Art Institute Scrapbooks,* the *Scrapbook on Art,* Artists, and the *Index of American Design.*

IN —ALLEN COUNTY PUBLIC LIBRARY, 900 Webster St, Fort Wayne, 46802. Paul Deane, Reader Services Dept Head; Kay Lynn Isca, Art Music & AV Dept Head
Holdings: Vols 1257

LA —R W NORTON ART GALLERY, Library, 4747 Creswell Ave, Shreveport, 71106. Jerry M Bloomer, Librn
Holdings: Vols 489 Cat

MA —OLD STURBRIDGE VILLAGE, Research Library, Sturbridge, 01566. Theresa Rini Percy, Librn
Holdings: Cat Mss Pix
Notes: New England, 1790-1850.

MO —SCHOOL OF THE OZARKS, Lois Brownell Research Library, Ralph Foster Museum, Point Lookout, 65726. Robert Esworthy, Librn
Holdings: Vols (1300) Cat
Notes: European and American antiques.

OH —PUBLIC LIBRARY OF CINCINNATI & HAMILTON COUNTY, Art & Music Dept, 800 Vine St, Cincinnati, 45202. R Jayne Craven, Head
Holdings: Vols (122,185) Cat Pix
Budget: ($56,100)

OH —GRANDVIEW HEIGHTS PUBLIC LIBRARY, 1685 W First Ave, Columbus, 43212. Kathryn M Hannon, Librn
Holdings: Vols (396) Cat

OH —MASSILLON PUBLIC LIBRARY, 208 Lincoln Way E, Massillon, 44646. Camille Leslie, Dir
Holdings: Vols 250 Cat
Notes: Specialty developed as member of Mideastern Ohio Library Organization, to supply other members on interlibrary loan. Covers all types of antiques and collectibles, with emphasis on American. No separate catalog.

VT —SHELBURNE MUSEUM, Library, Shelburne, 05482. Barbara Reenstierna, Librn
Holdings: Vols 200 Cat

ANTIQUITIES

CA —J PAUL GETTY MUSEUM, Photo Archives, 17985 Pacific Coast Hwy, Malibu, 90265. William Reeder, Cur
Holdings: Pix
Notes: Incl photographs of works of art at the Museum (180,000 cataloged, 500,000 uncataloged), incl ancient art, western European art (painting, sculpture, graphics) and European decorative arts, medieval and Renaissance to 19th century, and antiquities.

PA —UNIVERSITY OF PENNSYLVANIA, University Museum Library, 33 & Spruce Sts, Philadelphia, 19104. Jean S Adelman, Librn
Holdings: Vols (80,000) Cat Microforms
Notes: Emphasis on antiquities of all areas.

SC —UNIVERSITY OF SOUTH CAROLINA, Thomas Cooper Library, Columbia, 29208. Kenneth E Toombs, Dir of Libraries; Roger Mortimer, Rare Book Librn
Holdings: Vols 500 Cat
Notes: Particularly strong in landmark titles published in the 18th and 19th centuries.

ANTIQUITIES—COLLECTION AND PRESERVATION

PA —UNIVERSITY OF PENNSYLVANIA, University Museum Library, 33 & Spruce

ANTIQUITIES—COLLECTION AND PRESERVATION (cont.)

Sts, Philadelphia, 19104. Jean S Adelman, Librn
Holdings: Vols (80,000) Cat Microforms
Notes: Emphasis is on antiquities of all areas.

ANTIQUITIES, BIBLICAL see Bible—Antiquities

ANTIQUITIES, CHRISTIAN see Christian Antiquities

ANTIQUITIES, CLASSICAL see Classical Antiquities

ANTIQUITIES, ECCLESIASTICAL see Christian Antiquities

ANTIQUITIES, GRECIAN see Classical Antiquities; Greece—Antiquities

ANTIQUITIES, ROMAN see Classical Antiquities; Rome—Antiquities

ANTI-RUSSIAN PROPAGANDA see Propaganda, Anti-Russian

ANTISEMITISM

FL —UNIVERSITY OF FLORIDA LIBRARY, Isser and Rae Price Library of Judaica, 18 Libr East, Gainesville, 32611. Robert Singerman, Head Librn
Budget: ($30,000)
Notes: Total holdings estimated at 55,000 vols dealing with the political, social, economic and intellectual history of the Jews in the ancient, medieval and modern periods and in all geographic areas. The following areas are especially well represented by printed matter in all relevant languages: Bibliography, Festschriften, History, Bible, Judaism and Jewish theology, liturgy, responsa, rabbinical literature, Jewish law, Hebrew language and literature, Yiddish language and literature, anti-semitism, Zionism, Palestine and the *Yishuv*, and the State of Israel. German and American Judaica form a collecting emphasis with holdings for all the standard histories as well as histories of individual synagogues, institutions and local communities. Works in Hebrew and Yiddish comprise about 60 percent of the collection (estimated 30,000 vols). With few exceptions, holdingsare limited to nineteenth and twentieth century imprints, with complete sets of journals and thousands of ephemeral pamphlets, many of them commemorating anniversaries, enhancing the research value of the collection, the largest Judaica research library in the southeastern United States. Only about half of the collection is cataloged; the collection is a circulating one and vols may be borrowed on interlibrary loan. Incl the Leonard C Mishkin Collection (40,000 vols), the largest personal Judaica collection in the United States, the Shlomo Marenof Collection (3500 vols), and the inventory of Bernard Morgenstern's Lower East Side Book Store (8000 vols). Scholars should inquire in advance of their visit. *The Isser and Rae Price Library of Judaica* Report (circulation 2900 copies) is mailed gratis twice a year to all interested parties. Special catalogs:Pre-1881 Hebrew imprints recorded in a chronological card file.

MA —BRANDEIS UNIVERSITY, Goldfarb Library, 415 South St, Waltham, 02154. Bessie Hahn, Dir
Notes: Alfred

†NY —ANTI-DEFAMATION LEAGUE OF B'NAI B'RITH, 823 United Nations Plaza, New York, 10017.

NY —NEW YORK PUBLIC LIBRARY, Jewish Division, Fifth Ave & 42 St, New York, 10018. Leonard S Gold, Chief
Holdings: Vols (200,000) Cat Mss Microforms
Budget: ($33,383)
Notes: A collection of material in all languages on Judaism, Jewish history, literature and traditions from the earliest times to date and works in the Hebrew alphabet (mainly Hebrew and Yiddish) on a variety of subjects. The division has extensive files of Jewish periodicals and newspapers. The collection of rare Hebraica incl medieval texts, cabalistic works, ethical and philosophical tracts in book form. See *Dictionary Catalog of the Jewish Collection* (Boston: G K Hall, 1960), 14 vols. First Supplement (Boston: G K Hall, 1975), 8 vols.

NY —YIVO INSTITUTE FOR JEWISH RESEARCH, Library & Archives, 1048 Fifth Ave, New York, 10028. Dina Abramowicz, Librn; Marek Web, Archivist
Notes: Jews in contemporary world. Anti-Semitism. Many periodicals and pamphlets.

OH —HEBREW UNION COLLEGE-JEWISH INSTITUTE OF RELIGION, Klau Library, 3101 Clifton Ave, Cincinnati, 45220. David J Gilner, Reference Librn
Holdings: Cat
Notes: Extensive collection of 20th century ephemeral anti-Jewish works.

ANTISLAVERY see Slavery and Antislavery

ANTIVIVISECTION see Vivisection and Antivivisection

ANTROBUS, JOHN

MA —BOSTON UNIVERSITY, Mugar Memorial Library, Special Collections Dept, 771 Commonwealth Ave, Boston, 02215. Howard B Gotlieb, Dir
Holdings: Cat Mss Pix
Notes: Mss, correspondence, etc collected in depth; incl publications by or about.

ANTS

NY —AMERICAN MUSEUM OF NATURAL HISTORY, Library Services Dept, Central Park W & 79th St, New York, 10024. Nina J Root, Chairwoman; Mary Genett, Asst Librn for Reference Services
Notes: A major literature collection supplements the museum's entomology collections; perhaps the largest in the world.

ANZANIC LANGUAGE see Elamite Language

APACHE INDIANS

AZ —NORTHERN ARIZONA UNIVERSITY, Special Collection Library, CU Box 6022, Flagstaff, 86011. Peter M Whiteley, Coordr/Archivist; William Mullane, Librn
Notes: Apachean Languages and Music Collection. A music collection compiled by Werner Winter, Universitaet Kiel, Germany. Incl uses of language, stories, recipes, jokes, etc.

NM —ALBUQUERQUE PUBLIC LIBRARY, 501 Copper Ave NW, Albuquerque, 87102. Alan B Clark, Dir
Holdings: Vols (4000) Cat Microforms Records Maps VF
Notes: Large collection of materials on all aspects of New Mexico history and cultures. In-house index accesses VF materials and local and regional periodicals. Special emphasis on Indians of New Mexico and northeastern Arizona, partciularly the Navajo, Hopi, Pueblos and Apache. Reference copies of many works are housed at the Special Collections Library, 423 Central Ave NE, Albuquerque, NM 87102.

OK —US ARMY FIELD ARTILLERY SCHOOL LIBRARY, Morris Swett Library, Snow Hall, Fort Sill, 73503. Lester L Miller Jr, Chief Librn
Notes: Incl data on Fort Sill, Indian Territory, settlement of Kiowa, Apache and Commanche tribes, imprisonment of Geronimo, Oklahoma territory, settlement of Lawton. Unit histories, incl 10th Cavalry (Buffalo Soldiers, a black unit that built Fort Sill); working papers of Sheridan, Grierson and other commanders; Field Artillery School. Photographs on army subjects, Fort Sill, Indians, Indian Territory, settlement of Southwest Oklahoma.

APARTHEID see Segregation and Desegregation

APE PRINTS

MN —MAYO MEDICAL LIBRARY, History of Medicine Collection, Rochester, 55905. Nancy R Hensel, Librn
Holdings: Pix
Notes: The Comfort Collection of caricatures of physicians and scientists from *Vanity Fair.* Description: Mann, Ruth J: "The unheroic representation of heroes." *Mayo Clin Proc* 46:197-199, Mar 1971.

APES

NY —AMERICAN MUSEUM OF NATURAL HISTORY, Library Services Dept, Central Park W & 79th St, New York, 10024. Nina J Root, Chairwoman; Mary Genett, Asst Librn for Reference Services

OR —OREGON REGIONAL PRIMATE RESEARCH CENTER, Library, 505 NW 185 Ave, Beaverton, 97006. Isabel McDonald, Librn
Holdings: Vols (765) Cat Audiotapes 16mm Films Microforms
Notes: Incl small collection of dissertations and theses.

APHIDIDAE see Plant—Lice

APHIDS see Plant-Lice

APHORISMS, APOTHEGMS, EPIGRAMS, MAXIMS, AND PROVERBS

†CA —UNIVERSITY OF CALIFORNIA LOS ANGELES, Center for the Study of Comparative Folklore and Mythology, Los Angeles, 90024.
Notes: Archive, consisting of nearly 500,000 entries and cross-references, developed by Prof Wayland D Hand over the past 40 years as part of his monumental *Dictionary of American Popular Beliefs and* Superstitions. Entries have been drawn from both field collections and from printed and published sources. Analytical data stress both the historical component and the comparative approach. Of special interest is the emphasis on magical medicine, although natural and botanical medicine are also well represented.

CA —HUNTINGTON LIBRARY, Art Gallery & Botanical Gardens, 1151 Oxford Rd, San Marino, 91108. Robert L Middlekauff, Dir; Daniel H Woodward, Librn
Holdings: Vols 100 Cat
Notes: Refer to: Zall, P M "English Prose Jest Books in the Huntington Library: A Chronological Checklist (1535?-1799)," in *Shakespearean Research Opportunities*, no 4, 1968/69, pp 78-91, revised, 1983. Collections of prose anecdotes or tales with humorous intent incl apothegms and books that mix prose and verse, conventionally, in the 18th century.

IN —INDIANA UNIVERSITY, Institute for Sex Research Library, 416 Morrison Hall, Bloomington, 47401. Douglas Freeman, Collections and Services Librn; Joan Brewer, Information Services Librn
Holdings: Vols (62,000) Cat Mss Pix Phonorecords Audiotapes Slides Films Microforms
Budget: ($20,000)
Notes: One of the greatest and most extensive collections on sexual behavior, the library collects materials on all aspects of sex activity, with special emphasis on behavioral and social aspects. Also collects erotic literature and sexual ephemera. Incl 105 audiotapes, 23 vertical file drawers, 108 phonorecords, 55,000 pictures, 5000 slides, and 1700 films. Rich in French, German and American sources; also much Oriental. Semitraditional erotic poetry and song of

APHORISMS, APOTHEGMS, EPIGRAMS, MAXIMS, AND PROVERBS (cont.)

17th-18th century England. Bawdy limericks, double-entendre, puns, slang, erotic literature, graffiti, slang and special dictionaries, proverbs and sayings, epigrams and research materials of the Kinsey Studies, etc. Contact Information Service for: literature searching, preparation of bibliographies, permission to use collection. Limited photocopying.

MA —HARVARD UNIVERSITY LIBRARY, Widener Library, Cambridge, 02138.
Holdings: Cat

NC —UNIVERSITY OF NORTH CAROLINA, CHAPEL HILL, Wilson Library, Rare Book Collection, Chapel Hill, 27514. Paul S Koda, Cur of Rare Books
Holdings: Vols 2230 Cat
Notes: Incl two collections: The Jente Collection of Proverbs, 2000 items in many languages, printed from the 15th century to 1952; also volumes of critical and bibliographical material; and The Shedd Collection of Aphorisms, 229 books relating to aphorism, 1600-1920; most are in English, but many are in Spanish, French, German, and Latin.

OH —CLEVELAND PUBLIC LIBRARY, Fine Arts and Special Collections Department, 325 Superior Ave, Cleveland, 44114. Alice N Loranth, Head
Holdings: Vols 2800 Cat Mss
Notes: An outstanding colleciton of proverbs in the United States, international in scope but particularly strong in Spanish materials. Forms part of the Folklore Collection.
See also entry under Folklore

APICULTURE see Bees and Beekeeping

APOLLINAIRE, GUILLAUME

CA —FRANCIS BACON LIBRARY, 655 N Dartmouth Ave, Claremont, 91711. Elizabeth S Wrigley, Dir
Holdings: Mss Pix
Notes: Correspondence of Walter Arensberg with artists John Covert, Marcel Duchamp Francis Picabia and his wife Gabrielle Buffet Picabia, and psychiatrist Elmer Ernest Southard; Ms and draft of unpub Pantomime: A Quelle Heure un Train Partira-t-il pour Paris (1914) and ms and proof of ideogramme: Coeur Couronne et Miroir, with its published form in Les Soirees de Paris, by Guillaume Apollinaire (1880-1918); and Arensberg's miscellaneous correspondence with American literary figures (1920's-50's) including Bruce Bliven, Catherine Drinker Bowen, Kay Boyle, Witter Bynner, Edwin Corle, Helen A Keller, Lysander Kemp, Kenneth Macgowan, John Macy, Henry Miller, Lewis Mumford, Clifford Odets, Kenneth Patchen, Irving Stone, and William Carlos Williams. The Apollinaire ms has been described and reprinted in Apollinaire and the Faceless Man, by Willard Eugene Bohn(unpublished doctoral dissertation, University of Calif, Berkeley, ca 1973). It has also been reprinted with commentary in French by Willard Bohn by Bibliotheque Artistique and Litteraire, Fontefroide, 1982.

APOLLO MUSICAL CLUB OF CHICAGO

IL —CHICAGO HISTORICAL SOCIETY, Library, Clark St at North Ave, Chicago, 60614. Archie Motley, Manuscript Librn
Notes: Lyric Opera of Chicago and the Apollo Musical Club of Chicago, and in audio tapes of Herman Kogan's "Critic's Choice" radio programs.

APOLLONIA, ST.

MD —UNIVERSITY OF MARYLAND, BALTIMORE, Health Sciences Library, 111 S Greene St, Baltimore, 21201. Cyril C H Feng, Dir
Holdings: Vols (1000) Cat Mss Pix VF
Notes: The Clarence J Grieves Dental Historical Collection is one of the strongest collections of its kind in the United States. It includes some of the most significant early dental imprints; early records of the Maryland State Dental Association; and an excellent collection of prints on early dentistry and St Apollonia.

NY —NEW YORK UNIVERSITY DENTAL CENTER, John and Bertha E Waldmann Memorial Library, 345 E 24th St, New York, 10010. Roy C Johnson, Librn
Holdings: Vols 1350 Cat Mss Pix
Notes: Incl 300 vols published before the nineteenth century. Books and other historical dental materials from the Weinberger Collection, the Blum Collection, the Mestel St Apollonia Collection, and New York University College of Dentistry Archives. Also incl 9000 monographs.

APOPLEXY see Stroke

APOTHECARIES see Pharmacists

APOTHEGMS see Aphorisms, Apothegms, Epigrams, Maxims, and Proverbs

APPALACHIAN REGION

KY —BEREA COLLEGE, Hutchins Library, Berea, 40404. Gerald F Roberts, Librn Special Collections
Holdings: Vols (10,000) Cat Mss Maps Pix
Notes: Weatherford-Hammond Appalachian Collection is strong in Appalachian fiction. A bibliography of Appalachian fiction holdings has been distributed to selected academic libraries and Friends of Hutchins Library. Collection is also strong in history, ballads, folklore and religion.

KY —UNIVERSITY OF KENTUCKY COMMUNITY COLLEGES, Southeast Community College, Library, Learning Resource Center, Cumberland, 40823. Parker Boggs, Dir
Holdings: Vols (700) Cat Mss Maps Pix Slides Phonorecords Audiotapes Videotapes 16mm Films Filmstrips Microforms
Notes: Literature of southern Appalachia; fiction and non-fiction.

KY —MOREHEAD STATE UNIVERSITY, Johnson Camden Library, Morehead, 40351. Jack D Ellis, Dir
Holdings: Vols 2265 Cat

KY —CUMBERLAND COLLEGE, Norma P Hagan Memorial Library, 821 Walnut St, Williamsburg, 40769. Robert B Williams, Dir
Holdings: Vols 3500 Cat
Budget: ($3000)
Notes: Kentucky, Appalachia Collection.

NC —PACK MEMORIAL PUBLIC LIBRARY, North Carolina Collection, 67 Haywood St, Asheville, 28801. John Toms, Dept Head
Notes: Collection incl early ms accounts of western North Carolina; Civil War letters; letters, diary, and mss of Horace Kephart; mss of Thomas Dixon; Thomas Wolfe Collection; contemporary North Carolina authors; North Carolina censuses, 1790-1910; rare newspapers and runs of local newspapers, and clippings from Asheville newspapers, from 1920s; early maps; information on Cherokee Indians; approx 400 vols of North Carolina genealogy and file of unpublished genealogies. Collection concentrates on western North Carolina, with some general Appalachian materials. Incl 4000 local and state photographs, separate catalog.

NC —APPALACHIAN STATE UNIVERSITY, Belk Library, Appalachian Collection, Boone, 28608. Eric J Olson, Librn
Holdings: Vols (12,000) Cat Mss Maps Pix Slides Phonorecords Audiotapes Videotapes Films Microforms
Budget: ($4000)
Notes: The Appalachian Collection incl the Fry Collection of handmade quilts and coverlets; the York Collection of folk songs and ballads, plus tapes; the I G Greer Collection of Folk Songs and Ballads; the Amos Abrams ballad collection; artifacts, incl the Tatum Collection of household items, furniture, and farm implements; Daniel Boone loom; oral history tapes; the Jack Guy Collection of tapes of area music and photographs; and regional genealogy. This is a very comprehensive study on the Southern Appalachian Region. Separate catalog for the collection.

NC —WESTERN CAROLINA UNIVERSITY, Hunter Memorial Library, Cullowhee, 28723. James B Lloyd, Cur
Notes: Incl a regional ms collection documenting the social and natural history of Appalachia in general and western North Carolina in particular. Subject emphasis incl the Cherokee Indian, the establishment of the Great Smoky Mountains National Park, and the continuing use of Appalachian wilderness.

NC —MARS HILL COLLEGE, Memorial Library, Appalachian Room, Mars Hill, 28754. Richard Dillingham, Dir, Special Collections
Holdings: Vols (9600) Cat Mss Maps Pix Slides Phonorecords Audiotapes Microforms
Budget: ($4000)
Notes: Collection strong on local history, folklore, fiction. Incl Bascom Lamar Lunsford papers, books, sound recordings. Separate catalog.

PA —KING'S COLLEGE, D Leonard Corgan Library, 14 W Jackson St, Wilkes-Barre, 18711. Judith Tierney, Special Collections Librn
Holdings: Vols 850 Cat Mss Pix
Notes: The George Korson Folklore Archive. Separate catalog to books in collection. Books and periodicals relate to folklore generally; mss, 107 tapes and 70 disc recordings focus on folklore of the coal mining industry, 1918-1969. See Judith Tierney, comp. *A Description of the George Korson Folklore Archive* (Wilkes-Barre, Pa: King's College Press, 1973). Photocopying limited.

VA —VIRGINIA POLYTECHNIC INSTITUTE AND STATE UNIVERSITY LIBRARY, Blacksburg, 24061. Glenn L McMullen, Special Collections Librn
Holdings: Vols (2000) Cat Mss Maps Pix Audiotapes
Notes: Primarily Southwest Virginia materials. Collection incl ca 200 mss, account books and other archival records of nineteenth century area businesses and other mining operations; the extant archival records of several Southwest Virginia railroads, incl the Virginia and Tennessee Railroad and the Norfolk and Western Railroad; and papers of historically prominent Southwest Virginians, incl John Apperson, Dr Harvy Black, James P Charlton, W Graham Claytor, Henley Fugate, Clement D Johnston, Germanicus Kent, William Preston, J Hoge Tyler, and William C Wampler. Several oral history collections incl material on Appalachian customs and folklore, particularly in Patrick County.

VA —RADFORD UNIVERSITY, John Preston McConnell Library, Radford, 24142. Ann Swain, Librn
Holdings: Vols (7000) Cat Mss Maps Pix Slides Audiotapes
Notes: Southwest Virginia, black history, Virginiana and Appalachian books. The collection is built around, and organized with, the University Archives. Incl scrapbooks, clippings, etc.

WV —WEST VIRGINIA UNIVERSITY, Library, West Virginia and Regional History Collection, Morgantown, 26506. George P Parkinson Jr, Cur
Holdings: Vols 30,000 Cat Mss Maps Pix Audiotapes 16mm Films Filmstrips Microforms
Budget: ($20,000)
Notes: The West Virginia Collection contains over 10,000 linear ft of mss, broadsides, pictures, photographs, and other items relating to West Virginia and the Appalachian region. There are published guides to the collections.

APPALACHIAN REGION—FOLKLORE

DC —LIBRARY OF CONGRESS, American Folklife Center, Archive of Folk Culture,

APPALACHIAN REGION—FOLKLORE (cont.)

Washington, 20540.
Notes: 100 songs and ballads largely from the bituminous coal regions of Appalachia; songs recorded near Pottsville, PA. George Korson's original recordings and field notes are at King's College, Wilkes-Barre, PA.

KY —UNIVERSITY OF LOUISVILLE, Ekstrom Library, Photographic Archives, Louisville, 40292. J C Anderson, Cur; David G Horvath, Asst Cur
Holdings: Vols (750,000) Cat Pix Slides
Budget: ($60,000)
Notes: Photographs in three broad areas: works of outstanding photographers; examples of major developments in the art and technology of photography; photographs important as sociological, historical, or behavioral documents. Actors and actresses, Louisville's Macauley Theatre. Standard Oil of New Jersey Collection, 85,000 pictures of oil industry's effect on life in the 20th century (1943-1950, directed by Roy Stryker); Stryker's collection from Farm Security Administration series on rural conditions, 1934-1972. Caufield and Shook commercial photographs, Louisville area, 1920-1949. Jean Thomas "The Traipsin' Woman" photographs of Kentucky mountain folkways. Kate Matthews' (1870-1956) photographs incl prototypes for "Little Colonel" Series. Other collections described in unpublished brochure. Print duplication service.

NC —APPALACHIAN STATE UNIVERSITY, Belk Library, Appalachian Collection, Boone, 28608. Eric J Olson, Librn
Holdings: Vols (12,000) Cat Mss Maps Pix Slides Phonorecords Audiotapes
Budget: ($4000)
Notes: The Appalachian Collection incl the Fry Collectin of handmade quilts and coverlets; the York Collection of folk songs and ballads, plus tapes; the I G Greer Collection of Folk Songs and Ballads; the Amos Abrams ballad collection; artifacts, incl the Tatum Collection of household items, furniture, and farm implements; Daniel Boone loom; oral history tapes; the Jack Guy Collection of tapes of area music and photographs; and regional genealogy. This is a very comprehensive study on the Southern Appalachian Region. Separate catalog for the collection.

APPARATUS, ELECTRIC see Electric Apparatus and Appliances

APPARATUS, MEDICAL see Medical Instruments and Apparatus

APPARATUS, SCIENTIFIC see Scientific Instruments and Apparatus

APPARITIONS

NY —AMERICAN SOCIETY FOR PSYCHICAL RESEARCH LIBRARY, 5 W 73 St, New York, 10023. Rhea A White, Consultant to the Library
Holdings: Vols (7000) Cat Mss Pix
Budget: ($1500)
Notes: Incl books on spiritualism, as well as works in psychology, religion, philosophy, physics, anthropology, etc which have a possible bearing on parapsychology. An attempt is made to obtain all serious books on parapsychology in English.

OH —CLEVELAND PUBLIC LIBRARY, Fine Arts and Special Collections Department, 325 Superior Ave, Cleveland, 44114. Alice N Loranth, Head
Holdings: Vols (2500) Cat
Notes: Part of the Occult Sciences Collection. Emphasis is on historical treatises, folklore aspects and the classic texts pertaining to apparitions, ghosts, divinations, oracles, omens, witchcraft, magic, and sorcery in various civilizations. Astrology, palmistry, psychical research and contemporary manifestations are slmost entirely omitted.
See also entry under Folklore

RI —BROWN UNIVERSITY, John Hay Library, 20 Prospect St, Providence, 02912. Mark N Brown, Cur Mss
Holdings: Vols (900) // Mss
Notes: John William Graham Collection of Literature of Psychic Science; 350 predominantly late 19th and early 20th century books dealing with alchemy, black magic, dreams, demonology, church history, mysticism, mediumship, physical and somatic types of psychic experience. Collection described in *Index to Psychic* Science compiled by S R Morgan (Swarthmore, 1950). Also, the Damon Collection of Occult and Visionary Literature; 550 vols devoted to the development of western mysticism with particular emphasis on American and British thought, incl texts on alchemy, black magic, esoteric church history, dream interpretations, mysticism, witchcraft, the Kabbalah, and visionary testaments and manifestations of all types printed during the 16th to 20th centuries; and the Samuel Wyllys Papers; 125 mss, transcripts, and photocopies of legal and government papers relating to Indian affairs, colonial wars, civil and criminal cases, and the witchcraft trials of 1692-1693. Partially cataloged.

APPEARANCE SCIENCE

NY —ROCHESTER INSTITUTE OF TECHNOLOGY, Technical & Education Center of the Graphic Arts, Graphic Arts Information Service, One Lomb Memorial Dr, Rochester, 14623. Susan Clark, Technical Librn

APPELIN, ANNIE

AZ —NORTHERN ARIZONA UNIVERSITY, Special Collection Library, CU Box 6022, Flagstaff, 86011. Peter M Whiteley, Coordr/Archivist; William Mullane, Librn
Notes: Papers.

APPERSON, JOHN

VA —VIRGINIA POLYTECHNIC INSTITUTE AND STATE UNIVERSITY LIBRARY, Blacksburg, 24061. Glenn L McMullen, Special Collections Librn
Holdings: Vols (2000) Cat Mss Maps Pix Audiotapes
Notes: Primarily Southwest Virginia materials. Collection incl ca 200 mss, account books and other archival records of nineteenth century area businesses and other mining operations; the extant archival records of several Southwest Virginia railroads, incl the Virginia and Tennessee Railroad and the Norfolk and Western Railroad; and papers of historically prominent Southwest Virginians, incl John Apperson, Dr Harvy Black, James P Charlton, W Graham Claytor, Henley Fugate, Clement D Johnston, Germanicus Kent, William Preston, J Hoge Tyler, and William C Wampler. Several oral history collections incl material on Appalachian customs and folklore, particularly in Patrick County.

APPLEBY, JOHN T.

DC —GEORGETOWN UNIVERSITY, Library, Special Collections Div, 37 & O Sts NW, Washington, 20057. George M Barringer, Special Collections Librn; Nicholas B Sheetz, Mss Librn
Holdings: Mss Cat Pix
Notes: Mss of a number of Mr Appleby's works on English medieval history (principally his *England Without Richard*) and other subjects, some correspondence pertaining thereto, and a collection of photographs of Suffolk locales (some copies of 19th century prints); together with photographic copies of medieval mss.

APPLEBY, PAUL H.

NY —SYRACUSE UNIVERSITY LIBRARIES, Ernest S Bird Library, George Arents Research Library for Special Collections, Syracuse, 13210. Carolyn A Davis, Manuscripts Librn; Amy S Doherty, University Archivist; Mark F Weimer, Rare Book Librn
Notes: Papers of Paul H Appleby. He was Undersecretary of Agriculture under Pres Franklin D Roosevelt, Asst Dir of the US Bureau of the Budget under Roosevelt and Truman, and Dean of the Maxwell School at Syracuse University from 1947-1954.

APPLEWHITE, JAMES

NC —DUKE UNIVERSITY, William R Perkins Library, Rare Book Room, Durham, 27706. John L Sharpe, III, Cur
Notes: A collection of Duke University authors, established around 1963, with the writings of the students of William Blackburn and greatly enhanced by the gift of Professor Blackburn's collection. Represented are James Applewhite, Fred Chappell, Guy Davenport, Reynolds Price, William Styron, Frances Gray Patton, and Anne Tyler. Printed works are in the Rare Book Room and manuscripts are in the Manuscript Department.

APPLIANCES, ELECTRIC see Electric Apparatus and Appliances

APPLIED ART see Art Industries and Trade

APPLIED ELECTRICITY see Electricity, Applied

APPLIED MECHANICS see Mechanics, Applied

APPLIED PSYCHOLOGY see Psychology, Applied

APPLIED SCIENCE see Technology

APPRAISAL see Assessment; Valuation

APPRAISAL OF BOOKS see Bibliography—Best Books; Literature—History and Criticism

APPRECIATION OF ART see Aesthetics; Painting

APSAROKE INDIANS see Crow Indians

AQUACULTURE

AL —US FISH & WILDLIFE SERVICE, Southeastern Fish Cultural Laboratory, Route 3 Box 86, Marion, 36756.
Notes: This collection is cataloged as part of the Library of the US Fish and Wildlife Service, National Fisheries Center, Box 700, Kearneysville, WV 25430.

AR —US FISH & WILDLIFE SERVICE, Fish Farming Experimental Station, PO Box 860, Stuttgart, 72160. Joyce Cooper, Information Officer
Holdings: Vols (850)
Budget: ($2000)
Notes: Will loan or photocopy (up to 35 pages) with interlibrary loan forms.
See also entry under Fishes - Diseases and Pests

FL —FLORIDA DEPT OF NATURAL RESOURCES BUREAU OF MARINE RESEARCH, Library, 100 Eighth Ave SE, Saint Petersburg, 33701. Keir Gray, Archivist
Holdings: Vols (3400) Cat Maps Pix Slides 16mm Films Microforms
Budget: ($59,000)
Notes: The library supports the research of approx 50 biologists and technicians, with emphasis on the marine resources of Florida and nearby areas. An archives section houses original research data, reports, publications,, etc, developed by the scientific staff. Marine biological literature is received on exchange from laboratories and libraries throughout the world. There are approx 1400 journal

AQUACULTURE (cont.)

titles in the collection. Current titles received number approx 600. The 33,000 reprints are cataloged by author and subject. Current laboratory activities incl marine studies in aquaculture, descriptive biology, ecological studies, fisheries biology, and oceanography.

GA —UNIVERSITY OF GEORGIA, College of Agriculture, Coastal Plain Experiment Station Library, Moore Hwy, Tifton, 31793. Emory Cheek, Library Specialist
Holdings: Vols (13,500) Cat

ID —US FISH & WILDLIFE SERVICE, Hagerman Field Station, Route 1, Hagerman, 83332. Ilabell Casper, Librn

ME —BIGELOW LABORATORY FOR OCEAN SCIENCES & MAINE DEPT OF MARINE RESOURCES, Library, McKown Point, West Boothbay Harbor, 04575. Pamela Shephard-Lupo, Librn
Holdings: Vols Cat Periodicals
Budget: ($55,000)
Notes: This library presently serves two institutions. The Maine Dept of Marine Resources has maintained the library since 1957 and thus the majority of our holdings are geared to their needs, ie fish biology and stock assessment on a local, national and international level. In 1973 Bigelow Laboratory for Ocean Sciences came to West Boothbay Harbor and began to contribute to the library with a very specialized collection on the Gulf of Maine marine chemistry, phytoplankton and nutrient cycles.

NY —US FISH & WILDLIFE SERVICE, Tunison Laboratory of Fish Nutrition, Cortland, 13045.

OR —OREGON STATE UNIVERSITY, Marine Science Center, Library, Newport, 97365. Marilyn Guin, Librn
Holdings: Vols (8000) Cat Maps Microforms
Budget: ($15,000)
Notes: Collection emphasizes marine ecology, invertebrate zoology and marine algae. The portion of the collection concerned with fisheries emphasizes aquaculture. Collection is divided between the Marine Science Library and the Main OSU Library.

PA —US FISH & WILDLIFE SERVICE, National Fisheries Research and Development Laboratory, Wellsboro, 16901.
Notes: Approx 1050 books and 3000 reprints.

RI —UNIVERSITY OF RHODE ISLAND, International Center for Marine Resource Development, Library, Main Library Building, Kingston, 02881.
Holdings: Vols (13,000) Periodicals
Notes: Devoted to the development of marine resources in third world countries. Small-scale fisheries, anthropology of fishing peoples, coastal fisheries, aquaculture program planning. Approx 13,000 documents, 200 periodicals.

WV —US FISH & WILDLIFE SERVICE, National Fisheries Center, Technical Information Services, Route 3 Box 700, Kearneysville, 25430. Joyce A Mann-Grim, Librn
Holdings: Vols (22,900) Slides
Budget: $140,800
Notes: Collection topics incl fish virology, histology, bacteriology, immunology, nutrition and parasitology. Publish *Fish Health News*. Incl 20,000 reprints, 5000 slides.

AQUARIUMS

MD —NATIONAL AQUARIUM IN BALTIMORE, Pier 3, 501 East Pratt St, Baltimore, 21202. Lee Campbell, Librn
Notes: Staff members only.

PA —CARNEGIE LIBRARY OF PITTSBURGH, Science & Technology Dept, 4400 Forbes Ave, Pittsburgh, 15213. Catherine M Brosky, Dept Head
Notes: Except for certian special areas, such as entomology and ornithology and a few others that are emphasized, this general subject is of secondary interest. Incl both modern and classic works. Kept up to date in cooperation with the Library in Carnegie Museum of Natural History. Materials available on the various phyla, classes, orders and species. Abstracts, indexes, bibliographies, taxonomic manuals and standard reference books. Many journals and society publications complete from the beginning.

AQUATIC ANIMALS see Marine Fauna

AQUATIC BIRDS see Water Birds

AQUATIC ECOLOGY

CA —CALIFORNIA STATE UNIVERSITY, FULLERTON, Library, Box 4150, Fullerton, 92634. Linda Herman, Special Collections Librn
Holdings: Cat
Notes: Dr Leonard B Schultz Ichthyology Collection of 13,000 pieces incl books, pamphlets, articles and ephemera. It is supplemented by the Ecology of Bay and Estuarine Fishes Collections.

ME —BIGELOW LABORATORY FOR OCEAN SCIENCES & MAINE DEPT OF MARINE RESOURCES, Library, McKown Point, West Boothbay Harbor, 04575. Pamela Shephard-Lupo, Librn
Holdings: Vols Cat
Budget: ($55,000)
Notes: The library presently serves two institutions. The Maine Dept of Marine Resources has maintained the library since 1957 and thus the majority of our holdings are geared to their needs, ie fish biology and stock assessment on a local, national and international level. In 1973 Bigelow Laboratory for Ocean Sciences came to West Boothbay Harbor and began to contribute to the library with a very specialized collection on the Gulf of Maine marine chemistry, phytoplankton and nutrient cycles.

MO —US FISH & WILDLIFE SERVICE, Columbia National Fisheries Research Laboratory, Rte One, Columbia, 65201. Axie Hindman, Librn
Holdings: Vols (2000) Cat Microforms
Budget: ($7000)
Notes: Pesticides in aquatic biota; fisheries research; fresh-water ecology. Also incl collection in water pollution, acid rain, aquatic invertebrets, environment and 10,000 reprints.

TN —TENNESSEE VALLEY AUTHORITY (TVA), Norris Branch Library, Norris, 37828. Debra D Mills, Librn
Holdings: Vols (8000) Cat Microforms
Budget: ($35,000)

AQUATIC INSECTS see Insects, Aquatic

AQUATIC SPORTS

FL —INTERNATIONAL SWIMMING HALL OF FAME LIBRARY, 1 Hall of Fame Dr, Fort Lauderdale, 33316. Marion Washburn, Librn
Holdings: Vols (3000) Cat Mss Audiotapes Videotapes 16mm Films
Notes: All aspects of swimming: history, instruction, competition. Incl rare and out of print editions, complete set of *NCAA Swimming Guides* (1915-date), numerous periodicals (eg, *Swimming World*, 1951-date), and small collection of materials on related aquatic sports: diving, synchronized swimming, etc. Also have materials on Olympic Games, 1896-date, covering history, results, pictorial essays, programs, etc

IL —NATIONAL COUNCIL OF THE YMCAS, YMCA Historical Library, 6400 Shafer Ct, Rosemont, 60018. Eleanor R Murphy, Librn
Notes: Large collection, incl historical material, on basketball, wrestling, track and field, swimming, diving, scuba and volleyball.

MB —AQUATIC HALL OF FAME & MUSEUM OF CANADA, Library, 25 Poseidon Bay, Winnipeg, R3M 3E4, Can.
Notes: Aquatic sports, incl swimming, diving, water polo and synchronized swimming. Aquatic memorabilia; records covering Olympics, World Games, Pan-American Games, Commonwealth Games and Canadian Championships; coaching; record books. Collections on sailing and sailing ships, and yachts and yachting, incl books from the Cutty Sark Club of Winnipeg, covering sailing of the past.

AQUATIC TOXICOLOGY OF METALS AND METALLIC COMPOUNDS

MD —NATIONAL LIBRARY OF MEDICINE, 8600 Rockville Pike, Bethesda, 20209. Harold M Schoolinam, Actg Dir
Budget: ($46,400)

AQUEDUCTS

NY —JERVIS PUBLIC LIBRARY, 613 N Washington St, Rome, 13440. William A Dillon, Dir
Holdings: Vols (1500)// Cat Mss Maps Slides
Notes: John Bloomfield Jervis Collection contains personal library (1500 vols) and papers (1300 items) of chief engineer of Croton aqueduct and other waterworks, canals, and railroads circa 1825-1860. Papers available from Jervis Public Library.

AQUEOUS IONS

CA —UNIVERSITY OF CALIFORNIA, BERKELEY, Bancroft Library, Manuscripts Division, Berkeley, 94720. James D Hart, Dir
Notes: Extensive collections of papers and archives relative to the history of modern chemistry.

AQUINAS, ST. THOMAS see Thomas Aquinas, St.

ARAB CIVILIZATION see Civilization, Arab

ARAB LEAGUE

CA —HOOVER INSTITUTION ON WAR, REVOLUTION & PEACE, Stanford University, Stanford, 94305. Peter Duignan, Cur; Karen Fung, Deputy Cur
Holdings: Vols (100,000)
Notes: For full description of collection, see Hoover Institution entry under Near East.

ARAB ORTHODOX CHRISTIANS

†NJ —ANTIOCHIAN ORTHODOX CHRISTIAN ARCHDIOCESE OF NORTH AMERICA, Library, 358 Mountain Rd, Englewood, 07631.
Notes: History of Arab Orthodox Christians in North America.

ARABIA

CA —CALIFORNIA STATE POLYTECHNIC UNIVERSITY, POMONA, University Library, 3801 W Temple Ave, Pomona, 91768. Harold Schleiser, Actg Dir
Holdings: Vols (778) Cat Mss Pix Filmstrips
Budget: ($5500)
Notes: Arabia of the 18th and 19th centuries is featured in the collection, mainly in books of European and American travelers who incl descriptions of the horse of the desert in their writings. Interested in exchange programs with other libraries. Information of a list of holdings is available.
See also entry under Arabian Horses

DC —LIBRARY OF CONGRESS, African and Middle Eastern Division, Washington, 20540.
Holdings: Cat Mss Microforms
Notes: Near East: Over 105,000 vols, Arabic, Armenian, Turkish, Persian, and related languages. Special subject strengths incl Islamic philosophy, history, literature, economic and serial publications.

ARABIA—HISTORY see Arabic History

ARABIAN HORSES

CA —CALIFORNIA STATE POLYTECHNIC UNIVERSITY, POMONA, University

ARABIAN HORSES (cont.)

Library, 3801 W Temple Ave, Pomona, 91768. Harold Schleiser, Actg Dir
Holdings: Vols 2000 Cat Mss Pix Filmstrips
Budget: ($5500)
Notes: Among the finest Arabian horse collections in the world. Collector's items and rare books are featured, in addition to the working materials used in tracing pedigrees or in researching specific problems, such as immunodeficiency disease, which is endemic to the Arab breed. The collection is made available, upon request, to persons outside the academic community. Located on the site of the W K Kellogg Arabian Horse Ranch founded in 1926. Collection also incl the Ranch papers and copies of the papers of Kellogg dating from his purchase of the first Ranch herd. Official studbooks from 22 countries, numerous private studbooks, histories of the Arabian horse and backfiles of serial publications are also important segments of the collection. Interested in exchange programs with other libraries. Information or a list of holdings is available.

ARABIAN NIGHTS

NJ —PRINCETON UNIVERSITY, Library, Rare Books Dept, Princeton, 08544. Stephen Ferguson, Cur
Holdings: Vols 300 Cat
Notes: Refer to: James Holly Hanford, "Open Sesame: Notes on the *Arabian Nights* in English" in the *Princeton University Library Chronicle* XXVI, 1 (autumn, 1964) pp 48-56.

OH —CLEVELAND PUBLIC LIBRARY, Fine Arts and Special Collections Department, 325 Superior Ave, Cleveland, 44114. Alice N Loranth, Head
Holdings: Vols 753 Cat
Notes: An outstanding collection containing many versions, complete or partial, in 57 languages. Part of the folklore collection. *See also* entry under Folklore

ARABIC-AFRIKAANS DIALECT

MA —HARVARD UNIVERSITY LIBRARY, Cambridge, 02138.
Holdings: Cat

ARABIC FICTION see Fiction, Arabic

ARABIC HISTORY

NJ —PRINCETON UNIVERSITY, Library, Near East Collections, Princeton, 08540. James Weinberger, Cur
Holdings: Vols (100,000) Cat Mss Maps Phonorecords Audiotapes Microforms
Budget: ($72,000)
Notes: Princeton has the largest collection of Arabic mss in the US. Collections are particulary rich in classical Arabic and Persian texts, encompassing all the traditional genres. Of special note are the collections in Arabic and Persian literature, language, history, philosophy and theology and the religious sciences of Islam, both in ms and printed formats. A separate, additional collection of Arabic mss (about 2000 items) is being cataloged. It is especially rich in theology and philosophy of the classical Islamic period. Two printed catalogs are available: *Descriptive Catalog of the Garrett Collection of Arabic* Manuscripts, Philip K Hitti et al. (Princeton: Princeton Univ Press, 1938); and *Catalogue of Arabic Manuscripts (Yahuda Section) in the Garrett Collection, Princeton University,* Rudolph Mach (Princeton: Princeton Univ Press, 1977).

†PA —DROPSIE UNIVERSITY, Library, Broad & York Sts, Philadelphia, 19132.

TX —UNIVERSITY OF TEXAS LIBRARIES, Middle East Collection, PO Box P, Austin, 78712. Abazar Sepehri, Librn
Holdings: Vols (45,000) Cat Microforms
Notes: Arabic, Persian and Turkish materials in the humanities and social sciences. Incl 350 periodical and 45 newspaper titles from most of the countries of the Arab League, Turkey, Iran and Afghanistan.

UT —UNIVERSITY OF UTAH, Middle East Library, Salt Lake City, 84112. Ragai N Makar, Librn
Holdings: Vols 7000
Budget: ($40,000)
Notes: The Greek Mss on microfilm collection of the Patriarchal Library of Alexandria, Egypt. This incl about 1000 mss on microfilm about the history and theology of the Greek Orthodox Church. Collection described in Studies and Documents edited by Jacob Geerlings. Vol XXVI Catalog of MSS of the Patriarchal Library of Alexandria by T D Mosconas, Salt Lake City, University of Utah Press, 1965.

ARABIC LANGUAGE AND LITERATURE

AZ —UNIVERSITY OF ARIZONA, Library, Oriental Studies Collection, Tucson, 85721. Mary J McWhorter, Actg Head Librn
Holdings: Vols (95,000) Cat Microforms
Budget: ($30,000)
See also entry under Oriental Lanugages and Literatures

CA —LOS ANGELES PUBLIC LIBRARY, Foreign Languages Dept, 630 W Fifth St, Los Angeles, 90071. Sylva Manoogian, Principal Librn
Holdings: Vols 1076 Cat
Budget: ($41,500)

CA —UNIVERSITY OF CALIFORNIA, LOS ANGELES, Research Library, Near Eastern Collection, Los Angeles, 90024. Edward Shreeves, Chairman, Bibliographers Group; Dunning Wilson, Near Eastern Bibliographer
Holdings: Vols (200,000) Cat Mss Maps Microforms
Notes: Incl ancient cultures and history.

CA —HOOVER INSTITUTION ON WAR, REVOLUTION & PEACE, Stanford University, Stanford, 94305. Peter Duignan, Cur; Karen Fung, Deputy Cur
Holdings: Vols (100,000)
Notes: For full description of collection, see Hoover Institution entry under Near East

CT —YALE UNIVERSITY, Box 1603A, Yale Station, New Haven, 06520.
Holdings: Cat Mss

DC —LIBRARY OF CONGRESS, African and Middle Eastern Division, Washington, 20540.
Holdings: Cat Mss Microforms
Notes: Near East: Over 105,000 vols, Arabic, Armenian, Turkish, Persian, and related languages. Special subject strengths incl Islamic philosophy, history, literature, economic and serial publications.

IL —NORTHWESTERN UNIVERSITY, Melville J Herskovits Library of African Studies, Evanston, 60201. Hans E Panofsky, Cur
Notes: Collected in depth. Incl a complete set of the recordings by and on African authors assembled by the Transcription Centre, London. Also, about 3000 books and pamphlets on African languages.

MA —BOSTON PUBLIC LIBRARY, South End Branch, Multilingual Library, 685 Tremont St, Boston, 02118. Laura H Reyes, Librn
Holdings: Cat

MA —HARVARD UNIVERSITY LIBRARY, Widener Library, Middle Eastern Dept, Cambridge, 02138. David H Partington, Librn
Holdings: Cat Mss Microforms
Budget: ($55,000)
Notes: The library's published *Catalogue of Arabic, Persian, and Ottoman Turkish Books* (1968) lists some 30,000 volumes in Arabic; see also *Harvard Library Bulletin, XVI* (1968): pp 313-325; *Catalog of Arabic* Collections, 6 volumes, 1983.

MI —UNIVERSITY OF MICHIGAN, Graduate Library, Near East Dept, Ann Arbor, 48109. John A Eilts, Bibliographer
Holdings: Cat Mss Microforms
Notes: P L 480.

NJ —PRINCETON UNIVERSITY, Library, Near East Collections, Princeton, 08540. James Weinberger, Cur
Holdings: Vols (100,000) Cat Mss Maps Phonorecords Audiotapes Microforms
Budget: ($72,000)
Notes: Princeton has the largest collection of Arabic mss in the US. Collections are particularly rich in classical Arabic and Persian texts, encompassing all the traditional genres. Of special note are the collections in Arabic and Persian literature, language, history, philosophy and theology and the religious sciences of Islam, both in ms and printed formats. A separate, additional collection of Arabic mss (about 2000 items) is being cataloged. It is especially rich in theology and philosophy of the classical Islamic period. Two printed *Descriptive Catalog of the Garrett Collection of Arabic Manuscripts,* Philip K Hitti et al. (Princeton: Princeton Univ Press, 1938); and *Catalogue of Arabic Manuscripts (Yahuda Section) in the Garrett Collection, Princeton University,* Rudolf Mach (Princeton: Princeton Univ Press, 1977).

NY —COLUMBIA UNIVERSITY LIBRARIES, Rare Book & Manuscript Library, 801 Butler Library, 535 W 114 St, New York, 10027. Kenneth A Lohf, Librn
Holdings: Vols (5000) Cat
Notes: Incl the Arthur Jeffrey Collection. Have numerous photographic copies of Arabic mss in various Middle Eastern libraries. Restricted use.

NY —NEW YORK PUBLIC LIBRARY, Oriental Div, Fifth Ave & 42 St, New York, 10018. E Christian Filstrup, Chief
Holdings: Cat Mss Microforms
Budget: ($56,455)
Notes: Described in *Dictionary Catalog of the Oriental Collection,* The Research Libraries of the New York Public Library, 1960, 16 vols, and *First Supplement,* 1976, 8 vols (144,000 cards). This catalog incl 318, 000 entries for works in about 100 languages of the East, and all works in Western languages on Oriental subjects. The Oriental Collection numbers about 120,000 vols; its Arabic and Indic holdings and those on ancient Egypt and the ancient Near East are among the largest in the US. There is also a collection of 30,000 vols of PL 480 material from Egypt, Pakistan, and India to which there is main entry access, but which is not incorporated into the dictionary catalog. Other outstanding features of the Oriental Collection incl extensive holdings of Japanese technical and scientific periodicals; a unique collection of linguistic works, grammars, anddictionaries; and unusually good coverage of the field of Oriental religions and philosophies. The catalog contains numerous subject references to periodical articles in all languages. All entries are arranged alphabetically according to the Roman alphabet.

NY —NEW YORK PUBLIC LIBRARY, Donnell Foreign Language Library, 20 W 53 St, New York, 10019. Bosiljka Stevanovic, Supvr Librn
Holdings: Vols 617 Cat
Notes: Arabic collection incl Arabic authors of Arabic expression. No separate catalog.

NC —CUMBERLAND COUNTY PUBLIC LIBRARY, North Carolina Foreign Language Center, 328 Gillespie St, Fayetteville, 28301. Patrick M Valentine, Coordinator
Holdings: Vols 650 Cat
Budget: $500
Notes: The largest book collections are, in descending order of size, German Spanish, French, Japanese, Korean and Vietnamese, with fair sized collections in Italian, Russian, Chinese, Arabic, Greek, Hungarian, Polish, Hebrew, Thai, and Hindi. The Center has several shelves each of books in Bengali, Dutch, Marathi, Portuguese, Urdu, and Yiddish. Smaller collections of one to three shelves each incl Catalan, Croatian, Czech, Danish, Finnish, Gujarati, Icelandic, Kannada, Latin, Lithuanian, Malayalam, Norwegian, Panjabi, Persian (Farsi), Romanian, Slovak, Swedish, Tagalog, Tamil, Telegu, and Ukrianian. The Center has grammars, dictionaries and occasionally other readings in languages from Afrikaans and Albanian to Welsh, Yoruba and Zulu.

OH —HEBREW UNION COLLEGE-JEWISH INSTITUTE OF RELIGION, Klau Library,

ARABIC LANGUAGE AND LITERATURE (cont.)

3101 Clifton Ave, Cincinnati, 45220. David J Gilner, Reference Librn
Holdings: Cat Mss
Notes: About 6000 mss in Hebrew characters representing various languages, such as Hebrew, Ladino, Yiddish, Spanish, Italian, German; also mss in Arabic, Ethiopian, Chinese and Persian alphabets. Incl literary, archival, sermonic and halakhic mss.

OH —CLEVELAND PUBLIC LIBRARY, Fine Arts and Special Collections Department, 325 Superior Ave, Cleveland, 44114. Alice N Loranth, Head
Holdings: Vols 4000 Cat Mss Maps Microforms
Notes: Scholarly editions of classic Arabic texts, their versions in philosophy, religion, history, geography and literature are emphasized. Incl are the great dictionaries and encyclopedias, as well as 50 mss and over 50 facsimile editions of mss. Separate author entry entry catalog for titles written in Arabic. (2640 vols.)
See also entries under Near East; Manuscripts, Arabic; Oriental Languages and Literatures

OH —CLEVELAND PUBLIC LIBRARY, Foreign Literature Dept, 325 Superior Ave, Cleveland, 44114. Natalia Bezugloff, Head
Holdings: Vols 2280 Cat
Notes: A popular circulating collection containing classics and the standard works with emphasis on belles lettres, history and biography. A variety of other subjects such as learning languages, children's books, spoken phonodiscs and cassettes, periodicals, etc. Incl 210 emphemera.
See also entry under Foreign Language Collections

OH —OHIO STATE UNIVERSITY, Library, 1858 Neil Mall, Columbus, 43210. Dona Straley, Islamica Librn
Holdings: Vols (25,000) Cat Maps Microforms
Budget: ($30,000)
Notes: The bulk of the Arabic language collection is in the field of language and literature, with large and medium collections in the fields of Islamica and Middle East history. There are also approx 2000 Persian language vols and approx 3000 vols in Turkish. Scholarly translations of Arabic, Persian and Turkish materials are acquired when available. Substantial supporting collections of materials on Arabic language and literature, Islamica, and Middle East history in all of the major European languages are also held. Member of PL 480 program since 1975. No ms holdings. Incl modern Arabic fiction and literature, and foreign literature in Arabic translations.

TX —UNIVERSITY OF TEXAS LIBRARIES, Middle East Collection, PO Box P, Austin, 78712. Abazar Sepehri, Librn
Holdings: Vols (45,000) Cat Microforms
Notes: Arabic, Persian and Turkish materials in the humanities and social sciences. Incl 350 periodical and 45 newspaper titles from most of the countries of the Arab League, Turkey, Iran and Afghanistan.

UT —UNIVERSITY OF UTAH, Middle East Library, Salt Lake City, 84112. Ragai N Makar, Librn
Holdings: Vols 18,000
Budget: ($40,000)
Notes: Mt Sinai Arabic Manuscripts collection. This incl about 800 Arabic manuscripts on microfilm. This collection is incl in the catalogue *The Arabic Manuscripts of Mt Sinai* by Professor Aziz S Atiya. Baltimore, The Johns Hopkins Press, 1955. All the mss are on the history and theology of the Eastern Christian Church.

†UT —UNIVERSITY OF UTAH, Marriott Library, Salt Lake City, 84112.
Notes: Collection of Professor Aziz S Atiya, mostly in Arabic languages.

WA —UNIVERSITY OF WASHINGTON LIBRARIES, Suzzallo Library, Near East Section, FM-25, Seattle, 98195. Fawzi W Khoury, Head
Holdings: Vols (81,359) Cat Mss Maps Slides Phonorecords 16mm Films Filmstrips Microforms
Budget: ($52,752)
Notes: Incl a 2000 vol collection in Ottoman Turkish in the fields of language and literature and some Devlet and Vilayet Salnamehs.

ARABIC MANUSCRIPTS see Manuscripts, Arabic

ARABIC MEDICINE see Medicine, Arabic

ARABIC PERIODICALS see Periodicals, Arabic

ARABIC PHILOSOPHY see Philosophy, Arabic

ARABIC SCIENCE see Science, Arabic

ARABS—HISTORY see Arabic History

ARABS IN THE U.S.

MN —UNIVERSITY OF MINNESOTA, Immigration History Research Center, 826 Berry St, Saint Paul, 55114. Susan Griegs, Cur
Holdings: Vols (35,000) Mss Maps Pix Phonorecords Audiotapes 16mm Films Microforms
See also entry under US - Emigration and Immigration

†OH —ARAB-AMERICAN ASSOCIATION LIBRARY, PO Box 20041, Cincinnati, 45220.

PA —BALCH INSTITUTE FOR ETHNIC STUDIES, Library, 18 S Seventh St, Philadelphia, 19106. R Joseph Anderson, Library Dir
Holdings: Cat Microforms

ARACHNIDA

CA —UNIVERSITY OF CALIFORNIA, BERKELEY, Life Sciences Library, Entomology Library, 201 Wellman Hall, Berkeley, 94720. Nancy Axelrod, Librn
Holdings: Vols (12,000) Cat Microforms
Notes: A highly specialized collection limited to materials on insects, arachnida and animal parasites. Special emphasis is given to works on pest control, particularly on biological methods of control. The library's holdings in the field of parasitology emphasize medical parasitology. Incl over (17,000) pamphlets.

DC —SMITHSONIAN INSTITUTION LIBRARIES, Entomology Branch, Washington, 20560. Jean C Smith, Asst Dir for Bureau Services
Holdings: Vols (17,000) Cat Maps Pix

NY —CORNELL UNIVERSITY LIBRARIES, Comstock Memorial Library of Entomology, Ithaca, 14853. Edwin Spragg, Librn
Holdings: Vols (30,000) Cat Maps Pix Audiotapes Microforms
Budget: ($13,500)
Notes: Major topics: general and applied entomology. Minor topics: parasitology, medical entomology, ecology, zoological nomenclature and allied orders of arthropods. Separate catalog to the collection, also extensive collection of reprints. Apiculture material kept at nearby A R Mann Library.

NY —AMERICAN MUSEUM OF NATURAL HISTORY, Library Services Dept, Central Park W & 79th St, New York, 10024. Nina J Root, Chairwoman; Mary Genett, Asst Librn for Reference Services
Holdings: Vols (385,000) Cat Mss Maps Pix Slides Microforms
Notes: Nearly all collections are outstanding for depth of coverage and international range. Early and historic works, rare books, colored illustrations, and relevant serial publications supplement the modern scientific publications necessary to the researches of the scientific staff and the work of the educational division. Open to the public.

ARAMAIC LANGUAGE AND LITERATURE

NY —ALFRED UNIVERSITY, Herrick Memorial Library, Alfred, 14802. June E Brown, Head Librn
Holdings: Vols (1200) // Cat Mss
Notes: The Bergren Collection. A comprehensive collection on Biblical Studies in the Old and New Testaments. Includes material on the Dead Sea Scrolls, Eastern religions, and Hebrew and Aramaic languages.

NY —NEW YORK PUBLIC LIBRARY, Oriental Div, Fifth Ave & 42 St, New York, 10018. E Christian Filstrup, Chief
Holdings: Cat Mss Microforms
Budget: ($56,455)
Notes: Published catalog of holdings.

ARAMEAN LANGUAGE see Aramaic Language and Literature

ARANEIDA see Arachnida; Spiders

ARBITRATION, INDUSTRIAL

DC —US DEPT OF LABOR, Library, 200 Constitution Ave NW, Washington, 20210. Sabina Jacobson, Dir
Holdings: Vols (550,000) Cat

IA —UNIVERSITY OF IOWA, University Libraries, Iowa City, 52242. Robert A McCown, Mss Librn
Holdings: Mss
Notes: Two collections: labor arbitration case files, 1940-1970, of Clarence Milton Updegraff, consisting of briefs, decisions, correspondence, notes, transcripts of hearings, hearing statements, agreements, photographs and other material; and arbitration awards, 1963-1971, of the American Arbitration Association. 86 ft of mss.

NJ —RUTGERS, THE STATE UNIVERSITY OF NEW JERSEY, Institute of Management & Labor Relations, Ryders Lane & Clifton Ave, New Brunswick, 08903. Bernard F Downey, Librn
Holdings: Vols (18,530) Cat Slides Phonorecords 16mm Films Filmstrips
Budget: ($7300)
Notes: Separate card catalog for collection. Particular emphasis on dispute settlement. Strong collection on public sector labor relations, emphasizing New Jersey publications.

NY —CORNELL UNIVERSITY, New York State School of Industrial & Labor Relations, Martin P Catherwood Library, Ives Hall, Ithaca, 14853. Shirley F Harper, Dir
Holdings: Vols (150,000) Cat Mss Pix Phonorecords Microforms
Notes: Collection incl approx 1000 periodicals and union journals currently received, and ms collections of labor unions, arbitrators, and scholars. 6000 linear ft. *Library Catalog of the New York State School of Industrial and Labor Relations* (Boston: G K Hall, 1967), 12 volumes; *Cumulation of the Library Catalog Supplements of the New York State School of Industrial and Labor Relations* (Boston: G K Hall, 1976), 8 volumes.

TX —NORTH TEXAS STATE UNIVERSITY, Archives, NT Station Box 5188, Denton, 76203. Robert LaForte, University Archivist

ON —CANADA DEPT OF LABOUR, Library, Ottawa, K1A 0J2, Can. Monique Marchand, Chief Librn
Holdings: Vols (100,000) Cat Microforms

ARBITRATION, INTERNATIONAL

PA —SWARTHMORE COLLEGE, Peace Collection, Swarthmore, 19081. Jean R Soderlund, Cur of Peace Collection
Holdings: Vols (10,000) Cat Mss Pix Microforms
Notes: International arbitration has been one of the central subject emphases of the Peace Collection since its inception in 1930. A large proportion of the total book collection deals with international arbitration. In addition, major records and document collections in this area incl those of the Women's Peace Party (1915-1919), and its successor, the Women's International League for Peace and Freedom (1919-); the Lake Mohonk (New York) Arbitration

ARBITRATION, INTERNATIONAL (cont.)

Conferences (1895-1917); the American Peace Society and its branches (1828-1947); the World Peace Foundation (1911-); the Post War World Council (1942-1967); also, books and other materials on the Hague Peace Conferences of 1899 and 1907, and other peace congresses and conventions. The Peace Collection has been described in Downs 972, 978, 4633, and in Downs 1950-1961 Supplement 507 and 916. Fordescriptions of major document groups, see the *Guide to the Swarthmore College Peace Collection,* 2nd ed (1981).
See also entry under Pacifism - History.

ARBITRATION ASSOCIATION, AMERICAN see American Arbitration Association

ARBITRON RATINGS COMPANY

GA —UNIVERSITY OF GEORGIA, Libraries, Special Collections Division, Athens, 30602. Vesta Lee Gordon, Asst Dir for Special Collections
Notes: The Arbitron Collection of television and radio program ratings, 1949-date (except past year). In-depth, statistical analyses of the listening public by age, sex, county, some ethnic groups, farm population, listening preferences, etc. 26,302 bound vols. 2 reports, 1949-81. To be added to annually.

ARBORICULTURE

MA —HARVARD UNIVERSITY LIBRARY, Arnold Arboretum Library, 22 Divinty Ave, Cambridge, 02138. Barbara A Callahan, Librn
Holdings: Vols (89,239) Cat Mss Maps Pix Slides Microforms
Notes: Specializes in trees (arboriculture and dendrology). Horticultural Library maintained at the Arborway, Jamaica Plain, Mass.

MA —HARVARD UNIVERSITY, Arnold Arboretum, Horticultural Library, The Arborway, Jamaica Plain, 02130.
Holdings: Vols Pix Slides

NY —CARY ARBORETUM OF THE NEW YORK BOTANICAL GARDEN, Institute of Ecosystem Studies, Library, Box AB, Millbrook, 12545. Betsy Calvin, Librn
Holdings: Vols 10,000

ARBUS, DIANE

MD —UNIVERSITY OF MARYLAND, BALTIMORE COUNTY, Albin O Kuhn Library and Gallery, Edward L Bafford Photography Collection, 5401 Wilkens Ave, Baltimore, 21228. Tom Beck, Cur
Holdings: Pix
Notes: The Edward L Bafford Photography Collection contains more than 200,000 images, negatives, cameras and books representing the entire history and aesthetics of photography. Incl photographs of Diane Arbus.
See also entry under Photographs - Collections.

ARC WELDING see Welding

ARCHAEOLOGICAL SPECIMENS see Antiquities

ARCHAEOLOGY

AZ —FULTON-HAYDEN MEMORIAL LIBRARY, Dragoon, 85609. Mario Nick Klimiades, Librn
Holdings: Vols 17,000 Cat Mss Maps Pix Microforms
Budget: $3500
Notes: The Fulton-Hayden Memorial Library is a special collection of books about archaeology and ethnology specifically as they pertain to the western hemisphere and particularly to Mexico and the greater American Southwest.

AZ —NORTHERN ARIZONA UNIVERSITY, Special Collection Library, CU Box 6022, Flagstaff, 86011. Peter M Whiteley, Coordr/Archivist; William Mullane, Librn
Notes: John McGregor Collection; correspondence, papers, and class lectures of McGregor, an archaeologist. Correspondents incl A E Douglass, University of Ariz, and James Griffen, University of Michigan. Also incl reprints of articles about archaeology in Ariz, the US, and many foreign countries, 1881-1975.

AZ —ARIZONA STATE MUSEUM, Library, University of Arizona, Tucson, 85721. Hans R Bart, Museum Librn
Holdings: Vols (35,000) Cat Mss Maps Pix Slides Phonorecords Microforms

CA —PACIFIC SCHOOL OF RELIGION, Bade Institute of Biblical Archeology, 1798 Scenic Ave, Berkeley, 94709. Kay Schellhase, Cur
Holdings: Vols (2500) Cat Slides
Budget: ($700)
Notes: Syro-Palestinian archaeology.

CA —UNIVERSITY OF CALIFORNIA, BERKELEY, Humanities-Social Sciences Libraries, Anthropology Library, 230 Kroeber Hall, Berkeley, 94720. Dorothy A Koenig, Librn
Holdings: Vols (55,000) Cat Microforms
Notes: The library maintains general research collections covering all aspects of social and physical anthropology, anthropological linguistics and archaeology (excluding classical archaeology). Serials constitute the collection's special strength.

CT —YALE UNIVERSITY, Anthropology Library, Peabody Museum of Natural History, C-8 KBT, New Haven, 06511.
Holdings: Vols (16,000) Cat
Budget: ($11,000)

DC —LIBRARY OF CONGRESS, Geography and Map Division, Washington, 20540. John A Wolter, Chief
Notes: Ephraim George Squier's papers and maps of Central America. Maps are located in the Geography and Maps Division; mss in the Manuscripts Division.

DC —NATIONAL GEOGRAPHIC SOCIETY, Library, 1146 16th St NW, Washington, 20036. Susan Fifer Canby, Dir
Holdings: Vols (63,000) Cat Mss Maps Pix
Notes: Material concerning land, sea, and space exploration--past and present. All fields of anthropology, natural history, geography, etc.

DC —SMITHSONIAN INSTITUTION LIBRARIES, Anthropology Branch, Washington, 20560. Jean C Smith, Asst Dir for Bureau Services
Holdings: Vols (54,000) Cat Mss Maps Pix Slides Microforms
Budget: ($7041)
Notes: Physical anthropology, archaeology, ethnology, language and languages; Indians of both continents.

FL —HISTORICAL ASSOCIATION OF SOUTHERN FLORIDA, Charlton W Tebeau Library of Florida History, 101 W Flager St, Miami, 33130. Rebecca A Smith, Cur of Research Materials
Holdings: Vols (3000) Cat Mss Maps Pix Slides Audiotapes 16mm Films Microforms
Notes: History of Florida, with emphasis on southern area. Less extensively, history of the Caribbean area, especially as related to Florida. Florida materials incl anthropology, archaeology, Indians of south Florida, incl Seminole Indians, Dade County history, and a complete run of the newspaper *The American Eagle* (1906-date), printed by Koreshan Unity, Estero, Florida. Incl 300 feet of mss, 1500 maps, 75,000 pictures, 2000 slides, 125 audiotapes, 25 16mm films, 200 microforms, 50 feet of vertical files, and 7000 postcards. Work in progress on guide to ms collection and on indexing of photographs. Also incl books and journals on museum science: conservation and preservation of museum materials.

HI —BERNICE P BISHOP MUSEUM, Library, PO Box 19000-A, Honolulu, 96819. Cynthia Timberlake, Librn
Holdings: Vols (90,000) Cat Mss Maps Pix Slides Microforms
Budget: ($30,000)
Notes: Only American library devoted exclusively to the Pacific region. Collection reflects historical and contemporary research emphases of Bishop Museum; ie the natural and cultural history of the Pacific. Areas of concentration incl archaeology, ethnology, linguistics, voyages and explorations, history, vertebrate and invertebrate zoology, botany and museology. Strong special collections incl photographs, mss and archives, maps and art. Publications: Quarterly "Additions to the Catalog," *Dictionary Catalog of the* Library (9 vols and 2 suppl; Boston: G K Hall, 1964-69).

IL —FIELD MUSEUM OF NATURAL HISTORY, Library, Roosevelt Rd & Lake Shore Dr, Chicago, 60605. W Peyton Fawcett, Librn; Benjamin W Williams, Assoc Librn
Holdings: Vols (210,000) Cat
Budget: ($100,000)
Notes: Extensive collections--publications of learned societies and institutions and monographic works--in all fields of natural history, with emphasis on taxonomy and evolutionary biology; and on museum publications, American and foreign: anthropology, especially archaeology and ethnology of the Americas, Africa, East Asia, and Oceania; botany, particularly strong for the Americas; geology, chiefly paleontology and meteoritic studies; and zoology, worldwide (birds, fishes, insects, mammals, mollusks, reptiles and amphibians).

IL —NEWBERRY LIBRARY, 60 W Walton St, Chicago, 60610. Diana Haskell, Cur of Modern Mss
Holdings: Vols (1000) Cat Mss Pix
Notes: Western continent antiquities.

IL —UNIVERSITY OF ILLINOIS, URBANA/CHAMPAIGN, Library, Classics Library, 419A Main Library, Urbana, 61801. Suzanne N Griffiths, Librn
Holdings: Vols (10,000) Cat
Notes: Ancient history section of Classics Library is strong in numismatics and in inscription materials; also incl ancient archaeology.

IN —INDIANA UNIVERSITY, Art Museum Bldg, Fine Arts Bldg, Bloomington, 47401. Betty Jo Irvine, Fine Arts Librn
Holdings: Vols (57,000) Cat Pix Microforms
Budget: ($52,000)
Notes: Art forms relevant to the periods and places involved.

LA —TULANE UNIVERSITY, Howard-Tilton Memorial Library, Latin American Library, New Orleans, 70118. Thomas Niehaus, Dir
Holdings: Vols (150,000) Cat Mss Maps Pix Microforms VF
Budget: ($67,000)
Notes: *Catalog of the Latin American* Library (Boston: G K Hall, 1970, suppl. 1973,1975,1978); Downs 5338-41; suppl (1961), 2727, 2737. The Latin American Library is a general collection, but specializes in Central American, Mexican, and Brazilian materials. The disciplines which are most strongly represented are history, anthropology, and archaeology. The Viceregal Ecclesiastical Mexican Collection contains manuscripts from the colonial period. The France V Scholes Collection contains a large number of photoprints and microfilm of colonial documents from the archives of Spain and Mexico. The Merle Greene Robertson Rubbings Collection contains nearly five hundred rubbings of relief sculpture from Mayan archaeological sites in Mexico and Guatemala. The Photographic Collection contains photos of archaeological sites inMeso-America, of pre-Columbian Peruvian architecture, and a general group of historic photos from Latin America.

MD —JOHNS HOPKINS UNIVERSITY, Milton S Eisenhower Library, Charles & 34 Sts, Baltimore, 21218. Ann S Gwyn, Assistant Dir for Special Collections
Holdings: Vols 9100 Cat
Notes: Strong collection with some omissions. Not all excavation reports from Near East are included.

MD —CALVERT MARINE MUSEUM, Library, PO Box 97, Solomons, 20688.
Holdings: Uncat Mss Maps
Notes: Result of an ongoing project with the

ARCHAEOLOGY (cont.)

Nautical Archeological Associates to obtain information on the naval history of Patuxent River during the War of 1812.

†MA —UNIVERSITY OF MASSACHUSETTS AT AMHERST, Library, Amherst, 01003.
Notes: Classical art and archaeology. Special emphasis: Aegean area.

MA —HARVARD UNIVERSITY LIBRARY, Tozzer Library, 21 Divinity Ave, Cambridge, 02138. Nancy J Schmidt, Librn
Holdings: Vols (152,000) Cat Microforms
Budget: ($337,000)
Notes: (Formerly Peabody Museum Library). Believed to have the strongest collection in the United States for prehistoric archaeology generally, anthropology, and ethnology. Does not collect classical archaeology. Catalog, in 54 volumes, published in 1963, with 12-volume supplement in 1970, 5-volume supplement in 1971, 7-volume supplement in 1975, and 7-volume supplement in 1979, analyzes contents of serial publications. Quarterly journal, *Anthropological Literature, 1979-*. Described in *Harvard Library Bulletin*, III (1949): pp 94-101; J O Brew, *People and Projects of the Peabody Museum, 1866-1966* (Cambridge, Mass: The Museum, 1966), pp 57-59; and Nancy J Schmidt, Tozzer Library, Harvard University: *Special Libraries Association Boston Chapter News* Bulletin, 48, 2 (1982), pp 167-169.

MA —HARVARD UNIVERSITY LIBRARY, Botanical Museum Library, Cambridge, 02138.
Holdings: Vols (2400) Mss Pix
Notes: The Tina and Gordon Wisson Ethnomycological Collection, one of the most important modern collections, acquired as an adjunct to the Museum's Economic Botany Library of Oakes Ames. From 15th to 20th century, it deals with hallucinogenic mushrooms in art, religion, and folklore; chemistry, pharmacology, linguistics, archaeological artifacts of Mexico, Guatemala, India, Japan, China, etc. Personal papers, etc.

MO —UNIVERSITY OF MISSOURI-COLUMBIA, Museum of Art & Archaeology, Library, One Pickard Hall, Columbia, 65201. Ruth E Witt, Asst Dir
Holdings: Vols (4000)
Notes: Sales and exhibition catalogs, reports, bulletins, etc.

MO —UNIVERSITY OF MISSOURI-COLUMBIA, Ellis Library, Art, Archaeology and Music Dept, Columbia, 65201. Bonnie MacEwan, Librn
Holdings: Vols Cat
Notes: Good collection of Roman provincial archaeology.

MO —SCHOOL OF THE OZARKS, Lois Brownell Research Library, Ralph Foster Museum, Point Lookout, 65726. Robert Esworthy, Librn
Holdings: Vols (1300) Cat Mss Maps Pix
Notes: Archaeology of North America.

MO —WASHINGTON UNIVERSITY, Art & Architecture Library, Saint Louis, 63130. Imre Meszaros, Librn
Holdings: Vols (60,413) Cat Maps Pix Microforms
Budget: ($100,000)
Notes: Art and architecture of East Asia; rare books; archaeology; fashion design.

NE —NEBRASKA STATE HISTORICAL SOCIETY, Library, 1500 R St, Box 82554, Lincoln, 68501. M Ann Reinert, Library Dept Head
Holdings: Vols (100,000) Cat Maps Pix Microforms
Budget: ($200,000)
Notes: Primarily relating to Nebraska.
See also entry under Great Plains

NH —STRAWBERY BANKE, Thayer Cumings Historical Reference Library, Portsmouth, 03801. Nicole R Osborn, Librn
Holdings: Vols (2850) Cat Mss Maps Pix Microforms
Budget: ($1900)
Notes: The Library is a small, highly specialized library with holdings in American art, architecture and decorative arts. The collection is especially strong in the American decorative arts, with additional concentration in European decorative arts. In addition, the collection contains books on American painting, American architecture, archaeology, technology, maritime history and boatbuilding, landscape gardening and design, as well as books on local and regional history and social and material culture of the 17th-19th centuries. Collection of mss microfilm and documents is related to important properties and personages of Portsmouth and the surrounding area.

NJ —PRINCETON UNIVERSITY, Marquand Library, McCormick Hall, Princeton, 08544. Mary M Schmidt, Librn
Holdings: Vols (130,000) Cat Microforms
Notes: Especially strong in classical archaeology, medieval art and architecture, and photography history.

NJ —SETON HALL UNIVERSITY MUSEUM, Archaeological Research Center, S Orange Ave, South Orange, 07079. Herbert C Craft, Dir
Holdings: Vols (750) Cat
Notes: Primarily books and periodicals related to New Jersey and northeastern states prehistory and archaeology.

NM —AZTEC RUINS NATIONAL MONUMENT, Library, PO Box U, Aztec, 87410. William L Schart, Park Ranger
Holdings: Vols (500)// Cat Mss Maps Pix Slides
Notes: Archaeology of the Anasazi ruins.

NM —MUSEUM OF NEW MEXICO, Laboratory of Anthropology Library, PO Box 2087, Santa Fe, 87503. Laura Holt, Librn
Holdings: Vols (16,000) Cat Mss Maps
Notes: Southwestern archaeology, anthropology, ethnology. Noncirculating. Also incl the personal Library (2000 vols) of Sylvanus Morley, Meso-American archaeologist and historian. Some materials on Indians of Middle America.

NY —MUSEUM OF THE AMERICAN INDIAN, Library, 9 Westchester Square, Bronx, 10401. Mary B Davis, Librn
Holdings: Vols Cat
Notes: Incl information in Indians of North, Central, and South America; archaeology of North, Central, and South America; American Indian ethnology; anthropology, history.

NY —BUFFALO MUSEUM OF SCIENCE, Buffalo Society of Natural Sciences, Research Library, Humboldt Park, Buffalo, 14211. Marcia T Morrison, Chief Librn
Holdings: Vols 37,000 Cat Mss Pix
Notes: Natural sciences, anthropology, archaeology.

NY —CORNING MUSEUM OF GLASS LIBRARY, Corning, 14831. Norma P H Jenkins, Librn
Holdings: Vols (30,000) Cat Slides Videotapes Microforms
Notes: Extensive and comprehensive coverage of the art, archaeology, history and early manufacture of glass, with supporting materials in art, archaeology, and the decorative arts. Collection incl some 1800 manufacturers' trade catalogs on microfiche, 10,000 periodical vols and documents. 130 videotapes, 1000 microforms. Some incumabula. Research library primarily for use on the premises.

NY —AMERICAN NUMISMATIC SOCIETY LIBRARY, Broadway between 155 & 156 Sts, New York, 10032. Francis D Campbell Jr, Chief Librn
Holdings: Vols (50,000) Cat Mss Maps Pix Slides 16mm Films Microforms
Budget: ($6000)
Notes: Incl materials devoted to coins, medals, decorations, orders, tokens, paper money, seals, heraldry. Aids materials incl history, economic history, art history, archaeology, inscriptions and a number of encyclopedias and biographical dictionaries. Dictionary card catalog provides access to the materials: *Dictionary Catalogue of the Library of the American Numismatic* Society. (Boston: G K Hall, 1962). 6 vols and vol listing the auction catalogs in our collection; *First Supplement: 1962-1967;* Second Supplement: 1968-1972; Third Supplement: 1973-1977 (Boston: G K Hall, 1967, 1973, 1978). Noncirculating.

NY —EXPLORERS CLUB, James B Ford Memorial Library, 46 E 70 St, New York, 10021. Janet Baldwin, Librn
Holdings: Vols (24,000) Cat Maps
Notes: Additions to the collection depend upon gifts. Access by appointment only.

NY —METROPOLITAN MUSEUM OF ART, Thomas J Watson Library, Fifth Ave & 82 St, New York, 10028. William B Walker, Chief Librn
Holdings: Vols (250,000) Cat Mss Microforms
Notes: All fields of art: 1400 periodicals, incl bulletins and annual reports, catalogs, etc of American and foreign art societies, museums, etc; incl sales catalogs, exhibition catalogs, clipping file on individual artists and subjects, autograph letters. See *Library Catalog of the Metropolitan Museum of Art, New York,* second ed, rev and enl (Boston, G K Hall, 1980, 48 v and first supplement, 1982). Since 1980, holdings have been cataloged in RLIN.

NY —NEW YORK PUBLIC LIBRARY, Research Libraries, General Research Division, Fifth Ave & 42 St, New York, 10018. Rodney Phillips, Chief
Holdings: Vols (2,225,000) Cat Maps Pix Microforms
Budget: ($775,718)
Notes: Also strong in pictoral materials.

NY —NASSAU COUNTY MUSEUM, Sands Pt Preserve, Middleneck Rd, Sand Points, 11050.
Holdings: Vols (2500)
Notes: Collection contains almost every published reference on Long Island archaeology, ethnology, and geology, and incl most of those pertaining to the coastal New York area. Open by appointment. No photocopying.

NC —DUKE UNIVERSITY, William R Perkins Library, Rare Book Room, Durham, 27706. John L Sharpe, III, Cur
Notes: The Kanof collection of Judaic art contains more than 950 items on Jewish art, archaeology and symbolism.

NC —DUKE UNIVERSITY, Divinity School Library, Durham, 27706. Donn Michael Farris, Librn
Holdings: Vols (225,000)
Notes: Special collections and subject emphases in this library include: Archaeology, Egyptian; Archaeology, Middle Eastern; Art, Jewish; Bible; Bible-New Testament; Bible-Symbolism; Church Architecture; Egyptology; Fathers of the Church; Society of Friends; Great Britain-Religion-Methodism and Methodist Church; Hymns and Hymnals; Jansenists and Jansenism; Judaica; Mediaeval Christian Mysticism; Methodism and Methodist Church; Methodist Episcopal Church; Methodist Episcopal Church, South; Reformation; Religion-US-History; Rural Church; Theology-Great Britain-17th Century; Theology-Great Britain-18th Century; United Methodist Church; US-Church History; John Wesley.

NC —SOUTHEASTERN BAPTIST THEOLOGICAL SEMINARY LIBRARY, PO Box 752, Wake Forest, 27587. H Eugene McLeod, Librn
Holdings: Cat Maps Slides
Notes: Near Eastern archaeology related to biblical studies.

OH —CLEVELAND PUBLIC LIBRARY, History and Geography Department, 325 Superior Ave, Cleveland, 44114. JoAnn Petrello, Head
Holdings: Cat
Notes: General, exclusive of oriental archaeology in White Collection and biblical archaeology in the Social Sciences department. Especially strong in British and French archaeological serials.

OH —OHIO HISTORICAL SOCIETY, Archives Library Division, 1982 Velma Ave, Columbus, 43211. Dennis East, Division Chief
Holdings: Vols (96,000) Cat Mss Maps Pix Slides Microforms
Budget: ($18,000)
Notes: This library is the primary collection

ARCHAEOLOGY (cont.)

for Ohio. Most purchases are on the rare and op market. Collection area is early American history, esp relating to exploration into the Northwest Territory. Also, Ohio archaeology, natural history, and artifacts. Major media collections are books (96,000), newspapers (25,000 vols and 22,000 microfilm), pictures (50,000), maps (2500), manuscripts (1,500,000). Library is noncirculating except through interlibrary loan of microfilm.

OH —RUTHERFORD B HAYES LIBRARY, 1337 Hayes Ave, Fremont, 43420. Watt P Marchman, Dir
Holdings: Cat Mss
Notes: The Andrew E Douglass Collection. Index in collections; listed in *Guide to Manuscripts of the Ohio Historical Society*, 131.

OK —MUSEUM OF THE GREAT PLAINS, Research Center, 601 Ferris, PO Box 68, Lawton, 73502. Steve Wilson, Dir; Paula Williams, Special Collections
Notes: Anthropology; archaeology; ecology and history of Trans-Mississippi West, especially Great Plains. Reports and monographs of sites over Southern Plains.

†OR —LEWIS AND CLARK COLLEGE, Library, 615 SW Palatine Hill Rd, Portland, 97219.

PA —UNIVERSITY OF PENNSYLVANIA, University Museum Library, 33 & Spruce Sts, Philadelphia, 19104. Jean S Adelman, Librn
Holdings: Vols (80,000) Cat Microforms
Notes: World archaeology, with special emphasis on North and Central America, Egyptology, Sumerology, and the classical world. All holdings are listed in museum library catalog and are also listed in University of Pennsylvania main library (union) catalog.

PA —CARNEGIE LIBRARY OF PITTSBURGH, Science & Technology Dept, 4400 Forbes Ave, Pittsburgh, 15213. Catherine M Brosky, Dept Head
Notes: Of secondary interest in acquisitions because of the department's role in cooperating with Pittsburgh institutions and others across the Commonwealth in sharing resources, the cooperative acquisition of materials, and the provision of services and information. However, some aspects of the subject are emphasized. There are separate entries for each of these specialities in this vol.

PA —UNIVERSITY OF PITTSBURGH, Hillman Library, Pittsburgh, 15260. Glenora E Rossell, Head
Holdings: Vols 3695 Cat Microforms
Notes: The collection is very strong in pre-Columbian archaeology and Indian cultures from the historical and anthropological point of view. Emphasis on contemporary history, politics and socio-economical problems.

PA —UNIVERSITY OF PITTSBURGH, Henry Clay Frick Fine Arts Library, Pittsburgh, 15260. Anne W Gordon, Fine Arts Librn
Holdings: Vols (55,000) Cat Pix Slides Microforms
Notes: Emphasis is on the art of the Western World--architecture, sculpture, painting, minor arts, archaeology, with special strength in the Byzantine, early Christian, medieval, renaissance and modern periods. The Oriental field is represented, incl replicas of scrolls. Studio arts are also covered. Illuminated ms facsimiles. Extensive collections of slides and photographs for study of art history are available in the building but not administered by the art library.

SC —UNIVERSITY OF SOUTH CAROLINA, Institute of Archaeology and Anthropology, Research Report Library, Maxcy College, Columbia, 29208. Kenn Pinson, Ms Archivist
Holdings: Mss Maps Pix Slides
Notes: Reports of research performed by the Institute of Archeology and Anthropology. Incl four series: the *Institute of Archeology and Anthropology Notebook; Research Manuscript Series*; and *Anthropological Studies, Popular Series*. Partially cataloged.

SC —UNIVERSITY OF SOUTH CAROLINA, Thomas Cooper Library, Columbia, 29208. Kenneth E Toombs, Dir of Libraries; Roger Mortimer, Rare Book Librn
Holdings: Vols 500 Cat
Notes: Particularly strong in landmark titles published in the 18th and 19th centuries.

TN —CHUCALISSA MUSEUM, 1987 Indian Village Dr, Memphis, 38109. Gerald P Smith, Cur
Holdings: Vols (1100) Cat Mss
Budget: ($200)
Notes: Collection emphasizes midsouth archaeology, but incl some regional ethnographic and geological titles. Noncirculating.

TX —SOUTHERN METHODIST UNIVERSITY, DeGolyer Library, Box 396, SMU, Dallas, 75275. Clifton H Jones, Dir
Holdings: Vols (80,000) Cat Mss Maps Pix Slides Microforms
Notes: First editions of prominent authors; also of books in subject emphasis collections. All subjects listed in this vol are strong. Numerous collections of personal papers relating to subjects also.

UT —UNIVERSITY OF UTAH, Marriott Library, Special Collections, Salt Lake City, 84112. Gregory C Thompson, Cur
Notes: Utah and the West.

WI —MILWAUKEE PUBLIC MUSEUM, Reference Library, 800 W Wells St, Milwaukee, 53233. Judith Campbell Turner, Museum Librn
Holdings: Vols (90,000) Cat Maps Microforms

MB —ESKIMO MUSEUM, Library, Box 10, Churchill, R0B 0E0, Can. Brother J Volant, Cur
Holdings: Vols (300) Cat
Notes: Books on the North, mainly northern Canada; explorers' journals; Eskimo ethnology, archaeology, and art.

ON —NATIONAL MUSEUMS OF CANADA, Library Services Directorate, Ottawa, K1A 0M8, Can. Valerie Monkhouse, Director
Holdings: Vols (70,000) Cat Mss Maps Pix Slides Microforms
Budget: ($60,000)
Notes: Collection includes anthropology, archaeology, ethnology, folklore, history, Indians of North America, Inuit, linguistics of North American Indians, material history, military and naval history, museology. Research collection, interlibrary loans available, public may use on the premises.

ON —UNIVERSITY OF OTTAWA, Morisset Library, 65 Hastey St, Ottawa, K1N 9A5, Can. Yvon Richer, University Chief Librn
Holdings: Vols (17,000)
Notes: Incl monographs and 173 cataloged sets of periodicals. Only a small portion of this material is housed in Special Collections, but it is one of the strongest elements of our regular collection. Additional support, particularly in archaeology, philosophy and religion is also available at the affiliated St Paul University, 223 Main Street, Ottawa.

ON —ROYAL ONTARIO MUSEUM, Main Library and Archives, 100 Queen's Park, Toronto, M5S 2C6, Can. Julia Matthews, Head Librn
Holdings: Vols (85,000) Cat
Notes: Since January 1977, acquisitions have been entered in UTLAS.

ARCHAEOLOGY, BIBLICAL see Bible—Antiquities

ARCHAEOLOGY, CHRISTIAN see Christian Antiquities

ARCHAEOLOGY, CLASSICAL see Classical Antiquities

ARCHAEOLOGY, MARINE see Marine Archaeology

ARCHAEOLOGY PERIODICALS see Periodicals, Archaeological

ARCHER, FRED

CA —LOS ANGELES PUBLIC LIBRARY, Frances Howard Goldwyn Hollywood Regional Library, 1623 Ivar Ave, Los Angeles, 90028. Sally Dumaux, Librn
Holdings: Vols (100,000) Cat Mss Pix VF
Budget: ($60,000)
Notes: A general and a research collection covering motion pictures, radio broadcasting, and television. Over 2000 motion picture and television scripts. Biographical information on actors and actresses. Casts, credits, and other production information on over 1500 motion pictures from the 1920s to the present. Collections also include posters, lobby cards, souvenir programs, scrapbooks, vertical files, and over 3000 publicity stills. Including the following Special Collections: Fred Archer Collection, photographs, including the Hunchback of Notre Dame (1923), and personalities of the stage and screen, 1907-1930; Gilbert A Adrian, designer, sketches and photographs; Hazel Flynn, publicist, correspondence and photographs.

ARCHERY

CT —YALE UNIVERSITY, Box 1603A, Yale Station, New Haven, 06520.

DC —LIBRARY OF CONGRESS, Washington, 20540.

MA —UNIVERSITY OF MASSACHUSETTS AT AMHERST, Library, Amherst, 01002.

MA —HARVARD UNIVERSITY LIBRARY, Cambridge, 02138.

NY —NEW YORK PUBLIC LIBRARY, Research Libraries, General Research Division, Fifth Ave & 42 St, New York, 10018. Rodney Phillips, Chief

ARCHITECTS

AZ —NORTHERN ARIZONA UNIVERSITY, Special Collection Library, CU Box 6022, Flagstaff, 86011. Peter M Whiteley, Coordr/Archivist; William Mullane, Librn
Notes: Paul Schweikher Collection of original renderings and working drawings, from one of the most well-known of the Chicago architects. Schweikher was formerly head of the Architecture Departments at Yale and Carnegie-Mellon Universities. The collection is extensive and features most of his architectural drawings ever executed.

CA —CALIFORNIA STATE UNIVERSITY, LONG BEACH, Library, Dept of Special Collections & Archives, 1250 Bellflower Blvd, Long Beach, 90840. John Ahouse, Special Collections Librn
Holdings: Mss Phonorecords Audiotapes
Notes: Almost all of the papers, recordings, etc, published and unpublished, of Gerald V Strang.

CA —CALIFORNIA POLYTECHNIC STATE UNIVERSITY LIBRARY, Special Collections and University Archives, San Luis Obispo, 93407. Nancy E Loe, Head Librn
Holdings: Vols (100) Cat
Notes: Herpersonal papers covering her architectural career of forty years, which incl several Hearst estates as well as private residences in the California Arts and Crafts style. Incl Hearst/Morgan correspondence and telegrams; business correspondence, travel accounts, sketchbooks, awards, photographs and several hundred architectural drawings. Hearst Castle Collection incl 8500 architectural drawings for Hearst's residences at San Simeon, Jolon, Wyntoon, and Santa Monica and approx 100 vols of secondary source material. The Asilomar Collection contains 145 architectural drawings for the Morgan-designed YWCA facility near Monterey, California. Incl blueprints, diplomas, personal papers. Finding aid in progress. Incl 10,000 pieces of ms material, 10,000 architectural drawings and blueprints.

CA —STANFORD UNIVERSITY LIBRARIES, Cecil H Green Library, Stanford, 94305. Michael T Ryan, Cur

CT —YALE UNIVERSITY, Box 1603A, Yale Station, New Haven, 06520.
Holdings: Cat Pix
Notes: Yale architectural archives.

DC —GEORGETOWN UNIVERSITY, Library, Special Collections Div, 37 & O Sts

ARCHITECTS (cont.)

NW, Washington, 20057. George M Barringer, Special Collections Librn; Nicholas B Sheetz, Mss Librn
Holdings: Mss Cat Maps Pix
Notes: The Eric F Menke Collection. Incl the papers of the landscape architect Eric F Menke (1901-1980), and a large collection of mms, documents, and photographs pertaining to the history of Washington, DC. Also, the family archives of Richard X Evans incl papers of Robert Mills (1781-1855), architect.

IL —CHICAGO HISTORICAL SOCIETY, Library, Clark St at North Ave, Chicago, 60614. Archie Motley, Manuscript Librn
Notes: Chicago Architectural Archive contains the papers of Chicago architects Barry Byrne and Earl H Reed, the records of the Illinois Society of Architects, and the voluminous files of two leading Chicago architectural firms, Holabird & Root and Harry M Weese and Associates. Access to these collections is by arrangement with Frank Jewell, The Society's Curator of Architectural Collections.

IL —NORTHWESTERN UNIVERSITY, Library, Special Collections Dept, 1937 Sheridan Rd, Evanston, 60201. R Russell Maylone, Cur
Holdings: Vols 150 Cat Mss Pix
Notes: Works by and about Frank Lloyd Wright, with blueprints, letters, drawings, photographs, clippings, ephemera and mss.

IN —INDIANA HISTORICAL SOCIETY, Library, 315 W Ohio St, Indianapolis, 46202. Robert K O'Neill, Dir
Holdings: Vols Cat Mss Pix Microforms
Notes: Records and drawings of Indiana architects, contractors, and as well as records concerning structures created by non-Indiana professionals within the state. Types of material collected incl office files, correspondence, drawings, blueprints, photographs, personal papers, specifications, books and pamphlets. The collection incl approximately 14,000 drawings, along with another 10,000 on microfilm, from central Indiana architectural firms. Incl among the drawings are approximately 800 for Union Station, Indianapolis.

MA —SOCIETY FOR THE PRESERVATION OF NEW ENGLAND ANTIQUITIES, Library, 141 Cambridge St, Boston, 02114. Ellie Reichlin, Librn & Cur of Photographic Collections
Holdings: Vols (3000) // Cat Pix Microforms
Budget: ($75,000)
Notes: Architecture of the Northeast. Drawings (original designs); measured drawings; plot plans, etc. Over 7500 items, incl extensive collections of original designs by Ogden Codman, Jr (1890s-early 1900s); Arthur Little and Herbert Browne (1890s-1920s); Luther Briggs (1840s-1860s); Arland Dirlam (1930s-1960s), together with important examples of the work of Asher Benjamin, Richard Upjohn, and others. Measured drawings incl extensive holdings of work undertaken by HABS (Historic American Buildings Survey) in Massachusetts in the 1930s, 1940s under director Frank Chouteau Brown. Also represented are several residential and commercial commissions by F C Brown, not connected with HABS. Collection incl architectural pattern books, builders guides, 18th-19th century. Approx 350 volumes, English and American publications. Architectural drawings by approx 275 architects are in the collections. Architects represented, in addition to the ones named above, include Donald Millar,Thomas T Waterman, Norman Isham, John H Sturgis, and Gridley J F Bryant.

MA —MASSACHUSETTS INSTITUTE OF TECHNOLOGY, Institute Archives, Special Collections, Cambridge, 02139.
Notes: Papers of Howe, Manning and Almy, an architectural firm that started in 1913 as Lois Lilley Howe and Manning, was an unusual and successful partnership of women architects. The collection incl correspondence, financial data, reports, specifications, photographs, blueprints, drawings, and research material from the firm. Housing projects incl Mariemont, Ohio, as well as designs and renovations for New England especially in the Colonial Revival style. In addition, papers of William Robert Ware, architect and founder of MIT's School of Architecture and Urban Planning, the first such architectural training program in the United States. Incl unfinished biography of Ware. Unpublished finding aid, incl a correspondent index, available in the Institute Archives.

NV —UNIVERSITY OF NEVADA, RENO, University Library, Special Collections Dept, Reno, 89557. Robert E Blesse, Head
Holdings: Cat Mss Pix Drawings
Notes: Approximately 15,000 drawings, along with papers and photographs of three major Nevada architects. Frederic DeLongchamps, 1882-1969, was Nevada's most important for the first half of the 20th century designing many major public buildings. Edward S Parsons, Nevada's most prolific architect, did over 725 jobs between 1935 and 1983. Hewitt Wells designed the Washoe County Library, an internationally known building. These collections constitute the major holdings of the Nevada Architectural Archives.

NM —UNIVERSITY OF NEW MEXICO, Zimmerman Library, Albuquerque, 87131.
Holdings: Mss Pix
Notes: Entire professional library and archives of John Gaw Meem, architect of the Southwest. Incl pictures of many buildings taken by noted photographers.

NY —LANDMARK SOCIETY OF WESTERN NEW YORK, Wenrich Memorial Library, 130 Spring Rd, Rochester, 14608.
Holdings: Vols (2000) Cat Maps Pix Slide
Budget: ($500)
Notes: Paintings, slides, drawings, as well as the Society's archives of local architecture and information on preservation and restoration techniques. Much on preservation ordinances; legal, physical and financial aspects of building preservation; local and regional history especially of Rochester and Monroe County.

NY —UNIVERSITY OF ROCHESTER, Rush Rhees Library, Department of Rare Books and Special Collections, Rochester, 14627. Peter Dzwonkoski, Librn
Holdings: Cat Mss Pix
Notes: Claude Fayette Bragdon, 1866-1946. Correspondence, diaries, notebooks, scrapbooks, sketchbooks, posters, stage designs and architectural drawings. Some correspondence and all architectural drawings indexed. Unpublished guide. Also plans and drawings in other collections including Ellwanger and Barry Co Papers.

NC —UNIVERSITY OF NORTH CAROLINA, CHARLOTTE, J Murrey Atkins Library, UNCC Station, Charlotte, 28223. Robert F Brabham Jr, Special Collections Librn
Holdings: Cat Mss Pix
Notes: Papers of Charlotte, NC-area architects.

OR —UNIVERSITY OF OREGON LIBRARY, Special Collections Div, Eugene, 97403. Kenneth W Duckett, Curator
Holdings: Cat Mss
Notes: Over 30 mss collections of drawings and project files representing primarily Oregon architects, but also some architects outside the region, incl Paul Wiener, Herbert Congdon, Richard Smythe, and Auguste Noel. There are also collections of artists who specialized in architectural renderings, such as Louis Rosenberg, George T Plowman, and Claude R Butcher.
Publication: Martin Schmitt, comp, *Catalogue of Manuscripts in the University of Oregon Library* (Eugene: University of Oregon Books, 1971).
See also entry under Artists, American

SC —COLLEGE OF CHARLESTON LIBRARY, Special Collections Dept, Charleston, 29401.
Notes: Middleton Family Papers, 1809-1867 incl 34 architectural sketches and plans of Thomas Walker (1809), John Izard Middleton (1811), and William Middleton (1864); a color wheel and two maps, one of New England and the other of the Middle Atlantic States, drawn by Henry Middleton, Jr (1867).

TX —EL PASO PUBLIC LIBRARY, Southwest Collection, 501 N Oregon, El Paso, 79901. Mary A Sarber, Head
Holdings: Vols 12,000 Cat Mss Maps Pix Microforms
Budget: $11,000
Notes: 400 sets of architectural plans by El Paso firms of Trost and Trost, Percy McGhee, Frazer and Benner. Partial catalog of Trost and Trost buildings. See Engelbrecht, Lloyd C, and Engelbrecht, June-Marie F, *Henry C Trost: Architect of the Southwest* (El Paso Public Library Association, 1981).

AB —UNIVERSITY OF CALGARY, Libraries, Special Collections Div, 2500 University Dr, Calgary, T2N 1N4, Can.
Holdings: Cat Mss Pix Audiotapes 16mm Films Microforms
Notes: The Canadian Architectural Archives at the University of Calgary include collections of drawings, records, sketches, renderings, correspondence, project files of the following Canadian architects (qv separate entries): Raymond T Affleck, J Francis Brown and F Bruce Brown, J A Cawston, Arthur C Erickson, Long Mayell & Associates, Hugh McMillan Architects Ltd, Raymond Moriyama, John B Parkin Associates/NORR, Rule Wynn & Rule (Edmonton and Calgary). Stevenson Raines Barrett Hutton Seton & Partners, The Thom Partnership, Thompson Berwick Pratt & Partners, and H M Whiddington. Dates from 1891 to about 1974. The Archives also incl photographs, microfilmed material (16mm and 35mm, film strip and aperture cards), and Oral History Interviews on tape. Project lists and/or inventories are on hand.

ARCHITECTS, ALBERTA ASSOCIATION OF see Alberta Association of Architects

ARCHITECTURAL DESIGN see Architecture—Details

ARCHITECTURAL DESIGNS see Architecture—Designs and Plans

ARCHITECTURAL DETAILS see Architecture—Details

ARCHITECTURAL DRAWINGS

CA —CALIFORNIA POLYTECHNIC STATE UNIVERSITY LIBRARY, Special Collections and University Archives, San Luis Obispo, 93407. Nancy E Loe, Head Librn
Holdings: Vols (100) Cat
Notes: Herpersonal papers covering her architectural career of forty years, which incl several Hearst estates as well as private residences in the California Arts and Crafts style. Incl Hearst/Morgan correspondence and telegrams; business correspondence, travel accounts, sketchbooks, awards, photographs and several hundred architectural drawings. Hearst Castle Collection incl 8500 architectural drawings for Hearst's residences at San Simeon, Jolon, Wyntoon, and Santa Monica and approx 100 vols of secondary source material. The Asilomar Collection contains 145 architectural drawings for the Morgan-designed YWCA facility near Monterey, California. Incl blueprints, diplomas, personal papers. Finding aid in progress. Incl 10,000 pieces of ms material, 10,000 architectural drawings and blueprints.

CT —YALE UNIVERSITY, Box 1603A, Yale Station, New Haven, 06520.
Holdings: Cat Pix

DC —LIBRARY OF CONGRESS, Prints & Photographs Div, Washington, 20540.
Notes: Drawings by the Washington, DC architectural firm, Waggaman and Ray, early

ARCHITECTURAL DRAWINGS (cont.)

20th century. Contains presentation drawings, working sketches, renderings of structural and mechanical details, blueprints, and a small number of photographs and letters pertaining to 400 different projects. Incl 16,000 items.

DC —LIBRARY OF CONGRESS, Prints and Photographs Div, Historic American Buildings Survey, Washington, 20540.
Holdings: Cat Mss Pix Drawings
Notes: Details of some 17,000 American buildings in 81,000 photographs, 42,000 measured drawings and 44,000 pp of written documentation.

LA —TULANE UNIVERSITY, Howard-Tilton Memorial Library, Southeast Architectural Archives, 7001 Freret St, New Orleans, 70118. William R Cullison, Cur of Prints & Drawings
Notes: Southeast Architectural Archives Collection incl over 30,000 individual pieces. Drawings were made mostly by New Orleans practitioners, mostly for locations in and about the city; there are, however, some drawings by architects from outside New Orleans and some for buildings located elsewhere. Collection dates from about 1800 to the present day, with the majority of pieces falling between about 1835-1965.

MA —SOCIETY FOR THE PRESERVATION OF NEW ENGLAND ANTIQUITIES, Library, 141 Cambridge St, Boston, 02114. Ellie Reichlin, Librn & Cur of Photographic Collections
Holdings: Vols (3000) / / Cat Pix Microforms
Budget: ($75,000)
Notes: Architecture of the Northeast. Drawings (original designs); measured drawings; plot plans, etc. Over 7500 items, incl extensive collections of original designs by Ogden Codman, Jr (1890s-early 1900s); Arthur Little and Herbert Browne (1890s-1920s); Luther Briggs (1840s-1860s); Arland Dirlam (1930s-1960s), together with important examples of the work of Asher Benjamin, Richard Upjohn, and others. Measured drawings incl extensive holdings of work undertaken by HABS (Historic American Buildings Survey) in Massachusetts in the 1930s, 1940s under director Frank Chouteau Brown. Also represented are several residential and commercial commissions by F C Brown, not connected with HABS. Collection incl architectural pattern books, builders guides, 18th-19th century. Approx 350 volumes, English and American publications.

MT —MONTANA STATE UNIVERSITY, Library, Bozeman, 59717. Minnie Ellen Paugh, Special Collections Librn
Notes: 1500 drawing sets of Montana public and private buildings from the business files of architects: Link and Haire, Edwin G Osness, E F Link and Associates, John DeHass and Montana State Board of Architects.

NV —UNIVERSITY OF NEVADA, RENO, University Library, Special Collections Dept, Reno, 89557. Robert E Blesse, Head
Holdings: Cat Mss Pix
Notes: Approximately 15,000 drawings, along with papers and photographs of three major Nevada architects. Frederic DeLongchamps, 1882-1969, was Nevada's most important for the first half of the 20th century designing many major public buildings. Edward S Parsons, Nevada's most prolific architect, did over 725 jobs between 1935 and 1983. Hewitt Wells designed the Washoe County Library, an internationally known building. These collections constitute the major holdings of the Nevada Architectural Archives.

NY —COLUMBIA UNIVERSITY LIBRARIES, Avery Architectural and Fine Arts Library, 201 Avery Hall, New York, 10027. Angela Giral, Librn
Notes: Original drawings by architects or photographs of such architectural drawnings.

NY —STATE UNIVERSITY OF NEW YORK, COLLEGE AT PLATTSBURGH, Feinberg Library, Special Collections, 153 Hawkins Hall, Plattsburgh, 12901. Joseph G Swinyer, Librn
Holdings: Cat Mss Maps
See also entry under New York (State) - History

NY —LANDMARK SOCIETY OF WESTERN NEW YORK, Wenrich Memorial Library, 130 Spring Rd, Rochester, 14608.
Holdings: Vols (2000) Cat Maps Pix Slides
Budget: ($500)
Notes: Paintings, slides, drawings, as well as the Society's archives of local architecture and information on preservation and restoration techniques. Much on preservation ordinances; legal, physical and financial aspects of building preservation; local and regional history, especially of Rochester and Monroe County.

OR —UNIVERSITY OF OREGON LIBRARY, Architecture & Allied Arts Branch, Eugene, 97403. Reyburn R McCready, Head Librn
Holdings: Vols (35,000) Cat Pix Slides
Budget: ($57,000)
Notes: Incl 200,000 slides and student renderings on architecture and the arts, incl sculpture, painting, furniture, interior architecture, graphic arts, landscape, art history and art education.

OR —UNIVERSITY OF OREGON LIBRARY, Special Collections Div, Eugene, 97403. Kenneth W Duckett, Curator
Holdings: Cat Mss
Notes: Over 30 mss collections of drawings and project files representing primarily Oregon architects, but also some architects outside the region, incl Paul Wiener, Herbert Congdon, Richard Smythe, and Auguste Noel. There are also collections of artists who specialized in architectural renderings, such as Louis Rosenberg, George T Plowman, and Claude R Butcher.
Publication: Martin Schmitt, comp, *Catalogue of Manuscripts in the University of Oregon Library* (Eugene: University of Oregon Books, 1971).
See also entry under Artists, American

PA —PENNSYLVANIA DIV OF ARCHIVES & MANUSCRIPTS, State Archives, PO Box 1026, Harris, 17108. Roland M Baumann, Chief, History & Museums
Holdings: Vols (3000) / / Uncat Mss Maps Pix
Budget: ($40,000)
Notes: The Harmony Society (1785-1905), a German communistic and spiritual community, which immigrated to the US in 1805 and established their community in Harmony, Pennsylvania, moved to New Harmony, Indiana, and returned to Pennsylvania to set up the town of Economy, 20 miles north of Pittsburgh on the Ohio River. The Harmonists had a vast impact on the economy of the areas in which they lived. They were involved in agriculture, manufacturing and investing. 300,000 cu ft.
See also entry under Harmony Society and Harmonists.

WA —UNIVERSITY OF WASHINGTON LIBRARIES, Pacific Northwest Collection, Seattle, 98195. Andrew F Johnson, Librn
Holdings: Vols (50,000) Cat Maps Pix
Budget: ($12,000)
Notes: The Pacific Northwest Collection contains printed materials documenting the historic and contemporary life and culture of the region in a broad range of subject areas. The Pacific Northwest is defined as the geographic region including Washington, Oregon, Idaho, Montana, British Columbia, Yukon Territory, and Alaska. Printed materials including books, periodicals, government documents, maps, weekly and local regional newspapers, theses and dissertations, as well as photographs and architectural drawings are included in the Pacific Northwest Collection. Photographic works of over 200 photographers active in the Pacific Northwest, Alaska, and the Yukon Territory (Canada) during the period 1860-1930, including Asahel and Edward S Curtis, Eric Hegg, and Clark Kinsey, are represented in a print collection of more than 300,000 images. The architecturaldrawings collection includes over 19,000 original plans, drawings, sketches, renderings and blue prints pertaining to the history of architecture and urban planning and landscape gardening in the Pacific Northwest ca 1880-1940. Areas of particular strength are the holdings of over 1100 published journals of Pacific Northwest exploration expeditions, photographs of Northwest Coast Native Americans and of historic Seattle, newspapers issued within the Japanese-American relocation camps, 1942-1945, materials relating to the 1980 eruption of Mt St Helens, and Sanborne fire insurance maps for Washington. A unique feature of the Collection is the subject index to regional periodicals and local newspapers maintained by the PNW Collection staff; over 100 titles are currently indexed. G K Hall Company published a books catalog of the Pacific Northwest Collectionin 1973.

AB —UNIVERSITY OF CALGARY, Libraries, Special Collections Div, 2500 University Dr, Calgary, T2N 1N4, Can.
Holdings: Cat Mss Pix Audiotapes 16mm Films Microforms
Notes: The Canadian Architectural Archives at the University of Calgary include collections of drawings, records, sketches, renderings, correspondence, project files of the following Canadian architects (qv separate entries): Raymond T Affleck, J Francis Brown and F Bruce Brown, J A Cawston, Arthur C Erickson, Long Mayell & Associates, Hugh McMillan Architects Ltd, Raymond Moriyama, John B Parkin Associates/NORR, Rule Wynn & Rule (Edmonton and Calgary), Stevenson Raines Barrett Hutton Seton & Partners, The Thom Partnership, Thompson Berwick Pratt & Partners, and H M Whiddington. Dates from 1891 to about 1974. The Archives also incl photographs, microfilmed material (16mm and 35mm, film strip and aperture cards), and Oral History Interviews on tape. Project lists and/or inventories are on hand. Mss (2000 meters) and 400,000 audiotapes.

BC —UNIVERSITY OF VICTORIA, Maltwood Art Museum & Gallery, Finnerty Rd, Victoria, V8W 2Y2, Can. Martin Segger, Dir/Cur
Holdings: Vols 700
Notes: The Museum maintains a special archival collection of architectural plans and drawings, mainly of regional historic interest. Its library and archives are now housed and administered by the McPherson Library, University of Victoria.

ON —UNIVERSITY OF TORONTO, Thomas Fisher Rare Book Library, 120 Saint George St, Toronto, M5S 1A5, Can. Richard G Landon, Head
Notes: All currently published and most earlier major works on the fine and applied arts in Canada; Canadian art exhibition catalogues; limited editions illustrated by Canadian artists; 19th and 20th century architectural plans for buildings in Toronto and southern Ontario vicinity (ca 1700).

ARCHITECTURAL ENGINEERING

DC —LIBRARY OF CONGRESS, Prints and Photographs Div, Historic American Buildings Survey, Washington, 20540.
Holdings: Pix
Notes: Historic American Engineering Record, which has recorded 870 American engineering sites in 1500 sheets of measured drawings, 10,000 photographs, and 6,000 pages of written documentation.

NY —ENGINEERING SOCIETIES LIBRARY, 345 E 47 St, New York, 10017. S Kirk Cabeen, Dir
Holdings: Vols 250,000 Cat Maps 16mm Films Microforms
Notes: One of the largest, most comprehensive engineering libraries in the world. Covers all engineering disciplines; particularly strong in electrical and electronic, mechanical, mining and metallurgical, petroleum, chemical, industrial, air conditioning and refrigeration engineering. Incl Wheeler Collection of early materials on magnetism and electricity. 125,

ARCHITECTURAL ENGINEERING (cont.)

000 bound periodical volumes; 10,000 maps; 5000 serial subscriptions (many foreign-language). Virtually all materials abstracted in *Engineering Index* (1884-date) are incl in Library. Noncirculating, except to members of professional engineering societies which support the Library. See *Engineering Societies Library, New York, classed Subject Catalog and Index* (Boston: G K Hall, 1963); and *Supplements*, 1-10, 1964-1973.

PA —PENNSYLVANIA STATE UNIVERSITY, Engineering Library, 325 Hammond St, University Park, 16802. Tom Conkling, Librn
Holdings: Vols (60,000) Microforms
Notes: This collection includes substantial microform holdings and extensive runs of periodicals.

TX —UNIVERSITY OF TEXAS LIBRARIES, Richard W McKinney Engineering Library, 1.3 ECJ, Austin, 78712. Susan B Ardis, Librn
Holdings: Vols (83,548) Cat Microforms
Notes: Highway (transportation) engineering.

WI —MILWAUKEE SCHOOL OF ENGINEERING, Library, 500 E Kilbourn Ave, PO Box 644, Milwaukee, 53201. Mary Ann Schmidt, Head Librn
Holdings: Vols (34,500) Cat
Budget: ($215,800)

ARCHITECTURAL INSTITUTE OF CANADA, ROYAL see Royal Architectural Institute of Canada

ARCHITECTURAL PERIODICALS see Periodicals, Architectural

ARCHITECTURE

AL —AUBURN UNIVERSITY, Architecture & Fine Arts Library, Dudley Hall, Auburn, 36830. Larry Stafford, Librn
Holdings: Vols (18,000) Cat Mss Slides
Notes: Incl 30,000 slides.

AZ —ARIZONA STATE UNIVERSITY, Howe Architecture Library, Tempe, 85281.
Holdings: Vols 17,000 Cat Microforms

CA —UNIVERSITY OF CALIFORNIA, BERKELEY, Environmental Design Library, (The General Library), 210 Wurster Hall, Berkeley, 94720. Arthur B Waugh, Head
Holdings: Vols (90,000) Cat Pix Microforms
Budget: ($17,400)
Notes: A research collection devoted to the following aspects of the field of architecture: working details, drawing, theory, standards and professional practice; building materials, building types, earthquake resistant architecture, contemporary architecture of all countries, history of architecture, and architecture as a profession. A small rare book collection in the field of architecture is maintained. Approximately 1500 serials, incl many foreign-language titles, are currently being received. A collection of photographs (of buildings) and a slide collection are administered by the department of architecture.

†CA —WED ENTERPRISES, Research Library, 1401 Flower St, Glendale, 91201.
Notes: Popular art and architecture journals, pictorial material. Library is not open to the public.

CA —CALIFORNIA STATE UNIVERSITY, LONG BEACH, Library, Dept of Special Collections & Archives, 1250 Bellflower Blvd, Long Beach, 90840. John Ahouse, Special Collections Librn
Holdings: Mss Phonorecords Audiotapes
Notes: Almost all of the papers, recordings, etc, published and unpublished, of Gerald V Strang.

CA —UNIVERSITY OF CALIFORNIA, LOS ANGELES, Architecture & Urban Planning Library, 1302 Architecture Bldg, Los Angeles, 90024. Jon S Greene, Librn
Holdings: Vols (18,000) Cat
Budget: ($30,000)

CA —COGSWELL COLLEGE, Library, 600 Stockton St, San Francisco, 94108. Judith Carson-Croes, Dir
Holdings: Vols (12,000) Cat

CA —ESHERICK, HOMSEY, DODGE & DAVIS, Library, 2789 25th St, San Francisco, 94110. Elizabeth Walton, Librn
Holdings: Vols (2500) Cat Maps Pix Slides
Notes: General history of architecture; solar energy applications to architecture; residential architecture; zoo architecture; handbooks, codes, and standards; school and university architecture. Also incl is a large collection of product literature catalogs and samples (uncataloged).

CA —UNIVERSITY OF CALIFORNIA, SANTA BARBARA, Library, Dept of Special Collections, Santa Barbara, 93106. Christian F Brun, Head
Holdings: Vols (95,980) Cat Mss
Notes: The Pearl Chase Collections of Community Development and Conservation. Papers of outstanding California leaders in conservation, community planning, Indian affairs, national parks.

CA —UNIVERSITY OF CALIFORNIA, SANTA CRUZ, University Library, Special Collections, Santa Cruz, 95064. Rita Bottoms, Special Collections Librn; Margaret Felts, South Pacific Collection Bibliographer
Notes: General circulation.

CO —UNIVERSITY OF COLORADO, Libraries, Art & Architecture Library, Campus Box 184, Boulder, 80309. Liesel Nolan, Librn/Dept Head
Holdings: Vols (57,657) Cat Pix
Budget: ($39,000)
Notes: Special feature: art exhibition catalog collection 1963-1971, 1972-date. Good general collection with some special emphasis on environmental design, Islamic architecture, Indian art and South American Indian art. Fair collection of periodical backfiles in art and in architecture. Separate catalog for materials in collection. Rare books in main library, listed only in central union catalog.

CT —STOWE-DAY LIBRARY, 77 Forest St, Hartford, 06105. Diana J Royce, Librn
Holdings: Vols (15,000) Cat Mss Pix
Notes: 150,000 cataloged mss and publications concerning architecture, decorative arts, history and literature of the period 1840-1900, with emphasis on Nook Farm, Mark Twain, Harriet Beecher Stowe, Calvin E Stowe, Charles Dudley Warner, William Hooker Gillette, Isabella Beecher Hooker. Incl 5000 pictures.

CT —TRINITY COLLEGE LIBRARY, Watkinson Library, 300 Summit St, Hartford, 06106. Jeffrey Kaimowitz, Cur
Holdings: Vols 600 Cat
Notes: Incl J Cleveland Cady Collection.

DC —AMERICAN INSTITUTE OF ARCHITECTS, Library, 1735 New York Ave, Washington, 20006. Stephanie C Byrnes, Librn
Holdings: Vols (22,000) Cat Mss Pix Slides Microforms
Notes: Emphasis of current acquisitions is on American architecture and its practice. Incl the library of R M Hunt and considerable other material. Photocopying.

DC —NATIONAL ENDOWMENT FOR THE ARTS, Library, 1100 Pen Ave NW, Rm 213, Washington, 20506. Christine Morrison, Arts Librn
Holdings: Vols (6000) Cat
Notes: Incl arts and education and public policy in the arts.

DC —URBAN LAND INSTITUTE, Library, 1090 Vermont Ave, Washington, 20005. Ann Benson, Librn
Holdings: Vols (9000) Cat
Budget: ($6000)
Notes: Incl 200 serials.

GA —GEORGIA INSTITUTE OF TECHNOLOGY, Price Gilbert Memorial Library, 225 North Ave, Atlanta, 30332. Edward Graham Roberts, Dir
Holdings: Vols ($1,661,559) Cat Maps Slides Microforms
Budget: ($1,383,302)
Notes: Incl (4,307,996) patents and (568, 490) government documents.

IL —UNIVERSITY OF ILLINOIS, URBANA/CHAMPAIGN, Library, Ricker Library of Architecture & Art, 208 Architecture Bldg, 608 East Lorado Taft Dr, Champaign, 61820. Dee Wallace, Architecture & Art Librn
Holdings: Vols (46,873) Cat Pix
Budget: $24,400
Notes: Incl 32,901 mounted photos and reproductions. Cataloged. Also incl noncirculating collection of exhibition catalogs.

IL —CHICAGO PUBLIC LIBRARY, Art Section, Fine Arts Division, 78 E Washington St, Chicago, 60602. Rosalinda I Hack, Fine Arts Division Chief; Yvonne S Brown, Head, Art Section
Holdings: Vols 6000
Notes: Reference and circulating collection, with special emphasis on general architectural history, modern architecture, architecture of the United States, and Chicago architectural history. Collection is supported by the Chicago Architecture File, a card file that lists citations to information on buildings that have been recognized for their architectural significance. The section's picture collection has extensive documentation on Chicago area architecture, and incorporates a collection of architectural photographs by Stephen Beal. Archival copies of these photographs are to be found in Special Collections. The collection is also supplemented by the microform collections of *The Historic American Buildings Survey*, and *American Architectural Books*.

IL —LESTER B KNIGHT & ASSOCIATES, Library, 549 W Randolph St, Chicago, 60606. Clarita M Generao, Librn
Holdings: Vols (10,000) Cat Maps Slides
Notes: Collection is both technical and nontechnical; inc reports of the studies for our client companies, which incl European firms.

IL —NORTHBROOK PUBLIC LIBRARY, 1201 Cedar Lane, Northbrook, 60062. Carole Klein-Alexander, Head of Reference Service
Holdings: Vols 3650
Budget: $1000
Notes: Maintained as architecture center for North Suburban Library System's Coordinated Acquisitions Program through 1979. Library will attempt to maintain collection through its own budget.

IN —WILLARD LIBRARY, 21 First Ave, Evansville, 47710. Joan Elliott, Special Collections Librn
Holdings: Vols (1400) Cat
Budget: ($3500)
Notes: The Thrall Art Book Collection. Circulating collection of art books being purchased by special endowment. Emphasis on fine arts of all times and places, with particular reference to American artists, as well as European and American decorative arts and architecture. Noncirculating.

IN —BALL STATE UNIVERSITY, College of Architecture & Planning, Architecture Library, Muncie, 47306. Marjorie Hake Joyner, Librn
Holdings: Vols (25,000) Cat Maps Slides Microforms
Budget: ($17,360)
Notes: Strong emphasis on history of all aspects of architecture. Also, for other major areas, architecture and landscape architecture and planning 50,000 35 mm color slides, over half cataloged.

IN —UNIVERSITY OF NOTRE DAME, Architecture Library, Notre Dame, 46556. Geri Decker, Librn
Holdings: Cat Slides
Notes: Incl 26,000 slides.

IN —THE ART CENTER, Library, 120 St Joseph St, South Bend, 46601. Judy Oberhausen, Cur
Holdings: Vols (1010) Cat Slides
Notes: 500 slides. This Art Center has a specific, separate collection--"The Arts of the United States"--which has its own index and is geared toward American painting, graphics, architecture, design and decorative arts, from the 19th to the 20th century, and sculpture works on paper. Incl 32 periodical titles.

KY —UNIVERSITY OF LOUISVILLE, Allen R Hite Art Institute, Library, Belknap Campus, Louisville, 40292. Gail Gilbert, Librn
Holdings: Vols (40,000) Cat Pix
Budget: ($29,000)
Notes: Incl books on art, architecture,

ARCHITECTURE (cont.)

landscape architecture and gardening, prints, printing, illustrated books and brass rubbings. Library subscribes to 200 periodical titles in these and other areas. Collection circulates to faculty and staff only, with same restrictions placed on interlibrary loan. Library also has collections of bookplates, posters, original prints, hand-made Christmas cards and clippings file filling 56 VF drawers.

KY —KENTUCKY WESLEYAN COLLEGE LIBRARY, 3000 Frederica, Owensboro, 42301. Stuart Stiffler, Dir
Notes: The Dr and Mrs M David Orrahood Collection.

LA —LOUISIANA STATE UNIVERSITY, College of Design, Design Resource Center, 102 College of Design Bldg, Baton Rouge, 70803. Doris A Wheeler, Librn
Holdings: Vols 8500 Cat Maps Slides VF
Budget: $6000
Notes: Architecture, interior design, city planning, landscape architecture.

LA —R W NORTON ART GALLERY, Library, 4747 Creswell Ave, Shreveport, 71106. Jerry M Bloomer, Librn
Holdings: // Cat
Budget:

MD —UNIVERSITY OF MARYLAND, Architecture Library, College Park, 20742. Berna E Neal, Architecture Librn
Holdings: Vols (24,000) Cat
Budget: $30,000
Notes: Incl 600 vol collection on world expositions, 1851-1937. There is a slide collection independent of the library, curated by Elizabeth Alley.

MA —BOSTON PUBLIC LIBRARY, Copley Sq, Boston, 02117. Theresa D Cederholm, Cur of Fine Arts
Notes: Collection incl 138,000 titles (not incl multiple vols sets, serials, and unbound materials); VF on regional artists, architects, art organizations.

MA —SOCIETY FOR THE PRESERVATION OF NEW ENGLAND ANTIQUITIES, Library, 141 Cambridge St, Boston, 02114. Ellie Reichlin, Librn & Cur of Photographic Collections
Holdings: Vols (3000) // Cat Pix Microforms
Budget: ($75,000)
Notes: Architecture of the Northeast. Drawings (original designs); measured drawings; plot plans, etc. Over 7500 items, incl extensive collections of original designs by Ogden Codman, Jr (1890s-early 1900s); Arthur Little and Herbert Browne (1890s-1920s); Luther Briggs (1840s-1860s); Arland Dirlam (1930s-1960s), together with important examples of the work of Asher Benjamin, Richard Upjohn, and others. Measured drawings incl extensive holdings of work undertaken by HABS (Historic American Buildings Survey) in Massachusetts in the 1930s, 1940s under director Frank Chouteau Brown. Also represented are several residential and commercial commissions by F C Brown, not connected with HABS. Collection incl architectural pattern books, builders guides, 18th-19th century. Approx 350 volumes, English and American publications.

MA —HARVARD UNIVERSITY, Graduate School of Design, Frances Loeb Library, Gund Hall, Cambridge, 02138. James Hodgson, Librn
Holdings: Vols (225,000) Cat Mss Pix Slides Microforms
Budget: ($500,000)
Notes: Covers architecture, landscape architecture, city and regional planning, and urban design. Catalog, in 44 volumes, published in 1968, with 2-volume supplement in 1970, 5-volume supplement in 1974, and 3-volume supplement in 1979. It also analyzes periodical articles. Architecture collection described in *Harvard Library* Bulletin, VI (1952): pp 263-269. Noteworthy holdings incl those on Abbey of Cluny, Le Corbusier, amd Henry Hobson Richardson.

MA —MELROSE PUBLIC LIBRARY, 69 W Emerson St, Melrose, 02176. Diane E Shaw, Art Librn
Holdings: Vols (8500) Cat Pix Slides Microforms
Budget: ($6900)
Notes: Framed and unframed art reproductions (110), slides (2773), periodicals, clippings, sound recordings (3000). Incl the Mary Livermore Collection of Sacred Art, the Odlin Collection, and the Pierre Gendrot Collection of Fine Art.

MA —WELLESLEY COLLEGE, Art Library, Wellesley, 02181. Katherine D Finkelpearl, Art Librn
Holdings: Vols (30,000) Cat Pix Slides
Budget: ($22,000)
Notes: Primarily the art and architecture of Western Europe, the Far East, and classical antiquity. However, efforts are being made to expand the collection in the areas of photography, primitive art, and ancient (non-classical) art. The Art Department maintains a separate collection of 62,500 mounted pictures and 90,000 slides.

MI —UNIVERSITY OF MICHIGAN, Art and Architecture Library, 2106 Art and Architecture Bldg, Ann Arbor, 48109. Peggy Ann Kusnerz, Librn; Dot Shields, Asst Librn
Holdings: Vols (45,000)
Budget:
Notes: Incl 200 maps, 35,000 slides, vertical file, videocassettes, blueprints, Jens Jensen Landscape drawings, oral history, and 400 serial titles.

MI —CRANBROOK ACADEMY OF ART, 500 Lone Pine Rd, Box 801, Bloomfield Hills, 48013. Diane Gunn, Librn
Holdings: Vols (25,000) Slides

MI —UNIVERSITY OF DETROIT, Main Library, 4001 W McNichols Rd, Detroit, 48221.
Notes: Architecture Library was closed in 1981. Collection consolidated in main library.

MI —MONROE COUNTY LIBRARY SYSTEM, Bedford Branch, 8575 Jackman Road, Temperance, 48182. Paula Kaczmarek, Head, Bedford Branch
Holdings: Vols 6500 Cat Periodicals AV
Budget: $8000
Notes: Circulating general collection of popular art books, especially Western European and American painting; also includes technique, graphic arts, photography, sculpture, architecture. Periodicals held five years.

MN —MINNEAPOLIS COLLEGE OF ART & DESIGN, Library, 200 E 25 St, Minneapolis, 55404. Richard Kronstedt, Head Librn
Holdings: Vols 1300 Cat Slides
Notes: Emphasis on 20th century architecture and architects.

MN —UNIVERSITY OF MINNESOTA, Architecture Library, 89 Church St, Minneapolis, 55455. A Kristine Johnson, Librn
Holdings: Vols (27,000) Cat Mss
Budget: ($20,000)
Notes: Incl architecture, architectural history, landscape architecture, design methodology, housing, urban sociology, interior design, etc.

MN —WALKER ART CENTER, Staff Reference Library, Vineland Place, Minneapolis, 55403. Rosemary Furtak, Librn
Holdings: Vols 2600 Cat Pix Slides Films
Notes: Incl 5000 catalogs of individual artists; museum gallery catalogs--30,000 catalogs of major exhibitions from all over the world dating back to 1940. Vertical file material, tapes, slides, films.

MN —SAINT PAUL PUBLIC LIBRARY, Arts & Audiovisual Services, 90 W Fourth St, Saint Paul, 55102. Delores Sundbye, Supervising Librn
Holdings: Cat Pix Slides Phonorecords Audiotapes
Budget: ($20,000)
Notes: The Art and Music Dept incl 10,000 books on art and architecture, 4000 books on music and 10,000 cataloged music scores. Collection of 650 color reproduction, 10,000 mounted pictures and 500 exhibit catalogs. Complete set of first edition of Arundel Prints (color lithographic copies of Renaissance paintings, published by the Arundel Society, 1849-1897).

MO —UNIVERSITY OF MISSOURI-KANSAS CITY, General Library, 5100 Rockhill Road, Kansas City, 64110. Kenneth J LaBudde, Dir; Gordon Hendrickson, Assoc Dir; Marilyn Carbonell, Ref Librn
Holdings: Vols 25,000 Cat
Notes: 4121 current serial subscriptions. *See also* entry under Architecture - History.

MO —SAINT LOUIS PUBLIC LIBRARY, Art Dept, 1301 Olive St, Saint Louis, 63103. Martha Hilligoss, Librn
Holdings: Vols 6000 Cat Pix Slides

MO —WASHINGTON UNIVERSITY, Art & Architecture Library, Saint Louis, 63130. Imre Meszaros, Librn
Holdings: Vols (60,413) Cat Pix Microforms
Budget: ($100,000)
Notes: Art and architecture of East Asia; rare books; archaeology; fashion design.

NH —NEW HAMPSHIRE HISTORICAL SOCIETY, Library, 30 Park St, Concord, 03301. William Copeley, Assoc Librn
Holdings: Vols 500 Cat
Budget: ($9000)
Notes: New Hampshire and New England architecture.

NH —DARTMOUTH COLLEGE, Sherman Art Library, Hanover, 03755. Jeffrey L Horrell, Art Librn
Holdings: Vols (52,000) Cat
Notes: Incl art, architecture and photography. Access is available through OCLC and RLIN.

NJ —NEW JERSEY INSTITUTE OF TECHNOLOGY, Robert W Van Houten Library, 323 High St, Newark, 07102. Morton Snowhite, Librn
Holdings: Vols (128,000)

NJ —PRINCETON UNIVERSITY, Architecture Library, School of Architecture, Princeton, 08544. Frances Chen, Librn

NY —PRATT INSTITUTE LIBRARY, Art & Architecture Dept, 200 Willoughby Ave, Brooklyn, 11205. Sydney Star Keaveney, Prof
Holdings: Vols (30,000) Cat Pix Slides
Budget: ($50,000)
Notes: Art and architecture, incl sculpture, photography, painting, design, costume, and commercial art. Incl 60,000 art slides. Use restricted to Pratt faculty and students.

NY —STATE UNIVERSITY OF NEW YORK, COLLEGE AT BUFFALO, Lockwood Memorial Library, Art Dept, Buffalo, 14260. Florence S DaLuiso, Cur
Holdings: Vols (38,000) Cat Microforms
Budget: ($24,735)
Notes: Collection supports curriculum of the School of Fine Art. Incl 9000 exhibition catalogs. Recent acquisitions emphasize contemporary art and environmental design. The library by reciprocal agreement contains card catalog holdings of the Albright-Knox Art Gallery, Buffalo, New York. Books may be obtained on interlibrary loan.

NY —STATE UNIVERSITY OF NEW YORK, COLLEGE OF ARTS & SCIENCE AT GENESEO, Milne Library, Geneseo, 14454. William T Lane, Head of Information Services & Archivist
Holdings: // Cat Mss Pix Slides
Notes: The Carl Schmidt Collection on Local Architecture. Mss for Schmidt's books and folios on cobblestone architecture, Octagon House, Victorian architecture, colonial and post-colonial architecture, mouldings, etc. Notebooks; 2000 measured drawings of architecture and architectural detail in the Rochester, New York, area; 10, 000 slides. 60 ms storage boxes; 12 drawers of drawings.

NY —GENEVA HISTORICAL SOCIETY, James Luckett Memorial Archives, 543 S Main St, Geneva, 14456. Eleanore Clise, Librn

NY —CORNELL UNIVERSITY LIBRARIES, Collection of Regional History, Dept of Manuscripts and Univ Archives, Ithaca, 14853.
Notes: Incl papers, 1905-1908, 1912-1922, 1926-1935, 1938-1943, of the College of Architecture of Cornell University, NY. Incl notices, announcements, grades, attendance lists, financial statements, blueprints, scale drawings, newspaper clippings and other printed matter, and various correspondence.

ARCHITECTURE (cont.)

NY —CORNELL UNIVERSITY LIBRARIES, Fine Arts Library, Sibley Hall, Ithaca, 14853. Judith Holliday, Librn
Holdings: Vols (115,000) Cat Maps Pix

NY —QUEENS BOROUGH PUBLIC LIBRARY, Art & Music Div, 89-11 Merrick Blvd, Jamaica, 11432. Dorothea Wu, Head
Holdings: Vols (85,000) Cat Maps Pix Phonorecords Audiotapes Microforms
Budget: ($44,000)
Notes: The Picture Collection, covering all subjects, consists of approximately 1,500,000 pictures, mainly reproductions and clippings from books and magazines, photographs, and postcards on all subjects; The Framed Picture Collection, approx 180 framed pictures, mostly reproductions of paintings from various periods; and The Phonorecord and Cassette Collection consists of approx 3500 reference phonorecords and 6500 circulating records as well as 6000 reference cassettes and 1500 circulating cassettes.

NY —CITY UNIVERSITY OF NEW YORK, City College, Architecture Library, 3300 Broadway, New York, 10031. Sylvia Wright, Assoc Prof
Holdings: Vols (15,000) Cat Pix Microforms
Budget: ($15,000)
Notes: Architecture, landscape architecture, urban planning and other related areas. 11, 000 pamphlets.

NY —COLUMBIA UNIVERSITY LIBRARIES, Avery Architectural and Fine Arts Library, 201 Avery Hall, New York, 10027. Angela Giral, Librn
Holdings: Vols 100,000 Cat Mss Maps Pix
Notes: Have expanded periodical index on cards (on-line since 1979); also collection of 100,000 architectural drawings. Incl rare books, mss, original architectural drawings, etc. Restricted use: noncirculating.

NY —NEW YORK PUBLIC LIBRARY, Art, Prints, and Photographs Div, Fifth Ave & 42 St, New York, 10018. Donald Anderle, Chief
Holdings: Cat Mss Maps Pix

NY —UNIVERSITY CLUB, Library, One W 54 St, New York, 10019. Guy St Clair, Library Dir
Holdings: Vols (100,000) Cat Mss Maps Pix
Notes: A private library for the members of the University Club, their guests, and serious scholars upon written application to the Library Director.

NY —YIVO INSTITUTE FOR JEWISH RESEARCH, Library & Archives, 1048 Fifth Ave, New York, 10028. Dina Abramowicz, Librn; Marek Web, Archivist
Holdings: Cat Mss Pix Slides
Notes: Original works and reference materials, incl reproductions of 1500 objects; 500 slides. Separate catalog.

NY —LANDMARK SOCIETY OF WESTERN NEW YORK, Wenrich Memorial Library, 130 Spring Rd, Rochester, 14608.
Holdings: Vols (2000) Cat Maps Pix Slides
Budget: ($500)
Notes: Paintings, slides, drawings, as well as the Society's archives of local architecture and information on preservation and restoration techniques. Much on preservation ordinances; legal, physical and financial aspects of building preservation; local and regional history, especially of Rochester and Monroe County.

NY —UNIVERSITY OF ROCHESTER, Fine Arts Library and Gallery, Rochester, 14627. Stephanie J Frontz, Librn
Holdings: Vols (35,000) Cat
Budget: ($15,000)

NC —UNIVERSITY OF NORTH CAROLINA, CHAPEL HILL, Art Library, Art Classroom Studio Bldg, 079A, Chapel Hill, 27514. Philip A Rees, Art Librn
Holdings: Vols (47,000) Cat Microforms
Budget: ($52,000)
Notes: Emphasis on European and American art and architecture, ancient to modern. Special strengths: Rubens and 19th century French painting.

NC —NORTH CAROLINA STATE UNIVERSITY, Harry B Lyons Design Library, P. O. Box 7701, Raleigh, 27607. Maryellen LoPresti, Librn
Notes: Collection covers architecture, landscape architecture, design and related professions. Additional materials may be found on art, painting, sculpture, photography and solar energy design. The library presently houses a total of 28,000 books, periodical and serial volumes to support the curriculum. A product and trade literature file and a vertical file of pamplets are also locally cataloged in the library representing an additional 3000 items of materials available for use. A significant collection of over 50,000 cataloged slides primarily representing the areas of art and architectural history are also contained in the library facility. See *Directory of Special Libraries and Information Centers.*

NC —WAKE TECHNICAL COLLEGE, Library, Audio-Visual Dept, 9101 Fayetteville Road, Raleigh, 27603. James Gray, Librn; Horst Garloff, Audio-Visual Specialist
Holdings: Vols (32,332) Cat Maps Slides Phonorecords Audiotapes Videotapes 16mm Films Filmstrips Microforms

OH —CLEVELAND PUBLIC LIBRARY, Fine Arts and Special Collections Department, 325 Superior Ave, Cleveland, 44114. Alice N Loranth, Head
Holdings: Vols 9000 Cat Mss Pix Microforms
Notes: All periods of architecture are covered, with special emphasis on American and English architecture. Coverage incl good representation from all countries.

OH —OHIO STATE UNIVERSITY, Engineering Library, 2024 Neil Ave, Columbus, 43210. Mary Jo V Arnold, Librn
Holdings: Vols (132,000) Cat Microforms
Budget: ($110,000)

OH —DAYTON ART INSTITUTE LIBRARY, 405 W Riverview Ave, PO Box 941, Dayton, 45401. Helen L Pinkney, Librn and Assoc Cur
Holdings: Vols (23,220) Cat Mss Pix Slides Microforms VF
Budget: ($7000)
Notes: Incl museum catalogs and bulletins and collection of slides of stained glass.

OH —KENT STATE UNIVERSITY, Architecture Urban Studies Library, Kent, 44242.
Holdings: Vols 5500 Cat Slides Microforms
Budget: ($2000)

OK —HTB TECHNICAL INFORMATION CENTER, PO Box 1845, Oklahoma City, 73101. Retha Robertson, Librn
Holdings: Vols (100) Cat Documents Pix Slides Audiotapes 16mm Films Filmstrips VF
Notes: Architectural and engineering of the US, especially. Extensive photograph collection, incl 3000 slides.

OK —OKLAHOMA STATE UNIVERSITY, Library, Stillwater, 74708. Roscoe Rouse, Dir
Holdings: Vols 10,000 Cat
Notes: Underground construction.

OR —UNIVERSITY OF OREGON LIBRARY, Architecture & Allied Arts Branch, Eugene, 97403. Reyburn R McCready, Head Librn
Holdings: Vols (35,000) Cat Pix Slides
Budget: ($57,000)
Notes: Incl 200,000 slides and student renderings on architecture and the arts, incl sculpture, painting, furniture, interior architecture, graphic arts, landscape, art history and art education.

OR —SOUTHERN OREGON HISTORICAL SOCIETY, Jacksonville Museum Library, 206 N Fifth St, PO Box 480, Jacksonville, 97530. Richard H Engeman, Librn
Holdings: Vols (200) Cat Mss Maps Pix Slides 16mm Films
Budget: ($5200)

PA —TEMPLE UNIVERSITY, Engineering and Architecture Library, 12 & Norris Sts, Philadelphia, 19122. Raelaine Ballou, Librn
Holdings: Vols (12,000) Cat Microforms
Budget: ($13,500)

PA —CARNEGIE LIBRARY OF PITTSBURGH, Music and Art Dept, 4400 Forbes Ave, Pittsburgh, 15213. Ida Reed, Dept Head
Holdings: Vols 10,000 Cat Pix Slides

RI —PROVIDENCE PUBLIC LIBRARY, 150 Empire St, Providence, 02903. Lance J Bauer, Special Collections Librn
Holdings: Vols 2500 Cat Maps Pix
Notes: The Nickerson Architecture Collection incl some fine 17th and 18th century volumes, English style books of architectural details, a comprehensive collection of 18th and 19th century building styles in Europe and America and an extensive collection of contemporary works. Restricted use.

RI —RHODE ISLAND SCHOOL OF DESIGN, Library, Two College St, Providence, 02903. James A Findlay, Dir
Holdings: Vols (70,000) Cat Pix Slides
Budget: ($50,000)
Notes: Strong architecture and architectural history collection.

SC —CLEMSON UNIVERSITY, Emery A Gunnin Architectural Library, Lee Hall, Clemson, 29631. Leslie Abrams, Librn
Holdings: Vols (14,778) Cat Slides
Notes: Incl 2000 South Carolina planning documents. 56,000 slides.

TX —TEXAS STATE LIBRARY, Archives Div, 1201 Brazos, PO Box 12927, Capitol Sta, Austin, 78711. David B Gracy II, State Archivist

TX —UNIVERSITY OF TEXAS LIBRARIES, Architecture & Planning Library, PO Box P, Austin, 78712. Eloise F McDonald, Librn
Holdings: Vols (24,000) Cat Pix Microforms
Notes: Also 17,800 reports, incl 701 HUD reports.

TX —ROSENBERG LIBRARY, Galveston and Texas History Center, 2310 Sealy Ave, Galveston, 77550. Jane Kenamore, Archivist
Holdings: Mss Architectural drawings
Notes: Collection incl the Galveston Architecture Inventory, 1966-1967, photographs of Galveston buildings, and architectural drawings by Nicholas J Clayton.

TX —RICE UNIVERSITY, Fondren Library, 6100 S Main St, PO Box 1892, Houston, 77251. Dr Samuel M Carrington, Jr, University Librn
Holdings: Vols 6750 Cat
Budget: $15,200
Notes: Each serial title counted once.

VT —VERMONT TECHNICAL COLLEGE, Hartness Library, Randolph Center, 05061. Dewey Patterson, Library Dir
Holdings: Vols 3800 Cat

VT —SHELBURNE MUSEUM, Library, Shelburne, 05482. Barbara Reenstierna, Librn
Holdings: Vols 200 Cat Slides

VA —VIRGINIA POLYTECHNIC INSTITUTE & STATE UNIVERSITY, Architecture Library, Blacksburg, 24061. Robert E Stephenson, Architecture Librn
Holdings: Vols (46,000) Cat Microforms Cassettes Slides VF
Budget: ($57,700)

WA —SEATTLE PUBLIC LIBRARY, 1000 Fourth Ave, Seattle, 98104. Ronald A Dubberly, City Librn
Holdings: Vols 70,000 Cat Pix
Notes: Incl 28,000 photographs of Seattle and Pacific Northwest architecture and views. Balance of picture collection about 650,000 items.

WA —UNIVERSITY OF WASHINGTON LIBRARIES, Architecture-Urban Planning Library, 11, JO-30, Seattle, 98195. Betty L Wagner, Librn
Holdings: Vols (26,085) Cat Microforms
Budget: ($33,127)
Notes: Incl 5,241 microforms.

WI —UNIVERSITY OF WISCONSIN, MADISON, Kohler Art Library, 800 University Ave, Madison, 53706. William C Bunce, Chief; Louise Hunning, Ref Librn
Holdings: Vols (83,000) Cat Microforms
Notes: Incl over 10,000 exhibition and auction catalogs.

WI —UNIVERSITY OF WISCONSIN, MADISON, Memorial Library, 728 State St, Madison, 53706. Erwin K Welsch, Social Studies Bibliographer
Notes: A gift by Frank Morris Riley of many famous books on architecture.

WI —MILWAUKEE PUBLIC LIBRARY, 814 W Wisconsin Ave, Milwaukee, 53233.

ARCHITECTURE (cont.)

Donald J Sager, City Librn
Holdings: Vols (8700) Cat
Budget: ($10,661)
Notes: All periods of architecture with emphasis on American. Strength in Frank Lloyd Wright and Prairie School. Wisconsin Architectural Archive collections.

AB —SOUTHERN ALBERTA INSTITUTE OF TECHNOLOGY, Learning Resources Centre, 1301 16 Ave NW, Calgary, T2M 0L4, Can. Tom Skinner, Historian
Holdings: Vols (5000) Cat Pix Slides Films Audiotapes Filmstrips Videotapes
Notes: Serves Alberta College of Art (4-year professional course).

BC —VANCOUVER PUBLIC LIBRARY, Art Div, 750 Burrard St, Vancouver, V6Z 1X5, Can.
Holdings: Cat Pix
Notes: Book and pamphlet collection. Also, (1) Newspaper Clippings File: 31 drawers of relevant clippings from major newspapers, incl the *Sun, Province, Toronto Globe and Mail, Christian Science Monitor, New York* Times, etc on arts, music, architecture; incl biographical material (16 drawers). (2) Picture File about 500,000 pictures in 150 cabinet drawers, strong in architecture, costume, interior decoration, painting, sculpture, also portraits. (3) Exhibition Catalogs File: British Columbia and elsewhere. (4) Association and Organization File: organizations in the Lower Mainland in arts, music, city planning, etc, begun in 1940s; (5) Canadian Artists Index: begun in 1964, alphabetically by artist, with about 300,000 citationsto reproductions of work and biographical material on Canadian artist from the division's books and other sources; (6) Miscellaneous Index: material not covered in other special or published indexes, primarily of Canadian and local cultural events, hard-to-find informations, etc. Local newspapers, special Canadian publications and British film journals are the most regularly indexed items. (7) Song Index started in the 1930s. (8) Title Index to song collections and sheet music in the VPL collection, approx 100,000 entries.

MB —UNIVERSITY OF MANITOBA, Architecture & Fine Arts Library, Winnipeg, R3T 2N2, Can. Peter Anthony, Head
Holdings: Vols (50,000) Maps Pix
Notes: Incl over 1000 maps; 2000 pictures; 1000 microforms; 48 drawers of VF materials. Nearly 375 periodical titles; government publications.

ON —CANADIAN HOUSING INFORMATION CENTER, Canada Mortgage and Housing Corp, CMHC Annex Bldg Ground Floor, Montreal Rd, Ottawa, K1A 0P7, Can. Leslie Jones, Mgr
Holdings: Cat
Notes: General and domestic.

ON —METROPOLITAN TORONTO LIBRARY, Fine Arts Dept, 789 Yonge St, Toronto, M4W 2G8, Can. Alan Suddon, Head
Holdings: Vols (42,000) Cat Pix Microforms
Notes: Extensive collection.

ON —METROPOLITAN TORONTO LIBRARY, Science & Technology Dept, 789 Yonge St, Toronto, M4W 2G8, Can. Margaret Walshe, Head
Holdings: Vols (120,000) Cat
Notes: All aspects of technology of architecture and standards for the specialist, the student and the general public. The department gives high priority to Canadian material.

ON —UNIVERSITY OF TORONTO, Faculty of Architecture, Landscape Architecture Library, 230 College St, Toronto, M5S 1A1, Can. Pamela Manson-Smith, Librn
Holdings: Vols (14,401) Cat Slides

ON —UNIVERSITY OF WATERLOO, Library, Waterloo, N2L 3G1, Can. Susan Bellingham, Special Collections Librn
Notes: The Rosa Breithaupt Clark Collection of books on the history of architecture.

ARCHITECTURE—CONSERVATION AND RESTORATION

CA —UNIVERSITY OF CALIFORNIA, SANTA BARBARA, Library, Dept of Special Collections, Santa Barbara, 93106. Christian F Brun, Head
Holdings: Vols (95,980) Cat Mss
Notes: The Pearl Chase Collections of Community Development and Conservation. Papers of outstanding California leaders in conservation, community planning, Indian affairs, national parks.

MA —SOCIETY FOR THE PRESERVATION OF NEW ENGLAND ANTIQUITIES, Library, 141 Cambridge St, Boston, 02114. Ellie Reichlin, Librn & Cur of Photographic Collections
Holdings: Vols (3000) // Cat Pix Microforms
Budget: ($75,000)
Notes: Architecture of the Northeast. Drawings (original designs); measured drawings; plot plans, etc. Over 7500 items, incl extensive collections of original designs by Ogden Codman, Jr (1890s-early 1900s); Arthur Little and Herbert Browne (1890s-1920s); Luther Briggs (1840s-1860s); Arland Dirlam (1930s-1960s), together with important examples of the work of Asher Benjamin, Richard Upjohn, and others. Measured drawings incl extensive holdings of work undertaken by HABS (Historic American Buildings Survey) in Massachusetts in the 1930s, 1940s under director Frank Chouteau Brown. Also represented are several residential and commercial commissions by F C Brown, not connected with HABS. Collection incl architectural pattern books, builders guides, 18th-19th century. Approx 350 volumes, English and American publications.

NY —LANDMARK SOCIETY OF WESTERN NEW YORK, Wenrich Memorial Library, 130 Spring Rd, Rochester, 14608.
Holdings: Vols (2000) Cat Maps Pix Slides ($500)
Notes: Paintings, slides, drawings, as well as the Society's archives of local architecture and information on preservation and restoration techniques. Much on preservation ordinances; legal, physical and financial aspects of building preservation; local and regional history, especially of Rochester and Monroe County.

OR —SOUTHERN OREGON HISTORICAL SOCIETY, Jacksonville Museum Library, 206 N Fifth St, PO Box 480, Jacksonville, 97530. Richard H Engeman, Librn
Holdings: Vols (200) Cat Mss Maps Pix Slides 16mm Films
Budget: ($5200)

TX —SAN ANTONIO CONSERVATION SOCIETY, Library & Archives, Foundation Library, 107 King William St, San Antonio, 78204. Roland T Jones, Librn
Holdings: Vols (2500) Cat Mss Maps Pix Slides VF
Budget: ($1000)
Notes: San Antonio historic structures and their preservation. SACS Library is staffed entirely by volunteer members of the Society. Architectural plans with vertical files; 750 clippings. Limited hours.

ARCHITECTURE—DESIGNS AND PLANS

DC —LIBRARY OF CONGRESS, Prints and Photographs Div, Historic American Buildings Survey, Washington, 20540.
Holdings: Cat Mss Pix Drawings
Notes: Details of some 17,000 American buildings in 81,000 photographs, 42,000 measured drawings and 44,000 pp of written documentation.

IL —ART INSTITUTE OF CHICAGO, Ryerson & Burnham Libraries, Michigan Ave & Adams St, Chicago, 60603. Daphne C Roloff, Dir
Holdings: Vols (136,00) Cat Mss Slides Microforms
Budget: ($167,000)
Notes: Total collection incl 300,000 slides.

IN —INDIANA HISTORICAL SOCIETY, Library, 315 W Ohio St, Indianapolis, 46202. Robert K O'Neill, Dir
Holdings: Vols Cat Mss Pix Microforms
Notes: Records of Indiana architects, contractors, and engineers, as well as records concerning the structures created by non-Indiana professionals with the state. Types of material collected incl office files, correspondence, drawings, blueprints, photographs, personal papers, specifications, books and pamphlets. The collection incl approximately 14,000 drawings, along with another 10,000 on microfilm, from central Indiana architectural firms. Incl among the drawings are approximately 800 for Union Station, Indianapolis.

MA —SOCIETY FOR THE PRESERVATION OF NEW ENGLAND ANTIQUITIES, Library, 141 Cambridge St, Boston, 02114. Ellie Reichlin, Librn & Cur of Photographic Collections
Holdings: Vols (3000) // Cat Pix Microforms
Budget: ($75,000)
Notes: Architecture of the Northeast. Drawings (original designs); measured drawings; plot plans, etc. Over 7500 items, incl extensive collections of original designs by Ogden Codman, Jr (1890s-early 1900s); Arthur Little and Herbert Browne (1890s-1920s); Luther Briggs (1840s-1860s); Arland Dirlam (1930s-1960s), together with important examples of the work of Asher Benjamin, Richard Upjohn, and others. Measured drawings incl extensive holdings of work undertaken by HABS (Historic American Buildings Survey) in Massachusetts in the 1930s, 1940s under director Frank Chouteau Brown. Also represented are several residential and commercial commissions by F C Brown, not connected with HABS. Collection incl architectural pattern books, builders guides, 18th-19th century. Approx 350 volumes, English and American publications.

MO —UNIVERSITY OF MISSOURI-KANSAS CITY, General Library, State Historical Society of Missouri Manuscripts, 5100 Rockhill Road, Kansas City, 64110. Kenneth J LaBudde, Dir; Gordon Hendrickson, Assoc Dir
Holdings: Mss
Notes: Joint Collection Western Historical Manuscript Collection and the State Historical of Missouri Manuscripts, University of Missouri-Kansas City General Library, 5100 Rockhill Road, Kansas City, MO 64110. Ca 2,500 linear feet of manuscripts, blueprints and oral history tapes.
Notes: The manuscript collection includes material which documents the history, growth and development of Missouri, especially the Greater Kansas City area. The personal papers of business, civic, cultural, political and community leaders; local historians and other individuals of families from the area are within the collection as are the records of associations, organizations and institutions which reflect the history of the area. Prominent among the collections are the papers of Charles B. Wheeler, Jr., Charles N. Kimball, Arthur Mag, Oscar D. Nelson, Lou B. Holland, J. C. Nichols, Perry Cookingham, Blevins Davis and Daniel Macmorris and the records of the Kansas City Board of Trade. Architectural designs and plans for approximately 3,500 Kansas City buildings and the records of the Hoit, Price and Barnes architectural firm and the papers of Asa Beebe Cross, early Kansas City architect as well as a number of oral histories with Kansas City Jazz figures are in the collection.

ARCHITECTURE—DESIGNS AND PLANS (cont.)

SC —COLLEGE OF CHARLESTON LIBRARY, Special Collections Dept, Charleston, 29401.
Notes: William Martin Aiken Collection incl notebook, sketchbooks composed in Europe and the US, architectural designs, correspondence, miscellaneous printed material, and a photograph of Aiken; contains also collections of other architectural designs and building adornments; 34 architectural sketches and plans of Thomas Walker (1809), John Izard Middleton (1811), and William Middleton (1864).

TX —EL PASO PUBLIC LIBRARY, Southwest Collection, 501 N Oregon, El Paso, 79901. Mary A Sarber, Head
Holdings: Vols (12,000) Cat Mss Maps Pix Microforms
Budget: ($11,000)
Notes: 400 sets of plans, incl architectural plans, by El Paso firms of Trost and Trost, Percy McGhee, Frazer and Benner. Partial catalog of Trost and Trost buildings. See Engelbrecht, Lloyd C., and Engelbrecht, June-Marie F., *Henry C. Trost: Architect of the Southwest* (El Paso Public Library Association, 1981).

TX —SAN ANTONIO CONSERVATION SOCIETY, Library & Archives, Foundation Library, 107 King William St, San Antonio, 78204. Roland T Jones, Librn
Holdings: Vols (2500) Cat Mss Maps Pix Slides VF
Budget: ($1000)
Notes: San Antonio historic structures and their preservation. SACS Library is staffed entirely by volunteer members of the Society. Architectural plans with vertical files; 750 clippings. Limited hours.

UT —UNIVERSITY OF UTAH, Marriott Library, Special Collections, Salt Lake City, 84112. Gregory C Thompson, Cur
Notes: Collection of Utah Architects.

WA —UNIVERSITY OF WASHINGTON LIBRARIES, Pacific Northwest Collection, Seattle, 98195. Andrew F Johnson, Librn
Holdings: Vols (50,000) Cat Maps Pix
Budget: ($12,000)
Notes: The Pacific Northwest Collection contains printed materials documenting the historic and contemporary life and culture of the region in a broad range of subject areas. The Pacific Northwest is defined as the geographic region including Washington, Oregon, Idaho, Montana, British Columbia, Yukon Territory, and Alaska. Printed materials including books, periodicals, government documents, maps, weekly and local regional newspapers, theses and dissertations, as well as photogaphs and architectural drawings are included in the Pacific Northwest Collection. Photographic works of over 200 photographers active in the Pacific Northwest, Alaska, and the Yukon Territory (Canada) during the period 1860-1930, including Asahel and Edward S Curtis, Eric Hegg, and Clark Kinsey, are represented in a print collection of more than 300,000 images. The architecturaldrawings collection includes over 19,000 original plans, drawings, sketches, renderings and blue prints pertaining to the history of architecture and urban planning and landscape gardening in the Pacific Northwest ca 1880-1940. Areas of particular strength are the holdings of over 1100 published journals of Pacific Northwest exploration expeditions, photographs of Northwest Coast Native Americans and of historic Seattle, newspapers issued within the Japanese-American relocation camps, 1942-1945, materials relating to the 1980 eruption of Mt St Helens, and Sanborne fire insurance maps for Washington. A unique feature of the Collection is the subject index to regional periodicals and local newspapers maintained by the PNW Collection staff; over 100 titles are currently indexed. G K Hall Company published a books catalog of the Pacific Northwest Collectionin 1973.

ARCHITECTURE—DETAILS

MA —SOCIETY FOR THE PRESERVATION OF NEW ENGLAND ANTIQUITIES, Library, 141 Cambridge St, Boston, 02114. Ellie Reichlin, Librn & Cur of Photographic Collections
Holdings: Vols (3000) // Cat Pix Microforms
Budget: ($75,000)
Notes: Architecture of the Northeast. Drawings (original designs); measured drawings; plot plans, etc. Over 7500 items, incl extensive collections of original designs by Ogden Codman, Jr (1890s-early 1900s); Arthur Little and Herbert Browne (1890s-1920s); Luther Briggs (1840s-1860s); Arland Dirlam (1930s-1960s), together with important examples of the work of Asher Benjamin, Richard Upjohn, and others. Measured drawings incl extensive holdings of work undertaken by HABS (Historic American Buildings Survey) in Massachusetts in the 1930s, 1940s under director Frank Chouteau Brown. Also represented are several residential and commercial commissions by F C Brown, not connected with HABS. Collection incl architectural pattern books, builders guides, 18th-19th century. Approx 350 volumes, English and American publications.

NY —LANDMARK SOCIETY OF WESTERN NEW YORK, Wenrich Memorial Library, 130 Spring Rd, Rochester, 14608.
Holdings: Vols (2000) Cat Maps Pix Slides
Budget: ($500)
Notes: Paintings, slides, drawings, as well as the Society's archives of local architecture and information on preservation and restoration techniques. Much on preservation ordinances; legal, physical and financial aspects of building preservation; local and regional history, especially of Rochester and Monroe County.

SC —COLLEGE OF CHARLESTON LIBRARY, Special Collections Dept, Charleston, 29401.
Notes: William Martin Aiken Collection. Incl notebook, sketchbooks composed in Europe and the US, architectural designs, correspondence, miscellaneous printed material, and a photograph of Aiken; contains also collections of other architectural designs and building adornments.

MB —UNIVERSITY OF MANITOBA, Architecture & Fine Arts Library, Winnipeg, R3T 2N2, Can. Peter Anthony, Head
Holdings: Vols (54,000) Cat
Notes: Incl government publications.

ARCHITECTURE—HISTORY

CA —UNIVERSITY OF CALIFORNIA, BERKELEY, Environmental Design Library, (The General Library), 210 Wurster Hall, Berkeley, 94720. Arthur B Waugh, Head
Holdings: Vols (90,000) Cat Pix Microforms
Budget: ($17,000)
Notes: A research collection devoted to the following aspects of the field of architecture: working details, drawing, theory, standards and professional practice; building materials, building types, earthquake resistant architecture, contemporary architecture of all countries, history of architecture, and architecture as a profession. A small rare book collection in the field of architecture is maintained. Approximately 1500 serials, incl many foreign-language titles, are currently being received. A collection of photographs (of buildings) and a slide collection are administered by the department of architecture.

CA —ESHERICK, HOMSEY, DODGE & DAVIS, Library, 2789 25th St, San Francisco, 94110. Elizabeth Walton, Librn
Holdings: Vols (2500) Cat Maps Pix Slides
Notes: General history of architecture; solar energy applications to architecture; residential architecture; zoo architecture; handbooks, codes, and standards; school and university architecture. Also incl is a large collection of product literature catalogs and samples (uncataloged).

CA —STANFORD UNIVERSITY LIBRARIES, Art & Architecture Library, 102 Cummings Art Bldg, Stanford, 94305.
Alexander D Ross, Art Librarian
Holdings: Vols (110,000) Cat
Notes: Incl materials of scholarly interest on the history of the visual arts: painting, sculpture, architecture, drawing, printmaking, etc, for all regions and periods.

CT —STOWE-DAY LIBRARY, 77 Forest St, Hartford, 06105. Diana J Royce, Librn
Holdings: Vols (15,000) Cat Mss
Notes: Incl (6000) additional pamphlets. The entire collection covers architecture, decorative arts, history, literature, woman suffrage, and Harriet Beecher Stowe, through the 19th century.

CT —YALE UNIVERSITY, Art Library, 180 York St, New Haven, 06520. Nancy S Lambert, Art Librn
Holdings: Vols (80,000) Cat Slides
Notes: 100,000 photos and prints; 250,000 slides. There are, in addition to the subject library, about 75,000 books in the same fields in the University library. Slides and photographs are not loaned outside of the university. Books may be obtained on interlibrary loan. The Art Library is primarily for the use of the undergraduates and graduate students of the school of Art and Architecture. Incl environmental design and studio art. Emphasis on current publications and periodicals, and on research material. There is a vertical file of urban planning material and the collection contains some materials in this field, particularly as related to architecture.

DC —AMERICAN INSTITUTE OF ARCHITECTS, Library, 1735 New York Ave, Washington, 20006. Stephanie C Byrnes, Librn
Holdings: Vols (22,000) Cat Mss Pix Slides Microforms
Notes: Emphasis of current acquisitions is on American architecture and its practice. Incl the library of R M Hunt and considerable other material. Photocopying.

DC —LIBRARY OF CONGRESS, Washington, 20540.
Notes: Papers and working materials of Charles Eames (1907-1978), American architect and designer. Incl are original negatives and prints of the 106 educational films he created, business correspondence 1944 to 1978, some 400,000 color slides, 31, 000 black and white photographs, production materials for exhibits, and drawings for all his major furniture designs.

DC —LIBRARY OF CONGRESS, Prints & Photographs Div, Washington, 20540.
Notes: The Carnegie Survey of the Architecture of the South is a photographic record of the early buildings and gardens of Maryland, Virginia, the Carolinas, Georgia, Alabama, Louisiana, Florida and Mississippi, executed by Frances Benjamin Johnston between 1933 and 1940.

DC —LIBRARY OF CONGRESS, Prints and Photographs Div, Historic American Buildings Survey, Washington, 20540.
Holdings: Cat Mss Pix Drawings
Notes: Details of some 17,000 American buildings in 81,000 photographs, 42,000 measured drawings and 44,000 pp of written documentation.

IL —ART INSTITUTE OF CHICAGO, Ryerson & Burnham Libraries, Michigan Ave & Adams St, Chicago, 60603. Daphne C Roloff, Dir
Holdings: Vols 22,000 Cat Maps Slides Microforms
Budget: ($167,000)
Notes: Total collection incl 300,000 slides.

IL —CHICAGO PUBLIC LIBRARY, Art Section, Fine Arts Division, 78 E Washington St, Chicago, 60602. Rosalinda I Hack, Fine Arts Division Chief; Yvonne S Brown, Head, Art Section
Holdings: Vols 6000
Notes: Reference and circulating collection, with special emphasis on general architectural history, modern architecture,

ARCHITECTURE—HISTORY (cont.)

architecture of the United States, and Chicago architectural history. Collections is supported by the Chicago Architecture File, a card file that lists citations to information on buildings that been recognized for their architectural significance. The Section's picture Collection has extensive documentation on Chicago area architecture, and incorporates a collection of architectural photographs by Stephen Beal. Archival copies of these photographs are to be found in Special Collections. The collections is also supplemented by the microform collections of *The Historic American Buildings Survey,* and *American Architectural Books.*

IN —BALL STATE UNIVERSITY, College of Architecture & Planning, Architecture Library, Muncie, 47306. Marjorie Hake Joyner, Librn
Holdings: Vols (25,000) Cat Maps Slides Microforms
Budget: ($17,360)
Notes: Strong emphasis on history of all aspects of architecture. Also, for other major areas, architecture and landscape architecture and planning 50,000 35 mm color slides, over half cataloged.

MD —JOHNS HOPKINS UNIVERSITY, Milton S Eisenhower Library, Charles & 34 Sts, Baltimore, 21218. Ann S Gwyn, Assistant Dir for Special Collections
Holdings: Vols (18,000) Cat Maps
Notes: Strongest in ancient, Byzantine, and Renaissance art and architecture. Reference Library lacks some periodicals. Modern period being rapidly built up.

MD —JOHNS HOPKINS UNIVERSITY, Milton S Eisenhower Library, Special Collections, John Work Garrett Library, 4545 N Charles St, Baltimore, 21210. Jane Katz, Garrett Librn
Holdings: Vols 600 Cat
Notes: Early books on architecture. Vitruvius, Alberti, Scamozzi, Grapalus, Serlio, Vignola, ie, almost complete in all editions from 1496 on. Also French, German, Dutch and English authors. Downs (1961-70) 1745.

MD —MARYLAND HISTORICAL SOCIETY, Library, 201 W Monument St, Baltimore, 21201. William B Keller, Head Librn
Holdings: Mss Pix
Notes: Papers of Benjamin Henry Latrobe.

MA —HARVARD UNIVERSITY, Baker Library of the Graduate School of Business Administration, Kress Library of Business and Economics, Soldiers Field, Boston, 02163. Ruth E Rogers, Cur
Holdings: Cat
Notes: See *Journal of the Society of Architectural Historians,* XXIX (1970): pp 260-262.

MA —SOCIETY FOR THE PRESERVATION OF NEW ENGLAND ANTIQUITIES, Library, 141 Cambridge St, Boston, 02114. Ellie Reichlin, Librn & Cur of Photographic Collections
Holdings: Vols (3000) // Cat Pix Microforms
Budget: ($75,000)
Notes: Architecture of the Northeast. Drawings (original designs); measured drawings; plot plans, etc. Over 7500 items, incl extensive collections of original designs by Ogden Codman, Jr (1890s-early 1900s); Arthur Little and Herbert Browne (1890s-1920s); Luther Briggs (1840s-1860s); Arland Dirlam (1930s-1960s), together with important examples of the work of Asher Benjamin, Richard Upjohn, and others. Measured drawings incl extensive holdings of work undertaken by HABS (Historic American Buildings Survey) in Massachusetts in the 1930s, 1940s under director Frank Chouteau Brown. Also represented are several residential and commercial commissions by F C Brown, not connected with HABS. Collection incl architectural pattern books, builders guides, 18th-19th century. Approx 350 volumes, English and American publications.

MA —HARVARD UNIVERSITY, Harvard College Library, Fine Arts Library, Fogg Museum, 32 Quincy St, Cambridge, 02138. Wolfgang M Freitag, Librn
Holdings: Vols (202,000) Cat Mss Pix Slides
Budget: ($176,500)
Notes: All areas of art history, with emphasis on Italian primitives, Italian Renaissance, master drawings, Romanesque sculpture, architectural history, ms materials (particulary American artists'), conservation and restoration of art objects. Incl the Berenson repertory of photographs from the Harvard Center for Italian Renaissance Studies in Florence, and the Decimal Index to the Art of the Low Countries. Separate card catalogs for books, photographs and lantern slides, registers for ms holdings which are not incl in *National Union Catalog of Manuscript Collections.* Slides total over 230,000; over 745,000 pictures. *Fine Arts Library Catalogue* (14 volumes) and *Catalogue of Auction Sales Catalogues* (1 volume) (Boston: G K Hall, 1972); *A Guide to the Fine Arts Library* (Cambridge, Mass: 1971); *Guide to the Harvard Libraries,* microfiche edition of holdingscataloged through 1981 published 1984 (Munich/New York: Saur).

MN —UNIVERSITY OF MINNESOTA, Architecture Library, 89 Church St, Minneapolis, 55455. A Kristine Johnson, Librn
Holdings: Vols (27,000) Cat Mss
Budget: ($20,000)
Notes: Incl architecture, architectural history, landscape architecture, design methodology, housing, urban sociology, interior design, etc.

MO —UNIVERSITY OF MISSOURI-KANSAS CITY, General Library, State Historical Society of Missouri Manuscripts, 5100 Rockhill Road, Kansas City, 64110. Kenneth J LaBudde, Dir; Gordon Hendrickson, Assoc Dir
Notes: Joint Collection of Western Historical Manuscripts Collection. 50,000 individual blueprints sheets, representing over 3500 individual buildings, primarily in Kansas City.

NJ —PRINCETON UNIVERSITY, Marquand Library, McCormick Hall, Princeton, 08544. Mary M Schmidt, Librn
Holdings: Vols (130,000) Cat Microforms
Notes: Especially strong in classical archaeology, medieval art and architecture, and photography history.

NY —STATE UNIVERSITY OF NEW YORK, COLLEGE AT BUFFALO, Lockwood Memorial Library, Art Dept, Buffalo, 14260. Florence S DaLuiso, Cur
Holdings: Vols (38,000) Cat Microforms
Budget: ($24,735)
Notes: Collection supports curriculum of the School of Fine Art. Incl 9000 exhibition catalogs. Recent acquisitions emphasize contemporary art and environmental design. The library by reciprocal agreement contains card catalog holdings of the Albright-Knox Art Gallery, Buffalo, New York. Books may be obtained on interlibrary loan.

NY —STATE UNIVERSITY OF NEW YORK, COLLEGE OF ARTS & SCIENCE AT GENESEO, Milne Library, Geneseo, 14454. William T Lane, Head of Information Services & Archivist
Holdings: // Cat Mss Pix Slides
Notes: The Carl Schmidt Collection on Local Architecture. Mss for Schmidt's books and folios on cobblestone architecture, Octagon House, Victorian architecture, colonial and post-colonial architecture, mouldings, etc. Notebooks; 2000 measured drawings of architecture and architectural detail in the Rochester, New York, area; 10, 000 slides. 60 ms storage boxes; 12 drawers of drawings.

†NY —METROPOLITAN MUSEUM OF ART, Photograph & Slide Library, 82 St & Fifth Ave, New York, 10028. Margaret P Nolan, Chief Librn
Holdings: Cat Slides
Notes: Over 286,000 (125,000 in 2 x 2 color). The slides illustrate the history of architecture, sculpture, painting and the decorative arts from prehistoric times to the present. Incl a representative coverage of the Metropolitan Museum collections as well as objects from other museums and private collections. Slides available for rental to the public.

NY —NEW YORK HISTORICAL SOCIETY, Library, 170 Central Park W, New York, 10024. James Gregory, Librn
Holdings: Mss
Notes: 4 linear ft of correspondence and papers, 1842-1920, of Richard White (author) and of his son, Stanford White (architect). Incl in the papers are literary mss, ms music, 26 letters from James Russell Lowell and 11 letters from Thomas Bailey Aldrich.

NY —NEW YORK PUBLIC LIBRARY, Art, Prints, and Photographs Div, Fifth Ave & 42 St, New York, 10018. Donald Anderle, Chief
Holdings: Vols (150,000) Cat Mss Pix Microforms
Notes: History and design in the fine and applied arts. Architecture, painting, drawing, sculpture, costume, furniture, advertising art, prints, photography, crafts, and jewelry are among the subjects covered from ancient times to the present. See: New York Public Library *Dictionary Catalog of the Art and Architecture Division* (Boston, G K Hall, 1975), 30 vols. Holdings after that time are incl in the *Dictionary Catalog of the Research Libraries.* African Art and Afro-American Art are collected by the Schomburg Center for Research in Black Culture.

NY —LANDMARK SOCIETY OF WESTERN NEW YORK, Wenrich Memorial Library, 130 Spring Rd, Rochester, 14608.
Holdings: Vols (2000) Cat Maps Pix Slides
Budget: ($500)
Notes: Paintings, slides, drawings, as well as the Society's archives of local architecture and information on preservation and restoration techniques. Much on preservation ordinances; legal, physical and financial aspects of building preservation; local and regional history, especially Rochester and Monroe County.

NC —DUKE UNIVERSITY, East Campus Library, Durham, 27708. Betty Young, Librn
Notes: Special subject collections are Architecture-History and Art-History.

NC —NORTH CAROLINA STATE UNIVERSITY, Harry B Lyons Design Library, P. O. Box 7701, Raleigh, 27607. Maryellen LoPresti, Librn
Notes: Collection covers architecture, landscape architecture, design and related professions. Additional materials maybe found on art, painting sculpture photography and solar energy design. The library presently houses a total of 28,000 books, periodical and serial volumes to support the curriculum. A product and trade literature file and a vertical file of pamplets are also locally cataloged in the library representing an additional 3000 items of materials available for use. A significant collections of over 50,000 cataloged slides primarily representing the areas of art and architectural history are also contained in the library facility. See *Directory of Special Libraries and Information Centers.*

OH —PUBLIC LIBRARY OF CINCINNATI & HAMILTON COUNTY, Films and Recordings Center, 800 Vine St, Cincinnati, 45202. Robert Hudzik, Head
Holdings: Vols 2500 Cat Maps Pix Slides
Notes: There is a card catalog index and a printed subject index to the entire slide collection. Printed catalog does not break down Cincinnati History Collection. 2000 of the Cincinnati History Slides were originally on 3x4 glass slides and transferred to the more standard 2x2 size. Original slides are still in the collection. Use restricted to Cincinnati & Hamilton County and Fee Card Borrowers.

OH —OBERLIN COLLEGE LIBRARY, Clarence Ward Art Library, Allen Art Bldg, Oberlin, 44074. Jeffrey Weidman, Librn
Holdings: Vols (62,000) Cat Microforms
Notes: Strong in medieval European architecture and American architecture. Incl the Jefferson Collection, an almost complete duplication of the architectural books in

ARCHITECTURE—HISTORY (cont.)

Thomas Jefferson's library. Also incl Frederick B Artz Collection of books on architecture and gardening dating from the 16th through the 19th centuries. Significant holdings in early serials (see *ARLO Union List of Serials*).

OR —SOUTHERN OREGON HISTORICAL SOCIETY, Jacksonville Museum Library, 206 N Fifth St, PO Box 480, Jacksonville, 97530. Richard H Engeman, Librn
Holdings: Vols (200) Cat Mss Maps Pix Slides 16mm Films
Budget: ($5200)

PA —ATHENAEUM OF PHILADELPHIA, 219 S Sixth St, Philadelphia, 19106. Roger W Moss Jr, Librn
Holdings: Vols 15,000
Notes: Emphasis on 19th century architecture and decorative arts.

PA —FREE LIBRARY OF PHILADELPHIA, Art Dept, Logan Sq, Philadelphia, 19103. Marianne Promos, Head
Holdings: Cat
Notes: The Old Philadelphia Survey, 1931-1932, (368 measured drawings of principal 18th-century Philadelphia buildings bound in 14 vols), The Historic American Building Survey, 1933-1941, (9 vols of measured drawings 1668 through mid-19th century) and architectural pattern books from 16th century European through 19th-century American. Noncirculating, for use of graduate students and adult users in the department only.

PA —UNIVERSITY OF PITTSBURGH, Henry Clay Frick Fine Arts Library, Pittsburgh, 15260. Anne W Gordon, Fine Arts Librn
Holdings: Vols (55,000) Cat Pix Slides Microforms
Notes: Emphasis is on the art of the Western World--architecture, sculpture, painting, minor arts, archaeology, with special strength in the Byzantine, early Christian, medieval, renaissance and modern periods. The Oriental field is represented, incl replicas of scrolls. Studio arts are also covered. Illuminated ms facsimiles. Extensive collections of slides and photographs for study of art history are available in the building but not administered by the art library.

PA —PENNSYLVANIA STATE UNIVERSITY, Arts Library, 405 E Pattee Library, University Park, 18602. Jean Smith, Arts and Architecture Librn
Holdings: Vols (46,600) Cat
Notes: The Arts Library is supplemented by over 900 rare or early books from 1504 on art and architecture in The Special Collections area, and books on American architecture and current practice in The Architecture Reading Room.

RI —BROWN UNIVERSITY, John Carter Brown Library, Providence, 02912. Norman Fiering, Librn; Everett C Wilkie Jr, Bibliographer; Susan Danforth, Cur Maps & Prints
Notes: Architectural books known to have been in the Colonies before the American Revolution.

RI —PROVIDENCE PUBLIC LIBRARY, 150 Empire St, Providence, 02903. Lance J Bauer, Special Collections Librn
Holdings: Vols 2500 Cat Maps Pix
Notes: The Nickerson Architecture Collection incl some fine 17th and 18th century volumes, English style books of architectural details, a comprehensive collection of 18th and 19th century buildings styles in Europe and America and an extensive collection of contemporary works. Restricted use.

RI —RHODE ISLAND SCHOOL OF DESIGN, Library, Two College St, Providence, 02903. James A Findlay, Dir
Holdings: Vols (70,000) Cat Pix Slides
Budget: ($50,000)
Notes: Strong architecture and architectural history collection.

SC —COLLEGE OF CHARLESTON LIBRARY, Special Collections Dept, Charleston, 29401.
Notes: William Martin Aiken Collection. Incl notebook, sketchbooks composed in Europe and the US, architectural designs, correspondence, miscellaneous printed material, and a photograph of Aiken; contains also collections of other architectural designs and building adornments.

TX —UNIVERSITY OF TEXAS LIBRARIES, Architecture & Planning Library, PO Box P, Austin, 78712. Eloise F McDonald, Librn
Holdings: Vols (24,000) Cat

TX —EL PASO PUBLIC LIBRARY, Southwest Collection, 501 N Oregon, El Paso, 79901. Mary A Sarber, Head
Holdings: Vols (12,000) Cat Mss Maps Pix Microforms
Budget: ($11,000)
Notes: 400 sets of plans, incl architectural plans, by El Paso firms of Trost and Trost, Percy McGhee, Frazer and Benner. Partial catalog of Trost and Trost buildings. See Engelbrecht, Lloyd C., and Engelbrecht, June-Marie F., *Henry C. Trost: Architect of the Southwest* (El Paso Public Library Association, 1981).

WA —UNIVERSITY OF WASHINGTON LIBRARIES, Pacific Northwest Collection, Seattle, 98195. Andrew F Johnson, Librn
Holdings: Vols (50,000) Cat Maps Pix
Budget: ($12,000)
Notes: The Pacific Northwest Collection contains printed materials documenting the historic and contemporary life and culture of the region in a broad range of subject areas. The Pacific Northwest is defined as the geographic region including Washington, Oregon, Idaho, Montana, British Columbia, Yukon Territory, and Alaska. Printed materials including books, periodicals, government documents, maps, weekly and local regional newspapers, theses and dissertations, as well as photographs and architectural drawings are included in the Pacific Northwest Collection. Photographic works of over 200 photographers active in the Pacific Northwest, Alaska, and the Yukon Territory (Canada) during the period 1860-1930, including Asahel and Edward S Curtis, Eric Hegg, and Clark Kinsey, are represented in a print collection of more than 300,000 images. The architecturaldrawings collection includes over 19,000 original plans, drawings, sketches, renderings and blue prints pertaining to the history of architecture and urban planning and landscape gardening in the Pacific Northwest ca 1880-1940. Areas of particular strength are the holdings of over 1100 published journals of Pacific Northwest exploration expeditions, photographs of Northwest Coast Native Americans and of historic Seattle, newspapers issued within the Japanese-American relocation camps, 1942-1945, materials relating to the 1980 eruption of Mt St Helens, and Sanborne fire insurance maps for Washington. A unique feature of the Collection is the subject index to regional periodicals and local newspapers maintained by the PNW Collection staff; over 100 titles are currently indexed. G K Hall Company published a books catalog of the Pacific Northwest Collectionin 1973.

†WY —UNIVERSITY OF WYOMING, William Robertson Coe Library, Archives of Contemporary History, 13th & Ivinson, Laramie, 82071.
Notes: The papers of Victor Gondos. Incl journals and books, several hundred folders on military and archival history, his diaries from 1920-1974, and more than 1500 letters on historical research and architecture.

ON —UNIVERSITY OF WATERLOO, Library, Waterloo, N2L 3G1, Can. Susan Bellingham, Special Collections Librn
Notes: The Rosa Breithaupt Clark Collection of books on the history of architecture.

ARCHITECTURE—PLANS see Architecture—Designs and Plans; Architecture_History

ARCHITECTURE—RESTORATION see Architecture—Conservation and Restoration

ARCHITECTURE, AMERICAN

CA —STANFORD UNIVERSITY LIBRARIES, Cecil H Green Library, Stanford, 94305. Michael T Ryan, Cur
Holdings: Mss
Notes: Manuscript collections pertaining to the architect Frank Lloyd Wright.

DE —HENRY F DUPONT WINTERTHUR MUSEUM LIBRARY, Winterthur, 19735. Frank H Sommer, III, Head
Holdings: Cat
Notes: Strong collections.

DC —LIBRARY OF CONGRESS, Rare Book & Special Collections Div, Washington, 20540. William Matheson, Chief
Notes: The Division's general rare book collection contains substantial holdings relating to early American architecture. The collection incl early American imprints and British, French, and Italian books imported and used in the Colonies.

DC —LIBRARY OF CONGRESS, Washington, 20540.
Notes: Papers and working materials of Charles Eames (1907-1978), American architect and designer. Incl are original negatives and prints of the 106 educational films he created, business correspondence 1944 to 1978, some 400,000 color slides, 31, 000 black and white photographs, production materials for exhibits, and drawings for all his major furniture designs.

DC —LIBRARY OF CONGRESS, Prints & Photographs Div, Washington, 20540.
Holdings: 11,427 Items
Notes: The Joseph S Allen Collection of architectural photographs. Covering the period 1945 to 1967, the collection consists of photographs of churches, colleges, government buildings, residential structures, and historic monuments in 27 eastern and mid-western states. Also, the Carnegie Survey of the Architecture of the South is a photographic record of the early buildings and gardens of Maryland, Virginia, the Carolinas, Georgia, Alabama, Louisiana, Florida and Mississippi, executed by Frances Benjamin Johnston between 1933 and 1940. Also, the Pictorial Archives of Early American Architecture.

DC —LIBRARY OF CONGRESS, Prints and Photographs Div, Historic American Buildings Survey, Washington, 20540.
Holdings: Cat Mss Pix Drawings
Notes: Details of some 17,000 American buildings in 81,000 photographs, 42,000 measured drawings and 44,000 pp of written documentation.

KS —UNIVERSITY OF KANSAS, Kenneth Spencer Research Library, Kansas Collection, Lawrence, 66045. Sheryl K Williams, Cur
Holdings: Cat Mss Pix
Notes: Correspondence, drawings, and tracings of prominent architectural firms in Kansas, 1900-date. Photocopying dependent on condition and donor restrictions. Approximately 500 drawings and tracings. correspondence, drawings, etc, cataloged. Separate book catalog with inventories, provenance, etc, maintained. Architectural drawings incl.

KS —UNIVERSITY OF KANSAS, Kenneth Spencer Research Library, Special Collections Dept, Lawrence, 66045. Alexandra Mason, Librn
Holdings: Cat Mss Pix Slides
Notes: Two main groups: Willett-Pashley collection (working library of 19th century Chicago architectural firm): ca 800 volumes; cataloged. Frank Lloyd Wright collection (mss photographs, slides, books, clippings): ca 6 Hollinger boxes, photos, mss, magazines and books; cataloged. Noncirculating

LA —TULANE UNIVERSITY, Howard-Tilton Memorial Library, Southeast Architectural Archives, 7001 Freret St, New Orleans, 70118. William R Cullison, Cur of Prints & Drawings
Notes: Southeast Architectural Archives Collection incl over 30,000 individual pieces. Drawings were made mostly by New Orleans practitioners, mostly for locations in and about the city; there are, however, some drawings by architects from outside New Orleans and some for buildings located elsewhere. Collection dates from about 1800 to the present day, with the majority of pieces falling between about 1835-1965.

ARCHITECTURE, AMERICAN (cont.)

LA —LOUISIANA STATE UNIVERSITY, SHREVEPORT, Library-Archives, 8515 Youree Dr, Shreveport, 71129. Patricia L Meador, Archivist & Asst Librn
Notes: Archives incl catalogued manuscripts and records, 500 maps, more than 5000 photographs, 1000 architectural drawings, slides. The collection's primary emphasis is the history of North Louisiana, particularly Northwest Louisiana. The 1500 linear ft incl area plantation records and ledgers; personal papers of area pioneers, planters, legislators, politicians, educators, businessmen, and architects; papers and records of longtime (1919-1961) Caddo Parish Coroner, Willis P Butler; the Samuel G Wiener, Sr architectual records (1921-1976) with drawings and photographs; the Ted Flaxman architectual records (1919-1968); the papers (1860-1921) of architect Nathaniel S Allen; the collection of Dewey A Somdal,Shreveport architect, historian and collector, with emphasis on steamboats, travel on the Red River and Louisiana history, 1780-1972.

MD —MARYLAND HISTORICAL SOCIETY, Library, 201 W Monument St, Baltimore, 21201. William B Keller, Head Librn
Holdings: Vols (65,000) Cat Maps Pix Slides
Budget: ($8000)
Notes: Incl Benjamin H Latrobe (architectural) Papers.
See also entry under Maryland - History

NH —STRAWBERY BANKE, Thayer Cumings Historical Reference Library, Portsmouth, 03801. Nicole R Osborn, Librn
Holdings: Vols (2850) Cat Mss Maps Pix Microforms
Budget: ($1900)
Notes: The Library is a small, highly specialized library with holdings in American art, architecture and decorative arts. The collection is especially strong in the American decorative arts, with additional concentration in European decorative arts. In addition, the collection contains books on American painting, American architecture, archaeology, technology, maritime history and boatbuilding, landscape gardening and design, as well as books on local and regional history and social and material culture of the 17th-19th centuries. Collection of mss microfilm and documents is related to important properties and personages of Portsmouth and the surrounding area.

†NY —COLUMBIA UNIVERSITY LIBRARIES, Butler Library, Rare Book and Manuscript Library, 535 W 114 St, New York, 10027.
Notes: Located in the Avery Architectural Library. The architectural drawings of the New York firm of Kahn and Jacobs. A record of much of New York architecture from the 1890s through 1972. Incl works by Ely Jacques Kahn.

NY —MUSEUM OF THE CITY OF NEW YORK, Photo Archives, Fifth Ave & 103 St, New York, 10029. Esther Brumberg, Librn
Holdings: Mss Maps Pix
Notes: All aspects of New York City--history, costume, social life and customs, etc. Also, Byron Collection--about 10,000 prints, 1880-1930, of views of New York, commercial interiors, interiors and exteriors of private residences, social events, shipping, immigration; Wurts Collection--15,000 glass negatives, 1890-1940, mostly architectural; 100,000 Wurts Architectural Photographs, to be cataloged. Underhill Collection--about 900 glass negatives, mostly architectural, 1896-1936; McKim, Mead & White Collection--1000 glass negatives of the work of the firm, 1880-1915; and Berenice Abbott Collection, Changing New York--about 350 negatives taken by Miss Abbott for the Federal Arts Project, 1930s. Other FAP photographs incl a series on Coney Island, one on Harlem, Sewing Project, and Sabbath Studies.

NY —SYRACUSE UNIVERSITY LIBRARIES, Ernest S Bird Library, George Arents Research Library for Special Collections, Syracuse, 13210. Carolyn A Davis, Manuscripts Librn; Amy S Doherty, University Archivist; Mark F Weimer, Rare Book Librn
Notes: The George Arents Research Library for Special Collections at Syracuse University contains the papers of Harley James McKee, Lorimer Rich, Frederick Lear, Max Abramovitz, James I Arnold, Pietro Bulluschi, Claude Bragdon, Marcel Breuer, William Lescaze, Skidmore Owings & Merrill, Ralph Walker, Eric Fisher Wood, Minoru Yamasaki, Joseph Louis Young, and Archimedes Russell.

OH —CLEVELAND PUBLIC LIBRARY, Fine Arts and Special Collections Department, 325 Superior Ave, Cleveland, 44114. Alice N Loranth, Head
Holdings: Vols (9000) Cat Pix Plans Microforms
Notes: Part of the Architecture Collection, which incl all periods with special emphasis on American and English architecture. Coverage incl good representation from all countries. Original plans, drawings and elevations for five Cleveland area buildings by the architectural firm of Hubbell and Benes are housed as a special collection. 20 drawers of mounted pictures relatng to Cleveland.

OH —OBERLIN COLLEGE LIBRARY, Clarence Ward Art Library, Allen Art Bldg, Oberlin, 44074. Jeffrey Weidman, Librn
Holdings: Vols (62,000) Cat Microforms
Notes: Strong in medieval European architecture and American architecture. Incl the Jefferson Collection, an almost complete duplication of the architectural books in Thomas Jefferson's library. Also incl Frederick B Artz Collection of books on architecture and gardening dating from the 16th through the 19th centuries. Significant holdings in early serials (see *ARLO Union List of Serials).*

PA —ATHENAEUM OF PHILADELPHIA, 219 S Sixth St, Philadelphia, 19106. Roger W Moss Jr, Librn
Holdings: Vols 25,000 Mss
Notes: Incl 450 drawings of Thomas Ustick Walter from 1804-1887; nineteenth century architecture and decorative art; 30,000 mss drawings; 20,000 photographs; one billion mss.

PA —FREE LIBRARY OF PHILADELPHIA, Art Dept, Logan Sq, Philadelphia, 19103. Marianne Promos, Head
Holdings: Cat
Notes: The Old Philadelphia Survey, 1931-1932, (368 measured drawings of principal 18th-century Philadelphia buildings bound in 14 vols), The Historic American Building Survey, 1933-1941, (9 vols of measured drawings 1668 through mid-19th century) amd architectural pattern books from 16th-century European through 19th-century American. Noncirculating, for use of graduate students and adult users in the department only.

TX —ROSENBERG LIBRARY, Galveston and Texas History Center, 2310 Sealy Ave, Galveston, 77550. Jane Kenamore, Archivist
Holdings: Mss Architectural drawings
Notes: Collection incl the Galveston Architecture Inventory, 1966-1967, photographs of Galveston buildings, and architectural drawings by Nicolas J Clayton.

VA —COLONIAL WILLIAMSBURG FOUNDATION, Research Center Library, PO Drawer C, Williamsburg, 23187. John E Ingram, Research Archivist
Holdings: Vols (30,000) Cat Mss Maps Pix Microforms
Budget: ($20,000)
Notes: Virginia and the Chesapeake in the 17th-18th centuries. Particular strengths include social, economic, agricultural and architectural history. The collection encompasses over 6000 rare books, 18th Century music scores and 12,000 manuscripts, as well as a complete set of Virginia Colonial Records Project microfilm (1000 reels).

ARCHITECTURE, AMERICAN—PICTURES, ILLUSTRATIONS, ETC.

DC —LIBRARY OF CONGRESS, Prints & Photographs Div, Washington, 20540.
Notes: Joseph S Allen Collection of architectural photographs dating chiefly from 1945-1967.

ARCHITECTURE, BAROQUE

DC —LIBRARY OF CONGRESS, Prints & Photographs Div, Washington, 20540.
Notes: The Alfred Marie Collection contains drawings (copies) of French Renaissance and Baroque architecture.

ARCHITECTURE, BRITISH

IN —INDIANA UNIVERSITY, Lilly Library, Seventh St, Bloomington, 47405. William R Cagle, Librn
Holdings: Vols 200 Cat
Notes: Largely 19th century British architecture.

OH —CLEVELAND PUBLIC LIBRARY, Fine Arts and Special Collections Department, 325 Superior Ave, Cleveland, 44114. Alice N Loranth, Head
Holdings: Vols (9000) Cat Mss
Notes: All periods of architecture are covered, with special emphasis on American and English architecture. Coverage incl good representation from all countries.

ARCHITECTURE, BYZANTINE

MD —JOHNS HOPKINS UNIVERSITY, Milton S Eisenhower Library, Charles & 34 Sts, Baltimore, 21218. Ann S Gwyn, Assistant Dir for Special Collections
Holdings: Vols (18,000) Cat Maps
Notes: Strongest in ancient, Byzantine, and Renaissance art and architecture. Reference Library lacks some periodicals. Modern period being rapidly built up.

ARCHITECTURE, CALIFORNIA

CA —UNIVERSITY OF CALIFORNIA, DAVIS, Shields Library, Dept of Special Collections, Davis, 95616. Donald Kunitz, Head; C Danial Elliott, Asst Head
Holdings: Cat Mss Pix
Notes: The Baird Archive of California Art incl a section on California architecture, with photographs, clippings, research papers on specific buildings, and documentation compiled for the Historic American Buildings Survey. 1400 items. Described in Baird, Joseph A, Jr, *Northern California Art: An Interpretive Bibliography* (Davis, California, Library Associates, University of California, 1977).

CA —UNIVERSITY OF CALIFORNIA, LOS ANGELES, Research Library, Dept of Special Collections, 405 Hilgard Ave, Los Angeles, 90024. Edward Shreeves, Chairman, Bibliographers Group; David S Zeidberg, Head
Notes: 6000 photographs recording the work of Welton Becket; 600 photographs recording the work of Mark Daniels; the Richard J Neutra archive.

CA —PASADENA PUBLIC LIBRARY, Fine Arts Division, Reference Services, 285 E Walnut St, Pasadena, 91101. Anne Cain, Principal Librn
Holdings: Vols (10,000) Cat Pix Films
Notes: Plus clipping files and scrapbooks emphasizing Pasadena and California architecture; Greene & Greene, Architects. Incl over 130,000 pictures, 64 films. Special index of *Architectural Digest,* vols 1-III and VI-XII for southern California homes and architects.

CA —CALIFORNIA POLYTECHNIC STATE UNIVERSITY LIBRARY, Special Collections and University Archives, San Luis Obispo, 93407. Nancy E Loe, Head Librn
Holdings: Vols (100) Cat
Notes: Herpersonal papers covering her architectural career of forty years, which incl several Hearst estates as well as private residences in the California Arts and Crafts style. Incl Hearst/Morgan correspondence and telegrams; business correspondence, travel accounts, sketchbooks, awards, photographs and several hundred architectural drawings. Hearst Castle Collection incl 8500 architectural drawings

ARCHITECTURE, CALIFORNIA (cont.)

for Hearst's residences at San Simeon, Jolon, Wyntoon, and Santa Monica and approx 100 vols of secondary source material. The Asilomar Collection contains 145 architectural drawings for the Morgan-designed YWCA facility near Monterey, California. Incl blueprints, diplomas, personal papers. Finding aid in progress. Incl 10,000 pieces of ms material, 10,000 architectural drawings and blueprints.

ARCHITECTURE, CANADIAN

AB —UNIVERSITY OF CALGARY, Libraries, Special Collections Div, 2500 University Dr, Calgary, T2N 1N4, Can.
Holdings: Cat Mss Pix Audiotapes 16mm Films Microforms
Notes: The Canadian Architectural Archives at the University of Calgary include collections of drawings, records, sketches, renderings, correspondence, project files of the following Canadian architects (qv separate entries): Raymond T Affleck, J Francis Brown and F Bruce Brown, J A Cawston, Arthur C Erickson, Long Mayell & Associates, Hugh McMillan Architects Ltd, Raymond Moriyama, John B Parkin Associates/N O R R , Rule Wynn & Rule (Edmonton and Calgary), Stevenson Raines Barrett Hutton Seton & Partners, The Thom Partnership, Thompson Berwick Pratt & Partners, and H M Whiddington. Dates from 1891 to about 1974. The Archives also incl photographs, microfilmed material (16mm and 35mm, film strip and aperture cards), and Oral History Interviews on tape. Project lists and/or inventories are on hand.

BC —UNIVERSITY OF VICTORIA, Maltwood Art Museum & Gallery, Finnerty Rd, Victoria, V8W 2Y2, Can. Martin Segger, Dir/Cur
Holdings: Vols 700
Notes: The Museum maintains a special archival collection of architectural plans and drawings, mainly of regional historic interest. Its library and archives are now housed and administered by the McPherson Library, University of Victoria.

ON —UNIVERSITY OF TORONTO, Thomas Fisher Rare Book Library, 120 Saint George St, Toronto, M5S 1A5, Can. Richard G Landon, Head
Holdings: Vols (30,000) Mss
Budget: 5
Notes: All currently published and most earlier major works on the fine and applied arts in Canada; Canadian art exhibition catalogues; limited editions illustrated by Canadian artists; 19th and 20th century architectural plans for buildings in Toronto and southern Ontario vicinity (ca 1700).

ARCHITECTURE, CHICAGO

IL —CHICAGO PUBLIC LIBRARY, Art Section, Fine Arts Division, 78 E Washington St, Chicago, 60602. Rosalinda I Hack, Fine Arts Division Chief; Yvonne S Brown, Head, Art Section
Holdings: Vols 6000
Notes: Reference and circulating collection, with special emphasis on general architectural history, modern architecture, architecture of the United States, and Chicago architectural history. Collection is supported by the Chicago Architecture File, a card file that lists citations to information on buildings that have been recognized for their architectural significance. The section's picture collection has extensive documentation on Chicago area architecture, and incorporates a collection of architectural photographs by Stephen Beal. Archival copies of these photographs are to be found in Special Collections. The collection is also supplemented by the microform collections of *The Historic American Buildings Survey*, and *American Architectural Books*.

ARCHITECTURE, CHURCH see Church Architecture

ARCHITECTURE, CLUNIAC

MA —HARVARD UNIVERSITY, Graduate School of Design, Frances Loeb Library, Gund Hall, Cambridge, 02138. James Hodgson, Librn
Holdings: Cat Mss Pix
Notes: Materials deposited by Professor Kenneth J Conant, who was in charge of archaeological excavations at Cluny.

ARCHITECTURE, COUNTRY see Architecture, Domestic

ARCHITECTURE, DOMESTIC

CA —BURBANK PUBLIC LIBRARY, 110 N Glenoaks Blvd, Burbank, 91502. Mary Ann Grasso, Coordr; Barbara Stones, Coordr, Media Project
Holdings: Vols (32,000) Cat Clippings Pix VF
Notes: The

CA —CRAFT AND FOLK ART MUSEUM, Library, 5814 Wilshire Blvd, Los Angeles, 90036. Joan M Benedetti, Museum Librn
Holdings: Vols (2000) Slides VF
Notes: Incl 2000 books; 70 journal subscriptions; artists' biographical files: 6 file drawers; clipping files: 8 file drawers; 20,000 slides. Representation of the material culture of all people, traditional and contemporary expressions. Incl visual and printed information on ethnic, traditional, popular, decorative, idiosyncratic, and contemporary crafts as well as vernacular architecture, handmade houses, and design. Information about and for professional artists on health hazards, conservation, and career management. Anthropological and art historical works; exhibition catalogues; slides, photographs, audiocassettes; clipping and pamphlet files. Contemporary Slide Registry of Craftspeople and extensive biographical files of contemporary craft artists. Information and referral files of craft related galleries, shops, festivals, organizations, etc.

CA —MONTEREY PUBLIC LIBRARY, 625 Pacific St, Monterey, 93940. Ruth Kelly, Asst Library Dir
Holdings: Vols 500 Cat
Notes: French, Italian, Spanish and English country house architecture.

IN —INDIANA UNIVERSITY, Lilly Library, Seventh St, Bloomington, 47405. William R Cagle, Librn
Holdings: Vols 200 Cat
Notes: Largely 19th century British architecture.

WA —UNIVERSITY OF WASHINGTON LIBRARIES, Pacific Northwest Collection, Seattle, 98195. Andrew F Johnson, Librn
Holdings: Vols (50,000) Cat Maps Pix
Budget: ($12,000)
Notes: The Pacific Northwest Collection contains printed materials documenting the historic and contemporary life and culture of the region in a broad range of subject areas. The Pacific Northwest is defined as the geographic region including Washington, Oregon, Idaho, Montana, British Columbia, Yukon Territory, and Alaska. Printed materials including books, periodicals, government documents, maps, weekly and local regional newspapers, theses and dissertations, as well as photographs and architectural drawings are included in the Pacific Northwest Collection. Photographic works of over 200 photographers active in the Pacific Northwest, Alaska, and the Yukon Territory (Canada) during the period 1860-1930, including Asahel and Edward S Curtis, Eric Hegg, and Clark Kinsey, are represented in a print collection of more than 300,000 images. The architecturaldrawings collection includes over 19,000 original plans, drawings, sketches, renderings and blue prints pertaining to the history of architecture and urban planning and landscape gardening in the Pacific Northwest ca 1880-1940. Areas of particular strength are the holdings of over 1100 published journals of Pacific Northwest exploration expeditions, photographs of Northwest Coast Native Americans and of historic Seattle, newspapers issued within the Japanese-American relocation camps, 1942-1945, materials relating to the 1980 eruption of Mt St Helens, and Sanborne fire insurance maps for Washington. A unique feature of the Collection is the subject index to regional periodicals and local newspapers maintained by the PNW Collection staff; over 100 titles are currently indexed. G K Hall Company published a books catalog of the Pacific Northwest Collectionin 1973.

ARCHITECTURE, DUTCH

NJ —RUTGERS, THE STATE UNIVERSITY OF NEW JERSEY, Alexander Library, Special Collections and Archives, College Ave & Huntington St, New Brunswick, 08903. Ronald L Becker, Cur of Manuscripts and Rare Books
Holdings: Pix
Notes: The pictorial collection of Special Collections, dating from the 18th century to the present, incl foreign, US, and New Jersey material: portraits, local views, historical scenes. Special groups: George Washington and Benjamin Franklin engraved portraits; photos of New Jersey localities (among these about 10,000 postal cards).

ARCHITECTURE, ECCLESIASTICAL see Church Architecture

ARCHITECTURE, FRENCH

CA —SAN DIEGO PUBLIC LIBRARY, Art, Music & Recreation Sect, 820 E St, San Diego, 92101. Barbara A Tuhill, Supvr
Holdings: Vols 350 Cat
Notes: Special collection of books mainly on Spanish Mediterranean and Italian and French Renaissance architecture which was the private library of William Templeton Johnson, a local architect. For reference use only.

DC —LIBRARY OF CONGRESS, Prints & Photographs Div, Washington, 20540.
Notes: The Alfred Marie Collection contains drawings (copies) of French Renaissance and Baroque architecture.

ARCHITECTURE, GERMAN

MD —JOHNS HOPKINS UNIVERSITY, Milton S Eisenhower Library, Charles & 34 Sts, Baltimore, 21218. Ann S Gwyn, Assistant Dir for Special Collections
Holdings: Cat Mss
Notes: 100 mss of lectures on art and architecture, based on research done in Germany before World War II (many sites no longer extant).

ARCHITECTURE, INDIANA

IN —INDIANA HISTORICAL SOCIETY, Library, 315 W Ohio St, Indianapolis, 46202. Robert K O'Neill, Dir
Holdings: Vols Cat Mss Pix Microforms
Notes: Records and drawings of Indiana architects, contractors, and as well as records concerning structures created by non-Indiana professionals within the state. Types of material collected incl office files, correspondence, drawings, blueprints, photographs, personal papers, specifications, books and pamphlets. The collection incl approximately 14,000 drawings, along with another 10,000 on microfilm, from central Indiana architectural firms. Incl among the drawings are approximately 800 for Union Station, Indianapolis.

ARCHITECTURE, INSTITUTIONAL

†WY —UNIVERSITY OF WYOMING, William Robertson Coe Library, Archives of Contemporary History, 13th & Ivinson, Laramie, 82071.
Notes: The papers of Victor Gondos. Incl journals and books, several hundred folders on military and archival history, his diaries from 1920-1974, and more than 1500 letters on historical research and architecture.

ARCHITECTURE, ISLAMIC

CO —UNIVERSITY OF COLORADO, Libraries, Art & Architecture Library,

ARCHITECTURE, ISLAMIC (cont.)

Campus Box 184, Boulder, 80309. Liesel Nolan, Librn/Dept Head
Holdings: Vols (57,647) Cat Pix
Budget: ($39,000)
Notes: Special feature: art exhibition catalog collection 1963-1971, 1972-date. Good general collection with some special emphasis on environmental design, Islamic architecture, Indian art and South American Indian art. Fair collection of periodical backfiles in art and in architecture. Separate catalog for materials in collection. Rare books in main library, listed only in central union catalog.

MA —HARVARD UNIVERSITY, Harvard College Library, Fine Arts Library, Fogg Museum, 32 Quincy St, Cambridge, 02138. Wolfgang M Freitag, Librn
Holdings: Vols 4000
Notes: Books, slides, photographs, postcards, architectural plans, and drawings of historic sites.

ARCHITECTURE, ITALIAN

CA —SAN DIEGO PUBLIC LIBRARY, Art, Music & Recreation Sect, 820 E St, San Diego, 92101. Barbara A Tuhill, Supvr
Holdings: Vols 350 Cat
Notes: Special collection of books mainly on Spanish Mediterranean and Italian and French Renaissance architecture which was the private library of William Templeton Johnson, a local architect. For reference use only.

ARCHITECTURE, LATIN AMERICAN

AZ —ARIZONA STATE MUSEUM, Library, University of Arizona, Tucson, 85721. Hans R Bart, Museum Librn
Holdings: Vols 400 Cat
Notes: Art and architecture of Latin America, strong in pre-Columbian material but mainly Spanish Colonial from the 16th to the 18th century. This is a large private library which is being transferred to the ASM Library. Special catalog is planned.

DC —LIBRARY OF CONGRESS, Prints & Photographs Div, Washington, 20540.
Holdings: Cat Pix
Notes: The Archive of Hispanic Culture is a photographic reference collection for the study of Latin American art and architecture. The collection illustrates indigenous art works dating from the colonial period through the 20th century as well as artistically influential monuments in Spain, Portugal, the Phillipines, and the US.

LA —TULANE UNIVERSITY, Howard-Tilton Memorial Library, Latin American Library, New Orleans, 70118. Thomas Niehaus, Dir
Holdings: Vols (150,000) Cat Mss Maps Pix Microforms VF
Budget: ($67,000)
Notes: *Catalog of the Latin American* Library (Boston: G K Hall, 1970, suppl. 1973,1975,1978); Downs 5338-41; suppl (1961), 2727, 2737. The Latin American Library is a general collection, but specializes in Central American, Mexican, and Brazilian materials. The disciplines which are most strongly represented are history, anthropology, and archaeology. The Viceregal Ecclesiastical Mexican Collection contains manuscripts from the colonial period. The France V Scholes Collection contains a large number of photoprints and microfilm of colonial documents from the archives of Spain and Mexico. The Merle Greene Robertson Rubbings Collection contains nearly five hundred rubbings of relief sculpture from Mayan archaeological sites in Mexico and Guatemala. The Photographic Collection contains photos of archaeological sites inMeso-America, of pre-Columbian Peruvian architecture, and a general group of historic photos from Latin America.

ARCHITECTURE, LIBRARY see Library Architecture

ARCHITECTURE, MEDIEVAL

NJ —PRINCETON UNIVERSITY, Marquand Library, McCormick Hall, Princeton, 08544. Mary M Schmidt, Librn
Holdings: Vols (130,000) Cat Microforms
Notes: Especially strong in classical archaeology, medieval art and architecture, and photography history.

OH —OBERLIN COLLEGE LIBRARY, Clarence Ward Art Library, Allen Art Bldg, Oberlin, 44074. Jeffrey Weidman, Librn
Holdings: Vols (62,000) Cat Microforms
Notes: Strong in medieval European architecture and American architecture. Incl the Jefferson Collection, an almost complete duplication of the architectural books in Thomas Jefferson's library. Also incl Frederick B Artz Collection of books on architecture and gardening dating from the 16th through the 19th centuries. Significant holdings in early serials (see *ARLO Union List of Serials).*

ARCHITECTURE, MINNESOTA

MN —MINNEAPOLIS PUBLIC LIBRARY & INFORMATION CENTER, Minneapolis History Collection, 300 Nicollet Mall, Minneapolis, 55401. Dorothy M Burke, Librn
Holdings: Vols (20,000) Cat Mss Maps Pix Slides Phonorecords Audiotapes
Budget: ($850)
Notes: Collection contains print and film materials pertaining to Minneapolis, includes some Minnesota history. Also have 29 five-drawer legal files of clips and ephemeral materials, and direct access to the 119-file morgue of the old *Minneapolis Times,* a newspaper which ceased publishing in 1948. This is especially useful for items covering the 20s, 30s and 40s. Special card indexes to plates in architectural serials (local), houses, buildings, streets, parks, etc; also indexes to 10-20 local newspapers and magazines. Collection of about 60 neighborhood newspapers (current and retrospective) and about 1000 maps and atlases; nearly 250,000 pictures; early (1859-1920) city directories.

ARCHITECTURE, MOSLEM see Architecture, Islamic

ARCHITECTURE, NAVAL see Naval Architecture; Shipbuilding

ARCHITECTURE, NEW ENGLAND

MA —SOCIETY FOR THE PRESERVATION OF NEW ENGLAND ANTIQUITIES, Library, 141 Cambridge St, Boston, 02114. Ellie Reichlin, Librn & Cur of Photographic Collections
Holdings: Vols (3000) Cat Pix Microforms
Budget: ($75,000)
Notes: Photograph collections, all media (incl daguerreotypes, ambrotypes, etc, stereographic views, carte de visite) depicting New England buildings; interiors; street and town views; occupations; pastimes; transport and personalities. Covers 1840s-1930s, with some more recent additons. Amateur and professional photographers represented. Cataloged in part, otherwise arranged by localities, subject, personal name. Special collections incl: marine photographs by N L Stebbins and Henry Peabody (1880s-1920s); Boston and Albany railroad photographic archive, early 1900s; Quabbin Valley views; historic American Buildings Survey photographs (17th to early 19th century architecture) by Arthur Haskell; Baldwin Coolidge collection, and many others. Size: 500,000 prints, ca 75,000 negatives (glass plates and copy negs). These are cataloged. Some special indexes incllandscape design (arbors, conservatories, flower beds, bandstands etc); photographers represented; architects represented (partial), and pending, interiors (specific features of); occupations.

MA —OLD STURBRIDGE VILLAGE, Research Library, Sturbridge, 01566. Theresa Rini Percy, Librn
Holdings: Cat Pix
Notes: Before 1850.

†NY —COLUMBIA UNIVERSITY LIBRARIES, Butler Library, Rare Book and Manuscript Library, 535 W 114 St, New York, 10027.
Notes: Located in the Avery Architectural Library. The architectural drawings of the New York firm of Kahn and Jacobs. A record of much of New York architecture from the 1890s through 1972. Incl works by Ely Jacques Kahn.

ARCHITECTURE, NEW JERSEY

NJ —RUTGERS, THE STATE UNIVERSITY OF NEW JERSEY, Alexander Library, Special Collections and Archives, College Ave & Huntington St, New Brunswick, 08903. Ronald L Becker, Cur of Manuscripts and Rare Books
Holdings: Pix
Notes: The pictorial collection of Special Collections, dating from the 18th century to the present, incl foreign, US, and New Jersey material: portraits, local views, historical scenes. Special groups: George Washington and Benjamin Franklin engraved portraits; photos of New Jersey localities (among these about 10,000 postal cards).

ARCHITECTURE, NEW ORLEANS

LA —TULANE UNIVERSITY, Howard-Tilton Memorial Library, Southeast Architectural Archives, 7001 Freret St, New Orleans, 70118. William R Cullison, Cur of Prints & Drawings
Notes: Southeast Architectural Archives Collection incl over 30,000 individual pieces. Drawings were made mostly by New Orleans practitioners, mostly for locations in and about the city; there are, however, some drawings by architects from outside New Orleans and some for buildings located elsewhere. Collection dates from about 1800 to the present day, with the majority of pieces falling between about 1835-1965.

ARCHITECTURE, PRIMITIVE

CA —CRAFT AND FOLK ART MUSEUM, Library, 5814 Wilshire Blvd, Los Angeles, 90036. Joan M Benedetti, Museum Librn
Holdings: Vols (2000) Slides VF
Notes: Incl 2000 books; 70 journal subscriptions; artists' biographical files: 6 file drawers; clipping files: 8 file drawers; 20,000 slides. Representation of the material culture of all people, traditional and contemporary expressions. Incl visual and printed information on ethnic, traditional, popular, decorative, idiosyncratic, and contemporary crafts as well as vernacular architecture, handmade houses, and design. Information about and for professional artists on health hazards, conservation, and career management. Anthropological and art historical works; exhibition catalogues; slides, photographs, audiocassettes; clipping and pamphlet files. Contemporary Slide Registry of Craftspeople and extensive biographical files of contemporary craft artists. Information and referral files of craft related galleries, shops, festivals, organizations, etc.

ARCHITECTURE, RENAISSANCE

CA —SAN DIEGO PUBLIC LIBRARY, Art, Music & Recreation Sect, 820 E St, San Diego, 92101. Barbara A Tuhill, Supvr
Holdings: Vols 350 Cat
Notes: Special collection of books mainly on Spanish Mediterranean and Italian and French Renaissance architecture which was the private library of William Templeton Johnson, a local architect. For reference use only.

DC —LIBRARY OF CONGRESS, Prints & Photographs Div, Washington, 20540.
Notes: The Alfred Marie Collection contains drawings (copies) of French Renaissance and Baroque architecture.

LA —UNIVERSITY OF SOUTHERN LOUISIANA, Dupre Library, Jefferson Caffery Louisiana Room, 302 East St Mary Blvd, Lafayette, 70504. Cynthia J Rice, Louisiana Room Ref Librn
Holdings: Vols 20
Notes: Sixteenth and seventeenth century publications.

ARCHITECTURE, RENAISSANCE (cont.)

MD —JOHNS HOPKINS UNIVERSITY, Milton S Eisenhower Library, Charles & 34 Sts, Baltimore, 21218. Ann S Gwyn, Assistant Dir for Special Collections
Holdings: Vols (18,000) Cat Maps
Notes: Strongest in ancient, Byzantine, and Renaissance art and architecture. Reference Library lacks some periodicals. Modern period being rapidly built up.

ARCHITECTURE, RURAL see Architecture, Domestic

ARCHITECTURE, SCHOOL see School Buildings

ARCHITECTURE, SOUTHERN

DC —LIBRARY OF CONGRESS, Prints & Photographs Div, Washington, 20540.
Notes: The Carnegie Survey of the Architecture of the South is a photographic record of the early buildings and gardens of Maryland, Virginia, the Carolinas, Georgia, Alabama, Louisiana, Florida and Mississippi, executed by Frances Benjamin Johnston between 1933 and 1940.

ARCHITECTURE, SOUTHWESTERN

NM —ROSWELL PUBLIC LIBRARY, 301 N Pennsylvania Ave, Roswell, 88201. Sarah Beth Galloway, Library Dir
Holdings: Vols (2000) Cat Maps
Budget: $1000
Notes: Covers literature (fiction and nonfiction), history, biography, geography, law, architecture of Oklahoma, Texas, Colorado, New Mexico, Arizona and Northern Mexico.

TX —EL PASO PUBLIC LIBRARY, Southwest Collection, 501 N Oregon, El Paso, 79901. Mary A Sarber, Head
Holdings: Vols (12,000) Cat Mss Maps Pix Microforms
Budget: ($11,000)
Notes: 400 sets of plans, incl architectural plans, by El Paso firms of Trost and Trost, Percy McGhee, Frazer and Benner. Partial catalog of Trost and Trost buildings. See Engelbrecht, Lloyd C., and Engelbrecht, June-Marie F., *Henry C. Trost: Architect of the Southwest* (El Paso Public Library Association, 1981).

ARCHITECTURE, SPANISH

AZ —ARIZONA STATE MUSEUM, Library, University of Arizona, Tucson, 85721. Hans R Bart, Museum Librn
Holdings: Vols 250 Cat Mss
Notes: Art and architecture of Latin America, strong in pre-Columbian material but mainly Spanish Colonial from the 16th to the 18th century. This is a large private library which is being transferred to the ASM Library. Special catalog is planned.

CA —SAN DIEGO PUBLIC LIBRARY, Art, Music & Recreation Sect, 820 E St, San Diego, 92101. Barbara A Tuhill, Supvr
Holdings: Vols 350 Cat
Notes: Special collection of books mainly on Spanish Mediterranean and Italian and French Renaissance architecture which was the private library of William Templeton Johnson, a local architect. For reference use only.

ARCHITECTURE, SYNAGOGUE see Synagogue Architecture

ARCHITECTURE, TEXAS

TX —ROSENBERG LIBRARY, Galveston and Texas History Center, 2310 Sealy Ave, Galveston, 77550. Jane Kenamore, Archivist
Holdings: Mss Architectural drawings
Notes: Collection incl the Galveston Architecture Inventory, 1966-1967, photographs of Galveston buildings, and architectural drawings by Nicolas J Clayton.

ARCHITECTURE, THEATRE

ON —NATIONAL LIBRARY OF CANADA, 395 Wellington St, Ottawa, K1A 0N4, Can. Andre Preibish, Dir
Holdings: Vols 8000
Notes: Includes 100 serial titles, also programs, play bills etc on microfilm. Performing arts collection consists of Canadian titles received on legal deposit and purchased. Areas of concentration: Canadian theatre and dance; European and American performing arts tradition; theatre architecture; stage craft; costume history, dance history and notation etc.

ARCHIVES

IL —CENTER FOR RESEARCH LIBRARIES, 6050 S Kenwood Ave, Chicago, 60637. Donald B Simpson, Dir; Esther Smith, Collection Development Librn
Holdings: Microforms
Notes: Japanese foreign ministry archives 1868-1945, archives of army, navy, and other government agencies 1868-1945, Cabinet archives, Tokugawa documents, Okuma papers, other archival materials. Descriptive pamphlet available.

NE —NEBRASKA STATE HISTORICAL SOCIETY, Archives, 1500 R St, Box 82554, Lincoln, 68501. James E Potter, State Archivist
Holdings: Cat Mss Microforms
Budget: ($290,000)
Notes: Collection

NM —NEW MEXICO HIGHLANDS UNIVERSITY, Donnelly Library, National Ave, Las Vegas, 87701. Karen Jaggers, Assoc Librn
Holdings: // Mss Maps Microforms
Notes: The outstanding collection is the Arrott Collection on Fort Union, New Mexico, 1851-1891. Other collections incl Spanish Archives, Mexican Archives, Archdiocese of Santa Fe, Archivo del Parral; New Mexico Land Grants.

PA —UNIVERSITY OF PENNSYLVANIA, University Archives, North Arcade Franklin Field E-6, Philadelphia, 19104. Francis James Dallett, University Archivist
Notes: The University of Pennsylvania Archives holds the papers of 125 individuals, all with a University affiliation (former faculty, trustees, alumni, etc), some 175,000 individual biographical files of University-connected persons in the same categories who are deceased, as well as the non-current records and files of the academic and administrative divisions of the University and its predecessors beginning in 1740 (an overall collection of 8000 cubic feet). It is one of the six largest University Archives (of purely institutionally-related records) in the country. Sporadic reporting of holdings to NUCMUC have not been kept up in recent years. Severe staff limitations prevent more than reporting of additions to the collection to subject surveys and bibliographies.

TX —PANHANDLE-PLAINS HISTORICAL MUSEUM, Research Center, Box 967, WT Sta, Canyon, 79016. Claire R Kuehn, Archivist-Librn
Holdings: Microforms
Notes: Microfilm copies of correspondence, reports and miscellaneous documents and maps from the Archivo General de Indias, Seville, Spain, Mueso Naval, Madrid, archives in Mexico and other Latin American countries, dealing with expedition of Francisco Vazquez de Coronado.

†WY —UNIVERSITY OF WYOMING, William Robertson Coe Library, Archives of Contemporary History, 13th & Ivinson, Laramie, 82071.
Notes: The papers of Victor Gondos. Incl journals and books, several hundred folders on military and archival history, his diaries from 1920-1974, and more than 1500 letters on historical research and architecture.

ON —PUBLIC ARCHIVES OF CANADA, Library, 395 Wellington St, Ottawa, K1A 0N3, Can. Dawn E Monroe, Collections Development Officer
Holdings: Vols (80,000) Cat
Notes: Over the years, the Public Archives Library has assembled thousands of books and pamphlets relating to all aspects of Canadian history, from the founding of the country to the present day. The holdings incl journals of explorers and missionaries, accounts of the first voyageurs, as well as administrative, civil and military records. Also incl are basic reference works on the history, geography, politics and economics of Canada, the administration of New France, Canada's geographic and political history, transportation incl railways and navigation, immigration, Crown lands, religious groups and institutions. The Library's collection also has works covering other areas of interest such as archives and archives management, heraldry, genealogy, Canadian art, geographic indexes and sound and visual archives.

ARCHIVES, AUSTRIAN

DC —LIBRARY OF CONGRESS, Washington, 20540.
Notes: Project of a consortium to microfilm about 200,000 pp of material on Great Britain, France, Russia and Prussia, for the period 1848-1918 in the ms and documentary collections of the Austrian State Archives. The collection will incl among others, documents on the Austro-Prussian War of 1866, the treaty negotiations between France and Italy in 1868-1870, the Orient Question of 1877-1878, the persecution of Jews in Russia in 1882, the Congo Conference in Berlin, 1885-1887 and the British-Portuguese conflict in East Africa, 1889-1991.
Copies will be available at LC, the Center for Research Libraries, the Hampshire Inter-Library Center, and the libraries of Boston College, Yale, Harvard, Duke, Stanford and the University of Virginia.

IL —CENTER FOR RESEARCH LIBRARIES, 6050 S Kenwood Ave, Chicago, 60637. Donald B Simpson, Dir; Esther Smith, Collection Development Librn
Holdings: Microforms
Notes: 315 reels of microfilm to date. Microfilm of selected material in the Austrian state archives relating to Great Britain, France, Russia, Prussia and Turkey for the period 1848-1918.

MN —SAINT JOHN'S ABBEY & UNIVERSITY, Hill Monastic Manuscript Library, Collegeville, 56321. Julian G Plante, Dir
Holdings: Vols (61,000)
Notes: Films of 61,000 mss. The total number of codices or bound handwritten mss represents the holdings of several hundred libraries in Europe, mostly Austria, Spain, Ethiopia, West Germany, Portugal, and also Italy, Hungary, Poland, Great Britain, Belgium, Yugoslavia, France, Switzerland, and the Netherlands.

ARCHIVES, BRITISH

DC —LIBRARY OF CONGRESS, General Reading Rooms Division, Microform Reading Room, Washington, 20540.
Holdings: Cat Mss Maps Pix Microforms
Notes: Microform materials only in this LC Division. Works of individual authors; holdings of collections; archival records, etc, press releases and translations, etc.

IL —CENTER FOR RESEARCH LIBRARIES, 6050 S Kenwood Ave, Chicago, 60637. Donald B Simpson, Dir; Esther Smith, Collection Development Librn
Holdings: Microforms
Notes: Substansial quantities of microfilm from the Public Record Office, especially British Foreign Office records relating to China, the US, Russia, Mexico and Central America. Also smaller quantities of film from other repositories. No photocopying.

ARCHIVES, CANADIAN

ON —PUBLIC ARCHIVES OF CANADA, Library, 395 Wellington St, Ottawa, K1A 0N3, Can. Dawn E Monroe, Collections

ARCHIVES, CANADIAN (cont.)

Development Officer
Holdings: Vols (80,000) Cat
Notes: Over the years, the Public Archives Library has assembled thousands of books and pamphlets relating to all aspects of Canadian history, from the founding of the country to the present day. The holdings incl journals of explorers and missionaries, accounts of the first voyageurs, as well as administrative, civil and military records. Also incl are basic reference works on the history, geography, politics and economics of Canada, the administration of New France, Canada's geographic and political history, transportation incl railways and navigation, immigration, Crown lands, religious groups and institutions. The Library's collection also has works covering other areas of interest such as archives and archives management, heraldry, genealogy, Canadian art, geographic indexes and sound and visual archives.

ARCHIVES, CENTRAL AMERICAN

IL —CENTER FOR RESEARCH LIBRARIES, 6050 S Kenwood Ave, Chicago, 60637. Donald B Simpson, Dir; Esther Smith, Collection Development Librn
Notes: Substansial quantities of microfilm from the Public Record Office, especially British Foreign Office records relating to China, the US, Russia, Mexico and Central America. Also smaller quantities of film from other repositories. No photocopying.

ARCHIVES, ETHIOPIAN

MN —SAINT JOHN'S ABBEY & UNIVERSITY, Hill Monastic Manuscript Library, Collegeville, 56321. Julian G Plante, Dir
Notes: Films of 61,000 mss. The total number of codices or bound handwritten mss represents the holdings of several hundred libraries in Europe, mostly Austria, Spain, Ethiopia, West Germany, Portugal, and also Italy, Hungary, Poland, Great Britain, Belgium, Yugoslavia, France, Switzerland, and the Netherlands.

ARCHIVES, EUROPEAN

MN —SAINT JOHN'S ABBEY & UNIVERSITY, Hill Monastic Manuscript Library, Collegeville, 56321. Julian G Plante, Dir
Notes: Films of 61,000 mss. The total number of codices or bound handwritten mss represents the holdings of several hundred libraries in Europe, mostly Austria, Spain, Ethiopia, West Germany, Portugal, and also Italy, Hungary, Poland, Great Britain, Belgium, Yugoslavia, France, Switzerland, and the Netherlands.

ARCHIVES, FRENCH

IL —CENTER FOR RESEARCH LIBRARIES, 6050 S Kenwood Ave, Chicago, 60637. Donald B Simpson, Dir; Esther Smith, Collection Development Librn
Holdings: Microforms
Notes: Journal officiel and parlimentary proceedings, collections on revolutions of 1789, 1830, 1848. Political party proceedings. Statistical collections. Archival materials from Archives du Ministerere des Affaries Etrangeres. Newspaper backfiles.

ARCHIVES, FOREIGN

DC —LIBRARY OF CONGRESS, Manuscript Division, Washington, 20540. John C Broderick, Chief
Holdings: Cat Mss Pix Slides Microforms
Notes: Collections of the papers of most of the presidents, from George Washington through Calvin Coolidge, of many other statesmen, military, scientific, and literary leaders of numerous enterprises and institutions, totaling more than 35,000,000 pieces. Incl over 100 letters in the controversial series of "love letters" and "love poems" to and from President Harding and Mrs Hames (Carrie) Phillips, unpublished (except for some unauthorized phrases in newspapers) and under seal until the year 2014. Also, reproductions of mss in European archives relating to American history.

DC —LIBRARY OF CONGRESS, General Reading Rooms Division, Microform Reading Room, Washington, 20540.
Holdings: Cat Mss Maps Pix Microforms
Notes: Microform materials only in this LC Division. Works of individual authors; holdings of collections; archival records, etc, press releases and translations, etc.

MN —SAINT JOHN'S ABBEY & UNIVERSITY, Hill Monastic Manuscript Library, Collegeville, 56321. Julian G Plante, Dir
Holdings: Vols (61,000) Microfilms

ARCHIVES, GERMAN

DC —LIBRARY OF CONGRESS, General Reading Rooms Division, Microform Reading Room, Washington, 20540.
Holdings: Cat Mss Maps Pix Microforms
Notes: Microform materials only in this LC Division. Works of individual authors; holdings of collections; archival records, etc, press releases and translations, etc.

IL —CENTER FOR RESEARCH LIBRARIES, 6050 S Kenwood Ave, Chicago, 60637. Donald B Simpson, Dir; Esther Smith, Collection Development Librn
Holdings: Microforms
Notes: Over 10,000 reels of positive microfilm of captured German archives, principally of the German Foreign Ministry for the period 1867-1945, but also of other governmental agencies and army commands, etc, for period 1920-1945, mostly 1939-1945.

ARCHIVES, ITALIAN

DC —LIBRARY OF CONGRESS, General Reading Rooms Division, Microform Reading Room, Washington, 20540.
Holdings: Cat Mss Maps Pix Microforms
Notes: Microfilm materials only in this LC Division. Works of individual authors; holdings of collections; archival records, etc, press releases and translations, etc.

KS —UNIVERSITY OF KANSAS, Kenneth Spencer Research Library, Special Collections Dept, Lawrence, 66045. Alexandra Mason, Librn
Holdings: Mss Maps
Notes: Family, political, and business records from mainly Northern Italy, including the Rubenstein Collection of the papers of the Orsetti Family of Lucca, Tuscany, 1180-1850 (mostly before 1650), (117 linear ft), and the Graziani diplomatic papers.

ARCHIVES, JAPANESE

IL —CENTER FOR RESEARCH LIBRARIES, 6050 S Kenwood Ave, Chicago, 60637. Donald B Simpson, Dir; Esther Smith, Collection Development Librn
Holdings: Cat Microforms
Notes: Japanese foreign ministry archives 1868-1945, archives of army, navy, and other government agencies 1868-1945, Cabinet archives, Tokugawa docuemnts, Okuma papers, other archival materials. Descriptive pamphlet available.

ARCHIVES, MALTESE

MN —SAINT JOHN'S ABBEY & UNIVERSITY, Hill Monastic Manuscript Library, Collegeville, 56321. Julian G Plante, Dir
Notes: Films of 61,000 mss. The total number of codices or bound handwritten mss represents the holdings of several hundred libraries in Europe, mostly Austria, Spain, Ethiopia, West Germany, Portugal, and also Italy, Hungary, Poland, Great Britain, Belgium, Yugoslavia, France, Switzerland, and the Netherlands.

ARCHIVES, MEXICAN

DC —LIBRARY OF CONGRESS, General Reading Rooms Division, Microform Reading Room, Washington, 20540.
Holdings: Cat Mss Maps Pix Microfilm
Notes: Microfilm materials only in this LC Division. Works of individual authors; holdings of collections; archival records, etc, press releases and translations, etc.

TX —UNIVERSITY OF TEXAS LIBRARIES, Nettie Lee Benson Latin American Collection, Sid Richardson Hall 1.109, Austin, 78712. Laura Gutierrez-Witt, Head Librn
Holdings: Vols (450,000) Cat Mss Maps Pix Phonorecords Filmstrips Microforms
See also entry under Latin America

ARCHIVES, POLISH

MN —SAINT JOHN'S ABBEY & UNIVERSITY, Hill Monastic Manuscript Library, Collegeville, 56321. Julian G Plante, Dir
Notes: Films of 61,000 mss. The total number of codices or bound handwritten mss represents the holdings of several hundred libraries in Europe, mostly Austria, Spain, Ethiopia, West Germany, Portugal, and also Italy, Hungary, Poland, Great Britain, Belgium, Yugoslavia, France, Switzerland, and the Netherlands.

ARCHIVES, RUSSIAN

IL —CENTER FOR RESEARCH LIBRARIES, 6050 S Kenwood Ave, Chicago, 60637. Donald B Simpson, Dir; Esther Smith, Collection Development Librn
Notes: Substansial quantities of microfilm from the Public Record Office, especially British Foreign Office records relating to China, the US, Russia, Mexico and Central America. Also smaller quantities of film from other repositories. No photocopying.

ARCHIVES, SPANISH

DC —LIBRARY OF CONGRESS, General Reading Rooms Division, Microform Reading Room, Washington, 20540.
Holdings: Cat Mss Maps Pix Microforms
Notes: Microform materials only in this LC Division. Works of individual authors; holdings of collections; archival records, etc, press releases and translations, etc.

MN —SAINT JOHN'S ABBEY & UNIVERSITY, Hill Monastic Manuscript Library, Collegeville, 56321. Julian G Plante, Dir
Holdings: Vols (61,000) Microfilms
Notes: Films of 61,000 mss. The total number of codices or bound handwritten mss represents the holdings of several hundred libraries in Europe, mostly Austria, Spain, Ethiopia, West Germany, Portugal, and also Italy, Hungary, Poland, Great Britain, Belgium, Yugoslavia, France, Switzerland, and the Netherlands.

ARCHIVES, UKRAINIAN

NY —NEW YORK PUBLIC LIBRARY, Slavonic Div, Fifth Ave & 42 St, New York, 10018. Edward Kasinec, Chief
Holdings: Vols 180 // Cat Mss
Notes: The Ukrainian archive of Mykyta Shapoval consists mainly of the correspondence of General Mykola Shapoval (Army of the Ukrainian National Republic, 1917-1920) and of his family. Documents, mss, diaries relating to the activities and events of Ukrainians in Czechoslovakia and France are included. The material covers the period of the 1920s through 1950s.

ARCHIVES, U.S.

IL —CENTER FOR RESEARCH LIBRARIES, 6050 S Kenwood Ave, Chicago, 60637. Donald B Simpson, Dir; Esther Smith, Collection Development Librn
Holdings: Microforms
Notes: Over 25,000 reels of positive

ARCHIVES, U.S. (cont.)

microfilm of material in the National Archives, incl federal population censuses 1-10 complete, large quantities of State Department records, and other miscellaneous groups of material.

ARCHIVES, VATICAN see Vatican Archives

ARCHIVES MANAGEMENT

NJ —H M BAKER ASSOCIATES, Research Collection, 266 E Dudley Ave, Westfield, 07090. Helen Baker Cushman, Managing Associate
Holdings: Vols 2000 Cat Mss Maps Pix Slides
Notes: Baker Associates publishes *The Business History Letter* The Anniversary Manual, "Remember the Year," business histories and anniversary studies which are based on the contents of the collection. Emphasis of the collection is on industrial and business history.

ON —UNIVERSITY OF WESTERN ONTARIO, Schoool of Library and Information Science, Library, London, N6G 1H1, Can. Victoria Ripley, Librn
Holdings: Vols (50,000)
Notes: Auction and antiquarian booksellers' catalogs from Canadian, American and European firms, some dating back to the 18th century. A special strength is 19th and early 20th century American booksellers' catalogs, recently augmented by a collection of pre-1920 catalogs formed by the late H O Teisberg. Current emphasis is on Canadian catalogs.

ARCHONS OF COLOPHON

NY —COLUMBIA UNIVERSITY LIBRARIES, Rare Book & Manuscript Library, 801 Butler Library, 535 W 114 St, New York, 10027. Kenneth A Lohf, Librn
Holdings: Mss
Notes: Minutes and records of The Archons of Colophon, an elected social-professional group of administrative librarians of the Greater New York area. See the 50-year history, *The Archons of Colophon, 1909-1917 and 1926-1969:* "Much and Little Changed," by Lee Ash, New York, 1969 (54 pp, 500 copies). Incl 3000 items. Restricted use.

ARCTIC, CANADIAN see Canadian Arctic

ARCTIC EXPEDITIONS see Arctic Regions

ARCTIC FLORA see Botany—Arctic Regions

ARCTIC GAS PIPELINE

MB —UNIVERSITY OF MANITOBA, Elizabeth Dafoe Library, Government Publications Section, Winnipeg, R3T 2N2, Can. June Dutka, Head
Holdings: Vols 1300 // Uncat Maps Pix
Notes: The collection, which dates from 1975, consists of written direct testimonies and responses with supporting exhibits from over 100 oil and gas companies, Indian and native associations and concerned citizens groups. The content of these documents incl construction plans, financial statements, alternate corridors, and describes the social and economic impact of the Arctic Gas Pipeline in northern Canada. The *Biological Report Series* offers vital information on soils and vegetation, movements of porcupine, caribou herds, bird distribution and fisheries research. An index listing the various company exhibits accompanies this collection.

ARCTIC RACES

MB —UNIVERSITY OF MANITOBA, Elizabeth Dafoe Library, Archives and Special Collections Dept, Winnipeg, R3T 2N2, Can. Richard E Bennett, Dept Head; Corrado A Santoro, Reference Archivist
Notes: Arctic and Sub-Arctic cultural anthropology.

ARCTIC REGIONS

AK —UNIVERSITY OF ALASKA, Elmer E Rasmuson Library, Fairbanks, 99701. Robert H Geiman, Dir
Holdings: Vols Cat Mss Maps Pix Slides Phonoreocrds Audiotapes Film Microforms
Notes: The Alaska Collection is strong in all disciplines concerning Alaska. Main strengths are exploration and travel, pioneer memoirs, and materials on Alaska natives. Bulk of collection is in English with significant holdings in Russian, Native American, and European languages. Archival holdings incl 6000 cu ft of mss, 110,000 historic photographs, 2319 tape recordings, 727 films and videotapes, 200 rare maps and 1273 microfilms. Ms collection strongest in political and economic areas. A Guide to the Collections is available in hard copy and microfiche. About 1000 special collections, some 300 quite significant.

AK —ALASKA STATE LIBRARY, Alaska Historical Library Collection, Pouch G, Juneau, 99811. Phyllis Demuth, Readers Services Librn
Holdings: Vols (24,000) Cat Mss Maps Pix Slides Phonorecords Audiotapes 16mm Films Micorforms

CO —WORLD DATA CENTER A: GLACIOLOGY (SNOW AND ICE), CIRES, University of Colorado, Boulder, 80309. Ann M Brennan, Librn
Holdings: Vols 10,000 Maps Pix Microforms
Budget: $2000
Notes: Glaciology, all forms of snow and ice. Bibliographic information will be contained in a data file which will be fully searchable. Partially cataloged (UDC).

CT —YALE UNIVERSITY, Box 1603A, Yale Station, New Haven, 06520.

DC —NATIONAL ARCHIVES AND RECORDS SERVICE, Civil Archives Division, Washington, 20408.
Holdings: Vols (1500) Uncat
Notes: Repository for records created by federal government agencies engaged in Arctic and Antarctic activities, and for gifts of private papers relating to the regions. Collection maintained for reference use by staff and researchers only.

DC —NATIONAL GEOGRAPHIC SOCIETY, Library, 1146 16th St NW, Washington, 20036. Susan Fifer Canby, Dir
Holdings: Vols (63,000) Cat Mss Maps Pix
Notes: Material concerning land, sea, and space exploration--past and present. All fields of anthropology, natural history, geography, etc.

HI —PACIFIC SUBMARINE MUSEUM, Library, Naval Submarine Base, Pearl Harbor, 96860. Ray W de Yarmin, Cur
Holdings: Vols (1500) Cat Mss Maps Pix Slides Phonorecords 16mm Films
Budget: ($600)
Notes: Incl 3000 pictures. Extensive missile and torpedo collection; submarine models; salvage/deep-sea diver exhibit; Arctic exploration by submarines Worl War II submarine components. Research program for students, authors, lecturers, etc.

IL —NEWBERRY LIBRARY, 60 W Walton St, Chicago, 60610. Diana Haskell, Cur of Modern Mss
Holdings: Vols 500 Cat
Notes: Incl American, British, Spanish, Russian and French explorations. The E E Ayer Collection.

ME —BOWDOIN COLLEGE, Library, Brunswick, 04011. Dianne M Gutscher, Cur of Special Collections
Holdings: Vols 4000 Cat Mss Maps Pix
Notes: The papers (about 15,000 items) of Robert A Bartlett, arctic explorer and shipmaster for Admirals Robert E Peary and Donald B MacMillan, contain 10,000 mss, 23,000 photographs, clippings, diaries, 300 maps, logbooks and some printed material relating to Bartlett's arctic voyages. Also, Admiral MacMillan's personal library of about 4000 books relating to arctic exploration, several volumes of clippings, numerous scrapbooks, ms diaries, logbooks, and journals, photographs, maps, and other records.

MA —HARVARD UNIVERSITY LIBRARY, Cambridge, 02138.
Holdings: Cat

MA —PEABODY MUSEUM OF SALEM, Phillips Library, E India Sq, Salem, 01970. Gregor Trinkaus-Randall, Librn
Holdings: Vols (100,000) Cat Mss Maps Pix
Notes: Pacific and Arctic voyages.

MA —BOSTON COLLEGE LIBRARIES, Catherine B O'Connor Geophysics Library, Weston Observatory, Weston, 02193. F Clifford McElroy, Science Librn
Holdings: Vols (7813) Cat Maps Pix Microforms
Notes: This collection is being absorbed into the general collection.

MI —UNIVERSITY OF MICHIGAN, Library, Dept of Rare Books & Special Collections, Ann Arbor, 48109. Robert J Starring, Head
Holdings: Cat Mss Maps Pix
Notes: Includes over 100 books, mostly autographed presentation copies from polar explorers to donor William H Hobbs, and 62 scrapbooks, notebooks, albums, and made-up volumes of pamphlets, documents and correspondence, 11 relating to Admiral Peary. Also there are such primary records from Professor Hobbs' own expeditions as his journals, radio logs, purchase requisitions, pilot balloon ascension reports and graphs, and anemoscope records. In addition there are an estimated 3500 items of correspondence with explorers and other notables, 800 photographs, and maps.

MI —OLIVET COLLEGE, Burrage Library, Olivet, 49076. Chris Miko, Dir
Holdings: Vols (2000) Cat
Notes: The collection consists primarily of early printed voyages of the arctic and antarctic from the earliest times to the mid-20th century.

MN —UNIVERSITY OF MINNESOTA, DULUTH, Library & Learning Resources Service, Duluth, 55812. James V. Litha, Archivist
Holdings: Vols 1700 Cat Mss Maps Pix
Notes: The Voyageur Collection incl the Grace Lee Nute Papers. Books and materials relating to the Voyageur period (1650-1850) and the area of Northeastern Minnesota, Michigan, Wisconsin, Southern Canada. Emphasis on on all subjects listed in this volume. Incl materials about Arctic exploration.

NH —DARTMOUTH COLLEGE, Baker Memorial Library, Hanover, 03755.
Holdings: Cat Mss Maps Pix Audiotapes
Notes: The Vilhjalmur Stefansson Collection. First editions, mss and his own working library. Noncirculating. Also, 1200 atlases and 90,000 maps. Areas of special interest: historical cartography, polar regions, USSR, Alaska.

NH —US ARMY COLD REGIONS RESEARCH AND ENGINEERING LABORATORY, 72 Lyme Road, Hanover, 03755. Nancy Liston, Librn
Holdings: Cat Maps Microforms
Notes: The primary material consists of reports, documents, journal articles, cited in the library's "Bibliography on Cold Regions Science and Technology." About one third of the items cited in vols 1-22 are on microfilm or in report or reprint form; beginning with vol 23, all items are microfiched and sent to the library, which now has over 55,000 items on microfiche. These are indexed by author and subject in the annual volume of the Bibliography.

NJ —GLASSBORO STATE COLLEGE, Savitz Library, Stewart Room, Glassboro, 08028. Clara Kirner, Special Collection Librn
Holdings: Vols 22 Cat Mss Maps
Notes: Documents and mss of Isaac Israel Hayes, 1832-1881, dealing with his expeditions and personal life. Also, several items relating to Elisha Kent Kane, especially second Grinnel Expedition; mss of Charles Petersen's *Dr Kane's Voyage to the Polar Lands.*

ARCTIC REGIONS (cont.)

NY —COLUMBIA UNIVERSITY LIBRARIES, Rare Book & Manuscript Library, 801 Butler Library, 535 W 114 St, New York, 10027. Kenneth A Lohf, Librn
Holdings: 700 Cat
Notes: First editions, mss, letters and memorabilia relating to the exploration of the North and South Poles. 700 vols, 500 ms items. Restricted use.

NY —EXPLORERS CLUB, James B Ford Memorial Library, 46 E 70 St, New York, 10021. Janet Baldwin, Librn
Holdings: Vols (24,000) Cat Maps
Notes: Additions to the collection depend upon gifts. Access by appointment only. Collections incl the Ted Banks Collection; begun by Prof Harley H Bartlett, bequeathed to American Institute for Exploration, with additions by Prof Ted Bank II, and subsequently acquired by the Explorers Club. Incl field notes, diaries, and photographs of Bank, who led more than 30 scientific expeditions to the Arctic, Aleutians, Sea of Okhotsk, Japan, Taiwan, Southeast Asia and Africa.

NY —NEW YORK PUBLIC LIBRARY, Research Libraries, General Research Division, Fifth Ave & 42 St, New York, 10018. Rodney Phillips, Chief
Holdings: Vols (2,225,000) Cat Maps Pix Microforms
Budget: ($775,718)

OH —CLEVELAND PUBLIC LIBRARY, History and Geography Department, 325 Superior Ave, Cleveland, 44114. JoAnn Petrello, Head
Holdings: Cat Maps
Notes: Collection incl rare books.

RI —BROWN UNIVERSITY, John Carter Brown Library, Providence, 02912. Norman Fiering, Librn; Everett C Wilkie Jr, Bibliographer; Susan Danforth, Cur Maps & Prints
Holdings: Vols (40,000)
Notes: Exploration and discovery, incl the Bering Sea and Russian explorations of Alaska, to the search for Sir John Franklin (ca 1860).

VA —UNIVERSITY OF VIRGINIA, Alderman Library, Manuscripts Dept, Charlottesville, 22901. Edmund Berkeley Jr, Cur
Holdings: Cat Mss Pix
Notes: Papers of Edwin Swift Balch, author of *The North Pole* and *Bradley Land*, and *Antarctica*, and authority on the Cook-Peary controversy incl scrapbooks and correspondence.

WI —UNIVERSITY OF WISCONSIN, MADISON, Geophysical & Polar Research Center Library, Weeks Hall, 1215 W Dayton St, Madison, 53706. Alison N Mares, Librn
Holdings: Vols (1000) Cat Mss Maps Microforms
Notes: Collection incl large bibliography of Arctic and Antarctic subjects available. Library has some 1500 pamphlets; 500 maps, mostly bathymetric and geological; reprint collection from Cold Regions Research & Engineering Lab (CRREL); collection of Russian materials, dealing mainly with the Antarctic.

AB —ALPINE CLUB OF CANADA LIBRARY, Archives of the Canadian Rockies, Box 160, Banff, T0L 0C0, Can. E J Hart, Head Archivist
Holdings: Vols (2429) Cat Mss Maps Pix Slides Audiotapes
Budget: ($1000)
Notes: The Archives of the Canadian Rockies is the custodian of the library and archival collection of the Alpine Club of Canada. The materials cover mountaineering technique and attempts worldwide, incl the Alps, Rockies, Himalayas, Andes, etc. Subject areas incl history, personal records, mountain rescue and medicine, alpine flora and fauna, guide books, manuals and handbooks. A large part of the archival collection is concentrated on the Canadian Rocky Mountains, as the headquarters of The Alpine Club of Canada is in Banff, Alberta.

AB —GLENBOW-ALBERTA INSTITUTE, Historical Library & Archives, 130 9th Avenue SE, Calgary, T2G 0P3, Can. Leonard J Gottseleg, Chief Librn
Holdings: Vols (60,000) Cat Mss Maps Pix Microforms
Notes: Main emphasis is on Western Canadian history. Equally important emphasis is placed on the Canadian Arctic and Alaska, Northwest Coast explorations, Aboriginal peoples of the North and Canadian West, and the fur trade in the US Northwest.

MB —UNIVERSITY OF MANITOBA, Elizabeth Dafoe Library, Government Publications Section, Winnipeg, R3T 2N2, Can. June Dutka, Head
Holdings: Uncat Maps Pix Microforms
Notes: The Canadian National Energy Board's Polar Gas Project documentation provides an extremely useful source of information describing the proposed construction of the pipeline route which would generally pass from the Arctic Islands through the Northwest Territories, northern Manitoba and into Ontario, Canada.

MB —UNIVERSITY OF MANITOBA, Elizabeth Dafoe Library, Archives and Special Collections Dept, Winnipeg, R3T 2N2, Can. Richard E Bennett, Dept Head; Corrado A Santoro, Reference Archivist
Notes: Arctic and Sub-Arctic cultural anthropology.

ON —NATIONAL MUSEUMS OF CANADA, Library Services Directorate, Ottawa, K1A 0M8, Can. Valerie Monkhouse, Director
Holdings: Vols 500 // Maps
Notes: The personal library of R M Anderson, late Curator Emeritus of the Zoology Division, and leader of the Southern Party, Canadian Arctic Expedition, 1913-1918. The collection contains books on zoology (mainly ornithology and mammalogy), expeditions (some early and rare materials), and several runs of ornithological journals and numerous reprints. The collection is only partially cataloged.

ON —LAURENTIAN UNIVERSITY LIBRARY, Ramsey Lake Rd, Sudbury, P3E 2C6, Can. Suzanne Brunette, Special Collection Librn; Sue Vongpeisal, Head Librn
Notes: Materials on northern Canada, incl 2200 books and pamphlets, 60,000 press clippings on northern topics 75 series of periodicals and over 1500 maps, plus photographs and thousands of samples of arctic and subarctic plants incl mosses, lichens, algae and wood sections. Much of the material is in French.

ON —METROPOLITAN TORONTO LIBRARY, Canadian History Dept, Baldwin Room Section, 789 Yonge St, Toronto, M4W 2G8, Can. David B Kotin, Head
Holdings: Vols (52,000) Mss Pix
Notes: This collection consists of material on Canadian history, geography, travel, archaeology, genealogy, retrospective city and telephone directories, collective biographies, native peoples (excluding customs, rights and social conditions), Arctic regions, military history and theory. It is an extremely strong collection of both current and retrospective material. Particular strengths are national and local history (especially Ontario), Arctic regions, native peoples, travel (especially Ontario), and military history. Incl 78,000 historical pictures, 235 linear meters mss, 14,000 broadsides and 3800 bound newspapers.

ON —UNIVERSITY OF TORONTO, Thomas Fisher Rare Book Library, 120 Saint George St, Toronto, M5S 1A5, Can. Richard G Landon, Head
Holdings: Vols 30,000 Mss Maps Pix
Notes: Great variety of material relating to early exploration and settlement of Canada, including the search for the Northwest Passage and the subsequent exploration of the Arctic. Manuscript and printed material pertaining to the overland exploration of northwestern Canada and the Barren Lands. Manuscript and printed material documenting early emigration schemes and colonization attempts, including Selkirk's Red River settlement.

YT —YUKON ARCHIVES, Box 2703, Whitehorse, Y1A 3C6, Can. Miriam McTiernan, Territorial Archivist
Holdings: Vols (8000) Cat Mss Pix Phonorecords Audiotapes Videotapes 16mm Films Microforms
Budget: $15,000
Notes: Yukon and regional history and development. Incl also 500 mss; 10,000 maps; 30,000 pictures; 1200 microfilm rolls; 1115 oral history tapes, etc; Yukon newspapers.

ARCTIC REGIONS' LANGUAGES see Hyperborean Languages and Literatures

ARDIZZONE, EDWARD, 1900-1979

CA —UNIVERSITY OF CALIFORNIA, LOS ANGELES, Research Library, Dept of Special Collections, 405 Hilgard Ave, Los Angeles, 90024. Edward Shreeves, Chairman, Bibliographers Group; David S Zeidberg, Head
Holdings: Vols 150
Notes: 150 books written or illustrated by Ardizzone; watercolors for *Henry Esmond* and *Lucy Brown and Mr Grimes;* ink drawings for *Tim the Wanderer.*

IN —INDIANA UNIVERSITY, Lilly Library, Seventh St, Bloomington, 47405. William R Cagle, Librn
Notes: Contemporary with and depicting Lincoln; the War of 1812 and other periods. Incl significant mss of the modern cartoonists and caricaturists Ardizzone, Beerbohm, Fontane Fox, Kin Hubbard, Charles Bacon Jackson, McCutcheon, Messick, Nast, Rothenstein, Sendak, and many miscellaneous items.

ARDREY, ROBERT

MA —BOSTON UNIVERSITY, Mugar Memorial Library, Special Collections Dept, 771 Commonwealth Ave, Boston, 02215. Howard B Gotlieb, Dir
Holdings: Cat Mss
Notes: Mss, correspondence, etc collected in depth; incl publications by or about.

ARENDT, HANNAH

DC —LIBRARY OF CONGRESS, Manuscript Division, Washington, 20540. John C Broderick, Chief
Notes: Papers of Hannah Arendt; now unrestricted, except for the Judah L Magnes correspondence.

ARENSBERG, WALTER

CA —FRANCIS BACON LIBRARY, 655 N Dartmouth Ave, Claremont, 91711. Elizabeth S Wrigley, Dir
Holdings: Mss Pix
Notes: Correspondence of Walter Arensberg with artists John Covert, Marcel Duchamp Francis Picabia and his wife Gabrielle Buffet Picabia, and psychiatrist Elmer Ernest Southard; Ms and draft of unpub Pantomime: A Quelle Heure un Train Partira-t-il pour Paris (1914) and ms and proof of ideogramme: Coeur Couronne et Miroir, with its published form in Les Soirees de Paris, by Guillaume Apollinaire (1880-1918); and Arensberg's miscellaneous correspondence with American literary figures (1920's-50's) including Bruce Bliven, Catherine Drinker Bowen, Kay Boyle, Witter Bynner, Edwin Corle, Helen A Keller, Lysander Kemp, Kenneth Macgowan, John Macy, Henry Miller, Lewis Mumford, Clifford Odets, Kenneth Patchen, Irving Stone, and William Carlos Williams. The Apollinaire ms has been described and reprinted in Apollinaire and the Faceless Man, by Willard Eugene Bohn(unpublished doctoral dissertation, University of Calif, Berkeley, ca 1973). It has also been reprinted with commentary in French by Willard Bohn by Bibliotheque Artistique and Litteraire, Fontefroide, 1982.

ARENT, ARTHUR

MA —BOSTON UNIVERSITY, Mugar Memorial Library, Special Collections Dept, 771 Commonwealth Ave, Boston, 02215. Howard B Gotlieb, Dir
Holdings: Cat Mss

ARGENTINA

CA —UNIVERSITY OF CALIFORNIA, BERKELEY, University Library, Hispanic Collections, Berkeley, 94720. Gaston Somoshegyi-Szokol, Librn
Holdings: Vols (30,000)
Notes: General research collection. Main Library holdings are supplemented by subject coverage in branch libraries. Extensive government document holdings are maintained in the Government Documents Department.

CA —UNIVERSITY OF CALIFORNIA, RIVERSIDE, University Library, 4045 Canyon Crest Dr, Box 5900, Riverside, 92517.
Holdings: Vols 5000
Notes: General research collection in the humanities and social sciences, with special strengths in history, literature, folklore and economic conditions, especially 20th century. Significant collection of material about and by the Perons, incl complete set of *Mundo Peronista* (1951-1955).

CT —YALE UNIVERSITY, Sterling Memorial Library, Latin American Collections, New Haven, 06520. Lee H Williams Jr, Cur
Holdings: Vols (300,000) Cat Maps Pix Slides Phonorecords 16mm Films Filmstrips
See also entry under Latin America

MO —WASHINGTON UNIVERSITY, John M Olin Library, Campus Box 1061, St Louis, 63130.
Holdings: Vols (50,000) Cat
Notes: Strong collection. Much unusual material.

NY —AMERICAN MUSEUM OF NATURAL HISTORY, Library Services Dept, Central Park W & 79th St, New York, 10024. Nina J Root, Chairwoman; Mary Genett, Asst Librn for Reference Services

ARGENTINA—HISTORY

AZ —UNIVERSITY OF ARIZONA, Library, Tucson, 85721. W David Laird, Librn
Notes: Latin American materials in the University of Arizona Library system may be found in all of the campus libraries. The largest collection is located in the Main Library and concentrates primarily on the history, literature, political science and economics of Mexico, Panama, Columbia, Argentina, Brazil and Chile. Special Collections specializes in the colonial period in the areas of law, religion, and economics. They also incl numerous manuscript collections, photographs, and 4000 broadsides from Mexico covering the late 18th century through the 20th century revolutionary period. There are also strong map, music and phonorecord collections primarily on Mexico. The greatest collecting effort is current materials on contemporary Latin America. Materials are fully accessible through the main card catalog as there is no separate catalog of the collection.

CA —UNIVERSITY OF CALIFORNIA, BERKELEY, University Library, Hispanic Collections, Berkeley, 94720. Gaston Somoshegyi-Szokol, Librn
Holdings: Vols (15,000)
Notes: Strong research collection with extensive holdings on the Rosas-period the development of Argentine political thought, and the evolution of Argentine radicalism from 1890 to the 1930's.

CA —HOOVER INSTITUTION ON WAR, REVOLUTION & PEACE, Stanford University, Stanford, 94305. Milorad M Drachkovitch, Archivist
Holdings: Vols 1400 Pix
Notes: The Peron period in Argentina is represented by a wide range of published materials, especially the writings and speeches of Juan and Eva Peron, covering political, social and economic aspects of the regime. General description of the Latin American Collection and complete listing of the serial and newspaper holdings available in: Joseph W Bingaman, *Latin America: A Survey of Holdings at the Hoover Institution of War, Revolution and Peace*. Stanford, California: Hoover Institution, Stanford University, 1972. 96 pp.

CT —YALE UNIVERSITY, Box 1603A, Yale Station, New Haven, 06520.
Holdings: Cat
Notes: Incl about 500 vols of imprints from the Independence period.

IN —INDIANA UNIVERSITY, Lilly Library, Seventh St, Bloomington, 47405. William R Cagle, Librn
Holdings: Vols 2000 Cat Mss
Notes: Mostly from the Imprenta de los Ninos Expositos de Buenos Aires (Colleccion Antonio Santamaria de Buenos Aires) holdings, covering the entire period of the press life (1780-1825). The imprint collection reflects Buenos Aires development from its period as frontier outpost of the Spanish colonial empire to its emergence as an independent political, commercial, religious and intellectual force inclusively. Chronologically the material can be divided into four segments: (1) political, religious, and economic imprints prior to 1806; (2) material dealing with the English invasions of Buenos Aires and Montevideo, 1806-1807; (3) imprints dating from 1808-1810, largely concerning the events surrounding the Napoleonic invasion of Spain and the establishment of the first Junta Gubernativa of Buenos Aires (25 May 1810); and (4) the period of independence proper withits influence on the rest of the Spanish colonies of South America. An additional post-independence group of imprints deals with the struggle of the "Caudillos" through the dictatorial regime of Rosas. Mss cover years 1612-1944 but principally the independence period 1806-1823. 400 items.

MA —UNIVERSITY OF MASSACHUSETTS AT AMHERST, Library, Amherst, 01003.
Holdings: Cat Microforms
Notes: Latin American studies. Special strengths: Literature, history (especially Argentine history), anthropology. Newspapers on microfilm.

NE —AMERICAN HISTORICAL SOCIETY OF GERMANS FROM RUSSIA (AHSGR), 615 Twelfth St, Lincoln, 68502. Mary Lynn Tuck, Librn
Holdings: Vols (1900) Mss Maps Pix Phonorecords Videotapes Audiotapes Microforms VF
Notes: History of German people from Russia and history of people of German-Russian ancestory. Including times in Russia, Germany, US, Canada, Mexico, Argentina, Brazil, Paraguay, Korea, and Japan. This Society has fifty-six chapters in the United States. 1900 volumes, 100 maps; 500 mss; 1200 vertical files; 2000 pictures; 40,000 obituary files, 40,000 family group charts, 50 phonorecords, 20 videotapes, 50 audiotapes, 15 reel-to-reel tapes, 150 periodicals, 250 microforms, 250 family histories-published and unpublished.

NY —STATE UNIVERSITY OF NEW YORK, STONY BROOK, Melville Library, Dept of Special Collections, Stony Brook, 11794. Evert Volkersz, Head
Holdings: // Uncat
Notes: Pamphlets (380) of speeches by Juan and Eva Peron, as well as materials about them or promoting their regime. A list of titles is available.

PA —PENNSYLVANIA STATE UNIVERSITY, Fred Lewis Pattee Library, Library Hispanic Program, University Park, 16802. Donald C Henderson, Head
Holdings: Vols (50,000) Cat Mss
Budget: ($21,000)
Notes: Good general holdings focus on the Peron era with accessed pamphlet collection and elementary school textbooks of the period; supports doctoral programs.

TX —UNIVERSITY OF TEXAS LIBRARIES, Nettie Lee Benson Latin American Collection, Sid Richardson Hall 1.109, Austin, 78712. Laura Gutierrez-Witt, Head Librn
Holdings: Vols (450,000) Cat Mss Maps Pix Phonorecords Filmstrips Microforms
See also entry under Latin America.

ARGENTINE AUTHORS see Authors, Argentine

ARGENTINE LITERATURE

CT —YALE UNIVERSITY, Box 1603A, Yale Station, New Haven, 06520.
Holdings: Cat
Notes: The Tornquist Collection of Argentine authors.

PA —PENNSYLVANIA STATE UNIVERSITY, Fred Lewis Pattee Library, Library Hispanic Program, University Park, 16802. Donald C Henderson, Head
Holdings: Vols (50,000) Cat Mss
Budget: ($21,000)
Notes: A general collection with particular strength in gauchesque literature, backed by strong holdings in Argentine history and related fields, much acquired from American Antiquarian Society; supports doctoral programs.

TX —UNIVERSITY OF TEXAS LIBRARIES, Nettie Lee Benson Latin American Collection, Sid Richardson Hall 1.109, Austin, 78712. Laura Gutierrez-Witt, Head Librn
Holdings: Vols (450,000) Cat Mss Maps Pix Phonorecords Filmstrips
Notes: The library of Pedro Martinez Reales, emphasizing the literature of the Argentine gaucho, incl some 1500 books, pamphlets and articles, as well as 300 editions of the epic poem *Martin Fierro*. The literary papers of Julio Cortazar have recently been acquired.
See also entry under Latin America.

ARGOT see Cant; Slang

ARGUMENTATION see Logic

ARIAS see Songs—Collections

ARID REGIONS

AZ —DESERT BOTANICAL GARDEN, Richter Memorial Library, 1201 North Galvin Pkwy, Phoenix, 85008. J B Cole, Librn
Holdings: Vols (4000)
Notes: Emphasis on desert and arid regions ecology and horticulture.

CO —COLORADO STATE UNIVERSITY, Libraries, Fort Collins, 80523. Marjorie Rhoades, Engineering Sciences Librn
Holdings: Vols (6000) Cat
Budget: ($5000)
Notes: Water and Soil in Arid Regions (WASAR) is an index and guide to books, conference papers, journal articles, government documents and technical reports, mostly in English, within the appropriate subject areas and held by Colorado State University Libraries. The bibliographical citations are of selected items dealing with soils, water, arid lands, crops, foods and nutrition with certain economic, political, ecological and historical parameters also included. The information needs of developing countries and of those who serve them are the prime criteria for inclusion.

TX —TEXAS TECH UNIVERSITY, Library, Lubbock, 79409. David J Murrah, Assoc Dir for Special Collections

ARIEL (PERIODICAL)

AB —UNIVERSITY OF CALGARY, Libraries, Special Collections Div, 2500 University Dr, Calgary, T2N 1N4, Can.
Notes: Archives of the literary periodicals: *Tish, Imago, Ariel, Descant, Canadian Review Magazine* and *Canadian Short Story* Magazine.

ARIENS KAPPERS, CORNELIUS UBBO, 1877-1946

BC —UNIVERSITY OF VICTORIA, McPherson Library, Victoria, V8W 3H5, Can.

ARIOSTO, LODOVICO

CA —UNIVERSITY OF CALIFORNIA, BERKELEY, University Library, French and Italian Collections, Berkeley, 94720. Donald G Williams, Librn
Notes: Research collection with special strengths in early Italian literature (to 1400), and Italian literature of the Renaissance. Strong holdings for such authors as Dante, Petrarch, Boccaccio, Ariosto, Machiavelli, Tasso, and many others. The collections in the Main Library are complemented by significant incunabula, rare books and ms holdings in the Bancroft Library.

MA —HARVARD UNIVERSITY LIBRARY, Cambridge, 02138.
Holdings: Cat

NC —DUKE UNIVERSITY, William R Perkins Library, Durham, 27706. Elvin E Strowd, University Librn
Notes: The Mazzoni collection of approximately 23,000 books and 67,000 reprints and pamphlets is strong in, but not limited by any means to, Italian literature. A special aspect of this collection is a group of essays, studies, or small works published on the occasion of a marriage. These "per la nozze di" range from a poem published in post card form to a scientific or literary work. The manuscript catalog of the pamphlet collection has been published by the library in book form; the 23,000 volumes have been cataloged and are shelved in the library's bookstacks.

ARISTOPHANES

MA —HARVARD UNIVERSITY LIBRARY, Widener Library, Cambridge, 02138.
Holdings: Cat

NC —DUKE UNIVERSITY, William R Perkins Library, Durham, 27706. Elvin E Strowd, University Librn
Notes: The Spranger Collection of classical studies contains 2500 items. The principal dramatists, Euripides, Aeschylus, Aristophanes and Sophocles are fairly comprehensively covered by way of critical texts and studies up to 1968. Practically all the texts are represented by Loeb and Bude translations, and also Didot's 19th century series. Reference books includes a complete Pauly-Wissowa, Briquet, long runs of the Classical Review and Quarterly, the O E D and some 30 to 40 volumes of codex facsimiles of Euripides and others.

ARISTOTLE AND ARISTOTELIANISM

IN —INDIANA UNIVERSITY, Lilly Library, Seventh St, Bloomington, 47405. William R Cagle, Librn
Holdings: Vols 370 // Cat Mss
Notes: Largely commentaries, 15th-18th centuries.

PA —UNIVERSITY OF PENNSYLVANIA, Van Pelt Library, Rare Books Collection, 34 & Walnut Sts, Philadelphia, 19104. Daniel Traister, Special Collections Librn
Holdings: Vols 600 Cat Mss
Notes: Editions of 15th-17th centuries. See Downs 3722; (suppl) 1968, published catalog.

PA —UNIVERSITY OF PITTSBURGH, Hillman Library, Pittsburgh, 15260. Glenora E Rossell, Head
Holdings: Vols (11,550) Cat
Notes: The classics collection is particularly strong in Greek and Roman history, Greek philosophy, Greek and Latin language, and Greek epigraphy. In combination with the Frick Fine Arts collection it has a good collection in Greek and Roman art and archaeology. The collection of journals is also quite strong in these areas. There has been an emphasis in collecting books by and about Homer, Aristotle, Euripidies, Virgil, Cicero and Petronius. It has a unique collection of unpublished PhD dissertations and Master's theses on Petronius. It has a basic collection on Greek and Latin paleography and papyrology.

ON —UNIVERSITY OF TORONTO, Thomas Fisher Rare Book Library, 120 Saint George St, Toronto, M5S 1A5, Can. Richard G Landon, Head
Holdings: Vols 250 Cat Mss
Notes: Aristotle Collection containing important early editions of Aristotle; early commentaries on his works; several ms commentaries, the most important being Albert of Saxony's *Questiones in Aristotelis "De Caelo et Mundo"*, written in 1407, which is the earliest extant ms of this work.

ARITHMETIC—FOUNDATIONS

IL —UNIVERSITY OF ILLINOIS, URBANA/CHAMPAIGN, Library, Mathematics Library, 216 Altgeld Hall, Urbana, 61801. Nancy D Anderson, Librn
See also entry under Mathematics.

ARITHMETIC—TEXTBOOKS

PA —UNIVERSITY OF PITTSBURGH, Hillman Library, Special Collections Dept, 363 Hillman Library, Pittsburgh, 15260. Charles E Aston Jr, Coordinator
Holdings: Vols (13,480) Cat Mss
Notes: The John A Nietz Textbook Collection of primarily American textbooks in 3 areas; primary school books to 1900, secondary texts to ca 1930, and pedagogical books (1000 vols on the history and theory of education incl writings of the key figures in the field of education). Books are cataloged via an in-house computer printout and are accessible via name, title, subject, place, publisher and date. Late 18th and all of the 19th centuries are well represented. Important titles in each subject are discussed in John A Nietz's *Old Textbooks* (Pittsburgh, 1961) and in his *The Evolution of American Secondary School Textbooks* (Rutland, Vt, 1966). Collection also incl the papers (noncirculating) of Prof John A Nietz.

ARITHMETIC, MECHANICAL see Calculating Machines

ARIYOSHI, KOJI

GA —EMORY UNIVERSITY, Robert W Woodruff Library, Atlanta, 30322. Herbert Johnson, Dir
Holdings: Mss Pix Cat
Notes: The Philip J Jaffe Papers and books about communism and the Communist Party in the US, incl copies of rare magazines, private mss, the papers of such controversial figures as Anna Louise Strong, Agnes Smedley, Norman Bethune and Koji Ariyoshi, and documentation of the growth of Chinese communism. 36 linear ft mss.

ARIZONA

AZ —ARIZONA-SONORA DESERT MUSEUM, Library, Rte 9, Box 900, Tucson, 85743. Janice Hunter, Librn
Holdings: Vols (3000) Cat Pix Slide Videotapes 16mm Films
Notes: Ecology and natural history of the Southwest. Carr Collection on beavers. Incl 200 pictures, 5000 slides, 40 videotapes, and 6 films. Separate index of slides.

AZ —UNIVERSITY OF ARIZONA, University Library, Special Collections, Tucson, 85721. Louis A Hieb, Head
Holdings: Vols 30,000 Cat Mss Maps Pix Microforms
Budget: $40,000
Notes: The collection incl Arizona general periodicals and fiction, and books on the history, biography, travel, Indians, the arts, physical and natural resources, politics and government, business and industry, and social problems of Arizona. There are also over 450 processed manuscript collections varying in size from a single volume to hundreds of boxes. Also incl are the Arizona photograph and pamphlet collections. The collection is notably strong in official publications (territorial, state, county, and municipal) and selected US government documents. University of Arizona archival material (university publications, academic and administrative departmental files; photographs, faculty and biographical files and ephemera collections) are located in other departments of the library system.

NM —ALBUQUERQUE PUBLIC LIBRARY, 501 Copper Ave NW, Albuquerque, 87102. Alan B Clark, Dir
Holdings: Vols (4000) Cat Microforms Records Maps VF
Notes: Large collection of materials on all aspects of New Mexico history and cultures. In-house index accesses VF materials and local and regional periodicals. Special emphasis on Indians of New Mexico and northeastern Arizona, particularly the Navajo, Hopi, Pueblos and Apache. Reference copies of many works are housed at the Special Collections Library, 423 Central Ave NE, Albuquerque, NM 87102.

UT —UNIVERSITY OF UTAH, Marriott Library, Special Collections, Salt Lake City, 84112. Gregory C Thompson, Cur

ARIZONA—DESCRIPTION AND TRAVEL—VIEWS

CA —POMONA PUBLIC LIBRARY, Special Collections, 625 S Garey Ave, PO Box 2271, Pomona, 91766. David Streeter, Librn
Holdings: Uncat Slides
Notes: Contains 550 lantern slides (mostly of California) and 4200 color 35mm transparencies of world travel, 1960s. Also, the Burton Frasher Postal Card Collection of 60,000 negatives and prints of California, Arizona, Colorado, New Mexico, Nevada, and Utah; 30,000 world views; 8000 California views. There are also world views in nearly 1000 stereophotographs.

ARIZONA—GENEALOGY

AZ —CHURCH OF JESUS CHRIST OF LATTER DAY SAINTS, Arizona Branch Genealogical Library, 464 E First Ave, Mesa, 85204. Joseph Lindbloom, Dir
Holdings: Vols (14,000) Cat Mss Maps Pix Microforms
Notes: Incl 25,000 microfilms with access to 1,300,000 rolls of microfilm available on loan.

ARIZONA—GOVERNMENT PUBLICATIONS

AZ —PHOENIX PUBLIC LIBRARY, Arizona Room, 12 E McDowell, Phoenix, 85004. Jeannette Brush, Librn
Holdings: Vols (30,000) Cat Maps Pix
Budget: ($12,000)
See also entry under Arizona - History.

ARIZONA—HISTORY

AZ —NORTHERN ARIZONA UNIVERSITY, Special Collection Library, CU Box 6022, Flagstaff, 86011. Peter M Whiteley, Coordr/Archivist; William Mullane, Librn
Holdings: Cat Mss Maps Pix Slides Audiotapes Microforms
Notes: Northern Arizona history and Arizona economic history. Depository of Forest History Society of America; custodian for Northern Arizona Pioneers Historical Society Manuscript Collection. Also, (1) Apache County Record Book Collection; record book of mines located in the county, 1879-1881. (2) Arizona Historical Advisory Commission Collection; minutes of meetings, correspondence, and reports; (3) Arizona Statehood Proposal Collection; typed notes from Arizona newspapers, 1901-1910, regarding progress of passing the Arizona statehood proposal. (4) Arizona Tax Research Association Collection; reports on state institutions, 1940-1942; (5) Arizona Town Hall Collection; pamphlets and reports about the Arizona Town Hall, 1972-1974; (6) Bradshaw City,Arizona, Collection; copies of letters, newspaper articles, and unpublished papers about Bradshaw City and the Bradshaw Mountains in Central Arizona, 1957. (7) Betty Connelly Collection of four typescript articles by Janet Delano Lewis

ARIZONA—HISTORY (cont.)

concerning Northern Arizona. Incl two articles on the Indians living near Kingman, Ariz, ca 1918. (8) Francis L Decker Collection; correspondence files of many Northern Arizona companies concerning their finances and operating expenses, 1920's-1950's. (9) Marie Decker Collection; correspondence, diary calendars, 1971, 1978-1979, newspaper articles, property descriptions, maps, photographs, *Arizona* Highway magazines, and personal and business papers. (10) Flagstaff History Collection; handwritten history of Flagstaff by and unknown person, ca 1920-1930. (11) Flagstaff Water Use and Utilization CommissionCollection; minutes 1958-1976. (12) Flagstaff Weather Bureau Collection; weather records, 1898-1969. (13) Ernest Killebrew Collection; Cottonwood, Ariz, postal records, 1885-1912. (14) Mangum, Wall, Stoops, and Warden Collection; documents relative to the dispute surrounding the development of the Hart Prairie, in the San Francisco Mountains near Flagstaff, 1937-1975. Ione Morteson Collection; court proceedings of this owner of a maternity home vs the city of Phoenix, 1940. (15) Nogales, Ariz, Collection; letter from Arizona Governor Franklin concerning Nogales incurring a debt to build Nogales-Old Glory Road, 1897. Agreement of the townsmen to tax for the purpose of building the road, 1894. (16) Cornelius C Smith Collection; typescript of *Some Unpublished History of the Southwest,* by ColC C Smith. Incl are the stories of William S and Granville H Oury, brothers who arrived in Tucson, Ariz, in the 1850's. (17) Stewart and Doe Collection; outgoing correspondence (letter press book), 1888-1898, of this Flagstaff law firm. (18) Charles B Wilson, Jr, Collection; 130 volumes of Arizona Territorial sessions laws and state laws dating back to the First Territorial Legislature in 1864. (19) Billie Yost Collection; photocopy of the inquest into the death of Sam Dittenhoffer, which occurred at Red Lake, Coconino County, Ariz, in 1891. (20) Clifton, Ariz, Town Ordinances Collection; 1909-1945. (21) George E Babbitt Book Collection; concentrates on the history of Arizona and the Southwest. (22) Coconino County, Ariz, Board of Supervisors Collection; minutes concerning the tentative budget for the fiscal year ending June 30,1959. (23) Coconino Citizens Association Collection; correspondence, records, notes, and other material relating to the Association and their activities in Northern Ariz. (24) Flagstaff Bicentennial Centennial Commission Collection; catalogs, pamphlets, letters, reports of projets, newspaper articles, etc, 1975-1976. (25) Fredonia Public Library Collection; copies of the local history files from the Fredonia Public Library, incl many reminiscences of the early settlers, 1930's-1970's. (26) Museum of Northern Arizona Collection; proposed constitution and by-laws of the Northern Arizona Society of Science and Art (Museum of Northern Ariz), accompanied by letter from Grady Gammage, chairman, 1927.
See also entry under Southwest-History

AZ —FORT HUACHUCA HISTORICAL ASSOCIATION, Fort Huachuca, 85705. James P Finley, Dir
Holdings: Cat Mss Maps Pix Slides Microforms Artifacts
Notes: Voluminous collection of documents concerning Fort Huachuca, southeastern Arizona, Indians, pioneer settlements, and military history. About 50,000 manuscript pieces and documents.

AZ —PHOENIX PUBLIC LIBRARY, Arizona Room, 12 E McDowell, Phoenix, 85004. Jeannette Brush, Librn
Holdings: Vols (30,000) Cat Mss Maps Pix VF
Budget: $12,000
Notes: The Arizona Room incl the following collections: James McClintock Collection on Arizona history: books, pamphlets, clippings, letters, scrapbooks and photos, notably of the Rough Riders and their training in the Prescott area; Indians of the Southwest, Vertical files of clippings and pamphlets covering biography, local history organizations, law and politics in Phoenix, Maricopa County and Arizona; US, Arizona and Phoenix government documents; 2500 maps, National Forest maps, historical, climatological, geological, vegetation and flood plain maps, as well as a few old, rare or unique items; and a comprehensive collection of materials relating to the Superstition Mountains and the search for the Lost Dutchman Gold Mine and others.

AZ —SIERRA VISTA LIBRARY, 2950 E Tacoma St, Sierra Vista, 85635. Catherine Helmick, Acting Library Administrator
Holdings: Vols (350) Cat
Notes: Arizona and the Southwest: primarily history; some natural history, social life and customs, desert living, biography, and regional fiction.

AZ —ARIZONA STATE UNIVERSITY, Library, Arizona Collection, Tempe, 85281. Edward C Oetting, Head
Holdings: Vols Cat Mss Maps Pix Microforms
Notes: Resources

AZ —TOMBSTONE CITY LIBRARY, Box 218, Tombstone, 85638.
Holdings: Cat
Budget: ($1000)

AZ —ARIZONA DAILY STAR, Library, 4850 S Park Ave, PO Box 26807, Tucson, 85726. Elaine Y Raines, Librn; Michele R Canney, Asst Librn
Holdings: Cat Maps Pix Microforms
Budget: ($110,000)
Notes: Main resource is 1,800,000 piece clipping collection of Tucson and Arizona, from 1939. Holdings incl Tucson telephone books, from 1940; Tucson city directories, from 1918; 1500 books on Tucson and Arizona; daily newspaper (microfilm), from 1877. Index prepared by Univ of Arizona, 1953-1965 and 1979, with plans to index missing years. Picture collection (150,000) and VF of ephemera (5000 pieces) are valuable historical sources.

AZ —ARIZONA HERITAGE CENTER, Library, 949 E Second St, Tucson, 85719. Michael Weber, Dir
Notes: Espec with reference to Arizona, the West, and the Southwest.

AZ —ARIZONA STATE MUSEUM, Library, University of Arizona, Tucson, 85721. Hans R Bart, Museum Librn
Holdings: Vols (35,000) Cat Mss Maps Pix Slides Phonorecords Microforms

AZ —TUCSON PUBLIC LIBRARY, Arizona Collection, 200 S Sixth Ave, PO Box 27470, Tucson, 85726. Elaine Baarson, Librn
Holdings: Vols 4000 Cat
Budget: $1000

AZ —UNIVERSITY OF ARIZONA, University Library, Special Collections, Tucson, 85721. Louis A Hieb, Head
Holdings: Vols 30,000 Cat Mss Maps Pix Microforms
Budget: $40,000
Notes: The collection incl Arizona general periodicals and fiction, and books on the history, biography, travel, Indians, the arts, physical and natural resources, politics and government, business and industry, and social problems of Arizona. There are also over 450 processed manuscript collections varying in size from a single volume to hundreds of boxes. Also incl are the Arizona photograph and pamphlet collections. the collection is notably strong in official publications (territorial, state, county, and municipal) and selected US government documents. University of Arizona archival material (university publications, academic and administrative departmental files; photographs, faculty and biographical files and ephemera collections) are located in other departments of the library system.

CA —AZUSA PACIFIC COLLEGE, Marshburn Memorial Library, Citrus & Alosta, Azusa, 91702. Edward Peterman, Librn
Holdings: Vols (6000) Uncat
Budget: ($30,000)
Notes: Significant holdings in the George E Fullerton Library of California and Western Americana.

NM —ROSWELL PUBLIC LIBRARY, 301 N Pennsylvania Ave, Roswell, 88201. Sarah Beth Galloway, Library Dir
Holdings: Vols (2000) Cat Maps
Budget: $1000
Notes: Covers literature (fiction and nonfiction), history, biography, geography, of Oklahoma, Texas, Colorado, New Mexico and Arizona.

TX —UNIVERSITY OF TEXAS LIBRARIES, General Libraries, Barker Texas History Center, PO Box P, Austin, 78712. Don Carleton, Dir
Holdings: Vols (132,000) Cat Mss Maps Pix Slides Phonorecords Audiotapes Microforms
Notes: See description of collection under Texas-History.

TX —EL PASO PUBLIC LIBRARY, Southwest Collection, 501 N Oregon, El Paso, 79901. Mary A Sarber, Head
Holdings: Vols (12,000) Cat Mss Maps Pix
Budget: ($11,000)
Notes: Research collection includes rare books and mss journals, vertical files, index to El Paso newspapers, microfilmed newspapers, photographs, and architectural plans. Separate catalog. Limited to materials on Texas, New Mexico, Arizona and Mexico. Special collections of material by and about Tom Lea Jr, and Carl Hertzog. Aultman Collection of photographs includes 3500 on El Paso Southwest and 2500 on Mexican Revolution. Cited in Lovelace, Lisa, "The Southwest Collection of the El Paso Public Library". *Great Plains Journal,* vol 2, no 2, pp 161-166; Aultman, Otis A *Photographs from the Border: The Otis A Aultman Collection,* El Paso Public Library Association, 1977.

TX —ECTOR COUNTY LIBRARY, Texas-Southwest History & Genealogy Dept, 321 W 5th St, Odessa, 79761. Jan Carter, Head
Holdings: Vols (8500) Cat Maps Pix
Budget: ($4000)
Notes: A card catalog of Texas-History; Southwest, New-History; Oklahoma-History is located in the Texas-Southwest History Dept. A card file by subject is a guide to vertical file materials and Texas, New Mexico, Oklahoma, Arizona periodicals. The Texas-History collection has reference, closed shelf, and circulating books.

UT —UTAH STATE UNIVERSITY, Merrill Library, Department of Special Collections & Archives, Logan, 84322. A J Simmonds, Curator; Jeanie F Simmonds, Archivist; Bradford R Cole, Mss Librn
Holdings: Vols 4000 Cat
Notes: Books pamphlets, manuscripts on the history of Arizona and New Mexico. Complete holding of the Wallace bibliography citations. All books Cat.

ARIZONA-LABOR

AZ —NORTHERN ARIZONA UNIVERSITY, Special Collection Library, CU Box 6022, Flagstaff, 86011. Peter M Whiteley, Coordr/Archivist; William Mullane, Librn
Notes: All records of the central office of the Arizona AFL-CIO; ca 100 linear feet.

ARIZONA—MAPS

AZ —NORTHERN ARIZONA UNIVERSITY, Special Collection Library, CU Box 6022, Flagstaff, 86011. Peter M Whiteley, Coordr/Archivist; William Mullane, Librn
Notes: Approx 400 published and unpublished maps in the Northern Arizona Pioneer's Historical Society and NAU Collections, primarily relating to Northern Arizona. For exact holdings, see the "Arizona Index" in Special Collections.

AZ —ARIZONA STATE UNIVERSITY, University Library, Map Service, Tempe, 85281.
Holdings: Maps
Notes: 150,000 maps which cover the world, some concentration on Arizona and Southwest. Also some historical maps.

AZ —ARIZONA HISTORICAL SOCIETY, Research Library, Maps Section, 949 E

ARIZONA—MAPS (cont.)

Second St, Tucson, 85710.
Holdings: Maps
Notes: Historical maps of Arizona and the southwest. Ninety percent of collection is pre-1900. 1500 maps in the collection.

AZ —UNIVERSITY OF ARIZONA, Library, Map Collection, Tucson, 85721. Mary L Blakely, Map Librn
Holdings: Maps
Notes: 180,000 for world, special concentration of Arizona and Southwest maps.

OK —TULSA CITY-COUNTY LIBRARY, Business & Technology Dept, 400 Civic Center, Tulsa, 74103. Craig Buthod, Head
Notes: Original General Land Office survey maps for the states of Arizona, Arkansas, Colorado, Illinois, Indiana, Idaho, Kansas, Michigan, Missouri, Montana, Nebraska, Nevada, New Mexico, North Dakota, Ohio, Oklahoma, South Dakota, Utah and Wyoming. Incomplete coverage of each state.

ARIZONA—POLITICS AND GOVERNMENT

AZ —NORTHERN ARIZONA UNIVERSITY, Special Collection Library, CU Box 6022, Flagstaff, 86011. Peter M Whiteley, Coordr/Archivist; William Mullane, Librn
Notes: In various collections, incl: (1) Center for the Study of Democratic Institutions Collection; correspondence, minutes, by-laws, and policy statements, 1970's. Discussion papers, press releases, and promotional papers. Publications. (6 feet). (2) Reese Ling Collection; correspondence, 1912-1916. Incl files on the Arizona Securities and Investment Company, Navajo and Apache County Bank and Trust Company, Bullwacker Gold and Copper Company, McCabe Extension Mining Company of Arizona, Arizona Democratic Party, and Maricopa County Democratic Central Committee. Ling was a lawyer in Arizona. (3) Leonard Ritt Collection; County election data from Northern Arizona and New Mexico, collected for use in a study of Navajo voting patterns. 1950's-1970's. (4) St. Michaels, Ariz, Tally lists of the General Election held Sept 12, 1910 and of Road Bond Election held Jan 24, 1922 at St Michaels. (5) Harold S Sykes Collection; correspondence to Sykes, mayor of Flagstaff during the 1940's, concerning the building of a swimming pool in Flagstaff, 1947-1950. (6) Evangeline K Terheun Collection; correspondence of Mrs Terheun who was involved with the Republican Women's Club in the Phoenix Ariz, area, 1952-1964.

ARIZONA—RELIGIOUS LIFE AND CUSTOMS

AZ —NORTHERN ARIZONA UNIVERSITY, Special Collection Library, CU Box 6022, Flagstaff, 86011. Peter M Whiteley, Coordr/Archivist; William Mullane, Librn
Notes: Federated Community Church, Flagstaff, Ariz, Collection; correspondence records, 1886-1975. Incl record book of the Flagstaff Chautauqua Literary and Scientific Circle, 1887-1891. Financial records are restricted. Contact Special Collections Librarian for details on access.

ARIZONA—SOCIAL LIFE AND CUSTOMS

AZ —NORTHERN ARIZONA UNIVERSITY, Special Collection Library, CU Box 6022, Flagstaff, 86011. Peter M Whiteley, Coordr/Archivist; William Mullane, Librn
Notes: Flagstaff Community Concert Association Collection; membership lists, 1945-1955; brochures, 1940-1962.

ARIZONA AUTHORS see Authors, Arizona

ARIZONA PAGEANT

AZ —NORTHERN ARIZONA UNIVERSITY, Special Collection Library, CU Box 6022, Flagstaff, 86011. Peter M Whiteley, Coordr/Archivist; William Mullane, Librn
Notes: Arizona Pageant, a play done in Flagstaff in the 1930's. Incl sections on the Indians, Spanish, pioneers, and modern times.

ARIZONA PERSONNEL AND GUIDANCE ASSOCIATION

AZ —NORTHERN ARIZONA UNIVERSITY, Special Collection Library, CU Box 6022, Flagstaff, 86011. Peter M Whiteley, Coordr/Archivist; William Mullane, Librn
Notes: Collection contains copies of the first six issues of AzPGA Journal, the *Communicator*, most of the convention brochures, and a brief history of the association and copies of the by-laws and policies.

ARIZONA-SONORA COMMITTEE

AZ —NORTHERN ARIZONA UNIVERSITY, Special Collection Library, CU Box 6022, Flagstaff, 86011. Peter M Whiteley, Coordr/Archivist; William Mullane, Librn
Notes: Photocopied newspaper articles, notes, unpublished papers, and letters concerning the background, history and accomplishments of the Arizona-Sonora Committee which was studying the prospects of increasing trade between Arizona and Sonora, Mexico, early 1960's.

ARIZONA STATE DENTAL SOCIETY

AZ —NORTHERN ARIZONA UNIVERSITY, Special Collection Library, CU Box 6022, Flagstaff, 86011. Peter M Whiteley, Coordr/Archivist; William Mullane, Librn
Notes: Records, 1909-1967. Inventory available.

ARKANSAS

AR —UNIVERSITY OF ARKANSAS, Library, Special Collections Dept, Fayetteville, 72701. Michael J Dabrishus, Cur
Holdings: Vols (40,299) Cat Mss Maps Pix Phonorecords Audiotapes Microforms
Notes: Material pertaining to the political, governmental, economic, social, cultural, educational, religious, scientific and literary history of Arkansas, its people and its institutions, incl the "natural history", anthropological development, and folk traditions of the area, from prehistoric times to the present. Holdings described in: Samuel A Sizer, *A Guide to Selected Manuscript Collections in the University of Arkansas Library* (Fayetteville, Ark, 1976) and in supplementary catalogs, inventories, indexes and other unpublished finding aids in the library.

ARKANSAS—GENEALOGY

AR —NORTH ARKANSAS REGIONAL LIBRARY, 123 Jaycee Ave, Harrison, 72601. W L Larson, Librn
Holdings: Vols (2500) Cat Pix Microforms
Budget: $750
Notes: Incl 600 historical pictures and 50 reels of microfilm.

AR —CENTRAL ARKANSAS LIBRARY SYSTEM, Little Rock Public Library, 700 Louisiana, Little Rock, 72201. Roberta A Muelling, Librn
Holdings: Vols 2615 Cat
Budget: $2000
Notes: General genealogy collection with specialized materials pertaining to individual states. Arkansas material makes up the largest state collection. A separate catalog.

AR —HOT SPRING COUNTY LIBRARY, Ash & E Third, Malvern, 72104. Mary L Cheatham, Librn
Holdings: Vols 630 Cat Mss Maps Pix Microforms Phonorecords Videotapes
Budget: $500
Notes: Incl material on Arkansas as well as books written by Arkansas authors. Much of the material was given by Joseph W Hill, a collector of Arkansania.

AR —PUBLIC LIBRARY OF PINE BLUFF AND JEFFERSON COUNTY, Library System, 200 E Eighth Ave, Pine Bluff, 71601. Cora M Dorsett, Dir
Holdings: Vols 60 Cat Periodicals Microforms Maps VF
Notes: Census records, marriage records, cemetery records, county histories, mortality schedules, tax lists, city council minutes. Incls periodicals (10 titles), microforms (945 rolls), 474 family files, maps (53).

FL —ORLANDO PUBLIC LIBRARY, Local History & Genealogy Dept, 100 Block of Central Ave, Orlando, 32806. Eileen B Willis, Librn
Holdings: Vols 11,000 Cat Maps Microforms
Budget: $8000
Notes: Genealogy collection on Md, Del, W Va, NC, SC, Ala, Miss, La, Texas, Ark, Ky, Ohio, Ill, Ind, and Mich are well represented. Most other states are covered by smaller collections.
See also entry under Genealogy - Collections.

ARKANSAS—HISTORY

AR —UNIVERSITY OF CENTRAL ARKANSAS, Torreyson Library, Conway, 72032. Douglas A Green, Library Dir
Holdings: Vols 4000 Cat Mss Maps Pix Microforms
Budget: $1800
Notes: There is a separate catalog to the collection. Over 5800 state documents.

AR —UNIVERSITY OF ARKANSAS, Library, Special Collections Dept, Fayetteville, 72701. Michael J Dabrishus, Cur
Holdings: Vols (40,299) Cat Mss Maps Pix Phonorecords Audiotapes Microforms
Notes: Material pertaining to the political, governmental, economic, social, cultural, educational, religious, scientific and literary history of Arkansas, its people and its institutions, incl the "natural history", anthropological development, and folk traditions of the area, from prehistoric times to the present. Holdings described in: Samuel A Sizer, *A Guide to Selected Manuscript Collections in the University of Arkansas Library* (Fayetteville, Ark, 1976) and in supplementary catalogs, inventories, indexes and other unpublished finding aids in the library.

AR —NORTH ARKANSAS REGIONAL LIBRARY, 123 Jaycee Ave, Harrison, 72601. W L Larson, Librn
Holdings: Vols (2500) Cat Pix Microfilms
Budget: $750
Notes: Incl 600 historical pictures and 50 reels of microfilm.

AR —CENTRAL ARKANSAS LIBRARY SYSTEM, Little Rock Public Library, 700 Louisiana, Little Rock, 72201. Roberta A Muelling, Librn
Holdings: Vols 3156 Cat Maps Pix
Notes: The Arkansas Collection contains works by Arkansas authors as well as works about the state. Majority of the collection is history, biography, and literature. Smaller amounts of science material and juvenile works. An attempt is made to acquire every Arkansas-related book published.

AR —HOT SPRING COUNTY LIBRARY, Ash & E Third, Malvern, 72104. Mary L Cheatham, Librn
Holdings: Vols 1008 Cat Mss Maps Pix Phonorecords Videotapes Microforms
Budget: ($1000)
Notes: Incl material on Arkansas as well as books written by Arkansas authors.

AR —PUBLIC LIBRARY OF PINE BLUFF AND JEFFERSON COUNTY, Library System, 200 E Eighth Ave, Pine Bluff, 71601. Cora M Dorsett, Dir
Holdings: Vols 1589 Cat Mss Pix Maps Periodicals
Notes: Collection incl yearbooks, directories, county histories, biographies, Arkansas statutes, Arkansas criminal code, church histories, clippings. Incl manuscripts (37), pictures (1), maps (3), periodicals (3 titles).

ARKANSAS—HISTORY (cont.)

LA —LOUISIANA STATE UNIVERSITY, SHREVEPORT, Library-Archives, 8515 Youree Dr, Shreveport, 71129. Patricia L Meador, Archivist & Asst Librn
Notes: The collection's primary emphasis is the history of North Louisiana, particulary Northwest Louisiana.

MO —SPRINGFIELD-GREENE COUNTY PUBLIC LIBRARY, 397 E Central, PO Box 737, Springfield, 65801. Jewell Smith, Administrative Librn
Holdings: Vols 7100 Cat Maps Pix Microforms
Notes: Missouri and Ozarks collection. Incl uncataloged pamphlets. Special indexes have been prepared.

TX —AMARILLO PUBLIC LIBRARY, 413 E Fourth, Amarillo, 79101. Mary Kay Snell, Librn
Holdings: Vols Cat Mss Maps Pix
Notes: The southwest collections incl materials on the history of Texas, Louisiana, New Mexico, Arkansas, Missouri and Kansas. General subjects covered incl overland journeys, early narratives, early biographies, Indian captivities, outlaws, US government reports, Mississippi and Ohio Rivers, the Mexican War, reports of Catholic missionaries, Niles Register, early publications, fur trade, western trails, Texas Rangers, sheriffs and Texas as a sovereign state, buffalo hunting, Indian wars, cowboys, the arrival of farmers, fences, and towns. Over 1600 items which incl books, documents, maps, mss, pamphlets, unpublished theses, interviews and photographs. The three major collections are the William Henry Bush Collection, the Laurence J Fitzsimon Collection and the Calendar of John L McCarty.

TX —SOUTHERN METHODIST UNIVERSITY, DeGolyer Library, Box 396, SMU, Dallas, 75275. Clifton H Jones, Dir
Holdings: Vols (80,000) Cat Mss Maps Pix Slides Microforms

ARKANSAS—MAPS

†AR —UNIVERSITY OF ARKANSAS, Mullins Library, Reference Dept and Special Collections, Fayetteville, 72701.

OK —TULSA CITY-COUNTY LIBRARY, Business & Technology Dept, 400 Civic Center, Tulsa, 74103. Craig Buthod, Head
Notes: Original General Land Office survey maps for the states of Arizona, Arkansas, Colorado, Illinois, Indiana, Idaho, Kansas, Michigan, Missouri, Montana, Nebraska, Nevada, New Mexico, North Dakota, Ohio, Oklahoma, South Dakota, Utah and Wyoming. Incomplete coverage of each state.

ARKANSAS AUTHORS see Authors, Arkansas

ARKHAM HOUSE

†PA —PENNSYLVANIA STATE UNIVERSITY, Fred Lewis Pattee Library, Rare Books and Special Collections Dept, University Park, 16802. Charles Mann, Librn
Notes: Science fiction, 1000 paperbooks plus runs of Amazing Stories, Weird Tales, Startling Stories, etc. Arkham House. William Tenn (live!) in the English Department.

†UT —BRIGHAM YOUNG UNIVERSITY, Harold B Lee Library, Provo, 84602. Elizabeth Pope, Librn
Notes: Science Fiction-Fantasy Collection, extensive circulating collection. Arkham House near complete, non-circulating. Mysteries, westerns and gothic romances in general fiction. Edgar Rice Burroughs 1st edition collection does not circulate. Science fiction and fantasy art special collection.

WI —UNIVERSITY OF WISCONSIN, MADISON, Memorial Library, British & American Language & Literature Collection, 728 State St, Madison, 53706. Yvonne Schofer, Bibliographer
Holdings: Vols
Notes: A collection of mystery fiction mostly of the British Golden Age of the 20s and 30s, in original and reprint form; strong holdings for H Adams, J Rhode, A Upfield, and many others. Stacks. Substantial holdings also for fantasy and science fiction, mostly in stacks; Arkham House and A Derleth materials, restricted use only.

ARMADA, SPANISH, 1588 see Spanish Armada, 1588

ARMBRUSTER, EUGENE

NY —NEW YORK PUBLIC LIBRARY, Local History and Genealogy Div, Fifth Ave & 42 St, New York, 10018. Gunther E Pohl, Chief
Holdings: Vols (160,000) Cat Pix
Budget: ($38,548)
Notes: Incl Eugene Armbruster Collection of Long Island Photographic Views. See *United States Local History Catalog* (Boston: G K Hall, 1974), 2 vols.

ARMED SERVICES EDITIONS (BOOKS, WORLD WAR II, U.S.)

†AL —UNIVERSITY OF ALABAMA, Amelia Gayle Gorgas Library, PO Box S, University, 35486.
Notes: A rare, complete set of the Armed Services Editions of paperbacks issued for use of American forces overseas in World War II.

CA —UNIVERSITY OF CALIFORNIA, LOS ANGELES, Research Library, Dept of Special Collections, 405 Hilgard Ave, Los Angeles, 90024. Edward Shreeves, Chairman, Bibliographers Group; David S Zeidberg, Head
Holdings: Vols 860
Notes: 860 paperback editions of fiction and non-fiction printed especially for the armed forces during World War II.

DC —LIBRARY OF CONGRESS, Rare Book & Special Collections Div, Washington, 20540. William Matheson, Chief
Holdings: Vols 1322
Notes: A complete set of these paperbacks intended for overseas distribution only.

ARMENIA

CA —UNIVERSITY OF CALIFORNIA, LOS ANGELES, Research Library, Armenian Collection, 405 Hilgard Ave, Los Angeles, 90024. Edward Shreeves, Chairman, Bibliographers Group; Gia Aivazian, Armenian Bibliographer
Holdings: Vols (16,000) Mss Microforms Pix VF
Notes: Incl one of the largest collections in the US of publications in Armenian and relating to Armenia.

†DC —ARMENIAN ASSEMBLY CHARITABLE TRUST, Library and Information Center, 522 21 St, NW, Washington, 20006.

DC —CATHOLIC UNIVERSITY OF AMERICA, Mullen Library, ICOR/Semitics Library, Room 20, Washington, 20064. Monica J Blanchard, Librn
Holdings: Vols (200)
Notes: The bulk of the ICOR/Semitics Library collection belongs to the Institute of Christian Oriental Research which supports the work of the Corpus Scriptorum Christianorum Orientalium. The holdings are chiefly concerned with Christian Egypt and the Coptic Church, Syriac and Syrian patristic studies, and the Syriac and Arabic speaking eastern churches. There are less extensive holdings of Ethiopic, Armenian and Georgian material. ICOR titles are cataloged by the ICOR/Semitic Library, and ICOR holdings do not appear in the general catalogue of the University Library.

DC —LIBRARY OF CONGRESS, African and Middle Eastern Division, Washington, 20540.
Holdings: Cat Mss Microforms
Notes: Near East: Over 105,000 vols, Arabic, Armenian, Turkish, Persian, and related languages. Special subject strengths incl Islamic philosophy, history, literature, economic and serial publications.

MA —HARVARD UNIVERSITY LIBRARY, Widener Library, Middle Eastern Dept, Cambridge, 02138. David H Partington, Librn
Holdings: Vols (70,000) Cat
Budget: ($55,000)
Notes: The Middle Eastern Collections consist of separately housed and cataloged books in Arabic, Turkish, Persian, Kurdish, and Urdu. Approx 4000 titles are added per year in the principal subject fields of language, literature, Islamic studies, and the modern social science disciplines. The Armenian collection is especially strong in classical and medieval texts. Current Soviet Armenian materials are actively collected by the Widener Library Slavic Department.

†MO —NATIONAL ASSOCIATION FOR ARMENIAN STUDIES AND RESEARCH, 175 Mount Auburn St, Cambridge, 02138.

PA —UNIVERSITY OF PENNSYLVANIA, Van Pelt Library, Rare Books Collection, 34 & Walnut Sts, Philadelphia, 19104. Daniel Traister, Special Collections Librn

ARMENIA—HISTORY

CA —UNIVERSITY OF CALIFORNIA, LOS ANGELES, Research Library, Armenian Collection, 405 Hilgard Ave, Los Angeles, 90024. Edward Shreeves, Chairman, Bibliographers Group; Gia Aivazian, Armenian Bibliographer
Holdings: Vols (16,000) Mss Microforms Pix VF
Notes: Incl one of the largest collections in the US of publications in Armenian and relating to Armenia.

ARMENIA—RELIGION

CA —UNIVERSITY OF CALIFORNIA, LOS ANGELES, Research Library, Armenian Collection, 405 Hilgard Ave, Los Angeles, 90024. Edward Shreeves, Chairman, Bibliographers Group; Gia Aivazian, Armenian Bibliographer
Holdings: Vols (16,000) Mss
Notes: Incl one of the largest collections in the US of publications in Armenian and relating to Armenia.

ARMENIAN AMERICAN NEWSPAPERS see Newspapers, Armenian American

ARMENIAN FOLK MUSIC see Folk Music, Armenian

ARMENIAN LANGUAGE AND LITERATURE

CA —LOS ANGELES PUBLIC LIBRARY, Foreign Languages Dept, 630 W Fifth St, Los Angeles, 90071. Sylva Manoogian, Principal Librn
Holdings: Vols 801 Cat
Budget: ($41,500)

CA —UNIVERSITY OF CALIFORNIA, LOS ANGELES, Research Library, Armenian Collection, 405 Hilgard Ave, Los Angeles, 90024. Edward Shreeves, Chairman, Bibliographers Group; Gia Aivazian, Armenian Bibliographer
Holdings: Vols (16,000) Mss Microforms
Notes: Incl one of the largest collections in the US of publications in Armenian and relating to Armenia.

DC —LIBRARY OF CONGRESS, African and Middle Eastern Division, Washington, 20540.
Holdings: Cat Mss Microforms
Notes: Near East: Over 105,000 vols, Arabic, Armenian, Turkish, Persian, and related languages. Special subject strengths incl Islamic philosophy, history, literature, economic and serial publications.

MA —BOSTON PUBLIC LIBRARY, South End Branch, Multilingual Library, 685 Tremont St, Boston, 02118. Laura H Reyes, Librn
Holdings: Cat

MA —HARVARD UNIVERSITY LIBRARY, Widener Library, Middle Eastern Dept,

ARMENIAN LANGUAGE AND LITERATURE (cont.)

Cambridge, 02138. David H Partington, Librn
Holdings: Vols (70,000) Cat
Budget: ($55,000)
Notes: The Middle Eastern Collections consist of separately housed and cataloged books in Arabic, Turkish, Persian, Kurdish, and Urdu. Approx 4000 titles are added per year in the principal subject fields of language, literature, Islamic studies, and the modern social science disciplines. The Armenian collection is especially strong in classical and medieval texts. Current Soviet Armenian materials are actively collected by the Widener Library Slavic Department.

†MO —NATIONAL ASSOCIATION FOR ARMENIAN STUDIES AND RESEARCH, 175 Mount Auburn St, Cambridge, 02138.

NY —NEW YORK PUBLIC LIBRARY, Oriental Div, Fifth Ave & 42 St, New York, 10018. E Christian Filstrup, Chief
Holdings: Cat Mss Microforms
Budget: ($56,455)
Notes: Published catalog of holdings.

NY —NEW YORK PUBLIC LIBRARY, Donnell Foreign Language Library, 20 W 53 St, New York, 10019. Bosiljka Stevanovic, Supvr Librn
Holdings: Vols 152 Cat
Notes: Armenian collection incl Armenian authors of Armenian expression. No separate catalog.

OH —CLEVELAND PUBLIC LIBRARY, Foreign Literature Dept, 325 Superior Ave, Cleveland, 44114. Natalia Bezugloff, Head
Holdings: Vols 960 Cat
Notes: A popular circulating collection containing classics and the standard works with emphasis on belles lettres, history and biography. A variety of other subjects such as learning languages, art, spoken phonodiscs, etc.
See also entry under Foreign Language Collections

ARMENIAN MANUSCRIPTS see Manuscripts, Armenian

ARMENIAN NEWSPAPERS see Newspapers, Armenian; Newspapers, Armenian American

ARMENIANS IN THE U.S.

CA —UNIVERSITY OF CALIFORNIA, LOS ANGELES, Research Library, Armenian Collection, 405 Hilgard Ave, Los Angeles, 90024. Edward Shreeves, Chairman, Bibliographers Group; Gia Aivazian, Armenian Bibliographer
Holdings: Vols (16,000)
Notes: Incl one of the largest collections in the US of publications in Armenian and relating to Armenia.

MN —UNIVERSITY OF MINNESOTA, Immigration History Research Center, 826 Berry St, Saint Paul, 55114. Susan Griegs, Cur
Holdings: Vols (35,000) Mss Maps Pix Phonorecords Audiotapes 16mm Films Microforms
See also entry under US - Emigration and Immigration

PA —BALCH INSTITUTE FOR ETHNIC STUDIES, Library, 18 S Seventh St, Philadelphia, 19106. R Joseph Anderson, Library Dir
Holdings: Vols 400 Cat

ARMIES—MUSIC see War Songs

ARMIES—SUPPLIES see Military Supplies

ARMINIANISM

CA —POINT LOMA NAZARENE COLLEGE, Ryan Library, 3900 Lomaland Dr, San Diego, 92106. Esther Schandorff, Librn
Notes: Arminian-Wesleyan Theological Collection.

KY —ASBURY THEOLOGICAL SEMINARY, B L Fisher Library, Wilmore, 40390. D William Faupel, Dir of Library Services
Holdings: Vols 1000 Cat
Budget: ($72,000)
Notes: Special emphasis is on holiness from the Arminian-Wesleyan point of view, but other view points are also well represented.

ARMOR see Arms and Armor

ARMORED CARS (TANKS) see Tanks (Military Science)

ARMORED VEHICLES, MILITARY

VA —US ARMY TRANSPORTATION MUSEUM, Library, Bldg 300, Fort Eustis, 23604. Dennis P Mroczkowski, Museum Cur
Holdings: Vols (1254) Uncat Maps Pix 16mm Films
Budget: ($150)
Notes: Mainly US Army transportation from WW II on.

ARMORIAL BOOKPLATES see Bookplates

ARMORIC LANGUAGE AND LITERATURE see Breton Language and Literature

ARMOUR, RICHARD W.

CA —CLAREMONT COLLEGES, Ella Strong Denison Library, Scripps College, Claremont, 91711. Judy Harvey Sahak, Librn
Holdings: Cat Mss Pix
Notes: Includes manuscripts, typescripts, editor's correspondence, proof sheets, some drawings, etc of original and revised versions of 44 books.

CA —CALIFORNIA STATE UNIVERSITY, LONG BEACH, Library, Dept of Special Collections & Archives, 1250 Bellflower Blvd, Long Beach, 90840. John Ahouse, Special Collections Librn
Holdings: Vols 65 Mss
Notes: Incl complete inscribed first issues of his works.

MA —BOSTON UNIVERSITY, Mugar Memorial Library, Special Collections Dept, 771 Commonwealth Ave, Boston, 02215. Howard B Gotlieb, Dir
Holdings: Cat Mss Pix
Notes: Mss, correspondence, etc collected in depth; incl publications by or about.

ARMS, COATS OF see Heraldry

ARMS AND ARMOR

IL —BALZEKAS MUSEUM OF LITHUANIAN CULTURE, Research Library, 4012 S Archer Ave, Chicago, 60632. Jurgis Kasakaitis, Head Librn
Holdings: Vols 15,000 Cat Maps Pix Slides Phonorecords
Notes: Incl folklore, art, social life and customs, history, literature, poetry, anthropology, numismatics, armor, etc. All books published in Lithuanian, some in English on Lithuanian subjects. Incl newspaper clippings.

MA —LUCIUS BEEBE MEMORIAL LIBRARY, Main St, Wakefield, 01880.
Holdings: Vols (350) Cat
Notes: The Keough Collection of guns and arms and armor.

MO —SCHOOL OF THE OZARKS, Lois Brownell Research Library, Ralph Foster Museum, Point Lookout, 65726. Robert Esworthy, Librn
Holdings: Vols (1300) Cat
Notes: Firearms and weapons of the world.

NY —FORT ONTARIO HISTORIC SITE, Oswego, 13126. Shelley B Weinreb, Historic Site Mgr
Holdings: Vols (400) Cat Mss Maps Pix Slides
Notes: Primary focus is upon military activities at the mouth of the Oswego River and the utilization of fortifications (Fort Ontario, Fort Oswego, and Fort George) at that point which served to control the outlet of the traditional Mohawk-Oneida-Oswego route to the Great Lakes. A limited number of sources on fortification design, weapons, uniforms, and military equipment are included. Also incl 4000 slides and 400 pictures.

OK —US ARMY FIELD ARTILLERY SCHOOL LIBRARY, Morris Swett Library, Snow Hall, Fort Sill, 73503. Lester L Miller Jr, Chief Librn
Holdings: Vols (265,958) Documents Pix Maps Slides Microforms
Notes: Field artillery; artillery; ordnance; military history; military science; weapons and weapons systems; ammunition; ballistics; missiles; Field Artillery unit histories; military periodicals analytical index file (VF). Incl US and foreign artillery; survey data; photographs on army subjects.

WI —MILWAUKEE PUBLIC MUSEUM, Reference Library, 800 W Wells St, Milwaukee, 53233. Judith Campbell Turner, Museum Librn
Holdings: Vols (90,000) Cat Maps Microforms

ON —FORT MALDEN NATIONAL HISTORIC PARK, Library, 100 Laird Ave, Box 38, Amherstburg, N9V 2Z2, Can. Sally E Snyder, Librn
Holdings: Vols (400) Cat Mss Pix Slides
Notes: British and Canadian military life, weaponry, uniforms, from about 1760 to 1860.

ON —NATIONAL MUSEUMS OF CANADA, Library Services Directorate, Ottawa, K1A 0M8, Can. Valerie Monkhouse, Director
Holdings: Vols 12,000 Cat
Budget: ($60,000)
Notes: Collection includes; arms and armour, military aeronautics, military and naval arts and sciences, military and naval equipment, general military and naval history, military and naval history of Canada. Research collection, interlibrary loans available, public may use on the premises.

ARMS CONTROL

DC —US ARMS CONTROL & DISARMAMENT AGENCY, Library, George Washington Univ Special Collections, Washington, 21 St & Virginia Ave, NW, Rm 5851, Washington, 20451. Diane Ferguson, Librn
Holdings: Vols 4500 // Cat
Notes: Arms control, disarmament and related topics.

NY —HUDSON INSTITUTE, Library, Quaker Ridge Rd, Croton-on-Hudson, 10520. Mildred Schneck, Librn
Holdings: Vols (10,000) Cat
Budget: ($40,000)
Notes: Social sciences and world futures. About 30 percent of the collection emphasizes materials useful to our ongoing program of examining possible world futures: social and economic indicators, forecasts, current social problems, arms control and disarmament.

ARMSTRONG, CHARLOTTE

MA —BOSTON UNIVERSITY, Mugar Memorial Library, Special Collections Dept, 771 Commonwealth Ave, Boston, 02215. Howard B Gotlieb, Dir
Holdings: // Cat Mss Pix
Notes: Mss, correspondence, etc collected in depth; incl publications by or about.

ARMSTRONG, EDWIN HOWARD

NY —COLUMBIA UNIVERSITY LIBRARIES, Rare Book & Manuscript Library, 801 Butler Library, 535 W 114 St, New York, 10027. Kenneth A Lohf, Librn
Holdings: Mss
Notes: Some 200,000 papers tracing the career of Edwin Howard Armstrong, inventor of the FM radio, incl correspondence with many of the leading figures in the arts and sciences and numerous legal papers and documentation of his inventive work. Restricted use.

ARMSTRONG, FURST AND TILTON, ARCHITECTS

NY —CORNELL UNIVERSITY LIBRARIES, Collection of Regional History, Dept of Manuscripts and Univ Archives, Ithaca, 14853.
Notes: Incl records, (ca 1927-50)-ca 1955; blueprints, drawings, photos, pamphlets and other printed material. Unpublished guide available.

ARMSTRONG, MARGARET

CA —CALIFORNIA STATE UNIVERSITY, FULLERTON, Library, Box 4150, Fullerton, 92634. Linda Herman, Special Collections Librn
Holdings: Vols (6000) Uncat
Notes: History of bookbinding, with examples from 15th century to date and a strong emphasis on American trade cloth bindings, including those by Margaret Armstrong.

CA —UNIVERSITY OF CALIFORNIA, LOS ANGELES, Research Library, Dept of Special Collections, 405 Hilgard Ave, Los Angeles, 90024. Edward Shreeves, Chairman, Bibliographers Group; David S Zeidberg, Head
Notes: 425 examples of her decorated cloth bindings.

ARMSTRONG, TERENCE IAN FYTTON

BC —UNIVERSITY OF VICTORIA, McPherson Library, Victoria, V8W 3H5, Can.

ARMY see Military Art and Science; U.S. Army

ARMY LIFE see Soldiers' Life

ARMY SUPPLIES see Military Supplies

ARMY WAGONS see Vehicles, Military

ARNAZ, DESI

CA —SAN DIEGO STATE UNIVERSITY, Malcolm A Love Library, 5300 Campanile Dr, San Diego, 92182. D Dickinson, Univ Librn; Don L Bosseau, Dir
Notes: Desi Arnaz Collection of Film and Television Production Material. Includes films, television tapes, out-takes, scripts, correspondence, publicity material. (350 linear ft.)

ARNO, PETER

DC —LIBRARY OF CONGRESS, Prints & Photographs Div, Washington, 20540.
Notes: Swann Collection is strong in the work of contemporary cartoonists. Among the 400 artists represented are Peter Arno, Bil Canfield, Al Capp, Miguel Covarrubias, Louis Dalrymple, Whitney Darrow, Rube Goldberg, Thomas Nast, Jose Guadalupe Posada, Edward Sorel, and John Tenniel.

ARNOLD, BENEDICT

NY —HISTORICAL SOCIETY OF THE TARRYTOWNS, Library, One Grove St, Tarrytown, 10591. Adelaide R Smith, Cur
Holdings: Vols 30 Cat Maps Pix VF
Notes: Since the capture of Major Andre occurred in the Tarrytown area, 23 Sept 1780, we have comprehensive documentation and a variety of artifacts relating to this event. Our files cover the lives of the 3 captors, John Paulding, Isaac Van Wart and David Williams, as well as Major Andre. Limited material on Benedict Arnold.

ARNOLD, EDWIN G.

MO —HARRY S TRUMAN LIBRARY, Independence, 64050. Benedict K Zobrist, Dir
Holdings: Mss
Notes: Papers of Harry S Truman's administration; also papers of Edwin G Arnold, James P Aylword, Willa Mae Roberts. Approx 13,000,000 pages on hand.

ARNOLD, HENRY H.

DC —LIBRARY OF CONGRESS, Manuscript Division, Washington, 20540. John C Broderick, Chief
Holdings: Cat Mss Pix
Notes: Mss, papers, records, etc.

ARNOLD, JAMES I.

NY —SYRACUSE UNIVERSITY LIBRARIES, Ernest S Bird Library, George Arents Research Library for Special Collections, Syracuse, 13210. Carolyn A Davis, Manuscripts Librn; Amy S Doherty, University Archivist; Mark F Weimer, Rare Book Librn
Notes: The George Arents Research Library for Special Collections at Syracuse University contains the papers of Harley James McKee, Lorimer Rich, Frederick Lear, Max Abramovitz, James I Arnold, Pietro Bulluschi, Claude Bragdon, Marcel Breuer, William Lescaze, Skidmore Owings & Merrill, Ralph Walker, Eric Fisher Wood, Minoru Yamasaki, Joseph Louis Young, and Archimedes Russell.

ARNOLD, JULEAN HERBERT, 1876-1946

CA —HOOVER INSTITUTION ON WAR, REVOLUTION & PEACE, Stanford University, Stanford, 94305. Milorad M Drachkovitch, Archivist
Notes: Papers of Julean Herbert Arnold, 1905-1946, incl diary, correspondence, speeches and writings, reports, dispatches, instructions, memoranda, and other material relating to Arnold's service in the US Consular Service in China and as US Commercial Attache in China, to economic and political developments in China, and to American commercial and foreign policy interests in the Far East. 14 ms boxes.

ARNOLD, MATTHEW, 1822-1888

CA —CLAREMONT COLLEGES, Honnold Library, Ninth & Dartmouth, Claremont, 91711. Tania Rizzo, Special Collections Dept Head
Holdings: Vols 444 // Cat Mss
Notes: First and special editions, biographical and critical items, and his contributions to journals. 5 ALsS.

CA —UNIVERSITY OF CALIFORNIA, SANTA BARBARA, Library, Dept of Special Collections, Santa Barbara, 93106. Christian F Brun, Head
Holdings: Cat Mss Pix

CT —YALE UNIVERSITY, Box 1603A, Yale Station, New Haven, 06520.
Holdings: Cat Mss

VA —UNIVERSITY OF VIRGINIA, Alderman Library, Manuscripts Dept, Charlottesville, 22901. Edmund Berkeley Jr, Cur
Holdings: Vols 72 Cat Mss
Notes: The Arthur Kyle Davis-Matthew Arnold Collection consists of about 1500 copies of Arnold letters, plus about 110 original Arnold letters, assembled and purchased by Davis, long-time professor of English in the University of Virginia. The letters were used by Davis in preparing *Matthew Arnold's Letters: a Descriptive* Checklist (Charlottesville, Virginia: University Press of Virginia, 1968), which is also the best guide to the collection. Small portions of the collection have access restrictions.

ARNOLD, GEN. WILLIAM R.

†VA —GEORGE C MARSHALL RESEARCH FOUNDATION AND LIBRARY, Drawer 920, Lexington, 24450. Royster Lyle Jr, Cur Collections
Holdings: Cat Mss Maps Pix
Notes: Papers, incl personal correspondence, etc, especially with regard to service during World War II.

ARNONI, M. S.

MA —BOSTON UNIVERSITY, Mugar Memorial Library, Special Collections Dept, 771 Commonwealth Ave, Boston, 02215. Howard B Gotlieb, Dir
Holdings: Cat Mss Pix
Notes: Mss, correspondence, etc collected in depth; incl publications by or about.

ARNSTEIN, LEO

CT —YALE UNIVERSITY, Beinecke Rare Book & Manuscript Library, Osborn Collection, New Haven, 06520. Stephen R Parks, Cur
Holdings: Mss

ARNSTEIN, MARGARET

MA —BOSTON UNIVERSITY, Mugar Memorial Library, Special Collections Dept, 771 Commonwealth Ave, Boston, 02215. Howard B Gotlieb, Dir
Holdings: Cat Mss

AROMATIC PLANT PRODUCTS see Essences and Essential Oils

ARONSON, J. HUGO

MT —MONTANA HISTORICAL SOCIETY LIBRARY, 225 N Roberts St, Helena, 59601. Robert M Clark, Librn; Brian Cockhill, State Archivist
Holdings: Cat Mss
Notes: Personal, business, and political papers, 1924-1960.

AROOSTOOK WAR, 1839

ME —MAINE HISTORICAL SOCIETY, Library, 485 Congress St, Portland, 04101.
Holdings: Vols (60,000) Cat Mss Maps Pix
Notes: The Society's holdings cover all of Maine in its scope, with special emphasis on the Portland region.

ARRIGHI, MEL

MA —BOSTON UNIVERSITY, Mugar Memorial Library, Special Collections Dept, 771 Commonwealth Ave, Boston, 02215. Howard B Gotlieb, Dir
Holdings: Cat Mss

ARROWS see Bow and Arrow; Hunting with Bow and Arrow

ART

AL —AUBURN UNIVERSITY, Architecture & Fine Arts Library, Dudley Hall, Auburn, 36830. Larry Stafford, Librn
Holdings: Vols (18,000) Cat Mss Slides
Notes: Incl 30,000 slides.

AL —MONTGOMERY MUSEUM OF FINE ARTS, Library, 440 S McDonough St, Montgomery, 36104. Suzanne W Black, Librn
Holdings: Vols (1800) Cat
Notes: Exchange catalogs with 200 museums.

AZ —TUCSON PUBLIC LIBRARY, 200 S Sixth Ave, Tucson, 85726.
Notes: Fine Arts Room was closed. Materials now in general circulation.

AZ —YUMA CITY-COUNTY LIBRARY, 350 Third Ave, Yuma, 85364. Nancy R Cummings, Library Dir
Holdings: Vols 7000 Cat Phonorecords

CA —BERKELEY PUBLIC LIBRARY, Art and Music Div, 2090 Kittredge St, Berkeley, 97404. Diane Davenport, Reference
Holdings: Vols (20,000) Cat Pix Slides Audiotapes

CA —UNIVERSITY OF CALIFORNIA, BERKELEY, University Library, East Asiatic Library, Room 208, Durant Hall, Berkeley, 94720. Donald Shively, Head
Holdings: Vols (500,000) Cat Mss Maps Pix Microforms
Notes: Library materials are mainly on

ART (cont.)

humanities and social sciences covering the ancient and the modern periods and selectively in natural sciences; substantial in various fields but particularly notable in literary works, fine arts, rare books, folklore, wood-block printed editions, Chinese stone rubbings, Japanese old maps, first editions of Meiji literature, Buddhist texts, and Tibetan xylographs. Estimated 245,000 vols in Chinese, 215,000 vols in Japanese, 30,000 vols in Korean, 5000 in Manchu, Mongol or Tibetan.

†CA —WED ENTERPRISES, Research Library, 1401 Flower St, Glendale, 91201.
Notes: Popular art and architecture journals, pictorial material. Library is not open to the public.

CA —KINGS COUNTY LIBRARY, 401 N Douty St, Hanford, 93230. Ivan K Edelman, County Librn
Holdings: Vols 900 Cat

CA —UNIVERSITY OF CALIFORNIA, SAN DIEGO, Central University Library, Mandeville Dept of Special Collections, La Jolla, 92093. Lynda Corey Claassen, Head
Notes: Hispanic Collection: Approx 6000 vols describe cultures of Spain, Portugal, Mexico, Latin America, and South America. Works of literature, history, philosophy and art date from the 15th to the mid-19th century. Highlights of the collection include rare 18th century Spanish provincial dramas and works on the history of Seville and Andalusia.

CA —LOS ANGELES PUBLIC LIBRARY, Art, Music & Recreation Dept, 630 W Fifth St, Los Angeles, 90071. Melvin H Rosenberg, Mgr & Principal Librn
Holdings: Vols 65,000 Cat Pix
Budget: ($102,244)
Notes: See *Art in Los Angeles Scrapbook*, 1938-date.

CA —UNIVERSITY OF CALIFORNIA, LOS ANGELES, Art Library, Elmer Belt Library of Vinciana, 405 Hilgard Ave, Los Angeles, 90024. Joyce Pellerano Ludmer, Art Librn
Holdings: Vols (10,000) Cat Pix Microforms VF
Notes: The Renaissance, with emphasis on Leonardo da Vinci.

CA —UNIVERSITY OF CALIFORNIA, LOS ANGELES, Art Library, Los Angeles, 90024. Max Marmor, Library Assistant
Holdings: Pix Microforms
Notes: Art; Art History; Early Christian and Byzantine Art; Medieval Art; Apostolic Age to 1400; Iconography; Photo Archive; Christian Art and Symbolism.

CA —J PAUL GETTY MUSEUM, Research Library, 17985 Pacific Coast Highway, Malibu, 90265. Anne-Mieke Halbrook, Head Librn
Holdings: Vols (140,000) Cat
Notes: Western European paintings; French 18th century decorative art; classical art.

CA —J PAUL GETTY MUSEUM, Photo Archives, 17985 Pacific Coast Hwy, Malibu, 90265. William Reeder, Cur
Holdings: Pix
Notes: Incl photographs of works of art at the Museum (180,000 cataloged, 500,000 uncataloged), incl ancient art, western European art (painting, sculpture, graphics) and European decorative arts, medieval and Renaissance to 19th century, and antiquities.

CA —MONTEREY PENINSULA MUSEUM OF ART, Library, 559 Pacific St, Monterey, 93940. Rick Deragon, Asst Cur
Holdings: Vols (4000) Cat
Notes: Folk art is emphasized, although other arts are represented.

CA —OAKLAND PUBLIC LIBRARY, Art, Music and Recreation Section, 125 14 St, Oakland, 94612. Richard Colvig, Senior Librn
Holdings: Pix
Budget: ($500)
Notes: About 350,000 mounted pictures, posters, pictorial maps, postal cards, art reproductions, framed and unframed.

CA —PALO ALTO CITY LIBRARY, 1213 Newell Rd, Palo Alto, 94303. Mary Jo Levy, Dir
Holdings: Vols (6050) Cat

CA —PASADENA PUBLIC LIBRARY, Fine Arts Division, Reference Services, 285 E Walnut St, Pasadena, 91101. Anne Cain, Principal Librn
Holdings: Vols (10,000) Cat Pix Films
Notes: Library has 55 vertical drawers of pictures and clippings, constantly revised and added to. Incl over 130,000 pictures, 64 films.

CA —SACRAMENTO PUBLIC LIBRARY, 828 I St, Sacramento, 95814. Dorothy Harvey, Librn, Special Collections
Holdings: Vols (26,000) Cat Pix
Notes: Incl files, card indexes. Extensive collection on painters and their works.

CA —SAN DIEGO MUSEUM OF ART, Reference Library, PO Box 2107, Balboa Park, San Diego, 92112. Nancy J Andrews, Librn
Holdings: Vols 9000 Cat Slides
Notes: Incl 30,000 exhibition catalogs. Now cataloging bibliographies from all exhibition, sales and commercial gallery catalogs (15, 000). Library is noted for its collection of material on contemporary artists. Have 24 vertical files containing various material on individual artists. Have a catalog for slide collection, as well as a catalog of exhibition and sales catalogs. Incl 18,600 slides.

CA —SAN FRANCISCO ART INSTITUTE, Anne Bremer Memorial Library, 800 Chestnut St, San Francisco, 94133. Jeff Gunderson, Librn
Holdings: Vols (23,114) Cat Pix Slides Audiotapes 16mm Films Microforms
Budget: ($15,000)

CA —SANTA CRUZ PUBLIC LIBRARY, Art, Music, Film Dept, 224 Church St, Santa Cruz, 95060. Alma Westberg, Librn
Holdings: Vols 6500 Cat Pix
Budget: ($2200)
Notes: Over 2000 study prints.

CA —UNIVERSITY OF CALIFORNIA, SANTA CRUZ, University Library, Special Collections, Santa Cruz, 95064. Rita Bottoms, Special Collections Librn; Margaret Felts, South Pacific Collection Bibliographer

CA —CALIFORNIA INSTITUTE OF THE ARTS, Library, 24700 McBean Pkwy, Valencia, 91355. James Elrod, Dir
Holdings: Vols (61,000) Cat Slides
Budget: ($11,000)
Notes: Modern art, incl abstract, conceptual, concrete, environment, minimal, and pop art; art; dadaism; surrealism; happenings; and caricatures and cartoons. Slides (61,683).

CO —UNIVERSITY OF COLORADO, Libraries, Art & Architecture Library, Campus Box 184, Boulder, 80309. Liesel Nolan, Librn/Dept Head
Holdings: Vols (57,647) Cat Pix
Budget: ($39,000)
Notes: Special feature: art exhibition catalog collection 1963-1971, 1972-date. Good general collection with some special emphasis on environmental design, Islamic architecture, Indian art and South American Indian art. Fair collection of periodical backfiles in art and in architecture. Separate catalog for materials in collection. Rare books in main library, listed only in central union catalog.

CO —COLORADO SPRINGS FINE ARTS CENTER LIBRARY, 30 W Dale St, Colorado Springs, 80903. Roderick Dew, Librn
Holdings: Vols (20,000) Cat
Budget: ($4000)
Notes: Specialize in fine arts and anthropology of the Southwest. Incl auction and exhibition catalogs.

CT —MANCHESTER PUBLIC LIBRARY, 586 Main St, Manchester, 06040. John Jackson, Librn
Notes: Emphasis on fine arts.

CT —YALE UNIVERSITY, Art Library, 180 York St, New Haven, 06520. Nancy S Lambert, Art Librn
Holdings: Vols (80,000) Cat Slides
Notes: 100,000 photos and prints; 250,000 slides. There are, in addition to the subject library, about 75,000 books in the same fields in the University library. Slides and photographs are not loaned outside of the university. Books may be obtained on interlibrary loan. The Art Library is primarily for the use of the undergraduates and graduate students of the school of Art and Architecture. Incl environmental design and studio art. Emphasis on current publications and periodicals, and on research material. There is a vertical file of urban planning material and the collection contains some materials in this field, particularly as related to architecture.

CT —YALE UNIVERSITY, Yale Center for British Art, Rare Book Dept, New Haven, 06520. Joan Friedman, Cur
Notes: One of the greatest assemblages of British Art of the 17th-19th centuries.

CT —LYMAN ALLYN MUSEUM, Library, 100 Mohegan Ave, New London, 06320. Mrs D Dinsmore, Librn
Holdings: Vols 5550 Cat Maps Pix
Budget: $2000
Notes: Books on old Master Drawings and the Decorative Arts. Noncirculating library with emphasis on scholarly historical works and museum and exhibition catalogs. Also incl American museum bulletins (uncataloged).

CT —UNIVERSITY OF HARTFORD, Art School, Anne Bunce Cheney Library, 200 Bloomfield Ave, West Hartford, 06117. Jean J Miller, Art Librn
Holdings: Vols 12,800 Cat Pix Slides
Budget: $5500
Notes: Slide collection in Art History Dept.

DC —GEORGETOWN UNIVERSITY, Library, Special Collections Div, 37 & O Sts NW, Washington, 20057. George M Barringer, Special Collections Librn; Nicholas B Sheetz, Mss Librn

DC —NATIONAL ENDOWMENT FOR THE ARTS, Library, 1100 Pen Ave NW, Rm 213, Washington, 20506. Christine Morrison, Arts Librn
Holdings: Vols (6000) Cat
Notes: Incl arts and education and public policy in the arts.

†DC —SMITHSONIAN INSTITUTION LIBRARIES, Washington, 20560.
Notes: The published guide to the numerous Smithsonian Institution museums and deposits is one of the most helpful and successfully (and well-indexed) complementary vols that can be used with this edition of *Subject Collections.* Refer to Lynda Corey Claassen's *Finder's Guide to Prints and Drawings in the Smithsonian* Institution, 210 pp, (Washington: Smithsonian Institution Press, 1981), Los Angeles. An index of artists lists about 10, 000 names represented in the Smithsonian's collections in the Archives of American Art, Cooper-Hewitt Museum, Freer Gallery of Art, Hirshhorn Museum and Sculpture Garden, Museum of African Art, National Air and Space Museum, National Museum of American Art, National Museum of American History, National Museum of Natural History and National Museum of Man, National Portrait Gallery, Smithsonian Institution Archives, andSmithsonian Institution Libraries, and their subject departments, all of which are described.

FL —MIAMI-DADE PUBLIC LIBRARY SYSTEM, One Biscayne Blvd, Miami, 33132. Don Chauncey, AV Librn; Barbara Young, Art & Music Dept Librn
Holdings: Vols 18,000 Cat Pix Films
Notes: Index to color reproductions in reference books; Local artist vertical file; Picture file, portrait file, painting picture file, costume file (together 130,000 pictures); 1, 733 framed pictures, approximately half of which are available for public circulation.

FL —ORLANDO PUBLIC LIBRARY, 100 Block of Central Ave, Orlando, 32806. Helen M Struthers, AV Librn
Holdings: Cat Pix Slides
Budget: $150
Notes: The picture file collection (38,000 pictures) is made up of mounted pictures, pamphlets (10,000), and other vertical file material related to subjects in the Dewey 700's. 438 slides are available for circulation, as well as 340 framed art reproductions.

FL —RINGLING MUSEUM OF ART, Art Research Library, PO Box 1838, Sarasota, 33578. Lynell A Morr, Librn
Holdings: VOls (40,000) Cat
Budget: ($24,000)
Notes: Incl an additional 30,000 art auction catalogs, indexed 1970-date.

ART (cont.)

GA —ATLANTA COLLEGE OF ART LIBRARY, 1280 Peachtree St N E, Atlanta, 30309. Jean Haskell, Librn
Holdings: Vols (16,000) Cat Pix Slides Phonorecords Videotapes Microforms
Notes: Visual arts, with 20th-century emphasis. There is a catalog to the books and the exhibition catalogs.The library is the only collection devoted totally to the visual arts in the Atlanta area. Rare book collection and extensive artists' books collection.

GA —TELFAIR ACADEMY OF ARTS & SCIENCES, Library, 121 Barnard St, Savannah, 31401. Wilma Wierwill, Librn
Holdings: Vols 1150 Cat
Notes: American and German impressionists.

HI —BERNICE P BISHOP MUSEUM, Library, PO Box 19000-A, Honolulu, 96819. Cynthia Timberlake, Librn
Holdings: Vols (90,000) Cat Mss Maps Pix Slides Microforms
Budget: ($30,000)
Notes: Only American library devoted exclusively to the Pacific region. Collection reflects historical and contemporary research emphases of Bishop Museum; ie the natural and cultural history of the Pacific. Areas of concentration incl archaeology, ethnology, linguistics, voyages and explorations, history, vertebrate and invertebrate zoology, botany and museology. Strong special collections incl photographs, mss and archives, maps and art. Publications: Quarterly "Additions to the Catalog," *Dictionary Catalog of the* Library (9 vols and 2 suppl; Boston: G K Hall, 1964-69).

HI —HONOLULU ACADEMY OF ARTS, Robert Allerton Library, 900 S Beretania St, Honolulu, 96814. Anne T Seaman, Librn
Holdings: Vols (40,000) Cat Pix Slides
Notes: Incl 7000 pictures, 3000 slides, 16 VF drawers.

IL —UNIVERSITY OF ILLINOIS, URBANA/CHAMPAIGN, Library, Ricker Library of Architecture & Art, 208 Architecture Bldg, 608 East Lorado Taft Dr, Champaign, 61820. Dee Wallace, Architecture & Art Librn
Holdings: Vols (46,873) Cat
Budget: $35,800
Notes: Incl 32,901 mounted photos and reproductions. Cataloged. Also incl noncirculating collection of exhibition catalogs.

IL —ART INSTITUTE OF CHICAGO, Ryerson & Burnham Libraries, Michigan Ave & Adams St, Chicago, 60603. Daphne C Roloff, Dir
Holdings: Vols (136,000) Cat Mss Slides Microforms
Budget: ($167,000)
Notes: Subjects incl architecture (designs and plans, history); art exhibitions; art history; drawings; furniture; glassware; painting; sculpture; and silverware. Total collection incl 300,000 slides.

IL —CHICAGO PUBLIC LIBRARY, Art Section, Fine Arts Division, 78 E Washington St, Chicago, 60602. Rosalinda I Hack, Fine Arts Division Chief; Yvonne S Brown, Head, Art Section
Holdings: Vols 42,000
Notes: Reference and circulating collection of books, periodicals, exhibition catalogs, dissertations, picture collections, and microforms on all aspects of the visual arts. Major concentration of art history, especially European, with concentration on 19th and 20th century art movements and artists. We attempt to represent the works of recognized artists past and present. The Decorative Arts are well represented especially in the areas of antiques, interior decoration, and handicrafts. The collection is supplemented by a strong periodical collection, consisting of 330 current English and Foreign subscriptions, the majority of these titles we bind, as well as a strong bound retrospective collections. The visual arts is supported by a clipping File on Chicago Artists, a current exhibition catalogs collection, as well as by the microfilm collections of the*Chicago Art* Institute Scrapbooks, the *Scrapbook on Art,* Artists, and the *Index of American Design.*

IL —EVANSTON PUBLIC LIBRARY, 1703 Orrington Ave, Evanston, 60201. Linda Seckelson-Simpson, Librn
Holdings: Vols 31,000 Cat Pix Slides
Budget: $20,000
Notes: Functions as in-depth resource for fine and applied arts for the North Suburban Library System.

IN —INDIANA UNIVERSITY, Art Museum Bldg, Fine Arts Bldg, Bloomington, 47401. Betty Jo Irvine, Fine Arts Librn
Holdings: Vols (57,000) Cat Pix Microforms
Budget: ($52,000)
Notes: Art forms relevant to the periods and places involved.

IN —EVANSVILLE MUSEUM OF ARTS & SCIENCE, Henry B Walker Jr Memorial Art Library, 411 S E Riverside Dr, Evansville, 47713. John W Streetman III, Dir
Holdings: Vols 2050 Cat
Budget: $440,617
Notes: General Museum of Art, History and Science with a Koch Planetarium.

IN —WILLARD LIBRARY, 21 First Ave, Evansville, 47710. Joan Elliott, Special Collections Librn
Holdings: Vols (1400) Cat
Budget: ($3500)
Notes: The Thrall Art Book Collection. Circulating collection of art books being purchased by special endowment. Emphasis on fine arts of all times and places, with particular reference to American artists, as well as European and American decorative arts and architecture. Noncirculating.

IN —ALLEN COUNTY PUBLIC LIBRARY, 900 Webster St, Fort Wayne, 46802. Paul Deane, Reader Services Dept Head; Kay Lynn Isca, Art Music & AV Dept Head
Holdings: Vols 6000 Cat Pix Slides Phonorecords Audiotapes Films

IN —INDIANAPOLIS MUSEUM OF ART, Stout Reference Library, 1200 W 38 St, Indianapolis, 46208. Martha Blocker, Head Librn
Holdings: Vols (22,000) Cat
Notes: Incl 12,000 uncataloged art exhibition and sale catalogs, microforms, newspaper clippings, and slides (in separate Slide Library; Carolyn Metz, Cur)

IN —MORRISSON-REEVES LIBRARY, 80 N Sixth St, Richmond, 47374. Harriet E Bard, Librn
Holdings: Vols 3000 Cat Slides
Notes: Books on art covering a broad range of subject headings. Also, 1030 lantern slides of European sculpture, painting and architecture, particularly emphasizing the Italian Renaissance.

IN —THE ART CENTER, Library, 120 St Joseph St, South Bend, 46601. Judy Oberhausen, Cur
Holdings: Vols (1010) Cat Slides
Notes: 500 slides. This Art Center has a specific, separate collection--"The Arts of the United States"--which has its own index and is geared toward American painting, graphics, architecture, design and decorative arts, from the 19th to the 20th century, and sculpture works on paper. Incl 32 periodical titles.

IN —INDIANA STATE UNIVERSITY, Cunningham Memorial Library, Dept of Rare Books & Special Collections, Terre Haute, 47809. Lawrence J McCrank, Head
Holdings: Cat Maps Pix

IA —DES MOINES ART CENTER, Library, Greenwood Park, Des Moines, 50312. Peggy Buckley, Librn
Holdings: Vols 8400 Cat VF
Notes: Incl 12 vertical files.

KS —SOUTHWESTERN COLLEGE, Memorial Library, 100 College St, Winfield, 67156. Daniel L Nutter, Librn
Holdings: Vols 200 // Cat Pix
Notes: The Arthur Covey Art Collection. Arthur Covey was a noted American artist from the 1920s until his death in 1960 and was a graduate of Southwestern. His wife, Lois Lenski, noted author and illustrator of children's books, gave all of his paintings, materials, and library to the college in 1960.

KY —BOWLING GREEN PUBLIC LIBRARY, 1225 State St, Bowling Green, 42101. Karen A Turner, Dir
Holdings: Vols 1012 Cat Pix Slides Filmstrips Cassette Tapes

KY —UNIVERSITY OF KENTUCKY, Art Library, 4 Margaret I King Library, Lexington, 40506. Meg Shaw, Art Librn
Holdings: Vols 26,338

KY —SPEED ART MUSEUM, Library, 2035 S Third St, Louisville, 40208. Mary Jane Benedict, Librn
Holdings: Vols 12,000 Cat Mss Maps Pix

KY —UNIVERSITY OF LOUISVILLE, Allen R Hite Art Institute, Library, Belknap Campus, Louisville, 40292. Gail Gilbert, Librn
Holdings: Vols (40,000) Cat Pix
Budget: ($29,000)
Notes: Incl books on art, architecture, landscape architecture and gardening, prints, printing, illustrated books and brass rubbings. Library subscribes to 200 periodical titles in these and other areas. Collection circulates to faculty and staff only, with same restrictions placed on interlibrary loan. Library also has collections of bookplates, posters, original prints, hand-made Christmas cards and clippings file filling 56 VF drawers.

KY —KENTUCKY WESLEYAN COLLEGE LIBRARY, 3000 Frederica, Owensboro, 42301. Stuart Stiffler, Dir
Notes: The Dr and Mrs M David Orrahood Collection.

LA —JEFFERSON DAVIS PARISH LIBRARY, 118 West Plaquemine, Jennings, 70546. Trudy Patterson, Parish Librn
Holdings: Vols 550 Cat Pix

LA —NEW ORLEANS PUBLIC LIBRARY, Art & Music Div, 219 Loyola Ave, New Orleans, 70140. Marilyn Wilkins, Head
Holdings: Cat Pix
Budget: $23,500

LA —R W NORTON ART GALLERY, Library, 4747 Creswell Ave, Shreveport, 71106. Jerry M Bloomer, Librn
Holdings: Vols 3000 Cat
Notes: Extensive Art Reference section incl books and periodicals, monographs on artists, historical surveys of art from early times to the present, museum catalogs, exhibition catalogs. Large collection of art auction catalogs (mostly not yet cataloged).

ME —PORTLAND PUBLIC LIBRARY, 5 Monument Sq, Portland, 04101. Edward V Chenevert, Library Dir
Holdings: Vols (16,108)

ME —WILLIAM A FARNSWORTH LIBRARY & ART MUSEUM, 19 Elm St, Rockland, 04841. Marius B Peladeau, Dir
Holdings: Vols (4000) Cat Pix Microforms
Notes: Emphasis on American and European fine and decorative arts of all periods (largely modern). Other areas include marine history and Maine history (local); illustrated books and rare books also a part of our collection, which has its own catalog. Also, Louise Nevelsen, N C Wyeth Archives.

MD —BALTIMORE MUSEUM OF ART LIBRARY, Art Museum Dr, Baltimore, 21218. Anita Gilden, Librn
Holdings: Vols (40,000) Cat
Notes: General reference sources with emphasis on 19th and 20th century art and American decorative art. Incl prints and drawings. Photocopying.

MD —WALTERS ART GALLERY, Library & Manuscripts & Rare Book Collection, 600 N Charles St, Baltimore, 21201. Muriel L Toppan, Reference Librn; Lilian M C Randall, Cur of Mss & Rare Books
Holdings: Vols (80,000) Cat Mss
Budget: ($35,000)
Notes: The collection supports the gallery's collections of art objects which date from 4000 BC to the end of the 19th century. The collection of medieval and renaissance illuminated mss (782 in number), incunabula (about 1400) and rare books are considered art objects. There are card catalogs providing indexing to the collection. The mss are listed in De Ricci and the incunabula in Goff. Photocopying permitted for Reference Library materials only.

MA —ROBBINS LIBRARY, 700 Massachusetts Ave, Arlington, 02174. Peter L Fenton, Dir
Holdings: Cat Pix
Notes: 150,000 graphic works in all media,

ART (cont.)

emphasizing portrait prints from the 15th century to the present day.

MA —BOSTON PUBLIC LIBRARY, Copley Sq, Boston, 02117. Theresa D Cederholm, Cur of Fine Arts
Notes: Collection incl 138,000 titles (not incl multiple vols sets, serials, and unbound materials); VF on regional artists, architects, art organizations.

MA —BOSTON PUBLIC LIBRARY, Print Collection, Dartmouth St at Copley Sq, Boston, 02117. Sinclair H Hitchings, Keeper of Prints
Holdings: Cat
Notes: The collection of about 70,000 prints and 4500 drawings as well as a few oil paintings. There is a small collection of Old Master prints and drawings and a large and growing collection of French, British, and American prints (as well as some drawings) especially of the 19th century, also 18th and 20th century. Some German and Spanish artists are also represented. An overview of the entire collection appears in *Artist's* Proof, Vol XI. Arrangements can be made for professional photocopying.

MA —MASSACHUSETTS COLLEGE OF ART, Library, 364 Brookline Ave, Boston, 02215. Benjamin Hopkins, Head Librn
Holdings: Vols 45,000 Cat Slides
Notes: Incl 55,000 slides, 12 vertical file drawere of pictures.

MA —HARVARD UNIVERSITY, Harvard College Library, Fine Arts Library, Fogg Museum, 32 Quincy St, Cambridge, 02138. Wolfgang M Freitag, Librn
Holdings: Vols (202,000) Cat Mss Pix Slides
Budget: ($176,500)
Notes: All areas of art history, with emphasis on Italian primitives, Italian Renaissance, master drawings, Romanesque sculpture, architectural history, ms materials (particulary American artists'), conservation and restoration of art objects. Incl the Berenson repertory of photographs from the Harvard Center for Italian Renaissance Studies in Florence, and the Decimal Index to the Art of the Low Countries. Separate card catalogs for books, photographs and lantern slides, registers for ms holdings which are not incl in *National Union Catalog of Manuscript Collections.* Slides total over 230,000; over 745,000 pictures. *Fine Arts Library Catalogue* (14 volumes) and *Catalogue of Auction Sales Catalogues* (1 volume) (Boston: G K Hall, 1972); *A Guide to the Fine Arts Library* (Cambridge, Mass: 1971); *Guide to the Harvard Libraries,* microfiche edition of holdingscataloged through 1981 published 1984 (Munich/New York: Saur).

MA —BOSTON COLLEGE LIBRARIES, Chestnut Hill, 02167.

MA —DEDHAM PUBLIC LIBRARY, 43 Church St, Dedham, 02026. Murray F McDonald, Dir
Holdings: Vols 2001 Cat Pix

MA —MELROSE PUBLIC LIBRARY, 69 W Emerson St, Melrose, 02176. Diane E Shaw, Art Librn
Holdings: Vols (8500) Cat Pix Slides Phonorecords
Budget: ($6900)
Notes: Framed and unframed art reproductions (110), slides (2773), periodicals, clippings, sound recordings (3000). Incl the Mary Livermore Collection of Sacred Art, the Odlin Collection, and the Pierre Gendrot Collection of Fine Art.

MA —OSTERVILLE FREE LIBRARY, 43 Wianno Ave, Osterville, 02655. Barbara Baker, Dir
Holdings: Vols (700) Cat
Notes: Considered a "best collection on Cape Cod." Incl stereopticon slides.

MA —SPRINGFIELD CITY LIBRARY, Art & Music Dept, 220 State St, Springfield, 01103. Karen A Dorval, Supvr & Art Librn; Sylvia A Saint Amand, Music Librn
Holdings: Vols (22,500) Cat Pix Phonorecords Audiotapes Microforms
Budget: ($183,000)
Notes: Art: books (17,500), pamphlets (8000), pictures (120,000); music: books (5000), music scores (10,000), phonorecords (18,000), Audiocassettes (288 titles). Also microfilm (75 reels). Separate catalogs for art, music, and phonorecords and audiocassettes.

MA —WELLESLEY COLLEGE, Art Library, Wellesley, 02181. Katherine D Finkelpearl, Art Librn
Holdings: Vols (30,000) Cat Pix Slides
Budget: ($22,000)
Notes: Primarily the art and architecture of Western Europe, the Far East, and classical antiquity. However, efforts are being made to expand the collection in the areas of photography, primitive art, and ancient (non-classical) art. The Art Department maintains a separate collection of 62,500 mounted pictures and 90,000 slides.

MA —STERLING AND FRANCINE CLARK ART INSTITUTE LIBRARY, 225 South St, PO Box 8, Williamstown, 01267. Michael Rinehart, Librn
Holdings: Vols (77,000) Cat Pix Slides Microforms
Budget: ($105,000)
Notes: Primarily European art, 1300-present, and post-Columbian American art. Incl 850, 000 pictures, 80,000 slides, 400 microfilm reels, 25,000 auction sale catalogs, and Mary Ann Beinecke Decorative Art Collection.

MA —WORCESTER ART MUSEUM, Library, 55 Salisbury St, Worcester, 01609. Kathy Berg, Librn
Holdings: Vols (35,000) Cat Slides
Budget: ($16,000)

MI —UNIVERSITY OF MICHIGAN, Art and Architecture Library, 2106 Art and Architecture Bldg, Ann Arbor, 48109. Peggy Ann Kusnerz, Librn; Dot Shields, Asst Librn
Holdings: Vols (45,000)
Notes: Incl 200 maps, 35,000 slides, vertical file, videocassettes, blueprints, Jens Jensen Landscape drawings, oral history, and 400 serial titles.

MI —UNIVERSITY OF MICHIGAN, Fine Arts Library, Tappan Hall, Ann Arbor, 48109. Margaret Jensen, Fine Arts Librn; Joy Alexander, Cur Slide Collection
Holdings: Vols (50,000) Cat Slides Microforms
Notes: All aspects.

MI —CRANBROOK ACADEMY OF ART, 500 Lone Pine Rd, Box 801, Bloomfield Hills, 48013. Diane Gunn, Librn
Holdings: Vols 25,000 Slides
Notes: Incl 20,000 slides. Also information on metalsmithing and fiber arts (weaving).

MI —D'ARCY, MACMANUS, MASIUS, Library Information Center, 1725 N Woodward, PO Box 811, Bloomfield Hills, 48303. Lois W Collet, Dir, Library Information Services; Harriet Siden, Art Librn

MI —CENTER FOR CREATIVE STUDIES, College of Art and Design, (formerly Art School of the Society of Arts and Crafts), 245 E Kirby, Detroit, 48202. Jean Peyrat, Librn; Susan Campbell, Slide Librn
Holdings: Vols 15,500 Cat Pix Slides
Notes: Incl 50,000 pictures and 32,000 slides.

MI —DETROIT PUBLIC LIBRARY, Fine Arts Department, 5201 Woodward Ave, Detroit, 48202. Shirley Solvick, Chief
Holdings: Vols 60,000 Cat Pix
Budget: ($20,000)
Notes: Downs number 2882, 2923, 2938. Book collection covers all phases of art. Picture collection of over 500,000 items covers all subjects; especially strong in the fine and decorative arts, portraits, costume, and Detroit.

MI —MONROE COUNTY LIBRARY SYSTEM, Ellis Reference and Information Center, 3700 S Custer Rd, Monroe, 48161. Marie D Chulski, Head of Reference Services
Budget: $1000
Notes: 200 pieces of framed art, sculpture, pottery. Collection of original pieces of art from local artists. Acquired since 1976.

MI —MONROE COUNTY LIBRARY SYSTEM, Bedford Branch, 8575 Jackman Road, Temperance, 48182. Paula Kaczmarek, Head, Bedford Branch
Holdings: Vols 6500 Cat Periodicals AV
Budget: $8000
Notes: Circulating general collection of popular art books, especially Western European and American painting; also includes technique, graphic arts, photography, sculpture, architecture. Periodicals held five years.

MI —CAMPBELL-EWALD CO, Reference Center, 30400 Van Dyke, Warren, 48093. Susan Stepek, Mgr
Holdings: Vols 375 Cat Maps Pix
Notes: Collection intended for advertising agency personnel. Incl bound vols of periodicals, 36 vertical file drawers of pictures by subject, commercial art and photography annuals and current periodicals.

MN —MINNEAPOLIS COLLEGE OF ART & DESIGN, Library, 200 E 25 St, Minneapolis, 55404. Richard Kronstedt, Head Librn
Holdings: Vols (50,000) Cat Pix Slides
Notes: Incl art exhibition catalogs, collection emphasis on 20th century art and artists.

MN —MINNEAPOLIS PUBLIC LIBRARY & INFORMATION CENTER, Art, Music & Films Dept, 300 Nicollet Mall, Minneapolis, 55401. Mary Alice Walker, Music Specialist
Holdings: Vols (94,200) Cat Pix Slides
Budget: ($111,642)
Notes: Art collection incl 1,196,865 pictures; 46,560 slides; and 10,650 stereographs.

MN —WALKER ART CENTER, Staff Reference Library, Vineland Place, Minneapolis, 55403. Rosemary Furtak, Librn
Holdings: Vols 5000 Cat Pix
Notes: Incl 10,000 catalogs of individual artists; museum gallery catalogs-10,000 catalogs of major exhibitions from all over the world dating back to 1940. VF material and tapes.

MN —SAINT PAUL PUBLIC LIBRARY, Arts & Audiovisual Services, 90 W Fourth St, Saint Paul, 55102. Delores Sundbye, Supervising Librn
Holdings: Cat Pix Slides Phonorecords Audiotapes
Budget: ($20,000)
Notes: The Art and Music Dept incl 10,000 books on art and architecture, 4000 books on music and 10,000 cataloged music scores. Collection of 650 color reproduction, 10,000 mounted pictures and 500 exhibit catalogs. Complete set of first edition of Arundel Prints (color lithographic copies of Renaissance paintings, published by the Arundel Society, 1849-1897).

MO —UNIVERSITY OF MISSOURI-COLUMBIA, Museum of Art & Archaeology, Library, One Pickard Hall, Columbia, 65201. Ruth E Witt, Asst Dir
Holdings: Vols (4000)
Notes: Sales and exhibition catalogs, reports, bulletins, etc.

MO —THE NELSON-ATKINS MUSEUM OF ART, Kenneth & Helen Spencer Art Reference Library, 4525 Oak St, Kansas City, 64111. Stanley W Hess, Librn
Notes: Incl European painting and sculpture; ceramics; pottery; European and American decorative arts; porcelain; silver; furniture; ancient art; classical art; medieval art; modern art, 20th century; primitive art; tapestries; miniatures; period rooms/architecture; auction catalogs; and audition catalogs.

MO —UNIVERSITY OF MISSOURI-KANSAS CITY, General Library, 5100 Rockhill Road, Kansas City, 64110. Kenneth J LaBudde, Dir; Gordon Hendrickson, Assoc Dir; Marilyn Carbonell, Ref Librn
Holdings: Vols 25,000 Cat
Notes: 4121 current serial subscriptions.
See also entry under Architecture - History.

MO —SAINT LOUIS PUBLIC LIBRARY, Art Dept, 1301 Olive St, Saint Louis, 63103. Martha Hilligoss, Librn
Holdings: Vols 44,000 Cat Slides
Notes: Plus more than 1400 framed prints, 250 pieces of scuplture, 15,000 slides and 470,000 pictures.

MO —WASHINGTON UNIVERSITY, Art & Architecture Library, Saint Louis, 63130. Imre Meszaros, Librn
Holdings: Vols (60,413) Cat Maps Pix Microforms
Budget: ($100,000)
Notes: Art and architecture of East Asia; rare books; archaeology; fashion design.

ART (cont.)

NE —JOSLYN ART REFERENCE LIBRARY, Joslyn Art Museum, 2200 Dodge St, Omaha, 68102. Ann Birney, Librn; Marie Sedlacek, Cataloger-Slide Librn
Holdings: Vols (17,000) Cat Slides
Notes: Incl catalogs of exhibitions; materials on western US History, including early Omaha and Nebraska. Large collections of vertical files on artists; also mounted prints, reproductions and slides, 250 periodical titles.

NH —DARTMOUTH COLLEGE, Sherman Art Library, Hanover, 03755. Jeffrey L Horrell, Art Librn
Holdings: Vols (52,000) Cat
Notes: Incl art, architecture and photography. Access is available through OCLC and RLIN.

NH —STRAWBERY BANKE, Thayer Cumings Historical Reference Library, Portsmouth, 03801. Nicole R Osborn, Librn
Holdings: Vols (2850) Cat Mss Maps Pix Microforms
Budget: ($1900)
Notes: The Library is a small, highly specialized library with holdings in American art, architecture and decorative arts. The collection is especially strong in the American decorative arts, with additional concentration in European decorative arts. In addition, the collection contains books on American painting, American architecture, archaeology, technology, maritime history and boatbuilding, landscape gardening and design, as well as books on local and regional history and social and material culture of the 17th-19th centuries. Collection of mss microfilm and documents is related to important properties and personages of Portsmouth and the surrounding area.

NJ —ELIZABETH PUBLIC LIBRARY, Art & Music Dept, 11 S Broad St, Elizabeth, 07202. Roman Sawycky, Head
Holdings: Vols (20,000) Cat Pix Phonorecords 16mm Films Filmstrips
Budget: ($10,000)
Notes: Incl 200,000 pictures, 12,000 phonorecords and 700 films and filmstrips.

NJ —ENGLEWOOD LIBRARY, 31 Engle St, Englewood, 07631. N E Rhoades, Reference Librn
Holdings: Vols (8200) Cat

NJ —NEWARK PUBLIC LIBRARY, Art & Music Dept, 5 Washington St, Newark, 07101. William J Dane, Supv
Holdings: Vols (50,000) Cat Mss Maps Pix Slides Microforms VF
Notes: All phases of art and all periods of art history are covered in books and periodicals; supporting collections incl 1,000,000 illustrations, 2000 portfolios of plates, 15,000 fine prints, 15,000 slides, historic maps, manuscripts and book collection on the history of fine printing, posters and autographs, extensive vertical file.

NJ —PRINCETON UNIVERSITY, Library, Rare Books Dept, Princeton, 08544. Stephen Ferguson, Cur
Holdings: Vols (121,000) Cat

NY —NEW YORK STATE LIBRARY, Humanities Reference Service, Albany, 12230. Lee Stanton, Acting Assoc Librn
Holdings: Vols 40,000 Cat Pix
Notes: Incl 6500 titles (8000 volumes) in painting, 5600 titles (7000 volumes) in architecture.

NY —NEW YORK STATE COLLEGE OF CERAMICS AT ALFRED UNIVERSITY, Scholes Library, Harder Hall, Alfred, 14802. Bruce E Connolly, Library Dir
Holdings: Vols (70,000) Cat Mss Slides Microforms
Budget: ($134,000)
Notes: Very specialized collection incl all phases of the arts and sciences related to ceramics. Incl 1112 subscriptions.

†NY —SARAH LAWRENCE COLLEGE, Esther Raushenbush Library, 1 Meadway, Bronxville, 10708. Rose Ann Burstein, Librn

NY —BROOKLYN MUSEUM, Art Reference Library, 188 Eastern Parkway, Brooklyn, 11238.
Holdings: Vols (130,000)
Notes: Collection particularly strong in American Painting, Sculpture and Decorative Arts, African and Oceanic Art, Oriental Art, and Costume and Textiles. Special collection of original fashion sketches. Open by appointment.

NY —PRATT INSTITUTE LIBRARY, Art & Architecture Dept, 200 Willoughby Ave, Brooklyn, 11205. Sydney Star Keaveney, Prof
Holdings: Vols (30,000) Cat Pix Slides
Budget: ($50,000)
Notes: Art and architecture, incl sculpture, photography, painting, design, costume, and commercial art. Incl 60,000 art slides. Use restricted to Pratt faculty and students.

NY —STATE UNIVERSITY OF NEW YORK, COLLEGE AT BUFFALO, Lockwood Memorial Library, Art Dept, Buffalo, 14260. Florence S DaLuiso, Cur
Holdings: Vols (38,000) Cat Micorforms
Budget: ($24,735)
Notes: Collection supports curriculum of the School of Fine Art. Incl 9000 exhibition catalogs. Recent acquisitions emphasize contemporary art and environmental design. The library by reciprocal agreement contains card catalog holdings of the Albright-Knox Art Gallery, Buffalo, New York. Books may be obtained on interlibrary loan.

NY —CORNING MUSEUM OF GLASS LIBRARY, Corning, 14831. Norma P H Jenkins, Librn
Holdings: Vols (30,000) Cat Slides Videotapes
Notes: Extensive and comprehensive coverage of the art, archaeology, history and early manufacture of glass, with supporting materials in art, archaeology, and the decorative arts. Collection incl some 1800 manufacturers' trade catalogs on microfiche, 10,000 periodical vols and documents. 130 videotapes, 1000 microforms. Some incumabula. Research library primarily for use on the premises.

NY —GENEVA HISTORICAL SOCIETY, James Luckett Memorial Archives, 543 S Main St, Geneva, 14456. Eleanore Clise, Librn

NY —CORNELL UNIVERSITY LIBRARIES, Fine Arts Library, Sibley Hall, Ithaca, 14853. Judith Holliday, Librn
Holdings: Vols (115,000) Cat Maps Pix

NY —QUEENS BOROUGH PUBLIC LIBRARY, Art & Music Div, 89-11 Merrick Blvd, Jamaica, 11432. Dorothea Wu, Head
Holdings: Vols (85,000) Cat Maps Pix Phonorecords Audiotapes Microforms
Budget: ($44,000)
Notes: The Picture Collection, covering all subjects, consists of approximately 1,500,000 pictures, mainly reproductions and clippings from books and magazines, photographs, and postcards on all subjects; The Framed Picture Collection, approx 180 framed pictures, mostly reproductions of paintings from various periods; and The Phonorecord and Cassette Collection consists of approx 3500 reference phonorecords and 6500 circulating records as well as 1000 reference cassettes and 1500 circulating cassettes.

NY —STATE UNIVERSITY OF NEW YORK, COLLEGE AT NEW PALTZ, Sojourner Truth Library, New Paltz, 12561. W E Connors, Dir
Holdings: Vols 17,150
Notes: Art--education, history, studio.

NY —NEW ROCHELLE PUBLIC LIBRARY, Fine Arts Dept, Library Plaza, New Rochelle, 10801. Eugene L Mittelgluck, Library Dir
Holdings: Vols (13,000) Cat Pix Slides
Budget: ($10,000)
Notes: Incl (430,000) pictures and (6300) slides.
See also entries under Ballet and the Dance; Costume; Music.

NY —CITY UNIVERSITY OF NEW YORK, City College, Library, 138 St & Convent Ave, New York, 10031. Vira C Hinds, Assoc Prof
Notes: In general reference library.

NY —COLLECTORS CLUB, Library, 22 E 35 St, New York, 10016. Werner Elias, Librn
Holdings: Cat Mss Maps Pix Slides
Notes: Incl a special area of essays and proof which may be of interest to people desiring knowledge of art and engravers. Incl photographs of stamps. 100,000 items.

NY —COLUMBIA UNIVERSITY LIBRARIES, Avery Architectural & Fine Arts Library, 201 Avery Hall, New York, 10027. Roberta Blitz, Fine Arts Librn
Holdings: Vols 220,000
Notes: Restricted use: noncirculating.

NY —METROPOLITAN MUSEUM OF ART, Thomas J Watson Library, Fifth Ave & 82 St, New York, 10028. William B Walker, Chief Librn
Holdings: Vols (250,000) Cat Mss Microforms
Notes: All fields of art: 1400 periodicals, incl bulletins and annual reports, catalogs, etc of American and foreign art societies, museums, etc; incl sales catalogs, exhibition catalogs, clipping file on individual artists and subjects, autograph letters. See *Library Catalog of the Metropolitan Museum of Art, New York,* second ed, rev and enl (Boston, G K Hall, 1980, 48 v and first supplement, 1982). Since 1980, holdings have been cataloged in RLIN.

†NY —METROPOLITAN MUSEUM OF ART, Photograph & Slide Library, 82 St & Fifth Ave, New York, 10028. Margaret P Nolan, Chief Librn
Holdings: Cat
Notes: Incl 252,000 black and white photographs; 6000 color prints; 161,000 black and white slides (3 1/4 X 4), 125,000 color slides (2 X 2). Slides and photographs illustrate the history of architecture, sculpture, painting and the decorative arts; photographic records of the Metropolitan Museum collections. Slides available for rental; photographs available for reference; photographs of objects in the Metropolitan Museum available for sale.

NY —METROPOLITAN MUSEUM OF ART, Dept of Prints & Photographs, 82 St & Fifth Ave, New York, 10028. Colta Ives, Cur
Holdings: Vols (10,000)
Notes: Contained in a collection of 500,000 prints from 15th to 20th century. Approx 10, 000 illustrated books; European and American. No photocopying.

NY —NEW YORK PUBLIC LIBRARY, Art, Prints, and Photographs Div, Fifth Ave & 42 St, New York, 10018. Donald Anderle, Chief
Holdings: Vols 100,000 Cat Mss Pix Microforms

NY —NEW YORK PUBLIC LIBRARY, Mid-Manhattan Library, Art Collection, 455 Fifth Ave, New York, 10016.
Holdings: Vols 25,000 Cat Microforms
Budget: $36,000
Notes: College-oriented collection of architecture, fine and decorative arts.

†NY —UNION LEAGUE CLUB, Library, 38 E 37th St, New York, 10016. Jane Reed, Librn
Holdings: Vols (30,000)
Notes: Oriental, Chinese, Japanese, and Tibetan art and porcelain.

NY —UNIVERSITY CLUB, Library, One W 54 St, New York, 10019. Guy St Clair, Library Dir
Holdings: Vols (100,000) Cat Mss Maps Pix
Notes: A private library for the members of the University Club, their guests, and serious scholars upon written application to the Library Director.

NY —UNIVERSITY OF ROCHESTER, Fine Arts Library and Gallery, Rochester, 14627. Stephanie J Frontz, Librn
Holdings: Vols (35,000) Cat
Budget: ($15,000)

NY —SAINT BONAVENTURE UNIVERSITY, Friedsam Memorial Library, Saint Bonaventure, 14778. John Capozzi, OFM, Art Cur
Holdings: Vols 12,000 Cat
Budget: $2000
Notes: Collection is briefly described in *Art Tours and Detours in NY State,* by S Lane Faison (Random House, 1964).

NY —SKIDMORE COLLEGE, Lucy Scribner Library, Saratoga Springs, 12866. Jane Graves, Fine Arts Librn
Holdings: Vols 7500 Cat Pix Slides
Notes: Also 40,000 art slides.

NY —MUNSON-WILLIAMS-PROCTOR INSTITUTE, Reference Library, 310

ART (cont.)

Genessee St, Utica, 13502. Linda Lott, Librn
Holdings: Vols (16,000) Cat Slides
Notes: Mainly American art and history of art, especially 19th century. Incl 16,500 slides. Separate catalog.

NY —ELIZABETH SETON COLLEGE LIBRARY, Yonkers, 10701. Sr Margaret Sullivan, Librn

NY —YONKERS PUBLIC LIBRARY, Grinton I Will Library, 1500 Central Park Ave, Yonkers, 10701. Joan W Stevenson, Head of Fine Arts Dept
Holdings: Vols (12,000) Cat
Budget: ($36,000)
Notes: Incl periodicals, 70 titles (ca 15 yr back issues); 27 vertical file drawers (18 on artists & musicians); 1230 slides; 2200 music scores; cat; sheet music, ca 1200 titles; 140 libretti; 13,000 phonograph albums; cat; 1000 cassettes. Books, scores, phonograph albums, cassettes are cataloged. Rare collection of 57 test pressings of Geraldine Farrar, some of which have never been issued.

NC —UNIVERSITY OF NORTH CAROLINA, CHAPEL HILL, Art Library, Art Classroom Studio Bldg, 079A, Chapel Hill, 27514. Philip A Rees, Art Librn
Holdings: Vols (47,000) Cat Microforms
Budget: ($52,000)
Notes: Emphasis on European and American art and architecture, ancient to modern. Special strengths: Rubens and 19th century French painting.

NC —NORTH CAROLINA STATE UNIVERSITY, Harry B Lyons Design Library, P. O. Box 7701, Raleigh, 27607. Maryellen LoPresti, Librn
Notes: Collection covers architecture, landscape architecture, design and related professions. Additional materials may be found on art, painting, sculpture, photography and solar energy design. The library presently houses a total of 28,000 books, periodical and serial volumes to support the curriculum. A product and trade literature file and a vertical file of pamplets are also locally cataloged in the library representing an additional 3000 items of materials available for use. A significant collection of over 50,000 cataloged slides primarily representing the areas of art and architectural history are also contained in the library facility. See *Directory of Special Libraries and Information Centers.*

NC —SAINT MARY'S COLLEGE, Sarah Graham Kenan Library, 900 Hillsborough St, Raleigh, 27611.

NC —WAKE TECHNICAL COLLEGE, Library, Audio-Visual Dept, 9101 Fayetteville Road, Raleigh, 27603. James Gray, Librn; Horst Garloff, Audio-Visual Specialist
Holdings: Vols (32,332) Cat Maps Slides Phonorecords Audiotapes Videotapes 16mm Films Filmstrips Microforms

OH —OHIO UNIVERSITY, Vernon R Alden Library, Fine Arts Library, Athens, 45701. Anne Braxton, Fine Arts Librn
Holdings: Vols (40,000) Cat Pix Slides Microforms
Notes: Strong collection in history of film and photography; general art collection incl some 2000 exhibition catalogs.

OH —CINCINNATI ART MUSEUM, Library, Eden Park, Cincinnati, 45202. Patrician P Rutledge, Librn
Holdings: Vols (45,850) Cat Microforms
Notes: Art library containing all subjects on art-history, graphic arts, advertising art, etc; special strength in prints, ie engravings, etc. Near Eastern art and decorative arts are also strong. At least 90,000 art exhibition catalogs. Emphasis on artists of Cincinnati and vicinity in vertical file material.

OH —PUBLIC LIBRARY OF CINCINNATI & HAMILTON COUNTY, Art & Music Dept, 800 Vine St, Cincinnati, 45202. R Jayne Craven, Head
Holdings: Vols (122,185) Cat Pix
Budget: ($56,100)
Notes: Special collections: Eda Kuhn Loeb, "Artist and the Book, 1875-Date" (now shelved in Rare Book Room); music librettos (2345); exhibition catalogs (5474); large prints and posters (5051); Cincinnati artists vertical files; picture collection (673,906 clippings).

OH —CLEVELAND MUSEUM OF ART, Library, 11150 E Blvd, Cleveland, 44106. Jack Perry Brown, Librn
Holdings: Vols (120,000) Cat Pix Slides Microforms
Notes: 1500 serial titles incl museum bulletins. Also 200,000 slides; 250,000 photographs. Special photograph collections: Decimal Index Art of Low Countries (DIAL); Gernsheim Corpus Photographicum of drawings; Archive of Biblioteca Berenson; National Palace Collection, Victoria and Albert Museum. Index of Ohio artists.

OH —CLEVELAND PUBLIC LIBRARY, Fine Arts and Special Collections Department, 325 Superior Ave, Cleveland, 44114. Alice N Loranth, Head
Holdings: Vols (12,000) Cat Pix
Notes: The collection covers all periods and fields of art with special emphasis on contemporary and American art. 200 periodicals, incl bulletins of American museums. 50 VF drawers of art clippings and pictorical materials. Collection of original graphics by Cleveland artists, incl 129 prints from the Federal Art Project (WPA).

OH —GRANDVIEW HEIGHTS PUBLIC LIBRARY, 1685 W First Ave, Columbus, 43212. Kathryn M Hannon, Librn
Holdings: Vols 1764 Cat

OH —OHIO STATE UNIVERSITY, Fine Arts Library, 1813 N High St, Columbus, 43210. Susan Wyngaard, Head, Fine Arts Library
Holdings: Vols (75,000) Cat Microforms
Budget: ($60,000)
Notes: Also have 1000 uncataloged exhibition catalogs. Book collection strong in history of art especially in area of medieval & Northern Renaissance art. Good collection of portfolios. Photographic collections on microfiche. Receive Slavic titles, many on Byzantine frescoes. Online catalog. Decimal Index of the Art of the Low Countries, as well as Marburger Index; Index Photographique de i' Arten France; Alinari Archives on microfiche and other major microform collections in art.

OH —DAYTON ART INSTITUTE LIBRARY, 405 W Riverview Ave, PO Box 941, Dayton, 45401. Helen L Pinkney, Librn and Assoc Cur
Holdings: Vols (23,220) Cat Mss Pix Slides Microforms VF
Budget: ($7000)
Notes: Incl museum catalogs and bulletins and collection of slides of stained glass.

OH —OBERLIN COLLEGE LIBRARY, Clarence Ward Art Library, Allen Art Bldg, Oberlin, 44074. Jeffrey Weidman, Librn
Holdings: Vols (62,000) Cat Microforms
Notes: Incl approx 18,000 uncataloged exhibition catalogues and major sales catalogues. Significant holdings in early serials (see *ARLO Union List of Serials).*

OR —UNIVERSITY OF OREGON LIBRARY, Architecture & Allied Arts Branch, Eugene, 97403. Reyburn R McCready, Head Librn
Holdings: Vols (35,000) Cat Pix Slides
Budget: ($57,000)
Notes: Incl 200,000 slides and student renderings on architecture and the arts, incl sculpture, painting, furniture, interior architecture, graphic arts, landscape, art history and art education.
See also entry under Art, Oriental; Artists, American; East (Far East)

OR —LIBRARY ASSOCIATION OF PORTLAND, Art & Music Dept, 801 S W Tenth Ave, Portland, 97205. Barbara K Padden, Librn
Holdings: Vols Cat Pix Slides Phonorecords
Notes: Art book titles: 21,325; music book titles (incl dance books): 10,800; sheet music titles: 19,550; slides on art subjects: about 12,000; phonorecord albums: 27,000; picture clippings: about 2 million; color reproductions of old and modern masters: about 640.

PA —ALLIANCE COLLEGE, Washington Hall Library, Fullerton Ave, Cambridge Springs, 16403. Stanley J Kozaczka, Head Librn
Holdings: Vols (66,926) Cat Phonorecords Audiotapes 16mm Films Microforms
Budget: ($15,000)
Notes: Collection supports curriculum.

PA —EMMAUS PUBLIC LIBRARY, Ridge and Main Sts, Emmaus, 18049. Elaine B Timbers, Librn
Holdings: Cat

PA —FREE LIBRARY OF SPRINGFIELD TOWNSHIP, 1600 Paper Mill Rd, Philadelphia, 19118. Margaret Baroski, Librn
Holdings: Vols (50,000) Cat Pix Slides Audiotapes Microforms
Budget: ($165,753)
Notes: File of pictures, pamphlets, clippings, etc has separate index.

PA —LLOYD P JONES GALLERY, Gimbal Gym, Walnut & 37th St, Philadelphia, 19104.
Notes: Incl 83 works of art by R Tait McKenzie.

PA —PHILADELPHIA COLLEGE OF ART, Library, Broad & Spruce Sts, Philadelphia, 19102. Hazel Gustow, Dir
Holdings: Vols 25,000 Cat Periodicals Pix Slides Microforms VF
Budget: ($13,000)
Notes: Printed materials on the arts (history, techniques, aesthetics, etc.). Current buying incl most significant books coming into print or being reprinted, mainly in English. Incl about 22,000 titles, periodicals, 30 cabinets vertical file materials, etc.

PA —TEMPLE UNIVERSITY, Tyler School of Art, Beech & Penrose Aves, Philadelphia, 19126. Mary Ivy Bayard, Librn
Holdings: Vols 24,267 Cat Pix Microforms
Budget:
Notes: The art school branch of the main university library; supports a graduate program in the fine arts, incl some graduate courses in art history.

PA —UNIVERSITY OF PENNSYLVANIA, University Museum Library, 33 & Spruce Sts, Philadelphia, 19104. Jean S Adelman, Librn
Holdings: Vols (80,000) Cat
Notes: Emphasis on antiquitites of all areas.

PA —CARNEGIE LIBRARY OF PITTSBURGH, Music and Art Dept, 4400 Forbes Ave, Pittsburgh, 15213. Ida Reed, Dept Head
Holdings: Vols 47,000 Cat Pix Slides
Notes: Incl 300,000 pictures, 100,000 slides.

PA —UNIVERSITY OF PITTSBURGH, Henry Clay Frick Fine Arts Library, Pittsburgh, 15260. Anne W Gordon, Fine Arts Librn
Holdings: Vols (55,000) Cat Pix Slides Microforms
Notes: Emphasis in on the art of the Western World--architecture, sculpture, painting, minor arts, archaeology, with special strength in the Byzantine, early Christian, medieval, renaissance and modern periods. The Oriental field is represented, incl replicas of scrolls. Studio arts are also covered. Illuminated ms facsimiles. Extensive collections of slides and photographs for study of art history are avaiable in the building but not administered by the art library.

PA —READING PUBLIC MUSEUM & ART GALLERY, Museum Library, 19611 Museum Rd, Reading, 19611. Bruce Dietrich, Dir
Holdings: Vols 20,000 Cat
Notes: Also, some 400 art catalogs. Noncirculating. Open to public by appointment only.

PA —EASTERN COLLEGE, Frank Warner Memorial Library, Saint Davids, 19087. James L Sauer, Librn
Holdings: Uncat Mss Pix
Notes: The Harry C Goebel Collection. Incl Bruce Rogers printings (over 460); press books (about 350); oriental art (over 250); bookplates (with a separate collection of an almost complete set of bookplates designed by Edwin Davis French); Christmas Books; art and graphic arts (incl the French Graphic Arts Collection of Adolph DeMilly); first editions of Christopher Morley; Print Collection (1315 prints); Oriental art realia and artifacts.

ART (cont.)

PA —PENNSYLVANIA STATE UNIVERSITY, Arts Library, 405 E Pattee Library, University Park, 18602. Jean Smith, Arts and Architecture Librn
Holdings: Vols (46,600) Cat
Notes: Book and periodical collections support program in studio arts at undergraduate and masters levels.
See also entry under Art - History

RI —RHODE ISLAND SCHOOL OF DESIGN, Library, Two College St, Providence, 02903. James A Findlay, Dir
Holdings: Vols (70,000) Cat Pix Slides Phonorecords
Budget: ($50,000)
Notes: Incl 30,000 pictures, 92,000 slides, 1100 posters and color reproductions and 280,000 clippings.

SC —CLEMSON UNIVERSITY, Emery A Gunnin Architectural Library, Lee Hall, Clemson, 29631. Leslie Abrams, Librn
Holdings: Vols (14,778) Cat Slides
Notes: Incl 2000 South Carolina planning documents. 56,000 slides.

TN —STUDENTS' MUSEUM, Library, 516 Beaman St, Chihowee Park, Knoxville, 37914. Sylvia Gloeckner, Librn
Holdings: Vols 1200 Cat Mss Maps Pix Slides Phonorecords Audiotapes Videotapes
Notes: The materials are all related to objects, exhibitions, and programs of the Students' Museum. Incl 200 ms pieces, 100 maps, 1500 pictures, 5000 slides, etc.

TN —MEMPHIS ACADEMY OF ART, G Pillow Lewis Memorial Library, Overton Park, Memphis, 38112. Robert M Scarlett Jr, Librn; Bette R Callow, Slides Cur
Holdings: Vols 18,000 Cat Slides
Budget: $12,000
Notes: Incl 40,000 slides.

TN —THE BOTANICAL GARDENS AND FINE ARTS CENTER, Fine Arts Library, Forrest Park Drive, Nashville, 37205. Muriel H Connell, Librn
Holdings: Vols (3500) Cat Pix Slides
Budget: $2500

TX —UNIVERSITY OF TEXAS LIBRARIES, Fine Arts Library, PO Box P, Austin, 78712. Carole L Cable, Fine Arts Librn
Holdings: Vols (55,000) Cat Pix

TX —DALLAS PUBLIC LIBRARY, Fine Arts Div, 1515 Young St, Dallas, 75201. Richard L Waters, Acting Dir; Jane Holahan, Manager
Notes: Papers of John Rosenfield, eminent Dallas critic for 41 years.

TX —SOUTHERN METHODIST UNIVERSITY, DeGolyer Library, Box 396, SMU, Dallas, 75275. Clifton H Jones, Dir
Holdings: Vols (80,000) Cat Mss Maps Pix Slides Microforms
Notes: First editions of prominent authors; also of books in subject emphasis collection. All subjects listed in this vol are strong. Numerous collections of personal papers relating to subjects also.

TX —UNIVERSITY OF TEXAS, EL PASO, Library, Special Collections Dept, El Paso, 79968. Cesar Caballero, Dept Head
Holdings: Vols 6225 Cat
Budget: ($5000)
Notes: Art Books Collection. The collection was established to house rare and expensive editions.

TX —AMON CARTER MUSEUM, Library, 3510 Camp Bowie Blvd, PO Box 2365, Fort Worth, 76113. Nancy G Wynne, Librn
Holdings: Vols (25,000) Cat Mss Pix
Notes: The book collection, microfilm and photo archives have been built toward the goal of the interpretation of American history through art. At present, the greatest strengths are in Americana, Western Canadiana, bibliography, American exhibition catalogs and history of photography. Substantial books and files on American artists of the 19th and early 20th century, and particularly of Charles M Russell and Frederic Remington. Incl 25,000 pictures; 13,000 slides.
See also entries under Newspapers, American; Pictures - Collections.

UT —BRIGHAM YOUNG UNIVERSITY ART MUSEUM, Provo, 84602. J Cliff Allen, Dir
Notes: Contemporary American lithographs; J Alden Weir collection of paintings, prints, and drawings; 19th and 20th century American paintings, drawings and sculpture.

VT —JOHNSON STATE COLLEGE, John Dewey Library, Johnson, 05656. Paul Gallager, Library Dir
Holdings: Vols 4000 Cat Pix Slides
Notes: General art collection. Incl 3500 slides.

VA —VIRGINIA POLYTECHNIC INSTITUTE & STATE UNIVERSITY, Architecture Library, Blacksburg, 24061. Robert E Stephenson, Architecture Librn
Holdings: Vols (46,000) Cat Microforms VF
Budget: ($57,700)
Notes: Incl over 2000 planning reports.

VA —MARY WASHINGTON COLLEGE, E Lee Trinkle Library, Fredericksburg, 22401. Ruby Y Weinbrecht, Librn
Holdings: Vols 11,000 Cat
Budget: $10,000

VA —SWEET BRIAR COLLEGE, Library, Sweet Briar, 24595. John Jaffe, Librn
Holdings: Vols (5500) Cat Pix Slides
Budget: ($2000)

WA —SEATTLE PUBLIC LIBRARY, 1000 Fourth Ave, Seattle, 98104. Ronald A Dubberly, City Librn
Holdings: Vols 70,000 Cat Pix
Notes: Incl 28,000 photographs of Seattle and Pacific Northwest architecture architecture and views. Balance of picture collection about 650,000 items.

WA —UNIVERSITY OF WASHINGTON LIBRARIES, Art Library, 101 Art Bldg, DM-10, Seattle, 98195. Connie Okada, Librn
Holdings: Vols (33,595) Cat Pix
Budget: ($65,464)
Notes: Includes 7,500 photographs.

WV —HUNTINGTON ART GALLERIES, Library, Art Reference Library, Park Hills, Huntington, 25701. Mary McKernon, Librn
Holdings: Vols (3500) Cat Pix Slides
Notes: Large collection of pamphlets on glass and glass memorabilia. Includes literature on venetian, pressed, patterned, carnival, victorian, and depression glasses.

WI —UNIVERSITY OF WISCONSIN, MADISON, Kohler Art Library, 800 University Ave, Madison, 53706. William C Bunce, Chief; Louise Hunning, Ref Librn
Holdings: Vols (83,000) Cat Microforms
Notes: Incl over 10,000 exhibition and auction catalogs.

WI —MILWAUKEE ART MUSEUM, Library, 750 N Lincoln Memorial Dr, Milwaukee, 53202. Betty Karow, Librn
Holdings: Vols (15,000) Cat
Notes: Also, small collection on 19th century German painting and on Meissen porcelain.

WI —MILWAUKEE PUBLIC LIBRARY, 814 W Wisconsin Ave, Milwaukee, 53233. Donald J Sager, City Librn
Holdings: Vols Cat Pix Slides
Notes: The collection incl all fields of art, with emphasis on architecture, incl: Frank Lloyd Wright and local city planning documents; interior decoration; art history; American art; Oriental art; art instruction; decorative arts; numismatics and philately; photography, incl local photo archives and instruction manuals; costume; art exhibition and auction ctalogs; and local newspaper clippings on art subjects. Also, circulating mounted and framed art prints and sculpture reproductions.

AB —PETER WHYTE FOUNDATION, Gallery, Box 160, Banff, T0L 0C0, Can. Mary Andrews, Librn
Holdings: Vols (935)
Budget: ($800)
Notes: Small general colection with quite a bit on Canadian and American art, much of it donations from private collections.

AB —SOUTHERN ALBERTA INSTITUTE OF TECHNOLOGY, Learning Resources Centre, 1301 16 Ave NW, Calgary, T2M 0L4, Can. Tom Skinner, Historian
Holdings: Vols (5000) Cat Pix Slides Flims Audiotapes Filmstrips Videotapes
Notes: Serves Alberta College or Art (4-year professional course).

BC —VANCOUVER ART GALLERY, Library, 750 Hornby St, Vancouver, V6Z 2H7, Can. Catherine M Cowan, Librn
Holdings: Cat Microforms
Budget: $12,000
Notes: Canadian, American and British art. Contemporary Canadian emphasis, reference library only. Incl 7000 monographs, 15,000 exhibition catalogs, 1300 permanent collection catalogs, 3500 biographical files and 121 periodical subscriptions.

BC —VANCOUVER PUBLIC LIBRARY, Art Div, 750 Burrard St, Vancouver, V6Z 1X5, Can.
Holdings: Cat Pix
Notes: Book and pamphlet collection. Also, (1) Newspaper Clippings File: 31 drawers of relevant clippings from major newspapers, incl the *Sun, Province, Toronto Globe and Mail, Christian Science Monitor, New York* Times, etc on arts, music, architecture; incl biographical material (16 drawers). (2) Picture File about 500,000 pictures in 150 cabinet drawers, strong in architecture, costume, interior decoration, painting, sculpture, also portraits. (3) Exhibition Catalogs File: British Columbia and elsewhere. (4) Association and Organization File: organizations in the Lower Mainland in arts, music, city planning, etc, begun in 1940s; (5) Canadian Artists Index: begun in 1964, alphabetically by artist, with about 300,000 citations to reproductions of work and biographical material on Canadian artist from the division's books and other sources; (6) Miscellaneous Index: material not covered in other special or published indexes, primarily of Canadian and local cultural events, hard-to-find informations, etc. Local newspapers, special Canadian publications and British film journals are the most regularly indexed items. (7) Song Index started in the 1930s. (8) Title Index to song collections and sheet music in the VPL collection, approx 100,000 entries.

MB —UNIVERSITY OF MANITOBA, Architecture & Fine Arts Library, Winnipeg, R3T 2N2, Can. Peter Anthony, Head
Holdings: Vols (50,000) Exhibition Cat Pix
Notes: Incl over 775 pictures; 5 drawers of VF materials. Nearly 375 periodical titles.

ON —NATIONAL GALLERY OF CANADA, Library, National Museums of Canada, Ottawa, K1A 0M8, Can. J Hunter, Chief Librn

ON —METROPOLITAN TORONTO LIBRARY, Fine Arts Dept, 789 Yonge St, Toronto, M4W 2G8, Can. Alan Suddon, Head
Holdings: Vols(42,000) Cat Pix Microforms
Notes: Extensive collection.

ON —ROYAL ONTARIO MUSEUM, Main Library and Archives, 100 Queen's Park, Toronto, M5S 2C6, Can. Julia Matthews, Head Librn
Holdings: Vols (85,000) Cat
Notes: Since January 1977, acquisitions have been entered in UTLAS.

PQ —MCGILL UNIVERSITY, Blacker-Wood Library of Zoology & Ornithology, 3459 McTavish St, Montreal, H3A 1Y1, Can. Eleanor MacLean, Librn
Notes: Special features of collection incl: Robert Gurney Collection of reprints on Crustaceana; 3000 folders of letters from naturalists; over 9000 original paintings of wildlife; a small collection of falconry equipment; the archives of the Montreal Natural History Society; the archives of the North American Falconry Association; 156 17th-century feather pictures of birds and people. Does not incl entomology collection.

ART—ANALYSIS, INTERPRETATION, APPRECIATION see Aesthetics; Painting

ART—CATALOGS

AL —MONTGOMERY MUSEUM OF FINE ARTS, Library, 440 S McDonough St, Montgomery, 36104. Suzanne W Black, Librn
Holdings: Vols (1800) Cat
Notes: Exchange catalogs with 200 museums.

ART—CATALOGS (cont.)

CA —CRAFT AND FOLK ART MUSEUM, Library, 5814 Wilshire Blvd, Los Angeles, 90036. Joan M Benedetti, Museum Librn
Holdings: Vols (2000) Slides VF
Notes: Incl 2000 books; 70 journal subscriptions; artists' biographical files: 6 file drawers; clipping files: 8 file drawers; 20,000 slides. Representation of the material culture of all people, traditional and contemporary expressions. Incl visual and printed information on ethnic, traditional, popular, decorative, idiosyncratic, and contemporary crafts as well as vernacular architecture, handmade houses, and design. Information about and for professional artists on health hazards, conservation, and career management. Anthropological and art historical works; exhibition catalogues; slides, photographs, audiocassettes; clipping and pamphlet files. Contemporary Slide Registry of Craftspeople and extensive biographical files of contemporary craft artists. Information and referral files of craft related galleries, shops, festivals, organizations, etc.

CA —SAN DIEGO MUSEUM OF ART, Reference Library, PO Box 2107, Balboa Park, San Diego, 92112. Nancy J Andrews, Librn
Holdings: Vols 9000 Cat Slides
Notes: Incl 30,000 exhibition catalogs. Now cataloging bibliographies from all exhibition, sales and commercial gallery catalogs (15, 000). Library is noted for its collection of material on contemporary artists. Have 24 vertical files containing various material on individual artists. Have a catalog for slide collection, as well as a catalog of exhibition and sales catalogs. Incl 18,600 slides.

CA —SAN FRANCISCO ART INSTITUTE, Anne Bremer Memorial Library, 800 Chestnut St, San Francisco, 94133. Jeff Gunderson, Librn
Holdings: Vols (23,114) Cat Pix Slides Audiotapes 16mm Films Microforms
Budget: ($15,000)

CA —UNIVERSITY OF CALIFORNIA, SANTA BARBARA, Arts Library, Santa Barbara, 93106. William Treese, Art Librn
Notes: Incl 35,000 auction catalogs and 50, 000 exhibition catalogs. The UCSB Arts Library Art Exhibition Catalog (AEC) Collection. Incl catalogs in all areas of art, primarily US and European. Have computer-based indexing system. The Library "has... received national recognition as a leading collector and organizer of art exhibition catalogs." Is the University of California Archives for Auction Catalogs.

CA —CALIFORNIA INSTITUTE OF THE ARTS, Library, 24700 McBean Pkwy, Valencia, 91355. James Elrod, Dir
Holdings: Vols 7590 Cat
Budget: ($4000)
Notes: Modern art, incl abstract, conceptual, concrete, environment, minimal, and pop art; dadaism; surrealism; happenings; and caricatures and cartoons.

CO —COLORADO SPRINGS FINE ARTS CENTER LIBRARY, 30 W Dale St, Colorado Springs, 80903. Roderick Dew, Librn
Holdings: Vols (20,000) Cat
Budget: ($4000)
Notes: Specialize in fine arts and anthropology of the Southwest. Incl auction and exhibition catalogs.

CT —LYMAN ALLYN MUSEUM, Library, 100 Mohegan Ave, New London, 06320. Mrs D Dinsmore, Librn
Holdings: Vols (5550) Cat Maps Pix
Budget: $2000
Notes: Books on old Master Drawings and the Decorative Arts. Noncirculating library with emphasis on scholarly historical works and museum and exhibition catalogs. Also incl American museum bulletins (uncataloged).

FL —RINGLING MUSEUM OF ART, Art Research Library, PO Box 1838, Sarasota, 33578. Lynell A Morr, Librn
Holdings: Vols (40,000) Cat
Budget: ($24,000)
Notes: Incl an additional 30,000 art auction catalogs, indexed 1970-date.

IL —NORTHWESTERN UNIVERSITY, Library, Special Collections Dept, 1937 Sheridan Rd, Evanston, 60201. R Russell Maylone, Cur
Holdings: Vols 5300 //
Notes: Exhibition catalogs and ephemera arranged by artist, period, group or collection. Additional material cataloged for general collection.

IN —INDIANAPOLIS MUSEUM OF ART, Stout Reference Library, 1200 W 38 St, Indianapolis, 46208. Martha Blocker, Head Librn
Holdings: Vols (22,000) Cat
Notes: Incl 12,000 uncataloged art exhibition and sale catalogs, microforms, newspaper clippings, and slides (in separate Slide Library; Carolyn Metz, Cur).

LA —R W NORTON ART GALLERY, Library, 4747 Creswell Ave, Shreveport, 71106. Jerry M Bloomer, Librn
Holdings: Vols 3000 Cat
Notes: Extensive Art Reference section incl books and periodicals, monographs on artists, historical surveys of art from early times to the present, museum catalogs, exhibition catalogs. Large collection of art auction catalogs (mostly not yet cataloged).

MA —MUSEUM OF FINE ARTS, William Morris Hunt Memorial Library, Huntington Ave, Boston, 02115. Nancy S Allen, Librn
Holdings: Vols (100,000) Cat
Budget: ($70,000)
Notes: Strong collection of art auction catalogs, exhibition catalogs, and Asian language books on art history. Collection has about 100,000 pamphlet pieces also.

MA —HARVARD UNIVERSITY, Harvard College Library, Fine Arts Library, Fogg Museum, 32 Quincy St, Cambridge, 02138. Wolfgang M Freitag, Librn
Holdings: Vols (202,000) Cat Mss Pix Slides Microforms
Budget: ($176,500)
Notes: Catalog, in 15 volumes, published 1971, with supplementary volume listing auction catalogs. First supplement, 3 volumes, 1976. Incl 700,000 pictures; 220, 000 slides.

MA —STERLING AND FRANCINE CLARK ART INSTITUTE LIBRARY, 225 South St, PO Box 8, Williamstown, 01267. Michael Rinehart, Librn
Holdings: Vols (77,000) Cat Pix Slides Microforms
Budget: ($105,000)
Notes: Primarily European art, 1300-present, and post-Columbian American art. Incl 850, 000 pictures, 80,000 slides, 400 microfilm reels, 25,000 auction sale catalogs, and Mary Ann Beinecke Decorative Art Collection.

MA —WORCESTER ART MUSEUM, Library, 55 Salisbury St, Worcester, 01609. Kathy Berg, Librn
Holdings: Vols (35,000) Cat Slides
Budget: ($16,000)

MN —WALKER ART CENTER, Staff Reference Library, Vineland Place, Minneapolis, 55403. Rosemary Furtak, Librn
Holdings: Vols 5000 Cat
Notes: Incl 10,000 catalogs of individual artists; museum gallery catalogs-10,000 catalogs of major exhibitions from all over the world dating back to 1940. VF material and tapes.

MO —UNIVERSITY OF MISSOURI-COLUMBIA, Museum of Art & Archaeology, Library, One Pickard Hall, Columbia, 65201. Ruth E Witt, Asst Dir
Holdings: Vols (4000)
Notes: Sales and exhibition catalogs, reports, bulletins, etc.

MO —SAINT LOUIS ART MUSEUM, Richardson Memorial Library, Saint Louis, 63110. Ann B Abid, Librn
Holdings: Vols (30,000) Cat Pix Slides Microforms
Notes: Art history, incl decorative arts, catalogs, exhibitions, etc.

MO —UNIVERSITY OF MISSOURI-SAINT LOUIS, Thomas Jefferson Library, 8001 Natural Bridge Rd, Saint Louis, 63121.
Holdings: Uncat
Notes: Collection in boxes, currently inaccessible.

NE —JOSLYN ART REFERENCE LIBRARY, Joslyn Art Museum, 2200 Dodge St, Omaha, 68102. Ann Birney, Librn; Marie Sedlacek, Cataloger-Slide Librn
Holdings: Vols (17,000) Cat Slides
Notes: Incl catalogs of exhibitions and western US materials, especially early Omaha and Nebraska. Large collections of vertical files on subjects and artists; also mounted prints, reproductions, slides. filmstrips.

NY —ALBRIGHT-KNOX ART GALLERY, Art Reference Library, 1285 Elmwood Ave, Buffalo, 14222. Annette Masling, Librn
Holdings: Vols (20,000) Cat
Notes: Special strength in American 19th and 20th century art. Excellent collection of exhibition catalogs for contemporary art.

NY —METROPOLITAN MUSEUM OF ART, Thomas J Watson Library, Fifth Ave & 82 St, New York, 10028. William B Walker, Chief Librn
Holdings: Vols (250,000) Cat Mss Microforms
Notes: All fields of art: 1400 periodicals, incl bulletins and annual reports, catalogs, etc of American and foreign art societies, museums, etc; incl sales catalogs, exhibition catalogs, clipping file on individual artists and subjects, autograph letters. See *Library Catalog of the Metropolitan Museum of Art, New York,* second ed, rev and enl (Boston, G K Hall, 1980, 48 v and first supplement, 1982). Since 1980, holdings have been cataloged in RLIN.

NY —MUSEUM OF MODERN ART, Library, 11 W 53 St, New York, 10019. Clive Phillpot, Library Dir
Holdings: Vols 80,000 Cat Mss Microforms
Notes: Art of the 20th and latter half of the 19th century (painting, sculpture, drawings and prints, architecture, photography, film, design mixed media, artists' books). Special emphasis on Surrealist and Dada literature and art. Incl art exhibition catalogs. Photocopying restricted. See *Catalog of the Museum of Modern Art, New York City* (Boston: G K Hall, 1976), 14 vols.

NY —WHITNEY MUSEUM OF AMERICAN ART, Library, 945 Madison Ave, New York, 10021. May Castleberry, Librn
Holdings: 20,000 Uncat Pix
Notes: Vertical files on individual American artists; incl clippings, catalogs, exhibitions, letters, pictures, etc. Also, 1050 bound periodical titles.

OH —OHIO STATE UNIVERSITY, Fine Arts Library, 1813 N High St, Columbus, 43210. Susan Wyngaard, Head, Fine Arts Library
Holdings: Vols (75,000) Cat Microforms
Budget: ($60,000)
Notes: Also have 1000 uncataloged exhibition catalogs. Book collection strong in history of art especially in area of medieval & Northern Renaissance art. Good collection of portfolios. Photographic collections on microfiche. Receive Slavic titles, many on Byzantine frescoes. Online catalog. Decimal Index of the Art of the Low Countries, as well as Marburger Index; Index Photographique de i' Arten France; Alinari Archives on microfiche and other major microform collections in art.

OH —OBERLIN COLLEGE LIBRARY, Clarence Ward Art Library, Allen Art Bldg, Oberlin, 44074. Jeffrey Weidman, Librn
Holdings: Vols (62,000) Cat Microforms
Notes: Incl approx 18,000 uncataloged exhibition catalogues and major sales catalogues. Significant holdings in early serials (see *ARLO Union List of Serials).*

PA —PENNSYLVANIA ACADEMY OF THE FINE ARTS, ARCHIVES, Broad & Cherry Sts, Philadelphia, 19102. Marietta Bushnell, Librn
Holdings: Mss Pix
Notes: Incl material relating to the history of the school and museum, exhibition catalogs and records, limited biographical information about former students, faculty, and exhibitors. Open to serious scholars by appointment only.

PA —READING PUBLIC MUSEUM & ART GALLERY, Museum Library, 19611 Museum Rd, Reading, 19611. Bruce Dietrich, Dir
Holdings: Vols 20,000 Cat
Notes: Also, some 400 art catalogs.

ART—CATALOGS (cont.)

Noncirculating. Open to public by appointment only.

TN —HUNTER MUSEUM OF ART, Library, 10 Bluff View, Chattanooga, 37403. Diana Svarez, Cur of Education
Holdings: Vols (1300)
Notes: American art, and Architecture, Photography and World Art. It is a new and growing collection, especially strong in art catalogs of sales and exhibitions. Incl 38 subscriptions.

TX —FORT WORTH ART MUSEUM, Library, 1309 Montgomery St, Fort Worth, 76107. David Ryan, Dir
Holdings: Vols (3500) Cat Pix Slides Audiotapes Videotapes 16mm Films
Budget: ($5000)
Notes: 20th Century art of all countries and in all media to correspond with the scope of the museum. Extensive collection of exhibition catalogs.

WI —UNIVERSITY OF WISCONSIN, LA CROSSE, Murphy Library, 1631 Pine St, La Crosse, 54601. Edwin L Hill, Special Collections Librn
Holdings: Vols 200 Cat Pix
Notes: Art exhibition catalogs. Emphasis on major contemporary exhibitions.

WI —MILWAUKEE PUBLIC LIBRARY, 814 W Wisconsin Ave, Milwaukee, 53233. Donald J Sager, City Librn
Notes: The collection incl all fields of art, with emphasis on architecture, incl: Frank Lloyd Wright and local city planning documents; interior decoration; art history; American art; Oriental art; art instruction; decorative arts; numismatics and philately; photography, incl local photo archives and instruction manuals; costume; art exhibition and auction ctalogs; and local newspaper clippings on art subjects. Also, circulating mounted and framed art prints and sculpture reproductions.
See also entry under Art - Exhibitions

BC —VANCOUVER ART GALLERY, Library, 750 Hornby St, Vancouver, V6Z 2H7, Can. Catherine M Cowan, Librn
Holdings: Cat Pix Slides Microforms
Budget: $7700
Notes: Also 15,000 exhibition catalogs.

ON —NATIONAL GALLERY OF CANADA, Library, National Museums of Canada, Ottawa, K1A 0M8, Can. J Hunter, Chief Librn

ON —UNIVERSITY OF TORONTO, Art History Reference Library, Dept of Fine Art, 100 Saint George St, Toronto, M5S 1A1, Can. Andrea Retfalvi, Research Librn
Holdings: Vols (20,000) Cat Pix
Notes: The collection specializes in art history catalogs of various types: temporary exhibition catalogs, from the major institutions in Europe and North America; permanent collection catalogs, again for all the major institutions; dealer catalogs; and auction catalogs. The collection of auction catalogs is primarily French, covering 1870-1970, with particular strength from ca 1900 on. There is a catalog for all these types of catalogs. 90,000 photographs.

ART—CONSERVATION AND RESTORATION see Art Objects—Conservation and Restoration

ART—EXHIBITIONS

CA —SAN DIEGO MUSEUM OF ART, Reference Library, PO Box 2107, Balboa Park, San Diego, 92112. Nancy J Andrews, Librn
Holdings: Vols 9000 Cat Slides
Notes: Incl 30,000 exhibition catalogs. Now cataloging bibliographies from all exhibition, sales and commercial gallery catalogs (15, 000). Library is noted for its collection of material on contemporary artists. Have 24 vertical files containing various material on individual artists. Have a catalog for slide collection, as well as a catalog of exhibition and sales catalogs. Incl 18,600 slides.

CA —SAN FRANCISCO ART INSTITUTE, Anne Bremer Memorial Library, 800 Chestnut St, San Francisco, 94133. Jeff Gunderson, Librn
Holdings: Vols (23,144) Cat Pix Slides Audiotapes 16mm Films Microforms
Budget: ($15,000)

CA —UNIVERSITY OF CALIFORNIA, SANTA BARBARA, Arts Library, Santa Barbara, 93106. William Treese, Art Librn
Notes: Incl 35,000 auction catalogs and 50, 000 exhibition catalogs. The UCSB Arts Library Art Exhibition Catalog (AEC) Collection. Incl catalogs in all areas of art, primarily US and European. Have computer-based indexing system. The Library "has... received national recognition as a leading collector and organizer of art exhibition catalogs." Is the University of California Archives for Auction Catalogs.

CA —CALIFORNIA INSTITUTE OF THE ARTS, Library, 24700 McBean Pkwy, Valencia, 91355. James Elrod, Dir
Holdings: Vols (7950) Cat
Budget: ($4000)
Notes: Modern art, incl abstract, conceptual, concrete, environment, minimal, and pop art; dadaism; surrealism; happenings; and caricatures and cartoons.

CO —UNIVERSITY OF COLORADO, Libraries, Art & Architecture Library, Campus Box 184, Boulder, 80309. Liesel Nolan, Librn/Dept Head
Holdings: Vols (57,647) Cat Pix
Budget: ($39,000)
Notes: Special feature: art exhibition catalog collection 1963-1971, 1972-date. Good general collection with some special emphasis on environmental design, Islamic architecture, Indian art and South American Indian art. Fair collection of periodical backfiles in art and in architecture. Separate catalog for materials in collection. Rare books in main library, listed only in central union catalog.

CO —COLORADO SPRINGS FINE ARTS CENTER LIBRARY, 30 W Dale St, Colorado Springs, 80903. Roderick Dew, Librn
Holdings: Vols (20,000) Cat
Budget: ($4000)
Notes: Specialize in fine arts and anthropology of the Southwest. Incl auction and exhibition catalogs.

DC —NATIONAL GALLERY OF ART, Library, Sixth & Constitution Ave NW, Washington, 20565. J M Edelstein, Chief Librn
Holdings: Cat Mss Pix Slides Microforms
Notes: Incl art sale and exhibition catalogs, catalogs of private art collections, and photographic archives of western European and US art (798,229 photographs).

FL —RINGLING MUSEUM OF ART, Art Research Library, PO Box 1838, Sarasota, 33578. Lynell A Morr, Librn
Holdings: Vols (40,000) Cat
Budget: ($24,000)
Notes: Incl an additional 30,000 art auction catalogs, indexed 1970-date.

GA —ATLANTA COLLEGE OF ART LIBRARY, 1280 Peachtree St N E, Atlanta, 30309. Jean Haskell, Librn
Holdings: Vols (16,000) Cat Pix Slides Phonorecords Videotapes Microforms
Notes: Visual arts, with 20th-century emphasis. There is a catalog to the books and the exhibition catalogs.The library is the only collection devoted totally to the visual arts in the Atlanta area. Rare book collection and extensive artists' books collection.

IL —UNIVERSITY OF ILLINOIS, URBANA/CHAMPAIGN, Library, Ricker Library of Architecture & Art, 208 Architecture Bldg, 608 East Lorado Taft Dr, Champaign, 61820. Dee Wallace, Architecture & Art Librn
Holdings: Vols Cat Pix
Notes: Incl 32,901 mounted photos and reproductions. Cataloged. Also incl noncirculating collection of exhibition catalogs.

IL —ART INSTITUTE OF CHICAGO, Ryerson & Burnham Libraries, Michigan Ave & Adams St, Chicago, 60603. Daphne C Roloff, Dir
Holdings: Vols (136,000) Cat Mss Slides Microforms
Budget: ($167,000)
Notes: Total collection incl 300,000 slides.

IN —INDIANAPOLIS MUSEUM OF ART, Stout Reference Library, 1200 W 38 St, Indianapolis, 46208. Martha Blocker, Head Librn
Holdings: Vols (22,000) Cat
Notes: Incl 12,000 uncataloged art exhibition and sale catalogs, microforms, newspaper clippings, and slides (in separate Slide Library; Carolyn Metz, Cur).

LA —R W NORTON ART GALLERY, Library, 4747 Creswell Ave, Shreveport, 71106. Jerry M Bloomer, Librn
Holdings: Vols 3000 Cat
Notes: Extensive Art Reference section incl books and periodicals, monographs on artists, historical surveys of art from early times to the present, museum catalogs, exhibition catalogs. Large collection of art auction catalogs (mostly not yet cataloged).

MA —MUSEUM OF FINE ARTS, William Morris Hunt Memorial Library, Huntington Ave, Boston, 02115. Nancy S Allen, Librn
Holdings: Vols (100,000) Cat
Budget: ($70,000)
Notes: Strong collection of art auction catalogs, exhibition catalogs, and Asian language books on art history. Collection has about 100,000 pamphlet pieces also.

MA —WORCESTER ART MUSEUM, Library, 55 Salisbury St, Worcester, 01609. Kathy Berg, Librn
Holdings: Vols (35,000) Cat Slides
Budget: ($16,000)

MN —MINNEAPOLIS COLLEGE OF ART & DESIGN, Library, 200 E 25 St, Minneapolis, 55404. Richard Kronstedt, Head Librn
Notes: Incl art exhibition catalogs.

MN —WALKER ART CENTER, Staff Reference Library, Vineland Place, Minneapolis, 55403. Rosemary Furtak, Librn
Holdings: Vols 5000 Cat Pix
Notes: Incl 10,000 catalogs of individual artists; museum gallery catalogs-10,000 catalogs of major exhibitions from all over the world dating back to 1940. VF material and tapes.

MO —UNIVERSITY OF MISSOURI-COLUMBIA, Museum of Art & Archaeology, Library, One Pickard Hall, Columbia, 65201. Ruth E Witt, Asst Dir
Holdings: Vols (4000)
Notes: Sales and exhibition catalogs, reports, bulletins, etc.

MO —SAINT LOUIS ART MUSEUM, Richardson Memorial Library, Saint Louis, 63110. Ann B Abid, Librn
Holdings: Vols (30,000) Cat Pix Slides Microforms
Notes: Art history, incl decorative arts, catalogs, exhibitions, etc.

NY —STATE UNIVERSITY OF NEW YORK, COLLEGE AT BUFFALO, Lockwood Memorial Library, Art Dept, Buffalo, 14260. Florence S DaLuiso, Cur
Holdings: Vols (38,000) Cat Microforms
Budget: ($24,735)
Notes: Collection supports curriculum of the School of acquisitions emphasize contemporary art and environmental design. The library by reciprocal agreement contains card catalog holdings of the Albright-Knox Art Gallery, Buffalo, New York. Books may be obtained on interlibrary loan.

NY —AMERICAN CRAFT COUNCIL, Library and Artists Registry, 44 W 53 St, New York, 10019. Joanne Polster, Librn
Holdings: Vols 3300 Cat Pix Slides Films
Notes: Crafts and craft-related subjects, incl portfolios for approx 2000 contemporary American craftspeople consisting of biographical material and photographs, indexed by media, geographic location, and a visual index. Over 1500 exhibition catalogs. The collection incl 35mm slide kits available for purchase. Catagories covered are: exhibitions of ACC's American Craft Museum from 1958 to date; kits in all media: fiber, metal, wood, clay, glass and multimedia; kits covering crafts processes. The Library also holds catalogs of craft school and art centers offering craft courses; newsletters, by-laws, and other materials of craft organizations and groups; the Archives and Photo-Archives of the American Craft Museum. No photocopying.

ART—EXHIBITIONS (cont.)

NY —METROPOLITAN MUSEUM OF ART, Thomas J Watson Library, Fifth Ave & 82 St, New York, 10028. William B Walker, Chief Librn
Holdings: Vols (250,000) Cat Mss Microforms
Notes: All fields of art: 1400 periodicals, incl bulletins and annual reports, catalogs, etc of American and foreign art societies, museums, etc; incl sales catalogs, exhibition catalogs, clipping file on individual artists and subjects, autograph letters. See *Library Catalog of the Metropolitan Museum of Art, New York,* second ed, rev and enl (Boston, G K Hall, 1980, 48 v and first supplement, 1982). Since 1980, holdings have been cataloged in RLIN.

NY —MUSEUM OF MODERN ART, Library, 11 W 53 St, New York, 10019. Clive Phillpot, Library Dir
Holdings: Vols (80,000) Cat Mss Audiotapes Microforms VF
Notes: See *Catalog of the Library of the Museum of Modern Art, New York City* (Boston: G K Hall, 1976), 14 vols. Collection incl exhibition catalogs.

NY —SOHO CENTER FOR VISUAL ARTS, 110-112 Prince St, New York, 10012. Ronda Wall, Librn
Notes: Incl collection of current exhibition catalogs of contemporary artists since 1964 (formerly at Aldrich Museum of Contemporary Art).

NY —WHITNEY MUSEUM OF AMERICAN ART, Library, 945 Madison Ave, New York, 10021. May Castleberry, Librn
Holdings: 20,000 Uncat Pix
Notes: Vertical files on individual American artists; incl clippings, catalogs, exhibitions, letters, pictures, etc. Also, 1050 bound periodical titles.

NY —STATE UNIVERSITY OF NEW YORK, COLLEGE AT PURCHASE, Library, Lincoln Ave, Purchase, 10577. Robert W Evans, Dir
Holdings: Uncat Mss Pix
Notes: Gift of the artist, George Rickey, and his wife, whose collection of constructivist art works has also been given to the Neuberger Museum at the College at Purchase. The collection consists largely of over 1000 announcements and catalogs of exhibitions of constructivist works and material about the artists.

OH —OHIO UNIVERSITY, Vernon R Alden Library, Fine Arts Library, Athens, 45701. Anne Braxton, Fine Arts Librn
Holdings: Vols (40,000) Cat Pix Slides Microforms
Notes: Strong collection in history of film and photography; general art collection incl some 2000 exhibition catalogs.

OH —CINCINNATI ART MUSEUM, Library, Eden Park, Cincinnati, 45202. Patrician P Rutledge, Librn
Holdings: Vols (45,850) Cat Mss Microforms
Notes: Art library containing all subjects on art-history, graphic arts, advertising art, etc; special strength in prints, ie engravings, etc. Near Eastern art and decorative arts are also strong. At least 90,000 art exhibition catalogs. Emphasis on artists of Cincinnati and vicinity in vertical file material.

OH —PUBLIC LIBRARY OF CINCINNATI & HAMILTON COUNTY, Art & Music Dept, 800 Vine St, Cincinnati, 45202. R Jayne Craven, Head
Holdings: Vols (122,185) Cat Pix
Budget: ($56,000)
Notes: Special collections: Eda Kuhn Loeb, "Artist and the Book, 1875-Date" (now shelved in Rare Book Room); music librettos (2345); exhibition catalogs (5474); large prints and posters (5051); Cincinnati artists vertical files; picture collection (673,906 clippings).

OH —OHIO STATE UNIVERSITY, Fine Arts Library, 1813 N High St, Columbus, 43210. Susan Wyngaard, Head, Fine Arts Library
Holdings: Vols (75,000) Cat Microforms
Budget: ($60,000)
Notes: Also have 1000 uncataloged exhibition catalogs. Book collection strong in history of art especially in area of medieval & Northern Renaissance art. Good collection of portfolios. Photographic collections on microfiche. Receive Slavic titles, many on Byzantine frescoes. Online catalog. Decimal Index of the Art of the Low Countries, as well as Marburger Index; Index Photographique de i' Arten France; Alinari Archives on microfiche and other major microform collections in art.

OH —OBERLIN COLLEGE LIBRARY, Clarence Ward Art Library, Allen Art Bldg, Oberlin, 44074. Jeffrey Weidman, Librn
Holdings: Vols (62,000) Cat Microforms
Notes: Incl approx 18,000 uncataloged exhibition catalogues and major sales catalogues. Significant holdings in early serials (see *ARLO Union List of Serials).*

TN —HUNTER MUSEUM OF ART, Library, 10 Bluff View, Chattanooga, 37403. Diana Svarez, Cur of Education
Holdings: Vols (1300)
Notes: American art, and Architecture, Photography and World Art. It is a new and growing collection, especially strong in art catalogs of sales and exhibitions. Incl 38 subscriptions.

TN —THE BOTANICAL GARDENS AND FINE ARTS CENTER, Fine Arts Library, Forrest Park Drive, Nashville, 37205. Muriel H Connell, Librn
Holdings: Vols (3500) Uncat Slides Filmstrips
Budget: ($150)

TX —UNIVERSITY OF TEXAS LIBRARIES, Fine Arts Library, PO Box P, Austin, 78712. Carole L Cable, Fine Arts Librn
Holdings: Vols (55,000) Cat Pix
Notes: Emphasis is on historical as well as practical aspects.

TX —AMON CARTER MUSEUM, Library, 3510 Camp Bowie Blvd, PO Box 2365, Fort Worth, 76113. Nancy G Wynne, Librn
Holdings: Vols (25,000) Cat Mss Pix
Notes: The book collection, microfilm and photo archives have been built toward the goal of the interpretation of American history through art. At present, the greatest strengths are in Americana, Western Canadiana, bibliography, American exhibition catalogs and history of photography. Substantial books and files on American artists of the 19th and early 20th century, and particularly of Charles M Russell and Frederic Remington. Incl 25,000 pictures; 13,000 slides.
See also entries under Newspapers, American; Pictures - Collections.

TX —RICE UNIVERSITY, Art Library, 6100 S Main St, PO Box 1892, Houston, 77001. Jet Marie Prendeville, Librn
Holdings: Vols (41,335) Cat
Budget: ($28,100)
Notes: The Art Library collection covers all periods of Western Art with particular emphasis upon Classical Archaelogy, Medieval, Renaissance, and Modern Art and Architecture. The collection also offers representative coverage of film, photography, and Oriental art.

WI —MILWAUKEE ART MUSEUM, Library, 750 N Lincoln Memorial Dr, Milwaukee, 53202. Betty Karow, Librn
Holdings: Vols (15,000) Cat
Notes: Also, small collection on 19th century German painting and on Meissen porcelain.

WI —MILWAUKEE PUBLIC LIBRARY, 814 W Wisconsin Ave, Milwaukee, 53233. Donald J Sager, City Librn
Holdings: Vols Cat Pix Slides
Notes: A comprehensive collection of auction catalogs, incl price lists, from major world auction houses, as well as a selective collection of international exhibition catalogs, and a comprehensive collection of Milwaukee Art Center, Chicago Art Institute, NY. Metropolitan Museum of Art and NY Museum of Modern Art catalogs.

BC —VANCOUVER ART GALLERY, Library, 750 Hornby St, Vancouver, V6Z 2H7, Can. Catherine M Cowan, Librn
Budget: ($12,000)
Notes: Canadian, American and British Art. Incl 15,000 exhibition catalogs, 3500 biographical files.

BC —VANCOUVER PUBLIC LIBRARY, Art Div, 750 Burrard St, Vancouver, V6Z 1X5, Can.
Holdings: Cat Pix
Notes: *Exhibition Catalogs File.*
See also entry under Art.

ON —NATIONAL GALLERY OF CANADA, Library, National Museums of Canada, Ottawa, K1A 0M8, Can. J Hunter, Chief Librn

ON —UNIVERSITY OF TORONTO, Thomas Fisher Rare Book Library, 120 Saint George St, Toronto, M5S 1A5, Can. Richard G Landon, Head
Notes: All currently published and most earlier major works on the fine and applied arts in Canada; Canadian art exhibition catalogues; limited editions illustrated by Canadian artists; 19th and 20th century architectural plans for buildings in Toronto and southern Ontario vicinity (ca 1700).

ON —UNIVERSITY OF TORONTO, Art History Reference Library, Dept of Fine Art, 100 Saint George St, Toronto, M5S 1A1, Can. Andrea Retfalvi, Research Librn
Holdings: Vols (20,000) Cat Pix
Notes: The collection specializes in art history catalogs of various types: temporary exhibition catalogs, from the major institutions in Europe and North America; permanent collection catalogs, again for all the major institutions; dealer catalogs; and auction catalogs. The collection of auction catalogs is primarily French, covering 1870-1970, with particular strength from ca 1900 on. There is a catalog for all these types of catalogs. 90,000 photographs.

PQ —MUSEE D'ART CONTEMPORAIN, Bibliotheque, Cite du Havre, Montreal, H3C 3R4, Can. Isabelle Montplaisir, Librn
Holdings: Vols (5780) Cat Pix Slides Audiotapes Videotapes Microforms
Budget: ($12,000)
Notes: 7050 exhibition catalogs on a basic exchange from art galleries, museums, etc of many countries. Also 2000 pictures; 32,000 slides; and 2500 files relating to artists, galleries, museums, etc. Also, the Archives Paul-Emile Borduas (painter) of 12,500 items, incl his writings, correspondence, exhibition catalogs, etc. Plus 150 periodical subscriptions.

ART—GALLERIES AND MUSEUMS

NY —COLUMBIA UNIVERSITY LIBRARIES, Rare Book & Manuscript Library, 801 Butler Library, 535 W 114 St, New York, 10027. Kenneth A Lohf, Librn
Holdings: Mss
Notes: The Calvin S Hathaway Collection on the protection and salvaging of artisic and historic documents and art objects during and after two world wars. 6500 items. Restricted use.

ON —CANADIAN MUSEUMS ASSOCIATION, Resource Centre, 280 Metcalfe Suite 202, Ottawa, K2P 0G5, Can. Denis Roussel, Library Tech
Holdings: Vols (700) Cat Mss Slides Audiotapes
Budget: ($4000)
Notes: Emphasis on museology and administration of art galleries, museum techniques, etc. An extensive bibliography has been published containing articles and books contained in the library. The bibliography is supplemented as new titles are acquired. It is arranged alphabetically under relevant subject headings.

ART—HISTORY

CA —CALIFORNIA STATE UNIVERSITY, LONG BEACH, University Library, Reference Center, 1250 Bellflower Blvd, Long Beach, 90840. Henry J DuBois, Librn
Holdings: Cat Slides
Notes: Collection of 60,000 slides offers examples of virtually all types and periods of art, incl an extensive collection of slides of mss from the Bodleian Library, Oxford, a special series on Latin American art, another on the arts of the US Collection is cataloged using Fogg Museum classification. No photocopying.

ART—HISTORY (cont.)

CA —LOS ANGELES COUNTY MUSEUM OF ART, Art Research Library, 5905 Wilshire Blvd, Los Angeles, 90036. Eleanor C Hartman, Museum Librn
Holdings: Vols 63,900 Cat
Budget: ($25,000)
Notes: Incl 26,000 art auction catalogs.

CA —UNIVERSITY OF CALIFORNIA, LOS ANGELES, Art Library, Elmer Belt Library of Vinciana, 405 Hilgard Ave, Los Angeles, 90024. Joyce Pellerano Ludmer, Art Librn
Holdings: Vols (10,000) Cat Pix Microforms VF
Notes: The Renaissance, with emphasis on Leonardo da Vinci.

CA —UNIVERSITY OF CALIFORNIA, LOS ANGELES, Art Library, Los Angeles, 90024. Max Marmor, Library Assistant
Holdings: Pix Microforms
Notes: Art; Art History; Early Christian and Byzantine Art; Medieval Art; Apostolic Age to 1400; Iconography; Photo Archive; Christian Art and Symbolism.

CA —J PAUL GETTY MUSEUM, Photo Archives, 17985 Pacific Coast Hwy, Malibu, 90265. William Reeder, Cur
Holdings: Pix
Notes: Incl photographs of works of art at the Museum (180,000 cataloged, 500,000 uncataloged), incl ancient art, western European art (painting, sculpture, graphics) and European decorative arts, medieval and Renaissance to 19th century, and antiquities.

CA —MILLS COLLEGE LIBRARY, Oakland, 94613. Steven P Pandolfo, Librn
Holdings: Vols 500 Cat Pix
Notes: Early printed books with emphasis on works important for their illustrations, representative of the history of the book, and landmark volumes in the history of art.

CA —SAN FRANCISCO ART INSTITUTE, Anne Bremer Memorial Library, 800 Chestnut St, San Francisco, 94133. Jeff Gunderson, Librn
Holdings: Vols (23,114) Cat Pix Slides Audiotapes 16mm Films Microforms
Budget: ($15,000)

CA —SAN FRANCISCO STATE UNIVERSITY, Frank V de Bellis Collection, 1630 Holloway Ave, San Francisco, 94132. Serena de Bellis, Cur
Holdings: Vols (5000) Cat Mss Maps Pix
Notes: Rare and current materials. Emphasis on history, and history of the fine arts. General descriptive pamphlet: *The Frank V de Bellis Collection* (San Francisco, 1967).

CA —COLLEGE OF SAN MATEO, Library, 1700 W Hillsdale Blvd, San Mateo, 94402. Gregg T Atkins, Coordinator of Library Services
Holdings: Vols 4500 Cat Slides

CA —STANFORD UNIVERSITY LIBRARIES, Art & Architecture Library, 102 Cummings Art Bldg, Stanford, 94305. Alexander D Ross, Art Librarian
Holdings: Vols (110,000) Cat
Notes: Incl materials of scholarly interest on the history of the visual arts: painting, sculpture, architecture, drawing, printmaking, etc, for all regions and periods.

CT —YALE UNIVERSITY, Box 1603A, Yale Station, New Haven, 06520.

CT —YALE UNIVERSITY, Art Library, 180 York St, New Haven, 06520. Nancy S Lambert, Art Librn
Holdings: Vols (80,000) Cat Slides
Notes: 100,000 photos and prints; 250,000 slides. There are, in addition to the subject library, about 75,000 books in the same fields in the University library. Slides and photographs are not loaned outside of the university. Books may be obtained on interlibrary loan. The Art Library is primarily for the use of the undergraduates and graduate students of the school of Art and Architecture. Incl environmental design and studio art. Emphasis on current publications and periodicals, and on research material. There is a vertical file of urban planning material and the collection contains some materials in this field, particularly as related to architecture.

CT —YALE UNIVERSITY, Beinecke Rare Book & Manuscripts Library, Wall & High St, New Haven, 06520. Louis A Martz, Dir
Notes: Incl the Altschul Collection: The Arts of the French Book, 1838-1967. See *Yale Library Gazette*, October 1969 for description and catalog.

CT —LYMAN ALLYN MUSEUM, Library, 100 Mohegan Ave, New London, 06320. Mrs D Dinsmore, Librn
Holdings: Vols (5550) Cat Maps Pix
Budget: $2000
Notes: Books on old Master Drawings and the Decorative Arts. Noncirculating library with emphasis on scholarly historical works and museum and exhibition catalogs. Also incl American museum bulletins (uncataloged).

CT —UNIVERSITY OF HARTFORD, Art School, Anne Bunce Cheney Library, 200 Bloomfield Ave, West Hartford, 06117. Jean J Miller, Art Librn
Holdings: Vols 12,800 Cat Pix
Budget: $5500
Notes: Slide collection in Art History Dept.

DE —DELAWARE ART MUSEUM, Library, 2301 Kentmere Pkwy, Wilmington, 19806. Anne Hoslam, Librn
Holdings: Vols (25,000) Cat Mss
Notes: The collection is rich in the following subjects: Howard Pyle and his pupils; John Sloan and the eight; history of the book and printing; and English and American illustrated books. There is also a section on contemporary photography. Archival material on Albert Mumford Lindsay, Jerome Myers, Everett Shinn, Gayle Porter Hoskins, Frank Schoonover.

DC —CATHOLIC UNIVERSITY OF AMERICA, Mullen Library, 620 Michigan Ave NE, Washington, 20064. B Gutekunst, Humanities Librn
Holdings: Vols (20,000) Cat

DC —HARVARD UNIVERSITY, Dumbarton Oaks, Research Library, 1703 32nd St NW, Washington, 20007. Irene Vaslef, Librn
Holdings: Vols (91,000) Cat Maps Pix Slides Microforms
Budget: ($219,000)
Notes: Byzantine civilization (including art, archaeology, literature, history, religion, law, music, etc). Extensive supplemental material on Classical, Hellenistic, Medieval, Islamic, Medieval Slavic cultures. 62,000 b/w photographs, 25,000 slides and transparencies, 1000 microfilms of books and manuscripts. Printed description of collection in *Harvard Library Bulletin,* vol 19, no 1 (Jan 1971), pp 25-35 and vol 19, no 2 (April 1971), pp 204-214, pp 25-35 and vol 19, no 2 (April 1971), pp 204-214.

DC —SMITHSONIAN INSTITUTION, Hirshhorn Museum & Sculpture Garden Library, Eighth & Independence Ave SW, Washington, 20560. Anna Brooke, Librn
Holdings: Vols (12,000) Cat Pix Slides Microforms Audiotapes 16mm Films VF
Budget: ($79,000)
Notes: Twentieth century painting and sculpture. Incl 1200 pictures and 1300 slides.

DC —SMITHSONIAN INSTITUTION, Archives Div, Washington, 20560. William W Moss, Archivist
Holdings: Cat Mss
Notes: The Archives holds some of the records of the Hirshhorn Museum and Sculpture Garden, the Cooper-Hewitt Museum of Decorative Arts and Design, and the National Museum of American Art (formerly the National Collection of Fine Arts).

HI —HONOLULU ACADEMY OF ARTS, Robert Allerton Library, 900 S Beretania St, Honolulu, 96814. Anne T Seaman, Librn
Holdings: Vols (40,000) Cat Pix Slides Microforms

IL —ART INSTITUTE OF CHICAGO, Ryerson & Burnham Libraries, Michigan Ave & Adams St, Chicago, 60603. Daphne C Roloff, Dir
Holdings: Vols (136,000) Cat Mss Slides Microforms
Budget: ($167,000)
Notes: Subjects incl architecture (designs and plans, history); art exhibitions; art history; drawings; furniture; glassware; painting; sculpture; and silverware. Total collection incl 300,000 slides.

IL —CHICAGO PUBLIC LIBRARY, Art Section, Fine Arts Division, 78 E Washington St, Chicago, 60602. Rosalinda I Hack, Fine Arts Division Chief; Yvonne S Brown, Head, Art Section
Holdings: Vols 42,000
Notes: Reference and circulating collection of books, periodicals, exhibition catalogs, dissertations, picture collections, and microforms on all aspects of the visual arts. Major concentration of art history, especially European, with concentration on 19th and 20th century art movements and artists. We attempt to represent the works of recognized artists past and present. The Decorative Arts are well represented especially in the areas of antiques, interior decoration, and handicrafts. The collection is supplemented by a strong periodical collection, consisting of 330 current English and Foreign subscriptions, the majority of these titles we bind, as well as strong bound retrospective collections. The visual arts is supported by a clipping File on Chicago Artists, a current exhibition catalogs collection, as well as by the microfilm collections of the*Chicago Art Institute Scrapbooks,* the *Scrapbook on Art,* Artists, and the *Index of American Design.*

KY —UNIVERSITY OF LOUISVILLE, Allen R Hite Art Institute, Library, Belknap Campus, Louisville, 40292. Gail Gilbert, Librn
Holdings: Vols (40,000) Cat Pix
Budget: ($29,000)
Notes: Incl books on art, architecture, landscape architecture and gardening, prints, printing, illustrated books and brass rubbings. Library subscribes to 200 periodical titles in these and other areas. Collection circulates to faculty and staff only, with same restrictions placed on interlibrary loan. Library also has collections of bookplates, posters, original prints, hand-made Christmas cards and clippings file filling 56 VF drawers.

ME —WILLIAM A FARNSWORTH LIBRARY & ART MUSEUM, 19 Elm St, Rockland, 04841. Marius B Peladeau, Dir
Holdings: Vols (4000) Cat Pix Microforms
Notes: Emphasis on American and European fine and decorative arts of all periods (largely modern). Other areas include marine history and Maine history (local); illustrated books and rare books also a part of our collection, which has its own catalog. Also, Louise Nevelsen, N C Wyeth Archives.

MD —JOHNS HOPKINS UNIVERSITY, Milton S Eisenhower Library, Charles & 34 Sts, Baltimore, 21218. Ann S Gwyn, Assistant Dir for Special Collections
Holdings: Vols (18,000) Cat Maps
Notes: Strongest in ancient, Byzantine, and Renaissance art and architecture. Reference Library lacks some periodicals. Modern period being rapidly built up.

MD —WALTERS ART GALLERY, Library & Manuscripts & Rare Book Collection, 600 N Charles St, Baltimore, 21201. Muriel L Toppan, Reference Librn; Lilian M C Randall, Cur of Mss & Rare Books
Holdings: Vols (80,000) Cat Mss
Budget: ($35,000)
Notes: The collection supports the gallery's collections of art objects which date from 4000 BC to the end of the 19th century. The collection of medieval and renaissance illuminated mss (782 in number), incunabula (about 1400) and rare books are considered art objects. There are card catalogs providing indexing to the collection. The mss are listed in De Ricci and the incunabula in Goff. Photocopying permitted for Reference Library materials only.

MA —MUSEUM OF FINE ARTS, William Morris Hunt Memorial Library, Huntington Ave, Boston, 02115. Nancy S Allen, Librn
Holdings: Vols (100,000) Cat
Budget: ($70,000)
Notes: Strong collection of art auction catalogs, exhibition catalogs, and Asian language books on art history. Collection has about 100,000 pamphlet pieces also.

MA —HARVARD UNIVERSITY, Harvard College Library, Fine Arts Library, Fogg Museum, 32 Quincy St, Cambridge, 02138. Wolfgang M Freitag, Librn
Holdings: Vols (202,000) Cat Mss Pix Slides
Budget: ($176,500)
Notes: All areas of art history, with

ART—HISTORY (cont.)

emphasis on Italian primitives, Italian Renaissance, master drawings, Romanesque sculpture, architectural history, ms materials (particulary American artists'), conservation and restoration of art objects. Incl the Berenson repertory of photographs from the Harvard Center for Italian Renaissance Studies in Florence, and the Decimal Index to the Art of the Low Countries. Separate card catalogs for books, photographs and lantern slides, registers for ms holdings which are not incl in *National Union Catalog of Manuscript Collections.* Slides total over 230,000; over 745,000 pictures. *Fine Arts Library Catalogue* (14 volumes) and *Catalogue of Auction Sales Catalogues* (1 volume) (Boston: G K Hall, 1972); *A Guide to the Fine Arts Library* (Cambridge, Mass: 1971); *Guide to the Harvard Libraries,* microfiche edition of holdingscataloged through 1981 published 1984 (Munich/New York: Saur).

MA —MELROSE PUBLIC LIBRARY, 69 W Emerson St, Melrose, 02176. Diane E Shaw, Art Librn
Holdings: Vols (8500) Cat Pix Slides Phonorecords
Budget: ($6900)
Notes: Framed and unframed art reproductions (110), slides (2773), periodicals, clippings, sound recordings (3000). Incl the Mary Livermore Collection of Sacred Art, the Odlin Collection, and the Pierre Gendrot Collection of Fine Art.

MA —SWAIN SCHOOL OF DESIGN LIBRARY, 140 Orchard St, Sch add: 19 Hawthorn St, New Bedford, 02740. Martha Maier, Librn
Holdings: Vols 16,500 Cat Mss Slides
Notes: Small special file of material of artists of the New Bedford area, photographed and deposited with the Archives of American Art. 30,000 slides on art history.

MA —SMITH COLLEGE, Hillyer Art Library, Fine Arts Center, Northampton, 01063. Karen Harvey, Librn
Holdings: Vols (45,000) Cat Pix Slides

MA —BRANDEIS UNIVERSITY, Goldfarb Library, 415 South St, Waltham, 02154. Bessie Hahn, Dir
Notes: Leonardo da Vinci Collection. Comprised of over 1000 vols dealing with all aspects of Leonardo Da Vinci's life, art and engineering feats. The collection is fully catalogued and access is provided by the Special Collections card catalog and the Main Card Catalog.

MI —CENTER FOR CREATIVE STUDIES, College of Art and Design, (formerly Art School of the Society of Arts and Crafts), 245 E Kirby, Detroit, 48202. Jean Peyrat, Librn; Susan Campbell, Slide Librn
Holdings: Vols 15,500 Cat Pix Slides
Notes: Incl 50,000 pictures and 32,000 slides.

MI —MICHIGAN STATE UNIVERSITY, Art Library, East Lansing, 48824. Shirlee A Studt, Librn
Holdings: Vols (45,000) Cat
Notes: The Illuminated Manuscript Facsimile Collection includes examples of religious and secular works from the earliest codex to the age of printing. It has particular strengths in Carolingian, Ottonian, French Gothic and works from the British Isles. The facsimile collection is strengthened by related research materials (biographical material, critical studies, etc) The facsimile collection and related materials are part of a 45,000 volume separately housed and staffed collection on the visual and decorative arts (including photography) serving the curricular and research needs of the University community. A guide to full facsimiles in the collection is available in the Art Library and in the Special Collections division. A strong collection of architectural history.

MN —WALKER ART CENTER, Staff Reference Library, Vineland Place, Minneapolis, 55403. Rosemary Furtak, Librn
Holdings: Vols 5000 Cat Pix
Notes: Incl 10,000 catalogs of individual artists; museum gallery catalogs-10,000 catalogs of major exhibitions from all over the world dating back to 1940. VF material and tapes.

MO —UNIVERSITY OF MISSOURI-COLUMBIA, Ellis Library, Art, Archaeology and Music Dept, Columbia, 65201. Bonnie MacEwan, Librn
Holdings: Vols Cat
Notes: Rare art census reports published by 19th century European monument commissions.

MO —THE NELSON-ATKINS MUSEUM OF ART, Kenneth & Helen Spencer Art Reference Library, 4525 Oak St, Kansas City, 64111. Stanley W Hess, Librn

MO —SAINT LOUIS ART MUSEUM, Richardson Memorial Library, Saint Louis, 63110. Ann B Abid, Librn
Holdings: Vols (30,000) Cat Pix Slides Microforms
Notes: Art history, incl decorative arts, catalogs, exhibitions, etc.

MO —SAINT LOUIS UNIVERSITY, Pius XII Memorial Library, 3655 W Pine Blvd, Saint Louis, 63108. William Cole, Dir
Holdings: Vols 250 Cat Mss Slides //
Notes: Collection covers all areas of learning and European history from Classical Antiquity to early modern period. Researchers using collection receive assistance in paleography, bibliography and reference search.

MO —SPRINGFIELD ART MUSEUM, Reference Library, 1111 E Brookside Dr, Springfield, 65807. Greg G Thielen, Cur of Collections
Holdings: Vols 3000 Cat Pix Slides Art Reproductions
Notes: Art history and related fields. Growing emphasis on contemporary arts. Incl 1000 slides.

NJ —NEWARK PUBLIC LIBRARY, Art & Music Dept, 5 Washington St, Newark, 07101. William J Dane, Supv
Holdings: Vols (50,000) Cat Mss Maps Pix Slides Microforms VF
Notes: All phases of art and all periods of art history are covered in books and periodicals; supporting collections incl 1,000,000 illustrations, 2000 portfolios of plates, 15,000 fine prints, 15,000 slides, historic maps, manuscripts and book collection on the history of fine printing, posters and autographs, extensive vertical file.

NJ —PRINCETON UNIVERSITY, Marquand Library, McCormick Hall, Princeton, 08544. Mary M Schmidt, Librn
Holdings: Vols (130,000) Cat Microforms
Notes: Especially strong in classical archaeology, medieval art and architecture, and photography history.

NY —STATE UNIVERSITY OF NEW YORK, COLLEGE AT BUFFALO, Lockwood Memorial Library, Art Dept, Buffalo, 14260. Florence S DaLuiso, Cur
Holdings: Vols (38,000) Cat Microforms
Budget: ($24,735)
Notes: Collection supports curriculum of the School of Fine Art. Incl 9000 exhibition catalogs. Recent acquisitions emphasize contemporary art and environmental design. The library by reciprocal agreement contains card catalog holdings of the Albright-Knox Art Gallery, Buffalo, New York. Books may be obtained on interlibrary loan.

NY —STATE UNIVERSITY OF NEW YORK, COLLEGE AT NEW PALTZ, Sojourner Truth Library, New Paltz, 12561. W E Connors, Dir
Holdings: Vols 14,000
Notes: Art--education, history, studio.

NY —CITY UNIVERSITY OF NEW YORK, City College, Library, 138 St & Convent Ave, New York, 10031. Vira C Hinds, Assoc Prof
Notes: In general reference library.

NY —FRICK ART REFERENCE LIBRARY, 10 E 71 St, New York, 10021. Helen Sanger, Librn
Holdings: Vols (154,384) Cat Pix Per
Notes: History of painting, drawing, sculpture and illuminated mss of US and western Europe from 4th century AD to about 1860. 54,862 art auction catalogs; 420, 507 study photographs.

NY —METROPOLITAN MUSEUM OF ART, Thomas J Watson Library, Fifth Ave & 82 St, New York, 10028. William B Walker, Chief Librn
Holdings: Vols (250,000) Cat Mss Microforms
Notes: All fields of art: 1400 periodicals, incl bulletins and annual reports, catalogs, etc of American and foreign art societies, museums, etc; incl sales catalogs, exhibition catalogs, clipping file on individual artists and subjects, autograph letters. See *Library Catalog of the Metropolitan Museum of Art, New York,* second ed, rev and enl (Boston, G K Hall, 1980, 48 v and first supplement, 1982). Since 1980, holdings have been cataloged in RLIN.

NY —NEW YORK PUBLIC LIBRARY, Art, Prints, and Photographs Div, Fifth Ave & 42 St, New York, 10018. Donald Anderle, Chief
Holdings: Vols (150,000) Cat Mss Pix Microforms
Notes: History and design in the fine and applied arts. Architecture, painting, drawing, sculpture, costume, furniture, advertising art, prints, photography, crafts, and jewelry are among the subjects covered from ancient times to the present. See: New York Public Library *Dictionary Catalog of the Art and Architecture Division* (Boston, G K Hall, 1975), 30 vols. Holdings after that time are incl in the *Dictionary Catalog of the Research Libraries.* African Art and Afro-American Art are collected by the Schomburg Center for Research in Black Culture.

NY —MEMORIAL ART GALLERY LIBRARY, 490 University Ave, Rochester, 14607. Stephanie Frontz, Librn
Holdings: Vols 15,000 Cat

NY —VISUAL STUDIES WORKSHOP, Research Center, 31 Prince St, Rochester, 14607. Linn Underhill, Coordr; Robert Bretz, Librn
Holdings: Vols (8000) Cat Pix Slides Audiotapes Videotapes
Notes: Strong emphasis on photography (over 1,000,000 pictures) and the photographic arts in many subject areas incl in this volume. Heavy emphasis on early photographic processes and collections of examples of them. Also collections of individual photographers' works.

NC —UNIVERSITY OF NORTH CAROLINA, CHAPEL HILL, Art Library, Art Classroom Studio Bldg, 079A, Chapel Hill, 27514. Philip A Rees, Art Librn
Holdings: Vols (47,000) Cat Microforms
Budget: ($52,000)
Notes: Emphasis on European and American art and architecture, ancient to modern. Special strengths: Rubens and 19th century French painting.

NC —DUKE UNIVERSITY, East Campus Library, Durham, 27708. Betty Young, Librn
Notes: Special subject collections are Architecture-History and Art-History.

OH —CINCINNATI ART MUSEUM, Library, Eden Park, Cincinnati, 45202. Patrician P Rutledge, Librn
Holdings: Vols (45,850) Cat Mss Microforms
Notes: Art library containing all subjects on art-history, graphic arts, advertising art, etc; special strength in prints, ie engravings, etc. Near Eastern art and decorative arts are also strong. At least 90,000 art exhibition catalogs. Emphasis on artists of Cincinnati and vicinity in vertical file material.

OH —HEBREW UNION COLLEGE-JEWISH INSTITUTE OF RELIGION, Klau Library, 3101 Clifton Ave, Cincinnati, 45220. David J Gilner, Reference Librn
Holdings: Cat
Notes: Extensive collection of Jewish artists, primarily in the US and Israel; Jewish religious art, etc.

OH —OHIO STATE UNIVERSITY, Fine Arts Library, 1813 N High St, Columbus, 43210. Susan Wyngaard, Head, Fine Arts Library
Holdings: Vols (75,000) Cat Microforms
Budget: ($60,000)
Notes: Also have 1000 uncataloged exhibition catalogs. Book collection strong in history of art especially in area of medieval & Northern Renaissance art. Good

ART—HISTORY (cont.)

collection of portfolios. Photographic collections on microfiche. Receive Slavic titles, many on Byzantine frescoes. Online catalog. Decimal Index of the Art of the Low Countries, as well as Marburger Index; Index Photographique de i' Arten France; Alinari Archives on microfiche and other major microform collections in art.

OH —OBERLIN COLLEGE LIBRARY, Clarence Ward Art Library, Allen Art Bldg, Oberlin, 44074. Jeffrey Weidman, Librn
Holdings: Vols (62,000) Cat Microforms
Notes: Incl approx 18,000 uncataloged exhibition catalogues and major sales catalogues. Significant holdings in early serials (see *ARLO Union List of Serials).*

OH —TOLEDO MUSEUM OF ART, Reference Library, PO BOx 1013, Toledo, 43697. Carolyn Papsidera, Cur
Holdings: Vols 40,000 Cat
Notes: Plus 40,000 slides.

PA —BRYN MAWR COLLEGE, Canaday Library, Bryn Mawr, 19010. James Tanis, Dir
Notes: Baroque and Italian Renaissance painting and architecture; late antique and early Christian art; Flemish and Dutch painting 15th - 17th centuries; French painting 18th - 19th centuries. In Art and Archaeology Library.

PA —TEMPLE UNIVERSITY, Tyler School of Art, Beech & Penrose Aves, Philadelphia, 19126. Mary Ivy Bayard, Librn
Holdings: Vols 24,267 Cat Pix Microforms
Budget:
Notes: The art school branch of the main university library; supports a graduate program in the fine arts, incl some graduate courses in art history.

PA —UNIVERSITY OF PITTSBURGH, Henry Clay Frick Fine Arts Library, Pittsburgh, 15260. Anne W Gordon, Fine Arts Librn
Holdings: Vols (55,000) Cat Pix Slides Microforms
Notes: Emphasis is on the art of the Western World--architecture, sculpture, painting, minor arts, archaeology, with special strength in the Byzantine, early Christian, medieval, renaissance and modern periods. The Oriental field is represented, incl replicas of scrolls. Studio arts are also covered. Illuminated ms facsimiles. Extensive collections of slides and photographs for study of art history are available in the building but not administered by the art library.

PA —PENNSYLVANIA STATE UNIVERSITY, Arts Library, 405 E Pattee Library, University Park, 18602. Jean Smith, Arts and Architecture Librn
Holdings: Vols (46,600) Cat
Notes: Emphasis in Medieval and Byzantine, Italian Renaissance and Baroque. Includes photographs in Decimal Index of the Art of Low Countries; microfiche collections including Marburger Index and Index of American Design. Also fine print collection. *See also* entries under Architecture - History; Prints - Collections.

RI —RHODE ISLAND SCHOOL OF DESIGN, Library, Two College St, Providence, 02903. James A Findlay, Dir
Holdings: Vols (70,000) Cat Pix Slides Phonorecords
Budget: ($50,000)
Notes: Incl 30,000 pictures, 92,000 slides, 1100 posters and color reproductions and 280,000 clippings.

TN —MEMPHIS STATE UNIVERSITY, Slide Library, Jones Hall 220, Memphis, 38152. Belinda C Patterson, Slide Cur
Holdings: Slides Filmstrips
Budget: $3000
Notes: 90,000 slides for teaching art and architecture.

TX —UNIVERSITY OF TEXAS LIBRARIES, Fine Arts Library, PO Box P, Austin, 78712. Carole L Cable, Fine Arts Librn
Holdings: Vols (55,000) Cat Pix

TX —TEXAS A&M UNIVERSITY, Sterling C Evans Library, Special Collections Div, College Station, 77843. Donald H Dyal, Librn
Holdings: Vols 3500 Cat Mss Pix
Notes: Western art, art history, illustration.

TX —KIMBELL ART MUSEUM, Library, 3333 Camp Bowie Blvd, PO Box 9440, Fort Worth, 76107. Erika Esau, Librn
Holdings: Vols 25,000 Cat Slides 16mm Films Microforms
Budget: $70,000
Notes: Excl American and contemporary art. Incl 30,000 slides.

TX —MUSEUM OF FINE ARTS, Hirsch Library, 1001 Bissonnet, Houston, 77005. Linda Nelson Shearouse, Librn
Holdings: Vols 15,000 Cat
Notes: All areas of art history, but strongest in 20th century art. Also photgraphy.

TX —RICE UNIVERSITY, Art Library, 6100 S Main St, PO Box 1892, Houston, 77001. Jet Marie Prendeville, Librn
Holdings: Vols (41,335) Cat
Budget: ($28,100)
Notes: The Art Library collection covers all periods of Western Art with particular emphasis upon Classical Archaelogy, Medieval, Renaissance, and Modern Art and Architecture. The collection also offers representative coverage of film, photography, and Oriental art.

†TX —MCNAY ART INSTITUTE LIBRARY, San Antonio Museum Association, San Antonio, 78209.
Notes: The Robert L B Tobin Collections.

TX —TRINITY UNIVERSITY, Elizabeth Coates Maddux Library, 715 Stadium Dr, San Antonio, 78284. Richard Hume Werking, Library Dir; Craig Likness, Head Bibliographer
Notes: General reference.

VA —SWEET BRIAR COLLEGE, Library, Sweet Briar, 24595. John Jaffe, Librn
Holdings: Vols (5500) Cat Pix Slides
Budget: ($2000)

WI —MILWAUKEE PUBLIC LIBRARY, 814 W Wisconsin Ave, Milwaukee, 53233. Donald J Sager, City Librn
Holdings: Vols Cat Pix Slides
Notes: The collection incl all fields of art, with emphasis on architecture, incl: Frank Lloyd Wright and local city planning documents; interior decoration; art history; American art; Oriental art; art instruction; decorative arts; numismatics and philately; photography, incl local photo archives and instruction manuals; costume; art exhibition and auction ctalogs; and local newspaper clippings on art subjects. Also, circulating mounted and framed art prints and sculpture reproductions.
See also entry under Art.

AB —SOUTHERN ALBERTA INSTITUTE OF TECHNOLOGY, Learning Resources Centre, 1301 16 Ave NW, Calgary, T2M 0L4, Can. Tom Skinner, Historian
Holdings: Vols (7000) Cat Pix Slides Films Audiotapes Filmstrips Videotapes
Notes: Serves Alberta College of Art (4-year professional course). 60,000 individual cataloged slides.

ON —NATIONAL GALLERY OF CANADA, Library, National Museums of Canada, Ottawa, K1A 0M8, Can. J Hunter, Chief Librn
Budget: Vols (72,000)
Notes: History of art (postmediaeval, Western). Public reference only. Circulating only to gallery staff and on interlibrary loan. 1000 periodical titles currently received. 50, 000 pamphlets, mostly exhibition and sales catalogs (not cataloged). 40,000 items in documentation files: clippings, notices of exhibitions and other ephemera. Exchange of National Gallery publications with other art galleries. Special section on history of Canadian art. Emphasis of collection on painting, sculpture, graphic arts and photography. Study collection of photographs and slides. See *Catalogue of the National Gallery of Canada*, 8 vols (Boston: G K Hall, 1973) and *Supplement*, 6 vols (Boston: G K Hall, 1981).

ON —METROPOLITAN TORONTO LIBRARY, Fine Arts Dept, 789 Yonge St, Toronto, M4W 2G8, Can. Alan Suddon, Head
Holdings: Vols (42,000) Cat Pix Microforms
Notes: Extensive collection.

ON —UNIVERSITY OF TORONTO, Art History Reference Library, Dept of Fine Art, 100 Saint George St, Toronto, M5S 1A1, Can. Andrea Retfalvi, Research Librn
Holdings: Vols (20,000) Cat Pix
Notes: The collection specializes in art history catalogs of various types: temporary exhibition catalogs, from the major institutions in Europe and North America; permanent collection catalogs, again for all the major institutions; dealer catalogs; and auction catalogs. The collection of auction catalogs is primarily French, covering 1870-1970, with particular strength from ca 1900 on. There is a catalog for all these types of catalogs. 90,000 photographs.

ART—MANAGEMENT

CA —UNIVERSITY OF CALIFORNIA, LOS ANGELES, Graduate School of Management Library, UCLA Campus, Los Angeles, 90024. Robert Bellanti, Head Librn
Holdings: Vols (128,000) Cat Mss Microforms
Notes: The

ART—STUDY AND TEACHING

NY —STATE UNIVERSITY OF NEW YORK, COLLEGE AT NEW PALTZ, Sojourner Truth Library, New Paltz, 12561. W E Connors, Dir
Holdings: Vols 2000
Notes: Art--education, history, studio.

ART—TRADE see Art Industries and Trade

ART, ABSTRACT

CA —CALIFORNIA INSTITUTE OF THE ARTS, Library, 24700 McBean Pkwy, Valencia, 91355. James Elrod, Dir
Holdings: Vols (61,000) Slides
Budget: ($11,000)
Notes: Modern art, incl abstract, conceptual, concrete, environment, minimal, and pop art; art; dadaism; surrealism; happenings; and caricatures and cartoons. Slides (61,683).

NY —MUSEUM OF MODERN ART, Library, 11 W 53 St, New York, 10019. Clive Phillpot, Library Dir
Holdings: Vols (80,000) Cat Mss Audiotapes Microforms VF
Notes: See *Catalog of the Library of the Museum of Modern Art, New York City* (Boston: G K Hall, 1976), 14 vols. Collection incl exhibition catalogs.

ART, AFRICAN AND AFRO-AMERICAN

CA —CRAFT AND FOLK ART MUSEUM, Library, 5814 Wilshire Blvd, Los Angeles, 90036. Joan M Benedetti, Museum Librn
Holdings: Vols (2000) Slides VF
Notes: Incl 2000 books; 70 journal subscriptions; artists' biographical files: 6 file drawers; clipping files: 8 file drawers; 20,000 slides. Representation of the material culture of all people, traditional and contemporary expressions. Incl visual and printed information on ethnic, traditional, popular, decorative, idiosyncratic, and contemporary crafts as well as vernacular architecture, handmade houses, and design. Information about and for professional artists on health hazards, conservation, and career management. Anthropological and art historical works; exhibition catalogues; slides, photographs, audiocassettes; clipping and pamphlet files. Contemporary Slide Registry of Craftspeople and extensive biographical files of contemporary craft artists. Information and referral files of craft related galleries, shops, festivals, organizations, etc.

CA —FINE ARTS MUSEUMS OF SAN FRANCISCO, M H de Young Memorial Museum, Golden Gate Park, San Francisco, 94118. Jane Nelson, Librn
Holdings: Vols (30,000) Cat Slides
Budget: ($24,000)

DC —HOWARD UNIVERSITY, Moorland-Spingarn Research Center, 500 Howard

ART, AFRICAN AND AFRO-AMERICAN (cont.)

Place NW, Washington, 20059. Clifford L Muse, Jr, Acting Dir
Holdings: Vols (106,086) Mss Maps Pix Slides Phonorecords Audiotapes 16mm Films Filmstrips Microforms
Budget: ($854,753)
See also entry under Blacks

IN —INDIANA UNIVERSITY, Art Museum Bldg, Fine Arts Bldg, Bloomington, 47401. Betty Jo Irvine, Fine Arts Librn
Holdings: Vols (57,000) Cat Pix Microforms
Budget: ($52,000)
Notes: Art forms relevant to the periods and places involved.

MO —KANSAS CITY PUBLIC LIBRARY, 311 E 12, Kansas City, 64106. Daniel J Bradbury, Dir
Holdings: Vols 3500 Cat Mss Maps Pix Microforms
Notes: The John Ramos Collection.

MO —SAINT LOUIS ART MUSEUM, Richardson Memorial Library, Saint Louis, 63110. Ann B Abid, Librn
Holdings: Vols (30,000) Cat Pix Slides Microforms
Notes: Art history, incl decorative arts, catalogs, exhibitions, etc.

NY —BROOKLYN MUSEUM, Art Reference Library, 188 Eastern Parkway, Brooklyn, 11238.
Holdings: Vols (130,000)

NY —METROPOLITAN MUSEUM OF ART, Robert Goldwater Library, Fifth Ave at 82nd St, New York, 10028. Allan D Chapman, Librn
Holdings: Vols (27,000) Cat
Notes: Primitive art: African, Indians of the Americans (incl Pre-Columbian), Oceanic, Polynesian, etc. 150,000 photographs.

NY —NEW YORK PUBLIC LIBRARY, Schomburg Center for Research in Black Culture, 515 Lenox Ave, New York, 10037. Catherine J Lenix Hooker, Interim Administrator
Holdings: Vols (85,000) Cat Mss Maps Pix Slides Microforms Phonorecords Tapes Prints Broadsides
Notes: Materials in all formats about black people throughout the world. Extensive archival holdings, vertical files, Afro-American and African art. See *The Dictionary Catalog of the Schomburg* Collection, (Boston: G K Hall & Co., 1962), 9 vols. Since 1972 the Center's holdings have been included in the *Dictionary Catalog of the Research Libraries,* New York Public Library.

PA —SCHOOL DISTRICT OF PHILADELPHIA, Pedagogical Library, 21 St & Pkwy, Philadelphia, 19103. Helen E Howe, Librn; Patricia K Buck, Asst Librn
Holdings: Vols (47,000) Cat Pix Microforms
Budget: ($25,000)
Notes: Collection emphasis on public school education K-12 with the main areas including Afro-American history and culture, elementary and early childhood education, secondary education, educational administration, educational research, reading, school law, educational psychology. Special Collections: ERIC (140,000 documents), Archives of the School District of Philadelphia. Approx 500 periodical subscriptions.

PA —CARLOW COLLEGE, Grace Library, Fifth Ave, Pittsburgh, 15213. Joan M Mitchell, Dir of Library Services
Holdings: Vols (1786) Cat
Budget: ($500)
Notes: The Black Studies Collection consists of books which describe the Black experience in Africa and the United States, with special emphasis on slavery and contemporary Black literature and sociology.

ART, ALASKAN

AK —TONGASS HISTORICAL SOCIETY, Library, 629 Dock St, Ketchikan, 99901. Marjorie Anne Voss, Librn
Holdings: Vols 400 Cat Pix
Notes: Alaskan and regional history and art, as well as Northwest Coast Indian history and art. Extensive photograph collection.

ART, AMERICAN

CA —CALIFORNIA STATE UNIVERSITY, LONG BEACH, University Library, Reference Center, 1250 Bellflower Blvd, Long Beach, 90840. Henry J DuBois, Librn
Holdings: Cat Slides
Notes: Collection of 60,000 slides offers examples of virtually all types and periods of art, incl an extensive collection of slides of mss from the Bodleian Library, Oxford, a special series on Latin American art, another on the arts of the US Collection is cataloged using Fogg Museum classification. No photocopying.

CA —CRAFT AND FOLK ART MUSEUM, Library, 5814 Wilshire Blvd, Los Angeles, 90036. Joan M Benedetti, Museum Librn
Holdings: Vols (2000) Slides VF
Notes: Incl 2000 books; 70 journal subscriptions; artists' biographical files: 6 file drawers; clipping files: 8 file drawers; 20,000 slides. Representation of the material culture of all people, traditional and contemporary expressions. Incl visual and printed information on ethnic, traditional, popular, decorative, idiosyncratic, and contemporary crafts as well as vernacular architecture, handmade houses, and design. Information about and for professional artists on health hazards, conservation, and career management. Anthropological and art historical works; exhibition catalogues; slides, photographs, audiocassettes; clipping and pamphlet files. Contemporary Slide Registry of Craftspeople and extensive biographical files of contemporary craft artists. Information and referral files of craft related galleries, shops, festivals, organizations, etc.

CA —FINE ARTS MUSEUMS OF SAN FRANCISCO, M H de Young Memorial Museum, Golden Gate Park, San Francisco, 94118. Jane Nelson, Librn
Holdings: Vols Cat

DE —DELAWARE ART MUSEUM, Library, 2301 Kentmere Pkwy, Wilmington, 19806. Anne Hoslam, Librn
Holdings: Vols (25,000) Cat Mss
Notes: The collection is rich in the following subjects: Howard Pyle and his pupils; John Sloan and the eight; history of the book and printing; and English and American illustrated books. There is also a section on contemporary photography. Archival material on Albert Mumford Lindsay, Jerome Myers, Everett Shinn, Gayle Porter Hoskins, Frank Schoonover.

DC —SMITHSONIAN INSTITUTION, National Museum of American Art & the National Portrait Gallery Library, Eighth & F Sts, NW, Washington, 20560. Cecilia Chin, Librn
Holdings: Vols (47,000) Cat Microforms
Budget: ($60,000)
Notes: Subscribe to 600 foreign and domestic periodicals on art and American history. Holdings of older bound periodicals. Collection emphasizes American art, contemporary American and European painting, portraiture, American biography. Uncataloged material incl: 350 vertical file drawers of clippings, small catalogs and other ephemera on artists, art organizations, museums, etc; the "Ferdinand Perret Library"--180 scrapbooks with card index on California art and artists, incl clippings, catalogs, reproductions, etc; card bibliography of books and periodical literature on portraiture--international, retrospective and current--in progress. Mallett Library of Reproductions.

IN —WILLARD LIBRARY, 21 First Ave, Evansville, 47710. Joan Elliott, Special Collections Librn
Holdings: Vols (1400) Cat
Budget: ($3500)
Notes: The Thrall Art Book Collection. Circulating collection of art books being purchased by special endowment. Emphasis on fine arts of all times and places, with particular reference to American artists, as well as European and American decorative arts and architecture. Noncirculating.

IN —THE ART CENTER, Library, 120 St Joseph St, South Bend, 46601. Judy Oberhausen, Cur
Holdings: Vols (1010) Cat Slides
Notes: 500 slides. This Art Center has a specific, separate collection--"The Arts of the United States"--which has its own index and is geared toward American painting, graphics, architecture, design and decorative arts, from the 19th to the 20th century, and sculpture works on paper. Incl 32 periodical titles.

IA —CHARLES H MACNIDER MUSEUM, 303 Second St SE, Mason City, 50401. Richard E Leet, Museum Dir
Holdings: Vols 500 Cat Pix Slides
Budget: $500
Notes: The museum collection is designed to demonstrate the story of American art.

LA —R W NORTON ART GALLERY, Library, 4747 Creswell Ave, Shreveport, 71106. Jerry M Bloomer, Librn
Holdings: Vols 300 Cat
Notes: Monographs on artists and historical surveys of American art.

ME —WILLIAM A FARNSWORTH LIBRARY & ART MUSEUM, 19 Elm St, Rockland, 04841. Marius B Peladeau, Dir
Holdings: Vols (4000) Cat Pix Microforms
Notes: Emphasis on American and European fine and decorative arts of all periods (largely modern). Other areas include marine history and Maine history (local); illustrated books and rare books also a part of our collection, which has its own catalog. Also, Louise Nevelsen, N C Wyeth Archives.

MA —BROCKTON ART CENTER, Fuller Memorial Library, Oak St on Upper Porters Pond, Brockton, 02401. Carolina Costa, Librn
Holdings: Vols 500 Cat Slides
Notes: The Brockton Art Center's permanent collection is comprised of 19th and 20th century American works. The museum collection determines the library's areas of concentration.

MA —OLD STURBRIDGE VILLAGE, Research Library, Sturbridge, 01566. Theresa Rini Percy, Librn
Holdings: Cat Pix
Notes: Especially in New England, 1790-1850, incl painting, folk art, sculpture.

MA —STERLING AND FRANCINE CLARK ART INSTITUTE LIBRARY, 225 South St, PO Box 8, Williamstown, 01267. Michael Rinehart, Librn
Holdings: Vols (77,000) Cat Pix Slides Microforms
Budget: ($105,000)
Notes: Primarily European art, 1300-present, and post-Columbian American art. Incl 850, 000 pictures, 80,000 slides, 400 microfilm reels, 25,000 auction sale catalogs, and Mary Ann Beinecke Decorative Art Collection.

MI —EDISON INSTITUTE, Greenfield Village and Henry Ford Museum, Archives & Research Library, PO Box 1970, Dearborn, 48121. Steve Hamp, Dir; Joan W Gartland, Librn
Holdings: Vols 400,000 Cat Mss Maps Microforms
Notes: 400,000 vols incl pamphlets. The Archives and research library supports the program of Greenfield Village and the Henry Ford Museum. Special collections incl: automotive literature, ephemera, McGuffey Readers, trade catalogs, photographs and graphics.

NE —UNIVERSITY OF NEBRASKA-LINCOLN, Don L Love Library, University Archives and Special Collections, Lincoln, 68588. Joseph G Svoboda, University Archivist
Holdings: Pix Slides
Notes: R D Warden Collection of Charles Marion Russell. "Largest private collection of literature on Russell, 'The Cowboy Artist. '" 7000 items, incl first editions of every book and pamphlet by Russell and over 1000 periodical appearances of his art; 900 color prints; 142 drawings; color slides; scrapbooks about Russell and his family, from 1889.

NH —STRAWBERY BANKE, Thayer Cumings Historical Reference Library, Portsmouth, 03801. Nicole R Osborn, Librn
Holdings: Vols (2850) Cat Mss Maps Pix

ART, AMERICAN (cont.)

Microforms
Budget: ($1900)
Notes: The Library is small, highly specialized library with holdings in American art, architecture and decorative arts. The collection is especially strong in the American decorative arts, with additional concentration in European decorative arts. In addition the collection contains books on American painting, American architecture, archaeology, technology, maritime history and boatbuilding, landscape gardening and design as well as books on local and regional history and social and material culture of the 17th-19th centuries. Collection of mss, microfilm and documents is related to important properties and personages of Portsmouth and the surrounding area.

NJ —MONTCLAIR ART MUSEUM LIBRARY, 3 South Mountain Ave, PO Box 1582, Montclair, 07042. Edith A Rights, Librn
Holdings: Vols (10,000) Cat Pix Slides Audiotapes
Budget: ($3500)
Notes: American painting and sculpture. Incl 5000 pictures; 10,000 slides; posters. Audiotapes on American art and artists.

NJ —NEWARK MUSEUM LIBRARY, 49 Washington St, PO Box 540, Newark, 07101. Margaret DiSalvi, Librn
Holdings: Vols 4000 Cat Pix Slides
Notes: See *American Art in The Newark Museum; Paintings, Drawings and Sculpture* (a catalog of the collection).

NY —HISTORICAL SOCIETY OF EARLY AMERICAN DECORATION, 19 Dove St, Albany, 12210. Doris Fry, Dir; Laura Olf, Librn
Holdings: Cat Pix Slides
Notes: The Library is housed with the Museum Collection of the Society. Incl examples of 19th century American country painting on tin, stenciling on wood and tin, bronzing decoration on wood, English stencilled tin and wood, bronzed items, painted objects, reverse painting on glass and examples of other decorating techniques of the period. Also included is a large collection of painted recordings of designs from early articles. Many of these were done by Esther Stevens Brazer in the 1930s. Another large collection has been added since that time. The library material is related to this interest. See *The Decorator*, official publication of the Historical Society of Early American Decoration. Other publications: *The Ornamented Chair* and *The Ornamented Tray* (both ed by Zilla Rider Lea), *Antique Decorations* by Brazer.

NY —ADIRONDACK HISTORICAL ASSOCIATION, Museum Library, Blue Mountain Lake, 12812. Jerold Pepper, Librn
Holdings: Vols (7500) Cat Mss Maps Pix Phonorecords Audiotapes 16mm Films Microforms
Notes: Anything about the Adirondacks--history, people, economics, places, things. Strong in Adirondack art, outdoor recreation, logging, small boats. Resources incl more than 1000 maps, 40,000 pictures, 1600 microfilm reels, 576 linear ft of ms material, and 12 cabinets of VF ephemera, etc.

NY —ALBRIGHT-KNOX ART GALLERY, Art Reference Library, 1285 Elmwood Ave, Buffalo, 14222. Annette Masling, Librn
Holdings: Vols (20,000) Cat
Notes: Special strength in American 19th and 20th century art. Excellent collection of exhibition catalogs for contemporary art.

NY —SAINT LAWRENCE UNIVERSITY, Owen D Young Library, Canton, 13617. Mahlon Peterson, Librn
Holdings: Cat Mss Pix
Notes: Frederick Remington's correspondence with Poultney Bigelow and others is the most important part of this collection. Also incl is an extensive collection of magazines in which articles written and/or illustrated by Remington first appeared, a collection of prints of Remington paintings, and many books by and about Remington. There are some restrictions on use of this material. Over 400 items.

NY —NEW YORK STATE HISTORICAL ASSOCIATION, Library, Lake Rd, Cooperstown, 13326. Amy Barnum, Librn
Holdings: Vols (55,000) Cat Slides
Notes: Emphasis on folk art, native painting. Noncirculating.

NY —AMERICAN ACADEMY & INSTITUTE OF ARTS & LETTERS, Library, 633 W 155 St, New York, 10032. Casindania P Eaton, Librn; Nancy Johnson, Researcher
Notes: Works of members of the Academy only. Incl mss, letters, memorabilia, etc.

NY —NEW YORK HISTORICAL SOCIETY, Library, 170 Central Park W, New York, 10024. James Gregory, Librn
Holdings: Mss
Notes: Incl original mss, illustrative materials, etc.

NY —WHITNEY MUSEUM OF AMERICAN ART, Library, 945 Madison Ave, New York, 10021. May Castleberry, Librn
Holdings: Vols 10,000 Cat Mss Pix Microforms
Notes: American art is the essence of the library's entire collection; incl exhibition catalogs and 1050 bound periodical titles.

NY —MUNSON-WILLIAMS-PROCTOR INSTITUTE, Reference Library, 310 Genessee St, Utica, 13502. Linda Lott, Librn
Holdings: Cat Slides Monographs Exhibition Catalogues
Notes: Specifically 19th and 20th century American art and history of art. Incl 16,500 slides. Separate catalog.

NC —UNIVERSITY OF NORTH CAROLINA, CHAPEL HILL, Art Library, Art Classroom Studio Bldg, 079A, Chapel Hill, 27514. Philip A Rees, Art Librn
Holdings: Vols (47,000) Cat Microforms
Budget: ($52,000)
Notes: Emphasis on European and American art and architecture, ancient to modern. Special strengths: Rubens and 19th century French painting.

OH —CLEVELAND PUBLIC LIBRARY, Fine Arts and Special Collections Department, 325 Superior Ave, Cleveland, 44114. Alice N Loranth, Head
Holdings: Vols (12,000) Cat Pix
Notes: Part of the Art Collection, which covers all periods and fields of art with special emphasis on contemporary and American art. 200 periodicals, incl bulletins of American museums.

OK —NATIONAL COWBOY HALL OF FAME AND WESTERN HERITAGE, Library, 1700 NE 63 St, Oklahoma City, 73111. Esther Long, Librn
Holdings: Vols (8000) Uncat
Notes: Art of the American West. Covers western art and artists; rodeo and its history; cowboys; the cattle industry; and biographies on prominent westerners. Personal collection of Walter Brennen; collections of artists, Carl Link and James Earl Frazier.

OK —THOMAS GILCREASE INSTITUTE OF AMERICAN HISTORY & ART LIBRARY, 1400 North 25th West Ave, Tulsa, 74127. Sarah Hirsch, Librn
Holdings: Vols Cat Mss Maps Pix
Notes: Trans-Mississippi West, US, Indian and Hispanic history. The Gilcrease Library contains a total of about 40,000 mss; 10,000 imprints; 5000 photographs; 600 maps and 50,000 vols.

PA —INDEPENDENCE NATIONAL HISTORICAL PARK, Library, 313 Walnut St, Philadelphia, 19106. David C G Dutcher, Chief Historian; Shirley A Mays, Librn
Holdings: Vols 5000 Cat Mss Videotapes Films
Budget: ($25,000)
Notes: Emphasis on Pennsylvania and Philadelphia, incl arts and crafts to early 19th century. Incl some 2000 ms pieces; 25, 000 pictures; 3000 slides; 600 microfilm reels. No photocopying.

PA —PENNSYLVANIA ACADEMY OF THE FINE ARTS, ARCHIVES, Broad & Cherry Sts, Philadelphia, 19102. Marietta Bushnell, Librn
Holdings: Mss Pix
Notes: Incl material relating to the history of the school and museum, exhibition catalogs and records, limited biographical information about former students, faculty, and exhibitors. Open to serious scholars by appointment only.

PA —KING'S COLLEGE, D Leonard Corgan Library, 14 W Jackson St, Wilkes-Barre, 18711. Judith Tierney, Special Collections Librn
Notes: Approx 5 linear feet of completed questionnaires, clippings, brochures, and other material relating to artists and art organizations in the Wyoming Valley from 1808 to the present. Primarily biographical. Wyoming Valley Artists Files.

TN —HUNTER MUSEUM OF ART, Library, 10 Bluff View, Chattanooga, 37403. Diana Svarez, Cur of Education
Holdings: Vols (1300)
Notes: American art, and Architecture, Photography and World Art. It is a new and growing collection, especially strong in art catalogs of sales and exhibitions. Incl 38 subscriptions.

TN —THE BOTANICAL GARDENS AND FINE ARTS CENTER, Fine Arts Library, Forrest Park Drive, Nashville, 37205. Muriel H Connell, Librn
Holdings: Vols (3500) Uncat Slides Filmstrips
Budget: ($150)

TX —ABILENE CHRISTIAN UNIVERSITY, Margaret & Herman Brown Library, ACU Sta, Abilene, 79601. Callie Faye Milliken, Assoc Dir
Holdings: Cat
Notes: Dixie Vinson Art Collection. Books on painting and on American art make up part of the collection; the larger part of it is a circulating collection of framed art reproductions.

TX —TEXAS A&M UNIVERSITY, Sterling C Evans Library, Special Collections Div, College Station, 77843. Donald H Dyal, Librn
Notes: The Western Illustrators Collection is comprised of approximately 3500 illustrated books, pamphlets, and other items. The collection incl illustrated works by Charles Marion Russell, Frederic Sackrider Remington, and other artists of the American West. Numerous other artists of the West and Southwest are represented, many of them contemporary moderns. Quite a lot of the books have additional unique original drawings by the artists.

TX —EL PASO PUBLIC LIBRARY, Southwest Collection, 501 N Oregon, El Paso, 79901. Mary A Sarber, Head
Holdings: Vols (7000) Cat Pix
Budget: ($6000)
Notes: Emphasis on art and artists of the Southwest, particularly Tom Lea, Jr, and Southwestern Indian arts and crafts. 36 drawers of pictures. See Hinshaw, Glennis, and Lisabeth Lovelace, *A Bibliography of Writings and Illustrations by Tom Lea* (El Paso Public Library Association, 1971).

TX —AMON CARTER MUSEUM, Library, 3510 Camp Bowie Blvd, PO Box 2365, Fort Worth, 76113. Nancy G Wynne, Librn
Holdings: Vols (25,000) Cat Mss Pix
Notes: The book collection, microfilm and photo archives have been built toward the goal of the interpretation of American history through art. At present, the greatest strengths are in Americana, Western Canadiana, bibliography, American exhibition catalogs and history of photography. Substantial books and files on American artists of the 19th and early 20th century, and particularly of Charles M Russell and Frederic Remington. Incl 25,000 pictures; 13,000 slides.
See also entries under Newspapers, American; Pictures - Collections.

UT —BRIGHAM YOUNG UNIVERSITY ART MUSEUM, Provo, 84602. J Cliff Allen, Dir
Holdings: Vols 500
Notes: Contemporary American lithographs; J Alden Weir collection of paintings, prints, and drawings; 19th and 20th century American paintings, drawings and sculpture.

VT —SAINT JOHNSBURY ATHENAEUM, Library, 30 Main St, Saint Johnsbury, 05819.

ART, AMERICAN (cont.)

Jean F Marcy, Librn
Holdings: Vols (41,000) Cat
Notes: American artists of the late 19th century, with emphasis on artists whose works are in the Institution's art gallery.

VT —SHELBURNE MUSEUM, Library, Shelburne, 05482. Barbara Reenstierna, Librn
Holdings: Vols 600 Cat Slides

VA —COLONIAL WILLIAMSBURG FOUNDATION, Abby Aldrich Rockefeller Folk Art Center, PO Box C, Williamsburg, 23187. Anne E Watkins, Registrar
Holdings: Vols 1200 Cat Maps Pix Slides
Notes: American folk art emphasis.

WI —MILWAUKEE PUBLIC LIBRARY, 814 W Wisconsin Ave, Milwaukee, 53233. Donald J Sager, City Librn
Holdings: Vols Cat Pix Slides
Notes: The collection incl all fields of art, with emphasis on architecture, incl: Frank Lloyd Wright and local city planning documents; interior decoration; art history; American art; Oriental art; art instruction; decorative arts; numismatics and philately; photography, incl local photo archives and instruction manuals; costume; art exhibition and auction catalogs; and local newspaper clippings on art subjects. Also, circulating mounted and framed art prints and sculpture reproductions.
See also entry under Art.

BC —VANCOUVER ART GALLERY, Library, 750 Hornby St, Vancouver, V6Z 2H7, Can. Catherine M Cowan, Librn

ART, ANCIENT

IN —INDIANA UNIVERSITY, Art Museum Bldg, Fine Arts Bldg, Bloomington, 47401. Betty Jo Irvine, Fine Arts Librn
Holdings: Vols (57,000) Cat Pix Microforms
Budget: ($52,000)
Notes: Art forms relevant to the periods and places involved.

MA —WELLESLEY COLLEGE, Art Library, Wellesley, 02181. Katherine D Finkelpearl, Art Librn
Holdings: Vols (30,000) Cat Pix Slides
Budget: ($22,000)
Notes: Primarily the art and architecture of Western Europe, the Far East, and classical antiquity. However, efforts are being made to expand the collection in the areas of photography, primitive art, and ancient (non-classical) art. The Art Department maintains a separate collection of 62,500 mounted pictures and 90,000 slides.

MO —THE NELSON-ATKINS MUSEUM OF ART, Kenneth & Helen Spencer Art Reference Library, 4525 Oak St, Kansas City, 64111. Stanley W Hess, Librn

ART, APPLIED see Art Industries and Trade

ART, ARABIC

†NY —ARAB INFORMATION CENTER, League of Arab States, 747 Third Ave, New York, 10017.

ART, ASIAN

CA —ASIAN ART MUSEUM OF SAN FRANCISCO, Library, Golden Gate Park, San Francisco, 94118. Fred A Cline Jr, Librn
Holdings: Vols (16,000) Cat Mss Pix Microforms Clippings
Notes: The Avery Brundage Collection of Oriental Art. Emphasis on East Asian, Southeast Asian and East Indian art. Also building a microfilm library; collecting pictures and clipping files. Noncirculating. No interlibrary loans.

DC —FREER GALLERY OF ART, Library, 12th & Jefferson Dr SW, Washington, 20560. Ellen A Nollman, Librn

MI —UNIVERSITY OF MICHIGAN, Fine Arts Library, Tappan Hall, Ann Arbor, 48109. Margaret Jensen, Fine Arts Librn; Joy Alexander, Cur Slide Collection
Holdings: Vols (50,000) Cat Slides Microforms
Notes: The slide collection (250,000 slides) is owned and serviced by the History of Art Department; it is not part of the University of Michigan library system, but is used in conjunction with the library material, and housed in the same building.

MO —WASHINGTON UNIVERSITY, Art & Architecture Library, Saint Louis, 63130. Imre Meszaros, Librn
Holdings: Vols (60,413) Cat Maps Pix Microforms
Budget: ($100,000)
Notes: Art and architecture of East Asia; rare books; archaeology; fashion design.

WA —UNIVERSITY OF WASHINGTON LIBRARIES, East Asia Library, DO-27, Seattle, 98195. Karl Lo, Head
Holdings: Vols (300,000) Cat Microforms
Budget: ($200,000)
Notes: Southwest China: Joseph Rock Collection, ca 2000 vols; modern Chinese poetry, 1919 to date: ca 700 titles; Asian art, esp Japanese painting: 4097 vols; Tiao-yu-t'ai movement in the US: ca 400 items of periodicals and pamphlets; modern Korean poetry, ancient and modern: ca 1000 titles; Mu-yu-shu folk literature: ca 1000 items.

ART, BAROQUE

FL —RINGLING MUSEUM OF ART, Art Research Library, PO Box 1838, Sarasota, 33578. Lynell A Morr, Librn
Holdings: Vols (40,000) Cat
Budget: ($24,000)
Notes: Incl an additional 30,000 art auction catalogs, indexed 1970-date.

MA —SMITH COLLEGE, Hillyer Art Library, Fine Arts Center, Northampton, 01063. Karen Harvey, Librn
Holdings: Vols (45,000) Cat Pix Slides

OH —OBERLIN COLLEGE LIBRARY, Clarence Ward Art Library, Allen Art Bldg, Oberlin, 44074. Jeffrey Weidman, Librn
Holdings: Vols (62,000) Cat Microforms
Notes: Traditional strength in Northern and Southern Baroque. Have *Decimal Index to the Art of the Low Countries* (DIAL).

PA —BRYN MAWR COLLEGE, Canaday Library, Bryn Mawr, 19010. James Tanis, Dir
Notes: Baroque and Italian Renaissance painting and architecture; late antique and early Christian art; Flemish and Dutch painting 15th - 17th centuries; French painting 18th - 19th centuries. In Art and Archaeology Library.

ART, BELGIAN

IL —BLACK HAWK COLLEGE, Learning Resources Center, 6600 34 Ave, Moline, 61265. Donald C Rowland, Dir
Holdings: Vols 773 Cat Pix Audiotapes
Notes: Emphasis on fine arts. Entire college collection a gift of the Belgian Consul.

ART, BLACK see Art, African and Afro-American

ART, BOTANICAL

†CA —HUNTINGTON BOTANICAL GARDENS LIBRARY, 1151 Oxford Rd, San Marino, 91108. Ann Ravenscroft, Secretary
Holdings: Vols (8000)
Notes: Emphases on history of botanical science; papers and notes of American botanists and naturalists of The West; botanical illustration, etc. Subtropical horticulture, incl cacti and succulents of Australia, South Africa, and Mexico.

NY —NEW YORK BOTANICAL GARDEN LIBRARY, Bronx, 10458. Charles R Long, Asst Vice Pres & Dir
Notes: One of the largest botanical collections in the world. Over 900,000 items. Covers botany (150,000 vols), botanists (3000), horticulture (45,000) plant diseases (25,000), plant physiology (15,000), history of botany (1500), conservation of natural resources (15,000), gardening (13,000), paleobotany (7000), ecology (20,000), forestry (5000) medical botany (3000), agriculture (9000) and biology (20,000). Reference library; materials do not circulate, except for member circulating collection (1200) and standard inter-library loan. About 5000 vols uncataloged. Incl art, books, serials, pamphlets, archives and manuscripts, vertical files, microfiche and microfilm, nursery and seed catalogs, photographs, paintings, prints, drawings and engravings. Covers all areas of botanical sciences. This is an OCLC library with fullresource services incl photocopying and photography.

OH —GARDEN CENTER OF GREATER CLEVELAND, Eleanor Squire Library, 11030 East Blvd, Cleveland, 44106. Richard T Isaacson, Librn
Notes: The Warren C Corning Collection of Horticultural Classics. The Flowering Plant Index of Illustration and Information.

PA —HUNT INSTITUTE FOR BOTANICAL DOCUMENTATION, Hunt Botanical Library, Carnegie-Mellon University, Pittsburgh, 15213. Bernadette G Callery, Librn
Holdings: Vols 23,000 Cat Pix
Notes: Collection of primarily historical botany and plant taxonomy, especially 1730-1840. Includes approximately 500 15th through 17th century herbals, extensive collection of 18th and 19th century color-plate works, floras and monographic works, and other works on natural history, early gardening and horticulture, and travel, particularly that dealing with plant exploration and introduction. Extensive biographical materials, on people in plant sciences. Reference collection and extensive documentation in botanical bibliography, especially concerning books published before 1850. Includes as separate collections, the Strandell Collection of Linnaeana and the Michel Adanson Library. Over 800 items described in *Catalogue of Botanical Books in the Collection of Rachel McMasters Miller Hunt, 1477-1800* (Pittsburgh, 1958-1960).

ART, BRITISH

CT —YALE UNIVERSITY, Yale Center for British Art, Rare Book Dept, New Haven, 06520. Joan Friedman, Cur
Notes: One of the greatest assemblages of British Art of the 17th-19th centuries.

BC —VANCOUVER ART GALLERY, Library, 750 Hornby St, Vancouver, V6Z 2H7, Can. Catherine M Cowan, Librn

ART, BUDDHIST

CT —YALE UNIVERSITY, Box 1603A, Yale Station, New Haven, 06520.
Notes: A major collection of Tibetan Buddhist paintings, bronze images and books.

MA —HARVARD UNIVERSITY LIBRARY, Fine Arts Library, Rubel Asiatic Research Collection, Sackler Museum, 38 Quincy Street, Cambridge, 02138. Yen-Shew Lynn Chao, Librn
Holdings: Vols (12,000)
Notes: Rubel Asiatic Research Collection; specializes exclusively in the acquisition of Oriental language (Chinese, Japanese, and Korean) materials. Particular strengths incl the areas of Buddhist arts, Chinese bronzes and painting, Japanese painting and prints, and Chinese and Japanese ceramics. Also large holdings of oriental art periodicals, reprints, and exhibition and sales catalogs.

NY —INSTITUTE FOR ADVANCED STUDIES OF WORLD RELIGIONS (IASWR), Melville Memorial Library, State University of New York, Stony Brook, 11794. C T Shen, Dir
Holdings: Vols 1000 Cat Periodicals
Notes: Incl monographs and illustrated materials on Buddhist art in its many ethno-cultural expressions, viz architecture, calligraphy, ceremonial acts not excluding dance and drama, painting, sculpture, etc, of central, east, south, and southeast Asia. Refer inquiries to H G Robinson and L L Yang.
See also entry under Art, Oriental

ART, BYZANTINE

CA —UNIVERSITY OF CALIFORNIA, LOS ANGELES, Art Library, Los Angeles, 90024. Max Marmor, Library Assistant
Holdings: Pix Microforms
Notes: Art; Art History; Early Christian and Byzantine Art; Medieval Art; Apostolic Age to 1400; Iconography; Photo Archive; Christian Art and Symbolism.

DC —HARVARD UNIVERSITY, Dumbarton Oaks, Research Library, 1703 32nd St NW, Washington, 20007. Irene Vaslef, Librn
Holdings: Vols (91,000) Cat Maps Pix Slides Microforms
Budget: ($219,000)
Notes: Byzantine civilization (including art, archaeology, literature, history, religion, law, music, etc). Extensive supplemental material on Classical, Hellenistic, Medieval, Islamic, Medieval Slavic cultures. 62,000 b/w photographs, 25,000 slides and transparencies, 1000 microfilms of books and manuscripts. Printed description of collection in *Harvard Library Bulletin,* vol 19, no 1 (Jan 1971), pp 25-35 and vol 19, no 2 (April 1971), pp 204-214, pp 25-35 and vol 19, no 2 (April 1971), pp 204-214.

IL —ORIENTAL INSTITUTE, 1155 E 58th St, Chicago, 60637. John Larsen, Archivist
Notes: The Bernhard Moritz Collection. Fine examples of bindings as well as of Islamic calligraphy and writing materials--papyrus, parchment, papers, etc. Extensive collection is also in the Beatty Library in Dublin, Ireland; Victoria and Albert Museum in London; Libraries in East and West Germany.

MD —JOHNS HOPKINS UNIVERSITY, Milton S Eisenhower Library, Charles & 34 Sts, Baltimore, 21218. Ann S Gwyn, Assistant Dir for Special Collections
Holdings: Vols (18,000) Cat Maps
Notes: Strongest in ancient, Byzantine, and Renaissance art and architecture. Reference Library lacks some periodicals. Modern period being rapidly built up.

NY —SAINT VLADIMIRS' ORTHODOX THEOLOGICAL SEMINARY, 575 Scarsdale Rd, Yonkers, 10707. Paul D Garrett, Librn
Holdings: Vols (36,000) Pix
Notes: Incl 250 periodicals. A major source of materials on Orthodox Church theology. Much on works of art.

OH —OHIO STATE UNIVERSITY, Fine Arts Library, 1813 N High St, Columbus, 43210. Susan Wyngaard, Head, Fine Arts Library
Holdings: Vols (75,000) Cat Microforms
Budget: ($60,000)
Notes: Also have 1000 uncataloged exhibition catalogs. Book collection strong in history of art especially in area of medieval & Northern Renaissance art. Good collection of portfolios. Photographic collections on microfiche. Receive Slavic titles, many on Byzantine frescoes. Online catalog. Decimal Index of the Art of the Low Countries, as well as Marburger Index; Index Photographique de i' Arten France; Alinari Archives on microfiche and other major microform collections in art.

PA —UNIVERSITY OF PITTSBURGH, Henry Clay Frick Fine Arts Library, Pittsburgh, 15260. Anne W Gordon, Fine Arts Librn
Holdings: Vols (55,000) Cat Pix Slides Microforms
Notes: Emphasis is on the art of the Western World--architecture, sculpture, painting, minor arts, archaeology, with special strength in the Byzantine, early Christian, medieval, renaissance and modern periods. The Oriental field is represented, incl replicas of scrolls. Studio arts are also covered. Illuminated ms facsimiles. Extensive collections of slides and photographs for study of art history are available in the building but not administered by the art library.

ART, CALIFORNIA

CA —CRAFT AND FOLK ART MUSEUM, Library, 5814 Wilshire Blvd, Los Angeles, 90036. Joan M Benedetti, Museum Librn
Holdings: Vols (2000) Slides VF
Notes: Incl 2000 books; 70 journal subscriptions; artists' biographical files: 6 file drawers; clipping files: 8 file drawers; 20,000 slides. Representation of the material culture of all people, traditional and contemporary expressions. Incl visual and printed information on ethnic, traditional, popular, decorative, idiosyncratic, and contemporary crafts as well as vernacular architecture, handmade houses, and design. Information about and for professional artists on health hazards, conservation, and career management. Anthropological and art historical works; exhibition catalogues; slides, photographs, audiocassettes; clipping and pamphlet files. Contemporary Slide Registry of Craftspeople and extensive biographical files of contemporary craft artists. Information and referral files of craft related galleries, shops, festivals, organizations, etc.

DC —SMITHSONIAN INSTITUTION, National Museum of American Art & the National Portrait Gallery Library, Eighth & F Sts, NW, Washington, 20560. Cecilia Chin, Librn
Holdings: Vols (47,000) Cat Microforms
Budget: ($60,000)
Notes: The "Ferdinand Perret Library": 180 scrapbooks (with card index) on California art and artists, incl clippings, catalogs, reproductions, etc.

ART, CAMBODIAN

CA —SAN DIEGO PUBLIC LIBRARY, Art, Music & Recreation Sect, 820 E St, San Diego, 92101. Barbara A Tuhill, Supvr
Holdings: Vols 500 Cat Pix
Notes: Emphasis on Chinese, Japanese, Korean, and Cambodian art. Private library of Donal Hord, local sculptor. For reference use only.

ART, CANADIAN

AB —PETER WHYTE FOUNDATION, Gallery, Box 160, Banff, T0L 0C0, Can. Mary Andrews, Librn
Holdings: Vols (935)
Budget: ($800)
Notes: Small general collection, with quite a bit on Canadian and American art, much of it donations from private collections.

BC —VANCOUVER ART GALLERY, Library, 750 Hornby St, Vancouver, V6Z 2H7, Can. Catherine M Cowan, Librn

MB —UNIVERSITY OF MANITOBA, Elizabeth Dafoe Library, Archives and Special Collections Dept, Winnipeg, R3T 2N2, Can. Richard E Bennett, Dept Head; Corrado A Santoro, Reference Archivist
Notes: Bertram R Brooker Papers. Correspondence, diaries and daily notations, dramas, both published and unpublished, short stories and essays, and other literary works. Also 16 photographs mainly of Brooker, his family and fellow artists.

ON —NATIONAL GALLERY OF CANADA, Library, National Museums of Canada, Ottawa, K1A 0M8, Can. J Hunter, Chief Librn
Holdings: Vols (72,000)
Notes: History of art (postmediaeval, Western). Public reference only. Circulating only to gallery staff and on interlibrary loan. 1000 periodical titles currently received. 50, 000 pamphlets, mostly exhibition and sales catalogs (not cataloged). 40,000 items in documentation files: clippings, notices of exhibitions and other ephemera. Exchange of National Gallery publications with other art galleries. Special section on history of Canadian art. Emphasis of collection on painting, sculpture, graphic arts and photography. Study collection of photographs and slides. See *Catalogue of the National Gallery of Canada*, 8 vols (Boston: G K Hall, 1973) and *Supplement*, 6 vols (Boston: G K Hall, 1981).

ON —PUBLIC ARCHIVES OF CANADA, Library, 395 Wellington St, Ottawa, K1A 0N3, Can. Dawn E Monroè, Collections Development Officer
Holdings: Vols (80,000) Cat
Notes: The Library's collection related to material culture consists primarily of works on the history of fashion and clothing, architecture, crafts, traditional trades and technology. In the area of visual culture, there are works on the history of visual arts, the cinema, television and photgraphy.

ON —METROPOLITAN TORONTO LIBRARY, Fine Arts Dept, 789 Yonge St, Toronto, M4W 2G8, Can. Alan Suddon, Head
Holdings: Vols (42,000) Cat Pix Microforms
Notes: Extensive collection.

ON —UNIVERSITY OF TORONTO, Thomas Fisher Rare Book Library, 120 Saint George St, Toronto, M5S 1A5, Can. Richard G Landon, Head
Holdings: Vols (30,000) Mss
Notes: All currently published and most earlier major works on the fine and applied arts in Canada; Canadian art exhibition catalogues; limited editions illustrated by Canadian artists; 19th and 20th century architectural plans for buildings in Toronto and southern Ontario vicinity (ca 1700). Langdon Collection, named for donor, John E Langdon. Contains material on silver and silversmiths around the world with special emphasis on Canada.

PE —CONFEDERATION CENTRE ART GALLERY & MUSEUM, Art Reference Library, PO Box 848, Charlottetown, C1A 7L9, Can. David Webber, Dir
Holdings: Vols (3500) Cat Slides Phonorecords Audiotapes 16mm Films Filmstrips
Budget: ($2500)
Notes: Incl videotapes of local PEI artists; and 2000 slides.

ART, CEREMONIAL

NY —YIVO INSTITUTE FOR JEWISH RESEARCH, Library & Archives, 1048 Fifth Ave, New York, 10028. Dina Abramowicz, Librn; Marek Web, Archivist
Holdings: Cat Mss Pix Slides
Notes: Original works and reference materials, incl reproductions of 1500 objects; 500 slides. Separate catalog.

ART, CHINESE

CA —UNIVERSITY OF CALIFORNIA, BERKELEY, University Library, East Asiatic Library, Room 208, Durant Hall, Berkeley, 94720. Donald Shively, Head
Holdings: Vols 245,000 Cat Mss Maps Pix Microforms
Notes: Research

CA —SAN DIEGO PUBLIC LIBRARY, Art, Music & Recreation Sect, 820 E St, San Diego, 92101. Barbara A Tuhill, Supvr
Holdings: Vols 500 Cat Pix
Notes: Emphasis on Chinese, Japanese, Korean, and Cambodian art. Private library of Donal Hord, local sculptor. For reference use only.

CA —ASIAN ART MUSEUM OF SAN FRANCISCO, Library, Golden Gate Park, San Francisco, 94118. Fred A Cline Jr, Librn
Holdings: Vols (16,000) Cat Mss Pix Microforms Clippings
Notes: The Avery Brundage Collection of Oriental Art. Emphasis on East Asian, Southeast Asian and East Indian art. Also building a microform library; collecting pictures and clipping files. Noncirculating. No interlibrary loan.

CT —CONNECTICUT COLLEGE, Library, Mohegan Ave, New London, 06320. Brian Rogers, College Librn
Holdings: Vols 600 Cat
Notes: Holdings incl the Helen Carey Coudert Collection of nearly 500 books on Chinese and Japanese painting, sculpture and bronzes.

DC —FREER GALLERY OF ART, Library, 12th & Jefferson Dr SW, Washington, 20560. Ellen A Nollman, Librn

HI —HONOLULU ACADEMY OF ARTS, Robert Allerton Library, 900 S Beretania St, Honolulu, 96814. Anne T Seaman, Librn

IL —UNIVERSITY OF ILLINOIS, URBANA/CHAMPAIGN, Asian Library,

ART, CHINESE (cont.)

Urbana, 61801. William S Wong, Asian Librn
Holdings: Vols 82,000 Cat
Notes: South and West Asian Collection. Primarily a collection of South Asian and Middle Eastern language materials.

KS —OTTAWA UNIVERSITY, Myers Library, Ottawa, 66067. J Marion Rioth, Head Librn
Holdings: Vols 2350 Cat Maps Pix
Budget: $150
Notes: This started as a collection of studies about Chinese ceramics, art, and related areas. Incl 800 vols on general Asian studies. If this collection has any unique feature it is in the field of 19th century ceramics trade, especailly Chinese. There is a bibliography of the collection.

MA —HARVARD UNIVERSITY LIBRARY, Fine Arts Library, Rubel Asiatic Research Collection, Sackler Museum, 38 Quincy Street, Cambridge, 02138. Yen-Shew Lynn Chao, Librn
Holdings: Cat Mss Maps Pix Slides
Notes: Rubel Asiatic Research Collection; specializes exclusively in the acquisition of Oriental language (Chinese, Japanese, and Korean) materials. Particular strengths incl the areas of Buddhist arts, Chinese bronzes and painting, Japanese painting and prints, and Chinese and Japanese ceramics. Also large holdings of oriental art periodicals, reprints, and exhibition and sales catalogs.

MO —THE NELSON-ATKINS MUSEUM OF ART, Kenneth & Helen Spencer Art Reference Library, 4525 Oak St, Kansas City, 64111. Stanley W Hess, Librn
Notes: Strong in painting, furniture, ceramics, bronzes; journals, bulletins.

OH —OHIO UNIVERSITY, Vernon R Alden Library, Athens, 45701. Kent Mulliner, Africana Specialist
Notes: A collection of 634 vols of Chinese books covering a wide range of subjects incl art, culture, economics, geography, history, language, literature, martial arts, medical science, philosophy, and technology.

PA —EASTERN COLLEGE, Frank Warner Memorial Library, Saint Davids, 19087. James L Sauer, Librn
Holdings: Uncat Mss Pix
Notes: The Harry C Goebel Collection. Incl Bruce Rogers printings (over 460); press books (about 350); oriental art (over 250); bookplates (with a separate collection of an almost complete set of bookplates designed by Edwin Davis French); Christmas Books; art and graphic arts (incl the French Graphic Arts Collection of Adolph DeMilly); first editions of Christopher Morley; Print Collection (1315 prints); Oriental art realia and artifacts.

ART, CHRISTIAN see Christian Art and Symbolism

ART, CLASSICAL

CA —CALIFORNIA STATE UNIVERSITY, LONG BEACH, University Library, Reference Center, 1250 Bellflower Blvd, Long Beach, 90840. Henry J DuBois, Librn
Holdings: Cat Slides
Notes: Collection of 60,000 slides offers examples of virtually all types and periods of art, incl an extensive collection of slides of mss from the Bodleian Library, Oxford, a special series on Latin American art, another on the arts of the US Collection is cataloged using Fogg Museum classification. No photocopying.

CA —J PAUL GETTY MUSEUM, Research Library, 17985 Pacific Coast Highway, Malibu, 90265. Anne-Mieke Halbrook, Head Librn
Holdings: Vols (140,000) Cat

CT —YALE UNIVERSITY LIBRARY, Classical Art Slide Collection, Phelps Hall, Room 505, 344 College St, New Haven, 06520. Carla Lukas, Librn
Holdings: Cat Pix Slides
Notes: Nearly 25,000 slides of classical art.

DC —HARVARD UNIVERSITY, Dumbarton Oaks, Research Library, 1703 32nd St NW, Washington, 20007. Irene Vaslef, Librn
Holdings: Vols (91,000) Cat Maps Pix Slide Microforms
Budget: ($219,000)
Notes: Byzantine civilization (including art, archaeology, literature, history, religion, law, music, etc). Extensive supplemental material on Classical, Hellenistic, Medieval, Islamic, Medieval Slavic cultures. 62,000 b/w photographs, 25,000 slides and transparencies, 1000 microfilms of books and manuscripts. Printed description of collection in *Harvard Library Bulletin*, vol 19, no 1 (Jan 1971), pp 25-35 and vol 19, no 2 (April 1971), pp 204-214, pp 25-35 and vol 19, no 2 (April 1971), pp 204-214.

IN —INDIANA UNIVERSITY, Art Museum Bldg, Fine Arts Bldg, Bloomington, 47401. Betty Jo Irvine, Fine Arts Librn
Holdings: Vols (57,000) Cat Pix Microforms
Budget: ($52,000)

MO —THE NELSON-ATKINS MUSEUM OF ART, Kenneth & Helen Spencer Art Reference Library, 4525 Oak St, Kansas City, 64111. Stanley W Hess, Librn

TX —RICE UNIVERSITY, Art Library, 6100 S Main St, PO Box 1892, Houston, 77001. Jet Marie Prendeville, Librn
Holdings: Vols 7,040 Cat
Budget: ($28,100)
Notes: The Art Library collection covers all periods of Western Art with particular emphasis upon Classical Archaelogy, Medieval, Renaissance, and Modern Art and Architecture. The collection also offers representative coverage of film, photography, and Oriental art.

ART, CLUNIAC

MA —HARVARD UNIVERSITY, Graduate School of Design, Frances Loeb Library, Gund Hall, Cambridge, 02138. James Hodgson, Librn
Holdings: Cat Mss Pix
Notes: Materials deposited by Professor Kenneth J Conant, who was in charge of archaeological excavations at Cluny.

ART, COMMERCIAL see Commercial Art

ART, CONCEPTUAL

CA —CALIFORNIA INSTITUTE OF THE ARTS, Library, 24700 McBean Pkwy, Valencia, 91355. James Elrod, Dir
Holdings: Vols (61,000) Slides
Budget: ($11,000)
Notes: Modern art, incl abstract, conceptual, concrete, environment, minimal, and pop art; art; dadaism; surrealism; happenings; and caricatures and cartoons. Slides (61,683).

NY —MUSEUM OF MODERN ART, Library, 11 W 53 St, New York, 10019. Clive Phillpot, Library Dir
Holdings: Vols (80,000) Cat Mss Audiotapes Microforms VF
Notes: See *Catalog of the Library of the Museum of Modern Art, New York City* (Boston: G K Hall, 1976), 14 vols. Collection incl exhibition catalogs.

ART, CONCRETE

CA —CALIFORNIA INSTITUTE OF THE ARTS, Library, 24700 McBean Pkwy, Valencia, 91355. James Elrod, Dir
Holdings: Vols (48,300) Slides
Budget: ($8900)
Notes: Modern art, incl abstract, conceptual, concrete, environment, minimal, and pop art; dadaism; surrealism; happenings; and caricatures and cartoons.

ART, CONTEMPORARY see Art, Modern—20th Century

ART, CZECH

IL —CZECHOSLOVAK HERITAGE MUSEUM AND LIBRARY, 2701 S Harlem Ave, Berwyn, 60402.
Holdings: Vols 700
Notes: Incl 250 periodicals, 450 artifacts, 500 art works. A major resource for American-Czech and Slovak history. Much on Chicago's Czech community. Also collection of books written in "Schwabach."

NE —UNIVERSITY OF NEBRASKA-LINCOLN, Don L Love Library, Czech Heritage Collection, Lincoln, 68588. Joseph G Svoboda, University Archivist
Holdings: Vols (3000) Cat Mss Pix Audiotapes Microforms
Notes: The Czech Heritage Collection.

ART, DECORATIVE

CA —CRAFT AND FOLK ART MUSEUM, Library, 5814 Wilshire Blvd, Los Angeles, 90036. Joan M Benedetti, Museum Librn
Holdings: Vols (2000) Slides VF
Notes: Incl 2000 books; 70 journal subscriptions; artists' biographical files: 6 file drawers; clipping files: 8 file drawers; 20,000 slides. Representation of the material culture of all people, traditional and contemporary expressions. Incl visual and printed information on ethnic, traditional, popular, decorative, idiosyncratic, and contemporary crafts as well as vernacular architecture, handmade houses, and design. Information about and for professional artists on health hazards, conservation, and career management. Anthropological and art historical works; exhibition catalogues; slides, photographs, audiocassettes; clipping and pamphlet files. Contemporary Slide Registry of Craftspeople and extensive biographical files of contemporary craft artists. Information and referral files of craft related galleries, shops, festivals, organizations, etc.

CA —J PAUL GETTY MUSEUM, Research Library, 17985 Pacific Coast Highway, Malibu, 90265. Anne-Mieke Halbrook, Head Librn
Holdings: Vols (140,000) Cat
Notes: French 18th century.

CA —J PAUL GETTY MUSEUM, Photo Archives, 17985 Pacific Coast Hwy, Malibu, 90265. William Reeder, Cur
Holdings: Pix
Notes: Incl photographs of works of art at the Museum (180,000 cataloged, 500,000 uncataloged), incl ancient art, western European art (painting, sculpture, graphics) and European decorative arts, medieval and Renaissance to 19th century, and antiquities.

CT —STOWE-DAY LIBRARY, 77 Forest St, Hartford, 06105. Diana J Royce, Librn
Holdings: Vols (15,000) Cat Mss Pix
Notes: 150,000 cataloged mss and publications concerning architecture, decorative arts, history and literature of the period 1840-1900, with emphasis on Nook Farm, Mark Twain, Harriet Beecher Stowe, Calvin E Stowe, Charles Dudley Warner, William Hooker Gillette, Isabella Beecher Hooker. Incl 5000 pictures.

CT —LYMAN ALLYN MUSEUM, Library, 100 Mohegan Ave, New London, 06320. Mrs D Dinsmore, Librn
Holdings: Vols (5550) Cat Maps Pix
Budget: $2000
Notes: Books on old Master Drawing and the Decorative Arts. Noncirculating library with emphasis on scholarly historical works and museum and exhibition catalogs. Also incl American museum bulletins (uncataloged).

DE —HENRY F DUPONT WINTERTHUR MUSEUM LIBRARY, Winterthur, 19735. Frank H Sommer, III, Head
Holdings: Cat
Notes: Strong collections.

DC —NATIONAL SOCIETY, DAUGHTERS OF THE AMERICAN REVOLUTION, DAR Museum Reference Library, 1776 D St NW, Washington, 20006. Christine Minter-Dowd, Dir; Michael W Berry, Cur; Jean Martin, Registrar
Holdings: Vols (1600) Cat
Budget: ($500)
Notes: American decorative arts, 1700-1850, especially ceramics (incl British imports and Chinese export porcelain) and silverware.

IL —CHICAGO PUBLIC LIBRARY, Art Section, Fine Arts Division, 78 E Washington St, Chicago, 60602. Rosalinda I Hack, Fine Arts Division Chief; Yvonne S

ART, DECORATIVE (cont.)

Brown, Head, Art Section
Holdings: Vols 42,000
Notes: Reference and circulating collection of books, periodicals, exhibition catalogs, dissertations, picture collections, and microforms on all aspects of the visual arts. Major concentration of art history, especially European, with concentration on 19th and 20th century art movements and artists. We attempt to represent the works of recognized artists past and present. The Decorative Arts are well represented especially in the areas of antiques, interior decoration, and handicrafts. The collection is supplemented by a strong periodical collection, consisting of 330 current English and Foreign subscriptions, the majority of these titles we bind, as well as strong bound retrospective collections. The visual arts is supported by a clipping File on Chicago Artists, a current exhibition catalogs collection, as well as by the microfilm collections of the*Chicago Art Institute Scrapbooks,* the *Scrapbook on Art,* Artists, and the *Index of American Design.*

IN —WILLARD LIBRARY, 21 First Ave, Evansville, 47710. Joan Elliott, Special Collections Librn
Holdings: Vols (1400) Cat
Budget: ($3500)
Notes: The Thrall Art Book Collection. Circulating collection of art books being purchased by special endowment. Emphasis on fine arts of all times and places, with particular reference to American artists, as well as European and American decorative arts and architecture. Noncirculating.

IN —ALLEN COUNTY PUBLIC LIBRARY, 900 Webster St, Fort Wayne, 46802. Paul Deane, Reader Services Dept Head; Kay Lynn Isca, Art Music & AV Dept Head

IN —THE ART CENTER, Library, 120 St Joseph St, South Bend, 46601. Judy Oberhausen, Cur
Holdings: Vols (1010) Cat Slides
Notes: 500 slides. This Art Center has a specific, separate collection--"The Arts of the United States"--which has its own index and is geared toward American painting, graphics, architecture, design and decorative arts, from the 19th to the 20th century, and sculpture works on paper. Incl 32 periodical titles.

ME —WILLIAM A FARNSWORTH LIBRARY & ART MUSEUM, 19 Elm St, Rockland, 04841. Marius B Peladeau, Dir
Holdings: Vols (4000) Cat Pix Microforms
Notes: Emphasis on American and European fine and decorative arts of all periods (largely modern). Other areas include marine history and Maine history (local); illustrated books and rare books also a part of our collection, which has its own catalog. Also, Louise Nevelsen, N C Wyeth Archives.

ME —OLD YORK HISTORICAL SOCIETY, Library, PO Box 312, York, 03909. Eldridge H Pendleton, Dir of Collections
Holdings: Vols (3950) Cat Mss Maps Pix
Budget: $250
Notes: Maine history; York County Town Histories, Town of York Genealogies.

MD —BALTIMORE MUSEUM OF ART LIBRARY, Art Museum Dr, Baltimore, 21218. Anita Gilden, Librn
Holdings: Vols (40,000) Cat
Notes: General reference sources with emphasis on 19th and 20th century art and American decorative art. Incl prints and drawings. Photocopying.

MA —BOSTON PUBLIC LIBRARY, Copley Sq, Boston, 02117. Theresa D Cederholm, Cur of Fine Arts
Notes: Collection incl 138,000 titles (not incl multiple vols sets, serials, and unbound materials); VF on regional artists, architects, art organizations.

MA —HISTORIC DEERFIELD-POCUMTUCK VALLEY MEMORIAL ASSOCIATION, Libraries, Memorial St, Box 53, Deerfield, 01342. David R Proper, Librn
Holdings: Vols (6500) Cat Mss Maps Pix Slides Microforms
Notes: American decorative arts, from colonial times to date. Also, a substantial collection of sketches, patterns, mss, printed material, and color swatches relating to needlework, embroidery and related arts.

MA —OLD STURBRIDGE VILLAGE, Research Library, Sturbridge, 01566. Theresa Rini Percy, Librn
Holdings: Cat Mss Pix
Notes: New England, 1790-1850, incl ceramics, furniture, textiles, glass, metal work, etc.

MA —STERLING AND FRANCINE CLARK ART INSTITUTE LIBRARY, 225 South St, PO Box 8, Williamstown, 01267. Michael Rinehart, Librn
Holdings: Vols (77,000) Cat Pix Slides Microforms
Budget: ($105,000)
Notes: Primarily European art, 1300-present, and post-Columbian American art. Incl 850, 000 pictures, 80,000 slides, 400 microfilm reels, 25,000 auction sale catalogs, and Mary Ann Beinecke Decorative Art Collection.

MI —CRANBROOK ACADEMY OF ART, 500 Lone Pine Rd, Box 801, Bloomfield Hills, 48013. Diane Gunn, Librn
Holdings: Vols (25,000) Slides

MI —EDISON INSTITUTE, Greenfield Village and Henry Ford Museum, Archives & Research Library, PO Box 1970, Dearborn, 48121. Steve Hamp, Dir; Joan W Gartland, Librn
Holdings: Vols 400,000 Cat Mss Maps Microforms
Notes: 400,000 vols incl pamphlets. The Archives and research library supports the program of Greenfield Village and the Henry Ford Museum. Special collections incl: automotive literature, ephemera, McGuffey Readers, trade catalogs, photographs and graphics.

MI —DETROIT PUBLIC LIBRARY, Fine Arts Department, 5201 Woodward Ave, Detroit, 48202. Shirley Solvick, Chief
Holdings: Vols 60,000 Cat Pix
Budget: ($20,000)
Notes: Downs number 2882, 2923, 2938. Book collection covers all phases of art. Picture collection of over 500,000 items covers all subjects; especially strong in the fine and decorative arts, portraits, costume, and Detroit.

MI —MICHIGAN STATE UNIVERSITY, Art Library, East Lansing, 48824. Shirlee A Studt, Librn
Holdings: Vols (45,000) Cat
Notes: The Illuminated Manuscript Facsimile Collection includes examples of religious and secular works from the earliest codex to the age of printing. It has particular strengths in Carolingian, Ottonian, French Gothic and works from the British Isles. The facsimile collection is strengthened by related research materials (biographical material, critical studies, etc) The facsimile collection and related materials are part of a 45,000 volume separately housed and staffed collection on the visual and decorative arts (including photography) serving the curricular and research needs of the University community. A guide to full facsimiles in the collection is available in the Art Library and in the Special Collections division. A strong collection of architectural history.

MO —THE NELSON-ATKINS MUSEUM OF ART, Kenneth & Helen Spencer Art Reference Library, 4525 Oak St, Kansas City, 64111. Stanley W Hess, Librn
Notes: European and American.

MO —SAINT LOUIS ART MUSEUM, Richardson Memorial Library, Saint Louis, 63110. Ann B Abid, Librn
Holdings: Vols (30,000) Cat Pix Slides Microforms
Notes: Art history, incl decorative arts, catalogs, exhibitions, etc.

NH —NEW HAMPSHIRE HISTORICAL SOCIETY, Library, 30 Park St, Concord, 03301. William Copeley, Assoc Librn
Holdings: Vols 2000 Cat
Budget: ($9000)
Notes: New Hampshire and New England decorative arts.

NH —STRAWBERY BANKE, Thayer Cumings Historical Reference Library, Portsmouth, 03801. Nicole R Osborn, Librn
Holdings: Vols (2850) Cat Mss Maps Pix Microforms
Budget: ($1900)
Notes: The Library is a small, highly specialized library with holdings in American art, architecture and decorative arts. The collection is especially strong in the American decorative arts, with additional concentration in European decorative arts. In addition, the collection contains books on American painting, American architecture, archaeology, technology, maritime history and boatbuilding, landscape gardening and design, as well as books on local and regional history and social and material culture of the 17th-19th centuries. Collection of mss microfilm and documents is related to important properties and personages of Portsmouth and the surrounding area.

NJ —NEWARK MUSEUM LIBRARY, 49 Washington St, PO Box 540, Newark, 07101. Margaret DiSalvi, Librn
Holdings: Vols 4000 Cat Pix Slides

NY —HISTORICAL SOCIETY OF EARLY AMERICAN DECORATION, 19 Dove St, Albany, 12210. Doris Fry, Dir; Laura Olf, Librn
Holdings: Cat Pix Slides
Notes: The Library is housed with the Museum Collection of the Society. Incl examples of 19th century American country painting on tin, stenciling on wood and tin, bronzing decoration on wood, English stencilled tin and wood, bronzed items, painted objects, reverse painting on glass and examples of other decorating techniques of the period. Also included is a large collection of painted recordings of designs from early articles. Many of these were done by Esther Stevens Brazer in the 1930s. Another large collection has been added since that time. The library material is related to this interest. See *The Decorator,* official publication of the Historical Society of Early American Decoration. Other publications: *The Ornamented Chair* and *The Ornamented Tray* (both ed by Zilla Rider Lea), *Antique Decorations* by Brazer.

NY —BROOKLYN MUSEUM, Art Reference Library, 188 Eastern Parkway, Brooklyn, 11238.
Holdings: Vols (130,000)

NY —NEW YORK STATE HISTORICAL ASSOCIATION, Library, Lake Rd, Cooperstown, 13326. Amy Barnum, Librn
Holdings: Vols (55,000) Cat Mss Pix Slides Microforms
Notes: Emphasis on 19th-century American art. Noncirculating.

NY —CORNING MUSEUM OF GLASS LIBRARY, Corning, 14831. Norma P H Jenkins, Librn
Holdings: Vols (30,000) Cat Slides Videotapes Microfilms
Notes: Extensive and comprehensive coverage of the art, archaeology, history and early manufacture of glass, with supporting materials in art, archaeology, and the decorative arts. Collection incl some 1800 manufacturers' trade catalogs on microfiche, 10,000 periodical vols and documents. 130 videotapes, 1000 microforms. Some incumabula. Research library primarily for use on the premises.

NY —COLUMBIA UNIVERSITY LIBRARIES, Avery Architectural and Fine Arts Library, 201 Avery Hall, New York, 10027. Angela Giral, Librn
Holdings: Vols 7000
Notes: Restricted use: noncirculating.

†NY —METROPOLITAN MUSEUM OF ART, Photograph & Slide Library, 82 St & Fifth Ave, New York, 10028. Margaret P Nolan, Chief Librn
Holdings: Cat Slides
Notes: Over 286,000 (125,000 in 2 x 2 color). The slides illustrate the history of architecture, sculpture, painting and the decorative arts from prehistoric times to the present. Incl a representative coverage of the Metropolitan Museum collections as well as objects from other museums and private collections. Slides available for rental to the public.

NY —NEW YORK HISTORICAL SOCIETY, Library, 170 Central Park W, New York,

ART, DECORATIVE (cont.)

10024. James Gregory, Librn
Holdings: Mss
Notes: Incl original mss, illustrative materials, etc.

NY —LANDMARK SOCIETY OF WESTERN NEW YORK, Wenrich Memorial Library, 130 Spring Rd, Rochester, 14608.
Holdings: Vols (2000) Cat Maps Pix Slides
Budget: ($500)
Notes: Paintings, slides, drawings, as well as the Society's archives of local architecture and information on preservation and restoration techniques. Much on preservation ordinances; legal, physical and financial aspects of building preservation; local and regional history, especially of Rochester and Monroe County.

NC —NORTH CAROLINA STATE UNIVERSITY, Harry B Lyons Design Library, P. O. Box 7701, Raleigh, 27607. Maryellen LoPresti, Librn
Notes: Collection covers architecture, landscape architecture, design and related professions. Additional materials maybe found on art, painting sculpture photography and solar energy design. The library presently houses a total of 28,000 books, periodical and serial volumes to support the curriculum. A product and trade literature file and a vertical file of pamplets are also locally cataloged in the library representing an additional 3000 items of materials available for use. A significant collections of over 50,000 cataloged slides primarily representing the areas of art and architectural history are also contained in the library facility. See *Directory of Special Libraries and Information Centers*.

OH —CINCINNATI ART MUSEUM, Library, Eden Park, Cincinnati, 45202. Patrician P Rutledge, Librn
Holdings: Vols (45,850) Cat Microforms
Notes: Art library containing all subjects on art-history, graphic arts, advertising art, etc; special strength in prints, ie engravings, etc. Near Eastern art and decorative arts are also strong. At least 90,000 art exhibition catalogs. Emphasis on artists of Cincinnati and vicinity in vertical file material.

PA —ATHENAEUM OF PHILADELPHIA, 219 S Sixth St, Philadelphia, 19106. Roger W Moss Jr, Librn
Holdings: Vols (15,000)
Notes: Nineteenth century architecture and decorative arts.

PA —CHESTER COUNTY HISTORICAL SOCIETY, 225 N High St, West Chester, 19380. Rosemary B Philips, Librn; Jack McCarthy, Archivist; Laurie Rofini, Asst Archivist
Notes: Books, photographs, mss on early art, architecutre, material culture of Chester County. Especially large collection of paper dolls and paper toys (not limited to Chester County, Penn).

SC —CHARLESTON MUSEUM LIBRARY, 360 Meeting St, Charleston, 29403. John Brumgardt, Museum Dir
Holdings: Vols 30,000 Cat Mss Maps Pix

TX —AMON CARTER MUSEUM, Library, 3510 Camp Bowie Blvd, PO Box 2365, Fort Worth, 76113. Nancy G Wynne, Librn
Holdings: Vols (25,000) Cat Mss Pix
Notes: The book collection, microfilm and photo archives have been built toward the goal of the interpretation of American history through art. At present, the greatest strengths are in Americana, Western Canadiana, bibliography, American exhibition catalogs and history of photography. Substantial books and files on American artists of the 19th and early 20th century, and particularly of Charles M Russell and Frederic Remington. Incl 25,000 pictures; 13,000 slides.
See also entries under Art, American; Pictures - Collections.

VA —US NATIONAL PARK SERVICE, Harpers Ferry Center, Library, Harpers Ferry, 25425. David Nathanson, Chief Librn
Holdings: Vols 3000 Pix Slides Microforms Mss Trade Catalogs
Notes: Incl rare books and 900 trade catalogs.

VA —COLONIAL WILLIAMSBURG FOUNDATION, Abby Aldrich Rockefeller Folk Art Center, PO Box C, Williamsburg, 23187. Anne E Watkins, Registrar
Holdings: Vols (5000) Cat
Notes: American folk arts and crafts. Periodicals of current art, antiques, and history. Researchers wishing to use the library are requested to call the museum for an appointment.

WI —UNIVERSITY OF WISCONSIN, MADISON, Kohler Art Library, 800 University Ave, Madison, 53706. William C Bunce, Chief; Louise Hunning, Ref Librn
Holdings: Vols (83,000) Cat Microforms
Notes: Incl over 10,000 exhibition and auction catalogs.

WI —MILWAUKEE PUBLIC LIBRARY, 814 W Wisconsin Ave, Milwaukee, 53233. Donald J Sager, City Librn
Holdings: Vols 26,000 Cat
Budget: ($7000)
Notes: Strength in American and European decorative arts incl ceramics, glassware, jewelry, porcelain, silverware, furniture, interior decoration, textile arts and handicraft.

WI —MILWAUKEE PUBLIC MUSEUM, Reference Library, 800 W Wells St, Milwaukee, 53233. Judith Campbell Turner, Museum Librn
Holdings: Vols (90,000) Cat Maps Microforms

NS —NOVA SCOTIA MUSEUM, Library, 1747 Summer St, Halifax, B3H 3A6, Can. M S Whiteside, Librn
Holdings: Vols 2000
Notes: History of; emphases on European and North American.

ON —METROPOLITAN TORONTO LIBRARY, Fine Arts Dept, 789 Yonge St, Toronto, M4W 2G8, Can. Alan Suddon, Head
Holdings: Vols (42,000) Cat Pix Microforms
Notes: Extensive collection.

ART, EAST ASIAN see Art, Asian

ART, EAST INDIAN

CA —ASIAN ART MUSEUM OF SAN FRANCISCO, Library, Golden Gate Park, San Francisco, 94118. Fred A Cline Jr, Librn
Holdings: Vols (16,000) Cat Mss Pix Microforms Clippings
Notes: The Avery Brundage Collection of Oriental Art. Emphasis on East Asian, Southeast Asian and East Indian art. Also building a microform library; collecting pictures and clipping files. Noncirculating. No interlibrary loans.

CO —UNIVERSITY OF COLORADO, Libraries, Art & Architecture Library, Campus Box 184, Boulder, 80309. Liesel Nolan, Librn/Dept Head
Holdings: Vols (57,647) Cat Pix
Budget: ($39,000)
Notes: Special feature: art exhibition catalog collection 1963-1971, 1972-date. Good general collection with some special emphasis on environmental design, Islamic architecture, Indian art and South American Indian art. Fair collection of periodical backfiles in art and in architecture. Separate catalog for materials in collection. Rare books in main library, listed only in central union catalog.

MA —HARVARD UNIVERSITY LIBRARY, Fine Arts Library, Rubel Asiatic Research Collection, Sackler Museum, 38 Quincy Street, Cambridge, 02138. Yen-Shew Lynn Chao, Librn
Holdings: Cat Mss Maps Pix Slides
Notes: Rubel Asiatic Research Collection; specializes exclusively in the acquisition of Oriental language (Chinese, Japanese, and Korean) materials. Particular strengths incl the areas of Buddhist arts, Chinese bronzes and painting, Japanese painting and prints, and Chinese and Japanese ceramics; Indic art. Also large holdings of oriental art periodicals, reprints, and exhibition and sales catalogs.

MO —THE NELSON-ATKINS MUSEUM OF ART, Kenneth & Helen Spencer Art Reference Library, 4525 Oak St, Kansas City, 64111. Stanley W Hess, Librn
Notes: Building strength in sculpture and painting.

ART, ECCLESIASTICAL see Christian Art and Symbolism

ART, EGYPTIAN

NY —BROOKLYN MUSEUM, Wilbour Library of Egyptology, Eastern Parkway, Brooklyn, 11238. Diane Guzman, Librn
Holdings: Vols (30,000) Cat Maps
Notes: The Wilbour Library of Egyptology ranks as one of the world's finest, most complete collections of works on all aspects of the culture of Ancient Egypt (down to the Islamic conquest). A card catalog records authors, subjects, series and titles of all books, periodicals and and 12,000 pamphlets. A description of the collection, as of 1924, may be found in: William Burt Cook, Jr, *Catalogue of the Egyptological Library and other Books from the Collection of the Late Charles Edwin Wilbour* (Brooklyn, NY: Brooklyn Museum, 1924). Middle Eastern art formerly included, now transferred to the Brooklyn Museum.

ART, ENGLISH

CT —YALE UNIVERSITY, Yale Center for British Art, Rare Book Dept, New Haven, 06520. Joan Friedman, Cur
Notes: One of the greatest assemblages of British Art of the 17th-19th centuries.

UT —BRIGHAM YOUNG UNIVERSITY, Harold B Lee Library, Unversity Hill, Provo, 84602. Sterling Albrecht, Dir
Holdings: Vols 3000 Mss
Notes: Victorian books, autographed letters, mss and original drawings.

ART, ENVIRONMENTAL see Environment (Art)

ART, ESKIMO

AK —ALASKA STATE LIBRARY, Alaska Historical Library Collection, Pouch G, Juneau, 99811. Phyllis Demuth, Readers Services Librn
Holdings: Vols (24,000) Cat Mss Maps Pix Slides Phonorecords Audiotapes Videotapes 16mm Films Microforms

AK —TONGASS HISTORICAL SOCIETY, Library, 629 Dock St, Ketchikan, 99901. Marjorie Anne Voss, Librn
Holdings: Vols 400 Cat Pix
Notes: Alaskan and regional history and art, as well as Northwest Coast Indian history and art. Extensive photograph collection.

TX —AMON CARTER MUSEUM, Library, 3510 Camp Bowie Blvd, PO Box 2365, Fort Worth, 76113. Nancy G Wynne, Librn
Holdings: Vols (25,000) Cat Mss Pix
Notes: The book collection, microfilm and photo archives have been built toward the goal of the interpretation of American history through art. At present, the greatest strengths are in Americana, Western Canadiana, bibliography, American exhibition catalogs and history of photography. Substantial books and files on American artists of the 19th and early 20th century, and particularly of Charles M Russell and Frederic Remington. Incl 25,000 pictures; 13,000 slides.
See also entries under Newspapers, American; Pictures - Collections.

MB —ESKIMO MUSEUM, Library, Box 10, Churchill, R0B 0E0, Can. Brother J Volant, Cur
Holdings: Vols (300) Cat
Notes: Books on the North, mainly northern Canada; explorers' journals; Eskimo ethnology, archaeology, and art.

ON —NATIONAL GALLERY OF CANADA, Library, National Museums of Canada, Ottawa, K1A 0M8, Can. J Hunter, Chief Librn

ART, ETHNIC

CA —CRAFT AND FOLK ART MUSEUM, Library, 5814 Wilshire Blvd, Los Angeles,

ART, ETHNIC (cont.)

90036. Joan M Benedetti, Museum Librn
Holdings: Vols (2000) Slides VF
Notes: Incl 2000 books; 70 journal subscriptions; artists' biographical files: 6 file drawers; clipping files: 8 file drawers; 20,000 slides. Representation of the material culture of all people, traditional and contemporary expressions. Incl visual and printed information on ethnic, traditional, popular, decorative, idiosyncratic, and contemporary crafts as well as vernacular architecture, handmade houses, and design. Information about and for professional artists on health hazards, conservation, and career management. Anthropological and art historical works; exhibition catalogues; slides, photographs, audiocassettes; clipping and pamphlet files. Contemporary Slide Registry of Craftspeople and extensive biographical files of contemporary craft artists. Information and referral files of craft related galleries, shops, festivals, organizations, etc.

CT —YALE UNIVERSITY, Beinecke Rare Book & Manuscript Library, Osborn Collection, New Haven, 06520. Stephen R Parks, Cur
Holdings: Mss

MA —WELLESLEY COLLEGE, Art Library, Wellesley, 02181. Katherine D Finkelpearl, Art Librn
Holdings: Vols (30,000) Cat Pix Slides
Budget: ($22,000)
Notes: Primarily the art and architecture of Western Europe, the Far East, and classical antiquity. However, efforts are being made to expand the collection in the areas of photography, primitive art, and ancient (non-classical) art. The Art Department maintains a separate collection of 62,500 mounted pictures and 90,000 slides.

OH —CLEVELAND PUBLIC LIBRARY, Fine Arts and Special Collections Department, 325 Superior Ave, Cleveland, 44114. Alice N Loranth, Head
Holdings: Vols (16,000) Cat
Notes: Part of the Handicrafts Collection which incl crafts of many ethnic groups in Cleveland.

ART, EXPRESSIONISTIC

CA —STANFORD UNIVERSITY LIBRARIES, Cecil H Green Library, Stanford, 94305. Peter R Frank, Cur, CDP-Germanic Collection
Notes: Strong collection, with many first editions, rare journals, etc. The Cassirer Collection (correspondence, autographs and typescripts by Hasenclever, Meidner, printed material) in the Stanford Collection of German, Austrian and Swiss Culture, Special Collections Register of Manuscripts.

CT —YALE UNIVERSITY, Beinecke Rare Book & Manuscript Library, German Literature Collection, Box 1603A, Yale Sta, New Haven, 06520. Christa Sammons, Cur
Holdings: / / Cat Mss
Notes: Kurt Wolff Verlag. An archive of Kurt Wolff's business correspodence, chiefly from the German Expressionist period. 4000 ms pieces. Many of the items from this collection are printed in: Kurt Wolff, *Briefwechsel eines Verlegers, 1911-1963,* ed Bernhard Zeller and Ellen Otten (Frankfurt aM: Scheffler, 1966).

CT —UNIVERSITY OF CONNECTICUT, Library, Storrs, 06268. R H Schimmelpfeng, Dir of Special Collections
Holdings: Cat Microforms
Notes: 19th century drama, Expressionism, East German literature and literature since 1945 constitute major strengths in the collection. Coverge is maintained for 600 contemporary authors. Also noteworthy are holdings on popular culture of Austria and Germany, 18th and 19th century.

IL —NORTHWESTERN UNIVERSITY, Library, Special Collections Dept, 1937 Sheridan Rd, Evanston, 60201. R Russell Maylone, Cur
Holdings: Vols 2000 Cat
Notes: Espec German art and literature: books, periodicals, pamphlets, catalogs, ephemera.

MD —UNIVERSITY OF MARYLAND, Library, Rare Book Collection, College Park, 20742. Donald Farren, Assoc Dir for Special Collections
Holdings: Vols (10,000) Cat
Notes: Ranging from incunabula to modern first editions, the Rare Book Collection is particularly strong in materials relating to the history of France and in *exempla* of interest to students of bibliography. Related collections include sizable groups of books and other items relating to the Savoy, to *Expressionismus,* and to Pompeii. Pamphlet collections include many Mazarinades, many pamphlets relating to slavery and abolition, numerous French plays, and press books.

NY —MUSEUM OF MODERN ART, Library, 11 W 53 St, New York, 10019. Clive Phillpot, Library Dir
Holdings: Vols (80,000) Cat Mss Audiotapes Microforms VF
Notes: See *Catalog of the Library of the Museum of Modern Art, New York City* (Boston: G K Hall, 1976), 14 vols. Collection incl exhibition catalogs.

AB —UNIVERSITY OF ALBERTA, Cameron Library, The Bruce Peel Special Collections Room, Edmonton, T6G 2J8, Can. John Charles, Special Collections Librn
Holdings: Vols 1400 Cat
Notes: German expressionist drama.

ON —METROPOLITAN TORONTO LIBRARY, Literature Dept, 789 Yonge St, Toronto, M4W 2G8, Can. Katherine McCook, Head
Holdings: Vols (200) Cat
Notes: Books, periodicals, pamphlets, especially on French literature. Part of a collection on other international avant-garde literary movements.

ART, FOLK see Folk Art

ART, FRENCH

CA —FINE ARTS MUSEUMS OF SAN FRANCISCO, M H de Young Memorial Museum, Golden Gate Park, San Francisco, 94118. Jane Nelson, Librn
Holdings: Vols (25,000) Cat
Budget: ($4200)

NY —FRENCH INSTITUTE-ALLIANCE FRANCAISE, Library, 22 E 60 St, New York, 10022. Fred J Gitner, Librn
Holdings: Vols (40,000) Cat Phonorecords Audiotapes
Budget: ($23,000)
Notes: Special collections of art books, books about Paris. Rich in bibliographical, biographical and lexicographical works. Standard editions of all major French authors. Name has been changed from French Institute in the United States Library since merger with the Alliance Francaise de New York.

PA —BRYN MAWR COLLEGE, Canaday Library, Bryn Mawr, 19010. James Tanis, Dir
Notes: Baroque and Italian Renaissance painting and architecture; late antique and early Christian art; Flemish and Dutch painting 15th-17th centuries; French painting 18th-19th centuries. In Art and Archaeology Library.

ART, FRENCH CANADIAN

BC —CAPILANO COLLEGE, Media Centre, 2055 Purcell Way N, Vancouver, V7J 3H5, Can. Pat Biggins, Reference Librn
Holdings: Vols 600 Cat Maps Slides Phonorecords Audiotapes 16mm Films Filmstrips
Notes: Scope is general with emphasis on arts (in French).

ART, GERMAN

†CA —RIFKIND COLLECTION LIBRARY, 9454 Wilshire Blvd, Beverly Hills, 90212.
Notes: German art of the 20th century.

†NY —COLLEGE OF STATEN ISLAND, Saint George Campus Library, 130 Stuyvesant Place, Staten Island, 10301.
Notes: A good collection of unusual exhibition catalogs.

ART, GRAPHIC see Graphic Arts

ART, GREEK

DC —HARVARD UNIVERSITY, Dumbarton Oaks, Research Library, 1703 32nd St NW, Washington, 20007. Irene Vaslef, Librn
Holdings: Vols (91,000) Cat Maps Pix Slides Microforms
Budget: ($219,000)
Notes: Byzantine civilization (including art, archaeology, literature, history, religion, law, music, etc). Extensive supplemental material on Classical, Hellenistic, Medieval, Islamic, Medieval Slavic cultures. 62,000 b/w photographs, 25,000 slides and transparencies, 1000 microfilms of books and manuscripts. Printed description of collection in *Harvard Library Bulletin,* vol 19, no 1 (Jan 1971), pp 25-35 and vol 19, no 2 (April 1971), pp 204-214, pp 25-35 and vol 19, no 2 (April 1971), pp 204-214.

†MA —UNIVERSITY OF MASSACHUSETTS AT AMHERST, Library, Amherst, 01003.
Notes: Classical art and archaeology. Special emphasis: Aegean area.

MA —HARVARD UNIVERSITY LIBRARY, Widener Library, Modern Greek Collection, Cambridge, 02138. Evangelie Flessas, Librn
Holdings: Vols 80,000 Cat Mss Microforms

MA —SMITH COLLEGE, Hillyer Art Library, Fine Arts Center, Northampton, 01063. Karen Harvey, Librn
Holdings: Vols (45,000) Cat Pix Slides

ART, HAWAIIAN

HI —HONOLULU ACADEMY OF ARTS, Robert Allerton Library, 900 S Beretania St, Honolulu, 96814. Anne T Seaman, Librn
Holdings: Vols (40,000) Cat Pix Slides
Notes: Art, with reference also to Hawaiian art.

ART, HEBREW see Art, Jewish

ART, HOMOSEXUAL

NY —LESBIAN HERSTORY EDUCATIONAL FOUNDATION INC, Lesbian Herstory Archives, PO Box 1258, New York, 10116. Deborah Edel, Treasurer
Notes: Lesbian, feminist, and Gay books and periodicals on all aspects of Lesbian culture, photographs and slides of Lesbians and Lesbian art, records, tapes, graphics and crafts. Also, unpublished materials such as first drafts, term papers from Lesbian and Gay studies courses, diaries, letters, poetry, and conference notes.

ART, HORSE IN

VA —NATIONAL SPORTING LIBRARY, Chronicle of the Horse Bldg Publishing Offices, PO Box 1335, Middleburg, 22117. Judith Ozment, Librn
Holdings: Vols (11,000) Cat Mss Pix
Notes: Sporting art.

WV —SALEM COLLEGE, Library, Salem, 26426. Myron J Smith, Jr, Librn
Notes: Collection supports "the most complete equestrian studies program available anywhere". *Myron J Smith, Equestrian Studies:* the Salem College [Bibliographical] Guide to Sources in English, 1950-1980. Metuchen, NJ: Scarecrow Press, 1981; 4645 entries.

ART, IRISH

†IL —IRISH-AMERICAN CULTURAL ASSOCIATION LIBRARY, 10415 South Western, Chicago, 60643.
Notes: Irish literature, history, biography, art, music.

MA —BOSTON COLLEGE LIBRARIES, Thomas P O'Neill Library, Irish Collection, Chestnut Hill, 02167. Ralph Coffman, Cur
Holdings: Vols (10,000) Cat Mss Maps Pix
Notes: Nearly every aspect of Irish history and literature are covered in this collection. Items of special interest are the many papers of Patrick Andrew Collins, president of the

ART, IRISH (cont.)

Irish Land League, and letters of Jeremiah O'Donovan Rossa, poet, editor and leader in the Fenian and related organizations. Holdings also incl a facsimile of the famous illuminated ms of the Gospels, the *Book of* Kells; a complete vol of *Malton's Views of Dublin, 1799; The Ordinance Surveys;* a complete set of the *Irish Bulletin;* and Colgan's *Acta Sanctorum Hiberniae* describing the lives of the Irish saints.

ART, ISLAMIC

DC —FREER GALLERY OF ART, Library, 12th & Jefferson Dr SW, Washington, 20560. Ellen A Nollman, Librn

DC —HARVARD UNIVERSITY, Dumbarton Oaks, Research Library, 1703 32nd St NW, Washington, 20007. Irene Vaslef, Librn
Holdings: Vols (91,000) Cat Maps Pix Slides Microforms
Budget: ($219,000)
Notes: Byzantine civilization (including art, archaeology, literature, history, religion, law, music, etc). Extensive supplemental material on Classical, Hellenistic, Medieval, Islamic, Medieval Slavic cultures. 62,000 b/w photographs, 25,000 slides and transparencies, 1000 microfilms of books and manuscripts. Printed description of collection in *Harvard Library Bulletin,* vol 19, no 1 (Jan 1971), pp 25-35 and vol 19, no 2 (April 1971), pp 204-214, pp 25-35 and vol 19, no 2 (April 1971), pp 204-214.

IL —ORIENTAL INSTITUTE, 1155 E 58th St, Chicago, 60637. John Larsen, Archivist
Notes: The Bernhard Moritz Collection. Fine examples of bindings as well as of Islamic calligraphy and writing materials--papyrus, parchment, papers, etc. Extensive collection is also in the Beatty Library in Dublin, Ireland; Victoria and Albert Museum in London; Libraries in East and West Germany.

MA —HARVARD UNIVERSITY, Harvard College Library, Fine Arts Library, Fogg Museum, 32 Quincy St, Cambridge, 02138. Wolfgang M Freitag, Librn
Holdings: Vols 4000
Notes: Books, slides, photographs, postcards, architectural plans, and drawings of historic sites.

OH —CINCINNATI ART MUSEUM, Library, Eden Park, Cincinnati, 45202. Patrician P Rutledge, Librn
Holdings: Vols (45,850) Cat Microforms
Notes: Art library containing all subjects on art-history, graphic arts, advertising art, etc; special strength in prints, ie engravings, etc. Near Eastern art and decorative arts are also strong. At least 90,000 art exhibition catalogs. Emphasis on artists of Cincinnati and vicinity in vertical file material.

ART, ITALIAN

MA —BRANDEIS UNIVERSITY, Goldfarb Library, 415 South St, Waltham, 02154. Bessie Hahn, Dir
Notes: Leonardo da Vinci Collection. Comprised of over 1000 vols dealing with all aspects of Leonardo Da Vinci's life, art and engineering feats. The collection is fully catalogued and access is provided by the Special Collections card catalog and the Main Card Catalog.

†NY —ISTITUTO ITALIANO DI CULTURA LIBRARY, 686 Park Ave, New York, 10021.
Notes: Italian philosophy, social sciences concerning Italy, Italian language and literature, science and technology, Italian arts, history, geography and biography.

ART, ITALIAN RENAISSANCE

MA —HARVARD UNIVERSITY, Harvard College Library, Fine Arts Library, Fogg Museum, 32 Quincy St, Cambridge, 02138. Wolfgang M Freitag, Librn
Holdings: Vols (202,000) Cat Mss Pix Slides
Budget: ($176,500)
Notes: All areas of art history, with emphasis on Italian primitives, Italian Renaissance, master drawings, Romanesque sculpture, architectural history, ms materials (particulary American artists'), conservation and restoration of art objects. Incl the Berenson repertory of photographs from the Harvard Center for Italian Renaissance Studies in Florence, and the Decimal Index to the Art of the Low Countries. Separate card catalogs for books, photographs and lantern slides, registers for ms holdings which are not incl in *National Union Catalog of Manuscript Collections.* Slides total over 230,000; over 745,000 pictures. *Fine Arts Library Catalogue* (14 volumes) and *Catalogue of Auction Sales Catalogues* (1 volume) (Boston: G K Hall, 1972); *A Guide to the Fine Arts Library* (Cambridge, Mass: 1971); *Guide to the Harvard Libraries,* microfiche edition of holdingscataloged through 1981 published 1984 (Munich/New York: Saur).

MI —UNIVERSITY OF MICHIGAN, Fine Arts Library, Tappan Hall, Ann Arbor, 48109. Margaret Jensen, Fine Arts Librn; Joy Alexander, Cur Slide Collection
Holdings: Vols (50,000) Cat Slides Microforms
Notes: The slide collection (250,000 slides) is owned and serviced by the History of Art Department; it is not part of the University of Michigan library system, but is used in conjunction with the library material, and housed in the same building.

OH —OBERLIN COLLEGE LIBRARY, Clarence Ward Art Library, Allen Art Bldg, Oberlin, 44074. Jeffrey Weidman, Librn
Holdings: Vols (62,000) Cat Microforms
Notes: Traditional strength in Northern and Southern Baroque. Have *Decimal Index to the Art of the Low Countries* (DIAL).

PA —BRYN MAWR COLLEGE, Canaday Library, Bryn Mawr, 19010. James Tanis, Dir
Notes: Baroque and Italian Renaissance painting and architecture; late antique and early Christian art; Flemish and Dutch painting 15th - 17th centuries; French painting 18th - 19th centuries. In Art and Archaeology Library.

ART, JAPANESE

CA —SAN DIEGO PUBLIC LIBRARY, Art, Music & Recreation Sect, 820 E St, San Diego, 92101. Barbara A Tuhill, Supvr
Holdings: Vols 500 Cat Pix
Notes: Emphasis on Chinese, Japanese, Korean, and Cambodian art. Private library of Donal Hord, local sculptor. For reference use only.

CA —ASIAN ART MUSEUM OF SAN FRANCISCO, Library, Golden Gate Park, San Francisco, 94118. Fred A Cline Jr, Librn
Holdings: Vols (16,000) Cat Mss Pix Microforms Clippings
Notes: The Avery Brundage Collection of Oriental Art. Emphasis on East Asian, Southeast Asian and East Indian art. Also building a microform library; collecting pictures and clipping files. Noncirculating. No interlibrary loans.

CT —CONNECTICUT COLLEGE, Library, Mohegan Ave, New London, 06320. Brian Rogers, College Librn
Holdings: Vols 600 Cat
Notes: Holdings incl the Helen Carey Coudert Collection of nearly 500 books on Chinese and Japanese painting, sculpture and bronzes.

DC —FREER GALLERY OF ART, Library, 12th & Jefferson Dr SW, Washington, 20560. Ellen A Nollman, Librn

HI —HONOLULU ACADEMY OF ARTS, Robert Allerton Library, 900 S Beretania St, Honolulu, 96814. Anne T Seaman, Librn

MA —HARVARD UNIVERSITY LIBRARY, Fine Arts Library, Rubel Asiatic Research Collection, Sackler Museum, 38 Quincy Street, Cambridge, 02138. Yen-Shew Lynn Chao, Librn
Holdings: Cat Mss Maps Pix Slides
Notes: Rubel Asiatic Research Collection; specializes exclusively in the acquisition of Oriental language (Chinese, Japanese, and Korean) materials. Particular strengths incl the areas of Buddhist arts, Chinese bronzes and painting, Japanese painting and prints, and Chinese and Japanese ceramics. Also large holdings of oriental art periodicals, reprints, and exhibition and sales catalogs.

MA —BOSTON COLLEGE LIBRARIES, Thomas P O'Neill Library, Chestnut Hill, 02167. Frank J Seegraber, Special Collections Librn
Holdings: Vols 66 // Cat
Notes: The James W Morrissey Memorial Collection of Japanese Prints is composed of over 100 original prints and reproductions of Japanese artists of the 18th and 19th centuries, with others from the contemporary period. Available by appointment only.

MO —THE NELSON-ATKINS MUSEUM OF ART, Kenneth & Helen Spencer Art Reference Library, 4525 Oak St, Kansas City, 64111. Stanley W Hess, Librn
Notes: Strong in painting, sculpture, architecture and ceramics.

PA —EASTERN COLLEGE, Frank Warner Memorial Library, Saint Davids, 19087. James L Sauer, Librn
Holdings: Uncat Mss Pix
Notes: The Harry C Goebel Collection. Incl Bruce Rogers printings (over 460); press books (about 350); oriental art (over 250); bookplates (with a separate collection of an almost complete set of bookplates designed by Edwin Davis French); Christmas Books; art and graphic arts (incl the French Graphic Arts Collection of Adolph DeMilly); first editions of Christopher Morley; Print Collection (1315 prints); Oriental art realia and artifacts.

WA —UNIVERSITY OF WASHINGTON LIBRARIES, East Asia Library, DO-27, Seattle, 98195. Karl Lo, Head
Holdings: Vols (300,000) Cat Microforms
Budget: ($200,000)
Notes: Southwest China; Joseph Rock Collection, ca 2000 vols; modern Chinese poetry, 1919 to date: ca 700 titles; Asian art, esp Japanese painting: 4097 vols; Tiao-yu-t'ai movement in the US: ca 400 items of periodicals and pamphlets; modern Korean poetry, ancient and modern: ca 1000 titles; Mu-yu-shu folk literature: ca 1000 items.

PQ —MCGILL UNIVERSITY, McLennan Library, Rare Books and Special Collections Dept, 3459 McTavish St, Montreal, H3A 1Y1, Can.
Notes: 12,680 original prints and posters dating from the 16th century to the present. Prints representing many graphic techniques; special subject areas such as: early railways, Japanese woodblocks, Napoleon, early Canadian portraits.

ART, JEWISH

CA —JUDAH L MAGNES MEMORIAL MUSEUM, Morris Goldstein Library, 2911 Russell St, Berkeley, 94705. Jane Levy, Archivist
Holdings: Vols 10,000 Cat Mss Maps 16mm Films
Notes: Judaica, incl Hebrew manuscripts, Yiddish literature, and Jewish music and art.

CA —HEBREW UNION COLLEGE, Library, 3077 University Mall, Los Angeles, 90007. Barbara Gilbert, Head Librn
Holdings: Vols (300) Slides
Notes: Incl a collection of 8000 slides.

NY —LEO BAECK INSTITUTE, Library, 129 E 73 St, New York, 10021. Fred Grubel, Secretary & Dir
Holdings: Vols 6000 Cat Pix Microforms Drawings
Notes: History and philosophy of European German-speaking Jewry, 18th to 20th century. Publications: LBI Archives and Library News, free, 2 issues a year. Provides an update of collections. Also, LBI News incl more general info for members only. $35.00 per year dues.

NY —YIVO INSTITUTE FOR JEWISH RESEARCH, Library & Archives, 1048 Fifth Ave, New York, 10028. Dina Abramowicz, Librn; Marek Web, Archivist
Holdings: Cat Mss Pix Slides
Notes: Original works and reference

ART, JEWISH (cont.)

materials, incl reproductions of 1500 objects; 500 slides. Separate catalog.

NC —DUKE UNIVERSITY, William R Perkins Library, Rare Book Room, Durham, 27706. John L Sharpe, III, Cur
Notes: The Kanof collection of Judaic art contains more than 950 items on Jewish art, archaeology and symbolism.

NC —DUKE UNIVERSITY, Divinity School Library, Durham, 27706. Donn Michael Farris, Librn
Holdings: Vols (225,000)
Notes: Special collections and subject emphases in this library include: Archaeology, Egyptian; Archaeology, Middle Eastern; Art, Jewish; Bible; Bible-New Testament; Bible-Symbolism; Church Architecture; Egyptology; Fathers of the Church; Society of Friends; Great Britain-Religion-Methodism and Methodist Church; Hymns and Hymnals; Jansenists and Jansenism; Judaica; Mediaeval Christian Mysticism; Methodism and Methodist Church; Methodist Episcopal Church; Methodist Episcopal Church, South; Reformation; Religion-US-History; Rural Church; Theology-Great Britain-17th Century; Theology-Great Britain-18th Century; United Methodist Church; US-Church History; John Wesley.

OH —HEBREW UNION COLLEGE-JEWISH INSTITUTE OF RELIGION, Klau Library, 3101 Clifton Ave, Cincinnati, 45220. David J Gilner, Reference Librn
Holdings: Cat
Notes: Extensive collection of Jewish artists, primarily in the US and Israel; Jewish religious art, etc.

ART, KOREAN

CA —SAN DIEGO PUBLIC LIBRARY, Art, Music & Recreation Sect, 820 E St, San Diego, 92101. Barbara A Tuhill, Supvr
Holdings: Vols 500 Cat Pix
Notes: Emphasis on Chinese, Japanese, Korean, and Cambodian art. Private library of Donal Hord, local sculptor. For reference use only.

CA —ASIAN ART MUSEUM OF SAN FRANCISCO, Library, Golden Gate Park, San Francisco, 94118. Fred A Cline Jr, Librn
Holdings: Vols (16,000) Cat Mss Pix Microforms Clippings
Notes: The Avery Brundage Collection of Oriental Art. Emphasis on East Asian, Southeast Asian and East Indian art. Also building a microform library; collecting pictures and clippings files. Noncirculating. No interlibrary loans. Hours 1-4:45 (city holidays excepted).

DC —FREER GALLERY OF ART, Library, 12th & Jefferson Dr SW, Washington, 20560. Ellen A Nollman, Librn

MA —HARVARD UNIVERSITY LIBRARY, Fine Arts Library, Rubel Asiatic Research Collection, Sackler Museum, 38 Quincy Street, Cambridge, 02138. Yen-Shew Lynn Chao, Librn
Holdings: Cat Mss Maps Pix Slides
Notes: Rubel Asiatic Research Collection; specializes exclusively in the acquisition of Oriental language (Chinese, Japanese, and Korean) materials. Particular strengths incl the areas of Buddhist arts, Chinese bronzes and painting, Japanese painting and prints, and Chinese and Japanese ceramics. Also large holdings of oriental art periodicals, reprints, and exhibition and sales catalogs.

MO —THE NELSON-ATKINS MUSEUM OF ART, Kenneth & Helen Spencer Art Reference Library, 4525 Oak St, Kansas City, 64111. Stanley W Hess, Librn
Notes: Small collection with modest growth in painting, sculpture and ceramics.

ART, LATIN AMERICAN

AZ —ARIZONA STATE MUSEUM, Library, University of Arizona, Tucson, 85721. Hans R Bart, Museum Librn
Holdings: Vols 400 Cat
Notes: Art and architecture of Latin America, strong in pre-Columbian material but mainly Spanish Colonial from the 16th to the 18th century. This is a large private library which is being transferred to the ASM Library. Special catalog is planned.

AZ —TUCSON MUSEUM OF ART LIBRARY, 140 N Main, Tucson, 85705. Dorcas Worsley, Librn
Holdings: Vols (2000)
Budget: ($1500)
Notes: Extensive file of biographical and critical information on Arizona artists which is continually being increased. Subject card index to magazines on Western art and artists in magazines not indexed in *Art* Index 12 drawers in 1984, and continues to grow. Have a collection of 15,000 slides.

CA —CALIFORNIA STATE UNIVERSITY, LONG BEACH, University Library, Reference Center, 1250 Bellflower Blvd, Long Beach, 90840. Henry J DuBois, Librn
Holdings: Cat Slides
Notes: Collection of 60,000 slides offers examples of virtually all types and periods of art, incl an extensive collection of slides of mss from the Bodleian Library, Oxford, a special series on Latin American art, another on the arts of the US Collection is cataloged using Fogg Museum classification. No photocopying.

CA —FINE ARTS MUSEUMS OF SAN FRANCISCO, M H de Young Memorial Museum, Golden Gate Park, San Francisco, 94118. Jane Nelson, Librn
Holdings: Vols (30,000) Cat Slides
Budget: ($24,000)
Notes: Pre-Columbian art.

DC —LIBRARY OF CONGRESS, Prints & Photographs Div, Washington, 20540.
Holdings: Cat Pix

NY —MUSEUM OF MODERN ART, Library, 11 W 53 St, New York, 10019. Clive Phillpot, Library Dir
Holdings: Vols (80,000) Cat Mss Audiotapes Microforms VF
Notes: See *Catalog of the Library of the Museum of Modern Art, New York City* (Boston: G K Hall, 1976), 14 vols. Collection incl exhibition catalogs.

TX —UNIVERSITY OF TEXAS LIBRARIES, Nettie Lee Benson Latin American Collection, Sid Richardson Hall 1.109, Austin, 78712. Laura Gutierrez-Witt, Head Librn
Holdings: Vols (450,000) Cat Mss Maps Pix Phonorecords Filmstrips Microforms
See also entry under Latin America.

ART, LITURGICAL

NY —YIVO INSTITUTE FOR JEWISH RESEARCH, Library & Archives, 1048 Fifth Ave, New York, 10028. Dina Abramowicz, Librn; Marek Web, Archivist
Holdings: Cat Mss Pix Slides
Notes: Original works and reference materials, incl reproductins of 1500 objects; 500 slides. Separate catalog.

ART, MAINE

ME —WILLIAM A FARNSWORTH LIBRARY & ART MUSEUM, 19 Elm St, Rockland, 04841. Marius B Peladeau, Dir
Holdings: Vols (4000) Cat Pix Microforms
Notes: Emphasis on American and European fine and decorative arts of all periods (largely modern). Other areas include marine history and Maine history (local); illustrated books and rare books also a part of our collection, which has its own catalog. Also, Louise Nevelsen, N C Wyeth Archives.

ART, MASSACHUSETTS

MA —SWAIN SCHOOL OF DESIGN LIBRARY, 140 Orchard St, Sch add: 19 Hawthorn St, New Bedford, 02740. Martha Maier, Librn
Holdings: Vols 16,500 Cat Slides Clippings
Notes: Small special file of material of artists of the New Bedford area, photographed and deposited with the Archives of American Art. 30,000 slides on art history.

ART, MEDICAL

PA —PHILADELPHIA MUSEUM OF ART, Ars Medica Center, Parkway at Fairmount, Box 7646, Philadelphia, 19101. Ellen Jacobowutz; Ann Percy
Holdings: Cat Mss Maps Pix Slides
Notes: An international medical arts center of prints, drawings and photographs, related illustrative medical material, and a research reference center.

ART, MEDIEVAL

CA —UNIVERSITY OF CALIFORNIA, LOS ANGELES, Art Library, Los Angeles, 90024. Max Marmor, Library Assistant
Holdings: Pix Microforms
Notes: Art; Art History; Early Christian and Byzantine Art; Medieval Art; Apostolic Age to 1400; Iconography; Photo Archive; Christian Art and Symbolism.

CA —J PAUL GETTY MUSEUM, Photo Archives, 17985 Pacific Coast Hwy, Malibu, 90265. William Reeder, Cur
Holdings: Pix
Notes: Incl photographs of works of art at the Museum (180,000 cataloged, 500,000 uncataloged), incl ancient art, western European art (painting, sculpture, graphics) and European decorative arts, medieval and Renaissance to 19th century, and antiquities.

DC —CATHOLIC UNIVERSITY OF AMERICA, Mullen Library, 620 Michigan Ave NE, Washington, 20064. B Gutekunst, Humanities Librn
Holdings: Vols (20,000) Cat

DC —HARVARD UNIVERSITY, Dumbarton Oaks, Research Library, 1703 32nd St NW, Washington, 20007. Irene Vaslef, Librn
Holdings: Vols (91,000) Cat Maps Pix Slides Microforms
Budget: ($291,000)
Notes: Byzantine civilization (including art, archaeology, literature, history, religion, law, music, etc). Extensive supplemental material on Classical, Hellenistic, Medieval, Islamic, Medieval Slavic cultures. 62,000 b/w photographs, 25,000 slides and transparencies, 1000 microfilms of books and manuscripts. Printed description of collection in *Harvard Library Bulletin,* vol 19, no 1 (Jan 1971), pp 25-35 and vol 19, no 2 (April 1971), pp 204-214, pp 25-35 and vol 19, no 2 (April 1971), pp 204-214.

IN —INDIANA UNIVERSITY, Art Museum Bldg, Fine Arts Bldg, Bloomington, 47401. Betty Jo Irvine, Fine Arts Librn
Holdings: Vols (57,000) Cat Pix Microforms
Budget: ($52,000)
Notes: Art forms relevant to the periods and places involved.

MA —SMITH COLLEGE, Hillyer Art Library, Fine Arts Center, Northampton, 01063. Karen Harvey, Librn
Holdings: Vols (45,000) Cat Pix Slides

MO —THE NELSON-ATKINS MUSEUM OF ART, Kenneth & Helen Spencer Art Reference Library, 4525 Oak St, Kansas City, 64111. Stanley W Hess, Librn

NJ —PRINCETON UNIVERSITY, Marquand Library, McCormick Hall, Princeton, 08544. Mary M Schmidt, Librn
Holdings: Vols (130,000) Cat Microforms
Notes: Especially strong in classical archaeology, medieval art and architecture, and photography history.

NY —THE CLOISTERS, Metropolitan Museum of Art (Branch), Fort Tryon Park, New York, 10040. Suse C Childs, Librn
Holdings: Vols (5000) Cat Mss Pix Slides
Notes: A branch of the Metropolitan Museum of Art devoted solely to the literature of medieval art. Incl 16,000 slides and 5000 photographs with unique strengths in certain aspects of medieval art.

NY —METROPOLITAN MUSEUM OF ART, Thomas J Watson Library, Fifth Ave & 82 St, New York, 10028. William B Walker, Chief Librn
Holdings: Vols (250,000) Cat Mss Microforms
Notes: All fields of art: 1400 periodicals, incl bulletins and annual reports, catalogs, etc of American and foreign art societies, museums, etc; incl sales catalogs, exhibition catalogs, clipping file on individual artists and subjects, autograph letters. See *Library Catalog of the Metropolitan Museum of Art, New York,* second ed, rev and enl (Boston,

ART, MEDIEVAL (cont.)

G K Hall, 1980, 48 v and first supplement, 1982). Since 1980, holdings have been cataloged in RLIN.

OH —OHIO STATE UNIVERSITY, Fine Arts Library, 1813 N High St, Columbus, 43210. Susan Wyngaard, Head, Fine Arts Library
Holdings: Vols (75,000) Cat Microforms
Budget: ($60,000)
Notes: Also have 1000 uncataloged exhibition catalogs. Book collection strong in history of art especially in area of medieval & Northern Renaissance art. Good collection of portfolios. Photographic collections on microfiche. Receive Slavic titles, many on Byzantine frescoes. Online catalog. Decimal Index of the Art of the Low Countries, as well as Marburger Index; Index Photographique de i' Arten France; Alinari Archives on microfiche and other major microform collections in art.

PA —UNIVERSITY OF PITTSBURGH, Henry Clay Frick Fine Arts Library, Pittsburgh, 15260. Anne W Gordon, Fine Arts Librn
Holdings: Vols (55,000) Cat Pix Slides Microforms
Notes: Emphasis is on the art of the Western World--Architecture, sculpture, painting, minor arts, archaeology, with special strength in the Byzantine, early Christian, medieval, renaissance and modern periods. The Oriental field is represented, incl replicas of scrolls. Studio arts are also covered. Illuminated ms facsimiles. Extensive collections of slides and photographs for study of art history are available in the building but not administered by the art library.

ART, MEXICAN

CA —UNIVERSITY OF CALIFORNIA, SAN DIEGO, Central University Library, Mandeville Dept of Special Collections, La Jolla, 92093. Lynda Corey Claassen, Head
Notes: Hispanic Collection: Approx 6000 vols describe cultures of Spain, Portugal, Mexico, Latin America, and South America. Works of literature, history, philosophy and art date from the 15th to the mid-19th century. Highlights of the collection include rare 18th century Spanish provincial dramas and works on the history of Seville and Andalusia.

PA —TEMPLE UNIVERSITY LIBRARIES, Special Collections Dept, Rare Books & Mss Section, Philadelphia, 19122. Thomas M Whitehead, Cur
Holdings: Vols (200) Cat Mss Pix
Notes: The lithography collection emphasizes the technical process rather than the artistic medium and stresses the years 1800-1835. Significant are the early manuals, the Kubilius Louis Prang Collection and the documentation of early Mexican lithography. Some holdings are listed in the 1972 publication: *Aloys Senefelder 1771-1834: A Catalogue of Early Technical Literature and Selected Lithographs.* A register of the Mexican documents is available.

TX —UNIVERSITY OF TEXAS LIBRARIES, Nettie Lee Benson Latin American Collection, Sid Richardson Hall 1.109, Austin, 78712. Laura Gutierrez-Witt, Head Librn
Holdings: Vols (450,000) Cat Mss Maps Pix Phonorecords Filmstrips Microforms
See also entry under Latin America

TX —SOUTHERN METHODIST UNIVERSITY, DeGolyer Library, Box 396, SMU, Dallas, 75275. Clifton H Jones, Dir
Holdings: Vols (80,000) Cat Mss Maps Slides Microforms
Notes: First editions of prominent authors; also of books in subject emphasis collections. All subjects listed in this vol are strong. Numerous collections of personal papers relating to subjects also.

TX —EL PASO PUBLIC LIBRARY, Southwest Collection, 501 N Oregon, El Paso, 79901. Mary A Sarber, Head
Holdings: Vols (12,000) Cat Mss Maps Pix
Budget: ($11,000)
Notes: Limited to materials on Texas, New Mexico, Arizona, and Mexico. Special collections of material by and about Tom Lea Jr, and Carl Hertzog. Aultman Collection of photographs incl 3500 on El Paso and the Southwest and 2500 on the Mexican Revolution. Separate catalog. See Lovelace, Lisabeth, "The Southwest Collection of the El Paso Public Library," Great Plains Journal, 11:2, pp 161-166; and Aultman, Otis A, *Photographs from the Border: The Otis A Aultman Collection* (El Paso Public Library Association, 1977).

ART, MINIMAL

CA —CALIFORNIA INSTITUTE OF THE ARTS, Library, 24700 McBean Pkwy, Valencia, 91355. James Elrod, Dir
Holdings: Vols (61,000) Slides
Budget: ($11,000)
Notes: Modern art, incl abstract, conceptual, concrete, environment, minimal, and pop art; art; dadaism; surrealism; happenings; and caricatures and cartoons. Slides (61,683).

NY —STATE UNIVERSITY OF NEW YORK, COLLEGE AT PURCHASE, Library, Lincoln Ave, Purchase, 10577. Robert W Evans, Dir
Holdings: Uncat Mss Pix
Notes: Gift of the artist, George Rickey, and his wife, whose collection of constructivist art works has also been given to the Neuberger Museum at the College at Purchase. The collection consists largely of over 1000 announcements and catalogs of exhibitions of constructivist works and material about the artists.

ART, MODERN—20TH CENTURY

AZ —TUCSON MUSEUM OF ART LIBRARY, 140 N Main, Tucson, 85705. Dorcas Worsley, Librn
Holdings: Vols (2000)
Budget: ($1500)
Notes: Extensive file of biographical and critical information on Arizona artists which is continually being increased. Subject card index to magazines on Western art and artists in magazines not indexed in *Art* Index 12 drawers in 1984, and continues to grow. Have a collection of 15,000 slides.

CA —LA JOLLA MUSEUM OF CONTEMPORARY ART, Helen Palmer Geisel Art Reference Library, 700 Prospect St, La Jolla, 92037. Gail Richardson, Librn
Holdings: Vols 2000 Cat Slides

CA —CRAFT AND FOLK ART MUSEUM, Library, 5814 Wilshire Blvd, Los Angeles, 90036. Joan M Benedetti, Museum Librn
Holdings: Vols (2000) Slides VF
Notes: Incl 2000 books; 70 journal subscriptions; artists' biographical files: 6 file drawers; clipping files: 8 file drawers; 20,000 slides. Representation of the material culture of all people, traditional and contemporary expressions. Incl visual and printed information on ethnic, traditional, popular, decorative, idiosyncratic, and contemporary crafts as well as vernacular architecture, handmade houses, and design. Information about and for professional artists on health hazards, conservation, and career management. Anthropological and art historical works; exhibition catalogues; slides, photographs, audiocassettes; clipping and pamphlet files. Contemporary Slide Registry of Craftspeople and extensive biographical files of contemporary craft artists. Information and referral files of craft related galleries, shops, festivals, organizations, etc.

CA —SAN DIEGO MUSEUM OF ART, Reference Library, PO Box 2107, Balboa Park, San Diego, 92112. Nancy J Andrews, Librn
Holdings: Vols 9000 Cat Slides
Notes: Incl 30,000 exhibition catalogs. Now cataloging bibliographies from all exhibition, sales and commercial gallery catalogs (15, 000). Library is noted for its collection of material on contemporary artists. Have 24 vertical files containing various material on individual artists. Have a catalog for slide collection, as well as a catalog of exhibition and sales catalogs. Incl 18,600 slides.

CA —CALIFORNIA INSTITUTE OF THE ARTS, Library, 24700 McBean Pkwy, Valencia, 91355. James Elrod, Dir
Holdings: Vols (61,000) Cat Slides
Budget: ($11,000)
Notes: Modern art, incl abstract, conceptual, concrete, environment, minimal, and pop art; art; dadaism; surrealism; happenings; and caricatures and cartoons. Slides (61,683).

GA —ATLANTA COLLEGE OF ART LIBRARY, 1280 Peachtree St N E, Atlanta, 30309. Jean Haskell, Librn
Holdings: Vols (16,000) Cat Pix Slides Phonorecords Videotapes Microforms
Notes: Visual arts, with 20th-century emphasis. There is a catalog to the books and the exhibition catalogs.The library is the only collection devoted totally to the visual arts in the Atlanta area. Rare book collection and extensive artists' books collection.

IN —INDIANA UNIVERSITY, Art Museum Bldg, Fine Arts Bldg, Bloomington, 47401. Betty Jo Irvine, Fine Arts Librn
Holdings: Vols (57,000) Cat Pix Microforms
Budget: ($52,000)
Notes: Art forms relevant to the periods and places involved.

IA —UNIVERSITY OF IOWA, University Libraries, Iowa City, 52242. Frank Paluka, Head, Special Collections Dept
Holdings: Vols (13,170) Cat
Notes: See Arthur H Minters, "A Talk on Modern Art Periodicals", *Books at Iowa,* November 1967; also Timothy Shipe, "The Dada Archives", *Books at Iowa,* November 1983.

ME —WILLIAM A FARNSWORTH LIBRARY & ART MUSEUM, 19 Elm St, Rockland, 04841. Marius B Peladeau, Dir
Holdings: Vols (4000) Cat Pix Microforms
Notes: Emphasis on American and European fine and decorative arts of all periods (largely modern). Other areas include marine history and Maine history (local); illustrated books and rare books also a part of our collection, which has its own catalog. Also, Louise Nevelsen, N C Wyeth Archives.

MD —BALTIMORE MUSEUM OF ART LIBRARY, Art Museum Dr, Baltimore, 21218. Anita Gilden, Librn
Holdings: Vols (40,000) Cat VF
Notes: General reference sources with emphasis on 19th and 20th century art and American decorative art. Incl prints and drawings. Photocopying.

MI —KALAMAZOO INSTITUTE OF ARTS LIBRARY, 314 S Park St, Kalamazoo, 49006. Marianne Cavanaugh, Librn
Holdings: Vols (5000) Cat Slides
Budget: $2000
Notes: Incl (8000) slides. Vertical file on artists. Collection is supplemented by 55 current subscriptions to periodicals in visual arts. Emphasis is on 20th century art and on American art. Collection supports permanent collection in prints, paintings, photography, and sculpture.

MN —WALKER ART CENTER, Staff Reference Library, Vineland Place, Minneapolis, 55403. Rosemary Furtak, Librn
Holdings: Vols 5000 Cat Pix
Notes: Incl 10,000 catalogs of individual artists; museum gallery catalogs-10,000 catalogs of major exhibitions from all over the world dating back to 1940. VF material and tapes.

MO —THE NELSON-ATKINS MUSEUM OF ART, Kenneth & Helen Spencer Art Reference Library, 4525 Oak St, Kansas City, 64111. Stanley W Hess, Librn
Notes: European and American modern art.

MO —UNIVERSITY OF MISSOURI-SAINT LOUIS, Thomas Jefferson Library, 8001 Natural Bridge Rd, Saint Louis, 63121.
Holdings: Uncat
Notes: Collection in boxes, currently inaccessible.

NY —ALBRIGHT-KNOX ART GALLERY, Art Reference Library, 1285 Elmwood Ave, Buffalo, 14222. Annette Masling, Librn
Holdings: Vols (20,000) Cat
Notes: Special strength in American 19th and 20th century art. Excellent collection of exhibition catalogs for contemporary art.

NY —STATE UNIVERSITY OF NEW YORK, COLLEGE AT BUFFALO, Lockwood Memorial Library, Art Dept, Buffalo, 14260. Florence S DaLuiso, Cur
Holdings: Vols (38,000) Cat Microforms
Budget: ($24,735)
Notes: Collection supports curriculum of the

ART, MODERN—20TH CENTURY (cont.)

School of Fine Art. Incl 9000 exhibition catalogs. Recent acquistions emphasize contemporary art and environmental design. The library by reciprocal agreement contains card catalog holdings of the Albright-Knox Art Gallery, Buffalo, New York. Books may be obtained on interlibrary loan.

NY —HOFSTRA UNIVERSITY, Library, 1000 Fulton Ave, Hempstead, 11550. Charles R Andrews, Dean of Library Services
Holdings: / / Uncat Mss Pix
Notes: Howard L and Muriel Weingrow Collection of Avant-Garde Art and Literature. Incl 4000 items of foundation documents relating to all major art movements from Jugendstil and Art Nouveau periods to Pop and Op Art. No photocopying.

NY —AMERICAN CRAFT COUNCIL, Library and Artists Registry, 44 W 53 St, New York, 10019. Joanne Polster, Librn
Holdings: Vols 3300 Cat Pix Slides Films
Notes: Crafts and craft-related subjects, incl portfolios for approx 2000 contemporary American craftspeople consisting of biographical material and photographs, indexed by media, geographic location, and a visual index. Over 1500 exhibition catalogs. The collection incl 35mm slide kits available for purchase. Catagories covered are: exhibitions of ACC's American Craft Museum from 1958 to date; kits in all media: fiber, metal, wood, clay, glass and multimedia; kits covering crafts processes. The Library also holds catalogs of craft school and art centers offering craft courses; newsletters, by-laws, and other materials of craft organizations and groups; the Archives and Photo-Archives of the American Craft Museum. No photocopying.

NY —MUSEUM OF MODERN ART, Library, 11 W 53 St, New York, 10019. Clive Phillpot, Library Dir
Holdings: Vols 80,000 Cat Mss Microforms
Notes: Art of the 20th and latter half of the 19th century (painting, sculpture, drawings and prints, architecture, photography, film, design mixed media, artists' books). Special emphasis on Surrealist and Dada literature and art. Incl art exhibition catalogs. Photocopying restricted. See *Catalog of the Museum of Modern Art, New York City* (Boston: G K Hall, 1976), 14 vols.

NY —SOHO CENTER FOR VISUAL ARTS, 110-112 Prince St, New York, 10012. Ronda Wall, Librn
Notes: Incl collection of current exhibition catalogs of contemporary artists since 1964 (formerly at Aldrich Museum of Contemporary Art).

OH —CLEVELAND PUBLIC LIBRARY, Fine Arts and Special Collections Department, 325 Superior Ave, Cleveland, 44114. Alice N Loranth, Head
Holdings: Vols (12,000) Cat Pix
Notes: Part of the Art Collection, which covers all periods and fields of art with special emphasis on contemporary and American art. 200 periodicals, incl bulletins of American museums.

PA —PHILADELPHIA COLLEGE OF ART, Library, Broad & Spruce Sts, Philadelphia, 19102. Hazel Gustow, Dir
Holdings: Vols 25,000 Cat Periodicals Pix Slides Microforms VF
Notes: Printed materials on the arts (history, techniques, aesthetics, etc.). Current buying incl most significant books coming into print or being reprinted, mainly in English. Incl about 22,000 titles, periodicals, 30 cabinets vertical file materials, etc.

PA —UNIVERSITY OF PITTSBURGH, Henry Clay Frick Fine Arts Library, Pittsburgh, 15260. Anne W Gordon, Fine Arts Librn
Holdings: Vols (55,000) Cat Pix Slides Microforms
Notes: Emphasis is on the art of the Western World--Architecture, sculpture, painting, minor arts, archaeology, with special strength in the Byzantine, early Christian, medieval, renaissance and modern periods. The Oriental field is represented, incl replicas of scrolls. Studio arts are also covered. Illuminated ms facsimiles. Extensive collections of slides and photographs for study of art history are available in the building but not administered by the art library.

TX —FORT WORTH ART MUSEUM, Library, 1309 Montgomery St, Fort Worth, 76107. David Ryan, Dir
Holdings: Vols (3500) Cat Pix Slides Audiotapes Videotapes 16mm Films
Budget: ($5000)
Notes: 20th Century art of all countries and in all media to correspond with the scope of the museum. Extensive collection of exhibition catalogs.

WI —UNIVERSITY OF WISCONSIN, LA CROSSE, Murphy Library, 1631 Pine St, La Crosse, 54601. Edwin L Hill, Special Collections Librn
Holdings: Vols 200 Cat Pix
Notes: Art exhibition catalogs. Emphasis on major contemporary exhibitions.

ON —NATIONAL GALLERY OF CANADA, Library, National Museums of Canada, Ottawa, K1A 0M8, Can. J Hunter, Chief Librn

PQ —MUSEE D'ART CONTEMPORAIN, Bibliotheque, Cite du Havre, Montreal, H3C 3R4, Can. Isabelle Montplaisir, Librn
Holdings: Vols (5780) Cat Pix Slides Audiotapes Videotapes Microforms
Budget: ($12,000)
Notes: 7050 exhibition catalogs on a basic exchange from art galleries, museums, etc of many countries. Also 2000 pictures; 32,000 slides; and 2500 files relating to artists, galleries, museums, etc. Also, the Archives Paul-Emile Borduas (painter) of 12,500 items, incl his writings, correspondence, exhibition catalogs, etc. Plus 150 periodical subscriptions.

ART, MOSLEM see Art, Islamic

ART, NEAR EASTERN

†DC —MIDDLE EAST INSTITUTE, George Camp Keiser Library, 1761 N St, NW, Washington, 20036.

ART, NEW YORK (STATE)

NY —ALBANY INSTITUTE OF HISTORY & ART, McKinney Library, 125 Washington Ave, Albany, 12210. Daryl Severson, Actg Librn; Suzanne Roberson, Photographic Librn
Holdings: Vols 5000 Cat Mss Maps Pix
Notes: Local history of the Albany, New York area and arts related to it.

NY —HISTORICAL SOCIETY OF THE TARRYTOWNS, Library, One Grove St, Tarrytown, 10591. Adelaide R Smith, Cur
Notes: Collection incl portraits from easels of noted painters, such as the Beekman family; early subjects such as George Clinton and John Naylor; local notables such as Captain Nathan Cobb and John D Rockefeller. Several noteworthy paintings and prints; many demonstrate relationship between history and art.

ART, OCEANIC

CA —FINE ARTS MUSEUMS OF SAN FRANCISCO, M H de Young Memorial Museum, Golden Gate Park, San Francisco, 94118. Jane Nelson, Librn
Holdings: Vols (30,000) Cat Slides
Budget: ($24,000)

MO —SAINT LOUIS ART MUSEUM, Richardson Memorial Library, Saint Louis, 63110. Ann B Abid, Librn
Holdings: Vols (30,000) Cat Pix Slides Microforms
Notes: Art history, incl decorative arts, catalogs, exhibitions, etc.

NY —BROOKLYN MUSEUM, Art Reference Library, 188 Eastern Parkway, Brooklyn, 11238.
Holdings: Vols (130,000)

NY —METROPOLITAN MUSEUM OF ART, Robert Goldwater Library, Fifth Ave at 82nd St, New York, 10028. Allan D Chapman, Librn
Holdings: Vols (27,000) Cat
Notes: Primitive art: African, Indians of the Americans (incl Pre-Columbian), Oceanic, Polynesian, etc. 150,000 photographs.

ART, OHIO

OH —CINCINNATI ART MUSEUM, Library, Eden Park, Cincinnati, 45202. Patrician P Rutledge, Librn
Holdings: Vols (45,850) Cat Mss Microforms
Notes: Art library containing all subjects on art-history, graphic arts, advertising art, etc; special strength in prints, ie engravings, etc. Near Eastern art and decorative arts are also strong. At least 90,000 art exhibition catalogs. Emphasis on artists of Cincinnati and vicinity in vertical file material.

ART, ORIENTAL

CA —SAN DIEGO PUBLIC LIBRARY, Art, Music & Recreation Sect, 820 E St, San Diego, 92101. Barbara A Tuhill, Supvr
Holdings: Vols 500 Cat Pix
Notes: Emphasis on Chinese, Japanese, Korean, and Cambodian art. Private library of Donal Hord, local sculptor. For reference use only.

CA —ASIAN ART MUSEUM OF SAN FRANCISCO, Library, Golden Gate Park, San Francisco, 94118. Fred A Cline Jr, Librn
Holdings: Vols (16,000) Cat Mss Pix Microforms Clippings
Notes: The Avery Brundage Collection of Oriental Art. Emphasis on East Asian, Southeast Asian and East Indian art. Also building a microform library; collecting pictures and clipping files. Noncirculating. No interlibrary loans.

CT —CONNECTICUT COLLEGE, Library, Mohegan Ave, New London, 06320. Brian Rogers, College Librn
Holdings: Vols 600 Cat
Notes: Holdings incl the Helen Carey Coudert Collection of nearly 500 books on Chinese and Japanese painting, sculpture and bronzes.

DC —FREER GALLERY OF ART, Library, 12th & Jefferson Dr SW, Washington, 20560. Ellen A Nollman, Librn
Holdings: Cat Pix Slides
Notes: Incl 50,000 slides; 8000 photographs. Catalog published by G K Hall, Boston.

HI —HONOLULU ACADEMY OF ARTS, Robert Allerton Library, 900 S Beretania St, Honolulu, 96814. Anne T Seaman, Librn
Holdings: Vols (40,000) Cat Pix Slides

†MD —ASIAN CULTURAL EXCHANGE FOUNDATION LIBRARY, Towson State University, Towson, 21204.

MA —MUSEUM OF FINE ARTS, William Morris Hunt Memorial Library, Huntington Ave, Boston, 02115. Nancy S Allen, Librn
Holdings: Vols (100,000) Cat
Budget: ($70,000)
Notes: Strong collection of art auction catalogs, exhibition catalogs, and Asian language books on art history. Collection has about 100,000 pamphlet pieces also.

MA —HARVARD UNIVERSITY LIBRARY, Fine Arts Library, Rubel Asiatic Research Collection, Sackler Museum, 38 Quincy Street, Cambridge, 02138. Yen-Shew Lynn Chao, Librn
Holdings: Vols 12,000 Cat Pix Slides Microforms
Notes: Described in *Harvard Library Bulletin*, VIII (1954): pp 108-111. Also large holdings of oriental art periodicals, reprints, and exhibition and sales catalogs.

MA —WELLESLEY COLLEGE, Art Library, Wellesley, 02181. Katherine D Finkelpearl, Art Librn
Holdings: Vols (30,000) Cat Pix Slides
Budget: ($22,000)
Notes: Primarily the art and architecture of Western Europe, the Far East, and classical antiquity. However, efforts are being made to expand the collection in the areas of photography, primitive art, and ancient (non-classical) art. The Art Department maintains

ART, ORIENTAL (cont.)

a separate collection of 62,500 mounted pictures and 90,000 slides.

MO —THE NELSON-ATKINS MUSEUM OF ART, Kenneth & Helen Spencer Art Reference Library, 4525 Oak St, Kansas City, 64111. Stanley W Hess, Librn
Holdings: Vols (35,000)
Budget: ($210,000)
Notes: Strong in prints and drawings. Incl VF. Oriental art, especially Chinese and Japanese; exhibition catalogs; auction catalogs.

MO —SCHOOL OF THE OZARKS, Lois Brownell Research Library, Ralph Foster Museum, Point Lookout, 65726. Robert Esworthy, Librn
Holdings: Vols (1300) Cat
Notes: Oriental antiques and art.

NJ —NEWARK MUSEUM LIBRARY, 49 Washington St, PO Box 540, Newark, 07101. Margaret DiSalvi, Librn
Holdings: Vols 4000 Cat Pix Slides

NJ —PRINCETON UNIVERSITY, Library, Gest Oriental Library & East Asian Collections, 317 Palmer Hall, Princeton, 08544. D E Perushek, Cur
Holdings: Vols (370,000) Cat Mss Maps Pix Microforms
Notes: Materials collected are mostly in East Asian languages: Chinese, Japanese and Korean. Subject emphasis is on East Asia, China, Japan and Korea, their civilization and societies, languages, literature, philosophy, religion, history, politics and sociology. No historical period is excluded. The Gest Library also acquires works on East Asian art and archaeology that are of a general or cultural nature and primary textual sources (extensive collections on East Asian art and archaeology are held and maintained at the University Art Library). Works on historical and economic aspects of East Asian population are also acquired (while population censuses and vital statistics are held at the University Population Research Library). Subject areas in sciences and technology, except those materials dealing with indigenous developments and historical aspects, are excluded. Withregard to the Korean collection in a holding position with a minimum budget allocation, Western-language reference works in all fields of East Asian studies and Western-language monographs of importance on East Asian literature, language, and linguistics are collected. Preference is given to works in English. Emphasis is on current publications. All other Western-language works on East Asia are located elsewhere in the University Library system. The existing collections also incl books and manuscripts in the Manchu, Mongolian, and Tibetan languages. However, acquisitions in these languages are now made on a highly selective basis. Separate card catalogs are maintained for Chinese, Japanese, Korean, and Western-language collections. See also Chen, Frances M & Maureen H Donovan: Periodicals on Asia; Serials in the Princeton University Library inWestern Languages (Princeton: Princeton University Library, 1975).

NY —STATE UNIVERSITY OF NEW YORK AT ALBANY, Library, Special Collections Dept, 1400 Washington Ave, Albany, 12222. Marion P Munzer, Coordr
Notes: Correspondence (3 linear feet) of Ludwig Bachhofer, incl teaching and research notes; mss and published works; photographs of Oriental art. Part of the Library's German Exile Collection.
See also entry under Bachhofer, Ludwig

NY —BROOKLYN MUSEUM, Art Reference Library, 188 Eastern Parkway, Brooklyn, 11238.
Holdings: Vols (130,000)

NY —BUFFALO MUSEUM OF SCIENCE, Buffalo Society of Natural Sciences, Research Library, Humboldt Park, Buffalo, 14211. Marcia T Morrison, Chief Librn
Holdings: Vols 900 Cat Mss Pix
Notes: The Elizabeth W Hamlin Oriental Library of Art and Archaeology. Incl 75 scrolls.

NY —INSTITUTE FOR ADVANCED STUDIES OF WORLD RELIGIONS (IASWR), Melville Memorial Library, State University of New York, Stony Brook, 11794. C T Shen, Dir
Holdings: Vols 2000 Cat Periodicals
Notes: Incl monographs and illustrated materials on Buddhist, Hindu and Islamic arts of all parts of Asia. Refer inquiries to H G Robinson.
See also entry under Art, Buddhist

OR —UNIVERSITY OF OREGON LIBRARY, Special Collections Div, Eugene, 97403. Kenneth W Duckett, Curator
Holdings: Vols 984 // Cat
Notes: The Gertrude Bass Warner Memorial Library contains Chinese, Japanese, and Korean art books (mostly early c20) published in the Orient.

PA —UNIVERSITY OF PITTSBURGH, Henry Clay Frick Fine Arts Library, Pittsburgh, 15260. Anne W Gordon, Fine Arts Librn
Holdings: Vols (55,000) Cat Pix Slides Microforms
Notes: Emphasis is on the art of the Western World--architecture, sculpture, painting, minor arts, archeology, with special strength in the Byzantine, early Christian, medieval, renaissance and modern periods. The Oriental fields represented, incl replicas of scrolls. Studio arts are also covered. Illuminated ms facsimiles. Extensive collections of slides and photographs for study of art history are available in the building but not administered by the art library.

PA —EASTERN COLLEGE, Frank Warner Memorial Library, Saint Davids, 19087. James L Sauer, Librn
Holdings: Uncat Mss Pix
Notes: The Harry C Goebel Collection. Incl Bruce Rogers printings (over 460); press books (about 350); oriental art (over 250); bookplates (with a separate collection of an almost complete set of bookplates designed by Edwin Davis French); Christmas Books; art and graphic arts (incl the French Graphic Arts Collection of Adoph DeMilly); first editions of Christopher Morley; Print Collection (1315 prints); Oriental art realia and artifacts.

VA —SWEET BRIAR COLLEGE, Library, Sweet Briar, 24595. John Jaffe, Librn
Holdings: Vols (5500) Cat Pix Slides
Budget: ($2000)

WA —UNIVERSITY OF WASHINGTON LIBRARIES, East Asia Library, DO-27, Seattle, 98195. Karl Lo, Head
Holdings: Vols (300,000) Cat Microforms
Budget: ($200,000)
Notes: Southwest China: Joseph Rock Collection, ca 2000 vols; modern Chinese poetry, 1919 to date: ca 700 titles; Asian art, esp Japanese painting: 4097 vols; Tiao-yu-t'ai movement in the US: ca 400 items of periodicals and pamphlets; modern Korean poetry, ancient and modern: ca 1000 titles; Mu-yu-shu folk literature: ca 1000 items.

WI —MILWAUKEE PUBLIC LIBRARY, 814 W Wisconsin Ave, Milwaukee, 53233. Donald J Sager, City Librn
Notes: The collection incl all fields of art, with emphasis on architecture, incl: Frank Lloyd Wright and local city planning documents; interior decoration; art history; American art; Oriental art; art instruction; decorative arts; numismatics and philately; photography, incl local photo archives and instruction manuals; costume; art exhibition and auction ctalogs; and local newspaper clippings on art subjects. Also, circulating mounted and framed art prints and sculpture reproductions.

ART, PENNSYLVANIA

PA —KING'S COLLEGE, D Leonard Corgan Library, 14 W Jackson St, Wilkes-Barre, 18711. Judith Tierney, Special Collections Librn
Notes: Approx 5 linear feet of completed questionnaires, clippings, brochures, and other material relating to artist and art organizations in the Wyoming Valley from 1808 to the present. Primarily biographical. Wyoming Valley Artists Files.

ART, POLISH

CA —THE POLISH ARTS AND CULTURE FOUNDATION, 1290 Sutter St, San Francisco, 94109. Wanda Tomczykowska, President
Holdings: Vols (500)
Notes: Incl 400 posters, original paintings and valuable samples of folk art.

CA —STANFORD UNIVERSITY LIBRARIES, Cecil H Green Library, Stanford, 94305. Wojciech Zalewski, Cur, Russian & East European Collection
Holdings: Vols (200,000) Cat Maps Microforms
Budget: ($90,000)
Notes: Strong collection prior to 20th century, but Stanford University Libraries' collecting effort is coordinated with Hoover Institution, Stanford, and holdings are not duplicated. Collection descriptions: Wojciech Zalewski, *Russian Materials in the Main Library of Stanford University, A Collection* Survey (Stanford: Stanford University Libraries, 1974). Wojciech Zalerski, "Stanford University" in P L Horecky, ed, *East Central and Southeast Europe, A Handbook of Library and Archival Resources in North America* (Santa Barbara: Clio Press, 1976).

MI —SAINT MARY'S COLLEGE, Alumni Memorial Library, Orchard Lake, 48033. Sister Mary Ellen Lampe, Librn

PA —ALLIANCE COLLEGE, Washington Hall Library, Fullerton Ave, Cambridge Springs, 16403. Stanley J Kozaczka, Head Librn
Holdings: 23,000 Vols
Notes: Polish cultural history, art, music, and literature collection. Much on Poles in the US. Polish newspapers and literary periodicals of 19th century in microform.

ART, POLYNESIAN see Art, Oceanic

ART, POP see Pop Art

ART, PORTUGUESE

NY —HISPANIC SOCIETY OF AMERICA, Library, 613 W 155 St, New York, 10032. Martha M de Narvaez, Cur of Mss; Irene S Frye, Asst Librn
Holdings: Vols (150,000) Cat Mss Maps Pix Slides Phonorecords Microforms
Notes: History, art, literature and general culture of the Hispanic countries (where Spanish or Portuguese is spoken). Incl (18, 000) vols printed before 1701, incl (250) incunabula; over (100,000) later vols, plus thousands of periodicals. About (200,000) mss incl ms maps. Printed atlases are in the Book Collection. Some microfilms, chiefly of our early books. Engraved and printed separate maps; reference collection of over 100,000 photographs; slides: all in Department of Iconography, not in library. Catalogs: *Catalogue of the Hispanic Society of America* (Boston: G K Hall, 1962), 10 vols; *First Supplement* (Boston, 1970), 4 vols. Early books: *Printed Books 1468-1700;* Mss: *Catalogo de los Manuscritos Poeticos* Castellanos (15th-17th centuries; 3 vols); *Medieval Manuscripts in the Library; Golden Age Drama Manuscripts*(the latter in press).

ART, PRE-COLUMBIAN

AZ —ARIZONA STATE MUSEUM, Library, University of Arizona, Tucson, 85721. Hans R Bart, Museum Librn
Holdings: Vols 400 Cat
Notes: Art and architecture of Latin America, strong in pre-Columbian material but mainly Spanish Colonial from the 16th to the 18th century. This is a large private library which is being transferred to the ASM Library. Special catalog is planned.

AZ —TUCSON MUSEUM OF ART LIBRARY, 140 N Main, Tucson, 85705. Dorcas Worsley, Librn
Holdings: Vols (2000)
Budget: ($1500)
Notes: Extensive file of biographical and

ART, PRE-COLUMBIAN (cont.)

critical information on Arizona artists which is continually being increased. Subject card index to magazines on Western art and artists in magazines not indexed in *Art* Index 12 drawers in 1984, and continues to grow. Have a collection of 15,000 slides.

CA —FINE ARTS MUSEUMS OF SAN FRANCISCO, M H de Young Memorial Museum, Golden Gate Park, San Francisco, 94118. Jane Nelson, Librn
Holdings: Vols Cat Slides

DC —HARVARD UNIVERSITY, Dumbarton Oaks, Pre-Columbian Studies, 1703 32nd St NW, Washington, 20007. Elizabeth Boone, Dir
Holdings: Vols 14,000 Cat Slides Audiotapes Microforms

MO —SAINT LOUIS ART MUSEUM, Richardson Memorial Library, Saint Louis, 63110. Ann B Abid, Librn
Holdings: Vols (30,000) Cat Pix Slides Microforms
Notes: Art history, incl decorative arts, catalogs, exhibitions, etc.

NY —METROPOLITAN MUSEUM OF ART, Robert Goldwater Library, Fifth Ave at 82nd St, New York, 10028. Allan D Chapman, Librn
Holdings: Vols (27,000) Cat
Notes: Primitive art: African, Indians of the Americans (incl Pre-Columbian), Oceanic, Polynesian, etc. 150,000 photographs.

TX —UNIVERSITY OF TEXAS LIBRARIES, Nettie Lee Benson Latin American Collection, Sid Richardson Hall 1.109, Austin, 78712. Laura Gutierrez-Witt, Head Librn
Holdings: Vols (450,000) Cat Mss Maps Pix Phonorecords Filmstrips Microforms
See also entry under Latin America

ART, PRIMITIVE

AZ —HEARD MUSEUM, Library, 22 E Monte Vista Rd, Phoenix, 85004. Mary Graham, Librn
Holdings: Vols (40,000) Cat
Notes: Anthropology and primitive art. Incl 124 periodical titles and contemporary Native American Art.

IN —INDIANA UNIVERSITY, Art Museum Bldg, Fine Arts Bldg, Bloomington, 47401. Betty Jo Irvine, Fine Arts Librn
Holdings: Vols (57,000) Cat Pix Microforms
Budget: ($52,000)
Notes: Art forms relevant to the periods and places involved.

MA —WELLESLEY COLLEGE, Art Library, Wellesley, 02181. Katherine D Finkelpearl, Art Librn
Holdings: Vols (30,000) Cat Pix Slides
Budget: ($22,000)
Notes: Primarily the art and architecture of Western Europe, the Far East, and classical antiquity. However, efforts are being made to expand the collection in the areas of photography, primitive art, and ancient (non-classical) art. The Art Department maintains a separate collection of 62,500 mounted pictures and 90,000 slides.

MO —THE NELSON-ATKINS MUSEUM OF ART, Kenneth & Helen Spencer Art Reference Library, 4525 Oak St, Kansas City, 64111. Stanley W Hess, Librn
Notes: African, American, Indian, Mesoamerican, Oceanic.

NY —MUSEUM OF THE AMERICAN INDIAN, Library, 9 Westchester Square, Bronx, 10401. Mary B Davis, Librn
Holdings: Cat
Notes: Incl information in Indians of North, Central, and South America; archaeology of North, Central, and South America; American Indian ethnology; anthropology, history.

NY —METROPOLITAN MUSEUM OF ART, Robert Goldwater Library, Fifth Ave at 82nd St, New York, 10028. Allan D Chapman, Librn
Holdings: Vols (27,000) Cat
Notes: Primitive art: African, Indians of the Americans (incl Pre-Columbian), Oceanic, Polynesian, etc. 150,000 photographs.

WI —MILWAUKEE PUBLIC MUSEUM, Reference Library, 800 W Wells St, Milwaukee, 53233. Judith Campbell Turner, Museum Librn
Holdings: Vols (90,000) Cat Maps Microforms

ART, PSYCHEDELIC

DC —LIBRARY OF CONGRESS, Prints & Photographs Div, Washington, 20540.
Notes: Poster collection numbers about 70, 000 American and foreign items from the 1850s to the present. Incl *Art Nouveau* of World War I and World War II, WPA, propaganda, performing arts, and psychedelic posters.

ART, RENAISSANCE

CA —J PAUL GETTY MUSEUM, Research Library, 17985 Pacific Coast Highway, Malibu, 90265. Anne-Mieke Halbrook, Head Librn
Holdings: Vols (140,000) Cat

CA —J PAUL GETTY MUSEUM, Photo Archives, 17985 Pacific Coast Hwy, Malibu, 90265. William Reeder, Cur
Holdings: Pix
Notes: Incl photographs of works of art at the Museum (180,000 cataloged, 500,000 uncataloged), incl ancient art, western European art (painting, sculpture, graphics) and European decorative arts, medieval and Renaissance to 19th century, and antiquities.

FL —RINGLING MUSEUM OF ART, Art Research Library, PO Box 1838, Sarasota, 33578. Lynell A Morr, Librn
Holdings: Vols (40,000) Cat
Budget: ($24,000)
Notes: Incl an additional 30,000 art auction catalogs, indexed 1970-date.

IN —INDIANA UNIVERSITY, Art Museum Bldg, Fine Arts Bldg, Bloomington, 47401. Betty Jo Irvine, Fine Arts Librn
Holdings: Vols (57,000) Cat Pix Microforms
Budget: ($52,000)
Notes: Art forms relevant to the periods and places involved.

MD —JOHNS HOPKINS UNIVERSITY, Milton S Eisenhower Library, Charles & 34 Sts, Baltimore, 21218. Ann S Gwyn, Assistant Dir for Special Collections
Holdings: Vols (18,000) Cat Maps
Notes: Strongest in ancient, Byzantine, and Renaissance art and architecture. Reference Library lacks some periodicals. Modern period being rapidly built up.

MA —HARVARD UNIVERSITY, Harvard College Library, Fine Arts Library, Fogg Museum, 32 Quincy St, Cambridge, 02138. Wolfgang M Freitag, Librn
Holdings: Vols (202,000) Cat Mss Pix Slides
Budget: ($176,500)
Notes: All areas of art history, with emphasis on Italian primitives, Italian Renaissance, master drawings, Romanesque sculpture, architectural history, ms materials (particulary American artists'), conservation and restoration of art objects. Incl the Berenson repertory of photographs from the Harvard Center for Italian Renaissance Studies in Florence, and the Decimal Index to the Art of the Low Countries. Separate card catalogs for books, photographs and lantern slides, registers for ms holdings which are not incl in *National Union Catalog of Manuscript Collections.* Slides total over 230,000; over 745,000 pictures. *Fine Arts Library Catalogue* (14 volumes) and *Catalogue of Auction Sales Catalogues* (1 volume) (Boston: G K Hall, 1972); *A Guide to the Fine Arts Library* (Cambridge, Mass: 1971); *Guide to the Harvard Libraries,* microfiche edition of holdingscataloged through 1981 published 1984 (Munich/New York: Saur).

MO —SAINT LOUIS UNIVERSITY, Pius XII Memorial Library, 3655 W Pine Blvd, Saint Louis, 63108. William Cole, Dir
Holdings: Vols 250 Cat Mss Slides //
Notes: Collection covers all areas of learning and European history from Classical Antiquity to early modern period. Researchers using collection receive assistance in paleography, bibliography and reference search.

OH —OHIO STATE UNIVERSITY, Fine Arts Library, 1813 N High St, Columbus, 43210. Susan Wyngaard, Head, Fine Arts Library
Holdings: Vols (75,000) Cat Microforms
Budget: ($60,000)
Notes: Also have 1000 uncataloged exhibition catalogs. Book collection strong in history of art especially in area of medieval & Northern Renaissance art. Good collection of portfolios. Photographic collections on microfiche. Receive Slavic titles, many on Byzantine frescoes. Online catalog. Decimal Index of the Art of the Low Countries, as well as Marburger Index; Index Photographique de i' Arten France; Alinari Archives on microfiche and other major microform collections in art.

OH —OBERLIN COLLEGE LIBRARY, Clarence Ward Art Library, Allen Art Bldg, Oberlin, 44074. Jeffrey Weidman, Librn
Holdings: Vols (62,000) Cat Microforms

PA —BRYN MAWR COLLEGE, Canaday Library, Bryn Mawr, 19010. James Tanis, Dir
Notes: Baroque and Italian Renaissance painting and architecture; late antique and early Christian art; Flemish and Dutch painting 15th-17th centuries; French painting 18th-19th centuries. In Art and Archaeology Library.

PA —UNIVERSITY OF PITTSBURGH, Henry Clay Frick Fine Arts Library, Pittsburgh, 15260. Anne W Gordon, Fine Arts Librn
Holdings: Vols (55,000) Cat Pix Microforms
Notes: Emphasis is on the art of the Western World--Architecture, sculpture, painting, minor arts, archaeology, with special strength in the Byzantine, early Christian, medieval, renaissance and modern periods. The Oriental field is represented, incl replicas of scrolls. Studio arts are also covered. Illuminated ms facsimiles. Extensive collections of slides and photographs for study of art history are available in the building but not administered by the art library.

ON —NATIONAL GALLERY OF CANADA, Library, National Museums of Canada, Ottawa, K1A 0M8, Can. J Hunter, Chief Librn

ART, ROMAN

†MA —UNIVERSITY OF MASSACHUSETTS AT AMHERST, Library, Amherst, 01003.
Notes: Classical art and archaeology. Special emphasis: Aegean area.

MA —SMITH COLLEGE, Hillyer Art Library, Fine Arts Center, Northampton, 01063. Karen Harvey, Librn
Holdings: Vols (45,000) Cat

ART, RUSSIAN

CA —CALIFORNIA STATE UNIVERSITY, FRESNO, Henry Madden Library, Dept of Special Collections, Fresno, 93740. Ronald J Mahoney, Head
Holdings: Uncat
Notes: The Alexander Pronin Collection of Russian Postcards of approx 1500 Russian postcards, 1890-1920, illustrating Russian art, architecture and life. Approx 150 are partially used, incl various World War I censors' marks.

CA —STANFORD UNIVERSITY LIBRARIES, Cecil H Green Library, Stanford, 94305. Wojciech Zalewski, Cur, Russian & East European Collection
Holdings: Vols (200,000) Cat Maps Microforms
Budget: ($90,000)
Notes: Strong collection prior to 20th century, but Stanford University Libraries' collecting effort is coordinated with Hoover Institution, Stanford, and holdings are not duplicated. Collection descriptions: Wojciech Zalewski, *Russian Materials in the Main Library of Stanford University, A Collection* Survey (Stanford: Stanford University Libraries, 1974). Wojciech Zalerski, "Stanford University" in P L Horecky, ed, *East Central and Southeast Europe, A Handbook of Library and Archival*

ART, RUSSIAN (cont.)

Resources in North America (Santa Barbara: Clio Press, 1976).

NY —NEW YORK PUBLIC LIBRARY, Slavonic Div, Fifth Ave & 42 St, New York, 10018. Edward Kasinec, Chief
Holdings: Cat Microforms
Budget: ($62,153)
Notes: See: New York Public Library, Slavonic Div *Dictionary Catalog of the Slavonic Collection*, 2nd ed rev and enl (Boston: G K Hall, 1974), 44 vols; and New York Public Library, *Dictionary Catalog of the Research Libraries* (New York, 1972-).

NY —SAINT VLADIMIRS' ORTHODOX THEOLOGICAL SEMINARY, 575 Scarsdale Rd, Yonkers, 10707. Paul D Garrett, Librn
Holdings: Vols (36,000) Pix
Notes: Incl 250 periodicals. A major source of materials on Orthodox Church theology. Much on works of art.

ART, SCANDINAVIAN

IA —DES MOINES ART CENTER, Library, Greenwood Park, Des Moines, 50312. Georgeanne Kudron, Dir of Education
Holdings: Vols 175 // Uncat Mss
Notes: Pennington Collection. Primarily emphasis on Scandinavian weaving. *Seen by appointment only.* Inaccessable indefinitely due to building program.

ART, SERIAL see Minimal Art

ART, SEX IN see Sex in the Arts

ART, SLAVIC

DC —HARVARD UNIVERSITY, Dumbarton Oaks, Research Library, 1703 32nd St NW, Washington, 20007. Irene Vaslef, Librn
Holdings: Vols (91,000) Cat Maps Pix Slides Microforms
Budget: ($291,000)
Notes: Byzantine civilization (including art, archaeology, literature, history, religion, law, music, etc). Extensive supplemental material on Classical, Hellenistic, Medieval, Islamic, Medieval Slavic cultures. 62,000 b/w photographs, 25,000 slides and transparencies, 1000 microfilms of books and manuscripts. Printed description of collection in *Harvard Library Bulletin*, vol 19, no 1 (Jan 1971), pp 25-35 and vol 19, no 2 (April 1971), pp 204-214, pp 25-35 and vol 19, no 2 (April 1971), pp 204-214.

MA —HARVARD UNIVERSITY LIBRARY, Cambridge, 02138.

NY —NEW YORK PUBLIC LIBRARY, Slavonic Div, Fifth Ave & 42 St, New York, 10018. Edward Kasinec, Chief
Holdings: Cat Microforms
Budget: ($62,153)
Notes: See: New York Public Library, Slavic Div, *Dictionary Catalog of the Slavonic* Collection, 2nd ed, rev and enl (Boston G K Hall, 1974), 44 vols; and New York Public Library, *Dictionary Catalog of the Research* Libraries (New York, 1972-).

WA —UNIVERSITY OF WASHINGTON LIBRARIES, Suzzallo Library, Slavic & East European Section, FM-25, Seattle, 98195. Barbara A Galik, Head
Holdings: Vols (250,000) Cat Mss Maps Pix Phonorecords Audiotapes Microforms
Budget: ($85,000)
Notes: Strong research collections for Russia--USSR, including Central Asia, Eastern Europe and the Balkans, especially Yugoslavia and Poland. Holdings are strongest in Art, Russian with additional holdings listed under Art, individual country. There are extensive holdings of the publications of academies, major universities, and principal scholarly institutions, especially of long serial runs.

ART, SOUTH ASIAN

PA —UNIVERSITY OF PENNSYLVANIA, Van Pelt Library, South Asia Collection, 34 and Walnut Sts, Philadelphia, 19104. Kanta Bhatia, Bibliographer
Holdings: Pix Slides
Notes: South Asia Art Archive contains architecture, sculpture, terra cotta, coins, miniature paintings, and Baroque churches in India. Particularly strong in architecture and sculpture. 45,000 black and white photographs and 3000 color slides.

ART, SOUTHEAST ASIAN

CA —ASIAN ART MUSEUM OF SAN FRANCISCO, Library, Golden Gate Park, San Francisco, 94118. Fred A Cline Jr, Librn
Holdings: Vols (16,000) Cat Mss Pix Microforms Clippings
Notes: The Avery Brundage Collection of Oriental Art. Emphasis on East Asian, Southeast Asian and East Indian art. Also building a microform library; collecting pictures and clipping files. Noncirculating. No interlibrary loans.

DC —HOWARD UNIVERSITY, Founders Library, Bernard B Fall Collection (Southeast Asia Collection), Washington, 20059. Steven Ilsang Yoon, Cur
Holdings: Vols (6000) Cat Microforms
Budget: $15,000
Notes: The Bernard B Fall Collection has more than 6000 books, incl 1200 books purchased from the Kendric N Marshall Estate, 3000 items in vertical files, 300 pamphlets, and 800 microfilms, about Southeastern Asia and China. In addition, there are nearly 100 current periodicals and another 100 older periodicals about Indochina in the Collection.

IL —NORTHERN ILLINOIS UNIVERSITY, Founders Memorial Library, Southeast Asia Collection, Normal Rd, De Kalb, 60115. Lee S Dutton Dr, Cur
Holdings: Vols (34,000) Cat Maps Microforms
Notes: An extensive collection of books, periodicals, newspapers, maps, and microforms from or about Southeast Asia. Areas of concentration incl Thailand, Malaysia, Indonesia, Singapore, Brunei, Philippines, Laos, and Burma. Holdings (except rare books, maps, and microforms) are housed in a separate area collection within the Founders Library. A departmental card catalog and specialized reference collection support reference services. A Thai collection of several thousand vols is the largest vernacular component. Extensive Malaysia, Indonesia, Singapore, and Brunei holdings have been acquired through the NPAC program. A collection of Filipino-American newspapers, and a growing collection of children's literature in common and uncommon Southeast Asian languages are available. Resources are accessible to borrowers through OCLC.

MA —HARVARD UNIVERSITY LIBRARY, Fine Arts Library, Rubel Asiatic Research Collection, Sackler Museum, 38 Quincy Street, Cambridge, 02138. Yen-Shew Lynn Chao, Librn
Holdings: Cat Mss Maps Pix Slides
Notes: Rubel Asiatic Research Collection; specializes exclusively in the acquisition of Oriental language (Chinese, Japanese, and Korean) materials. Particular strengths incl the areas of Buddhist arts, Chinese bronzes and painting, Japanese painting and prints, and Chinese and Japanese ceramics. Also large holdings of oriental art periodicals, reprints, and exhibition and sales catalogs.

ART, SOUTHWESTERN

AZ —TUCSON MUSEUM OF ART LIBRARY, 140 N Main, Tucson, 85705. Dorcas Worsley, Librn
Holdings: Vols (2000)
Budget: ($1500)
Notes: Extensive file of biographical and critical information on Arizona artists which is continually being increased. Subject card index to magazines on Western art and artists in magazines not indexed in *Art* Index 12 drawers in 1984, and continues to grow. Have a collection of 15,000 slides.

TX —TEXAS A&M UNIVERSITY, Sterling C Evans Library, Special Collections Div, College Station, 77843. Donald H Dyal, Librn
Holdings: Vols 3500 Cat Mss Pix
Notes: The Western Illustrators Collection is comprised of approximately 3500 illustrated books, pamphlets, and other items. The collection incl illustrated works by Charles Marion Russell, Frederic Sackrider Remington, and other artists of the American West. Numerous other artists of the West and Southwest are represented, many of them contemporary moderns. Quite a lot of the books have additional unique original drawings by the artists.

TX —EL PASO PUBLIC LIBRARY, Southwest Collection, 501 N Oregon, El Paso, 79901. Mary A Sarber, Head
Holdings: Vols (12,000) Cat Mss Maps Pix
Budget: ($11,000)
Notes: Limited to materials on Texas, New Mexico, Arizona, and Mexico. Special collections of material by and about Tom Lea Jr, and Carl Hertzog. Aultman Collection of photographs incl 3500 on El Paso and the Southwest and 2500 on the Mexican Revolution. Separate catalog. See Lovelace, Lisabeth, "The Southwest Collection of the El Paso Public Library," Great Plains Journal, 11:2, pp 161-166; and Aultman, Otis A, *Photographs from the Border: The Otis A Aultman Collection* (El Paso Public Library Association, 1977).

ART, SPANISH

CA —UNIVERSITY OF CALIFORNIA, SAN DIEGO, Central University Library, Mandeville Dept of Special Collections, La Jolla, 92093. Lynda Corey Claassen, Head
Notes: Hispanic Collection: Approx 6000 vols describe cultures of Spain, Portugal, Mexico, Latin America, and South America. Works of literature, history, philosophy and art date from the 15th to the mid-19th century. Highlights of the collection include rare 18th century Spanish provincial dramas and works on the history of Seville and Andalusia.

NY —HISPANIC SOCIETY OF AMERICA, Library, 613 W 155 St, New York, 10032. Martha M de Narvaez, Cur of Mss; Irene S Frye, Asst Librn
Holdings: Vols (150,000) Cat Mss Maps Pix Slides Phonorecords Microforms
Notes: History, art, literature and general culture of the Hispanic countries (where Spanish or Portuguese is spoken). Incl (18, 000) vols printed before 1701, incl (250) incunabula; over (100,000) later vols, plus thousands of periodicals. About (200,000) mss incl ms maps. Printed atlases are in the Book Collection. Some microfilms, chiefly of our early books. Engraved and printed separate maps; reference collection of over 100,000 photographs; slides: all in Department of Iconography, not in library. Catalogs: *Catalogue of the Hispanic Society of America* (Boston: G K Hall, 1962), 10 vols; *First Supplement* (Boston, 1970), 4 vols. Early books: *Printed Books 1468-1700;* Mss: *Catalogo de los Manuscritos Poeticos* Castellanos (15th-17th centuries; 3 vols); *Medieval Manuscripts in the Library; Golden Age Drama Manuscripts*(the latter in press).

ART, SPANISH COLONIAL

AZ —TUCSON MUSEUM OF ART LIBRARY, 140 N Main, Tucson, 85705. Dorcas Worsley, Librn
Holdings: Vols (2000)
Budget: ($1500)
Notes: Extensive file of biographical and critical information on Arizona artists which is continually being increased. Subject card index to magazines on Western art and artists in magazines not indexed in *Art* Index 12 drawers in 1984, and continues to grow. Have a collection of 15,000 slides.

ART, STUDIO

NY —STATE UNIVERSITY OF NEW YORK, COLLEGE AT NEW PALTZ,

ART, STUDIO (cont.)

Sojourner Truth Library, New Paltz, 12561. W E Connors, Dir
Holdings: Vols 1000
Notes: Art--education, history, studio.

ART, SURREALISTIC

CA —CALIFORNIA INSTITUTE OF THE ARTS, Library, 24700 McBean Pkwy, Valencia, 91355. James Elrod, Dir
Holdings: Vols (61,000) Slides
Budget: ($11,000)
Notes: Modern art, incl abstract, conceptual, concrete, environment, minimal, and pop art; art; dadaism; surrealism; happenings; and caricatures and cartoons. Slides (61,683).

CT —YALE UNIVERSITY, Beinecke Rare Book & Manuscript Library, Osborn Collection, New Haven, 06520. Stephen R Parks, Cur
Holdings: Mss

IL —NORTHWESTERN UNIVERSITY, Library, Special Collections Dept, 1937 Sheridan Rd, Evanston, 60201. R Russell Maylone, Cur
Holdings: Vols 3000 Cat
Notes: Books, periodicals, pamphlets, catalogs, ephemera.

NY —MUSEUM OF MODERN ART, Library, 11 W 53 St, New York, 10019. Clive Phillpot, Library Dir
Holdings: Vols 80,000 Cat Mss Microforms
Notes: Art of the 20th and latter half of the 19th century (painting, sculpture, drawings and prints, architecture, photography, film, design mixed media, artists' books). Special emphasis on Surrealist and Dada literature and art. Incl art exhibition catalogs. Photocopying restricted. See *Catalog of the Museum of Modern Art, New York City* (Boston: G K Hall, 1976), 14 vols.

ON —METROPOLITAN TORONTO LIBRARY, Literature Dept, 789 Yonge St, Toronto, M4W 2G8, Can. Katherine McCook, Head
Holdings: Vols (200) Cat
Notes: Books, periodicals, pamphlets, especially on French literature. Part of a collection on other international avant-garde literary movements.

ON —VICTORIA UNIVERSITY, Library, 71 Queen's Park Crescent, Toronto, M5S 1K7, Can. Robert C Brandeis, Chief Librn
Holdings: Vols 5000
Notes: The Riese Collection, partially cataloged, containing presentation copies of works by modern and contemporary French authors. Strong in Surrealism.

ART, SWEDISH

OH —OBERLIN COLLEGE LIBRARY, Clarence Ward Art Library, Allen Art Bldg, Oberlin, 44074. Jeffrey Weidman, Librn
Holdings: Vols (62,000) Cat Microforms
Notes: Incl Swedish publications and original photographs of works of art collected by Prof Ellen Johnson. Also strong in publications of other parts of scandinavia.

ART, TIBETAN

CT —YALE UNIVERSITY, Box 1603A, Yale Station, New Haven, 06520.
Notes: A major collection of Tibetan Buddhist paintings, bronze images and books.

MA —HARVARD UNIVERSITY LIBRARY, Fine Arts Library, Rubel Asiatic Research Collection, Sackler Museum, 38 Quincy Street, Cambridge, 02138. Yen-Shew Lynn Chao, Librn
Holdings: Cat Mss Maps Pix Slides
Notes: Rubel Asiatic Research Collection; specializes exclusively in the acquisition of Oriental language (Chinese, Japanese, and Korean) materials. Particular strengths incl the areas of Buddhist arts, Chinese bronzes and painting, Japanese painting and prints, and Chinese and Japanese ceramics. Also large holdings of oriental art periodicals, reprints, and exhibition and sales catalogs.

NJ —NEWARK MUSEUM LIBRARY, 49 Washington St, PO Box 540, Newark, 07101. Margaret DiSalvi, Librn
Holdings: Vols 350 Cat Mss Maps Pix Slides
Notes: The Newark Museum has an outstanding collection of Tibetan religious books which are considered part of the museum's collections rather than the library's. The library's collections incl published books, pamphlets, etc, over 1000 photographs of Tibet and Tibetans, and many slides of Tibet and of the museum's collections. Have published a catalog of our Tibetan collections. See, *Catalogue of the Tibetan Collection and other Lamaist* Articles, 5-vols (Newark Museum, Newark, NJ), prepared by Eleanor Olson, Curator Emeritus of the Oriental Collections, 1950-1971.

ART, TYPOGRAPHIC

NY —ROCHESTER INSTITUTE OF TECHNOLOGY, Melbert B Cary Jr Graphic Arts Collection, School of Printing, One Lomb Memorial Drive, Rochester, 14623. David Pankow, Cur
Holdings: Vols (11,000) Cat
Notes: An extensive collection of the work of typographic artist Albert Schiller. Incl type pictures, their type forms, correspondence, sketches, books, proofs, and ephemera.

ART, UKRAINIAN

CT —UKRAINIAN MUSEUM AND LIBRARY, 161 Glenbrook Rd, Stamford, 06902. Wasyl Lencyk, Dir
Holdings: Vols (20,000)
Notes: Paintings, sculpture, engravings and easter eggs. About 60 Ukrainian painters.

MI —UKRAINIAN-AMERICAN ARCHIVES AND MUSEUM, 26601 Ryan Rd, Warren, 48091.
Notes: Historical relics, several thousand books, periodicals, manuscripts, etc. Christmas and Easter handicrafts.

NY —SHEVCHENKO SCIENTIFIC SOCIETY INC, 63 Fourth Ave, New York, 10003. Svitlana Andrushkiw, Librn
Holdings: Vols 3000
Notes: Supports graduate level research. The Society has a rare book and archival section which contains rare editions, mss, documents, photographs, some microforms. Society is in the process of establishing vertical files and full cataloging of all holdings. Collection consists of approx 35, 000 volumes. Basically a research, non-lending library. Graduate level researchers are welcome. To use library, make appointment by telephoning (212) 254-5130 or (212) 254-5239.

NY —UKRAINIAN MUSUEM, 203 Second Ave, New York, 10003. Maria Shust, Dir
Notes: Also over 1500 folk artifacts and works of art.

ART, WESTERN

AZ —TUCSON MUSEUM OF ART LIBRARY, 140 N Main, Tucson, 85705. Dorcas Worsley, Librn
Holdings: Vols (2000)
Budget: ($1500)
Notes: Extensive file of biographical and critical information on Arizona artists which is continually being increased. Subject card index to magazines on Western art and artists in magazines not indexed in *Art* Index 12 drawers in 1984, and continues to grow. Have a collection of 15,000 slides.

CO —DENVER PUBLIC LIBRARY, Western History Department, 1357 Broadway, Denver, 80203. Eleanor M Gehres, Head
Holdings: Vols (50,000) Cat Mss Maps Pix Audiotapes Microforms
Notes: Western US History. The department has a separate catalog, published in 1970 in 7 vols by G K Hall Co. First supplement published in 1975 in 1 vol. There is a subject index of some 3 million entries to newspapers and magazines of the Rocky Mountain region, added to daily. The Western Newspaper Microfilm Center contains approx 7000 reels of Western US newspapers. Collection has ca 275,000 negatives and prints of Western life; and ca 2500 maps, cataloged and classified.

TX —TEXAS A&M UNIVERSITY, Sterling C Evans Library, Special Collections Div, College Station, 77843. Donald H Dyal, Librn
Holdings: Vols 3500 Cat Mss Pix
Notes: Western art, art history, illustration.

ART, YUGOSLAVIAN

CA —STANFORD UNIVERSITY LIBRARIES, Cecil H Green Library, Stanford, 94305. Wojciech Zalewski, Cur, Russian & East European Collection
Holdings: Vols (200,000) Cat Maps Microforms
Budget: ($90,000)
Notes: Strong collection prior to 20th century, but Stanford University Libraries collecting effort is coordinated with Hoover Institution, Stanford, and holdings are not duplicated. Collection descriptions: Wojciech Zalewski, *Russian Materials in the Main Library of Stanford University, A Collection* Survey (Stanford: Stanford University Libraries, 1974). Wojciech Zalerski, "Stanford University" in P L Horecky, ed, *East Central and Southeast Europe, A Handbook of Library and Archival Resources in North America* (Santa Barbara: Clio Press, 1976).

ART AND DRUGS

CA —FITZ HUGH LUDLOW MEMORIAL LIBRARY, PO Box 99346, San Francisco, 94109. Michael R Aldrich, Exec Cur
Holdings: Vols 6000 Pix Slides
Notes: Collection stored. Important mail inquiries only. No interlibrary lending or telephone queries. Index to hundreds of drug-related illustrations, filed in several binders by topic (Cannabis, Hallucinogens, Cocaine, Music, etc). We have photostats of about 500 of the best illustrations available to researchers and writers as a graphics archive; copyright and reproduction permission must however be obtained by the user of publisher, in addition to a nominal fee (per illustration) paid to the Library. We also collect original art works, artifacts, paraphernalia, comic books, newspaper illustrations, and drug advertisements relating to psychoactive drug use and abuse. In addition we have available many illustrations pertinent to mythology (ancient and modern) peripherally related to drug history and folklore.

ART AUCTIONS

NY —STATE UNIVERSITY OF NEW YORK AT ALBANY, Library, Special Collections Dept, 1400 Washington Ave, Albany, 12222. Marion P Munzer, Coordr
Notes: Mss, publications, photographs relating to the work of Fritz Neugass as art correspondent for foreign newspapers and periodicals, specializing in the American art market (53 linear feet, 25 feet of auction catalogs). Part of the Library's German Exile Collection.
See also entry under Neugass, Fritz

ART GALLERIES see Art—Galleries and Museums

ART IN ADVERTISING see Commercial Art

ART INDUSTRIES AND TRADE

CA —CRAFT AND FOLK ART MUSEUM, Library, 5814 Wilshire Blvd, Los Angeles, 90036. Joan M Benedetti, Museum Librn
Holdings: Vols (2000) Slides VF
Notes: Incl 2000 books; 70 journal subscriptions; artists' biographical files: 6 file drawers; clipping files: 8 file drawers; 20,000 slides. Representation of the material culture of all people, traditional and contemporary expressions. Incl visual and printed information on ethnic, traditional, popular, decorative, idiosyncratic, and contemporary

ART INDUSTRIES AND TRADE (cont.)

crafts as well as vernacular architecture, handmade houses, and design. Information about and for professional artists on health hazards, conservation, and career management. Anthropological and art historical works; exhibition catalogues; slides, photographs, audiocassettes; clipping and pamphlet files. Contemporary Slide Registry of Craftspeople and extensive biographical files of contemporary craft artists. Information and referral files of craft related galleries, shops, festivals, organizations, etc.

CT —STOWE-DAY LIBRARY, 77 Forest St, Hartford, 06105. Diana J Royce, Librn
Holdings: Vols (15,000) Cat Mss
Notes: Incl (6000) additional pamphlets. The entire collection covers architecture, decorative arts, history, literature, woman suffrage, and Harriet Beecher Stowe, through the 19th century.

DE —HENRY F DUPONT WINTERTHUR MUSEUM LIBRARY, Winterthur, 19735. Frank H Sommer, III, Head
Holdings: Cat
Notes: Strong collections.

MI —UNIVERSITY OF MICHIGAN, Art and Architecture Library, 2106 Art and Architecture Bldg, Ann Arbor, 48109. Peggy Ann Kusnerz, Librn; Dot Shields, Asst Librn
Holdings: Vols (45,000)
Budget:
Notes: Incl 200 maps, 35,000 slides, vertical file, videocassettes, blueprints, Jens Jensen Landscape drawings, oral history, and 400 serial titles.

MI —CRANBROOK ACADEMY OF ART, 500 Lone Pine Rd, Box 801, Bloomfield Hills, 48013. Diane Gunn, Librn

NY —HISTORICAL SOCIETY OF EARLY AMERICAN DECORATION, 19 Dove St, Albany, 12210. Doris Fry, Dir; Laura Olf, Librn
Holdings: Cat Pix Slides
Notes: The Library is housed with the Museum Collection of the Society. Incl examples of 19th century American country painting on tin, stenciling on wood and tin, bronzing decoration on wood, English stencilled tin and wood, bronzed items, painted objects, reverse painting on glass and examples of other decorating techniques of the period. Also included is a large collection of painted recordings of designs from early articles. Many of these were done by Esther Stevens Brazer in the 1930s. Another large collection has been added since that time. The library material is related to this interest. See *The Decorator*, official publication of the Historical Society of Early American Decoration. Other publications: *The Ornamented Chair* and *The Ornamented Tray* (both ed by Zilla Rider Lea), *Antique Decorations* by Brazer.

NY —NEW YORK PUBLIC LIBRARY, Art, Prints, and Photographs Div, Fifth Ave & 42 St, New York, 10018. Donald Anderle, Chief

NY —ROCHESTER INSTITUTE OF TECHNOLOGY, Technical & Education Center of the Graphic Arts, Graphic Arts Information Service, One Lomb Memorial Dr, Rochester, 14623. Susan Clark, Technical Librn
Holdings: Vols (1500) Cat Microforms
Notes: Graphic arts (photographic and applied art aspects) with emphasis on science and technology of printing. Periodicals (265) and technical reports, pertinent to the graphic arts, are routinely scanned for articles of significant information content; articles are classified and keyworded, if needed, and the complete reference is published in *Graphic Arts Literature* Abstracts, a monthly publication of the Graphic Arts Research Center. All abstracted articles are microfilmed and in individual fiche jackets for easy storage and retrieval.

PA —TEMPLE UNIVERSITY, Tyler School of Art, Beech & Penrose Aves, Philadelphia, 19126. Mary Ivy Bayard, Librn
Holdings: Vols 24,267 Cat Pix Microforms
Budget:
Notes: The art school branch of the main university library; supports a graduate program in the fine arts, incl some graduate courses in art history.

TN —VANDERBILT UNIVERSITY, George Peabody College for Teachers, Education Library, Box 325, Nashville, 37203. Mary Beth Blalock, Librn
Notes: The Education Library collects in all areas relating to education with special emphasis on Child Study and Exceptional Children. The collection is strong in curriculum materials, physical education, applied art, psychology related to education and all areas of education. The Education Library is a Division of the Vanderbilt University Library.

VA —COLONIAL WILLIAMSBURG FOUNDATION, Abby Aldrich Rockefeller Folk Art Center, PO Box C, Williamsburg, 23187. Anne E Watkins, Registrar
Holdings: Vols 1200 Cat Maps Pix Slides
Notes: American folk art emphasis.

ON —METROPOLITAN TORONTO LIBRARY, Fine Arts Dept, 789 Yonge St, Toronto, M4W 2G8, Can. Alan Suddon, Head
Holdings: Vols (42,000) Cat Pix Microforms
Notes: Extensive collection.

ON —ROYAL ONTARIO MUSEUM, Main Library and Archives, 100 Queen's Park, Toronto, M5S 2C6, Can. Julia Matthews, Head Librn
Holdings: Vols (85,000) Cat
Notes: Since January 1977, acquisitions have been entered in UTLAS.

ON —UNIVERSITY OF TORONTO, Thomas Fisher Rare Book Library, 120 Saint George St, Toronto, M5S 1A5, Can. Richard G Landon, Head
Notes: All currently published and most earlier major works on the fine and applied arts in Canada; Canadian art exhibition catalogues; limited editions illustrated by Canadian artists; 19th and 20th century architectural plans for buildings in Toronto and southern Ontario vicinity (ca 1700).

ART NOUVEAU

DC —LIBRARY OF CONGRESS, Prints & Photographs Div, Washington, 20540.
Notes: Poster collection numbers about 70, 000 American and foreign items from the 1850s to the present. Incl *Art Nouveau* of World War I and World War II, WPA, propaganda, performing arts, and psychedelic posters.

IL —NORTHWESTERN UNIVERSITY, Library, Special Collections Dept, 1937 Sheridan Rd, Evanston, 60201. R Russell Maylone, Cur
Holdings: Cat
Notes: The collection includes 70 titles of the major Art Nouveau journals published in Belgium and France, amoung them *Van Nu en Straks, La Wallonie, La Jeune Revue Belgique, La Bosoche, Art et Decoration, L'Art Litteraire, Le Centaure, Le Chat-Noir, L'Ermitage, L'Estampe et l' Affiche, Gil Blas Illustree, Le Mercure de France, La Revue Contemporaine* and *Le Symboliste*.
Literature: Howe, Jeffery W, *Belgian and French Journals of the Fin-de-Siecle in the Northwestern University Library: A Bibliographical Study from an Art Historical Point of View* (Evanston: Northwestern University Library, 1977).

ART OBJECTS—CONSERVATION AND RESTORATION

CA —CRAFT AND FOLK ART MUSEUM, Library, 5814 Wilshire Blvd, Los Angeles, 90036. Joan M Benedetti, Museum Librn
Holdings: Vols (2000) Slides VF
Notes: Incl 2000 books; 70 journal subscriptions; artists' biographical files: 6 file drawers; clipping files: 8 file drawers; 20,000 slides. Representation of the material culture of all people, traditional and contemporary expressions. Incl visual and printed information on ethnic, traditional, popular, decorative, idiosyncratic, and contemporary crafts as well as vernacular architecture, handmade houses, and design. Information about and for professional artists on health hazards, conservation, and career management. Anthropological and art historical works; exhibition catalogues; slides, photographs, audiocassettes; clipping and pamphlet files. Contemporary Slide Registry of Craftspeople and extensive biographical files of contemporary craft artists. Information and referral files of craft related galleries, shops, festivals, organizations, etc.

MA —HARVARD UNIVERSITY, Harvard College Library, Fine Arts Library, Fogg Museum, 32 Quincy St, Cambridge, 02138. Wolfgang M Freitag, Librn
Holdings: Cat Mss Pix Slides
Notes: *Catalogue* of Library (15 volumes) published 1971. First supplement (3 volumes), 1976. Microfiche edition of holdings cataloged through 1981 published in 1984 (Munich/New York: K G Saur).

NY —NEW YORK STATE HISTORICAL ASSOCIATION, Library, Lake Rd, Cooperstown, 13326. Amy Barnum, Librn
Holdings: Vols (55,000) Cat Mss Pix Slides
Notes: Noncirculating.

NY —COLUMBIA UNIVERSITY LIBRARIES, Rare Book & Manuscript Library, 801 Butler Library, 535 W 114 St, New York, 10027. Kenneth A Lohf, Librn
Holdings: Mss
Notes: The Calvin S Hathaway Collection on the protection and salvaging of artisic and historic documents and art objects during and after two world wars. 6500 items. Restricted use.

ON —NATIONAL GALLERY OF CANADA, Library, National Museums of Canada, Ottawa, K1A 0M8, Can. J Hunter, Chief Librn

ON —NATIONAL MUSEUMS OF CANADA, Library Services Directorate, Ottawa, K1A 0M8, Can. Valerie Monkhouse, Director
Notes: Conservation and restoration of art objects.

ART PERIODICALS, EARLY see Periodicals, Art, Early

ART POVERA see Art, Conceptual

ART SONG

NY —NEW YORK PUBLIC LIBRARY, Performing Arts Research Center, Rodgers & Hammerstein Archives of Recorded Sound, 111 Amsterdam Ave, New York, 10023.
Holdings: // Audiotapes
Notes: Given by Mr and Mrs Arthur V Dusenberry in 1969, the 33 audiotapes comprise private recordings made by the great Norwegian soprano Kirsten Flagstad in Oslo subsequent to her retirement from the operatic stage. Virtually the whole of her German and Scandinavian art-song repertoire is included.

ARTE POVERA see Conceptual Art

ARTHRITIS

TX —HOUSTON ACADEMY OF MEDICINE-TEXAS MEDICAL CENTER, Library, Jesse H Jones Library Bldg, Houston, 77030. Elizabeth Borst White, Special Collections Librn
Holdings: Vols (1300) Mss Pix
Notes: Burbank Collection on Arthritis, Rheumatism and Gout. An exhaustive collection on arthritis and gout before 1957. Largely from the 16th-19th centuries (also a medical manuscript dated about 1450). Bound volumes of German, French and American offprints complement the monograph collection. In 1983 the Kevin Fraser Addition to this Collection included 130 titles published before 1900.

ARTHRITIS DEFORMANS IN CHILDREN see Rheumatoid Arthritis in Children

ARTHRITIS, JUVENILE RHEUMATOID see Rheumatoid Arthritis in Children

ARTHROPODA

FL —ARCHBOLD BIOLOGICAL STATION, Library, Rt 2, Box 180, Lake Placid, 33852.

ARTHROPODA (cont.)

Fred E Lohrer, Librn
Holdings: Vols (2000) Cat Periodicals

NY —CORNELL UNIVERSITY LIBRARIES, Comstock Memorial Library of Entomology, Ithaca, 14853. Edwin Spragg, Librn
Holdings: Vols (30,000) Cat Maps Pix Audiotapes Microforms
Budget: ($13,500)
Notes: Major topics: general and applied entomology. Minor topics: parasitology, medical entomology, ecology, zoological nomenclature and allied orders of arthropods. Separate catalog to the collection, also extensive collection of reprints. Apiculture material kept at nearby A R Mann Library.

ARTHUR, CHESTER ALAN

DC —LIBRARY OF CONGRESS, Manuscript Division, Washington, 20540. John C Broderick, Chief
Holdings: Cat Mss Pix

NY —COLUMBIA UNIVERSITY LIBRARIES, Rare Book & Manuscript Library, 801 Butler Library, 535 W 114 St, New York, 10027. Kenneth A Lohf, Librn
Notes: More than 32,000 items documenting the rise of William Russell Grace's shipping business and other materials relating to his career as mayor of New York. Incl records and correspondence relating to all aspects of the shipping business in New York and South America, mining interest in Peru and Chile, and transportation in Costa Rica and Nicaragua. Family memorabilia and photographs, materials concerning New York Politics, banking and insurance, real estate interests and Catholic charities, and letters from Chester A Arthur, John Jacob Astor, Andrew Carnegie, Grover Cleveland, Hamilton Fish, John Hay and J Pierpont Morgan. Restricted use.

ARTHUR, KING, AND LEGEND

CT —TRINITY COLLEGE LIBRARY, Watkinson Library, 300 Summit St, Hartford, 06106. Jeffrey Kaimowitz, Cur
Holdings: // Cat
Notes: Incl the Duncan B Macdonald Collection.

IL —NEWBERRY LIBRARY, 60 W Walton St, Chicago, 60610. Diana Haskell, Cur of Modern Mss
Holdings: Vols 1500 Cat
Notes: See Jane D Harding's *The Arthurian Legend: A Check List of Books in the Newberry Library.*

IL —WHEATON COLLEGE, Library, Marion E Wade Collection, Irving & Franklin Sts, Wheaton, 60187. Lyle Dorsett, Cur; Marjorie Mead, Associate Cur
Holdings: Vols (6500)
Notes: Extensive Marion E Wade Collection contains ancient and modern versions of the Arthurian legends, and numerous critical studies.

MA —HARVARD UNIVERSITY LIBRARY, Cambridge, 02138.
Holdings: Cat
Notes: Downs 3643. Medieval romances.

OH —CLEVELAND PUBLIC LIBRARY, Fine Arts and Special Collections Department, 325 Superior Ave, Cleveland, 44114. Alice N Loranth, Head
Holdings: Vols (3000) Cat Mss
Notes: Part of the Romances Collection, which incl critical studies, and early printed editions. The Arthurian and Charlemagne cycles, the Nibelungenlied and other Germanic titles, Amadis de Gaula and his numerous progeny, Alexander the Great, Barlaam and Joasaph, and the Seven Wise Masters of Rome are some of the strengths of the collection. Material in the Dewey/Brett Collection is classified by related cycles and their versions in various languages.
See also entry under Romances.

ARTHUR, TIMOTHY SHAY

FL —UNIVERSITY OF SOUTH FLORIDA, Library, Tampa, 33620. J B Dobkin, Special Collections Librn
Holdings: Vols Cat Mss Pix
Budget: ($7500)
Notes: The T S Arthur Collection. This collection currently contains over 200 volumes representing 130 titles by him. Incl in the collection are many serials edited by Arthur. The collection also contains a considerable body of unpublished bibliographical material relating to Arthur's works, as well as biographical material, original and facsimile Arthur manuscript items, etc.

ARTHUR GODFREY TIME (RADIO PROGRAM)

DC —LIBRARY OF CONGRESS, Motion Pictures, Broadcasting and Recorded Sound Div, Washington, 20540.
Notes: The *Arthur Godfrey Time* collection is comprised of broadcast recordings of the television and radio programs from the years 1949 to 1957 and recordings of several rehearsals and warm-ups.

ARTHUR GODFREY TIME (TELEVISION PROGRAM)

DC —LIBRARY OF CONGRESS, Motion Pictures, Broadcasting and Recorded Sound Div, Washington, 20540.
Notes: The *Arthur Godfrey Time* collection is comprised of broadcast recordings of the television and radio programs from the years 1949 to 1957 and recordings of several rehearsals and warm-ups.

ARTIFICIAL DEFORMITIES see Deformities

ARTIFICIAL FLIES see Flies, Artificial

ARTIFICIAL INTELLIGENCE

CA —INTERNATIONAL BUSINESS MACHINES RESEARCH LIBRARY, 5600 Cottle Rd, San Jose, 95193. Phil Grincewich, Mgr Technical Information
Holdings: Vols (13,500) Cat
Notes: Incl 21,000 vols of 770 journals. On-line search facility. Vols are divided into three libraries, Technical Research, Technical Information, and Programing. Not open to public.

NY —UNIVERSITY OF ROCHESTER, Carlson Library, Hutchison Hall, River Campus, Rochester, 14627. Michael W Poulin, Librn
Holdings: Vols (48,720) Cat Microforms
Notes: Strong collection in the field and related areas.

PA —ENSANIAN PHYSICOCHEMICAL INSTITUTE, Electrotopography Library, PO Box 98, Eldred, 16731. Elisabeth Anahid Ensanian, Chief Librn
Holdings: Cat Maps Slides
Notes: Electrotopographic sensors enable robotic systems to exhibit a very high degree of machine intelligence for total automated manufacturing of "critical metallurgical engineering components". With these sensors, robotic stations in the total automated manufacturing plant can handle or solve most quality control and reliability, on-production-line inspection and testing problems, after a suitable period of learning (establishment of the required *data bank* or multidimensional systems, product profile). ETG machine intelligence or "EXPERT SYSTEMS" can readily and, on-the-spot, determine the multidimensional rank of the product within its own parent product population, map out all of its mechanical properties nondestructively, predict service of fatigue life with over 90 percent reliability, and in the event that a given product is not up tospecifications, determine how best to save the investment; by determining a *reverse engineering* strategy (on-the-spot) and sending the part upstream with instructions for reprocessing so that it can be made to meet the required specifications. In the event a part cannot be reprocessed,then the ETC machine intelligence determines the optimum scrap classification for the defective part. ETC is a new science and technology; the institute has pioneered this field and coined the terms (ETG).

ARTIFICIAL KIDNEY

RI —MIRIAM HOSPITAL MEDICAL LIBRARY, 164 Summit Ave, Providence, 02906. Ann LeClaire, Dir of Library Services
Holdings: Cat Cassettes
Notes: Special collection on the renal system with emphasis on kidney transplantation and dialysis.

ARTIFICIAL LANGUAGES see Languages, Artificial

ARTIFICIAL MODIFICATION OF CLOUDS see Rainmaking

ARTIFICIAL ORGANS

MA —ABCOR, INC, Library, 850 Main St, Wilmington, 01887. Eileen Smith, Librn
Notes: Formerly engaged in biomedical engineering of artificial organs; contraceptive research; sustained-release drug preparations. No longer updated.

ARTIFICIAL SATELLITES

NJ —AT&T BELL LABORATORIES, Libraries and Information Systems Center, 600 Mountain Ave, Murray Hill, 07974. W D Penniman, Dir
Holdings: Vols (273,100) Cat Mss Audiotapes Videotapes Microforms
Budget: ($670,000)
Notes: Restricted use to AT&T employees.
Catalogs/*Indexes*: Bell Laboratories Library Network and Book Serial Catalogs; Bell Laboratories Translations. Bell Laboratories Library Network with New Jersey libraries located in Holmdel, Murray Hill, Piscataway, Whippany, Princeton, Short Hills, Summit, West Long Branch, Crawford Hill; libraries also in Allentown, Pennsylvania; Reading, Pennsylvania; New York, New York; Atlanta, Georgia; Columbus, Ohio; Naperville, Illinois; Indianapolis, Indiana; North Andover, Massachusetts.

ARTIFICIAL WEATHER CONTROL see Rainmaking; Weather Control

ARTILLERY

OK —US ARMY FIELD ARTILLERY SCHOOL LIBRARY, Morris Swett Library, Snow Hall, Fort Sill, 73503. Lester L Miller Jr, Chief Librn
Holdings: Vols 265,958 Documents Pix Maps Slides Microforms
Notes: Field artillery; artillery; ordnance; military history; military science; weapons and weapons systems; ammunition; ballistics; missiles; Field Artillery unit histories; military periodicals analytical index file (VF). Incl US and foreign artillery; survey data; historical material on the army in Indian Territory and settlement of the southwest; photographs on army subjects, Indian Territory, Oklahoma history, Indians of the southwest.

ARTISANS

NY —AMERICAN CRAFT COUNCIL, Library and Artists Registry, 44 W 53 St, New York, 10019. Joanne Polster, Librn
Holdings: Vols 3300 Cat Pix Slides Films
Notes: Crafts and craft-related subjects, incl portfolios for approx 2000 contemporary American craftspeople consisting of biographical material and photographs, indexed by media, geographic location, and a visual index. Over 1500 exhibition catalogs. The collection incl 35mm slide kits available for purchase. Catagories covered are: exhibitions of ACC's American Craft Museum from 1958 to date; kits in all

ARTISANS (cont.)

media: fiber, metal, wood, clay, glass and multimedia; kits covering crafts processes. The Library also holds catalogs of craft school and art centers offering craft courses; newsletters, by-laws, and other materials of craft organizations and groups; the Archives and Photo-Archives of the American Craft Museum. No photocopying.

ARTISANS' SAVINGS BANK OF WILMINGTON, DELAWARE

DE —HAGLEY MUSEUM AND LIBRARY, Eleutherian Mills-Hagley Foundation Inc, PO Box 3630, Greenville, 19807. Richmond D Williams, Dir; Heddy A Richter, Imprints Librn
Notes: Incl collections: Artisans' Savings Bank of Wilmington, Delaware (1861-1967; 150 cubic feet).

ARTISTS

MD —UNIVERSITY OF MARYLAND, BALTIMORE COUNTY, Albin O Kuhn Library and Gallery, 5401 Wilkens Ave, Baltimore, 21228. Ann Copeland, Special Collections Librn
Holdings: Vols (800) // Cat Pix
Notes: The Edgar and Kathleen Merkle Collection of 19th-century English graphic satire centers around the work of George E Cruikshank. Other artists represented incl Rowlandson, Gillray, Hogarth, and "Phiz." Rare items incl Cruikshank's lavish hand-colored film *Scraps and Sketches* (1828).

MN —WALKER ART CENTER, Staff Reference Library, Vineland Place, Minneapolis, 55403. Rosemary Furtak, Librn
Holdings: Vols 5000 Cat Pix
Notes: Incl 10,000 catalogs of individual artists; museum gallery catalogs-10,000 catalogs of major exhibitions from all over the world dating back to 1940. VF material and tapes.

NY —QUEENS BOROUGH PUBLIC LIBRARY, Art & Music Div, 89-11 Merrick Blvd, Jamaica, 11432. Dorothea Wu, Head
Holdings: Vols (85,000) Cat Maps Pix Phonorecords Audiotapes Microforms
Budget: ($44,000)
Notes: The Picture Collection, covering all subjects, consists of approximately 1,500,000 pictures, mainly reproductions and clippings from books and magazines, photographs, and postcards on all subjects; The Framed Picture Collection, approx 180 framed pictures, mostly reproductions of paintings from various periods; and The Phonorecord and Cassette Collection consists of approx 3500 reference phonorecords and 6500 circulating records as well as 1000 reference cassettes and 1500 circulating cassettes.

NY —AMERICAN CRAFT COUNCIL, Library and Artists Registry, 44 W 53 St, New York, 10019. Joanne Polster, Librn
Holdings: Vols 3300 Cat Pix Slides Films
Notes: Crafts and craft-related subjects, incl portfolios for approx 2000 contemporary American craftspeople consisting of biographical material and photographs, indexed by media, geographic location, and a visual index. Over 1500 exhibition catalogs. The collection incl 35mm slide kits available for purchase. Catagories covered are: exhibitions of ACC's American Craft Museum from 1958 to date; kits in all media: fiber, metal, wood, clay, glass and multimedia; kits covering crafts processes. The Library also holds catalogs of craft school and art centers offering craft courses; newsletters, by-laws, and other materials of craft organizations and groups; the Archives and Photo-Archives of the American Craft Museum. No photocopying.

NY —METROPOLITAN MUSEUM OF ART, Thomas J Watson Library, Fifth Ave & 82 St, New York, 10028. William B Walker, Chief Librn
Holdings: Vols (250,000) Cat Mss Microforms
Notes: All fields of art: 1400 periodicals, incl bulletins and annual reports, catalogs, etc of American and foreign art societies, museums, etc; incl sales catalogs, exhibition catalogs, clipping file on individual artists and subjects, autograph letters. See *Library Catalog of the Metropolitan Museum of Art, New York,* second ed, rev and enl (Boston, G K Hall, 1980, 48 v and first supplement, 1982). Since 1980, holdings have been cataloged in RLIN.

NY —MUSEUM OF MODERN ART, Library, 11 W 53 St, New York, 10019. Clive Phillpot, Library Dir
Holdings: Vols (80,000) Cat Mss Audiotapes Microforms VF
Notes: See *Catalog of the Library of the Museum of Modern Art, New York City* (Boston: G K Hall, 1976), 14 vols. Collection incl exhibition catalogs.

TX —UNIVERSITY OF TEXAS LIBRARIES, Fine Arts Library, PO Box P, Austin, 78712. Carole L Cable, Fine Arts Librn
Holdings: Vols (55,000) Cat Pix

BC —VANCOUVER PUBLIC LIBRARY, Art Div, 750 Burrard St, Vancouver, V6Z 1X5, Can.
Holdings: Cat Pix
Notes: Book and pamphlet collection. Also, (1) Newspaper Clippings File: 31 drawers of relevant clippings from major newspapers, incl the *Sun, Province, Toronto Globe and Mail, Christian Science Monitor, New York* Times, etc on arts, music, architecture; incl biographical material (16 drawers). (2) Picture File about 500,000 pictures in 150 cabinet drawers, strong in architecture, costume, interior decoration, painting, sculpture, also portraits. (3) Exhibition Catalogs File: British Columbia and elsewhere. (4) Association and Organization File: organizations in the Lower Mainland in arts, music, city planning, etc, begun in 1940s; (5) Canadian Artists Index: begun in 1964, alphabetically by artist, with about 300,000 citationsto reproductions of work and biographical material on Canadian artist from the division's books and other sources; (6) Miscellaneous Index: material not covered in other special or published indexes, primarily of Canadian and local cultural events, hard-to-find informations, etc. Local newspapers, special Canadian publications and British film journals are the most regularly indexed items. (7) Song Index started in the 1930s. (8) Title Index to song collections and sheet music in the VPL collection, approx 100,000 entries.

ON —NATIONAL GALLERY OF CANADA, Library, National Museums of Canada, Ottawa, K1A 0M8, Can. J Hunter, Chief Librn
Holdings: Vols (72,000)
Notes: History of art (postmediaeval, Western). Public reference only. Circulating only to gallery staff and on interlibrary loan. 1000 periodical titles currently received. 50, 000 pamphlets, mostly exhibition and sales catalogs (not cataloged). 40,000 items in documentation files: clippings, notices of exhibitions and other ephemera. Exchange of National Gallery publications with other art galleries. Special section on history of Canadian art. Emphasis of collection on painting, sculpture, graphic arts and photography. Study collection of photographs and slides. See *Catalogue of the National Gallery of Canada,* 8 vols (Boston: G K Hall, 1973) and *Supplement,* 6 vols (Boston: G K Hall, 1981).

ARTISTS—CATALOGS

MN —WALKER ART CENTER, Staff Reference Library, Vineland Place, Minneapolis, 55403. Rosemary Furtak, Librn
Holdings: Vols 5000 Cat Pix
Notes: Incl 10,000 catalogs of individual artists; museum gallery catalogs-10,000 catalogs of major exhibitions from all over the world dating back to 1940. VF material and tapes.

NY —WHITNEY MUSEUM OF AMERICAN ART, Library, 945 Madison Ave, New York, 10021. May Castleberry, Librn
Holdings: 20,000 Uncat Pix
Notes: Vertical files on individual American artists; incl clippings, catalogs, exhibitions, letters, pictures, etc. Also, 1050 bound periodical titles.

ARTISTS, ALASKAN

AK —Z J LOUSSAC PUBLIC LIBRARY, 524 W 6th Ave, Anchorage, 99501. Michael Catoggio, Alaskana Supervisor
Holdings: Vols 6000 Cat Mss Microforms
Budget: $30,000
Notes: Incl prints by Alaskan artists.

ARTISTS, AMERICAN

DC —SMITHSONIAN INSTITUTION, National Museum of American Art & the National Portrait Gallery Library, Eighth & F Sts, NW, Washington, 20560. Cecilia Chin, Librn
Holdings: Vols (47,000) Cat Microforms
Budget: ($60,000)
Notes: Subscribe to 600 foreign and domestic periodicals on art and American history. Holdings of older bound periodicals. Collection emphasizes American art, contemporary American and European painting, portraiture, American biography. Uncataloged material incl: 350 vertical file drawers of clippings, small catalogs and other ephemera on artists, art organizations, museums, etc; the "Ferdinand Perret Library"--180 scrapbooks with card index on California art and artists, incl clippings, catalogs, reproductions, etc; card bibliography of books and periodical literature on portraiture--international, retrospective and current--in progress. Mallett Library of Reproductions.

IN —INDIANA STATE UNIVERSITY, EVANSVILLE, Library, 8600 University Blvd, Evansville, 47712. Gina R Walker, Acting Archivist
Holdings: Uncat Mss
Notes: Papers, etc of the nationally known graphic arts specialist Herbert William Simpson (1904-1970), advertising man, type designer and calligrapher. Original examples of calligraphy and graphic design executed for commercial ads and occasional pieces for personal interest. Materials of about 1940-1970.

MA —HARVARD UNIVERSITY, Harvard College Library, Fine Arts Library, Fogg Museum, 32 Quincy St, Cambridge, 02138. Wolfgang M Freitag, Librn
Holdings: Vols (202,000) Cat Mss Pix Slides
Budget: ($176,500)
Notes: All areas of art history, with emphasis on Italian primitives, Italian Renaissance, master drawings, Romanesque sculpture, architectural history, ms materials (particulary American artists'), conservation and restoration of art objects. Incl the Berenson repertory of photographs from the Harvard Center for Italian Renaissance Studies in Florence, and the Decimal Index to the Art of the Low Countries. Separate card catalogs for books, photographs and lantern slides, registers for ms holdings which are not incl in *National Union Catalog of Manuscript Collections.* Slides total over 230,000; over 745,000 pictures. *Fine Arts Library Catalogue* (14 volumes) and *Catalogue of Auction Sales Catalogues* (1 volume) (Boston: G K Hall, 1972); *A Guide to the Fine Arts Library* (Cambridge, Mass: 1971); *Guide to the Harvard Libraries,* microfiche edition of holdingscataloged through 1981 published 1984 (Munich/New York: Saur).

MA —BRANDEIS UNIVERSITY, Goldfarb Library, 415 South St, Waltham, 02154. Bessie Hahn, Dir
Notes: James M Whistler Collection. 3 linear ft of correspondence to and from James McNeill Whistler, as well as newspaper clippings and other ephemera. A finding list to the collection can be found in Special Collections.

NE —UNIVERSITY OF NEBRASKA-LINCOLN, Don L Love Library, Lincoln, 68588. Joseph G Svoboda, University Archivist
Holdings: Vols (800) // Cat Mss Pix Slides 16mm Films
Notes: The R D Warden Collection

ARTISTS, AMERICAN (cont.)

pertaining to Charles M Russell, "The Cowboy Artist". Finding aid available.

NJ —MONTCLAIR ART MUSEUM LIBRARY, 3 South Mountain Ave, PO Box 1582, Montclair, 07042. Edith A Rights, Librn
Holdings: Vols (10,000) Cat Pix Slides Audiotapes
Budget: ($3500)
Notes: American painting and sculpture. Incl 5000 pictures; 10,000 slides; posters. Audiotapes on American art and artists.

NJ —MACCULLOCH HALL HISTORICAL MUSEUM, Morristown, 07960. Alice A Caulkins, Curator
Notes: The W Parsons Todd Collection.

NY —WHITNEY MUSEUM OF AMERICAN ART, Library, 945 Madison Ave, New York, 10021. May Castleberry, Librn
Holdings: 20,000 Uncat Pix
Notes: Vertical files on individual American artists; incl clippings, catalogs, exhibitions, letters, pictures, etc. Also, 1050 bound periodical titles.

OK —NATIONAL COWBOY HALL OF FAME AND WESTERN HERITAGE, Library, 1700 NE 63 St, Oklahoma City, 73111. Esther Long, Librn
Holdings: Vols (8000) Uncat
Notes: Art of the American West. Covers western art and artists; rodeo and its history; cowboys; the cattle industry; and biographies on prominent westerners. Personal collection of Walter Brennen; collections of artists, Carl Link and James Earl Frazier.

OR —UNIVERSITY OF OREGON LIBRARY, Special Collections Div, Eugene, 97403. Kenneth W Duckett, Curator
Holdings: Cat Mss
Notes: Incl artwork. Over 50 mss collections of artists and illustrators, about half being illustrators primarily for children's books, and several who specialized in architectural renderings. Collections usually contain some artwork in various stages of production and in various mediums. Correspondence and mss may also be included. Publication: Martin Schmitt, comp, *Catalogue of Manuscripts in the University of Oregon* Library (Eugene: University of Oregon Books, 1971).
See also entry under Illustrators, American; Architects

PA —BALCH INSTITUTE FOR ETHNIC STUDIES, Library, 18 S Seventh St, Philadelphia, 19106. R Joseph Anderson, Library Dir
Notes: Incl a catalogue of an exhibition of Samuel Brown's works.

ARTISTS, ARIZONA

AZ —TUCSON MUSEUM OF ART LIBRARY, 140 N Main, Tucson, 85705. Dorcas Worsley, Librn
Holdings: Vols (2000)
Budget: ($1500)
Notes: Extensive file of biographical and critical information on Arizona artists which is continually being increased. Subject card index to magazines on Western art and artists in magazines not indexed in *Art* Index 12 drawers in 1984, and continues to grow. Have a collection of 15,000 slides.

ARTISTS, CALIFORNIA

CA —UNIVERSITY OF CALIFORNIA, DAVIS, Shields Library, Dept of Special Collections, Davis, 95616. Donald Kunitz, Head; C Danial Elliott, Asst Head
Holdings: Vols 2800 Cat Mss Pix
Notes: The Baird Archive of California Art incl over 300 files of biographical information, monographs, exhibition catalogs, photographs, and contemporary commentary on individual artists, as well as reference and subject listings. Described in: Baird, Joseph A Jr, *Northern California Art; An Interpretive Bibliography* (Davis, California, Library Associates, University of California.)

CA —CRAFT AND FOLK ART MUSEUM, Library, 5814 Wilshire Blvd, Los Angeles, 90036. Joan M Benedetti, Museum Librn
Holdings: Vols (2000) Slides VF
Notes: Incl 2000 books; 70 journal subscriptions; artists' biographical files: 6 file drawers; clipping files: 8 file drawers; 20,000 slides. Representation of the material culture of all people, traditional and contemporary expressions. Incl visual and printed information on ethnic, traditional, popular, decorative, idiosyncratic, and contemporary crafts as well as vernacular architecture, handmade houses, and design. Information about and for professional artists on health hazards, conservation, and career management. Anthropological and art historical works; exhibition catalogues; slides, photographs, audiocassettes; clipping and pamphlet files. Contemporary Slide Registry of Craftspeople and extensive biographical files of contemporary craft artists. Information and referral files of craft related galleries, shops, festivals, organizations, etc.

CA —PASADENA PUBLIC LIBRARY, Fine Arts Division, Reference Services, 285 E Walnut St, Pasadena, 91101. Anne Cain, Principal Librn
Holdings: Vols (10,000) Cat Pix Films
Notes: Library has 55 vertical drawers of pictures and clippings, constantly revised and added to incl over 130,000 pictures, 64 films.

ARTISTS, CANADIAN

MB —UNIVERSITY OF MANITOBA, Elizabeth Dafoe Library, Archives and Special Collections Dept, Winnipeg, R3T 2N2, Can. Richard E Bennett, Dept Head; Corrado A Santoro, Reference Archivist
Notes: Bertram R Brooker Papers. Correspondence, diaries and daily notations, dramas, both published and unpublished, short stories and essays, and other literary works. Also 16 photographs mainly of Brooker, his family and fellow artists.

ON —NATIONAL GALLERY OF CANADA, Library, National Museums of Canada, Ottawa, K1A 0M8, Can. J Hunter, Chief Librn
Holdings: Vols (72,000)
Notes: History of art (postmediaeval, Western). Public reference only. Circulating only to gallery staff and on interlibrary loan. 1000 periodical titles currently received. 50, 000 pamphlets, mostly exhibition and sales catalogs (not cataloged). 40,000 items in documentation files: clippings, notices of exhibitions and other ephemera. Exchange of National Gallery publications with other art galleries. Special section on history of Canadian art. Emphasis of collection on painting, sculpture, graphic arts and photography. Study collection of photographs and slides. See *Catalogue of the National Gallery of Canada*, 8 vols (Boston: G K Hall, 1973) and *Supplement*, 6 vols (Boston: G K Hall, 1981).

ON —METROPOLITAN TORONTO LIBRARY, Fine Arts Dept, 789 Yonge St, Toronto, M4W 2G8, Can. Alan Suddon, Head
Holdings: Vols (42,000) Cat Pix Microforms
Notes: Extensive collection.

ON —UNIVERSITY OF TORONTO, Thomas Fisher Rare Book Library, 120 Saint George St, Toronto, M5S 1A5, Can. Richard G Landon, Head
Holdings: Vols (30,000) Mss
Notes: All currently published and most earlier major works on the fine and applied arts in Canada; Canadian art exhibition catalogues; limited editions illustrated by Canadian artists; 19th and 20th century architectural plans for buildings in Toronto and southern Ontario vicinity (ca 1700).

ARTISTS, CHICAGO

IL —CHICAGO PUBLIC LIBRARY, Art Section, Fine Arts Division, 78 E Washington St, Chicago, 60602. Rosalinda I Hack, Fine Arts Division Chief; Yvonne S Brown, Head, Art Section
Holdings: Vols 42,000
Notes: Reference and circulating collection of books, periodicals, exhibition catalogs, dissertations, picture collections, and microforms on all aspects of the visual arts. Major concentration of art history, especially European, with concentration on 19th and 20th century art movements and artists. We attempt to represent the works of recognized artists past and present. The Decorative Arts are well represented especially in the areas of antiques, interior decoration, and handicrafts. The collection is supplemented by a strong periodical collection, consisting of 330 current English and Foreign subscriptions, the majority of these titles we bind, as well as strong bound retrospective collections. The visual arts is supported by a clipping File on Chicago Artists, a current exhibition catalogs collection, as well as by the microfilm collections of the*Chicago Art Institute Scrapbooks*, the *Scrapbook on Art*, Artists, and the *Index of American Design*.

ARTISTS, CONTEMPORARY

NY —MUSEUM OF MODERN ART, Library, 11 W 53 St, New York, 10019. Clive Phillpot, Library Dir
Holdings: Vols (80,000) Cat Mss Audiotapes Microforms VF
Notes: See *Catalog of the Library of the Museum of Modern Art, New York City* (Boston: G K Hall, 1976), 14 vols. Collection incl exhibition catalogs.

ARTISTS, FRENCH

RI —PROVIDENCE PUBLIC LIBRARY, 150 Empire St, Providence, 02903. Lance J Bauer, Special Collections Librn
Holdings: Vols 400 / / Cat
Notes: The Wetmore Illustrated Books Collection. This historical collection of more than 400 volumes was given to Providence Public Library in 1955 by Newport, Rhode Island, Collector Edith Wetmore. An extremely fine collection of *livres d'artiste*, examples of fine illustration, printing and bindings. This collection incl the works of such notable artists as William Blake, Pablo Picasso, Giorgio DiChirico, Aubrey Beardsley, Jean Cocteau, William Hogarth, Raoul Dufy, Pierre Bonnard and numerous others. Although especially strong in the French illustrated books, English and German illustrated books are amply represented also. Partially cataloged. Material must be used in-house.

ARTISTS, HEBREW see Artists, Jewish

ARTISTS, JEWISH

NY —YIVO INSTITUTE FOR JEWISH RESEARCH, Library & Archives, 1048 Fifth Ave, New York, 10028. Dina Abramowicz, Librn; Marek Web, Archivist
Holdings: Cat Mss Slides
Notes: Original works and reference materials, incl reproductions of 1500 objects; 500 slides. Separate catalog.

OH —HEBREW UNION COLLEGE-JEWISH INSTITUTE OF RELIGION, Klau Library, 3101 Clifton Ave, Cincinnati, 45220. David J Gilner, Reference Librn
Holdings: Cat
Notes: Extensive collection of Jewish artists, primarily in the US and Israel; Jewish religious art, etc.

ARTISTS, NEW ENGLAND

MA —SOCIETY FOR THE PRESERVATION OF NEW ENGLAND ANTIQUITIES, Library, 141 Cambridge St, Boston, 02114. Ellie Reichlin, Librn & Cur of Photographic Collections
Holdings: Vols (3000) Cat Pix Microforms
Budget: ($75,000)
Notes: Incl two types of mss: (1) Family papers relating to historic properties administered by SPNEA. Ca 125 linear feet, incl the Codman family archive, 1700s-1960s, with associated family photograph collection. (2) Misc mss with emphasis on topics relating to building, interior designs, material culture (ca 3500 items, cataloged). For further information, an *Annotated*

ARTISTS, NEW ENGLAND (cont.)

Checklist to Special Collections of SPNEA Library is available. See also entry in *Architectural Records in Boston: A Guide to Architectural Research* (1983, Garland Publishing Co, New York). Additional collections incl prints, original artwork (largely by NE artists, engravers) relating to architectural subjects; maps; architectural periodicals (19th century).

ARTISTS, OHIO

OH —CLEVELAND MUSEUM OF ART, Library, 11150 E Blvd, Cleveland, 44106. Jack Perry Brown, Librn
Holdings: Vols (120,000) Cat Pix Slides Microforms
Notes: 1500 serial titles incl museum bulletins. Also 200,000 slides; 250,000 photographs. Special photograph collections: Decimal Index Art of Low Countries (DIAL); Gernsheim Corpus Photographicum of drawings; Archive of Biblioteca Berenson; National Palace Collection, Victoria and Albert Museum. Index of Ohio artists.

OH —CLEVELAND PUBLIC LIBRARY, 325 Superior Ave, Cleveland, 44114.
Holdings: Cat Maps Pix
Notes: Library collection in the subject departments incl: state and local history; city directories; business and industry; canals and waterworks; technology; local authors and artists; tourist and travel information (only advisory), vital statistics. Early Ohio pictures and historic maps. See also Western Reserve, Cleveland Public Library.

ARTISTS, PENNSYLVANIA

PA —KING'S COLLEGE, D Leonard Corgan Library, 14 W Jackson St, Wilkes-Barre, 18711. Judith Tierney, Special Collections Librn
Notes: Approx 5 linear feet of completed questionnaires, clippings, brochures, and other material relating to artist and art organizations in the Wyoming Valley from 1808 to the present. Primarily biographical. Wyoming Valley Artists Files.

ARTISTS, SLOVAK

OH —SLOVAK INSTITUTE, Saint Andrew's Abbey, 2900 King Dr, Cleveland, 44104. Rev Andrew Pier, Dir
Holdings: Vols (10,000)
Notes: Promotes cultural interests, especially work of Slovak authors, artists, and musicians through its Slovak Writers and Artists Association. Private library. Permission required.

ARTISTS' BOOKS

NY —ALBRIGHT-KNOX ART GALLERY, Art Reference Library, 1285 Elmwood Ave, Buffalo, 14222. Annette Masling, Librn
Holdings: Vols (20,000) Cat
Notes: Special strength in American 19th and 20th century art. Excellent collection of exhibition catalogs for contemporary art.

NY —MUSEUM OF MODERN ART, Library, 11 W 53 St, New York, 10019. Clive Phillpot, Library Dir
Holdings: Vols (80,000) Cat Mss Audiotapes Microforms VF
Notes: See *Catalog of the Library of the Museum of Modern Art, New York City* (Boston: G K Hall, 1976), 14 vols. Collection incl exhibition catalogs.

OH —OBERLIN COLLEGE LIBRARY, Clarence Ward Art Library, Allen Art Bldg, Oberlin, 44074. Jeffrey Weidman, Librn
Holdings: Vols (62,000) Cat Microforms
Notes: A growing collection of Artists' Books.

WA —UNIVERSITY OF WASHINGTON LIBRARIES, Suzzallo Library, Special Collections Division, Rare Book Collection, FM-25, Seattle, 98195. Gary Menges, Coordinator for Special Collections
Notes: Printing history, including early printed books and modern fine printing; book arts, including papermaking, decorated papers, bookbinding, book design, and artist's books; American literature, 19th century includes: Stephen Crane, Ralph Waldo Emerson, Nathaniel Hawthorne, Henry James, Henry Wadsworth Longfellow, Herman Melville, Frank Norris, Harriet Beecher Stowe and Walt Whitman and 20th century includes: Theodore Roethke; illustrated books, including emblem books, historical children's illustration, books illustrated with prints, and artist's books; costume history; voyages and travels; preservation of library materials.

ARTS, FINE see Art

ARTS, GRAPHIC see Graphic Arts

ARTS, USEFUL see Industrial Arts; Technology

ARTS, VISUAL see Visual Arts

ARTS AND TECHNOLOGY see Technology and the Arts

ARTS CLUB OF CHICAGO

†IL —NEWBERRY LIBRARY, 60 W Walton St, Chicago, 60610.
Notes: Archives.

ARTS IN EDUCATION

NY —STATE UNIVERSITY OF NEW YORK, STONY BROOK, Melville Library, Dept of Special Collections, Stony Brook, 11794. Evert Volkersz, Head

ARTS MANAGEMENT see Art—Management

ARTZYBASHEFF, BORIS

NY —COLUMBIA UNIVERSITY LIBRARIES, Rare Book & Manuscript Library, 801 Butler Library, 535 W 114 St, New York, 10027. Kenneth A Lohf, Librn
Holdings: Pix
Notes: Selected group of paintings, chiefly for the cover of Time magazine. Restricted use.

ARUBA

CT —YALE UNIVERSITY, Sterling Memorial Library, Latin American Collections, New Haven, 06520. Lee H Williams Jr, Cur
Holdings: Vols (300,000) Cat Maps Pix Slides Phonorecords 16mm Films Filmstrips
See also entry under Latin America

ARUNDEL PRINTS

MN —SAINT PAUL PUBLIC LIBRARY, Arts & Audiovisual Services, 90 W Fourth St, Saint Paul, 55102. Delores Sundbye, Supervising Librn
Holdings: Cat Pix
Budget: ($20,000)
Notes: Complete set of first edition of Arundel Prints, color lithographic copies of Renaissance paintings, published by the Arndel Society, 1849-1897.

ASBESTOS TOXICOLOGY

MD —NATIONAL LIBRARY OF MEDICINE, 8600 Rockville Pike, Bethesda, 20209. Harold M Schoolinam, Actg Dir
Budget: ($46,400)

ASBURY, SAMUEL E.

TX —STEPHEN F AUSTIN STATE UNIVERSITY, Ralph W Steen Library, Special Collections Dept, Box 13055, SFA Sta, Nacogdoches, 75962. Linda Cheves Nicklas, Special Collections Librn
Holdings: Mss Maps Pix
Budget: ($5000)
Notes: Incl personal and business papers, letters, diaries, and other records of East Texans and East Texas institutions and businesses. Major collections incl papers of Karl Wilson Baker, George L Crocket, Bennett Blake, McFarland-Russell family, Orton family, Samuel E Asbury; and records of Nacogdoches University, East Texas Historical Association, Kelly Plow Company and many local organizations; 60 Thomas J Rusk letters. Indexes, calendars and inventories are available. Description: SFASU, *A Guide to Special Collections,* 1980.

ASCETICAL THEOLOGY see Asceticism

ASCETICISM

TX —OBLATE SCHOOL OF THEOLOGY, Library, 285 Oblate Dr, San Antonio, 78216. James Maney, Libr Dir
Holdings: Vols (22,000) Cat
Budget: ($15,500)

ASCOLI, MAX

MA —BOSTON UNIVERSITY, Mugar Memorial Library, Special Collections Dept, 771 Commonwealth Ave, Boston, 02215. Howard B Gotlieb, Dir
Holdings: Mss Pix
Notes: Mss, correspondence, etc collected in depth; incl publications by or about. Files of the *Reporter* magazine of which Ascoli was editor and publisher.

ASDIC see Sonar

ASH, MARY K.

TX —NORTH TEXAS STATE UNIVERSITY, Archives, NT Station Box 5188, Denton, 76203. Robert LaForte, University Archivist
Notes: Part of Business Archive Project. Interviews with cosmetics entrepreneur (Mary Kay Cosmetics).

ASHANTI see Ghana

ASHBERY, RAY STEVENS, 1902-1974

NY —CORNELL UNIVERSITY LIBRARIES, Collection of Regional History, Dept of Manuscripts and Univ Archives, Ithaca, 14853.
Notes: Attorney, NY Assemblyman. Papers, 1930-ca 1971; 100 ft. Unpublished guide available. Restricted.

ASHER, DON

MA —BOSTON UNIVERSITY, Mugar Memorial Library, Special Collections Dept, 771 Commonwealth Ave, Boston, 02215. Howard B Gotlieb, Dir
Holdings: Cat Mss

ASHFORD, JEFFREY

MA —BOSTON UNIVERSITY, Mugar Memorial Library, Special Collections Dept, 771 Commonwealth Ave, Boston, 02215. Howard B Gotlieb, Dir
Holdings: Cat Mss

ASHLEY, FRED C.

†WA —WASHINGTON STATE UNIVERSITY, Library, Manuscripts, Archives & Special Collections, Pullman, 99164. John F Guido, Head
Holdings: Vols Cat Mss Maps Pix
Notes: The personal and political papers of Fred C Ashley, William Edward Carty, Knute Hill, Walter Franklin Horan, William Lon Johnson, Catherine May, and Austin Mires are amoung the holdings of the library. Most collections described in printed registers.

ASHTON-WARNER, SYLVIA

MA —BOSTON UNIVERSITY, Mugar Memorial Library, Special Collections Dept,

ASHTON-WARNER, SYLVIA (cont.)

771 Commonwealth Ave, Boston, 02215. Howard B Gotlieb, Dir
Holdings: Cat Mss Pix
Notes: Mss, correspondence, etc collected in depth; incl publications by or about.

ASIA

†CA —AMERICAN ACADEMY OF ASIAN STUDIES LIBRARY, 134-140 Church St, San Francisco, 94114.

†CA —ASIA FOUNDATION LIBRARY, 550 Kearny St, San Francisco, 94114.

†HI —EAST-WEST POPULATION INSTITUTE RESOURCE MATERIALS COLLECTION, 1777 East-West Rd, Honolulu, 96848.
Notes: Demography, population problems and policy in Hawaii, Asian countries and Pacific area, family planning programs, environment.

†HI —PACIFIC AND ASIAN AFFAIRS COUNCIL, Pacific House Library, 2004 University Ave, Honolulu, 96816.
Notes: Asia and the Pacific. Pacific and Asian foreign policy.

HI —UNIVERSITY OF HAWAII, Library, 2550 The Mall, Honolulu, 96822. Joyce Wright, Head, Asia Collection; Masato Matsu, Head, East Asia Vernacular Collection
Holdings: Vols 331,620
Notes: This collection includes materials from and about East, South and Southeast Asia in all languages. Holdings are shown in two card catalogs, one for East Asian language materials; the other, for western and other Asian languages. Emphasis is on the social sciences and humanities for the post-World War II period. Additional and supplementary retrospective western language materials are in the main library collection. *Resources for Research on Asia at the University of Hawaii and in Honolulu,* by G Raymond Nunn, Honolulu, 1965 (East West Center Library Occasional Paper, 1).

NY —CORNELL UNIVERSITY LIBRARIES, John M Olin Library, Wason Collection of China & the Chinese, Ithaca, 14853. James Cole, Cur; Paul P W Cheng, East Asia Librn
Notes: Incl Stein Collection, Pelliog Collection, Peking Library Collection, and information on Tuntun-Huang.

NY —STATE UNIVERSITY OF NEW YORK, COLLEGE AT NEW PALTZ, Sojourner Truth Library, World Study Center, New Paltz, 12561. Corinne Nyquist, Librn
Holdings: Vols (36,294) Cat Maps Pix
Notes: 36,294 volumes on Africa, Asia and the Near East, not incl reference books or pamphlets which have been integrated into the general collection.

†NY —ASIA SOCIETY LIBRARY, 725 Park Ave, New York, 10021.

NY —UNIVERSITY OF ROCHESTER, Rush Rhees Library, Rochester, 14627. Datta S Kharbas, Head
Holdings: Vols 100,000 Cat Maps Microforms
Notes: Area studies collection on East Asia and South Asia. Major emphasis is on social sciences and humanities. Over 57,000 volumes on East Asia, out of which 29,000 volumes are in Chinese and 15,000 in Japanese. Extensive holdings on Chinese and Japanese histories. Catalog of East Asian collection consisting of Chinese and Japanese language holdings published in 1968, with two subsequent supplements. Over 33,000 volumes on South Asia. Considerable depth in social sciences, history, politics and anthropology. Extensive holdings in Sanskrit, Hindi, and Marathi.

PA —BRYN MAWR COLLEGE, Canaday Library, Bryn Mawr, 19010. James Tanis, Dir
Notes: McBride Collection on Asia and Southeast Asia. Incl many rare books.

TX —UNIVERSITY OF TEXAS, Center for Asian Studies, Austin, 78712.
Notes: The Center for Asian Studies has a reading room where several hundred books in Asian studies (mostly in English) are available for reading there.

ASIA—COLONIZATION

NY —STATE UNIVERSITY OF NEW YORK, COLLEGE AT NEW PALTZ, Sojourner Truth Library, World Study Center, William J Haggerty Collection of French Colonial History, New Paltz, 12561. Corinne Nyquist, Librn
Holdings: Vols (19,153)// Uncat Mss Maps Pix
Notes: French colonial history. In 1966 this college acquired the research Library of the Comite Francais pour l'outre-mer. This library served the needs of a society in Paris whose membership incl French colonial administrators, scholars, and students. The more than 19,000 books and pamphlets and 135 sets of periodicals date from 1830, and cover the administration and development of the former colonies of France. Much of the material is economic, statistical, or agricultural, reflecting the interests of the collectors. British colonial history is well represented. Described in *Africana Library* Journal, Winter 1971.

ASIA—DESCRIPTION AND TRAVEL

MN —UNIVERSITY OF MINNESOTA, James Ford Bell Library, 309 19th Ave S, Minneapolis, 55455. John Parker, Cur
Holdings: Vols (11,000) Cat Mss Maps
Notes: Collection of original materials relating to European expansion, 1400-1800.

NY —EXPLORERS CLUB, James B Ford Memorial Library, 46 E 70 St, New York, 10021. Janet Baldwin, Librn
Holdings: Vols (24,000) Cat Maps
Notes: Additions to the collection depend upon gifts. Access by appointment only.

ASIA—ECONOMIC DEVELOPMENT

HI —BANK OF HAWAII, Information Ctr, PO Box 2900, Honolulu, 96846. Sally Campbell, Information Mgr
Holdings: Vols 4000 Cat Maps Pix
Notes: Economic reseach in developing areas of Hawaii, US Pacific Islands, Asian and other foreign coutries. Empahsis on economics, business statistics, demography, finance, banking, tourist industry, construction, domestic and foreign trade.

MA —HARVARD UNIVERSITY, Institute for International Development, Library, Coolidge Hall, 1737 Cambridge St, Cambridge, 02138. Barbara Mitchell, Librn
Holdings: Vols (17,000) Periodicals
Notes: Economic development, rural development, statistical material on selected underdeveloped countries. Incl 75 periodical titles.

ASIA—LANGUAGES see Oriental Languages and Literatures

ASIA—MAPS

CT —YALE UNIVERSITY, Box 1603A, Yale Station, New Haven, 06520.
Notes: Maps and atlas collection.

ASIA, CENTRAL

NY —COLUMBIA UNIVERSITY LIBRARIES, Lehman Library, Slavic and East Central European Collection, 420 W 118 St, New York, 10027. Nina Lencek, Bibliographer
Holdings: // Uncat
Notes: The Soviet Nationalities Collection consists of published materials in the Indo-European, Uralic, Altaic, Transcaucasian, and Paleo-Siberian languages of the Soviet Union and contains more than 14,000 volumes as well as current and discontinued periodical literature. The author/title catalog for this collection is in Russian translation except for Armenian books, which are cataloged in the original. The collection is circulating and available through interlibrary loan.

WA —UNIVERSITY OF WASHINGTON LIBRARIES, Suzzallo Library, Slavic & East European Section, FM-25, Seattle, 98195. Barbara A Galik, Head
Holdings: Vols (250,000) Cat Mss Maps Pix Phonorecords Audiotapes Microforms
Budget: ($85,000)
Notes: Strong research collections for Central Asia, especially Uzbekistan, Kazakhstan, Kirghizistan and Azerbaijan. Holdings are excellent in historical source materials, language, literature, geography, economics, the fine arts, and folklore. There are extensive holdings of the publications of academies, major universities, and principal scholarly institutions, especially of long serial runs.

ASIA, EAST

CA —UNIVERSITY OF CALIFORNIA, BERKELEY, University Library, East Asiatic Library, Room 208, Durant Hall, Berkeley, 94720. Donald Shively, Head
Holdings: Vols (500,000) Cat Mss Maps Pix Microforms
Notes: Research

CA —CLAREMONT COLLEGES, Honnold Library, Asian Studies Collection, Ninth & Dartmouth, Claremont, 91711. Frances D Wang, Cur
Holdings: Vols (69,658) Cat Mss Maps Pix Microforms
Budget: ($50,000)
Notes: Incl 62,476 vols in Chinese and Japanese; 6276 in Western languages. About 13,000 uncataloged. Collection incl artifacts, original mss, rare, original editions of Chinese, Japanese, Korean and Western language and literature, history, and archaeology, which are today totally unavailable to acquire. The most distinguished work is the collection of some 200 Chinese gazetteers (fang-chih) which is one of the best in the US. Another valuable collection is the Frederick McCormick Collection of 214 titles in 896 vols of movable-type editions of Korean printed books, 15th-19th centuries. The Western-language collection on the Far East is probably one of the strongest in the US. Recently added was a collection of Japanese books on Shinto (125 titles), periodicals, and artifacts. Separate catalog.

CA —UNIVERSITY OF CALIFORNIA, LOS ANGELES, Oriental Library, 405 Hilgard Ave, Los Angeles, 90024. Ik-Sam Kim, Head
Holdings: Vols (195,789) Cat
Budget: ($61,513)
Notes: Extensive collections in Chinese, Japanese, and Korean languages.

CT —TRINITY COLLEGE LIBRARY, 300 Summit St, Hartford, 06106. Ralph S Emerick, Librn
Holdings: Cat
Notes: Moore Collection of the Far East.

CT —YALE UNIVERSITY, American Oriental Society Library, 120 High St, New Haven, 06520. Rutherford B Rogers, Librarian
Holdings: Vols 22,000 Cat Mss
Notes: On deposit.

CT —CONNECTICUT COLLEGE, Library, Mohegan Ave, New London, 06320. Brian Rogers, College Librn
Holdings: Vols (382,000) Cat
Notes: Collection supports the Program in Asian Studies and the Department of Chinese and Japanese.

HI —UNIVERSITY OF HAWAII, Library, 2550 The Mall, Honolulu, 96822. Joyce Wright, Head, Asia Collection; Masato Matsu, Head, East Asia Vernacular Collection
Holdings: Vols 142,620 Cat Microforms
Notes: The Asia Collection holds materials from and relating to China, Japan, Korea, and Hong Kong in western and Asian languages. These are supplemented by additional western language works on the area in the main library and a large backlog of uncataloged East Asian language titles. A separate dictionary catalog, arranged by romanized entry, incl the Chinese, Japanese and Korean languages in one alphabet.

IL —SOUTHERN ILLINOIS UNIVERSITY, CARBONDALE, Delyte W Morris Library,

ASIA, EAST (cont.)

Carbondale, 62901.
Holdings: Vols (4100) Cat Maps Audiotapes Microforms
Notes: The Vietnamese collection has been transferred to the general library. It incl 1200 cataloged titles in the Vietnamese language, plus 56 Vietnamese language microfilms. A profile of the area emphasis on the collection appears from the following distribution of the 2987 titles entered in the holdings and accessions lists published by the Southern Illinois University Center for Vietnamese Studies: Vietnam, 1965; Cambodia and Laos, 63; Other Southeast Asia (incl Indonesia), 916; East Asia (mostly China), 246; General (reference works, bibliographies, etc), 197. Also over 1000 maps.

IL —CENTER FOR RESEARCH LIBRARIES, 6050 S Kenwood Ave, Chicago, 60637. Donald B Simpson, Dir; Esther Smith, Collection Development Librn
Holdings: Microfilm
Notes: Microfilms of newspaper backfiles, collections of printed materials and archival materials. Descriptive pamphlet available.

IL —FIELD MUSEUM OF NATURAL HISTORY, The Berthold Laufer Library, Roosevelt Rd & Lake Shore Dr, Chicago, 60605. W Peyton Fawcett, Librn
Notes: The part of the museum's collection of Berthold Laufer (1874-1934), Curator of Anthropology, dealing with the peoples of the pre-19th century Chinese Empire (incl Manchuria, Mongolia, Sinkiang and Tibet); their anthropology, art and religion; influences upon their cultures by those of India, Siberia, Japan, Indonesia, and Oceania--and vice versa. Incl about 500 books in Tibetan. About 2/3 of the collection is cataloged.

IL —MONMOUTH COLLEGE LIBRARY, Monmouth, 61462. Harris Hauge, Librn
Holdings: Vols 4500 Cat Maps Slides
Budget: $800
Notes: Collection supports an area studies program. PL 480 items supplement the collection.

IN —INDIANA UNIVERSITY, Lilly Library, Seventh St, Bloomington, 47405. William R Cagle, Librn
Holdings: Vols (2000) // Cat
Notes: The core of the collection is the specialized library of Charles R Boxer (1000 titles) dealing with the history of the Iberians in the East 16th-18th century. Mainly incl works on China, Japan and the Philippines during the period of their early intercourse with the West through 1800, as well as materials on the English and Dutch East India Companies, and the 17th century Anglo-Dutch naval wars. Special mention should be made of the valuable letters from missions by the Jesuits, and the works in this area by the Augustinians, Franciscans, and Dominicans, from the time of the arrival of the Iberians in Asia. The collection is a valuable source of information for the study of the European expansion into the area, including Southeast Asia.

KS —OTTAWA UNIVERSITY, Myers Library, Ottawa, 66067. J Marion Rioth, Head Librn
Holdings: Vols 2350 Cat Maps Pix
Budget: $150
Notes: This started as a collection of studies about Chinese ceramics, art, and related areas. Incl 800 vols on general Asian studies. If this collection has any unique feature it is in the field of 19th century ceramics trade, especially Chinese. There is a bibliography of the collection.

MD —UNIVERSITY OF MARYLAND, Library, East Asia Collection, College Park, 20742. Frank Joseph Shulman, Curator and Head
Holdings: Vols (90,000) // Mss
Notes: Japanese books, newspapers, periodicals, etc, of the Allied Occupation period (1945-1952), including files of censored publications. Books number 40,000; periodical titles, 13,000; newspaper titles, ca 16,500. The special collection relating to the Occupation period is supplemented by a growing collection (now ca 50,000 vols) of Chinese, Japanese, and Korean publications which form the basis of the University's general collection in East Asian language materials.

MA —CHILDREN'S MUSEUM, Resource Center, Museum Wharf, 300 Congress St, Boston, 02210. Marie Ariel, Librn; Maria Russell, Resource Services Mgr
Holdings: Vols 450 Cat Mss Slides Phonorecords Audiotapes Videotapes Filmstrips
Notes: Curriculum materials and materials for children and adults. Available for reference use by the public; borrowing privileges for Museum members; activity and curriculum kits available to public, schools and community groups for rental fee. Subject-related programs and services offered by Museum staff.

MA —HARVARD UNIVERSITY, Fairbank Center for East Asian Research, Library, 1737 Cambridge St, Cambridge, 02138. Nancy Hearst, Librn
Holdings: Vols (10,000) Mss Maps
Notes: Post-1949 China, particularly political and sociological developments. Also, post-1952 Japan. Partially cataloged.

MA —HARVARD UNIVERSITY LIBRARY, Harvard-Yenching Library, 2 Divinity Ave, Cambridge, 02138. Eugene W Wu, Librn
Holdings: Vols (640,000) Cat Mss Pix Microforms
Notes: Harvard's collection for publication in Chinese, Japanese, Korean, Manchu, Mongolian, Tibetan, and Vietnamese; general collection of works in these languages as well as a subject collection on East Asia. Literature, history, religion, philosophy and social sciences are emphasized; the natural sciences, in general, are not collected. Periodical collection of over 10,000 titles, 312 newspapers; 13,500 microfilm reels; and 3880 pieces of microfiche. See *Harvard Library Bulletin,* X (1956), 73-93. Three volumes of a *Classified Catalogue of Korean* Books have been published by the Library (1962, 1966 and 1980). *Japanese Collected Works and Series* in the Library published by Harvard-Yenching Institute. The Chinese and Japanese catalog, incl serials, is scheduled for publication in late 1984. Library also publishes the*Harvard-Yenching Library Bibliographical Series* and *Harvard-Yenching Library Occational Reference Notes.* Collection contains 4160 mss.

MI —UNIVERSITY OF MICHIGAN, Asia Library, Ann Arbor, 48109. Wei-Ying Wan, Head
Holdings: Vols 400,000 Cat Pix Microforms
Notes: Comprehensive coverage on East Asian social sciences and humanities; bibliographic, biographic and historical coverage on the sciences, technology, and medicine. Mostly in Chinese, Japanese, and Korean. Extensive holdings in Western languages in the Graduate Library collection. Also 21,190 microfilm reels and 17,280 microfiche.

MI —MICHIGAN STATE UNIVERSITY, International Library, East Asia Collection, East Lansing, 48824. Eugene deBenko, Librn
Holdings: Vols (34,000) Cat Mss Maps Phonorecords Audiotapes Microforms
Budget: ($11,000)
Notes: Priority given to East Asian publications on contemporary China, Japan and Korea. Principal subject emphasis on language, literature and history. Important resources also on politics and government, economics, anthropology, sociology, geography and agriculture.

MO —WASHINGTON UNIVERSITY, Art & Architecture Library, Saint Louis, 63130. Imre Meszaros, Librn
Holdings: Vols (60,413) Cat Maps Pix Microforms
Budget: ($100,000)
Notes: Art and architecture of East Asia; rare books; archaeology; fashion design.

MO —WASHINGTON UNIVERSITY, East Asian Library, 6600 Millbrook Blvd, Saint Louis, 63130. Sachiko Morrell, Librn
Holdings: Vols 96,000 Cat Microforms
Notes: See *Research Sources for Chinese and Japanese Studies: A List of Serials in Humanities and Social Sciences Held by Washington University Libraries*, comp by Ernest J Tsai (St. Louis; Washington Univ Libraries, 1976), 72 pp.

NJ —PRINCETON UNIVERSITY, Library, Gest Oriental Library & East Asian Collections, 317 Palmer Hall, Princeton, 08544. D E Perushek, Cur
Holdings: Vols (370,000) Cat Mss Maps Pix Microforms
Notes: Materials collected are mostly in East Asian languages: Chinese, Japanese and Korean. Subject emphasis is on East Asia, China, Japan and Korea, their civilization and societies, languages, literature, philosophy, religion, history, politics and sociology. No historical period is excluded. The Gest Library also acquires works on East Asian art and archaeology that are of a general or cultural nature and primary textual sources (extensive collections on East Asian art and archaeology are held and maintained at the University Art Library). Works on historical and economic aspects of East Asian population are also acquired (while population censuses and vital statistics are held at the University Population Research Library). Subject areas in sciences and technology, except those materials dealing with indigenous developments and historical aspects, are excluded. Withregard to the Korean collection in a holding position with a minimum budget allocation, Western-language reference works in all fields of East Asian studies and Western-language monographs of importance on East Asian literature, language, and linguistics are collected. Preference is given to works in English. Emphasis is on current publications. All other Western-language works on East Asia are located elsewhere in the University Library system. The existing collections also incl books and manuscripts in the Manchu, Mongolian, and Tibetan languages. However, acquisitions in these languages are now made on a highly selective basis. Separate card catalogs are maintained for Chinese, Japanese, Korean, and Western-language collections. See also Chen, Frances M & Maureen H Donovan: Periodicals on Asia; Serials in the Princeton University Library inWestern Languages (Princeton: Princeton University Library, 1975).

NY —NEW YORK PUBLIC LIBRARY, Oriental Div, Fifth Ave & 42 St, New York, 10018. E Christian Filstrup, Chief
Holdings: Cat Mss Microforms
Budget: ($56,455)
Notes: Described in *Dictionary Catalog of the Oriental Collection,* The Research Libraries of the New York Public Library, 1960, 16 vols, and *First Supplement,* 1976, 8 vols (144,000 cards). This catalog incl 318, 000 entries for works in about 100 languages of the East, and all works in Western languages on Oriental subjects. The Oriental Collection numbers about 120,000 vols; its Arabic and Indic holdings and those on ancient Egypt and the ancient Near East are among the largest in the US. There is also a collection of 30,000 vols of PL 480 material from Egypt, Pakistan, and India to which there is main entry access, but which is not incorporated into the dictionary catalog. Other outstanding features of the Oriental Collection incl extensive holdings of Japanese technical and scientific periodicals; a unique collection of linguistic works, grammars, anddictionaries; and unusually good coverage of the field of Oriental religions and philosophies. The catalog contains numerous subject references to periodical articles in all languages. All entries are arranged alphabetically according to the Roman alphabet.

NY —UNIVERSITY OF ROCHESTER, Rush Rhees Library, Rochester, 14627. Datta S Kharbas, Head
Holdings: Vols 100,000 Cat Maps Microforms
Notes: Area studies collection on East Asia and South Asia. Major emphasis is on social sciences and humanities. Over 57,000 volumes on East Asia, out of which 29,000 volumes are in Chinese and 15,000 in

ASIA, EAST (cont.)

Japanese. Extensive holdings on Chinese and Japanese histories. Catalog of East Asian collection consisting of Chinese and Japanese language holdings published in 1968, with two subsequent supplements. Over 33,000 volumes on South Asia. Considerable depth in social sciences, history, politics and anthropology. Extensive holdings in Sanskrit, Hindi, and Marathi.

OH —CLEVELAND PUBLIC LIBRARY, Fine Arts and Special Collections Department, 325 Superior Ave, Cleveland, 44114. Alice N Loranth, Head
Holdings: Cat Mss
Notes: Part of the Orientalia Collection. *See also* entry under Oriental Languages and Literatures.

PA —UNIVERSITY OF PITTSBURGH, East Asian Library, 234 Hillman Library, Pittsburgh, 15260. Thomas C Kuo, Cur
Holdings: Vols (118,000) Periodicals Microfilms
Budget: ($210,000)
Notes: Contains Chinese and Japanese language publications on all social sciences and humanities, with special emphasis on history and source materials on both traditional and modern China, as well as research materials on language, literature, history, anthropology, economics and sociology of modern Japan. Catalogs of Chinese local history, East Asian periodicals and serials, and microforms in the collection have been published by the library. Also, *A Brief Guide to the Use of the East Asian* Library (1983). Incl 1600 periodicals and 2900 reels of microfilms.

RI —BROWN UNIVERSITY, John Hay Library, 20 Prospect St, Providence, 02912. Mark N Brown, Cur Mss
Holdings: Vols (74,000) Cat Microforms
Budget: ($10,000)
Notes: East Asia Collection. The primary focus is on Chinese studies with a small segment of approx 700 vols devoted to Japanese studies. Major subject areas, in descending order of strength, are: literature (incl classics), history, geography, social sciences, philosophy and religion, fine arts, science and technology. This incl the personal collection (20,000 vols) formed by Harvard University Sinologist Dr Charles Sidney Gardner, which is especially rich in materials relating to the Ch'ing Dynasty (1644-1912). In addition to books, there are 500 reels of microfilm, plus runs of 8 Chinese newspapers and 26 current Chinese periodicals.

TX —UNIVERSITY OF TEXAS LIBRARIES, Asian Collection, PO Box P, Austin, 78712. Kevin Lin, Asian Librn; Merry Burlingham, South Asian Librn
Holdings: Vols (58,000) Cat Microforms
Notes: Anthropology, economics, government, history, and language and literature of China and Japan. Incl 250 periodical titles.

WA —UNIVERSITY OF WASHINGTON LIBRARIES, East Asia Library, DO-27, Seattle, 98195. Karl Lo, Head
Holdings: Vols (300,000) Cat Microforms
Budget: ($200,000)
Notes: Southwest China: Joseph Rock Collection, ca 2000 vols; modern Chinese poetry, 1919 to date: ca 700 titles; Asian art, esp Japanese painting; 1097 vols; Tiao-yu-t'ai movements in the US; ca 400 items of periodicals and pamphlets; modern Korean poetry, ancient and modern; ca 1000 titles; Mu-yu-shu folk literature: ca 1000 items.

WI —UNIVERSITY OF WISCONSIN, MADISON, Memorial Library, 728 State St, Madison, 53706. Erwin K Welsch, Social Studies Bibliographer

ASIA, EAST—COMMERCE

†CA —FAR EAST MERCHANTS ASSOCIATION, Femas Trade Library, 1597 Curtis St, Berkeley, 94702.
Notes: Trade with Far Eastern countries, esp China, Japan, Philippine Islands and Singapore.

ASIA, EAST—MAPS

CA —UNIVERSITY OF CALIFORNIA, BERKELEY, University Library, East Asiatic Library, Room 208, Durant Hall, Berkeley, 94720. Donald Shively, Head
Notes: Incl early Japanese maps, chiefly woodblock or copperplate, many in color, 17th through early 20th century.

ASIA, SOUTH

CA —UNIVERSITY OF CALIFORNIA, BERKELEY, University Library, 438 Main Library, Berkeley, 94720. Kenneth R Logan, South Asia Librn
Notes: South Asia collection (India, Pakistan, Bangladesh, Nepal, Sri Lanka) contain 150,000-200,000 titles. Covers at research level the social sciences and humanities in western languages and 20 South Asian languages. Subject areas: history, political science, lanugage and literature (especially strong in Hindi, Urdu, Tamil, Sanskrit and Nepali), art and art history, sociology, education, music, environmental design, philosophy and religion, anthropology, geography, national and local government publications. Formats: monographs, periodicals, newspapers, microforms, maps, sound recordings, video-tapes, pamphlets. Special strengths: modern Hindi literature; history of South Asian countries; government publications of India, late 19th and 20th centuries. Member of South Asia Microform Project; Participant in Library of Congress AcquisitionsPrograms for India, Pakistan, Nepal, and Bangladesh.

CA —CLAREMONT COLLEGES, Honnold Library, Asian Studies Collection, Ninth & Dartmouth, Claremont, 91711. Frances D Wang, Cur
Holdings: Vols (69,658) Cat Mss Maps Pix Microforms
Budget: ($50,000)
Notes: Incl 62,476 vols in Chinese and Japanese; 6276 in Western languages. About 13,000 uncataloged. Collection incl artifacts, original mss, rare, original editions of Chinese, Japanese, Korean and Western language and literature, history, and archaeology, which are today totally unavailable to acquire. The most distinguished work is the collection of some 200 Chinese gazetteers (fang-chih) which is one of the best in the US. Another valuable collection is the Frederick McCormick Collection of 214 titles in 896 vols of movable-type editions of Korean printed books, 15th-19th centuries. The Western-language collection on the Far East is probably one of the strongest in the US. Recently added was a collection of Japanese books on Shinto (125 titles), periodicals, and artifacts. Separate catalog.

CA —UNIVERSITY OF CALIFORNIA, LOS ANGELES, Research Library, Indo/Pacific Collection, 405 Hilgard Ave, Los Angeles, 90024. Edward Shreeves, Chairman, Bibliographers Group; Charlotte Spence, Indo/Pacific Bibliographer
Holdings: Vols Cat Mss Maps Pix Microforms
Notes: The South Asian collection has been developed on two levels. On the research level it focuses on (1) the cultural, economic, political and social history of India from about 1859 to 1947; (2) linguistic and literary studies, with particular emphasis given to Sanskrit and Pali; and (3) the history of the Portuguese experience in South Asia. On the teaching level, materials are collected which relate to India before 1859, and from 1947 to date, as well as materials relating to the other political entities of South Asia. A description of the South Asian collection is included in the May, 1977 issue of *The Librarian,* and in *South Asian Library Resources in North* America (1975).

DC —FREER GALLERY OF ART, Library, 12th & Jefferson Dr SW, Washington, 20560. Ellen A Nollman, Librn

DC —LIBRARY OF CONGRESS, African and Middle Eastern Division, Washington, 20540.
Holdings: Cat Mss Microforms
Notes: The Orientalia Division contains over 1,400,000 vols in Oriental languages. Chinese: more than 422,000 vols, espec strong in local histories and Ch'ing (1644-1911) period material. Japanese: over 574, 000 vols, espec strong in economics, statistics, history, literature; 12,000 government, learned society, and university periodical titles, espec strong in science, technology, and social sciences. Korean: 56, 000 vols, espec strong in social sciences and modern history. Hebraic: about 109,000 vols in Hebrew, Yiddish, Judeo-Arabic, Judeo-Persian, Ladino, Syriac, Ethiopic, espec strong in biblical subjects, responsa literature and socio-political aspects. Near Eastern: over 104,000 vols, Arabic, Armenian, Persian, Turkish, and fringe languages. Special subject strength Muslim theology, history and literature. Southern Asian: over 137,000 vols, literature of South and Southeast Asia from Pakistan to Philippines. Oriental maps are in the custody of Library's Geography & Map Division; pictorial materials, slides, etc, are in the custody of Prints & Photographs Division.

HI —UNIVERSITY OF HAWAII, Library, 2550 The Mall, Honolulu, 96822. Joyce Wright, Head, Asia Collection; Masato Matsu, Head, East Asia Vernacular Collection
Holdings: Vols 75,215 Cat Microforms
Notes: The Asia Collection holds material from and relating to Bangladesh, India, Nepal, Pakistan, and Sri Lanka in western and Asian languages. South Asian languages currently acquired: Bengali, Hindi, Marathi, Nepali, Pali, Prakrit, Sanskrit, Tamil. Period emphasis is post-World War II. Subject emphases: social sciences and the humanities (literature, economics, history, religion/philosophy). Holdings are supplemented by a large uncataloged backlog, much of it accessible through the Library of Congress Accessions Lists for the area and by over 7000 cataloged titles in the main library collection. *South Asian Library Resources in North America: A Survey Prepared for the Boston Conference,* 1974, ed by M L P Patterson (Zug, Switzerland: Tutes Documentation Compnay, 1975).(Bibliotheca Asiatica 12-), "University of Hawaii," pp 103-114.

IL —CENTER FOR RESEARCH LIBRARIES, 6050 S Kenwood Ave, Chicago, 60637. Donald B Simpson, Dir; Esther Smith, Collection Development Librn
Holdings: Microforms
Notes: Receive journals and monographs from India, Pakistan, Ceylon and Nepal, on PL 480. Buy newspapers and serials on microfilm. Collection begins 1969 in most cases. Have newspaper microfilms for some earlier years. There is also a South Asia Microform Project for which borrowing is restricted to members of the project but anyone may purchase copies when SAMP owns the negative. SAMP material cataloged; listed in SAMP Catalog and supplements. There are some 4,500 reels of microfilms and 25,000 microfiche.

IN —INDIANA UNIVERSITY, Lilly Library, Seventh St, Bloomington, 47405. William R Cagle, Librn
Holdings: Vols (2000) // Cat
Notes: Many of the vols are from the library of A E. Mss incl both his correspondence and writings and the papers of his biographer, Alan Denson.

MI —UNIVERSITY OF MICHIGAN, Graduate Library, South Asian Dept, Ann Arbor, 48109. Om P Sharma, Librn
Holdings: Vols (365,000) Cat Maps Slides Microforms
Notes: The major emphasis is on social sciences and humanities. Besides materials in classical languages, South Asian vernaculars being retained are Hindi, Bengali, Urdu, Marathi and Tamil; Strong in classical languages, especially Sanskrit, Pali, and Prakrit.

MI —MICHIGAN STATE UNIVERSITY, International Library, South and Southeast Asia Collection, East Lansing, 48824.

ASIA, SOUTH (cont.)

Clinton Lockert, Bibliographer
Holdings: Vols (58,000) Cat Mss Maps Audiotapes Microforms
Notes: Serials and monographs of South Asia received on PL 480 for India, Pakistan, Sri Lanka, and Nepal since 1968. Emphasis is upon Social Sciences, Humanities, and Science. Areas of strength are Anthropology and rural development. Only selected holdings were received.

MO —UNIVERSITY OF MISSOURI-COLUMBIA, Ellis Library, Ninth and Lowry, Columbia, 65201. Murari Lal Nagar, Librn
Holdings: Vols 100,000 Maps Microforms
Notes: The South Asia Studies Program at the University of Missouri-Columbia, is an interdepartmental, multi-disciplinary area studies program on India, Pakistan, Bangladesh, Sri Lanka and Nepal. Depository for the PL480 Program of the Library of Congress in many languages from South Asia. There are library resources in Sankskrit, Hindi, Bengali, Panjabi, and Malayalam. The library is particularly strong in Baroda, Bengal and the Punjab.

NY —NEW YORK PUBLIC LIBRARY, Oriental Div, Fifth Ave & 42 St, New York, 10018. E Christian Filstrup, Chief
Holdings: Cat Mss Microforms
Budget: ($56,455)
Notes: Described in *Dictionary Catalog of the Oriental Collection,* The Research Libraries of the New York Public Library, 1960, 16 vols, and *First Supplement,* 1976, 8 vols (144,000 cards). This catalog incl 318, 000 entries for works in about 100 languages of the East, and all works in Western languages on Oriental subjects. The Oriental Collection numbers about 120,000 vols; its Arabic and Indic holdings and those on ancient Egypt and the ancient Near East are among the largest in the US. There is also a collection of 30,000 vols of PL 480 material from Egypt, Pakistan, and India to which there is main entry access, but which is not incorporated into the dictionary catalog. Other outstanding features of the Oriental Collection incl extensive holdings of Japanese technical and scientific periodicals; a unique collection of linguistic works, grammars, anddictionaries; and unusually good coverage of the field of Oriental religions and philosophies. The catalog contains numerous subject references to periodical articles in all languages. All entries are arranged alphabetically according to the Roman alphabet.

NY —UNIVERSITY OF ROCHESTER, Rush Rhees Library, Rochester, 14627. Datta S Kharbas, Head
Holdings: Vols 100,000 Cat Maps Microforms
Notes: Area studies collection on East Asia and South Asia. Major emphasis is on social sciences and humanities. Over 57,000 volumes on East Asia, out of which 29,000 volumes are in Chinese and 15,000 in Japanese. Extensive holdings on Chinese and Japanese histories. Catalog of East Asian collection consisting of Chinese and Japanese language holdings published in 1968, with two subsequent supplements. Over 33,000 volumes on South Asia. Considerable in depth in social sciences, history, politics and anthropology. Extensive holdings in Sanskrit, Hindi, and Marathi.

NC —DUKE UNIVERSITY, William R Perkins Library, Durham, 27706. Elvin E Strowd, University Librn

OH —CLEVELAND PUBLIC LIBRARY, Fine Arts and Special Collections Department, 325 Superior Ave, Cleveland, 44114. Alice N Loranth, Head
Holdings: Vols 12,000 Cat Mss Microforms
Notes: Part of the Orientalia Collection. *See also* entries under India; Oriental Languages and Literatures.

PA —UNIVERSITY OF PENNSYLVANIA, Van Pelt Library, South Asia Collection, 34 and Walnut Sts, Philadelphia, 19104. Kanta Bhatia, Bibliographer
Holdings: Vols 160,000 Cat
Notes: Incl South Asia social sciences, history, politics, economics, anthropology and art. Extensive holdings in vernacular languages, especially Hindi, Tamil and Sanskrit.

TX —UNIVERSITY OF TEXAS LIBRARIES, Asian Collection, PO Box P, Austin, 78712. Kevin Lin, Asian Librn; Merry Burlingham, South Asian Librn
Holdings: Vols (58,000) Cat Microforms
Notes: Materials in Hindi, Sanskrit, Urdu, Prakrit, and Pali (acquired chiefly through the Special Foreign Acquisitions Program) and selected English-language materials incl Indian censuses and district gazetteers and Pakistani censuses.

WA —UNIVERSITY OF WASHINGTON LIBRARIES, Suzzallo Library, South Asian Section, Seattle, 98195. Irene M Joshi, Librn
Holdings: Vols (127,000) Maps Microforms Audiotapes
Notes: A nationally important collection of 127,000 vols incl approx 45,000 vols in South Asian languages and 22,000 uncataloged titles. The collection is especially strong in anthropology, classical Sanskrit literature, economic history, economics, history, linguistics, philosophy and political science. The microform holdings incl the Indian census from 1881, newspapers from 1838, legislative debates from 1854, development plans and serial titles. Twenty-eight newspapers and nearly 5000 serial titles are received from history, politics and government, Near Eastern and East Asian studies which also support South Asian studies. The Law Library has a collection of South Asian legal materials.

ASIA, SOUTHEAST

CA —UNIVERSITY OF CALIFORNIA, LOS ANGELES, Research Library, Indo/Pacific Collection, 405 Hilgard Ave, Los Angeles, 90024. Edward Shreeves, Chairman, Bibliographers Group; Charlotte Spence, Indo/Pacific Bibliographer
Holdings: Vols Cat Mss Maps Pix Microforms
Notes: The Southeast Asian collection has been developed on a combination of the research and teaching levels; it focuses on the cultural, economic, political and social history of the area from ancient times to the present day. Although all the individual countries of the region are represented, some priority is given to Malaysia, Singapore, Indonesia and the Philippines. The majority of the materials is in Western languages except for a collection of several thousand books in Thai, and a smaller collection of materials in Vietnamese, Indonesian, Malaysian, and the Philippine languages.

DC —HOWARD UNIVERSITY, Founders Library, Bernard B Fall Collection (Southeast Asia Collection), Washington, 20059. Steven Ilsang Yoon, Cur
Holdings: Vols (6000) Cat Microforms
Budget: $15,000
Notes: The Bernard B Fall Collection has more than 6000 books, incl 1200 books purchased from the Kendric N Marshall Estate, 3000 items in vertical files, 300 pamphlets, and 800 microfilms, about Southeastern Asia and China. In addition, there are nearly 100 current periodicals and another 100 older periodicals about Indochina in the Collection.

HI —UNIVERSITY OF HAWAII, Library, 2550 The Mall, Honolulu, 96822. Joyce Wright, Head, Asia Collection; Masato Matsu, Head, East Asia Vernacular Collection
Holdings: Vols 331,620 Cat Microforms
Notes: The Asia Collection holds materials from and about Southeast Asia: Brunei, Burma, Cambodia (Kampuchea), Indonesia, Laos, Malaysia, Philippines, Singapore, Thailand. Large contemporary Indonesian language collection. Several thousand vols in Thai and in Vietnamese. Minimal holdings in Burmese, Khmer, Lao languages. Social sciences and humanities emphasis for the post-World War II period. Western language coverage supplemented by retrospective holdings in the main library collection.

IL —SOUTHERN ILLINOIS UNIVERSITY, CARBONDALE, Delyte W Morris Library, Carbondale, 62901.
Holdings: Vols (4100) Cat Maps Audiotapes Microforms
Notes: The Vietnamese collection has been transferred to the general library. It incl 1200 cataloged titles in the Vietnamese language, plus 56 Vietnamese language microfilms. A profile of the area emphasis on the collection appears from the following distribution of the 2987 titles entered in the holdings and accessions lists published by the Southern Illinois University Center for Vietnamese Studies: Vietnam, 1965; Cambodia and Laos, 63; Other Southeast Asia (incl Indonesia), 916; East Asia (mostly China), 246; General (reference works, bibliographies, etc), 197. Also over 1000 maps.

IL —CENTER FOR RESEARCH LIBRARIES, 6050 S Kenwood Ave, Chicago, 60637. Donald B Simpson, Dir; Esther Smith, Collection Development Librn
Holdings: Microforms
Notes: Receive serials and monographs fromm Indonesia, Malaysia and Singapore under NPAC (formerly PL 480). Collection starts 1969 for Indonesia, 1971 for Malaysia, Singapore and Brunei. Buy 14 newspapers on microfilm. Also incl Southeast Asia Microform Project. Borrowing is restricted to members of the project.

IL —NORTHERN ILLINOIS UNIVERSITY, Founders Memorial Library, Southeast Asia Collection, Normal Rd, De Kalb, 60115. Lee S Dutton Dr, Cur
Holdings: Vols (34,000) Cat Mss Maps Microforms
Notes: An extensive collection of books, periodicals, newspapers, maps, and microforms from or about Southeast Asia. Areas of concentration incl Thailand, Malaysia, Indonesia, Singapore, Brunei, Philippines, Laos, and Burma. Holdings (except rare books, maps, and microforms) are housed in a separate area collection within the Founders Library. A departmental card catalog and specialized reference collection support reference services. A Thai collection of several thousand vols is the largest vernacular component. Extensive Malaysia, Indonesia, Singapore, and Brunei holdings have been acquired through the NPAC program. A collection of Filipino-American newspapers, and a growing collection of children's literature in common and uncommon Southeast Asian languages are available. Resources are accessible to borrowers through OCLC.

IN —INDIANA UNIVERSITY, Lilly Library, Seventh St, Bloomington, 47405. William R Cagle, Librn
Holdings: Vols (2000) // Cat
Notes: The core of the collection is the specialized library of Charles R Boxer (1000) dealing with the history of the Iberians in the East, 16th-18th century. Mainly incl works on China, Japan and the Philippines during the period of their early intercourse with the West through 1800, as well as materials on the English and Dutch East India Companies, and the 17th century Anglo-Dutch naval wars. Special mention should be made of the valuable letters from missions by the Jesuits, and the works in this area by the Augustinians, Franciscans, and Dominicans, from the time of the arrival of the Iberians in Asia. The collection is a valuable source of information for the study of the European expansion into the area, including Southeast Asia.

MI —UNIVERSITY OF MICHIGAN, Harlan Hatcher Graduate Library, Ann Arbor, 48109. Susan Go, Librn
Holdings: Vols (250,000) Cat Mss Maps Pix Slides Microforms
Notes: Incl in the Michigan Historical Collections (primarily archival material) are papers of Michiganders in southeast Asia, mostly the Philipines, eg papers of Joseph R Hayden, Frank Murphy and G Mennen Williams, also, on film, the selected papers of Philippines president Manuel Quezon. All aspects of the countries, cultures and peoples of Brunei, Burma, Khymer, Indonesia, Laos, Malaysia, Philippines, Singapore, Thailand, Portuguese Timor and Vietnam. Also the

ASIA, SOUTHEAST (cont.)

Malayo-Polynesian (Austronesian), Mon-Khmer (Austroasiatic), and Sino-Tibetan language groupings.

MI —MICHIGAN STATE UNIVERSITY, International Library, South and Southeast Asia Collection, East Lansing, 48824. Clinton Lockert, Bibliographer
Holdings: Vols (13,500) Cat Mss Mpas Pix Audiotapes Microforms
Notes: Emphasis is upon South Vietnam (1955-1962), Thailand (1964-1968) and MSU Vietnam Advisory Group, *Reports and Documents.* Extensive materials related to Thailand Project in Educational Planning, 1964-1968. Extensive holdings of the Institure of Pacific Relations.

†MN —UNIVERSITY OF MINNESOTA, Southeast Asia Resource Center, Minneapolis, 55455.

NY —CORNELL UNIVERSITY LIBRARIES, John M Olin Library, John M Echols Collection on Southeast Asia, Ithaca, 14853. Giok Po Oey, Curator
Holdings: Vols 167,000 Mss Maps Pix Audiotapes 16mm Films Microforms
Budget: $90,000
Notes: The John M Echols Collection on Southeast Asia is the largest collection of books, periodicals, newspapers, maps, and microforms in the world. Over 167,000 volumes in 1983. The Collection was named in honor of Professor John M Echols, in recognition of his outstanding assistance in its development over the past two decades. Holdings cataloged prior to January 1981 are listed in *Cornell University Libraries Southeast Asia Catalog* (G K Hall, 1976, First supplement, 1983), 10 vols. Monthly additions are listed in the collection's accessions list.

NY —NEW YORK PUBLIC LIBRARY, Oriental Div, Fifth Ave & 42 St, New York, 10018. E Christian Filstrup, Chief
Holdings: Cat Mss Microforms
Budget: ($56,455)
Notes: Described in *Dictionary Catalog of the Oriental Collection,* The Research Libraries of the New York Public Library, 1960, 16 vols, and *First Supplement,* 1976, 8 vols (144,000 cards). This catalog incl 318, 000 entries for works in about 100 languages of the East, and all works in Western languages on Oriental subjects. The Oriental Collection numbers about 120,000 vols; its Arabic and Indic holdings and those on ancient Egypt and the ancient Near East are among the largest in the US. There is also a collection of 30,000 vols of PL 480 material from Egypt, Pakistan, and India to which there is main entry access, but which is not incorporated into the dictionary catalog. Other outstanding features of the Oriental Collection incl extensive holdings of Japanese technical and scientific periodicals; a unique collection of linguistic works, grammars, anddictionaries; and unusually good coverage of the field of Oriental religions and philosophies. The catalog contains numerous subject references to periodical articles in all languages. All entries are arranged alphabetically according to the Roman alphabet. The Library currently collects for Southeast Asia in Western language materials only.

OH —OHIO UNIVERSITY, Vernon R Alden Library, Southeast Asia Collection, Athens, 45701. Lian The-Mulliner, Head
Holdings: Vols (68,000) Cat Maps Slides Phonorecords Videotapes 16mm Films Microforms
Budget: ($35,000)
Notes: Emphasis on Indonesia, Malaysia, Singapore, Brunei and the Philippines. Incl language and literature, history, civilization and culture, art, medicine, philosophy and economic conditions. Separate catalog.

OH —CLEVELAND PUBLIC LIBRARY, Fine Arts and Special Collections Department, 325 Superior Ave, Cleveland, 44114. Alice N Loranth, Head
Holdings: Vols 2000 Cat Mss Maps
Notes: Emphasis is on materials concerning Dutch East India. Complete runs of the Dutch serials and periodicals, such as the publications of the *Indisch Genootschnap, Instituut voor Taal-, Land- en Volkenkunde,* etc are the strengths of this collection.
See also entry under Oriental Languages and Literatures.

PA —BRYN MAWR COLLEGE, Canaday Library, Bryn Mawr, 19010. James Tanis, Dir
Notes: McBride Collection on Asia and Southeast Asia. Incl many rare books.

PA —UNIVERSITY OF PENNSYLVANIA, EDINBORO, Baron-Forness Library, Edinboro, 16444. Saul Weinstein, Dir of Libraries
Holdings: Vols 2339 Maps Pix Slides Microforms
Budget: $1500

PA —UNIVERSITY OF PITTSBURGH, Hillman Library, Pittsburgh, 15260. Glenora E Rossell, Head
Holdings: Vols (10,059) Cat
Notes: Emphasis is on cultural anthropology and archaeology.

ASIAN-AFRICAN POLITICS see Afro-Asian Politics

ASIAN AMERICANS

WI —STATE HISTORICAL SOCIETY OF WISCONSIN, Library, Newspaper and Periodicals Section, 816 State St, Madison, 53706. James P Danky, Librn
Notes: One of the largest collections of Asian American periodicals and newspapers in the US. Holdings described in *Asian American Periodicals and Newspapers: A Union List....* Madison, The Society, 1979. (ERIC Report ED 220 102).

ASIAN ART see Art, Asian

ASIAN DANCE

NY —NEW YORK PUBLIC LIBRARY, Performing Arts Research Center, Dance Collection, 111 Amsterdam Ave, New York, 10023. Genevieve Oswald, Cur
Holdings: Vols (40,000) Cat Mss Pix Audiotapes Videotapes 16mm Films Microforms
Budget: ($9,280)
Notes: Multi-media documentation of classical and traditional dance of Asia. Greatest strength in materials on India, Indonesia, and Japan; less well-represented are Sri Lanka, Malaysia, Pakistan, the Philippines, Thailand, Laos, Vietnam, Cambodia, Burma, and China. Intensive acquisitions program by the Collection's Asia Dance Project since 1975. By early 1978 Collection included: 307 books; 356 periodical articles; 77 manuscript vols on microfilm; 197 motion pictures and videotapes; periodicals from Japan, India, and China; photographs, programs, newspaper clippings, scrapbooks. Original documentation produced includes 35 hrs of taped oral interviews and 14 hrs of filmed or videotaped performance. Outstanding acquisitions are 73 mss vols (microfilm) on 15-17th cent Bugaku dance from the Japancse Imperial Household Library; the Claire Holt Collection of Indonesian materials(mss, letters, scrapbooks, over 2000 photographs). Also cataloged or indexed for inclusion in the catalog are an additional 670 books and 2835 periodical articles located in the NYPL's Theatre, Oriental, and Music Divisions. See also: US Works Progress Administration. New York (City), *Dance* Index. Published catalog: *Dictionary Catalog of the Dance Collection,* (Boston: G K Hall, 1974), 10 vols. Annual supplements: *Bibliographic Guide to Dance,* also published by G K Hall.

ASIAN MUSIC see Music, Asian

ASIAN NEWSPAPERS see Newspapers, Asian

ASIAN STUDIES

MD —UNIVERSITY OF MARYLAND, Library, East Asia Collection, College Park, 20742. Frank Joseph Shulman, Curator and Head
Holdings: Vols
Budget: $300
Notes: Very extensive (600) vertical files of Western-language newsletters and association bulletins published since the early 1960s that relate in whole or in part to Asian Studies. Some titles have been listed in Frank Joseph Shulman's Newsletters and Association Bulletins on Asia: An Annotated Guide to Current Academic Resources, *Asian Studies Professional Review,* vols 4 (1974-75) and 5 (1975-76). All disciplines covered. Most newsletters and bulletins are academically or culturally oriented; newsletters of the business world and of foreign embassies and their information centers are generally excluded. These files are believed to constitute the single most comprehensive collection of their kind in the world. This collection is not a component part of the University of Maryland Libraries, but all communications should beaddressed to Frank Joseph Shulman, c/o the University's East Asia Collection.

ASIANIC LANGUAGES

NY —NEW YORK PUBLIC LIBRARY, Oriental Div, Fifth Ave & 42 St, New York, 10018. E Christian Filstrup, Chief
Holdings: Cat Mss Microforms
Budget: ($56,455)
Notes: Published catalog of holdings.

†WA —UNIVERSITY OF WASHINGTON LIBRARIES, Seattle, 98195.

ASIANS IN THE U.S.

CA —UNIVERSITY OF CALIFORNIA, BERKELEY, University Library, East Asiatic Library, Room 208, Durant Hall, Berkeley, 94720. Donald Shively, Head
Notes: Incl early Japanese maps, chiefly woodblock or copperplate, many in color, 17th through early 20th century.

†CA —OAKLAND PUBLIC LIBRARY, Asian Library, 449 9th St, Oakland, 94612.

†NY —ASIAN AMERICAN RESOURCE CENTER, 199 Lafayette St, 7th Floor, New York, 10012.

PA —BALCH INSTITUTE FOR ETHNIC STUDIES, Library, 18 S Seventh St, Philadelphia, 19106. R Joseph Anderson, Library Dir
Holdings: Vols 620 Cat Mss Microforms Pix

ASIFA see International Animated Film Society (ASIFA)

ASIMOV, ISAAC

CA —SAN DIEGO STATE UNIVERSITY, Malcolm A Love Library, 5300 Campanile Dr, San Diego, 92182. D Dickinson, Univ Librn; Don L Bosseau, Dir
Holdings: Mss Audiotapes
Notes: Elizabeth Chater Collection in Science Fiction. Includes Tolkien Collection, fantasy, folklore, Gothic novels, mostly autographed first editions, some rare and scarce, includes manuscripts, graphics, cassette tapes. Examples: authors included, Isaac Asimov, Ray Bradbury, Joan Vinge, Greg Baer, Frederick Pohl, Andre Norton, etc. Examples of periodicals; Amazing Stories, Famous Fantastic Mysteries of the 1940s, The Black Cat, 1895. (3000 items)

MD —UNIVERSITY OF MARYLAND, BALTIMORE COUNTY, Albin O Kuhn Library and Gallery, 5401 Wilkens Ave, Baltimore, 21228. Ann Copeland, Special Collections Librn
Holdings: Cat Mss
Notes: Science fiction mss.
See also entry under Science Fiction.

MA —BOSTON UNIVERSITY, Mugar Memorial Library, Special Collections Dept, 771 Commonwealth Ave, Boston, 02215. Howard B Gotlieb, Dir
Holdings: Cat Mss Pix
Notes: Mss, correspondence, etc collected in depth; incl publications by or about.

ASKIN, JOHN

MI —DETROIT PUBLIC LIBRARY, Burton Historical Collection, 5201 Woodward Ave, Detroit, 48202. Alice Dalligan, Chief

ASKWITH, BETTY

MA —BOSTON UNIVERSITY, Mugar Memorial Library, Special Collections Dept, 771 Commonwealth Ave, Boston, 02215. Howard B Gotlieb, Dir
Holdings: Cat Mss
Notes: Mss, correspondence, etc collected in depth; incl publications by or about.

ASPINALL, WAYNE

†CO —UNIVERSITY OF DENVER, Penrose Library, 2150 E Evans, Denver, 80208.
Notes: Papers of Congressman Wayne Aspinall.

ASQUITH, LADY

DC —GEORGETOWN UNIVERSITY, Library, Special Collections Div, 37 & O Sts NW, Washington, 20057. George M Barringer, Special Collections Librn; Nicholas B Sheetz, Mss Librn
Holdings: Mss Cat Pix
Notes: The papers of the Irish man-of-letters Sir Shane Leslie (1885-1971) containing letters, mss, diaries, notebooks, clippings, and photographs. Extensive correspondence by Margot Asquith, countess of Oxford and Asquith; Lady Violet Bonham-Carter; Burke Cochran; Lord Alfred Douglas; Moreton Frewen; Cardinal Gasquet; Vyvyan Holland; Lady Leonie Leslie; Sir Wilfrid Meynell; Sir Horace Plunkett; John Quinn; Frederick Rolfe (Baron Corvo); and Elizabeth Russell, among others. Also incl are research files on Sir Winston Churchill (Leslie's first cousin); Leonard Jerome; Maria Anne Fitzherbet (wife of King George IV); Ghosts and Ghost stories; and Eton College.

ASSAMESE LANGUAGE AND LITERATURE

NY —NEW YORK PUBLIC LIBRARY, Oriental Div, Fifth Ave & 42 St, New York, 10018. E Christian Filstrup, Chief
Holdings: Cat Mss Microforms
Budget: ($56,455)
Notes: Published catalog of holdings. Currently collected in Western language materials only.

ASSASSINATION

DC —GEORGETOWN UNIVERSITY, Library, Special Collections Div, 37 & O Sts NW, Washington, 20057. George M Barringer, Special Collections Librn; Nicholas B Sheetz, Mss Librn
Holdings: Cat Mss Pix
Notes: Political assassinations, espec materials pertaining to the assassinations of John F Kennedy and Robert F Kennedy and the investigations thereof.

TX —TEXAS CHRISTIAN UNIVERSITY, Mary Couts Burnett Library, Fort Worth, 76129.
Notes: The Marguerite Oswald Collection (mother of Lee Harvey Oswald), incl the full Warren Commission Report, with her own annotations and comments. Also, some 200 vols, many inscribed or dedicated to her.

ASSAULT, CRIMINAL (AGAINST WOMEN) see Rape

ASSESSMENT

IL —INTERNATIONAL ASSOCIATION OF ASSESSING OFFICERS, Research & Technical Services Dept, 1313 E 60 St, Chicago, 60637. Stuart W Miller, Librn
Holdings: Vols 6000 Cat Documents Microforms
Budget: ($3500)
Notes: Extensive collection of materials relating to the property tax and its administration, incl assessment studies, reports of legislative and civic groups, manuals, judicial decisions and other works. Subscription information service available. Library is an OCLC member and lends on ILL. The Library is open to the public (at least 24 hours notice required) and accepts telephone inquiries.

ASSINIBOIN INDIANS

†IL —NEWBERRY LIBRARY, 60 W Walton St, Chicago, 60610.
Notes: Collection of color slides of the early 1950s. Photographs by the eight-year Superintendent of the Fort Belknap Indian Reservation in Montana, J W "Duke" Wellington, who was allowed to take pictures of some of the most important rituals of the Assiniboine and Gros Ventres Indians, dances, renewals, etc. An annotated collection.

MT —MONTANA STATE UNIVERSITY, Library, Bozeman, 59717. Minnie Ellen Paugh, Special Collections Librn
Holdings: Vols (7000) // Mss Maps Pix
Notes: Leggat-Donahoe Collection. Collection of Alexander Leggat of Butte, whose father was active in opening the mines. Mr Leggat's interests were mining, exploration, and the fur trade. There are excellent Indian materials in the collection. Also the manuscript and picture collections of James Willard Schultz, Harry James (about James Willard Schultz), and Olga Ross Hannon on Blackfeet Indian tepees. Land claim clase files and manuscripts about Blackfeet, Gros Ventre, Assiniboine and Crow Indians collected by Dr Thomas R Wessell, Edward E Barry and Dr Merrill G Burlingame.

ASSISTANCE TO UNDERDEVELOPED AREAS see Technical Assistance

ASSOCIATED PRESS

†OK —OKLAHOMA STATE UNIVERSITY, Library, Stillwater, 74074.
Notes: Papers of Paul Miller, chairman emeritus of the Gannett Company. Incl personal papers reflecting his career in journalism and as president of the Associated Press.

ASSOCIATION BOOKS

IN —INDIANA UNIVERSITY, Lilly Library, Seventh St, Bloomington, 47405. William R Cagle, Librn
Holdings: Vols 1000 Cat
Notes: Vols associated with people of literary and/or historical importance, largely in the Anglo-American world.

MD —ENOCH PRATT FREE LIBRARY, Humanities Dept, 400 Cathedral St, Baltimore, 21201. Neil R Jordahl, Librn
Holdings: Vols 4200 Cat Mss Pix
Notes: The definitive Mencken Collection; also incl over 2000 pamphlets. Mencken gave most of his books and papers to the library. Collection incl family papers, memorabilia, research notes, etc. Numerous presentation books given to Mencken, mostly inscribed.

MA —HARVARD UNIVERSITY LIBRARY, Houghton Library, Cambridge, 02138. F Thomas Noonan, Cur, Reading Room; Lawrence Dowler, Associate Librn
Holdings: Cat
Notes: See *Harvard Library Bulletin, XIII* (1959): pp 475-477.

NJ —PRINCETON UNIVERSITY, Library, Manuscript Collection, Nassau St, Princeton, 08540. Jean F Preston, Cur
Holdings: Vols 750 Cat Mss
Notes: Association items from the libraries of George Henry Boker (1823-1890) and Richard Palmer Blackmur (1904-1965).

NY —COLUMBIA UNIVERSITY LIBRARIES, Rare Book & Manuscript Library, 801 Butler Library, 535 W 114 St, New York, 10027. Kenneth A Lohf, Librn
Holdings: Mss Pix
Notes: The papers of Daniel Longwell, former editor at Doubleday and *Life*, incl his correspondence with many authors; also, nearly 400 first and inscribed editions, mss, and autograph letters. Much on the now defunct *Life* magazine. Restricted use.

ASSOCIATION FOOTBALL see Soccer

ASSOCIATION FOR THE BENEFIT OF COLORED ORPHANS OF NEW YORK CITY

NY —NEW YORK HISTORICAL SOCIETY, Library, 170 Central Park W, New York, 10024. James Gregory, Librn
Notes: The records, 1836-1865, of Association for the Benefit of Colored Orphans of NYC.

ASSOCIATION INTERNATIONALE DU FILM D'ANIMATION see International Animated Film Society (ASIFA)

ASSOCIATION OF AMERICAN GEOGRAPHERS

OH —UNIVERSITY OF CINCINNATI, Geology-Geography Library, 103 Old Tech Bldg ML 13, Cincinnati, 45221. Richard Spohn, Sr Library Assoc
Notes: Library is the depository for the Association of American Geographers Library.

ASSOCIATION OF AMERICAN RAILROADS

MS —UNIVERSITY OF SOUTHERN MISSISSIPPI, William David McCain Graduate Library, Box 5148, Southern Sta, Hattiesburg, 39406.
Holdings: Cat Mss
Notes: Office files of the General Secretary of the President's Conference Committee for the Federal Valuation of the Railraods. Incl correspondence, valuation orders, valuation reports and related exhibit information from railroads and switching companies for the period 1914-1937. A guide to the records is available for loan.

ASSOCIATION OF AMERICAN UNIVERSITY PRESSES

NY —COLUMBIA UNIVERSITY LIBRARIES, Rare Book & Manuscript Library, 801 Butler Library, 535 W 114 St, New York, 10027. Kenneth A Lohf, Librn
Holdings: Vols 340
Notes: One of the 6 university libraries selected for the deposit of copies of award books of the annual AAUP Book Shows; initial gift, 1965-1969. These are the 25 special award books. The library also has a complete file of the American Institute of Graphic Arts Fifty Books of the Year awards books. Restricted use.

ASSOCIATION OF CATHOLIC TRADE UNIONISTS

MI —WAYNE STATE UNIVERSITY, Walter P Reuther Library, Archives of Labor & Urban Affairs, Detroit, 48202. Philip Mason, Dir
Notes: The history of the labor movement in Detroit and Michigan. The records of the Wayne County and Michigan AFL-CIO, Association of Catholic Trade Unionists, and the Detroit Industrial Mission are housed in the Archives. The official files of August Scholle, as President of the Michigan AFL-CIO, complement the organizational records in the Archives.

ASSOCIATION OF FRATERNITY ADVISORS (AFA)

OH —BOWLING GREEN STATE UNIVERSITY, Jerome Library, Center for Archival Collections, Bowling Green, 43403. Paul D Yon, Dir; Elaine R Ezell, Reference Archivist; Nancy Steen, Rare Books Librn
Notes: Incl pamphlets. The archives of four national professional associations have been donated to the CAC, creating a special collecting area concerning student affairs in

ASSOCIATION OF FRATERNITY ADVISORS (AFA) (cont.)

higher education. The National Association for Women Deans, Counselors and Administrators (NAWDAC), the National Association of Student Personnel Administrators (NASPA), the American College Personnel Association (ACPA), and the Association of Fraternity Advisors (AFA), to date, have designated the CAC as the repository for their archives. These collections document the issues, professional education and activities of those employed within the student affairs area in colleges and universities in the US.

ASSOCIATION OF LITERARY MAGAZINES OF AMERICA

IN —INDIANA UNIVERSITY, Lilly Library, Seventh St, Bloomington, 47405. William R Cagle, Librn
Holdings: Mss Pix
Notes: Ms collection incl editorial and correspondence files of the following periodicals: *American Magazine*, 1906-15; *Athenaeum*, Jan 1853-Aug 1869 (Wm Hepworth Dixon); *Aylesford Review*, 1955-68; *Floating Bear*, 1961 (LeRoi Jones); *McClure's Magazine*, 1893-1925; *Northwest Review*, 1961-67 (Wm Worth); *Origin*, 1960-62 (Cid Corman); *Poetry*, 1945-80 (Henry Rago; Daryl Hine); *Tree*, 1969-74 (David Meltzer); *X: A Quarterly Review*, 1959-61; and *Yugen* 1958-61 (LeRoi Jones). Also, correspondence and papers of the Association of Literary Magazines of America, 1961-64 (164 items).

ASSOCIATIONS, INSTITUTIONS, ETC.

DC —AMERICAN SOCIETY OF ASSOCIATION EXECUTIVES, Information Central, 1575 Eye St NW, Washington, 20005. Cathy L Lalush, Mgr of Research and Info
Notes: Information regarding association management. Resources are designed to provide the association executive with the background knowledge for management decisions through case studies, research and statistical reports, bibliographies, and articles.

DC —SMITHSONIAN INSTITUTION, Archives Div, Washington, 20560. William W Moss, Archivist
Holdings: Cat Mss Pix
Notes: The Archives has been named the repository for the records of a number of professional societies, particularly those relating to natural history.

KY —ASBURY THEOLOGICAL SEMINARY, B L Fisher Library, Wilmore, 40390. D William Faupel, Dir of Library Services
Holdings: Uncat
Notes: A collection of 35 document boxes of publicity materials on nearly 300 service organizations (Christian, missionary, social, educational), fugitive materials which would serve as primary sources for a study of their history and work--form letter (strictly fund raising letters deleted), brochures, etc.

MI —GALE RESEARCH CO, Book Tower, Detroit, 48226. Annie Brewer, Librn
Holdings: Vols (65,000) Cat
Notes: Large collection of reference materials, incl computerized files used in the preparation of familiar contemporary reference books and guides to special fields.

ASSOCIATIONS, INTERNATIONAL see International Agencies

ASSURANCE (INSURANCE) see Insurance

ASSYRIANA

CA —CALIFORNIA STATE COLLEGE, STANISLAUS, Library, 801 W Monte Vista Ave, Turlock, 95380. J Carlyle Parker, Actg Library Dir
Holdings: Vols 100 // Uncat
Notes: The Sayad Collection of Assyriana consists of books in the Syriac dialect of the modern Assyrians, often called Nestorians, who are natives of northwestern Iran. Other books in English relating to the modern Assyrians are also in the collection. Also books on Mesopotamian civilizations.

ASSYRIOLOGY

MD —JOHNS HOPKINS UNIVERSITY, Milton S Eisenhower Library, Charles & 34 Sts, Baltimore, 21218. Ann S Gwyn, Assistant Dir for Special Collections
Holdings: Cat Mss Maps
Notes: Strong collection, espec in Biblical studies, Hebraica, and Assyriology, but with some omissions. Includes Leopold Strouse Rabbinical Library, with Hebrew and Oriental mss.

NJ —PRINCETON UNIVERSITY, Library, Rare Books Dept, Princeton, 08544. Stephen Ferguson, Cur
Holdings: Cat

OH —HEBREW UNION COLLEGE-JEWISH INSTITUTE OF RELIGION, Klau Library, 3101 Clifton Ave, Cincinnati, 45220. David J Gilner, Reference Librn
Holdings: Cat

ASSYRO-BABYLONIAN INSCRIPTIONS see Cuneiform Inscriptions

ASSYRO-BABYLONIAN LANGUAGE AND LITERATURE

CT —YALE UNIVERSITY, Sterling Memorial Library, Babylonian Collection, 120 High St, New Haven, 06520. William W Hallo, Cur
Holdings: Vols (12,000) Cat Mss Pix
Budget: $2500
Notes: 30,000 mss in form of Babylonian tablets; 6000 seals and other art objects from Mesopotamia and the rest of the Ancient Near East.

NY —NEW YORK PUBLIC LIBRARY, Oriental Div, Fifth Ave & 42 St, New York, 10018. E Christian Filstrup, Chief
Holdings: Cat Mss Microforms
Budget: ($56,455)
Notes: Published catalog of holdings.

ASSYRO-BABYLONIAN STUDIES see Assyriology

ASTAIRE, FRED AND ADELE

MA —BOSTON UNIVERSITY, Mugar Memorial Library, Special Collections Dept, 771 Commonwealth Ave, Boston, 02215. Howard B Gotlieb, Dir
Holdings: Cat Mss Memorabilia
Notes: Restricted

ASTEROIDS

CT —YALE UNIVERSITY, Dept of Astronomy Library, 260 Whitney Ave, Box 6666, New Haven, 06511.
Holdings: Cat Pix Slides
Notes: Over 3000 plates of asteroids, pictures taken with Yale telescopes in the Northern and Southern Hemispheres. Also about 65,000 stellar parallax plates and about 1000 (17 x 17 in) zone catalog plates recording some 200,000 star positions. There is also a collection of about 500 plates recording the location of the north celestial pole among the stars. Of this latter, only one other similar collection exists, at the Pulkova Observatory, near Leningrad.

ASTHMA

†CO —NATIONAL JEWISH HOSPITAL AND RESEARCH CENTER-NATIONAL ATHSMA CENTER, Gerald Tucker Memorial Medical Library, 3800 Colfax Ave, Denver, 80206. Helen-Ann Brown, Librn
Holdings: Vols (8500)
Notes: Allergy, asthma, immunology, research in molecular and cellular biology, medicine, tuberculosis and diseases of the chest.

ASTOR, JOHN JACOB

NY —COLUMBIA UNIVERSITY LIBRARIES, Rare Book & Manuscript Library, 801 Butler Library, 535 W 114 St, New York, 10027. Kenneth A Lohf, Librn
Notes: More than 32,000 items documenting the rise of William Russell Grace's shipping business and other materials relating to his career as mayor of New York. Incl records and correspondence relating to all aspects of the shipping business in New York and South America, mining interest in Peru and Chile, and transportation in Costa Rica and Nicaragua. Family memorabilia and photographs, materials concerning New York Politics, banking and insurance, real estate interests and Catholic charities, and letters from Chester A Arthur, John Jacob Astor, Andrew Carnegie, Grover Cleveland, Hamilton Fish, John Hay and J Pierpont Morgan. Restricted use.

ASTOR, MARY

MA —BOSTON UNIVERSITY, Mugar Memorial Library, Special Collections Dept, 771 Commonwealth Ave, Boston, 02215. Howard B Gotlieb, Dir
Holdings: Cat Mss Pix
Notes: Mss correspondence, etc collected in depth; incl publications by or about.

ASTOR, NANCY

DC —GEORGETOWN UNIVERSITY, Library, Special Collections Div, 37 & O Sts NW, Washington, 20057. George M Barringer, Special Collections Librn; Nicholas B Sheetz, Mss Librn
Holdings: Mss Pix
Notes: The papers of Christopher Sykes, biographer, journalist, and novelist; containing mss, letters, photographs, and drawings. With extensive correspondence from Harold Acton; Angela, Countess of Antrim; Sir John Betjeman; Ivy Compton-Burnett; Alick Dru; T S Eliot; Max Beerbohm; Graham Greene; John Hayward; Lord Patrick Kinross; Compton Mackenzie; Nancy Mitford; Anthony Powell; Dame Flora Robson; Cecil Roth; Sir John Russell; Osbert Sitwell; John Sparrow; Freya Stark; James Stern; and Evelyn Waugh, among others. Also, considerable research material about Evelyn Waugh, Adam von Trott, Robert Byron, Lady Nancy Astor; and the foundation of the state of Israel.

ASTRODYNAMICS

CA —ESL, SUBSIDIARY OF TRW, Research Library, 495 Java Dr, PO Box 3510, Sunnyvale, 94086. Verna Van Valzer, Head Librn
Holdings: Vols 200 Cat
Budget: $1000

ASTROGEOPHYSICS

CO —UNIVERSITY OF COLORADO, Libraries, Western Historical Collections, Boulder, 80309.
Holdings: Mss Slides Films
Notes: Papers of the world renowned space scientist and recipient of many honors, Walter Orr Roberts (1915-), who is currently associated with the University of Colorado as a professor of astrogeophysics. He has written extensively on solar activity and its effects on earth. The collection is comprised of correspondence with individuals and business and research organizations, reports, proposals and conference data, speeches, committee papers, studies, research notes, lectures and student papers plus a few personal papers, printed matter, films and slides. Also there are personal items which belonged to M Sydney Chapman and were given to Roberts. 40 boxes, 1940s-1970s. Typescript inventory is available.

CO —UNIVERSITY OF COLORADO, Duane Physical Laboratories G140, Mathematics-Physics Library, Boulder, 80309. Allen

ASTROGEOPHYSICS (cont.)

Wynne, Head Librn
Holdings: Vols Cat Microforms
Notes: All areas of mathematics and physics with special emphasis on astrophysics, astrogeophysics, theoretical high energy physics and theoretical computer science. Also basic astronomy. The most comprehensive general mathematics and physics collection in the Rocky Mountain area, although not having sufficient depth to allow doctoral research in some specific areas. Excellent bibliographic control for current and retrospective searching as complete runs of most major subject indexing and abstracting services are present. ILL for businesses through the Colorado Technical Reference Center in main library building.

ASTROLABES

PA —FRANKLIN INSTITUTE LIBRARY, 20 & The Parkway, Philadelphia, 19103. Miriam Padusis, Dir; Charles Wilt, Readers Servs Librn
Holdings: Vols (300,000) Cat Maps Pix Microforms

ASTROLOGY

AZ —AMERICAN FEDERATION OF ASTROLOGERS, Library, 6535 S Rural Rd, PO Box 22040, Tempe, 85282. Sara E Cooper, Librn
Notes: Publish educational and research books on astrology in the US. Issue quarterly booklist.

AZ —WORLD UNIVERSITY, Library, 711 E Blacklidge Dr, Tucson, 85719. Howard John Zitko, Cur
Holdings: Vols (15,000) Cat Mss Maps Audiotapes
Notes: Collection concerns what are generally called the "frontier sciences". No interlibrary loan.

CA —LOS ANGELES PUBLIC LIBRARY, Philosophy & Religion Dept, 630 W Fifth St, Los Angeles, 90071. Marilyn C Wherley, Librn
Holdings: Vols (500) Cat Long runs of periodicals some on microfiche
Budget: ($60,000)
Notes: Popular and scholarly works including monographs, serials and periodicals; standard reference tools.

CA —SAN DIEGO PUBLIC LIBRARY, Literature & Language Sect, 820 E St, San Diego, 92101. Alyce Archuleta, Senior Librn
Holdings: Cat
Notes: Old and current reference and circulating works on the subject. Incl complete works by Blavatsky, much by Rudolf Steiner, and C Zain. Strong in astrology, witchcraft, parapsychology.

IL —UNIVERSITY OF ILLINOIS, URBANA/CHAMPAIGN, Library, University Archives, 19 Library, 1408 W Gregory Drive, Urbana, 61801. Maynard Brichford, University Archivist
Holdings: Vols (5000) Cat
Budget: ($7000)
Notes: The Mandeville Collection in Parapsychology and Occult Sciences. Titles in the Merten J Mandeville Collection are purchased by funds from an endowment provided specifically for the collection on its establishment in 1966 by Merten J Mandeville, Professor Emeritus of Management, who donated 400 vols from his personal library as the nucleus of the collection. There are currently about 5000 titles in the collection, supplemented by related materials in the general collection. Topics include astrology, extrasensory perception, yoga, magic, satanism, faith healing, hypnosis, Eastern religions, witchcraft, fortune telling, reincarnation, flying saucers, ghosts, dreams, numerology, graphology, and mysticism. Biographies and reference books are a part of the collection as are journals devoted to the scientific study of parapsychology.

MI —APPLE TREE PRESS, Library, Box 1012, Flint, 48501. W D Chase, Editor/Librn
Holdings: Vols (1200) Uncat Mss Maps Pix Microforms

†NY —COLUMBIA UNIVERSITY LIBRARIES, Butler Library, Rare Book and Manuscript Library, 535 W 114 St, New York, 10027.
Notes: 76 vols of diaries of Lynn Thorndike, 1902-63. A record of his daily reading, progress in research and writing, European travels, relations with scholars and librarians, and other personal matters.

NY —NATIONAL ASTROLOGICAL SOCIETY, Library, New York, 10003.
Notes: Society became inactive in 1981. Library is in storage and not available for public use.

NY —NEW YORK PUBLIC LIBRARY, Research Libraries, Science and Technology Research Center, Fifth Ave & 42 St, New York, 10018.
Holdings: Vols (1,100,000) Cat Microforms
Budget: ($647,259)

RI —BROWN UNIVERSITY, John Hay Library, 20 Prospect St, Providence, 02912. Mark N Brown, Cur Mss
Holdings: Vols (5000) Cat Mss
Notes: History of Science Collection incl resources from several specific donor named collections of volumes printed from the 15th to 20th centuries. The significant volumes published before 1700 are unusually rich in Mathematica, Astronomy and Astrology (463 vols). Publications of the various scientific academies are well represented and include the *Philosophical Transactions of the Royal Society of London* (beginning in 1665) and *The American Journal of Science.*

VA —ASSOCIATION FOR RESEARCH & ENLIGHTENMENT, Library, 67 & Atlantic Avenue, PO Box 595, Virginia Beach, 23451. Stephen Jordan, Library Mgr
Holdings: Vols (1800) Cat
Notes: A R E Library Booklist incl 6000 items in 24 subject categories. This special collection is especially strong in the following subjects: astrology, spiritualism, reincarnation, healing arts, Theosophy, Atlantis, parapsychology and transpersonal psychology.

ASTROMETRY

DC —US NAVAL OBSERVATORY LIBRARY, 30th & Massachusetts Ave, NW, Washington, 20016. Brenda G Corbin, Librn
Holdings: Vols (75,000) Cat Mss Maps Pix Slides Microforms
Notes: Incl 1000 journals, with monograph and serial publications in the fields of celestial mechanics, fundamental astronomy, time determination, photographic astrometry and astrophysics, data processing, mathematics.

ASTRONAUTICAL CHARTS

DC —LIBRARY OF CONGRESS, Geography and Map Division, Washington, 20540. John A Wolter, Chief
Holdings: Cat Mss Maps Pix Slides Microforms
See also entry under Maps and Atlases - Collections

ASTRONAUTICAL INSTRUMENTS

MA —SMITHSONIAN INSTITUTION LIBRARIES, Astrophysical Observatory Branch, 60 Garden St, Cambridge, 02138. Joyce Rey, Librn
Holdings: Vols (10,000) Cat Maps Pix Microforms

PA —FRANKLIN INSTITUTE LIBRARY, 20 & The Parkway, Philadelphia, 19103. Miriam Padusis, Dir; Charles Wilt, Readers Servs Librn
Holdings: Vols (300,000) Cat Maps Pix Microforms

ASTRONAUTICS

CA —UNIVERSITY OF CALIFORNIA, LOS ANGELES, Engineering & Mathematical Sciences Library, 405 Hilgard, Los Angeles, 90024. Rosalee I Wright, Librn
Holdings: Vols (180,000) Cat Microforms
Notes: NACA and NASA report series and NASA microfiche depository of technical reports (inclusive); AAS publications (inclusive); AIAA journals and papers.

CA —SAN DIEGO PUBLIC LIBRARY, Science & Industry Section, 820 E St, San Diego, 92101. Joanne Anderson, Senior Librn
Budget: ($33,000)

FL —EMBRY-RIDDLE AERONAUTICAL UNIVERSITY, Regional Airport, Daytona Beach, 32014. M Judy Luther, Dir of Learning Resources

IL —UNIVERSITY OF ILLINOIS, URBANA/CHAMPAIGN, Library, 221 Engineering Hall, Urbana, 61801. William Mischo, Librn
Holdings: Vols (175,000) Cat Slides Microforms
Notes: Incl 3500 periodicals. Collection designed to serve teaching and research programs. Supports instructional faculty research. Also, 470 microfilm reels and 6000 microfiche sheets.

IN —PURDUE UNIVERSITY LIBRARIES, Engineering Library, A A Potter Engineering Center, West Lafayette, 47907. Edwin D Posey, Engineering Librn
Holdings: Vols (225,178) Cat Maps Audiotapes Microforms
Budget: ($300,000)

MA —UNIVERSITY OF MASSACHUSETTS AT AMHERST, Physical Sciences Library, Amherst, 01003. Siegfried Feller, Assoc Dir for Collection Development
Holdings: Vols Cat Microforms
Notes: Incl extensive holdings of journals, NACA and NASA publications, and AEC documents (microfiche).

MA —SMITHSONIAN INSTITUTION LIBRARIES, Astrophysical Observatory Branch, 60 Garden St, Cambridge, 02138. Joyce Rey, Librn
Holdings: Vols (10,000) Cat Maps Pix Microforms

NJ —PRINCETON UNIVERSITY, Library, Manuscript Collection, Nassau St, Princeton, 08540. Jean F Preston, Cur
Holdings: Cat Mss Maps Pix
Notes: Incl the collection of G Edward Pendray detailing the entry of the United States into the space age; much on early rocketry and the work of Richard H Goddard. Incl 71 boxes, 17 file drawers.

NY —AMERICAN INSTITUTE OF AERONAUTICS & ASTRONAUTICS, Technical Information Service, 555 West 57th St, New York, 10019. Patricia Marshall, Dir, Library Resources
Holdings: Vols (57,000) Cat Microforms
Notes: Basis or published literature input to NASA Information System; Special index--Semimonthly issues of *International Aerospace Abstracts* with cumulated annual indexes.

NY —AMERICAN MUSEUM-HAYDEN PLANETARIUM, Richard S Perkin Library, 81 St & Central Park W, New York, 10024. Sandra Kitt, Librn
Holdings: Vols (15,000) Cat Maps Pix Slides
Budget: ($8000)
Notes: Considered one of the strongest and most complete astronomy libraries on the east coast. Contains the Bliss Collection of Ancient Astronomical Instruments; also the Mt Wilson/Bloman Sky Survey to the 45 degree declination; the Lick Observatory Survey; *American Ephemeris and Nautical* Almanac, 1855-date.

PA —FRANKLIN INSTITUTE LIBRARY, 20 & The Parkway, Philadelphia, 19103. Miriam Padusis, Dir; Charles Wilt, Readers Servs Librn
Holdings: Vols (300,000) Cat Maps Pix Microforms

TX —DALLAS PUBLIC LIBRARY, Central Library, Humanities Division, 1515 Young St, Dallas, 75201. Richard L Waters, Acting Dir; Ron Boyd, Fiction Librn
Holdings: Vols Cat Microforms
Notes: Cited in Tymn, Marshall, Roger C Schlobin, and L W Currey. *A Research Guide to Science Fiction* New York: Garland, 1977. The science fiction collection now exceeds 8000 circulating vols. In addition, the Library purchased in 1983 the personal library and archives of Brian Aldiss

ASTRONAUTICS (cont.)

(which will be for reference use only). This collection consists of 350 books by Aldiss, 1900 other books by other science fiction writers, 800 issues of science fiction and fantasy periodicals, 100 vols concerning astronautics and space travel, over 1000 typescript pages of mss(incl 6 corrected mss), several sound recordings (incl BBC tapes), and a considerable amount of correspondence.

ASTRONAUTICS—BIOGRAPHY

DC —LIBRARY OF CONGRESS, Manuscript Division, Washington, 20540. John C Broderick, Chief
Notes: The American Institute of Aeronautics and Astronautics Archives incorporates primary source material documenting the history of aeronautics. Incl clippings, articles, questionnaires, printed matter, and original mss pertaining to individual aeronauts, the personal papers of balloonist Thaddeus S C Lowe, and a corporate file consisting entirely of printed information on aircraft companies. Incl 30, 000 items.

DC —SMITHSONIAN INSTITUTION LIBRARIES, National Air & Space Museum Branch, NASM Bldg, Sixth & Independence Ave SW, Washington, 20560. Frank A Pietropaoli, Branch Chief
Holdings: Vols (39,000) Cat Mss Maps Pix Slides Microforms
Notes: History of flight and aerospace development, incl biographical material on aviation pioneers, balloons and ballooning. Extensive photographic collection (600,000 pictures). Incl the Sherman Fairchild Collection of aeronautical photographs (transferred from the American Institute of Aeronautics and Astronautics). Also incl the Bella Landauer Aeronautical Sheet Music Collection (1500 pieces). 2000 films; 800,000 microforms; 9000 volumes bound.

ASTRONAUTICS—HISTORY

DC —LIBRARY OF CONGRESS, Manuscript Division, Washington, 20540. John C Broderick, Chief
Notes: The American Institute of Aeronautics and Astronautics Archives incorporates primary source material documenting the history of aeronautics. Incl clippings, articles, questionnaires, printed matter, and original mss pertaining to individual aeronauts, the personal papers of balloonist Thaddeus S C Lowe, and a corporate file consisting entirely of printed information on aircraft companies. Incl 30, 000 items.

DC —SMITHSONIAN INSTITUTION LIBRARIES, National Air & Space Museum Branch, NASM Bldg, Sixth & Independence Ave SW, Washington, 20560. Frank A Pietropaoli, Branch Chief
Holdings: Vols (39,000) Cat Mss Maps Pix Slides Microforms
Notes: History of flight and aerospace development, incl biographical material on aviation pioneers, balloons and ballooning. Extensive photographic collection (600,000 pictures). Incl the Sherman Fairchild Collection of aeronautical photographs (transferred from the American Institute of Aeronautics and Astronautics). Also incl the Bella Landauer Aeronautical Sheet Music Collection (1500 pieces). 2000 films; 800,000 microforms; 9000 volumes bound.

MD —JOHNS HOPKINS UNIVERSITY, Milton S Eisenhower Library, Charles & 34 Sts, Baltimore, 21218. Ann S Gwyn, Assistant Dir for Special Collections
Holdings: Cat Mss Pix Audiotapes
Notes: Almost entirely a ms collection. Personal papers, etc 144 linear ft.

ASTRONAUTS

DC —LIBRARY OF CONGRESS, Manuscript Division, Washington, 20540. John C Broderick, Chief
Holdings: Mss
Notes: Papers of John Glenn (90,000 pieces).

ASTRONOMERS

CA —UNIVERSITY OF CALIFORNIA, SANTA CRUZ, Shane Archives of Lick Observatory, Santa Cruz, 95064. Dorothy Schaumberg, Archivist
Notes: Dr Edward S Holden (first director of Lick Observatory) Collection of portraits of every famous astronomer from Galileo to the present. Open for scholarly research by appointment.

IL —UNIVERSITY OF CHICAGO LIBRARY, Dept of Special Collections, 1100 E 57 St, Chicago, 60637.
Notes: Miscellaneous research files, incl observation records of George Van Biesbroeck.

IA —HERBERT HOOVER PRESIDENTIAL LIBRARY, West Branch, 52358. Dale C Mayer, Archivist
Notes: Papers.

MA —HARVARD UNIVERSITY ARCHIVES, Nathan Marsh Pusey Library, Cambridge, 02138. Clark A Elliott, Associate Cur
Notes: Alistair Graham Walter Cameron's papers.

ASTRONOMICAL CLOCKS

PA —FRANKLIN INSTITUTE LIBRARY, 20 & The Parkway, Philadelphia, 19103. Miriam Padusis, Dir; Charles Wilt, Readers Servs Librn
Holdings: Vols 2400 Cat Mss
Notes: One of the finest collections of horology in the world.

ASTRONOMICAL GEOGRAPHY

NY —AMERICAN MUSEUM-HAYDEN PLANETARIUM, Richard S Perkin Library, 81 St & Central Park W, New York, 10024. Sandra Kitt, Librn
Holdings: Vols (15,000) Cat Maps Pix Slides
Budget: ($8000)
Notes: Considered one of the strongest and most complete astronomy libraries on the east coast. Contains the Bliss Collection of Ancient Astronomical Instruments; also the Mt Wilson/Bloman Sky Survey to the 45 degree declination; the Lick Observatory Survey; *American Ephemeris and Nautical* Almanac, 1855-date.

ASTRONOMICAL INSTRUMENTS

NY —AMERICAN MUSEUM-HAYDEN PLANETARIUM, Richard S Perkin Library, 81 St & Central Park W, New York, 10024. Sandra Kitt, Librn
Holdings: Vols (15,000) Cat Maps Pix Slides
Budget: ($8000)
Notes: Considered one of the strongest and most complete astronomy libraries on the east coast. Contains the Bliss Collection of Ancient Astronomical Instruments; also the Mt Wilson/Bloman Sky Survey to the 45 degree declination; the Lick Observatory Survey; *American Ephermeris and Nautical* Almanac, 1855-date.

ASTRONOMICAL OBSERVATORIES

CA —UNIVERSITY OF CALIFORNIA, SANTA CRUZ, University Library, Special Collections, Santa Cruz, 95064. Rita Bottoms, Special Collections Librn; Margaret Felts, South Pacific Collection Bibliographer
Holdings: Cat
Notes: Astronomy library. Incl all major astronomical and astrophysical journals and an extensive collection of domestic and foreign observatory publications. The book collection is particularly strong in stellar structure and evolution, stellar spectroscopy, the interstellar medium, galactic structure, external galaxies, general relativity and gravitational radiation, and high-energy astrophysics.

CA —UNIVERSITY OF CALIFORNIA, SANTA CRUZ, Shane Archives of Lick Observatory, Santa Cruz, 95064. Dorothy Schaumberg, Archivist
Notes: Extensive collection incl correspondence, portraits, pictures, memorabilia, logs and construction diaries, 1880s to present. Mary Lea Hegen Shane was an astronomer herself, and the arranging and cataloging of the collection was done by her. Archives open to scholars by appointment.

CT —YALE UNIVERSITY, Observatory Library, 260 Whitney Ave, Box 6666, New Haven, 06511.
Holdings: Vols (15,000) Cat Maps Pix
Budget: ($15,000)
Notes: Also an extensive collection of domestic and foreign observatory publications.

DC —SMITHSONIAN INSTITUTION, Archives Div, Washington, 20560. William W Moss, Archivist
Holdings: Cat Mss
Notes: The Archives holds the papers of Secretaries Samuel Pierpont Langley and Charles Greeley Abbot, as well as the records of the Smithsonian Astrophysical Observatory.

†MO —UNIVERSITY OF MISSOURI-COLUMBIA, Western Historical Manuscripts Collection, Columbia, 65201.
Notes: Papers of the Laws Observatory, 1877-1954.

PA —UNIVERSITY OF PITTSBURGH, Allegheny Observatory Library, Riverview Park, Pittsburgh, 15214. Paul Kubulnicky, Dir of Observatory
Holdings: Vols 800 Cat Mss Maps Pix Slides
Notes: This library has a strong collection of publications of other national and international observatories, received on exchange. Also in the collection are pertinent current journals and a weak gathering of contemporary monographs. The observatory also has cataloged its complete file of observational photographic plates.

ASTRONOMICAL PERIODICALS see Periodicals, Astronomical

ASTRONOMICAL PHOTOMETRY see Photometry, Astronomical

ASTRONOMICAL PHYSICS see Astrophysics

ASTRONOMICAL RESEARCH

CA —CALIFORNIA INSTITUTE OF TECHNOLOGY, Robert A Millikan Memorial Library, Archives, 1201 E California Blvd, Pasadena, 91125. Judith R Goodstein, Archivist
Notes: Correspondence and printed matter of William A Fowler, Nuclear Science Advisory Committee, 1977-1980; the National Academy of Science's Astronomy Survey Committee, 1979-1980; the National Science Foundation's Astronomy Advisory Committee, 1978-1979; and proceedings of the Pugwash Conference for the years 1960, 1962-1963.

ASTRONOMICAL SPECTROSCOPY see Astrophysics; Spectrum Analysis and Spectroscopy

ASTRONOMY

AZ —KITT PEAK NATIONAL OBSERVATORY, Library, 950 N Cherry, PO Box 26732, Tucson, 85726. Cathaleen Van Atta, Librn
Holdings: Vols (40,000) Cat
Budget: $20,000
Notes: This incl the auxiliary libraries on Kitt Peak Mountain, and at Cerro Tololo Interamerican Observatory at La Serena, Chile and Cerro Tololo, Chile.

CA —UNIVERSITY OF CALIFORNIA, BERKELEY, Science Libraries, Astronomy-Mathematics-Statistics-Computer Science Library, 100 Evans Hall, Berkeley, 94720. Kimiyo Hom, Head
Holdings: Vols (53,000) Cat Maps Microforms
Budget: ($117,301)
Notes: A research collection in the fields of

ASTRONOMY (cont.)

astronomy, mathematics, statistics and computer science. In the field of astronomy, emphasis is given to star charts, atlases and catalogs. In mathematics, the collection's strengths are in pure mathematics, mathematical statistics and probability theory. The computer science holdings emphasize the mathematics and theory of the field. The Library's serial holdings are particularly rich in foreign-language materials. Some 1300 serial titles are currently being received; over 4000 pamphlets. (Holdings in the AMSCS Library are complemented by approx 15,000 additional vols in the Main Library, as well as rare book materials in the The Bancroft Library.)

CA —UNIVERSITY OF CALIFORNIA, DAVIS, Physical Sciences Library, Davis, 95616. Scott Kennedy, Head
Holdings: Vols 2518 Cat

CA —GRIFFITH OBSERVATORY, Library, 2800 E Observatory Rd, Los Angeles, 90027. E C Krupp, Dir
Holdings: Vols Cat Pix Slides Phonorecords
Budget: ($1000)
Notes: No separate catalog. No photocopying.

CA —UNIVERSITY OF CALIFORNIA, LOS ANGELES, Engineering & Mathematical Sciences Library, 405 Hilgard, Los Angeles, 90024. Rosalee I Wright, Librn
Holdings: Vols (150,000) Cat Microforms
Notes: Library collects in the fields of engineering, astronomy, mathematics, and meteorology. About 2400 journal titles are currently received. Subject emphases in engineering: computers; electrical and electronic engineering; materials and metals; mathematical methods in engineering; control theory; systems science and engineering; mechanical and structural engineering; aerospace engineering and astronautics; nuclear engineeringl engineering aspects of energy and pollution. Incl engineering handbooks and material data compilations; ASTM and IEEE standards, SAE Aerospace Materials Specifications and Recommended Practices, and selected ASME Codes; 750,000 technical reports (mostly on Microform). Full depository for Dept of Energy (AEC, ERDA) and NASA; partial depository for NTIS (pollution, environment, meteorology, and bioengineering) since 1970.

CA —UNIVERSITY OF SOUTHERN CALIFORNIA, Seaver Science Library, University Park, Los Angeles, 90089. A Albert Baker, Head
Holdings: Vols (200,000) Microforms
Budget: ($700,000)
Notes: Includes technical reports (12,000), serial and periodical titles (3600).

CA —CALIFORNIA INSTITUTE OF TECHNOLOGY, Robert A Millikan Memorial Library, Archives, 1201 E California Blvd, Pasadena, 91125. Judith R Goodstein, Archivist
Notes: Correspondence and printed matter of William A Fowler, Nuclear Science Advisory Committee, 1977-1980; the National Academy of Science's Astronomy Survey Committee, 1979-1980; the National Science Foundation's Astronomy Advisory Committee, 1978-1979; and proceedings of the Pugwash Conference for the years 1960, 1962-1963.

CA —CALIFORNIA INSTITUTE OF TECHNOLOGY, Astrophysics Library, 1201 E California Blvd, Pasadena, 91125. Helen Zollars Knudsen, Astrophysics Librn
Holdings: Vols 20,000 Cat Pix Slides Films Microforms
Notes: Collection incl set of prints of the National Geographic/Palomar Sky Survey. Also incl complete set of American Ephemeris and Nautical Almanac from 1878 forward and observatory publications from worldwide sources. Over 64 leading journals, more than 100 observatory publications, and 120 pre-print series are indexed monthly in *Astronomy and Astrophysics Monthly* Index; observatory materials are listed in *Bibliography of Non-Commercial Publications of Observatories and Astronomical Societies.* Collection is not open to the public. Request permission to use the library in person by writing the chairman of the Astronomy Dept. Branch libraries at Owens Valley Radio Observatory, Big Pine, Calif; Palomar Mountain, Calif; Big Bear Solar Observatory, Fawnskin, Calif. Branch libraries are not open to the public. No public services of any kind are offered atbranch sites. Information available to public via written requests or by telephoned requests to Pasadena address.

CA —UNIVERSITY OF CALIFORNIA, SANTA CRUZ, University Library, Special Collections, Santa Cruz, 95064. Rita Bottoms, Special Collections Librn; Margaret Felts, South Pacific Collection Bibliographer
Holdings: Cat
Notes: Astronomy library. Incl all major astronomical and astrophysical journals and an extensive collection of domestic and foreign observatory publications. The book collection is particularly strong in stellar structure and evolution, stellar spectroscopy, the interstellar medium, galactic structure, external galaxies, general relativity and gravitational radiation, and high-energy astrophysics.

CO —UNIVERSITY OF COLORADO, Duane Physical Laboratories G140, Mathematics-Physics Library, Boulder, 80309. Allen Wynne, Head Librn
Holdings: Vols Cat Microforms
Notes: All areas of mathematics and physics with special emphasis on astrophysics, astrogeophysics, theoretical high energy physics and theoretical computer science. Also basic astronomy. The most comprehensive general mathematics and physics collection in the Rocky Mountain area, although not having sufficient depth to allow doctoral research in some specific areas. Excellent bibliographic control for current and retrospective searching as complete runs of most major subject indexing and abstracting services are present. ILL for businesses through the Colorado Technical Reference Center in main library building.

CT —YALE UNIVERSITY, Observatory Library, 260 Whitney Ave, Box 6666, New Haven, 06511.
Holdings: Vols (15,000) Cat Maps Pix
Budget: ($15,000)
Notes: Also an extensive collection of domestic and foreign observatory publications.

DC —GEORGETOWN UNIVERSITY, Library, Special Collections Div, 37 & O Sts NW, Washington, 20057. George M Barringer, Special Collections Librn; Nicholas B Sheetz, Mss Librn
Holdings: Mss Cat
Notes: The papers of Rev. John Hagen, SJ (1847-1930), noted Jesuit astronomer and a native of Austria. While in this country he was stationed at Prarie du Chien, Wisconsin and at Georgetown University, Washington, DC. In 1905 he has called to Rome by Pope Pius X and named Director of the Vatican Observatory. During his lifetime, Fr Hagen received numerous honors from the scientific community. The papers incl notebooks of calculations and observations kept by Fr Hagen.

DC —NATIONAL GEOGRAPHIC SOCIETY, Library, 1146 16th St NW, Washington, 20036. Susan Fifer Canby, Dir
Holdings: Vols (63,000) Cat Mss Maps Pix
Notes: Material concerning land, sea, and space exploration--past and present. All fields of anthropology, natural history, geography, etc.

DC —SMITHSONIAN INSTITUTION, Archives Div, Washington, 20560. William W Moss, Archivist
Holdings: Cat Mss
Notes: The Archives holds the papers of Secretaries Samuel Pierpont Langley and Charles Greeley Abbot, as well as the records of the Smithsonian Astrophysical Observatory.

DC —SMITHSONIAN INSTITUTION LIBRARIES, National Air & Space Museum Branch, NASM Bldg, Sixth & Independence Ave SW, Washington, 20560. Frank A Pietropaoli, Branch Chief
Holdings: Vols (39,000) Cat Mss Maps Pix Slides Microforms
Notes: Hisotry of flight and aerospace development, incl biographical material on aviation pioneers, balloons and ballooning. Extensive photographic collection (600,000 pictures). Incl the Sherman Fairchild Collection of aeronautical photographs (transferred from the American Insitute of Aeronautics and Astronautics). Also incl the Bella Landauer Aeronautical Sheet Music Collection (1500 pieces). 2000 films; 800,000 microforms; 4100 periodicals.

DC —SMITHSONIAN INSTITUTION LIBRARIES, Natural History Branch, Washington, 20560. Sylvia Churgin, Chief Librn
Holdings: Vols (2350) Cat Maps Pix

DC —US NAVAL OBSERVATORY LIBRARY, 30th & Massachusetts Ave, NW, Washington, 20016. Brenda G Corbin, Librn
Holdings: Vols (75,000) Cat Mss Maps Pix Slides Microforms
Notes: Incl 1000 journals, with monograph and serial publications in the fields of celestial mechanics, fundamental astronomy, time determination, photographic astrometry and astrophysics, data processing, mathematics.

GA —FERNBANK SCIENCE CENTER LIBRARY, 156 Heaton Park Dr NE, Atlanta, 30307. Mary Larsen, Librn; Janice MacLeod, Bibliographic Instructor
Holdings: Vols (12,000) Cat Maps Pix Slides Microforms
Budget: ($35,000)
Notes: Science with emphasis on astronomy, biology, outdoor education. Incl 5500 color slides; periodicals on microfilm.

IL —ADLER PLANETARIUM, Reference Library, 1300 S Lake Shore Dr, Chicago, 60605. Tim Blackman, Librn
Holdings: Vols (6500) Cat Maps
Budget: ($5000)
Notes: Noncirculating; no photocopying.

IL —UNIVERSITY OF CHICAGO LIBRARY, Dept of Special Collections, 1100 E 57 St, Chicago, 60637.
Notes: Miscellaneous research files, incl observation records of George Van Biesbroeck.

IL —NORTHWESTERN UNIVERSITY, Seeley G Mudd Library for Science & Engineering, 2233 Sheridan Rd, Evanston, 60201. Robert C Michaelson, Head
Holdings: Vols (200,000) Cat Microforms
Notes: Collection emphasizes graduate and research level material.

IN —PURDUE UNIVERSITY LIBRARIES, Physics Library, Physics Bldg, West Lafayette, 47907. Janet Huettner, Librn
Holdings: Vols (35,000) Cat Microforms

IN —PURDUE UNIVERSITY LIBRARIES, Geosciences Library, West Lafayette, 47907. Carolyn Lassoon, Librn
Holdings: Vols (15,000) Cat
Notes: Geosciences.

KY —UNIVERSITY OF KENTUCKY, Chemistry-Physics Library, 150 Chemistry-Physics Bldg, Lexington, 40506. Jane M Lane, Acting Librn
Holdings: Vols (41,500) Cat Audiotapes
Budget: ($164,700)
Notes: One shelflist is maintained. No record of volumes in each collection. Combined library has its own catalog, as well as entires in the public catalog in the main library.

MA —UNIVERSITY OF MASSACHUSETTS AT AMHERST, Physical Sciences Library, Amherst, 01003. Siegfried Feller, Assoc Dir for Collection Development
Holdings: Vols Cat Microforms
Notes: Incl extensive holdings of journals, NACA and NASA publications, and AEC documents (microfiche).

MA —HARVARD UNIVERSITY OBSERVATORY, John G Wolbach Library, 60 Garden St, Cambridge, 02138. Estelle W Karlin, Librn
Holdings: Vols (55,000) Cat Mss Maps Slides Microforms
Budget: ($60,000)
Notes: See *Harvard Library Bulletin,* V (1951): pp 102-111.

ASTRONOMY (cont.)

MA —SMITHSONIAN INSTITUTION LIBRARIES, Astrophysical Observatory Branch, 60 Garden St, Cambridge, 02138. Joyce Rey, Librn
Holdings: Vols (10,000) Cat Maps Pix Microforms

MA —TUFTS UNIVERSITY, Mathematics-Physics Library, Medford, 02155. Pauline Boucher, Librn
Holdings: Vols 400

MI —UNIVERSITY OF MICHIGAN, Library, Dept of Rare Books & Special Collections, Ann Arbor, 48109. Robert J Starring, Head
Holdings: Mss
Notes: Over 1200 mss chiefly in Arabic, but also in Persian, Turkish, Coptic, Syriac, Ethiopic, Hebrew, and Armenian. Incl the McGregor collection in mathematics and astronomy, The Tiflis collection, and portions of the Abdul Hamid and Yahuda collection.

MI —UNIVERSITY OF MICHIGAN, Physics-Astronomy Library, 290 Dennison Bldg, Ann Arbor, 48109. Jack W Weigel, Physical Sciences Librn
Holdings: Vols 17,000 Cat Maps Microforms
Budget: $22,000

MI —APPLE TREE PRESS, Library, Box 1012, Flint, 48501. W D Chase, Editor/Librn
Holdings: Vols (1200) Uncat Mss Maps Pix Microforms

MN —UNIVERSITY OF MINNESOTA, O Meredith Wilson Library, 309 19 Ave S, Minneapolis, 55455. Austin J McLean, Chief, Special Collections
Holdings: Vols (103)// Cat Mss
Notes: Basically mathematical astronomy with emphasis on eclipses. Particular strengths are the works of such authors as Delambre, Euclid, Newton, Ptolemy, and Rhaticus. Important in this respect are 6 of the 10 known printed editions of the Alphonsine Astronomical Tables.

MO —WASHINGTON UNIVERSITY, Physics Dept Library, 6600 Millbrook Blvd, Saint Louis, 63130. Betty Eickhoff, Librn

NJ —PRINCETON UNIVERSITY, Library, Rare Books Dept, Princeton, 08544. Stephen Ferguson, Cur
Holdings: Cat
Notes: Plus 1750 pamphlets (cataloged).

NM —NEW MEXICO STATE UNIVERSITY, Library, Box 3475, Las Cruces, 88003. James Dyke, Dir
Holdings: Vols 1200 Cat
Notes: Near complete collection of all astronomy PhD dissertations accepted by American universities from the early 1870s to date.

NM —UNIVERSITY OF CALIFORNIA, Los Alamos National Laboratory, Libraries, PO Box 1663, MSP 362, Los Alamos, 87545. J Arthur Freed, Head Librn
Holdings: Vols (800,000) Cat Films Microforms
Budget: ($700,000)
Notes: Incl 500,000 classified and unclassified reports. There are 25 branch libraries and a central collection. The Medical Library contains about 40,000 vols in the areas of biomedical research.

NY —CORNELL UNIVERSITY LIBRARIES, Physical Sciences Library, Clark Hall, Ithaca, 14853. Ellen S Thomas, Librn
Holdings: Vols (73,701) Cat Microforms
Budget: ($244,185)

NY —AMERICAN MUSEUM-HAYDEN PLANETARIUM, Richard S Perkin Library, 81 St & Central Park W, New York, 10024. Sandra Kitt, Librn
Holdings: Vols (15,000) Cat Maps Pix Slides
Budget: ($8000)
Notes: Considered one of the strongest and most complete astronomy libraries on the east coast. Contains the Bliss Collection of Ancient Astronomical Instruments; also the Mt Wilson/Bloman Sky Survey to the 45 degree declination; the Lick Observatory Survey; *American Ephemeris and Nautical* Almanac, 1855-date.

NY —COLUMBIA UNIVERSITY LIBRARIES, Physics Library, 810 Pupin, 535 W 114 St, New York, 10027. Mary Kay, Librn
Holdings: Vols 6000 Cat
Notes: Descriptive astronomy and astrophysics.

NY —NEW YORK PUBLIC LIBRARY, Research Libraries, Science and Technology Research Center, Fifth Ave & 42 St, New York, 10018.
Holdings: Vols (1,100,000) Cat Microforms
Budget: ($647,259)

NY —ROCHESTER MUSEUM & SCIENCE CENTER, Strasenburgh Planetarium, Todd Library, 663 East Ave, Rochester, 14607. Donald Hall, Dir
Holdings: Vols 550 Cat Maps Slides
Notes: Also, 8250 slides of astronomical and aeronautical subjects; 400 recordings; 150 celestial charts.

NY —UNIVERSITY OF ROCHESTER, Physics-Optics-Astronomy Library, Bausch & Lomb Bldg, River Campus, Rochester, 14627. Loretta Caren, Librn
Holdings: Vols (20,000) Cat
Notes: Strong research level collection in the field and related areas.

NY —DUDLEY OBSERVATORY LIBRARY, Union University, 69 Union Ave, Schenectady, 12308. Rita A Spencer, Acting Librn
Holdings: Vols 250 // Cat
Budget: $6000
Notes: Incl rare astronomical works. A partial list of holdings appeared in the *Annals of the Dudley Observatory,* vol 1, 1866. Currently preparing a checklist of holdings and have recently completed making a photographic record of title pages and bindings of all books in the collection. This collection is known to be the finest in any astronomical observatory in the United States (excluding the collections of the large university observatories which are housed in libraries separate from their observatories).

NY —US MILITARY ACADEMY LIBRARY, West Point, 10996. Robert E Schnare, Asst Librn, Special Collections
Holdings: Cat
Notes: An emphasis on astronomy, earliest imprint 1476, and general science within West Point Thayer Collection.

NC —SCHIELE MUSEUM OF NATURAL HISTORY, Library, 1500 E Garrison Blvd, Gastonia, 28052. Dot Gray, Librn; Margaret Summerill, Librn
Holdings: Vols (3800) Cat Maps Pix Slides Phonorecords Audiotapes 16mm Films Filmstrips Microforms
Budget: ($2800)
Notes: Listed on RECON computer with Library of Congress as Reference Center in Southeast in subject areas of natural sciences, aerospace and planetarium technology, and anthropology.

PA —FRANKLIN INSTITUTE LIBRARY, 20 & The Parkway, Philadelphia, 19103. Miriam Padusis, Dir; Charles Wilt, Readers Servs Librn
Holdings: Vols (300,000) Cat Maps Pix Microforms

PA —UNIVERSITY OF PENNSYLVANIA, Mathematics-Physics-Astronomy Library, 33 & Walnut Sts, Philadelphia, 19104. Marion A Kreiter, Librn
Holdings: Cat

PA —BUHL PLANETARIUM & INSTITUTE OF POPULAR SCIENCE, Staff Library, Allegheny Sq, Pittsburgh, 15212. Al DeSena, Dir
Holdings: Vols 1000 Cat Mss Maps Pix Slides Films
Notes: Science-oriented vols with several texts of historical value dating back to the 19th century.

PA —UNIVERSITY OF PITTSBURGH, Allegheny Observatory Library, Riverview Park, Pittsburgh, 15214. Paul Kubulnicky, Dir of Observatory
Holdings: Vols 8000 Cat Mss Maps Pix Slides
Notes: This library has a strong collection of publications of other national and international observatories, received on exchange. Also in the collection are pertinent current journals and a weak gathering of contemporary monographs. The observatory also has cataloged its complete file of observational photographic plates.

PA —READING SCHOOL DISTRICT PLANETARIUM, Library, 1211 Parkside Dr S, Reading, 19611. Bruce L Dietrich, Dir
Holdings: Vols (640) Cat Maps Pix Slides Phonorecords Audiotapes 16mm Films
Budget: ($1000)
Notes: Incl 400 maps, 1000 pictures, 7300 slides and 110 audiotapes.

PA —PENNSYLVANIA STATE UNIVERSITY, Physical Sciences Library, 230 Davey Laboratory, University Park, 16802. Cornelius J McKown, Librn
Notes: 77,317 items.

TX —UNIVERSITY OF TEXAS LIBRARIES, Physics-Mathematics-Astronomy Library, PO Box P, Austin, 78712. John Fandey, Librn
Holdings: Vols (55,000) Cat Microforms

TX —RICE UNIVERSITY, Fondren Library, 6100 S Main St, PO Box 1892, Houston, 77251. Dr Samuel M Carrington, Jr, University Librn
Holdings: Vols 2500 Cat
Budget: $15,200
Notes: Each serial title counted once.

UT —HANSEN PLANETARIUM LIBRARY, 15 S State St, Salt Lake City, 84101. Randall A Curtis, Librn; Sharon Johnston, Children's Librn
Holdings: Vols 1800 Cat Maps Pix Audiotapes
Budget: $1800

WI —UNIVERSITY OF CHICAGO, Yerkes Observatory Library, Yerkes Observatory, PO Box 258, Williams Bay, 53191. J Lola, Librn
Holdings: Vols 20,000 Cat

AB —CENTENNIAL PLANETARIUM, Library, PO Box 2100, 701 Eleventh St, Calgary, T2P 2M5, Can. Sig Wieser, Librn
Holdings: Vols (400) Uncat Pix Audiotapes 16mm Films
Notes: Also western Canadian aviation history with bias towards technology; and history of space technology.

MB —MANITOBA MUSEUM OF MAN & NATURE, Library, 190 Rupert Ave, Winnipeg, R3B 0N2, Can. V Hatten, Librn
Holdings: Vols (20,000) Cat Maps

MB —UNIVERSITY OF MANITOBA, Science Library, Machray Hall, Winnipeg, R3T 2N2, Can. V Simosko, Head
Holdings: Vols (90,000) Cat Microforms

ON —QUEEN'S UNIVERSITY, Douglas Library, Kingston, K7L 5C4, Can. William F E Morley, Cur, Special Collections
Holdings: Vols (802) Uncat
Notes: Riche-Covington Collection supports McNichol Collection (history of telecommunications), brings it up to date; also astrophysics, astronomy, solar radiation. Bibliography available.

ON —NATIONAL MUSEUMS OF CANADA, Library Services Directorate, Ottawa, K1A 0M8, Can. Valerie Monkhouse, Director
Holdings: Vols 15,500
Budget: $25,000
Notes: History and technology of agriculture, astronomy, aviation, chemistry, communications, computers, electrical engineering, exploration and surveying, fire prevention, forestry, industrial technology, mathematics, medicine, mining, photography, physics, printing, space and transportation. research collection, interlibrary loans available, public may use on the premises.

ON —ROYAL ASTRONOMICAL SOCIETY OF CANADA, Library, 252 College St, Toronto, M5T 1R7, Can. Phil Mozel, National Librn
Holdings: Vols 1200 Cat Maps Slides Films
Notes: Primarily oriented towards serious amateur astronomers although many books and periodicals of value to professional astronomers. Building an archive of Canadian astronomy.

ON —ROYAL ONTARIO MUSEUM, Main Library and Archives, 100 Queen's Park, Toronto, M5S 2C6, Can. Julia Matthews, Head Librn
Holdings: Vols (85,000) Cat
Notes: Since January 1977, acquisitions have been entered in UTLAS.

ASTRONOMY—ATLASES see Stars—Atlases

ASTRONOMY—HISTORY

CA —CALIFORNIA INSTITUTE OF TECHNOLOGY, Robert A Millikan Memorial Library, Archives, 1201 E California Blvd, Pasadena, 91125. Judith R Goodstein, Archivist
Notes: About 2000 items from the Palomar Collection and the Ted Watterson Collection, 1936-48, concerning the photographic history of the construction of the telescopes on Palomar Mountain. Many other Palomar and Mt Wilson pictures are in the Archive's central files.

CA —CALIFORNIA INSTITUTE OF TECHNOLOGY, Robert A Millikan Memorial Library, 1201 E California Blvd, Pasadena, 91125. Judith R Goodstein, Archivist
Holdings: Vols (2300) Cat
Notes: Emphasis on the period of Galileo and Kepler. Incl the Watson History of Science Collection and the Rocco Collection. Catalogs.

CA —SAN DIEGO STATE UNIVERSITY, Malcolm A Love Library, 5300 Campanile Dr, San Diego, 92182. D Dickinson, Univ Librn; Don L Bosseau, Dir
Holdings: Vols (1500) Cat Mss Maps Pix Slides 4200 Other Items
Notes: The Ernst Zinner Collection, incl 2 incunables, autographs of scientists, portraits, pictures of sundials, 31 ms letters.

CA —UNIVERSITY OF CALIFORNIA, SANTA CRUZ, University Library, Special Collections, Santa Cruz, 95064. Rita Bottoms, Special Collections Librn; Margaret Felts, South Pacific Collection Bibliographer
Holdings: Cat
Notes: Astronomy library. Incl all major astronomical and astrophysical journals and an extensive collection of domestic and foreign observatory publications. The book collection is particularly strong in stellar structure and evolution, stellar spectroscopy, the interstellar medium, galactic structure, external galaxies, general relativity and gravitational radiation, and high-energy astrophysics.

CA —UNIVERSITY OF CALIFORNIA, SANTA CRUZ, Shane Archives of Lick Observatory, Santa Cruz, 95064. Dorothy Schaumberg, Archivist
Notes: Extensive collection incl correspondence, portraits, pictures, memorabilia, logs and construction diaries, 1880s to present. Mary Lea Hegen Shane was an astronomer herself, and the arranging and cataloging of the collection was done by her. Archives open to scholars by appointment.

DC —GEORGETOWN UNIVERSITY, Library, Special Collections Div, 37 & O Sts NW, Washington, 20057. George M Barringer, Special Collections Librn; Nicholas B Sheetz, Mss Librn
Holdings: Vols 500// Uncat Mss Pix
Notes: Incl the records of the Georgetown University Observatory, 1841-1972, and a portion of its original library.

IL —ADLER PLANETARIUM, History of Astronomy Collection, 1300 S Lake Shore Dr, Chicago, 60605. Roderick Webster, Cur; Marjorie Webster, Cur; Sara Schechner Genuth, Asst Cur
Holdings: Vols (430) Uncat Mss Maps Pix
Notes: Historical astronomical, scientific instruments (1000). Price Photographic Archives (2800) containing prints of instruments.
See also entries under Navigation - History; Surveying - History; Horology.

IA —HERBERT HOOVER PRESIDENTIAL LIBRARY, West Branch, 52358. Dale C Mayer, Archivist
Notes: Unpublished papers of physicists and astronomers, 1917-1969.

KY —UNIVERSITY OF LOUISVILLE, Ekstrom Library, Rare Books & Special Collections, 2301 S Third St, Louisville, 40208. George T McWhorter, Cur; Delinda Stephens Buie, Asst Cur
Holdings: Vols 250 Uncat
Budget: ($1500)
Notes: The William Marshall Bullitt Collection of rare mathematics and astronomy books, incl first editions of Euclid, Copernicus, Euler, Gauss and others. Typed, annotated bibliography available.

MA —WELLESLEY COLLEGE, Margaret Clapp Library, College Archives, Wellesley, 02181.
Notes: Records of the Department of Astronomy of Wellesley College (1882-1955), 3 linear feet; also papers of Sarah Frances Whiting.

MI —UNIVERSITY OF MICHIGAN, Physics-Astronomy Library, 290 Dennison Bldg, Ann Arbor, 48109. Jack W Weigel, Physical Sciences Librn
Holdings: Cat Mss
Notes: Chiefly pre-1800 imprints.

†MO —UNIVERSITY OF MISSOURI-COLUMBIA, Western Historical Manuscripts Collection, Columbia, 65201.
Notes: Papers of the Laws Observatory, 1877-1954.

NY —AMERICAN INSTITUTE OF PHYSICS, Center for the History of Physics, Niels Bohr Library, 335 E 45 St, New York, 10017. John Aubry, Librn
Holdings: Vols (16,000) Cat Mss Pix Slides Phonorecords Audiotapes 16mm Films Microforms
Notes: The Library contains an extensive collection of published works relating to the history of modern physics and astronomy. Its archives incl letter, notebooks and other papers of physicists, as well as the records of leading American physics societies and institutions. Its collections of ms autobiographies, oral history interviews, and other tape recordings, and pictorial materials (incl unpublished film footage) are unrivaled in the field of history of science. It maintains the International Catalog of Sources for History of Physics and Astronomy. In addition, the Sources for History of Modern Astrophysics documents the history of 20th-century astrophysics. Incl some 400 hours of oral histroy interviews with astronomers, such as Bart Bok, S Chandrasekhar, Martin Schwarzschild, and A E Whitford. The project also organized and cataloged the papers of Henry NorrisRussell, Frank Schlesinger, Otto Struve, Ejnar Hertzsprung, Harlow Shapley, Charles Young, Robert Atkinson, Seth Chandler, Theodore Dunham, Jr, and G C McVittie.

NY —COLUMBIA UNIVERSITY LIBRARIES, Rare Book & Manuscript Library, 801 Butler Library, 535 W 114 St, New York, 10027. Kenneth A Lohf, Librn
Holdings: Vols (13,000) Mss Pix
Notes: History of mathematics and astronomy from the 15th to the 20th centuries. Autograph letters, mss, 275 mathematical instruments and 1200 portraits of mathematicians. Collection formed by David Eugene Smith. Restricted use.

NY —DUDLEY OBSERVATORY LIBRARY, Union University, 69 Union Ave, Schenectady, 12308. Rita A Spencer, Acting Librn
Holdings: Vols 250 // Cat
Budget: $4000
Notes: Incl rare astronomical works. A partial list of holdings appeared in the *Annals of the Dudley Observatory,* vol 1, 1866. Currently preparing a checklist of holdings and have recently completed making a photographic record of title pages and bindings of all books in the collection. This collection is known to be the finest in any astronomical observatory in the United States (excluding the collections of large university observatories which are housed in libraries separate from their observatories).

PA —FRANKLIN INSTITUTE LIBRARY, 20 & The Parkway, Philadelphia, 19103. Miriam Padusis, Dir; Charles Wilt, Readers Servs Librn
Holdings: Vols (300,000) Cat Maps Pix Microforms

PA —LIBRARY COMPANY OF PHILADELPHIA, 1314 Locust St, Philadelphia, 19107. Edwin Wolf II, Librn; Kenneth Finkel, Cur of Prints
Holdings: Vols (400,000) Cat Maps Pix
Budget: ($25,000)
Notes: American science and industry before 1860. Books, pamphlets, etc on science incl math, pysics, astronomy, and industry, incl business and engineering. Incl many 18th century books printed in England and France but used by American colonials in their study and research. Impossible to estimate the exact size of collection since it is not separated from general collection.

RI —BROWN UNIVERSITY, John Hay Library, 20 Prospect St, Providence, 02912. Mark N Brown, Cur Mss
Holdings: Vols (5000) Cat Mss
Notes: History of Science Collection inc resoruces from several specific donor named collections of volumes printed from the 15th to 20th centuries. The significant volumes published before 1700 are unusually rich in Mathematica, Astronomy and Astrology (463 vols). Publications of the various scientific academies are well represented and include the *Philosophical Transactions of the Royal Society of London* (beginning in 1665) and *The American Journal of Science.*

SC —COLLEGE OF CHARLESTON LIBRARY, Special Collections Dept, Charleston, 29401.
Notes: Papers record numerous scientific and technological studies covering a wide range of areas, particularly astronomical observations (often accompanied by drawings or photos) made in Charleston in the 1880s, at times in consultation with Lewis Reeve Gibbes. An inventor of scientific instruments, Fisher's work incl a "Machine for Ruling Diffraction Plates" for which a detailed description and photograph are provided. Incl in-depth record of Fisher's experiences, scientific and personal, of the 1886 Earthquake, accompanied by diagrams.

†ON —PUBLIC ARCHIVES OF CANADA, Library, 395 Wellington St, Ottawa, K1A 0N3, Can. Dawn E Monroe, Collections Dept Officer
Holdings: 4 Feet
Notes: Records of the Royal Astronomical Society of Canada, 1868-1968.

ON —ROYAL ASTRONOMICAL SOCIETY OF CANADA, Library, 252 College St, Toronto, M5T 1R7, Can. Phil Mozel, National Librn
Holdings: Vols 1200 Cat Maps Slides Films
Notes: Primarily oriented towards serious amateur astronomers although many books and periodicals of value to professional astronomers. Building an archive of Canadian astronomy.

ON —UNIVERSITY OF TORONTO, Thomas Fisher Rare Book Library, 120 Saint George St, Toronto, M5S 1A5, Can. Richard G Landon, Head
Holdings: Vols 4000 Cat Mss
Notes: Stillman Drake Galileo Collection, named for collector Prof Stillman Drake, University of Toronto. Comprises early editions of Galileo, of his precursors (Ptolemy and Copernicus) and of his contemporaries in the fields of astronomy and physical science. Also, the Science Collection is especially rich in works on Renaissance astronomy, physics and mechanics and has noteworthy holdings of works of English experimental scientists in the 17th and 18th centuries with excellent collections for the works of Robert Boyle, Robert Hooke, and Sir Isaac Newton. Includes virtually all important early editions of Euclid; alchemical works of the 18th century chemists like Lavoisier and Priestly; works on agriculture with special emphasis on British agriculture in the 18th century; and a variety of other worksimportant in the history of science in all its branches. In addition the Fisher Library has many other specialized scientific collections which are listed separately.

ASTRONOMY—OBSERVATORIES see Astronomical Observatories

ASTRONOMY—RESEARCH see Astronomical Research

ASTRONOMY—STUDY AND TEACHING

MA —WELLESLEY COLLEGE, Margaret Clapp Library, College Archives, Wellesley,

ASTRONOMY—STUDY AND TEACHING (cont.)

02181.
Notes: Records of the Department of Astronomy of Wellesley College (1882-1955), 3 linear feet; also papers of Sarah Frances Whiting.

ASTRONOMY, BIOLOGICAL see Biological Astronomy

ASTRONOMY, RADIO see Radio Astronomy

ASTROPHYSICS

AZ —KITT PEAK NATIONAL OBSERVATORY, Library, 950 N Cherry, PO Box 26732, Tucson, 85726. Cathaleen Van Atta, Librn
Holdings: Vols (40,000) Cat
Budget: $20,000
Notes: This incl the auxiliary libraries on Kitt Peak Mountain, and at Cerro Tololo Interamerican Observatory at La Serena, Chile and Cerro Tololo, Chile.

CA —UNIVERSITY OF CALIFORNIA, LOS ANGELES, Physics Library, 213 Kinsey Hall, Los Angeles, 90024. J Wally Pegram, Librn
Holdings: Vols (37,000) Cat
See also entry under Physics

CA —NASA, Ames Research Center, Libraries, Library Br 202-3, Moffett Field, 94035. Sarah Dueker, Chief, Library Branch
Holdings: Cat Audiotapes Microforms
Notes: Main library collections cover physical sciences, engineering and mathematical fields related to research programs in aeronautics-space research. Life sciences library collections cover medical, physiological, behavioral and biological sciences related to research programs. Also emphases on remote sensing of earth resources and the search for extraterrestrial life. 950 journal titles and 85,000 monographs. Reports collection includes 60, 000 hard copy reports and 900,000 microfiche.

CA —CALIFORNIA INSTITUTE OF TECHNOLOGY, Robert A Millikan Memorial Library, Archives, 1201 E California Blvd, Pasadena, 91125. Judith R Goodstein, Archivist
Holdings: Cat Mss Maps Pix Slides Phonorecords Audiotapes Videotapes 16mm Films Microforms
Notes: Ms sources for the history of astrophysics, cosmology, mathematical physics, experimental physics, radio astronomy, geophysics and biophysics. Collections incl the papers of: George Ellery Hale, Jesse Greenstein, H P Robertson, Richard Feynman, Paul Epstein, Max Delbruck, and Beno Gutenberg. Candid photos of physicists at meetings; etchings and photographs of Einstein; scientific medals; selected pieces of scientific apparatus (including the oil-drop machine constructed by Millikan at Caltech in the early 1920s); the reprint collection of Paul Epstein; over 3000 landmark books in the history of 20th century physics and mathematics. Printed publications include: Daniel Kevles, *Guide to the Microfilm Edition of the George Ellery Hale Papers* (Pasadena, Carnegie Institute of Washington and Caltech), 1968; Judith R Goodstein,*The Robert Andrews Millikan Collection at the California Institute of Technology: Guide to a Microfilm Edition* (Pasadena, Caltech), 1977; Judith R Goodstein and Carolyn Kopp, *The Theodore von Karman Collections at the California Institute of* Technology (Pasadena, Archives), 1981.

CA —CALIFORNIA INSTITUTE OF TECHNOLOGY, Astrophysics Library, 1201 E California Blvd, Pasadena, 91125. Helen Zollars Knudsen, Astrophysics Librn
Holdings: Vols 20,000 Cat Pix Slides Films Microforms
Notes: Collection incl set of prints of the National Geographic/Palomar Sky Survey. Also incl complete set of American Ephemeris and Nautical Almanac from 1878 forward and observatory publications from worldwide sources. Over 64 leading journals, more than 100 observatory publications, and 120 pre-print series are indexed monthly in *Astronomy and Astrophysics Monthly* Index; observatory materials are listed in *Bibliography of Non-Commercial Publications of Observatories and Astronomical Societies.* Collection is not open to the public. Request permission to use the library in person by writing the chairman of the Astronomy Dept. Branch libraries at Owens Valley Radio Observatory, Big Pine, Calif; Palomar Mountain, Calif; Big Bear Solar Observatory, Fawnskin, Calif. Branch libraries are not open to the public. No public services of any kind are offered atbranch sites. Information available to public via written requests or by telephoned requests to Pasadena address.

CA —UNIVERSITY OF CALIFORNIA, SANTA CRUZ, University Library, Special Collections, Santa Cruz, 95064. Rita Bottoms, Special Collections Librn; Margaret Felts, South Pacific Collection Bibliographer
Holdings: Cat
Notes: Astronomy library. Incl all major astronomical and astrophysical journals and an extensive collection of domestic and foreign observatory publications. The book collection is particularly strong in stellar structure and evolution, stellar spectroscopy, the interstellar medium, galactic structure, external galaxies, general relativity and gravitational radiation, and high-energy astrophysics.

CO —UNIVERSITY OF COLORADO, Duane Physical Laboratories G140, Mathematics-Physics Library, Boulder, 80309. Allen Wynne, Head Librn
Holdings: Vols Cat Microforms
Notes: All areas of mathematics and physics with special emphasis on astrophysics, astrogeophysics, theoretical high energy physics and theoretical computer science. Also basic astronomy. The most comprehensive general mathematics and physics collection in the Rocky Mountain area, although not having sufficient depth to allow doctoral research in some specific areas. Excellent bibliographic control for current and retrospective searching as complete runs of most major subject indexing and abstracting services are present. ILL for businesses through the Colorado Technical Reference Center in main library building.

CT —YALE UNIVERSITY, Box 1603A, Yale Station, New Haven, 06520.
Holdings: Mss
Notes: Papers of Rupert Wildt, professor of astrophysics.

CT —YALE UNIVERSITY, Observatory Library, 260 Whitney Ave, Box 6666, New Haven, 06511.
Holdings: Vols (15,000) Cat Maps Pix
Budget: ($15,000)
Notes: Also an extensive collection of domestic and foreign observatory publications.

DC —SMITHSONIAN INSTITUTION, Archives Div, Washington, 20560. William W Moss, Archivist
Holdings: Cat Mss
Notes: The Archives holds the papers of Secretaries Samuel Pierpont Langley and Charles Greeley Abbot, as well as the records of the Smithsonian Astrophysical Observatory.

DC —SMITHSONIAN INSTITUTION LIBRARIES, National Air & Space Museum Branch, NASM Bldg, Sixth & Independence Ave SW, Washington, 20560. Frank A Pietropaoli, Branch Chief
Holdings: Vols (39,000) Cat Mss Maps Pix Slides Microforms
Notes: History of flight and aerospace development, incl biographical material on aviation pioneers, balloons and ballooning. Extensive photographic collection (600,000 pictures). Incl the Sherman Fairchild Collection of aeronautical photographs (transferred from the American Institute of Aeronautics and Astronautics). Also incl the Bella Landauer Aeronautical Sheet Music Collection (1500 pieces). 2000 films; 800,000 microforms; 9000 volumes bound.

DC —US NAVAL OBSERVATORY LIBRARY, 30th & Massachusetts Ave, NW, Washington, 20016. Brenda G Corbin, Librn
Holdings: Vols (75,000) Cat Mss Maps Pix Slides Microforms
Notes: Incl 1000 journals, with monograph and serial publications in the fields of celestial mechanics, fundamental astronomy, time determination, photographic astrometry and astrophysics, data processing, mathematics.

IL —UNIVERSITY OF ILLINOIS, URBANA/CHAMPAIGN, Library, Physics/Astronomy Library, 204 Loomis Laboratory, 1110 West Green St, Urbana, 61801. Bernice Lord Hulsizer, Librn
Holdings: Vols (34,000) Cat
Budget: ($130,000)
Notes: Significant number of journals and books, nearly all on the research level. Incl IAU Symposia and IAU Telegrams.

IN —PURDUE UNIVERSITY LIBRARIES, Physics Library, Physics Bldg, West Lafayette, 47907. Janet Huettner, Librn
Holdings: Vols (35,000) Cat Microforms

MA —HARVARD UNIVERSITY OBSERVATORY, John G Wolbach Library, 60 Garden St, Cambridge, 02138. Estelle W Karlin, Librn
Holdings: Vols (55,000) Cat Mss Maps Slides Microforms
Budget: ($60,000)
Notes: See *Harvard Library Bulletin,* V (1951): pp 102-111.

MA —SMITHSONIAN INSTITUTION LIBRARIES, Astrophysical Observatory Branch, 60 Garden St, Cambridge, 02138 Joyce Rey, Librn
Holdings: Vols (10,000) Cat Maps Pix Microforms

NY —COLUMBIA UNIVERSITY LIBRARIES, Physics Library, 810 Pupin, 535 W 114 St, New York, 10027. Mary Kay, Librn
Holdings: Vols 6000 Cat
Notes: Descriptive astronomy and astrophysics.

NY —UNIVERSITY OF ROCHESTER, Physics-Optics-Astronomy Library, Bausch & Lomb Bldg, River Campus, Rochester, 14627. Loretta Caren, Librn
Holdings: Vols (20,000) Cat
Notes: Strong research level collection in the field and related areas.

PA —FRANKLIN INSTITUTE LIBRARY, 20 & The Parkway, Philadelphia, 19103. Miriam Padusis, Dir; Charles Wilt, Readers Servs Librn
Holdings: Vols (300,000) Cat Maps Pix Microforms

PA —UNIVERSITY OF PITTSBURGH, Physics Library, 208 Engineering Hall, Pittsburgh, 15260. Paul J Kobulnicky, Physical Sciences Librn
Holdings: Vols (25,000) Cat Microforms
Budget: ($100,000)
Notes: The Physics Library collection is both a graduate student research-level collection in basic experimental and theoretical physics with emphasis on solid-state, nuclear, upper-atmosphere, space, and crystallography, and also a collection in the earth and planetary sciences, serving both graduate and undergraduate students. The collection is cataloged in both the University of Pittsburgh, Hillman Library union catalog and in a separate catalog in the Physics Library.

ON —QUEEN'S UNIVERSITY, Douglas Library, Kingston, K7L 5C4, Can. William F E Morley, Cur, Special Collections
Holdings: Vols (802) Uncat
Notes: Riche-Covington Collection supports McNichol Collection (history of telecommunications), brings it up to date; also astrophysics, astronomy, solar radiation. Bibliography available.

ASTROPHYSICS—HISTORY

NY —AMERICAN INSTITUTE OF PHYSICS, Center for the History of Physics, Niels Bohr Library, 335 E 45 St, New York, 10017. John Aubry, Librn
Notes: The Sources for History of Modern

ASTROPHYSICS—HISTORY (cont.)

Astrophysics documents the history of 20th-century astrophysics. Incl some 400 hours of oral history interviews with astronomers, such as Bart Bok, S Chandrasekhar, Martin Schwarzschild, and A E Whitford. The project also organized and cataloged the papers of Henry Norris Russell, Frank Schlesinger, Otto Struve, Ejnar Hertzsprung, Harlow Shapley, Charles Young, Robert Atkinson, Seth Chandler, Theodore Dunham, Jr, and G C McVittie.

ASTRUC, GABRIEL

NY —NEW YORK PUBLIC LIBRARY, Performing Arts Research Center, Dance Collection, 111 Amsterdam Ave, New York, 10023. Genevieve Oswald, Cur
Holdings: Mss Pix
Budget: ($9,280)
Notes: The Gabriel Astruc papers, 1904-25 contain ca 1300 manuscripts, correspondence, and reports relating to the early activities of Diaghilev. Register published in *Bulletin of the New York Public Library,* v 75, no 8, Oct 1971. Holograph *Black Exercise Book,* 1909-11, by Diaghilev. Entire collection described in: *Dictionary Catalog of the Dance Collection,* published by G K Hall, Boston, 1974, 10 vols. Annual supplements: *Bibliographic Guide to Dance,* also published by G K Hall.

ATHEISM

CA —ATHEIST ASSOCIATION, Atheist Library, 3024 Fifth Ave, PO Box 2832, San Diego, 92112. James Hervey Johnson, Librn
Notes: The Atheist Library and the building at 3024 Fifth Ave were completely destroyed by fire in October of 1981. There is no library at this time.

MA —HARVARD UNIVERSITY LIBRARY, Cambridge, 02138.
Holdings: Cat

NY —UNIVERSITY OF ROCHESTER, Rush Rhees Library, Department of Rare Books and Special Collections, Rochester, 14627. Peter Dzwonkoski, Librn
Notes: Papers, etc, incl books by and about Clement William Scott.

TX —SOCIETY OF SEPARATIONISTS, Library, 2210 Hancock Dr, PO Box 2117, Austin, 78756. R Murray-O'Hair, Dir
Holdings: Vols (50,000)
Notes: Atheism, separation of church and state, biographical archives on Atheists, agnostics, humanists, and iconoclasts.

WI —UNIVERSITY OF WISCONSIN, MADISON, Memorial Library, 728 State St, Madison, 53706. Erwin K Welsch, Social Studies Bibliographer
Holdings: Vols 1500 Cat Microforms
Notes: British Atheism and Free Thought. The collection consists largely of pamphlets published by leading advocates of the Free Thought and Atheist movements in the 19th century, incl George Holyoake, Charles Bradlaugh, Annie Besant, Thomas Scott, Charles Southwell, Charles Robert Newman, and G W Foote. Also incl numerous vols of debates between freethinkers and religious spokesmen and several important periodicals: the only complete copies of Robert Taylor's *The Philalethean by Talasophron* (1833-1834), *The Atheist and Republican* (1841), *The Blasphemer* (1842), and *The Free Inquirer in Science, Politics, and Theology* (1850), as well as others such as *The Secular Chronicle* (1872-1879), *Our Corner* (1883-1888), and *The Reformer* (1897-1898). Finally, there are represented pamphlets of the types intended to reach a popular or working-class audiencewhich contain, on occasion, scurrilous illustrations. Many items in the collection were originally owned by Hypatia Bradlaugh Bonner, daughter of a leading 19th century English politician and freethinker.

ATHERTON, GERTRUDE

CA —SAN DIEGO STATE UNIVERSITY, Malcolm A Love Library, 5300 Campanile Dr, San Diego, 92182. D Dickinson, Univ Librn; Don L Bosseau, Dir
Notes: Collected works in first edition of certain prominent authors, as H G Wells, Somerset Maugham, William Dean Howells, Gertrude Atherton, Tom Stoppard, James Clavell, G A Henty, Henry Raup Wagner.

ATHLETES AND ATHLETICS

AL —TUSKEGEE INSTITUTE, Hallis Burke Frissel Library, Tuskegee Institute, 36088. Daniel Williams, Librn
Notes: The Robert Stewart Darnaby Collection on Blacks in American sports. Much on the Southern Intercollegiate Athletic Conference, incl historical materials. Large resources on Tuskegee athletics.

CA —FIRST INTERSTATE BANK, Athletic Foundation, 2141 W Adams, Los Angeles, 90018. W R Schroeder, Managing Dir
Notes: One of the most extensive library and museum collections relating to sports, the Olympic Games, etc. Bound vols of sports sections from several newspapers. Large collection of college and university annuals and yearbooks; souvenir publications from amateur, college, and professional sporting events. Also, large museum collection of sports memorabilia, ledger of halls of fame with thousands of names of outstanding athletes in all sports. Repository for the Association of Sports Museums and Halls of Fame. Noncirculating.

CO —UNITED STATES FIGURE SKATING ASSOCIATION, 20 First St, Colorado Springs, 80906.
Notes: Rule books and other publications on figure skating.

CT —YALE UNIVERSITY, Box 1603A, Yale Station, New Haven, 06520.
Notes: Papers of Walter Camp, father of American football and foremost authority on sports and physical fitness. 48 microfilm reels; incl also over 20,000 clippings, etc on sports, providing virtual history, 1866-1925. Published guide to the collection for sale.

DC —SMITHSONIAN INSTITUTION LIBRARIES, National Museum of American History Branch, Washington, 20560. Rhoda S Ratner, Branch Librn
Notes: Emphasis on history of American sports and recreation. Incl some 2000 baseball cards from cigarette and chewing-gum packets; 103 scrapbooks and other memorabilia about Joe Louis; much on bicycling and skating.

IL —NATIONAL COUNCIL OF THE YMCAS, YMCA Historical Library, 6400 Shafer Ct, Rosemont, 60018. Eleanor R Murphy, Librn
Notes: Large collection, incl historical material, on basketball, wrestling, track and field, swimming, diving, scuba and volleyball.

IL —UNIVERSITY OF ILLINOIS, URBANA/CHAMPAIGN, Library, Applied Life Studies Library, 1408 W Gregory Dr, Urbana, 61801.
Holdings: Vols (38,000) Cat Microforms
See also entry under Physical Education and Training.

IN —UNITED STATES TRACK AND FIELD HALL OF FAME, Angola, 46703.

IN —NATIONAL TRACK AND FIELD HALL OF FAME, USA National Office Athletics Congress, 155 W Washington, Indianapolis, 46204. Berny Wagner, National Coach/Coordr; Ollan Cassel, Exec Dir
Notes: Collection will be located in Hoosier Dome (South Capital Ave, Indianapolis) after its completion. Incl books, film, tapes, and memorabilia.

IN —UNIVERSITY OF NOTRE DAME, University Libraries, Notre Dame, 46556.
Notes: Very likely the largest collection of sporting materials in the world. Over 500 sports and games are represented in a half-million documents. All physical forms of records are included, and there is no geographical restriction. Major center for research into all aspects of games and sports.

KY —UNIVERSITY OF KENTUCKY, Margaret I King Library, Dept of Special Collections, Lexington, 40506. William Marshall, Head

MD —LACROSSE FOUNDATION HALL OF FAME AND LIBRARY, Newton H White Jr, Athletic Center, Homeswood, Baltimore, 21218. Ann Gwyn, Librn
Holdings: Microforms
Notes: Large collection of books and memorabilia.

MA —UNIVERSITY OF MASSACHUSETTS AT AMHERST, Library, Amherst, 01002.
Notes: Strong collections in physical education, sports studies, exercise, gymnastics, etc.

MA —HARVARD UNIVERSITY LIBRARY, Widener Library, Cambridge, 02138.
Notes: Extensive collection of all phases of sports. Incl the Fearing Collection on Angling and Fishing containing over 15,000 books, mss, photographs, etc.

MI —UNIVERSITY OF MICHIGAN, Bentley Historical Library, Michigan Historical Collections, 1150 Beal Ave, Ann Arbor, 48109. Francis X Blovin Jr, Dir
Notes: Substantial holdings relating to the University's Sports activities. Also, 93 scrapbooks on Joe Louis.

NY —NATIONAL BASEBALL HALL OF FAME AND MUSEUM, National Baseball Library, Cooperstown, 13326. Thomas R Heitz, Librn
Budget: ($6000)
Notes: The National Baseball Library incl the folowing special collections: Literature, a comprehensive collection of vols incl biographies, general histories, team and league histories, encyclopedias, directories, dictionaries, general reference materials, fiction, poetry, and children's books. Complete runs of *Baseball Digest, Baseball Magazine, Sport Magazine, Sports* Illustrated, team publications, and numerous other journals of interest to baseball researchers. A comprehensive collection of the public official documents of organized baseball for the major and minor leagues. Extensive runs of *The Sporting News, New York Clipper, Sporting Life* and other 19th and 20th century news publications. Current newspaper files are also available. A comprehensive collection of Spalding, Reach and other guides dating back to the 1870s. A comprehensivecollection of major league team publications, media guides, yearbooks and press releases. Biographical files: personal and career data on all major league players, past and present, as well as biographical data on managers, coaches, scouts, umpires, executives, broadcasters, sportswriters, authors and baseball personalities. The files contain an estimated 2,500,000 documents, questionnaires and news clippings. A file of minor league player record cards useful for tracing the careers of former baseball players, and several other collections of baseball-related items.

NY —CORNELL UNIVERSITY LIBRARIES, Collection of Regional History, Dept of Manuscripts and Univ Archives, Ithaca, 14853.
Notes: Scrapbook (1900) of Cornell University football clippings.

NY —COLUMBIA UNIVERSITY LIBRARIES, Rare Book & Manuscript Library, 801 Butler Library, 535 W 114 St, New York, 10027. Kenneth A Lohf, Librn
Notes: Restricted use. The Paul Magriel Boxing Collection on the history and literature of pugilism. The L S Alexander Gumby Collection, which incl 9 Joe Lewis scrapbooks, and much on Jack Johnson, Sugar Ray Robinson, Jackie Robinson. Much on Columbia sports and athletics. Good strengths in material on Columbia's sports figures, incl Lou Gehrig, Lou Little, etc.

NY —RACQUET & TENNIS CLUB, Library, 370 Park Ave, New York, 10022. Gerald Belliveau, Jr, Librn
Holdings: Vols (17,500) Cat
Budget: ($6000)
Notes: Specializes in court tennis, lawn tennis, early American sport. See *Dictionary Catalogue of the Library of Sports in the Racquet and Tennis Club* (Boston: G K Hall, 1971). Also, Robert W Henderson, *Early American Sport,* 3rd ed. (Cranbury, NJ: Fairleigh Dickinson University Press, 1977).

OH —PRO FOOTBALL HALL OF FAME, Library, 2121 Harrison Ave NW, Canton, 44708. Anne Mangus, Librn; Joe Horrigan,

ATHLETES AND ATHLETICS (cont.)

Cur
Notes: Incl materials on all aspects of professional football, with special emphasis on the 119 men enshrined in the Hall of Fame. Mainly a research library. Incl periodicals and a vast array of historical material and mementos. Incl 17,000 pictures, 1500 slides, 50 audiotapes, 1300 16mm films, 3000 game programs and and 500 team media guides.

OH —COLLEGE FOOTBALL HALL OF FAME, Library, PO Box 300, Kings Mills, 45034. Don Schumacher, Cur
Notes: College of Football History, tourist attraction. Museum of football memorabilia and publications. Library not open to public.

OH —NATIONAL FOOTBALL HALL OF FAME, Kings Island Dr, Kings Mills, 45034. Don Schumacher, Librn in Charge

OK —NATIONAL WRESTLING HALL OF FAME, 405 West Hall of Fame Ave, Stillwater, 74075.
Notes: Collection built around collegiate and amateur wrestling, incl Olympic competition, from the late 1890s to the present.

PA —CUMBERLAND COUNTY HISTORICAL SOCIETY, The Hamilton Library, 21 N Pitt St, PO Box 626, Carlisle, 17013. Cordelia M Neitz, Librn
Holdings: Vols 60 Mss Pix
Notes: Containing most of the magazines and journals published by the school, incl also yearbooks, commencement and other programs, illustrated brochures of the school, and several hundred photographs of classes, buildings, teaching facilities, school activities, athletes (Jim Thorpe being one) and athletic teams; one of the most complete collections of its kind in the US.

PA —UNIVERSITY OF PENNSYLVANIA, Archives and Records Center, North Facade - Franklin Field, Philadelphia, 19104. Mark Frazier Lloyd, Archivist
Notes: R Tait McKenzie's personal papers, and the J William White Collection of personal papers--sealed until 2016. Incl materials relating to McKenzie's sculpting and the sports medallions and medals which he sculpted. Biographical and reserved materials for two books about him. Incl 39 cu ft.

PA —PENNSYLVANIA STATE UNIVERSITY, Fred Lewis Pattee Library, University Park, 16802.
Notes: Numerous and large collections on many sports. Also, materials supporting every aspect of the program of the Center for Women and Sport, incl research into kinetics, endocrinology, physiology, psychology, etc.

TX —UNIVERSITY OF TEXAS LIBRARIES, General Libraries, PO Box P, Austin, 78713. Carolyn Bucknell, Asst Dir for Collection Development
Notes: Much on Texas' and the University's athletic programs and athletes.

WI —UNIVERSITY OF WISCONSIN, MADISON, Memorial Library, Rare Books Collection, 728 State St, Madison, 53706. Gretchen Lagana, Cur
Notes: Nearly 20,000 vols of books and serials.

BC —CANADIAN LACROSSE HALL OF FAME AND LIBRARY, Box 308, New Westminster, V3L 4Y6, Can. Archie W Miller, Cur
Notes: Incl a large collection of memorabilia, archival material and a small library of lacrosse around the world, particularly in Canada.

BC —BRITISH COLUMBIA SPORTS HALL OF FAME AND LIBRARY, BC Pavilion, Vancouver, V5K 4W3, Can.
Notes: British Columbia. Incl sports film collection.

ON —CANADIAN FOOTBALL HALL OF FAME, 58 Jackson St, West, Hamilton, L8P 1L4, Can. William McBride, Dir
Holdings: Vols Cat
Notes: History of Canadian football for 115 years. Incl programs, memorabilia, 200 16mm films of all Canadian championship games since 1950's. Also a museum and archives of Canadian Rugby Football Union with original minutes of meetings and photographs and artifacts.

ON —INTERNATIONAL HOCKEY HALL OF FAME AND MUSEUM, PO Box 82, York and Alfred Sts, Kingston, K7L 4V6, Can. Doug Nichols, Pres
Notes: Hockey books from 1886; scrapbooks, programs, guides, and magazines.

ON —UNIVERSITY OF WESTERN ONTARIO, Dept of Special Collections, London, N6A 5B9, Can. Beth Miller, Librn
Notes: Large and important collection on Canadian participation in pre-Olympic and other Game series. Incl minutes of annual meetings of the Athletic Union of Canada, 1884-1898, 1908-1954.

ON —CANADIAN SKI MUSEUM, 457A Sussex Dr, Ottawa, K1N 6Z4, Can. Sally Ingels, Librn
Notes: Mainly but not exclusively Canadian material. Artifacts used for displays.

ON —CANADA SPORTS HALL OF FAME, Exhibition Place, Toronto, M6K 3C3, Can. Cheryl Rielly, Librn
Notes: Incl sports library of John W Davies, supporter of Commonwealth Games in Canada.

ON —HOCKEY HALL OF FAME AND MUSEUM LIBRARY, Exhibition Place, Toronto, M6K 3C3, Can. M H Reid, Dir and Cur
Holdings: Uncat Pix Slides Audiotapes Videotapes 16mm Films
Notes: Incl scrapbooks of famous players; some biographical materials.

ON —UNIVERSITY OF WINDSOR, Leddy Library, Windsor, N9B 3P4, Can. P Jerome Malone, Librn
Notes: Human kinetics, with emphasis on the history, psychology, sociology, philosophy, and administration of sports and their organization. Also hold archival records, etc of numerous Canadian sports organizations: Canadian Intercollegiate Athletic Union (CIAU), Ontario-Quebec AA, Ontario Universities AA, etc. Local and Regional history. 40 feet of materials.

PQ —UNIVERSITY OF MONTREAL, Physical Education Library, Montreal, H3C 3J7, Can. Lisa Mayrand, Dir
Holdings: Vols 15,000
Notes: Perhaps Canada's largest university library sports collection. Collection is bilingual (in English and French). 441 periodical subscriptions, 890 periodical titles, 4000 microfiche and 317 microfilms. On line with Ottawa's SIRC data base (qv).

ATHLETIC MEDICINE see Sports Medicine

ATHLETIC UNION OF CANADA

ON —UNIVERSITY OF WESTERN ONTARIO, Dept of Special Collections, London, N6A 5B9, Can. Beth Miller, Librn
Notes: Large and important collection on Canadian participation in pre-Olympic and other Game series. Incl minutes of annual meetings of the Athletic Union of Canada, 1884-1898, 1908-1954.

ATHLETICS—MEDICAL ASPECTS see Sports Medicine

ATHLETICS—PHYSIOLOGICAL ASPECTS see Sports—Physiological Aspects

ATKINS, OLLIE

VA —GEORGE MASON UNIVERSITY, Fenwick Library, Special Collections Dept, 4400 University Drive, Fairfax, 22030. Ruth Kerns, Public Services Librn
Notes: The Ollie Atkins Photographic Collection. Atkins, award-winning photographer with the *Saturday Evening* Post, was also White House photographer under several administrations. The collection incl more than 15,000 prints, negatives, contact sheets, slides and 4000 images covering subjects of historical, artistic and social significance from 1948 to 1968.

ATKINSON, BROOKS

NY —NEW YORK PUBLIC LIBRARY, Performing Arts Research Center, Billy Rose Theatre Collection, 111 Amsterdam Ave, New York, 10023. Dorothy L Swerdlove, Cur
Holdings: Cat Mss Pix
Notes: Papers, scrapbooks, mss, photographs, memorabilia, etc.

ATKINSON, ROBERT

NY —AMERICAN INSTITUTE OF PHYSICS, Center for the History of Physics, Niels Bohr Library, 335 E 45 St, New York, 10017. John Aubry, Librn
Notes: The Sources for History of Modern Astrophysics documents the history of 20th-century astrophysics. Incl some 400 hours of oral history interviews with astronomers, such as Bart Bok, S Chandrasekhar, Martin Schwarzschild, and A E Whitford. The project also organized and cataloged the papers of Henry Norris Russell, Frank Schlesinger, Otto Struve, Ejnar Hertzsprung, Harlow Shapley, Charles Young, Robert Atkinson, Seth Chandler, Theodore Dunham, Jr, and G C McVittie.

ATLANTA CONSTITUTION (NEWSPAPER)

GA —EMORY UNIVERSITY, Robert W Woodruff Library, Special Collections Dept, Atlanta, 30322. Linda M Matthews, Head Special Collections; Virginia J H Cain, Processing Archivist; Richard H F Lindemann, Reference Archivist
Holdings: Cat Mss Pix Audiotapes
Notes: Extensive collection of papers of Henry W Grady, Corra Harris, Joel Chandler Harris, Julian LaRose Harris, Julia Collier Harris, Clark Howell, Ralph E McGill, and Harold H Martin, among others, most associated with the Atlanta *Constitution.* Descriptions and index available in repository.

ATLANTA, GEORGIA—POLITICS AND GOVERNMENT

GA —EMORY UNIVERSITY, Robert W Woodruff Library, Atlanta, 30322. Herbert Johnson, Dir
Notes: Personal papers of six Atlantans who played major parts in building the city's progressive image. Incl Joel Chandler Harris (1848-1908); William B Hartsfield, mayor, 1937-61; 1961; Richard H Rich (1901-1975), business leader; Eleonore Raoul Greene (b 1888), suffragist and organizer of the Atlanta League of Women Voters; Helen Bullard (1908-1979), public relations consultant; and Josephine Wilkins (d 1970) social reformer and founder of the Georgia Citizen's Fact Finding Movement in the 1930s.

ATLANTIC AND ST. LAWRENCE RAILROAD

ME —BOWDOIN COLLEGE, Library, Brunswick, 04011. Dianne M Gutscher, Cur of Special Collections
Holdings: Cat Mss
Notes: Atlantic and St Lawrence Railroad Papers. This archive of the first international railroad from Portland, Maine, to Montreal contains approximately 800 items for the years 1844-1889. It consists of the official records of the railroad, including committee reports, secretary's minutes, copybooks, miscellaneous notes, reports, leases, pamphlets and broadsides as well as correspondence.

ATLANTIC CITY, NEW JERSEY

NJ —ATLANTIC CITY FREE PUBLIC LIBRARY, Illinois & Pacific Aves, Atlantic City, 08401. Paul Nee, Adult Serv Librn
Holdings: Vols 500 Cat Maps Pix Mss Films Slides VF
Notes: Incl 2000 postcards.

ATLANTIC OCEAN

TX —SOUTHERN METHODIST UNIVERSITY, DeGolyer Library, Box 396, SMU, Dallas, 75275. Clifton H Jones, Dir
Holdings: Cat Mss Maps Pix
Notes: Transportation, especially railroads and trans-Atlantic steamboats.

ATLANTIC SALMON—FISHING

PA —LAFAYETTE COLLEGE, David Bishop Skillman Library, Easton, 18042. Dorothy Cieslicki, Librn
Holdings: Vols (825) Cat
Notes: Robert Tinsman Angling Collection. Incl 58 editions of Walton, *Compleat Angler*. Also, the Robert S Conahay, Jr, Atlantic Salmon Collection, which incl over 1000 hand-tied salmon and trout flies, many mounted and framed.

ATLANTIS

VA —ASSOCIATION FOR RESEARCH & ENLIGHTENMENT, Library, 67 & Atlantic Avenue, PO Box 595, Virginia Beach, 23451. Stephen Jordan, Library Mgr
Holdings: Vols (1800) Cat
Notes: A R E Library Booklist incl 6000 items in 24 subject categories. This special collection is especially strong in the following subjects: astrology, spiritualism, extrasensory perception, reincarnation, healing arts, Theosophy, Atlantis. Egerton Sykeo Collection of 2500 vols pertaining to Atlantis.

ATLAS POWDER COMPANY

DE —HAGLEY MUSEUM AND LIBRARY, Eleutherian Mills-Hagley Foundation Inc, PO Box 3630, Greenville, 19807. Richmond D Williams, Dir; Heddy A Richter, Imprints Librn
Notes: Records of E I du Pont de Nemours & Company (1801-1958; 2500 cubic feet). The collection traces the founding of the company in Paris, its evolution into an American partnership during the early nineteenth century and its first incorporation in 1899. Details concerning the financial and business negotiations which led to the founding of the company, the selection of a site for operations, the erection of the mills, and methods of manufacturing, production, marketing and labor relations are well described. Records of Atlas Powder Company (1912-1955; 500 cubic feet) document the history of one of the United States' largest manufacturers of gun powder which was split off from the Du Pont Company as a result of a 1912 antitrust case.

ATLASES see Maps and Atlases—Collections

ATLASES, ANATOMICAL see Anatomical Atlases

ATLASES, ASTRONOMICAL see Stars—Atlases

ATLASES, SURGICAL see Surgical Atlases

ATMOSPHERE

CO —US AIR FORCE ACADEMY, Library, USAF Academy, Colorado Springs, 80840. Reiner H Schaeffer, Dir
Holdings: Vols 6000 Cat Mss Maps Pix
Notes: The Colonel Richard Gimbel Aeronautical History Collection. Incl material from ancient myth to 1903 on manned flight: early scientific works on physical properties of the atmosphere, and imaginative literature on moon voyages. Collection is most complete in manned pioneer balloon ascents (1783ff). Also the Richard Upjohn Light Collection formerly at Culver Military Academy. Separate catalog, index to be published. 250 mss, 100 maps, 2000 pictures, 5000 prints, 7000 clippings.

CO —COLORADO STATE UNIVERSITY, Libraries, Fort Collins, 80523. Marjorie Rhoades, Engineering Sciences Librn
Holdings: Vols (8000) Cat
Budget: ($6000)
Notes: Atmosphere; upper atmosphere; atmospheric chemistry; atmospheric circulation; atmospheric radiation; atmospheric research; atmospheric thermodynamics; cloud physics; and clouds.

FL —UNIVERSITY OF MIAMI, Otto G Richter Library, PO Box 248214, Coral Gables, 33124. Frank Rodgers, Dir of Libraries
Holdings: Vols Microforms
Notes: The Rosenstiel School of Marine and Atmospheric Sciences Library is one of the major marine science collections in the United States and is especially strong in the literature of tropical oceanography. Special collections in the library incl 200 oceanographic atlases and more than 50 sets of the world's major expedition reports. The library also maintains a nautical chart collection. 3000 microforms; 1000 current subscriptions.

MD —NATIONAL OCEANIC & ATMOSPHERIC ADMINISTRATION, Library & Information Sciences Division, Central Library & Information Sciences Bldg, 6009 Executive Blvd, Rockville, 20852. Elizabeth J Yeates, Chief
Holdings: Vols (175,000) Cat Maps Microforms

NV —UNIVERSITY OF NEVADA, RENO, Desert Research Institute, PO Box 60220, Reno, 89557. Roberta Kiefer Orcutt, Librn
Holdings: Vols (10,480) Cat Maps Microforms
Notes: Incl materials in atmospheric physics, meteorology, climatology, weather modification, antarctic studies and related materials in basic sciences. Over 3000 microforms; also 1300 technical reports and 18,000 government publications.

NY —STATE UNIVERSITY OF NEW YORK AT ALBANY, Library, Special Collections Dept, 1400 Washington Ave, Albany, 12222. Marion P Munzer, Coordr
Notes: 28 linear feet of mss; 31 linear feet of pamphlets and periodicals; and 700 volumes from Vincent J Schaefer's personal library. Also, papers, photographs, publications, etc, dealing with his teaching and research on cloud seeding and other aspects of atmospheric science.
See also entries under Schaefer, Vincent J; Rainmaking

WA —UNIVERSITY OF WASHINGTON LIBRARIES, Suzzallo Library, Natural Sciences Library, FM-25, Seattle, 98195. Nancy G Blase, Head
Holdings: Vols (192,353) Cat
Budget: ($219,809)

ATMOSPHERE—RESEARCH see Atmospheric Research

ATMOSPHERE, UPPER

CA —UNIVERSITY OF CALIFORNIA, LOS ANGELES, Engineering & Mathematical Sciences Library, 405 Hilgard, Los Angeles, 90024. Rosalee I Wright, Librn
Notes: Collection includes WMO publications (comprehensive); IGY data series on surface observations, radiosonde and rawinsonde observations, upper wind observations, and radiation data (mostly in microform); selected government report or data series, eg from NOAA, NCC and AF Geophysics Laboratory.

CO —COLORADO STATE UNIVERSITY, Libraries, Fort Collins, 80523. Marjorie Rhoades, Engineering Sciences Librn
Holdings: Vols 8000 Cat
Budget: ($6000)

PA —UNIVERSITY OF PITTSBURGH, Physics Library, 208 Engineering Hall, Pittsburgh, 15260. Paul J Kobulnicky, Physical Sciences Librn
Holdings: Vols (25,000) Cat Microforms
Budget: ($100,000)
Notes: The Physics Library collection is both a graduate student research-level collection in basic experimental and theoretical physics with emphasis on solid-state, nuclear, upper-atmosphere, space, and crystallography, and also a collection in the earth and planetary sciences, serving both graduate and undergraduate students. The collection is cataloged in both the University of Pittsburgh, Hillman Library union catalog and in a separate catalog in the Physics Library.

ATMOSPHERIC ABSORPTION OF SOLAR RADIATION see Solar Radiation

ATMOSPHERIC RESEARCH

CO —COLORADO STATE UNIVERSITY, Libraries, Fort Collins, 80523. Marjorie Rhoades, Engineering Sciences Librn
Holdings: Vols 8000 Cat
Budget: ($6000)

IL —ILLINOIS STATE WATER SURVEY, Library, 605 E Springfield, Champaign, 61820. Marcia E Nelson, Head Librn
Holdings: Vols 22,000
Notes: Emphasis on Illinois and region.

ATOMIC BOMB

CA —HOOVER INSTITUTION ON WAR, REVOLUTION & PEACE, Stanford University, Stanford, 94305. Milorad M Drachkovitch, Archivist
Holdings: Mss
Notes: Papers of Eugene H Dooman, US diplomat, Counsellor of Embassy at Tokyo, 1937-41, and Special Assistant to the Assistant Secretary of State for Far Eastern Affairs, 1944-45, incl mss of writings, transcripts of speeches, correspondence, diaries and printed matter, 1913-1966, relating to US foreign policy in the Far East, US-Japanese relations, the decision to drop the atomic bomb on Japan. 1 1/2 ms boxes.

IL —UNIVERSITY OF CHICAGO LIBRARY, Dept of Special Collections, 1100 E 57 St, Chicago, 60637.
Holdings: Mss
Notes: Argonne National Laboratory deposit of 46 linear ft of materials dealing with the construction of Argonne and the Manhattan Project at the University of Chicago.

MA —MASSACHUSETTS INSTITUTE OF TECHNOLOGY, Institute Archives, Special Collections, Cambridge, 02139.
Notes: Papers of Bernard Feld, nuclear physicist at MIT and a world leader in disarmament activities. Graduate student under Leo Szilard and Enrico Fermi and continued as a physicist with the Manhattan Engineer District in Los Alamos, New Mexico. The collection incl extensive documentation of national and international arms control efforts which Feld initiated in the Cold War which followed the destruction of Hiroshima and Nagasaki. Founder and Editor-in-Chief of the Bulletin of Atomic Scientists.

MI —UNIVERSITY OF MICHIGAN, Libraries, Michigan Historical Collections, Ann Arbor, 48109. Mary Jo Pugh, Reference Archivist
Notes: Ralph A Sawyer's papers (1918-78). Incl material relating to his work as consultant at the test of the hydrogen bomb at the Naval Proving Grounds, Bikini Atoll.

NM —UNIVERSITY OF CALIFORNIA, Los Alamos National Laboratory, Libraries, PO Box 1663, MSP 362, Los Alamos, 87545. J Arthur Freed, Head Librn
Holdings: Vols (800,000) Cat Films Microforms
Budget: ($700,000)
Notes: Files of scientists who worked at Los Alamos during the early days of the Atomic Bomb Project (1943-1946).

OH —WILMINGTON COLLEGE, Peace Resource Center, Hiroshima/Nagasaki Memorial Collection, Pyle Center Box 1183, Wilmington, 45177. Helen Redding, Librn
Holdings: Vols 550 Cat Pix Slides Audiotapes Videotapes Film VF
Notes: A unique Japanese language collection dealing with the atomic bombings and nuclear issues in general. *Japanese A-*

ATOMIC BOMB (cont.)

Bomb Literature: An Annotated Bibliography lists each book in the Collection and gives a brief description in English.

ATOMIC ENERGY

CA —UNIVERSITY OF CALIFORNIA, BERKELEY, Bancroft Library, Manuscripts Division, Berkeley, 94720. James D Hart, Dir
Holdings: / / Cat Microforms
Notes: The Archive for the History of Quantum Physics contains tape-recorded interviews, microfilmed documents, and correspondence (largely unpublished), relating to the history of quantum and atomic physics. Coverage centers on the years 1900 to 1930. The Archive consists of some 300 reels of microfilm, in conjunction with the Office for History of Science, UC Berkeley. A catalog of about one-third of the holdings is incl in T S Kuhn, J L Heilbron, P Forman and L Allen, *Sources for the History of Quantum Physics* (Philadelphia: American Philosophical Society, 1967).

CT —WATERFORD PUBLIC LIBRARY, Millstone Power Plants Local Documents Room, 49 Rope Ferry Rd, Waterford, 06385. Vincent Juliano, Library Dir; Carolyn Greene, Millstone File Coordinator
Holdings: Uncat Mss
Notes: Collection is part of Nuclear Regulatory Commission's Local Public Document Room project and all materials are arranged by system developed by NRC/LPDR. No subject index is available. Additional materials on microfilm.

DC —GEORGETOWN UNIVERSITY, Library, Special Collections Div, 37 & O Sts NW, Washington, 20057. George M Barringer, Special Collections Librn; Nicholas B Sheetz, Mss Librn
Holdings: Cat
Notes: The papers incl a large quantity of Amrine's literary mss, together with correspondence, print and near print material relating to a number of subjects, most importantly, atomic energy research and development. Michael Amrine (1918-1974) began his career in journalism in 1934, working for a number of years with the Federation of Atomic Scientists while editing the *Bulletin* of Atomic Scientists. Amrine is the author of a number of books, incl *This Awesome Challenge* (1964). Correspondents incl: Albert Einstein, Hans Bethe, Harold Urey, Thomas Hart Benton and William Allen White. Other materials incl a collection of black and white still photographs relating to Amrine's research interests and tape recorded interviews, used as background for a number of his books.

ID —EG&G, INEL Technical Library, 1776 Science Center, Idaho Falls, 83401. Brent Jacobsen, Head Librn; Heather Redding, Ref Librn
Holdings: Vols (33,000) Cat Microforms
Notes: Energy research and development included in libraries collection. Incl over 500,000 AEC, ERDA, NRC, and foreign reports. Unclassified materials may be used by the public in the library by appointment or borrowed by interlibrary loan. Incl 12,000 bound documents, 520,000 microfiche, 400 periodical subscriptions.

ID —IDAHO STATE UNIVERSITY, Library, Pocatello, 83209. Gary Domitz, Social Science Librn
Holdings: Cat Mss Maps Pix
Notes: Extensive collection.

IA —IOWA STATE UNIVERSITY, Library, Ames, 50011. Warren B Kuhn, Dean of Library Services
Holdings: Cat Mss Microforms
Notes: Incl AEC and DOE technical reports; research notebooks of local scientists, and records of the Energy and Mineral Resources Research Institute (formerly AEC Ames Laboratory) since its establishment in 1942.

KS —WICHITA PUBLIC LIBRARY, 223 S Main, Wichita, 67202. Larry DePiesse, Head, Business & Technology Dept; Jayne F Young, Business & Technology Dept
Holdings: Vols 800 Cat
Budget: $700
Notes: 456 of our holdings are circulating books. The remaining 344 books are in a special non-circulating collection, the "Energy Collection." Includes solar, wind, nuclear, etc.

MA —HARVARD UNIVERSITY, Center for Middle Eastern Studies, Library, Coolidge Hall, 1737 Cambridge St, Cambridge, 02138. Barbara Mitchell, Librn
Holdings: Vols (5000) Periodicals
Notes: Some history of countries of the Middle East; increasingly emphasizes culture and politics of the current Middle Eastern area. Special collection of Energy Economics Research. Library currently receives 15 periodical titles.

MI —UNIVERSITY OF MICHIGAN, North Engineering Library, 1002 I St, Ann Arbor, 48109. Maurita Holland, Librn
Holdings: Vols (60,000) Cat Microforms
Budget: ($60,000)
Notes: Formerly a depository for US AEC technical reports, the library still acquires technical reports on microfiche (approx 12, 000 sheets per year) from the US DOE. As of 6/30/83, the library held 60,000 vols and 500,000 microforms (fiche and cards). The technical report collection, both full-size and microform, is uncataloged. A local "document catalog" lists reports by report number only.

NM —NATIONAL ATOMIC MUSEUM, Library & Public Document Room, Kirtland AFB-E, Albuquerque, 87115. Philip P Larragoite, Librn
Holdings: Vols (50) Cat
Budget: ($600)
Notes: Alternative energy resources.

NM —UNIVERSITY OF CALIFORNIA, Los Alamos National Laboratory, Libraries, PO Box 1663, MSP 362, Los Alamos, 87545. J Arthur Freed, Head Librn
Holdings: Vols (800,000) Cat Films Microforms
Budget: ($700,000)
Notes: Incl 500,000 classified and unclassified reports. There are 25 branch libraries and a central collection. The Medical Library contains about 40,000 vols in the areas of biomedical research.

NY —AMERICAN INSTITUTE OF PHYSICS, Center for the History of Physics, Niels Bohr Library, 335 E 45 St, New York, 10017. John Aubry, Librn
Notes: Papers and records.

NY —NEW YORK PUBLIC LIBRARY, Research Libraries, Science and Technology Research Center, Fifth Ave & 42 St, New York, 10018.
Holdings: Vols (1,100,000) Cat Microforms
Budget: ($647,259)

PA —FRANKLIN INSTITUTE LIBRARY, 20 & The Parkway, Philadelphia, 19103. Miriam Padusis, Dir; Charles Wilt, Readers Servs Librn
Holdings: Vols (300,000) Cat Maps Pix Microforms

PA —CARNEGIE LIBRARY OF PITTSBURGH, Science & Technology Dept, 4400 Forbes Ave, Pittsburgh, 15213. Catherine M Brosky, Dept Head
Holdings: Vols (380,000) Cat Maps Microforms
Budget: ($240,000)
Notes: Substantially complete DOE/AEC/ERDA documents in microform. Monographs, series, journals.
See also entry under Engineering.

†SD —SOUTH DAKOTA SCHOOL OF MINES & TECHNOLOGY, Devereaux Library, Rapid City, 57701.
Holdings: Vols 550 Cat Microforms

TN —TENNESSEE VALLEY AUTHORITY (TVA), Technical Library, 400 W Summit Hill Dr, E2 B7, Knoxville, 37902. Jesse C Mills, Chief Librn
Holdings: Vols (106,900) Cat Mss Maps Pix Audiotapes Microforms
Budget: ($2,025,000)
Notes: The Technical Library Headquarters Staff (order, cataloging, information, and administration) is located in Knoxville, Tenn. In addition there are branch libraries in Knoxville, Norris, and Chattanooga, Tennessee, and Muscle Shoals, Alabama.

TX —TEXAS STATE LIBRARY, Archives Div, 1201 Brazos, PO Box 12927, Capitol Sta, Austin, 78711. David B Gracy II, State Archivist

TX —SOUTHERN METHODIST UNIVERSITY, Fondren Library, Dallas, 75275. Curt Holleman, Librn for Collection Development

TX —RICE UNIVERSITY, Fondren Library, 6100 S Main St, PO Box 1892, Houston, 77251. Dr Samuel M Carrington, Jr, University Librn

ON —ATOMIC ENERGY OF CANADA LIMITED, Main Library, Technical Information Branch, Chalk River Nuclear Laboratories, Chalk River, K0J 1J0, Can. Harry Greenshields, Chief Librn
Holdings: Vols (128,700) Microforms
Budget: ($662,400)
Notes: The Main Library, Atomic Energy of Canada Limited, is the Canadian repository for the literature of nuclear science and technology. Its collections reflect both fundamental and nuclear aspects of biology, chemistry, electronics, engineering, mathematics, computers, metallurgy, physics and other specific areas of science involving nuclear technology with special emphasis on heavy water reactor systems. 512,000 research reports are available in paper copy and microfiche form. Incl US DOE, INIS and other offshore nuclear research reports. 386,000 microforms.

ON —RIO ALGOM LIMITED, Library, 120 Adelaide St W, Toronto, M5H 1W5, Can. Penny Lipman, Librn
Holdings: Vols (1500) Cat
Budget: ($7000)
Notes: Espec mining of uranium and copper; geology; mining methods; nuclear energy.

ATOMIC ENERGY—ACCIDENTS

DC —NATIONAL ARCHIVES AND RECORDS SERVICE, Civil Archives Division, Washington, 20408.
Notes: Records of the President's Commission on the Accident at Three Mile Island (May-December 1979).

ATOMIC ENERGY COMMISSION see U.s. Atomic Energy Commission

ATOMIC MEDICINE

NM —UNIVERSITY OF CALIFORNIA, Los Alamos National Laboratory, Libraries, PO Box 1663, MSP 362, Los Alamos, 87545. J Arthur Freed, Head Librn
Holdings: Vols (800,000) Cat Films Microforms
Budget: ($700,000)
Notes: Incl 500,000 classified and unclassified reports. There are 25 branch libraries and a central collection. The Medical Library contains about 40,000 vols in the areas of biomedical research.

TX —US AIR FORCE, School of Aerospace Medicine, Strughold Aeromedical Library, Brooks AFB, 78235. Fred W Todd, Chief Librn
Holdings: Vols (119,188) Cat Mss Maps Pix Microforms
Budget: ($499,000)
Notes: Aviation and space medicine and physiology, including the physiological effects of altitude and decompression. Biomedical and and human engineering. Military medicine, including chemical and biological warfare. Emergency medicine in both professional and technical areas. Radiobiology, including atomic medicine, nuclear medicine, and space radiation. Material not oriented to the School of Aerospace Medicine are excluded. Incl also 45,787 microforms and 142,371 technical documents.

ATOMIC NUCLEI see Nuclear Physics

ATOMIC PILES see Nuclear Reactors

ATOMIC POWER ENGINEERING see Nuclear Engineering

ATOMIC POWER PLANTS

CA —UNIVERSITY OF CALIFORNIA, LOS ANGELES, Engineering & Mathematical

ATOMIC POWER PLANTS (cont.)

Sciences Library, 405 Hilgard, Los Angeles, 90024. Rosalee I Wright, Librn
Notes: Complete depository of unclassified technical reports from AEC, ERDA, and DOE; selected IAEA publications, NRC dockets.

CT —WATERFORD PUBLIC LIBRARY, Millstone Power Plants Local Documents Room, 49 Rope Ferry Rd, Waterford, 06385. Vincent Juliano, Library Dir; Carolyn Greene, Millstone File Coordinator
Holdings: Uncat Mss
Notes: AEC-Northeast Utilities Reactor Plants I, II, and III, Waterford, Conn. Have 90 ft of archives. All documents relate to planning plants and their operation and expansion. Collection is part of Nuclear Regulatory Commission's Local Public Document Room project and all materials are arranged by system developed by NRC/LPDR. No subject index is available. Toll free assistance from NRC/LPDR, 800-638-8081. Additional materials on microfilm.

MI —MONROE COUNTY LIBRARY SYSTEM, Ellis Reference and Information Center, 3700 S Custer Rd, Monroe, 48161. Marie D Chulski, Head of Reference Services
Holdings: Microfiche Doucments
Notes: Detroit Edison nuclear power plant, Enrico Fermi II. All documents relating to planning plant's operation.

NJ —PUBLIC SERVICE ELECTRIC AND GAS CO, Nuclear Library, MC150A, PO Box 236, Hancocks Bridge, 08038. Virginia Swichel, Librn
Holdings: Vols (1000) Cat

NJ —PUBLIC SERVICE ELECTRIC & GAS CO, Library, 80 Park Place Plaza P3C, PO Box 570, Newark, 07101. Florine E Hunt, Corporate Librn
Holdings: Vols (20,000) Cat Microforms

†NY —COLUMBIA UNIVERSITY LIBRARIES, Butler Library, Rare Book and Manuscript Library, 535 W 114 St, New York, 10027.
Notes: Papers of the Citizen's Committee for the Protection of the Environment, Ossining, NY, whose activities are centered on the environmental hazards of Consolidated Edison's Indian Point nuclear power plants.

VA —UNIVERSITY OF VIRGINIA, Alderman Library, Manuscripts Dept, Charlottesville, 22901. Edmund Berkeley Jr, Cur
Holdings: Cat Mss Maps Pix
Notes: Papers of the Conservation Council of Virginia, and its chairman, the Central Atlantic Environment Center, the Virginia Electric and Power Co, the US Atomic Energy Commission, State Water Control Board Chairman, and members of the Governor's Council on the Environment focus on a variety of environmental issues particularly the location of a nuclear power plant on an alleged geological fault, water pollution and the Potomac River cleanup of the 1970s and state environmental goals regarding water and air pollution, preservation, and development.

ATOMIC SCIENTISTS

MA —MASSACHUSETTS INSTITUTE OF TECHNOLOGY, Institute Archives, Special Collections, Cambridge, 02139.
Notes: Papers of Bernard Feld, nuclear physicist at MIT and a world leader in disarmament activities. Graduate student under Leo Szilard and Enrico Fermi and continued as a physicist with the Manhattan Engineer District in Los Alamos, New Mexico. The collection incl extensive documentation of national and international arms control efforts which Feld initiated in the Cold War which followed the destruction of Hiroshima and Nagasaki. Founder and Editor-in-Chief of the Bulletin of Atomic Scientists.

ATOMIC THEORY

CA —INTERNATIONAL BUSINESS MACHINES RESEARCH LIBRARY, 5600 Cottle Rd, San Jose, 95193. Phil Grincewich, Mgr Technical Information
Holdings: Vols (13,500) Cat
Notes: Incl 21,000 vols of 770 journals. On-line search facility. Vols are divided into three libraries, Technical Research, Technical Information, and Programing. Not open to public.

ATOMIC WEAPONS

CA —UNIVERSITY OF CALIFORNIA, LIVERMORE, Lawrence Livermore National Laboratory, Library, PO Box 5500, Livermore, 94550. John B Verity, Library Mgr
Holdings: Vols (160,000) Cat 16mm Films Microforms
Budget: ($2,323,000)
Notes: The LLL library system includes a central collection in physics, chemistry, engineering, geology, mathematics, and computer science; and branch holdings in bio-medicine, environmental science, nuclear chemistry, energy research, theoretical physics, materials science, and nuclear weapons. Collections include 160,000 books, 145,000 technical reports, 530,000 reports on microfiche, and 3000 periodical subscriptions. LLL libraries are not open to the public. Unclassified materials may be borrowed on interlibrary loan.

DC —US ARMS CONTROL & DISARMAMENT AGENCY, Library, George Washington Univ Special Collections, Washington, 21 St & Virginia Ave, NW, Rm 5851, Washington, 20451. Diane Ferguson, Librn
Holdings: Vols 4500 // Cat
Notes: Arms control, disarmament and related topics.

NM —NATIONAL ATOMIC MUSEUM, Library & Public Document Room, Kirtland AFB-E, Albuquerque, 87115. Philip P Larragoite, Librn
Holdings: Vols 100 Cat Pix
Budget: ($600)
Notes: Nuclear weapons history.

NM —UNIVERSITY OF CALIFORNIA, Los Alamos National Laboratory, Libraries, PO Box 1663, MSP 362, Los Alamos, 87545. J Arthur Freed, Head Librn
Holdings: Vols (800,000) Cat Films Microforms
Budget: ($700,000)
Notes: Incl 500,000 classified and unclassified reports. There are 25 branch libraries and a central collection. The Medical Library contains about 40,000 vols in the areas of biomedical research.

ATOMIZATION (LIQUID)

IA —DELEVAN DIVISION OF COLT INDUSTRIES INC, Engineering Library, 811 Fourth St, PO Box 100, West Des Moines, 50265. G A Hartman, Librn
Holdings: Vols 2000 Cat Mss Slides Microforms
Budget: $400
Notes: Incl liquid atomization, droplet size measurement and representation, fuel nozzles for combustors, and spray nozzles for industrial and agricultural applications.

ATOMS, NUCLEI OF see Nuclear Physics

ATOMS FOR PEACE AWARD

MA —MASSACHUSETTS INSTITUTE OF TECHNOLOGY, Institute Archives, Special Collections, Cambridge, 02139.
Notes: Papers of executive secretary (1955-1969).

ATROCITIES see World War, 1939-1945—Atrocities

ATROPHY, MUSCULAR

NY —CORNELL UNIVERSITY MEDICAL COLLEGE, Samuel J Wood Library, 1300 York Ave, New York, 10021. Erich Meyerhoff, Dir
Holdings: Vols (9000) Cat Films
Notes: All aspects of muscle diseases.

NY —MUSCULAR DYSTROPHY ASSOCIATION, 810 Seventh Ave, New York, 10019. Marianthe Pappas, Librn
Holdings: Vols 8770 Cat
Budget: $55,000
Notes: All phases of muscular diseases. Incl some films.

ATSINA INDIANS

†IL —NEWBERRY LIBRARY, 60 W Walton St, Chicago, 60610.
Notes: Collection of color slides of the early 1950s. Photographs by the eight-year Superintendent of the Fort Belknap Indian Reservation in Montana, J W "Duke" Wellington, who was allowed to take pictures of some of the most important rituals of the Assiniboine and Gros Ventres Indians, dances, renewals, etc. An annotated collection.

MT —MONTANA STATE UNIVERSITY, Library, Bozeman, 59717. Minnie Ellen Paugh, Special Collections Librn
Holdings: Vols (7000) // Mss Maps Pix
Notes: Leggat-Donahoe Collection. Collection of Alexander Leggat of Butte, whose father was active in opening the mines. Mr Leggat's interests were mining, exploration, and the fur trade. There are excellent Indian materials in the collection. Also the manuscript and picture collections of James Willard Schultz, Harry James (about James Willard Schultz), and Olga Ross Hannon on Blackfeet Indian tepees. Land claim clase files and manuscripts about Blackfeet, Gros Ventre, Assiniboine and Crow Indians collected by Dr Thomas R Wessell, Edward E Barry and Dr Merrill G Burlingame.

ATTACK AND DEFENSE (MILITARY SCIENCE)

MN —UNIVERSITY OF MINNESOTA, O Meredith Wilson Library, 309 19 Ave S, Minneapolis, 55455. Austin J McLean, Chief, Special Collections
Holdings: Vols (410) Cat
Notes: Fortification from the Renaissance to 1800. Related materials on attack and defense and accounts of famous sieges.

ATTACK ON PEARL HARBOR, 1941 see Pearl Harbor, Attack on, 1941

ATTICA PRISON

†NY —COLUMBIA UNIVERSITY LIBRARIES, Butler Library, Rare Book and Manuscript Library, 535 W 114 St, New York, 10027.
Notes: The Papers of Dr David Abrahamsen, incl letters and mss. Contains letters from and interviews with family and friends of Richard M Nixon and 167 typed and handwritten letters sent by David Berkowitz to Dr Abrahamsen from Attica Prison during 1979-81.

ATWATER, WILBUR OLIN, 1844-1907

NY —CORNELL UNIVERSITY LIBRARIES, Collection of Regional History, Dept of Manuscripts and Univ Archives, Ithaca, 14853.
Notes: Agricultural and physiological chemist, professor of chemistry. Incl papers, 1876-1903; letter impression copybooks, student dissertations, notes on experiments, and much professional correspondence.

ATWELL, LESTER

MA —BOSTON UNIVERSITY, Mugar Memorial Library, Special Collections Dept, 771 Commonwealth Ave, Boston, 02215. Howard B Gotlieb, Dir
Holdings: Cat Mss

ATWOOD, MARY ANN

RI —BROWN UNIVERSITY, John Hay Library, 20 Prospect St, Providence, 02912. Mark N Brown, Cur Mss
Holdings: Vols (2000) Cat Mss
Notes: Several collections of religious history

ATWOOD, MARY ANN (cont.)

strong in material on Baptist, Congregational, and Unitarian Churches in the 19th century, incl the ms records some Rhode Island congregations plus the papers of Isaac Backus, Brown University presidents and faculty, Jones Very, Mary Ann Atwood, Thomas Ustick, and Charles King Newcomb; incl numerous ephemeral and pamphlet publications that relate to Baptist Church history, creed, biography, Sunday School literature and missions.

ATWOOD, MARY ANN SMITH

RI —BROWN UNIVERSITY, John Hay Library, 20 Prospect St, Providence, 02912. Mark N Brown, Cur Mss
Holdings: Mss
Notes: Two collections relating to the occult sciences: The Mary Ann Smith Atwood Collection--English theosophist and writer (700 items); and the S Foster Damon, 1893-1971, Collection--poet, dramatist and Professor of English at Brown University, (more than 15,000 items), unprocessed.

ATWOOD, R. FRANK

WA —WESTERN WASHINGTON UNIVERSITY, Center for Pacific Northwest Studies, High St, Bellingham, 98225. James W Scott, Dir
Holdings: Uncat Mss Maps Pix Slides Phonorecords Audiotapes Videotapes 16mm Films Filmstrips Microforms
Notes: Consists of the papers of R Frank Atwood, Bellingham attorney, who was formerly Minority Leader (Republican) in the Washington State Senate, retiring in 1974. The papers are almost exclusively political, with heavy emphasis on Washington state and on the district he represented, Whatcom County.

ATYPICAL CHILDREN see Exceptional Children

AUCHINCLOSS, LOUIS

†VA —UNIVERSITY OF VIRGINIA, Alderman Library, Manuscripts Dept, Charlottesville, 22901.
Notes: Papers, etc.

AUCTION CATALOGS see Catalogs, Auction

AUCTION CATALOGS, BOOKSELLERS' see Catalogs, Booksellers'—Auction

AUCTIONS, ART see Art Auctions

AUDEN, W. H.

AZ —UNIVERSITY OF ARIZONA, University Library, Special Collections, Tucson, 85721. Louis A Hieb, Head
Holdings: Vols (7000) Cat Mss Microforms
Budget: ($30,000)
Notes: The 20th century collection is dominated by the works of Auden, Durrell, Conrad, Hardy, D H Lawrence, and Yeats.

IL —NORTHWESTERN UNIVERSITY, Library, Special Collections Dept, 1937 Sheridan Rd, Evanston, 60201. R Russell Maylone, Cur
Holdings: (9000) Cat Mss
Notes: First, limited, special editions, letters, ephemera of major 20th century Anglo-Irish and English writers such as James Joyce, W B Yeats, T S Eliot, W H Auden and Lawrence Durrell, as well as representative minor writers. Correspondence files of James B Pinker & Sons, literary agents: 50,000 pieces, 1900-1934 inclusive.

IN —INDIANA UNIVERSITY, Lilly Library, Seventh St, Bloomington, 47405. William R Cagle, Librn
Notes: Writings by author W H Auden.

NV —UNIVERSITY OF NEVADA, RENO, University Library, Special Collections Dept, Reno, 89557. Robert E Blesse, Head
Holdings: Vols (240) Cat Other appearances 1500 Cat
Notes: Includes individual works by author in all editions including translations; also prefaces, introductions, published correspondence, appearances in anthologies, periodicals, etc. Bibliographical research collection, part of Modern Authors Collection.

NY —NEW YORK PUBLIC LIBRARY, Fifth Ave & 42 St, New York, 10018.
Notes: A Collection of original manuscripts and notebooks.

PA —SWARTHMORE COLLEGE, Library, Swarthmore, 19081. Michael J Durkan, Librn
Holdings: Vols 295 Cat Mss Pix
Notes: American and English editions of books written by Auden and translations made by him. It does not include critical works *about him*.

VA —SWEET BRIAR COLLEGE, Library, Sweet Briar, 24595. John Jaffe, Librn
Holdings: Vols 287 Cat Pix
Budget: $500
Notes: Incl first editions.

AUDIOLOGY

PA —EYE & EAR HOSPITAL OF PITTSBURGH, Blair-Lippincott Library, 230 Lothrop St, Pittsburgh, 15213. Bruce A Johnston, Medical Librn
Holdings: Vols (6000) Cat
Notes: Special emphasis on ophthalmology, otorhinolaryngology, audiology, and speech pathology.

AUDIOVISUAL EDUCATION AND INSTRUCTION

CA —LOS ANGELES PUBLIC LIBRARY, Central Library, Audio Visual Dept, 630 W Fifth St, Los Angeles, 90071. Richard V Partlow, Principal Librn
Budget: ($71,989)
Notes: Includes 16mm film (4300), VHS video (300), audio recordings (20,000), audio cassettes (5500), picture file (220,000 estimated clippings), filmstrips (60), periodicals (65). Material on all subject areas are included.

CO —SOCIAL SCIENCE EDUCATION CONSORTIUM, Resource & Demonstration Center (RDC), 855 Broadway, Boulder, 80302. Regina McCormick, Staff Assoc
Holdings: Vols (16,000) Cat Filmstrips Microforms
Notes: Contains over 15,000 elementary and secondary social studies textbooks, audiovisuals, games and simulations, professional books, and the complete ERIC microfiche collection. Staff available to travel to all parts of the US to consult on curriculum development, instructional methods, materials analysis and selection, evaluation, new materials, teaching strategies, and trends in the social studies.

DC —NATIONAL AUDIOVISUAL CENTER, General Services Administration, Information Services Section, National Audiovisual Center, Washington, 20409. Diana M Wade, Head, Information Services Section
Holdings: Slides Phonorecords Audiotapes Videotapes 16mm Films Filmstrips
Notes: The National Audiovisual Center was created under National Archives and Records Service of the General Services Administration to serve as the central clearinghouse for all Federal audiovisual materials and to make them available for public use through information and distribution services. Through the Center's distribution programs, the public has access to over 13,000 audiovisual materials covering a wide range of subjects.

IL —CHICAGO PUBLIC LIBRARY, Art Section, Fine Arts Division, 78 E Washington St, Chicago, 60602. Rosalinda I Hack, Fine Arts Division Chief; Yvonne S Brown, Head, Art Section
Holdings: Vols 2500
Notes: Reference and circulating collection of books, periodicals, pamphlets, and videotapes on all aspects of the dance eg ballet, social dance, square dance, jazz and folkdance. Focus of the collection is on ballet, history, biographies of dancers, and dance instruction. Subject is supplemented by a dance videotape collection, the *Folk Dance Index* a comprehensive index to descriptions of folkdances of all nations. Special Collections: Eliza Stigler Dance Collection of 200 dance books on ballet and dance history with particular emphasis on Spanish Dance. Ruth Page Archives: small collection of memorabilia documents the career of Ms Page. Reference collection of 85 dance videotapes that document notable dance performances, from the past and present by well known dancers and dance groups. Subject concentration is that of ballet, with some examples of ethnic dance. There is alsoa collection of tapes that document Chicago area dance groups, dancers, and choreographers. A file to the contents of the tapes is available.

IN —INDIANA UNIVERSITY, School of Education, Library, Bloomington, 47401. Adele Dendy, Head Librn
Holdings: Vols (35,000) Cat Pix Slides Phonorecords Microforms
Budget:
Notes: Library has complete ERIC collection of microfiche (277,308). 2098 non-ERIC items, 226 serials, and 22,823 nonprint items (housed in educational materials center). Emphasis on recent materials; the historic collections in education are located in the Main Library. The collection is geared to graduate level studies and research. A separate Teaching Materials Center includes 10,000 elementary and secondary textbooks. The Center also includes curriculum guides, supplementary materials and 17,823 nonprint teaching aids.

MA —NEW ENGLAND CONSERVATORY OF MUSIC, Harriet M Spaulding Library, 33 Gainsborough St, Boston, 02115.
Notes: Incl 55,000 books and music scores of New England composers; the Preston Collection of Musicians' Letters; Firestone Hour Collection of Music; and Vaughn Monroe Collection of Camel Caravan.

NH —PLYMOUTH STATE COLLEGE, Lamson Library, Plymouth, 03264. Phillip Wei, Dir of Library Services
Holdings: Cat Pix Microforms Films
Budget: ($30,000)
Notes: Incl 30,000 print and 87,000 nonprint items.

NY —STATE UNIVERSITY OF NEW YORK, COLLEGE AT BUFFALO, E H Butler Library, 1300 Elmwood Ave, Buffalo, 14222. Jerome Earley, Librn
Holdings: Vols 8918 Cat Maps Pix Slides Phonorecords Audiotapes Videotapes Filmstrips
Notes: Learning Systems is a multimedia collection incl all subjects on all intellectual levels from preschool through college. It combines a circulating collection of about 5000 items and a reserve collection of about 4000 items. In addition to software of many types, the room supplies the equipment on which to use the media materials. Pocket calculators are available for in-room use, as is a Kodak Instamatic Visualmaker for the student production of slides. Student teachers in the College's education programs use the large number of educational games in the collection. Other strengths in the collection include recorded music and lectures in psychology. Separate catalog.

NY —C W POST CENTER OF LONG ISLAND UNIVERSITY, B Davis Schwartz Memorial Library, Greenvale, 11548. Manju Prasad-Rao, Media Librn
Holdings: Pix Slides Phonorecords Audiotapes Videotapes 16mm Films Filmstrips
Budget: ($12,500)
Notes: The Center, while originally established for schools of Education and Library Science with a k-12 text and trade book collection and media, now incl a circulating non-print collection for the entire campus. (8000) Separate card catalog. Incl children's trade books (17,000); k-12

AUDIOVISUAL EDUCATION AND INSTRUCTION (cont.)

textbooks (1562 series); and k-12 curriculum guides (3053).

NY —EDUCATIONAL FILM LIBRARY ASSOCIATION, Film Reference Library, 45 John St, New York, 10038. Nadine Covert, Exec Dir
Holdings: Vols (2600) Cat Pix 16mm Films Filmstrips
Budget: ($1500)
Notes: Primarily a print collection emphasizing the documentary and educational film areas, but also film as art, animation and independent film in general. Maintain film title file of over 60,000 cards (primarily educational film titles), incl credit information, running time, release date, summary, and distributor. File is a mixture of EFLA evaluations, LC cards, etc. Subject file also separates film flyers by subject or topic. Maintain festivals file (film festivals, educational film festivals, etc); a film library administration file; a filmmakers file (with bio, credits, clippings, program notes); and a vertical file (incl information on grants, distribution, showcases, film activities in the metropolitan area and in major film centers around the country). Membership organization providing telephone, mail and in-person reference. Open to the generalpublic. Do not publish a catalog, but publish annual Film Library Administration bibliography of current or noteworthy reference books for $2.00.

NY —NEW YORK STATE DIVISION OF HUMAN RIGHTS, Reference Library, Two World Trade Center, Rm 5356, New York, 10047. Rosalind Spriggs, Librn
Holdings: Uncat
Notes: This special collection contains about 500 reels of tape recordings, produced by the division.

NC —APPALACHIAN STATE UNIVERSITY, Belk Library, Instructional Materials Center, Boone, 28608. Selma P Farthing, Librn
Holdings: Vols (31,847) Cat Pix Slides Phonorecords Audiotapes Videotapes Filmstrips Microforms 16mm Films
Budget: ($10,500)
Notes: Scope of the collection is life-long learning. Serving as a working laboratory for educators at all levels, we collect materials in every format available. The Instructional Materials Center has its own card catalog, and the holdings are also listed in the library's central catalog. Collection incl textbooks, children's literature, tests and computer software.

NC —TECHNICAL INSTITUTE OF ALAMANCE, Learning Resources Center, Jimmy Kerr Rd, PO Box 623, Haw River, 27258. Ron Plummer, Coordr
Holdings: Vols (230) Cat Slides Filmstrips Microforms

OH —UNIVERSITY OF CINCINNATI MEDICAL CENTER LIBRARIES, Media Resources Center, 231 Bethesda Ave, Cincinnati, 45267. Richard C Lucier, Head; Judy Milgrim, Media Coord
Holdings: Vols 3020 Cat Slides Audiotapes Videotapes 8mm Films Filmstrips Microforms 16mm Films Charts Models
Notes: The collection of the Media Resources Center consists of non-print instructional resources in the health sciences incl basic medical science, clinical medicine, pharmacy, and continuing medical education. The Media Resources Center has all the compatible equipment for the playback of these materials. All the materials are cataloged using National Library of Medicine as the authority, and a public catalog is available for patron use. The collection also incl 2200 audio-journal tapes on different medical specialties.

†PA —UNIVERSITY OF PITTSBURGH, Graduate School of Library & Information Sciences Library, L I S Bldg, Third Fl, Pittsburgh, 15260. Jean Kindlin, Librn
Holdings: Vols
Notes: Extensive collection on the historical development of school libraries, media services, and evaluation of materials for use in all types of schools. Incl 54,800 vols, 7524 bound periodicals, 630 periodical subscriptions.

PA —SHIPPENSBURG STATE COLLEGE, Lehman Library, Media/Curricular Center, Shippensburg, 17257. Gene R Hanson, Dir
Holdings: Vols 23,700 Cat Maps Pix Slides
Budget: ($20,000)
Notes: Extensive curriculum collection.

TN —CHATTANOOGA STATE TECHNICAL COMMUNITY COLLEGE, Augusta R Kolwyk Library, 4601 Amnicola Highway, Chattanooga, 37406. Victoria Leather, Dir

WI —UNIVERSITY OF WISCONSIN, EXTENSION, Bureau of AudioVisual Instruction, PO Box 2093, Madison, 53701. Hal Riehle, Dir
Holdings: Cat 16mm Films
Notes: 16mm educational films, 7500 titles (15,000 prints). Annotated catalog: *BAVI Film Reference Guide*. Selected titles in over 600 subject areas, pre-school through college and adult levels.

AUDITING

CA —COOPERS & LYBRAND, Library, 1000 W Sixth St, Los Angeles, 90017. Joan Schlimgen, Librn; Paula Edwalds, Technical Library Asst
Holdings: Vols 1500 Cat
Notes: Incl 200 periodicals.

OH —ERNST & WHINNEY, National Office Library, 2000 National City Ctr, Cleveland, 44114. Naomi Clifford, Librn
Holdings: Vols (5000) Cat
Notes: The collection consists of books, periodicals (350), and VF materials related to technical accounting and auditing and general business management. The emphasis is on current matters, not historical developments. AICPA and FASB publications are collected *in toto*.

ON —INSTITUTE OF CHARTERED ACCOUNTANTS OF ONTARIO, The Merrilees Library, 69 Bloor St E, Toronto, M4W 1B3, Can. Theresa Wolak, Librn
Holdings: Vols 197 Cat

AUDUBON, JOHN JAMES, 1785-1851

CT —YALE UNIVERSITY, Box 1603A, Yale Station, New Haven, 06520.

NJ —PRINCETON UNIVERSITY, Library, Manuscript Collection, Nassau St, Princeton, 08540. Jean F Preston, Cur
Holdings: Vols 166 Cat Mss Pix
Notes: Mss incl 3 prose works, 25 notes for animals in the *Quadrupeds*, over fifty letters, and several watercolors and oils. See *Princeton University Library Chronicle*, v 21, p 9-88. An unpublished typescript catalog of the mss is available for consultation.

NY —BUFFALO MUSEUM OF SCIENCE, Buffalo Society of Natural Sciences, Research Library, Humboldt Park, Buffalo, 14211. Marcia T Morrison, Chief Librn
Holdings: Vols 291 // Mss
Notes: First and rare editions of books in the history of science. *Milestones of Science* describes epochal books in the history of science as represented in the library of the Buffalo Society of Natural Sciences. Catalog compiled by Ruth A Sparrow. Buffalo Society of Natural Sciences. Collection Catalog no 1. Buffalo Museum of Science, Buffalo, New York, 1972. Colored frontispiece, 308 pages (of which 207 are plates). 100 limited numbered edition; 2000 regular edition. See especially no 68 Audubonia--letters, mss, autographs.

NY —NEW YORK HISTORICAL SOCIETY, Library, 170 Central Park W, New York, 10024. James Gregory, Librn
Holdings: Mss
Notes: Incl original mss, illustrative materials, etc.

RI —BROWN UNIVERSITY, John Hay Library, 20 Prospect St, Providence, 02912. Mark N Brown, Cur Mss
Holdings: Vols 50 // Cat Mss
Notes: Collection of John James Audubon's published works on birds and quadrupeds of America, incl the elephant folio edition of *Birds of America* (Edinburgh and London: 1827-1838). Some mss material.

TX —AMON CARTER MUSEUM, 3501 Camp Bowie Blvd, PO Box 2365, Fort Worth, 76113. Jan K Muhlert, Dir; Marni Sandweiss, Cur of Photographs
Holdings: Cat Pix
Notes: Emphasis of American prints dating from the sixteenth century through the twentieth century. Includes book illustrations, documentary records of important scientific explorations, renderings of landscape and city views, and fine art prints produced by artists seeking to exploit the expressive qualities inherent in the materials and techniques of the medium. Large collections of Audubon, Currier and Ives, nineteenth century city views, and early American modern fine art prints.

AUMONT, JEAN-PIERRE

MA —BOSTON UNIVERSITY, Mugar Memorial Library, Special Collections Dept, 771 Commonwealth Ave, Boston, 02215. Howard B Gotlieb, Dir
Holdings: Cat Mss Pix

AURELIUS, MARCUS see Marcus Aurelius

AUROBINDO see Sri Aurobindo

AUSTEN, JANE

CA —STANFORD UNIVERSITY LIBRARIES, Cecil H Green Library, Stanford, 94305. Michael T Ryan, Cur
Notes: In the Charlotte Ashley Felton Memorial Library.

MD —GOUCHER COLLEGE, Julia Rogers Library, Dulaney Valley Rd, Towson, 21204.
Holdings: Vols 1000
Notes: Alberta H Burke collection of books by and about Austen and her times.

AUSTIN, DANIEL BERRY

NY —BROOKLYN PUBLIC LIBRARY, Brooklyn Collection, Grand Army Plaza, Flatbush Ave and Eastern Parkway, Brooklyn, 11238.
Notes: Over 3000 books, pamphlets, and documents. Strong collections on the six original towns which made up Brooklyn. Also microfilm copies of defunct Brooklyn newspapers as well as recent issues of local community papers. A great treasure is the *Brooklyn Daily Eagle* morgue published from 1841-1955, the morgue's contents dating from 1904. Collection incl more than 25,000 photographs of people, places, and things from 1870 to the present; nearly a quarter of the photographs are by Geroge Brainard and Daniel Berry Austin. Further, there are more than 500 Brooklyn maps from the earliest times. Incl records of the Brooklyn Mercantile Library Association.

AUSTIN, MARY HUNTER

CA —CALIFORNIA STATE UNIVERSITY, LONG BEACH, Library, Dept of Special Collections & Archives, 1250 Bellflower Blvd, Long Beach, 90840. John Ahouse, Special Collections Librn
Holdings: Vols 45
Notes: Incl complete first issues of her works.

CA —UNIVERSITY OF SAN FRANCISCO, Richard A Gleeson Library, The Countess Bernardine Murphy Donohue Rare Book Room, San Francisco, 94117. D Steven Corey, Special Collections Librn
Holdings: Vols 85
Notes: First editions, minor mss, periodical appearances, ephemera.

CA —HUNTINGTON LIBRARY, Art Gallery & Botanical Gardens, 1151 Oxford Rd, San Marino, 91108. Robert L Middlekauff, Dir; Daniel H Woodward, Librn
Holdings: Vols 75 Mss Pix
Notes: Incl 600 literary mss, 219 letters, 400 photographs and ephemera.

AUSTIN, MARY HUNTER (cont.)

NY —CORNELL UNIVERSITY LIBRARIES, Collection of Regional History, Dept of Manuscripts and Univ Archives, Ithaca, 14853.
Notes: Letter, 1847; 1 item.

VA —UNIVERSITY OF VIRGINIA, Alderman Library, Clifton Waller Barrett Collection, Charlottesville, 22901. Joan St C Crane, Cur of American Literature Collections

AUSTIN, MOSES

TX —UNIVERSITY OF TEXAS LIBRARIES, General Libraries, Barker Texas History Center, PO Box P, Austin, 78712. Don Carleton, Dir

AUSTIN, STEPHEN F.

TX —UNIVERSITY OF TEXAS LIBRARIES, General Libraries, Barker Texas History Center, PO Box P, Austin, 78712. Don Carleton, Dir
Holdings: Vols (132,000) Cat Mss Maps Pix Slides
Notes: See description of entire collection under Texas-History.

AUSTIN, TEXAS—HISTORY

MS —UNIVERSITY OF SOUTHERN MISSISSIPPI, William David McCain Graduate Library, Box 5148, Southern Sta, Hattiesburg, 39406.
Holdings: Cat Mss Pix
Notes: Correspondence and records (1847-1892) relating to Alexander Melvorne Jackson's participation in the Mexican War, his service as Secretary of the State of the New Mexico Territory (1857-1861), and his participation in the Civil War on the side of the Confederacy. Among his correspondents were Albert Gallatin Brown, Reuben Davis, Miguel A Otero, Jacob Thompson, and John Ireland. Incl are photographs of Austin, Texas, ca 1890. 1.1 cubic feet holdings.

TX —AUSTIN PUBLIC LIBRARY, Austin History Center, 810 Guadalupe Street, PO Box 2287, Austin, 78768. Audray Bateman, Cur
Holdings: Vols 6080 Cat Mss Maps Pix Slides Microforms Clippings
Budget: $242,000
Notes: The Austin History Center collection incl approx 370 periodical titles; 69,678 printed items (programs, pamphlets, etc); 2800 scrapbooks and journals; 340 taped interviews, 92,000 mss; 752 maps; 80,000 pictures; 5000 slides; 94,000 clippings. All materials are cataloged. Books are cataloged with library's general collection, but all other materials are cataloged separately. A local newspaper, started in 1871, is in the process of being indexed from the beginning and the current newspaper index is kept up-to-date. A publication program under the name of the Waterloo Press has been sponsored by the Austin History Center Association. To date, 7 books have been produced from original material in the collection. 7 paperback compilations of articles on local history appearing weekly in the local newspaper have beenpublished.

AUSTIN, WARREN

VT —UNIVERSITY OF VERMONT, Guy W Bailey/David W Howe Library, Burlington, 05405. John Buehler, Asst Dir for Special Collections

AUSTRALIA

CA —LOS ANGELES STATE & COUNTY ARBORETUM, Plant Science Library, 301 N Baldwin Ave, Arcadia, 91006. Joan DeFato, Librn
Holdings: Vols (24,000) Cat 16mm Films
Budget: ($6000)
Notes: Emphasis on woody plants, particularly of Australia and South Africa. Botany is weighted toward taxonomy rather than plant physiology.

CA —UNIVERSITY OF CALIFORNIA, SANTA CRUZ, University Library, Special Collections, Santa Cruz, 95064. Rita Bottoms, Special Collections Librn; Margaret Felts, South Pacific Collection Bibliographer
Holdings: Vols (10,000) Cat
Notes: South Pacific Collection. Monographs, rare books, serials, documents and atlases which treat of the Pacific areas of Polynesia, Melanesia, Micronesia, Australia and New Zealand, but excluding western New Guinea (Irian Jaya), the Philippines and Southeast Asia. Approximately 10 percent of the titles are multi-volume documents such as parliamentary papers, legislative journals, official yearbooks, statistical sourcebooks, laws and statutes. The collection includes an exhaustive selection of current journals and monographic series from and about the Pacific: early serials, South Pacific Commission publications, US Government and US Trust Territory publications, serials from museums, universities and scholarly societies. Chief emphasis has been placed on acquisition of the literature of history, description and travel, ethnology andanthropology, literature and literary criticism, political and constitutional histories. Other extensive holdings are in the fields of geography and maps, voyages, mission histories, mythology and folklore, art, linguistics, and science fields of natural history, environmental studies, biology, zoology, botany, geology and astronomy. Printed catalog is available. This is an on-going, growing collection.

DC —EMBASSY OF AUSTRALIA, Library, 1601 Massachusetts Ave NW, Washington, 20036. Patricia Kay, Librn
Holdings: Vols 5000 Cat
Notes: Incl Australian government publications, legislation, statistics, and Australian newspapers and clippings, including federal and state.

NY —AMERICAN MUSEUM OF NATURAL HISTORY, Library Services Dept, Central Park W & 79th St, New York, 10024. Nina J Root, Chairwoman; Mary Genett, Asst Librn for Reference Services

NY —AUSTRALIAN CONSULATE-GENERAL, Australian Information Service, Reference Library, 636 Fifth Ave, New York, 10111. Jill Hutchison, Librn; Frank Long, Officer; Lynnette Shaw, Photo Librn & Press Asst
Holdings: Vols (9000) Cat Periodicals Mss Pix Slides 16mm Film VF
Notes: Books, pamphlets, bound periodical volumes, 1300 vertical files, 260 film titles, 2000 black and white photographs and 500 col slides; incl Australian federal government legislation, statistics, ministerial press releases and publications, Australian press clippings, newspapers, and magazines. Collection incl Australian history, law, politics and government, economics, flora and fauna, geography, social conditions, arts, science, literature, and the Aboriginals.

NY —BOOKS-ACROSS-THE-SEA, The English-Speaking Union, 16 E 69 St, New York, 10021. Catherine Nolan, Librn
Holdings: Vols (6500) Cat
Budget: ($25,000)
Notes: Deals mainly with humanities and social sciences of Great Britain, Australia, New Zealand, and Canada; adult books. Collection started in 1942; current titles added through exchange.

NY —NEW YORK PUBLIC LIBRARY, Research Libraries, General Research Division, Fifth Ave & 42 St, New York, 10018. Rodney Phillips, Chief
Holdings: Vols (2,225,000) Cat Maps Pix Microforms
Budget: ($775,718)
Notes: Strong for ethnology of Australian Aborigines.

PA —PENNSYLVANIA STATE UNIVERSITY, Fred Lewis Pattee Library, University Park, 16802.
Holdings: Cat Mss Maps Pix Slides Microforms
Notes: Described in *Australiana in the Pennsylvania State University Libraries*, compiled by Bruce Sutherland, edited by Mildred Treworgy, 390 pp.

AUSTRALIA—DESCRIPTION AND TRAVEL

NY —EXPLORERS CLUB, James B Ford Memorial Library, 46 E 70 St, New York, 10021. Janet Baldwin, Librn
Holdings: Vols (24,000) Cat Maps
Notes: Additions to the collection depend upon gifts. Access by appointment only. Collections incl the Ted Banks Collection; begun by Prof Harley H Bartlett, bequeathed to American Institute for Exploration, with additions by Prof Ted Bank II, and subsequently acquired by the Explorers Club. Incl field notes, diaries, and photographs of Bank, who led more than 30 scientific expeditions to the Arctic, Aleutians, Sea of Okhotsk, Japan, Taiwan, Southeast Asia and Africa.

AUSTRALIA—DESCRIPTION AND TRAVEL—VIEWS

NM —MUSEUM OF NEW MEXICO, Photo Archives, Box 2087, Santa Fe, 87503. Arthur L Olivas, Cur; Richard Rudisill, Photo Historian
Holdings: Cat Pix Slides
Budget: ($9000)
Notes: Extensive picture collections of Australia, New Zealand, China, India and the East taken in the 19th century. The Photo Archives contain approx 250,000 items, of which 200,000 are cataloged. The primary function of the archives is preserving significant historical material, and these pictures are mainly for research rather than for general browsing.

AUSTRALIA—DISCOVERY AND EXPLORATION

ON —UNIVERSITY OF TORONTO, Thomas Fisher Rare Book Library, 120 Saint George St, Toronto, M5S 1A5, Can. Richard G Landon, Head
Notes: Sheldon Collection of Australiana, named for collector William Sheldon. Especially rich in 19th century accounts of the exploration of the South Pacific and the interior of the Australian continent. Includes narratives of exiled Canadians who took part in the Rebellion of 1837 in Canada. Includes works on colonization and settlement, the gold-rush of the mid 19th century, and on the life of the indigenous peoples. Includes literature written by Australians or about Australia.

AUSTRALIA—ETHNOLOGY

ON —UNIVERSITY OF TORONTO, Thomas Fisher Rare Book Library, 120 Saint George St, Toronto, M5S 1A5, Can. Richard G Landon, Head
Holdings: Vols 1500 Uncat
Notes: Sheldon Collection of Australiana, named for collector William Sheldon. Especially rich in 19th century accounts of the exploration of the South Pacific and the interior of the Australian continent. Includes narratives of exiled Canadians who took part in the Rebellion of 1837 in Canada. Includes works on colonization and settlement, the gold-rush of the mid 19th century, and on the life of the indigenous peoples. Includes literature written by Australians or about Australia.

AUSTRALIA—GOVERNMENT PUBLICATIONS

PA —PENNSYLVANIA STATE UNIVERSITY, Fred Lewis Pattee Library, Documents Section, University Park, 16802. Diane H Smith, Head
Notes: Depository for US Government publications; depository for Pennsylvania documents; collect United Nations and related international and intergovernmental organization publications; selected publications from Australia, Great Britain, including Parliamentary Papers; census materials; a large microform collection,

AUSTRALIA—GOVERNMENT PUBLICATIONS (cont.)

including Department of Energy (formerly ERDA, AEC), Congressional publications, Patents, OAS, UN. Incl 900,000 documents. Australian publications, cataloged books.

AUSTRALIA—HISTORY

CA —UNIVERSITY OF CALIFORNIA, LOS ANGELES, Research Library, Indo/Pacific Collection, 405 Hilgard Ave, Los Angeles, 90024. Edward Shreeves, Chairman, Bibliographers Group; Charlotte Spence, Indo/Pacific Bibliographer
Holdings: Vols (60,000) Cat Mss Maps Pix Microforms
Notes: The Pacific area collection has been developed on a combination of the research and teaching levels. It focuses on the cultural, economic, political and social history of Australia, New Zealand and the various island groups. The accounts of the early European voyagers are well represented, with the highlight being the Captain Cook collection. An effort has also been made to collect the novels, poetry, drama, etc, of Australian and New Zealand authors.

NY —AUSTRALIAN CONSULATE-GENERAL, Australian Information Service, Reference Library, 636 Fifth Ave, New York, 10111. Jill Hutchison, Librn; Frank Long, Officer; Lynnette Shaw, Photo Librn & Press Asst
Holdings: Vols (9000) Cat Periodicals Mss Pix Slides 16mm Film VF
Notes: Books, pamphlets, bound periodical volumes, 1300 vertical files, 260 film titles, 2000 black and white photographs and 500 col slides; incl Australian federal government legislation, statistics, ministerial press releases and publications, Australian press clippings, newspapers, and magazines. Collection incl Australian history, law, politics and government, economics, flora and fauna, geography, social conditions, arts, science, literature, and the Aboriginals.

PA —PENNSYLVANIA STATE UNIVERSITY, Fred Lewis Pattee Library, University Park, 16802. Stuart Forth, Dean of Libraries
Holdings: Vols (10,000) Cat Mss Maps Pix
Notes: The Pennsylvania State University has for several years had a strong interest in the South Pacific, based on Australia but extending to New Zealand and other island groups, together with an interest in voyages of exploration and scientific discovery. The collection is particularly strong in literature but extends to history, political science, the arts and humanities generally. Holdings housed in Special Collections include the Moody gift of 90 prints and paintings, press collections including the Wattle Grove press, and Fanfrolico Press publications associated with Norman Lindsay. The special collection of Australiana is dedicated to Bruce Sutherland and was described in his publication *Australiana in the PSU Libraries* (Pennsylvania State University Libraries, 1969), 390 pp.

TX —SOUTHERN METHODIST UNIVERSITY, DeGolyer Library, Box 396, SMU, Dallas, 75275. Clifton H Jones, Dir
Notes: Small collection of first editions of prominent authors.

ON —UNIVERSITY OF TORONTO, Thomas Fisher Rare Book Library, 120 Saint George St, Toronto, M5S 1A5, Can. Richard G Landon, Head
Holdings: Vols 1500 Uncat
Notes: Sheldon Collection of Australiana, named for collector William Sheldon. Especially rich in 19th century accounts of the exploration of the South Pacific and the interior of the Australian continent. Includes narratives of exiled Canadians who took part in the Rebellion of 1837 in Canada. Includes works on colonization and settlement, the gold-rush of the mid 19th century, and on the life of the indigenous peoples. Includes literature written by Australians or about Australia.

AUSTRALIAN ABORIGINES—LANGUAGES see Australian Languages and Literature

AUSTRALIAN AUTHORS see Authors, Australian

AUSTRALIAN FOLKLORE see Folklore, Australian

AUSTRALIAN LANGUAGES AND LITERATURE

CA —UNIVERSITY OF CALIFORNIA, LOS ANGELES, Research Library, Indo/Pacific Collection, 405 Hilgard Ave, Los Angeles, 90024. Edward Shreeves, Chairman, Bibliographers Group; Charlotte Spence, Indo/Pacific Bibliographer
Holdings: Vols Cat Mss Maps Pix Microforms
Notes: The Pacific area collection has been developed on a combination of the research and teaching levels. It focuses on the cultural, economic, political and social history of Australia, New Zealand and the various island groups. The accounts of the early European voyagers are well represented, with the highlight being the Captain Cook collection. An effort has also been made to collect the novels, poetry, drama, etc, of Australian and New Zealand authors.

MS —UNIVERSITY OF MISSISSIPPI, John Davis Williams Library, University, 38677.
Notes: The folklore library of Professor Kenneth S Goldstein comprises more than 12,000 vols and 4500 phonodiscs. Incl a comprehensive 3000 vol collection of editions of collected folksongs and works about the evolution of the Anglo-American folksong, as well as works treating the folklore and folk life of Britain, Ireland, Canada, and Australia. The collection contains specialized holdings on children's lore and games, Afro-American folklore, and folklore theory. The phonodisc collection is rich in examples of American, English, Scottish, and Irish revival.

NY —AUSTRALIAN CONSULATE-GENERAL, Australian Information Service, Reference Library, 636 Fifth Ave, New York, 10111. Jill Hutchison, Librn; Frank Long, Officer; Lynnette Shaw, Photo Librn & Press Asst
Holdings: Vols (9000) Cat Periodicals Mss Pix Slides 16mm Film VF
Notes: Books, pamphlets, bound periodical volumes, 1300 vertical files, 260 film titles, 2000 black and white photographs and 500 col slides; incl Australian federal government legislation, statistics, ministerial press releases and publications, Australian press clippings, newspapers, and magazines. Collection incl Australian history, law, politics and government, economics, flora and fauna, geography, social conditions, arts, science, literature, and the Aboriginals.

PA —PENNSYLVANIA STATE UNIVERSITY, Fred Lewis Pattee Library, University Park, 16802. Stuart Forth, Dean of Libraries
Holdings: Vols (5000) Cat Phonorecords Microforms
Notes: Strong in Australian Literature, lesser holdings in Canadian, Caribbean, New Zealand, Indian and West African. Special collections of African Plays, Australian Literature.

ON —UNIVERSITY OF TORONTO, Thomas Fisher Rare Book Library, 120 Saint George St, Toronto, M5S 1A5, Can. Richard G Landon, Head
Notes: Sheldon Collection of Australiana, named for collector William Sheldon. Especially rich in 19th century accounts of the exploration of the South Pacific and the interior of the Australian continent. Includes narratives of exiled Canadians who took part in the Rebellion of 1837 in Canada. Includes works on colonization and settlement, the gold-rush of the mid 19th century, and on the life of the indigenous peoples. Includes literature written by Australians or about Australia.

AUSTRIA

CA —STANFORD UNIVERSITY LIBRARIES, Cecil H Green Library, Stanford, 94305. Peter R Frank, Cur, CDP-Germanic Collection
Notes: Extensive holdings, covering all aspects of Austrian culture and history of the Habsburg Empire up to the present. Especially strong for the period of Maria Theresia and Joseph II (rare Josephinica), 19th and 20th century. Rare material in the Stanford Collection of German, Austrian and Swiss Culture, Special Collections.
Description: "Narrative on a Good Meal: A Collection of Austriaca at Stanford University Libraries" by Peter R Frank.

CT —UNIVERSITY OF CONNECTICUT, Library, Storrs, 06268. R H Schimmelpfeng, Dir of Special Collections
Holdings: Cat Microforms
Notes: 19th century drama, Expressionism, East German literature and literature since 1945 constitute major strengths in the collection. Coverage is maintained for 600 contemporary authors. Also noteworthy are holdings on popular culture of Austria and Germany, 18th and 19th century.

AB —UNIVERSITY OF ALBERTA, Cameron Library, The Bruce Peel Special Collections Room, Edmonton, T6G 2J8, Can. John Charles, Special Collections Librn
Holdings: Vols 13,500
Notes: Library of the Juridisch-Politischer Leseverein, Vienna.

AUSTRIA—HISTORY

CA —HOOVER INSTITUTION ON WAR, REVOLUTION & PEACE, Stanford University, Stanford, 94305. Milorad M Drachkovitch, Archivist
Holdings: Mss Pix
Notes: Papers of G B Stockton, 1911-59, incl correspondence, dispatches, reports, clippings, and photographs, relating to activities of the Commission for Relief in Belgium, 1915-16, and of the American Relief Administration in Austria, 1919-20; to US and Florida politics, 1924-28; to US-Austrian relations, 1930-33; and to the establishment of the Jacksonville, Florida, Naval Air Base. 11 ms boxes.

CA —STANFORD UNIVERSITY LIBRARIES, Cecil H Green Library, Stanford, 94305. Peter R Frank, Cur, CDP-Germanic Collection
Holdings: Cat
Notes: Extensive holdings, covering Austrian history of the Habsburg Empire to the present. Especially strong for the period of Maria Theresia and Joseph II, 19th and 20th century. Extremely rich in the Josephinic pamphlets (Broschuren-Literatur), broadsheets of the Napoleonic Wars and of the Revolution 1848/1849, rare periodicals. This and other rare material in the Stanford Collection of German, Austrian and Swiss Culture, Special Collections. Over 4,000 vols entered in RLIN. Description: "Narrative on a Good Meal: A Collection of Austriaca at Stanford University Libraries" by Peter R Frank.

DC —LIBRARY OF CONGRESS, Washington, 20540.
Notes: Project of a consortium to microfilm about 200,000 pp of material on Great Britain, France, Russia and Prussia, for the period 1848-1918 in the ms and documentary collections of the Austrian State Archives. The collection will incl, among others, documents on the Austro-Prussian War of 1866, the treaty negotiations between France and Italy in 1868- 1870, the Orient Question of 1877-1878, the persecution of Jews in Russia in 1882, the Congo Conference in Berlin, 1884-1887 and the British-Portuguese conflict in East Africa, 1889-1891. Copies are available at LC, the Center for Research Libraries, the Hampshire Inter-Library Centger, and the libraries of Boston College, Yale, Harvard, Duke, Stanford and the University of Virginia.

AUSTRIA—HISTORY (cont.)

IL —CENTER FOR RESEARCH LIBRARIES, 6050 S Kenwood Ave, Chicago, 60637. Donald B Simpson, Dir; Esther Smith, Collection Development Librn
Holdings: Microforms
Notes: Microfilm of selected material in the Austrian state archives relating to Great Britain, France, Russian, Prussia and Turkey for the period 1848-1918. Also microfilm of the records of the Allied Commission for Austria, 1944-1953. Complete set of Austrian parlimentary proceedings.

IN —INDIANA UNIVERSITY, Lilly Library, Seventh St, Bloomington, 47405. William R Cagle, Librn
Holdings: Vols 300 // Cat

MA —HARVARD UNIVERSITY LIBRARY, Houghton Library, Cambridge, 02138. F Thomas Noonan, Cur, Reading Room; Lawrence Dowler, Associate Librn
Holdings: Vols 2600 Cat
Notes: Austrian Revolutionary Collection. See *1848 Austrian Revolutionary Broadsides and Pamphlets,* James E Walsh (Boston: G K Hall, 1976).

MA —BOSTON COLLEGE LIBRARIES, Thomas P O'Neill Library, Chestnut Hill, 02167. John D J Slinn, Librn of the Central Library
Holdings: Uncat Microforms
Notes: This collection is being absorbed into general collection.

†NY —AUSTRIAN INSTITUTE, 11 East 52 St, New York, 10022.

AB —UNIVERSITY OF ALBERTA, Cameron Library, The Bruce Peel Special Collections Room, Edmonton, T6G 2J8, Can. John Charles, Special Collections Librn
Holdings: Vols 13,500
Notes: Library of the Juridisch-Politischer Leseverein, Vienna.

AUSTRIA—IMPRINTS

CA —STANFORD UNIVERSITY LIBRARIES, Cecil H Green Library, Stanford, 94305. Peter R Frank, Cur, CDP-Germanic Collection
Holdings: Vols (47,620) Cat Maps
Notes: An emphasis in the Rare Book Collection. Also a sizable collection of works on the Austrian booktrade and libraries. *See also* entry under Austria.

AUSTRIA—LIBRARIES

MN —SAINT JOHN'S ABBEY & UNIVERSITY, Hill Monastic Manuscript Library, Collegeville, 56321. Julian G Plante, Dir
Holdings: Vols (33,000) Cat Mss Pix Slides Microforms
Notes: Films of 33,000 codices (bound mss). The total number of codices or bound handwritten mss represents the holdings of some 140 libraries in Europe, mostly Austria and Spain, but also Italy, Hungary, Poland, Great Britain, West Germany, Belgium, Yugoslavia, France, Switzerland and the Netherlands. Cataloging of the medieval and renaissance mss in our film collection is going on constantly; requests for information are welcome; in addition to our own card catalog, sources of information contained in these microfilmed mss derive from catalogs (sometimes published, sometimes not) of each library's collection or from unpublished inventories, shelflists, etc, in the possession of the respective library; an alphabetical index to these catalogs and inventories does not always exist; persons interested in the contents of a given collection can consult these catalogs andinventories which have been photographed for our collection; some of these are now available. Scope of collection: all mss handwritten before 1600 and a few selected ones thereafter. On rare occasions mss will not be filmed, eg, when original ms is in fragile state, loaned out on exhibition at time of filming, etc. For catalogs and other tools of access, see P O Kristeller, *Latin Manuscript Books before 1600*, 3rd ed (New York: Fordham University Press, 1965).

AUSTRIA—POLITICS AND GOVERNMENT

AB —UNIVERSITY OF ALBERTA, Cameron Library, The Bruce Peel Special Collections Room, Edmonton, T6G 2J8, Can. John Charles, Special Collections Librn
Holdings: Vols 13,500
Notes: Library of the Juridisch-Politischer Leseverein, Vienna.

AUSTRIAN LITERATURE

CA —STANFORD UNIVERSITY LIBRARIES, Cecil H Green Library, Stanford, 94305. Peter R Frank, Cur, CDP-Germanic Collection
Notes: Extensive collection of works by Austrian writers and secondary literature, literary periodicals, anthologies, and the like. Baroque items, especially rich in Josephinic literature, 19th and 20th century, with rare first editions. Autographs and typescripts (P Hanke, eg). Rare material in the Stanford Collection of German, Austrian and Swiss Culture, Special Collections. Description: "Narrative on a Good Meal: A Collection of Austriaca at Stanford University Libraries" by Peter R Frank.

CT —YALE UNIVERSITY, Beinecke Rare Book & Manuscript Library, German Literature Collection, Box 1603A, Yale Sta, New Haven, 06520. Christa Sammons, Cur
Holdings: Cat Mss
Notes: The Hermann Broch Archive, incl his mss and correspondence. New acquisitions yearly. Printed inventory; Sammons, Christa, "Hermann Broch Archive, Yale University Library," *Modern Austrian Literature* 5:3/4 (1972), pp 18-69.

MA —BRANDEIS UNIVERSITY, Goldfarb Library, 415 South St, Waltham, 02154. Bessie Hahn, Dir
Notes: Betty Kurth Collection: 2 linear ft of mss and book material relating to the author's first published book written pseudonymously in Vienna at the turn of the century. Apparently the book caused a controversy at the time. This collection is unprocessed, spring 1984.

†NY —AUSTRIAN INSTITUTE, 11 East 52 St, New York, 10022.

TX —RICE UNIVERSITY, Fondren Library, 6100 S Main St, PO Box 1892, Houston, 77251. Dr Samuel M Carrington, Jr, University Librn
Holdings: //
Notes: The Stephen K Swift Collection, incl Austro-Hungarian and Austrian history (3600 items). Has complete British Intelligence Service reports on Austria, 1945-1955; original charter from the Austrian Empire to the Hungarian government (ca 1527), with signature of Charles V. Also a 360 vol history of the city of Vienna.

AUSTRIAN-AMERICAN COMPOSERS see Composers, Austrian-American

AUSTRIANS IN THE U.S.

†NY —AUSTRIAN INSTITUTE, 11 East 52 St, New York, 10022.

PA —BALCH INSTITUTE FOR ETHNIC STUDIES, Library, 18 S Seventh St, Philadelphia, 19106. R Joseph Anderson, Library Dir
Holdings: Cat Microforms

AUSTRO-HUNGARIAN EMPIRE, 1867-1918—HISTORY

TX —RICE UNIVERSITY, Fondren Library, 6100 S Main St, PO Box 1892, Houston, 77251. Dr Samuel M Carrington, Jr, University Librn
Holdings: Vols 21,500 // Cat Maps Pix
Notes: The Austro-Hungarian Empire of Franz Josef. Historical and literary materials. Incl newspapers. Downs 2706.

AUSTRO-HUNGARIAN EMPIRE NEWSPAPERS see Newspapers, Austro-Hungarian Empire

AUSTRONESIAN LANGUAGES see Malay-Polynesian Languages

AUSTRO-PRUSSIAN WAR, 1866

DC —LIBRARY OF CONGRESS, Washington, 20540.
Notes: Project of a consortium to microfilm about 200,000 pp of material on Great Britain, France, Russia and Prussia, for the period 1848-1918 in the ms and documentary collections of the Austrian State Archives. The collection will incl, among others, documents on the Austro-Prussian War of 1866, the treaty negotiations between France and Italy in 1868-1870, the Orient Question of 1877-1878, the Congo Conference in Berlin, 1884-1887 and the British-Portuguese conflict in East Africa, 1889-1891. Copies are available at LC, the Center for Research Libraries, the Hampshire Inter-Library Center, and the libraries of Boston College, Yale, Harvard, Duke, Stanford and the University of Virginia.

AUTHORS

CO —NATIONAL WRITERS CLUB LIBRARY, 1450 S Havana, Suite 620, Aurora, 80012. Donald E Bower, Dir
Holdings: Vols 1000 Uncat Mss
Budget: ($5000)
Notes: Material of specific and special interest to writers.

†MA —BOSTON UNIVERSITY, Mugar Memorial Library, Special Collections Dept, 771 Commonwealth Avenue, Boston, 02215. Howard B Gotlieb, Dir
Notes: Extensive papers of mystery and science fiction writers, and film, radio and TV writers, performers, etc. 14 years of original Little Orphan Annie art. Collections built around papers of individuals are supplemented by their printed works.

MI —GALE RESEARCH CO, Book Tower, Detroit, 48226. Annie Brewer, Librn
Holdings: Vols (65,000) Cat
Notes: Large collection of reference materials, incl computerized files used in the preparation of familiar contemporary reference books and guides to special fields.

MN —UNIVERSITY OF MINNESOTA, O Meredith Wilson Library, 309 19 Ave S, Minneapolis, 55455. Austin J McLean, Chief, Special Collections
Notes: Extensive Mss collection incl numerous plays in varying states of completion never published and a voluminous amount of material on Shakespeare, also unpublished, as well as correspondence from 20th-century American and English writers.

NY —STATE UNIVERSITY OF NEW YORK AT ALBANY, Library, Special Collections Dept, 1400 Washington Ave, Albany, 12222. Marion P Munzer, Coordr
Notes: Mss and publications by and about Hans Natonek (15 linear feet). Part of the Library's German Exile Collection. *See also* entry under Natonek, Hans

WI —UNIVERSITY OF WISCONSIN, MILWAUKEE, Library, Box 604, Milwaukee, 53201. William C Roselle, Dir
Holdings: Uncat Mss
Notes: Correspondence of the *Little Review* with prominent 20th-century writers. Restricted use: Cataloged for use in Rare Book area only. No photocopying.

AUTHORS—PORTRAITS

CA —STANFORD UNIVERSITY LIBRARIES, Cecil H Green Library, Stanford, 94305. Michael T Ryan, Cur
Holdings: Cat Pix
Notes: The Dr and Mrs Leon Kolb Portrait Collection. Over 1600 portraits (engravings, etchings, mezzotints, lithographs) of rulers, statesmen, authors, scholars and other famous personages from ancient times to the 19th century. A Catalog of the collection, compiled by Dr Susan Lenkey, was published in 1972.

IN —INDIANA UNIVERSITY, Lilly Library, Seventh St, Bloomington, 47405. William R Cagle, Librn
Holdings: Cat Mss Maps Pix
Notes: Some strength in all periods of Americana. Special emphasis on contemporary works in the following areas: War of ideas leading to the American Revolution; War of 1812; Lincoln; Indiana History; US--Plains and Rockies. Strong collection of authors' portraits.

AUTHORS, ACADIAN

NS —UNIVERSITE SAINTE-ANNE, Library Louis R Comeau, PO Box 40, Church Point, B0W 1M0, Can. Neil Boucher, Director
Holdings: Vols (600) Cat Mss Maps Pix Slides 16mm Films
Notes: Material by and about Acadians. Incl 800 pictures, 3500 slides and over 300 films.

AUTHORS, AFRICAN

DC —HOWARD UNIVERSITY, Moorland-Spingarn Research Center, 500 Howard Place NW, Washington, 20059. Clifford L Muse, Jr, Acting Dir

IL —NORTHWESTERN UNIVERSITY, Melville J Herskovits Library of African Studies, Evanston, 60201. Hans E Panofsky, Cur
Notes: Collected in depth. Incl a complete set of the recordings by and on African authors assembled by the Transcription Centre, London. Also, about 3000 books and pamphlets on African languages.

NY —NEW YORK PUBLIC LIBRARY, Donnell Foreign Language Library, 20 W 53 St, New York, 10019. Bosiljka Stevanovic, Supvr Librn
Notes: African writings in French language incl in the French collection. No separate catalog.

AUTHORS, AGRARIAN see Agrarian Writers

AUTHORS, ALABAMA

AL —WHEELER BASIN REGIONAL LIBRARY, 504 Cherry St NE, PO Box 1766, Decatur, 35602. Margarete Lange, Reference Librn
Holdings: Vols (500) Cat Maps Pix Microforms
Notes: Incl Alabama history, politics, folklore, economy, archaeology, and books by Alabama authors.

AL —JACKSONVILLE STATE UNIVERSITY, University Library, Jacksonville, 36265. Thomas Freeman, Dir, Print Media
Holdings: Vols 2500 Cat Maps
Notes: Books and materials about Alabama and about or by Alabamians.

AL —ALABAMA PUBLIC LIBRARY SERVICE, 6030 Monticello Drive, Montgomery, 36130. Anthony W Miele, Dir
Holdings: Vols 2500 Cat 16mm Films Microforms
Notes: Alabamiana collection contains books about Alabama and by Alabama authors. Incl major Alabama newspapers on microfilm.

†AL —UNIVERSITY OF ALABAMA, Amelia Gayle Gorgas Library, PO Box S, University, 35486.
Notes: The Alabama Collection contains books about Alabama; by Alabama authors; scrapbooks, pamphlets, newspapers. Such ms collections as the Manly Family, Papers, 1819-1930; Samuel Townsend, Estate papers, 1827-90; Harry Mell Ayers, 19985-1964; and the Gorgas Family, papers 1821-1920.

AUTHORS, ALBANIAN

NY —NEW YORK PUBLIC LIBRARY, Donnell Foreign Language Library, 20 W 53 St, New York, 10019. Bosiljka Stevanovic, Supvr Librn
Holdings: Vols 163 Cat
Notes: Albanian collection incl Albanian authors of Albanian expression. No separate catalog.

AUTHORS, AMERICAN

CA —AZUSA PACIFIC COLLEGE, Marshburn Memorial Library, Citrus & Alosta, Azusa, 91702. Edward Peterman, Librn
Holdings: Vols (150) Uncat
Notes: The Odo B Stade Collection of Literary First Editions. No photocopying.

CA —STANFORD UNIVERSITY LIBRARIES, Cecil H Green Library, Stanford, 94305. Michael T Ryan, Cur
Holdings: Cat Mss Pix Audiotapes
Notes: American literature beginning with the period of Hawthorne and his contemporaries and incl the first editions of 20th century authors such as Robert Frost, William Faulkner, and John Steinbeck. Also, correspondence and literary mss of numerous British and American authors, incl Jack London, Ambrose Bierce, Bruce Bliven, John Steinbeck, John Galsworthy, Wallace Stegner, Janet Lewis (Mrs Yvor Winters), Somerset Maugham, and D H Lawrence.

CT —TRINITY COLLEGE LIBRARY, Watkinson Library, 300 Summit St, Hartford, 06106. Jeffrey Kaimowitz, Cur
Holdings: Cat
Notes: Incl Edward Albee, Rupert Brooke, Robert Browning, Walter De la Mare, Charles Dickens, Emily Dickinson, William Faulkner, Robert Frost, H Rider Haggard, Nathaniel Hawthorne, Rudyard Kipling, John Masefield, Edna St Vincent Millay, Marianne Moore, Kenneth Roberts, Edwin Arlington Robinson, Wallace Stevens, Robert Louis Stevenson, Algernon Charles Swinburne, William Makepeace Thackeray, Elinor Wylie, and other 19th and 20th century English & American writers and poets.

IL —NORTHWESTERN UNIVERSITY, Library, Special Collections Dept, 1937 Sheridan Rd, Evanston, 60201. R Russell Maylone, Cur
Holdings: Vols 11,000 Cat Mss Pix
Notes: First, limited, special editions, letters, ephemera of Walt Whitman and Mark Twain; also of major 20th century writers such as Faulkner, Hemingway, Hughes, Cullen, Moore, O'Neill. Incl the D R Wagner archive and a large number of avant-garde writers such as Eigner, Levy, Bukowski, Brautigan and Dorn. 15,000 "little magazines" (titles exclusive of runs in the general library collection). A portion of the personal library of Marguerite Wilkinson containing presentation copies and works inscribed by authors incl in her anthologies.

IN —INDIANA UNIVERSITY, Lilly Library, Seventh St, Bloomington, 47405. William R Cagle, Librn
Holdings: Cat Mss Pix
Notes: Extensive collections for all periods. Strong collection of portraits of authors.

KY —KENTUCKY WESLEYAN COLLEGE LIBRARY, 3000 Frederica, Owensboro, 42301. Stuart Stiffler, Dir
Notes: The Dr and Mrs M David Orrahood Collection.

MA —BOSTON UNIVERSITY, Mugar Memorial Library, Special Collections Dept, 771 Commonwealth Ave, Boston, 02215. Howard B Gotlieb, Dir
Holdings: Cat Mss Pix
Notes: Especially strong in modern writings See also names of individual authors.

MA —JOHN F KENNEDY LIBRARY, Columbia Point on Dorchester Bay, Boston, 02125. Joan L O'Connor, Cur
Holdings: Vols (1575) Cat Mss Maps Pix Slides Audiotapes Microforms
Notes: The papers of Ernest Hemingway. Incl mss for almost all his works, published and unpublished, and a large volume of correspondence, photographs (10,000), clippings, and scrapbooks. It covers his entire life. A complete catalog is available. No photocopying.

MA —SUFFOLK UNIVERSITY, College Library, Beacon Hill, Boston, 02114. Edmund G Hamann, College Librn
Holdings: Vols 2500 Cat
Budget: $2000
Notes: Special subject emphasis on black authors related to New England.

MA —HARVARD UNIVERSITY LIBRARY, Cambridge, 02138.
Holdings: Cat Mss
Notes: Particularly strong for New England authors.

MA —GREENFIELD COMMUNITY COLLGE, The Archibald MacLeish Collection, One College Dr, Greenfield, 01301. Margaret E C Howland, Cur
Holdings: Vols 1662 Cat Mss Pix Slides Phonorecords Audiotapes Videotapes
Notes: The only authorized collection in the world devoted exclusively to the study of Archibald MacLeish, the man, his works, and his life. Contains all his published works plus clippings, galley proofs, letters, memorabilia, playbills and programs, posters, etc. Separately housed. Open by appointment.

MA —ESSEX INSTITUTE, James Duncan Phillips Library, 132-34 Essex St, Salem, 01970. Prudence K Backman, Manuscript Librn
Notes: The Frazer Clark Collection of over 8000 Hawthorne pieces, incl over 300 editions of *The Scarlet Letter.* The Institute is now said to have the world's most comprehensive collection of Hawthorne, with much correspondence from Melville, Thoreau, etc.

MO —WASHINGTON UNIVERSITY, Libraries, Campus Box 1061, Saint Louis, 63130.
Notes: A collection of primary material.

NV —UNIVERSITY OF NEVADA, RENO, University Library, Special Collections Dept, Reno, 89557. Robert E Blesse, Head
Holdings: 30,000 Entries
Notes: Modern Authors Collection. A bibliographical research collection containing the writings of 174 British and American authors of fiction and poetry who published or became prominent after 1910. All published works are collected including anthology appearances, translations, prefaces, introductions, essays, and correspondence.

NY —ADELPHI UNIVERSITY, Library, Garden City, 11530. Jerome Yavarkovsky, Dean of Libraries
Holdings: Vols 149 Cat Mss
Notes: Expatriate American writers of the 1920s and 1930s, with primary emphasis on the works of Gertrude Stein and Laura Riding Jackson.

NY —COLUMBIA UNIVERSITY LIBRARIES, Rare Book & Manuscript Library, 801 Butler Library, 535 W 114 St, New York, 10027. Kenneth A Lohf, Librn
Holdings: Mss
Notes: Forty years of literary correspondence between the Harold Matson Literary Agency. Some 75,000 pieces written between 1937 and 1980. Restricted use.

NY —NEW YORK PUBLIC LIBRARY, Research Libraries, General Research Division, Fifth Ave & 42 St, New York, 10018. Rodney Phillips, Chief
Holdings: Vols (2,225,000) Cat Maps Pix Microforms
Budget: ($775,718)

NY —NEW YORK PUBLIC LIBRARY, Berg Collection of English & American Literature, Fifth Ave & 42 St, New York, 10018. Lola L Szladits, Cur
Holdings: Vols 20,000 Cat Mss
Notes: The preface to the Collection's G K Hall catalog, 1969, (5 vols), prints an outline of history and guide to the catalog: "The Berg Collection of English and American Literature is one of America's most celebrated collections of first editions, rare books, autograph letters, and mss. Among the 20,000 printed items and 50,000 mss, covering the entire range of English and American literature, there can be found rarities considered museum pieces by the book world. Irving, Hawthorne, Emerson, Thoreau, Whitman are represented in first editions as well as in mss. Mark Twain can be studied in depth by scholars who have not only correspondence but also the original mss of *A Connecticut Yankee in King Arthur's Court* and *Following the Equator,* besides many others, to consult. The policy of the Collection has been to acquire work of contemporaries. James RussellLowell's mss are next to ms poems by Robert Lowell. Gertrude Stein's printed works are followed by those of John Steinbeck. For the following 20th-century authors, the Collection is justly famous: Arnold Bennett, Joseph Conrad, George Gissing, Thomas Hardy, John Masefield, Bernard Shaw, Virginia Woolf, Lewis Carroll, Rudyard Kipling, and Robert Browning. The Irish

AUTHORS, AMERICAN (cont.)

Literary Renaissance survives in the papers of Lady Gregory."

NC —UNIVERSITY OF NORTH CAROLINA, CHAPEL HILL, Louis Round Wilson Academic Affairs Library, Southern Historical Collection, Chapel Hill, 27514. Carolyn Wallace, Librn
Notes: Manuscripts and papers of Walker Percy. Primarily mss from work on his published novels, etc.

NC —UNIVERSITY OF NORTH CAROLINA, CHARLOTTE, J Murrey Atkins Library, UNCC Station, Charlotte, 28223. Robert F Brabham Jr, Special Collections Librn
Holdings: Vols 2000 Cat
Notes: First and other significant editions of American writers, ca 1800-ca 1950, and children's books.

NC —DUKE UNIVERSITY, William R Perkins Library, Rare Book Room, Durham, 27706. John L Sharpe, III, Cur
Notes: A collection of Duke University authors, established around 1963, with the writings of the students of William Blackburn and greatly enhanced by the gift of Professor Blackburn's collection. Represented are James Applewhite, Fred Chappell, Guy Davenport, Reynolds Price, William Styron, Frances Gray Patton, and Anne Tyler. Printed works are in the Rare Book Room and manuscripts are in the Manuscript Department.

NC —UNIVERSITY OF NORTH CAROLINA, GREENSBORO, Walter Clinton Jackson Library, Special Collections Dept, 1000 Spring Garden St, Greensboro, 27412. Emilie W Mills, Librn
Holdings: Vols 1000 Cat Mss Pix
Notes: Selection of special or limited editions, collected works and anthologies by southern writers from the 1920s, who taught part-time or participated in arts forums on this campus during the 1950s and 1960s. Count incl works in special and general collections.

OH —OHIO STATE UNIVERSITY, William Oxley Thompson Memorial Library, 1858 Neil Ave Mall, Columbus, 43210. Robert A Tibbetts, Cur of Special Collections
Notes: The Charvat Collection of American Fiction, extended by a 1982 grant to incl works published during the first quarter of the 20th century.

OH —KENT STATE UNIVERSITY, Libraries, Dept of Special Collections, Kent, 44242. Dean H Keller, Cur
Notes: Manuscripts, etc.

OR —UNIVERSITY OF OREGON LIBRARY, Special Collections Div, Eugene, 97403. Kenneth W Duckett, Curator
Holdings: Cat Mss
Notes: 250 mss collections most often containing mss and correspondence with publishers, agents, and other authors. Incl the papers of authors of adventure stories and books, children's and young people's stories and books, mystery and detective stories and books, nonfiction articles and books, romance and confession stories and books, and Western stories and books. There are also papers of dramatists, jounalists, and poets. Publication: Martin Schmitt, Comp. *Catalogue of Manuscripts in the University of Oregon Library* (Eugene: University of Oregon Books, 1971).
See also entry under Children's Literature; Fiction, Western

PA —BRYN MAWR COLLEGE, Canaday Library, Bryn Mawr, 19010. James Tanis, Dir
Notes: Books and manuscripts from the library of *New Yorker* editor Katharine S White. Rare books: Stephen Crane, Willa Cather, H D, Robert Frost, Henry James, Marianne Moore, Gertrude Stein, Eudora Welty, Walt Whitman.

PA —UNIVERSITY OF PENNSYLVANIA, Van Pelt Library, Rare Books Collection, 34 & Walnut Sts, Philadelphia, 19104. Daniel Traister, Special Collections Librn
Notes: Primarily papers of modern American authors. Approx 2000 linear feet.

RI —BROWN UNIVERSITY, John Hay Library, 20 Prospect St, Providence, 02912. Mark N Brown, Cur Mss
Holdings: / / Mss
Notes: Papers of Winfield Townley Scott, poet, essayist, Literary Editor of the *Providence Journal*, and Instructor of English at Brown. Brown class of 1931. 32 portfolios of mss, typescripts and proofs of Scott's poetry and prose, and 8 literary notebooks. About 7000 pieces of correspondence, chiefly from American writers and publishers, and incl 700 letters and copies of letters from Scott, family correspondence, clippings, photographs, and tape recordings. Correspondents include most modern American writers. Register available.

RI —BROWN UNIVERSITY, John Hay Library, 20 Prospect St, Providence, 02912. Mark N Brown, Cur Mss
Holdings: Mss
Notes: Several large ms and University Archives collections relating to American literature. See entry for the Harris Collection of American Poetry and Plays. Includes the Winfield Townley Scott Collection (qv); the Margaret Emerson Bailey, 1880-1949, Collection; the Howard Blake, 1914-1960, Collection (50 items); the Anne Charlotte Lynch Botta, 1815-1891, Collection (100 items); the Thomas Holley Chivers, 1809-1858, Collection; the Harry Crosby, 1898-1929, Collection; the George William Curtis, 1824-1892, Collection (qv) (100 items); the David Cornel DeJong, 1905-1967, Collection; the Thomas Stearns Eliot, 1888-1965, Collection (115 items); the Hugh Bernard Fox, 1932- Collection (600 items); the Richard Watson Gilder, 1844-1909, Collection; the Paul Hamilton Hayne, 1830-1866, Collection; William Dean Howells, 1837-1920, Collection (113); the Arthur Crew Inman,1895-1963, Collection; the Howard Phillips Lovecraft, 1890-1937, Collection (qv) (4000 items); as well as numerous other collections involving writers of local, regional and national literature. Part of the Harris Collection of American Poetry and Plays.

RI —BROWN UNIVERSITY, John Hay Library, Harris Collection, Prospect St, Providence, 02912. Rosemary L Cullen, Cur
Holdings: Vols (200,000) Cat Mss Pix Phonorecords Microforms
Budget: ($15,000)
Notes: The Harris Collection of American Poetry and Plays is principally composed of American and Canadian poetry and plays, 17th century-date. Extensive holdings in songsters, gift books and annuals, hymnals, pageants, broadside verse, carriers' addresses, women poets, juvenile poetry, (incl Mother Goose and *The Night Before* Christmas), sheet music with lyrics, small press publications, fine printing, black poets, "little magazines," Yiddish-American literature. All movements or schools of American poetry are represented. Incl first editions of most American poets and playwrights, notably Whitman, Poe, Wallace Stevens, Eugene O'Neill, Edward Albee, Ezra Pound, T S Eliot, William Carlos Williams, Amy Lowell, Phyllis Wheatley, Robert Frost, Allen Ginsberg, Bliss Carman, and Stephen Foster sheet music. Also incl the Saunders Walt Whitman Collection (1300 vols); the LangdonCollection of Pageants (250 vols); the Asa Cushman Collection of plays in ms and prompt copies; the MacDougall Collection of Psalters and Hymnals; 4000 plays issued by Walter H Baker Co, Boston (1890-1957); the Vaxer Collection of Yiddish Poetry, Plays and Music (1700 vols). Collections incl 200,000 vols, 30,000 broadsides, 55,000 mss, 170,000 pieces of sheet music, 450 phonorecords, and 375 microfilm reels. See *Dictionary Catalog of the Harris Collection of American Poetry and Plays* (Boston: G K Hall, 1972), 13 vols; *Supplement* (1977), 3 vols. See also, *American Poetry, 1609-1900, A Collection on Microfilm, Segment I* (1609-1820); *Segment II* (1821-1850); *Segment III* (1851-1870) (Woodbridge, Conn: Research Publications). Separate catalog.

†UT —UNIVERSITY OF UTAH, Marriott Library, Salt Lake City, 84112.
Notes: Manuscripts and papers of historian-biographer Fawn M Brodie (d 1981). Incl taped interviews with Richard Nixon, and notes, clippings, reviews, articles, and about 400 books used in her researches on Nixon, Thomas Jefferson, and Sir Richard Burton, in preparation of their biographies.

VA —GEORGE MASON UNIVERSITY, Fenwick Library, Special Collections Dept, 4400 University Drive, Fairfax, 22030. Ruth Kerns, Public Services Librn
Notes: Some 275,000 items (incl administrative, play service and research, library and production records) pertaining to the WPA Federal Theatre Project, on permanent loan from the Library of Congress.

†WA —WASHINGTON STATE UNIVERSITY, Library, Manuscripts, Archives & Special Collections, Pullman, 99164. John F Guido, Head
Holdings: Cat Mss Maps Pix
Notes: The ms collection incl business and financial records of banks, breweries, insurance, land, lumber and livestock companies, trade and commodity associations; as well as the personal and professional papers of authors, aviators, educators, engineers, farmers, historians, pioneers, politicians and scientists; especially rich in documents relating to the exploration, settlement and development of the Palouse Country, the Inland Empire, the Columbia Basin and the Pacific Northwest. Described in *Selected Manuscript Resources in the Washington State University Library* (Pullman, 1974); and other published and unpublished inventories and registers.

WI —UNIVERSITY OF WISCONSIN, MADISON, Memorial Library, British & American Language & Literature Collection, 728 State St, Madison, 53706. Yvonne Schofer, Bibliographer
Notes: Archival research collection of first and other significant editions of the works of some 237 major 20th century English and American authors; American women writers, 1620-1900, incl Harriet Beecher Stowe, Emily Dickinson, Anne Bradstreet, Kate Chopin, Louisa May Alcott and Sarah Orne Jewett.

WI —UNIVERSITY OF WISCONSIN, MILWAUKEE, Library, Box 604, Milwaukee, 53201. William C Roselle, Dir
Holdings: Uncat Mss
Notes: Correspondence of the *Little Review* with prominent 20th-century writers.
Restricted use: Cataloged for use in Rare Book area only. No photocopying.

BC —SIMON FRASER UNIVERSITY, Library, Burnaby, V5A 1S6, Can. Percilla Groves, Special Collections Librn
Holdings: Cat Mss
Notes: Mss for published and unpublished works, plus a complete collection of published books, chapbooks and broadsides by Canadian and American writers, plus correspondence and business records of the British Columbia Press run by poet and teacher Barry McKinnon from 1972 to 1980.

AUTHORS, AMERICAN INDIAN

CA —LOS ANGELES PUBLIC LIBRARY, History Dept, 630 W Fifth St, Los Angeles, 90071. Leah Simon Kornbluth, Librn
Holdings: Vols (6000) Cat Maps Phonorecords Microforms
Budget: ($85,000)

AUTHORS, AMERICAN INDIAN (cont.)

Notes: The core of the American Indian collection is in the History Dept.; it includes descriptions of contemporary life, social commentary, legends, religious thought, political studies, as well as history and biography. There are sizeable sections of material outside the dept. as well; notable are anthropology in the Science Dept., art in the Art Dept., phonograph records in Audio-Visual. The History Dept.'s older holdings are particularly strong in folklore and descriptive accounts of Indian life. There are many full sets of monographs and society publications; the Bureau of American Ethnology Reports and Bulletins, the U.S. Office of Indian Affairs Reports, California Publications in American Archaeology and Ethnology among them, and the Indian Claims Commission Decisions and Expert Testimony on microfiche. Present acquisitions are strong in books written by Indian authors and material published by smaller and regional publishers. There are old and new journal runs and the History Dept. currently subscribes to 28 Indian periodicals. An index has been started within the last 2 years dealing with such topics as land tenure and claims, fishing rights, television programs, biographical information, etc. The material indexed is from periodicals, newspapers and books.

AUTHORS, ANGLO-IRISH

MA —BOSTON COLLEGE LIBRARIES, Thomas P O'Neill Library, Irish Collection, Chestnut Hill, 02167. Ralph Coffman, Cur
Holdings: Vols (10,000) Cat Mss Maps Pix
Notes: Nearly every aspect of Irish history and literature are covered in this collection. Items of special interest are the many papers of Patrick Andrew Collins, president of the Irish Land League, and letters of Jeremiah O'Donovan Rossa, poet, editor and leader in the Fenian and related organizations. Holdings also incl a facsimile of the famous illuminated ms of the Gospels, the *Book of* Kells; a complete vol of *Malton's Views of Dublin, 1799; The Ordinance Surveys;* a complete set of the *Irish Bulletin;* and Colgan's *Acta Sanctorum Hiberniae* describing the lives of the Irish saints.

NY —LE MOYNE COLLEGE, Library, Le Moyne Heights, Syracuse, 13214. James J Simonis, Dir; Annette M Monaco, Special Colelctions Librn
Holdings: Vols (1614) // Cat Mss Slides
Notes: Incl 614 monographs and 1000 pamphlets, reprint articles, and periodical issues. Represents the Irish Literature Collection, covering the modern Irish Literature period from 1880 to 1950, and the Rev William T Noon SJ Collection. Father Noon had James Joyce as his main interest. Manuscripts of Noon's books *Joyce and* Aquinas (Yale University, 1957) and *Poetry and Prayer* (Rutgers University, 1957) are incl. There are several hundred pieces of correspondence which incl authors who had similar interests. The collection also incl his class notes and cutouts from newspapers, pamphlets, periodical articles, many of which have notes written by him. Monographs are represented by an author file. Pamphlets and reprint articles are organized in boxes and numbered numerically.

ON —MCMASTER UNIVERSITY, Mills Memorial Library, Div of Archives & Research Collections, Hamilton, L8S 4L6, Can. G R Hill, Univ Librn
Holdings: Cat Mss
Notes: The main part of this collection consists of works from the Anglo-Irish renaissance, 1890-1939. There is also a small archival collection, as well as extensive runs of some Irish periodicals.

AUTHORS, ARABIC

NY —NEW YORK PUBLIC LIBRARY, Donnell Foreign Language Library, 20 W 53 St, New York, 10019. Bosiljka Stevanovic, Supvr Librn
Holdings: Vols 617 Cat
Notes: Arabic collection incl Arabic authors of Arabic expression. No separate catalog.

AUTHORS, ARGENTINE

CT —YALE UNIVERSITY, Box 1603A, Yale Station, New Haven, 06520.
Holdings: Cat
Notes: The Tornquist Collection of Argentine authors.

AUTHORS, ARIZONA

AZ —UNIVERSITY OF ARIZONA, Library, Tucson, 85721. W David Laird, Librn
Notes: Books, periodicals, mss pertaining to Arizona incl works of Arizona authors, state and territorial documents and documents of county and municipal governments in Arizona. Attempt completeness in printed works.

AUTHORS, ARKANSAS

AR —UNIVERSITY OF ARKANSAS, Library, Special Collections Dept, Fayetteville, 72701. Michael J Dabrishus, Cur
Holdings: Vols (40,299) Cat Mss Maps Pix Phonorecords Audiotapes Microforms
Notes: Material pertaining to the political, governmental, economic, social, cultural, educational, religious, scientific and literary history of Arkansas, its people and its institutions, incl the "natural history," anthropological development, and folk traditions of the area, from prehistoric tilmes to the present. Holdings described in: Samuel A Sizer, *A Guide to Selected Manuscript Collections in the University of Arkansas Library* (Fayetteville, Ark, 1976) and in supplementary catalogs, inventories, indexes and other unpublished finding aids in the library.

AR —CENTRAL ARKANSAS LIBRARY SYSTEM, Little Rock Public Library, 700 Louisiana, Little Rock, 72201. Roberta A Muelling, Librn
Holdings: Vols 3156 Cat Maps Pix
Notes: The Arkansas Collection contains works by Arkansas authors as well as works about the state. Majority of the collection is history, biography, and literature. Smaller amounts of science material and juvenile works. An attempt is made to acquire every Arkansas-related book published.

AR —HOT SPRING COUNTY LIBRARY, Ash & E Third, Malvern, 72104. Mary L Cheatham, Librn
Holdings: Vols 507 Cat Mss Maps Pix Microforms Phonorecords Videotapes
Budget: $500
Notes: Incl material on Arkansas as well as books written by Arkansas authors. Much of the material was given by Joseph W Hill, a collector of Arkansania.

AUTHORS, ARMENIAN

NY —NEW YORK PUBLIC LIBRARY, Donnell Foreign Language Library, 20 W 53 St, New York, 10019. Bosiljka Stevanovic, Supvr Librn
Holdings: Vols 152 Cat
Notes: Armenian collection incl Armenian authors of Armenian expression. No separate catalog.

AUTHORS, AUSTRALIAN

CA —UNIVERSITY OF CALIFORNIA, LOS ANGELES, Research Library, Indo/Pacific Collection, 405 Hilgard Ave, Los Angeles, 90024. Edward Shreeves, Chairman, Bibliographers Group; Charlotte Spence, Indo/Pacific Bibliographer
Holdings: Vols Cat Mss Maps Pix Microforms
Notes: The Pacific area collection has been developed on a combination of the research and teaching levels. It focuses on the cultural, economic, political and social history of Australia, New Zealand and the various island groups. The accounts of the early European voyagers are well represented, with the highlight being the Captain Cook collection. An effort has also been made to collect the novels, poetry, drama, etc, of Australian and New Zealand authors.

AUTHORS, BAPTIST

NY —AMERICAN BAPTIST HISTORICAL SOCIETY, Samuel Colgate Baptist Historical Library, 1106 S Goodman St, Rochester, 14620.
Holdings: Vols 65,000 Mss Pix Microforms
Notes: Baptist history, theology, and authors. Annual reports (250,000), 600 mss, 300 journal subscriptions; clippings. Incl, especially, the Henry Sweetser Burrage Collection of 17th and 18th century English Baptist materials; also the Danish Baptist Conference of America Archives. Publish *Baptist Bibliography*, 24 vols.

AUTHORS, BENGALI

NY —NEW YORK PUBLIC LIBRARY, Donnell Foreign Language Library, 20 W 53 St, New York, 10019. Bosiljka Stevanovic, Supvr Librn
Holdings: Vols 664 Cat
Notes: Bengali collection incl Bengali authors of Bengali expression. No separate catalog.

AUTHORS, BLACK

CA —UNIVERSITY OF CALIFORNIA, LOS ANGELES, Research Library, Dept of Special Collections, 405 Hilgard Ave, Los Angeles, 90024. Edward Shreeves, Chairman, Bibliographers Group; David S Zeidberg, Head
Holdings: Vols 1700
Notes: Incl 1.5 linear feet of ephemera in the Arthur B Spingarn Collection of Negro literature.

DC —HOWARD UNIVERSITY, Moorland-Spingarn Research Center, 500 Howard Place NW, Washington, 20059. Clifford L Muse, Jr, Acting Dir
Holdings: Vols (106,086) Cat Mss Maps Pix Slides Phonorecords Audiotapes 16mm Films Filmstrips Microforms
Budget: ($854,753)
Notes: *The Glenn Carrington Collection: A Guide to the Books, Manuscripts, Music and Recordings* (DC MSRC, 1977). *Dictionary Catalog of the Jesse E Moorland Collection of Negro Life and History,* 9 vols and Supplement, 3 vols (Boston: G K Hall, 1970, 1977). *Dictionary Catalog of the Arthur Spingarn Collection of Negro Authors,* 2 vols (Boston: G K Hall, 1970). Guide to Processed Collections in the Manuscript Division of the Moorland-Spingarn Research Center (DC, MSRC, 1983). The Moorland-Spingran Research Center is recognized as one of the largest and most comprehensive repositories in the world for the collection, preservation and dissemination of historical materials documenting from antiquity to the present the history and culture of Black people in Africa, Europe, the Caribbean and the US. Since 1973, the Research Center has greatly expanded its facilitiesand resources and currently provides research services in all aspects of library and archival research, including manuscripts, oral history, music, prints and photographs and general library materials. The Research Center also maintains professional zerographic, micrographic, photographic and similar reproduction laboratories.

DC —UNIVERSITY OF THE DISTRICT OF COLUMBIA, Mount Vernon Campus, Library & Media Services Div, 800 Mount Vernon Pl, NW, Washington, 20001. Lottie Wright, Librn
Holdings: Vols (1352) Uncat Pix Phonorecords Audiotapes Videotapes 16mm Films Microforms
Notes: The collection consists of limited print and nonprint materials related to the rise and development of Black culture in America. Collecting emphasis is being placed

AUTHORS, BLACK (cont.)

on first editions, works of major Black authors and significant minor ones, rare books, mss, and memorabilia. In keeping with the policy of acquiring books by and about Afro-Americans, the collection also contains 462 dissertations by Black PhD candidates at universities throughout the US.

IL —CHICAGO PUBLIC LIBRARY, G Woodson Regional Library, George C Hall Branch, 9525 S Halsted, Chicago, 60628. Steven C Newsome, Cur; Hattie L Power, Regional Library Dir
Holdings: Vols 8000 Cat Mss Audiotapes Microforms
Notes: The Vivian G Harsh Collection on Afro-American History and Literature, in the George Cleveland Hall Branch of the Chicago Public Library, contains books, in print and on microfilm, periodicals, recordings, tapes, pamphlets and mss. Specializes in Afro-Americana, but contains a sizeable number of books on Africa. Also contains these noteworthy items: *The Negro in Illinois: the Illinois Writers Project Files; The Chicago Afro-American Union Analytic Catalog; Big Boy Leaves Home*, by Richard Wright (an original typewritten ms); *The Big Sea*, by Langston Hughes (3 original typewritten mss of this work). 7800 vols on microfilm.

MA —SUFFOLK UNIVERSITY, College Library, Beacon Hill, Boston, 02114. Edmund G Hamann, College Librn
Holdings: Vols (2500) Cat
Budget: ($2000)
Notes: Special subject emphasis on black authors related to New England.

MA —AMERICAN ANTIQUARIAN SOCIETY LIBRARY, 185 Salisbury St, Worcester, 01609. Marcus A McCorison, Dir & Librn
Holdings: Cat Mss Pix
Notes: Rich in early writings of Black authors and in poetry, fiction, drama, and essays inspired by them, plus numerous newspaper and magazine files of Black publications. Many rare 18th century tracts on slavery; fine collections which illuminate the Black-White relationship, as well as documents dealing with the Black heritage (soldiers, religion, folklore, music).

MO —LINCOLN UNIVERSITY, Page Library, Chestnut St, Jefferson City, 65101.
Holdings: Vols (2000) Cat Phonorecords Filmstrips
Notes: Most books are early Negro writings on slavery and the Black experience. Ethnic Studies Center housed in the library. Has special collections of books, films, filmstrips and local oral history tapes relating to ethnicity and ethnic studies.

NY —NEW YORK PUBLIC LIBRARY, Schomburg Center for Research in Black Culture, 515 Lenox Ave, New York, 10037. Catherine J Lenix Hooker, Interim Administrator
Holdings: Vols (85,000) Cat Mss Maps Pix Slides Phonorecords Audiotapes Videotapes 16mm Films Filmstrips Microforms
See also entry under Black Studies

OK —LANGSTON UNIVERSITY, M B Tolson Black Heritage Library, Langston, 73050. Rosaland Savage, Cur
Holdings: Vols (4000) Cat Mss Maps Pix Slides Phonorecords Filmstrips Microforms
Budget: ($1000)
Notes: Main objective is to fill a large gap in the Afro-American academic community and to serve as a depository of Afro-Americana for research scholars in the Southwest.

PA —BALCH INSTITUTE FOR ETHNIC STUDIES, Library, 18 S Seventh St, Philadelphia, 19106. R Joseph Anderson, Library Dir
Holdings: Vols 100 Cat

PA —CARLOW COLLEGE, Grace Library, Fifth Ave, Pittsburgh, 15213. Joan M Mitchell, Dir of Library Services
Holdings: Vols (1786) Cat
Budget: ($500)
Notes: The Black Studies Collection consists of books which describe the Black experience in Africa and the United States, with special emphasis on slavery and contemporary Black literature and sociology.

RI —BROWN UNIVERSITY, John Hay Library, Harris Collection, Prospect St, Providence, 02912. Rosemary L Cullen, Cur
Holdings: Vols (200,000) Cat Mss Phonorecords Microforms
Budget: ($15,000)
Notes: The Harris Collection of American Poetry and Play is principally composed of American and Canadian poetry and plays, 17th century-date. Extensive holdings for Black poets. All movements or schools of American poetry are represented. Incl first editions of most American poets and playwrights. Collections incl 200,000 vols, 30,000 broadsides, 55,000 mss, 170,000 pieces of sheet music, 450 phonorecords, and 375 microfilm reels. See *Dictionary Catalog of the Harris Collection of American Poetry and Plays* (Boston: G K Hall), 1972, 13 vols, *Supplement* (1977), 3 vols. See also, *American Poetry*, 1609-1900, *A collection on Microfilm, Segment I (1609-1820); Segment II (1821-1850); Segment III* (1851-1870) (Woodbridge, Conn: Research Publications). Separate catalog.

RI —PROVIDENCE PUBLIC LIBRARY, 150 Empire St, Providence, 02903. Lance J Bauer, Special Collections Librn
Notes: The Edna Frazier Memorial Collection (South Providence Branch) is the largest public library collection in Rhode Island dedicated to Black Studies. Since 1969, the Collection has served the people of this area. Adults and children concerned with the heritage of Black people in America, their roles, culture, and accomplishments, have found a wealth of information here. From its initial 900 volumes, the Collection has grown to several thousand volumes incl noted works by Black authors, reference materials, sociological studies, poetry, music, sports, biographies, and titles no longer in print. The time span covered by the Collection is 1619 to the present. It contains materials on the Black Renaissance and the early Civil Rights movements of the '30s, '40s and '50s, in addition to the more well-known movements of the '60s and '70s. A unique feature of thiscollection is the large number of children's books it contains; these reflect the same concerns and interests as the larger adult collection. Another unique feature of this collection is that it does circulate. It is available to any resident of the state as a result of the Providence Public Library's role as Rhode Island's Principal Public Library.

TX —UNIVERSITY OF TEXAS LIBRARIES, General Libraries, PO Box P, Austin, 78713. Carolyn Bucknell, Asst Dir for Collection Development
Holdings: Cat Microforms

AUTHORS, BLIND

MA —PERKINS SCHOOL FOR THE BLIND, Samuel P Hayes Research Library, 175 N Beacon St, Watertown, 02172. Kenneth A Stuckey, Research Librn
Holdings: Vols (8000) Cat Mss Maps Pix Slides Microforms
Budget: ($30,000)
Notes: The Library holdings incl an extensive collection of over 18,000 books, serials, pamphlets, and newspaper clippings concerning the nonmedical aspects of blindness, books of fiction with blind and deaf-blind characters, books written by blind and deaf-blind authors, and photographs and art pictures of the blind. Incl examples of embossed and braille books.

AUTHORS, BRITISH

CA —UNIVERSITY OF CALIFORNIA, SANTA BARBARA, Library, Dept of Special Collections, Santa Barbara, 93106. Christian F Brun, Head
Notes: Most comprehensive Maugham collection on the west coast. Assembled and donated by Raymond Toole Stott, Maugham's official bibliographer and friend. Incl nearly all early rare books, first editions, unusual variants, and a series of letters from Maugham to Stott.

IN —INDIANA UNIVERSITY, Lilly Library, Seventh St, Bloomington, 47405. William R Cagle, Librn
Holdings: Vols 100 Cat Mss

KY —KENTUCKY WESLEYAN COLLEGE LIBRARY, 3000 Frederica, Owensboro, 42301. Stuart Stiffler, Dir
Notes: The Dr and Mrs M David Orrahood Collection.

MA —HARVARD UNIVERSITY LIBRARY, Cambridge, 02138.
Notes: Incl some 90 letters from A E Housman, as well as a few books from his library.

NY —ALFRED UNIVERSITY, Herrick Memorial Library, Alfred, 14802. June E Brown, Head Librn
Notes: The Evelyn Tennyson Openhym Collection of modern British literature and social history. Papers, incl correspondence of authors concerned with the business aspects of authorship. Gift of Evelyn Tennyson Openhym of Wellsville, NY. Also, 5300 volumes of British literature.
Notes: The earlier periods of British literature are represented in the Lilly Library only by high spots such as the editions of Chaucer and Gower printed by William Caxton in the fifteenth century, first editions of Spenser, Donner, and William Lilly, and the four seventeenth-century Shakespeare folios. Beginning with John Milton, the Lilly has numerous comprehensive author collections, among the notable of which might be mentioned Daniel Defoe, Laurence Sterne, and William Wordsworth. The Lilly's nineteenth-century holdings are strong in fiction and poetry but are especially so in drama, where the collection numbers more than 16,000 plays, with extensive supporting materials. The library's collection of works by twentieth-century authors, both major and minor, is too broad to attempt a list of specific names, though special mention might be made of both W. B. Yeats and Joseph Conrad, whose works have been collected in every discoverable printed form. Among the many authors represented in the library's manuscript collections are J. M. Barrie, Arnold Bennett, Joseph Conrad, John Galsworthy, D. H. Lawrence, J. M. Synge, George Russell ("AE"), W. Sommerset Maugham, Richard Hughes, Vita Sackville West, Harold Nicholson, Dylan Thomas, Stephen Spender, Harold Pinter, Ted Hughes, and Ian Hamilton Finlay. The library also houses the archives of the British publishing firm Calder and Boyars, which included Samuel Beckett among its authors. The study of modern British literature is further supplemented by a collection of more than 800 BBC radio scripts—drama, interviews, poetry—from the archives of Douglas Cleverdon, Lancelot Sieveking, and D. G. Bridson.

AUTHORS, BULGARIAN

NY —NEW YORK PUBLIC LIBRARY, Donnell Foreign Language Library, 20 W 53 St, New York, 10019. Bosiljka Stevanovic, Supvr Librn
Holdings: Vols 134 Cat
Notes: Bulgarian collection incl Bulgarian

AUTHORS, BULGARIAN (cont.)

authors of Bulgarian expression. No separate catalog.

AUTHORS, CALIFORNIA

CA —LOS ANGELES PUBLIC LIBRARY, Fiction Dept, 630 W 5th St, Los Angeles, 90071. Helene G Mochedlover, Dept Librn
Holdings: Vols 9500 Cat
Notes: Includes almost all hardcover novels and short stories published in US and England with California setting in whole or part. Annotated author card index and indexes by period and specific locale.

CA —CONTRA COSTA COUNTY LIBRARY, 1750 Oak Park Blvd, Pleasant Hill, 94523. Barbara Potter, Librn

CA —STOCKTON-SAN JOAQUIN COUNTY PUBLIC LIBRARY, California Reference Room, 605 N El Dorado St, Stockton, 95202.
Holdings: Vols (6300) Cat Maps Phonorecords Microforms
Budget: ($2000)
Notes: Emphasis on Stockton and San Joaquin County with lesser coverage of other Northern California cities and counties. Collection consists of books, periodicals, scrapbooks, and subject index of articles from about 60 books and periodicals dealing with California. Local history collection incl Stockton and San Joaquin County special reports and studies, vertical file materials by subject, an index to local newspapers, 1850-date (1899-1925 in progress), first editions of local authors, Harriet Chalmers Adams collection (qv).

AUTHORS, CANADIAN

RI —BROWN UNIVERSITY, John Hay Library, 20 Prospect St, Providence, 02912. Mark N Brown, Cur Mss
Holdings: Vols 2000 // Cat Mss
Notes: A nearly complete collection of the published speeches, historical writings, and novels, plus some autograph letters, of John Buchan, Lord Tweedsmuir, former Governor General of Canada. Also Harris Collection of American Poetry and Plays, principally composed of American and Canadian poetry and plays, 17th century to date. Extensive holdings in songsters, gift books and annuals, hymnals, pageants, broadside verse, carriers' addresses, women poets, juvenile poetry (incl Mother Goose and *The Night before* Christmas), sheet music with lyrics, small press publications, fine printing, black poets, "little magazines," Yiddish-American literature. All movements or schools of American poetry are represented. Incl first editions of most American poets and playwrights, notably Whitman, Poe, Wallace Stevens, Eugene O'Neill, Edward Albee, Ezra Pound, T S Eliot,William Carlos Williams, Amy Lowell, Phyllis Wheatley, Robert Frost, Allen Ginsberg, Bliss Carman, and Stephen Foster sheet music.

RI —BROWN UNIVERSITY, John Hay Library, Harris Collection, Prospect St, Providence, 02912. Rosemary L Cullen, Cur
Holdings: Vols (200,000) Cat Mss Phonorecords Microforms
Budget: ($15,000)
Notes: The Harris Collection of American Poetry and Plays is principally composed of American and Canadian poetry and plays, 17th century-date. Extensive holdings in songsters, gift books and annuals, hymnals, pageants, broadside verse, carriers' addresses, women poets, juvenile poetry (incl Mother Goose and *The Night Before* Christmas), sheet music with lyrics, small press publications, fine printing, black poets, "little magazines," Yiddish-American literature. All movements or schools of American poetry are represented. Collections incl 200,000 vols, 30,000 broadsides, 55,000 mss, 170,000 pieces of sheet music, 450 phonorecords, and 375 microfilm reels. See *Dictionary Catalog of the Harris Collection of American Poetry and Plays* (Boston: G K Hall, 1972), 13 vols; *Supplement* (1977), 3 vols. See also, *American Poetry*, 1609-1900,*A Collection on Microfilm, Segment I (1609-1820); Segment II (1821-1850); Segment III (1851-*1870) (Woodbridge, Conn: Research Publications). Separate catalog.

AB —UNIVERSITY OF CALGARY, Libraries, Special Collections Div, 2500 University Dr, Calgary, T2N 1N4, Can.
Holdings: Vols (5000) Cat Mss
Notes: The Division has extensive collections of the papers of modern Canadian authors (qv individuals), incl Hugh MacLennan, Mordecai Richler, Brian Moore, W O Mitchell, Cliff Faulknor, Christie Harris, Robert Kroetsch, Rudy Wiebe, Claude Peloquin, George Ryga, Andre Langevin, Malcolm Ross, Bruce Hutchison, John Mellor, Grant MacEwan, James Gray, Ernest Watkins, Len Peterson, Michael Cook, and Joanna Glass. The papers of musician Morris Surdin contain hundreds of Canadian Broadcasting Corporation scripts, and constitute a valuable addition to the purely literary ms collections. The Division's holdings also incl collections of scores by Canadian musicians R Murray Schafer and Bruce Mather. In addition, the records of the following Canadian publishing houses are on deposit: E C W Press, Hancock House Publishers Ltd and Coach House Press. The Division alsohouses small collections of letters and mss of Canadian poets such as Earle Birney and George Bowering as well as the archives of the literary periodicals *Tish, Imago, Ariel, Descant, Canadian Review Magazine,* and *Canadian Short Story Magazine.* The ms collections are complemented by a book collection of some 5000 vols.

BC —SIMON FRASER UNIVERSITY, Library, Burnaby, V5A 1S6, Can. Percilla Groves, Special Collections Librn
Holdings: Cat Mss
Notes: Mss for published and unpublished works, plus a complete collection of published books, chapbooks and broadsides by Canadian and American writers, plus correspondence and business records of the British Columbia Press run by poet and teacher Barry McKinnon from 1972 to 1980.

BC —VANCOUVER PUBLIC LIBRARY, Language & Literature Div, 750 Burrard St, Vancouver, V6Z 1X5, Can. B Kinnear, Head
Notes: General collection of poetry, drama criticism, novels, pamphlets. Index files of author biographies, poetry in periodicals, criticism in periodicals; also poetry index, both compiled by the staff to books unindexed periodicals. Partially cataloged. Also incl audiotapes.

BC —UNIVERSITY OF VICTORIA, McPherson Library, Victoria, V8W 3H5, Can.

MB —UNIVERSITY OF MANITOBA, Elizabeth Dafoe Library, Archives and Special Collections Dept, Winnipeg, R3T 2N2, Can. Richard E Bennett, Dept Head; Corrado A Santoro, Reference Archivist
Notes: Bertram R Brooker Papers. Correspondence, diaries and daily notations, dramas, both published and unpublished, short stories and essays, and other literary works. Also 16 photographs mainly of Brooker, his family and fellow artists.

NB —LEGISLATIVE LIBRARY, Legislative Bldg, Queen St, PO Box 6000, Fredericton, E3B 5H1, Can. Jocelyne LeBel, Dir
Holdings: Cat Pix Microforms
Notes: Incl also over 2000 items written by New Brunswickers on or about New Brunswick; with a full analytical catalog of New Brunswickiana. Largest collection of New Brunswick government documents.

NF —MEMORIAL UNIVERSITY OF NEWFOUNDLAND, University Library, Centre for Newfoundland Studies, Elizabeth Ave, Saint John's, A1C 5S7, Can. Anne Hart, Head
Holdings: Vols (48,000) Cat Maps Microforms
Budget: ($50,000)
Notes: Materials about Newfoundland, by Newfoundlanders, or published in Newfoundland, incl Labrador. Also, Saint Pierre and Miquelon. Bibliography of Newfoundland materials is being compiled (now over 7,000 items).

NS —DALHOUSIE UNIVERSITY LIBRARY, Halifax, B3H 4H8, Can.
Holdings: Vols (10,000) Cat
Notes: Extensive collection of Canadian small press publications with special strengths in poetry, drama, little magazines, poetry broadsides, and Atlantic Canada creative writing. Good holdings in various early Canadian literary periodicals and early Canadian small publishers, but main focus from 1970 to present. Also, a representative collection of the British, American and Canadian first editions and later editions of the important and popular humorist and Nova Scotian historian, Thomas Chandler Haliburton. Critical works, biographies of Haliburton, and prints of his major literary creation "Sam Slick" are incl in the collection.

NS —LEGISLATIVE LIBRARY OF NOVA SCOTIA, Province House, Halifax, B3J 2P8, Can. Ilga Leja, Librn
Holdings: Vols 11,000 Cat Mss Maps Pix Microforms
Notes: Part of the library's mandate is to collect all material relating to Nova Scotia and by Nova Scotia authors. This material is shelved separately from the rest of the collection (68,000 vols) and does not include Nova Scotia government documents, which are not cataloged under Dewey, as is the rest of the collection. The material is available through interlibrary loan whenever feasible.

ON —YORK UNIVERSITY, Scott Library, Downsview, M3J 2R2, Can. Hartwell Bowsfield, University Archivist
Notes: Papers of Margaret Laurence incl letters from readers, research notes, manuscripts of articles and stories, copies of lectures and addresses, diaries, financial records, and correspondence with contemporary Canadian authors.

ON —LONDON PUBLIC LIBRARIES & MUSEUMS, London Room, 305 Queen's Ave, London, N6B 1X2, Can. W Glen Curnoe, Librn
Holdings: Cat Mss Maps Pix Slides Phonorecords Audiotapes 16mm Films Microforms
Budget: ($3700)
Notes: History of Ontario, with emphasis on London and region, from early 19th century onward. Separate catalog books, films and microforms. Various subject indexes to materials. Special interest in London, Ontario authors and publishers.

ON —NATIONAL LIBRARY OF CANADA, 395 Wellington St, Ottawa, K1A 0N4, Can. Andre Preibish, Dir
Notes: Literary Manuscripts collection contains papers of several important Canadian authors writing in English and/or French eg Clare Bice (1909-1976), noted author and illustrator of children's books; Andre Giroux, novelist, writer for television and broadcaster; Roger Lemelin, well-known author of Au pied de la pente douce, Les Plouffe, and Pierre le magnifique; Gabrielle Roy (1909-1983), author of many novels, including Bonheur d'occasion, La Petite Poule d'Eau and Rue Deschambault; Laura Goodman Salverson (1890-1970), writer, public speaker and teacher; Phyllis Webb, poet.

ON —OTTAWA PUBLIC LIBRARY, 120 Metcalfe St, Ottawa, K1P 5M2, Can. Thomas Rooney, Librn
Notes: Ottawa subjects, imprints and authors.

PE —CONFEDERATION CENTRE PUBLIC LIBRARY, PO Box 7000, Charlottestown, C1A 8G8, Can. Elinor Vass, Cur of Special Collection
Holdings: Vols (1300) Cat Phonorecords Microforms
Notes: Material pertaining to PEI and works by PEI authors. The book and pamphlet collection of approximately 1300 items is cataloged and a separate catalogue is maintained. The microforms incl Prince Edward Island newspapers dating from 1792, PEI government documents and publications dating from 1770, 3 early census records, 1841, 1861 (incomplete) and 1881 at the

AUTHORS, CANADIAN (cont.)

Public Archives, PEI. The Prince Edward Island Heritage Foundation is preparing a vital statistics index (births, marriages, deaths) and a complete names index for the Island newspapers.

PQ —UNIVERSITY OF MONTREAL, Service des Bibliotheques, CP 6128, Succursale A, Montreal, H3C 3J7, Can. Arlette Joffe-Nicodeme, Directeur General
Holdings: Vols 4000 / /
Notes: The Louis Melzack Collection of Canadian Books and Manuscripts.

AUTHORS, CARIBBEAN

DC —HOWARD UNIVERSITY, Moorland-Spingarn Research Center, 500 Howard Place NW, Washington, 20059. Clifford L Muse, Jr, Acting Dir

AUTHORS, CATHOLIC

DC —GEORGETOWN UNIVERSITY, Library, Special Collections Div, 37 & O Sts NW, Washington, 20057. George M Barringer, Special Collections Librn; Nicholas B Sheetz, Mss Librn
Holdings: Vols 3000 Cat
Notes: Incl English Catholic works to 1700; American Catholic imprints to 1831; Belloc, Chesterton, and other more recent Catholic men of letters. See Downs Supplement 345.

IL —LOYOLA UNIVERSITY OF CHICAGO, E M Cudahy Memorial Library, 6525 N Sheridan Rd, Chicago, 60626.
Holdings: 300 Vols
Notes: A collection of Paul Claudel's works.

MA —BOSTON COLLEGE LIBRARIES, Chestnut Hill, 02167.
Notes: Personal library and papers of Hilaire Belloc (1870-1953), and first editions of his books. The largest collection of Belloc, incl materials that supported his literary and historical researches, an unpublished autobiography, and a wide correspondence with hundreds of notable acquintances, largely British authors, many of them Roman Catholics (since Belloc was one of England's most prominent among them).

MA —BOSTON COLLEGE LIBRARIES, Thomas P O'Neill Library, Chestnut Hill, 02167. Frank J Seegraber, Special Collections Librn
Holdings: Vols 1300 Cat Mss Pix Phonorecords Audiotapes Microforms
Notes: This, the most complete collection of Thompsoniana in existence, incl notebooks, mss, letters, and rare editions, and collateral material relating to poet, his times and his work. The notebooks are the chief source of clues to the identification of 300 of Thompson's unsigned contributions to periodicals. *An Account of the Books and Manuscripts of Francis Thompson,* ed by Rev Terence L Connolly (Boston College, 1937). Works of Wilfrid and Alice Meynell and their children, Viola, Sir Francis, and Everard, are incl in this collection. The items give a well-rounded view of this remarkable family as poets, fiction writers, essayists, biographers, prefacers, and editors. This collection incl mss, poems, correspondence, articles, and book reviews by Coventry Patmore, an English poet, essayist, and critic, and a good friend of Francis Thompson. Among thecorrespondents are Robert Browning, Alfred Tennyson, Matthew Arnold, Ralph Waldo Emerson, Nathaniel Hawthorne, Thomas Carlyle, and William Makepeace Thackeray. For reference use only, by arrangement with librarian.

AUTHORS, CHICANO

TX —UNIVERSITY OF TEXAS LIBRARIES, Nettie Lee Benson Latin American Collection, Sid Richardson Hall 1.109, Austin, 78712. Laura Gutierrez-Witt, Head Librn
Holdings: Vols (450,000) Cat Mss Maps Pix Slides Phonorecords Videotapes 16mm Films Filmstrips Microforms VF
Notes: The Mexican American Library Project has, since 1974, collected materials relating to all aspects of Spanish-speaking people in the US, with emphasis on Mexican Americans.
See also entry under Latin America

AUTHORS, CHINESE

NY —NEW YORK PUBLIC LIBRARY, Donnell Foreign Language Library, 20 W 53 St, New York, 10019. Bosiljka Stevanovic, Supvr Librn
Holdings: Vols 2273 Cat
Notes: Chinese collection incl Chinese authors of Chinese expression. No separate catalog.

AUTHORS, COLORADO

CO —FORT MORGAN PUBLIC LIBRARY, 414 Main, Fort Morgan, 80701. Jo Ann Kruglet, Dir
Holdings: Vols 500
Notes: Lute Johnson Collection contains books about Colorado by Colorado authors, many autographed, written at the turn of the century. Noncirculating. No photocopying. Also, 40 oral history tapes, collected during the Bicentennial, predominately about the history of Fort Morgan and Morgan County, Colorado.

AUTHORS, CONNECTICUT

CT —HARTFORD PUBLIC LIBRARY, Reference & General Reading Dept, 500 Main St, Hartford, 06103. Beverly A Loughlin, Admin Asst
Holdings: Vols (3000) Cat Mss Maps Pix Slides Phonorecords Audiotapes Videotapes 16mm Films
Notes: The Hartford Collection is a noncirculating multimedia collection encompassing Hartford: histories of businesses, churches, schools, and organizations; Hartford authors; and Hartford imprints. Separate catalog.

AUTHORS, CROATIAN

NY —NEW YORK PUBLIC LIBRARY, Donnell Foreign Language Library, 20 W 53 St, New York, 10019. Bosiljka Stevanovic, Supvr Librn
Holdings: Vols 124 Cat
Notes: Croatian collection incl Croatian authors of Croatian expression. No separate catalog.

AUTHORS, CUBAN

NY —NEW YORK PUBLIC LIBRARY, Donnell Foreign Language Library, 20 W 53 St, New York, 10019. Bosiljka Stevanovic, Supvr Librn

AUTHORS, DANISH

NY —NEW YORK PUBLIC LIBRARY, Donnell Foreign Language Library, 20 W 53 St, New York, 10019. Bosiljka Stevanovic, Supvr Librn
Holdings: Vols 364 Cat
Notes: Danish collection incl Danish authors of Danish expression. No separate catalog.

AUTHORS, DISTRICT OF COLUMBIA

DC —HOWARD UNIVERSITY, Moorland-Spingarn Research Center, 500 Howard Place NW, Washington, 20059. Clifford L Muse, Jr, Acting Dir

AUTHORS, DUTCH

NY —NEW YORK PUBLIC LIBRARY, Donnell Foreign Language Library, 20 W 53 St, New York, 10019. Bosiljka Stevanovic, Supvr Librn
Holdings: Vols 480 Cat
Notes: Dutch collection incl Dutch authors of Dutch expression. No separate catalog.

AUTHORS, ENGLISH

CA —FRANCIS BACON LIBRARY, 655 N Dartmouth Ave, Claremont, 91711. Elizabeth S Wrigley, Dir
Holdings: Vols 4000 Cat Mss Maps Pix Microforms
Notes: One of the widest collections of Bacon and Baconiana extant with secondary material, histories, chronicles, etc, of contemporary writers of the Elizabethan and Jacobean periods of English history; also journal articles, theses, and dissertations. Over 1000 titles in the STC and Wing periods; detailed collations of these vols published. Incl phonotapes. Published *Concordance to the Essays of Francis Bacon* (Detroit: Gale Research Co, 1973).

CA —STANFORD UNIVERSITY LIBRARIES, Cecil H Green Library, Stanford, 94305. Michael T Ryan, Cur
Holdings: Cat Mss Pix Audiotapes
Notes: The Charlotte Ashley Felton Memorial Library. English and American literature of the 19th and 20th centuries: American literature beginning with the period of Hawthorne and his contemporaries and incl the first editions of 20th century authors such as Robert Frost, William Faulkner, and John Steinbeck. The collection of British literature begins with Jane Austen's novels and the poetry of Lord Byron, Shelley, and Keats, and incl 20th century authors such as Somerset Maugham, Lawrence Durrell, D H Lawrence and Anthony Powell.

CT —LEE ASH, (personal collection), 66 Humiston Dr, Bethany, 06525.
Notes: A large collection of Baron Corvo's 1st editions, English and American, incl *Tarcissus,* and what is probably the only signed Corvo painting in the Western Hemisphere. Much ephemeral material and books, etc relating to Corvo. No mss materials. Also collections of Mervyn Peake, Quiller-Couch, Percy H Fitzgerald, Gavin Maxwell, etc.

CT —TRINITY COLLEGE LIBRARY, Watkinson Library, 300 Summit St, Hartford, 06106. Jeffrey Kaimowitz, Cur
Holdings: Cat
Notes: Incl Rupert Brooke, Robert Browning, Walter De la Mare, Charles Dickens, H Rider Haggard, Rudyard Kipling, John Masefield, Robert Louis Stevenson, Algernon Charles Swinburne, William Makepeace Thackeray, and other 19th and 20th century English and American writers and poets.

IL —NORTHWESTERN UNIVERSITY, Library, Special Collections Dept, 1937 Sheridan Rd, Evanston, 60201. R Russell Maylone, Cur
Holdings: Vols 9000 Cat Mss
Notes: First, limited, special editions, letters, ephemera of major 20th century Anglo-Irish and English writers such as James Joyce, W B Yeats, T S Eliot, W H Auden and Lawrence Durrell, as well as representative minor writers. Correspondence files of James B Pinker & Sons, literary agents: 50,000 pieces, 1900-1934 incl.

IN —INDIANA UNIVERSITY, Lilly Library, Seventh St, Bloomington, 47405. William R Cagle, Librn
Holdings: Cat Mss
Notes: The

MA —BOSTON UNIVERSITY, Mugar Memorial Library, Special Collections Dept, 771 Commonwealth Ave, Boston, 02215. Howard B Gotlieb, Dir
Holdings: Cat Mss Pix
Notes: Especially strong in modern writings.

MA —BOSTON COLLEGE LIBRARIES, Chestnut Hill, 02167.
Notes: Personal library and papers of Hilaire Belloc (1870-1953), and first editions of his books. The largest collection of Belloc, incl materials that supported his literary and historical researches, an unpublished autobiography, and a wide correspondence with hundreds of notable acquintances, largely British authors, many of them Roman Catholics (since Belloc was one of England's most prominent among them).

MA —BOSTON COLLEGE LIBRARIES, Thomas P O'Neill Library, Chestnut Hill, 02167. Frank J Seegraber, Special Collections Librn
Holdings: Vols 1300 Cat Mss Pix

AUTHORS, ENGLISH (cont.)

Phonorecords Audiotapes Microforms
Notes: This, the most complete collection of Thompsoniana in existence, incl notebooks, mss, letters, and rare editions, and collateral material relating to poet, his times and his work. The notebooks are the chief source of clues to the identification of 300 of Thompson's unsigned contributions to periodicals. *An Account of the Books and Manuscripts of Francis Thompson,* ed by Rev Terence L Connolly (Boston College, 1937). Works of Wilfrid and Alice Meynell and their children, Viola, Sir Francis, and Everard, are incl in this collection. The items give a well-rounded view of this remarkable family as poets, fiction writers, essayists, biographers, prefacers, and editors. This collection incl mss, poems, correspondence, articles, and book reviews by Coventry Patmore, an English poet, essayist, and critic, and a good friend of Francis Thompson. Among thecorrespondents are Robert Browning, Alfred Tennyson, Matthew Arnold, Ralph Waldo Emerson, Nathaniel Hawthorne, Thomas Carlyle, and William Makepeace Thackeray. For reference use only, by arrangement with librarian.

MO —WASHINGTON UNIVERSITY, Libraries, Special Collections Dept, Campus Box 1061, St Louis, 63130.
Notes: A major collection, incl books, mss, correspondence, literary papers, photographs, etc. Described in *Special Collections: an Annotated Guide to the Holdings of the Manuscript Division and the University Archives and Research Collection.*

NV —UNIVERSITY OF NEVADA, RENO, University Library, Special Collections Dept, Reno, 89557. Robert E Blesse, Head
Holdings: 30,000 Entries
Notes: Modern Authors Collection. A bibliographical research collection containing the writings of 174 British and American authors of fiction and poetry who published or became prominent after 1910. All published works are collected including anthology appearances, translations, prefaces, introductions, essays, and correspondence.

NY —NEW YORK PUBLIC LIBRARY, Research Libraries, General Research Division, Fifth Ave & 42 St, New York, 10018. Rodney Phillips, Chief
Holdings: Vols (2,225,000) Cat Maps Pix Microforms
Budget: ($775,718)

NY —NEW YORK PUBLIC LIBRARY, Berg Collection of English & American Literature, Fifth Ave & 42 St, New York, 10018. Lola L Szladits, Cur
Holdings: Vols 20,000 Cat Mss
Notes: The preface to the Collection's G K Hall catalog, 1969, (5 vols), prints an outline of history and guide to the catalog: "The Berg Collection of English and American Literature is one of America's most celebrated collections of first editions, rare books, autograph letters, and mss. Among the 20,000 printed items and 50,000 mss, covering the entire range of English and American literature, there can be found rarities considered museum pieces by the book world. Irving, Hawthorne, Emerson, Thoreau, Whitman are represented in first editions as well as in mss. Mark Twain can be studied in depth by scholars who have not only correspondence but also the original mss of *A Connecticut Yankee in King Arthur's Court* and *Following the Equator,* besides many others, to consult. The policy of the Collection has been to acquire work of contemporaries. James RussellLowell's mss are next to ms poems by Robert Lowell. Gertrude Stein's printed works are followed by those of John Steinbeck. For the following 20th-century authors, the Collection is justly famous: Arnold Bennett, Joseph Conrad, George Gissing, Thomas Hardy, John Masefield, Bernard Shaw, Virginia Woolf, Lewis Carroll, Rudyard Kipling, and Robert Browning. The Irish Literary Renaissance survives in the papers of Lady Gregory."

NY —UNIVERSITY OF ROCHESTER, Rush Rhees Library, Department of Rare Books and Special Collections, Rochester, 14627. Peter Dzwonkoski, Librn
Holdings: Vols 1200 // Cat
Notes: Collection of British authors published by the Leipzig firm of Bernhard Tauchnitz from 1840-1908. Much of the collection was originally in the library of the Kings of Hanover, and those vols are bound in cloth with the arms of the Royal Family. No photocopying permitted.

PA —BRYN MAWR COLLEGE, Canaday Library, Bryn Mawr, 19010. James Tanis, Dir
Notes: The Adelman Collection incl significant manuscript and printed material of the following authors: A E Housman, Laurence Housman, Ralph Hodgson, John Keats. Lewis Carroll: original drawings for and printed editions of *The Hunting of the* Snark. Rare books: Joseph Conrad, Walter De La Mare, James Hanley, W H Hudson, Rudyard Kipling, John Masefield, William Morris, Forrest Reid, Frank Swinnerton, Anthony Trollope, Virginia Woolf, William Butler Yeats.

PA —HAVERFORD COLLEGE, Magill Library, Quaker Collection, Haverford, 19041. Edwin B Bonner, Librn & Cur
Holdings: Vols 105 Cat
Notes: Rare books and mss of the English Renaissance period, especially contemporaries of Shakespeare.

PA —FREE LIBRARY OF PHILADELPHIA, Rare Book Dept, Logan Sq, Philadelphia, 19103. Marie E Korey, Rare Book Librn
Holdings: Cat
Notes: A collection of 400 selected first and early editions of major English writers incl J M Barrie, George Borrow, Robert and Elizabeth Barrett Browning, John Keats, John Milton, Stephen Phillips, Arthur W Pinaro, Robert Louis Stevenson, Alfred Lord Tennyson, William Makepeace Thackeray, and Anthony Trollope.

RI —BROWN UNIVERSITY, John Hay Library, 20 Prospect St, Providence, 02912. Mark N Brown, Cur Mss
Holdings: // Mss
Notes: The Koopman Collection, collected and donated by Philip D Sherman in memory of Harry Lyman Koopman. Incl Sherman's correspondence and private collection of more than 2000 mss relating to Victorian writers.

WI —UNIVERSITY OF WISCONSIN, MADISON, Memorial Library, British & American Language & Literature Collection, 728 State St, Madison, 53706. Yvonne Schofer, Bibliographer
Notes: Archival research collection of first and other significant editions of the works of some 237 major Twentieth Century English and American authors.

NS —DALHOUSIE UNIVERSITY LIBRARY, Halifax, B3H 4H8, Can.
Notes: The collection of numerous editions from Dr Henry Hicks, past president of Dalhousie.

AUTHORS, ESTONIAN

NY —NEW YORK PUBLIC LIBRARY, Donnell Foreign Language Library, 20 W 53 St, New York, 10019. Bosiljka Stevanovic, Supvr Librn
Holdings: Vols 186 Cat
Notes: Estonian collection incl Estonian authors of Estonian expression. No separate catalog.

AUTHORS, EXPATRIATE see Expatriate Writers, American

AUTHORS, FEMALE see Women Authors

AUTHORS, FINNISH

NY —NEW YORK PUBLIC LIBRARY, Donnell Foreign Language Library, 20 W 53 St, New York, 10019. Bosiljka Stevanovic, Supvr Librn
Holdings: Vols 274 Cat
Notes: Finnish collection incl Finnish authors of Finnish expression. No separate catalog.

AUTHORS, FLORIDA

FL —UNIVERSITY OF FLORIDA, Libraries, Special Collections, W University Ave, Gainesville, 32611. Sidney Ives, Librn & Rare Books
Holdings: Vols (8000) Cat Mss
Notes: Fiction by Florida writers, in ms when possible to obtain.

†FL —ORLANDO PUBLIC LIBRARY, Orlando, 32801.
Notes: Books by Floridians; books on Florida.

FL —FLORIDA STATE UNIVERSITY, Robert Manning Strozier Library, Special Collections Dept, Tallahassee, 32306. Opal M Free, Head, Special Collections
Holdings: Vols (12,301) Cat Microforms VF
Notes: Incl books by Floridians and about all aspects of Florida's development. Also fiction with Florida settings. Vertical file of 138,367 clippings and pamphlets. Non-circulating.

AUTHORS, FRENCH

IL —LOYOLA UNIVERSITY OF CHICAGO, E M Cudahy Memorial Library, 6525 N Sheridan Rd, Chicago, 60626.
Holdings: 300 Vols
Notes: A collection of Paul Claudel's works.

IN —INDIANA UNIVERSITY, Lilly Library, Seventh St, Bloomington, 47405. William R Cagle, Librn
Holdings: // Cat Mss Pix
Notes: Extensive collections of first editions from eighteenth to twentieth centuries. Literary papers and correspondence of Judith Jeanne Cladel, 1869-1927 (1589 items); letters of Jean Giono, 1895-1970, including the autograph manuscript of *Angelique* (1028 items); letters of Alexandre Dumas, 1824-1895 (307 items); letters of Henry Milon de Montherlant, 1895-1972 (111 items); letters of Romain Rolland, 1866-1944 (119 items); Mary Margaret Barr Koon Collection about Voltaire.

NY —FRENCH INSTITUTE-ALLIANCE FRANCAISE, Library, 22 E 60 St, New York, 10022. Fred J Gitner, Librn
Holdings: Vols (40,000) Cat Phonorecords Audiotapes
Budget: ($23,000)
Notes: Special collections of art books, books about Paris. Rich in bibliographical, biographical and lexicographical works. Standard editions of all major French authors. Name has been changed from French Institute in the United States Library since merger with the Alliance Francaise de New York.

NY —NEW YORK PUBLIC LIBRARY, Donnell Foreign Language Library, 20 W 53 St, New York, 10019. Bosiljka Stevanovic, Supvr Librn
Holdings: Vols 9420 Cat
Notes: Incl Haitian and African authors of French expression. No separate catalog.

UT —BRIGHAM YOUNG UNIVERSITY, Harold B Lee Library, Unversity Hill, Provo, 84602. Sterling Albrecht, Dir
Notes: Incl memorabilia.

AUTHORS, GEORGIA

GA —CARNEGIE LIBRARY, Henderson Room, 607 Broad St, Rome, 30161. Beatrice Millican, Librn
Holdings: Vols (2500) Cat 16mm Films
Budget: ($2700)
Notes: Our Georgia Collection is a collection of books about Georgia and by Georgians. We have a fiction and biography section with the histories of Georgia and ca 110 individual county histories. We also subscribe to the Atlanta *Constitution* and Rome, Georgia newspapers. We have the Rome *News-Tribune* on microfilm, 1951 to date, from 1921-1949 bound, and some few earlier Rome newspapers on microfilm.

AUTHORS, GERMAN

CA —STANFORD UNIVERSITY LIBRARIES, Cecil H Green Library,

AUTHORS, GERMAN (cont.)

Stanford, 94305. Peter R Frank, Cur, CDP-Germanic Collection
Holdings: Vols 4605 Cat
Notes: Library of Prof Rudolf Hildebran, Leipzig, the first large collection acquired by Stanford in 1895-1896, laid the foundation for an extensive German collection. Hildebrand's library is especially strong in German and Austrian philology (rare dictionaries, etc), but also in literary works. The collection is now especially strong for the period of the Reformation and Baroque, up to the present, with many rare editions, journals, almanacs, and the like. Sizable collections of women's working class and popular literature, dissertations and Schulschriften. Rare and valuable items in the Stanford Collection of German, Austrian and Swiss Culture, Special Collections. Catalog: *Katalog der Bibliothek des Herrn Prof Dr Rudolf Hildebrand.* Description: *The German Area Collection: A Stanford* Tradition by Peter R Frank.

CT —UNIVERSITY OF CONNECTICUT, Library, Storrs, 06268. R H Schimmelpfeng, Dir of Special Collections
Holdings: Cat Microforms
Notes: 19th century drama, Expressionism, East German literature and literature since 1945 constitute major strengths in the collection. Coverage is maintained for 600 contemporary authors. Also noteworthy are holdings on popular culture of Austria and Germany, 18th and 19th century.

NY —NEW YORK PUBLIC LIBRARY, Donnell Foreign Language Library, 20 W 53 St, New York, 10019. Bosiljka Stevanovic, Supvr Librn
Holdings: Vols 4303 Cat
Notes: German collection incl German authors of German expression. No separate catalog.

PA —BIBLIOGRAPHICAL CENTER OF GERMAN LITERATURE, University of Pittsburgh, Dept of Germanic Languages & Literatures, 102 Loeffler Bldg, Pittsburgh, 15260. Klaus W Jonas, Dir
Holdings: Cat Mss Pix Microforms
Notes: Center for the development of collections and bibliographical control of the record of publications, mss, correspondence, etc, by or relating to modern German authors. Special sections have been developed for Mann, Rilke, Hauptmann, Hesse, Broch, Sachs and others. Described by Professor Klaus W Jonas's "The German Literature Center in Pittsburgh," *Stechert-Hafner Book News*, vol 24, no 8, April 1970; "Documentation in Modern German Literature: A Progress Report," *Jahrbuch fuer Internationale Germanistik*, vol 4, no 2, 1972, and in *German and Austrian Contributions to World Literature* (1890-1970). Department of Germanic Languages and Literatures, University of Pittsburgh, 1983. 96 pp.

AUTHORS, GREEK (MODERN)

NY —NEW YORK PUBLIC LIBRARY, Donnell Foreign Language Library, 20 W 53 St, New York, 10019. Bosiljka Stevanovic, Supvr Librn
Holdings: Vols 1100 Cat
Notes: Greek collection incl Greek authors of Greek expression. No separate catalog.

AUTHORS, GUJARATI

NY —NEW YORK PUBLIC LIBRARY, Donnell Foreign Language Library, 20 W 53 St, New York, 10019. Bosiljka Stevanovic, Supvr Librn
Holdings: Vols 672 Cat
Notes: Gujarati collection incl Gujarati authors of Gujarati expression. No separate catalog.

AUTHORS, HAITIAN

DC —HOWARD UNIVERSITY, Moorland-Spingarn Research Center, 500 Howard Place NW, Washington, 20059. Clifford L Muse, Jr, Acting Dir

NY —NEW YORK PUBLIC LIBRARY, Donnell Foreign Language Library, 20 W 53 St, New York, 10019. Bosiljka Stevanovic, Supvr Librn
Notes: Haitian collection incl Haitian authors of Haitian expression. Haitian materials incl in the French collection. No separate catalog.

AUTHORS, HEBREW

NY —NEW YORK PUBLIC LIBRARY, Donnell Foreign Language Library, 20 W 53 St, New York, 10019. Bosiljka Stevanovic, Supvr Librn
Holdings: Vols 915 Cat
Notes: Hebrew collection incl Hebrew authors of Hebrew expression. No separate catalog.

AUTHORS, HINDI

NY —NEW YORK PUBLIC LIBRARY, Donnell Foreign Language Library, 20 W 53 St, New York, 10019. Bosiljka Stevanovic, Supvr Librn
Holdings: Vols 997 Cat
Notes: Hindi collection incl Hindi authors of Hindi expression. No separate catalog.

AUTHORS, HUNGARIAN

NY —NEW YORK PUBLIC LIBRARY, Donnell Foreign Language Library, 20 W 53 St, New York, 10019. Bosiljka Stevanovic, Supvr Librn
Holdings: Vols 1516 Cat
Notes: Hungarian collection incl Hungarian authors of Hungarian expression. No separate catalog.

AUTHORS, ILLINOIS

IL —CHICAGO PUBLIC LIBRARY, Special Collections Div, Cultural Center, 78 E Washington St, Chicago, 60602. Laura Linard, Cur
Holdings: Vols 400 Cat
Notes: Collect selectively in the area of Chicago writers, primarily literary figures. This collection primarily comprises first, early and private press editions of such authors as Eugene Field, Theodore Dreiser, Henry Blake Fuller, Maxwell Bodenheim, Floyd Dell, Ben Hecht, Sherwood Anderson, Carl Sandburg, Witter Bynner, Vincent Starrett, and Keith Preston. Several of these volumes are presentation and association copies.

IL —GALESBURG PUBLIC LIBRARY, 40 E Simmons St, Galesburg, 61401. Jane M Willenborg, Special Collections Librn
Holdings: Vols (6113) Cat Mss Maps Pix Slides Phonorecords Audiotapes
Budget: ($10,500)
Notes: Incl extensive collection of Illinois histories--state, county, city, town, and village; Illinois laws and statutes, 1829-1977; state and county atlases and plat books (listed in *United States Atlases,* vol II, Library of Congress, 1953); Lincoln books; works of Illinois authors; Civil War Illinois regimental histories; photographs of local interest (incl numerous photos of Carl Sandburg); and local newspapers and city directories on microfilm. Incl mss (26 ft), 79 maps, 4371 pictures, 3515 slides. 3053 negatives (some are duplicates of the photographs). Separate catalog. Restricted use: noncirculating; limited photocopying.

IL —QUINCY PUBLIC LIBRARY, 526 Jersey, Quincy, 62301. Michael G Garrison, Admin Librn
Holdings: Cat Mss Maps Pix Microforms
Notes: Local history and genealogy collection for city of Quincy and Adams County, Illinois. Incl Illinois and Adams County histories, area census records for 1820-1910 (microfilm), local cemetery records, probate papers and wills with index (microfilm), mss, church records (microfilm/microfiche), Quincy newspapers (1835-date), city directories, local atlases and plat books. Also incl over 250 books written by Quincy/Adams County authors. Collection does not circulate; reference only.

AUTHORS, INDIANA

IN —INDIANA UNIVERSITY, Lilly Library, Seventh St, Bloomington, 47405. William R Cagle, Librn
Holdings: Cat Mss Pix
Notes: Extensive holdings of first editions. Large collection of authors' portraits. Letters and manuscripts of many authors.
See also entry under Riley, James Whitcomb

IN —MONROE COUNTY PUBLIC LIBRARY, 303 E Kirkwood, Bloomington, 47401. Roberta Taylor, Indiana Room Librn
Holdings: Vols 1900 Cat Mss Maps Pix Microforms
Budget: $2500
Notes: The Indiana Collection also contains the following types of materials: books by and about Indiana authors, books and clippings about famous Indiana people, large vertical file containing clippings about state and local activities, Indiana magazines, and Monroe County on microfilm back to 1824. Indiana Federal Census Records on microfilm 1820-1910 (complete through 1850 for all counties, not complete thereafter except for Monroe County). Many Monroe County records of genealogical interest on microfilm and indexed. Special collections of oral histories, city directories, government documents, old atlases, photographs and slides (color transparencies), and historic preservation materials.

IN —INDIANA STATE UNIVERSITY, EVANSVILLE, Library, 8600 University Blvd, Evansville, 47712. Gina R Walker, Acting Archivist
Holdings: Vols (2500) Cat Mss Maps Pix
Notes: Restricted use: some items available on interlibrary loan.

IN —FRANKLIN COLLEGE OF INDIANA, Library, Special Collections Dept, Franklin, 46131. Mary Alice Medlicott, Cur
Holdings: Vols (12,000) Cat Mss Maps Pix
Budget: ($151,189)
Notes: David Demaree Banta Indiana Collection. Contains material relating to the area which became the Northwest Territory, the State of Indiana, its official publications; description, incl county and city histories, atlases and biographies; literary and scientific works of Hoosier authors. Printed catalog of collection available on request. Third edition of catalog is completed in manuscript.

IN —INDIANAPOLIS-MARION COUNTY PUBLIC LIBRARY, 40 E Saint Clair St, Indianapolis, 46204. Raymond E Gnat, Dir
Holdings: Vols 300 Cat
Notes: Reference only. Mostly first editions of Indiana authors. The Children's Division of the Library also has a collection (250 vols) of Indiana authors of children's books.

IN —INDIANA STATE LIBRARY, Indiana Div, 140 N Senate Ave, Indianapolis, 46204. Robert Logsdon, Acting Head
Holdings: Vols (60,541)
Budget: ($242,431)
Notes: Incl books, pamphlets (50,564), mss (3,000,000), microfilm (1641 reels), photographs (5000), records (37), audiotapes (22), films (107), slides (55 sets), maps (10, 160), VF (37), broadsides (920), newspapers (10,000 bound and wrapped files and 43,000 reels of microfilm). Collects information and materials both current and historical, about Indiana. Separate catalog for printed materials, separate indexes for mss, Indianapolis newspapers and pictures. Other indexes for smaller collections and special subjects.

IN —MUNCIE PUBLIC LIBRARY, 301 E Jackson St, Muncie, 47305. Arthur S Meyers, Librn
Holdings: Vols 1100 Cat
Notes: Mary Hough Goddard Memorial Reference Collection of Indiana Authors established in 1904. Collection contains material both by and about Indiana authors. It attempts to be representative rather than inclusive. Some vols are autographed, some are first editions. The collection is kept in a separate room and is noncirculating. Separate shelf list and accession book.

IN —INDIANA STATE UNIVERSITY, Cunningham Memorial Library, Dept of

AUTHORS, INDIANA (cont.)

Rare Books & Special Collections, Terre Haute, 47809. Lawrence J McCrank, Head
Holdings: Vols (2800) Cat Maps
Budget: ($1500)
Notes: The Indiana collection covers entire state with special emphasis on Terre Haute and the Wabash Valley in the following categories: first or special limited editions of major writers associated with Indiana for a significant portion of their productive lives; publications of private presses in Indiana; early Indiana imprints; other materials pertinent to Indiana, eg diaries, broadsides, early travel literature, etc; county, local and regional histories-chiefly 18th and 19th century; early atlases of Indiana locations; other materials (not rare) which depict the life of the state in a significant way in such areas as education, religion, industry, sports, social life, etc.

AUTHORS, IOWA

IA —DRAKE UNIVERSITY, Cowles Library, 28 St & University Ave, Des Moines, 50311.
Notes: 1200 pieces of correspondence of the Iowa novelist Philip Duffield Stong (1899-1957), mostly to and from his mother.

IA —UNIVERSITY OF IOWA, University Libraries, Iowa City, 52242. Frank Paluka, Head, Special Collections Dept
Holdings: Vols 5070 Cat Mss
Notes: Collection incl 440 mss. Myra Cao, "Some Children's Books by Iowa Writers", in *Books at Iowa*, Nov 1968. Also Frank Paluka, *Iowa Authors: A Bio-Bibliography of Sixty Native Writers* (1967).

IA —SIOUX CITY PUBLIC LIBRARY, 705 Sixth St, Sioux City, 51105. Betsy Thompson, Head Librn
Holdings: Vols 3700 Cat Mss Maps Pix Microforms
Notes: Emphasis on Sioux City and Iowa history, the Missouri River region. Microfilm copies of early newspapers, etc.

AUTHORS, IRISH

NY —LE MOYNE COLLEGE, Library, Le Moyne Heights, Syracuse, 13214. James J Simonis, Dir; Annette M Monaco, Special Colelctions Librn
Holdings: Vols (1614) // Cat Mss Slides
Notes: Incl 614 monographs and 1000 pamphlets, reprint articles, and periodical issues. Represents the Irish Literature Collection, covering the modern Irish Literature period from 1880 to 1950, and the Rev William T Noon SJ Collection. Father Noon had James Joyce as his main interest. Manuscripts of Noon's books *Joyce and Aquinas* (Yale University, 1957) and *Poetry and Prayer* (Rutgers University, 1957) are incl. There are several hundred pieces of correspondence which incl authors who had similar interests. The collection also incl his class notes and cutouts from newspapers, pamphlets, periodical articles, many of which have notes written by him. Monographs are represented by an author file. Pamphlets and reprint articles are organized in boxes and numbered numerically.

PA —BUCKNELL UNIVERSITY, Ellen Clarke Bertrand Library, Lewisburg, 17837. Ann de Klerk, Librn

BC —UNIVERSITY OF VICTORIA, McPherson Library, Victoria, V8W 3H5, Can.
Notes: Incl 9 cm, 1962; letters and mss by John Montague, editor; Peader O'Donnell; Liam Miller, Dolmen publisher; Aidan Higgins; Pearse Hutchinson; Val Iremonger; John Jordan; Tom Kinsella; James Liddy; John McGahern; Brian Moore; Richard Murphy; James Plunkett; Richard Weber; Leslie Dakin and Thomas McIntyre; and some miscellaneous writers.

AUTHORS, ITALIAN

CA —SAN FRANCISCO STATE UNIVERSITY, Frank V de Bellis Collection, 1630 Holloway Ave, San Francisco, 94132. Serena de Bellis, Cur
Holdings: Vols 3000 Cat Mss
Notes: There is a separate catalog of the collection which incl rare and current materials, with literature by Italian authors and medieval through contemporary literary criticism.

†NY —COLUMBIA UNIVERSITY LIBRARIES, Paterno Library, 1161 Amsterdam Ave, New York, 10027.
Notes: Italian literature and culture. One of the most extensive collections in the United States.

NY —NEW YORK PUBLIC LIBRARY, Donnell Foreign Language Library, 20 W 53 St, New York, 10019. Bosiljka Stevanovic, Supvr Librn
Holdings: Vols 1974 Cat
Notes: Italian collection incl Italian authors of Italian expression. No separate catalog.

AUTHORS, JAPANESE

FL —UNIVERSITY OF FLORIDA, Libraries, Gainesville, 32611. Ray Jones, Research Librn; Max Willocks, Librn
Holdings: Vols (2000)
Notes: An extensive collection of modern and premodern Japanese prose fiction in English translation and Japanese. Incl complete works of a number of important modern Japanese authors such as Yasunari Kawabata, Naoya Shiga, Junichiro Tanizaki, and Yukio Mishima.

NY —NEW YORK PUBLIC LIBRARY, Donnell Foreign Language Library, 20 W 53 St, New York, 10019. Bosiljka Stevanovic, Supvr Librn
Holdings: Vols 2653 Cat
Notes: Japanese collection incl Japanese authors of Japanese expression. No separate catalog.

AUTHORS, JAMAICAN

DC —HOWARD UNIVERSITY, Moorland-Spingarn Research Center, 500 Howard Place NW, Washington, 20059. Clifford L Muse, Jr, Acting Dir

AUTHORS, JEWISH

NY —YIVO INSTITUTE FOR JEWISH RESEARCH, Library & Archives, 1048 Fifth Ave, New York, 10028. Dina Abramowicz, Librn; Marek Web, Archivist
Holdings: Cat Mss Pix Slides
Notes: Emphasis is on immigration history. Incl archives of Jewish organizations which served immigrant masses, such as Educational Alliance, Hias, Hicem, Jewish Desertion Bureau and others. Yiddish language general and labor periodicals in originals and on microfilm. The Yiddish school movement in the US is covered, as well as other cultural activities in the field of the Yiddish theater, Literature and the arts. Correspondence of outstanding authors with parties in the US and abroad is an important source of information on Yiddish cultural life and communal affairs.

SC —COLLEGE OF CHARLESTON LIBRARY, Special Collections Dept, Charleston, 29401.
Notes: Collection contains materials from Ludwig Lewisohn and his former wife, Edna Manley, most of the latter dealing with her life with him. Among the items in the collection are their correspondence (1943-1945), Manley's diary which incl much material regarding Lewisohn's thoughts and experiences, typescript of his published book of translated Rilke poems, sheet music ms of a poem by Lewisohn, and a ten hour recorded interview with Manley regarding her life before, during and after their marriage (with transcript).

AUTHORS, KANSAS

KS —UNIVERSITY OF KANSAS, Kenneth Spencer Research Library, Kansas Collection, Lawrence, 66045. Sheryl K Williams, Cur
Holdings: Vols (92,000) Cat Mss Pix
Notes: Inclusiveness: Kansas-born authors, who write on regional themes or who maintain connections with Kansas and the Kansas region. Some materials are permanently deposited, others are gifts. William Inge, Richard Rhodes, Charles Bamfield Hoyt, Charles B Driscoll, Ed Howe, William Allen White, Guanetta Gordon, Langston Hughes and the archives of numerous literary and writers clubs.

KS —WICHITA PUBLIC LIBRARY, 223 S Main, Wichita, 67202. Richard Rademacher, Librn
Holdings: Vols (5560) Cat Pix
Notes: Books by Kansas authors and books about Kansas, old and new. Not loaned.

AUTHORS, KENTUCKY

KY —BOYD COUNTY PUBLIC LIBRARY, 1740 Central Ave, Ashland, 41101. Juliette Bryson, Dir
Holdings: Vols 264 Cat
Notes: Kentucky authors, with emphasis on books by and about Jesse Stuart.

KY —WESTERN KENTUCKY UNIVERSITY, Kentucky Library, Bowling Green, 42101. Riley Handy, Head, Special Collections; Connie Mills, Maps & Music Librn; Nancy Baird, Photographs Librn; Nancy Solley, Conservation Librn
Holdings: Vols (25,000) Cat Mss Maps Pix Microforms
Notes: Besides Kentucky history, other strengths are Mammoth Cave, South Union Shakers, Kentucky religion; and steamboat photos (3300 cataloged pictures); 8000 Kentucky postal cards, etc.

KY —HOPKINSVILLE COMMUNITY COLLEGE, Library, North Dr, Hopkinsville, 42240. Marjanna J Frising, Librn
Holdings: Vols 750 Cat Maps Pix Slides Microforms
Notes: Books about Kentucky and by Kentucky authors.

KY —UNIVERSITY OF KENTUCKY, Margaret I King Library, Dept of Special Collections, Lexington, 40506. William Marshall, Head
Holdings: Cat Mss Maps Pix Microforms
Notes: Kentucky history and travel. Incl the Samuel M Wilson Library, Kentucky imprints, Kentucky authors, biography and autobiography, regional history (Ohio Valley), Kentucky maps. Also sheet music, clippings, etc.

KY —FILSON CLUB, 118 W Breckinridge St, Louisville, 40203. Dorothy C Rush, Librn
Holdings: Vols (40,000) Cat Mss Maps Pix Microforms
Notes: Maintain a card catalog for books, pamphlets, maps and broadsides; separate catalog for newspapers incl a chronological file; and mss incl a chronological file. Collect anything about Kentucky, including Kentucky authors. Has file on Kentucky families.

KY —LOUISVILLE FREE PUBLIC LIBRARY, Fourth & York Sts, Louisville, 40203. Mark Harris, Head, Kentucky Division
Holdings: Vols 6000 Cat
Notes: Noncirculating.

KY —MIDWAY COLLEGE, Marrs Library, Stephens St, Midway, 40347. Kay Cordoves, Librn
Holdings: Vols (450) Cat
Notes: Incl books by Kentucky writers and Kentucky history.

KY —EASTERN KENTUCKY UNIVERSITY, Crabbe Library, Richmond, 40475. Sharon Brown McConnell, Cur
Holdings: Vols (10,000) Mss Maps Pix Microforms
Notes: The John Wilson Townsend Collection is a Kentuckiana collection and contains books, mss, letters, maps by Kentuckians and/or about Kentucky.

AUTHORS, KOREAN

NY —NEW YORK PUBLIC LIBRARY, Donnell Foreign Language Library, 20 W 53 St, New York, 10019. Bosiljka Stevanovic, Supvr Librn
Holdings: Vols 798 Cat
Notes: Korean collection incl Korean authors of Korean expression. No separate catalog.

AUTHORS, LATIN AMERICAN

NM —GALLUP PUBLIC LIBRARY, 115 W Hill Ave, Gallup, 87301. Octavia Fellin, Dir
Holdings: Vols 600 Cat

TX —UNIVERSITY OF TEXAS LIBRARIES, Nettie Lee Benson Latin American Collection, Sid Richardson Hall 1.109, Austin, 78712. Laura Gutierrez-Witt, Head Librn
Holdings: Vols (450,000) Cat Mss Maps Pix Phonorecords Filmstrips Microforms
See also entry under Latin America.

AUTHORS, LATVIAN

NY —NEW YORK PUBLIC LIBRARY, Donnell Foreign Language Library, 20 W 53 St, New York, 10019. Bosiljka Stevanovic, Supvr Librn
Holdings: Vols 174 Cat
Notes: Latvian collection incl Latvian authors of Latvian expression. No separate catalog.

AUTHORS, LITHUANIAN

NY —NEW YORK PUBLIC LIBRARY, Donnell Foreign Language Library, 20 W 53 St, New York, 10019. Bosiljka Stevanovic, Supvr Librn
Holdings: Vols 510 Cat
Notes: Lithuanian collection incl Lithuanian authors of Lithuanian expression. No separate catalog.

AUTHORS, LOUISIANA

LA —VERMILION PARISH LIBRARY, 200 North St, Abbeville, 70510. Mary Lou Hefley, Librn
Holdings: Vols (2000) Cat Phonorecords Filmstrips Microforms
Notes: Contains materials on various subjects on the state of Louisiana, and Louisiana Authors.

LA —LOUISIANA STATE LIBRARY, 760 Riverside N, PO Box 131, Baton Rouge, 70821. Harriet Callahan, Librn, Louisiana Section
Holdings: Vols (51,507) Cat Maps Pix Slides Microforms
Budget: ($12,000)
Notes: Louisiana history, folklore, customs, resources, industry, government, etc. Collection limited to books and materials about the state and by native and resident writers. Complete and historical depository for state documents (188,117 uncataloged). Huey Pierce Long materials, incl rare pamphlets and broadsides. Restricted use. 11,194 microfilm reels.

LA —LOUISIANA STATE UNIVERSITY, Troy H Middleton Library, Louisiana Room, Baton Rouge, 70803. Evangeline Mills Lynch, Head Librn; Ruth Murray, Associate Librn
Holdings: Vols (33,500) Cat Maps VF
Notes: Louisiana Collection of history, description and travel, biography, agriculture, literature, politics and government, folklore, anthropology, geography, geology, education, language, music and natural history. Especially large subject collections may be found on Louisiana, the history of the lower Mississippi Valley, Abraham Lincoln, Romance languages and literatures, sugar culture and technology, Southern history, petroleum engineering, plant pathology, micropaleontology, ornithology, and various aspects of crawfish life, biology and culture. Complete depository of Louisiana State Documents; extensive newspapers clipping files; separate card catalog; items listed in Louisiana Union Catalog; restricted use (research and reference). Incl both materials about Louisiana and by Louisianians without regard to subject. LSU Press Collection(preservation copy of each title kept for exhibit purposes only). LSU theses and dissertations from 1900-date. LSU Faculty Collection. Also, 1300 maps, 104 VF drawers, 250 boxes of uncataloged pamphlets.

LA —TULANE UNIVERSITY, Howard-Tilton Memorial Library, Special Collections Div, 7001 Freret St, New Orleans, 70118. Wilbur E Meneray, Librn
Holdings: Cat Mss
Notes: Published works, correspondence and literary manuscripts of 19th and 20th century Louisiana authors including French language writers.

NC —UNIVERSITY OF NORTH CAROLINA, CHAPEL HILL, Louis Round Wilson Academic Affairs Library, Southern Historical Collection, Chapel Hill, 27514. Carolyn Wallace, Librn
Notes: Manuscripts and papers of Walker Percy. Primarily mss from work on his published novels, etc.

TX —UNIVERSITY OF TEXAS LIBRARIES, General Libraries, PO Box P, Austin, 78713. Carolyn Bucknell, Asst Dir for Collection Development
Holdings: Cat Microforms

AUTHORS, MAINE

ME —MAINE STATE LIBRARY, Special Collections Dept, Cultural Bldg, Station 64, Augusta, 04333. Shirley Thayer, Librn
Holdings: Vols 5000
Budget: ($2,500,000)
Notes: A permanent collection of literary works by Maine authors and books about Maine. Non-circulating.

ME —LEWISTON PUBLIC LIBRARY, 118 Park St, Lewiston, 04240. Muriel P Landry, Actg Dir
Holdings: Vols 1547 Cat Mss Maps Pix
Notes: Collection comprised mostly of histories of Maine towns and cities. There is also much material on Maine writers. Local history is a special concern.

ME —UNIVERSITY OF MAINE AT ORONO, Raymond H Fogler Library, Special Collections Dept, Orono, 04469. Eric S Flower, Head
Holdings: Vols (9000) Mss Maps Pix Microforms
Budget: $4,000
Notes: State of Maine Collection. Books by Maine authors; Maine-related subjects and Maine imprints. Index to *Maine Times,* vol 1 to present. Index to *Down East,* vol 1 to present. Collection incl 6500 state documents dated 1820 to present; 2000 maps; postcards. Telephone inquiries welcomed (581-1686).

ME —PORTLAND PUBLIC LIBRARY, 5 Monument Sq, Portland, 04101. Edward V Chenevert, Library Dir
Holdings: Vols 8500 Cat Maps Pix Microforms
Notes: State of Maine Collection. Books by Maine authors or about Maine-related subjects, and Maine imprints. Maine and Portland government documents dating back to 1829. Collection strong in Maine history and Maine literature and poetry.

ME —WESTBROOK COLLEGE, Library, 716 Stevens Ave, Portland, 04103. Dorothy M Healy, Special Collections Librn
Holdings: Vols (3000) Cat Mss Pix Memorabilia
Notes: Collection incl work of Maine women writers. Many mss and scrapbooks are incl. Memorabilia of Mrs Robert E Peary, Mary Ellen Chase, Florence B Jacobs, Celia Thaxter, and Edna St Vincent Millay are notable items. Some rare books, ie Madame Wood novels, are part of the collection.

AUTHORS, MARATHI

NY —NEW YORK PUBLIC LIBRARY, Donnell Foreign Language Library, 20 W 53 St, New York, 10019. Bosiljka Stevanovic, Supvr Librn
Holdings: Vols 101 Cat
Notes: Marathi collection incl Marathi authors of Marathi expression. No separate catalog.

AUTHORS, MARYLAND

†MD —UNIVERSITY OF MARYLAND, Library, Marylandia Dept, College Park, 20742. Nancy K Walton, Head
Holdings: Vols 40,000 Cat Maps Audiotapes Microforms
Notes: Books, periodicals, maps, microforms, etc, on the history of the State and the University; works by Maryland authors; state, county, and municipal documents; University of Maryland theses and dissertations. State, county, and municipal documents are cataloged by subject. For a description of archival and manuscript materials in the Library, see entry under Maryland - Description and Travel - Views.

MD —TALBOT COUNTY FREE LIBRARY, Maryland Room, 100 W Dover St, Easton, 21601. Marguerite W Harvey, Cur
Holdings: Vols 3900 Cat Mss Maps Pix Slides Phonorecords Audiotapes Microforms
Notes: The Maryland Room of the Talbot County Free Library is probably the finest in the State outside of Baltimore. Incl history, description, Maryland authors, etc. Separate catalog. Collection described in *Guardian of Our Maryland Heritage: The Maryland Room, Talbot County Free Library* (Easton: The Library, 1968).

AUTHORS, MASSACHUSETTS

MA —JONES LIBRARY, 43 Amity St, Amherst, 01002. Daniel J Lombardo, Cur of Special Collections
Holdings: Vols 2768 Cat
Notes: Books by people born in Amherst or resident for more than 3 years; excluding publications by faculty members of the University of Massachusetts, Amherst College and Hampshire unless they come under the preceding clause. Incl a collection of Amherst imprints to the mid-20th century. Materials do not circulate.

MA —CONCORD FREE PUBLIC LIBRARY, 129 Main St, Concord, 01742. Rose Marie Mitten, Dir
Holdings: Cat Mss Maps Pix Slides
Notes: Extensive collection.

MA —GREENFIELD COMMUNITY COLLEGE, Pioneer Valley Resource Center, One College Drive, Greenfield, 01301. Margaret E C Howland, Dir; Carol Letson, Librn
Holdings: Vols 2000 Cat Mss Pix Phonorecords Videotapes 16mm Film Microforms
Notes: A special collection of primary and secondary material on the area surrounding the Connecticut River in Western Massachusetts. Covers every aspect of the Pioneer Valley, past and present, including art and artists, authors, census data, environment, ethnicity, geology, history, industry and commerce, literature, politics and government, etc. Separately housed. Open 20 hours a week.

MA —POLLARD MEMORIAL LIBRARY, 401 Merrimack St, Lowell, 01852. Walter V Hickey, Libr Asst
Holdings: Vols (3000) Cat Pix
Notes: Lowell History Collection. Most books were published in the late 1800s when Lowell was particularly prosperous. Holdings incl Lowell history, vital records, works by Lowell authors and biographies of former Lowell residents. Microfilm of Lowell newspapers from 1837 to the present, as well as City Directories from 1832. Also a full collection of Jack Kerouac's work. Also

AUTHORS, MASSACHUSETTS (cont.)

Town and County histories and published Genealogies, mostly from the late 1800's.

MA —BERKSHIRE ATHENAEUM, 1 Wendell Ave, Pittsfield, 01201. Ruth T Degenhardt, Head Local History & Literature
Holdings: Vols 800 Cat Mss Pix Slides
Budget: ($2000)
Notes: A representative collection of material by and about people who have produced literary works while residing in the Berkshires for a significant period of time. Collection is inclusive: all types of material on all types of authors, from the most famous to most obscure. Incl Oliver Wendell Holmes, William Cullen Bryant, Sinclair Lewis, and others. Also contains volumes from the personal library of Oliver Wendell Holmes (1809-1894).

MA —STOCKBRIDGE LIBRARY ASSOCIATION, Main St, Box H, Stockbridge, 01262. Rosemary Schmeyer, Librn
Holdings: Vols (1200) Cat Mss Maps Pix
Notes: The Historical Room contains approximately 1200 vols of genealogical reference, ie Massachusetts Soldiers and Sailors of the Revolution, Vital Statistics for towns in Massachusetts, local history, Indian history, books by and about Stockbridge residents, and a large collection of family papers of the Sedgwick and Field families among many others. These are being cataloged with the help of a special grant.

AUTHORS, MEXICAN

TX —EL PASO PUBLIC LIBRARY, Southwest Collection, 501 N Oregon, El Paso, 79901. Mary A Sarber, Head
Holdings: Vols 1723 Cat
Notes: Current and historical information about Mexican-Americans throughout the Southwest. Incl current social and economic writings about Mexican-Americans, Chicano literature, history and culture of Mexico from pre-Columbian times to the present, translations of Mexican authors.

AUTHORS, MEXICAN AMERICAN

TX —UNIVERSITY OF TEXAS LIBRARIES, Nettie Lee Benson Latin American Collection, Sid Richardson Hall 1.109, Austin, 78712. Laura Gutierrez-Witt, Head Librn
Holdings: Vols (450,000) Cat Slides 16mm Films Microforms
Notes: The Mexican American Library Project has, since 1974, collected materials relating to all aspects of Spanish-speaking people in the US, with emphasis on Mexican Americans.
See also entry under Latin America.

AUTHORS, MICHIGAN

MI —MITCHELL PUBLIC LIBRARY, 22 N Manning St, Hillsdale, 49242. Arlene Elliott, Head Librn
Holdings: Vols 500 Cat Maps Pix Microforms Newspapers
Notes: Emphasis on Hillsdale and surrounding counties. Incl local newspaper on both microfilm and in bound volumes; city and county directories; county plat books; local and family histories; and works of local authors. Newspapers being put on microfilm.

MI —LANSING PUBLIC LIBRARY, Local History Room, 401 S Capitol Ave, Lansing, 48914. Jane McClary, Local History Librn
Holdings: Vols (6000) Cat Mss Maps Pix Microforms VF

MI —OWOSSO PUBLIC LIBRARY, 502 W Main St, Owosso, 48867. Margaret A Bentley, Librn
Holdings: Vols 37 Cat Mss Pix
Notes: The library has accumulated as many titles as possible by James O Curwood. In conjunction with the area historical society, personnel have developed exhibits at the author's former studio, a rustic castle on the Shiawassee River. Since 1978, the anniversary of his birth has been celebrated annually by this community, with festivities and commemorations planned.

AUTHORS, MINNESOTA

MN —SAINT CLOUD STATE UNIVERSITY, Centennial Hall Learning Resources Center, Saint Cloud, 56301. John Berling, Dir
Holdings: Vols 1800 Cat Mss Maps Pix Slides Microforms
Notes: All available information about Minnesota authors.

MN —SAINT PAUL PUBLIC LIBRARY, Highland Park Branch Library, Perrie Jones Memorial Rm, 1974 Ford Pkwy, Saint Paul, 55116. Elizabeth Monigal
Holdings: Vols (1850) Cat //
Notes: Rare and interesting books from the 16th century to the present. Also collection of F Scott Fitzgerald and other St Paul authors.

AUTHORS, MISSISSIPPI

MS —UNIVERSITY OF SOUTHERN MISSISSIPPI, William David McCain Graduate Library, Box 5148, Southern Sta, Hattiesburg, 39406.
Holdings: Vols (12,000) Cat Mss Maps Pix Microforms
Notes: Mississippiana Collection, 1832 to date. Incl the papers of Theodore G Bilbo and William M Colmer, Paul B Johnson, Con Sellers, state government publications, the University of Southern Mississippi Archives, an oral history collection, and works on genealogy, geography, history and fiction. Mississippi newspapers on microfilm.

MS —FIRST REGIONAL LIBRARY, 59 Commerce St NW, Hernando, 38632. Jo Ann Wilroy, Asst Dir
Holdings: Vols 450 Cat Maps Pix
Notes: Materials about Mississippi or written by Mississippi authors.

MS —JACKSON METROPOLITAN LIBRARY SYSTEM, Information, Reference & Referral Div, 301 N State St, Jackson, 39201. Kathy Smith, Senior Ref Librn
Holdings: Vols 4500 Cat
Notes: Mississippi history, with emphasis on the city of Jackson. Also, files of Mississippi periodicals; Mississippi authors.

MS —MISSISSIPPI LIBRARY COMMISSION, 1221 Ellis Ave, Box 10700, Jackson, 39209. Gerald Buchanan, Asst Dir
Holdings: Vols 7000 Cat Videotapes
Notes: Circulating materials by or about Mississippi authors.

MS —MISSISSIPPI STATE UNIVERSITY, Mitchell Memorial Library, Box 5408, Mississippi State, 39762. Frances N Coleman, Head, Special Collections
Holdings: Vols (15,000) Cat Mss Maps Pix Microforms
Notes: Social and political history of Mississippi, incl University Archives (now separate branch). Microfilms of Protestant Church records. There are strong collections on history of the Southern States, Mississippi authors (especially Faulkner, Williams, Carter, Welty, and Young); also the John C Stennis Collection of over 2 million items, his books, papers, photographs, etc. Incl 400 collections of mss; papers of US Rep David R Bowen 1973-1983; papers of US Rep G V Montgomery 1967-.

NC —UNIVERSITY OF NORTH CAROLINA, CHAPEL HILL, Louis Round Wilson Academic Affairs Library, Southern Historical Collection, Chapel Hill, 27514. Carolyn Wallace, Librn
Notes: Manuscripts and papers of Walker Percy. Primarily mss from work on his published novels, etc.

AUTHORS, MODERN

CA —CALIFORNIA STATE UNIVERSITY, NORTHRIDGE, Delmar T Oviatt & South Libraries, 1811 Nordhoff St, Northridge, 91330. Donald L Read, Special Collections Dept
Holdings: Vols 2500 Cat
Notes: McDermott collection of contemporary writers of American fiction and poetry, signed, first editions. Emphasis is upon both established and new contemporary writers. Collection fully cataloged.

MO —WASHINGTON UNIVERSITY, Libraries, Special Collections Dept, Campus Box 1061, St Louis, 63130.
Notes: A major collection, incl books, mss, correspondence, literary papers, photographs, etc. Described in *Special Collections: an Annotated Guide to the Holdings of the Manuscript Division and the University Archives and Research Collection.*

AUTHORS, MONTANA

MT —UNIVERSITY OF MONTANA, Library, Missoula, 59801. Katherine Schaefer, Special Collections Librn
Notes: Mss, correspondence, first editions and miscellaneous items.

AUTHORS, NEBRASKA

MO —UNIVERSITY OF MISSOURI-COLUMBIA, Ellis Library, Language and Literature Dept, Columbia, 65201. Jeaneice Brewer, Librn
Holdings: Vols (3500) Cat
Notes: Consists of the personal library of John G Neihardt, 1881-1973, poet, literary critic, and lecturer. Lived among Omaha Indians and Ogalala Sioux Indians to study their character and history. Poet laureate of Nebraska. Literary editor of *St Louis* Post-Dispatch, 1926-38. Poet in residence and lecturer in English, U of Missouri, 1949-66. Manuscripts are housed separately in Western Historical Manuscripts Collection of Ellis Library.

NE —LINCOLN CITY LIBRARIES, Bennett Martin Public Library, 14 & N Sts, Lincoln, 68508. Carol J Connor, Dir
Holdings: Vols (4750) Cat Mss Maps Pix Slides Phonorecords Audiotapes Videotapes 16mm Films Filmstrips
Notes: Incl works by authors born in the state, resident in the state for a significant period of life, or resident in the state while producing a significant work. Also incl critical and biographical works about Nebraska authors; city, county, and state histories and documents; and other notebook materials. Incl first and other rare editions and a number of mss. Collection is noncirculating.

NE —NEBRASKA STATE HISTORICAL SOCIETY, Library, 1500 R St, Box 82554, Lincoln, 68501. M Ann Reinert, Library Dept Head
Holdings: Vols (100,000) Cat Maps Pix Microforms
Budget: ($200,000)
Notes: Collection of Nebraska authors, particularly Willa Cather and John G Neihardt.
See also entry under Great Plains

NE —OMAHA PUBLIC LIBRAY, Omaha, 68102. Michael Phipps, Dir
Holdings: Vols 2000 Cat Mss Maps Pix Microforms
Notes: Incl city, county and state histories and documents. Local scrapbooks and portfolios of pictures available. Census materials and local newspapers on microfilm. First editions and/or mss of Nebraska authors. Rare state and local serial titles in collection.

AUTHORS, NEWFOUNDLAND

NF —MEMORIAL UNIVERSITY OF NEWFOUNDLAND, University Library, Centre for Newfoundland Studies, Elizabeth Ave, Saint John's, A1C 5S7, Can. Anne Hart, Head
Holdings: Vols (48,000) Cat Maps Microforms
Budget: ($50,000)
Notes: Materials about Newfoundland, by Newfoundlanders, or published in Newfoundland, incl Labrador. Also, Saint Pierre and Miquelon. Bibliography of Newfoundland materials is being compiled (now over 7,000 items).

AUTHORS, NEW ENGLAND

MN —MINNEAPOLIS PUBLIC LIBRARY & INFORMATION CENTER, North Regional Branch Library, Ralph Waldo Emerson Room, 1315 Lowry Ave N, Minneapolis, 55411.
Holdings: Vols 4000 Cat Mss Pix
Notes: 19th century New England authors.

AUTHORS, NEW HAMPSHIRE

NH —KEENE STATE COLLEGE, Wallace E Mason Library, 229 Main St, Keene, 03431. Edward A Scott, Librn; Clifford Mead, Special Collections Librn
Holdings: Vols (2000) Cat Mss Maps Pix Audiotapes Microforms
Budget: ($7500)
Notes: New Hampshire history, genealogy, authors, imprints (especially Keene imprints), Keene State College materials, and newspapers (microfilm).

AUTHORS, NEW ZEALAND

CA —UNIVERSITY OF CALIFORNIA, LOS ANGELES, Research Library, Indo/Pacific Collection, 405 Hilgard Ave, Los Angeles, 90024. Edward Shreeves, Chairman, Bibliographers Group; Charlotte Spence, Indo/Pacific Bibliographer
Holdings: Vols Cat Mss Maps Pix Microforms
Notes: The Pacific area collection has been developed on a combination of the research and teaching levels. It focuses on the cultural, economic, political and social history of Australia, New Zealand and the various island groups. The accounts of the early European voyagers are well represented, with the highlight being the Captain Cook collection. An effort has also been made to collect the novels, poetry, drama, etc, of Australian and New Zealand authors.

AUTHORS, NORTH CAROLINA

NC —PACK MEMORIAL PUBLIC LIBRARY, North Carolina Collection, 67 Haywood St, Asheville, 28801. John Toms, Dept Head
Notes: Collection incl early ms accounts of western North Carolina; Civil War letters; letters, diary, and mss of Horace Kephart; mss of Thomas Dixon; Thomas Wolfe Collection; contemporary North Carolina authors; North Carolina censuses, 1790-1910; rare newspapers and runs of local newspapers, and clippings from Asheville newspapers, from 1920s; early maps; information on Cherokee Indians; approx 400 vols of North Carolina genealogy and file of unpublished genealogies. Collection concentrates on western North Carolina, with some general Appalachian materials. Incl 4000 local and state photographs, separate catalog.

NC —UNIVERSITY OF NORTH CAROLINA, CHAPEL HILL, Louis Round Wilson Academic Affairs Library, Southern Historical Collection, Chapel Hill, 27514. Carolyn Wallace, Librn

NC —GREENSBORO PUBLIC LIBRARY, 201 N Greene St, Drawer X-4, Greensboro, 27402. J Douglas Kerr, Caldwell Jones Librn
Holdings: Vols 8000 Cat Mss Maps Pix Microforms
Notes: Incl books by North Carolina authors and about North Carolina; a vertical file of pamphlets and newspaper clippings, microfilmed Federal Census of Population 1790-1910 for the state, some early maps of the state. There is a separate catalog to the collection.

NC —MARS HILL COLLEGE, Memorial Library, Appalachian Room, Mars Hill, 28754. Richard Dillingham, Dir, Special Collections
Notes: Collection strong on local history, folklore, fiction. Incl Bascom Lamar Lunsford papers, books, sound recordings. Separate catalog.

NC —ROWAN PUBLIC LIBRARY, History and Genealogy Dept, Salisbury, 28144. Philip Barton, Dir
Holdings: Vols (3000) Cat Mss Maps Microforms
Notes: Generally, the History and Genealogy Collection is composed of materials relating to local and North Carolina State history and materials for genealogical research. Primary emphasis is on genealogical research materials. The nucleus of the genealogical collection is the McCubbins Collection. The Collection consists primarily of deed abstracts of Rowan County. Another collection representing part of the genealogical research collection is the Smith Collection, consisting of notes and correspondence collected over a wide span of years about Smiths of the US. A recent addition is the Archibald Henderson Collection of literary works of North Carolinians, Transylvania materials and materials dealing with North Carolina State history and political science.

†NC —WAKE FOREST UNIVERSITY, Z Smith Reynolds Library, Box 7777, Reynold Sta, Winston-Salem, 27109. Richard J Murdoch, Rare Book Librn
Holdings: Cat

AUTHORS, NORTH DAKOTA

ND —UNIVERSITY OF NORTH DAKOTA, Chester Fritz Library, Dept of Special Collections, Grand Forks, 58202. Daniel F Rylance, Special Collections Coordr
Holdings: Vols (5500) Uncat Mss Maps Pix Microforms
Budget: ($2500)
Notes: Also the Orin G Libby Manuscript Collection (900 collections), and the Aandahl Collection of Western History on North Dakota and the Northern Great Plains. Emphasis on agriculture, politics, pioneering, Germans from Russia, etc. Guides to the collections available from the Coordinator of Special Collections.

SD —AUGUSTANA COLLEGE, Mikkelsen Library & Learning Resource Center, Center for Western Studies, Sioux Falls, 57197. Ronelle Thompson, Dir Library
Holdings: Vols (40,000) Cat Mss Maps Pix Slides Microforms
Budget: ($130,000)
Notes: Materials by and about the Dakotas and Dakotans.

AUTHORS, NORWEGIAN

NY —NEW YORK PUBLIC LIBRARY, Donnell Foreign Language Library, 20 W 53 St, New York, 10019. Bosiljka Stevanovic, Supvr Librn
Holdings: Vols 282 Cat
Notes: Norwegian collection incl Norwegian authors of Norwegian expression. No separate catalog.

AUTHORS, OHIO

†OH —OHIO NORTHERN UNIVERSITY, Heterick Memorial Library, 525 S Main St, Ada, 45810.

OH —PUBLIC LIBRARY OF CINCINNATI & HAMILTON COUNTY, Dept of Rare Books & Special Collections, 800 Vine St, Library Square, Cincinnati, 45202. Yeatman Anderson III, Cur
Holdings: Cat
Notes: Emphasis on Cincinnati and Ohio authors.

OH —CLEVELAND PUBLIC LIBRARY, 325 Superior Ave, Cleveland, 44114.
Holdings: Cat Maps Pix
Notes: Library collection in the subject departments incl: state and local history; city directories; business and industry; canals and waterworks; technology; local authors and artists; tourists and travel information (only advisory), vital statistics. Early Ohio pictures and historic maps. See also Western Reserve, Cleveland Public Library.

OH —OHIO HISTORICAL SOCIETY, Archives Library Division, 1982 Velma Ave, Columbus, 43211. Dennis East, Division Chief
Holdings: Vols (96,000) Cat Mss Maps Pix Slides Microforms
Budget: ($18,000)
Notes: This library is the primary collection for Ohio. Most purchases are on the rare and op market. Collecting area is early American history, esp relating to exploration into the Northwest Territory. Major subject areas are Ohio politics and government (8 presidents) military history (good collection of regimental histories and Ohio narratives of the Civil War), economic and social history, local history, esp county histories & atlases and city directories. Also, Ohio archaeology, natural history, artifacts. Major media collections are books (96,000), newspapers (25,000 vols and 22,000 microfilm), pictures (50,000), maps (2500), manuscripts (1,500,000). Library is noncirculating except through ILL of microfilm.

OH —COSHOCTON PUBLIC LIBRARY, 655 Main St, Coshocton, 43812. Susan Anderson, Librn
Holdings: Vols (875) Cat Mss Maps Pix Microforms
Budget: ($1000)
Notes: Local history and genealogy of Coshocton, Guernsey, Holmes, Knox, Tuscarawas, Licking and Muskingum counties. Incl published works, censuses (microfilm), cemetery index (Muskingum Co). Incl, for Coshocton Co, directories, newspapers, obituary and cemetery indexes, local authors and imprints, photographs, clippings, letters, personal papers. Building collection of histories and genealogies from areas of high migration to Coshocton Co.

OH —DAYTON & MONTGOMERY COUNTY PUBLIC LIBRARY, Dayton Collection, 215 E Third St, Dayton, 45402. Kevin Smith, Librn
Holdings: Vols (4500) Cat Mss Maps Pix
Notes: Contains materials on Dayton, Montgomery County and the Miami Valley, Ohio, area, incl materials relative to Dayton authors, inventors, political figures, etc, eg, Paul Laurence Dunbar, Wright Brothers, Clement Vallandigham, as well as materials on the geography, history, genealogy and political structure of the area.

AUTHORS, OKLAHOMA

OK —WILL ROGERS MEMORIAL LIBRARY, W Will Rogers Blvd, Box 157, Claremore, 74017. Reba N Collins, Dir
Holdings: Vols (2800) Cat Slides Phonorecords Audiotapes Videotapes 16mm Films Microforms
Notes: Thousands of original manuscripts, letters, photographs, plus many other personal items, all by or about Will Rogers. Library is available by appointment or special permission.

OK —OKLAHOMA DEPT OF LIBRARIES, Law Library, 109 State Capital, Oklahoma City, 73105. Robert Clark, Dir; Betty Brown, Okla Collection Librn; Virginia Collier, US Documents; Jan Blakely, State Documents; Blane Dessy, Library Science
Holdings: Vols 18,000 Cat
Notes: Noncirculating.

AUTHORS, OREGON

OR —UNIVERSITY OF OREGON LIBRARY, Special Collections Div, Eugene, 97403. Kenneth W Duckett, Curator
Holdings: Vols Cat Mss
Notes: Publication: Martin Schmitt, comp. *Catalogue of Manuscripts in the University of Oregon Library* (Eugene: University of Oregon Books, 1971). The Oregon Collection houses the published works of Oregon writers, c19-present.

OR —OREGON STATE LIBRARY, State Library Bldg, Salem, 97310. Alden Moberg, Oregoniana Consultant
Holdings: Vols 2200 Cat Pix
Notes: Oregon Collection incl published works of Oregonians. There are also files of clippings, biographical information, pictures.

WA —BELLINGHAM PUBLIC LIBRARY, 210 Central Ave, Bellingham, 98225. Claudia McCain, Dir
Holdings: Cat Mss Pix
Notes: Ella Higginson was a poet of the Pacific Coast who is claimed by Oregon and Washington. Her published writing was done

AUTHORS, OREGON (cont.)

in Bellingham. Collection of her works incl all her published poetry except for her first book, a miniature paper-bound brochure written in 1894. Published description of her collected works in *History of Oregon* Literature, by Alfred Powers (Metropolitan Press, 1935), pp 427-431.

AUTHORS, PANJABI

NY —NEW YORK PUBLIC LIBRARY, Donnell Foreign Language Library, 20 W 53 St, New York, 10019. Bosiljka Stevanovic, Supvr Librn
Holdings: Vols 213 Cat
Notes: Panjabi collection incl Panjabi authors of Panjabi expression. No separate catalog.

AUTHORS, PENNSYLVANIA

PA —MONTGOMERY COUNTY-NORRISTOWN PUBLIC LIBRARY, Swede & Elm Sts, Norristown, 19401. James G Gear, Exec Dir
Holdings: Vols 3000 Cat Mss Maps Pix Phonorecords Microforms
Notes: Emphasis is on Montgomery County and Norristown. Collection is retrospective and current. Local authors and publishers plus materials relating to local area are represented. Genealogies are not included in order not to duplicate the excellent collection of the Montgomery County Historical Society.

PA —FREE LIBRARY OF PHILADELPHIA, Central Children's Dept, Logan Sq, Philadelphia, 19103. Ellen Whitney, Head
Holdings: Vols (30,382) Cat Mss Pix
Notes: Special collections of children's literature dating from 1837 to the present are maintained by the Central Children's Department. These collections include Historical Bibliography, the Kathrine M McAlarney Collection of Illustrated Children's Books, the Folklore Collection, the Historical Collection which includes children's periodicals and the Series Collection. Featured in these non-circulating research collections are works of outstanding illustrators in the field of children's books, books by Philadelphia and Pennsylvania authors, books about Philadelphia and Pennsylvania people and places, and books published in Philadelphia and Pennsylvania. Included also are framed originals as well as manuscripts and typescripts by Evaline Ness, material for Lloyd Alexander books, Virginia Lee Burton, Marguerite (Lofft) deAngeli, Beatrice Schenk (Freedman) DeRegniers, Eulalie Osgood Grover, Carolyn Haywood, Elizabeth Hoffman Honness, Kristin (Eggleston) Hunter [on loan to Free Library], Margaret Oldroyd Hyde, Katherine Milhous, Scott O'Dell, Lucy Fitch Perkins, Elizabeth Blake Ripley, Tomi Ungerer, Hendrik Willem Van Loon and Lucille Wallower. *The Checklist of Children's* Books, 1837-1876, published in 1975 and available in limited supply in book form, but also available in microform from the Office of Work with Children, Free Library of Philadelphia, lists all books in Special Collections during this period at date of publication. These special collections supplement the Rosenbach Collection of Early American Children's Books, the American Sunday School Union Collection, the Elisabeth Ball Collection of Hornbooks, and other children's books published prior to 1837, all of which are housed in the Rare Book Department of the Free Library of Philadelphia.

PA —PENNSYLVANIA HORTICULTURAL SOCIETY, Library, 325 Walnut St, Philadelphia, 19106. Mary Lou Wolfe, Librn
Holdings: Vols (200) Cat Pix Slides
Notes: Books about horticulture published by Pennsylvanians, about Pennsylvania, or which bear a Philadelphia imprint. Descriptive catalog which highlights the collection: *From Seed to Flower: Philadelphia 1681-1876; A Horticultural Point of View* (Philadelphia: Pennsylvania Horticultural Society, 1976).

AUTHORS, PERSIAN

NY —NEW YORK PUBLIC LIBRARY, Donnell Foreign Language Library, 20 W 53 St, New York, 10019. Bosiljka Stevanovic, Supvr Librn
Holdings: Vols 159 Cat
Notes: Persian collection incl Persian authors of Persian expression. No separate catalog.

AUTHORS, POLISH

NY —NEW YORK PUBLIC LIBRARY, Donnell Foreign Language Library, 20 W 53 St, New York, 10019. Bosiljka Stevanovic, Supvr Librn
Holdings: Vols 1156 Cat
Notes: Polish collection incl Polish authors of Polish expression. No separate catalog.

AUTHORS, POLISH AMERICAN

IL —POLISH MUSEUM OF AMERICA, Library, 984 N Milwaukee Ave, Chicago, 60622. Donald Bilinski, OFM, Cur/Librn
Holdings: Vols (25,000) Cat Mss Maps Pix Slides Phonorecords 16mm Films Filmstrips Microforms
Notes: Material on Poland and Polish-Americans; works written by Polish-Americans, regardless of subject. About 80 percent of the works are in Polish. Extensive juvenile section in Polish for youngsters. The collection contains books not only of Poles in US but Poles beyond the borders of Poland. It contains Polish literature, incl translations into English.

AUTHORS, PORTUGUESE

NY —NEW YORK PUBLIC LIBRARY, Donnell Foreign Language Library, 20 W 53 St, New York, 10019. Bosiljka Stevanovic, Supvr Librn
Holdings: Vols 662 Cat
Notes: Portuguese collection incl Portuguese authors of Portuguese expression. No separate catalog.

RI —BROWN UNIVERSITY, John Hay Library, 20 Prospect St, Providence, 02912. Mark N Brown, Cur Mss
Notes: The Jose Rodrigues Migueis Collection of his works, personal library, correspondence, some manuscripts, diaries, drawings, notebooks, photographs, etc. Incl reprints, and thousands of newspaper clippings relating to him, Portugal's most important 20th century writer. Much of the correspondence is with Portuguese and other writers, academics, and political figures. Migueis was very active in modern Portuguese politics and Portuguese American studies.

AUTHORS, PUERTO RICAN

NY —NEW YORK PUBLIC LIBRARY, Donnell Foreign Language Library, 20 W 53 St, New York, 10019. Bosiljka Stevanovic, Supvr Librn
Notes: Puerto Rican collection incl Puerto Rican authors of Puerto Rican expression. No separate catalogs.

AUTHORS, RUMANIAN

NY —NEW YORK PUBLIC LIBRARY, Donnell Foreign Language Library, 20 W 53 St, New York, 10019. Bosiljka Stevanovic, Supvr Librn
Holdings: Vols 300 Cat
Notes: Rumanian collection incl Rumanian authors of Rumanian expression. No separate catalog.

AUTHORS, RUSSIAN

NY —NEW YORK PUBLIC LIBRARY, Donnell Foreign Language Library, 20 W 53 St, New York, 10019. Bosiljka Stevanovic, Supvr Librn
Holdings: Vols 8817 Cat
Notes: Russian collection incl Russian authors of Russian expression. No separate catalog.

AUTHORS, SCANDINAVIAN

WA —UNIVERSITY OF WASHINGTON LIBRARIES, Suzzallo Library, Scandinavian Collections, FM-25, Seattle, 98195. A Gerald Anderson, Librn
Holdings: Vols (50,000) Cat Mss Pix
Budget: ($15,546)
Notes: Research collections with emphasis on languages and literatures, and auxiliary strengths in history, political science, social science. Archival and other special materials relating to Scandinavian-Americans in the Pacific Northwest are located in other appropriate collections.

AUTHORS, SERBIAN

NY —NEW YORK PUBLIC LIBRARY, Donnell Foreign Language Library, 20 W 53 St, New York, 10019. Bosiljka Stevanovic, Supvr Librn
Holdings: Vols 291 Cat
Notes: Serbian collection incl Serbian authors of Serbian expression. No separate catalog.

AUTHORS, SLOVAK

OH —SLOVAK INSTITUTE, Saint Andrew's Abbey, 2900 King Dr, Cleveland, 44104. Rev Andrew Pier, Dir
Holdings: Vols (10,000)
Notes: Promotes cultural interests, especially work of Slovak authors, artists, and musicians through its Slovak Writers and Artists Association. Private library. Permission required.

AUTHORS, SOUTH CAROLINA

SC —MEDICAL UNIVERSITY OF SOUTH CAROLINA, Waring Historical Library, 171 Ashley Ave, Charleston, 29425. W Curtis Worthington, Jr, Dir; Anne K Donato, Cur
Holdings: Vols 6000 Cat Mss Pix Slides Microforms
Budget: ($3000)
Notes: The nucleus of our collections is the rare medical books that belonged to the Library of the Medical Society of South Carolina (a Charleston society founded in 1789, which started our college of medicine in 1824). Our special interest is the collection of South Carolina medical material and anything connected with the Medical University of South Carolina. We have old medical instruments and equipment, also.

AUTHORS, SOUTH DAKOTA

SD —NORTHERN STATE COLLEGE, Beulah Williams Library, Documents & Reference Dept, Aberdeen, 57401. Keith W Warne, Librn
Holdings: Vols 7000 Cat Maps Pix Microforms
Budget: $1000
Notes: Incl state documents, materials about South Dakota and the surrounding area and works by South Dakota residents.

SD —SOUTH DAKOTA HISTORICAL RESOURCE CENTER, Library, Soldiers Memorial Bldg, Pierre, 57501. Rosemary Evetts, Librn
Holdings: Vols 1020 Cat Mss Maps Pix
Budget: $2000
Notes: South Dakota state and territorial materials. Picture collection has been cataloged and numbers appoximately 20,000 items, of which we have negatives for about half. South Dakota materials include items on general state and territorial history, biographical, autobiographical, political, geological, economic and county and town materials.

SD —AUGUSTANA COLLEGE, Mikkelsen Library & Learning Resource Center, Center for Western Studies, Sioux Falls, 57197. Ronelle Thompson, Dir Library
Holdings: Vols (40,000) Cat Mss Maps Pix Slides Microforms
Budget: ($130,000)
Notes: The Center for Western Studies,

AUTHORS, SOUTH DAKOTA (cont.)

located in the Mikkelsen Library, is an archival and research agency of Augustana College. Dedicated to the history and culture of the Great Plains and the Trans-Mississippi West, the Center collects and preserves materials relating to Plains Indians, immigrant settlers, Norwegiana, Western Americana, Herbert Krause, Frederick Manfred, Donald Parker, Richard F Pettigrew, Augustana College, the Episcopal Diocese of South Dakota, the South Dakota District of the American Lutheran Church, the South Dakota Penitentiary and Minnehaha County.

AUTHORS, SPANISH

DC —LIBRARY OF CONGRESS, Manuscript Division, Washington, 20540. John C Broderick, Chief
Notes: 82 microfilm reels of the papers of Ortega Y Gasset, the originals being in Madrid.

NY —NEW YORK PUBLIC LIBRARY, Donnell Foreign Language Library, 20 W 53 St, New York, 10019. Bosiljka Stevanovic, Supvr Librn
Holdings: Vols 9959 Cat
Notes: Books of interest by and about the Dominican Republic, Puerto Rico and Cuba.

AUTHORS, SWEDISH

NY —NEW YORK PUBLIC LIBRARY, Donnell Foreign Language Library, 20 W 53 St, New York, 10019. Bosiljka Stevanovic, Supvr Librn
Holdings: Vols 356 Cat
Notes: Swedish collection incl Swedish authors of Swedish expression. No separate catalog.

AUTHORS, TAMIL

NY —NEW YORK PUBLIC LIBRARY, Donnell Foreign Language Library, 20 W 53 St, New York, 10019. Bosiljka Stevanovic, Supvr Librn
Holdings: Vols 205 Cat
Notes: Tamil collection incl Tamil authors of Tamil expression. No separate catalog.

AUTHORS, TELUGU

NY —NEW YORK PUBLIC LIBRARY, Donnell Foreign Language Library, 20 W 53 St, New York, 10019. Bosiljka Stevanovic, Supvr Librn
Holdings: Vols 140 Cat
Notes: Telugu collection incl Telugu authors of Telugu expression. No separate catalog.

AUTHORS, THAI (SIAMESE)

NY —NEW YORK PUBLIC LIBRARY, Donnell Foreign Language Library, 20 W 53 St, New York, 10019. Bosiljka Stevanovic, Supvr Librn
Holdings: Vols 581 Cat
Notes: Thai collection incl Thai authors of Thai expression. No separate catalog.

AUTHORS, TENNESSEE

TN —CHATTANOOGA-HAMILTON COUNTY, Bicentennial Library, Local History and Genealogy Dept, 1001 Broad St, Chattanooga, 37402. Clara W Swann, Librn
Holdings: Vols (24,561) Cat Mss Maps Pix Microforms
Budget: ($7000)
Notes: General emphasis on Tennessee history, with special attention to collection of items pertaining to Chattanooga (incl history, authors, artists, etc). Special indexes and clipping files supplement book collection. Tennessee census records on microfilm. Newspapers and county records on microfilm. All materials are noncirculating.

TN —UNIVERSITY OF TENNESSEE, MARTIN, Paul Meek Library, Martin, 38238. Joel A Stowers, Dir
Holdings: Vols (1000) Cat

TN —MIDDLE TENNESSEE STATE UNIVERSITY, Andrew L Todd Library, MTSU Box 13, Murfreesboro, 37132. John David Marshall, Head, Reference Dept
Holdings: Vols 6500 Cat
Notes: Tennesseeana and books by Tennessee authors.

TN —PUBLIC LIBRARY OF NASHVILLE & DAVIDSON COUNTY, Nashville Room, Eighth Ave N & Union, Nashville, 37203. David Marshall Stewart, Chief Librn
Holdings: Vols Cat
Notes: Books by Nashville authors. Nashville Room has separate catalog. All materials noncirculating.

AUTHORS, TEXAS

TX —UNIVERSITY OF TEXAS LIBRARIES, General Libraries, Barker Texas History Center, PO Box P, Austin, 78712. Don Carleton, Dir
Holdings: Vols (132,000) Cat Mss Maps Pix Slides Phonorecords Audiotapes Microforms
Notes: See description of entire collection under Texas-History.

TX —NORTH TEXAS STATE UNIVERSITY, Rare Book and Texana Collections, NT Station Box 5188, Denton, 76203. Kenneth Lavender, University Bibliographer
Notes: Larry McMurtry Collection. 64 typescripts; proofs; signed editions; ephemera. Typescripts incl undergraduate and graduate papers, drafts, notes.

TX —TEXAS WOMAN'S UNIVERSITY, Bralley Memorial Library, Box 23715, TWU Sta, Denton, 76204. Metta Nicewarner, Spec Collections Libn
Holdings: Uncat Mss Pix
Notes: The Claire Myers Owens Papers belong to the Texas author, religious philosopher, Zen Buddhist. Includes correspondence, edited mss, galleys and personal items.

TX —UNIVERSITY OF HOUSTON, M D Anderson Memorial Library, University Park, Houston, 77004. David Farmer, Cur, Special Collections; Jean Jackson, Assistant Cur
Holdings: Vols 200 Cat
Notes: The emphasis of this collection is on Houston writers of literature. The writers incl Cynthia McDonald, Leon Hale, Larry McMurtry, Beverly Lowry, Donald Barthelme and others who have resided or currently reside in the Houston area, and incl some writers who write about the Houston area although they do not live there.

AUTHORS, TURKISH

NY —NEW YORK PUBLIC LIBRARY, Donnell Foreign Language Library, 20 W 53 St, New York, 10019. Bosiljka Stevanovic, Supvr Librn
Holdings: Vols 155 Cat
Notes: Turkish collection incl Turkish authors of Turkish expression. No separate catalog.

AUTHORS, UKRAINIAN

NY —NEW YORK PUBLIC LIBRARY, Donnell Foreign Language Library, 20 W 53 St, New York, 10019. Bosiljka Stevanovic, Supvr Librn
Holdings: Vols 862 Cat
Notes: Ukrainian collection incl Ukrainian authors of Ukrainian expression. No separate catalog.

PA —SLAVIA LIBRARY, 418 W Nittany Ave, State College, 16801. W O Luciw, Founder & Dir; Jurij A Luciw, Asst Dir
Holdings: Vols (45,000) Mss Pix
Budget: ($3500)
Notes: Incl 5000 periodicals, 3000 av materials, 4000 artifacts, and 200 art works. Also 16,000 letters, etc from Slavic and other personages.

AUTHORS, URDU

NY —NEW YORK PUBLIC LIBRARY, Donnell Foreign Language Library, 20 W 53 St, New York, 10019. Bosiljka Stevanovic, Supvr Librn
Holdings: Vols 341 Cat
Notes: Urdu collection incl Urdu authors of Urdu expression. No separate catalog.

AUTHORS, UTAH

UT —PROVO CITY PUBLIC LIBRARY, 13 N 100 E, Provo, 84601. Larry Hortin, Dir
Holdings: Vols (600) Cat
Notes: Western states history with emphasis on Utah State and Utah County.

†UT —UNIVERSITY OF UTAH, Marriott Library, Salt Lake City, 84112.
Notes: Manuscripts and papers of historian-biographer Fawn M Brodie (d 1981). Incl taped interviews with Richard Nixon, and notes, clippings, reviews, articles, and about 400 books used in her researches on Nixon, Thomas Jefferson, and Sir Richard Burton, in preparation of their biographies.

AUTHORS, VERMONT

VT —TRINITY COLLEGE LIBRARY, Colchester Ave, Burlington, 05401.
Holdings: Vols (650) Cat
Budget: ($500)
Notes: "Vermont Collection" is chiefly a collection of Vermontiana book titles, many of which are cataloged and in most cases are available for general circulation. A limited number of special (fine/rare) titles are designated for in-house use only. Emphasis is upon Vermont history, works by and about Vermont authors, with some titles related to genealogy.

VT —LYNDON STATE COLLEGE LIBRARY, Lyndonville, 05851. Suzanne Gallagher, Head Librn
Holdings: Vols (1200) Cat Mss Maps Pix Microforms
Notes: Collection incl any and all works on Vermont and Vermonters as well as reports from state and local government agencies. Particular attention is paid to Northeast Kingdom.

VT —VERMONT DEPARTMENT OF LIBRARIES, Law & Documents Unit, 111 State St, Montpelier, 05602. Vivian Bryan, Librn
Holdings: Vols (42,000) Cat Maps Microforms
Budget: ($3000)
Notes: Vermontiana. Incl largest known collection of Vermont newspapers, authors and imprints. The library prepares and annual *Checklist of Available Vermont State* Publications.

AUTHORS, VIETNAMESE

NY —NEW YORK PUBLIC LIBRARY, Donnell Foreign Language Library, 20 W 53 St, New York, 10019. Bosiljka Stevanovic, Supvr Librn
Holdings: Vols 816 Cat
Notes: Vietnamese collection incl Vietnamese authors of Vietnamese expression. No separate catalog.

AUTHORS, VIRGINIA

VA —UNIVERSITY OF VIRGINIA, Alderman Library, Manuscripts Dept, Charlottesville, 22901. Edmund Berkeley Jr, Cur
Holdings: Cat Mss Pix
Notes: The Virginia Authors Collection includes extensive printed and manuscript material on the following authors: James Branch Cabell, ca 2500 items, unpublished guide available; John Esten Cooke, ca 2 feet of material; Ellen Glasgow, ca 2000 items, unpublished guide available; Mary Johnston, ca 4000 items; Frances Parkinson Keyes, ca 3000 items; Harry Edward Neal, ca 4500 items, unpublished guide available; Edgar Allan Poe, ca 10,000 documents and related items. Bibliography: Jon Carl Miller, *John Henry Ingram's Poe Collection at the University of Virginia* (Charlottesville: University of Virginia Press, 1960). Amelie Rives (Princess Troubetzskoy), ca 300 items, unpublished guide available; John Reuben Thompson, ca 500 items, unpublished guide

AUTHORS, VIRGINIA (cont.)

available; George Tucker, ca60 items. Also incl are letters of many other Virginia authors, such as Sherwood Anderson, Hawthorne Daniel, Murrell Edmunds, George Cary Eggleston, John Fox, Katie Letcher Lyle, John Pendleton Kennedy, Julian Rutherford Meade, Thomas Nelson Page, Virginius Dabney, Jane McClary, Clifford Dowdey, Peter Taylor, and others, some of whom are reported in other catagories.

See also entry under Journalists.

VA —RANDOLPH-MACON WOMAN'S COLLEGE, Lipscomb Library, Lynchburg, 24503. Frances White, Ref Librn
Holdings: Vols 1704 Cat Mss
Notes: Published writings by Virginia women.

VA —VIRGINIA COMMONWEALTH UNIVERSITY, James Branch Cabell Library, Richmond, 23284. Daniel Yanchisin, Special Collections Librn
Holdings: Vols 3600
Notes: A collection of approximately 3600 volumes by post 1945 American poets including some bibliography and criticism. 2000 books are cataloged and the remainder are accessible by author. The collection includes the library and archival holdings of two literary support organizations, New Virginia Review, Inc and the Poetry Society of Virginia.

AUTHORS, WASHINGTON (STATE)

WA —BELLINGHAM PUBLIC LIBRARY, 210 Central Ave, Bellingham, 98225. Claudia McCain, Dir
Holdings: Cat Mss Pix
Notes: Ella Higginson was a poet of the Pacific Coast who is claimed by Oregon and Washington. Her published writing was done in Bellingham. Collection of her works incl all her published poetry except for her first book, a miniature paper-bound brochure written in 1894. Published description of her collected works in *History of Oregon* Literature, by Alfred Powers (Metropolitan Press, 1935), pp 427-431.

WA —WASHINGTON STATE LIBRARY, Washington/Northwest Rm, State Library Bldg, Olympia, 98504. Nancy B Pryor, Research Consultant
Holdings: Vols 8000 Cat Mss Pix Microforms
Notes: Mss, photographs and microfilm largely limited to Washington territorial and state materials as is the file of pamphlets and newspaper clippings, which includes both historical and current material. The book collection incl works on the four Pacific Northwest States, Alaska, and British Columbia, and books by Washington authors.

AUTHORS, WEST INDIAN

DC —HOWARD UNIVERSITY, Moorland-Spingarn Research Center, 500 Howard Place NW, Washington, 20059. Clifford L Muse, Jr, Acting Dir

VI —COLLEGE OF THE VIRGIN ISLANDS, Ralph M Paiewonsky Library, Saint Thomas, 00802. Ernest C Wagner, Dir
Holdings: Vols 250 Cat
Notes: Novels and plays by West Indians.

AUTHORS, WISCONSIN

WI —UNIVERSITY OF WISCONSIN, MADISON, Cooperative Children's Book Center, Helen C White Hall, Rm 4290, 600 N Park St, Madison, 53706. Ginny Moore Kruse, Dir
Holdings: Vols (25,000) Cat
Notes: Cooperative Children's Book Center collections incl most US trade books published for children in last 24 months; first editions of recommended US children's trade books published since 1965; over 400 alternative press books published for children in US and Canada since 1970; children's books about Wisconsin and by Wisconsin authors and illustrators; representative 19th and early 20th century American children's books; 19th century children's periodicals; first and significant editions of Newbury and Caldecott Medal books; historical and contemporary toybooks; 75 vols of Mother Goose published since 1828; 160 vols of Thorton Burgess books, many first editions; ms and original artwork for Ellen Raskin's *The Westing Game* and *The Mysterious Disappearance of Leon (I Mean Noel);* juvenile mass market and traderomance fiction.

WI —MILWAUKEE PUBLIC LIBRARY, 814 W Wisconsin Ave, Milwaukee, 53233. Donald J Sager, City Librn
Holdings: Vols 800
Notes: Includes titles indexed in *Index To Fairy Tales, Myths and Legends* by Mary Huse Eastman and supplements and in Norma Olin Ireland's *Index to Fairy Tales* 1949-1972. Also titles indexed in *Index to Children's Poetry* and supplements by John and Sara Brewton. Dates of publication between 1850-1940 incl many of the old series books and textbooks. More than 150 past and present authors and illustrators represented.

AUTHORS, WOMEN see Women Authors

AUTHORS, WYOMING

WY —NATRONA COUNTY PUBLIC LIBRARY, 307 E Second St, Casper, 82601. Jo W Wilbert, Documents/Reference Librn
Holdings: Vols (2048) Cat Mss Maps Pix
Notes: The Wyoming Room houses a collection of materials about Wyoming and/or by Wyoming authors. The intent is to collect all possible material that relates to Wyoming. Incl city, county, and state documents.

AUTHORS, YIDDISH

NY —NEW YORK PUBLIC LIBRARY, Donnell Foreign Language Library, 20 W 53 St, New York, 10019. Bosiljka Stevanovic, Supvr Librn
Holdings: Vols 698 Cat
Notes: Yiddish collection incl Yiddish authors of Yiddish expression. No separate catalog.

NY —YIVO INSTITUTE FOR JEWISH RESEARCH, Library & Archives, 1048 Fifth Ave, New York, 10028. Dina Abramowicz, Librn; Marek Web, Archivist
Holdings: Vols 315,000 Mss Maps Pix Slides
Notes: The most extensive collection in existence of Yiddish books and periodicals. Covers American, European, Soviet, Israeli and other publications from 16th century to the present. Scholarship in the Yiddish field, as well as translations from Yiddish into other languages are incl. The archives division contains unpublished mss, correspondence and pictures, incl the library and archives of Max Weinreich.
Publications: *Guide to the YIVO Library, 1975; Guide to Major Collections in the YIVO Archives, 1973.*

AUTHORS LEAGUE OF AMERICA

NY —NEW YORK PUBLIC LIBRARY, Research Libraries, General Research Division, Fifth Ave & 42 St, New York, 10018. Rodney Phillips, Chief
Holdings: Vols (2,225,000) Cat Maps Pix Microforms
Budget: ($775,718)
Notes: Archives, memorabilia.

AUTHORSHIP

AZ —ARIZONA STATE UNIVERSITY, Library, Tempe, 85287. Marilyn Wurzburger, Special Collections Librn
Notes: Reflecting his roles of reporter, photographer and novelist, Ted Schwarz's papers cover subject areas such as investigative journalism, psychology, criminal justice, law, numismatics, visual communication, photography and writing as a career. Collection incl extensive research materials from the author's study and reporting of the "Hillside Strangler" case which deals with multiple personalities. Partially cataloged and indexed, the collection consists of 140 linear feet of multi-media materials: vols, magazines, newspaper articles, galley proofs, interviews and correspondence, reel-to-reel tapes, audiotapes and videotapes.

CO —NATIONAL WRITERS CLUB LIBRARY, 1450 S Havana, Suite 620, Aurora, 80012. Donald E Bower, Dir
Holdings: Vols 1000 Uncat Mss
Budget: ($5000)
Notes: Material on specific and special interest to writers.

FL —UNIVERSITY OF FLORIDA, Libraries, Special Collections, W University Ave, Gainesville, 32611. Sidney Ives, Librn & Rare Books
Holdings: Vols (8000) Cat Mss
Notes: Fiction by Florida writers, in ms when possible to obtain.

NY —GRADUATE CENTER OF THE CITY UNIVERSITY OF NEW YORK, William H and Gwynne K Crouse Library for Publishing Arts, 33 W 42 St, New York, 10036. Alfred H Lane, Dir
Notes: Recently established and still growing, but intended to become the authoritative source of materials in the field, of particular value in research about the publishing industry. Open to staff members of publishing houses, students, scholars, authors, printers, and booksellers. Primarily 20th century materials, and particularly useful for research on technical, financial, and historical matters. Much on the history of individual houses, economics of authorship; marketing and distribution of books; etc.

AUTO COURTS see Tourist Camps, Hotels, Etc.

AUTOCODES see Programming Languages (Electronic Computers)

AUTOGENIC TRAINING

VA —ASSOCIATION FOR RESEARCH & ENLIGHTENMENT, Library, 67 & Atlantic Avenue, PO Box 595, Virginia Beach, 23451. Stephen Jordan, Library Mgr
Holdings: Vols (3000) Cat
Notes: Emphasis on Christian, Buddhist, Hindu religions, mysticism, comparative religion, psychological approach to biofeedback, autogenics, etc.

AUTOGENOUS WELDING see Welding

AUTOMATIC COMPUTERS see Computers

AUTOGRAPHS—COLLECTIONS

CA —SAINT JOHN'S SEMINARY, Edward Laurence Doheny Memorial Library, The Estelle Doheny Collection, 5012 E Seminary Rd, Camarillo, 93010. Rita S Faulders, Cur
Notes: Incl letters and documents.

CA —CLAREMONT COLLEGES, Honnold Library, Ninth & Dartmouth, Claremont, 91711. Tania Rizzo, Special Collections Dept Head
Holdings: Vols 250 // Uncat Mss
Notes: Papers of Elbert A Wickes, 1884-1975, theatrical and lecture tour manager. Among his clients were Winston Churchill, William Butler Yeats, Houdini, Lowell Thomas, Vilhjalmur Stefansson, and Roy Chapman Andrews. He managed three American tours for the Abbey Players during the 1930s, was partner and producer of Fritz Leiber Shakespeare plays, the Water Follies of 1937, and the Affiliated Lyceum and Chautauquas Association. The collection is rich in autograph and photographic materials. There are 750 items relative to the Abbey Players. Card file and inventory available. Restricted use.

CT —YALE UNIVERSITY, Box 1603A, Yale Station, New Haven, 06520.

IL —SOUTHERN ILLINOIS UNIVERSITY, CARBONDALE, Delyte W Morris Library,

AUTOGRAPHS—COLLECTIONS (cont.)

Special Collections Dept, Carbondale, 62901. David V Koch, Cur of Special Collections; Louisa Bowen, Cur of Manuscripts
Holdings: // Cat Mss
Notes: Incl the Philip D Sang and the Alfred C Berol collections of documents of American presidents; the James S Schoff collection of letters of Civil War generals; and the Elbridge Gerry Collection of Elsie O and Philip D Sang. Separate catalogs exist for each collection.

IN —INDIANA UNIVERSITY, Lilly Library, Seventh St, Bloomington, 47405. William R Cagle, Librn
Holdings: // Mss
Notes: Letters and writings by Thomas Curtis Clark, 1909-1957; autographs collected by him; poems written by other authors. Writings by other authors present incl pieces by W H Auden, Witter Bynner, Harry Kemp, Vachel Lindsay, Edgar Lee Masters, Carl Sandburg, and Sara Teasdale. 761 items.

ME —BOWDOIN COLLEGE, Library, Brunswick, 04011. Dianne M Gutscher, Cur of Special Collections
Holdings: Vols Cat Mss
Notes: The Charles Livingston French Autograph Collection contains about 800 letters of illustrious French personalities, primarily of the 18th and 19th centuries, incl Balzac, Diderot, Rousseau, and Voltaire.

MD —JOHNS HOPKINS UNIVERSITY, Milton S Eisenhower Library, Charles & 34 Sts, Baltimore, 21218. Ann S Gwyn, Assistant Dir for Special Collections
Holdings: // Cat Mss
Notes: 7 scrapbooks of 1200 letters of Americans of the early 19th century: statesmen, writers, New York lawyers, women and clergymen, individually cataloged in manuscript room.

MD —JOHNS HOPKINS UNIVERSITY, Milton S Eisenhower Library, Special Collections, John Work Garrett Library, 4545 N Charles St, Baltimore, 21210. Jane Katz, Garrett Librn
Holdings: Vols Cat Mss Maps
Notes: The John Work Garrett Library incl 100 maps; 1500 autograph letters; early voyages and travels; Americana; early Maryland imprints and Marylandia; Bible collection; 17th century English Literature (4 Shakespeare folios, 2 quartos); ornithology and natural history (complete set of Gould's Birds); early illustrated books; 19th and 20th century adult and children's illustrated books; typography (Kent Currie), limited editions, incl Bruce Rogers proof sheets; Fowler Architectural Collection (has own book catalog); Sidney Lanier Personal Library, books he wrote and his ms music collection. Downs (1961-70) 444.

MA —AMHERST COLLEGE, Library, Amherst, 01002. John Lancaster, Special Collections Librn
Holdings: Cat Mss
Notes: These Signers of the Declaration of Independence documents are bound in one volume. Each signer is represented by at least one document.

MA —BOSTON UNIVERSITY, Mugar Memorial Library, Special Collections Dept, 771 Commonwealth Ave, Boston, 02215. Howard B Gotlieb, Dir
Holdings: Cat Mss
Notes: Especially strong in collections of modern authors, poets, journalists, musicians, actors and actresses, etc.

MA —WILLIAMS COLLEGE, Sawyer Library, Williamstown, 01267. Phyllis L Cutler, Dir
Holdings: Cat Mss Pix
Notes: Incl the Gates W McGarrah Collection of Presidential Autographs, originally assembled by William Henry Poor, containing handwritten letters and documents by every President from Washington to Theodore Roosevelt. The Library has numerous other presidential autograph pieces as well.

MO —WASHINGTON UNIVERSITY, Libraries, Special Collections Dept, Campus Box 1061, St Louis, 63130.
Notes: The Ira Adler Collection (of the noted bookman), incl his collection of mss, autographs, and correspondence of 19th and 20th century literary and historical figures.

NE —OMAHA PUBLIC LIBRARY, Omaha, 68102. Michael Phipps, Dir
Notes: Incl 832 autographs, chiefly attached to letters and documents. Prior to 1893, chiefly 19th century Americans. Byron Reed Collection.

NJ —NEWARK PUBLIC LIBRARY, Art & Music Dept, 5 Washington St, Newark, 07101. William J Dane, Supv
Holdings: Vols (50,000) Cat Mss Maps Pix Slides Microforms VF
Notes: All phases of art and all periods of art history are covered in books and periodicals; supporting collections incl 1,000,000 illustrations, 2000 portfolios of plates, 15,000 fine prints, 15,000 slides, historic maps, manuscripts and book collection on the history of fine printing, posters and autographs, extensive vertical file.

NY —COLUMBIA UNIVERSITY LIBRARIES, Rare Book & Manuscript Library, 801 Butler Library, 535 W 114 St, New York, 10027. Kenneth A Lohf, Librn
Notes: The Frederick C Schang Collection. About 650 calling cards of great and near-great celebrities. Most contain autographs or holograph notes. Restricted use.

NY —NEW YORK PUBLIC LIBRARY, Performing Arts Research Center, Billy Rose Theatre Collection, 111 Amsterdam Ave, New York, 10023. Dorothy L Swerdlove, Cur
Holdings: Cat
See also entry under Theatre - History.

NY —NEW YORK PUBLIC LIBRARY, Rare Books and Manuscripts Div, Fifth Ave & 42 St, New York, 10018. William L Joyce, Asst Dir; Susan E Davis, Cur of Mss
Holdings: Cat Mss
Budget: ($7161)
Notes: Incl autograph collections, and fraudulent signatures and documents.

NY —NEW YORK PUBLIC LIBRARY, Music Div, 111 Amsterdam Ave, New York, 10023. Frank C Campbell, Chief
Notes: Composers' autographs on microfilm. Works of 17-20th century composers. Major holdings: Bach, Handel, Beethoven. Incl mss.

NY —JERVIS PUBLIC LIBRARY, 613 N Washington St, Rome, 13440. William A Dillon, Dir
Holdings: // Cat Mss
Notes: Two autograph collections. (1) The Huntington Autograph Collection of 108 pieces (originals and typescript with index of signatories), 1689-1897, comprised of correspondence, printed documents, leases, deeds, proclamations, papers relating to slavery and apprenticing. Letters incl 24 from 6 signers of the Declaration of Independence (as Samuel Huntington, Roger Sherman, Robert Morris); 14 letters from and 4 proclamations of Governor Jonathan Trumball; numerous letters to Benjamin Huntington (2) The Thomas C Bright Autograph Collection of 169 pieces (originals and typescript with index of signatories), 1702-1872, comprised of correspondence, deeds, indentures, leases. Letters written during the Revolutionary era incl 22 letters from 11 signers of the Declaration of Independence; 2 letters from George Washington. Among the items are letters from Lafayette, Henry Clay,Horace Mann; autographs of men such as Charles Lamb, Noah Webster, John Jay. Letters concerning the feasibility of constructing Erie Canal included.

PA —HAVERFORD COLLEGE, Magill Library, Special Collections Dept, Haverford, 19041. Diana Alteu, Manuscripts Librn; E Rotau Sargent, Cricket Collection Librn
Holdings: Cat
Notes: The Charles Roberts autograph letters collection of some 20,000 pieces, incl many of scientists and literary and political figures.

PA —AMERICAN PHILOSOPHICAL SOCIETY, Library, 105 S Fifth St, Philadelphia, 19106. Edward C Carter II, Librn
Holdings: Cat Mss
Notes: Collection (as it was in 1970) is incl in *Catalog of Books in the American Philosophical Society Library* (Westport, Conn: Greenwood Publishing Corp, 1970) and *Catalog of Manuscripts in the American Philosophical Society Library* (Westport, Conn: Greenwood Publishing Corp, 1970). Both of these are reproductions of APS Library catalog cards, incl author, subject, and title entries.

PA —FREE LIBRARY OF PHILADELPHIA, Rare Book Dept, Logan Sq, Philadelphia, 19103. Marie E Korey, Rare Book Librn
Holdings: Uncat Mss
Notes: The John Frederick Lewis Collection of 1650 autograph letters of 17th and 18th century British engravers. Also, the Norman H and Charlotte A Strouse Collection of 100 selected autograph letters of presidents of the US.

PA —HISTORICAL SOCIETY OF PENNSYLVANIA, Library, 1300 Locust St, Philadelphia, 19107. David Fraser, Librn
Holdings: Vols (230,000) Mss Maps Pix Microforms
Notes: Incl over 14,000,000 ms pieces. The Library Company of Philadelphia mss are on deposit with the Historical Society of Pennsylvania. Many of the Society's rare books are on deposit with the Library Company. The Society maintains the collections of the Genealogical Society of Pennsylvania, incl some 20,000 printed genealogies, original mss, family, church, and civil records.

PA —WEST CHESTER UNIVERSITY, Francis Harvey Green Library, West Chester, 19380. R Gerald Schoelkopf, Special Collections Librn
Holdings: Vols 2000 Cat
Notes: The collection was begun in 1881 by Dr George Morris Philips and continued until his death in 1920. It contains autographs and inscriptions from practically all prominent English and American authors, as well as outstanding world figures in other fields. A small supplementary collection has been added since 1920.

RI —PROVIDENCE PUBLIC LIBRARY, 150 Empire St, Providence, 02903. Lance J Bauer, Special Collections Librn
Holdings: // Cat Mss
Notes: The Daniel Berkeley Updike Autograph Collection of 800 ms letters and historical documents, primarily New England, from late 17th to mid-19th century with emphasis on Rhode Island politics; American Revolution; French military figures; naval heroes of the Revolution, Tripolitan War and War of 1812; Civil War figures and US presidents. Illustrious personages represented incl: Henry David Thoreau, Daniel Webster, John Hay, Marquis de Lafayette, Henry Wadsworth Longfellow, and other notables. Material must be used in-house. Limited photocopying for educational purposes only.

SC —COLLEGE OF CHARLESTON LIBRARY, Special Collections Dept, Charleston, 29401.
Notes: Meltzer Music Collection incl autographed letters and/or photographs of composers and singers; it contains correspondence from C C Chaminade, Alphonse Daudet, Claude Debussy (1907), Emory Elgar (1916), George Gershwin (1928), J Massenet (1888, 1909), Felix Mendelsohn-Bartholdy (1839), Puccini (1911), and C Wolf-Ferrari (1911). Contains also a biography of Charles Henry Meltzer and newsclippings concerning the collection. One box.

TX —TEXAS STATE LIBRARY, Archives Div, 1201 Brazos, PO Box 12927, Capitol Sta, Austin, 78711. David B Gracy II, State Archivist

TX —UNIVERSITY OF HOUSTON-CLEAR LAKE CITY, Neumann Library, 2700 Bay Area Blvd, Houston, 77058.
Notes: The Dee Walker Poetry Collection. A collection of poetry books by mostly American and English authors, many autographed. Collected and subsequently donated to the College by the one-time alternate poet laureate of Texas.

TX —TEXAS TECH UNIVERSITY, Library, Lubbock, 79409. David J Murrah, Assoc Dir

AUTOGRAPHS—COLLECTIONS (cont.)

for Special Collections
Notes: The Samuel Weiselberg Memorial Autographs Collection of examples from distinguished historical and literary persons.

WA —SEATTLE PUBLIC LIBRARY, 1000 Fourth Ave, Seattle, 98104. Ronald A Dubberly, City Librn
Holdings: Cat Pix
Notes: Balch Autograph Collection of contemporary autographs (about 2000//) and photographs of newsworthy persons in all fields. Worldwide scope. Collection begun in late 1920's.

BC —UNIVERSITY OF VICTORIA, McPherson Library, Victoria, V8W 3H5, Can.
Notes: Incl 28 pges, 1828-59; 28 literary autographs of English lords incl, among others, Wellington, Peel, Palmerston, Disraeli, and George Cruikshank.

AUTOMATIC DATA PROCESSING see Electronic Data Processing

AUTOMATIC DATA PROCESSORS see Computers

AUTOMATIC DATA STORAGE see Information Storage and Retrieval Systems

AUTOMATIC DIGITAL COMPUTERS see Computers, Electronic

AUTOMATIC DRAFTING see Computer Graphics

AUTOMATIC FACTORIES see Automation

AUTOMATIC INDEXING see Indexing, Automatic

AUTOMATIC INFORMATION RETRIEVAL see Computers; Information Storage and Retrieval Systems

AUTOMATIC PRODUCTION see Automation

AUTOMATIC PROGRAMMING LANGUAGES see Programming Languages (Electronic Computers)

AUTOMATION

CA —BURROUGHS CORP, Library, 460 Sierra Madre Villa, Pasadena, 91107. Jean Robbins, Librn
Holdings: Vols 12,000 Cat
Notes: Computer theory and technology.

MA —HARVARD UNIVERSITY LIBRARY, John F Kennedy School of Government Library, Manpower and Industrial Relations Collection, Littauer Library, Cambridge, 02138. James C Damaskos, Librn
Holdings: Cat
Notes: Covers international aspects as well as US.

MA —MASSACHUSETTS INSTITUTE OF TECHNOLOGY, Institute Archives, Special Collections, Cambridge, 02139.
Notes: Papers of Norbert Wiener, renowned mathematician, was instrumental in the development of communication and control theories. He coined the word "cybernetics" to describe this new science. Professional papers document the development of this theory, his development as a mathematician, and his effective collaboration with students and colleagues including Vannevar Bush and John von Neumann. Unpublished finding aid with correspondent index is available in the Institute Archives.

NY —ENGINEERING SOCIETIES LIBRARY, 345 E 47 St, New York, 10017. S Kirk Cabeen, Dir
Holdings: Vols 250,000 Cat Maps 16mm Films Microforms
See also entry under Engineering.

NC —GREENSBORO PUBLIC LIBRARY, Business Library, 201 Greene St, Drawer X-4, Greensboro, 27402. Lebby B Lamb, Business Librn
Holdings: Vols (6000) Cat Microforms
Budget: ($12,000)

PA —ENSANIAN PHYSICOCHEMICAL INSTITUTE, Electrotopography Library, PO Box 98, Eldred, 16731. Elisabeth Anahid Ensanian, Chief Librn
Notes: Electrotopographic sensors enable robotic systems to exhibit a very high degree of machine intelligence for total automated manufacturing of "critical metallurgical engineering components." With these sensors, robotic stations in the total automated manufacturing plant can handle or solve most quality control and reliability, on-production-line inspection and testing problems, after a suitable period of learning (establishment of the required *data bank* or multidimensional systems, product profile). ETG machine intelligence or "Expert Systems" can readily and, on-the-spot, determine the multidimensional rank of the product within its own parent product population, map out all of its mechanical properties nondestructively, predict service of fatigue life with over 90 percent reliability, and in the event that a given product is not up tospecifications, determine how best to save the investment; by determining a *reverse engineering* strategy (on-the-spot) and sending the part upstream with instructions for reprocessing so that it can be made to meet the required specifications. In the event a part cannot be reprocessed,then the ETC machine intelligence determines the optimum scrap classification for the defective part. ETC is a new science and technology; the institute has pioneered this field and coined the terms (ETG).

PA —FRANKLIN INSTITUTE LIBRARY, 20 & The Parkway, Philadelphia, 19103. Miriam Padusis, Dir; Charles Wilt, Readers Servs Librn
Holdings: Vols (300,000) Cat Maps Pix Microforms

PA —UNIVERSITY OF PENNSYLVANIA, Towne Scientific Library, 220 S 33 St, Philadelphia, 19104. Charles Meyers, Librn
Holdings: Vols (65,000) Cat

PA —UNIVERSITY OF PENNSYLVANIA, Moore School of Electrical Engineering Library, 203 Moore School, 33 & Walnut Sts, Philadelphia, 19104. Charles Myers, Head Librn
Holdings: Vols (30,000) Cat Microforms

TX —UNIVERSITY OF TEXAS LIBRARIES, Richard W McKinney Engineering Library, 1.3 ECJ, Austin, 78712. Susan B Ardis, Librn
Holdings: Vols (83,548) Cat Microforms
Notes: Strong collection of industrial standards including Federal and Military standards and specifications.

ON —NATIONAL RESEARCH COUNCIL OF CANADA, Aeronautical/Mechanical Engineering Branch Library, Montreal Rd, Ottawa, K1A 0R6, Can. Louise Fletcher, Head
Notes: This branch library of the Canada Institute for Scientific and Technical Information (CISTI) of the National Research Council of Canada, Ottawa, has a collection strong in aeronautical engineering, automatic control, CAD/CAM, robotics, ocean, wind, and solar energy power, hydraulic and coastal engineering, icing, low temperature research, naval engineering, metals and metallurgy, incl composites, tribology, and air, railroad, marine transportation. Library supported the Council contribution to the development of the remote manipular Canadarm for NASA's Space Shuttle Orbiters and more recently, the Canadian Astronaut Program which will contribute payload specialists to NASA's Space Shuttle Program in 1984. 35, 000 monographs, 1200 serials. Report collection: over 500,000 items.

AUTOMATION—LIBRARIES see Libraries—Automation

AUTOMATION IN DOCUMENTATION see Information Storage and Retrieval Systems

AUTOMOBILE ACCIDENTS see Traffic Accidents

AUTOMOBILE DRIVERS

IL —UNIVERSITY OF ILLINOIS, URBANA/CHAMPAIGN, Library, Applied Life Studies Library, 1408 W Gregory Dr, Urbana, 61801.
Holdings: Vols (38,000) Cat Microforms
See also entry under Physical Education and Training.

MI —UNIVERSITY OF MICHIGAN, Transportation Research Institute, Library, 2901 Baxter Rd, Ann Arbor, 48109. Ann C Grimm, Librn
Holdings: Vols (57,000) Cat Mss Maps Pix Slides Microforms
Budget: ($25,000)

AUTOMOBILE ENGINEERING see Automotive Engineering

AUTOMOBILE EXHAUST GAS

MI —US ENVIRONMENTAL PROTECTION AGENCY, Motor Vehicle Emission Laboratory Library, 2565 Plymouth Rd, Ann Arbor, 48105. Debra Talsma, Librn
Holdings: // Uncat Microforms
Notes: No separate catalog. Collection described in: US EPA, Library System Branch, *Guide to EPA Libraries*, July, 1977. Collection includes 9500 technical reports on air pollution from mobile sources (especially automobiles); air pollution legislation (350 vols); fuel economy and conservation (800 technical reports); automobile engineering (300 vols); emission control technology for mobile source (8000 reports and papers); use of methanol and other alternative fuels in motor vehicles (600 technical reports).

AUTOMOBILE INDUSTRY AND TRADE

IN —HENRY BLOMMEL AUTOMOTIVE DATA COLLECTION, Library, Route 5, Connersville, 47331. Henry Blommel, Librn
Holdings: Uncat Pix
Notes: Automotive industry data.

MI —DETROIT PUBLIC LIBRARY, National Automotive History Collection, 5201 Woodward Ave, Detroit, 48202. Gloria Francis, Librn
Holdings: Vols (11,000) Pix
Notes: 11,000 volumes; 60,000 sales brochures; 300,000 photographs.

MI —CAMPBELL-EWALD CO, Reference Center, 30400 Van Dyke, Warren, 48093. Susan Stepek, Mgr
Holdings: Vols 300 Cat Pix
Notes: Bound auto trade publications, books and yearbooks, auto statistical services, pictures, ad collections from 1901: 50 vertical file drawers of clippings and pamphlets, auto booklets and catalogs, most categories from 1924, some from early 1900's. Around 100 current automotive periodical titles.

PA —FRANKLIN INSTITUTE LIBRARY, 20 & The Parkway, Philadelphia, 19103. Miriam Padusis, Dir; Charles Wilt, Readers Servs Librn
Holdings: Vols (300,000) Cat Maps Pix Microforms

PA —FREE LIBRARY OF PHILADELPHIA, Automobile Reference Collection, Logan Sq, Philadelphia, 19103. Louis G Helverson, Jr, Librn in Charge
Holdings: Vols (14,000) Cat Pix Slides
Notes: Collection is concerned with all aspects of automotive industry and its history. Includes shop manuals, instruction books, parts books, and periodicals dealing with all types of bicycles, tricylces and motor vehicles. Industry statistics, corporate annual reports, environmental problems, safety. Incl 18,000 pictures, 1700 slides, 648 microfilm reels, 23,000 sales catalogs, 5000 pieces of ephemera.

TX —NORTHWOOD INSTITUTE, Library, Box 58, Cedar Hill, 75104. Jennifer Cope, Librn
Holdings: Vols (200) Cat Audiotapes 16mm Films Filmstrips
Budget: ($1500)
Notes: Emphasis on automobile marketing, but incl the history of the automobile industry and biographies of people in the industry.

AUTOMOBILE INSURANCE see Insurance, Automobile

AUTOMOBILE MAINTENANCE see Automobiles—Maintenance and Repair

AUTOMOBILE RACING

IN —INDIANAPOLIS MOTOR SPEEDWAY, Hall of Fame Museum, 4790 W 16th St, Indianapolis, 46222. Jack L Martin, Dir
Holdings: Uncat Mss Maps Pix Slides Phonorecords Audiotapes 16mm Films
Notes: No photocopying.

AUTOMOBILE REPAIR see Automobiles—Maintenance and Repair

AUTOMOBILE SAFETY BELTS see Automobile Seat Belts

AUTOMOBILE SEAT BELTS

MI —UNIVERSITY OF MICHIGAN, Transportation Research Information Institute, Public Information Materials Center, 2901 Baxter Rd, Ann Arbor, 48109. Ann Grimm, Librn
Holdings: Vols (5000) Cat Print Materials Slides Phonorecords Audiotapes 16mm Films
Budget: ($200)
Notes: Collection of materials (mostly available free from originators) produced for public information campaigns on alcohol and highway safety, and adult and child restraint systems. Book catalogs to collection available (mailing list): *Alcohol/Safety Public Information Materials Catalog*, no 7. A C Grimm (UMTRI, June 1983); and *Restraint System Public Information Materials Catalog*, no 5, A C Grimm (UMTRI, June 1983).

AUTOMOBILES

CA —BLACKHAWK LIBRARY, 1975 San Ramon Valley Blvd, San Ramon, 94583. Gene Babow, Librn
Holdings: Vols 6800 Cat Mss Maps Pix Slides Microforms
Notes: Consists of books, magazines, catalogs, advertisements, photos, original drawings, clippings, VFs, from antiquity to future concepts, worldwide. Incl engineering and styling information; current projects. A rich and unique source of history and biography for the vehicle industry.

MI —UNIVERSITY OF MICHIGAN, Transportation Research Institute, Library, 2901 Baxter Rd, Ann Arbor, 48109. Ann C Grimm, Librn
Holdings: Vols (57,000) Cat Mss Maps Pix Slides Microforms
Budget: ($25,000)

MI —FLINT PUBLIC LIBRARY, 1026 E Kearsley St, Flint, 48502. Margaret Williams, Head, Business & Industry Dept
Holdings: Vols 1000 Cat Pix
Budget: $1000
Notes: Contains a large amount of noncataloged material such as owner's manuals, advertising brochures, press releases, etc. There is a separate shelf list for the collection, but not a separate author, title, subject catalog. There has been partial indexing of books, periodicals, and other materials contained in this collection.

NY —NEW YORK PUBLIC LIBRARY, Research Libraries, Science and Technology Research Center, Fifth Ave & 42 St, New York, 10018.
Holdings: Vols (1,100,000) Cat Microforms
Budget: ($647,259)

PA —FRANKLIN INSTITUTE LIBRARY, 20 & The Parkway, Philadelphia, 19103. Miriam Padusis, Dir; Charles Wilt, Readers Servs Librn
Holdings: Vols (300,000) Cat Maps Pix Microforms

PA —FREE LIBRARY OF PHILADELPHIA, Automobile Reference Collection, Logan Sq, Philadelphia, 19103. Louis G Helverson, Jr, Librn in Charge
Holdings: Vols (14,000) Cat Pix Slides
Notes: Collection is concerned with all aspects of automotive industry and its history. Includes shop manuals, instruction books, parts books, and periodicals dealing with all types of bicylces, tricylces and motor vehicles. Industry statistics, corporate annual reports, environmental problems, safety. Incl 18,000 pictures, 1700 slides, 648 microfilm reels, 23,000 sales catalogs, 5000 pieces of ephemera.

AUTOMOBILES—ACCIDENTS see Traffic Accidents

AUTOMOBILES—COLLECTORS AND COLLECTING

MI —HUDSON-ESSEX-TERRAPLANE CLUB LIBRARY, 5765 Munger Rd, Ypsilanti, 48197. Charles Liskow, Librn
Notes: Hudson-Essex-Terraplane car advertisements, parts books, owners' manuals, service procedure manuals, sales catalogs and brochures, color specifications, service bulletins, etc. Nominal charge is made for copies. No material will be loaned. About 12 feet shelf length holdings. Cataloged.

AUTOMOBILES—DESIGN AND CONSTRUCTION

MI —US ENVIRONMENTAL PROTECTION AGENCY, Motor Vehicle Emission Laboratory Library, 2565 Plymouth Rd, Ann Arbor, 48105. Debra Talsma, Librn
Holdings: // Uncat Microforms
Notes: No separate catalog. Collection described in: US EPA, Library System Branch, *Guide to EPA Libraries*, July, 1977. Collection includes 9500 technical reports on air pollution from mobile sources (especially automobiles); air pollution legislation (350 vols); fuel economy and conservation (800 technical reports); automobile engineering (300 vols); emission control technology for mobile source (8000 reports and papers); use of methanol and other alternative fuels in motor vehicles (600 technical reports).

MI —LANSING PUBLIC LIBRARY, Local History Room, 401 S Capitol Ave, Lansing, 48914. Jane McClary, Local History Librn
Holdings: Vols (6000) Cat Mss Maps Pix Microforms VF
Notes: Some 350-400 vols about automobiles and the automobile industry. Separate catalog.

MI —GENERAL MOTORS, Design Staff Library, General Motors Technical Center, Warren, 48090. Billie Delevich, Librn
Holdings: Vols 3500
Notes: Incl 130 magazine titles, 85 drawers of automotive catalogs.

OH —CLEVELAND PUBLIC LIBRARY, Science & Technology Dept, 325 Superior Ave, Cleveland, 44114. Jean Z Piety, Head
Holdings: Cat
Notes: Materials on automobile development, engineering and history. Manuals and catalogs.

AUTOMOBILES—DRIVING see Automobile Drivers

AUTOMOBILES—EXHAUST GAS see Automobile Exhaust Gas

AUTOMOBILES—HISTORY

CA —UNIVERSITY OF CALIFORNIA, LOS ANGELES, Research Library, Dept of Special Collections, 405 Hilgard Ave, Los Angeles, 90024. Edward Shreeves, Chairman, Bibliographers Group; David S Zeidberg, Head
Holdings: Cat Mss
Notes: Various collections, incl the Stuart A Work collection of automotive manuals, racing magazines, auto show brochures, etc; and the Ed Cray papers, incl correspondence, mss, etc, related to his history of General Motors Corporation.

CA —SAN DIEGO PUBLIC LIBRARY, Science & Industry Section, 820 E St, San Diego, 92101. Joanne Anderson, Senior Librn
Budget: ($33,000)
Notes: Primarily automotive history and shop manuals.

IN —AUBURN-CORD-DUESENBERG MUSEUM, Tri-Kappa Collection of Auburn Automotive Literature, 1600 S Wayne St, PO Box 271, Auburn, 46706. Skip Marketti, Exec Dir
Holdings: Vols 650 Cat Pix Slides Phonorecords Videotapes 16mm Films Periodicals Blueprints
Notes: Incl 4000 pictures. The literature collection is now being cataloged.

IN —INDIANAPOLIS MOTOR SPEEDWAY, Hall of Fame Museum, 4790 W 16th St, Indianapolis, 46222. Jack L Martin, Dir
Holdings: Uncat Mss Maps Pix Slides Phonorecords Audiotapes 16mm Films
Notes: No photocopying.

MI —UNIVERSITY OF MICHIGAN, Engineering-Transportation Library, 312 Undergraduate Library, Ann Arbor, 48109. Sharon A Balius, Assoc Librn
Holdings: Pix
Notes: The collection contains over 7000 automobile (domestic and foreign) advertisements and brochures from 1902 to the present. Also incl are over 1400 repair manuals for American cars dating from 1907 to the present.

MI —DETROIT PUBLIC LIBRARY, National Automotive History Collection, 5201 Woodward Ave, Detroit, 48202. Gloria Francis, Librn
Holdings: Vols (11,000) Pix
Notes: 11,000 volumes; 60,000 sales brochures; 300,000 photographs.

MI —ALFRED P SLOAN JR MUSEUM, 1221 E Kearsley St, Flint, 48503. Scott M Peters, Curator
Holdings: Uncat Pix
Notes: Catalogs, manuals, photographs of automotive companies. Centers about automobiles produced in our community with heavy emphasis on Buick and Chevrolet literature. Some information on predecessor companies such as carriage and wagon works. About 3000 pieces.

MI —LANSING PUBLIC LIBRARY, Local History Room, 401 S Capitol Ave, Lansing, 48914. Jane McClary, Local History Librn
Holdings: Vols (6000) Cat Mss Maps Pix Microforms VF
Notes: Some 350-400 vols about automobiles and the automobile industry. Separate catalog.

MI —R E OLDS MUSEUM LIBRARY, 240 Museum Drive, Lansing, 48933.
Notes: Emphasizes the contributions that Lansing has made to transportation history; materials on Oldsmobile, Reo, Star, Durant, and Bates cars. Incl books, manuals, magazines, advertisements, photographs, films, slides, audiotapes, videotapes, VF, and art reproductions.

MO —NATIONAL MUSEUM OF TRANSPORT, Reference Library, 3105 Barrett Station Rd, Saint Louis, 63122. John P Roberts, Secretary
Holdings: Vols (10,000) Cat Mss Maps Pix Slides

NH —NEW HAMPSHIRE HISTORICAL SOCIETY, Manuscripts Library, 30 Park St, Concord, 03301. Thomas E Camden, Cur
Holdings: Cat Mss Pix
Notes: Abbot-Downing Truck and Body Co records 1813-1945. Incl correspondence, account book, journals, ledgers, order books, accounts receivable, records of sales, balance sheet for New York branch, records of material mortgaged to Josiah E Fernald, banker, of Concord, New Hampshire, other financial papers, drawings, catalogs, and photos of vehicles, clippings, advertisements, and other papers of a firm based in Concord, New Hampshire, and manufacturing wagons, coaches, carriages, and motor-trucks. 33 linear feet, about 22,000 items.

NY —NEW YORK PUBLIC LIBRARY, Research Libraries, Science and Technology Research Center, Fifth Ave & 42 St, New

AUTOMOBILES—HISTORY (cont.)

York, 10018.
Holdings: Vols (1,100,000) Cat Microforms
Budget: ($647,259)

OH —CLEVELAND PUBLIC LIBRARY, Science & Technology Dept, 325 Superior Ave, Cleveland, 44114. Jean Z Piety, Head
Holdings: Cat
Notes: Materials on automobile development, engineering and history. Manuals and catalogs.

PA —FREE LIBRARY OF PHILADELPHIA, Automobile Reference Collection, Logan Sq, Philadelphia, 19103. Louis G Helverson, Jr, Librn in Charge
Holdings: Vols (14,000) Cat Pix Slidess
Notes: Collection is concerned with all aspects of automotive industry and its history. Includes shop manuals, instruction books, parts books, and periodicals dealing with all types of bicycles, tricycles and motor vehicles. Industry statistics, corporate annual reports, environmental problems, safety. Incl 18,000 pictures, 1700 slides, 648 microfilm reels, 23,000 sales catalogs, 5000 pieces of ephemera.

TX —NORTHWOOD INSTITUTE, Library, Box 58, Cedar Hill, 75104. Jennifer Cope, Librn
Holdings: Vols (200) Cat Audiotapes 16mm Films Filmstrips
Budget: ($1500)
Notes: Emphasis on automobile marketing, but incl the history of the automobile industry and biographies of people in the industry.

TX —SOUTHERN METHODIST UNIVERSITY, DeGolyer Library, Box 396, SMU, Dallas, 75275. Clifton H Jones, Dir
Holdings: Vols (80,000) Cat Mss Maps Pix Slides Microforms
Notes: First editions of prominent authors; also of books in subject emphasis collections. All subjects listed in this vol are strong. Numerous collections of personal papers relating to subjects also.

SK —WESTERN DEVELOPMENT MUSEUM, George Shepherd Library, 2935 Melville St, PO Box 1910, Saskatoon, S7K 3S5, Can. Warren Clubb, Research Coordr
Holdings: Vols (13,000) Documents Maps Pix Slides Audiotapes
Budget: $3500
Notes: Staff reference library. Open to the public although not a lending library. Extensive holdings of agricultural machinery catalogs, from Canadian and American manufacturers and distributors. Other holdings incl automobiles, avaition, museology and Western Canadian history. Partially cataloged.

AUTOMOBILES—INSURANCE see Insurance, Automobile

AUTOMOBILES—MAINTENANCE AND REPAIR

CA —LOS ANGELES PUBLIC LIBRARY, Science & Technology Dept, 630 W Fifth St, Los Angeles, 90071. Billie M Connor, Dept Head
Holdings: Vols 8000 Cat Microforms
Notes: Shop manuals for American and foreign made cars, trucks, motorcycles, and tractors. Specialized manuals on transmissions, air conditioning, air pollution control devices, electrical components, restoration prices, etc. Parts Lists Directories including flat rate and parts price manuals. Indexes include car and other motor vehicles repair manuals by make and model, road tests for specific models appearing in popular automotive periodicals, and an automobile illustration index.

CA —PASADENA PUBLIC LIBRARY, Business-Technology Division, 285 E Walnut St, Pasadena, 91101. Anne Cain, Librn for Reference Services
Holdings: Vols (19,000) Cat Microforms
Budget: ($35,000)
Notes: Investment and financial services (current and historical); trade and industrial directories; corporate annual reports; current economic statistics in business services and in state and federal government publications. Special index to directory collection.

CA —CONTRA COSTA COUNTY LIBRARY, 1750 Oak Park Blvd, Pleasant Hill, 94523. Barbara Potter, Librn
Holdings: Vols (18,000)

CA —SAN DIEGO PUBLIC LIBRARY, Science & Industry Section, 820 E St, San Diego, 92101. Joanne Anderson, Senior Librn
Budget: ($33,000)
Notes: Primarily automotive history and shop manuals.

FL —BREVARD COMMUNITY COLLEGE, Learning Resources Center, Cocoa Campus, Clearlake Rd, Cocoa, 32922. John S French, Ref Librn
Holdings: Vols 174 Cat
Notes: Most of collection comprised of repair manuals to support automotive instruction.

KS —WICHITA PUBLIC LIBRARY, 223 S Main, Wichita, 67202. Larry DePiesse, Head, Business & Technology Dept; Jayne F Young, Business & Technology Dept
Holdings: Vols 2452 Uncat
Budget: $1300
Notes: Unusual collection which dates back many years on every make of car for which repair manuals can be purchased. Lend only on money deposit. No interlibrary loans.

MI —DETROIT PUBLIC LIBRARY, National Automotive History Collection, 5201 Woodward Ave, Detroit, 48202. Gloria Francis, Librn
Holdings: Vols (11,000) Pix
Notes: 11,000 volumes; 60,000 sales brochures; 300,000 photographs.

MI —FLINT PUBLIC LIBRARY, 1026 E Kearsley St, Flint, 48502. Margaret Williams, Head, Business & Industry Dept
Holdings: Vols 1000 Cat Pix
Budget: $1000
Notes: Contains a large amount of noncataloged material such as owners' manuals, advertising brochures, press releases, etc. There is a separate shelf list for the collection, but not a separate author, title, subject catalog. There has been partial indexing of books, periodicals, and other materials contained in this collection.

MI —GENERAL MOTORS CORP, AC Spark Plug Div, Engineering Library, 1300 N Dort Hwy, Flint, 48556. Eileen L Lane, Librn
Holdings: Vols (150) Uncat Microforms
Notes: Incl *Thomas Register* microfiche catalogs (over 100); Society of Automotive Engineers *Transactions.* Over 150 automotive service manuals, allied and competitive; some foreign. Also 100 cartridges of microfilm on military specifications.

MI —GOGEBIC COMMUNITY COLLEGE, Alex D Chisholm Learning Resources Center, Greenbush & Jackson Rd, Ironwood, 49938. Charles Tetzlaff, Dir of Learning Resources
Holdings: Vols (20,000)

NH —NEW HAMPSHIRE VOCATIONAL-TECHNICAL COLLEGE, Library, Prescott Hill, Laconia, 03246. Patty Miller, Librn
Holdings: Vols 475 Cat Phonorecords Audiotapes Filmstrips Microforms Film Loops
Budget: $475

NC —TECHNICAL INSTITUTE OF ALAMANCE, Learning Resources Center, Jimmy Kerr Rd, PO Box 623, Haw River, 27258. Ron Plummer, Coordr
Holdings: Vols (480) Cat Pix Phonorecords Audiotapes Filmstrips Microforms

OH —CLEVELAND PUBLIC LIBRARY, Science & Technology Dept, 325 Superior Ave, Cleveland, 44114. Jean Z Piety, Head
Holdings: Cat
Notes: Materials on automobile development, engineering and history. Manuals and catalogs.

PA —FREE LIBRARY OF PHILADELPHIA, Automobile Reference Collection, Logan Sq, Philadelphia, 19103. Louis G Helverson, Jr, Librn in Charge
Holdings: Vols (14,000) Cat Pix Slides
Notes: Collection is concerned with all aspects of automotive industry and its history. Includes shop manuals, instruction books, parts books, and periodicals dealing with all types of bicylces, tricylces and motor vehicles. Industry statistics, corporate annual reports, environmental problems, safety. Incl 18,000 pictures, 1700 slides, 648 microfilm reels, 23,000 sales catalogs, 5000 pieces of ephemera.

PA —CARNEGIE LIBRARY OF PITTSBURGH, Science & Technology Dept, 4400 Forbes Ave, Pittsburgh, 15213. Catherine M Brosky, Dept Head
Notes: Automobile shop repair manuals for numerous makes and models.

SC —HORRY GEORGETOWN TECHNICAL COLLEGE, Library, Hwy 501, Box 1966, Conway, 29526. Barbara Brittain, Librn
Holdings: Vols (20,000) Cat Slides Microforms

SC —SUMTER TECHNICAL COLLEGE, Library, 506 Guignard Dr, Sumter, 29150. Fanny M Davis
Holdings: Vols (20,000) Cat Mss Maps Pix Slides Microforms
Budget: ($50,000)
Notes: Incl 300 books on automotive repair.

WI —MILWAUKEE PUBLIC LIBRARY, 814 W Wisconsin Ave, Milwaukee, 53233. Donald J Sager, City Librn
Holdings: Cat
Notes: Extensive collection of modern and historical automobile manuals, foreign and domestic.

BC —BURNABY PUBLIC LIBRARY, 4455 Alaska St, Burnaby, V5C 5T3, Can. Bryan L Bacon, Librn
Holdings: Vols 2000 Cat
Notes: Extensive collection of modern automobile manuals.

BC —NEW WESTMINSTER PUBLIC LIBRARY, 716 Sixth Ave, New Westminster, V3M 2B3, Can. Alan Woodland, Dir
Notes: Large collection of automobile service manuals.

ON —METROPOLITAN TORONTO LIBRARY, Science & Technology Dept, 789 Yonge St, Toronto, M4W 2G8, Can. Margaret Walshe, Head
Holdings: Vols (120,000) Cat Microforms VF
Notes: Large collection of shop manuals, from 1918. Manuals are collected for every make of car made or imported into Canada, with emphasis on North America makes.

AUTOMOBILES—MOTORS—EXHAUST see Automobile Exhaust Gas

AUTOMOBILES—REPAIRING see Automobiles—Maintenance and Repair

AUTOMOBILES—SAFETY MEASURES

MI —GENERAL MOTORS, Research Laboratories Library, General Motors Technical Center, Warren, 48090. Helene A Brown, Sr Librn
Holdings: Vols 100,000 Uncat Mss Microforms
Notes: Automotive safety information system.

AUTOMOBILES—SEAT BELTS see Automobile Seat Belts

AUTOMOBILES—SERVICING see Automobiles—Maintenance and Repair

AUTOMOBILES, ANTIQUE see Vintage Cars

AUTOMOBILES, MILITARY

VA —US ARMY TRANSPORTATION MUSEUM, Library, Bldg 300, Fort Eustis, 23604. Dennis P Mroczkowski, Museum Cur
Holdings: Vols (1254) Uncat Maps Pix 16mm Films
Budget: ($150)
Notes: Mainly US Army transportation from WW II on.

AUTOMOTIVE ENGINEERING

MI —UNIVERSITY OF MICHIGAN, Engineering-Transportation Library, 312

AUTOMOTIVE ENGINEERING (cont.)

Undergraduate Library, Ann Arbor, 48109. Maurita Holland, Librn
Holdings: Vols (400,000) Cat Microforms
Budget: ($225,000)

MI —US ENVIRONMENTAL PROTECTION AGENCY, Motor Vehicle Emission Laboratory Library, 2565 Plymouth Rd, Ann Arbor, 48105. Debra Talsma, Librn
Holdings: / / Uncat Microforms
Notes: No separate catalog. Collection described in: US EPA, Library System Branch, *Guide to EPA Libraries*, July, 1977. Collection includes 9500 technical reports on air pollution from mobile sources (especially automobiles); air pollution legislation (350 vols); fuel economy and conservation (800 technical reports); automobile engineering (300 vols); emission control technology for mobile source (8000 reports and papers); use of methanol and other alternative fuels in motor vehicles (600 technical reports).

MI —GENERAL MOTORS, Design Staff Library, General Motors Technical Center, Warren, 48090. Billie Delevich, Librn

NH —NEW HAMPSHIRE VOCATIONAL TECHNICAL COLLEGE, Library, 277 R Portsmouth Ave, Stratham, 03885. Nancy L Dodge, Librn
Budget: ($9500)

NY —NEW YORK CITY COMMUNITY COLLEGE, Voorhees Branch Library, 450 W 41 St, New York, 10036. Helena Haezeler, Branch Librn
Holdings: Vols 1500 Cat Videotapes Films
Notes: A selective bibliography is published occasionally.

NC —TECHNICAL INSTITUTE OF ALAMANCE, Learning Resources Center, Jimmy Kerr Rd, PO Box 623, Haw River, 27258. Ron Plummer, Coordr
Holdings: Vols (480) Cat Pix Phonorecords Audiotapes Filmstrips Microforms

PA —SOCIETY OF AUTOMOTIVE ENGINEERS, Library, 400 Commonwealth Dr, Warrendale, 15096. Janet Jedlicka, Librn
Holdings: Vols 200 Cat
Notes: 20,000 papers, 200 books. Incl all publications of the SAE since 1906.

VA —ENSCO, INC, Technical Library, 5400 Port Royal Rd, Springfield, 22151. Sue E Littlepage, Research Librn
Holdings: Vols (5000) Uncat Mss Maps Slides
Notes: Especially railroad technology and seismology.

AUTOMOTIVE ENGINEERING RESEARCH

IN —CUMMINS ENGINE CO, Information Center, 1000 Fifth St, Columbus, 47201. W E Poor, Tech Librn
Holdings: Vols 6000 Uncat Microforms
Notes: Incl Society of Automotive Engineers papers.

AUTOMOTIVE TRANSPORTATION see Transportation, Automotive

AUTOS-DA-FE

OH —HEBREW UNION COLLEGE-JEWISH INSTITUTE OF RELIGION, Klau Library, 3101 Clifton Ave, Cincinnati, 45220. David J Gilner, Reference Librn
Holdings: Cat Mss
Notes: Incl papal bulls, edicts of inquisitions, royal letters, inquisitorial instructions, sermons preached at the autos-da-fe held by the Portuguese Inquisition at Lisbon, Colombia, etc. Early and late histories.

AUTOSUGGESTION see Hypnotism; Mental Suggestion

AUTUMNAL CATARRH see Hay Fever

AVALLONE, MICHAEL

MA —BOSTON UNIVERSITY, Mugar Memorial Library, Special Collections Dept, 771 Commonwealth Ave, Boston, 02215. Howard B Gotlieb, Dir
Holdings: Cat Mss Pix
Notes: Mss, correspondence, etc collected in depth; incl publications by or about.

AVANT-GARDE MOVING PICTURES see Moving Pictures, Avant-Garde

AVANT-GARDE THEATRE see Experimental Theatre

AVERY INSTITUTE

SC —COLLEGE OF CHARLESTON LIBRARY, Special Collections Dept, Charleston, 29401.
Notes: This collection consists mostly of photocopied materials (correspondence, annual reports, financial records, etc) housed at the Amistad Research Center of Dillard University. Established and maintained through much of its history by the American Missionary Assn, this material reflects the organization's work in South Carolina beginning in the Reconstruction era. Incl also oral histories of graduates of Avery Institute.

AVESTA LANGUAGE AND LITERATURE

NY —NEW YORK PUBLIC LIBRARY, Oriental Div, Fifth Ave & 42 St, New York, 10018. E Christian Filstrup, Chief
Holdings: Cat Mss Microforms
Budget: ($56,455)
Notes: Published catalog of holdings.

AVIATION see Aeronautics

AVIATION EDUCATION RESOURCE CENTER

†SD —SOUTH DAKOTA SCHOOL OF MINES & TECHNOLOGY, Devereaux Library, Rapid City, 57701.
Holdings: Vols (3000) Uncat Maps Pix Slides Audiotapes 16mm Films Filmstrips
Notes: A somewhat limited Aviation Resource Center to an area approx 90,000 sq miles in breadth and width, covering western South Dakota; western North Dakota; western Nebraska; eastern Montana; eastern Wyoming; and northeast corner of Colorado. Materials incl are books, periodicals, posters, pictures, etc, from NASA, FAA and various aviation and aeronautics-related companies in the US.

AVIATION INDUSTRY see Airlines—History

AVIATION LAW see Aeronautics—Laws and Legislation

AVIATION MEDICINE see Aerospace Medicine

AVIATORS

DC —LIBRARY OF CONGRESS, Manuscript Division, Washington, 20540. John C Broderick, Chief
Notes: Papers and photographs of the Wright brothers.

DC —LIBRARY OF CONGRESS, Prints & Photographs Div, Washington, 20540.
Notes: Incl the great French collection of Albert and Gaston Tissandier, and the aeronautical biography files compiled by Jules Francois Dupuis-Delcourt. Ms materials are in the Manuscript Division.

MA —RADCLIFFE COLLEGE, Arthur & Elizabeth Schlesinger Library on the History of Women in America, 3 James St, Cambridge, 02138. Patricia Miller King, Dir; Eva Moseley, Cur of Mss
Notes: Correspondence and photographs of and about the aviator Amelia Earhart (1897-1937). Also, papers of her mother, Amy Otis Earhart, including letters from Amelia Earhart and and other aviators.

AVIONIC COMPONENTS see Electronic Industries; Electronic Instruments

AVOCADO

CA —UNIVERSITY OF CALIFORNIA, RIVERSIDE, University Library, Bio-Agricultural Library, Batchelor Hall, Riverside, 92521. Barbara Montanary, Head
Holdings: Vols (130,000) Cat Mss Maps Pix Microforms
Notes: The Bio-Agricultural Library (formerly the Library of Citrus Experiment Station of the University of California) is well known for its complete collections in the fields of the agriculture sciences. It is especially known for its emphasis on entomology, incl bio-control; botany, citriculture, plant sciences, nematology and plant pathology; arid and semi-arid lands research and subtropical agriculture. Specific areas of interest are avocados, dates, desert flora, jojoba, guayule and carob.

AVOCATIONS see Hobbies

AVOT, PIRKE

OH —HEBREW UNION COLLEGE-JEWISH INSTITUTE OF RELIGION, Klau Library, 3101 Clifton Ave, Cincinnati, 45220. David J Gilner, Reference Librn
Holdings: Cat
Notes: Excellent collection of Pirke Avot.

AXELBANK, HERMAN

CA —HOOVER INSTITUTION ON WAR, REVOLUTION & PEACE, Stanford University, Stanford, 94305. Milorad M Drachkovitch, Archivist
Notes: The Herman Axelbank Film Collection on Russian history. Much footage dating from about 1901-1921. Subjects incl Royal Family, Moscow and St Petersburg scenes, the Revolution and Civil War, espec good coverage of Leon Trotsky's role, Siberia, and the Far East. The first 28 of 266 reels have been received (April 1983).

AXES

†WA —WASHINGTON STATE UNIVERSITY, Library, Manuscripts, Archives & Special Collections, Pullman, 99164. John F Guido, Head
Holdings: Cat Mss Maps Pix
Notes: The Carl Parcher Russell papers, a vast resource (24,916 items; 45 linear feet) on American Indian and Western pioneer activities and artifacts. Much on the fur trade; pioneer life; mountain men and trapping; wildlife; primitive life in detail. Also the National Park Service, parks, monuments, etc. Described in *Carl Parcher Russell: An Indexed Register of His Scholarly and Professional Papers, 1920-1967, in the Washington State University* Library (Pullman, 1970), 149 pp.

AYDELOTTE, FRANK, 1880-1956

PA —FRIENDS HISTORICAL LIBRARY OF SWARTHMORE COLLEGE, Swarthmore, 19081. J William Frost, Dir
Holdings: Mss
Notes: Personal papers of Frank Aydelotte, noted educator, President of Swarthmore College, 1921-1940, and Director of the Institute for Advanced Study, 1939-1947. His official papers as President of Swarthmore are also included. Personal papers also pertain to his work as American Secretary to the Rhodes Trustees, Educational Advisor to the Guggenheim Foundation, and member of the Joint Anglo-American Committee of Inquiry on Palestine, 1946.

AYER, FREDERICK

MA —BOSTON UNIVERSITY, Mugar Memorial Library, Special Collections Dept, 771 Commonwealth Ave, Boston, 02215. Howard B Gotlieb, Dir
Holdings: Cat Mss

AYERS, HARRY MELL

†AL —UNIVERSITY OF ALABAMA, Amelia Gayle Gorgas Library, PO Box S, University, 35486.
Notes: The Alabama Collection contains

AYERS, HARRY MELL (cont.)

books about Alabama; by Alabama authors; scrapbooks, pamphlets, newspapers. Such ms collections as the Manly Family, Papers, 1819-1930; Samuel Townsend, Estate papers, 1827-90; Harry Mell Ayers, 1885-1964; and the Gorgas Family, papers 1821-1920.

AYLWORD, JAMES P.

MO —HARRY S TRUMAN LIBRARY, Independence, 64050. Benedict K Zobrist, Dir
Holdings: Mss
Notes: Papers of Harry S Truman's administration; also papers of Edwin G Arnold, James P Aylword, Willa Mae Roberts. Approx 13,000,000 pages on hand.

AYVAZIAN, L. FRED

MA —BOSTON UNIVERSITY, Mugar Memorial Library, Special Collections Dept, 771 Commonwealth Ave, Boston, 02215. Howard B Gotlieb, Dir
Holdings: Cat Mss

AZERBAIJANI LANGUAGE AND LITERATURE

NY —NEW YORK PUBLIC LIBRARY, Oriental Div, Fifth Ave & 42 St, New York, 10018. E Christian Filstrup, Chief
Holdings: Cat Mss Microforms
Budget: ($56,455)
Notes: Published catalog of holdings.

AZERI LANGUAGE see Azerbaijani Language and Literature

AZTEC LANGUAGE

CA —UNIVERSITY OF CALIFORNIA, LOS ANGELES, Research Library, Dept of Special Collections, 405 Hilgard Ave, Los Angeles, 90024. Edward Shreeves, Chairman, Bibliographers Group; David S Zeidberg, Head
Notes: Various collections, incl the John H Grepe and Byron McAfee collections.

AZTECS

CA —UNIVERSITY OF CALIFORNIA, LOS ANGELES, Research Library, Dept of Special Collections, 405 Hilgard Ave, Los Angeles, 90024. Edward Shreeves, Chairman, Bibliographers Group; David S Zeidberg, Head
Notes: Various collections on languages of the Aztec Indians, incl the John H Grepe and Byron McAfee Collections.

DC —LIBRARY OF CONGRESS, Manuscript Division, Washington, 20540. John C Broderick, Chief
Notes: The Hans P Kraus Collection of documents relating to colonial Spanish America, 1492-1819. Focusing on colonial Mexico, incl material on exploration, government, activities of the Inquisition, taxation and economic conditions, relations with the Indians and the French, and the impending loss of land to Anglo-American settlers. Also contains items concerning the history of Spanish Florida, Tezozomoc's chronicle on the history of the Aztecs, and mss describing the explorations of Amerigo Vespucci, Giovanni da Verrazzano, Alvar Nunez Cabeza de Vaca, Pedro de Ursua, and Lope de Aguirre.

TX —UNIVERSITY OF TEXAS LIBRARIES, Nettie Lee Benson Latin American Collection, Sid Richardson Hall 1.109, Austin, 78712. Laura Gutierrez-Witt, Head Librn
Holdings: Vols (450,000) Cat Mss Maps Pix Phonorecords Filmstrips Microforms
See also entry under Latin America.

TX —EL PASO PUBLIC LIBRARY, Mexican American Collection, 501 N Oregon, El Paso, 79901. Iris Espino, Librn
Notes: History and culture of Mexico from pre-Columbian times to the present.

AZUSA FOOTHILLS REGION

CA —AZUSA PACIFIC COLLEGE, Marshburn Memorial Library, Citrus & Alosta, Azusa, 91702. Edward Peterman, Librn
Holdings: Vols 5000 // Maps Pix
Notes: Azusa Foothill Citrus and Local History collection is related to the genesis of Azusa, the citrus industry, the Slauson and Macneil families, and such companies as the Azusa Land and Water Company, Azusa Electric Lighting and Power Company, Azusa Foothill Citrus Association, Azusa Agricultural Water Company, and the Azusa Foothill Citrus Company. Includes letters, ledges, etc.

B

BABBITT BROTHERS TRADING COMPANY

AZ —NORTHERN ARIZONA UNIVERSITY, Special Collection Library, CU Box 6022, Flagstaff, 86011. Peter M Whiteley, Coordr/Archivist; William Mullane, Librn
Notes: Financial records, 1888-1958. Incl records of numerous Babbitt ranches and businesses in Flagstaff and Northern Arizona. Inventory available.

BABBITT FAMILY

AZ —NORTHERN ARIZONA UNIVERSITY, Special Collection Library, CU Box 6022, Flagstaff, 86011. Peter M Whiteley, Coordr/Archivist; William Mullane, Librn
Notes: Collections on various members of the Babbitt Family: Gertrude Babbitt; correspondence and files concerning George, David, and Emma Babbitt, 1849-1929. Joseph Robert Babbitt, Sr; photocopied scrapbook belowing to him, incl miscellaneous receipts, some Babbitt Brothers Trading Company letters, letterheads and information on different businesses in Northern Arizona, 1884-1950. Also, George E Babbitt Book Collection concentrating on the history of Arizona and the Southwest; Rayma Babbitt Sharber Collection. Photocopy of unpublished mss, "Babbitt History," by Dean Smith, 1960's, and Babbitt family genealogical chart, 1821-1976.
See also entry under Babbitt Brothers Trading Company

BABCOCK, WILLIAM WAYNE

PA —TEMPLE UNIVERSITY LIBRARIES, Special Collections Dept, Conwellana-Templana Collection, 13 & Berks St, Philadelphia, 19122. Miriam I Crawford, Cur
Holdings: Vols 10 Cat Mss Pix Audiotapes
Budget: ($30,000)
Notes: W Wayne Babcock (1872-1963) was a surgeon and medical educator of international reputation. The introduction of spinal anesthesia and of steel wire sutures were among his innovations. His personal papers (unprocessed) include manuscripts, correspondence, journal articles, documents, and news clippings, chiefly on medical topics and experiences spanning the first half of the 20th century. 10 linear ft.

BABIES see Infants (Newborn)

BABINGTON, ANTHONY

MA —BOSTON UNIVERSITY, Mugar Memorial Library, Special Collections Dept, 771 Commonwealth Ave, Boston, 02215. Howard B Gotlieb, Dir
Holdings: Cat Mss
Notes: Mss correspondence, etc collected in depth; incl publications by or about.

BABITZ, SOL, 1911-1982

CA —UNIVERSITY OF CALIFORNIA, LOS ANGELES, Music Library, Schonberg Hall, Los Angeles, 90024. Stephen M Fry, Music Librn
Notes: Papers, recordings, correspondence, mss by Sol Babitz (1911-1982), Los Angeles violinist and music scholar.

BABOONS

OR —OREGON REGIONAL PRIMATE RESEARCH CENTER, Library, 505 NW 185 Ave, Beaverton, 97006. Isabel McDonald, Librn
Holdings: Vols (765) Cat Audiotapes 16mm Films Microforms
Notes: Incl small collection of dissertations and theses.

TX —SOUTHWEST FOUNDATION FOR RESEARCH AND EDUCATION LIBRARY, Preston C Northrup Memorial Library, Baboon Information Center, W Loop 410 at Military Dr, PO Box 28147, San Antonio, 78284. Dorothy M Brooks, Baboon
Notes: Principle field of research: Birth defects, atherosclerosis, reproductive physiology, cancer, genetics, organic chemistry, parasitology, primatology and behavioral sciences and their application to problems of drug abuse, alcoholism and ecology. Maintains the largest baboon colony in the world.

BABSON, NAOMI LANE

MA —BOSTON UNIVERSITY, Mugar Memorial Library, Special Collections Dept, 771 Commonwealth Ave, Boston, 02215. Howard B Gotlieb, Dir
Holdings: Cat Mss Pix
Notes: Mss, correspondence, etc collected in depth; incl publications by or about.

BABSON FAMILY

MA —BABSON COLLEGE, Horn Library, Babson Park, 02157. Elizabeth E Di Bartolomeis, Special Collections Librn
Notes: Collections of the Babson Family heirlooms, including books, memorabilia, and photographs which can be examined by special appointment.

BABY FOODS—HISTORY

MI —GERBER PRODUCTS COMPANY, Corporate Library, 445 State St, Fremont, 49412. Sherrie Anderson, Librn
Holdings: Vols (4270) Cat

BABYLONIAN INSCRIPTIONS see Cuneiform Inscriptions

BABYLONIAN LANGUAGE AND LITERATURE see Assyro-Babylonian Language and Literature

BABYLONICA

CT —YALE UNIVERSITY, Sterling Memorial Library, Babylonian Collection, 120 High St, New Haven, 06520. William W Hallo, Cur
Holdings: Vols (12,000) Cat Mss Pix
Budget: $2500
Notes: 30,000 mss in form of Babylonian tablets; 6000 seals and other art objects from Mesopotamia and the rest of the Ancient Near East.

NY —NEW YORK PUBLIC LIBRARY, Rare Books and Manuscripts Div, Fifth Ave & 42 St, New York, 10018. William L Joyce, Asst Dir; Susan E Davis, Cur of Mss
Holdings: Cat Mss
Budget: ($7161)

ON —NATIONAL LIBRARY OF CANADA, 395 Wellington St, Ottawa, K1A 0N4, Can. Andre Preibish, Dir
Notes: *The Jacob M Lowy Collection* over 2000 works of very rare Hebraica and Judaica. Among outstanding items are 30 incunabula - the first printed edition of the Babylonian Talmud, many editions of Flavius Josephus, including first edition of 1470 Early Bibles in many languages. *The Saul Hayes Collection* of Hebraic Manuscripts and microforms. Manuscripts from North Africa and the Orient; 300 reels of manuscripts held by libraries in Poland, USSR and Hungary. This collection is held in the Jacob M Lowy Room.

BACH, JOHANN SEBASTIAN, AND FAMILY

CT —YALE UNIVERSITY, Music Library, 98 Wall St, New Haven, 06520. Harold E Samuel, Librn
Holdings: Vols (118,000) Cat Mss Pix Phonorecords Audiotapes Microforms
Notes: General reference and research materials. Performing editions. Strong in theoretical literature, opera, 17-18th century music (incl mss), J S Bach and sons in early editions and mss, Russian liturgical music (Tkaczenko Collection), hymnology, American music. Also collection of musical pictures and portraits.

MI —UNIVERSITY OF MICHIGAN, School of Music, Music Library, Moore Bldg, Ann Arbor, 48109. Peggy Daub, Head
Holdings: Vols (90,000) Cat Mss Microforms
Notes: Reference and research materials, as well as performing editions. Rare materials (including the Stellfeld Collection) are strong in early editions of works by the sons of J S Bach and 18th-19th century opera scores, particularly French. Includes 1200 microfilms of important European and American primary sources. See L Cuyler, H David & G Sutherland: "The University of Michigans's Purchase of the Stellfeld Music Library," *MLA Notes* 12 (1954-5), 3-19.

NY —NEW YORK PUBLIC LIBRARY, Performing Arts Research Center, Rodgers & Hammerstein Archives of Recorded Sound, 111 Amsterdam Ave, New York, 10023.
Holdings: Audiotapes
Notes: Given by Miss Rosalyn Tureck, the collection consists of more than 500 hours on tape of performances by Miss Tureck, lectures and seminars on performance interpretation of Bach's music, and symposia and workshops of the International Bach Society.

NY —NEW YORK PUBLIC LIBRARY, Music Div, 111 Amsterdam Ave, New York, 10023. Frank C Campbell, Chief
Notes: Composers' autographs on microfilm. Works of 17th-20th century composers. Major holdings: Bach, Handel, Beethoven. Original music mss, association items, etc.

PA —LUTHERAN THEOLOGICAL SEMINARY, Krauth Memorial Library, 7301 Germantown Ave, Philadelphia, 19119. Rev David J Wartluft, Dir Libr
Holdings: Cat
Notes: The Otto Louis Schreiber Collection of Martin Luther and the Reformation in Numismatic Art. Also limited items in Melanchthon, Johann Sebastian Bach, and Anti-papal medals. This is most complete collection on the subject in America: 1000 items. A printed descriptive catalog is available.

BACHE, COMM. GEORGE M.

MD —US NAVAL ACADEMY, Nimitz Library, Annapolis, 21402. Alice S Creighton, Assistant Librn for Special Collections
Holdings: Mss Pix
Notes: Papers, etc.

BACHELLER, IRVING

NY —SAINT LAWRENCE UNIVERSITY, Owen D Young Library, Canton, 13617. Mahlon Peterson, Librn
Holdings: Cat Mss Pix Microforms
Notes: Colletion contains many autographed business and personal letters, 1890-1947, and all first editions of Bacheller's books, as well as photographs and newspaper clippings. Approx 400 items.

BACHHOFER, LUDWIG, 1894-1976

NY —STATE UNIVERSITY OF NEW YORK AT ALBANY, Library, Special Collections Dept, 1400 Washington Ave, Albany, 12222. Marion P Munzer, Coordr
Notes: Correspondence (3 linear feet) of Ludwig Bachhofer, incl teaching and research notes; mss and published works; photographs of Oriental art. Part of the Library's German Exile Collection.
See also entry under Art, Oriental

BACHMAN, JOHN

SC —COLLEGE OF CHARLESTON LIBRARY, Special Collections Dept, Charleston, 29401.
Notes: Papers of John Bachman, 1862.

BACHRACH, LOUIS FABIAN

NY —SYRACUSE UNIVERSITY LIBRARIES, Ernest S Bird Library, George

BACHRACH, LOUIS FABIAN (cont.)

Arents Research Library for Special Collections, Syracuse, 13210. Carolyn A Davis, Manuscripts Librn; Amy S Doherty, University Archivist; Mark F Weimer, Rare Book Librn
Notes: The George Arents Research Library for Special Collections at Syracuse University contains the papers of Margaret Bourke-White, Clara Sipprell, Gerda Peterich, Edward John Wall, Louis Fabian Bachrach, Joseph Costa (National Press Photographers Association), the University Archives Photographic Collection, and other misc photographs.

BACILLARIOPHYCEAE see Diatoms

BACILLARIOPHYTA see Diatoms

BACKGAMMON

NY —US MILITARY ACADEMY LIBRARY, West Point, 10996. Elaine B Eatroff, Rare Book Cur
Holdings: Vols 550 Cat Mss Pix
Notes: European imprints, beginning from the early 16th century, British, and American, incl: Hagedorn No 1, early chess periodicals. Incl: bibliography, collection of games, end games, history, openings, problems, and tournaments. Also, Chinese chess, Go, backgammon, and checkers. Chess sets, ephemera, etc.

BACKHOUSE, JOHN

NC —DUKE UNIVERSITY, William R Perkins Library, Manuscript Dept, Durham, 27706. Ellen Gartrell, Cur of Mss
Holdings: Cat Mss
Notes: Incl 50,000 items, 18th-20th centuries, representing the political, diplomatic, military, ecclesiastical, and economic affairs of Great Britain and the British Empire. Incl papers of William Wilberforce, William Smith, John Wilson Croker, John Backhouse, Malet Family, etc.

BACKPACKING

NY —ADIRONDACK HISTORICAL ASSOCIATION, Museum Library, Blue Mountain Lake, 12812. Jerold Pepper, Librn
Holdings: Vols (7500) Cat Mss Maps Pix Phonorecords Audiotapes 16mm Films Microforms
Notes: Anything about the Adirondacks--history, people, economics, places, things. Strong in Adirondack art, outdoor recreation, logging, small boats. Resources incl more than 1000 maps, 40,000 pictures, 1600 microfilm reels, 576 linear ft of ms material, and 12 cabinets of VF ephemera, etc.

WA —MOUNTAINEERS INC, Library, 300 3rd Ave West, Seattle, 98119. Verna M Ness, Library Cur
Holdings: Vols (3000) Cat
Notes: Collection incl some 19th century vols of Alpine information, incl the first issue of *The Alpine Journal* (1863). Bound serials of many important American climbing publications. Small sub-collections for American Alpine Club members and for The Mountaineer Foundation, the latter on conservation and ecology. In the main collection backpacking, skiing and natural history are also represented.

BACKUS, ISAAC

RI —BROWN UNIVERSITY, John Hay Library, 20 Prospect St, Providence, 02912. Mark N Brown, Cur Mss
Holdings: Vols (2000) Cat Mss
Notes: Several collections of religious history strong in material on Baptist, Congregational, and Unitarian Churches in the 19th century, incl the ms records some Rhode Island congregations plus the papers of Isaac Backus, Brown University presidents and faculty, Jones Very, Mary Ann Atwood, Thomas Ustick, and Charles King Newcomb; incl numerous ephemeral and pamphlet publications that relate to Baptist Church history, creed, biography, Sunday School literature and missions.

BACKWARD CHILDREN see Mentally Handicapped Children; Slow-Learning Children

BACON, EDMUND NORWOOD, 1910-

NY —CORNELL UNIVERSITY LIBRARIES, Collection of Regional History, Dept of Manuscripts and Univ Archives, Ithaca, 14853.
Notes: Papers, 1940-70; 9.3 ft. City planner.

BACON, ERNST

NY —SYRACUSE UNIVERSITY LIBRARIES, Ernest S Bird Library, George Arents Research Library for Special Collections, Syracuse, 13210. Carolyn A Davis, Manuscripts Librn; Amy S Doherty, University Archivist; Mark F Weimer, Rare Book Librn
Notes: American Music Collection. Papers of Ernst Bacon, Louis Krasner, Franklin Morris, William Henry Berwald, Earl George, and Arthur Polster.

BACON, SIR FRANCIS

CA —FRANCIS BACON LIBRARY, 655 N Dartmouth Ave, Claremont, 91711. Elizabeth S Wrigley, Dir
Holdings: Vols 4000 Cat Mss Maps Pix Microforms
Notes: One of the widest collections of Bacon and Baconiana extant with secondary material, histories, chronicles, etc, of contemporary writers of the Elizabethan and Jacobean periods of English history; also journal articles, theses, and dissertations. Over 1000 titles in the STC and Wing periods; detailed collations of these vols published. Incl phonotapes. Published *Concordance to the Essays of Francis Bacon* (Detroit: Gale Research Co, 1973).

CT —YALE UNIVERSITY, Box 1603A, Yale Station, New Haven, 06520.

MD —JOHNS HOPKINS UNIVERSITY, Milton S Eisenhower Library, George Peabody Collection, 17 E Mt Vernon Place, Baltimore, 21201. Lyn Hart, Peabody Librn
Notes: Emphasis on materials published before 1950. Strength is a good collection through the 19th century.

MA —HARVARD UNIVERSITY LIBRARY, Widener Library, Cambridge, 02138.
Holdings: Cat

NS —DALHOUSIE UNIVERSITY LIBRARY, Halifax, B3H 4H8, Can.
Holdings: Cat 283
Notes: The Bacon Collection consists primarily of books written by Bacon; incl a few written about him or related to him. Nearly all were printed before 1750; more than half of all the editions of his writings are to be found in the collection. The main collection was formed by Bacon's bibliographer Reginald W Gibson; it also incl items formerly in the libray of James Spedding, 19th editor of Bacon's work and items from other sources. Published catalog: *A short title catalogue of the Dalhousie Bacon Collection* by S E Sprott, Halifax: Dalhousie University Press, 1978.

ON —UNIVERSITY OF TORONTO, Thomas Fisher Rare Book Library, 120 Saint George St, Toronto, M5S 1A5, Can. Richard G Landon, Head
Holdings: Vols 220 Cat
Notes: First and early editions of Bacon's works; also Baconiana.

BACON, LEONARD

RI —UNIVERSITY OF RHODE ISLAND, Library, Special Collections, Kingston, 02881. David Maslyn, Head
Notes: Extensive collections.

BACOT, JOSEPHINE RHETT

SC —COLLEGE OF CHARLESTON LIBRARY, Special Collections Dept, Charleston, 29401.
Notes: Correspondence and papers of Josephine Rhett Bacot (incl mss and typescripts of her writings).

BACOT FAMILY

SC —COLLEGE OF CHARLESTON LIBRARY, Special Collections Dept, Charleston, 29401.
Notes: Contains genealogical and historical materials dealing with the Bacot, Barnwell, and Huger families; included are the correspondence and papers of Josephine Rhett Bacot (incl mss and typescripts of her writings), her husband Daniel Huger Bacot, and of their sons Daniel Huger Bacot and Walter Rhett Bacot, with numerous family members and friends.

BACTERIOLOGY

CA —UNIVERSITY OF CALIFORNIA, LOS ANGELES, Biomedical Library, Center for the Health Sciences, Los Angeles, 90024. Alison Bunting, Acting Biomedical Librn; Victoria Steele, Head, History & Special Collections Div
Holdings: Vols (400,000) Cat Slides Phonorecords Audiotapes Videotapes 16mm Films Microforms
Notes: The UCLA Biomedical Library serves primarily the Schools of Medicine, Dentistry, Nursing, and Public Health, the UCLA Medical Center, the Departments of Microbiology and Biology in the College of Letters and Science, and related institutes in biomedicine. The collections of the Library are broad in scope, designed not only to support the teaching and research needs of its many users, but also to function as a resource for the health sciences-biological field as a whole. The outstanding feature of the collection is the strength of its periodical holdings, both current and retrospective. The Library also has an excellent reference collection, a comprehensive historical section, and gives special emphasis to the fields of neuroscience, psychiatry, ophthalmology, radiation biology, molecular biology, and vertebrate zoology. Increased emphasis is being given to the acquisition of audiovisual materials.

DC —AMERICAN SOCIETY FOR MICROBIOLOGY, Archives, 1913 I Street NW, Washington, 20006. Donald Shay, Archivist
Notes: Collection of American and foreign books (texts, monographs, laboratory manuals, etc) on microbiology. 10,000 reprints are mostly old or connected to a past officer or award recipient. 150 theses incl American and foreign. Reprint collection incl Pratt collection on antibiotics, and C W Dodge collection on medical mycology. Ownership of all titles resides with the Society; Special Collections of University of Maryland Baltimore County serves as repository. The Society address is in Washington.

IA —IOWA STATE UNIVERSITY, Library, Ames, 50011. Warren B Kuhn, Dean of Library Services
Holdings: Cat
Notes: Extensive serial holdings.

IA —IOWA STATE UNIVERSITY, Library, Dept of Special Collections, Ames, 50011. Stanley M Yates, Head
Holdings: Mss Pix
Notes: Robert E Buchanan (1883-1973) Papers. Collection contains correspondence, reports, and printed matter relating to his career as a bacteriologist and administrator

BACTERIOLOGY (cont.)

who was head of the Iowa State University Bacteriology Department (1910-1948), first dean of the Graduate College (1919-1948), director of the Agriculture Experiment Station (1933-1948) and was editor of *Bergey's Manual.* 26 linear feet. Finding aid available.

MA —UNIVERSITY OF MASSACHUSETTS AT AMHERST, Library, Amherst, 01003. Siegfried Feller, Assoc Dir for Collection Development
Holdings: Cat
Notes: Microbiology, incl bacteriology, immunology, virology, and pathology.

NJ —RUTGERS, THE STATE UNIVERSITY OF NEW JERSEY, Waksman Institute of Microbiology, Library, PO Box 759, Piscataway, 08854. Helen Hoffman, Librn
Holdings: Vols (17,000) Cat
Budget: ($40,000)
Notes: Primarily concerned with basic research and applied microbiology. Little emphasis on clinical microbiology.

NY —ROCKEFELLER UNIVERSITY, Rockefeller Archive Center, Hillcrest, Pocantico Hills, North Tarrytown, 10591. Joseph W Ernst, Dir; J William Hess, Assoc Dir
Notes: Papers of Nobelist Edward L Tatum (1926-1975), who conducted essential research in the genetics and metabolism of bacteria, yeast, and molds.

PA —CARNEGIE LIBRARY OF PITTSBURGH, Science & Technology Dept, 4400 Forbes Ave, Pittsburgh, 15213. Catherine M Brosky, Dept Head
Notes: Of secondary interest in acquisitions because of the department's role in cooperating with Pittsburgh institutions and others across the Commonwealth in sharing resources, the cooperative acquisition of materials, and the provision of services and information. However, some aspects of the subject are emphasized. There are separate entries for each of these specialties in this vol.

WI —UNIVERSITY OF WISCONSIN, MADISON, College of Agricultural & Life Sciences, Steenbock Memorial Library, 550 Babcock Dr, Madison, 53706. Jan Kennedy, Dir
Holdings: Vols (186,312) Cat Docs

ON —AGRICULTURE CANADA, Research Branch, Neatby Library, Rm 3032, K W Neatby Bldg, CEF, Ottawa, K1A 0C6, Can. Marcel Charette, Library Technician
Holdings: Vols 1400 Cat

ON —ONTARIO MINISTRY OF HEALTH, Laboratory Services Branch, Library, Box 9000, Terminal A, Toronto, M5W 1R5, Can. Doris A Standing, Librn
Holdings: Vols (4000) Cat
Budget: ($50,000)
Notes: Medical laboratory technology and related subjects: microbiology; environmental bacteriology (limited to testing of milk, food and water for bacterial quality, etc); biological chemistry (clinical); mycology; parasitology; virology; immunology; serology; automated laboratory techniques; biohazard control.

BACTERIOLOGY—HISTORY

CT —YALE UNIVERSITY, Medical Historical Library, Klebs Collection, 333 Cedar St, New Haven, 06520. Ferenc A Gyorgyey, Librn
Notes: Incl the collection of Harvey Cushing, John Fulton and Arnold C Klebs, and historical collections of the Yale Medical Library.

MD —UNIVERSITY OF MARYLAND, BALTIMORE COUNTY, Albin O Kuhn Library and Gallery, 5401 Wilkens Ave, Baltimore, 21228. Ann Copeland, Special Collections Librn
Holdings: Vols (3000) Cat
Notes: The Archives of the American Society for Microbiology (ASM) are strong in 20th century English-language immunological and bacteriological works, incl nearly every edition of every major microbiological title published in England and the US. The reprint collection is also excellent, incl significant material published in non-bacteriological journals. The theses are largely European, pre-1900 inaugural dissertations. The collection also incl mss, proceedings, memorabilia and correspondence of the Society.

BACTERIOLOGY, AGRICULTURAL

IA —IOWA STATE UNIVERSITY, Library, Ames, 50011. Warren B Kuhn, Dean of Library Services
Holdings: Cat
Notes: Extensive serial holdings.

BACTRIAN LANGUAGE (OLD BACTRIAN) see Avesta Language and Literature

BADARRACO, JOSEPH R.

MO —WASHINGTON UNIVERSITY, Libraries, Special Collections Dept, Campus Box 1061, St Louis, 63130.
Notes: Papers of Joseph R Badarraco, espec files from his term as St Louis' president of the Board of Aldermen, 1972-75. Rich in City Plan Commission reports, etc, particularly redevelopment proposals and projects. Also records of Harland Bartholomew and Associates, early city planning firm active in St Louis and other cities.

BADE, WILLIAM FREDERIC, 1871-1936

BC —UNIVERSITY OF VICTORIA, McPherson Library, Victoria, V8W 3H5, Can.

BADEN-POWELL, SIR ROBERT

PQ —MCGILL UNIVERSITY, McLennan Library, Rare Books and Special Collections Dept, 3459 McTavish St, Montreal, H3A 1Y1, Can.
Notes: Incl scouting manuals, especially those of Sir Robert Baden-Powell, as well as some items on the history of scouting.

BADGER FAMILY

NY —CORNELL UNIVERSITY LIBRARIES, Collection of Regional History, Dept of Manuscripts and Univ Archives, Ithaca, 14853.
Notes: Record book, 1843-1919; incl legal, farm and household accounts; weather records; inventory of farm property; directions for making human and animal medical remedies and household preparations.

BADGES OF HONOR see Decorations of Honor; Insignia; Medals

BADLANDS OF SOUTH DAKOTA

†SD —SOUTH DAKOTA SCHOOL OF MINES & TECHNOLOGY, Devereaux Library, Rapid City, 57701.
Holdings: Vols (166,200) Cat Mss Maps Pix Microforms
Notes: Emphasis on the White River Badlands. The Museum has an extensive collection of reprint materials in this specific area (which is supportive of, and complimentary to, the resources of the Library).

BAER, GREG

CA —SAN DIEGO STATE UNIVERSITY, Malcolm A Love Library, 5300 Campanile Dr, San Diego, 92182. D Dickinson, Univ Librn; Don L Bosseau, Dir
Holdings: Mss Cassettes
Notes: Elizabeth Chater Collection in Science Fiction. Includes Tolkien Collection, fantasy, folklore, Gothic novels, mostly autographed first editions, some rare and scarce, includes manuscripts, graphics, cassette tapes. Examples: authors included, Isaac Asimov, Ray Bradbury, Joan Vinge, Greg Baer, Frederick Pohl, Andre Norton, etc. Examples of periodicals, Amazing Stories, Famous Fantastic Mysteries of the 1940s, The Black Cat, 1895. (3000 items)

BAHAISM

MA —HARVARD UNIVERSITY LIBRARY, Cambridge, 02138.
Holdings: Cat

MI —UNIVERSITY OF MICHIGAN, Graduate Library, Near East Dept, Ann Arbor, 48109. John A Eilts, Bibliographer
Holdings: Vols (150,000) Cat Mss Maps Microforms
Notes: Excludes Islam in the Far East, Judaism in general, though it does incl specifically Near Eastern Judaism. Incl Bahaism and Arab philosophy, fields of study connected with Islamic or Arabic studies, Turkish language and literature.

NY —NEW YORK PUBLIC LIBRARY, Oriental Div, Fifth Ave & 42 St, New York, 10018. E Christian Filstrup, Chief
Holdings: Cat Mss Microforms
Budget: ($56,455)
Notes: Described in *Dictionary Catalog of the Oriental Collection,* The Research Libraries of the New York Public Library, 1960, 16 vols (144,000 cards). This catalog incl 318,000 entries for works in Western languages of the east, and all works in Western languages on Oriental subjects.
See also entry under Oriental Languages and Literatures

BAHASA INDONESIA see Indonesian Language and Literature

BAHRAIN

CA —HOOVER INSTITUTION ON WAR, REVOLUTION & PEACE, Stanford University, Stanford, 94305. Peter Duignan, Cur; Karen Fung, Deputy Cur
Holdings: Vols (100,000)
Notes: For full description of collection, see Hoover Institution entry under Near East.

BAILEY, ALICE ANNE

CA —SAN DIEGO PUBLIC LIBRARY, Literature & Language Sect, 820 E St, San Diego, 92101. Alyce Archuleta, Senior Librn
Holdings: Vols (140) Cat

BAILEY, CAROLYN SHERWIN

CT —SOUTHERN CONNECTICUT STATE UNIVERSITY, Hilton C Buley Library, 501 Crescent St, New Haven, 06515. Elma B Wiacek, Special Collections Librn
Holdings: Vols 3000 Cat Mss
Notes: The Carolyn Sherwin Bailey Historical Collection of Children's Books. Incl holograph mss.

BAILEY, GEORGE

MA —BOSTON UNIVERSITY, Mugar Memorial Library, Special Collections Dept, 771 Commonwealth Ave, Boston, 02215. Howard B Gotlieb, Dir
Holdings: Cat Mss

BAILEY, JOSIAH W.

NC —DUKE UNIVERSITY, William R Perkins Library, Manuscript Dept, Durham, 27706. Ellen Gartrell, Cur of Mss
Holdings: Cat Mss
Notes: Papers, etc.

BAILEY, PARKER

CT —YALE UNIVERSITY, Music Library, 98 Wall St, New Haven, 06520. Harold E Samuel, Librn
Notes: Personal papers and musical mss.
See also entry under Music, American.

BAILEY, WARREN WORTH,1855-1928

NJ —PRINCETON UNIVERSITY, Library, Manuscript Collection, Nassau St, Princeton,

BAILEY, WARREN WORTH, 1855-1928 (cont.)

08540. Jean F Preston, Cur
Holdings: // Cat Mss
Notes: Incl 12 boxes; 1 carton of papers.

BAILLIE, JAMES L.

ON —UNIVERSITY OF TORONTO, Thomas Fisher Rare Book Library, 120 Saint George St, Toronto, M5S 1A5, Can. Richard G Landon, Head
Holdings: Vols 3000 Mss
Notes: Baillie Collection named for James L Baillie, Canadian ornithologist. Particularly significant for pamphlet and offprint material on both Canadian and American ornithology; extensive manuscript collection consisting of field notes compiled by J L Baillie recording his observations in Southern Ontario over a fifty-year period.

BAIN NEWS SERVICE

DC —LIBRARY OF CONGRESS, Prints & Photographs Div, Washington, 20540.
Notes: The George Grantham Bain Collection documents New York City sports events, theater, celebrities, crime, disasters, political activities, conventions, and public celebrations of the early 20th century with approximately 120,000 glass plate negatives and 240,000 photoprints acquired from the Bain News Service.

BAINBRIDGE, JOHN

MA —BOSTON UNIVERSITY, Mugar Memorial Library, Special Collections Dept, 771 Commonwealth Ave, Boston, 02215. Howard B Gotlieb, Dir
Holdings: Cat Mss Pix
Notes: Mss, correspondence, etc collected in depth; incl publications by or about.

BAIRD, SPENCER F.

DC —SMITHSONIAN INSTITUTION, Archives Div, Washington, 20560. William W Moss, Archivist
Holdings: Cat Mss Pix
Notes: The Archives holds the official records of Baird's tenure as Assistant Secretary and Secretary of the Smithsonian, 1850-1887, as well as the bulk of his personal papers, dated 1833-1889.

BAJA CALIFORNIA

CA —AZUSA PACIFIC COLLEGE, Marshburn Memorial Library, Citrus & Alosta, Azusa, 91702. Edward Peterman, Librn
Holdings: Vols (6000) Uncat
Budget: ($30,000)
Notes: Significant holdings in the George E Fullerton Library of California and Western Americana.

CA —UNIVERSITY OF CALIFORNIA, IRVINE, Library, Irvine, 92664. Roger Berry, Dept Head
Holdings: Cat Mss Maps Pix Slides
Notes: The Meadows Collection, an extensive collection of Californiana. Rich in material on the history of Orange County, Southern California and Baja, California. Incl more than 3500 vols, thousands of pieces of printed ephemera, over 10,000 mss items, significant runs of California historical periodicals and of rare early Orange County newspapers, maps and several hundred local historical photographs.

CA —UNIVERSITY OF CALIFORNIA, SAN DIEGO, Central University Library, Mandeville Dept of Special Collections, La Jolla, 92093. Lynda Corey Claassen, Head
Holdings: Vols 4000 Cat Mss Maps Pix
Notes: Baja California Collection. Research materials incl appoximately 1400 monographs, dissertations, magazines, manuscripts, maps, photographs, and newspapers that deal with all aspects of the region from Tijuana to Cabo San Lucas. Bibliography: *Baja California Bibliography,* Katherine M Silvera (La Jolla, 1968).

CA —UNIVERSITY OF CALIFORNIA, LOS ANGELES, William Andrews Clark Memorial Library, 2520 Cimarron St, Los Angeles, 90018.
Holdings: // Cat Mss
Notes: 18th and early 19th century mss, incl reports and correspondence on missions, Indians, New Mexico, Alta and Baja California.

CA —SAN DIEGO PUBLIC LIBRARY, 820 E St, San Diego, 92101. Rhoda E Kruse, Sr Librn
Holdings: Vols (13,500) Cat Mss Maps Pix
Budget: ($5000)
Notes: Baja California Collection. Index of *San Diego Union* Newspaper includes Baja California material. Noncirculating.
See also entry under California - History.

CA —CALIFORNIA ACADEMY OF SCIENCES, J W Mailliard Jr Library, Golden Gate Park, San Francisco, 94118. Ray Brian, Librn
Notes: Baja California natural history.

CA —UNIVERSITY OF SAN FRANCISCO, Richard A Gleeson Library, The Countess Bernardine Murphy Donohue Rare Book Room, San Francisco, 94117. D Steven Corey, Special Collections Librn
Holdings: Vols 3 Mss
Notes: Birth, marriage and death records for Mission Santa Rosalia de Mulege, 1718-1853.

BAKER, CHARLOTTE

CA —MILLS COLLEGE LIBRARY, Oakland, 94613. Steven P Pandolfo, Librn
Holdings: Vols (600) Cat Mss Pix
Notes: Incl ca 350 children's books featuring pigs as characters. The Charlotte Baker Papers incl the mss for eleven books and the artwork for fourteen books (over 200 finished drawings).

BAKER, F. SHERMAN

MA —BOSTON UNIVERSITY, Mugar Memorial Library, Special Collections Dept, 771 Commonwealth Ave, Boston, 02215. Howard B Gotlieb, Dir
Holdings: Cat Mss

BAKER, GEORGE BARR

CA —HOOVER INSTITUTION ON WAR, REVOLUTION & PEACE, Stanford University, Stanford, 94305. Milorad M Drachkovitch, Archivist
Holdings: Mss Pix
Notes: Papers of George Barr Baker, journalist. Incl correspondence, photos, and other papers relating to politics, relief agencies, and censorship. Unpublished register available in repository.

BAKER, GEORGE PIERCE

MA —HARVARD UNIVERSITY LIBRARY, Theatre Collection, Cambridge, 02138. Jeanne T Newlin, Cur
Notes: One of the largest existing collections of playbills, programs, prints, photographs, promptbooks, and other materials relating to the performing arts, the scope is worldwide; resources on the English-speaking stage of the 18th and 19th centuries are unequalled. Incl materials on ballet and modern dance, the circus, magic, minstrel shows, cinema, and pantomime. For description, see *Harvard Library Bulletin,* VI (1925): pp 281-301. Also, papers of Robert E Sherwood (1896-1955), John Mason Bowers, George Pierce Baker, Edward Sheldon, Percy Mackaye; Angus McBean collection of photographs of the London Stage, 1937-1965; Alix Jeffry collection of photographs of the Off-Broadway Theatre; and others.

BAKER, IRENE VICKERS

AZ —ARIZONA STATE UNIVERSITY, Library, Tempe, 85287. Marilyn Wurzburger, Special Collections Librn
Holdings: Vols (108) Pix
Notes: Collection covers various aspects of Children's Theatre from 1944 through the present. Areas of emphasis incl International and National Child Drama Associations, award-winning theatres, educational programs, regional groups and prominent figures in Children's Theatre incl: Irene Vickers Baker, Isabel Burger, Virginia Lee Comer, Rita Criste, Moses Goldberg, Kenneth Graham, Aurand Harris, Paul Kozelka, George Latshaw, Rosemary Musil, Sara Spencer, Winifred Ward, Susan Zeder and Lin Wright. Publications incl newsletters, research papers, bibliographies and records of the proceedings of the Children's Theatre Association of America. 80 linear feet of scripts, documents, publications, films, tapes (oral history) programs, correspondence, photographs, working papers and clippings. Partially indexed; finding guides available.

BAKER, JIM

OH —OHIO STATE UNIVERSITY, Library for Communication and Graphic Arts, 242 W 18th St, Columbus, 43210. Lucy S Caswell, Curator
Notes: Comic strip artists Hal Foster, Dudley T Fisher, Jr, Mark Szorady, Edwina Dumm, Jim Baker have original works in the library. Also new collections of original cartoons by Windsor McCay, John T McCutcheon, Dick Moores, Ned White, Walter Berndt, Jim Larrick, Carl Rose and Bill Crawford. Also a large collection of the work of illustrator Will Rannells. The Shel Dorf Collection incl historic comic strips and related materials. A small but growing collection of comic books, especially those featuring *Katy Keene,* is available in the library.

BAKER, KARL WILSON

TX —STEPHEN F AUSTIN STATE UNIVERSITY, Ralph W Steen Library, Special Collections Dept, Box 13055, SFA Sta, Nacogdoches, 75962. Linda Cheves Nicklas, Special Collections Librn
Holdings: Mss Maps Pix
Budget: ($5000)
Notes: Incl personal and business papers, letters, diaries, and other records of East Texans and East Texas institutions and businesses. Major collections incl papers of Karl Wilson Baker, George L Crocket, Bennett Blake, McFarland-Russell family, Orton family, Samuel E Asbury; and records of Nacogdoches University, East Texas Historical Association, Kelly Plow Company and many local organizations; 60 Thomas J Rusk letters. Indexes, calendars and inventories are available. Description: SFASU, *A Guide to Special Collections,* 1980.

BAKER, NEWTON D.

DC —LIBRARY OF CONGRESS, Manuscript Division, Washington, 20540. John C Broderick, Chief
Holdings: Cat Mss Pix
Notes: Mss, papers, records, etc.

BAKER, RAY STANNARD, 1870-1946

MA —JONES LIBRARY, 43 Amity St, Amherst, 01002. Daniel J Lombardo, Cur of Special Collections
Holdings: Vols 250 Cat Mss Pix
Notes: The Ray Stannard Baker Collection, incl books written under the name "David Grayson." Also periodicals, clippings, letters. Does no circulate. Unpublished guide available.

NJ —PRINCETON UNIVERSITY, Library, Manuscript Collection, Nassau St, Princeton, 08540. Jean F Preston, Cur
Holdings: // Cat Mss Pix
Notes: Incl 32 boxes. The papers cover the period 1905-1944. An unpublished typescript guide (14p) is available in the Library.

BAKER, WALTER H., CO.

RI —BROWN UNIVERSITY, John Hay Library, Harris Collection, Prospect St,

BAKER, WALTER H., CO. (cont.)

Providence, 02912. Rosemary L Cullen, Cur
Holdings: Vols (200,000) Cat Mss Pix Phonorecords Microforms
Budget: ($15,000)
Notes: The Harris Collection of American Poetry and Plays is principally composed of American and Canadian poetry and plays, 17th century-date. Extensive holdings in songsters, gift books and annuals, hymnals, pageants, broadside verse, carriers' addresses, women poets, juvenile poetry, (incl Mother Goose and *The Night Before Christmas*), sheet music with lyrics, small press publications, fine printing, black poets, "little magazines," Yiddish-American literature. All movements or schools of American poetry are represented. Incl first editions of most American poets and playwrights, notably Whitman, Poe, Wallace Stevens, Eugene O'Neill, Edward Albee, Ezra Pound, T S Eliot, William Carlos Williams, Amy Lowell, Phyllis Wheatley, Robert Frost, Allen Ginsberg, Bliss Carman, and Stephen Foster sheet music. Also incl the Saunders Walt Whitman Collection (1300 vols); the LangdonCollection of Pageants (250 vols); the Asa Cushman Collection of plays in ms and prompt copies; the MacDougall Collection of Psalters and Hymnals; 4000 plays issued by Walter H Baker Co, Boston (1890-1957); the Vaxer Collection of Yiddish Poetry, Plays and Music (1700 vols). Collections incl 200,000 vols, 30,000 broadsides, 55,000 mss, 170,000 pieces of sheet music, 450 phonorecords, and 375 microfilm reels. See *Dictionary Catalog of the Harris Collection of American Poetry and Plays* (Boston: G K Hall, 1972), 13 vols; *Supplement* (1977), 3 vols. See also, *American Poetry, 1609-1900, A Collection on Microfilm, Segment I* (1609-1820); *Segment II* (1821-1850); *Segment III* (1851-1870) (Woodbridge, Conn: Research Publications). Separate catalog.

BAKING

MB —CANADIAN GRAIN COMMISSION, Library, 303 Main St, Winnipeg, R3C 3G7, Can. Jim Blanchard, Librn
Holdings: Vols (7500) Cat Mss Maps Slides Microforms
Budget: ($20,000)

BAKST, LEON

NY —NEW YORK PUBLIC LIBRARY, Performing Arts Research Center, Billy Rose Theatre Collection, 111 Amsterdam Ave, New York, 10023. Dorothy L Swerdlove, Cur
Holdings: Cat
Notes: In addition to usual memorabilia and illustrative material, original designs from *Phaedra* and *Helen of Troy*, Considerably more Bakst designs in The Dance Collection, NYPL.

BALAENOPTERA see Whales and Whaling

BALAIC LANGUAGE see Palaic Language

BALANCE OF NATURE see Ecology

BALANCE OF PAYMENTS

DC —INTERNATIONAL MONETARY FUND AND WORLD BANK, Joint Bank-Fund Library, Washington, 20431. Maureen M Moore, Librn
Holdings: Vols Cat Films Microforms
Notes: Incl foreign trade and statistical bulletins and yearbooks, central bank reports and bulletins, budget papers, security yearbooks, economic development plans and reports on economic conditions from the 132 member countries. An index of periodical material compiled by the Library staff has been published as: *Economics and Finance; Index to Periodical Articles, 1947-1971;* First Supplement, 1972, 1973, 1974 (Second Supplement, 1975, 1976, 1977, in preparation), 5 vols. (Boston: G K Hall, 1972, 1975). Also, The Developing Areas: *A Classed Bibliography of the Joint Bank-Fund Library,* Vol 1: *Latin America and the* Caribbean; Vol 2: *Africa and the Middle* East; Vol 3: *Asia and Oceania* (Boston: G K Hall, 1976).

BALANCE SHEETS see Financial Statements

BALANCHINE, GEORGE, 1904-1983

NY —NEW YORK PUBLIC LIBRARY, Performing Arts Research Center, Dance Collection, 111 Amsterdam Ave, New York, 10023. Genevieve Oswald, Cur
Holdings: Vols (40,000) Cat Pix Audiotapes Videotapes 16mm Films
Budget: ($9,280)
Notes: Extensive biographical and visual material. Includes photographs, clippings, programs, scrapbooks, posters, tape-recorded interviews with associates of Mr Balanchine, motion pictures, videotapes, as well as drawings and stage designs. Much of the material relates to the New York City Ballet and productions of his ballets.
See also entry under New York City Ballet.

BALCH, EMILY GREENE

PA —SWARTHMORE COLLEGE, Peace Collection, Swarthmore, 19081. Jean R Soderlund, Cur of Peace Collection
Holdings: Vols (10,000) Mss Pix Microforms
Notes: Papers of E G Balch (1867-1961) include diaries and calendars (1876-1935), correspondence (1875-1957), autobiographical notes, poetry, manuscripts for articles and speeches, printed articles, subject files, clippings, and photographs.
See also entry under Pacifism - History.

BALCH FAMILY

PA —BALCH INSTITUTE FOR ETHNIC STUDIES, Library, 18 S Seventh St, Philadelphia, 19106. R Joseph Anderson, Library Dir
Notes: Mss, correspondence, etc collected in depth; incl publications by or about.

BALDWIN, FAITH

MA —BOSTON UNIVERSITY, Mugar Memorial Library, Special Collections Dept, 771 Commonwealth Ave, Boston, 02215. Howard B Gotlieb, Dir
Holdings: Cat Mss Pix
Notes: Mss, correspondence, etc collected in depth; incl publications by or about.

BALDWIN, JAMES

†MD —UNIVERSITY OF MARYLAND, Library, College Park, 20742. Donald Farren, Assoc Dir for Special Collections
Holdings: Cat
Notes: First appearances in book form, in anthologies, and in periodicals; subsequent editions, with differences in text, etc; works edited or translated; association items, especially with marginalia. Secondary works are generally excluded.

NV —UNIVERSITY OF NEVADA, RENO, University Library, Special Collections Dept, Reno, 89557. Robert E Blesse, Head
Holdings: Vols (107) Cat Other appearances 225 Cat
Notes: Includes individual works by author in all editions including translations; also prefaces, introductions, published correspondence, appearances in anthologies, periodicals, etc. Bibliographical research collection, part of Modern Authors Collection.

BALDWIN, ROGER NASH, 1884-1981

NJ —PRINCETON UNIVERSITY, Library, Manuscript Collection, Nassau St, Princeton, 08540. Jean F Preston, Cur
Holdings: Cat Mss Pix
Notes: Incl 42 boxes. The papers cover the period 1908-1981.

BALDWIN, T. W.

IL —UNIVERSITY OF ILLINOIS, URBANA/CHAMPAIGN, Library, 1408 W Gregory Drive, Urbana, 61801. Norman B Brown, Asst Dir for Special Collections
Holdings: Vols (5900)
Notes: Rare Book Room collection of Shakespeariana, incl vols of 16th, 17th, and 18th century texts of classical authors with commentaries. Bibles and prayer books, rhetorics and histories, in addition to 16th to 20th century editions of Shakespeare.

BALI see Indonesia

BALINESE LANGUAGE AND LITERATURE

NY —NEW YORK PUBLIC LIBRARY, Oriental Div, Fifth Ave & 42 St, New York, 10018. E Christian Filstrup, Chief
Holdings: / / Cat Mss Microforms
Budget: ($56,455)
Notes: Published catalog of holdings. Currently collected in Western language materials only.

BALKAN LANGUAGE

NY —NEW YORK PUBLIC LIBRARY, Oriental Div, Fifth Ave & 42 St, New York, 10018. E Christian Filstrup, Chief
Holdings: Cat Mss Microforms
Budget: ($56,455)
Notes: Published catalog of holdings.

BALKAN PENINSULA

†CA —UNIVERSITY OF SAN FRANCISCO, Richard A Gleeson Library, The Countess Bernardine Murphy Donohue Rare Book Room, San Francisco, 94117. D Steven Corey, Special Collections Librn
Notes: Some highly specialized materials.

WA —UNIVERSITY OF WASHINGTON LIBRARIES, Suzzallo Library, Slavic & East European Section, FM-25, Seattle, 98195. Barbara A Galik, Head
Holdings: Vols (250,000) Cat Mss Maps Pix Phonorecords Audiotapes Microforms
Budget: ($85,000)
Notes: Strong research collections for Yugoslavia, Bulgaria and Hungary. Holdings cover all aspects of life and culture and are execellent in historical source materials, language, literature, geography, economics, the fine arts, and folklore. There are extensive holdings of the publications of academies, major universities, and principal scholarly institutions, especially of long serial runs. Sizeable Slavic language collections are also to be found in the sciences among the branch libraries of the university.

BALKAN PENINSULA—HISTORY

WI —UNIVERSITY OF WISCONSIN, MADISON, Memorial Library, Slavic Studies Collection, 728 State St, Madison, 53706. Aleksander Rolich, Bibliographer for Slavic Studies; Robert P Gakovich, Slavic Cataloger; Valdis J Zeps, Baltic Studies Center
Holdings: Vols (25,000) Cat
Notes: The Balcanica collection in Memorial Library exceeds 25,000 volumes and active collecting continues at over 2000 titles per year in Bulgarian, Rumanian, Turkish and the languages of Yugoslavia. Many rare and unique titles are to be found in this collection, including serial titles, such as *Nova Vreme* (1897-1923, 1947-to date), *Nova Europa* (1920-1938), and unique Turkish Salnameh. The emphasis is on historical materials, but there is considerable strength in South Slavic literatures and linguistics. The Rumanian materials are of more recent vintage. A collection of post-World War II Yugoslav emigre and ethnic publications of 1500 volumes is split between Memorial Library and the Library of the Wisconsin Historical Society.

BALL, JOHN

MA —BOSTON UNIVERSITY, Mugar Memorial Library, Special Collections Dept,

BALL, JOHN (cont.)

771 Commonwealth Ave, Boston, 02215. Howard B Gotlieb, Dir
Holdings: Cat Mss
Notes: Mss, correspondence, etc collected in depth; incl publications by or about.

BALL, NELSON, 1940-

†ON —MCMASTER UNIVERSITY, Library, Hamilton, L8S 4L6, Can.
Notes: Nelson Ball manuscript poems, correspondence, and files relating to Weed and Flower Press, 1964-1967.

BALLADS

CA —UNIVERSITY OF CALIFORNIA, LOS ANGELES, Research Library, Dept of Special Collections, 405 Hilgard Ave, Los Angeles, 90024. Edward Shreeves, Chairman, Bibliographers Group; David S Zeidberg, Head
Holdings: Vols 800
Notes: 1800 American and British broadside ballads, ca 1790-1870; 800 volumes of ballads, primarily American and British.

CA —UNIVERSITY OF CALIFORNIA, LOS ANGELES, William Andrews Clark Memorial Library, 2520 Cimarron St, Los Angeles, 90018.
Notes: Extensive collection, first editions, etc.

CA —SAN DIEGO PUBLIC LIBRARY, Art, Music & Recreation Sect, 820 E St, San Diego, 92101. Barbara A Tuhill, Supvr
Holdings: Vols 132 Cat
Notes: A collection of gift sheet music has been organized into bound volumes by date of copyright covering popular songs from the 1800s through the 1950s. Each volume is arranged with a table of contents by title, and is also indexed in a special Song Title Index. Special volumes also cover the hits of World War I, ballads, religious songs and other subjects. Reference use only.

CT —YALE UNIVERSITY, Beincke Rare Book & Manuscript Library, Western Americana Collection, Wall & High St, New Haven, 06520. George Miles, Cur
Holdings: Cat
Notes: Incl California broadside ballads of the 19th century.

CT —CONNECTICUT COLLEGE, Library, Mohegan Ave, New London, 06320. Brian Rogers, College Librn
Holdings: Vols 450 Cat
Notes: Incl the Loraine Wyman Ballad Collection.

DC —LIBRARY OF CONGRESS, American Folklife Center, Archive of Folk Culture, Washington, 20540.
Notes: The Charles Todd and Robert Sonkin Collection of field recordings made in California migratory labor camps, 1940-41.

IL —NORTHWESTERN UNIVERSITY, Library, Special Collections Dept, 1937 Sheridan Rd, Evanston, 60201. R Russell Maylone, Cur
Holdings: Vols 500 Cat
Notes: 19th century English and Irish broadside ballads.

IA —UNIVERSITY OF IOWA, University Libraries, Iowa City, 52242. Frank Paluka, Head, Special Collections Dept
Holdings: // Cat
Notes: Collection incl 1050 items. See Harry Oster, "The Edwin Ford Piper Collection of Folksongs", *Books at Iowa,* Oct 1964. Also an unpublished thesis, Harold D Peterson, "Syllabus of the Ballad Collection of Edwin Ford Piper", June 1934, M A, Iowa.

KY —UNIVERSITY OF KENTUCKY, Margaret I King Library, Dept of Special Collections, Lexington, 40506. William Marshall, Head
Holdings: Cat Mss Pix Films Videotapes Audiotapes Phonorecords
Notes: Incl 95 boxes, musical instruments. Collection documents the career of John Jacob Niles as composer, artist and collector of ballads; period covered: 1887, 1905-1982. Unpublished inventory, correspondence.

MA —HARVARD UNIVERSITY LIBRARY, Cambridge, 02138.
Holdings: Cat
Notes: Catalog published in Harvard University Library, *Bibliographical* Contributions, 56 (1905).

NY —NEW YORK STATE LIBRARY, State Education Bldg Annex, Washington Ave, Albany, 12224.
Holdings: Vols (10,000) Cat
Notes: American poetry of more than 10,000 vols. Strong in minor poetry, extensive to 1900. Over 1300 broadside ballads.

NC —APPALACHIAN STATE UNIVERSITY, Belk Library, Appalachian Collection, Boone, 28608. Eric J Olson, Librn
Holdings: Vols (12,000) Cat Mss Maps Pix Slides Phonorecords Audiotapes
Budget: ($4000)
Notes: The Appalachian Collection incl the Fry Collectin of handmade quilts and coverlets; the York Collection of folk songs and ballads, plus tapes; the I G Greer Collection of Folk Songs and Ballads; the Amos Abrams ballad collection; artifacts, incl the Tatum Collection of household items, furniture, and farm implements; Daniel Boone loom; oral history tapes; the Jack Guy Collection of tapes of area music and photographs; and regional genealogy. This is a very comprehensive study on the Southern Appalachian Region. Separate catalog for the collection.

OH —CLEVELAND PUBLIC LIBRARY, Fine Arts and Special Collections Department, 325 Superior Ave, Cleveland, 44114. Alice N Loranth, Head
Holdings: Vols 2000 Cat mss
Notes: German, Romance language and Russian ballads represent the strength of this high quality collection, although the rarest items are in English. Collection incl 200 titles purchased from the Joliet library of Dijon when it was dispersed in 1922. Numerous chapbooks and political broadsides supplement the collection. Described in *English Ballads and Songs in the John G White Collection* by T J Holmes and G W Thayer (Cleveland: 1931). A "Spanish Ballad Index" (//) on cards and extensive indexes (//) for French, Provencal and Italian songs provide additional access to the early acquisitions.
See also entry under Folklore

PA —FREE LIBRARY OF PHILADELPHIA, Music Dept, Logan Sq, Philadelphia, 19103. Frederick James Kent, Head
Holdings: Vols 400 Cat
Notes: The Songster Collection contains songbooks of all types, campaign songsters, union songbooks and patriotic song collections, covering most of American music history. There is also a collection of 400 slip sheet and broadside ballads dating from the Civil War period.

PA —UNIVERSITY OF PITTSBURGH, Stephen Foster Memorial, Foster Hall Collection, Pittsburgh, 15260. Deane L Root, Cur
Holdings: Vols (1000) Cat Mss Pix Phonorecords VF //
Budget: ($50,000)
Notes: Collection comprises more than 10, 000 separate American items: original mss and letters; first editions, and early modern editions of Foster's music; personal possessions of the composer; books; magazine and newspaper articles; pictures and portraits; phonograph records; broadsides; and other material.

RI —BROWN UNIVERSITY, John Hay Library, Harris Collection, Prospect St, Providence, 02912. Rosemary L Cullen, Cur
Holdings: Vols (200,000) Cat Mss Pix Phonorecords Microforms
Budget: ($15,000)
Notes: The Harris Collection of American Poetry and Plays is principally composed of American and Canadian poetry and plays, 17th century-date. Extensive holdings in songsters, gift books and annuals, hymnals, pageants, broadside verse, carriers' addresses, women poets, juvenile poetry, (incl Mother Goose and *The Night Before* Christmas), sheet music with lyrics, small press publications, fine printing, black poets, "little magazines," Yiddish-American literature. All movements or schools of American poetry are represented. Incl first editions of most American poets and playwrights, notably Whitman, Poe, Wallace Stevens, Eugene O'Neill, Edward Albee, Ezra Pound, T S Eliot, William Carlos Williams, Amy Lowell, Phyllis Wheatley, Robert Frost, Allen Ginsberg, Bliss Carman, and Stephen Foster sheet music. Also incl the Saunders Walt Whitman Collection (1300 vols); the LangdonCollection of Pageants (250 vols); the Asa Cushman Collection of plays in ms and prompt copies; the MacDougall Collection of Psalters and Hymnals; 4000 plays issued by Walter H Baker Co, Boston (1890-1957); the Vaxer Collection of Yiddish Poetry, Plays and Music (1700 vols). Collections incl 200,000 vols, 30,000 broadsides, 55,000 mss, 170,000 pieces of sheet music, 450 phonorecords, and 375 microfilm reels. See *Dictionary Catalog of the Harris Collection of American Poetry and Plays* (Boston: G K Hall, 1972), 13 vols; *Supplement* (1977), 3 vols. See also, *American Poetry,* 1609-1900, *A Collection on Microfilm, Segment I* (1609-1820); *Segment II* (1821-1850); *Segment III* (1851-1870) (Woodbridge, Conn: Research Publications). Separate catalog.

RI —BROWN UNIVERSITY, John Hay Library, 20 Prospect St, Providence, 02912. Mary T Russo, Cur of Broadsides
Notes: Within this collection of poetry broadsides are numerous examples of early American ballads. Another separate collection of 5000 individual and 2000 bound slip sheets or slip ballads published from 1830 to 1870, record all aspects of everyday life and illustrate the manner in which people responded to political, military, social and economic events. Retrospective and current pieces are added annually. Partial catalog.

RI —PROVIDENCE PUBLIC LIBRARY, 150 Empire St, Providence, 02903. Lance J Bauer, Special Collections Librn
Holdings: Vols (7000) Cat Mss Maps Pix
Notes: The Harris Collection on the American Civil War and Slavery. Incl sheet music; Union and Confederate broadside ballads. The George W Potter and Alfred M Williams Memorial on Irish Culture. Covers various aspects of Irish culture in the English language with emphasis on 19th and 20th centuries. Incl over 1000 street ballads. Material must be used in-house. Photocopying when condition of material allows.

VT —MIDDLEBURY COLLEGE, Starr Library, Flanders Ballad Collection, Middlebury, 05753. Jennifer Post Quinn, Cur
Holdings: Vols (3000) Cat Mss Pix Phonorecords Audiotapes
Notes: Begun as Helen Hartness Flanders' private collection in 1930, given to Middlebury College, 1941. Incl over 9000 New England items recorded or transcribed since 1930: ballads and folk songs of British, American, French-Canadian, and Russian origin; religious songs; fiddle tunes; dance music. Incl research collection of folklore and folksong monographs, scores, tunebooks, journals. Reference: Quinn, Jennifer Post. *An Index to the Field Recordings in the Flanders Ballad Collection at Middlebury College, Middlebury, Vermont* Middlebury, VT, Middlebury College, 1983.
See also entry under Folk Songs; Songs - Collections.

VA —UNIVERSITY OF VIRGINIA, Alderman Library, Manuscripts Dept, Charlottesville, 22901. Edmund Berkeley Jr, Cur
Holdings: Cat Mss Pix
Notes: Virginia Folklore Collection (23,000 items) incl the following collection: Virginia WPA Folklore Files, compiled ca 1936-1943, under US Works Project Administration, ca 8000 items. Black and white folklore and folk music collected by field workers from informants throughout Virginia. Incl ms reports, phonorecords. Described in Rosenberg, Bruce A (comp) *The Folksongs of Virginia: A Checklist of the WPA Holdings in the Alderman Library, University of Virginia* (Charlottesville: University Press of Virginia, 1969); also,

BALLADS (cont.)

typescript and computer printed guides-Charles L Perdue Jr, and others (comps), *The White Folklore of the Virginia WPA Files: A Checklist...* (Charlottesville, 1973); Thomas Barden and others (comps), *Afro-American Folklore of the WPA Folklore Files in the Alderman Library...* (Charlottesville, 1973).

WI —UNIVERSITY OF WISCONSIN, MADISON, Memorial Library, British & American Language & Literature Collection, 728 State St, Madison, 53706. Yvonne Schofer, Bibliographer
Holdings: Vols (1000)// Cat
Notes: Arthur Beatty Collection. Consists of over 1000 volumes, principally in the English poetry of the Romantic period, strong in Coleridge, Tennyson, Swinburne, the prose of De Quincy and the folk poetry and balladry of Great Britain and Europe. Outstanding for its first and other editions of Wordsworth. About 200 titles in the Department of Rare Books and Special Collections; the rest is in stacks.

ON —VICTORIA UNIVERSITY, Library, 71 Queen's Park Crescent, Toronto, M5S 1K7, Can. Robert C Brandeis, Chief Librn
Holdings: Vols 350 // Cat
Notes: Includes many of the major works and collections.

BALLADS, BRITISH

DC —LIBRARY OF CONGRESS, American Folklife Center, Archive of Folk Culture, Washington, 20540.
Notes: The Sidney Robertson Cowell Collection of her folk music recordings, 1937 to 1957. Incl very unusual contributions by the Molokan community in the Potrero Hill neighborhood of San Francisco, a breakaway sect from the Russian Orthodox Church.

BALLADS, FOLK see Folk Music; Folk Songs

BALLADS, SLIP see Slip Ballads

BALLADS AND SONGS, IRISH see Irish Ballads and Songs

BALLANTYNE, R. M., 1825-1894

BC —UNIVERSITY OF VICTORIA, McPherson Library, Victoria, V8W 3H5, Can.

BALLET AND THE DANCE

AL —BIRMINGHAM PUBLIC LIBRARY, Art & Music Dept, 2020 Seventh Ave N, Birmingham, 35203. Jane Green, Librn
Holdings: Vols 1928 Cat Pix
Notes: The dance in all of its forms, particularly the ballet. See George Ray Stewart, *The Special Collections in the Birmingham Public Library* (MA thesis, Emory University, 1971).

CA —LOS ANGELES PUBLIC LIBRARY, Frances Howard Goldwyn Hollywood Regional Library, 1623 Ivar Ave, Los Angeles, 90028. Sally Dumaux, Librn
Holdings: Vols (100,000) Uncat Pix VF
Budget: ($60,000)
Notes: There is both a general and reference collection covering the history of dance, mainly Europe and the US. Special Collections: Gladys Littell - Ruth St Denis, 1880-1968, covering circa 1941-1957 incl photographs, programs, flyers, and brochures; Dance Programs, over 400 programs and playbills, mainly Los Angeles and New York from the 1930s to the present.

CA —MUSIC CENTER OPERATING CO, Music Center Archives, 135 N Grand Ave, Los Angeles, 90012. Fran Morris Rosman, Librn
Holdings: Uncat Mss Pix Slides Videotapes Filmstrips
Notes: History of music and the dance as developed and performed here. Extensive collection. Incl also the history of the performing arts.

CA —UNIVERSITY OF CALIFORNIA, LOS ANGELES, Research Library, Dept of Special Collections, 405 Hilgard Ave, Los Angeles, 90024. Edward Shreeves, Chairman, Bibliographers Group; David S Zeidberg, Head
Notes: Various collections, incl the Ernest Belcher, Gower Champion, Edward Gordon Craig, Mary Desti, Daniel Nagrin, Ruth St Denis, Southern California Folkdance Federation, and Arthur Todd Collections.

CA —MILLS COLLEGE LIBRARY, Oakland, 94613. Steven P Pandolfo, Librn
Holdings: Vols 500 Cat Pix
Notes: Jane Bourne Parton Collection of Books on the Dance. History of the dance with emphasis on Western ballet and modern dance. Incl works from 16th-20th centuries.

CA —CALIFORNIA INSTITUTE OF THE ARTS, Library, 24700 McBean Pkwy, Valencia, 91355. James Elrod, Dir
Holdings: Vols (61,000) Cat 16mm Films Videotapes Cat
Budget: ($2868)
Notes: Classical and modern dance forms. Incl 776 16mm films, 320 videotapes.

CT —YALE UNIVERSITY, Drama Library, 222 York St, Box 1903A, Yale Station, New Haven, 06520. Pamela C Jordan, Librn
Holdings: Vols (24,000) Cat Pix Slides Audiotapes
Budget: ($6000)
Notes: Book collection covers all phases of the dramatic arts: theatre, film, opera, dance, etc, with an emphasis on 20th century theatre. Incl audiotapes of Yale Drama School and Repertory Theatre productions, other plays and dramatic readings, and dialect tapes. Incl 1200 slides on costume design and 2000 slides on architecture, interiors, and furniture. Also incl more than 80,000 pictures on set and costume design.

DC —NATIONAL ENDOWMENT FOR THE ARTS, Library, 1100 Pen Ave NW, Rm 213, Washington, 20506. Christine Morrison, Arts Librn
Holdings: Vols (6000) Cat
Notes: Incl arts and education and public policy in the arts.

IL —CHICAGO PUBLIC LIBRARY, Art Section, Fine Arts Division, 78 E Washington St, Chicago, 60602. Rosalinda I Hack, Fine Arts Division Chief; Yvonne S Brown, Head, Art Section
Holdings: Vols 2500
Notes: Reference and circulating collection of books, periodicals, pamphlets, and videotapes on all aspects of the dance eg ballet, social dance, square dance, jazz and folkdance. Focus of the collection is on ballet, history, biographies of dancers, and dance instruction. Subject is supplemented by a dance videotape collection, the *Folk Dance Index* a comprehensive index to descriptions of folkdances of all nations. Special Collections: Eliza Stigler Dance Collection of 200 dance books on ballet and dance history with particular emphasis on Spanish Dance. Ruth Page Archives: small collection of memorabilia documents the career of Ms Page. Reference collection of dance video tapes that document notable dance performances, from the past and present by well known dancers and dance groups. Subject concentration is that of ballet, with some examples of ethnic dance. There is alsoa collection of tapes that document Chicago area dance groups, dancers, and choreographers. A file to the contents of the tapes is available.

IL —NEWBERRY LIBRARY, 60 W Walton St, Chicago, 60610. Carolyn A Sheehy, Administrator
Holdings: Cat Mss Pix Posters
Notes: Extensive holdings in the areas of dance history (including important first editions) and dance music. Newly formed Midwest Dance Archive contains the papers of Ann Barzel, Walter Camryn, Diana Huebert and Edna McRae.

IL —UNIVERSITY OF ILLINOIS, URBANA/CHAMPAIGN, Library, Applied Life Studies Library, 1408 W Gregory Dr, Urbana, 61801.
Holdings: Vols (38,000) Cat Pix Microforms
Notes: Contains books on ballet, contemporary dance, folk and national dances, ethnic dance, dance history, choreography, dance notation, dance therapy. Also collected are programs of dance concerts and performances of the 20th century.

IN —BUTLER UNIVERSITY, Jordan College of Music, Library, 4600 Sunset, Indianapolis, 46208. Phyllis J Schoonover, Librn
Holdings: Vols (5383) Cat Phonorecords Audiotapes
Budget: ($16,500)

KS —WICHITA PUBLIC LIBRARY, Art & Music Division, 223 S Main, Wichita, 67202. Leonard Messineo, Jr, Head, Art & Music Division; Deborah Hamilton, Special Collections Librn
Holdings: Uncat Audiotapes Videotape Pix
Notes: Alice Bauman Dance Symposia Collection. Contains 300 hours of audio tapes, 1 hour-long video tape, several hundred photographs, and fugitive material of the American Dance Symposia held in Wichita from 1968-1972. The symposia covered all dance idioms-ballet, modern, jazz, folk, ethnic, dance education and therapy-and featured such notable figures as Leonide Massine, Martha Hill, William Christensen, Alfonso Cimber, Toni Intravaia, James Clouser, Eleo Pomare, Juana de Laban, and many others. Characterized by the *Kansas City Star* as the "most distinguished faculties of fine artists ever assembled in the contemporary world of dance."

MA —HARVARD UNIVERSITY LIBRARY, Theatre Collection, Cambridge, 02138. Jeanne T Newlin, Cur
Holdings: Cat Mss Pix Slides Microforms
Notes: One of the largest existing collections of playbills, programs, prints, photographs, promptbooks, and other materials relating to the performing arts, the scope is worldwide; resources on the English-speaking stage of the 18th and 19th centuries are unequalled. Incl materials on ballet and modern dance, the circus, magic, minstrel shows, cinema, and pantomime. For description, see *Harvard Library Bulletin,* VI (1925): pp 281-301: *Dance Magazine,* December 1981, pp 47-53.

MA —SMITH COLLEGE, Werner Josten Library for the Performing Arts, Northampton, 01063. Marlene M Wong, Librn
Notes: Special collection: Einstein Collection of Music of the 16th-18th centuries copied in score by Alfred Einstein; 25,982 books, also 34,131 music scores, 42,405 phonorecords, 150 microforms. No photocopying.

MI —DETROIT PUBLIC LIBRARY, Music & Performing Arts Dept, 5201 Woodward, Detroit, 48202. Jean Currie Church, Cur
Holdings: Vols (1375) Cat Mss Pix
Notes: The E Azalia Hackley Collections document achievements of Blacks in the fields of music, dance, theatre, motion pictures, and broadcasting. World-wide in scope. Extensive clipping files arranged by personal names, titles and subjects. Incl musical scores (1500), recordings, and plays. No taping or other copying of recordings permitted.

MI —WESTERN MICHIGAN UNIVERSITY, Harper C Maybee Music and Dance Library, Dalton Center, Kalamazoo, 49008. Gregory Fitzgerald, Librn
Holdings: Vols 600
See also entry under Music.

NY —QUEENS BOROUGH PUBLIC LIBRARY, Art & Music Div, 89-11 Merrick Blvd, Jamaica, 11432. Dorothea Wu, Head
Holdings: Vols (85,000) Cat Maps Pix Phonorecords Audiotapes Microforms
Budget: ($44,000)
Notes: The Picture Collection, covering all subjects, consists of approximately 1,500,000 pictures, mainly reproductions and clippings from books and magazines, photographs, and postcards on all subjects; The Framed Picture Collection, approx 180 framed pictures, mostly reproductions of paintings from various periods; and The Phonorecord and Cassette Collection consists of approx 3500 reference phonorecords and 6500

BALLET AND THE DANCE (cont.)

circulating records as well as 1000 reference cassettes and 1500 circulating cassettes.

NY —NEW ROCHELLE PUBLIC LIBRARY, Fine Arts Dept, Library Plaza, New Rochelle, 10801. Eugene L Mittelgluck, Library Dir
Holdings: Vols (13,000) Cat Pix Slides
Budget: ($10,000)
Notes: Incl (430,000) pictures and (6300) slides.
See also entries under Art; Costume; Music.

NY —NANANNE PORCHER OSPREY DESIGNS, Library, 49 W 96 St, New York, 10028.
Notes: Lighting records for Lyric Opera of Chicago, 1961-1966; Dallas Civic Opera, 1959-1964; American Ballet Theatre, 1965-1966, 1971-1977; etc.

†NY —NEIGHBORHOOD PLAYHOUSE SCHOOL OF THE THEATRE, Irene Lewisohn Library, 340 E 54 St, New York, 10022. Alice G Owen, Librn
Holdings: Vols Cat Mss Pix
See also entry under Theatre - History

NY —NEW YORK PUBLIC LIBRARY, Performing Arts Research Center, Dance Collection, 111 Amsterdam Ave, New York, 10023. Genevieve Oswald, Cur
Holdings: Vols (40,000) Cat Mss Pix Audiotapes Videotapes 16mm Films Microforms
Budget: ($9,280)
Notes: Multi-media

NY —NEW YORK PUBLIC LIBRARY, Library & Museum of the Performing Arts, 111 Amsterdam Ave, New York, 10023. Elsie L Peck, Dance Specialist
Holdings: Vols (11,400) Cat Phonorecords Audiotapes
Budget: ($8675)
Notes: Circulating collection of books, scores, records and cassettes covering all areas of dance and related fields. Incl 8670 books and 1652 scores.

NY —SYRACUSE UNIVERSITY LIBRARIES, Music Collection, 222 Waverly Ave, Syracuse, 13210. Donald Seibert, Librn
Holdings: Vols 1349 // Cat
Notes: Collection of 19th century Italian opera and ballet librettos. An annotated catalog of the collection has been published by the Syracuse University Libraries: *19th Century Italian Opera and Ballet Libretti,* ed by Aubrey S Garlington. The catalog is arranged by title, with indices of composers, librettists, ballets, ballet creators, places of performance and publishers.

NC —UNIVERSITY OF NORTH CAROLINA, GREENSBORO, Walter Clinton Jackson Library, Special Collections Dept, 1000 Spring Garden St, Greensboro, 27412. Emilie W Mills, Librn
Holdings: Vols 2000// Cat
Notes: Incl 1000 pamphlets. The Homans Collection of historical materials acquired from Wellesley College, dating from 16th century to early 1900s. Emphasis on history of physical education for women. Incl early dance books and landmark works on all types of physical activity, training, theory; gymnastics books date from the 16th century.

NC —NORTH CAROLINA SCHOOL OF THE ARTS, Semans Library, PO Box 12189, Winston-Salem, 27107. William D VanHoven, Head Librn
Holdings: Vols (98,000) Cat Slides Microforms Phonorecords Films
Budget: ($105,000)
Notes: Incl clippings, pictures and programs.

OH —PUBLIC LIBRARY OF CINCINNATI & HAMILTON COUNTY, Art & Music Dept, 800 Vine St, Cincinnati, 45202. R Jayne Craven, Head
Holdings: Vols (122,185) Cat Pix
Budget: ($56,100)
Notes: Special collections: Eda Kuhn Loeb, "Artist and the Book, 1875-Date" (now shelved in Rare Book Room); music librettos (2345); exhibition catalogs (5474); large prints and posters (5051); Cincinnati artists vertical files; picture collection (673,906 clippings).

OH —OHIO STATE UNIVERSITY, William Oxley Thompson Memorial Library, 1858 Neil Ave Mall, Columbus, 43210. Robert A Tibbetts, Cur of Special Collections
Holdings: Cat Mss
Notes: Dance Notation Bureau collection, incl choreographic scores and papers on systems of notation. Emphasis on Labanotation.

OH —HEIDELBERG COLLEGE, Beeghly Library, Tiffin, 44883. Janice G Strickland, Dir
Holdings: Vols 199 Cat Pix //
Notes: The Pohlable Ballet Collection encompasses photographs, rare ballet prints, programs, periodicals and biographical volumes.

OK —UNIVERSITY OF OKLAHOMA, Drama Library, 550 Parrington Oval, Norman, 73019. Jan Seifert, Dir
Holdings: Vols (6683) Mss Pix Phonorecords
Notes: Incl VF material, newspaper clippings and magazine cut-outs covering the theatre and dance. Material dates from 1900. Collection of nearly 6000 plays.

OR —UNIVERSITY OF OREGON LIBRARY, Education-Psychology Dept, Eugene, 97403. Rose Marie Service, Head Dept Librn
Holdings: Microforms
Budget: ($4000)
Notes: General and research collection in health, physical education, recreation and dance incl serials. An important series is *Microforms Publications,* produced by the College of Health, Physical Education and Recreation, University of Oregon, which is comprised of 3632 microcards of microfiche of unpublished research of national significance.

OR —LIBRARY ASSOCIATION OF PORTLAND, Art & Music Dept, 801 S W Tenth Ave, Portland, 97205. Barbara K Padden, Librn
Holdings: Vols Cat Pix Slides Phonorecords
Notes: Art book titles: 21,325; music book titles (incl dance books): 10,800; sheet music titles: 19,550; slides on art subjects: about 12,000; phonorecord albums: 27,000; picture clippings: about 2 million; color reproductions of old and modern masters: about 640.

PA —UNIVERSITY OF PITTSBURGH, Hillman Library, Special Collection Dept, Anna Pavlova-Karl G Heinrich Collection, Pittsburgh, 15260. Charles Aston, Jr, Coordr
Holdings: Vols 153 Cat Mss
Notes: Acquired in 1967, consists of the "Mlle Anna Pavlova Memorial Ballet Library" formed by Karl Heinrich in conjunction with the Pittsburgh Civic Ballet and of printed books, scrapbooks, original sketches, posters and choreographic notes. In addition to the Pavlova-Heinrich Collection, the library owns a rare collection of material on the Burlesque Theatre. Skits which used dancers are part of this material. Incl 10 linear ft mss.

TX —SOUTHERN METHODIST UNIVERSITY, Fondren Library, McCord Theater Collection, Room 301, Dallas, 75275. Edyth Renshaw, Cur; Linda Sellers, Pub Serv
Holdings: Vols (2000) Uncat Mss Pix Slides Phonorecords
Notes: See *Theatre Collections in Libraries and Museums,* Gilder and Freedley (Theatre Arts, 1936). The McCord Theatre Collection encompasses the entire spectrum of the performing arts. The central purpose is to gather records of our regional theater before such ephemeral material is lost. Records of over two hundred early Texas theaters, some fragmentary and some relatively complete, are in the files. These records incl photographs of buildings, stagehands, orchestras, and performers. Local theatre history incl the once famous Dallas Little Theatre and the Margo Jones Theatre. The national theatre, opera, ballet, and circus archives incl pictures (some autographed), programs, posters, throw-aways, tear sheets, clippings, and letters. Our international archives are small, but we have some excellent material, eg, artifacts from Max Reinhardt's production of"The Miracle" which happened to go bankrupt in Dallas. After a few years the items were given to us. There are posters, tear sheets, souvenir programs, and other colorful items from Morris Gest and the Artef Collection. We have about 200 19th century English playbills and a few from the 18th century. There is a collection of modern English, French, and other European programs, many of them illustrated souvenir programs. Also, magazines on theater, cinema, and television (1800). Scrapbooks covering both southwest and Dallas theater, 1890s-1950s. Special Collections: artifacts and documents on puppets; masks; costume design; circus; and ballet and dance. The Harriet Bacon MacDonald Collection of over 200 photographs of musicians appearing in Dallas during the first three decades of the 20th century. Many autographed. Affiliated with Meadow Theatre of the Arts.

UT —UNIVERSITY OF UTAH, Marriott Library, Special Collections, Salt Lake City, 84112. Gregory C Thompson, Cur
Notes: Ballet-Utah. Records of Ballet West.

†WA —SEATTLE PUBLIC LIBRARY, Music Dept, Fourth & Madison, Seattle, 98104. Carolyn Holmquist, Head
Holdings: Vols 22,300 Cat
Notes: Books 11,000, music 10,000, dance 1300 vols, 14,000 phonorecords, 28,000 pieces of sheet music. Special indexes: symphony orchestra program notes. World, National and local premiere dates. Song titles in collections, 60,000 cards. Music literature, printed music and sheet music, and phonograph record collections all have separate catalogs.

BC —VANCOUVER PUBLIC LIBRARY, Art Div, 750 Burrard St, Vancouver, V6Z 1X5, Can.
Holdings: Cat Pix
Notes: Book and pamphlet collection. Also, (1) Newspaper Clippings File: 31 drawers of relevant clippings from major newspapers, incl the *Sun, Province, Toronto Globe and Mail, Christian Science Monitor, New York* Times, etc on arts, music, architecture; incl biographical material (16 drawers). (2) Picture File about 500,000 pictures in 150 cabinet drawers, strong in architecture, costume, interior decoration, painting, sculpture, also portraits. (3) Exhibition Catalogs File: British Columbia and elsewhere. (4) Association and Organization File: organizations in the Lower Mainland in arts, music, city planning, etc, begun in 1940s; (5) Canadian Artists Index: begun in 1964, alphabetically by artist, with about 300,000 citationsto reproductions of work and biographical material on Canadian artist from the division's books and other sources; (6) Miscellaneous Index: material not covered in other special or published indexes, primarily of Canadian and local cultural events, hard-to-find informations, etc. Local newspapers, special Canadian publications and British film journals are the most regularly indexed items. (7) Song Index started in the 1930s. (8) Title Index to song collections and sheet music in the VPL collection, approx 100,000 entries.

ON —YORK UNIVERSITY, Scott Library, Downsview, M3J 2R2, Can. Hartwell Bowsfield, University Archivist
Notes: The Dance in Canada Association's Jean A Chalmers Choreographic Archives, incl videotapes of works by Canadian choreographers, with technical and performance data on each work.

ON —NATIONAL LIBRARY OF CANADA, 395 Wellington St, Ottawa, K1A 0N4, Can. Andre Preibish, Dir
Holdings: Vols 8000
Notes: Includes 100 serial titles, also programs, play bills etc on microfilm. Performing arts collection consist of Canadian titles received on legal deposit and purchased. Areas of concentration: Canadian theatre and dance; European and American performing arts tradition; theatre architecture; stage craft; costume history, dance history and notation etc.

ON —METROPOLITAN TORONTO LIBRARY, Theatre Dept, 789 Yonge St, Toronto, M4W 2G8, Can. Heather

BALLET AND THE DANCE (cont.)

McCallum, Head
Notes: Theatre Department is one of eleven subject departments of the Metropolitan Toronto Library, which is generally acknowledged to be the most comprehensive of Canadian public library collections. The department balances book and nonbook materials in all areas of the performing arts except music. Although the major dance holdings are in the Theatre Department, some dance material is held in the Science Department (dance therapy, folk and ballroom dance); Music Department (music scores) and Audiovisual Department (commercially produced dance films). Production history is the special emphasis of the dance collection, as it is for all the material in the Theatre Department. The dance collection consists of 2500 programs, 2200 photographs, 2000 press clippings, 200 slides, 200 posters, 1800 books, 100 prints, 45 periodicals and 125 original stage designs. Also, papersdocumenting the work of John Fraser, as dance critic for the *Globe and* Mail (Toronto) 1972-75 and drama critic for the *Globe,* 1975-77 with some documentation of his earlier work in St John's and for the *Toronto Telegram.* Incl correspondence, notes and drafts for reviews, interviews, etc.

ON —SIRLS, Faculty of Human Kinetics & Leisure Studies, University of Waterloo, Waterloo, N2L 3G1, Can. Betty Smith, Database Mgr
Notes: Information Retrieval System for the Sociology of Leisure and Sport (SIRLS) is a computerized online database of about 13, 000 entries (1983). Incl dance as a leisure time activity.

ON —UNIVERSITY OF WATERLOO, Library, Waterloo, N2L 3G1, Can. Susan Bellingham, Special Collections Librn
Holdings: Vols (1000) Cat
Notes: Dance notation, choreography, ballet. Gift of Dr Henry H Crapo. Collection described in *A Catalogue of the Dance Collection in the Doris Lewis Rare Book* Room, University of Waterloo Library Bibliography #10, 1983.

PQ —UNIVERSITY OF MONTREAL, Physical Education Library, Montreal, H3C 3J7, Can. Lisa Mayrand, Dir
Holdings: Vols 15,000
Notes: Perhaps Canada's largest university library sports collection. Collection is bilingual (in English and French). 441 periodical subscriptions, 890 periodical titles, 4000 microfiche and 317 microfilms. On line with Ottawa's SIRC data base (qv).

BALLET AND THE DANCE—CANADA

ON —METROPOLITAN TORONTO LIBRARY, Theatre Dept, 789 Yonge St, Toronto, M4W 2G8, Can. Heather McCallum, Head
Notes: Theatre Department is one of eleven subject departments of the Metropolitan Toronto Library, which is generally acknowledged to be the most comprehensive of Canadian public library collections. The collection balances book and nonbook material in all areas of the performing arts. Production history is the special emphasis of the dance collection, as it is for all the material in the Theatre Department. This is supported by the department's extensive holdings of programs, posters, photographs and press clippings for Canadian productions and dancers, as well as a representative selection of material for non-Canadian dance. Important original stage designs in the collection incl work by Mstislav Dobujinsky for the Canadian ballet *Red Ear of Corn,* which was produced by Boris Volkoff in 1949; Maurice Strike's work for the National Ballet of Canada's productionof *Coppelia,* and Desmond Heeley's designs for that company's *Swan Lake.* Ms collections incl: The Boris Volkoff Collection (qv); papers of the Toronto dance teacher Bettina Byers; the papers of two Canadian dance critics, Ralph Hicklin and John Fraser; and the Mary Wigman Collection, consisting of xerox copies of letters exchanged between Miss Wigman and her Canadian pupil Judy Jarvis, and a taped conversation with Miss Wigman.

BALLET DANCERS see Dancers

BALLET RUSSE DE MONTE CARLO

NY —NEW YORK PUBLIC LIBRARY, Performing Arts Research Center, Dance Collection, 111 Amsterdam Ave, New York, 10023. Genevieve Oswald, Cur
Holdings: Vols (40,000) Cat Mss Pix 16mm Films
Budget: ($9,280)
Notes: Multi-media documentation, ca 1936-ca 1963. Extensive material, both written and visual, on dancers, choreographers, designers, and productions of the company as well as on its various directors, Rene Blum, Sergei Denham, and Leonide Massine. Collection includes programs, souvenir booklets, scrapbooks, clippings and reviews, photographs, stage and costume designs by artists such as Eugene Berman, Mstislav Dobuzhinskii, and Pavel Tchelitchew, tape-recorded interviews by and about former company members, motion pictures of company productions, many of them from the Leonide Massine Collection. Descriptions of items listed in *Dictionary Catalog of the Dance Collection,* published by G K Hall, Boston, 1974, 10 vols. Annual supplements: *Bibliographic Guide to Dance,* also published byG K Hall.

BALLETS RUSSES DE DIAGHILEV

NY —NEW YORK PUBLIC LIBRARY, Performing Arts Research Center, Dance Collection, 111 Amsterdam Ave, New York, 10023. Genevieve Oswald, Cur
Holdings: Vols (40,000) Cat Mss Pix
Budget: ($9,280)
Notes: Multi-media collection with extensive documentation on the company directed by Sergei Diaghilev (1872-1929) from 1909 until his death in 1929. Dancers such as Vaslav Nijinsky, Tamara Karsavina, Adolf Bolm, Leonide Massine, and Anna Pavlova, choreographers Michel Fokine, Bronislava Nijinska, George Balanchine, Nijinsky, and Massine, composers Stravinsky, Ravel, and Debussy, and painters Bakst, Benois, Gontcharova, Larionov, Tchelitchew, and Cocteau are well-represented. Collection includes extensive programs, clippings, photographs, manuscripts and letters, as well as stage and costume designs by Anisfeldt, Bakst, Bauchant, Chirico, Cocteau, Dobuzhinskii, Gontcharova, Larionov, and Pruna, and tape-recorded interviews by or about former company members. The Gabriel Astruc papers, 1904-25, contain ca 1300 manuscripts, correspondence, and reports relating tothe early activities of Diaghilev. Register published in *Bulletin of the New York Public Library,* v 75, no 8, Oct 1971. Holograph *Black Exercise Book,* 1909-11, by Diaghilev, and 195 holographs and typescripts written to Diaghilev. Entire collection described in: *Dictionary Catalog of the Dance Collection,* published by G K Hall, Boston, 1974, 10 vols. Annual supplements: *Bibliographic Guide to the* Dance, also published by G K Hall.

BALLINGER, WILLIAM PITT

TX —ROSENBERG LIBRARY, Galveston and Texas History Center, 2310 Sealy Ave, Galveston, 77550. Jane Kenamore, Archivist
Holdings: Cat Mss
Notes: William Pitt Ballinger, 1825-1888, lawyer of Galveston, Texas. Family correspondence, diaries, business papers, notebooks.

BALLINGER, WILLIAM S.

MA —BOSTON UNIVERSITY, Mugar Memorial Library, Special Collections Dept, 771 Commonwealth Ave, Boston, 02215. Howard B Gotlieb, Dir
Holdings: Cat Mss
Notes: Mss, correspondence, etc collected in depth; incl publications by or about.

BALLISTICS

OK —US ARMY FIELD ARTILLERY SCHOOL LIBRARY, Morris Swett Library, Snow Hall, Fort Sill, 73503. Lester L Miller Jr, Chief Librn
Holdings: Vols (265,958) Documents Pix Maps Slides Microforms
Notes: Field artillery; artillery; ordnance; military history; military science; weapons and weapons systems; ammunition; ballistics; missiles; Field Artillery unit histories; military periodicals analytical index file (VF). Incl US and foreign artillery; survey data; photographs on army subjects.

BALLOON PHOTOGRAPHY see Photography, Aerial

BALLOON PILOTS see Balloons and Balloonists

BALLOONS AND BALLOONISTS

CA —CLAREMONT COLLEGES, Norman F Sprague Memorial Library, 12 & Dartmouth, Claremont, 91711. David Kuhner, Librn
Holdings: Vols 4000 Cat Mss Maps Pix Phonorecords
Notes: Gift of Rev and Mrs John F B Carruthers of Pasadena, 1950. Emphasis on history of ballooning, early aviation, World War I and World War II military aviation, pioneer flyers and flights, women in aviation, cartoons, songs, memorabilia, some diaries and journals. Restricted use. Collection transferred here from Honnold Library.

CA —UNIVERSITY OF CALIFORNIA, LOS ANGELES, Research Library, Dept of Special Collections, 405 Hilgard Ave, Los Angeles, 90024. Edward Shreeves, Chairman, Bibliographers Group; David S Zeidberg, Head
Holdings: Pix
Notes: 3 linear feet of correspondence, photographs, and ephemera relating to pioneer men and women aviators, balloons, clippers, and the role of aviation in World Wars I and II, collected by Gregory.

CO —US AIR FORCE ACADEMY, Library, USAF Academy, Colorado Springs, 80840. Reiner H Schaeffer, Dir
Holdings: Vols 6000 Cat Mss Maps Pix
Notes: The Colonel Richard Gimbel Aeronautical History Collection. Incl material from ancient myth to 1903 on manned flight; early scientific works on physical properties of the atmosphere, and imaginative literature on moon voyages. Collection is most complete in manned pioneer balloon ascents (1783ff). Also the Richard Upjohn Light Collection formerly at Culver Military Academy. Separate catalog, index to be published. 250 mss, 100 maps, 2000 pictures, 5000 prints, 7000 clippings.

CO —DENVER PUBLIC LIBRARY, 1357 Broadway, Denver, 80203.
Holdings: Cat Maps Pix
Notes: The Ross-Barrett Historical Aeronautics Collection, incl ballooning. Also, on man in space, incl early (but not later) technical material.

DE —HAGLEY MUSEUM AND LIBRARY, Eleutherian Mills-Hagley Foundation Inc, PO Box 3630, Greenville, 19807. Richmond D Williams, Dir; Heddy A Richter, Imprints Librn
Notes: A very large collection of about 3000 vols, incl name rows rarities.

DC —LIBRARY OF CONGRESS, Rare Book & Special Collections Div, Washington, 20540. William Matheson, Chief
Notes: Selections from the Library of the Tissandier brothers, military balloonists and science journalists; particularly strong in the development of the idea of flight and the first decade of ballooning.

DC —LIBRARY OF CONGRESS, Manuscript Division, Washington, 20540. John C Broderick, Chief
Notes: The American Institute of

BALLOONS AND BALLOONISTS (cont.)

Aeronautics and Astronautics Archives incorporates primary source material documenting the history of aeronautics. Incl clippings, articles, questionnaires, printed matter, and original mss pertaining to individual aeronauts, the personal papers of balloonist Thaddeus S C Lowe, and a corporate file consisting entirely of printed information on aircraft companies. Incl 30, 000 items.

DC —LIBRARY OF CONGRESS, Prints & Photographs Div, Washington, 20540.
Notes: A collection of pictorial aeronautics assembled by Bella C Landauer (1874-1960). Incl aeronautical prints, drawings, posters, photographs, clippings, and printed ephemera dating from the 1780s to 1945, as well as portraits of early aeronauts and depictions of balloon ascents. Also, the great French collection of Albert and Gaston Tissandier, and the aeronautical biography files compiled by Jules Francois Dupuis-Delcourt. Ms materials are in the Manuscript Division.

DC —SMITHSONIAN INSTITUTION LIBRARIES, National Air & Space Museum Branch, NASM Bldg, Sixth & Independence Ave SW, Washington, 20560. Frank A Pietropaoli, Branch Chief
Holdings: Vols (39,000) Cat Mss Maps Pix Slides Microforms
Notes: History of flight and aerospace development, incl biographical material on aviation pioneers, balloons and ballooning. Extensive photographic collection (600,000 pictures). Incl the Sherman Fairchild Collection of aeronautical photographs (transferred from the American Institute of Aeronautics and Astronautics). Also incl the Bella Landauer Aeronautical Sheet Music Collection (1500 pieces). 2000 films; 800,000 microforms; 9000 volumes bound.

FL —EMBRY-RIDDLE AERONAUTICAL UNIVERSITY, Regional Airport, Daytona Beach, 32014. M Judy Luther, Dir of Learning Resources

MA —MASSACHUSETTS INSTITUTE OF TECHNOLOGY, Institute Archives, Special Collections, Cambridge, 02139.
Notes: Vail collection incl many early works on telecommunications, electricity, ballooning, aeronautics, and animal magnetism.

MI —UNIVERSITY OF MICHIGAN, Library, Dept of Rare Books & Special Collections, Ann Arbor, 48109. Robert J Starring, Head
Holdings: Cat Mss Maps Pix
Notes: Includes over 100 books, mostly autographed presentation copies from polar explorers to donor William H Hobbs, and 62 scrapbooks, notebooks, albums, and made-up volumes of pamphlets, documents and correspondence, 11 relating to Admiral Peary. Also there are such primary records from Professor Hobbs' own expeditions as his journals, radio logs, purchase requisitions, pilot balloon ascension reports and graphs, and anemoscope records. In addition there are an estimated 3500 items of correspondence with explorers and other notables, 800 photographs, and maps.

MN —UNIVERSITY OF MINNESOTA, O Meredith Wilson Library, 309 19 Ave S, Minneapolis, 55455. Austin J McLean, Chief, Special Collections
Holdings: Vols 1004
Notes: Publications on ballooning; also incl slides, pictures, films, memorabilia.

OH —AKRON-SUMMIT COUNTY PUBLIC LIBRARY, Science & Technology Div, 55 S Main St, Akron, 44326. Joyce McKnight, Head
Holdings: Vols 820 Cat Pix
Notes: The Lighter-Than-Air Society book collection is in the Akron Public Library, Incl foreign language books.

TX —SOUTHERN METHODIST UNIVERSITY, DeGolyer Library, Box 396, SMU, Dallas, 75275. Clifton H Jones, Dir
Holdings: Vols (80,000) Cat Mss Maps Pix Slides Microforms
Notes: First editions of prominent authors; also of books in subject emphasis collections. All subjects listed in this volume are strong. Numerous collections of personal papers relating to subjects also.

BALLROOM DANCING see Social Dancing

BAL'MONT, KONSTANTIN

CT —YALE UNIVERSITY, Box 1603A, Yale Station, New Haven, 06520.
Notes: Letters.

BALNEOLOGY

†CT —YALE UNIVERSITY, Medical Library, 333 Cedar St, New Haven, 06520.
Notes: Incl large world-wide pamphlet collection, arranged geographically, of resorts, etc, favorable to good health.

MD —MEDICAL & CHIRURGICAL FACULTY OF THE STATE OF MARYLAND, Library, 1211 Cathedral St, Baltimore, 21201. Joseph E Jensen, Librn
Holdings: Vols (10,000) // Cat Mss Maps Pix
See also entry under Medicine - History and Historic

†NY —MEDICAL RESEARCH LIBRARY OF BROOKLYN, Academy of Medicine of Brooklyn & The State University of New York Downstate Medical Center, 450 Clarkson St, Brooklyn, 11203. Kenneth E Moody, Dir
Notes: Extensive collection of 18th-19th century material.
See also entry under Medicine.

BALOCHI LANGUAGE see Baluchi Language

BALTIC LANGUAGES AND LITERATURES

NY —NEW YORK PUBLIC LIBRARY, Slavonic Div, Fifth Ave & 42 St, New York, 10018. Edward Kasinec, Chief
Holdings: Cat Microforms
Notes: Books and periodicals in Latvian and Lithuanian form one of the few collections of Baltic Language materials in the US. The emphasis is on language, literature, folklore and history. See New York Public Library, *Dictionary Catalog of the Slavonic* Collection (Boston: G K Hall, 1974), 44 vols.

BALTIC QUESTION see Baltic States

BALTIC STATES

CA —CLAREMONT COLLEGES, Honnold Library, Ninth & Dartmouth, Claremont, 91711. Franklin D Scott, Cur, Nordic Collection; Penelope Garris, Librn
Holdings: Vols (25,000) Cat Maps Pix Slides Audiotapes Videotapes Microforms
Notes: Nordic Collections are broadly inclusive, but emphasize history of Scandinavia, Baltic countries, and Hanseatic cities. Nucleus of collections from gifts and endowment of Waldemar Westergaard, supplemented with relevant collections of David Bjork, John H Wuorinen, Ingolf Olsen, Henry Steele Commager, Franklin Scott and other gifts and purchases. Eight vertical file drawers of news bulletins in English or vernaculars, 1941-. See: Franklin D Scott, "The Westergaard-Bjork Collection at the Honnold Library, the Claremont Colleges," *Scandinavian Studies,* 41 (1969), 346-354.

MA —HARVARD UNIVERSITY LIBRARY, Widener Library, Cambridge, 02138.
Holdings: Cat Mss Microforms
Notes: *Widener Library Shelflist* No 40 (1972) lists some 6500 volumes of the history, languages, and literatures of the Baltic states: Estonia, Latvia, Lithuania, and Livonia.

BALTIC STATES—HISTORY

NY —NEW YORK PUBLIC LIBRARY, Slavonic Div, Fifth Ave & 42 St, New York, 10018. Edward Kasinec, Chief
Holdings: Cat Microforms
Notes: See New York Public Library, *Dictionary Catalog of the Slavonic* Collection (Boston: G K Hall, 1974), 44 vols.

BALTIMORE, MARYLAND—HISTORY

MD —BALTIMORE STREETCAR MUSEUM, Transit Research Center, 1901 Falls Rd, PO Box 7184, Baltimore, 21218.
George F Nixon, Cur
Holdings: Cat Mss Pix Slides 16mm Films
Notes: Transit Research Center is devoted to the collection of memorabilia, photos, drawings, printed matter, etc, pertinent to public rail transportation in Baltimore and Maryland. Incl streetcar systems, interurban lines, and main line railroads in the area. Also incl bus history. Incl materials donated by The Baltimore Transit Co, United Railways and Electric Co, as well as private collections.

MD —JOHNS HOPKINS UNIVERSITY, Milton S Eisenhower Library, George Peabody Collection, 17 E Mt Vernon Place, Baltimore, 21201. Lyn Hart, Peabody Librn
Notes: Noncirculating.

MD —MARYLAND HISTORICAL SOCIETY, Library, 201 W Monument St, Baltimore, 21201. William B Keller, Head Librn
Holdings: Vols 65,000 Cat Mss Maps Pix Slides
Budget: $8000
Notes: Large collection of Maryland State Colonization Papers; Maryland and Baltimore business records; Baltimore & Ohio Railroad Papers; Baltimore Theatre records and programs (late 18th, early 19th century); Maryland lottery tickets; Benjamin H Latrobe (architectural) Papers; Maryland maps, plats, prints, newspapers; Baltimore history large collection (30,000 items Maryland local history and genealogy, 100, 000 mss); iron industry papers; Maryland currency; sheet music (8000 pieces, largely Baltimore publishers); Lester S Levy "Star-Spangled Banner" collection (probably the largest in the world--over 250 pieces).

MD —PEALE MUSEUM, Municipal Museum of Baltimore, 225 Holliday St, Baltimore, 21202. Nancy Brennan, Dir; Richard Flint, Cur Prints and Photos
Holdings: Cat Maps
Notes: Pictorial history of Baltimore. Collection of 100,000 items incl: T E Hambleton Collection of Historical Prints; A Aubrey Bodine Photographic Collection; John Dubas Collection of Photographs. Many original photographic negatives.

MD —UNIVERSITY OF BALTIMORE, Langsdale Library, 1420 Maryland Ave, Baltimore, 21201. Gerry Watkins, Head of Special Collections Dept
Notes: Photographs, plates and pictures of Baltimore and other areas (1890-1909); many on the Baltimore fire. Also incl the Baltimore Region Insitutional Studies Center Collections; 4500 cubic feet of papers, files, and records of various Baltimore institutions, both public and private.

MD —UNIVERSITY OF MARYLAND, BALTIMORE COUNTY, Albin O Kuhn Library and Gallery, 5401 Wilkens Ave, Baltimore, 21228. Ann Copeland, Special Collections Librn
Holdings: Vols (1500) Uncat Maps
Notes: The Edward G Howard Collection includes many 18th and 19th century first editions of foreign visitors' accounts of their travels through Baltimore and Maryland. These accounts provide excellent descriptions of Maryland history and culture. In addition to local histories and magazines, the collection also includes Francis Scott Key's personal copy of *Maryland in Liberia* and a strong section on the War of 1812. The collection is strong in 20th century material.

BALTIMORE AND OHIO RAILROAD

MD —MARYLAND HISTORICAL SOCIETY, Library, 201 W Monument St,

BALTIMORE AND OHIO RAILROAD (cont.)

Baltimore, 21201. William B Keller, Head Librn
Holdings: Cat Mss Maps Pix Slides Microforms
Notes: Espec relating to Maryland and Baltimore. Extensive collection.

MD —UNIVERSITY OF MARYLAND, Library, Archives & Manuscripts Dept, College Park, 20742. Mary A Boccaccio, Head
Holdings: Mss Pix
Notes: University of Maryland publications and archives; collections of organizational papers (eg Baltimore & Ohio Railroad; various organizations concerned iwth the Chesapeake Bay and environs; various labor unions, particularly those involving the tobacco industry), mostly associated with Maryland; collections of papers and mss associated with literary and public figures (eg, the late Senator Millard Tydings); oral histories relating to the archival and mss collections; associated memorabilia; photographs, mainly associated with Maryland. A guide to collections of personal, family, and organizational papers relating to Maryland is being prepared.

BALUCHI LANGUAGE

NY —NEW YORK PUBLIC LIBRARY, Oriental Div, Fifth Ave & 42 St, New York, 10018. E Christian Filstrup, Chief
Holdings: Cat Mss Microforms
Budget: ($56,455)
Notes: Published catalog of holdings.

BALZAC, HONORE DE

IL —UNIVERSITY OF CHICAGO LIBRARY, Dept of Special Collections, 1100 E 57 St, Chicago, 60637.
Notes: Croue Collection of Balzac's works.

NY —SYRACUSE UNIVERSITY LIBRARIES, Ernest S Bird Library, George Arents Research Library for Special Collections, Syracuse, 13210. Carolyn A Davis, Manuscripts Librn; Amy S Doherty, University Archivist; Mark F Weimer, Rare Book Librn
Holdings: Vols 2200 Cat Mss

BANCROFT, GEORGE

NY —CORNELL UNIVERSITY LIBRARIES, Collection of Regional History, Dept of Manuscripts and Univ Archives, Ithaca, 14853.
Holdings: Vols Pix
Notes: 1800-1891. Historian, diplomat. Incl papers, 1826-1941; letters, scrapbook, photo albums guest book, and miscellaneous business, legal and genealogical papers.

NY —NEW YORK PUBLIC LIBRARY, Rare Books and Manuscripts Div, Fifth Ave & 42 St, New York, 10018. William L Joyce, Asst Dir; Susan E Davis, Cur of Mss
Holdings: Mss
Budget: ($7161)
Notes: Incl personal and literary mss, papers, etc.

BAND MUSIC

AL —TROY STATE UNIVERSITY, Library, Troy, 36081. Kenneth Croslin, Dir of University Libraries
Holdings: Cat Phonorecords
Notes: Recordings of band music and original compositions of Paul Yoder performed at festivals in this country and abroad are gifts to the library. Also incl a collection of publishers' samples of band scores.

AZ —NORTHERN ARIZONA UNIVERSITY, Special Collection Library, CU Box 6022, Flagstaff, 86011. Peter M Whiteley, Coordr/Archivist; William Mullane, Librn
Notes: Dewitt Mytinger Collection; incl instrumental sheet music for all band instruments used by Mytinger when he was a US Army band leader. Contains good examples of 20th century popular music styles.

DC —LIBRARY OF CONGRESS, Washington, 20540.
Holdings: Pix
Notes: The Francis Maria Scala Collection. Scala led the US Marine Band, 1855-1871. Incl music, correspondence, clippings, programs, and photographs.

IL —UNIVERSITY OF ILLINOIS, URBANA/CHAMPAIGN, Library, Bands & Busch Instrument Collection, 1103 S Sixth St, Champaign, 61820. John Cranford, Librn
Holdings: Vols (8600) Cat Mss
Notes: Printed music, about 8400; plus the Sousa Library, 1900 vols, printed music about 1500; also the Clarke Library, 400 vols, printed music, approximately 375. No photocopying.

MD —PEABODY CONSERVATORY LIBRARY, 21 E Mt Vernon Place, Baltimore, 21202. Edwin A Quist, Librn
Holdings: Vols 70,000 Cat Mss Pix Phonorecords Audiotapes Videotapes Microforms
Budget: $30,000
Notes: The Peabody Conservatory Library, formerly a part of the Peabody Institute Library (now the George Peabody Library of the Johns Hopkins University) supplies the library needs of the faculty and student body of the Peabody Conservatory of Music. While the collection has numerous research capabilities, it is basically a collection of musical scores. The entire history of Western music is represented through collected editions, monumental anthologies, study scores, performing editions and a large collection of books and music periodicals. This collection is supplemented by a listening facility containing 14,000 discs and an ensembles library containing scores and parts of orchestral, band and chorus works.

†MD —UNIVERSITY OF MARYLAND, Library, American Bandmasters Association Research Center, College Park, 20742. Pearl Z Tubiash, Supvr
Holdings: Cat Pix Phonorecords Audiotapes
Notes: Materials on bands and band music; organizational and personal papers, with sizable collections relating to the careers of distinguished bandmasters, notably Edwin Franko Goldman.

MD —TOWSON STATE UNIVERSITY, Fine Arts Bldg, Room 457, Towson, 21204. Edwin L Gerhardt, Curator
Notes: The Gerhardt Library of Musical Information is a segregated representative collection of music literature, phonograph and tape recordings, pictures and artifacts. It incl special sections on Thomas Alva Edison and the phonograph, John Philip Sousa and bands, old popular songs and percussion. Most of the material is out of print and hard to find. It is *not* a collection of scores or manuscripts. A detailed outline is available upon request. Direct all correspondence to the curator, Edwin L Gerhardt, 4926 Leeds Ave, Baltimore, MD 21227, (301) 242-0328. *See also* entry under Sousa, John Philip

MS —UNIVERSITY OF SOUTHERN MISSISSIPPI, William David McCain Graduate Library, Box 5148, Southern Sta, Hattiesburg, 39406.
Holdings: Mss
Notes: The Paul Yoder Collection (1940-1980; 30 cubic feet) contains original musical scores and published copies of band music which Yoder composed or arranged. Some of the band music was written for foreign bands, especially Japanese. Catalog in progress.

NH —MANCHESTER HISTORIC ASSOCIATION, Library, 129 Amherst St, Manchester, 03104. Elizabeth Lessard, Librn
Holdings: Vols 45 // Cat
Notes: 45 band instrument books used by members of cornet band. The band books are part of the Walter Dignam Collection of Music. Dignam was a noted band leader of the 1840s and 1850s and his band accompanied the 4th New Hampshire Volunteer Regiment to the Civil War in 1863.

RI —BROWN UNIVERSITY, John Hay Library, 20 Prospect St, Providence, 02912. Mark N Brown, Cur Mss
Holdings: Uncat
Notes: The Sheet Music Collection concentrates on music of American imprint, incl 170,000 vocal pieces filed by title, plus 80,000 instrumental pieces filed by composers. Major strengths are in 19th century music, especially prior to 1830; Civil War music, both Union and Confederate; lithographic covers; World War I songs; political compaign music; and band music. An additional 100,000 pieces of American and European imprint remain unprocessed.

WI —UNIVERSITY OF WISCONSIN, MADISON, Memorial Library, Rare Books Collection, 728 State St, Madison, 53706. Gretchen Lagana, Cur
Holdings: Vols (12) // Mss Pix
Notes: Mss, part books, and photographs of the Brodhead Wisconsin Silver Cornet Band which during the latter parts of the Civil War, formed the band of the 1st Brigade, 3rd Division, 15th Army Corp, which marched across Georgia with General Sherman. Housed in the Dept of Rare Books and Special Collections.

BAND MUSIC, CIRCUS

WI —CIRCUS WORLD MUSEUM LIBRARY, 415 Lynn St, Baraboo, 53913. Robert L Parkinson, Research Center Dir
Holdings: Vols (1800) Cat Mss Pix Slides Phonorecords 16mm Films
Notes: Circus and "Wild West" shows. Owned by State Historical Society of Wisconsin. Incl 1800 books on circus subject; 400 route books; 1200 programs, 8000 circus lithographs, 20,000 photo negatives, 50,000 photo prints, heralds, couriers, tickets, letterheads, route cards, original circus artwork, records and documents of circus business, movies, newspaper ads, circus band music and periodicals of show business such as *Billboard, New York Clipper, White Tops,* Bandwagon, etc. Partially cataloged.

BANDITS see Brigands and Robbers

BANDMASTERS see Conductors (Music)

BANDMASTERS' ASSOCIATION, AMERICAN see American Bandmasters' Association

BANGLADESH

CA —UNIVERSITY OF CALIFORNIA, BERKELEY, University Library, 438 Main Library, Berkeley, 94720. Kenneth R Logan, South Asia Librn
Notes: South Asia collection (India, Pakistan, Bangladesh, Nepal, Sri Lanka) contain 150,000-200,000 titles. Covers at research level the social sciences and humanities in western languages and 20 South Asian languages. Subject areas: history, political science, lanugage and literature (especially strong in Hindi, Urdu, Tamil, Sanskrit and Nepali), art and art history, sociology, education, music, environmental design, philosophy and religion, anthropology, geography, national and local government publications. Formats: monographs, periodicals, newspapers, microforms, maps, sound recordings, video-tapes, pamphlets. Special strengths: modern Hindi literature; history of South Asian countries; government publications of India, late 19th and 20th centuries. Member of South Asia Microform Project; Participant in Library of Congress AcquisitionsPrograms for India, Pakistan, Nepal, and Bangladesh.

HI —UNIVERSITY OF HAWAII, Library, 2550 The Mall, Honolulu, 96822. Joyce Wright, Head, Asia Collection; Masato Matsu, Head, East Asia Vernacular Collection
Holdings: Vols 75,215 Cat Microforms
Notes: The Asia Collection holds material from and relating to Bangladesh, India, Nepal, Pakistan, and Sri Lanka in western and Asian languages. South Asian languages currently acquired: Bengali, Hindi, Marathi,

BANGLADESH (cont.)

Nepali, Pali, Prakrit, Sanskrit, Tamil. Period emphasis is post-World War II. Subject emphases: social sciences and the humanities (literature, economics, history, religion/philosophy). Holdings are supplemented by a large uncataloged backlog, much of it accessible through the Library of Congress Accessions Lists for the area and by over 7000 cataloged titles in the main library collection. *South Asian Library Resources in North America: A Survey Prepared for the Boston Conference,* 1974, ed by M L P Patterson (Zug, Switzerland: Tutes Documentation Compnay, 1975).(Bibliotheca Asiatica 12-), "University of Hawaii," pp 103-114.

IL —CENTER FOR RESEARCH LIBRARIES, 6050 S Kenwood Ave, Chicago, 60637. Donald B Simpson, Dir; Esther Smith, Collection Development Librn
Notes: Receive current monographs, serials and government documents on PL 480.

MI —UNIVERSITY OF MICHIGAN, Graduate Library, South Asian Dept, Ann Arbor, 48109. Om P Sharma, Librn
Holdings: Vols (365,000) Cat Maps Slides Microforms
Notes: The major emphasis is on social sciences and humanities. Besides materials in classical languages, South Asian vernaculars being retained are Hindi, Bengali, Urdu, Marathi and Tamil; strong in classical languages, especially Sanskrit, Pali, and Prakrit.

MI —MICHIGAN STATE UNIVERSITY, International Library, South and Southeast Asia Collection, East Lansing, 48824. Clinton Lockert, Bibliographer
Holdings: Vols (6000) // Cat Maps Microforms
Notes: Emphasis is upon South and Southeast Asia, especially Bangladesh and Vietnam (South). Attempt to collect extensively the economic and social development plans of the developing nations. Monographs and serials received on PL 480 from India, Pakistan, Sri Lanka and Nepal since 1968. Extensive holdings of Academy for Rural Development, Comilla, Bangladesh (1959-1976), and of the Michigan State University Vietnam Advisory Group (1955-1962). No additions to collection since 1976.

MO —UNIVERSITY OF MISSOURI-COLUMBIA, Ellis Library, Ninth and Lowry, Columbia, 65201. Murari Lal Nagar, Librn
Holdings: Vols 100,000 Maps Microforms
Notes: The South Asia Studies Program at the University of Missouri-Columbia, is an interdepartmental, multi-disciplinary area studies program on India, Pakistan, Bangladesh, Sri Lanka and Nepal. Depository for the PL480 Program of the Library of Congress in many languages from South Asia. There are library resources in Sankskrit, Hindi, Bengali, Panjabi, and Malayalam. The library is particularly strong in Baroda, Bengal and the Punjab.

TX —UNIVERSITY OF TEXAS LIBRARIES, General Libraries, PO Box P, Austin, 78713. Carolyn Bucknell, Asst Dir for Collection Development
Holdings: Cat Microforms

BANGS, GEORGE KENDRICK

VA —UNIVERSITY OF VIRGINIA, Alderman Library, Clifton Waller Barrett Collection, Charlottesville, 22901. Joan St C Crane, Cur of American Literature Collections
Notes: Papers.

BANISTER, MARGARET S.

MA —BOSTON UNIVERSITY, Mugar Memorial Library, Special Collections Dept, 771 Commonwealth Ave, Boston, 02215. Howard B Gotlieb, Dir
Holdings: Cat Mss

BANK, TED

NY —EXPLORERS CLUB, James B Ford Memorial Library, 46 E 70 St, New York, 10021. Janet Baldwin, Librn
Notes: Ted Banks Collection was begun by Prof Harley H Bartlett, bequeathed to American Institute for Exploration, with additions by Prof Ted Bank II, and subsequently acquired by the Explorers Club. Incl field notes, diaries, and photographs of Bank, who led more than 30 scientific expeditions to the Arctic, Aleutians, Sea of Okhotsk, Japan, Taiwan, Southeast Asia and Africa.

BANK NOTE ENGRAVING

NJ —NEWARK PUBLIC LIBRARY, Art & Music Dept, 5 Washington St, Newark, 07101. William J Dane, Supv
Holdings: Vols (15,000) Cat
Notes: Original prints and fine facsimiles in all major media from 16th century to contemporary times. Study and special exhibition collection of the traditional and current techniques of graphic art with emphasis on late 19th and 20th century artists; ancillary collections of Japanese prints and printed books, trade cards, music covers, greeting cards, bank notes and historic maps.

BANK OF CHARLESTON

SC —COLLEGE OF CHARLESTON LIBRARY, Special Collections Dept, Charleston, 29401.
Notes: Contains the Bank of Charleston, SC's ledgers for deposits, loans, bonds, stocks, real estate holdings, businesses' accounts, and accounts with the Bank of Liverpool and the Merchant's National Bank, 1837-1872; also contains a ledger of information regarding foreign investments.

BANK OF DELAWARE

DE —HAGLEY MUSEUM AND LIBRARY, Eleutherian Mills-Hagley Foundation Inc, PO Box 3630, Greenville, 19807. Richmond D Williams, Dir; Heddy A Richter, Imprints Librn
Notes: Bank of Delaware (1850-1940; 250 cubic feet).

DE —HISTORICAL SOCIETY OF DELAWARE, Library, 505 Market St Mall, Wilmington, 19801. Barbara E Benson, Library Dir
Holdings: Cat Mss Maps
Notes: Collection incl papers and other mss materials.

BANK OF SOUTH CAROLINA

SC —COLLEGE OF CHARLESTON LIBRARY, Special Collections Dept, Charleston, 29401.
Notes: Papers, 1816.

BANKERS ASSOCIATION, IOWA see Iowa Bankers Association

BANKHEAD, TALLULAH

NY —HAMPDEN-BOOTH THEATRE LIBRARY AT THE PLAYERS, 16 Gramercy Park, New York, 10003. Louis A Rachow, Librn/Cur
Holdings: Uncat Mss Pix
Notes: The Tallulah Bankhead Collection, incl mss, her correspondence, photographs, playbills, phonotapes, and memorabilia. 15 boxes; presently uncataloged. Described in *Theatre & Performing Arts Collections* (New York: Haworth Press, 1981).

BANKING see Banks and Banking

BANKOWSKY, RICHARD

MA —BOSTON UNIVERSITY, Mugar Memorial Library, Special Collections Dept, 771 Commonwealth Ave, Boston, 02215. Howard B Gotlieb, Dir
Holdings: Cat Mss

BANKS, CENTRAL see Banks and Banking, Central

BANKS, FRANK A.

†WA —WASHINGTON STATE UNIVERSITY, Library, Manuscripts, Archives & Special Collections, Pullman, 99164. John F Guido, Head
Holdings: Vols Cat Mss Maps Pix Microforms
Notes: Ms resources in the Washington State University Library for the study of Pacific Northwest history incl the personal papers of Frank A Banks, William Compton Brown, Enoch Albert Bryan, Ernest Otto Holland, William Lon Johnson, Catherine May, Lucullus Virgil McWhorter, Austin Mires, Carl Parcher Russell, Pierre Jean de Smet, Henry Harmon Spalding, Elkanah Walker, John McAdam Webster, Marcus Whitman, as well as many business records of banks, insurance firms and agencies, breweries, lumber mills, merchants, entrepreneurs and farmers. All ms collections are described in a catalog, a published register or an unpublished finding aid.

BANKS, LYNNE REID

MA —BOSTON UNIVERSITY, Mugar Memorial Library, Special Collections Dept, 771 Commonwealth Ave, Boston, 02215. Howard B Gotlieb, Dir
Holdings: Cat Mss

BANKS, NATHANIEL P.

DC —LIBRARY OF CONGRESS, Manuscript Division, Washington, 20540. John C Broderick, Chief
Holdings: Cat Mss Pix
Notes: Mss, papers, records, etc.

BANKS AND BANKING

AL —MOBILE PUBLIC LIBRARY, Special Collections Div, 701 Government St, Mobile, 36602.
Notes: The Mobile area; incl papers of the Forbes Trading Co, 1795-1840; Bank of Mobile papers, 1820-.

CA —UNIVERSITY OF CALIFORNIA, LOS ANGELES, Research Library, Dept of Special Collections, 405 Hilgard Ave, Los Angeles, 90024. Edward Shreeves, Chairman, Bibliographers Group; David S Zeidberg, Head
Notes: Various collections, incl collection of Roger Mennevee, editor of *Les documents politiques, diplomatiques et financiers,* and collection of Charles F Stern, incl mss, correspondence and clippings relating to his career as California Superintendent of Banks, Vice President of the First National Bank of Los Angeles, and co-owner of the Cuyamaca Water Company, San Diego.

CA —WELLS FARGO BANK, Library, 475 Sansome St, San Francisco, 94144. Alice Hunsacker, Asst VP and Mgr of Libr
Holdings: Vols (50,000) Cat

CO —AMERICAN NUMISMATIC ASSOCIATION LIBRARY, 818 N Cascade Ave, Colorado Springs, 80903. Nancy W Green, Librn
Holdings: Vols (20,000) Cat Slides
Notes: One of the largest numismatic libraries, the collection incl books, periodicals and auction catalogs on coins and coin collecting, medals, tokens, military orders and decorations, paper money, primitive money, banks and banking, seals and scarabs. ANA publishes a classified subject catalog of its collection and is open to the public for research and reference services. Only members may check books out.

CO —UNITED BANK OF DENVER, Information Center/Library, 1740 Broadway, Denver, 80217. Nancy Ransier, Marketing Research Analyst
Holdings: Vols 5000 Cat Audiotapes
Notes: 200 periodical titles in journals and newsletters.

DE —HAGLEY MUSEUM AND LIBRARY, Eleutherian Mills-Hagley Foundation Inc, PO Box 3630, Greenville, 19807. Richmond D Williams, Dir; Heddy A Richter, Imprints Librn
Notes: Incl collections: Artisans' Savings Bank of Wilmington, Delaware (1861-1967; 150 cubic feet), First Pennsylvania Banking and Trust Company (1850-1925; 500 cubic

BANKS AND BANKING (cont.)

feet), Philadelphia National Bank (1890-1935; 300 cubic feet), and Bank of Delaware (1850-1940; 250 cubic feet).

DC —EXPORT-IMPORT BANK OF THE UNITED STATES, EXIMBANK Library, 811 Vermont Ave NW, Washington, 20571. Theodora McGill, Librn; John Posniak, Asst Librn
Holdings: Vols (15,000) Maps Audiotapes
Notes: The library has almost a complete set of the Economist Intelligence unit of London's *Quarterly Economic Reviews*; various types of materials with general, economic and statistical data on virtually every country of the world; incl foreign government publications, publications of various international organizations, and US Government documents.

DC —INTERNATIONAL MONETARY FUND AND WORLD BANK, Joint Bank-Fund Library, Washington, 20431. Maureen M Moore, Librn
Holdings: Vols Cat Films Microforms
Notes: Incl foreign trade and statistical bulletins and yearbooks, central bank reports and bulletins, budget papers, security yearbooks, economic development plans and reports on economic conditions from the 132 member countries. An index of periodical material compiled by the Library staff has been published as: *Economics and Finance; Index to Periodical Articles, 1947-1971;* First Supplement, 1972, 1973, 1974 (Second Supplement, 1975, 1976, 1977, in preparation), 5 vols. (Boston: G K Hall, 1972, 1975). Also, The Developing Areas: *A Classed Bibliography of the Joint Bank-Fund Library,* Vol 1: *Latin America and the* Caribbean; Vol 2: *Africa and the Middle* East; Vol 3: *Asia and Oceania* (Boston: G K Hall, 1976).

GA —FEDERAL RESERVE BANK OF ATLANTA, Research Library, PO Box 1731, Atlanta, 30301. Leigh Watson Healy, Information Services Coord; Cynthia Walsh-Kloss, Assoc Librn
Holdings: Vols (12,000) Cat Mss Microforms
Notes: Collection specializes in banking, finance, economics, publications of the Federal Reserve Banks and Federal Reserve Board.

HI —BANK OF HAWAII, Information Ctr, PO Box 2900, Honolulu, 96846. Sally Campbell, Information Mgr
Holdings: Vols 4000 Cat Maps
Notes: Economics research in developing areas of Hawaii, US Pacific Islands, Asian and other foreign countries. Emphasis on economics, business statistics, demography, finance, banking, tourist industry, construction, domestic and foreign trade. Incl 1000 serial titles.

IL —CONTINENTAL ILLINOIS NATIONAL BANK & TRUST CO OF CHICAGO, Information Services Division, 231 S LaSalle St, Chicago, 60697. Susan J Montgomery, Mgr
Holdings: Vols (27,000) Cat Microforms

IL —FEDERAL RESERVE BANK OF CHICAGO, Library, 230 S La Salle St, PO Box 834, Chicago, 60690. Dorothy Phillips, Librn
Holdings: Vols (19,000) Cat
Notes: Restricted use: noncirculating. No photocopying.

IL —NORTHERN TRUST COMPANY LIBRARY, 50 S LaSalle St, Chicago, 60675. Marianne Lee, Head Librn
Holdings: Vols (2500) Cat Audiotapes Microforms

KS —UNIVERSITY OF KANSAS, Kenneth Spencer Research Library, Kansas Collection, Lawrence, 66045. Sheryl K Williams, Cur
Holdings: Vols (92,000) Cat Mss Maps Pix
Notes: Inventories of mss and photographs maintained with card catalog index. Papers of Kansas banking firms and local businees collected. Depository of official Kansas state publications since 1978; actual holdings extend into territorial period (1854-1861) with only occasional missing titles or vols. 4000 linear feet.

LA —LOUISIANA STATE UNIVERSITY, Middleton Library, Dept of Archives & Manuscripts, Room 202, Baton Rouge, 70803. M Stone Miller Jr, Head
Holdings: Cat Mss Maps Pix Microforms
Notes: History of Louisiana and lower Mississippi Valley, colonial through 20th century. Scope: political, social and literary history; economic history, incl forestry, banking, agriculture, transportation and trade; national, regional, and Louisiana history; military history. About 4,500,000 items.

MA —BANK OF NEW ENGLAND, 1 Washington Mall, Boston, 02108. Helen Mavareaf, Librn
Holdings: Vols (4500) Cat Microforms
Budget: ($18,000)
Notes: Annual reports of largest US banks; corporate financial reports on microfiche; Banking School theses from Stonier and Pacific Coast; industry studies.

MA —HARVARD UNIVERSITY, Graduate School of Business Administration, Baker Library, Soldiers Field, Boston, 02163. Mary V Chatfield, Librn; Florence Bartoshesky, Cur of Manuscripts and Archives
Holdings: Cat
Notes: US and foreign banking, central bank reports and bulletins, theses from Stonier Graduate School of Banking, American Bankers Association.

†MA —JOHN F KENNEDY LIBRARY, Columbia Point, Boston, 02125. Dan H Fenn Jr, Dir
Holdings: // Cat Mss
Notes: James P Warburg's personal papers and files relating to his banking career, the New Deal, World War II, and foreign policy, 1920-1969. 33 linear ft of mss. Holdings are described in "Historical Materials in the John F Kennedy Library". Copies may be obtained by writing the Research Archivist.

NY —KEY BANK N A, 60 State St, Albany, 12207. Joy Pauline Longo, Librn
Holdings: Vols 200 Cat

NY —CORNELL UNIVERSITY LIBRARIES, Graduate School of Management, Malott Hall, Ithaca, 14853. Betsy Ann Olive, Librn
Holdings: Vols (135,000) Cat Microforms
Budget: ($130,000)

NY —FEDERAL RESERVE BANK OF NEW YORK, Research Library, 33 Liberty St, Federal Reserve PO Sta, New York, 10045. Jean Deuss, Chief Librn
Holdings: Vols (60,000) Periodicals
Budget: ($115,000)
Notes: Collection incl (60,000 vols) and more than (1300) periodical titles.

NY —NEW YORK PUBLIC LIBRARY, Research Libraries, Economic & Public Affairs Div, Fifth Ave & 42 St, New York, 10018. Edward DiRoma, Chief
Holdings: Vols (1,500,000) Cat Microforms

NY —SALOMON BROTHERS, Library, One New York Plaza, 46th Floor, New York, 10004. Lydia P Davies, Library Mgr
Holdings: Vols (4750) Cat
Notes: Library contains a collection of reference sources relating to corporate finance, investment banking and international finance. Extensive domestic and international corporate documents on microfiche. 11,000 corporate document files; 406,700 microforms.

NC —GREENSBORO PUBLIC LIBRARY, Business Library, 201 Greene St, Drawer X-4, Greensboro, 27402. Lebby B Lamb, Business Librn
Holdings: Vols (6000) Cat Microforms
Budget: ($12,000)

NC —TECHNICAL INSTITUTE OF ALAMANCE, Learning Resources Center, Jimmy Kerr Rd, PO Box 623, Haw River, 27258. Ron Plummer, Coordr
Holdings: Vols (1025) Cat Pix Audiotapes Filmstrips Microforms
Notes: Accounting, banking & finance, business administration.

OH —CLEVELAND PUBLIC LIBRARY, Business, Economics and Labor Department, 325 Superior Ave, Cleveland, 44114. Joan Sorger, Head
Holdings: Cat
Notes: Currently receiving over 1700 periodicals and 1300 serial titles; 1000 individual trade, industrial and professional directories, worldwide; 324 file drawers annual reports of old companies, many local; 24 drawers historical information on Cleveland companies. Annual reports, 10-K's, Proxy Statements (disclosure SEC filings on fiche); over 200 loose-leaf services; 1700 current telephone and city directories. Emphasis on current material. Areas of special strength are banking, investments, marketing and management. Also strong insurance, accounting, real estate and transportation collections. Computerized sources available incl Dow Jones News Service and a variety of Dialog business-related databases.

OR —US BANCORP, Resource Library, PO Box 8837, Portland, 97208. K CannCasciato, Resource Librn; C Daley, Resource Librn
Holdings: Vols 2000 Cat Mss Maps Slides Phonorecords Audiotapes Videotapes 16mm Films Filmstrips
Budget: $12,000

PA —FEDERAL RESERVE BANK OF PHILADELPHIA, PO Box 66, Philadelphia, 19105. Aileen Boer, Librn
Holdings: Vols (10,000) Cat
Notes: Incl Philadelphia Bank Returns, 1890-date; other runs of important financial serials, etc. No photocopying.

PA —UNIVERSITY OF PENNSYLVANIA, Lippincott Library of the Wharton School, Philadelphia, 19104. Michael Halperin, Librn
Holdings: Cat
Notes: Long files of annual reports of central banks for most nations; large collection of central bank periodical publications. Extensive and long files of annual reports of US and foreign commercial banks. Long files of state banking laws and reports of banking commissions of many states.

TX —DALLAS PUBLIC LIBRARY, Central Research Library, Business & Technology Div, 1515 Young St, Dallas, 75201. Sarabeth Allen, Mgr
Holdings: Vols 6000 Cat
Budget: $2500
Notes: *Business History Collection; a* Checklist. Dallas, Texas: Business and Technology Div, Dallas Public Library, 1974. Published to serve as a subject (by corporate name) catalog. Interlibrary loans are invited.

VA —FEDERAL RESERVE BANK OF RICHMOND, Research Library, 701 E Byrd St, PO Box 27622, Richmond, 23261. Ruth M Eggleston Cannon, Librn
Holdings: Vols (20,000) Cat
Notes: Limited photocopying.

ON —CANADIAN HOUSING INFORMATION CENTER, Canada Mortgage and Housing Corp, CMHC Annex Bldg Ground Floor, Montreal Rd, Ottawa, K1A 0P7, Can. Leslie Jones, Mgr
Holdings: Cat

ON —CANADIAN IMPERIAL BANK OF COMMERCE, Information Centre, Commerce Court, Toronto, M5L 1A2, Can. Jane Cooney, Librn Head Office
Holdings: Vols (22,000) Cat Microforms
Notes: Canadian and international banking. Annual reports of Canadian chartered banks from 19th century. Government reports and proceedings on Canadian banking laws and legislation from mid-19th century. Central bank reports from around the world. All major Canadian and international banking periodicals.

ON —TORONTO CORPORATE INFORMATION CENTER, First Canadian Place, 15th Floor, Box 1, Toronto, L5P 1A2, Can. Rosale Kanshansky, Chief Librn
Holdings: Vols (10,000) Cat Maps
Notes: Canadian interests.

ON —TORONTO DOMINION BANK, Department of Economic Research, 55 King St W, Toronto, M5K 1A2, Can. Ruth P Smith, Librn
Holdings: Vols (6000) Cat

PQ —ROYAL BANK OF CANADA, Library, PO Box 6001, Montreal, H3C 3A9, Can. Anthea Downing, Chief Librn
Holdings: Cat Maps Microforms

BANKS AND BANKING—FOREIGN

IL —CENTER FOR RESEARCH LIBRARIES, 6050 S Kenwood Ave,

BANKS AND BANKING—FOREIGN (cont.)

Chicago, 60637. Donald B Simpson, Dir; Esther Smith, Collection Development Librn
Holdings: Vols 11,600 Uncat
Notes: Serial publications of foreign banks, both governmental and private. Selected titles from 1956, and some backfiles.

PA —UNIVERSITY OF PENNSYLVANIA, Lippincott Library of the Wharton School, Philadelphia, 19104. Michael Halperin, Librn
Holdings: Cat
Notes: Long files of annual reports of central banks for most nations; large collection of central bank periodical publications. Extensive and long files of annual reports of US and foreign commercial banks. Long files of state banking laws and reports of banking commissions of many states.

BANKS AND BANKING—HISTORY

†AL —MUSEUMS OF THE CITY OF MOBILE, Reference Library, 355 Government St, Mobile, 36602. Caldwell Delaney, Adminr

AZ —NORTHERN ARIZONA UNIVERSITY, Special Collection Library, CU Box 6022, Flagstaff, 86011. Peter M Whiteley, Coordr/Archivist; William Mullane, Librn
Notes: Various collections. (1) Bank of Northern Arizona Collection (Snowflake, Ariz); miscellaneous correspondence, receipts, checks, late 1890's-1909. (2) Loren Hesser Collection; Navajo-Apache Bank and Trust Company and Navajo County Bank, both in Winslow, Ariz. Incl miscellaneous, scattered records, 1900-1915.

DE —HISTORICAL SOCIETY OF DELAWARE, Library, 505 Market St Mall, Wilmington, 19801. Barbara E Benson, Library Dir
Notes: Bank of Delaware collection incl papers and other mss materials.

HI —BANK OF HAWAII, Information Ctr, PO Box 2900, Honolulu, 96846. Sally Campbell, Information Mgr
Holdings: Vols 4000 Cat Maps
Notes: Economics research in developing areas of Hawaii, US Pacific Islands, Asian and other foreign countries. Emphasis on economics, business statistics, demography, finance, banking, tourist industry, construction, domestic and foreign trade. Incl 1000 serial titles.

IN —PURDUE UNIVERSITY LIBRARIES, Graduate School of Management, Krannert Library, West Lafayette, 47907. Gordon Law, Librn
Holdings: Vols (7000) Cat Mss Maps Pix Microforms
Notes: The collection consists of books, journals and pamphlets dating from the early 16th to late 19th century, covering to a large degree the early literature in economic thought and business practices both here and abroad. No photocopying.

IA —IOWA STATE UNIVERSITY, Library, Dept of Special Collections, Ames, 50011. Stanley M Yates, Head
Holdings: Mss Pix
Notes: Iowa Bankers Association Records (1910-1973). Collection contains correspondence, printed matter, minutes, reports, financial records, photographs and newspaper clippings relatin to financial and economic conditions. Also contains files and photographs relating to crimes against Iowa banks. About 700 linear feet. Finding aid available.

MA —HARVARD UNIVERSITY, Baker Library of the Graduate School of Business Administration, Kress Library of Business and Economics, Soldiers Field, Boston, 02163. Ruth E Rogers, Cur
Holdings: Cat
Notes: Covers the progress of economic thought and the evolution of economic institutions and business life, with special strength in agriculture, banking, commerce, finance, industry, money, railroads, socialism, tariff. Restricted use: noncirculating. Collection available on microfilm: *Goldsmiths'-Kress Library of Economic Literature,* published by Research Publications, Inc. Downs 1477, 2704, 2712, 2719, 2727, Supplement 962, 963.

NY —COLUMBIA UNIVERSITY LIBRARIES, Rare Book & Manuscript Library, 801 Butler Library, 535 W 114 St, New York, 10027. Kenneth A Lohf, Librn
Holdings: Mss
Notes: Incl the Henry Parker Willis Collection. Strong on formation of the Federal Reserve System and papers, correspondence, about the Philippine National Bank, the Irish Banking Commission, the Banking Inquiry of 1925, the Banking Act of 1933, the New Zealand Monetary Commission, the Indian Currency Commission, etc. 22,500 items. Restricted use. Also more than 32,000 items documenting the rise of William Russell Grace's shipping business and other materials relating to his career as mayor of New York. Family memorabilia and photographs, materials concerning New York politics, banking and insurance, real estate interests and Catholic charities, and letters from Chester A Arthur, John Jacob Astor, Andrew Carnegie, Grover Cleveland, Hamilton Fish, John Hay and J Pierpont Morgan. Restricted use.

OH —RUTHERFORD B HAYES LIBRARY, 1337 Hayes Ave, Fremont, 43420. Watt P Marchman, Dir
Holdings: Cat Mss
Notes: The Andrew E Douglass Collection. Index in collections; listed in *Guide to Manuscripts of the Ohio Historical Society,* 131.

PA —AMERICAN PHILOSOPHICAL SOCIETY, Library, 105 S Fifth St, Philadelphia, 19106. Edward C Carter II, Librn
Holdings: Cat Microforms
Notes: The Stephen Girard Papers, 650 reels of microfilm.

SC —COLLEGE OF CHARLESTON LIBRARY, Special Collections Dept, Charleston, 29401.
Notes: (1) Bank of Charleston, SC's ledgers for deposits, loans, bonds, stocks, real estate holdings, businesses' accounts, and accounts with the Bank of Liverpool and the Merchant's National Bank, 1837-1872; also contains a ledger of information regarding foreign investments. (2) Bank of South Carolina, papers, 1816. (3) Bank of the United States papers, 1793-1818, incl stock indentures issued in Charleston.

†WA —WASHINGTON STATE UNIVERSITY, Library, Manuscripts, Archives & Special Collections, Pullman, 99164. John F Guido, Head
Holdings: Cat Mss Maps Pix
Notes: The ms collection incl business and financial records of banks, breweries, insurance, land, lumber and livestock companies, trade and commodity associations; as well as the personal and professional papers of authors, aviators, educators, engineers, farmers, historians, pioneers, politicians and scientists; especially rich in documents relating to the exploration, settlement and development of the Palouse Country, the Inland Empire, the Columbia Basin and the Pacific Northwest. Described in *Selected Manuscript Resources in the Washington State University Library* (Pullman, 1974); and other published and unpublished inventories and registers.

BANKS AND BANKING, CENTRAL

DC —INTERNATIONAL MONETARY FUND AND WORLD BANK, Joint Bank-Fund Library, Washington, 20431. Maureen M Moore, Librn
Holdings: Vols Cat Films Microforms
Notes: Incl foreign trade and statistical bulletins and yearbooks, central bank reports and bulletins, budget papers, security yearbooks, economic development plans and reports on economic conditions from the 132 member countries. An index of periodical material compiled by the Library staff has been published as: *Economics and Finance; Index to Periodical Articles, 1947-1971;* First Supplement, 1972, 1973, 1974 (Second Supplement, 1975, 1976, 1977, in preparation), 5 vols. (Boston: G K Hall, 1972, 1975). Also, The Developing Areas: *A Classed Bibliography of the Joint Bank-Fund Library,* Vol 1: *Latin America and the* Caribbean; Vol 2: *Africa and the Middle* East; Vol 3: *Asia and Oceania* (Boston: G K Hall, 1976).

IL —FEDERAL RESERVE BANK OF CHICAGO, Library, 230 S La Salle St, PO Box 834, Chicago, 60690. Dorothy Phillips, Librn
Holdings: Vols (19,000) Cat
Notes: Restricted use: noncirculating. No photocopying.

MA —HARVARD UNIVERSITY, Graduate School of Business Administration, Baker Library, Soldiers Field, Boston, 02163. Mary V Chatfield, Librn; Florence Bartoshesky, Cur of Manuscripts and Archives
Holdings: Cat
Notes: Central bank reports and bulletins.

BANNED BOOKS

CA —UNIVERSITY OF CALIFORNIA, SANTA BARBARA, Library, Dept of Special Collections, Santa Barbara, 93106. Christian F Brun, Head
Holdings: Vols 615 Cat
Notes: The Morris L Ernst Banned Books Collection.

BANNERMAN, HELEN

†IL —UNIVERSITY OF ILLINOIS LIBRARIES, Urbana, 61801.
Notes: The Mimi Kaplan Collection of materials relating to Helen Bannerman's *Little Black Sambo.* About 100 items covering 75 years of publishing, incl books, records, games puzzles, coloring books, etc, relating to the book which was withdrawn from many American public libraries in the early 1960's as a result of lobbying efforts of the Working Group for the Eradication of Color Prejudice.

BANNERS see Flags (Vexillology)

BANNING, MARGARET CULKIN

MA —BOSTON UNIVERSITY, Mugar Memorial Library, Special Collections Dept, 771 Commonwealth Ave, Boston, 02215. Howard B Gotlieb, Dir
Holdings: Cat Mss Pix
Notes: Mss, correspondence, etc collected in depth; incl publications by or about.

BAPTISM

NC —SOUTHEASTERN BAPTIST THEOLOGICAL SEMINARY LIBRARY, PO Box 752, Wake Forest, 27587. H Eugene McLeod, Librn
Holdings: Cat Microforms

BAPTISTS

†GA —GEORGIA SOUTHERN COLLEGE, Library, Landrum Box 8074, Statesboro, 30460.
Notes: Over 200 letters describing military and civilian activities of Spencer Houghton Cone and Spencer Wallace Cone. Spencer Houghton Cone, prominent 19th century Baptist minister who helped reconcile Northern and Southern church actions after the Civil War. His son, Spencer Wallace Cone's letters cover military tactics, etc.

IN —FRANKLIN COLLEGE OF INDIANA, Library, Special Collections Dept, Franklin, 46131. Mary Alice Medlicott, Cur
Holdings: Vols 1500 Cat Mss Maps Pix
Budget: ($151,189)
Notes: Indiana Baptist Collection. Contains minutes and record books of Baptist Churches and associations in Indiana; church histories and yearbooks, 1799 to the present time.

ME —BATES COLLEGE, George & Helen Ladd Library, Special Collections, Bardwell St, Lewiston, 04240. Mary Riley, Special Collections Librn
Holdings: Vols 380// Cat Mss
Notes: Free Will Baptists. Incl 23 mss.

BAPTISTS (cont.)

MD —JOHNS HOPKINS UNIVERSITY, Milton S Eisenhower Library, George Peabody Collection, 17 E Mt Vernon Place, Baltimore, 21201. Lyn Hart, Peabody Librn
Notes: Emphasis on materials published before 1950. Strength is a good collection through the 19th century.

NC —MOUNT OLIVE COLLEGE, Moye Library, Free Will Baptist Historical Collection, Mount Olive, 28365. Gary Fenton Barefoot, Librn
Holdings: Vols 800 Cat Mss Pix Audiotapes 8mm Films Microforms
Notes: Free Will Baptist history in general, with concentration in North Carolina and the South. The collection was begun in 1954 by joint action of the college and the Historical Commission of the North Carolina State Convention of Original Free Will Baptists. Collection is perhaps the best on the Free Will Baptist denomination in existance. Particular strength lies in the 225 vols of mss and printed minutes of associations, etc. Over 5000 clippings and pamphlets. The collection is housed and cataloged separately from the main library collection. Various special indexes (obituaries, churches, etc) are also maintained. Quite a number of vols and materials of associational value related to the General Baptists, Baptists, etc are also a part of the collection. The cataloged vols are represented in the North Carolina Union Catalog and in Starr's BaptistBibliography. In the case of Starr, however, holdings are only incl in the more recent vols.

NC —SOUTHEASTERN BAPTIST THEOLOGICAL SEMINARY LIBRARY, PO Box 752, Wake Forest, 27587. H Eugene McLeod, Librn
Holdings: Cat Microforms
Notes: Especially strong on early Baptists in England. Baptists in the US, to 1845, and the Southern Baptist Convention from 1845 to date.

NC —WAKE FOREST UNIVERSITY, Z Smith Reynolds Library, North Carolina Baptist Collection, PO Box 7777 Reynolda Station, Winston-Salem, 27109. John R Woodard, Jr, Dir
Notes: Baptist Historical Collection of papers, mss, speeches, etc, in 24 document boxes, covering the Southern Baptists, mainly the period 1963-1966. Other segments of the Brooks Hays papers are deposited at the John F Kennedy Library, Boston, and with the Historical Commission of the Southern Baptist Convention, Nashville, Tennessee.

PA —TEMPLE UNIVERSITY LIBRARIES, Special Collections Dept, Conwellana-Templana Collection, 13 & Berks St, Philadelphia, 19122. Miriam I Crawford, Cur
Holdings: Vols (2200) Cat Mss Maps Pix Slides Phonorecords Audiotapes Videotapes 16mm Films Microforms Art Reproductions VF
Budget: ($30,000)
Notes: The Conwellana Collection is a memorial to Dr Russell H Conwell, founder of Temple University and pastor of the Baptist Temple (Grace Baptists Church) of Philadelphia from 1882 to his death in 1925. The Collection contains almost all of his published works; his personal library of almost 2000 books, emphasizing Biblical and religious thoughts; mss both by Conwell and about his development of the institutional church; letters, including a large number written to his assistant pastor, Arthur E Harris; a near-complete bound set of his sermons and of the *Temple Review* of the Baptist Temple in which they appeared over a 36-year period; and an extensive file of articles, photographs and information on his activities. Card catalog of the Conwellana-Templana Collection incl books by and about Russell Conwell. Separate card files index his sermons, quotationsfrom his sermons, and items in the *Temple Review. Russell Herman Conwell, 1843-1925, A* Bibliography, by Maurice F Tauber (Philadelphia Temple University Library, 1935. 40 leaves mimeographed). *Russell Herman Conwell: The Individual and His Influence: Catalog of an Exhibition,* by Miriam I Crawford (Temple University General Alumni Association, 1977; unpaged).

RI —BROWN UNIVERSITY, John Hay Library, 20 Prospect St, Providence, 02912. Mark N Brown, Cur Mss
Holdings: Vols (2000) Cat Mss
Notes: Several collections of religious history strong in material on Baptist, Congregational, and Unitarian Churches in the 19th century, incl the ms records of some Rhode Island congregations plus the papers of Isaac Backus, Brown University presidents and faculty, Jones Very, Mary Ann Atwood, Thomas Ustick, and Charles King Newcomb; incl numerous ephemeral and pamphlet publications that relate to Baptist Church history, creed, biography, Sunday School literature and missions.
See also entry under Baptists - History.

TN —HISTORICAL COMMISSION-SUNDAY SCHOOL BOARD, Southern Baptist Convention, Dargan-Carver Library, 127 Ninth Ave N, Nashville, 37234. Howard Gallimore, Supvr
Holdings: Vols (10,000) Cat Mss Maps Pix Slides Phonorecords Audiotapes Videotapes 16mm Films Filmstrips Microforms
Budget: ($38,734)
Notes: Extensive holdings in proceedings and minutes of organized Baptist bodies; state conventions and associations, Baptist journals, and documentation of major Southern Baptist controversies. Material on Black, Russian, and other Baptists. Much on religious education and American religion. Large collection of Sunday School literature. Incl thousands of mss, pictures, slides, records, etc, and 12,000,000 pages on microforms.

TX —SOUTHWESTERN BAPTIST THEOLOGICAL SEMINARY, Roberts Library, 2001 W Seminary Dr, PO Box 22000-2E, Fort Worth, 76122. Keith C Wills, Dir
Holdings: Vols 79,000 Cat Mss Maps Pix Slides Phonorecords Audiotapes 16mm Films Filmstrips Microforms
Budget: $28,000
Notes: Roberts Library is the official depository for the Texas Baptist Historical Committee of the Baptist General Convention of Texas. This is in addition to emphasis upon this subject because of the Seminary curriculum and research activities. The largest Baptist library in the world.

WI —SEVENTH DAY BAPTIST HISTORICAL SOCIETY, Library, 3120 Kennedy Rd, PO Box 1678, Janesville, 53547. D Scott Smith, Historian
Holdings: Vols (600) Cat Mss Maps Pix
Notes: US Seventh Day Baptists Collection, incl records, letters. Established at Newport, Rhode Island, in 1671, this denomination is a part of the Free-Church evangelical movement in America. The General Conference was organized in 1801. The national and international headquarters of the Seventh Day Baptist denomination is located at Janesville, Wisconsin. Also have records, publications, etc of the denomination's mission in Shanghai, 1846-1950; further, materials (6 boxes) on the Church's work in Nyasaland (Malawi), 1895-1914, and then at a later period.

BAPTISTS—ENGLAND

AL —SAMFORD UNIVERSITY, Special Collections Library, 800 Lakeshore Dr, Birmingham, 35229. Annie Ford Wheeler, Acting Head Librn
Holdings: Vols 2500 Cat Mss Maps Pix Microforms
Notes: Baptist history in general and Alabama Baptist history in particular. Nucleus is Alabama Baptist Historical Collection. Incl 10,000 church associational minutes, 30,000 association minutes on microfilm, and 126,000 mss. Special catalogs and indexes maintained, and have a microfilm program for microfilming church records. Also a small collection of British Baptist history.

NY —AMERICAN BAPTIST HISTORICAL SOCIETY, Samuel Colgate Baptist Historical Library, 1106 S Goodman St, Rochester, 14620.
Holdings: Vols 65,000 Mss Pix Microforms
Notes: Baptist history, theology, and authors. Annual reports (250,000), 6000 mss, 300 journal subscriptions; clippings. Incl, especially, the Henry Sweetser Burrage Collection of 17th and 18th century English Baptist materials; also the Danish Baptist Conference of America Archives. Publish *Baptist Bibliography,* 24 vols.

NC —SOUTHEASTERN BAPTIST THEOLOGICAL SEMINARY LIBRARY, PO Box 752, Wake Forest, 27587. H Eugene McLeod, Librn
Holdings: Cat Microforms
Notes: Baptists in England, history, to 1850. Source materials on Baptists supplemented by the University Microfilms collection of *English Books,1475-1640,* based on Pollard and Redgrave's *Short Title Catalogue.*

BAPTISTS—HISTORY

AL —SAMFORD UNIVERSITY, Special Collections Library, 800 Lakeshore Dr, Birmingham, 35229. Annie Ford Wheeler, Acting Head Librn
Holdings: Vols 2500 Cat Mss Maps Pix Microforms
Notes: Baptist history in general and Alabama Baptist history in particular. Nucleus is Alabama Baptist Historical Collection. Incl 10,000 church associational minutes, 30,000 association minutes on microfilm, and 126,000 mss. Special catalogs and indexes maintained, and have a microfilm program for microfilming church records. Also a small collection of British Baptist history.
See also entry under Alabama - History

FL —FLORIDA BAPTISTS HISTORICAL SOCIETY, Library, Garwood Historical Collection, Stetson University Library, Box 1353, De Land, 32720.
Holdings: Vols 2500 Cat Mss Maps Filmstrips
Budget: $9000
Notes: Incl material on Baptist history, particularly in Florida. Separate catalog and incl in University Library catalog.

GA —AGNES SCOTT COLLEGE, McCain Library, E College Ave, Decatur, 30030. Judith Bourgeois Jensen, Librn
Holdings: Vols (945) Uncat
Budget: $300
Notes: The Frontier Religion Collection, which was given by Prof Walter Brownlow Posey, traces the effects of slavery on religion in the Old South Frontier prior to 1860. A catalog file (by author entry only) accompanies the collection at present. Noncirculating.

MS —MISSISSIPPI BAPTIST HISTORICAL COMMISSION, Leland Speed Library, Mississippi College, PO Box 51, Clinton, 39056. Alice G Cox, Librn; Jack W Gunn, Exec Secretary
Holdings: Vols (956) Cat Mss Maps Pix Slides Audiotapes Microforms VF
Notes: Principal objective is to collect and preserve primary historical materials about churches and other institutions affiliated with the Mississippi Baptist Convention. Incl 489 volumes of church minutes. 4000 folders of materials about various churches, individuals, etc. Card index to the (Mississippi) *Baptist Record* (in progress). Incl 165 slides, 153 audiotapes, 578 microforms. Available to researchers but materials do not circulate.

NY —AMERICAN BAPTIST HISTORICAL SOCIETY, Samuel Colgate Baptist Historical Library, 1106 S Goodman St, Rochester, 14620.
Holdings: Vols 65,000 Mss Pix Microforms
Notes: Baptist history, theology, and authors. Annual reports (250,000), 6000 mss, 300 journal subscriptions; clippings. Incl, especially, the Henry Sweetser Burrage Collection of 17th and 18th century English Baptist materials; also the Danish Baptist Conference of America Archives. Publish *Baptist Bibliography*, 24 vols.

BAPTISTS—HISTORY (cont.)

NC —MARS HILL COLLEGE, Memorial Library, Appalachian Room, Mars Hill, 28754. Richard Dillingham, Dir, Special Collections
Holdings: Vols (9600) Cat Mss Pix Doc
Budget: ($4000)
Notes: Incl literary society minutes from 1857-59.

NC —SOUTHEASTERN BAPTIST THEOLOGICAL SEMINARY LIBRARY, PO Box 752, Wake Forest, 27587. H Eugene McLeod, Librn
Holdings: Cat Microforms
Notes: Especially strong on early Baptists in England, Baptists in the US, to 1845, and the Southern Baptist Convention from 1845 to date.

NC —WAKE FOREST UNIVERSITY, Z Smith Reynolds Library, North Carolina Baptist Collection, PO Box 7777 Reynolda Station, Winston-Salem, 27109. John R Woodard, Jr, Dir
Holdings: Vols (7000) Cat Mss Maps Pix Slides Microforms
Budget: ($20,000)
Notes: The Ethel Taylor Crittenden Collection in Baptist History, emphasizes the Baptists of North Carolina in particular. Much, however, from other states, the Southern Baptist Convention and the American Baptist Convention. Also Negro, Primitive and Free-Will Baptist items. There is a general card file to all holdings, and alphabetical and chronological file (incl extinct churches), and special index files for biographical references; the NC Church file; vital statistics.

OH —KENT STATE UNIVERSITY, University Archives, Kent, 44242. Stephen C Morton, University Archivist
Holdings: Uncat Mss
Notes: Books and papers by A O Fuller, Cornelia Cowles Fuller, and Jeannette Fuller. Allen O Fuller was an ordained Baptist Minister in Northeastern, Ohio. The collection, in addition to periodical newspaper articles by A O Fuller, includes miscellaneous folders containing Fuller's religious and medical theories and other materials and two journals dated 1851-1854 and 1857.

OK —HILLSDALE FREE WILL BAPTIST COLLEGE, Library, Box 7208, Moore, 73153. Nancy Fogerson, Librn
Holdings: Vols 700 Uncat Mss Pix Audiotapes
Notes: Free Will Baptist Historical Collection.

RI —BROWN UNIVERSITY, John Hay Library, 20 Prospect St, Providence, 02912. Mark N Brown, Cur Mss
Holdings: Mss
Notes: Several collections relate directly to the history of Baptists and the Baptist Church in the United States. Incl the Isaac Backus Collection (qv); The Francis Wayland Collection (qv); The Asa Messer Collection (qv); the Roger Williams Collection (qv); as well as the records of the Baptists Church of Swansea, Massachusetts; the records of the Baptist Church in Warren, RI; and the ledgers of the Arkwright and Fiskeville (RI) Baptist Church, Scituate, RI. As Brown University was founded in 1764 by Baptists, University Archives contain substantial documentation as well. Also, the papers of James Manning, Baptist clergyman and first President of Brown University. More than 300 letters, documents, and mss for the period 1759 to 1794, about half of which are written or signed by Manning. Subjects incl the early history of Brown University, the Baptist religion in England andAmerica, the College Library, and the American Revolution. Register available.

SC —FURMAN UNIVERSITY, Library, James Buchanan Duke Bldg, Greenville, 29613. J Glenwood Clayton, Special Collection Librn
Holdings: Vols 1200 Cat Mss Maps Pix Microforms
Notes: Special Collection incl the Furman University archives and a very small amount of South Carolina material. Approx 85 percent of material is South Carolina Baptist records.

TN —HISTORICAL COMMISSION-SUNDAY SCHOOL BOARD, Southern Baptist Convention, Dargan-Carver Library, 127 Ninth Ave N, Nashville, 37234. Howard Gallimore, Supvr
Holdings: Vols (10,000) Cat Mss Maps Pix Slides Phonorecords Audiotapes Videotapes 16mm Films Filmstrips Microforms
Budget: ($38,734)
Notes: Extensive holdings in proceedings and minutes of organized Baptist bodies; state conventions and associations, Baptist journals, and documentation of major Southern Baptist controversies. Material on Black, Russian, and other Baptists. Much on religious education and American religion. Large collection of Sunday School literature. Incl thousands of mss, pictures, slides, records, etc, and 12,000,000 pages on microforms.

TX —SOUTHWESTERN BAPTIST THEOLOGICAL SEMINARY, Roberts Library, 2001 W Seminary Dr, PO Box 22000-2E, Fort Worth, 76122. Keith C Wills, Dir
Holdings: Vols 79,000 Cat Mss Maps Pix Slides Phonorecords Audiotapes 16mm Films Filmstrips Microforms
Budget: $28,000
Notes: Roberts Library is the official depository for the Texas Baptist Historical Committee of the Baptist General Convention of Texas. This is in addition to emphasis upon this subject because of the Seminary curriculum and research activities. The largest Baptist library in the world.

BAPTISTS—MISSIONS

RI —BROWN UNIVERSITY, John Hay Library, 20 Prospect St, Providence, 02912. Mark N Brown, Cur Mss
Holdings: Vols (2000) Cat Mss
Notes: Several collections of religious history strong in material on Baptist, Congregational, and Unitarian Churches in the 19th century, incl the ms records some Rhode Island congregations plus the papers of Isaac Backus, Brown University presidents and faculty, Jones Very, Mary Ann Atwood, Thomas Ustick, and Charles King Newcomb; incl numerous ephemeral and pamphlet publications that relate to Baptist Church history, creed, biography, Sunday School literature and missions.

TN —HISTORICAL COMMISSION-SUNDAY SCHOOL BOARD, Southern Baptist Convention, Dargan-Carver Library, 127 Ninth Ave N, Nashville, 37234. Howard Gallimore, Supvr
Holdings: Vols (10,000) Cat Mss Maps Pix Slides Phonorecords Audiotapes Videotapes 16mm Films Filmstrips Microforms
Budget: ($38,734)
Notes: Extensive holdings in proceedings and minutes of organized Baptist bodies; state conventions and associations, Baptist journals, and documentation of major Southern Baptist controversies. Material on Black, Russian, and other Baptists. Much on religious education and American religion. Large collection of Sunday School literature. Incl thousands of mss, pictures, slides, records, etc, and 12,000,000 pages on microforms.

BAPTY, WALTER, 1884-1973

BC —UNIVERSITY OF VICTORIA, McPherson Library, Victoria, V8W 3H5, Can.
Notes: Colonel, 2nd Battalion, Canadian Scottish Regiment. Mss of addresses, essays, lectures, documents, letters, telegrams and personal papers. Photographs of 2nd Battalion Canadian Scottish Regiment (1936-41).

BARACH, ALVAN LEROY

NY —CITY UNIVERSITY OF NEW YORK, City College, Morris R Cohen Library, North Academic Center, Convent Ave & 137th St, New York, 10031. Barbara J Dunlap, Archivist
Holdings: Mss Pix
Notes: The collection is by and about Dr Alvan Leroy Barach, graduate of the college and prominent physician of the 20th century. Inventor of the oxygen tent. The Alvan L Barach Collection at City College focuses on the nonmedical writings and letters of Dr Barach, although many of his medical publications are also there; incl four novels he wrote, one play, numerous poems, nearly 20 essays and a compilation of quotations; some of the foregoing is published and some is unpublished. The correspondence contains letters with family and friends from the early part of the century to the present. See *The Alvan L Barach Collection: Preliminary Inventory,* City College Archives. City College of New York, NY (1972).

BARAKA, IMAMU AMIRI see Jones, Leroi (Imamu Amiri Baraka), 1934-

BARBADOS

CT —YALE UNIVERSITY, Sterling Memorial Library, Latin American Collections, New Haven, 06520. Lee H Williams Jr, Cur
Holdings: Vols (300,000) Cat Maps Pix Slides Phonorecords 16mm Films Filmstrips
See also entry under Latin America

BARBARY CORSAIRS see Pirates and Piracy

BARBEE, DAVID RANKIN

DC —GEORGETOWN UNIVERSITY, Library, Special Collections Div, 37 & O Sts NW, Washington, 20057. George M Barringer, Special Collections Librn; Nicholas B Sheetz, Mss Librn
Holdings: Mss Cat
Notes: The papers of David Rankin Barbee, journalist with *The Washington Post* and authority on: Abraham Lincoln; the Lincoln assassination; Rose O'Neal Greenhow; and the Civil War. The collection incl, besides extensive correspondence with such historians as Albert J Beveridge, Henry Steele Commager, and Paul M Angle, all of Barbee's own research files and the mss of his works.

BARBERINI FAMILY

MA —HARVARD UNIVERSITY, Graduate School of Business Administration, Baker Library, Soldiers Field, Boston, 02163. Mary V Chatfield, Librn; Florence Bartoshesky, Cur of Manuscripts and Archives
Holdings: Cat Mss
Notes: Business papers; see *Harvard Alumni* Bulletin, XXII (1929), 62-66.

BARBOAR FAMILY

MA —NEW ENGLAND HISTORIC GENEALOGICAL SOCIETY, Library, 101 Newbury St, Boston, 02116. Ralph J Crandell, Dir
Notes: Family papers, likely to incl personal correspondence, diaries, business records, etc.

BARBOUR, HARRIOT BUXTON

MA —BOSTON UNIVERSITY, Mugar Memorial Library, Special Collections Dept, 771 Commonwealth Ave, Boston, 02215. Howard B Gotlieb, Dir
Holdings: // Cat Mss Pix
Notes: Mss, correspondence, etc collected in depth; incl publications by or about.

BARBOUR, JAMES

VA —UNIVERSITY OF VIRGINIA, Alderman Library, Manuscripts Dept, Charlottesville, 22901. Edmund Berkeley Jr, Cur
Holdings: Cat Mss
See also entry under Virginia - History

BARFIELD, OWEN

IL —WHEATON COLLEGE, Library, Marion E Wade Collection, Irving & Franklin Sts,

BARFIELD, OWEN (cont.)

Wheaton, 60187. Lyle Dorsett, Cur; Marjorie Mead, Associate Cur
Holdings: Vols (6500) Mss Pix Films Audiotapes Videotapes
Notes: Extensive Marion E Wade Collection of seven British authors incl books and papers of Owen Barfield. Items of special note are first editions (both British and American) of all Barfield works, as well as nearly all published and unpublished manuscripts, incl his "Great War" correspondence with C S Lewis. A member of Oxford's Inklings, Barfield has visited the Wade Collection several times.

BARGA FAMILY

IL —NEWBERRY LIBRARY, 60 W Walton St, Chicago, 60610. Diana Haskell, Cur of Modern Mss
Holdings: Cat Mss
Notes: Incl Parravicini, Strozzi, and Barga family papers. Restricted use: noncirculating.

BARGEO, C. F. see Angeli, Pietro (C. F. Bargeo)

BARGES

OH —PUBLIC LIBRARY OF CINCINNATI & HAMILTON COUNTY, Dept of Rare Books & Special Collections, 800 Vine St, Library Square, Cincinnati, 45202. Yeatman Anderson III, Cur
Holdings: Cat Mss Maps Pix Slides Microforms
Notes: Inland River Collection. Incl logbooks, account books, personal correspondence, diaries, etc. Also, a picture collection of 14,000 items (steamboats, towboats, river views, crews, construction, barges, etc.)

BARING, MAURICE

CT —YALE UNIVERSITY, Box 1603A, Yale Station, New Haven, 06520.
Holdings: Cat Mss

NY —HOFSTRA UNIVERSITY, Library, 1000 Fulton Ave, Hempstead, 11550. Charles R Andrews, Dean of Library Services

BARKER, EUGENE C.

TX —UNIVERSITY OF TEXAS LIBRARIES, General Libraries, Barker Texas History Center, PO Box P, Austin, 78712. Don Carleton, Dir

BARKER, FLORENCE

AZ —NORTHERN ARIZONA UNIVERSITY, Special Collection Library, CU Box 6022, Flagstaff, 86011. Peter M Whiteley, Coordr/Archivist; William Mullane, Librn
Notes: Florence Barker Collection. She was a missionary nurse on the Navajo, Havasupai, Acoma and Laguna Indian Reservations. Incl diaries, 1922-1927 (Immanuel Mission, Navajo Reservation), also some copied textual material of interest concerning the Immanuel Mission during the 1920's. Inventory available.

BARKER, GEORGE

NV —UNIVERSITY OF NEVADA, RENO, University Library, Special Collections Dept, Reno, 89557. Robert E Blesse, Head
Holdings: Vols (43) Cat Other appearances 475 Cat
Notes: Includes individual works by author in all editions including translations; also prefaces, introductions, published correspondence, appearances in anthologies, periodicals, etc. Bibliographical research collection, part of Modern Authors Collection.

BC —UNIVERSITY OF VICTORIA, McPherson Library, Victoria, V8W 3H5, Can.
Notes: Poet, artist. Correspondence, 1934-64; newspaper clippings, 1933-68; sketches, 1963-65; holographs and typescripts of essays, 1937-69; notebooks, holographs and typescripts of poetry, 1954-70; contracts, 1933-64; marked proofs.

BARKER, GEORGE FREDERICK, 1835-1910

PA —UNIVERSITY OF PENNSYLVANIA, University Archives, North Arcade Franklin Field E-6, Philadelphia, 19104. Francis James Dallett, University Archivist
Notes: His papers (1870-1900).

BARKLEY, ALBEN W.

KY —UNIVERSITY OF KENTUCKY, Margaret I King Library, Dept of Special Collections, Lexington, 40506. William Marshall, Head
Holdings: // Mss Pix Phonorecords Microforms
Notes: Public career of Vice President Barkley. 65,000 pieces.

BARLAAM AND JOSEPHAT

OH —CLEVELAND PUBLIC LIBRARY, Fine Arts and Special Collections Department, 325 Superior Ave, Cleveland, 44114. Alice N Loranth, Head
Holdings: Vols (3000) Cat Mss
Notes: Part of the Romances Collection, which incl critical studies, and early printed editions. The Arthurian and Charlemagne cycles, the Nibelungenlied and other Germanic titles, Amadis de Gaula and his numerous progeny, Alexander the Great, Barlaam and Joasaph, and the Seven Wise Masters of Rome are some of the strengths of the collection. Material in the Dewey/Brett Collection is classified by related cycles and their versions in various languages.
See also entry under Romances.

BARLOW, GEORGE, 1847-1913

BC —UNIVERSITY OF VICTORIA, McPherson Library, Victoria, V8W 3H5, Can.

BARLOW, JOEL

MA —HARVARD UNIVERSITY LIBRARY, Houghton Library, Cambridge, 02138. Rodney G Dennis, Cur of Manuscripts
Holdings: Cat Mss

BARNARD, ELLSWORTH

IN —INDIANA UNIVERSITY, Lilly Library, Seventh St, Bloomington, 47405. William R Cagle, Librn
Notes: Papers and correspondence of 1940 Republican presidential candidate Wendell Willkie. Bulk of material is for 1939-1944. Incl campaign-related correspondence, speeches, writings and publications, material on *One World*, scrapbooks, clippings, photographs, election memorabilia, etc; 500, 000 items. Correspondence, research notes, and ms of Willkie biography prepared by Ellsworth Barnard, 1907-: Collection relates to Professor Barnard's book *Wendell Willkie: Fighter for Freedon* (Northern Michigan University Press, 1966); 462 items. Also Willkie Clubs collection. Contains the presidential campaign files of the Associated Willkie Clubs of America, 1940. 64,417 items.
See also entry under Willkie, Wendell Lewis, 1892-1944.

BARNARD, HENRY

CT —TRINITY COLLEGE LIBRARY, Watkinson Library, 300 Summit St, Hartford, 06106. Jeffrey Kaimowitz, Cur
Holdings: Cat Mss Pix
Notes: Barnard papers; 7000 early American school books.

BARNARD, JOSEPH HENRY, M.D., 1804-1861

TX —UNIVERSITY OF TEXAS LIBRARIES, General Libraries, Barker Texas History Center, PO Box P, Austin, 78712. Don Carleton, Dir
Notes: Papers of Dr Joseph Henry Barnard (1804-1861), surgeon in the 1836 Texas Revolution. Incl names and statistics relative to the Battle of Coleto, 19 March 1836; also other professional and financial papers.

BARNES, BEN

TX —NORTH TEXAS STATE UNIVERSITY, Archives, NT Station Box 5188, Denton, 76203. Robert LaForte, University Archivist
Notes: Part of Oral History Collection. Interviews with former Speaker of Texas House of Representatives and Lt Governor.

BARNES, DJUNA

†MD —UNIVERSITY OF MARYLAND, Library, College Park, 20742. Donald Farren, Assoc Dir for Special Collections
Holdings: Cat
Notes: First appearances in book form, in anthologies, and in periodicals; subsequent editions, with differences in text, etc; works edited or translated; association items, especially with marginalia. Secondary works are generally excluded.

NV —UNIVERSITY OF NEVADA, RENO, University Library, Special Collections Dept, Reno, 89557. Robert E Blesse, Head
Holdings: // Vols 24 Cat Other appearances 75 Cat
Notes: Includes individual works by author in all editions including translations; also prefaces, introductions, published correspondence, appearances in anthologies, periodicals, etc. Bibliographical research collection, part of Modern Authors Collection.

BARNES, HARRY ELMER

PA —TEMPLE UNIVERSITY LIBRARIES, Special Collections Dept, Conwellana-Templana Collection, 13 & Berks St, Philadelphia, 19122. Miriam I Crawford, Cur
Holdings: Vols (22) // Cat Mss Pix
Budget: ($30,000)
Notes: Personal papers of Negley K Teeters. The published writings, manuscripts, correspondence, and research materials of Teeters, criminologist and faculty member of Temple University, covering the years 1927-1971. Contains extended correspondence with his co-author, Harry Elmer Barnes, from 1940 to 1968, and materials dealing with their investigation of the murder trial of Caryl Chessman, which failed to halt his execution in California in 1960. Incl copies of letters from Teeters to Barnes, originals of which are in the Western History Research Center of the University of Wyoming, and incl the Index to the Barnes Papers in that collection. *Descriptive Inventory of the Personal Papers of Negley K Teeters* (1896-1971), (Conwellana-Templana Collection, Temple University, 1971, addenda 1972 and 1974; 6 leaves; unpublished typescript).

WY —UNIVERSITY OF WYOMING, William Robertson Coe Library, Archives - American Heritage Center, PO Box 3412, Laramie, 82071.

BARNES, HAZEL

NE —UNIVERSITY OF NEBRASKA-LINCOLN, Don L Love Library, University Archives and Special Collections, Lincoln, 68588. Joseph G Svoboda, University Archivist
Notes: Virginia Faulkner was recognized as one of Nebraska's most distinguished writers and scholars. The Virginia Faulkner Collection, containing over 2000 titles, is housed in the Special Collections Department of Love Library. It is especially strong in twentieth century writers and in University of Nebraska Press publications. Of especial value to scholars are her extensive holdings of Willa Cather, Wright Morris, and John Neihardt. Her correspondence with S N Behrman, E B White, Edward Wagenknecht, Donald

BARNES, HAZEL (cont.)

Sutherland, Wright Morris, Louise Pound, Mari Sandoz, Hazel Barnes, Alfred A and Blanche Knopf, and others provide insight into the literary development of these figures, as well as chronicle the intellectual thought of the period. Amassed in a separate file, these letters are available to interested scholars.

BARNETT, CLAUDE A.

IL —CHICAGO HISTORICAL SOCIETY, Library, Clark St at North Ave, Chicago, 60614. Archie Motley, Manuscript Librn
Notes: Papers of founder and director of Associated Negro Press.

BARNUM, REV. FRANCIS A., S.J.

DC —GEORGETOWN UNIVERSITY, Library, Special Collections Div, 37 & O Sts NW, Washington, 20057. George M Barringer, Special Collections Librn; Nicholas B Sheetz, Mss Librn
Holdings: Vols (100) Cat Mss Maps Pix
Notes: A number of early Alaskan Mission imprints are included in the papers (1867-1920) of Rev Francis A Barnum, SJ, who served in Alaska ca 1890 and wrote an "Innuit" grammar.

BARNUM, P. T.

IL —NORTH PARK COLLEGE LIBRARY, 5125 N Spaulding Ave, Chicago, 60625. Dorothy-Ellen Gross, Dir
Holdings: Vols 200 Cat Mss
Notes: Collection consists of books, medals, other objects d'art (bottles, coins, etc), pictures, music and letters to and from Jenny Lind and P T Barnum.

BARODA

MO —UNIVERSITY OF MISSOURI-COLUMBIA, Ellis Library, Ninth and Lowry, Columbia, 65201. Murari Lal Nagar, Librn
Holdings: Vols 100,000 Maps Microforms
Notes: The South Asia Studies Program at the University of Missouri-Columbia, is an interdepartmental, multi-disciplinary area studies program on India, Pakistan, Bangladesh, Sri Lanka and Nepal. Depository for the PL480 Program of the Library of Congress in many languages from South Asia. There are library resources in Sankskrit, Hindi, Bengali, Panjabi, and Malayalam. The library is particularly strong in Baroda, Bengal and the Punjab.

BAROQUE ART see Art, Baroque

BAROQUE LITERATURE

CA —STANFORD UNIVERSITY LIBRARIES, Cecil H Green Library, Stanford, 94305. Peter R Frank, Cur, CDP-Germanic Collection
Notes: Library of Prof Rudolf Hildebran, Leipzig, the first large collection acquired by Stanford in 1895/1896, laid the foundation for an extensive German collection. Hildebrand's library is especially strong in German and Austrian philology (rare dictionaries, etc.), but also in literary works. The collection is now especially strong for the period of the Reformation and Baroque, up to the present, with many rare editions, journals, almanacs, and the like. Sizable collections of women's working class and popular literature, dissertations and Schulschriften. Rare and valuable items in the Stanford Collection of German, Austrian and Swiss Culture, Special Collections. Catalog: *Katalog der Bibliothek des Herrn Prof Dr Rudolf Hildebrand.* Description: *The German Area Collection: A Stanford* Tradition by Peter R Frank.

NC —DUKE UNIVERSITY, William R Perkins Library, Rare Book Room, Durham, 27706. John L Sharpe, III, Cur
Holdings: Vols 3600
Notes: Harold Jantz collection of German Baroque literature, consisting of 3600 volumes. Described in *German Baroque Literature: A Descriptive Catalogue of the Collection of Harold Jantz.* New Haven: Research Publications, Inc 1974. 2 vols.

BARREN LANDS (CANADA)

ON —UNIVERSITY OF TORONTO, Thomas Fisher Rare Book Library, 120 Saint George St, Toronto, M5S 1A5, Can. Richard G Landon, Head
Holdings: Vols 30,000 Cat Mss Pix Maps
Notes: Great variety of material relating to early exploration and settlement of Canada, including the search for the Northwest Passage and the subsequent exploration of the Arctic. Manuscript and printed material pertaining to the overland exploration of northwestern Canada and the Barren Lands. Manuscript and printed material documenting early emigration schemes and colonization attempts, including Selkirk's Red River settlement.

BARRETO, TOBIAS

WI —UNIVERSITY OF WISCONSIN, MADISON, Memorial Library, Ibero-American Studies Collection, 728 State St, Madison, 53706. Suzanne Hodgman, Bibliographer
Holdings: Vols (129) // Cat
Notes: An unusual collection of 129 volumes on Brazilian history, literature, and philosophy. Strongest in works published by members of the intellectual group known as the Escola do Recife, the leader of which was Tobias Barreto. The collection contains almost all of his works as well as most of the works, including many rare pamphlets, of Silvio Romero, Barreto's most illustrious disciple. No separate listing.

BARRETT, DAVID DEAN, 1892-1977

CA —HOOVER INSTITUTION ON WAR, REVOLUTION & PEACE, Stanford University, Stanford, 94305. Milorad M Drachkovitch, Archivist
Holdings: Mss Pix Phonorecords
Notes: Papers of David D Barrett, Colonel, US Army, chief of the US Dixie Mission to Chinese Communist forces, 1944, incl mss of writings, correspondence, printed matter, photographs and phonorecords, 1933-70, relating to the Dixie Mission and the military situation in China during World War II. 1/2 ms box, 4 envelopes, 2 phonorecords, 1 oversize box.

BARRETT, TONY

CA —UNIVERSITY OF CALIFORNIA, LOS ANGELES, Theater Arts Library, Los Angeles, 90024. Edward Shreeves, Chairman, Bibliographers Group; Audree Malkin, Head, Theater Arts Library
Notes: Tony Barrett (writer) Collection: extensive collection of material which spans both radio and television, incl such shows as *This is Your FBI, Suspense, Rin Tin Tin, Richard Diamond, Private Detective, The Cisco Kid, Peter Gunn, Burke's Law,* and *Mod Squad.* The material consists of various versions of the scripts, ideas, notes, research, production reports.

BARRIE, SIR JAMES MATTHEW, 1860-1937

CT —YALE UNIVERSITY, Box 1603A, Yale Station, New Haven, 06520.
Holdings: Cat Mss Pix

IN —INDIANA UNIVERSITY, Lilly Library, Seventh St, Bloomington, 47405. William R Cagle, Librn
Holdings: Vols 100 Cat Mss
Notes: First editions, etc. Mss include *Walker, London,* and *Peter Pan.*

MA —HARVARD UNIVERSITY LIBRARY, Houghton Library, Cambridge, 02138. Rodney G Dennis, Cur of Manuscripts
Holdings: Cat Mss
Notes: Manuscripts and personal papers.

NJ —PRINCETON UNIVERSITY, Library, Morris L Parrish Collection, Princeton, 08540. Alexander D Wainwright, Cur
Holdings: Vols 250 Cat Mss
Notes: Details may be found in: Walter Beinecke Jr, "Barrie in the Parrish Collection" in the *Chronicle* XVII, 2 (winter, 1956) pp 96-98.

BC —UNIVERSITY OF VICTORIA, McPherson Library, Victoria, V8W 3H5, Can.
Notes: Playwright. Incl six holograph letters to Thomas Lennox Gilmour mainly about his financial affairs.

BARRON, HETTY

SC —COLLEGE OF CHARLESTON LIBRARY, Special Collections Dept, Charleston, 29401.
Notes: Papers, 1840, incl warrant for sheriff's sale of Hetty Barron, a "free person of color," for non-payment of capitation tax, March 20, 1840.

BARRON, SAMUEL

VA —UNIVERSITY OF VIRGINIA, Alderman Library, Manuscripts Dept, Charlottesville, 22901. Edmund Berkeley Jr, Cur
Holdings: Cat Mss Maps Pix
Notes: Personal and official papers of Sir Andrew Snape Hamond and Graham Eden Hamond concern British naval operations during the American Revolution and in the Mediterranean during the Napoleonic Wars. Paul P Hoffman (ed) *Guide to the Naval Papers of Sir Andrew Snape Hamond . . . and Sir Graham Eden Hamond . . .* (Charlottesville, Va: Microfilm Publications, University of Virginia, 1966). Papers of US and Confederate naval officer Samuel Barron; US fleet surgeon and Brooklyn Navy Yard surgeon Gustavus R B Horner; US naval surgeon John S Whittle on a scientific expedition to the Pacific, 1838-1841; and US naval officer William Conway Whittle on West Indies and Mediterranean cruises, 1823-1831.

BARRY, DAVID

SD —SIOUXLAND HERITAGE MUSEUMS, Pettigrew Museum Library, 131 N Duluth Ave, Sioux Falls, 57104. Ms Lee N McLaird, Cur of Collections
Notes: Pettigrew Museum Library is a support service of the Siouxland Heritage Museums. US Senator R F Pettigrew established the core collection in 1926, covering natural history (incl North American Indian anthropology) and state-local history (concentrating on exploration and settlement to about 1900). The collection also incl the Senator's private papers (ca 1870-1926). Additions to the collection since 1926 have emphasized Plains Indian anthropology, state-local history, baseball and museology, supporting the work of the Museum staff. The collection is mostly cataloged and is inter-indexed with Augustana College, Sioux Falls College, and Sioux Falls Public libraries (as well as having its own catalog). The photograph collection includes prints by D F Barry as well as other photographs work with native peoples.

WI —DOUGLAS COUNTY HISTORICAL MUSEUM, 906 E Second St, Superior, 54880. James E Lundsted, Dir
Notes: Photographs by David Barry, of Sioux Indians at time of Custer fiasco, 1875-1888.

BARRY, JANE

MA —BOSTON UNIVERSITY, Mugar Memorial Library, Special Collections Dept, 771 Commonwealth Ave, Boston, 02215. Howard B Gotlieb, Dir
Holdings: Cat Mss

BARRY, JOHN

PA —PHILADELPHIA MARITIME MUSEUM, Library, 321 Chestnut St,

BARRY, JOHN (cont.)

Philadelphia, 19106. Dorothy H Mueller, Librn
Holdings: / / Mss
Notes: Hepburn Collection. Consists of the family papers of John Barry, Patrick Hayes, and the Sommers and Keene families of Philadelphia. Includes personal correspondence, financial and business papers, and diaries and journals. Dates range from 1723-1876. 300 ms pieces.

BARRY, JULIAN

MA —BOSTON UNIVERSITY, Mugar Memorial Library, Special Collections Dept, 771 Commonwealth Ave, Boston, 02215. Howard B Gotlieb, Dir
Holdings: Mss

BARRY FAMILY

BC —UNIVERSITY OF VICTORIA, McPherson Library, Victoria, V8W 3H5, Can.
Notes: Papers.

BARRYMORE, ETHEL

IN —INDIANA STATE UNIVERSITY, Cunningham Memorial Library, Dept of Rare Books & Special Collections, Terre Haute, 47809. Lawrence J McCrank, Head
Notes: The Debs Collection consists of aprox 7000 pieces of correspondence between Theodore Debs (brother of E V) and other persons, such as Sinclair Lewis, Upton Sinclair, Ethel Barrymore, Emma Goldman, Robert G Ingersoll, Carl Sandburg, Norman Thomas, Sacco and Vanzetti and many others. Many of the letters are from E V Debs to his brother; a good portion of these are from the federal penitentiary at Atlanta. Entire correspondence file has been microfilmed. 750 pamphlets cover all aspects of the labor movement, socialism and radical thought from the 19th century to appprox 1950. A collection ca 200 related books is also housed in the collection. See: J Robert Constantine and Gail Malmgreen, eds, *The Papers of Eugene V Debs, 1834-1945. A Guide to the Microfilm Edition.* NY: Microfilming Corp of America, 1983 (University Microfilms is the new distributer).

BARS see Restaurants, Lunch Rooms, Bars, Etc.

BARTH, GEORGE

PA —US ARMY MILITARY HISTORY INSTITUTE, Carlisle Barracks, 17013. Richard J Sommers, Chief Archivist-Historian
Holdings: Mss Cat
Notes: TheKorean War collection, personal correspondence, daily logs, recollections, and official papers of US officers and soldiers serving in the Korean War, incl Generals Edward Almond, George Barth Bruce Clarke, Matthew Ridgway, and Arthur Trudeau.

BARTH, JOHN

DC —LIBRARY OF CONGRESS, Manuscript Division, Washington, 20540. John C Broderick, Chief
Notes: His papers.

MO —WASHINGTON UNIVERSITY, Libraries, Campus Box 1061, Saint Louis, 63130.
Notes: A collection of primary material.

NV —UNIVERSITY OF NEVADA, RENO, University Library, Special Collections Dept, Reno, 89557. Robert E Blesse, Head
Holdings: Vols (35) Cat Other appearances 65 Cat
Notes: Includes individual works by author in all editions including translations; also prefaces, introductions, published correspondence, appearances in anthologies, periodicals, etc. Bibliographical research collection, part of Modern Authors Collection.

BARTHELME, DONALD

NV —UNIVERSITY OF NEVADA, RENO, University Library, Special Collections Dept, Reno, 89557. Robert E Blesse, Head
Holdings: Vols (34) Cat
Notes: Includes individual works by author in all editions including translations; also prefaces, introductions, published correspondence, appearances in anthologies, periodicals, etc. Bibliographical research collection, part of Modern Authors Collection. Other appearances 140 cataloged.

TX —UNIVERSITY OF HOUSTON, M D Anderson Memorial Library, University Park, Houston, 77004. David Farmer, Cur, Special Collections; Jean Jackson, Assistant Cur
Holdings: Vols (200) Cat
Notes: The emphasis of this collection is on Houston writers of literature. The writers incl Vassar Miller, Cynthia McDonald, Leon Hale, Larry McMurtry, Beverly Lowry, Donald Barthelme and others who have resided or currently reside in the Houston area, and incl some writers who write about the Houston area although they do not live there.

BARTHOLOMEW, HARLAND, AND ASSOCIATES

MO —WASHINGTON UNIVERSITY, Libraries, Special Collections Dept, Campus Box 1061, St Louis, 63130.
Notes: Papers of Joseph R Badarraco, espec files from his term as St Louis' president of the Board of Aldermen, 1972-75. Rich in City Plan Commission reports, etc, particularly redevelopment proposals and projects. Also records of Harland Bartholomew and Associates, early city planning firm active in St Louis and other cities.

BARTLETT, ADELBERT, 1887-1966

CA —UNIVERSITY OF CALIFORNIA, LOS ANGELES, Research Library, Dept of Special Collections, 405 Hilgard Ave, Los Angeles, 90024. Edward Shreeves, Chairman, Bibliographers Group; David S Zeidberg, Head
Notes: 11 linear feet of maps, photographs, memorabilia, and ephemera relating to the Near Eastern Relief Fund, of which he was the Los Angeles Director.

BARTLETT, DEWEY

OK —UNIVERSITY OF OKLAHOMA, Bizzell Memorial Library, Western History Collections, 401 W Brooks, Norman, 73069. John Ezell, Cur
Holdings: Vols Mss Pix Microforms Audiotapes Maps Newspapers Documents
Notes: Congressional Papers of Senator Dewey Bartlett.

BARTLETT, ELISHA, 1804-1855, AND FAMILY

†NY —UNIVERSITY OF ROCHESTER, Rush Rhees Library, History of Medicine Section, Rochester, 14627.
Notes: A collection of some 400 items, mostly letters and mss, relating to the Bartlett family of Rhode Island. Incl items concerning the medical career of Elisha Bartlett from 1832-1855; also correspondence with contemporary physicians and surgeons.

BARTLETT, ROBERT ABRAMS, 1875-1946

ME —BOWDOIN COLLEGE, Library, Brunswick, 04011. Dianne M Gutscher, Cur of Special Collections
Holdings: Mss
Notes: The papers (about 15,000 items) of Robert A Bartlett, arctic explorer and shipmaster for Admirals Robert E Peary and Donald B MacMillan, contain more than 15, 000 manuscripts, photographs, clippings, diaries, logbooks and some printed material relating to Bartlett's arctic voyages.

BARTLETT, TRUMAN H.

MA —BOSTON UNIVERSITY, Mugar Memorial Library, Special Collections Dept, 771 Commonwealth Ave, Boston, 02215. Howard B Gotlieb, Dir
Holdings: / / Mss Pix
Notes: Correspondence related to Abraham Lincoln sculpture, clippings about sculpture and sculptors of Lincoln.

BARTLETT ILLUSTRATIONS

ON —NATIONAL LIBRARY OF CANADA, 395 Wellington St, Ottawa, K1A 0N4, Can. Andre Preibish, Dir
Holdings: Vols 10,000
Notes: The collection on History and Art of the Book consists of over 10,000 volumes. Areas of concentration are: early imprints, special editions, examples of private presses works, book industry and trade books illustrating the aesthetic and technical aspects of the field, collection of books illustrated by Bartlett.

BARTOK, BELA

DC —LIBRARY OF CONGRESS, Music Division, Washington, 20540.
Notes: Mss in Koussevitzky Archives.

WA —UNIVERSITY OF WASHINGTON LIBRARIES, Music Library, DN-10, Seattle, 98195. David A Wood, Music Librn
Holdings: Vols (35,000) Cat Mss Microforms
Budget: ($11,700)
Notes: Incl 11 letters of Bela Bartok.

BARTOL FOUNDATION

PA —FRANKLIN INSTITUTE LIBRARY, Dept of Historical Programs, 20th St and Parkway, Philadelphia, 19103.
Notes: The atomic physics research records of the Bartol Foundation (1923-1940).

BARTON, ARTHUR G.

CA —CALIFORNIA POLYTECHNIC STATE UNIVERSITY LIBRARY, Special Collections and University Archives, San Luis Obispo, 93407. Nancy E Loe, Head Librn
Holdings: Mss
Notes: The Barton Collection incl the personal and professional papers of Arthur G Barton, a noted Southern California landscape architect, incl his office files, bids, and drawings and designs (collection in rough sorting stage). 55,000 pieces of ms material. 6000 landscape architecture designs and drawings.

BARTON, CLARA

DC —LIBRARY OF CONGRESS, Manuscript Division, Washington, 20540. John C Broderick, Chief
Holdings: Cat Mss Pix
Notes: Mss, papers, records, etc.

BARTON, GEORGE AARON, 1859-1942

MA —BRANDEIS UNIVERSITY, Goldfarb Library, 415 South St, Waltham, 02154. Bessie Hahn, Dir
Notes: 12 linear ft of correspondence by and to Professor George A Barton, noted Biblical scholar. This collection is unprocessed, spring 1984.

BARTON, HENRY

NY —AMERICAN INSTITUTE OF PHYSICS, Center for the History of Physics Niels Bohr Library, 335 E 45 St, New York, 10017. John Aubry, Librn
Notes: Papers and records.

BARTSCH, PAUL

DC —SMITHSONIAN INSTITUTION, Archives Div, Washington, 20560. William

BARTSCH, PAUL (cont.)

W Moss, Archivist
Holdings: Cat Mss Maps Pix Slides
Notes: The Archives has accessioned, processed and described the records of the US National Museum's Division of Mollusks, 1885-1951, principally outgoing correspondence from Honorary Curator William H Dall (qv). Curator Paul Bartsch and Assistant Curator Harold A Rhaeder covering the period 1885-1937.

BARUCH, BERNARD MANNES, 1870-1965

NJ —PRINCETON UNIVERSITY, Library, Manuscript Collection, Nassau St, Princeton, 08540. Jean F Preston, Cur
Holdings: Vols 31 Cat Mss Pix
Notes: Mss total 521 scrapbook volumes, 169 ms boxes, and 121 archival cartons. An unpublished 56p guide is available for consultation. The papers cover the period 1905-1965.

BARUS, CARL, 1856-1935

RI —BROWN UNIVERSITY, John Hay Library, 20 Prospect St, Providence, 02912. Mark N Brown, Cur Mss
Holdings: / / Mss
Notes: About 750 letters chiefly to Carl Barus from physicists in the US, Canada, and Europe; drafts of his contributions to scientific journals; University and faculty correspondence; and his autobiography in 269 typed pages with ms revisions. Register available.

BARZEL, ANN

IL —NEWBERRY LIBRARY, 60 W Walton St, Chicago, 60610. Carolyn A Sheehy, Administrator
Holdings: Cat Mss Pix Posters
Notes: Extensive holdings in the areas of dance history (including important first editions) and dance music. Newly formed Midwest Dance Archive contains the papers of Ann Barzel, Walter Camryn, Diana Huebert and Edna McRae.

BARZUN, JACQUES

†NY —COLUMBIA UNIVERSITY LIBRARIES, Butler Library, Rare Book and Manuscript Library, 535 W 114 St, New York, 10027.
Notes: Papers, correspondence, etc.

BASEBALL

DC —LIBRARY OF CONGRESS, Washington, 20540.
Holdings: Cat Mss Pix
Notes: The Arthur Mann papers, incl correspondence, 1923-1962, clippings and drafts and notes for books and articles, by the noted sports writer and baseball authority.

MA —BOSTON PUBLIC LIBRARY, Print Collection, Dartmouth St at Copley Sq, Boston, 02117. Sinclair H Hitchings, Keeper of Prints
Holdings: Cat
Notes: The Americana collection is especially strong in the 19th century. Incl 250 prints of American views, tradesmen's calling cards, illustrated diplomas and advertisements. Also in it is the McGreevey Baseball Collection of 225 photos, photoreproductions and paintings from the period 1870 to 1914. The American portrait collection contains 300 engravings, etchings and lithographs of prominent figures of the 18th and 19th century. In addition there are 200 portraits of Benjamin Franklin. Items cataloged by subject. Prints also by artist/ publisher.

MI —DETROIT PUBLIC LIBRARY, Burton Historical Collection, 5201 Woodward Ave, Detroit, 48202. Alice Dalligan, Chief
Notes: The extensive Ernie Harwell Collection on sports, incl baseball strength, espec the Detroit Tigers.

NY —NATIONAL BASEBALL HALL OF FAME AND MUSEUM, National Baseball Library, Cooperstown, 13326. Thomas R Heitz, Librn
Budget: ($6000)
Notes: The National Baseball Library incl the folowing special collections: Literature, a comprehensive collection of vols incl biographies, general histories, team and league histories, encyclopedias, directories, dictionaries, general reference materials, fiction, poetry, and children's books. Complete runs of *Baseball Digest, Baseball Magazine, Sport Magazine, Sports* Illustrated, team publications, and numerous other journals of interest to baseball researchers. A comprehensive collection of the public official documents of organized baseball for the major and minor leagues. Extensive runs of *The Sporting News, New York Clipper, Sporting Life* and other 19th and 20th century news publications. Current newspaper files are also available. A comprehensive collection of Spalding, Reach and other guides dating back to the 1870s. A comprehensivecollection of major league team publications, media guides, yearbooks and press releases. Biographical files: personal and career data on all major league players, past and present, as well as biographical data on managers, coaches, scouts, umpires, executives, broadcasters, sportswriters, authors and baseball personalities. The files contain an estimated 2,500,000 documents, questionnaires and news clippings. A file of minor league player record cards useful for tracing the careers of former baseball players, and several other collections of baseball-related items.

NY —NEW YORK PUBLIC LIBRARY, Research Libraries, General Research Division, Fifth Ave & 42 St, New York, 10018. Rodney Phillips, Chief
Holdings: Vols (2,225,000) Cat Maps Pix Microforms
Budget: ($775,718)
Notes: Incl Spalding Baseball Collections.

NY —RACQUET & TENNIS CLUB, Library, 370 Park Ave, New York, 10022. Gerald Belliveau, Jr, Librn
Holdings: Vols (17,500) Cat
Budget: ($6000)
Notes: Specializes in court tennis, lawn tennis, early American sport. See *Dictionary Catalogue of the Library of Sports in the Racquet and Tennis Club* (Boston: G K Hall, 1971). Also, Robert W Henderson, *Early American Sport,* 3rd ed. (Cranbury, NJ: Fairleigh Dickinson University Press, 1977).

OH —CLEVELAND PUBLIC LIBRARY, Social Sciences Department, 325 Superior Ave, Cleveland, 44114. Thelma Morris, Head
Holdings: Cat Pix
Notes: Incl 2000 vols of the Cahrles W Mears Baseball Collection. Magazines and newspapers from the late 1800s.

OK —SOCIETY FOR THE NORTH AMERICAN CULTURAL SURVEY, Dept of Geography, Oklahoma State University, Stillwater, 74078. John Rooney, Dir; Todd Zdorkowski, Asst
Notes: Producing a cultural survey of North American sports and games. John Rooney has published several books on the geography of sports. SWAC's current project involves mapping the continent-wide distributions and the participation patterns for the major and minor professional, college and high school sports.

SD —SIOUXLAND HERITAGE MUSEUMS, Pettigrew Museum Library, 131 N Duluth Ave, Sioux Falls, 57104. Ms Lee N McLaird, Cur of Collections
Notes: The collection includes the Records of Northern League Baseball.

BASEBALL CARDS

DC —SMITHSONIAN INSTITUTION LIBRARIES, National Museum of American History Branch, Washington, 20560. Rhoda S Ratner, Branch Librn
Notes: Emphasis on history of American sports and recreation. Incl some 2000 baseball cards from cigarette and chewing-gum packets; 103 scrapbooks and other memorabilia about Joe Louis; much on bicycling and skating.

NY —NATIONAL BASEBALL HALL OF FAME AND MUSEUM, National Baseball Library, Cooperstown, 13326. Thomas R Heitz, Librn
Notes: A file of minor league player records cards useful for tracing the careers of former baseball players.

BASEBALLS, SIGNED

NY —NATIONAL BASEBALL HALL OF FAME AND MUSEUM, National Baseball Library, Cooperstown, 13326. Thomas R Heitz, Librn
Notes: Collection of baseball-related items.

BASHKIR LANGUAGE

NY —NEW YORK PUBLIC LIBRARY, Oriental Div, Fifth Ave & 42 St, New York, 10018. E Christian Filstrup, Chief
Holdings: Cat Mss Microforms
Budget: ($56,455)
Notes: Published catalog of holdings.

BASKERVILLE, CHARLES

CT —YALE UNIVERSITY, Beinecke Rare Book & Manuscript Library, Osborn Collection, New Haven, 06520. Stephen R Parks, Cur
Holdings: Mss

NY —CITY UNIVERSITY OF NEW YORK, City College, Morris R Cohen Library, North Academic Center, Convent Ave & 137th St, New York, 10031. Barbara J Dunlap, Archivist
Holdings: Cat Mss Pix
Notes: Incl personal papers.

BASKETBALL

CA —UNIVERSITY OF CALIFORNIA, BERKELEY, Bancroft Library, Manuscripts Division, Berkeley, 94720. James D Hart, Dir
Notes: Wide scope but emphasis on the University's teams.

MA —NAISMITH MEMORIAL BASKETBALL HALL OF FAME, Edward J & Gena G Hickox Library, 460 Alden St, Box 175, Springfield, 01109. June Harrison Steitz, Librn
Holdings: Vols 2476 Cat Mss Pix Phonorecords 16mm Films
Budget: $2000
Notes: Incl 48 VF drawers of reports, documents, programs, pressbooks, etc; 20 VF drawers of pictures and photographs; complete sets of basketball rule books, NBA and ABA guides, Converse Basketball Yearbooks; minutes of NABC conventions; and complete basketball library of William G Mokray.

MA —SPRINGFIELD COLLEGE LIBRARY, Babson Library, Springfield, 01109. Henry Dutcher, Reference Librn
Holdings: Vols (130,000) Cat
Budget: ($65,000)

NY —COLUMBIA UNIVERSITY LIBRARIES, Rare Book & Manuscript Library, 801 Butler Library, 535 W 114 St, New York, 10027. Kenneth A Lohf, Librn
Notes: The L S Alexander Gumby Collection, which incl material on Blacks in sports. Restricted use.

NY —RACQUET & TENNIS CLUB, Library, 370 Park Ave, New York, 10022. Gerald Belliveau, Jr, Librn
Holdings: Vols (17,500) Cat
Budget: ($6000)
Notes: Specializes in court tennis, lawn tennis, early American sport. See *Dictionary Catalogue of the Library of Sports in the Racquet and Tennis Club* (Boston: G K Hall, 1971). Also, Robert W Henderson, *Early American Sport,* 3rd ed. (Cranbury, NJ: Fairleigh Dickinson University Press, 1977).

BASON, FRED

IN —INDIANA UNIVERSITY, Lilly Library, Seventh St, Bloomington, 47405. William R

BASON, FRED (cont.)

Cagle, Librn
Holdings: // Cat Mss
Notes: A collection of contracts and correspondence about those contracts for production or publication of sixty Maugham works, 1904-1973. 1696 items. A collection of correspondence and writings by and about Maugham collected by Grenville Cool of Watford, Herts, England. Incl are letters of Maugham to Fred Bason as well as articles, etc by Bason about WSM; also Robin Maugham's ms for *Somerset and All the Maughams*. Covers 1899-1970. 304 items. Incl first editions of Maugham's works. No photocopying.

BASQUE LANGUAGE AND LITERATURE

ID —UNIVERSITY OF IDAHO, Library, Dept of Special Collections & Archives, Moscow, 83843.
Holdings: Vols 2936 // Cat
Notes: Charles A Webbert, *The Basque Collection: A Preliminary Checklist* (University of Idaho Library Publication No 9, March 1971).

IL —NEWBERRY LIBRARY, 60 W Walton St, Chicago, 60610. Diana Haskell, Cur of Modern Mss
Holdings: Cat Maps
Notes: The bulk of the collection (about 15, 000 vols) is in the Prince Lucien Bonaparte group, which deals with western European linguistics. In this group the major rare categories are Etruscan and Basque linguistic studies, although the bulk of the group treats the major European languages and their dialects, ie French, German, English, Spanish, Italian and Russian. There is also strong representation in Gaelic linguistics, particularly Irish, Cornish, Welsh and Manx. In other collections of the library, there are major groups of books and mss dealing with American Indian languages and Philippine languages (about 4500 books and mss).

NV —UNIVERSITY OF NEVADA SYSTEM, Elko Community College, Learning Resources Center, Elko, 89801. Juanita R Karr, Dir
Holdings: Vols 400 Cat

NV —UNIVERSITY OF NEVADA, RENO, Noble H Getchell Library, Reno, 89557. William A Douglass, Coordinator
Holdings: Vols (15,000)
Notes: America's largest collection of Basque materials, both retrospective and current. Semi-annual *Newsletter*.

BASQUES

NV —UNIVERSITY OF NEVADA, RENO, Noble H Getchell Library, Reno, 89557. William A Douglass, Coordinator
Holdings: Vols (15,000)
Notes: America's largest collection of Basque materials, both retrospective and current. Semi-annual *Newsletter*.

BASS, PERKINS

NH —NEW HAMPSHIRE HISTORICAL SOCIETY, Library, 30 Park St, Concord, 03301. William Copeley, Assoc Librn
Holdings: Cat Mss Pix Audiotapes 16mm Films
Notes: Perkins Bass, lawyer, US Representative and Republican politician of NH. 60 linear feet of correspondence, speeches, press releases, scrapbooks, photos, memorabilia relating to public career 1935-62. Register available.

BASS, ROBERT P.

NH —DARTMOUTH COLLEGE, Baker Memorial Library, Hanover, 03755.
Holdings: Cat Mss
Notes: Personal papers.

BASSET, BRIAN

OH —OHIO STATE UNIVERSITY, Library for Communication and Graphic Arts, 242 W 18th St, Columbus, 43210. Lucy S Caswell, Curator
Notes: The original works of editorial cartoonists Art Poinier, Scott Willis, Brian Basset, Billy Ireland, Frank Williams, Charles Werner, Ned Beard, L D Warren, Edward D Kuekes, Ray Osrin, Mike Peters, Draper Hill, Eugene Craig and Bert Whitman.

BATAK LANGUAGE

NY —NEW YORK PUBLIC LIBRARY, Oriental Div, Fifth Ave & 42 St, New York, 10018. E Christian Filstrup, Chief
Holdings: // Cat Mss Microforms
Budget: ($56,455)
Notes: Published catalog of holdings.

BATCHELDER, JOHN DAVIS

DC —LIBRARY OF CONGRESS, Rare Book & Special Collections Div, Washington, 20540. William Matheson, Chief
Notes: Books, mss and other material assembled by John Davis Batchelder. The bulk of the collection is in the Rare Books Division. See description under Incunabula. Manuscript Division incl a few personal papers and his collection of 1500 autographs. The Music Division also has items from his collection.

BATEMAN, HARRY, 1882-1946

†CA —CALIFORNIA INSTITUTE OF TECHNOLOGY, Robert A Millikan Memorial Library, Archives, 1201 E California Blvd, Pasadena, 91125.
Notes: Papers.

BATES, FINIS L.

DC —GEORGETOWN UNIVERSITY, Library, Special Collections Div, 37 & O Sts NW, Washington, 20057. George M Barringer, Special Collections Librn; Nicholas B Sheetz, Mss Librn
Holdings: Mss Cat
Notes: The E H Swaim Collection. A collection of letters, affidavits, and photographs relating to the assassination of Abraham Lincoln and the subsequent career of John Wilkes Booth. Much of this material was gathered by Finis L Bates, Clarence True Wilson, and W P Campbell (whose research files were brought together by Swaim) and is for the most part by people who were involved in the events surrounding the assassination; members of the Booth family and their acquaintances; and individuals who claimed to have known Booth later in Texas and Oklahoma.

BATES, HERBERT E.

IL —ILLINOIS STATE UNIVERSITY, Milner Library, Dept of Special Collections, Normal, 61761. Robert Sokan, Librn
Notes: First editions, limited editions, ephemera, etc.

BATES, KATHARINE LEE

MA —FALMOUTH PUBLIC LIBRARY, 123 Katharine Lee Bates Rd, Falmouth, 02540. Ann M Haddad, Librn
Holdings: Vols 36 Cat
Notes: Incl books by the author.

BATES, SANFORD

TX —SAM HOUSTON STATE UNIVERSITY, Library, PO Box 2179, Huntsville, 77340. Chas Dwyer, Librn
Holdings: Vols 100
Notes: Incl the collection of Sanford Bates, head of the Federal Bureau of Prisons, 1930-1937. 1900 of the vols are now in circulation collection for Criminal Justice classes.

BATHE, GREVILLE

PA —SWARTHMORE COLLEGE, Library, Swarthmore, 19081. Michael J Durkan, Librn
Holdings: Vols 959 Cat Mss
Notes: This was the collection belonging to Greville Bathe. It is comprised of books on machines and steam engines published from the 16th-20th century. Also works on military engineering.

BATHS

†CT —YALE UNIVERSITY, Medical Library, 333 Cedar St, New Haven, 06520.
Notes: Incl large world-wide pamphlet collection, arranged geographically, of resorts, etc, favorable to good health.

†NY —MEDICAL RESEARCH LIBRARY OF BROOKLYN, Academy of Medicine of Brooklyn & The State University of New York Downstate Medical Center, 450 Clarkson St, Brooklyn, 11203. Kenneth E Moody, Dir
Notes: Extensive collection of 18th-19th century material.
See also entry under Medicine.

BATHYMETRY

CA —UNIVERSITY OF CALIFORNIA, SANTA BARBARA, Map and Imagery Laboratory, Santa Barbara, 93106. Larry Carver, Dept Head
Notes: Worldwide coverage of Landsat imagery donated by US Dept of Agriculture Aerial Photography Field Office. Consists of 153,000 scenes, covering most of the earth's surface between the years 1975 and 1980. Incl 300,000 maps, 1800 atlases, 9 globes, 300 relief models, 1,500,000 satellite imagery and aerial photographs, 700 reference books and gazetteers, 25 serials (titles received), and 21,000 microforms.

BATIK

NY —SOCIETY OF BATIK ARTISTS LIBRARY, 395 Riverside Dr, New York, 10025. Astrith Deyrup, Librn
Notes: Library dedicated to batik sources.

BATS

NY —AMERICAN MUSEUM OF NATURAL HISTORY, Library Services Dept, Central Park W & 79th St, New York, 10024. Nina J Root, Chairwoman; Mary Genett, Asst Librn for Reference Services
Holdings: Vols (385,000) Mss Maps Pix Slides

BATTA LANGUAGE (SUMATRA) see Batak Language

BATTERIES, DRY see Electric Batteries

BATTERIES, ELECTRIC see Electric Batteries

BATTERIES AND FUEL CELLS

IL —ARGONNE NATIONAL LABORATORY, Chemical Engineering Branch Library, 9700 S Cass Ave, Argonne, 60439. John P Frazier III, Librn
Notes: Incl 9000 vols monographs, 115 current journals, substantial collection of scientific and technical reports. Materials may be used by the public in the library by prior arrangement. Photocopies may be supplied for interlibrary loan, for which a processing and handling charge is made.

BATTLE, JOHN STEWART

VA —UNIVERSITY OF VIRGINIA, Alderman Library, Manuscripts Dept, Charlottesville, 22901. Edmund Berkeley Jr, Cur
Holdings: Cat Mss
See also entry under Virginia - History.

BATTLE OF GETTYSBURG, 1863 see Gettysburg, Battle of, 1863

BATTLE OF THE LITTLE BIG HORN, 1876 see Little Big Horn, Battle of the, 1876

BATTLE OF MONMOUTH see Monmouth, Battle of, 1778

BATTLE OF SHILOH, 1862 see Shiloh, Battle of, 1862

BATTLE OF THE BOXER AND THE ENTERPRISE see Boxer and the Enterprise (Battle)

BATTLE OF WATERLOO see Waterloo, Battle of, 1815

BATTLE SONGS see War Songs

BATTLES—PICTURES, ILLUSTRATIONS, ETC.

DC —LIBRARY OF CONGRESS, Prints & Photographs Div, Washington, 20540.
Holdings: Cat Pix
Notes: Civil War Photograph Collection incl

BATTLES—PICTURES, ILLUSTRATIONS, ETC. (cont.)

photographs commissioned by Mathew Brady and others. Brady employed 20 photographers at the height of his operations. His staff incl Alexander and James Gardner, James F Gibson, and Thomas C Roche.

BAUDELAIRE, CHARLES, 1821-1867

†TN —VANDERBILT UNIVERSITY, Library, Special Collections Dept, 419 21st Ave S, Nashville, 37203.
Notes: The Baudelaire Collection contains extensive materials by and about Charles Baudelaire.

BAUER, HAROLD, 1873-1951

DC —LIBRARY OF CONGRESS, Music Division, Washington, 20540.
Notes: Papers, music mss, and photographs.

BAUM, LYMAN FRANK

CA —UNIVERSITY OF SAN FRANCISCO, Richard A Gleeson Library, The Countess Bernardine Murphy Donohue Rare Book Room, San Francisco, 94117. D Steven Corey, Special Collections Librn
Holdings: Vols 725
Notes: Comprehensive collection icnl Oziana and multiple variant copies of all of the first editions, unique items, ephemera.

KY —UNIVERSITY OF LOUISVILLE, Ekstrom Library, Rare Books & Special Collections, 2301 S Third St, Louisville, 40208. George T McWhorter, Cur; Delinda Stephens Buie, Asst Cur
Holdings: Vols 150 Cat
Budget: ($1500)
Notes: The collection incl editions of the Oz books (incl those not written by Baum), Baum's pseudonymous works, the periodical *Baum Bugle,* and works about Baum and Oz. Incl clippings, dolls, posters.

NY —SYRACUSE UNIVERSITY LIBRARIES, Ernest S Bird Library, George Arents Research Library for Special Collections, Syracuse, 13210. Carolyn A Davis, Manuscripts Librn; Amy S Doherty, University Archivist; Mark F Weimer, Rare Book Librn
Holdings: Vols 250 Cat
Notes: The Russell McFall Collection.

BAUM, VICKI, 1888-1960

NY —STATE UNIVERSITY OF NEW YORK AT ALBANY, Library, Special Collections Dept, 1400 Washington Ave, Albany, 12222. Marion P Munzer, Coordr
Notes: Correspondence (0.3 linear feet) with Doubleday, Doran and Company regarding publishing of her writings. Part of the Library's German Exile Collection.

BAUMBACH, JONATHAN

MA —BOSTON UNIVERSITY, Mugar Memorial Library, Special Collections Dept, 771 Commonwealth Ave, Boston, 02215. Howard B Gotlieb, Dir
Holdings: Cat Mss

BAUMGARTNER, HOPE LEROY

CT —YALE UNIVERSITY, Music Library, 98 Wall St, New Haven, 06520. Harold E Samuel, Librn
Notes: Personal papers and musical mss. *See also* entry under Music, America.

BAVARIA—HISTORY

CA —CALIFORNIA STATE UNIVERSITY, FRESNO, Henry Madden Library, Dept of Special Collections, Fresno, 93740. Ronald J Mahoney, Head
Holdings: Vols 6 Uncat
Notes: The Joseph A Lowande Collection of Worldwide Rationing contains 20th century ration material from Germany and the United States. Especially strong on local rationing from Stadtamhof, Bavaria, 1915-1923.

MA —HARVARD UNIVERSITY LIBRARY, Widener Library, Cambridge, 02138. David E Silas, Specialist in Book Selection
Holdings: Cat

BAXT, GEORGE

MA —BOSTON UNIVERSITY, Mugar Memorial Library, Special Collections Dept, 771 Commonwealth Ave, Boston, 02215. Howard B Gotlieb, Dir
Holdings: Cat Mss
Notes: Mss, correspondence, etc collected in depth; incl publications by or about.

BAXTER, GEORGE, 1804-1867

CA —UNIVERSITY OF CALIFORNIA, LOS ANGELES, Research Library, Dept of Special Collections, 405 Hilgard Ave, Los Angeles, 90024. Edward Shreeves, Chairman, Bibliographers Group; David S Zeidberg, Head
Holdings: Vols 100 Pix
Notes: 100 books with color illustrations, and 100 color prints, printed by George Baxter.

ON —VICTORIA UNIVERSITY, Library, 71 Queen's Park Crescent, Toronto, M5S 1K7, Can. Robert C Brandeis, Chief Librn
Holdings: Vols (400) // Cat
Notes: A major collection of George Baxter's woodblock and metal plate prints and book illustration in watercolor and oil color. Listed in *Starr Collection of Baxter* Prints (Toronto: Ryerson Press, 1946).

BAXTER, PERCIVAL PROCTOR, 1876-1969

ME —MAINE STATE LIBRARY, Special Collections Dept, Cultural Bldg, Station 64, Augusta, 04333. Shirley Thayer, Librn
Holdings: // Mss Maps Pix
Budget: ($2,500,000)
Notes: Personal papers of Gov Percival Baxter, incl letters, scrapbooks, memorabilia. Subjects emphasized are state government, conservation, and Baxter State Park.

BAY, HOWARD

NY —NEW YORK PUBLIC LIBRARY, Performing Arts Research Center, Billy Rose Theatre Collection, 111 Amsterdam Ave, New York, 10023. Dorothy L Swerdlove, Cur
Holdings: Cat
Notes: In addition to the usual memorabilia and illustrative material, there is a large collection of original designs.

BAY, J. CHRISTIAN

CT —LEE ASH, (personal collection), 66 Humiston Dr, Bethany, 06525.
Holdings: Cat Mss Pix
Notes: Incl books, letters, ephemera, etc.

BAYH, BIRCH

IN —INDIANA UNIVERSITY, Lilly Library, Seventh St, Bloomington, 47405. William R Cagle, Librn
Notes: The papers of former US Senator Birch Evans Bayh (D-Ind), 1962-1980. Closed until 1990.

BAYLEY, C. I.

BC —UNIVERSITY OF VICTORIA, McPherson Library, Victoria, V8W 3H5, Can.
Notes: Bahamas Governor.

BAYLEY, EDWIN

†MA —JOHN F KENNEDY LIBRARY, Columbia Point, Boston, 02125. Dan H Fenn Jr, Dir
Holdings: // Cat Mss Microforms
Notes: Papers of JFK; microfilm copies (20 rolls) of papers of Public Information Director Edwin Bayley, General Counsel William Josephson; and records of the Peace Corps, 1961-1966. 2 linear ft of mss. Holdings are described in Historical Materials in the John F Kennedy Library. Copies may be obtained by writing the Research Archivist.

BAYLY, ADA ELLEN ('EDNA LYALL'), 1857-1902

CA —UNIVERSITY OF CALIFORNIA, LOS ANGELES, Research Library, Dept of Special Collections, 405 Hilgard Ave, Los Angeles, 90024. Edward Shreeves, Chairman, Bibliographers Group; David S Zeidberg, Head
Holdings: Vols 25 Cat Mss
Notes: 25 first and other editions of her books; 44 letters.

BAYLY, THOMAS

†CA —UNIVERSITY OF SAN FRANCISCO, Richard A Gleeson Library, The Countess Bernardine Murphy Donohue Rare Book Room, San Francisco, 94117. D Steven Corey, Special Collections Librn
Holdings: Vols (300) Cat
Notes: Largely from the Virtue-Cahill library in England, and the collection of Charles A Fracchia. Incl important works of Bayly, Cressy, Sergeant, and Worsley. Incl a contemporary manuscript of the trial of Father Garnet, accused of complicity in the Gunpowder Plot.

BAYNE, RT. REV. STEPHEN F.

†NY —GENERAL THEOLOGICAL SEMINARY, Saint Mark's Library, 175 Ninth Ave, New York, 10011.
Notes: The Bayne Collection of pamphllets, articles, correspondence, sermons and personal memorabilia of Episcopal Bishop Stephen F Bayne, eighth Dean of the General Theological Seminary in New York.

BAYNTON, WHARTON AND MORGAN

IL —UNIVERSITY OF ILLINOIS, URBANA/CHAMPAIGN, Library, Illinois Historical Survey Library, 1408 W Gregory Dr, 1A Library, Urbana, 61801.
Holdings: Vols 500 Cat Mss Maps Microforms
Notes: Colonial and Revolutionary Period--Medwest, particularly Illinois. Important ms collections (75 cubic feet) under this subject incl Baynton, Wharton and Morgan, papers, 1757-1799, 6 reels of microfilm. Guide to the collections published: Maynard J Brichford, Robert M Sutton, Dennis F Walle, *Manuscripts Guide to Collection at the University of Illinois at* Urbana-Champaign (Urbana, Chicago, London: University of Illinois Press, 1976).

BAYS

CA —CALIFORNIA STATE UNIVERSITY, FULLERTON, Library, Box 4150, Fullerton, 92634. Linda Herman, Special Collections Librn
Holdings: Cat
Notes: Dr Leonard B Schultz Ichthyology Collection of 13,000 pieces incl books, pamphlets, articles and ephemera. It is supplemented by the Ecology of Bay and Estuarine Fishes Collections.

BEACH, ALVAH AND ENOS

NY —SAINT LAWRENCE UNIVERSITY, Owen D Young Library, Canton, 13617. Mahlon Peterson, Librn
Holdings: Mss Pix
Notes: This collection consists of letters written home by two soldiers in the Union Army between 1861 and 1864. Approx 100 items.

BEACH, MRS. H. H. A.

DC —LIBRARY OF CONGRESS, Music Division, Washington, 20540.
Notes: The business papers and music mss of

BEACH, MRS. H. H. A. (cont.)

the Arthur P Schmidt Company. Numerous works by important composers.

BEACH, SYLVIA, 1887-1962

NJ —PRINCETON UNIVERSITY, Library, Manuscript Collection, Nassau St, Princeton, 08540. Jean F Preston, Cur
Holdings: Vols 1615 Cat Mss Pix
Notes: The book collection incl items from the Shakespeare and Company lending library. The mss are housed in about 300 ms boxes. See *Princeton University Library* Chronicle, v 26, p 7-12. An unpublished guide (55p) is available for consultation. Also incl 11 quartos from the David and Donald Maggin gift.

BEACH-DE-LA-MAR JARGON

MA —HARVARD UNIVERSITY LIBRARY, Cambridge, 02138.
Holdings: Cat

BEACH EROSION see Coasts

BEACH PROTECTION see Shore Protection

BEACHES—EROSION see Coasts

BEACHEY, LINCOLN

CA —SAN DIEGO AERO-SPACE MUSEUM, N Paul Whittier Historical Aviation Library, 2001 Pan American Plaza, Balboa Park, San Diego, 92101. B C Reynolds, Archivist
Holdings: // Uncat Microforms
Notes: 98 percent of this aeronautics and aerospace collection was destroyed by fire in early 1978. The only item saved was a large scrapbook of newspaper clippings (1913-14) compiled by Hillery Beachey.

BEADLE PUBLICATIONS

CT —YALE UNIVERSITY, Box 1603A, Yale Station, New Haven, 06520.
Holdings: Vols 3000 Cat
Notes: The Edward G Levy collection.

BEALS, CARLETON

MA —BOSTON UNIVERSITY, Mugar Memorial Library, Special Collections Dept, 771 Commonwealth Ave, Boston, 02215. Howard B Gotlieb, Dir
Holdings: Mss Pix Correspondence

BEALS, JESSIE TARBOX, 1870-1942

†MA —RADCLIFFE COLLEGE, Arthur & Elizabeth Schlesinger Library on History of Women in America, 3 James St, Cambridge, 02138.
Notes: Papers, etc.

NY —COLUMBIA UNIVERSITY LIBRARIES, Rare Book & Manuscript Library, 801 Butler Library, 535 W 114 St, New York, 10027. Kenneth A Lohf, Librn
Holdings: Mss
Notes: Papers of the Community Service Society of New York. Incl files, books, photographs (1000) and bound volumes of periodicals and conference proceedings. Among the papers are central and district administrative records, committee correspondence and minutes, and files of programs sponsored by the organization. Also more than 1000 photographs by Jessie Tarbox Beals and Lewis W Hine depicting conditions of the poor. 276,000 items. Restricted use.

BEAMISH, ROBERT E., M.D.

MB —UNIVERSITY OF MANITOBA, Elizabeth Dafoe Library, Archives and Special Collections Dept, Winnipeg, R3T 2N2, Can. Richard E Bennett, Dept Head; Corrado A Santoro, Reference Archivist
Notes: A collection of fifty-five reprints and copies of Dr Beamish's writings and speeches primarily in the areas of cardiology and heart disease. A list of titles is found with the collection.

BEAR, U.S. COAST GUARD CUTTER

CA —OAKLAND PUBLIC LIBRARY, Oakland History Room, 125 14th St, Oakland, 94612. William W Sturm, Librn
Holdings: Cat Mss Pix
Notes: Logbooks of the US Coast Guard Cutter *Bear*, from 1889 to 1932.

BEARD, CHARLES A. AND MARY

IL —SOUTHERN ILLINOIS UNIVERSITY, CARBONDALE, Delyte W Morris Library, Carbondale, 62901.
Holdings: Cat Mss Pix
Notes: The library and papers of John Dewey's colleague, George S Counts, authority on education in Russia; incl much correspondence with Charles and Mary Beard.

BEARD, DANIEL CARTER (UNCLE DAN)

TX —BOY SCOUTS OF AMERICA, Library, 1325 Walnut Hill Lane, Irving, 75062. Ann Lamont McVicar, Librn
Holdings: Vols (3000) Cat Pix Slides
Notes: Early and current books on the Boy Scouts of America, and on the subjects of scouts and scouting. Books by and about founders Baden-Powell, Seton, Beard.

BEARD, GEORGE MILLER

CT —YALE UNIVERSITY, Box 1603A, Yale Station, New Haven, 06520.
Holdings: Cat Mss

BEARD, MARY, 1876-1946

MA —SIMMONS COLLEGE ARCHIVES, 300 The Fenway, Boston, 02115. Megan Sniffin-Marinoff, College Archivist
Notes: Archives of the Simmons College School of Public Health Nursing (later reorganized into the School of Nursing) cover the years 1902-1970. Important correspondents in the collection incl M Adelaide Nutting, Mary Beard, Isabel Stewart, and Anne Hervey Strong, etc. Incl Strong's records of activity with regard to nursing education in the National Organization for Public Health Nursing, 1918-22. 1000 linear feet in institution, incl special collections nursing and photographs, nursing.

NY —CORNELL UNIVERSITY LIBRARIES, Collection of Regional History, Dept of Manuscripts and Univ Archives, Ithaca, 14853.
Notes: Nurse. Papers, ca 1926-40; 16 in.

BEARD, NED

OH —OHIO STATE UNIVERSITY, Library for Communication and Graphic Arts, 242 W 18th St, Columbus, 43210. Lucy S Caswell, Curator
Notes: The original works of editorial cartoonists Art Poinier, Scott Willis, Brian Basset, Billy Ireland, Frank Williams, Charles Werner, Ned Beard, L D Warren, Edward D Kuekes, Ray Osrin, Mike Peters, Draper Hill, Eugene Craig and Bert Whitman.

BEARDSLEY, AUBREY VINCENT, 1872-1898

NJ —PRINCETON UNIVERSITY, Library, Rare Books Dept, Princeton, 08544. Stephen Ferguson, Cur
Holdings: Vols 425 Cat Mss Pix
Notes: Incl in the collection are 6 boxes of mss and over 100 drawings. Described in *The Gallatin Beardsley Collection in the Princeton University Library: A Catalogue*, comp by A E Gallatin and Alexander D Wainwright, (Princeton, NJ: Princeton University Library, 1952). 43p.

NS —DALHOUSIE UNIVERSITY LIBRARY, Halifax, B3H 4H8, Can.
Notes: The collection of numerous editions from Dr Henry Hicks, past president of Dalhousie.

BEASTS see Domestic Animals; Zoology

BEAT MOVEMENT

CA —CALIFORNIA STATE UNIVERSITY, HAYWARD, Library, Hayward, 94542. Melissa Rose, Dir
Holdings: Vols (8000) Cat Phonorecords
Budget: $2469
Notes: Cover San Francisco Bay Area poetry publishing from early 1960s to date, incl key writers and works of the era of the Beat Generation. Incl books, periodicals, broadsides, records, with extensive collection of titles from Black Sparrow, Oyez, and Unicorn presses. Noncirculating.

CT —UNIVERSITY OF CONNECTICUT, Library, Storrs, 06268. R H Schimmelpfeng, Dir of Special Collections
Holdings: Cat Mss Pix Audiotapes
Notes: Focuses on poets brought to attention by Donald Allen's *New American Poetry* anthology: the Black Mountain, New York, San Francisco, Beat poets and their successors; the Postmodern American poets, such as Charles Olson, Robert Creeley, Robert Duncan, Allen Ginsberg, Edward Dorn, Frank O'Hara, Gary Snyder, LeRoi Jones/Imamu Baraka, and Denise Levertov.

IL —NORTHWESTERN UNIVERSITY, Library, Special Collections Dept, 1937 Sheridan Rd, Evanston, 60201. R Russell Maylone, Cur
Holdings: Vols 3000 Cat Mss
Notes: American Mid-Century Collection comprised of works by Beat movement and avant-garde writers publishing since the late 1940s. Incl the D R Wagner archive and such authors as Larry Eigner, D A Levy, Charles Bukowski, Ed Dorn, Robert Kelly, Jack Kerovac. Large collection of "little magazines", incl correspondence and production files of San Francisco Earthquake and Nova Broadcast, and all mss, correspondence, and production files for The Outsider.

RI —BROWN UNIVERSITY, John Hay Library, Harris Collection, Prospect St, Providence, 02912. Rosemary L Cullen, Cur
Holdings: Vols (200,000) Cat Mss Pix Phonorecords Microforms
Budget: ($15,000)
Notes: The Harris Collection of American Poetry and Plays is principally composed of American and Canadian poetry and plays, 17th century-date. Extensive holdings in songsters, gift books and annuals, hymnals, pageants, broadside verse, carriers' addresses, women poets, juvenile poetry, (incl Mother Goose and *The Night Before* Christmas), sheet music with lyrics, small press publications, fine printing, black poets, "little magazines," Yiddish-American literature. All movements or schools of American poetry are represented. Incl first editions of most American poets and playwrights, notably Whitman, Poe, Wallace Stevens, Eugene O'Neill, Edward Albee, Ezra Pound, T S Eliot, William Carlos Williams, Amy Lowell, Phyllis Wheatley, Robert Frost, Allen Ginsberg, Bliss Carman, and Stephen Foster sheet music. Also incl the Saunders Walt Whitman Collection (1300 vols); the LangdonCollection of Pageants (250 vols); the Asa Cushman Collection of plays in ms and prompt copies; the MacDougall Collection of Psalters and Hymnals; 4000 plays issued by Walter H Baker Co, Boston (1890-1957); the Vaxer Collection of Yiddish Poetry, Plays and Music (1700 vols). Collections incl 200,000 vols, 30,000 broadsides, 55,000 mss, 170,000 pieces of sheet music, 450 phonorecords, and 375 microfilm reels. See *Dictionary Catalog of the Harris Collection of American Poetry and Plays* (Boston: G K Hall, 1972), 13 vols; *Supplement* (1977), 3 vols. See also, *American Poetry, 1609-1900, A Collection on Microfilm, Segment I* (1609-1820); *Segment II* (1821-1850); *Segment III* (1851-

BEAT MOVEMENT (cont.)

1870) (Woodbridge, Conn: Research Publications). Separate catalog.
VA —UNIVERSITY OF VIRGINIA, Alderman Library, Rare Book Dept, Charlottesville, 22901. Julius P Barclay, Cur
Holdings: Vols (6500) Cat
Notes: The Marvin Tatum Collection of Contemporary Prose and Poetry contains some extremely rare items (mostly paperback). Some of Lawrence Ferlinghetti's earliest publications in mimeograph form are here. Posters, portfolios.

BEATSON, FINLAYSON, HOWATT AND PARTNERS

AB —UNIVERSITY OF CALGARY, Libraries, Special Collections Div, 2500 University Dr, Calgary, T2N 1N4, Can.
Holdings: Cat Mss Pix
Notes: 11,355 pictures; 45.5 mss. Collection consists of original working drawings and supporting project files representing every building type in the Southern Alberta region, particularly community projects, from 1957-82. Major projects are the Carseland Weir development, the University of Calgary Chemical Engineering Building, the Western Canada Pavilion at Expo '67, and the Selkirk, Manitoba, Civic Centre. In April 1982, the firm merged with that of Stevenson Raines Barrett Christie Hutton Seton & Partners. Inventories will be available shortly.
See also entry under Stevenson Raines (et al.) Architects.

BEATTY, MORGAN, 1902-1975

WY —UNIVERSITY OF WYOMING, William Robertson Coe Library, 13 & Ivinson, Laramie, 82071.
Notes: The papers of Morgan Beatty (1902-1975), an eminent newsman in print and broadcast journalism. Contains several thousand letters, many from prominent personalities, extensive background files of his "News of the World" and other broadcasts, and several thousand radio scripts and feature news stories.

BEAUCHAMP, WILLIAM

NY —NEW YORK STATE LIBRARY, State Education Bldg Annex, Washington Ave, Albany, 12224.
Notes: The papers of William Beauchamp (ca 1860-1930), consisting mainly of his notebooks and scrapbooks concerning the history of the Iroquois Indians. Incl 13 boxes material on Indian language, folklore, and place names, the Moravians, and New York State archeology.

BEAUHARNAIS, EUGENE DE, PRINCE D'EICHSTATT, 1781-1824

NJ —PRINCETON UNIVERSITY, Library, Manuscript Collection, Nassau St, Princeton, 08540. Jean F Preston, Cur
Holdings: Mss
Notes: The archive totals over 30,000 pieces. See *Princeton University Library Chronicle,* v 3, p 45-51. An unpublished typescript guide (9p) is available in the Library.

BEAULIEU, WILFRED

†MA —BOSTON PUBLIC LIBRARY, Copley Sq, Boston, 02117.
Notes: Archives of Wilfred Beaulieu, founder and editor of the Franco-American newspaper *Le Travailleur.*

BEAUMONT, WILLIAM

IL —UNIVERSITY OF CHICAGO LIBRARY, Dept of Special Collections, 1100 E 57 St, Chicago, 60637.
Notes: Personal papers.
MO —WASHINGTON UNIVERSITY, School of Medicine, Archives, 660 S Euclid Ave, Saint Louis, 63110. Paul G Anderson, Archivist
Holdings: Mss Pix Audiotapes
Budget: ($38,000)
Notes: Institutional records and papers of faculty of Washington University School of Medicine and its predecessors and associated hospitals. Contains records of St Louis Medical College, Missouri Medical Barnard Free Skin and Cancer Hospital, Barnes Hospital, St Louis Children's Hospital and Jewish Hospital of St Louis. Incl papers of William Beaumont, Joseph Erlanger, Leo Loeb, Evarts Graham, Edmund V Cowdry, Helen Graham, Carl V Moore, Margaret Smith and others. Oral history program. See also: Anderson, Paul G and Hoolihan, Christopher, eds. *Special Collections* (St Louis: Washington University School of Medicine, 1981). 960 linear feet.

BEAUREGARD, PIERRE GUSTAVE TOUTANT

NC —DUKE UNIVERSITY, William R Perkins Library, Manuscript Dept, Durham, 27706. Ellen Gartrell, Cur of Mss
Holdings: Cat Mss
Notes: Strong collection incl papers of many officers (eg Robert E Lee, P G T Beauregard), Confederate governments, and leaders (eg Jefferson Davis), thousands of letters and diaries from Union and Confederate soldiers and homefront.

THE BEAUTIFUL see Aesthetics

BEAUTY see Aesthetics

BEAUTY AIDS see Health and Beauty Aids

BEAUTY CULTURE

FL —BREVARD COMMUNITY COLLEGE, Learning Resources Center, Cocoa Campus, Clearlake Rd, Cocoa, 32922. John S French, Ref Librn
Holdings: Vols 82 Cat
Notes: All materials both print and nonprint supportive of instruction in cosmetology.
IN —INDIANA HISTORICAL SOCIETY, Library, 315 W Ohio St, Indianapolis, 46202. Robert K O'Neill, Dir
Holdings: Vols Cat Mss Pix
Notes: Materials on blacks in Indiana, from statehood to the present day. Incl books; letters; church and organization records; photographs. Incl records of the Madam C J Walker Company, a black cosmetics firm in Indianapolis.
PA —FRANKLIN INSTITUTE LIBRARY, 20 & The Parkway, Philadelphia, 19103. Miriam Padusis, Dir; Charles Wilt, Readers Servs Librn
Holdings: Vols (300,000) Cat Maps Pix Microforms

BEAVERS

AZ —ARIZONA-SONORA DESERT MUSEUM, Library, Rte 9, Box 900, Tucson, 85743. Janice Hunter, Librn
Holdings: Vols (3000) Cat Pix Slides Videotapes 16mm Films
Notes: Ecology and natural history of the Southwest. Carr Collection on beavers. Incl 200 pictures, 5000 slides, 40 videotapes, and 6 films. Separate index of slides.
†WA —WASHINGTON STATE UNIVERSITY, Library, Manuscripts, Archives & Special Collections, Pullman, 99164. John F Guido, Head
Holdings: Cat Mss Maps Pix
Notes: The Carl Parcher Russell papers, a vast resource (24,916 items; 45 linear feet) on American Indian and Western pioneer activities and artifacts. Much on the fur trade; pioneer life; mountain men and trapping; wildlife; primitive life in detail. Also the National Park Service, parks, monuments, etc. Described in *Carl Parcher Russell: An Indexed Register of His Scholarly and Professionsl Papers, 1920-1967, in the Washington State Unviversity* Library (Pullman, 1970), 149 pp.

BEAUVOIR, SIMONE DE

OH —OHIO STATE UNIVERSITY, William Oxley Thompson Memorial Library, 1858 Neil Ave Mall, Columbus, 43210. Robert A Tibbetts, Cur of Special Collections
Notes: Incl in the papers of Nelson Algren are 340 letters from Simone de Beauvoir written between the late 1940s and mid 1950s, and their joint Mexican trip diary of 1948.

BEBOP MUSIC see Jazz

BECHE-DE-MER JARGON see Beach-De-La-Mar Jargon

BECK, JAMES MONTGOMERY, 1861-1936

NJ —PRINCETON UNIVERSITY, Library, Manuscript Collection, Nassau St, Princeton, 08540. Jean F Preston, Cur
Holdings: // Cat Mss
Notes: Incl 46 volumes; 4 boxes; 3 cartons of papers.

BECK, JULIAN

CA —UNIVERSITY OF CALIFORNIA, DAVIS, Shields Library, Dept of Special Collections, Davis, 95616. Donald Kunitz, Head; C Danial Elliott, Asst Head
Holdings: Vols 2700 Cat Mss Pix Phonorecords Audiotapes Videotapes
Notes: Archives of the Living Theatre founded by Julian Beck and Judith Malina incl directing, lighting, and master scripts; correspondence; contracts; original art; programs; posters; reviews; photographs by Mantegna and Bissinger; performance notes and diagrams; music; Malina's diaries; published texts; financial records.

BECK, ROBERT K.

†IA —UNIVERSITY OF IOWA, Libraries, Iowa City, 52242.
Notes: Papers, etc.

BECK, WARREN

MA —BOSTON UNIVERSITY, Mugar Memorial Library, Special Collections Dept, 771 Commonwealth Ave, Boston, 02215. Howard B Gotlieb, Dir
Holdings: Cat Mss Pix
Notes: Mss, correspondence, etc collected in depth; incl publications by or about.

BECKER, HARRY J., 1909-1975

NY —CORNELL UNIVERSITY LIBRARIES, Collection of Regional History, Dept of Manuscripts and Univ Archives, Ithaca, 14853.
Notes: Hospital insurance consultant, educator. Papers, ca 1935-74; 175 ft.

BECKER, HOWARD I.

NY —UNION COLLEGE, Schaffer Library, Archives of Science and Technology, Schenectady, 12308. Ellen Fladger, Archivist
Notes: Papers etc.

BECKET, WELTON

CA —UNIVERSITY OF CALIFORNIA, LOS ANGELES, Research Library, Dept of Special Collections, 405 Hilgard Ave, Los Angeles, 90024. Edward Shreeves, Chairman, Bibliographers Group; David S Zeidberg, Head
Notes: 6000 photographs recording the work of Welton Becket; 600 photographs recording the work of Mark Daniels; the Richard J Neutra archive.

BECKETT, SAMUEL

CT —YALE UNIVERSITY, Box 1603A, Yale Station, New Haven, 06520.
MO —WASHINGTON UNIVERSITY, John M Olin Library, Campus Box 1061, St Louis,

BECKETT, SAMUEL (cont.)

63130.
Holdings: Vols 550
Notes: Extensive ms collection. First, later and special editions; copies corrected or inscribed by the author; books containing contributions; translations, biographies, critical studies and other printed materials; mss; proof material; ephemera; worksheets; typescripts; notebooks of titles written by Beckett. Described in *Special Collections: an Annotated Guide to the Holdings of the Manuscript Division and the University Archives and Research Collection.*

NY —NEW YORK PUBLIC LIBRARY, Performing Arts Research Center, Billy Rose Theatre Collection, 111 Amsterdam Ave, New York, 10023. Dorothy L Swerdlove, Cur
Holdings: Cat Mss Pix
Notes: Papers, scrapbooks, mss, photographs, memorabilia, etc.

OH —OHIO STATE UNIVERSITY, William Oxley Thompson Memorial Library, 1858 Neil Ave Mall, Columbus, 43210. Robert A Tibbetts, Cur of Special Collections
Holdings: Vols 160 Cat Mss

ON —MCMASTER UNIVERSITY, Mills Memorial Library, Div of Archives & Research Collections, Hamilton, L8S 4L6, Can. G R Hill, Univ Librn
Holdings: Vols 900 Cat Mss
Notes: The Theodore Besterman Collection. Collection described in *Library Research* News, vol 2, no 4, Oct 1973.

BECKFORD, WILLIAM, 1760-1844

CA —UNIVERSITY OF CALIFORNIA, LOS ANGELES, Research Library, Dept of Special Collections, 405 Hilgard Ave, Los Angeles, 90024. Edward Shreeves, Chairman, Bibliographers Group; David S Zeidberg, Head
Holdings: Vols 100
Notes: 100 first and other editions of his books.

CT —YALE UNIVERSITY, Box 1603A, Yale Station, New Haven, 06520.
Holdings: Cat Mss Pix
Notes: His writings, incl some mss, correspondence, etc, and numerous books from his library and with his annotations.

BECKHAM, BARRY

MA —BOSTON UNIVERSITY, Mugar Memorial Library, Special Collections Dept, 771 Commonwealth Ave, Boston, 02215. Howard B Gotlieb, Dir
Holdings: Cat Mss Pix
Notes: Mss, correspondence, etc collected in depth; incl publications by or about.

BEDBUGS

NY —AMERICAN MUSEUM OF NATURAL HISTORY, Library Services Dept, Central Park W & 79th St, New York, 10024. Nina J Root, Chairwoman; Mary Genett, Asst Librn for Reference Services
Notes: A major literature collection supplements the museum's entomology collections; perhaps the largest in the world.

BEDDING (HORTICULTURE) see Gardens and Gardening

BEDE, JEAN-ALBERT

†NY —COLUMBIA UNIVERSITY LIBRARIES, Butler Library, Rare Book and Manuscript Library, 535 W 114 St, New York, 10027.
Notes: Papers of Prof Jean-Albert Bede, with much emphasis on Francois Chateaubriand and Anatolo France.

BEDFORD, AGNES

IN —INDIANA UNIVERSITY, Lilly Library, Seventh St, Bloomington, 47405. William R Cagle, Librn
Notes: Incl more than 12,000 letters from the estate of Dorothy Shakespeare Pound, widow of Ezra Pound, ranging from 1900 to 1973, but concentrated between 1946 and 1953, the years of his confinement at St Elizabeth's Hospital. Large correspondence with his friend and mentor, Agnes Bedford, 1919-1968.

BC —SIMON FRASER UNIVERSITY, Library, Burnaby, V5A 1S6, Can. Percilla Groves, Special Collections Librn
Holdings: Cat Mss
Notes: Incl a collection of 75 letters from Ezra Pound to Agnes Bedford and five letters to Wyndham Lewis, 1950-1959, plus 46 letters to Denis Goacher, his literary agent, and 140 pages to Sinologist Willis Hawley with carbons of Hawley's letters to Pound, also graphics for *Confucius: The Great Digest and Unwobbling Pivet,* and for *The Cantos.*

BEDFORD-STUYVESANT DEVELOPMENT AND RESTORATION CORPORATIONS

MA —JOHN F KENNEDY LIBRARY, Columbia Point, Boston, 02125. Henry J Gwiazda II, Cur
Notes: The Burke Marshall papers, 50 archives boxes re civil rights, 1961-1964 and the Bedford-Stuyvesant Development and Restoration Corporations; the Joseph Dolan papers, 1 box; the Thomas Johnston papers, 3 boxes; the James Mc Shane papers, 2 boxes; the Frank Mankiewicz papers, 15 boxes; and the Scott Rafferty papers, 4 boxes.

BEDSPREADS see Coverlets

BEEBE, LUCIUS

NV —UNIVERSITY OF NEVADA, RENO, University Library, Special Collections Dept, Reno, 89557. Robert E Blesse, Head
Holdings: Vols (70) Cat Pix Mss
Notes: Works by author-historian Beebe. Includes a manuscript collection (1 cu ft) containing correspondence and clippings relating to his work.

BEEBE, WILLIAM

HI —UNIVERSITY OF HAWAII, Library, 2550 The Mall, Honolulu, 96822. David Kittelson, Hawaiian Cur
Holdings: Vols (65,000) Cat Microforms
Budget: ($2000)
Notes: This is a comprehensive collection of material published in and about Hawaii, including especially 20th century publications, and University of Hawaii publications and theses. The Collection publishes *Current Hawaiiana,* a quarterly bibliography of recently available publications. There is a separate Hawaiian Collection card catalog; it was published in 1963 by G K Hall as a 4-volume set.

BEECHER, HENRY WARD

CT —YALE UNIVERSITY, Box 1603A, Yale Station, New Haven, 06520.

BEECHER-STOWE FAMILY

MA —RADCLIFFE COLLEGE, Arthur & Elizabeth Schlesinger Library on the History of Women in America, 3 James St, Cambridge, 02138. Patricia Miller King, Dir; Eva Moseley, Cur of Mss
Holdings: Vols (23,000) Cat Mss Pix Microforms
Budget: ($300,000)
Notes: Ms collection incl Blackwell family, Beecher-Stowe family, Betty Friedan, Charlotte Perkins Gilman, Emma Goldman, Dr Alice Hamilton and the Hamilton family, the National Abortion Rights Action League, the National Organization for Women, Leonora O'Reilly, and the Women's Equity Action League.

BEEKEEPING see Bees and Beekeeping

BEEKMAN, E. M.

MA —BOSTON UNIVERSITY, Mugar Memorial Library, Special Collections Dept, 771 Commonwealth Ave, Boston, 02215. Howard B Gotlieb, Dir
Holdings: Cat Mss

BEER, THOMAS

CT —YALE UNIVERSITY, Box 1603A, Yale Station, New Haven, 06520.
Holdings: Cat Mss

BEER, WILLIAM

LA —TULANE UNIVERSITY, Howard-Tilton Memorial Library, Special Collections Div, 7001 Freret St, New Orleans, 70118. Wilbur E Meneray, Librn
Holdings: Cat Mss
Notes: Correspondence to and from Beer as librarian of the Howard Library, New Orleans.

BEER AND BREWING see Brewing

BEERBOHM, SIR MAX, 1872-1956

CA —UNIVERSITY OF CALIFORNIA, LOS ANGELES, William Andrews Clark Memorial Library, 2520 Cimarron St, Los Angeles, 90018.
Holdings: / / Cat Mss Pix
Notes: The Maj Ewing Collection of first editions, mss, association copies, and original drawings. See Book Club of California, *Quarterly News Letter,* Summer 1963.

CA —UNIVERSITY OF SAN FRANCISCO, Richard A Gleeson Library, The Countess Bernardine Murphy Donohue Rare Book Room, San Francisco, 94117. D Steven Corey, Special Collections Librn
Holdings: Vols 125 Cat Mss
Notes: Part of a larger collection of the 1890s. Incl 4 original caricatures and three mss.

CT —YALE UNIVERSITY, Box 1603A, Yale Station, New Haven, 06520.
Holdings: Cat Mss

DC —GEORGETOWN UNIVERSITY, Library, Special Collections Div, 37 & O Sts NW, Washington, 20057. George M Barringer, Special Collections Librn; Nicholas B Sheetz, Mss Librn
Holdings: Mss Pix
Notes: The papers of Christopher Sykes, biographer, journalist, and novelist; containing mss, letters, photographs, and drawings. With extensive correspondence from Harold Acton; Angela, Countess of Antrim; Sir John Betjeman; Ivy Compton-Burnett; Alick Dru; T S Eliot; Max Beerbohm; Graham Greene; John Hayward; Lord Patrick Kinross; Compton Mackenzie; Nancy Mitford; Anthony Powell; Dame Flora Robson; Cecil Roth; Sir John Russell; Osbert Sitwell; John Sparrow; Freya Stark; James Stern; and Evelyn Waugh, among others. Also, considerable research material about Evelyn Waugh, Adam von Trott, Robert Byron, Lady Nancy Astor; and the foundation of the state of Israel.

IN —INDIANA UNIVERSITY, Lilly Library, Seventh St, Bloomington, 47405. William R Cagle, Librn
Holdings: / / Cat Mss
Notes: Correspondence and drawings of Max Beerbohm, 1899-1944. Many cited in *An Exhibition of Books, Caricatures, Manuscripts, Letters, Memorabilia by Sir Max Beerbohm from the Collection of Alfred H Perrin, Cincinnati Public Library* (April 1965); 64 items. Also, first editions of Beerbohm appearances.

MA —HARVARD UNIVERSITY LIBRARY, Houghton Library, Cambridge, 02138. Rodney G Dennis, Cur of Manuscripts
Holdings: Cat Mss
Notes: See A E Gallatin's *Sir Max* Beerbohm (1944) and *Harvard Library* Bulletin, V (1951), 77-93, 221-241, and 338-361 for holdings.

NS —DALHOUSIE UNIVERSITY LIBRARY, Halifax, B3H 4H8, Can.
Holdings: Vols (305) Cat
Budget: s
Notes: Strong holdings of first and limited editions of Wilde's work are contained in the collection. Later editions, biographies

BEERBOHM, SIR MAX, 1872-1956 (cont.)

and critical studies, as well as first editions of contemporaries associated with Wilde, such as Lord Alfred Douglas, Frank Harris, Aubrey Beardsley and Max Beerbohm are well represented. Highlights incl: *Ravenna* (Oxford, 1878), and autogrpahed first editions of *Poems, An Ideal Husband, Importance of Being Earnest,* and *The Picture of Dorian Gray.*

ON —UNIVERSITY OF TORONTO, Thomas Fisher Rare Book Library, 120 Saint George St, Toronto, M5S 1A5, Can. Richard G Landon, Head
Holdings: Vols 5400 Cat Mss
Notes: Three collections. Duncan Collection is named for donor, Douglas Duncan, art dealer and collector,, Toronto. Contains first and subsequent important editions of Richard Aldington, Max Beerbohm, Norman Douglas, Aldoux Huxley, and D H Lawrence. Manuscripts by Beerbohm, Aldington, Lawrence, William Sharp. Endicott Collection named in honor of Norman J Endicott, Professor of English, University of Toronto, contains first and significant later editions of over fifty British writers whose major work falls into the period from 1880 to 1930. Fisher Collection named for donor, Charles B Fisher, contains first and significant editions of Kipling, Norman Douglas, and Lord Dunsany.

BEER-HOFFMANN, RICHARD

MA —HARVARD UNIVERSITY LIBRARY, Houghton Library, Cambridge, 02138. Rodney G Dennis, Cur of Manuscripts
Holdings: Cat Mss
Notes: Manuscripts and personal papers.

BEERS, CLIFFORD, 1876-1943

KS —MENNINGER FOUNDATION, Archives, 5600 W Sixth St, Box 829, Topeka, 66601. Alice Brand, Librn; Mark West, Archivist
Notes: 4 boxes, 1907-41. Beers founded the National Committee for Mental Hygiene and wrote *A Mind That Found Itself.* Consists primarily of personal and professional correspondence.

BEERS FAMILY

CT —YALE UNIVERSITY, Box 1603A, Yale Station, New Haven, 06520.
Holdings: Mss
Notes: Private and business papers of the Beers and Curtis Families, 1780-1909.

BEES AND BEEKEEPING

CA —UNIVERSITY OF CALIFORNIA, DAVIS, Shields Library, Dept of Special Collections, Davis, 95616. Donald Kunitz, Head; C Danial Elliott, Asst Head
Holdings: Cat Mss Pix Slides
Notes: Records of the American Beekeeping Federation (1940-1969) and the California State Beekeepers Association (1891-1973); manuscripts, patent papers, and daybooks of John S Harbison, pioneer California beekeeper; collection of beekeeping supply catalogs (late nineteenth century to the present); articles, correspondence, and working files on Harbison and Langstroth of Lee H Watkins; correspondence of John E Eckert (1936-1958) with apiculturalists from all over the world; correspondence, scrapbooks, clippings, and photographs of Max Clemens Richter, California beekeeper; miscellaneous articles and clippings on all aspects of beekeeping. 54,000 items. Described in: USDA Agricultural Research Service, *Beekeeping in the United States* (Agriculture Handbook no 335, rev ed 1977); and Johansson, Tag Sigvard *Kjell,Apicultural Literature Published in Canada and the United States* (New York, 1972).

DC —SMITHSONIAN INSTITUTION LIBRARIES, Entomology Branch, Washington, 20560. Jean C Smith, Asst Dir for Bureau Services
Holdings: Vols (17,000) Cat Maps Pix

FL —FLORIDA DEPARTMENT OF AGRICULTURE & CONSUMER SERVICES, Div of Plant Industry, Library, PO Box 1269, Gainesville, 32602. June B Jacobson, Librn; Alice Richards, Asst Librn
Holdings: Vols (11,455) Cat Mss Microforms
Budget: ($23,798)
Notes: Collection is primarily taxonomic. 464 periodical, current and antiquariat titles.

MA —UNIVERSITY OF MASSACHUSETTS AT AMHERST, Library, Amherst, 01003. Siegfried Feller, Assoc Dir for Collection Development
Holdings: Cat
Notes: Incl the Guy C Crampton Collection; also, extensive holdings on bees and beekeeping.

MI —MICHIGAN STATE UNIVERSITY, Libraries, Special Collections Div, East Lansing, 48824. Jannette Fiore, Librn
Holdings: Vols 324 Cat Mss
Notes: Works on bee-keeping, mostly before 1900, including books and some ms material from the library of Ray Stannard Baker.

NY —CORNELL UNIVERSITY LIBRARIES, Everett Franklin Phillips Beekeeping Library, Ithaca, 14853. Jan Olsen, Librn
Holdings: Vols 4200 Cat Mss
Notes: Incl collections of Moses Quimby, first commercial beekeeper in America, and Rev L L Langstroth.

NY —AMERICAN MUSEUM OF NATURAL HISTORY, Library Services Dept, Central Park W & 79th St, New York, 10024. Nina J Root, Chairwoman; Mary Genett, Asst Librn for Reference Services
Notes: A major literature collection supplements the museum's entomology collections; perhaps the largest in the world.

OH —OHIO STATE UNIVERSITY, William Oxley Thompson Memorial Library, 1858 Neil Ave Mall, Columbus, 43210. Robert A Tibbetts, Cur of Special Collections
Notes: Some 800 monographs, including almost all significant European and North American publications from the 18th century to the present on the subject of bees and beekeeping. A rich representation of relevant journals, pamphlets, and ephemeral material. The collection was that of the late William A Stephen.

PA —UNIVERSITY OF PENNSYLVANIA, Morris Arboretum Library, 9414 Meadowbrook Ave, Philadelphia, 19118.
Holdings: Vols 6000

WI —UNIVERSITY OF WISCONSIN, MADISON, College of Agricultural & Life Sciences, Steenbock Memorial Library, 550 Babcock Dr, Madison, 53706. Jan Kennedy, Dir
Holdings: Vols (186,312) Cat Docs
Notes: The Miller Collection, named for Charles C Miller (1831-1920), a popular writer on the subject of bee culture, was expanded into one of the most extensive collections of bee literature in English, French and German, after being acquired by the U of W, Madison. Only those materials considered rare are housed seperately in Steenbock Library, all other materials are integrated into the general collection.

ON —UNIVERSITY OF GUELPH, McLaughlin Library, Guelph, N1G 2W1, Can. Margaret Beckman, Head Librn; David Hull, Sciences Librn
Holdings: Vols 2200 Cat Mss Maps Pix Slides Phonorecords Audiotapes Videotapes 16mm Films Filmstrips Microforms
Budget: $5000
Notes: 2000 vols of bound journals (31 currently received); over 5000 reprints. Incl the 10,000 card bibliography of apiculture compiled by Dr Burton N Gates; also his extensive photographic collection and historic beekeeping equipment (the latter located in the Dept. of Environmental Biology).
See also entry under Agriculture

BEESON, JASPER LUTHER, 1867-1943

GA —GEORGIA COLLEGE, Ina Dillard Russell Library, Special Collections Dept, Milledgeville, 31061. Janice C Fennell, Dir of Libraries; Nancy Davis, Special Collections Assoc
Holdings: Uncat Mss
Notes: Beeson Collection of 67 folders of mss concerning Milledgeville, Baldwin County, Georgia, Georgia Normal and Industrial College.
See also entry under Beeson, Leola Selman, 1868-1962

BEESON, LEOLA SELMAN, 1868-1962

GA —GEORGIA COLLEGE, Ina Dillard Russell Library, Special Collections Dept, Milledgeville, 31061. Janice C Fennell, Dir of Libraries; Nancy Davis, Special Collections Assoc
Holdings: Uncat Mss
Notes: Beeson Collection of 67 folders of mss concerning Milledgeville, Baldwin County, Georgia, Georgia Normal and Industrial College.
See also entry under Beeson, Jasper Luther, 1867-1943

BEETHOVEN, LUDWIG VAN

DC —GEORGETOWN UNIVERSITY, Library, Special Collections Div, 37 & O Sts NW, Washington, 20057. George M Barringer, Special Collections Librn; Nicholas B Sheetz, Mss Librn
Holdings: Mss
Notes: Musical mss, incl a copyist's mss of the opening two movements of Beethoven's Ninth Symphony (1825); autograph mss of Rheinberger's Fantasie-Sonate fur die Orgel (before 1872); Gloetzner's Ave Regina and organ exercises; and a printed copy of his Mass, Op 12 (1910). Anton Gloetzner, Bavarian composer and musician, taught music at Georgetown College from 1873 to 1880.

NY —NEW YORK PUBLIC LIBRARY, Music Div, 111 Amsterdam Ave, New York, 10023. Frank C Campbell, Chief
Notes: Autographed music mss. First editions. Facsimiles of autographed music mss on microfilm.

TX —RICE UNIVERSITY, Fondren Library, Woodson Research Center, 6100 S Main St, PO Box 1892, Houston, 77251. Nancy Parker, Dir Woodson Research Center
Holdings: Vols 600// Cat
Notes: The Bartlett Beethoven Collection of books about the life and works of Beethoven, incl musicology, biography, studies of the composer by his contemporaries, and detailed studies of his compositions.

BEETLES

DC —SMITHSONIAN INSTITUTION LIBRARIES, Entomology Branch, Washington, 20560. Jean C Smith, Asst Dir for Bureau Services
Holdings: Vols (17,000) Cat Maps Pix

NY —AMERICAN MUSEUM OF NATURAL HISTORY, Library Services Dept, Central Park W & 79th St, New York, 10024. Nina J Root, Chairwoman; Mary Genett, Asst Librn for Reference Services
Notes: A major literature collection supplements the museum's entomology collections; perhaps the largest in the world.

BEHAN, BRENDAN

NV —UNIVERSITY OF NEVADA, RENO, University Library, Special Collections Dept, Reno, 89557. Robert E Blesse, Head
Holdings: Vols (33) Cat
Notes: Includes individual works by author in all editions including translations; also prefaces, introductions, published correspondence, appearances in anthologies, periodicals, etc. Bibliographical research collection, part of Modern Authors Collection. Other appearances 45 cataloged.

BEHAVIOR see Etiquette

BEHAVIOR (PSYCHOLOGY) see Animals, Habits and Behavior of; Human Behavior

BEHAVIOR GENETICS

AR —NATIONAL CENTER FOR TOXICOLOGICAL RESEARCH, Library,

BEHAVIOR GENETICS (cont.)

Jefferson, 72079. Susan Laney-Sheehan, Supvr Librn
Holdings: Vols (15,000) Cat Mss Slides Audiotapes 16mm Films Microforms
Notes: Incl (860) journal titles, (230) current subscriptions.

NY —CORNELL UNIVERSITY LIBRARIES, Collection of Regional History, Dept of Manuscripts and Univ Archives, Ithaca, 14853.
Notes: Incl records, 1929-32; programs, minutes, and newspaper clippings concerning the planning and financing of the 6th International Congress of Genetics held at Cornell University, NY in August, 1932.

BEHAVIOR OF CHILDREN see Children—Management

BEHAVIORAL SCIENCES

CA —HUMAN RESOURCES RESEARCH ORGANIZATION (HUMRRO), Western Div Library, 27857 Berwick Dr, Carmel, 93923. Dianalee Stickler, Librn
Notes: Citations for HumRRO reports appear in *HumRRO Bibliography of* Publications, 1971 and *HumRRO Bibliography of Publications and Presentations During FY,* 1972-77. Library is inactive.

CA —NASA, Ames Research Center, Libraries, Library Br 202-3, Moffett Field, 94035. Sarah Dueker, Chief, Library Branch
Holdings: Cat Audiotapes Microforms
Notes: Main library collections cover physical sciences, engineering and mathematical fields related to research programs in aeronautics-space research. Life sciences library collections cover medical, physiological, behavioral and biological sciences related to research programs. Also emphases on remote sensing of earth resources and the search for extraterrestrial life. 950 journal titles and 85,000 monographs. Reports collection includes 60, 000 hard copy reports and 900,000 microfiche.

DC —LIBRARY OF CONGRESS, Washington, 20540.
Notes: The Rudolf Dreikurs papers, incl material on the behavioral sciences and psychiatry.

MA —MCLEAN HOSPITAL MEDICAL LIBRARY, 115 Mill St, Belmont, 02178. Hector Bossange, Dir
Holdings: Vols 25,611 Cat
Notes: Extensive collection.

MA —BOSTON COLLEGE LIBRARIES, Chestnut Hill, 02167.

NY —COLUMBIA UNIVERSITY LIBRARIES, Whitney M Young Jr Memorial Library of Social Work, 420 W 118 St, New York, 10027. Tyrone Cannon, Librn
Holdings: Vols (118,646) Cat
Notes: The collection covers the history and philosophy of social work, social work methodology, and all aspects of social welfare services, especially child welfare, mental hygiene, correction, the aging, social security and medical care, rehabilitation, aspects and problems of civil rights and automation. There is also a substantial representation of literature in psychiatry and the behavioral and social sciences. The reference section includes more than 419 periodicals, publications issued by voluntary agencies, government publications, doctoral dissertations and masters' essays in the field and standard reference works. Reference service is available.

NY —COLUMBIA UNIVERSITY LIBRARIES, Teachers College, Milbank Memorial Library, 525 W 120 St, New York, 10027. Jane P Franck, Dir
Holdings: Vols (402,000) Cat Mss Pix Slides Microforms
Notes: Incl 3800 phonorecords and audiotapes; 900 filmstrips; 600 films; 1400 slides; 255,000 microforms; 575 mss; 50,000 photographs. Basic dictionary catalog of Teachers College Library (36 vols) has been published; with 5-volume supplement plus annual supplements.

NY —COLUMBIA UNIVERSITY LIBRARIES, Psychology Library, 409 Schermerhorn, New York, 10027. Barbara A List, Reference/Collection Development Librn
Holdings: Vols (25,000) Cat Microforms
Budget: ($23,300)
Notes: Incl material on animal physiology, cognition, psycholinguistics, learning theories, memory, perception, personality, sensation, sensorimotor activities, vision.

OH —CLEVELAND PSYCHIATRIC INSTITUTE, Karnosh Library, 1708 Aiken Ave, Cleveland, 44109. Anna L Harris, Librn
Holdings: Vols 5000 Cat

PA —UNIVERSITY OF PITTSBURGH, Graduate School of Business Library, 138 Mervis Hall, Pittsburgh, 15260. Susan Neuman, Head Librn
Holdings: Vols (36,000) Cat Microforms
Budget: ($40,000)
Notes: Incl material to support graduate programs in business administration, as well as faculty research. Reflects strongly the interest of business in the behavioral, social, and international aspects of management. 19, 000 microfiche cards, 1000 microfilm reels.

†RI —UNIVERSITY OF RHODE ISLAND, Library, Kingston, 02881.
Notes: Extensive collections.

TX —SOUTHWEST FOUNDATION FOR RESEARCH AND EDUCATION LIBRARY, Preston C Northrup Memorial Library, Baboon Information Center, W Loop 410 at Military Dr, PO Box 28147, San Antonio, 78284. Dorothy M Brooks, Baboon
Notes: Principle field of research: Birth defects, atherosclerosis, reproductive physiology, cancer, genetics, organic chemistry, parasitology, primatology and behavioral sciences and their application to problems of drug abuse, alcoholism and ecology. Maintains the largest baboon colony in the world.

WI —UNIVERSITY OF WISCONSIN, MADISON, Wisconsin Regional Primate Research Center, Primate Center Library, 1223 Capitol Court, Madison, 53715. Lawrence Jacobsen, Librn
Holdings: Vols (15,000) Cat Pix
Notes: Research in reproductive physiology, neurosciences, and behavior. Extensive subject orientated primate reprint file, audiovisual collection on primates. Current research uses approximately 25 species of nonhuman primates. Publications: *Primate Library Report*: print and non-print editions, biomonthly.

BEHAVIORAL SCIENCES—HISTORY

NY —CORNELL UNIVERSITY MEDICAL COLLEGE, Oskar Diethelm Historical Library, 525 E 68 St, New York, 10021. Phyllis Rubinton, Librn
Holdings: Vols (14,000) Cat Mss
Notes: History of psychiatry and the behavioral sciences. 14,000 historical vols, incl hospital annual reports and theses; 4000 reference vols. Library open to scholars and researchers by appointment. No photocopying.

BEHISTUN INSCRIPTIONS see Cuneiform Inscriptions

BEHN, APHRA

CA —UNIVERSITY OF CALIFORNIA, LOS ANGELES, William Andrews Clark Memorial Library, 2520 Cimarron St, Los Angeles, 90018.
Holdings: Cat
Notes: Extensive collection, first editions, etc.

BEHN, NOEL

MA —BOSTON UNIVERSITY, Mugar Memorial Library, Special Collections Dept, 771 Commonwealth Ave, Boston, 02215. Howard B Gotlieb, Dir
Holdings: Cat Mss

BEHREND, BERNARD A., 1875-1932

SC —CLEMSON UNIVERSITY, Libraries, Clemson, 29631. Michael F Kohl, Head of Special Collections
Holdings: // Uncat Mss Pix
Notes: Electricity, theoretical and applied to motors. Collected by Bernard A Behrend, 1875-1932, inventor of machinery and large electrical units. 29 cubic feet of material in English, German, and French, dating primarily from 1886-1932. The mss portion of this collection consists of numerous notebooks contains records of Mr Behrend's work and some scattered correspondence. Also incl pamphlets. Cited in *Manuscripts in US Depositories Relating to the History of Electrical Science and Technology* (Div of Electricity and Nuclear Energy, Smithsonian Institution, Washington, DC, 1973).

BEHRMAN, S. N.

NE —UNIVERSITY OF NEBRASKA-LINCOLN, Don L Love Library, University Archives and Special Collections, Lincoln, 68588. Joseph G Svoboda, University Archivist
Notes: Virginia Faulkner was recognized as one of Nebraska's most distinguished writers and scholars. The Virginia Faulkner Collection, containing over 2000 titles, is housed in the Special Collections Department of Love Library. It is especially strong in twentieth century writers and in University of Nebraska Press Publications. Of especial value to scholars are her extensive holdings of Willa Cather, Wright Morris and John Neihardt. Her correspondence with S N Behrman, E B White, Edward Wagenknecht, Donald Sutherland, Wright Morris, Louise Pound, Mari Sandoz, Hazel Barnes, Alfred A and Blanche Knopf, and others provide insight into the literary development of these figures, as well as chronicle the intellectual thought of the period. Amassed in a separate file, these letters are available to interested scholars.

BEISSEL, CONRAD

NY —COLUMBIA UNIVERSITY LIBRARIES, Rare Book & Manuscript Library, 801 Butler Library, 535 W 114 St, New York, 10027. Kenneth A Lohf, Librn
Holdings: Mss
Notes: Consisting of music mss of the Ephrata Community, by the founder of the community, Conrad Beissel. Restricted use.

BELASCO, DAVID

NY —NEW YORK PUBLIC LIBRARY, Performing Arts Research Center, Billy Rose Theatre Collection, 111 Amsterdam Ave, New York, 10023. Dorothy L Swerdlove, Cur
Holdings: Cat Mss Pix
Notes: Papers, scrapbooks, mss, photographs, memorabilia, etc.

BELCHER, EDWARD, 1799-1877

BC —UNIVERSITY OF VICTORIA, McPherson Library, Victoria, V8W 3H5, Can.

BELCHER, ERNEST

CA —UNIVERSITY OF CALIFORNIA, LOS ANGELES, Research Library, Dept of

BELCHER, ERNEST (cont.)

Special Collections, 405 Hilgard Ave, Los Angeles, 90024. Edward Shreeves, Chairman, Bibliographers Group; David S Zeidberg, Head
Notes: 3 linear feet of material relating to the dance.

BELCHER, PAGE HENRY

OK —UNIVERSITY OF OKLAHOMA, Bizzell Memorial Library, Western History Collections, 401 W Brooks, Norman, 73069. John Ezell, Cur
Holdings: Mss Pix Audio Videotapes Maps Newspapers Documents
Notes: US Representative. His papers. Guide available.

BELGIAN ART see Art, Belgian

BELGIAN CONGO see Zaire

BELGIAN LANGUAGES AND LITERATURE

GA —EMORY UNIVERSITY, Robert W Woodruff Library, Special Collections Dept, Atlanta, 30322. Linda M Matthews, Head Special Collections; Virginia J H Cain, Processing Archivist; Richard H F Lindemann, Reference Archivist
Holdings: Vols (16,000) Cat Mss Maps Pix Microforms

IL —BLACK HAWK COLLEGE, Learning Resources Center, 6600 34 Ave, Moline, 61265. Donald C Rowland, Dir
Holdings: Vols 773 Cat Pix Audiotapes
Notes: Emphasis on fine arts. Entire college collection a gift of the Belgian Consul.

†NY —BELGIAN CONSULATE GENERAL LIBRARY, 50 Rockefeller Plaza, New York, 10020.
Notes: Belgian history, art, cultures, and other aspects of Belgian life.

BELGIAN LITERATURE (FLEMISH) see Flemish Language and Literature

BELGIAN REVOLUTION, 1830-1839

CT —UNIVERSITY OF CONNECTICUT, Library, Storrs, 06268. R H Schimmelpfeng, Dir of Special Collections
Notes: Belgian revolution of 1830. The collection consists of primary sources, books and pamphlets, of the period, along with secondary materials. Two-thirds of the collection is in French, the rest in Dutch. An author/title checklist is also available.

BELGIANS IN THE U.S.

†NY —BELGIAN CONSULATE GENERAL LIBRARY, 50 Rockefeller Plaza, New York, 10020.
Notes: Belgian history, art, cultures, and other aspects of Belgian life.

PA —BALCH INSTITUTE FOR ETHNIC STUDIES, Library, 18 S Seventh St, Philadelphia, 19106. R Joseph Anderson, Library Dir
Notes: Ethnic Heritage Collection.

WI —UNIVERSITY OF WISCONSIN, GREEN BAY, Library/Learning Center, Green Bay, 54301. Marian A Gould, Acting Dir, Special Collections/University Archives
Holdings: Vols 100 Cat Mss Maps Pix Slides Audiotapes Videotapes
Notes: Belgian-American Research Collection deals with the Belgian-American Settlement in Brown, Door and Kewaunee counties of northeastern Wisconsin. Emphasis is on the rural life and commerical fishing activities in the Bay of Green Bay. Bibliography, *Belgian-American Research* Materials, is available on request.

BELGIUM—HISTORY

CA —HOOVER INSTITUTION ON WAR, REVOLUTION & PEACE, Stanford University, Stanford, 94305. Milorad M Drachkovitch, Archivist
Holdings: // Mss
Notes: Three collections: (1) Papers, 1908-1954, of Hugh Gibson, diplomat. Correspondence, diaries, journals and official papers, relating in part to the surrender of King Leopold of Belgium in 1940 and to relief activities in Europe following World War II. Correspondents incl Perrin C Galpin, Herbert Hoover, Ignace Jan Paderewski and Maurice Pate. Ca 80 ft finding aid in the repository. (2) Records of the Commission for Relief in Belgium, organized in 1914 under the chairmanship of Herbert Hoover, incl correspondence, reports, memoranda, accounts, pamphlets, bulletins and photographs, 1914-1924, relating to procurement of food and other supplies in the US and their distribution in German-occupied Belgium and northern France during and immediately after World War 1. 265 ft. (3) Papers of Brand Whitlock, author and US Ambassador to Belgium, 1913-22, incl writings,diaries, printed matter and photographs, 1913-34, relating to US--Belgian relations during World War I, work of the Commission for Relief in Belgium, and fictional writings of Brand Whitlock. 7 ms boxes, 1 oversize folder.

CT —UNIVERSITY OF CONNECTICUT, Library, Storrs, 06268. R H Schimmelpfeng, Dir of Special Collections
Holdings: Vols 700 Cat Pix
Notes: Belgian revolution of 1830. The collection consists of primary sources, books and pamphlets, of the period, along with secondary materials. Two-thirds of the collection is in French, the rest in Dutch. An author/title checklist is also available.

GA —EMORY UNIVERSITY, Robert W Woodruff Library, Special Collections Dept, Atlanta, 30322. Linda M Matthews, Head Special Collections; Virginia J H Cain, Processing Archivist; Richard H F Lindemann, Reference Archivist
Holdings: Vols (16,000) Cat Mss Maps Pix Microforms

IL —NORTHWESTERN UNIVERSITY, Library, Special Collections Dept, 1937 Sheridan Rd, Evanston, 60201. R Russell Maylone, Cur
Notes: Incl 2500 pamphlets dealing with the Brabant Revolution. Additional 14,000 pamphlets, legal documents, and periodical issues published in France 1787-1800.

IL —BLACK HAWK COLLEGE, Learning Resources Center, 6600 34 Ave, Moline, 61265. Donald C Rowland, Dir
Holdings: Vols 773 Cat Pix Audiotapes
Notes: Emphasis of fine arts. Entire college collection a gift of the Belgian consul.

†NY —BELGIAN CONSULATE GENERAL LIBRARY, 50 Rockefeller Plaza, New York, 10020.
Notes: Belgian history, art, cultures, and other aspects of Belgian life.

BELGIUM, COMMISSION FOR RELEIF IN see Commission for Relief in Belgium, 1914-1924

BELITT, BEN

MA —BOSTON UNIVERSITY, Mugar Memorial Library, Special Collections Dept, 771 Commonwealth Ave, Boston, 02215. Howard B Gotlieb, Dir
Holdings: Cat Mss
Notes: Mss, correspondence, etc collected in depht; incl publications by or about.

BELIZE

CT —YALE UNIVERSITY, Sterling Memorial Library, Latin American Collections, New Haven, 06520. Lee H Williams Jr, Cur
Holdings: Vols (300,000) Cat Maps Pix Slides Phonorecords 16mm Films Filmstrips
See also entry under Latin America

KS —UNIVERSITY OF KANSAS, Watson Library, Lawrence, 66045. George Jerkovich, Cur Slavic Collections
Notes: Over 6000 valuable Central American titles, of which fewer than half in a random sample are presently located in OCLC, and over half not incl in published holdings of the University of Texas or Tulane University. A special grant is supporting cataloging of the collection.

MA —PAN AMERICAN SOCIETY OF NEW ENGLAND, Shattuck Library, 152 North Street, Boston, 02109. Vivian Ingrao, Dir
Holdings: Vols (10,000) Cat Slides Phonorecords
Notes: Books on art, literature, history, and economy of Pan American countries.

BELL, ABRAHAM, AND SON

NY —STATE UNIVERSITY OF NEW YORK AT ALBANY, Library, Special Collections Dept, 1400 Washington Ave, Albany, 12222. Marion P Munzer, Coordr
Notes: Correspondence and financial records of Abraham Bell and Son, New York shipping line which exported cotton and brought back British and English immigrants in the 1830s and 1840s. Additional correspondence and papers of James W Bell from 1862-1917; James C Bell from 1864-1899; and Bell Brothers, a money-lending business in Yonkers (22 linear feet). Part of the Library's German Exile Collection.
See also entries under Shipping; Emigration and Immigration

BELL, ALEXANDER GRAHAM, 1847-1922

DC —LIBRARY OF CONGRESS, Manuscript Division, Washington, 20540. John C Broderick, Chief
Holdings: 140,000 Items
Notes: The papers of Alexander Graham Bell and his family. Incl Bell's diaries, correspondence, printed matter, financial and legal records, and several hundred vols of laboratory notebooks which record his daily work from 1865 to 1922. Also, materials of Alexander Melville Bell, Mabel Hubbard Bell, and Gilbert H Grosvenor.

BELL, BERT

OH —PRO FOOTBALL HALL OF FAME, Library, 2121 Harrison Ave NW, Canton, 44708. Anne Mangus, Librn; Joe Horrigan, Cur
Notes: Incl materials on all aspects of professional football, with special emphasis on the 119 men enshrined in the Hall of Fame. Mainly a research library. Incl periodicals and a vast array of historical material and mementos. Incl 17,000 pictures, 1500 slides, 50 audiotapes, 1300 16mm films, 3000 game programs and and 500 team media guides. Bert Bell Scrapbooks; Spalding Football guides.

BELL, CLIVE

NY —HOFSTRA UNIVERSITY, Library, 1000 Fulton Ave, Hempstead, 11550. Charles R Andrews, Dean of Library Services

ON —VICTORIA UNIVERSITY, Library, 71 Queen's Park Crescent, Toronto, M5S 1K7, Can. Robert C Brandeis, Chief Librn
Holdings: Vols Cat
Notes: A collection of first editions and others of Virginia Woolf and Bloomsbury writers: Clive Bell, Roger Fry, E M Forster, V Sackville-West, K Mansfield, etc. Contains a significant collection of Hogarth Press books, and many of those handprinted by the Woolfs.

BELL, MACKENZIE, 1856-1930

CA —UNIVERSITY OF CALIFORNIA, LOS ANGELES, Research Library, Dept of Special Collections, 405 Hilgard Ave, Los Angeles, 90024. Edward Shreeves, Chairman, Bibliographers Group; David S Zeidberg, Head
Holdings: Mss Pix
Notes: 6.5 linear feet of mss, correspondence, photographs, etc.

BELL, MARY HAYLEY

MA —BOSTON UNIVERSITY, Mugar Memorial Library, Special Collections Dept, 771 Commonwealth Ave, Boston, 02215. Howard B Gotlieb, Dir
Holdings: Cat Mss

BELL, VANESSA

IL —NORTHWESTERN UNIVERSITY, Library, Special Collections Dept, 1937 Sheridan Rd, Evanston, 60201. R Russell Maylone, Cur
Holdings: Mss
Notes: 79 letters to Vanessa Bell from J M Keynes.

BELL FAMILY

DC —LIBRARY OF CONGRESS, Manuscript Division, Washington, 20540. John C Broderick, Chief
Holdings: 140,000 Items
Notes: The papers of Alexander Graham Bell and his family. Incl Bell's diaries, correspondence, printed matter, financial and legal records, and several hundred vols of laboratory notebooks which record his daily work from 1865 to 1922. Also, materials of Alexander Melville Bell, Mabel Hubbard Bell, and Gilbert H Grosvenor.

BELL RINGING see Change Ringing; Handbell Ringing

BELL TELEPHONE LABORATORIES

NY —AMERICAN INSTITUTE OF PHYSICS, Center for the History of Physics, Niels Bohr Library, 335 E 45 St, New York, 10017. John Aubry, Librn
Notes: Physicist Karl Kelchner Darrow's professional correspondence (1928-73), diaries (1911-75), and early undergraduate notes, as well as materials on lectures, speeches, offprints, and family correspondence. Most of Dr Darrow's career was with the Bell Telephone Laboratories, and he was Secretary of the American Physical Society for 25 years.

BELLAH, JAMES WARNER

MA —BOSTON UNIVERSITY, Mugar Memorial Library, Special Collections Dept, 771 Commonwealth Ave, Boston, 02215. Howard B Gotlieb, Dir
Holdings: Cat Mss Pix
Notes: Mss, correspondence, etc collected in depth; incl publications by or about.

BELLAIRS, CARLYON WILFROY

PQ —MCGILL UNIVERSITY, McLennan Library, Rare Books and Special Collections Dept, 3459 McTavish St, Montreal, H3A 1Y1, Can.
Notes: 20,090 pamphlets on British historical, religious, and political material dating mainly from the 17th and 18th centuries, are housed in the Redpath Tracts Collection. Also the manuscripts of Carlyon Wilfroy Bellairs on early 20th century British politics and those of Henry Hardinge, first Viscount Hardinge of Lahore, are housed in the Manuscript Collection.

BELLAMY, EDWARD

MA —HARVARD UNIVERSITY LIBRARY, Houghton Library, Cambridge, 02138. Rodney G Dennis, Cur of Manuscripts
Holdings: Cat Mss
OH —ANTIOCH COLLEGE, Olive Kettering Library, Livermore St, Yellow Springs, 45387. Nina Myatt, Cur
Holdings: Cat Mss Pix
Notes: Personal papers, correspondence, 1920-1975. Mss, film out-takes, diaries, materials from Tennessee Valley Authority (Morgan was first chairman), Antioch College (Morgan was president 1920-1936), materials about Edward Bellamy (Morgan wrote biography of Bellamy, primary sources sent to Houghton Library at Harvard; only secondary sources here). About 175 file boxes.

BELLAMY, RALPH

CA —UNIVERSITY OF CALIFORNIA, LOS ANGELES, Theater Arts Library, Los Angeles, 90024. Edward Shreeves, Chairman, Bibliographers Group; Audree Malkin, Head, Theater Arts Library
Notes: Ralph Bellamy (actor) Collection: shooting script (pts 1-7), production material, press clippings, and periodical articles relating to the television miniseries *Winds of War.* Miscellaneous periodical articles, letters and clippings relating to his career.

BELLES LETTRES see Literature

BELLIGERENT OCCUPATION see Military Occupation

BELLINGHAM BAY IMPROVEMENT COMPANY

WA —WESTERN WASHINGTON UNIVERSITY, Center for Pacific Northwest Studies, High St, Bellingham, 98225. James W Scott, Dir
Holdings: // Maps Pix
Notes: Bellingham Bay Improvement Company Collection. The records of 6 companies formerly operative in NW Washington: Bellingham Bay Coal Co; Bellingham Bay & British Columbia Railroad Co; Bellingham Bay Improvement Co; Bellingham Bay Lumber Co; Bellingham Terminals and Railroad Co; Bellingham Securitites Syndicate. The records cover 1864-1942. Officers of the companies incl many important PNW businessmen incl P B Cornwall, Joshua Green, J J Donovan and J H Bloedel. A published listing and description is available: *Informational Paper* 1 of the Center for PNW Studies. Partially cataloged.

BELLOC, HILAIRE

DC —GEORGETOWN UNIVERSITY, Library, Special Collections Div, 37 & O Sts NW, Washington, 20057. George M Barringer, Special Collections Librn; Nicholas B Sheetz, Mss Librn
Holdings: Mss
Notes: The Archives of the Gallery of Living Catholic Authors was founded in 1932 by Sister Mary Joseph of the Sisters of Loretto to focus attention on modern Catholic literature, and to provide a depository for manuscripts, letters, photographs, and books by contemporary Catholic writers. Contains material by hundreds of writers, incl Hilaire Belloc, Roy Campbell, Padraic Colum, Eric Gill, Paul Horgan, Mary Lavin, Marie Belloc Lowndes, Kathleen Norris, Alred Noyes, Sheila Kaye-Smith, Sigrid Undset, and Evelyn Waugh, to name only a few.
MA —BOSTON COLLEGE LIBRARIES, Chestnut Hill, 02167.
Notes: Personal library and papers of Hilaire Belloc (1870-1953), and first editions of his books. The largest collection of Belloc, incl materials that supported his literary and historical researches, an unpublished autobiography, and a wide correspondence with hundreds of notable acquintances, largely British authors, many of them Roman Catholics (since Belloc was one of England's most prominent among them).
NY —HOFSTRA UNIVERSITY, Library, 1000 Fulton Ave, Hempstead, 11550. Charles R Andrews, Dean of Library Services
Notes: Strong Collection. Incl some mss.

BELLOW, SAUL

CA —UNIVERSITY OF CALIFORNIA, DAVIS, Shields Library, Dept of Special Collections, Davis, 95616. Donald Kunitz, Head; C Danial Elliott, Asst Head
Holdings: Vols Uncat Mss Pix
Notes: Business papers of off-Broadway literary and theatrical agent, Toby Cole, for the years 1957-73. Incl mss by Saul Bellow and Sam Shepherd, among others. 4000 pix.
NV —UNIVERSITY OF NEVADA, RENO, University Library, Special Collections Dept, Reno, 89557. Robert E Blesse, Head
Holdings: Vols (97) Cat
Notes: Includes individual works by author in all editions including translations; also prefaces, introductions, published correspondence, appearances in anthologies, periodicals, etc. Bibliographical research collection, part of Modern Authors Collection. Other appearances 225 cataloged.

BELLOWS, GEORGE WESLEY

MA —AMHERST COLLEGE, Library, Amherst, 01002. John Lancaster, Special Collections Librn
Holdings: // Cat Mss Pix
Notes: American painter. 6 Hollinger boxes of ms material, etc.

BELLS

MI —GUILD OF CARILLONNEURS IN NORTH AMERICA, Archives, 900 Burton Tower, University of Michigan, Ann Arbor, 48109. William De Turk, Archivist
Holdings: Mss Pix Phonorecords
Notes: Emphasis is on carillons.
NY —SOCIETAS CAMPANARIORUM (SOCIETY OF BELL-RINGERS), Campanological Library, Riverside Church, 490 Riverside Dr, New York, 10027. James R Lawson, Librn
Holdings: Vols 1000 Cat
Notes: One of the largest collections of books, pamphlets, periodicals, etc on bells and bell music (chimes, carillons, change-ringing, handbells, electronic carillons, etc) in North America. Examined by appointment only.
ON —NATIONAL LIBRARY OF CANADA, 395 Wellington St, Ottawa, K1A 0N4, Can. Andre Preibish, Dir
Notes: Books, papers, and artifacts from Percival Price, renowned authority on campanology and first Dominion carilloneur (1927-39). Incl designs of bells and bell towers around the world, sound recordings, programs, etc. Some bells. About a third of the collection refers to Canadian carillons and carilloneurs.

BELLUSCHI, PIETRO

NY —SYRACUSE UNIVERSITY LIBRARIES, Ernest S Bird Library, George Arents Research Library for Special Collections, Syracuse, 13210. Carolyn A Davis, Manuscripts Librn; Amy S Doherty, University Archivist; Mark F Weimer, Rare Book Librn
Notes: The George Arents Research Library for Special Collections at Syracuse University contains the papers of Harley James McKee, Lorimer Rich, Frederick Lear, Max Abramovitz, James I Arnold, Pietro Bulluschi, Claude Bragdon, Marcel Breuer, William Lescaze, Skidmore Owings & Merrill, Ralph Walker, Eric Fisher Wood, Minoru Yamasaki, Joseph Louis Young, and Archimedes Russell.

BELOGORSKII, N.

CA —HOOVER INSTITUTION ON WAR, REVOLUTION & PEACE, Stanford University, Stanford, 94305. Milorad M Drachkovitch, Archivist
Holdings: // Mss Pix
Notes: Memoirs, supplemented by letters and photos, of Nikolai Vsevolodovich Shinkarenko, who used the pseudonym N Belogorskii. Memoirs deal mainly with the Russian Revolution.

BELOUTCHI LANGUAGE see Baluchi Language

BENCHLEY, NATHANIEL

MA —BOSTON UNIVERSITY, Mugar Memorial Library, Special Collections Dept, 771 Commonwealth Ave, Boston, 02215. Howard B Gotlieb, Dir
Holdings: Cat Mss Pix
Notes: Mss, correspondence, etc collected in depth; incl publications by or about.

BENCHLEY, ROBERT

CA —UNIVERSITY OF CALIFORNIA, LOS ANGELES, Theater Arts Library, Los

BENCHLEY, ROBERT (cont.)

Angeles, 90024. Edward Shreeves, Chairman, Bibliographers Group; Audree Malkin, Head, Theater Arts Library
Holdings: Cat Mss Pix
Notes: Script Collection, Screenplays: a collection of more than 32,636 unpublished scripts for American, British and some foreign language films. An important part of the collection is the Metro-Goldwyn-Mayer Screenplay Collection which covers the period 1924-1947. Incl are the *Andy Hardy, Dr Kildare,* and *Maisie* film series which are virtually complete, and a number of short features, such as *Robert Benchley Series, Pete Smith Specialties,* and *Our Gang* Comedies. Also incl the *Thin Man* series.

MA —BOSTON UNIVERSITY, Mugar Memorial Library, Special Collections Dept, 771 Commonwealth Ave, Boston, 02215. Howard B Gotlieb, Dir
Holdings: Mss Pix Correspondence

NY —NEW YORK PUBLIC LIBRARY, Performing Arts Research Center, Billy Rose Theatre Collection, 111 Amsterdam Ave, New York, 10023. Dorothy L Swerdlove, Cur
Holdings: Cat Mss Pix
Notes: Papers, scrapbooks, mss, photographs, memorabilia, etc.

BENDER, ALBERT M.

CA —MILLS COLLEGE LIBRARY, Oakland, 94613. Steven P Pandolfo, Librn
Holdings: Vols (65) Cat Mss
Notes: Books and ephemera from the Cuala Press; ms correspondence between Albert M Bender and the Yeats family.

BENDER, JAN

OH —WITTENBERG UNIVERSITY, Thomas Library, Springfield, 45501. Betty Beatty, Dir
Holdings: Vols (1000) Mss
Notes: No photocopying.

BENEDICTINES

MN —SAINT JOHN'S UNIVERSITY, Alcuin Library, Collegeville, 56321. Michael Kathman, Dir
Holdings: Vols (300,000) Cat Maps Slides Phonorecords Audiotapes Videotapes Filmstrips Microforms
Budget: ($176,000)
Notes: St John's University is operated by St John's Abbey. The library contains a large collection of works by and about Benedictine monks.

NC —BELMONT ABBEY COLLEGE, Abbot Vincent Taylor Library, Belmont, 28012. Marjorie McDermott, Dir
Holdings: Vols 3500 Cat Pix
Notes: The Benedictine Collection contains books and periodicals written and published by Benedictine monks and nuns, and books which deal with the Benedictine monastic life. Incl are many rare volumes published in the last 200 years, and several journals published by European abbeys, some of which are difficult to locate elsewhere. The collection is limited exclusively to *Benedictine* monasticism. As far as we know, it is the only collection of its type in the entire South. It is housed in a special room in the library. Access to the collection is through the main card catalog.

PA —HOLY TRINITY BENEDICTINE BYZANTINE RITE MONESTERY, PO Box 990, Butler, 16002.

BENES, EDUARD

CA —UNIVERSITY OF CALIFORNIA, BERKELEY, University Library, Slavic Collections, Berkeley, 94720. Edward Kasinec, Librn
Holdings: Vols 1917 Cat Pix
Notes: The Masaryk-Benes Library is a rich resource for the study of Czechoslovak and European history, especially for the period 1918-1939. It contains Masaryk's own works in original and later editions, as well as in translation (231 volumes), and books about Tomas and Jan Masaryk and family (573). Benes is represented by his own writings (100) and items about him and his family (69). Miscellaneous titles (335) on Slavic problems, and on the history of Czechoslovakia, complete the monograph collection. The balance consists of periodical articles, reprints, and newspaper clippings. Publication dates range from 1883 to 1945, with the bulk of the material published during 1920-1940.

IL —UNIVERSITY OF ILLINOIS, URBANA/CHAMPAIGN, Slavic and East European Library, Urbana, 61801. Marianna Tax Choldin, Head
Holdings: Vols (35,000) Cat
Notes: Extensive coverage.

MA —HARVARD UNIVERSITY LIBRARY, Widener Library, Slavic Collections, Cambridge, 02138. Hugh M Olmsted, Slavic Dept Head
Holdings: Cat

BENESH NOTATION

NY —NEW YORK PUBLIC LIBRARY, Performing Arts Research Center, Dance Collection, 111 Amsterdam Ave, New York, 10023. Genevieve Oswald, Cur
Holdings: Vols (36,752) Cat Mss Pix Videotapes 16mm Films Microforms
Notes: Multi-media collection with full documentation on various systems devised to record dance movement. Includes historical treatises and technical manuals from the 15th century to the present; manuals describing notation systems of Arbeau, Feuillet, Saint-Leon, Zorn, Stepanov, Morris, Laban, Benesh, Eshkol-Wachmann, Sutton, and others; over 250 dance notation scores, chiefly in Laban or Benesh notation, recording the choreography of specific dances--ballets, modern dance works, musical comedies, folk and social dances. Visual documentation recording and preserving the choreography of contemporary dance works is privided by 2640 motion pictures and 773 videotapes.

BENET, LAURA

NY —CITY UNIVERSITY OF NEW YORK, BROOKLYN COLLEGE, Library, Manuscripts Collection, Bedford Ave & Ave H, Brooklyn, 11210.
Notes: Her diaries, 1944-1948, 1950, 1952, 1954 and 1955.

BENET, STEPHEN VINCENT

CT —YALE UNIVERSITY, Box 1603A, Yale Station, New Haven, 06520.
Holdings: Cat Mss

NV —UNIVERSITY OF NEVADA, RENO, University Library, Special Collections Dept, Reno, 89557. Robert E Blesse, Head
Holdings: // Vols (83) Cat Other appearances 290 Cat
Notes: Includes individual works by author in all editions including translations; also prefaces, introductions, published correspondence, appearances in anthologies, periodicals, etc. Bibliographical research collection, part of Modern Authors Collection.

VA —UNIVERSITY OF VIRGINIA, Alderman Library, Clifton Waller Barrett Collection, Charlottesville, 22901. Joan St C Crane, Cur of American Literature Collections
Notes: Papers.

BENET, WILLIAM ROSE

CT —YALE UNIVERSITY, Box 1603A, Yale Station, New Haven, 06520.
Holdings: Cat Mss

BENEVOLENT INSTITUTIONS see Charitable Uses, Trusts, and Foundations

BENEZET, ANTHONY

†PA —FRIENDS HISTORICAL LIBRARY OF SWARTHMORE COLLEGE, Swarthmore, 19081.
Notes: Mss and published works by Anthony Benezet, Lucretia Mott, John Woolman; proceedings of antislavery societies; materials on the movement in Great Britian and America. Poetry incl.

BENFORD, GREGORY

†CA —UNIVERSITY OF CALIFORNIA, RIVERSIDE, Library, PO Box 5900, Riverside, 92507. George Slusser, Librn
Notes: Large slide collections of science fiction art, and hold the Gregory Benford mss.

BENGAL

MO —UNIVERSITY OF MISSOURI-COLUMBIA, Ellis Library, Ninth and Lowry, Columbia, 65201. Murari Lal Nagar, Librn
Holdings: Vols 100,000 Maps Microforms
Notes: The South Asia Studies Program at the University of Missouri-Columbia, is an interdepartmental, multi-disciplinary area studies program on India, Pakistan, Bangladesh, Sri Lanka and Nepal. Depository for the PL480 Program of the Library of Congress in many languages from South Asia. There are library resources in Sankskrit, Hindi, Bengali, Panjabi, and Malayalam. The library is particularly strong in Baroda, Bengal and the Punjab.

BENGALI LANGUAGE AND LITERATURE

DC —LIBRARY OF CONGRESS, African and Middle Eastern Division, Washington, 20540.
Holdings: Cat Mss Microforms
Notes: Southern Asian: over 137,000 vols of literature of the area from Pakistan to the Philippines.

HI —UNIVERSITY OF HAWAII, Library, 2550 The Mall, Honolulu, 96822. Joyce Wright, Head, Asia Collection; Masato Matsu, Head, East Asia Vernacular Collection
Holdings: Vols 75,215 Cat Microforms
Notes: The Asia Collection holds material from and relating to Bangladesh, India, Nepal, Pakistan, and Sri Lanka in western and Asian languages. South Asian languages currently acquired: Bengali, Hindi, Marathi, Nepali, Pali, Prakrit, Sanskrit, Tamil. Period emphasis is post-World War II. Subject emphases: social sciences and the humanities (literature, economics, history, religion/philosophy). Holdings are supplemented by a large uncataloged backlog, much of it accessible through the Library of Congress Accessions Lists for the area and by over 7000 cataloged titles in the main library collection. *South Asian Library Resources in North America: A Survey Prepared for the Boston Conference,* 1974, ed by M L P Patterson (Zug, Switzerland: Tutes Documentation Company, 1975). (Bibliotheca Asiatica 12-), University of Hawaii, pp 103-114.

MI —UNIVERSITY OF MICHIGAN, Graduate Library, South Asian Dept, Ann Arbor, 48109. Om P Sharma, Librn
Holdings: Vols (365,000) Cat Maps Slides Microforms
Notes: The major emphasis is on social sciences and humanities. Besides materials in classical languages, South Asian vernaculars being retained are Hindi, Bengali, Urdu, Marathi and Tamil; strong in classical languages, especially Sanskrit, Pali, and Prakrit.

MI —MICHIGAN STATE UNIVERSITY, International Library, South and Southeast Asia Collection, East Lansing, 48824. Clinton Lockert, Bibliographer
Holdings: //Vols 55,700 Cat Mss Maps Audiotapes Microforms
Notes: Serials and monographs of South Asia received on PL 480 for India, Pakistan, Sri Lanka, and Nepal since 1968. Emphasis in upon Social Sciences, Humanitites, and Science. Areas of strength are Anthropology

BENGALI LANGUAGE AND LITERATURE (cont.)

and rural development. This subject has been de-emphasized, additions are not being made.

MO —UNIVERSITY OF MISSOURI-COLUMBIA, Ellis Library, Ninth and Lowry, Columbia, 65201. Murari Lal Nagar, Librn
Holdings: Vols 100,000 Maps Microforms
Notes: The South Asia Studies Program at the University of Missouri-Columbia, is an interdepartmental, multi-disciplinary area studies program on India, Pakistan, Bangladesh, Sri Lanka and Nepal. Depository for the PL480 Program of the Library of Congress in many languages from South Asia. There are library resources in Sankskrit, Hindi, Bengali, Panjabi, and Malayalam. The library is particularly strong in Baroda, Bengal and the Punjab.

NY —NEW YORK PUBLIC LIBRARY, Oriental Div, Fifth Ave & 42 St, New York, 10018. E Christian Filstrup, Chief
Holdings: Cat Mss Microforms
Budget: ($56,455)
Notes: Published catalog of holdings.

NY —NEW YORK PUBLIC LIBRARY, Donnell Foreign Language Library, 20 W 53 St, New York, 10019. Bosiljka Stevanovic, Supvr Librn
Holdings: Vols 664 Cat
Notes: Bengali collection incl Bengali authors of Bengali expression. No separate catalog.

BENGOUGH, JOHN WILSON, 1851-1923

ON —MCMASTER UNIVERSITY, Mills Memorial Library, Div of Archives & Research Collections, Hamilton, L8S 4L6, Can. G R Hill, Univ Librn
Holdings: // Mss Pix
Notes: Mss of prose works, poetry, scrapbooks, and cartoons by the Canadian political cartoonist John Wilson Bengough.

BENHAM, GEN. HENRY WASHINGTON

OH —RUTHERFORD B HAYES LIBRARY, 1337 Hayes Ave, Fremont, 43420. Watt P Marchman, Dir
Holdings: Cat Mss Pix
Notes: Papers of Gen H W Benham, largely business and American military. Index with the collection. Listed in *Guide to Manuscripts of the Ohio Historical Society,* 32. (1 linear foot).

BENIN

DC —HOWARD UNIVERSITY, Moorland-Spingarn Research Center, 500 Howard Place NW, Washington, 20059. Clifford L Muse, Jr, Acting Dir

BENJAMIN, ASHER

MA —SOCIETY FOR THE PRESERVATION OF NEW ENGLAND ANTIQUITIES, Library, 141 Cambridge St, Boston, 02114. Ellie Reichlin, Librn & Cur of Photographic Collections
Holdings: Vols (3000) // Cat Pix Microforms
Budget: ($75,000)
Notes: Architecture of the Northeast. Drawings (original designs, measured drawings, plot plans, etc). Over 7500 items, incl extensive collections of original designs by Ogden Codman, Jr (1890s-early 1900s); Arthur Little and Herbert Browne (1890s-1920s); Luther Briggs (1840s-1860s); Arland Dirlam (1930s-1960s), together with important examples of the work of Asher Benjamin, Richard Upjohn, and others. Measured drawings incl extensive holdings of work undertaken by HABS (Historic American Buildings Survey) in Massachusetts in the 1930s, 1940s under director Frank Chouteau Brown. Also represented are several residential and commercial commissions by F C Brown, not connected with HABS. Collection incl architectural pattern books, builders guides, 18th-19th century. Approx 350 volumes, English and American publications.

BENNET, SEN. WALLACE

UT —UNIVERSITY OF UTAH, Marriott Library, Special Collections, Salt Lake City, 84112. Gregory C Thompson, Cur
Holdings: Cat Mss Microfilm Film Oral History
Notes: Papers.

BENNETT, ARNOLD, 1867-1931

CA —UNIVERSITY OF CALIFORNIA, LOS ANGELES, Research Library, Dept of Special Collections, 405 Hilgard Ave, Los Angeles, 90024. Edward Shreeves, Chairman, Bibliographers Group; David S Zeidberg, Head
Holdings: Vols 125 Cat Mss
Notes: 125 first and other editions of his books; 20 letters; 8 mss.

NY —HOFSTRA UNIVERSITY, Library, 1000 Fulton Ave, Hempstead, 11550. Charles R Andrews, Dean of Library Services
Notes: Strong collection. Incl some mss.

OH —OHIO UNIVERSITY, Vernon R Alden Library, Department of Archives and Special Collections, Athens, 45701. Gary A Hunt, Head
Holdings: Vols 158 Cat
Notes: A comprehensive collection of first and other important editions.

BENNETT, G. C.

NM —MUSEUM OF NEW MEXICO, Photo Archives, Box 2087, Santa Fe, 87503. Arthur L Olivas, Cur; Richard Rudisill, Photo Historian
Holdings: Cat Pix Slides
Notes: Extensive collection of his work.

BENNETT, HAL

MA —BOSTON UNIVERSITY, Mugar Memorial Library, Special Collections Dept, 771 Commonwealth Ave, Boston, 02215. Howard B Gotlieb, Dir
Holdings: Cat Mss

BENNETT, JACK

MA —BOSTON UNIVERSITY, Mugar Memorial Library, Special Collections Dept, 771 Commonwealth Ave, Boston, 02215. Howard B Gotlieb, Dir
Holdings: Cat Mss

BENNETT, JOHN, 1938-

RI —BROWN UNIVERSITY, John Hay Library, 20 Prospect St, Providence, 02912. Mark N Brown, Cur Mss
Holdings: Vols 83 Mss
Notes: Records of the Vagabond Press, containing approximately 3000 items. Vagabond magazine, chapbooks, etc, were published and edited, 1965-80, by John Bennett (1938-).

BENNETT, JOHN M., 1942-

MO —WASHINGTON UNIVERSITY, Libraries, Special Collections Dept, Campus Box 1061, St Louis, 63130.
Notes: A major collection, incl mss, correspondence, literary papers, photographs, etc. Described in *Special Collections: an Annotated Guide to the Holdings of the Manuscript Division and the University Archives and Research Collection.*

BENNY, JACK, 1894-1974

CA —UNIVERSITY OF CALIFORNIA, LOS ANGELES, Research Library, Dept of Special Collections, 405 Hilgard Ave, Los Angeles, 90024. Edward Shreeves, Chairman, Bibliographers Group; David S Zeidberg, Head
Holdings: Mss Pix Phonorecords Films
Notes: 39 linear feet of scripts, mss, and ephemera, incl recordings, films, and 6000 photographs. Business and personal records, 1935-1955, are sealed until 1988. No photocopying.

BENNY, JACK, RADIO SHOW

WA —GONZAGA UNIVERSITY, Crosby Library, East 502 Boone Ave, Spokane, 99258. Robert Burr, Dir
Notes: Books, records, memorabilia and papers, incl Jack Benny Radio Show scripts.

BENSON, ARTHUR CHRISTOPHER, 1862-1925

CA —UNIVERSITY OF CALIFORNIA, LOS ANGELES, Research Library, Dept of Special Collections, 405 Hilgard Ave, Los Angeles, 90024. Edward Shreeves, Chairman, Bibliographers Group; David S Zeidberg, Head
Holdings: Vols 50 Cat Mss
Notes: 50 first and other editions of his books; 50 letters, mss, and typescripts.

NY —HOFSTRA UNIVERSITY, Library, 1000 Fulton Ave, Hempstead, 11550. Charles R Andrews, Dean of Library Services

BENSON, EDWARD FREDERIC, 1867-1940

CA —UNIVERSITY OF CALIFORNIA, LOS ANGELES, Research Library, Dept of Special Collections, 405 Hilgard Ave, Los Angeles, 90024. Edward Shreeves, Chairman, Bibliographers Group; David S Zeidberg, Head
Holdings: Vols 100 Mss
Notes: 100 first and other editions of his books; holograph drafts of three novels and 95 stories.

NY —HOFSTRA UNIVERSITY, Library, 1000 Fulton Ave, Hempstead, 11550. Charles R Andrews, Dean of Library Services

BENSON, FRANK

MA —ESSEX INSTITUTE, James Duncan Phillips Library, 132-34 Essex St, Salem, 01970. Prudence K Backman, Manuscript Librn
Holdings: Mss
Notes: Papers of Essex County artist.

BENSON, JOHN HOWARD, 1901-1956

IL —NEWBERRY LIBRARY, 60 W Walton St, Chicago, 60610. Diana Haskell, Cur of Modern Mss
Holdings: Cat Mss
Notes: His correspondence with Herman Cohen concerning editions of Arrighi's *L'Operina* (1522) and Palatino's *The Instruments of Writing* (1540). The collection includes engraved slates.

BENSON, ROBERT HUGH

NY —HOFSTRA UNIVERSITY, Library, 1000 Fulton Ave, Hempstead, 11550. Charles R Andrews, Dean of Library Services
Notes: Strong collection. Incl some mss.

BENT, WILLIAM

CO —DENVER PUBLIC LIBRARY, 1357 Broadway, Denver, 80203.
Notes: Correspondence, papers, pictures, diaries, etc.

BENTINCK, WILLIAM

WI —UNIVERSITY OF WISCONSIN, MADISON, Memorial Library, South Asian Collection, 728 State St, Madison, 53706. Jack C Wells, Bibliographer
Holdings: Cat Microforms
Notes: Public and private papers as Governor of Madras, India.

BENTLEY, ARTHUR FISHER, 1870-1957

IN —INDIANA UNIVERSITY, Lilly Library, Seventh St, Bloomington, 47405. William R

BENTLEY, ARTHUR FISHER, 1870-1957 (cont.)

Cagle, Librn
Holdings: // Mss
Notes: Writings, 1891-1956 and correspondence, 1896-1952, of Arthur Fisher Bentley. 8586 items; gift of AFB, 1953. Fully cataloged and accessible through ms card catalog. Correspondence of Bentley with friends; and correspondence of his widow Imogene (Shaw) Bentley after AFB's death, 1876-1969. 6188 items; uncataloged; gift of Mrs Bentley, 1972.

BENTLEY, NICOLAS

DC —GEORGETOWN UNIVERSITY, Library, Special Collections Div, 37 & O Sts NW, Washington, 20057. George M Barringer, Special Collections Librn; Nicholas B Sheetz, Mss Librn
Holdings: Mss Cat
Notes: The literary papers of author and art curator, James Laver (1899-1975), and those of his wife, the actress Veronica Turleigh; consisting of letters, with a considerable number written by Lady Cnythia Asquith; Clifford Box; Enid Bagnold; Nicholas Bentley; Violet Clifton; Desmond MacCarthy; Sir Edward Marsh; Sir Francis Meynell; Kate O'Brien; Dorothy L Sayers; Andre Simon; Enid Starkie; A J A Symons; Angela Thirkell; and Alec Waugh.

BENTLEY, RICHARD, PUBLISHERS (LONDON)

CA —UNIVERSITY OF CALIFORNIA, LOS ANGELES, Research Library, Dept of Special Collections, 405 Hilgard Ave, Los Angeles, 90024. Edward Shreeves, Chairman, Bibliographers Group; David S Zeidberg, Head
Holdings: Cat Mss
Notes: 8 linear feet of correspondence, records, mss, and publications, 1829-1898, incl a run of Bentley's *List of the Principal* Publications.

BENTLEY, WILLIAM

PA —ALLEGHENY COLLEGE, Lawrence Lee Pelletier Library, Meadville, 16335. Margaret L Moser, Librn
Holdings: Vols 1746 Cat
Notes: Part of the original gift to this library, listed in *Catalogus Bibliothecae Collegii* Alleghaniensis, by Timothy Alden, 1823. Downs 180.

BEOWULF

GA —EMORY UNIVERSITY, Robert W Woodruff Library, Atlanta, 30322. Herbert Johnson, Dir
Holdings: Cat Mss
Notes: The extensive personal library of Kemp Malone (1889-1971), a leading authority on Old English; incl 66 editions of Beowulf.

BERBERS

NV —UNIVERSITY OF NEVADA, RENO, Noble H Getchell Library, Reno, 89557. William A Douglass, Coordinator
Holdings: Vols (15,000)
Notes: America's largest collection of Basque materials, both retrospective and current. Semi-annual *Newsletter.*

BERCKMAN, EVELYN

MA —BOSTON UNIVERSITY, Mugar Memorial Library, Special Collections Dept, 771 Commonwealth Ave, Boston, 02215. Howard B Gotlieb, Dir
Holdings: Cat Mss
Notes: Mss, correspondence, etc collected in depth; incl publications by or about.

BERENSON, BERNARD

MA —HARVARD UNIVERSITY, Harvard College Library, Fine Arts Library, Fogg Museum, 32 Quincy St, Cambridge, 02138. Wolfgang M Freitag, Librn
Holdings: Vols (202,000) Cat Mss Pix Slides
Budget: ($176,500)
Notes: All areas of art history, with emphasis on Italian primitives, Italian Renaissance, master drawings, Romanesque sculpture, architectural history, ms materials (particulary American artists'), conservation and restoration of art objects. Incl the Berenson repertory of photographs from the Harvard Center for Italian Renaissance Studies in Florence, and the Decimal Index to the Art of the Low Countries. Separate card catalogs for books, photographs and lantern slides, registers for ms holdings which are not incl in *National Union Catalog of Manuscript Collections.* Slides total over 230,000; over 745,000 pictures. *Fine Arts Library Catalogue* (14 volumes) and *Catalogue of Auction Sales Catalogues* (1 volume) (Boston: G K Hall, 1972); *A Guide to the Fine Arts Library* (Cambridge, Mass: 1971); *Guide to the Harvard Libraries,* microfiche edition of holdingscataloged through 1981 published 1984 (Munich/New York: Saur).

BERG, ALBAN

DC —LIBRARY OF CONGRESS, Music Division, Washington, 20540.
Notes: Papers and recordings of composer Arnold Schoenberg. Extensive correspondence with other composers, writers, etc.

†NY —SYRACUSE UNIVERSITY LIBRARIES, Ernest S Bird Library, Syracuse, 13210.
Notes: Louis Krasner Collection, with original scores by classic composers, also an original death mask of Alban Berg made by Anna Mahler.

BERG, ERNST JULIUS

NY —UNION COLLEGE, Schaffer Library, Archives of Science and Technology, Schenectady, 12308. Ellen Fladger, Archivist
Notes: Papers etc.

BERGEN, EDGAR

CA —UNIVERSITY OF SOUTHERN CALIFORNIA, Edward L Doheny Memorial Library, Archives of Performing Arts, University Park, Los Angeles, 90089. Robert Knutson, Librn
Holdings: Mss Pix
Notes: Personal collection of papers, pictures, etc.

BERGER, THOMAS

MA —BOSTON UNIVERSITY, Mugar Memorial Library, Special Collections Dept, 771 Commonwealth Ave, Boston, 02215. Howard B Gotlieb, Dir
Holdings: Cat Mss
Notes: Mss, correspondence, etc collected in depth; incl publications by or about.

VA —UNIVERSITY OF VIRGINIA, Alderman Library, Clifton Waller Barrett Collection, Charlottesville, 22901. Joan St C Crane, Cur of American Literature Collections
Notes: Papers.

BERGERY, GASTON

CA —HOOVER INSTITUTION ON WAR, REVOLUTION & PEACE, Stanford University, Stanford, 94305. Milorad M Drachkovitch, Archivist
Holdings: Mss
Notes: Papers of Gaston Bergery, French attorney, diplomat, author, journalist, politician, with service as Secretary-General for the Inter-Allied Commission for Reparations, 1918-1924, Director of the Cabinet of the Ministry of Foreign Affairs, 1924-25, and French Ambassador to Moscow, 1941, incl correspondence, telegrams, reports, memoranda, lists, speeches and writings, posters, leaflets, and other material, 1924-1973, relating to his government service in France and broad, his literary and legal careers, French political events and foreign relations, France during World War II, and his activities in the Fron Populaire. Primarily in French. 28 ms boxes.

BERGQUIST, LAURA

MA —BOSTON UNIVERSITY, Mugar Memorial Library, Special Collections Dept, 771 Commonwealth Ave, Boston, 02215. Howard B Gotlieb, Dir
Holdings: Mss

BERING SEA

NY —EXPLORERS CLUB, James B Ford Memorial Library, 46 E 70 St, New York, 10021. Janet Baldwin, Librn
Notes: Ted Banks Collection was begun by Prof Harley H Bartlett, bequeathed to American Institute for Exploration, with additions by Prof Ted Bank II, and subsequently acquired by the Explorers Club. Incl field notes, diaries, and photographs of Bank, who led more than 30 scientific expeditions to the Arctic, Aleutians, Sea of Okhotsk, Japan, Taiwan, Southeast Asia and Africa.

BERING SEA CONTROVERSY

NY —AMERICAN MUSEUM OF NATURAL HISTORY, Library Services Dept, Central Park W & 79th St, New York, 10024. Nina J Root, Chairwoman; Mary Genett, Asst Librn for Reference Services

TX —SOUTHERN METHODIST UNIVERSITY, DeGolyer Library, Box 396, SMU, Dallas, 75275. Clifton H Jones, Dir
Holdings: Vols (80,000) Cat Mss Maps Pix Slides Microforms
Notes: First editions of prominent authors; also of books in subject emphasis collections. All subjects listed in the vol are strong. Numerous collections of personal papers relating to subjects also.

BERKELEY, GEORGE

CT —YALE UNIVERSITY, Box 1603A, Yale Station, New Haven, 06520.
Holdings: Mss

BERKELEY FAMILY

VA —UNIVERSITY OF VIRGINIA, Alderman Library, Manuscripts Dept, Charlottesville, 22901. Edmund Berkeley Jr, Cur
Holdings: Cat Mss Maps Pix
Notes: 19th century Virginia Family Papers Collections enable a researcher to obtain an excellant picture of the economic and social interactions on large plantations in Virginia during the 19th century. They are invaluable as research sources in the study of slavery, women's history, economic history, agrarian and political history.

BERKOWITZ, DAVID

†NY —COLUMBIA UNIVERSITY LIBRARIES, Butler Library, Rare Book and Manuscript Library, 535 W 114 St, New York, 10027.
Notes: The Papers of Dr David Abrahamsen, incl letters and mss. Contains letters from and interviews with family and friends of Richard M Nixon and 167 typed and handwritten letters sent by David Berkowitz to Dr Abrahamsen from Attica Prison during 1979-81.

BERKSHIRE MUSIC FESTIVAL

MA —LENOX LIBRARY ASSOCIATION, Main St, Lenox, 01240. Denis J Lesieur, Dir
Holdings: Mss Pix
Notes: Repository for the official records of the Berkshire Music Festival, located in Lenox, Mass, ca 1934- (11 linear feet).

BERKSON, WILLIAM

CT —UNIVERSITY OF CONNECTICUT, Library, Storrs, 06268. George F Butterick,

BERKSON, WILLIAM (cont.)

Cur of Literary Archives
Holdings: Mss
Notes: Repository for his papers.

BERLIN, IRVING

IN —INDIANA UNIVERSITY, Lilly Library, Seventh St, Bloomington, 47405. William R Cagle, Librn
Holdings: / / Uncat
Notes: In the Starr Collection of American Sheet Music.

BERLIN SAMOAN CONFERENCE

DE —UNIVERSITY OF DELAWARE, Hugh M Morris Library, S College Ave, Newark, 19711. T Stuart Dick, Special Collections
Holdings: Cat Mss Pix
Notes: The George Handy Bates Samoan Papers (about 400 items). Calendared mss Berlin Samoan Conference Papers. Downs 5382.

BERLINER, EMILE

DC —LIBRARY OF CONGRESS, Motion Pictures, Broadcasting and Recorded Sound Div, Washington, 20540.
Notes: Recordings, photographs, correspondence, scrapbooks and other memorabilia concerning the invention of the lateral cut disc gramophone record, basis of the modern recording industry, Emile Berliner (1851-1929). Devised word "Gramophone," and invented acoustic tiling.

BERLINER GRAMOPHONE RECORDS

DC —LIBRARY OF CONGRESS, Motion Pictures, Broadcasting and Recorded Sound Div, Washington, 20540.
Holdings: Cat
Notes: 133 Berliner Gramophone Co records, 1896-1900; 31 Zonophone records, 1899-1904; 2 rare Vitaphone records, 1899; 67 Eldridge R Johnson records, 1900-1901; and 30 Victor Talking Machine Co records, 1902-1909.

BERLIOZ, HECTOR

NY —COLUMBIA UNIVERSITY LIBRARIES, Rare Book & Manuscript Library, 801 Butler Library, 535 W 114 St, New York, 10027. Kenneth A Lohf, Librn
Holdings: Vols 400 Cat Mss Pix
Notes: Incl 31,000 items. Books about his time and correspondence, mss and printed ephemera relating to Berlioz and 19th century art and literature. Restricted use.

BERMANT, CHAIM

MA —BOSTON UNIVERSITY, Mugar Memorial Library, Special Collections Dept, 771 Commonwealth Ave, Boston, 02215. Howard B Gotlieb, Dir
Holdings: Cat Mss
Notes: Mss, correspondence, etc collected in depth; incl publications by or about.

BERNARD, CLAUDE

†MA —FRANCIS A COUNTWAY LIBRARY OF MEDICINE, Boston, 02115.
VA —MARY WASHINGTON COLLEGE, E Lee Trinkle Library, Fredericksburg, 22401. Ruby Y Weinbrecht, Librn
Holdings: Vols 42 Cat

BERNARD OF CLAIRVAUX, ST.

CT —YALE UNIVERSITY, Box 1603A, Yale Station, New Haven, 06520.
Holdings: Cat Mss
Notes: A collection of 65 items by him and others ofhis order, relating to all aspects of the Cistercian Rule, incl four manuscripts, 21 incunabula, and 40 other books printed before 1665.
MI —WESTERN MICHIGAN UNIVERSITY, Dwight B Waldo Library, Institute of Cistercian Studies Library, Kalamazoo, 49008. Beatrice H Beck, Librn
Notes: Collection contains mss and early editions of Cistercian liturgy and authors, especially Bernard of Clairvaux. Ms sources of Cistercian documentary history, abbey histories and charters.

BERNAYS, EDWARD

DC —LIBRARY OF CONGRESS, Manuscript Division, Washington, 20540. John C Broderick, Chief
Holdings: Cat Mss Pix
Notes: Mss, papers, records, etc.

BERNDT, WALTER

OH —OHIO STATE UNIVERSITY, Library for Communication and Graphic Arts, 242 W 18th St, Columbus, 43210. Lucy S Caswell, Curator
Notes: Original cartoons by Winsor McCay, John T McCutcheon, Dick Moores, Ned White, Walter Berndt, Jim Larrick, Carl Rose and Bill Crawford.

BERNFELD, SIEGFRIED, 1892-1953

DC —LIBRARY OF CONGRESS, Manuscript Division, Washington, 20540. John C Broderick, Chief
Holdings: Cat Mss
Notes: The papers of Siegfried Bernfeld, one of Freud's pupils and associates.

BERNSTEIN, DAVID

NY —STATE UNIVERSITY OF NEW YORK, BINGHAMTON, Glenn G Bartle Library, Binghamton, 13901. Marion Hanscom, Special Collections Librn
Notes: Papers, correspondence, etc of the Washington, DC speech writer and journalist.

BERNSTEIN, KARL

NY —NEW YORK PUBLIC LIBRARY, Performing Arts Research Center, Billy Rose Theatre Collection, 111 Amsterdam Ave, New York, 10023. Dorothy L Swerdlove, Cur
Holdings: Cat
See also entry under Theatre - History.

BERNSTEIN, LEONARD

DC —LIBRARY OF CONGRESS, Music Division, Washington, 20540.
Notes: Music mss.

BERNSTEIN, PHILIP

NY —UNIVERSITY OF ROCHESTER, Rush Rhees Library, Department of Rare Books and Special Collections, Rochester, 14627. Peter Dzwonkoski, Librn
Holdings: Vols Mss
Notes: Correspondence, drafts of sermons, speeches and other records that relate to Bernstein's career as a rabbi of Temple Brith Kodesh (Rochester, NY), as head of the Committee on Army and Navy Religious Activities of the National Jewish Welfare Board during World War II, as the advisor on Jewish Affairs to the US Army Commanders in Europe following the War, as President of the Central Conference of American Rabbis, and as Chairman of the American Israel Public Affairs Committee.

BEROUHI LANGUAGE see Brahui Language

BERRIGAN, DANIEL AND PHILIP

NY —CORNELL UNIVERSITY LIBRARIES, John M Olin Library, Dept of Rare Books, Ithaca, 14853. Donald D Eddy, Librn
Holdings: Cat Mss Pix
Notes: Incl newspaper clippings.

BERRY, BURTON YOST, 1901-

IN —INDIANA UNIVERSITY, Lilly Library, Seventh St, Bloomington, 47405. William R Cagle, Librn
Holdings: Mss Pix
Notes: Papers of diplomat Burton Yost Berry, 1925-1971. Incl correspondence; diaries; newspaper clippings, photographs, diplomatic reports, etc 6381 items.

BERRY, CHARLES WALTER

IL —ILLINOIS STATE UNIVERSITY, Milner Library, Dept of Special Collections, Normal, 61761. Robert Sokan, Librn
Holdings: Vols 210 Cat Mss Pix
Notes: The Lucas collection contains 4 vols of correspondence between Lucas and his childhood friend, Charles Walter Berry; three volumes of holograph mss, and 29 vols of ephemera, eg, printed poems for special occasions, incribed dinner menus, short, humorous notes, etc.

BERRYMAN, CLIFFORD

DC —GEORGE WASHINGTON UNIVERSITY, Gelman Library, 2130 H St NW, Washington, 20052.
Holdings: Uncat Pix
Notes: Original drawings of editorial and political cartoons by Clifford Berryman, covering the period of ca 1892-1949. Berryman was cartoonist for the Washington *Post* from 1896-1908 and then for the Washington *Star* from 1908 until his death in 1949. Library also holds cartoons of George Y Coffin (qv).

BERRYMAN, JOHN, 1914-1972

MN —UNIVERSITY OF MINNESOTA, O Meredith Wilson Library, 309 19 Ave S, Minneapolis, 55455. Austin J McLean, Chief, Special Collections
Notes: Extensive Mss collection incl numerous plays in varying states of completion never published and a voluminous amount of material on Shakespeare, also unpublished, as well as correspondence from 20th-century American and English writers.
MO —WASHINGTON UNIVERSITY, Libraries, Special Collections Dept, Campus Box 1061, St Louis, 63130.
Notes: A small but significant collection.
NV —UNIVERSITY OF NEVADA, RENO, University Library, Special Collections Dept, Reno, 89557. Robert E Blesse, Head
Holdings: Vols (24) Cat Other appearances 250 Cat
Notes: Includes individual works by author in all editions including translations; also prefaces, introductions, published correspondence, appearances in anthologies, periodicals, etc. Bibliographical research collection, part of Modern Authors Collection.
†NY —COLUMBIA UNIVERSITY LIBRARIES, Butler Library, Rare Book and Manuscript Library, 535 W 114 St, New York, 10027.
Notes: John Berryman Collection.

BERTHIER, LOUIS ALEXANDRE, 1752-1815

NJ —PRINCETON UNIVERSITY, Library, Manuscript Collection, Nassau St, Princeton, 08540. Jean F Preston, Cur
Holdings: Vols 24 Cat Mss Maps
Notes: About 100 of the French cartographer Louis Alexandre Berthier's maps and associated papers involving French campaigns in the Revolutionary War form the manuscript section of the collection. See *Princeton University Library Chronicle,* v 1, no 1, p 3-8. An unpublished guide (25p) of the manuscripts and map section of the collection is available for consultation. See *The American Campaigns of Rochambeau's* Army, ed by Howard C Rice, Jr and Anne S K Brown (Princeton, 1972).

BERTON, PIERRE, 1920-

ON —MCMASTER UNIVERSITY, Mills Memorial Library, Div of Archives &

BERTON, PIERRE, 1920- (cont.)

Research Collections, Hamilton, L8S 4L6, Can. G R Hill, Univ Librn
Holdings: / / Mss
Notes: Pierre Berton's mss and research files. Collection partially described in *Library Research News*, vol 2, no 5, May 1974.

BERWALD, WILLIAM HENRY

NY —SYRACUSE UNIVERSITY LIBRARIES, Ernest S Bird Library, George Arents Research Library for Special Collections, Syracuse, 13210. Carolyn A Davis, Manuscripts Librn; Amy S Doherty, University Archivist; Mark F Weimer, Rare Book Librn
Notes: American Music Collection. Papers of Ernst Bacon, Louis Krasner, Franklin Morris, William Henry Berwald, Earl George, and Arthur Polster.

BERYLLIUM

OH —BRUSH WELLMAN, Technical Library, 17876 Saint Clair Ave, Cleveland, 44110. Nancie Skonezny, Tech Librn
Holdings: Vols 1000 Cat
Notes: Beryllium technology--its metals, alloys and ceramics. Incl approx 5000 uncat government documents and international technical reports.

PA —CABOT CORPORATION, Reading Technology Library, PO Box 1296, Reading, 19603. Pamela L Hehr, Librn
Holdings: Vols (3800) Cat Mss Slides Microforms
Notes: Copper-beryllium and special metals and alloys. Incl 2100 patents, 9000 reports and articles.

BESANT, ANNIE

CA —SAN DIEGO PUBLIC LIBRARY, Literature & Language Sect, 820 E St, San Diego, 92101. Alyce Archuleta, Senior Librn
Holdings: Vols (140) Cat

BEST BOOKS see Bibliography—Best Books

BEST SELLERS

MA —BRANDEIS UNIVERSITY, Goldfarb Library, 415 South St, Waltham, 02154. Bessie Hahn, Dir
Notes: The American Best Sellers Collection consists of 48 linear feet of the top ten annual best sellers of popular literature from 1900-1975. Access to this collection is through the Main Card Catalog and Special Collections Catalog.

NY —GRADUATE CENTER OF THE CITY UNIVERSITY OF NEW YORK, William H and Gwynne K Crouse Library for Publishing Arts, 33 W 42 St, New York, 10036. Alfred H Lane, Dir
Notes: Recently established and still growing, but intended to become the authoritative source of materials in the field, of particular value in research about the publishing industry. Open to staff members of publishing houses, students, scholars, authors, printers, and booksellers. Primarily 20th century materials, and particularly useful for research on technical, financial, and historical matters. Much on the history of individual houses, economics of authorship; marketing and distribution of books; etc.

VA —UNIVERSITY OF VIRGINIA, Alderman Library, Rare Book Dept, Charlottesville, 22901. Julius P Barclay, Cur
Holdings: Vols 1200 / / Cat
Notes: The Mrs Robert Coleman Taylor Collection of First Editions of American Best Sellers (Fiction). Almost without exception, these books are in mint and fine condition. Scope: 1752-1949. Incl very rare early American fiction.

BESTON, HENRY, 1888-1968

ME —BOWDOIN COLLEGE, Library, Brunswick, 04011. Dianne M Gutscher, Cur of Special Collections
Holdings: Vols 150 Cat Mss Pix Clippings
Notes: Incl books and manuscripts by Elizabeth Coatsworth Beston.

BESTON FAMILY PAPERS

ME —BOWDOIN COLLEGE, Library, Brunswick, 04011. Dianne M Gutscher, Cur of Special Collections
Holdings: Mss Pix
Notes: Beston Family Papers. The Beston Collection contains printed works, mss (10, 000), correspondence and ephemera relating to the late Henry Beston and his wife Elzabeth Coatsworth Beston of Chimney Farm, Nobleboro, Maine. Mrs Beston is a widely known author of children's books.

BESTOR, ARTHUR

IL —UNIVERSITY OF ILLINOIS, URBANA/CHAMPAIGN, Library, University Archives, 19 Library, 1408 W Gregory Drive, Urbana, 61801. Maynard Brichford, University Archivist
Holdings: Cat Mss Maps Pix Slides Microforms
Notes: Papers, archival records, etc.

BETA RAYS

TX —RICE UNIVERSITY, Fondren Library, 6100 S Main St, PO Box 1892, Houston, 77251. Dr Samuel M Carrington, Jr, University Librn
Holdings: Mss Pix
Notes: Papers of Fred Terry Rogers (1931-1956; 9 linear ft); incl researches in Beta ray spectrography.

BETATRON

IL —UNIVERSITY OF ILLINOIS, URBANA/CHAMPAIGN, Library, University Archives, 19 Library, 1408 W Gregory Drive, Urbana, 61801. Maynard Brichford, University Archivist
Holdings: Mss
Notes: Papers of Donald W Kerst, incl correspondence on the betatron, 1943-1952.

BETHE, HANS

DC —LIBRARY OF CONGRESS, Manuscript Division, Washington, 20540. John C Broderick, Chief
Notes: Correspondence in the J Robert Oppenheimer Collection.

NY —CORNELL UNIVERSITY LIBRARIES, Collection of Regional History, Dept of Manuscripts and Univ Archives, Ithaca, 14853.
Notes: Physicist, professor of physics. Incl papers, 1935-42; calculations, notes, professional correspondence, related reports and printed matter. Restricted.

BETHUNE, MARY MCLEOD

LA —AMISTAD RESEARCH CENTER, 400 Esplanade Ave, New Orleans, 70116. Clifton H Johnson, Exec Dir; Florence E Borders, Senior Archivist
Holdings: Vols (10,000) Cat Mss Pix Audiotapes Microforms
Budget: ($315,000)
Notes: In addition 8,000,000 ms pieces, 10, 000 pictures, 3500 microforms, and 500 audiotapes. Amistad Research Center is an historical research library. Originally established at Fisk University, in Nashville, by the American Missionary Association (AMA), this research center on Black American History consists of mss, photographs, clippings, books, pamphlets, taped speeches, and interviews; also, the papers of such leaders as W E B DuBois, Countee Cullen, and Mary McLeod Bethune. Also materials on other American minorities, such as Native Americans, Asian Americans, Hispanics, etc.

BETHUNE, NORMAN

GA —EMORY UNIVERSITY, Robert W Woodruff Library, Atlanta, 30322. Herbert Johnson, Dir
Holdings: Mss Pix Cat
Notes: The Philip J Jaffe Papers and books about communism and the Communist Party in the US, incl copies of rare magazines, private mss, the papers of such controversial figures as Anna Louise Strong, Agnes Smedley, Norman Bethune and Koji Ariyoshi, and documentation of the growth of Chinese communism. 36 linear ft mss.

BETJEMAN, SIR JOHN

DC —GEORGETOWN UNIVERSITY, Library, Special Collections Div, 37 & O Sts NW, Washington, 20057. George M Barringer, Special Collections Librn; Nicholas B Sheetz, Mss Librn
Holdings: Mss Pix
Notes: The papers of Christopher Sykes, biographer, journalist, and novelist; containing mss, letters, photographs, and drawings. With extensive correspondence from Harold Acton; Angela, Countess of Antrim; Sir John Betjeman; Ivy Compton-Burnett; Alick Dru; T S Eliot; Max Beerbohm; Graham Greene; John Hayward; Lord Patrick Kinross; Compton Mackenzie; Nancy Mitford; Anthony Powell; Dame Flora Robson; Cecil Roth; Sir John Russell; Osbert Sitwell; John Sparrow; Freya Stark; James Stern; and Evelyn Waugh, among others. Also, considerable research material about Evelyn Waugh, Adam von Trott, Robert Byron, Lady Nancy Astor; and the foundation of the state of Israel.

NV —UNIVERSITY OF NEVADA, RENO, University Library, Special Collections Dept, Reno, 89557. Robert E Blesse, Head
Holdings: Vols (140) Cat Other appearance 680 Cat
Notes: Includes individual works by author in all editions including translations; also prefaces, introductions, published correspondence, appearances in anthologies, periodicals, etc. Bibliographical research collection, part of Modern Authors Collection.

BC —UNIVERSITY OF VICTORIA, McPherson Library, Victoria, V8W 3H5, Can.
Notes: Incl 21 meters, 1913-1971. The personal archive of poet laureate, writer and public figure, Sir John Betjeman, covering mainly the years from 1930 on, but incl some notes, sketches, poems, etc from his schooldays, as well as some correspondence and memorabilia from his Oxford years. Consisting largely of correspondence inward: 1926-71 (containing many enclosures, such as photographs, pamphlets, mss, drawings, reports, plans, contracts, scripts, clippings, bills, etc); professional: from publishers, editors, radio and TV producers, etc; public: from literary, arts, preservation and other societies; from religious and civic bodies; from interested individuals, aspiring poets and fans; personal: from a long list of important contemporaries incl many famous in the arts; business: from banks, agents and commercial establishments; family. correspondence outward: drafts orcarbon copies; Poems: mss, published and unpublished; Prose: mss of articles, book reviews, lectures, prefaces, radio broadcasts, etc; proof; notebooks; sketchbooks; diaries (1935-36; 1941-42); desk diaries (1959; 1965-68); account books; miscellanea.

BETON see Concrete

BETTER BUSINESS BUREAU OF METROPOLITAN CHICAGO

IL —CHICAGO HISTORICAL SOCIETY, Library, Clark St at North Ave, Chicago, 60614. Archie Motley, Manuscript Librn
Notes: Business history acquisitions incl the records of the Illinois Manufacturers' Association; customer complaint files of the Better Business Bureau of Metropolitan Chicago; Chicago Board of Underwriters; papers of George S Bowen, Illinois capitalist; and Ernest J Stevens.

BETTER GOVERNMENT ASSOCIATION

IL —CHICAGO HISTORICAL SOCIETY, Library, Clark St at North Ave, Chicago,

BETTER GOVERNMENT ASSOCIATION (cont.)

60614. Archie Motley, Manuscript Librn
Notes: Election and topical files. 30 linear ft.

BETTING see Gambling

BETTS, DORIS

MA —BOSTON UNIVERSITY, Mugar Memorial Library, Special Collections Dept, 771 Commonwealth Ave, Boston, 02215. Howard B Gotlieb, Dir
Holdings: Cat Mss Pix
Notes: Mss, correspondence, etc, collected in depth; incl publications by or about.

BEVERAGES

IN —HURTY-PECK LIBRARY OF BEVERAGE LITERATURE, 5650 W Raymond Street, PO Box 41167, Indianapolis, 46208. Ben Wilson, Librn
Holdings: Vols (6000) Cat //
Notes: The most comprehensive collection, in English, in the world on beverages of all types. History, manufacture, formulae, customs. Books on beer and brewing; cocoa and chocolate; coffee; liquors and spirits; soft drinks; tea; and wine.

NY —CULINARY INSTITUTE OF AMERICA, Katharine Angell Library, North Rd, Hyde Park, 12538. Gertrude Trani, Asst Librn
Holdings: Vols (23,000) Cat Slides Videotapes 16mm Films Filmstrips
Notes: Culinary arts, incl cookery, beverages, and food service management. AV materials housed in separate Learning Resources Center. Henry Woods, Dir.

BEVERIDGE, ALBERT J.

DC —LIBRARY OF CONGRESS, Manuscript Division, Washington, 20540. John C Broderick, Chief
Holdings: Cat Mss Pix
Notes: Mss, papers, records, etc.

BEWICK, THOMAS, 1753-1828

CA —UNIVERSITY OF CALIFORNIA, LOS ANGELES, Research Library, Dept of Special Collections, 405 Hilgard Ave, Los Angeles, 90024. Edward Shreeves, Chairman, Bibliographers Group; David S Zeidberg, Head
Holdings: Vols 125 Cat
Notes: 125 books by and illustrated by Bewick; 16 original woodblocks.

CT —TRINITY COLLEGE LIBRARY, Watkinson Library, 300 Summit St, Hartford, 06106. Jeffrey Kaimowitz, Cur
Notes: Part of ornithology collection.

IL —NEWBERRY LIBRARY, 60 W Walton St, Chicago, 60610. Diana Haskell, Cur of Modern Mss
Holdings: Cat Pix
Notes: Perhaps the largest collection of Bewick blocks (150) in a public collection; mainly birds and quadrupeds. Also some 25 Bewick drawings from from which blocks were engraved. Newberry Library published for the Cherryburn Press a portfolio of 100 prints from the original blocks printed by R Hunter Middleton, with introduction by J M Wells.

KS —UNIVERSITY OF KANSAS, Kenneth Spencer Research Library, Special Collections Dept, Lawrence, 66045. Alexandra Mason, Librn
Notes: In Ellis Collection of Ornithology and Natural History. Especially strong in birds. Noncirculating. Bird books described in Mengel, Robert M, comp. *A Catalogue of the Ellis Collection of Ornithological Books in the University of Kansas Libraries,* Lawrence, Kansas. Volume 1, A-B, 1972. (Univ of Kansas Publications, Library Series, 33); Volume 2, C-D, 1983. (Univ of Kansas Publications, Library Series, 48).

MO —SAINT LOUIS PUBLIC LIBRARY, Gardner Rare Book Room, 1301 Olive St, Saint Louis, 63103. Julanne M Good, Supervisor; Martha Riley, Rare Books Librn
Holdings: Vols Cat Mss
Budget: ($5573)
Notes: Collection of books on wood engraving and book illustration in that medium, including some notable books illustrated by Thomas Bewick, the famous nineteenth century wood engraver. Largely the gift of Leonard Blake, a private collector, although an occasional purchase is made. Noncirculating.

BEXAR ARCHIVES

TX —UNIVERSITY OF TEXAS LIBRARIES, General Libraries, Barker Texas History Center, PO Box P, Austin, 78712. Don Carleton, Dir
Holdings: Vols (132,000) Cat Mss Maps Pix Slides Phonorecords Audiotapes Microforms
Notes: Bexar Archives: records kept by Spanish and Mexican officials in San Antonio, 1717-1836. The collection was transferred to the University of Texas by the Commissioners' Court of Bexar County in 1899. Incl records relating to governmental administration and to all aspects of military, ecclesiastical and civil life in Spanish and Mexican Texas. Over 250,000 ms pages and 4000 printed pages; also, a microfilm edition (172 reels) published by the University of Texas Library, 1967-1971.

BEYER, CLARA M.

MA —RADCLIFFE COLLEGE, Arthur & Elizabeth Schlesinger Library on the History of Women in America, 3 James St, Cambridge, 02138. Patricia Miller King, Dir; Eva Moseley, Cur of Mss
Notes: Incl the audiotapes and transcripts of the Women in the Federal Government Oral History Project, also papers of Clara M Beyer, Martha May Eliot, MD, Elizabeth Holtzman, Jeannette Rankin, Edith Nourse Rogers, and Mary Elizabeth Switzer.

BEYER, WALTER

CA —UNIVERSITY OF CALIFORNIA, LOS ANGELES, Research Library, Dept of Special Collections, 405 Hilgard Ave, Los Angeles, 90024. Edward Shreeves, Chairman, Bibliographers Group; David S Zeidberg, Head
Holdings: Mss Pix
Notes: 23 linear feet of correspondence, ephemera, slides, etc, concerning Walter Beyer's work as an engineer at Paramount Pictures, the development of VistaVision, the Motion Picture Research Council, and Universal Pictures.

BEYLE, MARIE HENRI see Stendhal (Marie Henri Beyle)

BHANG

CA —FITZ HUGH LUDLOW MEMORIAL LIBRARY, PO Box 99346, San Francisco, 94109. Michael R Aldrich, Exec Cur
Holdings: Vols (500) Cat Mss Maps Pix Slides Phonorecords Audiotapes Videotapes
Notes: Collection stored. Important mail inquiries only. No interlibrary lending or telephone queries. Emphasizes historical, literary aspects of cannabis use, as well as sociology, chemistry, pharmacology, botany, legal aspects. Incl complete archives of the California Marijuana Initiative, 1972-74, and many documents from the international marijuana law reform movement. Also incl a sizeable collection of phonograph records, artwork, rolling papers, smoking paraphernalia and research artifacts related to cannabis.

BHATTACHARYA, BHABANI

MA —BOSTON UNIVERSITY, Mugar Memorial Library, Special Collections Dept, 771 Commonwealth Ave, Boston, 02215. Howard B Gotlieb, Dir
Holdings: Cat Mss Pix
Notes: Mss, correspondence, etc collected in depth; incl publications by or about.

BHOTANTA LANGUAGE see Tibetan Language and Literature

BHUTAN

CA —UNIVERSITY OF CALIFORNIA, BERKELEY, University Library, 438 Main Library, Berkeley, 94720. Kenneth R Logan, South Asia Librn
Notes: South Asia collection (India, Pakistan, Bangladesh, Nepal, Sri Lanka) contain 150,000-200,000 titles. Covers at research level the social sciences and humanities in western languages and 20 South Asian languages. Subject areas: history, political science, lanugage and literature (especially strong in Hindi, Urdu, Tamil, Sanskrit and Nepali), art and art history, sociology, education, music, environmental design, philosophy and religion, anthropology, geography, national and local government publications. Formats: monographs, periodicals, newspapers, microforms, maps, sound recordings, videotapes, pamphlets. Special strengths: modern Hindi literature; history of South Asian countries; government publications of India, late 19th and 20th centuries. Member of South Asia Microform Project; Participant in Library of Congress AcquisitionsPrograms for India, Pakistan, Nepal, and Bangladesh.

MI —UNIVERSITY OF MICHIGAN, Graduate Library, South Asian Dept, Ann Arbor, 48109. Om P Sharma, Librn
Holdings: Vols (365,000) Cat Maps Slides Microforms
Notes: The major emphasis is on social sciences and humanities. Besides materials in classical languages, South Asian vernaculars being retained are Hindi, Bengali, Urdu, Marathi and Tamil; strong in classical languages, especially Sanskrit, Pali, and Prakrit.

BHUTAN LANGUAGE see Tibetan Language and Literature

BIBAUD, MAXIMILIEN, 1824-1887

PQ —CONCORDIA UNIVERSITY LIBRARIES, 1455 de Maisonneuve Blvd W, Montreal, H3G 1M8, Can. Martin Cohen, Special Collections Librn
Holdings: Vols 60 // Cat Mss
Notes: The Maximilien Bibaud Collection contains the author's memoirs and correspondence as well as his writing on diverse subjects such as religion, theology, Canadian, European and ancient history, and the French language. 51 vols of ms material.

BIBB, HENRY

ON —CHATHAM PUBLIC LIBRARY, 120 Queen St, Chatham, N7M 2G6, Can. Arlene Mason, Head of Reference
Holdings: Vols 20 Cat
Notes: Books, pamphlets, and articles on Henry Bibb, William King, Martin Delaney, and John Brown and their work in the Chatham, Ont region.

BIBBENS FAMILY

NY —CORNELL UNIVERSITY LIBRARIES, Collection of Regional History, Dept of Manuscripts and Univ Archives, Ithaca, 14853.
Holdings: Microforms
Notes: Bibbens Family of Weedsport, NY. Incl papers, 1766-1961; one diary incl genealogical data and obituaries; Bible records of births, deaths, and marriages of Bibbens and related families.

BIBLE

CA —BIOLA UNIVERSITY, Rose Memorial Library, 13800 Biola Ave, La Mirada, 90639. A Lawrence Marshburn
Holdings: Vols (178,000) Cat Maps Pix Microforms
Budget: ($430,000)
Notes: Biblical and evangelical materials.

BIBLE (cont.)

CA —LOS ANGELES PUBLIC LIBRARY, Philosophy & Religion Dept, 630 W Fifth St, Los Angeles, 90071. Marilyn C Wherley, Librn
Holdings: Vols 6900 Cat Includes long runs of periodicals, some on microfilm
Budget: ($60,000)
Notes: Comprehensive collection of English versions of the Bible and related materials, and reference works, such as commentaries, dictionaries, atlases, concordances etc.

CT —YALE UNIVERSITY, Box 1603A, Yale Station, New Haven, 06520.

DC —LIBRARY OF CONGRESS, African and Middle Eastern Division, Washington, 20540.
Holdings: Cat Mss Microforms
Notes: Hebraica: about 109,000 vols in Hebrew, Yiddish, Judeo-Arabic, Judeo-Persian, Ladino, Syriac, Ethiopic; espec strong in Biblical subjects, responsa literature, and socio-political aspects.

FL —UNIVERSITY OF FLORIDA LIBRARY, Isser and Rae Price Library of Judaica, 18 Libr East, Gainesville, 32611. Robert Singerman, Head Librn
Budget: ($30,000)
Notes: Total holdings estimated at 55,000 vols dealing with the political, social, economic and intellectual history of the Jews in the ancient, medieval and modern periods and in all geographic areas. The following areas are especially well represented by printed matter in all relevant languages: Bibliography, Festschriften, History, Bible, Judaism and Jewish theology, liturgy, responsa, rabbinical literature, Jewish law, Hebrew language and literature, Yiddish language and literature, anti-semitism, Zionism, Palestine and the *Yishuv*, and the State of Israel. German and American Judaica form a collecting emphasis with holdings for all the standard histories as well as histories of individual synagogues, institutions and local communities. Works in Hebrew and Yiddish comprise about 60 percent of the collection (estimated 30,000 vols). With few exceptions, holdingsare limited to nineteenth and twentieth century imprints, with complete sets of journals and thousands of ephemeral pamphlets, many of them commemorating anniversaries, enhancing the research value of the collection, the largest Judaica research library in the southeastern United States. Only about half of the collection is cataloged; the collection is a circulating one and vols may be borrowed on interlibrary loan. Incl the Leonard C Mishkin Collection (40,000 vols), the largest personal Judaica collection in the United States, the Shlomo Marenof Collection (3500 vols), and the inventory of Bernard Morgenstern's Lower East Side Book Store (8000 vols). Scholars should inquire in advance of their visit. *The Isser and Rae Price Library of Judaica* Report (circulation 2900 copies) is mailed gratis twice a year to all interested parties. Special catalogs:Pre-1881 Hebrew imprints recorded in a chronological card file.

KS —SAINT MARY COLLEGE, Library, Leavenworth, 66048. Therese Deplazes, Special Collections Librn
Holdings: Vols 2000 Cat Mss Pix
Notes: The Sir John J and Mary Craig Collection of Holy Scripture shows how the Bible looked in the hands of the people through twenty centuries. In the Craig Collection and the general collection are originals and facsimiles of complete Bibles and parts of Holy Scripture, from Torah to modern exegesis, incl ms leaves, antiphonals, scrolls, codices, incunabula, early and later printed books, and bound periodicals, in ninety languages, thirty of which are languages of North and South American Indians.

MD —JOHNS HOPKINS UNIVERSITY, Milton S Eisenhower Library, George Peabody Collection, 17 E Mt Vernon Place, Baltimore, 21201. Lyn Hart, Peabody Librn
Holdings: Vols 2000

MA —HARVARD UNIVERSITY, Harvard Divinity School, Andover-Harvard Theological Library, 45 Francis Ave, Cambridge, 02138. Maria Grossmann, Librn
Holdings: Vols (370,000) Vols

MA —NEW ENGLAND QUAKER RESEARCH LIBRARY, PO Box 655, North Amherst, 01059. Francis W Holmes, Librn
Holdings: Vols (6000) Cat Mss Pix Slides Phonorecords Audiotapes Microforms
Budget: ($300)
Notes: No photocopying on premises. Subject emphases: Quakers and Quaker concerns; Pacifism; Racism; Feminism; Religion; Bible; Poverty.

MA —BRANDEIS UNIVERSITY, Goldfarb Library, 415 South St, Waltham, 02154. Bessie Hahn, Dir
Holdings:
Budget:
Notes: George Barton Correspondence. Consists of 12 linear ft of correspondence by and to Professor George A Barton, noted Biblical scholar. This collection is unprocessed.

NY —ALFRED UNIVERSITY, Herrick Memorial Library, Alfred, 14802. June E Brown, Head Librn
Holdings: Vols (1200) // Cat Mss
Notes: The Bergren Collection. A comprehensive collection on Biblical Studies in the Old and New Testaments. Includes material on the Dead Sea Scrolls, Eastern religions, and Hebrew and Aramaic languages.

NY —BUFFALO & ERIE COUNTY PUBLIC LIBRARY, Rare Book Room, Lafayette Sq, Buffalo, 14203. William H Loos, Cur
Holdings: Vols 200 Cat

NY —AMERICAN BIBLE SOCIETY LIBRARY, 1865 Broadway, New York, 10023. Boyd Daniels, Coordr Libr Servs
Holdings: Vols 36,500 Cat Mss Microforms
Notes: Catalogs exist for books of scripture and for reference works on books relating to the Bible and its influence, its history, its translations, etc. The library contains Bibles and parts published in over 1650 languages.

NY —GENERAL THEOLOGICAL SEMINARY, Saint Marks Library, 175 Ninth Ave, New York, 10011. David Green, Dir
Holdings: Vols (200,000) Cat Mss Maps Pix Slides Microforms

NY —YESHIVA UNIVERSITY, Library, 500 West 185th Street, New York, 10033. Pearl Berger
Holdings: Cat

†NY —COLGATE ROCHESTER DIVINITY SCHOOL, Ambrose Swasey Library, 1100 S Goodman St, Rochester, 14620.
Notes: Incl introductions and commentaries as well as special monographs on various portions of the Bible; works in German, French, English and other languages.

NC —DUKE UNIVERSITY, Divinity School Library, Durham, 27706. Donn Michael Farris, Librn
Holdings: Vols (225,000)
Notes: Special collections and subject emphases in this library include: Archaeology, Egyptian; Archaeology, Middle Eastern; Art, Jewish; Bible; Bible-New Testament; Bible-Symbolism; Church Architecture; Egyptology; Fathers of the Church; Society of Friends; Great Britain-Religion-Methodism and Methodist Church; Hymns and Hymnals; Jansenists and Jansenism; Judaica; Mediaeval Christian Mysticism; Methodism and Methodist Church; Methodist Episcopal Church; Methodist Episcopal Church, South; Reformation; Religion-US-History; Rural Church; Theology-Great Britain-17th Century; Theology-Great Britain-18th Century; United Methodist Church; US-Church History; John Wesley.

NC —SOUTHEASTERN BAPTIST THEOLOGICAL SEMINARY LIBRARY, PO Box 752, Wake Forest, 27587. H Eugene McLeod, Librn
Holdings: Cat Slides Microforms

TX —ABILENE CHRISTIAN UNIVERSITY, Margaret & Herman Brown Library, ACU Sta, Abilene, 79601. Callie Faye Milliken, Assoc Dir
Holdings: Vols (4000) Cat
Notes: Sewell Bible Library. This collection is strong in general reference books in religion, 19th and 20th century church history, and religious education. The personal library of ACU's fourth president, Jesse P Sewell, has been augmented by gifts from friends and purchases by the Library.

TX —OBLATE SCHOOL OF THEOLOGY, Library, 285 Oblate Dr, San Antonio, 78216. James Maney, Libr Dir
Holdings: Vols (22,000) Cat
Budget: ($15,500)

WI —SAINT FRANCIS SEMINARY, SCHOOL OF PASTOR MINISTRY, Salzmann Library, 3257 S Lake Dr, Milwaukee, 53207. Lawrence Miech, Librn
Holdings: Vols (65,000) Cat
Budget: ($27,000)

ON —HURON COLLEGE, Silcox Memorial Library, 1349 Western Rd, London, N6G 1H3, Can. Pamela MacKay, Chief Librn
Holdings: Vols (120,000) Cat
Notes: Covers Bible, church history, church music, liturgics, pastoralia, religious education, philosophy of religion, religious studies, systematics. 200 periodical subscriptions including foreign language materials. Rare books collection of 750 volumes, including collections of sermons, commentaries, particularly rare bibles, many in foreign languages in archives.

ON —TORONTO SCHOOL OF THEOLOGY, Consortium of Libraries, University of Toronto, Toronto, M5S 1A5, Can. R Grane Bracewell, Library Coordr
Holdings: Cat
Notes: A consortium of 7 theological college and faculty libraries at the University of Toronto.

BIBLE—ANTIQUITIES

CA —PACIFIC SCHOOL OF RELIGION, Bade Institute of Biblical Archeology, 1798 Scenic Ave, Berkeley, 94709. Kay Schellhase, Cur
Holdings: Vols (2500) Cat
Budget: ($700)
Notes: Syro-Palestinian archaeology.

MA —HARVARD UNIVERSITY, Harvard Divinity School, Andover-Harvard Theological Library, 45 Francis Ave, Cambridge, 02138. Maria Grossmann, Librn
Holdings: Vols (370,000) Cat
Notes: Periodicals and serials dealing with Biblical archeology and its scholarship, and church history. Additions to the monograph collections.

MA —BRANDEIS UNIVERSITY, Goldfarb Library, 415 South St, Waltham, 02154. Bessie Hahn, Dir
Notes: 12 linear ft of correspondence by and to Professor George A Barton, noted Biblical scholar. This collection is unprocessed, spring 1984.

NY —NEW YORK PUBLIC LIBRARY, Jewish Division, Fifth Ave & 42 St, New York, 10018. Leonard S Gold, Chief
Holdings: Vols (200,000) Cat Mss Microforms
Budget: ($33,383)
Notes: A collection of material in all languages on Judaism, Jewish history, literature and traditions from the earliest times to date and works in the Hebrew alphabet (mainly Hebrew and Yiddish) on a variety of subjects. The division has extensive files of Jewish periodicals and newspapers. The collection of rare Hebraica incl medieval texts, cabalistic works, ethical and philosophical tracts in book form. See *Dictionary Catalog of the Jewish Collection* (Boston: G K Hall, 1960), 14 vols. First Supplement (Boston: G K Hall, 1975), 8 vols.

NC —DUKE UNIVERSITY, William R Perkins Library, Rare Book Room, Durham, 27706. John L Sharpe, III, Cur
Notes: The Kanof collection of Judaic art contains more than 950 items on Jewish art, archaeology and symbolism.

NC —DUKE UNIVERSITY, Divinity School Library, Durham, 27706. Donn Michael Farris, Librn

BIBLE—ARCHAEOLOGY see Bible—Antiquities

BIBLE—CODICES see Bible—Manuscripts

BIBLE—COMMENTARIES

†NY —COLGATE ROCHESTER DIVINITY SCHOOL, Ambrose Swasey Library, 1100 S

BIBLE—COMMENTARIES (cont.)

Goodman St, Rochester, 14620.
Notes: Incl introductions and commentaries as well as special monographs on various portions of the Bible; works in German, French, English and other languages.

ON —HURON COLLEGE, Silcox Memorial Library, 1349 Western Rd, London, N6G 1H3, Can. Pamela MacKay, Chief Librn
Holdings: Vols (120,000) Cat
Notes: Covers Bible, church history, church music, liturgics, pastoralia, religious education, philosophy of religion, religious studies, systematics. 200 periodical subscriptions including foreign language materials. Rare books collection of 750 volumes, including collections of sermons, commentaries, particularly rare bibles, many in foreign languages in archives.

BIBLE—CRITICISM, HIGHER see Bible—Criticism, Interpretation, Etc.

BIBLE—CRITICISM, INTERPRETATION, ETC.

CA —LOS ANGELES PUBLIC LIBRARY, Philosophy & Religion Dept, 630 W Fifth St, Los Angeles, 90071. Marilyn C Wherley, Librn
Holdings: Vols 6900 Cat Includes long runs of periodicals, some on microfilm
Budget: ($60,000)
Notes: Comprehensive collection of English versions of the Bible and related materials, and reference works, such as commentaries, dictionaries, atlases, concordances etc.

DC —LIBRARY OF CONGRESS, African and Middle Eastern Division, Washington, 20540.
Holdings: Cat Mss Microforms
Notes: Herbraica: about 109,000 vols in Hebrew, Yiddish, Judeo-Arabic, Judeo-Persian, Ladino, Syriac, Ethiopic; espec strong in Biblical subjects, responsa literature, and socio-political aspects.

MD —JOHNS HOPKINS UNIVERSITY, Milton S Eisenhower Library, George Peabody Collection, 17 E Mt Vernon Place, Baltimore, 21201. Lyn Hart, Peabody Librn
Notes: Noncirculating.

NE —MIDLAND LUTHERAN COLLEGE LIBRARY, Ninth & Irving Sts, Fremont, 68025. Thomas Boyle, Librn
Holdings: Vols 1000 Cat

NY —UNION THEOLOGICAL SEMINARY, Library, 3041 Broadway at Reinhold Niebuhr Place, New York, 10027. Richard D Spoor, Dir
Holdings: Vols (580,000) Cat Mss Microforms
Budget: ($750,000)

†NY —COLGATE ROCHESTER DIVINITY SCHOOL, Ambrose Swasey Library, 1100 S Goodman St, Rochester, 14620.
Notes: Incl introductions and commentaries as well as special monographs on various portions of the Bible; works in German, French, English and other languages.

NC —SOUTHEASTERN BAPTIST THEOLOGICAL SEMINARY LIBRARY, PO Box 752, Wake Forest, 27587. H Eugene McLeod, Librn
Holdings: Cat

OH —HEBREW UNION COLLEGE-JEWISH INSTITUTE OF RELIGION, Klau Library, 3101 Clifton Ave, Cincinnati, 45220. David J Gilner, Reference Librn
Holdings: Cat Mss

OH —CLEVELAND PUBLIC LIBRARY, Social Sciences Department, 325 Superior Ave, Cleveland, 44114. Thelma Morris, Head
Notes: Strong collection of important editions of and books about the Bible, the Reformation, and patrology.

OK —MIDWEST CHRISTIAN COLLEGE, Library, 6600 N Kelley Ave, Oklahoma City, 73111. Jean Cavett, Dir
Holdings: Vols (7000) Cat Pix Phonorecords Audiotapes Filmstrips Microforms
Notes: The Restoration Movement (Independent Christian Church) to restore the Church to its New Testament form. Incl churches called "Christian Churches," "Churches of Christ," "Disciples of Christ," and a few called just "Christ's Church."

OR —MULTNOMAH SCHOOL OF THE BIBLE, Library, 8435 NE Gilsan St, Portland, 97220. James F Scott, Dir of Library; Susan Johnson, Asst Librn
Holdings: Vols (40,686) Cat Slides Phonorecords Audiotapes Filmstrips
Budget: ($33,950)
Notes: Multnomah School of the Bible is an evangelical school that educates students through a program of instruction having the Bible as its center. It supports this centralized Bible major with several ancillary, pertinent supporting minors, ie, Christian education, pastoral, missions and New Testament Greek.

PA —LUTHERAN THEOLOGICAL SEMINARY, Krauth Memorial Library, 7301 Germantown Ave, Philadelphia, 19119. Rev David J Wartluft, Dir Libr
Holdings: Vols 10,200 Cat

PA —TEMPLE UNIVERSITY LIBRARIES, Special Collections Dept, Conwellana-Templana Collection, 13 & Berks St, Philadelphia, 19122. Miriam I Crawford, Cur
Holdings: Vols (2200) Cat Mss
Budget: ($30,000)
Notes: The Conwellana Collection is a memorial to Dr Russell H Conwell, founder of Temple University and pastor of the Baptist Temple (Grace Baptists Church) of Philadelphia from 1882 to his death in 1925. The Collection contains almost all of his published works; his personal library of almost 2000 books, emphasizing Biblical and religious thoughts; mss both by Conwell and about his development of the institutional church; letters, including a large number written to his assistant pastor, Arthur E Harris; a near-complete bound set of his sermons and of the *Temple Review* of the Baptist Temple in which they appeared over a 36-year period; and an extensive file of articles, photographs and information on his activities. Card catalog of the Conwellana-Templana Collection incl books by and about Russell Conwell. Separate card files index his sermons, quotations from his sermons, and items in the *Temple Review. Russell Herman Conwell, 1843-1925, A* Bibliography, by Maurice F Tauber (Philadelphia Temple University Library, 1935. 40 leaves mimeographed). *Russell Herman Conwell: The Individual and His Influence: Catalog of an Exhibition,* by Miriam I Crawford (Temple University General Alumni Association, 1977; unpaged).

PA —DUQUESNE UNIVERSITY, Library, Pittsburgh, 15282. Dena F Jacobson, Music and Reference Librn
Holdings: Vols 3000 Cat
Notes: Main emphasis of collection is on history of Jewish philosophy in the Middle Ages and relationship between Jewish and Christian scholars; collection incl works by 14th century writer Nicolas de Lyra and general Judaica, history of the Jews, theology, Bible texts and commentaries, literature, grammatical works and dictionaries, etc.

TX —SOUTHWESTERN BAPTIST THEOLOGICAL SEMINARY, Roberts Library, 2001 W Seminary Dr, PO Box 22000-2E, Fort Worth, 76122. Keith C Wills, Dir
Holdings: Vols 73,000 Cat Mss Audiotapes Filmstrips Microforms
Budget: $20,000

TX —LUBBOCK CHRISTIAN COLLEGE, Moody Library, 5601 W 19, Lubbock, 79407. Becky Vickers, Librn
Holdings: Vols (9000) Cat Microforms
Budget: ($6000)
Notes: Emphasis on materials related to Church of Christ. No separate catalog.

†ON —METROPOLITAN TORONTO LIBRARY, Social Sciences Dept, 789 Yonge St, Toronto, M4W 2G8, Can. Abdus Salam, Head
Holdings: Vols Cat Maps Phonorecords Audiotapes 16mm Films
Notes: The collection is strong in history and philosophy of religion and comparative religions; literature of all the major religions of the world; works on the devotional and practical aspects of religion; and books on such scared scripture as the Bible. In addition, our holdings contain many denominational studies on religion in Canada, as well as more than 300 congregational histories, particularly Ontario churches and synagogues.

PQ —BISHOP'S UNIVERSITY, John Bassett Memorial Library, Laurie Allison Room for Special Collections, Lennoxville, J1M 1Z7, Can. Germain Belisle, Chief Librn
Holdings: Vols 10,000
Notes: Partially cataloged. Relates to ecclesiastical subjects, dating from as early as the 16th century, largely concerned with the history of the Church of England in Canada and elsewhere.

BIBLE—EXEGESIS see Bible—Commentaries

BIBLE—FICTION see Bible—History of Biblical Events—Fiction

BIBLE—FOLKLORE see Folklore, Jewish

BIBLE—HIGHER CRITICISM see Bible—Criticism, Interpretation, Etc.

BIBLE—HISTORY

MA —BRANDEIS UNIVERSITY, Goldfarb Library, 415 South St, Waltham, 02154. Bessie Hahn, Dir
Notes: George Barton Correspondence. Consists of 12 linear ft of correspondence by and to Professor George A Barton, noted Biblical scholar. This collection is unprocessed, spring 1984.

NY —AMERICAN BIBLE SOCIETY LIBRARY, 1865 Broadway, New York, 10023. Boyd Daniels, Coordr Libr Servs
Holdings: Vols 36,500 Cat Mss Microforms
Notes: Catalogs exist for books of scripture and for reference works on books relating to the Bible and its influence, its history, its translations, etc. The library contains Bibles and parts published in over 1650 languages.

BIBLE—HISTORY OF BIBLICAL EVENTS—FICTION

CA —BIOLA UNIVERSITY, Rose Memorial Library, 13800 Biola Ave, La Mirada, 90639. A Lawrence Marshburn
Holdings: Vols (178,000) Cat Maps Pix Microforms
Budget: ($430,000)
Notes: Biblical and evangelical materials.

BIBLE—INTERPRETAION see Bible—Commentaries; Bible—Criticism, Interpretation, Etc.

BIBLE—LAW see Jewish Law

BIBLE—LITERARY CRITICISM see Bible—Criticism, Interpretation, Etc.

BIBLE—MANUSCRIPTS

MI —UNIVERSITY OF MICHIGAN, Library, Dept of Rare Books & Special Collections, Ann Arbor, 48109. Robert J Starring, Head
Notes: Mss in Greek, Latin, Coptic, Hebrew, Ethiopic, Armenian, and Syriac. The Greek New Testament Mss. (51 mss and 4 papyri) are listed in K W Clark, *A descriptive catalogue of Greek New Testament manuscripts in America* (The University of Chicago Press, 1937): pp 275-340. Described also by Merrill M Parvis, *The Importance of the Michigan manuscript collections for New Testament Textual Studies, in New Testament Manuscript Studies,* ed by M M Parvis and A P Wikgren (The University of Chicago Press, 1950): pp 125-36.

NC —DUKE UNIVERSITY, William R Perkins Library, Rare Book Room, Durham, 27706. John L Sharpe, III, Cur
Notes: Greek mss, 87 in number, dating from the 10th to the 12th centuries, incl 24 New Testament mss.

BIBLE—NEW TESTAMENT

CA —UNIVERSITY OF CALIFORNIA, SANTA BARBARA, Library, Dept of Special Collections, Santa Barbara, 93106. Christian F Brun, Head
Holdings: Vols (340) Cat Mss Pix
Notes: Incl 105 Greek New Testaments from the Isaac Foot Collection; and Archives (235 vols, uncataloged) of the Lockman Foundation, which specializes in support of the Bible and religious translations, simplified Bible, etc.

IL —WHEATON COLLEGE, Buswell Memorial Library, Wheaton, 60187. Paul Snezek, Library Dir
Holdings: Mss Cat
Notes: Ngbaka Tribe. Material consists of word lists, a conversation manual, a dictionary and the translated New Testament. All of the material collected by Zaire Missionary pioneer, Theodore B Wallin.

MA —HARVARD UNIVERSITY, Harvard Divinity School, Andover-Harvard Theological Library, 45 Francis Ave, Cambridge, 02138. Maria Grossmann, Librn
Holdings: Vols (370,000) Cat

NC —DUKE UNIVERSITY, Divinity School Library, Durham, 27706. Donn Michael Farris, Librn
Holdings: Vols (225,000)
Notes: Special collections and subject emphases in this library include: Archaeology, Egyptian; Archaeology, Middle Eastern; Art, Jewish; Bible; Bible-New Testament; Bible-Symbolism; Church Architecture; Egyptology; Fathers of the Church; Society of Friends; Great Britain-Religion-Methodism and Methodist Church; Hymns and Hymnals; Jansenists and Jansenism; Judaica; Mediaeval Christian Mysticism; Methodism and Methodist Church; Methodist Episcopal Church; Methodist Episcopal Church, South; Reformation; Religion-US-History; Rural Church; Theology-Great Britain-17th Century; Theology-Great Britain-18th Century; United Methodist Church; US-Church History; John Wesley.

NC —SOUTHEASTERN BAPTIST THEOLOGICAL SEMINARY LIBRARY, PO Box 752, Wake Forest, 27587. H Eugene McLeod, Librn
Holdings: Cat

OK —MIDWEST CHRISTIAN COLLEGE, Library, 6600 N Kelley Ave, Oklahoma City, 73111. Jean Cavett, Dir
Holdings: Vols (7000) Cat Pix Phonorecords Audiotapes Filmstrips Microforms
Notes: The Restoration Movement (Independent Christian Church) to restore the Church to its New Testament form. Incl churches called "Christian Churches," "Churches of Christ," "Disciples of Christ," and a few called just "Christ's Church."

OR —MULTNOMAH SCHOOL OF THE BIBLE, Library, 8435 NE Gilsan St, Portland, 97220. James F Scott, Dir of Library; Susan Johnson, Asst Librn
Holdings: Vols (40,686) Cat Slides Phonorecords Audiotapes Filmstrips
Budget: ($33,950)
Notes: Multnomah School of the Bible is an evangelical school that educates students through a program of instruction having the Bible as its center. It supports this centralized Bible major with several ancillary, pertinent supporting minors, ie, Christian education, pastoral, missions and New Testament Greek.

BIBLE—NEW TESTAMENT—MANUSCRIPTS

IL —UNIVERSITY OF CHICAGO LIBRARY, Dept of Special Collections, 1100 E 57 St, Chicago, 60637.
Notes: Edgar J Goodspeed Collection of New Testament mss.

MI —UNIVERSITY OF MICHIGAN, Library, Dept of Rare Books & Special Collections, Ann Arbor, 48109. Robert J Starring, Head
Holdings: Mss
Notes: The majority (51 mss and 4 papyri) in Greek. Other mss in Coptic, Armenian, Syriac, and Ethiopic.

BIBLE—OLD TESTAMENT

†CA —HEBREW UNION COLLEGE, Jewish Institute of Religion, 3077 University Ave, Los Angeles, 90007.
Notes: Bible, Talmud, Rabbinics, Jewish history, philosophy, art and communal science, Hebrew literature, religion, Zionism.

FL —UNIVERSITY OF FLORIDA LIBRARY, Isser and Rae Price Library of Judaica, 18 Libr East, Gainesville, 32611. Robert Singerman, Head Librn
Budget: ($30,000)
Notes: Total holdings estimated at 55,000 vols dealing with the political, social, economic and intellectual history of the Jews in the ancient, medieval and modern periods and in all geographic areas. The following areas are especially well represented by printed matter in all relevant languages: Bibliography, Festschriften, History, Bible, Judaism and Jewish theology, liturgy, responsa, rabbinical literature, Jewish law, Hebrew language and literature, Yiddish language and literature, anti-semitism, Zionism, Palestine and the *Yishuv,* and the State of Israel. German and American Judaica form a collecting emphasis with holdings for all the standard histories as well as histories of individual synagogues, institutions and local communities. Works in Hebrew and Yiddish comprise about 60 percent of the collection (estimated 30,000 vols). With few exceptions, holdingsare limited to nineteenth and twentieth century imprints, with complete sets of journals and thousands of ephemeral pamphlets, many of them commemorating anniversaries, enhancing the research value of the collection, the largest Judaica research library in the southeastern United States. Only about half of the collection is cataloged; the collection is a circulating one and vols may be borrowed on interlibrary loan. Incl the Leonard C Mishkin Collection (40,000 vols), the largest personal Judaica collection in the United States, the Shlomo Marenof Collection (3500 vols), and the inventory of Bernard Morgenstern's Lower East Side Book Store (8000 vols). Scholars should inquire in advance of their visit. *The Isser and Rae Price Library of Judaica* Report (circulation 2900 copies) is mailed gratis twice a year to all interested parties. Special catalogs:Pre-1881 Hebrew imprints recorded in a chronological card file.

IL —HEBREW THEOLOGICAL COLLEGE, Saul Silber Memorial Library, 7135 N Carpenter Rd, Skokie, 60077. Leah Mishkin, Head Librn/Cur
Holdings: Vols (58,000) Cat Mss Microforms
Notes: Main subject is rabbinics (Halachic literature). We also have a large and important Holocaust Collection.

IA —UNIVERSITY OF IOWA, University Libraries, Iowa City, 52242.
Holdings: Vols 1850 Mss
Notes: The Leo W Schwarz Collection, a valuable and rare group of books dealing with Hasidic literature, a portion on Old Testament studies and works on Jewish history, philosophy and culture, the Jews in Nazi Germany, Jewish folklore and the history of the Jews in the US. Incl about 850 books in Hebrew and 1000 in other languages, mss of several of Schwarz's books and articles, correspondence, notes, and background research relating to his publications.

MA —HARVARD UNIVERSITY, Harvard Divinity School, Andover-Harvard Theological Library, 45 Francis Ave, Cambridge, 02138. Maria Grossmann, Librn
Holdings: Vols (370,000) Cat

NY —NEW YORK PUBLIC LIBRARY, Jewish Division, Fifth Ave & 42 St, New York, 10018. Leonard S Gold, Chief
Holdings: Vols (200,000) Cat Mss Microforms
Budget: ($33,383)
Notes: A collection of material in all languages on Judaism, Jewish history, literature and traditions from the earliest times to date and works in the Hebrew alphabet (mainly Hebrew and Yiddish) on a variety of subjects. The division has extensive files of Jewish periodicals and newspapers. The collection of rare Hebraica incl medieval texts, cabalistic works, ethical and philosophical tracts in book form. See *Dictionary Catalog of the Jewish Collection* (Boston: G K Hall, 1960), 14 vols. First Supplement (Boston: G K Hall, 1975), 8 vols.

NC —SOUTHEASTERN BAPTIST THEOLOGICAL SEMINARY LIBRARY, PO Box 752, Wake Forest, 27587. H Eugene McLeod, Librn
Holdings: Cat

BIBLE—PHILOLOGY

CA —PACIFIC SCHOOL OF RELIGION, Bade Institute of Biblical Archeology, 1798 Scenic Ave, Berkeley, 94709. Kay Schellhase, Cur
Notes: The textual materials are a part of the archeology collection.

MD —JOHNS HOPKINS UNIVERSITY, Milton S Eisenhower Library, Charles & 34 Sts, Baltimore, 21218. Ann S Gwyn, Assistant Dir for Special Collections
Holdings: Vols 4000 Cat
Notes: The August Dillmann Collection of Oriental Literature. Very strong and complete collection of Ethiopic until 1900. Dillman was the greatest scholar in his field. Catalog published at Johns Hopkins. Also contains Biblical philology.

BIBLE—PROPHECIES

MI —ANDREWS UNIVERSITY, James White Library, Berrien Springs, 49104. Marley H Soper, Dir
Holdings: Cat Mss Pix
Notes: Advent Source Collection. Deals with prophecy of the Bible and the Advent hope in historical context. About 3700 items. Materials gathered by Dr L R Froom in the preparation of his four-volume set entitled *Prophetic Faith of Our Fathers.* ca 1964-1954. Not availabe by interlibrary loan, but may be used at this library.

OK —MIDWEST CHRISTIAN COLLEGE, Library, 6600 N Kelley Ave, Oklahoma City, 73111. Jean Cavett, Dir
Holdings: Vols (7000) Cat Pix Phonorecords Audiotapes Filmstrips Microforms
Notes: The Restoration Movement (Independent Christian Church) to restore the Church to its New Testament form. Incl churches called "Christian Churches," "Churches of Christ," "Disciples of Christ," and a few called just "Christ's Church."

BIBLE—SYMBOLISM see Symbolism in the Bible

BIBLE—TRANSLATIONS

AZ —NORTHERN ARIZONA UNIVERSITY, Special Collection Library, CU Box 6022, Flagstaff, 86011. Peter M Whiteley, Coordr/Archivist; William Mullane, Librn
Notes: Faye and Faith Hill Edgerton Collection; mss and notes of the translation of the New Testament into the Apache and Navajo languages, 1940's-1960's.

IL —WHEATON COLLEGE, Buswell Memorial Library, Wheaton, 60187. Paul Snezek, Library Dir
Holdings: Vols 50 Mss
Notes: 12 linear feet of mss material related to the *Living Bible* translation, *The Bible Story Book. Related Topics:* Bible-Translations.

KS —SAINT MARY COLLEGE, Library, Leavenworth, 66048. Therese Deplazes, Special Collections Librn
Notes: The Sir John J and Mary Craig Collection of Holy Scripture shows how the Bible looked in the hands of the people through twenty centuries. In the Craig Collection and the general collection are originals and facsimiles of complete Bibles and parts of Holy Scripture, from Torah to

BIBLE—TRANSLATIONS (cont.)

modern exegesis, incl ms leaves, antiphonals, scrolls, codices, incunabula, early and later printed books, and bound periodicals, in ninety languages, thirty of which are languages of North and South American Indians.

MI —ALBION COLLEGE, Stockwell Memorial Library, 602 E Cass St, Albion, 49224. Charles H Held, Librn
Holdings: Uncat
Notes: European Reformation Bibles and Bibles in non-European languages.

NY —AMERICAN BIBLE SOCIETY LIBRARY, 1865 Broadway, New York, 10023. Boyd Daniels, Coordr Libr Servs
Holdings: Vols 36,500 Cat Mss Microforms
Notes: Catalogs exit for books of scripture and for reference works on books relating to the Bible and its influence, its history, its translations, etc. The library contains Bibles and parts published in over 1650 languages.

ON —QUEEN'S UNIVERSITY, Douglas Library, Kingston, K7L 5C4, Can. William F E Morley, Cur, Special Collections
Holdings: Vols 1050 Uncat
Notes: Incl 1050 codex copies and printed editions of the Old and New Testament in about 50 different languages, half of which are in non-Roman alphabets. Does not incl Commentaries. Partial description in *Exhibit of Bibles from the Collection in Douglas* Library. Canadian National Exhibition 1949 (Kingston, 1949). Checklist available.

ON —HURON COLLEGE, Silcox Memorial Library, 1349 Western Rd, London, N6G 1H3, Can. Pamela MacKay, Chief Librn
Holdings: Vols (28,000) Cat
Budget: ($24,710)
Notes: Covers Bible, church history, church music, liturgics, pastoralia, religious education, philosophy of religion, religious studies, systematics. 95 periodical subscriptions including foreign language materials. Rare books collection of 750 volumes, including collections of sermons, commentaries, particularly rare bibles, many in foreign languages.

ON —NATIONAL LIBRARY OF CANADA, 395 Wellington St, Ottawa, K1A 0N4, Can. Andre Preibish, Dir
Notes: *The Jacob M Lowy Collection* over 2000 works of very rare Hebraica and Judaica. Among outstanding items are 30 incunabula - the first printed edition of the Babylonian Talmud, many editions of Flavius Josephus, including first edition of 1470 Early Bibles in many languages. *The Saul Hayes Collection* of Hebraic Manuscripts and microforms. Manuscripts from North Africa and the Orient; 300 reels of manuscripts held by libraries in Poland, USSR and Hungary. This collection is held in the Jacob M Lowy Room.

†ON —METROPOLITAN TORONTO LIBRARY, Social Sciences Dept, 789 Yonge St, Toronto, M4W 2G8, Can. Abdus Salam, Head
Holdings: Vols Cat Maps Phonorecords Audiotapes 16mm Films Microforms
Notes: Strong collection on folklore, education, religion, anthropology. Also includes bibles in Canadian Indian languages.

ON —VICTORIA UNIVERSITY, Library, 71 Queen's Park Crescent, Toronto, M5S 1K7, Can. Robert C Brandeis, // Chief Librn
Holdings: Vols (1000) // Cat Mss Maps Pix
Notes: Collection consists of books, pamphlets, and government report mainly dealing with North American Indians and western explorations and missionary enterprises among the Indian tribes in Canada. Incl Indian Bibles and hymnbooks, and mss and vols by Peter Jones (an Indian missionary) and James Evans (inventor of the Cree syllabic alphabet).

BIBLE—VERSIONS

CA —PACIFIC SCHOOL OF RELIGION, Bade Institute of Biblical Archeology, 1798 Scenic Ave, Berkeley, 94709. Kay Schellhase, Cur
Notes: The textual materials are a part of the archeology collection.

CA —BIOLA UNIVERSITY, Rose Memorial Library, 13800 Biola Ave, La Mirada, 90639. A Lawrence Marshburn
Holdings: Vols (178,000) Cat Maps Pix Microforms
Budget: ($430,000)
Notes: Biblical and evangelical materials.

CA —LOS ANGELES PUBLIC LIBRARY, Philosophy & Religion Dept, 630 W Fifth St, Los Angeles, 90071. Marilyn C Wherley, Librn
Holdings: Vols 6900 Cat Includes long runss of periodicals, some on microfilm
Budget: ($60,000)
Notes: Comprehensive collection of English versions of the Bible and related materials, and reference works, such as commentaries, dictionaries, atlases, concordances etc.

CA —UNIVERSITY OF CALIFORNIA, SANTA BARBARA, Library, Dept of Special Collections, Santa Barbara, 93106. Christian F Brun, Head
Holdings: Vols (340) Cat Mss Pix
Notes: Incl 105 Greek New Testaments from the Isaac Foot Collection; and Archives (235 vols, uncataloged) of the Lockman Foundation, which specializes in support of the Bible and religious translations, simplified Bible, etc.

IL —WHEATON COLLEGE, Buswell Memorial Library, Wheaton, 60187. Paul Snezek, Library Dir
Holdings: Vols 50 Mss
Notes: 12 linear feet of mss material related to the *Living Bible* translation, *The Bible Story Book.*

IN —INDIANA UNIVERSITY, Lilly Library, Seventh St, Bloomington, 47405. William R Cagle, Librn
Holdings: Cat
Notes: First editions of early versions of the Bible.

IN —VOLHYNIAN BIBLIOGRAPHIC CENTER, 307 N Overhill Drive, Bloomington, 47401. Max Boyko, Mgr
Notes: Collect materials on Volhynia in Western Ukraine. Compile and publish bibliographies on the region.

KS —SAINT MARY COLLEGE, Library, Leavenworth, 66048. Therese Deplazes, Special Collections Librn
Notes: The Sir John J and Mary Craig Collection of Holy Scripture shows how the Bible looked in the hands of the people through twenty centuries. In the Craig Collection and the general collection are originals and facsimiles of complete Bibles and parts of Holy Scripture, from Torah to modern exegesis, incl ms leaves, antiphonals, scrolls, codices, incunabula, early and later printed books, and bound periodicals, in ninety languages, thirty of which are languages of North and South American Indians.

MD —JOHNS HOPKINS UNIVERSITY, Milton S Eisenhower Library, Special Collections, John Work Garrett Library, 4545 N Charles St, Baltimore, 21210. Jane Katz, Garrett Librn
Holdings: Vols 500 Cat
Notes: Hoffmann Biblical Collection: editions of the Bible in various languages used in research on the origins of the English Bible. Also 2 Luther Bibles, 1522 and 1523, and a pre-Luther one, 1485.

NY —ALFRED UNIVERSITY, Herrick Memorial Library, Alfred, 14802. June E Brown, Head Librn
Holdings: Vols (1200) // Cat Mss
Notes: The Bergren Collection. A comprehensive collection on Biblical Studies in the Old and New Testaments. Includes material on the Dead Sea Scrolls, Eastern relilgions, and Hebrew and Aramaic languages.

NY —STATE UNIVERSITY OF NEW YORK, COLLEGE AT BUFFALO, Lockwood Memorial Library, Main St, Buffalo, 14260. Stanton F Biddle, Assoc Dir
Holdings: Vols 48,000 Cat Pix
Notes: About half of the collection donated by the Orthodox Catholic Alliance of Buffalo, New York. The collection is devoted chiefly to the world of Byzantium in both its secular and religious phases; Greek Patristic literature and its interpretation; and the tradition of the Greek Bible and its antecedents. As support for these subjects the pagan literature of late antiquity is strongly represented, as well as the Hellenistic and Roman background of the East Christian world and its relations with its neighbors in the Near East, in Eastern Europe, and in the Latin West.

NY —AMERICAN BIBLE SOCIETY LIBRARY, 1865 Broadway, New York, 10023. Boyd Daniels, Coordr Libr Servs
Holdings: Vols 36,500 Cat Mss Microforms
Notes: Catalogs exist for books of scripture and for reference works on books relating to the Bible and its influence, its history, its translations, etc. The library contains Bibles and parts published in over 1650 languages.

NC —DUKE UNIVERSITY, Divinity School Library, Durham, 27706. Donn Michael Farris, Librn

PA —FREE LIBRARY OF PHILADELPHIA, Rare Book Dept, Logan Sq, Philadelphia, 19103. Marie E Korey, Rare Book Librn
Holdings: Vols (750) Cat
Notes: Early and important editions of the Bible in numerous languages.

PA —NORTHEASTERN CHRISTIAN JR COLLEGE, Whitworth Library, 1860 Montgomery Ave, Villanova, 19085. Robert S Brown, Librn
Holdings: Vols 30 Uncat
Budget: $300

TX —TEXAS CHRISTIAN UNIVERSITY, Mary Couts Burnett Library, Fort Worth, 76129.
Holdings: Vols 975 Cat
Notes: Editions of the Bible before the King James version.

ON —QUEEN'S UNIVERSITY, Douglas Library, Kingston, K7L 5C4, Can. William F E Morley, Cur, Special Collections
Holdings: Vols 1050 Uncat
Notes: Incl 1050 codex copies and printed editions of the Old and New Testament in about 50 different languages, half of which are in non-Roman alphabets. Does not incl Commentaries. Partial description in *Exhibit of Bibles from the Collection in Douglas* Library. Canadian National Exhibition 1949 (Kingston, 1949). Checklist available.

ON —HURON COLLEGE, Silcox Memorial Library, 1349 Western Rd, London, N6G 1H3, Can. Pamela MacKay, Chief Librn
Holdings: Vols (28,000) Cat
Budget: ($24,710)
Notes: Covers Bible, church history, church music, liturgics, pastoralia, religious education, philosophy of religion, religious studies, systematics. 95 periodical subscriptions including foreign language materials. Rare books collection of 750 volumes, including collections of sermons, commentaries, particularly rare bibles, many in foreign languages.

ON —NATIONAL LIBRARY OF CANADA, 395 Wellington St, Ottawa, K1A 0N4, Can. Andre Preibish, Dir
Notes: *The Jacob M Lowy Collection* over 2000 works of very rare Hebraica and Judaica. Among outstanding items are 30 incunabula - the first printed edition of the Babylonian Talmud, many editions of Flavius Josephus, including first edition of 1470 Early Bibles in many languages. *The Saul Hayes Collection* of Hebraic Manuscripts and microforms. Manuscripts from North Africa and the Orient; 300 reels of manuscripts held by libraries in Poland, USSR and Hungary. This collection is held in the Jacob M Lowy Room.

BIBLES AND PRAYER BOOKS

CA —SAINT JOHN'S SEMINARY, Edward Laurence Doheny Memorial Library, The Estelle Doheny Collection, 5012 E Seminary Rd, Camarillo, 93010. Rita S Faulders, Cur
Notes: Bibles, incl Gutenberg Bible, vol I.

CA —UNIVERSITY OF CALIFORNIA, DAVIS, Shields Library, Dept of Special Collections, Davis, 95616. Donald Kunitz, Head; C Danial Elliott, Asst Head
Holdings: Vols 200 Cat Mss
Notes: A selection of Bibles in various formats and languages, incl New Testament, Gospels, Greek, 12th and 14th centuries; the

BIBLES AND PRAYER BOOKS (cont.)

earliest Latin Bible produced by Koburger, 1478; Tyndale's New Testament, 1525, the first New Testament printed in English; Tremellius Latin Bible, London, 1585; the first Geneva Bible without the Apocryphia, 1599; the London Polyglot Bible, 1657, and others.

CA —BIOLA UNIVERSITY, Rose Memorial Library, 13800 Biola Ave, La Mirada, 90639. A Lawrence Marshburn
Holdings: Vols (178,000) Cat Maps Pix Microforms
Budget: ($430,000)
Notes: Biblical and evangelical materials.

CA —LOS ANGELES PUBLIC LIBRARY, Philosophy & Religion Dept, 630 W Fifth St, Los Angeles, 90071. Marilyn C Wherley, Librn
Holdings: Vols 6900 Cat Includes long runs of periodicals, some on microfilm
Budget: ($60,000)
Notes: Comprehensive collection of English versions of the Bible and related materials, and reference works, such as commentaries, dictionaries, atlases, concordances etc.

CT —TRINITY COLLEGE LIBRARY, Watkinson Library, 300 Summit St, Hartford, 06106. Jeffrey Kaimowitz, Cur
Holdings: Cat Mss
Notes: Incl Books of Hours and incunabula.

CT —YALE UNIVERSITY, Box 1603A, Yale Station, New Haven, 06520.

DC —GEORGETOWN UNIVERSITY, Library, Special Collections Div, 37 & O Sts NW, Washington, 20057. George M Barringer, Special Collections Librn; Nicholas B Sheetz, Mss Librn
Holdings: Vols 750 Cat
Notes: Incl Downs 1038.

DC —LIBRARY OF CONGRESS, Rare Book & Special Collections Div, Washington, 20540. William Matheson, Chief
Holdings: Vols 1471 Cat
Notes: Contains notable examples of Bibles, the Old and New Testaments, individual books of the Bible, and psalm books from 1501 to the present. Many are notable for their fine bindings, illustrations, rarity, typography and textual importance. Other examples are found in the Incunabula collections, Medieval and Renaissance Manuscripts Collection, Rosenwald Collection. Miniature Case, etc.

FL —FLORIDA SOUTHERN COLLEGE, Roux Library, Johnson at McDonald, Lakeland, 33802. Larry Stallings, Special Collections Librn
Holdings: Vols (5100) Cat Mss
Notes: Incl Florida church histories and minutes of District Conventions. Methodist-related books and hymnals, and many old Bibles, are included. Separate indexes.

FL —FLORIDA STATE UNIVERSITY, Robert Manning Strozier Library, Special Collections Dept, Tallahassee, 32306. Opal M Free, Head, Special Collections
Holdings: Vols (12,254) Cat
Notes: Incl 65 uncataloged volumes in the Carothers Memorial Collection: The Julia Stover and Milton Washington Carothers Collection of Bibles and Rare Books given to honor their memory by their son, Milton Stover Carothers. Noncirculating. No photocopying.

IL —JESUIT-KRAUSS-MCCORMICK LIBRARY, 1100 E 55th St, Chicago, 60615. Donald Vorp, Dir; Elvire Hilgert, Librn
Holdings: Vols (375,000) Microforms
Notes: Collections contain merger of Jesuit Library, Lutheran School of Theology of Chicago (Krauss Library), and McCormick Theological Seminary. Jesuit: Sermones Thesaurus Novi de Tempore (anonymous, Strassbourg 1486); Opera Omnia (Jean Gerson, Strassbourg 1488), 3 vols; Summa Rosella Casuum (Venice 1495); moral theology (major figures of 16th and 17th century scholasticism); early modern editions of patristics and canon law regarding procedures and organzation of the Catholic Church, incl treatises and multi-volume commentaries. Krauss: Archives of Lutheran Church in America and its predecessors; Reformation imprints; early printed versions of the Bible (L Franklin Gruber Collection); German and Scandanavian (Swedish, Danish, Finnish) theology; Lutheran Church of America document depository. McCormick: Presbyteriana; historical record of Synod of Illinois, UnitedPresbyterian Church of USA; Church Federation of Chicago archives prior to 1969; USA imprints of the Bible (Simms Collection).

IL —NEWBERRY LIBRARY, 60 W Walton St, Chicago, 60610. Diana Haskell, Cur of Modern Mss
Holdings: Vols 10,300 Cat Mss
Notes: Early Bibles and editions of Bible or parts therof. Restricted use.

IL —UNIVERSITY OF CHICAGO LIBRARY, Dept of Special Collections, 1100 E 57 St, Chicago, 60637.
Notes: English Bibles.

IN —INDIANA UNIVERSITY, Lilly Library, Seventh St, Bloomington, 47405. William R Cagle, Librn
Holdings: Cat
Notes: First editions of early versions of the Bible.

KS —BAKER UNIVERSITY, Library, Quayle Rare Bible Collection, Eighth St, Baldwin City, 66006. John Forbes, Dir
Holdings: Vols (600) Cat Mss
Notes: This collection of rare Bibles was given by Bishop William A Quayle (1860-1925), representative collection of books and other writings before advent (in the western world) of printing by moveable type, incunabula. Biblical works since 1501, and a few non-Biblical works since 1500. See *The William Alfred Quayle Bible Collection: A Self-Guided Tour Manual* (preliminary ed) by Ray Firestone. Persons desiring to visit the collection are advised to make an appointment or phone ahead to Baker University (913-594-6451 ext 414) to assure that collection is open.

KS —SAINT MARY COLLEGE, Library, Leavenworth, 66048. Therese Deplazes, Special Collections Librn
Notes: The Sir John J and Mary Craig Collection of Holy Scripture shows how the Bible looked in the hands of the people through twenty centuries. In the Craig Collection and the general collection are originals and facsimiles of complete Bibles and parts of Holy Scripture, from Torah to modern exegesis, incl ms leaves, antiphonals, scrolls, codices, incunabula, early and later printed books, and bound periodicals, in ninety languages, thirty of which are languages of North and South American Indians.

KY —BEREA COLLEGE, Hutchins Library, Berea, 40404. Gerald F Roberts, Librn Special Collections
Holdings: Vols (9000) Cat Mss Microforms Phonorecords
Notes: The Rare Bible Collection. See Ira J Martin, "The Rare Bibles at Berea College," 1968. 3 vols (unpublished).

MD —JOHNS HOPKINS UNIVERSITY, Milton S Eisenhower Library, Special Collections, John Work Garrett Library, 4545 N Charles St, Baltimore, 21210. Jane Katz, Garrett Librn
Holdings: Vols 500 Cat
Notes: Hoffmann Biblical Collection: editions of the Bible in various languages used in research on the origins of the English Bible. Also 2 Luther Bibles, 1522 and 1523, and a pre-Luther one, 1485. Also 600 Bibles and devotional works, 16th-19th century, part of the Nikulas Ottenson Collection of Icelandic and Old Norse literature.

MA —EPISCOPAL DIOCESE OF MASSACHUSETTS, Diocesan Library, 1 Joy St, Boston, 02108. Mark J Duffy, Archivist; Margaret A Dempsey, Asst Archivist
Holdings: Mss Pix
Budget: $37,000
Notes: Official material of the Diocese of Massachusetts, incl parish histories, biographies and writings of bishops and clergymen; prayer books and hymnals of the American Church; Americana; colonial Church histories; materials relating to the Society for the Propagation of the Gospel (SPG); 18th and 19th century pamphlets.

MA —GORDON COLLEGE, Winn Library, Vining Collection, 255 Grapevine Rd, Wenham, 01984. John Beauregard, Dir
Holdings: Vols 400 Cat
Notes: The Vining Collection (of rare books). Early English Bibles, first editions of most.

†MA —WILLIAMS COLLEGE, Chapin Library of Rare Books, PO Box 426, Williamstown, 01267. Robert L Volz, Custodian
Holdings: Vols 380 Cat
Notes: No material available on interlibrary loan.

MA —AMERICAN ANTIQUARIAN SOCIETY LIBRARY, 185 Salisbury St, Worcester, 01609. Marcus A McCorison, Dir & Librn
Holdings: Cat
Notes: Almost every American printing of the Bible to 1820; incl two editions of the Eliot Indian Bible; also the first Hawaiian Bible.

MI —ALBION COLLEGE, Stockwell Memorial Library, 602 E Cass St, Albion, 49224. Charles H Held, Librn
Holdings: Uncat
Notes: European Reformation Bibles and Bibles in non-European languages.

MI —UNIVERSITY OF MICHIGAN, Library, Dept of Rare Books & Special Collections, Ann Arbor, 48109. Robert J Starring, Head
Holdings: Cat
Notes: Noteworthy editions of Bibles from the 15th to the 20th centuries, incl the William C Hollands Collection.

MI —DETROIT PUBLIC LIBRARY, Rare Books Department, 5201 Woodward Ave, Detroit, 48202.
Holdings: Vols 400 Cat Mss
Notes: Significant editions of the Bible from 15th to 20th century, with a few earlier mss.

NJ —DREW UNIVERSITY, Library, Madison, 07940. Caroline Coughlin, Assoc Dir
Notes: The Maser Collection of the *Book of Common Prayer.* Incl 152 versions, ranging from a 1522 *Psalter and Hymnal of the Sarum Use* to the 1977 version of the prayer book of the Protestant Episcopal Church of the USA.

NY —NEW YORK STATE LIBRARY, State Education Bldg Annex, Washington Ave, Albany, 12224.
Notes: Incl catechisms, etc in American Indian languages.

NY —AMERICAN BIBLE SOCIETY LIBRARY, 1865 Broadway, New York, 10023. Boyd Daniels, Coordr Libr Servs
Holdings: Vols 36,500 Cat Mss Microforms
Notes: Catalogs exist for books of scripture and for reference works on books relating to the Bible and its influence, its history, its translations, etc. The library contains Bibles and parts published in over 1650 languages.

NY —GENERAL THEOLOGICAL SEMINARY, Saint Marks Library, 175 Ninth Ave, New York, 10011. David Green, Dir
Holdings: Vols (200,000) Cat
Notes: Extensive collection.

NY —NEW YORK PUBLIC LIBRARY, Rare Books and Manuscripts Div, Fifth Ave & 42 St, New York, 10018. William L Joyce, Asst Dir; Francis O Mattson, Curator
Holdings: Cat
Budget: ($7161)
Notes: The Lenox Collection of early Bibles, incl the first copy of the Gutenberg Bible to be brought to this country (1847).

NY —PIERPONT MORGAN LIBRARY, 29 E 36 St, New York, 10016. Paul Needham, Cur
Notes: One of the largest collections, with many rarities, unique works and mss.

NY —UNION THEOLOGICAL SEMINARY, Library, 3041 Broadway at Reinhold Niebuhr Place, New York, 10027. Richard D Spoor, Dir
Holdings: Vols (580,000) Cat Mss Microforms
Budget: ($750,000)

OH —CASE WESTERN RESERVE UNIVERSITY, M A Baxter School of Information and Library Science, 10900

BIBLES AND PRAYER BOOKS (cont.)

Euclid Ave, Cleveland, 44106. Bettina MacAyeal, Librn; Gretchen Larson, Librn
Holdings: Vols (1100)
Notes: Incl collection of 1100 historical children's books and periodicals, housed in the Special Collections Dept of Freiberger Library, and can be used by the public. Incl *The Holy Bible Abridged* published by Isaiah Thomas in 1786, *The Life and Strange Surprising Adventures of Robinson Crusoe* of 1790, and a *Cinderella* dated 1809. There are examples of the work of illustrators Walter Crane, Randolph Caldecott, Kate Greenaway and Maurice Boutet de Monvel. The periodical collection incl a complete run of St. Nicholas Magazine.

OH —CLEVELAND PUBLIC LIBRARY, Social Sciences Department, 325 Superior Ave, Cleveland, 44114. Thelma Morris, Head
Notes: Strong collection of imporatant editions of and books about the Bible, the Reformation, and patrology.

PA —DICKINSON COLLEGE, Boyd Lee Spahr Library, W High St, Carlisle, 17013. Yates M Forbis, Dir
Notes: The Edwin Willoughby Collection of English Bibles, 1549-1716.

PA —TEMPLE UNIVERSITY LIBRARIES, Special Collections Dept, Rare Books & Mss Section, Philadelphia, 19122. Thomas M Whitehead, Cur
Holdings: Vols 300 Cat
Notes: Incl the J S Ladd Thomas Collection. Noteworthy editions of the Bible, 15th and 20th centuries; psalters and prayer books; strength in English and American Bibles.

PA —UNIVERSITY OF PENNSYLVANIA, Van Pelt Library, Rare Books Collection, 34 & Walnut Sts, Philadelphia, 19104. Daniel Traister, Special Collections Librn
Holdings: Vols 155 Cat Mss
Notes: Bibles of the 15th to the 20th centuries. See Downs 1039.

RI —BROWN UNIVERSITY, John Carter Brown Library, Providence, 02912. Norman Fiering, Librn; Everett C Wilkie Jr, Bibliographer; Susan Danforth, Cur Maps & Prints
Notes: Incl Bibles printed in Europe and America until 1800.

TX —SLOVANSKA PODPORUJICI JEDNOTA STATU TEXAS, Slavonic Benevolent Order of the State of Texas, SPJST Library, Archives, Museum, 520 N Main St, Temple, 76501. Otto Hanus, Cur-Librn; Thelma Bartosh, Asst Cur-Librn
Holdings: Vols 70 Cat
Notes: This collection contains old Czech and Svabach bibles, prayer books, postillas and kancionals, some from the year 1530.

WI —SEVENTH DAY BAPTIST HISTORICAL SOCIETY, Library, 3120 Kennedy Rd, PO Box 1678, Janesville, 53547. D Scott Smith, Historian
Holdings: Cat Mss Maps Pix
Notes: Julies Sachse Collection. Ephrata Community records (1729-1883). Original music mss, some illuminated; samples of early printing of Bibles and books form an important part of this collection. Some material also on Snow Hill, daughter colony, et al. About 500 items; incl artifacts. Much of this collection now in Pennsylvania State Archives, Pennsylvania Historical and Museum Commission, Philadelphia.

ON —QUEEN'S UNIVERSITY, Douglas Library, Kingston, K7L 5C4, Can. William F E Morley, Cur, Special Collections
Holdings: Vols 1050 Uncat
Notes: Incl 1050 codex copies and printed editions of the Old and New Testament in about 50 different languages, half of which are in non-Roman alphabets. Does not incl Commentaries. Partial description in *Exhibit of Bibles from the Collection in Douglas* Library. Canadian National Exhibition 1949 (Kingston, 1949). Checklist available.

ON —WYCLIFFE COLLEGE, Leonard Library, 5 Hoskin Ave, Toronto, M5S 1H7, Can. Adrienne Taylor, Librn; Gayle Ford, Library Technician
Holdings: Vols (47,000) Cat Microforms
Budget: ($11,000)
Notes: Collection of early and rare books of prayer books, sermons, Bibles. Basic reference collection of standard theological dictionaries, encyclopedias, commentaries. Homiletics collection including 19th century works. Strong in church history, Evengelical Anglicanism, English Reformation, Wycliffe studies.

BIBLICAL ARAMAIC LANGUAGE see Aramaic Language and Literature

BIBLICAL ARCHAEOLOGY see Bible—Antiquities

BIBLICAL LAW see Jewish Law

BIBLICAL MANUSCRIPTS see Bible—Manuscripts

BIBLICAL RESEARCH see Bible—Criticism, Interpretation, Etc.

BIBLIOGRAPHICAL CENTERS

PA —BIBLIOGRAPHICAL CENTER OF GERMAN LITERATURE, University of Pittsburgh, Dept of Germanic Languages & Literatures, 102 Loeffler Bldg, Pittsburgh, 15260. Klaus W Jonas, Dir
Holdings: Cat Mss Pix Microforms
Notes: Center for the development of collections and bibliographical control of the record of publications, mss, correspondence, etc, by or relating to modern German authors. Special sections have been developed for Mann, Rilke, Hauptmann, Hesse, Broch, Sachs and others. Described by Professor Klaus W Jonas's "The German Literature Center in Pittsburgh," *Stechert-Hafner Book News*, vol 24, no 8, April 1970; "Documentation in Modern German Literature: A Progress Report," *Jahrbuch fuer Internationale Germanistik*, vol 4, no 2, 1972, and in *German and Austrian Contributions to World Literature* (1890-1970). Department of Germanic Languages and Literatures, University of Pittsburgh, 1983. 96 pp.

BIBLIOGRAPHY

CA —UNIVERSITY OF CALIFORNIA, BERKELEY, Humanities-Social Sciences Libraries, Library School Library, 2 South Hall, Berkeley, 94720. Virginia Pratt, Head
Holdings: Vols (41,500) Cat Microforms
Notes: Research collection with special strengths in general library science; history of libraries; history of printing and book arts, and publishing; information systems and services; history, criticism, and bibliography of children's literature. The collections in printing and the book arts are complemented by significant holdings both in the Main Library and in the Bancroft Library. Incl collection of 5000 pamphlets.

CA —CLAREMONT COLLEGES, Honnold Library, Ninth & Dartmouth, Claremont, 91711. Tania Rizzo, Special Collections Dept Head
Holdings: Vols (70,000) Cat VF
Notes: Books on typography, bibliography, and history of printing; incunabula; specimen books; fine press books, esp Kelmscott, Doves, Daniel, Mosher, Grabhorn, Nash, and Arion presses and many Southern California printers. A comprehensive collection of Zamorano Club publications and keepsakes, partial source for George E Fulleton, *The Zamorano Club: The First Half Century* (Los Angeles, 1978). Extensive files of ephemera. Fine bindings and fore-edge paintings. Samples of Oriental type and printing.

CA —UNIVERSITY OF CALIFORNIA, SAN DIEGO, Central University Library, Mandeville Dept of Special Collections, La Jolla, 92093. Lynda Corey Claassen, Head
Notes: The Reference Collection: More than 2500 bibliographies guides, and catalogues to rare book and manuscript collections, auction records, histories of book collecting, and important works on the social and technological history of books and printing are included.

CA —UNIVERSITY OF CALIFORNIA, LOS ANGELES, Research Library, Medieval and Renaissance Collection, 405 Hilgard Ave, Los Angeles, 90024. Edward Shreeves, Chairman, Bibliographers Group; Frances K Zeitlin, Medievan and Renaissance Bibliographer
Notes: Early printing history, catalogs of ms collection. Incorporates part of the reference library of the antiquarian bookselling firm of Ulrice Hoepli of Milan.

CA —BIBLIOGRAPHIC RESEARCH LIBRARY, 964 Chapel Hill Way, San Jose, 95122. Robert B Harmon, Bibliographer
Holdings: Vols 759 Uncat Microforms
Budget: $500
Notes: Private research library emphasizing bibliography, political science, John Steinbeck and Ernest Hemingway.

CO —BIBLIOGRAPHICAL CENTER FOR RESEARCH, Rocky Mountain Region, Inc, Library, 1777 S Bellaire, Suite G 150, Denver, 80222. J Segal, Exec Dir
Holdings: Cat
Notes: Library automation, data bases, information retrieval, union catalogs, etc.

CT —LEE ASH, (personal collection), 66 Humiston Dr, Bethany, 06525.

CT —TRINITY COLLEGE LIBRARY, Watkinson Library, 300 Summit St, Hartford, 06106. Jeffrey Kaimowitz, Cur
Holdings: Cat

CT —YALE UNIVERSITY, Box 1603A, Yale Station, New Haven, 06520.

CT —UNIVERSITY OF CONNECTICUT, Library, Storrs, 06268. R H Schimmelpfeng, Dir of Special Collections
Holdings: Vols 310 Cat
Notes: Comprehensive collection of the first editions and reprints of the bibliographical and historical writings of the Chilean bibliographer, Jose Toribio Medina.

DC —LIBRARY OF CONGRESS, Rare Book & Special Collections Div, Washington, 20540. William Matheson, Chief
Notes: The Henry Harrisse Collection comprises works and bibliographies relating to Americana, incl the author's own interleaved and profusely annotated copies of his writings on the Columbus period, together with volumes containing his correspondence with bibliographers and collectors of the latter part of the 19th century.

†DC —LIBRARY OF CONGRESS, Washington, 20540.
Notes: The Library of Congress's collections are matched by no library in the world.

IL —CHICAGO PUBLIC LIBRARY, Special Collections Div, Cultural Center, 78 E Washington St, Chicago, 60602. Laura Linard, Cur
Holdings: Vols 1000 Cat
Notes: Author and subject bibliographies, retrospective and current rare books and manuscripts collections catalogs, bookdealers' catalogs, catalogs of private collections (primarily sale or auction catalogs published in hardbound or deluxe editions).

IL —NEWBERRY LIBRARY, John M Wing Foundation on the History of Printing, 60 W Walton St, Chicago, 60610. Diana Haskell, Cur of Modern Mss
Holdings: Vols (30,000) Cat Mss
Budget: ($50,000)
Notes: The collection covers printing and printing history of Western Europe and the Americas from its invention to the present. It is particularly rich in incunabula (about 2000); the works of the great printers, among others Aldus, Bodoni, Baskerville, and Rogers. Printed catalog: *A Dictionary* Catalogue. (Boston: G K Hall, 1961); *Supplements* (1981). Brief descriptions: James M Wells, "The John M Wing Foundation of the Newberry Library," *The Book Collector, VIII,* 2 (Summer 1959), pp 157-162; Lawrece W Towner, *An Uncommon Collection of Uncommon* Collections (Chicago: The Newberry Library, 1977), pp 25-26.

IL —NEWBERRY LIBRARY, John M Wing Foundation on the History of Printing, 60 W Walton St, Chicago, 60610. Diana Haskell, Cur of Modern Mss
Holdings: Cat Mss
Notes: Several thousand local, national,

BIBLIOGRAPHY (cont.)

subject bibliographies in the humanities. Good historical holdings, incl library catalogs, early bibliographic and learned journals, early bibliographies and reference works.

IN —INDIANA STATE UNIVERSITY, Cunningham Memorial Library, Dept of Rare Books & Special Collections, Terre Haute, 47809. Lawrence J McCrank, Head
Holdings: Vols 500 Cat
Budget: $500
Notes: The Reference Collection of the Rare Books and Special Collections Department holds bibliographies and reference works related specifically to the department's collections in lexicography, Indiana local and regional history, education, travel and discovery, etc, and on the book arts, eg, printing, typography, paper making, illustration, conservation and binding. Includes several facsimile editions of famous codices.

KS —UNIVERSITY OF KANSAS, Kenneth Spencer Research Library, Special Collections Dept, Lawrence, 66045. Alexandra Mason, Librn
Holdings: Cat Mss
Notes: Early bibliography in Summerfield renaissance collection, later throughout various collections; large reference collection. Some ms catalogs of private libraries, many printed catalogs of libraries. Noncirculating.

LA —R W NORTON ART GALLERY, Library, 4747 Creswell Ave, Shreveport, 71106. Jerry M Bloomer, Librn
Holdings: Vols 1450 Cat

MD —JOHNS HOPKINS UNIVERSITY, Milton S Eisenhower Library, Charles & 34 Sts, Baltimore, 21218. Ann S Gwyn, Assistant Dir for Special Collections
Holdings: Vols Cat Mss Microforms
Notes: Standard bibliographical reference works. Also the personal library of bibliophile Leonard L Mackall, plus 46 drawers of his letters and correspondence.

MD —JOHNS HOPKINS UNIVERSITY, Milton S Eisenhower Library, George Peabody Collection, 17 E Mt Vernon Place, Baltimore, 21201. Lyn Hart, Peabody Librn
Holdings: Vols 6000
Notes: Noncirculating.

MA —HARVARD UNIVERSITY LIBRARY, Widener Library, Cambridge, 02138.
Holdings: Cat Microforms
Notes: *Widener Library Shelflist* No 7 (1966) lists 25,999 vols classified in Bibliography; this does not incl subject bibliographies.

MA —HARVARD UNIVERSITY LIBRARY, Law School Library, Langdell Hall, Cambridge, 02138. Harry S Martin III, Librn
Holdings: Cat Mss Maps Pix Slides
Notes: Downs 1687, 1763, 1774, 1776-1779, 1782-1784, 1790-1793, 1809, 1764, 1768, 1796; Downs Supplement 789. Comprehensive collection of English common law, American Law (historical and current), foreign law, comparative law, international law, Roman law and Canon law. Over a million vols.

MA —AMERICAN ANTIQUARIAN SOCIETY LIBRARY, 185 Salisbury St, Worcester, 01609. Marcus A McCorison, Dir & Librn
Notes: Extensive bibliographic notes concerning Thomas W Streeter's collection of Americana.

MI —UNIVERSITY OF MICHIGAN, Graduate Library, Ann Arbor, 48109. Janet White, Reference Librn
Holdings: Cat Microforms
Notes: Extensive bibliography collection constituting the current and historical book record of most nations.

MI —GALE RESEARCH CO, Book Tower, Detroit, 48226. Annie Brewer, Librn
Holdings: Vols (65,000) Cat
Notes: Large collection of reference materials, incl computerized files used in the preparation of familiar contemporary reference books and guides to special fields.

MI —MICHIGAN STATE UNIVERSITY, Libraries, Special Collections Div, East Lansing, 48824. Jannette Fiore, Librn
Holdings: Mss
Notes: Outstanding collection of over 100, 000 items, including Douglas C McMurtrie's published pamphlets and monographs, with manuscript, typescript, galleys, etc, material for the unfinished *History of Printing in the United States,* and his vast correspondence on printing and its history. Supported by a collection of works on printing.

MO —WASHINGTON UNIVERSITY, John M Olin Library, Campus Box 1061, St Louis, 63130.
Holdings: Vols Cat Microforms
Notes: Strongest in subject, individual and analytical bibliography.

NY —NEW YORK STATE LIBRARY, State Education Bldg Annex, Washington Ave, Albany, 12224.
Holdings: Vols 15,100 Cat
Notes: Extensive collection of national catalogs and general and subject bibliographies.

NY —BUFFALO & ERIE COUNTY PUBLIC LIBRARY, Rare Book Room, Lafayette Sq, Buffalo, 14203. William H Loos, Cur
Holdings: Vols 550 Cat

NY —CORNELL UNIVERSITY LIBRARIES, John M Olin Library, History of Science Collections, Ithaca, 14853. Lillian A Clark, Administrative Supervisor; David W Corson, History of Science Librn
Notes: Very extensive collection of history, biography and bibliography.
See also entry under Science - History

NY —COLUMBIA UNIVERSITY LIBRARIES, Rare Book & Manuscript Library, 801 Butler Library, 535 W 114 St, New York, 10027. Kenneth A Lohf, Librn

NY —GRADUATE CENTER OF THE CITY UNIVERSITY OF NEW YORK, William H and Gwynne K Crouse Library for Publishing Arts, 33 W 42 St, New York, 10036. Alfred H Lane, Dir
Notes: Recently established and still growing, but intended to become the authoritative source of materials in the field, of particular value in research about the publishing industry. Open to staff members of publishing houses, students, scholars, authors, printers, and booksellers. Primarily 20th century materials, and particularly useful for research on technical, financial, and historical matters. Much on the history of individual houses, economics of authorship; marketing and distribution of books; etc.

NY —GROLIER CLUB OF NEW YORK LIBRARY, 47 E 60 St, New York, 10022. Robert Nikirk, Librn
Holdings: Cat
Notes: Subject strength.

NY —NEW YORK ACADEMY OF MEDICINE, Library, 2 E 103 St, New York, 10029. Brett A Kirkpatrick, Librn
Holdings: Vols Cat
Notes: Incl works on general bibliography with emphasis on medical bibliography.

NY —NEW YORK PUBLIC LIBRARY, Research Libraries, General Research Division, Fifth Ave & 42 St, New York, 10018. Rodney Phillips, Chief
Holdings: Vols (2,225,000) Cat Maps Pix Microforms
Budget: ($775,718)
Notes: Strong in all fields.

NY —NEW YORK PUBLIC LIBRARY, Music Div, 111 Amsterdam Ave, New York, 10023. Frank C Campbell, Chief

NY —UNIVERSITY CLUB, Library, One W 54 St, New York, 10019. Guy St Clair, Library Dir
Holdings: Vols (100,000) Cat Mss Maps Pix
Notes: A private library for the members of the University Club, their guests, and serious scholars upon written application to the Library Director. Holds the Edward Larocque Tinker Collection of Illustrated Books Between the Two World Wars, A Milton Runyon Collection on the History of Printing and Publishing, the Frederic R Coudert "Les Bibliophiles des Paris" Collection, The University Club Rare Book Collection, and the Frederick G Rudge Collection of Books Designed by William E Rudge and Bruce Rogers.

NC —DUKE UNIVERSITY, William R Perkins Library, Durham, 27706. Elvin E Strowd, University Librn

OH —CASE WESTERN RESERVE UNIVERSITY, M A Baxter School of Information and Library Science, 10900 Euclid Ave, Cleveland, 44106. Bettina MacAyeal, Librn; Gretchen Larson, Librn
Holdings: Vols (15,000) Cat
Budget: ($40,000)
Notes: Western Reserve University merged with Case Institute of Technology to form Case Western Reserve University. The University Libraries do have a library science collection, but the Library Science Library is a separate department on campus, and does not have the same address. Noncirculating historical children's literature collection is established and cataloged.

OK —UNIVERSITY OF TULSA, McFarlin Library, Dept of Rare Books and Special Collections, 600 S College, Tulsa, 74104. David Farmer, Dir; Toby Murray, Archivist; Caroline Swinson, Cur of Manuscripts & Art
Holdings: Cat
Notes: Incl the John Bennett Shaw Collection of Books About Books.

†PA —UNIVERSITY OF PITTSBURGH, Graduate School of Library & Information Sciences Library, L I S Bldg, Third Fl, Pittsburgh, 15260. Jean Kindlin, Librn
Notes: Extensive collection on the historical development of school libraries, media services, and evaluation of materials for use in all types of schools. Incl 54,800 vols, 7524 bound periodicals, 630 periodical subscriptions.

TX —TEXAS STATE LIBRARY, Archives Div, 1201 Brazos, PO Box 12927, Capitol Sta, Austin, 78711. David B Gracy II, State Archivist

TX —AMON CARTER MUSEUM, Library, 3510 Camp Bowie Blvd, PO Box 2365, Fort Worth, 76113. Nancy G Wynne, Librn
Holdings: Vols (25,000) Cat Mss Pix
Notes: The book collection, microfilm and photo archives have been built toward the goal of the interpretation of American history through art. At present, the greatest strengths are in Americana, history of photography, bibliography and American exhibition catalogs.

TX —RICE UNIVERSITY, Fondren Library, 6100 S Main St, PO Box 1892, Houston, 77251. Dr Samuel M Carrington, Jr, University Librn
Holdings: Vols 9000 Cat

TX —UNIVERSITY OF HOUSTON, M D Anderson Memorial Library, University Park, Houston, 77004. David Farmer, Cur, Special Collections; Jean Jackson, Assistant Cur
Holdings: Vols 225
Notes: The collection follows, to a degree, the checklist prepared by Charles Heartman in 1942 (supplement, 1946), but contains many items not included by Heartman.

ON —QUEEN'S UNIVERSITY, Douglas Library, Kingston, K7L 5C4, Can. William F E Morley, Cur, Special Collections
Holdings: Vols 6980 Cat Mss Pix
Notes: Subject strength of the collections is in Canadiana.

ON —UNIVERSITY OF TORONTO, Massey College, Robertson Davies Library, 4 Devonshire Place, Toronto, M5S 2E1, Can. Desmond G Neill, Librn
Holdings: Vols (12,000) Cat Mss Microforms
Notes: Library contains Bibliography Room (11 hand presses, type and equipment) and Papermaking Room. Book collections incl Ruari McLean Collection of 19th-century books on, and representative of, color printing (approx 4300 items).

BIBLIOGRAPHY—BEST BOOKS

IN —INDIANA UNIVERSITY, Lilly Library, Seventh St, Bloomington, 47405. William R Cagle, Librn
Holdings: / / Cat
Notes: First editions, largely from the J K Lilly Collection.

MA —HISTORIC DEERFIELD-POCUMTUCK VALLEY MEMORIAL ASSOCIATION, Libraries, Memorial St,

BIBLIOGRAPHY—BEST BOOKS (cont.)

Box 53, Deerfield, 01342. David R Proper, Librn
Holdings: Vols (17,000) Cat Mss Maps Pix Microforms
Notes: Local and regional history, especially western Massachusetts. Also, remnants of several collections of books available to early Deerfield and Greenfield residents.

BIBLIOGRAPHY—COLLECTIONS

†DC —LIBRARY OF CONGRESS, Washington, 20540.
Notes: The Library of Congress's collections are matched by no library in the world.

BIBLIOGRAPHY—EARLY PRINTED BOOKS—15TH CENTURY see Incunabula

BIBLIOGRAPHY—HISTORY

ON —UNIVERSITY OF WESTERN ONTARIO, Schoool of Library and Information Science, Library, London, N6G 1H1, Can. Victoria Ripley, Librn
Holdings: Vols (50,000)
Notes: Auction and antiquarian booksellers' catalogs from Canadian, American and European firms, some dating back to the 18th century. A special strength is 19th and early 20th century American booksellers' catalogs, recently augmented by a collection of pre-1920 catalogs formed by the late H O Teisberg. Current emphasis is on Canadian catalogs.

BIBLIOGRAPHY—LIMITED EDITIONS

CA —SAN DIEGO PUBLIC LIBRARY, Wangenheim Rm, 820 E St, San Diego, 92101. Eileen Boyle, Librn
Holdings: Vols (7500)
Notes: A collection on the history of the book and the development of printing with specimens ranging from Babylonian tablets to cassettes.

CO —DENVER PUBLIC LIBRARY, Douglas Collection of Fine Printing, 1357 Broadway, Denver, 80203.
Holdings: Vols 1700 Cat
Notes: Books from private presses, limited editions and books about private presses. Incl a complete set of vols from William Morris' Kelmscott Press and a virtually complete collection of Ashendene Press books. Most major presses are well represented and minor presses have representative works in the collection.

CT —TRINITY COLLEGE LIBRARY, Watkinson Library, 300 Summit St, Hartford, 06106. Jeffrey Kaimowitz, Cur
Holdings: Cat
Notes: Incl the Mrs John G McCarthy Collection.

CT —YALE UNIVERSITY, Box 1603A, Yale Station, New Haven, 06520.

FL —FLORIDA STATE UNIVERSITY, Robert Manning Strozier Library, Special Collections Dept, Tallahassee, 32306. Opal M Free, Head, Special Collections
Holdings: Vols (12,254) Cat
Notes: Noncirculating. No photocopying.

IL —CHICAGO PUBLIC LIBRARY, Special Collections Div, Cultural Center, 78 E Washington St, Chicago, 60602. Laura Linard, Cur
Holdings: Vols (1000) Cat
Notes: A general collection on the history of typography, including a specimen collection of works printed before 1700, books about books, private press productions (primarily Chicago), limited editions, illustrated and extra-illustrated books and fine bindings. Outstanding items described in *Treasures of The Chicago Public Library,* compiled by Thomas A Orlando and Marie Gecik, 1977, pp 6-29.

IL —NORTHWESTERN UNIVERSITY, Library, Special Collections Dept, 1937 Sheridan Rd, Evanston, 60201. R Russell Maylone, Cur
Holdings: Vols 20,000 Cat
Notes: First, limited, special editions, works about, and ephemera of the major authors of the 20th century as well as representative minor writers. Incl English, American, French, and German authors and to a lesser extent Italian, Spanish, and other European writers. Extensive collections of Lawrence Durrell, T S Eliot, William Faulkner, Robert Graves, Ernest Hemingway, James Joyce, Karl Kraus, D H Lawrence, Hugh MacDiarmid, Henry Miller, Anais Nin, Ezra Pound, Gertrude Stein, H G Wells, W B Yeats. Additional 5000 Private Press books. 15,000 "little magazine" titles (exclusive of runs in the general library collections).

MA —BOSTON UNIVERSITY, Mugar Memorial Library, Special Collections Dept, 771 Commonwealth Ave, Boston, 02215. Howard B Gotlieb, Dir
Holdings: Cat
Notes: Extensive collection; especially works of authors who have deposited their papers and mss with the library.

NY —UNIVERSITY CLUB, Library, One W 54 St, New York, 10019. Guy St Clair, Library Dir
Holdings: Vols (100,000) Cat Mss Maps Pix
Notes: A private library for the members of the University Club, their guests, and serious scholars upon written application to the Library Director. Holds the Edward Larocque Tinker Collection of Illustrated Books Between the Two World Wars, A Milton Runyon Collection on the History of Printing and Publishing, the Frederic R Coudert "Les Bibliophiles des Paris" Collection, The University Club Rare Book Collection, and the Frederick G Rudge Collection of Books Designed by William E Rudge and Bruce Rogers.

PA —TEMPLE UNIVERSITY LIBRARIES, Special Collections Dept, Rare Books & Mss Section, Philadelphia, 19122. Thomas M Whitehead, Cur
Holdings: Vols (3000) Cat Mss
Notes: Extensive holdings of modern English and American literature, late 19th, 20th centuries. First and limited editions, association copies, supported by mss holdings. Special sub-collections of Walter de la Mare, Joseph Conrad, Robert Louis Stevenson, Joel Chandler Harris, E H W Meyerstein, Thackeray, George MacDonald, W W Gibson, John Masefield, Tennyson, Sir Walter Scott.

PA —UNIVERSITY OF PITTSBURGH, Hillman Library, Special Collections Dept, 363 Hillman Library, Pittsburgh, 15260. Charles E Aston Jr, Coordinator
Holdings: Vols 3000 Cat
Notes: Limited editions of 20th-century British and U S authors; also a representative collection of Limited Editions Club imprints.

RI —BROWN UNIVERSITY, John Hay Library, Harris Collection, Prospect St, Providence, 02912. Rosemary L Cullen, Cur
Holdings: Vols (200,000) Cat Mss Pix Phonorecords Microforms
Budget: ($15,000)
Notes: The Harris Collection of American Poetry and Plays is principally composed of American and Canadian poetry and plays, 17th century-date. Extensive holdings in songsters, gift books and annuals, hymnals, pageants, broadside verse, carriers' addresses, women poets, juvenile poetry, (incl Mother Goose and *The Night Before* Christmas), sheet music with lyrics, small press publications, fine printing, black poets, "little magazines," Yiddish-American literature. All movements or schools of American poetry are represented. Incl first editions of most American poets and playwrights, notably Whitman, Poe, Wallace Stevens, Eugene O'Neill, Edward Albee, Ezra Pound, T S Eliot, William Carlos Williams, Amy Lowell, Phyllis Wheatley, Robert Frost, Allen Ginsberg, Bliss Carman, and Stephen Foster sheet music. Also incl the Saunders Walt Whitman Collection (1300 vols); the LangdonCollection of Pageants (250 vols); the Asa Cushman Collection of plays in ms and prompt copies; the MacDougall Collection of Psalters and Hymnals; 4000 plays issued by Walter H Baker Co, Boston (1890-1957); the Vaxer Collection of Yiddish Poetry, Plays and Music (1700 vols). Collections incl 200,000 vols, 30,000 broadsides, 55,000 mss, 170,000 pieces of sheet music, 450 phonorecords, and 375 microfilm reels. See *Dictionary Catalog of the Harris Collection of American Poetry and Plays* (Boston: G K Hall, 1972), 13 vols; *Supplement* (1977), 3 vols. See also, *American Poetry,* 1609-1900, *A Collection on Microfilm, Segment I* (1609-1820); *Segment II* (1821-1850); *Segment III* (1851-1870) (Woodbridge, Conn: Research Publications). Separate catalog.

NS —MOUNT SAINT VINCENT UNIVERSITY, Library, 166 Bedford Hwy, Halifax, B3M 2J6, Can. Lucian Bianchini, University Librn
Holdings: Vols 7000 Cat
Budget: ($125,000)
Notes: The MacDonald Collection consists of 19th and 20th century English and American literature, fine bindings, a few examples of fore-edge paintings, limited editions, first editions, and autographed copies.

BIBLIOGRAPHY—MICROSCOPIC AND MINIATURE EDITIONS

DC —LIBRARY OF CONGRESS, Rare Book & Special Collections Div, Washington, 20540. William Matheson, Chief
Holdings: Vols 1596 Cat
Notes: The Rare Book Division has custody of all of the Library's miniature books (ie, books less than 10 centimeters in both height and width) with the exception of those assigned to various subject collections. The dates range from the 15th century to present and incl imprints of virtually every country.

IN —INDIANA UNIVERSITY, Lilly Library, Seventh St, Bloomington, 47405. William R Cagle, Librn
Holdings: Uncat Mss
Notes: The Elisabeth Ball Collection consists of more than 7000 books and many manuscripts from the late seventeenth to the early twentieth centuries. Strengths incl Newberry and other early imprints, chapbooks, horn books, harlequinades, street cries, and miniature books.

ME —PORTLAND PUBLIC LIBRARY, 5 Monument Sq, Portland, 04101. Edward V Chenevert, Library Dir
Holdings: Vols 17 Cat
Notes: The Yellow Kid Press is privately operated by David W Serette. Specialty is miniature books.

MD —JOHNS HOPKINS UNIVERSITY, Milton S Eisenhower Library, Special Collections, John Work Garrett Library, 4545 N Charles St, Baltimore, 21210. Jane Katz, Garrett Librn
Holdings: Vols 87 // Cat
Notes: Early 19th century. Incl runs of Diamond Classics and Diamond Poets. No photocopying.

MN —UNIVERSITY OF MINNESOTA, O Meredith Wilson Library, 309 19 Ave S, Minneapolis, 55455. Austin J McLean, Chief, Special Collections
Holdings: Vols 230 Cat
Notes: Miniature editions from 16th century to modern finely printed volumes. Partially cataloged, but complete listing available in Division. No photocopying.

MN —COLLEGE OF SAINT CATHERINE, Library, 2004 Randolph Ave, Saint Paul, 55105. Sister Mary William Brady, Archivist
Holdings: Vols 250 Uncat
Notes: Marcella and Catherine Hurley Miniature Book Collection. Separate title listing.

†NY —COLUMBIA UNIVERSITY LIBRARIES, Butler Library, Rare Book and Manuscript Library, 535 W 114 St, New York, 10027.

NC —DUKE UNIVERSITY, William R Perkins Library, Rare Book Room, Durham, 27706. John L Sharpe, III, Cur
Notes: Miniature books collection of 100 volumes less than 10 cm tall.

OH —HEBREW UNION COLLEGE-JEWISH INSTITUTE OF RELIGION, Klau Library, 3101 Clifton Ave, Cincinnati, 45220. David J Gilner, Reference Librn
Holdings: Cat
Notes: Incl editions of the Pentateuch, Psalms, the Haggadah, prayerbooks, etc.

BIBLIOGRAPHY—MICROSCOPIC AND MINIATURE EDITIONS (cont.)

OH —CLEVELAND PUBLIC LIBRARY, Fine Arts and Special Collections Department, 325 Superior Ave, Cleveland, 44114. Alice N Loranth, Head
Holdings: Vols 115 Cat Mss
Notes: Incl several dictionaries, Bibles, and Omar Khayyam editions.
See also entry under Rare Books.

BIBLIOGRAPHY—PAPERBACK EDITIONS

†AL —UNIVERSITY OF ALABAMA, Amelia Gayle Gorgas Library, PO Box S, University, 35486.
Notes: A rare, complete set of the Armed Services Editions of paperbacks issued for use of American forces overseas in World War II.

CA —UNIVERSITY OF CALIFORNIA, LOS ANGELES, Research Library, Dept of Special Collections, 405 Hilgard Ave, Los Angeles, 90024. Edward Shreeves, Chairman, Bibliographers Group; David S Zeidberg, Head
Notes: Various collections, incl almanacs, comic books, commercial catalogs, fantasy fiction, pulp magazines, trade cards, and 19th century American paperbacks.

DC —LIBRARY OF CONGRESS, Rare Book & Special Collections Div, Washington, 20540. William Matheson, Chief
Notes: The division has an archival set of the Dell paperback books published from 1943-76.

NY —GRADUATE CENTER OF THE CITY UNIVERSITY OF NEW YORK, William H and Gwynne K Crouse Library for Publishing Arts, 33 W 42 St, New York, 10036. Alfred H Lane, Dir
Notes: Recently established and still growing, but intended to become the authoritative source of materials in the field, of particular value in research about the publishing industry. Open to staff members of publishing houses, students, scholars, authors, printers, and booksellers. Primarily 20th century materials, and particularly useful for research on technical, financial, and historical matters. Much on the history of individual houses, economics of authorship; marketing and distribution of books; etc.

BIBLIOGRAPHY, BOTANICAL

PA —HUNT INSTITUTE FOR BOTANICAL DOCUMENTATION, Hunt Botanical Library, Carnegie-Mellon University, Pittsburgh, 15213. Bernadette G Callery, Librn
Holdings: Vols 23,000 Cat Pix
Notes: Collection of primarily historical botany and plant taxonomy, especially 1730-1840. Includes approximately 500 15th through 17th century herbals, extensive collection of 18th and 19th century color-plate works, floras and monographic works, and other works on natural history, early gardening and horticulture, and travel, particularly that dealing with plant exploration and introduction. Extensive biographical materials, on people in plant sciences. Reference collection and extensive documentation in botanical bibliography, especially concerning books published before 1850. Includes as separate collections, the Strandell Collection of Linnaeana and the Michel Adanson Library. Over 800 items described in *Catalogue of Botanical Books in the Collection of Rachel McMasters Miller Hunt, 1477-1800* (Pittsburgh, 1958-1960).

BIBLIOGRAPHY, CRITICAL see Literature—History and Criticism

BIBLIOGRAPHY, NATIONAL

MI —UNIVERSITY OF MICHIGAN, Graduate Library, Ann Arbor, 48109. Janet White, Reference Librn
Holdings: Cat Microforms
Notes: Extensive bibliography collection constituting the current and historical book record of most nations.

NY —NEW YORK STATE LIBRARY, State Education Bldg Annex, Washington Ave, Albany, 12224.
Holdings: Vols (15,100) Cat
Notes: Extensive collection of national catalogs and general and subject bibliographies.

BIBLIOPHILY see Book Collecting and Book Collectors

BICE, CLARE, 1909-1976

ON —NATIONAL LIBRARY OF CANADA, 395 Wellington St, Ottawa, K1A 0N4, Can. Andre Preibish, Dir
Notes: Literary Manuscripts collection contains papers of several important Canadian authors writing in English and/or French eg Clare Bice (1909-1976), noted author and illustrator of children's books; Andre Giroux, novelist, writer for television and broadcaster; Roger Lemelin, well-known author of Au pied de la pente douce, Les Plouffe, and Pierre le magnifique; Gabrielle Roy (1909-1983), author of many novels, including Bonheur d'occasion, La Petite Poule d'Eau and Rue Deschambault; Laura Goodman Salverson (1890-1970), writer, public speaker and teacher; Phyllis Webb, poet.

BICULTURALISM—CANADA

PQ —CONCORDIA UNIVERSITY LIBRARIES, Vanier Library, 7141 Sherbrooke St SW, Montreal, H3G 1M8, Can. Martin Cohen, Collections Coordinator
Holdings: Uncat Mss
Notes: Dr J B Rudnyckyj was on the Royal Commission on Bilingualism and Biculturalism in Canada. His papers deal with bilingualism, multi-culturalism, minorities, languages. 400 boxes.

BICYCLES AND TRICYCLES

CA —CLAREMONT COLLEGES, Honnold Library, Ninth & Dartmouth, Claremont, 91711. Tania Rizzo, Special Collections Dept Head
Holdings: Vols 100 Uncat Pix Periodicals Ephemera Scrapbooks
Notes: Charles Sigmund Frey Memorial Bicycle Collection, donated by Ruth Frey Axe. Publications from 1870s to present, incl history, advertising, magazines, guidebooks, humor, fiction, and children's books.

PA —FREE LIBRARY OF PHILADELPHIA, Automobile Reference Collection, Logan Sq, Philadelphia, 19103. Louis G Helverson, Jr, Librn in Charge
Holdings: Vols (14,000) Cat Pix Slides
Notes: Collection is concerned with all aspects of automotive industry and its history. Includes shop manuals, instruction books, parts books, and periodicals dealing with all types of bicycles, tricycles and motor vehicles. Industry statistics, corporate annual reports, environmental problems, safety. Incl 18,000 pictures, 1700 slides, 648 microfilm reels, 23,000 sales catalogs, 5000 pieces of ephemera.

BICYCLING see Cycling

BIDDLE, MRS. FRANCIS see Chapin, Katherine Garrison, 1890-1977

BIDDLE, NICHOLAS

DC —LIBRARY OF CONGRESS, Manuscript Division, Washington, 20540. John C Broderick, Chief
Holdings: Cat Mss Pix
Notes: Mss, papers, records, etc.

BIDPAI

OH —CLEVELAND PUBLIC LIBRARY, Fine Arts and Special Collections Department, 325 Superior Ave, Cleveland, 44114. Alice N Loranth, Head
Holdings: Vols (700) Cat Mss
Notes: Part of the Fables Collection, which is strong in Medieval European and Oriental works. Numerous rare and early editions of Reynard the Fox (200 vols), Panchatantra, Bidpai, Hitopadesa, etc, are incl. Aesop and the modern fabulists are incl only by representative editions.
See also entry under Fables; Oriental Languages and Literatures

BIEBER, MARGARET

LA —TULANE UNIVERSITY, Howard-Tilton Memorial Library, Special Collections Div, 7001 Freret St, New Orleans, 70118. Wilbur E Meneray, Librn
Notes: Major collection.

BIEMILLER, ANDREW JOHN

OK —UNIVERSITY OF OKLAHOMA, Bizzell Memorial Library, Western History Collections, 401 W Brooks, Norman, 73069. John Ezell, Cur
Holdings: Mss Pix Maps Documents
Notes: US Representative. His papers. Guide available.

BIERCE, AMBROSE

CA —STANFORD UNIVERSITY LIBRARIES, Cecil H Green Library, Stanford, 94305. Michael T Ryan, Cur
Holdings: Vols Cat
Notes: Also incl correspondence and literary mss.

VA —UNIVERSITY OF VIRGINIA, Alderman Library, Clifton Waller Barrett Collection, Charlottesville, 22901. Joan St C Crane, Cur of American Literature Collections

BIERY, GALEN A.

WA —WESTERN WASHINGTON UNIVERSITY, Center for Pacific Northwest Studies, High St, Bellingham, 98225. James W Scott, Dir
Holdings: Mss Pix Videotapes
Notes: The Galen A Biery Collection. One of the Pacific Northwest's best-known and most active local historians. Incl in the collection are the copy books of the Sehome Coal Co which flourished in the 1870s and 1880s, and a variety of business records of the Pacific American Fisheries Co. See also entry for Archie W Shiels. Partially cataloged.
See also entry under Archie W Shiels

BIG BLUE BOOKS

MI —MICHIGAN STATE UNIVERSITY, Libraries, Special Collections Div, East Lansing, 48824. Jannette Fiore, Librn
Notes: The Russel B Nye Popular Culture Collection in the Michigan State Univ Libraries incl over (45,000) items. Most of the collection is organized into 4 categories: comic art, popular fiction, popular information materials and materials relating to the popular performing arts. About 3900 items. Almanacs, Blue Books, and works popularizing knowledge or offering self-help and how-to advice. There are ca 350 issues of 100 19th and 20th century almanacs. The Blue Books incl ca 2000 Little Blue Books, over 600 Big Blue Books and a good number of issues of the various Haldeman-Julius magazines. In addition to almanacs and Blue Books, Popular Information incl books of advice on etiquette, life and love, how-to-succeed books, popular history, science and biography, and several hundred public schooltextbooks from the 19th and early 20th centuries.

BIG BROTHERS

NY —ROCKEFELLER UNIVERSITY, Rockefeller Archive Center, Hillcrest, Pocantico Hills, North Tarrytown, 10591. Joseph W Ernst, Dir; J William Hess, Assoc Dir
Notes: Papers relative to the Rockefeller Family, Foundations, University, and other specific enterprises and contributions to

BIG BROTHERS (cont.)

particular areas of social, physical, educational, and historic reform, preservation, conservation, or development. Extensive records of administrative, financial, physical, or intellectual relationships.

BIG DRY WASH, BATTLE OF, 1882

AZ —NORTHERN ARIZONA UNIVERSITY, Special Collection Library, CU Box 6022, Flagstaff, 86011. Peter M Whiteley, Coordr/Archivist; William Mullane, Librn
Notes: Letters concerning placement of monument at the Battle of Big Dry Wash, last major Indian battle in Arizona, 1882, located near the Mogollon Rim. Incl letters written by W C Barnes, author of *Arizona Place Names,* and E G Miller, former Coconino National Forest supervisor, 1929-1934.

BIG GAME FISHING see Game Fishing

BIG-LITTLE BOOKS

CA —UNIVERSITY OF CALIFORNIA, DAVIS, Shields Library, Dept of Special Collections, Davis, 95616. Donald Kunitz, Head; C Danial Elliott, Asst Head
Holdings: Vols 230 Cat
Notes: Unique literary form from the 1930s; incl Charlie Chan, Popeye, Tom Mix, Buck Rogers, Little Orphan Annie, the Lone Ranger, and many more.

DC —LIBRARY OF CONGRESS, Rare Book & Special Collections Div, Washington, 20540. William Matheson, Chief
Notes: The Big Little Books published by the Whitman Publishing Company of Racine, Wisconsin are the largest part of this collection. Also represented are books similar in format to the Big Little Books such as the Big Big Books, Better Little Books, and Chubby Little Books.

†IL —NORTHWESTERN UNIVERSITY, Library, Special Collections Dept, Evanston, 60201. R Russell Maylone, Librn
Notes: ca 100 Big-Little books. Some fanzines. Comic books, 8500.

†KS —UNIVERSITY OF KANSAS, Spencer Research Library, Dept of Special Collections, Lawrence, 66045. Alexandra Mason, Librn
Notes: Extensive science fiction, 6 ft of fanzines, 500 Big-Little Books, extensive series books, James E Gunn and Lloyd Biggle special collections in the Dept of Special Collections.

†MI —MICHIGAN STATE UNIVERSITY, Libraries, East Lansing, 48824. Jannette Flore, Librn
Notes: Good samples of Big-Little Books, foreign comics, dime novels, pulps, TV scripts, underground comics. SFWA and Clarion depository.

MN —UNIVERSITY OF MINNESOTA, Libraries, Children's Literature Research Collections, 109 Walter Library, Minneapolis, 55455. Karen Nelson Hoyle, Cur
Holdings: Vols 561 Cat
Notes: Kerlan Collection. No photocopying.

NY —MUSEUM OF CARTOON ART LIBRARY, Comly Avenue, Rye Brook, 10573.
Notes: Original comics and cartoon art, 60, 000 pieces. 800 animated cartoons. Disney collection extensive. Samples of Big-Little Books, foreign comics, fanzines, cartoon related games, posters, pulps, undergrounds. Hal Foster, Walt Kelly, Gene Byrns, Tad Dorgan, Chester Gould extensive original art collections.

OH —BOWLING GREEN STATE UNIVERSITY, Library, Popular Culture Library, Bowling Green, 43403.
Notes: Extensive holdings of Big-Little books, comic books, matchbook covers, picture postcards, personal scrapbooks, trading cards, posters, magazines, film pressbooks, juvenile series novels and popular literature.

BIGELOW, JOHN

NY —NEW YORK PUBLIC LIBRARY, Rare Books and Manuscripts Div, Fifth Ave & 42 St, New York, 10018. William L Joyce, Asst Dir; Susan E Davis, Cur of Mss
Holdings: Mss
Budget: ($7161)
Notes: Incl personal and literary mss, papers, etc.

BIGELOW, POULTNEY

NY —SAINT LAWRENCE UNIVERSITY, Owen D Young Library, Canton, 13617. Mahlon Peterson, Librn
Holdings: Cat Mss Pix
Notes: Frederick Remington's correspondence with Poultney Bigelow and others is the most important part of this collection. Also incl is an extensive collection of magazines in which articles written and/or illustrated by Remington first appeared, a collection of prints of Remington paintings, and many books by and about Remington. There are some restrictions on use of this material. Over 400 items.

BIGELOW FAMILY

NY —UNION COLLEGE, Schaffer Library, Schenectady, 12308. Ann Seemann, Librn; Ellen Fladger, Archivist
Holdings: Vols 20 linear feet // Indexed Mss
Notes: Letters to and copies of letters from John Bigelow and Bigelow Family correspondence, 1816-1911. Photocopies may be supplied upon written request only.

BIGGLE, LLOYD

†KS —UNIVERSITY OF KANSAS, Spencer Research Library, Dept of Special Collections, Lawrence, 66045. Alexandra Mason, Librn
Notes: Extensive science fiction, 6 ft of fanzines, 500 Big-Little Books, extensive series books, James E Gunn and Lloyd Biggle special collections in the Dept of Special Collections.

BIGLER, HENRY WILLIAM

AZ —NORTHERN ARIZONA UNIVERSITY, Special Collection Library, CU Box 6022, Flagstaff, 86011. Peter M Whiteley, Coordr/Archivist; William Mullane, Librn
Notes: Henry William Bigler Collection. He was a Mormon pioneer with the Mormon Battalion, and was present at the Sutter gold discovery in Calif; incl journal, 1846-1853 (original in the Henry E Huntington Library).

BILBO, SEN. THEODORE G.

MS —UNIVERSITY OF SOUTHERN MISSISSIPPI, William David McCain Graduate Library, Box 5148, Southern Sta, Hattiesburg, 39406.
Holdings: Cat Mss Pix
Notes: Papers, 1915-47. Approx 1200 linear feet, incl correspondence, subject films, clippings, photographs, and memorabilia. Bilbo served two terms as Governor of Mississippi (1916-1920, 1928-1932) and was a United States Senator from 1935 until his death in 1947. His papers cover a wide range of subjects relating to Mississippi, the South and the US as a whole during these years.

BILINGUALISM

MI —UNIVERSITY OF MICHIGAN, English Language Institute/Linguistics Library, 1013 N University Bldg, Ann Arbor, 48109. Patricia M Aldridge, Librn
Holdings: Vols (4500) Cat Maps VF Videotapes
Notes: The collection on teaching English as a foreign language is fairly complete; in modern language study it is also quite good. Supporting subjects are linguistics and English grammar; psychology, American culture, education, foreign student adjustment, and bibliography are covered.

BILINGUALISM—CANADA

PQ —CONCORDIA UNIVERSITY LIBRARIES, Vanier Library, 7141 Sherbrooke St SW, Montreal, H3G 1M8, Can. Martin Cohen, Collections Coordinator
Holdings: Uncat Mss
Notes: Dr J B Rudnyckyj was on the Royal Commission on Bilingualism and Biculturalism in Canada. His papers deal with bilingualism, multi-culturalism, minorities, languages. 400 boxes.

BILLBOARDS

NJ —FAIRLEIGH DICKINSON UNIVERSITY, Friendship Library, 285 Madison Ave, Madison, 07940. James Fraser, Library Dir; Renee Weber, Cur
Holdings: Vols 1200 Cat Mss Pix Slides Phonorecords 16mm Films
Notes: Official depository for the Outdoor Advertising industry. Collection initiated in August 1972. About 100,000 items. It is the concern of the Outdoor Advertising Association of America that this collection become the definitive collection on the industry in this country. Incl 20,000 mss, 10, 000 pictures, 30,000 slides. 15 original billboards.

BILLINGS, JOHN SHAW

†MD —JOHNS HOPKINS UNIVERSITY, Institute of the History of Medicine, 1900 E Monument St, Baltimore, 21205.
Holdings: Vols (50,000) Cat

BILUCHI LANGUAGE see Baluchi Language

BINAC COMPUTER

DE —HAGLEY MUSEUM AND LIBRARY, Eleutherian Mills-Hagley Foundation Inc, PO Box 3630, Greenville, 19807. Richmond D Williams, Dir; Heddy A Richter, Imprints Librn
Notes: Records of the Sperry-Univac Company (1940-1975; 400 cubic feet) document the early development and rapid growth of the computer industry. The collection incl technical and administrative documents relating to the ENIAC, BINAC and UNIVAC computers.

BINDER, STEVE

CA —UNIVERSITY OF CALIFORNIA, LOS ANGELES, Theater Arts Library, Los Angeles, 90024. Edward Shreeves, Chairman, Bibliographers Group; Audree Malkin, Head, Theater Arts Library
Notes: Steve Binder (producer) Collection: various annotated versions of scripts, guest spots, memos, correspondence and production material for television shows filmed before live audiences, such as *The Flip Wilson Show, The Andy Williams Show, The Carol Burnett Show, The Mac Davis Show, The Lucy Show, The Danny Kaye Show,* and *The Liza Minnelli Show.*

BINDING OF BOOKS see Bookbinding and Bookbinders

BINDINGS, FINE see Bookbinding and Bookbinders

BING, SIR RUDOLF

MA —BOSTON UNIVERSITY, Mugar Memorial Library, Special Collections Dept, 771 Commonwealth Ave, Boston, 02215. Howard B Gotlieb, Dir
Holdings: Cat Mss Pix

BINGHAM, JOHN A.

OH —OHIO HISTORICAL SOCIETY, Archives Library Division, 1982 Velma Ave, Columbus, 43211. Dennis East, Division Chief
Notes: His papers.

BINI, LUCIO, 1908-1964

KS —MENNINGER FOUNDATION, Archives, 5600 W Sixth St, Box 829, Topeka, 66601. Alice Brand, Librn; Mark West, Archivist
Notes: 1 box, 1935-63. Bini assisted Ugo Cerletti in the development of electroshock therapy. Incl correspondence, research notes, and clinical records.

BIOASSAY see Biological Assay

BIOASSAY, WATER QUALITY see Water Quality Bioassay

BIOCHEMISTRY see Biological Chemistry

BIOELECTRICITY—HISTORY

MN —BAKKEN LIBRARY OF ELECTRICITY IN LIFE, 3537 Zenith Ave S, Minneapolis, 55416. John Edward Senior, Dir

BIOENERGETICS

AZ —WORLD UNIVERSITY, Library, 711 E Blacklidge Dr, Tucson, 85719. Howard John Zitko, Cur
Holdings: Vols (15,000) Cat Mss Maps Audiotapes
Notes: Collection concerns what are generally called the "frontier sciences." No interlibrary loan.

MN —BAKKEN LIBRARY OF ELECTRICITY IN LIFE, 3537 Zenith Ave S, Minneapolis, 55416. John Edward Senior, Dir
Notes: Books (including periodicals, manuscripts, and archival materials) and instrument collection. 1500 instruments (focus-18th and 19th centuries). Relating to the history of electrophysiology.

VA —ASSOCIATION FOR RESEARCH & ENLIGHTENMENT, Library, 67 & Atlantic Avenue, PO Box 595, Virginia Beach, 23451. Stephen Jordan, Library Mgr
Holdings: Vols (3000) Cat
Notes: Emphasis on Christian, Buddhist, Hindu religions, mysticism, comparative religion, psychological approach to biofeedback, autogenics, etc.

BIOENGINEERING

NY —ENGINEERING SOCIETIES LIBRARY, 345 E 47 St, New York, 10017. S Kirk Cabeen, Dir
Holdings: Vols 250,000 Cat Maps 16mm Films Microforms
Notes: One of the largest, most comprehensive engineering libraries in the world. Covers all engineering disciplines; particularly strong in electrical and electronic, mechanical, mining and metallurgical, petroleum, chemical, industrial, air conditioning and refrigeration engineering. Incl Wheeler Collection of early materials on magnetism an electricity. 125, 000 bound periodical volumes; 10,000 maps; 5000 serial subscriptions (many foreign-language). Virtually all materials abstracted in *Engineering Index* (1884-date) are incl in Library. Noncirculating, except to members of professional engineering societies which support the Library. See *Engineering Societies Library, New York, Classed Subject Catalog and Index* (Boston: G K Hall, 1963); and *Supplements,* 1-10, 1964-1973.

PA —UNIVERSITY OF PENNSYLVANIA, Towne Scientific Library, 220 S 33 St, Philadelphia, 19104. Charles Meyers, Librn
Holdings: Vols (65,000) Cat

PA —PENNSYLVANIA STATE UNIVERSITY, Engineering Library, 325 Hammond St, University Park, 16802. Tom Conkling, Librn
Holdings: Vols (60,000) Microforms
Notes: This collection includes substantial microform holdings and extensive runs of periodicals.

WI —UNIVERSITY OF WISCONSIN, MADISON, College of Agricultural & Life Sciences, Steenbock Memorial Library, 550 Babcock Dr, Madison, 53706. Jan Kennedy, Dir
Holdings: Vols (186,312) Cat Docs
Notes: Collection incl basic and applied research in biochemistry, plant and animal genetics.

BIOETHICS

DC —CENTER FOR BIOETHICS, Library, Kennedy Institute, Georgetown University, 3520 Prospect St NW, Washington, 20057. Doris Goldstein, Dir; Judith Mistichelli, Senior Librn
Holdings: Vols (8200)
Notes: Largest library of its kind. Incl 31, 000 journal articles on applied ethics. Produces computer database *Bioethicsline,* available through MEDLARS; and the printed annual *Bibliography of Bioethics.* Other library publications are: *New Titles in* Bioethics (monthly); *Scope Notes* series on current topics.

DC —GEORGETOWN UNIVERSITY, Library, Special Collections Div, 37 & O Sts NW, Washington, 20057. George M Barringer, Special Collections Librn; Nicholas B Sheetz, Mss Librn
Holdings: Mss Cat Pix
Notes: Papers of Andre E Hellegers, obstetrician, gynecologist and leading authority in bioethics. The major bulk of the papers concerns Dr Helleger's directorship of the Joseph and Rose Kennedy Institute for Ethics, 1971-1979. Incl are numerous publications and mss written by Hellegers and others on abortion, birth control, population research, and bioethics.

IN —SAINT VINCENT HOSPITAL & HEALTH CARE CENTER, Garceau Library, 20001 W 86 St, Indianapolis, 46260. Virginia Durkin, Librn
Holdings: Vols (7500) Cat

MA —BOSTON COLLEGE LIBRARIES, School of Nursing, Library, Cushing Hall, Chestnut Hill, 02167. Mary L Pekarski, Librn
Holdings: Vols 30,000 Cat Slides Audiotapes Videotapes Filmstrips Microforms
Budget: $24,650
Notes: This collection is being absorbed in the general collection.

BIOFEEDBACK TRAINING

VA —ASSOCIATION FOR RESEARCH & ENLIGHTENMENT, Library, 67 & Atlantic Avenue, PO Box 595, Virginia Beach, 23451. Stephen Jordan, Library Mgr
Holdings: Vols (3000) Cat
Notes: Emphasis on Christian, Buddhist, Hindu religions, mysticism, comparative religion, psychological approach to biofeedback, autogenics, etc.

BIOFUEL

NY —CARY ARBORETUM OF THE NEW YORK BOTANICAL GARDEN, Library, Box AB, Millbrook, 12545. Fred Strum, Librn
Notes: This collection of alternative energy sources consists of publications concerned with solar energy, wind power, biofuel, methanol, small hydroelectric projects, and wood power.

BIOGENESIS see Life—Origin

BIOGRAPHY—COLLECTIONS

CA —CRAFT AND FOLK ART MUSEUM, Library, 5814 Wilshire Blvd, Los Angeles, 90036. Joan M Benedetti, Museum Librn
Holdings: Vols (2000) Slides VF
Notes: Incl 2000 books; 70 journal subscriptions; artists' biographical files: 6 file drawers; clipping files: 8 file drawers; 20,000 slides. Representation of the material culture of all people, traditional and contemporary expressions. Incl visual and printed information on ethnic, traditional, popular, decorative, idiosyncratic, and contemporary crafts as well as vernacular architecture, handmade houses, and design. Information about and for professional artists on health hazards, conservation, and career management. Anthropological and art historical works; exhibition catalogues; slides, photographs, audiocassettes; clipping and pamphlet files. Contemporary Slide Registry of Craftspeople and extensive biographical files of contemporary craft artists. Information and referral files of craft related galleries, shops, festivals, organizations, etc.

CA —LOS ANGELES PUBLIC LIBRARY, Municipal Reference Library, Rm 530, City Hall E, 200 N Main St, Los Angeles, 90012. C Grimsley, Senior Librn
Holdings: Vols (86,000) Cat
Budget: ($33,000)
Notes: Emphasis on cities over 500,000 with special collection of municipal documents from large cities. Biographical material on local government officials.

†CA —HUNTINGTON BOTANICAL GARDENS LIBRARY, 1151 Oxford Rd, San Marino, 91108. Ann Ravenscroft, Secretary
Holdings: Vols (8000)
Notes: Emphases on history of botanical science; papers and notes of American botanists and naturalists of The West; botanical illustration, etc. Subtropical horticulture, incl cacti and succulents of Australia, South Africa, and Mexico.

CA —THE HAGGIN MUSEUM, Petzinger Library of Californiana, 1201 N Pershing Ave, Stockton, 95203. Diane Freggiaro, Librn/Archivist
Holdings: Vols (7000) Cat Mss Maps Pix Slides Audiotapes 16mm Films
Notes: The Petzinger Library is open by appointment only. Special emphasis on Stockton and San Joaquin County and Valley area, local biography, agriculture, agricultural history, industrial history, farm machinery (especially Holt Manufacturing Co, Stockton). There is a photograph collection of 8500 pictures, and extensive manuscript holdings (about 17,000 pieces).

DC —LIBRARY OF CONGRESS, Prints & Photographs Div, Washington, 20540.
Notes: Incl the great French collection of Albert and Gaston Tissandier, and the aeronautical biography files compiled by Jules Francois Dupuis-Delcourt. Ms materials are in the Manuscript Division.

DC —SMITHSONIAN INSTITUTION, National Museum of American Art & the National Portrait Gallery Library, Eighth & F Sts, NW, Washington, 20560. Cecilia Chin, Librn
Holdings: Vols (47,000) Cat Microforms
Budget: ($60,000)
Notes: Subscribe to 600 foreign and domestic periodicals on art and American history. Holdings of older bound periodicals. Collection emphasizes American art, contemporary American and European painting, portraiture, American biography. Uncataloged material incl 500 vertical file drawers of clippings, small catalogs and other ephemera on artists, art organizations, museums, etc; mss and archival material on American artists; the "Ferdinand Perret Library"--180 scrapebooks with card index on California art and artists, incl clippings, catalogs, reproductions, etc; card bibliography of books and periodical literature on portraiture--international, retrospective and current--in progress.

DC —SMITHSONIAN INSTITUTION LIBRARIES, General Library, Washington, 20560. Mary Claire Grey, Chief Cent Ref & Loan Servs
Holdings: Vols (79,000) Cat Mss Maps Pix Slides Microforms

IL —SOUTHERN ILLINOIS UNIVERSITY, CARBONDALE, Delyte W Morris Library, Carbondale, 62901.
Holdings: Vols (14,000) Cat
Notes: The Wilhelm Kosch Collection of German Literature, History, Biography, etc. A scholar's working library, especially strong in German monographs and standard editions from the late 19th century through the 1940s. There are some runs of German periodicals and serials. No separate catalog or index. Not maintained as a separate collection.

BIOGRAPHY—COLLECTIONS (cont.)

IL —NEWBERRY LIBRARY, 60 W Walton St, Chicago, 60610. Diana Haskell, Cur of Modern Mss
Holdings: Cat

LA —LOUISIANA STATE UNIVERSITY, Troy H Middleton Library, Louisiana Room, Baton Rouge, 70803. Evangeline Mills Lynch, Head Librn; Ruth Murray, Associate Librn
Holdings: Vols (33,500) Cat Maps VF
Notes: Louisiana Collection of history, description and travel, biography, agriculture, literature, politics and government, folklore, anthropology, geography, geology, education, language, music and natural history. Especially large subject collections may be found on Louisiana, the history of the lower Mississippi Valley, Abraham Lincoln, Romance languages and literatures, sugar culture and technology, Southern history, petroleum engineering, plant pathology, micropaleontology, ornithology, and various aspects of crawfish life, biology and culture. Complete depository of Louisiana State Documents; extensive newspapers clipping files; separate card catalog; items listed in Louisiana Union Catalog; restricted use (research and reference). Incl both materials about Louisiana and by Louisianians without regard to subject. LSU Press Collection(preservation copy of each title kept for exhibit purposes only). LSU theses and dissertations from 1900-date. LSU Faculty Collection. Also, 1300 maps, 104 VF drawers, 250 boxes of uncataloged pamphlets.

LA —R W NORTON ART GALLERY, Library, 4747 Creswell Ave, Shreveport, 71106. Jerry M Bloomer, Librn
Holdings: Cat

MD —JOHNS HOPKINS UNIVERSITY, Milton S Eisenhower Library, George Peabody Collection, 17 E Mt Vernon Place, Baltimore, 21201. Lyn Hart, Peabody Librn
Holdings: Vols 15,000
Notes: Noncirculating.

MA —NEW ENGLAND HISTORIC GENEALOGICAL SOCIETY, Library, 101 Newbury St, Boston, 02116. Ralph J Crandell, Dir
Holdings: Vols (250,000) Mss Maps Microforms Pix
Notes: New England genealogy. Especially strong Massachusetts, Maine, and New Hampshire, although all states are well represented, as are the relevancies of each subject listed in this volume with regard to British antecedent and contemporary history. Special strengths in local history and biography, obituaries, etc, incl parish registers, censuses, British and American. 3125 linear ft of mss.

MA —AMERICAN ANTIQUARIAN SOCIETY LIBRARY, 185 Salisbury St, Worcester, 01609. Marcus A McCorison, Dir & Librn
Holdings: Vols 15,000 Cat
Notes: Incl heraldry, biography, etc. Numerous special indexes and clipping files supplement the book collection.

MI —GALE RESEARCH CO, Book Tower, Detroit, 48226. Annie Brewer, Librn
Holdings: Vols (65,000) Cat
Notes: Large collection of reference materials, incl computerized files used in the preparation of familiar contemporary reference books and guides to special fields.

MI —CENTRAL MICHIGAN UNIVERSITY, Clarke Historical Library, Mount Pleasant, 48859. William H Mulligan, Jr, Dir; William Miles, Biography Collections Librn
Holdings: Vols 600
Notes: Biography collection of books written during campaigns of both successful and unsuccessful candidates for presidential nomination.

MN —MAYO MEDICAL LIBRARY, History of Medicine Collection, Rochester, 55905. Nancy R Hensel, Librn
Holdings: Vols (18,000) Cat Mss Maps Pix Slides
Notes: The collection consists of over 18,000 vols, 6500 of which are considered source materials (rare or reprint editions of classics). 4308 items from Garrison-Morton are available in the collection. Appropriate bibliographies, biographies and histories of medicine are a part of the collection. Fields of collecting interest are anesthesiology, dermatology, cardiology, neurology, immunology and radiology. Eight medical incunabula. Also, 800 vols of the Walter C Alvarez Collection of autobiographies of the physically and mentally handicapped. Collection described: Mann, Ruth J: "The Shelf of Walter C Alvarez, MD," *Mayo Clin* Proc 47: 125-127, Feb 1972.

NY —GRADUATE CENTER OF THE CITY UNIVERSITY OF NEW YORK, William H and Gwynne K Crouse Library for Publishing Arts, 33 W 42 St, New York, 10036. Alfred H Lane, Dir
Notes: Recently established and still growing, but intended to become the authoritative source of materials in the field, of particular value in research about the publishing industry. Open to staff members of publishing houses, students, scholars, authors, printers, and booksellers. Primarily 20th century materials, and particularly useful for research on technical, financial, and historical matters. Much on the history of individual houses, economics of authorship; marketing and distribution of books; etc.

NY —NEW YORK GENEALOGICAL & BIOGRAPHICAL SOCIETY, Library, 122 E 58 St, New York, 10022. James P Gregory, Librn
Holdings: Vols 63,500 Cat Mss Maps Microforms
Notes: The Society has copied and has in its ms collections a great many church records from all parts of New York State and several from adjacent states; and many very valuable ms genealogies and family Bible records which have never been published. The Society library is noncirculating and one of the principal genealogical reference libraries in the country. It has accumulated in its collections approximately 63 thousand vols on genealogy, local history and biography. In addition it has a rapidly expanding microfilm division which presently numbers over 2000 reels and keeps four microfilm readers in continuous use.

NY —NEW YORK HISTORICAL SOCIETY, Library, 170 Central Park W, New York, 10024. James Gregory, Librn
Holdings: Vols 7000 Cat Mss Maps Pix Slides Microforms
Budget: $20,000
Notes: The Ethel Taylor Crittenden Collection in Baptist History emphasizes the Baptists of North Carolina in particular. Much, however, from other states, the Southern Baptist Convention and the American Baptist Convention. Also Negro, Primitive and Free-Will Baptist items. There is a general card file to all holdings, an alphabetical and chronological file (incl extinct churches), and special index files for biographical references; the NC Church file; vital statistics.

NY —UNIVERSITY CLUB, Library, One W 54 St, New York, 10019. Guy St Clair, Library Dir
Holdings: Vols (100,000) Cat Mss Maps Pix
Notes: A private library for the members of the University Club, their guests, and serious scholars upon written application to the Library Director.

OH —CLEVELAND PUBLIC LIBRARY, Literature Dept, 325 Superior Ave, Cleveland, 44114. Evelyn Ward, Head
Holdings: Vols Cat Microforms Phonorecords
Notes: Comprehensive collection of literary texts, with a large body of literary history, criticism and biography. Strong in drama and poetry. Many first editions, books from special presses, and rarities. Microprint. Reference aids.

RI —BROWN UNIVERSITY, John Hay Library, Anne S K Brown Military Collection, 20 Prospect St, Providence, 02912. Richard B Harrington, Cur
Notes: The Anne S K Brown Military Collection has been formed over the past forty or more years by Mrs John Nicholas Brown, now of Newport, and contains approximately 40,000 volumes and 60,000 prints, drawings and watercolors as well as a number of oil paintings and about 5000 miniature model soldiers. At its beginning (and still today) the emphasis or focus of this collection has been upon the history of, and the accurate contemporary illustration of, military and naval uniforms of all nations from the early XVII century to the present. In the course of time, however, the collection has come to incl also a vast and related amount of material on military and naval history, military and naval arts and tactics, wars, campaigns, ceremonies, biography, portraits and caricatures of this and earlier periods. It has been probably the largest private collection of such a nature inthe world, and it contains much ms and graphic documentation which is unique. It has been useful to numerous scholars and historians, editors, filmmakers and publishers for research and for illustrative material and has also contributed to many museum exhibitions. In 1982 the entire collection, with its complete card catalog and subject index, has been presented to Brown University, where it is located in the John Hay Library. Special requests are taken care of by phone, mail and appointments with the curator.

RI —PROVIDENCE ATHENAEUM, 251 Benefit St, Providence, 02903. Sally Duplaix, Dir
Holdings: Vols 15,000 Cat
Notes: Strong 19th cnetury English and American emphasis.

SC —WOFFORD COLLEGE, Sandor Teszler Library, N Church St, Spartanburg, 29301. Frank J Anderson, Librn
Holdings: Vols 200 Cat
Notes: Mainly 19th century, incl biographies of 19th century Methodist preachers. Listed in: *Biography,* compiled by Elizabeth Sabin and edited by Frank J Anderson (Wofford College Library. Special Collections Checklist no 4), Spartanburg, S C: Wofford Library Press, 1970; 31 pp, mimeo. Also, Methodist hymnals from the early 1800's to date.

BIOGRAPHY—DICTIONARIES

IL —ENCYCLOPAEDIA BRITANNICA, Editorial Library, 310 S Michigan Ave, Chicago, 60604. Terry Miller, Editorial Librn
Holdings: Vols (25,000) Cat Maps Microforms
Budget: ($80,000)
Notes: This collection is not open to the general public, but photocopies of materials will be made. Collection contains all major and most minor encyclopedias and dictionaries. A large collection of atlases and statisical data on all foreign countries is maintained.

MI —GALE RESEARCH CO, Book Tower, Detroit, 48226. Annie Brewer, Librn
Holdings: Vols (65,000) Cat
Notes: Large collection of reference materials, incl computerized files used in the preparation of familiar contemporary reference books and guides to special fields.

OH —CLEVELAND PUBLIC LIBRARY, General Reference Dept, 325 Superior Ave, Cleveland, 44114. Donald Tipka, Head
Holdings: Vols (5500) Cat Microforms
Notes: Geographical and occupational biographic directories. Noncirculating.

BIOLOGICAL ASSAY

CA —CALIFORNIA STATE UNIVERSITY, FULLERTON, Library, Box 4150, Fullerton, 92634. Linda Herman, Special Collections Librn
Holdings: Cat
Notes: Dr Leonard B Schultz Ichthyology Collection of 13,000 pieces incl books, pamphlets, articles and ephemera. It is supplemented by the Ecology of Bay and Estuarine Fishes Collections.

BIOLOGICAL ASTRONOMY

NY —NEW YORK PUBLIC LIBRARY, Research Libraries, Science and Technology

BIOLOGICAL ASTRONOMY (cont.)

Research Center, Fifth Ave & 42 St, New York, 10018.
Holdings: Vols (1,100,000) Cat Microforms
Budget: ($647,259)

BIOLOGICAL CHEMISTRY

AR —NATIONAL CENTER FOR TOXICOLOGICAL RESEARCH, Library, Jefferson, 72079. Susan Laney-Sheehan, Supvr Librn
Holdings: Vols (15,000) Cat Mss Slides Audiotapes 16mm Films Microforms
Notes: Incl (860) journal titles, (230) current subscriptions.

CA —UNIVERSITY OF CALIFORNIA, BERKELEY, Bancroft Library, Manuscripts Division, Berkeley, 94720. James D Hart, Dir
Holdings: Cat Mss Pix
Notes: Correspondence and papers (37 boxes; 73 cartons) of the eminent German biochemist and Nobel Prize winner Emil Fischer. Incl his labor notebooks and notebooks of many of his students. Many of his speeches and other writings are represented. The collection also contains subject files relating to his many scientific discoveries as well as items reflecting his involvement in scientific societies.

CA —UNIVERSITY OF CALIFORNIA, DAVIS, Health Sciences Library, Davis, 95616. Marjan Merala, Health Sciences Librn
Holdings: Vols (164,000) Cat Microforms
Budget: ($509,737)
Notes: Human medicine: ca 82,000 vols; veterinary medicine: ca 19,700 vols; allied sciences (biochemistry, physiology, etc); reference works: ca 62,300 vols.

CA —BECKMAN INSTRUMENTS, Research Library, 2500 Harbor Blvd, Fullerton, 92634. Jean R Miller, Librn
Holdings: Vols (7000) Cat Slides Audiotapes Videotapes Microforms
Budget: ($9000)
Notes: Strong collections in scientific and analytic instrumentation, electrochemistry, analytical chemistry, optics and spectroscopy, chromatography, clinical chemistry and biochemistry.

CA —UNIVERSITY OF CALIFORNIA, LOS ANGELES, Biomedical Library, Center for Health Sciences, Los Angeles, 90024. Louise Darling, Biomedical Librn

CA —UNIVERSITY OF CALIFORNIA, LOS ANGELES, Chemistry Library, 4238 Young Hall, Los Angeles, 90024. Marion C Peters, Chemistry Librn
Holdings: Vols (55,600) Cat Microforms
Notes: (768) current serials subscriptions; special collection of 450 volumes on the history of chemistry; US Chemical Patents since 1952 on microforms; Sadtler Standard Spectra; UCLA biochemistry and chemistry theses.

CA —NASA, Ames Research Center, Libraries, Library Br 202-3, Moffett Field, 94035. Sarah Dueker, Chief, Library Branch
Holdings: Cat Audiotapes Microforms
Notes: Main library collections cover physical sciences, engineering and mathematical fields related to research programs in aeronautics-space research. Life sciences library collections cover medical, physiological, behavioral and biological sciences related to research programs. Also emphases on remote sensing of earth resources and the search for extraterrestrial life. 950 journal titles and 85,000 monographs. Reports collection includes 60, 000 hard copy reports and 900,000 microfiche.

CA —CALIFORNIA INSTITUTE OF TECHNOLOGY, Millikan Library 1-32, Biology Library, Pasadena, 91125. Dana L Roth, Biology Librn
Holdings: Vols 36,000 Cat
Budget: $144,000

CA —UNIVERSITY OF CALIFORNIA, RIVERSIDE, University Library, Bio-Agricultural Library, Batchelor Hall, Riverside, 92521. Barbara Montanary, Head
Holdings: Vols (130,000) Cat Mss Maps Pix Microforms
Notes: The Bio-Agricultural Library (formerly the Library of Citrus Experiment Station of the University of California) is well known for its complete collections in the fields of the agriculture sciences. It is especially known for its emphasis on entomology, incl bio-control; botany, citriculture, plant sciences, nematology and plant pathology; arid and semi-arid lands research and subtropical agriculture. Specific areas of interest are avocados, dates, desert flora, jojoba, guayule and carob.

CT —YALE MEDICAL LIBRARY, 333 Cedar St, New Haven, 06510.
Holdings: Vols (334,215) Cat Mss Pix Slides Microforms
Budget: ($361,650)
Notes: Incl films, audiotapes, artifacts, etc.

DE —UNIVERSITY OF DELAWARE, Agriculture Library, 2 Townsend Hall, Newark, 19717. Frederick Getze, Assoc Librn
Holdings: Vols (32,500) Cat Pix Microforms
Notes: Strong in entomology and ornamental horticulture. Extensive collection of state agriculture documents for each US state and Puerto Rico. Library subscribes to 600 serials (English and foreign).

FL —ARCHBOLD BIOLOGICAL STATION, Library, Rt 2, Box 180, Lake Placid, 33852. Fred E Lohrer, Librn
Holdings: Vols (2000) Cat Periodicals

IL —UNIVERSITY OF ILLINOIS, URBANA/CHAMPAIGN, Chemistry Library, 255 Noyes Laboratory, Urbana, 61801. Lucille M Wert, Chemistry Librn; Susan Eilering, Asst Chemistry Librn
Holdings: Vols (150,000) Cat Microforms
Budget: ($224,660)
Notes: The collection incl monographs, treatises and serials in all languages covering all aspects of biochemistry. It includes materials on chemistry of natural products, medicinal chemistry and pharmacology. It is desigend to serve the instructional and research needs of the School of Chemical Sciences and the University community.

IN —INDIANA UNIVERSITY, Chemistry Library, Chemistry Bldg, Rm One, Bloomington, 47405. Gary Wiggins, Head Librn
Holdings: Vols (55,000) Cat Slides Microforms
Budget: ($157,000)

IN —PURDUE UNIVERSITY LIBRARIES, Biochemistry Library, West Lafayette, 47907. Martha J Bailey, Librn
Holdings: Vols (10,398) Cat Slides Microforms
Budget: ($36,025)

IA —IOWA STATE UNIVERSITY, Library, Ames, 50011. Warren B Kuhn, Dean of Library Services
Holdings: Cat
Notes: Extensive serial holdings.

LA —LOUISIANA STATE UNIVERSITY, Chemistry Library, Virginia Rice Williams Hall, Baton Rouge, 70803.
Holdings: Vols (40,000) Cat Mss Microforms
Notes: Incl chemical patents, 1955-date. With 700 journals.

MD —JOHNS HOPKINS UNIVERSITY, Milton S Eisenhower Library, Charles & 34 Sts, Baltimore, 21218. Ann S Gwyn, Assistant Dir for Special Collections
Holdings: Vols (46,500) Cat
Notes: Very strong in all biological fields except taxonomy. Strongest in molecular biology, cell physiology and premedical areas. Strong in journals, espec in biochemistry. Many long runs of rare journals. Natural science not as strong as biochemistry. Contemporary monographs better than earlier ones.

MD —UNIVERSITY OF MARYLAND, White Memorial Library, College Park, 20742. Elizabeth W McElroy, Head
Holdings: Vols (48,000) Cat Microforms
Budget: ($193,000)
Notes: Current periodicals. Have own card catalog, which is included also in the total university catalog.

MA —FRANCIS A COUNTWAY LIBRARY OF MEDICINE, Boston Medical Library/Harvard Medical Library, 10 Shattuck St, Boston, 02115. C Robin LeSueur, Librn; Richard J Wolfe, Cur, Rare Books & Manuscripts
Holdings: Vols (500,000) Cat Mss Maps Pix Microforms
Notes: Combines resources of the Harvard Medical School and the Boston Medical Library. Strong in serials and medical history in all fields of medicine, incl incunabula, non-medical books by doctors, travel books by doctors. 500,000 medical dissertations and theses. Special strength in all medical subjects listed in this volume.

MA —HARVARD UNIVERSITY LIBRARY, Biological Laboratories Library, 16 Divinity Ave, Cambridge, 02138. Dorothy Solbrig, Librn
Holdings: Vols (20,000) Cat Films
Notes: Materials in all areas of biology, emphasizing biochemistry and cellular and developmental biology. There is little in systematic biology and morphology.

MA —MASSACHUSETTS INSTITUTE OF TECHNOLOGY, Institute Archives, Special Collections, Cambridge, 02139.
Notes: Collection incl over 100 oral history interviews with scientists, legislators, lobbyists, environmentalists, journalists, university administration, and citizen review board members concerned with recombinant DNA technology. Also incl are audiotapes, videotapes, and printed material collected in preparations for oral history interviews.

MI —WARNER-LAMBERT/PARKE-DAVIS, Research Library, 2800 Plymouth Rd, Ann Arbor, 48106. Katherine C Owen, Mgr, Library Services
Holdings: Vols (27,977) Cat

MI —LAFAYETTE CLINIC LIBRARY, 951 E Lafayette, Detroit, 48207. Nancy E Ward, Librn
Holdings: Vols (7000) Cat
Notes: Special emphasis on the biological aspects, causes and treatment of mental illness.

MN —UNIVERSITY OF MINNESOTA, Bio-Medical Library, Diehl Hall, Minneapolis, 55455. Gertrude Foreman, Acting Dir
Holdings: Vols (263,361)
Budget: ($500,000)

NY —ALBERT EINSTEIN COLLEGE OF MEDICINE, D Samuel Gottesman Library, 1300 Morris Park Ave, Bronx, 10461. Charlotte K Lindner, Dir

NY —NEW YORK BOTANICAL GARDEN LIBRARY, Bronx, 10458. Charles R Long, Asst Vice Pres & Dir
Holdings: Vols 2000 Cat VF
Budget: ($356,000)
Notes: Over 900,000 items, incl books, serials, pamphlets, archives and manuscripts, vertical files, microfiche and microfilm, nursery and seed catalogs, photographs, paintings, prints, drawings and engravings. Covering all areas of botanical sciences.

NY —COLD SPRING HARBOR LABORATORY, Library, PO Box 100, Cold Spring Harbor, 11724. Susan Gensel, Library Dir; Genemary Falvey, Librn
Holdings: Vols (30,000)
Budget: ($103,500)
Notes: The highly technical collection is comprised of 20,000 serial vols and 10,000 monographs. The library receives 500 current serial titles. Subjects covered incl molecular and cellular biology, virology, biochemistry, microbiology, oncology, neurobiology, biological risk assessment and genetic engineering/biotechnology. Special collections in eugenics and genetics are primarily historical dealing with the development of genetics in the US which had its beginnings here.

NY —BOYCE THOMPSON INSTITUTE FOR PLANT RESEARCH, Library, Cornell University, Tower Rd, Ithaca, 14853. Greta Colavito, Librn
Holdings: Vols (5300) Cat
Budget: ($46,000)
Notes: Mainly plant physiology, biochemistry, entomology, air and water pollution, pesticides, and plant pathology.

NY —COLUMBIA UNIVERSITY LIBRARIES, Biological Sciences Library, 601 Fairchild, New York, 10027. Barbara A List, Reference/Collection Development

BIOLOGICAL CHEMISTRY (cont.)

Librn
Holdings: Vols 38,000 Cat
Notes: Incl biochemistry and molecular biology.

NY —CORNELL UNIVERSITY MEDICAL COLLEGE, Samuel J Wood Library, 1300 York Ave, New York, 10021. Erich Meyerhoff, Dir
Holdings: Vols (9000) Cat Films
Notes: All aspects of muscle diseases.

NY —MUSCULAR DYSTROPHY ASSOCIATION, 810 Seventh Ave, New York, 10019. Marianthe Pappas, Librn
Holdings: Vols 8770 Cat
Budget: $55,000
Notes: All phases of muscular diseases. Incl some films.

NY —NEW YORK PUBLIC LIBRARY, Research Libraries, Science and Technology Research Center, Fifth Ave & 42 St, New York, 10018.
Holdings: Vols (1,100,000) Cat Microforms
Budget: ($647,259)

NY —UNIVERSITY OF ROCHESTER, Carlson Library, Hutchison Hall, River Campus, Rochester, 14627. Michael W Poulin, Librn
Holdings: Vols (48,720) Cat Microforms
Notes: Strong collection in the field and related areas.

NY —REVLON HEALTH CARE GROUP, Information Services, One Scarsdale Ave, Tuckahoe, 10707. Rena Radovich, Manager
Holdings: Cat
Notes: Book vols & periodicals.

NY —MASONIC MEDICAL RESEARCH LIBRARY, 2150 Bleecker St, Utica, 13501. Irma A Tuttle, Librn
Holdings: Vols (2000) Cat Slides Microforms
Notes: Biochemical gerontology collection represents 10 percent of total holdings in basic medical research fields of physiology, pharmacology, vision and circulation. Incl 16,000 periodicals.

NC —UNIVERSITY OF NORTH CAROLINA, CHAPEL HILL, Zoology Dept Library, Wilson Hall 046A, Chapel Hill, 27514. John B Darling, Librn
Holdings: Vols (31,000) Cat
Notes: Collection incl theses and dissertations.

NC —NATIONAL INSTITUTE OF ENVIRONMENTAL HEALTH SCIENCES, Library, PO Box 12233, Research Triangle Park, 27709. W Davenport Robertson, Head Librn
Holdings: Vols (9000) Cat Mss Microforms
Notes: The subject, "environmental health," incl toxicology, carcinogenesis, pharmacology, genetics, biophysics, and biochemistry. Special emphasis is placed on cell biology. The collection does not include works on pollution control or law. In addition to the collection there are some 2500 vols in the laboratories. The library has an automated catalog.

ND —UNIVERSITY OF NORTH DAKOTA, Harley E French Medical Library, Grand Forks, 58202. David W Boilard, Dir; Lila Pedersen, Asst Dir
Holdings: Vols (56,000) Cat
Budget: ($206,000)
Notes: 1075 current periodical subscriptions.

OH —OHIO STATE UNIVERSITY, Biological Sciences Library, 1735 Neil Ave, Columbus, 43210. Victoria Welborn, Librn
Holdings: Vols (85,000) Cat Mss Maps Microforms

OK —CIVIL AERO MEDICAL INSTITUTE LIBRARY (CAMI), PO Box 25082, AAC 64D1, Oklahoma City, 73125. Darrell R Goulden, Medical Librn
Holdings: Vols 8500 Cat Mss
Notes: Aviation and aerospace medicine. About 175 current periodicals.

PA —CARDEZA FOUNDATION, Tocantins Memorial Library, 1015 Walnut St, Philadelphia, 19107. Doris Riso, Librn
Holdings: Vols 1800 Cat Mss Pix
Notes: Extensive collection of hematology. Mss of the late hematologist, Leandro M Tocantins, renowned for his work in coagulation. Part of the Jefferson University. Currently 39 periodicals in the field of hematology and related biochemistry and immunology are received.

PA —FRANKLIN INSTITUTE LIBRARY, 20 & The Parkway, Philadelphia, 19103. Miriam Padusis, Dir; Charles Wilt, Readers Servs Librn
Holdings: Vols (300,000) Cat Maps Pix Microforms

PA —UNIVERSITY OF PITTSBURGH, Langley Library, A-217 Langley Hall, Pittsburgh, 15260. D L Johnston, Librn
Holdings: Vols (14,000) Cat
Budget: ($30,000)

PA —PENNSYLVANIA STATE UNIVERSITY, Fred Lewis Pattee Library, University Park, 16802.
Notes: Numerous and large collections on many sports. Also, materials supporting every aspect of the program of the Center for Women and Sport, incl research into kinetics, endocrinology, physiology, psychology, etc.

TX —UNIVERSITY OF TEXAS LIBRARIES, Science Library, PO Box P, Austin, 78712. Betty White, Librn
Holdings: Vols (103,000) Cat Microforms

TX —UNIVERSITY OF TEXAS LIBRARIES, John W Mallet Chemistry Library, Welch Hall 2132, Austin, 78712. A E Skinner, Chemistry Librn
Holdings: Vols (44,000) Cat Microforms
Notes: Described in *The John W Mallet Chemistry Library (The University of Texas at Austin)* (Austin: The General Libraries, 1975).

VT —UNIVERSITY OF VERMONT, Chemistry/Physics Library, Burlington, 05405. Craig A Robertson, Librn
Holdings: Vols (23,000) Cat Microforms
Notes: The collection consists largely of periodicals, having about 12,000 bound periodical volumes. The number of periodical titles currently received is approximately 210.

ON —AGRICULTURE CANADA, Research Branch, Neatby Library, Rm 3032, K W Neatby Bldg, CEF, Ottawa, K1A 0C6, Can. Marcel Charette, Library Technician
Holdings: Vols 2100 Cat

ON —ONTARIO MINISTRY OF HEALTH, Laboratory Services Branch, Library, Box 9000, Terminal A, Toronto, M5W 1R5, Can. Doris A Standing, Librn
Holdings: Vols (4000) Cat
Budget: ($50,000)
Notes: Medical laboratory technology and related subjects: microbiology; environmental bacteriology (limited to testing of milk, food and water for bacterial quality, etc); biological chemistry (clinical); mycology; parasitology; virology; immunology; serology; automated laboratory techniques; biohazard control.

BIOLOGICAL OCEANOGRAPHY see Marine Ecology

BIOLOGICAL PERIODICALS see Periodicals, Biological

BIOLOGICAL PHYSICS

†AZ —UNIVERSITY OF ARIZONA, Library, Tucson, 85721.
Notes: The Pierre Lecomte du Nouy Collection incl scarce, original editions of the works of contemporary scientists and thinkers, editions of his own works, his mss, and many volumes inscribed to him.

CA —NASA, Ames Research Center, Libraries, Library Br 202-3, Moffett Field, 94035. Sarah Dueker, Chief, Library Branch
Holdings: Cat Audiotapes Microforms
Notes: Main library collections cover physical sciences, engineering and mathematical fields related to research programs in aeronautics-space research. Life sciences library collections cover medical, physiological, behavioral and biological sciences related to research programs. Also emphases on remote sensing of earth resources and the search for extraterrestrial life. 950 journal titles and 85,000 monographs. Reports collection includes 60, 000 hard copy reports and 900,000 microfiche.

CA —CALIFORNIA INSTITUTE OF TECHNOLOGY, Robert A Millikan Memorial Library, Archives, 1201 E California Blvd, Pasadena, 91125. Judith R Goodstein, Archivist
Holdings: Vols (3000) Cat Mss Maps Pix Slides Phonorecords Audiotapes Videotapes 16mm Films Microforms
Notes: Ms sources for the history of astrophysics, cosmology, mathematical physics, experimental physics, radio astronomy, geophysics and biophysics. Collections incl the papers of: George Ellery Hale, Jesse Greenstein, H P Robertson, Richard Feynman, Paul Epstein, Max Delbruck, and Beno Gutenberg. Candid photos of physicists at meetings; etchings and photographs of Einstein; scientific medals; selected pieces of scientific apparatus (including the oil-drop machine constructed by Millikan at Caltech in the early 1920s); the reprint collection of Paul Epstein; over 3000 landmark books in the history of 20th century physics and mathematics. Printed publications include: Daniel Kevles, *Guide to the Microfilm Edition of the George Ellery Hale Papers* (Pasadena, Carnegie Institute of Washington and Caltech), 1968; Judith R Goodstein, *The Robert Andrews Millikan Collection at the California Institute of Technology: Guide to a Microfilm Edition* (Pasadena, Caltech), 1977; Judith R Goodstein and Carolyn Kopp, *The Theodore von Karman Collections at the California Institute of* Technology (Pasadena, Archives), 1981.

CT —YALE MEDICAL LIBRARY, 333 Cedar St, New Haven, 06510.
Holdings: Vols (334,215) Cat Mss Pix Slides Microforms
Budget: ($361,650)
Notes: Incl films, audiotapes, artifacts, etc.

CT —YALE UNIVERSITY, Kline Science Library, Kline Biology Tower Rm C-8, PO Box 6666, New Haven, 06511. Richard J Dionne, Head
Holdings: Vols (175,480) Cat 16mm Films Microforms
Budget: ($340,000)
Notes: Comprehensive collection on biological sciences, physics and chemistry. Incl Evans Collection of Bryology and Lichenology (with catalog cards in both Kline Science Library and Sterling Memorial Library). Also incl AEC reports (hardcopy and microform) to 1970.

FL —ARCHBOLD BIOLOGICAL STATION, Library, Rt 2, Box 180, Lake Placid, 33852. Fred E Lohrer, Librn
Holdings: Vols (2000) Cat Periodicals

IL —UNIVERSITY OF ILLINOIS, URBANA/CHAMPAIGN, Library, Biology Library, 101 Burrill Hall, 407 S Goodwin, Urbana, 61801. Elisabeth B Davis, Librn
Holdings: Vols (115,000) Cat Microforms
Budget: ($200,000)
Notes: The Biology Library incl books, periodicals, and reference works that cover the fields of anatomy, biophysics, botany, ecology, entomology, genetics, immunology, microbiology, physiology and zoology. About three-quarters of the total collection is made up of journals and other serials representing 2000 distinctive titles. The serial list is comprehensive for the biological sciences, contains most of the major international titles and consists of complete runs for almost all titles. Additional materials (approx 90,000 vols) in the biological sciences are available in the Natural History Survey Library and the bookstacks at the Main Library on the Urbana campus. Professional assistance is available for reference service, online searching, and library instruction. Interlibrary loan service is provided. Photocopying.

IA —IOWA STATE UNIVERSITY, Library, Ames, 50011. Warren B Kuhn, Dean of Library Services
Holdings: Cat
Notes: Extensive serial holdings.

MD —US ARMED FORCES RADIOBIOLOGY RESEARCH INSTITUTE, Naval Medical Command, Bethesda, 20014. Nannette M Pope, Head,

BIOLOGICAL PHYSICS (cont.)

Library Division
Holdings: Vols (50,000)
Budget: ($150,000)
Notes: Collection consists of monographs, technical reports, serials, and microfiche related to radiation effects on human and animal biology.

MA —MASSACHUSETTS INSTITUTE OF TECHNOLOGY, Research Laboratory of Electronics, Document Room 36-412, Cambridge, 02139. J E Woore, Head
Holdings: Vols (15,000)
Notes: Incl World War II technical reports on radar. Current electromagnetism and electronic engineering, radar, etc.

MA —MASSACHUSETTS INSTITUTE OF TECHNOLOGY, Institute Archives, Special Collections, Cambridge, 02139.
Notes: Collection incl over 100 oral history interviews with scientists, legislators, lobbyists, environmentalists, journalists, university administration, and citizen review board members concerned with recombinant DNA technology. Also incl are audiotapes, videotapes, and printed material collected in preparations for oral history interviews.

NY —NEW YORK PUBLIC LIBRARY, Research Libraries, Science and Technology Research Center, Fifth Ave & 42 St, New York, 10018.
Holdings: Vols (1,100,000) Cat Microforms
Budget: ($647,259)

NC —NATIONAL INSTITUTE OF ENVIRONMENTAL HEALTH SCIENCES, Library, PO Box 12233, Research Triangle Park, 27709. W Davenport Robertson, Head Librn
Holdings: Vols (9000) Cat Mss Audiotapes Microforms
Notes: The subject, "environmental health," incl toxicology, carcinogenesis, pharmacology, genetics, biophysics, and biochemistry. Special emphasis is placed on cell biology. The collection does not incl works on pollution control or law. In addition to the collection there are some 2500 vols in the laboratories. The library has an automated catalog.

OH —OHIO STATE UNIVERSITY, Biological Sciences Library, 1735 Neil Ave, Columbus, 43210. Victoria Welborn, Librn
Holdings: Vols (85,000) Cat Mss Maps Microforms

PA —UNIVERSITY OF PITTSBURGH, Langley Library, A-217 Langley Hall, Pittsburgh, 15260. D L Johnston, Librn
Holdings: Vols (14,000) Cat
Budget: ($30,000)

BIOLOGICAL RISK ASSESSMENT

NY —COLD SPRING HARBOR LABORATORY, Library, PO Box 100, Cold Spring Harbor, 11724. Susan Gensel, Library Dir; Genemary Falvey, Librn
Holdings: Vols (30,000)
Budget: ($103,500)
Notes: The highly technical collection is comprised of 20,000 serial vols and 10,000 monographs. The library receives 500 current serial titles. Subjects covered incl molecular and cellular biology, virology, biochemistry, microbiology, oncology, neurobiology, biological risk assessment and genetic engineering/biotechnology. Special collections in eugenics and genetics are primarily historical dealing with the development of genetics in the US which had its beginnings here.

BIOLOGICAL SCIENCES

MA —WELLESLEY COLLEGE, Margaret Clapp Library, College Archives, Wellesley, 02181.
Notes: Records of the Departments of Astronomy, Biological Sciences, Botany, Chemistry, Geology, Physics, Zoology, and individuals connected with these departments at Wellesley College (27 linear feet).

MN —BAKKEN LIBRARY OF ELECTRICITY IN LIFE, 3537 Zenith Ave S, Minneapolis, 55416. John Edward Senior, Dir
Notes: Books (including periodicals, manuscripts, and archival materials) and instrument collection. 1500 instruments (focus-18th and 19th centuries). Relating to the history of biological sciences.

PA —UNIVERSITY OF PENNSYLVANIA, Bio-Medical Library, Johnson Pavilion/G2, Philadelphia, 19104. Eleanor Goodchild, Librn
Holdings: Vols (139,000) Cat Slides Audiotapes Videotapes

BIOLOGICAL WARFARE

DC —CENTER FOR BIOETHICS, Library, Kennedy Institute, Georgetown University, 3520 Prospect St NW, Washington, 20057. Doris Goldstein, Dir; Judith Mistichelli, Senior Librn
Holdings: Vols (8200)
Notes: Largest library of its kind. Incl 31, 000 journal articles on applied ethics. Produces computer database *Bioethicsline,* available through MEDLARS; and the printed annual *Bibliography of Bioethics.* Other library publications are: *New Titles in* Bioethics (monthly); *Scope Notes* series on current topics.

BIOLOGISTS

DC —LIBRARY OF CONGRESS, Manuscript Division, Washington, 20540. John C Broderick, Chief
Notes: Papers of Barry Commoner, biologist and ecologist.

IN —INDIANA UNIVERSITY, Lilly Library, Seventh St, Bloomington, 47405. William R Cagle, Librn
Notes: Collections incl papers of geneticists and biologists, most notably those of Nobel Prize winner Hermann Joseph Muller, 1890-1967 and Tracy Morton Sonneborn, 1905-1981. Also papers of plant geneticists Ralph Cleland, 1892-1971, and Paul Weatherwax, 1888-1976.

NY —ROCKEFELLER UNIVERSITY, Rockefeller Archive Center, Hillcrest, Pocantico Hills, North Tarrytown, 10591. Joseph W Ernst, Dir; J William Hess, Assoc Dir
Notes: Papers of Edward L Tatum, Rockefeller University professor. Conducted research in the genetics and metabolism of bacteria, yeasts, and molds. In 1958, he was joint recipient, with Joshua Lederberg and George Beadle, of the Nobel Prize in medicine and physiolgy.

BIOLOGY

CA —UNIVERSITY OF CALIFORNIA, DAVIS, General Library, Davis, 95616. Bernard Kreissman, University Librn; C Danial Elliott, Asst Head, Dept Special Collections
Holdings: Vols 21,767

CA —UNIVERSITY OF CALIFORNIA, LOS ANGELES, Biomedical Library, Center for the Health Sciences, Los Angeles, 90024. Alison Bunting, Acting Biomedical Librn; Victoria Steele, Head, History & Special Collections Div
Holdings: Vols (400,000) Cat Slides Phonorecords Audiotapes Videotapes 16mm Films Microforms
Notes: The UCLA Biomedical Library serves primarily the Schools of Medicine, Dentistry, Nursing, and Public Health, the UCLA Medical Center, the Departments of Microbiology and Biology in the College of Letters and Science, and related institutes in biomedicine. The collections of the Library are broad in scope, designed not only to support the teaching and research needs of its many users, but also to function as a resource for the health sciences-biological field as a whole. The outstanding feature of the collection is the strength of its periodical holdings, both current and retrospective. The Library also has an excellent reference collection, a comprehensive historical section, and gives special emphasis to the fields of neuroscience, psychiatry, ophthalmology, radiation biology, molecular biology, and vertebrate zoology. Increased emphasis is being given to the acquisition of audiovisual materials.

CA —UNIVERSITY OF SOUTHERN CALIFORNIA, Seaver Science Library, University Park, Los Angeles, 90089. A Albert Baker, Head
Holdings: Vols (200,000) Microforms
Budget: ($700,000)
Notes: Includes technical reports (12,000), serial and periodical titles (3600).

CA —UNIVERSITY OF SOUTHERN CALIFORNIA, Allan Hancock Foundation, Hancock Library of Biology and Oceanography, Los Angeles, 90007. Kimberly Douglas, Librn
Holdings: Vols (16,000) Cat Maps
Notes: Mostly marine, but incl some land expeditions. Covers all geographical areas. Also incl serial collection of 80,000 vols.

CA —CALIFORNIA INSTITUTE OF TECHNOLOGY, Millikan Library 1-32, Biology Library, Pasadena, 91125. Dana L Roth, Biology Librn
Holdings: Vols 36,000 Cat
Budget: $144,000

CA —CONTRA COSTA COUNTY LIBRARY, 1750 Oak Park Blvd, Pleasant Hill, 94523. Barbara Potter, Librn
Holdings: Vols (18,000)

CA —CALIFORNIA STATE POLYTECHNIC UNIVERSITY, POMONA, University Library, 3801 W Temple Ave, Pomona, 91768. Harold Schleiser, Actg Dir
Notes: General reference materials on agricultural business management, agricultural engineering, animal science, horticulture and plant and soil science.

CA —UNIVERSITY OF CALIFORNIA, RIVERSIDE, University Library, Bio-Agricultural Library, Batchelor Hall, Riverside, 92521. Barbara Montanary, Head
Holdings: Vols (130,000) Cat Mss Maps Pix Microforms
Notes: The Bio-Agricultural Library (formerly the Library of Citrus Experiment Station of the University of California) is well known for its complete collections in the fields of the agriculture sciences. It is especially known for its emphasis on entomology, incl bio-control; botany, citriculture, plant sciences, nematology and plant pathology; arid and semi-arid lands research and subtropical agriculture. Specific areas of interest are avocados, dates, desert flora, jojoba, guayule and carob.

CT —YALE UNIVERSITY, Kline Science Library, Kline Biology Tower Rm C-8, PO Box 6666, New Haven, 06511. Richard J Dionne, Head
Holdings: Vols (175,480) Cat 16mm Films Microforms
Budget: ($340,000)
Notes: Comprehensive collection on biological sciences, physics, and chemistry. Incl Evans Collection of Bryology and Lichenology (with catalog cards in both Kline Science Library and Sterling Memorial Library). Also incl AEC reports (hardcopy and microform) to 1970.

†DC —CATHOLIC UNIVERSITY OFF AMERICA, Nursing & Biology Library, Washington, 20064. N L Powell, Head
Holdings: Vols (17,000) Cat Microforms

DC —MALCOLM GROW USAF MEDICAL CENTER, Medical Library, Box 3097, Andrews AFB, Washington, 20331. Eunice M Lyon, Librn
Holdings: Vols (10,000) Maps Pix Slides Audiotapes Microforms
Budget: ($31,000)

DC —SMITHSONIAN INSTITUTION, Archives Div, Washington, 20560. William

BIOLOGY (cont.)

W Moss, Archivist
Holdings: Cat Mss Pix Slides
Notes: The Archives holds the records of the Smithsonian's National Museum of Natural History.
See also entries under Natural History; Botany; Invertebrate Zoology; Entomology; Ornithology; Paleobiology; Ichthyology

DC —SMITHSONIAN INSTITUTION, Smithsonian Tropical Research Institute, Washington, 20560. Carol Jopling, Chief Librn
Holdings: Vols (22,000) Cat Mss Maps Pix Slides 16mm Films Microforms
Budget: ($70,000)
Notes: Smithsonian Institution, Smithsonian Tropical Research Institute is located in Balboa, Panama.

FL —UNIVERSITY OF FLORIDA, Institute of Food & Agricultural Sciences, Hume Library, Gainesville, 32611. Albert C Strickland, Librn
Holdings: Vols (135,000) Cat Mss Microforms
Notes: Including journals and monographs, this collection is a general agricultural one. The emphasis is on tropical agriculture, especially Latin America. Entomology is very strong. The library offers on-line information retrieval using Lockheed and SDC data bases.

FL —ARCHBOLD BIOLOGICAL STATION, Library, Rt 2, Box 180, Lake Placid, 33852. Fred E Lohrer, Librn
Holdings: Vols (2000) Cat Periodicals

FL —FLORIDA INSTITUTE OF TECHNOLOGY, Library, 150 W University Blvd, PO Box 1150, Melbourne, 32901. L L Henson, Dir of Libraries
Holdings: Vols 2500 Cat Maps Pix

FL —FLORIDA DEPT OF NATURAL RESOURCES BUREAU OF MARINE RESEARCH, Library, 100 Eighth Ave SE, Saint Petersburg, 33701. Keir Gray, Archivist
Holdings: Vols (3400) Cat Maps Pix Slides 16mm Films Microforms
Budget: ($59,000)
Notes: The library supports the research of approx 50 biologists and technicians, with emphasis on the marine resources of Florida and nearby areas. An archives section houses original research data, reports, publications,, etc, developed by the scientific staff. Marine biological literature is received on exchange from laboratories and libraries throughout the world. There are approx 1400 journal titles in the collection. Current titles received number approx 600. The 33,000 reprints are cataloged by author and subject. Current laboratory activities incl marine studies in aquaculture, descriptive biology, ecological studies, fisheries biology, and oceanography.

GA —FERNBANK SCIENCE CENTER LIBRARY, 156 Heaton Park Dr NE, Atlanta, 30307. Mary Larsen, Librn; Janice MacLeod, Bibliographic Instructor
Holdings: Vols (12,000) Cat Maps Pix Slides Microforms
Budget: ($35,000)
Notes: Science with emphasis on astronomy, biology, outdoor education. Incl 5500 color slides; periodicals on microfilm.

GA —GEORGIA INSTITUTE OF TECHNOLOGY, Price Gilbert Memorial Library, 225 North Ave, Atlanta, 30332. Edward Graham Roberts, Dir
Holdings: Vols (1,661,559) Cat Maps Slides Microforms
Budget: ($1,383,302)
Notes: Incl (4,307,996) patents and (568, 490) government documents.

IL —ARGONNE NATIONAL LABORATORY, Library, Technical Information Services Dept, 9700 Cass Ave, Argonne, 60439. Hillis L Griffin, Dir
Notes: The ANL library system consists of eight branch libraries with centralized processing services. The entire collection numbers 70,000 monographic titles, 3700 journal titles, and over 1 million scientific and technical reports. Materials may be used by the public in the library by prior arrangement. Photocopies may be supplied for interlibrary loan, for which a processing and handling charge is made. The branch libraries are: Biological and Medical Research; Chemical Engineering; Chemistry; Mathematics/Physics/Computer Science; Reactor Science/Engineering; Materials Science; Solid State Physics; High-Energy Physics/Environmental Sciences.

IL —NORTHWESTERN UNIVERSITY, Seeley G Mudd Library for Science & Engineering, 2233 Sheridan Rd, Evanston, 60201. Robert C Michaelson, Head
Holdings: Vols (200,000) Cat Microforms
Notes: Collection emphasizes graduate and research level material.

IL —UNIVERSITY OF ILLINOIS, URBANA/CHAMPAIGN, Library, Biology Library, 101 Burrill Hall, 407 S Goodwin, Urbana, 61801. Elisabeth B Davis, Librn
Holdings: Vols (115,000) Cat Microforms
Budget: ($200,000)
Notes: The Biology Library incl books, periodicals, and reference works that cover the fields of anatomy, biophysics, botany, ecology, entomology, genetics, immunology, microbiology, physiology and zoology. About three-quarters of the total collection is made up of journals and other serials representing 2000 distinctive titles. The serial list is comprehensive for the biological sciences, contains most of the major international titles and consists of complete runs for almost all titles. Additional materials (approx 90,000 vols) in the biological sciences are available in the Natural History Survey Library and the bookstacks at the Main Library on the Urbana campus. Professional assistance is available for reference service, online searching, and library instruction. Interlibrary loan service is provided. Photocopying.

IN —INDIANA UNIVERSITY, Biology Library, Jordan Hall, Bloomington, 47405. Steven Sowell, Head
Holdings: Vols (105,461) Cat
Notes: 109,900 reprints on genetics.

IN —INDIANA STATE UNIVERSITY, Science Library, Terre Haute, 47809. Susan J Thompson, Science Librn
Holdings: Vols (40,000) Cat Microforms
Budget: ($160,846)

IN —PURDUE UNIVERSITY LIBRARIES, Life Sciences Library, Lilly Hall of Life Sciences, West Lafayette, 47907. Martha J Bailey, Librn
Holdings: Vols (73,404) Cat Microforms
Budget: ($223,445)
Notes: Incl materials in agronomy, animal sciences, botany, entomology, forestry, horticulture, biological sciences and agricultural engineering.

KY —UNIVERSITY OF KENTUCKY, Agriculture Library, Agricultural Science Center North, Lexington, 40546. Antoinette P Powell, Head Librn
Holdings: Vols (90,000) Cat Maps Microforms
Budget: ($110,582)

ME —COLLEGE OF THE ATLANTIC, Thorndike Library, Bar Harbor, 04609. Marcie L Dworak, Libr Dir
Notes: A rebuilding, fire-destroyed library (1983).

MD —JOHNS HOPKINS UNIVERSITY, Milton S Eisenhower Library, Charles & 34 Sts, Baltimore, 21218. Ann S Gwyn, Assistant Dir for Special Collections
Holdings: Vols (46,500) Cat
Notes: Very strong in all biological fields except taxonomy. Strongest in molecular biology, cell physiology and premedical areas. Strong in journals, espec in biochemistry. Many long runs of rare journals. Natural science not as strong as biochemistry. Contemporary monographs better than earlier ones.

MD —SMITHSONIAN ENVIRONMENTAL RESEARCH CENTER, Branch Library, 12441 Parklawn Dr, Rockville, 20852. Angela N Haggins, Chief
Holdings: Vols (3300) Cat Maps Pix Slides

MA —UNIVERSITY OF MASSACHUSETTS AT AMHERST, Library, Amherst, 01003. Siegfried Feller, Assoc Dir for Collection Development
Holdings: Cat
Notes: Genetics and developmental biology.

MA —HARVARD UNIVERSITY LIBRARY, Biological Laboratories Library, 16 Divinity Ave, Cambridge, 02138. Dorothy Solbrig, Librn
Holdings: Vols (20,000) Cat Films
Notes: Materials in all areas of biology, emphasizing biochemistry and cellular and developmental biology. There is little in systematic biology and morphology.

MA —BOSTON COLLEGE LIBRARIES, Science Library, Devlin Hall, Chestnut Hill, 02167. F Clifford McElroy, Science Librn
Holdings: Vols (54,508) Cat Maps Microforms
Budget: ($94,270)
Notes: Library is being absorbed into the general collection.

MI —UNIVERSITY OF MICHIGAN, Biological Station Library, Pellston, 49769. Patricia B Devlin, Librn
Holdings: Vols (10,000) Cat Mss Maps Pix Microforms

MN —UNIVERSITY OF MINNESOTA, Bio-Medical Library, Diehl Hall, Minneapolis, 55455. Gertrude Foreman, Acting Dir
Holdings: Vols (263,361)
Budget: ($500,000)

MO —WASHINGTON UNIVERSITY, Biology Library, 6600 Millbrook Blvd, Saint Louis, 63130. Betty S Galyon, Librn
Holdings: Vols (40,407) Cat

NH —DARTMOUTH COLLEGE, Dartmouth-Hitchcock Medical Center, Dana Biomedical Library, Hanover, 03756. Shirley J Grainger, Librn
Holdings: Vols (146,611) Cat Mss Phonorecords Audiotapes Videotapes Microforms
Budget: ($280,000)

NJ —PRINCETON UNIVERSITY, Library, Rare Books Dept, Princeton, 08544. Stephen Ferguson, Cur
Holdings: Cat

NJ —ORTHO PHARMACEUTICAL CORP, Hartman Library, U S Highway 202, Raritan, 08869. June Bente, Mgr
Holdings: Vols (15,000) Cat Microforms

NY —NEW YORK BOTANICAL GARDEN LIBRARY, Bronx, 10458. Charles R Long, Asst Vice Pres & Dir
Holdings: Vols 20,000 Cat Mss Pix Slides Microforms VF
Budget: ($356,000)
Notes: One of the largest botanical collections in the world. Covers botany (150, 000 vols), botanists (3000), horticulture (45, 000), plant diseases (25,000), plant physiology (15,000), history of botany (1500), conservation of natural resources (15,000), gardening (13,000), paleobotany (7000), ecology (20,000), forestry (5000), medical botany (3000), agriculture (9000) and biology (20,000). Reference library; materials do not circulate, except via standard inter-library loan. About 5000 vols uncataloged. Incl archives, art and vertical files. An OCLC library.

NY —CORNELL UNIVERSITY LIBRARIES, Albert R Mann Library, Ithaca, 14853. Henry T Murphy, Librn
Holdings: Vols 100,000 Cat Microforms
Notes: Especially strong in plant sciences.

NY —AMERICAN MUSEUM OF NATURAL HISTORY, Library Services Dept, Central Park W & 79th St, New York, 10024. Nina J Root, Chairwoman; Mary Genett, Asst Librn for Reference Services
Holdings: Vols (385,000) Cat Mss Maps Pix Slides Microforms
Notes: Nearly all collections are outstanding for depth of coverage and international range. Early and historic works, rare books, colored illustrations, and relevant serial publications necessary to the researches of the scientific staff and the work of the educational division. Open to the public.

NY —COLUMBIA UNIVERSITY LIBRARIES, Biological Sciences Library, 601 Fairchild, New York, 10027. Barbara A List, Reference/Collection Development Librn
Holdings: Vols 38,000 Cat
Notes: Incl biochemistry and molecular biology.

BIOLOGY (cont.)

NY —ROCKEFELLER UNIVERSITY, Rockefeller Archive Center, Hillcrest, Pocantico Hills, North Tarrytown, 10591. Joseph W Ernst, Dir; J William Hess, Assoc Dir
Notes: Papers of Edward L Tatum, Rockefeller University professor. Conducted research in the genetics and metabolism of bacteria, yeasts, and molds. In 1958, he was joint recipient, with Joshua Lederberg and George Beadle, of the Nobel Prize in medicine and physiology.

NY —UNIVERSITY OF ROCHESTER, Carlson Library, Hutchison Hall, River Campus, Rochester, 14627. Michael W Poulin, Librn
Holdings: Vols (48,720) Cat Microforms
Notes: Strong collection in the field and related areas.

NY —STATE UNIVERSITY OF NEW YORK, STONY BROOK, Biology Library, Stony Brook, 11794. Doris Williams, Biology Librn
Holdings: Vols 625 // Uncat
Notes: Raymond Pearl Collection. The collection contains reprints collected by Raymond Pearl, founder of the *Quarterly Review of Biology*. The reprints are indexed by author and arranged by twenty subjects relating to biology and the history of science.

NC —DUKE UNIVERSITY, Biology-Forestry Library, Durham, 27706. Bertha Livingstone, Librn
Holdings: Vols 143,474

OH —LLOYD LIBRARY & MUSEUM, 917 Plum St, Cincinnati, 45202. John B Griggs, Librn
Notes: General holdings in biology and natural sciences.

OH —SAINT THOMAS INSTITUTE, Library, 1842 Madison Rd, Cincinnati, 45206. Sister M Virgil Ghering, O P Librn
Holdings: Vols 8000 Cat
Budget: ($39,878)

OH —CLEVELAND PUBLIC LIBRARY, Science & Technology Dept, 325 Superior Ave, Cleveland, 44114. Jean Z Piety, Head
Holdings: Cat
Notes: Collection covers the environmental sciences concerned with the Great Lakes-St Lawrence drainage basins. Emphasis is on limnology, ecology, meteorology, hydraulics, biology, pollution of air and water, natural history and general research. Most of the material indexed has been donated by numerous agencies around the Great Lakes. Also, card index file and a file of approx 2000 documents. The card index file incl references to material in the total department collection, as well as to specific documents housed in the filing cabinets.

OH —OHIO STATE UNIVERSITY, Biological Sciences Library, 1735 Neil Ave, Columbus, 43210. Victoria Welborn, Librn
Holdings: Vols (85,000) Cat Mss Maps Microforms

PA —DELAWARE VALLEY COLLEGE, Joseph Krauskopf Library, Doylestown, 18901. Constance Shook, Dir

PA —CARNEGIE LIBRARY OF PITTSBURGH, Science & Technology Dept, 4400 Forbes Ave, Pittsburgh, 15213. Catherine M Brosky, Dept Head
Holdings: Vols (380,000) Cat Maps Microforms
Budget: ($240,000)
Notes: Currently acquiring general monographs and journals. Incl many older sets and titles.

PA —CARNEGIE-MELLON UNIVERSITY, Mellon Institute Library, 4400 Fifth Ave, Pittsburgh, 15213. Mary J Volk, Librn
Holdings: Vols (60,000) Cat
Notes: Emphasis is on chemistry and biological sciences, with material at the graduate and research level.

PA —UNIVERSITY OF PITTSBURGH, Langley Library, A-217 Langley Hall, Pittsburgh, 15260. D L Johnston, Librn
Holdings: Vols (14,000) Cat
Budget: ($147,170)

PA —PENNSYLVANIA STATE UNIVERSITY, Fred Lewis Pattee Library, Life Sciences Library, University Park, 16802. Keith Roe, Head
Notes: This collection is strong in periodical runs, particularly European learned societies and agriculture. It contains extensive collections of Experiment Station publications and has developed specialties in Mycology and Fusaria. There is also a special collection of 1105 glass slides on early Pennsylvania lumbering.

SC —UNIVERSITY OF SOUTH CAROLINA, Thomas Cooper Library, Columbia, 29208. Kenneth E Toombs, Dir of Libraries; Roger Mortimer, Rare Book Librn
Holdings: Vols 1250 Cat
Notes: Especially for 1750-1850.

TX —UNIVERSITY OF TEXAS LIBRARIES, Science Library, PO Box P, Austin, 78712. Betty White, Librn
Holdings: Vols (103,000) Cat Microforms

TX —UNIVERSITY OF TEXAS, Marine Science Institute Library, Port Aransas, 78373. Ruth Grundy, Librn
Holdings: Vols (45,000) Cat Maps Pix
Budget: ($70,000)
Notes: Current researches in marine science, especially concerning the Gulf of Mexico, the Texas Coastal Zone, and the Continental Shelf. Incl journals.

†VA —VIRGINIA COMMONWEALTH UNIVERSITY/MEDICAL COLLEGE OF VIRGINIA, Tompkins-McCaw Library, Box 667, MCV Sta, Richmond, 23298. J Craig McLean, Asst Dir of University Libraries
Holdings: Vols (155,000) Cat Mss Microforms
Budget: ($281,200)
Notes: Graduate sciences (biomedical emphasis). All newly cataloged books and journals are reported in the *Abridged Book* Catalog. Citations are limited to main entry and two subject entries. The catalog is cumulated monthly in 42x microfiche format. A cumulated Union Catalog covering 6 years and parts of 5 library collections is in preparation.

WA —UNIVERSITY OF WASHINGTON LIBRARIES, Suzzallo Library, Natural Sciences Library, FM-25, Seattle, 98195. Nancy G Blase, Head
Holdings: Vols (192,353)
Budget: ($219,809)

ON —AGRICULTURE CANADA, Research Branch, Neatby Library, Rm 3032, K W Neatby Bldg, CEF, Ottawa, K1A 0C6, Can. Marcel Charette, Library Technician
Holdings: Vols 2100 Cat

ON —NATIONAL LIBRARY OF CANADA, 395 Wellington St, Ottawa, K1A 0N4, Can. Andre Preibish, Dir
Holdings: Vols 10,000
Notes: Includes 130 serial titles, theses, pamphlets, government publications relating to family and marriage. The following disciplines covered: anthropology, psychology and psychiatry, law, economics, religion, sociology, demography, education, political science and biology. Earliest title 1630.

PQ —MCGILL UNIVERSITY, Botany-Genetics Library, 1205 McGregor Ave, Montreal, H3A 1B1, Can. Eleanor MacLean, Librn
Holdings: Vols (21,000)

BIOLOGY—CLASSIFICATION

NY —AMERICAN MUSEUM OF NATURAL HISTORY, Library Services Dept, Central Park W & 79th St, New York, 10024. Nina J Root, Chairwoman; Mary Genett, Asst Librn for Reference Services
Holdings: Vols (385,000) Cat Mss Maps Pix Slides Microforms
Notes: Nearly all collections are outstanding for depth of coverage and international range. Early and historic works, rare books, colored illustrations, and relevant serial publications supplement the modern scientific publications necessary to the researches of the scientific staff and the work of the educational division. Open to the public.

BIOLOGY—ECOLOGY see Ecology

BIOLOGY—HISTORY

NY —CORNELL UNIVERSITY LIBRARIES, John M Olin Library, History of Science Collections, Ithaca, 14853. Lillian A Clark, Administrative Supervisor; David W Corson, History of Science Librn
Holdings: Vols (33,000) Cat
Notes: Early printed source materials in all biological sciences, 16th through 19th centuries. Incl Adelmann Collection in the History of Embryology and Anatomy, Hill Collection in North American ornithology, and extensive collection of 16th-19th century medical dissertations. Noncirculating.
See also entry under Science - History

NY —AMERICAN MUSEUM OF NATURAL HISTORY, Library Services Dept, Central Park W & 79th St, New York, 10024. Nina J Root, Chairwoman; Mary Genett, Asst Librn for Reference Services
Notes: Nearly all collections are outstanding for depth of coverage and international range. Early and historic works, rare books, colored illustrations, and relevant serial publications necessary to the researches of the scientific staff and the work of the educational division. Open to the public.

OH —CLEVELAND MEDICAL LIBRARY ASSOCIATION/CASE WESTERN RESERVE UNIVERSITY, Cleveland Health Sciences Library, Historical Division, Allen Memorial Medical Library, 11000 Euclid Ave, Cleveland, 44106. Glen Jenkins, Rare Book Librarian & Archivist
Holdings: Vols 2000 Cat Mss Slides
Notes: History of Biology Collection.

BIOLOGY, DEVELOPMENTAL

CA —STANFORD UNIVERSITY, Hopkins Marine Station Library, Cabrillo Point, Pacific Grove, 93950. Alan Baldridge, Librn

IA —IOWA STATE UNIVERSITY, Library, Ames, 50011. Warren B Kuhn, Dean of Library Services
Holdings: Cat
Notes: Extensive serial holdings supplement this strong collection.

MA —HARVARD UNIVERSITY LIBRARY, Biological Laboratories Library, 16 Divinity Ave, Cambridge, 02138. Dorothy Solbrig, Librn
Holdings: Vols (20,000) Cat Films
Notes: Materials in all areas of biology, emphasizing biochemistry and cellular and developmental biology. There is little in systematic biology and morphology.

NY —UNIVERSITY OF ROCHESTER, Carlson Library, Hutchison Hall, River Campus, Rochester, 14627. Michael W Poulin, Librn
Holdings: Vols (48,720) Cat Microforms
Notes: Strong collection in the field and related areas.

BIOLOGY, EVOLUTIONARY

CA —RANCHO SANTA ANA BOTANIC GARDEN LIBRARY, 1500 N College Ave, Claremont, 91711. Beatrice M Beck, Librn
Notes: Incl emphasis on California flora, floras of the world, evolutionary biology and ethnobotany.

BIOLOGY, MOLECULAR see Molecular Biology

BIOLOGY, ORAL see Oral Biology

BIOLOGY, RADIATION see Radiobiology

BIOMATHEMATICS

CA —UNIVERSITY OF CALIFORNIA, BERKELEY, Life Sciences Libraries, Public Health Library, 42 Earl Warren Hall, Berkeley, 94720. Thomas J Alexander, Librn
Holdings: Vols (75,000) Cat Microforms
Notes: Research collection covering all aspects of public health. Health Department annual reports from all 50 states are acquired, as well as such reports from all California health units and from major US cities. Serial publications issued by Health Departments in the 13 western states are being received.

BIOMECHANICS see Human Engineering

BIOMEDICAL ENGINEERING

CA —REES-STEALY MEDICAL CLINIC LIBRARY, 2001 Fourth Ave, San Diego, 92101. Margaret O'Rourke, Librn
Holdings: Vols 6600 Cat Tapes

†HI —PACIFIC BIO-MEDICAL RESEARCH CENTER, 41 Ahui St, Honolulu, 96813.

IN —MILES LABORATORIES, Library Resources and Services, 1127 Myrtle St, PO Box 40, Elkhart, 46515. Allam Hagopian, Mgr
Holdings: Vols (16,500) Cat Audiotapes Microforms
Notes: Incl files of pharmaceutical product advertising pieces, extensive literature files on company related drugs; domestic and international marketing files. 32,000 bound periodicals.

IA —IOWA STATE UNIVERSITY, College of Veterinary Medicine, Veterinary Medical Library, Ames, 50011. Sara R Peterson, Librn
Holdings: Vols (17,000) Cat Microforms
Notes: Incl comparative and veterinary medicine with emphasis in the fields of mammalian anatomy and physiology, laboratory animal medicine, pathology, toxicology, biomedical engineering and clinical veterinary medicine. Incl 2000 uncataloged German theses.

MA —RAYTHEON CO, Research Div, Library, 131 Spring St, Lerington, 02193. Martha C Adamson, Head Librn
Holdings: Vols (5000) Cat
Notes: 6000 technical reports, 200 journal subscriptions.

MA —INSTRUMENTATION LABORATORY, Library, 113 Hartwell Ave, Lexington, 02173. Jacqueline R Kates, Librn
Holdings: Vols (6000) Cat Microforms Reprints

MA —ABCOR, INC, Library, 850 Main St, Wilmington, 01887. Eileen Smith, Librn
Notes: Formerly engaged in biomedical engineering of artificial organs; contraceptive research; sustained-release drug preparations. No longer updated.

MI —WAYNE STATE UNIVERSITY, Vera Parshall Shiffman Medical Library, 4325 Brush St, Detroit, 48201. Faith Van Toll, Acting Head Librn
Holdings: Vols (158,612)
Budget: ($381,153)
Notes: Resource Library in Greater Midwest Regional Medical Library Network Program.

NJ —BECTON, DICKINSON & CO, Corporate Library/Information Center, Rutherford, 07070. Lynda M Wiseman, Corporate Librn
Holdings: Vols (3500) Cat Microforms
Notes: Open to the public by appointment and ILL.

NY —UNIVERSITY OF ROCHESTER, Engineering Library, Gavett Hall, River Campus, Rochester, 14627. Isabel Kaplan, Librn
Holdings: Vols (25,000) Cat
Notes: Stong collection in the field and related areas.

NC —DUKE UNIVERSITY, School of Engineering, Library, Durham, 27706. Eric J Smith, Librn
Holdings: Vols (72,000) Cat Microforms
Budget: ($110,000)

TX —UNIVERSITY OF TEXAS LIBRARIES, Richard W McKinney Engineering Library, 1.3 ECJ, Austin, 78712. Susan B Ardis, Librn
Holdings: Vols (83,548) Cat Microforms

WI —MARQUETTE UNIVERSITY, Memorial Library, 1415 W Wisconsin Ave, Milwaukee, 53233. Jay Kirk, Health Sciences Librn
Notes: Supports curriculum and research.

BIOMEDICINE

MD —US ARMED FORCES RADIOBIOLOGY RESEARCH INSTITUTE, Naval Medical Command, Bethesda, 20014. Nannette M Pope, Head, Library Division
Holdings: Vols (50,000)
Budget: ($150,000)
Notes: Collection consists of monographs, technical reports, serials, and microfiche related to radiation effects on human and animal biology.

NY —CORNELL UNIVERSITY, New York State College of Veterinary Medicine, Flower Veterinary Library, Ithaca, 14853. Susanne Whitaker, Librn
Holdings: Vols (74,000) Cat
Notes: Veterinary college library; incl biomedical publications as well as purely veterinary titles.

TX —US AIR FORCE, School of Aerospace Medicine, Strughold Aeromedical Library, Brooks AFB, 78235. Fred W Todd, Chief Librn
Holdings: Vols (119,188) Cat Mss Maps Pix Microforms
Budget: ($499,000)
Notes: Aviation and space medicine and physiology, including the physiological effects of altitude and decompression. Biomedical and and human engineering. Military medicine, including chemical and biological warfare. Emergency medicine in both professional and technical areas. Radiobiology, including atomic medicine, nuclear medicine, and space radiation. Material not oriented to the School of Aerospace Medicine are excluded. Incl also 45,787 microforms and 142,371 technical documents.

BIOMETEOROLOGY

CT —YALE UNIVERSITY, Forestry Library, 205 Prospect St, New Haven, 06511. Joseph A Miller, Librn
Holdings: Vols (115,000) Cat Microforms
Notes: Forestry is construed broadly to incl underlying or closely related social, physical, and biological sciences.

†CT —YALE UNIVERSITY, Medical Library, 333 Cedar St, New Haven, 06520.
Notes: Incl large world-wide pamphlet collection, arranged geographically, of resorts, etc, favorable to good health.

BC —CANADIAN FORESTRY SERVICE, Pacific Forest Research Centre, Library, 506 West Burnside Rd, Victoria, V8Z 1M5, Can. Alice Solyma, Librn
Holdings: Vols (60,500) Cat Microforms
Notes: Incl forest meteorology and also a general meteorology collection.

BIONICS see Cybernetics

BIONOMICS see Ecology

BIOPHYSICS see Biological Physics

BIOSSAT, BRUCE, 1910-1974

MA —BOSTON UNIVERSITY, Mugar Memorial Library, Special Collections Dept, 771 Commonwealth Ave, Boston, 02215. Howard B Gotlieb, Dir
Holdings: // Cat Mss Pix
Notes: Mss, correspondence, etc collected in depth; incl publications by or about.

BIOTECHNOLOGY see Cybernetics; Human Engineering

BIRCH SOCIETY see John Birch Society

BIRCHARD, SARDIS

OH —RUTHERFORD B HAYES LIBRARY, 1337 Hayes Ave, Fremont, 43420. Watt P Marchman, Dir
Holdings: Vols 100 Cat Mss Maps Pix
Notes: Sardis Birchard was the bachelor uncle and one-time guardian of Rutherford B Hayes. Incl 4 linear feet of correspondence, diary, account books, cash books, notes, deeds, tax records and receipts.

BIRCH-BARK CANOES see Canoes and Canoeing

BIRD, ROBERT MONTGOMERY

PA —UNIVERSITY OF PENNSYLVANIA, Van Pelt Library, Rare Books Collection, 34 & Walnut Sts, Philadelphia, 19104. Daniel Traister, Special Collections Librn
Holdings: Vols 50 Cat Mss
Notes: American physician, playwright and novelist. 20 boxes of mss of plays and poems, incl first editions. See Downs (Supp) 1668-9. Descriptive case file available in library.

BIRD, WILLIAM

IN —INDIANA UNIVERSITY, Lilly Library, Seventh St, Bloomington, 47405. William R Cagle, Librn
Holdings: Vols 155 Cat Mss
Notes: First editions, etc. Mss incl significant correspondence files with William Bird, T S Eliot, D G Bridson, John Quinn, et al.
See also entry under Press Books - Three Mountains Press

BIRDNESTS see Birds—Eggs and Nests

BIRDS

CA —UNIVERSITY OF CALIFORNIA, BERKELEY, Museum of Vertebrate Zoology, Grinnell-Miller Library, Berkeley, 94720.
Holdings: Vols (2000) Cat
Notes: Vertebrate zoology, with emphasis on birds and mammals of the Pacific States.

CA —LOS ANGELES PUBLIC LIBRARY, Science & Technology Dept, 630 W Fifth St, Los Angeles, 90071. Billie M Connor, Dept Head
Holdings: Vols 2250 Cat
Notes: Extensive collection of handbooks, identification manuals and monographs. Many classical illustrated works, materials on domesticated birds.

CA —WESTERN FOUNDATION OF VERTEBRATE ZOOLOGY, Library, 1100 Glendon Ave, Los Angeles, 90024. Lloyd F Kiff, Dir
Holdings: Vols (4000) Uncat Mss Pix Slides 16mm Films
Budget: ($10,000)
Notes: This is probably the third largest collection on birds in the Western US. It incl the combined resources of 10 former private libraries on this topic, plus additions made by us during the past 20 years. There is special emphasis on oology, or the study of bird eggs. The collection is freely available for use by any interested researcher.

CA —CALIFORNIA ACADEMY OF SCIENCES, J W Mailliard Jr Library, Golden Gate Park, San Francisco, 94118. Ray Brian, Librn
Notes: Downs No 2160.

CT —TRINITY COLLEGE LIBRARY, Watkinson Library, 300 Summit St, Hartford, 06106. Jeffrey Kaimowitz, Cur
Holdings: Vols (7000) Cat
Notes: Incl the Ostrom Enders and Gurdon Russell Collections of Ornithology.

CT —YALE UNIVERSITY, Box 1603A, Yale Station, New Haven, 06520.
Holdings: Cat Mss Pix
See also entry under Ornithology.

CT —YALE UNIVERSITY, Ornithology Library, Peabody Museum of Natural History, 170 Whitney Ave, New Haven, 06520. Eleanor Stickney, Senior Museum Asst
Holdings: Vols 8200 Cat Mss Pix Slides
Notes: The William R Coe Collection is held in this library. There is also a reprint collection of 10,000. Incl 120 journals.

DC —SMITHSONIAN INSTITUTION LIBRARIES, Natural History Branch, Washington, 20560. Sylvia Churgin, Chief Librn
Holdings: Vols 4600 Cat Maps Pix Slides

FL —EVERGLADES NATIONAL PARK, South Florida Research Center, PO Box 279, Homestead, 33030. Gary Hendrix, Librn
Holdings: Vols (5500) Cat Microforms
Notes: Emphasis on South Florida, birds, water problems. This is a special reference collection maintained for the Park Staff only. Noncirculating. Estuaries. ILL available.

FL —ARCHBOLD BIOLOGICAL STATION, Library, Rt 2, Box 180, Lake Placid, 33852. Fred E Lohrer, Librn
Holdings: Vols (2000) Cat Periodicals

BIRDS (cont.)

IL —FIELD MUSEUM OF NATURAL HISTORY, Edward E Ayer Ornithology Library Collection, Roosevelt Rd & Lake Shore Dr, Chicago, 60605. W Peyton Fawcett, Librn
Holdings: Vols 3500 Cat
Notes: John T Zimmer's concluding note: "In the works cataloged...there are, approximately, 50,995 plates of birds (39,888 in colors and 11,107 plain), 39,347 text figures of ornithological subjects (987 in colors and 38,360 plain), and 1981 plates of birds' eggs (1914 in colors and 67 plain)." Downs 2333.

IN —INDIANA CENTRAL UNIVERSITY, Krannert Memorial Library, 1400 E Hanna Ave, Indianapolis, 46227. Florabelle Wilson, Librn
Holdings: Vols 244 Cat
Notes: The Wilfrid Goodman Collection consists of books and periodicals about birds, their lives and habits. Major emphasis is on birds of the Americas, but collection incl some volumes on birds of other continents.

IA —IOWA STATE UNIVERSITY, Library, Dept of Special Collections, Ames, 50011. Stanley M Yates, Head
Holdings: / / Mss
Notes: Frederic Leopold has observed and recorded over 35 years the nesting habits of wood ducks along the Mississippi River near Burlington, Iowa. Collection includes his notebooks.

KS —UNIVERSITY OF KANSAS, Kenneth Spencer Research Library, Special Collections Dept, Lawrence, 66045. Alexandra Mason, Librn
Holdings: Vols 5000 Cat Mss Pix
Notes: Ralph Ellis Collection. Special strengths: John Gould, Thomas Bewick. Many color plate books, Gould and other drawings, prints. 15th century to 1945, especially 19th century. Noncirculating. See Mengel, Robert M, comp *A Catalogue of the Ellis Collection of Ornithological Books in the University of Kansas Libraries*, Lawrence, Kansas. Volume 1, A-B, 1972. (University of Kansas Publications. Library series, 33) xxix, 259pp.; v. 2, C-D, 1983. (Univ of Kansas Publications, Libr Series, 48) 176 pp.

LA —LOUISIANA STATE UNIVERSITY, Troy H Middleton Library, Baton Rouge, 70803. Lance E Dickson, Acting Dir
Holdings: Vols (3000) Cat Maps Pix
Notes: Noncirculating collection.

LA —R W NORTON ART GALLERY, Library, 4747 Creswell Ave, Shreveport, 71106. Jerry M Bloomer, Librn
Holdings: Cat
Notes: Many rare works, such as Audubon's elephant folio ed of *The Birds of America*, (also the octavo edition), Catesby, John Gould (a complete collection), Alexander Wilson and Rex Brasher.

MA —UNIVERSITY OF MASSACHUSETTS AT AMHERST, Library, Amherst, 01003. Siegfried Feller, Assoc Dir for Collection Development
Holdings: Cat
Notes: Incl the Arthur Cleveland Bent Ornithology Collection.

MA —HARVARD UNIVERSITY, Museum of Comparative Zoology, Library, 26 Oxford St, Cambridge, 02138. Eva S Jonas, Librn
Holdings: Cat Mss Pix Microforms

†MA —WILLIAMS COLLEGE, Chapin Library of Rare Books, PO Box 426, Williamstown, 01267. Robert L Volz, Custodian
Holdings: Vols 250 Cat
Notes: Color plate bird books. No material available on interlibrary loan.

MI —UNIVERSITY OF MICHIGAN, Museums Library, Ann Arbor, 48109. Patricia B Yocum, Librn
Holdings: Vols 11,000 Cat

NY —CORNELL UNIVERSITY LIBRARIES, Albert R Mann Library, Ithaca, 14853. Henry T Murphy, Librn
Holdings: Vols 4000 Cat Pix Microforms
Notes: There are about 1500 additional vols in the Ornithology Library, a branch of the Mann Library, at the Cornell Laboratory of Ornithology. About 75 percent of these are duplicates of the Mann Library collection.

NY —AMERICAN MUSEUM OF NATURAL HISTORY, Library Services Dept, Central Park W & 79th St, New York, 10024. Nina J Root, Chairwoman; Mary Genett, Asst Librn for Reference Services
Holdings: Vols (385,000) Cat Mss Maps Pix Slides Microforms
Notes: Nearly all collections are outstanding for depth of coverage and international range. Early and historic works, rare books, colored illustrations, and relevant serial publications supplement the modern scientific publications necessary to the researches of the scientific staff and the work of the educational division. Open to the public.

OH —CLEVELAND PUBLIC LIBRARY, Science & Technology Dept, 325 Superior Ave, Cleveland, 44114. Jean Z Piety, Head
Holdings: Cat Pix
Notes: Comprehensive collection of books and journals.

OH —OHIO HISTORICAL SOCIETY, Archives Library Division, 1982 Velma Ave, Columbus, 43211. Dennis East, Division Chief
Holdings: Vols 800 Cat
Notes: Collection based on the William L Dawson Library; more than local coverage; good for scarce periodicals. Supports Natural History Division of the Society.

PA —ZOOLOGICAL SOCIETY OF PHILADELPHIA, Library, 34 & Girard Ave, Philadelphia, 19104. Alyssa N Scheuermann, Librn
Holdings: Vols (1000) Cat
Notes: Photocopying with permission.

PA —PENNSYLVANIA STATE UNIVERSITY, Fred Lewis Pattee Library, Special Collections Dept, University Park, 16802. Charles Mann, Chief, Special Collections
Holdings: Vols (122,533) Cat
Budget: ($37,000)
Notes: 19th century illustrated works on birds.

RI —BROWN UNIVERSITY, John Hay Library, 20 Prospect St, Providence, 02912. Mark N Brown, Cur Mss
Holdings: Vols (5000) Cat Mss
Notes: History of Science Collection incl resources from several specific donor named collections of volumes printed from the 15th to 20th centuries. The significant volumes published before 1700 are unusually rich in Mathematics, Astronomy and Astrology (463 vols). Publications of the various scientific academies are well represented and include the *Philosophical Transactions of the Royal Society of London* (beginning in 1665) and *The American Journal of Science.* Collection of John James Audubon's published works on birds and quadrupeds of America, incl the elephant folio edition of *Birds of America* (Edinburgh and London: 1827-1838) and some mss material.

SC —UNIVERSITY OF SOUTH CAROLINA, Thomas Cooper Library, Columbia, 29208. Kenneth E Toombs, Dir of Libraries; Roger Mortimer, Rare Book Librn
Holdings: Vols 500 Cat
Notes: Especially rare items, incl the Elephant folio Audubon, and rare editions of Cotesby, Wilson, Selby, Gould and Brasher. *See also* entry under Natural History.

TN —PUBLIC LIBRARY OF NASHVILLE & DAVIDSON COUNTY, Nashville Room, Eighth Ave N & Union St, Nashville, 37203. Mary Glenn Hearne, Head
Holdings: Vols 300/ / Uncat Mss Maps Pix
Notes: A 60-year collection of books, journals, diaries, and notes on birds, kept by Harry C Monk. It incl 1916-1966 Nashville bird sightings; 1922-1974 correspondence with Mrs Amelia Laskey of Nashville; book blurbs; government documents; Tennessee Ornithological Society minutes, finance, and membership reports. Partially cataloged. *The Carrie Mae Weil Ornithological Collection* (Nashville: Public Library of Nashville and Davidson County, 1977).

WI —MILWAUKEE PUBLIC LIBRARY, 814 W Wisconsin Ave, Milwaukee, 53233. Donald J Sager, City Librn
Holdings: Vols 5000 Cat
Notes: Owns a set of Audubon Prints, also Gould's *Birds of Australia,* Catesby, Selby, Wilson, Edwards, and Brasher.

WI —MILWAUKEE PUBLIC MUSEUM, Reference Library, 800 W Wells St, Milwaukee, 53233. Judith Campbell Turner, Museum Librn
Holdings: Vols (90,000) Cat Maps Microforms

ON —NATIONAL MUSEUMS OF CANADA, Library Services Directorate, Ottawa, K1A 0M8, Can. Valerie Monkhouse, Director
Holdings: Vols (90,000) Cat Mss Microforms
Budget: ($81,000)
Notes: Emphasis on Canadian and circumpolar natural history. Collection incl botany, herpetology, ichthyology, invertebrate zoology, malacology, mammology, mineralogy, ornithology, paleobiology, zooarchaeology. Exceptional collections in lichenology, bryology, malacology, ornithology. Research collection, interlibrary loans available, public may use on the premises.

BIRDS—EGGS AND NESTS

CA —WESTERN FOUNDATION OF VERTEBRATE ZOOLOGY, Library, 1100 Glendon Ave, Los Angeles, 90024. Lloyd F Kiff, Dir
Holdings: Vols (4000) Uncat Mss Pix Slides 16mm Films
Budget: ($10,000)
Notes: This is probably the third largest collection on birds in the Western US. It incl the combined resources of 10 former private libraries on this topic, plus additions made by us during the past 20 years. There is special emphasis on oology, or the study of bird eggs. The collection is freely available for use by any interested researcher.

BIRDS—FLIGHT see Flight—History

BIRDS—NESTS see Birds—Eggs and Nests

BIRDS—PICTURES, ILLUSTRATIONS, ETC. see Color Plates—Bird Books

BIRDS, AQUATIC see Water Birds

BIRDSALL AND SON

ON —UNIVERSITY OF TORONTO, Thomas Fisher Rare Book Library, 120 Saint George St, Toronto, M5S 1A5, Can. Richard G Landon, Head
Holdings: Vols 25 Cat
Notes: Birdsall Collection of about 3000 finishing tools acquired from the British firm, Birdsall & Son, Northampton, England. Earliest tools date back to the 18th century; majority are 19th century. Includes small number of volumes bound by the firm; also manufacturers' catalogues of finishing tools. Collection described in Evans, E and R Grover, *The Birdsall Collection of Bookbinders' Finishing Tools* (Toronto, University of Toronto Library, 1972).

BIRDWELL, RUSSELL, 1913-1977

CA —UNIVERSITY OF CALIFORNIA, LOS ANGELES, Research Library, Dept of Special Collections, 405 Hilgard Ave, Los Angeles, 90024. Edward Shreeves, Chairman, Bibliographers Group; David S Zeidberg, Head
Holdings: Mss Pix
Notes: 33 linear feet of the film publicist's personal papers and memorabilia.

BIRGE, RAYMOND T., 1887-

CA —UNIVERSITY OF CALIFORNIA, BERKELEY, Bancroft Library, Manuscripts Division, Berkeley, 94720. James D Hart, Dir
Notes: Papers.

BIRIUKOVA, YULIA

ON —METROPOLITAN TORONTO LIBRARY, Theatre Dept, 789 Yonge St,

BIRIUKOVA, YULIA (cont.)

Toronto, M4W 2G8, Can. Heather McCallum, Head
Notes: The Boris Volkoff Collection documents the Russian-born dancer's 45 year career in Canada and his important contribution to the development of Canadian ballet. The collection incl scrapbooks, costume and set designs (incl original stage designs by Mstislav Dobujinsky for the Canadian ballet *Red Ear of Corn,* produced by Volkoff in 1949), photographs, programs, correspondence, choreographic notebooks, and a portrait of Boris Volkloff painted by Yulia Biriukova.

BIRMINGHAM, ENGLAND

PA —TEMPLE UNIVERSITY, Samuel Paley Library, Berks & 13 Sts, Philadelphia, 19122.
Notes: Collection of works of the City of Birmingham School of Printing (England). Books and ephemera of the students and Leonard Jay, Master Printer. Also the William Danner Collection of periodical issues from amateur printers and presses.

BIRMINGHAM, JOHN, 1951-

CT —LEE ASH, (personal collection), 66 Humiston Dr, Bethany, 06525.
Notes: First editions, mss, ephemera, memorabilia, correspondence.

BIRMINGHAM, STEPHEN

MA —BOSTON UNIVERSITY, Mugar Memorial Library, Special Collections Dept, 771 Commonwealth Ave, Boston, 02215. Howard B Gotlieb, Dir
Holdings: Cat Mss Pix
Notes: Mss, correspondence, etc collected in depth; incl publications by or about.

BIRMINGHAM WATER WORKS

AL —BIRMINGHAM PUBLIC LIBRARY, Dept of Archives & Mss, 2020 Seventh Ave N, Birmingham, 35203. Marvin Y Whiting, Archivist & Cur
Holdings: Cat Docs Mss Photos
Notes: Collected records, 1883-1952, incl company correspondence, financial reports, operations records, scrapbooks, and photographs documenting the history of the company.

BIRNEY, EARLE

AB —UNIVERSITY OF CALGARY, Libraries, Special Collections Div, 2500 University Dr, Calgary, T2N 1N4, Can.
Notes: The Division houses small collections of letters and mss of Canadian poets such as Earle Birney and George Bowering.

BIROHI LANGUAGE see Brahui Language

BIRTH, REGISTERS OF see Registers of Births, Etc.

BIRTH CONTROL

CA —WOMEN'S HISTORY RESEARCH CENTER, Microfilm Library, 2325 Oak St, Berkeley, 94708. Laura X, Librn
Holdings: Mss Pix Microforms
Notes: Incl material (150 subject files) on physical and mental health and illnesses; sex roles; biology; women and the life cycle; birth/population control; sex and sexuality; black and Third World women. Collection at University of Wyoming. Archive of Contemporary History, PO Box 3334, Laramie, Wyoming 82701, c/o David Crosson. Research inquiries accepted. Microfilm of collection (14 reels and reel guides) available at many universities and through Women's History Research Center, 2325 Oak St, Berkeley, CA 94708. No collections housed at this address.

CA —UNIVERSITY OF CALIFORNIA, SANTA BARBARA, Library, Dept of Special Collections, Santa Barbara, 93106. Christian F Brun, Head
Holdings: Vols 1550 Cat Mss
Notes: The Marie Stopes Collection.

DC —CENTER FOR BIOETHICS, Library, Kennedy Institute, Georgetown University, 3520 Prospect St NW, Washington, 20057. Doris Goldstein, Dir; Judith Mistichelli, Senior Librn
Holdings: Vols 8200
Notes: Largest library of its kind. Incl 31, 000 journal articles. Collects in the following subject areas: applied ethics; medical ethics; philosophy of medicine; science, technology and society; sociology of medicine; patient-physician care; sexuality; contraception; abortion; population policy; reproductive technologies; in vitro fertilization; genetic counseling and screening; genetic engineering; mental organ transplantation; death and dying; "baby doe" issues; euthanasia; suicide; use of chemical and biological weapons. Produces computer database *Bioethicsline,* available through MEDLARS; and the printed annual *Bibliography of Bioethics.* Other library publications are: *New Titles in Bioethics* (monthly); *Scope Notes* series on current topics.

DC —LIBRARY OF CONGRESS, Manuscript Division, Washington, 20540. John C Broderick, Chief

IL —SOUTHERN ILLINOIS UNIVERSITY, CARBONDALE, Delyte W Morris Library, Carbondale, 62901.
Holdings: Cat Mss Pix
Notes: Incl the papers of Drs William Josephus and Victor Robinson; with the papers of Theodore A Schroeder. Much on sex instruction and birth control.

MA —RADCLIFFE COLLEGE, Arthur & Elizabeth Schlesinger Library on the History of Women in America, 3 James St, Cambridge, 02138. Patricia Miller King, Dir; Eva Moseley, Cur of Mss
Notes: Books, pamphlets, clippings; also oral history interviews in the Family Planning Oral History Project, and numerous mss collections, espec those of the Birth Control League of Massachusetts, Mary (Steichen) Calderone, MD (1904-), Edna (Rankin) McKinnon (1893-1978), and Florence Clothier, MD (1903-).

MA —ABCOR, INC, Library, 850 Main St, Wilmington, 01887. Eileen Smith, Librn
Notes: Formerly engaged in biomedical engineering of artificial organs; contraceptive research; sustained-release drug preparations. No longer updated.

NY —MATERNITY CENTER ASSOCIATION, Library, 48 E 92 St, New York, 10028. Esther Hanchett, Acting Librn
Holdings: Vols 2000 Cat
Notes: No photocopying.

NY —PLANNED PARENTHOOD FEDERATION OF AMERICA, Katharine Dexter McCormick Library, 810 Seventh Ave, New York, 10019. Gloria A Roberts, Head Librn
Holdings: Vols (4000) Cat
Notes: Birth control, teenagers, contraception and contraceptive research, family planning, religion and birth control.

NY —UNIVERSITY OF ROCHESTER, Rush Rhees Library, Department of Rare Books and Special Collections, Rochester, 14627. Peter Dzwonkoski, Librn
Holdings: Cat Mss
Notes: Correspondence, reports, articles written by Wile on birth control (including many letters from Margaret Sanger), left and right handedness, sex education, child development, and mental hygiene.

NY —STATE UNIVERSITY OF NEW YORK, STONY BROOK, Melville Library, Dept of Special Collections, Stony Brook, 11794. Evert Volkersz, Head
Holdings: Cat
Notes: Emphasis on Marie Stopes and her work for birth control.

WI —PLANNED PARENTHOOD OF WISCONSIN, Maurice Ritz Resource Library & Bookstore, 1135 W State St, Milwaukee, 53233. Ann McIntyre, Librn
Holdings: Vols (2500) Cat Pix Slides Phonorecords 16mm Films Filmstrips VF
Notes: Special emphasis on family planning and reproductive health, birth control and contraception.

BIRTH CONTROL—HISTORY

NY —PLANNED PARENTHOOD FEDERATION OF AMERICA, Katharine Dexter McCormick Library, 810 Seventh Ave, New York, 10019. Gloria A Roberts, Head Librn
Holdings: Vols (4000) Cat
Notes: History of the birth control movement.

BIRTH CONTROL AND RELIGION see Religion and Birth Control

BIRTH RECORDS see Registers of Births, Etc.

BIRTH-RATE see Population

BISBEE DEPORTATION

AZ —NORTHERN ARIZONA UNIVERSITY, Special Collection Library, CU Box 6022, Flagstaff, 86011. Peter M Whiteley, Coordr/Archivist; William Mullane, Librn
Notes: Photocopies of government publications and published articles concerning World War I and the Bisbee Deportation, 1917. Covers period 1917-1920, 1950's-1970's.

BISCAILUZ, EUGENE WARREN, 1883-

CA —UNIVERSITY OF CALIFORNIA, LOS ANGELES, Research Library, Dept of Special Collections, 405 Hilgard Ave, Los Angeles, 90024. Edward Shreeves, Chairman, Bibliographers Group; David S Zeidberg, Head
Holdings: Vols 45 Pix
Notes: Incl 17 linear feet of correspondence, photographs, and scrapbooks relating to his career as the first superintendent of the California State Highway Patrol and Sheriff of Los Angeles County.

BISEXUALITY

IN —INDIANA UNIVERSITY, Institute for Sex Research Library, 416 Morrison Hall, Bloomington, 47401. Douglas Freeman, Collections and Services Librn; Joan Brewer, Information Services Librn
Holdings: Vols (62,000) Cat Mss Pix Phonorecords Audiotapes Slides
Budget: ($20,000)
Notes: One of the greatest and most extensive collections on sexual behavior, the library collects materials on all aspects of sex activity, with special emphasis on behavioral and social aspects. Also collects erotic literature and sexual ephemera. Incl 105 audiotapes, 23 vertical file drawers, 108 phonorecords, 55,000 pictures, 5000 slides, and 1700 films. Rich in French, German and American sources; also much Oriental. Semitraditional erotic poetry and song of 17th-18th century England. Bawdy limericks, double-entendre, puns, slang, erotic literature, graffiti, slang and special dictionaries, proverbs and sayings, epigrams and research materials of the Kinsey Studies, etc. Contact Information Service for: literature searching, preparation of bibliographies, permission to use collection. Limited photocopying.

BISHOP, ELIZABETH

MO —WASHINGTON UNIVERSITY, Libraries, Special Collections Dept, Campus Box 1061, St Louis, 63130.
Notes: A small but significant collection.

NV —UNIVERSITY OF NEVADA, RENO, University Library, Special Collections Dept, Reno, 89557. Robert E Blesse, Head
Holdings: Vols 26 Cat Other appearances 375 Cat
Notes: Includes individual works by author in all editions including translations; also prefaces, introductions, published

BISHOP, ELIZABETH (cont.)

correspondence, appearances in anthologies, periodicals, etc. Bibliographical research collection, part of Modern Authors Collection.

NY —VASSAR COLLEGE, Library, Rare Books & Manuscripts Collection, Box 20, Poughkeepsie, 12601. Lisa Browar, Cur
Notes: An extensive collection of Elizabeth Bishop's papers, incl notebooks, mss, drafts, galleys, etc, as well as correspondence and business files, with files of letters from Cummings, Toklas, Dylan Thomas, and Eudora Welty.

BISHOP, JIM

NY —SAINT BONAVENTURE UNIVERSITY, Friedsam Memorial Library, Saint Bonaventure, 14778. John Capozzi, OFM, Art Cur
Holdings: Mss
Notes: 47 file boxes of original typescripts (6000 pp), proof sheets, and photos of his 20-some works. Also, copies of his books in various foreign languages.

BISHOP, LEONARD

MA —BOSTON UNIVERSITY, Mugar Memorial Library, Special Collections Dept, 771 Commonwealth Ave, Boston, 02215. Howard B Gotlieb, Dir
Holdings: Cat Mss Pix
Notes: Mss, correspondence, etc collected in depth; incl publications by or about.

BISHOP, MICHAEL

†PA —TEMPLE UNIVERSITY LIBRARY, Philadelphia, 19122. Thomas M Whitehead, Librn
Notes: More than 100 cubic ft of mss, incl papers of Michael Bishop, Ben Bova, Jack Dann, Gardner Dozois, Lloyd Eshback, Tom Purdom, Pamela Sargent, John Varley, and George Zebrowski.

BISHOP HILL COMMUNITY

IL —UNIVERSITY OF ILLINOIS, URBANA/CHAMPAIGN, Library, Illinois Historical Survey Library, 1408 W Gregory Dr, 1A Library, Urbana, 61801.
Holdings: Vols 50 Cat Mss Maps Pix Microforms
Notes: Communitarianism in America. The ms material, contained in 30 separate collections (10 cubic feet), concentrates on the period 1840-70. It incl correspondence, records, minutes, ledgers and diaries. Communal societies such as Bishop Hill, Brook Farm, New Harmony, the North American Phalanx and the Sodus Bay Phalanx are represented. Among the correspondents are Albert Brisbane, Parke Godwin, Sarah Grimke, Richard Owen, Robert Owen, Robert Dale Owen, and George Ripley. Numerous pictures. Guide to the collections published in 1976.

BISMARK, OTTO FURST VON, 1815-1898

MA —BRANDEIS UNIVERSITY, Goldfarb Library, 415 South St, Waltham, 02154. Bessie Hahn, Dir
Notes: Edward Lasker Collection. Consists of 21 linear ft of mss material, correspondence and contemporary pamphlets. Eduard Lasker was a political leader during the Bismarck regime in Germany. A finding list to the collection is located in Special Collections.

BISON, AMERICAN

TX —AMARILLO PUBLIC LIBRARY, 413 E Fourth, Amarillo, 79101. Mary Kay Snell, Librn
Holdings: Vols Cat Mss Maps Pix
Notes: The southwest collections incl materials on the history of Texas, Louisiana, New Mexico, Arkansas, Missouri and Kansas. General subjects covered incl overland journeys, early narratives, early biographies, Indian captivities, outlaws, US government reports, Mississippi and Ohio Rivers, the Mexican War, reports of Catholic missionaries, Niles Register, early publications, fur trade, western trails, Texas Rangers, sheriffs and Texas as a sovereign state, buffalo hunting, Indian wars, cowboys, the arrival of farmers, fences, and towns. Over 1600 items which incl books, documents, maps, mss, pamphlets, unpublished theses, interviews and photographs. The three major collections are the William Henry Bush Collection, the Laurence J Fitzsimon Collection and the Calendar of John L McCarty.

TX —UNIVERSITY OF TEXAS LIBRARIES, General Libraries, Barker Texas History Center, PO Box P, Austin, 78712. Don Carleton, Dir

†WA —WASHINGTON STATE UNIVERSITY, Library, Manuscripts, Archives & Special Collections, Pullman, 99164. John F Guido, Head
Holdings: Cat Mss Maps Pix
Notes: The Carl Parcher Russell papers, a vast resource (24,916 items; 45 linear feet) on American Indian and Western pioneer activities and artifacts. Much on the fur trade; pioneer life; mountain men and trapping; wildlife; primitive life in detail. Also the National Park Service, parks, monuments, etc. Described in *Carl Parcher Russell: An Indexed Register of His Scholarly and Professional Papers, 1920-1967, in the Washington State University* Library (Pullman, 1970), 140 pp.

BISSETT, BILL, 1939-

BC —SIMON FRASER UNIVERSITY, Library, Burnaby, V5A 1S6, Can. Percilla Groves, Special Collections Librn
Holdings: Cat Mss
Notes: Typescripts, carbons, with some holographs, of books and poems by the Vancouver poet, Bill Bissett, 782 leaves mss, plus some photographs.

BITTING, KATHERINE GOLDEN

DC —LIBRARY OF CONGRESS, Rare Book & Special Collections Div, Washington, 20540. William Matheson, Chief
Notes: The Katherine Golden Bitting Gastronomic Library. The collection comprises materials on the sources, preparation and consumption of foods from the earliest times to the present day, embracing the whole range of human interest in food. Incl an important 15th century Italian ms, a large number of early French, Italian, English and German works (incl incunabula) and a range of early American cookbooks and works on domestic science. Regional cookbooks and works on the chemistry, bacteriology and preservation of food are strongly represented among titles of more recent date. The majority of the volumes in the collection are described in Mrs Bitting's *Gastronomic Bibliography* (San Francisco, 1939). Also, personal library of Elizabeth Robins Pennell, magazine journalist and wife of artist Joseph Pennell, incl about 430 cookbooks in English, French and German16th to 18th century, described in Mrs. Pennell's *My Cookery Books* (Boston, Houghton-Mifflin, 1903).

BITTLE, CAMILLA

MA —BOSTON UNIVERSITY, Mugar Memorial Library, Special Collections Dept, 771 Commonwealth Ave, Boston, 02215. Howard B Gotlieb, Dir
Holdings: Cat Mss Pix
Notes: Mss, correspondence, etc collected in depth; incl publications by or about.

BITUMINOUS COAL see Coal

BIXBY, WILLIAM K., 1857-1931

MO —WASHINGTON UNIVERSITY, Libraries, Special Collections Dept, Campus Box 1061, St Louis, 63130.
Notes: Papers of the prominent American industrialist and collector's papers, nearly 2000 items. Incl Bixby's personal papers, materials relating to the St Louis Burns Club, and a large group of Eugene Field's materials; also, autographs, mss, and correspondence of literary and historical figures.

BLACK, CHARLES

OK —MUSEUM OF THE GREAT PLAINS, Research Center, 601 Ferris, PO Box 68, Lawton, 73502. Steve Wilson, Dir; Paula Williams, Special Collections
Notes: Papers of Charles Black about law and politics in early Lawton.
See also entry under Oklahoma - History

BLACK, ELINOR, M.D.

MB —UNIVERSITY OF MANITOBA, Elizabeth Dafoe Library, Archives and Special Collections Dept, Winnipeg, R3T 2N2, Can. Richard E Bennett, Dept Head; Corrado A Santoro, Reference Archivist
Notes: Misc collection of speeches, journal articles, administrative bulletins, covering 1941-71. Former head, Dept Obstetrics & Gynaecology, University of Manitoba. 6 folders.

BLACK, GEORGE

MB —UNIVERSITY OF MANITOBA, Elizabeth Dafoe Library, Archives and Special Collections Dept, Winnipeg, R3T 2N2, Can. Richard E Bennett, Dept Head; Corrado A Santoro, Reference Archivist
Notes: Handwritten notes of George Black, official representative of the Manitoba government on board the steamer "Assiniboine" despatched by the government to give relief to settlers in distress owing to high water flooding. April 23, 1897.

BLACK, HARVY

VA —VIRGINIA POLYTECHNIC INSTITUTE AND STATE UNIVERSITY LIBRARY, Blacksburg, 24061. Glenn L McMullen, Special Collections Librn
Holdings: Vols (2000) Cat Mss Maps Pix Audiotapes
Notes: Primarily Southwest Virginia materials. Collection incl ca 200 mss, account books and other archival records of nineteenth century area businesses and other mining operations; the extant archival records of several Southwest Virginia railroads, incl the Virginia and Tennessee Railroad and the Norfolk and Western Railroad; and papers of historically prominent Southwest Virginians, incl John Apperson, Dr Harvy Black, James P Charlton, W Graham Claytor, Henley Fugate, Clement D Johnston, Germanicus Kent, William Preston, J Hoge Tyler, and William C Wampler. Several oral history collections incl material on Appalachian customs and folklore, particularly in Patrick County.

BLACK, KNOX CHARLTON

WY —UNIVERSITY OF WYOMING, William Robertson Coe Library, Archives - American Heritage Center, PO Box 3412, Laramie, 82071.
Notes: Papers of Knox Charlton Black, incl those of a 12-year period when he worked on a cable important to television.

BLACK, WILLIAM

NJ —PRINCETON UNIVERSITY, Library, Morris L Parrish Collection, Princeton, 08540. Alexander D Wainwright, Cur
Holdings: Vols 17
Notes: The collection contains over 6500 vols, as well as many theatre programs, playbills, photographs, clippings and other miscellanea. Parrish's goal was to assemble in both the English and the American first editions, in the original condition as issued,

BLACK, WILLIAM (cont.)

everything that a given author published. He was also interested in a high standard of condition for his books. Many additions have been acquired since the Parrish collection came to the Library as a bequest in 1944. The collection is an assemblage of author collections, consisting of books by: William Harrison Ainsworth, James Matthew Barrie, William Black, The Brontes, William Wilkie Collins, Dinah Mulock Craik, Marie de la Ramee ("Ouida"), Benjamin Disraeli, Charles Dickens, Charles Dodgson, George du Maurier, George Eliot (ie Mary Ann Evans), Elizabeth Gaskell, Thomas Hardy, Thomas Hughes,Charles Kingsley, Charles Lever, Edward George Earle Bulwer-Lytton, Mary Maxwell, George Meredith, Charles Reade, Walter Scott, Robert Louis Stevenson, William Makepeace Thackeray, Trollope Family, Ellen Wood, and Charlotte Yonge.

NY —SAINT LAWRENCE UNIVERSITY, Owen D Young Library, Canton, 13617. Mahlon Peterson, Librn
Holdings: Cat Mss Pix
Notes: Collection consists of letters sent to Edith O'Dell Black and Pomeroy Burton of the New York *World* from 1903 to 1944. Also incl are works by Alexander Black, a novelist, and manuscripts which he wrote for "picture plays," the forerunners of the modern moving pictures. Approx 350 items.

BLACK ACTORS AND ACTRESSES

CA —UNIVERSITY OF CALIFORNIA, LOS ANGELES, Research Library, Dept of Special Collections, 405 Hilgard Ave, Los Angeles, 90024. Edward Shreeves, Chairman, Bibliographers Group; David S Zeidberg, Head
Notes: The George P Johnson Negro Film Collection reflects the early involvement of Blacks in the moving picture industry and lists some 1400 Black actors and actresses.

†MD —MARYLAND HISTORICAL SOCIETY, Library, 201 W Monument St, Baltimore, 21201.
Notes: Eubie Blake's personal and professional archive. Incl the Baltimore-born pianist, composer, and songwriter's collection of songs and instrumental pieces in mss, extensive documentation of his collaboration with Noble Sissle, Flournog Miller, Milton Reddie, and others. The Broadway musical comedy, Shuffle Along, is represented in box office records, programs, scores and parts, photographs, and sheet music. Blake's involvement with other productions is similarly documented.

NY —SYRACUSE UNIVERSITY LIBRARIES, Ernest S Bird Library, George Arents Research Library for Special Collections, Syracuse, 13210. Carolyn A Davis, Manuscripts Librn; Amy S Doherty, University Archivist; Mark F Weimer, Rare Book Librn

BLACK ART see Art, African and Afro-American

BLACK AUTHORS see Authors, Black

BLACK CULTURE

DC —HOWARD UNIVERSITY, Moorland-Spingarn Research Center, 500 Howard Place NW, Washington, 20059. Clifford L Muse, Jr, Acting Dir

MO —LINCOLN UNIVERSITY, Page Library, Chestnut St, Jefferson City, 65101.
Holdings: Vols (2000) Cat Phonorecords Filmstrips
Notes: Most books are early Negro writings on slavery and the Black experience. Ethnic Studies Center housed in the Library. It has special collections of books, films, filmstrips and local oral history tapes relating to ethnicity and ethnic studies. A part-time administrator is to be in charge.

NJ —PRINCETON UNIVERSITY, Firestone Library, Afro-American Studies Collection, Princeton, 08540. William Wellburn, Cur
Holdings: Vols (2000) Cat Pix Phonorecords Audiotapes Microforms
Notes: Our emphasis is primarily Afro-American: catalogs of other collections, biographical and vertical files, reference materials, indexes, bibliographies and serials.

NY —NEW YORK PUBLIC LIBRARY, Schomburg Center for Research in Black Culture, 515 Lenox Ave, New York, 10037. Catherine J Lenix Hooker, Interim Administrator
Holdings: Vols (85,000) Cat Mss Maps Pix Slides Phonorecords Audiotapes Videotapes 16mm Films Filmstrips Microforms
See also entry under Black Studies

PA —SCHOOL DISTRICT OF PHILADELPHIA, Pedagogical Library, 21 St & Pkwy, Philadelphia, 19103. Helen E Howe, Librn; Patricia K Buck, Asst Librn
Holdings: Vols (47,000) Cat Pix Microforms
Budget: ($25,000)
Notes: Collection emphasis on public school education K-12 with the main areas including Afro-American history and culture, elementary and early childhood education, secondary education, educational administration, educational research, reading, school law, educational psychology. Special Collections: ERIC (140,000 documents), Archives of the School District of Philadelphia. Approx 500 periodical subscriptions.

RI —BROWN UNIVERSITY, John Hay Library, Harris Collection, Prospect St, Providence, 02912. Rosemary L Cullen, Cur
Holdings: Vols (200,000) Cat Mss Pix Phonorecords Microforms
Budget: ($15,000)
Notes: The Harris Collection of American Poetry and Plays is principally composed of American and Canadian poetry and plays, 17th century-date. Extensive holdings in songsters, gift books and annuals, hymnals, pageants, broadside verse, carriers' addresses, women poets, juvenile poetry, (incl Mother Goose and *The Night Before* Christmas), sheet music with lyrics, small press publications, fine printing, black poets, "little magazines," Yiddish-American literature. All movements or schools of American poetry are represented. Incl first editions of most American poets and playwrights, notably Whitman, Poe, Wallace Stevens, Eugene O'Neill, Edward Albee, Ezra Pound, T S Eliot, William Carlos Williams, Amy Lowell, Phyllis Wheatley, Robert Frost, Allen Ginsberg, Bliss Carman, and Stephen Foster sheet music. Also incl the Saunders Walt Whitman Collection (1300 vols); the LangdonCollection of Pageants (250 vols); the Asa Cushman Collection of plays in ms and prompt copies; the MacDougall Collection of Psalters and Hymnals; 4000 plays issued by Walter H Baker Co, Boston (1890-1957); the Vaxer Collection of Yiddish Poetry, Plays and Music (1700 vols). Collections incl 200,000 vols, 30,000 broadsides, 55,000 mss, 170,000 pieces of sheet music, 450 phonorecords, and 375 microfilm reels. See *Dictionary Catalog of the Harris Collection of American Poetry and Plays* (Boston: G K Hall, 1972), 13 vols; *Supplement* (1977), 3 vols. See also, *American Poetry,* 1609-1900, *A Collection on Microfilm, Segment I* (1609-1820); *Segment II* (1821-1850); *Segment III* (1851-1870) (Woodbridge, Conn: Research Publications). Separate catalog.

TX —UNIVERSITY OF TEXAS LIBRARIES, General Libraries, PO Box P, Austin, 78713. Carolyn Bucknell, Asst Dir for Collection Development
Holdings: Cat Microforms

BLACK DEATH

MD —MEDICAL & CHIRURGICAL FACULTY OF THE STATE OF MARYLAND, Library, 1211 Cathedral St, Baltimore, 21201. Joseph E Jensen, Librn
Holdings: Vols (10,000) // Cat Mss Maps Pix
See also entry under Medicine - History and Historic

TX —UNIVERSITY OF TEXAS, DALLAS, Health Science Center, Reference Dept & History of Health Sciences Dept, 5323 Harry Hines Blvd, Dallas, 75235. Helen Mayo, Head
Holdings: Vols (10,000) Cat Pix Slides Audiotapes Videotapes Microforms
Notes: History of Medicine collection contains ca 10,000 vols. This total is comprised of pre-1900 journals, primary materials in the History of Medicine and the History of Science, and secondary studies in these two areas. The major strengths of this collection are in the areas of epidemics and plagues, military medicine, and collected works of famous medical pioneers. Incl in this collection are the medical journals published by the county medical societies in Texas, local publications by Dallas County medical organizations, and ephemeral material in a similar vein. The university archives contain all theses and dissertations form UTHSCD and miscellaneous institutional documents circulated by the school's administration.

BLACK FOLKLORE see Folklore, Black

BLACK FRIARS see Dominicans

BLACK HAWK WAR, 1832

IL —AUGUSTANA COLLEGE, Library, Rock Island, 61201. Marjorie M Miller, Special Collections Librn
Holdings: Vols 2000 Cat Mss
Notes: The John Hauberg Upper Mississippi Valley Collection. Incl strong collection of immigrant guide books for the Midwestern states. Fine collection relative to the Sauk and Fox tribes and Black Hawk in particular.

WI —HOARD HISTORICAL MUSEUM, Fort Atkinson Historical Society, 407 Merchant Ave, Fort Atkinson, 53538. Hannah Werwath Swart, Cur
Holdings: Vols (4663) Cat Mss Maps Pix Slides
Notes: Entirely devoted to books, mss, etc, concerning the local history of Fort Atkinson and Jefferson County, with particular emphasis on the Black Hawk War.

BLACK HILLS REGION

†SD —SOUTH DAKOTA SCHOOL OF MINES & TECHNOLOGY, Devereaux Library, Rapid City, 57701.
Holdings: Vols (3786) Cat Mss Maps Pix Audiotapes Microforms
Notes: This special collection, in general, relates to the Black Hills area of South Dakota and Wyoming, especially mining and exploration of the area; the West River area of South Dakota, primarily county histories; and South Dakota Territorial and State materials. There are also specialized areas of this collection: (1) *Marion N Bruce* Collection. Documents, correspondence, books and periodicals dealing with weather modification in South Dakota; (2) *Mildred Fielder Collection.* Mss, pictures, books and periodicals from an author whose special area was the Black Hills. Most of her work on railroads, mines, trails, etc, relates to historical aspects. Collection incl research materials, galley proofs and final copies of her various publications; (3) *Cleophas C O'Harra Collection.* Mss, pictures, books and original source materials, primarily related to the Black Hills area andexpeditions thereto. Much of the data was collected for a book on the Black Hills which was never published; and (4) *Caving* Collection. Maps of various caves in Black Hills area, being kept current and updated by members of the Paha Sapa Grotto. Also, some books and periodicals on caving in general.

SD —AUGUSTANA COLLEGE, Mikkelsen Library & Learning Resource Center, Center for Western Studies, Sioux Falls, 57197. Ronelle Thompson, Dir Library
Notes: The Center for Western Studies, located in the Mikkelsen Library, is an archival and research agency of Augustana College. Dedicated to the history and culture of the Great Plains and the Trans-Mississippi West, the Center collects and preserves materials relating to Plains Indians,

BLACK HILLS REGION (cont.)

immigrant settlers, Norwegiana, Western Americana, Herbert Krause, Frederick Manfred, Donald Parker, Richard F Pettigrew, Augustana College, the Episcopal Diocese of South Dakota, the South Dakota District of the American Lutheran Church, the South Dakota Penitentiary and Minnehaha County.

BLACK HISTORY see Blacks—History

BLACK HOLES (ASTRONOMY)

NY —UNIVERSITY OF ROCHESTER, Physics-Optics-Astronomy Library, Bausch & Lomb Bldg, River Campus, Rochester, 14627. Loretta Caren, Librn
Holdings: Vols (20,000) Cat
Notes: Strong research level collection in the field and related areas.

BLACK ILLUSTRATORS see Illustrators, Black

BLACK LEAD see Graphite

BLACK LITERATURE

CT —YALE UNIVERSITY, Box 1603A, Yale Station, New Haven, 06520.
Holdings: Cat Mss Pix Microforms

DC —HOWARD UNIVERSITY, Moorland-Spingarn Research Center, 500 Howard Place NW, Washington, 20059. Clifford L Muse, Jr, Acting Dir
Holdings: Vols (106,086) Cat Mss Maps Pix Slides Phonorecords Audiotapes 16mm Films Filmstrips Microforms
Budget: ($854,753)
Notes: *The Glenn Carrington Collection: A Guide to the Books, Manuscripts, Music and Recordings* (DC MSRC, 1977). *Dictionary Catalog of the Jesse E Moorland Collection of Negro Life and History,* 9 vols and Supplement, 3 vols (Boston: G K Hall, 1970, 1977). *Dictionary Catalog of the Arthur Spingarn Collection of Negro Authors,* 2 vols (Boston: G K Hall, 1970). Guide to Processed Collections in the Manuscript Division of the Moorland-Spingarn Research Center (DC, MSRC, 1983). The Moorland-Spingran Research Center is recognized as one of the largest and most comprehensive repositories in the world for the collection, preservation and dissemination of historical materials documenting from antiquity to the present the history and culture of Black people in Africa, Europe, the Caribbean and the US. Since 1973, the Research Center has greatly expanded its facilitiesand resources and currently provides research services in all aspects of library and archival research, including manuscripts, oral history, music, prints and photographs and general library materials. The Research Center also maintains professional zerographic, micrographic, photographic and similar reproduction laboratories.

IL —CHICAGO PUBLIC LIBRARY, G Woodson Regional Library, George C Hall Branch, 9525 S Halsted, Chicago, 60628. Steven C Newsome, Cur; Hattie L Power, Regional Library Dir
Holdings: Vols 8000 Cat Mss Audiotapes Microforms
Notes: The Vivian G Harsh Collection on Afro-American History and Literature, in the George Cleveland Hall Branch of the Chicago Public Library, contains books, in print and on microfilm, periodicals, recordings, tapes, pamphlets and mss. Specializes in Afro-Americana, but contains a sizeable number of books on Africa. Also contains these noteworthy items: *The Negro in Illinois: the Illinois Writers Project Files; The Chicago Afro-American Union Analytic Catalog; Big Boy Leaves Home,* by Richard Wright (an original typewritten ms); *The Big Sea,* by Langston Hughes (3 original typewritten mss of this work). 7800 vols on microfilm.

MD —PRINCE GEORGE'S COUNTY MEMORIAL LIBRARY SYSTEM, Oxon Hill Branch Library, Sojourner Truth Collection, 6200 Oxon Hill Rd, Oxon Hill, 20745. Cherie Phillips Barnett, Librn
Holdings: Vols (3000) Cat Mss Pix Films Phonorecords Microforms VF
Budget: ($3500)
Notes: The Sojourner Truth Collection on Blacks in America is a representative collection of materials by and about Black Americans, their historical problems and accomplishments. The collection, containing certain unique and rare items, emphasizes the Black woman, the Black family, slavery and anti-slavery, Black literature, Blacks in the military and slave narratives. Also incl current US government publications concerning the Black American. A supportive collection of films, recordings, paperbacks, and periodicals is available. Programs, displays, and bibliographies are prepared in order to develop interest in the collection.

NJ —PRINCETON UNIVERSITY, Firestone Library, Afro-American Studies Collection, Princeton, 08540. William Wellburn, Cur
Holdings: Vols (2000) Cat Pix Phonorecords Audiotapes Microforms
Notes: Our emphasis is primarily Afro-American: catalogs of other collections, biographical and vertical files, reference materials, indexes, bibliographies and serials.

NJ —PRINCETON UNIVERSITY, Library, Manuscript Collection, Nassau St, Princeton, 08540. Jean F Preston, Cur
Notes: Special collection on American Negro History and Culture.

NY —NEW YORK PUBLIC LIBRARY, Schomburg Center for Research in Black Culture, 515 Lenox Ave, New York, 10037. Catherine J Lenix Hooker, Interim Administrator
Holdings: Vols (85,000) Cat Mss Maps Pix Slides Phonorecords Audiotapes Videotapes 16mm Films Filmstrips Microforms
See also entry under Black Studies

NY —NEW YORK PUBLIC LIBRARY, Mid-Manhattan Library, Literature and Language Dept, 455 Fifth Ave, New York, 10016. Eric Steele, Sr Principal Librn
Holdings: Vols (160,000) Cat Phonorecords Microforms Audiotapes
Budget: ($92,000)
Notes: Extensive collection of works, criticism and biographies of major and minor American writers for undergraduate study; special attention directed towards Black American literature. Collection includes material on the teaching of literature, the techniques of creative writing, and the history of the theater when relevant to the study of dramatic literature. Substantial or complete runs of the major journals. Representative collection of literary magazines. Recordings of prose, poetry and drama.

OH —AKRON-SUMMIT COUNTY PUBLIC LIBRARY, 55 S Main St, Akron, 44326. Steven Hawk, Dir
Holdings: Vols (1200)
Notes: Known as the Schomburg Collection: consists of microfilms of 11 magazines related to black history, 1824-1963 (73 reels).

PA —TEMPLE UNIVERSITY LIBRARIES, Special Collections Dept, Rare Books & Mss Section, Philadelphia, 19122. Thomas M Whitehead, Cur
Holdings: Vols (10,000) Mss Pix
Notes: "The Charles Blockson Afro-American Historical Collection". Curated by Charles Blockson. The Private Library of Charles Blockson established as a collection at Temple University. Approximately 25,000 items of Afro-American literature, history of slavery and African and Caribbean history and culture. Selective catalog (exhibition) available.

PA —CARLOW COLLEGE, Grace Library, Fifth Ave, Pittsburgh, 15213. Joan M Mitchell, Dir of Library Services
Holdings: Vols (1786) Cat
Budget: ($500)
Notes: The Black Studies Collection consists of books which describe the Black experience in Africa and the United States, with special emphasis on slavery and contemporary Black literature and sociology.

RI —BROWN UNIVERSITY, John Hay Library, Harris Collection, Prospect St, Providence, 02912. Rosemary L Cullen, Cur
Holdings: Vols (200,000) Cat Mss Pix Phonorecords Microforms
Budget: ($15,000)
Notes: The Harris Collection of American Poetry and Plays is principally composed of American and Canadian poetry and plays, 17th century-date. Extensive holdings in songsters, gift books and annuals, hymnals, pageants, broadside verse, carriers' addresses, women poets, juvenile poetry, (incl Mother Goose and *The Night Before* Christmas), sheet music with lyrics, small press publications, fine printing, black poets, "little magazines," Yiddish-American literature. All movements or schools of American poetry are represented. Incl first editions of most American poets and playwrights, notably Whitman, Poe, Wallace Stevens, Eugene O'Neill, Edward Albee, Ezra Pound, T S Eliot, William Carlos Williams, Amy Lowell, Phyllis Wheatley, Robert Frost, Allen Ginsberg, Bliss Carman, and Stephen Foster sheet music. Also incl the Saunders Walt Whitman Collection (1300 vols); the LangdonCollection of Pageants (250 vols); the Asa Cushman Collection of plays in ms and prompt copies; the MacDougall Collection of Psalters and Hymnals; 4000 plays issued by Walter H Baker Co, Boston (1890-1957); the Vaxer Collection of Yiddish Poetry, Plays and Music (1700 vols). Collections incl 200,000 vols, 30,000 broadsides, 55,000 mss, 170,000 pieces of sheet music, 450 phonorecords, and 375 microfilm reels. See *Dictionary Catalog of the Harris Collection of American Poetry and Plays* (Boston: G K Hall, 1972), 13 vols; *Supplement* (1977), 3 vols. See also, *American Poetry,* 1609-1900, *A Collection on Microfilm, Segment I* (1609-1820); *Segment II* (1821-1850); *Segment III* (1851-1870) (Woodbridge, Conn: Research Publications). Separate catalog.

TX —UNIVERSITY OF TEXAS LIBRARIES, General Libraries, PO Box P, Austin, 78713. Carolyn Bucknell, Asst Dir for Collection Development
Holdings: Cat Microforms

BLACK MAGIC

CA —LOS ANGELES PUBLIC LIBRARY, Philosophy & Religion Dept, 630 W Fifth St, Los Angeles, 90071. Marilyn C Wherley, Librn
Holdings: Vols 250 Cat
Budget: ($60,000)
Notes: Scholarly and popular materials as part of the occult sciences collection.

RI —BROWN UNIVERSITY, John Hay Library, 20 Prospect St, Providence, 02912. Mark N Brown, Cur Mss
Holdings: Vols (900) // Mss
Notes: John William Graham Collection of Literature of Psychic Science; 350 predominantly late 19th and early 20th century books dealing with alchemy, black magic, dreams, demonology, church history, mysticism, mediumship, physical and somatic types of psychic experience. Collection described in *Index to Psychic* Science compiled by S R Morgan (Swarthmore, 1950). Also, the Damon Collection of Occult and Visionary Literature; 550 vols devoted to the development of western mysticism with particular emphasis on American and British thought, incl texts on alchemy, black magic, esoteric church history, dream interpretations, mysticism, witchcraft, the Kabbalah, and visionary testaments and manifestations of all types printed during the 16th to 20th centuries; and the Samuel Wyllys Papers; 125 mss, transcripts, and photocopies of legal and government papers relating to Indianaffairs, colonial wars, civil and criminal cases, and the witchcraft trials of 1692-1693. Partially cataloged.

BLACK MASS see Satanism

BLACK MOUNTAIN COLLEGE

NC —NORTH CAROLINA DIV OF ARCHIVES & HISTORY, 109 E Jones St,

BLACK MOUNTAIN COLLEGE (cont.)

Raleigh, 27611.
Notes: Archive of administrative, student, and all other records of Black Mountain College, which was located at Black Mountain, North Carolina, 1933-1956.

BLACK MOUNTAIN POETS

†CT —UNIVERSITY OF CONNECTICUT, Library, Storrs, 06268.

BC —SIMON FRASER UNIVERSITY, Library, Burnaby, V5A 1S6, Can. Percilla Groves, Special Collections Librn
Holdings: Vols (12,000) Cat Mss
Notes: This collection concentrates on avant-garde American poetry since World War II. Incl some Canadian poetry (particularly West Coast poets), some British and certain of the International Concrete school. It particularly features the Black Mountain and San Francisco schools and those American and Canadian poets influenced by them. There is a relatively complete collection of works. There is a relatively complete collection of books by Ezra Pound (qv) and William Carlos Williams together with considerable criticism on both. Also incl certain underground newspapers and 1600 little magazines.

BLACK MOUNTAIN REVIEW

MO —WASHINGTON UNIVERSITY, Libraries, Special Collections Dept, Campus Box 1061, St Louis, 63130.
Notes: A small but significant collection.

BLACK MUSIC see Blacks—Songs; Music—Blacks; Music, Afro-American

BLACK MUSLIMS

DC —HOWARD UNIVERSITY, Moorland-Spingarn Research Center, 500 Howard Place NW, Washington, 20059. Clifford L Muse, Jr, Acting Dir
Holdings: Vols (106,086) Mss Maps Pix Slides Phonorecords Audiotapes 16mm Films Filmstrips Microforms
Budget: ($854,753)
See also entry under Blacks

BLACK NATIONALISM

DC —HOWARD UNIVERSITY, Moorland-Spingarn Research Center, 500 Howard Place NW, Washington, 20059. Clifford L Muse, Jr, Acting Dir
Holdings: Vols (106,086) Mss Maps Pix Slides Phonorecords Audiotapes 16mm Films Filmstrips Microforms
Budget: ($854,753)
See also entry under Blacks

MI —UNIVERSITY OF MICHIGAN, Dept of Rare Books & Special Collections, Ann Arbor, 48109. Edward C Weber, Head, Labadie Collection
Holdings: Vols (40,000) Cat
Notes: Strongest in domestic movements from the 1960s on. Incl records, tapes.

BLACK NEWSPAPERS see Newspapers, Black

BLACK PERIODICALS see Periodicals, Black

BLACK POETS see Poets, Black

BLACK PSYCHOLOGY see Psychology, Black

BLACK PUBLICATIONS

DC —HOWARD UNIVERSITY, Moorland-Spingarn Research Center, 500 Howard Place NW, Washington, 20059. Clifford L Muse, Jr, Acting Dir

DC —LIBRARY OF CONGRESS, General Reading Rooms Division, Microform Reading Room, Washington, 20540.
Holdings: Cat Mss Maps Pix Microforms
Notes: Microform materials only in this LC Division. Works of individual authors; holdings of collections; archival records, etc, press releases and translations, etc.

IL —JOHNSON PUBLISHING CO, Library, 820 S Michigan Ave, Chicago, 60605. Pamela J Cash, Librn
Holdings: Vols 8000 Cat Maps Microforms
Notes: Incl all publications of Johnson Publishing Company and many more Black publications.

MA —AMERICAN ANTIQUARIAN SOCIETY LIBRARY, 185 Salisbury St, Worcester, 01609. Marcus A McCorison, Dir & Librn
Holdings: Cat Mss Pix
Notes: Rich in early writings of Black authors and in poetry, fiction, drama, and essays inspired by them, plus numerous newspaper and magazine files of Black publications. Many rare 18th century tracts on slavery; fine collections which illuminate the Black-White relationship, as well as documents dealing with the Black heritage (soldiers, religion, folklore, music).

MO —LINCOLN UNIVERSITY, Page Library, Chestnut St, Jefferson City, 65101.
Holdings: Vols (2000) Cat Phonorecords Filmstrips
Notes: Most books are early Negro writings on slavery and the Black experience. Ethnic Studies Center housed in the Library. It has special collections of books, films, filmstrips and local oral history tapes relating to ethnicity and ethnic studies. A part-time administrator is to be in charge.

BLACK SONGS see Blacks—Songs

BLACK STUDIES

AR —UNIVERSITY OF ARKANSAS, John Brown Watson Memorial Library, Pine Bluff, 71601. Vitory Davis, Librn
Holdings: Vols 3044 Cat Pix Microforms
Notes: Collection is comprised mainly of books and materials of a sociological nature, with history and literature being the next two areas respectively containing the most materials. The entire collection deals mainly with materials by and about Black Americans.

CA —LOS ANGELES PUBLIC LIBRARY, Social Sciences Dept, 630 W Fifth St, Los Angeles, 90071. Marilyn C Wherley, Principal Librn
Holdings: Vols 5000 Cat Microforms
Budget: ($150,000)
Notes: Black Studies Collection. Pamphlets, bibliographies, indexes, periodicals, with some historical runs on microfilm, strong collection on slavery and anti-slavery, abolition, civil rights movements, with emphasis on the black experience in the United States. No separate catalog.

CA —COLLEGE OF SAN MATEO, Library, 1700 W Hillsdale Blvd, San Mateo, 94402. Gregg T Atkins, Coordinator of Library Services
Holdings: Vols 500 Cat

DC —HOWARD UNIVERSITY, Moorland-Spingarn Research Center, 500 Howard Place NW, Washington, 20059. Clifford L Muse, Jr, Acting Dir

DC —UNIVERSITY OF THE DISTRICT OF COLUMBIA, Mount Vernon Campus, Library & Media Services Div, 800 Mount Vernon Pl, NW, Washington, 20001. Lottie Wright, Librn
Holdings: Vols (1352) Uncat Pix Phonorecords Audiotapes Videotapes 16mm Films Microforms
Notes: The collection consists of limited print and nonprint materials related to the rise and development of Black culture in America. Collecting emphasis is being placed on first editions, works of major Black authors and significant minor ones, rare books, mss, and memorabilia. In keeping with the policy of acquiring books by and about Afro-Americans, the collection also contains 462 dissertations by Black PhD candidates at universities throughout the US.

GA —UNIVERSITY OF GEORGIA, Libraries, Special Collections Division, Athens, 30602. Vesta Lee Gordon, Asst Dir for Special Collections
Notes: The Arbitron Collection of television and radio program ratings, 1949-date (except past year). In-depth, statistical analyses of the listening public by age, sex, county, some ethnic groups, farm population, listening preferences, etc. 26,302 bound vols. 2 reports, 1949-81. To be added to annually.

GA —MARTIN LUTHER KING, JR, CENTER FOR NONVIOLENT SOCIAL CHANGE, INC, King Library and Archives, 449 Auburn Ave, Atlanta, 30312. D Louise Cook, Dir of Library and Archives
Holdings: Vols 4000 Cat Mss Audiotapes Microforms
Notes: The philosophy of Martin Luther King and the movement he led. Emphasis on obscure information and ephemeral pieces. Oral history project has over 500 tapes. Incl collection of mss of various civil rights organizations of the 1950s and 1960s. All materials are noncirculating.

IL —CHICAGO PUBLIC LIBRARY, G Woodson Regional Library, George C Hall Branch, 9525 S Halsted, Chicago, 60628. Steven C Newsome, Cur; Hattie L Power, Regional Library Dir
Holdings: Vols 8000 Cat Mss Audiotapes Microforms
Notes: The Vivian G Harsh Collection on Afro-American History and Literature, in the George Cleveland Hall Branch of the Chicago Public Library, contains books, in print and on microfilm, periodicals, recordings, tapes, pamphlets and mss. Specializes in Afro-Americana, but contains a sizeable number of books on Africa. Also contains these noteworthy items: *The Negro in Illinois: the Illinois Writers Project Files; The Chicago Afro-American Union Analytic Catalog; Big Boy Leaves Home*, by Richard Wright (an original typewritten ms); *The Big Sea*, by Langston Hughes (3 original typewritten mss of this work). 7800 vols on microfilm.

MA —HARVARD UNIVERSITY LIBRARY, Widener Library, Cambridge, 02138.
Holdings: Mss Microforms
Notes: A *Guide* was published by the library in 1976. Resources incl numerous mss, notably those of Higginson, Sumner, Villard, and Booker T Washington.

MA —SIMON'S ROCK OF BARD COLLEGE, Library, Alford Rd, Great Barrington, 01230. Ruth D Jones, Cataloger
Holdings: Vols 2400 Cat
Notes: The DuBois Collection, in honor of W E B DuBois, a native of Great Barrington, incl books describing or highly influenced by the Black experience. Emphasis is on US materials, but books about countries with predominantly Black populations are included. Access through main catalog or DuBois Collection shelflist.

MI —WASHTENAW COMMUNITY COLLEGE, Learning Resource Center, P.O. Box D-1, Ann Arbor, 48106. Adella Scott, Dir

MO —KANSAS CITY PUBLIC LIBRARY, 311 E 12, Kansas City, 64106. Daniel J Bradbury, Dir
Holdings: Vols 3500 Cat Mss Maps Pix Microforms
Notes: The John Ramos Collection.

NJ —PRINCETON UNIVERSITY, Library, Manuscript Collection, Nassau St, Princeton, 08540. Jean F Preston, Cur
Notes: Special collection on American Negro History and Culture.

NY —NEW YORK CITY TECHNICAL COLLEGE, Library, 300 Jay St, Brooklyn, 11201. Catherine T Brody, Chief Librn
Holdings: Vols 2700 Cat Maps Pix Films Phonorecords Audiotapes Microforms
Notes: Three bibliographies of the collection *available--Black Perspectives.* (Community College Press of the Faculty-Student Association for NYCCC, Inc, 1971). *A Guide to the Afro-American Resources at the Library of the New York City Community College* introduces students to the collection and annotates important reference materials. Afro-American Studies--A Guide to Resources in the Namm Library.

NY —NEW YORK PUBLIC LIBRARY, Schomburg Center for Research in Black Culture, 515 Lenox Ave, New York, 10037.

BLACK STUDIES (cont.)

Catherine J Lenix Hooker, Interim Administrator
Holdings: Vols (85,000) Cat Mss Maps Pix Slides Phonorecords Audiotapes Videotapes 16mm Films Filmstrips Microforms
Notes: Materials in all formats about Black peoples throughout the world. Extensive archival holdings, vertical files, Afro-American and African art. Collections incl 182 groups of mss, 100,000 photographs, 6500 slides, 5600 phonorecords, 2300 audiotapes, and over 30,000 microforms. Described in *The Dictionary Catalog of the Schomburg Collection*, 9 vols, and supplements to 1974, 7 vols (Boston: G K Hall, 1962-1975); and *Bibliographic Guide to Black Studies* (Boston: G K Hall). Since 1972, the Center's holdings have been incl in the *Dictionary Catalog of the Research Libraries, New York Public Library*.

PA —LIBRARY COMPANY OF PHILADELPHIA, 1314 Locust St, Philadelphia, 19107. Edwin Wolf II, Librn; Kenneth Finkel, Cur of Prints
Holdings: Vols (400,000) Cat Mss Maps Pix
Budget: ($25,000)
Notes: With the collection of The Historical Society of Pennsylvania, one of the richest collections of mss, books and other materials on the slave trade, the abolition movement and other chapters of Blacks in the New World. Incl printed material on the history of Blacks in the US, the West Indies, and Africa, to 1906.

PA —CARLOW COLLEGE, Grace Library, Fifth Ave, Pittsburgh, 15213. Joan M Mitchell, Dir of Library Services
Holdings: Vols (1786) Cat
Budget: ($500)
Notes: The Black Studies Collection consists of books which describe the Black experience in Africa and the United States, with special emphasis on slavery and contemporary Black literature and sociology.

PA —UNIVERSITY OF PITTSBURGH, Hillman Library, Pittsburgh, 15260.
Holdings: Vols (5279) Cat Microforms
Notes: Special emphasis of the Afro-American Collection is on the blacks in the United States; incl materials on Africa south of the Sahara and Caribbean area of the world.

RI —PROVIDENCE PUBLIC LIBRARY, 150 Empire St, Providence, 02903. Lance J Bauer, Special Collections Librn
Notes: The Edna Frazier Memorial Collection (South Providence Branch) is the largest public library collection in Rhode Island dedicated to Black Studies. Since 1969, the Collection has served the people of this area. Adults and children concerned with the heritage of Black people in America, their roles, culture, and accomplishments, have found a wealth of information here. From its initial 900 volumes, the Collection has grown to several thousand volumes incl noted works by Black authors, reference materials, sociological studies, poetry, music, sports, biographies, and titles no longer in print. The time span covered by the Collection is 1619 to the present. It contains materials on the Black Renaissance and the early Civil Rights movements of the '30s, '40s and '50s, in addition to the more well-known movements of the '60s and '70s. A unique feature of thiscollection is the large number of children's books it contains; these reflect the same concerns and interests as the larger adult collection. Another unique feature of this collection is that it does circulate. It is available to any resident of the state as a result of the Providence Public Library's role as Rhode Island's Principal Public Library.

SC —WOFFORD COLLEGE, Sandor Teszler Library, N Church St, Spartanburg, 29301. Frank J Anderson, Librn
Holdings: Vols 1000 Cat
Notes: Books ranging through the Dewey classes relating to the black experience in America. 19th and 20th century imprints, incl recently reprinted 19th century works.

TX —FORT WORTH PUBLIC LIBRARY, Southeast Branch, 4300 E Berry, Fort Worth, 76105. Michael Roseborough, Special Collections Librn
Holdings: Vols 2500 Cat Mss Pix Phonorecords Audiotapes Filmstrips
Budget: ($6000)
Notes: Studies Collection incl most titles by and about Blacks published since 1972, plus many older titles on Afro-American history. Library also maintains up-to-date index to more than 20 Black periodicals.

VA —VIRGINIA UNION UNIVERSITY, William J Clark Library, 1500 N Lombardy St, Richmond, 23220. Verdelle V Bradley, Librn
Holdings: Vols 9905 Cat Pix Slides Phonorecords Audiotapes Filmstrips Microforms
Notes: Incl 1369 microforms. Special collection on slavery is not cataloged; oral history tapes of Black Virginians, especially in religious contexts.

BLACKBURN, JOHN

MA —BOSTON UNIVERSITY, Mugar Memorial Library, Special Collections Dept, 771 Commonwealth Ave, Boston, 02215. Howard B Gotlieb, Dir
Holdings: Cat Mss
Notes: Mss, correspondence, etc collected in depth; incl publications by or about.

BLACKBURN, PAUL, 1926-1971

CA —UNIVERSITY OF CALIFORNIA, SAN DIEGO, Central University Library, Mandeville Dept of Special Collections, La Jolla, 92093. Lynda Corey Claassen, Head; Michael Davidson, Cur, Archive for New Poetry
Holdings: Vols 450 Cat Mss Pix Audiotapes
Notes: An extensive collection of modern English-language poetry published since World War II, the Archive contains over 28, 000 books, over 1000 magazine titles, and some 900 tapes and records. The Archive maintains substantial collections of papers from Paul Blackburn, Charles Reznikoff, Lew Welch, Jerome Rothenberg, Louis Zukofsky, and other major contemporary American poets.

MO —WASHINGTON UNIVERSITY, Libraries, Special Collections Dept, Campus Box 1061, St Louis, 63130.
Notes: A small but significant collection.

NY —STATE UNIVERSITY OF NEW YORK, STONY BROOK, Melville Library, Dept of Special Collections, Stony Brook, 11794. Evert Volkersz, Head
Holdings: Cat Mss

BLACKBURN, WILLIAM

NC —DUKE UNIVERSITY, William R Perkins Library, Manuscript Dept, Durham, 27706. Ellen Gartrell, Cur of Mss
Holdings: Cat Mss
Notes: Papers, correspondence, etc.

BLACKFOOT INDIANS

CT —YALE UNIVERSITY, Box 1603A, Yale Station, New Haven, 06520.
Holdings: Cat Mss Pix

MT —MONTANA STATE UNIVERSITY, Library, Bozeman, 59717. Minnie Ellen Paugh, Special Collections Librn
Holdings: Vols (7000) // Mss Maps Pix
Notes: Leggat-Donahoe Collection. Collection of Alexander Leggat of Butte, whose father was active in opening the mines. Mr Leggat's interests were mining, exploration, and the fur trade. There are excellent Indian materials in the collection. Also the manuscript and picture collections of James Willard Schultz, Harry James (about James Willard Schultz), and Olga Ross Hannon on Blackfeet Indian tepees. Land claim clase files and manuscripts about Blackfeet, Gros Ventre, Assiniboine and Crow Indians collected by Dr Thomas R Wessell, Edward E Barry and Dr Merrill G Burlingame.

BLACKFOOT INDIANS—PICTURES, ILLUSTRATIONS, ETC.

NM —MUSEUM OF NEW MEXICO, Photo Archives, Box 2087, Santa Fe, 87503. Arthur L Olivas, Cur; Richard Rudisill, Photo Historian
Holdings: Cat Pix Slides
Budget: ($9000)
Notes: 200,000

BLACKMORE, RICHARD DODDRIDGE

VA —UNIVERSITY OF VIRGINIA, Alderman Library, Manuscripts Dept, Charlottesville, 22901. Edmund Berkeley Jr, Cur
Holdings: Vols 23 Cat Mss
Notes: The Atcheson Laughlin Hench Memorial Collection of Richard Doddridge Blackmore manuscripts consists of ca 1035 items, 1812-1973, by, about, and relating to the English poet, novelist, and agricultural experimenter. The collection chiefly contains correspondence but also includes bills; exercises; examination questions and answers from Exeter College, Oxford; proofs for the novels *Cradock Nowell* and *Perlycross*; a patent; and some printed materials. An additional part of the collection consists of miscellanea from the files of Atcheson L Hench, longtime University of Virginia professor of English, who acquired the major portion of this collection and presented it to the Library. The most significant part of the collection is the correspondence which illuminates the most important facets of Blackmore's life: his strong family ties; his fruit growing andgardening; his novels and poetry, and his negotiations with editors, illustrators, and publishers. An unpublished register is available in the repository.

BLACKMUR, RICHARD PALMER, 1904-1965

DE —UNIVERSITY OF DELAWARE, Hugh M Morris Library, S College Ave, Newark, 19711. T Stuart Dick, Special Collections
Holdings: Cat Mss Pix
Notes: Manuscripts, etc, incl literary correspondence.

NJ —PRINCETON UNIVERSITY, Library, Manuscript Collection, Nassau St, Princeton, 08540. Jean F Preston, Cur
Holdings: Vols 300 Cat Mss
Notes: The Richard Blackmur book collection incl association items from the author's library. His personal papers occupy 70 ms boxes.

BLACKS

AL —TUSKEGEE INSTITUTE, Hallis Burke Frissel Library, Tuskegee Institute, 36088. Daniel Williams, Librn
Notes: The Robert Stewart Darnaby Collection on Blacks in American sports. Much on the Southern Intercollegiate Athletic Conference, incl historical materials. Large resources on Tuskegee athletics.

AR —UNIVERSITY OF ARKANSAS, John Brown Watson Memorial Library, Pine Bluff, 71601. Vitory Davis, Librn
Holdings: Vols 3044 Cat Pix Microforms
Notes: Collection is comprised mainly of books and materials of a sociological nature, with history and literature being the next two areas respectively containing the most materials. The entire collection deals mainly with materials by and about Black Americans.

CA —ACADEMY OF MOTION PICTURE ARTS & SCIENCES, Margaret Herrick Library, 8949 Wilshire Blvd, Beverly Hills, 90211. Linda Harris Mehr, Library Administrator
Notes: The Black American Film History Collection, the first permanent collection of material related to Blacks in American motion pictures.

CA —UNIVERSITY OF CALIFORNIA, LOS ANGELES, Research Library, Dept of Special Collections, 405 Hilgard Ave, Los Angeles, 90024. Edward Shreeves, Chairman, Bibliographers Group; David S Zeidberg, Head
Holdings: Cat Mss Pix
Notes: Various collections, incl American

BLACKS (cont.)

Civil Liberties Union; Ralph J Bunche papers; Civil Rights Movements in the US; George P Johnson Negro Film Collection; and Arthur B Springarn collection of Negro Literature.

CA —CALIFORNIA HISTORICAL SOCIETY, Schubert Hall Library, 2099 Pacific Ave, San Francisco, 94109. Bruce L Johnson, Library Dir
Holdings: Vols (50,000) Cat Mss Maps Pix
Notes: Incl (8500) mss collections; strong collections on theatre, trade catalogs, Black history, early California imprints, Gold Rush, sheet music, business history, printing, publishing, and Taylor and Taylor Co (publishers) Archives. Incl 300,000 pix.

CT —YALE UNIVERSITY, Box 1603A, Yale Station, New Haven, 06520.
Holdings: Cat Mss Microforms
Notes: James Weldon Johnson Memorial Collection of Negro Arts and Letters. Large monograph and newspaper holdings in Sterling Library.

DC —DISTRICT OF COLUMBIA PUBLIC LIBRARY, Martin Luther King Memorial Library, Black Studies Div, 901 G St NW, Washington, 20001. Alice Robinson, Chief
Holdings: Vols (12,000) Cat Phonorecords Microforms
Budget: ($14,000)
Notes: The Black Studies Division was established with the opening of the Martin Luther King Memorial Library in 1972. The collection consists of books and other materials in all subject areas by and about Black Americans and other people of African descent throughout the world. The collection provides primary resource information to a broad range of patrons, from the general reader to the scholarly researcher. A separate catalog for the collection is located in the division. All materials are non-circulating.

DC —HOWARD UNIVERSITY, Moorland-Spingarn Research Center, 500 Howard Place NW, Washington, 20059. Clifford L Muse, Jr, Acting Dir
Holdings: Vols (106,086) Cat Mss Maps Pix Slides Phonorecords Audiotapes 16mm Films Filmstrips Microforms
Budget: ($854,753)
Notes: *The Glenn Carrington Collection: A Guide to the Books, Manuscripts, Music and Recordings* (DC MSRC, 1977). *Dictionary Catalog of the Jesse E Moorland Collection of Negro Life and History*, 9 vols and Supplement, 3 vols (Boston: G K Hall, 1970, 1977). *Dictionary Catalog of the Arthur Spingarn Collection of Negro Authors*, 2 vols (Boston: G K Hall, 1970). Guide to Processed Collections in the Manuscript Division of the Moorland-Spingarn Research Center (DC, MSRC, 1983). The Moorland-Spingran Research Center is recognized as one of the largest and most comprehensive repositories in the world for the collection, preservation and dissemination of historical materials documenting from antiquity to the present the history and culture of Black people in Africa, Europe, the Caribbean and the US. Since 1973, the Research Center has greatly expanded its facilitiesand resources and currently provides research services in all aspects of library and archival research, including manuscripts, oral history, music, prints and photographs and general library materials. The Research Center also maintains professional zerographic, micrographic, photographic and similar reproduction laboratories.

DC —LIBRARY OF CONGRESS, Rare Book & Special Collections Div, Washington, 20540. William Matheson, Chief
Notes: Pamphlets by black authors assembled by Library employee, Daniel Murray, on slavery, emancipation and the black experience in the US. LC Information Bulletin, January 8, 1974, 1315.

DC —LIBRARY OF CONGRESS, Manuscript Division, Washington, 20540. John C Broderick, Chief
Notes: The papers of Booker T Washington; Roy Wilkins; NAACP; National Urban League.

GA —ATLANTA UNIVERSITY CENTER, Woodruff Library, 111 Chestnut St SW, Atlanta, 30314. Minnie H Clayton, Division Director
Holdings: Vols (25,000) Cat Mss Photographs VF Microforms
Notes: Incl 25,000 books and rare books, mss, 7,500 linear feet of institutional/organizational records, individual papers, photographs, verticle file of ephemera, microforms, artifacts and memorabilia. Card catalog; preliminary inventories, guide to archival holdings.

IL —CHICAGO PUBLIC LIBRARY, G Woodson Regional Library, George C Hall Branch, 9525 S Halsted, Chicago, 60628. Steven C Newsome, Cur; Hattie L Power, Regional Library Dir
Holdings: Vols 8000 Cat Mss Audiotapes Microforms
Notes: The Vivian G Harsh Collection on Afro-American History and Literature, in the George Cleveland Hall Branch of the Chicago Public Library, contains books, in print and on microfilm, periodicals, recordings, tapes, pamphlets and mss. Specializes in Afro-Americana, but contains a sizeable number of books on Africa. Also contains these noteworthy items: *The Negro in Illinois: the Illinois Writers Project Files; The Chicago Afro-American Union Analytic Catalog; Big Boy Leaves Home*, by Richard Wright (an original typewritten ms); *The Big Sea*, by Langston Hughes (3 original typewritten mss of this work). 7800 vols on microfilm.

IL —JOHNSON PUBLISHING CO, Library, 820 S Michigan Ave, Chicago, 60605. Pamela J Cash, Librn
Holdings: Vols 8000 Cat Maps Microforms
Notes: Incl all publications of Johnson Publishing Company and many more Black publications.

IN —INDIANA STATE UNIVERSITY, EVANSVILLE, Library, 8600 University Blvd, Evansville, 47712. Gina R Walker, Acting Archivist
Holdings: Cat Mss Pix Phonorecords Audiotapes
Notes: A small but continuing collection of mss, clippings, pictures, records, tape recordings to document the story of the blacks of this southwestern Indiana region. Restricted use: noncirculating.

IN —MORRISSON-REEVES LIBRARY, 80 N Sixth St, Richmond, 47374. Harriet E Bard, Librn

KY —LOUISVILLE FREE PUBLIC LIBRARY, Western Branch, Fourth and York Sts, Louisville, 40203. Larry Rees, Mgr of Extension Services
Holdings: Vols 5000 Cat Mss Maps Pix
Notes: Includes some Joseph S Cotter ms items; also clippings.

LA —AMISTAD RESEARCH CENTER, 400 Esplanade Ave, New Orleans, 70116. Clifton H Johnson, Exec Dir; Florence E Borders, Senior Archivist
Holdings: Vols (10,000) Cat Mss Pix Audiotapes Microforms
Budget: ($315,000)
Notes: In addition, 8,000,000 ms pieces, 10, 000 pictures, 3500 microforms, and 500 audiotapes. Amistad Research Center is an historical research library devoted to the collection and use of primary source materials on the history of America's ethnic minorities, with particular emphasis on Afro-Americans, American Indians, and immigrant groups. Among the larger institutional collections held are the archives and records of the American Missionary Association, the American Home Missionary Society, the Race Relations Dept of the Anti-Defamation League, the Catholic Committee of the South, and the National Association of Human Rights Workers, (formerly NAIRO, National Association of Intergroup Related Officials). Also, private papers of the Harlem Renaissance poet, Countee Cullen; educator and civil rights leader, Mary McLeod Bethune;20th century civil rights lawyer, Alexander P Tureaud; 19th century Black attorney and judge, George Ruffin; founder and director of Operation Crossroads Africa, Dr James H Robinson; and over 70 others.

MD —PRINCE GEORGE'S COUNTY MEMORIAL LIBRARY SYSTEM, Oxon Hill Branch Library, Sojourner Truth Collection, 6200 Oxon Hill Rd, Oxon Hill, 20745. Cherie Phillips Barnett, Librn
Holdings: Vols (3000) Cat Mss Pix Films Phonorecords Microforms VF
Budget: ($3500)
Notes: The Sojourner Truth Collection on Blacks in America is a representative collection of materials by and about Black Americans, their historical problems and accomplishments. The collection, containing certain unique and rare items, emphasizes the Black woman, the Black family, slavery and anti-slavery, Black literature, Blacks in the military and slave narratives. Also incl current US government publications concerning the Black American. A supportive collection of films, recordings, paperbacks, and periodicals is available. Programs, displays, and bibliographies are prepared in order to develop interest in the collection.

MA —UNIVERSITY OF MASSACHUSETTS AT AMHERST, Library, Archives and Manuscripts, Amherst, 01003. Siegfried Feller, Assoc Dir for Collection Development
Holdings: Mss
Notes: Papers, 1926-1972. Personal and professional correspondence, 1926-1972; administrative and teaching records pertaining to his career, especially his presidencies of Fort Valley State College (1939-1945) and Lincoln University (1945-1957), and later career at Atlanta University (1957-1971); reserch data; manuscripts of published and unpublished speeches, articles, and books; Bond family papers. Incl correspondence of James Bond (1863-1929) detailing social and race conditions in Kentucky. *The Horace Mann Bond Papers, 1830 (1926-72) 1979; a Guide*, by Barbara S Meloni, Rita Norton, and Katherine Emerson, 1982.

MA —FRANCIS A COUNTWAY LIBRARY OF MEDICINE, Boston Medical Library/Harvard Medical Library, 10 Shattuck St, Boston, 02115. C Robin LeSueur, Librn; Richard J Wolfe, Cur, Rare Books & Manuscripts
Holdings: Vols (200) Cat Mss Pix
Notes: The Frantz Fanon Collection, dealing with the subject of black psychology.

MA —RADCLIFFE COLLEGE, Arthur & Elizabeth Schlesinger Library on the History of Women in America, 3 James St, Cambridge, 02138. Patricia Miller King, Dir; Eva Moseley, Cur of Mss

MA —BOSTON COLLEGE LIBRARIES, Chestnut Hill, 02167.
Notes: The archives of the Citywide Coordinating Council of Boston, Mass, established in 1975 to monitor the desegregation of the Boston school system and to foster public awareness in the implementation of the court's desegregation orders. Incl the collection of transcripts of School Committee meetings; the central files, reflecting the functioning of the council office; and the files of the senior staff, containing the key administrative records of the Council.

MA —AMERICAN ANTIQUARIAN SOCIETY LIBRARY, 185 Salisbury St, Worcester, 01609. Marcus A McCorison, Dir & Librn
Holdings: Cat Mss Pix
Notes: Rich in early writings of Black authors and in poetry, fiction, drama, and essays inspired by them, plus numerous newspaper and magazine files of Black publications. Many rare 18th century tracts on slavery; fine collections which illuminate the Black-White relationship, as well as documents dealing with the Black heritage (soldiers, religion, folklore, music).

MI —CENTRAL MICHIGAN UNIVERSITY, Clarke Historical Library, Mount Pleasant, 48859. William H Mulligan, Jr, Dir; William Miles, Biography Collections Librn
Holdings: Vols 900
Notes: Wilbert Wright Collection of Africana and Afro-Americana.

MN —MINNESOTA HISTORICAL SOCIETY LIBRARY, 690 Cedar St, Saint

BLACKS (cont.)

Paul, 55101. Patricia C Harpole, Chief of Reference Library; Bonnie G Wilson, Head of Special Libraries
Notes: Oral History Collection contains tapes of representatives of ethnic groups in Minnesota interviewed as a part of special projects incl Blacks, Mexican-Americans, Finns in northern Minnesota, and Jews in Minneapolis.

MS —TOUGALOO COLLEGE, L Zenobia Coleman Library, Tougaloo, 39174. Virgia Brocks-Shedd, Acting Dir
Budget: ($142,650)
Notes: Civil rights cases and legal papers; lawsuits; Mississippi, 1960-1968. Local attorneys have donated papers of cases they have handled, espec attorneys of two government-funded legal services offices. Individual collections: Jerry W Ward, Lance Jeffers, (Ret) Lt Col Jesse Johnson on Blacks in the military. Incl VF holdings of articles from 1930 and on.

NJ —PRINCETON UNIVERSITY, Firestone Library, Afro-American Studies Collection, Princeton, 08540. William Wellburn, Cur
Holdings: Vols (2000) Cat Pix Phonrecords Audiotapes Microforms
Notes: Our emphasis is primarily Afro-American: catalogs of other collections, biographical and vertical files, reference materials, indexes, bibliographies and serials.

NY —COLUMBIA UNIVERSITY LIBRARIES, Rare Book & Manuscript Library, 801 Butler Library, 535 W 114 St, New York, 10027. Kenneth A Lohf, Librn
Notes: Pamphlets, clippings, pictures and mss. The L S Alexander Gumby Collection on the American Negro. 5000 items. Also the Paul Magriel Boxing Collection on the history and literature of pugilism. The L S Alexander Gumby Collection, which incl 9 Joe Lewis scrapbooks, and much on Jack Johnson, Sugar Ray Robinson, and Jackie Robinson. Restricted use.

NY —NEW YORK PUBLIC LIBRARY, Schomburg Center for Research in Black Culture, 515 Lenox Ave, New York, 10037. Catherine J Lenix Hooker, Interim Administrator
Holdings: Vols (85,000) Cat Mss Maps Pix Slides Phonorecords Audiotapes Videotapes 16mm Films Filmstrips Microforms
Notes: Materials in all formats about Black peoples throughout the world. Extensive archival holdings, vertical files, Afro-American and African art. Collections incl 182 groups of mss, 100,000 photographs, 6500 slides, 5600 phonorecords, 2300 audiotapes, and over 30,000 microforms. Described in *The Dictionary Catalog of the Schomburg Collection,* 9 vols, and supplements to 1974, 7 vols (Boston: G K Hall, 1962-1975); and *Bibliographic Guide to Black Studies* (Boston: G K Hall). Since 1972, the Center's holdings have been incl in the *Dictionary Catalog of the Research Libraries, New York Public Library.*

NY —YWCA NATIONAL BOARD, Library, 726-730 Broadway, New York, 10012. Elizabeth Norris, Librn
Holdings: Vols (3000) Cat Mss
Budget: ($2400)
Notes: Women and their contemporary interests.

NC —UNIVERSITY OF NORTH CAROLINA, CHAPEL HILL, Louis Round Wilson Academic Affairs Library, Southern Historical Collection, Chapel Hill, 27514. Carolyn Wallace, Librn
Notes: The papers of Algernon Lee Butler, former judge of the United States Court for the Eastern District of North Carolina (1959-1975).

NC —DUKE UNIVERSITY, William R Perkins Library, Durham, 27706. Elvin E Strowd, University Librn
Notes: The Race and Race Relations collection contains books, pamphlets, letters, and manuscripts dealing with Southern problems with the Negro and the subject of race generally.

OK —LANGSTON UNIVERSITY, M B Tolson Black Heritage Library, Langston, 73050. Rosaland Savage, Cur
Holdings: Vols (4000) Cat Mss Maps Pix Slides Microforms Filmstrips Phonorecords
Budget: ($1000)
Notes: Main objective is to fill a large gap in the Afro-American academic community and to serve as a depository of Afro-Americana for research scholars in the Southwest.

PA —LUZERNE COUNTY COMMUNITY COLLEGE, Library, Prospect St & Middle Rd, Nanticoke, 18634. Robert N Cohee, Library Dir
Holdings: Vols (900) Cat Maps Phonorecords Audiotapes 16mm Films Filmstrips
Budget: ($26,000)
Notes: Limited number of volumes in Ethnic Collection.

PA —BALCH INSTITUTE FOR ETHNIC STUDIES, Library, 18 S Seventh St, Philadelphia, 19106. R Joseph Anderson, Library Dir
Holdings: Vols 3200 Cat Mss Pix Microforms

PA —FREE LIBRARY OF PHILADELPHIA, Social Science and History Dept, Logan Sq, Philadelphia, 19103. William Handley, Head
Holdings: Vols 1500 Cat
Notes: Incl Historical Collection.

†PA —TEMPLE UNIVERSITY LIBRARIES, Special Collections Dept, Urban Archives Center, Philadelphia, 19122. Thomas Whitehead, Cur of Mss
Holdings: Cat
Notes: Incl the records of several separate collections which are deposited in the Urban Archives Center. Many collections contain photographs, maps and pamphlets, in addition to manuscripts. All collections in the Urban Archives are separately cataloged.

PA —UNIVERSITY OF PITTSBURGH, Hillman Library, Archives of Industrial Society, 363 Hillman Library, Pittsburgh, 15260. Frank A Zabrosky, Cur
Holdings: Mss Pix Audiotapes Microforms
Notes: Unique collections: NAACP, Pittsburgh Chap Records, 1940-1966; Urban League of Pittsburgh Records, 1915-1940.

RI —PROVIDENCE PUBLIC LIBRARY, 150 Empire St, Providence, 02903. Lance J Bauer, Special Collections Librn
Notes: The Edna Frazier Memorial Collection (South Providence Branch) is the largest public library collection in Rhode Island dedicated to Black Studies. Since 1969, the Collection has served the people of this area. Adults and children concerned with the heritage of Black people in America, their roles, culture, and accomplishments, have found a wealth of information here. From its initial 900 volumes, the Collection has grown to several thousand volumes incl noted works by Black authors, reference materials, sociological studies, poetry, music, sports, biographies, and titles no longer in print. The time span covered by the Collection is 1619 to the present. It contains materials on the Black Renaissance and the early Civil Rights movements of the '30s, '40s and '50s, in addition to the more well-known movements of the '60s and '70s. A unique feature of thiscollection is the large number of children's books it contains; these reflect the same concerns and interests as the larger adult collection. Another unique feature of this collection is that it does circulate. It is available to any resident of the state as a result of the Providence Public Library's role as Rhode Island's Principal Public Library.

SC —SOUTH CAROLINA STATE COLLEGE, Miller F Whittaker Library, College Ave, PO Box 1991, Orangeburg, 29117. Barbara Williams Jenkins, Dir
Holdings: Vols 5910 Cat Maps Pix Microforms
Notes: Afro-American historical background.

TN —FISK UNIVERSITY, Library, Special Collections, 17 & Jackson St, Nashville, 37203. Ann Allen Shockley, Assoc Librn
Holdings: Vols 45,000 Cat Mss Pix Slides Phonorecords Audiotapes Videotapes Filmstrips Microforms
Notes: There is an author catalog in the Special Collections Room. A published catalog has been done, *Dictionary Catalog of the Negro Collection,* 6 vols, Greenwood Press, 1974. The collection includes all aspects of the Negro in America, Africa, and the Caribbean. Oral history tapes, archival and ms collections, newspapers, magazines and journals.

TX —EAST TEXAS STATE UNIVERSITY, James G Gee Library, Special Collections Dept, East Texas Station, Commerce, 75428. James Conrad, Dept Head
Holdings: Vols (3500) Cat Mss Pix Slides
Notes: The books on Black Literature (with the exception of those on Texas folklore) and Slavery in the US have been transferred to the general stack area of the library; however, our collection of county histories of Texas, which is still housed in the Special Collections, continues to grow. In addition, we have acquired sizeable collections of books on Texas folklore and Texas placenames; and World War II posters. Another new area is printing arts in Texas. There is a separate dictionary card catalog for the book collection in the Special Collections Department.

TX —BISHOP COLLEGE, Southwest Research Center Library, 3837 Simpson-Stuart Rd, Dallas, 75241.
Holdings: Vols 3,000
Notes: History and current status of Blacks in the Southwestern US.

VA —VIRGINIA UNION UNIVERSITY, William J Clark Library, 1500 N Lombardy St, Richmond, 23220. Verdelle V Bradley, Librn
Holdings: Vols 9905 Cat Pix Slides Phonorecords Audiotapes Filmstrips Microforms
Notes: Incl 1369 microforms. Special collection on slavery is not cataloged; oral history tapes of Black Virginians, especially in religious contexts.

WA —SEATTLE PUBLIC LIBRARY, Douglass-Truth Branch, 23 & E Yesler Way, Seattle, 98104. Marcia Myers, Branch Librn
Holdings: Vols 5500 Cat Pix Phonorecords
Notes: Focus is on the Afro-American experience in the US, with emphasis on the Pacific Northwest, incl works of local Black authors. Incl 5500 cataloged volumes, 2200 pamphlets and pictures, 300 recordings, 32 periodical subscriptions.

†WA —UNIVERSITY OF WASHINGTON LIBRARIES, Seattle, 98195.

WI —STATE HISTORICAL SOCIETY OF WISCONSIN, Library, Newspaper and Periodicals Section, 816 State St, Madison, 53706. James P Danky, Librn
Notes: One of the largest collections of US and Canadian Black newspapers and periodicals in the US dating from the early 19th century to the present. Holdings described in *Black Periodicals: A Union List of Holdings in Libraries of the University of Wisconsin and the Library of the State Historical Society of Wisconsin* (Second Edition 1979). (ERIC Report ED 192800).

BLACKS—AFRICA

DC —HOWARD UNIVERSITY, Moorland-Spingarn Research Center, 500 Howard Place NW, Washington, 20059. Clifford L Muse, Jr, Acting Dir

PA —LIBRARY COMPANY OF PHILADELPHIA, 1314 Locust St, Philadelphia, 19107. Edwin Wolf II, Librn; Kenneth Finkel, Cur of Prints
Holdings: Vols (400,000) Cat Mss Maps Pix
Budget: ($25,000)
Notes: With the collection of The Historical Society of Pennsylvania, one of the richest collections of mss, books and other materials on the slave trade, the abolition movement and other chapters of Blacks in the New World. Incl printed material on the history of Blacks in the US, the West Indies, and Africa, to 1906.

TN —FISK UNIVERSITY, Library, Special Collections, 17 & Jackson St, Nashville, 37203. Ann Allen Shockley, Assoc Librn
Holdings: Vols 45,000 Cat Mss Pix Slides Phonorecords Audiotapes Videotapes Filmstrips Microforms
Notes: There is an author catalog in the

BLACKS—AFRICA (cont.)

Special Collections Room. A published catalog has been done, *Dictionary Catalog of the Negro Collection,* 6 vols, Greenwood Press, 1974. The collection includes all aspects of the Negro in America, Africa, and the Caribbean. Oral history tapes, archival and ms collections, newspapers, magazines and journals.

BLACKS—ART see Art, African and Afro-American

BLACKS—CARIBBEAN

DC —HOWARD UNIVERSITY, Moorland-Spingarn Research Center, 500 Howard Place NW, Washington, 20059. Clifford L Muse, Jr, Acting Dir

BLACKS—EDUCATION

DC —HOWARD UNIVERSITY, Moorland-Spingarn Research Center, 500 Howard Place NW, Washington, 20059. Clifford L Muse, Jr, Acting Dir

DC —LIBRARY OF CONGRESS, Manuscript Division, Washington, 20540. John C Broderick, Chief
Holdings: 135,200 Items
Notes: Correspondence, reports, student and financial records, subject files, scrapbooks, clippings, photographs, printed matter, and other memorabilia of Nannie Helen Burroughs (1878-1961).

MA —UNIVERSITY OF MASSACHUSETTS AT AMHERST, Library, Archives and Manuscripts, Amherst, 01003. Siegfried Feller, Assoc Dir for Collection Development
Holdings: Mss
Notes: Papers, 1926-1972. Personal and professional correspondence, 1926-1972; administrative and teaching records pertaining to his career, especially his presidencies of Fort Valley State College (1939-1945) and Lincoln University (1945-1957), and later career at Atlanta University (1957-1971); research data; manuscripts of published and unpublished speeches, articles, and books; Bond family papers. Incl correspondence of James Bond (1863-1929) detailing social and race conditions in Kentucky. *The Horace Mann Bond Papers, 1830 (1926-72) 1979; a Guide,* by Barbara S Meloni, Rita Norton, and Katherine Emerson, 1982.

MS —UNIVERSITY OF SOUTHERN MISSISSIPPI, William David McCain Graduate Library, Box 5148, Southern Sta, Hattiesburg, 39406.
Holdings: Uncat Mss
Notes: Records (1967-1975; 2 cubic feet) of the Mississippi Association of Educators concerning the merger of the predominantly Black, Mississippi Teachers Association and the predominantly White, Mississippi Education Association. The collection incl correspondence, minutes of meetings, conference hearings, resolutions, proposals and constitutions from various state education associations.

RI —BROWN UNIVERSITY, John Hay Library, 20 Prospect St, Providence, 02912. Mark N Brown, Cur Mss
Holdings: Mss
Notes: Papers of Black educator John Brown Watson (1872-1942), President of Leland College, Louisiana (1923-1928) and Arkansas Agricultural, Mechanical and Normal College (1928-1942). Correspondents incl Booker T Washington, John Hope, Mary M Bethune, Florence M Read, W E B DuBois, Benjamin E Mays, S H Archer, C G Woodson, Rufus Clement, Mordecai Johnson, Hale Woodruff, Trevor Arnett, Langston Hughes, Lucy H Tapley, Channing Tobias, and Joe Louis.

SC —COLLEGE OF CHARLESTON LIBRARY, Special Collections Dept, Charleston, 29401.
Notes: Laing School Collection consists of photocopied material from the papers of the Pennsylvania Abolition Society housed at the Historical Society of Pennsylvania, dealing with the establishment (1866), maintenance and eventual relinquishing of the Laing School to the local Public School Board (1940). Collection guide available. Also, Avery Institute Collection, consisting of photocopied materials from the collection housed at Amistad Research Center of Dillard University. The Institute was established and maintained through much of its history by the American Missionary Assn. Also oral histories of Avery Institute graduates.

BLACKS—HISTORY

AL —BIRMINGHAM PUBLIC LIBRARY, Dept of Archives & Mss, 2020 Seventh Ave N, Birmingham, 35203. Marvin Y Whiting, Archivist & Cur
Holdings: Mss Audiotapes
Notes: Black history. Incl materials of the Alabama Council on Human Relations and the Alabama Commission on Interracial Cooperation. 6400 ms pieces.

CA —ACADEMY OF MOTION PICTURE ARTS & SCIENCES, Margaret Herrick Library, 8949 Wilshire Blvd, Beverly Hills, 90211. Linda Harris Mehr, Library Administrator
Notes: The Black American Film History Collection, the first permanent collection of material related to Blacks in American motion pictures.

CA —LOS ANGELES PUBLIC LIBRARY, Philosophy & Religion Dept, 630 W Fifth St, Los Angeles, 90071. Marilyn C Wherley, Librn
Holdings: Vols 175 Cat
Budget: ($60,000)
Notes: Comprehensive coverage of scholarly and popular material on the religious experience of Black Americans including history and impact of the Black Church with emphasis on California and the Southwest. Part of the more general Black History and Culture collection.

CT —STOWE-DAY LIBRARY, 77 Forest St, Hartford, 06105. Diana J Royce, Librn
Holdings: Vols (15,000) Cat Mss Pix
Notes: 150,000 cataloged mss and publications concerning architecture, decorative arts, history and literature of the period 1840-1900, with emphasis on Nook Farm, Mark Twain, Harriet Beecher Stowe, Calvin E Stowe, Charles Dudley Warner, William Hooker Gillette, Isabella Beecher Hooker. Incl 5000 pictures.

DC —GEORGETOWN UNIVERSITY, Library, Special Collections Div, 37 & O Sts NW, Washington, 20057. George M Barringer, Special Collections Librn; Nicholas B Sheetz, Mss Librn
Holdings: Mss Cat Pix
Notes: The papers of Rev Patrick F Healy, SJ (1836-1910), Georgetown University's twenty-eighth president from 1873-1882 - a period of great quantitative and qualitative expansion for the college. Healy was born in Georgia, the son of an Irish plantation owner and a mulatto slave, and is reportedly the first black in the United States to hold a PhD. The papers consist of correspondence (1853-1906), diaries (18 7, 1879-80, 1891-1906), academic notebooks and misc documents. Also incl is material regarding Bishop James A Healy, photographs of the Healy brothers, and newspaper clippings about the Healy family.

DC —HOWARD UNIVERSITY, Moorland-Spingarn Research Center, 500 Howard Place NW, Washington, 20059. Clifford L Muse, Jr, Acting Dir
Holdings: Vols (106,086) Cat Mss Maps Pix Slides Phonorecords Audiotapes 16mm Films Filmstrips Microforms
Budget: ($854,753)
Notes: *The Glenn Carrington Collection: A Guide to the Books, Manuscripts, Music and Recordings* (DC MSRC, 1977). *Dictionary Catalog of the Jesse E Moorland Collection of Negro Life and History,* 9 vols and Supplement, 3 vols (Boston: G K Hall, 1970, 1977). *Dictionary Catalog of the Arthur Spingarn Collection of Negro Authors,* 2 vols (Boston: G K Hall, 1970). Guide to Processed Collections in the Manuscript Division of the Moorland-Spingarn Research Center (DC, MSRC, 1983). The Moorland-Spingarn Research Center is recognized as one of the largest and most comprehensive repositories in the world for the collection, preservation and dissemination of historical materials documenting from antiquity to the present the history and culture of Black people in Africa, Europe, the Caribbean and the US. Since 1973, the Research Center has greatly expanded its facilitiesand resources and currently provides research services in all aspects of library and archival research, including manuscripts, oral history, music, prints and photographs and general library materials. The Research Center also maintains professional xerographic, micrographic, photographic and similar reproduction laboratories.

DC —LIBRARY OF CONGRESS, Rare Book & Special Collections Div, Washington, 20540. William Matheson, Chief
Notes: Daniel Murray Pamphlet Collection on Afro-American history, 1850-1920, pertains chiefly to slavery and the abolitionist movement.

DC —LIBRARY OF CONGRESS, Manuscript Division, Washington, 20540. John C Broderick, Chief
Holdings: Cat Mss
Notes: More than 5000 Frederick Douglass items, principally letters addressed to him; mss by Douglass, etc. Transferred from the National Park Service collections. Also the papers of Roy Wilkins.

DC —UNIVERSITY OF THE DISTRICT OF COLUMBIA, Mount Vernon Campus, Library & Media Services Div, 800 Mount Vernon Pl, NW, Washington, 20001. Lottie Wright, Librn
Holdings: Vols (1352) Uncat Pix Phonorecords Audiotapes Videotapes 16mm Films Microforms
Notes: The collection consists of limited print and nonprint materials related to the rise and development of Black culture in America. Collecting emphasis is being placed on first editions, works of major Black authors and significant minor ones, rare books, mss, and memorabilia. In keeping with the policy of acquiring books by and about Afro-Americans,, the collection also contains 462 dissertations by Black PhD candidates at universities throughout the US.

FL —BETHUNE-COOKMAN COLLEGE LIBRARY, Daytona Beach, 32015. Albert M Bethune, Jr, College Archivist
Notes: Papers and private library of the historian, Joseph Henry Taylor.

IL —CHICAGO HISTORICAL SOCIETY, Library, Clark St at North Ave, Chicago, 60614. Archie Motley, Manuscript Librn
Notes: Twentieth century black history holdings incl these papers: Afro-American Patrolmen's League, Chicago (black policemen's organization); Claude A Barnett (founder and Director of the Associated Negro Press); Brotherhood of Sleeping Car Porters-Chicago Division (labor union) and the Brotherhood's Ladies Auxiliary; Archibald J Carey, Jr (African, Methodist Episcopal minister, Illinois state senator, chairman of the American Negro Emancipation Centennial Commission in Illinois); William Levi Dawson (lawyer, US Representative); Thyra Edwards (social worker, writer); George Washington Ellis (lawyer, author, Secretary to the US Legation in Liberia, Assistant Corporation Counsel, Chicago); Irene McCoy Gaines(social worker, Negro clubwoman, President of the Chicago Council of Negro Organizations, civil rights activist, Republican Party activist); Arthur W Mitchell (lawyer, US Representative, first Negro Democrat to serve in Congress); Milton P Webster (Chicago Division, Brotherhood of Sleeping Car Porters, civil rights activist, member Fair Employment Practices Commission).

IL —CHICAGO PUBLIC LIBRARY, G Woodson Regional Library, George C Hall Branch, 9525 S Halsted, Chicago, 60628. Steven C Newsome, Cur; Hattie L Power, Regional Library Dir
Holdings: Vols 8000 Cat Mss Audiotapes

BLACKS—HISTORY (cont.)

Microforms
Notes: The Vivian G Harsh Collection on Afro-American History and Literature, in the George Cleveland Hall Branch of the Chicago Public Library, contains books, in print and on microfilm, periodicals, recordings, tapes, pamphlets and mss. Specializes in Afro-Americana, but contains a sizeable number of books on Africa. Also contains these noteworthy items: *The Negro in Illinois: the Illinois Writers Project Files; The Chicago Afro-American Union Analytic Catalog; Big Boy Leaves Home,* by Richard Wright (an original typewritten ms); *The Big Sea,* by Langston Hughes (3 original typewritten mss of this work). 7800 vols on microfilm.

†IL —UNIVERSITY OF ILLINOIS LIBRARIES, Urbana, 61801.
Notes: The Mimi Kaplan Collection of materials relating to Helen Bannerman's *Little Black Sambo.* About 100 items covering 75 years of publishing, incl books, records, games puzzles, coloring books, etc, relating to the book which was withdrawn from many American public libraries in the early 1960's as a result of lobbying efforts of the Working Group for the Eradication of Color Prejudice.

IN —INDIANA HISTORICAL SOCIETY, Library, 315 W Ohio St, Indianapolis, 46202. Robert K O'Neill, Dir
Holdings: Vols Cat Mss Pix
Notes: Materials on blacks in Indiana, from statehood to the present day. Incl books; letters; church and organization records; photographs. Incl records of the Madam C J Walker Company, a black cosmetics firm in Indianapolis.

KS —SAINT MARY COLLEGE, Library, Leavenworth, 66048. Therese Deplazes, Special Collections Librn
Holdings: Vols 310 Cat Mss

LA —AMISTAD RESEARCH CENTER, 400 Esplanade Ave, New Orleans, 70116. Clifton H Johnson, Exec Dir; Florence E Borders, Senior Archivist
Notes: Originally established at Fisk University, in Nashville, by the American Missionary Association (AMA), this research center on Black American History consists of mss, photographs, clippings, books, pamphlets, taped speeches and interviews; also, the papers of such leaders as W E B DuBois, Countee Cullen, and Mary McLeod Bethune. Also materials on other American minorities, such as Native Americans, Asian Americans, Hispanics, etc.

ME —BOWDOIN COLLEGE, Library, Brunswick, 04011. Dianne M Gutscher, Cur of Special Collections
Holdings: Mss Pix
Notes: The Oliver Otis Howard Papers consist of more than 150,000 pieces of correspondence, articles, lectures, and ephemera for the period 1843-1908, covering his services as a Civil War officer, as founder of the Freedmen's Bureau, as president of Howard University, and as superintendent of the US Military Academy at West Point.

MD —UNIVERSITY OF MARYLAND, BALTIMORE COUNTY, Albin O Kuhn Library and Gallery, 5401 Wilkens Ave, Baltimore, 21228. Ann Copeland, Special Collections Librn
Holdings: Vols 600// Uncat Mss
Notes: Major items in the Hugh Davis Graham papers on southern history include *Southern School News,* Southern Regional Council publications, and reports on civil rights and integration in the 1950s and 1960s.

MA —UNIVERSITY OF MASSACHUSETTS AT AMHERST, Library, Archives and Manuscripts, Amherst, 01003. Siegfried Feller, Assoc Dir for Collection Development
Holdings: Mss
Notes: Papers, 1926-1972. Personal and professional correspondence, 1926-1972; administrative and teaching records pertaining to his career, especially his presidencies of Fort Valley State College (1939-1945) and Lincoln University (1945-1957), and later career at Atlanta University (1957-1971); reserch data; manuscripts of published and unpublished speeches, articles, and books; Bond family papers. Incl correspondence of James Bond (1863-1929) detailing social and race conditions in Kentucky. *The Horace Mann Bond Papers, 1830 (1926-72) 1979; a Guide,* by Barbara S Meloni, Rita Norton, and Katherine Emerson, 1982.

MA —BOSTON COLLEGE LIBRARIES, Chestnut Hill, 02167.
Notes: The archives of the Citywide Coordinating Council of Boston, Mass, established in 1975 to monitor the desegregation of the Boston school system and to foster public awareness in the implementation of the court's desegregation orders. Incl the collection of transcripts of School Committee meetings; the central files, reflecting the functioning of the council office; and the files of the senior staff, containing the key administrative records of the Council.

MI —DETROIT PUBLIC LIBRARY, Burton Historical Collection, 5201 Woodward Ave, Detroit, 48202. Alice Dalligan, Chief

MI —CENTRAL MICHIGAN UNIVERSITY, Clarke Historical Library, Mount Pleasant, 48859. William H Mulligan, Jr, Dir; William Miles, Biography Collections Librn
Holdings: Vols 900
Notes: Wilbert Wright Collection of Africana and Afro-Americana.

MO —KANSAS CITY PUBLIC LIBRARY, 311 E 12, Kansas City, 64106. Daniel J Bradbury, Dir
Holdings: Vols 3500 Cat Mss Maps Pix Microforms
Notes: The John Ramos Collection.

NJ —PRINCETON UNIVERSITY, Firestone Library, Afro-American Studies Collection, Princeton, 08540. William Wellburn, Cur
Holdings: Vols (2000) Cat Pix Phonorecords Audiotapes Microforms
Notes: Our emphasis is primarily Afro-American: catalogs of other collections, biographical and vertical files, reference materials, indexes, bibliographies and serials.

NJ —PRINCETON UNIVERSITY, Library, Manuscript Collection, Nassau St, Princeton, 08540. Jean F Preston, Cur
Notes: Special collection on American Negro History and Culture.

NY —NEW YORK HISTORICAL SOCIETY, Library, 170 Central Park W, New York, 10024. James Gregory, Librn
Notes: The records, 1836-1865, of Association for the Benefit of Colored Orphans of NYC.

NY —NEW YORK PUBLIC LIBRARY, Schomburg Center for Research in Black Culture, 515 Lenox Ave, New York, 10037. Catherine J Lenix Hooker, Interim Administrator
Holdings: Vols (85,000) Cat Mss Maps Pix Slides Phonorecords Audiotapes Videotapes 16mm Films Filmstrips Microforms
See also entry under Blacks

NC —UNIVERSITY OF NORTH CAROLINA, CHARLOTTE, J Murrey Atkins Library, UNCC Station, Charlotte, 28223. Robert F Brabham Jr, Special Collections Librn
Holdings: Cat Mss Pix
Notes: Papers of Harry Golden, editor of the *Carolina Israelite;* of Julius Chambers relating to the Swann v Charlotte/ Mecklenburg Board of Education case, which established the constitutionality of busing to achieve racial integration of the public schools; of Frederick Douglas Alexander, first black city councilman in Charlotte, NC in the 20th century; and of T J Reddy, a member of the Charlotte 3, a group of black men accused of burning a riding stable and killing horses.

NC —DUKE UNIVERSITY, William R Perkins Library, Durham, 27706. Elvin E Strowd, University Librn
Notes: The Race and Race Relations collection contains books, pamphlets, letters, and manuscripts dealing with Southern problems with the Negro and the subject of race generally.

NC —DUKE UNIVERSITY, William R Perkins Library, Manuscript Dept, Durham, 27706. Ellen Gartrell, Cur of Mss
Holdings: Cat Mss
Notes: Especially US South, incl slavery and slave trade, abolition movement, freedmen, civil rights. Notable are papers of black educator Charles N Hunter, many plantation records, and British antislavery papers of William Wilberforce and William Smith. Also, papers of Robert S Rankin, member US Civil Rights Commission 1960-69 and North Carolina Advisory Committee to US Commission; Boyte Family Papers; NCCLU Papers; Earnest S Cox Papers on 20th century Negro migration to Africa; papers of US senators, congressmen, others.

NC —DUKE UNIVERSITY, William R Perkins Library, Rare Book Room, Durham, 27706. John L Sharpe, III, Cur
Notes: A vast collection composed primarily of pamphlets recording the views of 18th and 19th century America (both northern and southern) and Europe toward slavery.

OH —AKRON-SUMMIT COUNTY PUBLIC LIBRARY, 55 S Main St, Akron, 44326. Steven Hawk, Dir
Holdings: Vols (1200)
Notes: Known as the Schomburg Collection: consists of microfilms of 11 magazines related to black history, 1824-1963 (73 reels).

OH —CLEVELAND PUBLIC LIBRARY, History and Geography Department, 325 Superior Ave, Cleveland, 44114. JoAnn Petrello, Head
Holdings: Cat
Notes: Extensive collection. Full runs of periodicals.

PA —HISTORICAL SOCIETY OF PENNSYLVANIA, Library, 1300 Locust St, Philadelphia, 19107. David Fraser, Librn
Holdings: Vols (230,000) Mss Maps Pix Microforms
Notes: Incl over 14,000,000 ms pieces. The Library Company of Philadelphia mss are on deposit with the Historical Society of Pennsylvania. Many of the Society's rare books are on deposit with the Library Company. The Society maintains the collections of the Genealogical Society of Pennsylvania, incl some 20,000 printed genealogies, original mss, family, church, and civil records.

PA —LIBRARY COMPANY OF PHILADELPHIA, 1314 Locust St, Philadelphia, 19107. Edwin Wolf II, Librn; Kenneth Finkel, Cur of Prints
Holdings: Vols (400,000) Cat Mss Maps Pix
Budget: ($25,000)
Notes: With the collection of The Historical Society of Pennsylvania, one of the richest collections of mss, books and other materials on the slave trade, the abolition movement and other chapters of Blacks in the New World. Incl printed material on the history of Blacks in the US, the West Indies, and Africa, to 1906.

PA —SCHOOL DISTRICT OF PHILADELPHIA, Pedagogical Library, 21 St & Pkwy, Philadelphia, 19103. Helen E Howe, Librn; Patricia K Buck, Asst Librn
Holdings: Vols (47,000) Cat Pix Microforms
Budget: ($25,000)
Notes: Collection emphasis on public school education K-12 with the main areas including Afro-American history and culture, elementary and early childhood education, secondary education, educational administration, educational research, reading, school law, educational psychology. Special Collections: ERIC (140,000 documents), Archives of the School District of Philadelphia. Approx 500 periodical subscriptions.

PA —FRIENDS HISTORICAL LIBRARY OF SWARTHMORE COLLEGE, Swarthmore, 19081. J William Frost, Dir
Holdings: Vols (35,000) Cat Mss Pix Microforms
Notes: Library's collection contain information on the history and doctrine of the Society of Friends, Quaker contributions to literature, science, business, education, and government, plus their reform efforts in peace, Indian rights, women's rights, and

BLACKS—HISTORY (cont.)

abolition of slavery. Among the more than 250 mss collections are several which describe Quaker antislavery work, aid to freedmen, and schools established to educate Blacks.

RI —BROWN UNIVERSITY, John Hay Library, Harris Collection, Prospect St, Providence, 02912. Rosemary L Cullen, Cur
Holdings: Vols (200,000) Cat Mss
Budget: ($15,000)
Notes: The Harris Collection of American Poetry and Plays is principally composed of American and Canadian poetry and plays, 17th century-date. Extensive holdings in songsters, gift books and annuals, hymnals, pageants, broadside verse, carriers' addresses, women poets, juvenile poetry, (incl Mother Goose and *The Night Before* Christmas), sheet music with lyrics, small press publications, fine printing, black poets, "little magazines," Yiddish-American literature. All movements or schools of American poetry are represented. Incl first editions of most American poets and playwrights, notably Whitman, Poe, Wallace Stevens, Eugene O'Neill, Edward Albee, Ezra Pound, T S Eliot, William Carlos Williams, Amy Lowell, Phyllis Wheatley, Robert Frost, Allen Ginsberg, Bliss Carman, and Stephen Foster sheet music. Also incl the Saunders Walt Whitman Collection (1300 vols); the LangdonCollection of Pageants (250 vols); the Asa Cushman Collection of plays in ms and prompt copies; the MacDougall Collection of Psalters and Hymnals; 4000 plays issued by Walter H Baker Co, Boston (1890-1957); the Vaxer Collection of Yiddish Poetry, Plays and Music (1700 vols). Collections incl 200,000 vols, 30,000 broadsides, 55,000 mss, 170,000 pieces of sheet music, 450 phonorecords, and 375 microfilm reels. See *Dictionary Catalog of the Harris Collection of American Poetry and Plays* (Boston: G K Hall, 1972), 13 vols; *Supplement* (1977), 3 vols. See also, *American Poetry*, 1609-1900, *A Collection on Microfilm, Segment I* (1609-1820); *Segment II* (1821-1850); *Segment III* (1851-1870) (Woodbridge, Conn: Research Publications). Separate catalog.

RI —BROWN UNIVERSITY, John Carter Brown Library, Providence, 02912. Norman Fiering, Librn; Everett C Wilkie Jr, Bibliographer; Susan Danforth, Cur Maps & Prints
Notes: Works documenting slavery and slave trade in European possessions in the New World until 1833. Particular strengths are British and French abolition movements in the early nineteenth century. (Little material on slavery in what became the United States).

SC —COLLEGE OF CHARLESTON LIBRARY, Special Collections Dept, Charleston, 29401.
Notes: (1) Avery Institute Collection consists mostly of photocopied materials (correspondence, annual reports, financial records, etc) housed at the Amistad Research Center of Dillard University. Established and maintained through much of its history by the American Missionary Assn, this material reflects the organization's work in South Carolina beginning in the Reconstruction era. Incl also oral histories of graduates of Avery Institute. (2) The Laing School Collection consists of photocopied material from the papers of the Pennsylvania Abolition Society housed at the Historical Society of Pennsylvania, dealing with the establishment (1866), maintenance and eventual relinquishing of the Laing School to the local Public School Board (1940). (3) The Septima Poinsette Clark Papers contain personal papers, recorded interviews anddiscussions, numerous writings for speeches and/or publications, various honorary degrees and awards, and materials reflecting Septima Poinsette Clark's activities as educator and civil rights activist, among them papers from Alpha Kappa Alpha Sorority, Benedict College, Black Women's Community, Charleston County Public School Board of Trustees, Hampton Institute, Highlander Center, League of Women Voters of Charleston County, National Association for the Advancement of Colored People, National Association of College Women, National Association of Negro Women, Neighborhood Legal Assistance Program, Old Bethel United Methodist Church, Penn Community Services, Southern Christian Leadership Conference, United Methodist Women, US Commission on Civil Rights, and The Young Women's Christian Association of Greater Charleston. Correspondents incl Ralph Abernathy, Algernon Black, Gerald Ford, Myles Horton, Hubert H Humphrey, Coretta Scott King, Martin Luther King, Jr, Allard Lowenstein, Justine Wise Polier, Dick Riley, Joseph P Riley, Jr, Theodore Stern, and Strom Thurmond. Incl also material relating to Martin Luther King, Jr, Esau Jenkins, and Rosa Parks. The collection contains, among others, photographs of Ralph Abernathy, Benedict College of Charleston, Highlander, Jesse Jackson, Esau Jenkins, Coretta Scott King, Martin Luther King, Jr, Poinsette family, Bernice Robinson, Hosea Williams, and Andrew Young.
See also entries under Plantation Records; Slavery in the U.S.

TX —BISHOP COLLEGE, Southwest Research Center Library, 3837 Simpson-Stuart Rd, Dallas, 75241.
Holdings: Vols 3,000
Notes: History and current status of Blacks in the Southwestern US.

VA —ARLINGTON COUNTY LIBRARIES, Virginiana Collection, 1015 N Quincy St, Arlington, 22201. Sara Collins, Librn
Holdings: Vols (6800) Cat Mss Maps Pix Audiotapes Microforms Videotapes VF
Notes: Collection incl books, magazines, pamphlets, clippings and maps on Virginia history, especially local history of the northern Virginia area. Incl a number of rare pamphlets and leaflets concerning Arlington County history in the early part of the century, as well as county and state documents on matters of current concern. One feature is the Oral and Video History collection, aimed at collecting personal recollections and programs on Arlington's development and history from all members of the community, including Blacks. A special community archive project is collecting and organizing manuscripts of collections donated by individuals and community groups. Researchers should make an appointment for use of special materials.

VA —UNIVERSITY OF VIRGINIA, Alderman Library, Manuscripts Dept, Charlottesville, 22901. Edmund Berkeley Jr, Cur
Holdings: Cat Mss Pix
Notes: Material in over 420 collections documents the history and culture of Afro-Americans incl letters and narratives by slaves and masters, plantation accounts, letters from Liberian immigrants, folklore, literture, the desegregation movement in Virginia in the 1960s and 1970s and the "massive resistance" of Virginia political leaders. Michael F Plunkett (ed) *A Guide to Materials on the History, Literature, and Culture of Afro-Americans in the Manuscripts Department, University of Virginia Library.*

BLACKS—LATIN AMERICAN

DC —HOWARD UNIVERSITY, Moorland-Spingarn Research Center, 500 Howard Place NW, Washington, 20059. Clifford L Muse, Jr, Acting Dir

BLACKS—MUSIC see Blacks—Songs; Music—Blacks

BLACKS—RELIGIOUS LIFE AND CUSTOMS

CA —LOS ANGELES PUBLIC LIBRARY, Philosophy & Religion Dept, 630 W Fifth St, Los Angeles, 90071. Marilyn C Wherley, Librn
Holdings: Vols 175 Cat
Budget: ($60,000)
Notes: Comprehensive coverage of scholarly and popular material on the religious experience of Black Americans including history and impact of the Black Church with emphasis on California and the Southwest. Part of the more general Black History and Culture collection.

DC —HOWARD UNIVERSITY, Moorland-Spingarn Research Center, 500 Howard Place NW, Washington, 20059. Clifford L Muse, Jr, Acting Dir

DC —LIBRARY OF CONGRESS, American Folklife Center, Archive of Folk Culture, Washington, 20540.
Notes: Georgia vernacular architecture, food customs, storytelling, and gospel singing traditions, in local black and white communities. Thousands of color transparencies, etc.

PA —SCHOOL DISTRICT OF PHILADELPHIA, Pedagogical Library, 21 St & Pkwy, Philadelphia, 19103. Helen E Howe, Librn; Patricia K Buck, Asst Librn
Holdings: Vols (47,000) Cat Pix Microforms
Budget: ($25,000)
Notes: Collection emphasis on public school education K-12 with the main areas including Afro-American history and culture, elementary and early childhood education, secondary education, educational administration, educational research, reading, school law, educational psychology. Special Collections: ERIC (140,000 documents), Archives of the School District of Philadelphia. Approx 500 periodical subscriptions.

TN —HISTORICAL COMMISSION-SUNDAY SCHOOL BOARD, Southern Baptist Convention, Dargan-Carver Library, 127 Ninth Ave N, Nashville, 37234. Howard Gallimore, Supvr
Holdings: Vols (10,000) Cat Mss Maps Pix Slides Phonorecords Audiotapes Videotapes 16mm Films Filmstrips Microforms
Budget: ($38,734)
Notes: Extensive holdings in proceedings and minutes of organized Baptist bodies; state conventions and associations, Baptist journals, and documentation of major Southern Baptist controversies. Material on Black, Russian, and other Baptists. Much on religious education and American religion. Large collection of Sunday School literature. Incl thousands of mss, pictures, slides, records, etc, and 12,000,000 pages on microforms.

VA —UNIVERSITY OF VIRGINIA, Alderman Library, Manuscripts Dept, Charlottesville, 22901. Edmund Berkeley Jr, Cur
Holdings: Cat Mss Pix
Notes: Virginia Folklore Collection (23,000 items) incl the following collection: Virginia WPA Folklore Files, compiled ca 1936-1943, under US Works Project Administration, ca 8000 items. Black and white folklore and folk music collected by field workers from informants throughout Virginia. Incl ms reports, phonorecords. Described in Rosenberg, Bruce A (comp) *The Folksongs of Virginia: A Checklist of the WPA Holdings in the Alderman Library, University of Virginia* (Charlottesville: University Press of Virginia, 1969); also, typescript and computer printed guides-Charles L Perdue Jr, and others (comps), *The White Folklore of the Virginia WPA Files: A Checklist...* (Charlottesville, 1973); Thomas Barden and others (comps), *Afro-American Folklore of the WPA Folklore Files in the Alderman Library...* (Charlottesville, 1973).

BLACKS—SOCIAL LIFE AND CUSTOMS

DC —HOWARD UNIVERSITY, Moorland-Spingarn Research Center, 500 Howard Place NW, Washington, 20059. Clifford L Muse, Jr, Acting Dir

DC —LIBRARY OF CONGRESS, American Folklife Center, Archive of Folk Culture, Washington, 20540.
Notes: Georgia vernacular architecture, food customs, storytelling, and gospel singing traditions, in local black and white

BLACKS—SOCIAL LIFE AND CUSTOMS (cont.)

communities. Thousands of color transparencies, etc.

NJ —PRINCETON UNIVERSITY, Firestone Library, Afro-American Studies Collection, Princeton, 08540. William Wellburn, Cur
Holdings: Vols (2000) Cat Pix Phonorecords Audiotapes Microforms
Notes: Our emphasis is primarily Afro-American: catalogs of other collections, biographical and vertical files, reference materials, indexes, bibliographies and serials.

NY —NEW YORK PUBLIC LIBRARY, Schomburg Center for Research in Black Culture, 515 Lenox Ave, New York, 10037. Catherine J Lenix Hooker, Interim Administrator
Holdings: Vols (85,000) Cat Mss Maps Pix Slides Phonorecords Audiotapes Videotapes 16mm Films Filmstrips Microforms
See also entry under Blacks

BLACKS—SONGS

DC —LIBRARY OF CONGRESS, American Folklife Center, Archive of Folk Culture, Washington, 20540.
Notes: Georgia vernacular architecture, food customs, storytelling, and gospel singing traditions, in local black and white communities. Thousands of color transparencies, etc.

MI —DETROIT PUBLIC LIBRARY, Music & Performing Arts Dept, 5201 Woodward, Detroit, 48202. Jean Currie Church, Cur
Holdings: Vols (1375) Cat Mss Pix
Notes: The E Azalia Hackley Collections document achievements of Blacks in the fields of music, dance, theatre, motion pictures, and broadcasting. World-wide in scope. Extensive clipping files arranged by personal names, titles and subjects. Incl musical scores (1500), recordings, and plays. No taping or other copying of recordings permitted.

NY —BARNARD A & MORRIS N YOUNG LIBRARY OF EARLY AMERICAN POPULAR MUSIC, 270 Riverside Dr, New York, 10025. Morris N Young, Cur
Holdings: Cat Mss Pix Phonorecords Audiotapes Microforms
Notes: 48,000 items of American popular music, mostly 1790-1910. Incl books, serials, sheet music, broadsides, anthologies, air checks, broadcasting and music business memorabilia, and correspondence.

NY —NEW YORK PUBLIC LIBRARY, Schomburg Center for Research in Black Culture, 515 Lenox Ave, New York, 10037. Catherine J Lenix Hooker, Interim Administrator
Notes: A repository for 10,000 phonodiscs and 2000 tapes covering African and West Indian folk music, early blues, and jazz.

RI —BROWN UNIVERSITY, John Hay Library, Harris Collection, Prospect St, Providence, 02912. Rosemary L Cullen, Cur
Holdings: Vols (200,000) Cat Mss Pix Phonorecords Microforms
Budget: ($15,000)
Notes: The Harris Collection of American Poetry and Plays is principally composed of American and Canadian poetry and plays from the 17th century to the present. Extensive holdings in songsters and sheet music with lyrics (170,000 pieces). Incl large collection of Stephen Foster sheet music, music by Rhode Island composers and lyricists, and a large collection of music by and relating to Afro-American, from the 19th and 20th centuries. See *Dictionary Catalog of the Harris Collection of American Poetry and Plays* (Boston: G K Hall, 1972), 13 vols, Supplement (1977), 3 vols. Separate catalog.

BLACKS—WEST INDIES

DC —HOWARD UNIVERSITY, Moorland-Spingarn Research Center, 500 Howard Place NW, Washington, 20059. Clifford L Muse, Jr, Acting Dir

PA —LIBRARY COMPANY OF PHILADELPHIA, 1314 Locust St, Philadelphia, 19107. Edwin Wolf II, Librn; Kenneth Finkel, Cur of Prints
Holdings: Vols (400,000) Cat Mss Maps Pix
Budget: ($25,000)
Notes: With the collection of The Historical Society of Pennsylvania, one of the richest collections of mss, books and other materials on the slave trade, the abolition movement and other chapters of Blacks in the New World. Incl printed material on the history of Blacks in the US, the West Indies, and Africa, to 1906.

BLACKS AS AUTHORS see Authors, Black

BLACKS IN BUSINESS

IN —INDIANA HISTORICAL SOCIETY, Library, 315 W Ohio St, Indianapolis, 46202. Robert K O'Neill, Dir
Holdings: Vols Cat Mss Pix
Notes: Materials on blacks in Indiana, from statehood to the present day. Incl books; letters; church and organization records; photographs. Incl records of the Madam C J Walker Company, a black cosmetics firm in Indianapolis.

BLACKS IN CANADA

PA —BALCH INSTITUTE FOR ETHNIC STUDIES, Library, 18 S Seventh St, Philadelphia, 19106. R Joseph Anderson, Library Dir
Notes: Ethnic Heritage Collection.

ON —CHATHAM PUBLIC LIBRARY, 120 Queen St, Chatham, N7M 2G6, Can. Arlene Mason, Head of Reference
Holdings: Vols 35 Cat Mss Maps Slides Microforms
Notes: Black abolitionist papers (microfilm), books, articles, pamphlets, and theses. Chatham papers from 1841. Mss cover the Dresden settlement of Josiah Henson and the Elgin Settlement of William King at Buxton and Chatham, Ont.

BLACKS IN MOVING PICTURES

CA —ACADEMY OF MOTION PICTURE ARTS & SCIENCES, Margaret Herrick Library, 8949 Wilshire Blvd, Beverly Hills, 90211. Linda Harris Mehr, Library Administrator
Notes: The Black American Film History Collection, the first permanent collection of material related to Blacks in American motion pictures.

CA —UNIVERSITY OF CALIFORNIA, LOS ANGELES, Research Library, Dept of Special Collections, 405 Hilgard Ave, Los Angeles, 90024. Edward Shreeves, Chairman, Bibliographers Group; David S Zeidberg, Head
Notes: The George P Johnson Negro Film Collection reflects the early involvement of Blacks in the moving picture industry and lists some 1400 Black actors and actresses.

MI —DETROIT PUBLIC LIBRARY, Music & Performing Arts Dept, 5201 Woodward, Detroit, 48202. Jean Currie Church, Cur
Holdings: Vols (1375) Cat Mss Pix
Notes: The E Azalia Hackley Collections document achievements of Blacks in the fields of music, dance, theatre, motion pictures, and broadcasting. World-wide in scope. Extensive clipping files arranged by personal names, titles and subjects. Incl musical scores (1500), recordings, and plays. No taping or other copying of recordings permitted.

BLACKS IN MUSIC see Blacks—Songs; Music—Blacks

BLACKS IN SPORTS

AL —TUSKEGEE INSTITUTE, Hallis Burke Frissel Library, Tuskegee Institute, 36088. Daniel Williams, Librn
Notes: The Robert Stewart Darnaby Collection on Blacks in American sports. Much on the Southern Intercollegiate Athletic Conference, incl historical materials. Large resources on Tuskegee athletics.

NY —COLUMBIA UNIVERSITY LIBRARIES, Rare Book & Manuscript Library, 801 Butler Library, 535 W 114 St, New York, 10027. Kenneth A Lohf, Librn
Notes: Restricted use. The Paul Magriel Boxing Collection on the history and literature of pugilism. The L S Alexander Gumby Collection, which incl 9 Joe Lewis scrapbooks, and much on Jack Johnson, Sugar Ray Robinson, and Jackie Robinson.

BLACKS IN THE PERFORMING ARTS

CA —UNIVERSITY OF CALIFORNIA, LOS ANGELES, Research Library, Dept of Special Collections, 405 Hilgard Ave, Los Angeles, 90024. Edward Shreeves, Chairman, Bibliographers Group; David S Zeidberg, Head
Holdings: Cat Mss Pix Slides
Notes: *George Johnson Collection:* A valuable collection of clippings about Blacks in the moving picture industry and lists some 1400 Black actors and actresses.

CT —YALE UNIVERSITY, Box 1603A, Yale Station, New Haven, 06520.
Holdings: Cat Mss Pix
Notes: The James Weldon Johnson Memorial Collection of American Negro Arts and Letters. Incl mss and pictures.

DC —HOWARD UNIVERSITY, Founders Library, Channing Pollock Theatre Collection, 500 Howard Place NW, Washington, 20059. Marilyn Mahanand, Librn
Holdings: Vols (16,440) Cat Mss Maps Pix Slides Microforms
Notes: Much on the Black Theatre.

MI —DETROIT PUBLIC LIBRARY, Music & Performing Arts Dept, 5201 Woodward, Detroit, 48202. Jean Currie Church, Cur
Holdings: Vols (1375) Cat Mss Pix
Notes: The E Azalia Hackley Collections document achievements of Blacks in the fields of music, dance, theatre, motion pictures, and broadcasting. World-wide in scope. Extensive clipping files arranged by personal names, titles and subjects. Incl musical scores (1500), recordings, and plays. No taping or other copying of recordings permitted.

NY —NEW YORK PUBLIC LIBRARY, Performing Arts Research Center, Billy Rose Theatre Collection, 111 Amsterdam Ave, New York, 10023. Dorothy L Swerdlove, Cur
Holdings: Cat

OK —LANGSTON UNIVERSITY, M B Tolson Black Heritage Library, Langston, 73050. Rosaland Savage, Cur
Holdings: Vols (4000) Cat Mss Maps Pix Slides Microforms Filmstrips Phonorecords
Budget: ($1000)
Notes: Main objective is to fill a large gap in the Afro-American academic community and to serve as a depository of Afro-Americana for research scholars in the Southwest.

BLACKSMITHING

MA —OLD STURBRIDGE VILLAGE, Research Library, Sturbridge, 01566. Theresa Rini Percy, Librn
Holdings: Cat Mss

BLACKSTONE, SIR WILLIAM

CT —YALE UNIVERSITY, Law Library, 127 Wall St, New Haven, 06520. Morris L Cohen, Librn

DC —LIBRARY OF CONGRESS, Law Library, 101 Independence Ave, SE, Washington, 20540. Carleton W Kenyon, Dir
Holdings: Vols 500
Notes: William Blackstone Collection. Nearly 85 per cent of the publications cited in *The William Blackstone Collection in the Yale Law Library: A Bibliographic* Catalogue, Catherine S Eller (Yale University Press, New Haven, 1938), are represented.

NY —NEW YORK STATE LIBRARY, Law Library, Cultural Education Center, Empire State Plaza, Albany, 12230. Stephanie

BLACKSTONE, SIR WILLIAM (cont.)

Welden, State Law Librn
Holdings: Cat
Notes: An almost complete collection of English and American editions of the commentaries.

BLACKWELL FAMILY

MA —RADCLIFFE COLLEGE, Arthur & Elizabeth Schlesinger Library on the History of Women in America, 3 James St, Cambridge, 02138. Patricia Miller King, Dir; Eva Moseley, Cur of Mss
Holdings: // Cat Mss Microforms
Notes: Papers are mainly those of Elizabeth Blackwell (1821-1910), physician, and Antoinette Louisa (Brown) Blackwell (1825-1921), minister and author. Also incl: Henry Brown Blackwell (1825-1909), Lucy Stone (1818-1893), Alice Stone Blackwell (1857-1950). The Blackwell Family Papers are divided between the Schlesinger Library and the Library of Congress. Two of the collections are available on microfilm. Inventories published by G K Hall in 1984 (see Hamilton Family for citation).

BLAGDEN, SIR CHARLES

CT —YALE UNIVERSITY, Box 1603A, Yale Station, New Haven, 06520.
Holdings: Cat Mss
Notes: The papers of Sir Charles Blagden, ca 1777-1820, many of them relating to his secretaryship of the Royal Society.

BLAIR, WALTER

NC —DUKE UNIVERSITY, William R Perkins Library, Jay B Hubbell Center for American Literary Historiography, Durham, 27706. Erma Whittington, Librn
Notes: 77,312 items, including manuscripts, pictures, clippings, and correspondence. "The objective of the Center is to gather the papers and materials of significant scholars and critics in American literary history." The Center is a part of the Perkins Library Manuscripts Department.

BLAIR FAMILY PAPERS

DC —LIBRARY OF CONGRESS, Manuscript Division, Washington, 20540. John C Broderick, Chief

BLAIR-LEE FAMILIES

NJ —PRINCETON UNIVERSITY, Library, Manuscript Collection, Nassau St, Princeton, 08540. Jean F Preston, Cur
Holdings: Mss Pix
Notes: The Blair-Lee Families Collection, which deals in large part with American political and naval history of the period 1733-1916, fills 291 ms boxes. It incl the papers of Francis Preston Blair, Sr, Samuel Phillips Lee, Elizabeth Blair Lee, and Blair Lee. An unpublished partial typescript guide (75p) is available in the library.

BLAISE, CLARK, 1940-

AB —UNIVERSITY OF CALGARY, Libraries, Special Collections Div, 2500 University Dr, Calgary, T2N 1N4, Can.
Holdings: Mss
Notes: Correspondence and mss (4 meters) for short stories, novels, articles and reviews, 1960-75.

BLAKE, BENNETT

TX —STEPHEN F AUSTIN STATE UNIVERSITY, Ralph W Steen Library, Special Collections Dept, Box 13055, SFA Sta, Nacogdoches, 75962. Linda Cheves Nicklas, Special Collections Librn
Holdings: Mss Maps Pix
Budget: ($5000)
Notes: Incl personal and business papers, letters, diaries, and other records of East Texans and East Texas institutions and businesses. Major collections incl papers of Karl Wilson Baker, George L Crocket, Bennett Blake, McFarland-Russell family, Orton family, Samuel E Asbury; and records of Nacogdoches University, East Texas Historical Association, Kelly Plow Company and many local organizations; 60 Thomas J Rusk letters. Indexes, calendars and inventories are available. Description: SFASU, *A Guide to Special Collections,* 1980.

BLAKE, EUBIE

†MD —MARYLAND HISTORICAL SOCIETY, Library, 201 W Monument St, Baltimore, 21201.
Notes: Eubie Blake's personal and professional archive. Incl the Baltimore-born pianist, composer, and songwriter's collection of songs and instrumental pieces in mss, extensive documentation of his collaboration with Noble Sissle, Flournog Miller, Milton Reddie, and others. The Broadway musical comedy, Shuffle Along, is represented in box office records, programs, scores and parts, photographs, and sheet music. Blake's involvement with other productions is similarly documented.

BLAKE, KATHERINE

MA —BOSTON UNIVERSITY, Mugar Memorial Library, Special Collections Dept, 771 Commonwealth Ave, Boston, 02215. Howard B Gotlieb, Dir
Holdings: Cat Mss Pix
Notes: Mss, correspondence, etc collected in depth; incl publications by or about.

BLAKE, WILLIAM, 1757-1827

CA —CLAREMONT COLLEGES, Honnold Library, Ninth & Dartmouth, Claremont, 91711. Tania Rizzo, Special Collections Dept Head
Holdings: Vols 25 // Cat
Notes: The William W Clary Collection. First, limited, and special editions of books, pamphlets, offprints by or about him.

CA —UNIVERSITY OF CALIFORNIA, SAN DIEGO, Central University Library, Mandeville Dept of Special Collections, La Jolla, 92093. Lynda Corey Claassen, Head
Holdings: Vols 220 Cat
Notes: Facsimiles and important editions of his work and illustrations.

CA —UNIVERSITY OF CALIFORNIA, RIVERSIDE, University Library, 4045 Canyon Crest Dr, Box 5900, Riverside, 92517.
Holdings: Vols 900
Notes: Works by and about Blake, incl some contemporary printed editions and all the Trianon Press facsimiles of his illuminated books.

CA —UNIVERSITY OF CALIFORNIA, SANTA CRUZ, University Library, Special Collections, Santa Cruz, 95064. Rita Bottoms, Special Collections Librn; Margaret Felts, South Pacific Collection Bibliographer
Notes: The archives of Trianon Press. All major publications of the Press. Under the direction of Arnold Fawcus from the late 1940s through the 1970s, Trianon Press was noted for its replica editions of the works of early authors with special emphasis on the works of William Blake Marcel Duchamp.

CT —TRINITY COLLEGE LIBRARY, 300 Summit St, Hartford, 06106. Ralph S Emerick, Librn
Holdings: Cat

CT —YALE UNIVERSITY, Box 1603A, Yale Station, New Haven, 06520.

CT —CONNECTICUT COLLEGE, Library, Mohegan Ave, New London, 06320. Brian Rogers, College Librn
Holdings: Vols 250 Cat
Notes: Incl Blake Trust publications.

FL —UNIVERSITY OF MIAMI, Otto G Richter Library, PO Box 248214, Coral Gables, 33124. Frank Rodgers, Dir of Libraries
Holdings: Vols 400 Cat
Notes: Incl all of the Trianon Press facsimiles on William Blake works.

MA —HARVARD UNIVERSITY LIBRARY, Houghton Library, Cambridge, 02138. F Thomas Noonan, Cur, Reading Room; Lawrence Dowler, Associate Librn
Holdings: Cat
Notes: See *Harvard Library Bulletin,* XIX (1971): pp 117-139.

MA —BOSTON COLLEGE LIBRARIES, Chestnut Hill, 02167.

NJ —PRINCETON UNIVERSITY, Library, Rare Books Dept, Princeton, 08544. Stephen Ferguson, Cur
Holdings: Vols 250 Cat
Notes: The Library has "one of the great Blake collections in the United States." It is described by Gerald E Bentley Jr in the *Princeton University Library Chronicle* XXXV, 3 (spring, 1974) p 324. Also consult under Princeton the index to G Bentley's *Blake Books* (Oxford, 1977) (Ex Z8103.B4. 1977). The collection is based on the gift of Mrs Gerald B Lambert of Princeton in 1960 and was augmented by the bequest of Caroline Newton in 1974. The Library has illuminated works and type-printed works. For particulars refer to: Charles Ryskamp, "A Blake Collection for Princeton" in the *Princeton University Library Chronicle* XXI, 3 (spring, 1960) pp 172-175 as well as Charles Ryskamp. *William Blake, Engraver: A Descriptive Catalog of an Exhibition.* (Princeton: Princeton University Library, 1969) 61 pp(Ex) ND497.B5.R95. Also see: Charles Ryskamp, "*Songs of Innocence* and Miss Caroline Newton's Blake Collection" in the *Princeton University Library Chronicle* XXIX, 2 (winter, 1968) pp 150-155.

NY —ADELPHI UNIVERSITY, Library, Garden City, 11530. Jerome Yavarkovsky, Dean of Libraries
Holdings: Vols 130 Cat
Notes: Incl Trianon Press Facsimiles.

†NC —WAKE FOREST UNIVERSITY, Z Smith Reynolds Library, Box 7777, Reynold Sta, Winston-Salem, 27109. Richard J Murdoch, Rare Book Librn
Holdings: Vols 66 Cat
Notes: Incl most of the Blake Trust publications.

RI —BROWN UNIVERSITY, John Hay Library, 20 Prospect St, Providence, 02912. Mark N Brown, Cur Mss
Holdings: Vols 300 Cat
Notes: William Blake Collection of biographical and critical works, plus books and music illustrated by Blake, formed by the noted scholar, S Foster Damon, supplemented by resources in the Harry Lyman Koopman Collection and purchases of the facsimile editions published by the Trianon Press.

†TN —MEMPHIS STATE UNIVERSITY, American Blake Foundation Research Library, Memphis, 38152.
Notes: Blake's art, editions of his works, biography, bibliography, original engravings, his followers, auction catalogs, poetry criticism.

WA —UNIVERSITY OF WASHINGTON LIBRARIES, Suzzallo Library, Special Collections Division, Rare Book Collection, FM-25, Seattle, 98195. Gary Menges, Coordinator for Special Collections
Notes: Extensive collection; includes first editions.

WI —UNIVERSITY OF WISCONSIN, MILWAUKEE, Library, Box 604, Milwaukee, 53201. William C Roselle, Dir
Holdings: Vols (68,000) Cat Mss Phonorecords Audiotapes
Notes: Special strengths of the literature collection include Shakespeare Research Collection (1800 volumes). 17th Century Collection (600 volumes), William Blake, James Joyce, Howard Fast (English-language editions and unique collection of foreign-language editions and unique collection of foreign-language translations), contemporary small press poetry publications, etc.

PQ —MCGILL UNIVERSITY, McLennan Library, Rare Books and Special Collections Dept, 3459 McTavish St, Montreal, H3A 1Y1, Can.
Notes: 1583 items. Blake's literary work, engravings, drawings, facsimiles of coloured books, and works about Blake and his

BLAKE, WILLIAM, 1757-1827 (cont.)

followers. A catalogue is available: A Catalogue of the Lawrence Lande Blake Collection in the Department of Rare Books and Special Collections of the McGill University Libraries. Montreal, 1983.

BLANCHFIELD, FLORENCE

MA —BOSTON UNIVERSITY, Mugar Memorial Library, Special Collections Dept, 771 Commonwealth Ave, Boston, 02215. Howard B Gotlieb, Dir
Holdings: Cat Mss Pix

BLANCHARD, JONATHAN

IL —WHEATON COLLEGE, Buswell Memorial Library, Wheaton, 60187. Paul Snezek, Library Dir
Holdings: Mss Pix
Notes: Blanchard's papers, correspondence, books and photographs. Also a complete set of the periodical Christian Cynosure. *Related Topics:* Anti-slavery, Abolitionists, Secret Societies, Wheaton College.

BLANKFORT, MICHAEL

MA —BOSTON UNIVERSITY, Mugar Memorial Library, Special Collections Dept, 771 Commonwealth Ave, Boston, 02215. Howard B Gotlieb, Dir
Holdings: Cat Mss
Notes: Mss correspondence, etc collected in depth; incl publications by or about.

BLASER, ROBIN, 1925-

BC —SIMON FRASER UNIVERSITY, Library, Burnaby, V5A 1S6, Can. Percilla Groves, Special Collections Librn
Holdings: Cat Mss
Notes: Galley proofs, proof sheets with corrections, of translation of Nerval's *Les* chimeres; mss and correspondence related to *Image-Nations 1-12* and *The Stadium of the* Mirror qv *Pacific Nation.* Also letters of Charles Olson to Robin Blaser.

BLATNIK, JOHN A.

MN —MINNESOTA HISTORICAL SOCIETY LIBRARY, 690 Cedar St, Saint Paul, 55101. Patricia C Harpole, Chief of Reference Library; Bonnie G Wilson, Head of Special Libraries
Notes: Materials by such well-known figures as Hubert H. Humphrey, Eugene J. McCarthy, Orville L Freeman, Maurice H. Stans, Donald M Fraser, Albert H Quie, Clark MacGregor and John A Blatnik. A list of these holdings is on file in the Audio-Visual Library, the tapes are housed in the MHS Research Center, 1500 Mississippi Street, St Paul, Minn.

BLATTY, WILLIAM PETER

DC —GEORGETOWN UNIVERSITY, Library, Special Collections Div, 37 & O Sts NW, Washington, 20057. George M Barringer, Special Collections Librn; Nicholas B Sheetz, Mss Librn
Holdings: Mss
Notes: Mss of a number of William Peter Blatty's novels and screenplays, incl the first draft of *John Goldfarb, Please Come Home* and a draft screenplay of *The Exorcist.*

BLAU, HERBERT

NY —NEW YORK PUBLIC LIBRARY, Performing Arts Research Center, Billy Rose Theatre Collection, 111 Amsterdam Ave, New York, 10023. Dorothy L Swerdlove, Cur
Holdings: Cat
Notes: Actors Repertory Theatre, San Francisco and Repertory Theatre at Lincoln Center.

BLAUSTEIN, JULIAN

MA —BOSTON UNIVERSITY, Mugar Memorial Library, Special Collections Dept, 771 Commonwealth Ave, Boston, 02215. Howard B Gotlieb, Dir
Holdings: Cat Mss Pix
Notes: Mss, correspondence, etc collected in depth; incl publications by or about.

BLAVATSKY, MME. HELENA PETROVNA

CA —SAN DIEGO PUBLIC LIBRARY, Literature & Language Sect, 820 E St, San Diego, 92101. Alyce Archuleta, Senior Librn
Holdings: Cat
Notes: Old and current reference and circulating works on the subject. Incl complete works by Blavatsky, much by Rudolf Steiner, and C Zain. Strong in astrology, witchcraft, parapsychology.

BLAZONRY see Heraldry

BLEICHROEDER, GERSON VON

MA —HARVARD UNIVERSITY, Baker Library of the Graduate School of Business Administration, Kress Library of Business and Economics, Soldiers Field, Boston, 02163. Ruth E Rogers, Cur
Holdings: Cat Mss
Notes: Archives and personal papers of major 19th century German banker; see *Harvard Library Bulletin,* XXI (1973), 221-222.

BLESSED VIRGIN MARY see Mary, Virgin

BLESSINGTON, MARGUERITE, COUNTESS OF, 1789-1849

CA —UNIVERSITY OF CALIFORNIA, LOS ANGELES, Research Library, Dept of Special Collections, 405 Hilgard Ave, Los Angeles, 90024. Edward Shreeves, Chairman, Bibliographers Group; David S Zeidberg, Head
Holdings: Vols Cat Mss
Notes: 40 first and other editions of her books; 30 letters and mss.

BLIMPS (AERONAUTICS)

OH —AKRON-SUMMIT COUNTY PUBLIC LIBRARY, Science & Technology Div, 55 S Main St, Akron, 44326. Joyce McKnight, Head
Holdings: Vols 820 Cat Pix
Notes: The Lighter-Than-Air Society book collection is in the Akron Public Library. Incl foreign language books.

BLIND

BC —UNIVERSITY OF BRITISH COLUMBIA, Charles Crane Memorial Library, 2075 Westbrook Hall, Vancouver, V6T 1W5, Can. Paul E Thiele, Librn
Holdings: Vols (25,000) Cat Maps Phonorecords Audiotapess
Notes: This is a special library serving blind, visually inpaired and physically handicapped college and university students with books and materials in Braille (approx 25,000 vols) phonotape (4000 Vols); various other phono media incl cassette and disc (approx 3000 vols), large type (300 vols) and print materials. We offer recording services and copying of prerecorded material plus transcription of print into Braille or Large Type. Also incl 12 Contour maps. Library uses BRF message service; BIF Communication #TB-18; ENVOY 100; Electronic Mail #CIANE.

BLIND—EDUCATION—READING see Blind—Printing and Writing Systems

BLIND—PRINTING AND WRITING SYSTEMS

MO —WASHINGTON UNIVERSITY, John M Olin Library, Campus Box 1061, St Louis, 63130.
Holdings: Vols (1300)
Notes: The Philip M Arnold Semeiology Collection is concerned with the study of signs and symbols. Topics incl cryptography; artificial memory; decipherment of unknown languages; universal languages; early developments in stenography, telegraphy; and communication systems for the blind, the deaf and the mute; and various forms of nonverbal communication. Limited photocopying. Noncirculating.

BLIND, BOOKS AND RECORDINGS FOR THE

CA —THEOSOPHICAL BOOK ASSOCIATION FOR THE BLIND, Baker Memorial Library, Route 2 Krotona 54, Ojai, 93023. Dennis Gotsehalk, Dir
Holdings: Vols 1200
Notes: Free lending library for the blind; Braille books, tapes, cassettes concerning philosophy, religion and theosophical.

DC —LIBRARY OF CONGRESS, National Library Service for Blind Physically Handicapped, 1291 Taylor St NW, Washington, 20542. Frank Kunt Cylke, Director; Hylda Kamisar, Head Reference Section
Holdings: Cat
Budget: $35,099,000
Notes: The Library of Congress National Library Service for the Blind and Physically Handicapped administers a free national library service to provide reading materials for persons who cannot read or use conventional print because of visual or physical handicapping conditions. The materials are distributed through a cooperating network of 56 regional and more than 100 subregional (local) libraries. Titles issued in multiple copies under this program total 5100 in braille, 11,200 on disc recordings, and 9700 on cassettes. Additional titles in braille and on tape are made available through a national volunteer program. Other special materials incl books in foreign languages in both braille and recorded form. Other special collections incl a musiccollection for the blind and physically handicapped and a print reference collection on blindness and physical handicapping conditions. The following publications describe the program: *Reading is for Everyone, Fact Sheet; Books for Blind and Physically Handicapped Individuals,* and *A Music Library for Blind and Physically Handicapped Individuals.*

NY —NEW YORK STATE LIBRARY, Library for the Blind and Visually Handicapped, Cultural Education Center, Empire State Plaza, Albany, 12230.
Holdings: Cat
Notes: Small collection of New York Point books retained to preserve specimens of now defunct print for blind readers.

NY —JEWISH BRAILLE INSTITUTE OF AMERICA, 110 E 30St, New York, 10016. Richard Borgersen, Library Dir
Holdings: Vols (50,000) Cat Audiotapes
Budget: ($75,000)
Notes: A worldwide circulating library of English and Hebrew Braille, English, Hebrew and Yiddish tape talking books and English and Hebrew large type books. All books sent free of charge. Loan period 90 days.

NY —JEWISH GUILD FOR THE BLIND, Cassette Library, 15 W 65 St, New York, 10023. Bruce Edward Massis, Dir
Holdings: Cat Audiotapes
Budget: $115,000
Notes: This 40,000 audiocassette library records and circulates fiction and non-fiction best sellers in their unabridged form on standard cassettes to blind and physically handicapped persons free of charge worldwide.

NY —WILLARD PSYCHIATRIC CENTER, Patients Library, Willard, 14588. Helen Bunting, Chief Library Services
Holdings: Vols (23,025) Cat Phonorecords

TX —TEXAS STATE LIBRARY, Division for the Blind & Physically Handicapped, 1201 Brazos, Austin, 78711. Dale Propp, Librn
Holdings: Cat
Notes: Books and magazines on phonograph

BLIND, BOOKS AND RECORDINGS FOR THE (cont.)

discs, cassette and open-reel tapes, braille and large type. All materials are provided free to all people in Texas who cannot read conventional print or who cannot hold a book. Talking books, 130,702; cassettes, 45, 447; large-type books, 11,505; braille, 150, 000. Tape-duplicating and limited braille copying. Information and referral program.

WA —WASHINGTON LIBRARY FOR THE BLIND AND PHYSICALLY HANDICAPPED, 821 Lenora St, Seattle, 98129. Jan Ames, Regional Librn
Holdings: Vols 159,485 Cat Phonorecords Audiotapes
Notes: Serves blind, visually impaired, physically handicapped, and learning disabled. A Regional Library and a Machine Agency for the State of Washington. Incl 19, 655 Braille volumes, 59,600 cassette volumes, 99,885 recorded disc volumes, plus collections in large print and ink print reference materials.

BC —UNIVERSITY OF BRITISH COLUMBIA, Charles Crane Memorial Library, 2075 Westbrook Hall, Vancouver, V6T 1W5, Can. Paul E Thiele, Librn
Holdings: Vols (25,000) Cat Maps Phonorecords Akudiotapes
Notes: This is a special library serving blind, visually inpaired and physically handicapped college and university students with books and materials in Braille (approx 25,000 vols) phonotape (4000 Vols); various other phono media incl cassette and disc (approx 3000 vols), large type (300 vols) and print materials. We offer recording services and copying of prerecorded material plus transcription of print into Braille or Large Type. Also incl 12 Contour maps. Library uses BRF message service; BIF Communication #TB-18; ENVOY 100; Electronic Mail #CIANE.

ON —CANADIAN NATIONAL INSTITUTE FOR THE BLIND, National Library, 1929 Bayview Ave, Toronto, M4G 3E8, Can. Francoise Herbert, Dir, Library Services
Notes: Separate catalog for the Braille Recreational Library, and the braille books in Transcription Services. The CNIB Library circulates braille and talking books to registered blind readers across Canada, and provides services to transcribe materials into braille or recorded form for registered blind students, and others, upon request. Tapes, 19,481 titles and 8900 are in braille.

BLIND, MUSIC FOR THE

DC —LIBRARY OF CONGRESS, National Library Service for Blind Physically Handicapped, 1291 Taylor St NW, Washington, 20542. Frank Kunt Cylke, Director; Hylda Kamisar, Head Reference Section
Holdings: Cat
Budget: ($434,000)
Notes: Collection of instructional recordings, music scores, and books about music in large print and braille. Instructional recordings incl recorded books, recorded methods for the guitar, piano, and other instruments, lectures, master classes, rehearsals, and a small collection of slow tapes for piano. Large print and braille books incl college texts, biographies, histories, and music appreciation and other general interest books. The collection consists of over 30,000 items. The publication series, *Music and* Musicians, lists holdings by medium and by instrument. All material available on free loan to blind and partially sighted persons or physically handicapped persons not able to read conventional printed materials.

ON —CANADIAN NATIONAL INSTITUTE FOR THE BLIND, National Library, 1929 Bayview Ave, Toronto, M4G 3E8, Can. Francoise Herbert, Dir, Library Services
Holdings: Scores 15,000

BLIND AUTHORS see Authors, Blind

BLIND DEAF

MA —PERKINS SCHOOL FOR THE BLIND, Samuel P Hayes Research Library, 175 N Beacon St, Watertown, 02172. Kenneth A Stuckey, Research Librn
Holdings: Vols (8000) Cat Mss Maps Pix Microforms
Budget: ($30,000)
Notes: The Library holdings incl an extensive collection of over 18,000 books, serials, pamphlets, and newspaper clippings concerning the nonmedical aspects of blindness, books of fiction with blind and deaf-blind characters, books written by blind and deaf-blind authors, and photographs and art pictures of the blind. Incl examples of embossed and braille books.

BLINDNESS

DC —LIBRARY OF CONGRESS, National Library Service for Blind Physically Handicapped, 1291 Taylor St NW, Washington, 20542. Frank Kunt Cylke, Director; Hylda Kamisar, Head Reference Section
Holdings: Vols 3000 Cat
Notes: A reference collection about blindness and physical handicapping conditions. Excludes medicine. Collection consists of books, periodicals and vertical file items. Available for use by libraries, organizations, and indiviuals. Inquiries accepted by correspondence, telephone, or in person.

MA —PERKINS SCHOOL FOR THE BLIND, Samuel P Hayes Research Library, 175 N Beacon St, Watertown, 02172. Kenneth A Stuckey, Research Librn
Holdings: Vols (8000) Cat Mss Maps Pix Slides Microforms
Budget: ($30,000)
Notes: The Library holdings incl an extensive collection of over 18,000 books, serials, pamphlets, and newspaper clippings concerning the nonmedical aspects of blindness, books of fiction with blind and deaf-blind characters, books written by blind and deaf-blind authors, and photographs and art pictures of the blind. Incl examples of embossed and braille books.

NY —AMERICAN FOUNDATION FOR THE BLIND, M C Migel Memorial Library and Information Center, 15 W 16 St, New York, 10011. Diane Wolfe, Head Librn & Info Ctr Coordr; Marguerite Levine, Supvr Archives
Holdings: Vols 35,000 Cat
Notes: Published catalog: American Foundation for the Blind. *Dictionary catalog of the M C Migel Memorial Library, New York City.* (Boston: G K Hall & Co, 1966, 2 vols). Incl collection of mss and photographs reflecting non-medical activities in behalf of the blind in the United States. Information center lends books about blindness and visual impairment to professionals, students, the media, researchers and the general public in person or through the mail; offers research assistance to professionals, students, scholars and writers; provides information through regularly updated bibliographies.

NY —NATIONAL SOCIETY FOR THE PREVENTION OF BLINDNESS, Conrad Berens Library, 79 Madison Ave, New York, 10016. Dede Silverston, Librn
Holdings: Vols (3000) Cat
Notes: Includes complete and up-to-date ophthalmology collection. Current vertical file of 21 drawers on phases of eye care.

OR —OREGON STATE SCHOOL FOR THE BLIND, Library, 700 Church St SE, Salem, 97310. Delphie Schuberg, Librn
Holdings: Vols 200 Cat
Notes: Professional materials related to visually and multiply handicapped children.

BC —UNIVERSITY OF BRITISH COLUMBIA, Charles Crane Memorial Library, 2075 Westbrook Hall, Vancouver, V6T 1W5, Can. Paul E Thiele, Librn
Holdings: Vols (25,000) Cat Maps Phonorecords Audiotapes
Notes: This is a special library serving blind, visually inpaired and physically handicapped college and university students with books and materials in Braille (approx 25,000 vols) phonotape (4000 Vols); various other phono media incl cassette and disc (approx 3000 vols), large type (300 vols) and print materials. We offer recording services and copying of prerecorded material plus transcription of print into Braille or Large Type. Also incl 12 Contour maps. Library uses BRF message service; BIF Communication #TB-18; ENVOY 100; Electronic Mail #CIANE.

ON —CANADIAN NATIONAL INSTITUTE FOR THE BLIND, National Library, 1929 Bayview Ave, Toronto, M4G 3E8, Can. Francoise Herbert, Dir, Library Services
Budget: ($28,000)
Notes: Small library (printed) on research of the social aspects of the blind.

BLINDNESS IN LITERATURE

MA —PERKINS SCHOOL FOR THE BLIND, Samuel P Hayes Research Library, 175 N Beacon St, Watertown, 02172. Kenneth A Stuckey, Research Librn
Holdings: Vols (8000) Cat Mss Maps Pix Microforms
Notes: The Library holdings incl an extensive collection of over 18,000 books, serials, pamphlets, and newspaper clippings concerning the nonmedical aspects of blindness, books of fiction with blind and deaf-blind characters, books written by blind and deaf-blind authors, and photographs and art pictures of the blind. Incl examples of embossed and braille books.

BLISH, JAMES

IN —INDIANA UNIVERSITY, Lilly Library, Seventh St, Bloomington, 47405. William R Cagle, Librn
Notes: First editions. Ms collections incl papers of writer Fritz Leiber, Jr, 1910- , containing correspondence with many authors and manuscript notes, etc, of several Leiber writings, 1932-1974. 1500 items. Papers of reviewer and critic William Anthony Parker White (Tony Boucher) which incl sizeable correspondence files with Ray Bradbury, etc, as well as reviews and manuscripts of Boucher's own writings. Letters to editor and fantastic fiction writer Lin Carter from Lyon Sprague de Camp (ca 200 items) and from various other writers (293 items). Letters, 1966-1972, from James Blish to editors at Doubleday (30 items). Letters, 1966-1976, from Roger Zelazny to editors at Doubleday (44 items).

BLISS, RALPH K.

IA —IOWA STATE UNIVERSITY, Library, Dept of Special Collections, Ames, 50011. Stanley M Yates, Head
Holdings: / / Mss
Notes: Ralph K Bliss was director of the ISU Extension Service and was active in state conservation and state agricultural planning. 20 linear ft, finding aid available.

BLIVEN, BRUCE

CA —FRANCIS BACON LIBRARY, 655 N Dartmouth Ave, Claremont, 91711. Elizabeth S Wrigley, Dir
Holdings: Mss Pix
Notes: Arensberg's miscellaneous correspondence with American literary figures (1920's-50's) including Bruce Bliven, Catherine Drinker Bowen, Kay Boyle, Witter Bynner, Edwin Corle, Helen A Keller, Lysander Kemp, Kenneth Macgowan, John Macy, Henry Miller, Lewis Mumford, Clifford Odets, Kenneth Patchen, Irving Stone, and William Carlos Williams.

CA —STANFORD UNIVERSITY LIBRARIES, Cecil H Green Library, Stanford, 94305. Michael T Ryan, Cur
Holdings: Vols Cat
Notes: Also incl correspondence and literary mss.

BLIXEN, KAREN

NV —UNIVERSITY OF NEVADA, RENO, University Library, Special Collections Dept, Reno, 89557. Robert E Blesse, Head
Holdings: Vols (50) Cat
Notes: Includes individual works by author

BLIXEN, KAREN (cont.)

in all editions including translations; also prefaces, introductions, published correspondence, appearances in anthologies, periodicals, etc. Bibliographical research collection, part of Modern Authors Collection. Other appearances 50 cataloged.

BLOCH, ERNEST, 1880-1959

AZ —UNIVERSITY OF ARIZONA, Center for Creative Photography, 843 E University Blvd, Tucson, 85721. James Enyeart, Dir; Terence Pitts, Cur and Librn
Notes: Center has significant collections consisting of more than 25 photographs plus other archival material such as negatives, contact sheets, work prints, correspondence, financial records, diaries, project files, etc. Inventories of the collections are available to researchers. Published guides available for some collections.

CA —UNIVERSITY OF CALIFORNIA, BERKELEY, Humanities-Social Sciences Libraries, Music Library, 24 Morrison Hall, Berkeley, 94720. Michael A Keller, Head Librn
Holdings: Cat Mss
Notes: Special collection of Ernest Bloch materials incl sketches and autograph scores of some 30 works, correspondence, memorabilia, etc.

DC —LIBRARY OF CONGRESS, Music Division, Washington, 20540.
Notes: The Ernest Bloch Collection incl music mss, personal papers, and voice recordings of the Swiss-born composer.

IL —NORTHWESTERN UNIVERSITY, Music Library, 1937 Sheridan Rd, Evanston, 60201. Don L Roberts, Head Music Librn
Holdings: Uncat Mss
Notes: Materials in the moldenhauer Archive. 9 music mss; about 30 letters and documents.

BLOCKBOOKS

DC —LIBRARY OF CONGRESS, Rare Book & Special Collections Div, Washington, 20540. William Matheson, Chief
Holdings: Cat Pix
Notes: Ten examples from the Lessing J Rosewald Collection.

NY —INSTITUTE FOR ADVANCED STUDIES OF WORLD RELIGIONS (IASWR), Melville Memorial Library, State University of New York, Stony Brook, 11794. C T Shen, Dir
Holdings: Vols 250 Microforms
Notes: 250 actual xylographic prints, but also some 5000 modern reproductions of Tibetan xylographic prints. All available on microfiche. Refer inquiries to H G Robinson, J Abritis.
See also entries under Tibetan Buddhism; Kanjur; Tanjur; Tibetan Language and Literature

BLOND, GEORGE

MA —BOSTON UNIVERSITY, Mugar Memorial Library, Special Collections Dept, 771 Commonwealth Ave, Boston, 02215. Howard B Gotlieb, Dir
Holdings: Cat Mss

BLONDEAU, BARBARA

NY —VISUAL STUDIES WORKSHOP, Research Center, 31 Prince St, Rochester, 14607. Linn Underhill, Coordr; Robert Bretz, Librn
Holdings: Vols (8000) Cat Pix Slides Audiotapes Videotapes
Notes: Strong emphasis on photography (over 1,000,000 pictures) and the photographic arts in many subject areas incl in the volume. Heavy emphasis on early photographic processes and collections of examples of them. Also collections of individual photographers' work.

BLOOD

CT —YALE MEDICAL LIBRARY, 333 Cedar St, New Haven, 06510.
Notes: A special subject emphasis.

MA —INSTRUMENTATION LABORATORY, Library, 113 Hartwell Ave, Lexington, 02173. Jacqueline R Kates, Librn
Holdings: Vols (6000) Cat Microforms Reprints

PA —CARDEZA FOUNDATION, Tocantins Memorial Library, 1015 Walnut St, Philadelphia, 19107. Doris Riso, Librn
Holdings: Vols 1800 Cat Mss Pix
Notes: Extensive collection of hematology. Mss of the late hematologist, Leandro M Tocantins, renowned for his work in coagulation. Part of the Jefferson University. Currently 39 periodicals in the field of hematology and related biochemistry and immunology are received.

TX —HOUSTON ACADEMY OF MEDICINE-TEXAS MEDICAL CENTER, Library, Jesse H Jones Library Bldg, Houston, 77030. Elizabeth Borst White, Special Collections Librn
Holdings: Vols (250) Cat
Notes: Historic texts and classic works are collected with emphasis on surgical intervention in cardivascular disorders and on replacement with artificial materials or transplantation. About 55 of the titles are 19th century works on hematology.

MB —UNIVERSITY OF MANITOBA, Elizabeth Dafoe Library, Archives and Special Collections Dept, Winnipeg, R3T 2N2, Can. Richard E Bennett, Dept Head; Corrado A Santoro, Reference Archivist
Notes: Correspondence, reports and various papers of Dr Bruce H Chown. Haemolitic diseases of the newborn, especially erthroblastosis fetalis and the maternal Rh-factor. Incl correspondence with Dr Louis Diamond of Boston. Also incl are human anthropological blood group studies of Eskimo, Indian and Canadian-Japanese communities.

BLOOD—CIRCULATION

MA —AVCO EVERETT RESEARCH LABORATORY, INC, Library, 2385 Revere Beach Parkway, Everett, 02149. Lorraine T Nazzaro, Librn
Holdings: Vols (24,000) Cat Maps Microforms
Budget: ($150,000)
Notes: Incl 50,000 reports.

NY —MASONIC MEDICAL RESEARCH LIBRARY, 2150 Bleecker St, Utica, 13501. Irma A Tuttle, Librn
Holdings: Vols (2000) Cat Slides Microforms
Notes: Biochemical gerontology collection represents 10 percent of total holdings in basic medical research fields of physiology, pharmacology, vision and circulation. Incl 16,000 periodicals.

BLOOD—CIRCULATION—RESEARCH see Cardiovascular Research

BLOOD—COAGULATION

PA —CARDEZA FOUNDATION, Tocantins Memorial Library, 1015 Walnut St, Philadelphia, 19107. Doris Riso, Librn
Holdings: Vols 1800 Cat Mss Pix
Notes: Extensive collection of hematology. Mss of the late hematologist, Leandro M Tocantins, renowned for his work in coagulation. Part of the Jefferson University. Currently 39 periodicals in the field of hematology and related biochemistry and immunology are received.

BLOOD—DIALYSIS see Artificial Kidney

BLOOD—JURISPRUDENCE see Forensic Hematology

BLOOD PRESSURE, HIGH see Hypertension

BLOOD VESSELS—SURGERY

†TN —SAINT THOMAS HOSPITAL, Health Sciences Library, Box 380, Nashville, 37202. Dee Platt, Dir
Holdings: Vols (2600) Cat Slides

TX —HOUSTON ACADEMY OF MEDICINE-TEXAS MEDICAL CENTER, Library, Jesse H Jones Library Bldg, Houston, 77030. Elizabeth Borst White, Special Collections Librn
Holdings: Vols (250) Cat
Notes: Historic texts and classic works are collected with emphasis on surgical intervention in cardiovascular disorders and on replacement with artificial materials or transplantation. About 55 of the titles are 19th century works on hematology.

BLOODWORTH, DENNIS

MA —BOSTON UNIVERSITY, Mugar Memorial Library, Special Collections Dept, 771 Commonwealth Ave, Boston, 02215. Howard B Gotlieb, Dir
Holdings: Cat Mss Pix
Notes: Mss, correspondence, etc collected in depth; incl publications by or about.

BLOOMER, AMELIA

DC —LIBRARY OF CONGRESS, Manuscript Division, Washington, 20540. John C Broderick, Chief
Notes: Susan B Anthony's papers in the Manuscript Division incl scrapbooks, correspondence, speeches, and related material. Diaries from the years 1865-1906 contain brief comments regarding her lecture tours on behalf of woman suffrage and referrences to such associates as Amelia Bloomer, Lucretia Mott, and Lucy Stone.

BLOOMSBURY GROUP

NY —HOFSTRA UNIVERSITY, Library, 1000 Fulton Ave, Hempstead, 11550. Charles R Andrews, Dean of Library Services
Notes: Strong collection. Incl some mss.

†WA —WASHINGTON STATE UNIVERSITY, Library, Manuscripts, Archives & Special Collections, Pullman, 99164. John F Guido, Head
Holdings: Vols Mss Pix
Notes: The library of Virginia and Leonard Woolf (from Monk's House and Victoria Sq) forms the nucleus of the collection, which incorporates the library of Sir Leslie Stephen, Virginia's father. Leonard's interests are reflected by works concerning the Labour Party, the Fabian Society, as well as Ceylon. Their interest in printing and publishing works of significance is reflected by the collection of Hogarth Press publications (1917-1941). Incl works by Virginia and Leonard Woolf, the Bloomsbury Group, as well as by other friends--eg, Elizabeth Robins, Victoria Sackville-West, Harold Nicholson, etc. Many of these are unique copies, ie, of association and texual interest. Other 20th century English authors incl the Sitwells, Margaret Sackville, Rose Macaulay, D H Lawrence, John Masefield, Rupert Croft-Cooke, and Charles Williams. Partiallycataloged.

BLOSSOM, FREDERICK AUGUSTUS, 1878-1974

CT —LEE ASH, (personal collection), 66 Humiston Dr, Bethany, 06525.
Holdings: Cat Mss Pix
Notes: Librarian, teacher, translator, radical. Anything by or about him or his colleagues.

BLOUNT, WILLIAM, 1749-1800

DC —LIBRARY OF CONGRESS, Manuscript Division, Washington, 20540. John C Broderick, Chief
Holdings: Cat Mss

BLOW FAMILY, 1732-1890

VA —COLLEGE OF WILLIAM AND MARY, Earl Gregg Swem Library, Williamsburg, 23185. Margaret C Cook, Cur of Manuscripts & Rare Books
Holdings: // Cat Mss
Notes: Family papers from Tower Hill

BLOW FAMILY, 1732-1890 (cont.)

plantation in Sussex County, Virginia, beginning with Indian deeds to the property in 1730s. Particularly significant are papers of Richard Blow (1746-1833), merchant and shipowner. Important source for study of Virginia economic history during the Revolution and early national periods. 42, 562 etems.

BLUCHER, WALTER HAROLD, 1901-

NY —CORNELL UNIVERSITY LIBRARIES, Collection of Regional History, Dept of Manuscripts and Univ Archives, Ithaca, 14853.
Notes: City planner. Papers, 1934-70; 31 ft. Detroit, MI.

BLUE BOOKS see Big Blue Books; Little Blue Books

BLUE RIDGE INSTITUTE FOR SOUTHERN COMMUNITY SERVICE EXECUTIVES

FL —FLORIDA STATE UNIVERSITY, Robert Manning Strozier Library, Special Collections Dept, Tallahassee, 32306. Opal M Free, Head, Special Collections
Holdings: Vols 4091 Mss Pix
Notes: Catalog of the collection: *A List of the Records of the Blue Ridge Institute for Southern Community Service Executives, 1927-1977, on Deposit in the Florida State University Library,* 1977. Consists of proceedings, presentations not incl in proceedings, correspondence, invitations and invitation lists. photographs, and other records. Non-circulating.

BLUE SKY LAWS see Securities

BLUES (SONGS, ETC.)

IL —CHICAGO PUBLIC LIBRARY, Music Section, Fine Arts Division, 78 E Washington St, Chicago, 60602. Rosalinda I Hack, Fine Arts Division Chief; Richard C Schwegel, Head, Music Section
Notes: Strong collection of books, dissertations, and periodicals. Chicago Blues Archive consists primarily of recordings and video cassettes, small but growing.

NM —NEW MEXICO STATE UNIVERSITY, Library, Box 3475, Las Cruces, 88003. James Dyke, Dir
Holdings: Vols 4000 // Cat
Notes: Jazz, Blues, and music history. Collection of music periodicals and monographs of the 1930s, 1940s and 1950s.

NY —NEW YORK PUBLIC LIBRARY, Schomburg Center for Research in Black Culture, 515 Lenox Ave, New York, 10037. Catherine J Lenix Hooker, Interim Administrator
Notes: A repository for 10,000 phonodiscs and 2000 tapes covering African and West Indian folk music, early blues, and jazz.

TN —COUNTRY MUSIC FOUNDATION, Library & Media Center, 4 Music Sq E, Nashville, 37203. Charlie Seemann, Dir
Holdings: Vols (6000) Mss Pix Slides Phonorecords Audiotapes Videotapes 16mm Films Microforms
Notes: The largest collection in the world dealing with American country music. Related subject areas are also included--Anglo-American folksong, popular music in general (soul, jazz, rock and roll, rhythm and blues, etc), recorded sound technology, music law.

BLUMENFELD, LILLIAN RIFKIN

PA —KING'S COLLEGE, D Leonard Corgan Library, 14 W Jackson St, Wilkes-Barre, 18711. Judith Tierney, Special Collections Librn
Holdings: Uncat Mss Pix Audiotapes
Notes: Personal papers of Lillian Rifkin Blumenfeld, educator in the early progressive schools in the US, including correspondence, diaries, articles, poems, clippings, photographs and tapes, 1937-1981.

BLUNDEN, EDMUND CHARLES, 1896-1974

CA —UNIVERSITY OF CALIFORNIA, LOS ANGELES, Research Library, Dept of Special Collections, 405 Hilgard Ave, Los Angeles, 90024. Edward Shreeves, Chairman, Bibliographers Group; David S Zeidberg, Head
Holdings: Vols 125 Cat
Notes: 125 first and other editions of his books; 25 letters.

IL —ILLINOIS STATE UNIVERSITY, Milner Library, Dept of Special Collections, Normal, 61761. Robert Sokan, Librn
Notes: First editions, limited editions, ephemera, etc.

IA —UNIVERSITY OF IOWA, University Libraries, Iowa City, 52242. Frank Paluka, Head, Special Collections Dept
Holdings: Vols 290 Cat Mss Pix
Notes: Collection incl 600 mss. See Henry Clark Lacey, *The Iowa Blunden Collection: A Catalogue,* M A Thesis, Iowa 1967.

MA —AMHERST COLLEGE, Library, Amherst, 01002. John Lancaster, Special Collections Librn
Holdings: Vols (500) Uncat Mss
Notes: Concentration on the Georgian poets Lascelles Abercrombie, Edmund Blunden, W H Davies, John Drinkwater, Wilfrid Gibson, Harold Monro, Edward Thomas.

NY —HOFSTRA UNIVERSITY, Library, 1000 Fulton Ave, Hempstead, 11550. Charles R Andrews, Dean of Library Services
Notes: Strong collection. Incl some mss.

OH —OHIO UNIVERSITY, Vernon R Alden Library, Department of Archives and Special Collections, Athens, 45701. Gary A Hunt, Head
Holdings: Vols 10,191 Uncat Mss
Notes: The Edmund Blunden Collection of Romantic and Modern Literature, being the private library assembled by Blunden during 6 decades of active collecting. The bulk of the collection (6,264 titles) consists of English imprints from the period 1750-1850, concentrating on literature but also incl contemporary works on art, natural history, philosophy and other subjects important for understanding the background of English Romanticism. Among the authors most heavily represented by first and other early editions are: Allington, Barnes, Bloomfield, Byron, Clare, Coleridge, Cowper, Dyer, Edgeworth, Goldsmith, Hazlitt, Hunt, Lamb, Landor, Scott, Thompson and Wordsworth. Books written by Blunden himself, together with his Georgian contemporaries (particularly W H Davies, Walter De la Mare, and Sigfried Sassoon) form a second major area of strength. Many ofthe modern books are inscribed to Blunden, and nearly all the volumes in the collection bear his annotations.

BLUNTSCHLI, J. C.

MD —JOHNS HOPKINS UNIVERSITY, Milton S Eisenhower Library, Charles & 34 Sts, Baltimore, 21218. Ann S Gwyn, Assistant Dir for Special Collections
Holdings: // Cat Mss
Notes: Incl part of library of J C Bluntschi, his complete works, mss and notebooks. Annotated works and mss of Francis Lieber. Ms lecture notes of Edouard Laboulaye.

BLYDEN, EDWARD, 1857-1908

VI —COLLEGE OF THE VIRGIN ISLANDS, Ralph M Paiewonsky Library, Saint Thomas, 00802. Ernest C Wagner, Dir
Holdings: Vols 25 Cat Microforms

BOAL FAMILY

PA —PENNSYLVANIA STATE UNIVERSITY, Fred Lewis Pattee Library, Special Collections Dept, University Park, 16802. Charles Mann, Chief, Special Collections
Holdings: // Mss Microforms
Notes: Papers from the Columbus family--116 microfilm reels; Boal family papers--94.5 feet. Principally 1700-date. Listed in *Columbus and Related Family Papers, 1451-1902; An Inventory of the Boal Collection,* by D C Henderson and R L Garner. (Pennsylvania State University Press, 1974), 94 pp. No photocopying.

BOARD GAMES

RI —PROVIDENCE PUBLIC LIBRARY, 150 Empire St, Providence, 02903. Lance J Bauer, Special Collections Librn
Holdings: 542 Vols
Notes: The Edward B Hanes Checkers Collection. Incl scarce periodicals on draughts and imprints in many languages dating from 1694.

BOARDING HOUSES see Hotels, Taverns, Etc.

BOARDMAN, TRUE

CA —UNIVERSITY OF CALIFORNIA, LOS ANGELES, Theater Arts Library, Los Angeles, 90024. Edward Shreeves, Chairman, Bibliographers Group; Audree Malkin, Head, Theater Arts Library
Notes: True Boardman (writer) Collection: Covering the years 1934-1977, the collection consists of material for radio and television, incl scripts, treatments, pre-production and production material.

BOAS, FRANZ

PA —AMERICAN PHILOSOPHICAL SOCIETY, Library, 105 S Fifth St, Philadelphia, 19106. Edward C Carter II, Librn
Holdings: Cat Mss
Notes: The Boas Family Papers, incl 60,000 pieces of correspondence of Franz Boas'. Also 600 groups of items in honor of Dr Boas, chiefly field notes, lexical files, dictionaries, texts, etc concerning the American Indian and, especially, Indian linguistics. Numerous papers of other anthropologists are also in the APS Library: Sylvanus G Morley, Frans M Olbrechts, Ely S Parker, Elsie Clews Parson, Paul Radin, Frank G Speck, etc. See *A Guide to Manuscripts Relating to the American Indian in the Library of the American Philosophical Society,* by John F Freeman and Murphy D Smith (1966).

BC —UNIVERSITY OF VICTORIA, McPherson Library, Victoria, V8W 3H5, Can.
Notes: Anthropologist Franz. Incl types mss *Indian Legends of the North Pacific Coast of America,* a translation by Dietrich Bertz of anthropologist Franz Boas' *Indianische Sagen von der Nord-Pacifischen Ku06ste* Amerikas.

BOAT FITTINGS see Boats and Boating—Equipment and Supplies

BOAT HANDLING see Boats and Boating

BOAT RACING see Rowing

BOATNER, HAYDON L. 1900-

CA —HOOVER INSTITUTION ON WAR, REVOLUTION & PEACE, Stanford University, Stanford, 94305. Milorad M Drachkovitch, Archivist
Holdings: Mss
Notes: Papers of Maj Gen Haydon L Boatner, USA, 1941-1974, incl correspondence, memoranda, reports, studies, orders, maps, notes, and printed matter relating to military policy and operations in the China-Burma-India Theatre during World War II. 5 ms boxes.

BOATS, PT see PT Boats

BOATS AND BOATING

CT —PERROT MEMORIAL LIBRARY, 90 Sound Beach Ave, Old Greenwich, 06870. Michael F Hagan, Dir
Holdings: Vols 215 Cat Pix

BOATS AND BOATING (cont.)

ME —ANTIQUE BOAT SOCIETY, Archives & Library, Learning Place, Manset, 04656. Admiral E R Welles, Cur
Holdings: Vols (200) Uncat Maps Pix
Notes: Data relative to mariner items that have aged 25 years or more, designs of boats and accessories, charts, pictures, books and sometimes original items themselves. This is a research library with no lending. Researchers should telephone (204) 244-5015 to make arrangements.

MD —CALVERT MARINE MUSEUM, Library, PO Box 97, Solomons, 20688.
Holdings: Vols (2000) Uncat Mss Maps Pix Slides Audiotapes Magazines
Notes: Vessel lists of boats built in the county; lists of vessels owned in Calvert County, ships papers, half models, building plans and blueprints, artifacts, shipyard papers (correspondence, material lists, etc) and contracts. See also entries under Shipwrecks and US--History--War of 1812.

MA —ABBOT PUBLIC LIBRARY, 235 Pleasant St, Marblehead, 01945. Genevieve A Moloney, Dir
Holdings: Vols 762 Cat

NH —STRAWBERY BANKE, Thayer Cumings Historical Reference Library, Portsmouth, 03801. Nicole R Osborn, Librn
Holdings: Vols (2850) Cat Mss Maps Microforms
Budget: ($1900)
Notes: The Library is a small, highly specialized library with holdings in American art, architecture and decorative arts. The collection is especially strong in the American decorative arts, with additional concentration in European decorative arts. In addition, the collection contains books on American painting, American architecture, archaeology, technology, maritime history and boatbuilding, landscape gardening and design, as well as books on local and regional history and social and material culture of the 17th-19th centuries. Collection of mss microfilm and documents is related to important properties and personages of Portsmouth and the surrounding area.

NY —NEW YORK HISTORICAL SOCIETY, Library, 170 Central Park W, New York, 10024. James Gregory, Librn
Notes: Randall J LeBoeuf Jr's collection of Robert Fulton and related material, 1764-1857, consisting of correspondence, drawings, legal papers, etc, relating to steam engines and boats, canals, and torpedoes. The correspondents incl John Quincy Adams, Henry Clay, De Witt Clinton, Albert Gallatin, Benjamin H Latrobe, James Madison, James Monroe, John Livingston, Robert R Livingston, and William Thornton. Also incl are Fulton's expense and note book, 1803-1808, and Robert R Livingston's receipt book, 1808-1812. Approx 215 items, cataloged.

OH —RUTHERFORD B HAYES LIBRARY, 1337 Hayes Ave, Fremont, 43420. Watt P Marchman, Dir
Holdings: Vols 500 Cat Mss Maps Pix Slides
Notes: The Great Lakes Marine Collection, incl the Capt Frank E Hamilton Collection; Great Lakes boats and shipping. Incl 300 charts; over 20,000 pictures (with 2500 negatives, 30 glass plates). Index and findings aids with the collection.

RI —PROVIDENCE PUBLIC LIBRARY, 150 Empire St, Providence, 02903. Lance J Bauer, Special Collections Librn
Holdings: Vols 225 // Uncat Pix
Notes: A fine collection of books, technical drawings, photographs, pamphlets and other ephemera concerned with naval architecture from the library of Alfred S Brownell. An important highlight of this collection are 11 ship models of Atlantic fishing craft, 9 of which were built by Brownell; these models are permanently on display. Incl 550 technical drawings, photographs, indexed.

TN —PT BOATS MUSEUM & LIBRARY, PO Box 109, Memphis, 38101. J M "Boats" Newberry, Librn
Holdings: Vols (2000) Uncat Maps Pix Slides Phonorecords Audiotapes 16mm Films Microforms Videotapes
Budget: ($25,000)
Notes: PT Boats, Inc is an 8000-man organization of PT boat veterans, families, modelers and history buffs who have donated a sizable collection of artifacts and records pertaining to their PT boat service. The collection also contains an 80-foot Elco PT boat and a 78-foot Higgins PT boat, both restored. National headquarters and archives are in Memphis, and the display collection is located on board the USS Massachusetts at Battleship Cove, Fall River, Mass, 02721. To use the library, write PT Boat Coordinator, William C Hindle and/or Don Rhoads, Chief Administrative Officer in Memphis. Memphis headquarters has some 10,000 photos and line drawings with specifications.

†WA —WASHINGTON STATE UNIVERSITY, Library, Manuscripts, Archives & Special Collections, Pullman, 99164. John F Guido, Head
Holdings: Cat Mss Maps Pix
Notes: The Carl Parcher Russell papers, a vast resource (24,916 items; 45 linear feet) on American Indian and Western pioneer activities and artifacts. Much on the fur trade; pioneer life; mountain men and trapping; wildlife; primitive life in detail. Also the National Park Service, parks, monuments, etc. Described in *Carl Parcher Russell: An Indexed Register of His Scholarly and Professional Papers, 1920-1967, in the Washington State University* Library (Pullman, 1970), 149 pp.

BC —VANCOUVER PUBLIC LIBRARY, Science & Technology Div, 750 Burrard St, Vancouver, V6Z 1X5, Can. P Haffenden, Head, Science & Technology Div
Holdings: Cat
Notes: Plus special indexes, incl Organization and Association File (primarily local, British Columbian, and Canadian), begun in 1950s, expanded since 1960s; Government Documents File; Chart File; Ship Index (a source of pictures, historical and current information; engineering data, plans, etc); Boat Plans Index.

BOBBS-MERRILL COMPANY, INDIANAPOLIS

IN —INDIANA UNIVERSITY, Lilly Library, Seventh St, Bloomington, 47405. William R Cagle, Librn
Holdings: // Mss Pix
Notes: Papers of publisher Bobbs-Merrill, 1885-1957. Primary period covered is after 1910. Arranged alphabetically by author. Incl bound volumes of stockholders meetings; minutes of board of directors; general ledgers; record of publications by title, 1897-1906, etc 131,056 items.

BOCCA, GEOFFREY

MA —BOSTON UNIVERSITY, Mugar Memorial Library, Special Collections Dept, 771 Commonwealth Ave, Boston, 02215. Howard B Gotlieb, Dir
Holdings: Cat Mss
Notes: Mss, correspondence, etc collected in depth; incl publications by or about.

BOCCACCIO, GIOVANNI

CA —UNIVERSITY OF CALIFORNIA, BERKELEY, University Library, French and Italian Collections, Berkeley, 94720. Donald G Williams, Librn
Notes: Research collection with special strengths in early Italian literature (to 1400), and Italian literature of the Renaissance. Strong holdings for such authors as Dante, Petrarch, Boccaccio, Ariosto, Machiavelli, Tasso, and many others. The collections in the Main Library are complemented by significant incunabula, rare books and ms holdings in the Bancroft Library.

CT —YALE UNIVERSITY, Box 1603A, Yale Station, New Haven, 06520.
Notes: Incl 15th century editions.

NC —DUKE UNIVERSITY, William R Perkins Library, Durham, 27706. Elvin E Strowd, University Librn
Notes: The Mazzoni collection of approximately 23,000 books and 67,000 reprints and pamphlets is strong in, but not limited by any means to, Italian literature. A special aspect of this collection is a group of essays, studies, or small works published on the occasion of a marriage. These "per la nozze di" range from a poem published in post card form to a scientific or literary work. The manuscript catalog of the pamphlet collection has been published by the library in book form; the 23,000 volumes have been cataloged and are shelved in the library's bookstacks.

PA —UNIVERSITY OF PENNSYLVANIA, Van Pelt Library, Rare Books Collection, 34 & Walnut Sts, Philadelphia, 19104. Daniel Traister, Special Collections Librn
Holdings: Cat
Notes: Strong collections of 15th and 16th century imprints, especially Boccaccio and Tasso.

BODE, HENDRIK WADE, 1905-

MA —HARVARD UNIVERSITY ARCHIVES, Nathan Marsh Pusey Library, Cambridge, 02138. Clark A Elliott, Associate Cur
Notes: His papers (1936-1974).

BODENREFORM see Single Tax

BODKY, ERWIN, 1896-1958

NY —STATE UNIVERSITY OF NEW YORK AT ALBANY, Library, Special Collections Dept, 1400 Washington Ave, Albany, 12222. Marion P Munzer, Coordr
Notes: Correspondence, music mss, programs, and articles of Erwin Bodky. Letters to his fiancee during his service in the German army during World War I are of interest (4 linear feet).
See also entries under Musicology; World War, 1914-1918.

BODMER, KARL

MN —JAMES JEROME HILL REFERENCE LIBRARY, Fourth St at Market St, Saint Paul, 55106. Virgil F Massman, Dir
Holdings: Cat Pix
Notes: Comprehensive collection of works about Karl Bodmer. Also, 80 hand-colored plates.

UT —UNIVERSITY OF UTAH, Marriott Library, Special Collections, Salt Lake City, 84112. Gregory C Thompson, Cur
Notes: A majority of the books listed in H R Wagner's *The Plains and Rockies* are found in Rare Books as are the works of George Catlin, Karl Bodmer, Edward Curtis, and McKenny and Hall. Some of these are so rare that they must be used under restricted conditions.

BODY, HUMAN

MI —UNIVERSITY OF MICHIGAN, Transportation Research Institute, Library, 2901 Baxter Rd, Ann Arbor, 48109. Ann C Grimm, Librn
Holdings: Vols (57,000) Cat Mss Pix Slides Microforms
Budget: ($25,000)

BODY AND MIND see Mind and Body

BODY AND SOUL (PHILOSOPHY) see Mind and Body

BODY SNATCHING

NY —NEW YORK ACADEMY OF MEDICINE, Library, 2 E 103 St, New York, 10029. Brett A Kirkpatrick, Librn
Holdings: Vols Cat
Notes: The Fenwick Beekman Collection on the criminals of 1829.

BOEHME, JAKOB

MD —JOHNS HOPKINS UNIVERSITY, Milton S Eisenhower Library, Charles & 34 Sts, Baltimore, 21218. Ann S Gwyn,

BOEHME, JAKOB (cont.)

Assistant Dir for Special Collections
Holdings: Vols Cat
Notes: The Osler Collection (Tudor and Stuart Club) contains original editions of Shelley, Milton, Keats, Donne, Defoe, Thomas Fuller, Golden Book of Marcus Aurelius (1559). A collection of his articles made by Walt Whitman. 17th and 18th century commonplace books in English and French, in ms. Most English translations of Jakob Boehme. Cards in main catalog. Also, not included in the above figure, Pollard and Redgrave's and Wing's Early English Books on microfilm.

BOEING COMPANY

MA —MASSACHUSETTS INSTITUTE OF TECHNOLOGY, Institute Archives, Special Collections, Cambridge, 02139.
Notes: Correspondence, newsletters, fact-sheets, newspaper and magazine articles, books and reports of the Citizens' League Against the Sonic Boom, established in 1967 by William Shurcliff to oppose the sonic boom, stop commercial supersonic transport production, and influence public opinion and policy decisions on the SST. Major correspondents incl Bo Lundberg, Richard Wiggs, several US congressmen, and CLASB members.

BOERS see Afrikaners

BOGAN, LOUISE, 1897-1970

MA —AMHERST COLLEGE, Library, Amherst, 01002. John Lancaster, Special Collections Librn
Holdings: Vols 35 Cat Mss
Notes: Chiefly correspondence and manuscripts (8 ft), with related printed books.

MO —WASHINGTON UNIVERSITY, Libraries, Special Collections Dept, Campus Box 1061, St Louis, 63130.
Notes: A small but significant collection.

NV —UNIVERSITY OF NEVADA, RENO, University Library, Special Collections Dept, Reno, 89557. Robert E Blesse, Head
Holdings: Vols (23) Cat Other appearances 450 Cat
Notes: Includes individual works by author in all editions including translations; also prefaces, introductions, published correspondence, appearances in anthologies, periodicals, etc. Bibliographical research collection, part of Modern Authors Collection.

NJ —PRINCETON UNIVERSITY, Library, Manuscript Collection, Nassau St, Princeton, 08540. Jean F Preston, Cur
Holdings: Vols 24 Cat
Notes: Incl mss and typescripts of her prose writings; 5 ms boxes.

OH —MIAMI UNIVERSITY, King Library, Walter Havighurst Special Collections Library, Oxford, 45056. Helen Ball, Cur of Special Collections
Holdings: Vols 1500 Uncat
Notes: The working library of the poet and critic Louise Bogan (1897-1970). Includes first editions of modern poetry, autographed by the writers, and annotated by Miss Bogan. Formerly listed as at Western College, which has become part of Miami University.

BOGGS, THOMAS HALE

LA —TULANE UNIVERSITY, Howard-Tilton Memorial Library, Special Collections Div, 7001 Freret St, New Orleans, 70118. Wilbur E Meneray, Librn
Holdings: Cat Mss Pix Audiotapes Videotapes
Notes: Papers of Louisiana politicians, including Thomas Hale Boggs, Felix Edward Hebert, Sam Houston Jones and deLesseps Story Morrison.

BOHEMIA

NE —UNIVERSITY OF NEBRASKA-LINCOLN, Don L Love Library, Czech Heritage Collection, Lincoln, 68588. Joseph G Svoboda, University Archivist
Holdings: Vols (3000) Cat Mss Pix Audiotapes Microforms
Notes: The Czech Heritage Collection.

NY —NEW YORK PUBLIC LIBRARY, Slavonic Div, Fifth Ave & 42 St, New York, 10018. Edward Kasinec, Chief
Holdings: Vols (28,000) Cat Microforms
Notes: Emphasis is on the humanities and social sciences, but government documents and publications of learned societies are also well represented. Materials in both languages, ie, Czech and Slovak, are collected. See New York Public Library, *Dictionary Catalog of the Slavonic* Collection (Boston: G K Hall, 1974, 44 vols).

BOHEMIA—HISTORY

IL —UNIVERSITY OF ILLINOIS, URBANA/CHAMPAIGN, Slavic and East European Library, Urbana, 61801. Marianna Tax Choldin, Head
Holdings: Vols (35,000) Cat Mss Maps Microforms
Notes: Extensive coverage.

BOHEMIAN LANGUAGE see Czech Language and Literature

BOHR, NIELS

DC —LIBRARY OF CONGRESS, Motion Pictures, Broadcasting and Recorded Sound Div, Washington, 20540.
Notes: Disc recordings of Dr J Robert Oppenheimer's lectures and interviews. Incl a 3-hour discussion between Niels Bohr and Dr Oppenheimer taped in Denmark in 1958 and a conference held at Seven Springs Farm in Mount Kisco, NY, that featured addresses by Nicolas Nabokov and Robert Lowell.

NY —AMERICAN INSTITUTE OF PHYSICS, Center for the History of Physics, Niels Bohr Library, 335 E 45 St, New York, 10017. John Aubry, Librn
Holdings: Cat Mss Maps Pix Microforms

BOISEN, ANTON T., 1876-1965

KS —MENNINGER FOUNDATION, Archives, 5600 W Sixth St, Box 829, Topeka, 66601. Alice Brand, Librn; Mark West, Archivist
Notes: 2 boxes, 1920-65. His published works incl *The Exploration of the Inner World and Religion in Crisis and Custom.* The collection contains case histories, mss, lecture notes, correspondence, and published material.

BOK, BART

NY —AMERICAN INSTITUTE OF PHYSICS, Center for the History of Physics, Niels Bohr Library, 335 E 45 St, New York, 10017. John Aubry, Librn
Notes: The Sources for History of Modern Astrophysics documents the history of 20th-century astrophysics. Incl some 400 hours of oral history interviews with astronomers, such as Bart Bok, S Chandrasekhar, Martin Schwarzschild, and A E Whitford. The project also organized and cataloged the papers of Henry Norris Russell, Frank Schlesinger, Otto Struve, Ejnar Hertzsprung, Harlow Shapley, Charles Young, Robert Atkinson, Seth Chandler, Theodore Dunham, Jr, and G C McVittie.

BOKER, GEORGE HENRY, 1823-1890

NJ —PRINCETON UNIVERSITY, Library, Manuscript Collection, Nassau St, Princeton, 08540. Jean F Preston, Cur
Holdings: Vols 450 Cat Mss
Notes: The George Henry Boker book collection, incl association items from the author's library. Mss total 7 ms boxes of poems and plays and over 100 letters. A typescript list (4p) of the mss is available for consultation.

BOLGER, RAY

CA —UNIVERSITY OF SOUTHERN CALIFORNIA, Edward L Doheny Memorial Library, Archives of Performing Arts, University Park, Los Angeles, 90089. Robert Knutson, Librn
Holdings: Mss Pix
Notes: Personal collection of papers, pictures, etc.

BOLIVAR, SIMON

DC —LIBRARY OF CONGRESS, General Reading Rooms Division, Microform Reading Room, Washington, 20540.
Holdings: Cat Mss Maps Pix Microforms
Notes: Microform materials only in this L C Division. Works of individual authors; holdings of collections; archival records, etc, press releases and translations, etc.

BOLIVIA

NY —COLUMBIA UNIVERSITY LIBRARIES, Rare Book & Manuscript Library, 801 Butler Library, 535 W 114 St, New York, 10027. Kenneth A Lohf, Librn
Holdings: Mss
Notes: The papers of Professor Carter Goodrich, economic historian, incl his papers as chairman of the governing body of the International Labor Office, 1939-1945; chief of the United Nations economic mission in Vietnam, 1955-1956; and special representative to Bolivia for the Secretary-General of the United Nations, 1952-1953. About 28,000 items. Restricted use.

NC —DUKE UNIVERSITY, William R Perkins Library, Durham, 27706. Elvin E Strowd, University Librn

PA —UNIVERSITY OF PITTSBURGH, Hillman Library, Pittsburgh, 15260. Glenora E Rossell, Head
Holdings: Vols (172,000) Cat Microforms
Notes: The Bolivian collection incl all subject areas, but is particularly strong in history, politics, economics, sociology, and literature. It contains very good coverage of the Chaco War, boundry problems and political and social history of this century, especially for the revolutionary and post-revolutionary periods. 11

RI —BROWN UNIVERSITY, John Hay Library, 20 Prospect St, Providence, 02912. Mark N Brown, Cur Mss
Holdings: Vols 3500 // Cat Mss Maps
Notes: George Earl Church Collection--formed by a civil engineer, explorer and Fellow of the Royal Geographic Society, who specialized in railroad construction. Although part of the collection is devoted to American Revolutionary and Civil War history, the majority, over 2000 volumes, pertains to Central and South America. The imprints, which are predominantly 18th century, include Lima, Madrid, Rome, Mexico City, Seville, Barcelona, Lisbon, and Cadiz as well as *Nova orbis regionum as insularum veteribus incognitarum* (Basle: 1537). Major subject areas are: anthropology, commerce, economics, engineering, ethnology, geography, history, law, mineral resources, railroad surveys, voyages of exploration and dictionaries of the South American Indian languages. The most significant ms is historical account of the Bolivian mining town of Potosi fromp1545-1737.

TX —UNIVERSITY OF TEXAS LIBRARIES, Nettie Lee Benson Latin American Collection, Sid Richardson Hall 1.109, Austin, 78712. Laura Gutierrez-Witt, Head Librn
Holdings: Vols (450,000) Cat Mss Maps Pix Phonorecords Filmstrips Microforms
See also entry under Latin America

BOLIVIA—HISTORY

IN —INDIANA UNIVERSITY, Lilly Library, Seventh St, Bloomington, 47405. William R Cagle, Librn
Holdings: Vols 2500 Cat Mss
Notes: Probably one of the most complete collections of Bolivia's history from the declaration of independence (1826), and the establishment of the press there through the beginning of the 20th century. A dynamic view of the most important legal, political,

BOLIVIA—HISTORY (cont.)

economic, and religious aspects of the organization of Bolivia as an independent nation. The collection is complemented by like material issued during the colonial period when Bolivia was part of the Viceroy of Peru and later as part of Rio de la Plata. Ms holdings cover primarily 1810-1826 and consist mostly of Spanish Army related material. 610 items.

TX —UNIVERSITY OF TEXAS LIBRARIES, Nettie Lee Benson Latin American Collection, Sid Richardson Hall 1.109, Austin, 78712. Laura Gutierrez-Witt, Head Librn
Holdings: Vols (450,000) Cat Mss Maps Pix Phonorecords Microforms
Notes: Private collection of Diego Munoz relating to Chile, Bolivia, Peru and Ecuador. Incl extensive coverage of the laws of Chile and of the Congress of Chile during the 19th century; also, 200 volumes of works of Jose Toribio Medina.
See also entry under Latin America.

BOLIVIA—POLITICS AND GOVERNMENT

MA —BRANDEIS UNIVERSITY, Goldfarb Library, 415 South St, Waltham, 02154. Bessie Hahn, Dir
Notes: Lora Collection on Bolivian Politics. Approx 500 books and pamphlets dealing with Bolivian politics from the early to mid-20th century. The thrust of this collection is in the 1950s period. An author-title card catalog can be found in the Special Collections Card Catalog.

BOLIVIAN LITERATURE

PA —UNIVERSITY OF PITTSBURGH, Hillman Library, Pittsburgh, 15260. Glenora E Rossell, Head
Holdings: Vols (172,000) Cat Microforms
Notes: A general collection of Latin American literature, with emphasis on Cuba, Mexico, Chile, Guatemala, Ecuador, Peru, Bolivia, and Argentina. The holdings on Bolivian, Ecuadorian, and Cuban literature are extremely good. Very strong in contemporary literature of the whole area.

TX —UNIVERSITY OF TEXAS LIBRARIES, Nettie Lee Benson Latin American Collection, Sid Richardson Hall 1.109, Austin, 78712. Laura Gutierrez-Witt, Head Librn
Holdings: Vols (450,000) Cat Mss Maps Pix Phonorecords Filmstrips Microforms
See also entry under Latin America

BOLIVIAN NEWSPAPERS see Newspapers, Bolivian

BOLL, HEINRICH

MA —BOSTON UNIVERSITY, Mugar Memorial Library, Special Collections Dept, 771 Commonwealth Ave, Boston, 02215. Howard B Gotlieb, Dir
Notes: Collection moved to Cologne, West Germany.

BOLLINGEN FOUNDATION

DC —LIBRARY OF CONGRESS, Rare Book & Special Collections Div, Washington, 20540. William Matheson, Chief
Notes: An archival set of the Foundation's publications, supporting the papers of the Foundation in the Library's Manuscript Division. Focused originally on writings of Carl Jung on myth, symbol, and the collective unconsciousness, but expanded to incl "works that increase human consciousness" in aesthetics, cultural and art history, philosophy, poetry, psychology, and religion.

BOLSHEVISM see Communism and Anticommunism

BOLT FAMILY

CA —UNIVERSITY OF THE PACIFIC, Holt-Atherton Pacific Center for Western Studies, Stockton, 95211. Hiram L Davis, Dir of Libraries
Holdings: // Uncat Mss Pix Slides
Notes: The Bolt family papers comprise primarily the diaries of Beatrice Rebecca (French) Bolt, and the papers of her husband, Dr Richard Arthur Bolt (1880-1959), a noted US child health authority. 19 linear ft (42 document boxes).

BOLTON, HERBERT EUGENE

TX —UNIVERSITY OF TEXAS LIBRARIES, General Libraries, Barker Texas History Center, PO Box P, Austin, 78712. Don Carleton, Dir

BOMBS, FLYING see Guided Missiles

BON (TIBETAN RELIGION)

†NY —INSTITUTE FOR ADVANCED STUDIES OF WORLD RELIGIONS (IASWR), Library, State University of New York at Stony Brook, Stony Brook, 11794. C T Shen, Librn
Holdings: Vols 4400 Mss Microforms

BON MOTS see Wit and Humor

BONAPARTE, JOSEPH

MD —JOHNS HOPKINS UNIVERSITY, Milton S Eisenhower Library, Charles & 34 Sts, Baltimore, 21218. Ann S Gwyn, Assistant Dir for Special Collections
Holdings: // Cat Mss
Notes: About 90 letters to Francis Lieber. Cards in mss catalog.

BONCOMPAGNI—LUDOVISI, BALDASSARE, 1821-1894

NY —CORNELL UNIVERSITY LIBRARIES, John M Olin Library, History of Science Collections, Ithaca, 14853. Lillian A Clark, Administrative Supervisor; David W Corson, History of Science Librn
Holdings: Vols 3200 // Uncat Mss
Notes: Boncompagni Archive: papers of Baldassare Boncompagni-Ludovisi (1821-1894) relating to his research in the history of mathematics, mostly from 1859 to 1894. Unpublished draft checklist exists.

BOND, HORACE MANN, 1904-1972

MA —UNIVERSITY OF MASSACHUSETTS AT AMHERST, Library, Archives and Manuscripts, Amherst, 01003. Siegfried Feller, Assoc Dir for Collection Development
Holdings: Mss
Notes: Papers, 1926-1972. Personal and professional correspondence, 1926-1972; administrative and teaching records pertaining to his career, especially his presidencies of Fort Valley State College (1939-1945) and Lincoln University (1945-1957), and later career at Atlanta University (1957-1971); research data; manuscripts of published and unpublished speeches, articles, and books; Bond family papers. Incl correspondence of James Bond (1863-1929) detailing social and race conditions in Kentucky. *The Horace Mann Bond Papers, 1830 (1926-72) 1979; a Guide,* by Barbara S Meloni, Rita Norton, and Katherine Emerson, 1982.

BOND, JAMES, 1863-1929

MA —UNIVERSITY OF MASSACHUSETTS AT AMHERST, Library, Archives and Manuscripts, Amherst, 01003. Siegfried Feller, Assoc Dir for Collection Development
Holdings: Mss
Notes: Papers, 1926-1972. Personal and professional correspondence, 1926-1972; administrative and teaching records pertaining to Horace Mann Bond's career, especially his presidencies of Fort Valley State College (1939-1945) and Lincoln University (1945-1957), and later career at Atlanta University (1957-1971); research data; manuscripts of published and unpublished speeches, articles, and books; Bond family papers. Incl correspondence of James Bond (1863-1929) detailing social and race conditions in Kentucky. *The Horace Mann Bond Papers, 1830 (1926-72) 1979; a* Guide, by Barbara S Meloni, Rita Norton, and Katherine Emerson, 1982.

BONE, HOMER T.

WA —UNIVERSITY OF WASHINGTON LIBRARIES, Suzzallo Library, Manuscripts Section, FM-25, Seattle, 98195. Karyl Winn, Librn
Notes: One linear foot, circa 1932-1944.

BONE TRANSPLANTS see Transplantation of Organs, Tissues, Etc.

BONHAM-CARTER, LADY VIOLET

DC —GEORGETOWN UNIVERSITY, Library, Special Collections Div, 37 & O Sts NW, Washington, 20057. George M Barringer, Special Collections Librn; Nicholas B Sheetz, Mss Librn
Holdings: Mss Cat Pix
Notes: The papers of the Irish man-of-letters Sir Shane Leslie (1885-1971) containing letters, mss, diaries, notebooks, clippings, and photographs. Extensive correspondence by Margot Asquith, countess of Oxford and Asquith; Lady Violet Bonham-Carter; Burke Cochran; Lord Alfred Douglas; Moreton Frewen; Cardinal Gasquet; Vyvyan Holland; Lady Leonie Leslie; Sir Wilfrid Meynell; Sir Horace Plunkett; John Quinn; Frederick Rolfe (Baron Corvo); and Elizabeth Russell, among others. Also incl are research files on Sir Winston Churchill (Leslie's first cousin); Leonard Jerome; Maria Anne Fitzherbet (wife of King George IV); Ghosts and Ghost stories; and Eton College.

BONI, ALBERT, 1892-1981

CA —UNIVERSITY OF CALIFORNIA, LOS ANGELES, Research Library, Dept of Special Collections, 405 Hilgard Ave, Los Angeles, 90024. Edward Shreeves, Chairman, Bibliographers Group; David S Zeidberg, Head
Notes: The Albert Boni Collection covers the early history of photography, incl an extensive collection of early photographic books and 19th century photographic images.

BONNER, JAMES C., 1904-

GA —GEORGIA COLLEGE, Ina Dillard Russell Library, Special Collections Dept, Milledgeville, 31061. Janice C Fennell, Dir of Libraries; Nancy Davis, Special Collections Assoc
Holdings: Uncat Mss
Notes: 86 folders containing photographs, documents, letters, etc, concerning Milledgeville, Georgia, and the South.

BONNER, PRICILLA

CA —UNIVERSITY OF CALIFORNIA, LOS ANGELES, Theater Arts Library, Los Angeles, 90024. Edward Shreeves, Chairman, Bibliographers Group; Audree Malkin, Head, Theater Arts Library
Notes: Pricilla Bonner (actress) Collection: motion picture production stills and portraits, 1920-1930; clippings from her career in silent films.

BONTEMPS, ARNA WENDELL

NY —SYRACUSE UNIVERSITY LIBRARIES, Ernest S Bird Library, George Arents Research Library for Special Collections, Syracuse, 13210. Carolyn A Davis, Manuscripts Librn; Amy S Doherty, University Archivist; Mark F Weimer, Rare Book Librn
Notes: Correspondence, writings and memorabilia.

BONUS ARMY (U.S.), 1932

CA —UNIVERSITY OF CALIFORNIA, LOS ANGELES, Research Library, Dept of Special Collections, 405 Hilgard Ave, Los Angeles, 90024. Edward Shreeves, Chairman, Bibliographers Group; David S Zeidberg, Head
Notes: 5 linear feet incl in the Pelham Davis Glassford collection.

BOOBY TRAPS (MILITARY SCIENCE) see Mines, Military and Submarine

BOOK ART see Artists' Books

BOOK CENSORSHIP see Censorship

BOOK CLUB OF CALIFORNIA

CA —SOLANO COUNTY LIBRARY, John F Kennedy Library, Donovan J McCune Collection, 505 Santa Clara St, Vallejo, 94590.
Holdings: Vols 150 //
Notes: The Donovan J McCune Collection (3000) vols //.

OK —UNIVERSITY OF TULSA, McFarlin Library, Dept of Rare Books and Special Collections, 600 S College, Tulsa, 74104. David Farmer, Dir; Toby Murray, Archivist; Caroline Swinson, Cur of Manuscripts & Art
Notes: Complete collection of publications issued by the Book Club of California.

BONNER, MARY

SC —COLLEGE OF CHARLESTON LIBRARY, Special Collections Dept, Charleston, 29401.
Notes: Contains biographical and family history material of Wendell Mitchel Levi; invertebrate anatomy course notes from the College of Charleston; University of Chicago Law School casebooks; correspondence concerning pigeons and camellias; notes, photographs, mss, typescripts, and galleys of published works; and other materials relating to pigeons and camellias. Among the more prominent correspondents are B F Skinner, Madame Chiang Kai-Shek, and Mary Bonner.

BOOK CLUBS

DC —LIBRARY OF CONGRESS, Washington, 20540.
Holdings: Cat Mss Pix
Notes: Book-of-the-Month Club records, incl official correspondence and readers' reports. See *LC Information Bulletin,* 25 May 1964, pp 232-233. Incl archives.

NY —COLUMBIA UNIVERSITY LIBRARIES, Rare Book & Manuscript Library, 801 Butler Library, 535 W 114 St, New York, 10027. Kenneth A Lohf, Librn
Notes: Limited Editions Club.

NY —GRADUATE CENTER OF THE CITY UNIVERSITY OF NEW YORK, William H and Gwynne K Crouse Library for Publishing Arts, 33 W 42 St, New York, 10036. Alfred H Lane, Dir
Notes: Recently established and still growing, but intended to become the authoritative source of materials in the field, of particular value in research about the publishing industry. Open to staff members of publishing houses, students, scholars, authors, printers, and booksellers. Primarily 20th century materials, and particularly useful for research on technical, financial, and historical matters. Much on the history of individual houses, economics of authorship; marketing and distribution of books; etc.

†ON —UNIVERSITY OF WESTERN ONTARIO, School of Library and Information Science, Special Collections Room, London, N6A 5B9, Can.
Holdings: Vols 776
Notes: A representative collection incl early materials of private presses and fine press books. Also incl publications of bibliophile clubs and societies.

BOOK COLLECTING AND BOOK COLLECTORS

CA —UNIVERSITY OF CALIFORNIA, SAN DIEGO, Central University Library, Mandeville Dept of Special Collections, La Jolla, 92093. Lynda Corey Claassen, Head
Notes: The Reference Collection: More than 2500 bibliographies guides, and catalogues to rare book and manuscript collections, auction records, histories of book collecting, and important works on the social and technological history of books and printing are included.

IL —NEWBERRY LIBRARY, 60 W Walton St, Chicago, 60610. Diana Haskell, Cur of Modern Mss
Holdings: Vols 1000 Cat
Notes: Special emphasis on book catalogs, incl private collectors, and on book collector's societies. The Library published Archer Taylor's *Book Catalogues: Their Subjects and Uses,* which used the collection extensively.

IN —INDIANA UNIVERSITY, Lilly Library, Seventh St, Bloomington, 47405. William R Cagle, Librn
Notes: The Lilly Library collection of incunables (books printed before January 1501) now numbers over 700 titles and is being added to on a selective basis, primarily in the major works of the humanities and sciences. Presses from the sixteenth century to the present are well represented, and to aid the user there is a separate printers and presses file which will lead to the major books of all periods from Gutenberg to Grabhorn. It is a selective rather than a comprehensive collection.

MO —WASHINGTON UNIVERSITY, Libraries, Special Collections Dept, Campus Box 1061, St Louis, 63130.
Notes: The Ira Adler Collection of the noted bookman incl his collection of mss, autographs, and correspondence of 19th and 20th century literary and historical figures.

NY —MANHASSET PUBLIC LIBRARY, 30 Onderdonk Ave, Manhasset, 11030. Sylvia Levin, Dir
Holdings: Vols 400
Notes: A checklist of the collection is available.

NY —GRADUATE CENTER OF THE CITY UNIVERSITY OF NEW YORK, William H and Gwynne K Crouse Library for Publishing Arts, 33 W 42 St, New York, 10036. Alfred H Lane, Dir
Notes: Recently established and still growing, but intended to become the authoritative source of materials in the field, of particular value in research about the publishing industry. Open to staff members of publishing houses, students, scholars, authors, printers, and booksellers. Primarily 20th century materials, and particularly useful for research on technical, financial, and historical matters. Much on the history of individual houses, economics of authorship; marketing and distribution of books; etc.

NY —GROLIER CLUB OF NEW YORK LIBRARY, 47 E 60 St, New York, 10022. Robert Nikirk, Librn
Notes: Subject strength.

OK —UNIVERSITY OF TULSA, McFarlin Library, Dept of Rare Books and Special Collections, 600 S College, Tulsa, 74104. David Farmer, Dir; Toby Murray, Archivist; Caroline Swinson, Cur of Manuscripts & Art
Holdings: Vols 2500
Notes: The only known extant lending library from the 19th century. It was formed by British subjects in Oporto, Portugal between 1820-1890. 70 percent not in Sadlier.

PA —FREE LIBRARY OF PHILADELPHIA, Rare Book Dept, Logan Sq, Philadelphia, 19103. Marie E Korey, Rare Book Librn
Holdings: Cat Mss Pix
Notes: The A Edward Newton Collection of his own writings and publications including 350 books, periodicals, proof sheets, manuscripts, autograph letters, association copies and memorabilia. The gift of Swift Newton.

SC —WOFFORD COLLEGE, Sandor Teszler Library, N Church St, Spartanburg, 29301. Frank J Anderson, Librn
Holdings: Vols (500) Cat
Budget: ($500)
Notes: Books about the history and practice of printing, hand papermaking, bookbinding, book collecting, fine press and private press books used in conjunction with instruction at the Wofford Library Press, an experimental and bibliographic press which has been in operation since 1969. Collection contains materials on printmaking methods and related graphic arts.

ON —UNIVERSITY OF WESTERN ONTARIO, Schoool of Library and Information Science, Library, London, N6G 1H1, Can. Victoria Ripley, Librn
Holdings: Vols (50,000)
Notes: Auction and antiquarian booksellers' catalogs from Canadian, American and European firms, some dating back to the 18th century. A special strength is 19th and early 20th century American booksellers' catalogs, recently augmented by a collection of pre-1920 catalogs formed by the late H O Teisberg. Current emphasis is on Canadian catalogs.

BOOK DESIGN

CT —TRINITY COLLEGE LIBRARY, Watkinson Library, 300 Summit St, Hartford, 06106. Jeffrey Kaimowitz, Cur
Holdings: Cat Pix
Notes: Incl Trumbull-Prime Collection of early illustrated books; also material on all aspects of book design.

IL —CHICAGO PUBLIC LIBRARY, Special Collections Div, Cultural Center, 78 E Washington St, Chicago, 60602. Laura Linard, Cur
Holdings: Vols (1000) Cat
Notes: A general collection on the history of typography, including a specimen collection of works printed before 1700, books about books, private press productions (primarily Chicago), limited editions, illustrated and extra-illustrated books and fine bindings. Outstanding items described in *Treasures of The Chicago Public Library,* compiled by Thomas A Orlando and Marie Gecik, 1977, pp 6-29.

IL —NEWBERRY LIBRARY, 60 W Walton St, Chicago, 60610. Diana Haskell, Cur of Modern Mss
Holdings: Cat Mss
See also entry under Printing - History.

IN —PURDUE UNIVERSITY LIBRARIES, Special Collections Dept, West Lafayette, 47907. Keith Dowden, Asst Dir, Special Collections
Holdings: Vols 925 Cat Mss Pix
Notes: Bruce Rogers Collection. Incl book design examples and books about fine printing. The nucleus of the collection of Bruce Rogers' own collection left to his alma mater, Purdue University. Some unique material.

ME —BOWDOIN COLLEGE, Library, Brunswick, 04011. Dianne M Gutscher, Cur of Special Collections
Holdings: Vols
Notes: The Frederic Wilson Main Collection contains several hundred books, pamphlets, and clippings relating to the art of printing and bookmaking. Most major contemporary presses are represented, and it incl examples of the typographic work of Bruce Rogers, Frederic W Goudy, Daniel Berkeley Updike, and Rudolph Ruzicka, to mention only a few.

†MD —UNIVERSITY OF MARYLAND, Library, R D Remley Collection, College Park, 20742. Donald Farren, Cur Rare Books
Holdings: Vols (2000) Cat
Notes: *Exempla* and secondary works in the areas of typography, calligraphy, book design, book illustration, the history of books, and of publishing, etc. Catalog entries for designers, printing types, private presses, etc.

NJ —PRINCETON UNIVERSITY, Library, Graphic Arts Collection, Princeton, 08540. Dale Roylance, Cur
Notes: Sinclair Hamilton Collection. One of

BOOK DESIGN (cont.)

the largest collections of American Illustrated Books in the US. 2 vols published; catalog available. Also, large collection of illustrated books of all countries, for all periods.

NY —COLUMBIA UNIVERSITY LIBRARIES, Rare Book & Manuscript Library, 801 Butler Library, 535 W 114 St, New York, 10027. Kenneth A Lohf, Librn
Holdings: Vols (15,000) Cat
Notes: Incl allied crafts. Book arts, graphic arts and typographic libraries. Restricted use: noncirculating.

†NY —COLUMBIA UNIVERSITY LIBRARIES, Butler Library, Rare Book and Manuscript Library, 535 W 114 St, New York, 10027.
Notes: More than 1,000 examples of the books designed by Ernst Reichl from the 1930s to the 1970s. Each volume incl his handwritten notes giving details on the binding and design and the problems he encountered. Also copies of Reichl's own writings, two early diaries and two scrapbooks.

NY —GRADUATE CENTER OF THE CITY UNIVERSITY OF NEW YORK, William H and Gwynne K Crouse Library for Publishing Arts, 33 W 42 St, New York, 10036. Alfred H Lane, Dir
Notes: Recently established and still growing, but intended to become the authoritative source of materials in the field, of particular value in research about the publishing industry. Open to staff members of publishing houses, students, scholars, authors, printers, and booksellers. Primarily 20th century materials, and particularly useful for research on technical, financial, and historical matters. Much on the history of individual houses, economics of authorship; marketing and distribution of books; etc.

NY —GROLIER CLUB OF NEW YORK LIBRARY, 47 E 60 St, New York, 10022. Robert Nikirk, Librn
Notes: Subject strength.

NY —VISUAL STUDIES WORKSHOP, Research Center, 31 Prince St, Rochester, 14607. Linn Underhill, Coordr; Robert Bretz, Librn
Holdings: Vols (8000) Cat Pix Slides Audiotapes Videotapes
Notes: Strong emphasis on photography (over 1,000,000 pictures) and the photographic arts in many subject areas incl in this volume. Heavy emphasis on early photographic processes and collections of examples of them. Also collections of individual photographers' works.

NC —UNIVERSITY OF NORTH CAROLINA, GREENSBORO, Walter Clinton Jackson Library, Special Collections Dept, 1000 Spring Garden St, Greensboro, 27412. Emilie W Mills, Librn
Holdings: Vols 1000 Cat
Notes: Examples of American trade bindings from the early 19th century up to including work of artists Margaret Armstrong, Will Bradley, Charles Buckles Falls, T B Meteyard, Amy Richards, Bruce Rodgers, Amy Sacker and the work of the Decorative Designers group.

WA —UNIVERSITY OF WASHINGTON LIBRARIES, Suzzallo Library, Special Collections Division, Rare Book Collection, FM-25, Seattle, 98195. Gary Menges, Coordinator for Special Collections
Notes: Printing history, including early printed books and modern fine printing; book arts, including papermaking, decorated papers, bookbinding, book design, and artist's books; American literature, 19th century includes: Stephen Crane, Ralph Waldo Emerson, Nathaniel Hawthorne, Henry James, Henry Wadsworth Longfellow, Herman Melville, Frank Norris, Harriet Beecher Stowe and Walt Whitman and 20th century includes: Theodore Roethke; illustrated books, including emblem books, historical children's illustration, books illustrated with prints, and artist's books; costume history; voyages and travels; preservation of library materials.

ON —UNIVERSITY OF TORONTO, Massey College, Robertson Davies Library, 4 Devonshire Place, Toronto, M5S 2E1, Can. Desmond G Neill, Librn
Holdings: Vols (12,000) Cat Mss Microforms
Notes: Library contains Bibliography Room (11 hand presses, type and equipment) and Papermaking Room. Book collections incl Ruari McLean Collection of 19th-century books on, and representative of, color printing (approx 4300 items).

BOOK DESIGN, CZECH

IL —UNIVERSITY OF ILLINOIS, URBANA/CHAMPAIGN, Slavic and East European Library, Urbana, 61801. Marianna Tax Choldin, Head
Holdings: Vols (35,000) Cat
Notes: Extensive coverage.

BOOK ILLUSTRATION see Illustration of Books

BOOK JACKETS

IL —CENTER FOR RESEARCH LIBRARIES, 6050 S Kenwood Ave, Chicago, 60637. Donald B Simpson, Dir; Esther Smith, Collection Development Librn
Holdings: Vols 45,000 Uncat
Notes: Fairly comprehensive collection of books for children and juveniles published in US since 1950, and a few earlier titles. Most retain their original dust jackets.

MA —HARVARD UNIVERSITY, Harvard College Library, Fine Arts Library, Fogg Museum, 32 Quincy St, Cambridge, 02138. Wolfgang M Freitag, Librn
Holdings: Cat
Notes: See *Fine Arts Library Newsletter*, March 1970.

NY —GRADUATE CENTER OF THE CITY UNIVERSITY OF NEW YORK, William H and Gwynne K Crouse Library for Publishing Arts, 33 W 42 St, New York, 10036. Alfred H Lane, Dir
Notes: Recently established and still growing, but intended to become the authoritative source of materials in the field, of particular value in research about the publishing industry. Open to staff members of publishing houses, students, scholars, authors, printers, and booksellers. Primarily 20th century materials, and particularly useful for research on technical, financial, and historical matters. Much on the history of individual houses, economics of authorship; marketing and distribution of books; etc.

BOOK MATCH COVERS see Matchcovers

BOOK OF COMMON PRAYER

CT —YALE UNIVERSITY, Box 1603A, Yale Station, New Haven, 06520.

MA —EPISCOPAL DIOCESE OF MASSACHUSETTS, Diocesan Library, 1 Joy St, Boston, 02108. Mark J Duffy, Archivist; Margaret A Dempsey, Asst Archivist
Holdings: Mss Pix
Budget: $37,000
Notes: Official material of the Diocese of Massachusetts, incl parish histories, biographies and writings of bishops and clergymen; prayer books and hymnals of the American Church; Americana; colonial Church histories; materials relating to the Society for the Propagation of the Gospel (SPG); 18th and 19th century pamphlets.

NJ —DREW UNIVERSITY, Library, Madison, 07940. Caroline Coughlin, Assoc Dir
Notes: The Maser Collection of the *Book of Common Prayer*. Incl 152 versions, ranging from a 1522 *Psalter and Hymnal of the Sarum Use* to the 1977 version of the prayer book of the Protestant Episcopal Church of the USA.

NY —GENERAL THEOLOGICAL SEMINARY, Saint Marks Library, 175 Ninth Ave, New York, 10011. David Green, Dir
Holdings: Vols (200,000) Cat
Notes: Extensive collection.

BOOK-OF-THE-MONTH CLUB

DC —LIBRARY OF CONGRESS, Washington, 20540.
Holdings: Cat Mss Pix
Notes: Book-of-the-Month Club records, incl official correspondence and readers' reports. See *LC Information Bulletin*, 25 May 1964, pp 232-233.

BOOK PUBLISHING INDUSTRY see Publishers and Publishing

BOOK REPAIRING see Books—Conservation and Restoration

BOOK TRADE see Publishers and Publishing

BOOKBINDING AND BOOKBINDERS

CA —SAINT JOHN'S SEMINARY, Edward Laurence Doheny Memorial Library, The Estelle Doheny Collection, 5012 E Seminary Rd, Camarillo, 93010. Rita S Faulders, Cur

CA —CLAREMONT COLLEGES, Ella Strong Denison Library, Scripps College, Claremont, 91711. Judy Harvey Sahak, Librn
Holdings: Vols (10,000) Cat Mss Pix
Notes: Emphasizes the history of the book and fine printing; includes illuninated manuscripts, incunabula, fine bindings, representative examples of modern fine presses, first editions, and literary ALS.

CA —CALIFORNIA STATE UNIVERSITY, FULLERTON, Library, Box 4150, Fullerton, 92634. Linda Herman, Special Collections Librn
Holdings: Vols (6000) Uncat
Notes: History of bookbinding, with examples from 15th century to date and a strong emphasis on American trade cloth bindings, including those by Margaret Armstrong.

CA —UNIVERSITY OF CALIFORNIA, LOS ANGELES, Research Library, Dept of Special Collections, 405 Hilgard Ave, Los Angeles, 90024. Edward Shreeves, Chairman, Bibliographers Group; David S Zeidberg, Head
Holdings: Vols 15,000
Notes: Incl examples of French Romantic bindings, English 19th century trade bindings; 425 bindings designed by Margaret Armstrong, correspondence concerning and more than 100 examples of Decorative Designers bindings.

CA —MILLS COLLEGE LIBRARY, Oakland, 94613. Steven P Pandolfo, Librn
Holdings: Vols 400 Cat
Notes: Works on the history and technique of hand bookbinding. Examples of fine binding, 17th-20th centuries. Florence Walter Studio of Hand Bookbinding incl equipment and fine tools.

CA —SAN DIEGO PUBLIC LIBRARY, Wangenheim Rm, 820 E St, San Diego, 92101. Eileen Boyle, Librn
Holdings: Vols (7500)
Notes: A collection on the history of the book and the development of printing with specimens ranging from Babylonian tablets to cassettes.

CA —SAN DIEGO STATE UNIVERSITY, Malcolm A Love Library, 5300 Campanile Dr, San Diego, 92182. D Dickinson, Univ Librn; Don L Bosseau, Dir
Holdings: 500 Items
Notes: Wallace Pearce history of Book Binding Collection. Includes rarities, fine printing examples of all phases of book production design, publiction and preservation.

CA —HUNTINGTON LIBRARY, Art Gallery & Botanical Gardens, 1151 Oxford Rd, San Marino, 91108. Robert L Middlekauff, Dir; Daniel H Woodward, Librn
Holdings: Mss Maps Pix Slides Microforms
Notes: Approx 350,000 rare books, 250,000 reference books, manuscript collection of nearly 2,500,000 pieces and between 200, 000 and 300,000 prints, rare photographs and other related materials. The fullest

BOOKBINDING AND BOOKBINDERS (cont.)

available survey is now *Guide to Literary Manuscripts in the Huntington Library,* a 539-page handlist published by the Library in 1979.

CA —STANFORD UNIVERSITY LIBRARIES, Cecil H Green Library, Stanford, 94305. Michael T Ryan, Cur
Holdings: Vols (12,000) Cat
Notes: The Morgan A & Aline D Gunst Memorial Library. The book arts in every century with some of the best examples. Strong collection of examples of California printers and graphic artists. Complete or nearly complete collections of works by the Kelmscott, Doves, Ashendene, Colt, Grabhorn, and Grabhorn-Hoyem presses.

CT —TRINITY COLLEGE LIBRARY, Watkinson Library, 300 Summit St, Hartford, 06106. Jeffrey Kaimowitz, Cur
Holdings: Cat
Notes: Incl the Mrs John G McCarthy Collection.

IL —CHICAGO PUBLIC LIBRARY, Special Collections Div, Cultural Center, 78 E Washington St, Chicago, 60602. Laura Linard, Cur
Holdings: Vols (1000) Cat
Notes: A general collection on the history of typography, including a specimen collection of works printed before 1700, books about books, private press productions (primarily Chicago), limited editions, illustrated and extra-illustrated books and fine bindings. Outstanding items described in *Treasures of The Chicago Public Library,* compiled by Thomas A Orlando and Marie Gecik, 1977, pp 6-29.

IL —DE PAUL UNIVERSITY, Library, 2323 N Seminary, Chicago, 60614. Kathryn De Graff, Special Collections Librn
Holdings: Vols (170)// Uncat
Notes: The Louis Silver Collection. Incl materials describing the history of printing, typography, book binding, book plates, bibliographies, exhibition catalogs, private collections, and subject-related periodicals.

IL —NEWBERRY LIBRARY, John M Wing Foundation on the History of Printing, 60 W Walton St, Chicago, 60610. Diana Haskell, Cur of Modern Mss
Holdings: Vols (30,000) Cat Mss
Budget: ($50,000)
Notes: The collection covers printing and printing history of Western Europe and the Americas from its invention to the present. It is particularly rich in incunabula (about 2000); the works of the great printers, among others Aldus, Bodoni, Baskerville, and Rogers. Bindings by Reichenbach, Devome, Payne, Cobden-Sanderson, Powell, et al. Printed catalog *A Dictionary* Catalogue. (Boston G K Hall, 1961); *Supplements* (1981). Brief descriptions: James M Wells, "The John M Wing Foundation of The Newberry Library," *The Book Collector,* VIII, 2 (Summer 1959), pp 157-162; Lawrence W Towner, *An Uncommon Collection of Uncommon* Collections (Chicago: The Newberry Library, 1977), pp 25-26.

IN —INDIANA UNIVERSITY, Lilly Library, Seventh St, Bloomington, 47405. William R Cagle, Librn
Holdings: // Cat Mss
Notes: 39 British bindings of the 1970s commissioned to show "the range of present activity." Also representative 20th century French and some 19th and 20th century Czech.

KY —UNIVERSITY OF KENTUCKY, Margaret I King Library, Dept of Special Collections, Lexington, 40506. William Marshall, Head
Holdings: Cat Mss Pix Slides Microforms
Notes: Comprehensive collection of books on typography and history of printing; fine press books (incl Lexington imprints); ms books and illumination, paleography; mss of W A Dwiggins (gift of C H Griffith); James Anderson papers; bookbinding; 2 hand-presses and working collection for summer seminars in hand-press printing; bookplates, bookmarks, book jackets, etc.

ME —BOWDOIN COLLEGE, Library, Brunswick, 04011. Dianne M Gutscher, Cur of Special Collections
Holdings: Vols 1200 // Cat
Notes: Susan Dwight Bliss Collection. Housed in a handsome Baroque library, the Bliss Collection contains 1200 volumes relating primarily to the fine arts, French and English history and literature and travel. It is particularly noted for its many examples of fine and elaborate European bindings by such masters as Riviere, Chambolle-Duru, Zaehnsdorf, Michel, Gruel, Bradstreet, Taffin and others.

MA —BOSTON PUBLIC LIBRARY, Print Collection, Dartmouth St at Copley Sq, Boston, 02117. Sinclair H Hitchings, Keeper of Prints
Holdings: Vols (500) Cat
Notes: Fine illustrated books, mainly English, of the 18th, 19th and 20th centuries, containing original prints or photographs. Also, 250 books with fore-edge paintings and books with fine bindings. No photocopying.

†MA —CLARK UNIVERSITY, Robert Hutchings Goddard Library, Worcester, 01610. Dorothy Mosa Kowski, Rare Books Librn
Holdings: Vols Cat Mss
Notes: Rare books, first editions, mss, incunabula (50), bindings, fore-edge paintings.

MI —DETROIT PUBLIC LIBRARY, Rare Books Department, 5201 Woodward Ave, Detroit, 48202.
Holdings: Vols 500 Cat Mss Pix
Notes: Incl fine bindings and some 200 books on the subject of bookbinding as well as specimens. An index of binders represented in the collection is maintained. Restricted use. Reference collection.

NJ —FAIRLEIGH DICKINSON UNIVERSITY, Friendship Library, 285 Madison Ave, Madison, 07940. James Fraser, Library Dir; Renee Weber, Cur
Holdings: Vols 100 Cat Mss Pix
Notes: Books printed and bound by Loyd Haberly; also original drawings and sketches for illustrated bindings and page layouts for various books. Private funds are provided for purchase of books on the subject of Haberly's interests: hand binding and fine printing, not only his own.

NY —GROLIER CLUB OF NEW YORK LIBRARY, 47 E 60 St, New York, 10022. Robert Nikirk, Librn
Notes: Subject strength.

NY —GUILD OF BOOK WORKERS, Library, 521 Fifth Avenue, New York, 10175. Stanley E Cushing, Librn
Holdings: Vols 500 Cat
Notes: History and techniques of hand bookbinding. Library maintained as a service to members of the Guild of Book Workers.

NY —NEW YORK PUBLIC LIBRARY, Spencer Collection, Fifth Ave & 42 St, New York, 10018. Joseph T Rankin, Cur
Holdings: Vols (8000) Cat Mss
Notes: Rare illustrated and illuminated mss and books, in fine bindings, in all languages, of all countries, and of all periods, constituting the development of book illustration and the book arts the world around. See *Dictionary Catalog and Shelf List of the Spencer Collection,* New York Public Library, 1970. 2 vols, $155.

NY —MARGARET WOODBURY STRONG MUSEUM, 1 Manhattan Square, Rochester, 14607.
Holdings: Vols (20,000) Periodicals
Notes: The Margaret Woodbury Strong Museum Library contains a collection of approx 20,000 books, periodicals and ephemera of and concerning the 19th and early 20th centuries. A large part of the library's holdings reflect the interests of Margaret Strong and her family: domestic life and literature of the 19th century and world travel, with particular emphasis on the Orient. The library's resources are available to all visitors for research. Book stacks and rare book storage are not open for browsing and do not circulate, but facilities are provided in reading room for study.

NY —ROCHESTER INSTITUTE OF TECHNOLOGY, Melbert B Cary Jr Graphic Arts Collection, School of Printing, One Lomb Memorial Drive, Rochester, 14623. David Pankow, Cur
Holdings: Vols (11,000) Cat Mss Pix
Notes: Incl the Bernard C Middleton Collection.

NY —UNIVERSITY OF ROCHESTER, Rush Rhees Library, Department of Rare Books and Special Collections, Rochester, 14627. Peter Dzwonkoski, Librn
Holdings: Vols 1000 Cat
Notes: Collection of 19th and early 20th century trade bindings, chiefly in publishers' cloth from the period 1850-1914. No photocopying.

NY —VISUAL STUDIES WORKSHOP, Research Center, 31 Prince St, Rochester, 14607. Linn Underhill, Coordr; Robert Bretz, Librn
Holdings: Vols (8000) Cat Pix Slides Audiotapes Videotapes
Notes: Strong emphasis on photography (over 1,000,000 pictures) and the photographic arts in many subject areas incl in the volume. Heavy emphasis on early photographic processes and collections of examples of them. Also collections of individual photographers' works.

PA —BRYN MAWR COLLEGE, Canaday Library, Bryn Mawr, 19010. James Tanis, Dir
Notes: Frederick E Maser Collection of American book bindings, 1680-1910, and supporting reference materials.

SC —UNIVERSITY OF SOUTH CAROLINA, Thomas Cooper Library, Columbia, 29208. Kenneth E Toombs, Dir of Libraries; Roger Mortimer, Rare Book Librn
Holdings: Vols 1000 Cat
Notes: Collection contains examples of bookmaking for the 15th-20th centuries, especially, noteworthy bindings and fore-edge paintings.

SC —WOFFORD COLLEGE, Sandor Teszler Library, N Church St, Spartanburg, 29301. Frank J Anderson, Librn
Holdings: Vols (500) Cat
Budget: ($500)
Notes: Books about the history and practice of printing, hand papermaking, bookbinding, book collecting, fine press and private press books in conjuction with instruction at the Wofford Library Press, experimental and bibliographic press which has been in operation since 1969. Collection contains materials on printmaking methods and methods and related graphic arts.

TX —ROSENBERG LIBRARY, Fox Rare Book Room, 2310 Sealy Ave, Galveston, 77550. Fernando Basilza, Rare Book Librn
Holdings: Vols (2000) Cat Mss Pix
Notes: The Col Milo Pitcher Fox and Agnes Peel Fox Rare Book Room contains 2000 Vols incunabula, first printings, and modern fine printing. Incl clay tablets. horn books, parchment material, illuminated books and mss, fine printing (principally 15th-18th centuries), fine binding, fore-edge paintings, etc.

VA —UNIVERSITY OF VIRGINIA, Alderman Library, Rare Book Dept, Charlottesville, 22901. Julius P Barclay, Cur
Notes: The Oscar Ogg Collection of Book Arts covers calligraphy, letterforms, typography, printing, and graphic arts. Contains early writing books and printed works, as well as modern manuals and other works on printing, publishing, and promotion through graphic arts. The Dept also has the Edward L Stone Collection of Printing Specimens, 3000 items. Contains materials tracing the history of printing, inks, binding styles and materials, types.

WA —UNIVERSITY OF WASHINGTON LIBRARIES, Suzzallo Library, Special Collections Division, Rare Book Collection, FM-25, Seattle, 98195. Gary Menges, Coordinator for Special Collections
Holdings: Vols (12,000) Cat Maps
Notes: American, British, French, German and Italian books printed before 1800, chiefly in the fields of history and literature. Fine bindings and illustrated works are represented. Incl incunabula, emblemata, history of travel, and first editions of the works of major poets; Spenser, Blake,

BOOKBINDING AND BOOKBINDERS (cont.)

Whitman, Yeates, Roethke, etc. Material on marbling also.

NS —DALHOUSIE UNIVERSITY LIBRARY, Halifax, B3H 4H8, Can.
Holdings: Vols 127 Uncat
Notes: The Cockerell Collection of Fine Bindings is a representative collection of fine bindings from the 15th to 19th century assembled by Douglas Cockerell, famous English bookbinder. Most of the bindings are done in calf, but there are also examples of morroco, pigskin, sheepskin, vellum and fishskin. English, Scottish, French and Italian designs are represented; ornamentation is by blind and gold tooling, and with wrought silver or brass clasps and decorations. Restricted to reference use.

NS —MOUNT SAINT VINCENT UNIVERSITY, Library, 166 Bedford Hwy, Halifax, B3M 2J6, Can. Lucian Bianchini, University Librn
Holdings: Vols 7000 Cat
Budget: ($125,000)
Notes: The MacDonald Collection consists of 19th and 20th century English and American literature, fine bindings, a few examples of fore-edge painting, limited editions, first editions, and autographed copies.

ON —UNIVERSITY OF TORONTO, Thomas Fisher Rare Book Library, 120 Saint George St, Toronto, M5S 1A5, Can. Richard G Landon, Head
Holdings: Vols 25 Cat
Notes: Birdsall Collection of about 3000 finishing tools acquired from the British firm, Birdsall & Son, Northampton, England. Earliest tools date back to the 18th century; majority are 19th century. Includes small number of volumes bound by the firm; also manufacturers' catalogues of finishing tools. Collection described in Evans, E and R Grover, *The Birdsall Collection of Bookbinders' Finishing Tools* (Toronto, University of Toronto Library, 1972). Pantazzi Collection, named for donor Sybille Pantazzi, Librn, Art Gallery of Ontario. Small collection of signed English publishers' bindings, 1846-1880, chiefly designed by John Leighton.

BOOKBINDING AND BOOKBINDERS, ISLAMIC

IL —ORIENTAL INSTITUTE, 1155 E 58th St, Chicago, 60637. John Larsen, Archivist
Notes: The Bernhard Moritz Collection. Fine examples of bindings as well as of Islamic calligraphy and writing materials--papyrus, parchment, papers, etc. Extensive collection is also in the Beatty Library in Dublin, Ireland; Victoria and Albert Museum in London; Libraries in East and West Germany.

BOOKKEEPING—HISTORY

IN —PURDUE UNIVERSITY LIBRARIES, Graduate School of Management, Krannert Library, West Lafayette, 47907. Gordon Law, Librn
Notes: An important resource at the Krannert Library is its Special Collection of Business and Economics, consisting of some 8000 rare pre-20th century strengths in books, journals, tracts and pamphlets covering primarily the early literature of economic thought and business practices in America and abroad, 1500-1870. A catalog was issued in 1979.

MA —HARVARD UNIVERSITY, Baker Library of the Graduate School of Business Administration, Kress Library of Business and Economics, Soldiers Field, Boston, 02163. Ruth E Rogers, Cur
Holdings: Cat Mss
Notes: For 16th-century materials, see *Business History Review,* XXXIV (1960): pp 327-334.

NY —SAINT JOHN'S UNIVERSITY, Special Collections Dept, Grand Central & Utopia Pkwys, Jamaica, 11439. Szilvia E Szmuk, Librn
Holdings: Vols 160 // Cat
Notes: The Joseph C Myer Collection consists of books, issues of journals, and ledgers from the early 16th through the early 20th century. A very large part of the collection is 17th and 18th century French, English, and German titles on methods of bookkeeping and business practices. Many of these volumes are in fine and unusual bindings which have been recently restored. Nophotocopying.

BOOKMARKS

KY —UNIVERSITY OF KENTUCKY, Margaret I King Library, Dept of Special Collections, Lexington, 40506. William Marshall, Head
Holdings: Cat Mss Pix Slides Microforms
Notes: Comprehensive collection of books on typography and history of printing; fine press books (incl Lexington imprints); ms books and illumination, paleography; mss of W A Dwiggins (gift of C H Griffith); James Anderson papers; bookbinding; 2 hand-presses and working collection for summer seminars in hand-press printing; bookplates, bookmarks, book jackets. etc.

BOOKPLATES

CA —CLAREMONT COLLEGES, Ella Strong Denison Library, Scripps College, Claremont, 91711. Judy Harvey Sahak, Librn
Holdings: 50 Cat
Notes: About 5000 examples of bookplates, the Louise Seymour Jones Collections. Includes her papers.

CA —CLAREMONT COLLEGES, Honnold Library, Ninth & Dartmouth, Claremont, 91711. Tania Rizzo, Special Collections Dept Head
Holdings: Vols 164 Cat Periodicals
Notes: Charles R and Hanna F Flack Collection of and about bookplates and related arts. Over 1000 mounted bookplates. Restricted use.

CA —UNIVERSITY OF CALIFORNIA, LOS ANGELES, Research Library, Dept of Special Collections, 405 Hilgard Ave, Los Angeles, 90024. Edward Shreeves, Chairman, Bibliographers Group; David S Zeidberg, Head
Holdings: Vols 200
Notes: 200 books about bookplates; 10,000 examples in various collections.

CA —UNIVERSITY OF SAN FRANCISCO, Richard A Gleeson Library, The Countess Bernardine Murphy Donohue Rare Book Room, San Francisco, 94117. D Steven Corey, Special Collections Librn
Holdings: Vols 35
Notes: The Louise E Winterburn collection of royal bookplates plus other vols of bookplates arranged by subject.

CA —UNIVERSITY OF CALIFORNIA, SANTA BARBARA, Library, Dept of Special Collections, Santa Barbara, 93106. Christian F Brun, Head
Holdings: Vols 150 Cat Pix
Notes: Special collections of 18th-10th century bookplates.

CT —YALE UNIVERSITY, Box 1603A, Yale Station, New Haven, 06520.

CT —UNIVERSITY OF CONNECTICUT, Library, Storrs, 06268. R H Schimmelpfeng, Dir of Special Collections
Holdings: Cat Mss Pix
Notes: Consists of Clare Ryan Talbot, Mary Alice Ercolini, and Major Weaver-Hazelton collections of books, periodicals, and mounted specimens of bookplates.

IL —DE PAUL UNIVERSITY, Library, 2323 N Seminary, Chicago, 60614. Kathryn De Graff, Special Collections Librn
Holdings: Vols (170)// Uncat
Notes: The Louis Silver Collection. Incl materials describing the history of printing, typography, book binding, book plates, bibliographies, exhibition catalogs, private collections, and subject-related periodicals.

IL —MILLIKIN UNIVERSITY, Staley Library, 1184 W Main St, Decatur, 62522. Charles E Hale, Librn
Holdings: Vols 100 Uncat
Notes: In addition, over 5000 bookplates.

KY —UNIVERSITY OF KENTUCKY, Margaret I King Library, Dept of Special Collections, Lexington, 40506. William Marshall, Head
Holdings: Cat Mss Pix Slides Microforms
Notes: Comprehensive collection of books on typography and history of printing; fine press books (incl Lexington imprints); ms books and illunination, paleography; mss of W A Dwiggins (gift of C H Griffith); James Anderson papers; bookbinding; 2 hand-presses and working collection for summer seminars in hand-press printing; bookplates, bookmarks, book jackets, etc.

KY —UNIVERSITY OF LOUISVILLE, Allen R Hite Art Institute, Library, Belknap Campus, Louisville, 40292. Gail Gilbert, Librn
Holdings: Vols (40,000) Cat Pix
Budget: ($29,000)
Notes: Incl books on art, architecture, landscape architecture and gardening, prints, printing, illustrated books and brass rubbings. Library subscribes to 200 periodical titles in these and other areas. Collection circulates to faculty and staff only, with same restrictions placed on interlibrary loan. Library also has collections of bookplates, posters, original prints, hand-made Christmas cards and clippings file filling 56 VF drawers.

LA —TULANE UNIVERSITY, Howard-Tilton Memorial Library, Special Collections Div, 7001 Freret St, New Orleans, 70118. Wilbur E Meneray, Librn
Holdings: Vols 350
Notes: Major collection, incl 11,000 bookplates.

MA —AMERICAN ANTIQUARIAN SOCIETY LIBRARY, 185 Salisbury St, Worcester, 01609. Marcus A McCorison, Dir & Librn
Holdings: Cat
Notes: The largest and choicest collection anywhere , of which 3000 date between 1674 and 1830.

MI —UNIVERSITY OF MICHIGAN, Library, Dept of Rare Books & Special Collections, Ann Arbor, 48109. Robert J Starring, Head
Holdings: Cat Pix
Notes: In addition to 3967 bookplates on mounts, there are over 7000 catalog cards indexing bookplates in books.

MI —DETROIT PUBLIC LIBRARY, Rare Books Department, 5201 Woodward Ave, Detroit, 48202.
Holdings: Vols 190 Cat
Notes: 9000 plates and 190 books on ex-libris. Restricted use. Reference collection.

NH —DARTMOUTH COLLEGE, Baker Memorial Library, Hanover, 03755.
Holdings: Uncat
Notes: Noncirculating.

NJ —MONTCLAIR ART MUSEUM LIBRARY, 3 South Mountain Ave, PO Box 1582, Montclair, 07042. Edith A Rights, Librn
Holdings: Vols (10,000) Cat Pix Slides Audiotapes
Budget: ($3500)

NJ —RUTGERS, THE STATE UNIVERSITY OF NEW JERSEY, Alexander Library, Special Collections and Archives, College Ave & Huntington St, New Brunswick, 08903. Ronald L Becker, Cur of Manuscripts and Rare Books
Holdings: Uncat
Notes: Bookplates date from the 18th through the 20th century; about 4000 examples. There is also some literature on the subject.

NJ —PRINCETON UNIVERSITY, Library, Graphic Arts Collection, Princeton, 08540. Dale Roylance, Cur
Holdings: Vols 373
Notes: Also a collection of 12,000 individual bookplates.

NY —NEW YORK STATE LIBRARY, State Education Bldg Annex, Washington Ave, Albany, 12224.
Holdings: Vols 260
Notes: Over 11,000 bookplates, and 260 reference books on ex-libris.

NY —COLUMBIA UNIVERSITY LIBRARIES, Rare Book & Manuscript Library, 801 Butler Library, 535 W 114 St,

BOOKPLATES (cont.)

New York, 10027. Kenneth A Lohf, Librn
Notes: 23,600 American and foreign bookplates, incl Columbia University Association bookplates and groups of Libraries', Societies' and Children's plates. 18th through 20th century.

NY —GROLIER CLUB OF NEW YORK LIBRARY, 47 E 60 St, New York, 10022. Robert Nikirk, Librn
Notes: Subject strength.

NY —UNIVERSITY OF ROCHESTER, Rush Rhees Library, Department of Rare Books and Special Collections, Rochester, 14627. Peter Dzwonkoski, Librn
Holdings: Vols 20,000 Cat
Notes: Three collections formed by Donald Bean Gilchrist, Maude Motley, and Louis J Bailey. Includes personal as well as institutional plates; also books on bookplates.

OH —KENT STATE UNIVERSITY, Libraries, Dept of Special Collections, Kent, 44242. Dean H Keller, Cur
Holdings: Vols 160 Cat
Notes: Approx 30,000 bookplates.

PA —FREE LIBRARY OF PHILADELPHIA, Rare Book Dept, Logan Sq, Philadelphia, 19103. Marie E Korey, Rare Book Librn
Holdings: Uncat
Notes: The James Somers Smith Collection of 2400 institutional, armorial, and pictorial bookplates.

PA —EASTERN COLLEGE, Frank Warner Memorial Library, Saint Davids, 19087. James L Sauer, Librn
Holdings: Uncat Mss Pix
Notes: The Harry C Goebel Collection. Incl Bruce Rogers printings (over 460); press books (about 350); oriental art (over 250); bookplates (with a separate collection of an almost complete set of bookplates designed by Edwin Davis French); Christmas Books; art and graphic arts (incl the French Graphic Arts Collection of Adolph DeMilly); first editions of Christopher Morley; Print Collection (1315 prints); Oriental art realia and artifacts.

RI —BROWN UNIVERSITY, John Hay Library, 20 Prospect St, Providence, 02912. Mark N Brown, Cur Mss
Holdings: / / Uncat
Notes: Sonia J Lustig Collection of some 5000 individual and institutional bookplates dating from 17th to 20th century; indexed by owner and designer.

TX —FORT WORTH PUBLIC LIBRARY, Arts Division, 300 Taylor St, Fort Worth, 76102. Heather Gobel, Head
Holdings: Vols 35 Cat
Notes: Nucleus collection (800 bookplates) received as a gift to the Fort Worth Public Library Arts Division in 1957 from the late Mrs Nancy Taylor, Fort Worth Rare Book Dealer. Designs range from those used over 300 years ago in the 1650's to the modern. In addition to individual plates, books containing designs include Italian, German, French, British, & American.

WI —UNIVERSITY OF WISCONSIN, MADISON, Memorial Library, Rare Books Collection, 728 State St, Madison, 53706. Gretchen Lagana, Cur
Holdings: / /
Notes: Doane-Davidson Bookplate Collection. This collection of approximately 10,000 bookplates is composed of two collections originally belonging to Gilbert H Doane and Flora Davidson. There are extensive separate collections of University of Wisconsin libraries bookplates, medical, animal, and punning plates, as well as the plates of two Boston engravers: Sidney Lawton Smith and Joseph Winfield Spenceley. The collection is indexed. Housed in the Dept of Rare Books and Special Collections.

BOOKPLATES, JEWISH

OH —HEBREW UNION COLLEGE-JEWISH INSTITUTE OF RELIGION, Klau Library, 3101 Clifton Ave, Cincinnati, 45220. David J Gilner, Reference Librn
Notes: Incl the Philip Goodman Collection of some 7000 bookplates of Jewish interest. Description in: *College and Research* Libraries, no 5, May 1969, p 166.

BOOKPLATES, PHYSICIANS'

CT —YALE UNIVERSITY, Medical Historical Library, 333 Cedar St, New Haven, 06510. Ferenc A Gyorgyey, Librn
Holdings: Uncat
Notes: About 3000 bookplates. Many of medical iconography. The Warren S Lowenhaupt Collection.

FL —UNIVERSITY OF MIAMI, School of Medicine, Louis Calder Memorial Library, PO Box 520875, Miami, 33152. Henry L Lemkau, Jr, Dir
Holdings: Vols (127,843) Cat Mss Maps Pix Slides
Budget: ($915,000)
Notes: Ophthalmology Branch Library of 6969 vols incl in total count; University of Miami School of Medicine dissertations; 209 medical medallions; physicians' bookplates; postage stamps with medical themes.

MN —MAYO MEDICAL LIBRARY, History of Medicine Collection, Rochester, 55905. Nancy R Hensel, Librn
Holdings: Pix
Notes: Over 300 bookplates of physicians and medical institutions. Listed. Collection described: Mann, Ruth J: "Of bookplates, books, and their owners." *Mayo Clin Proc* 46:358-360, May 1971.

BOOKS—APPRAISAL see Bibliography—Best Books; Literature—History and Criticism

BOOKS—CARE see Books—Conservation and Restoration

BOOKS—CENSORSHIP see Censorship

BOOKS—CONSERVATION AND RESTORATION

IL —NEWBERRY LIBRARY, 60 W Walton St, Chicago, 60610. Bonnie Jo Cullison, Preservation Librn
Holdings: Vols 700 Cat Slides
Budget: $350
Notes: Book and ms conservation and restoration; also 1500 slides and 1300 reports.

†NY —COLUMBIA UNIVERSITY LIBRARIES, Butler Library, Rare Book and Manuscript Library, 535 W 114 St, New York, 10027.
Notes: Files relating to the American Library Association's Special Committee to Aid Italian Libraries' assistance to Italian libraries to help restore books, mss and other library materials after the 1966 floods in Florence.

WA —UNIVERSITY OF WASHINGTON LIBRARIES, Suzzallo Library, Special Collections Division, Rare Book Collection, FM-25, Seattle, 98195. Gary Menges, Coordinator for Special Collections
Notes: Printing history, including early printed books and modern fine printing; book arts, including papermaking, decorated papers, bookbinding, book design, and artist's books; American literature, 19th century includes: Stephen Crane, Ralph Waldo Emerson, Nathaniel Hawthorne, Henry James, Henry Wadsworth Longfellow, Herman Melville, Frank Norris, Harriet Beecher Stowe and Walt Whitman and 20th century includes: Theodore Roethke; illustrated books, including emblem books, historical children's illustration, books illustrated with prints, and artist's books; costume history; voyages and travels; preservation of library materials.

ON —UNIVERSITY OF WESTERN ONTARIO, Schoool of Library and Information Science, Library, London, N6G 1H1, Can. Victoria Ripley, Librn
Holdings: Vols (50,000)
Notes: Auction and antiquarian booksellers' catalogs from Canadian, American and European firms, some dating back to the 18th century. A special strength is 19th and early 20th century American booksellers' catalogs, recently augmented by a collection of pre-1920 catalogs formed by the late H O Teisberg. Current emphasis is on Canadian catalogs.

BOOKS—LIMITED EDITIONS see Bibliography—Limited Editions

BOOKS—PRESERVATION, REPAIRING, RESTORATION see Books—Conservation and Restoration

BOOKS—REVIEWS—INDEXES

MI —GALE RESEARCH CO, Book Tower, Detroit, 48226. Annie Brewer, Librn
Holdings: Vols (65,000) Cat
Notes: Large collection of reference materials, incl computerized files used in the preparation of familiar contemporary reference books and guides to special fields.

BOOKS, BEST see Bibliography—Best Books

BOOKS, EMBOSSED see Embossed Books

BOOKS, ILLUSTRATED see Illustrated Books

BOOKS, TALKING see Talking Books

BOOKS ABOUT BOOKS

†AL —UNIVERSITY OF ALABAMA, Amelia Gayle Gorgas Library, PO Box S, University, 35486.
Notes: A rare, complete set of the Armed Services Editions of paperbacks issued for use of American forces overseas in World War II.

CA —UNIVERSITY OF CALIFORNIA, BERKELEY, Humanities-Social Sciences Libraries, Library School Library, 2 South Hall, Berkeley, 94720. Virginia Pratt, Head
Holdings: Vols (41,500) Cat Microforms
Notes: Research collection with special strengths in general library science; history of libraries; history of printing and book arts, and publishing; information systems and services; history, criticism, and bibliography of children's literature. The collections in printing and the book arts are complemented by significant holdings both in the Main Library and in the Bancroft Library. Incl collection of 5000 pamphlets.

CA —CLAREMONT COLLEGES, Ella Strong Denison Library, Scripps College, Claremont, 91711. Judy Harvey Sahak, Librn
Holdings: Vols (10,000) Cat Mss Pix
Notes: Emphasizes the history of the book and fine printing; includes illuminated manuscripts, incuabula, fine bindings, representative examples of modern fine presses, first editions, and literary ALS.

CA —CALIFORNIA STATE UNIVERSITY, FULLERTON, Library, Box 4150, Fullerton, 92634. Linda Herman, Special Collections Librn
Holdings: Vols (4600) Cat
Notes: Press books and fine printing of the 20th century incl vols from the Grabhorn Press of San Francisco (Dr William B Langsdorf Anniversary Collection; 613 vols) and the Fine Arts Press of Santa Ana, Calif (67 vols). It is supplemented by a group of related collections on printing, binding, and book history reference, which incl representative examples of most modern fine presses.

CA —UNIVERSITY OF CALIFORNIA, SAN DIEGO, Central University Library, Mandeville Dept of Special Collections, La Jolla, 92093. Lynda Corey Claassen, Head
Notes: The Reference Collection: More than 2500 bibliographies guides, and catalogues to rare book and manuscript collections, auction records, histories of book collecting, and important works on the social and technological history of books and printing are included.

BOOKS ABOUT BOOKS (cont.)

CA —UNIVERSITY OF CALIFORNIA, LOS ANGELES, Research Library, Dept of Special Collections, 405 Hilgard Ave, Los Angeles, 90024. Edward Shreeves, Chairman, Bibliographers Group; David S Zeidberg, Head
Holdings: Vols (15,000) Cat
Notes: Includes examples of French Romantic bindings, English 19th century bindings (in the Michael Sadleir Collection of 19th Century English Fiction), a collection of bindings designed by Margaret Armstrong, as well as specimens of fine leather bindings. Restricted use: scholarly research only.

CA —UNIVERSITY OF CALIFORNIA, LOS ANGELES, Research Library, Medieval and Renaissance Collection, 405 Hilgard Ave, Los Angeles, 90024. Edward Shreeves, Chairman, Bibliographers Group; Frances K Zeitlin, Medievan and Renaissance Bibliographer
Notes: Early printing history, catalogs of ms collections. Incorporates the reference library of the antiquarian bookselling firm of Ulrice Hoepli of Milan.

CA —MILLS COLLEGE LIBRARY, Oakland, 94613. Steven P Pandolfo, Librn
Holdings: Vols 1000 Cat
Notes: Books on typography, the history of books and printing, bookbinding and papermaking. Representative examples of fine printing, 15th-20th centuries.

CA —SAN DIEGO PUBLIC LIBRARY, Wangenheim Rm, 820 E St, San Diego, 92101. Eileen Boyle, Librn
Holdings: Vols (7500) Cat
Notes: A collection on the history of the book and the development of printing with specimens ranging from Babylonian tablets to cassettes.

CA —UNIVERSITY OF CALIFORNIA, SANTA BARBARA, Library, Dept of Special Collections, Santa Barbara, 93106. Christian F Brun, Head
Holdings: Vols 11,000 Cat Mss Pix
Notes: Skofield Printers Collection. History of printing, examples of fine printing.

CA —STANFORD UNIVERSITY LIBRARIES, Cecil H Green Library, Stanford, 94305. Michael T Ryan, Cur
Holdings: Vols (12,000) Cat
Notes: The Morgan A & Aline D Gunst Memorial Library. The book arts in every century with some of the best examples. Strong collection of examples of California printers and graphic artists. Complete or nearly complete collections of works by the Kelmscott, Doves, Ashendene, Colt, Grabhorn, and Grabhorn-Hoyem presses.

CA —SOLANO COUNTY LIBRARY, John F Kennedy Library, Donovan J McCune Collection, 505 Santa Clara St, Vallejo, 94590.
Holdings: Vols 850 //
Notes: The Donovan J McCune Collection (3000) vols //.

CT —LEE ASH, (personal collection), 66 Humiston Dr, Bethany, 06525.
Holdings: Mss Maps Pix
Notes: Incl books, letters, ephemera, prints, etc.

CT —TRINITY COLLEGE LIBRARY, Watkinson Library, 300 Summit St, Hartford, 06106. Jeffrey Kaimowitz, Cur
Holdings: Cat Pix
Notes: Incl Trumbull-Prime Collection of early illustrated books; also material on all aspects of book design.

CT —YALE UNIVERSITY, Box 1603A, Yale Station, New Haven, 06520.
Notes: Collection of the arts of the book.

DE —DELAWARE ART MUSEUM, Library, 2301 Kentmere Pkwy, Wilmington, 19806. Anne Hoslam, Librn
Holdings: Vols (25,000) Cat Mss
Notes: The collection is rich in the following subjects: Howard Pyle and his pupils; John Sloan and the eight; history of the book and printing; and English and American illustrated books. There is also a section on contemporary photography. Archival material on Albert Mumford Lindsay, Jerome Myers, Everett Shinn, Gayle Porter Hoskins, Frank Schoonover.

FL —FLORIDA STATE UNIVERSITY, Robert Manning Strozier Library, Special Collections Dept, Tallahassee, 32306. Opal M Free, Head, Special Collections
Holdings: Vols (12,254) Cat
Notes: Cuneiform tablets, ostraka, papyri to illustrate the history of writing, printing, and the book through the ages. Noncirculating. No photocopying.

IL —CHICAGO PUBLIC LIBRARY, Special Collections Div, Cultural Center, 78 E Washington St, Chicago, 60602. Laura Linard, Cur
Holdings: Vols (1000) Cat
Notes: A general collection on the history of typography, including a specimen collection of works printed before 1700, books about books, private press productions (primarily Chicago), limited editions, illustrated and extra-illustrated books and fine bindings. Outstanding items described in *Treasures of The Chicago Public Library,* compiled by Thomas A Orlando and Marie Gecik, 1977, pp 6-29.

IL —DE PAUL UNIVERSITY, Library, 2323 N Seminary, Chicago, 60614. Kathryn De Graff, Special Collections Librn
Holdings: Vols (170)// Uncat
Notes: The Louis Silver Collection. Incl materials describing the history of printing, typography, book binding, book plates, bibliographies, exhibition catalogs, private collections, and subject-related periodicals.

IL —NEWBERRY LIBRARY, John M Wing Foundation on the History of Printing, 60 W Walton St, Chicago, 60610. Diana Haskell, Cur of Modern Mss
Holdings: Vols (30,000) Cat Mss
Budget: ($50,000)
Notes: The collection covers printing and printing history of Western Europe and the Americas from its invention to the present. It is particularly rich in incunabula (about 2000); the works of the great printers, among others Aldus, Bodoni, Baskerville, and Rogers. Printed catalog: *A Dictionary* Catalogue. (Boston: G K Hall, 1961); *Supplements* (1981). Brief descriptions: James M Wells, "The John M Wing Foundation of the Newberry Library," *The Book Collector, VIII,* 2 (Summer 1959), pp 157-162; Lawrece W Towner, *An Uncommon Collection of Uncommon* Collections (Chicago: The Newberry Library, 1977), pp 25-26.

IL —ORIENTAL INSTITUTE, 1155 E 58th St, Chicago, 60637. John Larsen, Archivist
Notes: The Bernhard Moritz Collection. Fine examples of bindings as well as of Islamic calligraphy and writing materials--papyrus, parchment, papers, etc. Extensive collection is also in the Beatty Library in Dublin, Ireland; Victoria and Albert Museum in London; Libraries in East and West Germany.

IL —NORTHERN ILLINOIS UNIVERSITY, Founders Memorial Library, Rare Books and Special Collections Dept, De Kalb, 60115. William R DuBois, Dept Head
Holdings: Vols (450) Cat
Notes: Works on the history of books and printing and representative examples of fine printing. Includes more than 50 titles published in Chicago by Way & Williams.

IN —INDIANA UNIVERSITY, Lilly Library, Seventh St, Bloomington, 47405. William R Cagle, Librn
Holdings: Mss
Notes: The Lilly Library collection of incunables (books printed before January 1501) now numbers over 700 titles and is being added to on a selective basis, primarily in the major works of the humanities and sciences. Presses from the sixteenth century to the present are well represented, and to aid the user there is a separate printers and presses file which will lead to the major books of all periods from Gutenberg to Grabhorn. It is a selective rather than a comprehensive collection.

KY —UNIVERSITY OF KENTUCKY, Margaret I King Library, Dept of Special Collections, Lexington, 40506. William Marshall, Head
Holdings: Cat Mss Pix Slides Microforms
Notes: Comprehensive collection of books on typography and history of printing; fine press books (incl Lexington imprints); ms books and illumination, paleography; mss of W A Dwiggins (gift of C H Griffith); James Anderson papers; bookbinding; 2 hand-presses and working collection for summer seminars in hand-press printing; bookplates, bookmarks, book jackets, etc.

†MD —UNIVERSITY OF MARYLAND, Library, R D Remley Collection, College Park, 20742. Donald Farren, Cur Rare Books
Holdings: Vols (2000) Cat
Notes: *Exempla* and secondary works in the areas of typography, calligraphy, book design, book illustration, the history of books, and of publishing etc. Catalog entries for designers, printing types, private presses, etc.

MA —BOSTON UNIVERSITY, Mugar Memorial Library, Special Collections Dept, 771 Commonwealth Ave, Boston, 02215. Howard B Gotlieb, Dir
Holdings: Vols Cat

MI —DETROIT PUBLIC LIBRARY, Rare Books Department, 5201 Woodward Ave, Detroit, 48202.
Holdings: Cat
Notes: Incl bibliographies, exhibit catalogs, booksellers' catalogs, auction catalogs, books about collecting, book arts, printing history, etc. Restricted use. Reference collection.

MI —MICHIGAN STATE UNIVERSITY, Libraries, Special Collections Div, East Lansing, 48824. Jannette Fiore, Librn
Holdings: Mss
Notes: Outstanding collection of over 100, 000 items, including Douglas C McMurtrie's published pamphlets and monographs, with manuscript, typescript, galleys, etc, material for the unfinished *History of Printing in the United States,* and his vast correspondence on printing and its history. Supported by a collection of works on printing.

MO —KANSAS CITY PUBLIC LIBRARY, 311 E 12, Kansas City, 64106. Daniel J Bradbury, Dir
Holdings: Vols 1500 Cat
Notes: Graphics arts collection contains the "rare book" section of the library with emphasis on book arts and printing. Additions made as desired items become available.

MO —SAINT LOUIS PUBLIC LIBRARY, Gardner Rare Book Room, 1301 Olive St, Saint Louis, 63103. Julanne M Good, Supervisor; Martha Riley, Rare Books Librn
Holdings: Vols 1300 Cat Mss
Budget: ($5573)
Notes: Collection of rare materials, 350 specimen leaves and supporting reference materials on history of the book, history of printing, bibliography, book collecting, book and document conservation, papermaking, and bookbinding. The 350 specimen leaves are from illuminated manuscript books and incunabula. Noncirculating.

NJ —PRINCETON UNIVERSITY, Library, Graphic Arts Collection, Princeton, 08540. Dale Roylance, Cur
Notes: Sinclair Hamilton Collection. One of the largest collections of American Illustrated Books in the US. 2 vols published; catalog available. Also, large collection of illustrated books of all countries, for all periods.

NY —PRATT INSTITUTE, Library Science Library, 200 Willoughby Ave, Brooklyn, 11205. Margot Karp, Library Science Librn
Holdings: Vols (10,000) Cat Microforms
Budget: ($15,000)
Notes: Separate catalog.

NY —BUFFALO & ERIE COUNTY PUBLIC LIBRARY, Rare Book Room, Lafayette Sq, Buffalo, 14203. William H Loos, Cur
Holdings: Vols 550 Cat

NY —MANHASSET PUBLIC LIBRARY, 30 Onderdonk Ave, Manhasset, 11030. Sylvia Levin, Dir
Holdings: Vols 400
Notes: A checklist of the collection is available.

NY —COLUMBIA UNIVERSITY LIBRARIES, Rare Book & Manuscript Library, 801 Butler Library, 535 W 114 St, New York, 10027. Kenneth A Lohf, Librn
Holdings: Vols (15,000) Cat
Notes: Covers all phases of bookmaking,

BOOKS ABOUT BOOKS (cont.)

bookbinding, book illustrations, book design, development of writing, paper, type, etc. Books about books as well as examples of fine printing.

NY —GRADUATE CENTER OF THE CITY UNIVERSITY OF NEW YORK, William H and Gwynne K Crouse Library for Publishing Arts, 33 W 42 St, New York, 10036. Alfred H Lane, Dir
Notes: Recently established and still growing, but intended to become the authoritative source of materials in the field, of particular value in research about the publishing industry. Open to staff members of publishing houses, students, scholars, authors, printers, and booksellers. Particularly useful for research on technical, financial, and historical matters. Much on the history of individual houses, economics of authorship; marketing and distribution of books; etc. Primarily 20th century material in hard form or microfilm, incl books, pamphlets, reprints, translations, dissertations, periodicals, indexing and abstracting services, yearbooks, reports and directories of organizations, publishers' and antiquarian dealers' catalogs (particularly those who deal in books about books), periodicals, legislative materials, and clippingspertaining to the book industry. Sections of the library deal with printing, incl typography, specimen books, history of printing and printing techniques, book design and small press and alternative publishing.

NY —GROLIER CLUB OF NEW YORK LIBRARY, 47 E 60 St, New York, 10022. Robert Nikirk, Librn
Holdings: Cat
Notes: Subject strength.

NY —R R BOWKER CO, Frederick G Melcher Library, 205 E 42nd St, New York, 10036. Nancy Dvorin, Librn
Holdings: Vols (15,000) Cat
Notes: Also have an 80-drawer vertical file. No photocopying.

NY —VISUAL STUDIES WORKSHOP, Research Center, 31 Prince St, Rochester, 14607. Linn Underhill, Coordr; Robert Bretz, Librn
Holdings: Vols (9000) Cat Pix Slides Audiotapes Videotapes
Notes: Strong emphasis on photography (over 1,000,000 pictures) and the photographic arts in many subject areas incl in this volume. Heavy emphasis on early photographic processes and collections of examples of them. Also collections of individual photographers' works.

NC —UNIVERSITY OF NORTH CAROLINA, CHAPEL HILL, Wilson Library, Rare Book Collection, Chapel Hill, 27514. Paul S Koda, Cur of Rare Books
Holdings: Vols 1000 Cat Mss
Notes: The Hanes Collection of the History of the Book consists of Sumerian and Babylonian clay tablets, papyri in Eqyptian and in Greek, stone inscriptions, 24 olas, manuscripts, and 600 items of 16th, 17th, and 18th century printing, incl many landmarks in the history of printing. It also contains many books about books, incl some rare bibliographies, histories of presses and technology, and books on collecting.

OH —OHIO UNIVERSITY, Vernon R Alden Library, Department of Archives and Special Collections, Athens, 45701. Gary A Hunt, Head
Holdings: Vols 1000 Mss Maps Pix Phonorecords Audiotapes
Notes: History of books and printing, chiefly in England from Caxton through the 19th century.

OH —KENT STATE UNIVERSITY, Libraries, Dept of Special Collections, Kent, 44242. Dean H Keller, Cur
Holdings: Vols 750 Cat

OK —UNIVERSITY OF TULSA, McFarlin Library, Dept of Rare Books and Special Collections, 600 S College, Tulsa, 74104. David Farmer, Dir; Toby Murray, Archivist; Caroline Swinson, Cur of Manuscripts & Art
Holdings: Cat
Notes: Incl the John Bennett Shaw Collection of Books About Books.

PA —FREE LIBRARY OF PHILADELPHIA, Rare Book Dept, Logan Sq, Philadelphia, 19103. Marie E Korey, Rare Book Librn
Holdings: Cat Mss Pix
Notes: The A Edward Newton Collection of his own writings and publications including 350 books, periodicals, proof sheets, manuscripts, autograph letters, association copies and memorabilia. The gift of Swift Newton.

PA —EASTERN COLLEGE, Frank Warner Memorial Library, Saint Davids, 19087. James L Sauer, Librn
Holdings: Uncat Mss Pix
Notes: The Harry C Goebel Collection. Incl Bruce Rogers printings (over 460); press books (about 350); oriental art (over 250); bookplates (with a separate collection of an almost complete set of bookplates designed by Edwin Davis French); Christmas Books; art and graphic arts (incl the French Graphic Arts Collection of Adolph DeMilly); first editions of Christopher Morley; Print Collection (1315 prints); Oriental art realia and artifacts.

PA —PENNSYLVANIA STATE UNIVERSITY, Fred Lewis Pattee Library, Special Collections Dept, University Park, 16802. Charles Mann, Chief, Special Collections
Holdings: Vols (122,533) Cat Mss Maps Pix Slides Phonorecords Audiotapes Videotapes 16mm Films Microforms
Budget: ($37,000)
Notes: Special Collections and Rare Books includes several collections described separately. The holdings are particularly strong in literature, the 18th century, aeronautics, facsimiles, atlases. 19th century illustrated works on birds, botany and traveller's views. Special strengths are Emblem Books, Utopias, Fantastic Fiction, Australiana, Fine Presses, Labor Archives, Lanscape Architecture, Pennsylvaniana. These collectons are strengthened by parallel holdings in the open stacks. It also includes the collections of the Penn State Room. Several mimeographed lists are available. Audiotapes are listed in *Voices and Events. A Catalog of Audio Tapes* (Pennsylvania State University Libraries, 1975), 45 pp.

RI —UNIVERSITY OF RHODE ISLAND, Library, Special Collections, Kingston, 02881. David Maslyn, Head
Notes: Extensive collections.

RI —BROWN UNIVERSITY, John Hay Library, 20 Prospect St, Providence, 02912. Mark N Brown, Cur Mss
Holdings: Vols 9000 Cat, Mss Pix
Notes: The Koopman Collection contains examples of the work of five centuries of fine printers and representative works by modern fine presses such as Kelmscott, Doves, Ashendene and Merrymount. Also incl are examples of ancient writing, illuminated manuscript books, fine bindings, first editions of American and British authors, auction catalogues of sales of significant collections, photographs of American and British authors, and museum objects once owned by various authors. Also a general working collection of Books on Books reference material.

SC —WOFFORD COLLEGE, Sandor Teszler Library, N Church St, Spartanburg, 29301. Frank J Anderson, Librn
Holdings: Vols (500) Cat
Budget: ($500)
Notes: Books about the history and practice of printing, hand papermaking, bookbinding, book collecting, fine press and private press books used in conjuctionn with instruction at the Wofford Library Press, an experimental and bibliographic press which has been in operation since 1969. Collection contains materials on printmaking methods and related graphic arts.

TX —UNIVERSITY OF TEXAS, EL PASO, Library, Special Collections Dept, El Paso, 79968. Cesar Caballero, Dept Head
Holdings: Vols 1370 Cat
Budget: ($5000)
Notes: Carl Hertzog Collection. More than three hundred books produced by the prominent printer/book designer Carl Hertzog and over a thousand books on books about books, typography, and the history of printing make up this collection. It also contains many Southwestern classics by Frank Dobie and Tom Lea.

TX —ROSENBERG LIBRARY, Fox Rare Book Room, 2310 Sealy Ave, Galveston, 77550. Fernando Basilza, Rare Book Librn
Holdings: Vols (2000) Cat Mss Pix
Notes: The Col Milo Pitcher Fox and Agnes Peel Fox Rare Book Room contains 2000 vols incunabula, first printings, and modern fine printing. Incl clay tablets, horn books, parchment material, illuminated books and mss, fine printing (principally 15th-18th centuries), fine binding, fore-edge paintings, etc.

TX —UNIVERSITY OF HOUSTON, M D Anderson Memorial Library, University Park, Houston, 77004. David Farmer, Cur, Special Collections; Jean Jackson, Assistant Cur
Holdings: Vols 150 Cat
Notes: This relatively young collection is not a collection of cornerstone books in printing history, fine printing or presses, but rather a collection of technical manuals, specimen books, and literature on the processes of bookmaking.

VA —UNIVERSITY OF VIRGINIA, Alderman Library, Rare Book Dept, Charlottesville, 22901. Julius P Barclay, Cur
Holdings: Vols (6500)// Mss
Notes: The Oscar Ogg Collection of Book Arts covers calligraphy, letterforms, typography, printing, and graphic arts. Contains early writing books and printed works, as well as modern manuals and other works on printing, publishing, and promotion through graphic arts. The Dept also has the Edward L Stone Collection of Printing Specimens, 3000 items. Contains materials tracing the history of printing, inks, binding styles and materials, types; some very rare incunabula, and Aldine Press books, Bodoni Printings, Bewick illustrations, an important collection of William Blake, and Boccaccio. Also the Tompkins Collection (2000 vols), and the Stevens Watts Collection (900 vols).

VA —SWEET BRIAR COLLEGE, Library, Sweet Briar, 24595. John Jaffe, Librn
Holdings: Vols (600) Cat
Budget: ($2000)

WA —UNIVERSITY OF WASHINGTON LIBRARIES, Suzzallo Library, Special Collections Division, Rare Book Collection, FM-25, Seattle, 98195. Gary Menges, Coordinator for Special Collections
Holdings: Vols (12,000) Cat Maps
Notes: American, British, French, German and Italian books printed before 1800, chiefly in the fields of history and literature. Fine bindings and illustrated works are represented. Inc incunabula, emblemata, history of travel, and first editions of the works of major poets: Spenser, Blake, Whitman, Yeats, Roethke, etc.

WI —MILWAUKEE PUBLIC LIBRARY, 814 W Wisconsin Ave, Milwaukee, 53233. Donald J Sager, City Librn
Holdings: Vols 5000 Cat
Notes: Extensive collection of author, imprint, subject, press, library, bibliographies.

PR —LA CASA DEL LIBRO, Library, Calle del Cristo 255, PO Box 2265, San Juan, 00903. David Jackson McWilliams, Dir
Holdings: Vols 5000 Uncat Mss Maps Slides
Notes: History and art of the book.

MB —UNIVERSITY OF MANITOBA, Elizabeth Dafoe Library, Archives and Special Collections Dept, Winnipeg, R3T 2N2, Can. Richard E Bennett, Dept Head; Corrado A Santoro, Reference Archivist
Holdings: // Uncat Mss
Notes: The Dysart Memorial Library collection of rare books representative of the development and the art of book-making and fine printing, with several illuminated mss and examples of the works of famous printers from the 15th century to the present day.

ON —QUEEN'S UNIVERSITY, Douglas Library, Kingston, K7L 5C4, Can. William F E Morley, Cur, Special Collections
Holdings: Vols 6980 Cat Mss Pix
Notes: Subject strength of the collections.
See also entry under Printing - History.

BOOKS ABOUT BOOKS (cont.)

ON —UNIVERSITY OF WESTERN ONTARIO, Schoool of Library and Information Science, Library, London, N6G 1H1, Can. Victoria Ripley, Librn
Holdings: Vols (50,000)
Notes: Auction and antiquarian booksellers' catalogs from Canadian, American and European firms, some dating back to the 18th century. A special strength is 19th and early 20th century American booksellers' catalogs, recently augmented by a collection of pre-1920 catalogs formed by the late H O Teisberg. Current emphasis is on Canadian catalogs.

ON —NATIONAL LIBRARY OF CANADA, 395 Wellington St, Ottawa, K1A 0N4, Can. Andre Preibish, Dir
Holdings: Vols 10,000
Notes: The collection on History and Art of the Book consists of over 10,000 volumes. Areas of concentration are: early imprints, special editions, examples of private presses works, book industry and trade books illustrating the aesthetic and technical aspects of the field, collection of books illustrated by Bartlett.

ON —METROPOLITAN TORONTO LIBRARY, Fine Arts Dept, 789 Yonge St, Toronto, M4W 2G8, Can. Alan Suddon, Head
Holdings: Vols (42,000)
Notes: Extensive collection.

PQ —MCGILL UNIVERSITY, McLennan Library, Rare Books and Special Collections Dept, 3459 McTavish St, Montreal, H3A 1Y1, Can.
Notes: Several thousand books on the history of the book to be found in the Reference Collection and especially in the William Colgate History of Printing Collection.

BOOKS, ARTISTS' see Artists' Books

BOOKS FOR CHILDREN see Children's Literature

BOOKS FOR SIGHT SAVING see Sight-Saving Books

BOOKS FOR THE ARMED SERVICES

†AL —UNIVERSITY OF ALABAMA, Amelia Gayle Gorgas Library, PO Box S, University, 35486.
Notes: A rare, complete set of the Armed Services Editions of paperbacks issued for use of American forces overseas in World War II.

CA —UNIVERSITY OF CALIFORNIA, LOS ANGELES, Research Library, Dept of Special Collections, 405 Hilgard Ave, Los Angeles, 90024. Edward Shreeves, Chairman, Bibliographers Group; David S Zeidberg, Head
Notes: 860 paperback editions of fiction and non-fiction printed especially for the armed forces during World War II.

DC —LIBRARY OF CONGRESS, Rare Book & Special Collections Div, Washington, 20540. William Matheson, Chief
Notes: A complete set of these paperbacks intended for overseas distribution only.

BOOKS FOR THE BLIND see Blind, Books and Recordings for the

BOOKS IN PARTS

IL —DE PAUL UNIVERSITY, Library, 2323 N Seminary, Chicago, 60614. Kathryn De Graff, Special Collections Librn
Holdings: Vols (598) Uncat Pix
Budget: $1500
Notes: The Jack Davidson and Nathan Schwartz Collection. Numerous editions of Dickens' works in the original publishers parts, first complete editions, first American editions and special editions. Also about 300 books about Dickens incl *The Dickension,* 500 prints, posters and photographs, an interesting collection of memorabilia such as figurines, etc. The extra-illustrated volumes, with over 7000 illustrations, were prepared by Mr Bradford, the original owner of the collection, and contain the conceptions of scenes and characters in Dickens' novels by various illustrators.

IL —NEWBERRY LIBRARY, John M Wing Foundation on the History of Printing, 60 W Walton St, Chicago, 60610. Diana Haskell, Cur of Modern Mss
Holdings: Vols (30,000) Cat Mss
Budget: ($50,000)
Notes: The collection covers printing and printing history of Western Europe and the Americas from its invention to the present. It is particularly rich in incunabula (about 2000); the works of the great printers, among others Aldus, Bodoni, Baskerville, and Rogers. Printed catalog: *A Dictionary* Catalogue. (Boston: G K Hall, 1961); *Supplements* (1981). Brief descriptions: James M Wells, "The John M Wing Foundation of the Newberry Library," *The Book Collector, VIII,* 2 (Summer 1959), pp 157-162; Lawrece W Towner, *An Uncommon Collection of Uncommon* Collections (Chicago: The Newberry Library, 1977), pp 25-26.

NY —NEW YORK PUBLIC LIBRARY, Rare Books and Manuscripts Div, Fifth Ave & 42 St, New York, 10018. William L Joyce, Asst Dir; Bernard McTigue, Cur, Arents Collection
Budget: Cat Mss Pix
Notes: The Arents Collection of Books in Parts consists of 12,000 pieces, most in English, printed in England and America from the 18th to the 20th century, of works that appeared piecemeal over a period of time and are preserved in original wrappers. Special subjects: Holograph manuscripts of some of the books, original drawings by illustrators (John Leech, Thomas Rowlandson, George Cruikshank, and others); autograph letters relating to the books and their illustrators, incl Dickens, Thackeray, Ainsworth, Trollope, Collins, Kate Greenaway, etc. See: *The Arents Collection of Books in Parts and Associated Literature: a Complete Checklist.* NY, 1957; Supplement, 1964.

OH —OHIO UNIVERSITY, Vernon R Alden Library, Department of Archives and Special Collections, Athens, 45701. Gary A Hunt, Head
Holdings: Vols 25 Cat
Notes: Books originally issued in monthly or weekly parts; mostly 19th century English novels, incl 10 by Charles Dickens.

BOOKS OF KNOWLEDGE see Encyclopedias and Dictionaries

BOOKS PRIVATELY PRINTED see Press Books

BOOKSELLERS AND BOOKSELLING

CA —UNIVERSITY OF CALIFORNIA, LOS ANGELES, Research Library, Dept of Special Collections, 405 Hilgard Ave, Los Angeles, 90024. Edward Shreeves, Chairman, Bibliographers Group; David S Zeidberg, Head
Holdings: Cat Mss
Notes: Various collections, incl archives of Dawson's Book Store, Los Angeles; F S Ellis, London; Holmes Book Company, Los Angeles; Henry Stevens of Vermont, London; Zeitlin and Ver Brugge, Los Angeles; 125 booksellers sample books. Also 8 linear feet of the Antiquarian Booksellers Association of America (ABAA), Southern California Chapter, archives; related papers, posters, etc, that refer to various aspects of international antiquarian bookselling.

CA —STANFORD UNIVERSITY LIBRARIES, Cecil H Green Library, Stanford, 94305. Peter R Frank, Cur, CDP-Germanic Collection
Notes: An emphasis in the Rare Book Collection. Also a sizable collection of works on the Austrian booktrade and libraries.

IN —INDIANA UNIVERSITY, Lilly Library, Seventh St, Bloomington, 47405. William R Cagle, Librn
Holdings: Mss
Notes: Correspondence and financial records of the Elkin Mathews, Ltd, firm, booksellers of Takeley, Bishops Stortford, England, 1927-1958. 69,334 items. Uncataloged but chronologically arranged. Correspondence, book orders, and invoices for Phoenix Book Shop, New York, NY, 1962-1980, with yearly additions. 30,000 items. The David Anton Randall papers incl his files while working for Scribner's in New York, as well as much correspondence, etc with John Carter concerning the English scene. 900 items. J K Lilly's personal papers contain correspondence with numerous dealers on purchase and availability of rare books and mss. Files arranged alphabetically by dealer. 25,000 items. Correspondence and business files of Joseph the Provider, Santa Barbara, California 1970-1982. (ca 9700 items)

MS —UNIVERSITY OF SOUTHERN MISSISSIPPI, William David McCain Graduate Library, Box 5148, Southern Sta, Hattiesburg, 39406.
Holdings: Uncat Mss
Notes: The personal and business records (1913-1953; 15 cubic feet) of the noted bookseller, Charles F Heartman. Incl correspondence, auction and book catalogs, the Heartman Historical Series, and copies of articles, pamphlets and books written or published by Heartman.

NY —STATE UNIVERSITY OF NEW YORK, COLLEGE AT BUFFALO, Poetry/Rare Books Collection, 420 Capen Hall, Buffalo, 14260. Robert J Bertholf, Cur
Notes: Extensive archive of Jack Shoemaker, a prominent bookseller, publisher, and poet. Incl mss, work sheets, correspondence, ephemera, and business records of the Sand Dollar and Unicorn bookshops and the Maya Press. Also incl mss and letters of prominent modern poets.

†NY —COLUMBIA UNIVERSITY LIBRARIES, Butler Library, Rare Book and Manuscript Library, 535 W 114 St, New York, 10027.
Notes: The files of Gramercy Bookshop in New York, 1940-79.

NY —GRADUATE CENTER OF THE CITY UNIVERSITY OF NEW YORK, William H and Gwynne K Crouse Library for Publishing Arts, 33 W 42 St, New York, 10036. Alfred H Lane, Dir
Notes: Recently established and still growing, but intended to become the authoritative source of materials in the field, of particular value in research about the publishing industry. Open to staff members of publishing houses, students, scholars, authors, printers, and booksellers. Primarily 20th century materials, and particularly useful for research on technical, financial, and historical matters. Much on the history of individual houses, economics of authorship; marketing and distribution of books; etc.

NY —GROLIER CLUB OF NEW YORK LIBRARY, 47 E 60 St, New York, 10022. Robert Nikirk, Librn
Notes: Archive of the noted bookseller, covering the years of his US career.

NY —R R BOWKER CO, Frederick G Melcher Library, 205 E 42nd St, New York, 10036. Nancy Dvorin, Librn
Holdings: Vols (15,000) Cat
Notes: Also have an 80-drawer vertical file. No photocopying.

OK —UNIVERSITY OF TULSA, McFarlin Library, Dept of Rare Books and Special Collections, 600 S College, Tulsa, 74104. David Farmer, Dir; Toby Murray, Archivist; Caroline Swinson, Cur of Manuscripts & Art
Notes: The Robert Frost Collection, assembled by the late John Kohn, a friend of Frost and proprietor of Seven Gables Book Shop in New York. Incl all first editions of Frost's works, his appearances in anthologies and periodicals, translations into other languages, and critical works.

PA —TEMPLE UNIVERSITY LIBRARIES, Special Collections Dept, Rare Books & Mss Section, Philadelphia, 19122. Thomas M Whitehead, Cur
Holdings: Vols 500 Cat Mss Pix
Notes: Collection of archives of bookselling activities in the Philadelphia area. Collection inlcudes archives of the William J Campbell

BOOKSELLERS AND BOOKSELLING (cont.)

firm (1850-1950), Leary & Co (1840-1968) and other selected manuscript and printed materials.

VT —UNIVERSITY OF VERMONT, Guy W Bailey/David W Howe Library, Burlington, 05405. John Buehler, Asst Dir for Special Collections
Notes: Manuscripts and printed material on Henry Stevens of Vermont.

ON —UNIVERSITY OF WESTERN ONTARIO, Schoool of Library and Information Science, Library, London, N6G 1H1, Can. Victoria Ripley, Librn
Holdings: Vols (50,000)
Notes: Auction and antiquarian booksellers' catalogs from Canadian, American and European firms, some dating back to the 18th century. A special strength is 19th and early 20th century American booksellers' catalogs, recently augmented by a collection of pre-1920 catalogs formed by the late H O Teisberg. Current emphasis is on Canadian catalogs.

BOOKSELLERS' AUCTION CATALOGS see Catalogs, Booksellers'—Auction

BOOKSELLERS' CATALOGS see Catalogs, Booksellers'

BOONE, DANIEL

KY —UNIVERSITY OF KENTUCKY, Margaret I King Library, Dept of Special Collections, Lexington, 40506. William Marshall, Head
Holdings: Vols 75 Uncat
Notes: Collection confined to novels with a Kentucky background only (Indian fighting, political intrigue, adventure in the "wilds" of Kentucky); 30 other novels relating to Western adventures.

BOORSTEIN, DANIEL JOSEPH

DC —LIBRARY OF CONGRESS, Manuscript Division, Washington, 20540. John C Broderick, Chief
Notes: The papers of Daniel J Boorstein.

BOOT AND SHOEMAKERS UNION

PA —PENNSYLVANIA STATE UNIVERSITY, Fred Lewis Pattee Library, Labor History Collection, University Park, 16802. Peter Gottlieb, Archivist
Holdings: Cat Mss
Notes: Trade union's archives, etc.

BOOTH, EDWIN

CA —UNIVERSITY OF CALIFORNIA, DAVIS, Shields Library, Dept of Special Collections, Davis, 95616. Donald Kunitz, Head; C Danial Elliott, Asst Head
Holdings: Uncat Mss Pix
Notes: Photographs, clippings, and correspondence of personalities of American and British theatre in the 19th and 20th centuries, such as Edwin Booth, Joseph Jefferson, Julia Marlowe, E H Sothern, Ellen Terry, Henry Irving, McKee Rankin, Fanny Davenport, and Zero Mostel.

CA —CALIFORNIA STATE UNIVERSITY, NORTHRIDGE, Delmar T Oviatt & South Libraries, 1811 Nordhoff St, Northridge, 91330. Donald L Read, Special Collections Dept
Holdings: Vols 22 Cat Mss Pix
Notes: Collection acquired from the actor's great-granddaughter, Mrs Edwina Booth Cutting. incl 13 mss, 128 pictures.

NY —HAMPDEN-BOOTH THEATRE LIBRARY AT THE PLAYERS, 16 Gramercy Park, New York, 10003. Louis A Rachow, Librn/Cur
Holdings: Cat Mss Pix
Notes: Incl his correspondence (1500 letters), 500 documents (promptbooks, diaries, ledgers, scrapbooks), photographs, playbills, and personal mementos. Letters and records concern his theatre experiences on the 19th-century American and English stages and business matters in the theatre, with numerous letters from friends, colleagues, and business acquaintances. Original draft of his Proclamation "To the People of the United States" upon the assassination of President Abraham Lincoln by John Wilkes Booth. Ledgers and journals of Booth's Theatre, 1867-1874. Ledgers and journals of the Booth-Barrett and Booth-Modjeska tours, 1886-1891. Incl 75 Shakespeare prompt books and numerous playbills, programs and photographs; 100 letters, dated January 1885, from prominent Washingtonians incl President Chester A Arthur, members of his Cabinet, and members of the Congress requestingBooth to return to the stage in Washington. Collection described in *Wilson Library Bulletin* (April 1964), pp 656-659; *Theatre Survey,* vol 14, no 1, May 1973, pp 72-111; and *Performing Arts Resources,* vol 3 (New York: Theatre Library Association, 1976), pp 98-142. Described in *Theatre & Performing Arts* Collections (New York: Haworth Press, 1981).

NY —NEW YORK PUBLIC LIBRARY, Performing Arts Research Center, Billy Rose Theatre Collection, 111 Amsterdam Ave, New York, 10023. Dorothy L Swerdlove, Cur
Holdings: Cat Pix
Notes: Important collection of prompt books, pictures, letters, and other memorabilia.

BOOTH, JOHN WILKES

DC —GEORGETOWN UNIVERSITY, Library, Special Collections Div, 37 & O Sts NW, Washington, 20057. George M Barringer, Special Collections Librn; Nicholas B Sheetz, Mss Librn
Holdings: Mss Cat
Notes: The E H Swaim Collection. A collection of letters, affidavits, and photographs relating to the assassination of Abraham Lincoln and the subsequent career of John Wilkes Booth. Much of this material was gathered by Finis L Bates, Clarence True Wilson, and W P Campbell (whose research files were brought together by Swaim) and is for the most part by people who were involved in the events surrounding the assassination; members of the Booth family and their acquaintances; and individuals who claimed to have known Booth later in Texas and Oklahoma.

IA —UNIVERSITY OF IOWA, University Libraries, Iowa City, 52242. Frank Paluka, Head, Special Collections Dept
Holdings: Vols 4620 Cat Pix
Notes: See "The Judge and His Lincoln," by Harry J Lytle in the *Lincoln Herald,* Oct-Dec 1942 and "John Wilkes Booth in the Bollinger Lincoln Collection," by Ronald L Fingerson in *Books at Iowa,* April 1965. Also "James W Bollinger as a Collection of Lincolniana", *Books at Iowa,* April 1982.

NY —HAMPDEN-BOOTH THEATRE LIBRARY AT THE PLAYERS, 16 Gramercy Park, New York, 10003. Louis A Rachow, Librn/Cur
Holdings: Cat Mss Pix
Notes: One folder of mss, playbills, and photographs.

BOOTH, JOSEPH

WI —SEVENTH DAY BAPTIST HISTORICAL SOCIETY, Library, 3120 Kennedy Rd, PO Box 1678, Janesville, 53547. D Scott Smith, Historian
Holdings: Uncat Mss Maps Pix Slides
Notes: Nyasaland (Malawi) Collection. These materials (1895-1914) deal with the founding of Baptist work in Central Africa by Joseph Booth, his influence on John Chilembwa and others in the Blantyre area and in the northern provinces of the country. Founded by Seventh Day Baptists, the mission was sold to Seventh-Day Adventists and then later (1947) reopened with the help of native leaders who had remained Seventh Day Baptists. Incl correspondence, reports, ledgers, deeds. NUCMC - MS 72-1226.

BOOTHE, CHARLES B.

CA —HOOVER INSTITUTION ON WAR, REVOLUTION & PEACE, Stanford University, Stanford, 94305. Milorad M Drachkovitch, Archivist
Holdings: / / Mss
Notes: Letters, copies of telegrams and misc newspaper clippings relating to the Chinese Revolution and especially to an American conceived plan for financing a revolution to overthrow the Ch'ing Dynasty. Principal correspondents incl Boothe, Homer Lea, a friend of Boothe and military adviser to Sun Yat-sen, W W Allen, a friend of Boothe and a New York consulting engineer, Yung Wing, a well-known Chinese-American of Hartford, Conn. Charles B Hill and Sun Yat-sen. Unpublished inventory at repository.

BOOTS AND SHOES

NY —UNIVERSITY OF ROCHESTER, School of Medicine and Dentistry, Edward G Miner Library, 601 Elmwood Ave, Rochester, 14642. Lucretia McClure, Medical Librn; Janet Brady Berk, History of Medicine Librn
Holdings: Slides
Notes: Very rare historical collection of some 300 glass slides, most of which relate to human gait, the foot, footwear, and myodynamics.

BOOTS AND SHOES—TRADE AND MANUFACTURE

NH —MANCHESTER HISTORIC ASSOCIATION, Library, 129 Amherst St, Manchester, 03104. Elizabeth Lessard, Librn
Notes: McElwain Shoe Company (1894-): Materials related to Massachusetts Institute of Technology, Trade Associations in the leather and shoe manufacturing industry, and personal correspondence of executives including J F Mcelwain, founder (2 document boxes and 1 Hollinger storage box).

NY —GEORGE F JOHNSON MEMORIAL LIBRARY, 1001 Park St, Endicott, 13760. S Judson Locke, Dir
Holdings: Pix
Notes: The Endicott-Johnson Shoe Company. Incl reports, company newspapers, clippings, pictures, etc. Original of periodical, *E J Worker's Review.*

BORCHARDT, SELMA M.

MI —WAYNE STATE UNIVERSITY, Walter P Reuther Library, Archives of Labor & Urban Affairs, Detroit, 48202. Philip Mason, Dir
Notes: The records of the American Federation of Teachers, as well as the files of the Detroit, Toledo, East Detroit, and other Federations of Teachers, are now preserved in the Archives. The personal papers of several teacher union leaders, incl Arthur Elder, Selma M Borchardt, Henry R Linville, Mary Herrick, and others are important supplements to the national union's file.

BORDEN, GAIL

TX —ROSENBERG LIBRARY, Galveston and Texas History Center, 2310 Sealy Ave, Galveston, 77550. Jane Kenamore, Archivist
Holdings: Cat Mss
Notes: Gail Borden Jr, 1801-1874, first collector of customs at Galveston and secretary and agent for the Galveston City Company. Inventor of condensed milk and founder of the Borden Milk Company. Papers relate to business, family, and records kept by Borden as customs collector.

BORDEN, MARY

MA —BOSTON UNIVERSITY, Mugar Memorial Library, Special Collections Dept,

BORDEN, MARY (cont.)

771 Commonwealth Ave, Boston, 02215. Howard B Gotlieb, Dir
Holdings: // Cat Mss Pix
Notes: Mss, correspondence, etc collected in depth; incl publications by or about.

BORDER LIFE see Frontier and Pioneer Life

BORDER STUDIES

AZ —UNIVERSITY OF ARIZONA, University Library, Special Collections, Tucson, 85721. Louis A Hieb, Head
Notes: The Southwestern Collection is a research collection of materials relating to the larger cultural, historical and environmental context. Particular emphasis is placed on the borderlands and the Mexican state of Sonora.

TX —UNIVERSITY OF TEXAS, EL PASO, Library, Special Collections Dept, El Paso, 79968. Cesar Caballero, Dept Head
Budget: ($6000)
Notes: Border Studies Manuscript Collection. Incl 20 linear ft, unpublished conference papers, research reports, articles and other ephemera. This collection was established to support the development of a Border Studies Program at U T El Paso. The collection is currently in the process of being indexed.

TX —SAINT MARY'S UNIVERSITY, Library, 2700 Cincinnati Ave, San Antonio, 78284. Anita C Saxine, Special Collections Librn
Notes: Spanish Colonial History of the Texas Borderlands incl the Spanish archives of Laredo, 1749-1850. Two bibliographical guides to materials in Special Collections were compiled by Anita C Saxine in 1983: *Reference Sources in Spanish Colonial History of Texas* (Academic Library Guide, no 12, 27 pp); *Penisular War, 1807-1814 by Contemporary Observers* (Academic Library Guide, no 13, 18 pp).

BORDERLAND COAL COMPANY

VA —UNIVERSITY OF VIRGINIA, Alderman Library, Manuscripts Dept, Charlottesville, 22901. Edmund Berkeley Jr, Cur
Holdings: Cat Mss
Notes: Papers, 1901-1934, of the Borderland Coal Company, a Mingo County, West Virginia and Pike County, Kentucky bituminous porducer.

BORDUAS, PAUL-EMILE

PQ —MUSEE D'ART CONTEMPORAIN, Bibliotheque, Cite du Havre, Montreal, H3C 3R4, Can. Isabelle Montplaisir, Librn
Holdings: Vols (5780) Cat Pix Slides Audiotapes Videotapes Microforms
Budget: ($12,000)
Notes: 7050 exhibition catalogs on a basic exchange from art galleries, museums, etc of many countries. Also 2000 pictures; 32,000 slides; and 2500 files relating to artists, galleries, museums, etc. Also, the Archives Paul-Emile Borduas (painter) of 12,500 items, incl his writings, correspondence, exhibition catalogs, etc. Plus 150 periodical subscriptions.

BOREN, LYLE H.

OK —UNIVERSITY OF OKLAHOMA, Bizzell Memorial Library, Western History Collections, 401 W Brooks, Norman, 73069. John Ezell, Cur
Holdings: Mss Pix Documents Maps Newspapers
Notes: US Representative. His papers.

BORGES, JORGE LUIS

VA —UNIVERSITY OF VIRGINIA, Alderman Library, Charlottesville, 22901.
Holdings: Vols 650

BORGLUM, GUTZON

DC —LIBRARY OF CONGRESS, Manuscript Division, Washington, 20540. John C Broderick, Chief
Holdings: Cat Mss Pix
Notes: Mss, papers, records, etc.

BORLAND, HAL AND BARBARA

CT —YALE UNIVERSITY, Box 1603A, Yale Station, New Haven, 06520.
Holdings: Cat Mss

BORN, ERNEST

†CA —UNIVERSITY OF SAN FRANCISCO, Richard A Gleeson Library, The Countess Bernardine Murphy Donohue Rare Book Room, San Francisco, 94117. D Steven Corey, Special Collections Librn
Notes: Some highly specialized materials.

BORN, LEONARD

CA —UNIVERSITY OF CALIFORNIA, DAVIS, Shields Library, Dept of Special Collections, Davis, 95616. Donald Kunitz, Head; C Danial Elliott, Asst Head
Holdings: Uncat Mss Pix
Notes: Food technology files, 1943-1959, involving the research of Leonard Born on the irradiation of foods, cold sterilization, and algae production. Also, mss, correspondence, photographs, and clippings on various aspects of growing and processing fruit and vegetables, with an emphasis on canning. 3800 items.

BORN, MAX, 1882-1970

NY —LEO BAECK INSTITUTE, Library, 129 E 73 St, New York, 10021. Fred Grubel, Secretary & Dir
Notes: His papers (1925-1935, ca 1962-1970).

BORNEO

NY —CORNELL UNIVERSITY LIBRARIES, John M Olin Library, John M Echols Collection on Southeast Asia, Ithaca, 14853. Giok Po Oey, Curator
Holdings: Vols (135,000) Cat Mss Maps Pix Microforms
Budget: ($63,500)
Notes: Additions published in monthly *John M Echols Collection on Southeast Asia Accessions List* (Ithica: Cornell University, Southeast Asia Program, 1959-). Described partially in the following publications: Anderson, Benedict R *Bibliography of Indonesia Publications; Newspapers, Non-government Periodicals and Bulletins 1945-1958 at Cornell University.* Ithaca, NY: Cornell University, Southeast Asia Program, 1959 (datapaper no 33); Echols, John M *Preliminary Checklist of Indonesian Imprints (1945-1949), with Cornell University* Holdings. Ithaca, NY: Cornell University, Modern Indonesia Project, 1965; Leigh, Michael B *Checklist of Holdings on Borneo in the Cornell University Libraries.* 1966. (Data paper, no 62); Lev, Daniel SA *Bibliography of Indonesian Government Documents and Selected indonesian Writings on Government in the Cornell University Library,* 1958 (data paper no 31); Thung, Yvonne and John M Echols, *A Checklist of Indonesian Serials in the Cornell University Library, 1945-1970* (Ithaca: Cornell University, Southest Asia Program, 1973) (Data Ppaer no 89); and Nakamura, Mitsuo, *Checklist of Microfilm Holdings on he Japanese Occupation of Indonesia in the Cornell University Library, Watson Collection* (Ithica, 1970). Holdings through June 1975 listed in *Cornell University Libraries Southeast Asia Catalog* (Boston: G K Hall, 1976), vols 2, 4, and 7.

BORNEO (KALIMANTAN) see Indonesia

BORNEO, SOUTHERN see Indonesia

BOROUGH, REUBEN WARRINER, 1883-1970

CA —UNIVERSITY OF CALIFORNIA, LOS ANGELES, Research Library, Dept of Special Collections, 405 Hilgard Ave, Los Angeles, 90024. Edward Shreeves, Chairman, Bibliographers Group; David S Zeidberg, Head
Notes: 27 linear feet of unprocessed mss and correspondence relating to his political activities.

BORROW, GEORGE

CT —TRINITY COLLEGE LIBRARY, 300 Summit St, Hartford, 06106. Ralph S Emerick, Librn
Holdings: // Cat

BOSKOVIC, RUDJER JOSIP

CA —UNIVERSITY OF CALIFORNIA, BERKELEY, Bancroft Library, Manuscripts Division, Berkeley, 94720. James D Hart, Dir
Holdings: Cat Mss
Notes: The personal papers and correspondence (2000 pieces) of Rudjer Josip Boskovic, an important Yugoslav, 18th-century Jesuit mathematician and natural philosopher. Of particular importance are 180 textual mss dealing with subjects in the field of mechanics. A register of the collection has been prepared. The collection is complemented by extensive holdings of Boskovic's published works.

BOSONE, REP. REVA BECK

UT —UNIVERSITY OF UTAH, Marriott Library, Special Collections, Salt Lake City, 84112. Gregory C Thompson, Cur
Holdings: Cat Mss Microfilm Film Oral History
Notes: Papers.

BOSSUET, JACQUES-BENIGNE

CA —UNIVERSITY OF CALIFORNIA, LOS ANGELES, William Andrews Clark Memorial Library, 2520 Cimarron St, Los Angeles, 90018.
Holdings: Cat
Notes: Original editions.

MA —HARVARD UNIVERSITY LIBRARY, Widener Library, Cambridge, 02138.
Holdings: Cat
Notes: See *Harvard Library Notes,* II (1925-26), 60-62, 90.

NY —PIERPONT MORGAN LIBRARY, 29 E 36 St, New York, 10016. Herbert Cahoon, Librn

BOSTON—CITY RECORDS

†MA —BOSTON PUBLIC LIBRARY, Copley Sq, Boston, 02117.
Holdings: Cat Microforms
Notes: Microform Publication: Records of the Town and City of Boston from 1634 to 1914. 225 reels.

BOSTON—CULTURE

MA —BOSTON UNIVERSITY, Mugar Memorial Library, Special Collections Dept, 771 Commonwealth Ave, Boston, 02215. Howard B Gotlieb, Dir
Notes: Personal collection of Arthur Fiedler, incl 6000 scores and sound recordings, manuscripts, photographs, memorabilia, library, and test pressings of Fiedler's performances.

BOSTON—DESCRIPTION—VIEWS

MA —BOSTON PUBLIC LIBRARY, Print Collection, Dartmouth St at Copley Sq, Boston, 02117. Sinclair H Hitchings, Keeper of Prints
Holdings: Maps Pix Slides
Notes: The Boston Pictorial Archive (especially strong from 1850 to 1910) contains views, aerial views, buildings, and events depicted in fine art prints, 19th and 20th century photos, and early 20th century postcards: 18 original town plans, 3000 old photos, 600 old glass negatives, 2500 old postcards, 100 prints, 100 stereopticon views. Material of the 18th and 20th century

BOSTON—DESCRIPTION—VIEWS (cont.)

is also incl to a lesser degree. Items are cataloged by subject matter. Prints are also cataloged by artist and/or by publisher.

BOSTON—GOVERNMENT PUBLICATIONS

MA —BOSTON PUBLIC LIBRARY, Government Documents Department, Boston, 02117. V Lloyd Jameson, Cur
Holdings: Maps Microforms
Notes: We maintain our own subject index to Boston City Documents published since the 1960s.

BOSTON—HISTORY

MA —BOSTONIAN SOCIETY, Library, 206 Washington St, Boston, 02109. Thomas W Parker, Dir; Mary Leen, Librn
Holdings: Vols (5000) Cat Mss Maps Pix Slides
Budget: $200

MA —BOSTON PUBLIC LIBRARY, Rare Books and Manuscripts, Copley Square, Boston, 02117. Laura V Monti, Keeper of Rare Books
Holdings: Cat Mss
Notes: Records of the Boston Municipal Court from the 18th century.

MA —BOSTON COLLEGE LIBRARIES, Chestnut Hill, 02167.
Notes: The archives of the Citywide Coordinating Council of Boston, Mass, established in 1975 to monitor the desegregation of the Boston school system and to foster public awareness in the implementation of the court's desegregation orders. Incl the collection of transcripts of School Committee meetings; the central files, reflecting the functioning of the council office; and the files of the senior staff, containing the key administrative records of the Council.

MA —BOSTON COLLEGE LIBRARIES, Thomas P O'Neill Library, Brehaut Bostonian Collection, Chestnut Hill, 02167. Frank J Seegraber, Special Collections Librn
Holdings: Cat Mss Maps Pix
Notes: Over 5000 items, incl 85 scrapbooks, and 100 maps of Boston and vicinity, 1850-1900. Emphasis on political history, incl the Boston fire, 1872; Boston police strike, 1919; development of the Boston transit system; career of James Michael Curley. For reference use only, by arrangement with librarian.

BOSTON—PICTURES, ILLUSTRATIONS, ETC.

DC —LIBRARY OF CONGRESS, Prints & Photographs Div, Washington, 20540.
Notes: The Charles Henry Currier Collection of photographs of homes, offices, factories, charitable institutions, and recreational organizations in the Boston area, 1890s-1910s.

BOSTON AND ALBANY RAILROAD

MA —SOCIETY FOR THE PRESERVATION OF NEW ENGLAND ANTIQUITIES, Library, 141 Cambridge St, Boston, 02114. Ellie Reichlin, Librn & Cur of Photographic Collections
Notes: Boston and Albany Railroad Archive (1890s-1920s): original negatives with prints of stations, structures along rail lines, views of construction. 1500 pieces.

BOSTON BUILDING DEPARTMENT

MA —SOCIETY FOR THE PRESERVATION OF NEW ENGLAND ANTIQUITIES, Library, 141 Cambridge St, Boston, 02114. Ellie Reichlin, Librn & Cur of Photographic Collections
Notes: Photographs by W W Campbell of so-called "dilapidated" buildings, mainly residential, in virtually all Boston neighborhoods focusing on sources of complaint. Some owner and address information incl.

BOSTON COOKING SCHOOL

MA —SIMMONS COLLEGE ARCHIVES, 300 The Fenway, Boston, 02115. Megan Sniffin-Marinoff, College Archivist
Notes: (I) Minutes of the Industrial Committee of the Woman's Education Association (1873-1929) from Feb 15, 1872 to Dec 5, 1882. Primarily concerned with the Committee's development of the Boston Cooking School. Figuring prominently in the minutes are Maria Parloa (1843-1909), one of the first instructors at the school, and Mary Johnson Bailey Lincoln (1844-1921), under whose leadership the Boston Cooking School began to attain a national reputation. For further information on these women, see *Notable American Women.* The Committee's relationship with the NY Diet Kitchen, the North Bennett St Industrial School (Boston), and the Massachusetts Institute of Technology also are discussed in the minutes. In addition to organizing a school for cooking, the Committee concerned itself with the education for women in dressmaking, nursing, phonography, andwoodcarving (based on the Cincinnati carving school). (II) Account books of the Household Aid Co (The Domestic Economy Committee) of the Woman's Education Association from August, 1903 to May, 1905. Organized by the Association of Collegiate Alumnae and the Woman's Education Association, the company was a cooperative residence for 20 servants with a training and placement program and a mediation service to deal with employers.

BOSTON MERCANTILE LIBRARY ASSOCIATION

MA —BOSTON UNIVERSITY, Mugar Memorial Library, Special Collections Dept, 771 Commonwealth Ave, Boston, 02215. Howard B Gotlieb, Dir
Holdings: // Cat Mss Phonorecords
Notes: Correspondence and scrapbooks.

BOSTON POPS ORCHESTRA

MA —BOSTON UNIVERSITY, Mugar Memorial Library, Special Collections Dept, 771 Commonwealth Ave, Boston, 02215. Howard B Gotlieb, Dir
Notes: Personal collection of Arthur Fiedler, incl 6000 scores and sound recordings, manuscripts, photographs, memorabilia, library, and test pressings of Fiedler's performances.

BOSTON PUBLIC LATIN SCHOOL

MA —HARVARD UNIVERSITY LIBRARY, Widener Library, Cambridge, 02138.
Holdings: // Cat
Notes: See *Harvard Alumni Bulletin,* XXXVII (1935), 834-839.

BOSTON SCHOOL COMMITTEE

MA —BOSTON SCHOOL COMMITTEE, Administration Library, 77 Ave Louis Pasteur, Boston, 02115. Polly Kaufman, Coordinating Dir; Barbara Elam, Coordinating Dir
Holdings: Vols (12,000) Cat Microfiche
Budget: ($10,000)
Notes: Collection incl file of Boston School Committee Documents, 1845-date and Minutes of Boston School Committee, 1869-date. Also, ERIC research materials, current index to journals, 100 periodicals on education.

BOSTON SOCIETY OF NATURAL HISTORY

MA —MUSEUM OF SCIENCE, Library, Science Park, Boston, 02114. Edward D Pearce, Librn
Holdings: Cat Mss Pix
Notes: 19th, 20th century American. In English language. Downs 2298. Archives of the Boston Society of Natural History.

BOSTON SYMPHONY ORCHESTRA

DC —LIBRARY OF CONGRESS, Music Division, Washington, 20540.
Notes: Music mss and papers of Charles Loeffler, composer and concert master of the Boston Symphony Orchestra.

MA —BOSTON UNIVERSITY, Mugar Memorial Library, Special Collections Dept, 771 Commonwealth Ave, Boston, 02215. Howard B Gotlieb, Dir
Notes: Scores of Italian operas (19th century) in contemporary copies. Deposit from archives of the Boston Symphony Orchestra.

BOSWELL, JAMES

CT —YALE UNIVERSITY, Box 1603A, Yale Station, New Haven, 06520.
Holdings: Cat Mss

IL —NORTHWESTERN UNIVERSITY, Library, Special Collections Dept, 1937 Sheridan Rd, Evanston, 60201. R Russell Maylone, Cur
Holdings: Vols 900 Cat
Notes: The Elmer A Smith Memorial Collection contains works of Samuel Johnson and those of his contemporaries touching upon him, especially Boswell. Additional material in general collections.

NC —UNIVERSITY OF NORTH CAROLINA, CHAPEL HILL, Wilson Library, Rare Book Collection, Chapel Hill, 27514. Paul S Koda, Cur of Rare Books
Holdings: Vols 300 Cat
Notes: The Whitaker Collection of Samuel Johnson and James Boswell contains 600 first and rare editions of the writings of Johnson and his friends. Important works of James Boswell, as well as Chesterfield, Goldsmith, and Fanny Burney are included, as well as reference, critical, and bibliographical material.

VA —VIRGINIA COMMONWEALTH UNIVERSITY, James Branch Cabell Library, Richmond, 23284. Daniel Yanchisin, Special Collections Librn

BOSWORTH, ALLAN

MA —BOSTON UNIVERSITY, Mugar Memorial Library, Special Collections Dept, 771 Commonwealth Ave, Boston, 02215. Howard B Gotlieb, Dir
Holdings: Cat Mss
Notes: Mss, correspondence, etc collected in depth; incl publications by or about.

BOTANIC MEDICINE see Medicine, Botanic

BOTANICAL EXPLORATION

BC —VANDUSEN GARDENS LIBRARY, 5251 Oak St, Vancouver, V6M 4H1, Can. Mary Nickel, Librn
Holdings: Vols (2100)

BOTANICAL GARDEN, MISSOURI see Missouri Botanical Garden, St. Louis

BOTANICAL GARDENS see Gardens and Gardening

BOTANICAL ILLUSTRATION

CA —CALIFORNIA STATE UNIVERSITY, HAYWARD, Library, Hayward, 94542. Melissa Rose, Dir

FL —FLORIDA DEPT OF STATE, Florida State Archives, Florida Photographic Collection, R A Gray Bldg, Tallahassee, 32301. Mrs Allen Morris, Archives Supervisor
Holdings: Maps Pix Slides Films Audiotapes
Notes: 500 photographs of Florida flora, made by Charles A Mosier, Charles Torrey Simpson and J K Small, famous naturalists, mostly in South Dade County. Added March, 1983, 2200 glass and nitrate negatives by J K Small.

BOTANICAL ILLUSTRATION (cont.)

IN —BUTLER UNIVERSITY, Irwin Library, Hugh Thomas Miller Rare Book Room, 4600 Sunset Ave, Indianapolis, 46208. Gisela Terrell, Rare Books Librn
Holdings: Uncat
Notes: The Jeanette S Pelton Botanical Print Collection. A collection tracing the history and development of botanical illustration from the 15th through the mid-19th century. *See also* entry under Prints - Collections

ME —BOWDOIN COLLEGE, Library, Brunswick, 04011. Dianne M Gutscher, Cur of Special Collections
Holdings: Mss
Notes: The Kate Furbish collection of the "Flora of Maine" consists of her watercolor sketches of specimens collected between 1870 and 1908 (16 folio volumes).

PA —HUNT INSTITUTE FOR BOTANICAL DOCUMENTATION, Hunt Botanical Library, Carnegie-Mellon University, Pittsburgh, 15213. Bernadette G Callery, Librn
Holdings: Vols (23,000) Cat Pix
Notes: Collection of primarily historical botany and plant taxonomy, especially 1730-1840. Includes approximately 500 15th through 17th century herbals, extensive collection of 18th and 19th century color-plate works, floras and monographic works, and other works on natural history, early gardening and horticulture, and travel, particularly that dealing with plant exploration and introduction. Extensive biographical materials, on people in plant sciences. Reference collection and extensive documentation in botanical bibliography, especially concerning books published before 1850. Includes as separate collections, the Strandell Collection of Linnaeana and the Michel Adanson Library. Over 800 items described in *Catalogue of Botanical Books in the Collection of Rachel McMasters Miller Hunt, 1477-1800* (Pittsburgh, 1958-1960).

PA —PENNSYLVANIA STATE UNIVERSITY, Fred Lewis Pattee Library, Special Collections Dept, University Park, 16802. Charles Mann, Chief, Special Collections
Holdings: Vols (122,533) Cat Mss Maps Pix Slides Phonorecords Audiotapes 16mm Films Microforms
Budget: ($37,000)
Notes: Special Collections and Rare Books includes several collections described separately. The holdings are particularly strong in literature, the 18th century, aeronautics, facsimiles, atlases, 19th century illustrated works on birds, botany and traveller's views. Special strengths are Emblem Books, Utopias, Fantastic Fiction, Australiana, Fine Presses, Labor Archives, Landscape Architecture, Pennsylvaniana. These collections are strengthened by parallel holdings in the open stacks. It also includes the collections of the Penn State Room. Several mimeographed lists are available. Audiotapes are listed in *Voices and Events, A Catalog of Audio Tapes* (Pennsylvania State University Libraries, 1975), 45 pp.

BOTANICAL PERIODICALS see Periodicals, Botanical

BOTANISTS

†CA —HUNTINGTON BOTANICAL GARDENS LIBRARY, 1151 Oxford Rd, San Marino, 91108. Ann Ravenscroft, Secretary
Holdings: Vols (8000)
Notes: Emphases on history of botanical science; papers and notes of American botanists and naturalists of The West; botanical illustration, etc. Subtropical horticulture, incl cacti and succulents of Australia, South Africa, and Mexico.

IA —IOWA STATE UNIVERSITY, Library, Dept of Special Collections, Ames, 50011. Stanley M Yates, Head
Holdings: Vols 49 // Cat Mss
Notes: Louis H Pammel (1862-1931) was professor of botany (1889-1931) and head of department of botany. Collection incl correspondence, collected works, speeches, interviews and articles. Collection is 39 linear feet. Important in conservation movement; founder of Iowa State Park System; teacher and friend of George Washington Carver.

KS —UNIVERSITY OF KANSAS, Kenneth Spencer Research Library, Special Collections Dept, Lawrence, 66045. Alexandra Mason, Librn
Holdings: Vols 5600 Cat Mss
Notes: About 2600 items before 1800. Espec strong in herbals, medical botany, Linnaeus, early American botanists (William Darlington, C S Rafinesque). Incl material from T J Fitzpatrick collection. Noncirculating.

NY —NEW YORK BOTANICAL GARDEN LIBRARY, Bronx, 10458. Charles R Long, Asst Vice Pres & Dir
Holdings: Vols (385,000) Cat Mss Pix Slides Microforms VF
Budget: ($356,000)
Notes: One of the largest botanical collections in the world. Covers botany (150,000 vols), botanists (3000), horticulture (45,000), plant diseases (25,000), plant physiology (15,000), history of botany (1500), conservation of natural resources (15,000), gardening (13,000), paleobotany (7000), ecology (20,000), forestry (5000), medical botany (3000), agriculture (9000) and biology (20,000). Reference library; materials do not circulate, except via standard inter-library loan. About 5000 vols uncataloged. Incl archives, art and vertical files. An OCLC library.

†NC —UNIVERSITY OF NORTH CAROLINA, CHAPEL HILL, Department of Botany Library, 301 Coker Hall 010-A, Chapel Hill, 27514. William R Burk, Botany Librn
Notes: The mycology collection incl some 6000 pamphlets. It contains papers of the following scientists: William C Coker, John N Couch, Lindsay F Olive, mycologists; also, Victor A Greulach, plant pathologist. The mycology catalog is in preparation (1983), and will provide author, title, and subject access.

PA —HUNT INSTITUTE FOR BOTANICAL DOCUMENTATION, Hunt Botanical Library, Carnegie-Mellon University, Pittsburgh, 15213. Bernadette G Callery, Librn
Holdings: Vols (23,000) Cat Pix
Notes: Collection of primarily historical botany and plant taxonomy, especially 1730-1840. Includes approximately 500 15th through 17th century herbals, extensive collection of 18th and 19th century color-plate works, floras and monographic works, and other works on natural history, early gardening and horticulture, and travel, particularly that dealing with plant exploration and introduction. Extensive biographical materials, on people in plant sciences. Reference collection and extensive documentation in botanical bibliography, especially concerning books published before 1850. Includes as separate collections, the Strandell Collection of Linnaeana and the Michel Adanson Library. Over 800 items described in *Catalogue of Botanical Books in the Collection of Rachel McMasters Miller Hunt, 1477-1800* (Pittsburgh, 1958-1960).

BOTANISTS—PORTRAITS

PA —HUNT INSTITUTE FOR BOTANICAL DOCUMENTATION, Portrait Collection, Carnegie-Mellon University, Pittsburgh, 15213. Michael T Stieber, Archivist
Holdings: Cat Pix
Notes: Approximately 25,000 photos of over 13,000 botanists, horticulturists and botanical artists. Collection partially described in *Biographical Dictionary of Botanists Represented in the Hunt Institute Portrait Collection*, edited by Theodore Bossert (Boston: G K Hall, 1972). A revised and expanded edition is in process. It will include an additional 2,000 names, and a detailed description of each portrait. Also included will be a catalogue of over 450 group portraits and an index of names of persons portrayed.

BOTANISTS, AMERICAN

KS —UNIVERSITY OF KANSAS, Kenneth Spencer Research Library, Special Collections Dept, Lawrence, 66045. Alexandra Mason, Librn
Holdings: Vols (5600) Cat Mss
Notes: About (2600) items before 1800. Especially strong in herbals, medicine, botany, Linnaeus, early American botanists (William Darlington, C S Refinesque). Incl material from T J Fitzpatrick collection. Noncirculating.

BOTANY

AL —BIRMINGHAM BOTANICAL GARDENS, Horace Hammond Memorial Library, 2612 Lane Park Road, Birmingham, 35223. Ida Burns, Librn
Holdings: Vols 2800 Cat Pix Films Slides VF

†AK —UNIVERSITY OF ALASKA, Museum Herbarium, 907 Yucan Dr, Fairbanks, 99701.

CA —LOS ANGELES STATE & COUNTY ARBORETUM, Plant Science Library, 301 N Baldwin Ave, Arcadia, 91006. Joan DeFato, Librn
Holdings: Vols (24,000) Cat 16mm Films
Budget: ($6000)
Notes: Emphasis on woody plants, particularly of Australia and South Africa. Botany is weighted toward taxonomy rather than plant physiology.

CA —RANCHO SANTA ANA BOTANIC GARDEN LIBRARY, 1500 N College Ave, Claremont, 91711. Beatrice M Beck, Librn
Holdings: Vols 30,000 Cat Maps Microforms
Notes: Incl emphasis on California flora, floras of the world, evolutionary biology and ethnobotany.

CA —UNIVERSITY OF CALIFORNIA, DAVIS, General Library, Davis, 95616. Bernard Kreissman, University Librn; C Danial Elliott, Asst Head, Dept Special Collections
Holdings: Vols 15,747
Budget: $18,000

CA —UNIVERSITY OF CALIFORNIA, SAN DIEGO, Central University Library, Mandeville Dept of Special Collections, La Jolla, 92093. Lynda Corey Claassen, Head
Notes: Hill Collection: One of the most distinguished collections on early voyages to all parts of the Pacific Ocean, these materials include more than 2000 accounts of and commentaries on important voyages from the 16th to the mid 19th century, plus extensive anthropological, botanical, and zoological reports made by scientists who accompanied the explorers.

CA —R MITCHEL BEAUCHAMP BOTANICAL LIBRARY, 1843 E 16th St, National City, 92050.
Notes: Survey and exploration reports. American seed and bulb catalogues, 1960-date.

CA —CALIFORNIA STATE POLYTECHNIC UNIVERSITY, POMONA, University Library, 3801 W Temple Ave, Pomona, 91768. Harold Schleiser, Actg Dir
Notes: General reference materials on agricultural business management, agricultural engineering, animal science, horticulture and plant and soil science.

CA —CALIFORNIA ACADEMY OF SCIENCES, J W Mailliard Jr Library, Golden Gate Park, San Francisco, 94118. Ray Brian, Librn
Notes: Downs No 2160.

†CA —HUNTINGTON BOTANICAL GARDENS LIBRARY, 1151 Oxford Rd,

BOTANY (cont.)

San Marino, 91108. Ann Ravenscroft, Secretary
Notes: Emphases on history of botanical science; papers and notes of American botanists and naturalists of The West; botanical illustration, etc. Subtropical horticulture, incl cacti and succulents of Australia, South Africa, and Mexico.

CA —SANTA BARBARA BOTANIC GARDEN, Library, 1212 Mission Canyon Rd, Santa Barbara, 93105. Margaret Connors, Librn
Holdings: Vols 5500 Cat Mss Maps Slides
Notes: Botany and horticulture with emphasis on California native flora. Restricted to use by the staff and members of the Garden; limited use by public is permitted. Incl seed catalogs.

CO —HORTICULTURAL ART SOCIETY OF COLORADO SPRINGS, Library, Orchard House, 3202 Chambers Way, Colorado Springs, 80904. Ernestine H Fagan, Librn
Holdings: Vols (950)
Notes: Horticulture of the Pikes Peak Region.

CO —DENVER BOTANIC GARDENS, Helen Fowler Library, 909 York St, Denver, 80206. Solange G Gignac, Librn
Holdings: Vols (13,500) Cat Pix Slides
Budget: ($15,000)

CT —YALE UNIVERSITY, Kline Science Library, Kline Biology Tower Rm C-8, PO Box 6666, New Haven, 06511. Richard J Dionne, Head
Holdings: Vols (175,000) Cat 16mm Films Microforms
Budget: ($340,000)
Notes: Comprehensive collection on biological sciences, physics, and chemistry. Incl Evans Collection of Bryology and Lichenology (with catalog cards in both Kline Science Library and Sterling Memorial Library). Also incl AEC reports (hardcopy and microform) to 1970.

DE —WILMINGTON GARDEN CENTER LIBRARY, 503 Market Street Mall, Wilmington, 19801. Bonnie J Swan Day, Admin Asst; Karen Bidus, Librn
Holdings: Vols (1500)
Notes: Library open to the public, only circulates to members.

†DC —CATHOLIC UNIVERSITY OFF AMERICA, Nursing & Biology Library, Washington, 20064. N L Powell, Head
Holdings: Vols (17,000) Cat Microforms

DC —LIBRARY OF CONGRESS, Manuscript Division, Washington, 20540. John C Broderick, Chief
Notes: The papers of Luther Burbank (1849-1926), incl approximately 10,000 items range in date over much of his life span. Contains correspondence, writings, scientific notes and records, ledgers, account books, scrapbooks, photographs, and journal reprints and other printed matter.

DC —SMITHSONIAN INSTITUTION, Archives Div, Washington, 20560. William W Moss, Archivist
Holdings: Cat Mss Pix
Notes: The Archives holds the records of the National Museum of Natural History's Division of Plants and the Department of Botany, 1870-1970, as well as correspondence of botanists incl Joseph Nelson Rose and William Ralph Maxon.

DC —SMITHSONIAN INSTITUTION, Smithsonian Tropical Research Institute, Washington, 20560. Carol Jopling, Chief Librn
Holdings: Vols (22,000) Cat Mss Maps Pix Slides 16mm Films Microforms
Budget: ($70,000)
Notes: Smithsonian Institution, Smithsonian Tropical Research Institute is located in Balboa, Panama.

DC —SMITHSONIAN INSTITUTION LIBRARIES, Botany Branch, Washington, 20560. Ruth Schallert, Branch Librn
Holdings: Vols (21,000) Cat Mss Maps Pix Microforms
Notes: Taxonomic botany; with the J D Smith Collection of general botany, the Dawson Collection on algae, and the Hitchcock-Chase Collection on grasses.

DC —US NATIONAL ARBORETUM, Library, 3501 New York Ave NE, Washington, 20002. Judi Ho, Librn
Holdings: Vols (6000) Cat Microforms
Notes: Separate catalog. Botany and horticulture, especially of woody plants. Library is a branch of the National Agricultural Library. No photocopying.

FL —UNIVERSITY OF FLORIDA, Institute of Food & Agricultural Sciences, Hume Library, Gainesville, 32611. Albert C Strickland, Librn
Holdings: Vols (135,000) Cat Mss Microforms
Notes: Including journals and monographs, this collection is a general agricultural one. The emphasis is on tropical agriculture, especially Latin America. Entomology is very strong. The library offers on-line information retrieval using Lockheed and SDC data bases.

FL —RARE FRUIT COUNCIL INTERNATIONAL, 13609 Old Cutler Rd, Miami, 33158. Fred Frazer, Pres; Louise Garavatlia, Librn
Holdings: Vols (300)
Notes: Not open to the public.

GA —UNIVERSITY OF GEORGIA, College of Agriculture, Coastal Plain Experiment Station Library, Moore Hwy, Tifton, 31793. Emory Cheek, Library Specialist
Holdings: Vols (13,500) Cat

HI —BERNICE P BISHOP MUSEUM, Library, PO Box 19000-A, Honolulu, 96819. Cynthia Timberlake, Librn
Holdings: Vols (90,000) Cat Mss Maps Pix Slides Microforms
Budget: ($30,000)
Notes: Only American library devoted exclusively to the Pacific region. Collection reflects historical and contemporary research emphases of Bishop Museum; ie the natural and cultural history of the Pacific. Areas of concentration incl archaeology, ethnology, linguistics, voyages and explorations, history, vertebrate and invertebrate zoology, botany and museology. Strong special collections incl photographs, mss and archives, maps and art. Publications: Quarterly "Additions to the Catalog," *Dictionary Catalog of the* Library (9 vols and 2 suppl; Boston: G K Hall, 1964-69).

HI —PACIFIC TROPICAL BOTANICAL GARDEN, PO Box 340, Lawal, Kavai, 96765. Dr Clark Dalton, Librn

IL —ILLINOIS NATURAL HISTORY SURVEY LIBRARY, 196 Natural Resources Bldg, Champaign, 61820. Carla G Heister, Librn
Holdings: Vols (36,000) Cat Microforms
Budget: ($25,500)
Notes: A Research and Science Branch of the State of Illinois, the Natural History Survey maintains a library of books, journals and reports on various aspects of natural history. Material is collected in all major languages. The library maintains its own exchange arrangements with some 600 worldwide institutions and organizations. Interlibrary loans and photocopy services are available through the University of Illinois Library. Publications issued regularly by the Survey incl *Biological Notes, The Bulletin, and Circulars.*

IL —FIELD MUSEUM OF NATURAL HISTORY, Library, Roosevelt Rd & Lake Shore Dr, Chicago, 60605. W Peyton Fawcett, Librn; Benjamin W Williams, Assoc Librn
Holdings: Vols (210,000) Cat
Budget: ($100,000)
Notes: Extensive collections--publications of learned societies and institutions and monographic works--in all fields of natural history, with emphasis on taxonomy and evolutionary biology; and on museum publications, American and foreign: anthropology, especially archaeology and ethnology of the Americas, Africa, East Asia, and Oceania; botany, particularly strong for the Americas; geology, chiefly paleontology and meteoritic studies; and zoology, worldwide (birds, fishes, insects, mammals, mollusks, reptiles and amphibians).

IL —UNIVERSITY OF CHICAGO LIBRARIES, John Crerar Library Collections, 1100 E 57th St, Chicago, 60637. Robert Rosenthal, Special Collections Librn
Notes: The John Crerar Library's extensive science, medicine, and engineering collections have been transferred in trust to the University of Chicago Libraries. Incl rare books and special collections as listed here.

IL —MORTON ARBORETUM, Sterling Morton Library, Lisle, 60532. Ian MacPhail, Librn
Holdings: Vols (20,000) Cat Maps Pix
Budget: ($10,000)
Notes: The library is especially concerned with the literature of woody plants (trees and shrubs) of north temperate zones but has substantial holdings in the taxonomy and systematics of plants in general, both wild and cultivated, flora of different parts of the world, and a growing collection on plant monographs. Also about 2000 pictures. Described in *The Morton Arboretum* Quarterly, vol 9, no 4 (Winter 1973), pp 56-61.

IL —UNIVERSITY OF ILLINOIS, URBANA/CHAMPAIGN, Library, Biology Library, 101 Burrill Hall, 407 S Goodwin, Urbana, 61801. Elisabeth B Davis, Librn
Holdings: Vols (115,000) Cat Microforms
Budget: ($200,000)
Notes: The Biology Library incl books, periodicals, and reference works that cover the fields of anatomy, biophysics, botany, ecology, entomology, genetics, immunology, microbiology, physiology and zoology. About three-quarters of the total collection is made up of journals and other serials representing 2000 distinctive titles. The serial list is comprehensive for the biological sciences, contains most of the major international titles and consists of complete runs for almost all titles. Additional materials (approx 90,000 vols) in the biological sciences are available in the Natural History Survey Library and the bookstacks at the Main Library on the Urbana campus. Professional assistance is available for reference service, online searching, and library instruction. Interlibrary loan service is provided. Photocopying.

IN —INDIANA UNIVERSITY, Biology Library, Jordan Hall, Bloomington, 47405. Steven Sowell, Head
Holdings: Vols (105,461) Cat

IN —UNIVERSITY OF NOTRE DAME, University Libraries, Notre Dame, 46556.
Notes: The collection (4000 items) has many editions dating back to the 16th century and incl many works written by Edward L Greene, one of the foremost botanists of his time and a professor of botany at Notre Dame. The collection is exceptionally rich in fine and rare editions of classical botanical herbaria, published before and Carolus Linnaeus (1708-1778).

IN —PURDUE UNIVERSITY LIBRARIES, Life Sciences Library, Lilly Hall of Life Sciences, West Lafayette, 47907. Martha J Bailey, Librn
Holdings: Vols (73,404) Cat Microforms
Budget: ($223,445)
Notes: Incl materials in agronomy, animal sciences, botany, entomology, forestry, horticulture, biological sciences and agricultural engineering.

IA —IOWA STATE UNIVERSITY, Library, Ames, 50011. Warren B Kuhn, Dean of Library Services
Holdings: Cat Mss
Notes: Specific strengths: botanical taxonomy, ferns, mycology and plant pathology. Extensive serial holdings.

†IA —UNIVERSITY OF IOWA, Botany - Chemistry Library, Iowa City, 52242.
Holdings: Vols (60,000)

KS —UNIVERSITY OF KANSAS, Science Library, 6040 Malott Hall, Lawrence, 66045. Sharon R Cook, Asst Science Librn
Holdings: Vols Cat Maps Microforms
Notes: Incl US Geological Survey topographical maps.

KS —UNIVERSITY OF KANSAS, Kenneth Spencer Research Library, Special Collections Dept, Lawrence, 66045. Alexandra Mason, Librn
Holdings: Vols 5600 Cat Mss
Notes: About 2600 items before 1800. Espec

BOTANY (cont.)

strong in herbals, medical botany, Linnaeus, early American botanists (William Darlington, C S Rafinesque). Incl material from T J Fitzpatrick collection. Noncirculating.

LA —LOUISIANA STATE UNIVERSITY, Troy H Middleton Library, E A McIlhenny Natural History Collection, Baton Rouge, 70803. Kathryn N Morgan, Cur
Holdings: Vols (6000) Maps Pix
Notes: Collection of rare and valuable works on natural history with emphasis on ornithology and botany. Noncirculating collection open to researchers and vistors.

†MD —PUBLIC LIBRARY OF ANNAPOLIS, 1410 West St, Annapolis, 21401.
Notes: Collection at Annapolis branch, and at Glen Burnie branch.

MD —US DEPT OF AGRICULTURE, National Agricultural Library, 10301 Baltimore Blvd, Beltsville, 20705. Joseph H Howard, Director
Notes: Worldwide coverage of all aspects of agriculture and related fields. Crop ecology, agro-climatic analogs; air pollution effects. Agronomy: agricultural and tropical and desert agriculture. For use by the staff of the USDA. Incl in the former collections of American Institute of Crop Ecology.

MD —NATIONAL LIBRARY OF MEDICINE, 8600 Rockville Pike, Bethesda, 20209. Harold M Schoolinam, Actg Dir
Holdings: Vols (3,150,000) Cat Mss Audiotapes Videotapes 16mm Films Filmstrips Microforms
Budget: ($46,400)
Notes: The world's largest medical library. Materials are collected exhaustively in some 40 biomedical areas and, to a lesser degree, in related subject areas such as general chemistry, physics, zoology, botany, and instrumentation. Holdings include 80,000 monographic volumes, pre-1871; 368,000 monographic volumes, 1871-present; 545,000 bound serial volumes; 281,000 theses; 172, 000 pamphlets; 822,000 manuscripts; 32,000 microforms; 5000 audiovisuals; and 72,000 prints and photographs. Pre-1871 material is in a separate historical collection. Approximately 26,000 serial titles are currently received.

MA —UNIVERSITY OF MASSACHUSETTS AT AMHERST, Library, Amherst, 01003. Siegfried Feller, Assoc Dir for Collection Development
Holdings: Cat
Notes: Botanical taxonomy, physiology, pathology and mycology.

MA —MASSACHUSETTS HORTICULTURAL SOCIETY, 300 Massachusetts Ave, Boston, 02115. Becky Ellis, Librn
Holdings: Vols (37,000)
Notes: Garden history, pomology, flora, landscape design. Print collection of many centuries; nursery catalogues from the mid-18th century. In storage, remodeling, will be available in about a year. Open to the public.

MA —HARVARD UNIVERSITY LIBRARY, Farlow Reference Library, 20 Divinity Ave, Cambridge, 02138. Geraldine C Kaye, Librn
Holdings: Vols (60,000) Cat Mss Serials Pix Microforms
Notes: The Farlow Reference Library provides complete coverage of the systematic literature on algae, bryophytes, fungi, and lichens. Established by bequest of Professor William G Farlow, it is one of the most extensive cryptogamic botany libraries in the US. Books do not circulate.

MA —HARVARD UNIVERSITY LIBRARY, Arnold Arboretum Library, 22 Divinty Ave, Cambridge, 02138. Barbara A Callahan, Librn
Holdings: Vols (89,239) Cat Mss Maps Pix Slides Microforms
Notes: Specializes in trees (arboriculture and dendrology). Horticultural Library maintained at The Arborway, Jamaica Plain, Mass. Arnold Arboretum and Gray Herbarium Libraries hold one of the nation's largest collections (149,000 items).

MA —HARVARD UNIVERSITY LIBRARY, Gray Herbarium Library, 22 Divinity Ave, Cambridge, 02138. Barbara A Callahan, Librn
Holdings: Vols (61,445) Cat Pix Microforms
Notes: Flowering plants and ferns are emphasized. *Gray Herbarium Index,* 10 volumes (published 1968) reproduces 265, 000 cards giving names and literature citations of newly described or established vascular plants of the Western Hemisphere. One of the nation's strongest collections (149,000 items).

MA —NEW ENGLAND WILD FLOWER SOCIETY, INC, Lawrence Newcomb Library, Hemenway Rd, Framingham, 01701. Mary M Walker, Librn
Holdings: Vols (2500)
Budget: ($1000)
Notes: Incl 15,000 slides (35mm) and 4 vertical files.

MA —SMITH COLLEGE, Library, Northampton, 01063. Ruth Mortimer, Cur of Rare Books
Holdings: Vols 145 // Cat
Notes: Thornton Collection of 15-19th century herbals, early microscopy, Linneaus, biography.

MA —HARVARD UNIVERSITY, Harvard Forest Library, Petersham, 01366. Catherine M Danahar, Librn
Notes: Tropical botany.

MA —WELLESLEY COLLEGE, Margaret Clapp Library, College Archives, Wellesley, 02181.
Notes: Records of the Departments of Astronomy, Biological Sciences, Botany, Chemistry, Geology, Physics, Zoology, and individuals connected with these departments at Wellesley College (27 linear feet).

MI —UNIVERSITY OF MICHIGAN, Museums Library, Ann Arbor, 48109. Patricia B Yocum, Librn
Holdings: Vols 11,000 Cat Pix Microforms
Notes: Taxonomy.

MI —UNIVERSITY OF MICHIGAN, Matthaei Botanical Gardens, 1800 N Dixboro Rd, Ann Arbor, 48105. Annie Hannan, Collections Botanist
Holdings: Vols (1750)
Notes: Computer inventory of indoor collections. 30 scientific (botanical) journals.

MI —MICHIGAN STATE UNIVERSITY, Science Library, East Lansing, 48824. Carole S Armstrong, Head
Holdings: Vols 18,900 Cat
Notes: Collection has 390 journal titles with 9300 vols and 9600 monographs.

MN —UNIVERSITY OF MINNESOTA, Landscape Arboretum, Andersen Horticultural Library, 3675 Arboretum Drive, Box 39, Chanhassen, 55317. June Rogier, Head
Holdings: Vols (8000)

MN —MINNEAPOLIS PUBLIC LIBRARY & INFORMATION CENTER, 300 Nicollet Mall, Minneapolis, 55401. Richard J Hofstad, Athenaeum Librn
Holdings: Vols 700 Cat Pix
Notes: Incl rare books in natural history. Emphasis on botany and ornithology.

MS —GULF COAST RESEARCH LABORATORY, Gordon Gunter Library, E Beach Rd, Ocean Springs, 39564. Malcolm Ware, Sr, Librn
Holdings: Vols (9000) Uncat Mss Pix Microforms
Notes: Also have reprint collection of 30,000 cataloged reprints, indexed by card catalog, on all aspects of marine biology.

MO —MISSOURI BOTANICAL GARDEN LIBRARY, PO Box 299, Saint Louis, 63166. M R Crosby, Dir of Research
Holdings: Vols 82,000 Cat Pix Microforms
Notes: Incl 80,000 pamphlets and reprints and George Engelmann's botanical notebooks and correspondence, incl 6000 letters. Also, over 800 environmental impact statements.

†NH —UNIVERSITY OF NEW HAMPSHIRE, Biological Science Library, Kendall Hall, Durham, 03824. Lloyd Heldgard, Librn
Holdings: Vols (45,000)

NH —DARTMOUTH COLLEGE, Dartmouth-Hitchcock Medical Center, Dana Biomedical Library, Hanover, 03756. Shirley J Grainger, Librn
Holdings: Vols (146,611) Cat Mss Phonorecords Audiotapes Videotapes Microforms
Budget: ($280,000)

NY —NEW YORK BOTANICAL GARDEN LIBRARY, Bronx, 10458. Charles R Long, Asst Vice Pres & Dir
Holdings: Vols 150,000 Cat Mss Pix Slides Microforms VF
Budget: ($356,000)
Notes: One of the largest botanical collections in the world. Over 900,000 items. Covers botany (150,000 vols), botanists (3000), horticulture (45,000) plant diseases (25,000), plant physiology (15,000), history of botany (1500), conservation of natural resources (15,000), gardening (13,000), paleobotany (7000), ecology (20,000), forestry (5000) medical botany (3000), agriculture (9000) and biology (20,000). Reference library; materials do not circulate, except for member circulating collection (1200) and standard inter-library loan. About 5000 vols uncataloged. Incl art, books, serials, pamphlets, archives and manuscripts, vertical files, microfiche and microfilm, nursery and seed catalogs, photographs, paintings, prints, drawings and engravings. Covers all areas of botanical sciences. This is an OCLC library with fullresource services incl photocopying and photography.

NY —BROOKLYN BOTANIC GARDEN, 1000 Washington Ave, Brooklyn, 11225. Marie Giasi, Librn
Notes: A reference library of approx 55,000 vols of horticultural and botanical interest. Also, all publications of the Garden, incl annual reports, quarterly magazine "Plants & Gardens," pamphlets, newsletters, contributions and handbook series.

NY —BOYCE THOMPSON INSTITUTE FOR PLANT RESEARCH, Library, Cornell University, Tower Rd, Ithaca, 14853. Greta Colavito, Librn
Holdings: Vols (5300) Cat
Budget: ($46,000)
Notes: Mainly plant physiology, biochemistry, entomology, air and water pollution, pesticides, and plant pathology.

NY —AMERICAN MUSEUM OF NATURAL HISTORY, Library Services Dept, Central Park W & 79th St, New York, 10024. Nina J Root, Chairwoman; Mary Genett, Asst Librn for Reference Services
Notes: The Ernest Thompson Seton Diaries incl hundreds of examples of flora and fauna in drawings and sketches. Nearly all collections of the museum are outstanding for depth of coverage and international range. Early and historic works, rare books, colored illustrations, and relevant serial publications supplement the modern scientific publications necessary to the researches of the scientific staff and the work of the educational division. Open to the public.
See also entry under Ecology

NY —PLANTING FIELDS ARBORETUM HORTICULTURAL LIBRARY, Oyster Bay, 11771. Elizabeth K Reilley, Dir; Helen S Moskowitz, Librn
Holdings: Vols 4500
Notes: Incl periodicals and vertical file materials.

NY —GARDEN CENTER OF ROCHESTER INC, Library, 5 Castle Park, Rochester, 14620. Dorothea Baschnagel, Librn
Holdings: Vols (3000)
Notes: Gardening and home landscaping; plant identification; decorative use of plants; 19th century gardening. 700 bound periodicals, 30 periodical subscriptions.

NY —STATE UNIVERSITY OF NEW YORK, COLLEGE OF ENVIRONMENTAL SCIENCE AND FORESTRY, F Franklin Moon Library, Syracuse, 13210. Donald F Webster, Librn
Holdings: Vols (86,430) Cat
Budget: ($120,000)

†NC —UNIVERSITY OF NORTH CAROLINA, CHAPEL HILL, Department of Botany Library, 301 Coker Hall 010-A, Chapel Hill, 27514. William R Burk, Botany Librn
Notes: The mycology collection incl some

BOTANY (cont.)

6000 pamphlets. It contains papers of the following scientists: William C Coker, John N Couch, Lindsay F Olive, mycologists; also, Victor A Greulach, plant pathologist. The mycology catalog is in preparation (1983), and will provide author, title, and subject access.

OH —LLOYD LIBRARY & MUSEUM, 917 Plum St, Cincinnati, 45202. John B Griggs, Librn
Notes: Botany, with emphasis on morphology and taxonomy; plant chemistry and floras. Much Linnean literature, incl original editions.

OH —OHIO STATE UNIVERSITY, Biological Sciences Library, 1735 Neil Ave, Columbus, 43210. Victoria Welborn, Librn
Holdings: Vols (85,000) Cat Mss Maps Microforms

OH —HOLDEN ARBORETUM, Warren H Corning Library, 9500 Sperry Rd, Mentor, 44060. Paul C Spector, Dir of Education
Holdings: Vols (5500) // Cat
Notes: Extensive collection of horticultural classics, floras, herbals and monographs prior to 1850. Primarily European works.

OH —THE DAWES ARBORETUM LIBRARY, 7770 Jacksontown Rd SE, Newark, 43055. Alan D Cook, Senior Horticulturist
Holdings: Vols 5000

OR —OREGON STATE UNIVERSITY, Library, Corvallis, 97331. Melvin George, Dir
Holdings: Vols 13,500 Cat Pix

PA —ACADEMY OF NATURAL SCIENCES LIBRARY, 19 Benjamin Franklin Parkway, Philadelphia, 19103.
Holdings: Vols (180,000) Cat Mss Maps Pix Slides Microforms
Notes: Incl (250,000) mss. Described in *Academy of Natural Sciences of Philadelphia: Catalog* (Boston: G K Hall, 1972); *Guide to the Manuscript Collections in the Academy of Natural Sciences of* Philadelphia, by Venia T Phillips (Philadelphia: Academy of Natural Sciences, 1963).

PA —UNIVERSITY OF PENNSYLVANIA, Bio-Medical Library, Johnson Pavilion/G2, Philadelphia, 19104. Eleanor Goodchild, Librn
Holdings: Vols (139,000) Cat Slides Audiotapes Videotapes

PA —UNIVERSITY OF PENNSYLVANIA, Morris Arboretum Library, 9414 Meadowbrook Ave, Philadelphia, 19118.
Holdings: Vols 6000

PA —ZOOLOGICAL SOCIETY OF PHILADELPHIA, Library, 34 & Girard Ave, Philadelphia, 19104. Alyssa N Scheuermann, Librn
Holdings: Vols (500) Cat
Notes: Photocopying with permission.

PA —CARNEGIE LIBRARY OF PITTSBURGH, Science & Technology Dept, 4400 Forbes Ave, Pittsburgh, 15213. Catherine M Brosky, Dept Head
Holdings: Vols (380,000) Cat Maps Microforms
Budget: ($240,000)
Notes: Now of secondary importance, this subject was extensively developed from 1902 to 1945. Abstracts, indexes, bibliographies and the important reference books. There are some old and rare items in the original and some important compilations, sets and journals are available. Covers plant classification, physiology, nutrition, breeding, pathology, structural botany, plant chemistry, economic botany, plant history and geography.

PA —WEST CHESTER UNIVERSITY, Francis Harvey Green Library, West Chester, 19380. R Gerald Schoelkopf, Special Collections Librn
Holdings: Vols 1700 Cat Maps
Notes: The collection was the personal library of Dr William Darlington (1782-1863), Chester County botanist. It incl many titles of important botanical works in English and Latin published between 1800 and 1860. Also contains bound volumes of early scientific journals. A herbarium of plant specimens forms an adjunct to the collection.

RI —UNIVERSITY OF RHODE ISLAND, Library, Special Collections, Kingston, 02881. David Maslyn, Head

TN —THE BOTANICAL GARDENS, Minnie Ritchie and Joel Owsley Cheek Memorial Library, Forrest Park Drive, Nashville, 37205. Richard C Page, Dir Botanical Gardens
Holdings: Vols (3500) Cat Pix Slides
Budget: $2500

TX —UNIVERSITY OF TEXAS LIBRARIES, Science Library, PO Box P, Austin, 78712. Betty White, Librn
Holdings: Vols (103,000) Cat Microforms

TX —TEXAS A&M UNIVERSITY, Sterling C Evans Library, Special Collections Div, College Station, 77843. Donald H Dyal, Librn
Holdings: Vols (400) Cat
Notes: The E J Dyksterhuis Collection on American forestry, range science, ecology and botany (compiled by Professor Emeritus E J Dyksterhuis).

TX —SOUTHERN METHODIST UNIVERSITY, Fondren Library, Dallas, 75275. Curt Holleman, Librn for Collection Development

TX —UNIVERSITY OF TEXAS, Marine Science Institute Library, Port Aransas, 78373. Ruth Grundy, Librn
Holdings: Vols (45,000) Cat Maps Pix
Budget: ($70,000)
Notes: Current researches in marine science, especially concerning the Gulf of Mexico, the Texas Coastal Zone, and the Continental Shelf. Incl journals.

VA —NORFOLK BOTANICAL GARDENS LIBRARY, Airport Rd, Norfolk, 23518. Marian Cole, Librn
Holdings: Vols 1903 Cat Pix

WA —UNIVERSITY OF WASHINGTON LIBRARIES, Suzzallo Library, Natural Sciences Library, FM-25, Seattle, 98195. Nancy G Blase, Head
Holdings: Vols (192,353) Cat
Budget: ($219,809)

WI —UNIVERSITY OF WISCONSIN, MADISON, College of Agricultural & Life Sciences, Steenbock Memorial Library, 550 Babcock Dr, Madison, 53706. Jan Kennedy, Dir
Holdings: Vols (34,000)
Notes: Extensive general agricultural collection supporting the College of Agricultural and Life Sciences in agronomy, dairy science, agricultural engineering, entomology, botany, natural resources, nutrition, forestry, genetics, veterinary science, meat and animal science, poultry science, and soils. Collection includes USDA, USDI, experiment station and state documents.

WI —US FOREST SERVICE, Forest Products Laboratory Library, Box 5130, Madison, 53705. Roger Schurmer, Librn; Dr Regis Miller, Librn; Dr Harold H Burdsall, Jr, Librn
Holdings: Cat
See also entries under Herbaria; Mycology; Wood.

WI —MILWAUKEE PUBLIC MUSEUM, Reference Library, 800 W Wells St, Milwaukee, 53233. Judith Campbell Turner, Museum Librn
Holdings: Vols (90,000) Cat Maps Microforms

AB —CANADIAN FORESTRY SERVICE, Northern Forest Research Centre Library, 5320 122nd, Edmonton, T6H 3S5, Can. David J S Robinson, Librn
Holdings: Vols (7000) Cat Microforms
Budget: ($25,000)
Notes: Also 23,000 government documents, 2600 research reports, 3000 pamphlets and reprints.

†BC —UNIVERSITY OF BRITISH COLUMBIA, Botanic Garden, 6501 NW Marine Dr, Vancouver, V6T 1W5, Can. Roy I Taylor, Dir

MB —AGRICULTURE CANADA, Research Station Library, 195 Dafoe Rd, Winnipeg, R3T 2M9, Can. Mike Malyk, Librn
Holdings: Vols (8000) Cat
Notes: Incl the Buller Botanical Library. 5000 bound jounals, 5000 unbound journals, 200 periodicals, 12,000 government publications, 30,000 reprints. Founded 1926.

MB —MANITOBA MUSEUM OF MAN & NATURE, Library, 190 Rupert Ave, Winnipeg, R3B 0N2, Can. V Hatten, Librn
Holdings: Vols (20,000) Cat

MB —UNIVERSITY OF MANITOBA, Science Library, Machray Hall, Winnipeg, R3T 2N2, Can. V Simosko, Head
Holdings: Vols (90,000) Cat Microforms

ON —ROYAL BOTANICAL GARDENS, Library, Box 399, Hamilton, L8N 3H8, Can. Ina Vrugtman, Librn
Holdings: Vols (5000) Cat
Budget: ($13,000)
Notes: Botany and ornamental horticulture. Incl 10,000 slides. Periodicals are not yet union listed. Collection of nursery and seed trade catalogs; *Gray Herbarium Index;* Centre for Canadian Historical Horitcultural Studies. The library is located in the headquarters building of the Royal Botanical Gradens, 680 Plains Road West (Highway No 2) Burlington, Ontario. Phone: (416) 527-1158. Road West (Highway No 2) Burlington, Ontario. Phone: (416) 527-1158.

ON —AGRICULTURE CANADA, Research Branch, Neatby Library, Rm 3032, K W Neatby Bldg, CEF, Ottawa, K1A 0C6, Can. Marcel Charette, Library Technician
Holdings: Vols 1600 Cat

ON —AGRICULTURE CANADA, Plant Research Library, Research Branch, Central Experimental Farm 49, Ottawa, K1A 0C6, Can. Mrs E Gavora, Librn
Holdings: Vols (10,500) Cat Maps Microforms
Notes: One of the most extensive botanical collections in Canada, especially in the taxonomy of higher plants and fungi. Contains many of the basic works from the starting point of botany in 1753 to date. Major botanical works of Linnaeus and others, covering flora of land areas of most parts of the world.

ON —NATIONAL MUSEUMS OF CANADA, Library Services Directorate, Ottawa, K1A 0M8, Can. Valerie Monkhouse, Director
Holdings: Vols (90,000) Cat Mss Microforms
Budget: ($81,000)
Notes: Emphasis on Canadian and circumpolar natural history. Collection incl botany, herpetology, ichthyology, invertebrate zoology, malacology, mammology, mineralogy, ornithology, paleobiology, zooarchaeology. Exceptional collections in lichenology, bryology, malacology, ornithology. Research collection, interlibrary loans available, public may use on the premises.

ON —ROYAL ONTARIO MUSEUM, Main Library and Archives, 100 Queen's Park, Toronto, M5S 2C6, Can. Julia Matthews, Head Librn
Holdings: Vols (85,000) Cat
Notes: Since January 1977, acquisitions have been entered in UTLAS.

PQ —MCGILL UNIVERSITY, Botany-Genetics Library, 1205 McGregor Ave, Montreal, H3A 1B1, Can. Eleanor MacLean, Librn
Holdings: Vols (21,000) Cat

BOTANY—ARCTIC REGIONS

ON —NATIONAL MUSEUMS OF CANADA, Library Services Directorate, Ottawa, K1A 0M8, Can. Valerie Monkhouse, Director
Notes: Emphasis on Canadian and circumpolar natural history. Collection incl botany, herpetology, ichthyology, invertebrate zoology, malacology, mammology, mineralogy, ornithology, paleobiology, zooarchaeology. Exceptional collections in lichenology, bryology, malacology, ornithology. Research collection, interlibrary loans available, public may use on the premises.

BOTANY—AUSTRALIA

CA —LOS ANGELES STATE & COUNTY ARBORETUM, Plant Science Library, 301

BOTANY—AUSTRALIA (cont.)

N Baldwin Ave, Arcadia, 91006. Joan DeFato, Librn
Holdings: Vols (26,000)
Notes: Emphasis on woody plants, particularly of Australia and South Africa. Botany is weighted toward taxonomy rather than plant physiology.

†CA —HUNTINGTON BOTANICAL GARDENS LIBRARY, 1151 Oxford Rd, San Marino, 91108. Ann Ravenscroft, Secretary
Holdings: Vols (8000)
Notes: Emphases on history of botanical science; papers and notes of American botanists and naturalists of The West; botanical illustration, etc. Subtropical horticulture, incl cacti and succulents of Australia, South Africa, and Mexico.

BOTANY—BIOGRAPHY see Botanists

BOTANY—CALIFORNIA

CA —RANCHO SANTA ANA BOTANIC GARDEN LIBRARY, 1500 N College Ave, Claremont, 91711. Beatrice M Beck, Librn
Notes: Incl emphasis on California flora, floras of the world, evolutionary biology and ethnobotany.

CA —R MITCHEL BEAUCHAMP BOTANICAL LIBRARY, 1843 E 16th St, National City, 92050.
Notes: Survey and exploration reports. American seed and bulb catalogues, 1960-date.

CA —STRYBING ARBORETUM SOCIETY, Golden Gate Park Library, Jane Gates, Librn, 9th Ave at Lincoln Way, San Francisco, 94122.
Holdings: Vols (10,000)

CA —SANTA BARBARA BOTANIC GARDEN, Library, 1212 Mission Canyon Rd, Santa Barbara, 93105. Margaret Connors, Librn
Notes: Incl 1000 nursery and seed catalogs. Especially strong on California native plants.

BOTANY—CANADA

ON —AGRICULTURE CANADA, Library Division, Plant Research Library, 49 Central Experimental Farm Bldg, Ottawa, K1A 0C6, Can. Eva Gavora, Plant Research Librn
Holdings: (15,000) Items
Notes: Emphasis on flora of North America.

BOTANY—CLASSIFICATION

CA —LOS ANGELES STATE & COUNTY ARBORETUM, Plant Science Library, 301 N Baldwin Ave, Arcadia, 91006. Joan DeFato, Librn
Holdings: Vols (24,000) Cat 16mm Films
Budget: ($6000)
Notes: Emphasis on woody plants, particularly of Australia and South Africa. Botany is weighted toward taxonomy rather than plant physiology.

IA —IOWA STATE UNIVERSITY, Library, Ames, 50011. Warren B Kuhn, Dean of Library Services
Holdings: Cat Mss
Notes: Specific strenghts: botanical taxonomy, ferns, mycology and plant pathology. Extensive serial holdings.

MA —UNIVERSITY OF MASSACHUSETTS AT AMHERST, Library, Amherst, 01003. Siegfried Feller, Assoc Dir for Collection Development
Holdings: Cat
Notes: Botanical taxonomy, physiology, pathology and mycology.

MA —HARVARD UNIVERSITY LIBRARY, Gray Herbarium Library, 22 Divinity Ave, Cambridge, 02138. Barbara A Callahan, Librn
Holdings: Vols (61,445) Cat Mss Maps Pix Microforms
Notes: Downs 2325. Research in evolutionary and systematic botany.

MI —UNIVERSITY OF MICHIGAN, Museums Library, Ann Arbor, 48109. Patricia B Yocum, Librn
Holdings: Vols 11,000 Cat Pix Microforms
Notes: Taxonomy.

MI —UNIVERSITY OF MICHIGAN, Herbarium Library, University Herbarium, 2003 N University Bldg, Ann Arbor, 48109. Robert L Shaffer, Dir, Herbarium
Holdings: Vols (22,000) Cat Mss Maps Microforms
Notes: Systematic Botany including floristics, revisions and monographs in all groups of plants. Collection incl maps, mss (fieldbooks, correspondence, etc), photographs, microfiches, and approx 100, 000 reprints that are not officially part of the University Library. These are indexed and are available to qualified scholars. Incl botanical libraries of Parke, Davis & Co, Harley H Bartlett, Bruce Fink (lichens), Howard A Kelly (mycology).

PA —CARNEGIE LIBRARY OF PITTSBURGH, Science & Technology Dept, 4400 Forbes Ave, Pittsburgh, 15213. Catherine M Brosky, Dept Head
Notes: Now of secondary importance, this subject was extensively developed from 1902 to 1945. Abstracts, indexes, bibliographies and the important reference books. There are some old and rare items in the original and some important compilations, sets and journals are available. Covers plant classification, physiology, nutrition, breeding, pathology, structural botany, plant chemistry, economic botany, plant history and geography.

PA —HUNT INSTITUTE FOR BOTANICAL DOCUMENTATION, Hunt Botanical Library, Carnegie-Mellon University, Pittsburgh, 15213. Bernadette G Callery, Librn
Holdings: Vols (23,000) Cat Pix
Notes: Collection of primarily historical botany and plant taxonomy, especially 1730-1840. Includes approximately 500 15th through 17th century herbals, extensive collection of 18th and 19th century color-plate works, floras and monographic works, and other works on natural history, early gardening and horticulture, and travel, particularly that dealing with plant exploration and introduction. Extensive biographical materials, on people in plant sciences. Reference collection and extensive documentation in botanical bibliography, especially concerning books published before 1850. Includes as separate collections, the Strandell Collection of Linnaeana and the Michel Adanson Library. Over 800 items described in *Catalogue of Botanical Books in the Collection of Rachel McMasters Miller Hunt, 1477-1800* (Pittsburgh, 1958-1960).

ON —AGRICULTURE CANADA, Plant Research Library, Research Branch, Central Experimental Farm 49, Ottawa, K1A 0C6, Can. Mrs E Gavora, Librn
Holdings: Vols (10,500) Cat Maps Microforms
Notes: One of the most extensive botanical collections in Canada, especially in the taxonomy of higher plants and fungi. Contains many of the basic works from the starting point of botany in 1753 to date. Major botanical works of Linnaeus and others, covering flora of land areas of most parts of the world.

BOTANY—COLORADO

CO —HORTICULTURAL ART SOCIETY OF COLORADO SPRINGS, Library, Orchard House, 3202 Chambers Way, Colorado Springs, 80904. Ernestine H Fagan, Librn
Holdings: Vols (950)
Notes: Horticulture of the Pikes Peak Region.

†CO —DENVER BOTANIC GARDENS, Helen Fowler Library, 909 York St, Denver, 80206. Solange G Gignac, Librn
Notes: Emphasis on Bromeliada Literature; horticulture; Colorado, Oregon, and Rocky Mountains Region botany; landscape architecture; juvenile horticultural and botanical literature. Incl over 5000 pamphlets on botany and horticulture; also, 197 watercolors of Colorado wildflowers by Emma Irvine, and 250 of Oregon by Lillian Hallock.

BOTANY—ECOLOGY

FL —ARCHBOLD BIOLOGICAL STATION, Library, Rt 2, Box 180, Lake Placid, 33852. Fred E Lohrer, Librn
Holdings: Cat Slides
Notes: Florida natural history. Emphasis on south central peninsular Florida. Habitats, plants, vertebrates, land use changes. About 8000 2x2 color transparencies and 35mm films.

NV —FORESTA INSTITUTE FOR OCEAN AND MOUNTAIN STUDIES, Library, 6205 Franktown Rd, Carson City, 89701. Shannon Porter, Librn
Holdings: Vols (3000) Cat Mss Maps Pix Slides
Notes: Material on plant, animal, and human ecology with special emphasis on far western US and Nevada ecology and environmental problems. Also hold about 2000 reprints, pamphlets, reports, etc.

ND —NORTHERN PRAIRIE WILDLIFE RESEARCH CENTER, Library, PO Box 1747, Jamestown, 58401.
Holdings: Vols (2500) Cat Pix Slides
Budget: ($10,000)
Notes: Wildlife management and research, incl avian biology, plant and animal ecology as related to wetlands and prairies, waterfowl research, and effects of predators on waterfowl.

WI —UNIVERSITY OF WISCONSIN, MADISON, College of Agricultural & Life Sciences, Steenbock Memorial Library, 550 Babcock Dr, Madison, 53706. Jan Kennedy, Dir
Holdings: Vols (186,312) Cat Docs Microforms
Notes: Collection includes plant and animal ecology to support horticulture, plant pathology, forestry, and wildlife ecology programs.

BOTANY—HAWAII

HI —PACIFIC TROPICAL BOTANICAL GARDEN, PO Box 340, Lawal, Kavai, 96765. Dr Clark Dalton, Librn

BOTANY—HISTORY

CA —RANCHO SANTA ANA BOTANIC GARDEN LIBRARY, 1500 N College Ave, Claremont, 91711. Beatrice M Beck, Librn
Holdings: Vols 30,000 Cat Maps Microforms
Notes: Incl emphasis on California flora, floras of the world, evolutionary biology and ethnobotany.

†CA —HUNTINGTON BOTANICAL GARDENS LIBRARY, 1151 Oxford Rd, San Marino, 91108. Ann Ravenscroft, Secretary
Notes: Emphases on history of botanical science; papers and notes of American botanists and naturalists of The West; botanical illustration, etc. Subtropical horticulture, incl cacti and succulents of Australia, South Africa, and Mexico.

†CT —UNIVERSITY OF CONNECTICUT LIBRARY, Special Collections Dept, Storrs, 06268. Richard H Schimmelpfeng, Dir of Special Collections

IL —MORTON ARBORETUM, Sterling Morton Library, Lisle, 60532. Ian MacPhail, Librn
Holdings: Vols (22,000)
Notes: Emphasis is on Woody plants. Print collection of 3000 pieces; 2000 botanical and horticultural rare books; Linnaeana. The Jens Jensen Archive of letters, photographs, blueprints, landscape plans.

MD —US DEPT OF AGRICULTURE, National Agricultural Library, 10301 Baltimore Blvd, Beltsville, 20705. Joseph H Howard, Director
Notes: Worldwide coverage of all aspects of agriculture and related fields. Crop ecology, agro-climatic analogs; air pollution effects. Agronomy: agricultural and tropical and desert agriculture. For use by the staff of the USDA. Incl in the former collections of American Institute of Crop Ecology.

MA —MASSACHUSETTS HORTICULTURAL SOCIETY, 300 Massachusetts Ave, Boston, 02115. Becky Ellis, Librn
Holdings: Vols (37,000)
Notes: Garden history, pomology, flora, landscape design. Print collection of many

BOTANY—HISTORY (cont.)

centuries; nursery catalogues from the mid-18th century. In storage, remodeling, will be available in about a year. Open to the public.

MA —HARVARD UNIVERSITY LIBRARY, Arnold Arboretum Library, 22 Divinty Ave, Cambridge, 02138. Barbara A Callahan, Librn
Holdings: Vols (89,239) Cat Mss Maps Pix Slides Microforms
Notes: Specializes in trees (arboriculture and dendrology). Horticultural Library maintained at The Arborway. Jamaica Plain, Mass.

MA —HARVARD UNIVERSITY LIBRARY, Gray Herbarium Library, 22 Divinity Ave, Cambridge, 02138. Barbara A Callahan, Librn
Holdings: Vols 56,278 Cat Mss Maps Pix Microforms
Notes: Downs 2325. Research in evolutionary and systematic botany.

MA —HERB SOCIETY OF AMERICA, Library, 2 Independence Court, Concord, 01742. Julie Macksoud, Exec Dir
Holdings: Vols (600)

MI —UNIVERSITY OF MICHIGAN, Library, Dept of Rare Books & Special Collections, Ann Arbor, 48109. Robert J Starring, Head
Holdings: Cat Mss Pix
Notes: Chiefly pre-1800 imprints.

MO —MISSOURI BOTANICAL GARDEN LIBRARY, PO Box 299, Saint Louis, 63166. M R Crosby, Dir of Research
Holdings: Cat
Notes: Sturtevant Collection of pre-Linnean (pre-1753) books and Linnean collection. Also George Engelmann's correspondence with famous botanists and 6000 letters discussing botanical species. Also 60 vols of his notes and beautifully drawn sketches from his extensive studies on Cactaceae, Coniferae, Yucca, Agave, Isoetes, etc.

NY —NEW YORK BOTANICAL GARDEN LIBRARY, Bronx, 10458. Charles R Long, Asst Vice Pres & Dir
Holdings: Vols 1500 Cat Mss Pix Slides Microforms VF
Budget: ($356,000)
Notes: One of the largest botanical collections in the world. Covers botany (150, 000 vols), botanists (3000), horticulture (45, 000), plant diseases (25,000), plant physiology (15,000), history of botany (1500), conservation of natural resources (15,000), gardening (13,000), paleobotany (7000), ecology (20,000), forestry (5000), medical botany (3000), agriculture (9000) and biology (20,000). Reference library; materials do not circulate, except via standard inter-library loan. About 5000 vols uncataloged. Incl archives, art and vertical files. An OCLC library.

NY —CORNELL UNIVERSITY LIBRARIES, John M Olin Library, History of Science Collections, Ithaca, 14853. Lillian A Clark, Administrative Supervisor; David W Corson, History of Science Librn
Notes: Very extensive collection of history, biography and bibliography.
See also entry under Science - History

OH —OHIO UNIVERSITY, Vernon R Alden Library, Department of Archives and Special Collections, Athens, 45701. Gary A Hunt, Head
Holdings: Mss
Notes: Botanical notebooks, mss and printed documents of Manasseh Cutler, dating from 1776-1822.

OH —CLEVELAND PUBLIC LIBRARY, Science & Technology Dept, 325 Superior Ave, Cleveland, 44114. Jean Z Piety, Head
Holdings: Cat
Notes: Many early volumes.

OH —GARDEN CENTER OF GREATER CLEVELAND, Eleanor Squire Library, 11030 East Blvd, Cleveland, 44106. Richard T Isaacson, Librn
Notes: The Warren C Corning Collection of Horticultural Classics. The Flowering Plant Index of Illustration and Information.

PA —BRYN MAWR COLLEGE, Canaday Library, Bryn Mawr, 19010. James Tanis, Dir
Holdings: Vols 5000 Cat Mss Pix
Notes: Rare books: Michaelis, Zirkle (Botony) and Castle (Ornithology and Botanical Illustration) Collections.

PA —LIBRARY COMPANY OF PHILADELPHIA, 1314 Locust St, Philadelphia, 19107. Edwin Wolf II, Librn; Kenneth Finkel, Cur of Prints
Holdings: Vols (400,000) Cat Maps Pix
Budget: ($25,000)
Notes: American science and industry before 1860. Books, pamphlets, etc on science incl math, pysics, astronomy, and industry, incl business and engineering. Incl many 18th century books printed in England and France but used by American colonials in their study and research. Impossible to estimate the exact size of collection since it is not separated from general collection.

PA —HUNT INSTITUTE FOR BOTANICAL DOCUMENTATION, Hunt Botanical Library, Carnegie-Mellon University, Pittsburgh, 15213. Bernadette G Callery, Librn
Holdings: Vols (23,000) Cat Pix
Notes: Collection of primarily historical botany and plant taxonomy, especially 1730-1840. Includes approximately 500 15th through 17th century herbals, extensive collection of 18th and 19th century color-plate works, floras and monographic works, and other works on natural history, early gardening and horticulture, and travel, particularly that dealing with plant exploration and introduction. Extensive biographical materials, on people in plant sciences. Reference collection and extensive documentation in botanical bibliography, especially concerning books published before 1850. Includes as separate collections, the Strandell Collection of Linnaeana and the Michel Adanson Library. Over 800 items described in *Catalogue of Botanical Books in the Collection of Rachel McMasters Miller Hunt, 1477-1800* (Pittsburgh, 1958-1960).

PA —PENNSYLVANIA STATE UNIVERSITY, Fred Lewis Pattee Library, Special Collections Dept, University Park, 16802. Charles Mann, Chief, Special Collections
Holdings: Vols 89 Uncat
Budget: ($37,000)
Notes: Gift of Robert E Dengler, it includes early editions of the work of the Greek botanists, beginning with the *editio princeps* of 1483.

RI —BROWN UNIVERSITY, John Hay Library, 20 Prospect St, Providence, 02912. Mark N Brown, Cur Mss
Holdings: // Mss
Notes: Solomon Drowne papers. He was a physician and Professor of Botany at Brown, Class of 1773. Mss incl accounts, invoices, receipts; originals and copies of prose and poetry; notes of Dr Drowne; sketches and valentines; political, legal, and military documents; and ships' papers. Subjects incl Colonial and Revolutionary history of Rhode Island and Brown University; medicine and botany 1770-1834; the early history of Morgantown, Virginia; Union, Pennsylvania; and Marietta, Ohio; business and trade in the Colonial period; and the Continental Congress. Correspondence with most persons of importance in his time.

TX —UNIVERSITY OF TEXAS LIBRARIES, Science Library, PO Box P, Austin, 78712. Betty White, Librn
Holdings: Vols (103,000) Cat Microforms

WI —UNIVERSITY OF WISCONSIN, MADISON, Memorial Library, Rare Books Collection, 728 State St, Madison, 53706. Gretchen Lagana, Cur
Holdings: Vols 142 Cat

BOTANY—ILLUSTRATION see Botanical Illustration

BOTANY—MEDITERRANEAN REGION

CA —STRYBING ARBORETUM SOCIETY, Golden Gate Park Library, Jane Gates, Librn, 9th Ave at Lincoln Way, San Francisco, 94122.
Holdings: Vols (10,000)

BOTANY—MEXICO

†CA —HUNTINGTON BOTANICAL GARDENS LIBRARY, 1151 Oxford Rd, San Marino, 91108. Ann Ravenscroft, Secretary
Holdings: Vols (8000)
Notes: Emphasis on history of botanical science; papers and notes of American botanists and naturalists of The West; botanical illustration, etc. Subtropical horticulture, incl cacti and succulents of Australia, South Africa, and Mexico.

BOTANY—NORTH CAROLINA

SC —COLLEGE OF CHARLESTON LIBRARY, Special Collections Dept, Charleston, 29401.
Notes: Specimens collected in Summerville, SC, and Flat Rock, NC, 1883-1884.

BOTANY—OREGON

†CO —DENVER BOTANIC GARDENS, Helen Fowler Library, 909 York St, Denver, 80206. Solange G Gignac, Librn
Notes: Emphasis on Bromeliada Literature; horticulture; Colorado, Oregon, and Rocky Mountains Region botany; landscape architecture; juvenile horticultural and botanical literature. Incl over 5000 pamphlets on botany and horticulture; also, 197 watercolors of Colorado wildflowers by Emma Irvine, and 250 of Oregon by Lillian Hallock.

BOTANY—PATHOLOGY see Plant Diseases

BOTANY—PENNSYLVANIA

PA —PENNSYLVANIA HORTICULTURAL SOCIETY, Library, 325 Walnut St, Philadelphia, 19106. Mary Lou Wolfe, Librn
Notes: Publications: *Selected Books From the Library of the Pennsylvania Horticultural Society*, 1976; *From Seed to Flower, Philadelphia 1681-1876*, 1976.

BOTANY—PHYSIOLOGY see Plant Physiology

BOTANY—SOUTH AFRICA

CA —LOS ANGELES STATE & COUNTY ARBORETUM, Plant Science Library, 301 N Baldwin Ave, Arcadia, 91006. Joan DeFato, Librn
Holdings: Vols (26,000)
Notes: Emphasis on woody plants, particularly of Australia and South Africa. Botany is weighted toward taxonomy rather than plant physiology.

†CA —HUNTINGTON BOTANICAL GARDENS LIBRARY, 1151 Oxford Rd, San Marino, 91108. Ann Ravenscroft, Secretary
Holdings: Vols (8000)
Notes: Emphases on history of botanical science; papers and notes of American botanists and naturalists of The West; botanical illustration, etc. Subtropical horticulture, incl cacti and succulents of Australia, South Africa, and Mexico.

BOTANY—SOUTH CAROLINA

SC —COLLEGE OF CHARLESTON LIBRARY, Special Collections Dept, Charleston, 29401.
Notes: Specimens collected in Summerville, SC, and Flat Rock, NC, 1883-1884.

BOTANY—TAXONOMY see Botany—Classification

BOTANY—U.S.

MA —HARVARD UNIVERSITY LIBRARY, Gray Herbarium Library, 22 Divinity Ave, Cambridge, 02138. Barbara A Callahan, Librn
Notes: Arnold Arboretum and Gray Herbarium Libraries hold one of the nation's largest collections (149,000 items).

†PA —LIBRARY COMPANY OF PHILADELPHIA, 1314 Locust St, Philadelphia, 19107. Edwin Wolf II, Librn
Holdings: Vols (450,000)

BOTANY, AGRICULTURAL see Botany, Economic

BOTANY, ECONOMIC

KY —UNIVERSITY OF KENTUCKY, Agriculture Library, Agricultural Science Center North, Lexington, 40546. Antoinette P Powell, Head Librn
Holdings: Vols (90,000) Cat Maps Microforms
Budget: ($110,582)

MA —HARVARD UNIVERSITY LIBRARY, Arnold Arboretum Library, 22 Divinty Ave, Cambridge, 02138. Barbara A Callahan, Librn
Holdings: Vols (89,239) Cat Mss Maps Pix Slides Microforms
Notes: Specializes in trees (arboriculture and dendrology). Horticultural Library maintained at The Arborway, Jamaica Plain, Mass.

PA —CARNEGIE LIBRARY OF PITTSBURGH, Science & Technology Dept, 4400 Forbes Ave, Pittsburgh, 15213. Catherine M Brosky, Dept Head
Notes: Now of secondary importance, this subject was extensively developed from 1902 to 1945. Abstracts, indexes, bibliographies and the important reference books. There are some old and rare items in the original and some important compilations, sets and journals are available. Covers plant classification, physiology, nutrition, breeding, pathology, structural botany, plant chemistry, economic botany, plant history and geography.

BOTANY, FOSSIL see Paleobotany

BOTANY, MEDICAL

CA —UNIVERSITY OF SOUTHERN CALIFORNIA, School of Medicine, Norris Medical Library, 2025 Zonal Ave, Los Angeles, 90033. Nelson J Gilman, Librn
Holdings: Vols 275 Cat
Budget: $200
Notes: The Collection of American Indian Ethnopharmacology.

CT —YALE UNIVERSITY, Medical Historical Library, Klebs Collection, 333 Cedar St, New Haven, 06520. Ferenc A Gyorgyey, Librn
Notes: The Arnold Carl Klebs Medical Collection books, pamphlets, etc, incl the library of his father, Edwin T A Klebs, pathologist. Strong in bibliography of early printed medical books, herbals, plague tracts, inoculation, vaccination and tubercular diseases.

†CT —UNIVERSITY OF CONNECTICUT LIBRARY, Special Collections Dept, Storrs, 06268. Richard H Schimmelpfeng, Dir of Special Collections

GA —MEDICAL COLLEGE OF GEORGIA, Library, Laney Walker Blvd, Augusta, 30902. Dorothy H Mims, Librn for Special Collections
Holdings: Vols (2500) Cat
Notes: Special collection of late 18th and early 19th century medical works, incl texts and atlases of medical botany.

IL —UNIVERSITY OF ILLINOIS AT CHICAGO, Library of the Health Sciences, 1750 W Polk St, PO Box 7509, Chicago, 60612. Robert J Adelsperger, Cur, Special Collections
Holdings: Vols (6000) Cat Mss
Notes: Emphasis on pharmacopoeias, formularies and dispensatories, and American and foreign herbals. Description of collection in *Pharmacopeias, Formularies,* Dispensatories (Chicago: Library of the Health Sciences, 1975).

KS —UNIVERSITY OF KANSAS, Kenneth Spencer Research Library, Special Collections Dept, Lawrence, 66045. Alexandra Mason, Librn
Holdings: Vols (5600) Cat Mss
Notes: About 2600 items before 1800. Espec strong in herbals, medical botany, Linnaeus, early American botanists (William Darlington, C S Rafinesque). Incl material from T J Fitzpatrick collection. Noncirculating.

MA —MASSACHUSETTS COLLEGE OF PHARMACY AND ALLIED HEALTH SCIENCES, Sheppard Library, 179 Longwood Ave, Boston, 02115. Barbara M Hill, Librn
Holdings: Vols (56,000) Cat Mss Pix Slides Microforms
Notes: Worldwide representation.

MA —HARVARD UNIVERSITY LIBRARY, Botanical Museum Library, Cambridge, 02138.
Holdings: Vols (2400) Mss Pix
Notes: The Tina and Gordon Wisson Ethnomycological Collection, one of the most important modern collections, acquired as an adjunct to the Museum's Economic Botany Library of Oakes Ames. From 15th to 20th century, it deals with hallucinogenic mushrooms in art, religion, and folklore; chemistry, pharmacology, linguistics, archaeological artifacts of Mexico, Guatemala, India, Japan, China, etc. Personal papers, etc.

MI —UNIVERSITY OF MICHIGAN, Herbarium Library, University Herbarium, 2003 N University Bldg, Ann Arbor, 48109. Robert L Shaffer, Dir, Herbarium
Holdings: Vols 2311 Cat
Notes: Gift from Parke Davis and Co in 1933. Many volumes are rare and noncirculating; for scholarly research only. Other items added through gifts and purchase.

MN —UNIVERSITY OF MINNESOTA, Owen H Wangensteen Historical Library of Biology & Medicine, Diehl Hall, Minneapolis, 55455. Judith Overmier, Cur
Holdings: Vols (35,000) Cat
Budget: ($80,000)
Notes: Incl History and Historic.

MN —3M COMPANY, 3M Center, Riker Laboratories, Saint Paul, 55101.
Holdings: Vols (6100) Cat
Budget: ($13,000)
Notes: Covers medical and pharmaceutical chemistry and medical botany. Incl 2600 books (175 drug directories) and 3500 bound journal vols.

NY —NEW YORK BOTANICAL GARDEN LIBRARY, Bronx, 10458. Charles R Long, Asst Vice Pres & Dir
Holdings: Vols 3000 Cat Mss Pix Slides Microforms VF
Budget: ($356,000)
Notes: One of the largest botanical collections in the world. Covers botany (150, 000 vols), botanists (3000), horticulture (45, 000), plant diseases (25,000), plant physiology (15,000), history of botany (1500), conservation of natural resources (15,000), gardening (13,000), paleobotany (7000), ecology (20,000), forestry (5000), medical botany (3000), agriculture (9000) and biology (20,000). Reference library; materials do not circulate, except via standard inter-library loan. About 5000 vols uncataloged. Incl archives, art and vertical files. An OCLC library.

OH —LLOYD LIBRARY & MUSEUM, 917 Plum St, Cincinnati, 45202. John B Griggs, Librn
Notes: Extensive holdings on drug plants, plant drugs, pharmacognosy, and plant chemistry.

OH —CLEVELAND MEDICAL LIBRARY ASSOCIATION/CASE WESTERN RESERVE UNIVERSITY, Cleveland Health Sciences Library, Historical Division, Allen Memorial Medical Library, 11000 Euclid Ave, Cleveland, 44106. Glen Jenkins, Rare Book Librarian & Archivist
Holdings: Vols 500 Cat
Notes: Partially described in Fisch, Ruth B and Max H, "The Marshall Collection of Herbals in the Cleveland Medical Library" (checklist), *Bulletin of the History of* Medicine, 1947, vol 21, pp 224-261.

OH —MIAMI UNIVERSITY, King Library, Walter Havighurst Special Collections Library, Oxford, 45056. Helen Ball, Cur of Special Collections
Holdings: Vols 150
Notes: American 19th century botanical medicine. Incl pamphlets, periodicals and ephemera.

PA —PENNSYLVANIA HOSPITAL HISTORICAL LIBRARY, Eighth & Spruce Sts, Philadelphia, 19107. Caroline Morris, Librn
Holdings: Vols (12,963) // Cat Mss
Notes: First medical library in US. Rich in runs of 19th century medical journals. Some early botany books. Some incunabula. Printed catalog was made in 1876. This collection is important because it reflects the history of medicine by the nature of the materials that were acquired. However, *no attempt is made to keep a current history of medicine library.*

BOTANY, SYSTEMATIC see Botany—Classification

BOTHWELL, JEAN

MA —BOSTON UNIVERSITY, Mugar Memorial Library, Special Collections Dept, 771 Commonwealth Ave, Boston, 02215. Howard B Gotlieb, Dir
Holdings: // Cat Mss Pix
Notes: Mss, correspondence, etc collected in depth; incl publications by or about.

BOTKIN, BENJAMIN A.

NE —UNIVERSITY OF NEBRASKA-LINCOLN, Don L Love Library, Lincoln, 68588. Joseph G Svoboda, University Archivist
Holdings: Vols (8000) // Uncat Mss Pix Slides Phonorecords Audiotapes Microforms
Notes: This is an extensive collection belonging to the folklorist Benjamin A Botkin, about 500 linear ft, consisting of various types of materials. Main emphasis is American folklore, although folklore of all nations is incl.

BOTKINE, SERGE

CA —HOOVER INSTITUTION ON WAR, REVOLUTION & PEACE, Stanford University, Stanford, 94305. Milorad M Drachkovitch, Archivist
Holdings: // Mss
Notes: Archives of the Imperial Russian Consulate General, Leipzig, Germany, consisting of correspondence (1830-1876), reports (1878-1914) on conditions and events in Germany, and circulars (1860-1914) of the Russian Foreign Office concerning the consular service; together with memoranda (1919-1924) on political questions affecting Russians in Bolshevik Russia, reports (1922-1930) on the condition of Russian emigre groups, memoranda (1924-1928) concerning the situation of emigres in Germany, and copies of confidential reports (1921-1926) of Russian diplomatic representatives in various countries addressed to the senior Russian representative in Paris. 10 ft.

BOTSFORD, TALITHA

NY —CORNELL UNIVERSITY LIBRARIES, Collection of Regional History, Dept of Manuscripts and Univ Archives, Ithaca, 14853.
Notes: Artist. Water colors and pen-and ink sketches, 1950-71; 8 map case drawers.

BOTSWANA

DC —HOWARD UNIVERSITY, Moorland-Spingarn Research Center, 500 Howard Place NW, Washington, 20059. Clifford L Muse, Jr, Acting Dir

OH —OHIO UNIVERSITY, Vernon R Alden Library, Athens, 45701. Kent Mulliner, Africana Specialist
Holdings: Vols (30,000) Cat Maps Microforms
Notes: Major emphasis on South Africa, East Africa, and Nigeria. Incl extensive collection of government reports and newspapers on microfilm.

BOTTOMLEY, GORDON

NY —HOFSTRA UNIVERSITY, Library, 1000 Fulton Ave, Hempstead, 11550.

BOTTOMLEY, GORDON (cont.)

Charles R Andrews, Dean of Library Services
Notes: Strong collection. Incl some mss.
BC —UNIVERSITY OF VICTORIA, McPherson Library, Victoria, V8W 3H5, Can.

BOUCHER, TONY see White, William Anthony Parker (Tony Boucher)

BOUCICAULT, DION

FL —UNIVERSITY OF SOUTH FLORIDA, Library, Tampa, 33620. J B Dobkin, Special Collections Librn
Holdings: Cat Mss
Notes: The theatre of Dion Boucicault; almost exclusively manuscript materials (a major collection) but with a very few published plays or works by or about Boucicault.

BOUCK, WILLIAM C., 1786-1859

NY —CORNELL UNIVERSITY LIBRARIES, Collection of Regional History, Dept of Manuscripts and Univ Archives, Ithaca, 14853.
Holdings: Mss Microforms
Notes: Governor of NY, 1843-44; postmaster, sheriff, assemblyman, construction contractor. Considerable correspondence concerning official duties, canal construction projects and problems, legal, personal, and family business, and sale of lands. Legal documents of Bouck, his father, Christian, and his grandfather, William.

BOUDINOT FAMILY

NJ —PRINCETON UNIVERSITY, Library, Manuscript Collection, Nassau St, Princeton, 08540. Jean F Preston, Cur
Holdings: Vols 40 Cat Mss
Notes: The mss occupy 7 ms boxes. Most of the material relates to Elias Boudinot (1740-1821).

BOUDREAU, FRANK GEORGE

NY —NEW YORK ACADEMY OF MEDICINE, Library, 2 E 103 St, New York, 10029. Brett A Kirkpatrick, Librn
Holdings: Uncat Mss Pix
Notes: Collection of personal papers of Frank George Boudreau, incl correspondence, from his birth to his early years as health officer in Ohio, through his international experience at the League of Nations, and as President of the Milbank Memorial Fund. Much on epidemiology, public health, and public medicine. Collection described in Lee Ash's "Frank George Boudreau, 18 July 1886-14 February 1970," *The Academy Bookman*, (New York Academy of Medicine, Friends of the Rare Book Room), Vol 26, No 1, 1973, pp 6-7.

BOUHOURS, DOMINIQUE

CA —UNIVERSITY OF CALIFORNIA, LOS ANGELES, William Andrews Clark Memorial Library, 2520 Cimarron St, Los Angeles, 90018.
Holdings: // Cat
Notes: Original editions.

BOUNDARIES

ME —BOWDOIN COLLEGE, Library, Brunswick, 04011. Dianne M Gutscher, Cur of Special Collections
Holdings: Mss
Notes: The Charles S Daveis Papers consist of about 400 items of correspondence, addresses, and documents, 1808-1864, of this Portland, Maine, lawyer who was active in the settlement of the dispute with Great Britain over Maine's northeastern boundary.
NY —NEW YORK PUBLIC LIBRARY, Research Libraries, American History Div, Fifth Ave & 42 St, New York, 10018.
Holdings: Vols (20,000) Cat Maps Microforms
Notes: Encompasses all countries of Latin America. Outstanding collection of materials on Mexico and material on boundary disputes among countries of the Western Hemisphere. Local history materials for Latin America are incl. See *Dictionary Catalog of the History of Americas* Collections (Boston: G K Hall, 1961), 28 vols.

BOURASSA, HENRI

AB —UNIVERSITY OF CALGARY, Library, Calgary, T2N 1N4, Can. Apollonia Steele, Special Collections Librn
Holdings: Cat
Notes: With a strengthened collection of materials on French Canada, incl many runs of periodicals and an extensive amount of early pamphlets, incl those of Henri Bourassa and other political figures.

BOURBON FAMILY

WI —UNIVERSITY OF WISCONSIN, MADISON, Memorial Library, Rare Books Collection, 728 State St, Madison, 53706. Gretchen Lagana, Cur
Notes: The Wight Collection, acquired in 1943, consists of about 1000 volumes related to the Bourbon family and pretenders to the throne of France. Willard Ward Wight's *Louis XVII, A Bibliography* (1915) serves as a partial guide to the collection.

BOURDUE, CHOLLET AND BOURDUE

SC —COLLEGE OF CHARLESTON LIBRARY, Special Collections Dept, Charleston, 29401.
Notes: Contains mss copies of letters sent by Edward Simons, of the counting house of Keating Simons & Sons, informing Donald Rowe, Stephen Elliot, Benjamin Seabrook, Benjamin Alston, Louisa Ingraham, Ellis Emanuel, William Maynard, John Carter, and Admiral Blanding that their notes payable to Bourdue, Chollet & Bourdue were stolen, May 26 or 27, 1821.

BOURJAILY, VANCE NYE, 1922-

ME —BOWDOIN COLLEGE, Library, Brunswick, 04011. Dianne M Gutscher, Cur of Special Collections
Holdings: Vols Cat Mss
Notes: The literary archives of this prominent contemporary American novelist, the collection contains ms and printed materials, as well as several hundred pieces of correspondence, and a file of reviews and clippings.

BOURKE-WHITE, MARGARET

NY —SYRACUSE UNIVERSITY LIBRARIES, Ernest S Bird Library, George Arents Research Library for Special Collections, Syracuse, 13210. Carolyn A Davis, Manuscripts Librn; Amy S Doherty, University Archivist; Mark F Weimer, Rare Book Librn
Notes: Correspondence, writings, photographs.

BOURNEUF, PHILIP

MA —BOSTON UNIVERSITY, Mugar Memorial Library, Special Collections Dept, 771 Commonwealth Ave, Boston, 02215. Howard B Gotlieb, Dir
Holdings: Cat Mss Pix

BOUTAN LANGUAGE see Tibetan Language and Literature

BOUTWELL, ALBERT

AL —BIRMINGHAM PUBLIC LIBRARY, Dept of Archives & Mss, 2020 Seventh Ave N, Birmingham, 35203. Marvin Y Whiting, Archivist & Cur
Holdings: Cat Mss //
Notes: Collected papers, 1963-1967 for Albert Boutwell, first mayor of Birmingham, Alabama under the mayor-council form of government. His administration was dominated by several concerns: the Civil Rights Movement, the growth of police surveillance powers within the community, the effort to revitalize the inner city, and stimulate economic growth. Correspondence, memoranda, reports, and other documents are organized by subject categories.

BOVA, BEN

†PA —TEMPLE UNIVERSITY LIBRARY, Philadelphia, 19122. Thomas M Whitehead, Librn
Notes: More than 100 cubic ft of mss, incl papers of Michael Bishop, Ben Bova, Jack Dann, Gardner Dozois, Lloyd Eshback, Tom Purdom, Pamela Sargent, John Varley, and George Zebrowski.

BOW AND ARROW

CT —YALE UNIVERSITY, Box 1603A, Yale Station, New Haven, 06520.
DC —LIBRARY OF CONGRESS, Washington, 20540.
MA —UNIVERSITY OF MASSACHUSETTS AT AMHERST, Library, Amherst, 01002.
MA —HARVARD UNIVERSITY LIBRARY, Cambridge, 02138.
NY —MUSEUM OF THE AMERICAN INDIAN, Library, 9 Westchester Square, Bronx, 10401. Mary B Davis, Librn
Holdings: Vols Cat
Notes: Incl information in Indians of North, Central, and South America; archaeology of North, Central, and South America; American Indian ethnology; anthropology, history.
NY —NEW YORK PUBLIC LIBRARY, Research Libraries, General Research Division, Fifth Ave & 42 St, New York, 10018. Rodney Phillips, Chief

BOWDOIN, JAMES, 1752-1811

ME —BOWDOIN COLLEGE, Library, Brunswick, 04011. Dianne M Gutscher, Cur of Special Collections
Holdings: Vols 2550 // Cat Mss
Notes: Library of James Bowdoin (1752-1811), preserved with his papers as a unit, incl 2000 pamphlets; supplemented with 550 additional volumes from the library of Governor James Bowdoin (1726-1790).

BOWEN, CATHERINE DRINKER

CA —FRANCIS BACON LIBRARY, 655 N Dartmouth Ave, Claremont, 91711. Elizabeth S Wrigley, Dir
Holdings: Mss Pix
Notes: Walter Arensberg's miscellaneous correspondence with American literary figures (1920's-50's) including Bruce Bliven, Catherine Drinker Bowen, Kay Boyle, Witter Bynner, Edwin Corle, Helen A Keller, Lysander Kemp, Kenneth Macgowan, John Macy, Henry Miller, Lewis Mumford, Clifford Odets, Kenneth Patchen, Irving Stone, and William Carlos Williams.

BOWEN, DAVID R.

MS —MISSISSIPPI STATE UNIVERSITY, Mitchell Memorial Library, Box 5408, Mississippi State, 39762. Frances N Coleman, Head, Special Collections
Holdings: Mss
Notes: Papers of Us Rep David R Bowen 1973-1983.

BOWEN, ELIAS, 1791-1871

NY —CORNELL UNIVERSITY LIBRARIES, Collection of Regional History, Dept of Manuscripts and Univ Archives, Ithaca, 14853.
Notes: Methodist clergyman. Papers, 1820-52; many letters, mainly relating to subjects of religious nature.

BOWEN, ELIZABETH

NV —UNIVERSITY OF NEVADA, RENO, University Library, Special Collections Dept,

BOWEN, ELIZABETH (cont.)

Reno, 89557. Robert E Blesse, Head
Holdings: Vols (94) Cat Other appearances 150 Cat
Notes: Includes individual works by author in all editions including translations; also prefaces, introductions, published correspondence, appearances in anthologies, periodicals, etc. Bibliographical research collection, part of Modern Authors Collection.

BOWEN, GEORGE S.

IL —CHICAGO HISTORICAL SOCIETY, Library, Clark St at North Ave, Chicago, 60614. Archie Motley, Manuscript Librn
Notes: Business history acquisitions incl the records of the Illinois Manufacturers' Association; customer complaint files of the Better Business Bureau of Metropolitan Chicago; Chicago Board of Underwriters; papers of George S Bowen, Illinois capitalist; and Ernest J Stevens.

BOWEN, JOHN

MA —BOSTON UNIVERSITY, Mugar Memorial Library, Special Collections Dept, 771 Commonwealth Ave, Boston, 02215. Howard B Gotlieb, Dir
Holdings: Cat Mss Pix
Notes: Mss, correspondence, etc collected in depth; incl publications by or about.

BOWERING, GEORGE

AB —UNIVERSITY OF CALGARY, Libraries, Special Collections Div, 2500 University Dr, Calgary, T2N 1N4, Can.
Notes: The Division houses small collections of letters and mss of Canadian poets such as Earle Birney and George Bowering.

BOWERS, CLAUDE GERNADE, 1878-1958

IN —INDIANA UNIVERSITY, Lilly Library, Seventh St, Bloomington, 47405. William R Cagle, Librn
Holdings: // Mss Pix
Notes: Papers of Claude G Bowers, (1878-1958), newspaperman, author, ambassador to Spain, 1933-1936, and ambassador to Chile, 1939-1953. Collection incl diaries, materials relating to both ambassadorships, particularly important for Spanish Civil War period; speeches; some original political cartoons; awards, medals, etc; newspaper clippings, etc, 1868-1972. 18,386 items.

BOWERS, LAMONT MONTGOMERY

NY —STATE UNIVERSITY OF NEW YORK, BINGHAMTON, Glenn G Bartle Library, Binghamton, 13901. Marion Hanscom, Special Collections Librn
Notes: Papers, correspondence, etc of the former aide to the Rockefeller enterprises. Incl much on the Colorado mine strikes.

BOWERS, LLOYD WHEATON, 1859-1910

DC —GEORGETOWN UNIVERSITY, Library, Special Collections Div, 37 & O Sts NW, Washington, 20057. George M Barringer, Special Collections Librn; Nicholas B Sheetz, Mss Librn
Holdings: Mss Cat
Notes: Correspondence of a semi-official nature from Lloyd Wheaton Bowers' (1859-1910) term as Solicitor-General of the United States from 1909-1910. The bulk of the material is composed of inquiries pertaining to government positions and appointments, especially relating to federal judgeship in Chicago. Other material relates to various cases handled by Bowers. Incl is correspondence from Felix Frankfurter, Joseph Choate, George Wickersham and Clarence Darrow, among others.

BOWERS, RAYMOND

NY —CORNELL UNIVERSITY LIBRARIES, Manuscript and Archives Division, Ithaca, 14853. H Thomas Hickerson, Special Collections Librn
Notes: Raymond Bowers' papers, 1950-78.

BOWES, MAJOR

DC —LIBRARY OF CONGRESS, Motion Pictures, Broadcasting and Recorded Sound Div, Washington, 20540.
Notes: The *Amateur Hour* Collection consists of original radio recordings of the Major Bowes series (1935-1944) and disc, tape, and television coverage of the Ted Mack series (1948-1968). Incl applications to appear on the program and accompanying correspondence and news clippings.

BOWKER, RICHARD ROGERS

NY —CITY UNIVERSITY OF NEW YORK, City College, Morris R Cohen Library, North Academic Center, Convent Ave & 137th St, New York, 10031. Barbara J Dunlap, Archivist
Holdings: // Uncat Mss Pix
Notes: Collection of materials by and about R R Bowker, publisher. Composed of correspondence from 1860-1933, the essays, orations, exams and papers he wrote as a student and general memorabilia. Incl are examples of publications he founded while a student. Housed in the City College Archives in Cohen Library; 2 linear feet of mss.

NY —NEW YORK PUBLIC LIBRARY, Rare Books and Manuscripts Div, Fifth Ave & 42 St, New York, 10018. William L Joyce, Asst Dir; Susan E Davis, Cur of Mss
Holdings: Mss
Budget: ($7161)
Notes: Incl personal and literary mss, papers, etc.

BOWLES, PAUL FREDERIC

NV —UNIVERSITY OF NEVADA, RENO, University Library, Special Collections Dept, Reno, 89557. Robert E Blesse, Head
Holdings: Vols (96) Cat
Notes: Includes individual works by author in all editions including translations; also prefaces, introductions, published correspondence, appearances in anthologies, periodicals, etc. Bibliographical research collection, part of Modern Authors Collection. Other appearances 175 cataloged.

BOWMAN, ISAIAH

MD —JOHNS HOPKINS UNIVERSITY, Milton S Eisenhower Library, Charles & 34 Sts, Baltimore, 21218. Ann S Gwyn, Assistant Dir for Special Collections
Holdings: Cat Mss
Notes: Collected papers, 1904-1948. Correspondence incl council on Foreign Relations, 1931-1949, and American Geographical Society, 1915-1950. Together, about 10,000 ms pieces. Restricted access; apply in advance.

BOXER AND THE ENTERPRISE (BATTLE)

CT —LEE ASH, (personal collection), 66 Humiston Dr, Bethany, 06525.
Holdings: Cat Mss Pix
Notes: Mss, notes, letters, pictures, memorabilia, ephemera, etc about this War of 1812 seafight off Monhegan Island, Maine.

BOXING

CA —LOS ANGELES PUBLIC LIBRARY, Art, Music & Recreation Dept, 630 W Fifth St, Los Angeles, 90071. Melvin H Rosenberg, Mgr & Principal Librn
Notes: Large collection.

KY —UNIVERSITY OF KENTUCKY, Margaret I King Library, Dept of Special Collections, Lexington, 40506. William Marshall, Head

MI —UNIVERSITY OF MICHIGAN, Bentley Historical Library, Michigan Historical Collections, 1150 Beal Ave, Ann Arbor, 48109. Francis X Blovin Jr, Dir
Notes: Substantial holdings relating to the University's Sports activities. Also, 93 scrapbooks on Joe Louis.

NY —COLUMBIA UNIVERSITY LIBRARIES, Rare Book & Manuscript Library, 801 Butler Library, 535 W 114 St, New York, 10027. Kenneth A Lohf, Librn
Notes: Restricted use. The Paul Magriel Boxing Collection on the history and literature of pugilism. The L S Alexander Gumby Collection, which incl 9 Joe Lewis scrapbooks, and much on Jack Johnson, Sugar Ray Robinson, Jackie Robinson and Paul Robeson.

WI —MILWAUKEE PUBLIC LIBRARY, 814 W Wisconsin Ave, Milwaukee, 53233. Donald J Sager, City Librn
Holdings: Vols 2210 Cat
Notes: Boxing collection incl most of the important works from 1900 to date, including Fleischer's *Ring Boxing Encyclopedia and Record Book* (30 vols). *See also* entry under Sports.

BOY SCOUTS OF AMERICA

NM —BOY SCOUTS OF AMERICA, Ernest Thompson Seton Memorial Library, Philmont Scout Ranch & Explorer Base, Cimarron, 87714. Eleanor Pratt, Dir of Museums
Holdings: Vols (3000) Cat Mss Maps Pix
Notes: Along with Seton's library, his writings (books, articles, short stories, Birchbark Roll, Indian Woodbadge work with young people), approx 3000 study skins of birds and small animals. Also approx 3000 of his pen and ink, water color and oil paintings. This collection was given to the Boy Scouts of America by Seton's widow. The museum, library, collections room and laboratory were built for BSA by Mr L O Crosby of Picayune, Mississippi. (See also the diaries at the library of the American Museum of Natural History, New York, NY.) The 33 volumes of Seton's journals (diaries) were given to the American Museum of Natural History by Joseph F Cullman 3rd; he also had copies made for the Seton Memorial Library. Our second museum is the Kit Carson Museum, a living history museum, open June, July and August.

NY —CORNELL UNIVERSITY LIBRARIES, Collection of Regional History, Dept of Manuscripts and Univ Archives, Ithaca, 14853.
Notes: Records, 1965-72; Louis Agassiz Fuertes Council; .7 ft.

NY —AMERICAN MUSEUM OF NATURAL HISTORY, Library Services Dept, Central Park W & 79th St, New York, 10024. Nina J Root, Chairwoman; Mary Genett, Asst Librn for Reference Services
Holdings: Cat Mss Pix Microforms
Notes: The Ernest Thompson Seton diaries. Thousands of pages of an unpublished 67-year diary record of one of the world's most famous naturalists, the gift of Joseph F Cullman III, a Trustee of the Museum. Preserved in 35 protective cases, the gift incl unpublished diaries, notebooks, and some other writings. The diary begins 12 June 1879; the last entries were written in hospital, just a month before Seton's death in 1946. Literally hundreds of examples of flora and fauna are pictured in the diaries in original pencil, pen-and-ink, and watercolor sketches, on nearly every page. Research will reveal information on the Indian sign language, the Boy Scouts of America, the Woodcraft League of America, and the wilderness of Canada, Florida, Texas, the West and Southwest, etc.

NY —ROCKEFELLER UNIVERSITY, Rockefeller Archive Center, Hillcrest, Pocantico Hills, North Tarrytown, 10591. Joseph W Ernst, Dir; J William Hess, Assoc Dir
Notes: Papers relative to the Rockefeller Family, Foundations, University, and other specific enterprises and contributions to particular areas of social, physical, educational, and historic reform,

BOY SCOUTS OF AMERICA (cont.)

preservation, conservation, or development. Extensive records of administrative, financial, physical, or intellectual relationships.

TX —BOY SCOUTS OF AMERICA, Library, 1325 Walnut Hill Lane, Irving, 75062. Ann Lamont McVicar, Librn
Holdings: Vols 3000 Cat Pix Slides
Notes: Early and current books on the Boy Scouts of America, and on the subjects of scouts and scouting. Books by and about founders Baden-Powell, Seton, Beard.

BOYCE, JESSE L.

AZ —NORTHERN ARIZONA UNIVERSITY, Special Collection Library, CU Box 6022, Flagstaff, 86011. Peter M Whiteley, Coordr/Archivist; William Mullane, Librn
Notes: C E Boyce's General Merchandise Store, Williams, Ariz. Financial records, 1895-1919.

BOYD, MALCOLM

MA —BOSTON UNIVERSITY, Mugar Memorial Library, Special Collections Dept, 771 Commonwealth Ave, Boston, 02215. Howard B Gotlieb, Dir
Holdings: Cat Mss Pix
Notes: Mss, correspondence, etc collected in depth; incl publications by or about.

BOYER, ALDEN SCOTT

NY —INTERNATIONAL MUSEUM OF PHOTOGRAPHY AT GEORGE EASTMAN HOUSE, Archives, 900 East Ave, Rochester, 14607. Rachel Stuhlman, Head Librn
Holdings: Vols (30,000) Cat Mss Microforms
Budget: ($104,000)
Notes: History, aesthetics and technology of photography and cinematography, incl the Gabriel Cromer, Josef Maria Eder, Alden Scott Boyer, Louis Walton Sipley/3M Collections, and the James Card Collection from 1893. Covers photographic, especially cinematographic history; also hundreds of negatives of Edward Muybridge as well as his notebooks. Incl 450,000 pictures and slides. Also the Lewis Hine Collection of social documentary photography.

BOYER, CHARLES

CA —UNIVERSITY OF CALIFORNIA, LOS ANGELES, Research Library, Dept of Special Collections, 405 Hilgard Ave, Los Angeles, 90024. Edward Shreeves, Chairman, Bibliographers Group; David S Zeidberg, Head
Holdings: Mss Pix
Notes: 1 linear foot of photographs, scrapbooks, and ephemera.

BOYLE, KAY

CA —FRANCIS BACON LIBRARY, 655 N Dartmouth Ave, Claremont, 91711. Elizabeth S Wrigley, Dir
Holdings: Mss Pix
Notes: Arensberg's miscellaneous correspondence with American literary figures (1920's-50's) including Bruce Bliven, Catherine Drinker Bowen, Kay Boyle, Witter Bynner, Edwin Corle, Helen A Keller, Lysander Kemp, Kenneth Macgowan, John Macy, Henry Miller, Lewis Mumford, Clifford Odets, Kenneth Patchen, Irving Stone, and William Carlos Williams.

IL —SOUTHERN ILLINOIS UNIVERSITY, CARBONDALE, Delyte W Morris Library, Special Collections Dept, Carbondale, 62901. David V Koch, Cur of Special Collections; Louisa Bowen, Cur of Manuscripts
Holdings: Vols 140 Cat Mss
Notes: Personal and literary papers approx 30 linear feet, unprocessed.

MO —WASHINGTON UNIVERSITY, Libraries, Special Collections Dept, Campus Box 1061, St Louis, 63130.
Notes: A small but significant collection.

BOYLE, ROBERT, 1627-1691

CA —UNIVERSITY OF CALIFORNIA, LOS ANGELES, William Andrews Clark Memorial Library, 2520 Cimarron St, Los Angeles, 90018.
Holdings: Cat
Notes: Extensive collection, first editions, etc.

CT —YALE UNIVERSITY, Medical Historical Library, 333 Cedar St, New Haven, 06510. Ferenc A Gyorgyey, Librn
Holdings: Vols 250 Cat
Notes: See John F Fulton, *A Bibliography of the Honourable Robert Boyle*, 2d ed Oxford: Clarendon Press, 1961. (Based on this collection; holdings noted.)

MA —HARVARD UNIVERSITY LIBRARY, Houghton Library, Cambridge, 02138. Rodney G Dennis, Cur of Manuscripts
Holdings: Cat Mss

NY —CORNELL UNIVERSITY LIBRARIES, John M Olin Library, History of Science Collections, Ithaca, 14853. Lillian A Clark, Administrative Supervisor; David W Corson, History of Science Librn
Holdings: Vols (33,000) Cat
Notes: Comprehensive collection of lifetime editions of Boyle's published writings, all subjects. Incl Doris and Ellis H Robison Collection of the works of Robert Boyle (175 vols). Noncirculating.

PA —UNIVERSITY OF PENNSYLVANIA, Van Pelt Library, Edgar Fahs Smith Memorial Collection in the History of Chemistry, 3420 Walnut St, Philadelphia, 19104. Arnold W Thackray, Cur
Holdings: Vols 180 Cat Mss
Notes: The Smith Collection, 15,000 vols, is one of the most comprehensive collections on the history of chemistry in North America, covering chemistry and its allied disciplines, from the Renaissance to the early 20th century. The Collection's traditional strengths lie in classical history of chemistry, ie pre-1800. However acquisitions over the past 15 years have substantially built up the post-1800 holdings, especially in areas of chemical technology. News of the Collection may be found in the Center's twice yearly newsletter *CHOC News* which is available free of charge to interested persons. A convenient description is provided in Herbert S Klickstein, "Edgar Fahs Smith-His Contributions to the History of Chemistry," *Chymia,* 5 (1959), 11-30. A published catalog of our holdings now needs considerable revision, due to continued *acquisitions:Catalog of the Edgar Fahs Smith Memorial Collection* (Boston: G K Hall and Co, 1960). Portions of our manuscript collection have been described in Norman P Zacour and Rudolf Hirsch, *Catalogue of the Manuscripts in the Libraries of the University of Pennsylvania to 1800* (Philadelphia: University of Pennsylvania Press, 1965), 231-243; and R Hirsch, "Catalogue of Manuscripts...Supplement a (5) ," *Library Chronicle,* 37 (1971), 91-115.

WI —UNIVERSITY OF WISCONSIN, MADISON, Memorial Library, History of Science Collection, 728 State St, Madison, 53706. John Neu, Bibliographer
Holdings: Cat
Notes: The collection of the works of Robert Boyle is one of the most complete in any institution. It contains many rare first editions, including Boyle's first publication, as well as many variant editions. Also incl items not recorded in Fulton's bibliography of Boyle. Restricted use: Rare Book Department.

ON —UNIVERSITY OF TORONTO, Thomas Fisher Rare Book Library, 120 Saint George St, Toronto, M5S 1A5, Can. Richard G Landon, Head
Holdings: Vols 4000
Notes: The Science Collection is especially rich in works on Renaissance astronomy, physics and mechanics and has noteworthy holdings of works of English experimental scientists in the 17th and 18th centuries with excellent collections of the works of Robert Boyle, Robert Hooke, and Sir Isaac Newton. Includes virtually all important early editions of Euclid; alchemical works of the 16th and 17th centuries together with the works of 18th century chemists like Lavoisier and Priestly; works on agriculture with special emphasis on British agriculture in the 18th century; and a variety of other works important in the history of science in all its branches. In addition the Fisher Library has many other specialized scientific collections which are listed separately.

BOYLESVE, RENE

MN —CARLETON COLLEGE LIBRARY, Northfield, 55057.
Holdings: Vols 7000 Cat
Notes: Books and periodicals relating to French literature of the second half of the 19th century, incl the French symbolist and decadent writers and critical works about them. Major writers are well represented as are some of the relatively minor figures, such as Paul Adam, Rene Boylesve, Abel Hermant, Pierre Louys, and others. The collection incl 69 plays written and produced in the period.

BOYS—EMPLOYMENT see Children—Employment; Youth—Employment

BOYS—SOCIETIES AND CLUBS

IL —NATIONAL COUNCIL OF THE YMCAS, YMCA Historical Library, 6400 Shafer Ct, Rosemont, 60018. Eleanor R Murphy, Librn
Holdings: Vols (15,000) Cat
Notes: Early young men's societies. Incl very little primary material; mainly published material. Societies incl are very varied, such as the Young Men's Christian Union of Boston; the Society for Reformation of Manners, 1657-1690; Society for Suppression of Vice; and the Woman's Seamen's Friend Society. In addition, there are early bound periodicals, essays, etc, for the guidance and "betterment" of young men. Separate catalog.

BOYS' CLUBS see Boys—Societies and Clubs

BOYTE FAMILY

NC —DUKE UNIVERSITY, William R Perkins Library, Manuscript Dept, Durham, 27706. Ellen Gartrell, Cur of Mss
Holdings: Cat Mss
Notes: Papers of Robert S Rankin, member US Civil Right Commission 1960-69 and North Carolina Advisory Committee to US Commission; Boyte Family Papers; NCCLU Papers; Earnest S Cox Papers on 20th century Negro migration to Africa; papers of US senators, congressmen, others.

BRABANT REVOLUTION

IL —NORTHWESTERN UNIVERSITY, Library, Special Collections Dept, 1937 Sheridan Rd, Evanston, 60201. R Russell Maylone, Cur
Notes: Incl 2500 pamphlets dealing with the Brabant Revolution. Additional 14,000 pamphlets, legal documents, and periodical issues published in France 1787-1800.

BRACE, GERALD WARNER

MA —BOSTON UNIVERSITY, Mugar Memorial Library, Special Collections Dept, 771 Commonwealth Ave, Boston, 02215. Howard B Gotlieb, Dir
Holdings: Cat Mss Pix
Notes: Mss, correspondence, etc collected in depth; incl publications by or about.

BRACHYGRAPHY see Shorthand

BRACKETT, LEIGH

NM —EASTERN NEW MEXICO UNIVERSITY, Golden Library, Special Collections, Portales, 88130. Mary Jo

BRACKETT, LEIGH (cont.)

Walker, Special Collections Librn
Holdings: Vols 11,940 Cat Mss Pix Audiotapes
Notes: Incl 700 magazine titles (10,318 issues), 11,940 vols, mss and correspondences of the following science fiction writers: Jack Williamson, Edmond Hamilton, Leigh Brackett, Forrest J Ackerman and Piers Anthony (Jacob), plus *Astounding/Analog* ms files (1954-1975). Also serves as a depository for Science Fiction Writers of America. Incl separate catalog for published books and unpublished registers to personal papers. The Williamson Register is being prepared for publication. Collection is described in *Anatomy of* Wonder, by Neil Barron (NY: Bowker, 1981); and *Special Collections, II* (winter, 1982), pp 49-57.

BRACKISH WATER BIOLOGY see Marine Biology

BRADBURY, RAY, 1920—

CA —UNIVERSITY OF CALIFORNIA, LOS ANGELES, Research Library, Dept of Special Collections, 405 Hilgard Ave, Los Angeles, 90024. Edward Shreeves, Chairman, Bibliographers Group; David S Zeidberg, Head
Holdings: Vols 60 Cat Mss
Notes: 60 books; 1.5 linear feet of correspondence, mss, and ephemera.

CA —SAN DIEGO STATE UNIVERSITY, Malcolm A Love Library, 5300 Campanile Dr, San Diego, 92182. D Dickinson, Univ Librn; Don L Bosseau, Dir
Holdings: Mss Cassettes
Notes: Elizabeth Chater Collection in Science Fiction. Includes Tolkien Collection, fantasy, folklore, Gothic novels, mostly autographed first editions, some rare and scarce, includes manuscripts, graphics, cassette tapes. Examples: authors included, Isaac Asimov, Ray Bradbury, Joan Vinge, Greg Baer, Frederick Pohl, Andre Norton, etc. Examples of periodicals, Amazing Stories, Famous Fantastic Mysteries of the 1940s, The Black Cat, 1895. (3000 items)

IN —INDIANA UNIVERSITY, Lilly Library, Seventh St, Bloomington, 47405. William R Cagle, Librn
Holdings: Cat Mss Pix
Notes: First editions. Ms collections include letters by Bradbury to producer Sidney Carrol in 1959, letters to his editors at Doubleday and Co, 1949-1976 (123 items); copyright agreements and correspondence between editors and literary agents at Harold Matson Company relating to Bradbury; and a sizeable correspondence file with reviewer and mystery fiction critic William Anthony Parker White (Tony Boucher).
See also entry under White, William Anthony Parker (Tony Boucher).

NV —UNIVERSITY OF NEVADA, RENO, University Library, Special Collections Dept, Reno, 89557. Robert E Blesse, Head
Holdings: Vols (157) Cat Other appearances 400 Cat
Notes: Includes individual works by author in all editions including translations; also prefaces, introductions, published correspondence, appearances in anthologies, periodicals, etc. Bibliographical research collection, part of Modern Authors Collection.

NY —COLUMBIA UNIVERSITY LIBRARIES, Rare Book & Manuscript Library, 801 Butler Library, 535 W 114 St, New York, 10027. Kenneth A Lohf, Librn
Holdings: Mss
Notes: Forty years of literary correspondence between the Harold Matson Literary Agency and numerous notable authors. Restricted use.

OH —BOWLING GREEN STATE UNIVERSITY, Jerome Library, Center for Archival Collections, Bowling Green, 43403. Paul D Yon, Dir; Elaine R Ezell, Reference Archivist; Nancy Steen, Rare Books Librn
Holdings: Vols 1000 Cat Mss Pamphlets Periodicals Tapes Phonodiscs Pix Posters
Budget: ($3000)
Notes: The William F Nolan Collection of manuscripts books, pamphlets, periodicals, records, and memorabilia. The most extensive collection of Bradbury material in existence.

BRADEMAS, REP. JOHN, 1927-

DC —LIBRARY OF CONGRESS, Manuscript Division, Washington, 20540. John C Broderick, Chief
Notes: Papers of Congressman John Brademas. About 361,000 items.

BRADEN, HUB

CA —UNIVERSITY OF CALIFORNIA, LOS ANGELES, Theater Arts Library, Los Angeles, 90024. Edward Shreeves, Chairman, Bibliographers Group; Audree Malkin, Head, Theater Arts Library
Notes: Hub Braden Collection: 24 (30" x 40") sketches from *Cleopatra;* 100 costume sketches and production notes for the *Lorenzo and Henrietta Music Show;* miscellaneous television scripts, photographs, programs.

BRADEN, SPRUILLE

†NY —COLUMBIA UNIVERSITY LIBRARIES, Butler Library, Rare Book and Manuscript Library, 535 W 114 St, New York, 10027.
Notes: The papers of Spruille Braden, American diplomat in Latin American affairs and American representative at the Chaco Peace Conference.

BRADFORD, WILLIAM, PRINTER

NY —NEW YORK HISTORICAL SOCIETY, Library, 170 Central Park W, New York, 10024. James Gregory, Librn

BRADLEE, CHARLES

†IL —NEWBERRY LIBRARY, Chicago, 60610.
Notes: Charles Bradlee was a music publisher in Boston and used Graupner and Ashton plates. His music, from the J Francis Driscoll Collection.

BRADLEY, AMY MORRIS

NC —DUKE UNIVERSITY, William R Perkins Library, Manuscript Dept, Durham, 27706. Ellen Gartrell, Cur of Mss
Holdings: Cat Mss
Notes: Numerous collection contain personal or professional papers of women, especially in southern US, eg Lucy Randolph Mason, Alliance for Guidance of Rural Youth, Amy Morris Bradley, Carson McCullers, Campbell Family.

BRADLEY, J. GARDNER

NY —CORNELL UNIVERSITY LIBRARIES, Collection of Regional History, Dept of Manuscripts and Univ Archives, Ithaca, 14853.
Notes: Incl papers, 1879-1964; 70 ft. Coal operator.

BRADLEY, MARION ZIMMER

MA —BOSTON UNIVERSITY, Mugar Memorial Library, Special Collections Dept, 771 Commonwealth Ave, Boston, 02215. Howard B Gotlieb, Dir
Holdings: Mss

BRADLEY, NORMAN

MS —MISSISSIPPI STATE UNIVERSITY, Mitchell Memorial Library, Box 5408, Mississippi State, 39762. Frances N Coleman, Head, Special Collections
Holdings: Mss
Notes: Papers of Norman Bradley, editor of *The Chattanooga Post* and *The Chattanooga* Times.

BRADLEY, OMAR

PA —US ARMY MILITARY HISTORY INSTITUTE, Carlisle Barracks, 17013. Richard J Sommers, Chief Archivist-Historian
Holdings: Mss, Cat
Notes: The World War II collection, personal letters, daily logs, reminiscences, speeches, and official papers of American officers and soldiers serving in the European, Mediterranean, Middle Eastern, China-Burma-India, Southwest Pacific, and Central Pacific Theaters and in the Zone of the Interior during the Second World War. Most of these collections are manuscripts of General officers, incl Omar Bradley, Stephen Chamberlin, Lewis Hershey, John Lucas, William Simpson, and Brehon Somervell.

BRADLEY, SCULLEY, 1897-

NC —DUKE UNIVERSITY, William R Perkins Library, Jay B Hubbell Center for American Literary Historiography, Durham, 27706. Erma Whittington, Librn
Notes: 77,312 items, including manuscripts, pictures, clippings, and correspondence. "The objective of the Center is to gather the papers and materials of significant scholars and critics in American literary history." The Center is a part of the Perkins Library Manuscripts Department.

BRADLEY, WILL

NC —UNIVERSITY OF NORTH CAROLINA, GREENSBORO, Walter Clinton Jackson Library, Special Collections Dept, 1000 Spring Garden St, Greensboro, 27412. Emilie W Mills, Librn
Notes: All but nine of the titles published by Way and Williams of Chicago, 1895-1898. First, variant editions, many autographed by authors or publisher. Many association items. Letters to Chauncey Williams from William Allen White, Maxfield Parrish, Charles Lummis, Opie Read, etc. Photographs of Williams and several authors. Original artwork by Parrish, Will Bradley and ephemeral printing incl in the scrapbook compiled by Chauncey L Williams, ca 1919. Major part of the collection the gift of John M Williams in memory of Chauncey L Williams.

BRADSHAW, HERBERT CLARENCE

†NC —DUKE UNIVERSITY, William R Perkins Library, Durham, 27706.
Notes: Papers. Over 39,000 items in the archives of this area journalist, author, and civic leader.
See also entry under Journalists.

BRADSTREET, ANNE

WI —UNIVERSITY OF WISCONSIN, MADISON, Memorial Library, British & American Language & Literature Collection, 728 State St, Madison, 53706. Yvonne Schofer, Bibliographer
Holdings: Vols 2200 Mss Microforms Documents Periodicals
Notes: A collection of primary and secondary materials for nine major American women writers: Anne Bradstreet; Louisa May Alcott, Emily Dickinson, Kate Chopin, Mary Williams Freeman, Margaret Fuller, Sarah Orne Jewett, Charlotte Perkins Gilman, Harriet Beecher Stowe. Primary materials also collected for a list of less well known authors together with manuscripts and archives of letters of special research interest. Variety of holdings: fiction, poetry, drama, biography and autobiography, letters, memoirs, diaries, travel, domestic economy and other kinds of writings by women mostly of the 19th century. Held in Dept of Rare Books and Special Collections.

BRADY, MATHEW B., 1823?-1896

DC —LIBRARY OF CONGRESS, Prints & Photographs Div, Washington, 20540.
Holdings: Cat Pix
Notes: The Brady-Handy Collection consists

BRADY, MATHEW B., 1823?-1896 (cont.)

of some 10,000 negatives from the files of photographers Levin C Handy (1855?-1932) and Mathew B Brady (1823?-1896), most of which are portrait photographs and views of Washington, DC from the 19th and early 20th centuries. Incl portraits of Congressmen and government leaders (1855-90). Civil War Photograph Collection incl photographs commissioned by Mathew B Brady and others.

BRAGDON, CLAUDE FAYETTE, 1866-1946

NY —HAMPDEN-BOOTH THEATRE LIBRARY AT THE PLAYERS, 16 Gramercy Park, New York, 10003. Louis A Rachow, Librn/Cur
Holdings: Mss Pix
Notes: Numerous promptbooks and annotated scripts, official company records of Walter Hampden, Inc, letters and correspondence dating from 1896, photographs and clippings, and blueprints and sketches of productions by Claude Bragdon. 55 boxes of indexed material. Described in *The Players Bulletin* (autumn 1968), pp 15-16. Described in *Theatre & Performing Arts Collections* (New York: Haworth Press, 1981).

NY —UNIVERSITY OF ROCHESTER, Rush Rhees Library, Department of Rare Books and Special Collections, Rochester, 14627. Peter Dzwonkoski, Librn
Holdings: Cat Mss Pix
Notes: Claude Fayette Bragdon, 1866-1946. Correspondence, diaries, notebooks, scrapbooks, sketchbooks, posters, stage designs and architectural drawings. Some correspondence and all architectural drawings indexed. Unpublished guide.

NY —SYRACUSE UNIVERSITY LIBRARIES, Ernest S Bird Library, George Arents Research Library for Special Collections, Syracuse, 13210. Carolyn A Davis, Manuscripts Librn; Amy S Doherty, University Archivist; Mark F Weimer, Rare Book Librn
Notes: The George Arents Research Library for Special Collections at Syracuse University contains the papers of Harley James McKee, Lorimer Rich, Frederick Lear, Max Abramovitz, James I Arnold, Pietro Bulluschi, Claude Bragdon, Marcel Breuer, William Lescaze, Skidmore Owings & Merrill, Ralph Walker, Eric Fisher Wood, Minoru Yamasaki, Joseph Louis Young, and Archimedes Russell.

BRAHE, TYCHO

CA —CALIFORNIA INSTITUTE OF TECHNOLOGY, Robert A Millikan Memorial Library, 1201 E California Blvd, Pasadena, 91125. Judith R Goodstein, Archivist
Holdings: Vols (2300) Cat
Notes: Emphasis on the period of Galileo and Kepler. Incl the Watson History of Science Collection and the Rocco Collection. Catalogs.

BRAHMANISM

AZ —WORLD UNIVERSITY, Library, 711 E Blacklidge Dr, Tucson, 85719. Howard John Zitko, Cur
Holdings: Vols (15,000) Cat Mss Maps Audiotapes
Notes: Collection concerns what are generally called the "frontier sciences." No interlibrary loan.

BRAHMS, JOHANNES

DC —LIBRARY OF CONGRESS, Music Division, Washington, 20540.
Notes: A large collection of letters from Brahms to Robert Keller.

NY —NEW YORK PUBLIC LIBRARY, Music Div, 111 Amsterdam Ave, New York, 10023. Frank C Campbell, Chief

BRAHUI LANGUAGE

NY —NEW YORK PUBLIC LIBRARY, Oriental Div, Fifth Ave & 42 St, New York, 10018. E Christian Filstrup, Chief
Holdings: Cat Mss Microforms
Budget: ($56,455)
Notes: Published catalog of holdings.

BRAIDISM see Hypnotism

BRAILLE SYSTEM see Blind—Printing and Writing Systems

BRAILOWSKY, ALEXANDER

MA —BOSTON UNIVERSITY, Mugar Memorial Library, Special Collections Dept, 771 Commonwealth Ave, Boston, 02215. Howard B Gotlieb, Dir
Holdings: Cat Mss Pix
Notes: Mss, correspondence, etc collected in depth; incl publications by or about.

BRAIN

KS —KANSAS NEUROLOGICAL INSTITUTE, Menninger Professional Library, 3107 W 21 St, Topeka, 66604. Richard Gray, Librn

MI —LAFAYETTE CLINIC LIBRARY, 951 E Lafayette, Detroit, 48207. Nancy E Ward, Librn
Holdings: Vols (7000) Cat
Notes: Special emphasis on the biological aspects, causes and treatment of mental illness. Also geriatrics.

BRAIN—BLOOD VESSELS—DISEASES see Cerebrovascular Disease

BRAIN—LOCALIZATION OF FUNCTIONS

MO —WASHINGTON UNIVERSITY, School of Medicine, Library, 660 South Euclid Ave, Saint Louis, 63110. Christopher Hoolihan, Rare Book Librn
Holdings: Vols (12,000) Cat
Budget: ($40,000)
Notes: Growing collection of classics in the localization of brain function published from the 17th to 20th centuries.

BRAIN—PATHOLOGY

CT —YALE UNIVERSITY, School of Medicine, Section of Neuropathology Library, Brain Tumor Registry, New Haven, 06520. Dr Elias Manuelidis, Cur
Holdings: Cat Slides
Notes: The Ernest Sachs Collection of about 8000 microscopic slides of brain tumors. Also the Harvey Cushing Collection of 800 jars of brain tissue in Formalin, and about 2500 microscopic slides. Another collection, belonging to the Pathology Department, consists of brain sections from about 100 monkeys, with 30 slides from each brain. Not cataloged, in boxes and inaccessible.

BRAIN DEATH

MD —NATIONAL LIBRARY OF MEDICINE, 8600 Rockville Pike, Bethesda, 20209. Harold M Schoolinam, Actg Dir
Budget: ($46,400)

BRAIN FUNCTION LOCALIZATION see Brain—Localization of Functions

BRAINARD, GEORGE

NY —BROOKLYN PUBLIC LIBRARY, Brooklyn Collection, Grand Army Plaza, Flatbush Ave and Eastern Parkway, Brooklyn, 11238.
Notes: Over 3000 books, pamphlets, and documents. Strong collections on the six original towns which made up Brooklyn. Also microfilm copies of defunct Brooklyn newspapers as well as recent issues of local community papers. A great treasure is the *Brooklyn Daily Eagle* morgue published from 1841-1955, the morgue's contents dating from 1904. Collection incl more than 25,000 photographs of people, places, and things from 1870 to the present; nearly a quarter of the photographs are by George Brainard and Daniel Berry Austin. Further, there are more than 500 Brooklyn maps from the earliest times. Incl records of the Brooklyn Mercantile Library Association.

NY —CORNELL UNIVERSITY LIBRARIES, Collection of Regional History, Dept of Manuscripts and Univ Archives, Ithaca, 14853.
Holdings: Vol 1
Notes: General store accounts, 1848-1850.

BRAINWASHING

CA —GRADUATE THEOLOGICAL UNION LIBRARY, New Religious Movements Research Collection, Public Services and Special Collections Dept, 2400 Ridge Road, Berkeley, 94709. Diane Choquette, Dept Head
Holdings: Vols (3000) Mss Pix
Notes: Begun in 1977, the collection focuses on religious movements new to America since 1960, and unorthodox religious movements resurgent since 1960. American forms of Hinduism, Buddhism, Sikhism, and Sufism are included along with occultism, Neo-Paganism, esoteric and alternative forms of Christianity, feminist spirituality, and human potential movements having a spiritual aspect. Legal issues, such as deprogramming, and the question of church/state relations are an important part of the collection. The Library is a depository for publications of the Unification Church in America, the Church of Scientology, and the International Society for Krishna Consciousness (America). The responses of mainstream religions and concerned citizens groups are also included. Besides 3000 monographs, the library has 400 periodical titles, 200 posters from the San FranciscoBay Area, 1965-77, 300 research papers, and 31 linear feet of ephemera.

BRAITHWAITE, WILLIAM S.

ME —COLBY COLLEGE, Miller Library, Alfred King Champman Room, Waterville, 04901.
Holdings: Mss
Notes: Papers, etc.

BRAKHAGE, STAN

MO —WASHINGTON UNIVERSITY, Libraries, Special Collections Dept, Campus Box 1061, St Louis, 63130.
Notes: A small but significant collection.

BRANCH, EDGAR MARQUIS

NC —DUKE UNIVERSITY, William R Perkins Library, Jay B Hubbell Center for American Literary Historiography, Durham, 27706. Erma Whittington, Librn
Notes: 77,312 items, including manuscripts, pictures, clippings, and correspondence. "The objective of the Center is to gather the papers and materials of significant scholars and critics in American literary history." The Center is a part of the Perkins Library Manuscripts Department.

BRAND, MAX

†CA —UNIVERSITY OF CALIFORNIA, BERKELEY, Bancroft Library, Berkeley, 94720. James D Hart, Director
Notes: Underground comics, 500. Max Brand and H Rider Haggard Collections.

CA —CALIFORNIA STATE UNIVERSITY, FULLERTON, Library, Box 4150, Fullerton, 92634. Kathy Morris, Archivist
Notes: All Star Trek scripts. Some fanzines and undergrounds. Circulating paperback collections of mysteries, science fiction and westerns. Extensive pulps. Max Brand collection.

BRAND BOOKS

IL —NEWBERRY LIBRARY, 60 W Walton St, Chicago, 60610. Diana Haskell, Cur of Modern Mss
Holdings: Vols 300 Cat Mss
Notes: Books incl brand books, accounts of

BRAND BOOKS (cont.)

cowboy life in late 19th, early 20th century America, biographies, Indian-White relations. Material kept in Ayer and Graff Collections; incl newspaper clippings.

OR —UMATILLA COUNTY LIBRARY, 214 N Main St, Pendleton, 97801. Barbara L Bishop, Dir
Holdings: Vols (675) Cat Mss Pix Audiotapes 16mm Films Microforms
Notes: Oregon history, especially Umatilla County. Lee Moorehouse photos (glass negatives)--1004 negatives, use restricted to professional photographers, copies may be made on premises only, also 3 rolls of microfilm of Moorehouse photos. Dr William McKay papers, 1830-1900, 14 folders, uncataloged, letters, coroner's reports (1885-86), miscellaneous papers, notes, memos and rough drafts, Army statements, receipts, accounts and business and personal receipts, accounts, 8 letters written by Donald McKay, one letter written December 7, 1880, by William F Cody. Early brands of Eastern Oregon, 1/2 reel microfilm. Some cassette recordings of interviews with early pioneers.

TX —UNIVERSITY OF TEXAS LIBRARIES, General Libraries, Barker Texas History Center, PO Box P, Austin, 78712. Don Carleton, Dir
Holdings: Vols (132,000) Cat Mss Maps Pix Slides Phonorecords Audiotapes Microforms
Notes: See description of entire collection under Texas-History.

BRAND NAMES see Business Names; Trademarks

BRANDEIS, LOUIS DEMBITZ, 1856-1941

MA —HARVARD UNIVERSITY LIBRARY, Law School Library, Langdell Hall, Cambridge, 02138. Erika S Chadbourn, Cur of Mss
Holdings: Cat Mss
Notes: Judicial papers. Typed inventory in repository. Inclusive dates, 1881-1966.

MA —BRANDEIS UNIVERSITY, Goldfarb Library, 415 South St, Waltham, 02154. Bessie Hahn, Dir
Notes: Approx 500 books and periodical articles by and about Justice Louis D Brandeis. Incl also are 72 linear ft of correspondence to and from Louis D Brandeis and his wife, Alice. A card catalog to the books and pamphlets can be found in Special Collections, as well as a finding list to some of the correspondence.

BRANDING IRONS see Brand Books

BRANDON, THOMAS J.

NY —MUSEUM OF MODERN ART, Dept of Film, 11 W 53 St, New York, 10019. Eileen Bowser, Cur
Holdings: Mss
Notes: Special collections: D W Griffith: personal papers and scrapbooks (cataloged); Carl Lerner Collection: notebooks, scripts, letters (cataloged); Harry McWilliams Collection: promotional and advertising material; Merritt Crawford Collection: documents and letters on early film history (cataloged); Thomas J Brandon Collection: documents and letters on the US labor movement and independent filmmaking, scripts, unpublished mss and research material (partially cataloged). Also, special material relating to Robert Flaherty, Helen Van Dongen, Thomas Ince, Paul Terry, G W Pabst, film censorship. Extensive clipping files and scripts on motion pictures. Partially cataloged.

BRANDT, KARL

MA —BOSTON UNIVERSITY, Mugar Memorial Library, Special Collections Dept, 771 Commonwealth Ave, Boston, 02215. Howard B Gotlieb, Dir
Holdings: Cat Mss
Notes: Mss, correspondence, etc collected in depth; incl publications by or about.

BRANIGIN, ROGER DOUGLAS, 1902-1975

IN —FRANKLIN COLLEGE OF INDIANA, Library, Special Collections Dept, Franklin, 46131. Mary Alice Medlicott, Cur
Holdings: Cat Mss Pix
Budget: ($151,189)
Notes: Governor Roger D Branigan papers. Incl correspondence reports, mementos, and pictures of Roger Douglas Branigan, mostly from the years 1964-1968, while he was governor of the State of Indiana. Considerable additional material from the years prior to 1964 and subsequent to 1968 have recently been added. A finding aid for use with the collection is available; 414 ft, 193 boxes.

BRANSON, EUGENE CUNNINGHAM, 1861-1933

NC —UNIVERSITY OF NORTH CAROLINA, CHAPEL HILL, Wilson Library, Rare Book Collection, Chapel Hill, 27514. Paul S Koda, Cur of Rare Books
Holdings: Cat Mss
Notes: 160 letterfile boxes of the extensive correspondence of Eugene Cunningham Branson, Professor of Rural Economics at the University of North Carolina from 1914-1933.

BRASHER, JOHN LAKIN

NC —DUKE UNIVERSITY, William R Perkins Library, Manuscript Dept, Durham, 27706. Ellen Gartrell, Cur of Mss
Holdings: Cat Mss
Notes: Methodist Church Papers (records of local and regional units) also many personal and professional papers of clergy, missionaries and laymen, 19th-20th centuries, eg Methodist John Lakin Brasher (holiness movement leader), Carlyle Marney (Southern Baptist minister), Methodist Bishop James Cannon, missionary Martha Foster Crawford.

BRASSES

KY —UNIVERSITY OF LOUISVILLE, Allen R Hite Art Institute, Library, Belknap Campus, Louisville, 40292. Gail Gilbert, Librn
Holdings: Cat Pix //
Budget: ($29,000)
Notes: Incl books on brass rubbings, monumental brasses and closely related topics. Also portfolios and transactions of the Monumental Brass Society, London, England. Collection circulates to faculty and staff only, with these same restrictions placed on interlibrary loans.

BRAY, WILLIAM C.

CA —UNIVERSITY OF CALIFORNIA, BERKELEY, Bancroft Library, Manuscripts Division, Berkeley, 94720. James D Hart, Dir
Notes: Correspondence and papers relative to the history of modern chemistry.

BRAYMAN, MASON

IL —CHICAGO HISTORICAL SOCIETY, Library, Clark St at North Ave, Chicago, 60614. Archie Motley, Manuscript Librn
Notes: Papers of Ninian Edwards and Edward Coles (Illinois Governors); Mason Brayman, attorney and Union Army officer.

BRAZER, ESTHER STEVENS

NY —HISTORICAL SOCIETY OF EARLY AMERICAN DECORATION, 19 Dove St, Albany, 12210. Doris Fry, Dir; Laura Olf, Librn
Holdings: Cat Pix Slides
Notes: The Library is housed with the Museum Collection of the Society. Incl examples of 19th century American country painting on tin, stenciling on wood and tin, bronzing decoration on wood, English stencilled tin and wood, bronzed items, painted objects, reverse painting on glass and examples of other decorating techniques of the period. Also included is a large collection of painted recordings of designs from early articles. Many of these were done by Esther Stevens Brazer in the 1930s. Another large collection has been added since that time. The library material is related to this interest. See *The Decorator,* official publication of the Historical Society of Early American Decoration. Other publications: *The Ornamented Chair* and *The Ornamented Tray* (both ed by Zilla Rider Lea), *Antique Decorations* by Brazer.

BRAZIL

CA —UNIVERSITY OF CALIFORNIA, BERKELEY, University Library, Hispanic Collections, Berkeley, 94720. Gaston Somoshegyi-Szokol, Librn
Holdings: Vols (40,000)
Notes: General research collection in the humanities and social sciences, with special strengths in history, literature, economics, and political developments. Main Library holdings are supplemented by subject coverage in branch libraries. Extensive government document holdings are maintained in the Documents Department.

CA —UNIVERSITY OF CALIFORNIA, RIVERSIDE, University Library, 4045 Canyon Crest Dr, Box 5900, Riverside, 92517.
Holdings: Vols 2,500
Notes: General research collection in the humanities and social sciences, with special strengths in history, literature, folklore and economic conditions, chiefly 20th century.

CT —YALE UNIVERSITY, Sterling Memorial Library, Latin American Collections, New Haven, 06520. Lee H Williams Jr, Cur
Holdings: Vols (300,000) Cat Maps Pix Slides Phonorecords 16mm Films Filmstrips
See also entry under Latin America

MO —WASHINGTON UNIVERSITY, John M Olin Library, Campus Box 1061, St Louis, 63130.
Holdings: Vols (50,000) Cat
Notes: Strong collection. Much unusual material.

NY —AMERICAN MUSEUM OF NATURAL HISTORY, Library Services Dept, Central Park W & 79th St, New York, 10024. Nina J Root, Chairwoman; Mary Genett, Asst Librn for Reference Services

NY —STATE UNIVERSITY OF NEW YORK, STONY BROOK, Melville Library, Stony Brook, 11794. John B Smith, Dir
Holdings: Vols 11,000 Cat
Notes: The Brasiliana Collection of literature and all fields of the social sciences.

NC —DUKE UNIVERSITY, William R Perkins Library, Durham, 27706. Elvin E Strowd, University Librn
Notes: The collection on Brazil is made up of several thousand volumes dealing with Brazil, including files of the publications of many Brazilian learned societies; additions are ongoing.

BRAZIL—DESCRIPTION AND TRAVEL

†DC —CATHOLIC UNIVERSITY OF AMERICA, Oliveira Lima Library, Washington, 20064.
Notes: Brazilian and Portuguese history, literature, church history, Portuguese colonial expansion, Portuguese diplomatic history, Brazilian travel.

BRAZIL—ECONOMIC CONDITIONS

CA —UNIVERSITY OF CALIFORNIA, RIVERSIDE, University Library, 4045 Canyon Crest Dr, Box 5900, Riverside, 92517.
Holdings: Vols 2,500
Notes: General research collection in the humanities and social sciences, with special strengths in history, literature, folklore and economic conditions, chiefly 20th century.

BRAZIL—HISTORY

AZ —UNIVERSITY OF ARIZONA, Library, Tucson, 85721. W David Laird, Librn
Notes: Latin American materials in the University of Arizona Library system may be found in all of the campus libraries. The largest collection is located in the Main Library and concentrates primarily on the history, literature, political science and economics of Mexico, Panama, Colombia, Argentina, Brazil and Chile. Special Collections specializes in the colonial period in the areas of law, religion, and economics. They also incl numerous manuscript collections, photographs, and 4000 broadsides from Mexico covering the late 18th century through the 20th century revolutionary period. There are also strong map, music and phonorecord collections primarily on Mexico. The greatest collecting effort is current materials on contemporary Latin America. Materials are fully accessible through the main card catalog as there is no separate catalog of the collection.

CA —UNIVERSITY OF CALIFORNIA, BERKELEY, University Library, Hispanic Collections, Berkeley, 94720. Gaston Somoshegyi-Szokol, Librn
Notes: General research collection in the humanities and social sciences, with special strengths in history, literature, economics, and political developments. Main Library holdings are supplemented by subject coverage in branch libraries. Extensive government document holdings are maintained in the Documents Department.

CA —UNIVERSITY OF CALIFORNIA, LOS ANGELES, Research Library, Dept of Special Collections, 405 Hilgard Ave, Los Angeles, 90024. Edward Shreeves, Chairman, Bibliographers Group; David S Zeidberg, Head
Holdings: Cat Mss Periodicals
Notes: 1000 issues of newspapers, 1881-1965; 360 items published by the Apostolado Positivista do Brazil, ca 1900-1967.

CA —UNIVERSITY OF CALIFORNIA, RIVERSIDE, University Library, 4045 Canyon Crest Dr, Box 5900, Riverside, 92517.
Holdings: Vols 2,500
Notes: General research collection in the humanities and social sciences, with special strengths in history, literature, folklore and economic conditions, chiefly 20th century.

†DC —CATHOLIC UNIVERSITY OF AMERICA, Oliveira Lima Library, Washington, 20064.
Notes: Brazilian and Portuguese history, literature, church history, Portuguese colonial expansion, Portuguese diplomatic history, Brazilian travel.

FL —UNIVERSITY OF MIAMI, Otto G Richter Library, PO Box 248214, Coral Gables, 33124. Frank Rodgers, Dir of Libraries
Holdings: Vols 2000
Notes: Incl valuable collection of books, rare offprints, microfilms, and miscellaneous items pertaining to colonial Brazil from the collection of Dr Bailey W Diffie (2000 vols).

IN —INDIANA UNIVERSITY, Lilly Library, Seventh St, Bloomington, 47405. William R Cagle, Librn
Holdings: Vols (40,000) Cat Mss Maps
Notes: Research and rare book collection (Bernardo Mendel) of first or only editions, mostly printed in Latin America, from the discovery of the New World through 1830. Special strength in discoveries and exploration, history (mainly period of independence), Inquisition, missionary works by the Augustinians, Dominicans, Franciscans, and the Jesuits, and the history of the Catholic Church in these countries. Major geographic concentration is on the three great viceroyalties of Mexico (ca 10, 000 titles, plus over 10,000 official Mexican broadsides), Peru (2000 titles), and Argentina (4000 titles), incl in Argentina a substantial amount of printings from the Imprenta de Ninos Expositos, and the Coleccion Santamarina. A special Bolivian Collection (2500 titles), mostly history, from the establishment of the press there, ca 1826, through the beginning of the 20th century. Part of the Mendel Collection is the select Bibliotheca Boxeriana from Charles R Boxer (1000 titles) on European expansion into Asia, and into the New World, mainly Brazil, during the 16th-18th centuries. The collection is supplemented by substantial material from the private collection of Josiah K Lilly.
See also entries under Spain - History; Portugal - History; Mexico - History.

KS —UNIVERSITY OF KANSAS, Kenneth Spencer Research Library, Special Collections Dept, Lawrence, 66045. Alexandra Mason, Librn
Holdings: Vols 500 Uncat Mss
Notes: Boehrer Collection. Portuguese and Brazilian history in first half of 19th century, incl over 4000 mss. Noncirculating.

LA —TULANE UNIVERSITY, Howard-Tilton Memorial Library, Latin American Library, New Orleans, 70118. Thomas Niehaus, Dir
Holdings: Vols (150,000) Cat Mss Maps Pix Microforms VF
Budget: ($67,000)
Notes: *Catalog of the Latin American* Library (Boston: G K Hall, 1970, suppl. 1973,1975,1978); Downs 5338-41; suppl (1961), 2727, 2737. The Latin American Library is a general collection, but specializes in Central American, Mexican, and Brazilian materials. The disciplines which are most strongly represented are history, anthropology, and archaeology. The Viceregal Ecclesiastical Mexican Collection contains manuscripts from the colonial period. The France V Scholes Collection contains a large number of photoprints and microfilm of colonial documents from the archives of Spain and Mexico. The Merle Greene Robertson Rubbings Collection contains nearly five hundred rubbings of relief sculpture from Mayan archaeological sites in Mexico and Guatemala. The Photographic Collection contains photos of archaeological sites inMeso-America, of pre-Columbian Peruvian architecture, and a general group of historic photos from Latin America.

NE —AMERICAN HISTORICAL SOCIETY OF GERMANS FROM RUSSIA (AHSGR), 615 Twelfth St, Lincoln, 68502. Mary Lynn Tuck, Librn
Holdings: Vols (1900) Mss Maps Pix Phonorecords Videotapes Audiotapes Microforms VF
Notes: History of German people from Russia and history of people of German-Russian ancestory. Including times in Russia, Germany, US, Canada, Mexico, Argentina, Brazil, Paraguay, Korea, and Japan. This Society has fifty-six chapters in the United States. 1900 volumes, 100 maps; 500 mss; 1200 vertical files; 2000 pictures; 40,000 obituary files, 40,000 family group charts, 50 phonorecords, 20 videotapes, 50 audiotapes, 15 reel-to-reel tapes, 150 periodicals, 250 microforms, 250 family histories-published and unpublished.

NY —CORNELL UNIVERSITY LIBRARIES, John M Olin Library, Ithaca, 14853.
Holdings: Vols (190,000) Cat Mss Maps 16mm Films Microforms
See also entry under South America.

NC —DUKE UNIVERSITY, William R Perkins Library, Durham, 27706. Elvin E Strowd, University Librn
Notes: The collection on Brazil is made up of several thousand volumes dealing with Brazil, including files of the publications of many Brazilian learned societies; additions are ongoing.

TX —UNIVERSITY OF TEXAS LIBRARIES, Nettie Lee Benson Latin American Collection, Sid Richardson Hall 1.109, Austin, 78712. Laura Gutierrez-Witt, Head Librn
Holdings: Vols (450,000) Mss
Notes: Over 1,000,000 ms pages containing the business records, 1830-1960, of the St John d'el Rey Mining Company, which operates gold and iron ore mines in Brazil.

WI —UNIVERSITY OF WISCONSIN, MADISON, Memorial Library, Ibero-American Studies Collection, 728 State St, Madison, 53706. Suzanne Hodgman, Bibliographer
Holdings: Vols (129) / / Cat
Notes: An unusual collection of 129 volumes on Brazilian history, literature, and philosophy. Strongest in works published by members of the intellectual group known as the Escola do Recife, the leader of which was Tobias Barreto. The collection contains almost all of his works as well as most of the works, including many rare pamphlets, of Silvio Romero, Barreto's most illustrious disciple. No separate listing.

WI —UNIVERSITY OF WISCONSIN, MADISON, Memorial Library, Ibero-American Studies Collection, 728 State St, Madison, 53706. Suzanne Hodgman, Bibliographer
Holdings: Vols (230,000) Cat Maps Pix Phonorecords Microforms
Budget: ($50,000)
Notes: Materials on Latin America, Spain, and Portugal may be found in all the campus libraries. The largest single collection is located in the Memorial Library, and the above holdings and budget statements refer only to this collection. Strongest holdings are in language and literature and in history, although many other disciplines in the humanities and social sciences are well represented: political science, sociology, economics, anthropology, statistics, etc. Geographically, primary emphasis is on Brazil. The collection of materials on the history of Portugal is outstanding and that of Portuguese language and literature is one of the largest in the US. The collection is fully integrated into the general collections of the libraries. There is no separate catalog.

BRAZIL—LAWS, STATUTES, ETC.

AZ —UNIVERSITY OF ARIZONA, Library, Tucson, 85721. W David Laird, Librn
Notes: The greatest strength of this collection is in long back-runs of periodicals.

BRAZIL—RELIGION

†DC —CATHOLIC UNIVERSITY OF AMERICA, Oliveira Lima Library, Washington, 20064.
Notes: Brazilian and Portuguese history, literature, church history, Portuguese colonial expansion, Portuguese diplomatic history, Brazilian travel.

WI —UNIVERSITY OF WISCONSIN, MADISON, Memorial Library, Ibero-American Studies Collection, 728 State St, Madison, 53706. Suzanne Hodgman, Bibliographer
Holdings: Vols (394) Uncat
Notes: Brazilian Positivist Collection. The collection consists of a nearly complete set of the official publications of the Positivist Church of Brazil. It includes first editions of pamphlets and booklets from the late 19th century, in addition to later reprints. A typescript listing of the collection is available. Collection is housed in the Rare Book Department.

BRAZILIAN FOLKLORE see Folklore, Brazilian

BRAZILIAN LANGUAGE see Portuguese Language and Literature—Brazil

BRAZILIAN LITERATURE

AZ —UNIVERSITY OF ARIZONA, Library, Tucson, 85721. W David Laird, Librn
Notes: The greatest strength of this collection is in long back-runs of periodicals.

†DC —CATHOLIC UNIVERSITY OF AMERICA, Oliveira Lima Library, Washington, 20064.
Notes: Brazilian and Portuguese history, literature, church history, Portuguese colonial expansion, Portuguese diplomatic history, Brazilian travel.

MO —WASHINGTON UNIVERSITY, John M Olin Library, Campus Box 1061, St Louis, 63130.
Holdings: Vols (50,000) Cat
Notes: Strong collection. Much unusual material.

BRAZILIAN LITERATURE (cont.)

NY —STATE UNIVERSITY OF NEW YORK, STONY BROOK, Melville Library, Stony Brook, 11794. John B Smith, Dir
Holdings: Vols 11,000 Cat
Notes: The Brasiliana Collection of literature and all fields of the social sciences.

PA —PENNSYLVANIA STATE UNIVERSITY, Fred Lewis Pattee Library, Library Hispanic Program, University Park, 16802. Donald C Henderson, Head
Holdings: Vols (50,000) Cat Mss
Budget: ($21,000)
Notes: A general coverage of all periods, backed by collections in history and related fields; supports doctoral programs.

WI —UNIVERSITY OF WISCONSIN, MADISON, Memorial Library, Ibero-American Studies Collection, 728 State St, Madison, 53706. Suzanne Hodgman, Bibliographer
Holdings: Vols (230,000) Cat Maps Pix Phonorecords Microforms
Budget: ($50,000)
Notes: Materials on Latin America, Spain, and Portugal may be found in all the campus libraries. The largest single collection is located in the Memorial Library, and the above holdings and budget statements refer only to this collection. Strongest holdings are in language and literature and in history, although many other disciplines in the humanities and social sciences are well represented: political science, sociology, economics, anthropology, statistics, etc. Geographically, primary emphasis is on Brazil. The collection of materials on the history of Portugal is outstanding and that of Portuguese language and literature is one of the largest in the U.S. The collection is fully integrated into the general collections of the libraries. There is no separate catalog.

BRAZILIAN PERIODICALS see Periodicals, Brazilian

BREAD AND PUPPET THEATRE

CA —UNIVERSITY OF CALIFORNIA, DAVIS, Shields Library, Dept of Special Collections, Davis, 95616. Donald Kunitz, Head; C Danial Elliott, Asst Head
Holdings: Cat Mss Pix Videotapes 16mm Films
Notes: A collection of correspondence, reviews, programs, posters, and newsletters document the performance of the Bread and Puppet Theatre formed in 1962 by Peter Schumann. 260 items.

VT —UNIVERSITY OF VERMONT, Guy W Bailey/David W Howe Library, Burlington, 05405. John Buehler, Asst Dir for Special Collections
Notes: The papers of the Bread and Puppet Theatre of Glover, Vermont for the years 1962-1972.

BREADSTUFFS see Flour and Feed Trade

BREAN, HERBERT

MA —BOSTON UNIVERSITY, Mugar Memorial Library, Special Collections Dept, 771 Commonwealth Ave, Boston, 02215. Howard B Gotlieb, Dir
Holdings: Cat Mss

BREAST—CANCER

NY —YWCA NATIONAL BOARD, Library, 726-730 Broadway, New York, 10012. Elizabeth Norris, Librn
Holdings: Vols (3000) Cat Mss
Budget: ($2400)
Notes: Women and their contemporary interests.

BREATHING see Respiration

BRECHT, ARNOLD, 1884-1977

NY —STATE UNIVERSITY OF NEW YORK AT ALBANY, Library, Special Collections Dept, 1400 Washington Ave, Albany, 12222. Marion P Munzer, Coordr
Notes: Photocopies of correspondence of Arnold Brecht, incl lectures and teaching notes on law and political science; mss and articles (15 linear feet). Part of the Library's German Exile Collection.

BRECHT, BERTOLT

MA —HARVARD UNIVERSITY LIBRARY, Houghton Library, Cambridge, 02138. Rodney G Dennis, Cur of Manuscripts
Holdings: Cat Mss

BREEDER REACTORS see Nuclear Technology

BREEDING, CROP see Crop Breeding

BREEDING, STOCK see Stock and Stockbreeding

BREESE, WILLIAM E., JR.

NC —WESTERN CAROLINA UNIVERSITY, Hunter Memorial Library, Cullowhee, 28723. James B Lloyd, Cur
Notes: The papers of former North Carolina state senators William E Breese, Jr (1875-1939), W Frank Forsyth (1913-70), and Carl Dan Killian, Sr (1903-76).

BRELIS, DEAN

MA —BOSTON UNIVERSITY, Mugar Memorial Library, Special Collections Dept, 771 Commonwealth Ave, Boston, 02215. Howard B Gotlieb, Dir
Holdings: Cat Mss Pix
Notes: Mss, correspondence, etc collected in depth; incl publications by or about.

BRENT, ROMNEY

NY —HAMPDEN-BOOTH THEATRE LIBRARY AT THE PLAYERS, 16 Gramercy Park, New York, 10003. Louis A Rachow, Librn/Cur
Holdings: Cat Mss
Notes: Numerous letters by actors and actresses to Romney Brent. Also, a large collection of letters pertaining to Romney Brent's foreign tours as an American Specialist (actor, producer, and lecturer) for the United States Department of State in 1967-1968. Two folders.

NY —NEW YORK PUBLIC LIBRARY, Performing Arts Research Center, Billy Rose Theatre Collection, 111 Amsterdam Ave, New York, 10023. Dorothy L Swerdlove, Cur
Holdings: Cat Mss Pix
Notes: Papers, scrapbooks, mss, photographs, memorabilia, etc.

BRENTANO, FRANZ

MA —HARVARD UNIVERSITY LIBRARY, Houghton Library, Cambridge, 02138. F Thomas Noonan, Cur, Reading Room; Lawrence Dowler, Associate Librn
Holdings: Cat Mss
Notes: Mss and personal papers.

BRERETON, F. S.

MS —UNIVERSITY OF SOUTHERN MISSISSIPPI, William David McCain Graduate Library, Box 5148, Southern Sta, Hattiesburg, 39406.
Holdings: Vols 18
Notes: The Lena Y de Grummond Collection of Children's Literature. Incl the Robert L Dartt Collection of over 1800 books for boys from the late 19th and early 20th centuries. Extensive Henty (over 550 vols), Alger, Brereton, Castlemon, Fenn, Kingston, Optic, and Stratemeyer holdings. Catalog in progress.

BRETHREN, UNITED see Moravian Church and Moravians

BRETON LANGUAGE AND LITERATURE

MA —HARVARD UNIVERSITY LIBRARY, Houghton Library, Cambridge, 02138. F Thomas Noonan, Cur, Reading Room; Lawrence Dowler, Associate Librn
Holdings: Cat
Notes: Downs: 3743.

BRETT, SIMON

MA —BOSTON UNIVERSITY, Mugar Memorial Library, Special Collections Dept, 771 Commonwealth Ave, Boston, 02215. Howard B Gotlieb, Dir
Holdings: Cat Mss

BREUER, MARCEL

NY —SYRACUSE UNIVERSITY LIBRARIES, Ernest S Bird Library, George Arents Research Library for Special Collections, Syracuse, 13210. Carolyn A Davis, Manuscripts Librn; Amy S Doherty, University Archivist; Mark F Weimer, Rare Book Librn
Notes: The George Arents Research Library for Special Collections at Syracuse University contains the papers of Harley James McKee, Lorimer Rich, Frederick Lear, Max Abramovitz, James I Arnold, Pietro Bulluschi, Claude Bragdon, Marcel Breuer, William Lescaze, Skidmore Owings & Merrill, Ralph Walker, Eric Fisher Wood, Minoru Yamasaki, Joseph Louis Young, and Archimedes Russell.

BREWER, GEORGE AND GRACE

MI —WAYNE STATE UNIVERSITY, Walter P Reuther Library, Archives of Labor & Urban Affairs, Detroit, 48202. Philip Mason, Dir
Notes: The politics of 20th century America are mirrored in the collections of Patrick V McNamara, US Senator; Charles Diggs, US Representative from Michigan; Ofield Dukes, aide to Vice-President Hubert H Humphrey; and George and Grace Brewer, Socialist Party workers and assistants to Eugene V Debs.

BREWER, WILLIAM HENRY

CT —YALE UNIVERSITY, Box 1603A, Yale Station, New Haven, 06520.
Holdings: Mss
Notes: Mss, notebooks, correspondence and memorabilia, 1848-1910.

BREWING

CA —UNIVERSITY OF CALIFORNIA, DAVIS, General Library, Davis, 95616. Bernard Kreissman, University Librn; C Danial Elliott, Asst Head, Dept Special Collections
Notes: Liquor distillation; brewing industry. Only limited materials. Major emphasis for collections is wine and wine making.

CA —UNIVERSITY OF SAN FRANCISCO, Richard A Gleeson Library, The Countess Bernardine Murphy Donohue Rare Book Room, San Francisco, 94117. D Steven Corey, Special Collections Librn
Holdings: Vols 55 Mss
Notes: Archive for Tamalpai Press, propietor, Roger Levenson. Complete collection, plus the archival business files of the firm, extensive ephemera.

IN —HURTY-PECK LIBRARY OF BEVERAGE LITERATURE, 5650 W Raymond Street, PO Box 41167, Indianapolis, 46208. Ben Wilson, Librn
Holdings: Vols (6000) Cat //
Notes: The most comprehensive collection, in English, in the world on beverages of all types. History, manufacture, formulae,

BREWING (cont.)

customs. Books on beer and brewing; cocoa and chocolate; coffee; liquors and spirits; soft drinks; tea; and wine.

MB —CANADIAN GRAIN COMMISSION, Library, 303 Main St, Winnipeg, R3C 3G7, Can. Jim Blanchard, Librn
Holdings: Vols (7500) Cat Mss Maps Slides Microforms
Budget: ($20,000)

BREWING—HISTORY

DC —US BREWERS ASSOCIATION, Research Library, 1750 K St NW, Washington, 20006.
Holdings: Vols (2000)
Notes: Extensive collection of early brewing periodicals, as well as some early technical works. Partially cataloged. Not a technical library.

BRICKER, JOHN W.

OH —OHIO HISTORICAL SOCIETY, Archives Library Division, 1982 Velma Ave, Columbus, 43211. Dennis East, Division Chief
Notes: Papers; governor 1939-1945; US senator, 1947-1959.

BRICKER AMENDMENT

NJ —PRINCETON UNIVERSITY, Library, Manuscript Collection, Nassau St, Princeton, 08540. Jean F Preston, Cur
Holdings: Mss
Notes: 3 cartons of papers. The collection relates to the Bricker Amendment and the treaty-making power of the United States, 1952-57.

BRIDGES

MA —AMERICAN ANTIQUARIAN SOCIETY LIBRARY, 185 Salisbury St, Worcester, 01609. Marcus A McCorison, Dir & Librn
Holdings: Vols 5200 Cat
Notes: Incl the Thomas Winthrop Streeter Collection on Transportation. The finest and most complete documentation of early American railroads, canals, bridges, turnpikes, and harbors in existence.

ON —ROADS & TRANSPORTATION ASSOCIATION OF CANADA, Library, 1765 St Laurent Blvd, Ottawa, K1G 3V4, Can. Charles James, Librn
Holdings: Vols (18,000) Cat
Budget: ($8000)
Notes: All areas of ground transportation and road construction.

BRIDGES—HISTORY

IN —PURDUE UNIVERSITY LIBRARIES, Graduate School of Management, Krannert Library, West Lafayette, 47907. Gordon Law, Librn
Notes: An important resource at the Krannert Library is its Special Collection of Business and Economics, consisting of some 8000 rare pre-20th century strengths in books, journals, tracts and pamphlets covering primarily the early literature of economic thought and business practices in America and abroad, 1500-1870. A catalog was issued in 1979.

MA —AMERICAN ANTIQUARIAN SOCIETY LIBRARY, 185 Salisbury St, Worcester, 01609. Marcus A McCorison, Dir & Librn
Holdings: Cat Mss Maps Pix
Notes: Outstanding collection, especially for early period, primarily to 1840; thereafter for States of the East and Midwest to the Civil War. Over 6000 items. Incl the Thomas Winthrop Streeter Collection of Transportation; much on the history of canals, bridges, turnpikes, and harbors.

MI —UNIVERSITY OF MICHIGAN, Engineering-Transportation Library, 312 Undergraduate Library, Ann Arbor, 48109. Sharon A Balius, Assoc Librn
Holdings: Mss Pix
Notes: Incl the personal and business papers of Charles Ellet, Jr, designer and builder of 3 wire suspension bridges in the US.

MO —WASHINGTON UNIVERSITY, Libraries, Special Collections Dept, Campus Box 1061, St Louis, 63130.
Notes: Terminal Railroad Association Records (1889-date), of more than 450 original tracings of the Eads Bridge (1874-date). Drawings show in fine and complete detail all the design features of this internationally known St Louis landmark.

NY —NEW YORK CITY MUNICIPAL ARCHIVES, Dept of Records and Information Services, 31 Chambers, New York, 10007. Idilio Gracia, Director
Notes: The Brooklyn Bridge Drawings Collection (1869-ca 1950), consisting of approximately 10,000 original plans, drawings, and notes.

BRIDGES, COVERED see Covered Bridges

BRIDGES, RAILROAD see Railroad Bridges

BRIDGES, ROBERT

SC —UNIVERSITY OF SOUTH CAROLINA, Thomas Cooper Library, Columbia, 29208. Kenneth E Toombs, Dir of Libraries; Roger Mortimer, Rare Book Librn
Holdings: Vols 150 Cat
Notes: Perhaps one of the most complete collections of first editions available.

BRIDGES ADAMS, W.

AB —UNIVERSITY OF CALGARY, Library, Calgary, T2N 1N4, Can. Apollonia Steele, Special Collections Librn
Holdings: Cat Mss Pix
Notes: Incl the books and papers of W Bridges Adams, Shakespearian actor, director and historian. Mr Bridges Adams was Director of the Stratford-upon-Avon Festival from 1919 to 1934 and was the author of two major works, *The British Theatre and the Irresistable Theatre*. Extensive correspondence with well-known literary and musical figures.

BRIDGMAN, P.W.

MA —HARVARD UNIVERSITY ARCHIVES, Nathan Marsh Pusey Library, Cambridge, 02138. Clark A Elliott, Associate Cur
Holdings: Cat Mss Pix
Notes: Correspondence, notebooks and mss of the Nobel Prize winning physicist (1882-1961).

BRIDSON, DOUGLAS GEOFFREY

IN —INDIANA UNIVERSITY, Lilly Library, Seventh St, Bloomington, 47405. William R Cagle, Librn
Holdings: Vols (700) Cat Mss
Notes: Collection of BBC radio scripts. Ms holdings incl correspondence, manuscripts of writings and scrapbooks of Douglas Geoffrey Bridson, BBC producer and writer.

BRIEFHAND see Shorthand

BRIEFS, GOETZ A., 1889-1974

DC —GEORGETOWN UNIVERSITY, Library, Special Collections Div, 37 & O Sts NW, Washington, 20057. George M Barringer, Special Collections Librn; Nicholas B Sheetz, Mss Librn
Holdings: Mss Cat
Notes: Papers of Goetz A Briefs (1889-1974), economist and educator, who lived in Germany (1915-1934) and in the United States (1934-1974). In addition to teaching, Briefs held official positions in both governments. The papers incl correspondence and mss, principally in the field of economics and the "ethos problem." The bulk of the material dates from Brief's immigration to the United States in 1934.

BRIGANDS AND ROBBERS

IL —NEWBERRY LIBRARY, 60 W Walton St, Chicago, 60610. Diana Haskell, Cur of Modern Mss
Holdings: Vols 150 Cat
Notes: The collection falls into two groups, Western Americana (which includes some pictures, biographies, broadsides and rare pamphlets) and English (mostly 18th and 19th century broadsides and poems).

BRIGGS, LUTHER

MA —SOCIETY FOR THE PRESERVATION OF NEW ENGLAND ANTIQUITIES, Library, 141 Cambridge St, Boston, 02114. Ellie Reichlin, Librn & Cur of Photographic Collections
Notes: Architectual drawing for buildings in Dorchester, Nahant, Boston, and other Massachusetts cities.

VT —UNIVERSITY OF VERMONT, Guy W Bailey/David W Howe Library, Burlington, 05405. John Buehler, Asst Dir for Special Collections
Notes: Papers of Paul Brigham (1746-1824), lieutenant governor of Vermont, 1796-1813, 1815-20.

BRIGHT CHILDREN see Gifted Children

BRIGHTFIELD, MYRON FRANKLIN

CA —UNIVERSITY OF CALIFORNIA, LOS ANGELES, Research Library, Dept of Special Collections, 405 Hilgard Ave, Los Angeles, 90024. Edward Shreeves, Chairman, Bibliographers Group; David S Zeidberg, Head
Notes: 17 linear feet of Berkeley English professor's research notes and mss on Victorian England; syllabi and other course material.

BRILLOUIN, LEON

NY —AMERICAN INSTITUTE OF PHYSICS, Center for the History of Physics, Niels Bohr Library, 335 E 45 St, New York, 10017. John Aubry, Librn
Notes: Papers and records.

BRINGHURST, JOSEPH

ME —BOWDOIN COLLEGE, Library, Brunswick, 04011. Dianne M Gutscher, Cur of Special Collections
Holdings: Cat Mss
Notes: The Charles Brockden Brown Papers contain 159 letters and mss relating to America's first professional novelist. There are 54 letters from Brown to Joseph Bringhurst, and 105 letters and mss from the Bringhurst-Deborah Ferris correspondence.

BRINNIN, JOHN MALCOLM

DE —UNIVERSITY OF DELAWARE, Hugh M Morris Library, S College Ave, Newark, 19711. T Stuart Dick, Special Collections
Holdings: Cat Mss
Notes: Manuscripts, etc incl literary correspondence with such figures as John Ashbery, Elizabeth Bishop, Kay Boyle, Truman Capote, Richard Eberhart, TS Eliot, Denise Levertov, Robert Lowell, James Merrill, Howard Moss, Bill Read, Allan Tate, Dylan Thomas, and Richard Wilbur. Incl typescripts of most of John Malcolm Brinnin's own work.

BRINTON, DANIEL GARRISON

PA —UNIVERSITY OF PENNSYLVANIA, University Museum Library, 33 & Spruce Sts, Philadelphia, 19104. Jean S Adelman, Librn
Holdings: Vols (2000) Cat Mss
Notes: Incl the Daniel Garrison Brinton collection of about 2000 vols, on aboriginal American linguistics and ethnology. Espec strong in Maya language materials.

BRINTON FAMILY

DE —UNIVERSITY OF DELAWARE, Hugh M Morris Library, S College Ave, Newark, 19711. T Stuart Dick, Special Collections
Holdings: / / Mss
Notes: Personal and business letters and

BRINTON FAMILY (cont.)

receipts of six generations of the Brintons of Philadelphia, a Quaker family (1786-1930) prominent in mercantile and medical circles. Incl are household receipts for the 1808-1827 period.

BRISBANE, ALBERT, 1809-1890

IL —UNIVERSITY OF ILLINOIS, URBANA/CHAMPAIGN, Library, Illinois Historical Survey Library, 1408 W Gregory Dr, 1A Library, Urbana, 61801.
Holdings: Vols 50 Cat Mss Maps Pix Microforms
Notes: Communitarianism in America. The ms material, contained in 30 separate collections (10 cubic feet), concentrates on the period 1840-70. It incl correspondence, records, minutes, ledgers and diaries. Communal societies such as Bishop Hill, Brook Farm, New Harmony, the North American Phalanx and the Sodus Bay Phalanx are represented. Among the correspondents are Albert Brisbane, Parke Godwin, Sarah Grimke, Richard Owen, Robert Owen, Robert Dale Owen, and George Ripley. Numerous pictures. Guide to the collections published in 1976.

NY —SYRACUSE UNIVERSITY LIBRARIES, Ernest S Bird Library, George Arents Research Library for Special Collections, Syracuse, 13210. Carolyn A Davis, Manuscripts Librn; Amy S Doherty, University Archivist; Mark F Weimer, Rare Book Librn
Notes: Papers and memorabilia, incl ms writings. Papers 1840-1936 (1/2 linear foot).

BRISSON, FREDERICK

CA —UNIVERSITY OF CALIFORNIA, LOS ANGELES, Theater Arts Library, Los Angeles, 90024. Edward Shreeves, Chairman, Bibliographers Group; Audree Malkin, Head, Theater Arts Library
Notes: Russell/Brisson Collection (Rosalind Russell, actress and her husband, Frederick Brisson, producer): screenplays and television scripts in various versions, treatments, production material, programs, business records, personal and business correspondence, accounting records, awards, certificates, scrapbooks, press clippings, magazine interviews, posters, playbills, portraits, production stills, fashion and publicity stills, tapes and 35mm films.

BRITISH ACTORS ORPHANAGE FUND

NY —HAMPDEN-BOOTH THEATRE LIBRARY AT THE PLAYERS, 16 Gramercy Park, New York, 10003. Louis A Rachow, Librn/Cur
Holdings: // Uncat Mss
Notes: The British Actors Orphanage Fund was incorporated in Los Angeles, California, in July 1940 "To promote and effect the transfer of male and female minor orphans of deceased British actors and actresses from their present home or homes in Great Britain to America... and to provide and pay for their complete maintenance, housing and schooling therein, during the pendency of the present war between Great Britain and Germany, to the end that these orphans may be removed from the horrors and perils of such war. "The duties and activities of the Fund came to a successful conclusion in 1946 when forty-eight of the original fifty-four orphans returned to England and the remaining six either became self-supporting or their care was assumed by others. The collection consists of copies of the charter and by-laws, minutes, journals and ledgers, children's travel arrangements, working files and preliminary and general correspondence for the years 1940–1946 featuring such luminaries as Noel Coward, Dame May Whitty, Boris Karloff, Maurice Evans, Cole Porter, Peggy Wood and Margaret Webster.

BRITISH-AMERICAN TOBACCO COMPANY

NC —DUKE UNIVERSITY, William R Perkins Library, Manuscript Dept, Durham, 27706. Ellen Gartrell, Cur of Mss
Holdings: Cat Mss
Notes: Tobacco culture, marketing, trade, especially US South, 19th-20th century, incl papers of Duke Family, Richard H Wright, British-American Tobacco Co, James A Thomas, Edward J Parrish, United Cigarette Machine Co; also tobacco advertising (trade cards, etc).

BRITISH ART see Art, British

BRITISH ARCHITECTURE see Architecture, British

BRITISH AUTHORS see Authors, British

BRITISH BALLADS see Ballads, British

BRITISH BROADCASTING COMPANY (BBC)

IL —WHEATON COLLEGE, Buswell Memorial Library, Wheaton, 60187. Paul Snezek, Library Dir
Holdings: Mss
Notes: A collection of over 200 films and 30 sound recordings. *Related Topics:* BBC.

IN —INDIANA UNIVERSITY, Lilly Library, Seventh St, Bloomington, 47405. William R Cagle, Librn
Holdings: Vols (700) Cat Mss
Notes: Extensive collection of scripts. Ms holdings incl the papers of Lance Sieveking, BBC producer; Douglas Geoffrey Bridson, BBC producer and writer; and Douglas Cleverdon, producer. All three were most closely connected with The Third Program. Scripts for many of these programs are in the collection as well as extensive correspondence regarding programming.

BRITISH COLUMBIA

WA —WASHINGTON STATE LIBRARY, Washington/Northwest Rm, State Library Bldg, Olympia, 98504. Nancy B Pryor, Research Consultant
Holdings: Vols 8000 Cat Mss Maps Pix Microforms
Notes: Mss, photographs and microfilm largely limited to Washington territorial and state materials as is the file of pamphlets and newspaper clippings, which includes both historical and current material. The book collection incl works on the four Pacific Northwest States, Alaska, and British Columbia, and books by Washington authors.

WA —UNIVERSITY OF WASHINGTON LIBRARIES, Pacific Northwest Collection, Seattle, 98195. Andrew F Johnson, Librn
Holdings: Vols (50,000) Cat Mss Maps Pix
Budget: ($12,000)
Notes: The Pacific Northwest Collection contains printed materials documenting the historic and contemporary life and culture of the region in a broad range of subject areas. The Pacific Northwest is defined as the geographic region including Washington, Oregon, Idaho, Montana, British Columbia, Yukon Territory, and Alaska. Printed materials including books, periodicals, government documents, maps, weekly and local regional newspapers, theses and dissertations, as well as photographs and architectural drawings are included in the Pacific Northwest Collection. Photographic works of over 200 photographers active in the Pacific Northwest, Alaska, and the Yukon Territory (Canada) during the period 1860-1930, including Asahel and Edward S Curtis, Eric Hegg, and Clark Kinsey, are represented in a print collection of more than 300,000 images. The architecturaldrawings collection includes over 19,000 original plans, drawings, sketches, renderings and blue prints pertaining to the history of architecture and urban planning and landscape gardening in the Pacific Northwest ca 1880-1940. Areas of particular strength are the holdings of over 1100 published journals of Pacific Northwest exploration expeditions, photographs of Northwest Coast Native Americans and of historic Seattle, newspapers issued within the Japanese-American relocation camps, 1942-1945, materials relating to the 1980 eruption of Mt St Helens, and Sanborne fire insurance maps for Washington. A unique feature of the Collection is the subject index to regional periodicals and local newspapers maintained by the PNW Collection staff; over 100 titles are currently indexed. G K Hall Company published a books catalog of the Pacific Northwest Collectionin 1973.

BC —KAMLOOPS MUSEUM & ARCHIVES, Reference Library, 207 Seymour St, Kamloops, V2C 2E7, Can. Kem Favrholdt, Curator
Holdings: Vols (900) Cat Mss Maps Pix Slides Audiotapes Microforms
Budget: ($500)
Notes: British Columbia in general, but concentrating on the Thompson Valley drainage basin. Incl history of the Kamloops District up to 1914, of Kamloops, 1914-1945.

BC —DAVID THOMPSON UNIVERSITY CENTRE, Library, Nelson, V1L 3C7, Can. Ronald J Welwood, Dir
Holdings: Vols 2000 Cat Mss Pix Microforms
Budget: $1000
Notes: Especially Nelson and Central Kootenay District of British Columbia. Emphasis on historical, social, and economic materials. Collection described in *Kootenaiana: A Listing of Books, Government Publications, Monographs, Journals, Pamphlets, etc, Relating to the Kootenay Area...Located in the Libraries of Notre Dame University...up to 31 March* 1976, ed by W J Welwood (Nelson: Notre Dame Univ of Nelson, Library, etc, 1976), 167 pp.

BC —UNIVERSITY OF BRITISH COLUMBIA, Library, Special Collections Div, 1956 Main Mall, Vancouver, V6T 1Y3, Can. Anne Yandle, Head
Holdings: Vols Cat Mss Maps Pix Slides

BC —LEGISLATIVE LIBRARY (PROVINCIAL), Parliament Bldgs, Victoria, V8V 1X4, Can. J H MacEachern, Head, Government Documents Division
Holdings: Vols Cat Microforms
Notes: Documents, newspapers, magazines, etc.

BRITISH COLUMBIA—HISTORY

CA —UNIVERSITY OF CALIFORNIA, BERKELEY, Bancroft Library, Manuscripts Division, Berkeley, 94720. James D Hart, Dir
Holdings: Vols Mss Maps Pix Slides Microforms
Notes: Approxi. twelve million pieces, with primary emphasis on California, with a lesser emphasis on the other Pacific States, incl. Alaska and the Province of British Columbia. In general, the Bancroft Library seeks to acquire historical and biographical works and primary source materials, documenting: the development of a geographic area or political unit; man and his activities, and his impact on the land and on his institutions. Methodological and theoretical work and texts in the physical and biological sciences are not collected, as a rule; exceptions here are publications essential to the study of an area's historical development and those providing general

BRITISH COLUMBIA—HISTORY (cont.)

background information. Hubert Howe Bancroft's own distinguished holdings, assembled 1860-1880, constitute the core of the collection. The Bancroft Library's collections are noncirculating. A. G. K. Hall catalog has been published. The Bolton Collection (146,000 pages of archival material) contains ms. materials for the history of the Pacific Coast and the Southwest, gathered by Herbert Eugene Bolton. There is a comprehensive key to the arrangement of the collection.

WA —WESTERN WASHINGTON UNIVERSITY, Center for Pacific Northwest Studies, High St, Bellingham, 98225. James W Scott, Dir
Holdings: Cat Mss Maps Pix
Notes: The Percival R Jeffcott Collection of Local History is particularly rich in photographic materials, incl about 1800 negatives and about 1100 photographs, which deal with pioneer settlement and economic and cultural developments in Whatcom County, Washington, and a few adjacent areas, such as the Lower Mainland of British Columbia to the north and neighboring counties of Washington to the south and west. Incl also ms versions of Jeffcott's published works: *Nooksack Tales and Trails, Chechaco and Sourdough and Blanket Bill Jarman* and numerous unpublished papers and workbooks. A small collection of Jeffcott materials is housed in the Washington State Historical Society, Tacoma, and for this there is an unpublished inventory. An inventory of the present collection is being prepared for publication by the Center for Pacific Northwest Studies.

WA —WASHINGTON STATE HISTORICAL SOCIETY LIBRARY, 315 N Stadium Way, Tacoma, 98403. Frank L Green, Librn
Holdings: Vols 15,000 Cat Mss Maps Pix Microforms
Notes: Scope is entire Pacific Northwest, with emphasis on Washington.

AB —GLENBOW-ALBERTA INSTITUTE, Historical Library & Archives, 130 9th Avenue SE, Calgary, T2G 0P3, Can. Leonard J Gottseleg, Chief Librn
Holdings: Vols (60,000) Cat Mss Maps Pix Microforms
Notes: Main emphasis is on Western Canadian history. Equally important emphasis is placed on the Canadian Arctic and Alaska, Northwest Coast explorations, Aboriginal peoples of the North and Canadian West, and the fur trade in the US Northwest.

BC —SELKIRK COLLEGE, Library, PO Box 1200, Castlegar, V1N 3J1, Can. John Mansbridge, Dir
Holdings: Vols 1000 Cat Mss Maps Pix Microforms
Notes: The West Kootenay History Collection is particularly rich in works on the Doukhobor people. The West Kootenay area of BC is bounded on the south by the US border, on the north by the Trans-Canada Highway, on the east by Kootenay Lake, and on the west by the Okanagan Valley.

BC —KAMLOOPS MUSEUM & ARCHIVES, Reference Library, 207 Seymour St, Kamloops, V2C 2E7, Can. Kem Favrholdt, Curator
Holdings: Vols (900) Cat Mss Maps Pix Slides Audiotapes Microforms
Budget: ($500)
Notes: British Columbia in general, but concentrating on the Thompson Valley drainage basin. Incl history of the Kamloops District up to 1914, of Kamloops, 1914-1945.

BC —VANCOUVER ISLAND REGIONAL LIBRARY, 10 Strickland St, Nanaimo, V9R 5G7, Can. R W Reeves, Librn
Holdings: Vols 2200 Cat Pix Microforms
Notes: Emphasis on British Columbia history, especially Vancouver Island. Incl pamphlets and 150 microforms.

BC —NEW WESTMINSTER PUBLIC LIBRARY, 716 Sixth Ave, New Westminster, V3M 2B3, Can. Alan Woodland, Dir
Holdings: Cat Mss Maps Pix Slides Microforms
Notes: Attempts to gather as much information as possible about the history of the city of New Westminster. Collection based on almost complete run of *Columbian* Newspaper (1861-date); *The Weekly Columbian Newspaper* (1902-1954), and other newspapers and documents. Indexing of the *Columbian Newspaper* is taking place slowly. Have 25 maps, 1800 pictures, 110 slides, microforms, newspaper. Copies of photographs and documents are made when these become available.

BC —PRINCE RUPERT LIBRARY, 101 W Sixth Ave, Prince Rupert, V8J 1Y9, Can. Denise St Arnaud, City Librn
Holdings: Vols 270 Cat Mss Audiotapes 16mm Films
Notes: This collection of Northwest History deals chiefly with this area but extends to parts of Alaska and the Queen Charlotte Islands and BC inland and north. Noncirculating.

BC —TERRACE PUBLIC LIBRARY, 4610 Park Ave, Terrace, V8G 1V6, Can. Ed Curell, Librn; Gillian Campbell, Librn, Terrace Collection
Holdings: Vols (270) Cat
Budget: ($250)
Notes: The collection is limited to books and pamphlets relating to Terrace, Skeena, and Nass River District history and geography. Emphasis on art and sociology of the Niska and Tsimshian and lives of early missionaries.

BC —BRITISH COLUMBIA SPORTS HALL OF FAME AND LIBRARY, BC Pavilion, Vancouver, V5K 4W3, Can.
Notes: Sporting history. Incl sports film collection.

BC —UNIVERSITY OF BRITISH COLUMBIA, Library, Special Collections Div, 1956 Main Mall, Vancouver, V6T 1Y3, Can. Anne Yandle, Head
Holdings: Vols Cat Mss Maps Pix Slides

BC —VANCOUVER COMMUNITY COLLEGE, Langara Library, 100 W 49 Ave, Vancouver, V5Y 2Z6, Can. Mary Anne Epp, Librn
Holdings: Vols (70,000) Cat Maps Slides Audiotapes 16mm Films Microforms

BC —VANCOUVER PUBLIC LIBRARY, History & Government Div, 750 Burrard St, Vancouver, V6Z 1X5, Can.
Holdings: Vols 5000 Cat Microforms
Notes: Geographical limits of the collection are the present area of British Columbia, Oregon and Washington Territory to 1846, some Alberta material for approach to the mountain barrier and its exploration, pre-1898 Yukon Territory and the Klondike gold rush, Alaska pre-1867, Bering Sea fur seal arbitration issue. The chronological limit is 1950. Incl 500 maps, 25 atlases.

BC —MARITIME MUSEUM OF BRITISH COLUMBIA, 28 Bastion Sq, Victoria, V8W 1H9, Can. C H Shaw, Dir
Holdings: Vols (2500) Cat Mss Maps Pix Slides Microforms
Budget: ($110,000)
Notes: Also 4000 registration cards; 6000 pictures.

BRITISH COLUMBIA PRESS

BC —SIMON FRASER UNIVERSITY, Library, Burnaby, V5A 1S6, Can. Percilla Groves, Special Collections Librn
Holdings: Cat Mss
Notes: Mss for published and unpublished works, plus a complete collection of published books, chapbooks and broadsides by Canadian and American writers, plus correspondence and business records of the British Columbia Press run by poet and teacher Barry McKinnon from 1972 to 1980.

BRITISH COMMONWEALTH OF NATIONS see Commonwealth of Nations

BRITISH EMPIRE GAMES

ON —UNIVERSITY OF WESTERN ONTARIO, Dept of Special Collections, London, N6A 5B9, Can. Beth Miller, Librn
Notes: Large and important collection on Canadian participation in pre-Olympic and other Game series. Incl minutes of annual meetings of the Athletic Union of Canada, 1884-1898, 1908-1954.

BRITISH FOLK MUSIC see Folk Music, British

BRITISH FOLK SONGS see Folk Songs, British

BRITISH FOLKLORE see Folklore, British

BRITISH DOMINIONS see Commonwealth of Nations

BRITISH GUIANA see Guyana

BRITISH HONDURAS see Belize

BRITISH IN PORTUGAL

OK —UNIVERSITY OF TULSA, McFarlin Library, Dept of Rare Books and Special Collections, 600 S College, Tulsa, 74104. David Farmer, Dir; Toby Murray, Archivist; Caroline Swinson, Cur of Manuscripts & Art
Holdings: Vols 2500
Notes: The only known extant lending library from the 19th century. It was formed by British subjects in Oporto, Portugal between 1820-1890. 70 percent not in Sadlier.

BRITISH IN THE U.S.

NY —STATE UNIVERSITY OF NEW YORK AT ALBANY, Library, Special Collections Dept, 1400 Washington Ave, Albany, 12222. Marion P Munzer, Coordr
Notes: Correspondence and financial records of Abraham Bell and Son, New York shipping line which exported cotton and brought back British and English immigrants in the 1830s and 1840s. Additional correspondence and papers of James W Bell from 1862-1917; James C Bell from 1864-1899; and Bell Brothers, a money-lending business in Yonkers (22 linear feet). Part of the Library's German Exile Collection.

NY —NEW YORK HISTORICAL SOCIETY, Library, 170 Central Park W, New York, 10024. James Gregory, Librn
Holdings: Mss
Notes: Incl original mss, illustrative materials, etc.

PA —SWARTHMORE COLLEGE, Library, Swarthmore, 19081. Michael J Durkan, Librn
Holdings: Vols 1450 Cat Maps Pix
Notes: Accounts of travel in the US by English visitors.

BRITISH LAW see Law, British

BRITISH MILITARY HISTORY see Military History, British

BRITISH MUSIC HALLS

GA —UNIVERSITY OF GEORGIA, Libraries, Special Collections Division, Athens, 30602. Vesta Lee Gordon, Asst Dir for Special Collections
Notes: Theater Collection contains the Paris Music Hall set and costume designs with original drawings by Erte, Barbier, Zig and

BRITISH MUSIC HALLS (cont.)

others; British Music Hall Papers; European toy theater collection; Charles Coburn papers; television script collection; Tennessee Williams papers. Collection contains 16,000 pieces.

BRITISH NEWSPAPERS see Newspapers, British

BRITISH NOBILITY see Great Britain—Nobility

BRITISH PAINTING see Painting, British

BRITISH PERIODICALS see Periodicals, British; Periodicals, Irish

BRITISH POETRY see English Poetry

BRITISH TOGOLAND see Ghana

BRITISH TRACTS

CT —YALE UNIVERSITY, Box 1603A, Yale Station, New Haven, 06520.
Notes: A large collection, especially political, economic, religious.

MO —UNIVERSITY OF MISSOURI-COLUMBIA, Ellis Library, Special Collections Dept, Ninth & Lowry, Columbia, 65201. Margaret A Howell, Head, Special Collections
Holdings: Vols 20,000 //
Notes: 17th, 18th and 19th century English tracts-religious, political and historical. Also British tracts.

ON —QUEEN'S UNIVERSITY, Douglas Library, Kingston, K7L 5C4, Can. William F E Morley, Cur, Special Collections
Holdings: Vols 3200
Notes: Predominantly 18th century British pamphlets, but the collection does have pamphlets from ca 1590 to ca 1830.

BRITISH WEST INDIES see West Indies

BRITTAIN, VERA MARY, 1896-1970

ON —MCMASTER UNIVERSITY, Mills Memorial Library, Div of Archives & Research Collections, Hamilton, L8S 4L6, Can. G R Hill, Univ Librn
Holdings: // Mss Pix
Notes: Mss and typescripts of all books, reviews, lectures, articles. Also correspondence and diaries. Collection described in McMaster University *Library Research News*, vol 4, nos 3, 4, 5.

BRITTEN, BENJAMIN

DC —LIBRARY OF CONGRESS, Music Division, Washington, 20540.
Notes: Mss in Koussevitzky Archives.

BRITTON, LIONEL

IL —SOUTHERN ILLINOIS UNIVERSITY, CARBONDALE, Delyte W Morris Library, Special Collections Dept, Carbondale, 62901. David V Koch, Cur of Special Collections; Louisa Bowen, Cur of Manuscripts
Holdings: Cat Mss
Notes: Personal papers incl the mss of his books and plays, 1936-1950, 6 linear ft.

BROADCAST SCRIPTS see Moving Pictures—Scripts; Radio Scripts; Television Scripts

BROADCASTING see International Broadcasting; Radio Broadcasting; Television Broadcasting

BROADSHEETS see Broadsides—Collections

BROADSIDES—COLLECTIONS

CA —UNIVERSITY OF CALIFORNIA, LOS ANGELES, Research Library, Dept of Special Collections, 405 Hilgard Ave, Los Angeles, 90024. Edward Shreeves, Chairman, Bibliographers Group; David S Zeidberg, Head
Notes: Various collections, incl Italian Broadsides (ca 1676-1821); 158 French Political Broadsides (1793-1871); American and British broadside ballads; Victorial broadsides; posters (World War I and II, travel film); political broadsides (Californian, Mexican, student protest of the 60s).

CA —STANFORD UNIVERSITY LIBRARIES, Cecil H Green Library, Stanford, 94305. Peter R Frank, Cur, CDP-Germanic Collection
Notes: Stanford's holdings in all branches of the field of history are strong, from Medieval times to the present. Extensive collection of regional and city histories, regional historical journals, of historical material both for the Federal Republic of Germany and the German Democratic Republic. Broadsheet collection for the Revolution 1848/1849. Extensive collection of works on military affairs, the workers' and women's movements. Many rare items in the Stanford Collection of German, Austrian and Swiss Culture. Description: "The German Area Collection: A German Tradition" by Peter R Frank.

CT —YALE UNIVERSITY, Box 1603A, Yale Station, New Haven, 06520.

CT —YALE UNIVERSITY, Beincke Rare Book & Manuscript Library, Western Americana Collection, Wall & High St, New Haven, 06520. George Miles, Cur
Holdings: Cat
Notes: Incl California broadside ballads of the 19th century.

CT —UNIVERSITY OF CONNECTICUT, Library, Storrs, 06268. R H Schimmelpfeng, Dir of Special Collections
Holdings: // Cat
Notes: The collection incl 1900 Italian books, about 4400 contemporary periodicals, and more than 7000 broadsides, the latter not yet cataloged. A checklist of the author file is available. The collection does not incl the secondary sources which are cataloged for the general library.

DC —LIBRARY OF CONGRESS, Rare Book & Special Collections Div, Washington, 20540. William Matheson, Chief
Holdings: Cat
Notes: The collection represents over 28,000 separate pieces from US (chiefly), Europe and South America, ranging in date from 1527 to present. Especially rich in Americana owing to collections of Peter Force and Ebenezer Hazard; eg contains nearly 200 items printed (or photostats of) in Virginia before 1800. Contains 246 broadsides relating exclusively to the Continental Congress and 21 concerned with the Constitutional Convention of 1787. Several subject collections: carriers' addresses, Lincoln material, poetry, etc. The Division's card catalog with its three-fold approach (geographical, author/title, and chronological) has been published by G K Hall: US Library of Congress, Rare Book Division. *Catalog of Broadsides in the Rare Book Division, Library of Congress* (Boston: 1972), 4 vols.

GA —UNIVERSITY OF GEORGIA, Libraries, Special Collections Division, Athens, 30602. Vesta Lee Gordon, Asst Dir for Special Collections
Holdings: Vols 7300 Maps
Notes: The Confederate Imprints Collection, arranged by Crandell numbers, also incl 500 sheets of music, approx 350 broadsides and approx 1600 newspapers.

IL —SOUTHERN ILLINOIS UNIVERSITY, CARBONDALE, Delyte W Morris Library, Special Collections Dept, Carbondale, 62901. David V Koch, Cur of Special Collections; Louisa Bowen, Cur of Manuscripts
Holdings: Vols 93 Cat
Notes: Also 152 broadsides and cards from the Cuala Press and the Press of John Henry Nash.

IL —CHICAGO HISTORICAL SOCIETY, Library, Clark St at North Ave, Chicago, 60614. Robert L Brubaker, Librn
Holdings: Cat
Notes: About 14,000 pieces, dating from the 18th century to the present, concerning Chicago, the Midwest, and American history. Especially strong for politics, the Civil War, World War I, labor, transportation, expositions in Chicago, theatre, and literary posters of the Art Nouveau period.

IL —CHICAGO PUBLIC LIBRARY, Special Collections Div, Cultural Center, 78 E Washington St, Chicago, 60602. Laura Linard, Cur
Holdings: Mss Pix
Notes: Special Collections maintains a scarce collection of theatre broadsides, playbills, programs and other ephemera for Chicago productions, 1880-1930 as well as a recently acquired collection of contemporary material (1971-1981). These are described in *Treasures of The Chicago Public Library*, compiled by Thomas A Orlando and Marie Gecik, 1977, pp 121-33. The Archives of the Publicity Department of the Goodman Theatre (formerly of the Art Institute of Chicago) are maintained by Special Collections at The Chicago Public Library. We also have a nearly complete collection of the plays of Kenneth Sawyer Goodman, after whom the Goodman Theatre is named. Some unique pre-fire material is also to be found in these collections.A finding aid to these collections has been prepared.

IL —NORTHWESTERN UNIVERSITY, Library, Special Collections Dept, 1937 Sheridan Rd, Evanston, 60201. R Russell Maylone, Cur
Notes: Broadsides from the Siege of Paris, 1870, the Paris Commune, 1871, and the Communes beyond Paris, 1871. Broadside poems produced in England and America during the 20th century. 500 19th century English and Irish street ballads.

IL —ILLINOIS STATE HISTORICAL SOCIETY, Library, Old State Capitol, Springfield, 62706. Roger D Bridges, Head Librn
Holdings: Vols (146,000) Cat Mss Maps Pix Microforms
Budget: ($40,000)
Notes: Incl 8 million mss, nearly 2000 maps, 180,000 pictures and 60,000 microfilm reels. Downs 2546, 2606, 2612, 187, 188. See also *Guide to the Microfilm Edition of the Pierre Menard Collection in the Illinois State Historical Library*. Separate catalogs (card) for printed material, mss, broadsides.

IN —INDIANA UNIVERSITY, Lilly Library, Seventh St, Bloomington, 47405. William R Cagle, Librn
Holdings: Vols 6000 // Cat
Notes: Research and rare book collection (Bernardo Mendel) of first or only editions, mostly printed in Latin America, from the discovery of the New World through 1830. Special strength in discoveries and exploration, history (mainly period of independence), Inquisition, missionary works by the Augustinians, Dominicans, Franciscans, and the Jesuits, and the history of the Catholic Church in these countries. Major geographic concentration is on the three great viceroyalties of Mexico (ca. 10,000 titles, plus over 10,000 official Mexican broadsides), Peru (2000 titles), and Argentina (4000 titles), incl. in Argentina a substantial amount of printings from the Imprenta de Ninos Expositos, and the Coleccion Santamarina. A special Bolivian Collection (2500 titles), mostly history, from the establishment of the press there, ca. 1826, through the beginning of the 20th century. Part of the Mendel Collection is the select Bibliotheca Boxeriana from Charles R. Boxer (1000 titles) on European expansion into Asia, and into the New World, mainly Brazil, during the 16th-18th centuries. The collection is supplemented by substantial material from the private collection of Josiah K. Lilly. See also entries under Spain-History, Portugal-History, and Mexico-History.

BROADSIDES—COLLECTIONS (cont.)

KS —UNIVERSITY OF KANSAS, Kenneth Spencer Research Library, Special Collections Dept, Lawrence, 66045. Alexandra Mason, Librn
Holdings: Vols 4400 Uncat Mss
Notes: William Griffith Collection on Central America, especially Guatemalan imprints, late 18th to mid-20th century, incl many newpapers and broadsides. Noncirculating.

KY —WESTERN KENTUCKY UNIVERSITY, Kentucky Library, Bowling Green, 42101. Riley Handy, Head, Special Collections; Connie Mills, Maps & Music Librn; Nancy Baird, Photographs Librn; Nancy Solley, Conservation Librn
Holdings: Vols (25,000) Cat Mss Maps Pix Microforms
Notes: Besides Kentucky history, other strengths are Mammoth Cave, South Union Shakers, Kentucky religion; and steamboat photos (3300 cataloged pictures); 8000 Kentucky postal cards, etc.

KY —UNIVERSITY OF KENTUCKY, Margaret I King Library, Dept of Special Collections, Lexington, 40506. William Marshall, Head
Holdings: Uncat
Notes: Nearly 3000 broadside sheets. English, Irish, American; a few in other languages. Card index by title.

MD —UNIVERSITY OF BALTIMORE, Langsdale Library, 1420 Maryland Ave, Baltimore, 21201. Gerry Watkins, Head of Special Collections Dept
Notes: Broadsides and posters from the 1848 Paris Revolution (0.25 cubic feet).

MA —WENHAM HISTORICAL ASSOCIATION AND MUSEUM, Timothy Pickering Library, 132 Main St, Wenham, 01984. Eleanor E Thompson, Dir
Holdings: Vols (1000) Cat Mss Pix
Notes: Incl books and broadsides on agriculture from 1800s.

MA —AMERICAN ANTIQUARIAN SOCIETY LIBRARY, 185 Salisbury St, Worcester, 01609. Marcus A McCorison, Dir & Librn
Holdings: Vols 60,000 Cat
Notes: Sixty percent of the total of books and pamphlets known to have been printed in the United States before 1821. Source of Readex Microprint Corp project called *Early American Imprints, 1639-1800,* a Microprint edition of every extant book, pamphlet and broadside printed in what is now the United States. Keyed to Evans *American* Bibliography it reprints in full the texts of nearly 50,000 titles and includes all of Shipton's revision of Evans. A second series, keyed to Shaw and Shoemaker's *American* Bibliography, will bring these Microprint reproductions up to 1820. One of the great strengths of the collection is its broadsides and American newspapers, the best anywhere. From it emerged Clarence Brigham's monumental *History and Bibliography of American Newspapers,* 1690-1820, which locates every surviving copy of every newspaper printed in the United States before 1821. ReadexSociety's collections extend beyond 1820, in special strengths, to the turn of the century. The collection incl unusual strengths in Amateur Newspapers (about 50,000 issues), and Bolivian, Chilean, and West Indian newspapers. Incl up to 1876.

MI —DETROIT PUBLIC LIBRARY, Burton Historical Collection, 5201 Woodward Ave, Detroit, 48202. Alice Dalligan, Chief

NH —DARTMOUTH COLLEGE, Baker Memorial Library, Hanover, 03755.
Holdings: Cat
Notes: About 1600. Espec New Hampshire. Noncirculating.

NJ —RUTGERS, THE STATE UNIVERSITY OF NEW JERSEY, Alexander Library, Special Collections and Archives, College Ave & Huntington St, New Brunswick, 08903. Ronald L Becker, Cur of Manuscripts and Rare Books
Holdings: Uncat
Notes: Largely American, 17th-20th century; 5000 items.

NY —NEW YORK STATE LIBRARY, State Education Bldg Annex, Washington Ave, Albany, 12224.
Holdings: Cat
Notes: Printed handbills and posted announcements of historic and everday events; Theater performances; auctions; advertisements; land sales; slave sales, reward posters for runaways; inducements to enlist for military service. Over 2000 pieces. Also over 3000 poetic broadside ballads.

NY —QUEENS BOROUGH PUBLIC LIBRARY, Long Island Div, 89-11 Merrick Blvd, Jamaica, 11432. Nicholas Falco, Head
Holdings: Vols 22,000 Cat Mss Maps Pix Microforms
Budget: ($13,000)
Notes: Files of Long Island community newspapers, with strong holdings for Queens Borough. Also, 550 glass negatives of Long Island scenes, 1895-1915; with 32,750 other pictures; 5300 maps; 36,000 ms pieces. Extensive name indexes of births, deaths and marriages mainly from 19th century Long Island books and newspapers. Many cemetery records, etc. 60 VF drawers of clippings; over 500 broadsides, 1795-date, relating to Long Island, with chronological and community name indexes; books published by Marion Press, a private press in Jamaica, NY.

NY —BARNARD A & MORRIS N YOUNG LIBRARY OF EARLY AMERICAN POPULAR MUSIC, 270 Riverside Dr, New York, 10025. Morris N Young, Cur
Holdings: Cat Mss Pix Phonorecords Audiotapes Microforms
Notes: 48,000 items of American popular music, mostly 1790-1910. Incl books, serials, sheet music, broadsides, anthologies, air checks, broadcasting and music business memorabilia, and correspondence.

NY —NEW YORK ACADEMY OF MEDICINE, Library, 2 E 103 St, New York, 10029. Brett A Kirkpatrick, Librn
Notes: Neinken Collection of 2000 Italian broadsides from 16th-19th centuries.

NY —NEW YORK PUBLIC LIBRARY, Rare Books and Manuscripts Div, Fifth Ave & 42 St, New York, 10018. William L Joyce, Asst Dir; Francis O Mattson, Curator
Holdings: Cat
Budget: ($7161)
Notes: About 20,000 broadsides. The broadside file is an appendix to the Division's 21-volume dictionary catalog published by G K Hall.

NY —NEW YORK PUBLIC LIBRARY, Music Div, 111 Amsterdam Ave, New York, 10023. Frank C Campbell, Chief
Holdings: Vols (300,000) Cat Mss Pix Microforms
Notes: Described in *Dictionary Catalog of the Music Collection, The Research Libraries of the New York Public Library,* 33 vols (532,000 cards), 1964, $2190; Supplement 1, 1 vol (17,000 cards), 1966, $100. Also, *Bibliographic Guide to Music,* 2 vols, 1975-1976, $70 ea. Literature pertaining to virtually all musical subjects, and scores covering the broadest range of musical style and history are represented in this catalog. Incl 1821 broadsides.

NC —DUKE UNIVERSITY, William R Perkins Library, Durham, 27706. Elvin E Strowd, University Librn
Notes: Books, serials and pamphlets (2,820, 527); music scores (31,551); motion pictures (285); microforms (1,055,627); tapes, cassettes and phonorecords, the library is a depository for Radio Canada International recordings, (2289); and manuscripts, US Government publications, maps, and broadsides, additions in all formats are ongoing.

NC —DUKE UNIVERSITY, William R Perkins Library, Rare Book Room, Durham, 27706. John L Sharpe, III, Cur
Notes: Broadside collection of approximately 8500 items. Primarily 19th century American imprints ranging from auction lists to military orders. Also, Thomas J Wise collection has works of Byron, Coleridge, Dryden, Pope, and Hardy incl 135 political and religious broadsides, mostly of the 17th century.

†NC —WAKE FOREST UNIVERSITY, Z Smith Reynolds Library, Box 7777, Reynold Sta, Winston-Salem, 27109. Richard J Murdoch, Rare Book Librn
Holdings: Vols 200 Cat
Notes: Confederate broadside verse.

OH —HEBREW UNION COLLEGE-JEWISH INSTITUTE OF RELIGION, Klau Library, 3101 Clifton Ave, Cincinnati, 45220. David J Gilner, Reference Librn
Holdings: Uncat
Notes: Incl 5000 posters, broadsides, leaflets and various ephemera, mostly from Israel and the US. Subjects incl charity, politics, religion, culture, education, theater, Zionism, anti-Semitism, all of Jewish content.

OH —OHIO HISTORICAL SOCIETY, Archives Library Division, 1982 Velma Ave, Columbus, 43211. Dennis East, Division Chief
Holdings: Vols (96,000) Cat Mss Maps Pix Slides Microforms
Budget: ($18,000)
Notes: This library is the primary collection for Ohio. Most purchases are on the rare and op market. Collecting area is early American history, esp relating to exploration into the Northwest Territory. Major subject areas are Ohio politics and government (8 presidents) military history (good collection of regimental histories and Ohio narratives of the Civil War), economic and social history, local history, esp county histories & atlases and city directories. Also, Ohio archaeology, natural history, artifacts. Major media collections are books (96,000), newspapers (25,000 vols and 22,000 microfilm), pictures (50,000), maps (2500), manuscripts (1,500,000). Library is noncirculating except through interlibrary loan of microfilm.

OR —UNIVERSITY OF OREGON LIBRARY, Special Collections Div, Eugene, 97403. Kenneth W Duckett, Curator
Holdings: Vols 1,000 Cat
Notes: Mostly on Pacific Northwest subjects, 1847-1920.

PA —BALCH INSTITUTE FOR ETHNIC STUDIES, Library, 18 S Seventh St, Philadelphia, 19106. R Joseph Anderson, Library Dir

PA —FREE LIBRARY OF PHILADELPHIA, Theatre Collection, Logan Sq, Philadelphia, 19103. Geraldine Duclow, Librn-in-Charge
Holdings: Vols (1,250,000) Uncat Pix
Notes: The Theatre Collection contains books, magazines, playbills, broadsides, posters, photographs, and other memorabilia covering theatre, motion pictures, minstrels, vaudeville, circus, radio and television. The Library's Philadelphia Theatre Index lists the major productions here since 1855, and partially indexes the collection of local playbills which date back to 1803. There are also programs from many other cities, incl New York; some from London date back to 1800. Early film companies as well as the present movie industry are represented by advertising materials and over 30,000 film stills. The Lubin Film Co (1910-1916) Archive has been established with over 600 photographs and related items. Circus programs and route books date back to 1900. There are minstrel programs as early as 1865. Most significant are the mss from Philadelphia's Dumont Minstrels. Variousfiles contain autographs, photographs, newspaper articles and reviews in all pertinent subject areas. Noncirculating.

PA —LIBRARY COMPANY OF PHILADELPHIA, 1314 Locust St, Philadelphia, 19107. Edwin Wolf II, Librn; Kenneth Finkel, Cur of Prints
Holdings: Vols (450,000) Cat Maps Pix
Notes: American broadsides to 1880. Incl American Judaica broadsides printed from 1718 to 1875.

BROADSIDES—COLLECTIONS (cont.)

PA —FRIENDS HISTORICAL LIBRARY OF SWARTHMORE COLLEGE, Swarthmore, 19081. J William Frost, Dir
Holdings: Vols (35,000) Cat
Notes: Library has numerous broadsides, mostly from Britain and America, some published as early as the mid-17th century. Many are public statements issued by official Quaker organizations, particularly yearly meetings. A number of antislavery broadsides, mostly non-Quaker, are included.

RI —BROWN UNIVERSITY, John Hay Library, Harris Collection, Prospect St, Providence, 02912. Rosemary L Cullen, Cur
Holdings: Vols (200,000) Cat Mss Phonorecords Microforms
Budget: ($15,000)
Notes: See *Dictionary Catalog of the Harris Collection of American Poetry and Plays* (Boston: G K Hall, 1972), 13 vols; *Supplement* (1977), 3 vols. See also, *American Poetry,* 1609-1900, *A Collection on Microfilm, Segment I (1609-1820); Segment II (1821-1850); Segment III* (1851-1870) (Woodbridge, Conn: Research Publications). Separate catalog.

RI —BROWN UNIVERSITY, John Hay Library, 20 Prospect St, Providence, 02912. Mary T Russo, Cur of Broadsides
Holdings: Vols (35,000)
Notes: This is a major collection of broadside material. Its strength lies in the area of American Poetry represented by 28,000 pieces ranging from 18th and 19th century ephemeral verse to contemporary broadsides displaying the work of modern poets. All major figures are represented as well as the work of lesser and unknown poets. The Beat Movement, Black Mountain School, Concrete poetry and Poetry of the Harlem Renaissance are represented as well as that of the young black poets published by the Detroit Broadside Press and a good selection of poetry by women. The collection includes 1200 Carriers' Addresses, 7,000 slip or sheet ballads as well as rewards of merit. War posters, postcards and greetings cards. Historical material appears in the Rider and Drowne broadsides which contain mainly Rhode Island material and the John Hay and Lincoln Collections. The Koopman Collection is strong in finely printed broadsides relating to the history of printing. A general category contains miscellaneous pieces. Retrospective and current pieces are added annually. Partial catalog.

RI —PROVIDENCE PUBLIC LIBRARY, 150 Empire St, Providence, 02903. Lance J Bauer, Special Collections Librn
Holdings: Vols 5000 Cat Mss Maps Pix
Notes: The Harris Collection on the American Civil War and Slavery. Incl 18th and 19th century books, rare pamphlets, and periodicals concerning slavery and the slave trade, and origins, progress and results of the Civil Civil War; also regimental histories; military and naval tactics; personal narratives; women's accounts of the Civil War; works on abolition; sheet music; Union and Confederate broadside ballads; Confederate imprints; *The Liberator* from 1843 through the Civil War; and over 85 editions of *Uncle Tom's Cabin* in 14 languages. Excellent primary and secondary sources for the study of the Civil War and slavery. Material must be used in-house. Photocopying when condition of material allows.

TX —UNIVERSITY OF TEXAS LIBRARIES, General Libraries, Barker Texas History Center, PO Box P, Austin, 78712. Don Carleton, Dir

VA —UNIVERSITY OF VIRGINIA, Alderman Library, Tracy W McGregor Collection, Charlottesville, 22901. William H Runge, Cur
Holdings: Vols 18,000 Cat Mss Maps Pix Microforms
Notes: Library spans 15th-20th century, concentrating on Southeastern American history. Rare collection of books on early exploration and travel; foundation of the Virginia Colony; Civil War. Books in foreign languages. Collection cataloged by date of publication. Special shelflist. Published descriptions: William H Runge, "The Tracy W McGregor Library and Its Founder," *The University of Virginia News Letter* vol 39, no 11, July 15, 1963; *Description of the Tracy W McGregor Library, University of Virginia, With Rules for Its Use and a Biographical Sketch of Its Founder* (Charlottesville: Tracy W McGregor Library, 1951).

VA —VIRGINIA STATE LIBRARY, 12 & Capitol Sts, Richmond, 23219.
Holdings: Cat
Notes: About 3350 items, mostly Virginia, Civil War and the Confederacy. and Southern history.

WV —WEST VIRGINIA UNIVERSITY, Library, West Virginia and Regional History Collection, Morgantown, 26506. George P Parkinson Jr, Cur
Holdings: Vols 30,000 Cat Mss Maps Pix Audiotapes 16mm Films Filmstrips Microforms
Budget: ($20,000)
Notes: The West Virginia Collection contains over 10,000 linear ft of mss, broadsides, pictures, photographs, and other items relating to West Virginia and the Appalachian region. There are published guides to the collections.

BC —SIMON FRASER UNIVERSITY, Library, Burnaby, V5A 1S6, Can. Percilla Groves, Special Collections Librn
Holdings: Cat Mss
Notes: Mss for published and unpublished works, plus a complete collection of published books, chapbooks and broadsides by Canadian and American writers, plus correspondence and business records of the British Columbia Press run by poet and teacher Barry McKinnon from 1972 to 1980.

ON —QUEEN'S UNIVERSITY, Douglas Library, Kingston, K7L 5C4, Can. William F E Morley, Cur, Special Collections
Holdings: Cat
Notes: Canadian Broadside Collection. 1500 broadsides, incl posters.

ON —METROPOLITAN TORONTO LIBRARY, Canadian History Dept, Baldwin Room Section, 789 Yonge St, Toronto, M4W 2G8, Can. David B Kotin, Head
Holdings: Vols (52,000) Mss Pix
Notes: This collection consists of material on Canadian history, geography, travel, archaeology, genealogy, retrospective city and telephone directories, collective biographies, native peoples (excluding customs, rights and social conditions), Arctic regions, military history and theory. It is an extremely strong collection of both current and retrospective material. Particular strengths are national and local history (especially Ontario), Arctic regions, native peoples, travel (especially Ontario), and military history. Incl 78,000 historical pictures, 235 linear meters mss, 14,000 broadsides and 3800 bound newspapers.

BROCH, HERMANN

CT —YALE UNIVERSITY, Beinecke Rare Book & Manuscript Library, German Literature Collection, Box 1603A, Yale Sta, New Haven, 06520. Christa Sammons, Cur
Holdings: Cat Mss
Notes: The Hermann Broch Archive, incl his mss and correspondence. New acquisitions yearly. Printed inventory; Sammons, Christa, "Hermann Broch Archive, Yale University Library," *Modern Austrian Literature* 5:3/4 (1972), pp 18-69.

PA —BIBLIOGRAPHICAL CENTER OF GERMAN LITERATURE, University of Pittsburgh, Dept of Germanic Languages & Literatures, 102 Loeffler Bldg, Pittsburgh, 15260. Klaus W Jonas, Dir
Holdings: Cat Mss Pix Microforms
Notes: Center for the development of collections and bibliographical control of the record of publications, mss, correspondence, etc, by or relating to modern German authors. Special sections have been developed for Mann, Rilke, Hauptmann, Hesse, Broch, Sachs and others. Described by Professor Klaus W Jonas's "The German Literature Center in Pittsburgh," *Stechert-Hafner Book News,* vol 24, no 8, April 1970; "Documentation in Modern German Literature: A Progress Report," *Jahrbuch fuer Internationale Germanistik,* vol 4, no 2, 1972, and in *German and Austrian Contributions to World Literature* (1890-1970). Department of Germanic Languages and Literatures, University of Pittsburgh, 1983. 96 pp.

BRODIE, FAWN M., ?-1981

UT —UNIVERSITY OF UTAH, Marriott Library, Special Collections, Salt Lake City, 84112. Gregory C Thompson, Cur
Notes: Manuscripts and papers of historian-biographer Fawn M Brodie (d 1981). Incl taped interviews with Richard Nixon, and notes, clippings, reviews, articles, and about 400 books used in her researches on Nixon, Thomas Jefferson, and Sir Richard Burton, in preparation of their biographies.

BRODMAN, ESTELLE

†NY —COLUMBIA UNIVERSITY LIBRARIES, Butler Library, Rare Book and Manuscript Library, 535 W 114 St, New York, 10027.
Notes: The papers of Dr Estelle Brodman, incl letters, mss, reports, and conference papers.

BROHKI LANGUAGE see Brahui Language

BROMELIACEAE

†CO —DENVER BOTANIC GARDENS, Helen Fowler Library, 909 York St, Denver, 80206. Solange G Gignac, Librn
Notes: Emphasis on Bromeliada Literature; horticulture; Colorado, Oregon, and Rocky Mountains Region botany; landscape architecture; juvenile horticultural and botanical literature. Incl over 5000 pamphlets on botany and horticulture; also, 197 watercolors of Colorado wildflowers by Emma Irvine, and 250 of Oregon by Lillian Hallock.

BROMBERG, CONRAD

MA —BOSTON UNIVERSITY, Mugar Memorial Library, Special Collections Dept, 771 Commonwealth Ave, Boston, 02215. Howard B Gotlieb, Dir
Holdings: Cat Mss Pix
Notes: Mss, correspondence, etc collected in depth; incl publications by or about.

BRONSON, ARTHUR

IL —CHICAGO HISTORICAL SOCIETY, Library, Clark St at North Ave, Chicago, 60614. Archie Motley, Manuscript Librn
Notes: Papers of real estate developer Arthur Bronson.

BRONSON, BETTY

CA —UNIVERSITY OF CALIFORNIA, LOS ANGELES, Theater Arts Library, Los Angeles, 90024. Edward Shreeves, Chairman, Bibliographers Group; Audree Malkin, Head, Theater Arts Library
Notes: Betty Bronson (actress, silent period) Collection: scripts, photographs, clippings, playbills, artwork, scrapbooks, sheet music, correspondence, legal papers, diaries,

BRONSON, BETTY (cont.)

journals, and mss relating to the career of Betty Bronson.

BRONTE, CHARLOTTE AND EMILY

MA —HARVARD UNIVERSITY LIBRARY, Houghton Library, Cambridge, 02138. Rodney G Dennis, Cur of Manuscripts
Holdings: Cat Mss

BRONTE FAMILY

NJ —PRINCETON UNIVERSITY, Library, Morris L Parrish Collection, Princeton, 08540. Alexander D Wainwright, Cur
Holdings: Vols 585
Notes: A sizable section of the Parrish collection, with more than 585 vols. Ninety-eight volumes are books from the libraries of the Brontes. See Morris L Parrish, *Victorian Lady Novelists,* (London, 1933) (Ex) 04705. 692.

BRONZES

MI —KALAMAZOO INSTITUTE OF ARTS LIBRARY, 314 S Park St, Kalamazoo, 49006. Marianne Cavanaugh, Librn
Holdings: Vols (5000) Cat Slides
Budget: $2000
Notes: Incl (8000) slides. Vertical file on artists. Collection is supplemented by 55 current subscriptions to periodicals in visual arts. Emphasis is on 20th century art and on American art. Collection supports permanent collection in prints, paintings, photography, and sculpture.

BRONZING

NY —HISTORICAL SOCIETY OF EARLY AMERICAN DECORATION, 19 Dove St, Albany, 12210. Doris Fry, Dir; Laura Olf, Librn
Holdings: Cat Pix Slides
Notes: The Library is housed with the Museum Collection of the Society. Incl examples of 19th century American country painting on tin, stenciling on wood and tin, bronzing decoration on wood, English stencilled tin and wood, bronzed items, painted objects, reverse painting on glass and examples of other decorating techniques of the period. Also included is a large collection of painted recordings of designs from early articles. Many of these were done by Esther Stevens Brazer in the 1930s. Another large collection has been added since that time. The library material is related to this interest. See *The Decorator,* official publication of the Historical Society of Early American Decoration. Other publications: *The Ornamented Chair* and *The Ornamented Tray* (both ed by Zilla Rider Lea), *Antique Decorations* by Brazer.

BROOK FARM

IL —UNIVERSITY OF ILLINOIS, URBANA/CHAMPAIGN, Library, Illinois Historical Survey Library, 1408 W Gregory Dr, 1A Library, Urbana, 61801.
Holdings: Vols 50 Cat Mss Maps Pix Microforms
Notes: Communitarianism in America. The ms material, contained in 30 separate collections (10 cubic feet), concentrates on the period 1840-70. It incl correspondence, records, minutes, ledgers and diaries. Communal societies such as Bishop Hill, Brook Farm, New Harmony, the North American Phalanx and the Sodus Bay Phalanx are represented. Among the correspondents are Albert Brisbane, Parke Godwin, Sarah Grimke, Richard Owen, Robert Owen, Robert Dale Owen, and George Ripley. Numerous pictures. Guide to the collections published in 1976.

RI —BROWN UNIVERSITY, John Hay Library, 20 Prospect St, Providence, 02912. Mark N Brown, Cur Mss
Holdings: // Mss
Notes: Charles King Newcomb, Rhode Island Transcendentalist, member of Brook Farm community, and Brown Class of 1837. Incl 2 ms boxes of letters for the period 1802 to 1849 written by Mrs Rhoda M Newcomb, incl letters to her son Charles King Newcomb while he was in theological seminary from 1838 to 1840, and while he lived at Brook Farm from 1841 to 1846. Also 11 ms volumes of his Commonplace Book and 27 ms journals containing thoughts on principles of life, nature, Shakespeare, and scholarship. Members of the community at Brook Farm as well as the literati of Concord, Massachusetts, and those of Providence, especially Sarah Helen Whitman, Margaret Fuller, R W Emerson, and Bronson Alcott, are discussed.

BROOKE, JOCELYN

IL —ILLINOIS STATE UNIVERSITY, Milner Library, Dept of Special Collections, Normal, 61761. Robert Sokan, Librn
Notes: First editions, limited editions, ephemera, etc.

MO —WASHINGTON UNIVERSITY, Libraries, Special Collections Dept, Campus Box 1061, St Louis, 63130.
Notes: A small but significant collection.

BROOKE, RUPERT

CT —LEE ASH, (personal collection), 66 Humiston Dr, Bethany, 06525.
Holdings: Mss Pix
Notes: First editions, mss, ephemera, memorabilia.

CT —TRINITY COLLEGE LIBRARY, Watkinson Library, 300 Summit St, Hartford, 06106. Jeffrey Kaimowitz, Cur
Holdings: Cat
Notes: First editions, etc.

NH —DARTMOUTH COLLEGE, Baker Memorial Library, Hanover, 03755.
Holdings: Vols 600 Cat Mss
Notes: Noncirculating collection of first editions, ephemera, biography, criticism, memorabilia. Also, books from Brooke's library. Strong collection. Incl some mss.

NY —ALFRED UNIVERSITY, Herrick Memorial Library, Alfred, 14802. June E Brown, Head Librn
Notes: The Evelyn Tennyson Openhym Collection of modern British literature and social history.

NY —HOFSTRA UNIVERSITY, Library, 1000 Fulton Ave, Hempstead, 11550. Charles R Andrews, Dean of Library Services

NC —UNIVERSITY OF NORTH CAROLINA, GREENSBORO, Walter Clinton Jackson Library, Special Collections Dept, 1000 Spring Garden St, Greensboro, 27412. Emilie W Mills, Librn
Holdings: Vols 50 Cat
Notes: First, variant and limited editions donated in memory of Gerald D McDonald; includes Brooke's copy of George Herbert's *Poems* with his penciled annotations.

BROOKER, BERTRAM R., 1888-1955

MB —UNIVERSITY OF MANITOBA, Elizabeth Dafoe Library, Archives and Special Collections Dept, Winnipeg, R3T 2N2, Can. Richard E Bennett, Dept Head; Corrado A Santoro, Reference Archivist
Notes: Bertram R Brooker Papers. Correspondence, diaries and daily notations, dramas, both published and unpublished, short stories and essays, and other literary works. Also 16 photographs mainly of Brooker, his family and fellow artists.

BROOKHOUSE, CHRISTOPHER

MA —BOSTON UNIVERSITY, Mugar Memorial Library, Special Collections Dept, 771 Commonwealth Ave, Boston, 02215. Howard B Gotlieb, Dir
Holdings: Cat Mss

BROOKHOUSER, FRANK, 1912-1975

PA —TEMPLE UNIVERSITY LIBRARIES, Special Collections Dept, Conwellana-Templana Collection, 13 & Berks St, Philadelphia, 19122. Miriam I Crawford, Cur
Holdings: Vols 6 // Cat Mss Pix
Notes: Frank Brookhouser, news reporter, columnist, and film and book critic, emphasized the human interest in his stories, which included daily columns in the Philadelphia newspapers from 1936 to 1975 and a large number of magazine stories. Philadelphia and its people provide the focus for much of his writing.

BROOKLYN, NEW YORK

NY —CITY UNIVERSITY OF NEW YORK, BROOKLYN COLLEGE, Library, Special Collections Div, Bedford Ave & Ave H, Brooklyn, 11210. Antoinette Ciolli, Chief
Holdings: Cat
Notes: The Brooklyniana Collection is composed of books, clippings, and maps on the history and culture of Brooklyn and its neighborhoods.

BROOKLYN, NEW YORK—FICTION

NY —STATE UNIVERSITY OF NEW YORK, STONY BROOK, Melville Library, Dept of Special Collections, Stony Brook, 11794. Evert Volkersz, Head
Holdings: Vols Uncat
Notes: A growing collection of fiction and literature with Long Island, incl Queens and Brooklyn, as a fictional setting.

BROOKLYN, NEW YORK—HISTORY

NY —BROOKLYN PUBLIC LIBRARY, Brooklyn Collection, Grand Army Plaza, Flatbush Ave and Eastern Parkway, Brooklyn, 11238.
Notes: More than 3000 books, pamphlets, and documents cover such topics as history, religion, literature, and politics. Microfilm copies of now defunct Brooklyn daily newspapers as well as recent issues of local Brooklyn papers. Incl the morgue of the *Brooklyn Daily Eagle* (1841-1955). Also, more than 25,000 photographs of Brooklyn people, places, and things dating from 1870 to the present, incl those by George Brainard and Daniel Berry Austin. Old town records, vertical files, maps, and institutional archives.

NY —KINGSBOROUGH HISTORICAL SOCIETY, Kingsborough Community College, 2001 Oriental Blvd, Brooklyn, 11235.

NY —LONG ISLAND HISTORICAL SOCIETY, 128 Pierrepont St, at Clinton St, Brooklyn, 11201.
Notes: Books and pamphlets relating to the history of Brooklyn. Over 350 newspapers and periodical resources, incl *The Long Island Star* (1809-1863) and *Williamsburgh* Gazette (1835-1853). 10,000 photographs, paintings, prints, and broadsides. More than 1400 mss collections relating primarily to Brooklyn, dating from 1650 to 1980s. 750 maps and atlases, artifacts, archives, and Decorative Arts collections. Two published guides to Manuscripts: *Calendar of Manuscripts: 1783-1783,* LIHS by Karin N Mango, 1980. Also, *A Guide to Brooklyn Manuscripts in the Long Island Historical* Society. Prepared by Brooklyn Rediscovery, a program of the Brooklyn Educational and Cultural Alliance, 1980. Also, guide to Museum Exhibit, *Brooklyn Before the Bridge - American paintings from the Long Island Historical Society.* Published by Brooklyn Museum, 1982.

NY —SAINT FRANCIS COLLEGE, The James A Kelly Institute for Local Historical Studies, 180 Remsen St, Brooklyn, 11201.
Notes: 250 cubic feet of records of the six original towns of Brooklyn dating from 1643 to 1898. Incl original Dutch patents, minutes of town meetings, assessment and census rolls, court records, wills, property transactions, account books, and school and highway records. Also incl papers of prominent Brooklyn political figures, maps, photographs, vertical files, and theses on Brooklyn history.

NY —SOCIETY FOR THE PRESERVATION OF WEEKSVILLE AND BEDFORD-

BROOKLYN, NEW YORK—HISTORY (cont.)

STUYVESANT HISTORY, PO Box 120, St John's Station, Brooklyn, 11213.

BROOKLYN, NEW YORK—NEWSPAPERS see Newspapers, Brooklyn

BROOKLYN, NEW YORK—PICTURES, ILLUSTRATIONS, ETC.

NY —BROOKLYN PUBLIC LIBRARY, Brooklyn Collection, Grand Army Plaza, Flatbush Ave and Eastern Parkway, Brooklyn, 11238.
Notes: More than 3000 books, pamphlets, and documents cover such topics as history, religion, literature, and politics. Microfilm copies of now defunct Brooklyn daily newspapers as well as recent issues of local Brooklyn papers. Incl the morgue of the *Brooklyn Daily Eagle* (1841-1955). Also, more than 25,000 photographs of Brooklyn people, places, and things dating from 1870 to the present, incl those by George Brainard and Daniel Berry Austin. Old town records, vertical files, maps, and institutional archives.

NY —LONG ISLAND HISTORICAL SOCIETY, 128 Pierrepont St, at Clinton St, Brooklyn, 11201.
Notes: Books and pamphlets relating to the history of Brooklyn. Over 350 newspapers and periodical resources, incl *The Long Island Star* (1809-1863) and *Williamsburgh* Gazette (1835-1853). 10,000 photographs. Paintings, prints, and broadsides. More than 1400 mss collections relating primarily to Brooklyn, dating from 1650 to 1980s. 750 maps and atlases, artifacts, archives, and Decorative Arts collections. Two published guides to Manuscripts: *Calendar of Manuscripts: 1783-1783,* LIHS by Karin N Mango, 1980. Also, *A Guide to Brooklyn Manuscripts in the Long Island Historical* Society. Prepared by Brooklyn Rediscovery, a program of the Brooklyn Educational and Cultural Alliance, 1980. Also, guide to Museum Exhibit, *Brooklyn Before the Bridge - American paintings from the Long Island Historical Society.* Published by Brooklyn Museum, 1982.

BROOKLYN BRIDGE

NJ —RUTGERS, THE STATE UNIVERSITY OF NEW JERSEY, Alexander Library, Special Collections and Archives, College Ave & Huntington St, New Brunswick, 08903. Ronald L Becker, Cur of Manuscripts and Rare Books
Notes: Roebling Family (1823-) incl the papers of John A Roebling, Washington A Roebling, and Ferdinand W Roebling and the John A Roebling's Son Company incl materials relating to the Brooklyn Bridge and other bridge construction.

NY —NEW YORK CITY MUNICIPAL ARCHIVES, Dept of Records and Information Services, 31 Chambers, New York, 10007. Idilio Gracia, Director
Notes: The Brooklyn Bridge Drawings Collection (1869-ca 1950), consisting of approximately 10,000 original plans, drawings, and notes.

BROOKLYN DAILY EAGLE

NY —BROOKLYN PUBLIC LIBRARY, Brooklyn Collection, Grand Army Plaza, Flatbush Ave and Eastern Parkway, Brooklyn, 11238.
Notes: More than 3000 books, pamphlets, and documents cover such topics as history, religion, literature, and politics. Microfilm copies of now defunct Brooklyn daily newspapers as well as recent issues of local Brooklyn papers. Incl the morgue of the *Brooklyn Daily Eagle* (1841-1955). Also, more than 25,000 photographs of Brooklyn people, places, and things dating from 1870 to the present, incl those by George Brainard and Daniel Berry Austin. Old town records, vertical files, maps, and institutional archives.

BROOKLYN MERCANTILE LIBRARY ASSOCIATION

NY —BROOKLYN PUBLIC LIBRARY, Brooklyn Collection, Grand Army Plaza, Flatbush Ave and Eastern Parkway, Brooklyn, 11238.
Notes: Over 3000 books, pamphlets, and documents. Strong collections on the six original towns which made up Brooklyn. Also microfilm copies of defunct Brooklyn newspapers as well as recent issues of local community papers. A great treasure is the *Brooklyn Daily Eagle* morgue published from 1841-1955, the morgue's contents dating from 1904. Collection incl more than 25,000 photographs of people, places, and things from 1870 to the present; nearly a quarter of the photographs are by George Brainard and Daniel Berry Austin. Further, there are more than 500 Brooklyn maps from the earliest times. Incl records of the Brooklyn Mercantile Library Association.

BROOKS, CHARLES STEPHENS, 1878-1934

BC —UNIVERSITY OF VICTORIA, McPherson Library, Victoria, V8W 3H5, Can.

BROOKS, CLEANTH

MS —UNIVERSITY OF SOUTHERN MISSISSIPPI, William David McCain Graduate Library, Box 5148, Southern Sta, Hattiesburg, 39406.
Holdings: Vols 3500 Ucnat
Notes: The personal library of Yale professor emeritus, Cleanth Brooks, who has been one of the leading literary critics of this century. The collection dates from the 18th century to the present and is particularly strong in 20th century american literature and criticism.

BROOKS, VAN WYCK

DC —GEORGETOWN UNIVERSITY, Library, Special Collections Div, 37 & O Sts NW, Washington, 20057. George M Barringer, Special Collections Librn; Nicholas B Sheetz, Mss Librn
Holdings: Uncat Mss Pix
Notes: Substantial correspondence between Brooks and Theodore Maynard; virtually complete run of Brooks' publications, presented to Maynard.

NY —COLUMBIA UNIVERSITY LIBRARIES, Rare Book & Manuscript Library, 801 Butler Library, 535 W 114 St, New York, 10027. Kenneth A Lohf, Librn
Holdings: Mss
Notes: Numerous letters. Restricted use.

PA —UNIVERSITY OF PENNSYLVANIA, Van Pelt Library, Rare Books Collection, 34 & Walnut Sts, Philadelphia, 19104. Daniel Traister, Special Collections Librn
Holdings: Vols 60 Cat Mss
Notes: Mss and first editions, with literary correspondence. See (Pennsylvania) *Library* Chronicle. Vol 31, no 1 Winter 1965, p 25. "The Van Wyck Brooks Collection." Descriptive case file available in library.

BROSCHUEREN-LITERATUR

CA —STANFORD UNIVERSITY LIBRARIES, Cecil H Green Library, Stanford, 94305. Peter R Frank, Cur, CDP-Germanic Collection
Notes: Extensive holdings, covering Austrian history of the Habsburg Empire to the present. Especially strong for the period of Maria Theresia and Joseph II, 19th & 20th century. Extremely rich in the Josephinic pamphlets (Broschuren-Literatur), broadsheets of the Napoleonic Wars and of the Revolution 1848/1849, rare periodicals. This and other rare material in the Stanford Collection of German, Austrian and Swiss Culture, Special Collections. Over 4,000 vols entered in RLIN. Description: "Narrative on a Good Meal: A Collection of Austriaca at Stanford University Libraries" by Peter R Frank.

BROTHELS see Prostitution

BROTHERHOOD OF PAINTERS, DECORATORS AND PAPERHANGERS UNION

PA —PENNSYLVANIA STATE UNIVERSITY, Fred Lewis Pattee Library, Labor History Collection, University Park, 16802. Peter Gottlieb, Archivist
Holdings: Cat Mss
Notes: Trade union's archives, etc.

BROTHERHOOD OF SLEEPING CAR PORTERS

IL —CHICAGO HISTORICAL SOCIETY, Library, Clark St at North Ave, Chicago, 60614. Archie Motley, Manuscript Librn
Notes: Papers of Chicago Division of the Brotherhood of Sleeping Car Porters.

BROUGHTON, JAMES

OH —KENT STATE UNIVERSITY, Libraries, Dept of Special Collections, Kent, 44242. Dean H Keller, Cur
Holdings: Vols 75 Mss Pix Audiotapes 16mm Films

BROUN, HEYWOOD

MI —WAYNE STATE UNIVERSITY, Walter P Reuther Library, Archives of Labor & Urban Affairs, Detroit, 48202. Philip Mason, Dir
Notes: The most recent national labor union to place its records in the Archives is the American Newspaper Guild. The collection contains many personal papers and writings of Heywood Broun. The records of local Guild offices are being collected and those from the Detroit Newspaper Guild have already been obtained.

BROWDER, EARL

MI —MICHIGAN STATE UNIVERSITY, Labor and Industrial Relations Library, East Lansing, 48824. Martha Jane Soltow, Librn
Holdings: Cat Microforms
Notes: This material is composed primarily of special collections of papers on microfilm or microfiche.

BROWN, ADELAIDE

CA —STANFORD UNIVERSITY LIBRARIES, Lane Medical Library, Stanford University, Medical Center, Stanford, 94305. Peter Stangl, Librn
Notes: Adelaide Brown, papers on sanitation and prenatal care.

BROWN, ALBERT GALLATIN

MS —UNIVERSITY OF SOUTHERN MISSISSIPPI, William David McCain Graduate Library, Box 5148, Southern Sta, Hattiesburg, 39406.
Holdings: Cat Mss Pix
Notes: Correspondence and records (1847-1892) relating to Alexander Melvorne Jackson's participation in the Mexican War, his service as Secretary of the State of the New Mexico Territory (1857-1861), and his participation in the Civil War on the side of the Confederacy. Among his correspondents were Albert Gallatin Brown, Reuben Davis, Miguel A Otero, Jacob Thompson, and John Ireland. Incl are photographs of Austin, Texas, ca 1890.

BROWN, CHARLES BROCKDEN, 1771-1810

ME —BOWDOIN COLLEGE, Library, Brunswick, 04011. Dianne M Gutscher, Cur of Special Collections
Holdings: Cat Mss
Notes: The Charles Brockden Brown Papers

BROWN, CHARLES BROCKDEN, 1771-1810 (cont.)

contain 159 letters and mss relating to America's first professional novelist. There are 54 letters from Brown to Joseph Bringhurst, and 105 letters and mss from the Bringhurst-Deborah Ferris correspondence.

OH —KENT STATE UNIVERSITY, Libraries, Dept of Special Collections, Kent, 44242. Dean H Keller, Cur
Holdings: Vols 85 Cat Mss Microforms
Notes: Material by and about Brown brought together as an aid in preparing an edition of his works.

VA —UNIVERSITY OF VIRGINIA, Alderman Library, Clifton Waller Barrett Collection, Charlottesville, 22901. Joan St C Crane, Cur of American Literature Collections
Notes: Papers.

BROWN, DEAN

AZ —UNIVERSITY OF ARIZONA, Center for Creative Photography, 843 E University Blvd, Tucson, 85721. James Enyeart, Dir; Terence Pitts, Cur and Librn
Notes: Center has significant collections consisting of more than 25 photographs plus other archival material such as negatives, contact sheets, work prints, correspondence, financial records, diaries, project files, etc. Inventories of the collections are available to researchers. Published guides available for some collections.

BROWN, EDGAR A., 1888-1975

SC —CLEMSON UNIVERSITY, Libraries, Clemson, 29631. Michael F Kohl, Head of Special Collections
Holdings: // Cat Mss Pix Audiotapes Videotapes
Notes: Edgar A Brown papers. There is a folder title listing to the the collection. Senator Brown served 50 years in the South Carolina General Assembly, and was for some time a member of the Democratic National Committee. Approximately 125 cubic ft of mss; 200 photos; 29 scrapbooks and memorabilia.

BROWN, ESTHER LUCILE

MA —BOSTON UNIVERSITY, Mugar Memorial Library, Special Collections Dept, 771 Commonwealth Ave, Boston, 02215. Howard B Gotlieb, Dir
Holdings: Cat Mss

BROWN, FRANK CHOUTEAU

MA —SOCIETY FOR THE PRESERVATION OF NEW ENGLAND ANTIQUITIES, Library, 141 Cambridge St, Boston, 02114. Ellie Reichlin, Librn & Cur of Photographic Collections
Holdings: Vols (3000) // Cat Pix Microforms
Budget: ($75,000)
Notes: Architecture of the Northeast. Drawings (original designs, measured drawings, plot plans, etc). Over 7500 items, incl extensive collections of original designs by Ogden Codman, Jr (1890s-early 1900s); Arthur Little and Herbert Browne (1890s-1920s); Luther Briggs (1840s-1860s); Arland Dirlam (1930s-1960s), together with important examples of the work of Asher Benjamin, Richard Upjohn, and others. Measured drawings incl extensive holdings of work undertaken by HABS (Historic American Buildings Survey) in Massachusetts in the 1930s, 1940s under director Frank Chouteau Brown. Also represented are several residential and commercial commissions by F C Brown, not connected with HABS. Collection incl architectural pattern books, builders guides, 18th-19th century. Approx 350 volumes, English and American publications.

NC —DUKE UNIVERSITY, William R Perkins Library, Manuscript Dept, Durham, 27706. Ellen Gartrell, Cur of Mss
Holdings: Cat Mss
Notes: Papers of Frank C Brown and colleagues, much of which later published in *The Frank C Brown Collection of North Carolina Folklore* (7 vols, Durham, 1952-64). Incl correspondence, texts, recordings, clippings, quilt blocks.

BROWN, FRED R., 1888-1966

NY —STATE UNIVERSITY OF NEW YORK AT ALBANY, Library, Special Collections Dept, 1400 Washington Ave, Albany, 12222. Marion P Munzer, Coordr
Notes: Fred R Brown's correspondence, mss, photographs, and maps. He was a Methodist missionary to China from 1910-31 (6 linear feet). Part of the Library's German Exile Collection.
See also entries under Missions - China; Missionaries; China - History.

BROWN, GEORGE H.

NH —PLYMOUTH STATE COLLEGE, Lamson Library, Plymouth, 03264. Phillip Wei, Dir of Library Services
Holdings: Uncat Mss Pix
Budget: ($30,000)
Notes: More than 80 folders. All photocopies remain the property of library unless specific permission given in advance by copyright owner. Collection importance is letters to George H Browne, founder of Browne and Nichols School, Boston, during Franconia period 1915-1920 and a few typescripts of poems from same period. List of holdings available upon request. Depository from current New Hampshire state publications. Early mss and varia on town of Plymouth.

BROWN, GEORGE M.

MI —UNIVERSITY OF MICHIGAN, Engineering-Transportation Library, 312 Undergraduate Library, Ann Arbor, 48109. Sharon A Balius, Assoc Librn
Holdings: Mss
Notes: Brown was an employee of the Pere (Flint and Pere) Marquette Railroad from 1867 to 1891. The collection incl business and personal papers, 1859-1901.

BROWN, H. C.

IN —PURDUE UNIVERSITY LIBRARIES, Chemistry Library, West Lafayette, 47907. John Pinzelik, Librn
Holdings: Vols 49,900 Cat Microforms
Budget: $142,800
Notes: Archives of H C Brown, 1979 Nobel Laureate in Chemistry.

BROWN, HARRY

MO —WASHINGTON UNIVERSITY, Libraries, Special Collections Dept, Campus Box 1061, St Louis, 63130.
Notes: A small but significant collection.

BROWN, HERBERT CHILDS, 1882-1927

NY —CORNELL UNIVERSITY LIBRARIES, Collection of Regional History, Dept of Manuscripts and Univ Archives, Ithaca, 14853.
Notes: "Personal Memoranda and Diary Transcript of War Service in 1917, 1918, and 1919"; 1 item.

BROWN, IVOR

MA —BOSTON UNIVERSITY, Mugar Memorial Library, Special Collections Dept, 771 Commonwealth Ave, Boston, 02215. Howard B Gotlieb, Dir
Holdings: Cat Mss
Notes: Mss, correspondence, etc collected in depth; incl publications by or about.

BROWN, J. C.

AZ —NORTHERN ARIZONA UNIVERSITY, Special Collection Library, CU Box 6022, Flagstaff, 86011. Peter M Whiteley, Coordr/Archivist; William Mullane, Librn
Notes: Letter written by J C Brown about some mineral claims near the Gap Trading Post (located some 110 miles north of Flagstaff, Ariz), 1937.

BROWN, J. FRANCIS AND F. BRUCE

AB —UNIVERSITY OF CALGARY, Libraries, Special Collections Div, 2500 University Dr, Calgary, T2N 1N4, Can.
Holdings: Cat
Notes: Collection consists of 48 original drawings, renderings and watercolors of Toronto architects J Francis Brown and his son F Bruce Brown. Of particular interest is the set of drawings by J Francis Brown for the British Columbia Parliament Building Competition 1891. An inventory is on hand.

BROWN, JAMES OLIVER

NY —COLUMBIA UNIVERSITY LIBRARIES, Rare Book & Manuscript Library, 801 Butler Library, 535 W 114 St, New York, 10027. Kenneth A Lohf, Librn
Holdings: Mss
Notes: Publications and papers, by and about his literary agency. Incl 200,000 items. Restricted use.

BROWN, JAMES S.

AZ —NORTHERN ARIZONA UNIVERSITY, Special Collection Library, CU Box 6022, Flagstaff, 86011. Peter M Whiteley, Coordr/Archivist; William Mullane, Librn
Notes: Brown was a Northern Arizona Mormon pioneer and missionary. Collection incl diary, 1875-1877.

BROWN, JOHN

OH —HUDSON LIBRARY & HISTORICAL SOCIETY, Library, 22 Aurora St, Hudson, 44236. Thomas L Vince, Dir
Holdings: Vols 78 Cat Mss Maps Pix Slides
Notes: The John Brown Collection was acquired mainly from the collection of Dr Clarence S Gee of Lockport, New York, formerly of Hudson, who began collecting John Brown material in 1924, when he learned that Brown (a one-time resident of Hudson) had been baptized in his church in 1816. Incl four original John Brown letters, 12 boxes of mss, the standard genealogy of the Brown family as drawn up by Dr Gee and much collateral family correspondence and documents. No catalog as yet. Inquiries, students, scholars are welcome.

ON —CHATHAM PUBLIC LIBRARY, 120 Queen St, Chatham, N7M 2G6, Can. Arlene Mason, Head of Reference
Holdings: Vols 20 Cat
Notes: Books, pamphlets, and articles on Henry Bibb, William King, Martin Delaney, and John Brown and their work in the Chatham, Ont region.

BROWN, JOHN MASON

MA —HARVARD UNIVERSITY LIBRARY, Theatre Collection, Cambridge, 02138. Jeanne T Newlin, Cur
Notes: One of the largest existing collections of playbills, programs, prints, photographs, promptbooks, and other materials relating to the performing arts, the scope is worldwide; resources on the English-speaking stage of the 18th and 19th centuries are unequalled. Incl materials on ballet and modern dance, the circus, magic, minstrel shows, cinema, and pantomime. For description, see *Harvard Library Bulletin,* VI (1925): pp 281-301. Also, papers of Robert E Sherwood (1896-1955), John Mason Bowers, George Pierce Baker, Edward Sheldon, Percy Mackaye; Angus McBean collection of photographs of the London Stage, 1937-1965; Alix Jeffry collection of photographs of the Off-Broadway Theatre; and others.

BROWN, MARGARET WISE

RI —WESTERLY PUBLIC LIBRARY, Broad St, Westerly, 02891. David J Panciera, Library Dir
Holdings: Vols 100// Uncat Mss Pix
Notes: The Margaret Wise Brown Collection

BROWN, MARGARET WISE (cont.)

of books, correspondence, etc, was donated to the library in 1957. At present the library owns the most complete collection of the famous author and illustrator's works of children's picture books. There is a listing of the books, but no listing of the other material at present.

BROWN, MURIEL W., 1892-

KS —MENNINGER FOUNDATION, Archives, 5600 W Sixth St, Box 829, Topeka, 66601. Alice Brand, Librn; Mark West, Archivist
Notes: 5 boxes, 1930-77. Incl correspondence, mss, publications, and miscellaneous materials related to parent education.

BROWN, PHILLIP KING

CA —STANFORD UNIVERSITY LIBRARIES, Lane Medical Library, Stanford University, Medical Center, Stanford, 94305. Peter Stangl, Librn
Notes: Phillip King Brown's papers on health insurance and socialized medicine.

BROWN, REAGAN

†TX —TEXAS A&M UNIVERSITY, Library, University Archives, College Station, 77843.
Notes: Papers of Reagan Brown, former Texas Agriculture Commissioner.

BROWN, ROSEL GEORGE

†LA —TULANE UNIVERSITY, Libraries, Rare Books Dept, New Orleans, 70118. Sylvia V Metzinger, Librn
Notes: Science fiction, 1000 vols and growing. Rosel George Brown and Robert A Heinlein special collections.

BROWN, SAMUEL

PA —BALCH INSTITUTE FOR ETHNIC STUDIES, Library, 18 S Seventh St, Philadelphia, 19106. R Joseph Anderson, Library Dir
Notes: Incl a catalogue of an exhibition of Samuel Brown's works.

BROWN, STUART E., JR.

VA —UNIVERSITY OF VIRGINIA, Alderman Library, Manuscripts Dept, Charlottesville, 22901. Edmund Berkeley Jr, Cur
Notes: Papers and notes of Stuart E Brown, Jr.
See also entry under Virginia History

BROWN, VAUGHAN

WA —WESTERN WASHINGTON UNIVERSITY, Center for Pacific Northwest Studies, High St, Bellingham, 98225. James W Scott, Dir
Holdings: Mss Maps Pix
Notes: The Vaughan Brown Collection. Vaughan Brown, a retired attorney, is a former Postmaster of Bellingham and a former member of the house and senate of Washington State, retiring from the latter in the 1950s. This voluminous collection consists of political papers and materials in large part, covering state and local matters. Rural electrification is one of the major topics covered, and there is much illustrative campaign literature, largely Democratic, but incl some Republican. Personal, financial and legal papers are also included. Mainly Pacific Northwest--especially Washington and, in particular Whatcom County, but also some items of Arkansas, home of O P Brown, his father, some of whose papers are included. Partially cataloged.

BROWN, GEN. WILLIAM CAREY

CO —UNIVERSITY OF COLORADO, Libraries, Western Historical Collections, Boulder, 80309.
Holdings: // Cat Mss Maps Pix
Notes: The collection contains correspondence, diaries, military papers, maps, publications, scrapbooks, addresses, photographs, and newspaper clippings relating to Gen William Carey Brown's military career, which incl campaigns against the Indians, service in the Spanish-American War and the Philippine Insurrection, and participation in the Mexican Punitive Expedition. The materials, in 49 boxes, covers virtually all of Brown's life (1854-1939). A published guide is available.

BROWN, WILLIAM COMPTON

†WA —WASHINGTON STATE UNIVERSITY, Library, Manuscripts, Archives & Special Collections, Pullman, 99164. John F Guido, Head
Holdings: Vols Cat Mss Maps Pix Microforms
Notes: Ms resources for the study of Pacific Northwest Indians incl the papers of historians William Compton Brown, Carl Parcher Russell, and Lucullus Virgil McWhorter; and missionaries Henry Harmon Spalding, Elkanah Walker and Marcus Whitman. A few of these resources have been described in the following publications: *William Compton Brown: A Calendar of His Papers in the Washington State University Library* (Pullman, 1966); *Carl Parcher Russell: An Indexed Register of His Scholarly and Professional Papers, 1920-1967, in the Washington State University* Library (Pullman, 1970); *The Papers of Lucullus Virgil McWhorter*, compiled by Nelson A Ault (Pullman, 1959).

BROWN, WILLIAM H.

NM —MUSEUM OF NEW MEXICO, Photo Archives, Box 2087, Santa Fe, 87503. Arthur L Olivas, Cur; Richard Rudisill, Photo Historian
Holdings: Cat Pix Slides
Notes: Extensive collection of his work.

BROWN, ADM. WILSON

MD —US NAVAL ACADEMY, Nimitz Library, Annapolis, 21402. Alice S Creighton, Assistant Librn for Special Collections
Holdings: Mss Pix
Notes: Papers, etc.

BROWN AND IVES

RI —RHODE ISLAND HISTORICAL SOCIETY, Library, 121 Hope St, Providence, 02906. Paul R Campbell, Library Dir
Holdings: Mss
Budget: ($200,000)
Notes: The Brown and Ives collection of manufacturing records. Incl the records of the Brown and Ives firm; their principal management agency, the firm of Goddard Brothers; and cotton mills owned by Brown and Ives. Collection incl 1000 mss.

BROWN FAMILY

NY —CORNELL UNIVERSITY LIBRARIES, Collection of Regional History, Dept of Manuscripts and Univ Archives, Ithaca, 14853.
Notes: Chiefly Baker, Barker, Bloom, Brown letters (1827-74), Chapel, Coshun, Fanning, Furber, Green, Ketchum, Kilmer, Livingston, O'Daniels, Pew families.

OH —OHIO UNIVERSITY, Vernon R Alden Library, Athens, 45701. Kent Mulliner, Africana Specialist
Notes: The Brown Family Papers, containing over 400 letters written by members of the Brown family, early settlers in Athens County, Ohio. Most of the letters deal with the Civil War, in particular activities of the Ohio 36th Regiment, the West Virginia 4th Regiment, and the Kentucky campaigns.

BROWN-SEQUARD, CHARLES EDWARD, 1817-1894

KS —UNIVERSITY OF KANSAS MEDICAL CENTER, College of Health Sciences & Hospital, Clendening History of Medicine Library, Rainbow Blvd at 39th, Kansas City, 66103. Robert P Hudson, Chmn/Cur
Notes: Papers, 1835-92. 135 items. Physiologist, endocrinologist and neurologist. Correspondence, cards, poems, notes and other papers, written by Brown-Seguard to members of his fmaily. In English and French. Access restricted. Gift of Dr Brown-Seguard's great-great granddaughter, Mrs George Stumpf.

BROWNE, HABLOT KNIGHT (PHIZ)

MD —UNIVERSITY OF MARYLAND, BALTIMORE COUNTY, Albin O Kuhn Library and Gallery, 5401 Wilkens Ave, Baltimore, 21228. Ann Copeland, Special Collections Librn
Holdings: Vols (800) Cat Pix
Notes: The Edgar and Kathleen Merkle Collection of 19th-century English graphic satire centers around the work of George E Cruikshank. Other artists represented incl Rowlandson, Gillray, Hogarth, and "Phiz." Rare items incl Cruikshank's lavish hand-colored film *Scraps and Sketches* (1828).

BROWNE, JOHN ROSS

CA —UNIVERSITY OF THE PACIFIC, Holt-Atherton Pacific Center for Western Studies, Stockton, 95211. Hiram L Davis, Dir of Libraries
Holdings: Vols 22 // Cat Mss
Notes: A collection of all the major works of John Ross Browne, 19th century American author, plus the bulk of his minor works. Some unpublished manuscripts and letters.

BROWNE, MAURICE

MI —UNIVERSITY OF MICHIGAN, Library, Dept of Rare Books & Special Collections, Ann Arbor, 48109. Robert J Starring, Head
Holdings: Cat Mss Pix
Notes: Extensive holdings of books on the theatre. Also, in the Charles Sanders Collection, about 14,000 British and American playbills and programs mostly of the 19th century, as well as scrapbooks, posters, and about 750 photographs and prints of actors and actresses. In the Ellen Van Volkenburg--Maurice Browne Collection, about 4000 photographs of stage productions and friends and associates, as well as programs, posters, scrapbosk of mounted clippings, about 200 original stage and costume designs, promptbooks, and play manuscripts, representing the American and British careers of his husband-wife team from 1912 to about 1940. The Chicago Little Theatre, 1912-1917, is well represented. Also contains more than 6000 items of correspondence with theatrical and literary figures. Another collection contains 143 Alfred Lunt letters, mainly from 1909-1915.

BROWNELL, GEORGE M., 1899-1979

MB —UNIVERSITY OF MANITOBA, Elizabeth Dafoe Library, Archives and Special Collections Dept, Winnipeg, R3T 2N2, Can. Richard E Bennett, Dept Head; Corrado A Santoro, Reference Archivist
Notes: A collection fo twenty-two reprints and copies of Dr Brownell's writings and speeches (1927-1974) pertaining primarily to geological studies such as surveying with the scintillometer and berylometer, various Manitoba mineral deposits, etc. A biographcial chronology of Dr Brownell is also incl.

BROWNING, ROBERT AND ELIZABETH BARRETT

AZ —UNIVERSITY OF ARIZONA, University Library, Special Collections, Tucson, 85721. Louis A Hieb, Head
Holdings: Vols (7000) Cat Mss Microforms
Budget: ($30,000)
Notes: The major collection of 19th century authors are Byron, Dickens, Scott, Thackeray, Trollope, the Brownings, Stevens, Tennyson, and Wordsworth.

BROWNING, ROBERT AND ELIZABETH BARRETT (cont.)

CA —CLAREMONT COLLEGES, Ella Strong Denison Library, Scripps College, Claremont, 91711. Judy Harvey Sahak, Librn
Holdings: Vols 1100 Cat Mss Pix
Notes: Gift of the Pacific Coast Browning Foundation, the collection includes all but one of the first editions of the Brownings, letters, manuscripts, and association items. The letters are described in *The Brownings* Correspondence by Philip Kelley.

CA —UNIVERSITY OF CALIFORNIA, LOS ANGELES, William Andrews Clark Memorial Library, 2520 Cimarron St, Los Angeles, 90018.
Holdings: Cat
Notes: Extensive collection, first editions, etc.

CA —MILLS COLLEGE LIBRARY, Oakland, 94613. Steven P Pandolfo, Librn
Holdings: Vols 100 Cat Mss Pix
Notes: First editions; some correspondence, pictures, association items.

CT —TRINITY COLLEGE LIBRARY, Watkinson Library, 300 Summit St, Hartford, 06106. Jeffrey Kaimowitz, Cur
Holdings: Cat
Notes: First editions, etc.

CT —YALE UNIVERSITY, Box 1603A, Yale Station, New Haven, 06520.
Holdings: Cat Mss

MA —BOSTON UNIVERSITY, Mugar Memorial Library, Special Collections Dept, 771 Commonwealth Ave, Boston, 02215. Howard B Gotlieb, Dir
Holdings: Cat
Notes: Correspondence incl publications by or about.

MA —HARVARD UNIVERSITY LIBRARY, Houghton Library, Cambridge, 02138. Rodney G Dennis, Cur of Manuscripts
Holdings: Cat Mss

TX —BAYLOR UNIVERSITY, Armstrong Browning Library, 700 Speight, Box 6336, Waco, 76706. Jack W Herring, Dir
Holdings: Vols 10,000 Cat Mss Pix Slides Phonorecords 16mm Films Filmstrips Microforms
Notes: Largest Browning collection in the world. Contains books that belonged to the Brownings (300); letters written by Browning (1100); letters written by Elizabeth B Browning; letters written to the Brownings; furniture from the Brownings' homes; jewelry which belonged to the Brownings; 51 stained-glass windows depicting poems; music composed to accompany the poems (1500 pieces), etc. Noncirculating. Publish "Studies in Browning and His Circle" (semi-annual).

VA —ROANOKE CITY PUBLIC LIBRARY, Virginia Room, 706 S Jefferson St, Roanoke, 24011. Alice Carol Tuckwiller, Librn
Holdings: Vols 142 // Cat

BROWNING FAMILY

NJ —GLASSBORO STATE COLLEGE, Savitz Library, Stewart Room, Glassboro, 08028. Clara Kirner, Special Collection Librn
Notes: Papers.

BROWNLOW, LOUIS

†MA —JOHN F KENNEDY LIBRARY, Columbia Point, Boston, 02125. Dan H Fenn Jr, Dir
Holdings: // Cat Mss
Notes: Louis Brownlow's papers relating to government reorganization during the Roosevelt administration, the District of Columbia, the Public Administration Clearing House, and other topics; manuscript material for books, articles and lectures; and personal and family papers, 1902-1963. 30 linear ft of mss. Holdings are described in "Historical Materials in the John F Kennedy Library." Copies may be obtained by writing the Research Archivist.

BRUCE FAMILY

VA —UNIVERSITY OF VIRGINIA, Alderman Library, Manuscripts Dept, Charlottesville, 22901. Edmund Berkeley Jr, Cur
Holdings: Cat Mss Maps Pix
Notes: 19th century Virginia Family Papers Collections enable a researcher to obtain an excellent picture of the economic and social interactions on large plantations in Virginia during the 19th century. They are invaluable as research sources in the study of slavery, women's history, economic history, agrarian and political history.

BRUGUIERE, FRANCIS

NY —NEW YORK PUBLIC LIBRARY, Performing Arts Research Center, Billy Rose Theatre Collection, 111 Amsterdam Ave, New York, 10023. Dorothy L Swerdlove, Cur
Holdings: Cat Mss Pix
Notes: Papers, scrapbooks, mss, photographs, memorabilia, etc.

BRUNDAGE, AVERY

IL —UNIVERSITY OF ILLINOIS, URBANA/CHAMPAIGN, Library, University Archives, 19 Library, 1408 W Gregory Drive, Urbana, 61801. Maynard Brichford, University Archivist
Holdings: Vols (1663)// Cat Mss Pix
Notes: The Avery Brundage Collection. Incl his papers and material on amateur athletics, Olympic games, and sports. Published guide is available: *Avery Brundage Collection,* 1908-1975 (Cologne: Karl Hofmann Schorndorf, 1977). 517,000 ms pieces. There is also a collection on Olympic sports and other aspects of sports kept in the Brundage Room.

BRUNDAGE, PERCIVAL FLACK, 1892-1979

†DC —LIBRARY OF CONGRESS, Manuscript Division, Washington, 20540.
Notes: The papers, etc, of Percival Flack Brundage.

BRUNEI

HI —UNIVERSITY OF HAWAII, Library, 2550 The Mall, Honolulu, 96822. Joyce Wright, Head, Asia Collection; Masato Matsu, Head, East Asia Vernacular Collection
Holdings: Vols 331,620 Cat Microforms
Notes: The Asia Collection holds materials from and about Southeast Asia: Brunei, Burma, Cambodia (Kampuchea), Indonesia, Laos, Malaysia, Philippines, Singapore, Thailand. Large contemporary Indonesian language collection. Several thousand vols in Thai and in Vietnamese. Minimal holdings in Burmese, Khmer, Lao languages. Social sciences and humanities emphasis for the post-World War II period. Western language coverage supplemented by retrospective holdings in the main library collection.

IL —CENTER FOR RESEARCH LIBRARIES, 6050 S Kenwood Ave, Chicago, 60637. Donald B Simpson, Dir; Esther Smith, Collection Development Librn
Holdings: Vols Cat Microforms
Notes: Receive serials and monographs fromm Indonesia, Malaysia and Singapore under NPAC (formerly PL 480). Collection starts 1969 for Indonesia, 1971 for Malaysia, Singapore and Brunei. Buy 14 newspapers on microfilm. Also incl Southeast Asia Microform Project. Borrowing is restricted to members of the project.

IL —NORTHERN ILLINOIS UNIVERSITY, Founders Memorial Library, Southeast Asia Collection, Normal Rd, De Kalb, 60115. Lee S Dutton Dr, Cur
Holdings: Vols (34,000) Cat Mss Maps Microforms
Notes: An extensive collection of books, periodicals, newspapers, maps, and microforms from or about Southeast Asia. Areas of concentration incl Thailand, Malaysia, Indonesia, Singapore, Brunei, Philippines, Laos, and Burma. Holdings (except rare books, maps, and microforms) are housed in a separate area collection within the Founders Library. A departmental card catalog and specialized reference collection support reference services. A Thai collection of several thousand vols is the largest vernacular component. Extensive Malaysia, Indonesia, Singapore, and Brunei holdings have been acquired through the NPAC program. A collection of Filipino-American newspapers, and a growing collection of children's literature in common and uncommon Southeast Asian languages are available. Resources are accessible to borrowers through OCLC.

MI —UNIVERSITY OF MICHIGAN, Harlan Hatcher Graduate Library, Ann Arbor, 48109. Susan Go, Librn
Holdings: Vols (250,000) Cat Mss Maps Pix Slides Microforms
Notes: Incl in the Michigan Historical Collections (primarily archival material) are papers of Michiganders in southeast Asia, mostly the Philipines, eg papers of Joseph R Hayden, Frank Murphy and G Mennen Williams, also, on film, the selected papers of Philippines president Manuel Quezon. All aspects of the countries, cultures and peoples of Brunei, Burma, Khymer, Indonesia, Laos, Malaysia, Philippines, Singapore, Thailand, Portuguese Timor and Vietnam. Also the Malayo-Polynesian (Austronesian), Mon-Khmer (Austroasiatic), and Sino-Tibetan language groupings.

NY —CORNELL UNIVERSITY LIBRARIES, John M Olin Library, John M Echols Collection on Southeast Asia, Ithaca, 14853. Giok Po Oey, Curator
Holdings: Vols (167,000) Cat Mss Maps Pix Microforms
Budget: ($90,000)
Notes: Additions published in the collection's monthly accessions list (Ithaca: Cornell University, Southeast Asia Program, 1959-). Holdings through December 1980 listed in *Cornell University Libraries Southeast Asia Catalog* (Boston: G K Hall, 1976, First supplement, 1983), 10 vols.

OH —OHIO UNIVERSITY, Vernon R Alden Library, Southeast Asia Collection, Athens, 45701. Lian The-Mulliner, Head
Holdings: Vols (68,000) Cat Maps Slides Phonorecords Videotapes 16mm Films Filmstrips Microforms
Budget: ($35,000)
Notes: Emphasis on Indonesia, Malaysia, Singapore, Brunei and the Philippines. Incl language and literature, history, civilization and culture, art, medicine, philosophy and economic conditions. Separate catalog.

BRUTALITY see Cruelty

BRUTUS, DENNIS

IL —NORTHWESTERN UNIVERSITY, Melville J Herskovits Library of African Studies, Evanston, 60201. Hans E Panofsky, Cur
Holdings: Vols (85,000) Mss
Budget: ($70,000)
Notes: Papers, etc. Mostly southern Africa. *See also* entry under Africa.

BRY, THEODORE AND JOHANN DE

NY —NEW YORK PUBLIC LIBRARY, Rare Books and Manuscripts Div, Fifth Ave & 42 St, New York, 10018. William L Joyce, Asst Dir; Francis O Mattson, Curator
Holdings: Cat
Budget: ($7161)
Notes: Incl one of the most extensive collections of De Bry and Hulsius and one of the finest sets of Canadian Jesuit Relations. Most editions of Columbus' "Letter."

BRYAN, CHARLES W., JR., 1890-1966

MO —WASHINGTON UNIVERSITY, Libraries, Special Collections Dept, Campus Box 1061, St Louis, 63130.
Notes: Papers of Charles W Bryan Jr, incl correspondence, personal journals, scrapbooks, photographs, and printed material associated with the Federal Shipbuilding Company from 1917 to 1948,

BRYAN, CHARLES W., JR., 1890-1966 (cont.)

and as president of the Pullman Standard Car Manufacturing Company from 1950 to 1958.

BRYAN, ENOCH ALBERT

†WA —WASHINGTON STATE UNIVERSITY, Library, Manuscripts, Archives & Special Collections, Pullman, 99164. John F Guido, Head
Holdings: Vols Cat Mss Maps Pix Microforms
Notes: Ms resources in the Washington State University Library for the study of pacific Northwest history incl the personal papers of Frank A Banks, William Compton Brown, Enoch Albert Bryan, Ernest Otto Holland, William Lon Johnson, Catherine May, Lucullus Virgil McWhorter, Austin Mires, Carl Parcher Russell, Pierre Jean de Smet, Henry Harmon Spalding, Elkanah Walker, John McAdam Webster, Marcus Whitman, as well as many business records of banks, insurance firms and agencies, breweries, lumber mills, merchants, entrepreneurs and farmers. All ms collections are described in a catalog, a published register or an unpublished finding aid.

BRYAN, WILLIAM JENNINGS

OH —RUTHERFORD B HAYES LIBRARY, 1337 Hayes Ave, Fremont, 43420. Watt P Marchman, Dir
Notes: Correspondence in the Lyman-Lincoln Collection.

BRYAN-WHITEFIELD FAMILY

SC —COLLEGE OF CHARLESTON LIBRARY, Special Collections Dept, Charleston, 29401.
Notes: Incl indenture for the sale of a tract of land in Prince Willliam Parish, Granville County, SC, granted to Hugh Bryan by King George II and given to Rev George Whitefield and then by Rev Whitefield to Mary Bryan, Nov 24, 1752. Incl also a plat of the tract dated Dec 29, 1747.

BRYANT, LAURA, 1878-1961

NY —CORNELL UNIVERSITY LIBRARIES, Collection of Regional History, Dept of Manuscripts and Univ Archives, Ithaca, 14853.
Holdings: Pix
Notes: Music and singing teacher. Papers, ca 1895-1961; miscellaneous teaching materials and correspondence, personal letters, diaries, notebooks, scrapbooks, concert programs, musical scores, albums, and greeting cards.

BRYANT, WILLIAM CULLEN

MA —WILLIAMS COLLEGE, Sawyer Library, Williamstown, 01267. Phyllis L Cutler, Dir
Holdings: Vols 450 Cat Mss
Budget: $500

NY —NEW YORK PUBLIC LIBRARY, Rare Books and Manuscripts Div, Fifth Ave & 42 St, New York, 10018. William L Joyce, Asst Dir; Susan E Davis, Cur of Mss
Holdings: Mss
Budget: ($7161)
Notes: Incl personal and literary mss, papers, etc.

NC —DUKE UNIVERSITY, William R Perkins Library, Rare Book Room, Durham, 27706. John L Sharpe, III, Cur
Notes: William Cullen Bryant collection, loan of Dr Ernest Risley. Includes not only a number of 19th and 20th century editions of the poet's works and various books about him, but also several interesting letters written by Bryant.

VA —UNIVERSITY OF VIRGINIA, Alderman Library, Clifton Waller Barrett Collection, Charlottesville, 22901. Joan St C Crane, Cur of American Literature Collections
Notes: Papers.

BRYCE, GEORGE, 1844-1931

MB —UNIVERSITY OF MANITOBA, Elizabeth Dafoe Library, Archives and Special Collections Dept, Winnipeg, R3T 2N2, Can. Richard E Bennett, Dept Head; Corrado A Santoro, Reference Archivist
Notes: Unpublished work, *An Illustrated History of Winnipeg* by Bryce.

BRYOLOGY

CT —YALE UNIVERSITY, Kline Science Library, Kline Biology Tower Rm C-8, PO Box 6666, New Haven, 06511. Richard J Dionne, Head
Holdings: Vols (175,480) Cat 16mm Films Microforms
Budget: ($340,000)
Notes: Comprehensive collection on biological sciences, physics, and chemistry. Incl Evans Collection of Bryology and Lichenology (with catalog cards in both Kline Science Library and Sterling Memorial Library). Also incl AEC reports (hardcopy and microform) to 1970.

MO —MISSOURI BOTANICAL GARDEN LIBRARY, PO Box 299, Saint Louis, 63166. M R Crosby, Dir of Research
Holdings: Vols 1000 Cat Mss Maps Pix Microforms
Notes: The William Campbell Steere Collection of Bryology, incl 4000 reprints and pamphlets.

BRYOPHYTES

MA —HARVARD UNIVERSITY LIBRARY, Farlow Reference Library, 20 Divinity Ave, Cambridge, 02138. Geraldine C Kaye, Librn
Holdings: Vols (60,000) Cat Mss Serials Pix Microforms
Notes: The Farlow Reference Library provides complete coverage of the systematic literature on algae, bryophytes, fungi, and lichens. Established by bequest of Professor William G Farlow, it is one of the most extensive cryptogamic botany libraries in the US. Books do not circulate.

MI —UNIVERSITY OF MICHIGAN, Herbarium Library, University Herbarium, 2003 N University Bldg, Ann Arbor, 48109. Robert L Shaffer, Dir, Herbarium
Holdings: Vols (22,000) Cat Mss Maps Microforms
Notes: Systematic Botany including floristics, revisions and monographs in all groups of plants. Collection incl maps, mss (fieldbooks, correspondence, etc), photographs, microfiches, and approx 100, 000 reprints that are not officially part of the University Library. These are indexed and are available to qualified scholars. Incl botanical libraries of Parke, Davis & Co, Harley H Bartlett, Bruce Fink (lichens), Howard A Kelly (mycology).

ON —NATIONAL MUSEUMS OF CANADA, Library Services Directorate, Ottawa, K1A 0M8, Can. Valerie Monkhouse, Director
Holdings: Vols (90,000) Cat Mss Microforms
Budget: ($81,000)
Notes: Emphasis on Canadian and circumpolar natural history. Collection incl botany, herpetology, ichthyology, invertebrate zoology, malacology, mammology, mineralogy, ornithology, paleobiology, zooarchaeology. Exceptional collections in lichenology, bryology, malacology, ornithology. Research collection, interlibrary loans available, public may use on the premises.

BUBONIC PLAGUE see Plague

BUBONIDAE see Owls

BUCCANEERS see Pirates and Piracy

BUCHAN, JOHN, 1ST BARON TWEEDSMUIR, 1875-1940

CT —YALE UNIVERSITY, Box 1603A, Yale Station, New Haven, 06520.

IL —ILLINOIS STATE UNIVERSITY, Milner Library, Dept of Special Collections, Normal, 61761. Robert Sokan, Librn
Notes: First editions, limited editions, ephemera, etc.

NY —ALFRED UNIVERSITY, Herrick Memorial Library, Alfred, 14802. June E Brown, Head Librn
Notes: The Evelyn Tennyson Openhym Collection of modern British literature and social history. Papers, incl correspondence of authors concerned with the business aspects of authorship. Gift of Evelyn Tennyson Openhym of Wellsville, NY. Also, 5300 volumes of British literature.

RI —BROWN UNIVERSITY, John Hay Library, 20 Prospect St, Providence, 02912.
Mark N Brown, Cur Mss
Holdings: Vols 2000 // Cat Mss
Notes: A nearly complete collection of the published speeches, historical writings and novels, plus some autograph letters of John Buchan, Lord Tweedsmuir, former Governor General of Canada.

ON —QUEEN'S UNIVERSITY, Douglas Library, Kingston, K7L 5C4, Can. William F E Morley, Cur, Special Collections
Holdings: Vols 5000 Cat Mss
Notes: Bound mss and typescripts of more than 30 novels and other writings. Almost all published editions of Buchan's works and a strong Scottish collection. Augmented by new editions of works by Buchan as well as works about him. Also works by Buchan's widow, Lady Susan Tweedsmuir. Described in *A Checklist of Works by and about John Buchan in the John Buchan Collection, Queen's University*, compiled by B C Wilmont (Kingston, Douglas Library, 1958).

BUCHMAN, FRANK N. D., 1878-1961

DC —LIBRARY OF CONGRESS, Manuscript Division, Washington, 20540. John C Broderick, Chief
Holdings: 357,000 Items
Notes: The records of Moral Re-Armament, incl the personal papers of its founder, Frank N D Buchman.

BUCHANAN, HANDASYDE

DC —GEORGETOWN UNIVERSITY, Library, Special Collections Div, 37 & O Sts NW, Washington, 20057. George M Barringer, Special Collections Librn; Nicholas B Sheetz, Mss Librn
Holdings: Mss
Notes: Extensive collection of books, manuscripts, and correspondence by novelist Evelyn Waugh. Incl his letters to Graham Greene, Leonard Russell, Douglas Woodruff, Handasyde Buchanan, and Christopher Sykes. Also present are Syke's own papers containing research material about Waugh.

BUCHANAN, JAMES

PA —HISTORICAL SOCIETY OF PENNSYLVANIA, Library, 1300 Locust St, Philadelphia, 19107. David Fraser, Librn
Holdings: Vols (230,000) Mss Maps Pix Microforms
Notes: Incl over 14,000,000 ms pieces. The Library Company of Philadelphia mss are on deposit with the Historical Society of Pennsylvania. Many of the Society's rare books are on deposit with the Library Company. The Society maintains the collections of the Genealogical Society of Pennsylvania, incl some 20,000 printed genealogies, original mss, family, church, and civil records.

BUCHANAN, ROBERT E., 1883-1973

IA —IOWA STATE UNIVERSITY, Library, Dept of Special Collections, Ames, 50011. Stanley M Yates, Head
Holdings: // Mss
Notes: Robert E Buchanan (1883-1973) Papers. Collection contains correspondence, reports, and printed matter relating to his

BUCHANAN, ROBERT E., 1883-1973 (cont.)

career as a bacteriologist and administrator who was head of the Iowa State University Bacteriology Department (1910-1948), first dean of the Graduate College (1919-1948), director of the Agriculture Experiment Station (1933-1948) and was editor of *Bergey's Manual*. 26 linear feet. Finding aid available.

BUCHER, LLOYD M., 1927-

CA —HOOVER INSTITUTION ON WAR, REVOLUTION & PEACE, Stanford University, Stanford, 94305. Milorad M Drachkovitch, Archivist
Holdings: Mss Pix
Notes: Papers of Lloyd M Bucher, Commander, US Navy, and Commander of the USS *Pueblo*, incl correspondence, newspaper clippings, reports, copies of court inquiries, photographs, plaques, memorabilia, and other materials, 1970-75, relating to the *Pueblo* incident and its aftermath. Incl is a typewritten manuscript of his memoirs, entitled "Bucher, My Story." 68 ms boxes, 1 oversize package.

BUCK, PEARL S.

VA —RANDOLPH-MACON WOMAN'S COLLEGE, Lipscomb Library, Lynchburg, 24503. Frances White, Ref Librn
Holdings: Vols 150 Letters Pix//
Notes: Life-long correspondence from Miss Buck to Randolph-Macon Woman's College class mate Emma Edmunds White.

WV —PEARL S BUCK BIRTHPLACE FOUNDATION, Library, Box 126, Hillsboro, 24946. David C Hyer, Cur
Notes: The birthplace and repository for the 303 mss and personal possessions of Pearl S Buck (Nobel Prize winner of 1938). Materials are temporarily stored (Jan 1978) at West Virginia Wesleyan College until suitable storage can be arranged here. They are not accessible to the general public.

BUCK, TIM

ON —UNIVERSITY OF TORONTO, Thomas Fisher Rare Book Library, 120 Saint George St, Toronto, M5S 1A5, Can. Richard G Landon, Head
Holdings: Vols 2500 Mss Pix Phonorecords
Notes: Kenny Collection named for original collector, Robert Kenny of Toronto. Chiefly material on and by the Labor Progressive Party and the Communist Party of Canada, including their constitutions, reports of national conventions, leaflets, posters, election material, ephemera. Manuscript material of A E Smith, Tim Buck and other Canadian communists.

BUCKET SHOPS see Speculation

BUCKINGHAM, HARRY

OK —MUSEUM OF THE GREAT PLAINS, Research Center, 601 Ferris, PO Box 68, Lawton, 73502. Steve Wilson, Dir; Paula Williams, Special Collections
Notes: Business papers.
See also entry under Oklahoma - History

BUCKLEY, JAMES

NY —SAINT JOHN'S UNIVERSITY, Special Collections Dept, Grand Central & Utopia Pkwys, Jamaica, 11439. Szilvia E Szmuk, Librn
Holdings: Uncat Pix Videotapes
Notes: Books, press releases, pamphlets, campaign materials. No photocopying.

BUCKNILL, SIR JOHN C., 1817-1897

DC —GEORGETOWN UNIVERSITY, Library, Special Collections Div, 37 & O Sts NW, Washington, 20057. George M Barringer, Special Collections Librn; Nicholas B Sheetz, Mss Librn
Holdings: Mss Cat Pix
Notes: Scrapbook containing photographs, correspondence, and drawings compiled by Sir John C Bucknill (1817-1897), distinguished English physician who was most noted for his work with the insane. The scrapbook contains photographs of Thomas Carlyle, Charles Darwin, Charles Dickens, Thomas Huxley, Alfred Tennyson, and William Makepeace Tackery, among others. Correspondence incl letters from John Bright, J A Clarke, Sir John Duke Coleridge, and Edward A Seymour.

BUCKS COUNTY PLAYHOUSE

PA —UNIVERSITY OF PITTSBURGH, Special Collections Dept, Curtis Theatre Collection, 363 Hillman Library, Pittsburgh, 15260. Jeanette Blanco, Cur
Holdings: Mss Documents Pix
Notes: Production records of Bucks County Playhouse and New York City; memorabilia. Catalog in process.

BUDDHA AND BUDDHISM

AZ —WORLD UNIVERSITY, Library, 711 E Blacklidge Dr, Tucson, 85719. Howard John Zitko, Cur
Holdings: Vols (15,000) Cat Mss Maps Audiotapes
Notes: Collection concerns the "frontier sciences." No interlibrary loan.

CA —GRADUATE THEOLOGICAL UNION LIBRARY, New Religious Movements Research Collection, Public Services and Special Collections Dept, 2400 Ridge Road, Berkeley, 94709. Diane Choquette, Dept Head
Holdings: Vols (3000) Mss Pix
Notes: Begun in 1977, the collection focuses on religious movements new to America since 1960, and unorthodox religious movements resurgent since 1960. American forms of Hinduism, Buddhism, Sikhism, and Sufism are included along with occultism, Neo-Paganism, esoteric and alternative forms of Christianity, feminist spirituality, and human potential movements having a spiritual aspect. Legal issues, such as deprogramming, and the question of church/state relations are an important part of the collection. The Library is a depository for publications of the Unification Church in America, the Church of Scientology, and the International Society for Krishna Consciousness (America). The responses of mainstream religions and concerned citizens groups are also included. Besides 3000 monographs, the library has 400 periodical titles, 200 posters from the San FranciscoBay Area, 1965-77, 300 research papers, and 31 linear feet of ephemera.

†CA —INSTITUTE OF BUDDHISTS STUDIES LIBRARY, 2717 Haste St, Berkeley, 94704.

CA —UNIVERSITY OF CALIFORNIA, BERKELEY, University Library, East Asiatic Library, Room 208, Durant Hall, Berkeley, 94720. Donald Shively, Head
Holdings: Vols (500,000) Cat Mss Maps Pix Microforms
Notes: The largest collection of Japanese-language materials at any American University. Subject coverage is universal in scope, but works in the humanities and the social sciences predominate. All historical periods are represented. The East Asiatic Library (like the Library of Congress) serves as a full depository for Japanese Government publications. The Library maintains a distinguished rare book collection, comprising, for instance, ancient woodblock color maps, manuscripts, early Buddhist Sutras, and rare and early editions. Outstanding resources include: the Murakami Collection of Meiji Literature; the Mitsui Library; and the Japanese Military Map Collection. Western-language materials in related fields are located in the Main Library. A G K Hall catalog of East Asiatic Library holdings has been published. Also, a small (1250 vols) but importantcollection of Tibetan-language research materials in the fields of Buddhist Studies, and Tibetan historical/social conditions. Holdings incl a rare collection of writings from the oldest surviving school of Tibetan Buddhism (The Rin-Chen-Gter-Mdzod Collection), consisting of a monumental corpus of Tantric literature spanning ten centuries of composition. The collections are complemented by related holdings in the Main Library and in the South/Southeast Asia Library Service.

CA —LOS ANGELES PUBLIC LIBRARY, Philosophy & Religion Dept, 630 W Fifth St, Los Angeles, 90071. Marilyn C Wherley, Librn
Holdings: Vols 450 Cat
Budget: ($60,000)
Notes: Historical, theological, and biographical works relating to the religion. Many English translations of sacred works with revelent criticism. Includes scholarly and popular materials on comparative religions. Emphasis on groups active in Southern California including much ephemera.

CA —UNIVERSITY OF CALIFORNIA, LOS ANGELES, Oriental Library, 405 Hilgard Ave, Los Angeles, 90024. Ik-Sam Kim, Head
Holdings: Vols 20,000
Notes: Art, archaeology, literature and history related to Buddhism.

DC —BUDDHIST VIHARA SOCIETY LIBRARY, 5017 16 St, NW, Washington, 20011. Bhikkhu Ajita, Librn
Holdings: Vols 1000 Cat
Notes: Buddhism and related subjects.

HI —UNIVERSITY OF HAWAII, Library, 2550 The Mall, Honolulu, 96822. Joyce Wright, Head, Asia Collection; Masato Matsu, Head, East Asia Vernacular Collection
Holdings: Vols (400,000) Cat Microforms
Notes: The Asia Collection includes materials from and relating to Japan in all languages. In addition to the cataloged Japanese language volumes (above), there are an estimated 15,000 not yet processed. No figures are available for western language volumes about Japan, which are supplemented by retrospective materials in the main library collection. Scope: social sciences and humanities. Subject strengths: Japanese history, especially Tokugawa period, Buddhism, Ryukyus and Satsuma (Sakamaki Collection), Hokkaido. *Catalog of the Glenn Shaw Collection at the East West Center Library*, by H Arai & M Gibu, Honolulu, 1967 (East West Center Library Occasional Paper No 8); *Research Resources on Hokkaido, Sakhalen and the Kuriles at the East-West Center Library*, by M Matsui and K Shimanaka, Honolulu, 1967 (East West Center Library Occasional Paper No 9);*Ryukyuan Research Resources at the University of Hawaii*, by Shunzo Sakamaki, Honolulu, 1965 (Ryukyuan Research Center. Research Series No 1).

MD —JOHNS HOPKINS UNIVERSITY, Milton S Eisenhower Library, Charles & 34 Sts, Baltimore, 21218. Ann S Gwyn, Assistant Dir for Special Collections
Holdings: Vols 1000// Cat Mss
Notes: Incl numerous rare texts and unusual pamphlets. History, politics, geography, philosophy. Chiefly in German, also French and English. Incl more than Buddhist texts.

MD —JOHNS HOPKINS UNIVERSITY, Milton S Eisenhower Library, George Peabody Collection, 17 E Mt Vernon Place, Baltimore, 21201. Lyn Hart, Peabody Librn
Notes: Emphasis on materials published before 1950. Strength is a good collection through the 19th century.

MA —HARVARD UNIVERSITY LIBRARY, Harvard-Yenching Library, 2 Divinity Ave, Cambridge, 02138. Eugene W Wu, Librn
Holdings: Cat Mss
Notes: Particularly strong in Japanese-language and Tibetan publications.

NY —AMERICAN BUDDHIST ACADEMY, Library, 332 Riverside Dr, New York, 10025. Tomoe Murata Arai, Librn
Holdings: Vols 5000 Cat
Notes: Largest Sutra collection in the US. Half of Japanese collection on Shin Buddhism. Incl some titles on general philosophy and Eastern thought. About 800 titles in English, 2000 in Japanese. Collection for reference use only.

BUDDHA AND BUDDHISM (cont.)

NY —NEW YORK PUBLIC LIBRARY, Oriental Div, Fifth Ave & 42 St, New York, 10018. E Christian Filstrup, Chief
Holdings: Cat Mss Microforms
Budget: ($56,455)
Notes: Described in *Dictionary Catalog of the Oriental Collection,* The Research Libraries of the New York Public Library, 1960, 16 vols, and *First Supplement,* 1976, 8 vols (144,000 cards). This catalog incl 318, 000 entries for works in about 100 languages of the East, and all works in Western languages on Oriental subjects. The Oriental Collection numbers about 120,000 vols. Unusually good coverage of Oriental religions and philosophies.

NY —INSTITUTE FOR ADVANCED STUDIES OF WORLD RELIGIONS (IASWR), Melville Memorial Library, State University of New York, Stony Brook, 11794. C T Shen, Dir
Holdings: Vols 40,000 Cat Periodicals Mss Maps Microforms
Notes: Buddhism and related subjects in history, art, etc, in English, European and Asian languages. Buddhist Canon: Chinese version in Chinese, Japanese, and Korean editions; Tibetan version in Peking Derge, Tog, eds and Mongolian translation; Pali version in Burmese, Cambodian, Devanagari, Roman, Sinhalese, Thai and Vietnamese editions and some translations. Some rare editions of Chinese canonical texts. 6000 volumes modern and growing reprint collection of Tibetan post-canonical works obtained through the Library of Congress. Collection incl extensive reference and research facilities in about 30 languages for the study of Buddhism, its thought, history, culture, art and societal role (refer inquiries to H G Robinson and L L Yang). Microforms: Chinese mss from Tun-Huang in the British Museum and Bibliotheque Nationale. Collected works in microficheeditions in Cambodian, Chinese, Sanskrit, and Tibetan. Chinese: Sung Chi-Sha Tsang in 2558 fiche; Snar-thang Kanjur in 2404 fiche; Sde-dge-Kanjur in 1730 fiche. Sanskrit: IASWR Buddhist Sanskrit mss, 471 titles in 1167 fiche; and others (refer inquiries to J Abritis).
See also entries under Art, Buddhist; Tantrism, Buddhist; Tibetan Buddhism

NC —UNIVERSITY OF NORTH CAROLINA, CHARLOTTE, J Murrey Atkins Library, UNCC Station, Charlotte, 28223. Robert F Brabham Jr, Special Collections Librn
Notes: Part of the Suzuki Collection of books on Mahayana Buddhism. It incl 10 vols and 25 paintings and sketches of Himalayan scenes. Cataloged.

OH —CLEVELAND PUBLIC LIBRARY, Fine Arts and Special Collections Department, 325 Superior Ave, Cleveland, 44114. Alice N Loranth, Head
Holdings: Vols (7000) Cat Mss
Notes: Part of the Oriental Religion Collection. Emphasis is on religious texts in their original languages and Western translations. Treatises on religious beliefs and practices are also incl. Strong holdings in Buddhism, Egyptian religion, Hinduism, Judaica, Lamaistic texts, Islam, Sikhism and Zoroastrianism. Works on primitive religion cover aspects of animism, totemism, fetishism, etc. Special emphasis on Islam in China.
See also entries under Religion, Oriental; Religion, Primitive.

RI —BROWN UNIVERSITY, John Hay Library, 20 Prospect St, Providence, 02912. Mark N Brown, Cur Mss
Holdings: Vols (53) //
Notes: Indic Manuscripts Collection: Codices written in Burmese, Cambodian, Telugu, Skandhas, Bengali, and Sinhalese script on palm leaves, encased within wood covers, some lacquered. Subjects include: Buddhist canon, Pali grammar and lexicons, epics, dance drama, and a treatise on midwifery. Recorded in *A Census of Indic Manuscripts in the United States and Canada* compiled by Horace I Poleman (New Haven: American Oriental Society, 1938).

VA —ASSOCIATION FOR RESEARCH & ENLIGHTENMENT, Library, 67 & Atlantic Avenue, PO Box 595, Virginia Beach, 23451. Stephen Jordan, Library Mgr
Holdings: Vols (3000) Cat
Notes: Emphasis on Christian, Buddhist, Hindu religions, mysticism, comparative religion, psychological approach to biofeedback, autogenics, etc.

WI —UNIVERSITY OF WISCONSIN, MADISON, Memorial Library, Rare Books Collection, 728 State St, Madison, 53706. Gretchen Lagana, Cur
Holdings: Vols (3000) Cat Maps Pix
Budget: $4000
Notes: Welch Collection of comprehensive and outstanding materials on Buddhism.

BUDDHIST ART see Art, Buddhist

BUDDHIST TANTRISM see Tantrism, Buddhist

BUDGELL, EUSTACE

TX —SAN ANTONIO COLLEGE, Library, 1001 Howard St, San Antonio, 78284. James O Wallace, Dir
Notes: His works.

BUDGETING

DC —METROPOLITAN WASHINGTON COUNCIL OF GOVERNMENTS, Research Library, 1875 Eye St NW, Suite 200, Washington, 20006. Suan Kalish, Librn
Holdings: Vols (3000) Cat Microforms
Notes: Contains (on 75 reels of microfilm) archives of Maryland-National Park and Planning Commission, archives of the Council of Governments, and audits and financial reports of local governments (1950-date). Also incl annual reports, planning reports and budgets from each jurisdiction (1973-date).

NY —STATE UNIVERSITY OF NEW YORK AT ALBANY, Library, Special Collections Dept, 1400 Washington Ave, Albany, 12222. Marion P Munzer, Coordr
Notes: Howard F Miller's correspondence, lecture outlines, reports, relating to academic and administrative career in public budgeting (8.6 linear feet).
See also entries under Miller, Howard F; Finance, Public

VA —UNITED WAY OF AMERICA INFORMATION CENTER, 701 North Fairfax St, United Way Plaza, Alexandria, 22314. Henry M Smith, Dir; Barbara L Owen, Librn
Holdings: Vols (1200) Cat Microforms
Notes: Incl 5000 research reports and studies on microfiche; 100 vertical file drawers. Services primarily for United Way organizations--United Funds, Community Chests, Health and Welfare Planning Councils.

BUDGETS, MUNICIPAL see Municipal Budgets

BUDGETS, TIME see Time Allocation

BUECHNER, FREDERIC

IL —WHEATON COLLEGE, Buswell Memorial Library, Wheaton, 60187. Paul Snezek, Library Dir
Holdings: Vols 40 Cat Mss
Notes: Literary papers of Frederic Buechner, author of eleven novels and nine nonfiction on works dealing with religious topics. Also, the C S Lewis papers, in the Wade Collection. In addition to the 25 feet of manuscripts and correspondence, there are books, dissertations, and non-print media, including a CBS production of one book.

BUFFALO, AMERICAN see Bison, American

BUFFALO, NEW YORK—HISTORY

NY —STATE UNIVERSITY OF NEW YORK, COLLEGE AT BUFFALO, Library, The Francis E Fronczak Collection, Buffalo, 14222. Lucien E Palmieri, Head Collections Dept
Holdings: 1000 Vols
Notes: Collection of Buffalo's noted Polish-American, Francis E Fronczak.

BUFFALO HUNTING

TX —AMARILLO PUBLIC LIBRARY, 413 E Fourth, Amarillo, 79101. Mary Kay Snell, Librn
Notes: John L McCarty, newspaper editor, author, artist, and businessman in Amarillo and Dalhart, Texas. Papers incl 4030 notes, interviews, photographs unpublished theses, clippings, and historical editions. A wide variety of subjects incl buffalo hunting, Indian wars, cowboys and the open range, the arrival of the farmers, fences, and and towns. His work begins around the turn of the century and ranges through the depression years, the Dust Bowl, and soil and water conservation studies.

BUFFALO SOLDIERS

OK —US ARMY FIELD ARTILLERY SCHOOL LIBRARY, Morris Swett Library, Snow Hall, Fort Sill, 73503. Lester L Miller Jr, Chief Librn
Notes: Incl data on Fort Sill, Indian Territory, settlement of Kiowa, Apache and Commanche tribes, imprisonment of Geronimo, Oklahoma territory, settlement of Lawton. Unit histories, incl 10th Cavalry (Buffalo Soldiers, a black unit that built Fort Sill); working papers of Sheridan, Grierson and other commanders; Field Artillery School. Photographs on army subjects, Fort Sill, Indians, Indian Territory, settlement of Southwest Oklahoma.

BUGBEE, LESTER G.

TX —UNIVERSITY OF TEXAS LIBRARIES, General Libraries, Barker Texas History Center, PO Box P, Austin, 78712. Don Carleton, Dir

BUGENHAGEN, JOHANN

CA —STANFORD UNIVERSITY LIBRARIES, Cecil H Green Library, Stanford, 94305. Peter R Frank, Cur, CDP-Germanic Collection
Notes: Extensive holdings in the field of Reformation and Counter-Reformation. First and early editions by Luther, Melanchthon, Bugenhagen, Cochleus, Eck, Hutten, Reuchlin, and minor figures in Special Collections.

BUGS

NY —AMERICAN MUSEUM OF NATURAL HISTORY, Library Services Dept, Central Park W & 79th St, New York, 10024. Nina J Root, Chairwoman; Mary Genett, Asst Librn for Reference Services
Notes: A major literature collection supplements the museum's entomology collections; perhaps the largest in the world.

BUILDING

MI —UNIVERSITY OF DETROIT, Main Library, 4001 W McNichols Rd, Detroit, 48221.
Notes: Architecture Library was closed in 1981. Collection consolidated in main library.

NH —NEW HAMPSHIRE TECHNICAL INSTITUTE, Paul E Farnum Library, 5 Fan Rd, Concord, 03301. Wm John Hare, Librn
Holdings: Vols 908 Cat Slides Filmstrips
Budget: $800
Notes: Architectural Engineering Technology.

PA —FRANKLIN INSTITUTE LIBRARY, 20 & The Parkway, Philadelphia, 19103. Miriam Padusis, Dir; Charles Wilt, Readers Servs Librn
Holdings: Vols (300,000) Cat Maps Pix Microforms

WA —UNIVERSITY OF WASHINGTON LIBRARIES, Architecture-Urban Planning

BUILDING (cont.)

Library, 11, JO-30, Seattle, 98195. Betty L Wagner, Librn
Holdings: Vols (26,085) Cat Microforms
Budget: ($33,127)

ON —METROPOLITAN TORONTO LIBRARY, Science & Technology Dept, 789 Yonge St, Toronto, M4W 2G8, Can. Margaret Walshe, Head
Holdings: Vols (120,000) Cat
Notes: All aspects of technology for the specialist, the student, and the general public. The department gives high priority to Canadian material.

BUILDING—HISTORY

MA —SOCIETY FOR THE PRESERVATION OF NEW ENGLAND ANTIQUITIES, Library, 141 Cambridge St, Boston, 02114. Ellie Reichlin, Librn & Cur of Photographic Collections
Notes: Architecture of the Northeast. Drawings (original designs, measured drawings, plot plans, etc). Over 7500 items, incl extensive collections of original designs by Ogden Codman, Jr (1890s-early 1900s); Arthur Little and Herbert Browne (1890s-1920s); Luther Briggs (1840s-1860s); Arland Dirlam (1930s-1960s), together with important examples of the work of Asher Benjamin, Richard Upjohn, and others. Measured drawings incl extensive holdings of work undertaken by HABS (Historic American Buildings Survey) in Massachusetts in the 1930s, 1940s under director Frank Chouteau Brown. Also represented are several residential and commercial commissions by F C Brown, not connected with HABS. Collection incl architectural pattern books, builders guides, 18th-19th century. Approx 350 volumes, English and American publications.

BUILDING—MATERIALS see Building Materials

BUILDING, EARTHQUAKE-PROOF see Earthquakes and Buildings

BUILDING, IRON AND STEEL

NY —EASTMAN KODAK COMPANY, Kodak Park Div, Engineering Library, Bldg 23, Rochester, 14650. Raymond Curtin, Librn
Holdings: Vols (14,000) Uncat Microforms
Notes: The library is not open to the public. Use of the library for reference purposes may be requested and appointments may be obtained through the librarian.

BUILDING INDUSTRY see Construction Industry

BUILDING MATERIALS

CA —UNIVERSITY OF CALIFORNIA, BERKELEY, Environmental Design Library, (The General Library), 210 Wurster Hall, Berkeley, 94720. Arthur B Waugh, Head
Holdings: Vols (90,000) Cat Pix Microforms
Budget: ($17,400)
Notes: A research collection devoted to the following aspects of the field of architecture: working details, drawing, theory, standards and professional practice; building materials, building types, earthquake resistant architecture, contemporary architecture of all countries, history of architecture, and architecture as a profession. A small rare book collection in the field of architecture is maintained. Approximately 1500 serials, incl many foreign-language titles, are currently being received. A collection of photographs (of buildings) and a slide collection are administered by the department of architecture.

DE —HAGLEY MUSEUM AND LIBRARY, Eleutherian Mills-Hagley Foundation Inc, PO Box 3630, Greenville, 19807. Richmond D Williams, Dir; Heddy A Richter, Imprints Librn
Notes: Records of the Lukens Steel Co of Coatsville, Pa (1798-1944; 750 cubic feet) incl administrative, accounting, payroll, production and sales records documenting the history of one of America's oldest iron and steel companies. Records of the Phoenix Steel Corporation (1827-1962; 335 cubic feet) incl minute books, financial records, payroll and production records documenting the history of this important Delaware Valley steel producer. Also, Alan Wood Steel Company of Conshohocken, Pa (1728-1937; 250 cubic feet).

NY —NEW YORK STATE COLLEGE OF CERAMICS AT ALFRED UNIVERSITY, Scholes Library, Harder Hall, Alfred, 14802. Bruce E Connolly, Library Dir
Holdings: Vols (70,000) Cat Mss Slides Microforms
Budget: ($134,000)
Notes: Very specialized collection incl all phases of the arts and sciences related to ceramics. Incl 1112 subscriptions.

PA —FRANKLIN INSTITUTE LIBRARY, 20 & The Parkway, Philadelphia, 19103. Miriam Padusis, Dir; Charles Wilt, Readers Servs Librn
Holdings: Vols (300,000) Cat Maps Pix Microforms

BUILDING STANDARDS see Standards and Specifications

BUILDING TRADES

IN —PURDUE UNIVERSITY LIBRARIES, Graduate School of Management, Krannert Library, West Lafayette, 47907. Gordon Law, Librn
Notes: An important resource at the Krannert Library is its Special Collection of Business and Economics, consisting of some 8000 rare pre-20th century strengths in books, journals, tracts and pamphlets covering primarily the early literature of economic thought and business practices in America and abroad, 1500-1870. A catalog was issued in 1979.

MI —GOGEBIC COMMUNITY COLLEGE, Alex D Chisholm Learning Resources Center, Greenbush & Jackson Rd, Ironwood, 49938. Charles Tetzlaff, Dir of Learning Resources
Holdings: Vols (20,000)

NY —COLUMBIA UNIVERSITY LIBRARIES, Avery Architectural and Fine Arts Library, 201 Avery Hall, New York, 10027. Angela Giral, Librn
Holdings: Vols
Notes: Books published by American architectural firms picturing their own buildings. Directories of architects and companies in the building trades. Also incl ledgers, account books, collections of letters and other documents produced by architects, builders or others in the building trades.

NY —YONKERS PUBLIC LIBRARY, Information Services, 7 Main St, Yonkers, 10701. Martita Schwarz, Dept Head
Holdings: Vols (21,500) Cat Maps Microforms
Budget: ($30,000)

BUILDINGS

CA —UNIVERSITY OF CALIFORNIA, BERKELEY, Environmental Design Library, (The General Library), 210 Wurster Hall, Berkeley, 94720. Arthur B Waugh, Head
Holdings: Vols (90,000) Cat Pix Microforms
Budget: ($17,400)
Notes: A research collection devoted to the following aspects of the field of architecture: working details, drawing, theory, standards and professional practice; building materials, building types, earthquake resistant architecture, contemporary architecture of all countries, history of architecture, and architecture as a profession. A small rare book collection in the field of architecture is maintained. Approximately 1500 serials, incl many foreign-language titles, are currently being received. A collection of photographs (of buildings) and a slide collection are administered by the department of architecture.

NY —COLUMBIA UNIVERSITY LIBRARIES, Avery Architectural and Fine Arts Library, 201 Avery Hall, New York, 10027. Angela Giral, Librn
Notes: Souvenir books of pictures of single American cities, towns, resorts, expositions, etc, places featuring buildings. They vary in size, are frequently in paper covers and the plates are usually photographic. Date from ca 1880-1940. Guidebooks to cities are also available. Also, books published by American architectural firms picturing their own buildings. Directories of architects and companies in the building trades.

NY —ENGINEERING SOCIETIES LIBRARY, 345 E 47 St, New York, 10017. S Kirk Cabeen, Dir
Holdings: Vols 250,000 Cat Maps 16mm Films Microforms
Notes: One of the largest, most comprehensive engineering libraries in the World. Covers all engineering disciplines; particularly strong in electrical and electronic, mechanical, mining and metallurgical, petroleum, chemical, industrial, air conditioning and refrigeration engineering. Incl Wheeler Collection of early materials on magnetism and electricity. 125, 000 bound periodical volumes; 10,000 maps; 5000 serial subscriptions (many foreign-language). Virtually all materials abstracted in *Engineering Index* (1884-date) are incl in Library. Noncirculating, except to members of professional engineering societies which support the Library. See *Engineering Societies Library, New York, Classed Subject Catalog and Index* (Boston: G K Hall, 1963); and *Supplements*, 1-10, 1964-1973.

PA —CARNEGIE LIBRARY OF PITTSBURGH, Science & Technology Dept, 4400 Forbes Ave, Pittsburgh, 15213. Catherine M Brosky, Dept Head
Notes: Collection incl material on general construction, carpentry, masonry, plumbing, heating, air conditioning, corrosion and painting and numerous other building trades. Sweets Architectural File complete except for a few years. *Car Builders Encyclopedia of American Practice*, most editions since 1879.

ON —UNIVERSITY OF TORONTO, Thomas Fisher Rare Book Library, 120 Saint George St, Toronto, M5S 1A5, Can. Richard G Landon, Head
Holdings: Vols 30,000 Mss
Notes: All currently published and most earlier major works on the fine and applied arts in Canada; Canadian art exhibition catalogues; limited editions illustrated by Canadian artists; 19th and 20th century architectural plans for buildings in Toronto and southern Ontario vicinity (ca 1700).

BUILDINGS—DAMPNESS see Dampness in Buildings

BUILDINGS—DETAILS see Architecture—Details

BUILDINGS—MATERIALS see Building Materials

BUILDINGS, COLLEGE see Universities and Colleges—Buildings

BUILDINGS, HISTORIC AMERICAN, SURVEY see Historic American Buildings Survey

BUILDINGS, HISTORICAL see Historic Houses, Etc.

BUILDINGS, LIBRARY see Library Architecture

BUILDINGS, RESTORATION OF see Architecture—Conservation and Restoration

BUILDINGS, SCHOOL see School Buildings

BUKOWSKI, CHARLES, 1920-

AZ —UNIVERSITY OF ARIZONA, University Library, Special Collections,

BUKOWSKI, CHARLES, 1920- (cont.)

Tucson, 85721. Louis A Hieb, Head
Holdings: Vols (7000) Cat Mss Microforms
Budget: ($30,000)
Notes: In the 20th century, the major emphasis is Bukowski, Wakoski, Wilder, Reznikoff, Ginzberg, Ferlinghetti, Snyder, Whalen, Everson, Joyce Carol Oates, and Kurt Vonnegut.

CA —UNIVERSITY OF CALIFORNIA, SANTA BARBARA, Library, Dept of Special Collections, Santa Barbara, 93106. Christian F Brun, Head
Holdings: Mss
Notes: Collection of books, correspondence, paintings.

FL —UNIVERSITY OF MIAMI, Otto G Richter Library, PO Box 248214, Coral Gables, 33124. Frank Rodgers, Dir of Libraries
Holdings: Cat
Notes: Innovative and experimental writing of the 1960s and 1970s. Incl generous proportion of press books--Black Sparrow, Auerhahn, and many others; also other private publications ranging from the best to the least attractive. Format includes postcards and broadsides as well as periodical and book form. Writers incl Charles Bukowski, Diane Wakoski, Jerome Rothenberg, Clayton Eshleman, and many of their contemporaries.

OH —OHIO UNIVERSITY, Vernon R Alden Library, Department of Archives and Special Collections, Athens, 45701. Gary A Hunt, Head
Holdings: Vols 156 Cat Mss
Notes: Chiefly Bukowski's books (in all editions) and periodical appearances, but also typescripts, galleys, drawings, letters, and tape recordings. About 500 items.

BULGARIA

CA —UNIVERSITY OF CALIFORNIA, BERKELEY, University Library, Slavic Collections, Berkeley, 94720. Edward Kasinec, Librn
Holdings: Vols (210,000) Cat Maps Microforms
Budget: ($40,000)
Notes: Strong research collections for Bulgaria, Czechoslovakia, Poland, Russia-USSR, and Yugoslavia. Holdings are excellent in economics, folklore, history, linguistics, and literature. Publications issued by academies, major universities, and principal scholarly institutions are well represented. Extensive periodical holdings have been built up, largely as a result of early exchange arrangements. More than 4000 Slavic-language serials are currently being received. Farmington Plan and PL480 commitments have augmented Yugoslav resources. Sizable Slavic-language collections are to be found in Branch Libraries as well, in such subjects as agriculture, biology, earth sciences, forestry, and mathematics.

IL —UNIVERSITY OF ILLINOIS, URBANA/CHAMPAIGN, Slavic and East European Library, Urbana, 61801. Marianna Tax Choldin, Head
Holdings: Vols (9200) Cat
Notes: Extensive coverage.

NY —NEW YORK PUBLIC LIBRARY, Slavonic Div, Fifth Ave & 42 St, New York, 10018. Edward Kasinec, Chief
Holdings: Vols 8300 Cat Microforms
Notes: Emphasis is on the humanities, but history is also well represented. Periodicalss, learned society publications and public documents are represented. See New York Public Library, *Dictionary Catalog of the Slavonic Collection* (Boston: G K Hall, 1974), 44 vols.

WI —UNIVERSITY OF WISCONSIN, MADISON, Memorial Library, Slavic Studies Collection, 728 State St, Madison, 53706. Aleksander Rolich, Bibliographer for Slavic Studies; Robert P Gakovich, Slavic Cataloger; Valdis J Zeps, Baltic Studies Center
Holdings: Vols (25,000) Cat
Notes: The Balcanica collection in Memorial Library exceeds 25,000 volumes and active collecting continues at over 2000 titles per year in Bulgarian, Rumanian, Turkish and the languages of Yugoslavia. Many rare and unique titles are to be found in this collection, including serial titles, such as *Nova Vreme* (1897-1923, 1947-to date), *Nova Europa* (1920-1939), and unique Turkish Salnameh. The emphasis is on historical materials, but there is considerable strength in South Slavic literatures and linguistics. The Rumanian materials are of more recent vintage.

BULGARIA—HISTORY

CA —UNIVERSITY OF CALIFORNIA, LOS ANGELES, Library, Slavic Collection, 405 Hilgard Ave, Los Angeles, 90024. Edward Shreeves, Chairman, Bibliographers Group; Leon Ferder, Slavic Bibliographer
Holdings: Vols (250,000) Cat Maps Microforms
Notes: The entire range of humanities, social sciences, and the arts. One of the most comprehensive US collections for material not only on Russia and the Soviet Union, but also on Bulgaria, Czechoslovakia, Poland, Yugoslavia, the non-Slavic countries of Eastern Europe (Romania, Hungary, Albania) and Soviet Central Asia. Holdings in Russian and Slavic linguistics, Russian literature, and Russian history are particularly strong, covering all periods. The collections are described in some detail in Paul Horecky's book on US Slavic collections.

CA —HOOVER INSTITUTION ON WAR, REVOLUTION & PEACE, Stanford University, Stanford, 94305. Milorad M Drachkovitch, Archivist
Holdings: Mss Pix
Notes: Papers of William A Drayton, 1913-1946, incl correspondence, reports, memoranda, speeches and writings, photographs, and other materials, relating to Serbia, during and after World War I, and W A Drayton's activities as an American volunteer in the Serbian Army, member of the Serbian Delegation to Paris Peace Conference, and Inter-Allied Commissioner of Bulgarian Atrocities Commission. 2 ms boxes.

CA —STANFORD UNIVERSITY LIBRARIES, Cecil H Green Library, Stanford, 94305. Wojciech Zalewski, Cur, Russian & East European Collection
Holdings: Vols (200,000) Cat Maps Microforms
Budget: ($90,000)
Notes: Strong collection prior to 20th century, but Stanford University Libraries' collecting effort is coordinated with Hoover Institution, Stanford, and holdings are not duplicated. Collection descriptions: Wojciech Zalewski, *Russian Materials in the Main Library of Stanford University, A Collection* Survey (Stanford: Stanford University Libraries, 1974). Wojciech Zalerski, "Stanford University" in P L Horecky, ed, *East Central and Southeast Europe, A Handbook of Library and Archival Resources in North America* (Santa Barbara: Clio Press, 1976).

IN —INDIANA UNIVERSITY, University Libraries, Bloomington, 47401. Murlin Croucher, Librn for Slavic Studies
Holdings: Vols (300,000) Cat Maps Microforms
Budget: ($63,000)
Notes: The collection, established after World War II, covers material of, and on, the Soviet Union (55 percent) and Eastern Europe (45 percent) in the languages of the area and in western European languages as well. Material is chiefly in the fields of humanities and social sciences. Many other Slavic and East European books are located in the Lilly Library (rare book library).

MA —HARVARD UNIVERSITY LIBRARY, Widener Library, Slavic Collections, Cambridge, 02138. Hugh M Olmsted, Slavic Dept Head
Holdings: Cat Microforms
Notes: Bulgarian history shelflist through June, 1976 lists 2552 titles (earlier version was incl in *Widener Library Shelflist,* volumes 28-31, 1971). The collections continue to be developed actively, and are strong both in current and in antiquarian materials. See also *East Central and Southeast Europe; A Handbook of Library and Archival Resources in North America,* edited by P L Horecky and D H Kraus, 1976, pp 115-118.

NY —NEW YORK PUBLIC LIBRARY, Slavonic Div, Fifth Ave & 42 St, New York, 10018. Edward Kasinec, Chief
Holdings: Cat Microforms
Notes: See New York Public Library, *Dictionary Catalog of the Slavonic* Collection (Boston: G K Hall, 1974), 44 vols.

OH —OHIO STATE UNIVERSITY, William Oxley Thompson Memorial Library, Hilander Room, 1858 Neil Ave Mall, Columbus, 43210. Predrag Matejic, Cur; G Koolemans Beynen, Slavic Bibliographer
Holdings: Vols (200,000) Cat Maps Microforms
Budget: ($45,000)
Notes: Area studies of Central, Southeastern and Eastern Europe. Emphasis on on Slavic literatures, languages and history. At present economics, sociology, law (Russian only) have been added. Within this framework the following priorities have been established: Material in Russian problems; then Medieval Slavic (Cyrillic); then Polish, then Serbo-Croatian, then Bulgarian, and now Romanian. Special attention is paid to serials, bibliographies, ms descriptions and dictionaries (incl biographical and encyclopedias). Apart from materials in native languages, materials in the following languages are acquired: Old Church Slavonic, Greek, English, French, German, Italian, a few in Scandinavian languages, incl Finnish, and a few in Baltic languages. The Hillandar Room holds approx 2000 Slavic mss, 1050 from Hilandar Monastery, Mount Athos, on microform and a related referencecollection.

BULGARIA—IMPRINTS

DC —LIBRARY OF CONGRESS, Rare Book & Special Collections Div, Washington, 20540. William Matheson, Chief
Notes: The liturgical and religious works, grammars, readers, calendars, simple arithmetics, and other works that kept Bulgarian national consciousness alive during Turkish domination. The total is more than a third of all Bulgarian-language publications appearing in the "Bulgarian Renaissance" (1802-77).

BULGARIAN ACADEMY AND UNIVERSITY PUBLICATIONS

IL —UNIVERSITY OF ILLINOIS, URBANA/CHAMPAIGN, Slavic and East European Library, Urbana, 61801. Marianna Tax Choldin, Head
Holdings: Vols (9200) Cat
Notes: Extensive coverage.

BULGARIAN CHURCH SLAVIC LANGUAGE see Church Slavic Languages and Literature

BULGARIAN LANGUAGE—OLD BULGARIAN see Church Slavic Languages and Literature

BULGARIAN LANGUAGE AND LITERATURE

CA —UNIVERSITY OF CALIFORNIA, LOS ANGELES, Library, Slavic Collection, 405 Hilgard Ave, Los Angeles, 90024. Edward Shreeves, Chairman, Bibliographers Group; Leon Ferder, Slavic Bibliographer
Holdings: Vols (250,000) Cat
Notes: The Slavic Collection at UCLA consists of materials from and relating to Russia and the Soviet Union, Poland, Czechoslovakia, Yugoslavia, Bulgaria, the Sorbians in East Germany, and works by

BULGARIAN LANGUAGE AND LITERATURE (cont.)

Slavic emigres. The collection contains nearly 250,000 vols, and is particularly strong in linguistics, literature, history and social sciences, and reference materials. Slavic materials are collected in hard copy and microform, and incl monographs, serials (incl newspapers), reference works, proceedings of Slavistic congresses and symposia, and also *Festschriften* and dissertations.

CA —STANFORD UNIVERSITY LIBRARIES, Cecil H Green Library, Stanford, 94305. Wojciech Zalewski, Cur, Russian & East European Collection
Holdings: Vols (200,000) Cat Maps Microforms
Budget: ($90,000)
Notes: Strong collection prior to 20th century, but Stanford University Libraries' collecting effort is coordinated with Hoover Institution, Stanford, and holdings are not duplicated. Collection descriptions: Wojciech Zalewski, *Russian Materials in the Main Library of Stanford University, A Collection* Survey (Stanford: Stanford University Libraries, 1974). Wojciech Zalerski, "Stanford University" in P L Horecky, ed, *East Central and Southeast Europe, A Handbook of Library and Archival Resources in North America* (Santa Barbara: Clio Press, 1976).

DC —LIBRARY OF CONGRESS, Rare Book & Special Collections Div, Washington, 20540. William Matheson, Chief
Notes: The liturgical and religious works, grammars, readers, calendars, simple arithmetics, and other works that kept Bulgarian national consciousness alive during Turkish domination. The total is more than a third of all Bulgarian-language publications appearing in the "Bulgarian Renaissance" (1802-77).

IL —UNIVERSITY OF ILLINOIS, URBANA/CHAMPAIGN, Slavic and East European Library, Urbana, 61801. Marianna Tax Choldin, Head
Holdings: Vols (9200) Cat
Notes: Extensive coverage.

MA —HARVARD UNIVERSITY LIBRARY, Widener Library, Slavic Collections, Cambridge, 02138. Hugh M Olmsted, Slavic Dept Head
Holdings: Cat Microforms
Notes: Bulgarian literature shelflist through June, 1976 lists 3444 titles (earlier version was incl in *Widener Library Shelflist,* volumes 28-31, 1971). The language and literature collections continue to be developed actively, and are strong both in current and in antiquarian materials. See also *Harvard Library Notes,* III (1940), pp 295-302, and IV (1941), p 36.

NY —NEW YORK PUBLIC LIBRARY, Donnell Foreign Language Library, 20 W 53 St, New York, 10019. Bosiljka Stevanovic, Supvr Librn
Holdings: Vols 134 Cat
Notes: Bulgarian collection incl Bulgarian authors of Bulgarian expression. No separate catalog.

NY —NEW YORK PUBLIC LIBRARY, Slavonic Div, Fifth Ave & 42 St, New York, 10018. Edward Kasinec, Chief
Holdings: Cat Microforms
Notes: See New York Public Library, *Dictionary Catalog of the Slavonic* Collection (Boston: G K Hall, 1974), 44 vols.

OH —CLEVELAND PUBLIC LIBRARY, Foreign Literature Dept, 325 Superior Ave, Cleveland, 44114. Natalia Bezugloff, Head
Holdings: Vols 1630 Cat
Notes: A popular circulating collection containing classics and the standard works with emphasis on belles lettres, history and biography. A variety of other subjects such as learning languages, how to do books, art, children's books, spoken phonodiscs and cassettes, periodicals, etc.
See also entry under Foreign Language Collections

OH —OHIO STATE UNIVERSITY, William Oxley Thompson Memorial Library, 1858 Neil Ave, Columbus, 43210. A Robert Thorson, Head, Circulation Dept
Holdings: Cat Mss Microforms
Notes: This collection presently contains films of 2000 mss from the Hilandar Monastery, Mt Athos. Expansion will add Byzantine, Bulgarian, Russian and Valachian mss on film.

WI —UNIVERSITY OF WISCONSIN, MADISON, Memorial Library, Slavic Studies Collection, 728 State St, Madison, 53706. Aleksander Rolich, Bibliographer for Slavic Studies; Robert P Gakovich, Slavic Cataloger; Valdis J Zeps, Baltic Studies Center
Holdings: Vols (25,000) Cat
Notes: The Balcanica collection in Memorial Library exceeds 25,000 volumes and active collecting continues at over 2000 titles per year in Bulgarian, Rumanian, Turkish and the languages of Yugoslavia. Many rare and unique titles are to be found in this collection, including serial titles, such as *Nova Vreme* (1897-1923, 1947-to date), *Nova Europa* (1920-1939), and unique Turkish Salnameh. The emphasis is on historical materials, but there is considerable strength in South Slavic literatures and linguistics. The Rumanian materials are of more recent vintage.

BULGARIAN PERIODICALS see Periodicals, Bulgarian

BULGARIANS IN THE U.S.

MN —UNIVERSITY OF MINNESOTA, Immigration History Research Center, 826 Berry St, Saint Paul, 55114. Susan Griegs, Cur
Holdings: Vols (35,000) Mss Maps Pix Phonorecords Audiotapes 16mm Films Microforms
See also entry under US - Emigration and Immigration.

BULLARD, ARTHUR, 1879-1929

NJ —PRINCETON UNIVERSITY, Library, Manuscript Collection, Nassau St, Princeton, 08540. Jean F Preston, Cur
Holdings: // Cat Mss Pix
Notes: 20 boxes. The papers cover the period, 1905-1929. An unpublished typescript guide (10p) is available in the Library.

BULLARD, FREDERIC LAURISTON

MA —BOSTON UNIVERSITY, Mugar Memorial Library, Special Collections Dept, 771 Commonwealth Ave, Boston, 02215. Howard B Gotlieb, Dir
Holdings: Cat Mss
Notes: Correspondence, notebooks and clippings related to Abraham Lincoln collected in depth.

BULLETIN OF ATOMIC SCIENTISTS

NY —STATE UNIVERSITY OF NEW YORK AT ALBANY, Library, Special Collections Dept, 1400 Washington Ave, Albany, 12222. Marion P Munzer, Coordr
Notes: Eugene I Rabinowitch's correspondence and administrative files dealing with his academic and publishing career; editorship of the *Bulletin of Atomic* Scientists, establishment of the Center for Science and the Study of Society at the State University of New York at Albany (16 linear feet).

BULLEY, STANLEY

BC —UNIVERSITY OF VICTORIA, McPherson Library, Victoria, V8W 3H5, Can.
Notes: Letters from Gustav Holst and R Vaughan Williams to Stanley Bulley.

BULLFIGHTING

CA —LOS ANGELES PUBLIC LIBRARY, 630 W Fifth St, Los Angeles, 90071. Wyman Jones, City Librn
Notes: The George Smith Collection, with prints, posters and other materials, has been integrated into the general collection.

IN —INDIANA UNIVERSITY, Lilly Library, Seventh St, Bloomington, 47405. William R Cagle, Librn
Holdings: // Cat Mss
Notes: Correspondence of Roy Campbell, 1931-1936, primarily with his wife and his publisher, concerning publication of writings, Campbell's bullfighting, and his finances. Incl 13 ms writings, some apparently unpublished. 150 items. Library's holdings incl published first editions of Campbell's works.

BULLOCK, WYNN

AZ —UNIVERSITY OF ARIZONA, Center for Creative Photography, 843 E University Blvd, Tucson, 85721. James Enyeart, Dir; Terence Pitts, Cur and Librn
Notes: Center has significant collections consisting of more than 25 photographs plus other archival material such as negatives, contact sheets, work prints, correspondence, financial records, diaries, project files, etc. Inventories of the collections are available to researchers. Published guides available for some collections.

BULLS, PAPAL

MA —COLLEGE OF THE HOLY CROSS, Dinand Library, College St, Worcester, 01610. James M Mahoney, Cur of Special Collection
Holdings: Uncat Mss Pix
Notes: 48 signed papal documents and letters of 31 popes, 1181-1946; about 100 portrait engravings of the popes. Restricted use.

BULLS AND BEARS see Stock Exchanges

BUNBURY, HENRY, 1750-1811

DC —LIBRARY OF CONGRESS, Prints & Photographs Div, Washington, 20540.
Notes: The British Cartoon collection contains 10,000 British political caricatures and satires dating from the 17th through mid 19th centuries. Incl the work of Henry Bunbury, George Cruikshank, Issac Cruikshank, Matthew Darly, James Gillray, and Thomas Rowlandson.

BUNCHE, RALPH JOHNSON, 1904-1972

CA —UNIVERSITY OF CALIFORNIA, LOS ANGELES, Research Library, Dept of Special Collections, 405 Hilgard Ave, Los Angeles, 90024. Edward Shreeves, Chairman, Bibliographers Group; David S Zeidberg, Head
Holdings: Cat Mss Pix
Notes: 200 linear feet of mss, correspondence, photographs, memorabilia, and research notes relating to his professional career.

DC —HOWARD UNIVERSITY, Moorland-Spingarn Research Center, 500 Howard Place NW, Washington, 20059. Clifford L Muse, Jr, Acting Dir
Holdings: Vols (106,086) Mss Maps Pix Slides Phonorecords Audiotapes 16mm Films Filmstrips Microforms
Budget: ($854,753)
See also entry under Blacks

BUNTING, BASIL

MO —WASHINGTON UNIVERSITY, John M Olin Library, Campus Box 1061, St Louis, 63130.
Notes: Extensive collection of printed material, some correspondence and mss.

BUNYAN, JOHN

CA —UNIVERSITY OF CALIFORNIA, LOS ANGELES, William Andrews Clark Memorial Library, 2520 Cimarron St, Los

BUNYAN, JOHN (cont.)

Angeles, 90018.
Holdings: Cat
Notes: Original editions.

IL —WHEATON COLLEGE, Buswell Memorial Library, Wheaton, 60187. Paul Snezek, Library Dir
Holdings: Vols 350 Cat
Notes: Primarily a collection of Nineteenth century first editions. *Related Topics:* Pilgrim's Progress.

NY —NEW YORK PUBLIC LIBRARY, Rare Books and Manuscripts Div, Fifth Ave & 42 St, New York, 10018. William L Joyce, Asst Dir; Francis O Mattson, Curator
Holdings: Cat
Budget: ($7161)
Notes: Literary first editions. Incl notable collections of Shakespeare, Milton, Walton, Bunyan and Whitman (The Oscar Lion Collection).

AB —UNIVERSITY OF ALBERTA, Cameron Library, The Bruce Peel Special Collections Room, Edmonton, T6G 2J8, Can. John Charles, Special Collections Librn
Holdings: Vols 285 Cat
Notes: Incl early editions, illustrated editions and translations of his works.

BUNYAN, PAUL

MN —UNIVERSITY OF MINNESOTA, Libraries, Children's Literature Research Collections, 109 Walter Library, Minneapolis, 55455. Karen Nelson Hoyle, Cur
Holdings: Vols 138 Cat Mss Maps Pix Phonorecords
Notes: Paul Bunyan Collection, incl correspondence, advertisements, etc. Kerlan Collection.

BURACK, ABRAHAM

MA —BOSTON UNIVERSITY, Mugar Memorial Library, Special Collections Dept, 771 Commonwealth Ave, Boston, 02215. Howard B Gotlieb, Dir
Holdings: Cat Correspondence

BURBANK, ELBRIDGE AYER

IL —NEWBERRY LIBRARY, 60 W Walton St, Chicago, 60610. Diana Haskell, Cur of Modern Mss
Holdings: Cat Mss Pix
Notes: Inventoried collection of 1572 items, incl 346 letters from various Indian villages of the West and Southwest. Approx 1200 crayon drawings and 26 oil paintings of Indians and Indian life.

BURBANK, LUTHER, 1849-1926

CA —UNIVERSITY OF CALIFORNIA, DAVIS, Shields Library, Dept of Special Collections, Davis, 95616. Donald Kunitz, Head; C Danial Elliott, Asst Head
Holdings: Cat Mss
Notes: Correspondence between Luther Burbank and E J Wickson, regarding Burbank's developments and Wickson's writing about him. Also extracts from Burbank's scrapbooks (Wickson's copies), articles on Burbank. 287 items.

CA —SANTA ROSA-SONOMA COUNTY FREE PUBLIC LIBRARY, Third & E Sts, Santa Rosa, 95404. Audrey Herman, Librn
Holdings: Vols 91 Cat Pix Clippings
Notes: Picture collection is indexed.

DC —LIBRARY OF CONGRESS, Manuscript Division, Washington, 20540. John C Broderick, Chief
Notes: The papers of Luther Burbank (1849-1926), incl approximately 10,000 items range in date over much of his life span. Contains correspondence, writings, scientific notes and records, ledgers, account books, scrapbooks, photographs, and journal reprints and other printed matter.

BURDICK, EUGENE

MA —BOSTON UNIVERSITY, Mugar Memorial Library, Special Collections Dept, 771 Commonwealth Ave, Boston, 02215. Howard B Gotlieb, Dir
Holdings: Cat Mss Pix
Notes: Mss, correspondence, etc collected in depth; incl publications by or about.

BUREAU OF APPLIED SOCIAL RESEARCH

NY —COLUMBIA UNIVERSITY LIBRARIES, Lehman Library, Bureau of Applied Social Research Archive, 420 W 118th St, New York, 10027. David Lewis, Librn
Holdings: / / Mss
Notes: Comprised of files relating to projects and studies undertaken by the bureau between its opening in 1935 and its closing in 1977. Files incl proposals, drafts, interim reports, codebooks, final reports, and articles and books which were published as a result of a specific study. The collection does not circulate.

†NY —COLUMBIA UNIVERSITY LIBRARIES, Butler Library, Rare Book and Manuscript Library, 535 W 114 St, New York, 10027.
Notes: Papers, etc, of Paul F Lazarsfeld.

BUREAU OF MUNICIPAL RESEARCH

NY —ROCKEFELLER UNIVERSITY, Rockefeller Archive Center, Hillcrest, Pocantico Hills, North Tarrytown, 10591. Joseph W Ernst, Dir; J William Hess, Assoc Dir
Notes: Papers relative to the Rockefeller Family, Foundations, University, and other specific enterprises and contributions to particular areas of social, physical, educational, and historic reform, preservation, conservation or development. Extensive records of administrative, financial, physical, or intellectual relationships.

BURGER, ISABEL

AZ —ARIZONA STATE UNIVERSITY, Library, Tempe, 85287. Marilyn Wurzburger, Special Collections Librn
Holdings: Vols (108) Pix
Notes: Collection covers various aspects of Children's Theatre from 1944 through the present. Areas of emphasis incl International and National Child Drama Associations, award-winning theatres, educational programs, regional groups and prominent figures in Children's Theatre incl: Irene Vickers Baker, Isabel Burger, Virginia Lee Comer, Rita Criste, Moses Goldberg, Kenneth Graham, Aurand Harris, Paul Kozelka, George Latshaw, Rosemary Musil, Sara Spencer, Winifred Ward, Susan Zeder and Lin Wright. Publications incl newsletters, research papers, bibliographies and records of the proceedings of the Children's Theatre Association of America. 80 linear feet of scripts, documents, publications, films, tapes (oral history) programs, correspondence, photographs, working papers and clippings. Partially indexed; finding guides available.

BURGESS, FRANK GELETT

†MA —WILLIAMS COLLEGE, Chapin Library of Rare Books, PO Box 426, Williamstown, 01267. Robert L Volz, Custodian
Holdings: Vols 50 Cat
Notes: No material available on interlibrary loan.

BURGESS, ANTHONY

MO —WASHINGTON UNIVERSITY, Libraries, Special Collections Dept, Campus Box 1061, St Louis, 63130.
Notes: A small but significant collection.

BURGESS, THORNTON

WI —UNIVERSITY OF WISCONSIN, MADISON, Cooperative Children's Book Center, Helen C White Hall, Rm 4290, 600 N Park St, Madison, 53706. Ginny Moore Kruse, Dir
Holdings: Vols (25,000) Cat
Notes: Cooperative Children's Book Center collections incl most US trade books published for children in last 24 months; first editions of recommended US children's trade books published since 1965; over 400 alternative press books published for children in US and Canada since 1970; children's books about Wisconsin and by Wisconsin authors and illustrators; representative 19th and early 20th century American children's books; 19th century children's periodicals; first and significant editions of Newbury and Caldecott Medal books; historical and contemporary toybooks; 75 vols of Mother Goose published since 1828; 160 vols of Thorton Burgess books, many first editions; ms and original artwork for Ellen Raskin's *The Westing Game* and *The Mysterious Disappearance of Leon (I Mean Noel);* juvenile mass market and traderomance fiction. There are several extra-illustrated volumes in the Burgess Collection; each copy is inscribed by Burgess to Roy W Oppegard.

BURGESS, W. STARLING

RI —US NAVAL WAR COLLEGE, Historical Collection & Museum, Newport, 02841. Anthony S Nicolosi, Dir; Evelyn Cherpak, Cur
Holdings: Mss
Notes: Research files relating to the development of counter measures for the German acoustic torpedo done for the US Navy Special Devices Division, ASDEVLANT and the accelerometer development under the Damage Control Research Project, Stevens Institute of Technology. Incl are blueprints of designs, calculations, test data, reports, correspondence, memoranda and technical publications. The collection is rich in materials relating to scientific/technical naval inventions and developments.

BURIAL STATISTICS see Registers of Births, Etc.; Vital Statistics

BURIAT LANGUAGE AND LITERATURE

NY —NEW YORK PUBLIC LIBRARY, Oriental Div, Fifth Ave & 42 St, New York, 10018. E Christian Filstrup, Chief
Holdings: Cat Mss Microforms
Budget: ($56,455)
Notes: Published catalog of holdings.

BURKE, EDMUND

CA —UNIVERSITY OF CALIFORNIA, SANTA BARBARA, Library, Dept of Special Collections, Santa Barbara, 93106. Christian F Brun, Head
Holdings: Cat Mss Pix

CT —YALE UNIVERSITY, Beinecke Rare Book & Manuscript Library, Osborn Collection, New Haven, 06520. Stephen R Parks, Cur
Holdings: Mss

NY —UNIVERSITY OF ROCHESTER, Rush Rhees Library, Department of Rare Books and Special Collections, Rochester, 14627. Peter Dzwonkoski, Librn
Holdings: Vols 150 Cat
Notes: No photocopying.

BURKE, JACKSON

MA —BOSTON UNIVERSITY, Mugar Memorial Library, Special Collections Dept, 771 Commonwealth Ave, Boston, 02215. Howard B Gotlieb, Dir
Holdings: Mss

BURKE, KENNETH

MO —WASHINGTON UNIVERSITY, Libraries, Special Collections Dept, Campus Box 1061, St Louis, 63130.
Notes: A small but significant collection.

BURKE AND HARE (RESURRECTION MEN)

NY —NEW YORK ACADEMY OF MEDICINE, Library, 2 E 103 St, New York, 10029. Brett A Kirkpatrick, Librn
Holdings: Vols Cat
Notes: The Fenwick Beekman Collection on the criminals of 1829.

BURKHOLZ, HERBERT

MA —BOSTON UNIVERSITY, Mugar Memorial Library, Special Collections Dept, 771 Commonwealth Ave, Boston, 02215. Howard B Gotlieb, Dir
Holdings: Mss Tape Recordings

BURLEIGH, GEORGE SHEPHERD, 1821-1903

RI —BROWN UNIVERSITY, John Hay Library, 20 Prospect St, Providence, 02912. Mark N Brown, Cur Mss
Holdings: // Mss
Notes: Three ms boxes and 29 notebooks of George S Burleigh, containing letters for the period 1839 to 1903 reflecting his interests in Transcendentalism; the anti-slavery, temperance, and woman's liberation movements; the Sabbath Question; and the publication of his writing in reform periodicals. Two manuscript boxes and 29 notebooks contain poems by Burleigh.

BURLEIGH, HARRY

PA —ERIE COUNTY HISTORICAL SOCIETY LIBRARY, 417 State St, Erie, 16501. Helen Andrews, Librn
Notes: Original research materials in 16 legal size drawers, including Pennsylvania Population Company papers, Old Erie Academy papers, Erie Street railway papers, Harry Burleigh (black singer & composer) transcripts and research papers; also four letter size drawers with old account books.

BURLESON, OMAR

TX —ABILENE CHRISTIAN UNIVERSITY, Margaret & Herman Brown Library, ACU Sta, Abilene, 79601. Callie Faye Milliken, Assoc Dir
Notes: The Omar Burleson Congressional Papers. Includes correspondence, hearings, books, memorabilia.

BURLESQUE (THEATRE)

NY —HAMPDEN-BOOTH THEATRE LIBRARY AT THE PLAYERS, 16 Gramercy Park, New York, 10003. Louis A Rachow, Librn/Cur
Holdings: Mss Pix
Notes: Nearly 300 burlesque scripts and vaudeville skits, music in ms, 25 photographs in character, two song books of the period, a notebook of stage gags and repartee, typescript of biography of Chuck Callahan (30 pages), and a number of ephemeral pieces, stage money, programs, etc. 4 boxes of indexed material. Described in *The Players Bulletin,* Spring 1966, pp 20-21; and *Performing Arts Resources* vol 3 (New York: Theatre Library Association, 1976), pp 143-150. Described in *Theatre & Performing Arts Collections* (New York: Haworth Press, 1981).

NY —NEW YORK PUBLIC LIBRARY, Performing Arts Research Center, Billy Rose Theatre Collection, 111 Amsterdam Ave, New York, 10023. Dorothy L Swerdlove, Cur
Holdings: Cat Mss

PA —UNIVERSITY OF PITTSBURGH, Hillman Library, Special Collection Dept, Anna Pavlova-Karl G Heinrich Collection, Pittsburgh, 15260. Charles Aston, Jr, Coordr
Holdings: Vols 135 Cat
Notes: Acquired in 1967, consists of the "Mlle Anna Pavlowa Memorial Ballet Library" formed by Karl Heinrich in conjunction with the Pittsburgh Civic Ballet and of printed books, scrapbooks, original sketches, posters and choreographic notes. In addition to the Pavlowa-Heinrich Collection, the library owns a rare collection of material on the Burlesque Theatre. Skits which used dancers are part of this material. Incl 10 ft linear mss.
See also entry under Theatre - History

PA —UNIVERSITY OF PITTSBURGH, Special Collections Dept, Curtis Theatre Collection, 363 Hillman Library, Pittsburgh, 15260. Jeanette Blanco, Cur
Holdings: Vols (4000) Cat Mss Pix Slides Microforms VF
Notes: The legitimate theatre of plays, musicals and vaudeville, chiefly of New York City and Pittsburgh, from 1865, and other US, community, summer, college and foreign theatre. Incl 500,000 programs, 12, 000 pictures, 300 posters, the Oliver P Merriman Scrapbooks and 300 other scrapbooks, clippings and other ephemera. Vols incl over 3000 acting editions and playscripts. Separate collections: Ralph G Allen Burlesque Skits Collection; Michael Ellis Papers; William P Halstead Theatre Collection; Kenyon Family Papers; Philip Dunning Playscripts Collection; Pittsburgh Playhouse Records; Pittsburgh Savoyards Records. Noncirculating.

BURLINGHAM, CHARLES CULP, 1858-1959

MA —HARVARD UNIVERSITY LIBRARY, Law School Library, Langdell Hall, Cambridge, 02138. Erika S Chadbourn, Cur of Mss
Holdings: Cat Mss
Notes: Personal papers. Typed inventory in repository. Inclusive dates: 1876-1960.

BURLINGTON RAILROAD

IL —NEWBERRY LIBRARY, 60 W Walton St, Chicago, 60610. Diana Haskell, Cur of Modern Mss
Holdings: Uncat Mss Maps Pix
Notes: Collection is richest for the years 1870 to 1895. There is little material of a "working nature," ie payrolls, lists of employees, track of engine construction and maintenance, nor any policy statements, but there are many records of financial and administrative structure. Approx 400 sq ft of archives. Printed descriptive list: *Guide to the Burlington Archives in the Newberry* Library, Elisabeth Jackson and Carolyn Curtis (Chicago: The Newberry Library, 1949).

BURMA

HI —UNIVERSITY OF HAWAII, Library, 2550 The Mall, Honolulu, 96822. Joyce Wright, Head, Asia Collection; Masato Matsu, Head, East Asia Vernacular Collection
Holdings: Vols 331,620 Cat Microforms
Notes: The Asia Collection holds materials from and about Southeast Asia: Brunei, Burma, Cambodia (Kampuchea), Indonesia, Laos, Malaysia, Philippines, Singapore, Thailand. Large contemporary Indonesian language collection. Several thousand vols in Thai and in Vietnamese. Minimal holdings in Burmese, Khmer, Lao languages. Social sciences and humanities emphasis for the post-World War II period. Western language coverage supplemented by retrospective holdings in the main library collection.

IL —NORTHERN ILLINOIS UNIVERSITY, Founders Memorial Library, Southeast Asia Collection, Normal Rd, De Kalb, 60115. Lee S Dutton Dr, Cur
Holdings: Vols (34,000) Cat Maps Microforms
Notes: An extensive collection of books, periodicals, newspapers, maps, and microforms from or about Southeast Asia. Areas of concentration incl Thailand, Malaysia, Indonesia, Singapore, Brunei, Philippines, Laos, and Burma. Holdings (except rare books, maps, and microforms) are housed in a separate area collection within the Founders Library. A departmental card catalog and specialized reference collection support reference services. A Thai collection of several thousand vols is the largest vernacular component. Extensive Malaysia, Indonesia, Singapore, and Brunei holdings have been acquired through the NPAC program. A collection of Filipino-American newspapers, and a growing collection of children's literature in common and uncommon Southeast Asian languages are available. Resources are accessible to borrowers through OCLC.

MI —UNIVERSITY OF MICHIGAN, Harlan Hatcher Graduate Library, Ann Arbor, 48109. Susan Go, Librn
Holdings: Vols (250,000) Cat Mss Maps Pix Slides Microforms
Notes: Incl in the Michigan Historical Collections (primarily archival material) are papers of Michiganders in southeast Asia, mostly the Philipines, eg papers of Joseph R Hayden, Frank Murphy and G Mennen Williams, also, on film, the selected papers of Philippines president Manuel Quezon. All aspects of the countries, cultures and peoples of Brunei, Burma, Khymer, Indonesia, Laos, Malaysia, Philippines, Singapore, Thailand, Portuguese Timor and Vietnam. Also the Malayo-Polynesian (Austronesian), Mon-Khmer (Austroasiatic), and Sino-Tibetan language groupings.

NY —CORNELL UNIVERSITY LIBRARIES, John M Olin Library, John M Echols Collection on Southeast Asia, Ithaca, 14853. Giok Po Oey, Curator
Holdings: Vols (167,000) Cat Mss Maps Pix Microforms
Budget: ($90,000)
Notes: Additions published in the collection's monthly accessions list (Ithaca: Cornell University, Southeast Asia Program, 1959-). Holdings through December 1980 listed in *Cornell University Libraries Southeast Asia Catalog* (Boston: G K Hall, 1976, First supplement, 1983), 10 vols.

BURMAN, BEN LUCIEN

MA —BOSTON UNIVERSITY, Mugar Memorial Library, Special Collections Dept, 771 Commonwealth Ave, Boston, 02215. Howard B Gotlieb, Dir
Holdings: Cat Mss

BURMESE LANGUAGE AND LITERATURE

DC —LIBRARY OF CONGRESS, African and Middle Eastern Division, Washington, 20540.
Holdings: Cat Mss Microforms
Notes: Southern Asian: over 137,000 vols of literature of the area from Pakistan to the Philippines.

HI —UNIVERSITY OF HAWAII, Library, 2550 The Mall, Honolulu, 96822. Joyce Wright, Head, Asia Collection; Masato Matsu, Head, East Asia Vernacular Collection
Holdings: Vols 331,620 Cat Microforms
Notes: The Asia Collection holds materials from and about Southeast Asia: Brunei, Burma, Cambodia (Kampuchea), Indonesia, Laos, Malaysia, Philippines, Singapore, Thailand. Large contemporary Indonesian language collection. Several thousand vols in Thai and in Vietnamese. Minimal holdings in Burmese, Khmer, Lao languages. Social sciences and humanities emphasis for the post-World War II period. Western language coverage supplemented by retrospective holdings in the main library collection.

NY —CORNELL UNIVERSITY LIBRARIES, John M Olin Library, John M Echols Collection on Southeast Asia, Ithaca, 14853. Giok Po Oey, Curator
Holdings: Vols (167,000) Cat Mss Maps Pix Microforms
Budget: ($90,000)
Notes: Additions published in the collection's monthly accessions list (Ithaca: Cornell University, Southeast Asia Program, 1959-). Holdings through December 1980 listed in *Cornell University Libraries*

BURMESE LANGUAGE AND LITERATURE (cont.)

Southeast Asia Catalog (Boston: G K Hall, 1976, First supplement, 1983), 10 vols.

NY —NEW YORK PUBLIC LIBRARY, Oriental Div, Fifth Ave & 42 St, New York, 10018. E Christian Filstrup, Chief
Holdings: Cat Mss Microforms
Budget: ($56,455)
Notes: Published catalog of holdings. Currently collected in Western language materials only.

BURNET, DAVID GOUVERNEUR

TX —ROSENBERG LIBRARY, Galveston and Texas History Center, 2310 Sealy Ave, Galveston, 77550. Jane Kenamore, Archivist
Holdings: Cat Mss
Notes: Papers of David G Burnett (1789-1870), first President of the Republic of Texas. Correspondence relating to personal, family, business, military, and political matters, land tax receipts, and two private notebooks.

BURNET, GILBERT, 1643-1715

PA —TEMPLE UNIVERSITY LIBRARIES, Special Collections Dept, Rare Books & Mss Section, Philadelphia, 19122. Thomas M Whitehead, Cur
Holdings: Cat
Notes: An extensive collection, incl 137 titles. A list of the tracts, sermons, and books is available.

BURNETT, FRANCES HODGSON, 1849-1924

NY —STATE UNIVERSITY OF NEW YORK, STONY BROOK, Melville Library, Dept of Special Collections, Stony Brook, 11794. Evert Volkersz, Head
Holdings: Vols 26 Uncat
Notes: Photocopying.

BURNETT, WHIT, 1899-1973

NJ —PRINCETON UNIVERSITY, Library, Manuscript Collection, Nassau St, Princeton, 08540. Jean F Preston, Cur
Holdings: Mss Cat
Notes: The Whit Burnett Collection, which deals in large part with *Story: The Magazine of the Short Story*, fills 163 boxes and 9 cartons. See *Princeton University Library* Chronicle, v 27, p 107-12. Part of the collection has been indexed on 3 X 5 cards.

BURNEY FAMILY

CT —YALE UNIVERSITY, Beinecke Rare Book & Manuscript Library, Osborn Collection, New Haven, 06520. Stephen R Parks, Cur
Holdings: Mss

BURNS, DAVID

NY —NEW YORK PUBLIC LIBRARY, Performing Arts Research Center, Billy Rose Theatre Collection, 111 Amsterdam Ave, New York, 10023. Dorothy L Swerdlove, Cur
Holdings: Cat Mss Pix
Notes: Papers, scrapbooks, mss, photographs, memorabilia, etc.

BURNS, MRS. GAVIN HAMILTON, 1858-1924

BC —UNIVERSITY OF VICTORIA, McPherson Library, Victoria, V8W 3H5, Can.
Notes: Daughter of Senator W J Macdonald. Letters from Louisa Blum, Laura H Richards (mother of Pearl Craigie, John Oliver Hobbes pseud); Craigie ephemera, 1906-11; Ethel Jenner Rosenberg; Warburg Family; Mrs Wilhelmina Stirling and Rev E F W Hudson.

BURNS, GEORGE

CA —UNIVERSITY OF CALIFORNIA, LOS ANGELES, Theater Arts Library, Los Angeles, 90024. Edward Shreeves, Chairman, Bibliographers Group; Audree Malkin, Head, Theater Arts Library
Holdings: Cat Mss Pix
Notes: Television scripts of *The George Burns Show,* 232 episodes, 1958-1959.

CA —UNIVERSITY OF SOUTHERN CALIFORNIA, Edward L Doheny Memorial Library, Archives of Performing Arts, University Park, Los Angeles, 90089. Robert Knutson, Librn
Holdings: Mss Pix
Notes: Personal collection of papers, pictures, etc.

BURNS, JOHN

CA —CALIFORNIA STATE UNIVERSITY, NORTHRIDGE, Delmar T Oviatt & South Libraries, 1811 Nordhoff St, Northridge, 91330. Donald L Read, Special Collections Dept
Holdings: Vols 2000 Uncat
Notes: Partial contents: Liberal Publication Dept, London. Pamphlets and leaflets (1893-1903; 1905-1914), Fabian tracts (1884-1904), Irish Loyal and Patriotic Union. Pamphlets and leaflets (1887). Particularly strong in letters from John Burns' personal correspondence (approx 100). Entire collection, 20 linear feet. Indexed in *Century of Change, 1815-1914; A Collection of Original Pamphlets, Tracts, Posters, Holograph Letters, Manuscripts, Etc.* Guernsey, Channel Islands: Guernsey Books, 1972.

BURNS, ROBERT

IL —NORTHERN ILLINOIS UNIVERSITY, Founders Memorial Library, Rare Books and Special Collections Dept, De Kalb, 60115. William R DuBois, Dept Head
Holdings: Vols 160 Cat
Notes: Noncirculating.

IA —GRAND LODGE OF IOWA, AF & AM Iowa Masonic Library, 813 First Ave SE, Cedar Rapids, 52406. Tom Eggleston, Librn
Holdings: Vols 250 Cat

MA —HARVARD UNIVERSITY LIBRARY, Houghton Library, Cambridge, 02138. Rodney G Dennis, Cur of Manuscripts
Holdings: Cat Mss

MO —WASHINGTON UNIVERSITY, Libraries, Special Collections Dept, Campus Box 1061, St Louis, 63130.
Notes: Papers of the prominent American industrialist and collector's papers, nearly 2000 items. Incl Bixby's personal papers, materials relating to the St Louis Burns Club, and a large group of Eugene Field's materials; also, autographs, mss, and correspondence of literary and historical figures.

NV —UNIVERSITY OF NEVADA, RENO, University Library, Special Collections Dept, Reno, 89557. Robert E Blesse, Head
Holdings: Vols (650) Uncat
Notes: First and early editions, books about Burns, Scotland, his contemporaries. Publication: Robert Burns, an exhibition... University of Nevada Press, Bibliographic Series no 1, 1962.

NH —DARTMOUTH COLLEGE, Baker Memorial Library, Hanover, 03755.
Holdings: Cat Pix
Notes: Incl ephemera, first editions, etc. Noncirculating.

NC —DAVIDSON COLLEGE, E H Little Library, Davidson, 28036. Leland M Park, Dir; Chalmers G Davidson, Dir
Holdings: Cat

RI —PROVIDENCE ATHENAEUM, 251 Benefit St, Providence, 02903. Sally Duplaix, Dir
Holdings: Vols 455 Cat
Notes: Books by and about Burns. Collection of Charles Bradley given to library in 1920.

BC —UNIVERSITY OF BRITISH COLUMBIA, Library, Special Collections Div, 1956 Main Mall, Vancouver, V6T 1Y3, Can. Anne Yandle, Head
Holdings: Vols Cat Mss
Notes: Books by Burns, about Burns and his works, by and about his contemporaries and followers, and about contemporary Scotland.

BURNS, VINCENT G.

DC —GEORGETOWN UNIVERSITY, Library, Special Collections Div, 37 & O Sts NW, Washington, 20057. George M Barringer, Special Collections Librn; Nicholas B Sheetz, Mss Librn
Holdings: Mss Cat
Notes: Collection concerning the literary career of Vincent G Burns, author, lecturer and poet. Incl are manuscripts, published poetry, programs and handbills, correspondence from Burns to various public officials, newspaper clippings and published works inscribed by Burns. During his literary career, Burns was named Maryland's Poet Laureate.

BURNSIDE, R.H.

NY —NEW YORK PUBLIC LIBRARY, Performing Arts Research Center, Billy Rose Theatre Collection, 111 Amsterdam Ave, New York, 10023. Dorothy L Swerdlove, Cur
Holdings: Cat Mss Pix
Notes: Papers, scrapbooks, mss, photographs, memorabilia, etc.

BURR, AARON, 1756-1836

NJ —AARON BURR ASSOCIATION LIBRARY, RD 1, RT 33, Box 429, Hightstown-Freehold Rd, Hightstown, 08520. Samuel E Burr, Jr, Librn
Holdings: Vols 100 Cat Pix Microforms
Notes: Materials concerning Col Aaron Burr, his life, his career and members of his immediate family. Incl some materials on his daughter, Mrs Theodosia Burr Alston, Jefferson Davis and Mrs Jefferson Davis (Varina Howell Davis). Open to the public by appointment only.

NJ —PRINCETON UNIVERSITY, Library, Manuscript Collection, Nassau St, Princeton, 08540. Jean F Preston, Cur
Holdings: Vols 421 Mss
Notes: Mss total 5 boxes. See *Princeton University Library Chronicle*, v 18, p 223-24. An unpublished guide (34 p) of the manuscript section is available for consultation.

BURR, GEORGE ELBERT

CO —DENVER PUBLIC LIBRARY, Western History Department, 1357 Broadway, Denver, 80203. Eleanor M Gehres, Head
Holdings: Cat Pix
Notes: Etchings, watercolors, drawings and other works of George Elbert Burr. Burr's correspondence with Cyrus Boutwell, art dealer, and other mss relating to Burr.

BURR-PURKITT FAMILY

MO —WASHINGTON UNIVERSITY, Libraries, Special Collections Dept, Campus Box 1061, St Louis, 63130.
Notes: Family and business correspondence.

BURR-WILKINSON CONSPIRACY

IL —NEWBERRY LIBRARY, 60 W Walton St, Chicago, 60610. Diana Haskell, Cur of Modern Mss
Holdings: Cat Mss
Notes: Incl the Everett D Graff Collection materials.

BURRITT, MAURICE CHASE, 1883-1959

NY —CORNELL UNIVERSITY LIBRARIES, Collection of Regional History, Dept of Manuscripts and Univ Archives, Ithaca, 14853.
Holdings: Vols Pix
Notes: Agriculturist, editor, author, banker, farm owner/operator, and appointee to several government agricultural positions. Incl papers, 1832-(1902-1959); journal, diaries, notebooks, scrapbooks of editorials and articles, inventories; farm, family, and

BURRITT, MAURICE CHASE, 1883-1959 (cont.)

personal accounts; general correspondence, photo album and loose photographs.

BURROUGHS, EDGAR RICE

CA —UNIVERSITY OF CALIFORNIA, RIVERSIDE, University Library, 4045 Canyon Crest Dr, Box 5900, Riverside, 92517.
Holdings: Vols (30,000)
Notes: The Eaton Collection of science fiction and fantasy materials, incl 5,600 pulp magazines; also horror, supernatural, and Gothic mystery fiction; boys' books; utopian and dystopian fiction, imaginary voyages, future war and lost race fiction; large holdings in French language science fiction and fantasy; critical and scholarly works pertaining to these genres; videotapes of science fiction/fantasy films and shooting scripts. Collection covers science fiction/fantasy literature from the 16th-17th centuries to the present. Strong individual author collections of Jules Verne, H Rider Haggard, H G Wells, Edgar Rice Burroughs, and Philip K Dick. For a complete description of the collection see: George Slusser, "The J Lloyd Eaton Collection," *Special Collections*, II, 1/2, 25-38 (1983), and*Dictionary Catalog of the J Lloyd Eaton Collection of Science Fiction and Fantasy* Literature (Boston: G K Hall) 1982.

KY —UNIVERSITY OF LOUISVILLE, Ekstrom Library, Rare Books & Special Collections, 2301 S Third St, Louisville, 40208. George T McWhorter, Cur; Delinda Stephens Buie, Asst Cur
Holdings: Vols 5000 // Mss Pix
Notes: The Edgar Rice Burroughs Collection has been augmented with archival materials from the Burroughs family, incl autographed copies with illustrations by the author, original art and sculpture and primary source materials. It has become the largest institutional collection of Burroughs in existence. Research by appointment. *Library Review 30* gives a bibliographic description of this collection and is available upon request.
See also entry under Fanzines

†UT —BRIGHAM YOUNG UNIVERSITY, Harold B Lee Library, Provo, 84602. Elizabeth Pope, Librn
Notes: Science Fiction-Fantasy Collection, extensive circulating collection. Arkham House near complete, non-circulating. Mysteries, westerns and gothic romances in general fiction. Edgar Rice Burroughs 1st edition collection does not circulate. Science fiction and fantasy art special collection.

MB —UNIVERSITY OF WINNIPEG, Library, 515 Portage Ave, Winnipeg, R3B 2E9, Can. W R Converse, Chief Librn
Holdings: Vols (1800) Cat Microforms
Notes: Collection incl all major science fiction writers, all science fiction classics, *Amazing Stories Monthly* and *Amazing Stories Quarterly*. Also incl fantasy, eg, Edgar Rice Burroughs' Tarzan stories, as well as his Martian stories. Collection will very soon incl all science fiction periodicals on microfilm.

BURROUGHS, JOHN, 1837-1921

NY —VASSAR COLLEGE, Library, Rare Books & Manuscripts Collection, Box 20, Poughkeepsie, 12601. Lisa Browar, Cur
Notes: John Burroughs' 53 notebooks comprising his manuscript journals, 1876 to 1921. Devoted principally to his observations of nature, with many comments of literary and political observations.

VA —UNIVERSITY OF VIRGINIA, Alderman Library, Clifton Waller Barrett Collection, Charlottesville, 22901. Joan St C Crane, Cur of American Literature Collections
Notes: Papers.

BURROUGHS, NANNIE HELEN, 1878-1961

DC —LIBRARY OF CONGRESS, Manuscript Division, Washington, 20540. John C Broderick, Chief
Holdings: 135,200 Items
Notes: Correspondence, reports, student and financial records, subject files, scrapbooks, clippings, photographs, printed matter, and other memorabilia of Nannie Helen Burroughs (1878-1961).

BURROUGHS, WILLIAM S.

AZ —ARIZONA STATE UNIVERSITY, Library, Tempe, 85287. Marilyn Wurzburger, Special Collections Librn
Notes: The William S Burroughs Collection consists of four feet of mss dating from 1938, incl source material and sometimes several drafts of many of Burroughs' major works: *Soft Machine, Revised Boy Scout Manual, APO-33, Exterminator!, Port of Saints, Ah Pook Is Here, Wild Boys, Unspeakable Mr Hart, Book of Breething, Last Words of Dutch Schultz;* with also the *Naked Lunch* filmscript, two vols of dream notes, and some seventy other small mss and fragments. Also incl three feet of clippings and source material assembled by Burroughs, much of it during the Beat Hotel period with Byron Gysin in Paris. Present are Burroughs' copies of some 100 magazines containing his work and a partial set of translations of Burroughs' books. This is a growing collection, the only extensive collection of Burroughs material publicly available. Annotated inventory, no published guide.

NY —COLUMBIA UNIVERSITY LIBRARIES, Rare Book & Manuscript Library, 801 Butler Library, 535 W 114 St, New York, 10027. Kenneth A Lohf, Librn
Holdings: Mss
Notes: Forty years of literary correspondence between the Harold Matson Literary Agency and numerous notable authors. Restricted use.

BURT, BRADLEY BENEDICT

NY —STATE UNIVERSITY OF NEW YORK, COLLEGE AT OSWEGO, Penfield Library, Oswego, 13126. Anne Commerton, Dir
Holdings: // Uncat Mss
Notes: Burt was a lawyer interested in the history of Oswego. The collection consists of correspondence, financial records, legal papers, and material collected about the history of Oswego. 17 1/2 linear inches of mss.

BURT FAMILY

NJ —PRINCETON UNIVERSITY, Library, Manuscript Collection, Nassau St, Princeton, 08540. Jean F Preston, Cur
Holdings: Vols 84 Cat Mss
Notes: Incl books and mss by Katherine, Nathaniel and Struthers Burt. Mss occupy over 44 ms boxes.

BURTON, CLARENCE MONROE, 1853-1932

MI —DETROIT PUBLIC LIBRARY, Burton Historical Collection, 5201 Woodward Ave, Detroit, 48202. Alice Dalligan, Chief
Notes: Materials illustrating the history of Detroit. The resources of the Burton Historical Collections consist of almost 250, 000 volumes, 13,000 cataloged pamphlets, 4800 bound newspaper volumes, 6800 scrapbooks, 325 broadsides, 500 periodical subscriptions, over 4000 maps, about 20,000 reels of microfilm, 600 microfiche and microcards, about 43,000 pictures, 7400 negatives, 9300 feet of City and County archives, and 5000 feet of personal and business papers. Transcripts have been made of pertinent records in foreign archives relating to early Michigan history. There are extensive files of newspaper clippings, biographical sketches, pictures, photographs, and ephemera-such items as menus, advertising cards, playbills, and election handbills. The holdings are listed in the *Union Catalog of Manuscripts.*

BURTON, HAROLD HITZ, 1888-1964

DC —LIBRARY OF CONGRESS, Manuscript Division, Washington, 20540. John C Broderick, Chief
Notes: Papers; additions, 1977- .

ME —BOWDOIN COLLEGE, Library, Brunswick, 04011. Dianne M Gutscher, Cur of Special Collections
Holdings: Vols Mss Pix
Notes: The Harold Hitz Burton Supreme Court Collection contains about 175 volumes, incl presentation copies from Felix Frankfurter, Hugo Black, and others of that stature, and Supreme Court procedural rules and legal texts with the Justice's annotations. Also part of the collection are about 100 letters, many speeches, and autographed presentation photographs of fellow Justices.

BURTON, POMEROY

NY —SAINT LAWRENCE UNIVERSITY, Owen D Young Library, Canton, 13617. Mahlon Peterson, Librn
Holdings: Cat Mss Pix
Notes: Collection consists of letters sent to Edith O'Dell Black and Pomeroy Burton of the New York *World* from 1903 to 1944. Also incl are works by Alexander Black, a novelist, and manuscripts which he wrote for "picture plays," the forerunners of the modern moving pictures. Approx 350 items.

BURTON, SIR RICHARD, 1821-1890

CT —LEE ASH, (personal collection), 66 Humiston Dr, Bethany, 06525.
Holdings: Cat Mss Pix
Notes: Incl books, letters, ephemera, etc.

NY —SYRACUSE UNIVERSITY LIBRARIES, Ernest S Bird Library, George Arents Research Library for Special Collections, Syracuse, 13210. Carolyn A Davis, Manuscripts Librn; Amy S Doherty, University Archivist; Mark F Weimer, Rare Book Librn
Notes: His correspondence, papers and works (0.5 linear feet).

†UT —UNIVERSITY OF UTAH, Marriott Library, Salt Lake City, 84112.
Notes: Manuscripts and papers of historian-biographer Fawn M Brodie (d 1981). Incl taped interviews with Richard Nixon, and notes, clippings, reviews, articles, and about 400 books used in her researches on Nixon, Thomas Jefferson, and Sir Richard Burton, in preparation of their biographies.

BURTON, ROBERT, 1577-1640

CA —CLAREMONT COLLEGES, Honnold Library, Ninth & Dartmouth, Claremont, 91711. Tania Rizzo, Special Collections Dept Head
Holdings: Vols 345 // Cat Mss
Notes: First six editions of the *Anatomy of* Melancholy, 1621-1652; original editions of Renaissance and later authors cited by Burton. Original gift of Paul Jordan Smith supplemented by purchase of parts of library of Edward Bensly. See Downs Suppl 1791. Paul Jordan-Smith, *Burton's Anatomy of Melancholy and Burtoniana* (Claremont, 1959).

BURUNDI

DC —HOWARD UNIVERSITY, Moorland-Spingarn Research Center, 500 Howard Place NW, Washington, 20059. Clifford L Muse, Jr, Acting Dir

BUS LINES see Motor Bus Lines

BUSCH, FRITZ, 1890-1951

IN —INDIANA UNIVERSITY, Lilly Library, Seventh St, Bloomington, 47405. William R Cagle, Librn
Holdings: // Cat Mss
Notes: Library of the conductor Fritz Busch, largely orchestral scores and parts. Many scores have ms annotations in the hand of

BUSCH, FRITZ, 1890-1951 (cont.)

the conductor. Many non-annotated printings of scores and tape copies of recordings by Fritz Busch are in the Indiana University School of Music Library.

BUSES see Motor Buses

BUSH, VANNEVAR

DC —LIBRARY OF CONGRESS, Washington, 20540.
Holdings: Vols 18,000
Notes: Personal papers, scientific and general correspondence, subject files, speeches and articles, laboratory notebooks, files and notebooks concerning inventions and patents, research notes and mss for books.

MA —MASSACHUSETTS INSTITUTE OF TECHNOLOGY, Institute Archives, Special Collections, Cambridge, 02139.
Notes: Papers of Norbert Wiener, renowned mathematician, was instrumental in the development of communication and control theories. He coined the word "cybernetics" to describe this new science. Professional papers document the development of this theory, his development as a mathematician, and his effective collaboration with students and colleagues including Vannevar Bush and John von Neumann. Unpublished finding aid with correspondent index is available in the Institute Archives.

BUSHMAN, JOHN

AZ —NORTHERN ARIZONA UNIVERSITY, Special Collection Library, CU Box 6022, Flagstaff, 86011. Peter M Whiteley, Coordr/Archivist; William Mullane, Librn
Notes: Diaries and journals, 1871-1923, Joseph City, Ariz. Mormon history.
See also entry under Bushman Family

BUSHMAN FAMILY

AZ —NORTHERN ARIZONA UNIVERSITY, Special Collection Library, CU Box 6022, Flagstaff, 86011. Peter M Whiteley, Coordr/Archivist; William Mullane, Librn
Notes: Land patents certificates of Jesse Bushman and John Bushman in Navajo county, Ariz, 1917, 1924, 1948.
See also entry under Bushman, John

BUSINESS

AL —UNIVERSITY OF ALABAMA, Business Library, Box 2937, University, 35486. Dorothy Eady Brown, Librn; Linda Suttle Harris, Ref Librn and Data Base Searcher
Holdings: Vols (105,000) Cat Microforms
Budget: ($60,000)
Notes: Incl 90,000 corporation reports and 38,500 microforms.

CA —ARMSTRONG COLLEGE, Library, 2222 Harold Way, Berkeley, 94704. Carroll R Phillips, Librn
Holdings: Vols 20,000 Cat
Notes: 5,000 law volumes cataloged. Also have file of annual reports from top 1000 US companies.

CA —LOS ANGELES PUBLIC LIBRARY, Business & Economic Dept, 630 W 5th St, Los Angeles, 90071. Joan Bartel, Principal Librn
Notes: Annual reports in hard copy of corporations traded on the New York, American, OTC, and Pacific Exchanges, are received on a current basis. All are retained for 5 years; S&P 500 companies and some western companies indefinitely. Annual reports and 10-Ks for New York American Stock Exchange corporations are available in microfiche, 1970-1976. Beginning with 1977, 10-K reports for all US publicly traded corporations are collected. Beginning in 1980, annual reports for all US publicly traded companies are collected on microfiche. Standard sources of information on corporations are available, current and retrospective.

CA —UNIVERSITY OF CALIFORNIA, LOS ANGELES, Graduate School of Management Library, UCLA Campus, Los Angeles, 90024. Robert Bellanti, Head Librn
Holdings: Vols (128,000) Cat Mss Microforms
Notes: The UCLA Graduate School of Management Library serves the instructional and research needs of students and faculty in the Graduate School of Management. The collection is broad in scope covering all aspects of business and management; emphasis is placed on in-depth collecting in the Graduate School of Management's core curriculum areas: accounting, behavioral and organizational science, business economics, computers and information science, production and operations management, public/not-for-profit management and urban land economics. The Library receives 2500 current periodical and serial titles and has strong retrospective holdings. The collection of uncataloged hard-copy annual reports of U.S. and foreign corporations numbers over 80,000. The library also holds over 160,000 microforms of annual and 10K reports of U.S. corporations, journals and newspapers. Special collections include the Robert E. Gross collection of Rare Books in Business and Economics (2,500 imprints prior to 1800), the microfilm of the University of London Goldsmiths' Library of Economic Literature and the Harvard Kress Library of Business and Economics of Printed books through 1850, a corporate history collection of over 3000 volumes, and the microfilm Business History Collection (primary source material representing the American economy during the 20th century).

CA —UNIVERSITY OF SOUTHERN CALIFORNIA, Crocker Business Library, Hoffman Hall, University Park, Los Angeles, 90007. Judith A Truelson, Head Librn
Holdings: Vols (100,000) Cat Microforms
Notes: The Roy P Crocker Library of Business Administration, located in Hoffman Hall, houses more than 100,000 volumes and regularly receives approximately 1500 trade, financial, economics, labor, and general business periodicals and newspapers. The areas of subject concentration include business economics, finance and investments, general management/management theory, international business, finance and management, marketing/food marketing, and quantitative business analysis.

CA —ALAMEDA COUNTY LIBRARY SYSTEM, Business & Government Library, 2201 Broadway, Oakland, 94612. David Lewallen, Manager
Holdings: Vols (10,000) Cat Maps Microforms
Budget: ($50,000)

CA —PASADENA PUBLIC LIBRARY, Business-Technology Division, 285 E Walnut St, Pasadena, 91101. Anne Cain, Librn for Reference Services
Holdings: Vols (19,000) Cat Microforms
Budget: ($35,000)
Notes: Investment and financial services (current and historical); trade and industrial directories; corporate annual reports; current economic statistics in business services and in state and federal government publications. Special index to directory collection.

CA —CONTRA COSTA COUNTY LIBRARY, 1750 Oak Park Blvd, Pleasant Hill, 94523. Lyn Talme, Business Specialist
Holdings: Vols (7000)
Notes: Incl 76 periodicals, 1000 corporate annual reports, and 316 telephone directories.

CA –CALIFORNIA STATE POLYTECHNIC UNIVERSITY, POMONA, University Library, 3801 W Temple Ave, Pomona, 91768. Harold Schleiser, Actg Dir
Notes: General reference materials on agricultural business management, agricultural engineering, animal science, horticulture and plant and soil science.

CA —SACRAMENTO PUBLIC LIBRARY, 828 I St, Sacramento, 95814. Dorothy Harvey, Librn, Special Collections
Holdings: Vols (8000) Cat
Budget: ($16,000)
Notes: Incl 800 periodicals and services. Emphasis is on business subjects and economics and labor. Technology not incl. Incl about 1000 corporation reports.

CA —GOLDEN GATE UNIVERSITY, One Embarcadero Center, No 216, San Francisco, 94111. Jeanne Nichols, Librn
Notes: World Trade Libraries and archives.

CA —STANFORD UNIVERSITY, Graduate School of Business, J Hugh Jackson Library, Stanford, 94305.
Holdings: Vols (316,994) Cat Microforms
Budget: ($255,000)
Notes: Incl 590,027 microforms, 300,000 corporate reports, and 2344 periodical subscriptions. Library Publications: *Selected Additions to the J Hugh Jackson Library* (bimonthly); and *Catalog of Jackson Library Periodicals and Annuals on Standing Order* (annual).

CO —UNIVERSITY OF COLORADO, Business Research Div, Travel Reference Center, Boulder, 80309. C R Goeldner, Librn; Karen Duea, Librn
Holdings: Vols (8000) Uncat

CT —AMERICAN CAN CO, Business Information Center, American Lane, Greenwich, 06830. Estelle Adler, Mgr
Holdings: Vols (6000) Cat Microforms

CT —UNIVERSITY OF CONNECTICUT, HARTFORD, School of Business Administration, Library, 39 Woodland St, Hartford, 06105.
Holdings: Vols (17,000) Cat Audiotapes Microforms
Notes: Incl 8 vertical file drawers of pamphlets, etc; 60 of annual reports.

CT —YALE UNIVERSITY, Social Science Library, 140 Prospect St, New Haven, 06520. Billie I Salter, Librn
Holdings: Vols (40,000) Cat Microforms
See also entry under Social Sciences.

CT —STAMFORD'S PUBLIC LIBRARY, Ferguson Library, Adult Services Dept, 96 Broad St, Stamford, 06901. Ernest A DiMattia Jr, Dir; Doris Goodlett, Head Adult Servs
Holdings: Vols (29,500) Cat

DC —AMERICAN SOCIETY OF ASSOCIATION EXECUTIVES, Information Central, 1575 Eye St NW, Washington, 20005. Cathy L Lalush, Mgr of Research and Info
Notes: Information regarding association management. Resources are designed to provide the association executive with the background knowledge for management decisions through case studies, research and statistical reports, bibliographies, and articles.

DC —EXPORT-IMPORT BANK OF THE UNITED STATES, EXIMBANK Library, 811 Vermont Ave NW, Washington, 20571. Theodora McGill, Librn; John Posniak, Asst Librn
Holdings: Vols (15,000) Maps Audiotapes
Notes: The library has almost a complete set of the Economist Intelligence unit of London's *Quarterly Economic Reviews*; various types of materials with general, economic and statistical data on virtually every country of the world; incl foreign government publications, publications of various international organizations, and US Government documents.

FL —MIAMI-DADE PUBLIC LIBRARY SYSTEM, Miami Public Library, One Biscayne Blvd, Miami, 33132. Edward

BUSINESS (cont.)

Oswald, Business Librn
Holdings: Vols 12,000 Cat
Notes: Incl 300 journals, on-line reference searching, import-export statistics and international business materials.

GA —ATLANTA PUBLIC LIBRARY, Ivan Allen Jr Dept of Science, Industry & Government, One Margaret Mitchell Square, Atlanta, 30303. William D Munro, Head
Holdings: Vols (15,000) Cat Microforms
Budget: ($180,000)
Notes: This colletion incl on microfiche annual reports and Securities Exchange Commission 10-K reports for some 11,000 companies from 1976 to date; current and retrospective stock quotations, stock reports, corporate and industry records and directories and supporting looseleaf services; information file on Atlanta's largest 15,000 with annual updates; and current plat maps for the five county Metro-Atlanta area. Atlanta and Georgia business history sections are being developed. Most material in this collection is noncirculating.

HI —BANK OF HAWAII, Information Ctr, PO Box 2900, Honolulu, 96846. Sally Campbell, Information Mgr
Holdings: Vols 4000 Cat Maps
Notes: Economics research in developing areas of Hawaii, US Pacific Islands, Asian and other foreign countries. Emphasis on economics, business statistics, demography, finance, banking, tourist industry, construction, domestic and foreign trade. Incl 1000 serial titles.

HI —HAWAII PACIFIC COLLEGE, Meader Library, 1060 Bishop St, Honolulu, 96813. Barbara Burton Hoefler, Head Librn
Holdings: Vols 450 Cat
Notes: The Hawaii Society of Certified Public Accountants has given us a collection of approximately 450 items. This collection has been cataloged and added to the regular collection, but we maintain a separate card catalog drawer with author cards and analytics for the collection. It is a growing collection.

IL —CENTER FOR RESEARCH LIBRARIES, 6050 S Kenwood Ave, Chicago, 60637. Donald B Simpson, Dir; Esther Smith, Collection Development Librn
Holdings: Vols Cat
Notes: Very extensive holdings of older scientific journals, especially in medicine, applied science, technology, industry and trade. Currently 5,000 titles.

IL —CHICAGO PUBLIC LIBRARY, Business/Science/Technology Div, Science/Technology Information Center, 425 North Michigan Ave, Chicago, 60611. Lynda Sanford, Head; John R Moore, Environment Collection Coordinator & Engineering Librn
Holdings: Vols 60,000
Budget: $205,000
Notes: Collection incl all subject areas of business within HB-HJ Library of Congress classifications scheme. Emphases are on current materials in management, careers, investments, and reference. Collection is also strong in labor history. 2200 periodical titles; 60,000 vols monographs.

IL —CONTINENTAL ILLINOIS NATIONAL BANK & TRUST CO OF CHICAGO, Information Services Division, 231 S LaSalle St, Chicago, 60697. Susan J Montgomery, Mgr
Holdings: Vols (27,700) Cat Microforms

IL —FEDERAL RESERVE BANK OF CHICAGO, Library, 230 S La Salle St, PO Box 834, Chicago, 60690. Dorothy Phillips, Librn
Holdings: Vols (19,000) Cat
Notes: Restricted use; noncirculating. No photocopying.

IL —ILLINOIS BELL TELEPHONE CO, Library, 225 W Randolph St, Chicago, 60606. Marguerite J Krynicki, Head Librn
Holdings: Vols (11,000) Cat

IL —MONTGOMERY WARD CORPORATE LIBRARY, One Montgomery Ward Plaza, Chicago, 60671. Barbara J Burnett, Librn
Holdings: Vols (1300) Cat Mss Pix

IL —NORTHWESTERN UNIVERSITY, Joseph Schaffner Library, 339 E Chicago Ave, Chicago, 60611. Dorothy E Olson, Librn
Holdings: Vols 62,300 Cat Microforms
Notes: Plus 2600 microforms; 5100 pamphlets.

IL —NORTHWESTERN UNIVERSITY, Library, 1935 Sheridan Rd, Evanston, 60201. Patricia Bush, Management Librn
Holdings: Vols (43,900) Cat Microforms
Notes: Library has a current and historical collection of 5600 bound vols of corporation annual reports representing coverage of 2500 corporations, primarily industrials. Many date to beginning of the 20th century. Annual reports for 1200 corporations are currently received. Also available since 1973 is a microfiche collection of annual reports to shareholders and 10-K reports of corporations listed on the New York Stock Exchange.

IL —SCHAUMBURG TOWNSHIP PUBLIC LIBRARY, 32 W Library Lane, Schaumburg, 60194. Michael Madden, Librn
Holdings: Vols (20,000) Cat
Budget: ($60,000)
Notes: Maintained as business and economics subject center under the North Suburban Library System's Coordinated Acquisitions Program.

IN —INDIANA UNIVERSITY, Business-School of Public and Environmental Affairs (SPEA), Bloomington, 47405. Michael Parrish, Dir
Holdings: Vols (100,000)
Budget: ($200,000)
Notes: Collection covers all phases of business, public administration and environment.

IN —CUMMINS ENGINE CO, Information Center, 1000 Fifth St, Columbus, 47201. W E Poor, Tech Librn
Holdings: Vols 1800 Cat

IN —MILES LABORATORIES, Library Resources and Services, 1127 Myrtle St, PO Box 40, Elkhart, 46515. Allam Hagopian, Mgr
Holdings: Vols (16,500) Cat Audiotapes Microforms
Notes: Incl files of pharmaceutical product advertising pieces, extensive literature files on company related drugs; domestic and international marketing files. 32,000 bound periodicals.

IN —ELI LILLY AND COMPANY, Business Library, 307 E McCarty St, Indianapolis, 46206. Helen E Loftus, Dept Head
Holdings: Vols 8500 Cat
Notes: No photocopying.

IN —CABOT CORP, Stellite Div, Technical Library, 1020 W Park Ave, Kokomo, 46901. Betty Hollis, Librn
Holdings: Vols (10,000) Cat Slides Microforms
Notes: Emphasis on metallurgy. Incl 12,000 internal technical reports, 4 Lektriever units.

IN —PURDUE UNIVERSITY LIBRARIES, Graduate School of Management, Krannert Library, West Lafayette, 47907. Gordon Law, Librn
Holdings: Vols (142,727) Cat Microforms
Budget: ($69,700)
Notes: There is an extensive collection of corporate reports and labor information material (some 115,000 items). Over 2500 periodicals are currently received.

KY —KENTUCKY WESLEYAN COLLEGE LIBRARY, 3000 Frederica, Owensboro, 42301. Stuart Stiffler, Dir
Notes: The Dr and Mrs M David Orrahood Collection.

LA —ETHYL CORP, Information & Library Services, Gulf States Rd, PO Box 2246, Baton Rouge, 70821. Lois M Skinner, Chemist-Librn
Holdings: Vols (15,000) Cat

†LA —TULANE UNIVERSITY, Graduate School of Business Administration, New Orleans, 70118.

ME —THOMAS COLLEGE, Marriner Library, W River Rd, Waterville, 04901. Richard A Boudreau, Librn
Holdings: Vols 19,064 Cat Microforms
Budget: $24,000

MD —UNIVERSITY OF BALTIMORE, Langsdale Library, 1420 Maryland Ave, Baltimore, 21201. Gerry Watkins, Head of Special Collections Dept
Holdings: Cat Mss Maps
Notes: Incl the entire stock (10,000 vols) of Peter Decker, New York antiquarian bookdealer (acquired in 1970); incl Peter Decker's mss of his published works and his records as a dealer in Americana.

MA —BANK OF NEW ENGLAND, 1 Washington Mall, Boston, 02108. Helen Mavareaf, Librn
Holdings: Vols (4500) Cat Microforms
Budget: ($18,000)
Notes: Annual reports of largest US banks; corporate financial reports on microfiche; Banking School theses from Stonier and Pacific Coast; industry studies.

MA —BOSTON PUBLIC LIBRARY, Kirstein Business Branch, 20 City Hall Ave, Boston, 02108. Joseph E Walsh, Business Branch Librn
Holdings: Vols 42,900 Cat
Notes: City and telephone directories, trade directories, investment manuals and services, law reporting services, trade periodicals and newspapers, government periodicals, periodical indexes, books on all aspects of business incl accounting, advertising, banking, retail and wholesale trade, marketing, real estate, etc. No separate catalog or index to the collection. Also annual reports to stockholders and 10K reports to SEC for all companies listed on NYSE and AMEX.

MA —HARVARD UNIVERSITY, Graduate School of Business Administration, Baker Library, Soldiers Field, Boston, 02163. Mary V Chatfield, Librn; Florence Bartoshesky, Cur of Manuscripts and Archives

MA —RAYTHEON SERVICE CO, Library, Spencer Laboratory, 2 Wayside Rd, Burlington, 01803. Jean C Cameron, Librn
Holdings: Vols (1400) Cat
Notes: Collection emphasizes business and management.

MA —HARVARD UNIVERSITY, Graduate School of Education, Monroe C Gutman Library, 6 Appian Way, Cambridge, 02138. Susan S Baughman, Associate Librn
Holdings: Vols (150,000) Cat Mss Microforms
Budget: ($95,000)
Notes: A comprehensive research collection that seeks to acquire all scholarly works published in the English language in the fields of education, educational administration, educational psychology, and human development. Selective coverage in the related areas of counseling and psychology, business administration, finance, forecasting, statistical analysis and survey design, public and social policy, linguistics, demographics, and international and economic development. Incl 4000 educational and psychological tests.

MA —BOSTON COLLEGE LIBRARIES, Thomas P O'Neill Library, Chestnut Hill, 02167. John D J Slinn, Librn of the Central Library
Holdings: Vols 62,000 Cat Maps Audiotapes Filmstrips Microforms
Budget: ($120,000)

MA —NICHOLS COLLEGE, Conant Library, Dudley, 01570. Cheryl S Nelson, Dir
Holdings: Vols 65,000 Phonorecords Audiotapes Videotapes Films Microforms
Notes: Incl 65,000 books, 1500 microforms, 750 records, 12 films, 120 videotapes, 300 audiotapes.

MA —MASSACHUSETTS MUTUAL LIFE INSURANCE CO, Library, 1295 State St, Springfield, 01111. Yvette Jensen, Librn
Holdings: Vols 350 Cat

MA —WESTERN NEW ENGLAND COLLEGE, Churchill Library, 1215 Wilbraham Rd, Springfield, 01119. Glenn Johnson, Librn
Holdings: Vols 12,000 Cat Phonorecords Audiotapes 16mm Films Microforms

MI —UNIVERSITY OF MICHIGAN, Graduate School of Business Administration, Business Administration Library, Institute for International Commerce Reading Rm, Ann Arbor, 48109. Carol Holbrook, Dir
Holdings: Vols Cat Microforms
Notes: Also incl annual reports and 10k's.

MI —WASHTENAW COMMUNITY COLLEGE, Learning Resource Center, P.O. Box D-1, Ann Arbor, 48106. Adella Scott, Dir

BUSINESS (cont.)

MI —WESTERN MICHIGAN UNIVERSITY, Business Library, N Hall, Kalamazoo, 49008. David H McKee, Head
Holdings: Vols (71,977) Cat Phonorecords Microforms
Notes: Incl 14,570 vols of bound periodicals, 33,041 monographs, 14,605 government documents, 1796 microfilm and 7u965 microfiche/microcards. Large collection of corporate annual reports is separate.

MI —NORTHWOOD INSTITUTE, Strosacker Library, 3225 Cook Rd, Midland, 48640. Catherine Chen, Head Librn
Holdings: Vols 3000 Cat Maps Microforms
Budget: $30,000
Notes: Business and management, incl economics and economic history. Audiovisual materials are located in the Griswold Communications Center.

MI —MONROE COUNTY LIBRARY SYSTEM, Ellis Reference and Information Center, Dorsch Memorial Branch, 18 E First St, Monroe, 48161. Mary Jo Garmire, Head, Dorsch Memorial Branch
Holdings: Vols Periodicals Microforms
Budget: $25,000
Notes: Collection contains 1200 circulating volumes, 200 reference volumes, 95 business periodical and newspaper subscriptions, 710 microfilms and 10,725 microfiche. Annual Reports and 10K Reports for Fortune 500 corporations and local firms as available are included in 18 drawers of vertical file materials on corporations and business related topics. The collection concentrates on investments, finance, small business, mutual funds, stock market information, management, insurance and marketing. *Business Index COM* and *Business Periodicals Index* aid in access to the collection. The library publishes a quarterly newsletter included with the Monroe County Chamber of Commerce mailings to all members highlighting additions to the collection and programs of interest to the local business community. Regularly scheduled speakers, exhibits and other programsrelating to business collection topics encourage use of the collection. MCLS also publishes the Monroe County Industrial Directory in cooperation with the Monroe County Chamber of Commerce.

MN —MINNEAPOLIS PUBLIC LIBRARY & INFORMATION CENTER, Business & Economics Dept, 300 Nicollet Mall, Minneapolis, 55401. Mary Lawson, Librn
Notes: Separate card catalog, telephone reference service, and directory service. Incl periodical titles; large files of corporation annual reports; VF of local company histories and annual reports; domestic and foreign telephone directories; historical US stock quotations, 1891-date; local OTC quotations, 1933-date; indexes and abstracting services; looseleaf reference services.

MN —JAMES JEROME HILL REFERENCE LIBRARY, Fourth St at Market St, Saint Paul, 55106. Virgil F Massman, Dir
Holdings: Vols 60,000 Cat
Budget: ($170,000)
Notes: A good standard collection of books by standard authors.

MN —SAINT PAUL PUBLIC LIBRARY, Science and Industry Room, 90 W Fourth St, Saint Paul, 55102. Virginia B Stavn, Supvr
Holdings: Vols 20,000 Cat Microforms Audiotapes
Budget: ($79,500)
Notes: Corporate annual reports and proxy statements of all companies listed on New York and American Stock Exchanges and 6000 OTC companies from 1978-date. 10-K's from 1981-date. Reports of 2500 foreign companies 1980-date. Investment manuals and services.

MO —UNIVERSITY OF MISSOURI-KANSAS CITY, General Library, 5100 Rockhill Road, Kansas City, 64110. Kenneth J LaBudde, Dir; Pamela Jenkins, Business Librn
Holdings: Vols 67,500
Notes: Incl many microforms, cataloged. (4121 current serial subscriptions).

MO —WADDELL & REED, INC, Research Library, One Crown Center, PO Box 1343, Kansas City, 64141. Betty J Howerton, Head Librn
Holdings: Vols (45,000) Cat Microforms
Budget: ($10,000)
Notes: Annual and Interim Reports; Wall Street Journal Stock Quotes.

MO —SAINT LOUIS PUBLIC LIBRARY, Humanities & Social Science Dept, 1301 Olive Blvd, Saint Louis, 63103. Edna J Reinhold, Librn
Holdings: Vols 16,000 Cat

NH —DARTMOUTH COLLEGE, Feldberg Business & Engineering Library, Hanover, 03755. Phyllis E Jaynes, Librn
Holdings: Vols 35,000 Cat Microforms
Budget: $42,000
Notes: Largely current materials. 12 serial titles.

NH —NEW HAMPSHIRE COLLEGE, Harry A B and Gertrude C Shapiro Library, 2500 N River Rd, Manchester, 03104. Richard Pantano, Dir
Holdings: Vols (66,000) Cat Maps Slides Audiotapes Videotapes 16mm Films Filmstrips Microforms
Budget: ($133,173)
Notes: Library is a selective US Government Documents depository, and New Hampshire State Documents depository. Subscribe to microfiche SEC 10K reports to AMEX and NYSE (1975-), as well as AMEX and NYSE company annual reports (1977-); AICPA publications and cassettes. Strong collections in accounting; business; business education; computers; hotel and restaurant management; and social service.

NJ —TRENTON FREE PUBLIC LIBRARY, Business & Technology Dept, 120 Academy St, Trenton, 08608. Richard D Rebecca, Principal Librn
Holdings: Vols (9000) Cat Microforms
Notes: Books, vertical files, annual reports on paper and microfiche, government documents related to dept on paper and fiche. Incl 400 telephone directories. Interlibrary Loan (photocopies) available.

NY —BROOKLYN PUBLIC LIBRARY, Business Library, 280 Cadman Plaza W, Brooklyn, 11201. Sylvia Mechanic, Business Librn
Holdings: Vols (107,000) Cat
Notes: Library received about 1800 periodicals, 3000 serials, 2700 directories, 1600 telephone books from all over the world with a complete back file on microfilm for greater New York. Library is a selective US Government Documents depository. Subscribes to microfiche SEC 10K reports for AMEX, NYSE and OTC from 1976 to date; annual reports for earlier years. Transnational annual reports, on fiche from 1982-to date. 78 vertical file trays; Sanborn maps for Brooklyn, special collection of corporation histories. Publish monthly newsletter, *Service to Business and Industry* with our Science Division.

NY —BUFFALO & ERIE COUNTY PUBLIC LIBRARY, Business and Labor Dept, Lafayette Sq, Buffalo, 14203. Joyce Davoli, Dept Head
Holdings: Vols (62,000) Cat
Notes: Incl bound periodicals; 41 drawers VF materials; US government depository, active microfiche collection of annual reports of companies listed on the American and New York Stock Exchanges. Also, New York State Data Center Affiliate for US Census; depository for mortgage disclosure statistics for Erie and Niagara Counties.

NY —CORNELL UNIVERSITY LIBRARIES, Graduate School of Management, Malott Hall, Ithaca, 14853. Betsy Ann Olive, Librn
Holdings: Vols (135,000) Cat Microforms
Budget: ($130,000)

NY —BERNARD M BARUCH COLLEGE (CUNY), Library, 156 E 25 St, New York, 10010. Alan Weiner, Head of Reference

NY —COLUMBIA UNIVERSITY LIBRARIES, Thomas J Watson Library of Business & Economics, Box 130, Uris Hall, New York, 10027. Jane E Winland, Librn
Holdings: Vols 340,000 Microforms
Notes: The Marvin Scudder Financial Collection (corporation reports). Research material and documents pertaining to the financial histories of over one-half million corporations, domestic and foreign, for a period from 1821 to date. Incl annual reports, proxy statements, prospectuses, listing statements, brokerage house reports. Special catalog for the collection is by name of corporation only. Annual reports of listed corporations are in microform from 1951 or year of listing (if later) to the present. This collection is not open to the public unless they apply for library privileges through the Information Office in Butler Library, Room 234.

NY —CONFERENCE BOARD, Information Service Library, 845 Third Ave, New York, 10022. Tamsen M Hernandez, Dir
Holdings: Vols 25,000 Cat Microforms
Notes: Heavily directed to collection of government materials and corporate data.

NY —INTERNATIONAL PAPER CO, Corporate Information Center, 77 W 45 St, New York, 10036. Elizabeth Skerritt, Corporate Librn
Holdings: Vols 1570 Cat Maps Pix Slides Audiotapes Microforms
Notes: Extensive statistics and VF on paper industry.

NY —MUTUAL LIFE INSURANCE CO OF NEW YORK, Corporate Library, 1740 Broadway, New York, 10028. Marion Koshar, Librn
Holdings: Vols (6000) Cat Periodicals Microforms
Notes: Incl Mutual's company history and archives; over 200 periodical titles.

NY —NEW YORK PUBLIC LIBRARY, Research Libraries, Economic & Public Affairs Div, Fifth Ave & 42 St, New York, 10018. Edward DiRoma, Chief
Holdings: Vols (1,500,000) Cat Microforms
Notes: Strong collection on national and international level.

NY —NEW YORK PUBLIC LIBRARY, Mid-Manhattan Library, Science & Business Dept, 455 Fifth Ave, New York, 10016. Frederick E Dusold, Sr Principal Librn
Holdings: Vols (31,000) Cat Audiotapes Microforms
Budget: ($55,000)
Notes: Undergraduate level collection with duplicate reference and circulating copies of books. 80 drawers of pamphlet material. Standard business and financial services. 560 periodicals.

NY —NEW YORK PUBLIC LIBRARY, Research Libraries, General Research Div, Fifth Ave & 42 St, New York, 10018. Keith McKinney, Assistant Div Chief
Holdings: Cat
Notes: Current periodicals. Subjects incl advertising, business and professional periodicals, international affairs, labor and trade unions, political and social sciences, humanities in general. Division holds 10,000 titles.

NY —RESEARCH INSTITUTE OF AMERICA, Editorial Library, 589 Fifth Ave, New York, 10017. Jamie Russell, Librn
Holdings: Vols 3500
Notes: Not open to public.

NY —STANDARD & POOR'S CORP, Library, 25 Broadway, New York, 10004. Walter Nixon, Ref Librn
Holdings: Vols (22,000) Cat Microforms
Notes: Library has 800,000 microforms.

†NY —TECHNICAL CAREER INSTITUTE LIBRARY, 320 W 31st Street, New York, 10001. Michael Brent, Librn
Holdings: Vols (3500)

NY —UNIVERSITY OF ROCHESTER, Graduate School of Management Library, Rush Rhees Library, Rochester, 14627. Edward Wass; Janet Prentice; Datta Kharbas
Holdings: Vols (108,000) Cat Microforms
Budget: ($84,500)
Notes: Incl a reference collection, a geographical file on economic conditions, an industry file of statistics and trends, research reports and working papers, more than 2600 hardcopy annual reports. Several microfiche or microcard Collections of Corporate reports dating from the 1950s to the present and over 900 management and economics periodicals.

NY —GENERAL ELECTRIC CO, Main Library, One River Rd, Schenectady, 12345. Julia Hewitt, Mgr
Holdings: Vols (56,000) Cat

BUSINESS (cont.)

NY —ELIZABETH SETON COLLEGE LIBRARY, Yonkers, 10701. Sr Margaret Sullivan, Librn

NC —GREENSBORO PUBLIC LIBRARY, Business Library, 201 Greene St, Drawer X-4, Greensboro, 27402. Lebby B Lamb, Business Librn
Holdings: Vols 8000 Cat Microforms
Budget: $15,000

NC —TECHNICAL INSTITUTE OF ALAMANCE, Learning Resources Center, Jimmy Kerr Rd, PO Box 623, Haw River, 27258. Ron Plummer, Coordr
Holdings: Vols (1025) Cat Pix Audiotapes Filmstrips Microforms
Notes: Accounting, banking & finance, business administration.

NC —WAKE TECHNICAL COLLEGE, Library, Audio-Visual Dept, 9101 Fayetteville Road, Raleigh, 27603. James Gray, Librn; Horst Garloff, Audio-Visual Specialist
Holdings: Vols (32,332) Cat Maps Slides Phonorecords Audiotapes Videotapes 16mm Films Filmstrips Microforms

OH —AKRON-SUMMIT COUNTY PUBLIC LIBRARY, Business, Labor & Government Div, 55 S Main St, Akron, 44326. William G Johnson, Head
Holdings: Vols (10,000) Cat Microforms
Budget: ($20,000)

OH —PUBLIC LIBRARY OF CINCINNATI & HAMILTON COUNTY, Government and Business Dept, 800 Vine St, Cincinnati, 45202. Paul T Hudson, Head
Holdings: Vols 120,000 Cat
Notes: Department receives over 1200 periodical and loose-leaf service titles, 1500 serial titles and over 1500 telephone directories. Subjects include political science, especially foreign relations, economics, law, public administration and business management. Dept houses Murray Seasongood collection of local government. Dept has extensive census material from 1790. Library is a full depository for US Government Publications, 1884 to date.

OH —ALCAN ALUMINUM CORP, Library, 100 Erieview Plaza, Cleveland, 44114. Winifred B Bowes, Librn
Holdings: Vols 3000 Cat

OH —CLEVELAND PUBLIC LIBRARY, Business, Economics and Labor Department, 325 Superior Ave, Cleveland, 44114. Joan Sorger, Head
Holdings: Vols (115,703) Cat
Notes: Currently receiving over 1700 periodicals and 1300 serial titles; 1000 individual trade, industrial and professional directories, worldwide; 324 file drawers annual reports of old companies, many local; 24 drawers historical information on Cleveland companies. Annual reports, 10-K's, Proxy Statements (disclosure SEC filings on fiche); over 200 loose-leaf services; 1700 current telephone and city directories. Emphasis on current material. Areas of special strength are banking, investments, marketing and management. Also strong insurance, accounting, real estate and transportation collections. Computerized sources available incl Dow Jones News Service and a variety of Dialog business-related databases.

PA —DREXEL UNIVERSITY LIBRARIES, W W Hagerty Library, 32 & Chestnut Sts, Philadelphia, 19104. R L Snyder, Dir
Holdings: Vols (66,500) Cat Microforms
Budget: ($82,000)
Notes: Incl 25,000 microforms of annual reports of companies traded on the NYSE and ASE.

PA —FREE LIBRARY OF PHILADELPHIA, Mercantile Library, 1021 Chestnut St, Philadelphia, 19107. James B Woy, Librn
Holdings: Vols 47,000 Cat Maps Microforms
Budget: $50,000

PA —LIBRARY COMPANY OF PHILADELPHIA, 1314 Locust St, Philadelphia, 19107. Edwin Wolf II, Librn; Kenneth Finkel, Cur of Prints
Holdings: Vols (400,000) Cat Maps Pix
Budget: ($25,000)
Notes: American science and industry before 1860. Books, pamphlets, etc on science incl math, pysics, astronomy, and industry, incl business and engineering. Incl many 18th century books printed in England and France but used by American colonials in their study and research. Impossible to estimate the exact size of collection since it is not separated from general collection.

PA —UNIVERSITY OF PENNSYLVANIA, Lippincott Library of the Wharton School, Philadelphia, 19104. Michael Halperin, Librn
Holdings: Vols 188,217 Cat Microforms
Budget: ($135,152)
Notes: Espec source material and statistical data.

PA —CARNEGIE LIBRARY OF PITTSBURGH, Science & Technology Dept, 4400 Forbes Ave, Pittsburgh, 15213. Catherine M Brosky, Dept Head
Notes: About 25,000 trade catalogs emphasizing American business and industry with a few foreign ones.

PA —UNIVERSITY OF PITTSBURGH, Graduate School of Business Library, 138 Mervis Hall, Pittsburgh, 15260. Susan Neuman, Head Librn
Holdings: Vols (36,000) Cat Microforms
Budget: ($40,000)
Notes: Incl material to support graduate programs in business administration, as well as faculty research. Reflects strongly the interest of business in the behavioral, social and international aspects of management. 19, 000 microfiche cards, 1000 microfilm reels.

PA —SCRANTON PUBLIC LIBRARY, Vine & N Washington Sts, Scranton, 18503. Thomas McHale, Dir
Holdings: Vols (975) Cat
Budget: ($6000)

†RI —UNIVERSITY OF RHODE ISLAND, Library, Kingston, 02881.
Notes: Extensive collections.

RI —BRYANT COLLEGE, Edith M Hodgson Memorial Library, Rte 7, Douglas Pike, Smithfield, 02917. John P Hannon, Dir
Holdings: Vols (103,000) Cat Phonorecords Audiotapes Videotapes 16mm Films Filmstripts Microforms
Budget: $50,000
Notes: Incl 6000 bound periodical vols, 250 phonorecords, 220 audiotapes, 120 videotapes, 30 16mm films, 150 filmstrips and 7500 microforms.

SC —HORRY GEORGETOWN TECHNICAL COLLEGE, Library, Hwy 501, Box 1966, Conway, 29526. Barbara Brittain, Librn
Holdings: Vols (20,000) Cat Maps Slides Microforms

SC —SUMTER TECHNICAL COLLEGE, Library, 506 Guignard Dr, Sumter, 29150. Fanny M Davis
Holdings: Vols (20,000) Cat Mss Maps Pix Slides Microforms
Budget: ($500,000)
Notes: Incl 293 books on business.

SD —MINUTEMAN GRADUATE CENTER LIBRARY, RR 3, Box 3050, Rapid City, 57701. Laura K Dickson, Librn
Holdings: Vols (8000) Cat Microforms
Budget: ($11,000)
Notes: Library mainly for use of Air Force officers and civilians enrolled in the Minuteman Education Program (MMEP), Ellsworth Air Force Base, SD. Limited public use. Interlibrary loans permitted.

TX —SOUTHWESTERN PUBLIC SERVICE CO, Library, PO Box 1261, Amarillo, 79170. Gloria Branham, Librn
Holdings: Vols (2500) Cat 16mm Films

TX —UNIVERSITY OF TEXAS LIBRARIES, General Libraries, PO Box P, Austin, 78713. Carolyn Bucknell, Asst Dir for Collection Development
Holdings: Cat Microforms

TX —NORTHWOOD INSTITUTE, Library, Box 58, Cedar Hill, 75104. Jennifer Cope, Librn
Holdings: Vols 1000 Cat Slides Audiotapes Videotapes 16mm Films Filmstrips
Budget: $5000

TX —SOUTHERN UNION CO, Library, Inter-First II, Suite 1800, Dallas, 75270. Charles Woodard, Research Librn
Holdings: Vols (100) Cat
Notes: Incl periodicals (43 subscriptions), and annual reports (1500).

TX —FORT WORTH PUBLIC LIBRARY, 300 Taylor St, Fort Worth, 76102. John R McCracken, Manager
Holdings: Vols 6000 Cat
Budget: $29,550
Notes: Business, incl business services.

TX —ECTOR COUNTY LIBRARY, Department of Business and Technology, 321 W 5th St, Odessa, 79760. Pat Jones, Dept Head
Holdings: Vols 2000 Cat
Notes: 25,000 Corporate Annual Reports microfilmed reports are complete from 1978-1983. 200 vertical files, 30 periodicals. Collection includes the subjects of Business, Management, Real Estate Accounting, Land Economics, Labor Economics, Finance, Personal Finance and Environmental Economics. Also included are stock and dividend reports, commodities and bond reports as well as business rankings. All items are referenced and cataloged.

TX —UNITED SERVICES AUTOMOBILE ASSOCIATION, Library, USAA Bldg, San Antonio, 78288. Fran Day, Librn
Holdings: Vols (3600) Cat
Notes: Principally property and casualty insurance. 300 subscriptions.

TX —SOUTHWEST TEXAS STATE UNIVERSITY, Library, San Marcos, 78666. Bob Harris, Special Collections Librn
Holdings: / / Uncat
Notes: American textbooks to 1918. Liberal arts, education, business.

VT —NATIONAL LIFE INSURANCE CO LIBRARY, Montpelier, 05602. Saba L Foster, Chief Librn
Holdings: Vols (6250) Cat Mss Maps Pix
Budget: ($58,100)
Notes: Includes general reference, business, and government documents.

WA —SEATTLE PUBLIC LIBRARY, 1000 Fourth Ave, Seattle, 98104. Ronald A Dubberly, City Librn
Holdings: Cat

WA —UNIVERSITY OF WASHINGTON LIBRARIES, Business Administration Library, DJ-10, Seattle, 98195. Anne B Passarelli, Head
Holdings: Vols (41,500) Cat
Budget: ($101,500)

WI —BLACKHAWK TECHNICAL INSTITUTE, PO Box 5009, 6004 Prairie Rd, Janesville, 53547. Grace M Sweeney, Libn
Holdings: Vols 10,000
Budget: $1800

WI —MILWAUKEE PUBLIC LIBRARY, 814 W Wisconsin Ave, Milwaukee, 53233. Donald J Sager, City Librn
Holdings: Vols (13,456) Cat
Notes: Incl over 1600 periodicals and serial titles and more than 100 abstracting and indexing services in major fields of business, science, and technology. Strong general reference.

WY —US AIR FORCE INSTITUTE OF TECHNOLOGY, Library, Dept 9 Bldg 831, FE, Warren AFB, 82001. Patricia A Johnson, Librn
Holdings: Vols (7000) Cat Microforms
Budget: ($9000)
Notes: The Library supports graduate programs for students (Air Force Missile-Combat Crewmen) seeking a Master of Business Administration Degree. Civilian students and other military personnel are also admitted.

BC —VANCOUVER PUBLIC LIBRARY, Business and Economics Div, 750 Burrard St, Vancouver, V6Z 1X5, Can. Barbara Bell, Librn
Notes: Incl numerous special files for *Quick Reference, Subject Clippings, Companies* (information of major Canadian, US and international corporations; index to new British Columbia and Canadian company corporations, 1951 to 1978; 160,000 cards); company file, *Province Index* and *Association File* (particulars of Canadian trade and professional associations). *International Collection of Trade* directories and telephone books.

MB —UNIVERSITY OF MANITOBA, Faculty of Administrative Studies, Administrative Studies Library, Winnipeg,

BUSINESS (cont.)

R3T 2N2; Can. Judith Head, Librn
Holdings: Vols (15,000) Cat Microfiche
Notes: Incl 11,000 microfiche, cataloged; annual reports of 800 companies.

ON —QUEEN'S UNIVERSITY, Douglas Library, Kingston, K7L 5C4, Can. William F E Morley, Cur, Special Collections
Holdings: Mss Maps Pix
Notes: About 3500 linear feet of mss materials with special emphasis on families and businesses of eastern Ontario; Presbyterian Church; Canadian politics and public affairs, university and city of Kingston records, literary figures.

ON —MACLEAN HUNTER LIBRARY, Maclean Hunter Bldg, 777 Day St, Toronto, M5W 1A7, Can. Theresa Butcher, Librn
Holdings: Vols 1500 Cat Pix
Notes: Mainly a resource for the journalists of the *Financial Post,* Canada's foremost financial paper. The library is basically made up of vertical files divided into (1) general subject files, (2) Canadian public companies, (3) biographical (mainly photographic). The *Financial Post* (weekly) is completely clipped. The Toronto *Globe and Mail* (daily) and other Canadian publications are selectively clipped. In addition, the library houses all Maclean-Hunter publications (over 80 and constantly growing). The *Financial Post* is indexed by the library staff.

ON —METROPOLITAN TORONTO LIBRARY, Business Dept, 789 Yonge St, Toronto, M4W 2G8, Can. Patricia Dye, Head
Holdings: Vols (63,682) Cat Microforms
Budget: ($508,800)
Notes: Economics and business management. Concentration on small businesses. Extensive current and historical information on Canadian corporations. Collection of domestic and international trade directories. Statistics collection. Approximately 1000 current periodicals and up-dating services. "A Focus on Business and Finance Libraries," in Special Libraries Association, Business and Finance Division, *BFD Newsletter,* no 44, Winter 1977, 99 13-15.

ON —TORONTO DOMINION BANK, Department of Economic Research, 55 King St W, Toronto, M5K 1A2, Can. Ruth P Smith, Librn
Holdings: Vols (6000) Cat

ON —WILFRID LAURIER UNIVERSITY, Library, (Formerly Waterloo Lutheran University), 75 University Ave W, Waterloo, N2L 3C5, Can. Erich R W Schultz, Librn
Holdings: Vols 37,000 Cat Microforms
Budget: $63,400

BUSINESS—BIOGRAPHY

DE —HAGLEY MUSEUM AND LIBRARY, Eleutherian Mills-Hagley Foundation Inc, PO Box 3630, Greenville, 19807. Richmond D Williams, Dir; Heddy A Richter, Imprints Librn
Holdings: Vols 25,000 Pamphlets Mss
Notes: 20,000 cubic feet of mss and archives. Our very strong collection documents American business history with a special emphasis on the development of the Mid-Atlantic region. Book and ms collections are especially strong in the chemical, iron and steel, leather, railway, coal, and petroleum industries from 1830 to 1950.

MA —HARVARD UNIVERSITY, Graduate School of Business Administration, Baker Library, Soldiers Field, Boston, 02163. Mary V Chatfield, Librn; Florence Bartoshesky, Cur of Manuscripts and Archives
Holdings: Vols (75,000) Cat Mss Pix
Notes: Baker Library strong in historical aspects of business and economics incl original company records, company histories, business biographies, histories of industries, etc; 16,000 pictures. Ms collection of more than 75,000 incl original records of business firms from 1400 (Medici Collection) to present; especially strong in 19th century. New England enterprises, textile firms, international trade, China trade, railroads, papers of several Northeast merchant families, 19th century small business. Also incl pictures, trade cards, clipper ship cards, money, trade catalogs, business cartoons, prices current and exhibit items. See Robert W Lovett and Eleanor C Bishop, compilers, *Business Manuscripts in Baker Library* (Boston: The Library, 1978), 382 pp. Mss are described in the*National Union Catlog of Manuscript Collections* and in Hamer's *A Guide to Archives and Manuscripts in the United States.* Restricted use: Manuscripts noncirculating. Downs: 1636, 2122, 2616, 2675, 2677, 2698, 2700, 2701, 2702, 2706, 2708, 2711, 2713-15, 2716, 2717-18, 2721-26, 2734, 2737, 2774, 2814, 4300, 5162: Supplement 964, 965, 968, 998.

BUSINESS—DIRECTORIES

NY —BROOKLYN PUBLIC LIBRARY, Business Library, 280 Cadman Plaza W, Brooklyn, 11201. Sylvia Mechanic, Business Librn
Holdings: Vols (107,000) Cat
Notes: Library received about 1800 periodicals, 3000 serials, 2700 directories, 1600 telephone books from all over the world with a complete back file on microfilm for greater New York. Library is a selective US Government Documents depository. Subscribes to microfiche SEC 10K reports for AMEX, NYSE and OTC from 1976 to date; annual reports for earlier years. Transnational annual reports, on fiche from 1982-to date. 78 vertical file trays; Sanborn maps for Brooklyn, special collection of corporation histories. Publish monthly newsletter, *Service to Business and Industry* with our Science Division.

PA —UNIVERSITY OF PENNSYLVANIA, Lippincott Library of the Wharton School, Philadelphia, 19104. Michael Halperin, Librn
Holdings: Cat Microforms
Notes: All major US business directories of large firms. Industrial directories for most states, incl many state export directories. International export, import and industrial directories, as well as many country industrial directories. Industrial directories for many specific US industries.

ON —METROPOLITAN TORONTO LIBRARY, Business Dept, 789 Yonge St, Toronto, M4W 2G8, Can. Patricia Dye, Head
Holdings: Vols (63,682) Cat Microforms
Budget: ($508,800)
Notes: Extensive current and historical information with emphasis on Canadian companies incl annual reports, clippings and pamphlets files, and a collection of business and trade directories. Also international directories. Approximately 1000 current periodicals, and up-dating services giving corporation information.

BUSINESS—HISTORY

CA —UNIVERSITY OF SOUTHERN CALIFORNIA, Crocker Business Library, Hoffman Hall, University Park, Los Angeles, 90007. Judith A Truelson, Head Librn
Holdings: Vols (100,000) Cat Microforms
Notes: The Roy P Crocker Library of Business Administration, located in Hoffman Hall, houses more than 100,000 volumes and regularly receives approximately 1500 trade, financial, economics, labor, and general business periodicals and newspapers. The areas of subject concentration include business economics, finance and investments, general management/management theory, international business, finance and management, marketing/food marketing, and quantitative business analysis.

CA —POMONA PUBLIC LIBRARY, Special Collections, 625 S Garey Ave, PO Box 2271, Pomona, 91766. David Streeter, Librn
Holdings: Uncat Mss
Notes: 165 linear feet of Pomona Valley business records incl 16 water companies and 28 citrus companies; diaries; clubs and organizations; Laura Ingalls Wilder.

CA —CALIFORNIA HISTORICAL SOCIETY, Schubert Hall Library, 2099 Pacific Ave, San Francisco, 94109. Bruce L Johnson, Library Dir
Holdings: Vols (50,000) Cat Mss Maps Pix
See also entry under California - History.

CA —STANFORD UNIVERSITY, Graduate School of Business, J Hugh Jackson Library, Stanford, 94305.
Holdings: Vols (316,994) Cat Microforms
Budget: ($255,000)
Notes: Incl 590,027 microforms, 300,000 corporate reports, and 2344 periodical subscriptions. Library Publications: *Selected Additions to the J Hugh Jackson Library* (bimonthly); and *Catalog of Jackson Library Periodicals and Annuals on Standing Order* (annual).

CO —COLORADO HISTORICAL SOCIETY, Research Collections, 1300 Broadway, Denver, 80203. Catherine Kane, Head Public Service and Access
Holdings: Mss
Budget:
Notes: Strong ms holdings in western and Colorado business history in such areas as mining, water, transportation, sugar industry.

DE —HAGLEY MUSEUM AND LIBRARY, Eleutherian Mills-Hagley Foundation Inc, PO Box 3630, Greenville, 19807. Richmond D Williams, Dir; Heddy A Richter, Imprints Librn
Holdings: Vols 25,000 Pamphlets Mss
Notes: Our very strong collection documents American business history, with a special emphasis on the development of the Mid-Atlantic region. Book and ms collections are especially strong in the chemical, iron and steel, leather, railway, coal and petroleum industries from 1830 to 1950. Incl 20,000 cubic feet of mss and archives.

DC —SMITHSONIAN INSTITUTION LIBRARIES, Business & Industry Collections, Washington, 20560.
Notes: The Warshaw Collection of illustrative materials.

HI —BERNICE P BISHOP MUSEUM, Library, PO Box 19000-A, Honolulu, 96819. Cynthia Timberlake, Librn
Holdings: Vols (90,000) Cat Mss Maps Pix Slides Microforms
Budget: ($30,000)
Notes: Only American library devoted exclusively to the Pacific region. Collection reflects historical and contemporary research emphases of Bishop Museum; ie the natural and cultural history of the Pacific. Areas of concentration incl archaeology, ethnology, linguistics, voyages and explorations, history, vertebrate and invertebrate zoology, botany and museology. Strong special collections incl photographs, mss and archives, maps and art. Publications: Quarterly "Additions to the Catalog," *Dictionary Catalog of the* Library (9 vols and 2 suppl; Boston: G K Hall, 1964-69).

IL —CHICAGO HISTORICAL SOCIETY, Library, Clark St at North Ave, Chicago, 60614. Archie Motley, Manuscript Librn
Notes: Twentieth century business holdings incl these papers: Better Business Bureau of Metropolitan Chicago; George S Bowen (wool merchant, utilities company president, mayor of Elgin); the Bowen family; Chicago Rock Island and Pacific Railway Company; Chicago Surface Lines (papers of the CLS and predecessor Chicago and surburban street railway companies); Chicago Underwriters Association; George Dillwyn Cook (banker, industrialist, President Mexican Mineral Railroad Co); Charles Hull Ewing (real estate and investment executive); Goldenberg Furniture Co, Chicago; Gottlieb and Schwartz (Chicago law firm, Harry N Gottlieb and Charles K Schwartz); Lake Michigan Mortgage Co, Chicago; Thomas Leeming (attorney, member of Chicago law firm Eckert, Peterson and Leeming); Levi Z Leiter Estate (Joseph Leiter, executor) and Levi Z Leiter (merchant, real estate investor, Chicago civic and philanthropic leader); Sterling Morton (industrialist, philanthropist, teletype company executive, Chairman of the Board Morton Salt Co); Morton family (Sterling Morton, Joy Morton, and other Morton family men and women; industrialists, government officials and philanthropists); Potter Palmer Estate and Potter Palmer (merchant, real estate

BUSINESS—HISTORY (cont.)

investor, Chicago civic leader) and his wife Bertha Honore Palmer (Chicago socialite, civic leader, President Board of Lady Managers World's Columbian Exposition); Holman D Pettibone (Chicago Title and Trust Co); Henry S Robbins (attorney, counsel for the Chicago Board of Trade); Arthur Rubloff (chairman Arthur Rubloff & Co, Chicago, international realtors, Chicago civic leader); John Calvin Welling (Illinois Central Railroad executive); John PaulWelling; the Welling family (real estate and other investments).

IL —NORTHERN ILLINOIS REGIONAL HISTORY CENTER, Sven Parson Hall, Northern Illinois University, De Kalb, 60115. Glen Gildemeister, Dir
Holdings: Cat Mss Maps Pix Slides Phonorecords Audiotapes 16mm Films Microforms
Notes: "A research center for advanced research in the humanities. This northern area of Illinois (excluding Cook County) has been virtually untouched by collecting agencies and we hope to fill that void. We will be strong in agribusiness, agricultural implement business, and hybrid farming mechanics....Will be primarily a ms repository, but [have] already taken responsibility for many artifacts and books, some rare."

IN —PURDUE UNIVERSITY LIBRARIES, Graduate School of Management, Krannert Library, West Lafayette, 47907. Gordon Law, Librn
Holdings: Vols (7000) Cat Mss Maps Pix Microforms
Notes: The collection consists of books, journals and pamphlets dating from the early 16th to late 19th century, covering to a large degree the early literature in economic thought and business practices both here and abroad. No photocopying.

MA —HARVARD UNIVERSITY, Baker Library of the Graduate School of Business Administration, Kress Library of Business and Economics, Soldiers Field, Boston, 02163. Ruth E Rogers, Cur
Holdings: Vols 32,000 Cat Mss Microforms
Notes: Four volumes of catalog have been published (1940-1967). For description see *Business History Review,* XXXIV (1960), 474-494; *Harvard Library Notes,* III (1940), 316-319, and *Kress Library Publication,* No 1 (1939); also *Harvard Business School* Bulletin, Feb 1982. Scope of library is business and economics prior to 1850.

MA —HARVARD UNIVERSITY, Graduate School of Business Administration, Baker Library, Soldiers Field, Boston, 02163. Mary V Chatfield, Librn; Florence Bartoshesky, Cur of Manuscripts and Archives
Holdings: Vols (75,000) Cat Mss Pix
Notes: Baker Library strong in historical aspects of business and economics incl original company records, company histories, business biographies, histories of industries, etc; 16,000 pictures. Ms collection of more than 75,000 incl original records of business firms from 1400 (Medici Collection) to present; especially strong in 19th century. New England enterprises, textile firms, international trade, China trade, railroads, papers of several Northeast merchant families, 19th century small business. Also incl pictures, trade cards, clipper ship cards, money, trade catalogs, business cartoons, prices current and exhibit items. See Robert W Lovett and Eleanor C Bishop, compilers, *Business Manuscripts in Baker Library* (Boston: The Library, 1978), 382 pp. Mss are described in the*National Union Catlog of Manuscript Collections* and in Hamer's *A Guide to Archives and Manuscripts in the United States.* Restricted use: Manuscripts noncirculating. Downs: 1636, 2122, 2616, 2675, 2677, 2698, 2700, 2701, 2702, 2706, 2708, 2711, 2713-15, 2716, 2717-18, 2721-26, 2734, 2737, 2774, 2814, 4300, 5162: Supplement 964, 965, 968, 998.

MA —STONEHILL COLLEGE, Donahue Hall, Washington St, North Easton, 02356. Louise M Kenneally, Archivist & Special Collections Librn
Notes: The Arnold B Tofias Industrial Archives; 2000 linear feet of records and correspondence of the Ames Shovel Company of North Easton, Mass. About 800 shovels and other artifacts. Covers the period 1774-1956.

MO —WASHINGTON UNIVERSITY, John M Olin Library, Lindell & Skinker Blvd, Saint Louis, 63130. Beryl H Manne, Archivist
Holdings: Mss Pix Audiotapes 16mm Films Filmstrips Microforms
Notes: The University Archives and Research collection at the John M Olin Library of Washington University is a growing ms archives collecting original source material pertaining to 20th century political, business, and social welfare history of the St Louis metropolitan area. Incl the personal papers of prominent St Louis politicians, businessmen, engineers, educators, scientists, architects. Holdings especially strong in municipal and county governmental affairs.

NJ —NEW JERSEY HISTORICAL SOCIETY, Library and Museum, 230 Broadway, Newark, 07104. Joan C Hull, Exec Dir; Barbara S Irwin, Library Dir; Alan R Fraser, Cur
Holdings: Mss
Budget: ($100,000)
Notes: For mss materials, see Morris & Skemer, *Guide to the Manuscript Collections of the New Jersey Historical* Society, 1979. Incl annual reports, trade catalogs, printed materials, manuscripts.

NJ —H M BAKER ASSOCIATES, Research Collection, 266 E Dudley Ave, Westfield, 07090. Helen Baker Cushman, Managing Associate
Holdings: Vols 5000 Cat Mss Maps Pix Slides Periodicals
Notes: Baker Associates publishes *The Business History Letter,* The Anniversary Manual, "Remember the Year," business histories and anniversary studies which are based on the contents of the collection. Emphasis of the collection is on industrial and business history.

NY —SAINT JOHN'S UNIVERSITY, Special Collections Dept, Grand Central & Utopia Pkwys, Jamaica, 11439. Szilvia E Szmuk, Librn
Holdings: Vols 160 // Cat
Notes: The Joseph C Myer Collection consists of books, issues of journals, and ledgers from the early 16th through the early 20th century. A very large part of the collection is 17th and 18th century French, English, and German titles on methods of bookkeeping and business practices. Many of these volumes are in fine and unusual bindings which have been recently restored. No photocopying.

NY —NEW YORK PUBLIC LIBRARY, Research Libraries, Economic & Public Affairs Div, Fifth Ave & 42 St, New York, 10018. Edward DiRoma, Chief
Holdings: Vols (1,500,000) Cat Microforms

OK —UNIVERSITY OF OKLAHOMA, Bizzell Memorial Library, Bass Collection in Business History, 401 W Brooks, Norman, 73069. Daniel Wren, Cur
Holdings: Vols 18,862 Cat Pix

PA —AMERICAN PHILOSOPHICAL SOCIETY, Library, 105 S Fifth St, Philadelphia, 19106. Edward C Carter II, Librn
Holdings: // Microforms
Notes: 650 reels of microfilm of the papers of Stephen Girard.

PA —TEMPLE UNIVERSITY LIBRARIES, Special Collections Dept, Rare Books & Mss Section, Philadelphia, 19122. Thomas M Whitehead, Cur
Holdings: Vols 500 Cat Mss
Notes: Extensive collection of printed books and mss, 900 AD-1900 AD; Cochran History of Business Collection. Original documents, ledgers, contracts, business letters, indentures, statutes, etc. Emphasis on Italy, 13th-17th centuries. Partial listings and descriptions published in the *Temple University Library Bulletin,* 1950-1963. Catalog in preparation.

PA —FRIENDS HISTORICAL LIBRARY OF SWARTHMORE COLLEGE, Swarthmore, 19081. J William Frost, Dir
Holdings: Vols (35,000) Cat Mss Pix Microforms
Notes: Library's collection contain information on the history and doctrine of the Society of Friends, Quaker contributions to literature, science, business, education, and government, plus their reform efforts in peace, Indian rights, women's rights, and abolition of slavery. Incl in the more than 250 mss collections are account books and correspondence of artisans and merchants. Of particular significance are the personal papers of the industrialist Joseph Wharton.

TX —DALLAS PUBLIC LIBRARY, Central Research Library, Business & Technology Div, 1515 Young St, Dallas, 75201. Sarabeth Allen, Mgr
Holdings: Vols 6000 Cat
Budget: $2500
Notes: *Business History Collection; a* Checklist. Dallas, Texas: Business and Technology Div, Dallas Public Library, 1974. Published to serve as a subject (by corporate name) catalog. Interlibrary loans are invited.

TX —SOUTHERN METHODIST UNIVERSITY, DeGolyer Library, Box 396, SMU, Dallas, 75275. Clifton H Jones, Dir
Holdings: Vols (80,000) Cat Mss Maps Pix Slides Microforms
Notes: First editions of prominent authors; also of books in subject emphasis collections. All subjects listed in this vol are strong. Numerous collections of personal papers relating to subjects also.

TX —NORTH TEXAS STATE UNIVERSITY, Archives, NT Station Box 5188, Denton, 76203. Robert LaForte, University Archivist
Notes: The Business Archive Project conducts interviews with business and labor leaders to preserve records of business enterprises which have contributed to economic growth in Texas. The Oral History Collection provides administrative and technical assistance and houses the original tapes and transcripts. Incl interviews with Mary K Ash (Mary Kay Cosmetics), Frank Cuellar, Sr (El Chico Corporation), Bettie C Graham (Liquid Paper Corp), Cecil H Green (Texas Instruments), C B and Jerry Owens (Owens Country Sausage), and others. In 1980 incl over 4000 pages of transcripts.

†WA —WASHINGTON STATE UNIVERSITY, Library, Manuscripts, Archives & Special Collections, Pullman, 99164. John F Guido, Head
Holdings: Cat Mss Maps Pix
Notes: The ms collection incl business and financial records of banks, breweries, insurance, land, lumber and livestock companies, trade and commodity associations; as well as the personal and professional papers of authors, aviators, educators, engineers, farmers, historians, pioneers, politicians, and scientists; especially rich in documents relating to the exploration, settlement and development of the Palouse Country, the Inland Empire, the Columbia Basin and the Pacific Northwest. Described in *Selected Manuscript Resources in the Washington State University Library* (Pullman, 1974); and other published and unpublished inventories and registers.

SK —UNIVERSITY OF SASKATCHEWAN, Library, Saskatoon, S7N 0W0, Can. S Perkins, Librn
Notes: Extensive microfiche collection of annual reports of Ontario-registered (1967-) and federally-registered companies. Some pre-1967 annual reports (papercopy). Complete set of *Annual Financial Review* Canadian, Houstons Standard Publications, 1901-1941.

BUSINESS—PICTURES, ILLUSTRATIONS, ETC.

DC —SMITHSONIAN INSTITUTION LIBRARIES, Business & Industry Collections, Washington, 20560.
Notes: The Warshaw Collection of illustrative materials.

BUSINESS—REPORTS

MA —HARVARD UNIVERSITY, Graduate School of Business Administration, Baker Library, Soldiers Field, Boston, 02163. Mary V Chatfield, Librn; Florence Bartoshesky, Cur of Manuscripts and Archives
Notes: Corporate reports; company annual reports, both domestic and foreign; SEC filings; material dates from 19th century forward.

MI —MONROE COUNTY LIBRARY SYSTEM, Ellis Reference and Information Center, Dorsch Memorial Branch, 18 E First St, Monroe, 48161. Mary Jo Garmire, Head, Dorsch Memorial Branch
Holdings: Vols Periodicals Microforms
Budget: $25,000
Notes: Collection contains 1200 circulating volumes, 200 reference volumes, 95 business periodical and newspaper subscriptions, 710 microfilms and 10,725 microfiche. Annual Reports and 10K Reports for Fortune 500 corporations and local firms as available are included in 18 drawers of vertical file materials on corporations and business related topics. The collection concentrates on investments, finance, small business, mutual funds, stock market information, management, insurance and marketing. *Business Index COM* and *Business Periodicals Index* aid in access to the collection. The library publishes a quarterly newsletter included with the Monroe County Chamber of Commerce mailings to all members highlighting additions to the collection and programs of interest to the local business community. Regularly scheduled speakers, exhibits and other programsrelating to business collection topics encourage use of the collection. MCLS also publishes the Monroe County Industrial Directory in cooperation with the Monroe County Chamber of Commerce.

BUSINESS—STATISTICS

DC —US BUREAU OF THE CENSUS, Library, Federal Office Bldg 3, Rm 2451, Washington, 20233. Betty Baxtresser, Chief, ASD Library Branch
Holdings: Cat Microforms
Notes: Emphases on statistics of agriculture, business, construction, economics, foreign trade, governments, housing, industry, population, transportation, statistical methodology, and data processing. Library holdings are largely current materials covering the Bureau's programs. Outdated materials are withdrawn regularly.

NY —NEW YORK PUBLIC LIBRARY, Research Libraries, Economic & Public Affairs Div, Fifth Ave & 42 St, New York, 10018. Edward DiRoma, Chief
Holdings: Vols (1,500,000) Cat Microforms
Notes: Statistical publications from US and foreign countries.

ON —METROPOLITAN TORONTO LIBRARY, Business Dept, 789 Yonge St, Toronto, M4W 2G8, Can. Patricia Dye, Head
Holdings: Vols (63,682) Cat Microforms
Budget: ($508,800)
Notes: Extensive current and historical information with emphasis on Canadian companies incl annual reports, clippings and pamphlets files, and a collection of business and trade directories. Also international directories. Approximately 1000 current periodicals, and up-dating services giving corporation information.

BUSINESS—STUDY AND TEACHING see Business Education

BUSINESS, CHOICE OF see Vocational Guidance

BUSINESS, WOMEN IN see Women in Business

BUSINESS ADMINISTRATION see Business

BUSINESS CARDS see Advertising Cards

BUSINESS CORPORATIONS see Corporations

BUSINESS CYCLES

IN —PURDUE UNIVERSITY LIBRARIES, Graduate School of Management, Krannert Library, West Lafayette, 47907. Gordon Law, Librn
Holdings: Vols (142,727) Cat Microforms
Budget: ($69,700)
Notes: There is an extensive collection of corporate reports and labor information material (some 115,000 items). Over 2500 periodicals are currently received.

BUSINESS EDUCATION

NH —NEW HAMPSHIRE COLLEGE, Harry A B and Gertrude C Shapiro Library, 2500 N River Rd, Manchester, 03104. Richard Pantano, Dir
Holdings: Vols (66,000) Cat Maps Slides Audiotapes Videotapes 16mm Films Filmstrips Microforms
Budget: ($133,173)
Notes: Library is a selective US Government Documents depository, and New Hampshire State Documents depository. Subscribe to microfiche SEC 10K reports to AMEX and NYSE (1975-), as well as AMEX and NYSE company annual reports (1977-); AICPA publications and cassettes. Strong collections in accounting; business; business education; computers; hotel and restaurant management; and social service.

RI —BRYANT COLLEGE, Edith M Hodgson Memorial Library, Rte 7, Douglas Pike, Smithfield, 02917. John P Hannon, Dir
Holdings: Vols (82,000) / / Cat Phonorecords Audiotapes Videotapes 16mm Films Filmstrips Microforms
Budget: $50,000
Notes: Incl 6000 bound periodical vols, 250 phonorecords, 220 audiotapes, 120 videotapes, 30 16mm films, 150 filmstrips and 7500 microforms.

BUSINESS EDUCATION—HISTORY

IL —NEWBERRY LIBRARY, John M Wing Foundation on the History of Printing, 60 W Walton St, Chicago, 60610. Diana Haskell, Cur of Modern Mss
Holdings: Cat Mss Pix
Budget: $800
Notes: Incl writing speciman books and about 7000 ms pieces on American handwriting, espec the Spencerian hand, and the history of business schools.

BUSINESS ENTERPRISES, FOREIGN

MA —HARVARD UNIVERSITY, Graduate School of Business Administration, Baker Library, Soldiers Field, Boston, 02163. Mary V Chatfield, Librn; Florence Bartoshesky, Cur of Manuscripts and Archives
Notes: International business enterprises.

MI —UNIVERSITY OF MICHIGAN, Graduate School of Business Administration, Business Administration Library, Institute for International Commerce Reading Rm, Ann Arbor, 48109. Carol Holbrook, Dir
Holdings: Cat
Notes: International business.

BUSINESS ENTERPRISES, INTERNATIONAL see International Business Enterprises

BUSINESS LAW

AL —UNIVERSITY OF ALABAMA, Business Library, Box 2937, University, 35486. Dorothy Eady Brown, Librn; Linda Suttle Harris, Ref Librn and Data Base Searcher
Holdings: Vols (105,000) Cat Microforms
Budget: ($60,000)
Notes: Incl 90,000 corporation reports and 38,500 microforms.

CA —UNIVERSITY OF CALIFORNIA, DAVIS, Law Library, Davis, 95616. Mortimer D Schwartz, Librn
Holdings: Vols (225,000) Cat
Budget: ($211,177)

MI —WAYNE STATE UNIVERSITY, Arthur Neef Law Library, Detroit, 48202. Georgia Clark, Law Librn
Holdings: Vols (165,587) Cat Microforms

BUSINESS LOSSES

CT —HARTFORD INSURANCE GROUP, Loss Control Dept Library, Hartford Plaza, Hartford, 06115. Laurice Klemarczyk, Librn

BUSINESS NAMES

NY —TOBACCO MERCHANTS ASSOCIATION OF THE US, Howard S Cullman Library, Suite 705, 1220 Broadway, New York, 10001. R Robert Sengstacken, Dir Information Servs
Holdings: Vols (3000)
Notes: Tobacco Industry. Trademark and brand files for tobacco products and smoker's articles. Incl 150 subscriptions, 30 VF.

BUSINESS NEWSPAPERS see Newspapers, Business

BUSINESS PSYCHOLOGY see Psychology, Industrial

BUSINESS RESEARCH see Economic Research

BUSINESS TEACHERS

RI —BRYANT COLLEGE, Edith M Hodgson Memorial Library, Rte 7, Douglas Pike, Smithfield, 02917. John P Hannon, Dir
Holdings: Vols (103,000) Cat Phonorecords Audiotapes Videotapes 16mm Films Filmstrips Microforms
Budget: ($175,000)
Notes: Incl 6000 bound periodical vols, 250 phonorecords, 220 audiotapes, 120 videotapes, 30 16mm films, 150 filmstrips and 7500 microforms.

BUSINESSWOMEN see Women in Business

BUSTERUD, JOHN A.

CA —HOOVER INSTITUTION ON WAR, REVOLUTION & PEACE, Stanford University, Stanford, 94305. Milorad M Drachkovitch, Archivist
Holdings: Mss
Notes: Papers of John A Busterud, US attorney and public official, Deputy Assistant Secretary of Defense for Environmental Quality, 1971-72, Chairman of the Council on Environmental Quality, Executive Office of the President, 1972-77, incl correspondence, speeches and writings, memoranda, reports, studies, printed matter, and other material, 1972-77, relating to his government service in the US and to international and domestic energy and environmental programs. 22 ms boxes.

BUTCHART, HARVEY

AZ —NORTHERN ARIZONA UNIVERSITY, Special Collection Library, CU Box 6022, Flagstaff, 86011. Peter M Whiteley, Coordr/Archivist; William Mullane, Librn
Notes: Harvey Butchart, Grand Canyon hiker and explorer, former NAU professor; photography of "Grand Canyon Trail Notes, 1957-1969."

BUTLER, ALGERNON LEE

NC —UNIVERSITY OF NORTH CAROLINA, CHAPEL HILL, Louis Round Wilson Academic Affairs Library, Southern Historical Collection, Chapel Hill, 27514. Carolyn Wallace, Librn
Notes: The papers of Algernon Lee Butler, former judge of the United States Court for the Eastern District of North Carolina (1959-1975).

BUTLER, MICHAEL

MA —BOSTON UNIVERSITY, Mugar Memorial Library, Special Collections Dept, 771 Commonwealth Ave, Boston, 02215. Howard B Gotlieb, Dir
Holdings: Cat Mss Pix
Notes: Mss, correspondence, etc collected in depth, incl publications by or about. Incl scripts, scores, correspondence, publicity, and other material relative to the history of "Hair".

BUTLER, NICHOLAS MURRAY

NY —COLUMBIA UNIVERSITY LIBRARIES, Rare Book & Manuscript Library, 801 Butler Library, 535 W 114 St, New York, 10027. Kenneth A Lohf, Librn
Holdings: Mss
Notes: Correspondence, private papers and memorabilia. Incl 360,000 items. Restricted use.

BUTLER, PIERCE

IL —NEWBERRY LIBRARY, John M Wing Foundation on the History of Printing, 60 W Walton St, Chicago, 60610. Diana Haskell, Cur of Modern Mss
Holdings: Vols (30,000) Cat Mss
Budget: ($50,000)
Notes: The collection covers printing and printing history of Western Europe and the Americas from its invention to the present. It is particularly rich in incunabula (about 2000); the works of the great printers, among others Aldus, Bodoni, Baskerville, and Rogers. Printed catalog: *A Dictionary* Catalogue. (Boston: G K Hall, 1961); *Supplements* (1981). Its first custodian was Pierce Butler, who established the basic collecting policy. Brief descriptions: James M Wells, "The John M Wing Foundation of the Newberry Library," *The Book Collector,* VIII 2 (Summer 1959), pp 157-162; Lawrence W Towner, *An Uncommon Collection of Uncommon Collections* (Chicago: The Newberry Library, 1977), pp 25-26.

BUTLER, PIERCE (LIBRARIAN)

CT —LEE ASH, (personal collection), 66 Humiston Dr, Bethany, 06525.
Notes: Material by and about him.

BUTLER, SAMUEL, 1835-1902

CA —CLAREMONT COLLEGES, Honnold Library, Ninth & Dartmouth, Claremont, 91711. Tania Rizzo, Special Collections Dept Head
Holdings: Vols 87 / / Cat
Notes: First editions of all of Butler's books and music; many pamphlets, leaflets, cards, and tracts. Typed bibliography by Paul Jordan-Smith, donor. Restricted use.

†MA —WILLIAMS COLLEGE, Chapin Library of Rare Books, PO Box 426, Williamstown, 01267. Robert L Volz, Custodian
Holdings: Vols 200 Cat Mss Pix
Notes: Incl 150 mss, approx 1000 pictures and glass photographic negatives. No material available on interlibrary loan.

BUTLER, WILLIS P.

LA —LOUISIANA STATE UNIVERSITY, SHREVEPORT, Library-Archives, 8515 Youree Dr, Shreveport, 71129. Patricia L Meador, Archivist & Asst Librn
Notes: Archives incl catalogued manuscripts and records, 500 maps, more than 5000 photographs, 1000 architectural drawings, slides. The collection's primary emphasis is the history of North Louisiana, particularly Northwest Louisiana. The 1500 linear ft incl area plantation records and ledgers; personal papers of area pioneers, planters, legislators, politicians, educators, businessmen, and architects; papers and records of longtime (1919-1961) Caddo Parish Coroner, Willis P Butler; the Samuel G Wiener, Sr architectural records (1921-1976) with drawings and photographs; the Ted Flaxman architectural records (1919-1968); the papers (1860-1921) of architect Nathaniel S Allen; the collection of Dewey A Somdal,Shreveport architect, historian and collector, with emphasis on steamboats, travel on the Red River and Louisiana history, 1780-1972.

BUTLERS see Servants

BUTOR, MICHEL

MO —SOUTHWEST MISSOURI STATE UNIVERSITY, Duane G Meyer Library, 901 S National, Box 175, Springfield, 65804. Robert D Harvey, Dir
Holdings: Cat Mss
Notes: Materials by and about Michel Butor. 810 items, incl letters, clippings, articles, programs, etc.

BUTTERFLIES AND MOTHS

†CT —UNIVERSITY OF CONNECTICUT LIBRARY, Special Collections Dept, Storrs, 06268. Richard H Schimmelpfeng, Dir of Special Collections

DC —SMITHSONIAN INSTITUTION LIBRARIES, Entomology Branch, Washington, 20560. Jean C Smith, Asst Dir for Bureau Services
Holdings: Vols (17,000) Cat Maps Pix

MA —AMHERST COLLEGE, Library, Amherst, 01002. John Lancaster, Special Collections Librn
Holdings: Vols 1402 Cat Maps Pix

MI —MICHIGAN STATE UNIVERSITY, Libraries, Special Collections Div, East Lansing, 48824. Jannette Fiore, Librn
Holdings: Vols 40 Cat
Notes: Works before 1850.

NY —AMERICAN MUSEUM OF NATURAL HISTORY, Library Services Dept, Central Park W & 79th St, New York, 10024. Nina J Root, Chairwoman; Mary Genett, Asst Librn for Reference Services
Holdings: Vols (385,000) Cat Mss Maps Pix Slides Microforms
Notes: Nearly all collections are outstanding for depth of coverage and international range. Early and historic works, rare books, colored illustrations, and relevant serial publications supplement the modern scientific publications necessary to the researchers of the scientific staff and the work of the educational division. Open to the public.

†TX —UNIVERSITY OF TEXAS LIBRARIES, General Libraries, Humanities Research Center, PO Box 7219, Austin, 78712. John Chalmers, Librn
Notes: A collection of the works of Vladimir Nabokov. Contains almost 500 items, incl his English and Russian language books, translations, periodicals and publications about him. Also incl some of his entomological writings. Nabokov was an authority on certain species of butterflies.

NS —NOVA SCOTIA MUSEUM, Library, 1747 Summer St, Halifax, B3H 3A6, Can. M S Whiteside, Librn
Holdings: Vols 800 Cat
Notes: Emphasis on Lepidoptera.

BUTZ, EARL L.

IN —PURDUE UNIVERSITY LIBRARIES, Special Collections Dept, West Lafayette, 47907. Keith Dowden, Asst Dir, Special Collections
Notes: Papers of Earl L Butz relating to his service as Secretary of Agriculture under Presidents Nixon and Ford (1971-76).

BUYERS' GUIDES see Consumer Education

BUZKASHI

WV —SALEM COLLEGE, Library, Salem, 26426. Myron J Smith, Jr, Librn
Notes: Collection supports "the most complete equestrian studies program available anywhere." *Myron J Smith, Equestrian Studies:* the Salem College (Bibliographical) Guide to Sources in English, 1950-1980. Metuchen, NJ: Scarecrow Press, 1981; 4645 entries.

BYE, GEORGE T.

NY —COLUMBIA UNIVERSITY LIBRARIES, Rare Book & Manuscript Library, 801 Butler Library, 535 W 114 St, New York, 10027. Kenneth A Lohf, Librn
Holdings: Mss
Notes: Publications and papers, by and about, predecessor of and absorbed by the literary agency of James Oliver Brown. Restricted use.

BYELORUSSIA—HISTORY

DC —WOODROW WILSON INTERNATIONAL CENTER FOR SCHOLARS, Kennan Institute for Advanced Russian Studies, 1000 Jefferson Dr SW, Washington, 20560. V David Zdenek, Librn
Holdings: Vols 50
Notes: Incl materials on Russians, Ukrainians, Byelorussians, and on other Soviet republics.

NJ —BYELORUSSIAN INSTITUTE OF ARTS AND SCIENCES, INC, 230 Springfield Ave, Rutherford, 07070.
Holdings: Vols 2000 Mss
Notes: Incl Byelorussian art, pictures, and music on types.

BYELORUSSIAN LANGUAGE AND LITERATURE

NJ —BYELORUSSIAN INSTITUTE OF ARTS AND SCIENCES, INC, 230 Springfield Ave, Rutherford, 07070.
Holdings: Vols 4000

NY —NEW YORK PUBLIC LIBRARY, Slavonic Div, Fifth Ave & 42 St, New York, 10018. Edward Kasinec, Chief
Holdings: Vols 2260 Cat Microforms
Budget: ($62,153)
Notes: Subject strength is in literature, incl the literature of the early 20th century. Linguistics and folklore are also well represented. The collection of early Byelorussian newspapers is quite strong. See New York Public Library, *Dictionary Catalog of the Slavonic Collection* (Boston: G K Hall, 1974), 44 vols.

OH —CLEVELAND PUBLIC LIBRARY, Foreign Literature Dept, 325 Superior Ave, Cleveland, 44114. Natalia Bezugloff, Head
Holdings: Vols 600 Cat
Notes: A popular circulating collection containing classics and the standard works with emphasis on belles lettres, history and biography. A variety of other subjects such as learning languages, children's books, spoken phonodiscs, etc.
See also entry under Foreign Language Collections

BYELORUSSIAN MUSIC see Music, Byelorussian

BYELORUSSIANS IN THE U.S.

MN —UNIVERSITY OF MINNESOTA, Immigration History Research Center, 826 Berry St, Saint Paul, 55114. Susan Griegs, Cur
Holdings: Vols (35,000) Mss Maps Pix Phonorecords Audiotapes 16mm Films Microforms
See also entry under US - Emigration and Immigration

NJ —BYELORUSSIAN INSTITUTE OF ARTS AND SCIENCES, INC, 230 Springfield Ave, Rutherford, 07070.
Holdings: Vols 2000 Mss
Notes: Incl Byelorussian art, pictures, and music on types.

BYERS, BETTINA

ON —METROPOLITAN TORONTO LIBRARY, Theatre Dept, 789 Yonge St, Toronto, M4W 2G8, Can. Heather McCallum, Head
Notes: Theatre Department is one of eleven subject departments of the Metropolitan Toronto Library, which is generally acknowledged to be the most comprehensive of Canadian public library collections. The collection balances book and nonbook material in all areas of the performing arts. Production history is the special emphasis of the dance collection, as it is for all the material in the Theatre Department. This is supported by the department's extensive holdings of programs, posters, photographs and press clippings for Canadian productions and dancers, as well as a representative selection of material for non-Canadian dance. Important original stage designs in

BYERS, BETTINA (cont.)

the collection incl work by Mstislav Dobujinsky for the Canadian ballet *Red Ear of Corn,* which was produced by Boris Volkoff in 1949; Maurice Strike's work for the National Ballet of Canada's productionof *Coppelia,* and Desmond Heeley's designs for that company's *Swan Lake.* Ms collections incl: The Boris Volkoff Collection (qv); papers of the Toronto dance teacher Bettina Byers; the papers of two Canadian dance critics, Ralph Hicklin and John Fraser; and the Mary Wigman Collection, consisting of xerox copies of letters exchanged between Miss Wigman and her Canadian pupil Judy Jarvis, and a taped conversation with Miss Wigman.

BYERS, CLOVIS E., 1899-1973

CA —HOOVER INSTITUTION ON WAR, REVOLUTION & PEACE, Stanford University, Stanford, 94305. Milorad M Drachkovitch, Archivist
Holdings: Mss
Notes: Papers of Lt Gen Clovis E Byers, 1917-1961, incl correspondence, memoranda, diaries, speeches and writings, clippings, personnel records, and audiovisual matter, relating to his military career in the Pacific theater during World War II, in the army of occupation in Japan, in the Korean War, and in the North Atlantic Treaty Organization (NATO) command in Europe. 40 ms boxes.

BYERS, WILLIAM NEWTON

CO —DENVER PUBLIC LIBRARY, 1357 Broadway, Denver, 80203.
Notes: Correspondence, papers, pictures, diaries, etc.

BYFIELD, BARBARA NINDE

MA —BOSTON UNIVERSITY, Mugar Memorial Library, Special Collections Dept, 771 Commonwealth Ave, Boston, 02215. Howard B Gotlieb, Dir
Holdings: Mss

BYNNER, WITTER, 1881-1968

CA —FRANCIS BACON LIBRARY, 655 N Dartmouth Ave, Claremont, 91711. Elizabeth S Wrigley, Dir
Holdings: Mss Pix
Notes: Arensberg's miscellaneous correspondence with American literary figures (1920's-50's) including Bruce Bliven, Catherine Drinker Bowen, Kay Boyle, Witter Bynner, Edwin Corle, Helen A Keller, Lysander Kemp, Kenneth Macgowan, John Macy, Henry Miller, Lewis Mumford, Clifford Odets, Kenneth Patchen, Irving Stone, and William Carlos Williams.

CA —UNIVERSITY OF CALIFORNIA, LOS ANGELES, Research Library, Dept of Special Collections, 405 Hilgard Ave, Los Angeles, 90024. Edward Shreeves, Chairman, Bibliographers Group; David S Zeidberg, Head
Holdings: Vols 30
Notes: Incl 600 letters, mostly photocopies.

IN —INDIANA UNIVERSITY, Lilly Library, Seventh St, Bloomington, 47405. William R Cagle, Librn
Notes: Writings by author Witter Bynner.

BYNUM, BEN

TX —NORTH TEXAS STATE UNIVERSITY, Archives, NT Station Box 5188, Denton, 76203. Robert LaForte, University Archivist
Notes: Part of Oral History Collection. Interviews 1971-1975 with member of Texas legislature.

BY-PRODUCTS see Waste Products

BYRD, HARRY FLOOD

VA —UNIVERSITY OF VIRGINIA, Alderman Library, Manuscripts Dept, Charlottesville, 22901. Edmund Berkeley Jr, Cur
Holdings: Cat Mss Pix
Notes: The papers of Virginia Senator Harry Flood Byrd, Sr, comprising material from 1916 to 1966, incl extensive correspondence (business and political), memoranda, documents, reports and other material accumulated while Senator Byrd served in the Virginia senate, as governor, and as US Senator.
See also entry under U.S. Congress.

BYRD, WILLIAM

MA —HARVARD UNIVERSITY LIBRARY, Widener Library, Cambridge, 02138.
Holdings: Cat Mss
Notes: See *Harvard Library Bulletin,* XIV (1960), 343-365.

BYRNE, BARRY

IL —CHICAGO HISTORICAL SOCIETY, Library, Clark St at North Ave, Chicago, 60614. Archie Motley, Manuscript Librn
Notes: Chicago Architectural Archive contains the papers of Chicago architects Barry Byrne and Earl H Reed, the records of the Illinois Society of Architects, and the voluminous files of two leading Chicago architectural firms, Holabird & Root and Harry M Weese and Associates. Access to these collections is by arrangement with Frank Jewell, The Society's Curator of Architectural Collections.

BYRNE, DONN

CA —HUNTINGTON LIBRARY, Art Gallery & Botanical Gardens, 1151 Oxford Rd, San Marino, 91108. Robert L Middlekauff, Dir; Daniel H Woodward, Librn

†CA —STANFORD UNIVERSITY LIBRARIES, Stanford, 94305.
Notes: In collection of English and American Literature.

DC —LIBRARY OF CONGRESS, Washington, 20540.

†MA —BOSTON PUBLIC LIBRARY, Copley Sq, Boston, 02117.

MA —HARVARD UNIVERSITY LIBRARY, Cambridge, 02138.

NH —DARTMOUTH COLLEGE, Baker Memorial Library, Hanover, 03755.

NY —NEW YORK PUBLIC LIBRARY, Fifth Ave & 42 St, New York, 10018.

†TX —UNIVERSITY OF TEXAS LIBRARIES, General Libraries, Humanities Research Center, PO Box 7219, Austin, 78712. John Chalmers, Librn
Notes: Incl his papers, etc, and correspondence with publishers, writers, and other literary figures.

VA —UNIVERSITY OF VIRGINIA, Alderman Library, Charlottesville, 22901.

BYRNES, JAMES F., 1882-1972

SC —CLEMSON UNIVERSITY, Libraries, Clemson, 29631. Michael F Kohl, Head of Special Collections
Holdings: / / Cat Mss Pix
Notes: James F Byrnes Papers. Byrnes served as Congressman, US Senator, US Supreme Court Justice, Director of Office of Economic Stabilization, Director of Office of War Mobilization, US Secretary of State, and Governor of South Carolina. Approximately 95,000 papers have been indexed by name and date. Folder analyses give access to the remainder. Incl approx 183,000 mss items; 300 pictures; 32 scrapbooks; phonograph records and tape recordings; notebooks.

BYRON, GEORGE GORDON, LORD

AZ —UNIVERSITY OF ARIZONA, University Library, Special Collections, Tucson, 85721. Louis A Hieb, Head
Holdings: Vols (7000) Cat Mss Microforms
Budget: ($30,000)
Notes: The major collection of 19th century authors are Byron, Dickens, Scott, Thackeray, Trollope, the Brownings, Stevens, Tennyson, and Wordsworth.

CA —UNIVERSITY OF CALIFORNIA, LOS ANGELES, William Andrews Clark Memorial Library, 2520 Cimarron St, Los Angeles, 90018.
Holdings: Cat Mss
Notes: Extensive collection, first editions, etc.

CA —STANFORD UNIVERSITY LIBRARIES, Cecil H Green Library, Stanford, 94305. Michael T Ryan, Cur
Holdings: Vols (23,000) Cat
Notes: The Charlotte Ashley Felton Memorial Library. Incl first editions.

CT —YALE UNIVERSITY, Box 1603A, Yale Station, New Haven, 06520.
Holdings: Cat Mss

IL —NORTHERN ILLINOIS UNIVERSITY, Founders Memorial Library, Rare Books and Special Collections Dept, De Kalb, 60115. William R DuBois, Dept Head
Holdings: Vols 135 Cat
Notes: Noncirculating.

IN —INDIANA UNIVERSITY, Lilly Library, Seventh St, Bloomington, 47405. William R Cagle, Librn
Holdings: Vols 270 Cat
Notes: First editions, etc of Lord George Gordon Byron.

MD —JOHNS HOPKINS UNIVERSITY, Milton S Eisenhower Library, Charles & 34 Sts, Baltimore, 21218. Ann S Gwyn, Assistant Dir for Special Collections
Holdings: Vols Cat
Notes: Strong in Romantic poets, particularly Byron (Dickey Collection). First editions.

MA —HARVARD UNIVERSITY LIBRARY, Houghton Library, Cambridge, 02138. Rodney G Dennis, Cur of Manuscripts
Holdings: Cat Mss

NC —DUKE UNIVERSITY, William R Perkins Library, Rare Book Room, Durham, 27706. John L Sharpe, III, Cur
Holdings: Vols 200
Notes: Various editions of Byron's works, including many in T J Wise's bibliography, as well as some not included by Wise.

OH —OHIO UNIVERSITY, Vernon R Alden Library, Department of Archives and Special Collections, Athens, 45701. Gary A Hunt, Head
Holdings: Vols (10,191) Uncat Mss
Notes: The Edmund Blunden Collection of Romantic and Modern Literature, being the private library assembled by Blunden during 6 decades of active collecting. The bulk of the collection (6,264 titles) consists of English imprints from the period 1750-1850, concentrating on literature but also incl contemporary works on art, natural history, philosophy and other subjects important for understanding the background of English Romanticism. Among the authors most heavily represented by first and other early editions are: Allington, Barnes, Bloomfield, Byron, Clare, Coleridge, Cowper, Dyer, Edgeworth, Goldsmith, Hazlitt, Hunt, Lamb, Landor, Scott, Thompson and Wordsworth. Books written by Blunden himself, together with his Georgian contemporaries (particularly W H Davies, Walter De la Mare, and Sigfried Sassoon) form a second major area of strength. Many ofthe modern books are inscribed to Blunden, and nearly all the volumes in the collection bear his annotations.

PA —UNIVERSITY OF PENNSYLVANIA, Van Pelt Library, Rare Books Collection, 34 & Walnut Sts, Philadelphia, 19104. Daniel Traister, Special Collections Librn
Holdings: Vols 75 Uncat Mss
Notes: A collection of first editions, ms letters, many unpublished, incl an early Byron will and the sale catalog of his library. See (University of Pennsylvania) *Library* Chronicle, Vol 33, No 1, 1967. Marshall, William H The Byron Collection in Memory of Meyer Davis, Jr.

BYRON, ROBERT

DC —GEORGETOWN UNIVERSITY, Library, Special Collections Div, 37 & O Sts NW, Washington, 20057. George M Barringer, Special Collections Librn; Nicholas B Sheetz, Mss Librn
Holdings: Mss Pix
Notes: The papers of Christopher Sykes,

BYRON, ROBERT (cont.)

biographer, journalist, and novelist; containing mss, letters, photographs, and drawings. With extensive correspondence from Harold Acton; Angela, Countess of Antrim; Sir John Betjeman; Ivy Compton-Burnett; Alick Dru; T S Eliot; Max Beerbohm; Graham Greene; John Hayward; Lord Patrick Kinross; Compton Mackenzie; Nancy Mitford; Anthony Powell; Dame Flora Robson; Cecil Roth; Sir John Russell; Osbert Sitwell; John Sparrow; Freya Stark; James Stern; and Evelyn Waugh, among others. Also, considerable research material about Evelyn Waugh, Adam von Trott, Robert Byron, Lady Nancy Astor; and the foundation of the state of Israel.

BYZANTINE ART see Art, Byzantine

BYZANTINE EMPIRE

DC —HARVARD UNIVERSITY, Dumbarton Oaks, Research Library, 1703 32nd St NW, Washington, 20007. Irene Vaslef, Librn
Holdings: Vols (91,000) Cat Maps Pix Slides Microforms
Budget: ($219,000)
Notes: Byzantine civilization (including art, archaeology, literature, history, religion, law, music, etc). Extensive supplemental material on Classical, Hellenistic, Medieval, Islamic, Medieval Slavic cultures. 62,000 b/w photographs, 25,000 slides and transparencies, 1000 microfilms of books and manuscripts. Printed description of collection in *Harvard Library Bulletin,* vol 19, no 1 (Jan 1971), pp 25-35 and vol 19, no 2 (April 1971), pp 204-214, pp 25-35 and vol 19, no 2 (April 1971), pp 204-214.

NY —STATE UNIVERSITY OF NEW YORK, COLLEGE AT BUFFALO, Lockwood Memorial Library, Main St, Buffalo, 14260. Stanton F Biddle, Assoc Dir
Holdings: Vols 48,000 Cat Pix
Notes: About half of the collection donated by the Orthodox Catholic Alliance of Buffalo, New York. The collection is devoted chiefly to the world of Byzantium in both its secular and religious phases; Greek Patristic literature and its interpretation; and the tradition of the Greek Bible and its antecedents. As support for these subjects the pagan literature of late antiquity is strongly represented, as well as the Hellenistic and Roman background of the East Christian world and its relations with its neighbors in the Near East, in Eastern Europe, and in the Latin West.

OH —UNIVERSITY OF CINCINNATI, Classics Library, 320 Blegen, Cincinnati, 45221. Jean Susorney Wellington, Classics Librn; Eugenia Foster, Modern Greek Cur
Holdings: Vols (110,000) Cat Mss Maps Microforms
Notes: Niove Kyparissiotis. *The Modern Greek Collection in the Library of the University of Cincinnati; a Catalog.* Athens: Hestia Press, for the University of Cincinnati, 1960; also *Catalog of the Modern Greek Collection at the University of* Cincinnati, 5 vols. (Boston; G K Hall, 1978).

PA —UNIVERSITY OF PENNSYLVANIA, Lea Library, 3420 Walnut St, Philadelphia, 19104. Daniel Traister, Special Collections Librn
Holdings: Vols (20,000) Cat Mss
Notes: Collection incl works on Church history, the history of jurisprudence political theory, Byzantine history, the Crusades and medieval urban history. See Downs 4241, 4234.

WA —UNIVERSITY OF WASHINGTON LIBRARIES, Suzzallo Library, Manuscripts Section, FM-25, Seattle, 98195. Karyl Winn, Librn
Notes: More than 600 monographs and serials on Byzantine studies from the library of the late professor Paul Alexander. His Jewish studies collection is included.

BYZANTINE LANGUAGES AND LITERATURES

OH —OHIO STATE UNIVERSITY, William Oxley Thompson Memorial Library, 1858 Neil Ave, Columbus, 43210. A Robert Thorson, Head, Circulation Dept
Holdings: Cat Mss Microforms
Notes: This collection presently contains films of 2000 mss from the Hilandar Monastery, Mt Athos. Expansion will add Byzantine, Bulgarian, Russian and Valachian mss on film.

BYZANTINE RITE (CATHOLIC CHURCH) see Catholic Church—Byzantine Rite

BYZANTINE STUDIES

DC —HARVARD UNIVERSITY, Dumbarton Oaks, Research Library, 1703 32nd St NW, Washington, 20007. Irene Vaslef, Librn
Holdings: Vols (91,000) Cat Maps Pix Slides Microforms
Budget: ($219,000)
Notes: Byzantine civilization (including art, archaeology, literature, history, religion, law, music, etc). Extensive supplemental material on Classical, Hellenistic, Medieval, Islamic, Medieval Slavic cultures. 62,000 b/w photographs, 25,000 slides and transparencies, 1000 microfilms of books and manuscripts. Printed description of collection in *Harvard Library Bulletin,* vol 19, no 1 (Jan 1971), pp 25-35 and vol 19, no 2 (April 1971), pp 204-214, pp 25-35 and vol 19, no 2 (April 1971), pp 204-214.

NY —STATE UNIVERSITY OF NEW YORK, COLLEGE AT BUFFALO, Lockwood Memorial Library, Main St, Buffalo, 14260. Stanton F Biddle, Assoc Dir
Holdings: Vols 48,000 Cat Pix
Notes: About half of the collection donated by the Orthodox Catholic Alliance of Buffalo, New York. The collection is devoted chiefly to the world of Byzantium in both its secular and religious phases; Greek Patristic literature and its interpretation; and the tradition of the Greek Bible and its antecedents. As support for these subjects the pagan literature of late antiquity is strongly represented, as well as the Hellenistic and Roman background of the East Christian world and its relations with its neighbors in the Near East, in Eastern Europe, and in the Latin West.

WA —UNIVERSITY OF WASHINGTON LIBRARIES, Suzzallo Library, Manuscripts Section, FM-25, Seattle, 98195. Karyl Winn, Librn
Notes: More than 600 monographs and serials on Byzantine studies from the library of the late professor Paul Alexander. His Jewish studies collection is included.

C

CABALA

MA —HEBREW COLLEGE, Jacob & Rose Grossman Library and Lawrence Jay & Anne Cable Rubenstein Library, 43 Hawes St, Brookline, 02146. Maurice Tuchman, Librn
Holdings: Vols 600 Cat Mss
Notes: Hassidic and Cabalistic literature.

NY —NEW YORK PUBLIC LIBRARY, Jewish Division, Fifth Ave & 42 St, New York, 10018. Leonard S Gold, Chief
Holdings: Vols (200,000) Cat Mss Microforms
Budget: ($33,383)
Notes: A collection of material in all languages on Judaism, Jewish history, literature and traditions from the earliest times to date and works in the Hebrew alphabet (mainly Hebrew and Yiddish) on a variety of subjects. The division has extensive files of Jewish periodicals and newspapers. The collection of rare Hebraica incl medieval texts, cabalistic works, ethical and philosophical tracts in book form. See *Dictionary Catalog of the Jewish Collection* (Boston: G K Hall, 1960), 14 vols. First Supplement (Boston: G K Hall, 1975), 8 vols.

RI —BROWN UNIVERSITY, John Hay Library, 20 Prospect St, Providence, 02912. Mark N Brown, Cur Mss
Holdings: Vols (900) // Mss
Notes: John William Graham Collection of Literature of Psychic Science--350 predominantly late 19th and early 20th century books dealing with alchemy, black magic, dreams, demonology, church history, mysticism, mediumship, physical and somatic types of psychic experience. Collection described in *Index to Psychic* Science compiled by S R Morgan (Swathmore, 1950). Also, the Damon Collection of Occult and Visionary Literature--550 vols devoted to the development of western mysticism with particular emphasis on American and British thought, incl texts on alchemy, black magic, esoteric church history, dream interpretations, mysticism, witchcraft, the Kabbalah, and visionary testaments and manifestations of all types printed during the 16th to 20th centuries; and the Samuel Wyllys Papers--125 mss, transcripts, and photocopies of legal and government papers relating to Indianaffairs, colonial wars, civil and criminal cases, and the witchcraft trials of 1692-1693. Partially cataloged.

CABARETS see Music Halls (Variety Theatres, Cabarets, Night Clubs, Etc.)

CABBALA see Cabala

CABELL, EARLE

TX —NORTH TEXAS STATE UNIVERSITY, Archives, NT Station Box 5188, Denton, 76203. Robert LaForte, University Archivist
Notes: Part of Oral History Collection. Interviews with dairyman, mayor of Dallas 1961-65, member of US House of Representatives 1965-73.

CABELL, JAMES BRANCH, 1879-1958

CA —UNIVERSITY OF CALIFORNIA, LOS ANGELES, Research Library, Dept of Special Collections, 405 Hilgard Ave, Los Angeles, 90024. Edward Shreeves, Chairman, Bibliographers Group; David S Zeidberg, Head
Holdings: Vols 80 Cat
Notes: Restricted use: scholarly research only.

CA —UNIVERSITY OF CALIFORNIA, SANTA BARBARA, Library, Dept of Special Collections, Santa Barbara, 93106. Christian F Brun, Head
Holdings: Vols 600 Mss Pix
Notes: The John Coulthard Collection.

CT —YALE UNIVERSITY, Box 1603A, Yale Station, New Haven, 06520.
Holdings: Cat Mss

KY —UNIVERSITY OF LOUISVILLE, Ekstrom Library, Rare Books & Special Collections, 2301 S Third St, Louisville, 40208. George T McWhorter, Cur; Delinda Stephens Buie, Asst Cur

MI —UNIVERSITY OF MICHIGAN, Library, Dept of Rare Books & Special Collections, Ann Arbor, 48109. Robert J Starring, Head
Holdings: Vols (170) Cat Ms Audiotapes Microforms
Notes: Many first editions. There are also over 2500 manuscript items, including 7 Cabell holograph letters; the archives of the Cabell Society, chiefly comprising correspondence of donor Julius Rothman, founder of the Society and editor of *The* Cabellian, with Cabell scholars; and the papers of Joe Lee Davis, president of the Cabell Society and advisory editor of *The* Cabellian.

MI —DETROIT PUBLIC LIBRARY, Rare Books Department, 5201 Woodward Ave, Detroit, 48202.
Holdings: Vols 126 Cat Mss
Notes: The Frances Joan Brewer collection, incl Cabell-Brewer correspondence pertaining to the preparation of Mrs Brewer's bibliography of the works of Cabell. Restricted use. Reference collection.

NC —UNIVERSITY OF NORTH CAROLINA, CHAPEL HILL, Wilson Library, Rare Book Collection, Chapel Hill, 27514. Paul S Koda, Cur of Rare Books
Holdings: Cat
Notes: Fully representative collection.

†NC —WAKE FOREST UNIVERSITY, Z Smith Reynolds Library, Box 7777, Reynold Sta, Winston-Salem, 27109. Richard J Murdoch, Rare Book Librn
Holdings: Vols 89 Cat

PA —FREE LIBRARY OF PHILADELPHIA, Rare Book Dept, Logan Sq, Philadelphia, 19103. Marie E Korey, Rare Book Librn
Holdings: Vols (400) Uncat Mss
Notes: The D Jacques Benoliel Collection incl first and important editions, periodicals, autograph letters, biographical and critical reference works.

VA —UNIVERSITY OF VIRGINIA, Alderman Library, Clifton Waller Barrett Collection, Charlottesville, 22901. Joan St C Crane, Cur of American Literature Collections
Holdings: Vols 550 Cat Mss
Notes: Materials by and about him. First editions, 600 manuscripts, etc. No published description (for Barrett Library collection); Rare Book Dept Collection: Matthew J Bruccoli, *Notes on the Cabell Collections at the University of Virginia*, Vol II of Frances J Brewer's *James Branch Cabell: A Bibliography of His Writings, Biography and* Criticism (Charlottesville: University of Virginia Press, 1957).

VA —VIRGINIA COMMONWEALTH UNIVERSITY, James Branch Cabell Library, Richmond, 23284. Daniel Yanchisin, Special Collections Librn
Notes: A collection of materials centered on novelist James Branch Cabell: almost 100 books and pamphlets by Cabell--first editions, revised vols and reprints; 20 books to which he contributed; 22 books in part or completely about him; bound magazines, containing over 225 original stories by Cabell and magazine articles about him; several letters.

VA —COLLEGE OF WILLIAM AND MARY, Earl Gregg Swem Library, Williamsburg, 23185. Margaret C Cook, Cur of Manuscripts & Rare Books
Holdings: Vols 266 // Cat
Notes: First and subsequent editions of James Branch Cabell.

CABELL, JOSEPH CARRINGTON

VA —UNIVERSITY OF VIRGINIA, Alderman Library, Manuscripts Dept, Charlottesville, 22901. Edmund Berkeley Jr, Cur
Holdings: Cat Mss Maps Pix
Notes: 19th century Virginia Family Papers Collections enable a researcher to obtain an excellent picture of the economic and social interactions on large plantations in Virginia during the 19th century. They are invaluable as research sources in the study of slavery, women's history, economic history, agrarian and political history.

CABLE, GEORGE WASHINGTON

LA —TULANE UNIVERSITY, Howard-Tilton Memorial Library, Special Collections Div, 7001 Freret St, New Orleans, 70118. Wilbur E Meneray, Librn
Holdings: Cat Mss Pix
Notes: Correspondence to and from Cable, literary manuscripts and published works.

MA —HARVARD UNIVERSITY LIBRARY, Houghton Library, Cambridge, 02138. Rodney G Dennis, Cur of Manuscripts
Holdings: Cat Mss

OH —BOWLING GREEN STATE UNIVERSITY, Jerome Library, Center for Archival Collections, Bowling Green, 43403. Paul D Yon, Dir; Elaine R Ezell, Reference Archivist; Nancy Steen, Rare Books Librn
Holdings: Vols 88 Cat
Budget: ($3000)
Notes: Various editions and printings of most of Cable's works as well as several volumes of criticism.

VA —UNIVERSITY OF VIRGINIA, Alderman Library, Clifton Waller Barrett Collection, Charlottesville, 22901. Joan St C Crane, Cur of American Literature Collections
Notes: Papers.

CABLE CARS AND RAILROADS see Railroads, Cable Car

CABLES

NJ —AT&T BELL LABORATORIES, Libraries and Information Systems Center, 600 Mountain Ave, Murray Hill, 07974. W D Penniman, Dir
Holdings: Vols (273,100) Cat Mss Audiotapes Videotapes Microforms
Budget: ($670,000)
Notes: Restricted use to AT&T employees. Catalogs/*Indexes*: Bell Laboratories Library Network and Book Serial Catalogs; Bell Laboratories Translations. Bell Laboratories Library Network with New Jersey libraries located in Holmdel, Murray Hill, Piscataway, Whippany, Princeton, Short Hills, Summit, West Long Branch, Crawford Hill; libraries also in Allentown, Pennsylvania; Reading, Pennsylvania; New York, New York; Atlanta, Georgia; Columbus, Ohio; Naperville, Illinois; Indianapolis, Indiana; North Andover, Massachusetts.

OH —PREFORMED LINE PRODUCTS CO, Research & Engineering Library, 660 Beta Drive, Mayfield Village, (Mailing add: PO Box 91129, Cleveland, 44101). Edwina T Barron, Librn
Holdings: Vols (11,500) Cat Mss Pix Microfiche VF
Budget: ($30,500)
Notes: Library covering research and engineering fields emphasizing this subject. Aerodynamic characteristics and electrical characteristics of power cables, communication cables (including fiber optics), cable support systems, as well as associated fittings and hardware; in service behavior of manufactured products and materials as it relates to its static and dynamic forces and environmental conditions; oceanographic cable fittings and terminations.

WY —UNIVERSITY OF WYOMING, William Robertson Coe Library, Archives - American Heritage Center, PO Box 3412, Laramie, 82071.
Notes: Papers of Knox Charlton Black, incl those of a 12-year period when he worked on a cable important to television.

CABRAL, OLGA

MA —BOSTON UNIVERSITY, Mugar Memorial Library, Special Collections Dept,

CABRAL, OLGA (cont.)

771 Commonwealth Ave, Boston, 02215. Howard B Gotlieb, Dir
Holdings: Cat Mss
Notes: Mss, correspondence, etc collected in depth; incl publications by or about.

CABS see Carriage, Cart, and Wagon Making

CACTI AND SUCCULENTS

AZ —DESERT BOTANICAL GARDEN, Richter Memorial Library, 1201 North Galvin Pkwy, Phoenix, 85008. J B Cole, Librn
Holdings: Vols (4000)
Notes: Emphasis on desert and arid regions ecology and horticulture.

†CA —HUNTINGTON BOTANICAL GARDENS LIBRARY, 1151 Oxford Rd, San Marino, 91108. Ann Ravenscroft, Secretary
Notes: Emphases on history of botanical science; papers and notes of American botanists and naturalists of The West; botanical illustration, etc. Subtropical horticulture, incl cacti and succulents of Australia, South Africa, and Mexico.

CA —SANTA BARBARA BOTANIC GARDEN, Library, 1212 Mission Canyon Rd, Santa Barbara, 93105. Margaret Connors, Librn
Notes: Incl 1000 nursery and seed catalogs. Especially strong on California native plants.

CADAVER IN ART

MA —HARVARD UNIVERSITY LIBRARY, Widener Library, Cambridge, 02138.
Holdings: Cat Pix Slides

CAD-CAM see Computer Aided Design-Computer Aided Manufacturing

CADMAN, CHARLES WAKEFIELD

PA —PENNSYLVANIA STATE UNIVERSITY, Arts Library, 405 E Pattee Library, University Park, 16802. Daniel Zager, Music Librn
Holdings: Mss Phonorecords
Notes: Mss, published scores, personal papers, and some recordings of the American composer Charles Wakefield Cadman.

CADY, ELIAS W.

NY —CORNELL UNIVERSITY LIBRARIES, Collection of Regional History, Dept of Manuscripts and Univ Archives, Ithaca, 14853.
Notes: NY State assemblyman, farmer, born 1792. Incl papers, 1801-57; much personal and professional correspondence.

CAFES see Hotels, Taverns, Etc.; Restaurants, Lunch Rooms, Bars, Etc.

CAGE, JOHN

TX —NORTH TEXAS STATE UNIVERSITY, Audio Center, Box 5188, NT Station, Denton, 76203. Morris Martin, Music Librn
Notes: Emphasis on Contemporary and Avant Garde music. More than 450 musical compositions (mostly manuscript, many multi-media). This is an archive of materials published in, or submitted for publication to, the contemporary music magazine *Source, the Music of the Avant Garde* which appeared from 1967-1977 (although bearing dates only through 1973). Composers represented are the editors (Larry Austin and Stanley Lunetta), John Cage, Steve Reich, Pauline Oliveros, Harry Partch, Morton Feldman, Lukas Foss, Barney Childs, David Cope, Peter Garland, Philip Glass, Ben Johnston, Alcides Lanza, Alvin Lucier, David Rosenboom, Dane Rudhyar, and Nicolas Slonimsky.

CAIN, NOBLE, 1896-1977

†KS —FRIENDS UNIVERSITY, Library, 2100 University Ave, Wichita, 67213.
Notes: Printed music, mss, and memorabilia of Noble Cain.

CAIRD, JANET

MA —BOSTON UNIVERSITY, Mugar Memorial Library, Special Collections Dept, 771 Commonwealth Ave, Boston, 02215. Howard B Gotlieb, Dir
Holdings: Cat Mss

CAIRNS, HUNTINGTON

DC —LIBRARY OF CONGRESS, Manuscript Division, Washington, 20540. John C Broderick, Chief
Holdings: Cat Mss Pix
Notes: Mss, papers, records, etc.

CAJUNS

LA —LOUISIANA STATE UNIVERSITY, Library, Baton Rouge, 70803. Anna H Perrault, Humanities Bibliographer
Holdings: Vols (1000) Cat Microforms
Budget: ($500)

NH —ASSOCIATION CANADO-AMERICAIN (FRATERNAL LIFE INSURANCE SOCIETY), Institute Canado-Americain, 52 Concord St, Manchester, 03101. Robert A Beaudoin, Librn
Holdings: Vols (40,000) Cat Mss Maps Pix Slides Phonorecords Audiotapes Microforms
Budget: ($2000)
Notes: Contains books, pamphlets, mss, university dissertations, newspapers, manuscripts, periodicals, and archives of various other societies (active of defunct). Subjects covered incl art, music, literature, folklore, religion, politics, sociology, history, etc of the French in France, Canada, and US (especially New England's Franco-Americans, Louisiana's Cajuns, and Quebec's French-Canadians). There is also an extensive collection of genealogical works dealing with Quebec Acadia, and New England Francophones. Articles dealing with the library are: "The Library of the Association Canado-Americaine" by Edward B Ham in *Modern Language Notes*, vol LII, no 7, November 1937 and a bilingual article "Appel d'un jeune aux jeunes en faveur de al Bibliotheque ACA" by Robert B Perreault in *Le Canado-Americain*, nouvelle serie, vol 1, no 5, julliet-aout-septembre 1975, pp 18-19.

CALAMITIES see Disasters and Disaster Relief

CALCULATING MACHINES

DE —HAGLEY MUSEUM AND LIBRARY, Eleutherian Mills-Hagley Foundation Inc, PO Box 3630, Greenville, 19807. Richmond D Williams, Dir; Heddy A Richter, Imprints Librn
Notes: Sperry Univac has deposited a large amount of historical records. Approximately 2000 cubic feet of records, files and photographs that document the invention and development of computers and the rapid growth of the industry were officially released by Sperry Corporation to the Library. The collection includes technical and legal documents relating to the ENIAC and UNIVAC computers as well as records of the founding of the E Remington Typewriter Company and other predecessor companies of the Sperry organization, such as The Library Bureau, Kardex, Rodic Rubber and the Powers Accounting Machinery Company. Thus our knowledge of the Sperry predecessors dates back in this collection to 1902.

CALCULATORS see Calculating Machines

CALDECOTT, RANDOLPH, 1846-1886

CA —UNIVERSITY OF CALIFORNIA, LOS ANGELES, Research Library, Dept of Special Collections, 405 Hilgard Ave, Los Angeles, 90024. Edward Shreeves, Chairman, Bibliographers Group; David S Zeidberg, Head
Holdings: Vols 60
Notes: Incl 9 original drawings for *A Farmer Went Trotting.*

OH —CASE WESTERN RESERVE UNIVERSITY, M A Baxter School of Information and Library Science, 10900 Euclid Ave, Cleveland, 44106. Bettina MacAyeal, Librn; Gretchen Larson, Librn
Holdings: Vols (1100)
Notes: Incl collection of 1100 historical children's books and periodicals, housed in the Special Collections Dept of Freiberger Library, and can be used by the public. Incl *The Holy Bible Abridged* published by Isaiah Thomas in 1786, *The Life and Strange Surprising Adventures of Robinson Crusoe* of 1790, and a *Cinderella* dated 1809. There are examples of the work of illustrators Walter Crane, Randolph Caldecott, Kate Greenaway and Maurice Boutet de Monvel. The periodical collection incl a complete run of St. Nicholas Magazine.

CALDECOTT MEDAL BOOKS

FL —FLORIDA STATE UNIVERSITY, Robert Manning Strozier Library, Special Collections Dept, Tallahassee, 32306. Opal M Free, Head, Special Collections
Holdings: Vols 45 Uncat
Notes: Noncirculating.

MI —WAYNE STATE UNIVERSITY, Kresge Library (Education), Detroit, 48202. Theodore Manheim, Librn
Holdings: Vols (65,000) Cat Mss Microforms
Budget: ($2000)
Notes: The Eloise Ramsey Collection (10, 000 vols). See, *The Eloise Ramsey Collection of Literature for Young People: A Catalogue;* compiled by Joan Cusenza (Detroit: Wayne State University Libraries, 1967). Besides the Ramsey Collection, which is housed separately and does not circulate, the Education Library has approx 55,000 volumes of children's and young adults' literature, with a very large picture-book collection, a large poetry collection; all with special emphasis on urban and ethnic materials.

MN —UNIVERSITY OF MINNESOTA, Libraries, Children's Literature Research Collections, 109 Walter Library, Minneapolis, 55455. Karen Nelson Hoyle, Cur
Holdings: Vols (550) Cat Mss Pix
Notes: Incl first editions, mss, and illustrations for children's books. Newbery and Caldecott award books and honor books and their translations; Mildred L Batchelder Award nominees in original and US editions; Minnesota; Dakota and Ojibway Indian tribes; languages other than English; correspondence between authors and illustrators and Dr Irvin Kerlan, Kerlan Collection. 350 volumes are in translation.

TX —DALLAS PUBLIC LIBRARY, Central Library, Humanities Division, 1515 Young St, Dallas, 75201. Richard L Waters, Acting Dir; Muriel W Brown, Children's Literature Specialist; Rosemarie Dunlap, Assistant to Children's Literature Specialist
Holdings: Vols (56,000) Cat Mss Pix Microforms
Notes: Incl Mother Goose Books, autographed Newbery and Caldecott winners, books important in the history of children's literature, foreign language books, and Texas books in addition to a general collection.

WI —UNIVERSITY OF WISCONSIN, MADISON, Cooperative Children's Book Center, Helen C White Hall, Rm 4290, 600 N Park St, Madison, 53706. Ginny Moore Kruse, Dir
Holdings: Vols (25,000) Cat
Notes: Cooperative Children's Book Center collections incl most US trade books published for children in last 24 months; first editions of recommended US children's trade books published since 1965; over 400 alternative press books published for children in US and Canada since 1970; children's books about Wisconsin and by Wisconsin authors and illustrators; representative 19th and early 20th century American children's books; 19th century children's periodicals; first and significant editions of Newbury and Caldecott Medal books; historical and contemporary toybooks; 75 vols of Mother

CALDECOTT MEDAL BOOKS (cont.)

Goose published since 1828; 160 vols of Thorton Burgess books, many first editions; ms and original artwork for Ellen Raskin's *The Westing Game* and *The Mysterious Disappearance of Leon (I Mean Noel);* juvenile mass market and traderomance fiction.

CALDER AND BOYARS, PUBLISHERS

IN —INDIANA UNIVERSITY, Lilly Library, Seventh St, Bloomington, 47405. William R Cagle, Librn
Holdings: Vols 500 Cat Mss
Notes: Publisher's file copies. Papers, 1950-1975 of the firm and it's predecessor John Calder Publishers, including correspondence with authors, translators, agents, etc, financial records, book design and production material, etc (ca 250,000 items).

CALDERONE, MARY (STEICHEN), 1904-

MA —RADCLIFFE COLLEGE, Arthur & Elizabeth Schlesinger Library on the History of Women in America, 3 James St, Cambridge, 02138. Patricia Miller King, Dir; Eva Moseley, Cur of Mss
Notes: Books, pamphlets, clippings; also oral history interviews in the Family Planning Oral History Project, and numerous mss collections, espec those of the Birth Control League of Massachusetts, Mary (Steichen) Calderone, MD (1904-), Edna (Rankin) McKinnon (1893-1978), and Florence Clothier, MD (1903-).

CALEDONIA WRITING SERIES ARCHIVE

BC —SIMON FRASER UNIVERSITY, Library, Burnaby, V5A 1S6, Can. Percilla Groves, Special Collections Librn
Holdings: Cat Mss
Notes: Mss for published and unpublished works, plus a complete collection of published books, chapbooks and broadsides by Canadian and American writers, plus correspondence and business records of the British Columbia Press run by poet and teacher Barry McKinnon from 1972 to 1980.

CALDWELL, CHARLES

KY —UNIVERSITY OF LOUISVILLE, Kornhauser Health Sciences Library, 520 S Preston St, PO Box 35260, Louisville, 40292. Leonard M Eddy, Dir; Sherrill R McConnell, Archivist
Holdings: Vols 100 Cat Mss
Notes: Phrenology and the Charles Caldwell Collection. Have phrenological and head charts. See E Horine, *Sketch and Guide to the Writings of Charles Caldwell* (1960).

CALDWELL, ERSKINE

DE —UNIVERSITY OF DELAWARE, Hugh M Morris Library, S College Ave, Newark, 19711. T Stuart Dick, Special Collections
Holdings: Cat Mss Pix
Notes: Manuscripts, etc, incl literary correspondence.

NV —UNIVERSITY OF NEVADA, RENO, University Library, Special Collections Dept, Reno, 89557. Robert E Blesse, Head
Holdings: // Vols (133) Cat Other appearances 220 Cat
Notes: Includes individual works by author in all editions including translations; also prefaces, introductions, published correspondence, appearances in anthologies, periodicals, etc. Bibliographical research collection, part of Modern Authors Collection.

NH —DARTMOUTH COLLEGE, Baker Memorial Library, Hanover, 03755.
Holdings: Cat Mss Pix
Notes: First editions, ephemera, etc, incl scrapbooks (microfilm available). Noncirculating.

VA —UNIVERSITY OF VIRGINIA, Alderman Library, Manuscripts Dept, Charlottesville, 22901. Edmund Berkeley Jr, Cur
Holdings: Cat Mss
Notes: 175 items, incl papers, 1925-1980, mss and correspondence.

CALENDARS

IL —UKRAINIAN NATIONAL MUSEUM, Library, 2453 W Chicago Ave, Chicago, 60622. Emil Basiuk, Librn
Notes: Department has been organized in collaboration with the Ukrainian Librarians of America Association, Ukrainian Bibliographic-Reference Center. Interlibrary loans. Collection of books and pamphlets incl material in Ukrainian and other languages on Ukrainian history, geography, literature, language, art, social sciences, religion and Ukrainian fiction. Large collection of Ukrainian calendars and almanacs. Around 100 current periodicals. Collection of serials and monographs of the Ukrainian scholarly institutions, collection of publications of the Institute for the Study of the USSR. There is a large collection of Ukrainian postcards showing all aspects of Ukrainian civilization and culture.

MI —APPLE TREE PRESS, Library, Box 1012, Flint, 48501. W D Chase, Editor/Librn
Holdings: Vols (1200) Uncat Mss Maps Pix Microforms

NY —MORRIS N & CHESLEY V YOUNG LIBRARY OF MNEMONICS, 270 Riverside Dr, New York, 10025. Morris N Young, Cur
Holdings: Cat Mss Maps Pix Phonorecords Audiotapes 16mm Films Microforms
Notes: Collection of 5000 books, pamphlets, pictures, memorabilia, etc incl medieval art of memory; psychology of memory, forgetting and reading; medical aspects of memory, amnesia, dyslexia; biomedical aspects of learning and memory; information storage, retrieval and cybernetics; memory prodigies, lightning calculators, calendars; remembrance cups and memory mementos. All languages. Memorabilia incl engravings, posters, programs, advertisements, birthday cards, teaching cards, ASLs, and Mark Twain's Memory Builder game and other games. Items range from 1410 to 1980s.

CALHOUN, JAMES EDWARD, 1796-1889

DC —GEORGETOWN UNIVERSITY, Library, Special Collections Div, 37 & O Sts NW, Washington, 20057. George M Barringer, Special Collections Librn; Nicholas B Sheetz, Mss Librn
Holdings: Mss
Notes: Correspondnece of William Oswald Dundas. Outgoing letters addressed chiefly to Edward I Devitt, SJ (1841-1920), archivist and professor of history at Georgetown College and Henry J Shandelle, SJ (1848-1925), librarian and professor of English and philosophy; extensive recollections of student life at Georgetown 1856-58 and of life in Washington during the 1850's. Incoming correspondence incl letters from James Edward Calhoun (1796-1889) of South Carolina, cousin and brother-in-law of John C Calhoun and a member of Long's expedition of 1819-1820; and official letters from various public officials, incl Sen James Vardaman of Mississippi, Gov William Hodges Mann of Virginia, and Robert Bacon, all in connection with Dundas' attempts to obtain a roster of Confederate troops for Fr Devitt. Family correspondence sundry family documents and personalreminiscences complete the collection.

CALHOUN, JOHN C., 1782-1850

SC —CLEMSON UNIVERSITY, Libraries, Clemson, 29631. Michael F Kohl, Head of Special Collections
Holdings: Cat Mss //
Notes: John C Calhoun Papers. About 200 items. Indexed by author and date.

CALIFORNIA

CA —UNIVERSITY OF CALIFORNIA, BERKELEY, Institute of Transportation Studies Library, Library, 412 McLaughlin Hall, Berkeley, 94720.
Holdings: Vols (82,000)
Budget: ($215,000)
Notes: US Department of Transportation depository through NTIS.

CA —UNIVERSITY OF CALIFORNIA, BERKELEY, Bancroft Library, Manuscripts Division, Berkeley, 94720. James D Hart, Dir
Holdings: Vols Mss Maps Pix Slides Microforms
Notes: Approx 12 million pieces, with primary emphasis on California, with a lesser emphasis on the other Pacific States, incl Alaska and the Province of British Columbia. In general, the Bancroft Library seeks to acquire historical and biographical works and primary source materials, documenting: the development of a geographic area or political unit; man and his institutions. Methodological and theoretical works and texts in the physical and biological sciences are not collected, as a rule; exceptions here are publications essential to the study of an area's historical development and those providing general background information. Hubert Howe Bancroft's own distinguished holdings, assembled 1860-1880, constitute the core of the collection. The Bancroft Library's collections are noncirculating. A G K Hall catalog has been published. The Bolton Collection(146,000 pages of archival material) contains ms materials for the history of the Pacific Coast and the Southwest, gathered by Herbert Eugene Bolton. There is a comprehensive key to the arrangement of the collection.

CA —FRESNO COUNTY FREE LIBRARY, 2420 Mariposa St, Fresno, 93721. Linda J Goff, Local History Librn
Holdings: Vols 3250 Cat Mss Maps Pix Microforms
Notes: Primary emphasis is on the central San Joaquin Valley, with particular attention to Fresno County. Incl local oral history transcripts.

CA —CALIFORNIA STATE UNIVERSITY, FULLERTON, Library, Box 4150, Fullerton, 92634. Linda Herman, Special Collections Librn
Holdings: Vols (5000)
Notes: California history stressing Orange County is basis of a group of collections including citrus, water, school annuals, and education. The Orange County Historical Society archives/depository supplement these holdings. Incl 4500 periodical issues, 165 boxes of ephemera, 20 audiotapes, 300 maps and 1000 pictures.

CA —LAKE COUNTY LIBRARY, 200 Park St, Lakeport, 95453. Kathleen Jansen, Librn
Holdings: Vols (300) Cat Maps Pix
Notes: Large collection of books, articles, and reports on geothermal resources, especially in California. Partially cataloged.

CA —LOS ANGELES PUBLIC LIBRARY, History Dept, 630 W 5th St, Los Angeles, 90071. Bettye H Ellison, Librn in Charge, California Room
Holdings: Vols 8000 Cat Pix
Notes: The California Collection is a reference and circulating collection consisting of state, county and city histories, volumes of travel and description, periodicals, and publications of state and local historical societies. Over 260,000 historic photographs from the turn of the century to the mid-1950s. Portraits are incl. The majority of the views are of Los Angeles and Southern California. Special subject and biographical indexes provide references to a wide variety of California related books, periodicals and Los Angeles area newspapers. A separate index is maintained for photographs.

CA —UNIVERSITY OF CALIFORNIA, LOS ANGELES, Music Library, Schonberg Hall, Los Angeles, 90024. Stephen M Fry, Music Librn
Notes: The Philip Kahgan Collection of

CALIFORNIA (cont.)

music films, letters, programs, and photographs important to the Southern California classical music scene. Incl 16mm "home movies" of more than thirty renowned conductors and performers during Hollywood Bowl rehearsals in the late 1930s. Incl Kahgan correspondence, memorabilia, 35 scrapbooks, etc.

CA —SAINT MARY'S COLLEGE, Library, Moraga, 94575. Brother Casimir Reichlin, Dir of the Library; Brother Richard Lemberg FSC, Asst Librn
Notes: The Leonard Verbarg library of over 800 books on Western Americana, especially California. Incl vertical files containing over 1100 entries related to Californiana in the form of clippings and correspondence amassed during editorship of "The Knave" page of local history in the *Oakland Tribune.*

CA —ASSOCIATION OF BAY AREA GOVERNMENTS, MTC/ABAG Library, 101 Eighth St, Oakland, 94607. Diane Gillman, Information Coord
Notes: Concentrates heavily on the nine-county Bay Area region. About 10,000 monographs and serials. Title catalog, OCLC/ATS. Central collection of documents for six transit properties in Bay Area.

CA —OAKLAND PUBLIC LIBRARY, Oakland History Room, 125 14th St, Oakland, 94612. William W Sturm, Librn
Holdings: Vols (20,000) Cat Mss Maps Pix Microforms
Notes: The Oakland History Room Collection is a reference collection of books, pamphlets, periodicals, pictures, and newspaper clippings. California items incl as much biographical material as possible clipped from the *Oakland Tribune, Oakland Post, California Voice,* the *Montclarion,* and *Alameda Times-Star.* (Library no longer clips *San Francisco Chronicle* or *Examiner*). These clippings are filed by subjects. An index of all the subjects with many cross references are made. An index of articles from about 75 magazines dealing with California subjects is kept up to date. The log books of the Coast Guard Cutter *Bear* from 1889 to 1932 are in the collection. The Jack London collection is listed separately. Ms pages and letters from Joaquin Miller and a fewmiscellaneous letters from other authors are also incl. A set of George Sterling, both inscribed and not inscribed, is owned by the Room.

CA —SUNKIST GROWERS, Research Library, 760 E Sunkist St, Ontario, 91761. Martha C Nemeth, Librn
Holdings: Vols (1500) Cat
Budget: ($10,000)
Notes: Technology of citrus fruit and citrus fruit products, primarily Californian. Strong in organic and food chemistry, with additional coverage of food technology, essential oils, microbiology and environmental protection.

CA —PALO ALTO CITY LIBRARY, 1213 Newell Rd, Palo Alto, 94303. Mary Jo Levy, Dir
Holdings: Vols (1125) Cat
Notes: Incl newspapers.

CA —PASADENA PUBLIC LIBRARY, 285 E Walnut St, Pasadena, 91101. Carolyn Garner, Librn II
Holdings: Vols 3000 Cat Maps Pix
Notes: California collection described in Gertrude Stoughton, *The Books of* California. 1968. Old Pasadena newspapers 1883-date. *Pasadena Star-News* on microfilm 1910-date. Selected California documents. Pasadena local history and biography.

CA —CALIFORNIA STATE LIBRARY, Library & Courts Bldg, 914 Capitol Mall, Sacramento, 95809. Gary Kurutz, Head of Special Collections
Holdings: Vols (60,000) Cat Mss Maps Pix Microforms
Budget: ($41,550)
Notes: 150,000 photographs; 600 cu ft of mss; 4000 maps; 70,000 reels on microfilm; 8000 bound vols California newspapers; 500 prints of lithographs on California newpapers; 1000 posters; and vertical file materials.

CA —SAN DIEGO PUBLIC LIBRARY, 820 E St, San Diego, 92101. Rhoda E Kruse, Sr Librn
Holdings: Vols (13,500) Cat Mss Maps Pix
Budget: ($5000)
Notes: Also 450 bound periodicals. Incl extensive local history; papers of Foss and Kelly families; some material on John D Spreckels; papers of Southern California Exposition, San Diego 200th Anniversary Committee; Census microfilms; registers of voters 1866-1909; *San Diego Union* Index, which also incl material on Baja Califorina; records of Little Landers Colony, a 1910 Utopian group founded in the Tia Juana River Valley.

CA —SAN JOSE PUBLIC LIBRARY, 180 W San Carlos St, San Jose, 95113. Homer Fletcher, Dir
Holdings: Vols (11,000) Cat Mss Maps Pix Slides Microforms
Notes: Extensive collection of California.

CT —YALE UNIVERSITY, Box 1603A, Yale Station, New Haven, 06520.
Holdings: Cat Mss

CALIFORNIA—BIOGRAPHY

CA —LOS ANGELES PUBLIC LIBRARY, Municipal Reference Library, Rm 530, City Hall E, 200 N Main St, Los Angeles, 90012. C Grimsley, Senior Librn
Holdings: Vols (86,000) Cat
Budget: ($33,000)
Notes: Emphasis on cities over 500,000 with special collection of municipal documents from large cities. Biographical material on local government officials.

CA —OAKLAND PUBLIC LIBRARY, Oakland History Room, 125 14th St, Oakland, 94612. William W Sturm, Librn
Holdings: Vols (20,000) Cat Mss Maps Pix Microforms
Notes: The Oakland History Room Collection is a reference collection of books, pamphlets, periodicals, pictures, and newspaper clippings. California items incl as much biographical material as possible clipped from the *Oakland Tribune, Oakland Post, California Voice,* the *Montclarion,* and *Alameda Times-Star.* (Library no longer clips *San Francisco Chronicle* or *Examiner*). These clippings are filed by subjects. An index of all the subjects with many cross references are made. An index of articles from about 75 magazines dealing with California subjects is kept up to date. The log books of the Coast Guard Cutter *Bear* from 1889 to 1932 are in the collection. The Jack London collection is listed separately. Ms pages and letters from Joaquin Miller and a fewmiscellaneous letters from other authors are also incl. A set of George Sterling, both inscribed and not inscribed, is owned by the Room.

CALIFORNIA—CENSUSES

CA —POMONA PUBLIC LIBRARY, Special Collections, 625 S Garey Ave, PO Box 2271, Pomona, 91766. David Streeter, Librn
Holdings: Cat Maps Microforms
Notes: Complete California census through 1900 on microfilm and 1850 California census index.

CA —SAN DIEGO PUBLIC LIBRARY, 820 E St, San Diego, 92101. Rhoda E Kruse, Sr Librn
Notes: Incl complete California census microfilms, incomplete from other states. Noncirculating.

CALIFORNIA—DESCRIPTION AND TRAVEL—VIEWS

CA —UNIVERSITY OF CALIFORNIA, LOS ANGELES, Research Library, Dept of Special Collections, 405 Hilgard Ave, Los Angeles, 90024. Edward Shreeves, Chairman, Bibliographers Group; David S Zeidberg, Head
Holdings: Cat Mss Pix
Notes: 2 million pictures, incl original photographs and ephemera of California people and places, images by California Pictorialists, and news photographs from the morgues of the *Los Angeles Daily News* and the *Los Angeles Times.*

CA —POMONA PUBLIC LIBRARY, Special Collections, 625 S Garey Ave, PO Box 2271, Pomona, 91766. David Streeter, Librn
Holdings: Uncat Slides
Notes: Contains 550 lantern slides (mostly of California) and 4200 color 35mm transparencies of world travel, 1960s. Also, the Burton Frasher Postal Card Collection of 60,000 negatives and prints of California, Arizona, Colorado, New Mexico, Nevada, and Utah; 30,000 world views; 8000 California views. There are also world views in nearly 1000 stereographs.

CA —CALIFORNIA HISTORICAL SOCIETY, Schubert Hall Library, 2099 Pacific Ave, San Francisco, 94109. Bruce L Johnson, Library Dir
Holdings: Vols (50,000) Cat Mss Maps Pix
Notes: San Francisco CHS Photographic Archives holds 300,000 images on California statewide; CHS Title Insurance and Trust Corporation Collection of Historical Photographs in Los Angeles contains 20,000 photographs centered around pictures of Southern California by noted photographer C C Pierce. Copies of photographs by other pioneer Los Angeles photographers, such as Godfrey, Wolfenstein and Parker are incl, as well as 2000 glass plate negatives of local Indians by George Wharton James.

CA —UNIVERSITY OF CALIFORNIA, SANTA CRUZ, University Library, Special Collections, Santa Cruz, 95064. Rita Bottoms, Special Collections Librn; Margaret Felts, South Pacific Collection Bibliographer

CA —WHITTIER COLLEGE, Wardman Library, Whittier, 90608. Christine Erdmann, Special Collections Librn
Holdings: // Cat Pix
Notes: Aerial photographs of California, 1927-1963. 100,000 aerial photo negatives (40,000 nitrate-base), 300,000 aerial photo prints, 1000 photomosaics, 750 orthophoto maps. Concentration in California, particularly in the Los Angeles region, and elsewhere in metropolitan areas. Many flights are among the earliest available and cover areas since developed. Sequential photos often allow documentation of the history of development or of natural effects. Prints may be borrowed for 2-week periods. Purchase of prints only through Teledyne-Geotronics, Long Beach, California. An inventory list of flights can be purchased through the Dept of Geology.

CALIFORNIA—EARTHQUAKES

CA —ASSOCIATION OF BAY AREA GOVERNMENTS, MTC/ABAG Library, 101 Eighth St, Oakland, 94607. Diane Gillman, Information Coord
Notes: Concentrates heavily on the nine-county Bay Area region. About 10,000 monographs and serials. Title catalog, OCLC/ATS. Central collection of documents for six transit properties in Bay Area. Incl material on hazardous geographic environments.

CA —POMONA PUBLIC LIBRARY, Special Collections, 625 S Garey Ave, PO Box 2271, Pomona, 91766. David Streeter, Librn
Holdings: Cat Mss Maps
Notes: Some 4000 maps. Strong for Pomona Valley area: tract maps, water company maps; depository for USGS California topographic maps; California earthquake fault maps.

NY —VISUAL STUDIES WORKSHOP, Research Center, 31 Prince St, Rochester, 14607. Linn Underhill, Coordr; Robert Bretz, Librn
Holdings: Vols (8000) Cat Pix Slides Audiotapes Videotapes
Notes: Strong emphasis on photography (over 1,000,000 pictures) and the photographic arts in many subject areas incl in this volume. Heavy emphasis on early photographic processes and collections of examples of them. Also collections of individual photographers' works.

CALIFORNIA—FICTION

CA —LOS ANGELES PUBLIC LIBRARY, Fiction Dept, 630 W 5th St, Los Angeles, 90071. Helene G Mochedlover, Dept Librn
Holdings: Vols 9500 Cat
Notes: Includes almost all hardcover novels and short stories published in US and England with California setting in whole or part. Annotated author card index and indexes by period and specific locale.

CA —POMONA PUBLIC LIBRARY, Special Collections, 625 S Garey Ave, PO Box 2271, Pomona, 91766. David Streeter, Librn
Holdings: Vols 114
Notes: Emphasizes the novels with settings in the Pomona-San Bernardino Vallies (Inland Empire). Growth is anticipated.

CALIFORNIA—FLOWERS

CA —RANCHO SANTA ANA BOTANIC GARDEN LIBRARY, 1500 N College Ave, Claremont, 91711. Beatrice M Beck, Librn
Holdings: Vols 30,000 Cat Maps Microforms
Notes: Incl emphasis on California flora, floras of the world, evolutionary biology and ethnobotany.

CA —POMONA PUBLIC LIBRARY, Special Collections, 625 S Garey Ave, PO Box 2271, Pomona, 91766. David Streeter, Librn
Holdings: // Uncat Pix Slides
Notes: Brooking Tatum collection of California Flora: 125 8x10 color prints and 50 35mm color transparencies; Estella E Howes water color paintings of local flora (98 paintings); Cyril Albritt oil painting.

CA —STRYBING ARBORETUM SOCIETY, Golden Gate Park Library, Jane Gates, Librn, 9th Ave at Lincoln Way, San Francisco, 94122.
Holdings: Vols (10,000)

CALIFORNIA—GENEALOGY

CA —AZUSA PACIFIC COLLEGE, Marshburn Memorial Library, Citrus & Alosta, Azusa, 91702. Edward Peterman, Librn
Holdings: Vols (1000) // Uncat Maps Pix
Notes: Macneil Family Collection on Local History. These items relate to the Slauson, Macneil and Wilcox families, incl photographs, diaries, letters, maps, books, and financial and legal documents.

CA —SONS OF THE REVOLUTION IN THE STATE OF CALIFORNIA, Library, 600 S Central Ave, Glendale, 91204. Richard E Coe, Library Dir
Holdings: Vols 22,000 Mss
Notes: Incl 5000 mss and 2000 family histories. Partially cataloged.

CA —LONG BEACH PUBLIC LIBRARY, 101 Pacific Ave, Long Beach, 90802. Douglas Kermode, Librn
Holdings: Vols (700) Cat Mss Maps Pix
Notes: Records the development of Long Beach from its beginnings as a city (ca 1887). Picture file (ca 3400) and negative collection from local Winstead Bros, Photographers (ca 10,000).

CA —LOS ANGELES PUBLIC LIBRARY, Genealogy & Local History Dept, 630 W 5th St, Los Angeles, 90071. Lucile Lipman, Sr Librn
Holdings: Vols (55,000) Cat Mss Maps Pix Microforms
Budget: ($16,000)
Notes: Complete California census on microfilm, Great Registers (voter records) on microfilm, Depository library for materials published by California State Society of the Daughters of the Revolution. Local histories and biography are included in History Dept. California collection.

CA —MODESTO-STANISLAUS COUNTY FREE LIBRARY, 1500 I St, Modesto, 95354. Andrew L La Mance, Special Collections Librn
Holdings: Microforms
Budget: $1000
Notes: Incl 1,500 cataloged Census records (microfilm) and periodicals.

CA —POMONA PUBLIC LIBRARY, Special Collections, 625 S Garey Ave, PO Box 2271, Pomona, 91766. David Streeter, Librn
Holdings: Cat Maps Microforms
Notes: Complete California census through 1900 on microfilm; 1850 California Census index; reconstructed passenger lists; overland arrivals. Scattered censuses on microfilm from other states. All printed indexes to US Census; general US research collection. Basic heraldry and coats-of-arms.

CALIFORNIA—GOLD RUSH see Gold Rush, California

CALIFORNIA—GOVERNMENT DOCUMENTS

CA —LOS ANGELES PUBLIC LIBRARY, Social Sciences Dept, 630 W Fifth St, Los Angeles, 90071. Marilyn C Wherley, Principal Librn
Holdings: Vols 3000 Cat
Budget: ($150,000)
Notes: Serials, including state legislative manuals and rosters of public officials. Complete depository for California legislative materials dating from 1850 to present. 10, 000 uncataloged pieces.

CA —UNIVERSITY OF CALIFORNIA, LOS ANGELES, Research Library, Public Affairs Service, 405 Hilgard Ave, Los Angeles, 90024. Edward Shreeves, Chairman, Bibliographers Group; Eugenia Eaton, Head, Public Affairs Service
Holdings: Microforms
Notes: Depository for the official publications of California cities and counties, the state of California, the United States government, the United Nations and some of its specialized agencies (including the Food and Agricultural Organization and UNESCO), and such regional organizations as the European Communities and Organization of American States. Selected publications of other American cities and counties, of the other states and possessions of the United States, of interstate organizations, and of foreign governments (with emphasis on major world powers, Africa, Latin America and the Near and Middle East) and intergovernmental organizations.

CA —CONTRA COSTA COUNTY LIBRARY, Documents Section, 1750 Oak Park Blvd, Pleasant Hill, 94523. Carmen Miller, Documents Librn
Holdings: Vols (65,000) Uncat Maps Microforms
Budget: ($5000)
Notes: Depository for documents of California (since 1947) and the US (since 1964).

CA —CALIFORNIA STATE ARCHIVES, 1020 O St, Room 130, Sacramento, 95814. John F Burns, Chief of Archives; Joseph Samora, Head of Reference
Holdings: Mss Pix Maps Microforms
Notes: 55,000 cubic feet of records, papers, photographs, maps and microforms; cataloged. Historical records of the California executive, legislative and judicial branches of government, as well as selected records of six counties and several school districts.

NC —DUKE UNIVERSITY, William R Perkins Library, Public Documents and Maps Department, Durham, 27706. Jaia Barrett, Head
Holdings: Vols Maps Pamphlets Microforms
Notes: A selective depository for US Government publications since 1890, the Department currently holds well over 500, 000 items, plus publications of the European Community (a depository collection), the League of Nations, the UN and UN-affiliated agencies. Other international organizations, publications are acquired also, as are state government publications, especially from the Southeast, California, New York and Illinois. The Documents Department holds services the major map collections of Perkins Library. These collections include topographic, geologic, and special subject maps which are worldwide in coverage. The department is a depository for the US Defense Mapping Agency and the US Geological Survey. In addition, there are many other maps of general and specific interest, including US and foreign road maps. As appropriate, maps are also held in the Perkins Library's Rare BookRoom and Manuscript Department. Atlases are shelved in the Reference Department and in the bookstacks of Perkins Library.

CALIFORNIA—HISTORY

CA —ANAHEIM PUBLIC LIBRARY, 500 W Broadway, Anaheim, 92805.
Holdings: Vols (2000) Cat Mss Maps Pix Microforms
Notes: Our specialty is local history, especially that of Anaheim and Orange County. In addition to many books on California, we have photographs, maps, directories, organization histories, ephemera, journals; books published by The Fine Arts Press, Santa Ana; periodicals, original minute books and records of the Los Angeles Vineyard Society. The Walt Disney Archives has designated the library as an official depository of material on Walt Disney, with an emphasis on Disneyland. This collection incl Disney books, Disney periodicals, press releases, operating manuals, guide-books, posters, photographs, Disney character merchandise and examples of ephemeral materials such as tickets, hand-bills, and advertising matter.

CA —ARCADIA PUBLIC LIBRARY, 20 W Duarte Rd, Arcadia, 91006. James M Domney, City Librn

CA —HUMBOLDT STATE UNIVERSITY, Library, Arcata, 95521. Erich F Schimps, Assoc Librn
Holdings: Vols 2500 Cat Mss Maps Pix Microforms
Notes: Contains materials relating to any aspect of Humboldt County. Also incl neighboring regions and counties if the material contributes to the knowledge and understanding of Humboldt County. Author catalog for the book collection; all cataloged items are listed in the main public catalog.

CA —AZUSA PACIFIC COLLEGE, Marshburn Memorial Library, Citrus & Alosta, Azusa, 91702. Edward Peterman, Librn
Holdings: Vols 5000 // Maps Pix
Notes: Azusa Foothill Citrus and Local History collection is related to the genesis of Azusa, the citrus industry, the Slauson and Macneil families, and such companies as the Azusa Land and Power Company, Azusa Electric Lighting and Power Company, Azusa Foothill Citrus Association, Azusa Agricultural Water Company, and the Azusa Foothill Citrus Company. Includes letters, ledgers, etc.

CA —KERN COUNTY LIBRARY SYSTEM, 1315 Truxtun Ave, Bakersfield, 93301. Mary Hanel, Historical Librn
Holdings: Vols 5000 Microforms
Notes: Primarily Kern County history, but collection also covers California and the bordering western states. Microfilm collection consists chiefly of local newspapers, some dating back to 1866, indexed from 1936-present.

CA —UNIVERSITY OF CALIFORNIA, BERKELEY, Bancroft Library, Manuscripts Division, Berkeley, 94720. James D Hart, Dir
Holdings: Vols Mss Maps Pix Slides Microforms
Notes: Approxi. twelve million pieces, with primary emphasis on California, with a lesser emphasis on the other Pacific States, incl. Alaska and the Province of British Columbia. In general, the Bancroft Library seeks to acquire historical and biographical works and primary source materials, documenting: the development of a geographic area or political unit; man and his activities, and his impact on the land and on his institutions. Methodological and theoretical work and texts in the physical and biological sciences are not collected, as a rule; exceptions here are publications essential to the study of an area's historical development and those providing general background information. Hubert Howe Bancroft's own distinguished holdings, assembled 1860-1880,

CALIFORNIA—HISTORY (cont.)

constitute the core of the collection. The Bancroft Library's collections are noncirculating. A. G. K. Hall catalog has been published. The Bolton Collection (146,000 pages of archival material) contains ms. materials for the history of the Pacific Coast and the Southwest, gathered by Herbert Eugene Bolton. There is a comprehensive key to the arrangement of the collection.

CA —BURBANK PUBLIC LIBRARY, 110 N Glenoaks Blvd, Burbank, 91502. Mary Ann Grasso, Coordr; Barbara Stones, Coordr, Media Project
Holdings: Vols (2600) Cat Maps Pix
Notes: Strong in Grabhorn Press imprints and other California press items of historical interest. Also, strong collection of pamphlets and ephemera concerning California. Separate catalog in preparation. Collection well described in "The Burbank Western History Collection", by Thomas F Parker, in *California Librarian* (April 1965).

CA —SAINT JOHN'S SEMINARY, Edward Laurence Doheny Memorial Library, The Estelle Doheny Collection, 5012 E Seminary Rd, Camarillo, 93010. Rita S Faulders, Cur

CA —CLAREMONT COLLEGES, Honnold Library, Ninth & Dartmouth, Claremont, 91711. Tania Rizzo, Special Collections Dept Head
Holdings: Vols 15,000 Cat Mss Maps Pix VF Periodicals
Notes: Early and contemporary imprints. Also, additions interpretative of modern scene. Incl William Smith Mason and William McPherson collections.

CA —UNIVERSITY OF CALIFORNIA, DAVIS, Shields Library, Dept of Special Collections, Davis, 95616. Donald Kunitz, Head; C Danial Elliott, Asst Head
Holdings: Cat Mss Pix
Notes: The California Promotional Collection incl pamphlets and newspapers promoting California in the 19th and 20th centuries, with items on tourism, irrigation, real estate investment, agriculture, growth and lure of cities and counties (2200 items). The Lindley Papers document life in Sacramento during the second half of the 19th century, with family papers, photograhs, and memorabilia (356 items). The Wolfskill Collection of scrapbooks, memorbilia and family papers, relate to John R Wolfskill, early settler in Solano County (1842) (1150 items). The Pierce Papers contain general and family correspondence, business and legal papers, photographs and related printed material of an early Davis, California, family, as well as material relating to the purchase of the University of California, Davis, and to the California Almond Growers' Exchange (1075 items). The Shields Collectiondocuments the career of California Superior Court Judge Peter J Shields of Sacramento, his 49 years on the bench and his relationship with prominent political figures (1050 items).

CA —DEATH VALLEY NATIONAL MONUMENT, Library, Death Valley, 92328. Shirley Harding, Cur/Librn
Holdings: Vols 3000 Cat Mss Maps Pix Slides
Notes: Death Valley (History, Archeology, Geology, Natural History, etc). Reference Library only.

CA —EUREKA-HUMBOLDT COUNTY LIBRARY, 636 F St, Eureka, 95503. Dierdre Sockbeson, Reference Librn
Holdings: Vols (5000) Cat Mss Maps Pix Microforms
Budget: ($5000)
Notes: Humboldt County history, with particular emphasis on Indians of northwest California. Do not offer telephone reference service.

CA —CALIFORNIA STATE UNIVERSITY, FRESNO, Henry Madden Library, Dept of Special Collections, Fresno, 93740. Ronald J Mahoney, Head
Holdings: Vols 6200 Cat Mss Maps Pix
Notes: California history, with emphasis on San Joaquin Valley and Sierra Nevada.

CA —CALIFORNIA STATE UNIVERSITY, FULLERTON, Library, Box 4150, Fullerton, 92634. Linda Herman, Special Collections Librn
Holdings: Vols 4300 Uncat Mss Maps Pix Audiotapes
Notes: California history stressing Orange County is basis of a group of collections including citrus, water, school annuals, and education. The Orange County Historical Society archives/depository supplement these holdings. Incl 4500 periodical issues, 165 boxes of ephemera, 20 audiotapes, 300 maps and 1000 pictures.

CA —GLENDALE PUBLIC LIBRARY, 222 E Harvard St, Glendale, 91205. Barbara Boyd, Special Collections Librn
Holdings: Cat Mss Maps Pix Slides Audiotapes Microforms
Budget: ($8000)
Notes: Emphasis on the city of Glendale.

CA —SONS OF THE REVOLUTION IN THE STATE OF CALIFORNIA, Library, 600 S Central Ave, Glendale, 91204. Richard E Coe, Library Dir
Holdings: Vols 22,000 Mss
Notes: Incl 5000 mss and 2000 family histories. Partially cataloged.

CA —CALIFORNIA STATE UNIVERSITY, HAYWARD, Library, Hayward, 94542. Melissa Rose, Dir
Holdings: Vols (14,000) // Cat Mss Pix
Budget: ($7408)
Notes: Jensen Family Papers (about 3000 leaves) consisting of letters, journals, original watercolors, are the papers of a pioneer German family (Jensen-Hensen) who settled in the 1860s in the Hayward-Castro Valley, Calif, area. Covering the approx period 1830-1920, the collection incl both sides of the correspondence, a large part of which is written in German script.

CA —HAYWARD AREA HISTORICAL SOCIETY, 22701 Main St, Hayward, 94541. Eugene G Hirtle Jr, Cur
Holdings: Vols Mss Pix Audiotapes Videotapes Microforms
Notes: History of Hayward, Alameda County and California. Partially cataloged. Incl city and county records, oral history audiotapes.

CA —HEMET PUBLIC LIBRARY, 510 E Florida Ave, Hemet, 92343. James P Boulton, Chief Librn
Holdings: Vols (3000) Cat Mss Maps Pix
Notes: Special emphasis on southern California and Indians of the Southwest. Local newspaper collection from 1907 to date.

CA —UNIVERSITY OF CALIFORNIA, IRVINE, Library, Irvine, 92664. Roger Berry, Dept Head
Holdings: Cat Mss Maps Pix Slides
Notes: The Meadows Collection, an extensive collection of Californiana. Rich in material on the history of Orange County, Southern California and Baja, California. Incl more than 3500 vols, thousands of pieces of printed ephemera, over 10,000 mss items, significant runs of California historical periodicals and of rare early Orange County newspapers, maps and several hundred local historical photographs.

CA —COPLEY NEWSPAPERS, James S Copley Library, 1134 Kline St, PO Box 1530, La Jolla, 92038. Richard Reilly, Cur; Suzanne Carnes, Librn
Holdings: Vols (10,000) Cat
Notes: Collection incl materials on American Revolutionary period and California and western Americana. Library open to graduate students who obtain reading privileges from curator or librarian.

CA —UNIVERSITY OF CALIFORNIA, SAN DIEGO, Central University Library, Mandeville Dept of Special Collections, La Jolla, 92093. Lynda Corey Claassen, Head
Notes: Several rare and extremely valuable books dealing with the discovery and early history of the San Diego region.

CA —LAKE COUNTY LIBRARY, 200 Park St, Lakeport, 95453. Kathleen Jansen, Librn
Holdings: Vols (300) Cat Maps Pix
Notes: Primarily materials dealing with the history of Lake County, California. Special collection incl the 8000 page notebooks of the County Historian, with an extensive index. Partially cataloged.

CA —CALIFORNIA STATE UNIVERSITY, LONG BEACH, Library, Dept of Special Collections & Archives, 1250 Bellflower Blvd, Long Beach, 90840. John Ahouse, Special Collections Librn
Holdings: Vols (5000) Cat Mss Maps Pix VF
Notes: Incorporates the former library of Philip B Bekeart.

CA —LONG BEACH PUBLIC LIBRARY, 101 Pacific Ave, Long Beach, 90802. Douglas Kermode, Librn
Holdings: Vols (700) Cat Mss Maps Pix
Notes: Records the development of Long Beach from its beginnings as a city (ca 1887). Picture file (ca 3400) and negative collection from local Winstead Bros, Photographers (ca 10,000).

CA —LONG BEACH PUBLIC LIBRARY, Science and Technology Dept, 101 Pacific Ave, Long Beach, 90802. James Jackson, Librn
Holdings: Vols 2000 Uncat Mss Maps Pix Slides
Notes: California Petroleum Industry Collection incl 2000 government publications, 700 petroleum company documents, 750 pamphlets, 1000 tool catalogs and brochures, 93 periodical titles, mss, 400 maps, 3000 pictures, and slides. Cataloged and indexed. Open to serious researchers by appointment.

CA —LONG BEACH PUBLIC LIBRARY, Historic Sites Section, Rancho Los Cerritos, 4600 Virginia Rd, Long Beach, 90807. Ellen Calomiris, Historical Cur
Holdings: Vols (3000) Cat Mss Maps Pix Audiotapes
Budget: $1000
Notes: Emphasis on rancho, Long Beach, and Southern California history; incl materials on the westward movement. Incl 250 maps and 3000 pictures. Additional historic site: Rancho Los Alamitos, 6400 Bixby Hill Rd, Long Beach, Calif, 90815.

CA —LONG BEACH PUBLIC LIBRARY, Literature & History Dept, 101 Pacific Ave, Long Beach, 90802. Harriet J Friis, Head
Holdings: Vols Pamphlets Documents Pix Maps Periodicals Audiotapes Microforms
Notes: Collection documents the history and continuing development of Long Beach. Publications of the City of Long Beach are incl, as well as a selective index to the Long Beach *Independent* and other local newspapers. Also incl material on the steamship *Queen Mary.* Items in the collection do not circulate. Incl city directories.

CA —LOS ANGELES PUBLIC LIBRARY, History Dept, 630 W 5th St, Los Angeles, 90071. Bettye H Ellison, Librn in Charge, California Room
Holdings: Vols 10,000 Cat Pix
Budget: ($85,000)
Notes: The California Collection is a reference and circulating collection consisting of state, county and city histories, volumes of travel and description, periodicals, and publications of state and local historical societies. Historic photographs are predominantly portraits of early Southern Californians and streets and buildings--about 235,000 photographs.

CALIFORNIA—HISTORY (cont.)

Special subject and biographical indexes provide references to a wide variety of California related books, periodicals and Los Angeles area newspapers. A separate index is maintained for photographs.

CA —LOS ANGELES PUBLIC LIBRARY, Philosophy & Religion Dept, 630 W Fifth St, Los Angeles, 90071. Marilyn C Wherley, Librn
Holdings: Vols 2350 Cat Includes long runs of major periodicals and newspapers, many on microfilm
Budget: ($60,000)
Notes: History, theology, biography, California missions, the church in the Southwest. Includes both popular and scholarly works.

CA —LOS ANGELES PUBLIC LIBRARY, Frances Howard Goldwyn Hollywood Regional Library, 1623 Ivar Ave, Los Angeles, 90028. Sally Dumaux, Librn
Holdings: Vols (100,000) Cat Pix VF
Budget: ($60,000)
Notes: Special Collections: Francis William Vreeland, local artist, incl correspondence, working papers, scrapbooks, photographs; Gladys Littell Collection incl Hollywood Bowl Sunrise Services 1920s-1940s, Hollywood Conservatory of Music, 1920s, Hollywood Chamber of Commerce, incl correspondence, programs, working papers, and photographs; Holly Leaves, Hollywood, Calif, 1916-1930.

CA —OCCIDENTAL COLLEGE, Library, 1600 Campus Rd, Los Angeles, 90041. Michael C Sutherland, Special Collections Librn
Holdings: Vols 300 // Cat
Notes: Max and Virginia Hayward Collection of Californiana.

CA —UNIVERSITY OF CALIFORNIA, LOS ANGELES, Research Library, Dept of Special Collections, 405 Hilgard Ave, Los Angeles, 90024. Edward Shreeves, Chairman, Bibliographers Group; David S Zeidberg, Head
Holdings: Vols 20,000 Cat Mss Pix Microforms
Notes: Founded on the Cowan collection, all aspects of California history are covered, but the emphasis is on Southern California. Incl 20,000 books, 900,000 mss, 500 maps, 60, 000 pictures, 1200 pieces of sheet music, 50 linear feet of ephemera, 10 linear feet of photographs, 1.5 million news photographs; personal papers of many individuals and families, incl the Cole family, John Randolph Haynes, Franklin Hichborn, Carey McWilliams, William Starke Rosecrans.

CA —MILL VALLEY PUBLIC LIBRARY, Lucretia Hanson Little History Room, 375 Throckmorton Ave, Mill Valley, 94941. Thelma Percy, Head Librn
Holdings: Vols 1300 Cat Mss Maps Oral Histories Slides Audiotapes Periodicals Newspaper Index

CA —SAN FERNANDO VALLEY HISTORICAL SOCIETY, Mark R Harrington Library, 10940 Sepulveda Blvd, Mission Hills, 91345. Elva Meline, Cur
Holdings: Vols (2000) Cat Maps Pix Slides Audiotapes
Notes: California history, with emphasis on San Fernando Valley. Incl 50 linear feet of periodicals, pamphlets and clippings. ally

CA —MCHENRY MUSEUM OF ART & HISTORY, Library, 1402 I St, Modesto, 95354. Heidi L Warner, Cur
Holdings: Cat Mss Maps Pix Slides Audiotapes Videotapes Filmstrips
Notes: Original documents pertaining to Stanislaus County history, incl court cases, school records, county records, pictures, pioneer family histories, oral histories, all books on local history, original mss and diaries of local pioneers. Incl several thousand pictures and 1200 slides.

CA —MODESTO-STANISLAUS COUNTY FREE LIBRARY, 1500 I St, Modesto, 95354. Andrew L La Mance, Special Collections Librn
Holdings: Vols 2000 Cat Maps Pix Slides Microforms
Budget: $1500
Notes: History of Modesto and Stanislaus County, incl government documents, newspaper clippings, microfilms. Also genealogical materials, incl census records (microfilm) and periodicals.

CA —SAINT MARY'S COLLEGE, Library, Moraga, 94575. Brother Casimir Reichlin, Dir of the Library; Brother Richard Lemberg FSC, Asst Librn
Holdings: Cat Mss Maps Pix Slides Audiotapes Microforms
Notes: Sources for local history. In the area of purview are four communities: Orinda, Lafayette, Morgana, Canyon, all in Western Contra Costa County, California within the grant boundaries of Rancho Laguna de los Palos Colorados. Incl 800 mss, 600 maps, 100 pictures, 800 slides, 60 audiotapes, and 100 microforms. No catalog. Index to 6-vol abstract to land titles (to 1920s) and index to surnames in trial records (60 yrs).

CA —OAKLAND PUBLIC LIBRARY, Oakland History Room, 125 14th St, Oakland, 94612. William W Sturm, Librn
Holdings: Vols (20,000) Cat Mss Maps Pix Microforms
Notes: The Oakland History Room Collection is a reference collection of books, pamphlets, periodicals, pictures, and newspaper clippings. California items incl as much biographical material as possible clipped from the *Oakland Tribune, Oakland Post, California Voice,* the *Montclarion,* and *Alameda Times-Star.* (Library no longer clips *San Francisco Chronicle* or *Examiner*). These clippings are filed by subjects. An index of all the subjects with many cross references are made. An index of articles from about 75 magazines dealing with California subjects is kept up to date. The log books of the Coast Guard Cutter *Bear* from 1889 to 1932 are in the collection. The Jack London collection is listed separately. Ms pages and letters from Joaquin Miller and a fewmiscellaneous letters from other authors are also incl. A set of George Sterling, both inscribed and not inscribed, is owned by the Room.

CA —PASADENA PUBLIC LIBRARY, 285 E Walnut St, Pasadena, 91101. Carolyn Garner, Librn II
Holdings: Vols 3000 Cat Maps Pix
Notes: California collection described in Gertrude Stoughton, *The Books of* California. 1968. Old Pasadena newspapers 1883-date. *Pasadena Star-News* on microfilm 1910-date. Selected California documents. Pasadena local history and biography.

CA —CONTRA COSTA COUNTY LIBRARY, 1750 Oak Park Blvd, Pleasant Hill, 94523. Thomas F Gates, History Specialist
Holdings: Vols (2000) Cat Maps Pix
Notes: Covers Contra Costa County and northern California history, Gold Rush memoirs, California Indian studies, county history reprints. Newspaper clippings, ephemera.

CA —POMONA PUBLIC LIBRARY, Special Collections, 625 S Garey Ave, PO Box 2271, Pomona, 91766. David Streeter, Librn
Holdings: Vols 43,000 Cat Mss Maps Pix Slides Audiotapes Microforms
Notes: Collections consist of printed materials; manuscripts; diaries; oral history interviews; photographs (100,000 images); societies and organizations; Pomona Valley business records. 48 linear feet of city records: Acessors records 1888-1933; various police records (Police Docket, Civil Docket) 1891-1960. Considerable emphasis on the Pomona Valley Region (Los Angeles-San Bernadino Counties).

CA —A K SMILEY PUBLIC LIBRARY, 125 W Vine St, Redlands, 92373. Larry E Burgess, Archivist
Holdings: Vols (3500) Mss Maps Pix Phonorecords Microforms
Budget: ($45,000)
Notes: Emphasis on San Bernadino County and the Redlands area. Especially prized is *The Citrographic*, 1887-1908 (bound vols and microfilm) edited by Scipio Craig, prominent in state, national, and newspaper circles. The ms collection (250,000 pieces) incl the Smily Family papers, much on water development, and onthe citrus industry. The photograph collection (over 5000) covers the history of the area; there are many stereographs and glass slides. The collection on Indians of California and the Southwest was begun from a special gift by Andrew Carnegie honoring his friend, Albert K Smiley.

CA —RICHMOND PUBLIC LIBRARY, Civic Center Plaza, Richmond, 94804. Rosa Casazza, Specialist
Holdings: Vols 400 Cat Mss Maps Pix
Notes: Especially of the Richmond area, but also West Contra Costa County. Also, archives of the Richmond Art Center, 1936-date.

CA —ROSEMEAD PUBLIC LIBRARY, 8800 Valley Blvd, Rosemead, 91770. Sally Colby, Ref Librn
Holdings: Vols 11,012 Cat Mss
Budget: $7500
Notes: Los Angeles County Public Library System cooperates with the Oral History Program, Claremont Colleges, Claremont, California, in the policy, planning, interviewing and funding of oral histories on the San Gabriel Valley and greater Los Angeles area. Collection incl 25 mss (cataloged). Also, a collection of 19th century newspapers. No photocopying.

CA —CALIFORNIA STATE LIBRARY, Library & Courts Bldg, 914 Capitol Mall, Sacramento, 95809. Gary Kurutz, Head of Special Collections
Holdings: Vols (60,000) Cat Mss Maps Pix Microforms
Budget: ($41,550)
Notes: 150,000 photographs; 600 cu ft of mss; 4000 maps; 70,000 reels on microfilm; 8000 bound vols California newspapers; 500 prints of lithographs on California newpapers; 1000 posters; and vertical file materials.

CA —SACRAMENTO PUBLIC LIBRARY, 828 I St, Sacramento, 95814. Dorothy Harvey, Librn, Special Collections
Holdings: Vols 2800 Cat Maps Pix
Notes: Incl reports, studies, histories, yearbooks, guidebooks. *Sacramento Bee* and *Sacramento Union* are indexed 1905 to 1937 and 1974 to date; clipping file contains selected clippings and ephemera; picture file contains black and white photos of Sacramento buildings, streets, and events. A depository for city and county documents was established in 1975; the collection now contains 4000 documents.

CA —MONTEREY COUNTY LIBRARY, 26 Central Ave, Salinas, 93901. Ruth Forsberg, Ref Librn
Holdings: Vols 3000 Cat Maps Pix Slides
Notes: Emphasis on local history.

CA —SAN BERNARDINO COUNTY HISTORICAL ARCHIVES, 104 W Fourth St, San Bernardino, 92415.
Notes: San Bernardino County records.

CA —SAN BERNARDINO COUNTY LIBRARY, 104 W Fourth St, San Bernardino, 92415.
Holdings: Cat Mss Maps Pix
Budget: ($3000)

CA —SAN DIEGO HISTORICAL SOCIETY, Research Archives, Casa de Balboa 1649 El Prado, Balboa Park PO Box 81825, San Diego, 92138. Sylvia Arden, Head Librn & Archivist
Holdings: Cat Mss Maps Pix Audiotapes
Notes: Emphasis on San Diego County and early materials of Riverside and Imperial counties. Over 10,000 photographs also.

CA —SAN DIEGO PUBLIC LIBRARY, 820 E St, San Diego, 92101. Rhoda E Kruse, Sr Librn
Holdings: Vols (13,500) Cat Mss Maps Pix Microforms
Budget: ($5087)
Notes: Also 450 bound periodicals. Incl extensive local history; papers of Foss and Kelly families; some material on John D Spreckels; papers of Southern California Exposition, San Diego 200th Anniversary Committee; Census microfilms; registers of voters 1866-1909; *San Diego Union* Index, which also incl material on Baja Califorina; records of Little Landers Colony, a 1910 Utopian group founded in the Tia Juana River Valley.

CALIFORNIA—HISTORY (cont.)

CA —CALIFORNIA DIVISION OF MINES AND GEOLOGY LIBRARY, Ferry Bldg, Rm 2022, San Francisco, 94111. Angela Brunton, Librn
Holdings: Vols (28,500) Cat Mss Maps Pix Microforms
Budget: ($5650)
Notes: Incl theses on California geology; publications of USGS and USBM, state governments (other than California) concerning mining and geology; publications of foreign governments concerning geology and mining; history of mining in California.

CA —CALIFORNIA HISTORICAL SOCIETY, Schubert Hall Library, 2099 Pacific Ave, San Francisco, 94109. Bruce L Johnson, Library Dir
Holdings: Vols (50,000) Cat Mss Maps Pix
Notes: Incl 8500 collections of mss, 300,000 photographs in San Francisco Photographic Archives and 20,000 at CHS History Center, Los Angeles. Areas of strength incl rare books, early voyages, Mexican War, Gold Rush, overland narrative, Indians, county and municipal histories, histories of industries and corporations, 20th-century social history, trade catalogs, ethnic history, women's history, early California imprints, posters, newspapers, history of printing and publishing, ephemera.

CA —THE POLISH ARTS AND CULTURE FOUNDATION, 1290 Sutter St, San Francisco, 94109. Wanda Tomczykowska, President
Holdings: (1500) Vols
Notes: Incl much on the Polish contribution to California.

CA —SOCIETY OF CALIFORNIA PIONEERS, Library, 456 McAllister St, San Francisco, 94102. Grace E Baker, Librn
Holdings: Vols (12,000) Cat Mss Maps Pix Microforms
Notes: California history, especially the gold rush and the San Francisco earthquake, Sherman collection of early California music, business letterheads of early California firms, San Francisco City Directories 1850-1944, records of California Battalion 1846-47, ms material on overland diaries, ships' logs and passenger lists. Also, large photograph collection.

†CA —UNIVERSITY OF SAN FRANCISCO, Richard A Gleeson Library, The Countess Bernardine Murphy Donohue Rare Book Room, San Francisco, 94117. D Steven Corey, Special Collections Librn
Notes: Some highly specialized materials.

CA —SAN JOSE HISTORICAL MUSEUM, Repository, 635 Phelan Ave, San Jose, 95112. Mignon Gibson, Museum Dir
Holdings: Cat Mss Maps Pix Phonorecords 16mm Films
Notes: Collection of about 2500 cu ft relates to the history of the Santa Clara Valley. Holdings incl Spanish documents from Pueblo de San Jose, ca 1790-1840: Spanish and Mexican landgrant maps for the area; official city and county records, from 1860s on; local newspapers, from 1878 on; maps; personal papers of prominent local figures; local business and organizational records; miscellaneous ephemera; and over 4000 historic photographs. Limited photocopying.

CA —SAN JOSE PUBLIC LIBRARY, 180 W San Carlos St, San Jose, 95113. Homer Fletcher, Dir
Holdings: Vols (11,000) Cat Mss Maps Pix Slides Microforms
Notes: Extensive collection of Californiana.

CA —HUNTINGTON LIBRARY, Art Gallery & Botanical Gardens, 1151 Oxford Rd, San Marino, 91108. Robert L Middlekauff, Dir; Daniel H Woodward, Librn
Holdings: Mss Maps Pix Slides Microforms
Notes: Approx 350,000 rare books, 250,000 reference books, manuscript collection of nearly 2,500,000 pieces and between 200, 000 and 300,000 prints, rare photographs and other related materials. The fullest available survey is now *Guide to Literary Manuscripts in the Huntington Library*, a 539-page handlist published by the Library in 1979.

CA —UNIVERSITY OF CALIFORNIA, SANTA BARBARA, Library, Dept of Special Collections, Santa Barbara, 93106. Christian F Brun, Head
Holdings: Cat Mss Pix
Notes: J J Mitchell Collection.

CA —UNIVERSITY OF SANTA CLARA, Michel Orradre Library, Santa Clara, 95053. Alice Whistler, Ref Librn
Holdings: Vols Cat Maps Pix Microforms

CA —SANTA ROSA-SONOMA COUNTY FREE PUBLIC LIBRARY, Third & E Sts, Santa Rosa, 95404. Audrey Herman, Librn
Holdings: Vols 1200 Cat Maps Pix
Notes: Sonoma County primarily. There is a separate card index (primarily biographical) to the county histories. Incl 180 maps, 4714 pictures.

CA —HOOVER INSTITUTION ON WAR, REVOLUTION & PEACE, Stanford University, Stanford, 94305. Milorad M Drachkovitch, Archivist
Holdings: Mss
Notes: Correspondence, questionnaires, student education records, and other miscellaneous items pertaining to the National Japanese American Student Relocation Council, 1942-1946. 101 cartons and 17 drawers of index cards.

CA —HOOVER INSTITUTION ON WAR, REVOLUTION & PEACE, Stanford University, Stanford, 94305. Milorad M Drachkovitch, Archivist
Notes: The New Left Politics Collection consists of monographs and serials on the New Left that are cataloged. In addition, the collection subscribes to numerous underground newspapers and has obtained special subject collections such as the Free Speech Movement at Berkeley 1964-1965, SNCC and Mississippi Summer 1964, and the insurrection at San Francisco State College in 1968-1969. There is also a good collection on the French student revolts of 1968. The collection is a supervised one and not open to browsers. Interested students and scholars are welcome. Only limited photocopying is permitted.

CA —STANFORD UNIVERSITY LIBRARIES, Cecil H Green Library, Stanford, 94305. Michael T Ryan, Cur
Holdings: Vols Cat Mss Pix Audiotapes
Notes: Manuscript Collections incl papers of the Progressive period in California; papers of New Almaden quicksilver mines; papers of J Arthur Younger (office records); comprehensive collection of personal, business and legal papers of Goodwin J Knight, and miscellaneous Californiana. Farm labor materials incl papers gathered by Ernesto Galarza, Fr Victor Salandini, and Fr James Vizzard.
See also entry under Chicano Studies

CA —THE HAGGIN MUSEUM, Petzinger Library of Californiana, 1201 N Pershing Ave, Stockton, 95203. Diane Freggiaro, Librn/Archivist
Holdings: Vols (7000) Cat Mss Maps Pix Slides Audiotapes 16mm Films
Notes: The Petzinger Library is open by appointment only. Special emphasis on Stockton and San Joaquin County and Valley area, local biography, agriculture, agricultural history, industrial history, farm machinery (especially Holt Manufacturing Co, Stockton). There is a photograph collection of 8500 pictures, and extensive manuscript holdings (about 17,000 pieces).

CA —STOCKTON-SAN JOAQUIN COUNTY PUBLIC LIBRARY, California Reference Room, 605 N El Dorado St, Stockton, 95202.
Holdings: Vols (6300) Cat Maps Phonorecords Microforms
Budget: ($2000)
Notes: Emphasis on Stockton and San Joaquin County with lesser coverage of other Northern California cities and counties. Collection consists of books, periodicals, scrapbooks, and subject index of articles from about 60 books and periodicals dealing with California. Local history collection incl Stockton and San Joaquin County special reports and studies, vertical file materials by subject, an index to local newspapers, 1850-date (1899-1925 in progress), first editions of local authors, Harriet Chalmers Adams collection (qv).

CA —UNIVERSITY OF THE PACIFIC, Holt-Atherton Pacific Center for Western Studies, Stockton, 95211. Hiram L Davis, Dir of Libraries
Holdings: Vols (15,000) Cat Mss Maps Pix Slides
Budget: ($1000)
Notes: The Stuart Library of Western Americana contains a strong basic collection of published material on California history plus numerous special collections of unpublished material.

CA —VALENCIA PUBLIC LIBRARY, 23743 W Valencia Blvd, Valencia, 91355. Naomi Richards, Ref Librn
Holdings: Vols 2000 Uncat
Notes: Arthur B and Margarite Perkins Collection of local history of the Santa Clarita Valley area. Collection not indexed or cataloged.

CA —TULARE COUNTY FREE LIBRARY, 200 W Oak St, Visalia, 93277. Mary Ann Terstette, Historical Librn
Holdings: Vols 2800 Cat Mss Maps Pix Microforms
Notes: Emphasis on Tulare County area.

CA —LOS ANGELES HARBOR COLLEGE, Library, 1111 Figueroa Pl, Wilmington, 90744. Elizabeth Campbell, Librn
Holdings: Vols 250 Cat Mss Maps Pix Slides Microforms
Notes: Los Angeles Harbor Area history, incl San Pedro, Wilmington, Terminal Island, Lomita, Harbor City, Catalina Island, Dead Man's Island. Also incl memorabilia.

CT —YALE UNIVERSITY, Beincke Rare Book & Manuscript Library, Western Americana Collection, Wall & High St, New Haven, 06520. George Miles, Cur
Holdings: Cat Mss Maps Pix
Notes: Incl much historical ephemeral material.

IN —INDIANA UNIVERSITY, Lilly Library, Seventh St, Bloomington, 47405. William R Cagle, Librn
Holdings: // Cat Mss
Notes: First editions and early accounts, including 1000 issues of California gold rush newspapers.

MO —WASHINGTON UNIVERSITY, John M Olin Library, Campus Box 1061, St Louis, 63130.
Holdings: Vols (1800) Cat Mss
Notes: Incl material from the Arthur C Hoskins, Richard S Hawes, Ernst C Krohn, George N Meissner, Stratford Lee Morton, and Edgar M Queeny collections; strong in early travel literature of the US and Latin America; accounts of exploration in the Mississippi Valley and Trans-Mississippi West; miscellaneous accounts of history, pioneer life, and travel in the Ohio Valley, Old Southwest, and California; material on the American Indian; 18th century American music; early American imprints.

NY —SAINT LAWRENCE UNIVERSITY, Owen D Young Library, Canton, 13617. Mahlon Peterson, Librn
Holdings: Mss
Notes: Collection consists of letters written home to New York State from the California gold fields and from New Orleans and Memphis during the Civil War. Approx 90 items.

NY —NEW YORK HISTORICAL SOCIETY, Library, 170 Central Park W, New York, 10024. James Gregory, Librn
Notes: One of the largest collections in the East of California newspapers printed in the 1850s.

RI —BROWN UNIVERSITY, John Hay Library, 20 Prospect St, Providence, 02912. Mark N Brown, Cur Mss
Holdings: Vols 350 // Uncat
Notes: Eberstadt Collection of Narratives of California Pioneers--personal narratives written by pioneers who crossed the Plains to California after the discovery of gold in 1849. A large portion of the books were printed in late 19th and early 20th centuries and deal with: Indian contacts, captivities, frontier lore, travel routes, topography, fauna and flora, outlaws, traders and trappers, and frontier army life.

CALIFORNIA—IMPRINTS

CA —UNIVERSITY OF CALIFORNIA, LOS ANGELES, Research Library, Dept of Special Collections, 405 Hilgard Ave, Los Angeles, 90024. Edward Shreeves, Chairman, Bibliographers Group; David S Zeidberg, Head
Holdings: Vols 13,500 Cat
Notes: 13,500 books, serials, and directories published in Southern California.

CA —CALIFORNIA HISTORICAL SOCIETY, Schubert Hall Library, 2099 Pacific Ave, San Francisco, 94109. Bruce L Johnson, Library Dir
Holdings: Vols (50,000) Cat Mss Maps Pix
See also entry under California - History

CT —YALE UNIVERSITY, Box 1603A, Yale Station, New Haven, 06520.

CALIFORNIA—INDUSTRIES

CA —CALIFORNIA STATE UNIVERSITY, FRESNO, Henry Madden Library, Dept of Special Collections, Fresno, 93740. Ronald J Mahoney, Head
Holdings: Vols (3400) Cat Maps Pix
Notes: Books and pamphlets relating to the history and development of viticulture and enology. Emphasizes pre-1920 worldwide imprints. Incl 900 merchants' catalogs, 1400 pamphlets, 200 wine lists, 750 periodical issues, and ephemera. Partially cataloged.

CA —POMONA PUBLIC LIBRARY, Special Collections, 625 S Garey Ave, PO Box 2271, Pomona, 91766. David Streeter, Librn
Holdings: Uncat Mss
Notes: 165 linear feet of Pomona Valley business records incl 16 water companies and 28 citrus companies; diaries; clubs and organizations; Laura Ingalls Wilder.

WA —URS ENGINEERS, Library, 2615 Fourth Ave, Seattle, 98121. Jill Phelps, Librn
Holdings: Vols (3100) Cat
Budget: ($5000)
Notes: Environmental impact assessment, hazardous materials disposal, oil spill cleanup and environmental effects of waterborne pollutants, especially with regard to California and the Western environment.

CALIFORNIA—LOCAL HISTORY

CA —AZUSA PACIFIC COLLEGE, Marshburn Memorial Library, Citrus & Alosta, Azusa, 91702. Edward Peterman, Librn
Holdings: Vols 5000 // Maps Pix
Notes: Azusa Foothill Citrus and Local History collection is related to the genesis of Azusa, the citrus industry, the Slauson and Macneil families, and such companies as the Azusa Land and Water Company, Azusa Electric Lighting and Power Company, Azusa Foothill Citrus Association, Azusa Agricultural Water Company, and the Azusa Foothill Citrus Company. Includes letters, ledgers, etc.

CA —UNIVERSITY OF CALIFORNIA, RIVERSIDE, University Library, 4045 Canyon Crest Dr, Box 5900, Riverside, 92517.
Holdings: Vols Cat Mss Maps Pix
Notes: Emphasis on Riverside City and County, early materials on San Bernardino, and on the Mojave and Colorado Deserts. Over 5,000 photographs.

CA —SAN JOSE PUBLIC LIBRARY, 180 W San Carlos St, San Jose, 95113. Homer Fletcher, Dir

CALIFORNIA—MAPS

CA —KERN COUNTY LIBRARY SYSTEM, 1315 Truxtun Ave, Bakersfield, 93301. Mary Haas, Geology, Mining, Petroleum Librn
Notes: Deals with California and western states primarily. Incl 5000 maps.

†CA —UNIVERSITY OF CALIFORNIA, BERKELEY, General Library, Map Room, Berkeley, 94720.
Notes: Emphasis on US, particularly California and the West.

CA —CALIFORNIA STATE UNIVERSITY, CHICO, Library, Government Publications and Maps, Chico, 95929. William Stuve, Librn
Holdings: Vols (64,600)

†CA —CALIFORNIA STATE UNIVERSITY, FRESNO, Library, Reference Dept, Fresno, 93740.

CA —CALIFORNIA STATE UNIVERSITY, LONG BEACH, Reference Center, 1250 Bellflower Blvd, Long Beach, 90840.
Notes: Incl 22,544 maps and 550 atlases. The map collection is especially strong in California topographical maps.

CA —LOS ANGELES PUBLIC LIBRARY, History Dept, 630 W Fifth St, Los Angeles, 90071. Dorothy Mewshaw, Librn, Map Rm
Holdings: Vols (3000) Cat Maps
Budget: ($85,000)
Notes: The Mary Helen Peterson Collection of Maps and Atlases. World wide coverage, including topographic, political and special purpose maps. Depository for US Geologic Survey topographical maps, Defense Mapping Agency, and National Ocean Survey. Maps of Los Angeles City and County.

CA —UNIVERSITY OF CALIFORNIA, LOS ANGELES, Research Library, Dept of Special Collections, 405 Hilgard Ave, Los Angeles, 90024. Edward Shreeves, Chairman, Bibliographers Group; David S Zeidberg, Head
Holdings: Maps
Notes: 600 historical maps of early California and ranchos maps of Southern California; 75 real estate, insurance, and zoning atlases of Los Angeles and vicinity.

CA —POMONA PUBLIC LIBRARY, Special Collections, 625 S Garey Ave, PO Box 2271, Pomona, 91766. David Streeter, Librn
Holdings: Cat Mss Maps
Notes: Some 4000 maps. Strong for Pomona Valley area: tract maps, water company maps; depository for USGS California topographic maps; California earthquake fault maps.

CA —CALIFORNIA STATE ARCHIVES, 1020 O St, Room 130, Sacramento, 95814. John F Burns, Chief of Archives; Joseph Samora, Head of Reference
Holdings: Vols (19)
Notes: A special collection of Spanish and Mexican land grants, ca 1784-1846.

CA —CALIFORNIA STATE LIBRARY, Library & Courts Bldg, 914 Capitol Mall, Sacramento, 95809. Gary Kurutz, Head of Special Collections
Holdings: Vols (60,000) Cat Mss Maps Pix Microforms
Budget: ($41,550)
Notes: 150,000 photographs; 600 cu ft of mss; 4000 maps; 70,000 reels on microfilm; 8000 bound vols California newspapers; 500 prints of lithographs on California newpapers; 1000 posters; and vertical file materials.

†CA —SAN DIEGO STATE UNIVERSITY, Geography Dept, Map Library, San Diego, 92182.

CA —UNIVERSITY OF CALIFORNIA, SANTA BARBARA, Map and Imagery Laboratory, Santa Barbara, 93106. Larry Carver, Dept Head
Notes: California imagery collection: 250, 000 frames of high/medium altitude color infrared color, B/W aerial photography, specializing in the tri-county area, the Central Valley and the Pacific Coast.

CALIFORNIA—NATURAL RESOURCES

CA —STRYBING ARBORETUM SOCIETY, Golden Gate Park Library, Jane Gates, Librn, 9th Ave at Lincoln Way, San Francisco, 94122.
Holdings: Vols (10,000)

†TX —UNIVERSITY OF TEXAS, EL PASO, Library, El Paso, 79968.
Notes: Significant collections of water resources information about Texas and California.

CALIFORNIA—PICTURES, ILLUSTRATIONS, ETC.

CA —CALIFORNIA STATE UNIVERSITY, LONG BEACH, Library, Dept of Special Collections & Archives, 1250 Bellflower Blvd, Long Beach, 90840. John Ahouse, Special Collections Librn
Holdings: Mss Maps Pix VF
Notes: Emphasis on Long Beach, bibliography available.

CA —UNIVERSITY OF CALIFORNIA, LOS ANGELES, Research Library, Dept of Special Collections, 405 Hilgard Ave, Los Angeles, 90024. Edward Shreeves, Chairman, Bibliographers Group; David S Zeidberg, Head
Notes: 150 images of San Francisco Chinatown and the Mother Lode country, taken by Louis J Stellman, a San Francisco photographer.

CALIFORNIA—POLITICS AND GOVERNMENT

CA —CLAREMONT COLLEGES, Honnold Library, Ninth & Dartmouth, Claremont, 91711. Tania Rizzo, Special Collections Dept Head
Holdings: Vols 200 Cat Mss Pix
Notes: The papers of former Democratic Congressman Jerry Voorhis, from the 1930s to present, occupying nearly 100 document boxes. The papers reflect his life and career, incl biographical material, the history of the Voorhis School for Boys, his involvement in the Dies Committee, and his wide-ranging interests in American economic and social issues, such as cooperatives, monopolies and cartels, Latin American relations, consumers, and senior citizens. Books by and about him, with research files. Correspondence with political leaders. Inventory available. Restricted use.

CA —UNIVERSITY OF CALIFORNIA, DAVIS, Shields Library, Dept of Special Collections, Davis, 95616. Donald Kunitz, Head; C Danial Elliott, Asst Head
Holdings: Cat Mss Pix
Notes: The Shields Collection documents the career of California Superior Court Judge Peter J Shields of Sacramento, his 49 years on the bench and his relationship with prominent political figures. 1050 items.

CA —LOS ANGELES PUBLIC LIBRARY, Municipal Reference Library, Rm 530, City Hall E, 200 N Main St, Los Angeles, 90012. C Grimsley, Senior Librn
Holdings: Vols (86,000) Cat
Budget: ($33,000)
Notes: Emphasis on cities over 500,000 with special collection of municipal documents from large cities. Biographical material on local governmental officials.

CA —UNIVERSITY OF CALIFORNIA, LOS ANGELES, Research Library, Dept of Special Collections, 405 Hilgard Ave, Los Angeles, 90024. Edward Shreeves, Chairman, Bibliographers Group; David S Zeidberg, Head
Notes: Personal papers of many individuals and families, incl Eugene Warren Biscailuz, Katherine Philipps Edson, John Randolph Haynes, Franklin Hichborn, Carey McWilliams, William Starke Rosecrans, and Philip David Swing.

CA —UNIVERSITY OF CALIFORNIA, LOS ANGELES, Research Library, Public Affairs Service, 405 Hilgard Ave, Los Angeles, 90024. Edward Shreeves, Chairman, Bibliographers Group; Eugenia Eaton, Head, Public Affairs Service
Notes: Political campaign materials of the United States from 1920. Particularly strong for campaigns from the 1940s to the 1980s. Focus is on United States, California, and Los Angeles area candidates and issues. Mostly ephemeral materials (flyers, brochures, publicity releases, pamphlets, etc).

†CA —UNIVERSITY OF SOUTHERN CALIFORNIA, University Library, Archives of Performing Arts, Los Angeles, 90089. Robert Knutson, Librn
Holdings: Mss
Notes: Ronald Reagan's personal, moving picture, and political papers.

CA —CALIFORNIA STATE ARCHIVES, 1020 O St, Room 130, Sacramento, 95814. John F Burns, Chief of Archives; Joseph Samora, Head of Reference
Holdings: Mss Maps Pix Microforms
Notes: 55,000 cubic feet of records, papers,

CALIFORNIA—POLITICS AND GOVERNMENT (cont.)

photographs, maps and microforms; cataloged. Historical records of the California executive, legislative and judicial branches of government, as well as selected records of six counties and several school districts.

CA —SAN BERNARDINO COUNTY LIBRARY, 104 W Fourth St, San Bernardino, 92415.
Holdings: ($3000)

OK —UNIVERSITY OF OKLAHOMA, Bizzell Memorial Library, Western History Collections, 401 W Brooks, Norman, 73069. John Ezell, Cur
Holdings: Mss Documents Newspapers Pix Maps
Notes: Stage actress, Helen Gahagan Douglas, US Representative. Her papers. Guide available.

CALIFORNIA—PROMOTION

CA —UNIVERSITY OF CALIFORNIA, DAVIS, Shields Library, Dept of Special Collections, Davis, 95616. Donald Kunitz, Head; C Danial Elliott, Asst Head
Holdings: Cat Mss Pix
Notes: The California Promotional Collection incl pamphlets and newspapers promoting California in the 19th and 20th centuries, with items on tourism, irrigation, real estate investment, agriculture, growth and lure of cities and counties (2200 items). The Lindley Papers document life in Sacramento during the second half of the 19th century, with family papers, photograhs, and memorabilia (356 items). The Wolfskill Collection of scrapbooks, memorbilia and family papers, relate to John R Wolfskill, early settler in Solano County (1842) (1150 items). The Pierce Papers contain general and family correspondence, business and legal papers, photographs and related printed material of an early Davis, California, family, as well as material relating to the purchase of the University of California, Davis, and to the California Almond Growers' Exchange (1075 items). The Shields Collectiondocuments the career of California Superior Court Judge Peter J Shields of Sacramento, his 49 years on the bench and his relationship with prominent political figures (1050 items).

CA —CALIFORNIA POLYTECHNIC STATE UNIVERSITY LIBRARY, Special Collections and University Archives, San Luis Obispo, 93407. Nancy E Loe, Head Librn
Holdings: Vols 100 Cat Mss Pix Slides
Notes: The Fairs Collection incl 56,000 mss materials (correspondence, scrapbooks, legislative opinions, and memoranda), photographs and slides documenting the Western Fairs Association of Sacramento, California, and the management and growth of fairs in California and around the world (materials in rough sorting stage).

CALIFORNIA—RELIGIOUS LIFE AND CUSTOMS

CA —LOS ANGELES PUBLIC LIBRARY, Philosophy & Religion Dept, 630 W Fifth St, Los Angeles, 90071. Marilyn C Wherley, Librn
Holdings: Vols 2500 Cat
Budget: ($60,000)
Notes: Historical, theological and biographical works on all major world religions including materials on leading cults and sects, especially in California. Particular strengths in Christianity, oriental religions and comparative religions. Includes many serials, periodicals, and special indexes.

CALIFORNIA—SEALS

CA —LOS ANGELES PUBLIC LIBRARY, Genealogy & Local History Dept, 630 W 5th St, Los Angeles, 90071. Lucile Lipman, Sr Librn
Holdings: Pix
Budget: ($16,000)
Notes: Collection of California city and county seals.

CALIFORNIA—SOCIAL CONDITIONS

CA —LOS ANGELES PUBLIC LIBRARY, Social Sciences Dept, 630 W Fifth St, Los Angeles, 90071. Marilyn C Wherley, Principal Librn
Holdings: Vols 165,000 Cat Microforms
Budget: ($150,000)
Notes: Incl government documents, pamphlets, statistics, social problems, planning, etc. Popular and scholarly works.

CALIFORNIA—SOCIAL LIFE AND CUSTOMS

†CA —JEWISH FEDERATION COUNCIL OF GREATER LOS ANGELES, Jewish Community Library, 6505 Wilshire Blvd, Los Angeles, 90048.
Notes: Jewish culture, life in America. Incl historical documents and pictures pertaining to the history of the Jewish community in Los Angeles and vicinity.

CA —LOS ANGELES PUBLIC LIBRARY, Philosophy & Religion Dept, 630 W Fifth St, Los Angeles, 90071. Marilyn C Wherley, Librn
Holdings: Vols 175 Cat
Budget: ($60,000)
Notes: Comprehensive coverage of scholarly and popular material on the religious experience of Black Americans including history and impact of the Black Church with emphasis on California and the Southwest. Part of the more general Black History and Culture collection.

CA —LOS ANGELES PUBLIC LIBRARY, Philosophy & Religion Dept, 630 W Fifth St, Los Angeles, 90071. Marilyn C Wherley, Librn
Holdings: Vols 2500 Cat
Budget: ($60,000)
Notes: Historical, theological and biographical works on all major world religions including materials on leading cults and sects, especially in California. Particular strengths in Christianity, oriental religions and comparative religions. Includes many serials, periodicals, and special indexes.

CA —CALIFORNIA POLYTECHNIC STATE UNIVERSITY LIBRARY, Special Collections and University Archives, San Luis Obispo, 93407. Nancy E Loe, Head Librn
Holdings: Vols (100) Cat
Notes: Herpersonal papers covering her architectural career of forty years, which incl several Hearst estates as well as private residences in the California Arts and Crafts style. Incl Hearst/Morgan correspondence and telegrams; business correspondence, travel accounts, sketchbooks, awards, photographs and several hundred architectural drawings. Hearst Castle Collection incl 8500 architectural drawings for Hearst's residences at San Simeon, Jolon, Wyntoon, and Santa Monica and approx 100 vols of secondary source material. The Asilomar Collection contains 145 architectural drawings for the Morgan-designed YWCA facility near Monterey, California. Incl blueprints, diplomas, personal papers. Finding aid in progress. Incl 10,000 pieces of ms material, 10,000 architectural drawings and blueprints.

DC —LIBRARY OF CONGRESS, American Folklife Center, Archive of Folk Culture, Washington, 20540.
Notes: The Charles Todd and Robert Sonkin Collection of field recordings made in California migratory labor camps, 1940-41.

CALIFORNIA, LOWER see Baja California

CALIFORNIA ALMOND GROWERS' EXCHANGE

CA —UNIVERSITY OF CALIFORNIA, DAVIS, Shields Library, Dept of Special Collections, Davis, 95616. Donald Kunitz, Head; C Danial Elliott, Asst Head
Holdings: Cat Mss Pix
Notes: The California Promotional Collection incl pamphlets and newspapers promoting California in the 19th and 20th centuries, with material relating to the California Almond Growers' Exchange.

CALIFORNIA ALMONDS see Almonds, California

CALIFORNIA ART see Art, California

CALIFORNIA ARTISTS see Artists, California

CALIFORNIA COMPOSERS see Composers, California

CALIFORNIA CHANNEL ISLANDS

†CA —SANTA BARBARA BOTANIC GARDEN LIBRARY, 1212 Mission Canyon Road, Santa Barbara, 93105. Margaret Connors, Librn
Holdings: Vols (5000)
Notes: Especially strong on California native plants.

CALIFORNIA GOLD RUSH see Gold Rush, California

CALIFORNIA INSTITUTE OF TECHNOLOGY

CA —CALIFORNIA INSTITUTE OF TECHNOLOGY, Robert A Millikan Memorial Library, Archives, 1201 E California Blvd, Pasadena, 91125. Judith R Goodstein, Archivist
Notes: The Lee A DuBridge papers, incl 228 boxes of correspondence, documents, reports, and memorabilia reflecting his tenure as head of MIT Radiation Laboratory, 1940-1946; as president of Caltech, 1946-1969; and his participation in professional and governmental organizations.

CALIFORNIA MIGRANT MINISTRY

MI —WAYNE STATE UNIVERSITY, Walter P Reuther Library, Archives of Labor & Urban Affairs, Detroit, 48202. Philip Mason, Dir
Notes: Insights into national problems of discrimination and poverty can ve found in the records and papers of the United Farm Workers Organizing Committee and its Director, Cesar Chavez; the California Migrant Ministry; and the Citizen's Crusade Against Poverty, now preserved in the Archives.

CALIFORNIA MUSIC see Music, California

CALIFORNIA NEWSPAPERS see Newspapers, California

CALIFORNIA POETRY see Poetry, California

CALIFORNIA STATE BEEKEEPERS' ASSOCIATION

CA —UNIVERSITY OF CALIFORNIA, DAVIS, Shields Library, Dept of Special Collections, Davis, 95616. Donald Kunitz, Head; C Danial Elliott, Asst Head
Holdings: Cat Mss Pix Slides
Notes: Records of the California State Beekeepers Association (1891-1973) (1600 items). Described in: USDA Agricultural Research Service, *Beekeeping in the United* States (Agricultural Handbook, no 335, rev ed 1977); and Johansson, Tag Sigvard Kjell, *Apicultural Literature Published in Canada and the United States* (New York, 1972).

CALLAGHAN, MORLEY

IL —ILLINOIS STATE UNIVERSITY, Milner Library, Dept of Special Collections, Normal, 61761. Robert Sokan, Librn
Notes: First editions, limited editions, ephemera, etc.

CALLAHAN, CHUCK

NY —HAMPDEN-BOOTH THEATRE LIBRARY AT THE PLAYERS, 16 Gramercy Park, New York, 10003. Louis A Rachow, Librn/Cur
Holdings: Mss Pix
Notes: Nearly 300 burlesque scripts and vaudeville skits, music in ms, 25 photographs in character, two song books of the period, a notebook of stage gags and repartee, typescript of biography of Chuck Callahan (30 pages), and a number of ephemeral pieces, stage money, programs, etc. 4 boxes of indexed material. Described in *The Players Bulletin,* Spring 1966, pp 20-21; and *Performing Arts Resources* vol 3 (New York: Theatre Library Association, 1976), pp 143-150. Described in *Theatre & Performing Arts Collections* (New York: Haworth Press, 1981).

CALLAHAN, HARRY

AZ —UNIVERSITY OF ARIZONA, Center for Creative Photography, 843 E University Blvd, Tucson, 85721. James Enyeart, Dir; Terence Pitts, Cur and Librn
Notes: Center has significant collections consisting of more than 25 photographs plus other archival material such as negatives, contact sheets, work prints, correspondence, financial records, diaries, project files, etc. Inventories of the collections are available to researchers. Published guides available for some collections.

CALLEY, LT. WILLIAM

UT —UNIVERSITY OF UTAH, Marriott Library, Special Collections, Salt Lake City, 84112. Gregory C Thompson, Cur
Notes: Papers of George Latimer, attorney for Lt William Calley. Complete record of court-martial trial 1968-1973.

CALLIGRAPHY AND CALLIGRAPHERS

†CA —SAN FRANCISCO PUBLIC LIBRARY, San Francisco, 94102.

CA —STANFORD UNIVERSITY LIBRARIES, Cecil H Green Library, Stanford, 94305. Michael T Ryan, Cur
Holdings: Vols (12,000) Cat
Notes: The Morgan A & Aline D Gunst Memorial Library. The book arts in every century with some of the best examples of California printers and graphic artists. Complete or nearly complete collections of works by the Kelmscott, Doves, Ashendene, Colt, Grabhorn, and Grabhorn-Hoyem presses.

IL —NEWBERRY LIBRARY, John M Wing Foundation on the History of Printing, 60 W Walton St, Chicago, 60610. Diana Haskell, Cur of Modern Mss
Holdings: Vols (30,000) Cat Mss
Budget: ($50,000)
Notes: The collection covers printing and printing history of Western Europe and the Americas from its invention to the present. It is particularly rich in incunabula (about 2000); the works of the great printers, among others Aldus, Bodoni, Baskerville, and Rogers. Excellent collection of European and American calligraphy including Arrighi, Beauchesne, Jarry Johnston, Spencer, et al. Printed catalog: *A Dictionary Catalogue.* (Boston: G K Hall, 1961); *Supplements* (1981). Brief descriptions: James M Wells, "The John M Wing Foundation of the Newberry Library," *The Book Collector,* VIII, 2 (Summer 1959), pp 157-162; Lawrence W Towner, *An Uncommon Collection* (Chicago: The Newberry Library, 1977), pp 25-26.

IL —ORIENTAL INSTITUTE, 1155 E 58th St, Chicago, 60637. John Larsen, Archivist
Notes: The Bernhard Moritz Collection. Fine examples of bindings as well as of Islamic calligraphy and writing materials--papyrus, parchment, papers, etc. Extensive collection is also in the Beatty Library in Dublin, Ireland; Victoria and Albert Museum in London; Libraries in East and West Germany.

IN —INDIANA STATE UNIVERSITY, EVANSVILLE, Library, 8600 University Blvd, Evansville, 47712. Gina R Walker, Acting Archivist
Holdings: Uncat Mss
Notes: Papers, etc of the nationally known graphic arts specialist Herbert William Simpson (1904-1970), advertising man, type designer and calligrapher. Original examples of calligraphy and graphic design executed for commercial ads and occasional pieces for personal interest. Materials of about 1940-1970.

MD —JOHNS HOPKINS UNIVERSITY, Milton S Eisenhower Library, George Peabody Collection, 17 E Mt Vernon Place, Baltimore, 21201. Lyn Hart, Peabody Librn

†MD —UNIVERSITY OF MARYLAND, Library, R D Remley Collection, College Park, 20742. Donald Farren, Cur Rare Books
Holdings: Vols (2000) Cat
Notes: *Exempla* and secondary works in the areas of typography, calligraphy, book design, book illustration, the history of books, and of publishing, etc. Catalog entries for designers, printing types, private presses, etc.

MA —HARVARD UNIVERSITY LIBRARY, Widener Library, Cambridge, 02138.
Holdings: Cat Mss
Notes: English copybooks of the 18th century are desribed in *Harvard Library* Bulletin, XIV (1960), 12-19.

MA —HARVARD UNIVERSITY LIBRARY, Houghton Library, Printing and Graphic Arts Dept, Cambridge, 02138. Eleanor M Garvey, Cur
Notes: Collection incl illustrated books, fine printing, type specimens, illuminated and calligraphic manuscripts, and drawings for book illustration.

MN —MINNEAPOLIS COLLEGE OF ART & DESIGN, Library, 200 E 25 St, Minneapolis, 55404. Richard Kronstedt, Head Librn

NY —COLUMBIA UNIVERSITY LIBRARIES, Rare Book & Manuscript Library, 801 Butler Library, 535 W 114 St, New York, 10027. Kenneth A Lohf, Librn
Holdings: Vols (16,000)
Notes: The Plimpton Collection. One of the best collections in existence. Particularly rich in American examples, but most of the old masters are well represented.

PA —FREE LIBRARY OF PHILADELPHIA, Rare Book Dept, Logan Sq, Philadelphia, 19103. Marie E Korey, Rare Book Librn
Holdings: Vols (5600) Uncat Mss
Notes: A collection of printed writing books (200), as well as the David N Carvalho Collection of examples of handwriting from the 9th to the 20th century.

VA —UNIVERSITY OF VIRGINIA, Alderman Library, Rare Book Dept, Charlottesville, 22901. Julius P Barclay, Cur
Holdings: Vols (6500) // Mss
Notes: The Oscar Ogg Collection of Book Arts covers calligraphy, letterforms, typography, printing, and graphic arts. Contains early writing books and printed works, as well as modern manuals and other works on printing, publishing, and promotion through graphic arts. The Dept also has the Edward L Stone Collection of Printing Specimens, 3000 items. Contains materials tracing the history of printing, inks, binding styles and materials, types. Also the Tompkins Collection (2000 vols), and the Stevens Watts collection (900 vols).

CALLIGRAPHY AND CALLIGRAPHERS, CHINESE

IL —UNIVERSITY OF ILLINOIS, URBANA/CHAMPAIGN, Asian Library, Urbana, 61801. William S Wong, Asian Librn
Holdings: Vols 130,000 Cat
Notes: East Asian Collection. Primarily a collection of Chinese, Japanese, and Korean language materials.

CALLING CARDS

NY —COLUMBIA UNIVERSITY LIBRARIES, Rare Book & Manuscript Library, 801 Butler Library, 535 W 114 St, New York, 10027. Kenneth A Lohf, Librn
Holdings: Mss
Notes: The Frederick C Schang Collection. About 650 calling cards of great and near-great celebrities. Most contain autographs or holograph notes. Restricted use.

CALLOWAY, CAB

MA —BOSTON UNIVERSITY, Mugar Memorial Library, Special Collections Dept, 771 Commonwealth Ave, Boston, 02215. Howard B Gotlieb, Dir
Holdings: Cat Pix
Notes: Mss, correspondence, scores arranged for his band, etc collected in depth; incl publications by or about him.

CALLOWAY, ERNEST AND DEVERNE

MO —UNIVERSITY OF MISSOURI-SAINT LOUIS, Thomas Jefferson Library, Manuscript and Historical Society Collection, 8001 Natural Bridge Rd, Saint Louis, 63121.

CALMUCK LANGUAGE see Kalmuck Language

CALVIN, JOHN, AND CALVINISM

DC —FOLGER SHAKESPEARE LIBRARY, 201 E Capitol St, Washington, 20003. Philip A Knachel, Acting Dir
Notes: A major collection.
See also entry under Reformation.

IL —NEWBERRY LIBRARY, 60 W Walton St, Chicago, 60610. Diana Haskell, Cur of Modern Mss
Holdings: Cat

MD —JOHNS HOPKINS UNIVERSITY, Milton S Eisenhower Library, George Peabody Collection, 17 E Mt Vernon Place, Baltimore, 21201. Lyn Hart, Peabody Librn
Notes: Noncirculating.

WI —UNIVERSITY OF WISCONSIN, MADISON, Memorial Library, Western European Humanities Collection, 728 State St, Madison, 53706. Charles Szabo, Bibliographer
Holdings: Vols (5000) Cat
Notes: Tank Collection. The core of this extensive collection is its works on theology, the largest portion of which deals with Calvinism. Practically all the printed sermons of the major Calvinist preachers of the 18th century are represented. Includes many 16th and 17th century sermons. About a third of the collection deals with Church history; not only are Calvinist histories represented but also 18th century histories of Methodists, Quakers, and Moravians. Supplements the Montauban Collection (French Protestantism) and the Chwalibog Collection (theology).

CAMAC, CHARLES NICOLL BANCKER, 1868-1940

KS —UNIVERSITY OF KANSAS MEDICAL CENTER, College of Health Sciences & Hospital, Clendening History of Medicine Library, Rainbow Blvd at 39th, Kansas City, 66103. Robert P Hudson, Chmn/Cur
Notes: Papers, 1906-28. 1 vol. Physician and educator. Correspondence, invoices, press notices and reviews, photos, and other papers relating to Camac's book, *Epoch-making Contributions to Medicine, Surgery and the Allied Sciences* (1909). Correspondents incl N W Green of W B Saunders Company, Camac's publisher, and American and English physicians.

CAMBODIA

HI —UNIVERSITY OF HAWAII, Library, 2550 The Mall, Honolulu, 96822. Joyce Wright, Head, Asia Collection; Masato

CAMBODIA (cont.)

Matsu, Head, East Asia Vernacular Collection
Holdings: Vols 331,620 Cat Microforms
Notes: The Asia Collection holds materials from and about Southeast Asia: Brunei, Burma, Cambodia (Kampuchea), Indonesia, Laos, Malaysia, Philippines, Singapore, Thailand. Large contemporary Indonesian language collection. Several thousand vols in Thai and in Vietnamese. Minimal holdings in Burmese, Khmer, Lao languages. Social sciences and humanities emphasis for the post-World War II period. Western language coverage supplemented by retrospective holdings in the main library collection.

IL —SOUTHERN ILLINOIS UNIVERSITY, CARBONDALE, Delyte W Morris Library, Carbondale, 62901.
Holdings: Vols (4100) Cat Maps Audiotapes Microforms
Notes: The Vietnamese collection has been transferred to the general library. It incl 1200 cataloged titles in the Vietnamese language, plus 56 Vietnamese language microfilms. A profile of the area emphasis on the collection appears from the following distribution of the 2987 titles entered in the holdings and accessions lists published by the Southern Illinois University Center for Vietnamese Studies: Vietnam, 1965; Cambodia and Laos, 63; Other Southeast Asia (incl Indonesia), 916; East Asia (mostly China), 246; General (reference works, bibliographies, etc), 197. Also over 1000 maps.

MI —UNIVERSITY OF MICHIGAN, Harlan Hatcher Graduate Library, Ann Arbor, 48109. Susan Go, Librn
Holdings: Vols (250,000) Cat Mss Maps Pix Slides Microforms
Notes: Cambodia's name was recently changed to Khymer. Incl in the Michigan Historical Collections (primarily archival material) are papers of Michiganders in southeast Asia, mostly the Philipines, eg papers of Joseph R Hayden, Frank Murphy and G Mennen Williams, also, on film, the selected papers of Philippines president Manuel Quezon. All aspects of the countries, cultures and peoples of Brunei, Burma, Khymer, Indonesia, Laos, Malaysia, Philippines, Singapore, Thailand, Portuguese Timor and Vietnam. Also the Malayo-Polynesian (Austronesian), Mon-Khmer (Austroasiatic), and Sino-Tibetan language groupings.

NY —CORNELL UNIVERSITY LIBRARIES, John M Olin Library, John M Echols Collection on Southeast Asia, Ithaca, 14853. Giok Po Oey, Curator
Holdings: Vols (167,000) Cat Mss Maps Pix Microforms
Budget: ($90,000)
Notes: Additions published in the collection's monthly accessions list (Ithaca: Cornell University, Southeast Asia Program, 1959-). Holdings through December 1980 listed in *Cornell University Libraries Southeast Asia Catalog* (Boston: G K Hall, 1976, First supplement, 1983), 10 vols.

CAMBODIA—HISTORY

CA —HOOVER INSTITUTION ON WAR, REVOLUTION & PEACE, Stanford University, Stanford, 94305. Milorad M Drachkovitch, Archivist
Holdings: Maps Pix
Notes: Papers of Ambassador Philip D Sprouse, incl printed matter, news clippings, maps, invitations, programs of various events, diplomatic list, and photographs relating to the George C Marshall Mission to China, 1945-1946, activities of Philip D Sprouse as US Ambassador to Cambodia, 1962-1964, cultural and political aspects of recent Cambodian history. 2 ms boxes.

CAMBODIAN ART see Art, Cambodian

CAMBODIAN LITERATURE see Khmer Language and Literature

CAMELLIA

PA —LONGWOOD GARDENS, INC, Library, Kennett Square, 19348. Enola Jane N Teeter, Librn

SC —COLLEGE OF CHARLESTON LIBRARY, Special Collections Dept, Charleston, 29401.
Notes: Contains biographical and family history material of Wendell Mitchel Levi; invertebrate anatomy course notes from the College of Charleston; University of Chicago Law School casebooks; correspondence concerning pigeons and camellias; notes, photographs, mss, typescripts, and galleys of published works; and other materials relating to pigeons and camellias. Among the more prominent correspondents are B F Skinner, Madame Chiang Kai-Shek, and Mary Bonner.

CAMERON, ALISTAIR GRAHAM WALTER, 1925-

MA —HARVARD UNIVERSITY ARCHIVES, Nathan Marsh Pusey Library, Cambridge, 02138. Clark A Elliott, Associate Cur
Notes: Alistair Graham Walter Cameron's papers.

CAMERON, ANNE

BC —SIMON FRASER UNIVERSITY, Library, Burnaby, V5A 1S6, Can. Percilla Groves, Special Collections Librn
Holdings: Cat Mss
Notes: Playscripts, prose and poetry mss, correspondence, proofs and notebooks of the British Columbia poet and playwright.

CAMEROON

DC —HOWARD UNIVERSITY, Moorland-Spingarn Research Center, 500 Howard Place NW, Washington, 20059. Clifford L Muse, Jr, Acting Dir

SC —UNIVERSITY OF SOUTH CAROLINA, Thomas Cooper Library, Columbia, 29208. Kenneth E Toombs, Dir of Libraries; Roger Mortimer, Rare Book Librn
Holdings: Vols 200 Cat
Notes: Farmington Plan Assignment.

CAMOENS, LUIS DE

CA —CALIFORNIA STATE UNIVERSITY, HAYWARD, Library, Hayward, 94542. Melissa Rose, Dir
Holdings: Vols 200 Cat
Budget: ($7408)
Notes: Editions in several languages, incl early printings of works by and about Camoens. Most of the collection was originally in the library of Henry Hart, San Francisco scholar whose extensive writings in the field of early voyages and travels include a biography of Camoens. Noncirculating.

CT —UNIVERSITY OF CONNECTICUT, Library, Storrs, 06268. R H Schimmelpfeng, Dir of Special Collections
Holdings: Vols 258 Cat

MA —HARVARD UNIVERSITY LIBRARY, Widener Library, Cambridge, 02138. Ellen H Brow, Specialist in Book Selection
Holdings: Cat

CAMP, ELISHA, 1786-1866

NY —CORNELL UNIVERSITY LIBRARIES, Collection of Regional History, Dept of Manuscripts and Univ Archives, Ithaca, 14853.
Holdings: Mss
Notes: Politician, land agent and owner, newspaper editor, banker. Incl 38 pieces, mainly of mss drafts of handbills, editorials, and speeches.

CAMP, JOHN NEWBOLD 'HAPPY'

OK —UNIVERSITY OF OKLAHOMA, Bizzell Memorial Library, Western History Collections, 401 W Brooks, Norman, 73069. John Ezell, Cur
Holdings: Vols Mss Pix Maps Microforms
Notes: John Newbold "Happy" Camp, US Representative, papers. Guide available.

CAMP, WALTER

CT —YALE UNIVERSITY, Box 1603A, Yale Station, New Haven, 06520.
Notes: Papers of Walter Camp, father of American football and foremost authority on sports and physical fitness. 48 microfilm reels; incl also over 20,000 clippings, etc on sports, providing virtual history, 1866-1925. Published guide to the collection for sale.

CAMPAIGN SONGS

RI —BROWN UNIVERSITY, John Hay Library, 20 Prospect St, Providence, 02912. Mary T Russo, Cur of Broadsides
Notes: Within this collection of poetry broadsides are numerous examples of early American ballads. Another collection of 5000 separate and 2000 bound slip sheets or slip ballads published from 1830 to 1870, record all aspects of everyday life and illustrate the manner in which people responded to political, military, social and economic events. Civil War ballads are included. Retrospective pieces are added annually. Partial catalog.

CAMPANOLOGY

NY —SOCIETAS CAMPANARIORUM (SOCIETY OF BELL-RINGERS), Campanological Library, Riverside Church, 490 Riverside Dr, New York, 10027. James R Lawson, Librn
Holdings: Vols 1000 Cat
Notes: One of the largest collections of books, pamphlets, periodicals, etc on bells and bell music (chimes, carillons, change-ringing, handbells, electronic carillons, etc) in North America. Examined by appointment only.

ON —NATIONAL LIBRARY OF CANADA, 395 Wellington St, Ottawa, K1A 0N4, Can. Andre Preibish, Dir
Notes: Books, papers, and artifacts from Percival Price, renowned authority on campanology and first Dominion carilloneur (1927-39). Incl designs of bells and bell towers around the world, sound recordings, programs, etc. Some bells. About a third of the collection refers to Canadian carillons and carilloneurs.

CAMPBELL, E. SIMMS

MA —BOSTON UNIVERSITY, Mugar Memorial Library, Special Collections Dept, 771 Commonwealth Ave, Boston, 02215. Howard B Gotlieb, Dir
Holdings: Cat Pix
Notes: Cartoons, drawings, correspondence, etc collected in depth; incl publications by or about.

CAMPBELL, LILY BESS, 1883-1968

CA —UNIVERSITY OF CALIFORNIA, LOS ANGELES, Research Library, Dept of Special Collections, 405 Hilgard Ave, Los Angeles, 90024. Edward Shreeves, Chairman, Bibliographers Group; David S Zeidberg, Head
Notes: 7.5 linear feet of UCLA English professor's letters, photographs, and papers.

CAMPBELL, R. WRIGHT

MA —BOSTON UNIVERSITY, Mugar Memorial Library, Special Collections Dept, 771 Commonwealth Ave, Boston, 02215. Howard B Gotlieb, Dir
Holdings: Cat Mss

CAMPBELL, ROY, 1902-1957

DC —GEORGETOWN UNIVERSITY, Library, Special Collections Div, 37 & O Sts NW, Washington, 20057. George M Barringer, Special Collections Librn; Nicholas B Sheetz, Mss Librn
Holdings: Mss
Notes: The Archives of the Gallery of Living Catholic Authors was founded in 1932 by Sister Mary Joseph of the Sisters of Loretto to focus attention on modern Catholic literature, and to provide a depository for manuscripts, letters, photographs, and books by contemporary Catholic writers. Contains material by hundreds of writers, incl Hilaire Belloc, Roy Campbell, Padraic Colum, Eric

CAMPBELL, ROY, 1902-1957 (cont.)

Gill, Paul Horgan, Mary Lavin, Marie Belloc Lowndes, Kathleen Norris, Alred Noyes, Sheila Kaye-Smith, Sigrid Undset, and Evelyn Waugh, to name only a few.

IN —INDIANA UNIVERSITY, Lilly Library, Seventh St, Bloomington, 47405. William R Cagle, Librn
Holdings: // Cat Mss
Notes: Correspondence of Roy Campbell, 1931-1936, primarily with his wife and his publisher, concerning publication of writings, Campbell's bullfighting, and his finances. Incl 13 ms writings, some apparently unpublished. 150 items. Library's holdings incl published first editions of Campbell's works.

NV —UNIVERSITY OF NEVADA, RENO, University Library, Special Collections Dept, Reno, 89557. Robert E Blesse, Head
Holdings: // Vols (40) Cat Other appearances 260 Cat
Notes: Includes individual works by author in all editions including translations; also prefaces, introductions, published correspondence, appearances in anthologies, periodicals, etc. Bibliographical research collection, part of Modern Authors Collection.

CAMPBELL, THOMAS

MA —BOSTON UNIVERSITY, Mugar Memorial Library, Special Collections Dept, 771 Commonwealth Ave, Boston, 02215. Howard B Gotlieb, Dir
Holdings: // Mss
Notes: 27 letters; mss, proofs and related items.

OH —OHIO UNIVERSITY, Vernon R Alden Library, Department of Archives and Special Collections, Athens, 45701. Gary A Hunt, Head
Holdings: Vols 71 Cat
Notes: First and later editions of Campbell's published works.

CAMPBELL, WILLIAM W.

NY —NEW YORK HISTORICAL SOCIETY, Library, 170 Central Park W, New York, 10024. James Gregory, Librn
Notes: The papers of historian and judge William W Campbell; business papers of Benjamin Maverick Mumford, insurance broker and ship owner. About 2300 items.

CAMPBELL BOOKSTORE, PHILADELPHIA

PA —TEMPLE UNIVERSITY, Samuel Paley Library, Berks & 13 Sts, Philadelphia, 19122.
Notes: Archives of the William J Campbell Bookstore, Philadelphia, from mid-19th century.

CAMPBELL FAMILY

NC —DUKE UNIVERSITY, William R Perkins Library, Manuscript Dept, Durham, 27706. Ellen Gartrell, Cur of Mss
Holdings: Cat Mss
Notes: Papers, etc.

CAMPBELLITES see Disciples of Christ

CAMPING

MA —APPALACHIAN MOUNTAIN CLUB, 5 Joy St, Boston, 02108. Fran Belcher, Librn
Holdings: Vols (6500) Cat Maps Pix Slides
Budget: ($3000)
Notes: Mountaineering, espec the White Mountains. Bound editions of other countries, mountaineering journals.

MA —HARVARD UNIVERSITY, Harvard Forest Library, Petersham, 01366. Catherine M Danahar, Librn
Holdings: Cat
Notes: Emphasis on National Forest recreation, with related subjects incl wildlife and economics.

CAMPION, JOHN F.

CO —UNIVERSITY OF COLORADO, Libraries, Western Historical Collections, Boulder, 80309.
Holdings: // Cat Mss Maps
Notes: Papers of John F Campion (1849-1916), who mined in California and Nevada before striking it rich in the 1880s in Leadville, Colorado. He owned Reindeer, Caribou, and Ibex (better known as Little Johnny) mining companies. He was the vice-president of the Denver National Bank and the Denver, Northwestern and Pacific Railroad, and was a founder of Colorado's sugar beet industry. The collection focuses on his Leadville mining activities, covering the period from 1887 to 1922. A guide is available to the 14 boxes of material. Typescript inventory is available.

CAMRYN, WALTER

IL —NEWBERRY LIBRARY, 60 W Walton St, Chicago, 60610. Carolyn A Sheehy, Administrator
Holdings: Cat Mss Pix Posters
Notes: Extensive holdings in the areas of dance history (including important first editions) and dance music. Newly formed Midwest Dance Archive contains the papers of Ann Barzel, Walter Camryn, Diana Huebert and Edna McRae.

CAMPS—WATER PROGRAMS see Aquatic Sports

CANADA

CT —YALE UNIVERSITY, Box 1603A, Yale Station, New Haven, 06520.

†MA —HARVARD UNIVERSITY, Harvard College Library, Cambridge, 02138.
Notes: Depository for Canadian documents. Library collection supports academic and research activities in Canadian studies.

MI —UNIVERSITY OF MICHIGAN, Graduate Library, Ann Arbor, 48109. Janet White, Reference Librn
Holdings: Cat
Notes: Espec French Canadian aspects of Canadian civilization, language, and literature.

NY —AMERICAN MUSEUM OF NATURAL HISTORY, Library Services Dept, Central Park W & 79th St, New York, 10024. Nina J Root, Chairwoman; Mary Genett, Asst Librn for Reference Services
Holdings: Cat Mss Pix Microforms
Notes: The Ernest Thompson Seton diaries. Thousands of pages of an unpublished 67-year diary record of one of the world's most famous naturalists, the gift of Joseph F Cullman III, a Trustee of the Museum. Preserved in 35 protective cases, the gift incl unpublished diaries, notebooks, and some other writings. The diary begins 12 June 1879; the last entries were written in hospital, just a month before Seton's death in 1946. Literally hundreds of examples of flora and fauna are pictured in the diaries in original pencil, pen-and-ink, and watercolor sketches, on nearly every page. Research will reveal information on the Indian sign language, the Boy Scouts of America, the Woodcraft League of America, and the wilderness of Canada, Florida, Texas, the West and Southwest, etc.

NY —BOOKS-ACROSS-THE-SEA, The English-Speaking Union, 16 E 69 St, New York, 10021. Catherine Nolan, Librn
Holdings: Vols (6500) Cat
Budget: ($25,000)
Notes: Deals mainly with humanities and social sciences of Great Britain, Australia, New Zealand, and Canada; adult books. Collection started in 1942; current titles added through exchange.

NC —DUKE UNIVERSITY, William R Perkins Library, Durham, 27706. Elvin E Strowd, University Librn

OH —CASE WESTERN RESERVE UNIVERSITY, Kulas Music Library, 11118 Bellflower Rd, Cleveland, 44106. Timothy Robson, Music Librn
Notes: Containing deposit of a collection of some 800 records of music and the spoken word in French, English, and Spanish presented by Radio Canada International in Montreal.

BC —NEW WESTMINSTER PUBLIC LIBRARY, 716 Sixth Ave, New Westminster, V3M 2B3, Can. Alan Woodland, Dir
Holdings: Cat Mss Maps Pix Slides Microforms
Notes: Attempts to gather as much information as possible about the history of the city of New Westminster. Collection based on almost complete run of *Columbian* Newspaper (1861-date); *The Weekly Columbian Newspaper* (1902-1954), and other newspapers and documents. Indexing of the *Columbian Newspaper* is taking place slowly. Have 25 maps, 1800 pictures, 110 slides, microforms, newspaper. Copies of photographs and documents are made when these become available.

BC —LEGISLATIVE LIBRARY (PROVINCIAL), Parliament Bldgs, Victoria, V8V 1X4, Can. J H MacEachern, Head, Government Documents Division
Holdings: Vols Cat Microforms

ON —QUEEN'S UNIVERSITY, Douglas Library, Kingston, K7L 5C4, Can. William F E Morley, Cur, Special Collections
Notes: Canadiana (humanities). Edith and Lorne Pierce Collection; incl 15,000 Canadian pamphlets and about 50,000 vols, cataloged. Also Canadian paper collection: broadsides and posters, sheet music, programmes, greeting cards, maps, etc.

ON —LIBRARY OF PARLIAMENT, Parliament Bldgs, Ottawa, K1A 0A9, Can. Erik J Spicer, Parliamentary Librn
Holdings: Vols (350,000) Cat Mss Maps Pix Microforms
Notes: Also 2,000 bound vols of Canadian pamphlet collection. Older material (19th century and earlier) not available on interlibrary loan.

ON —NATIONAL FILM BOARD, CANADA, Tunney's Pasture Area, Ottawa, K1A 0M9, Can.
Notes: Photo library of 225,000 Canadian images, incl 33,000 slides.

ON —NATIONAL MUSEUMS OF CANADA, Library Services Directorate, Ottawa, K1A 0M8, Can. Valerie Monkhouse, Director
Holdings: Vols (70,000) Cat Mss Maps Pix Slides Microforms
Budget: ($60,000)
Notes: Collection includes anthropology, archaeology, ethnology, folklore, history, Indians of North America, Inuit, linguistics of North American Indians, material history, military and naval history, museology. Research collection, interlibrary loans available, public may use on the premises.

†ON —TRENT UNIVERSITY, Peterborough, K9J 7B8, Can.
Notes: Canadiana; Canadian literature (Shell Collection); native studies; Trent Valley region.

ON —METROPOLITAN TORONTO LIBRARY, Canadian History Dept, Baldwin Room Section, 789 Yonge St, Toronto, M4W 2G8, Can. David B Kotin, Head
Holdings: Vols (52,000) Mss Pix
Notes: This collection consists of material on Canadian history, geography, travel, archaeology, genealogy, retrospective city and telephone directories, collective biographies, native peoples (excluding customs, rights and social conditions), Arctic regions, military history and theory. It is an extremely strong collection of both current and retrospective material. Particular strengths are national and local history (especially Ontario), Arctic regions, native peoples, travel (especially Ontario), and military history. Incl 78,000 historical pictures, 235 linear meters mss, 14,000 broadsides and 3800 bound newspapers.

ON —NORTH YORK PUBLIC LIBRARY, Canadiana Collection, 35 Fairview Mall Dr, Willowdale, M2J 4S4, Can. Ian C Ross, Head
Holdings: Vols (70,000) Cat Microforms
Notes: Special areas of interest: history, particularly Ontario local history; historical societies; art; printing; bibliography; genealogy; education; native peoples; Canadian literature, poetry and criticism. Special collections incl Newton MacTavish

CANADA (cont.)

Collection (150 vols; 3 linear ft mss); North York Public Library Archives; Graphic Publishers of Ottawa (150 vols); Douglas C McMurtrie printing collection (300 items); and post-Confederation literary mss and correspondence (10 linear ft). Partially cataloged. Publications: *Genealogy and Family History Catalogue* (Library, 1978); *Reader, Lover of Books, Lover of Heaven: A Catalogue ... of the Book Arts in Ontario* (1978) and *Reader, Lover of Books*, Vol 2 (1981).

PQ —ROYAL BANK OF CANADA, Library, PO Box 6001, Montreal, H3C 3A9, Can. Anthea Downing, Chief Librn
Holdings: Cat Maps Microforms

CANADA—ARTS

ON —YORK UNIVERSITY, Scott Library, Downsview, M3J 2R2, Can. Hartwell Bowsfield, University Archivist
Notes: The Jean A Chalmers Choreographic Archives of works by Canadian choreographers, along with background information and technical and performance data on each work. A continuing deposit donated by the Ontario Arts Council.

CANADA—DESCRIPTION AND TRAVEL

MN —UNIVERSITY OF MINNESOTA, James Ford Bell Library, 309 19th Ave S, Minneapolis, 55455. John Parker, Cur
Holdings: Vols (11,000) Cat Mss Maps
Notes: Collection of original materials relating to European expansion, 1400-1800.

AB —PETER WHYTE FOUNDATION, Archives of the Canadian Rockies, Box 160, Banff, T0L 0C0, Can. Mary Andrews, ACR Librn
Holdings: Vols (4247) Cat Mss Maps Pix Slides Phonorecords Audiotapes Videotapes 16mm Films Filmstrips Microforms
Budget: ($1500)
Notes: Collect all available material which touches on the Rocky Mountains of Canada (from the US border to the Peace River in the north; from the west of Calgary on the east to the town of Revelstoke, BC on the west). This material incl history (the early explorers, Indians, construction of the railroads, mountaineering, and development of the national parks), natural history (geology, botany, wildlife) and poetry and fiction with the Rockies as a setting. Collect maps of the area, photographs, tape recordings of the pioneers. We also house on our premises the Alpine Club of Canada's library, which is one of the most comprehensive collections on the subject of mountaineering worldwide. Noncirculating.

NT —NORTHWEST TERRITORIES PUBLIC LIBRARY SERVICES, Bos 1100, Hay River, X0E 0R0, Can.
Holdings: Vols (1235) Cat Maps Audiotapes
Notes: Originally intended to provide items of historical significance on the Northwest Territories. It contains a number of first editions, some of which have since become available in reprint form. Copies of material in relevant native languages and on learning languages.

ON —UNIVERSITY OF GUELPH, Library, Guelph, N1G 2W1, Can. Margaret Beckman, Chief Librn; Ellen Pearson, Ref Librn
Holdings: Vols 5000 Cat Mss Maps Pix Slides Phonorecords Audiotapes 16mm Films Microforms
Notes: Early travel and exploration in Canada. Special Archival Collection of the Canadian Guide. Special catalogs can be produced for any part of collections from automated library records. (All records for all formats are in machine readable form.)
See also entry under Canada - History

ON —QUEEN'S UNIVERSITY, Douglas Library, Kingston, K7L 5C4, Can. William F E Morley, Cur, Special Collections
Holdings: Vols (50,000) Cat Mss Maps Pix Microforms
Budget: ($12,000)
Notes: The Edith and Lorne Pierce Collection of Canadiana. Also over 15,000 titles in Canadian Pamphlet Collection. Strong in humanities and social sciences, special strength in English and French Canadian literature; discovery and exploration narratives; Loyalists; War of 1812; opening of the West; local history, 19th century pamphlets and association items. Described in *A Catalogue of Canadian Manuscripts Collected by Lorne Pierce and Presented to Queen's University* (Toronto: Ryerson, 1946); and in *Canadiana 1698-1900 in the Possession of the Douglas* Library, comp by Janet S Porteous, foreword by Lorne Pierce (Kingston, 1932). Many more recent published studies on parts of the collection.

ON —PUBLIC ARCHIVES OF CANADA, Library, 395 Wellington St, Ottawa, K1A 0N3, Can. Dawn E Monroe, Collections Development Officer
Holdings: Vols (80,000) Cat
Notes: Over the years, the Public Archives Library has assembled thousands of books and pamphlets relating to all aspects of Canadian history, from the founding of the country to the present day. The holdings incl journals of explorers and missionaries, accounts of the first voyageurs, as well as administrative, civil and military records. Also incl are basic reference works on the history, geography, politics and economics of Canada, the administration of New France, Canada's geographic and political history, transportation incl railways and navigation, immigration, Crown lands, religious groups and institutions. The Library's collection also has works covering other areas of interest such as archives and archives management, heraldry, genealogy, Canadian art, geographic indexes and sound and visual archives.

ON —LAURENTIAN UNIVERSITY LIBRARY, Ramsey Lake Rd, Sudbury, P3E 2C6, Can. Suzanne Brunette, Special Collection Librn; Sue Vongpeisal, Head Librn
Notes: Materials on northern Canada, incl 2200 books and pamphlets, 60,000 press clippings on northern topics 75 series of periodicals and over 1500 maps, plus photographs and thousands of samples of arctic and subarctic plants incl mosses, lichens, algae and wood sections. Much of the material is in French.

ON —METROPOLITAN TORONTO LIBRARY, Canadian History Dept, Baldwin Room Section, 789 Yonge St, Toronto, M4W 2G8, Can. David B Kotin, Head
Holdings: Vols (52,000) Mss Pix
Notes: This collection consists of material on Canadian history, geography, travel, archaeology, genealogy, retrospective city and telephone directories, collective biographies, native peoples (excluding customs, rights and social conditions), Arctic regions, military history and theory. It is an extremely strong collection of both current and retrospective material. Particular strengths are national and local history (especially Ontario), Arctic regions, native peoples, travel (especially Ontario), and military history. Incl 78,000 historical pictures, 235 linear meters mss, 14,000 broadsides and 3800 bound newspapers.

ON —VICTORIA UNIVERSITY, Library, 71 Queen's Park Crescent, Toronto, M5S 1K7, Can. Robert C Brandeis, Chief Librn
Holdings: Vols (5000) Cat
See also entry under Canada - History

PQ —MCGILL UNIVERSITY, McLennan Library, Rare Books and Special Collections Dept, 3459 McTavish St, Montreal, H3A 1Y1, Can.
Notes: Numerous primary sources, eg, maps, manuscripts, guide books, personal narratives. This material can be found throughout the collections, particularly in Canadian Pamphlets, Manuscripts, Maps, Topography, and the Lawrence Lande Collection of Canadiana. Catalogues are available for the last-named collection: The Lawrence Lande Collection of Canadiana in the Redpath Library of McGill University: a Bibliography. Montreal, 1965. Rare and Unusual Canadiana: First Supplement to the Lande Bibliography. Montreal, 1971.

PQ —MCGILL UNIVERSITY, McLennan Library, Rare Books and Special Collections Dept, 3459 McTavish St, Montreal, H3A 1Y1, Can.
Notes: 5524 sheet maps, 370 atlases, 571 folded maps, 629 guide books, 248 reference books. The coverage is worldwide, specializing in North America, Canada, Quebec, Montreal. Includes a collection of guide books from the 1800s to the present day, as well as a reference collection; there is also a large collection of modern topographical literature with worldwide coverage, and an important collection of postcards particularly of Montreal and the Province of Quebec. A finding list is available for 19th century guide books on Canada: A Preliminary Guide to Nineteenth Century Canadian Guide Books: a Survey of the Holdings of the McLennan Library with an Historical Introduction. Montreal, 1982.

CANADA—DIRECTORIES

ON —METROPOLITAN TORONTO LIBRARY, Canadian History Dept, 789 Yonge St, Toronto, M4W 2G8, Can.
Notes: Bell Canada Telephone Historical Collection of 448 reels of microfilm of Ontario and Quebec telephone books from 1878 to 1979. The collection will be updated. Toronto city directories from 1868-1949 are available also.

CANADA—DISCOVERY AND EXPLORATION

MN —UNIVERSITY OF MINNESOTA, James Ford Bell Library, 309 19th Ave S, Minneapolis, 55455. John Parker, Cur
Holdings: Vols (10,000) Cat Mss Maps
Notes: Collection of original materials relating to European expansion, 1400-1800.

AB —PETER WHYTE FOUNDATION, Archives of the Canadian Rockies, Box 160, Banff, T0L 0C0, Can. Mary Andrews, ACR Librn
Holdings: Vols (4247) Cat Mss Maps Pix Slides Phonorecords Audiotapes Videotapes 16mm Films Filmstrips Microforms
Budget: ($1500)
Notes: Collect all available material which touches on the Rocky Mountains of Canada (from the US border to the Peace River in the north; from the west of Calgary on the east to the town of Revelstoke, BC on the west). This material incl history (the early explorers, Indians, construction of the railroads, mountaineering, and development of the national parks), natural history (geology, botany, wildlife) and poetry and fiction with the Rockies as a setting. Collect maps of the area, photographs, tape recordings of the pioneers. We also house on our premises the Alpine Club of Canada's library, which is one of the most comprehensive collections on the subject of mountaineering worldwide. Noncirculating.

MB —HUDSON'S BAY CO, Library, 77 Main St, Winnipeg, R3C 2R1, Can. Carol Preston, Librn Hudson's Bay House
Holdings: Vols (6000) Cat Mss Maps Pix Slides
Notes: Main purpose is to provide research materials for production of the historical quarterly *The Beaver*, and to answer inquiries about the Company's history. Incl 250,000 pictures and 7000 VF pieces. No published catalog, but Library maintains author/subject/title card catalog. Limited photocopying. Mss of HBC Archives held by the Manitoba Provincial Archives. Published descriptions: Dowdall, Judi, "Hudson's Bay Company Library," *Canadian Library* Journal, June 1974, p 179; Preston, Carol, "Hudson's Bay Company Library," *Manitoba Library Association Bulletin*, June 1976, pp 24-25.

NS —DALHOUSIE UNIVERSITY LIBRARY, Halifax, B3H 4H8, Can.
Holdings: Cat Pix
Notes: Approx 2000 lithographs, steel engravings, fine prints and illustrated historical maps from the 18th and 19th centuries are in the collection. Subject

CANADA—DISCOVERY AND EXPLORATION (cont.)

coverage is primarily of Nova Scotia, New Brunswick, Prince Edward Island, and Newfoundland scenery, street scenes, and portrayals of prominent people, buildings and events. Generally rich in illustrations of the working and social life of the period. Artists represented incl: J E Woolford, J F W Desbarres, William Eagar, William Bartlett and Richard Short. Historical maps incl some of the earliest visual depictions of the Atlantic coast. Material available for editorial reproduction. Print fee charged. No loans.

ON —QUEEN'S UNIVERSITY, Douglas Library, Kingston, K7L 5C4, Can. William F E Morley, Cur, Special Collections
Holdings: Vols (50,000) Cat Mss Maps Pix Microforms
Budget: ($12,000)
Notes: The Edith and Lorne Pierce Collection of Canadiana. Also over 15,000 titles in Canadian Pamphlet Collection. Strong in humanities and social sciences, special strength in English and French Canadian literature; discovery and exploration narratives; Loyalists; War of 1812; opening of the West; local history, 19th century pamphlets and association items. Described in *A Catalogue of Canadian Manuscripts Collected by Lorne Pierce and Presented to Queen's University* (Toronto: Ryerson, 1946); and in *Canadiana 1698-1900 in the Possession of the Douglas* Library, comp by Janet S Porteous, foreword by Lorne Pierce (Kingston, 1932). Also later books and articles on parts of the collection.

ON —UNIVERSITY OF TORONTO, Thomas Fisher Rare Book Library, 120 Saint George St, Toronto, M5S 1A5, Can. Richard G Landon, Head
Holdings: Vols (30,000) Mss Maps Pix
Notes: Great variety of material relating to early exploration and settlement of Canada, including the search for the Northwest Passage and the subsequent exploration of the Arctic. Manuscript and printed material pertaining to the overland exploration of northwestern Canada and the Barren Lands. Manuscript and printed material documenting early emigration schemes and colonization attempts, including Selkirk's Red River settlement.

CANADA—ECONOMIC CONDITIONS

MB —UNIVERSITY OF MANITOBA, Elizabeth Dafoe Library, Archives and Special Collections Dept, Winnipeg, R3T 2N2, Can. Richard E Bennett, Dept Head; Corrado A Santoro, Reference Archivist
Notes: Correspondence, minutes of executive and annual meetings, membership lists, annual reports, financial records and investigative reports on foods, durgs, prices, marketing schemes, loans and many other consumer-oriented topics. Also files on the Winnipeg and Fort Garry Branches of CAC (Manitoba).

ON —CANADA, DEPT OF EMPLOYMENT & IMMIGRATION LIBRARY, Ottawa, K1A 0J9, Can. P E Sunder-Raj, Dir Library Services
Holdings: Vols (15,000) // Cat

ON —ENERGY, MINES & RESOUCES CANADA, Headquarters, 580 Booth St, Ottawa, K1A 0E4, Can. F B Scollie, Chief Librn
Holdings: Vols (65,000) Cat Microforms
Budget: ($200,000)
Notes: EMR Libraries Network includes the Headquarters, Conservation and Non-Petroleum Branch, and Petroleum Incentives Branch. Topics incl energy and mineral economics, especially Canadian.

ON —CANADIAN IMPERIAL BANK OF COMMERCE, Information Centre, Commerce Court, Toronto, M5L 1A2, Can. Jane Cooney, Librn Head Office
Holdings: Vols (22,000) Cat Microforms
Notes: Emphasis on current information and major historical documents. Incl material on all sectors of the Canadian economy with emphasis on industry. Sources incl all provincial governments, the federal government and commercial publishers. 2000 current periodicals and annuals, incl a representative selection of Canadian trade journals and Canadian and foreign business, financial and management periodicals. Also incl a complete file of Statistics Canada documents and 1500 clipping files.

PQ —ROYAL BANK OF CANADA, Library, PO Box 6001, Montreal, H3C 3A9, Can. Anthea Downing, Chief Librn
Holdings: Cat Maps Microforms

CANADA—EMIGRATION AND IMMIGRATION

PA —BALCH INSTITUTE FOR ETHNIC STUDIES, Library, 18 S Seventh St, Philadelphia, 19106. R Joseph Anderson, Library Dir
Holdings: Vols 385 Cat

ON —CANADA, DEPT OF EMPLOYMENT & IMMIGRATION LIBRARY, Ottawa, K1A 0J9, Can. P E Sunder-Raj, Dir Library Services
Holdings: Vols (15,000) // Cat

†ON —METROPOLITAN TORONTO LIBRARY, Social Sciences Dept, 789 Yonge St, Toronto, M4W 2G8, Can. Abdus Salam, Head
Holdings: Vols Cat Maps Phonorecords Audiotapes 16mm Films Microforms
Notes: Collection is both current and historical. Strong in immigrants' guides, government reports and statistics, analyses, histories and studies of ethnic groups. Strong on the Underground Railroad.

CANADA—ENGLISH-FRENCH RELATIONS

PQ —CONCORDIA UNIVERSITY LIBRARIES, Vanier Library, 7141 Sherbrooke St SW, Montreal, H3G 1M8, Can. Martin Cohen, Collections Coordinator
Holdings: Uncat Mss
Notes: Dr J B Rudnyckyj was on the Royal Commission on Bilingualism and Biculturalism in Canada. His papers deal with bilingualism, multi-culturalism, minorities, languages. 400 boxes.

CANADA—FOREIGN RELATIONS

ON —CANADA DEPT OF EXTERNAL AFFAIRS, Library Services Div, 125 Sussex Dr, Ottawa, K1A 0G2, Can. Ruth Margaret Thompson, Dir
Holdings: Vols (40,000) Cat Maps Phonorecords Audiotapes Microforms
Notes: Incl 1000 maps, 250,000 microforms, and 550,000 documents.

ON —CANADIAN INSTITUTE OF INTERNATIONAL AFFAIRS, 15 King's College Circle, Toronto, M5S 2V9, Can. Jane Barrett, Librn
Holdings: Vols (23,000) Cat Mss Microforms Books VF
Budget: ($8800)
Notes: Incl both historical and current material on all subjects relevant to a study of Canadian foreign relations.

†ON —METROPOLITAN TORONTO LIBRARY, Social Sciences Dept, 789 Yonge St, Toronto, M4W 2G8, Can. Abdus Salam, Head
Holdings: Vols Cat Maps Phonorecords Audiotapes 16mm Films Microforms
Notes: Strong collection emphasizing historical and current aspects of Canadian foreign relations. Areas of special emphasis include Canadian-US relations and Canadian-Great Britain relations. Complete holdings of Canadian and British Treaties from 1686.

CANADA—FRENCH-ENGLISH RELATIONS see Canada—English-French Relations

CANADA—GENEALOGY

MA —FREE PUBLIC LIBRARY, Genealogy Room, 613 Pleasant St, Bedford, 02740. Paul A Cyr, Librn
Holdings: Vols (10,000) Cat Mss Maps Pix Microforms
Budget: ($1000)
Notes: Extensive collection on the history and genealogy of New England, with a strong emphasis on southeastern Massachusetts. Materials incl books, periodicals, mss, microfilms, and pictures of New England life. Unique features of the collection incl the *Leonard Papers* ms of vital records of early Bristol County, *Repertoires des Mariages* of Province Quebec, Canada, and a collection on the Society of Friends, or Quakers.

MA —SPRINGFIELD CITY LIBRARY, Genealogy and Local History Dept, 220 State St, Springfield, 01103. Joseph Carvalho III, Supervisor
Holdings: Vols (17,000) Cat Mss Maps Pix Microforms
Budget: ($8000)
Notes: New England, Massachusetts, local history (Springfield), and genealogy collections. collections. 18,000 pictures, 3200 microforms, ca 15,000 clippings, pamphlets, etc (280 ft of vertical files).

ON —LONDON PUBLIC LIBRARIES & MUSEUMS, London Room, 305 Queen's Ave, London, N6B 1X2, Can. W Glen Curnoe, Librn
Holdings: Cat Mss Maps Pix Slides Phonorecords Audiotapes 16mm Films Microforms
Budget: ($3700)
Notes: History of Ontario, with emphasis on London and region, from early 19th century onward. Separate catalog books, films and microforms. Various subject indexes to materials. Special interest in London, Ontario authors and publishers.

ON —PUBLIC ARCHIVES OF CANADA, Library, 395 Wellington St, Ottawa, K1A 0N3, Can. Dawn E Monroe, Collections Development Officer
Holdings: Vols (80,000) Cat
Notes: The Public Archives Library holds a wide variety of printed sources for those wishing to conduct genealogical research. Most often consulted are those manuals referred to in the pamphlet produced by the Public Archives titled *Tracing Your Ancestors in Canada* (Ottawa: Public Archives, 1983). In addition, those wishing to conduct research overseas may obtain the titles of certain specialized guides by contacting the Library. The Library also has various lists and and bibliographies of the few genealogies which have been published to date. The Library's collection incl most of the ancestral genealogies listed in these bibliographies and these works may be consulted on the premises. The information they contain varies greatly and ranges from a simple listing of the names of common ancestors to complete family histories.

ON —METROPOLITAN TORONTO LIBRARY, Canadian History Dept, Baldwin Room Section, 789 Yonge St, Toronto, M4W 2G8, Can. David B Kotin, Head
Holdings: Vols (52,000) Mss Pix
Notes: This collection consists of material on Canadian history, geography, travel, archaeology, genealogy, retrospective city and telephone directories, collective biographies, native peoples (excluding customs, rights and social conditions), Arctic regions, military history and theory. It is an extremely strong collection of both current and retrospective material. Particular strengths are national and local history (especially Ontario), Arctic regions, native peoples, travel (especially Ontario), and military history. Incl 78,000 historical pictures, 235 linear meters mss, 14,000 broadsides and 3800 bound newspapers.

ON —NORTH YORK PUBLIC LIBRARY, Canadiana Collection, 35 Fairview Mall Dr, Willowdale, M2J 4S4, Can. Ian C Ross, Head
Holdings: Vols (70,000) Cat Microforms
See also entry under Canada.

PQ —BIBLIOTHEQUE DE LA VILLE DE MONTREAL, Montreal City Library, Salle Gagnon Collection, 1210 Sherbrooke St E, Montreal, H2L 1L9, Can. Daniel Olivier,

CANADA—GENEALOGY (cont.)

Dept Head
Holdings: Vols (44,055) Cat Mss Maps Slides Microforms
Budget: ($30,000)
Notes: Marriage records of Roman Catholic parishes of Province of Quebec; censuses; deeds; family histories; etc.

PQ —BIBLIOTHEQUE DES ARCHIVES NATIONALES DU QUEBEC, CP 10450, Sainte-Foy, G1V 4N1, Can. Collete Barry, Dir
Holdings: Vols (50,000) Cat Mss Maps Pix Microforms
Budget: ($25,000)
Notes: Dictionary catalog on cards (unpublished). Official Quebec documents published before 1867.

CANADA—GOVERNMENT PUBLICATIONS

CT —YALE UNIVERSITY LIBRARY, Government Documents Center, 38 Mansfield St, PO Box 2491, Yale Sta, New Haven, 06520. Sandra K Peterson, Documents Librn
Holdings: Microforms
Notes: Canadian depository.

KY —UNIVERSITY OF KENTUCKY, Margaret I King Library, Government Publications Dept, Lexington, 40506. Sandra McAninch, Head
Holdings: Cat
Notes: Depository since 1956. Incl papers.

†MA —HARVARD UNIVERSITY, Harvard College Library, Cambridge, 02138.
Notes: Depository for Canadian documents. Library collection supports academic and research activities in Canadian studies.

NY —NEW YORK STATE LIBRARY, State Education Bldg Annex, Washington Ave, Albany, 12224.
Holdings: Cat Microforms
Notes: Official depository of New York State publications; regional depository of US documents, also in microfilm; depository for Canadian government docuements; strong collections of state documents, New York City documents; British sessional papers; also League of Nations, United Nations, OAS documents. Extensive holdings of other domestic and foreign publications. Congressional serial set, incl hearings (1946-date).

NY —NEW YORK PUBLIC LIBRARY, Research Libraries, Economic & Public Affairs Div, Fifth Ave & 42 St, New York, 10018. Edward DiRoma, Chief
Holdings: Vols (1,500,000) Cat Microforms
Notes: Full depository.

NC —DUKE UNIVERSITY, William R Perkins Library, Durham, 27706. Elvin E Strowd, University Librn

OR —UNIVERSITY OF OREGON LIBRARY, Documents Section, Eugene, 97403. Tom Stave, Section Head; John Shuler, Documents Librn
Holdings: Vols 24,000
Notes: Depository for Canadian government publications.

PA —UNIVERSITY OF PITTSBURGH, Hillman Library, Pittsburgh, 15260. Mary E Miller, Documents Librn
Notes: Selective depository, since 1968. Earlier materials were transferred into this separate collection. Only federal government printers are incl.

AB —ALBERTA ATTORNEY GENERAL, Law Library, Fourth Floor North Wing, Bowker Bldg 9833-109 St, Edmonton, T5K 2E8, Can. Andrew Balazs, Departmental Librn
Holdings: Vols (13,000) Cat Audiotapes
Budget: ($121,620)
Notes: Emphasis is on Canadian law. But if the solicitors can not find a Canadian precedent, they consult English law. If there is no precedent in English law they consult Commonwealth law, and if there is no precedent there either, then they consult American law. Therefore, the Library does have all the basic Canadian and certain basic English Commonwealth, and a very small number of American texts, as well as the basic Canadian and English law reports. There is one Australian law report. Besides texts (monographs), the Library subscribes to Albertan and Canadian legislative publications like bills, orders, votes and proceedings, Hansard, and Debates of the House of Commons. Assistance is available to users' from the simplest to the most complex legal research questions.

AB —UNIVERSITY OF ALBERTA, John Weir Memorial Law Library, Law Centre, Second Floor, Edmonton, T6G 2H5, Can. Lillian MacPherson, Law Librn
Holdings: Vols (140,000) Cat Maps Audiotapes Microforms
Budget: ($400,000)
Notes: Emphases on Canadian Government Publications, oil and gas, Canadian and US, UK, Australia, New Zealand primary materials. Separate catalog.

BC —VANCOUVER PUBLIC LIBRARY, Science & Technology Div, 750 Burrard St, Vancouver, V6Z 1X5, Can. P Haffenden, Head, Science & Technology Div
Notes: We have a comprehensive collection of Canadian and British Columbian government documents in the Science and Technology subject areas as well as a selection of documents from other governments.

BC —LEGISLATIVE LIBRARY (PROVINCIAL), Parliament Bldgs, Victoria, V8V 1X4, Can. J H MacEachern, Head, Government Documents Division
Holdings: Vols 1,000,000 Cat Microforms
Notes: Depository for British Columbia, Canada (incl Statistics Canada), Ontario. Selective depository for Quebec. Receive the "partial set" of US exchange publications. On microfiche: Canada - Microlog; US - CIS; Great Britain - House of Commons papers and bills, command papers. Publications from other jurisdictions ordered selectively in fields of law, labor, ecinimics, public administration, political science, etc.

ON —LIBRARY OF PARLIAMENT, Parliament Bldgs, Ottawa, K1A 0A9, Can. Erik J Spicer, Parliamentary Librn
Notes: Interlibrary loan restricted.

ON —NATIONAL LIBRARY OF CANADA, 395 Wellington St, Ottawa, K1A 0N4, Can. Andre Preibish, Dir
Notes: Over 1,100,000 Canadian federal and provincial government publications; about 800,000 documents from other countries, plus extensive microform collections. Strong in pre-Confederation as well as post-Confederation documents.

†ON —METROPOLITAN TORONTO LIBRARY, Social Sciences Dept, 789 Yonge St, Toronto, M4W 2G8, Can. Abdus Salam, Head
Holdings: Vols Cat Maps Phonorecords Audiotapes 16mm Films Microforms
Notes: The collection is a full depository for Canadian federal and Ontario provincial publications and contains an exhaustive collection of publications from the various Canadian provinces. It includes statutes, gazettes, legislative debates, journals, reports, etc. Also extensive holdings for the US and Great Britain; comprehensive holdings of treaties for Canada, Great Britain and the US; selected publications for other foreign countries. Types of publications emphasized are statutory laws, treaties, legislative proceedings, government directories and manuals, statistical materials and national yearbooks. Large collection of UN materials; full depository for UNESCO publications; selected publications of various international organizations. The collection is cited in Canada, National Library, Resources Survey *Section,Research Collections of Official Publications in Canada* (Ottawa: Supply and Services Canada, 1976).

SK —SASKATCHEWAN LEGISLATIVE LIBRARY, 234 Legislative Bldg, Regina, S4S 0B3, Can. Marian Powell, Librn
Holdings: Cat Microforms
Notes: Government publication; of Saskatchewan, Ontario, Canada, and full exchange with the US. This is a Depository Library. Listed in Microlog.

CANADA—HISTORY

CT —YALE UNIVERSITY, Box 1603A, Yale Station, New Haven, 06520.

IL —WHEATON COLLEGE, Buswell Memorial Library, Wheaton, 60187. Paul Snezek, Library Dir
Holdings: Mss
Notes: The collection includes mss, correspondence, lecture tapes, (40), (25 linear feet). 1945 UN conference on International Organization, Canadian Rebellion, 1837-1838, Wheaton Scholastic Society.

IN —ALLEN COUNTY PUBLIC LIBRARY, Fred J Reynolds Historical Genealogy Collection, 900 Webster St, Fort Wayne, 46802. Rick J Ashton, Dir; Michael B Clegg, Manager
Holdings: Vols 200,000 Cat Mss Maps Pix Microforms
Notes: Incl state, county, regional, town and church histories. All census schedules and port of entry records released by the federal government are in the microfilm collection of 40,000 reels. The collection contains parish registers and publications of British parish register societies. Canadian, English, Scotch, Irish and Welsh records are well represented. The heraldry collection is housed with the genealogy collection. Allen County Public Library is and has been the depository for the North American Association of Directory Publishers since 1964.

†MA —BOSTON PUBLIC LIBRARY, Copley Sq, Boston, 02117.
Notes: Archives of Wilfred Beaulieu, founder and editor of the Franco-American newspaper *Le Travailleur.*

MA —BOSTON PUBLIC LIBRARY, Rare Books and Manuscripts, Copley Square, Boston, 02117. Laura V Monti, Keeper of Rare Books
Notes: Significant material, in volume, is devoted to economic and political relationships between New England and the Maritime Provinces in the 18th Century; much on Abolitionists and the antisalvery movement. Described in *Canadian Manuscripts in the Boston Public Library* (Boston: G K Hall), 1 vol. Incl about 17,000 items.

MA —HARVARD UNIVERSITY LIBRARY, Widener Library, Cambridge, 02138. Carolyn Fawcett, Specialist in Book Selection
Holdings: Vols 19,000 Cat
Notes: 19,000 volumes on Canadian history and literature. Both French and English materials are well represented.

MA —SPRINGFIELD CITY LIBRARY, Genealogy and Local History Dept, 220 State St, Springfield, 01103. Joseph Carvalho III, Supervisor
Holdings: Vols (17,000) Cat Mss Maps Pix Microforms
Budget: ($8000)
Notes: New England, Massachusetts, local history (Springfield), and genealogy collections. collections. 18,000 pictures, 3200 microforms, ca 15,000 clippings, pamphlets, etc (280 ft of vertical files).

MA —AMERICAN ANTIQUARIAN SOCIETY LIBRARY, 185 Salisbury St, Worcester, 01609. Marcus A McCorison, Dir & Librn
Holdings: Vols 1300 Cat
Notes: Incl the collection of Dr Gabriel Nadeau.

MN —UNIVERSITY OF MINNESOTA, DULUTH, Library & Learning Resources Service, Duluth, 55812. James V. Litha, Archivist
Holdings: Vols (1700) Cat Mss Maps Pix
Notes: The Voyageur Collection incl the Grace Lee Nute Papers. Books and materials relating to the Voyageur period (1650-1850) and the area of Northeastern Minnesota, Michigan, Wisconsin, Southern Canada. Emphasis on all subjects listed in this volume.

NE —AMERICAN HISTORICAL SOCIETY OF GERMANS FROM RUSSIA (AHSGR), 615 Twelfth St, Lincoln, 68502. Mary Lynn Tuck, Librn
Holdings: Vols (1900) Mss Maps Pix Phonorecords Videotapes Audiotapes Microforms VF
Notes: History of German people from

CANADA—HISTORY (cont.)

Russia and history of people of German-Russian ancestory. Including times in Russia, Germany, US, Canada, Mexico, Argentina, Brazil, Paraguay, Korea, and Japan. This Society has fifty-six chapters in the United States. 1900 volumes, 100 maps; 500 mss; 1200 vertical files; 2000 pictures; 40,000 obituary files, 40,000 family group charts, 50 phonorecords, 20 videotapes, 50 audiotapes, 15 reel-to-reel tapes, 150 periodicals, 250 microforms, 250 family histories-published and unpublished.

NY —ALFRED UNIVERSITY, Herrick Memorial Library, Alfred, 14802. June E Brown, Head Librn
Notes: The Howells/Frechette Collection. Family documents, 7000 letters of William Cooper Howells (American consul to Quebec, later to Toronto), William Dean Howells, his sister Annie Frechette, Achille Frechette (official translator, Canadian House of Commons), and Louis Frechette (poet laureate of Canada).

NY —NEW YORK PUBLIC LIBRARY, Research Libraries, American History Div, Fifth Ave & 42 St, New York, 10018.
Holdings: Vols 15,000 Cat Maps Microforms
Notes: Local, provincial and general histories of Canada.

NY —STATE UNIVERSITY OF NEW YORK, COLLEGE AT PLATTSBURGH, Feinberg Library, Special Collections, 153 Hawkins Hall, Plattsburgh, 12901. Joseph G Swinyer, Librn
Holdings: Vols (1000) Cat Mss Maps Pix Phonorecords Microforms
See also entry under New York (State) - History

NY —UNIVERSITY OF ROCHESTER, Rush Rhees Library, Department of Rare Books and Special Collections, Rochester, 14627. Peter Dzwonkoski, Librn
Holdings: // Cat Mss
Notes: Jean Frederic Phelypeaux, Comte de Maurepas. Manuscripts relating to the French in Canada and Louisiana in the mid-18th century.

NC —DUKE UNIVERSITY, William R Perkins Library, Rare Book Room, Durham, 27706. John L Sharpe, III, Cur
Notes: Lionel Stevenson collection of more than 500 titles and manuscripts dealing with literary life in Canada. Primarily in the fields of poetry and fiction in English, but also in literary criticism, drama, essays, history and travel. Almost all are first editions, published in Canada. Many are the writers' presentation copies to Professor Stevenson. Manuscripts are housed in the Manuscript Department.

PA —BALCH INSTITUTE FOR ETHNIC STUDIES, Library, 18 S Seventh St, Philadelphia, 19106. R Joseph Anderson, Library Dir

PA —UNIVERSITY OF PENNSYLVANIA, Van Pelt Library, Rare Books Collection, 34 & Walnut Sts, Philadelphia, 19104. Daniel Traister, Special Collections Librn
Holdings: Vols 2500 //
Notes: Robert Dechert Collection: early exploration, 17th and 18th centuries; western Americana, 19th century; Canadiana, incl Jesuit relations.

RI —BROWN UNIVERSITY, John Hay Library, 20 Prospect St, Providence, 02912. Mark N Brown, Cur Mss
Holdings: Vols 2000 Cat Mss
Notes: A nearly complete collection of the published speeches, historical writings, and novels, plus some autographed letters, of John Buchan, Lord Tweedsmuir, former Governor General of Canada.

†RI —UNION SAINT-JEAN-BAPTISTE, Bibliotheque Mallet, Woonsocket, 02895.
Notes: Emphasis on genealogy, French parish histories; theses and dissertations on French Canadian topics.

TX —AMON CARTER MUSEUM, Library, 3510 Camp Bowie Blvd, PO Box 2365, Fort Worth, 76113. Nancy G Wynne, Librn
Holdings: Vols (25,000) Cat Mss Pix
Notes: The book collection, microfilm and photo archives have been built toward the goal of the interpretation of American history through art. At present, the greatest strengths are in Americana, Western Canadiana, bibliography, American exhibition catalogs and history of photography. Substantial books and files on American artists of the 19th and early 20th century, and particularly of Charles M Russell and Frederic Remington. Incl 25,000 pictures; 13,000 slides.
See also entries under Art, American; Pictures - Collections.

WI —STATE HISTORICAL SOCIETY OF WISCONSIN, Library, 816 State St, Madison, 53706. James L Hansen, Reference Librn
Holdings: Vols (25,000) Cat Maps Microforms
Notes: Selective depository for Canadian national and provincial documents.

AB —ALPINE CLUB OF CANADA LIBRARY, Archives of the Canadian Rockies, Box 160, Banff, T0L 0C0, Can. E J Hart, Head Archivist
Holdings: Vols (2429) Cat Mss Maps Pix Slides Audiotapes
Budget: ($1000)
Notes: The Archives of the Canadian Rockies is the custodian of the library and archival collection of the Alpine Club of Canada. The materials cover mountaineering technique and attempts worldwide, incl the Alps, Rockies, Himalayas, Andes, etc. Subject areas incl history, personal records, mountain rescue and medicine, alpine flora and fauna, guide books, manuals and handbooks. A large part of the archival collection is concentrated on the Canadian Rocky Mountains, as the headquarters of The Alpine Club of Canada is in Banff, Alberta.

AB —PETER WHYTE FOUNDATION, Archives of the Canadian Rockies, Box 160, Banff, T0L 0C0, Can. Mary Andrews, ACR Librn
Holdings: Vols (4247) Cat Mss Maps Pix Slides Phonorecords Audiotapes Videotapes 16mm Films Filmstrips Microforms
Budget: ($1500)
Notes: Collect all available material which touches on the Rocky Mountains of Canada (from the US border to the Peace River in the north; from west of Calgary on the east to the town of Revelstoke, BC on the west). This material incl history (the early explorers, Indians, construction of the railroads, mountaineering, and development of the national parks), natural history (geology, botany, wildlife) and poetry and fiction with the Rockies as a setting. Collect maps of the area, photographs, tape recordings of the pioneers. We also house on our premises the Alpine Club of Canada's library, which is one of the most comprehensive collections on the subject of mountaineering worldwide. Noncirculating.

AB —CENTENNIAL PLANETARIUM, Library, PO Box 2100, 701 Eleventh St, Calgary, T2P 2M5, Can. Sig Wieser, Librn
Holdings: Vols (400) Uncat Pix Audiotapes 16mm Films
Notes: Also western Canadian aviation history with bias towards technology; and history of space technology.

AB —GLENBOW-ALBERTA INSTITUTE, Historical Library & Archives, 130 9th Avenue SE, Calgary, T2G 0P3, Can. Leonard J Gottseleg, Chief Librn
Holdings: Vols (60,000) Cat Mss Maps Pix Microforms
Notes: Main emphasis is on Western Canadian history. Equally important emphasis is placed on the Canadian Arctic and Alaska, Northwest Coast explorations, Aboriginal peoples of the North and Canadian West, and the fur trade in the US Northwest.

AB —UNIVERSITY OF CALGARY, Library, Calgary, T2N 1N4, Can. Apollonia Steele, Special Collections Librn
Holdings: Cat
Notes: With a strengthened collection of materials on French Canada, incl many runs of periodicals and an extensive amount of early pamphlets, incl those of Henri Bourassa and other political figures.

AB —UNIVERSITY OF ALBERTA, Cameron Library, The Bruce Peel Special Collections Room, Edmonton, T6G 2J8, Can. John Charles, Special Collections Librn
Notes: The Canadian West, especially; incl 1000 items from the Rutherford Collection.

BC —DAVID THOMPSON UNIVERSITY CENTRE, Library, Nelson, V1L 3C7, Can. Ronald J Welwood, Dir
Holdings: Vols 2000 Cat Mss Pix Microforms
Budget: $1000
Notes: Especially Nelson and Central Kootenay District of British Columbia. Emphasis on historical, social, and economic materials. Collection described in *Kootenaiana: A Listing of Books, Government Publications, Monographs, Journals, Pamphlets, etc, Relating to the Kootenay Area ... Located in the Libraries of Notre Dame University ... up to 31 March* 1976, ed by W J Welwood (Nelson: Notre Dame Univ of Nelson, Library, etc, 1976), 167 pp.

BC —PRINCE RUPERT LIBRARY, 101 W Sixth Ave, Prince Rupert, V8J 1Y9, Can. Denise St Arnaud, City Librn
Holdings: Vols 270 Cat Mss Audiotapes 16mm Films
Notes: This collection of Northwest History deals chiefly with this area but extends to parts of Alaska and the Queen Charlotte Islands and BC inland and north. Noncirculating.

BC —TERRACE PUBLIC LIBRARY, 4610 Park Ave, Terrace, V8G 1V6, Can. Ed Curell, Librn; Gillian Campbell, Librn, Terrace Collection
Holdings: Vols (270) Cat
Budget: ($250)
Notes: The collection is limited to books and pamphlets relating to Terrace, Skeena, and Nass River District history and geography. Emphasis on art and sociology of the Niska and Tsimshian and lives of early missionaries.

BC —LEGISLATIVE LIBRARY (PROVINCIAL), Parliament Bldgs, Victoria, V8V 1X4, Can. J H MacEachern, Head, Government Documents Division
Holdings: Cat Maps Microforms

MB —ESKIMO MUSEUM, Library, Box 10, Churchill, R0B 0E0, Can. Brother J Volant, Cur
Holdings: Vols (300) Cat
Notes: Books on the North, mainly northern Canada; explorers' journals; Eskimo ethnology, archaeology, and art.

MB —MANITOBA MENNONITE HISTORICAL SOCIETY, Reimer Historical Library, Box 1136, Steinbach, R0A 2A0, Can. Peter Goertzen, Manager
Holdings: Vols (2500) Cat Mss Maps Pix Phonorecords
Notes: Mennonite history and teachings. Also incl material on pioneer settlers in Manitoba. Incl 1000 mss and 600 pictures.

MB —HUDSON'S BAY CO, Library, 77 Main St, Winnipeg, R3C 2R1, Can. Carol Preston, Librn Hudson's Bay House
Holdings: Vols (6000) Cat Mss Maps Pix Slides
Notes: Main purpose is to provide research materials for production of the historical quarterly *The Beaver,* and to answer inquiries about the Company's history. Incl 250,000 pictures and 7000 VF pieces. No published catalog, but Library maintains author/subject/title card catalog. Limited photocopying. Mss of HBC Archives held by the Manitoba Provincial Archives. Published descriptions: Dowdall, Judi, "Hudson's Bay Company Library," *Canadian Library* Journal, June 1974, p 179; Preston, Carol, "Hudson's Bay Company Library," *Manitoba Library Association Bulletin*, June 1976, pp 24-25.

MB —MANITOBA MUSEUM OF MAN & NATURE, Library, 190 Rupert Ave, Winnipeg, R3B 0N2, Can. V Hatten, Librn
Holdings: Vols (20,000) Cat Maps Slides Audiotapes Videotapes Microforms
Notes: Human and natural history of Manitoba.

MB —UNIVERSITY OF MANITOBA, Saint John's College, Library, 400 Dysart Rd,

CANADA—HISTORY (cont.)

Winnipeg, R3T 2M5, Can. Patrick D Wright, Head
Holdings: Vols (45,600) Cat
Notes: Canadian literature and history.

†MB —UNIVERSITY OF MANITOBA, Library, Winnipeg, R3T 2N2, Can.
Notes: Complete research archive of ninety years of the Winnipeg *Times*, defunct in 1980. Millions of newspaper clippings, indexed and in chronological order; about one million photographs, identified and dated; 10,000 books, etc.

MB —UNIVERSITY OF WINNIPEG, Library, 515 Portage Ave, Winnipeg, R3B 2E9, Can. W R Converse, Chief Librn
Holdings: Vols (5500) Cat
Notes: The Ashdown Collection. Not inclusive, as more Canadiana is elsewhere in the Library.

NB —LEGISLATIVE LIBRARY, Legislative Bldg, Queen St, PO Box 6000, Fredericton, E3B 5H1, Can. Jocelyne LeBel, Dir
Holdings: Cat Pix Microforms
Notes: Incl also over 2000 items written by New Brunswickers on or about New Brunswick; with a full analytical catalog of New Brunswickiana. Largest collection of New Brunswick government documents.

NB —MOUNT ALLISON UNIVERSITY, Ralph Pickard Bell Library, Sackville, E0A 3C0, Can. M Fancy, Librn
Notes: The Winthrop P Bell Collection. Canadian Maritime Provinces.

NT —NORTHWEST TERRITORIES PUBLIC LIBRARY SERVICES, Bos 1100, Hay River, X0E 0R0, Can.
Holdings: Vols (1235) Cat Maps Audiotapes
Notes: Originally intended to provide items of historical significance on the Northwest Territories. It contains a number of first editions, some of which have since become available in reprint form. Copies of material in relevant native languages and on learning languages.

NS —UNIVERSITE SAINTE-ANNE, Library Louis R Comeau, PO Box 40, Church Point, B0W 1M0, Can. Neil Boucher, Director
Holdings: Vols (600) Cat Mss Maps Pix Slides 16mm Films
Notes: Material by and about Acadians. Incl 800 pictures, 3500 slides and over 300 films.

NS —DALHOUSIE UNIVERSITY LIBRARY, Halifax, B3H 4H8, Can.
Holdings: Vols (2000)
Notes: Nova Scotia history pamphlets. Compiled by a Nova Scotia newspaper editor, J J Stewart, the pamphlet collection provides a comprehensive view of Nova Scotia society in the 19th century, religious, political, educational, economic, and moral issues are all hotly debated in the collection's pamphlets. Many unique items are to be found in the collection.

ON —CHATHAM PUBLIC LIBRARY, 120 Queen St, Chatham, N7M 2G6, Can. Arlene Mason, Head of Reference
Holdings: Mss Maps Pix Slides Microforms
Notes: Collection incl books on Black history, especially the Underground Railroad pertaining to the Chatham and Windsor area; many articles, and a few pictures of these subjects; also Indians of Kent County. Kent County and Southern Ontario History is also a subject of this collection, especially United Empire Loyalists in Southern Ontario. There are a number of books on Natural History of Ontario.

ON —YORK UNIVERSITY, Scott Library, Downsview, M3J 2R2, Can. Hartwell Bowsfield, University Archivist
Notes: A collection of 10,000 Canadian pamphlets, providing a continuum of information about political and cultural events in Canada, especially Quebec and Ontario between 1880 and 1950.

ON —UNIVERSITY OF GUELPH, McLaughlin Library, Guelph, N1G 2W1, Can. Margaret Beckman, Head Librn; David Hull, Sciences Librn
Holdings: Vols 30,000 Cat Maps Mss Pix Slides Phonorecords Audiotapes Videotapes 16mm Films Microforms
Notes: Documents and monographs. 150 periodical titles. Special catalogs can be produced for any part of the collection. *See also* entry under Canada - Description and Travel; Ontario - History; Theatre - Canada

ON —QUEEN'S UNIVERSITY, Douglas Library, Kingston, K7L 5C4, Can. William F E Morley, Cur, Special Collections
Holdings: Vols (50,000) Cat Mss Maps Pix Microforms
Budget: ($12,000)
Notes: The Edith and Lorne Pierce Collection of Canadiana. Also over 15,000 titles in Canadian Pamphlet Collection. Strong in humanities and social sciences, special strength in English and French Canadian literature; discovery and exploration narratives; Loyalists; War of 1812; opening of the West; local history, 19th century pamphlets and association items. Described in *A Catalogue of Canadian Manuscripts Collected by Lorne Pierce and Presented to Queen's University* (Toronto: Ryerson, 1946); and in *Canadiana 1698-1900 in the Possession of the Douglas* Library, comp by Janet S Porteous, foreword by Lorne Pierce (Kingston, 1932). Also later books and articles on parts of the collection. About 3500 linear feet of mss material with special emphasis on families and businesses of eastern Ontario; Presbyterian Church; Canadian politics and public affairs, university and city of Kingston records; literary figures.

ON —LONDON PUBLIC LIBRARIES & MUSEUMS, London Room, 305 Queen's Ave, London, N6B 1X2, Can. W Glen Curnoe, Librn
Holdings: Cat Mss Maps Pix Slides Phonorecords Audiotapes 16mm Films
Budget: ($3700)
Notes: History of Ontario, with emphasis on London and region, from early 19th century onward. Separate catalog for books, films and microforms. Various subject indexes to materials. Special interest in London, Ontario authors and publishers.

ON —LIBRARY OF PARLIAMENT, Parliament Bldgs, Ottawa, K1A 0A9, Can. Erik J Spicer, Parliamentary Librn
Holdings: Vols (350,000) Cat Mss Maps Pix Microforms
Notes: Also 2,000 bound vols of Canadian pamphlet collection. Older material (19th century and earlier) not available on interlibrary loan.

ON —NATIONAL LIBRARY OF CANADA, 395 Wellington St, Ottawa, K1A 0N4, Can. Andre Preibish, Dir
Holdings: Vols 44,000 Documents
Budget: $50,000
Notes: Includes 400 serials titles. Collection aims to be comprehensive and covers all aspects of Canadian history. The library has received all Canadian titles on legal deposit since 1950; intensive acquisition of earlier works and those published abroad. In addition, the collection is supported by representative resources for American, British and French history.

ON —NATIONAL MUSEUMS OF CANADA, Library Services Directorate, Ottawa, K1A 0M8, Can. Valerie Monkhouse, Director
Holdings: Vols (70,000) Cat Mss Maps Pix Slides Microforms
Budget: ($60,000)
Notes: Collection includes anthropology, archaeology, ethnology, folklore, history, Indians of North America, Inuit, linguistics of North American Indians, material history, military and naval history, museology. Research collection, interlibrary loans available, public may use on the premises.

ON —PUBLIC ARCHIVES OF CANADA, Library, 395 Wellington St, Ottawa, K1A 0N3, Can. Dawn E Monroe, Collections Development Officer
Holdings: Vols (80,000) Cat
Notes: Over the years, the Public Archives Library has assembled thousands of books and pamphlets relating to all aspects of Canadian history, from the founding of the country to the present day. The holdings incl journals of explorers and missionaries, accounts of the first voyageurs, as well as administrative, civil and military records. Also incl are basic reference works on the history, geography, politics and economics of Canada, the administration of New France, Canada's geographic and political history, transportation incl railways and navigation, immigration, Crown lands, religious groups and institutions. The Library's collection also has works covering other areas of interest such as archives and archives management, heraldry, genealogy, Canadian art, geographic indexes and sound and visual archives.

†ON —TRENT UNIVERSITY, Peterborough, K9J 7B8, Can.
Notes: Canadiana; Canadian literature (Shell Collection); native studies; Trent Valley region.

ON —ANGLICAN CHURCH OF CANADA, Chancellor R V Harris Memorial Library, 600 Jarvis St, Toronto, M4Y 2J6, Can. Alice Marie Hedderick, Librn
Holdings: Vols (2000) Cat Maps Pix
Notes: Reference Library for the National headquarters of the Anglican Church of Canada. Most significant part of the collection is in reference, periodicals and VF materials.

ON —CANADA SPORTS HALL OF FAME, Exhibition Place, Toronto, M6K 3C3, Can. Cheryl Rielly, Librn
Notes: Incl sports library of John W Davies, supporter of Commonwealth Games in Canada.

ON —CANADIAN INSTITUTE OF INTERNATIONAL AFFAIRS, 15 King's College Circle, Toronto, M5S 2V9, Can. Jane Barrett, Librn
Holdings: Vols (23,000) Cat Mss Microforms Books VF
Budget: ($8800)
Notes: Incl both historical and current material on all subjects relevant to a study of Canadian Foreign relations.

ON —METROPOLITAN TORONTO LIBRARY, Canadian History Dept, Baldwin Room Section, 789 Yonge St, Toronto, M4W 2G8, Can. David B Kotin, Head
Holdings: Vols (52,000) Mss Pix
Notes: This collection consists of material on Canadian history, geography, travel, archaeology, genealogy, retrospective city and telephone directories, collective biographies, native peoples (excluding customs, rights and social conditions), Arctic regions, military history and theory. It is an extremely strong collection of both current and retrospective material. Particular strengths are national and local history (especially Ontario), Arctic regions, native peoples, travel (especially Ontario), and military history. Incl 78,000 historical pictures, 235 linear meters mss, 14,000 broadsides and 3800 bound newspapers.

ON —ROYAL ONTARIO MUSEUM, Main Library and Archives, 100 Queen's Park, Toronto, M5S 2C6, Can. Julia Matthews, Head Librn
Holdings: Vols (85,000) Cat
Notes: Since January 1977, acquisitions have been entered in UTLAS.

ON —UNIVERSITY OF TORONTO, Thomas Fisher Rare Book Library, 120 Saint George St, Toronto, M5S 1A5, Can. Richard G Landon, Head
Holdings: Vols (30,000) Mss Maps Pix
Notes: Great variety of material relating to early exploration and settlement of Canada, including the search for the Northwest Passage and the subsequent exploration of the Arctic. Manuscript and printed material pertaining to the overland exploration of northwestern Canada and the Barren Lands. Manuscript and printed material documenting early emigration schemes and colonization attempts, including Selkirk's Red River settlement.

ON —VICTORIA UNIVERSITY, Library, 71 Queen's Park Crescent, Toronto, M5S 1K7, Can. Robert C Brandeis, Chief Librn
Holdings: Vols (5000) Cat
Notes: The collection is very strong in 19th-20th century poetry, drama and fiction; it contains gazetteers, travel books, biographies, and works on history and

CANADA—HISTORY (cont.)

geography. Nucleus of collection listed in James, C C, *A Bibliography of Canadian Poetry (English)* (Victoria University Library Publication No 1, Toronto, 1899); and Horning, L E, and Burpee, L J, *A Bibliography of Canadian Fiction (English)* (Victoria University Library Publications No 2, Toronto, 1904).

ON —NORTH YORK PUBLIC LIBRARY, Canadiana Collection, 35 Fairview Mall Dr, Willowdale, M2J 4S4, Can. Ian C Ross, Head
Holdings: Vols (70,000) Cat Microforms
See also entry under Canada.

PQ —SPECIAL LIBRARY FOR LA SOCIETE HISTORIQUE DU SAGUENAY, 930 est, Jacques-Cartier, PO Box 456, Chicoutimi, G7H 5C8, Can. Roland Belanger, Archivist
Holdings: Vols 850 Uncat Mss Maps Pix
Notes: All concerning the history and geography of the Saguenay Region. Incl about 50,000 pictures.

PQ —BISHOP'S UNIVERSITY, John Bassett Memorial Library, Laurie Allison Room for Special Collections, Lennoxville, J1M 1Z7, Can. Germain Belisle, Chief Librn
Holdings: Vols 2500 Cat Microforms
Notes: The Hon C Gordon MacKinnon Collection of Canadiana. Books and pamphlets dealing with Canadian history and biography, including such rare and valuable items as Joseph Bouchette's *The British Dominions in North America* (1832); George Munro Grant's *Picturesque Canada* (1882); George Heriot's *Travels Through the Canadas* (1807); and Alexander MacKenzie's *Voyage from Montreal* (1801), to cite but a few examples.

PQ —BIBLIOTHEQUE DE LA VILLE DE MONTREAL, Montreal City Library, Salle Gagnon Collection, 1210 Sherbrooke St E, Montreal, H2L 1L9, Can. Daniel Olivier, Dept Head
Holdings: Vols (44,055) Cat Mss Maps Slides Microforms
Budget: ($30,000)

PQ —CONCORDIA UNIVERSITY LIBRARIES, 1455 de Maisonneuve Blvd W, Montreal, H3G 1M8, Can. Martin Cohen, Special Collections Librn
Holdings: Vols 60 // Cat Mss
Notes: The Maximilien Bibaud Collection contains the author's memoirs and correspondence as well as his writing on diverse subjects such as religion, theology, Canadian, European and ancient history, and the French language. 51 vols of ms materials.

PQ —MCGILL UNIVERSITY, McLennan Library, Rare Books and Special Collections Dept, 3459 McTavish St, Montreal, H3A 1Y1, Can.
Notes: Numerous primary sources, eg, maps, manuscripts, personal narratives, pamphlets, early Canadian imprints. This material can be found throughout the collection, particularly in Canadian Pamphlets, Manuscripts, Maps, and the Lawrence Lande Collection of Canadiana. Catalogues are available for the last-named collection: The Lawrence Lande Collection of Canadiana in the Redpath Library of McGill Unversity: a Bibliography. Montreal, 1965. Rare and Unusual Canadiana: First Supplement to the Lande Bibliography. Montreal, 1971.

PQ —UNIVERSITY OF MONTREAL, Service des Bibliotheques, CP 6128, Succursale A, Montreal, H3C 3J7, Can. Arlette Joffe-Nicodeme, Directeur General
Holdings: Vols 1250 //
Notes: The Louis Melzack Collection of Canadian Books and Manuscripts and the L F Georges Baby Collection of Canadian Books.

PQ —BIBLIOTHEQUE DES ARCHIVES NATIONALES DU QUEBEC, CP 10450, Sainte-Foy, G1V 4N1, Can. Collete Barry, Dir
Holdings: Vols (50,000) Cat Mss Maps Pix Microforms
Budget: ($25,000)
Notes: Dictionary catalog on cards (unpublished). Official Quebec documents published before 1867.

SK —MOOSE JAW PUBLIC LIBRARY, Archives, 461 Langdon Crescent, Moose Jaw, S6H 0X6, Can. Fay Hutchinson
Holdings: Vols 2769 Cat 3500 Mss Maps Pix Slides Microforms VF
Budget: $2400
Notes: Emphasis on Moose Jaw and surrounding area.

SK —SASKATCHEWAN ARCHIVES BOARD, University of Regina, Regina, S4S 0A2, Can. Ian E Wilson, Provincial Archivist
Holdings: Mss Maps Pix Audiotapes Videotapes 16mm Films Microforms
Budget: $900,000
Notes: The Saskatchewan Archives Board attempts to document the history of the area now the Province of Saskatchewan and its communities through all archival media. Collection incl 5800 meters of mss, 4800 maps, 250,000 pictures, 10,000 architectural drawings, 4400 audiotapes, 1648 16mm films and 9400 microfilm reels. Individual collections are listed in *The Union List of Manuscripts in Canadian Repositories* (Ottawa, 1975 & 1976). Detailed catalogs, indexes and inventories are available in two offices. (Second office is located at University of Saskatchewan, Saskatoon, Sask S7N 0W0 Canada.)

SK —SASKATCHEWAN LEGISLATIVE LIBRARY, 234 Legislative Bldg, Regina, S4S 0B3, Can. Marian Powell, Librn
Holdings: Vols 1825 Cat
Notes: Western Canadiana and Canadian history.

SK —UNIVERSITY OF REGINA, Campion College, Library, Regina, S4S 0A2, Can. Myfanwy Truscott, Librn
Holdings: Vols (500,000) Cat
Budget: ($100,000)

SK —UNIVERSITY OF SASKATCHEWAN, Library, Saskatoon, S7N 0W0, Can. S Perkins, Librn
Holdings: Vols 18,000 Cat Mss
Budget: $13,000
Notes: Shortt Collection. Emphasis on the Canadian prairies: the fur trade; religious history; social, economic and political development; explorations, including the Northwest passage; and local histories. The collection also includes rare pre-confederation items, especially on Upper and Lower Canada.

SK —WESTERN DEVELOPMENT MUSEUM, George Shepherd Library, 2935 Melville St, PO Box 1910, Saskatoon, S7K 3S5, Can. Warren Clubb, Research Coordr
Holdings: Vols (13,000) Documents Maps Pix Slides Audiotapes
Budget: $3500
Notes: Staff reference library. Open to the public although not a lending library. Extensive holdings of agricultural machinery catalogs, from Canadian and American manufacturers and distributors. Other holdings incl automobiles, aviation, museology and Western Canadian history. Partially cataloged.

YT —YUKON ARCHIVES, Box 2703, Whitehorse, Y1A 3C6, Can. Miriam McTiernan, Territorial Archivist
Holdings: Vols (8000) Cat Mss Maps Pix Phonorecords Audiotapes Videotapes 16mm Films Microforms
Budget: $15,000
Notes: Yukon and regional history and development. Incl also 500 mss; 10,000 maps; 30,000 pictures; 1200 microfilm rolls; 1115 oral history tapes, etc; Yukon newspapers.

CANADA—HISTORY—TO 1763 (NEW FRANCE)

DC —GEORGETOWN UNIVERSITY, Library, Special Collections Div, 37 & O Sts NW, Washington, 20057. George M Barringer, Special Collections Librn; Nicholas B Sheetz, Mss Librn
Holdings: Cat Mss Maps
Notes: New France, to 1763.

ON —ONTARIO MINISTRY OF TOURISM & RECREATION, Huronia Historical Resource Centre, PO Box 160, Midland, L4R 4K8, Can. M Quealey, Supervisor, Library Services
Holdings: Vols 11,000 Cat Mss Maps Pix Slides Phonorecords Audiotapes Filmstrips Microforms Videotapes
Notes: Reference collection; interlibrary loan; non-circulating. Research facility for reconstruction of historic sites: Historic Naval and Military Establishments, 19th century British base on the Great Lakes; and Sainte-Marie among the Hurons, an early 17th century French Jesuit mission to the Huron Indians. Also, local history collection and archaeological reports for Simcoe County, Ont, Canada.

CANADA—HISTORY—WAR OF 1812

ON —FORT MALDEN NATIONAL HISTORIC PARK, Library, 100 Laird Ave, Box 38, Amherstburg, N9V 2Z2, Can. Sally E Snyder, Librn
Holdings: Vols (150) Cat Mss Maps Pix Slides Microforms

CANADA—HISTORY—REBELLION, 1837-1838

ON —FORT MALDEN NATIONAL HISTORIC PARK, Library, 100 Laird Ave, Box 38, Amherstburg, N9V 2Z2, Can. Sally E Snyder, Librn
Holdings: Vols (150) Cat Mss Maps Pix Slides Microforms

CANADA—HISTORY, MILITARY

ON —NATIONAL DEFENCE HEADQUARTERS, Directorate of History, Ottawa, K1A 0K2, Can. Peter Greig, Collections Dept
Holdings: Vols (5000) Cat Mss Maps Microforms
Notes: History of the Canadian Armed Forces. The document collection dates from the Second World War and later periods, WW II papers are being transferred to the Public Archives of Canada where earlier ones have already gone. The holdings of regulations for the RCN, Canadian Army and the RCAF (before 1964) and those for the Canadian Armed Forces (since that date) are comprehensive. Admiralty Fleet Orders, 1910-1964, are held. These are listed in *Union List of Manuscripts in Canadian* Repostitories.

ON —NATIONAL MUSEUMS OF CANADA, Library Services Directorate, Ottawa, K1A 0M8, Can. Valerie Monkhouse, Director
Holdings: Vols 12,000 Cat
Budget: $60,000
Notes: Collection includes; arms and armour, military aeronautics, military and naval arts and sciences, military and naval equipment, general military and naval history, military and naval history of Canada. Research collection, interlibrary loans available, public may use on the premises.

ON —PUBLIC ARCHIVES OF CANADA, Library, 395 Wellington St, Ottawa, K1A 0N3, Can. Dawn E Monroe, Collections Development Officer
Holdings: Vols (80,000) Cat
Notes: Military strategy and naval construction are areas which are well documented in the Rare Book Collection. Among the most interesting titles are Vauban's *Traite de l'attaque des places* (Paris: Chez Barrois l'aine et Magimel, 1790? xxxci, 242 pp) and *Traite de la Defense des places* (Paris: Chez Charles-Antoine Jombert, 1769, xvi, 3, 334, 2 pp). The Library also holds field exercise manuals such as that produced by the British War Office and titled *Rules and Regulations for the Formation, Field-exercise and Movements, of His Majesty's Forces.* (A new ed War-Office, printed and sold by J Walter. London: Printed by Luke Hansard, 1799, xxiii, (1) 377 pp).

CANADA—INDUSTRY

ON —CANADIAN IMPERIAL BANK OF COMMERCE, Information Centre,

CANADA—INDUSTRY (cont.)

Commerce Court, Toronto, M5L 1A2, Can. Jane Cooney, Librn Head Office
Holdings: Vols (22,000) Cat Microforms
Notes: Emphasis on current information and major historical documents. Incl material on all sectors of the Canadian economy with emphasis on industry. Sources incl all provincial governments, the federal government and commercial publishers. 2000 current periodicals and annuals, incl a representative selection of Canadian trade journals and Canadian and foreign business, financial and management periodicals. Also incl a complete file of Statistics Canada documents and 1500 clipping files.

CANADA—LIBRARIES

ON —UNIVERSITY OF WESTERN ONTARIO, Schoool of Library and Information Science, Library, London, N6G 1H1, Can. Victoria Ripley, Librn
Holdings: Vols (50,000)
Notes: Auction and antiquarian booksellers' catalogs from Canadian, American and European firms, some dating back to the 18th century. A special strength is 19th and early 20th century American booksellers' catalogs, recently augmented by a collection of pre-1920 catalogs formed by the late H O Teisberg. Current emphasis is on Canadian catalogs.

CANADA—MAPS

ON —UNIVERSITY OF TORONTO, Thomas Fisher Rare Book Library, 120 Saint George St, Toronto, M5S 1A5, Can. Richard G Landon, Head
Holdings: Vols (30,000) Mss Maps Pix
Notes: Great variety of material relating to early exploration and settlement of Canada, including the search for the Northwest Passage and the subsequent exploration of the Arctic. Manuscript and printed material pertaining to the overland exploration of northwestern Canada and the Barren Lands. Manuscript and printed material documenting early emigration schemes and colonization attempts, including Selkirk's Red River settlement. Also a large group of fire insurance plans for cities, town, and villages across Canada, 1876-1973.

PQ —MCGILL UNIVERSITY, McLennan Library, Rare Books and Special Collections Dept, 3459 McTavish St, Montreal, H3A 1Y1, Can.
Notes: 5524 sheet maps, 370 atlases, 571 folded maps, 629 guide books, 248 reference books. The coverage is worldwide, specializing in North America, Canada, Quebec, Montreal. Includes a collection of guide books from the 1800s to the present day, as well as a reference collection; there is also a large collection of modern topographical literature with worldwide coverage, and an important collection of postcards particularly of Montreal and the Province of Quebec. A finding list is available for 19th century guide books on Canada: A Preliminary Guide to Nineteenth Century Canadian Guide Books: a Survey of the Holdings of the McLennan Library with an Historical Introduction. Montreal, 1982.

CANADA—MINORITIES

PA —BALCH INSTITUTE FOR ETHNIC STUDIES, Library, 18 S Seventh St, Philadelphia, 19106. R Joseph Anderson, Library Dir
Holdings: Vols 100 Cat

ON —PUBLIC ARCHIVES OF CANADA, Library, 395 Wellington St, Ottawa, K1A 0N3, Can. Dawn E Monroe, Collections Development Officer
Holdings: Vols (80,000) Cat
Notes: The Public Archives Library has collected certain published documents, general works and specialized studies pertinent to the study of the historical and sociological development of native peoples. These documents incl accounts of the trips made by missionaries, explorers and others into Inuit or Amerindian territory, territory, specialized bibliographies, and ethnographic reference works incl dictionaries of native languages, studies on customs and and habits, and specialized periodicals.

ON —CANADIAN ASSOCIATION IN SUPPORT OF THE NATIVE PEOPLES, Library, 277 Victoric St, Toronto, M5V 1W2, Can. Frances Davidson-Arnott, Librn
Holdings: Vols 4000 Cat Mss Maps Pix Slides Microforms
Notes: Native peoples of North America, especially of Canada.

†ON —METROPOLITAN TORONTO LIBRARY, Social Sciences Dept, 789 Yonge St, Toronto, M4W 2G8, Can. Abdus Salam, Head
Holdings: Vols Cat Maps Phonorecords Audiotapes 16mm Films Microfilms
Notes: Collection is both current and historical. Strong in immigrants' guides, government reports and statistics, analyses, histories and studies of ethnic groups. Strong on the Underground Railroad.

†SK —UNIVERSITY OF REGINA, Library, Regina, S4S 0A2, Can. Margarett Hammond, Librn
Notes: Native peoples of North America, especially of Canada. Collection formerly held by Canadian Association in Support of the Native Peoples.

CANADA—NURSING

ON —CANADIAN NURSES' ASSOCIATION, 50 The Driveway, Ottawa, K2P 1E2, Can. Linda Solomon Shiff, Librn Mgr
Holdings: Vols 1200 Cat
Notes: National nursing library; repository of studies by Canadian nurses or about nursing in Canada. Incl 475 subscriptions to periodicals.

CANADA—PICTURES, ILLUSTRATIONS, ETC.

NS —DALHOUSIE UNIVERSITY LIBRARY, Halifax, B3H 4H8, Can.
Holdings: Cat Pix
Notes: Approx 2000 lithographs, steel engravings, fine prints and illustrated historical maps from the 18th and 19th centuries are in the collection. Subject coverage is primarily of Nova Scotia, New Brunswick, Prince Edward Island, and Newfoundland scenery, street scenes, and portrayals of prominent people, buildings and events. Generally rich in illustrations of the working and social life of the period. Artists represented incl: J E Woolford, J F W Desbarres, William Eagar, William Bartlett and Richard Short. Historical maps incl some of the earliest visual depictions of the Atlantic coast. Material available for editorial reproduction. Print fee charged. No loans.

†ON —METROPOLITAN TORONTO LIBRARY, 789 Yonge St, Toronto, M4W 2G8, Can.
Notes: Over 15,000 drawings, prints, and paintings, and over 50,000 photographs of Canadian scenes, as well as portraits from the 18th century on. Particularly strong in material relating to the Toronto area from the founding in 1793.

CANADA—POLITICS AND GOVERNMENT

NC —DUKE UNIVERSITY, William R Perkins Library, Durham, 27706. Elvin E Strowd, University Librn

PA —BALCH INSTITUTE FOR ETHNIC STUDIES, Library, 18 S Seventh St, Philadelphia, 19106. R Joseph Anderson, Library Dir

AB —UNIVERSITY OF CALGARY, Libraries, Special Collections Div, 2500 University Dr, Calgary, T2N 1N4, Can.
Holdings: Mss
Notes: The papers reflect Ernest Watkins' activities as lawyer, politician and writer in Canada and Britain and include correspondence, speeches, broadcasts, as well as mss of books, articles, plays, short stories and novels.

BC —UNIVERSITY OF VICTORIA, McPherson Library, Victoria, V8W 3H5, Can.
Notes: Byron Johnson (1890-1964); Premier of British Columbia. Incl correspondence; reports; clippings; ephemera; photographs (1914-57).

MB —UNIVERSITY OF MANITOBA, Elizabeth Dafoe Library, Archives and Special Collections Dept, Winnipeg, R3T 2N2, Can. Richard E Bennett, Dept Head; Corrado A Santoro, Reference Archivist
Notes: Newsclippings of articles, editorials and feature columns (all dated) from newspapers across Canada concerning not only national activities of the Liberal and Cooperative Commonwealth Federation but their efforts in Manitoba, Saskatchewan and Alberta.

ON —YORK UNIVERSITY, Scott Library, Downsview, M3J 2R2, Can. Hartwell Bowsfield, University Archivist
Notes: Literary and political papers of Canadian playwright, theatre director, and teacher Herman Voaden, leading exponent of Canadian national drama, and the concept of "Symphonic theatre," encompassing all the living arts, collection covers 1897-1975, incl personal papers, diaries, etc. Over 700 playbills, 1926-1945, etc.

ON —YORK UNIVERSITY, Scott Library, Downsview, M3J 2R2, Can. Hartwell Bowsfield, University Archivist
Notes: A collection of 10,000 Canadian pamphlets, providing a continuum of information about political and cultural events in Canada, especially Quebec and Ontario between 1880 and 1950.

ON —QUEEN'S UNIVERSITY, Douglas Library, Kingston, K7L 5C4, Can. William F E Morley, Cur, Special Collections
Holdings: Cat Mss Pix
Notes: The papers of Dr John J Deutsch, incl the correspondence, notes, memoranda and other files accumulated by him during his career. Also, about 3500 linear feet of mss material with special emphasis on families and businesses of eastern Ontario; Presbyterian Church; Canadian politics and public affairs, university and city of Kingston records, literary figures.

ON —PUBLIC ARCHIVES OF CANADA, Library, 395 Wellington St, Ottawa, K1A 0N3, Can. Dawn E Monroe, Collections Development Officer
Holdings: Vols (80,000) Cat
Notes: The Public Archives Library has a wealth of material on the history of government, incl a great deal of published legislation which makes it possible to trace the nation's constitutional history. There are also many manuals, monographs and periodical articles documenting the evolution of the government organizations which have adminstered Canada. Supplementing these are treaties and printed works, incl both primary and secondary sources, on the relationships between Canada and its parent countries.

ON —PUBLIC ARCHIVES OF CANADA, Library, 395 Wellington St, Ottawa, K1A 0N3, Can. Dawn E Monroe, Collections Development Officer
Notes: William Lyon Mackenzie King Collection. About 4000 vols. This Canadian Prime Minister, the longest serving of any of our leaders, left a large legacy of documents. Several small transfers of material have been received from the King papers in the Manuscript Division although those items integral to the collection have been retained within the Papers. The largest part of the publiched materials remain at King's study in Laurier House. The Library is in the process of cataloging the collection.

†ON —METROPOLITAN TORONTO LIBRARY, Social Sciences Dept, 789 Yonge St, Toronto, M4W 2G8, Can. Abdus Salam, Head
Holdings: Vols Cat Maps Phonorecords Audiotapes 16mm Films Microforms
Notes: Extensive collection emphasizing historical and current aspects of Canadian

CANADA—POLITICS AND GOVERNMENT (cont.)

politics and government. Special areas such as Canadian Constitutional history and law, and Canadian political parties and movements are well covered.

PQ —MCGILL UNIVERSITY, McLennan Library, Rare Books and Special Collections Dept, 3459 McTavish St, Montreal, H3A 1Y1, Can.
Notes: 3000 books and pamphlets on the social, political, and economic history of Quebec.

CANADA—POPULATION

ON —CANADIAN ASSOCIATION IN SUPPORT OF THE NATIVE PEOPLES, Library, 277 Victoric St, Toronto, M5V 1W2, Can. Frances Davidson-Arnott, Librn
Holdings: Vols 4000 Cat Mss Maps Pix Slides Microforms
Notes: Native peoples of North America, especially of Canada.

†SK —UNIVERSITY OF REGINA, Library, Regina, S4S 0A2, Can. Margarett Hammond, Librn
Notes: Native peoples of North America, especially of Canada. Collection formerly held by Canadian Association in Support of the Native Peoples.

CANADA—RACIAL GROUPS

PA —BALCH INSTITUTE FOR ETHNIC STUDIES, Library, 18 S Seventh St, Philadelphia, 19106. R Joseph Anderson, Library Dir
Notes: Ethnic Heritage Collection.

MB —MANITOBA MUSEUM OF MAN & NATURE, Library, 190 Rupert Ave, Winnipeg, R3B 0N2, Can. V Hatten, Librn
Holdings: Vols (20,000) Cat

ON —PUBLIC ARCHIVES OF CANADA, Library, 395 Wellington St, Ottawa, K1A 0N3, Can. Dawn E Monroe, Collections Development Officer
Holdings: Vols (80,000) Cat
Notes: The Public Archives Library has collected certain published documents, general works and specialized studies pertinent to the study of the historical and sociological development of native peoples. These documents incl accounts of the trips made by missionaries, explorers and others into Inuit or Amerindian territory, territory, specialized bibliographies, and ethnographic reference works incl dictionaries of native languages, studies on customs and and habits, and specialized periodicals.

ON —CANADIAN ASSOCIATION IN SUPPORT OF THE NATIVE PEOPLES, Library, 277 Victoric St, Toronto, M5V 1W2, Can. Frances Davidson-Arnott, Librn
Holdings: Vols 4000 Cat Mss Maps Pix Slides Microforms
Notes: Native peoples of North America, especially of Canada.

†ON —METROPOLITAN TORONTO LIBRARY, Social Sciences Dept, 789 Yonge St, Toronto, M4W 2G8, Can. Abdus Salam, Head
Holdings: Vols Cat Maps Phonorecords Audiotapes 16mm Films Microforms
Notes: Collection is both current and historical. Strong in immigrants' guides, government reports and statistics, analyses, histories and studies of ethnic groups. Strong on the Underground Railroad.

†SK —UNIVERSITY OF REGINA, Library, Regina, S4S 0A2, Can. Margarett Hammond, Librn
Notes: Native peoples of North America, especially of Canada. Collection formerly held by Canadian Association in Support of the Native Peoples.

CANADA—RELIGION

PA —BALCH INSTITUTE FOR ETHNIC STUDIES, Library, 18 S Seventh St, Philadelphia, 19106. R Joseph Anderson, Library Dir
Holdings: Cat Microforms

ON —ANGLICAN CHURCH OF CANADA, Chancellor R V Harris Memorial Library, 600 Jarvis St, Toronto, M4Y 2J6, Can. Alice Marie Hedderick, Librn
Holdings: Vols (2000) Cat Maps Pix
Notes: Reference Library for the National headquarters of the Anglican Church of Canada. Most significant part of the collection is in reference, periodicals and VF materials.

ON —TORONTO SCHOOL OF THEOLOGY, Consortium of Libraries, University of Toronto, Toronto, M5S 1A5, Can. R Grane Bracewell, Library Coordr
Holdings: Cat
Notes: A consortium of 7 theological college and faculty libraries at the University of Toronto.

CANADA—SOCIAL LIFE AND CUSTOMS

NC —DUKE UNIVERSITY, William R Perkins Library, Durham, 27706. Elvin E Strowd, University Librn

BC —UNIVERSITY OF VICTORIA, McPherson Library, Victoria, V8W 3H5, Can.
Notes: Subject files of Reg Fife, organizer of the Centennial Voyageur Canoe Pageant: background, correspondence, weather; civic ceremonies; TV setups, personnel files, operating manual, itinerary, photographs, trial races, ephemera and notes.

MB —UNIVERSITY OF MANITOBA, Elizabeth Dafoe Library, Archives and Special Collections Dept, Winnipeg, R3T 2N2, Can. Richard E Bennett, Dept Head; Corrado A Santoro, Reference Archivist
Notes: Photographs of western prairie Canada as collected by Heather Robertson from archives and museums across Canada for use in her book *Salt from the Earth.* Pictures are between 1880-1915, showing such things as immigrant families, farms, towns and city life on the prairies, churches, schools, railroads, homestead residences and other aspects of life in the developing Canadian West.

ON —YORK UNIVERSITY, Scott Library, Downsview, M3J 2R2, Can. Hartwell Bowsfield, University Archivist
Notes: A collection of 10,000 Canadian pamphlets, providing a continuum of information about political and cultural events in Canada, especially Quebec and Ontario between 1880 and 1950. Also the Jean A Chalmers Choreographic Archives of works by Canadian choreographers, along with background information and technical and performance data on each work. A continuing deposit donated by the Ontario Arts Council.

ON —NATIONAL FILM BOARD, CANADA, Tunney's Pasture Area, Ottawa, K1A 0M9, Can.
Notes: Photo library of 225,000 Canadian images, incl 33,000 slides.

ON —TORONTO SCHOOL OF THEOLOGY, Consortium of Libraries, University of Toronto, Toronto, M5S 1A5, Can. R Grane Bracewell, Library Coordr
Notes: A consortium of 7 theological college and faculty libraries at the University of Toronto.

PQ —MCGILL UNIVERSITY, McLennan Library, Rare Books and Special Collections Dept, 3459 McTavish St, Montreal, H3A 1Y1, Can.
Notes: 3000 books and pamphlets on the social, political, and economic history of Quebec.

CANADA—STATISTICS

ON —STATISTICS CANADA LIBRARY, R H Coats Bldg, Tunney's Pasture, Ottawa, K1A 0T6, Can. G Ellis, Chief Librn
Holdings: Vols 100,000 Cat Microforms
Notes: Statistics--Canadian and foreign.

CANADA—STUDY AND TEACHING

OH —CASE WESTERN RESERVE UNIVERSITY, Kulas Music Library, 11118 Bellflower Rd, Cleveland, 44106. Timothy Robson, Music Librn
Notes: Containing deposit of a collection of some 800 records of music and the spoken word in French, English, and Spanish presented by Radio Canada International in Montreal.

CANADA LABOR PROGRESSIVE PARTY see Labor Progressive Party, Canada

CANADAY, JOHN

†VA —UNIVERSITY OF VIRGINIA, Alderman Library, Manuscripts Dept, Charlottesville, 22901.
Notes: Papers, etc.

CANADIAN ANTHROPOLOGY see Anthropology, Canadian

CANADIAN ARCHITECTURE see Architecture, Canadian

CANADIAN ARCHIVES see Archives, Canadian

CANADIAN ARCTIC

AB —GLENBOW-ALBERTA INSTITUTE, Historical Library & Archives, 130 9th Avenue SE, Calgary, T2G 0P3, Can. Leonard J Gottseleg, Chief Librn
Holdings: Vols (60,000) Cat Mss Maps Pix Microforms
Notes: Main emphasis is on Western Canadian history. Equally important emphasis is placed on the Canadian Arctic and Alaska, Northwest Coast explorations, Aboriginal peoples of the North and Canadian West, and fur trade in the US Northwest.

ON —LAURENTIAN UNIVERSITY LIBRARY, Ramsey Lake Rd, Sudbury, P3E 2C6, Can. Suzanne Brunette, Special Collection Librn; Sue Vongpeisal, Head Librn
Notes: Materials on northern Canada, incl 2200 books and pamphlets, 60,000 press clippings on northern topics 75 series of periodicals and over 1500 maps, plus photographs and thousands of samples of arctic and subarctic plants incl mosses, lichens, algae and wood sections. Much of the material is in French.

CANADIAN ARCTIC EXPEDITION, 1913-1918

ON —NATIONAL MUSEUMS OF CANADA, Library Services Directorate, Ottawa, K1A 0M8, Can. Valerie Monkhouse, Director
Holdings: Vols 500 // Maps
Notes: The personal library of R M Anderson, late Curator Emeritus of the Zoology Division, and leader of the Southern Party, Canadian Arctic Expedition, 1913-1918. The collection contains books on zoology (mainly ornithology and mammalogy), expeditions (some early and rare materials), and several runs of ornithological journals and numerous reprints. The collection is only partially cataloged.

CANADIAN ART see Art, Canadian

CANADIAN ARTISTS see Artists, Canadian

CANADIAN ASSOCIATION IN SUPPORT OF NATIVE PEOPLES

ON —NATIONAL MUSEUMS OF CANADA, Library Services Directorate, Ottawa, K1A 0M8, Can. Valerie Monkhouse, Director
Holdings: Vols 6000 //Cat Mss Maps Pix Slides Microforms
Notes: Ethnology, archaeology, folk-lore, linguistics, etc. Also 13,500 periodical titles;

CANADIAN ASSOCIATION IN SUPPORT OF NATIVE PEOPLES (cont.)

vertical files of Canadian Association in Support of Native Peoples (microfilm); over 22,000 items covering every facet of contemporary native life. Mss, pictures and theses are held in Archives (National Museum of Man).

CANADIAN ASSOCIATION OF PHYSICISTS

†ON —PUBLIC ARCHIVES OF CANADA, Library, 395 Wellington St, Ottawa, K1A 0N3, Can. Dawn E Monroe, Collections Dept Officer
Notes: Records.

CANADIAN AUTHORS see Authors, Canadian

CANADIAN BROADCASTING CORPORATION (CBC)

AB —UNIVERSITY OF CALGARY, Libraries, Special Collections Div, 2500 University Dr, Calgary, T2N 1N4, Can.
Holdings: Vols (5000) Cat Mss
Notes: The Division has extensive collections of the papers of modern Canadian authors (qv individuals), incl Hugh MacLennan, Mordecai Richler, Brian Moore, W O Mitchell, Cliff Faulknor, Christie Harris, Robert Kroetsch, Rudy Wiebe, Claude Peloquin, George Ryga, Andre Langevin, Malcolm Ross, Bruce Hutchison, John Mellor, Grant MacEwan, James Gray, Ernest Watkins, Len Peterson, Michael Cook, and Joanna Glass. The papers of musician Morris Surdin contain hundreds of Canadian Broadcasting Corporation scripts, and constitute a valuable addition to the purely literary ms collections. The Division's holdings also incl collections of scores by Canadian musicians R Murray Schafer and Bruce Mather. In addition, the records of the following Canadian publishing houses are on deposit: E C W Press, Hancock House Publishers Ltd and Coach House Press. The Division alsohouses small collections of letters and mss of Canadian poets such as Earle Birney and George Bowering as well as the archives of the literary periodicals *Tish, Imago, Ariel, Descant, Canadian Review Magazine,* and *Canadian Short Story Magazine.* The ms collections are complemented by a book collection of some 5000 vols.

MB —UNIVERSITY OF MANITOBA, Elizabeth Dafoe Library, Archives and Special Collections Dept, Winnipeg, R3T 2N2, Can. Richard E Bennett, Dept Head; Corrado A Santoro, Reference Archivist
Notes: Radio broadcast entitled "The Search for Frederick Philip Grove". Aired in September 1962. Four reel-to-reel tapes.

ON —CANADIAN BROADCASTING CORP, Head Office Library, 1500 Bronson Ave, PO Box 8478, Ottawa, K1G 3J5, Can. Normand Deschamps, Librn
Holdings: Vols (6400) Cat
Budget: ($18,000)
Notes: Emphasis on radio and television broadcasting. No holdings on technical aspects.

PQ —CONCORDIA UNIVERSITY LIBRARIES, 1455 de Maisonneuve Blvd W, Montreal, H3G 1M8, Can. Martin Cohen, Special Collections Librn
Holdings: Cat Mss
Notes: Collection of 14,000 English language radio drama scripts broadcast over the Canadian Broadcasting Corp from 1930s to date. Presently being accessed by computer. Contains two sections: the main collection is the Esse W Ljungh Collection: besides plays, incl CBC memos, correspondence, etc; the second is the T Frank Willis Collection and consists of the scipts, letters and memos of the late producer.

CANADIAN DRAMA

NY —NEW YORK PUBLIC LIBRARY, Performing Arts Research Center, Billy Rose Theatre Collection, 111 Amsterdam Ave, New York, 10023. Dorothy L Swerdlove, Cur
Holdings: Cat

RI —BROWN UNIVERSITY, John Hay Library, Harris Collection, Prospect St, Providence, 02912. Rosemary L Cullen, Cur
Holdings: Vols (200,000) Cat Mss Phonorecords Microforms
Budget: ($15,000)
Notes: The Harris Collection of American Poetry and Plays is principally composed of American and Canadian poetry and plays, 17th century-date. Extensive holdings in songsters, gift books and annuals, hymnals, pageants, broadside verse, carriers' addresses, women poets, juvenile poetry, (incl Mother Goose and *The Night Before* Christmas), sheet music with lyrics, small press publications, fine printing, black poets, "little magazines," Yiddish-American literature. All movements or schools of American poetry are represented. Incl first editions of most American poets and playwrights, notably Whitman, Poe, Wallace Stevens, Eugene O'Neill, Edward Albee, Ezra Pound, T S Eliot, William Carlos Williams, Amy Lowell, Phyllis Wheatley, Robert Frost, Allen Ginsberg, Bliss Carman, and Stephen Foster sheet music. Also incl the Saunders Walt Whitman Collection (1300 vols); the LangdonCollection of Pageants (250 vols); the Asa Cushman Collection of plays in ms and prompt copies; the MacDougall Collection of Psalters and Hymnals; 4000 plays issued by Walter H Baker Co, Boston (1890-1957); the Vaxer Collection of Yiddish Poetry, Plays and Music (1700 vols). Collections incl 200,000 vols, 30,000 broadsides, 55,000 mss, 170,000 pieces of sheet music, 450 phonorecords, and 375 microfilm reels. See *Dictionary Catalog of the Harris Collection of American Poetry and Plays* (Boston: G K Hall, 1972), 13 vols; *Supplement* (1977), 3 vols. See also, *American Poetry,* 1609-1900, *A Collection on Microfilm, Segment I* (1609-1820); *Segment II* (1821-1850); *Segment III* (1851-1870) (Woodbridge, Conn: Research Publications). Separate catalog.

AB —UNIVERSITY OF ALBERTA, Cameron Library, The Bruce Peel Special Collections Room, Edmonton, T6G 2J8, Can. John Charles, Special Collections Librn
Holdings: Vols 1000
Notes: Catalog in preparation by drama department.

BC —VANCOUVER PUBLIC LIBRARY, Language & Literature Div, 750 Burrard St, Vancouver, V6Z 1X5, Can. B Kinnear, Head
Notes: Good general collection of drama and dramatic criticism, supplemented by biographical clippings and indexed critical periodical material, compiled by the staff. Incl play sets, audiotapes, books and pamphlets.

NS —DALHOUSIE UNIVERSITY LIBRARY, Halifax, B3H 4H8, Can.
Holdings: Vols (10,000) Cat
Notes: Extensive collection of Canadian small press publications with special strengths in poetry, drama, little magazines, poetry broadsides, and Atlantic Canada creative writing. Good holdings in various early Canadian literary periodicals and early Canadian small publishers, but main focus from 1970 to present.

ON —YORK UNIVERSITY, Scott Library, Downsview, M3J 2R2, Can. Hartwell Bowsfield, University Archivist
Notes: Literary and political papers of Canadian playwright, theatre director, and teacher Herman Voaden, leading exponent of Canadian national drama, and the concept of "Symphonic theatre," encompassing all the living arts, collection covers 1897-1975, incl personal papers, diaries, etc. Over 700 playbills, 1926-1945, etc.

ON —METROPOLITAN TORONTO LIBRARY, Theatre Dept, 789 Yonge St, Toronto, M4W 2G8, Can. Heather McCallum, Head
Holdings: Vols (30,500) Mss Pix Slides Phonorecords Microforms
Notes: The Theatre Department is one of eleven subject departments of the Metropolitan Toronto Library, which is generally acknowledged to be the most comprehensive of Canadian public library collections. The department balances book and non book materials in all areas of the performing arts except music: theatre and drama, moving pictures, dance, television and radio programming, and varieties of popular entertainment such as circus, music hall, vaudeville, puppetry and pantomime. The department's substantial holdings of rare books include over 75 court festival books. The collection is international in scope and is particularly strong in materials relating to Canadian theatre history and drama. Non-book holdings include extensive files of newspaper clippings, playbills, programs, production and publicity photographs, posters, and original stage designs, all of which document for the most part the history of Canadian theatre and dance companies, a large collection of British and American theatre portrait engravings, and a representative selection of 19th century, Japanese woodblock prints. Special collections relating to the history of the performing arts in Canada include the records of the Taverner Company which played Eastern Canada and the United States in the late 19th century, Toronto's Grand Opera House, the Marks Brothers touring company, film actor Ned Sparks, the Canadian-born actress Judith Evelyn, Toronto's Crest Theatre, the Canadian Players, Montreal Repertory Theatre, dancer/teacher Boris Volkoff, the Dumbells, the Canadian all-soldier concert party which originated in France in 1917, and vaudeville performer Charles Manny.

ON —VICTORIA UNIVERSITY, Library, 71 Queen's Park Crescent, Toronto, M5S 1K7, Can. Robert C Brandeis, Chief Librn
Holdings: Vols (5000) Cat
See also entry under Canada - History

CANADIAN DRAMA LEAGUE

†ON —METROPOLITAN TORONTO LIBRARY, Theatre Dept, Toronto, M4W 2G8, Can.
Notes: Papers documenting the history of the Canadian Drama League.

CANADIAN FICTION

NC —DUKE UNIVERSITY, William R Perkins Library, Rare Book Room, Durham, 27706. John L Sharpe, III, Cur
Notes: Lionel Stevenson collection of more than 500 titles and manuscripts dealing with literary life in Canada. Primarily in the fields of poetry and fiction in English, but also in literary criticism, drama, essays, history and travel. Almost all are first editions, published in Canada. Many are the writers' presentation copies to Professor Stevenson. Manuscripts are housed in the Manuscript Department.

OH —CASE WESTERN RESERVE UNIVERSITY, Kulas Music Library, 11118 Bellflower Rd, Cleveland, 44106. Timothy Robson, Music Librn
Notes: Selected as a full depository for recordings of Radio Canada International.

CANADIAN FICTION (cont.)

Includes some 800 recordings of music and the spoken word in French, English, and Spanish. Literary, cultural, and political materials are included.

BC —UNIVERSITY OF VICTORIA, McPherson Library, Victoria, V8W 3H5, Can.

ON —UNIVERSITY OF TORONTO, Thomas Fisher Rare Book Library, 120 Saint George St, Toronto, M5S 1A5, Can. Richard G Landon, Head
Holdings: Vols (30,000) Mss
Notes: Comprehensive collection of first and as many subsequent editions as may be obtained of works of Canadian fiction, poetry, and drama. Large collections of Canadian literary papers; papers of Margaret Atwood, Earle Birney, Ernest Buckler, Leonard Cohen, Mavis Gallant, Dennis Lee, Raymond Souster, Josef Skvorecky, and many others.

ON —VICTORIA UNIVERSITY, Library, 71 Queen's Park Crescent, Toronto, M5S 1K7, Can. Robert C Brandeis, Chief Librn
Holdings: Vols (5000) Cat
Notes: The collection of very strong in 19th-20th century poetry, drama and fiction; it contains gazetteers, travel books, biographies, and works on history and geography. Nucleus of collection listed in James C C, *A Bibliography of Canadian Poetry (English)* (Victoria University Library Publication No 1, Toronto, 1899); and Horning, L E, and Burpee, L J, *A Bibliography of Canadian of Canadian Fiction (English)* (Victoria University Library Publication No 2, Toronto, 1904).

CANADIAN FOLKLORE see Folklore, Canadian

CANADIAN INDIANS see Indians of North America and Mexico—Canada

CANADIAN INTERCOLLEGIATE ATHLETIC UNION (CIAU)

ON —UNIVERSITY OF WINDSOR, Leddy Library, Windsor, N9B 3P4, Can. P Jerome Malone, Librn
Notes: Human kinetics, with emphasis on the history, psychology, sociology, philosophy, and administration of sports and their organization. Also hold archival records, etc of numerous Canadian sports organizations: Canadian Intercollegiate Athletic Union (CIAU), Ontario-Quebec AA, Ontario Universities AA, etc. Local and Regional history. 40 feet of materials.

CANADIAN LANGUAGE AND LITERATURE

CT —YALE UNIVERSITY, Beinecke Rare Book & Manuscript Library, Osborn Collection, New Haven, 06520. Stephen R Parks, Cur
Holdings: Mss

MA —HARVARD UNIVERSITY LIBRARY, Widener Library, Cambridge, 02138. Carolyn Fawcett, Specialist in Book Selection
Holdings: Vols 19,000 Cat
Notes: 19,000 volumes on Canadian history and literature. Both French and English materials are well represented.

NC —DUKE UNIVERSITY, William R Perkins Library, Rare Book Room, Durham, 27706. John L Sharpe, III, Cur
Notes: Lionel Stevenson collection of more than 500 titles and manuscripts dealing with literary life in Canada. Primarily in the fields of poetry and fiction in English, but also in literary criticism, drama, essays, history and travel. Almost all are first editions, published in Canada. Many are the writers' presentation copies to Professor Stevenson. Manuscripts are housed in the Manuscript Department.

PA —PENNSYLVANIA STATE UNIVERSITY, Fred Lewis Pattee Library, University Park, 16802. Stuart Forth, Dean of Libraries
Holdings: Vols (5000) Cat Phonorecords Microforms
Notes: Strong in Australian literature, lesser holdings in Canadian, Caribbean, New Zealand, Indian and West African. Special collections of African Plays, Australian Literature.

RI —BROWN UNIVERSITY, John Hay Library, 20 Prospect St, Providence, 02912. Mark N Brown, Cur Mss
Notes: A nearly complete collection of the published speeches, historical writings, and novels, plus some autograph letters, of John Buchan, Lord Tweedsmuir, former Governor General of Canada. Also Harris Collection of American Poetry and Plays, principally composed of American and Canadian poetry and plays, 17th century to date. Extensive holdings in songsters, gift books and annuals, hymnals, pageants, broadside verse, carriers' addresses, women poets, juvenile poetry (incl Mother Goose and *The Night Before* Christmas), sheet music with lyrics, small press publications, fine printing, black poets, "little magazine," Yiddish-American literature. All movements or schools of American poetry are represented. Incl first editions of most American poets and playwrights, notably Whitman, Poe, Wallace Stevens, Eugene O'Neill, Edward Albee, Ezra Pound, T S Eliot,William Carlos Williams, Amy Lowell, Phyllis Wheatley, Robert Frost, Allen Ginsberg, Bliss Carman, and Stephen Foster sheet music.
See also entry under Canadian Poetry

TX —UNIVERSITY OF TEXAS LIBRARIES, General Libraries, PO Box P, Austin, 78713. Carolyn Bucknell, Asst Dir for Collection Development
Holdings: Cat Microforms

AB —PETER WHYTE FOUNDATION, Archives of the Canadian Rockies, Box 160, Banff, T0L 0C0, Can. Mary Andrews, ACR Librn
Holdings: Vols (4247) Cat Mss Maps Pix Slides Phonorecords Audiotapes Videotapes 16mm Films Filmstrips Microforms
Budget: ($1500)
Notes: Collect all available material which touches on the Rocky Mountains of Canada (from the US border to the Peace River in the north; from west of Calgary on the east to the town of Revelstoke, BC on the west). This material incl history (the early explorers, Indians, construction of the railroads, mountaineering, and development of the national parks), natural history (geology, botany, wildlife) and poetry and fiction with the Rockies as a setting. Collect maps of the area, photographs, tape recordings of the pioneers. We also house on our premises the Alpine Club of Canada's library, which is one of the most comprehensive collections on the subject of mountaineering worldwide. Noncirculating.

BC —UNIVERSITY OF BRITISH COLUMBIA, Library, Special Collections Div, 1956 Main Mall, Vancouver, V6T 1Y3, Can. Anne Yandle, Head
Holdings: Vols Cat Mss

BC —VANCOUVER PUBLIC LIBRARY, Language & Literature Div, 750 Burrard St, Vancouver, V6Z 1X5, Can. B Kinnear, Head
Holdings: Audiotapes Books Pamphlets
Notes: Canadian Literature: general collection of poetry, drama, criticism, novels, pamphlets. Index files of Canadian author biographies, poetry in periodicals, criticism in periodicals; also poetry index, both compiled by the staff to books and unindexed periodicals. Partially cataloged.

MB —UNIVERSITY OF MANITOBA, Elizabeth Dafoe Library, Archives and Special Collections Dept, Winnipeg, R3T 2N2, Can. Richard E Bennett, Dept Head; Corrado A Santoro, Reference Archivist
Notes: Artist, playwright, novelist, essayist Bertram R Brooker's correspondence (1910-1955); diaries and daily notations (1905-1938); dramas; published and unpublished novels both complete and incomplete; short stories and essays; poetry; literary reviews and announcements; and articles on advertising. Separated from the collections are 16 photographs, mainly of Brooker, his family and fellow artists. Also, separated is a private library of approx 300 titles cataloged "RBR."

MB —UNIVERSITY OF WINNIPEG, Library, 515 Portage Ave, Winnipeg, R3B 2E9, Can. W R Converse, Chief Librn
Holdings: Vols (5500) Cat
Notes: The Ashdown Collection. Not inclusive, as more Canadiana is elsewhere in the Library.

ON —YORK UNIVERSITY, Scott Library, Downsview, M3J 2R2, Can. Hartwell Bowsfield, University Archivist
Notes: Papers of Margaret Laurence incl letters from readers, research notes, manuscripts of articles and stories, copies of lectures and addresses, diaries, financial records, and correspondence with contemporary Canadian authors.

ON —QUEEN'S UNIVERSITY, Douglas Library, Kingston, K7L 5C4, Can. William F E Morley, Cur, Special Collections
Holdings: Vols (50,000) Cat Mss Maps Pix Microforms
Budget: ($12,000)
Notes: The Edith and Lorne Pierce Collection of Canadiana. Also over 15,000 titles in Canadian Pamphlet Collection. Strong in humanities and social sciences, special strength in English and French Canadian literature; discovery and exploration narratives; Loyalists; War of 1812; opening of the West; local history, 19th century pamphlets and association items. Described in *A Catalogue of Canadian Manuscripts Collected by Lorne Pierce and Presented to Queen's University* (Toronto: Ryerson, 1946); and in *Canadiana 1698-1900 in the Possession of the Douglas* Library, comp by Janet S Porteous, foreword by Lorne Pierce (Kingston, 1932). Also later books and articles on parts of the collection.

ON —NATIONAL LIBRARY OF CANADA, 395 Wellington St, Ottawa, K1A 0N4, Can. Andre Preibish, Dir
Holdings: Vols 34,000
Notes: Includes 350 serial titles. The Library has been receiving on legal deposit all current literary works in English and French published in Canada since 1950. Intensive acquisition of earlier works and those published abroad. The collection aims to be comprehensive. In addition, the collection is supported by representative resources for English, American, French and Commonwealth Literature.

†ON —TRENT UNIVERSITY, Peterborough, K9J 7B8, Can.
Notes: Canadiana; Canadian literature (Shell Collection); native studies; Trent Valley region.

ON —UNIVERSITY OF TORONTO, Thomas Fisher Rare Book Library, 120 Saint George St, Toronto, M5S 1A5, Can. Richard G Landon, Head
Holdings: Vols (30,000) Mss
Notes: Comprehensive collection of first and as many subsequent editions as may be obtained of works of Canadian fiction, poetry, and drama. Large collections of Canadian literary papers; papers of Margaret Atwood, Earle Birney, Ernest Buckler, Leonard Cohen, Mavis Gallant, Dennis Lee, Raymond Souster, Josef Skvorecky, and many others.

ON —UNIVERSITY OF TORONTO, Massey College, Robertson Davies Library, 4 Devonshire Place, Toronto, M5S 2E1, Can. Desmond G Neill, Librn
Holdings: Vols (15,500) Uncat
Notes: Canadian literature in English, especially fiction and poetry.

ON —NORTH YORK PUBLIC LIBRARY, Canadiana Collection, 35 Fairview Mall Dr, Willowdale, M2J 4S4, Can. Ian C Ross, Head
Holdings: Vols (70,000) Cat Microforms
See also entry under Canada.

PQ —BIBLIOTHEQUE DE LA VILLE DE MONTREAL, Montreal City Library, Salle Gagnon Collection, 1210 Sherbrooke St E, Montreal, H2L 1L9, Can. Daniel Olivier, Dept Head
Holdings: Vols (44,055) Cat Mss Maps Slides Microforms
Budget: ($30,000)

CANADIAN LANGUAGE AND LITERATURE (cont.)

PQ —UNIVERSITY OF MONTREAL, Service des Bibliotheques, CP 6128, Succursale A, Montreal, H3C 3J7, Can. Arlette Joffe-Nicodeme, Directeur General
Holdings: Vols 4000 //
Notes: The Louis Melzack Collection of Canadian Books and Manuscripts.

CANADIAN LAW see Law, Canadian

CANADIAN MUSIC see Music, Canadian

CANADIAN MUSICIANS see Musicians, Canadian

CANADIAN NEWSPAPERS see Newspapers, Canadian

CANADIAN NORTH

ON —LAURENTIAN UNIVERSITY LIBRARY, Ramsey Lake Rd, Sudbury, P3E 2C6, Can. Suzanne Brunette, Special Collection Librn; Sue Vongpeisal, Head Librn
Notes: Materials on northern Canada, incl 2200 books and pamphlets, 60,000 press clippings on northern topics 75 series of periodicals and over 1500 maps, plus photographs and thousands of samples of arctic and subarctic plants incl mosses, lichens, algae and wood sections. Much of the material is in French.

CANADIAN NORTHWEST—HISTORY

AB —GLENBOW-ALBERTA INSTITUTE, Historical Library & Archives, 130 9th Avenue SE, Calgary, T2G 0P3, Can. Leonard J Gottseleg, Chief Librn
Holdings: Vols (60,000) Cat Mss Maps Pix Microforms
Notes: Main emphasis is on Western Canadian history. Equally important emphasis is placed on the Canadian Arctic and Alaska, Northwest Coast explorations, Aboriginal peoples of the North and Canadian West, and the fur trade in the US Northwest.

AB —UNIVERSITY OF ALBERTA, Cameron Library, The Bruce Peel Special Collections Room, Edmonton, T6G 2J8, Can. John Charles, Special Collections Librn
Notes: The Canadian West, especially; incl 1000 items from the Rutherford Collection.

CANADIAN NORTHWEST MOUNTED POLICE see Royal Canadian Northwest Mounted Police

CANADIAN PERIODICALS see Periodicals, Canadian

CANADIAN PLAYERS

ON —METROPOLITAN TORONTO LIBRARY, Theatre Dept, 789 Yonge St, Toronto, M4W 2G8, Can. Heather McCallum, Head
Notes: Special collections relating to the history of the performing arts in Canada incl the records of the Taverner Company which played Eastern Canada and the United States in the late 19th century, Toronto's Grand Opera House, the Marks Brothers touring company, film actor Ned Sparks, the Canadian-born actress Judith Evelyn, Crest Theatre (Toronto), the Canadian Players, Montreal Repertory Theatre, dancer/teacher Boris Volkoff, The Dumbells, the Canadian all-soldier concert party which originated in France in 1917, and vaudeville performer Charles Manny.

CANADIAN POETRY

NC —DUKE UNIVERSITY, William R Perkins Library, Rare Book Room, Durham, 27706. John L Sharpe, III, Cur
Notes: Lionel Stevenson collection of more than 500 titles and manuscripts dealing with literary life in Canada. Primarily in the fields of poetry and fiction in English, but also in literary criticism, drama, essays, history and travel. Almost all are first editions, published in Canada. Many are the writers' presentation copies to Professor Stevenson. Manuscripts are housed in the Manuscript Department.

OH —CASE WESTERN RESERVE UNIVERSITY, Kulas Music Library, 11118 Bellflower Rd, Cleveland, 44106. Timothy Robson, Music Librn
Notes: Selected as a full depository for recordings of Radio Canada International. Includes some 800 recordings of music and the spoken word in French, English, and Spanish. Literary, cultural, and political materials are included.

RI —BROWN UNIVERSITY, John Hay Library, Harris Collection, Prospect St, Providence, 02912. Rosemary L Cullen, Cur
Holdings: Vols (200,000) Cat Mss Phonorecords Microforms
Budget: ($15,000)
Notes: The Harris Collection of American Poetry and Plays is principally composed of American and Canadian poetry and plays, 17th century-date. Extensive holdings in songsters, gift books and annuals, hymnals, pageants, broadside verse, carriers' addresses, women poets, juvenile poetry, (incl Mother Goose and *The Night Before* Christmas), sheet music with lyrics, small press publications, fine printing, black poets, "little magazines," Yiddish-American literature. All movements or schools of American poetry are represented. Incl first editions of most American poets and playwrights, notably Whitman, Poe, Wallace Stevens, Eugene O'Neill, Edward Albee, Ezra Pound, T S Eliot, William Carlos Williams, Amy Lowell, Phyllis Wheatley, Robert Frost, Allen Ginsberg, Bliss Carman, and Stephen Foster sheet music. Also incl the Saunders Walt Whitman Collection (1300 vols); the LangdonCollection of Pageants (250 vols); the Asa Cushman Collection of plays in ms and prompt copies; the MacDougall Collection of Psalters and Hymnals; 4000 plays issued by Walter H Baker Co, Boston (1890-1957); the Vaxer Collection of Yiddish Poetry, Plays and Music (1700 vols). Collections incl 200,000 vols, 30,000 broadsides, 55,000 mss, 170,000 pieces of sheet music, 450 phonorecords, and 375 microfilm reels. See *Dictionary Catalog of the Harris Collection of American Poetry and Plays* (Boston: G K Hall, 1972), 13 vols; *Supplement* (1977), 3 vols. See also, *American Poetry,* 1609-1900, *A Collection on Microfilm, Segment I* (1609-1820); *Segment II* (1821-1850); *Segment III* (1851-1870) (Woodbridge, Conn: Research Publications). Separate catalog.

BC —VANCOUVER PUBLIC LIBRARY, Language & Literature Div, 750 Burrard St, Vancouver, V6Z 1X5, Can. B Kinnear, Head
Notes: General collection of poetry, drama criticism, novels, pamphlets. Index files of author biographies, poetry in periodicals, criticism in periodicals; also poetry index, both compiled by the staff to books unindexed periodicals. Partially cataloged. Also incl audiotapes.

MB —UNIVERSITY OF MANITOBA, Elizabeth Dafoe Library, Archives and Special Collections Dept, Winnipeg, R3T 2N2, Can. Richard E Bennett, Dept Head; Corrado A Santoro, Reference Archivist
Notes: Artist, playwright, novelist, essayist Bertram R Brooker's correspondence (1910-1955); diaries and daily notations (1905-1938); dramas; published and unpublished novels both complete and incomplete; short stories and essays; poetry; literary reviews and announcements; and articles on advertising. Separated from the collections are 16 photographs, mainly of Brooker, his family and fellow artists. Also, separated is a private library of approx 300 titles cataloged "RBR."

NS —DALHOUSIE UNIVERSITY LIBRARY, Halifax, B3H 4H8, Can.
Holdings: Vols 10,000 Cat
Notes: Extensive collection of Canadian small press publications with special strengths in poetry, drama, little magazines, poetry broadsides, and Atlantic Canada creative writing. Good holdings in various early Canadian literary periodicals and early Canadian small publishers, but main focus from 1970 to present.

ON —QUEEN'S UNIVERSITY, Douglas Library, Kingston, K7L 5C4, Can. William F E Morley, Cur, Special Collections
Holdings: Vols Cat
Notes: Incl F R Scott Collection, incl Canadian poetry and poetry magazines. (650) uncat. Checklist of holdings is available.

ON —UNIVERSITY OF TORONTO, Thomas Fisher Rare Book Library, 120 Saint George St, Toronto, M5S 1A5, Can. Richard G Landon, Head
Holdings: Vols (30,000) Mss
Notes: Comprehensive collection of first and as many subsequent editions as may be obtained of works of Canadian fiction, poetry, and drama. Large collections of Canadian literary papers; papers of Margaret Atwood, Earle Birney, Ernest Buckler, Leonard Cohen, Mavis Gallant, Dennis Lee, Raymond Souster, Josef Skvorecky, and many others.

ON —VICTORIA UNIVERSITY, Library, 71 Queen's Park Crescent, Toronto, M5S 1K7, Can. Robert C Brandeis, Chief Librn
Holdings: Vols (5000)
Notes: The collection is very strong in 19th-20th century poetry, drama and fiction; it contains gazetteers, travel books, biographies, and works on history and geography. Nucleus of collection listed in James, C C, *A Bibliography of Canadian Poetry (English)* (Victoria University Library Publication No 1, Toronto, 1899); and Horning, L E and Burpee, L J, *A Bibliography of Canadian Fiction (English)* (Victoria University Library Publication No 2, Toronto, 1904). Collection incl mss and vols by Canadian writers Helena Coleman, Raymond Knister, and Marjorie L C Pickthall and letters of Bliss Carman, and Duncan Campbell Scott.

ON —NORTH YORK PUBLIC LIBRARY, Canadiana Collection, 35 Fairview Mall Dr, Willowdale, M2J 4S4, Can. Ian C Ross, Head
Holdings: Vols (70,000) Cat Microforms
See also entry under Canada.

CANADIAN POETS see Poets, Canadian

CANADIAN REVIEW MAGAZINE

AB —UNIVERSITY OF CALGARY, Libraries, Special Collections Div, 2500 University Dr, Calgary, T2N 1N4, Can.
Notes: Archives of the literary periodicals: *Tish, Imago, Ariel, Descant, Canadian Review Magazine* and *Canadian Short Story* Magazine.

CANADIAN ROCKY MOUNTAINS

AB —ALPINE CLUB OF CANADA LIBRARY, Archives of the Canadian Rockies, Box 160, Banff, T0L 0C0, Can. E J Hart, Head Archivist
Holdings: Vols (2429) Cat Mss Maps Pix Slides Audiotapes
Budget: ($1000)
Notes: The Archives of the Canadian Rockies is the custodian of the library and archival collection of the Alpine Club of Canada. The materials cover mountaineering technique and attempts worldwide, incl the Alps, Rockies, Himalayas, Andes, etc. Subject areas incl history, personal records, mountain rescue and medicine, alpine flora and fauna, guide books, manuals and handbooks. A large part of the archival collection is concentrated on the Canadian Rocky Mountains, as the headquarters of The Alpine Club of Canada is in Banff, Alberta.

AB —PETER WHYTE FOUNDATION, Archives of the Canadian Rockies, Box 160, Banff, T0L 0C0, Can. Mary Andrews, ACR Librn
Holdings: Vols (4247) Cat Mss Maps Pix Slides Phonorecords Audiotapes Videotapes

CANADIAN ROCKY MOUNTAINS (cont.)

16mm Films Filmstrips Microforms
Budget: ($1500)
Notes: Collect all available material which touches on the Rocky Mountains of Canada (from the US border to the Peace River in the north; from the west of Calgary on the east to the town of Revelstoke, BC on the west). This material incl history (the early explorers, Indians, construction of the railroads, mountaineering, and development of the national parks), natural history (geology, botany, wildlife) and poetry and fiction with the Rockies as a setting. Collect maps of the area, photographs, tape recordings of the pioneers. We also house on our premises the Alpine Club of Canada's library, which is one of the most comprehensive collections on the subject of mountaineering worldwide. Noncirculating.

CANADIAN SHORT STORY MAGAZINE

AB —UNIVERSITY OF CALGARY, Libraries, Special Collections Div, 2500 University Dr, Calgary, T2N 1N4, Can.
Notes: Archives of the literary periodicals: *Tish, Imago, Ariel, Descant, Canadian Review Magazine* and *Canadian Short Story* Magazine.

CANADIAN SOCIETY FOR CHEMICAL ENGINEERING

ON —MCMASTER UNIVERSITY, Mills Memorial Library, Div of Archives & Research Collections, Hamilton, L8S 4L6, Can. G R Hill, Univ Librn
Holdings: Mss
Notes: Typescripts of articles submitted to *Canadian Journal of Chemical Engineering*, 1965. No photocopying.

CANADIAN STUDIES see Canada—Study and Teaching

CANADIAN UNION OF STUDENTS

ON —MCMASTER UNIVERSITY, Mills Memorial Library, Div of Archives & Research Collections, Hamilton, L8S 4L6, Can. G R Hill, Univ Librn
Holdings: / / Mss
Notes: Office files, correspondence, financial records, briefs, and reports of the Canadian Union of Students and its predecessor the National Federation of Canadian University Students. No photocopying.

CANADIAN WEST

AB —PETER WHYTE FOUNDATION, Archives of the Canadian Rockies, Box 160, Banff, T0L 0C0, Can. Mary Andrews, ACR Librn
Holdings: Vols (4247) Cat Mss Maps Pix Slides Phonorecords Audiotapes Videotapes 16mm Films Filmstrips Microforms
Budget: ($1500)
Notes: Collect all available material which touches on the Rocky Mountains of Canada (from the US border to the Peace River in the north; from the west of Calgary on the east to the town of Revelstoke, BC on the west). This material incl history (the early explorers, Indians, construction of the railroads, mountaineering, and development of the national parks), natural history (geology, botany, wildlife) and poetry and fiction with the Rockies as a setting. Collect maps of the area, photographs, tape recordings of the pioneers. We also house on our premises the Alpine Club of Canada's library, which is one of the most comprehensive collections on the subject of mountaineering worldwide. Noncirculating.

MB —UNIVERSITY OF MANITOBA, Elizabeth Dafoe Library, Archives and Special Collections Dept, Winnipeg, R3T 2N2, Can. Richard E Bennett, Dept Head; Corrado A Santoro, Reference Archivist
Notes: Photographs of western prairie Canada as collected by Heather Robertson from archives and museums across Canada for use in her book *Salt from the Earth.* Pictures are between 1880-1915, showing such things as immigrant families, farms, towns and city life on the prairies, churches, schools, railroads, homestead residences and other aspects of life in the developing Canadian West.

ON —QUEEN'S UNIVERSITY, Douglas Library, Kingston, K7L 5C4, Can. William F E Morley, Cur, Special Collections
Holdings: Vols (50,000) Cat Mss Maps Pix Microforms
Budget: ($12,000)
Notes: The Edith and Lorne Pierce Collection of Canadiana. Also over 15,000 titles in Canadian Pamphlet Collection. Strong in humanities and social sciences, special strength in English and French Canadian literature; discovery and exploration narratives; Loyalists; War of 1812; opening of the West; local history, 19th century pamphlets and association items. Described in *A Catalogue of Canadian Manuscripts Collected by Lorne Pierce and Presented to Queen's University* (Toronto: Ryerson, 1946); and in *Canadiana 1698-1900 in the Possession of the Douglas* Library, comp by Janet S Porteous, foreword by Lorne Pierce (Kingston, 1932). Also later books and articles on parts of the collection.

CANADIAN WOMEN see Women, Canadian

CANADIANA

ON —NATIONAL LIBRARY OF CANADA, 395 Wellington St, Ottawa, K1A 0N4, Can. Andre Preibish, Dir
Holdings: Vols 18,000
Notes: The collection contains 42 incunabula. The core collection consists of early Canadiana (1752-1867) and 16th and 17th century books on Canada. The books printed in native languages are a very valuable part of the collection. Canadian Livres d'Artistes collection of limited editions and Canadian *livres d'artistes* received on legal deposit as well as examples of private press publications from other countries also form part of the Rare Book collection.

CANADIANS IN THE U.S.

CT —THOMPSON LIBRARY, Rte 193, Box 188, Thompson, 06277. Ted Perch, Librn
Holdings: Audiotapes
Notes: Information on French Canadians in Connecticut. Part of the Library's oral history project of the Quinebaug River Valley.

PA —BALCH INSTITUTE FOR ETHNIC STUDIES, Library, 18 S Seventh St, Philadelphia, 19106. R Joseph Anderson, Library Dir
Notes: Ethnic Heritage Collection.

CANALS

DC —LIBRARY OF CONGRESS, Rare Book & Special Collections Div, Washington, 20540. William Matheson, Chief
Notes: Important holdings relating to subjects such as railroads and canals. Material by and about Robert Fulton is particularly strong. The division contains many pre-Civil War technical manuals.

MA —STURGIS LIBRARY, Rte 6A, Barnstable, 02630. Susan R Klein, Chief Librn
Holdings: Vols (1500) Cat Mss Maps Microforms
Budget: ($1000)
Notes: Lothrop Room Collection of genealogy and history is considered to be the finest on Cape Cod. No printed vital records for the County of Barnstable, but 37 books of handwritten *Genealogical Notes of Cape Cod Families* (1620-1850), also on microfilm. Also incl is the Stanley W Smith Collection of books, pamphlets and manuscript materials (mostly original land deeds, all Cape Cod oriented, some of them Indian and dating from the early 1700s). The Percy F Rex Collection represents a unique library of Cape Cod literature. Many rarities, incl early sermons preached on the Cape and pamphlets on Cape Cod canal, etc.

MA —UNIVERSITY OF LOWELL, Library, One University Ave, Lowell, 01854. Martha Mayo, Special Collections Librn
Holdings: Vols 3000 Cat Mss Maps Pix
Notes: The Locks and Canals Collection consist of the 19th century engineering library of the Proprietors of the Locks and Canals on Merrimack River 1793-present. This collection also contains 5000 photographs and 8000 architectural and engineering drawings.

MA —AMERICAN ANTIQUARIAN SOCIETY LIBRARY, 185 Salisbury St, Worcester, 01609. Marcus A McCorison, Dir & Librn
Holdings: Vols 5200 Cat
Notes: Incl the Thomas Winthrop Streeter Collection on Transportation. The finest and most complete documentation of early American railroads, canals, bridges, turnpikes, and harbors in existence.

NY —NEW YORK STATE LIBRARY, State Education Bldg Annex, Washington Ave, Albany, 12224.
Notes: Books, pamphlets, and manuscripts with particular emphasis on The New York State Canal System. Contains Dewitt Clinton and Genet items. Not a separate collection.

NY —BUFFALO & ERIE COUNTY HISTORICAL SOCIETY, 25 Nottingham Court, Buffalo, 14216. Herman Sass, Librn
Notes: Emphasis om the Erie Canal and the region. In various resources departments. No separate catalog.

NY —NEW YORK PUBLIC LIBRARY, Research Libraries, Science and Technology Research Center, Fifth Ave & 42 St, New York, 10018.
Holdings: Vols (1,100,000) Cat Microforms
Budget: ($647,259)

NY —UNIVERSITY OF ROCHESTER, Rush Rhees Library, Department of Rare Books and Special Collections, Rochester, 14627. Peter Dzwonkoski, Librn
Notes: Drawings (20) for structures for enlarged Erie Canal after 1840.

NY —CANAL MUSEUM, Research Library, 318 Erie Blvd E, Syracuse, 13202. Todd S Weseloh, Librn & Archivist
Holdings: Vols 6000 Uncat Mss Maps Pix Slides
Notes: Collections on American Canals, English Canals and Panama Canal. Main focus on canals of New York State from 1793 to present. Engineering, finance, maintenance, construction, canal life, canal boats and impact of canals on New York. Limited genealogical value. 954 linear feet mss, 46,000 photos and slides, 7000 mss, maps and plans.

OH —BOWLING GREEN STATE UNIVERSITY, Jerome Library, Institute for Great Lakes Research, Bowling Green, 43403. Richard J Wright, Dir
Holdings: Vols (2500) Cat Mss Maps Pix Slides Phonorecords Audiotapes Videotapes 16mm Films Microforms
Budget: ($8300)
Notes: About 50 major ms collections, most of them processed; several thousand minor ms items, unprocessed. 100,000 pictures, incl several thousand film and glass plate negatives. Microforms of government vessel registries, vessel passages, 1500 maps, some mss. 6000 naval architectural drawings, 600 vols of scrapbooks. 140 periodical titles, current and op. Author/title/subject catalog.

OH —CLEVELAND PUBLIC LIBRARY, 325 Superior Ave, Cleveland, 44114.
Holdings: Cat Maps Pix
Notes: Library collection in the subject departments incl: state and local history; city directories; business and industry; canals and waterworks; technology; local authors and artists; tourist and travel information (only advisory), vital statistics. Early Ohio pictures and historic maps. See also Western Reserve, Cleveland Public Library.

VA —MARINERS MUSEUM, Library, Newport News, 23606. Ardie L Kelly, Librn

CANALS (cont.)

Holdings: Vols (60,000) Cat Mss Maps Pix Slides
Notes: Incl collections of over 150,000 photographs of merchant ships, naval vessels, sailing ships, lighthouses, portraits of naval men, harbors, canals, etc, and maps, ships' papers, and log books. Catalogs of various parts of the collection published by G K Hall, Boston.

CANALS—FINANCE

MA —HARVARD UNIVERSITY, Baker Library of the Graduate School of Business Administration, Kress Library of Business and Economics, Soldiers Field, Boston, 02163. Ruth E Rogers, Cur
Holdings: Cat
Notes: Corporation Records Division: Active file of annual reports of over 20,000 corporations, US and foreign; SEC reports, and other financial documents. Large collection of older material, especially railroads and canals; financial services. Mainly noncirculating.

CANALS—HISTORY

DE —HISTORICAL SOCIETY OF DELAWARE, Library, 505 Market St Mall, Wilmington, 19801. Barbara E Benson, Library Dir
Holdings: Cat Mss Maps Pix Slides Microforms
Notes: Collection incl papers and other mss materials.

IN —PURDUE UNIVERSITY LIBRARIES, Graduate School of Management, Krannert Library, West Lafayette, 47907. Gordon Law, Librn
Notes: An important resource at the Krannert Library is its Special Collection of Business and Economics, consisting of some 8000 rare pre-20th century strengths in books, journals, tracts and pamphlets covering primarily the early literature of economic thought and business practices in America and abroad, 1500-1870. A catalog was issued in 1979.

MA —HARVARD UNIVERSITY, Baker Library of the Graduate School of Business Administration, Kress Library of Business and Economics, Soldiers Field, Boston, 02163. Ruth E Rogers, Cur
Notes: An extensive collection. Historical emphasis on railroads and canals.

MA —AMERICAN ANTIQUARIAN SOCIETY LIBRARY, 185 Salisbury St, Worcester, 01609. Marcus A McCorison, Dir & Librn
Holdings: Cat Mss Maps Pix
Notes: Outstanding collection, especially for early period, primarily to 1840; thereafter for States of the East and Midwest to the Civil War. Over 6000 items. Incl the Thomas Winthrop Streeter Collection of Transportation; much on the history of canals, bridges, turnpikes, and harbors.

MI —UNIVERSITY OF MICHIGAN, Engineering-Transportation Library, 312 Undergraduate Library, Ann Arbor, 48109. Sharon A Balius, Assoc Librn
Holdings: Mss Pix
Notes: The Canal Collection contains 3000 items, incl annual reports, pamphlets and documents, predominantly from the 19th century, for the US and Canada. In addition, there are materials relating to the Panama Canal and to other proposed interoceanic routes.

NY —STATE UNIVERSITY OF NEW YORK, COLLEGE OF ARTS & SCIENCE AT GENESEO, Milne Library, Geneseo, 14454. William T Lane, Head of Information Services & Archivist
Holdings: Vols (3900) Cat Maps Pix Slides Microforms
Budget: ($1000)
Notes: Genesee Valley Historical Collection. County, town, village, family and church histories for the counties of Allegany, Genesee, Livingston, Monroe, Orleans and Wyoming. Materials on the Seneca Indians, Genesee Valley Canal, and the geology of western New York state.

NY —NEW YORK HISTORICAL SOCIETY, Library, 170 Central Park W, New York, 10024. James Gregory, Librn
Notes: Randall J Leboeuf Jr's collection of Robert Fulton and related material, 1974-1857, consisting of correspondence, drawings, legal papers, etc, relating to steam engines and boats, canals, and torpedoes. The correspondents incl John Quincy Adams, Henry Clay, De Witt Clinton, Albert Gallatin, Benjamin H Latrobe, James Madison, James Monroe, John Livingston, Robert R Livingston, and William Thornton. Also incl are Fulton's expense and note book, 1803-1808, and Robert R Livingston's receipt book, 1808-1812. Approx 215 items, cataloged.

NY —JERVIS PUBLIC LIBRARY, 613 N Washington St, Rome, 13440. William A Dillon, Dir
Holdings: Vols (1500) // Cat Mss Maps Slides
Notes: John Bloomfiled Jervis Collection contains personal library (1500 vols) and papers (1300 items) of chief engineer of Croton aqueduct and other waterworks, canals, and railroads circa 1825-1860. Papers available on microfilm; indexes to papers available from Jervis Public Library.

PA —PENNSYLVANIA STATE UNIVERSITY, Fred Lewis Pattee Library, Special Collections Dept, University Park, 16802. Charles Mann, Chief, Special Collections
Holdings: Vols (1976) Cat Mss Pix Slides
Budget: ($37,000)
Notes: Includes The Beaver Collection (576 vols) in honor of James Beaver, Governor of Pennsylvania, mostly county histories, atlases and Regimental Civil War histories; John M Read Pamphlets (1400 titles), 1830-1890, relating to canals, railroads and civil law. No photocopying.

CANALS—LOCKS see Locks (Hydraulic Engineering)

CANALS, INTEROCEANIC

MI —UNIVERSITY OF MICHIGAN, Engineering-Transportation Library, 312 Undergraduate Library, Ann Arbor, 48109. Sharon A Balius, Assoc Librn
Notes: The Canal Collection contains 3000 items, incl annual reports, pamphlets and documents, predominantly from the 19th century, for the US and Canada. In addition, there are materials relating to the Panama Canal and to other proposed interoceanic routes.

CANARESE LANGUAGE see Kanarese Language and Literature

CANCER

CA —UNIVERSITY OF CALIFORNIA, LOS ANGELES, Biomedical Library, Center for the Health Sciences, Los Angeles, 90024. Alison Bunting, Acting Biomedical Librn; Victoria Steele, Head, History & Special Collections Div
Holdings: Vols (400,000) Cat Slides Phonorecords Audiotapes Videotapes 16mm Films Microforms

Notes: The UCLA Biomedical Library serves primarily the Schools of Medicine, Dentistry, Nursing, and Public Health, the UCLA Medical Center, the Departments of Microbiology and Biology in the College of Letters and Science, and related institutes in biomedicine. The collections of the Library are broad in scope, designed not only to support the teaching and research needs of its many users, but also to function as a resource for the health sciences-biological field as a whole. The outstanding feature of the collection is the strength of its periodical holdings, both current and retrospective. The Library also has an excellent reference collection, a comprehensive historical section, and gives special emphasis to the fields of neuroscience, psychiatry, ophthalmology, radiation biology, molecular biology, and vertebrate zoology. Increased emphasis is being given to the acquisition of audiovisual materials.

†CT —YALE UNIVERSITY, Medical Library, 333 Cedar St, New Haven, 06520.
Notes: An extensive collection.

MD —FREDERICK MEMORIAL HOSPITAL, Walter F Prior Medical Library, W Seventh St, Frederick, 21701. Linda A Collenberg, Librn
Holdings: Vols 900 Cat

MA —FRANCIS A COUNTWAY LIBRARY OF MEDICINE, Boston Medical Library/Harvard Medical Library, 10 Shattuck St, Boston, 02115. C Robin LeSueur, Librn; Richard J Wolfe, Cur, Rare Books & Manuscripts
Holdings: Cat Pix Microforms

MA —SOUTHWOOD COMMUNITY HOSPITAL, Medical Library, 111 Dedham St, Norfolk, 02056.
Holdings: Vols (800) Cat Audiotapes Filmstrips
Budget: ($4500)
Notes: The present emphasis is on human and animal research, diagnosis and treatment. Journals cataloged v 1-12, 1948-59; v 13, 1960-.

NY —COLD SPRING HARBOR LABORATORY, Library, PO Box 100, Cold Spring Harbor, 11724. Susan Gensel, Library Dir; Genemary Falvey, Librn
Holdings: Vols (30,000)
Budget: ($103,500)
Notes: The highly technical collection is comprised of 20,000 serial vols and 10,000 monographs. The library receives 500 current serial titles. Subjects covered incl molecular and cellular biology, virology, biochemistry, microbiology, oncology, neurobiology, biological risk assessment and genetic engineering/biotechnology. Special collections in eugenics and genetics are primarily historical dealing with the development of genetics in the US which had its beginnings here.

NY —MEMORIAL SLOAN KETTERING CANCER CENTER, Lee Coombe Memorial Library, 1275 York Ave, New York, 10021. Angelina Harmon, Dir
Holdings: Vols (25,000) Cat Mss Pix Slides Phonorecords Audiotapes Videotapes 16mm Films Microforms
Budget: ($450,000)
Notes: Incl an developing archives collection, with some rare materials. An extensive bibliography of the institution's professional staff is maintained along with reprints. The main collection is concentrated in cancer and related fields of research and therapy.

NY —SLOAN-KETTERING INSTITUTE FOR CANCER RESEARCH, Donald S Walker Laboratory, C P Rhoads Memorial Library, 145 Boston Post Rd, Rye, 10580. Alison Morrow, Librn
Holdings: Vols (9300) Cat Films Microforms
Budget: $90,000
Notes: Cancer and allied diseases.

TX —UNIVERSITY OF TEXAS, M D Anderson Hospital and Tumor Institute, Research Medical Library, Texas Medical Center, Houston, 77030. Marie Harvin, Research Medical Librn
Holdings: Vols (48,000) Cat
Notes: Library attempts to collect every publication in all languages related to clinical cancer (or oncology). Aim is an exhaustive collection in this field. Collect heavily (research level) in pathology, radiology, nuclear medicine, genetics and cell biology.

TX —SOUTHWEST FOUNDATION FOR RESEARCH AND EDUCATION

CANCER (cont.)

LIBRARY, Preston C Northrup Memorial Library, Baboon Information Center, W Loop 410 at Military Dr, PO Box 28147, San Antonio, 78284. Dorothy M Brooks, Baboon
Notes: Principle field of research: Birth defects, atherosclerosis, reproductive physiology, cancer, genetics, organic chemistry, parasitology, primatology and behavioral sciences and their application to problems of drug abuse, alcoholism and ecology. Maintains the largest baboon colony in the world.

CANCER RESEARCH

AR —NATIONAL CENTER FOR TOXICOLOGICAL RESEARCH, Library, Jefferson, 72079. Susan Laney-Sheehan, Supvr Librn
Holdings: Vols (15,000) Cat Mss Slides Audiotapes 16mm Films Microforms
Notes: Incl (860) journal titles, (230) current subscriptions.

IL —ARGONNE NATIONAL LABORATORY, Biological and Medical Research Branch Library, 9700 S Cass Ave, Argonne, 60439. Rebecca Smith, Librn
Notes: Incl 14,000 vols monographs, 250 current journals. Materials may be used by the public in the library by prior arrangement. Photocopies may be supplied for interlibrary loan, for which a processing and handling charge is made.

ME —JACKSON LABORATORY, Research Laboratory, Bar Harbor, 04609.
Notes: "Subject: *Strain Bibliography* of inbred strains of mice, transplantable tumors, and named genes in mice ..." *Mouse News* Letter. Database discontinued 1984, and has become an archival record.

MA —SOUTHWOOD COMMUNITY HOSPITAL, Medical Library, 111 Dedham St, Norfolk, 02056.
Holdings: Vols (800) Cat Audiotapes Filmstrips
Budget: ($4500)
Notes: The present emphasis is on human and animal research, diagnosis and treatment. Journals cataloged v 1-19, 1941-59; v 20, 1960-.

NE —UNIVERSITY OF NEBRASKA MEDICAL CENTER, Library, 42 & Dewey Ave, Omaha, 68105. Robert M Braude, Dir
Notes: Eppley Institute research collection on cancer now part of Medical Center Library.

NY —ALBERT EINSTEIN COLLEGE OF MEDICINE, D Samuel Gottesman Library, 1300 Morris Park Ave, Bronx, 10461. Charlotte K Lindner, Dir

NY —MEMORIAL SLOAN KETTERING CANCER CENTER, Lee Coombe Memorial Library, 1275 York Ave, New York, 10021. Angelina Harmon, Dir
Holdings: Vols (25,000) Cat Mss Pix Slides Phonorecords Audiotapes Videotapes 16mm Films Microforms
Budget: ($450,000)
Notes: Incl an developing archives collection, with some rare materials. An extensive bibliography of the institution's professional staff is maintained along with reprints. The main collection is concentrated in cancer and related fields of research and therapy.

TN —SAINT JUDE CHILDREN'S RESEARCH HOSPITAL, Medical Library, 323 N Lauderdale, PO Box 318, Memphis, 38101. Mary Edith Walker, Librn; Cindy Suter, Asst Librn
Holdings: Vols (10,000)
Notes: The collection of pediatric oncology is intermingled with general clinical and research materials. Published description of collection in *International Directory of Specialized Cancer Research and Treatment* Establishments (Geneva: International Union Against Cancer, 1976), p 442.

CANE, MELVILLE

NY —COLUMBIA UNIVERSITY LIBRARIES, Rare Book & Manuscript Library, 801 Butler Library, 535 W 114 St, New York, 10027. Kenneth A Lohf, Librn
Holdings: Mss
Notes: Copyright and libel lawyer, lyric poet. A collection of his literary papers, incl books, correspondence, ms, files, literary collections and memorabilia. Restricted use.

CANFIELD, BIL

DC —LIBRARY OF CONGRESS, Prints & Photographs Div, Washington, 20540.
Notes: Swann Collection is strong in the work of contemporary cartoonists. Among the 400 artists represented are Peter Arno, Bil Canfield, Al Capp, Miguel Covarrubias, Louis Dalrymple, Whitney Darrow, Rube Goldberg, Thomas Nast, Jose Guadalupe Posada, Edward Sorel, and John Tenniel.

CANFIELD, ELI H., 1817-1898

RI —BROWN UNIVERSITY, John Hay Library, 20 Prospect St, Providence, 02912. Mark N Brown, Cur Mss
Holdings: // Mss
Notes: Eli H Canfield mss reflect issues of the day and incl the subjects of missions, religious education, temperance, and Reconstruction. There are also 300 letters from Canfield to his son and grandchildren; letters from Europe and the South during and after the Civil War; and papers relating to Christ Church, Brooklyn. Register available. See "The Rev Eli Canfield (1817-1898): Low-church Yankee Episcopalian," ed by William G McLoughlin Jr, in *Books at* Brown, vol XXIII (1969), pp 135-68.

VT —MARTHA CANFIELD MEMORIAL FREE LIBRARY, Russell Vermontiana Collection, Arlington, 05250. D L Thomas, Cur; M L Thomas, Cur
Holdings: Cat Mss
Notes: Russell Collection of Vermontiana. 260 pamphlet boxes (nonbook items). Special railroad collection (unindexed). Also 250 diaries, ledgers, account books and minute books, 1757-1940. Not all briefed. Incl 1000 mss, 100 maps, 300 pictures, Canfield family and Dorothy Canfield Fisher papers.

CANIFF, MILTON

OH —OHIO STATE UNIVERSITY, Library for Communication and Graphic Arts, 242 W 18th St, Columbus, 43210. Lucy S Caswell, Curator
Notes: 5,000 ORIGINAL CARTOONS (INCLUDING *DICKIE *DARE, *TERRY AND THE *PIRATES, *MALE *CALL AND *STEVE *CANYON); 300,000 PAGES CORRESPONDENCE, BUSINESS RECORDS, RESEARCH FILES, ETC.; PHOTOGRAPHS.

CANNABIS see Marijuana

CANNERIES

IN —INDIANA UNIVERSITY, Lilly Library, Seventh St, Bloomington, 47405. William R Cagle, Librn
Holdings: // Mss
Notes: Papers of an Indianapolis cannery, the Columbia Conserve Company, 1903-1953. Incl correspondence; minutes of the Council, annual meetings, and stockholders; stock certificate books; account books and general ledgers; sales reports; production records; and some printed matter about the company. 56,321 items.

CANNING, GEORGE

MA —HARVARD UNIVERSITY LIBRARY, Houghton Library, Cambridge, 02138. Rodney G Dennis, Cur of Manuscripts
Holdings: Cat Mss

CANNING AND PRESERVING

CA —UNIVERSITY OF CALIFORNIA, DAVIS, Shields Library, Dept of Special Collections, Davis, 95616. Donald Kunitz, Head; C Danial Elliott, Asst Head
Notes: Food technology files, 1943-1959, involving the research of Leonard Born on the irradiation of foods, cold sterilization, and algae production. Also, mss, correspondence, photographs, and clippings on various aspects of growing and processing fruit and vegetables, with an emphasis on canning. 3800 items.

CANNON, IDA

MA —SIMMONS COLLEGE ARCHIVES, 300 The Fenway, Boston, 02115. Megan Sniffin-Marinoff, College Archivist
Notes: Archives of the Simmons College School of Public Health Nursing (later reorganized into the School of Nursing) cover the years 1902-1970. Important correspondents in the collection incl M Adelaide Nutting, Mary Beard, Isabel Stewart, and Anne Hervey Strong, etc. Incl Strong's records of activity with regard to nursing education in the National Organization for Public Health Nursing, 1918-22. 1000 linear feet in institution, incl special collections nursing and photographs, nursing.

CANNON, JAMES

NC —DUKE UNIVERSITY, William R Perkins Library, Manuscript Dept, Durham, 27706. Ellen Gartrell, Cur of Mss
Holdings: Cat Mss
Notes: Especially US South, eg Methodist Church Papers (records of local and regional units) also many personal and professional papers of clergy, missionaries and laymen, 19th-20th centuries, eg Methodist John Lakin Brasher (holiness movement leader), Carlyle Marney (Southern Baptist minister), Methodist Bishop James Cannon, missionary Martha Foster Crawford.

CANNONS see Ordnance

CANOES AND CANOEING

NY —ADIRONDACK HISTORICAL ASSOCIATION, Museum Library, Blue Mountain Lake, 12812. Jerold Pepper, Librn
Holdings: Vols (7500) Cat Mss Maps Pix Phonorecords Audiotapes 16mm Films Microforms
Notes: Anything about the Adirondacks--history, people, economics, places, things. Strong in Adirondack art, outdoor recreation, logging, small boats. Resources incl more than 1000 maps, 40,000 pictures, 1600 microfilm reels, 576 linear ft of ms material, and 12 cabinets of VF ephemera, etc.

CANON LAW

CA —UNIVERSITY OF CALIFORNIA, BERKELEY, School of Law, Library, Berkeley, 94720. Stephan G Kuttner, Dir, Canon Law Collection
Holdings: Vols (23,000) Cat Mss Microforms
Notes: Entirely supported by the R D and S M Robbins Endowment, the Robbins Canon Law Collection emphasizes particularly Roman Catholic, Eastern and Anglican canon law. Additional subject areas being developed are ecclesiastical history and institutions, historical and contemporary church and state relations, and ecumenical studies. Library is in process of obtaining complete microfilms of all medieval canon and Roman law mss held by the Vatican Library.

DC —CATHOLIC UNIVERSITY OF AMERICA, Canon Law Library, 300B Mullen Library, Washington, 20064. R Bruce Miller, Librn
Holdings: Vols (22,000)
Notes: The collection includes extensive 16th, 17th, and 18th century works in both Latin and Italian. There are many printed editions of pre-16th century sources. Both the 19th and 20th century materials are well represented. This collection is also rich in materials relating to the Second Vatican Council and its aftermath and is up-to-date on the new (1983) Code of Canon Law. Current periodical subscriptions to journals in English, German, French, Italian, and Spanish.

CANON LAW (cont.)

DC —LIBRARY OF CONGRESS, Law Library, 101 Independence Ave, SE, Washington, 20540. Carleton W Kenyon, Dir
Notes: The Canon Law Collection contains mss, early printed sources, contemporary works, and periodicals pertaining mostly to the canon law of the Roman Catholic church.

IL —JESUIT-KRAUSS-MCCORMICK LIBRARY, 1100 E 55th St, Chicago, 60615. Donald Vorp, Dir; Elvire Hilgert, Librn
Notes: Collection contains merger of Jesuit Library, Lutheran School of Theology of Chicago (Krauss Library), and McCormick Theological Seminary. Jesuit: Sermones Thesaurus Novi de Tempore (anonymous, Strassbourg 1486); Opera Omnia (Jean Gerson, Strassbourg 1488), 3 vols; Summa Rosella Casuum (Venice 1495); moral theology (major figures of 16th and 17th century scholasticism); early modern editions of patristics and canon law regarding procedures and organzation of the Catholic Church, incl treatises and multi-volume commentaries.
See also entries under Religion; Lutheran Church; Presbyterian Church

IL —NORTHWESTERN UNIVERSTIY, School of Law, Library, 357 E Chicago Ave, Chicago, 60611. George S Grossman, Dir
Holdings: Cat Mss
Notes: Comprehensive collections of Anglo-American and foreign (especially European) law; Roman and Canon law (selective); international law; European Common Market; Williams Collection of Legal Instruments (AD 1300-1700); George W Shaw Collection of Early European Law. Incl 500 ms legal documents.

KS —UNIVERSITY OF KANSAS, Kenneth Spencer Research Library, Special Collections Dept, Lawrence, 66045. Alexandra Mason, Librn
Holdings: Vols 1400 Cat Mss
Notes: Especially strong in 16th century French and Italian juris consults, consilia, and commentaries on the C I C. Noncirculating.

MA —HARVARD UNIVERSITY LIBRARY, Law School Library, Langdell Hall, Cambridge, 02138. Harry S Martin III, Librn
Holdings: Cat Mss Maps Pix Slides
Notes: Downs 1687, 1763, 1774, 1776-1779, 1782-1784, 1790-1793, 1809, 1764, 1768, 1798; Downs Supplement 789. Comprehensive collection of English common law, American Law (historical and current), foreign law, comparative law, international law, Roman law and Canon law. Over a million vols.

MO —SAINT LOUIS UNIVERSITY, Pius XII Memorial Library, 3655 W Pine Blvd, Saint Louis, 63108. William Cole, Dir
Holdings: Slides Microforms
Notes: Collection covers all areas of learning and European history from Classical Antiquity to early modern period. Researchers using collection receive assistance in paleography, bibliography and reference search. Approx 10,000 1000-foot reels of microfilm (not counting master negatives) reproducing Vatican Library's Latin, Greek, Hebrew, Arabic and Ethiopic mss. Some 8000 100-foot reels of microfilm (again not counting master negative) reproducing rare and out of print books relating to subject areas in the mss. Over 50, 000 color slides of medieval and Renaissance mss illuminations. A reference collection of modern materials relating to ms research.

NY —UNION THEOLOGICAL SEMINARY, Library, 3041 Broadway at Reinhold Niebuhr Place, New York, 10027. Richard D Spoor, Dir
Holdings: Vols (580,000) Cat Mss Microforms
Budget: ($750,000)

PA —UNIVERSITY OF PENNSYLVANIA, Lea Library, 3420 Walnut St, Philadelphia, 19104. Daniel Traister, Special Collections Librn
Notes: Medieval church history, particularly strong in canon law. See Downs 4234, 4241.

PA —UNIVERSITY OF PENNSYLVANIA, Biddle Law Library, 3400 Chestnut St, Philadelphia, 19104. Elizabeth S. Kelly, Libn
Holdings: Vols (350,000) Cat
Notes: Comprehensive collection of Anglo-American law. Legal materials from selected foreign countries, particularly in Common Market area. International law incl UN documents and other regional organizations. Substantial holdings in historical sources particularly early English law and Canon law.

TX —OBLATE SCHOOL OF THEOLOGY, Library, 285 Oblate Dr, San Antonio, 78216. James Maney, Libr Dir
Holdings: Vols (22,000) Cat
Budget: ($15,500)

AB —UNIVERSITY OF ALBERTA, Cameron Library, The Bruce Peel Special Collections Room, Edmonton, T6G 2J8, Can. John Charles, Special Collections Librn
Holdings: Vols 3800
Notes: Salzburg Collections.

CANONS, FUGUES, ETC.

MA —BOSTON PUBLIC LIBRARY, Music Division, 666 Boylston St, Box 286, Boston, 02117. Ruth Bleecker, Cur of Music
Holdings: Vols 32 Cat Mss
Notes: Thomas Warren's working collection of 32 ms vols of catches, canons, and glees, 1763-1794, incl 2277 compositions, probably half unpublished.

CANS see Containers

CANTOR, EDDIE, 1892-1964

CA —UNIVERSITY OF CALIFORNIA, LOS ANGELES, Research Library, Dept of Special Collections, 405 Hilgard Ave, Los Angeles, 90024. Edward Shreeves, Chairman, Bibliographers Group; David S Zeidberg, Head
Holdings: Mss Pix
Notes: 30 linear feet of personal papers, memorabilia, and working papers related to his life and career.

CANYON DEL MUERTO

AZ —NORTHERN ARIZONA UNIVERSITY, Special Collection Library, CU Box 6022, Flagstaff, 86011. Peter M Whiteley, Coordr/Archivist; William Mullane, Librn
Notes: Day Family Collection. They were Anglo traders on the eastern Navajo reservation. Correspondence, files of trading and other activities of Sam, Anna, Charles, and Sam Day, Jr, 1880's-1930's. Incl unpublished mss on Navajo ceremonies and correspondence relating to the looting of Canyon del Muerto.

CAPE CANAVERAL, FLORIDA

FL —FLORIDA DEPT OF COMMERCE, Research Library, 408 Fletcher Bldg, Tallahassee, 32301. Dennis Hitchens, Librn
Holdings: Vols (3000) Cat Mss Maps VF
Budget: ($6000)
Notes: Collect materials related to the 2 divisions of the Florida Dept of Commerce. Economic Development and Tourism, incl titles on Florida (historical and current), international trade, transportation, education, employment, management, industrial development and business. The Florida and US documents collection covers population, manufacturing, employment, agriculture, retail trade, wholesale trade and labor. VF incl files on every city and county, especially local economic data, SIC coded material, out-of-state information, county files, Florida specific material and general subject material. 100 VF drawers.

CAPE COD, MASSACHUSETTS

MA —STURGIS LIBRARY, Rte 6A, Barnstable, 02630. Susan R Klein, Chief Librn
Holdings: Vols (1500) Cat Mss Maps Microforms
Budget: ($1000)
Notes: Lothrop Room Collection of genealogy and history is considered to be the finest on Cape Cod. No printed vital records for the County of Barnstable, but 37 books of handwritten *Genealogical Notes of Cape Cod Families* (1620-1850), also on microfilm. Also incl is the Stanley W Smith Collection of books, pamphlets and manuscript materials (mostly original land deeds, all Cape Cod oriented, some of them Indian and dating from the early 1700s). The Percy F Rex Collection represents a unique library of Cape Cod literature. Many rarities, incl early sermons preached on the Cape and pamphlets on Cape Cod canal, etc.

MA —CAPE COD MUSEUM OF NATURAL HISTORY, Clarence L Hay Library, Rte 6A, Brewster, 02631. Eileen R Bush, Librn
Holdings: Vols (4000) Cat Maps Pix Slides Phonorecords
Budget: ($1900)
Notes: No photocopying.

MA —FALMOUTH PUBLIC LIBRARY, 123 Katharine Lee Bates Rd, Falmouth, 02540. Ann M Haddad, Librn
Holdings: Vols 46 Cat
Notes: Incl Joseph C Lincoln novels about Cape Cod area and people.

MA —CAPE COD NATIONAL SEASHORE, Reference Library, Park Headquarters S, Wellfleet, 02663. Virginia Osborn, Librn
Holdings: Vols (3000) Cat Mss Maps Pix Slides Phonorecords 16mm Films
Budget: ($2000)
Notes: Cape Cod natural and human history.

CAPE HATTERAS, NORTH CAROLINA

NC —NATIONAL PARK SERVICE, Cape Hatteras National Seashore, Reference Library, Rte 1, Box 675, Manteo, 27954.
Holdings: Cat Mss Maps Pix
Notes: US Lifesaving Service, records and annual reports.

CAPE KENNEDY, FLORIDA see Cape Canaveral, Florida

CAPE VERDE

DC —HOWARD UNIVERSITY, Moorland-Spingarn Research Center, 500 Howard Place NW, Washington, 20059. Clifford L Muse, Jr, Acting Dir
Notes: Cape Verde Islands.

MI —MICHIGAN STATE UNIVERSITY, International Library, Sahel Documentation Center, East Lansing, 48824. Eugene deBenko, Librn; Learthen Dorsey, Librn
Holdings: Vols (5100) Cat Mss Maps Pix Slides Phonorecords Audiotapes Videotapes Microforms
Budget: ($8000)
Notes: See description under The Sahel.

CAPITAL AND LABOR see Industrial Relations

CAPITAL EXPORTS AND IMPORTS see Investments, Foreign

CAPITAL OUTPUT RATIOS see Cost Effectiveness

CAPITAL PUNISHMENT

NY —NEW YORK STATE LIBRARY, State Education Bldg Annex, Washington Ave, Albany, 12224.
Notes: Incl all but 30 of the titles in English listed in the L C bibliography of 1912, and practically all periodical articles. It has also about 60 titles before 1912 not in the bibliography.

PA —FRIENDS HISTORICAL LIBRARY OF SWARTHMORE COLLEGE, Swarthmore, 19081. J William Frost, Dir
Holdings: Vols (31,340) Cat Mss Pix
Notes: Incl works on prison conditions, capital punishment, and works by and about Quaker prison reformers, Elizabeth Fry, John Howard, Richard Vaux, Roberts Vaux, American Friends Service Sommittee, and others.

CAPITALIZATION (FINANCE) see Securities; Valuation

CAPOTE, TRUMAN

DC —LIBRARY OF CONGRESS, Manuscript Division, Washington, 20540. John C Broderick, Chief
Holdings: Cat Mss
Notes: Papers and mss, incl some unpublished. Access only through special permission of the chief of the division.

NV —UNIVERSITY OF NEVADA, RENO, University Library, Special Collections Dept, Reno, 89557. Robert E Blesse, Head
Holdings: Vols (86) Cat Other appearances 160 Cat
Notes: Includes individual works by author in all editions including translations; also prefaces, introductions, published correspondence, appearances in anthologies, periodicals, etc. Bibliographical research collection, part of Modern Authors Collection.

CAPP, AL

DC —LIBRARY OF CONGRESS, Prints & Photographs Div, Washington, 20540.
Notes: Swann Collection is strong in the work of contemporary cartoonists. Among the 400 artists represented are Peter Arno, Bil Canfield, Al Capp, Miguel Covarrubias, Louis Dalrymple, Whitney Darrow, Rube Goldberg, Thomas Nast, Jose Guadalupe Posada, Edward Sorel, and John Tenniel.

MA —BOSTON UNIVERSITY, Mugar Memorial Library, Special Collections Dept, 771 Commonwealth Ave, Boston, 02215. Howard B Gotlieb, Dir
Holdings: Cat
Notes: Original cartoons collected in depth; incl publications by or about.

CAPTIVE ANIMALS see Wild Animals, Captive

CAPTIVE WILD ANIMALS see Wild Animals, Captive

CAPUTO, PHILIP

MA —BOSTON UNIVERSITY, Mugar Memorial Library, Special Collections Dept, 771 Commonwealth Ave, Boston, 02215. Howard B Gotlieb, Dir
Holdings: Cat Mss

CAR WORKERS see Railroads—Employees

CARAS, ROGER

MA —BOSTON UNIVERSITY, Mugar Memorial Library, Special Collections Dept, 771 Commonwealth Ave, Boston, 02215. Howard B Gotlieb, Dir
Holdings: Cat Mss Pix
Notes: Mss, correspondence, etc, collected in depth; incl publications by or about.

CARBIDES

MI —GENERAL ELECTRIC COMPANY, Carboloy Systems Department, Library, Box 237, GPO, Detroit, 48232.
Holdings: Vols (4500) Cat Maps Slides 16mm Films Filmstrips Microforms
Budget: ($5000)
Notes: Collection covers cemented carbide cutting tools, powder metallurgy, metal cutting, metal working, machining, and related subjects. Also numerical control, statistics (related to the cutting tool industry) and general management. Incl 500 maps, 4000 slides, 61 films, 261 filmstrips, 700 microfiche, 7000 patents, and 300 periodical titles.

CARBINES see Rifles

CARBON

MI —ACHESON COLLOIDS, Library, 511 Port St, Port Huron, 48060. Myles T Musgrave, Librn
Holdings: Vols (5000) Cat Mss Maps Slides Microforms
Notes: Incl some original items and records of Dr E G Acheson, inventor of process of manufacturing (electric-furnace) artificial graphite and Carborundum. Incl materials on industrial manufacture and uses of graphite (natural and artificially produced) and related carbon materials, especially as solid lubricants in films, liquids, greases, etc. Incl extensive patent collection (US and foreign).

CARBON, ACTIVATED

TX —ICI AMERICAS, Darco Experimental Laboratory, Library, Drawer U, Marshall, 75670. Tim Butler, Business Manager
Holdings: Vols 4800 Cat
Notes: Activated carbon: uses, applications, origin, and development. No photocopying.

CARBON-14

CA —UNIVERSITY OF CALIFORNIA, BERKELEY, Bancroft Library, Manuscripts Division, Berkeley, 94720. James D Hart, Dir
Notes: Extensive collections of papers and archives relative to the history of modern chemistry.

CARBON ISOTOPES see Carbon

CARBONATED BEVERAGES

IN —HURTY-PECK LIBRARY OF BEVERAGE LITERATURE, 5650 W Raymond Street, PO Box 41167, Indianapolis, 46208. Ben Wilson, Librn
Holdings: Vols (6000) Cat //
Notes: The most comprehensive collection, in English, in the world on beverages of all types. History, manufacture, formulae, customs. Books on beer and brewing; cocoa and chocolate; coffee; liquors and spirits; soft drinks; tea; and wine.

CARBONATED WATERS see Mineral Waters

CARBORUNDUM

MI —ACHESON COLLOIDS, Library, 511 Port St, Port Huron, 48060. Myles T Musgrave, Librn
Holdings: Vols (5000) Cat Mss Maps Slides Microforms
Notes: Incl some original items and records of Dr E G Acheson, inventor of process of manufacturing (electric-furnace) artificial graphite and Carborundum. Incl materials on industrial manufacture and uses of graphite (natural and artificially produced) and related carbon materials, especially as solid lubricants in films, liquids, greases, etc. Incl extensive patent collection (US and foreign).

CARCINOGENS

NE —UNIVERSITY OF NEBRASKA MEDICAL CENTER, Library, 42 & Dewey Ave, Omaha, 68105. Robert M Braude, Dir
Notes: Eppley Institute research collection on cancer now part of Medical Center Library.

CARCINOMA see Cancer; Tumors

CARD, JAMES

NY —INTERNATIONAL MUSEUM OF PHOTOGRAPHY AT GEORGE EASTMAN HOUSE, Archives, 900 East Ave, Rochester, 14607. Rachel Stuhlman, Head Librn
Holdings: Vols (30,000) Cat Mss Microforms
Budget: ($104,000)
Notes: History, aesthetics and technology of photography and cinematography, incl the Gabriel Cromer, Josef Maria Eder, Alden Scott Boyer, Louis Walton Sipley/3M Collections, and the James Card Collection from 1893. Covers photographic, especially cinematographic history; also hundreds of negatives of Edward Muybridge as well as his notebooks. Incl 450,000 pictures and slides. Also the Lewis Hine Collection of social documentary photography.

CARD GAMES see Cards

CARDIAC DISEASES see Cardiovascular System—Diseases; Heart—Diseases

CARDIOLOGY

AL —UNIVERSITY OF ALABAMA, BIRMINGHAM, Lister Hill Library of the Health Sciences, University Sta, Birmingham, 35294. Richard B Fredericksen, Dir

RI —MIRIAM HOSPITAL MEDICAL LIBRARY, 164 Summit Ave, Providence, 02906. Ann LeClaire, Dir of Library Services
Holdings: Cat Cassettes
Notes: Special collection on the renal system with emphasis on kidney transplantation and dialysis.

TX —AMERICAN HEART ASSOCIATION, Library, 7320 Greenville Ave, Dallas, 75231. Katie Trickey, Librn; Barbara Lightfoot, Info Spec
Holdings: Vols (4000) Cat
Budget: ($20,000)
Notes: Cardiovascular diseases.

CARDIOLOGY—HISTORY

MN —MAYO MEDICAL LIBRARY, History of Medicine Collection, Rochester, 55905. Nancy R Hensel, Librn
Holdings: Vols (18,000) Cat Mss Maps Pix Slides
Notes: The collection consists of over 18,000 vols, 6500 of which are considered source material (rare or reprint editions of classics). 4308 items from Garrison-Morton are available in the collection. Appropriate bibliographies, biographies and histories of medicine are a part of the collection. Fields of collecting interest are anesthesiology, dermatology, cardiology, neurology, immunology and radiology. Eight medical incunabula.

NY —NEW YORK ACADEMY OF MEDICINE, Library, 2 E 103 St, New York, 10029. Brett A Kirkpatrick, Librn
Holdings: Vols Cat
Notes: Incl Robert L Levy Collection of (122 vols) in cardiology.

TX —HOUSTON ACADEMY OF MEDICINE-TEXAS MEDICAL CENTER, Library, Jesse H Jones Library Bldg, Houston, 77030. Elizabeth Borst White, Special Collections Librn
Holdings: Vols (250) Cat
Notes: Historic texts and classic works are collected with emphasis on surgical intervention in cardiovascular disorders and on replacement with artificial materials of transplantation. About 55 of the titles are 19th century works on hematology.

CARDIOVASCULAR RESEARCH

TX —HOUSTON ACADEMY OF MEDICINE-TEXAS MEDICAL CENTER, Library, Jesse H Jones Library Bldg, Houston, 77030. Elizabeth Borst White, Special Collections Librn
Holdings: Vols (250) Cat
Notes: Historic texts and classic works are collected with emphasis on surgical intervention in cardiovascular disorders and on replacement with artificial materials of transplantation. About 55 of the titles are 19th century works on hematology.

CARDIOVASCULAR SYSTEM

MA —HARVARD MEDICAL SCHOOL, New England Primate Research Center Library, 1 Pine Hill Dr, Southborough, 01772. Sydney Fingold, Librn
Holdings: Vols (4000)

NY —MASONIC MEDICAL RESEARCH LIBRARY, 2150 Bleecker St, Utica, 13501. Irma A Tuttle, Librn
Holdings: Vols (2000) Cat Slides Microforms

CARDIOVASCULAR SYSTEM (cont.)

Notes: Biochemical gerontology collection represents 10 percent of total holdings in basic medical research fields of physiology, pharmacology, vision and circulation. Incl 16,000 periodicals.

TX —SOUTHWEST FOUNDATION FOR RESEARCH AND EDUCATION LIBRARY, Preston C Northrup Memorial Library, Baboon Information Center, W Loop 410 at Military Dr, PO Box 28147, San Antonio, 78284. Dorothy M Brooks, Baboon
Notes: Principle field of research: Birth defects, atherosclerosis, reproductive physiology, cancer, genetics, organic chemistry, parasitology, primatology and behavioral sciences and their application to problems of drug abuse, alcoholism and ecology. Maintains the largest baboon colony in the world.

CARDIOVASCULAR SYSTEM—DISEASES

MA —FRANCIS A COUNTWAY LIBRARY OF MEDICINE, Boston Medical Library/ Harvard Medical Library, 10 Shattuck St, Boston, 02115. C Robin LeSueur, Librn; Richard J Wolfe, Cur, Rare Books & Manuscripts
Holdings: Cat

CARDIOVASCULAR SYSTEM—RESEARCH see Cardiovascular Research

CARDOZO, FRANCIS LEWIS, 1836-1903

DC —LIBRARY OF CONGRESS, Manuscript Division, Washington, 20540. John C Broderick, Chief
Notes: Papers.

CARDS

CT —YALE UNIVERSITY, Box 1603A, Yale Station, New Haven, 06520.
Notes: Playing cards from about 1440 to the present.

DC —LIBRARY OF CONGRESS, Prints & Photographs Div, Washington, 20540.
Notes: Playing Card Collection.

IN —INDIANA UNIVERSITY, Lilly Library, Seventh St, Bloomington, 47405. William R Cagle, Librn
Holdings: Vols 140 // Ct
Notes: American card games of the late 19th century.

LA —LOUISIANA STATE UNIVERSITY, Troy H Middleton Library, Baton Rouge, 70803. Lance E Dickson, Acting Dir
Notes: About two thirds of all the known books and other materials published on the subject of poker. Some 500 pieces. Gift of former Judge Oliver P "Ike" Carriere, of New Orleans.

MI —DETROIT PUBLIC LIBRARY, Burton Historical Collection, 5201 Woodward Ave, Detroit, 48202. Alice Dalligan, Chief

OH —CINCINNATI ART MUSEUM, Library, Eden Park, Cincinnati, 45202. Patrician P Rutledge, Librn
Holdings: Vols (45,850) Cat Mss Microforms
Notes: Art library containing all subjects on art--history, graphic arts, advertising art, etc; special strength in prints, ie engravings, etc. Near Eastern art and decorative arts are also strong. At least 90,000 art exhibition catalogs. Emphasis on artists of Cincinnati and vicinity in vertical file material.

CARDS, ADVERTISING see Advertising Cards

CARDS, GREETING see Greeting Cards

CARDS, VISITING see Visiting Cards

CARE OF SOULS see Pastoral Counseling; Pastoral Theology

CAREERS see Professions; Vocational Guidance

CAREY, ARCHIBALD J., JR.

IL —CHICAGO HISTORICAL SOCIETY, Library, Clark St at North Ave, Chicago, 60614. Archie Motley, Manuscript Librn
Notes: Papers of Minister and Illinois legislator.

CAREY, JAMES

MI —WAYNE STATE UNIVERSITY, Walter P Reuther Library, Archives of Labor & Urban Affairs, Detroit, 48202. Philip Mason, Dir
Notes: Papers, etc of James Carey, Secretary-Treasurer of the CIO.

CAREY, MATHEW

NY —HOFSTRA UNIVERSITY, Library, 1000 Fulton Ave, Hempstead, 11550. Charles R Andrews, Dean of Library Services
Notes: Strong collection. Incl some mss.

CARIBBEAN AREA

CT —YALE UNIVERSITY, Sterling Memorial Library, Latin American Collections, New Haven, 06520. Lee H Williams Jr, Cur
Holdings: Vols (300,000) Cat Maps Pix Slides Phonorecords 16mm Films Filmstrips
See also entry under Latin America

DC —HOWARD UNIVERSITY, Moorland-Spingarn Research Center, 500 Howard Place NW, Washington, 20059. Clifford L Muse, Jr, Acting Dir
Holdings: Vols (106,086) Cat Mss Maps Pix Slides Phonorecords Audiotapes 16mm Films Filmstrips Microforms
Budget: ($854,753)
Notes: *The Glenn Carrington Collection: A Guide to the Books, Manuscripts, Music and Recordings* (DC MSRC, 1977). *Dictionary Catalog of the Jesse E Moorland Collection of Negro Life and History,* 9 vols and Supplement, 3 vols (Boston: G K Hall, 1970, 1977). *Dictionary Catalog of the Arthur Spingarn Collection of Negro Authors,* 2 vols (Boston: G K Hall, 1970). Guide to Processed Collections in the Manuscript Division of the Moorland-Spingarn Research Center (DC, MSRC, 1983). The Moorland-Spingran Research Center is recognized as one of the largest and most comprehensive repositories in the world for the collection, preservation and dissemination of historical materials documenting from antiquity to the present the history and culture of Black people in Africa, Europe, the Caribbean and the US. Since 1973, the Research Center has greatly expanded its facilitiesand resources and currently provides research services in all aspects of library and archival research, including manuscripts, oral history, music, prints and photographs and general library materials. The Research Center also maintains professional zerographic, micrographic, photographic and similar reproduction laboratories.

FL —UNIVERSITY OF MIAMI, Otto G Richter Library, PO Box 248214, Coral Gables, 33124. Frank Rodgers, Dir of Libraries
Notes: Unique special collections on Cuba, the Cuban exiles and Jamaica are supported by a growing general Caribbean collection. See *Catalog of the Cuban and Caribbean Library, University of Miami,* (Boston: G K Hall, 1977).

FL —UNIVERSITY OF FLORIDA, Libraries, Special Collections, W University Ave, Gainesville, 32611. Sidney Ives, Librn & Rare Books
Holdings: Cat Mss Maps
Notes: This collection, of manuscripts only, deals especially with Haiti, revolutionary period and after. Also a very large group of notaries' papers useful for research in trade and slavery, etc.

FL —ARCHBOLD BIOLOGICAL STATION, Library, Rt 2, Box 180, Lake Placid, 33852. Fred E Lohrer, Librn
Holdings: Vols (2000) Cat Periodicals

FL —HISTORICAL ASSOCIATION OF SOUTHERN FLORIDA, Charlton W Tebeau Library of Florida History, 101 W Flager St, Miami, 33130. Rebecca A Smith, Cur of Research Materials
Holdings: Vols (3000) Cat Mss Maps Pix Slides Audiotapes 16mm Films Microforms
Notes: History of Florida, with emphasis on southern area. Less extensively, history of the Caribbean area, especially as related to Florida. Florida materials incl anthropology, archaeology, Indians of south Florida, incl Seminole Indians, Dade County history, and a complete run of the newspaper *The American Eagle* (1906-date), printed by Koreshan Unity, Estero, Florida. Incl 300 feet of mss, 1500 maps, 75,000 pictures, 2000 slides, 125 audiotapes, 25 16mm films, 200 microforms, 50 feet of vertical files, and 7000 postcards. Work in progress on guide to ms collection and on indexing of photographs. Also incl books and journals on museum science: conservation and preservation of museum materials.

GA —FEDERAL RESERVE BANK OF ATLANTA, Research Library, PO Box 1731, Atlanta, 30301. Leigh Watson Healy, Information Services Coord; Cynthia Walsh-Kloss, Assoc Librn
Holdings: Vols (40,000) Cat Maps Microforms
Notes: Emphasis on banking and economics of the area.

MA —BOSTON COLLEGE LIBRARIES, Thomas P O'Neill Library, Nicholas M Williams Ethnological Collection, Chestnut Hill, 02167. Frank J Seegraber, Special Collections Librn
Holdings: Vols 10,000 // Cat Mss
Notes: Collection emphasizes Caribbeana, especially Jamaica, to 1940. Incl discovery, exploration and natural history of the British, French and Spanish settlements; the slave question; piracy. There are over 6000 mss, 5000 of which are Anansi folk tales recorded by native school children. Also small ancillary sections of Africana and Judaica. For reference use only, by arrangement with librarian.

NY —HAMILTON COLLEGE, Daniel Burke Library, Special Collections Dept, Clinton, 13323. Frank K Lorenz, Cur
Holdings: Vols 1300 Cat Mss Maps Pix
Notes: The Beinecke Lesser Antilles Collection. Specialized works on the smaller islands of the West Indies, incl history, travel literature, flora and fauna, anthropology. Incl numerous rare items in many languages.

NY —RESEARCH INSTITUTE FOR THE STUDY OF MAN, Library, 162 E 78 St, New York, 10021. Judith Selakoff, Librn
Holdings: Vols (14,500) Cat Mss Maps VF
Notes: The non-Hispanic Caribbean. Incl material on all aspects of life in non-Hispanic Caribbean, with primary emphasis on anthropology and the social sciences.

PA —UNIVERSITY OF PITTSBURGH, Hillman Library, Pittsburgh, 15260.
Holdings: Vols (5279) Cat Microforms
Notes: Special emphasis of the Afro-American Collection is on the blacks in the United States; incl materials of Africa south of the Sahara and Caribbean area of the world.

TN —FISK UNIVERSITY, Library, Special Collections, 17 & Jackson St, Nashville, 37203. Ann Allen Shockley, Assoc Librn
Holdings: Vols 45,000 Cat Mss Pix Slides Phonorecords Audiotapes Videotapes Filmstrips Microforms
Notes: There is an author catalog in the Special Collections Room. A published catalog has been done, *Dictionary Catalog of the Negro Collection,* 6 vols, Greenwood Press, 1974. The collection includes all aspects of the Negro In America, Africa, and the Caribbean. Oral history tapes, archival and ms collections, newspapers, magazines and journals.

TX —UNIVERSITY OF TEXAS LIBRARIES, Nettie Lee Benson Latin American Collection, Sid Richardson Hall 1.109, Austin, 78712. Laura Gutierrez-Witt, Head Librn
Holdings: Vols (450,000) Cat Mss Maps Pix Phonorecords Filmstrips Microforms
See also entry under Latin America

†TX —TRINITY UNIVERSITY, Library, 715 Stadium Dr, San Antonio, 78284.
Holdings: Vols (10,000)
Notes: The library of Professor Ronald

CARIBBEAN AREA (cont.)

Hilton on Latin America and the Carribbean. Incl 270 audiotapes of interviews with prominent Latin Americans, 34 autograph letters, and photographs of Cuba during the Spanish-American War.

PR —CARIBBEAN REGIONAL LIBRARY, General Library, University of Puerto Rico, Rio Piedras, (Mailing add: PO Box 21917, University Station, San Juan, 00931). Carmen M Costa de Ramos, Librn
Holdings: Vols (115,605) Cat Pix Maps Microforms
Notes: Collection is specialized in the Caribbean with emphasis in the areas of interest to developing countries: social sciences, politics, economics, labor, education, commerce, tourism, literature, etc. The *Current Caribbean Bibliography* is compiled at the Caribbean Regional Library, with card contributions from all countries of the Caribbean; it also lists all the new additions to the library.

VI —COLLEGE OF THE VIRGIN ISLANDS, Ralph M Paiewonsky Library, Saint Thomas, 00802. Ernest C Wagner, Dir
Holdings: Cat Mss Maps Pix
Notes: Incl a number of rare books and broadsides (The collection of H Lee Platt of St Croix, 175 vols).

VI —VIRGIN ISLANDS BUREAU OF LIBRARIES, MUSEUMS & ARCHAEOLOGICAL SERVICES, Enid M Baa Library & Archives, Von Scholten Collection, PO Box 390, Saint Thomas, 00801. June A V Lindqvist, Cur
Holdings: Vols (13,000) Cat Mss Maps Pix Microforms
Notes: Caribbeana, with emphasis on the Virgin Islands. Library collects in all aspects of Virgin Islands life, incl natural and cultural history. Collection is especially strong in Danish West Indian and Virgin Islands newspapers and in dissertations on Caribbean subjects. Library is a full depository for USVI documents. Auxilliary collections are located in the Bureau's libraries in St Croix and St John.

CARIBBEAN AREA NEWSPAPERS see Newspapers, Caribbean Area

CARIBBEAN LANGUAGES AND LITERATURES

DC —HOWARD UNIVERSITY, Moorland-Spingarn Research Center, 500 Howard Place NW, Washington, 20059. Clifford L Muse, Jr, Acting Dir

MO —DRURY COLLEGE, Library, Springfield, 65802. Judith Armstrong, Dir
Holdings: Vols 260 Cat
Notes: No separate catalog or index. Confined to prose and poetry.

NY —HAMILTON COLLEGE, Daniel Burke Library, Special Collections Dept, Clinton, 13323. Frank K Lorenz, Cur
Holdings: Vols 1300 Cat Mss Maps Pix
Notes: The Beinecke Lesser Antilles Collection. Specialized works on the smaller islands of the West Indies, incl history, travel literature, flora and fauna, anthropology. Incl numerous rare items in many languages.

TX —UNIVERSITY OF TEXAS LIBRARIES, Nettie Lee Benson Latin American Collection, Sid Richardson Hall 1.109, Austin, 78712. Laura Gutierrez-Witt, Head Librn
Holdings: Vols (450,000) Cat Mss Maps Pix Phonorecords Filmstrips Microforms
See also entry under Latin America.

VI —COLLEGE OF THE VIRGIN ISLANDS, Ralph M Paiewonsky Library, Saint Thomas, 00802. Ernest C Wagner, Dir
Holdings: Vols 1200 Cat Microforms
Budget: $3500
Notes: Incl novels, poetry and plays written by Caribbean authors and critical writings of the works of these authores. We are acquiring all materials on Caribbean literature in English.

CARICATURES AND CARTOONS

AZ —NORTHERN ARIZONA UNIVERSITY, Special Collection Library, CU Box 6022, Flagstaff, 86011. Peter M Whiteley, Coordr/Archivist; William Mullane, Librn
Notes: Carol Jones Collection. Scrapbooks belonging to Mrs Jones, her mother, and grandmother, 1880's-1940's. One scrapbook contains World War II Reg Manning cartoons appearing in the *Arizona Republic.*

CA —UNIVERSITY OF CALIFORNIA, SAN DIEGO, Central University Library, Mandeville Dept of Special Collections, La Jolla, 92093. Lynda Corey Claassen, Head
Holdings: Vols 301 // Uncat Mss Pix
Notes: The Paul F Conrad collection of political cartoons. He is the Pulitzer Prize-winning cartoonist of the Los Angeles *Times* (1964 and 1971).

CA —UNIVERSITY OF CALIFORNIA, LOS ANGELES, Theater Arts Library, Los Angeles, 90024. Edward Shreeves, Chairman, Bibliographers Group; Audree Malkin, Head, Theater Arts Library
Notes: Scripts, posters, comic books, music, models, original sketches, research, drawings, cels, storyboards, and films of cartoon producer Walter Lantz. Extensive collection. Also, a collection of original comic books, color comic books, storyboards, and posters illustrated by Clyde Geronimi.

CA —FITZ HUGH LUDLOW MEMORIAL LIBRARY, PO Box 99346, San Francisco, 94109. Michael R Aldrich, Exec Cur
Holdings: Vols (6000) Pix Slides
Notes: Collection stored. Important mail inquiries only. No interlibrary lending or telephone queries. Index to hundreds of drug-related illustrations, filed in several binders by topic (Cannabis, Hallucinogens, Cocaine, Music, etc). We have photostats of about 500 of the best illustrations available to researchers and writers as a graphics archive; copyright and reproduction permission must however be obtained by the user of publisher, in addition to a nominal fee (per illustration) paid to the Library. We also collect original art works, artifacts, paraphernalia, comic books, newspaper illustrations, and drug advertisements relating to psychoactive drug use and abuse. In addition we have available many illustrations pertinent to mythology (ancient and modern) peripherally related to drug history and folklore.

CA —HOOVER INSTITUTION ON WAR, REVOLUTION & PEACE, Stanford University, Stanford, 94305. Milorad M Drachkovitch, Archivist
Holdings: // Mss
Notes: Papers, 1903-1939, of Louis Raemaekers, Belgian artist and cartoonist. Correspondence relating to business and art work, World War I sketches, drawings, cartoons, watercolors, ink drawings, clippings, invitations and honors, and photos. 27 ft. Unpublished finding aid in repository.

CA —CALIFORNIA INSTITUTE OF THE ARTS, Library, 24700 McBean Pkwy, Valencia, 91355. James Elrod, Dir
Holdings: Vols (61,000) Slides
Budget: ($11,000)
Notes: Modern art, incl abstract, conceptual, concrete, environment, minimal, and pop art; art; dadaism; surrealism; happenings; and caricatures and cartoons. Slides (61,683).

CT —LEWIS WALPOLE LIBRARY, 154 Main St, Farmington, 06032. Catherine Jestin, Librn
Holdings: Cat Mss Maps Pix Slides Microforms
Notes: Research center for English eighteenth-century studies. A department of Yale University Library. Scholars may visit by appointment only.

CT —TRINITY COLLEGE LIBRARY, Watkinson Library, 300 Summit St, Hartford, 06106. Jeffrey Kaimowitz, Cur
Holdings: Cat
Notes: Incl the Sherman P Haight Cruikshank Collection.

CT —YALE UNIVERSITY, Medical Historical Library, 333 Cedar St, New Haven, 06510. Ferenc A Gyorgyey, Librn
Holdings: Cat Pix
Notes: The Clements C Fry Collection of Medical Prints and Drawings. About 2000 items. Also, about 3000 bookplates of physicians, many of medical interest.

DC —GEORGETOWN UNIVERSITY, Library, Special Collections Div, 37 & O Sts NW, Washington, 20057. George M Barringer, Special Collections Librn; Nicholas B Sheetz, Mss Librn
Holdings: Cat Mss Maps Pix Slides Phonorecords Audiotapes
Notes: Includes the papers (1912-49) of Sen Robert F Wagner; the archives (1903-) of the American Political Science Association and of its local Washington chapter; the archives of the Center for Public Financing of elections; a collection of several hundred political cartoons by Eric Smith; and other smaller collections.

DC —GEORGE WASHINGTON UNIVERSITY, Gelman Library, 2130 H St NW, Washington, 20052.
Holdings: // Uncat Mss Pix
Notes: Original drawings of editorial and political cartoons by George Y Coffin, covering the period ca 1884-1896. Coffin drew for *Puck, Harper's Weekly,* and other periodicals and was staff cartoonist for the Washington *Post* until 1895. The collection also includes Coffin's diaries, scrapbooks, and notebooks. Library also holds cartoons by Clifford Berryman (pv).

DC —HOWARD UNIVERSITY, Moorland-Spingarn Research Center, 500 Howard Place NW, Washington, 20059. Clifford L Muse, Jr, Acting Dir
Holdings: Vols (106,086) Mss Maps Pix Slides Phonorecords Audiotapes 16mm Films Filmstrips Microforms
Budget: ($854,753)
See also entry under Blacks

DC —LIBRARY OF CONGRESS, Prints & Photographs Div, Washington, 20540.
Notes: Incl the Caroline and Erwin Swann Collection of caricatures and cartoons. Strong in the work of modern artists from the middle of the 19th century. *The New Yorker* Collection contains original cartoons and cover illustrations from the magazine, mid-20th century. The Gary Yonker Collection of political propaganda posters, late 1960s to present. Strongest for US materials but incl about 50 other countries' work. Over 4500 items, arranged geographically.

IL —NORTHWESTERN UNIVERSITY, Library, Special Collections Dept, 1937 Sheridan Rd, Evanston, 60201. R Russell Maylone, Cur
Holdings: Cat
Notes: John T McCutcheon drawings of political carttons from the *Chicago Tribune.* 560 original drawings.

IN —INDIANA UNIVERSITY, Lilly Library, Seventh St, Bloomington, 47405. William R Cagle, Librn
Holdings: Uncat Mss
Notes: Contemporary with and depicting Lincoln; the War of 1812 and other periods. Incl significant mss of the modern cartoonists and caricaturists Ardizzone, Beerbohm, Fontane Fox, Kin Hubbard, Charles Bacon Jackson, McCutcheon, Messick, Nast, Rothenstein, Sendak, and many miscellaneous items.
See also entry under Animation (Cinematography)

IN —UNIVERSITY OF EVANSVILLE, Clifford Memorial Library & Learning Resources, 1800 Lincoln Ave, Evansville, 47714. P Grady Morein, University Librn
Holdings: Vols 45 // Uncat Mss
Notes: Incl approximately 10,000 cartoons by Karl K Knecht.

IN —BUTLER UNIVERSITY, Irwin Library, Hugh Thomas Miller Rare Book Room, 4600 Sunset Ave, Indianapolis, 46208. Gisela Terrell, Rare Books Librn
Holdings: Cat Mss Pix
Notes: *Gaar Williams/Kin Hubbard* Collection. This collection was presented to the library by Blanche Stillson in 1964. It contains original cartoons and other drawings, books (many of them inscribed), magazines, letters and other manuscripts, photographs, and memorabilia by both Hoosier cartoonists and humorists. A catalogue of the Gaar Williams ("Abe Martin") items was printed in 1981. It is available upon request.

CARICATURES AND CARTOONS (cont.)

IN —PURDUE UNIVERSITY LIBRARIES, Special Collections Dept, West Lafayette, 47907. Keith Dowden, Asst Dir, Special Collections
Holdings: Mss Pix
Notes: John T McCutcheon Collection. Incl 800 cartoons, clippings and photographs.

IA —UNIVERSITY OF IOWA, University Libraries, Iowa City, 52242. Frank Paluka, Head, Special Collections Dept
Holdings: Cat Mss Pix
Notes: Collection incl 6000 cartoons and 4 file drawers of ms material by Ding. An extensive subject index is located in the library. See The Sui Ding Darling Cartoon Collection, in the *Iowa Alumni Review,* Dec 1963.

KS —UNIVERSITY OF KANSAS, Kenneth Spencer Research Library, Kansas Collection, Lawrence, 66045. Sheryl K Williams, Cur
Holdings: Cat
Notes: The Albert T Reid Cartoon Collection. Nucleus of collection was Reid's personal collection of political and comic cartoons. Later cartoonists presented samples of their work. Bill Mauldin, Rollin Kirby, Daniel B Dowling, Thomas Nast, and other political cartoonists are represented. Comic strips from the late 1920s and 1930s also. The collection of cartoons is cataloged and represented in the Kansas Collection card catalog. A separate book catalog is maintained also. For description see: *Albert T Reid Cartoon Collection.* Lawrence, Kan, Published for the Journalistic Historical Center, University of Kansas, ca 1957. Originally maintained by the Journalistic Historical Center, William Allen White School of Journalism, the collection was transferred to the Kansas Collection, Kenneth Spencer Library in 1969.

KS —WICHITA STATE UNIVERSITY, Ablah Library, Box 68, Wichita, 67208. Michael T Kelly, Cur of Special Collections
Notes: Includes work by Gene Bassett, Ed Batchelor, Jack Bender, Douglas Borgstedt, Paul Conrad, William H Crawford, Dan Dowling, Karl S Hubenthal and others.

KY —WESTERN KENTUCKY UNIVERSITY, Kentucky Library, Bowling Green, 42101. Riley Handy, Head, Special Collections; Connie Mills, Maps & Music Librn; Nancy Baird, Photographs Librn; Nancy Solley, Conservation Librn
Holdings: Vols (25,000) Cat Mss Maps Pix Microforms
Notes: Besides Kentucky history, other strengths are Mammoth Cave, South Union Shakers, Kentucky religion; and steamboat photos (3300 cataloged pictures); 8000 Kentucky postal cards, etc.

MA —BOSTON PUBLIC LIBRARY, Print Collection, Dartmouth St at Copley Sq, Boston, 02117. Sinclair H Hitchings, Keeper of Prints
Holdings: Cat
Notes: The caricature collection incl 300 American prints (colonial period to 1900), 65 of these are by Thomas Nast; 400 English prints (mostly 18th century) many by Thomas Rowlandson and James Gillray; and several thousand 19th century French items, large numbers of them by Daumier. Items are cataloged by artist when known; or else by publisher or country. In addition, the American caricatures are arranged chronologically.

MA —AMERICAN ANTIQUARIAN SOCIETY LIBRARY, 185 Salisbury St, Worcester, 01609. Marcus A McCorison, Dir & Librn
Holdings: Cat Maps Pix
Notes: Over 6000 American prints, arranged by lithographer. Incl political caricatures and cartoons, maps, sheet music. Also advertising cards, Valentines, etc.

MI —MICHIGAN STATE UNIVERSITY, Libraries, Special Collections Div, East Lansing, 48824. Jannette Fiore, Librn
Holdings: Vols 23,500 Cat
Notes: Approximatley 21,000 comic books, cataloged, with anthologies and collections of comics, caricature, politcal cartoons, and standard reference tools.

MN —MAYO MEDICAL LIBRARY, History of Medicine Collection, Rochester, 55905. Nancy R Hensel, Librn
Holdings: Pix
Notes: The Dr Howard F Polley Cartoon Collection, over 70 cartoons featured in newspapers nationally that relate to the Mayo Clinic and Rochester.

MS —UNIVERSITY OF SOUTHERN MISSISSIPPI, William David McCain Graduate Library, Box 5148, Southern Sta, Hattiesburg, 39406.
Holdings: Cat Pix
Notes: The Association of American Editorial Cartoonists Collection, 1968 to date. More than 3400 items by more than 200 artists. The collection, founded in 1968, incl members from the United States, Canada and Mexico. Incl (but not limited) cartoons by Gene Basset, Charles Brooks, Bill Daniels, Syd Hoff, Bob Howie, Jim Ivey, Jack Jurden, Jon Kennedy, Reg Manning, John Milt Morris, John Pierotti, Eldon Pletcher, Arthur Poineier, John Riedell, Robbie Robinson, John Shevchik, John Stampone, Ed Valtman, L D Warren and Richard Yardley.

NJ —MACCULLOCH HALL HISTORICAL MUSEUM, Morristown, 07960. Alice A Caulkins, Curator
Notes: The W Parsons Todd Collection.

NY —NEW YORK STATE ARCHIVES, 9049 Cultural Education Center, Albany, 12230. Richard Andress, Archivist
Holdings: Vols 40,000
Notes: Scripts read by the Motion Picture Division of the NYS Education Departments for the purposes of rating and approval, with orders by Department for deletions or changes in dialogue. Between 1910-1966 all moving pictures shown in New York were reviewed by this Board. Incl animated cartoon films. 54,000 items.

NY —NATIONAL BASEBALL HALL OF FAME AND MUSEUM, National Baseball Library, Cooperstown, 13326. Thomas R Heitz, Librn
Notes: A representative collection of cartoon art related to baseball.

NY —NEW YORK PUBLIC LIBRARY, Performing Arts Research Center, Billy Rose Theatre Collection, 111 Amsterdam Ave, New York, 10023. Dorothy L Swerdlove, Cur
Holdings: Cat
Notes: A large collection of original caricatures, many of which appeared in the *New Yorker* magazine, 1925-1962. Published description: Frueh, Alfred J, *Frueh on the Theatre; Theatrical Caricatures, 1906-1962,* (New York Public Library, 1972).
See also entry under Sardi's Restaurant.

NY —SCHOLASTIC MAGAZINES, Editorial Library, 730 Broadway, New York, 10003. Lucy Evankow, Chief Librn
Notes: Political cartoons back to the 40s-50s.

NY —UNIVERSITY OF ROCHESTER, Rush Rhees Library, Department of Rare Books and Special Collections, Rochester, 14627. Peter Dzwonkoski, Librn
Notes: Original drawings by Thomas Nast; also World War II political cartoons by Elmer Messher, cartoonist for Rochester, New York newspaper.

NY —MUSEUM OF CARTOON ART LIBRARY, Comly Avenue, Rye Brook, 10573.
Notes: Original comics and cartoon art, 60, 000 pieces. 800 animated cartoons. Disney collection extensive. Samples of Big-Little Books, foreign comics, fanzines, cartoon related games, posters, pulps, undergrounds. Hal Foster, Walt Kelly, Gene Byrns, Tad Dorgan, Chester Gould extensive original art collections.

†NY —SYRACUSE UNIVERSITY LIBRARIES, E S Bird Library, George Arents Research Library, Rm 600, Syracuse, 13210. Mr Sidney Huttner, Librn
Notes: Samples or selections of cartoon art, comic strips, Disney, fantasy, fanzines, horror (Ackerman mss), mystery pulps, series books and westerns.

OH —OHIO STATE UNIVERSITY, Library for Communication and Graphic Arts, 242 W 18th St, Columbus, 43210. Lucy S Caswell, Curator

Notes: 5,000 original cartoons (including Dickie Dare, Terry and the Pirates, Male Call and Steve Canyon); 300,000 pages correspondence, business records, research files, etc.; photographs.

PA —BALCH INSTITUTE FOR ETHNIC STUDIES, Library, 18 S Seventh St, Philadelphia, 19106. R Joseph Anderson, Library Dir

PA —FREE LIBRARY OF PHILADELPHIA, Rare Book Dept, Logan Sq, Philadelphia, 19103. Marie E Korey, Rare Book Librn
Holdings: Uncat Pix
Notes: The Alfred Bendiner Collection of 920 caricatures which incl original art, prints, books and periodicals of European and American origin.

RI —BROWN UNIVERSITY, John Hay Library, McLellan Lincoln Collection, 20 Prospect St, Providence, 02912. Jennifer B Lee, Special Collections Librn
Holdings: Vols (15,000) Cat Mss Pix Phonorecords
Notes: Prints, arranged according to Meserve numbers, contain most of the known photographs of Lincoln, rare engravings, caricatures, Currier and Ives prints, and original oil portraits done by artists of Lincoln's day, as well as original paintings of Lincoln's deathbed by Alonzo Chappel and Alexander Ritchie; some original drawings, as well as a scrapbook of Thomas Nast's Civil War sketches.

RI —BROWN UNIVERSITY, John Hay Library, Anne S K Brown Military Collection, 20 Prospect St, Providence, 02912. Richard B Harrington, Cur
Holdings: Vols (40,000) Cat Mss Pix
Notes: The Anne S K Brown Military Collection has been formed over the past forty or more years by Mrs John Nicholas Brown, now of Newport, and contains approximately 40,000 volumes and 60,000 prints, drawings and water-colours as well as a number of oil paintings and about 5000 miniature model soldiers. At its beginning (and still today) the emphasis or focus of this collection has been upon the history of - and the accurate contemporary illustration of - military and naval uniforms of all nations from the early XVII century to the present. In the course of time, however, the collection has come to incl also a vast and related amount of material on military and naval history, military and naval arts and tactics, wars, campaigns, ceremonies, biography, portraits and caricatures of this and earlier periods. It has been probably the largest private collection of such a nature inthe world, and it contains much ms and graphic documentation which is unique. It has been useful to numerous scholars and historians, editors, film-makers and publishers for research and for illustrative material and has also contributed to many museum exhibitions. In 1982 the entire collection, with its complete card-catalogue and subject index, has been presented to Brown University, where it is located in the John Hay Library. Special requests are taken care of by phone, mail and appointments with the curator.

TX —FORT WORTH PUBLIC LIBRARY, Arts Division, 300 Taylor St, Fort Worth, 76102. Heather Gobel, Head
Holdings: Uncat
Notes: Original cartoon art. Emphasis is on editorial, political, historical events cartoons. Nucleus collection comprised of original Hal Coffman Cartoons rendered for the editorial pages of the *Fort Worth Star-Telegram* from October 10, 1939, until his death on August 31, 1958. 4575 pieces.

VA —UNIVERSITY OF VIRGINIA, Alderman Library, Manuscripts Dept, Charlottesville, 22901. Edmund Berkeley Jr, Cur
Holdings: Cat
Notes: This library contains a number of collections of cartoons, chiefly but not

CARICATURES AND CARTOONS (cont.)

exclusively political, by a number of artists. The more important collections are: (1) The Fred O Seibel Collection: editorial page cartoons in the Richmond *Times-Dispatch*, 1926-1968. Incl are ca 3500 drawings, plus his research files. Unpublished guides; (2) Bernard M Meeks Collection: 326 original drawings assembled by a collector. Includes drawings by Herbert Block, Walt Disney, Thomas Nast, Jay N "Ding" Darling, Jimmy Hatlo, Rube Goldberg, James Thurber, etc; (3) Oscar Edward Cesare Collection: 232 cartoons for New York City newspapers and periodicals, 1912-1943, including such subjects as US politics, international relations, labor unrest, World Wars I & II; (4) Art Wood Collection: 625 drawings by the long-time cartoonist for the Richmond *News-Leader*; (5) Harry F Byrd: over 500original drawings, many by Fred O Seibel, but including almost every artist working during the Virginia Senator's years in Washington. The great majority of the cartoons concern Senator Byrd and his political positions or ambitions, but other subjects, many of national interest, are included; (6) Hugh Scott Collection: ca 75 cartoons by various artists, chiefly concerning the Pennsylvania senator and his political positions or ambitions, but many of national interest. Other cartoonists represented in the collection by one or more drawings include: Milt Caniff, Gib Crockett, Dan Dowling, Jeff MacNelly, Gus Mager, Charles Schultz, Richard Q Yardley, and Draper Hill.

†VA —VIRGINIA COMMONWEALTH UNIVERSITY, James Branch Cabell Library, Special Collections Dept, 901 Park Avenue, Richmond, 23284. Daniel A Yanchisin, Librn
Notes: Books and original works of caricatures and cartoons.

WY —UNIVERSITY OF WYOMING, William Robertson Coe Library, 13 & Ivinson, Laramie, 82071.
Notes: 2000 volumes of popular humor, incl books of cartoons, humorous novels, and the like.

WY —UNIVERSITY OF WYOMING, William Robertson Coe Library, Archives - American Heritage Center, PO Box 3412, Laramie, 82071.
Notes: Music manuscripts of Carl W Stalling, writer of music for such cartoons as "Mickey Mouse," "Silly Symphonies," "Three Little Pigs," "Bugs Bunny," "Looney Tunes," and other productions of Walt Disney and Warner Brothers. Incl 1300 complete original scores, more than 2000 sheets of other music, and many other materials.

†ON —METROPOLITAN TORONTO LIBRARY, Theatre Dept, Toronto, M4W 2G8, Can.
Notes: Incl ballet caricatures by Nikolai and Sergei Legat, St Petersburg, 1902-1905.

CARICATURES AND CARTOONS—MUSIC

WY —UNIVERSITY OF WYOMING, William Robertson Coe Library, Archives - American Heritage Center, PO Box 3412, Laramie, 82071.
Notes: Music manuscripts of Carl W Stalling, writer of music for such cartoons as "Mickey Mouse," "Silly Symphonies," "Three Little Pigs," "Bugs Bunny," "Looney Tunes," and other productions of Walt Disney and Warner Brothers. Incl 1300 complete original scores, more than 2000 sheets of other music, and many other materials.

CARICATURISTS AND CARTOONISTS

CA —UNIVERSITY OF CALIFORNIA, SAN DIEGO, Central University Library, Mandeville Dept of Special Collections, La Jolla, 92093. Lynda Corey Claassen, Head
Holdings: Vols 301 // Uncat Mss Pix
Notes: The Paul F Conrad collection of political cartoons. He is the Pulitzer Prize-winning cartoonist of the Los Angeles *Times* (1964 and 1971).

CA —UNIVERSITY OF CALIFORNIA, LOS ANGELES, Research Library, Dept of Special Collections, 405 Hilgard Ave, Los Angeles, 90024. Edward Shreeves, Chairman, Bibliographers Group; David S Zeidberg, Head
Holdings: Vols (1000) Cat Mss Pix
Notes: Various collections, incl books illustrated by George Cruikshank; mss, scrapbooks, etc, of George McManus, creator of *Maggie and Jiggs;* original cartoons by *L A Times* political satirist Bruce Russell; original drawings by Theodor Geisel (Dr Seuss); first issues of comic books; miscellaneous comic books.

CA —UNIVERSITY OF CALIFORNIA, LOS ANGELES, Theater Arts Library, Los Angeles, 90024. Edward Shreeves, Chairman, Bibliographers Group; Audree Malkin, Head, Theater Arts Library
Notes: Scripts, posters, comic books, music, models, original sketches, research, drawings, cels, storyboards, and films of cartoon producer Walter Lantz. Extensive collection. Also, a collection of original comic books, color comic books, storyboards, and posters illustrated by Clyde Geronimi.

DC —GEORGETOWN UNIVERSITY, Library, Special Collections Div, 37 & O Sts NW, Washington, 20057. George M Barringer, Special Collections Librn; Nicholas B Sheetz, Mss Librn
Holdings: Cat Mss Maps Pix Slides Phonorecords Audiotapes
Notes: Includes the papers (1912-49) of Sen Robert F Wagner; the archives (1903-) of the American Political Science Association and of its local Washington chapter; the archives of the Center for Public Financing of Elections; a collection of several hundred political cartoons by Eric Smith; and other smaller collections.

IL —NORTHWESTERN UNIVERSITY, Library, Special Collections Dept, 1937 Sheridan Rd, Evanston, 60201. R Russell Maylone, Cur
Holdings: Cat
Notes: John T McCutcheon drawings of political cartoons from the *Chicago Tribune*. 560 original drawings.

IN —INDIANA UNIVERSITY, Lilly Library, Seventh St, Bloomington, 47405. William R Cagle, Librn
Holdings: Uncat Mss
Notes: Contemporary with and depicting Lincoln; the War of 1812 and other periods. Incl significant mss of the modern cartoonists and caricaturists Ardizzone, Beerbohm, Fontane Fox, Kin Hubbard, Charles Bacon Jackson, McCutcheon, Messick, Nast, Rothenstein, Sendak, and many miscellaneous items.

IN —BUTLER UNIVERSITY, Irwin Library, Hugh Thomas Miller Rare Book Room, 4600 Sunset Ave, Indianapolis, 46208. Gisela Terrell, Rare Books Librn
Holdings: Cat Mss Pix
Notes: *Gaar Williams/Kin Hubbard* Collection. This collection was presented to the library by Blanche Stillson in 1964. It contains original cartoons and other drawings, books (many of them inscribed), magazines, letters and other manuscripts, photographs, and memorabilia by both Hoosier cartoonists and humorists. A catalogue of the Gaar Williams ("Abe Martin") items was printed in 1981. It is available upon request.

†KS —UNIVERSITY OF KANSAS, Spencer Research Library, Lawrence, 66045. Sheryl K Williams, Asst Librn
Notes: Original art by Albert T Reid and 600 other cartoonists, in the Kansas Collection.

KS —WICHITA STATE UNIVERSITY, Ablah Library, Box 68, Wichita, 67208. Michael T Kelly, Cur of Special Collections
Notes: Includes work by Gene Bassett, Ed Batchelor, Jack Bender, Douglas Borgstedt, Paul Conrad, William H Crawford, Dan Dowling, Karl S Hubenthal and others.

NJ —MACCULLOCH HALL HISTORICAL MUSEUM, Morristown, 07960. Alice A Caulkins, Curator
Notes: The W Parsons Todd Collection.

NC —UNIVERSITY OF NORTH CAROLINA, CHARLOTTE, J Murrey Atkins Library, UNCC Station, Charlotte, 28223. Robert F Brabham Jr, Special Collections Librn
Holdings: Cat
Notes: 1059 cartoons by Eugene G Payne, Pulitier Prize-winning cartoonist of *The Charlotte Observer*.

OH —OHIO STATE UNIVERSITY, Library for Communication and Graphic Arts, 242 W 18th St, Columbus, 43210. Lucy S Caswell, Curator
Notes: 5,000 original cartoons (including Dickie Dare, Terry and the Pirates, Male Call and Steve Canyon); 300,000 pages correspondence, business records, research files, etc.; photographs.

OH —RUTHERFORD B HAYES LIBRARY, 1337 Hayes Ave, Fremont, 43420. Watt P Marchman, Dir
Holdings: Cat Mss Pix
Notes: Correspondence, diary (1860-61), literary mss, account book, scrapbooks, sketches, caricatures, clippings, designs and misc printed matter of Thomas Nast.

TX —FORT WORTH PUBLIC LIBRARY, Arts Division, 300 Taylor St, Fort Worth, 76102. Heather Gobel, Head
Holdings: Uncat
Notes: Original cartoon art. Emphasis is on editorial, political, historical events cartoons. Nucleus collection comprised of original Hal Coffman cartoons rendered for the editorial pages of the *Fort Worth Star-Telegram* from October 10, 1939, until his death on August 31, 1958. 4575 pieces.

VA —UNIVERSITY OF VIRGINIA, Alderman Library, Manuscripts Dept, Charlottesville, 22901. Edmund Berkeley Jr, Cur
Holdings: Cat
Notes: This library contains a number of collections of cartoons, chiefly but not exclusively political, by a number of artists. The more important collections are: (1) The Fred O Seibel Collection: editorial page cartoons in the Richmond *Times-Dispatch*, 1926-1968. Incl are ca 3500 drawings, plus his research files. Unpublished guides; (2) Bernard M Meeks Collection: 326 original drawings assembled by a collector. Includes drawings by Herbert Block, Walt Disney, Thomas Nast, Jay N "Ding" Darling, Jimmy Hatlo, Rube Goldberg, James Thurber, etc; (3) Oscar Edward Cesare Collection: 232 cartoons for New York City newspapers and periodicals, 1912-1943, including such subjects as US politics, international relations, labor unrest, World Wars I & II; (4) Art Wood Collection: 625 drawings by the long-time cartoonist for the Richmond *News-Leader*; (5) Harry F Byrd: over 500original drawings, many by Fred O Seibel, but including almost every artist working during the Virginia Senator's years in Washington. The great majority of the cartoons concern Senator Byrd and his political positions or ambitions, but other subjects, many of national interest, are included; (6) Hugh Scott Collection: ca 75 cartoons by various artists, chiefly concerning the Pennsylvania senator and his political positions or ambitions, but many of national interest. Other cartoonists represented in the collection by one or more drawings include: Milt Caniff, Gib Crockett, Dan Dowling, Jeff MacNelly, Gus Mager, Charles Schultz, Richard Q Yardley, and Draper Hill.

WI —MILWAUKEE PUBLIC LIBRARY, 814 W Wisconsin Ave, Milwaukee, 53233. Donald J Sager, City Librn
Notes: Ross Lewis, Pulitzer Prize winning cartoonist for the *Milwaukee Journal*. Original cartoons.

ON —MCMASTER UNIVERSITY, Mills Memorial Library, Div of Archives & Research Collections, Hamilton, L8S 4L6, Can. G R Hill, Univ Librn
Holdings: // Mss Pix
Notes: Mss of prose works, poetry, scrapbooks, and cartoons by the Canadian political cartoonist John Wilson Bengough.

CARILLONS

MI —GUILD OF CARILLONNEURS IN NORTH AMERICA, Archives, 900 Burton Tower, University of Michigan, Ann Arbor, 48109. William De Turk, Archivist
Holdings: Mss Pix Phonorecords
Notes: Emphasis is on carillons.

NY —SOCIETAS CAMPANARIORUM (SOCIETY OF BELL-RINGERS), Campanological Library, Riverside Church, 490 Riverside Dr, New York, 10027. James R Lawson, Librn
Holdings: Vols 1000 Cat
Notes: One of the largest collections of books, pamphlets, periodicals, etc on bells and bell music (chimes, carillons, change-ringing, handbells, electronic carillons, etc) in North America. Examined by appointment only.

CARLISLE INDIAN SCHOOL

CT —YALE UNIVERSITY, Box 1603A, Yale Station, New Haven, 06520.
Holdings: Cat Mss Pix
Notes: Incl Gen Richard Henry Pratt Papers.

PA —CUMBERLAND COUNTY HISTORICAL SOCIETY, The Hamilton Library, 21 N Pitt St, PO Box 626, Carlisle, 17013. Cordelia M Neitz, Librn
Holdings: Vols 60 Mss Pix
Notes: Containing most of the magazines and journals published by the school, incl also yearbooks, commencement and other programs, illustrated brochures of the school, and several hundred photographs of classes, buildings, teaching facilities, school activities, athletes (Jim Thorpe being one) and athletic teams; one of the most complete collections of its kind in the US.

CARLSON, CHESTER F.

NY —NEW YORK PUBLIC LIBRARY, Rare Books and Manuscripts Div, Fifth Ave & 42 St, New York, 10018. William L Joyce, Asst Dir; Susan E Davis, Cur of Mss
Holdings: Cat Mss
Budget: ($7161)
Notes: The personal and scientific papers of Chester F Carlson, inventor of xerography.

CARLTON, WILL

NY —UNIVERSITY OF ROCHESTER, Rush Rhees Library, Department of Rare Books and Special Collections, Rochester, 14627. Peter Dzwonkoski, Librn
Holdings: Cat Mss
Notes: Correspondents include Robert Underwood Johnson, Will Carlton, Henry Mills Alden, Richard Watson Gilder; Howell's proof of article on Henrik Ibsen (1906).

CARLUCCI, FRANK C.

DC —GEORGETOWN UNIVERSITY, Library, Special Collections Div, 37 & O Sts NW, Washington, 20057. George M Barringer, Special Collections Librn; Nicholas B Sheetz, Mss Librn
Holdings: Mss Cat
Notes: The archives of the Commission on Security and Economic Assistance, chaired by Frank C Carlucci, consist of memberships correspondence files; papers generated or solicited by the Commission; minutes from Commission meetings and public hearings; and drafts of the Commission's final report.

CARLYLE, THOMAS, 1795-1881

CA —UNIVERSITY OF CALIFORNIA, SANTA CRUZ, University Library, Special Collections, Santa Cruz, 95064. Rita Bottoms, Special Collections Librn; Margaret Felts, South Pacific Collection Bibliographer
Notes: The Norman and Charlotte Strouse Collection. Extensive collection, noncirculating. Scholarly research only.

CT —YALE UNIVERSITY, Box 1603A, Yale Station, New Haven, 06520.
Holdings: Cat Mss

IL —ILLINOIS STATE UNIVERSITY, Milner Library, Dept of Special Collections, Normal, 61761. Robert Sokan, Librn
Notes: First editions, limited editions, ephemera, etx.

ME —BOWDOIN COLLEGE, Library, Brunswick, 04011. Dianne M Gutscher, Cur of Special Collections
Holdings: Vols 1500 // Mss
Notes: All first and authorized editions, much criticism and biography; several hundred pamphlets and periodical articles. Incl Isaac Watson Dyer's notes for the *Bibliography of Thomas Carlyle,* 1928, and 24 autograph letters, signed, of Carlyle to William Graham, 1820-1854.

MA —HARVARD UNIVERSITY LIBRARY, Widener Library, Cambridge, 02138.
Holdings: Cat Mss
Notes: See Harvard University Library, *Bibliographical Contributions,* 26 (1888). Incl books given by Carlyle to the library.

MI —UNIVERSITY OF MICHIGAN, Library, Dept of Rare Books & Special Collections, Ann Arbor, 48109. Robert J Starring, Head
Holdings: Vols 646 Cat Mss Pix
Notes: Partially described in *A Catalogue of the Dr Samuel A Jones Collection* (University of Michigan, General Library Publication no 1).

ON —MCMASTER UNIVERSITY, Mills Memorial Library, Div of Archives & Research Collections, Hamilton, L8S 4L6, Can. G R Hill, Univ Librn
Holdings: // Mss
Notes: A collection of 262 ms letters from Thomas Carlyle to his brother Alexander in Canada, incl letters to and among other family members. Published in Marrs, Edwin W, *The Letters of Thomas Carlyle to His Brother Alexander* (Cambridge, Mass: Belknap Press, 1968).

CARMAN, ALBERT P., 1861-1946

IL —UNIVERSITY OF ILLINOIS, URBANA/CHAMPAIGN, Library, University Archives, 1408 W Gregory Drive, Urbana, 61801. Maynard Brichford, Univ Archivist
Notes: Papers.

CARMAN, BLISS

MA —HARVARD UNIVERSITY LIBRARY, Widener Library, Cambridge, 02138.
Holdings: Cat Mss
Notes: Bibliography by William Inglis Morse published in 1941.

RI —BROWN UNIVERSITY, John Hay Library, Harris Collection, Prospect St, Providence, 02912. Rosemary L Cullen, Cur
Holdings: Vols (200,000) Cat Mss Pix Phonorecords Microforms
Budget: ($15,000)
Notes: The Harris Collection of American Poetry and Plays is principally composed of American and Canadian poetry and plays, 17th century-date. Extensive holdings in songsters, gift books and annuals, hymnals, pageants, broadside verse, carriers' addresses, women poets, juvenile poetry, (incl Mother Goose and *The Night Before* Christmas), sheet music with lyrics, small press publications, fine printing, black poets, "little magazines," Yiddish-American literature. All movements or schools of American poetry are represented. Incl first editions of most American poets and playwrights, notably Whitman, Poe, Wallace Stevens, Eugene O'Neill, Edward Albee, Ezra Pound, T S Eliot, William Carlos Williams, Amy Lowell, Phyllis Wheatley, Robert Frost, Allen Ginsberg, Bliss Carman, and Stephen Foster sheet music. Also incl the Saunders Walt Whitman Collection (1300 vols); the LangdonCollection of Pageants (250 vols); the Asa Cushman Collection of plays in ms and prompt copies; the MacDougall Collection of Psalters and Hymnals; 4000 plays issued by Walter H Baker Co, Boston (1890-1957); the Vaxer Collection of Yiddish Poetry, Plays and Music (1700 vols). Collections incl 200,000 vols, 30,000 broadsides, 55,000 mss, 170,000 pieces of sheet music, 450 phonorecords, and 375 microfilm reels. See *Dictionary Catalog of the Harris Collection of American Poetry and Plays* (Boston: G K Hall, 1972), 13 vols; *Supplement* (1977), 3 vols. See also, *American Poetry,* 1609-1900, *A Collection on Microfilm, Segment I* (1609-1820); *Segment II* (1821-1850); *Segment III* (1851-1870) (Woodbridge, Conn: Research Publications). Separate catalog.

BC —UNIVERSITY OF VICTORIA, McPherson Library, Victoria, V8W 3H5, Can.

CARMICHAEL, HOAGLAND (HOAGY)

IN —INDIANA UNIVERSITY, Lilly Library, Seventh St, Bloomington, 47405. William R Cagle, Librn
Holdings: // Uncat Mss
Notes: In the Starr Collection of American Sheet Music.

CARMICHAEL, ROBERT

IL —UNIVERSITY OF ILLINOIS, URBANA/CHAMPAIGN, Library, University Archives, 19 Library, 1408 W Gregory Drive, Urbana, 61801. Maynard Brichford, University Archivist
Holdings: Cat Mss Maps Pix Slides Microforms
Notes: Papers, archival records, etc.

CARNAP, RUDOLF

PA —UNIVERSITY OF PITTSBURGH, Hillman Library, Pittsburgh, 15260.
Notes: Economic and philosophical papers of the English scholar Frank Plumpton Ramsey (1903-1930), incl mss of published and unpublished writings, reading notes, etc. Significant because of his work in modern mathematics, logic, probability, and economics. Complementary to the Library's holdings of the papers of the logical empiricists, Rudolf Carnap and Hans Reichenback.

CARNATACA LANGUAGE see Kanarese Language and Literature

CARNE, FREDERICK, 1856-1933

BC —UNIVERSITY OF VICTORIA, McPherson Library, Victoria, V8W 3H5, Can.
Notes: Businessman. Transcripts of collection of letters home by a Canadian soldier in the First World War.

CARNEGIE, ANDREW

CT —LEE ASH, (personal collection), 66 Humiston Dr, Bethany, 06525.
Holdings: Cat Mss Pix
Notes: Incl books, letters, ephemera, etc.

DC —LIBRARY OF CONGRESS, Manuscript Division, Washington, 20540. John C Broderick, Chief
Holdings: Cat Mss Pix
Notes: Mss, papers, records, etc.

NY —COLUMBIA UNIVERSITY LIBRARIES, Rare Book & Manuscript Library, 801 Butler Library, 535 W 114 St, New York, 10027. Kenneth A Lohf, Librn
Notes: More than 32,000 items documenting the rise of William Russell Grace's shipping business and other materials relating to his career as mayor of New York. Incl records and correspondence relating to all aspects of the shipping business in New York and South America, mining interest in Peru and Chile, and transportation in Costa Rica and Nicaragua. Family memorabilia and photographs, materials concerning New York Politics, banking and insurance, real estate interests and Catholic charities, and letters from Chester A Arthur, John Jacob Astor, Andrew Carnegie, Grover Cleveland, Hamilton Fish, John Hay and J Pierpont Morgan. Restricted use.

CARNEGIE ENDOWMENT FOR INTERNATIONAL PEACE

DC —GEORGE WASHINGTON UNIVERSITY, Gelman Library, 2130 H St

CARNEGIE ENDOWMENT FOR INTERNATIONAL PEACE (cont.)

NW, Washington, 20052.
Holdings: Vols (50,000)// Cat Mss Microforms
Notes: The Carnegie Endowment for International Peace library was purchased in 1950. The collection has been cataloged and assimilated in the University Library and the Law Library's holdings. It includes monographs, a few bound manuscripts, conference proceedings, and periodicals. Certain periodicals are available on microfilm through Clearwater Publishing Co. Holdings are catalogued individually.

NY —COLUMBIA UNIVERSITY LIBRARIES, Rare Book & Manuscript Library, 801 Butler Library, 535 W 114 St, New York, 10027. Kenneth A Lohf, Librn
Holdings: Mss
Notes: Archival material of the Carnegie Endowment for International Peace through 1954. Incl 712,500 items. Restricted use.

CARNIVALS (CIRCUS) see Amusement Parks; Circus

CAROB

CA —UNIVERSITY OF CALIFORNIA, RIVERSIDE, University Library, Bio-Agricultural Library, Batchelor Hall, Riverside, 92521. Barbara Montanary, Head
Holdings: Vols (130,000) Cat Mss Maps Pix Microforms
Notes: The Bio-Agricultural Library (formerly the Library of Citrus Experiment Station of the University of California) is well known for its complete collections in the fields of the agriculture sciences. It is especially known for its emphasis on entomology, incl bio-control; botany, citriculture, plant sciences, nematology and plant pathology; arid and semi-arid lands research and subtropical agriculture. Specific areas of interest are avocados, dates, desert flora, jojoba, guayule and carob.

CAROLS

CT —YALE UNIVERSITY, Box 1603A, Yale Station, New Haven, 06520.
Notes: Especially French carols.

ON —UNIVERSITY OF TORONTO, Thomas Fisher Rare Book Library, 120 Saint George St, Toronto, M5S 1A5, Can. Richard G Landon, Head
Holdings: Vols 300 Cat
Notes: Noels Collection of French carols and hymns in a variety of dialects, 18th and 19th centuries.

CAROLS—INDEXES

OH —CLEVELAND PUBLIC LIBRARY, Fine Arts and Special Collections Department, 325 Superior Ave, Cleveland, 44114. Alice N Loranth, Head
Notes: 71 drawers of index cards, incl 37 drawers of songs, 31 drawers of hymns and 3 drawers of Christmas carols. A "Spanish Ballad Index" on cards is in the Special Collections were extensive indexes for French, Provencal and Italian songs are also maintained.

CARPATHO-RUTHENIA—HISTORY

NY —SAINT VLADIMIRS' ORTHODOX THEOLOGICAL SEMINARY, 575 Scarsdale Rd, Yonkers, 10707. Paul D Garrett, Librn
Holdings: Vols 1500 Mss

PA —HOLY TRINITY BENEDICTINE BYZANTINE RITE MONESTERY, PO Box 990, Butler, 16002.

PA —BYZANTINE CATHOLIC SEMINARY LIBRARY, 3605 Perrysville Ave, Pittsburgh, 15214.
Holdings: 12,500 Vols Mss

CARPATHO-RUTHENIAN NEWSPAPERS see Newspapers, Carpatho-Ruthenian

CARPATHO-RUTHENIANS IN THE U.S.

MN —UNIVERSITY OF MINNESOTA, Immigration History Research Center, 826 Berry St, Saint Paul, 55114. Susan Griegs, Cur
Holdings: Vols (35,000) Mss Maps Pix Phonorecords Audiotapes 16mm Films Microforms
See also entry under US - Emigration and Immigration

NY —SAINT VLADIMIRS' ORTHODOX THEOLOGICAL SEMINARY, 575 Scarsdale Rd, Yonkers, 10707. Paul D Garrett, Librn
Holdings: Vols 1500 Mss

PA —UNIVERSITY OF PITTSBURGH, Hillman Library, Archives of Industrial Society, 363 Hillman Library, Pittsburgh, 15260. Frank A Zabrosky, Cur
Holdings: Mss Documents Newspapers Audiotapes Microforms
Notes: Unique collections: Carpatho-Ruthenian Microforms Project (200 reels of microfilms containing newspapers, almanacs and other serials); United Russian Orthodox Brotherhood Association, Records, 1915-1973.

CARPENTER, CYRUS C.

IA —STATE HISTORICAL SOCIETY OF IOWA LIBRARY, 402 Iowa Ave, Iowa City, 52240. Darold J Brown, Librn
Holdings: Cat
Notes: Thousands of individual items and smaller collections. Two hundred larger collections incl the papers of Cyrus C Carpenter, Jonathan P Dolliver, Gilbert Haugen, W W Waymack, Ephraim Adams, A C Dodge, Dorothy Houghton, Jesse Macy, Agnes Samuelson, Donald Johnson, Jack Miller, Ruth Sayre, Samuel Kirkwood, Thomas McKnight, Robert Lucas, Dwight McCarty, William Larrabee. Includes church, school, company and organization records, Civil War materials.

CARPENTER, ISAAC W., 1893-

NJ —PRINCETON UNIVERSITY, Library, Manuscript Collection, Nassau St, Princeton, 08540. Jean F Preston, Cur
Holdings: Mss Pix
Notes: The collection fills 3 cartons. The papers, which cover the years 1954-61, may be read by qualified scholars, but written permission is required for quoting.

CARPENTER, MATTHEW HALE

IL —LOYOLA UNIVERSITY OF CHICAGO, E M Cudahy Memorial Library, 6525 N Sheridan Rd, Chicago, 60626.
Notes: Incl letters from Matthew Hale Carpenter, lawyer and US Senator from Wisconsin, to Murat Halstead, prominent 19th century journalist, war correspondent, author and editor. Also, other letters and collection of clipped signatures of prominent individuals.

CARPENTRY

PA —CARNEGIE LIBRARY OF PITTSBURGH, Science & Technology Dept, 4400 Forbes Ave, Pittsburgh, 15213. Catherine M Brosky, Dept Head
Notes: Collection incl material on general construction, carpentry, masonry, plumbing, heating, air conditioning, corrosion and painting and numerous other building trades. Sweets Architectural File complete except for a few years. *Cat Builders Encyclopedia of American Practice,* most editions since 1879.

WI —UNIVERSITY OF WISCONSIN-STOUT, Library Learning Center, Menomonie, 54751. Philip Sawin Jr, Coll Develop Librn
Notes: This collection is a major one, including the Verne C Fryklund Papers. The program was begun in 1883 as an original purpose of the University. The collection contains original editions on sloyd, a 19th century Swedish system of manual training based on wood carving and carpentry.

CARPETBAG RULE see Reconstruction (U.S., 1863-1877)

CARRANZA, VENUSTIANO

CA —CLAREMONT COLLEGES, Honnold Library, Ninth & Dartmouth, Claremont, 91711. Tania Rizzo, Special Collections Dept Head
Holdings: Cat Mss Pix Scrapbooks
Notes: Correspondence, mss, documents, clippings, photographs, and ephemera, 2200 pieces, some in carbon copies, of Jose Maytorena, from 1882-1947. Important correspondents incl Venustiano Carranza, Francisco Madero, and Alvaro Obregon, among many others. Guy T McCreary, *A Primary Study of the Revolutionary, Governor, General, Jose maria Maytorena and the Mexican Revolution* 1910-1916 (thesis, 1967) based on this collection. Restricted use.

CARREL, ALEXIS

DC —GEORGETOWN UNIVERSITY, Library, Special Collections Div, 37 & O Sts NW, Washington, 20057. George M Barringer, Special Collections Librn; Nicholas B Sheetz, Mss Librn
Holdings: Mss Cat Pix Slides
Notes: The papers of Alexis Carrel, consisting of correspondence, experimental records and notebooks, mss of articles and books, reprints of articles, scrapbooks, and photographs of a professional and personal nature. Alexis Carrel (1873-1944), noted research scientist in medicine, is most remembered for his accomplishments in perfecting arterial surgery, cellular physiology, organ transplants in animals, and cancer research. In 1912 he was awarded a Nobel Prize for his work in the field of physiology. Dr Carrel was also the author of *Man, the Unknown.* Correspondence incl letters from Harvey Cushing, John Dewey, Charles A Lindbergh, Sinclair Lewis, Paul Claudel, Philippe Bunau-Varilla, William Durant, and Upton Sinclair. The papers also incl notes and other material generated by Rev Joseph Durkin, SJ in writing his biography of Carrel entitled*Hope for Our* Times. Specimen and apparatus collection located at medical school.

DC —GEORGETOWN UNIVERSITY, Medical Center, John Vinton Dahlgren Memorial Library, 3900 Reservoir Rd NW, Washington, 20057. Clementine Pellegrino, Librn
Holdings: Vols (1000) Cat Mss Pix Slides
Notes: The Alexis Carrel Collection. Medical research of man and society. Biological specimens. Numerous specimens of Dr Carrel's work in transplantation of blood vessels, kidney, thyroid and other organs; considerable data on tissue cultivation. Mss collection located at Special Collections Division.

CARRERA ANDRADE, JORGE, 1903-

NY —STATE UNIVERSITY OF NEW YORK, STONY BROOK, Melville Library, Dept of Special Collections, Stony Brook, 11794. Evert Volkersz, Head
Holdings: Vols 85 Cat Mss

CARRIAGE, CART, AND WAGON MAKING

MI —ALFRED P SLOAN JR MUSEUM, 1221 E Kearsley St, Flint, 48503. Scott M Peters, Curator
Holdings: Uncat Pix
Notes: Catalogs, manuals, photographs of automotive companies. Centers about automobiles produced in our community with heavy emphasis on Buick and Chevrolet literature. Some information on predecessor companies such as carriage and wagon works. About 3000 pieces.

TX —PANHANDLE-PLAINS HISTORICAL MUSEUM, Research Center, Box 967, WT Sta, Canyon, 79016. Claire R Kuehn, Archivist-Librn
Holdings: Vols 85 Cat
Budget: $300
Notes: Supplements Museum's wagon and carriage collection. Incl periodicals and catalogs.

CARRIAGES AND CARTS

NH —NEW HAMPSHIRE HISTORICAL SOCIETY, Manuscripts Library, 30 Park St,

CARRIAGES AND CARTS (cont.)

Concord, 03301. Thomas E Camden, Cur
Holdings: Cat Mss Pix
Notes: Abbot-Downing Truck and Body Co records 1813-1945. Incl correspondence, account book, journals, ledgers, order books, accounts receivable, records of sales, balance sheet for New York branch, records of material mortgaged to Josiah E Fernald, banker, of Concord, New Hampshire, other financial papers, drawings, catalogs, and photos of vehicles, clippings, advertisements, and other papers of a firm based in Concord, New Hampshire, and manufacturing wagons, coaches, carriages, and motor-trucks. 33 linear feet, about 22,000 items.

OK —MUSEUM OF THE GREAT PLAINS, Research Center, 601 Ferris, PO Box 68, Lawton, 73502. Steve Wilson, Dir; Paula Williams, Special Collections
Notes: Large holdings of hardware and agricultural catalogs and trade periodicals dating 1869 to 1926. Collection incl over 2000 photographs of wagons and carriages from various manufacturer's catalogs and trade periodicals. Catalogs and periodicals are indexed. Collections are described in Vol 17 (1978) Great Plains Journal published by the Museum.

CARRIER CORPORATION

NY —CORNELL UNIVERSITY LIBRARIES, Collection of Regional History, Dept of Manuscripts and Univ Archives, Ithaca, 14853.
Notes: Incl publications, 1913-(1915-1962); technical bulletins and manuals, photos and historical sketches.

CARRIERS' ADDRESSES

DC —LIBRARY OF CONGRESS, Rare Book & Special Collections Div, Washington, 20540. William Matheson, Chief
Holdings: Cat
See also entry under Broadsides - Collections

NJ —RUTGERS, THE STATE UNIVERSITY OF NEW JERSEY, Alexander Library, Special Collections and Archives, College Ave & Huntington St, New Brunswick, 08903. Ronald L Becker, Cur of Manuscripts and Rare Books
Budget: Vols 125 Uncat
Notes: Largely 19th century.

NY —NEW YORK HISTORICAL SOCIETY, Library, 170 Central Park W, New York, 10024. James Gregory, Librn
Holdings: Mss
Notes: Incl original mss, illustrative materials, etc.

RI —BROWN UNIVERSITY, John Hay Library, Harris Collection, Prospect St, Providence, 02912. Rosemary L Cullen, Cur
Holdings: Vols (200,000) Cat Mss Phonorecords Microforms
Budget: ($15,000)
Notes: The Harris Collection of American Poetry and Plays is principally composed of American and Canadian poetry and plays, 17th century-date. Extensive holdings in songsters, gift books and annuals, hymnals, pageants, broadside verse, carriers' addresses, women poets, juvenile poetry (incl Mother Goose and *The Night Before* Christmas), sheet music with lyrics, small press publications, fine printing, black poets, "little magazines", Yiddish-American literature. See *Dictionary Catalog of the Harris Collection of American Poetry and* Plays (Boston: G K Hall, 1972), 13 vols; *Supplement* (1977), 3 vols. See also, *American Poetry,* 1690-1900, *A Collection on Microfilm, Segment 1 (1609-1820); Segment II (1821-1850); Segment III* (1851-1870) (Woodbridge, Conn: Research Publications). Separate catalog.

RI —BROWN UNIVERSITY, John Hay Library, 20 Prospect St, Providence, 02912. Mary T Russo, Cur of Broadsides
Holdings: Vols (1200)
Notes: These single sheets of American verse presented by newsboys on New Year's Day are part of the Broadside Collection. Ranging from 1772 to 1950, they are useful for the study of American verse, American printing and American social life. Retrospective pieces are added annually. Partial catalog.

CARRIGHAR, SALLY

MA —BOSTON UNIVERSITY, Mugar Memorial Library, Special Collections Dept, 771 Commonwealth Ave, Boston, 02215. Howard B Gotlieb, Dir
Holdings: Cat Mss
Notes: Mss, correspondence, etc collected in depth; incl publications by or about.

CARRINGTON, ELAINE

NY —NEW YORK PUBLIC LIBRARY, Performing Arts Research Center, Billy Rose Theatre Collection, 111 Amsterdam Ave, New York, 10023. Dorothy L Swerdlove, Cur
Holdings: Cat
See also entry under Radio.

CARROLL, CHARLES, OF CARROLLTON, MARYLAND

CA —UNIVERSITY OF SAN FRANCISCO, Richard A Gleeson Library, The Countess Bernardine Murphy Donohue Rare Book Room, San Francisco, 94117. D Steven Corey, Special Collections Librn
Holdings: Vols 200 Mss
Notes: Present are a number of ms ledgers and letters concenring various aspects of his extensive business dealing and a great deal of secondary background material.

CARROLL, GLADYS HASTY

MA —BOSTON UNIVERSITY, Mugar Memorial Library, Special Collections Dept, 771 Commonwealth Ave, Boston, 02215. Howard B Gotlieb, Dir
Holdings: Cat Mss Pix
Notes: Mss, correspondence, etc collected in depth; incl publications by or about.

CARROLL, ABP. JOHN

DC —GEORGETOWN UNIVERSITY, Library, Special Collections Div, 37 & O Sts NW, Washington, 20057. George M Barringer, Special Collections Librn; Nicholas B Sheetz, Mss Librn
Notes: Historical archives of the Maryland Province. Incl the letters of Abp John Carroll and Fr John McElroy.

CARROLL, LEWIS (CHARLES LUTWIDGE DODGSON), 1832-1898

CA —UNIVERSITY OF CALIFORNIA, LOS ANGELES, Research Library, Dept of Special Collections, 405 Hilgard Ave, Los Angeles, 90024. Edward Shreeves, Chairman, Bibliographers Group; David S Zeidberg, Head
Holdings: Vols 120 Cat Mss
Notes: 150 books; 4 letters; ephemera relating to Lewis Carroll (Charles Lutwidge Dodgson), 1832-1898.

MA —HARVARD UNIVERSITY LIBRARY, Houghton Library, Cambridge, 02138. F Thomas Noonan, Cur, Reading Room; Lawrence Dowler, Associate Librn
Holdings: Cat Mss
Notes: Bibliography by Flora V Livingston published in 1932.

NJ —PRINCETON UNIVERSITY, Library, Morris L Parrish Collection, Princeton, 08540. Alexander D Wainwright, Cur
Notes: For particulars refer to: Warren Weaver, "The Parrish Collection of Carrolliana" in the Chronicle XVII, 2 (winter, 1956) pp 85-91. The collection incl some 580 vols. The collection contains not only the books published under the name Lewis Carroll, but also the more scholarly works and mathematical treatises published under the name Charles L Dodgson. See, as well, the following catalogs prepared by Parrish, based on his collection. Morris L Parrish, *List of the Writings of Carroll Collected by Morris L Parrish* (Pine Valley, NJ, 1929) and *Supplementary List* (Pine Valley, NJ, 1933).

NY —COLUMBIA UNIVERSITY LIBRARIES, Rare Book & Manuscript Library, 801 Butler Library, 535 W 114 St, New York, 10027. Kenneth A Lohf, Librn
Holdings: Cat Mss
Notes: Mss, editions of *Alice,* and other publications. Restricted use.

NY —NEW YORK UNIVERSITY, Elmer Holmes Bobst Library, 70 Washington Sq S, New York, 10012.
Notes: The Alfred C Berol Collection.

NY —PIERPONT MORGAN LIBRARY, 29 E 36 St, New York, 10016. Herbert Cahoon, Librn
Notes: The superb collection of Arthur A Houghton, Jr. Books, mss, memorabilia, etc.

OH —CLEVELAND PUBLIC LIBRARY, Children's Literature Dept, 325 Superior Ave, Cleveland, 44114. Ruth M Hadlow, Head
Holdings: Vols 150 Cat
Notes: Biographies of the author and various editions of his writings incl several first editions. No attempt to be exhaustive.

PA —BRYN MAWR COLLEGE, Canaday Library, Bryn Mawr, 19010. James Tanis, Dir
Notes: Manuscript and printed material in the Adelman Collection.

CARRUTH, HAYDEN

VT —UNIVERSITY OF VERMONT, Guy W Bailey/David W Howe Library, Burlington, 05405. John Buehler, Asst Dir for Special Collections
Notes: The papers of Hayden Carruth (1921-), poet and poetry editor for the *Hudson* Review.

CARS (AUTOMOBILES) see Automobiles

CARS, ARMORED (TANKS) see Tanks (Military Science)

CARSON, JOSEPHINE

MA —BOSTON UNIVERSITY, Mugar Memorial Library, Special Collections Dept, 771 Commonwealth Ave, Boston, 02215. Howard B Gotlieb, Dir
Holdings: Cat Mss Correspondence

CARSON, RACHEL

CT —YALE UNIVERSITY, Box 1603A, Yale Station, New Haven, 06520.
Holdings: Mss
Notes: Her manuscripts, papers and correspondence.

CARSON, ROBERT

MA —BOSTON UNIVERSITY, Mugar Memorial Library, Special Collections Dept, 771 Commonwealth Ave, Boston, 02215. Howard B Gotlieb, Dir
Holdings: Cat Mss Pix
Notes: Mss correspondence, etc collected in depth; incl publications by or about.

CARSON, TAHOE LUMBER AND FLUMING COMPANY

NV —UNIVERSITY OF NEVADA, RENO, University Library, Special Collections Dept, Reno, 89557. Robert E Blesse, Head
Holdings: Vols (100) Cat Pix Mss
Notes: Books, manuscripts (115 cu ft), photographs (500), dealing with Lake Tahoe and the surrounding region. Included are papers of organizations concerned with the environmental quality of the lake, eg, the Lake Tahoe Area Council records, the Tahoe Regional Planning Association records. Records of two 19th-20th century business involved with logging and lumber production in the Tahoe region, the Carson, Tahoe Lumber and Fluming Company, and the El Dorado Wood and Flume Company. Photographs include many early 19th

CARSON, TAHOE LUMBER AND FLUMING COMPANY (cont.)

century views of the lake and structures surrounding it.

CARSON, WILLIAM G. B.

MO —WASHINGTON UNIVERSITY, Libraries, Special Collections Dept, Campus Box 1061, St Louis, 63130.
Notes: Family and business correspondence.

CARSON AND COLORADO RAILROAD

NV —UNIVERSITY OF NEVADA, RENO, University Library, Special Collections Dept, Reno, 89557. Robert E Blesse, Head
Holdings: Vols (150) Cat Mss Pix Maps
Notes: Includes 370 cu ft manuscripts, 2000 photographs. Major collection include papers of Nevada railroad companies Virginia and Truckee, Carson and Colorado, Eureka and Palisade, and Nevada Copper Belt. Materials are collected which deal with the history and development of railroads within Nevada and those which have run through the state.

CARTELS

CA —CLAREMONT COLLEGES, Honnold Library, Ninth & Dartmouth, Claremont, 91711. Tania Rizzo, Special Collections Dept Head
Holdings: Vols 200 Cat Mss Pix
Notes: The papers of former Democratic Congressman Jerry Voorhis, from the 1930s to present, occupying nearly 100 document boxes. The papers reflect his life and career, incl biographical material, the history of the Voorhis School for Boys, his involvement in the Dies Committee, and his wide-ranging interests in American economic and social issues, such as cooperatives, monopolies and cartels, Latin American relations, consumers, and senior citizens. Books by and about him, with research files. Correspondence with political leaders. Inventory available. Restricted use.

CARTER, ELLIOT

DC —LIBRARY OF CONGRESS, Music Division, Washington, 20540.
Notes: Music Mss.

CARTER, ERNEST TROW

CT —YALE UNIVERSITY, Music Library, 98 Wall St, New Haven, 06520. Harold E Samuel, Librn
Notes: Personal papers and musical mss. *See also* entry under Music, American.

CARTER, HODDING II AND BETTY WERLEIN

MS —MISSISSIPPI STATE UNIVERSITY, Mitchell Memorial Library, Box 5408, Mississippi State, 39762. Frances N Coleman, Head, Special Collections
Holdings: Mss
Notes: Papers of the editor/publisher of the Greenville, Mississippi *Delta* Democrat-Times.

CARTER, JOHN

†DC —LIBRARY OF CONGRESS, Manuscript Division, Washington, 20540.
Notes: The papers, etc, of John Carter.

IN —INDIANA UNIVERSITY, Lilly Library, Seventh St, Bloomington, 47405. William R Cagle, Librn
Holdings: Mss
Notes: The David Anton Randall papers incl his files while working for Scribner's in New York, as well as much correspondence, etc with John Carter concerning the English scene. 900 items.

CARTER, LIN

IN —INDIANA UNIVERSITY, Lilly Library, Seventh St, Bloomington, 47405. William R Cagle, Librn
Notes: First editions. Ms collections incl papers of writer Fritz Leiber, Jr, 1910- , containing correspondence with many authors and manuscript notes, etc, of several Leiber writings, 1932-1974. 1500 items. Papers of reviewer and critic William Anthony Parker White (Tony Boucher) which incl sizeable correspondence files with Ray Bradbury, etc, as well as reviews and manuscripts of Boucher's own writings. Letters to editor and fantastic fiction writer Lin Carter from Lyon Sprague de Camp (ca 200 items) and from various other writers (293 items). Letters, 1966-1972, from James Blish to editors at Doubleday (30 items). Letters, 1966-1976, from Roger Zelazny to editors at Doubleday (44 items).

CARTER, GEN. MARSHALL S.

†VA —GEORGE C MARSHALL RESEARCH FOUNDATION AND LIBRARY, Drawer 920, Lexington, 24450. Royster Lyle Jr, Cur Collections
Holdings: Cat Mss Maps Pix
Notes: Papers, incl personal correspondence, etc, especially with regard to service during World War II.

CARTER, MARY

MA —BOSTON UNIVERSITY, Mugar Memorial Library, Special Collections Dept, 771 Commonwealth Ave, Boston, 02215. Howard B Gotlieb, Dir
Holdings: Cat Mss

CARTER, MARY 'POLLY'

KS —SAINT MARY COLLEGE, Library, Leavenworth, 66048. Therese Deplazes, Special Collections Librn
Notes: Holographs of American personalities, mostly of Colonial, Revolutionary, Confederacy periods, and 19th Century. Incl ms letters, deeds, petitions, wills, slave papers. Holographs of Col Philip Marsteller (one of George Washington's pall bearers), family papers of Richard, Mary and Edward Cutts; love letters to Mary "Polly" Carter, Frank Ellery (grandson of William Ellery, signer of the Declaration of Independence), letters of Connie Mack and Babe Ruth, of some American authors.

CARTER-KARIS

IL —NORTHWESTERN UNIVERSITY, Melville J Herskovits Library of African Studies, Evanston, 60201. Hans E Panofsky, Cur
Holdings: Vols (85,000) Mss
Budget: ($70,000)
Notes: Papers, etc. Mostly southern Africa. *See also* entry under Africa.

CARTER-SMITH FAMILY

VA —UNIVERSITY OF VIRGINIA, Alderman Library, Manuscripts Dept, Charlottesville, 22901. Edmund Berkeley Jr, Cur
Holdings: Cat Mss Maps Pix
Notes: 19th century Virginia Family Papers Collections enable a researcher to obtain an excellent picture of the economic and social interactions on large plantations in Virginia during the 19th century. They are invaluable as research sources in the study of slavery, women's history, economic history, agrarian and political history.

CARTERET BOOK CLUB, NEWARK, N.J.

NY —GROLIER CLUB OF NEW YORK LIBRARY, 47 E 60 St, New York, 10022. Robert Nikirk, Librn
Notes: Archives and a complete run of publications of this now defunct fraternity of bibliophiles.

CARTES-DE-VISITES—COLLECTIONS

†NY —COLUMBIA UNIVERSITY LIBRARIES, Butler Library, Rare Book and Manuscript Library, 535 W 114 St, New York, 10027.

NY —VISUAL STUDIES WORKSHOP, Research Center, 31 Prince St, Rochester, 14607. Linn Underhill, Coordr; Robert Bretz, Librn
Holdings: Vols (8000) Cat Pix Slides Audiotapes Videotapes
Notes: Strong emphasis on photography (over 1,000,000 pictures) and the photographic arts in many subject areas incl in this volume. Heavy emphasis on early photographic processes and collections of examples of them. Also collections of individual photographers' works.

†TX —UNIVERSITY OF TEXAS LIBRARIES, General Libraries, Humanities Research Center, PO Box 7219, Austin, 78712. John Chalmers, Librn

CARTLAND, BARBARA

MA —BOSTON UNIVERSITY, Mugar Memorial Library, Special Collections Dept, 771 Commonwealth Ave, Boston, 02215. Howard B Gotlieb, Dir
Holdings: Mss Pix
Notes: Mss, correspondence.

CARTOBIBLIOGRAPHY

PA —FREE LIBRARY OF PHILADELPHIA, Social Science and History Dept, Map Collection, Logan Sq, Philadelphia, 19103.
Holdings: Vols (30,000) Cat Mss Mapss
Notes: Map collection incl atlases, maps, pamphlets, and aerial views. Incl a representative collection of early atlases (1534-1827). The collection emphasizes the Philadelphia, Pennsylvania and Delaware Valley areas in particular and the eastern seaboard in general. Low altitude oblique aerial photographs have been transferred to the Print and Picture Dept; high altitude vertical aerial photographs have been retained; some volumes and pamphlets reassigned within the Social Science and History Dept.

CARTOGRAPHY

AL —SAMFORD UNIVERSITY, Special Collections Library, 800 Lakeshore Dr, Birmingham, 35229. Annie Ford Wheeler, Acting Head Librn
Holdings: Cat Maps
Notes: Emphases: early maps of Alabama and the Southeast; local maps of Ireland which support Irish history and genealogy collection; some early atlases and bibliographies; basic works on cartography and map bibliography. Incl about 3000 maps. Published catalog of the collection.

CA —CALIFORNIA STATE UNIVERSITY, FULLERTON, Library, Box 4150, Fullerton, 92634. Linda Herman, Special Collections Librn
Holdings: Vols 480 Maps
Notes: Collection documents history of map-making including 1500 rare maps pre-1901.

CA —UNIVERSITY OF CALIFORNIA, LOS ANGELES, Map Library, Los Angeles, 90024. Carlos B Hagen, Head
Holdings: Vols (5566) Cat Maps Pix
Notes: The Library is a depository for the publications of many world-wide mapping agencies. The collection incl 507,097 maps of all areas of the world (subject and topographic maps, nautical and aeronautical charts, historical maps, and city plans), gazetteers, atlases, aerial photographs, periodicals and other basic cartographic reference tools. Incl 2550 atlases; 10,424 aerial maps; 1035 technical reports; and 311 (titles) serials subscriptions.

DC —LIBRARY OF CONGRESS, Geography and Map Division, Washington, 20540. John A Wolter, Chief
Holdings: Cat Mss Maps Pix Slides Microforms
Notes: *Cartographic Materials.* One of the largest cartographic collections in the world, all-inclusive in coverage. Early original manuscript maps, navigation charts by Italian, Portuguese, and Spanish 15th, 16th, and 17th-century cartographers; the Hummel

CARTOGRAPHY (cont.)

& Warner Collections of rare manuscript and printed maps and atlases of China and Korea from the 17th, 18th, and 19th centuries; manuscript and printed maps of colonial America, the Revolutionary War, the War of 1812, the Civil War, and wars of the 20th century; individual sheets of large and medium-scale set maps and charts published in the 19th and 20th centuries, including official topographic, geologic, soil, mineral, and resource maps, and nautical and aeronautical charts for most countries of the world; special subject maps of the world and its various political entities; maps of the United States and the separateStates; county maps and plans of cities and towns, and the Sanborn Fire Insurance Maps, dating back to 1866 for some 13,000 cities in the United States. Atlases include earliest printed editions of Ptolemy's Geography (1482), and representative volumes of leading atlas publishers of the last five centuries covering individual continents, countries, states, counties, cities, and the world. Total: 3,800, 000 maps, 49,000 atlases, 400 globes and 2000 relief models. See *The Geography and Map Division: A Guide to Its Collections and Services,* rev ed, 1975 (LC 5.2:SE6/ 975).

DC —NATIONAL GEOGRAPHIC SOCIETY, Library, 1146 16th St NW, Washington, 20036. Susan Fifer Canby, Dir
Holdings: Vols (63,000) Cat Mss Maps Pix
Notes: Material concerning land, sea, and space exploration--past and present. All fields of anthropology, natural history, geography, etc.

IL —NEWBERRY LIBRARY, 60 W Walton St, Chicago, 60610. Diana Haskell, Cur of Modern Mss
Notes: Collections concerned with US historical county boundary data file, 1790-1970.

KS —UNIVERSITY OF KANSAS, Kenneth Spencer Research Library, Map Library, Lawrence, 66045. Richard L Embers, Map Cur
Holdings: Cat
Budget: ($3000)
Notes: (234,000 maps; 2500 books, atlases and gazetteers). A very strong collection for post-1900 maps in over 40 basic subjects. Depository for USGS and DMA. Maps are available for every country in the world with particular strength in North American, European, and East Asian maps. Excellent holdings for Kansas and the Mid-west. Library also has a large collection of books and serials dealing with cartography. Guide for readers available upon request.

MI —UNIVERSITY OF MICHIGAN, Harlan Hatcher Graduate Library, Map Room, Ann Arbor, 48109. James O Minton, Map Librn
Notes: The collection consists of approx 300, 000 sheet maps incl maps and charts received on deposit from the US Geological Survey, Defense Mapping Agency, and the National Ocean Service. The collection also incl approx 5000 reference volumes related to cartography, surveying, and mapping, with emphasis on place-name literature (gazetteers, dictionaries), books on how to use and interpret maps, carto-bibliographies, and state (provincial, etc), regional, national, and international atlases. The collection is strongest geographically in materials of Michigan, Midwest, Anglo-America, and Europe; chronologically, 1850-date; and thematically, in topographic and geologic maps, although all subjects are collected. The collection maintains a separate catalog of holdings. Reference volumes are fully cataloged and classified.

MI —UNIVERSITY OF MICHIGAN, William L Clements Library, Ann Arbor, 48109. John C Dann, Dir
Notes: The William L. Clements Library of Americana is a non-circulating rare book library of original source material, printed and manuscript, dealing with America, from the discovery period into the late nineteenth century. The collection includes approximately 55,000 books and pamphlets, 550 linear feet of manuscripts, 4,100 volumes of newspapers, 36,000 maps, 40,000 pieces of sheet music, and 1,000 prints. The collection is strongest for the period of the American Revolution, and includes the papers of Thomas Gage, Sir Henry Clinton, and the Earl of Shelburne. Other areas of strength include antislavery, cartography and geography, discovery and exploration, American Indians, The Civil War, tune-books, sermons and orations, and the War of 1812. There are selective research collections dealing with Christopher Columbus, Thomas Paine, Benjamin Franklin, George Washington, Thomas Jefferson, and the Federalist Papers. Publications describing the collections of the library are: Author/Title catalog of Americana 1493-1860 in the William L. Clements Library... 7 volumes, Boston, G. K. Hall, 1970; Guide to the manuscript collections of the William L. Clements Library, by Arlene P. Shy 3d edition, Boston, G. K. Hall, 1978; Guide to the manuscript maps in the William L. Clements Library, compiled by Christian Burn, Ann Arbor, U. of Michigan, 1959; and Research catalog of maps of America, to 1860 in the William L. Clements Library...,edited by Douglas W. Marshall, 4 volumes, Boston, G. K. Hall, 1972.

NJ —HAMMOND, Editorial Department Library, 515 Valley St, Maplewood, 07040. Ernest J Dupuy, Librn
Holdings: Vols (10,000) Cat Maps Pix
Notes: Also about 15,000 maps; 50 vertical file drawers of administrative, census, national parks, highway, and related materials. No photocopying.

NY —NEW YORK PUBLIC LIBRARY, Map Division, Fifth Ave & 42 St, New York, 10018. Alice Judson, Librn
Holdings: Vols (33,000) Cat Mss Maps Microforms
Notes: Incl 11,000 atlases and 354,000 maps. European maps from 1600. American from 1800 are in the Map Div; earlier maps are in the Rare Book Div. This collection incl topographical surveys, detailed plans of American cities; large-scale maps of all foreign countries; up-to-date road maps. There are atlases, gazetteers, and postal guides, and an index to periodical articles about maps. The collection of the history of cartography, the techniques of map making, and of county atlases of the US is exceptionally strong. See *Dictionary Catalog of the Map Division,* The Research Libraries of the New York Public Library, 10X14, est 175,000 cards, 10 vols, $730.

OH —PUBLIC LIBRARY OF CINCINNATI & HAMILTON COUNTY, Map Collection, History Dept, 800 Vine St, Cincinnati, 45202. Carl G Marquette Jr, Librn
Holdings: Vols (1775) Cat Maps
Budget: ($4000)
Notes: The collection consists of 137,951 maps (uncataloged); 1250 atlases, with emphasis on Ohio county atlases, national atlases and facsimiles of important cartographic works; 125 bibliographies of maps or collections of maps and atlases; 400 gazetteers and other works, monographs series and journals (partially cataloged) relating to cartography and maps. The library is a depository for USGS and Defense Mapping Agency. Concentration of maps is Ohio, Hamilton County and Cincinnati. No catalog for flat maps.

OH —UNIVERSITY OF CINCINNATI, Geology-Geography Library, 103 Old Tech Bldg ML 13, Cincinnati, 45221. Richard Spohn, Sr Library Assoc
Holdings: Vols (2000) Cat Maps
Budget: ($6000)
Notes: Collection covers only physical geography and cartography.

OK —SOCIETY FOR THE NORTH AMERICAN CULTURAL SURVEY, Dept of Geography, Oklahoma State University, Stillwater, 74078. John Rooney, Dir; Todd Zdorkowski, Asst
Notes: Has produced a cultural atlas of North America incl 309 pages of maps and supporting text. Maps were gathered from the geographical, historical and cultural source-literatures; many were redrafted to add new information or to alter the format for this publication. Of particular interest may be the maps of perception and behavior.

OR —UNIVERSITY OF OREGON, Map Library, Eugene, 97403. Peter L Stark, Map Librarian
Holdings: Cat Maps Pix
Budget: ($4000)
Notes: 2500 atlases, 247,000 maps, 330,000 aerial photos. Specializations for maps are Pacific Northwest, Latin America and West Africa. Incl topographic maps. Specialization for aerial photos is Oregon. Separate catalog and index. Atlases are fully cataloged; maps are classified with shelf list cards; aerial photographs are fully indexed.

WA —UNIVERSITY OF WASHINGTON LIBRARIES, Geography Library, Humanities and Social Science Dept, 415 Smith Hall, DP-10, Seattle, 98195. Joan Christ, Asst Librn
Holdings: Vols (15,701) Cat
Budget: ($18,627)

WI —STATE HISTORICAL SOCIETY OF WISCONSIN, Archives, 816 State St, Madison, 53706. Harold L Miller, Reference Archivist
Holdings: Vols 2500 Cat Maps
Notes: Incl 25,000 sheet maps and 2500 atlases. Collection specializes in maps of Wisconsin, its counties, and its cities, but also is strong in coverage of adjacent states of Middle West and North America as a whole. We also have a collection of European atlases from the 16th through 18th centuries, and many maps of North American areas prior to 1800. There is a separate card catalog of the map collection, and a descriptive brochure is available upon request. Maps and atlases are noncirculating.

WI —UNIVERSITY OF WISCONSIN, MADISON, Geography Library, 280 Science Hall, Madison, 53706. Miriam E Kerndt, Librn
Holdings: Vols (40,000) Cat Microforms
Budget: ($35,000)
Notes: Geography Library collects books, journals, and atlases in all fields of regional and systematic geography to support research and university teaching. Popular works, travel accounts, and tourist literature are not collected. Maps are collected in a separate Map and Air Photo Library in the same building.

WI —UNIVERSITY OF WISCONSIN, MILWAUKEE, American Geographical Society Collection, 2311 E Hartford Ave, PO Box 399, Milwaukee, 53201. Roman Drazniowsky, Cur
Holdings: Vols (196,800)
Budget: ($270,000)
Notes: Current geographical publications. Annually 10 issues. The largest special collection in geography, cartography, and related fields in the Western Hemisphere. Incl 6469 atlases; 385,610 maps; 72 globes; 33,700 pamphlets; 79,000 photographs; 99, 000 Landsat Images. Catalog published by G K Hall, Boston.

BC —UNIVERSITY OF BRITISH COLUMBIA, Library, Special Collections Div, 1956 Main Mall, Vancouver, V6T 1Y3, Can. Anne Yandle, Head
Holdings: Vols Cat Maps
Notes: Emphasis on cartography of North America and historical Japanese maps.

CARTOGRAPHY (cont.)

ON —QUEEN'S UNIVERSITY, Map and Air Photo Library, Mackintosh-Corry Hall, Kingston, K7L 5C4, Can. M B McBurney, Chief Librn; Kathryn Harding, Senior Technician
Holdings: Cat Maps
Notes: Major interest in Canadian maps. Incl text and journals on cartography and photogrammetry; history of cartography collection (facsimile maps and atlases, as well as text and journals).

ON —UNIVERSITY OF TORONTO, Library, Map Library, 130 St George St, Toronto, M5S 1A5, Can. Joan Winearls, Map Librn
Holdings: Vols (10,376) Cat Maps
Notes: A collection of 183,000 current topographic and thematic maps for all parts of the world; strong in Canada, Ontario, Toronto, Europe, US, parts of Latin America and Africa, Near East and Far East. Good atlas and cartography collection; 205,283 aerial photos, 1977-date, for Toronto, 1952-date for southern Ontario and parts of northern Ontario; files maintained of the following: publishers catalogs; maps clipped from newspapers and reports; articles on cartography, particularly the history of cartography; and base maps. In-house bibliographies on Toronto maps, climate and map interpretation. Map catalog is separate and housed only in the Map Library. Equipment, facilities for use of materials.

PQ —MCGILL UNIVERSITY, McLennan Library, Rare Books and Special Collections Dept, 3459 McTavish St, Montreal, H3A 1Y1, Can.
Notes: 5524 sheet maps, 370 atlases, 571 folded maps, 629 guide books, 248 reference books. The coverage is worldwide, specializing in North America, Canada, Quebec, Montreal. Includes a collection of guide books from the 1800s to the present day, as well as a reference collection; there is also a large collection of modern topographical literature with worldwide coverage, and an important collection of postcards particularly of Montreal and the Province of Quebec. A finding list is available for 19th century guide books on Canada: A Preliminary Guide to Nineteenth Century Canadian Guide Books: a Survey of the Holdings of the McLennan Library with an Historical Introduction. Montreal, 1982.

CARTOGRAPHY—HISTORY

AL —BIRMINGHAM PUBLIC LIBRARY, 2020 Seventh Ave N, Birmingham, 35203. Virginia K Scott, Librn
Holdings: Vols (2000) Cat Maps Pix
Notes: History and development of cartography. 19th-century US atlases. Maps of eastern US with most emphasis on southeastern US. The Rucker Agee Map Collection incl over 2000 maps. See *The Rucker Agee Collection of the Birmingham Public Library*, Birmingham Public Library, 1964; *Atlas Maior, Sive Cosmographia Blaviana, Qva Solvm, Salvm, Coelvm, Accvratissime Describvntvr*, Birmingham Public Library, nd; 1570-1970. *An Exhibit in Commemoration of the 400th Anniversary of Publication by Abraham Ortelius of Theatrum Orbis Terrarum; the World's First Atlas*, Birmingham Public Library, 1970; George Ray Stewart, *The Special Collections In the Birmingham Public Library*, MA thesis, Emory University, 1971; and *A List of Nineteenth Century Maps of the State of Alabama*, Birmingham Library, 1973.

CA —CALIFORNIA STATE UNIVERSITY, FULLERTON, Library, Box 4150, Fullerton, 92634. Linda Herman, Special Collections Librn
Holdings: Vols (1300) Cat Maps
Notes: The Collection for the History of Cartography incl 1087 pre-1900 maps and related books. Also 6 display catalogs from annual rare map exhibits. No photocopying. Noncirculating.

CT —LEE ASH, (personal collection), 66 Humiston Dr, Bethany, 06525.
Holdings: Cat Mss Pix
Notes: Incl books, letters, ephemera, etc.

DC —LIBRARY OF CONGRESS, Geography and Map Division, Washington, 20540. John A Wolter, Chief
Holdings: Cat Mss Maps Pix Slides Microforms
Notes: Early original ms maps, navigation charts by Italian, Portuguese, and Spanish 15th, 16th, and 17th-century cartographers; the Hummel and Warner Collections of rare ms and printed maps and atlases of China and Korea from the 17th, 18th, and 19th centuries: ms and printed maps of colonial America and the Revolutionary War. Atlases incl earliest printed editions of Ptolemy's Geography (1482). Rare printed maps of North America. 167 works produced between 1750 and 1790 incl copies of *A Map of the Most Inhabited Part of Virginia* by Joshua Fry and Peter Jefferson (1755 and 1775 editions), John Montresor's *A Map of the Province of New York* (1777), William Gerard De Brahm's *A Map of South Carolina and a Part of Georgia* (1757), and *A Plan of the City of Philadelphia* (1776) by Benjamin Easburn.

IL —NEWBERRY LIBRARY, Hermon Dunlap Smith Center, 60 W Walton St, Chicago, 60610. David Buisseret, Head
Holdings: Vols 4000 Cat
Notes: The Hermon Dunlap Smith Center for the History of Cartography is a separately funded research and teaching center within the library. Holdings listed do not incl maps and atlases.

IL —UNIVERSITY OF ILLINOIS, URBANA/CHAMPAIGN, Library, Map & Geography Library, 418 Main Library, Urbana, 61801. David Cobb, Librn
Holdings: Vols (14,500) Cat Maps Pix Microforms
Notes: Maps (over 325,000) of almost all types, incl topographic, soil, transportation, economic, hydrographic, weather, city, pictorial, and historical maps, are collected. Coverage is excellent for Illinois and for most parts of the United States and Canada. Good maps are available for Europe, Central America and the ocean areas. The early map collection is rich in maps of Illnois, Italy, and the western hemisphere. A large number of publishers' catalogs, particularly of foreign map publishings are kept on file. The collection of aerial photographs provides complete and sequential coverage of the State of Illinois from the late 1930s to the present. Much of the coverage is stereoscopic. Other map resources on the campus include about 50,000 geologic and topographic maps and aerial photographs in the Geology Library, a wall map collection in the Geography Department, severalhundred early maps and atlases of the Illinois area in the Illinois Historical Survey, and geologic and topographic maps and aerial photographs in the Civil Engineering Department. Publication: *Biblio* (bi-monthly acquisitions list).

KS —UNIVERSITY OF KANSAS, Kenneth Spencer Research Library, Special Collections Dept, Lawrence, 66045. Alexandra Mason, Librn
Holdings: Vols 550 Cat Mss Maps
Notes: Particularly interested in the development of the cartography of the Americas. Collection incl about 700 reference books, 900 antiquarian sheet maps, and over 100 atlases. Noncirculating. See Smith, Thomas R, *Maps of the 16th to 19th Centuries in the University of Kansas* Library, Lawrence: University of Kansas Libraries, 1963, covers about half of the sheet-map holdings.

MA —HARVARD UNIVERSITY, Harvard College Library, Map Collection, Cambridge, 02138. Frank E Trout, Cur
Holdings: Cat Mss Maps
Notes: Harvard Map Collection is comprehensive in global coverage and historical depth. Incl books on history and science of cartography, gazetteers, topographic maps, urban plans, and thematic atlases.

MI —UNIVERSITY OF MICHIGAN, William L Clements Library, Ann Arbor, 48109. John C Dann, Dir
Notes: The William L. Clements Library of Americana is a non-circulating rare book library of original source material, printed and manuscript, dealing with America, from the discovery period into the late nineteenth century. The collection includes approximately 55,000 books and pamphlets, 550 linear feet of manuscripts, 4,100 volumes of newspapers, 36,000 maps, 40,000 pieces of sheet music, and 1,000 prints. The collection is strongest for the period of the American Revolution, and includes the papers of Thomas Gage, Sir Henry Clinton, and the Earl of Shelburne. Other areas of strength include antislavery, cartography and geography, discovery and exploration, American Indians, The Civil War, tune-books, sermons and orations, and the War of 1812. There are selective research collections dealing with Christopher Columbus, Thomas Paine, Benjamin Franklin, George Washington, Thomas Jefferson, and the Federalist Papers. Publications describing the collections of the library are: Author/Title catalog of Americana 1493-1860 in the William L. Clements Library... 7 volumes, Boston, G. K. Hall, 1970; Guide to the manuscript collections of the William L. Clements Library, by Arlene P. Shy 3d edition, Boston, G. K. Hall, 1978; Guide to the manuscript maps in the William L. Clements Library, compiled by Christian Burn, Ann Arbor, U. of Michigan, 1959; and Research catalog of maps of America, to 1860 in the William L. Clements Library...,edited by Douglas W. Marshall, 4 volumes, Boston, G. K. Hall, 1972.

NH —DARTMOUTH COLLEGE, Baker Memorial Library, Hanover, 03755.
Holdings: Cat Mss Maps
Notes: 1200 atlases and 90,000 maps. Areas of special interest: historical cartography, polar regions, USSR, Alaska, New Hampshire.

OH —PUBLIC LIBRARY OF CINCINNATI & HAMILTON COUNTY, Map Collection, History Dept, 800 Vine St, Cincinnati, 45202. Carl G Marquette Jr, Librn
Holdings: Vols (1775) Cat Maps
Budget: ($4000)
Notes: The collection consists of 137,951 maps (uncataloged); 1250 atlases, with emphasis on Ohio county atlases, national atlases and facsimiles of important cartographic works; 125 bibliographies of maps or collections of maps and atlases; 400 gazetteers and other works, monographs series and journals (partially cataloged) relating to cartography and maps. The library is a depository for USGS and Defense Mapping Agency. Concentration of maps is Ohio, Hamilton County and Cincinnati. No catalog for flat maps.

PA —FREE LIBRARY OF PHILADELPHIA, Social Science and History Dept, Map Collection, Logan Sq, Philadelphia, 19103.
Holdings: Vols (30,000) Cat Mss Maps
Notes: Map collection incl atlases, maps, pamphlets, and aerial views. Incl a representative collection of early atlases (1534-1827). The collection emphasizes the Philadelphia, Pennsylvania and Delaware Valley areas in particular and the eastern seaboard in general. Low altitude oblique aerial photographs have been transferred to the Print and Picture Dept; high altitude vertical aerial photographs have been

CARTOGRAPHY—HISTORY (cont.)

retained; some volumes and pamphlets reassigned within the Social Science and History Dept.

TX —UNIVERSITY OF TEXAS, ARLINGTON, Library, PO Box 19497, Arlington, 76019. Chas Colley, Dir Special Collections
Holdings: Uncat Maps Slides
Notes: The collection focuses on the history of cartography in general, specializing in the discovery and exploration of North America, with special emphasis on Texas and the American West. The collection consists of thousands of rare maps and atlases dating from 1493, coupled with an extensive collection of related reference works and primary works on exploration and discovery.

NS —DALHOUSIE UNIVERSITY LIBRARY, Halifax, B3H 4H8, Can.
Holdings: Cat Pix
Notes: Approx 2000 lithographs, steel engravings, fine prints and illustrated historical maps from the 18th and 19th centuries are in the collection. Subject coverage is primarily of Nova Scotia, New Brunswick, Prince Edward Island, and Newfoundland scenery, street scenes, and portrayals of prominent people, buildings and events. Generally rich in illustrations of the working and social life of the period. Artists represented incl: J E Woolford, J F W Desbarres, William Eagar, William Bartlett and Richard Short. Historical maps incl some of the earliest visual depictions of the Atlantic coast. Material available for editorial reproduction. Print fee charged. No loans.

CARTOON MUSIC see Caricatures and Cartoons—Music

CARTOONISTS see Caricaturists and Cartoonists

CARTOONS see Caricatures and Cartoons

CARTS see Carriages and Carts

CARTULARIES

WI —UNIVERSITY OF WISCONSIN, MADISON, Memorial Library, Rare Books Collection, 728 State St, Madison, 53706. Gretchen Lagana, Cur
Holdings: Microforms
Notes: Photostats of the equivalent of 61 reels of microfilm (as well as the microfilms themselves). Originals in the Archivio di Stato in Genoa. These are registers or cartularies of the Genoese notaries beginning in 1154 AD. Supplements LC's collection of Pandects of Genoese Notaries to 1300.

CARTULARIES, GENOESE

DC —LIBRARY OF CONGRESS, General Reading Rooms Division, Microform Reading Room, Washington, 20540.
Holdings: Cat Mss Maps Pix Microforms
Notes: Microform materials only in this LC Division. Works of individual authors; holdings of collections; archival records, etc, press releases and translations, etc.

CARTWRIGHT, WILBURN

OK —UNIVERSITY OF OKLAHOMA, Bizzell Memorial Library, Western History Collections, 401 W Brooks, Norman, 73069. John Ezell, Cur
Holdings: Vols Mss Newspapers Maps Documents
Notes: US Representative. His papers. Guide available (1985).

CARTY, WILLIAM EDWARD

†WA —WASHINGTON STATE UNIVERSITY, Library, Manuscripts, Archives & Special Collections, Pullman, 99164. John F Guido, Head
Holdings: Vols Cat Mss Maps Pix
Notes: The personal and political papers of Fred C Ashley, William Edward Carty, Knute Hill, Walter Franklin Horan, William Lon Johnson, Catherine May, and Austin Mires are among the holdings of the library. Most collections described in printed registers.

CARUS, PAUL

IL —SOUTHERN ILLINOIS UNIVERSITY, CARBONDALE, Delyte W Morris Library, Special Collections Dept, Carbondale, 62901. David V Koch, Cur of Special Collections; Louisa Bowen, Cur of Manuscripts
Holdings: Vols 140 Cat Mss Pix
Notes: Twenty collections related to 20th century American philosophy incl company archives, 1886-1930, 72 linear feet. The archive of Dr Paul Carus and the Open Court Publishing Company of LaSalle, Illinois, major publishing center for philosophy for more than 30 years, consist of more than 100,000 letters and ms pages. Dr Carus and his associates conducted a voluminous correspondence with philosophers, scientists, and men of letters throughout the world, so that the archives offer a major source of historical study of philosophy from 1888 to 1920. There is correspondence with John Dewey and C S Pierce, whose early writings were published by Open Court, J M Baldwin, Couturat, DeVries, Höffding, Husserl, Eucken, Harnack, Hasegawa, Levy-Bruhl, Lovejoy, Lombroso, Lutoslawski, Mach, Morgan, Poincare, Royce, Sarton, Suzuki, Thorndike.

CARUSO, ENRICO

MD —PEABODY CONSERVATORY LIBRARY, 21 E Mt Vernon Place, Baltimore, 21202. Edwin A Quist, Librn
Notes: Incl mss and memorabilia. Library formerly a part of Peabody Institute Library.

CARVER, CLIFFORD NICKELS, 1891-1965

NJ —PRINCETON UNIVERSITY, Library, Manuscript Collection, Nassau St, Princeton, 08540. Jean F Preston, Cur
Holdings: // Cat Mss
Notes: Incl 18 cartons of papers.

CARVER, GEORGE WASHINGTON

MO —US NATIONAL PARK SERVICE, G W Carver National Monument, Box 38, Diamond, 64840. Lawrence A Blake, Historian
Holdings: Vols 200 Cat Mss Pix Audiotapes
Notes: Original mss and research dealing with Carver's life and influence. Archive collection on microfilm.

CARY, JOYCE

NV —UNIVERSITY OF NEVADA, RENO, University Library, Special Collections Dept, Reno, 89557. Robert E Blesse, Head
Holdings: Vols (58) Cat
Notes: Includes individual works by author in all editions including translations; also prefaces, introductions, published correspondence, appearances in anthologies, periodicals, etc. Bibliographical research collection, part of Modern Authors Collection. Other appearances 130 cataloged.

CARY, MRS. MELBERT

NY —CARY ARBORETUM OF THE NEW YORK BOTANICAL GARDEN, Institute of Ecosystem Studies, Library, Box AB, Millbrook, 12545. Betsy Calvin, Librn
Holdings: Vols 10,000

CASANOVA DE SEINGALT, GIOVANNI GIACOMO

VA —RANDOLPH-MACON COLLEGE, Walter Hines Page Library, Ashland, 23005. Flavia Reed Owen, Librn
Holdings: Vols 3000
Notes: Collection incl books of Casanova and other minor 18th-century European authors-Ange Goudar, Sara Goudar, Justienne Wynne. Descriptions of collection in *Cassanoviana: An Annotated Bibliography of Jacques Casanova de Seingalt and of Works Concerning Him*, by J Rives Childs (Vienna: C M Nebehay, 1956, for the Casanova Society of Virginia) and in *Casanova Gleanings*, ed by J Rives Childs (Horn, Austria: Ferdinand Berger, 1958-).

VA —UNIVERSITY OF VIRGINIA, Alderman Library, Manuscripts Dept, Charlottesville, 22901. Edmund Berkeley Jr, Cur
Holdings: Cat Mss
Notes: Papers of J Rives Childs, author and diplomat; incl research material from his work on Casanova, about 7600 items.

CASE, CLIFFORD P., 1904-

NJ —RUTGERS, THE STATE UNIVERSITY OF NEW JERSEY, Alexander Library, Special Collections and Archives, College Ave & Huntington St, New Brunswick, 08903. Ronald L Becker, Cur of Manuscripts and Rare Books
Holdings: // Mss
Notes: Papers, etc (500 linear feet).

CASE FAMILY

ME —COLBY COLLEGE, Miller Library, Colby Archives, Waterville, 04901.
Holdings: Mss
Notes: Family papers or other correspondence.

CASEMENT, DAN

KS —KANSAS STATE UNIVERSITY, Library, Special Collections & University Archives, Manhattan, 66506. Antonia Q Pigno, Coordr; John J Vander Velde, Librn; Anthony R Crawford, Univ Archivist
Holdings: Vols 25// Cat Mss
Notes: Dan Casement, 1868-1953, was a wealthy Manhattan rancher. He graduated from Princeton in 1890. During the years 1897-1901 he helped his father, Jack, build a railroad across Costa Rica. Jack had built the Union Pacific across the US. Dan Casement opposed the New Deal, incl the Agricultural Adjustment Act; he wrote articles and made radio speeches against them. Most of the 2500 letters congratulate him on his stand.

CASEY, ROBERT R.

TX —TEXAS A&M UNIVERSITY, Sterling C Evans Library, University Archives, College Station, 77843. Charles R Schultz, University Archivist
Holdings: Mss
Notes: The Archives of Modern Politics: the papers of Robert R Casey, 1958-1976.

CASSILL, R. V.

MA —BOSTON UNIVERSITY, Mugar Memorial Library, Special Collections Dept, 771 Commonwealth Ave, Boston, 02215. Howard B Gotlieb, Dir
Holdings: Cat Mss
Notes: Mss, correspondence, etc collected in depth; incl publications by or about.

CASSIRER, ERNST

CT —YALE UNIVERSITY, Box 1603A, Yale Station, New Haven, 06520.

CASSIRER (PUBLISHERS)

CA —STANFORD UNIVERSITY LIBRARIES, Cecil H Green Library, Stanford, 94305. Peter R Frank, Cur, CDP-Germanic Collection
Notes: Strong collection, with many first editions, rare journals, etc. The Cassirer Collection (correspondence, autographs and typescripts by Hasenclever, Meidner, printed material) in the Stanford Collection of German, Austrian and Swiss Culture, Special Collections Register of Manuscripts.

CASSYD, SYD

CA —UNIVERSITY OF CALIFORNIA, LOS ANGELES, Theater Arts Library, Los

CASSYD, SYD (cont.)

Angeles, 90024. Edward Shreeves, Chairman, Bibliographers Group; Audree Malkin, Head, Theater Arts Library
Notes: Syd Cassyd Collection. He was the first president of the National Academy of Television Arts and Sciences. Collection contains material relating to his career, 1935-1977; incl screenplay, television and radio scripts; treatments; pre-production and production material; production stills, portraits, souvenir motion picture programs; awards programs; clippings; personal notes.

CASTELNUOVO-TEDESCO, MARIO

†IL —NORTHWESTERN UNIVERSITY, Music Library, 1937 Sheridan Rd, Evanston, 60201.
Notes: Materials in the Moldenhauer Archive. Uncataloged, Incl music mss, letters and documents.

CASTELVETRO, GIACOPO

IL —NEWBERRY LIBRARY, 60 W Walton St, Chicago, 60610. Diana Haskell, Cur of Modern Mss
Holdings: Cat Mss
Notes: Collection consists of 9 mss vols, diplomatic documents collected and annotated by Castelvetro.

CASTIGLIONE, BALDASSARE

OH —CLEVELAND PUBLIC LIBRARY, Fine Arts and Special Collections Department, 325 Superior Ave, Cleveland, 44114. Alice N Loranth, Head
Holdings: Vols 102 Cat
Notes: Special strength. Early and rare 16th-20th century editions, translations, and revisions. Separate edition catalog maintained.
See also entry under Rare Books.

CASTILIAN LANGUAGE see Spanish Language and Literature

CASTINGS, METAL see Metal Castings

CASTLE, IRENE FOOTE, 1893-1969

NY —CORNELL UNIVERSITY LIBRARIES, Collection of Regional History, Dept of Manuscripts and Univ Archives, Ithaca, 14853.
Notes: Actress, dancer. Incl papers, (1916-23)-1946, pertaining mostly to her film career; legal documents, correspondence, 2 scrapbooks of newspaper and magazine clippings, publicity galleys and loose clippings.

CASTLEMON, HARRY see Fosdick, Charles Austin

CASTLES

DC —GEORGETOWN UNIVERSITY, Library, Special Collections Div, 37 & O Sts NW, Washington, 20057. George M Barringer, Special Collections Librn; Nicholas B Sheetz, Mss Librn
Holdings: Mss Cat
Notes: A collection of 242 medieval Latin and Catalan charters previously belonging to Frederick C Scheuch, ranging in date from 1261 to 1690. The documents comprise the archives of the Sala family who owned the castle of Montorroell in Catalonia, Spain. See Joseph J Gwara, Jr's *The Sala Family Archives: A Handlist of Medieval and Early Modern Catalonian Manuscripts.*

CASTRO, FIDEL, 1927-

CA —HOOVER INSTITUTION ON WAR, REVOLUTION & PEACE, Stanford University, Stanford, 94305. Milorad M Drachkovitch, Archivist
Holdings: Vols (1600) Mss Pix Microfilm
Notes: About 1600 titles on contemporary Cuba. Intensive collecting of political, social and economic works covering the Castro period, especially writings and speeches of Castro and Guevara. Some 30 periodical and newspaper titles currently received from the island. General description of the Latin American Collection and complete listing of the serial and newspaper holdings available in: Joseph W Bingaman, *Latin America: a Survey of Holdings at the Hoover Institution on War, Revolution and Peace.* Stanford, California: Hoover Institution, Stanford University, 1972. 96 pp.

NY —COLUMBIA UNIVERSITY LIBRARIES, Rare Book & Manuscript Library, 801 Butler Library, 535 W 114 St, New York, 10027. Kenneth A Lohf, Librn
Holdings: Mss
Notes: Materials on Castro's Cuba in the Herbert Matthews and Lee Lockwood papers. Restricted use.

CASUALTY INSURANCE see Insurance, Casualty

CATABAPTISTS see Anabaptists

CATALAN LANGUAGE AND LITERATURE

CA —UNIVERSITY OF CALIFORNIA, BERKELEY, University Library, Hispanic Collections, Berkeley, 94720. Gaston Somoshegyi-Szokol, Librn
Holdings: Vols (7000)
Notes: In 1981, as a member of the RLG the Library accepted primary responsibility for collecting Catalan language materials in depth. Every effort is now being made to develop the already extensive Catalan collection.

MA —HARVARD UNIVERSITY LIBRARY, Widener Library, Cambridge, 02138. Ellen H Brow, Specialist in Book Selection
Holdings: Cat
Notes: Incl in *Widener Library Shelflist* No 41 (1972); also a collection of 10,000 *goigs* and *gozos.*

NY —HISPANIC SOCIETY OF AMERICA, Library, 613 W 155 St, New York, 10032. Martha M de Narvaez, Cur of Mss; Irene S Frye, Asst Librn
Holdings: Vols (150,000) Cat Mss Maps Pix Slides Phonorecords Microforms
Notes: History, art, literature and general culture of the Hispanic countries (where Spanish or Portuguese is spoken). Incl (18,000) vols printed before 1701, incl (250) incunabula; over (100,000) later vols, plus thousands of periodicals. About (200,000) mss incl ms maps. Printed atlases are in the Book Collection. Some microfilms, chiefly of our early books. Engraved and printed separate maps; reference collection of over 100,000 photographs; slides: all in Department of Iconography, not in library. Catalogs: *Catalogue of the Hispanic Society of America* (Boston: G K Hall, 1962), 10 vols; *First Supplement* (Boston, 1970), 4 vols. Early books: *Printed Books 1468-1700;* Mss: *Catalogo de los Manuscritos Poeticos* Castellanos (15th-17th centuries; 3 vols); *Medieval Manuscripts in the Library; Golden Age Drama Manuscripts*(the latter in press).

CATALONIA—HISTORY

DC —GEORGETOWN UNIVERSITY, Library, Special Collections Div, 37 & O Sts NW, Washington, 20057. George M Barringer, Special Collections Librn; Nicholas B Sheetz, Mss Librn
Holdings: Mss Cat
Notes: A collection of 242 medieval Latin and Catalan charters previously belonging to Frederick C Scheuch, ranging in date from 1261 to 1690. The documents comprise the archives of the Sala family who owned the castle of Montorroell in Catalonia, Spain. See Joseph J Gwara, Jr's *The Sala Family Archives: A Handlist of Medieval and Early Modern Catalonian Manuscripts.*

CATALOGS, ART DEALERS'

CA —LOS ANGELES COUNTY MUSEUM OF ART, Art Research Library, 5905 Wilshire Blvd, Los Angeles, 90036. Eleanor C Hartman, Museum Librn
Holdings: Vols 63,900 Cat
Budget: ($34,000)
Notes: Incl 26,000 art auction catalogs.

FL —RINGLING MUSEUM OF ART, Art Research Library, PO Box 1838, Sarasota, 33578. Lynell A Morr, Librn
Holdings: Vols (40,000) Cat
Budget: ($24,000)
Notes: Incl an additional 30,000 art auction catalogs, indexed 1970-date.

IL —NORTHWESTERN UNIVERSITY, Library, Special Collections Dept, 1937 Sheridan Rd, Evanston, 60201. R Russell Maylone, Cur
Holdings: Vols 5300
Notes: Exhibition catalogs and ephemera arranged by artist, period, group or collection. Additional material cataloged for general collection.

IN —INDIANAPOLIS MUSEUM OF ART, Stout Reference Library, 1200 W 38 St, Indianapolis, 46208. Martha Blocker, Head Librn
Holdings: Vols (22,000) Cat
Notes: Incl 12,000 uncataloged art exhibition and sale catalogs, microforms, newspaper clippings, and slides (in separate Slide Library; Carolyn Metz, Cur)

MO —THE NELSON-ATKINS MUSEUM OF ART, Kenneth & Helen Spencer Art Reference Library, 4525 Oak St, Kansas City, 64111. Stanley W Hess, Librn

NY —ALBRIGHT-KNOX ART GALLERY, Art Reference Library, 1285 Elmwood Ave, Buffalo, 14222. Annette Masling, Librn
Holdings: Vols (20,000) Cat
Notes: Special strength in American 19th and 20th century art. Excellent collection of exhibition catalogs for contemporary art.

NY —METROPOLITAN MUSEUM OF ART, Thomas J Watson Library, Fifth Ave & 82 St, New York, 10028. William B Walker, Chief Librn
Holdings: Vols (250,000) Cat Mss Microforms
Notes: All fields of art: 1400 periodicals, incl bulletins and annual reports, catalogs, etc of American and foreign art societies, museums, etc; incl sales catalogs, exhibition catalogs, clipping file on individual artists and subjects, autograph letters. See *Library Catalog of the Metropolitan Museum of Art, New York,* second ed, rev and enl (Boston, G K Hall, 1980, 48 v and first supplement, 1982). Since 1980, holdings have been cataloged in RLIN.

WI —UNIVERSITY OF WISCONSIN, MADISON, Kohler Art Library, 800 University Ave, Madison, 53706. William C Bunce, Chief; Louise Hunning, Ref Librn
Holdings: Vols (83,000) Cat Microforms
Notes: Incl over 10,000 exhibition and auction catalogs.

ON —UNIVERSITY OF TORONTO, Thomas Fisher Rare Book Library, 120 Saint George St, Toronto, M5S 1A5, Can. Richard G Landon, Head
Notes: All currently published and most earlier major works on the fine and applied arts in Canada; Canadian art exhibition catalogues; limited editions illustrated by Canadian artists; 19th and 20th century architectural plans for buildings in Toronto and southern Ontario vicinity (ca 1700).

ON —UNIVERSITY OF TORONTO, Art History Reference Library, Dept of Fine Art, 100 Saint George St, Toronto, M5S 1A1, Can. Andrea Retfalvi, Research Librn
Holdings: Vols (20,000) Cat Pix
Notes: The collection specializes in art history catalogs of various types: temporary exhibition catalogs, from the major institutions in Europe and North America; permanent collection catalogs, again for all the major institutions; dealer catalogs; and auction catalogs. The collection of auction catalogs is primarily French, covering 1870-1970, with particular strength from ca 1900 on. There is a catalog for all these types of catalogs. 90,000 photographs.

CATALOGS, AUCTION

AZ —NORTHERN ARIZONA UNIVERSITY, Special Collection Library,

CATALOGS, AUCTION (cont.)

CU Box 6022, Flagstaff, 86011. Peter M Whiteley, Coordr/Archivist; William Mullane, Librn
Notes: Art Dealer and Art Auction Catalogues Collection; mostly contains catalogs from dealer, Sotheby Parke Bernet, 1972. Other art dealers are also represented. Art work of all types and periods are incl. Catalogs dated 1970-1972.

CA —UNIVERSITY OF CALIFORNIA, SAN DIEGO, Central University Library, Mandeville Dept of Special Collections, La Jolla, 92093. Lynda Corey Claassen, Head
Notes: The Reference Collection: More than 2500 bibliographies guides, and catalogues to rare book and manuscript collections, auction records, histories of book collecting, and important works on the social and technological history of books and printing are included.

CA —UNIVERSITY OF CALIFORNIA, SANTA BARBARA, Arts Library, Santa Barbara, 93106. William Treese, Art Librn
Notes: Incl 35,000 auction catalogs and 50, 000 exhibition catalogs. The UCSB Arts Library Art Exhibition Catalog (AEC) Collection. Incl catalogs in all areas of art, primarily US and European. Have computer-based indexing system. The Library "has... received national recognition as a leading collector and organizer of art exhibition catalogs." Is the University of California Archives for Auction Catalogs.

CT —YALE UNIVERSITY, Art Library, 180 York St, New Haven, 06520. Nancy S Lambert, Art Librn
Holdings: Cat

DE —HENRY F DUPONT WINTERTHUR MUSEUM LIBRARY, Winterthur, 19735. Frank H Sommer, III, Head
Notes: Strong collections.

FL —RINGLING MUSEUM OF ART, Art Research Library, PO Box 1838, Sarasota, 33578. Lynell A Morr, Librn
Holdings: Vols (40,000) Cat
Budget: ($24,000)
Notes: Incl an additional 30,000 art auction catalogs, indexed 1970-date.

IL —NORTHWESTERN UNIVERSITY, Library, Special Collections Dept, 1937 Sheridan Rd, Evanston, 60201. R Russell Maylone, Cur
Holdings: Vols 5000
Notes: Catalogs arranged by bookseller, dealer or auction house.

KS —UNIVERSITY OF KANSAS, Kenneth Spencer Research Library, Special Collections Dept, Lawrence, 66045. Alexandra Mason, Librn
Holdings: Uncat
Notes: Several thousand catalogs, Mostly 19th and 20th century, some earlier. Incl auction catalogs. Noncirculating.

MA —HARVARD UNIVERSITY, Harvard College Library, Fine Arts Library, Fogg Museum, 32 Quincy St, Cambridge, 02138. Wolfgang M Freitag, Librn
Holdings: Vols (202,000) Cat Mss Pix Slides
Budget: ($176,500)
Notes: All areas of art history, with emphasis on Italian primitives, Italian Renaissance, master drawings, Romanesque sculpture, architectural history, ms materials (particulary American artists'), conservation and restoration of art objects. Incl the Berenson repertory of photographs from the Harvard Center for Italian Renaissance Studies in Florence, and the Decimal Index to the Art of the Low Countries. Separate card catalogs for books, photographs and lantern slides, registers for ms holdings which are not incl in *National Union Catalog of Manuscript Collections.* Slides total over 230,000; over 745,000 pictures. *Fine Arts Library Catalogue* (14 volumes) and *Catalogue of Auction Sales Catalogues* (1 volume) (Boston: G K Hall, 1972); *A Guide to the Fine Arts Library* (Cambridge, Mass: 1971); *Guide to the Harvard Libraries,* microfiche edition of holdingscataloged through 1981 published 1984 (Munich/New York: Saur).

MA —STERLING AND FRANCINE CLARK ART INSTITUTE LIBRARY, 225 South St, PO Box 8, Williamstown, 01267. Michael Rinehart, Librn
Holdings: Vols (77,000) Cat Pix Slides Microforms
Budget: ($105,000)
Notes: Primarily European art, 1300-present, and post-Columbian American art. Incl 850, 000 pictures, 80,000 slides, 400 microfilm reels, 25,000 auction sale catalogs, and Mary Ann Beinecke Decorative Art Collection.

MA —AMERICAN ANTIQUARIAN SOCIETY LIBRARY, 185 Salisbury St, Worcester, 01609. Marcus A McCorison, Dir & Librn
Holdings: Cat
Notes: Collection was the basis for *American Manuscripts 1763-1815,* Cripe and Campbell (Wilmington, Del, 1977).

MI —DETROIT PUBLIC LIBRARY, Rare Books Department, 5201 Woodward Ave, Detroit, 48202.
Holdings: Cat
Notes: Incl bibliographies, exhibit catalogs, booksellers' catalogs, auction catalogs, books about collecting, book arts, printing history, etc. Restricted use. Reference collection.

MO —THE NELSON-ATKINS MUSEUM OF ART, Kenneth & Helen Spencer Art Reference Library, 4525 Oak St, Kansas City, 64111. Stanley W Hess, Librn
Notes: Auction and exhibition catalogs.

NY —C W POST CENTER OF LONG ISLAND UNIVERSITY, B Davis Schwartz Memorial Library, Greenvale, 11548. Jean Goldberg, Special Collections Librn
Notes: William Randolph Hearst Collection, incl photographs.

NY —FRICK ART REFERENCE LIBRARY, 10 E 71 St, New York, 10021. Helen Sanger, Librn
Holdings: Vols (154,384) Cat Pix Per
Notes: History of painting, drawing, sculpture and illuminated mss of US and western Europe from 4th century AD to about 1860. 54,862 art auction catalogs; 420, 507 study photographs.

PA —PENNSYLVANIA STATE UNIVERSITY, Fred Lewis Pattee Library, Special Collections Dept, University Park, 16802. Charles Mann, Chief, Special Collections
Holdings: Vols (6230) Cat
Budget: ($37,000)
Notes: Includes nearly complete runs of Anderson Galleries, Parke-Bernet, and Sotheby/Parke-Bernet on microfilm.

WI —UNIVERSITY OF WISCONSIN, MADISON, Kohler Art Library, 800 University Ave, Madison, 53706. William C Bunce, Chief; Louise Hunning, Ref Librn
Holdings: Vols (83,000) Cat Microforms
Notes: Incl over 10,000 exhibition and auction catalogs.

WI —MILWAUKEE PUBLIC LIBRARY, 814 W Wisconsin Ave, Milwaukee, 53233. Donald J Sager, City Librn
Holdings: Cat
Notes: Comprehensive collection of major US and British auction houses, incl price lists.

ON —UNIVERSITY OF WESTERN ONTARIO, Schoool of Library and Information Science, Library, London, N6G 1H1, Can. Victoria Ripley, Librn
Holdings: Vols (50,000)
Notes: Auction and antiquarian booksellers' catalogs from Canadian, American and European firms, some dating back to the 18th century. A special strength is 19th and early 20th century American booksellers' catalogs, recently augmented by a collection of pre-1920 catalogs formed by the late H O Teisberg. Current emphasis is on Canadian catalogs.

ON —UNIVERSITY OF TORONTO, Art History Reference Library, Dept of Fine Art, 100 Saint George St, Toronto, M5S 1A1, Can. Andrea Retfalvi, Research Librn
Holdings: Vols (20,000) Cat Pix
Notes: The collection specializes in art history catalogs of various types: temporary exhibition catalogs, from the major institutions in Europe and North America; permanent collection catalogs, again for all the major institutions; dealer catalogs; and auction catalogs. The collection of auction catalogs is primarily French, covering 1870-1970, with particular strength from ca 1900 on. There is a catalog for all these types of catalogs. 90,000 photographs.

CATALOGS, BOOKSELLERS'

CT —YALE UNIVERSITY, Box 1603A, Yale Station, New Haven, 06520.

DC —GEORGETOWN UNIVERSITY, Library, Special Collections Div, 37 & O Sts NW, Washington, 20057. George M Barringer, Special Collections Librn; Nicholas B Sheetz, Mss Librn
Holdings: Vols 2000 Cat
Notes: Reference file, fairly comprehensive for major dealers from 1970.

†DC —LIBRARY OF CONGRESS, Washington, 20540.
Notes: The Library of Congress's collections are matched by no library in the world.

IL —CHICAGO PUBLIC LIBRARY, Special Collections Div, Cultural Center, 78 E Washington St, Chicago, 60602. Laura Linard, Cur
Holdings: Vols (1000) Cat
Notes: Author and subject bibliographies, retrospective and current rare books and manuscripts collections catalogs, bookdealers' catalogs, catalogs of private collections (primarily sale or auction catalogs published in hardbound or deluxe editions).

IL —NORTHWESTERN UNIVERSITY, Library, Special Collections Dept, 1937 Sheridan Rd, Evanston, 60201. R Russell Maylone, Cur
Holdings: Vols 7000
Notes: Catalogs arranged by dealer or auction house.

KS —UNIVERSITY OF KANSAS, Kenneth Spencer Research Library, Special Collections Dept, Lawrence, 66045. Alexandra Mason, Librn
Holdings: Uncat
Notes: Several thousand catalogs, Mostly 19th and 20th century, some earlier. Incl auction catalogs. Noncirculating.

MA —HARVARD UNIVERSITY LIBRARY, Cambridge, 02138.
Holdings: Cat

MA —AMERICAN ANTIQUARIAN SOCIETY LIBRARY, 185 Salisbury St, Worcester, 01609. Marcus A McCorison, Dir & Librn
Holdings: Vols 45,000 Cat
Notes: Collection was the basis for *American Manuscripts 1763-1815,* Cripe and Campbell (Wilmington, Del, 1977).

MI —DETROIT PUBLIC LIBRARY, Rare Books Department, 5201 Woodward Ave, Detroit, 48202.
Holdings: Cat
Notes: Incl bibliographies, exhibit catalogs, booksellers' catalogs, auction catalogs, books about collecting, book arts, printing history, etc. Restricted use. Reference collection.

MS —UNIVERSITY OF SOUTHERN MISSISSIPPI, William David McCain Graduate Library, Box 5148, Southern Sta, Hattiesburg, 39406.
Holdings: Uncat Mss
Notes: 15 cubic feet. The personal and business records (1913-1953) of the noted bookseller, Charles F Heartman. Incl correspondence, auction and book catalogs, the Heartman Historical Series, and copies of articles, pamphlets and books written or published by Heartman.

NY —GRADUATE CENTER OF THE CITY UNIVERSITY OF NEW YORK, William H and Gwynne K Crouse Library for Publishing Arts, 33 W 42 St, New York, 10036. Alfred H Lane, Dir
Notes: Recently established and intended as a source of 20th century materials, in hard form or microfilm, incl books, pamphlets, reprints, translations, dissertations, periodicals, indexing and abstracting services, yearbooks, reports and directories of organizations, publishers' and antiquarian dealers' catalogs (particularly those who deal in books about books), periodicals, legislative materials, and clippings pertaining to the book industry. Sections of the library deal with printing, including typography, specimen books, history of printing and

CATALOGS, BOOKSELLERS' (cont.)

printing techniques, book design and small press and alternative publishing.

NY —GROLIER CLUB OF NEW YORK LIBRARY, 47 E 60 St, New York, 10022. Robert Nikirk, Librn
Notes: Catalogs representative of the genre from the earliest times. Also, archive copies of the Scribner Rare Book Shop, NYC.

NY —NEW YORK PUBLIC LIBRARY, Research Libraries, General Research Division, Fifth Ave & 42 St, New York, 10018. Rodney Phillips, Chief
Holdings: Vols (2,225,000) Cat Maps Pix Microforms
Budget: ($775,718)

PA —PENNSYLVANIA STATE UNIVERSITY, Fred Lewis Pattee Library, Special Collections Dept, University Park, 16802. Charles Mann, Chief, Special Collections
Holdings: Vols (6230) Cat
Budget: ($37,000)
Notes: Includes nearly complete runs of Anderson Galleries, Parke-Bernet, in hard copies, and Sotheby/Parke-Bernet on microfilm.

RI —BROWN UNIVERSITY, John Hay Library, 20 Prospect St, Providence, 02912. Mark N Brown, Cur Mss
Holdings: Vols 5000 Uncat
Notes: A rapidly-growing collection of twentieth century auction and antiquarian booksellers catalogs from American, British, Dutch, French, German, and Italian firms.

WI —MILWAUKEE PUBLIC LIBRARY, 814 W Wisconsin Ave, Milwaukee, 53233. Donald J Sager, City Librn
Holdings: Cat
Notes: Incl all major US and British dealers.

ON —UNIVERSITY OF WESTERN ONTARIO, Schoool of Library and Information Science, Library, London, N6G 1H1, Can. Victoria Ripley, Librn
Holdings: Vols (50,000)
Notes: Auction and antiquarian booksellers' catalogs from Canadian, American and European firms, some dating back to the 18th century. A special strength is 19th and early 20th century American booksellers' catalogs, recently augmented by a collection of pre-1920 catalogs formed by the late H O Teisberg. Current emphasis is on Canadian catalogs.

CATALOGS, BOOKSELLERS'—AUCTION

CT —YALE UNIVERSITY, Box 1603A, Yale Station, New Haven, 06520.

DC —GEORGETOWN UNIVERSITY, Library, Special Collections Div, 37 & O Sts NW, Washington, 20057. George M Barringer, Special Collections Librn; Nicholas B Sheetz, Mss Librn
Holdings: Vols 1500 Cat
Notes: Incl long runs of sales at Sotheby-Parke-Bernet and its antecedents; Sotheby's (London) from 1960 onwards; working reference file.

MA —AMERICAN ANTIQUARIAN SOCIETY LIBRARY, 185 Salisbury St, Worcester, 01609. Marcus A McCorison, Dir & Librn
Holdings: Vols 14,000 Cat
Notes: Collection was the basis for *American Manuscripts 1763-1815,* Cripe and Campbell (Wilmington, Del, 1977). 18th century-present.

NY —NEW YORK PUBLIC LIBRARY, Research Libraries, General Research Division, Fifth Ave & 42 St, New York, 10018. Rodney Phillips, Chief
Holdings: Vols (2,225,000) Cat Maps Pix Microforms
Budget: ($775,718)

RI —BROWN UNIVERSITY, John Hay Library, 20 Prospect St, Providence, 02912. Mark N Brown, Cur Mss
Holdings: Vols 5000 Uncat
Notes: A rapidly-growing collection of twentieth century auction and antiquarian booksellers catalogs from American, British, Dutch, French, German, and Italian firms.

CATALOGS, COLLEGE

CA —CALIFORNIA STATE UNIVERSITY, LONG BEACH, Reference Center, 1250 Bellflower Blvd, Long Beach, 90840.
Budget: $8000
Notes: Fiche collection contains 3767 catalogs, supplemented by 600 hard copy catalogs, primarily California institutions. Also selectively from all other states.

CA —LOS ANGELES PUBLIC LIBRARY, Social Sciences Dept, 630 W Fifth St, Los Angeles, 90071. Marilyn C Wherley, Principal Librn
Holdings: Vols (3000) Cat Microforms
Budget: ($150,000)
Notes: Major foreign catalogs, hard copy or microfiche, college catalogs on microfiche, and nearly complete collection of California catalogs.

CA —SAN DIEGO PUBLIC LIBRARY, Social Sciences Section, 820 E St, San Diego, 92101. Margaret E Queen, Supvr
Budget: ($36,000)
Notes: Excellent microfiche collection of current university and college catalogs from throughout the US, print copies of most California and San Diego college catalogs. Also, good collection of educational directories and guides. The collection is indexed by state and name of institution.

DC —CHRONICLE OF HIGHER EDUCATION, INC, 1333 New Hampshire Ave NW, Suite 500, Washington, 20036. Edith H Uunila, Sr Editor
Holdings: Cat Pix
Notes: *Chronicle of Higher Education* published weekly. Library is for editorial research.

IL —CENTER FOR RESEARCH LIBRARIES, 6050 S Kenwood Ave, Chicago, 60637. Donald B Simpson, Dir; Esther Smith, Collection Development Librn
Holdings: Vols 125,000 Uncat
Notes: Both US and foreign institutions, dates early 19th century to present, incl many administrative reports.

IL —CHICAGO PUBLIC LIBRARY, Business/Science/Technology Div, Science/Technology Information Center, 425 North Michigan Ave, Chicago, 60611. Lynda Sanford, Head; John R Moore, Environment Collection Coordinator & Engineering Librn
Budget: $15,000
Notes: Books on careers complemented by Education/Philosophy Information Center's collection of college catalogs and guides and Business Information Center's collections. Over 500 titles; 3 VF cabinets pamphlet materials.

MA —NORTHEASTERN UNIVERSITY LIBRARIES, Center for International Higher Education Documentation, 360 Huntington Ave, Boston, 02115. Solveig M Turner, Dir; Nieves F Farin, Head Collection Development Librn
Notes: Collection based on files of the International Encyclopedia of Higerh Education. Emphasis on international higher education. Subjects incl: national systems of higher education (administrative concerns, planning, enrollments, equivalences of credentials). Also incl international university catalogs. Extensive subject index maintained.

NY —NEW YORK STATE LIBRARY, State Education Bldg Annex, Washington Ave, Albany, 12224.
Holdings: Vols 100,000 Cat Microforms
Notes: Emphasis is on American education, particularly New York State. Strong retrospective file of college catalogs. Textbooks excluded. Microform holdings incl ERIC, Manpower Research, Pacesetters in innovation.

NY —NEW YORK PUBLIC LIBRARY, Mid-Manhattan Library, History and Social Sciences Dept, 455 Fifth Ave, New York, 10016. Robert Sheehan, Sr Principal Librn
Holdings: Vols 20,000 Cat Audiotapes Microforms
Budget: $16,700
Notes: Strong undergraduate level collection with duplicate reference and circulating copies of books in many instances. Good collection of college catalogs incl some foreign catalogs. 65 vertical file drawers; 250 periodicals. ERIC index and microfiche collection from 1966.

NY —NEW YORK PUBLIC LIBRARY, Mid-Manhattan Library, Education Collection, 455 Fifth Ave, New York, 10016.
Holdings: Vols (31,000) Cat Audiotapes Microforms
Budget: ($22,550)
Notes: Strong undergraduate level collection of reference and circulating books. Good collection of current college catalogs incl some foreign catalogs. 32 vertical file drawers; 250 periodicals; ERIC index and microfiche collection from 1966.

NC —DUKE UNIVERSITY, William R Perkins Library, Rare Book Room, Durham, 27706. John L Sharpe, III, Cur
Notes: American college catalog collection. Early college catalogs.

NC —FORSYTH COUNTY PUBLIC LIBRARY, Adult Continuing Education (ACE) Div, 660 W Fifth St, Winston-Salem, 27101. Ann R Gehlen, Librn
Holdings: Vols 3500 Phonorecords Audiotapes Videotapes 16mm Films Filmstrips Microforms
Budget: $6900
Notes: Special Emphasis on high school equivalency preparation, adult new readers, improvement in language and math, secretarial skills, job- hunting techniques, college alternatives, test preparation, and support to independent study in popular subject areas. Extensive pamphlet files of up-to-date career information, indexed. Some 600 bound college catalogs plus national microfiche collection. Current local job openings on microfiche. Information and referral files maintained to relevant local resources (courses, etc). Partially cataloged.

OH —AKRON-SUMMIT COUNTY PUBLIC LIBRARY, 55 S Main St, Akron, 44326. Steven Hawk, Dir
Holdings: Vols 5000 Uncat
Notes: Catalogs are current ones only, from degree granting colleges, universities and junior colleges in the US, Canada and Australia. Often incl specific catalogs from a college. In addition the division has 600 catalogs and brochures from non-degree granting schools in the US.

OR —UNIVERSITY OF OREGON LIBRARY, Education-Psychology Dept, Eugene, 97403. Rose Marie Service, Head Dept Librn
Holdings: Vols 60,500 Cat Microforms
Notes: Collection includes complete National Microfilm Library College Catalog Collection from 1974-75 to the present, numbering approximately 12,800 catalogs. Additional historical collection of 60,000 paper catalogs published prior to 1974, including over 2500 schools and dating back as far as the middle 1800s. Several hundred current paper catalogs kept on hand from West Coast colleges, major national universities, and some foreign colleges.

†ON —METROPOLITAN TORONTO LIBRARY, Social Sciences Dept, 789 Yonge St, Toronto, M4W 2G8, Can. Abdus Salam, Head
Holdings: Vols Cat Maps Phonorecords Audiotapes 16mm Films Microforms
Notes: Extensive collection of current university and college catalogs from throughout the US and Canada, as well as selected foreign universities. Also extensive collection of educational directories and guides.

CATALOGS, COMMERCIAL

AZ —NORTHERN ARIZONA UNIVERSITY, Special Collection Library, CU Box 6022, Flagstaff, 86011. Peter M Whiteley, Coordr/Archivist; William Mullane, Librn
Notes: Old Miner and Hardware Dealer Catalog Collection; contains mining equipment and hardware catalogs from all over the US, representing many different companies. Types of catalogs incl log machinery, mining, furniture, plumbing goods, explosives, tolls, and all types of machinery, 1900's-1970's.

CATALOGS, COMMERCIAL (cont.)

NY —NEW YORK CITY COMMUNITY COLLEGE, Voorhees Branch Library, 450 W 41 St, New York, 10036. Helena Haezeler, Branch Librn
Notes: Collection of product catalogs.

CATALOGS, FILM see Moving Pictures—Catalogs

CATALOGS, LIBRARY see Library Catalogs

CATALOGS, MAIL ORDER see Mail Order Catalogs

CATALOGS, MANUSCRIPT

NY —COLUMBIA UNIVERSITY LIBRARIES, Rare Book & Manuscript Library, 801 Butler Library, 535 W 114 St, New York, 10027. Kenneth A Lohf, Librn
Holdings: Vols 5000 Cat
Notes: 5000 vols of catalogs of ms collections in the US, Europe, Great Britain, France, Germany, Italy and other countries of the Western World.

CATALOGS, MUSIC TRADE

CA —INSTITUTE OF THE AMERICAN MUSICAL, Library, 121 N Detroit St, Los Angeles, 90036. Miles Kreuger, Cur
Holdings: Cat Mss Maps Pix Slides Phonorecords
Notes: Reference materials on the American musical theatre and motion pictures incl 40, 000 phonograph records, sound tapes, and cylinders dating back to the 1890s; record catalogs to 1900; thousands of theatre and film programs, periodicals, sheet music and vocal scores as early as 1830; thousands of motion picture press books and over 200,000 stills from 1914 to the present; every musical comedy script published in America and dozens in ms form, original or photocopy materials from the archives of movie palaces, films and record companies, incl discographies of many major Broadway and Hollywood stars; and thousands of books on theatre, film, broadcasting, world's fairs and other allied areas of showmanship.

MI —DETROIT PUBLIC LIBRARY, Music & Performing Arts Dept, 5201 Woodward, Detroit, 48202. Agatha Pfeiffer Kalkanis, Chief
Notes: Collection of discographical material--500 discographies, manufacturers' catalogs, indexes to reviews, histories of recording industry, runs of American and European record magazines.

NY —NEW YORK PUBLIC LIBRARY, Performing Arts Research Center, Rodgers & Hammerstein Archives of Recorded Sound, 111 Amsterdam Ave, New York, 10023.
Holdings: Vols VF
Notes: Major collection of record manufacturers' catalogs from the 1890's to the present.

CATALOGS, NURSERY

CA —UNIVERSITY OF CALIFORNIA, DAVIS, Shields Library, Dept of Special Collections, Davis, 95616. Donald Kunitz, Head; C Danial Elliott, Asst Head
Holdings: Vols 6500 Cat
Notes: Nursery catalogs from the US and foreign countries dating from late 19th century to the present. An estimated 650 nurseries and/or growers are represented in the collection.

CATALOGS, POSTAGE STAMP

DC —SMITHSONIAN INSTITUTION LIBRARIES, National Museum of American History Branch, Washington, 20560. Rhoda S Ratner, Branch Librn
Holdings: Vols 7500 Cat Mss Maps Pix
Notes: International in scope. Covers all phases of philately and postal history. Incl auction and dealers' catalogs.

CATALOGS, STAR see Stars—Catalogs

CATALOGS, TRADE see Trade Catalogs—Collections

CATALOGS, UNION

CO —BIBLIOGRAPHICAL CENTER FOR RESEARCH, Rocky Mountain Region, Inc, Library, 1777 S Bellaire, Suite G 150, Denver, 80222. J Segal, Exec Dir
Holdings: Cat
Notes: Library automation, data bases, information retrieval, union catalogs, etc.

PA —BIBLIOGRAPHICAL CENTER OF GERMAN LITERATURE, University of Pittsburgh, Dept of Germanic Languages & Literatures, 102 Loeffler Bldg, Pittsburgh, 15260. Klaus W Jonas, Dir
Holdings: Cat Mss Pix Microforms
Notes: Center for the development of collections and bibliographical control of the record of publications, mss, correspondence, etc, by or relating to modern German authors. Special sections have been developed for Mann, Rilke, Hauptmann, Hesse, Broch, Sachs and others. Described by Professor Klaus W Jonas's "The German Literature Center in Pittsburgh," *Stechert-Hafner Book News*, vol 24, no 8, April 1970; "Documentation in Modern German Literature: A Progress Report," *Jahrbuch fuer Internationale Germanistik*, vol 4, no 2, 1972, and in *German and Austrian Contributions to World Literature* (1890-1970). Department of Germanic Languages and Literatures, University of Pittsburgh, 1983. 96 pp.

CATALOGS, UNIVERSITY see Catalogs, College

CATALYSIS

IL —ARGONNE NATIONAL LABORATORY, Chemistry Branch Library, 9700 S Cass Ave, Argonne, 60439. Betty Guttman, Librn
Notes: Incl 20,000 vols monographs, 190 current journals. Materials may be used by the public in the library by prior arrangement. Photocopies may be supplied for interlibrary loan, for which a processing and handling charge is made.

MD —JOHNS HOPKINS UNIVERSITY, Milton S Eisenhower Library, Charles & 34 Sts, Baltimore, 21218. Ann S Gwyn, Assistant Dir for Special Collections
Holdings: Vols (30,000) Cat
Notes: Very strong in all branches of chemistry, particularly in all pure research fields. Less emphasis on industrial application. Incl small but important Lelia Emmett Collection on catalysis: Complete long runs in theoretical fields back to 19th and some to 18th centuries.

PA —FRANKLIN INSTITUTE LIBRARY, 20 & The Parkway, Philadelphia, 19103. Miriam Padusis, Dir; Charles Wilt, Readers Servs Librn
Holdings: Vols (300,000) Cat Maps Pix Microforms

CATARRH, AUTUMNAL see Hay Fever

CATASTROPHES see Disasters and Disaster Relief

CATCHES see Glees, Catches, Rounds, Etc.

CATECHISMS AND CATECHETICS

PA —LUTHERAN THEOLOGICAL SEMINARY, Krauth Memorial Library, 7301 Germantown Ave, Philadelphia, 19119. Rev David J Wartluft, Dir Libr
Holdings: Vols 1000 Cat
Notes: A collection of catechisms of the Lutheran Church, chiefly Luther's catechisms and interpretations thereof, in various languages, dating from the Reformation to the present.

TX —OBLATE SCHOOL OF THEOLOGY, Library, 285 Oblate Dr, San Antonio, 78216. James Maney, Libr Dir
Holdings: Vols (22,000) Cat
Budget: ($15,500)

CATEGORIES see Logic

CATHER, WILLA

CA —UNIVERSITY OF SAN FRANCISCO, Richard A Gleeson Library, The Countess Bernardine Murphy Donohue Rare Book Room, San Francisco, 94117. D Steven Corey, Special Collections Librn
Holdings: Vols 35
Notes: Virtually complete collection.

CT —YALE UNIVERSITY, Box 1603A, Yale Station, New Haven, 06520.
Notes: Incl correspondence.

IL —NEWBERRY LIBRARY, 60 W Walton St, Chicago, 60610. Diana Haskell, Cur of Modern Mss
Holdings: Cat Mss

MI —DETROIT PUBLIC LIBRARY, Rare Books Department, 5201 Woodward Ave, Detroit, 48202.
Holdings: Vols 76 Cat
Notes: Restricted use. Reference collection.

NE —UNIVERSITY OF NEBRASKA-LINCOLN, Don L Love Library, University Archives and Special Collections, Lincoln, 68588. Joseph G Svoboda, University Archivist
Notes: Virginia Faulkner was recognized as one of Nebraska's most distinguished writers and scholars. The Virginia Faulkner Collection, containing over 2000 titles, is housed in the Special Collections Department of Love Library. It is especially strong in twentieth century writers and in University of Nebraska Press publications. Of especial value to scholars are her extensive holdings of Willa Cather, Wright Morris, and John Neihardt. Her correspondence with S N Behrman, E B White, Edward Wagenknecht, Donald Sutherland, Wright Morris, Louise Pound, Mari Sandoz, Hazel Barnes, Alfred A and Blanche Knopf, and others provide insight into the literary development of these figures, as well as chronicle the intellectual thought of the period. Amassed in a separate file, these letters are available to interested scholars.

NE —WILLA CATHER HISTORICAL CENTER, Nebraska State Historical Society, Library, 338 N Webster St, Red Cloud, 68970. Ann E Billesbach, Cur
Holdings: Cat Pix VF
Notes: Over 1000 books; 1300 photographs; over 15 linear feet vertical files incl articles, clippings, etc; 150 reels microfiche; 250 pieces of correspondence.

NV —UNIVERSITY OF NEVADA, RENO, University Library, Special Collections Dept, Reno, 89557. Robert E Blesse, Head
Holdings: // Vols (77) Cat Other appearances 200 Cat
Notes: Includes individual works by author in all editions including translations; also prefaces, introductions, published correspondence, appearances in anthologies, periodicals, etc. Bibliographical research collection, part of Modern Authors Collection.

PA —BRYN MAWR COLLEGE, Canaday Library, Bryn Mawr, 19010. James Tanis, Dir
Notes: Rare books and manuscripts.

TX —SOUTHERN METHODIST UNIVERSITY, DeGolyer Library, Box 396, SMU, Dallas, 75275. Clifton H Jones, Dir
Holdings: Vols (80,000) Cat Mss Maps Pix Slides Microforms
Notes: First editions of prominent authors; also of books in subject emphasis collections. All subjects listed in this vol are strong. Numerous collections of personal papers relating to subjects also.

VA —UNIVERSITY OF VIRGINIA, Alderman Library, Clifton Waller Barrett Collection, Charlottesville, 22901. Joan St C Crane, Cur of American Literature Collections
Holdings: Vols 300
Notes: Holograph of fragment of unpublished novel "Hard Punishment".

CATHERWOOD, MARY HARTWELL

IL —NEWBERRY LIBRARY, 60 W Walton St, Chicago, 60610. Diana Haskell, Cur of Modern Mss
Holdings: Vols 152 Cat Mss
Notes: Incl mss, notebooks, scrapbooks. Restricted use: noncirculating.

IN —INDIANA UNIVERSITY, Lilly Library, Seventh St, Bloomington, 47405. William R Cagle, Librn
Holdings: Vols 12 Cat Mss
Notes: Letters of midwestern novelist Mary Catherwood to Mary Elizabeth (Riley) Payne, sister of James Whitcomb Riley. The letters date 1880-1902 and reflect the long friendship of the two women, with occasional reference to Catherwood's writings. 79 items. Library's holdings incl first editions of Catherwood's works.

CATHOLIC CHURCH

CA —AZUSA PACIFIC COLLEGE, Marshburn Memorial Library, Citrus & Alosta, Azusa, 91702. Edward Peterman, Librn
Holdings: Vols 1500 Uncat
Notes: The Monsignor Francis J Weber Collection on American Catholic Church History incl biographies, reference works, theological studies, scholarly journals, monograph series, and the complete works of some Catholic historians. No photocopying.

CA —UNIVERSITY OF CALIFORNIA, BERKELEY, School of Law, Library, Berkeley, 94720. Stephan G Kuttner, Dir, Canon Law Collection
Holdings: Vols (23,000) Cat Mss Microforms
Notes: Entirely supported by the R D and S M Robbins Endowment, the Robbins Canon Law Collection emphasizes particularly Roman Catholic, Eastern and Anglican canon law. Additional subject areas being developed are ecclesiastical history and institutions, historical and contemporary church and state relations, and ecumenical studies. Library is in process of obtaining complete microfilms of all medieval canon and Roman law mss held by the Vatican Library.

CA —LOS ANGELES PUBLIC LIBRARY, Philosophy & Religion Dept, 630 W Fifth St, Los Angeles, 90071. Marilyn C Wherley, Librn
Holdings: Vols 2350 Cat Includes long runs of major periodicals and newspapers, many on microfilm
Budget: ($60,000)
Notes: History, theology, biography, California missions, the church in the Southwest. Includes both popular and scholarly works.

CA —UNIVERSITY OF CALIFORNIA, LOS ANGELES, Research Library, Dept of Special Collections, 405 Hilgard Ave, Los Angeles, 90024. Edward Shreeves, Chairman, Bibliographers Group; David S Zeidberg, Head
Notes: Various single mss and service books. The Orsini family papers, 13th to 20th century, incl material relating to their relationships with the Catholic Church and the Papal Throne.

†CA —UNIVERSITY OF SAN FRANCISCO, Richard A Gleeson Library, The Countess Bernardine Murphy Donohue Rare Book Room, San Francisco, 94117. D Steven Corey, Special Collections Librn
Holdings: Vols (1500)
See also entries under Theology and Great Britain - History

GA —EMORY UNIVERSITY, Candler School of Theology, Pitts Theology Library, Atlanta, 30322. Channing Jeschke, Librn; Anita K Delaries, Curator
Notes: 10 linear feet of ms and printed material (1822-92) documenting the life of Cardinal Henry Edward Manning (1808-92). The most notable items are his sermons, sermon notes and speeches; items on Archdiocese of Westminster. Finding aid available.

IL —JESUIT-KRAUSS-MCCORMICK LIBRARY, 1100 E 55th St, Chicago, 60615. Donald Vorp, Dir; Elvire Hilgert, Librn
Holdings: Vols (375,000) Microforms
Notes: Collection contains merger of Jesuit Library, Lutheran School of Theology of Chicago (Krauss Library), and McCormick Theological Seminary. Jesuit: Sermones Thesaurus Novi de Tempore (anonymous, Strassbourg 1486); Opera Omnia (Jean Gerson, Strassbourg 1488), 3 vols; Summa Rosella Casuum (Venice 1495); moral theology (major figures of 16th and 17th century scholasticism); early modern editions of patristics and canon law regarding procedures and organzation of the Catholic Church, incl treatises and multi-volume commentaries.
See also entries under Religion; Lutheran Church; Presbyterian Church

IN —SAINT MARY-OF-THE-WOODS COLLEGE, College Library, Saint Mary-of-the-Woods, 47876. Sister Emily Walsh, SP, Administrator
Holdings: Vols 2500 Cat
Notes: Catholic Americana. Principally notable books of the last century no longer used today.

MD —LOYOLA/NOTRE DAME LIBRARY, 200 Winston Ave, Baltimore, 21212. Jack Ray, Dir
Holdings: Vols (215,000)

MD —SAINT MARY'S SEMINARY & UNIVERSITY, School of Theology Library, 5400 Roland Ave, Baltimore, 21210. David Siemen, Dir
Holdings: Vols (170,000) Cat Mss Maps Pix Audiotapes Videotapes Microforms

MO —SAINT LOUIS UNIVERSITY, Pius XII Memorial Library, Vatican Film Library Collection, 3655 W Pine Blvd, Saint Louis, 63108. Charles J Ermatinger, Librn
Holdings: Mss Slides Microforms
Notes: Vatican Film Library has 75 percent of the Greek, Latin and western European vernacular holdings in the Vatican Library, plus all the Hebrew, Arabic and Ethiopic holdings on film. Covers 5th-19th centuries. Sizable collection of western European books. In addition, has largest collection on the work of the Jesuits in Latin America, the US and the Philippines, filmed from European Jesuit archives. Excellent catalogs and guides to all collections. Also, 50,608 slides of illuminated mss; 26,470 reels of microfilm.

NE —CREIGHTON UNIVERSITY, Reinert/Alumni Library, California at 24th St, Omaha, 68178. Raymond B Means, Dir
Holdings: Vols (19,175) Cat Mss
Budget: ($14,100)
Notes: In addition to English, Latin and Greek predominate in the collection. Emphasis on Catholic religion, history and saints.

OR —UNIVERSITY OF PORTLAND, Wilson W Clark Memorial Library, 5000 N Willamette Blvd, PO Box 03017, Portland, 97203. Rev Joseph P Browne, CSC, Dir
Holdings: Vols (12,000) Cat
Budget: $6000
Notes: Emphasis on Catholic theology.

TX —UNIVERSITY OF SAINT THOMAS, Saint Mary's Seminary, Cardinal Beran Library, 9845 Memorial Dr, Houston, 77024. Constance Walker, Librn
Holdings: Vols 37,500 Cat Phonorecords Audiotapes Microforms
Budget: $60,000
Notes: Library for the Graduate School of Theology.

TX —OBLATE SCHOOL OF THEOLOGY, Library, 285 Oblate Dr, San Antonio, 78216. James Maney, Libr Dir
Holdings: Vols (22,000) Cat
Budget: ($15,500)

WI —UNIVERSITY OF WISCONSIN, MADISON, Memorial Library, Western European Humanities Collection, 728 State St, Madison, 53706. Charles Szabo, Bibliographer
Notes: Chwalibog Collection. Contemporary editions of the principal European theologians of the 17th and 18th centuries. The bulk of the collection consists of standard sets of Roman Catholic writers such as Bossuet, Fenelon, and Cardinal Fleury. There are also a number of rare and unusual items dealing with other Christian denominations. There is also a good representation of titles by the philosophers of the 18th century enlightenment. Supplements the Tank Collection (Calvinism) and the Montauban Collection (French Protestantism).

WI —SAINT FRANCIS SEMINARY, SCHOOL OF PASTOR MINISTRY, Salzmann Library, 3257 S Lake Dr, Milwaukee, 53207. Lawrence Miech, Librn
Holdings: Vols (42,000) Cat
Budget: ($11,800)

MB —UNIVERSITY OF MANITOBA, Saint Paul's College Library, Winnipeg, R3T 2M6, Can. Rev H J Drake, SJ, Head

ON —TORONTO SCHOOL OF THEOLOGY, Consortium of Libraries, University of Toronto, Toronto, M5S 1A5, Can. R Grane Bracewell, Library Coordr
Holdings: Cat
Notes: A consortium of 7 theological college and faculty libraries at the University of Toronto.

CATHOLIC CHURCH—BYZANTINE RITE

PA —HOLY TRINITY BENEDICTINE BYZANTINE RITE MONESTERY, PO Box 990, Butler, 16002.

PA —SLOVAK EASTERN CATHOLIC SYNOD OF AMERICA, 515 W Main, Monongahela, 15063.
Holdings: 1500 Vols
Notes: Promotes use of the Byzantine Rite among Slovak-Americans. Special interest in St Cyril and St Methodius.

PA —BYZANTINE CATHOLIC SEMINARY LIBRARY, 3605 Perrysville Ave, Pittsburgh, 15214.
Holdings: 12,500 Vols Mss

CATHOLIC CHURCH—EDUCATION

CT —SACRED HEART UNIVERSITY, Library, 5229 Park Ave, PO Box 6460, Bridgeport, 06606. Roch-Josef di Lisio, Actg Dir
Holdings: Vols 1200 Cat
Notes: The John A Rycenga Memorial Collection on American Catholic Higher Education.

OH —KENT STATE UNIVERSITY, University Archives, Kent, 44242. Stephen C Morton, University Archivist
Holdings: Uncat Mss Maps Phonorecords Filmstrips Microforms
Notes: Collection on deposit. Correspondence and other papers, printed materials of the Diocese of Youngstown dealing with the National Newman Foundation and Apostolate, and the National Catholic Welfare Conference. Some material restricted. Records of High Schools of the Diocese are also part of the collection.

CATHOLIC CHURCH—HISTORY

CA —LOS ANGELES PUBLIC LIBRARY, Philosophy & Religion Dept, 630 W Fifth St, Los Angeles, 90071. Marilyn C Wherley, Librn
Holdings: Vols 2350 Cat Includes long runs of major periodicals and newspapers, many on microfilm
Budget: ($60,000)
Notes: History, theology, biography, California missions, the church in the Southwest. Includes both popular and scholarly works.

CA —UNIVERSITY OF CALIFORNIA, LOS ANGELES, Research Library, Dept of Special Collections, 405 Hilgard Ave, Los Angeles, 90024. Edward Shreeves, Chairman, Bibliographers Group; David S Zeidberg, Head
Holdings: Mss
Notes: Various single mss and service books. The Orsini family papers, 13th to 20th century, incl material relating to their relationships with the Catholic Church and the Papal Throne.

CA —UNIVERSITY OF CALIFORNIA, LOS ANGELES, Research Library, Western

CATHOLIC CHURCH—HISTORY (cont.)

European Collection, Los Angeles, 90024. Edward Shreeves, Chairman, Bibliographers Group; Mary E Greco, Western European Bibliographer
Holdings: Mss Maps Pix Microforms
Notes: Good general coverage.

DC —CATHOLIC UNIVERSITY OF AMERICA, Mullen Library, 620 Michigan Ave NE, Washington, 20064. B Gutekunst, Humanities Librn
Holdings: Vols (20,000) Cat

DC —DOMINICAN HOUSE OF STUDIES, Dominican College Library, 487 Michigan Ave NE, Washington, 20017. J Raymond Vandegrift, OP, Librn
Holdings: Vols (5000) Cat
Budget: ($1350)
Notes: The Dominican Order (its history, spirituality, government, liturgy), its members (directories, biographies, bibliographies, lives of saints) and works written by Dominicans: incunabula, rare books, dissertations, periodicals (2300 vols), monographs. Incl periodicals either about the Order or edited by Dominicans. Does not incl titles about the congregations of Dominican Sisters. The Library's catalog contains analytics for Dominican contributors to monographs.

DC —GEORGETOWN UNIVERSITY, Library, Special Collections Div, 37 & O Sts NW, Washington, 20057. George M Barringer, Special Collections Librn; Nicholas B Sheetz, Mss Librn
Holdings: Mss Pix
Notes: The papers of Rev Edward Devitt, SJ (1841-1920) who, during his years in the Society, taught at Gonzaga College, Woodstock College, Holy Cross and Georgetown. He was also, at one time, rector of Boston College and editor of the *Woodstock Letters*. Fr Devitt also gained wide recognition as an historian of early Catholic history in the United States. The papers incl a series of diaries (1865-1920), a commonplace book of verse and sundry documents, in addition to numerous notes, mss and published material. Also incl in the papers is the last revision of Rev Thomas Hughes's, SJ *History of the Society of Jesus in North America* with related correspondence and miscellaneous photographs.

DC —GEORGETOWN UNIVERSITY, Woodstock Theological Center Library, Box 37445, Washington, 20013. Thomas a Marshall, SJ, Librn
Holdings: Vols (165,000)
Notes: Works by Jesuit authors, from the 16th century on.

DC —LIBRARY OF CONGRESS, Law Library, 101 Independence Ave, SE, Washington, 20540. Carleton W Kenyon, Dir
Notes: The Canon Law Collection contains mss, early printed sources, contemporary works, and periodicals pertaining mostly to the canon law of the Roman Catholic church.

GA —EMORY UNIVERSITY, Candler School of Theology, Pitts Theology Library, Atlanta, 30322. Channing Jeschke, Librn; Anita K Delaries, Curator
Notes: 10 linear feet of ms and printed material (1822-92) documenting the life of Cardinal Henry Edward Manning (1808-92). The most notable items are his sermons, sermon notes and speeches; items on Archdiocese of Westminster. Finding aid available.

IN —INDIANA UNIVERSITY, Lilly Library, Seventh St, Bloomington, 47405. William R Cagle, Librn
Holdings: Vols (40,000) Cat Mss Maps
Notes: Research and rare book collection (Bernardo Mendel) of first or only editions, mostly printed in Latin America, from the discovery of the New World through 1830. Special strength in discoveries and exploration, history (mainly period of independence), Inquisition, missionary works by the Augustinians, Dominicans, Franciscans, and the Jesuits, and the history of the Catholic Church in these countries. Major geographic concentration is on the three great viceroyalties of Mexico (ca 10, 000 titles, plus over 10,000 official Mexican broadsides), Peru (2000 titles), and Argentina (4000 titles), incl in Argentina a substantial amount of printings from the Imprenta de Ninos Expositos, and the Coleccion Santamarina. A special Bolivian Collection (2500 titles), mostly history, from the establishment of the press there, ca 1826, through the beginning of the 20th century. Part of the Mendel Collection is the select Bibliotheca Boxeriana from Charles R Boxer (1000 titles) on European expansion into Asia, and into the New World, mainly Brazil, during the 16th-18th centuries. The collection is supplemented by substantial material from the private collection of Josiah K Lilly.
See also entries under Spain - History, Portugal - History, and Mexico - History

MD —MOUNT SAINT MARY'S COLLEGE, Hugh J Phillips Library, Emmitsburg, 21727. Stephen Rockwood, Librn
Holdings: Vols (140,000) Cat Mss Maps Pix
Notes: Early Catholic Americana, especially for western Maryland.

MO —SAINT LOUIS UNIVERSITY, Pius XII Memorial Library, 3655 W Pine Blvd, Saint Louis, 63108. William Cole, Dir
Holdings: Slides Microforms
Notes: Collection covers all areas of learning and European history from Classical Antiquity to early modern period. Researchers using collection receive assistance in paleography, bibliography and reference search. Approx 10,000 1000-foot reels of microfilm (not counting master negatives) reproducing Vatican Library's Latin, Greek, Hebrew, Arabic and Ethiopic mss. Some 8000 100-foot reels of microfilm (again not counting master negative) reproducing rare and out of print books relating to subject areas in the mss. Over 50, 000 color slides of medieval and Renaissance mss illuminations. A reference collection of modern materials relating to ms research.

NM —NEW MEXICO HIGHLANDS UNIVERSITY, Donnelly Library, National Ave, Las Vegas, 87701. Karen Jaggers, Assoc Librn
Holdings: Vols (5000) Cat Mss Maps Pix Microforms
Notes: The outstanding collection is the Arrott Collection on Fort Union, New Mexico, 1851-1891. Other collections incl Spanish Archives, Mexican Archives, Archdiocese of Santa Fe, Archivo del Parral; New Mexico Land Grants.

NY —GENERAL THEOLOGICAL SEMINARY, Saint Marks Library, 175 Ninth Ave, New York, 10011. David Green, Dir
Holdings: Vols (200,000) Cat Mss Maps Pix Slides Microforms
Notes: Extensive collection.

NC —BELMONT ABBEY COLLEGE, Abbot Vincent Taylor Library, Belmont, 28012. Marjorie McDermott, Dir
Holdings: Vols (10,000) Cat Mss Pix
Notes: Patristics (incl Migne's *Patrologie*), Roman Catholic Church history, philosophy, literature (American and British), and both US and North Carolina history. A substantial number of the books date from the 15th, 16th, and 17th centuries. Most of the source material in Catholic studies particularly could not be obtained elsewhere in the Southeast.

PA —SAINT JOSEPH'S UNIVERSITY, Drexel Library, 5600 City Ave, Philadelphia, 19131. Josephine Savaro, Dir of Library
Notes: The collection of Martin I J Griffin (1842-1911), leading figure in Catholic historiography, and founder of the American Catholic Historical Society of Philadelphia. Correspondence, scrapbooks, and pamphlets.

TX —ABILENE CHRISTIAN UNIVERSITY, Margaret & Herman Brown Library, ACU Sta, Abilene, 79601. Callie Faye Milliken, Assoc Dir
Holdings: Vols 3000// Cat
Notes: Lambert Collection on Catholicism and Mormonism.

WI —SAINT FRANCIS SEMINARY, SCHOOL OF PASTOR MINISTRY, Salzmann Library, 3257 S Lake Dr, Milwaukee, 53207. Lawrence Miech, Librn
Holdings: Vols (65,000) Cat
Budget: ($27,000)

CATHOLIC CHURCH—HISTORY—MIDDLE AGES see Church History—Middle Ages

CATHOLIC CHURCH—MISSIONS

CA —LOS ANGELES PUBLIC LIBRARY, Philosophy & Religion Dept, 630 W Fifth St, Los Angeles, 90071. Marilyn C Wherley, Librn
Holdings: Vols 2350 Cat Includes long runs of major periodicals and newspapers, many on microfilm
Budget: ($60,000)
Notes: History, theology, biography, California missions, the church in the Southwest. Includes both popular and scholarly works.

DC —GEORGETOWN UNIVERSITY, Library, Special Collections Div, 37 & O Sts NW, Washington, 20057. George M Barringer, Special Collections Librn; Nicholas B Sheetz, Mss Librn

†WA —WASHINGTON STATE UNIVERSITY, Library, Manuscripts, Archives & Special Collections, Pullman, 99164. John F Guido, Head
Holdings: // Mss Maps Pix
Notes: Papers, 1821-1873, covering Father De Smet's early sojourns at Whitemarsh and St Louis, his founding of the Rocky Mountain Missions, his long service as Procurator and Socius of the Missouri Province, and his many travels. Correspondence with his family in Belgium, mss of his published journals, 2 small maps, sketches and engravings used to illustrate his books. Incl about 100 small pencil sketches by Father Nicholas Point depicting the 1841 journey from Westport to Saint Mary's Mission in the Bitterroot Valley. Described in *The Record*, 30 (1969) 6-40; and 32 (1971) 47-63.

CATHOLIC CHURCH, BYZANTINE RITE see Catholic Church—Byzantine Rite

CATHOLIC CHURCH EXTENSION SOCIETY

IL —LOYOLA UNIVERSITY OF CHICAGO, E M Cudahy Memorial Library, 6525 N Sheridan Rd, Chicago, 60626.
Holdings: Mss
Notes: Correspondence and other papers of the Catholic Church Extension Society covering the years 1905-1962. The Society was established in 1905 and has played an important role in domestic missionary work, particularly in the subsidization of church construction and Newman Center projects. To be used under the direct supervision of the archivist at all times. Incl 10,000 photos.

CATHOLIC CHURCH IN CANADA

PA —BALCH INSTITUTE FOR ETHNIC STUDIES, Library, 18 S Seventh St, Philadelphia, 19106. R Joseph Anderson, Library Dir

†RI —UNION SAINT-JEAN-BAPTISTE, Bibliotheque Mallet, Woonsocket, 02895.
Notes: Emphasis on genealogy, French parish histories; theses and dissertations on French Canadian topics.

MB —UNIVERSITY OF MANITOBA, Saint Paul's College Library, Winnipeg, R3T 2M6, Can. Rev H J Drake, SJ, Head

ON —TORONTO SCHOOL OF THEOLOGY, Consortium of Libraries, University of Toronto, Toronto, M5S 1A5, Can. R Grane Bracewell, Library Coordr
Holdings: Cat
Notes: A consortium of 7 theological college and faculty libraries at the University of Toronto.

CATHOLIC CHURCH IN GREAT BRITAIN

DC —GEORGETOWN UNIVERSITY, Library, Special Collections Div, 37 & O Sts

CATHOLIC CHURCH IN GREAT BRITAIN (cont.)

NW, Washington, 20057. George M Barringer, Special Collections Librn; Nicholas B Sheetz, Mss Librn
Holdings: Mss Cat
Notes: A portion of the papers of Bishop William Bernard Ullathorne (1806-1889), incl correspondence to and from other English prelates such as Nicholas Cardinal Wiseman (1802-1865) and Henry Ededward Cardinal Manning (1808-1892).

MA —BOSTON COLLEGE LIBRARIES, Chestnut Hill, 02167.
Holdings: Vols 10,345 Mss Maps Pix
Notes: The library and personal papers of Hilaire Belloc (1870-1953), whose writings on a wide range of subjects: history, travel, politics, economics, religion, social conditions and in a variety of literary forms: biography, fiction, essays, poetry, children's literature reflect both an uncommon versatility and a prophetic vision. For reference use only, by arrangement with librarian. Also 151 literary mss, over 8000 letters, notebooks, sketches, music.

MO —SAINT LOUIS UNIVERSITY, Pius XII Memorial Library, 3655 W Pine Blvd, Saint Louis, 63108. William Cole, Dir
Holdings: Vols Mss Pamphlets //
Notes: Fundamental source material for the study of every aspect of Catholic religious, political, and social thought during nearly five hundred years of English, Scottish, and Irish history (early sixteenth century to modern times). Approx 2220 vols do not appear in card catalog and researchers must write ahead to make arrangements, since these vols are not readily available for public use. Incl (5000) mss. Partially cataloged.

CATHOLIC CHURCH IN MEXICO

TX —UNIVERSITY OF TEXAS LIBRARIES, Nettie Lee Benson Latin American Collection, Sid Richardson Hall 1.109, Austin, 78712. Laura Gutierrez-Witt, Head Librn
Holdings: Vols (450,000) Cat Mss Maps Pix Phonorecords Filmstrips Microforms
See also entry under Latin America

CATHOLIC CHURCH IN THE AMERICAS

DC —GEORGETOWN UNIVERSITY, Library, Special Collections Div, 37 & O Sts NW, Washington, 20057. George M Barringer, Special Collections Librn; Nicholas B Sheetz, Mss Librn

TX —AMARILLO PUBLIC LIBRARY, 413 E Fourth, Amarillo, 79101. Mary Kay Snell, Librn
Holdings: Vols Cat Mss Maps Pix
Notes: The southwest collections incl materials on the history of Texas, Louisiana, New Mexico, Arkansas, Missouri and Kansas. General subjects covered incl overland journeys, early narratives, early biographies, Indian captivities, outlaws, US government reports, Mississippi and Ohio Rivers, the Mexican War, reports of Catholic missionaries, Niles Register, early publications, fur trade, western trails, Texas Rangers, sheriffs and Texas as a sovereign state, buffalo hunting, Indian wars, cowboys, the arrival of farmers, fences, and towns. Over 1600 items which incl books, documents, maps, mss, pamphlets, unpublished theses, interviews and photographs. The three major collections are the William Henry Bush Collection, the Laurence J Fitzsimon Collection and the Calendar of John L McCarty.

TX —UNIVERSITY OF TEXAS LIBRARIES, Nettie Lee Benson Latin American Collection, Sid Richardson Hall 1.109, Austin, 78712. Laura Gutierrez-Witt, Head Librn
Holdings: Vols (450,000) Cat Mss Maps Pix Phonorecords Filmstrips Microforms
See also entry under Latin America

CATHOLIC CHURCH IN THE U.S.

AZ —NORTHERN ARIZONA UNIVERSITY, Special Collection Library, CU Box 6022, Flagstaff, 86011. Peter M Whiteley, Coordr/Archivist; William Mullane, Librn
Notes: Mary Sweitzer Collection; typed ms of the history of the Catholic Church in Flagstaff, Ariz, probably written ca 1955.

CA —AZUSA PACIFIC COLLEGE, Marshburn Memorial Library, Citrus & Alosta, Azusa, 91702. Edward Peterman, Librn
Holdings: Vols 1500 Uncat
Notes: The Monsignor Francis J Weber Collection on American Catholic Church History incl biographies, reference works, theological studies, scholarly journals, monograph series, and the complete works of some Catholic historians. No photocopying.

DC —GEORGETOWN UNIVERSITY, Library, Special Collections Div, 37 & O Sts NW, Washington, 20057. George M Barringer, Special Collections Librn; Nicholas B Sheetz, Mss Librn

DC —GEORGETOWN UNIVERSITY, Woodstock Theological Center Library, Box 37445, Washington, 20013. Thomas a Marshall, SJ, Librn
Holdings: Vols (165,000)
Notes: Works by Jesuit authors, from the 16th century on.

MA —BOSTON COLLEGE LIBRARIES, Chestnut Hill, 02167.
Holdings: Vols Pix
Notes: 1900-1950: The library and personal papers of David Goldstein, 1870-1958, street preacher, former Socialist. Incl posters, clippngs, articles, debates and speeches, chiefly on Communism, Socialism, the American labor movement, and Catholic social thought in the US, 1900-1950. For reference use only, by arrangement with the librarian. 52 vols, 37 linear ft correspondence, scrapbooks, pictures //. 1925-1975: Over 8000 items. Books, periodicals, pamphlets, religious articles and related materials on the whole spectrum of American Catholic life in an era of profound change, with particular reference to public and private devotions, language usage, religious life, parish structure, education, role of the laity, etc, before and after the Second Vatican Council. For reference use only, by appointment.

MO —SAINT LOUIS UNIVERSITY, Pius XII Memorial Library, 3655 W Pine Blvd, Saint Louis, 63108. William Cole, Dir
Holdings: Vols (1503) Microfiche Uncat //
Notes: Pamphlets drawn from all periods of United States history, with concentration between the years 1820-1970. There is a printed bibliographic guide to the collection.

PA —BALCH INSTITUTE FOR ETHNIC STUDIES, Library, 18 S Seventh St, Philadelphia, 19106. R Joseph Anderson, Library Dir
Holdings: Vols 200 Cat

CATHOLIC CHURCH IN THE U.S. —HISTORY

DC —GEORGETOWN UNIVERSITY, Library, Special Collections Div, 37 & O Sts NW, Washington, 20057. George M Barringer, Special Collections Librn; Nicholas B Sheetz, Mss Librn
Holdings: Cat
Notes: Papers of John Gilmary Shea (1824-1892), noted Catholic historian and linguist of Indian languages who published over two hundred titles during his lifetime. The papers incl correspondence to Shea, manuscripts and notes reflecting his research, collected documents and manuscripts, and various photographs. Correspondence written to Shea incl letters from George Bancroft, Francis Parkman, Jared Sparks, Harriet Beecher Stowe, E B O'Callahan, Hanry Schoolcraft, Charles White, D D, Charles Currier, P T Barnum, Frederick Douglass, Thomas A Edison, Oliver Wendell Holmes, as well as noted members of the Church hierarchy. A long span of correspondence from Shea to the historian, Edmund Mallet contains many insights into Shea's life and work. Photographs incl likenesses of Elizabeth Seton, Isaac Hecker and George Bancroft. Also incl in the papers are numerous documents andmss concerning Shea's work in the field of Native American history, language, and culture.

DC —GEORGETOWN UNIVERSITY, Library, Special Collections Div, 37 & O Sts NW, Washington, 20057. George M Barringer, Special Collections Librn; Nicholas B Sheetz, Mss Librn
Holdings: Mss Cat
Notes: Correspondence, mss, reviews, and clippings, comprising the papers of J. Herman Schauinger, historian of early United States Catholic history. Incl is Xeroxed and transcribed research material on Fr Stephen Badin, Bishop Benoit J Flaget, Bishop Jean B M David, Orestes Brownson, and William Gaston.

KS —SAINT MARY COLLEGE, Library, Leavenworth, 66048. Therese Deplazes, Special Collections Librn
Holdings: Cat Mss Pix
Notes: Catholic Church in Vicariate Apostolic established July 19, 1850, became the Diocese of Leavenworth, May 22, 1877, became the Archdiocese of Kansas City, Kansas 1955-date.

NC —BELMONT ABBEY COLLEGE, Abbot Vincent Taylor Library, Belmont, 28012. Marjorie McDermott, Dir
Holdings: Vols (1000) Cat
Notes: Consists of books dealing with the history of North and South Carolina from colonial times to the present. Incl are several county histories, some early newspapers, and a strong section on the history of religion (especially the Roman Catholic Church) in the two states.

OH —KENT STATE UNIVERSITY, University Archives, Kent, 44242. Stephen C Morton, University Archivist
Holdings: Uncat Mss Maps Pix Phonorecords Filmstrips Microforms
Notes: Diocese of Youngstown Chancery Office and Parish Files. Collection on deposit. Some materials are restricted. Contains materials on the second Vatican Council and Council Review Days, Cathedral records and plans, parochial school photography collection, Canon Law collection. The parish records are especially valuable for researching births, marriages, and deaths. A large amount of ethnic material is also found in the files.

PA —SAINT JOSEPH'S UNIVERSITY, Drexel Library, 5600 City Ave, Philadelphia, 19131. Josephine Savaro, Dir of Library
Notes: The collection of Martin I J Griffin (1842-1911), leading figure in Catholic historiography, and founder of the American Catholic Historical Society of Philadelphia. Correspondence, scrapbooks, and pamphlets.

PA —KING'S COLLEGE, D Leonard Corgan Library, 14 W Jackson St, Wilkes-Barre, 18711. Judith Tierney, Special Collections Librn
Notes: Collection focuses on the histories of the various parishes in the Roman Catholic Diocese of Scranton, Pennsylvania and other churches in northeastern Pennsylvania. Collection indexed by name, location, denomination, and ethnic group. 9 linear ft.

VT —SAINT MICHAEL'S COLLEGE, Durick Library, Winooski, 05404. Joseph Popecki, Dir; Henry Nadeau, Head of Archives & Special Collections
Holdings: Vols (5000) Cat
Notes: French Canadian genealogy, Irish genealogy, art, a complete set of Jesuit Relations and allied documents with a deluxe binding.

CATHOLIC CLUB

NY —AMERICAN IRISH HISTORICAL SOCIETY, Library, 991 Fifth Ave, New York, 10028. Lisa M Hottin, Cur; William D Griffin, Librn
Holdings: Vols (20,000) Cat Maps Pix Slides
Notes: Archives and Manuscripts: The documents and papers of Friends of Irish Freedom, The Land League, the Society of the Friendly Sons of St Patrick, the Catholic Club, and the Guild of Catholic Lawyers. The papers of New York State Supreme

CATHOLIC CLUB (cont.)

Court Justice Daniel F Cohalan. This is the largest and most complete collection of over 20,000 American Irish and Irish history, biography and literature in the United States. Incl American-Irish Newspaper collections dating from 1811, the most comprehensive in the US; 1000 rare books and special editions. Special collections incl regular exhibits of Irish or American Irish interest incl mss, letters, books, photographs and memorabilia. Permanent collection of representative works of Irish painters.

CATHOLIC COMMITTEE OF THE SOUTH

LA —AMISTAD RESEARCH CENTER, 400 Esplanade Ave, New Orleans, 70116. Clifton H Johnson, Exec Dir; Florence E Borders, Senior Archivist
Holdings: Vols (10,000) Cat Mss Pix Audiotapes Microforms
Budget: ($315,000)
Notes: In addition, 8,000,000 ms pieces, 10, 000 pictures, 3500 microforms, and 500 audiotapes. Amistad Research Center is an historical research library devoted to the collection and use of primary source materials on the history of America's ethnic minorities, with particular emphasis on Afro-Americans, American Indians, and immigrant groups. Among the larger institutional collections held are the archives and records of the American Missionary Association, the American Home Missionary Society, the Race Relations Dept of the Anti-Defamation League, the Catholic Committee of the South, and the National Association of Human Rights Workers, (formerly NAIRO, National Association of Intergroup Related Officials). Also, private papers of the Harlem Renaissance poet, Countee Cullen; educator and civil rights leader, Mary McLeod Bethune;20th century civil rights lawyer, Alexander P Tureaud; 19th century Black attorney and judge, George Ruffin; founder and director of Operation Crossroads Africa, Dr James H Robinson; and over 70 others.

CATHOLIC IMPRINTS

DC —GEORGETOWN UNIVERSITY, Library, Special Collections Div, 37 & O Sts NW, Washington, 20057. George M Barringer, Special Collections Librn; Nicholas B Sheetz, Mss Librn
Holdings: Vols 1000 Cat
Notes: Incl American Catholic imprints to 1831.

IL —JESUIT-KRAUSS-MCCORMICK LIBRARY, 1100 E 55th St, Chicago, 60615. Donald Vorp, Dir; Elvire Hilgert, Librn
Notes: Collection contains merger of Jesuit Library, Lutheran School of Theology of Chicago (Krauss Library), and McCormick Theological Seminary. Jesuit: Sermones Thesaurus Novi de Tempore (anonymous, Strassbourg 1486); Opera Omnia (Jean Gerson, Strassbourg 1488), 3 vols; Summa Rosella Casuum (Venice 1495); moral theology (major figures of 16th and 17th century scholasticism); early modern editions of patristics and canon law regarding procedures and organzation of the Catholic Church, incl treatises and multi-volume commentaries.
See also entries under Religion; Lutheran Church; Presbyterian Church

CATHOLIC LITERATURE

DC —GEORGETOWN UNIVERSITY, Library, Special Collections Div, 37 & O Sts NW, Washington, 20057. George M Barringer, Special Collections Librn; Nicholas B Sheetz, Mss Librn
Holdings: Mss
Notes: The Archives of the Gallery of Living Catholic Authors was founded in 1932 by Sister Mary Joseph of the Sisters of Loretto to focus attention on modern Catholic literature, and to provide a depository for manuscripts, letters, photographs, and books by contemporary Catholic writers. Contains material by hundreds of writers, incl Hilaire Belloc, Roy Campbell, Padraic Colum, Eric Gill, Paul Horgan, Mary Lavin, Marie Belloc Lowndes, Kathleen Norris, Alred Noyes, Sheila Kaye-Smith, Sigrid Undset, and Evelyn Waugh, to name only a few.

IL —JESUIT-KRAUSS-MCCORMICK LIBRARY, 1100 E 55th St, Chicago, 60615. Donald Vorp, Dir; Elvire Hilgert, Librn
Notes: Collection contains merger of Jesuit Library, Lutheran School of Theology of Chicago (Krauss Library), and McCormick Theological Seminary. Jesuit: Sermones Thesaurus Novi de Tempore (anonymous, Strassbourg 1486); Opera Omnia (Jean Gerson, Strassbourg 1488), 3 vols; Summa Rosella Casuum (Venice 1495); moral theology (major figures of 16th and 17th century scholasticism); early modern editions of patristics and canon law regarding procedures and organzation of the Catholic Church, incl treatises and multi-volume commentaries.
See also entries under Religion; Lutheran Church; Presbyterian Church

MA —BOSTON COLLEGE LIBRARIES, Thomas P O'Neill Library, Chestnut Hill, 02167. Frank J Seegraber, Special Collections Librn
Holdings: Vols 1300 Cat Mss Pix Phonorecords Audiotapes Microforms
Notes: This, the most complete collection of Thompsoniana in existence, incl notebooks, mss, letters, and rare editions, and collateral material relating to poet, his times and his work. The notebooks are the chief source of clues to the identification of 300 of Thompson's unsigned contributions to periodicals. *An Account of the Books and Manuscripts of Francis Thompson,* ed by Rev Terence L Connolly (Boston College, 1937). Works of Wilfrid and Alice Meynell and their children, Viola, Sir Francis, and Everard, are incl in this collection. The items give a well-rounded view of this remarkable family as poets, fiction writers, essayists, biographers, prefacers, and editors. This collection incl mss, poems, correspondence, articles, and book reviews by Coventry Patmore, an English poet, essayist, and critic, and a good friend of Francis Thompson. Among thecorrespondents are Robert Browning, Alfred Tennyson, Matthew Arnold, Ralph Waldo Emerson, Nathaniel Hawthorne, Thomas Carlyle, and William Makepeace Thackeray. For reference use only, by arrangement with librarian.

CATHOLIC MOVEMENT (ANGLICAN COMMUNION) see Anglo-Catholicism

CATHOLIC NEWSPAPERS see Newspapers, Catholic

CATHOLIC PERFECTION see Perfection (Catholic)

CATHOLIC SPIRITUAL LIFE see Spiritual Life—Catholic Authors

CATHOLICS IN ENGLAND

DC —GEORGETOWN UNIVERSITY, Library, Special Collections Div, 37 & O Sts NW, Washington, 20057. George M Barringer, Special Collections Librn; Nicholas B Sheetz, Mss Librn
Holdings: Cat Mss
Notes: The papers of the English author, journalist, and historian Douglas Woodruff (1897-1978), containing correspondence, mss, and photographs. Incl is considerable material concerning his years at Oxford University; his editorship for many years of The "Tablet"; English Catholic society in general and English Catholic literature in particular. Also present are research files on the Tichborne Claimant, one of the most famous cases of impersonation in English legal history. There is extensive correspondence from such figures as: Hilaire Belloc; Tom Burns; Rev Martin D'Arcy, SJ; Christopher Dawson; Sir Roy Harrod; Christopher Hollis; Msgr Ronald Knox; Sir Shane Leslie; Sir Arnold Lunn; Rebecca West; and Evelyn Waugh.

DC —GEORGETOWN UNIVERSITY, Library, Special Collections Div, 37 & O Sts NW, Washington, 20057. George M Barringer, Special Collections Librn; Nicholas B Sheetz, Mss Librn
Holdings: Mss Cat
Notes: The papers of the journalist and author, Count Michael de la Bedoyere, who edited for many years the English periodical, "The Catholic Herald." Contains for the most part correspondence from contributors and readers.

GA —EMORY UNIVERSITY, Candler School of Theology, Pitts Theology Library, Atlanta, 30322. Channing Jeschke, Librn; Anita K Delaries, Curator
Notes: 10 linear feet of ms and printed material (1822-92) documenting the life of Cardinal Henry Edward Manning (1808-92). The most notable items are his sermons, sermon notes and speeches; items on Archdiocese of Westminster. Finding aid available.

IL —NEWBERRY LIBRARY, 60 W Walton St, Chicago, 60610. Diana Haskell, Cur of Modern Mss
Holdings: Vols 10,000 Cat
Notes: History and literature of Catholics in England. Incl 500 ms pieces.

MO —SAINT LOUIS UNIVERSITY, Pius XII Memorial Library, 3655 W Pine Blvd, Saint Louis, 63108. William Cole, Dir
Holdings: Vols Mss Pamphlets / /
Notes: Fundamental source material for the study of every aspect of Catholic religious, political, and social thought during nearly five hundred years of English, Scottish, and Irish history (early sixteenth century to modern times). Approx 2220 vols do not appear in card catalog and researchers must write ahead to make arrangements, since these vols are not readily available for public use. Incl (5000) mss. Partially cataloged.

CATHOLICS IN THE U.S.

DC —GEORGETOWN UNIVERSITY, Library, Special Collections Div, 37 & O Sts NW, Washington, 20057. George M Barringer, Special Collections Librn; Nicholas B Sheetz, Mss Librn
Notes: Historical archives of the Maryland Province. Incl the letters of Abp John Carroll and Fr John McElroy.

OH —GREENE COUNTY DISTRICT LIBRARY, 76 E Market St, PO Box 520, Xenia, 45385. Julie M Overton, Local History Coordr
Notes: Collection of papers of Raymond Higgins, editor emeritus of the Xenia Daily Gazette, and historian for the Xenia area until the mid-1970's. Correspondence includes letters written in response to his historical column and are unusually good depictions of Xenia's Catholic population in the 1920's and 1930's.

PA —SAINT JOSEPH'S UNIVERSITY, Drexel Library, 5600 City Ave, Philadelphia, 19131. Josephine Savaro, Dir of Library
Notes: The collection of Martin I J Griffin (1842-1911), leading figure in Catholic historiography, and founder of the American Catholic Historical Society of Philadelphia. Correspondence, scrapbooks, and pamphlets.

CATLEDGE, TURNER

MS —MISSISSIPPI STATE UNIVERSITY, Mitchell Memorial Library, Box 5408, Mississippi State, 39762. Frances N Coleman, Head, Special Collections
Holdings: Mss
Notes: Papers of Turner Catledge, editor of *The New York Times.*

CATLIN, GEORGE EDWARD GORDON, 1896-

UT —UNIVERSITY OF UTAH, Marriott Library, Special Collections, Salt Lake City, 84112. Gregory C Thompson, Cur
Notes: A majority of the books listed in H R

CATLIN, GEORGE EDWARD GORDON, 1896- (cont.)

Wagner's *The Plains and Rockies* are found in Rare Books as are the works of George Catlin, Karl Bodmer, Edward Curtis, and McKenny and Hall. Some of these are so rare that they must be used under restricted conditions.

ON —MCMASTER UNIVERSITY, Mills Memorial Library, Div of Archives & Research Collections, Hamilton, L8S 4L6, Can. G R Hill, Univ Librn
Holdings: / / Mss
Notes: Correspondence, mss and typescripts of some published books and all unpublished work; mss and typescripts of articles, speeches, diaries, journals, and family papers.

CATS AND CATLORE

CA —GLENDALE PUBLIC LIBRARY, 222 E Harvard St, Glendale, 91205. Barbara Boyd, Special Collections Librn
Holdings: Cat Mss Pix
Budget: ($8,000)
Notes: Large collection of books, pamphlets, mss, histories, pictures, and studbooks concerning cats.

CA —POMONA PUBLIC LIBRARY, Laura Ingalls Wilder Room, 625 S Garey, PO Box 2271, Pomona, 91766. Kerry Stafford, Children's Librn
Holdings: Cat
Notes: Mostly 20th century dolls dressed in national costumes; some antique dolls; also doll house furniture; cat and angel doll collections. 663 dolls.

CT —LEE ASH, (personal collection), 66 Humiston Dr, Bethany, 06525.

CT —YALE UNIVERSITY, Box 1603A, Yale Station, New Haven, 06520.
Holdings: Pix

NM —THOMAS BRANIGAN MEMORIAL LIBRARY, 200 E Picacho Ave, Las Cruces, 88001. Don Dresp, Dir
Notes: Eunice Mannen Collection (cat).

CATSKILL MOUNTAINS

NY —GREENE COUNTY HISTORICAL SOCIETY, Vedder Memorial Library, RD, Coxsackie, 12051. Raymond Beecher, Librn
Holdings: Vols (3500) Cat Mss Maps Pix Slides
Budget: ($500)
Notes: Collection strong in Greene County, the mid-Hudson region and the Catskill Mountains. County newspapers, pictorial county file, very large mss collection for region, incl Greene County mss, 1800-1900.

CATT, CARRIE CHAPMAN

DC —LIBRARY OF CONGRESS, Rare Book & Special Collections Div, Washington, 20540. William Matheson, Chief
Notes: See description of collection under: Women--Suffrage.

DC —LIBRARY OF CONGRESS, Manuscript Division, Washington, 20540. John C Broderick, Chief
Notes: The papers of Carrie Chapman Catt date chiefly from 1890-1920 and pertain to her efforts to secure voting rights for women. Material from after 1920 relates to her world peace movement activities.

CATTLE—HERD REGISTERS

IA —IOWA STATE UNIVERSITY, Library, Ames, 50011. Warren B Kuhn, Dean of Library Services
Holdings: Cat
Notes: Substantial serial holdings.

CATTLE—MARKETING see Cattle Trade

CATTLE COUNTRY

MT —MONTANA HISTORICAL SOCIETY LIBRARY, 225 N Roberts St, Helena, 59601. Robert M Clark, Librn; Brian Cockhill, State Archivist
Holdings: Vols 3000 Cat
Budget: ($2500)
Notes: The Ames and Margaret Booth Teakel Range Life Memorial Collection (cowboy and cattle range subjects). The scope of this collection includes the entire West, not just Montana and contiguous states. Also, L A Huffman Collection; incl 1100 photographs.

ND —THEODORE ROOSEVELT NATIONAL PARK, Library, PO Box 7, Medora, 58645. Susan Snow, Librn; Miki Hellickson, Chief Naturalist
Holdings: Vols (1500) Cat Mss Maps Pix Slides Audiotapes 16mm Films
Budget: ($5000)
Notes: Theodore Roosevelt, cattle country history, natural history. Also 2400 pictures and 2200 slides.

OK —NATIONAL COWBOY HALL OF FAME AND WESTERN HERITAGE, Library, 1700 NE 63 St, Oklahoma City, 73111. Esther Long, Librn
Holdings: Vols (8000) Uncat
Notes: Art of the American West. Covers western art and artists; rodeo and its history; cowboys; the cattle industry; and biographies on prominent westerners. Personal collection of Walter Brennen; collections of artists, Carl Link and James Earl Frazier.

TX —HARDIN-SIMMONS UNIVERSITY, Richardson Library, Abilene, 79601. Joe F Dahlstrom, Dir
Holdings: Vols (10,000) Cat Mss Maps Pix Microforms
Notes: Special collection name is Richardson Research Center, named in honor of Dr Rupert N Richardson. Collect in the areas of his own research interests, especially that portion of the US that was once a part of Mexico. Emphases on the history of ranching, railroads, discovery and exploration, Texas county histories, etc. Incl 350 items printed and/or designed by El Paso printer Carl Hertzog; the Judge R C Crane collection of Texana and a similar collection of Louise Kelley's; and the Research Publication's Western Americana collection (microfilm).

TX —TEXAS A&M UNIVERSITY, Sterling C Evans Library, Special Collections Div, College Station, 77843. Donald H Dyal, Librn
Holdings: Vols 9000
Notes: The Jeff Dykes (and other) Range Livestock Industry Collection.

TX —TEXAS TECH UNIVERSITY, Library, Lubbock, 79409. David J Murrah, Assoc Dir for Special Collections

CATTLE MARKETS see Stockyards

CATTLE RANGES see Stock Ranges

CATTLE TRADE

AZ —NORTHERN ARIZONA UNIVERSITY, Special Collection Library, CU Box 6022, Flagstaff, 86011. Peter M Whiteley, Coordr/Archivist; William Mullane, Librn
Notes: Various collections, incl (1) Arizona Cattle Feeders Association; correspondence (some from Carl Hayden, US Senator from Arizona) concerning grain sorghum reserves in Arizona, 1965. (2) M O Dumas Collection; photocopied typescript of "My First Roundup" (1896), by M O Dumas. Incl names of man on roundup and cattle brands represented, 1960. Also incl some historical information, ie, short summary of Martha Summerhayes' book *Vanished Arizona,* about her trip to Arizona in 1874. (3) Giglas Collection; correspondence, financial records, minutes, 1920's-1950's of the Horseshoe Land and Livestock Company and Hennessey Sheep Company, Flagstaff, Ariz (7 linear feet). (4) Livestock Inspector of Flagstaff, Ariz, Collection; monthly report of the Livestock Inspector, 1893-1895. (5) Arizona Cattle Growers Association Collection; Miscellaneousscattered financial records, 1927-1934, and meeting programs, 1939, 1963, 1976, 1977. Incl unpublished paper, "Arizona Cattle Growers: The Pre-Corporate Years, 1903-1923."

AZ —ARIZONA STATE UNIVERSITY, Library, Arizona Collection, Tempe, 85281. Edward C Oetting, Head
Holdings: Cat Mss
Notes: Papers of 50 individuals associated with Arizona politics, business, mines, and cattle ranching.

AZ —ARIZONA HERITAGE CENTER, Library, 949 E Second St, Tucson, 85719. Michael Weber, Dir
Notes: Espec with reference to Arizona, the West, and the Southwest.

CO —COLORADO HISTORICAL SOCIETY, Research Collections, 1300 Broadway, Denver, 80203. Catherine Kane, Head Public Service and Access
Holdings: Cat Mss Pix Microforms
Budget:
Notes: Correspondence and business records of cattle companies and cattlemen and railroads gathered as part of the Western Range Cattle Industry Study. Also, correspondence and records of companies, organizations and related materials arranged by state (1850-1945). About 50,000 items.

KS —FORT HAYS KANSAS STATE UNIVERSITY, Forsyth Library, Western Collection, 600 Park St, Hays, 67601. Esta Lou Riley, Archivist/Special Collections Librn
Holdings: Vols Cat VF
Budget: ($1000)
Notes: Kansas material, emphasizing Western Kansas; the cattle industry of the Great Plains area to pre-World War I.

MO —UNIVERSITY OF MISSOURI-KANSAS CITY, General Library, Snyder Collection of Americana, 5100 Rockhill Road, Kansas City, 64110. Kenneth J LaBudde, Dir; Robert Paustian, Asst Dir
Holdings: Vols 25,000 Cat
Notes: Nucleus was Robert M Snyder, Jr Americana Collection of some 14,000 items. Contains printed materials on 19th-century American history, especially the Trans-Mississippi West. Strengths include the history of Kansas City and Jackson County, Missouri, Kansas and Missouri county and state histories, American frontier religion (esp the Mormons and Alexander Campbell's Disciples of Christ), the history of railroads and transportation, the cattle trade, 19th-Century biography and autobiography, North American Indians and early Kansas and Missouri imprints.

TX —AMARILLO PUBLIC LIBRARY, 413 E Fourth, Amarillo, 79101. Mary Kay Snell, Librn
Holdings: Vols 1210 Cat Maps Filmstrips VF
Notes: The Meat Industry Collection contains documents, periodicals, pamphlets, AV materials on the production of processing and marketing of cattle, swine, sheep, poultry and rabbits. Most of the collection circulates except for the magazines.

TX —PANHANDLE-PLAINS HISTORICAL MUSEUM, Research Center, Box 967, WT Sta, Canyon, 79016. Claire R Kuehn, Archivist-Librn
Holdings: Vols 8000 Cat Mss Maps Pix Microforms
Budget: $2000
Notes: History of the Texas Panhandle. Incl interviews with early settlers taken over a 50-year period, ranch records, and business records relating to the Texas Panhandle and surrounding states.

TX —TEXAS A&M UNIVERSITY, Sterling C Evans Library, Special Collections Div, College Station, 77843. Donald H Dyal, Librn
Holdings: Vols (16,000) Mss Pix
Notes: Jeff Dykes Range Livestock Collection (incl a 600-item collection of J Frank Dobie works). Part of the Dobie Collection is described in Dykes, Jeff C *My Dobie Collection* (College Station, Tex: Friends of the Texas A & M University Library).

UT —UNIVERSITY OF UTAH, Marriott Library, Special Collections, Salt Lake City, 84112. Gregory C Thompson, Cur

VA —VIRGINIA POLYTECHNIC INSTITUTE AND STATE UNIVERSITY LIBRARY, Blacksburg, 24061. Glenn L McMullen, Special Collections Librn
Notes: Collection largely consists of nineteenth century and early twentieth century imprints, emphasizing the role of native Virginians in the development of the

CATTLE TRADE (cont.)

trans-Mississippi West, particularly Texas; cowboys and the cattle industry; outlaws and lawlessness; and emigrants' guidebooks to states, cities, and regions in the West.

CATTLE TRADE—HISTORY

IL —NEWBERRY LIBRARY, 60 W Walton St, Chicago, 60610. Diana Haskell, Cur of Modern Mss
Holdings: Cat
Notes: To about 1910.

KS —UNIVERSITY OF KANSAS, Kenneth Spencer Research Library, Kansas Collection, Lawrence, 66045. Sheryl K Williams, Cur
Holdings: Vols (92,000) Cat Mss Maps Pix
Notes: All aspects of the American West and trans-Mississippi history, especially the plains region. Overland diaries, cartographic history, Indians, emigration and immigration, printing history, cattle industry, agriculture and farm life, conservation are some special interests, in addition to the usual political, economic, military and social interests.

MT —MONTANA HISTORICAL SOCIETY LIBRARY, 225 N Roberts St, Helena, 59601. Robert M Clark, Librn; Brian Cockhill, State Archivist
Holdings: Vols 3000 Cat
Budget: ($2500)
Notes: The Ames and Margaret Booth Teakel Range Life Memorial Collection (cowboy and cattle range subjects). The scope of this collection includes the entire West, not just Montana and contiguous states. Also, L A Huffman Collection; incl 1100 photographs.

NE —KEARNEY STATE COLLEGE, Calvin T Ryan Library, Kearney, 68847. John Mayeski, Dir; Anita Norman, Reference Librn
Holdings: Vols 1700 Cat Mss Maps Pix Slides Microforms
Notes: Collection attempts to cover total historical development of Nebraska. Special strengths of the collection incl overland journeys, Pony Express, sod houses, and the Union Pacific. Special consideration has been given to Indians of Nebraska and the cattle industry. The collection is well supported by the library's general strength of Western Americana.

ND —THEODORE ROOSEVELT NATIONAL PARK, Library, PO Box 7, Medora, 58645. Susan Snow, Librn; Miki Hellickson, Chief Naturalist
Holdings: Vols (1500) Cat Mss Maps Pix Slides Audiotapes 16mm Films
Budget: ($5000)
Notes: Theodore Roosevelt, cattle country history, natural history. Also 2400 pictures and 2200 slides.

OK —NATIONAL COWBOY HALL OF FAME AND WESTERN HERITAGE, Library, 1700 NE 63 St, Oklahoma City, 73111. Esther Long, Librn
Holdings: Vols (8000) Uncat
Notes: Art of the American West. Covers western art and artists; rodeo and its history; cowboys; the cattle industry; and biographies on prominent westerners. Personal collection of Walter Brennen; collections of artists, Carl Link and James Earl Frazier.

TX —UNIVERSITY OF TEXAS LIBRARIES, General Libraries, Barker Texas History Center, PO Box P, Austin, 78712. Don Carleton, Dir
Holdings: Vols (132,000) Cat Mss Maps Pix Slides Phonorecords Audiotapes Microforms
Notes: See description of collection under Texas-History.

TX —AMON CARTER MUSEUM, Library, 3510 Camp Bowie Blvd, PO Box 2365, Fort Worth, 76113. Nancy G Wynne, Librn
Holdings: Vols (25,000) Cat Mss Pix
Notes: The book collection, microfilm and photo archives have been built toward the goal of the interpretation of American history through art. At present, the greatest strengths are in Americana, Western Canadiana, bibliography, American exhibition catalogs and history of photography. Substantial books and files on American artists of the 19th and early 20th century, and particularly of Charles M Russell and Frederic Remington. Incl 25,000 pictures; 13,000 slides.
See also entries under Newspapers, American and Pictures-Collections

UT —UTAH STATE UNIVERSITY, Merrill Library, Department of Special Collections & Archives, Logan, 84322. A J Simmonds, Curator; Jeanie F Simmonds, Archivist; Bradford R Cole, Mss Librn
Holdings: Vols 1000 Uncat Pics
Notes: Books and pamphlets on the history of Western Grazing (cattle and sheep). Incl manuscript of W P A produced history of Grazing, 1540-1936. All supported by 800 photographs in Pictures-Collections (General) qv.

WY —UNIVERSITY OF WYOMING, William Robertson Coe Library, Western History Research Center, Laramie, 82071. Gene M Gressley, Dir, Asst to Pres
Holdings: Vols (35,000) Cat Mss Maps Pix Microforms
Notes: The Western History Research Center of the University of Wyoming's William Robertson Coe Library has sizable ms collections in several areas pertaining to the history and development of the American West. Principal ms collection areas incl; cattle industry history, western literature, mining and petroleum history, transportation history, conservation history, water resources history, and related western history topics. The collections are supplemented by a fine Western Americana book collection cataloged by the main library but located at the Western History Research Center.

CAUCASUS

IN —INDIANA UNIVERSITY, Lilly Library, Seventh St, Bloomington, 47405. William R Cagle, Librn
Holdings: // Cat Mss
Notes: Emphasis on travel. Incl Russo-Turkish relations; Georgia and the Caucasus.

CAVAGNA FAMILY

†IL —UNIVERSITY OF ILLINOIS, URBANA/CHAMPAIGN, Library, Special Collections Div, Urbana, 61801.
Notes: Incl mss of the Cavagna Family in Italy.

CAVANAGH, JEROME

MI —WAYNE STATE UNIVERSITY, Walter P Reuther Library, Archives of Labor & Urban Affairs, Detroit, 48202. Philip Mason, Dir
Notes: Many personal ms collections in the Archives document individual strivings, accomplishments, and frustrations in developing a higher quality of urban life. The papers of Jerome Cavanagh, former Mayor of Detroit; George Edwards, former Detroit Housing Commissioner, Detroit Police Commissioner, and Michigan Supreme Court Justice; and Edward Connor, former Director of the Citizen's Housing and Planning Council of Detroit, are just 3 important collections concerning governmental, law enforcement, and social problems in a major metropolitan area of the country.

CAVE MAPS

†SD —SOUTH DAKOTA SCHOOL OF MINES & TECHNOLOGY, Devereaux Library, Rapid City, 57701.
Holdings: Vols 1000 Cat Mss Maps Microforms Audiotapes
Notes: Microfilm copy (complete set) of the US Bureau of Mines "Mine Map Depository (Denver)" material. Also, there are about a half-dozen periodicals that we subscribe to that relate to this subject (in general or specifically). Lastly, there are a few private collections, of varying size, that we are in process of acquiring for this area. Have collection of cave maps, also. Further, oral history program underway.

CAVES AND CAVERNS

NY —AMERICAN MUSEUM OF NATURAL HISTORY, Library Services Dept, Central Park W & 79th St, New York, 10024. Nina J Root, Chairwoman; Mary Genett, Asst Librn for Reference Services

†SD —SOUTH DAKOTA SCHOOL OF MINES & TECHNOLOGY, Devereaux Library, Rapid City, 57701.
Holdings: Vols (3786) Cat Mss Maps Pix Audiotapes Microforms
Notes: This special collection, in general, relates to the Black Hills area of South Dakota and Wyoming, especially mining and exploration of the area; the West River area of South Dakota, primarily county histories; and South Dakota Territorial and State materials. There are also specialized areas of this collection: (1) *Marion N Bruce* Collection. Documents, correspondence, books and periodicals dealing with weather modification in South Dakota; (2) *Mildred Fielder Collection*. Mss, pictures, books and periodicals from an author whose special area was the Black Hills. Most of her work on railroads, mines, trails, etc, relates to historical aspects. Collection incl research materials, galley proofs and final copies of her various publications; (3) *Cleophas C O'Harra Collection*. Mss, pictures, books and original source materials, primarily related to the Black Hills area andexpeditions thereto. Much of the data was collected for a book on the Black Hills which was never published; and (4) *Caving* Collection. Maps of various caves in Black Hills area, being kept current and updated by members of the Paha Saha Grotto. Also, some books and periodicals on caving in general.

CAWSTON, JOHN ALEXANDER

AB —UNIVERSITY OF CALGARY, Libraries, Special Collections Div, 2500 University Dr, Calgary, T2N 1N4, Can.
Holdings: Cat // Pix Microforms
Notes: Collection of 3500 architectural drawings--entirely on 35mm microfiche--by Alberta architect John Alexander Cawston, from 1946 to 1968. Represents all types of community buildings, as well as private residences, hotels, motels, and apartment buildings.

CAXTON, WILLIAM

CT —YALE UNIVERSITY, Box 1603A, Yale Station, New Haven, 06520.

CAYAKS see Canoes and Canoeing

CAYCE, EDGAR

AZ —WORLD UNIVERSITY, Library, 711 E Blacklidge Dr, Tucson, 85719. Howard John Zitko, Cur
Holdings: Vols (15,000) Cat Mss Maps Audiotapes
Notes: Collection concerns the "frontier sciences." No interlibrary loan.

VA —ASSOCIATION FOR RESEARCH & ENLIGHTENMENT, Library, 67 & Atlantic Avenue, PO Box 595, Virginia Beach, 23451. Stephen Jordan, Library Mgr
Holdings: Vols (250) Cat Audiotapes
Notes: Book collection plus Edgar Cayce Collection of Readings-384 looseleaf binders with typescripts of 14,250 discourses and answers given by him in response to questions while in a trance state. Readings cover period 1903 to September 1944. Subjects range from "Attitudes and Emotions" through "World Affairs" and "Yoga." Medical files cover common ailments from "Acne" and "Arthritis" through "Whooping Cough."

CEARD, HENRI

RI —BROWN UNIVERSITY, John Hay Library, 20 Prospect St, Providence, 02912. Mark N Brown, Cur Mss
Holdings: Mss
Notes: ALS by Zola, 1864-1901, 77 of which

CEARD, HENRI (cont.)

were addressed to Henri Ceard, novelist and playwright.

CELEBES see Indonesia

CELEBRITIES

CA —CLAREMONT COLLEGES, Honnold Library, Ninth & Dartmouth, Claremont, 91711. Tania Rizzo, Special Collections Dept Head
Holdings: Vols (250) // Uncat Mss Doc Pix Scrapbooks
Notes: Papers of Elbert A Wickes, 1884-1975, theatrical and lecture tour manager. Among his clients were Winston Churchill, William Butler Yeats, Houdini, Lowell Thomas, Vilhjalmur Stefansson, and Roy Chapman Andrews. He managed three American tours for the Abbey Players during the 1930s, was partner and producer of Fritz Leiber Shakespeare plays, the Water Follies of 1937, and the Affiliated Lyceum and Chautauquas Association. The collection is rich in autograph and photographic materials. There are 750 items relative to the Abbey Players. Card file and inventory available. Restricted use.

CA —STANFORD UNIVERSITY LIBRARIES, Cecil H Green Library, Stanford, 94305. Michael T Ryan, Cur
Holdings: Cat Pix
Notes: The Dr and Mrs Leon Kolb Portrait Collection. Over 1600 portraits (engravings, etchings, mezzotints, lithographs) of rulers, statesmen, authors, scholars and other famous personages from ancient times to the 19th century. A catalog of the collection, compiled by Dr Susan Lenkey, was published in 1972.

DC —HOWARD UNIVERSITY, Moorland-Spingarn Research Center, 500 Howard Place NW, Washington, 20059. Clifford L Muse, Jr, Acting Dir
Holdings: Vols (106,086) Mss Maps Pix Slides Phonorecords Audiotapes 16mm Films Filmstrips Microforms
Budget: ($854,753)
See also entry under Blacks

NY —COLUMBIA UNIVERSITY LIBRARIES, Rare Book & Manuscript Library, 801 Butler Library, 535 W 114 St, New York, 10027. Kenneth A Lohf, Librn
Holdings: Mss
Notes: The Frederick C Schang Collection. About 650 calling cards of great and near-great celebrities. Most contain autographs or holograph notes. Restricted use.

NY —NEW YORK PUBLIC LIBRARY, Performing Arts Research Center, Rodgers & Hammerstein Archives of Recorded Sound, 111 Amsterdam Ave, New York, 10023.
Holdings: Cat Tapes
Notes: A collection of taped interviews, representing over 400 prominent figures. Incl are voices of Richard Nixon, Billy Graham, Maurice Chevalier, Sammy Davis, Jr, Dr Albert Sabin, etc.

TX —TEXAS TECH UNIVERSITY, Library, Lubbock, 79409. David J Murrah, Assoc Dir for Special Collections
Notes: The Samuel Weiselberg Memorial Autographs Collection of examples from distinguished historical and literary persons.

CELESTIAL MECHANICS see Mechanics, Celestial

CELESTIAL NORTH POLE see North Pole, Celestial

CELL, VOLTAIC see Electric Batteries

CELLER, REP. EMANUEL

DC —LIBRARY OF CONGRESS, Manuscript Division, Washington, 20540. John C Broderick, Chief
Notes: Papers of Representative Emanuel Celler.

CELLO

DC —LIBRARY OF CONGRESS, Music Division, Washington, 20540.
Holdings: Cat Mss Maps Pix Slides Microforms
Notes: Incl the Whittall Foundation of Stradivari instruments (3 violins, viola, cello).

CELLS

MA —UNIVERSITY OF MASSACHUSETTS AT AMHERST, Library, Amherst, 01003. Siegfried Feller, Assoc Dir for Collection Development
Holdings: Cat
Notes: Special emphasis on cellular, developmental and physiological zoology.

MA —HARVARD UNIVERSITY LIBRARY, Biological Laboratories Library, 16 Divinity Ave, Cambridge, 02138. Dorothy Solbrig, Librn
Holdings: Vols (20,000) Cat Films
Notes: Materials in all areas of biology, emphasizing biochemistry and cellular and developmental biology. There is little in systematic biology and morphology.

NY —ALBERT EINSTEIN COLLEGE OF MEDICINE, D Samuel Gottesman Library, 1300 Morris Park Ave, Bronx, 10461. Charlotte K Lindner, Dir

NC —NATIONAL INSTITUTE OF ENVIRONMENTAL HEALTH SCIENCES, Library, PO Box 12233, Research Triangle Park, 27709. W Davenport Robertson, Head Librn
Holdings: Vols (9000) Cat Mss Audiotapes Microforms
Notes: The subject, "environmental health," incl toxicology, carcinogenesis, pharmacology, genetics, biophysics, and biochemistry. Special emphasis is placed on cell biology. The collection does not incl works on pollution control or law. In addition to the collection there are some 2500 vols in the laboratories. The library has an automated catalog.

TX —UNIVERSITY OF TEXAS, M D Anderson Hospital and Tumor Institute, Research Medical Library, Texas Medical Center, Houston, 77030. Marie Harvin, Research Medical Librn
Holdings: Vols (48,000) Cat
Notes: Library attempts to collect every publication in all languages related to clinical cancer (or oncology). Aim is an exhaustive collection in this field. Collect heavily (research level) in pathology, radiology, nuclear medicine, genetics and cell biology.

ON —AGRICULTURE CANADA, Research Branch, Neatby Library, Rm 3032, K W Neatby Bldg, CEF, Ottawa, K1A 0C6, Can. Marcel Charette, Library Technician
Holdings: Vols 500 Cat
Notes: Mycotoxins. All phases of cell biology.

CELLULOSE

NY —STATE UNIVERSITY OF NEW YORK, COLLEGE OF ENVIRONMENTAL SCIENCE AND FORESTRY, F Franklin Moon Library, Syracuse, 13210. Donald F Webster, Librn
Holdings: Vols (86,430) Cat
Budget: ($120,000)

CELTIBERI

NV —UNIVERSITY OF NEVADA, RENO, Noble H Getchell Library, Reno, 89557. William A Douglass, Coordinator
Holdings: Vols (15,000)
Notes: America's largest collection of Basque materials, both retrospective and current. Semi-annual *Newsletter*.

CELTIC LANGUAGE AND LITERATURE

CA —SONOMA STATE UNIVERSITY, Salazar Library, 1801 E Cotati Ave, Rohnert Park, 94928. Sandra Walton, Librn
Holdings: Vols (650)
Notes: The W W Lyman Collection of Celtic literature, consisting of Irish, Scottish and Welsh fiction, poetry and plays.

CT —YALE UNIVERSITY, Box 1603A, Yale Station, New Haven, 06520.

DC —CATHOLIC UNIVERSITY OF AMERICA, Mullen Library, 620 Michigan Ave NE, Washington, 20064. B Gutekunst, Humanities Librn
Holdings: Vols 4500 Cat

IL —NEWBERRY LIBRARY, 60 W Walton St, Chicago, 60610. Diana Haskell, Cur of Modern Mss
Holdings: Cat
Notes: Incl Irish history and literature to 1900. Also, a collection on Gaelic linguistics, particularly Irish, Cornish, Welsh and Manx.

MA —HARVARD UNIVERSITY LIBRARY, Widener Library, Cambridge, 02138.
Holdings: Cat Mss Microforms
Notes: *Widener Library Shelflist* No 25 (1970) lists 8147 titles in Celtic languages and literatures, of which some 4800 are Welsh and 2000 are Irish. See *Harvard Library Bulletin*, I (1947), 52-65. There is also a Celtic seminar room in Widener Library containing 1200 vols. For microfilms of Irish mss, see *Harvard Library Bulletin*, VIII (1954), 111-114.

MA —BOSTON COLLEGE LIBRARIES, Thomas P O'Neill Library, Irish Collection, Chestnut Hill, 02167. Ralph Coffman, Cur
Holdings: Vols (10,000) Cat Mss Maps Pix
Notes: Nearly every aspect of Irish history and literature are covered in this collection. Items of special interest are the many papers of Patrick Andrew Collins, president of the Irish Land League, and letters of Jeremiah O'Donovan Rossa, poet, editor and leader in the Fenian and related organizations. Holdings also incl a facsimile of the famous illuminated ms of the Gospels, the *Book of Kells*; a complete vol of *Malton's Views of Dublin, 1799; The Ordinance Surveys;* a complete set of the *Irish Bulletin;* and Colgan's *Acta Sanctorum Hiberniae* describing the lives of the Irish saints.

NY —AMERICAN IRISH HISTORICAL SOCIETY, Library, 991 Fifth Ave, New York, 10028. Lisa M Hottin, Cur; William D Griffin, Librn
Holdings: Vols (20,000) Cat Maps Pix Slides
Notes: Archives and Manuscripts: The documents and papers of Friends of Irish Freedom, The Land League, the Society of the Friendly Sons of St Patrick, the Catholic Club, and the Guild of Catholic Lawyers. The papers of New York State Supreme Court Justice Daniel F Cohalan. This is the largest and most complete collection of over 20,000 American Irish and Irish history, biography and literature in the United States. Incl American-Irish Newspaper collections dating from 1811, the most comprehensive in the US; 1000 rare books and special editions. Special collections incl regular exhibits of Irish or American Irish interest incl mss, letters, books, photographs and memorabilia. Permanent collection of representative works of Irish painters.

OH —CLEVELAND PUBLIC LIBRARY, Fine Arts and Special Collections Department, 325 Superior Ave, Cleveland, 44114. Alice N Loranth, Head
Holdings: Vols 1000 Cat
Notes: Medieval texts, translations, folk-songs, linguistics are emphasized. The important scholarly journals, and the serials and publications of the Cymmrodorian Society, Irish Texts Society, Ossianic Society, etc, are well represented.
See also entry under Folklore; Literature, Medieval

WI —UNIVERSITY OF WISCONSIN, MADISON, Memorial Library, British & American Language & Literature Collection, 728 State St, Madison, 53706. Yvonne Schofer, Bibliographer
Holdings: Cat Mss Maps
Notes: An extensive collection of Celtic materials acquired from 1914 onward. Includes important philological and historical journals, the principal editions of texts, and photostats of the Royal Irish Academy's collection of manuscripts, held in Rare Books and Special Collections Dept. Approximately 60 17th and 18th century maps.

NS —SAINT FRANCIS XAVIER UNIVERSITY, Angus L MacDonald Library, Antigonish, B0H 1C0, Can.

CELTIC LANGUAGE AND LITERATURE (cont.)

Maureen Lonergan, Librn
Holdings: Vols 5298 Cat Mss Maps Pix Phonorecords Audiotapes
Notes: Books on or about Scotland and Scottish people; books and pamphlets dealing with Scottish immigrants to Canada; books written in Gaelic; complete file of *MacTalla* (Gaelic newspaper published in Cape Breton); reports and records of Scottish societies. Separate catalog. See "The Saint Francis Xavier University Celtic Collection," by Calum I N MacLeod in *Special Collections in Canadian Libraries* (Ottawa: Canadian Library Assn, 1963) (Occasional Paper, 53).

CEMETERIES—RECORDS

NE —KEENE MEMORIAL LIBRARY, 1030 N Broad St, Fremont, 68025. William S McDermott, Dir
Holdings: Vols (10) Cat
Notes: Cemetery indexes compiled from gravestones, etc, for all cemeteries in Dodge and Washington counties. The project will incl surrounding counties in the future. These indexes are also available at the Nebraska State Historical Society, Lincoln.

OH —CLEVELAND PUBLIC LIBRARY, General Reference Dept, 325 Superior Ave, Cleveland, 44114. Donald Tipka, Head
Notes: Approximately 800,000 entries. Microfilm and computer printout of death notices from Cleveland newspapers: 1833-1975, 1976-date, index by computer; also cemetery records to 1939 for Cuyahoga County cemeteries. Photocopying.

RI —PROVIDENCE PUBLIC LIBRARY, 150 Empire St, Providence, 02903. Lance J Bauer, Special Collections Librn
Notes: The Arnold Collection (Knight Memorial Library) consists of tombstone records, family notes, probate records, newspaper clippings, and books relating to Rhode Island genealogy and history. The core of the collection consists of the tombstone records and family notes. The greater part of this material has been typed from mss information that was gathered by James Arnold. The tombstone records are arranged in loose-leaf folders by cities and towns of Rhode Island. The family notes are also arranged in loose-leaf folders, but alphabetically by family name. All this material has been indexed. Because of its uniqueness, the core collection is invaluable to anyone searching for local genealogical information.

CENSORSHIP

CA —CALIFORNIA STATE UNIVERSITY, FRESNO, Henry Madden Library, Dept of Special Collections, Fresno, 93740. Ronald J Mahoney, Head
Holdings: Uncat
Notes: The Alexander Pronin Collection of Russian Postcards of approx 1500 Russian postcards, 1890-1920, illustrating Russian art, architecture and life. Approx 150 are partially used, incl various World War I censors' marks.

CA —HUNTINGTON LIBRARY, Art Gallery & Botanical Gardens, 1151 Oxford Rd, San Marino, 91108. Robert L Middlekauff, Dir; Daniel H Woodward, Librn
Notes: Incl the Larpent Collection of English manuscript plays submitted to the Lord Chamberlain for approval after the Licensing Act of 1737--the year and reason the phrase "legitimate stage" came into use. Refer to MacMillian, Dougald, *Catalogue of the Larpent Plays in the Huntington Library* (San Marino, Calif: 1939).

CA —UNIVERSITY OF CALIFORNIA, SANTA BARBARA, Library, Dept of Special Collections, Santa Barbara, 93106. Christian F Brun, Head
Holdings: Vols 615 Cat
Notes: The Morris L Ernst Banned Books Collection.

IL —CENTER FOR RESEARCH LIBRARIES, 6050 S Kenwood Ave, Chicago, 60637. Donald B Simpson, Dir; Esther Smith, Collection Development Librn
Holdings: Vols Cat Microforms
Notes: Microfilm holdings of newspapers, official gazette. Microfilm and reprint of Imperial and National Diet proceedings. Archival material, Tokugwa period forward. Microfilm of annual reports of over 2,000 companies, 1872-1945. Meiji and Taisho prefectural statistics. Prange collection of censored periodicals, occupation period. Fairly complete collection of records of the International Military Tribunal for the Far East. 520 current periodical subscriptions. Descriptive pamphlet available.

IL —NEWBERRY LIBRARY, 60 W Walton St, Chicago, 60610. Diana Haskell, Cur of Modern Mss
Notes: John M Wing History of Printing collection. Incl some 1100 French edicts, 17th-19th century, regulating the printing and publishing industries.

†IL —UNIVERSITY OF ILLINOIS LIBRARIES, Urbana, 61801.
Notes: The Mimi Kaplan Collection of materials relating to Helen Bannerman's *Little Black Sambo*. About 100 items covering 75 years of publishing, incl books, records, games puzzles, coloring books, etc, relating to the book which was withdrawn from many American public libraries in the early 1960's as a result of lobbying efforts of the Working Group for the Eradication of Color Prejudice.

MD —UNIVERSITY OF MARYLAND, Library, East Asia Collection, College Park, 20742. Frank Joseph Shulman, Curator and Head
Holdings: Vols (90,000) // Mss
Notes: Japanese books, newspapers, periodicals, etc, of the Allied Occupation period (1945-1952), including files of censored publications. Books number 40,000; periodical titles, 13,000; newspaper titles, ca 16,500. The special collection relating to the Occupation period is supplemented by a growing collection (now ca 50,000 vols) of Chinese, Japanese, and Korean publications which form the basis of the University's general collection in East Asian language materials.

MA —HARVARD UNIVERSITY LIBRARY, Law School Library, Langdell Hall, Cambridge, 02138. Harry S Martin III, Librn
Holdings: Cat

MN —UNIVERSITY OF MINNESOTA, O Meredith Wilson Library, 309 19 Ave S, Minneapolis, 55455. Austin J McLean, Chief, Special Collections
Holdings: Vols (576) Uncat Pix Slides Phonorecords
Notes: Published writings of Henry Miller in all languages are contained in this collection, along with information about him, his work, and censorship as it relates to his career. A complete listing is available in the Division.

NY —NEW YORK STATE ARCHIVES, 9049 Cultural Education Center, Albany, 12230. Richard Andress, Archivist
Notes: Records of the New York State Education Department's former Motion Picture Division 1921 to 1965, which exercised censorship control over all films offered for public viewing in New York State. Incl large collection of film scripts. 54, 000 items.

†NY —STATE UNIVERSITY OF NEW YORK, COLLEGE AT BROCKPORT, Brockport, 14420.
Notes: Microfilm copy of the Lord Chamberlain's *Daybooks*, registers of plays licensed for presentation in London from 1824-1903. Originals in British Museum. Some other miscellaneous material is incl from the Lord Chamberlain's office.

NY —GRADUATE CENTER OF THE CITY UNIVERSITY OF NEW YORK, William H and Gwynne K Crouse Library for Publishing Arts, 33 W 42 St, New York, 10036. Alfred H Lane, Dir
Notes: Recently established and still growing, but intended to become the authoritative source of materials in the field, of particular value in research about the publishing industry. Open to staff members of publishing houses, students, scholars, authors, printers, and booksellers. Primarily 20th century materials, and particularly useful for research on technical, financial, and historical matters. Much on the history of individual houses, economics of authorship; marketing and distribution of books; etc.

NY —MUSEUM OF MODERN ART, Dept of Film, 11 W 53 St, New York, 10019. Eileen Bowser, Cur
Holdings: Mss Pix
Notes: Papers, correspondence, scrapbooks, pictures, etc. Partially cataloged.

†ON —UNIVERSITY OF WESTERN ONTARIO, School of Library and Information Science, Special Collections Room, London, N6A 5B9, Can.
Holdings: Vols 70,000 Cat
Notes: Representive collection of books and pamphlets censored on moral, political, and religious grounds. Complemented by reference works in the School's main library.

CENSORSHIP OF THE PRESS see Liberty of the Press

CENSUSES

CA —UNIVERSITY OF CALIFORNIA, BERKELEY, University Library, Government Documents Department, 350 Library Annex, Berkeley, 94720. Suzanne Gold, Collection Dept Librn
Holdings: Vols (314,000) Cat Microforms
Budget: ($85,115)
Notes: General collection of government documents, historical and current, on the federal and state levels; as well as international and foreign documents. The Library's holdings are particularly strong in foreign statistics and censuses, and US Congress. The Government Documents Department serves as a full depository for GPO, NASA, State of California, EEC, GATT, IAEA, United Nations, UNESCO, Rand Corporation (non-classified), IBRD, OECD, ILO, UNITAR, ITC, and CE. Selective depository, PL-480 Programs, or gift or exchange arrangements obtain for the states of Michigan and Washington and for Canada, India, Pakistan and Indonesia. Incl microfilm and 300,000 fiche, cards, and prints.

CA —LOS ANGELES PUBLIC LIBRARY, Social Sciences Dept, 630 W Fifth St, Los Angeles, 90071. Marilyn C Wherley, Principal Librn
Holdings: Vols 800 Cat Maps
Budget: ($150,000)
Notes: Nearly complete set of US Census, mainly population and housing statistics, current reports, from 1790. Depository (selective) since 1891. No separate catalog.

CA —POMONA PUBLIC LIBRARY, Special Collections, 625 S Garey Ave, PO Box 2271, Pomona, 91766. David Streeter, Librn
Holdings: Cat Maps Microforms
Notes: Complete California census through 1900 on microfilm and 1850 California census index.

DC —METROPOLITAN WASHINGTON COUNCIL OF GOVERNMENTS, Research Library, 1875 Eye St NW, Suite 200, Washington, 20006. Suan Kalish, Librn
Holdings: Vols (3000) Cat Microforms
Notes: Contains (on 75 reels of microfilm) archives of Maryland-National Park and Planning Commission, archives of the Council of Governments, and audits and financial reports of local governments (1950-date). Also incl annual reports, planning reports and budgets from each jurisdiction (1973-date).

DC —US BUREAU OF THE CENSUS, Library, Federal Office Bldg 3, Rm 2451, Washington, 20233. Betty Baxtresser, Chief, ASD Library Branch
Holdings: Cat Mss Maps Microforms
Notes: Publications and related source materials issued by the Bureau of the Census and its predecessor organizations from 1790 to the present. Also, reports based upon surveys conducted by the Bureau for other governmental agencies. Papers by Census staff members, providing a rich source of

CENSUSES (cont.)

material on statistical methods, population and other Bureau-related matters are important.

FL —ORLANDO PUBLIC LIBRARY, Local History & Genealogy Dept, 100 Block of Central Ave, Orlando, 32806. Eileen B Willis, Librn
Holdings: Vols 11,000 Cat Maps Microforms
Budget: $8000
Notes: The

FL —FLORIDA STATE UNIVERSITY, Robert Manning Strozier Library, Tallahassee, 32306. Judith Depew, Head, Documents-Maps Dept
Holdings: Vols (680,000) Uncat Microforms
Notes: A depository for Florida, GPO, NASA, UN, and UNESCO documents, with standing orders for British, ILO, OAS, IMF; selected documents are purchased from various government levels. The collection incl historical as well as current material, especially Florida, US, Great Britain. The Library's holdings are strong in congressional bills and hearings, decennial censuses, and British Sessional papers. Number of volumes incl microprint and microfiche, but not cataloged documents and microfilm.

GA —UNIVERSITY OF GEORGIA, Libraries, Special Collections Division, Athens, 30602. Vesta Lee Gordon, Asst Dir for Special Collections
Notes: The Arbitron Collection of television and radio program ratings, 1949-date (except past year). In-depth, statistical analyses of the listening public by age, sex, county, some ethnic groups, farm population, listening preferences, etc. 26,302 bound vols. 2 reports, 1949-81. To be added to annually.

IL —BARTON-ASCHMAN ASSOCIATES, Library, 820 Davis St, Evanston, 60204.
Holdings: Vols (9000) Cat Mss Microforms

MD —JOHNS HOPKINS UNIVERSITY, Milton S Eisenhower Library, George Peabody Collection, 17 E Mt Vernon Place, Baltimore, 21201. Lyn Hart, Peabody Librn
Notes: Emphasis on materials published before 1950. Strength is a good collection through the 19th century.

MA —UNIVERSITY OF MASSACHUSETTS AT AMHERST, Library, Amherst, 01003. Siegfried Feller, Assoc Dir for Collection Development
Holdings: Cat Microforms
Notes: Microform collections of materials in other American libraries.

MA —NEW ENGLAND HISTORIC GENEALOGICAL SOCIETY, Library, 101 Newbury St, Boston, 02116. Ralph J Crandell, Dir
Notes: Large collection of printed British and American parish registers; some American ms parish records. Strong collection of early censuses, incl the Massachusetts Direct Tax Record of 1798, actually a census of Maine and Massachusetts and more informative than the Federal decennial record of early national censuses. Earlier similarly useful records incl the Accounts of Pay for King Philip's War (1675-1676) kept by John Hull, War Treasurer.

MI —OAKLAND COUNTY REFERENCE LIBRARY, 1200 N Telegraph Rd, Pontiac, 48053. Phyllis Jose, Library Dir
Holdings: Vols (11,000) Cat
Budget: ($34,000)

MO —UNIVERSITY OF MISSOURI-COLUMBIA, Museum of Anthropology Archives, 104 Swallow Hall, Columbia, 65201. Lawrence H Feldman, Museum Dir
Holdings: Vols (30) Cat Mss Maps Slides Microforms
Notes: Copies of Latin American and colonial mss. Many of the ms copies are of census, or census-like, documents of late colonial Verapaz; a few are from Sonsonate, El Salvador or Chiapas, Mexico. Additional material in the archives incl an original Eskimo manuscript (ca 1930) and an original Diegueno Yuman card vocabulary (ca 1964) and the Museum archives (papers on old accession systems, etc). Uncataloged microfilm copies of colonial Otomi and other vocabularies are also part of the collection. A catalog of material in this collection will appear in the Annual Report of the Museum of Anthropology, beginning with 1976-77 volume.

NJ —PRINCETON UNIVERSITY, Office of Population Research, Library, 21 Prospect Ave, Princeton, 08540. Thomas Holzmann, Librn
Holdings: Vols (25,000) Cat Mss Maps Microforms
Notes: The library is attached to the Office of Population Research, which publishes the *Population Index*. Library is particularly strong in statistical materials, such as worldwide population censuses and vital statistics; it is less strong in the biomedical aspects of population research. Incl 10,000 reprints, pamphlets, mss, etc. ILL requests should be addressed to Princeton University Library, Interlibrary Services.

NY —ST LAWRENCE COUNTY HISTORICAL LIBRARY & ARCHIVES ASSOCIATION, Library, 3 E Main St, PO Box 506, Canton, 13617. John Baule, County Librn
Holdings: Vols (600) Uncat Mss Pix Audiotapes Microforms
Notes: Genealogical Research Collection: Saint Lawrence County printed and manuscript records, military records, diaries, account books, burial, church, school records. Complete "Alms House" of county records (1825-1975). Many scrapbooks, census microfilm, court records, etc. Housed in the Silas Wright House and Museum.

NC —PACK MEMORIAL PUBLIC LIBRARY, North Carolina Collection, 67 Haywood St, Asheville, 28801. John Toms, Dept Head
Notes: Collection incl early ms accounts of western North Carolina; Civil War letters; letters, diary, and mss of Horace Kephart; mss of Thomas Dixon; Thomas Wolfe Collection; contemporary North Carolina authors; North Carolina censuses, 1790-1910; rare newspapers and runs of local newspapers, and clippings from Asheville newspapers, from 1920s; early maps; information on Cherokee Indians; approx 400 vols of North Carolina genealogy and file of unpublished genealogies. Collection concentrates on western North Carolina, with some general Appalachian materials. Incl 4000 local and state photographs, separate catalog.

OH —PUBLIC LIBRARY OF CINCINNATI & HAMILTON COUNTY, Government and Business Dept, 800 Vine St, Cincinnati, 45202. Paul T Hudson, Head
Holdings: Vols 120,000 Cat
Notes: Department receives over 1200 periodical and loose-leaf service titles, 1500 serial titles and over 1500 telephone directories. Subjects include political science, especially foreign relations, economics, law, public administration and business management. Dept houses Murray Seasongood collection of local government. Dept has extensive census material from 1790. Library is a full depository for US Government Publications, 1884 to date.

PA —LANCASTER MENNONITE CONFERENCE HISTORICAL SOCIETY LIBRARY, 2215 Millstream Rd, Lancaster, 17602. Lloyd Zeager, Librn; David J Smucker, Genealogist
Holdings: Vols (55,000) Cat Mss Maps Pix Microforms
Budget: ($3186)
Notes: Specializes in southeastern Pennsylvania genealogy and history. Genealogical card file of over 200,000 cards. Cemetery records for all Lancaster County, Pa, cemeteries. Periodical index compiled from historical, genealogical, and theological periodicals. Census records on microfilm for 1790, 1800, 1810, 1820, 1830, 1840, 1850, 1860, 1870, 1880, 1900, and 1910 for Lancaster County and incomplete census records for other southeastern Pennsylvania counties. Complete 1850 for Pennsylvania.

PA —HISTORICAL SOCIETY OF PENNSYLVANIA, Library, 1300 Locust St, Philadelphia, 19107. David Fraser, Librn
Holdings: Vols (230,000) Mss Maps Pix Microforms
Notes: Incl over 14,000,000 ms pieces. The Library Company of Philadelphia mss are on deposit with the Historical Society of Pennsylvania. Many of the Society's rare books are on deposit with the Library Company. The Society maintains the collections of the Genealogical Society of Pennsylvania, incl some 20,000 printed genealogies, original mss, family, church, and civil records.

PA —PENNSYLVANIA STATE UNIVERSITY, Fred Lewis Pattee Library, Documents Section, University Park, 16802. Diane H Smith, Head
Notes: Depository for US Government publications; depository for Pennsylvania documents; collect United Nations and related international and intergovernmental organization publications; selected publications from Australia, Great Britain, including Parliamentary Papers; census materials; a large microform collection, including Department of Energy (formerly ERDA, AEC), Congressional publications, Patents, OAS, UN. Incl 900,000 documents. Censuses books and microforms, some cataloged.

TX —UNIVERSITY OF TEXAS LIBRARIES, Population Research Center Library, 1701 Main Bldg Tower, Austin, 78712. Doreen S Goyer, Librn
Holdings: Vols (20,000) Cat Microforms
Budget: ($3000)
Notes: The International Census Collection contains population censuses of 200 nations and territories, current and retrospective. Combined holdings of several University of Texas libraries constitute 80 percent of the items cited in the *International Population Census Bibliography* (6 volumes and 1 supplement), and the *IPCB, Revision and Update: 1945-1977,* with the majority of items in the Population Research Center. The *Handbook of National Population Censuses, Latin America and the Caribbean, North America, and Oceania* (1983) aids the researcher in the use of foreign censuses.

CENSUSES, AGRICULTURAL see Agriculture—Statistics

CENTER FOR PUBLIC FINANCING OF ELECTIONS

DC —GEORGETOWN UNIVERSITY, Library, Special Collections Div, 37 & O Sts NW, Washington, 20057. George M Barringer, Special Collections Librn; Nicholas B Sheetz, Mss Librn
Holdings: Cat Mss Maps Pix Slides Phonorecords Audiotapes
Notes: Includes the papers (1912-49) of Sen Robert F Wagner; the archives (1903-) of the American Political Science Association and of its local Washington chapter; the archives of the Center for Public Financing of Elections; a collection of several hundred political cartoons by Eric Smith; and other smaller collections.

CENTRAL AFRICAN EMPIRE

DC —HOWARD UNIVERSITY, Moorland-Spingarn Research Center, 500 Howard Place NW, Washington, 20059. Clifford L Muse, Jr, Acting Dir

CENTRAL AFRICAN REPUBLIC see Central African Empire

CENTRAL AMERICA

KS —UNIVERSITY OF KANSAS, Kenneth Spencer Research Library, Special Collections Dept, Lawrence, 66045. Alexandra Mason, Librn
Holdings: Vols 4400 Uncat Mss
Notes: William Griffith Collection on Central America, especially Guatemalan imprints, late 18th to mid-20th century, incl many newpapers and broadsides. Noncirculating.

CENTRAL AMERICA—DESCRIPTION AND TRAVEL

DC —LIBRARY OF CONGRESS, Geography and Map Division, Washington, 20540. John

CENTRAL AMERICA—DESCRIPTION AND TRAVEL (cont.)

A Wolter, Chief
Notes: Ephraim George Squier's papers and maps of Central America. Maps are located in the Geography and Maps Division; mss in the Manuscripts Division.

MN —UNIVERSITY OF MINNESOTA, James Ford Bell Library, 309 19th Ave S, Minneapolis, 55455. John Parker, Cur
Holdings: Vols (11,000) Cat Mss Maps
Notes: Collection of original materials relating to European expansion, 1400-1800.

CENTRAL AMERICA—HISTORY

CA —UNIVERSITY OF CALIFORNIA, BERKELEY, Bancroft Library, Manuscripts Division, Berkeley, 94720. James D Hart, Dir
Holdings: Vols Cat Mss Maps Pix Slides Microforms
Notes: Primary emphasis on Mexico, with a lesser emphasis on the Central American Republics. In general, The Bancroft Library seeks to acquire historical and biographical works and primary source materials, documenting: the development of a geographic area or political unit; man and his activities and his impact on the land and on his institutions. Methodological and theoretical works, and texts in the physical and biological sciences, are not collected, as a rule; exceptions here are publications essential to the study of an area's historical development, and those providing general background information. The Bancroft Library's collections are noncirculating. A G K Hall catalog has been published.

CA —UNIVERSITY OF CALIFORNIA, SAN DIEGO, Central University Library, Mandeville Dept of Special Collections, La Jolla, 92093. Lynda Corey Claassen, Head
Holdings: Vols (2400) Cat Mss Maps
Notes: The Hill Collection of Pacific Voyages, including reports and commentaries of important voyages in the Pacific, from those of Magellan and Sir Francis Drake to exploration through the first half of the 19th century. Includes many rare overland accounts to the Pacific across North America, Mexico, and Panama.
Bibliography: Silveira de Braganza, Ronald, *The Hill Collection of Pacific Voyages* (La Jolla: Calif, 1974-1983).

DE —UNIVERSITY OF DELAWARE, Hugh M Morris Library, S College Ave, Newark, 19711. T Stuart Dick, Special Collections
Holdings: // Mss
Notes: Personal and business papers of the Potter Family, a Philadelphia merchant family prominent in the import trade with Central America, particularly Nicaragua (1801-1943).

DC —LIBRARY OF CONGRESS, Manuscript Division, Washington, 20540. John C Broderick, Chief
Notes: The Harkness Collection contains documents relating to the first 200 years of Spanish rule in Mexico and Peru.

IL —CENTER FOR RESEARCH LIBRARIES, 6050 S Kenwood Avc, Chicago, 60637. Donald B Simpson, Dir; Esther Smith, Collection Development Librn
Holdings: Microforms
Notes: British Foreign Office and US State Dept records relating to Mexico and Central America.

LA —TULANE UNIVERSITY, Howard-Tilton Memorial Library, Latin American Library, New Orleans, 70118. Thomas Niehaus, Dir
Holdings: Vols (150,000) Cat Mss Maps Pix Microforms VF
Budget: ($67,000)
Notes: *Catalog of the Latin American* Library (Boston: G K Hall, 1970, suppl. 1973,1975,1978); Downs 5338-41; suppl (1961), 2727, 2737. The Latin American Library is a general collection, but specializes in Central American, Mexican, and Brazilian materials. The disciplines which are most strongly represented are history, anthropology, and archaeology. The Viceregal Ecclesiastical Mexican Collection contains manuscripts from the colonial period. The France V Scholes Collection contains a large number of photoprints and microfilm of colonial documents from the archives of Spain and Mexico. The Merle Greene Robertson Rubbings Collection contains nearly five hundred rubbings of relief sculpture from Mayan archaeological sites in Mexico and Guatemala. The Photographic Collection contains photos of archaeological sites inMeso-America, of pre-Columbian Peruvian architecture, and a general group of historic photos from Latin America.

RI —BROWN UNIVERSITY, John Hay Library, 20 Prospect St, Providence, 02912. Mark N Brown, Cur Mss
Holdings: Vols 3500// Cat Mss Maps
Notes: George Earl Church Collection--formed by a civil engineer, explorer and Fellow of the Royal Geographic Society, who specialized in railroad construction. Although part of the collection is devoted to American Revoltionary and Civil War history, the majority, over 2000 volumes, pertains to Central and South America. The imprints, which are predominantly 18th century, include Lima, Madrid, Rome, Mexico City, Seville, Barcelona, Lisbon, and Cadiz as well as *Nova orbis regionum ac insularum veteribus incognitarum* (Basle:1537). Major subject areas are: anthropology, commerce, economics, engineering, ethnology, geography, history, law, mineral resources, railroad surveys, voyages of exploration and dictionaries of the South American Indian languages. The most significant ms is an historical account of the Bolivian mining town of Potosi from 1545-1737.

TX —UNIVERSITY OF TEXAS LIBRARIES, Nettie Lee Benson Latin American Collection, Sid Richardson Hall 1.109, Austin, 78712. Laura Gutierrez-Witt, Head Librn
Holdings: Vols (450,000) Cat Mss Maps Pix Videotapes Microforms
Notes: Private library of Arturo Taracena Flores, providing extensive coverage of all Central American countries. Incl nearly all Guatemala imprints, 1800-1964; also incl broadsides.
See also entry under Latin America

CENTRAL AMERICA—IMPRINTS

†KS —UNIVERSITY OF KANSAS, Watson Memorial Library, Lawrence, 66045.

CENTRAL ARIZONA PROJECT

AZ —NORTHERN ARIZONA UNIVERSITY, Special Collection Library, CU Box 6022, Flagstaff, 86011. Peter M Whiteley, Coordr/Archivist; William Mullane, Librn
Notes: Jay Price Collection; correspondence, files, and reports pertaining to *Forestry* Topics, 1950's. Incl information on watershed and forest management for the Salt River and Central Arizona Projects as part of the Arizona Water Resource Committee files, 1956-1960; and files of the Soil Conservation Society, Arizona Chapter, 1956-1957 (2 feet).

CENTRAL ASIA see Asia, Central

CENTRAL BANKS AND BANKING see Banks and Banking, Central

CENTRAL EUROPE

CO —UNIVERSITY OF SOUTHERN COLORADO, Library, 2200 Bonforte Blvd, Pueblo, 81001.
Holdings: Vols (4000) Cat Mss Maps Pix Phonorecords Audiotapes
Budget: ($10,000)
Notes: Yugoslavian; especially Slovenian history and culture. The collection was inaugurated in 1969. Besides published titles, 2800 in English, and 900 in Slavic languages, there are memorabilia, organizational records, and newspapers, magazines, and music. There is a separate card catalog of items in the collection. Colorado has had a number of Slavic colonies and this collection attempts to recapture the history of these early settlers. Incl sheet music and phonorecords.

NY —JOZEF PILSUDSKI INSTITUTE FOR RESEARCH IN THE MODERN HISTORY OF POLAND, INC, 381 Park Ave, South, New York, 10016.
Holdings: 12,000 Vols Mss Maps Pix Archive
Notes: Said to be the fourth largest Polish collection of documents in the world outside of Poland. Materials emphasize history since 1863. Incl 2000 periodicals.

CENTRAL INSTITUTE FOR THE DEAF

MO —WASHINGTON UNIVERSITY, School of Medicine, Library, 660 South Euclid Ave, Saint Louis, 63110. Christopher Hoolihan, Rare Book Librn
Holdings: Vols 850
Budget: $30000
Notes: The CID/Max A Goldstein Collection in Speech and Hearing. Incl some of the earliest and most of the classic books. Also materials of the Central Institute for the Deaf (CID). Collection being cataloged. All items cataloged are in OCLC data base.

CENTRAL NEW ENGLAND RAILROAD

NY —COLGATE UNIVERSITY, Everett Needham Case Library, Hamilton, 13346. Bruce M Brown, Collections Librn
Notes: New York State railroads. Incl timetables, maps, pictures, clippings, letters and misc materials. Extensive collection on Central New England Railroad.

CERAM, C.W. see Marek, Kurt (C.w. Ceram)

CERAMIC DESIGN

NY —FASHION INSTITUTE OF TECHNOLOGY, Edward C Blum Design Laboratory, 227 W 27 St, New York, 10001. Laura Sinderbrand, Dir
Holdings: Cat Pix Slides
Notes: The largest resource of it kind consisting of 4 million indexed swatches and 300 swatch books, jacquard point paper, croquis, quilts, rug samples, laces, embroideries, and color swatch cards. A collection of international scope incl antique and contemporary textiles; woven and printed patterns created for apparel and home furnishings which may be adapted to china, giftware, floor covering, wallpaper, and package design. A comprehensive research facility comprised of over one million articles of dress dating from the 17th Century to the present, incl men's, women's, children's clothes, furs, foundation garments and lingerie, as well as an outstanding grouping of 19th and 20th century designer clothing. Accessories as diverse as hats, handbags, gloves, hosiery, shoes, shawls, and costume jewelry offer an additonal resource to this international collection.

CERAMIC INDUSTRIES

GA —GEORGIA INSTITUTE OF TECHNOLOGY, Price Gilbert Memorial Library, 225 North Ave, Atlanta, 30332. Edward Graham Roberts, Dir
Holdings: Vols (1,661,559) Cat Maps Slides Microforms
Budget: ($1,383,302)
Notes: Incl (126,998) maps, (4,307,996) patents and (568,490) government documents.

CERAMIC METALS

IL —UNIVERSITY OF ILLINOIS, URBANA/CHAMPAIGN, Library, 221 Engineering Hall, Urbana, 61801. William Mischo, Librn
Holdings: Vols (175,000) Cat Slides

CERAMIC METALS (cont.)

Microforms
Notes: Incl 3500 periodicals. Collection designed to serve teaching and research programs. Supports instructional faculty research. Also, 470 microfilm reels and 6000 microfiche sheets. Incl ceramic engineering.

NY —NEW YORK STATE COLLEGE OF CERAMICS AT ALFRED UNIVERSITY, Scholes Library, Harder Hall, Alfred, 14802. Bruce E Connolly, Library Dir
Holdings: Vols (70,000) Cat Mss Slides Microforms
Budget: ($134,000)
Notes: Very specialized collection incl all phases of the arts and sciences related to ceramics. Incl 1112 subscriptions.

OH —BRUSH WELLMAN, Technical Library, 17876 Saint Clair Ave, Cleveland, 44110. Nancie Skonezny, Tech Librn
Holdings: Vols 1000 Cat
Notes: Beryllium technology--its metals, alloys and ceramics. Incl approx 5000 uncat government documents and international technical reports.

CERAMIC TECHNOLOGY see Ceramics

CERAMICS

CA —CALIFORNIA COLLEGE OF ARTS & CRAFTS, Meyer Library, Broadway at College, Oakland, 94618. Robert L Harper, Head Librn
Holdings: Vols (29,132) Cat Pix
Budget: ($10,000)
Notes: All fields of arts and crafts.

DC —NATIONAL SOCIETY, DAUGHTERS OF THE AMERICAN REVOLUTION, DAR Museum Reference Library, 1776 D St NW, Washington, 20006. Christine Minter-Dowd, Dir; Michael W Berry, Cur; Jean Martin, Registrar
Holdings: Vols (1600) Cat
Budget: ($500)
Notes: American decorative arts, 1700-1850, especially ceramics (incl British imports and Chinese export porcelain) and silverware.

GA —GEORGIA INSTITUTE OF TECHNOLOGY, Price Gilbert Memorial Library, 225 North Ave, Atlanta, 30332. Edward Graham Roberts, Dir
Holdings: Vols (1,661,559) Cat Maps Slides Microforms
Budget: ($1,383,302)
Notes: Incl (126,998) maps, (4,307,996) patents and (568,490) government documents.

IL —UNIVERSITY OF ILLINOIS, URBANA/CHAMPAIGN, Library, 221 Engineering Hall, Urbana, 61801. William Mischo, Librn
Holdings: Vols (175,000) Cat Slides Microforms
Notes: Incl 3500 periodicals. Collection designed to serve teaching and research programs. Supports instructional faculty research. Also, 470 microfilm reels and 6000 microfiche sheets. Incl ceramic engineering.

IA —IOWA STATE UNIVERSITY, Library, Ames, 50011. Warren B Kuhn, Dean of Library Services
Holdings: Cat
Notes: Extensive serial holdings.

KY —UNIVERSITY OF KENTUCKY, Robert E Shaver Library of Engineering, 355 Anderson Hall, Lexington, 40506. Russell H Powell, Engineering Librn
Holdings: Vols (48,000) Cat Microforms

MA —OLD STURBRIDGE VILLAGE, Research Library, Sturbridge, 01566. Theresa Rini Percy, Librn
Holdings: Vols (23,000) Cat Mss Pix
Notes: Hand and mechanized methods and products in New England, 1790-1850: agriculture, ceramics, leatherwork, metal-work, mill-work, needlework, printing, textile crafts and manufacture, woodworking.

MA —NORTON COMPANY, Library, 1 New Bond St, Worcester, 01606. Joan K Chaffey, Librn
Holdings: Cat
Notes: Abrasive industry collection. High performance materials.

MI —CRANBROOK ACADEMY OF ART, 500 Lone Pine Rd, Box 801, Bloomfield Hills, 48013. Diane Gunn, Librn
Holdings: Vols (25,000) Slides

MO —THE NELSON-ATKINS MUSEUM OF ART, Kenneth & Helen Spencer Art Reference Library, 4525 Oak St, Kansas City, 64111. Stanley W Hess, Librn

NM —MUSEUM OF NEW MEXICO, Museum of International Folk Art Library, 706 Camino Lejo, Santa Fe, 87501. Judith Sellars, Librn
Holdings: Vols (8000) Cat
Notes: Folk art of all countries, incl such subjects as costume, ceramics, textiles, furniture. Restricted use; noncirculating.

NY —NEW YORK STATE COLLEGE OF CERAMICS AT ALFRED UNIVERSITY, Scholes Library, Harder Hall, Alfred, 14802. Bruce E Connolly, Library Dir
Holdings: Vols (70,000) Cat Mss Slides Microforms
Budget: ($134,000)
Notes: Very specialized collection incl all phases of the arts and sciences related to ceramics. Incl 1112 subscriptions.

NY —NEW YORK PUBLIC LIBRARY, Art, Prints, and Photographs Div, Fifth Ave & 42 St, New York, 10018. Donald Anderle, Chief
Holdings: Cat Mss Pix

NY —SYBRON CORP, Pfaudler Co, Technical Library, PO Box 1600, Rochester, 14603. Candice Johnson, Librn
Holdings: Vols (1700) Cat Slides Phonorecords Microforms
Notes: Glass and ceramic science.

NC —MINT MUSEUM OF ART, Delhom-Gambrell Reference Library, 501 Hempstead Place, Charlotte, 28207. Sara H Wolf, Librn
Holdings: Vols (3430) Cat Pix Slides
Notes: Library has added 2 private collections on Oriental ceramics (approx 800 volumes, not cataloged) and on decorative arts, mostly French Ceramics (approx 500 volumes, not cataloged). No photocopying.

NC —NORTH CAROLINA STATE UNIVERSITY, D H Hill Library, Box 7111, Raleigh, 27695. I T Littleton, Dir
Holdings: Vols 1380 Cat
Budget: $3000
Notes: Incl monographs in materials engineering.

OH —CLEVELAND PUBLIC LIBRARY, Fine Arts and Special Collections Department, 325 Superior Ave, Cleveland, 44114. Alice N Loranth, Head
Holdings: Vols (16,000) Cat
Notes: Part of the Handicrafts Collection, which incl crafts of many ethnic groups in Cleveland.

OH —OHIO STATE UNIVERSITY, Materials Engineering Library, Watts Hall, 2041 N College Road, Columbus, 43210. Mary Jo V Arnold, Librn
Holdings: Vols (15,000) Cat Microforms
Budget: ($30,000)

OH —TOLEDO-LUCAS COUNTY PUBLIC LIBRARY, 325 Michigan St, Toledo, 43624. Ardath Danford, Dir
Holdings: Vols (2000) Cat Pix Pamphlets
Notes: As complete as possible in fields of history, manufacture and technology. Antique and art glass collections are in Art Division.

PA —FRANKLIN INSTITUTE LIBRARY, 20 & The Parkway, Philadelphia, 19103. Miriam Padusis, Dir; Charles Wilt, Readers Servs Librn
Holdings: Vols (300,000) Cat Maps Pix Microforms

PA —PHILADELPHIA COLLEGE OF ART, Library, Broad & Spruce Sts, Philadelphia, 19102. Hazel Gustow, Dir
Holdings: Vols 25,000 Cat Periodicals Pix Slides Microforms VF
Notes: Printed materials on the arts (history, techniques, aesthetics, etc.). Current buying incl most significant books coming into print or being reprinted, mainly in English. Incl about 22,000 titles, periodicals, 30 cabinets vertical file materials, etc.

PA —PENNSYLVANIA STATE UNIVERSITY, Earth & Mineral Sciences Library, 105 Deike Bldg, University Park, 16802. Emilie McWilliams, Head Librn
Holdings: Vols (58,000) Cat Maps Microforms
Budget: ($49,750)
Notes: This collection includes substantial numbers of geological maps, and strong periodical holdings including microform.

RI —RHODE ISLAND SCHOOL OF DESIGN, Library, Two College St, Providence, 02903. James A Findlay, Dir
Holdings: Vols (70,000) Cat
Budget: ($50,000)

TN —COMBUSTION ENGINEERING, Metallurgical Materials Library, 911 W Main St, Chattanooga, 37402. Nell T Holder, Tech Librn
Holdings: Vols (10,000) Cat Microforms
Notes: Metallurgical research and development.

WI —MILWAUKEE ART MUSEUM, Library, 750 N Lincoln Memorial Dr, Milwaukee, 53202. Betty Karow, Librn
Notes: Also, small collection on 19th century German painting and on Meissen porcelain.

WI —MILWAUKEE PUBLIC LIBRARY, 814 W Wisconsin Ave, Milwaukee, 53233. Donald J Sager, City Librn
Holdings: Vols Cat
Notes: Strength in American and European decorative arts incl ceramics, glassware, jewelry, porcelain, silverware, furniture, interior decoration, textile arts and handicraft.
See also entry under Art, Decorative.

CERAMICS, CHINESE

KS —OTTAWA UNIVERSITY, Myers Library, Ottawa, 66067. J Marion Rioth, Head Librn
Holdings: Vols 2350 Cat Maps Pix
Budget: $150
Notes: This started as a collection of studies about Chinese ceramics, art, and related areas. Incl 800 vols on general Asian studies. If this collection has any unique feature it is in the field of 19th century ceramics trade, especially Chinese. There is a bibliography of the collection.

CEREAL CHEMISTRY

NY —BORDEN FOODS INC, Research Centre Library, 600 N Franklin St, Syracuse, 13204. Carol Lenz-Taylor, Librn
Holdings: Vols (1800) Cat
Notes: Incl 10 vertical file drawers and 6100 patents.

MB —CANADIAN GRAIN COMMISSION, Library, 303 Main St, Winnipeg, R3C 3G7, Can. Jim Blanchard, Librn
Holdings: Vols (7500) Cat Mss Maps Slides Microforms
Budget: ($20,000)

CEREBRAL DEATH see Brain Death

CEREBRAL HEMORRHAGE see Stroke

CEREBRAL LOCALIZATION see Brain—Localization of Functions

CEREBRAL PALSY

CT —NEWINGTON CHILDREN'S HOSPITAL, Professional Library, 181 E Cedar St, Newington, 06111. Jean Long, Librn
Holdings: Vols (3500) Cat
Budget: ($6500)

KS —KANSAS NEUROLOGICAL INSTITUTE, Menninger Professional Library, 3107 W 21 St, Topeka, 66604. Richard Gray, Librn
Holdings: Vols 125
Notes: Incl development disabilities; special education; nursing care for the handicapped; programs for the mentally retarded; behavioral psychology; supervision in mental health/mental retardation; staff training in mental health/mental retardation.

CEREBRAL PARALYSIS see Cerebral Palsy

CEREBROVASCULAR DISEASE

KS —KANSAS NEUROLOGICAL INSTITUTE, Menninger Professional

CEREBROVASCULAR DISEASE (cont.)

Library, 3107 W 21 St, Topeka, 66604. Richard Gray, Librn

TX —AMERICAN HEART ASSOCIATION, Library, 7320 Greenville Ave, Dallas, 75231. Katie Trickey, Librn; Barbara Lightfoot, Info Spec
Holdings: Vols (4000) Cat
Budget: ($20,000)

CEREMONIES see Etiquette

CERF, BENNETT

†NY —COLUMBIA UNIVERSITY LIBRARIES, Butler Library, Rare Book and Manuscript Library, 535 W 114 St, New York, 10027.
Notes: The Bennett Cerf Collection.

CERF, JAY H.

CA —HOOVER INSTITUTION ON WAR, REVOLUTION & PEACE, Stanford University, Stanford, 94305. Milorad M Drachkovitch, Archivist
Holdings: Mss
Notes: Papers, correspondence, etc.

CERLETTI, UGO, 1877-1963

KS —MENNINGER FOUNDATION, Archives, 5600 W Sixth St, Box 829, Topeka, 66601. Alice Brand, Librn; Mark West, Archivist
Notes: 30 boxes, 1905-63. Incl mss, publications, correspondence, research notes, and miscellaneous materials. Nearly all of the papers in the collection are written in Italian.

CERMETS see Ceramic Metals

CERTAINTY see Probabilities (Statistics)

CERVANTES, ALPHONSO J.

MO —WASHINGTON UNIVERSITY, Libraries, Special Collections Dept, Campus Box 1061, St Louis, 63130.
Notes: St Louis Mayoral Papers Collection: Papers of Aloys P Kaufmann, 1944-49; Raymond R Tucker, 1953-65; Alphonso J Cervantes, 1965-73; John H Poelker, 1973-77; James F Conway, 1977-81.

CERVANTES, MIGUEL DE

CA —UNIVERSITY OF CALIFORNIA, BERKELEY, University Library, Hispanic Collections, Berkeley, 94720. Gaston Somoshegyi-Szokol, Librn
See also entry under Spanish Language and Literature.

DC —LIBRARY OF CONGRESS, Rare Book & Special Collections Div, Washington, 20540. William Matheson, Chief
Notes: Based on important gifts, the collection now holds almost 100 Spanish editions, 150 English and 43 French translations, translations in 26 other languages of *Don Quixote,* and distinguished editions from the 20th century. US Library of Congress, *Works by Miguel de Cervantes Savedra in the Library of Congress,* (Washington, 1960). QJLC, vol 39, no 1, Winter 1982, 17-33.

KS —UNIVERSITY OF KANSAS, Kenneth Spencer Research Library, Special Collections Dept, Lawrence, 66045. Alexandra Mason, Librn
Holdings: Vols 200 Cat
Notes: Largely from the library of Sir William Stirling-Maxwell. Very strong in editions of *Don Quixote,* especially 17th-18th centuries. Noncirculating.

MA —HARVARD UNIVERSITY LIBRARY, Houghton Library, Cambridge, 02138. F Thomas Noonan, Cur, Reading Room; Lawrence Dowler, Associate Librn
Holdings: Cat
Notes: See *Harvard Library Bulletin,* I (1947), 306-310.

NY —NEW YORK PUBLIC LIBRARY, Research Libraries, General Research Division, Fifth Ave & 42 St, New York, 10018. Rodney Phillips, Chief
Holdings: Vols (2,225,000) Cat Maps Pix Microforms
Budget: ($775,718)

OH —OHIO STATE UNIVERSITY, William Oxley Thompson Memorial Library, 1858 Neil Ave Mall, Columbus, 43210. Robert A Tibbetts, Cur of Special Collections
Holdings: Vols 800 Cat
Notes: Incl 114 items in Talfourd P Linn Collection. Published catalog: Dorothy Petersen Ackerman. *A Catalogue of the Talfourd P Linn Collection of Cervantes Materials on Deposit in the Ohio State University Libraries.* Columbus: Ohio State University Press, 1963. 90 pp.

ON —QUEEN'S UNIVERSITY, Douglas Library, Kingston, K7L 5C4, Can. William F E Morley, Cur, Special Collections
Holdings: Vols 6980 Cat Mss Pix
Notes: Subject strength of the collections.

CESARE, OSCAR

†VA —UNIVERSITY OF VIRGINIA, Library, Charlottesville, 22901.
Notes: Bernard Meeks original cartoons and drawings collection, 326 items incl some original comic strip art. Fred O Seibel collection of ca 6000 original drawings, and cartoonists' working papers and files. Additional collection of editorial cartoons by Oscar Cesare, Jeff MacNelly, Art Wood, etc. Examples of almost all political and many comic artists working in he mid-20th century.

CETACEA

MA —OLD DARTMOUTH HISTORICAL SOCIETY, 18 Johnny Cake Hill, New Bedford, 02740. Richard C Kugler, Dir
Holdings: Vols (15,000) Mss Maps Pix Microforms
Budget: ($5000)
Notes: Whaling Museum Library contains one of the most comprehensive collections of printed and manuscript material ever assembled on the history of the whaling industry. Although primary emphasis is on American participation in this industry, foreign works are well-represented. Particularly noteworthy are the 5000 rare books and pamphlets assembled by the distinguished whaling scholar, Charles F Batchelder. Also, material on merchant ships and the natural history of whales. Incl 750 ft mss, 1070 log books, 650 maps, 25,000 pix and 25,000 pix, and 1800 microforms.

CETE see Cetacea

CETOMORPHA see Cetacea

CHACO BOREAL WAR, 1932-1935 see Chaco War, 1932-1935

CHACO PEACE CONFERENCE

†NY —COLUMBIA UNIVERSITY LIBRARIES, Butler Library, Rare Book and Manuscript Library, 535 W 114 St, New York, 10027.
Notes: The papers of Spruille Braden, American diplomat in Latin American affairs and American representative at the Chaco Peace Conference.

CHACO WAR, 1932-1935

PA —UNIVERSITY OF PITTSBURGH, Hillman Library, Pittsburgh, 15260.
Holdings: Vols (5000) Cat

CHAD

DC —HOWARD UNIVERSITY, Moorland-Spingarn Research Center, 500 Howard Place NW, Washington, 20059. Clifford L Muse, Jr, Acting Dir

MI —MICHIGAN STATE UNIVERSITY, International Library, Sahel Documentation Center, East Lansing, 48824. Eugene deBenko, Librn; Learthen Dorsey, Librn
Holdings: Vols (5100) Cat Mss Maps Pix Slides Phonorecords Audiotapes Videotapes Microforms
Budget: ($8000)
Notes: See description under The Sahel.

CHADIC LANGUAGES

NY —NEW YORK PUBLIC LIBRARY, Oriental Div, Fifth Ave & 42 St, New York, 10018. E Christian Filstrup, Chief
Holdings: Cat Mss Microforms
Budget: ($56,455)
Notes: Published catalog of holdings.

CHADWICK, GEORGE W.

DC —LIBRARY OF CONGRESS, Music Division, Washington, 20540.
Notes: The business papers and music mss of the Arthur P Schmidt Company. Numerous works by important composers.

CHAFEE, ZECHARIAH, JR., 1885-1957

MA —HARVARD UNIVERSITY LIBRARY, Law School Library, Langdell Hall, Cambridge, 02138. Erika S Chadbourn, Cur of Mss
Holdings: Cat Mss
Notes: Personal-professional papers. Typed inventory in repository. Inclusive dates: 1898-1957.

RI —BROWN UNIVERSITY, John Hay Library, 20 Prospect St, Providence, 02912. Mark N Brown, Cur Mss
Holdings: / / Mss
Notes: The Zechariah Chafee, Jr, mss, 400 papers relating to the Commission on the Freedom of the Press, 1943 to 1947. Incl correspondence, notes, memoranda, reports, clippings, reviews, and articles. Also 450 pieces of correspondence, 1915-1957, relating to Brown University.

CHAGATAI LANGUAGE see Jagataic Language and Literature

CHAIKIN, JOSEPH

OH —KENT STATE UNIVERSITY, Libraries, Dept of Special Collections, Kent, 44242. Dean H Keller, Cur
Holdings: Mss

CHAIN REACTION PILES see Nuclear Reactors

CHAISSON, JOHN R., 1916-1972

CA —HOOVER INSTITUTION ON WAR, REVOLUTION & PEACE, Stanford University, Stanford, 94305. Milorad M Drachkovitch, Archivist
Holdings: Mss Pix
Notes: Papers of Lt Gen John R Chaisson, 1940-1967, incl correspondence, photographs and printed matter relating to his service in the US Marine Corps during World War II, in China during 1948-1949, and during the war in Vietnam. 1 ms box.

CHAKRAVARTY, AMIYA

MA —BOSTON UNIVERSITY, Mugar Memorial Library, Special Collections Dept, 771 Commonwealth Ave, Boston, 02215. Howard B Gotlieb, Dir
Notes: Correspondence with literary and public figures.

CHALDAIC LANGUAGE see Aramaic Language and Literature

CHALDEAN LANGUAGE see Aramaic Language and Literature

CHALDEE LANGUAGE see Aramaic Language and Literature

CHALDIAN LANGUAGE see Vannic Language

CHALMERS, ALLAN KNIGHT

MA —BOSTON UNIVERSITY, Mugar Memorial Library, Special Collections Dept,

CHALMERS, ALLAN KNIGHT (cont.)

771 Commonwealth Ave, Boston, 02215.
Howard B Gotlieb, Dir
Holdings: // Cat Mss Pix
Notes: Mss, correspondence, etc collected in depth; incl publications by or about.

CHAMBER MUSIC

CA —UNIVERSITY OF CALIFORNIA, LOS ANGELES, Music Library, Schonberg Hall, Los Angeles, 90024. Stephen M Fry, Music Librn
Notes: Incl ca 28,000 scores and parts. Broad collection for 1 to 9 instruments.

CA —OAKLAND PUBLIC LIBRARY, Art, Music and Recreation Section, 125 14 St, Oakland, 94612. Richard Colvig, Senior Librn
Holdings: Vols (5000) Cat Phonorecords Audiotapes
Budget: ($6700)
Notes: 10,000 scores, incl chamber music, instrumental music (piano and organ collections especially strong), miniature scores, opera scores, songs and song collections; 30,000 octavos (anthems and choral music of all kinds); 5000 books about music; 8000 phonorecords; and audiocassettes.

CA —PASADENA PUBLIC LIBRARY, Alice Coleman Batchelder Music Library, Reference Services, 285 E Walnut, Pasadena, 91101. Anne Cain, Principal Librn
Holdings: Vols (8012) Cat Pix
Notes: Separate record catalog of over 10, 000 phonorecords; over 4400 music scores. Special index of songs in collection. Over 150,000 pictures.

CA —SANTA CRUZ PUBLIC LIBRARY, Art, Music, Film Dept, 224 Church St, Santa Cruz, 95060. Alma Westberg, Librn
Holdings: Vols (1500) Cat Mss
Budget: ($750)
Notes: The music collection is in a catalog separate from the general one. It consists of approx 1700 cataloged books about music; 2100 bound, cataloged books of music incl opera and musical comedy scores; 2700 pieces of sheet music which incl sacred, art and popular songs, and instrumental solos. Good collection of chamber music from baroque to contemporary composers. Also a special collection of 10,000 pieces of American popular sheet music of the period from the 1860s to 1970s incl songs of California. The record collection, primarily classical, consists of about 5500 records.

DC —LIBRARY OF CONGRESS, Music Division, Washington, 20540.
Notes: Elizabeth Sprague Coolidge Foundation Collection incl music mss of 20th century chamber music and her papers and photographs.

IL —AURORA PUBLIC LIBRARY, 1 Benton St, Aurora, 60506. Mary E Clark, Head Librn
Holdings: Vols (23,000) Cat
Notes: Plus 1000 pieces of early popular sheet music (uncataloged). Collection espec strong in vocal and piano music and in chamber music.

IN —INDIANA UNIVERSITY, Lilly Library, Seventh St, Bloomington, 47405. William R Cagle, Librn
Holdings: Cat
Notes: Extensive holdings of American sheet music; first editions of works by great composers (operas, symphonies, chamber music, etc); scores annotated for performances conducted by Fritz Busch.

MD —UNIVERSITY OF MARYLAND, BALTIMORE COUNTY, Albin O Kuhn Library and Gallery, 5401 Wilkens Ave, Baltimore, 21228. Larry Wilt, Collection Management Librn
Holdings: Vols (3000) Cat
Notes: Collection incl musical monuments, collected editions, full scores, performing editions and study scores. Particularly strong in performing editions of chamber music (classical and romantic periods). Coverage of modern period incl Igor Stravinski, John Cage, Charles Ives, Karlheinz Stockhausen, Kenneth Gabino, Mauricio Kagel, Stuart Smith, Herbert Brun. Recent collecting has emphasized graphic notation in music.

MA —BOSTON PUBLIC LIBRARY, Music Division, 666 Boylston St, Box 286, Boston, 02117. Ruth Bleecker, Cur of Music
Holdings: Vols (100,000) Cat Mss Pix Microforms
Notes: The Allen A Brown Music Library is the nucleus of the collection. There is a *Dictionary Catalog of the Music Collection* (Boston: G K Hall, 1976; 24 vols). Incl music scores.

OH —CLEVELAND PUBLIC LIBRARY, Fine Arts and Special Collections Department, 325 Superior Ave, Cleveland, 44114. Alice N Loranth, Head
Holdings: Vols 1750 Cat
Notes: Incl scores and parts for chamber music for trios to nonets and various combinations of instruments. Indexed by types of combinations.

OH —OBERLIN COLLEGE, Oberlin Conservatory of Music, Mary M Vial Library, Oberlin, 44074. John E Druesedow Jr, Dir
Holdings: Vols (75,000) Cat Phonorecords Audiotapes Filmstrips Microforms
Budget: ($60,000)
Notes: Special emphases; history and literature of the organ; music before 1700; music since 1950; music education; opera; American music; chamber and solistic music. Published catalog: *Mr and Mrs C W Best Collection of Autographs in the Mary M Vial Music Library of the Oberlin College Conservatory of Music* (Oberlin, Ohio: Oberlin College, 1967).

PA —BALA CYNWYD LIBRARY, Old Lancaster Rd & N Highland Ave, Bala Cynwyd, 19004. Rosalind Leighton, Reference Librn
Holdings: Vols (450) Cat Phonorecords Audiotapes

PA —FREE LIBRARY OF PHILADELPHIA, Music Dept, Drinker Library of Choral Music, Logan Sq, Philadelphia, 19103. Frederick James Kent, Head
Holdings: Cat Mss
Budget: ($27,754)
Notes: The collection has approx 18,000 sets of chamber music parts for ensembles.

TX —NORTH TEXAS STATE UNIVERSITY, Audio Center, Box 5188, NT Station, Denton, 76203. Morris Martin, Music Librn
Notes: Supports wide range of music curricula and research with over 100,000 volumes incl music books, periodicals, scores, sheet music of all kinds, chamber music, recordings.

CHAMBERLAIN, JOSHUA LAWRENCE, 1828-1914

ME —BOWDOIN COLLEGE, Library, Brunswick, 04011. Dianne M Gutscher, Cur of Special Collections
Holdings: Mss Pix
Notes: (1) The Chamberlain Papers consist of 1900 mss pieces of correspondence, addresses, lecture notes, diaries, and clippings relating to Chamberlain's career in the United States Army (1862-1865), as governor of Maine (1867-1870), and as president of Bowdoin College (1871-1883).

CHAMBERLAIN AND LYMAN BROWN THEATRICAL AGENCY

NY —NEW YORK PUBLIC LIBRARY, Performing Arts Research Center, Billy Rose Theatre Collection, 111 Amsterdam Ave, New York, 10023. Dorothy L Swerdlove, Cur
Holdings: Cat Mss Pix
Notes: Papers, scrapbooks, mss, photographs, memorabilia, etc.

CHAMBERLEN, PETER

WI —SEVENTH DAY BAPTIST HISTORICAL SOCIETY, Library, 3120 Kennedy Rd, PO Box 1678, Janesville, 53547. D Scott Smith, Historian
Holdings: Vols 200 Uncat Mss Pix
Notes: English Seventh Day Baptists Collection. These materials have to do with early and middle years of Baptist movement (1662-1920) in England, incl work of John James, Joseph Stennett, Peter Chamberlen, et al, Sabbatarians or Seventh Day Baptists. About 300 items incl record books, tracts, correspondence.

CHAMBERLIN, STEPHEN

PA —US ARMY MILITARY HISTORY INSTITUTE, Carlisle Barracks, 17013. Richard J Sommers, Chief Archivist-Historian
Holdings: Mss Cat
Notes: The World War II collection, personal letters, daily logs, reminiscences, speeches, and official papers of American officers and soldiers serving in the European, Mediterranean, Middle Eastern, China-Burma-India, Southwest Pacific, and Central Pacific Theaters and in the Zone of the Interior during the Second World War. Most of these collections are manuscripts of General officers, incl Omar Bradley, Stephen Chamberlin, Lewis Hershey, John Lucas, William Simpson, and Brehon Somervell.

CHAMBERS, EVERETT

MA —BOSTON UNIVERSITY, Mugar Memorial Library, Special Collections Dept, 771 Commonwealth Ave, Boston, 02215. Howard B Gotlieb, Dir
Holdings: Cat Mss Pix
Notes: Mss, correspondence, etc collected in depth; incl publications by or about.

CHAMBERS, JULIUS

NC —UNIVERSITY OF NORTH CAROLINA, CHARLOTTE, J Murrey Atkins Library, UNCC Station, Charlotte, 28223. Robert F Brabham Jr, Special Collections Librn
Holdings: Cat Mss
Notes: Papers of Julius Chambers relating to the Swann v Charlotte/Mecklenburg Board of Education case, which established the constitutionality of busing to achieve racial integration of the public schools.

CHAMBERS, ROBERT W.

NY —COLGATE UNIVERSITY, Everett Needham Case Library, Hamilton, 13346. Bruce M Brown, Collections Librn
Holdings: Vols 98 Uncat Mss

CHAMBRUN, RENE

CA —HOOVER INSTITUTION ON WAR, REVOLUTION & PEACE, Stanford University, Stanford, 94305. Milorad M Drachkovitch, Archivist
Holdings: // Mss
Notes: The Rene Chambrun Collection. Depositions concerning the government of Marshall Petain and Pierre Laval, by persons who held important official positions in France during the German occupation. Unpublished register available in repository.

CHAMPIGNONS see Mushrooms

CHAMPION, GOWER, 1921-1980

CA —UNIVERSITY OF CALIFORNIA, LOS ANGELES, Research Library, Dept of Special Collections, 405 Hilgard Ave, Los Angeles, 90024. Edward Shreeves, Chairman, Bibliographers Group; David S Zeidberg, Head
Holdings: Mss Pix
Notes: 1 linear foot of scripts and related materials for musicals he directed.

CHAMPLAIN, HELENE

PA —DICKINSON COLLEGE, Boyd Lee Spahr Library, W High St, Carlisle, 17013. Yates M Forbis, Dir
Holdings: Mss Pix Audiotapes
Notes: The Sandburg-Champlain collection of mss, letters, books, photographs, and memorabilia. Incl some 200 vols with

CHAMPLAIN, HELENE (cont.)

references to Sandburg or his friends, or contain pieces written by Sandburg. Memorabilia incl eye-shade, audiotapes, etc by Sandburg and Miss Champlain.

CHAMPLAIN VALLEY, NEW YORK

NY —STATE UNIVERSITY OF NEW YORK, COLLEGE AT PLATTSBURGH, Feinberg Library, Special Collections, 153 Hawkins Hall, Plattsburgh, 12901. Joseph G Swinyer, Librn
Holdings: Vols (1000) Cat Mss Maps Pix Phonorecords Microforms
See also entry under New York (State) - History

CHANCE COMPOSITION (MUSIC)

CA —CALIFORNIA INSTITUTE OF THE ARTS, Library, 24700 McBean Pkwy, Valencia, 91355. James Elrod, Dir
Holdings: Vols (61,000) Cat Phonorecords Audiotapes
Budget: ($500)
Notes: Incl 11,656 audiotapes. Cataloged.

CHANCE MUSIC see Chance Composition (Music)

CHANDLER, ALBERT BENJAMIN

KY —UNIVERSITY OF KENTUCKY, Margaret I King Library, Dept of Special Collections, Lexington, 40506. William Marshall, Head
Holdings: Cat Mss Pix Film Audiotapes
Notes: Collection incl papers relating to his legal practice, 2 terms as Kentucky's governor, US senator from Kentucky, commissioner of baseball as well as family and personal files. Period covered: 1920-1973. Unpublished inventory.

CHANDLER, GEORGE

CA —AMERICAN FILM INSTITUTE, Louis B Mayer Library, 2021 N Western Ave, PO Box 27999, Los Angeles, 90027. Anne G Schlosser, Dir
Holdings: Vols (3500) Cat

CHANDLER, RAYMOND, 1888-1959

CA —CLAREMONT COLLEGES, Honnold Library, Ninth & Dartmouth, Claremont, 91711. Tania Rizzo, Special Collections Dept Head
Notes: Working papers of Irving Wallace and his family. Incl audio and video taped interviews with Wallace, Marlene Dietrich, Raymond Chandler, and Pablo Picasso.

CA —UNIVERSITY OF CALIFORNIA, LOS ANGELES, Research Library, Dept of Special Collections, 405 Hilgard Ave, Los Angeles, 90024. Edward Shreeves, Chairman, Bibliographers Group; David S Zeidberg, Head
Holdings: Vols 330 Cat Mss Pix
Notes: 18 linear feet of books, correspondence, mss, and foreign paperback editions.

OH —KENT STATE UNIVERSITY, Libraries, Dept of Special Collections, Kent, 44242. Dean H Keller, Cur
Holdings: Vols 232 Cat

CHANDLER, THOMAS ALBERTER

OK —UNIVERSITY OF OKLAHOMA, Bizzell Memorial Library, Western History Collections, 401 W Brooks, Norman, 73069. John Ezell, Cur
Holdings: Mss Documents
Notes: US Representative. His papers. Guide available.

CHANDLER, SETH

NY —AMERICAN INSTITUTE OF PHYSICS, Center for the History of Physics, Niels Bohr Library, 335 E 45 St, New York, 10017. John Aubry, Librn
Notes: The Sources for History of Modern Astrophysics documents the history of 20th-century astrophysics. Incl some 400 hours of oral history interviews with astronomers, such as Bart Bok, S Chandrasekhar, Martin Schwarzschild, and A E Whitford. The project also organized and cataloged the papers of Henry Norris Russell, Frank Schlesinger, Otto Struve, Ejnar Hertzsprung, Harlow Shapley, Charles Young, Robert Atkinson, Seth Chandler, Theodore Dunham, Jr, and G C McVittie.

CHANDLER, WILLIAM E.

NH —NEW HAMPSHIRE HISTORICAL SOCIETY, Manuscripts Library, 30 Park St, Concord, 03301. Thomas E Camden, Cur
Holdings: Cat Mss
Notes: William E Chandler (1835-1917), lawyer, politician, and US Senator from Concord, New Hampshire. Papers incl correspondence, family records, diaries, documents, articles, speeches, and newspaper clippings, relating to Chandler's political career, especially as Assistant Secretary of the Treasury (1865-67), secretary of the Republican National Committee (1868, 1872, 1876), Secretary of the Navy (1882-1885), US Senator (1887-1901), and as president of the Spanish Treaty Claims Commission (1901-1907). 22 linear feet, about 25,000 items.

CHANDRASEKHAR, S.

IL —UNIVERSITY OF CHICAGO LIBRARY, Dept of Special Collections, 1100 E 57 St, Chicago, 60637.
Notes: Papers.

NY —AMERICAN INSTITUTE OF PHYSICS, Center for the History of Physics, Niels Bohr Library, 335 E 45 St, New York, 10017. John Aubry, Librn
Notes: The Sources for History of Modern Astrophysics documents the history of 20th-century astrophysics. Incl some 400 hours of oral history interviews with astronomers, such as Bart Bok, S Chandrasekhar, Martin Schwarzschild, and A E Whitford. The project also organized and cataloged the papers of Henry Norris Russell, Frank Schlesinger, Otto Struve, Ejnar Hertzsprung, Harlow Shapley, Charles Young, Robert Atkinson, Seth Chandler, Theodore Dunham, Jr, and G C McVittie.

CHANEY, RALPH W.

OR —UNIVERSITY OF OREGON, Library, Eugene, 97403. Kenneth W Duckett, Curator
Notes: Ralph W Chaney's books; about 12, 000 letters; and mss for books and articles. Largely concerned with various aspects of paleontology, paleobotany, and the fossil Redwoods.

CHANGE RINGING

MI —GUILD OF CARILLONNEURS IN NORTH AMERICA, Archives, 900 Burton Tower, University of Michigan, Ann Arbor, 48109. William De Turk, Archivist
Holdings: Mss Pix Phonorecords
Notes: Emphasis is on carillons.

NY —SOCIETAS CAMPANARIORUM (SOCIETY OF BELL-RINGERS), Campanological Library, Riverside Church, 490 Riverside Dr, New York, 10027. James R Lawson, Librn
Holdings: Vols 1000 Cat
Notes: One of the largest collections of books, pamphlets, periodicals, etc on bells and bell music (chimes, carillons, change-ringing, handbells, electronic carillons, etc) in North America. Examined by appointment only.

CHANNEL IMPROVEMENTS see Stream Channelization

CHANNELIZATION, STREAM see Stream Channelization

CHANNING, WILLIAM ELLERY (THE YOUNGER)

MA —CONCORD FREE PUBLIC LIBRARY, 129 Main St, Concord, 01742. Rose Marie Mitten, Dir
Holdings: Cat Mss Pix
Notes: A close friend of Emerson, Alcott, and Thoreau.

CHANUTE, OCTAVE, 1832-1910

WY —UNIVERSITY OF WYOMING, William Robertson Coe Library, 13 & Ivinson, Laramie, 82071.
Notes: The papers of Octave Chanute (1832-1910), pioneer railroad engineer and prominent aeronautic pioneer. Incl several hundred aviation photographs, letters, articles, pamphlets, speeches, and clippings, particularly on early-day gliders, with which Chanute was greatly involved.

CHAPBOOKS

CA —CLAREMONT COLLEGES, Ella Strong Denison Library, Scripps College, Claremont, 91711. Judy Harvey Sahak, Librn
Holdings: Vols 452 Cat
Notes: Early books for children published 1790 to early 20th century. Emphasis on moralistic and didactic literature of 1790s-1840s, tracts, alphabet books, school books, readers, chap books, horn books, verse and riddles. 150 vols uncataloged.

CA —UNIVERSITY OF CALIFORNIA, LOS ANGELES, Research Library, Dept of Special Collections, 405 Hilgard Ave, Los Angeles, 90024. Edward Shreeves, Chairman, Bibliographers Group; David S Zeidberg, Head
Holdings: Vols 1000
Notes: 1000 British chapbooks, incl some with music.

CA —HUNTINGTON LIBRARY, Art Gallery & Botanical Gardens, 1151 Oxford Rd, San Marino, 91108. Robert L Middlekauff, Dir; Daniel H Woodward, Librn
Holdings: Vols 100 Cat
Notes: Refer to: Zall, P M "English Prose Jest Books in the Huntington Library: A Chronological Checklist (1535?-1799)," in *Shakespearean Research Opportunities*, no 4, 1968/69, pp 78-91, revised, 1983. Collections of prose anecdotes or tales with humorous intent incl apothegms and books that mix prose and verse, conventionally, in the 18th century.

CT —YALE UNIVERSITY, Box 1603A, Yale Station, New Haven, 06520.

IL —NORTHWESTERN UNIVERSITY, Library, Special Collections Dept, 1937 Sheridan Rd, Evanston, 60201. R Russell Maylone, Cur
Holdings: Vols 650 Cat
Notes: English chapbooks of the early 19th century.

IN —INDIANA UNIVERSITY, Lilly Library, Seventh St, Bloomington, 47405. William R Cagle, Librn
Holdings: Vols 2000 Uncat
Notes: The Elisabeth Ball Collection consists of more than 7,000 books and many manuscripts from the late seventeenth to the early twentieth centuries. Strengths include Newbery and other early imprints, chapbooks, horn books, harlequinades, street cries, and miniature books.

KY —UNIVERSITY OF KENTUCKY, Margaret I King Library, Dept of Special Collections, Lexington, 40506. William Marshall, Head
Holdings: Uncat
Notes: About 400 items--English, American, Irish; a few in other languages. Partial index file.

MA —HARVARD UNIVERSITY LIBRARY, Widener Library, Cambridge, 02138.
Holdings: Cat
Notes: Catalog published in Harvard University Library, *Bibliographical* Contributions, 56 (1905).

MO —SAINT LOUIS PUBLIC LIBRARY, Gardner Rare Book Room, 1301 Olive St, Saint Louis, 63103. Julanne M Good, Supervisor; Martha Riley, Rare Books Librn
Holdings: Vols 200 // Cat
Notes: Collection incl 150 miniature chapbooks printed in the US and in Great Britain between ca 1790 and 1880, and 2 pre-1550 printed broadsides. Noncirculating.

CHAPBOOKS (cont.)

NH —DARTMOUTH COLLEGE, Baker Memorial Library, Hanover, 03755.
Holdings: Vols 350 Cat
Notes: Primarily New Hampshire imprints. Noncirculating.

NY —NEW YORK PUBLIC LIBRARY, Research Libraries, General Research Division, Fifth Ave & 42 St, New York, 10018. Rodney Phillips, Chief
Holdings: Vols (2,225,000) Cat Maps Pix Microforms
Budget: ($775,718)

NY —STATE UNIVERSITY OF NEW YORK, STONY BROOK, Melville Library, Dept of Special Collections, Stony Brook, 11794. Evert Volkersz, Head
Holdings: Vols 150 Uncat
Notes: Early 19th century English chapbooks.

OH —CLEVELAND PUBLIC LIBRARY, Fine Arts and Special Collections Department, 325 Superior Ave, Cleveland, 44114. Alice N Loranth, Head
Holdings: Vols 1730 Cat
Notes: Incl a large number of English as well as specimens in French, Spanish, Italian, German, Russian and other European languages. A fair collection of English and French broadsides and street slip ballads of the late 18th and early 19th century supplements the chapbook collection. Unique in the USA is the collection of 130 Russian chapbooks.
See also entry under Folklore

BC —SIMON FRASER UNIVERSITY, Library, Burnaby, V5A 1S6, Can. Percilla Groves, Special Collections Librn
Holdings: Cat Mss
Notes: Mss for published and unpublished works, plus a complete collection of published books, chapbooks and broadsides by Canadian and American writers, plus correspondence and business records of the British Columbia Press run by poet and teacher Barry McKinnon from 1972 to 1980.

CHAPIN, CHARLES V., 1856-1941

RI —BROWN UNIVERSITY, John Hay Library, 20 Prospect St, Providence, 02912. Mark N Brown, Cur Mss
Holdings: // Mss
Notes: Three boxes of correspondence of Charles V Chapin and mss, 1900-1939, chiefly with workers in public health in America, Europe, and Australia about Dr Chapin's work in communicable diseases.

CHAPIN, CORNELIA VAN AUKEN, 1893- ?

MA —RADCLIFFE COLLEGE, Arthur & Elizabeth Schlesinger Library on the History of Women in America, 3 James St, Cambridge, 02138. Patricia Miller King, Dir; Eva Moseley, Cur of Mss
Notes: Correspondence, writings, etc of the sculptor Harriet Goodhue Hosmer. (1830-1908). Probably largest collection of her papers. Available on microfilm. Inventory published by G K Hall; see Hamilton Family for citation. Also papers of Alma Kline and Cornelia Van Auken Chapin (1893-).

CHAPIN, KATHERINE GARRISON, 1890-1977

DC —GEORGETOWN UNIVERSITY, Library, Special Collections Div, 37 & O Sts NW, Washington, 20057. George M Barringer, Special Collections Librn; Nicholas B Sheetz, Mss Librn
Holdings: Cat
Notes: The papers of the poet and essayist Katherine Garrison Chapin (1890-1977), wife of former Attorney-General Francis Biddle. Containing mss, photographs, and correspondence. Also present is her extensive poetry library with many of the volumes bearing presentation inscriptions by the authors.

CHAPLAINS, HOSPITAL see Chaplains and Chaplaincy

CHAPLAINS AND CHAPLAINCY

CA —HOOVER INSTITUTION ON WAR, REVOLUTION & PEACE, Stanford University, Stanford, 94305. Milorad M Drachkovitch, Archivist
Notes: Papers of Paul W Frillmann, chaplain of the American Volunteer Group ("Flying Tigers"), 1941-45, and US consular official in China and Hong Kong, 1946-50, incl correspondence, memoranda, orders, notes and photos, 1941-69, relating to activities of the American Volunteer Group in China during World War II, US foreign relations with China, 1946-50, and conditions in China during the civil war. 3 ms boxes, 3 framed certificates.

SC —BAPTIST MEDICAL CENTER, Amelia White Pitts Memorial Library, Taylor at Marion Sts, Columbia, 29220. Lois W Smith, Medical Librn
Holdings: Vols (3000) Cat

CHAPLIN, CHARLES

NY —NEW YORK PUBLIC LIBRARY, Performing Arts Research Center, Billy Rose Theatre Collection, 111 Amsterdam Ave, New York, 10023. Dorothy L Swerdlove, Cur
Holdings: Cat Mss Pix
Notes: Papers, scrapbooks, mss, photographs, memorabilia, etc.

CHAPMAN, CHAUNCEY BREWSTER, JR., 1919-1980

DC —GEORGETOWN UNIVERSITY, Library, Special Collections Div, 37 & O Sts NW, Washington, 20057. George M Barringer, Special Collections Librn; Nicholas B Sheetz, Mss Librn
Holdings: Cat
Notes: Papers of Chauncey Brewster Chapman, Jr (1919-1980), attorney, from his early legal career in private practice and his years in the Department of Interior where he served as solicitor for territories from 1967-1979. The bulk of the papers concerns judicial and legal matters in regard to territories outside the United States, as well as internal departmental affairs. Of particular interest is material concerning Samoa from 1969-1980.

CHAPMAN, JOHN

MA —LEOMINSTER PUBLIC LIBRARY, 30 West St, Leominster, 01453.
Holdings: Mss Pix
Notes: Index. Material about the legendary John (Johnny Appleseed) Chapman.

CHAPMAN, JOHN JAY

MA —HARVARD UNIVERSITY LIBRARY, Houghton Library, Cambridge, 02138. Rodney G Dennis, Cur of Manuscripts
Holdings: Cat Mss

CHAPMAN, M. SYDNEY

CO —UNIVERSITY OF COLORADO, Libraries, Western Historical Collections, Boulder, 80309.
Holdings: Mss Slides Films
Notes: Papers of the world renowned space scientist and recipient of many honors, Walter Orr Roberts (1915-), who is currently associated with the University of Colorado as a professor of astro-geophysics. He has written extensively on solar activity and its effects on earth. The collection is comprised of correspondence with individuals and business and research organizations, reports, proposals and conference data, speeches, committee papers, studies, research notes, lectures and student papers plus a few personal papers, printed matter, films and slides. Also there are personal items which belonged to M Sydney Chapman and were given to Roberts. 60 boxes, 1940s-1970s. Typescript inventory is available.

CHAPPELL, FRED

NC —DUKE UNIVERSITY, William R Perkins Library, Rare Book Room, Durham, 27706. John L Sharpe, III, Cur
Notes: A collection of Duke University authors, established around 1963, with the writings of the students of William Blackburn and greatly enhanced by the gift of Professor Blackburn's collection. Represented are James Applewhite, Fred Chappell, Guy Davenport, Reynolds Price, William Styron, Frances Gray Patton, and Anne Tyler. Printed works are in the Rare Book Room and manuscripts are in the Manuscript Department.

CHARACTER TESTS

CT —YALE UNIVERSITY, Medical Historical Library, 333 Cedar St, New Haven, 06510. Ferenc A Gyorgyey, Librn

IL —UNIVERSITY OF ILLINOIS, URBANA/CHAMPAIGN, Library, University Archives, 19 Library, 1408 W Gregory Drive, Urbana, 61801. Maynard Brichford, University Archivist
Holdings: Vols (6000) Cat
Budget: $1500
Notes: The Odell Test Collection contains 3150 items comprising intelligence, achievement, subject, and character and personality tests. Almost every educational and psychological test of consequence prior to the early 1950s is included. The collection is located in the Education and Social Science Library and is integrated into a comprehensive collection of current and recent standardized tests. The indexing of the collection follows the scheme created and used by Oscar K Buros in his *Mental Measurement Yearbooks* and in the predecessors to the Yearbooks which appeared in the Rutgers Studies in Education series. The collection was a gift in 1960 of Charles Watters Odell, Professor Emeritus of Education. No photocopying.

CHARCOAL, ACTIVATED see Carbon, Activated

CHARCOT, JEAN MARTIN

MA —FRANCIS A COUNTWAY LIBRARY OF MEDICINE, Boston Medical Library/Harvard Medical Library, 10 Shattuck St, Boston, 02115. C Robin LeSueur, Librn; Richard J Wolfe, Cur, Rare Books & Manuscripts
Holdings: Mss
Notes: Incl 10,000 glass negatives of neurological patients.

CHARGED PARTICLE ACCELERATORS see Particle Accelerators

CHARITABLE INSTITUTIONS see Charitable Uses, Trusts, and Foundations

CHARITABLE USES, TRUSTS, AND FOUNDATIONS

CT —HARTFORD PUBLIC LIBRARY, Reference & General Reading Dept, 500 Main St, Hartford, 06103. Beverly A Loughlin, Admin Asst
Holdings: Vols (3000) Cat Mss Maps Pix Slides Phonorecords Audiotapes Videotapes 16mm Films
Notes: Collection is a Foundation Center cooperative collection of Grant-in-Aid for the state of Connecticut, with such holdings as soft and hard copy, IRS apperture cards, comsearch microfiche and other periodicals in support of their subject area.

†DC —ARMENIAN ASSEMBLY CHARITABLE TRUST, Library and Information Center, 522 21 St, NW, Washington, 20006.

†IN —NORTH AMERICAN ISLAMIC TRUST INC, Library, 10900 West Washington St, Indianapolis, 46227.

KS —WICHITA PUBLIC LIBRARY, Reference Dept, 223 S Main, Wichita, 67202. Myrna Hudson, General Ref Librn
Holdings: Vols 30 Cat Aperture Cards
Notes: The library is a local affliate of the

CHARITABLE USES, TRUSTS, AND FOUNDATIONS (cont.)

Foundation Center. The core collection is (30) reference volumes, plus aperture cards of the IRS 990 forms filed in Kansas. This core collection is supplemented by circulating materials in the General Collections area.

MI —MONROE COUNTY LIBRARY SYSTEM, Ellis Reference and Information Center, 3700 S Custer Rd, Monroe, 48161. Bernard Margolis, Dir
Holdings: Vols 500 Cat Microforms Periodicals
Budget: $5000
Notes: Incl all types of current and historical materials on foundations, foundation reports, grants-in-aid, fund raising, grant writing, sample file, periodicals, booklist, etc.

NY —COLUMBIA UNIVERSITY LIBRARIES, Rare Book & Manuscript Library, 801 Butler Library, 535 W 114 St, New York, 10027. Kenneth A Lohf, Librn
Notes: More than 32,000 items documenting the rise of William Russell Grace's shipping business and other materials relating to his career as mayor of New York. Incl records and correspondence relating to all aspects of the shipping business in New York and South America, mining interest in Peru and Chile, and transportation in Costa Rica and Nicaragua. Family memorabilia and photographs, materials concerning New York Politics, banking and insurance, real estate interests and Catholic charities, and letters from Chester A Arthur, John Jacob Astor, Andrew Carnegie, Grover Cleveland, Hamilton Fish, John Hay and J Pierpont Morgan. Restricted use.

NY —THE FOUNDATION CENTER, Library, 888 Seventh Ave, New York, 10106. Candace Kuhta, Coordr, Public Services
Holdings: Vols (2500) Cat Microforms
Budget: ($12,000)
Notes: 200,000 Foundation IRS returns on aperture cards; 500 annual reports. All available material on foundations, both current and historical. Private foundation tax returns; annual reports; books, pamphlets, and articles on foundations and philanthropy. Publish *The Foundation Directory, The Foundation Grants Index, Source Book Profiles, National Data Book, Foundation Grants to Individuals, Comsearch Printouts, Corporate Foundation Profiles, America's voluntary spirit.* Washington Library, 1001 Connecticut Ave, NW. Field offices: Foundation Center--Cleveland, 739 National City Bank Bldg, 629 Euclid Ave, Cleveland, Ohio 44114; Foundation Center--San Francisco, 312 Sutter St, San Francisco, Calif 94108. Over 130 regional depositories of foundation information and reports, in all states, Mexico, Puerto Rico, Canada, the Virgin Islands and England.

NY —ROCKEFELLER UNIVERSITY, Rockefeller Archive Center, Hillcrest, Pocantico Hills, North Tarrytown, 10591. Joseph W Ernst, Dir; J William Hess, Assoc Dir
Notes: The Rockefeller Archive Center, a division of The Rockefeller University, preserves and makes available to scholars the records of the University, the Rockefeller Foundation, the Rockefeller Brothers Fund, members of the family, and those of other individuals and organizations associated with their endeavors. Collections at the Center document a century of philanthropy by legions of associated social and scientific pioneers, providing a unique window into the past.

NY —UNIVERSITY OF ROCHESTER, Rush Rhees Library, Department of Rare Books and Special Collections, Rochester, 14627. Peter Dzwonkoski, Librn
Holdings: Vols Cat Mss Pix
Notes: The manuscript and printed records of several Rochester, NY civic and charitable organizations including the Hillside Children's Center (founded in 1837 as the Rochester Orphan Asylum), Rochester's Children Nursery (founded in 1847 as the Rochester Home for the Friendless), Rochester Female Charitable Society (founded in 1822), YWCA of Rochester and Monroe County (founded in 1883), and Planned Parenthood of Rochester and Monroe County (founded in 1932).

NC —CAMPBELL COLLEGE, Carrie Rich Memorial Library, Box 98, Buies Creek, 27506. Helen Sistrunk, Asst to Dir
Holdings: Vols 8500 Cat Mss
Budget: $5600

NC —DUKE UNIVERSITY, William R Perkins Library, Manuscript Dept, Durham, 27706. Ellen Gartrell, Cur of Mss
Holdings: Cat Mss
Notes: Papers of the Duke Endowment (1924-).

PA —LIBRARY COMPANY OF PHILADELPHIA, 1314 Locust St, Philadelphia, 19107. Edwin Wolf II, Librn; Kenneth Finkel, Cur of Prints
Holdings: Vols (450,000) Cat
Notes: Significant collection of works on early American charities. See *American Philanthropy, 1731-1860* by Cornelia S King (Gailand, 1984).

WA —SEATTLE PUBLIC LIBRARY, Education Dept, 1000 Fourth Ave, Seattle, 98104. Jean Coberly, Head
Holdings: Cat Microforms

†WA —UNIVERSITY OF WASHINGTON LIBRARIES, Seattle, 98195.

CHARITIES see Charitable Uses, Trusts, and Foundations

CHARLEMAGNE CYCLE

OH —CLEVELAND PUBLIC LIBRARY, Fine Arts and Special Collections Department, 325 Superior Ave, Cleveland, 44114. Alice N Loranth, Head
Holdings: Vols (3000) Cat Mss
Notes: Part of the Romances Collection, which incl critical studies, and early printed editions. The Arthurian and Charlemagne cycles, the Nibelungenlied and other Germanic titles, Amadis de Gaula and his numerous progeny, Alexander the Great, Barlaam and Joasaph, and the Seven Wise Masters of Rome are some of the strengths of the collection. Material in the Dewey/Brett Collection is classified by related cycles and their versions in various languages.
See also entry under Romances.

CHARLES I, KING OF ENGLAND

IN —INDIANA UNIVERSITY, Lilly Library, Seventh St, Bloomington, 47405. William R Cagle, Librn
Holdings: Vols 970 // Cat
Notes: Incl contemporary printings of government publications.

CHARLES II, KING OF ENGLAND

CT —YALE UNIVERSITY, Art Library, 180 York St, New Haven, 06520. Nancy S Lambert, Art Librn
Holdings: Cat Mss
Notes: "24 letters written by the youthful Charles II before his ascent to the British throne in 1660...addressed to Theobald Taaffee." See *New York Times*, 15 May 1971.

IN —INDIANA UNIVERSITY, Lilly Library, Seventh St, Bloomington, 47405. William R Cagle, Librn
Holdings: Vols (570) // Cat Mss
Notes: Incl contemporary printings of government publication. Mss incl papers of Ignatius White, Marquis d'Albeville. 1653-1690, 335 items.

CHARLES X, KING OF FRANCE

NY —CORNELL UNIVERSITY LIBRARIES, John M Olin Library, Dept of Rare Books, Ithaca, 14853. Donald D Eddy, Librn
Holdings: // Mss
Notes: Charles X (Santerre) Collection. See Lynn Manuela Welch, "The Santerres and King Charles the Tenth" in *The Cornell Library Journal*, Autumn 1969.

CHARLESTON, SOUTH CAROLINA—HISTORY

SC —COLLEGE OF CHARLESTON LIBRARY, Special Collections Dept, Charleston, 29401.
Notes: (1) Papers of the Charleston High School 1843-1976, (for white boys until recently), one of the nation's oldest public institutions of secondary education, dating from 1839. Also papers of The Memminger School (for white girls until recently); two black schools: Avery Institute (1866-1940) and Laing School (1866-1980). (2) South Carolina Court of Common Pleas Papers, 1948-1760, 1810. (3) Charleston history papers incl papers of Charleston County's Citizen's Council, Office of County Clerk, 1700-1936, Charleston Daily Courier, 1864; Charleston Library Society, 1762; Charleston, SC, Appeals Court, 1849; Chamber of Commerce, 1823-1839 and 1858; City Council, 1832-1859 and 1867; and Voter Registration Notice, 1815.

CHARLOT, ANDRE, 1882-1956

CA —UNIVERSITY OF CALIFORNIA, LOS ANGELES, Research Library, Dept of Special Collections, 405 Hilgard Ave, Los Angeles, 90024. Edward Shreeves, Chairman, Bibliographers Group; David S Zeidberg, Head
Notes: 24 linear feet of scripts, music, photographs, business papers, and programs pertaining to his reviews for the London stage.

CHARLOT, JEAN

HI —UNIVERSITY OF HAWAII, Library, 2550 The Mall, Honolulu, 96822. David Kittelson, Hawaiian Cur
Notes: Art, books, manuscripts, and correspondence; incl his shorthand diaries, published and unpublished research, and a nearly complete collection of Charlot prints. Also a large collection of letters to and from fellow artists in France, Mexico, and the United States.

CHARLOTTE THREE

NC —UNIVERSITY OF NORTH CAROLINA, CHARLOTTE, J Murrey Atkins Library, UNCC Station, Charlotte, 28223. Robert F Brabham Jr, Special Collections Librn
Holdings: Cat
Notes: Papers of Harry Golden, editor of the *Carolina Israelite;* of Julius Chambers relating to the Swann v Charlotte/Mecklenburg Board of Education case, which established the constitutionality of busing to achieve racial integration of the public schools; of Frederick Douglas Alexander, first black city councilman in Charlotte, NC in the 20th century; and of T J Reddy, a member of the Charlotte 3, a group of black men accused of burning a riding stable and killing horses.

CHARLTON, JAMES P.

VA —VIRGINIA POLYTECHNIC INSTITUTE AND STATE UNIVERSITY LIBRARY, Blacksburg, 24061. Glenn L McMullen, Special Collections Librn
Holdings: Vols (2000) Cat Mss Maps Pix Audiotapes
Notes: Primarily Southwest Virginia materials. Collection incl ca 200 mss, account books and other archival records of nineteenth century area businesses and other mining operations; the extant archival records of several Southwest Virginia railroads, incl the Virginia and Tennessee Railroad and the Norfolk and Western Railroad; and papers of historically prominent Southwest Virginians, incl John Apperson, Dr Harvy Black, James P Charlton, W Graham Claytor, Henley

CHARLTON, JAMES P. (cont.)

Fugate, Clement D Johnston, Germanicus Kent, William Preston, J Hoge Tyler, and William C Wampler. Several oral history collections incl material on Appalachian customs and folklore, particularly in Patrick County.

CHARMS

OH —CLEVELAND PUBLIC LIBRARY, Fine Arts and Special Collections Department, 325 Superior Ave, Cleveland, 44114. Alice N Loranth, Head
Holdings: Vols (1600) Cat
Notes: Part of the Witchcraft Collection, which incl witchcraft, magic, sorcery, magical manuals, devil worship, incantations, charms, talismans, amulets and spells. Contemporary urban practices are almost entirely omitted.
See also entry under Folklore; Witchcraft

CHARTERIS, LESLIE

MA —BOSTON UNIVERSITY, Mugar Memorial Library, Special Collections Dept, 771 Commonwealth Ave, Boston, 02215. Howard B Gotlieb, Dir
Holdings: Cat Mss Pix
Notes: Mss, correspondence, etc collected in depth; incl publications by or about.

CHARTERS

MA —HARVARD UNIVERSITY LIBRARY, Houghton Library, Cambridge, 02138. F Thomas Noonan, Cur, Reading Room; Lawrence Dowler, Associate Librn
Holdings: Cat Mss
Notes: *Harvard Library Notes,* II (1924), p 84, gives account of 800 English charters, from the 12th to the 17th century.

PA —PENNSYLVANIA ECONOMY LEAGUE, Eastern Div Library, 215 S Broad St, Philadelphia, 19107. Ellen Brennan, Librn
Holdings: Vols (15,000) Cat Maps
Notes: Public finance, charters, constitutions, public education.

CHARTOGRAPHY see Cartography

CHARTS, NAUTICAL see Nautical Charts

CHARTS, PORTOLAN see Portolan Charts

CHARTULARIES see Cartularies

THE CHASE see Hunting

CHASE, DANA B.

NM —MUSEUM OF NEW MEXICO, Photo Archives, Box 2087, Santa Fe, 87503. Arthur L Olivas, Cur; Richard Rudisill, Photo Historian
Holdings: Cat Pix Slides
Notes: Extensive collection of his work.

CHASE, ILKA

MA —BOSTON UNIVERSITY, Mugar Memorial Library, Special Collections Dept, 771 Commonwealth Ave, Boston, 02215. Howard B Gotlieb, Dir
Holdings: Cat Mss
Notes: Mss, correspondence, etc collected in depth; incl publications by or about.

CHASE, MARY ELLEN

ME —WESTBROOK COLLEGE, Library, 716 Stevens Ave, Portland, 04103. Dorothy M Healy, Special Collections Librn
Holdings: Vols (3000) Cat Mss Pix
Notes: Collection incl work of Maine women writers. Many mss and scrapbooks are incl. Memorabilia of Mrs Robert E Peary, Mary Ellen Chase, Florence B Jacobs, Celia Thaxter, and Edna St Vincent Millay are notable items. Some rare books, ie Madame Wood novels, are part of the collection.

MA —BOSTON UNIVERSITY, Mugar Memorial Library, Special Collections Dept, 771 Commonwealth Ave, Boston, 02215. Howard B Gotlieb, Dir
Holdings: Cat Mss
Notes: Mss, correspondence, incl publications by.

CHASE, PEARL

CA —UNIVERSITY OF CALIFORNIA, SANTA BARBARA, Library, Dept of Special Collections, Santa Barbara, 93106. Christian F Brun, Head
Holdings: Vols (95,980) Cat Mss
Notes: The Pearl Chase Collections of Community Development and Conservation. Papers of outstanding California leaders in conservation, community planning, Indian affairs, national parks.

CHASE, SALMON P.

DC —LIBRARY OF CONGRESS, Manuscript Division, Washington, 20540. John C Broderick, Chief
Notes: Papers; additions, 1977- .

OH —RUTHERFORD B HAYES LIBRARY, 1337 Hayes Ave, Fremont, 43420. Watt P Marchman, Dir
Notes: Correspondence in the Lyman-Lincoln Collection.

PA —HISTORICAL SOCIETY OF PENNSYLVANIA, Library, 1300 Locust St, Philadelphia, 19107. David Fraser, Librn
Holdings: Vols (230,000) Mss Maps Pix Microforms
Notes: Incl over 14,000,000 ms pieces. The Library Company of Philadelphia mss are on deposit with the Historical Society of Pennsylvania. Many of the Society's rare books are on deposit with the Library Company. The Society maintains the collections of the Genealogical Society of Pennsylvania, incl some 20,000 printed genealogies, original mss, family, church, and civil records.

CHASE, STANLEY

CA —UNIVERSITY OF CALIFORNIA, LOS ANGELES, Research Library, Dept of Special Collections, 405 Hilgard Ave, Los Angeles, 90024. Edward Shreeves, Chairman, Bibliographers Group; David S Zeidberg, Head
Holdings: Mss Pix
Notes: 29 linear feet of scripts and related materials for Broadway, moving picture and television productions.

CHASE-JOHNSON PAPERS

ME —BOWDOIN COLLEGE, Library, Brunswick, 04011. Dianne M Gutscher, Cur of Special Collections
Notes: Besides a general collection of 13,000 volumes relating to the state of Maine, there are also many ms collections touching on the political, economic, and social history of Maine. These incl Chase-Johnson Papers; 8000 mss relating to these two Brunswick families.

CHASIDISM see Hasidism

CHATEAUBRIAND, FRANCOIS AUGUSTE RENE, VICOMTE DE, 1768-1848

NJ —PRINCETON UNIVERSITY, Library, Rare Books Dept, Princeton, 08544. Stephen Ferguson, Cur
Holdings: Vols 300 Cat

†NY —COLUMBIA UNIVERSITY LIBRARIES, Butler Library, Rare Book and Manuscript Library, 535 W 114 St, New York, 10027.
Notes: Papers of Prof Jean-Albert Bede, with much emphasis on Francois Chateaubriand and Anatolo France.

WI —UNIVERSITY OF WISCONSIN, MADISON, Memorial Library, 728 State St, Madison, 53706. Erwin K Welsch, Social Studies Bibliographer
Notes: Chateaubriand Manuscripts: a collection of ms pages from Francois-Rene de Chateaubriand's *Memoires d'outre-tombe.* Rare Books Dept.

CHATEAUX see Castles

CHAUCER, GEOFFREY

CO —UNIVERSITY OF COLORADO, Libraries, Special Collections, Boulder, 80309. Nora J Quinlan, Head
Holdings: Cat Mss
Notes: The Germaine Dempster Collection, incl 6 boxes of Germaine Dempster notes, notebooks, mss, reprints, microfilms and correspondence.

IL —UNIVERSITY OF CHICAGO LIBRARY, Dept of Special Collections, 1100 E 57 St, Chicago, 60637.
Notes: Life records of Geoffrey Chaucer and *Canterbury Tales* in transcripts and photostats.

KS —SAINT MARY COLLEGE, Library, Leavenworth, 66048. Therese Deplazes, Special Collections Librn
Holdings: Vols 90 Cat

MA —HARVARD UNIVERSITY LIBRARY, Houghton Library, Cambridge, 02138. Rodney G Dennis, Cur of Manuscripts
Holdings: Cat Mss

TX —UNIVERSITY OF TEXAS LIBRARIES, General Libraries, PO Box P, Austin, 78713. Carolyn Bucknell, Asst Dir for Collection Development
Holdings: Cat Microforms

CHAUTAUQUAS

IA —UNIVERSITY OF IOWA, University Libraries, Iowa City, 52242. Frank Paluka, Head, Special Collections Dept
Holdings: // Mss Pix
Notes: The Redpath Chautauqua Collection comprises 900 linear feet of ms materials, etc. See Robert A McCown, "Records of the Redpath Chautauqua," in *Books at Iowa,* Nov 1973.

CHAVEZ, CESAR

MI —WAYNE STATE UNIVERSITY, Walter P Reuther Library, Archives of Labor & Urban Affairs, Detroit, 48202. Philip Mason, Dir
Notes: Insights into national problems of discrimination and poverty can ve found in the records and papers of the United Farm Workers Organizing Committee and its Director, Cesar Chavez; the California Migrant Ministry; and the Citizen's Crusade Against Poverty, now preserved in the Archives.

CHAVEZ, J. FRANCISCA

AZ —NORTHERN ARIZONA UNIVERSITY, Special Collection Library, CU Box 6022, Flagstaff, 86011. Peter M Whiteley, Coordr/Archivist; William Mullane, Librn
Notes: J Francisco Chavez Collection; photocopied report and journal by Chavez of his march while in command of the escort to the civil officers of the Arizona Territory from Santa Fe, New Mexico to Fort Whipple, Ariz, 1864.

CHECKERS

NY —BROOKLYN PUBLIC LIBRARY, Art & Music Div, Grand Army Plaza, Brooklyn, 11238. Sue H Sharma, Chief
Holdings: Vols (4500) Cat Mss
Notes: "One of the finest collections of literature on chess and checkers in the world...incl some of the rarest books that exist on the subject..." Second largest collection of its kind, after that of the Cleveland Public Library. Incl private collections of William T Call (checkers), Melvin Brown, and R H Rimington-Wilson. Books are in many languages, from the 15th century to date. Incl many valuable mss, complete runs of most of the best-known periodicals, and over 100 scrapbooks of newspaper and periodical clippings. Many first editions and rare titles.

CHECKERS (cont.)

NY —US MILITARY ACADEMY LIBRARY, West Point, 10996. Elaine B Eatroff, Rare Book Cur
Holdings: Vols 150 Cat
Notes: Part of the Robert Sinnott chess collection, which incl runs of early periodicals, early European, British, and American imprints, mss, and ephemera.

OH —CLEVELAND PUBLIC LIBRARY, Fine Arts and Special Collections Department, 325 Superior Ave, Cleveland, 44114. Alice N Loranth, Head
Holdings: Vols 2600 Cat Mss Pix Microforms
Notes: Comprehensive research and reference collection on checkers, documents the history, development and technical aspects of the game and incl records of competitions, tournaments and players; all variations of checkers are represented.
See also entry under Chess

RI —PROVIDENCE PUBLIC LIBRARY, 150 Empire St, Providence, 02903. Lance J Bauer, Special Collections Librn
Holdings: Vols 542 // Uncat
Notes: The Edward B Hanes Checkers Collection. Incl scarce periodicals on draughts and imprints in numerous languages dating from 1694, indexed.. Material must be used in-house. Photocopying when condition of material allows.

CHEEVER, JOHN, 1912-1982

MA —BRANDEIS UNIVERSITY, Goldfarb Library, 415 South St, Waltham, 02154. Bessie Hahn, Dir
Notes: Approx 6 linear ft of original mss of John Cheever. Access to the material is through the Special Collections Card Catalog.

CHEEVER, SAMUEL

NY —CORNELL UNIVERSITY LIBRARIES, Collection of Regional History, Dept of Manuscripts and Univ Archives, Ithaca, 14853.
Notes: Papers, 1813-1939; 7 ft.

CHEKHOV PUBLISHING COMPANY

IL —NATIONAL COUNCIL OF THE YMCAS, YMCA Historical Library, 6400 Shafer Ct, Rosemont, 60018. Eleanor R Murphy, Librn
Holdings: Vols (15,000) Cat Mss Pix
Notes: YMCA work in Russia and with Russian emigres in Europe. See Edward Kasinec, "The YMCA National Board Historical Library," *Slavic Bibliographic and Documentation Center Newsletter*, Washington, DC, November 1971, no 5, page 9. No separate catalog. Collection incl virtually complete files of Russian language publications of the YMCA Press (Prague-Berlin, and Paris, after 1925), and the Chekhov Publishing House (NY, 1951-56), along with its archives, correspondence, etc. Some primary material is restricted. Application should be made to librarian for permission.

CHELONIA see Turtles and Tortoises

CHEMEHUEVI INDIANS

AZ —COLORADO RIVER INDIAN TRIBES MUSEUM/LIBRARY, Rte One, Box 23-B, Parker, 85344. Priscilla Johnson, Librn
Holdings: Cat Mss Maps Pix Slides Audiotapes Micorforms
Notes: Library deals with the four tribes of the Colorado River Indian Reservation: Mojave, Chemehuevi, Navajo, and Hopi. Emphasis is also given to the prehistoric cultures of this area; Patayan and Hohokam. Library collections include original manuscripts and other documents, photographs, oral history tape recordings, cultural items and artifacts. Copies of many documents relating to the reservation are in bound volumes, microfilm, and photocopies. Photos relative to the reservation from various other collections are copied in our collection . Of particular interest is the museum basket collection which incl about 1000 Chemehuevi baskests--the largest Chemehuevi basket collection. Other artifacts give special emphasis to the Mojave culture.

CHEMICAL ANALYSIS see Chemistry, Analytic

CHEMICAL DYNAMICS see Dynamics, Chemical

CHEMICAL ENGINEERING

AL —NATIONAL FERTILIZER DEVELOPMENT CENTER, Tennessee Valley Authority Technical Library, TVA National Fertilizer Development Center, Muscle Shoals, 35660. Shirley G Nichols, Librn
Holdings: Vols (32,000) Cat Mss Maps Pix Slides Microforms
Notes: One of the most complete collections of material on fertilizer as it relates to agriculture, agro-economics, chemistry, chemical engineering, etc, in the country.

AL —TUSKEGEE INSTITUTE, School of Engineering Library, Tuskegee Institute, 36088. Frances F Davis, Librn
Holdings: Vols 355 Cat
Budget: $3000

CA —UNIVERSITY OF CALIFORNIA, DAVIS, Physical Sciences Library, Davis, 95616. Scott Kennedy, Head
Holdings: Vols (170,000) Cat
Notes: Collection covers aeronautical, agricultural, chemical, civil, electrical, mechanical, water science, hydrology, nuclear reactor, extensive cold regions collection in vertical file drawers, and computer science engineering academic programs. Good strength in journal runs.

CA —CALIFORNIA INSTITUTE OF TECHNOLOGY, Chemical Engineering Library, Pasadena, 91109. April Olsen, Librn
Holdings: Vols 3000 Cat

CA —CALIFORNIA STATE POLYTECHNIC UNIVERSITY, POMONA, University Library, 3801 W Temple Ave, Pomona, 91768. Harold Schleiser, Actg Dir
Notes: General reference materials on aerospace, chemical, civil, electrical, electronics, industrial, mechanical and manufacturing engineering.

CT —ROGERS CORP, Lurie Library, One Technology Drive, Rogers, 06263. Myrna D Riquier, Librn; Nini S Davis, Librn
Holdings: Vols (650) Cat
Notes: Emphasis on materials science, plastics, polymers, resins.

GA —GEORGIA INSTITUTE OF TECHNOLOGY, Price Gilbert Memorial Library, 225 North Ave, Atlanta, 30332. Edward Graham Roberts, Dir
Holdings: Vols (1,661,559) Cat Maps Slides Microforms
Budget: ($1,383,302)
Notes: Incl (4,307,996) patents and (568, 490) government documents.

IL —ARGONNE NATIONAL LABORATORY, Library, Technical Information Services Dept, 9700 Cass Ave, Argonne, 60439. Hillis L Griffin, Dir
Notes: The ANL library system consists of eight branch libraries with centralized processing services. The entire collection numbers 70,000 monographic titles, 3700 journal titles, and over 1 million scientific and technical reports. Materials may be used by the public in the library by prior arrangement. Photocopies may be supplied for interlibrary loan, for which a processing and handling charge is made. The branch libraries are: Biological and Medical Research; Chemical Engineering; Chemistry; Mathematics/Physics/Computer Science; Reactor Science/Engineering; Materials Science; Solid State Physics; High-Energy Physics/Environmental Sciences.

IL —UNIVERSITY OF ILLINOIS, URBANA/CHAMPAIGN, Chemistry Library, 255 Noyes Laboratory, Urbana, 61801. Lucille M Wert, Chemistry Librn; Susan Eilering, Asst Chemistry Librn
Holdings: Vols (150,000) Cat Microforms
Budget: ($224,660)
Notes: The collection incl monographs, treatises and serials in all languages covering all aspects of industrial chemistry and chemical engineering. It is designed to serve the needs of the School of Chemical Sciences and the University community.

IN —INTERNATIONAL MINERALS & CHEMICAL CORP, R & D Library, 1331 S First St, PO Box 207, Terre Haute, 47808. Ruth Smedlund, Librn
Holdings: Vols (50,000) Cat

IN —PURDUE UNIVERSITY LIBRARIES, Engineering Library, A A Potter Engineering Center, West Lafayette, 47907. Edwin D Posey, Engineering Librn
Holdings: Vols (225,178)
Budget: ($300,000)

IA —IOWA STATE UNIVERSITY, Library, Ames, 50011. Warren B Kuhn, Dean of Library Services
Holdings: Cat
Notes: Extensive serial holdings.

KY —UNIVERSITY OF KENTUCKY, Robert E Shaver Library of Engineering, 355 Anderson Hall, Lexington, 40506. Russell H Powell, Engineering Librn
Holdings: Vols (48,000) Cat Microforms

LA —ETHYL CORP, Information & Library Services, Gulf States Rd, PO Box 2246, Baton Rouge, 70821. Lois M Skinner, Chemist-Librn
Holdings: Vols (15,000) Cat

LA —LOUISIANA STATE UNIVERSITY, Chemistry Library, Virginia Rice Williams Hall, Baton Rouge, 70803.
Holdings: Vols (40,000) Cat Mss Microforms
Notes: Incl chemical patents, 1955-date. With 700 journals.

LA —PPG INDUSTRIES, Chemical Div, Technical Information, P O Box 1000, Lake Charles, 70602. Theresa Leboeuf, Service Coordinator
Holdings: Vols 10,000 Cat

MA —UNIVERSITY OF MASSACHUSETTS AT AMHERST, Physical Sciences Library, Amherst, 01003. Siegfried Feller, Assoc Dir for Collection Development
Holdings: Vols Cat Microforms
Notes: Extensive journal holdings, incl chemical engineering.

MA —STONE & WEBSTER ENGINEERING CORP, Technical Information Center, Library, 245 Summer St, PO Box 2325, Boston, 02107. Nancy M Pellini, Mgr
Holdings: Vols (10,000) Cat Pix Microforms
Notes: Also over 1200 periodicals. Extensive vertical file collection, and 5 on-line system for search.

MI —UNIVERSITY OF MICHIGAN, Engineering-Transportation Library, 312 Undergraduate Library, Ann Arbor, 48109. Maurita Holland, Librn
Holdings: Vols (400,000) Cat Microforms
Budget: ($225,000)

NJ —EXXON RESEARCH AND ENGINEERING CO, Linden Information Center, PO Box 121, Linden, 07036. PA Lorenz, Section Head
Holdings: Vols (40,000) Cat Maps Pix Microforms
Notes: No photocopying.

NJ —WITCO CHEMICAL CORP, Corporate Research Center Library, 100 Bauer Dr, Oakland, 07436. Jo Therese Smith, Mgr, Information Services
Holdings: Vols (9000) Cat
Budget: ($52,000)

NY —WESTRECO INC, Research Library, 555 S Fourth St, Fulton, 13069. Janice Burns, Research Librn
Holdings: Vols 38 Cat Periodicals VF
Notes: Food Science and Technology collection of about (1200) books and pamphlets. Back files of periodicals retained up to 20 years.

NY —COLUMBIA UNIVERSITY LIBRARIES, Engineering Library, 422 Mudd Bldg, New York, 10027.
Holdings: Vols (177,000) Cat
Notes: All aspects of engineering--aeronautical, industrial mining, civil, chemical, mechanical, electrical, nuclear.

CHEMICAL ENGINEERING (cont.)

Incl applied mathematics and applied physical sciences. Over (1,000,000) technical reports.

NY —ENGINEERING SOCIETIES LIBRARY, 345 E 47 St, New York, 10017. S Kirk Cabeen, Dir
Holdings: Vols 250,000 Cat Maps 16mm Films Microforms
Notes: One of the largest, most comprehensive engineering libraries in the world. Covers all engineering disciplines; particularly strong in electrical and electronic, mechanical, mining and metallurgical, petroleum, chemical, industrial, air conditioning and refrigeration engineering. Incl Wheeler Collection of early materials on magnetism and electricity. 125, 000 bound periodical volumes; 10,000 maps; 5000 serial subscriptions (many foreign-language). Virtually all materials abstracted in *Engineering Index* (1884-date) are incl in Library. Noncirculating, except to members of professional engineering societies which support the Library. See *Engineering Societies Library, New York, Classed Subject Catalog and Index* (Boston: G K Hall, 1963); and *Supplements*, 1-10, 1964-1973.

NY —NEW YORK PUBLIC LIBRARY, Research Libraries, Science and Technology Research Center, Fifth Ave & 42 St, New York, 10018.
Holdings: Vols (1,100,000) Cat Microforms
Budget: ($647,259)

NY —NEW YORK PUBLIC LIBRARY, Mid-Manhattan Library, Science & Business Dept, 455 Fifth Ave, New York, 10016. Frederick E Dusold, Sr Principal Librn
Holdings: Vols (110,000) Cat Microforms
Budget: ($134,000)
Notes: All works are in English. Material is current; policy precludes archival collecting. Collection is geared toward the undergraduate college student, with consideration given to the professional, the lay reader and the beginning graduate student. Collection incl monographs, texts, treatises, standard reference works and periodicals in agriculture, horticulture, home economics, crafts, engineering, industrial chemistry, construction and other technologies. Books are available for circulation in addition to an extensive reference collection.

NY —EASTMAN KODAK COMPANY, Kodak Park Div, Engineering Library, Bldg 23, Rochester, 14650. Raymond Curtin, Librn
Holdings: Vols (14,000) Uncat Microforms
Notes: The library is not open to the public. Use of the library for reference purposes may be requested and appointments may be obtained through the librarian.

NY —UNIVERSITY OF ROCHESTER, Engineering Library, Gavett Hall, River Campus, Rochester, 14627. Isabel Kaplan, Librn
Holdings: Vols (25,000) Cat
Notes: Strong collection in the field and related areas.

OH —PPG INDUSTRIES, Chemical Div, Research Library, PO Box 31, Barberton, 44203. Diane Danko, Chemical Information Specialist
Holdings: Vols (20,000) Cat Microforms
Notes: Organic, inorganic, analytical and agricultural chemistry, with special emphasis on applied and chemical engineering.

OH —EMERY INDUSTRIES, Research Library, 4900 Este Ave, Cincinnati, 45232. B A Bernard, Librn
Holdings: Cat
Notes: Special subjects: fatty acids and organic chemical derivatives, ozone, plasticizers, polymers, synthetic lubricants.

OH —UNIVERSITY OF CINCINNATI, Engineering Library, 880 Baldwin Hall, Cincinnati, 45221. Dorothy Furber Byers, Head
Holdings: Vols (50,000) Cat Videotapes Microforms
Budget: ($100,000)
Notes: Have NASA and DOE microfiche collections.

PA —CENTER FOR THE HISTORY OF CHEMISTRY, EF Smith Hall, D-6 University of Pennsylvania, 215 S 34 St, Philadelphia, 19104. Prof Arnold Thackray, Dir
Notes: Established in 1982 and jointly sponsored by the American Chemical Society, the American Institute of Chemical Engineers, and The University of Pennsylvania, the Center's purpose is to "discover and disseminate information about historical resources, and to encourage research, scholarship, and popular writing in the history of chemistry, chemical engineering, and the chemical process industries.". The Center is associated with the Edgar Fahs Smith Memorial Collection in the History of Chemistry.

PA —FRANKLIN INSTITUTE LIBRARY, 20 & The Parkway, Philadelphia, 19103. Miriam Padusis, Dir; Charles Wilt, Readers Servs Librn
Holdings: Vols (300,000) Cat Maps Pix Microforms
Notes: Book budget, $20,000; periodicals, $160,000.

PA —UNIVERSITY OF PENNSYLVANIA, Towne Scientific Library, 220 S 33 St, Philadelphia, 19104. Charles Meyers, Librn
Holdings: Vols (65,000) Cat

PA —CARNEGIE LIBRARY OF PITTSBURGH, Science & Technology Dept, 4400 Forbes Ave, Pittsburgh, 15213. Catherine M Brosky, Dept Head
Holdings: Vols (380,000) Cat Maps Microforms
Budget: ($240,000)
See also entry under Engineering.

PA —ROCKWELL INTERNATIONAL, General Industries Operations, Technical Information Center, 400 N Lexington Ave, Pittsburgh, 15208. Kathleen H Witkowski, Library Coordr
Holdings: Vols Cat Microforms Mss Documents Periodicals VF
Budget: ($5100)

PA —PENNSYLVANIA STATE UNIVERSITY, Physical Sciences Library, 230 Davey Laboratory, University Park, 16802. Cornelius J McKown, Librn
Notes: 77,317 items.

SC —CRYOVAC TECHNICAL LIBRARY, PO Box 464, Duncan, 29334. M M Ezell, Libn
Holdings: Vols (6000) Cat
Notes: Library supports corporate research, development, and engineering. Incl materials on chemical and mechanical engineering, polymers and polymerization, plastics, and food packaging. 175 periodical titles received. Library open by appointment or through ILL.

SC —SONOCO PRODUCTS CO, Research Laboratory, Technical Information Center, One N Second St, Hartsville, 29550. Ken Chavis, Dir
Holdings: Vols (4000) Cat Mss Slides Microforms
Notes: Restricted to Sonoco employees. No photocopying.

†SD —SOUTH DAKOTA SCHOOL OF MINES & TECHNOLOGY, Devereaux Library, Rapid City, 57701.
Holdings: Vols (166,200) Cat Maps Audiotapes Filmstrips Microforms
Budget: ($70,000)
Notes: Supportive collection incl an almost complete set of US Geological Survey materials (incl early Territorial Surveys); a microfilm copy (complete set) of the US Bureau of Mines "Mine Map Depository (Denver)" material; periodicals and technical reports (NASA, ACRL, JPL, etc) in engineering and geology; extensive government document materials (NBS, Bureau of Mines, etc).

TX —UNIVERSITY OF TEXAS LIBRARIES, John W Mallet Chemistry Library, Welch Hall 2132, Austin, 78712. A E Skinner, Chemistry Librn
Holdings: Vols (44,000) Cat Microforms
Notes: Described in *The John W Mallet Chemistry Library (The University of Texas at Austin)* (Austin: The General Libraries, 1975).

TX —RICE UNIVERSITY, Fondren Library, 6100 S Main St, PO Box 1892, Houston, 77251. Dr Samuel M Carrington, Jr, University Librn
Holdings: Vols 2295 Cat
Budget: $27,800
Notes: Each serial title counted once.

WA —UNIVERSITY OF WASHINGTON LIBRARIES, Chemistry-Pharmacy Library, BG-10, Seattle, 98195. Heidi Mercado, Librn
Holdings: Vols (47,500) Cat Microforms
Budget: ($195,000)
Notes: All aspects of chemical engineering such as plastics, polymers, fermentation, head and mass transfer, petroleum, etc are included.
See also entry under Chemistry.

AB —SOUTHERN ALBERTA INSTITUTE OF TECHNOLOGY, Learning Resources Centre, 1301 16 Ave NW, Calgary, T2M 0L4, Can. Tom Skinner, Historian
Holdings: Vols (40,000) Cat Maps Pix Slides Films Videotapes Microforms
Budget: ($50,000)
Notes: Wide range of current technical information about electronics and engineering (mechanical, electrical, chemical); emphasis on vocational-technical material. Incl (50,000) slides, (300) videotapes, and (500) films.

ON —MCMASTER UNIVERSITY, Mills Memorial Library, Div of Archives & Research Collections, Hamilton, L8S 4L6, Can. G R Hill, Univ Librn
Notes: Typescripts of articles submitted to *Canadian Journal of Chemical Engineering*, 1965-. No photocopying.

PQ —NORANDA RESEARCH CENTRE, Library, 240 Hymus Blvd, Pointe-Claire, H9R 1G5, Can. Shirley Courtis, Librn
Holdings: Vols (7000)

CHEMICAL INDUSTRIES

DC —MANUFACTURING CHEMISTS' ASSOCIATION, Library, 1825 Connecticut Ave NW, Washington, 20009. Rose Clark, Librn
Holdings: Vols 3000 Cat
Notes: Incl extensive files on the business and trade aspects of the chemical industry; also, environmental and health aspects.

PA —CENTER FOR THE HISTORY OF CHEMISTRY, EF Smith Hall, D-6 University of Pennsylvania, 215 S 34 St, Philadelphia, 19104. Prof Arnold Thackray, Dir
Notes: Established in 1982 and jointly sponsored by the American Chemical Society, the American Institute of Chemical Engineers, and The University of Pennsylvania, the Center's purpose is to "discover and disseminate information about historical resources, and to encourage research, scholarship, and popular writing in the history of chemistry, chemical engineering, and the chemical process industries.". The Center is associated with the Edgar Fahs Smith Memorial Collection in the History of Chemistry.

CHEMICAL PERIODICALS see Periodicals, Chemical

CHEMICAL TECHNOLOGY see Chemistry, Technical

CHEMICAL WARFARE

IN —INDIANA UNIVERSITY, Lilly Library, Seventh St, Bloomington, 47405. William R Cagle, Librn
Holdings: Vols (2000) // Cat
Notes: The core of the collection is the specialized library of Charles R Boxer (1000 titles) dealing with the history of the Iberians in the East 16th-18th century. Mainly incl works on China, Japan and the Philippines during the period of their early intercourse with the West through 1800, as well as materials on the English and Dutch East India Companies, and the 17th century Anglo-Dutch naval wars. Special mention should be made of the valuable letters from missions by the Jesuits, and the works in this area by the Augustinians, Franciscans, and

CHEMICAL WARFARE (cont.)

Dominicans, from the time of the arrival of the Iberians in Asia. The collection is a valuable source of information for the study of the European expansion into the area, including Southeast Asia.

CHEMICALS—MANUFACTURE AND INDUSTRY

DE —HAGLEY MUSEUM AND LIBRARY, Eleutherian Mills-Hagley Foundation Inc, PO Box 3630, Greenville, 19807. Richmond D Williams, Dir; Heddy A Richter, Imprints Librn
Notes: Records of E I du Pont de Nemours & Company (1801-1958; 2500 cubic feet). The collection traces the founding of the company in Paris, its evolution into an American partnership during the early nineteenth century and its first incorporation in 1899. Details concerning the financial and business negotiations which led to the founding of the company, the selection of a site for operations, the erection of the mills, and methods of manufacturing, production, marketing and labor relations are well described. Records of Atlas Powder Company (1912-1955; 500 cubic feet) document the history of one of the United States' largest manufacturers of gun powder which was split off from the Du Pont Company as a result of a 1912 antitrust case.

DC —MANUFACTURING CHEMISTS' ASSOCIATION, Library, 1825 Connecticut Ave NW, Washington, 20009. Rose Clark, Librn
Holdings: Vols 3000 Cat
Notes: Incl extensive files on the business and trade aspects of the chemical industry; also, environmental and health aspects.

CHEMISTRY

AL —NATIONAL FERTILIZER DEVELOPMENT CENTER, Tennessee Valley Authority Technical Library, TVA National Fertilizer Development Center, Muscle Shoals, 35660. Shirley G Nichols, Librn
Holdings: Vols (32,000) Cat Mss Maps Pix Slides Microforms
Notes: One of the most complete collections of material on fertilizer as it relates to agriculture, agro-economics, chemistry, chemicl engineering, etc, in the country.

CA —UNION OIL CO OF CALIFORNIA, Library, 376 S Valencia Ave, Brea, 92621. Barbara Orosz, Head Librn
Holdings: Vols (40,000) Cat Maps Microforms Books Documents Journals

CA —UNIVERSITY OF CALIFORNIA, DAVIS, Physical Sciences Library, Davis, 95616. Scott Kennedy, Head
Holdings: Vols 17,498 Cat Microforms
Budget: ($14,250)
Notes: Strong in journal runs and reference materials. Nuclear chemistry represented by microcopy depository collection of US Dept of Energy (AEC and ERDA) (est 462,574). Sadtler standard spectra and other spectral compilations available. Access to online reference bases. Biochemistry better represented in Shields and Health Sciences Libraries of the Davis campus.

CA —UNIVERSITY OF CALIFORNIA, LOS ANGELES, Chemistry Library, 4238 Young Hall, Los Angeles, 90024. Marion C Peters, Chemistry Librn
Holdings: Vols (55,600) Cat Microforms
Notes: (768) current serials subscriptions; special collection of 450 volumes on the history of chemistry; US Chemical Patents since 1952 on microforms; Sadtler Standard Spectra; UCLA biochemistry and chemistry theses. Collection strengths incl analytical, biological, inorganic, organic and physical chemistry.

CA —UNIVERSITY OF SOUTHERN CALIFORNIA, Seaver Science Library, University Park, Los Angeles, 90089. A Albert Baker, Head
Holdings: Vols (200,000) Microforms
Budget: ($700,000)
Notes: Includes technical reports (12,000), serial and periodical titles (3600).

CA —CONTRA COSTA COUNTY LIBRARY, 1750 Oak Park Blvd, Pleasant Hill, 94523. Barbara Potter, Librn
Holdings: Vols (18,000)

CA —UNIVERSITY OF CALIFORNIA, RIVERSIDE, Physical Sciences Library, Riverside, 92517. Richard W Vierich, Librn
Holdings: Vols (89,000) Cat Microforms
Budget: ($347,000)

CA —INTERNATIONAL BUSINESS MACHINES RESEARCH LIBRARY, 5600 Cottle Rd, San Jose, 95193. Phil Grincewich, Mgr Technical Information
Holdings: Vols (13,500) Cat
Notes: Extensive collection of polymer chemistry and analytical organic chemistry. Incl 21,000 vols of 770 journals. On-line search facility. Volumes are divided into three libraries, Technical Research, Technical Information, and Programing. Not open to public.

CO —IBM, Boulder Library, PO Box 1900, Boulder, 80302. Beverly Jorman, Library Mgr
Holdings: Vols (10,000) Cat Microforms
Notes: Emphasis in chemistry, physics, computer sciences and technology.

CO —COLORADO SCHOOL OF MINES, Arthur Lakes Library, 14 & Illinois Sts, Golden, 80401. Hartley K Phinney, Jr, Head Librn
Holdings: Vols (270,557) Cat Microforms

CT —YALE UNIVERSITY, Kline Science Library, Kline Biology Tower Rm C-8, PO Box 6666, New Haven, 06511. Richard J Dionne, Head
Holdings: Vols (175,480) Cat 16mm Films Microforms
Budget: ($340,000)
Notes: Comprehensive collection on biological sciences, physics, and chemistry. Incl Evans Collection of Bryology and Lichenology (with catalog cards in both Kline Science Library and Sterling Memorial Library). Also inc AEC reports (hardcopy and micrform) to 1970.

CT —YALE UNIVERSITY, Chemistry Library, Sterling Chemistry Laboratory, 225 Prospect St, PO Box 6666, New Haven, 06511. Deborah A Paolillo, Librn
Holdings: Vols (15,000)
Budget: ($52,500)

†DC —CATHOLIC UNIVERSITY OFF AMERICA, Nursing & Biology Library, Washington, 20064. N L Powell, Head
Holdings: Vols (16,000) at
Notes: Espec strong in organometallic, Moessbauer and physical chemistry.

FL —UNIVERSITY OF FLORIDA, Chemistry Library, 216 Leigh Hall, Gainesville, 32611. Carol A Drum, Librn
Holdings: Vols 30,000 Cat
Budget: $35,600

GA —GEORGIA INSTITUTE OF TECHNOLOGY, Price Gilbert Memorial Library, 225 North Ave, Atlanta, 30332. Edward Graham Roberts, Dir
Holdings: Vols (1,661,559) Cat Maps Slides Microforms
Budget: ($1,383,302)
Notes: Incl (4,307,996) patents and (568, 490) government documents.

ID —EG&G, INEL Technical Library, 1776 Science Center, Idaho Falls, 83401. Brent Jacobsen, Head Librn; Heather Redding, Ref Librn
Holdings: Vols (33,000) Cat Microforms
Notes: Energy research and development included in libraries collection. Incl over 500,000 AEC, ERDA, NRC, and foreign reports. Unclassified materials may be used by the public in the library by appointment or borrowed by interlibrary loan. Incl 12,000 bound documents, 520,000 microfiche, 400 periodical subscriptions.

IL —ARGONNE NATIONAL LABORATORY, Library, Technical Information Services Dept, 9700 Cass Ave, Argonne, 60439. Hillis L Griffin, Dir
Notes: The ANL library system consists of eight branch libraries with centralized processing services. The entire collection numbers 70,000 monographic titles, 3700 journal titles, and over 1 million scientific and technical reports. Materials may be used by the public in the library by prior arrangement. Photocopies may be supplied for interlibrary loan, for which a processing and handling charge is made. The branch libraries are: Biological and Medical Research; Chemical Engineering; Chemistry; Mathematics/Physics/Computer Science; Reactor Science/Engineering; Materials Science; Solid State Physics; High-Energy Physics/Environmental Sciences.

IL —UNIVERSITY OF CHICAGO LIBRARIES, John Crerar Library Collections, 1100 E 57th St, Chicago, 60637. Robert Rosenthal, Special Collections Librn
Notes: The John Crerar Library's extensive science, medicine, and engineering collections have been transferred in trust to the University of Chicago Libraries. Incl rare books and special collections as listed here.

IL —NORTHWESTERN UNIVERSITY, Seeley G Mudd Library for Science & Engineering, 2233 Sheridan Rd, Evanston, 60201. Robert C Michaelson, Head
Holdings: Vols (200,000) Cat Microforms
Notes: Collection emphasizes graduate and research level material.

IL —UNIVERSITY OF ILLINOIS, URBANA/CHAMPAIGN, Chemistry Library, 255 Noyes Laboratory, Urbana, 61801. Lucille M Wert, Chemistry Librn; Susan Eilering, Asst Chemistry Librn
Holdings: Vols (150,000) Cat Microforms
Budget: ($224,660)
Notes: Collection incl monographs, treatises and serials in all languages covering all the fields of chemistry, biochemsitry and chemical engineering. Its major strength is its journal collections. It is designed to serve the needs of the School of Chemical Sciences and the University Community.

IN —INDIANA UNIVERSITY, Chemistry Library, Chemistry Bldg, Rm One, Bloomington, 47405. Gary Wiggins, Head Librn
Holdings: Vols (55,000) Cat Slides Microforms
Budget: ($157,000)

IN —MILES LABORATORIES, Library Resources and Services, 1127 Myrtle St, PO Box 40, Elkhart, 46515. Allam Hagopian, Mgr
Holdings: Vols (16,500) Cat Audiotapes Microforms
Notes: Incl files of pharmaceutical product advertising pieces, extensive literature files on company related drugs; domestic and international marketing files. 32,000 bound periodicals.

IN —BRISTOL-MYERS PHARMACEUTICAL R&D DIVISION, Scientific Information Dept, 2404 W Pennsylvania St, Evansville, 47721. Alice Weisling, Mgr
Holdings: Vols 33,000 Cat Microforms

IN —ELI LILLY AND COMPANY, Scientific Library, 307 E McCarty St, Indianapolis, 46285. Adele Hoskin, Chief Librn
Holdings: Vols (35,000) Cat Microforms
Notes: Drug product information (1.7 million cards); drug encyclopedias, foreign and domestic; foreign pharmacopoeias. Restricted use: company employees and approved outsiders.

IN —INDIANA STATE UNIVERSITY, Science Library, Terre Haute, 47809. Susan J Thompson, Science Librn
Holdings: Vols (40,000) Cat Microforms
Budget: ($160,846)

IN —INTERNATIONAL MINERALS & CHEMICAL CORP, R & D Library, 1331 S First St, PO Box 207, Terre Haute, 47808. Ruth Smedlund, Librn
Holdings: Vols (50,000) Cat

IN —PURDUE UNIVERSITY LIBRARIES, Chemistry Library, West Lafayette, 47907. John Pinzelik, Librn
Holdings: Vols 49,900 Cat Microforms
Budget: $142,800
Notes: Archives of H C Brown, 1979 Nobel Laureate in Chemistry.

IA —IOWA STATE UNIVERSITY, Library, Ames, 50011. Warren B Kuhn, Dean of Library Services
Holdings: Cat Mss
Notes: Extensive serial holdings.

†IA —UNIVERSITY OF IOWA, Botany - Chemistry Library, Iowa City, 52242.
Holdings: Vols (60,000)

CHEMISTRY (cont.)

KY —UNIVERSITY OF KENTUCKY, Chemistry-Physics Library, 150 Chemistry-Physics Bldg, Lexington, 40506. Jane M Lane, Acting Librn
Holdings: Vols (41,500) Cat Audiotapes
Budget: ($164,700)
Notes: One shelflist is maintained. No records of volumes in each collection. Combined library has its own catalog, as well as entries in the public catalog in the main library.

LA —ETHYL CORP, Information & Library Services, Gulf States Rd, PO Box 2246, Baton Rouge, 70821. Lois M Skinner, Chemist-Librn
Holdings: Vols (15,000) Cat

LA —LOUISIANA STATE UNIVERSITY, Chemistry Library, Virginia Rice Williams Hall, Baton Rouge, 70803.
Holdings: Vols (40,000) Cat Mss Microforms
Notes: Incl chemical patents, 1955-date. With 700 journals.

LA —PPG INDUSTRIES, Chemical Div, Technical Information, P O Box 1000, Lake Charles, 70602. Theresa Leboeuf, Service Coordinator
Holdings: Vols 10,000 Cat

ME —COLLEGE OF THE ATLANTIC, Thorndike Library, Bar Harbor, 04609. Marcie L Dworak, Libr Dir
Notes: A rebuilding, fire-destroyed library (1983).

MD —JOHNS HOPKINS UNIVERSITY, Milton S Eisenhower Library, Charles & 34 Sts, Baltimore, 21218. Ann S Gwyn, Assistant Dir for Special Collections
Holdings: Vols (30,000) Cat
Notes: Very strong in all branches of chemistry, particularly in all pure research fields. Less emphasis on industrial application. Incl small but important Lelia Emmett Collection on catalysis. Complete long runs in theoretical fields back to 19th and some to 18th centuries.

MD —US DEPT OF AGRICULTURE, National Agricultural Library, 10301 Baltimore Blvd, Beltsville, 20705. Joseph H Howard, Director
Notes: Worldwide coverage of all aspects of agriculture and related fields. Crop ecology, agro-climatic analogs; air pollution effects. Agronomy: agricultural and tropical and desert agriculture. For use by the staff of the USDA. Incl in the former collections of American Institute of Crop Ecology.

MD —NATIONAL LIBRARY OF MEDICINE, 8600 Rockville Pike, Bethesda, 20209. Harold M Schoolinam, Actg Dir
Holdings: Vols (3,150,000) Cat Mss Audiotapes Videotapes 16mm Films Filmstrips Microforms
Budget: ($46,400)
Notes: The world's largest medical library. Materials are collected exhaustively in some 40 biomedical areas and, to a lesser degree, in related subject areas such as general chemistry, physics, zoology, botany, and instrumentation. Holdings include 82,000 monographic volumes, pre-1871; 438,000 monographic volumes, 1871-present; 714,000 bound serial volumes; 281,000 theses; 172, 000 pamphlets; 1,207,000 manuscripts; 156, 000 microforms; 12,000 audiovisuals; and 75, 000 prints and photographs. Pre-1871 material is in a separate historical collection. Approximately 24,000 serial titles are currenlty received.

MD —UNIVERSITY OF MARYLAND, White Memorial Library, College Park, 20742. Elizabeth W McElroy, Head
Holdings: Vols (48,000) Cat Microforms
Budget: ($193,000)
Notes: Current periodicls. Have own card catalog, which is included also in the total university catalog.

MA —UNIVERSITY OF MASSACHUSETTS AT AMHERST, Physical Sciences Library, Amherst, 01003. Siegfried Feller, Assoc Dir for Collection Development
Holdings: Vols Cat Microforms
Notes: Extensive journal holdings, incl chemical engineering.

MA —FRANCIS A COUNTWAY LIBRARY OF MEDICINE, Boston Medical Library/Harvard Medical Library, 10 Shattuck St, Boston, 02115. C Robin LeSueur, Librn; Richard J Wolfe, Cur, Rare Books & Manuscripts
Holdings: Vols (500,000) Cat Mss Maps Pix Microforms
Notes: Combines resources of the Harvard Medical School and the Boston Medical Library. Strong in serials and medical history in all fields of medicine, incl incunabula, non-medical books by doctors, travel books by doctors. 500,000 medical dissertations and theses. Special strength in all medical subjects listed in this volume.

MA —HARVARD UNIVERSITY LIBRARY, Converse Memorial Library, Chemistry Library, 12 Oxford St, Cambridge, 02138. Ludmila Birladeanu, Supv
Holdings: Vols (50,000) Cat Microforms
Budget: ($110,000)
Notes: Also 13,000 bound periodical vols; 23,000 foreign chemical theses.

MA —BOSTON COLLEGE LIBRARIES, Science Library, Devlin Hall, Chestnut Hill, 02167. F Clifford McElroy, Science Librn
Holdings: Vols (54,508) Cat Maps Microforms
Budget: ($94,270)
Notes: Library is being absorbed into the general collection.

MA —TUFTS UNIVERSITY, Chemistry Library, Medford, 02155. Wayne Powell, Science-Engineering Librn
Holdings: Vols 12,500 Cat Microforms

MA —WELLESLEY COLLEGE, Margaret Clapp Library, College Archives, Wellesley, 02181.
Notes: Records of the Departments of Astronomy, Biological Sciences, Botany, Chemistry, Geology, Physics, Zoology, and individuals connected with these departments at Wellesley College (27 linear feet).

MA —NORTON COMPANY, Library, 1 New Bond St, Worcester, 01606. Joan K Chaffey, Librn
Holdings: Cat
Notes: Abrasive industry collection.

MI —WARNER-LAMBERT/PARKE-DAVIS, Research Library, 2800 Plymouth Rd, Ann Arbor, 48106. Katherine C Owen, Mgr, Library Services
Holdings: Vols (27,977) Cat

MI —UNIVERSITY OF MICHIGAN, Chemistry-Pharmacy Library, 2000 Chemistry Bldg, Ann Arbor, 48109. Stephen C Lucchetti, Librn
Holdings: Vols (50,000) Cat Microforms
Budget: ($130,000)
Notes: Incl 15,000 edge-notched cards of spectra. Comp Access provided to Lockheed, and CAS Online.

MS —UNIVERSITY OF SOUTHERN MISSISSIPPI, William David McCain Graduate Library, Box 5148, Southern Sta, Hattiesburg, 39406.
Holdings: Mss
Notes: Collections incl the research records (1934-1977) of Dr James S Long and the research records and organizational records of the American Tung Oil Institute and its predecessor organizations. 33 cubic feet of mss.
See also entries under Long, Dr James S; American Tung Oil Institute.

MS —GULF COAST RESEARCH LABORATORY, Gordon Gunter Library, E Beach Rd, Ocean Springs, 39564. Malcolm Ware, Sr, Librn
Holdings: Vols (9000) Uncat Mss Pix Microforms
Notes: Also have reprint collection of 30,000 cataloged reprints, indexed by card catalog, on all aspects of marine biology.

NV —UNIVERSITY OF NEVADA, RENO, Physical Sciences Library, Chemistry Bldg, Rm 316, Reno, 89557. Roberta Kiefer Orcutt, Librn
Holdings: Vols (24,000) Cat Slides Microforms

NJ —NUODEX, INC, Library, PO Box 365, Piscataway, 08854. J Carnahan, Librn
Holdings: Vols (4000) Cat Microforms
Budget: $30,000
Notes: Industrial chemistry. Open to public by appointment.

NJ —PRINCETON UNIVERSITY, Library, Rare Books Dept, Princeton, 08544. Stephen Ferguson, Cur
Holdings: Cat

NJ —GAF CORP, Library, Technical Information Services, 1361 Alps Rd, Wayne, 07470. Ira Naznitsky, Mgr Tech Info Serv; Helen H Carini, Supvr Libr
Holdings: Vols 8000 Cat
Budget: $100,000

NY —CORNELL UNIVERSITY LIBRARIES, Physical Sciences Library, Clark Hall, Ithaca, 14853. Ellen S Thomas, Librn
Holdings: Vols (73,701) Cat Microforms
Budget: ($244,185)

NY —NEW YORK PUBLIC LIBRARY, Research Libraries, Science and Technology Research Center, Fifth Ave & 42 St, New York, 10018.
Holdings: Vols (1,100,000) Cat Microforms
Budget: ($647,259)

NY —NEW YORK SOCIETY LIBRARY, 53 E 79 St, New York, 10021. Mark Piel, Librn
Notes: Incl Governor John Winthrop's Collection on chemistry and alchemy (part of which is at the New York Academy of Medicine Library).

NY —EASTMAN KODAK COMPANY, Research Library, Research Laboratories, Bldg 83, Rochester, 14650. E W Kraus, Head
Holdings: Vols 9800 Cat Microforms

NY —UNIVERSITY OF ROCHESTER, Carlson Library, Hutchison Hall, River Campus, Rochester, 14627. Michael W Poulin, Librn
Holdings: Vols (48,720) Cat Microforms
Notes: Strong collection in the field and related areas.

NY —REVLON HEALTH CARE GROUP, Information Services, One Scarsdale Ave, Tuckahoe, 10707. Rena Radovich, Manager
Holdings: Cat
Notes: Book vols & periodicals.

NC —DUKE UNIVERSITY, Chemistry Library, Durham, 27706. Kitty Porter, Librn

NC —R J REYNOLDS TOBACCO CO, Scientific Information Services Library, Bowman Gray Technical Center, BGTC 611-12/205, Winston-Salem, 27102. Nellie W Sizemore, Librn
Holdings: Vols 5000 Cat Microforms

OH —EMERY INDUSTRIES, Research Library, 4900 Este Ave, Cincinnati, 45232. B A Bernard, Librn
Holdings: Cat
Notes: Special subjects: fatty acids and organic chemical derivatives, ozone, plasticizers, polymers, synthetic lubricants.

OH —LLOYD LIBRARY & MUSEUM, 917 Plum St, Cincinnati, 45202. John B Griggs, Librn
Notes: Extensive holdings in plant chemistry and pharmaceutical chemistry.

OH —PUBLIC LIBRARY OF CINCINNATI & HAMILTON COUNTY, Science & Technology Dept, 800 Vine St, Cincinnati, 45202. Rosemary Gaiser, Head
Holdings: Vols (250,000) Cat
Notes: Pure and applied science. Incl over 1600 periodicals and serial titles and more than 100 abstracting and indexing services in major fields of science and technology.

OH —SAINT THOMAS INSTITUTE, Library, 1842 Madison Rd, Cincinnati, 45206. Sister M Virgil Ghering, O P Librn
Holdings: Vols 10,000 Cat
Budget: ($39,878)

OH —SDS BIOTECH CORP, PO Box 348, Painesville, 44077. Violet Forgach, Business Librn
Holdings: Cat Pix Microforms

OK —OKLAHOMA STATE UNIVERSITY, Library, Stillwater, 74708. Roscoe Rouse, Dir
Holdings: Vols 27,703 Cat Microforms

OR —OREGON STATE UNIVERSITY, Library, Corvallis, 97331. Melvin George, Dir
Holdings: Vols 21,000 Cat Pix

PA —LEHIGH UNIVERSITY LIBRARIES, Mart Science & Engineering Library, Bethlehem, 18015.
Holdings: Mss
Notes: Papers of Dr William J Wiswesser on his system for encoding all possible chemical compounds.

CHEMISTRY (cont.)

PA —DELAWARE VALLEY COLLEGE, Joseph Krauskopf Library, Doylestown, 18901. Constance Shook, Dir

PA —COLLEGE OF PHYSICIANS OF PHILADELPHIA, Library, 19 S 22 St, Philadelphia, 19103. Anthony Aguirre, Libr Dir
Holdings: Vols (316,223) // Cat Mss Microforms
Budget: ($1,096,557)
Notes: Incl 13,515 pamphlets; 1435 mss; 326,367 reports, dissertations, and reprints. Strong historical and bibliographical collections, as well as current materials. Medical documentation service provides current alerting, incl abstracting, etc.

PA —FRANKLIN INSTITUTE LIBRARY, 20 & The Parkway, Philadelphia, 19103. Miriam Padusis, Dir; Charles Wilt, Readers Servs Librn
Holdings: Vols (300,000) Cat Maps Pix Microforms

PA —CARNEGIE LIBRARY OF PITTSBURGH, Science & Technology Dept, 4400 Forbes Ave, Pittsburgh, 15213. Catherine M Brosky, Dept Head
Holdings: Vols (380,000) Cat Maps Microforms
Budget: ($240,000)
Notes: Area of primary interest with more than 80,000 vols relating directly to chemistry. Attempts to acquire journals in Chemical Abstracts. Incl literature guides, history and biography, encyclopedias, handbooks, dictionaries, tables, directories, compendia, annual reviews, abstracts, indexes and bibliographies relating to organic, inorganic, analytical and general chemistry. Special endowment fund established by Pittsburgh Section, American Chemical Society.

PA —CARNEGIE-MELLON UNIVERSITY, Mellon Institute Library, 4400 Fifth Ave, Pittsburgh, 15213. Mary J Volk, Librn
Holdings: Vols (60,000) Cat
Notes: Emphasis is on chemistry and biological sciences, with material at the graduate and research level.

PA —PENNSYLVANIA STATE UNIVERSITY, Physical Sciences Library, 230 Davey Laboratory, University Park, 16802. Cornelius J McKown, Librn
Holdings: Vols (80,000) Cat Microforms

PA —MERCK SHARP & DOHME, Research Laboratories, Literature Resource Center, West Point, 19486. Evelyn W Armstrong, Dir, Literature Resource Centers
Holdings: Cat Microforms
Notes: Monographs (3000) and journals (15, 000 vols).

†RI —UNIVERSITY OF RHODE ISLAND, Library, Kingston, 02881.
Notes: Extensive collections.

SC —UNIVERSITY OF SOUTH CAROLINA, Thomas Cooper Library, Columbia, 29208. Kenneth E Toombs, Dir of Libraries; Roger Mortimer, Rare Book Librn
Holdings: Vols 1250 Cat
Notes: Especially for 1750-1850.

†SD —SOUTH DAKOTA SCHOOL OF MINES & TECHNOLOGY, Devereaux Library, Rapid City, 57701.
Holdings: Vols (166,200) Cat Maps Audiotapes Filmstrips Microforms
Notes: Supportive collection incl periodicals and technical reports (NASA, ACRL, JPL, etc); and extensive government document materials (NBS, Dept of Commerce, HEW, etc).

TN —COMBUSTION ENGINEERING, Metallurgical Materials Library, 911 W Main St, Chattanooga, 37402. Nell T Holder, Tech Librn
Holdings: Vols (10,000) Cat
Notes: Metallurgical research and development. 350 serials and periodicals, 800 translations of foreign articles. 250,000 US Government Reports. MF Collection C-E Technical reports ASME.

TX —TEXAS STATE LIBRARY, Archives Div, 1201 Brazos, PO Box 12927, Capitol Sta, Austin, 78711. David B Gracy II, State Archivist

TX —UNIVERSITY OF TEXAS LIBRARIES, John W Mallet Chemistry Library, Welch Hall 2132, Austin, 78712. A E Skinner, Chemistry Librn
Holdings: Vols (44,000) Cat Microforms
Notes: Described in *The John W Mallet Chemistry Library (The University of Texas at Austin)* (Austin: The General Libraries, 1975).

TX —RICE UNIVERSITY, Fondren Library, 6100 S Main St, PO Box 1892, Houston, 77251. Dr Samuel M Carrington, Jr, University Librn
Holdings: Vols 6050 Cat
Budget: $64,800
Notes: Each serial title counted once.

TX —UNIVERSITY OF TEXAS, Marine Science Institute Library, Port Aransas, 78373. Ruth Grundy, Librn
Holdings: Vols (45,000) Cat Maps Pix
Budget: ($70,000)
Notes: Current researches in marine science, especially concerning the Gulf of Mexico, the Texas Coastal Zone, and the Continental Shelf. Incl journals.

VT —UNIVERSITY OF VERMONT, Chemistry/Physics Library, Burlington, 05405. Craig A Robertson, Librn
Holdings: Vols (23,000) Cat Microforms
Notes: The collection consists largely of periodicals, having about 12,000 bound periodical volumes. The number of periodical titles currently received is approximately 210.

WA —BATTELLE-PACIFIC NORTHWEST LABORTORIES, Technical Library, PO Box 999, Richland, 99352. Wayne Snyder, Librn
Holdings: Vols (50,000) Cat Microforms
Budget: ($500,000)
Notes: Holdings: 50,000 books; 35,000 bound periodical volumes; 200,000 technical reports; 200,000 technical reports in microform. Subscriptions: 1800 journals and other serials. Services: interlibrary loans; literature searching; translation; library open to public with restrictions.

WA —UNIVERSITY OF WASHINGTON LIBRARIES, Chemistry-Pharmacy Library, BG-10, Seattle, 98195. Heidi Mercado, Librn
Holdings: Vols (47,500) Cat Microforms
Budget: ($195,000)
Notes: All aspects of analytical, inorganic, organic and physical chemistry are covered. *See also* entry under Chemical Engineering.

WI —UNIVERSITY OF WISCONSIN, MADISON, Memorial Library, Rare Books Collection, 728 State St, Madison, 53706. Gretchen Lagana, Cur
Notes: Incl the William A Cole Collection of 18th-19th century chemical books, many in original languages and translations. Library is strong in 16th-17th century works through the Duveen Collection on Alchemy and Early Chemistry.

WI —UNIVERSITY OF WISCONSIN, MADISON, Chemistry Library, 2361 Farrington Daniels Chemistry Bldg, 1101 University Ave, Madison, 53706. Kendall Rouse, Chemistry Librn
Holdings: Vols (35,000) Cat Microforms
Budget: ($174,000)

WI —MILWAUKEE PUBLIC LIBRARY, 814 W Wisconsin Ave, Milwaukee, 53233. Donald J Sager, City Librn
Holdings: Vols (30,000) Cat
Notes: Strong collection acquired to support state interlibrary loan. Covers all the pure and applied sciences. Incl over (1600) periodicals and serial titles and more than (100) abstracting and indexing services in major fields of science and technology. Strong general reference service.

AB —SHERRITT RESEARCH CENTRE, Library, Sherritt Gordon Mines Ltd, Fort Saskatchewan, T8L 2P2, Can. D Sim, Librn
Holdings: Vols (7000)
Budget: $20,000

MB —UNIVERSITY OF MANITOBA, Science Library, Machray Hall, Winnipeg, R3T 2N2, Can. V Simosko, Head
Holdings: Vols (90,000) Cat Microforms

ON —ONTARIO RESEARCH FOUNDATION, Library, Sheridan Park, Mississauga, L5K 1B3, Can. Carl K Wei, Librn
Holdings: Vols (13,000) Cat
Budget: ($14,000)

ON —METROPOLITAN TORONTO LIBRARY, Science & Technology Dept, 789 Yonge St, Toronto, M4W 2G8, Can. Margaret Walshe, Head
Holdings: Vols (120,000) Cat
Notes: All aspects of science for the specialist, the student, and the general public. The department gives high priority to Canadian materials.

PQ —SERVICE DE LA DOCUMENTATION ET DES RENSEIGNEMENTS MINISTERE DE L'ENERGIE ET DES RESSOURCES, 2000B, chemin Sainte-Foy, 7th floor, Quebec, G1R 4X7, Can. Normand Guerette, Dir
Holdings: Vols (114,800) Slides Videotapes
Notes: In 1979, the Bibliotheque du ministere des Richesses naturelles du Quebec merged with the Bibliotheque du ministere des Terres et Forets. The result of this merger was the creation of the service de la Documentation et des Renseignements du ministere de l'Energie et des Ressources.
Publications: Info-Biblio Terres et Forets; Mines; Energy.

CHEMISTRY—HISTORY

CA —UNIVERSITY OF CALIFORNIA, BERKELEY, Bancroft Library, Manuscripts Division, Berkeley, 94720. James D Hart, Dir
Notes: Extensive collections of papers and archives relative to the history of modern chemistry.

CA —UNIVERSITY OF CALIFORNIA, LOS ANGELES, Chemistry Library, 4238 Young Hall, Los Angeles, 90024. Marion C Peters, Chemistry Librn
Holdings: Vols (55,600) Cat Microforms
Notes: (768) current serials subscriptions; special collection of 450 volumes on the history of chemistry; US Chemical Patents since 1952 on microforms; Sadtler Standard Spectra; UCLA biochemistry and chemistry theses. Collection strengths incl analytical, biological, inorganic, organic and physical chemistry.

DE —HAGLEY MUSEUM AND LIBRARY, Eleutherian Mills-Hagley Foundation Inc, PO Box 3630, Greenville, 19807. Richmond D Williams, Dir; Heddy A Richter, Imprints Librn
Notes: Records of E I du Pont de Nemours & Company (1801-1958; 2500 cubic feet). The collection traces the founding of the company in Paris, its evolution into an American partnership during the early nineteenth century and its first incorporation in 1899. Details concerning the financial and business negotiations which led to the founding of the company, the selection of a site for operations, the erection of the mills, and methods of manufacturing, production, marketing and labor relations are well described. Records of Atlas Powder Company (1912-1955; 500 cubic feet) document the history of one of the United States' largest manufacturers of gun powder which was split off from the Du Pont Company as a result of a 1912 antitrust case.

DE —UNIVERSITY OF DELAWARE, Hugh M Morris Library, S College Ave, Newark, 19711. T Stuart Dick, Special Collections
Holdings: Vols (2100) Cat Mss
Notes: The Unidel History of Chemistry Collection. 60 percent of the collection deals with chemistry prior to 1780. Particularly strong in alchemical works incl some 6 alchemical mss. Also works on mining, medicine and pharmacy. Notable chemical pioneers of the 1780-1860 period are well represented by such men as Lavoisier, Avogardo, Chaptal, Davy, Faraday, Fourcroy, Liebig and Volta. Majority of the collection in French and Italian.

KS —UNIVERSITY OF KANSAS, Kenneth Spencer Research Library, Special Collections Dept, Lawrence, 66045. Alexandra Mason, Librn
Holdings: Cat Mss Maps Pix
Notes: Ellis Collection of Ornithology, natural history and voyages and travels;

CHEMISTRY—HISTORY (cont.)

botanical literature from Fitzpatrick collection (especially medical botany, early American botanists, renaissance herbals, Matthioli); some early chemistry and mathematics; scientific voyages and travels; De Beer collection of offprints in embryology, endocrinology, and systematic zoology; D'Arcy Wentworth Thompson collection of separates in natural history and classics; Herrick, Coghill and Roofe collections in neurology. Noncirculating.

MA —HARVARD UNIVERSITY LIBRARY, Converse Memorial Library, Chemistry Library, 12 Oxford St, Cambridge, 02138. Ludmila Birladeanu, Supv
Holdings: Vols (50,000) Cat Microforms
Budget: ($110,000)
Notes: Also 13,000 bound periodical vols; 23,000 foreign chemical theses.

MI —UNIVERSITY OF MICHIGAN, Library, Dept of Rare Books & Special Collections, Ann Arbor, 48109. Robert J Starring, Head
Holdings: Cat Mss Pix
Notes: Chiefly pre-1800 imprints.

NY —CORNELL UNIVERSITY LIBRARIES, John M Olin Library, History of Science Collections, Ithaca, 14853. Lillian A Clark, Administrative Supervisor; David W Corson, History of Science Librn
Holdings: Vols (33,000) Cat
Notes: Early printed source materials in all physical sciences, 16th through 19th centuries. Incl Robison Collection of the works of Robert Boyle (175 vols) and Lavoisier Collection (2000 vols, 500 mss). Very extensive holdings in chemistry from Boyle to immediate successors of Lavoisier. Noncirculating.
See also entries under Robert Boyle; Antoine Lavoisier; Science - History.

NY —AMERICAN INSTITUTE OF PHYSICS, Center for the History of Physics, Niels Bohr Library, 335 E 45 St, New York, 10017. John Aubry, Librn
Holdings: Cat Mss Maps Pix Microforms

NY —CHEMISTS' CLUB LIBRARY, 52 E 41 St, New York, 10017. Elsie Lim, Librn
Holdings: Pix
Notes: Incl a large vertical file collection of portraits of chemists.

NY —US MILITARY ACADEMY LIBRARY, West Point, 10996. Egon A Weiss, Librn
Holdings: Mss
Notes: Records of the Department of Chemistry, Mechanics, and Physics (1881-1971), of the US Military Academy at West Point. 9.75 ft of mss.

OH —OHIO UNIVERSITY, Vernon R Alden Library, Department of Archives and Special Collections, Athens, 45701. Gary A Hunt, Head
Holdings: Vols 1737 Uncat Pix
Notes: The J W Morgan Collection in the History of Chemistry and Science. The emphasis in upon chemistry. Ranges from 16th to 20th centuries, with greatest strength in 18th and 19th centuries, and in American and British imprints. See Moss, Roger W, Jr. *The Morgan Collection in the History of Chemistry: A Checklist* (Athens, Ohio University Library, 1965).

PA —CENTER FOR THE HISTORY OF CHEMISTRY, EF Smith Hall, D-6 University of Pennsylvania, 215 S 34 St, Philadelphia, 19104. Prof Arnold Thackray, Dir
Notes: Established in 1982 and jointly sponsored by the American Chemical Society, the American Institute of Chemical Engineers, and The University of Pennsylvania, the Center's purpose is to "discover and disseminate information about historical resources, and to encourage research, scholarship, and popular writing in the history of chemistry, chemical engineering, and the chemical process industries.". The Center is associated with the Edgar Fahs Smith Memorial Collection in the History of Chemistry.

PA —UNIVERSITY OF PENNSYLVANIA, Van Pelt Library, Edgar Fahs Smith Memorial Collection in the History of Chemistry, 3420 Walnut St, Philadelphia, 19104. Arnold W Thackray, Cur
Holdings: Vols (15,000) Cat Mss Pix
Notes: The Smith Collection, 15,000 vols, is one of the most comprehensive collections on the history of chemistry in North America, covering chemistry and its allied disciplines, from the Renaissance to the early 20th century. The Collection's traditional strengths lie in classical history of chemistry, ie pre-1800. However acquisitions over the past 15 years have substantially built up the post-1800 holdings, especially in areas of chemical technology. News of the Collection may be found in the Center's twice yearly newsletter *CHOC News* which is available free of charge to interested persons. A convenient description is provided in Herbert S Klickstein, "Edgar Fahs Smith-His Contributions to the History of Chemistry," *Chymia,* 5 (1959), 11-30. A published catalog of our holdings now needs considerable revision, due to continued *acquisitions:Catalog of the Edgar Fahs Smith Memorial Collection* (Boston: G K Hall and Co, 1960). Portions of our manuscript collection have been described in Norman P Zacour and Rudolf Hirsch, *Catalogue of the Manuscripts in the Libraries of the University of Pennsylvania to 1800* (Philadelphia: University of Pennsylvania Press, 1965), 231-243; and R Hirsch, "Catalogue of Manuscripts...Supplement a (5) ," *Library Chronicle,* 37 (1971), 91-115.

WI —UNIVERSITY OF WISCONSIN, MADISON, Memorial Library, History of Science Collection, 728 State St, Madison, 53706. John Neu, Bibliographer
Holdings: Cat Mss
Notes: Major research collection of primary and secondary materials in the history of chemistry and alchemy. Includes the Dennis I Duveen Collection, the William A Cole Collection, and the collections of Joseph Priestley and Robert Boyle. See John Neu, ed, *Chemical, Medical and Pharmaceutical Books Printed before 1800 in the Collections of the University of Wisconsin Libraries* (Madison and Milwaukee: University of Wisconsin Press, 1965); Dennis I Duveen, *Bibliotheca Alchemica et Chemica: An Annotated Catalogue of Printed Books on Alchemy, Chemistry and Cognate Subjects in the Library of Dennis I Duveen* (London: Dawsons of Pall Mall, 1965). Restricted use: Rare Book Department.

ON —UNIVERSITY OF TORONTO, Thomas Fisher Rare Book Library, 120 Saint George St, Toronto, M5S 1A5, Can. Richard G Landon, Head
Holdings: Vols 4000
Notes: The Science Collection is especially rich in works on Renaissance astronomy, physics and mechanics and has noteworthy holdings of works of English experimental scientists in the 17th and 18th centuries with excellent collections of the works of Robert Boyle, Robert Hooke, and Sir Isaac Newton. Includes virtually all important early editions of Euclid; alchemical works of the 16th and 17th centuries together with the works of 18th century chemists like Lavoisier and Priestly; works on agriculture with special emphasis on British agriculture in the 18th century; and a variety of other works important in the history of science in all its branches. In addition the Fisher Library has many other specialized scientific collections which are listed separately.

CHEMISTRY—STUDY AND TEACHING

NY —US MILITARY ACADEMY LIBRARY, West Point, 10996. Egon A Weiss, Librn
Holdings: Mss
Notes: Records of the Department of Chemistry, Mechanics, and Physics (1881-1971), of the US Military Academy at West Point. 9.75 ft of mss.

CHEMISTRY, AGRICULTURAL see Agricultural Chemistry

CHEMISTRY, ANALYTIC

AR —NATIONAL CENTER FOR TOXICOLOGICAL RESEARCH, Library, Jefferson, 72079. Susan Laney-Sheehan, Supvr Librn
Holdings: Vols (15,000) Cat Mss Slides Audiotapes 16mm Films Microforms
Notes: Incl (860) journal titles, (230) current subscriptions.

CA —UNIVERSITY OF CALIFORNIA, BERKELEY, Bancroft Library, Manuscripts Division, Berkeley, 94720. James D Hart, Dir
Notes: Extensive collections of papers and archives relative to the history of modern chemistry.

CA —BECKMAN INSTRUMENTS, Research Library, 2500 Harbor Blvd, Fullerton, 92634. Jean R Miller, Librn
Holdings: Vols (7000) Cat Slides Audiotapes Videotapes Microforms
Budget: ($9000)
Notes: Strong collections in scientific and analytic instrumentation, electrochemistry, analytical chemistry, optics and spectroscopy, chromatography, clinical chemistry and biochemistry.

CA —UNIVERSITY OF CALIFORNIA, LOS ANGELES, Chemistry Library, 4238 Young Hall, Los Angeles, 90024. Marion C Peters, Chemistry Librn
Holdings: Vols (55,600) Cat Microforms
Notes: (768) current serials subscriptions; special collection of 450 volumes on the history of chemistry; US Chemical Patents since 1952 on microforms; Sadtler Standard Spectra; UCLA biochemistry and chemistry theses. Collection strengths incl analytical, biological, inorganic, organic and physical chemistry.

IL —UNIVERSITY OF ILLINOIS, URBANA/CHAMPAIGN, Chemistry Library, 255 Noyes Laboratory, Urbana, 61801. Lucille M Wert, Chemistry Librn; Susan Eilering, Asst Chemistry Librn
Holdings: Vols (150,000) Cat Microforms
Budget: ($224,660)
Notes: Collection incl monographs, treatises and serials in all languages covering all the fields of chemistry. Its major holdings are in the area of spectroscopy. It is designed to serve the instructional and research needs of the School of Chemical Sciences and the University Community.

IN —INDIANA UNIVERSITY, Chemistry Library, Chemistry Bldg, Rm One, Bloomington, 47405. Gary Wiggins, Head Librn
Holdings: Vols (55,000) Cat Slides Microforms
Budget: ($157,000)

IA —ARCHER DANIELS MIDLAND, Research Library, PO Box 340, Clinton, 52732. Carol L Kolk, Research Librn
Holdings: Vols 2200 Cat Microforms
Notes: Card index to patent file. Keydex index to Research Experiment Reports.

MA —US DEPT OF HEALTH, EDUCATION & WELFARE, Public Health Service, FDA Winchester Engineering Analytical Center, 109 Holton St, Winchester, 01890. Lisa Leone, Librn
Holdings: Vols (3000) Mss Maps Audiotapes

NY —WESTRECO INC, Research Library, 555 S Fourth St, Fulton, 13069. Janice Burns, Research Librn
Holdings: Vols 44 Cat Periodicals VF
Notes: Food Science and Technology collection of about (1200) books and pamphlets. Back files of periodicals retained up to 20 years.

NY —BORDEN FOODS INC, Research Centre Library, 600 N Franklin St, Syracuse, 13204. Carol Lenz-Taylor, Librn
Holdings: Vols (1800) Cat
Notes: Incl 10 vertical file drawers and 6100 patents.

OH —PPG INDUSTRIES, Chemical Div, Research Library, PO Box 31, Barberton, 44203. Diane Danko, Chemical Information Specialist
Holdings: Vols (20,000) Cat Microforms
Notes: Organic, inorganic, analytical and agricultural chemistry, with special emphasis on applied and chemical engineering.

PA —FRANKLIN INSTITUTE LIBRARY, 20 & The Parkway, Philadelphia, 19103. Miriam Padusis, Dir; Charles Wilt, Readers Servs Librn
Holdings: Vols (300,000) Cat Maps Pix Microforms

CHEMISTRY, ANALYTIC (cont.)

PA —CARNEGIE LIBRARY OF PITTSBURGH, Science & Technology Dept, 4400 Forbes Ave, Pittsburgh, 15213. Catherine M Brosky, Dept Head
Holdings: Vols (380,000) Cat Maps Microforms
Budget: ($240,000)
See also entry under Chemistry.

PA —UNIVERSITY OF PITTSBURGH, Chemistry Library, 200 Alumni Hall, Pittsburgh, 15260. Paul J Kobulnicky, Physical Sciences Librn
Holdings: Vols (20,000) Cat Microforms
Budget: ($100,000)
Notes: This library has traditionally limited its collection to pure chemistry. Complete spectral files with index.

WI —UNIVERSITY OF WISCONSIN, MADISON, Chemistry Library, 2361 Farrington Daniels Chemistry Bldg, 1101 University Ave, Madison, 53706. Kendall Rouse, Chemistry Librn
Holdings: Vols (35,000) Cat Microforms
Budget: ($174,000)

ON —AGRICULTURE CANADA, Research Branch, Neatby Library, Rm 3032, K W Neatby Bldg, CEF, Ottawa, K1A 0C6, Can. Marcel Charette, Library Technician
Holdings: Vols 1800 Cat

CHEMISTRY, BIOLOGICAL see Biological Chemistry

CHEMISTRY, BOTANICAL see Botanical Chemistry

CHEMISTRY, DETERGENT

MN —ECONOMICS LABORATORY INFORMATION CENTER, Osborn Bldg, Saint Paul, 55102. Dona M Bradt, Librn

CHEMISTRY, HEAVY ELEMENT

IL —ARGONNE NATIONAL LABORATORY, Chemistry Branch Library, 9700 S Cass Ave, Argonne, 60439. Betty Guttman, Librn
Notes: Incl 20,000 vols monographs, 190 current journals. Materials may be used by the public in the library by prior arrangement. Photocopies may be supplied for interlibrary loan, for which a processing and handling charge is made.

CHEMISTRY, INDUSTRIAL see Chemical Engineering; Chemistry, Technical

CHEMISTRY, INORGANIC

CA —UNIVERSITY OF CALIFORNIA, LOS ANGELES, Chemistry Library, 4238 Young Hall, Los Angeles, 90024. Marion C Peters, Chemistry Librn
Holdings: Vols (55,600) Cat Microforms
Notes: (768) current serials subscriptions; special collection of 450 volumes on the history of chemistry; US Chemical Patents since 1952 on microforms; Sadtler Standard Spectra; UCLA biochemistry and chemistry theses. Collection strengths incl analytical, biological, inorganic, organic and physical chemistry.

IL —ARGONNE NATIONAL LABORATORY, Chemistry Branch Library, 9700 S Cass Ave, Argonne, 60439. Betty Guttman, Librn
Notes: Incl 20,000 vols monographs, 190 current journals. Materials may be used by the public in the library by prior arrangement. Photocopies may be supplied for interlibrary loan, for which a processing and handling charge is made.

IL —UNIVERSITY OF ILLINOIS, URBANA/CHAMPAIGN, Chemistry Library, 255 Noyes Laboratory, Urbana, 61801. Lucille M Wert, Chemistry Librn; Susan Eilering, Asst Chemistry Librn
Holdings: Vols (150,000) Cat Microforms
Budget: ($224,660)
Notes: Collection incl monographs, treatises and serials in all languages covering all the fields of chemistry. It is designed to serve the instructional and research needs of the School of Chemical Science and the University Community.

NY —UNIVERSITY OF ROCHESTER, Carlson Library, Hutchison Hall, River Campus, Rochester, 14627. Michael W Poulin, Librn
Holdings: Vols (48,720) Cat Microforms
Notes: Strong collection in the field and related areas.

OH —PPG INDUSTRIES, Chemical Div, Research Library, PO Box 31, Barberton, 44203. Diane Danko, Chemical Information Specialist
Holdings: Vols (20,000) Cat Microforms
Notes: Organic, inorganic, analytical and agricultural chemistry, with special emphasis on applied and chemical engineering.

OH —SDS BIOTECH CORP, PO Box 348, Painesville, 44077. Violet Forgach, Business Librn
Holdings: Cat Pix Microforms

PA —FRANKLIN INSTITUTE LIBRARY, 20 & The Parkway, Philadelphia, 19103. Miriam Padusis, Dir; Charles Wilt, Readers Servs Librn
Holdings: Vols (300,000) Cat Maps Pix Microforms

PA —CARNEGIE LIBRARY OF PITTSBURGH, Science & Technology Dept, 4400 Forbes Ave, Pittsburgh, 15213. Catherine M Brosky, Dept Head
Holdings: Vols (380,000) Cat Maps Microforms
Budget: ($240,000)
Notes: Area of primary interest with more than 80,000 vols relating directly to chemistry. Attempts to acquire journals in Chemical Abstracts. Incl literature guides, history and biography, encyclopedias, handbooks, dictionaries, tables, directories, compendia, annual reviews, abstracts, indexes and bibliographies relating to organic, inorganic, analytical and general chemistry. Special endowment fund established by Pittsburgh Section, American Chemical Society.

PA —UNIVERSITY OF PITTSBURGH, Chemistry Library, 200 Alumni Hall, Pittsburgh, 15260. Paul J Kobulnicky, Physical Sciences Librn
Holdings: Vols (20,000) Cat Microforms
Budget: ($100,000)
Notes: This library has traditionally limited its collection to pure chemistry. Complete spectral files with index.

WI —UNIVERSITY OF WISCONSIN, MADISON, Chemistry Library, 2361 Farrington Daniels Chemistry Bldg, 1101 University Ave, Madison, 53706. Kendall Rouse, Chemistry Librn
Holdings: Vols (35,000) Cat Microforms
Budget: ($174,000)

ON —AGRICULTURE CANADA, Research Branch, Neatby Library, Rm 3032, K W Neatby Bldg, CEF, Ottawa, K1A 0C6, Can. Marcel Charette, Library Technician
Holdings: Vols 3000 Cat

PQ —NORANDA RESEARCH CENTRE, Library, 240 Hymus Blvd, Pointe-Claire, H9R 1G5, Can. Shirley Courtis, Librn
Holdings: Vols (7000)

CHEMISTRY, LASERS IN see Lasers in Chemistry

CHEMISTRY, MARINE

ME —BIGELOW LABORATORY FOR OCEAN SCIENCES & MAINE DEPT OF MARINE RESOURCES, Library, McKown Point, West Boothbay Harbor, 04575. Pamela Shephard-Lupo, Librn
Holdings: Vols Cat Periodicals
Budget: ($55,000)
Notes: This library presently serves two institutions. The Maine Dept of Marine Resources has maintained the library since 1957 and thus the majority of our holdings are geared to their needs, ie fish biology and stock assessment on a local, national and international level. In 1973 Bigelow Laboratory for Ocean Sciences came to West Boothbay Harbor and began to contribute to the library with a very specialized collection on the Gulf of Maine marine chemistry. phytoplankton and nutrient cycles.

TX —UNIVERSITY OF TEXAS, Marine Science Institute Library, Port Aransas, 78373. Ruth Grundy, Librn
Holdings: Vols (45,000) Cat Maps Pix
Budget: ($70,000)
Notes: Current researches in marine science, especially concerning the Gulf of Mexico, the Texas Coastal Zone, and the Continental Shelf. Incl journals.

CHEMISTRY, MEDICAL AND PHARMACEUTICAL

CA —BECKMAN INSTRUMENTS, Research Library, 2500 Harbor Blvd, Fullerton, 92634. Jean R Miller, Librn
Holdings: Vols (7000) Cat Slides Audiotapes Videotapes Microforms
Budget: ($9000)
Notes: Strong collections in scientific and analytic instrumentation, electrochemistry, analytical chemistry, optics and spectroscopy, chromatogaphy, clinical chemistry and biochemistry.

MA —MASSACHUSETTS COLLEGE OF PHARMACY AND ALLIED HEALTH SCIENCES, Sheppard Library, 179 Longwood Ave, Boston, 02115. Barbara M Hill, Librn
Holdings: Vols (56,000) Cat Mss Pix Slides Microforms
Notes: Worldwide representation.

MN —UNIVERSITY OF MINNESOTA, Bio-Medical Library, Diehl Hall, Minneapolis, 55455. Gertrude Foreman, Acting Dir
Holdings: Vols (263,361)
Budget: ($500,000)

MN —3M COMPANY, 3M Center, Riker Laboratories, Saint Paul, 55101.
Holdings: Vols (6100) Cat
Budget: ($13,000)
Notes: Covers medical and pharmaceutical chemistry and medical botany. Incl 2600 books (175 drug directories) and 3500 bound journal vols.

NJ —BERLEX LABORATORIES, Research & Development Library, 110 E Hanover Ave, Cedar Knolls, 07927. Lorene Lingelbach, Librn
Holdings: Vols (10,000) Cat Microforms
Notes: The library was established in 1972 by consolidating the collections of companies which merged with Berlex Laboratories. 425 periodical titles are received currently.

NY —LONG ISLAND UNIVERSITY, Brooklyn Center, Pharmacy Library Collection, University Plaza, Brooklyn, 11201. Barbara Chanton, Dir & Health Sciences Librn
Holdings: Vols (17,500) Cat Mss
Notes: Pharmacy, drug abuse, hospital pharmacy, medicinal chemistry.

CHEMISTRY, ORGANIC

CA —UNIVERSITY OF CALIFORNIA, BERKELEY, Bancroft Library, Manuscripts Division, Berkeley, 94720. James D Hart, Dir
Notes: Extensive collections of papers and archives relative to the history of modern chemistry.

CA —UNIVERSITY OF CALIFORNIA, LOS ANGELES, Chemistry Library, 4238 Young Hall, Los Angeles, 90024. Marion C Peters, Chemistry Librn
Holdings: Vols (55,600) Cat Microforms
Notes: (768) current serials subscriptions; special collection of 450 volumes on the history of chemistry; US Chemical Patents since 1952 on microforms; Sadtler Standard Spectra; UCLA biochemistry and chemistry theses. Collection strengths incl analytical, biological, inorganic, organic and physical chemistry.

CA —SUNKIST GROWERS, Research Library, 760 E Sunkist St, Ontario, 91761. Martha C Nemeth, Librn
Holdings: Vols (1500) Cat
Budget: ($10,000)
Notes: Technology of citrus fruit and citrus

CHEMISTRY, ORGANIC (cont.)

fruit products, primarily Californian. Strong in organic and food chemistry, with additional coverage of food technology, essential oils, microbiology and environmental protection.

CA —INTERNATIONAL BUSINESS MACHINES RESEARCH LIBRARY, 5600 Cottle Rd, San Jose, 95193. Phil Grincewich, Mgr Technical Information
Holdings: Vols (13,500) Cat
Notes: Extensive collection of polymer chemistry and analytical organic chemistry. Incl 21,000 vols of 770 journals. On-line search facility. Volumes are divided into three libraries, Technical Research, Technical Information, and Programing. Not open to public.

CT —UPJOHN CO, D S Gilmore Library, 410 Sacketts Point Rd, North Haven, 06473. A M Nashu, Supvr
Holdings: Vols 6000 Cat
Budget: $60,000

IL —UNIVERSITY OF ILLINOIS, URBANA/CHAMPAIGN, Chemistry Library, 255 Noyes Laboratory, Urbana, 61801. Lucille M Wert, Chemistry Librn; Susan Eilering, Asst Chemistry Librn
Holdings: Vols (150,000) Cat Microforms
Budget: ($224,660)
Notes: Collection incl monographs, treatises and serials in all languages covering all the fields of chemistry. It is designed to support the instructional and research needs of the School of Chemical Sciences and the University Community.

MI —THE UPJOHN COMPANY, Corporate Technical Library, 301 Henrietta St, Kalamazoo, 49001. Lorraine Schulte, Manager
Holdings: Cat Microforms Audiotape Videotape Books Journals

NJ —WITCO CHEMICAL CORP, Corporate Research Center Library, 100 Bauer Dr, Oakland, 07436. Jo Therese Smith, Mgr, Information Services
Holdings: Vols (9000) Cat
Budget: ($52,000)

NJ —ORTHO PHARMACEUTICAL CORP, Hartman Library, U S Highway 202, Raritan, 08869. June Bente, Mgr
Holdings: Vols (15,000) Cat Microforms

NY —UNIVERSITY OF ROCHESTER, Carlson Library, Hutchison Hall, River Campus, Rochester, 14627. Michael W Poulin, Librn
Holdings: Vols (48,720) Cat Microforms
Notes: Strong collection in the field and related areas.

NY —SCHENECTADY CHEMICALS INC, W H Wright Research Center, Library, 2750 Balltown Rd, Schenectady, 12309. Elizabeth H Groot, Mgr Tech Information Serv
Holdings: Vols (1000) Cat Microforms
Notes: Also incl patents. Open by appointment only.

OH —PPG INDUSTRIES, Chemical Div, Research Library, PO Box 31, Barberton, 44203. Diane Danko, Chemical Information Specialist
Holdings: Vols (20,000) Cat Microforms
Notes: Organic, inorganic, analytical and agricultural chemistry, with special emphasis on applied and chemical engineering.

OH —FERRO CORP, Ferro Chemical Library, 7050 Krick Rd, Bedford, 44146. Mary Jane Campbell, Librn
Holdings: Vols 3500 Cat Audiotapes Microforms
Notes: Incl audiotapes (10) and microforms (52,750).

OH —EMERY INDUSTRIES, Research Library, 4900 Este Ave, Cincinnati, 45232. B A Bernard, Librn
Holdings: Cat
Notes: Special subjects: fatty acids and organic chemical derivatives, ozone, plasticizers, polymers, synthetic lubricants.

OH —SDS BIOTECH CORP, PO Box 348, Painesville, 44077. Violet Forgach, Business Librn
Holdings: Cat Pix Microforms

PA —FRANKLIN INSTITUTE LIBRARY, 20 & The Parkway, Philadelphia, 19103. Miriam Padusis, Dir; Charles Wilt, Readers Servs Librn
Holdings: Vols (300,000) Cat Maps Pix Microforms

PA —CARNEGIE LIBRARY OF PITTSBURGH, Science & Technology Dept, 4400 Forbes Ave, Pittsburgh, 15213. Catherine M Brosky, Dept Head
Holdings: Vols (380,000) Cat Maps Microforms
Budget: ($240,000)
Notes: Area of primary interest with more than 80,000 vols relating directly to chemistry. Attempts to acquire journals in Chemical Abstracts. Incl literature guides, history and biography, encyclopedias, handbooks, dictionaries, tables, directories, compendia, annual reviews, abstracts, indexes and bibliographies relating to organic, inorganic, analytical and general chemistry. Special endowment fund established by Pittsburgh Section, American Chemical Society.

PA —UNIVERSITY OF PITTSBURGH, Chemistry Library, 200 Alumni Hall, Pittsburgh, 15260. Paul J Kobulnicky, Physical Sciences Librn
Holdings: Vols (20,000) Cat Microforms
Budget: ($100,000)
Notes: This library has traditionally limited its collection to pure chemistry. Complete spectral files with index.

TX —ECTOR COUNTY LIBRARY, Department of Business and Technology, 321 W 5th St, Odessa, 79760. Pat Jones, Dept Head
Holdings: Vols 100 Cat

TX —SOUTHWEST FOUNDATION FOR RESEARCH AND EDUCATION LIBRARY, Preston C Northrup Memorial Library, Baboon Information Center, W Loop 410 at Military Dr, PO Box 28147, San Antonio, 78284. Dorothy M Brooks, Baboon
Notes: Principle field of research: Birth defects, atherosclerosis, reproductive physiology, cancer, genetics, organic chemistry, parasitology, primatology and behavioral sciences and their application to problems of drug abuse, alcoholism and ecology. Maintains the largest baboon colony in the world.

WI —UNIVERSITY OF WISCONSIN, MADISON, Chemistry Library, 2361 Farrington Daniels Chemistry Bldg, 1101 University Ave, Madison, 53706. Kendall Rouse, Chemistry Librn
Holdings: Vols (35,000) Cat Microforms
Budget: ($174,000)

ON —AGRICULTURE CANADA, Research Branch, Neatby Library, Rm 3032, K W Neatby Bldg, CEF, Ottawa, K1A 0C6, Can. Marcel Charette, Library Technician
Holdings: Vols 3000 Cat
Notes: On microcards: *Beilsteins Handbuch der Organischen Chemie,* vols 1-31.

CHEMISTRY, ORGANIC—SYNTHESIS

OH —MONSANTO CO, Library, Polymer Products Division, 260 Springside Dr, Akron, 44313. J P Ferrin, Librn
Holdings: Vols 1500 Cat Microforms
Notes: Literature on organic synthesis.

CHEMISTRY, PATHOLOGICAL see Chemistry, Medical and Pharmaceutical

CHEMISTRY, PHARMACEUTICAL see Chemistry, Medical and Pharmaceutical

CHEMISTRY, PHYSICAL AND THEORETICAL

CA —UNIVERSITY OF CALIFORNIA, SAN DIEGO, Central University Library, Mandeville Dept of Special Collections, La Jolla, 92093. Lynda Corey Claassen, Head
Notes: Papers of Harold Clayton Urey (1893-1981), winner of the 1934 Nobel Prize in chemistry for his discovery of Deuterium. Incl files concerning the Emergency Committee of Atomic Scientists, 1946-49; also some material on the Rosenberg/Sobell spy cases; also on his works as science advisor to John F Kennedy (president-elect).

CA —UNIVERSITY OF CALIFORNIA, LOS ANGELES, Chemistry Library, 4238 Young Hall, Los Angeles, 90024. Marion C Peters, Chemistry Librn
Holdings: Vols (55,600) Cat Microforms
Notes: (768) current serials subscriptions; special collection of 450 volumes on the history of chemistry; US Chemical Patents since 1952 on microforms; Sadtler Standard Spectra; UCLA biochemistry and chemistry theses. Collection strengths incl analytical, biological, inorganic, organic and physical chemistry.

CA —INTERNATIONAL BUSINESS MACHINES RESEARCH LIBRARY, 5600 Cottle Rd, San Jose, 95193. Phil Grincewich, Mgr Technical Information
Holdings: Vols (13,500) Cat
Notes: Incl 21,000 vols of 770 journals. On-line search facility. Vols are divided into three libraries, Technical Research, Technical Information, and Programing. Not open to public.

CT —YALE UNIVERSITY, Box 1603A, Yale Station, New Haven, 06520.
Holdings: Mss
Notes: Papers of Rupert Wildt, professor of astrophysics.

†DC —CATHOLIC UNIVERSITY OFF AMERICA, Nursing & Biology Library, Washington, 20064. N L Powell, Head
Holdings: Vols (16,000) Cat
Notes: Espec Strong in organometallic, Moessbauer and physical chemistry.

IL —ARGONNE NATIONAL LABORATORY, Chemistry Branch Library, 9700 S Cass Ave, Argonne, 60439. Betty Guttman, Librn
Holdings: Vols (20,000)
Notes: Incl monographs, 190 current journals. Materials may be used by the public in the library by prior arrangement. Photocopies may be supplied for interlibrary loan, for which a processing and handling charge is made.

IL —UNIVERSITY OF ILLINOIS, URBANA/CHAMPAIGN, Chemistry Library, 255 Noyes Laboratory, Urbana, 61801. Lucille M Wert, Chemistry Librn; Susan Eilering, Asst Chemistry Librn
Holdings: Vols (150,000) Cat Microforms
Budget: ($224,660)
Notes: Collection incl monographs, treatises and serials in all languages covering all the fields of chemistry. It is designed to support the instructional and research needs of the School of Chemical Sciences and the University Community.

IN —INDIANA UNIVERSITY, Chemistry Library, Chemistry Bldg, Rm One, Bloomington, 47405. Gary Wiggins, Head Librn
Holdings: Vols (55,000) Cat Slides Microforms
Budget: ($157,000)

MD —UNIVERSITY OF MARYLAND, White Memorial Library, College Park, 20742. Elizabeth W McElroy, Head
Holdings: Vols (48,000) Cat Microforms
Budget: ($193,000)
Notes: Current periodicals. Have own card catalog, which is included also in the total university catalog.

NY —UNIVERSITY OF ROCHESTER, Carlson Library, Hutchison Hall, River Campus, Rochester, 14627. Michael W Poulin, Librn
Holdings: Vols (48,720) Cat Microforms
Notes: Strong colleciton in the field and related areas.

PA —FRANKLIN INSTITUTE LIBRARY, 20 & The Parkway, Philadelphia, 19103. Miriam Padusis, Dir; Charles Wilt, Readers Servs Librn
Holdings: Vols (300,000) Cat Maps Pix Microforms

PA —CARNEGIE LIBRARY OF PITTSBURGH, Science & Technology Dept, 4400 Forbes Ave, Pittsburgh, 15213. Catherine M Brosky, Dept Head
Holdings: Vols (380,000)
Budget: ($240,000)
Notes: Area of primary interest with more than 80,000 vols relating directly to chemistry. Attempts to acquire journals in Chemical Abstracts. Incl literature guides,

CHEMISTRY, PHYSICAL AND THEORETICAL (cont.)

history and biography, encyclopedias, handbooks, dictionaries, tables, directories, compendia, annual reviews, abstracts, indexes and bibliographies relating to organic, inorganic, analytical and general chemistry. Special endowment fund established by Pittsburgh Section, American Chemical Society.

PA —UNIVERSITY OF PITTSBURGH, Chemistry Library, 200 Alumni Hall, Pittsburgh, 15260. Paul J Kobulnicky, Physical Sciences Librn
Holdings: Vols (20,000) Cat Microforms
Budget: ($100,000)
Notes: This library has traditionally limited its collection to pure chemistry. Complete spectral files with index.

WI —UNIVERSITY OF WISCONSIN, MADISON, Chemistry Library, 2361 Farrington Daniels Chemistry Bldg, 1101 University Ave, Madison, 53706. Kendall Rouse, Chemistry Librn
Holdings: Vols (35,000) Cat Microforms
Budget: ($174,000)

ON —AGRICULTURE CANADA, Research Branch, Neatby Library, Rm 3032, K W Neatby Bldg, CEF, Ottawa, K1A 0C6, Can. Marcel Charette, Library Technician
Holdings: Vols 600 Cat

CHEMISTRY, SYNTHETIC see Chemistry, Organic—Synthesis

CHEMISTRY, TECHNICAL

NC —TECHNICAL INSTITUTE OF ALAMANCE, Learning Resources Center, Jimmy Kerr Rd, PO Box 623, Haw River, 27258. Ron Plummer, Coordr
Holdings: Vols 225 Cat Pix Microforms

OH —PPG INDUSTRIES, Chemical Div, Research Library, PO Box 31, Barberton, 44203. Diane Danko, Chemical Information Specialist
Holdings: Vols (20,000) Cat Microforms
Notes: Organic, inorganic, analytical and agricultural chemistry, with special emphasis on applied and chemical engineering.

OH —PUBLIC LIBRARY OF CINCINNATI & HAMILTON COUNTY, Science & Technology Dept, 800 Vine St, Cincinnati, 45202. Rosemary Gaiser, Head
Holdings: Vols (250,000) Cat
Notes: Pure and applied science. Incl over 1600 periodicals and serial titles and more than 100 abstracting and indexing services in major fields of science and technology.

PA —FRANKLIN INSTITUTE LIBRARY, 20 & The Parkway, Philadelphia, 19103. Miriam Padusis, Dir; Charles Wilt, Readers Servs Librn
Holdings: Vols (300,000) Cat Maps Pix Microforms

PA —UNIVERSITY OF PENNSYLVANIA, Van Pelt Library, Edgar Fahs Smith Memorial Collection in the History of Chemistry, 3420 Walnut St, Philadelphia, 19104. Arnold W Thackray, Cur
Holdings: Vols (15,000) Cat Mss Pix
Notes: The Smith Collection, 15,000 vols, is one of the most comprehensive collections on the history of chemistry in North America, covering chemistry and its allied disciplines, from the Renaissance to the early 20th century. The Collection's traditional strengths lie in classical history of chemistry, ie pre-1800. However acquisitions over the past 15 years have substantially built up the post-1800 holdings, especially in areas of chemical technology. News of the Collection may be found in the Center's twice yearly newsletter *CHOC News* which is available free of charge to interested persons. A convenient description is provided in Herbert S Klickstein, "Edgar Fahs Smith-His Contributions to the History of Chemistry," *Chymia,* 5 (1959), 11-30. A published catalog of our holdings now needs considerable revision, due to continued *acquisitions:Catalog of the Edgar Fahs Smith Memorial Collection* (Boston: G K Hall and Co, 1960). Portions of our manuscript collection have been described in Norman P Zacour and Rudolf Hirsch, *Catalogue of the Manuscripts in the Libraries of the University of Pennsylvania to 1800* (Philadelphia: University of Pennsylvania Press, 1965), 231-243; and R Hirsch, "Catalogue of Manuscripts...Supplement a (5) ," *Library Chronicle,* 37 (1971), 91-115.

PA —CARNEGIE LIBRARY OF PITTSBURGH, Science & Technology Dept, 4400 Forbes Ave, Pittsburgh, 15213. Catherine M Brosky, Dept Head
Holdings: Vols (380,000) Cat Maps Microforms
Budget: ($240,000)
Notes: Incl many journals, especially those in metallurgy with particular reference to iron and steel, petroleum, plastics, paper, rubber, etc. Encyclopedias, general reference books, abstracts, indexes and bibliographies.

SC —CRYOVAC TECHNICAL LIBRARY, PO Box 464, Duncan, 29334. M M Ezell, Libn
Holdings: Vols (6000) Cat
Notes: Library supports corporate research, development, and engineering. Incl materials on chemical and mechanical engineering, polymers and polymerization, plastics, and food packaging. 175 periodical titles received. Library open by appointment or through ILL.

TX —ECTOR COUNTY LIBRARY, Department of Business and Technology, 321 W 5th St, Odessa, 79760. Pat Jones, Dept Head
Holdings: Vols 100 Cat

ON —METROPOLITAN TORONTO LIBRARY, Science & Technology Dept, 789 Yonge St, Toronto, M4W 2G8, Can. Margaret Walshe, Head
Holdings: Vols (120,000) Cat
Notes: All aspects of technology for the specialist, the student, and the general public. The departmment gives high priority ot Canadian material.

CHEMISTRY, TEXTILE see Textile Chemistry

CHEMISTRY, THEORETICAL see Chemistry, Physical and Theoretical

CHEMISTRY OF FOOD see Food—Analysis

CHEMISTS

GA —EMORY UNIVERSITY, Robert W Woodruff Library, Special Collections Dept, Atlanta, 30322. Linda M Matthews, Head Special Collections; Virginia J H Cain, Processing Archivist; Richard H F Lindemann, Reference Archivist
Notes: Correspondence and other materials of Charles Holmes Herty (1867-1937), who was known for his work in applying chemistry to the improvement of industry and who served as president of the American Chemical Association; items reflect Herty's naval stores and other forestry products. 300,000 items.

NY —CHEMISTS' CLUB LIBRARY, 52 E 41 St, New York, 10017. Elsie Lim, Librn
Holdings: Pix
Notes: Incl a large vertical file collection of portraits of chemists.

PA —UNIVERSITY OF PITTSBURGH, Chemistry Library, 200 Alumni Hall, Pittsburgh, 15260. Paul J Kobulnicky, Physical Sciences Librn
Holdings: Vols (20,000) Cat Microforms
Budget: ($100,000)
Notes: This library has traditionally limited its collection to pure chemistry. Complete spectral files with index.

CHENEY, JOHN VANCE

IL —NEWBERRY LIBRARY, 60 W Walton St, Chicago, 60610. Diana Haskell, Cur of Modern Mss
Holdings: Vols 500 Uncat Mss
Notes: Restricted use: noncirculating.

CHENNAULT, CLAIRE LEE

CA —HOOVER INSTITUTION ON WAR, REVOLUTION & PEACE, Stanford University, Stanford, 94305. Milorad M Drachkovitch, Archivist
Holdings: / / Mss
Notes: Papers, 1941-1954, of Claire Lee Chennault, civilian flyer and Army Air Force officer in China. Correspondence, diaries, mss of writings, articles, combat reports, group field orders, flight material, radiograms, memoranda, press comments and clippings, and other papers relating to the American Volunteer Group ("Flying Tigers"), China Air Task Force, US 14th Air Force, Civil Air Transports, incl, "Plan for the Modernization of Chinese Air Force" and Freedom Cause. Correspondents incl Allied and Chinese authorities. Ca 5 ft (ca 7800 items). Detailed inventory in the repository.

CHEREMIS LANGUAGE see Cheremissian Language and Literature

CHEREMISSIAN LANGUAGE AND LITERATURE

NY —NEW YORK PUBLIC LIBRARY, Slavonic Div, Fifth Ave & 42 St, New York, 10018. Edward Kasinec, Chief
Holdings: Cat Microforms
Notes: See New York Public Library, *Dictionary Catalog of the Stavonic* Collection (Boston: G K Hall, 1974), 44 vols.

CHEROKEE INDIANS

DC —LIBRARY OF CONGRESS, Manuscript Division, Washington, 20540. John C Broderick, Chief
Holdings: Cat Mss

GA —CARNEGIE LIBRARY, Henderson Room, 607 Broad St, Rome, 30161. Beatrice Millican, Librn
Holdings: Cat Maps 16mm Films
Budget: ($2700)
Notes: There is a special catalog to the Indian collection. The collection (5000 items) includes, books, maps, excerpts of other books, copies of documents, etc.

NC —PACK MEMORIAL PUBLIC LIBRARY, North Carolina Collection, 67 Haywood St, Asheville, 28801. John Toms, Dept Head
Notes: Collection incl early ms accounts of western North Carolina; Civil War letters; letters, diary, and mss of Horace Kephart; mss of Thomas Dixon; Thomas Wolfe Collection; contemporary North Carolina authors; North Carolina censuses, 1790-1910; rare newspapers and runs of local newspapers, and clippings from Asheville newspapers, from 1920s; early maps; information on Cherokee Indians; approx 400 vols of North Carolina genealogy and file of unpublished genealogies. Collection concentrates on western North Carolina, with some general Appalachian materials. Incl 4000 local and state photographs, separate catalog.

NC —MUSEUM OF THE CHEROKEE INDIAN, Library, PO Box 770-A, Cherokee, 28719. Juanita H Hughes, Archivist
Holdings: Vols 1400 Cat Mss Microforms
Budget: $500

NC —WESTERN CAROLINA UNIVERSITY, Hunter Memorial Library, Cullowhee, 28723. James B Lloyd, Cur
Notes: Incl a regional ms collection documenting the social and natural history of Appalachia in general and western North Carolina in particular. Subject emphasis incl the Cherokee Indian, the establishment of the Great Smokey Mountains National Park, and the continuing use of Appalachian wilderness.

OK —OKLAHOMA HISTORICAL SOCIETY, Library, Historical Bldg, Oklahoma City, 73105. Andrea Clark, Dir, Library Resources Division
Holdings: Vols (43,000) Cat Mss Maps Pix Microforms
Notes: The Society also has the Indian Archives Collection of 2,500,000 pieces (Mary Lee Boyle, Archivist). This is an

CHEROKEE INDIANS (cont.)

extensive collection of records, particularly of the Five Civilized Tribes. Incl tribal rolls, agency reports, manuscripts, etc.

OK —CHEROKEE NATIONAL HISTORICAL SOCIETY, Archives & Library, PO Box 515 TSA-LA-GI, Tahlequah, 74464. Duane King, Dir
Holdings: Vols (1000) Uncat Mss Maps Pix Slides Audiotapes Microforms
Notes: An embryonic collection, directly or indirectly related to Cherokee history, culture and genealogy. Slide collection depicts copies of material from the collection, from the Cherokee National Museum Village (Cherokee, 1650 AD) and the Cultural Theatre ("Trail of Tears Drama"). Newspaper collection incl several hundred newspapers dating back to 1762, each of which contains some reference to the Cherokees. The Cherokee National Archives also contains the non-current 1975 files of the Cherokee Nation of Oklahoma and the Keeler Collection (papers and personal files of W W Keeler, former Principal Chief of the Cherokee Nation for 26 years).

OK —THOMAS GILCREASE INSTITUTE OF AMERICAN HISTORY & ART LIBRARY, 1400 North 25th West Ave, Tulsa, 74127. Sarah Hirsch, Librn
Holdings: Vols Cat Mss Maps Pix
Notes: Trans-Mississippi West, US, Indian and Hispanic history. The Gilcrease Library contains a total of about 40,000 mss; 10,000 imprints; 5000 photographs; 600 maps and 50,000 vols.

OK —UNIVERSITY OF TULSA, McFarlin Library, Dept of Rare Books and Special Collections, 600 S College, Tulsa, 74104. David Farmer, Dir; Toby Murray, Archivist; Caroline Swinson, Cur of Manuscripts & Art
Holdings: Cat
Notes: The Indian collection of John W Shleppey. Indian materials of some 6000 bibliographic items, excl of mss and photographs. Emphasis on Indian Territory imprints, laws, Cherokee and Choctaw tribes, etc.

CHESAPEAKE AND DELAWARE CANAL

DE —HISTORICAL SOCIETY OF DELAWARE, Library, 505 Market St Mall, Wilmington, 19801. Barbara E Benson, Library Dir
Holdings: Cat Mss Maps Microforms
Notes: Collection incl papers and other mss materials.

CHESAPEAKE BAY

DE —HAGLEY MUSEUM AND LIBRARY, Eleutherian Mills-Hagley Foundation Inc, PO Box 3630, Greenville, 19807. Richmond D Williams, Dir; Heddy A Richter, Imprints Librn
Holdings: Vols (25,000)
Notes: The Library's large collection of trade catalogs are fully accessible through our card catalog with further access provided by a chronological file. The collection emphasizes the products of Delaware Valley and Chesapeake area manufacturers and distributors in the chemical, iron and steel, leather, railway and petroleum industries from 1880 to 1920.

MD —UNIVERSITY OF MARYLAND, Library, Archives & Manuscripts Dept, College Park, 20742. Mary A Boccaccio, Head
Holdings: Mss Pix
Notes: University of Maryland publications and archives; collections of organizational papers (eg, Baltimore & Ohio Railroad; various organizations concerned with the Chesapeake Bay and environs; various labor unions, particularly those involving the tobacco industry), mostly associated with Maryland; collections of papers and mss associated with literary and public figures (eg, the Senator Millard Tydings); oral histories relating to the archival and mss collections; associated memorabilia; photographs, mainly associated with Maryland. A guide to collections of personal family, and organizational papers relating to Maryland is being prepared.

VA —COLONIAL WILLIAMSBURG FOUNDATION, Research Center Library, PO Drawer C, Williamsburg, 23187. John E Ingram, Research Archivist
Holdings: Vols (30,000) Cat Mss Maps Pix Microforms
Budget: ($20,000)
Notes: Virginia and the Chesapeake in the 17th-18th centuries. Particular strengths include social, economic, agricultural and architectural history. The collection encompasses over 6000 rare books, 18th Century music scores and 12,000 manuscripts, as well as a complete set of Virginia Colonial Records Project microfilm (1000 reels).

CHESAPEAKE BAY—HISTORY

DE —HAGLEY MUSEUM AND LIBRARY, Eleutherian Mills-Hagley Foundation Inc, PO Box 3630, Greenville, 19807. Richmond D Williams, Dir; Heddy A Richter, Imprints Librn
Holdings: Vols (25,000)
Notes: The Library's large collection of trade catalogs are fully accessible through our card catalog with further access provided by a chronological file. The collection emphasizes the products of Delaware Valley and Chesapeake area manufacturers and distributors in the chemical, iron and steel, leather, railway and petroleum industries from 1880 to 1920.

MD —WASHINGTON COLLEGE, Clifton M Miller Library, Chestertown, 21620.
Notes: Archive-library of source material, incl primary sources in microform, on the Chesapeake Bay during the American Revolutinary period.

CHESS

CA —LOS ANGELES PUBLIC LIBRARY, Art, Music & Recreation Dept, 630 W Fifth St, Los Angeles, 90071. Melvin H Rosenberg, Mgr & Principal Librn
Notes: Large collection.

CA —SAN DIEGO PUBLIC LIBRARY, Art, Music & Recreation Sect, 820 E St, San Diego, 92101. Barbara A Tuhill, Supvr
Holdings: Vols 850 Cat
Notes: Incl are books by famous grandmasters, records of tournament games and Russian publications. An extensive periodical collection from many foreign countries is also available. For reference use only.

†CA —UNIVERSITY OF SAN FRANCISCO, Richard A Gleeson Library, The Countess Bernardine Murphy Donohue Rare Book Room, San Francisco, 94117. D Steven Corey, Special Collections Librn
Notes: Some highly specialized materials.

KY —UNIVERSITY OF LOUISVILLE, Ekstrom Library, Rare Books & Special Collections, 2301 S Third St, Louisville, 40208. George T McWhorter, Cur; Delinda Stephens Buie, Asst Cur
Holdings: Vols 300 Cat
Budget: $50
Notes: The Muir-Hogenauer Chess Collection. Gift from Mr Walter Muir.

MA —HARVARD UNIVERSITY LIBRARY, Widener Library, Cambridge, 02138.
Holdings: // Cat
Notes: See *Harvard Library Notes,* 1 (1922), 191-195.

NJ —PRINCETON UNIVERSITY, Library, Rare Books Dept, Princeton, 08544. Stephen Ferguson, Cur
Notes: Cook Chess Collection. In all over 2000 vols. Complete list of collection published in *Princeton University Library Classified List* IV (1920) pp 3585-3608. (ExB)0639.7373.5 vol 6. Separate off-print of the list has call number COOK 0639.7377. For particulars refer to: Albrecht Buschke, "Chess Libraries in America" in *Chronicle* II, 4 (June, 1941) 147-52. Article's emphasis is on Eugene B Cook collection. Spackman Collection: For particulars see: Albrecht Buschke, "The Spackman Collection of Chess Books" in the *Chronicle* XIX, 1 (autumn, 1957) pp 62-64. The Spackman collection incl more than 500 chess books and magazines.

NY —BROOKLYN PUBLIC LIBRARY, Art & Music Div, Grand Army Plaza, Brooklyn, 11238. Sue H Sharma, Chief
Holdings: Vols (4500) Cat Mss
Notes: "One of the finest collections of literature on chess and checkers in the world...incl some of the rarest books that exist on the subject...." Second largest collection of its kind, after that of the Cleveland Public Library. Incl private collections of William T Call (checkers), Melvin Brown, and R H Rimington-Wilson. Books are in many languages, from the 15th century to date. Incl many valuable mss, complete runs of most of the best-known periodicals, and over 100 scrapbooks of newspaper and periodical clippings. Many first editions and rare titles.

NY —NEW YORK PUBLIC LIBRARY, Research Libraries, General Research Division, Fifth Ave & 42 St, New York, 10018. Rodney Phillips, Chief
Holdings: Vols (2,225,000) Cat Maps Pix Microforms
Budget: ($775,718)

NY —US MILITARY ACADEMY LIBRARY, West Point, 10996. Elaine B Eatroff, Rare Book Cur
Holdings: Vols 550 Cat Mss Pix
Notes: European imprints, beginning from the early 16th century, British, and American, incl: Hagedorn No 1, early chess periodicals. Incl: bibliography, collection of games, end games, history, openings, problems, and tournaments. Also, Chinese chess, Go, backgammon, and checkers. Chess sets, ephemera, etc.

OH —CLEVELAND PUBLIC LIBRARY, Fine Arts and Special Collections Department, 325 Superior Ave, Cleveland, 44114. Alice N Loranth, Head
Holdings: Vols 25,600 Cat Mss Pix
Notes: The most extensive research and reference library on chess and checkers in existence. Incl monographs, periodicals, chess and checkers columns, mss, archival materials, tournament files, 1200 uncataloged tournaments, etc. Documents the history, development and technical aspects of the games, and incl records of competitions, tournaments and players. Significant references to the games in the literature of other subjects, such as history, philosophy, religion and literature are also collected, as are other related move games. Unpublished bibliographic compilations, rare and limited editions, 1000 mss, facsimile reproductions and copies of mss. Special indexes and separate edition catalog of author entries maintained. Described in Cleveland Public Library, White Collection of Folk-lore and Orientalia, *Catalog of the Chess Collection (Incl Checkers),*(Boston: Q K Hll, 1964), 2 vols (Intro by George J Maciuszko). Loranth, A N: "Die Schachsammlung des John G White Department of Folklore, Orientalia and Chess in der Cleveland Public Library," Schachwissenschaftliche Forschungen, Nr 5 (Jan 1975), pp 147-158.

PA —FREE LIBRARY OF PHILADELPHIA, Social Science and History Dept, Logan Sq, Philadelphia, 19103. William Handley, Head
Holdings: Vols 1700 Cat
Notes: With the Willing Collection of Chess Books as nucleus. Incl 97 periodical sets.

WI —UNIVERSITY OF WISCONSIN, MADISON, Memorial Library, Rare Books Collection, 728 State St, Madison, 53706. Gretchen Lagana, Cur
Holdings: Vols 800// Cat
Notes: A collection of rare and valuable chess books dating from the 15th century to about 1900 which was donated by Peter G Toepfer. Described in *Catalogue of Works on Chess in the Collection of Peter G* Toepfer (Milwuakee: Privately printed, 1910), and *UW Library News,* vol 17 (1972), pp 1-5.

†ON —METROPOLITAN TORONTO LIBRARY, 789 Yonge St, Toronto, M4W 2G8, Can.
Notes: Good subject strengths.

CHESSMAN, CARYL

PA —TEMPLE UNIVERSITY LIBRARIES, Special Collections Dept, Conwellana-Templana Collection, 13 & Berks St, Philadelphia, 19122. Miriam I Crawford, Cur
Holdings: Mss Pix Documents Newsclippings
Budget: ($30,000)
Notes: Personal papers of Negley K Teeters. The published writings, manuscripts, correspondence, and research materials of Teeters, criminologist and faculty member of Temple University, covering the years 1927-1971. Contains extended correspondence with his co-author, Harry Elmer Barnes, from 1940 to 1968, and materials dealing with their investigation of the murder trial of Caryl Chessman, which failed to halt his execution in California in 1960. Incl copies of letters from Teeters to Barnes, originals of which are in the Western History Research Center of the University of Wyoming, and incl the Index to the Barnes Papers in that collection. *Descriptive Inventory of the Personal Papers of Negley K Teeters* (1896-1971), (Conwellana-Templana Collection, Temple University, 1971, addenda 1972 and 1974; 6 leaves; unpublished typescript).

CHESSON, WILFRID HUGH

DC —GEORGETOWN UNIVERSITY, Library, Special Collections Div, 37 & O Sts NW, Washington, 20057. George M Barringer, Special Collections Librn; Nicholas B Sheetz, Mss Librn
Holdings: Mss Cat
Notes: Mss diaries and scrapbooks kept by Wilfrid Hugh Chesson, editor and reviewer, regarding his professional and private life as a literary entrepreneur. The diaries, interesting for their literary style alone, contain references to numerous literary figures incl G K Chesterton, Grant Richards, Jospeh Conrad, and T Fisher Unwin, among others.

CHESTERTON, GILBERT KEITH

DC —GEORGETOWN UNIVERSITY, Library, Special Collections Div, 37 & O Sts NW, Washington, 20057. George M Barringer, Special Collections Librn; Nicholas B Sheetz, Mss Librn
Holdings: Vols 400 Cat Mss

IL —WHEATON COLLEGE, Library, Marion E Wade Collection, Irving & Franklin Sts, Wheaton, 60187. Lyle Dorsett, Cur; Marjorie Mead, Associate Cur
Holdings: Vols (6500) Mss Pix Audiotapes Videotapes
Notes: Extensive Marion E Wade Collection of seven British authors incl the John Sullivan library.

IN —UNIVERSITY OF NOTRE DAME, University Libraries, Notre Dame, 46556.
Notes: This collection (2000 items) contains almost all of the published material in John Sullivan's bibliography which is the standard work on Chesterton. In terms of books by the author, this is one of the largest collections in the country. It contains original photographs, autograph mss and original artistic drawngs by Chesterton, in addition to signed and inscribed first editions. The collection is particularly strong in foreign translations of Chesterton's works, British and American first editons, and editions containing the author's book illustration art.

NY —HOFSTRA UNIVERSITY, Library, 1000 Fulton Ave, Hempstead, 11550. Charles R Andrews, Dean of Library Services
Notes: Strong collection. Incl some mss.

CHEVASSU, MAURICE AUGUSTE, 1877-1957

NY —CORNELL UNIVERSITY LIBRARIES, Collection of Regional History, Dept of Manuscripts and Univ Archives, Ithaca, 14853.
Notes: French surgeon, author and editor of medical publications. Incl 265 letters and notes to Chevassu.

CHEW, BENJAMIN, 1722-1810

PA —LIBRARY COMPANY OF PHILADELPHIA, 1314 Locust St, Philadelphia, 19107. Edwin Wolf II, Librn; Kenneth Finkel, Cur of Prints
Notes: "Cliveden," estate of the Chew Family, Germantown, Pa, books. The volumes, which constitute the only private library in America in its original state and setting since the 18th century, includes the law library of Benjamin Chew (1722-1810), Chief Justice of Pennsylvania. Some books removed from Cliveden to the Library Company's collections.

CHIAKULAS, CHARLES

MI —WAYNE STATE UNIVERSITY, Walter P Reuther Library, Archives of Labor & Urban Affairs, Detroit, 48202. Philip Mason, Dir
Notes: Papers, etc of Charles Chiakulas, a labor leader active in the Chicago Community Center, peace organizations, and the Justice for Cyprus Committee.

CHIANG, MADAME MEI-LING (SUNG)

SC —COLLEGE OF CHARLESTON LIBRARY, Special Collections Dept, Charleston, 29401.
Notes: Contains biographical and family history material of Wendell Mitchel Levi; invertebrate anatomy course notes from the College of Charleston; University of Chicago Law School casebooks; correspondence concerning pigeons and camellias; notes, photographs, mss, typescripts, and galleys of published works; and other materials relating to pigeons and camellias. Among the more prominent correspondents are B F Skinner, Madame Chiang Kai-Shek, and Mary Bonner.

CHIAROSCURO

MN —MINNEAPOLIS COLLEGE OF ART & DESIGN, Library, 200 E 25 St, Minneapolis, 55404. Richard Kronstedt, Head Librn

NJ —NEWARK PUBLIC LIBRARY, Art & Music Dept, 5 Washington St, Newark, 07101. William J Dane, Supv
Notes: On all forms of artistic expression, particularly on the use of light.

CHICACHAS INDIANS see Chickasaw Indians

CHICAGO

IL —CHICAGO HISTORICAL SOCIETY, Library, Clark St at North Ave, Chicago, 60614. Robert L Brubaker, Librn
Holdings: Vols (150,000) Cat Mss Maps Pix Slides Microfilm

IL —CHICAGO TRANSIT AUTHORITY, Anthon Memorial Library, Merchandise Mart Plaza, PO Box 3555, Chicago, 60654. Joseph Benson, Dir
Holdings: Vols (10,000) Cat Maps Slides Microforms
Budget: ($27,200)
Notes: Urban transportation. Use of collection by appointment with Librarian.

IL —LAKE FOREST COLLEGE, Donnelley Library, Lake Forest, 60045. Arthur H Miller Jr, College Librn
Holdings: Vols (500) Cat Maps
Budget: ($1200)
Notes: Focus on development of suburban fringe areas, particularly Lake Co, Ill. and Chicago region: local documents (plans, transit, zoning maps, etc), US documents, and special studies of suburban issues, such as historic preservation and land use.

CHICAGO—DESCRIPTION

IL —CHICAGO HISTORICAL SOCIETY, Library, Clark St at North Ave, Chicago, 60614. Robert L Brubaker, Librn
Holdings: Vols (150,000) Cat Mss Maps Pix Slides Microfilm
Notes: Extensive holdings concerning the Chicago area form the 17th century to the present, incl ms and printed narratives of travel and description; about 4000 ,maps of Chicago plus other maps of the Midwest; numerous prints and photographs showing buildings, streets, and other views; and other materials.
See also entry under Chicago - History

CHICAGO—FIRE, 1871

IL —CHICAGO HISTORICAL SOCIETY, Library, Clark St at North Ave, Chicago, 60614. Archie Motley, Manuscript Librn
Notes: Materials on the Haymarket Riot, Chicago, 1886 and on the Chicago Fire of 1871.

CHICAGO—FIRE, 1903

IL —CHICAGO HISTORICAL SOCIETY, Library, Clark St at North Ave, Chicago, 60614. Archie Motley, Manuscript Librn

CHICAGO—GOVERNMENT PUBLICATIONS

IL —NORTHWESTERN UNIVERSITY, Library, Government Publications Dept, Evanston, 60201. Robert W Baumgartner, Head
Notes: Collection consists of US federal documents (depository library since 1876); state documents (emphasis on Illinois); municipal documents (emphasis on Evanston and Chicago); documents of international organizations (emphasis on United Nations, United Nations specialized agencies, Organization of American States, European Communities). Collection consists of publications of 44 international organizations. Shelflist maintained in the Government publications not incl in the library's general catalog.

CHICAGO—HAYMARKET SQUARE RIOT, 1886

IL —CHICAGO HISTORICAL SOCIETY, Library, Clark St at North Ave, Chicago, 60614. Archie Motley, Manuscript Librn
Notes: Materials on the Haymarket Riot, Chicago, 1886 and on the Chicago Fire of 1871.

CHICAGO—HISTORY

IL —CHICAGO HISTORICAL SOCIETY, Library, Clark St at North Ave, Chicago, 60614. Robert L Brubaker, Librn
Holdings: Vols (150,000) Cat Mss Maps Pix Slides Microfilm
Notes: Incl Chicago imprints, periodicals, and newspapers; Chicago city, telephone, and commercial directories; catalogs of Chicago mail order houses and special industries and stores; paper and archives of Chicago leaders and organizations (4,000, 000 items); nagatives and photographs from Chicago newspaper morgues, 1900-1965 (250,000); photographs from Chicagoland-in-Pictures, a project for historical photography sponsored by the Society and the Chicago Area Camera Clubs Association since 1948 (22,000); daguerreotypes, ambrotypes, tintypes, sterographs, other photographic materials, engravings, lithographs, prints in other media (228,000); clippings from major Chicago newspapers since the 1930s (50, 000); trade and advertising cards (6000); programs of Chicago theatres (5000); early sheetmusic concerning Chicago or published in Chicago (4600); fiction with a Chicago locale. Also, the papers of Ralph G Newman, relative to his Abraham Lincoln Book Shop and other business and public service ventures. Also, membership records of the South Shore Country Club and papers of other Chicago-area activities.

IL —CHICAGO PUBLIC LIBRARY, Special Collections Div, Cultural Center, 78 E

CHICAGO—HISTORY (cont.)

Washington St, Chicago, 60602. Laura Linard, Cur
Holdings: Mss Maps Pix Slides Microforms
Notes: A vast amount of material on Chicago neighborhood history is housed at several locations in The Chicago Public Library system. A centralized program for organizing, storing and accessing this material was begun by the Special Collections Division in 1977. Major neighborhood collections which have been organized and are now accessible to researchers include: The Papers of the Calumet Pioneer Historical Society, The Calumet Region Community Collection. The Lawndale-Crawford Community Collection, The Papers of the Lawndale-Crawford Historical Association, and the Historic Pullman Collection (all of these collections are housed in the Special Collections Division). Also, the Ravenswood-Lake View Community Collection and the Papers of the Ravenswood-Lake View Historical Association are located at the Hild Regional Library and are open foruse by appointment. Several other neighborhood collections are still housed at branch libraries and are currently being organized. Principal contact person for these neighborhood collections is Robert Marshall, Archivist.

IL —NEWBERRY LIBRARY, 60 W Walton St, Chicago, 60610. Diana Haskell, Cur of Modern Mss
Holdings: Cat Mss Maps Pix Slides
Notes: Midwest Manuscript Collection specializes in the papers of local literary, political, and socially prominent figures. Over 200,000 pieces. Restricted use: noncirculating.

IL —LAKE FOREST COLLEGE, Donnelley Library, Lake Forest, 60045. Arthur H Miller Jr, College Librn
Holdings: Vols (1500) Mss Microforms
Notes: Book holdings (largely post-Fire) incl Chicago poetry, prose, historical writing, social topics, and World's Columbian Exposition. The Capt Joseph Medill Patterson Library and Archive (received 1983) incl working papers relating to the *Chicago Tribune* and general material on the Patterson family. *Tribune* complete on film.

IL —SCHAUMBURG TOWNSHIP PUBLIC LIBRARY, 32 W Library Lane, Schaumburg, 60194. Michael Madden, Librn
Notes: Illinois Setting Collection. Maintains reference and circulating collection of current and out-of-print materials in history, economics, business, biography, art, architecture representing entire state with special emphasis on Chicago. Materials for both adults and children, includes slides, dioramas, and realia as well as books, manuscripts, and maps.

CHICAGO—IMPRINTS

IL —CHICAGO PUBLIC LIBRARY, Special Collections Div, Cultural Center, 78 E Washington St, Chicago, 60602. Laura Linard, Cur
Holdings: Vols (800) Cat
Budget: ($3000)
Notes: The Special Collections Division endeavors to collect all Chicago imprints produced before 1900, and all Chicago private press productions 1900-50. An imprint is defined as any printed item; thus we have a fine collection of pre-fire theatre broadsides and other ephemeral material. Private presses well-represented are Black Cat Press, Norman Press, Normandie House, Americana House, Covici-McGee and Lakeside Press. An exceptional collection of books and keepsakes designed by Norman Forgue. We actively purchase in this area. Outstanding items in the Chicago Imprints Inventory are described in*Treasures of The Chicago Public Library,* compiled by Thomas A Orlando and Marie Gecik, 1977, pp 93-120.

IL —UNIVERSITY OF ILLINOIS AT CHICAGO, Library of the Health Sciences, 1750 W Polk St, PO Box 7509, Chicago, 60612. Robert J Adelsperger, Cur, Special Collections
Holdings: Vols (6000) Cat
Notes: Books, monographs, and periodicals concerning medicine published in Chicago prior to 1871. Described in *A Catalog of Prefire Chicago Imprints (1844-1871)* (Chicago: Library of the Health Sciences, 1976).

IL —NORTHERN ILLINOIS UNIVERSITY, Founders Memorial Library, Rare Books and Special Collections Dept, De Kalb, 60115. William R DuBois, Dept Head
Holdings: Vols (450) Cat
Notes: Works on the history of books and printing and representative examples of fine printing. Includes more than 50 titles published in Chicago by Way & Williams.

CHICAGO—POLITICS AND GOVERNMENT

IL —CHICAGO HISTORICAL SOCIETY, Library, Clark St at North Ave, Chicago, 60614. Robert L Brubaker, Librn
Holdings: Vols (150,000) Cat Mss Maps Pix Microforms
Notes: Early municipal documents, incl some not in the Municipal Reference Library, and selected later documents; archives of the City Club of Chicago, the Illinois League of Women Voters, Independent Voters of Illinosi, and other organizations; papers of Chicago aldermen and other political leaders from Chicago; broadsides concerning political campaigns; ward maps; and other publications.

IL —MUNICIPAL REFERENCE LIBRARY, City Hall, Rm 1004, Chicago, 60602. Joyce Malden, Librn
Holdings: Vols (68,000) Cat Maps Microforms
Budget: ($60,000)

CHICAGO—SOCIAL LIFE AND CUSTOMS

IL —CZECHOSLOVAK HERITAGE MUSEUM AND LIBRARY, 2701 S Harlem Ave, Berwyn, 60402.
Holdings: Vols 350
Notes: Incl 250 periodicals, 100 artifacts. A major resource for American-Czech and Slovak history. Much on Chicago's Czech community. Also collection of books written in "Schwabach".

CHICAGO—WORLD'S COLUMBIAN EXPOSITION, 1893

IL —CHICAGO PUBLIC LIBRARY, Special Collections Div, Cultural Center, 78 E Washington St, Chicago, 60602. Laura Linard, Cur
Holdings: Vols (300) Cat Mss Pix Slides
Notes: The Chicago Public Library received deposit copies of World's Columbian Exposition publications from the Department of Publicity and Promotion, several of which are still uncataloged and not included in the NUC-Pre 1956 Imprints. The Papers of James W Ellsworth, prominent Chicago financier and member of the Board of Directors of the Exposition, are here (finding aid available). Outstanding items in the World's Columbian collections are described in *Treasures of The Chicago Public Library*, compiled by Thomas A Orlando and Marie Gecik, 1977, pp 111-20.

CHICAGO, BURLINGTON AND QUINCY RAILROAD

NE —NEBRASKA STATE HISTORICAL SOCIETY, Archives, 1500 R St, Box 82554, Lincoln, 68501. James E Potter, State Archivist
Holdings: / / Uncat Mss Maps Pix
Notes: Agriculture, reclamation, and irrigation on the Great Plains from 1910 to 1957. Collection of Val Kuska, agricultural development for the CB&O Railroad.

CHICAGO ARTISTS see Artists, Chicago

CHICAGO BOARD OF TRADE

IL —CHICAGO BOARD OF TRADE, Library, 141 W Jackson Blvd, Chicago, 60604. Darlene Appleman, Librn
Holdings: Vols (3500) Cat Micriforms
Notes: Incl materials on commodity exhanges, commodities that are traded on futures ecchanges, finance, and agricultural exonomics. *Commodity Futures Trading. A* Bibliography is published annually. The archives of the Chicago Board of Trade are located in the Manuscript Collection at the University of Illinois at Chicago Circle Campus, a published catalog. *The Archives of the Chicago Board of Trade, 1859-1925,* is available from the Chicago Board of Trade.

CHICAGO BOARD OF UNDERWRITERS

IL —CHICAGO HISTORICAL SOCIETY, Library, Clark St at North Ave, Chicago, 60614. Archie Motley, Manuscript Librn
Notes: Business history acquisitions incl the records of the Illinois Manufacturers' Association; customer complaint files of the Better Business Bureau of Metropolitan Chicago; Chicago Board of Underwriters; papers of George S Bowen, Illinois capitalist; and Ernest J Stevens.

CHICAGO COMMITTEE TO DEFEND THE BILL OF RIGHTS

IL —CHICAGO HISTORICAL SOCIETY, Library, Clark St at North Ave, Chicago, 60614. Archie Motley, Manuscript Librn
Notes: Papers of Chicago Committee to Defend the Bill of Rights.

CHICAGO CUBS

IL —CHICAGO HISTORICAL SOCIETY, Library, Clark St at North Ave, Chicago, 60614. Archie Motley, Manuscript Librn
Notes: Papers of Chicago Cubs 1874-1901.

CHICAGO DAILY NEWS (NEWSPAPER)

IL —NEWBERRY LIBRARY, 60 W Walton St, Chicago, 60610. Diana Haskell, Cur of Modern Mss
Holdings: Cat Mss
Notes: Working and private papers of *Daily* News editors and feature writers: E P Bell; C Binder; R Casey; C H Dennis; J Drury; V F Lawson; L Lewis; P S Mowrer; H V O'Brien; K Preston; H J Smith. Restricted use; noncirculating. Housed in the Midwest Manuscripts Collection.

CHICAGO FIRE OF 1871 see Chicago—Fire, 1871

CHICAGO HEARING SOCIETY

IL —CHICAGO HISTORICAL SOCIETY, Library, Clark St at North Ave, Chicago, 60614. Archie Motley, Manuscript Librn
Notes: Papers, 1916-1976.

CHICAGO IN LITERATURE

IL —CHICAGO HISTORICAL SOCIETY, Library, Clark St at North Ave, Chicago, 60614. Robert L Brubaker, Librn
Holdings: Vols (150,000) Cat Mss Maps Pix Slides Microfilm

CHICAGO INTER-STUDENT CATHOLIC ACTION

IL —LOYOLA UNIVERSITY OF CHICAGO, E M Cudahy Memorial Library, 6525 N Sheridan Rd, Chicago, 60626.
Notes: Papers and some photos, 1927-65, documenting the history of this student group.

CHICAGO JOURNALISM REVIEW

IL —CHICAGO HISTORICAL SOCIETY, Library, Clark St at North Ave, Chicago, 60614. Archie Motley, Manuscript Librn
Notes: Publishing and literary collections

CHICAGO JOURNALISM REVIEW (cont.)

incl these papers: *Chicago Journalism* Review; *Chicago Seed*; *The Chicagoan*; Friends of American Writers, Chicago literary group; Emmett Dedmon (Chicago newspaper executive, journalist, author); Interviews of 97 Chicago journalists conducted by students in Northwestern University's Medill School.

CHICAGO LITERARY RENAISSANCE

IL —NEWBERRY LIBRARY, 60 W Walton St, Chicago, 60610. Diana Haskell, Cur of Modern Mss
Holdings: Cat Mss Pix
Notes: Incl papers of Floyd Dell, Sherwood Anderson and others.

CHICAGO LITTLE THEATRE

MI —UNIVERSITY OF MICHIGAN, Library, Dept of Rare Books & Special Collections, Ann Arbor, 48109. Robert J Starring, Head
Holdings: Cat Mss Pix
Notes: Extensiveholdings of books on the theatre. Also, in the Charles Sanders Collection, about 14,000 British and American playbills and programs mostly of the 19th century, as well as scrapbooks, posters, and about 750 photographs and prints of actors and actresses. In the Ellen Van Volkenburg-Maurice Browne Collection, about 4000 photographs of stage productions and friends and associates, as well as programs, posters, scrapbooks of mounted clippings, about 200 original stage and costume designs, promptbooks, and play manuscripts, representing the American and British careers of this husband-wife team from 1912 to about 1940. The Chicago Little Theatre, 1912-1917, is well represented. Also contains more than 6000 items of correspondence with theatrical and literary figures. Another collection contains 143 Alfred Lunt letters, mainly from 1901-1915.

CHICAGO NEWSPAPERS see Newspapers, Chicago

CHICAGO SEED

IL —CHICAGO HISTORICAL SOCIETY, Library, Clark St at North Ave, Chicago, 60614. Archie Motley, Manuscript Librn
Notes: Publishing and literary collections incl these papers: *Chicago Journalism* Review; *Chicago Seed*; *The Chicagoan*; Friends of American Writers, Chicago literary group; Emmett Dedmon (Chicago newspaper executive, journalist, author); Interviews of 97 Chicago journalists conducted by students in Northwestern University's Medill School.

CHICAGO SEVEN TRIAL, 1969-1970

IL —CHICAGO HISTORICAL SOCIETY, Library, Clark St at North Ave, Chicago, 60614. Archie Motley, Manuscript Librn
Notes: Correspondence and papers of Julius H Hoffman, judge at Chicago Seven Conspiracy Trial.

PA —TEMPLE UNIVERSITY, Samuel Paley Library, Berks & 13 Sts, Philadelphia, 19122.
Notes: Archives of the magazine, *Seven* Days, which first appeared in 1975 and was considered the successor of *Ramparts*. Leading editor was David Dellinger, one of the defendants in the Chicago Conspiracy Trial. Incl office files, correspondence, editorial files, and a selection of Dellinger's papers relating to *Seven Days*.

CHICAGO SURFACE LINES

IL —CHICAGO HISTORICAL SOCIETY, Library, Clark St at North Ave, Chicago, 60614. Archie Motley, Manuscript Librn
Notes: Papers of Chicago Surface Lines and predecessor Chicago and Surburban Street Railway Companies.

CHICAGO TRIBUNE (NEWSPAPER)

IL —LAKE FOREST COLLEGE, Donnelley Library, Lake Forest, 60045. Arthur H Miller Jr, College Librn
Holdings: Vols (1500) Mss Microforms
Notes: Book holdings (largely post-Fire) incl Chicago poetry, prose, historical writing, social topics, and World's Columbian Exposition. The Capt Joseph Medill Patterson Library and Archive (received 1983) incl working papers relating to the *Chicago Tribune* and general material on the Patterson family. *Tribune* complete on film.

CHICAGO WOMEN'S CLUB

IL —CHICAGO HISTORICAL SOCIETY, Library, Clark St at North Ave, Chicago, 60614. Robert L Brubaker, Librn
Notes: Papers.

CHICAGO WOMEN'S LIBERATION UNION

IL —CHICAGO HISTORICAL SOCIETY, Library, Clark St at North Ave, Chicago, 60614. Archie Motley, Manuscript Librn
Notes: Papers of Chicago Women's Liberation Union.

CHICAGOAN (MAGAZINE)

IL —CHICAGO HISTORICAL SOCIETY, Library, Clark St at North Ave, Chicago, 60614. Archie Motley, Manuscript Librn
Notes: Publishing and literary collections incl these papers: *Chicago Journalism* Review; *Chicago Seed*; *The Chicagoan*; Friends of American Writers, Chicago literary group; Emmett Dedmon (Chicago newspaper executive, journalist, author); Interviews of 97 Chicago journalists conducted by students in Northwestern University's Medill School.

CHICANO AUTHORS see Authors, Chicano

CHICANO STUDIES

AZ —ARIZONA STATE UNIVERSITY, Library, Arizona Collection, Tempe, 85281. Edward C Oetting, Head
Notes: Biographical file for references to Chicanos in early Arizona newspapers.

†CA —ANAHEIM PUBLIC LIBRARY, 500 W Broadway, Anaheim, 92805.

CA —CALIFORNIA STATE UNIVERSITY, FULLERTON, Library, Box 4150, Fullerton, 92634. Alfredo H Zuniga, Coord
Notes: Some materials on the subject; not maintained as a separate collection.

CA —LOS ANGELES PUBLIC LIBRARY, Social Sciences Dept, 630 W Fifth St, Los Angeles, 90071. Marilyn C Wherley, Principal Librn
Holdings: Vols 10,000 Microforms
Budget: ($150,000)
Notes: Emphasis on minorities; immigration policies, background and social problems of ethnic minorities in the US and the Southwest in particular. Incl periodicals, government publications and documents, popular and scholarly works on Blacks, Hispanics and Asians predominantly.

CA —UNIVERSITY OF CALIFORNIA, LOS ANGELES, Research Library, Dept of Special Collections, 405 Hilgard Ave, Los Angeles, 90024. Edward Shreeves, Chairman, Bibliographers Group; David S Zeidberg, Head
Holdings: // Uncat Mss
Notes: Personal papers, clippings, and reports relating to the problems of the Mexican American, 1930-1940. The Zoot-Suit Riots are incl in the Cary McWilliams Collection.

CA —STANFORD UNIVERSITY LIBRARIES, Cecil H Green Library, Stanford, 94305. Michael T Ryan, Cur
Notes: Ms collections of individuals and organizations whose activities have influenced public policy issues pertaining to Mexican Americans. Collections incl: the Mexican American Legal Defense Educational Fund (MALDEF) archives, the Centro de Accion Social Autonomo (CASA) records, the Ernesto Galarza papers, the Bert Corona papers, the Manuel Ruiz Jr papers, the Eduardo Queredo papers and the Edward Valenzuela papers.

GA —UNIVERSITY OF GEORGIA, Libraries, Special Collections Division, Athens, 30602. Vesta Lee Gordon, Asst Dir for Special Collections
Notes: The Arbitron Collection of television and radio program ratings, 1949-date (except past year). In-depth, statistical analyses of the listening public by age, sex, county, some ethnic groups, farm population, listening preferences, etc. 26,302 bound vols. 2 reports, 1949-81. To be added to annually.

TX —UNIVERSITY OF TEXAS LIBRARIES, Nettie Lee Benson Latin American Collection, Sid Richardson Hall 1.109, Austin, 78712. Laura Gutierrez-Witt, Head Librn
Holdings: Vols (450,000) Cat Mss Maps Pix Slides Phonorecords Videotapes 16mm Films Filmstrips Microforms VF
Notes: The Mexican American Library Project has, since 1974, collected materials relating to all aspects of Spanish-speaking people in the US, with emphasis on Mexican Americans.

TX —EL PASO PUBLIC LIBRARY, Mexican American Collection, 501 N Oregon, El Paso, 79901. Iris Espino, Librn
Holdings: Vols 3000 Cat
Notes: Current and historical information about Mexican-Americans throughout the US. Incl current social and economic writings about Mexican-Americans, Chicano literature, history and culture of Mexico from pre-Columbian times to the present, translations of Mexican authors, and Mexicans in current society.

TX —UNIVERSITY OF TEXAS, EL PASO, Library, Chicano Services Section, El Paso, 79968. Juan Sandoval, Chicano Services Librn
Holdings: Vols 1300
Budget: $6500
Notes: Chicano Services Section. Incl 396 AV items.

TX —FORT WORTH PUBLIC LIBRARY, North Branch, 601 Park St, Fort Worth, 76106. Betty M Hennington, Branch Head
Holdings: Vols 1000 Cat Phonorecords Audiotapes Filmstrips
Notes: Collection is entirely non-fiction. Although an effort is made to have novels by Mexican-American authors, these are not included in this collection. The criteria for the collection is anything written about Mexican Americans or books in which a large portion is devoted to the Mexican American. The history of Mexico until 1920 is included, but there are no books dealing with the history of Mexico since that time. Travel books are not included. An effort is made to obtain all current materials and to acquire retrospective materials when available, especially in the field of education and teaching.

CHICASA INDIANS see Chickasaw Indians

CHICHACHA INDIANS see Chickasaw Indians

CHICKASAW INDIANS

OK —OKLAHOMA HISTORICAL SOCIETY, Library, Historical Bldg, Oklahoma City, 73105. Andrea Clark, Dir, Library Resources Division
Holdings: Vols (43,000) Cat Mss Maps Pix Microforms
Notes: The Society also has the Indian Archives Collection of 2,500,000 pieces (Mary Lee Boyle, Archivist). This is an extensive collection of records, particularly of the Five Civilized Tribes. Incl tribal rolls, agency reports, manuscripts, etc.

CHICKENS see Poultry

CHICKESAW INDIANS see Chickasaw Indians

CHIDSEY, DONALD BARR

MA —BOSTON UNIVERSITY, Mugar Memorial Library, Special Collections Dept,

CHIDSEY, DONALD BARR (cont.)

771 Commonwealth Ave, Boston, 02215. Howard B Gotlieb, Dir
Holdings: Cat Mss Pix
Notes: Mss, Correspondence, etc collected in depth; incl publications by or about.

CHIKASAW INDIANS see Chickasaw Indians

CHILD, DANIEL AND MOSES

NY —SAINT LAWRENCE UNIVERSITY, Owen D Young Library, Canton, 13617. Mahlon Peterson, Librn
Holdings: Mss
Notes: Records of the land business of James Moon of Middleton, Pa, who owned part of Macomb's Purchase in northern New York. He sold this land to settlers through his relatives and agents, Daniel and Moses Child. The collection, incl maps, deeds, accounts and correspondence, covers the years 1818-1855 and numbers approx 100 items.

CHILD, LYDIA MARIA (FRANCIS), 1802-1880

MA —RADCLIFFE COLLEGE, Arthur & Elizabeth Schlesinger Library on the History of Women in America, 3 James St, Cambridge, 02138. Patricia Miller King, Dir; Eva Moseley, Cur of Mss
Notes: Author, editor, abolitionist, woman's rights advocate. Books by and about Lydia Maria Child, and several hundred letters in various mss collections, espec two of Child herself and that of Ellis Gray Loring. Also copy of microfiche edition of Child's correspondence.

NY —HOFSTRA UNIVERSITY, Library, 1000 Fulton Ave, Hempstead, 11550. Charles R Andrews, Dean of Library Services
Notes: Strong collection. Incl some mss.

†NY —UNIVERSITY OF ROCHESTER, Rush Rhees Library, Rochester, 14627.

CHILD AND PARENT see Parent and Child

CHILD BEHAVIOR see Children—Management

CHILD DEVELOPMENT

CA —CENTER FOR EARLY EDUCATION, Laura M Ellis Memorial Library, 563 N Alfred St, Los Angeles, 90048. Janice M Eastman, Librn
Holdings: Vols 2000 Cat
Budget: ($10,000)
Notes: Child development, birth to 12 years: psychological aspects, especially from psychoanalytic literature; materials written for laypersons, teachers and child care workers. Medical aspects generally excluded. Incl periodicals in field.

CA —LOS ANGELES PUBLIC LIBRARY, Social Sciences Dept, 630 W Fifth St, Los Angeles, 90071. Marilyn C Wherley, Principal Librn
Holdings: Vols (3000) Cat Microforms
Budget: ($150,000)
Notes: Collection incl government publications, agency reports, statistics, yearbooks, directories, pamphlets, bibliographies, child and adolescent psychology theories and history. Parent-children relations, deliquency, poplular and scholarly works.

CA —REISS-DAVIS CHILD STUDY CENTER, Research Library, 3200 Motor Ave, Los Angeles, 90034. Lee Freehling, Librn
Holdings: Vols (12,000) Cat
Notes: Child study, child psychiatry, psychoanalysis, clinical psychology, psychiatric social work. Incl 500 audiotapes; 25 16mm Films.

CT —YALE MEDICAL LIBRARY, 333 Cedar St, New Haven, 06510.
Holdings: Vols (334,215) Cat Mss Pix Slides Microforms
Budget: ($361,650)
Notes: Incl films, audiotapes, artifacts, etc.

CT —YALE UNIVERSITY, Medical Historical Library, 333 Cedar St, New Haven, 06510. Ferenc A Gyorgyey, Librn

DC —GEORGETOWN UNIVERSITY, Library, Special Collections Div, 37 & O Sts NW, Washington, 20057. George M Barringer, Special Collections Librn; Nicholas B Sheetz, Mss Librn
Notes: Archives of information used for compilation of *The American Heritage School Dictionary* (1972).

IL —UNIVERSITY OF ILLINOIS, URBANA/CHAMPAIGN, Library, Home Economics Library, 314 Bevier Hall, Champaign, 61820. Barbara C Swain, Librn
Holdings: Vols 4568 Cat
Notes: Human development and family ecology.

IL —INSTITUTE FOR PSYCHOANALYSIS, McLean Library, 180 N Michigan Ave, Chicago, 60601. Glenn Miller, Librn
Holdings: Vols (10,000) Cat Mss Pix Audiotapes Videotapes 16mm Films Microforms
Budget: ($87,000)
Notes: The collection is the data base for the *Chicago Psychoanalytic Literature Index*, a computer-generated quarterly subject guide to books, monographs, journals, symposia, tapes, films, and unpublished material indexed to a depth determined by the quality of the data. The *Index* is published by the Institute in Chicago; a sample is available on request.

IN —PURDUE UNIVERSITY LIBRARIES, Consumer & Family Sciences Library, Stone Hall W, West Lafayette, 47907. Emily Alward, Librn
Holdings: Vols (14,000) Cat

KS —JOHNSON COUNTY MENTAL HEALTH CENTER, John R Keach Memorial Library, 6000 Lamar Ave, Mission, 66202. Krista Hilton-Ross, Librn
Holdings: Vols (1000) Cat Mss

KS —KANSAS NEUROLOGICAL INSTITUTE, Menninger Professional Library, 3107 W 21 St, Topeka, 66604. Richard Gray, Librn
Holdings: Vols 300
Notes: Incl development disabilities; special education; nursing care for the handicapped; programs for the mentally retarded; behavioral psychology; supervision in mental health/mental retardation; staff training in mental health/mental retardation.

MD —NATIONAL LIBRARY OF MEDICINE, 8600 Rockville Pike, Bethesda, 20209. Harold M Schoolinam, Actg Dir
Budget: ($46,400)
Notes: Archives of the Society for Research in Child Development.

MA —CHILDREN'S MUSEUM, Resource Center, Museum Wharf, 300 Congress St, Boston, 02210. Marie Ariel, Librn; Maria Russell, Resource Services Mgr
Holdings: Vols (200) Cat Slides Phonorecords
Notes: Multimedia collection of books, games and other teaching materials for early childhood, displayed in the Resource Center and available for reference use by public with borrowing privileges for Resource Center members; Museum-developed multimedia kits available to schools for rental fee; reference collection of games and kits developed from recycled materials; subject-related programs and services available by Museum staff. Collection emphasis on child study and early childhood education materials.

NY —BANK STREET COLLEGE OF EDUCATION LIBRARY, 610 W 112 St, New York, 10025. Eleanor Kule Seid, Library Dir
Holdings: Vols (90,000) Cat Microforms
Notes: Education, guidance, psychology, educational psychology, curricula, textbooks, Black Studies, etc. All subjects are integrated in one professional collection; in addition there are two separately cataloged and shelved collections: Children's and Elementary Curriculum Materials.

NY —COLUMBIA UNIVERSITY LIBRARIES, Psychology Library, 409 Schermerhorn, New York, 10027. Barbara A List, Reference/Collection Development Librn
Holdings: Vols (25,000) Cat Microforms
Budget: ($23,300)
Notes: Incl material on animal physiology, cognition, psycholinguistics, learning theories, memory, perception, personality, sensation, sensorimotor activities, vision.

NY —ASTOR HOME FOR CHILDREN, Professional Library, 36 Mills St, Rhinebeck, 12572. William J Nichols, Librn
Holdings: Vols (2850) Cat Mss Audiotapes
Notes: Child psychiatry with emphasis on child mental health, encompassing child psychology, residential treatment centers, social work and related areas.

NY —UNIVERSITY OF ROCHESTER, Rush Rhees Library, Department of Rare Books and Special Collections, Rochester, 14627. Peter Dzwonkoski, Librn
Holdings: Cat Mss
Notes: Correspondence, reports, articles written by Wile on birth control (including many letters from Margaret Sanger), left and right handedness, sex education, child development, and mental hygiene.

NY —ELIZABETH SETON COLLEGE LIBRARY, Yonkers, 10701. Sr Margaret Sullivan, Librn

PA —CARLOW COLLEGE, Grace Library, Fifth Ave, Pittsburgh, 15213. Joan M Mitchell, Dir of Library Services
Holdings: Vols (1050) Cat
Budget: ($800)

TN —VANDERBILT UNIVERSITY, George Peabody College for Teachers, Education Library, Box 325, Nashville, 37203. Mary Beth Blalock, Librn
Holdings: Vols (192,541) Cat Pix Slides Phonorecords Filmstrips Microforms
Budget: ($59,000)
Notes: The Education Library (192,541 vols) collects in all areas relating to education with special emphasis on Child Study and Exceptional Children. Special funds are available for continuing purchases in these areas. The collection is strong in curriculum materials, physical education, applied art, psychology related to education and all areas of education. Amoung special papers are over 300 papers by and about Jean Piaget and an extensive author and subject file referring to the location of these papers and books and journal articles by and about Piaget in the rest of the Education Library collection. The Education Library is a Division of the Vanderbilt University Library.

ON —UNIVERSITY OF GUELPH, Library, Guelph, N1G 2W1, Can. Margaret Beckman, Chief Librn; Ellen Pearson, Ref Librn
Holdings: Vols 30,000 Cat Audiotapes Videotapes 16mm Films Microforms
Budget: ($21,500)
Notes: 320 periodical titles. Special catalogs can be produced for any part of the collection. Additional historical material in archives on early rural movements, such as the women's institutes.
See also entry under Rural Sociology

†ON —METROPOLITAN TORONTO LIBRARY, Social Sciences Dept, 789 Yonge St, Toronto, M4W 2G8, Can. Abdus Salam, Head
Holdings: Vols Cat Maps Phonorecords Audiotapes 16mm Films Microforms
Notes: Includes books on general psychology and its history. Also, a strong collection of the works of individual psychologists and critical works about them. The following specialized areas of psychology are also well covered: child psychology, psychology and mental health, and parapsychology.

PQ —HOPITAL SAINTE-JUSTINE POUR LES ENFANTS, Centre d'Information sur la Sante de l'Enfant, 3175 Cote Sainte-Catherine, Montreal, H3T 1C5, Can. Louis LucLecompte, Librn
Holdings: Vols (7000) Cat Audiotapes Videotapes 16mm Films Microforms
Budget: ($11,000)
Notes: 40 percent of collection in French.

CHILD LABOR see Children—Employment; Youth—Employment

CHILD PLACING see Adoption

CHILD PSYCHIATRY

CA —CENTER FOR EARLY EDUCATION, Laura M Ellis Memorial Library, 563 N

CHILD PSYCHIATRY (cont.)

Alfred St, Los Angeles, 90048. Janice M Eastman, Librn
Holdings: Vols 2000 Cat
Budget: ($10,000)
Notes: Child development, birth to 12 years: psychological aspects, especially from psychoanalytic literature; materials written for laypersons, teachers and child care workers. Medical aspects generally excluded. Incl periodicals in field.

CA —REISS-DAVIS CHILD STUDY CENTER, Research Library, 3200 Motor Ave, Los Angeles, 90034. Lee Freehling, Librn
Holdings: Vols (12,000) Cat
Notes: Child study, child psychiatry, psychoanalysis, clinical psychology, psychiatric social work. Incl 500 audiotapes; 25 16mm Films.

CA —LANGLEY PORTER PSYCHIATRIC INSTITUTE LIBRARY, University of California, 401 Parnassus Ave Box 13-B, San Francisco, 94143. Lisa M Dunkel, Librn
Holdings: Vols (11,700) Cat
Notes: Attempt to cover, selectively, literature in psychiatry, psychoanalysis, clinical psychology, and allied fields for an institute which is involved in clinical work, training and research.

CT —CONNECTICUT VALLEY HOSPITAL, Hallock Medical Library, Silver St, Middletown, 06457. Mildred Asbell, Medical Librn
Holdings: Vols (3400) Cat

CT —NEWINGTON CHILDREN'S HOSPITAL, Professional Library, 181 E Cedar St, Newington, 06111. Jean Long, Librn
Holdings: Vols (3500) Cat
Budget: ($6500)

IL —INSTITUTE FOR PSYCHOANALYSIS, McLean Library, 180 N Michigan Ave, Chicago, 60601. Glenn Miller, Librn
Holdings: Vols (10,000) Cat Mss Pix Audiotapes Videotapes 16mm Films Microforms
Budget: ($87,000)
Notes: The collection is the data base for the *Chicago Psychoanalytic Literature Index*, a computer-generated quarterly subject guide to books, monographs, journals, symposia, tapes, films, and unpublished material indexed to a depth determined by the quality of the data. The *Index* is published by the Institute in Chicago; a sample is available on request.

IL —JACKSONVILLE STATE HOSPITAL, Training & Research Library, 1201 S Main St, Jacksonville, 62650. Lois E Wells, Librn
Notes: Concerned particularly with developmental disabilities.

KS —JOHNSON COUNTY MENTAL HEALTH CENTER, John R Keach Memorial Library, 6000 Lamar Ave, Mission, 66202. Krista Hilton-Ross, Librn
Budget: Vols (1000) Cat Mss

KS —KANSAS NEUROLOGICAL INSTITUTE, Menninger Professional Library, 3107 W 21 St, Topeka, 66604. Richard Gray, Librn
Holdings: Vols 256 Cat
Notes: Incl development disabilities; special education; nursing care for the handicapped; programs for the mentally retarded; behavioral psychology; supervision in mental health/mental retardation; staff training in mental health/mental retardation.

KY —UNIVERSITY OF LOUISVILLE, Kornhauser Health Sciences Library, 520 S Preston St, PO Box 35260, Louisville, 40292. Leonard M Eddy, Dir; Sherrill R McConnell, Archivist
Holdings: Vols 300 Cat
Notes: History of child psychiatry in the 20th century.

MD —NATIONAL LIBRARY OF MEDICINE, 8600 Rockville Pike, Bethesda, 20209. Harold M Schoolinam, Actg Dir
Budget: ($46,400)
Notes: Archives of the Society for Research in Child Development.

NY —ASTOR HOME FOR CHILDREN, Professional Library, 36 Mills St, Rhinebeck, 12572. William J Nichols, Librn
Holdings: Vols (2850) Cat Mss Audiotapes
Notes: Child psychiatry with emphasis on child mental health, encompassing child psychology, residential treatment centers, social work and related areas.

RI —EMMA PENDLETON BRADLEY HOSPITAL, Austin T and June Rockwell Levy Library, 1011 Veterans Memorial Parkway, Riverside, 02915. Carolyn A Waller, Librn
Holdings: Vols 4000 Cat Audiotapes
Budget: ($9866)
Notes: This collection, although small, contains both landmark and current book titles related to the interdisciplinary field of child mental health. Because Bradley Hospital has had a 52-year intense concern with child behavior problems, the bound journal collection is comprehensive. A present major emphasis is acquisition and development of bibliographies to undergird research in child psychiatry.

WA —WESTERN STATE HOSPITAL, Library, Fort Steilacoom, 98494. Neal Van Der Voorn, Librn
Holdings: Vols (5900) Cat Audiotapes
Notes: Collection incl 5500 journal vols, 1800 pamphlets and 420 audiotapes.

CHILD PSYCHOLOGY see Child Psychiatry; Child Development

CHILD REARING see Children—Management

CHILD STUDY see Child Development

CHILD WELFARE

AL —BIRMINGHAM PUBLIC LIBRARY, Southern Women's Archives, 2020 Park Place, Birmingham, 35203. Theresa A Ceravolo, Archivist
Holdings: Cat Mss
Notes: Monthly legislative reports, 1981-1983, which discuss Alabama legislative and, to some extent, US Congress activities regarding abortion, domestic violence, child support, and other related issues.

CA —HOOVER INSTITUTION ON WAR, REVOLUTION & PEACE, Stanford University, Stanford, 94305. Milorad M Drachkovitch, Archivist
Holdings: Mss
Notes: Records of the White House Conference on Child Health and Protection, established in 1930 by President Herbert Hoover to investigate child welfare in the US, incl correspondence, reports, memoranda, expense statements and pamphlets, 1909-1950, relating to the physical and social conditions of children in the US, the status of school health education and health service programs, and proposals for the promotion of child welfare. Incl reports of the American Child Welfare Association. 143 ms boxes. 5 posters.

NJ —NEW JERSEY HISTORICAL SOCIETY, Library and Museum, 230 Broadway, Newark, 07104. Joan C Hull, Exec Dir; Barbara S Irwin, Library Dir; Alan R Fraser, Cur
Budget: ($100,000)
Notes: Records of eight Newark orphanages and child service organizations dating back to 1847. Incl records, casebooks, registers, adoption contracts, minutes of meetings, financial and administrative records, case studies by student interns in social work, and related printed materials.

NY —COLUMBIA UNIVERSITY LIBRARIES, Whitney M Young Jr Memorial Library of Social Work, 420 W 118 St, New York, 10027. Tyrone Cannon, Librn
Holdings: Vols (118,646) Cat
Notes: The collection covers the history and philosophy of social work, social work methodology, and all aspects of social welfare services, especially child welfare, mental hygiene, correction, the aging, social security and medical care, rehabilitation, aspects and problems of civil rights and automation. There is also a substantial representation of literature in psychiatry and the behavioral and social sciences. The reference section includes more than 419 periodicals, publications issued by voluntary agencies, government publications, doctoral dissertations and masters' essays in the field and standard reference works. Reference service is available.

WI —UNIVERSITY OF WISCONSIN, MADISON, School of Social Work, Virginia L Franks Library, 425 Henry Mall, Rm 230, Madison, 53706. Thurston Davini, Librn
Holdings: Vols 12,000 Cat Journals
Budget: $16,000
Notes: Special emphasis on social gerontology, child abuse/foster care.

ON —ONTARIO MINISTRY OF COMMUNITY & SOCIAL SERVICES, Library, 880 Bay St, Rm 663, Toronto, M7A 1E9, Can. Sandra Walsh, Chief Librn
Holdings: Vols (30,000) Cat Slides Videotapes 16mm Films Microforms

CHILDBIRTH

NY —MATERNITY CENTER ASSOCIATION, Library, 48 E 92 St, New York, 10028. Esther Hanchett, Acting Librn
Holdings: Vols 2000 Cat
Notes: No photocopying.

CHILDE, W. R.

BC —UNIVERSITY OF VICTORIA, McPherson Library, Victoria, V8W 3H5, Can.

CHILDHOOD DISEASES see Children—Diseases

CHILDHOOD IN POETRY

FL —FLORIDA STATE UNIVERSITY, Robert Manning Strozier Library, Childhood in Poetry Collection, Tallahassee, 32306. Frederick Korn, Cur
Holdings: Vols (25,000) Cat
Notes: The Childhood in Poetry Collection consists of the books of all the great poets and hundreds of minor poets of all periods, in first or other early and illustrated editions, in children's periodicals and "juveniles." There are more than 300 hymnals, incl the personal collection of Dr Robert Lowry, author of "Shall We Gather at the River" and other popular hymns. There are also nearly 500 annuals and gift books. The Collection is strong, as well, in works of criticism, biography and reference. An eleven-volume, illustrated catalog (1967-1980) is available from Gale Research. Over 200,000 poems are listed in a key-word index, keyed to the books in which they apppear. The nucleus of the Collection was assembled as the lifetime leisure activity of the donor, John Mackay Shaw, who now serves as curator emeritus. His object has been to gather in one place thebooks in which poems relating to childhood first appeared.

CHILDREN

IL —UNIVERSITY OF ILLINOIS, URBANA/CHAMPAIGN, Library, Home Economics Library, 314 Bevier Hall, Champaign, 61820. Barbara C Swain, Librn
Holdings: Vols 4568 Cat
Notes: Human development and family ecology.

†MA —HARVARD UNIVERSITY LIBRARY, Judaica Dept, Cambridge, 02138. Charles Berlin, Librn
Notes: Harvard's Judaica Collections have been helped by a special grant from the S H and Helen R Scheuer Family Foundation (NY) to develop its Jewish children's literature collection to encourage research in literature for and about Jewish children.

NY —BANK STREET COLLEGE OF EDUCATION LIBRARY, 610 W 112 St, New York, 10025. Eleanor Kule Seid, Library Dir
Holdings: Vols (80,000) Cat Microforms
Budget: ($29,000)
Notes: Education, guidance, psychology,

CHILDREN (cont.)

educational psychology, curricula, textbooks, Black Studies, etc. All subjects are integrated in one professional collection; in addition there are two separately cataloged and shelved collections: Children's and Elementary Curriculum Materials.

NY —ROCKEFELLER UNIVERSITY, Rockefeller Archive Center, Hillcrest, Pocantico Hills, North Tarrytown, 10591. Joseph W Ernst, Dir; J William Hess, Assoc Dir
Notes: Papers relative to the Rockefeller Family, Foundations, University, and other specific enterprises and contributions to particular areas of social, physical, educational, and historic reform, preservation, conservation, or development. Extensive records of administrative, financial, physical, or intellectual relationships.

OH —OHIO STATE UNIVERSITY, Home Economics Library, Campbell Hall Rm 325, 1787 Neil Ave, Columbus, 43210. Neosha Mackey, Librn
Holdings: Vols (14,000) Cat Microforms
Notes: Separate catalog. Also, book catalog: *Catalog of the Home Economics Library* (Boston: G K Hall, 1976), 3 vols.

PA —UNIVERSITY OF PITTSBURGH, Hillman Library, Pittsburgh, 15260. Glenora E Rossell, Head
Holdings: Vols (18,600) Cat
Notes: Especially strong in social theory, social history, social groups, criminology and urban sociology. Emphasis is currently being given to administration of justice, sociology of the child, sociology of the aged, sociology of education and sociology of religion. This collection is strengthened by the US government publications depository collection, the partial UN depository collection, the Canadian government publications collection and the collection of the Social Work Library.

RI —EMMA PENDLETON BRADLEY HOSPITAL, Austin T and June Rockwell Levy Library, 1011 Veterans Memorial Parkway, Riverside, 02915. Carolyn A Waller, Librn
Holdings: Vols 4000 Cat Audiotapes
Budget: ($9866)
Notes: This collection, although small, contains both landmark and current book titles related to the interdisciplinary field of child mental health. Because Bradley Hospital has had a 52-year intense concern with child behavior problems, the bound journal collection is comprehensive. A present major emphasis is acquisition and development of bibliographies to undergird research in child psychiatry.

PQ —HOPITAL SAINTE-JUSTINE POUR LES ENFANTS, Centre d'Information sur la Sante de l'Enfant, 3175 Cote Sainte-Catherine, Montreal, H3T 1C5, Can. Louis LucLecompte, Librn
Holdings: Vols (7000) Cat Audiotapes Videotapes 16mm Films Microforms
Budget: ($11,000)
Notes: 40 percent of collection in French.

CHILDREN—CARE AND HYGIENE

CA —UNIVERSITY OF CALIFORNIA, BERKELEY, Life Sciences Libraries, Public Health Library, 42 Earl Warren Hall, Berkeley, 94720. Thomas J Alexander, Librn
Holdings: Vols (75,000) Cat Microforms
Notes: Research collection covering all aspects of public health. Health Department annual reports from all 50 states are acquired, as well as such reports from all California health units and from major US cities. Serial publications issued by Health Departments in the 13 western states are being received.

CA —HOOVER INSTITUTION ON WAR, REVOLUTION & PEACE, Stanford University, Stanford, 94305. Milorad M Drachkovitch, Archivist
Holdings: Mss
Notes: Records of the White house Conference on Child Health and Protection, established in 1930 by President Herbert Hoover to investigate child welfare in the US, incl correspondence, reports, memoranda, expense statements and pamphlets, 1909-1950, relating to the physical and social conditions of children in the US, the status of school health education and health service programs, and proposals for the promotion of child welfare. Incl reports of the American Child Welfare Association. 143 ms boxes, 5 posters.

KS —KANSAS NEUROLOGICAL INSTITUTE, Menninger Professional Library, 3107 W 21 St, Topeka, 66604. Richard Gray, Librn
Holdings: Vols 100
Notes: Incl development disabilities; special education; nursing care for the handicapped; programs for the mentally retarded; behavioral psychology; supervision in mental health/mental retardation; staff training in mental health/mental retardation.

MI —UNIVERSITY OF MICHIGAN, Public Health Library, Ann Arbor, 48109. Mary Townsend, Head
Holdings: Vols (55,000) Cat Maps Pix
Budget: ($24,000)

NY —ASTOR HOME FOR CHILDREN, Professional Library, 36 Mills St, Rhinebeck, 12572. William J Nichols, Librn
Holdings: Vols (2850) Cat Mss Audiotapes
Notes: Child psychiatry with emphasis on child mental health, encompassing child psycology, residential treatment centers, social work and related areas.

NC —TECHNICAL INSTITUTE OF ALAMANCE, Learning Resources Center, Jimmy Kerr Rd, PO Box 623, Haw River, 27258. Ron Plummer, Coordr
Holdings: Vols (796) Cat Slides Audiotapes 16mm Films Filmstrips Microforms
Notes: Incl children's games.

WI —UNIVERSITY OF WISCONSIN, MADISON, College of Agricultural & Life Sciences, Steenbock Memorial Library, 550 Babcock Dr, Madison, 53706. Jan Kennedy, Dir
Holdings: Vols (186,312) Cat Docs
Notes: Collection supports the School of Family Resources and Consumer Sciences in areas of textiles and fashion design, interior decorating, consumer science, and nutrition; USDA documents and experiment station publications.

CHILDREN—CHARITIES see Child Welfare

CHILDREN—DISEASES

CA —UNIVERSITY OF CALIFORNIA, BERKELEY, Life Sciences Libraries, Public Health Library, 42 Earl Warren Hall, Berkeley, 94720. Thomas J Alexander, Librn
Holdings: Vols (75,000) Cat Microforms
Notes: Research collection covering all aspects of public health. Department annual reports from all 50 states are acquired, as well as such reports from all California health units and from major US cities. Serial publications issued by Health Departments in the 13 western states are being received.

GA —MEDICAL COLLEGE OF GEORGIA, Library, Laney Walker Blvd, Augusta, 30902. Dorothy H Mims, Librn for Special Collections
Holdings: Vols (2500)// Cat
Notes: Special collection of late 18th and early 19th century medical books, incl classics on diseases of children and advice to mothers on care of children.

MD —MEDICAL & CHIRURGICAL FACULTY OF THE STATE OF MARYLAND, Library, 1211 Cathedral St, Baltimore, 21201. Joseph E Jensen, Librn
Holdings: Vols (10,000) // Cat Mss Maps Pix
See also entry under Medicine - History and Historic

TN —SAINT JUDE CHILDREN'S RESEARCH HOSPITAL, Medical Library, 323 N Lauderdale, PO Box 318, Memphis, 38101. Mary Edith Walker, Librn; Cindy Suter, Asst Librn
Holdings: Vols (10,000)
Notes: The collection of pediatric oncology is intermingled with general clinical and research materials. Published description of collection in *International Directory of Specialized Cancer Research and Treatment* Establishments (Geneva: International Union Against Cancer, 1976), p 442.

CHILDREN—EDUCATION see Education of Children

CHILDREN—EMPLOYMENT

CA —HOOVER INSTITUTION ON WAR, REVOLUTION & PEACE, Stanford University, Stanford, 94305. Milorad M Drachkovitch, Archivist
Holdings: Mss
Notes: Papers of Alice Park, 1883-1957, incl diaries, correspondence, pamphlets, clippings, and leaflets, relating to Pacifism and the peace movement, the Ford Peace Ship Expedition of 1915-1916, feminism, socialism, the labor movement, prison reform, child labor legislation, civil liberties, and a variety of other reform movements in the US 30 ms boxes, 3 envelopes.

DC —INTERNATIONAL LABOR ORGANIZATION, International Labor Office, Washington Branch Library, 1750 New York Ave NW, Rm 330, Washington, 20006. Karen J Mark, Librn
Holdings: Vols (13,500) Cat Pix 16mm Films Monographs
Notes: Wide range of titles dealing with worldwide labor and social matters. The library contains ILO publications and documentation only, dating back to 1919. Also, a collection of ILO films and photos. See *Subject Guide to Publications of the ILO, 1919-1964* and *ILO Catalogue of Publications in Print, 1982* (ILO).

DC —LIBRARY OF CONGRESS, Manuscript Division, Washington, 20540. John C Broderick, Chief
Notes: Records and photographs of the National Child Labor Committee, 1904-53.

IL —LOYOLA UNIVERSITY OF CHICAGO, E M Cudahy Memorial Library, 6525 N Sheridan Rd, Chicago, 60626.
Notes: Dorr E Felt Pamphlet and Clipping Collection. Emphasizes political and economic issues, 1902-35, and documents Illinois Manufacturers Association Conference, September 8-9, 1919; Air Board of Chicago, April 16, 1921-August 1, 1930; Allied Debts to the US, May 15, 1923-September 30, 1926; Bolshevism, Communism, "Red" Russia, 1924-27; Child Labor Bill, March 30, 1915, 1914-20; Labor, March, 1902-March, 1932; Railroad Strike, August 25, 1916-August 7, 1920; The War, August, 1914-October 23, 1930; War Industries Commission, June, 1918-November 23, 1928. A pamphlet list is available for each topic.

RI —SLATER MILL HISTORIC SITE, SMHS Library, Roosevelt Ave, Pawtucket, 02962. TE Leary, Cur
Holdings: Vols 500 Mss Maps Pix Oral History
Budget: $500
Notes: Lewis Hine photos of child labor in RI (1909-1912).

CHILDREN—HEALTH see Children—Care and Hygiene

CHILDREN—HYGIENE see Children—Care and Hygiene

CHILDREN—INSTITUTIONAL CARE

NY —ROCKEFELLER UNIVERSITY, Rockefeller Archive Center, Hillcrest, Pocantico Hills, North Tarrytown, 10591. Joseph W Ernst, Dir; J William Hess, Assoc Dir
Notes: The Rockefeller Archive Center, a division of Rockefeller University, preserves and makes available to scholars the records of the University, the Rockefeller Foundation, the Rockefeller Brothers Fund, members of the family, and those of other individuals and organizations associated with their endeavors. Collections at the Center

CHILDREN—INSTITUTIONAL CARE (cont.)

document a century of philanthropy by legions of associated social and scientific pioneers, providing a unique window into the past.

CHILDREN—MANAGEMENT

NJ —NEW JERSEY HISTORICAL SOCIETY, Library and Museum, 230 Broadway, Newark, 07104. Joan C Hull, Exec Dir; Barbara S Irwin, Library Dir; Alan R Fraser, Cur
Budget: ($100,000)
Notes: Records of eight Newark orphanages and child service organizations dating back to 1847. Incl records, casebooks, registers, adoption contracts, minutes of meetings, financial and administrative records, case studies by student interns in social work, and related printed materials.

CHILDREN—PROTECTION see Child Welfare

CHILDREN—RECREATION see Games

CHILDREN—TRAINING see Children—Management

CHILDREN, DEAF—EDUCATION see Deaf and Deafness—Education

CHILDREN, EXCEPTIONAL see Exceptional Children

CHILDREN, FOLKLORE OF see Folklore of Children

CHILDREN, FOREIGN see Children in Foreign Countries

CHILDREN, RETARDED see Exceptional Children; Mentally Handicapped Children; Slow-Learning Children

CHILDREN AS PERFORMERS

NY —NEW YORK PUBLIC LIBRARY, General Library of the Performing Arts at Lincoln Center, 111 Amsterdam Ave, New York, 10023. Elizabeth Long, Children's Performing Arts Specialist
Holdings: Vols 28,000 Cat Phonorecords Audiotapes Filmstrips
Notes: A collection of performing arts materials (music, dance, drama) for children, ages 7-11, and adults working with children. Incl over 10,000 phonorecords and audiotapes.

CHILDREN IN FOREIGN COUNTRIES

†MA —HARVARD UNIVERSITY LIBRARY, Judaica Dept, Cambridge, 02138. Charles Berlin, Librn
Notes: Harvard's Judaica Collections have been helped by a special grant from the S H and Helen R Scheuer Family Foundation (NY) to develop its Jewish children's literature collection to encourage research in literature for and about Jewish children.

NY —US COMMITTEE FOR UNICEF, Information Center on Children's Cultures, 331 E 38 St, New York, 10016. Melinda Greenblatt, Chief Librn
Holdings: Vols (17,500) Cat Pix Slides Films Filmstrips
Notes: Social and cultural aspects of lives of children from developing countries. Especially strong in the area of school textbooks from Near Eastern Asian, African, Latin American, Caribbean, and Pacific Area countries; holidays and celebrations related to children all over the world; children's books in English which describe child life in other countries. Especially strong collection of folklore, and folklore of children, from all regions mentioned above.

CHILDREN'S BOOKS see Children's Literature; Illustrated Books, Children's

CHILDREN'S BOOK PUBLISHING

NY —GRADUATE CENTER OF THE CITY UNIVERSITY OF NEW YORK, William H and Gwynne K Crouse Library for Publishing Arts, 33 W 42 St, New York, 10036. Alfred H Lane, Dir
Notes: Recently established and still growing, but intended to become the authoritative source of materials in the field, of particular value in research about the publishing industry. Open to staff members of publishing houses, students, scholars, authors, printers, and booksellers. Primarily 20th century materials, and particularly useful for research on technical, financial, and historical matters. Much on the history of individual houses, economics of authorship; marketing and distribution of books; etc.

CHILDREN'S CLOTHING—PATTERN DESIGN

CA —CARLSBAD CITY LIBRARY, 1250 Elm Ave, Carlsbad, 92008. Clifford E Lange, Library Dir
Holdings: Vols (2297) Cat
Notes: Collection of sewing patterns. Catalogs of the patterns have been made up with complete information on size, etc, and have been divided into subject areas, such as gift ideas, toys, dolls, women's clothes, men's clothes, children's clothes, etc. Also patterns for knitted and crocheted wearing apparel. Incl patterns for children's costumes, historical fashions and antique dolls.

CHILDREN'S DISEASES see Children—Diseases

CHILDREN'S HOMES see Children—Institutional Care

CHILDREN'S ILLUSTRATED BOOKS see Illustrated Books, Children's

CHILDREN'S LIBRARIES see Libraries, Children's; School Libraries

CHILDREN'S LITERATURE

CA —UNIVERSITY OF CALIFORNIA, BERKELEY, Humanities-Social Sciences Libraries, Education-Psychology Library, 2600 Tolman Hall, Berkeley, 94720. Sonya Kaufman, Acting Head
Holdings: Vols (110,000)
Notes: General research collection in fields of education and psycology. Education collection's emphases are in the areas of administration, policy planning, higher education, science and math education, language and literacy. Serial holdings are strong. The library receives approx 2200 current serial titles in education and psychology.

CA —CALIFORNIA STATE UNIVERSITY, LONG BEACH, Reference Center, 1250 Bellflower Blvd, Long Beach, 90840.
Holdings: Vols 20,557
Budget: $2000
Notes: Juvenile books.

CA —LOS ANGELES PUBLIC LIBRARY, Children's Literature Dept, 630 W 5th St, Los Angeles, 90071. Serenna Day, Sr Librn
Holdings: Vols (2120) Cat Phonorecords Filmstrips
Notes: Also includes reference collection, covering some 50 years of published folklore and modern fairy tales. Includes extensive Mother Goose collection, examples of the work of such outstanding illustrators as Edmund Dulac and Arthur Rackham. Many volumes out of print. Index to titles of stories in collections.

CA —UNIVERSITY OF CALIFORNIA, LOS ANGELES, Research Library, Dept of Special Collections, 405 Hilgard Ave, Los Angeles, 90024. Edward Shreeves, Chairman, Bibliographers Group; David S Zeidberg, Head
Holdings: Vols Cat
Notes: 2500 selected modern juveniles, international in scope, 1900 to date. Also 12, 000 volumes, principally British and American, with emphasis on ca 1775-1840, incl a collection of Harris and Newbery imprints; and 25 linear feet of mss, correspondence, illustrations, and memorabilia of Holling Clancey Holling and Lucille Webster Holling, authors and illustrators of modern children's books.

CA —MILLS COLLEGE LIBRARY, Oakland, 94613. Steven P Pandolfo, Librn
Holdings: Vols 600 Cat Mss Pix
Notes: Incl ca 350 children's books featuring pigs as characters. The Charlotte Baker Papers incl the mss for eleven books and the artwork for fourteen books (over 200 finished drawings).

CA —POMONA PUBLIC LIBRARY, Special Collections, 625 S Garey Ave, PO Box 2271, Pomona, 91766. David Streeter, Librn
Holdings: Vols 559
Notes: Clara J Webber collection of children's books. Emphasis on Laura Ingalls Wilder award winners; Caldecott and Newberry award books; contemporary pop-up-books; miscellaneous early children's books.

CA —SAN FRANCISCO ACADEMY OF COMIC ART, Library, 2850 Ulloa, San Francisco, 94116.
Notes: Incl largest collection of pulp magazines in US. Paper copies of all major American newspapers, emphasis on Hearst papers. Extensive collection of Sherlockiana and a member of the National Sherlockiana Society. Also extensive collection of early motion picture tapes, books, magazines and posters. 19th and early 20th century children's books also in the holdings. Collection incl 1,000,000 comic strips, 22, 000 comic books, 12,500 hard cover mystery books, 8000 hard cover science fiction books and copies of all science fiction pulp magazines.

CA —SAN FRANCISCO STATE UNIVERSITY, J Paul Leonard Library, 1630 Holloway Ave, San Francisco, 94132. Susan Quinlan, Curriculum Librn
Holdings: Vols (49,246) Cat Phonorecords Audiotapes 8mm Films Microforms
Budget: ($8500)
Notes: The young people's collection or children's literature collection of 17,843 vols incl books with reading and interest levels ranging from preschool through senior high school. The Marguerite Archer collection of historical children's books contains an additional 3000 vols. Have 19,755 textbooks, 5150 curriculum guides, 1970 pamphlets. Collection emphasizes instructional materials that can be utitlized in the school classroom. Professional books and journals and other media relating to educational history, philosophy, research, theories of teaching, etc are in the main collection.

CA —SAN JOSE PUBLIC LIBRARY, 180 W San Carlos St, San Jose, 95113. Homer Fletcher, Dir
Holdings: Vols (8800) Cat
Notes: General collection of representative children's books, the major part published between 1870 and 1930. Strongest areas are popular series (Alger, Baum, Finley, Optic, etc), history and *travel*. Includes work of Art Nouveau illustrators, almost complete run of St Nicholas Magazine, and several other children's magazines of the period. For reference use in library only.

CA —STANFORD UNIVERSITY LIBRARIES, Cecil H Green Library, Stanford, 94305. Michael T Ryan, Cur
Holdings: Vols (10,000)
Notes: The Mary L Schofield Collection of Children's Literature.

CO —UNIVERSITY OF COLORADO, Libraries, Special Collections, Boulder, 80309. Nora J Quinlan, Head
Holdings: Vols Uncat Mss
Notes: George Creamer Collection. Over two thousand books on 19th century English literature (Dickens), and 19th and 20th centuries British and American book illustration. In addition, approx 250 children's illustrated books. In addition, the Epsteen Collection.

†CO —DENVER BOTANIC GARDENS, Helen Fowler Library, 909 York St, Denver, 80206. Solange G Gignac, Librn
Notes: Emphasis on Bromeliada Literature;

CHILDREN'S LITERATURE (cont.)

horticulture; Colorado, Oregon, and Rocky Mountains Region botany; landscape architecture; juvenile horticultural and botanical literature. Incl over 5000 pamphlets on botany and horticulture; also, 197 watercolors of Colorado wildflowers by Emma Irvine, and 250 of Oregon by Lillian Hallock.

CT —SOUTHERN CONNECTICUT STATE UNIVERSITY, Hilton C Buley Library, 501 Crescent St, New Haven, 06515. Elma B Wiacek, Special Collections Librn
Holdings: Vols 3000 Cat Mss
Notes: The Carolyn Sherwin Bailey Historical Collection of Children's Books. Incl holograph mss.

CT —CONNECTICUT COLLEGE, Library, Mohegan Ave, New London, 06320. Brian Rogers, College Librn
Holdings: Vols 2600
Notes: Holdings incl the Helen Gildersleeve Collection of Children's Literature. Principally 19th and 20th century to 1960.

†CT —UNIVERSITY OF CONNECTICUT LIBRARY, Special Collections Dept, Storrs, 06268. Richard H Schimmelpfeng, Dir of Special Collections
Notes: Good and unusual collection.

DC —GEORGETOWN UNIVERSITY, Library, Special Collections Div, 37 & O Sts NW, Washington, 20057. George M Barringer, Special Collections Librn; Nicholas B Sheetz, Mss Librn
Holdings: Mss Cat Pix
Notes: A collection of books, mss, letters, clippings, photographs and tapes by and about the British author Arthur Ransome (1884-1967). Ransome is best known for his children's books and his works on Russia. Also, personalized papers, files, art work, etc of Lynd Ward and his wife, May McNeer.

DC —LIBRARY OF CONGRESS, Rare Book & Special Collections Div, Washington, 20540. William Matheson, Chief
Holdings: Vols 17,348 Cat
Notes: The Juvenile Collection covers the early 18th century to the present and is particularly strong in fiction. Authors extensively represented are: Alcott, Alger, Abbott, Goodrich, Fosdick, Lothrop and McGuffey. Approx 100 unique titles issued before 1820.

DC —LIBRARY OF CONGRESS, Children's Literature Center, Washington, 20540. Sybille Jagusch, Chief
Holdings: Vols 117,809 Cat Microforms
Notes: English language children's books.

FL —FLORIDA STATE UNIVERSITY, Robert Manning Strozier Library, Childhood in Poetry Collection, Tallahassee, 32306. Frederick Korn, Cur
Holdings: Vols (25,000) Cat
Notes: The Childhood in Poetry Collection consists of the books of all the great poets and hundreds of minor poets of all periods, in first or other early and illustrated editions, in children's periodicals and "juveniles." There are more than 300 hymals, incl the personal collection of Dr Robert Lowry. author of "Shall We Gather at the River" and other popular hymns. There are also nearly 500 annuals and gift books. The Collection is strong, as well, in works of criticism, biography and reference. An eleven-volume, illustrated catalog (1967-1980) is available from Gale Research. Over 200,000 poems are listed in a key-word index, keyed to the books in which they appear. The nucleus of the Collection was assembled as the lifetime leisure activity of the donor, John Mackay Shaw, who now serves as curator emeritus. His object has been togather in one place the books in which poems relating to childhood first appeared.

FL —FLORIDA STATE UNIVERSITY, Robert Manning Strozier Library, Special Collections Dept, Tallahassee, 32306. Opal M Free, Head, Special Collections
Holdings: Uncat Mss Pix Tapes
Notes: The Lois Lenski collection contains 867 items, many first editions of books written and illustrated by Miss Lenski and other editions of her books, incl foreign-language editions: books illustrated by Lois Lenski; books containing selections from her works; articles by and about her; original drawings, block prints, lithographs, rough sketches. Many items autographed. Two editions of a catalog of the collection, *The Lois Lenski Collection in the Florida State University Library,* were published in 1966, both limited editions and now out-of-print. Noncirculating. No photocopying.

FL —UNIVERSITY OF SOUTH FLORIDA, Library, Tampa, 33620. J B Dobkin, Special Collections Librn
Holdings: Vols 7000 Cat
Budget: ($7500)
Notes: The Harry K Hudson Collection of American Juvenile Series Books of boys' and girls' fiction issued in series in the 19th and first part of the 20th century. Comprehensive coverage of boys' series books, incl many specimens in original dust jackets (approximately 5000 volumes total). Complimentary collection of girls' series books under development; current holdings approx 2000 volumes. Books arranged by series with in-house finding aids rather than card catalog access. Collection contains book material only.

IL —SOUTHERN ILLINOIS UNIVERSITY, CARBONDALE, Delyte W Morris Library, Carbondale, 62901.
Holdings: Vols 6000 Cat
Notes: Historical Children's Book Collection. Incl trade books, textbooks, and periodicals; mainly American and English publications, late 18th century through 20th century.

IL —CENTER FOR RESEARCH LIBRARIES, 6050 S Kenwood Ave, Chicago, 60637. Donald B Simpson, Dir; Esther Smith, Collection Development Librn
Holdings: Vols 50,000 Uncat
Notes: Fairly comprehensive collection of books for children and juveniles published in US since 1950, and a few earlier titles. Most retain their original dust jackets.

IL —CHICAGO PUBLIC LIBRARY, Thomas Hughes Children's Library, 78 E Washington St, Chicago, 60602. Lillian R New, Head
Holdings: Vols 3000 Cat
Notes: This special collection was developed at the Central Library to answer reference and information requests from both adults and children who were unable to find obscure materials related to children's books in the neighborhood branch library collections. Limited in its inclusion of rare children's books, but it has a good representation of out-of-print titles, series books of the 1910's like the *Hardy Boys* stories, early ethnic books for children of the 1930s and 40s, and illustrated editions of children's classics, incl those of Mother Goose, Hans Christian Andersen, and the Grimm brothers, and a collection of Chicago Area Authors and Illustrators.

IL —UNIVERSITY OF CHICAGO LIBRARY, Dept of Special Collections, 1100 E 57 St, Chicago, 60637.
Notes: Books for children, mostly 19th century. Incl Encyclopedia Britannica Collection.

IL —NORTHERN ILLINOIS UNIVERSITY, Founders Memorial Library, Rare Books and Special Collections Dept, De Kalb, 60115. William R DuBois, Dept Head
Holdings: Vols (1000)
Budget: ($5000)
Notes: Mass-appeal publications, ca 1865-1920. Includes Horatio Alger, "Oliver Optic" and other popular writers.

IL —SCOTT, FORESMAN & CO, Editorial Library, 1900 E Lake Ave, Glenview, 60025. S Donal Robertson, Head Librn
Holdings: Vols (30,000) Phonorecords Audiotapes Microforms
Notes: A general collection, fairly heavy in the areas of education and children's literature. Study and teaching of reading is probably the largest single section of the collection.

IL —ILLINOIS STATE UNIVERSITY, Milner Library, Dept of Special Collections, Normal, 61761. Robert Sokan, Librn
Holdings: Vols (170) Uncat Mss Pix Audiotapes
Notes: Correspondence (1935-1957) to Lois Lenski concerning her doll and toy collection and her books for children; correspondence (1956-1970) from Lois Lenski to Milner Library concerning additions to the collection; bookmarks and Christmas cards designed by Miss Lenski; photograph albums; sketchbooks; scrapbooks (contain photographs, correspondence and sketches); original illustrations; handwritten mss (*Houseboat Girl*, 1957, and *Corn Farm* Boy, 1953); typewritten mss (*Coal Camp* Girl, 1959); articles, plays and speeches written by Miss Lenski; newspaper and magazine clippings; and a tape recording entitled *A Talk with Lois Lenski.*

IL —UNIVERSITY OF ILLINOIS, URBANA/CHAMPAIGN, Library, University Archives, 19 Library, 1408 W Gregory Drive, Urbana, 61801. Maynard Brichford, University Archivist
Holdings: Vols 30,000 Cat
Budget: $7400
Notes: The School Collection consists of fiction and nonfiction for children and young adults. Included are children's classics, easy readers, picture books, folk literature and mythology. In addition to the Newbery and Caldecott winners, national award-winning books which encompass the areas of literature, science and the social sciences are collected. Current representative children's magazines are also part of the collection. A reference collection relevant to the study of children's literature is maintained. An exellent representation of historical children's literature dating back to 1800 is part of the School Collection. Special reprint collections are *Classics of Children's Literature 1621-1932* and the *Osborne Collection of Early Children's Books.* Children's materials from 1600-1800 are in the Rare Book Room.

IN —INDIANA UNIVERSITY, Lilly Library, Seventh St, Bloomington, 47405. William R Cagle, Librn
Holdings: Uncat Mss
Notes: The Elisabeth Ball Collection consists of more than 7000 books and many manuscripts from the late seventeenth to the early twentieth centuries. Strengths include Newbery and other early imprints, chapbooks, horn books, harlequinades, street cries, and miniature books. Mss that are not part of the Ball collection incl some original illustrations for 19th and 20th century books.

IN —INDIANA STATE UNIVERSITY, EVANSVILLE, Library, 8600 University Blvd, Evansville, 47712. Gina R Walker, Acting Archivist
Holdings: Vols 150 Cat
Notes: Building a repesentative collection of children's books and early texts for use by faculty and students of Teacher Education and English Departments. Restricted use: noncirculating.

IN —INDIANAPOLIS-MARION COUNTY PUBLIC LIBRARY, Children's Div, PO Box 211, Indianapolis, 46206. Margaret Barks, Librn
Holdings: Vols 408 Cat
Notes: Indiana Collection incl 245 vols of children's books by Indiana authors and 163 vols of books about Indiana.

IN —BALL STATE UNIVERSITY, Library Science Library, Muncie, 47306. Audrey W Collins, Librn
Holdings: Vols 32,645 Cat
Notes: The Elizabeth Ball Collection of Children's Books in English. The children's collection includes a historical collection of approximately 667 volumes published primarily in the second half of the nineteenth century. Separate catalog.

IA —UNIVERSITY OF IOWA, University Libraries, Iowa City, 52242. Frank Paluka, Head, Special Collections Dept
Holdings: Vols 5070 Cat Mss
Notes: Collection incl 440 mss. See Bernice E Leary's "Milestones in Children's Books," in *Books at Iowa,* April 1970, and Myra Cao, "Some Children's Books by Iowa Writers," in *Books at Iowa,* Nov 1968. Also Frank Paluka, *Iowa Authors: A Bio-Bibliography of Sixty Native Writers* (1967).

CHILDREN'S LITERATURE (cont.)

KS —EMPORIA STATE UNIVERSITY, William Allen White Library, Emporia, 66801. Mary E Bogan, Special Collections Librn
Holdings: Vols (2015) Cat Mss Pix
Notes: The May Massee Collection of children's books edited by Miss Massee over a period of 40 years. Incl manuscripts, proofs, galleys, original art work, dummies, research notes, correspondence, research notes, reminiscences, ephemera, memorabilia, and audiovisual materials based on books published by her. A book catalog of the collection was published in 1979. Copies of this publication may be purchased from the William Allen White Library. *The May Massee Collection: Creative Publishing for Children, 1923-1963, a Checklist,* Dr George V Hodowanec, editor. William Allen White Library, Emporia State University, 1979. (2320 pieces of art work, 18 linear feet of other materials included in the library holdings.)

KS —EMPORIA STATE UNIVERSITY, William Allen White Library, Emporia, 66801. Mary E Bogan, Special Collections Librn
Holdings: Vols (625)
Notes: The Children's Literature Collection contains approx 29,000 children's books and books about Children's Literature. The books in this collection circulate. The William Allen White Children's Book Award Collection and Archives includes the books which have appeared on the White Award Master Lists since 1952 and a special display of those books which have won this award as well as photographs of the authors who have been recipients of the White Award which was the first statewide reader's choice award. The White Award Archives contains manuscripts, original art work, audiotapes, videotapes, photographs, information about the authors, correspondence, Master Lists, bookmarks, voting report forms, tally sheets, publicity and other records related to the White Award. The book collection is cataloged but the archives are not cataloged. (36 linear feet.) Acumulative listing of books which have appeared on White Award Master Lists since 1952-1953 is available for purchase from the William Allen White Library. *The William Allen White Children's Book Award: Books on the Master Lists.* Mary E Bogan, Editor. William Allen White Library, Emporia State University.

KS —UNIVERSITY OF KANSAS, Kenneth Spencer Research Library, Special Collections Dept, Lawrence, 66045. Alexandra Mason, Librn
Holdings: Vols 7000 Cat
Notes: Late 18th to early 20th century, mostly English and American. Noncirculating.

KY —UNIVERSITY OF KENTUCKY, Education Library, Dickey Hall Room 205, Lexington, 40506. Larry Greenwood, Librn
Holdings: Vols 48,000 Cat Microforms
Budget: $6500
Notes: Professional books, model children's and young people's collection, curriculum materials and guides and ERIC collection (297,000 microfiche).

ME —BOWDOIN COLLEGE, Library, Brunswick, 04011. Dianne M Gutscher, Cur of Special Collections
Holdings: Vols Mss
Notes: The Abbott Memorial Collection contains almost every first edition, as well as later ones, of Jacob Abbott's Rollo series and many other children's stories; the Kellogg Collection contains more than 80 volumes of the adventure stories for boys written by Elijah Kellogg (1813-1901); the Charles Asbury Stephens Collection consists of 40 volumes of his writings and 2350 mss of his books, correspondence, speeches and other related items; the Kate Douglas Wiggin Collection consists of her personal library and incl books, mss, clippings, and ephemeral items; the Beston Collection contains printed works, mss, correspondence, and ephemera relating to Henry Beston and his wife, Elizabeth Coatsworth, a widely known author of children's books.

ME —SOUTH PORTLAND PUBLIC LIBRARY, 482 Broadway, South Portland, 04106. Carol Scheffler, Cataloger
Holdings: Vols 1900 Mss Pix
Notes: Papers and books of James Otis Kaler, famous Maine children's author of the 19th century, author of *Toby Tyler.* Also, other books, pre-1920. Separate shelflist.

MD —PRINCE GEORGE'S COUNTY MEMORIAL LIBRARY SYSTEM, Hyattsville Branch Library, 6530 Adelphi Rd, Hyattsville, 20782. Edward Talbert, Librn
Holdings: Vols 2345 Cat Mss Pix
Budget: $1400

MA —AMHERST COLLEGE, Library, Amherst, 01002. John Lancaster, Special Collections Librn
Notes: Collections relating to the life of Samuel Griswold Goodrich, author who wrote as "Peter Parley".

MA —BRANDEIS UNIVERSITY, Goldfarb Library, 415 South St, Waltham, 02154. Bessie Hahn, Dir
Notes: Dime Novel and Juvenile Literature Collection. Over 1000 dime novels, an extensive collection of the works of Horatio Alger, Harry Castlemon, Oliver Optic and other boys and girls literature of the 19th and early 20th century. Access to this collection is through the card catalog in Special Collections.

MA —WELLESLEY FREE LIBRARY, 530 Washington St, Box 308, Wellesley, 02181. Anne L. Reynolds, Dir
Holdings: Vols 858 Cat
Notes: The Ruth Hill Viguers Memorial collection of children's books, old and new, American and foreign.

MA —AMERICAN ANTIQUARIAN SOCIETY LIBRARY, 185 Salisbury St, Worcester, 01609. Marcus A McCorison, Dir & Librn
Holdings: Vols 8000 Cat
Notes: From 1821-1876, incl McLaughlin brothers' imprints.

MA —WORCESTER STATE COLLEGE, Learning Resources Center, 486 Chandler St, Worcester, 01602. William G Piekarski, Special Collections Librn
Holdings: Vols 8000 Cat

MI —DETROIT PUBLIC LIBRARY, Language and Literature Dept, 5201 Woodward Ave, Detroit, 48202. Ann Rabjohns, Chief
Holdings: Vols 4000 //
Notes: Reference collection of children's literature encompassing many subjects. Half of it is cataloged. Chiefly 19th and early 20th century material, illustrating the history of writing for children, incl classics, oddities, and types or titles popular at a particular time. Historical Collection in Language and Literature Department. Rare children's books in Rare Book Room.

MI —WAYNE STATE UNIVERSITY, Kresge Library (Education), Detroit, 48202. Theodore Manheim, Librn
Holdings: Vols (65,000) Cat Mss Microforms
Budget: ($2000)
Notes: The Eloise Ramsey Collection (10, 000 vols). See, *The Eloise Ramsey Collection of Literature for Young People: A Catalogue;* compiled by Joan Cusenza (Detroit: Wayne State University Libraries, 1967). Besides the Ramsey Collection, which is housed separately and does not circulate, the Education Library has approx 55,000 volumes of children's and young adults' literature, with a very large picture-book collection, a large poetry collection; all with special emphasis on urban and ethnic materials.

MI —MICHIGAN STATE UNIVERSITY, Libraries, Special Collections Div, East Lansing, 48824. Jannette Fiore, Librn
Notes: The Russel B Nye Popular Culture Collection in the Michigan State Univ Libraries incl over (45,000) items. Most of the collection is organized into 4 categories: comic art, popular fiction, popular information materials and materials relating to the popular performing arts. Popular fiction in the collection is organized into juvenile, detective-mystery, and science fiction, westerns and women's fiction. In addition, there is a sample collection of dime novels and story papers (ca 400 issues representing nearly 100 titles). Pulp magazines which fall into none of the separate categories are housed with the dime novels and story papers. Juvenile Fiction: ca 4000 vols. Emphasis is on juvenile series fiction of the 19th and 20th centuries, with nearly 200 girls and 300 boys series represented. 19th-century "Sunday School" books andboth fiction and non-fiction scouting books are also included. Western Fiction: An exceptionally fine institutional collection, with over 3000 novels (most published between 1900 and 1950), almost all hardbound and in dust jackets, and nearly 500 pulp magazine issues representing more than fifty titles. The most important pulp runs are Street and Smith's *Western Story* Magazine and Warner Publications's *Ranch* Romances. Women's Fiction: Over 3000 novels and ca 1000 issues of romance, confession and movie magazines and pulps from the 1920s through the 1970s. Most of the novels are in the romance category, with over 2000 Harlequin novels, a good representation of other modern best-selling romances, and several dozen titles from late 19th-century romance series. Science Fiction: ca 3000 books and periodicals. MSU is a depository for the Science Fiction Writersof America, which contributes review copies of new books. The bulk of the collection is periodicals, with 71 titles represented. Most issues come from the period from the late 1940s to the present. The collection subscribes to most major science fiction magazines and holds a fanzine collection which now numbers over 2500. Detective-Mystery Fiction: ca 3500 novels, in paper and hardback, and pulps representing 28 titles from 1920-1950. Complete runs of *The London Mystery* Magazine and *Ellery Queen's Mystery* Magazine are included, along with a large sample collection of the more sensational detective and crime fiction magazines from the 1930s through the present.

MI —AQUINAS COLLEGE, Learning Resource Center, 1607 Robinson Rd SE, Grand Rapids, 49506. Larry Zysk, Dir
Holdings: Vols (55)// Cat
Notes: Mother Goose in all languages. Built on a collection began as a gift from a former Grand Rapids teacher, Miss Coye.

MI —CENTRAL MICHIGAN UNIVERSITY, Clarke Historical Library, Mount Pleasant, 48859. William H Mulligan, Jr, Dir; William Miles, Biography Collections Librn
Notes: Lucile Clarke Memorial Children's Library. Strength in British and American pre-1920 material.

MN —UNIVERSITY OF MINNESOTA, Libraries, Children's Literature Research Collections, 109 Walter Library, Minneapolis, 55455. Karen Nelson Hoyle, Cur
Holdings: Vols (40,000) Cat Mss Pix
Notes: Incl first editions, mss, and illustrations for children's books. Newbery and Caldecott award books and honor books and their translations; Mildred L Batchelder Award nominees in original and US editions. Kerlan Collection.

MN —COLLEGE OF SAINT CATHERINE, Library, 2004 Randolph Ave, Saint Paul, 55105. Sister Elizabeth Delmore, Library Dir
Holdings: Vols 2100 Cat Mss Pix Phonorecords Audiotapes
Budget: $500
Notes: The Ruth Sawyer Collection. Also personal letters, medals.

MS —UNIVERSITY OF SOUTHERN MISSISSIPPI, William David McCain Graduate Library, Box 5148, Southern Sta, Hattiesburg, 39406.
Holdings: Vols (20,000) Mss Pix
Notes: The Lena Y de Grummond Collection. Literary mss, correspondence and original illustrations for children's books, original editions of children's books and magazines, 1530-date. Approx 2100 feet. Incl works by over 900 authors and

CHILDREN'S LITERATURE (cont.)

illustrators, among them Kate Greenaway, Randolph Caldecott, Maud and Miska Petersham, Merritt Mauzey, Berta and Elmer Hader, Scott O'Dell, Lois Lenski, Roger Duvoisin, Lynd Ward, Taro Yashima, Marcia Brown, Adrienne Adams, Madeleine L'Engle, Barbara Cooney and Nonny Hogrogian. Robert L Dartt Collection of over 1800 books for boys from the late 19th and early 20th centuries. Extensive Henty (over 550 vols), Alger, Brereton, Castlemon, Fenn, Kingston, Optic, and Stratemeyer holdings. Catalog in progress.

MO —SAINT LOUIS PUBLIC LIBRARY, Gardner Rare Book Room, 1301 Olive St, Saint Louis, 63103. Julanne M Good, Supervisor; Martha Riley, Rare Books Librn
Holdings: Vols 25,000 Cat
Budget: $7400
Notes: Children's books and adult readings concerning the juvenile materials.

NE —KEENE MEMORIAL LIBRARY, Children's Library, 1030 N Broad St, Fremont, 68025. Mary Scheele, Children's Librn
Holdings: Vols (35,000) Cat Phonorecords Filmstrips
Budget: ($10,000)
Notes: Keene Memorial Library (Fremont Public Library) combined with former Nebraska Library Commission Juvenile collection. It is a working collection, nearly all 20th century, English-language materials. Strengths incl multiple editions of standard children's titles, such as Robin Hood, tales of King Arthur, and examples of the work of most children's book illustrators from 1900 to present.

NH —PLYMOUTH STATE COLLEGE, Lamson Library, Plymouth, 03264. Phillip Wei, Dir of Library Services
Holdings: Cat Pix Microforms Films
Budget: ($30,000)
Notes: Incl 30,000 prints and 87,000 nonprint items.

NJ —SOMERSET COUNTY LIBRARY, Northbridge & Vogt Dr, Box 6700, Bridgewater, 08807. Elizabeth Griesbach, Head Reference Librn
Holdings: Vols (2500) Cat Mss Maps Pix Audiotapes
Notes: Historical and modern history; state (NJ) depository documents; juvenile collection; New Jersey periodicals; vertical files (26 drawers); and landmark survey on each county municipality. Separate catalog in New Jersey Room. Restricted use; noncirculating.

NY —PRATT INSTITUTE LIBRARY, 200 Willoughby Ave, Brooklyn, 11205. Tad G Kumatz, Asst Dir
Holdings: Vols 8500 Cat Pix //
Budget: ($135,000)
Notes: Incl about 765 historical children's books. 1830-1920. Also, numerous books autographed by Anne Carroll Moore, first Children's Librarian at Pratt Institute Library.

NY —EASTCHESTER HISTORICAL SOCIETY LIBRARY, Box 37, Eastchester, 10709. Madeline D Schaeffer, Librn
Holdings: Vols (6000) Cat Mss Maps Pix Slides
Notes: New York State history with emphasis on Westchester County and local area. Also children's literature, 1750-1910, and juvenile textbooks, 1790-1910. No photocopying.

NY —C W POST CENTER OF LONG ISLAND UNIVERSITY, B Davis Schwartz Memorial Library, Greenvale, 11548. Manju Prasad-Rao, Media Librn
Holdings: Pix Slides Phonorecords Audiotapes Videotapes 16mm Films Filmstrips
Budget: ($12,500)
Notes: The Center, while originally established for schools of Education and Library Science with a k-12 text and trade book collection and media, now incl a circulating non-print collection for the entire campus. (8000) Separate card catalog. Incl children's trade books (17,000); k-12 textbooks (1562 series); and k-12 curriculum guides (3053).

NY —BANK STREET COLLEGE OF EDUCATION LIBRARY, 610 W 112 St, New York, 10025. Eleanor Kule Seid, Library Dir
Holdings: Vols (80,000) Cat Microforms
Budget: ($29,000)
Notes: Education, guidance, psychology, educational psychology, curricula, textbooks, Black Studies, etc. All subjects are integrated in one professional collection; in addition there are two separately cataloged and shelved collections: Children's and Elementary Curriculum Materials.

NY —CHILDREN'S BOOK COUNCIL, Library, 67 Irving Place, New York, 10003.
Holdings: Vols (4,000) Cat
Notes: Besides award-winning books. the Children's Book Council maintains a non-circulating examination collection of children's books published by CBC members during the past year, adding books of the current year as they are published. Collection also incl critical and historical studies of children's books; bibliographies, selection aids and other reference books; biographies of authors and illustrators; facsimile editions and catalogs of collections and exhibitions; and books about publishing, writing, and storytelling. There is an author/title card catalog and a separate illustrator card catalog for this collection. No photocopying.

NY —CITY UNIVERSITY OF NEW YORK, City College, Library, 138 St & Convent Ave, New York, 10031. Vira C Hinds, Assoc Prof
Holdings: Vols (35,000) Cat
Budget: ($9173)
Notes: Education, incl juveniles (10,437), textbooks, and ERIC collection. Separate author catalog.

NY —COLUMBIA UNIVERSITY LIBRARIES, Teachers College, Milbank Memorial Library, 525 W 120 St, New York, 10027. Jane P Franck, Dir
Holdings: Vols 2900 Cat
Notes: Historical collection of children's books mostly from the 19th century. A few titles from late 18th and early 20th. Many foreign as well as US titles.

†NY —COLUMBIA UNIVERSITY LIBRARIES, Butler Library, Rare Book and Manuscript Library, 535 W 114 St, New York, 10027.
Notes: A collection of the art work of Tibor Gergely, containing 2,824 watercolors, pen-and-ink drawings, and sketches. Gergely is best known for his illustrations of the popular Golden Book Series for children.

NY —SCHOLASTIC MAGAZINES, Editorial Library, 730 Broadway, New York, 10003. Lucy Evankow, Chief Librn

NY —US COMMITTEE FOR UNICEF, Information Center on Children's Cultures, 331 E 38 St, New York, 10016. Melinda Greenblatt, Chief Librn
Holdings: Vols (17,500) Cat Pix Slides Films Filmstrips
Notes: Social and cultural aspects of lives of children from developing countries. Especially strong in the area of school textbooks from Near Eastern Asian, African, Latin American, Caribbean, and Pacific Area countries; holidays and celebrations related to children all over the world; children's books in English which describe child life in other countries. Especially strong collection of folklore, and folklore of children, from all regions mentioned above.

NY —VASSAR COLLEGE, Library, Rare Books & Manuscripts Collection, Box 20, Poughkeepsie, 12601. Lisa Browar, Cur
Notes: Predominantly 19th and early 20th centuries.

NY —MARGARET WOODBURY STRONG MUSEUM, 1 Manhattan Square, Rochester, 14607.
Holdings: Vols (20,000) Periodicals
Notes: The Margaret Woodbury Strong Museum Library contains a collection of approx 20,000 books, periodicals and ephemera of and concerning the 19th and early 20th centuries. A large part of the library's holdings reflect the interests of Margaret Strong and her family: domestic life and literature of the 19th century and world travel, with particular emphasis on the Orient. The library's resources are available to all visitors for research. Book stacks and rare book storage are not open for browsing and do not circulate, but facilities are provided in reading room for study.

NY —STATE UNIVERSITY OF NEW YORK, STONY BROOK, Melville Library, Dept of Special Collections, Stony Brook, 11794. Evert Volkersz, Head
Holdings: Vols 2500
Notes: English and American children's literature, early 19th century to present. Partially catalogued.

NC —APPALACHIAN STATE UNIVERSITY, Belk Library, Instructional Materials Center, Boone, 28608. Selma P Farthing, Librn
Holdings: Vols (31,847) Cat Pix Slides Phonorecords Audiotapes Videotapes Filmstrips Microforms 16mm Films
Budget: ($10,500)
Notes: Scope of the collection is life-long learning. Serving as a working laboratory for educators at all levels, we collect materials in every format available. The Instructional Materials Center has its own card catalog, and the holdings are also listed in the library's central catalog. Collection incl textbooks, children's literature, tests and computer software.

NC —UNIVERSITY OF NORTH CAROLINA, CHARLOTTE, J Murrey Atkins Library, UNCC Station, Charlotte, 28223. Robert F Brabham Jr, Special Collections Librn
Holdings: Vols 500 Cat Mss
Notes: Principally American and English. Strength of the collection is US, 1800-1850. Incl 200 vols from the collection of Elizabeth Botteme Lewis. Also incl first editions of Andrew Lang's fairy books, several series of books for boys (early 20th century), and 1960s comic books. Also incl small collection of papers of and ephemera collected by Wilbur Macey Stone, collector and writer about historical children's books.

NC —UNIVERSITY OF NORTH CAROLINA, GREENSBORO, Walter Clinton Jackson Library, Special Collections Dept, 1000 Spring Garden St, Greensboro, 27412. Emilie W Mills, Librn
Holdings: Vols 2500
Notes: The Lois Lenski Collection of Early American Children's Books Incl miniature books, letters, valentines, panoramas, hornbooks, toy books dating from the 18th century, which were part of Miss Lenski's personal collection. Emphasis is on the 19th century. Some foreign imprints and foreign language editions are incl and some very rare items. Also, a collection of 300 vols presented by Mary V Graver, of Danville, Va, in memory of Mary Frances Kennon Johnson.

OH —OHIO UNIVERSITY, Vernon R Alden Library, Department of Archives and Special Collections, Athens, 45701. Gary A Hunt, Head
Holdings: Vols (1400) Uncat
Notes: A miscellaneous collection of children's books by American and English authors, with most imprint dates in the period 1870-1930; numerous series books. Authors incl Jacob Abbott (196 v), "Oliver Optic" (84 v), Horatio Alger (89 v), J H Ewing (53 v), Martha Finley (47 v), G A Henty (46 v), Frank V Webster (38 v), and many others.

OH —BOWLING GREEN STATE UNIVERSITY, Library, Popular Culture Library, Bowling Green, 43403.
Notes: Extensive holdings of Big-Little books, comic books, matchbook covers, picture postcards, personal scrapbooks, trading cards, posters, magazines, film pressbooks, juvenile series novels and popular literature.

OH —HEBREW UNION COLLEGE-JEWISH INSTITUTE OF RELIGION, Klau Library, 3101 Clifton Ave, Cincinnati, 45220. David J Gilner, Reference Librn
Holdings: Cat
Notes: The Jewish Holocaust (1939-1945)

CHILDREN'S LITERATURE (cont.)

collection. Incl large collections of memorial books, curricula and juvenile fiction.

OH —CASE WESTERN RESERVE UNIVERSITY, M A Baxter School of Information and Library Science, 10900 Euclid Ave, Cleveland, 44106. Bettina MacAyeal, Librn; Gretchen Larson, Librn
Holdings: Vols (1100)
Notes: Incl collection of 1100 historical children's books and periodicals, housed in the Special Collections Dept of Freiberger Library, and can be used by the public. Incl *The Holy Bible Abridged* published by Isaiah Thomas in 1786, *The Life and Strange Surprising Adventures of Robinson Crusoe* of 1790, and a *Cinderella* dated 1809. There are examples of the work of illustrators Walter Crane, Randolph Caldecott, Kate Greenaway and Maurice Boutet de Monvel. The periodical collection incl a complete run of St. Nicholas Magazine.

OH —CLEVELAND PUBLIC LIBRARY, Children's Literature Dept, 325 Superior Ave, Cleveland, 44114. Ruth M Hadlow, Head
Holdings: Cat Phonorecords
Notes: A general collection with special attention to the demands of adults working with children, eg, college students and teachers. Other titles of special significance are retained to provide a sequence of children's literature. Incl book/cassette and book/record combinations.

OK —OKLAHOMA DEPT OF LIBRARIES, 200 NE 18 St, Oklahoma City, 73105. Susan Galloway, Public Library Consultant for Children's Services
Holdings: Vols 2500 Cat
Budget: $1800
Notes: A basic juvenile collection, for use with the current publications in the *Juvenile Review Collection*. Based on titles incl in *Children's Catalog* and *Junior High School* Catalog. Also 2000-4000 current publications retained for 2 years. File of related reviews and evaluations retained. Author catalog only. Uncirculating.

OR —UNIVERSITY OF OREGON LIBRARY, Special Collections Div, Eugene, 97403. Kenneth W Duckett, Curator
Holdings: Vols (11,500) Cat Mss Pix
Notes: Collection contains 250,000 pieces, incl original mss, correspondence, dummy books, and original illustrations from Harriet Stratemayer Adams, Clyde Bulla, Ruth Robinson Carroll, Edgar and Ingri d'Aulaire, James Daugherty, Roger Duvoisin, Leonard Everett Fisher, Jean Fritz, Hardie Gramatky, Berta and Elmer Hader, Holling C Holling, Evelyn Sibley Lampman, Maud Hart Lovelace, James Marshall, Walt Morey, Clare Newberry, Scott O'Dell, Lucille Ogle, Willy Pogany, Kate Seredy, Yoshiko Uchida, Lynd Ward, Kurt Wiese and many others. Incl 5,000 vols uncat of c19-c20 children's books in the Ogle collection. Publication: Martin Schmitt, Comp. *Catalogue of Manuscripts in the University of Oregon* Library (Eugene: University of Oregon Books, 1971).

PA —DREXEL UNIVERSITY LIBRARIES, Library Science Library, 32 & Chestnut Sts, Philadelphia, 19104. Timothy LaBorie, Librn
Holdings: Vols 7500
Budget: $2100
Notes: Incl Children's literature and school library materials in book and multimedia formats.

PA —FREE LIBRARY OF PHILADELPHIA, Central Children's Dept, Logan Sq, Philadelphia, 19103. Ellen Whitney, Head
Holdings: Vols (30,382) Cat Mss Pix
Notes: Special collections of children's literature dating from 1837 to the present are maintained by the Central Children's Department. These collections include Historical Bibliography, the Kathrine M McAlarney Collection of Illustrated Children's Books, the Folklore Collection, the Historical Collection which includes children's periodicals and the Series Collection. Featured in these non-circulating research collections are works of outstanding illustrators in the field of children's books, books by Philadelphia and Pennsylvania authors, books about Philadelphia and Pennsylvania people and places, and books published in Philadelphia and Pennsylvania. Included also are framed originals as well as manuscripts and typescripts by Evaline Ness, material for Lloyd Alexander books, Virginia Lee Burton, Marguerite (Lofft) deAngeli, Beatrice Schenk (Freedman) DeRegniers, EulalieOsgood Grover, Carolyn Haywood, Elizabeth Hoffman Honness, Kristin (Eggleston) Hunter [on loan to Free Library], Margaret Oldroyd Hyde, Katherine Milhous, Scott O'Dell, Lucy Fitch Perkins, Elizabeth Blake Ripley, Tomi Ungerer, Hendrik Willem Van Loon and Lucille Wallower. *The Checklist of Children's* Books, 1837-1876, published in 1975 and available in limited supply in book form, but also available in microform from the Office of Work with Children, Free Library of Philadelphia, lists all books in Special Collections during this period at date of publication. These special collections supplement the Rosenbach Collection of Early American Children's Books, the American Sunday School Union Collection, the Elisabeth Ball Collection of Hornbooks, and other children's books published prior to 1837, all of which are housed in the Rare Book Department of the Free Library ofPhiladelphia.

PA —CARNEGIE LIBRARY OF PITTSBURGH, Children's Dept, 4400 Forbes Ave, Pittsburgh, 15213. Amy Kellman, Head
Holdings: Vols 2000 Cat
Notes: Historical children's books. Strong in folk tales.

†PA —UNIVERSITY OF PITTSBURGH, Graduate School of Library & Information Sciences Library, L I S Bldg, Third Fl, Pittsburgh, 15260. Jean Kindlin, Librn
Notes: History collection of children's literature, 5000 volumes. Archives of Mr Rogers Neighborhood television series.

RI —BROWN UNIVERSITY, John Hay Library, Harris Collection, Prospect St, Providence, 02912. Rosemary L Cullen, Cur
Holdings: Vols (200,000) Cat Mss Pix Phonorecords Microforms
Budget: ($15,000)
Notes: The Harris Collection of American Poetry and Plays is principally composed of American and Canadian poetry and plays, 17th century-date. Extensive holdings in songsters, gift books and annuals, hymnals, pageants, broadside verse, carriers' addresses, women poets, juvenile poetry, (incl Mother Goose and *The Night Before* Christmas), sheet music with lyrics, small press publications, fine printing, black poets, "little magazines," Yiddish-American literature. All movements or schools of American poetry are represented. Incl first editions of most American poets and playwrights, notably Whitman, Poe, Wallace Stevens, Eugene O'Neill, Edward Albee, Ezra Pound, T S Eliot, William Carlos Williams, Amy Lowell, Phyllis Wheatley, Robert Frost, Allen Ginsberg, Bliss Carman, and Stephen Foster sheet music. Also incl the Saunders Walt Whitman Collection (1300 vols); the LangdonCollection of Pageants (250 vols); the Asa Cushman Collection of plays in ms and prompt copies; the MacDougall Collection of Psalters and Hymnals; 4000 plays issued by Walter H Baker Co, Boston (1890-1957); the Vaxer Collection of Yiddish Poetry, Plays and Music (1700 vols). Collections incl 200,000 vols, 30,000 broadsides, 55,000 mss, 170,000 pieces of sheet music, 450 phonorecords, and 375 microfilm reels. See *Dictionary Catalog of the Harris Collection of American Poetry and Plays* (Boston: G K Hall, 1972), 13 vols; *Supplement* (1977), 3 vols. See also, *American Poetry*, 1609-1900, *A Collection on Microfilm, Segment I* (1609-1820); *Segment II* (1821-1850); *Segment III* (1851-1870) (Woodbridge, Conn: Research Publications). Separate catalog.

RI —PROVIDENCE PUBLIC LIBRARY, 150 Empire St, Providence, 02903. Lance J Bauer, Special Collections Librn
Holdings: Vols 2000 Cat Mss Pix
Notes: The Edith Wetmore Collection of Books for Children. Collection spans 400 years in 20 languages, incl Japanese and Arabic, with primary emphasis on 19th and 20th century books in English. First editions of many important children's writers with many important children's illustrators represented. In addition, this collection is rich in scarce ephemeral material such as chapbooks, toybooks, peepshows, nursery rhymes and London street cries. Material must be used in-house. Photocopying when condition of material allows.
See also entry under Black Studies

RI —WESTERLY PUBLIC LIBRARY, Broad St, Westerly, 02891. David J Panciera, Library Dir
Holdings: Vols 100// Uncat Mss Pix
Notes: The Margaret Wise Brown Collection of books, correspondence, etc, was donated to the library in 1957. At present the library owns the most complete collection of the famous author and illustrator's works of children's picture books. There is a listing of the books, but no listing of the other material at present.

SC —UNIVERSITY OF SOUTH CAROLINA, Thomas Cooper Library, Columbia, 29208. Kenneth E Toombs, Dir of Libraries; Roger Mortimer, Rare Book Librn
Holdings: Vols 1200 Cat
Notes: Very strong for English language editions for the 18th, 19th and early 20th centuries.

SC —FRANCIS MARION COLLEGE, James A Rogers Library, Florence, 29501. H Paul Dove, Dir; Roger K Hux, Special Collections Librn
Holdings: Vols (600) Cat Mss Audiotapes Microforms
Notes: The Pee Dee Region of South Carolina. Emphasis on Colonial and Revolutionary periods, rice and indigo culture, plantations. Includes old rural church library with children's books.

SC —WOFFORD COLLEGE, Sandor Teszler Library, N Church St, Spartanburg, 29301. Frank J Anderson, Librn
Holdings: Vols 500 Uncat
Notes: Principally children's books of late 19th and early 20th century, incl SC textbooks and Sunday School tracts. Described in: *Children's Literature,* compiled by Elizabeth Sabin (Wofford College Library. Special Collections Checklist no 3), Spartanburg, SC: Wofford Library Press, 1970; 32 pp, mimeo. (Does not incl later acquistitions.)

TN —GEORGE PEABODY COLLEGE FOR TEACHERS, Education Library, Science Library, Peabody College, Box 325, Nashville, 32703. Mary Beth Blalock, Librn
Holdings: Vols (28,493) Cat
Budget: ($14,000)
Notes: Incl collection of adolescent and children's literature. There are separate catalogs for this collection and the library science collection.

TX —SAINT EDWARD'S UNIVERSITY, Curriculum Materials Collection, 3001 S Congress, Austin, 78704. Joseph Sprug, Director
Holdings: Vols 850 Cat
Notes: Collection consists of French, German, Spanish (300 titles), and other languages.

TX —WEST TEXAS STATE UNIVERSITY, Cornette Library, PO Box 748 WT Sta, Canyon, 79016. Alan D Gabehart, Circulation Librn
Holdings: Vols 6400 Cat Microforms
Notes: Includes microform collections.

TX —DALLAS PUBLIC LIBRARY, Central Library, Humanities Division, 1515 Young St, Dallas, 75201. Richard L Waters, Acting Dir; Muriel W Brown, Children's Literature Specialist; Rosemarie Dunlap, Assistant to Children's Literature Specialist
Holdings: Vols (56,000) Cat Mss Pix Microforms
Budget: $26,000
Notes: Incl Mother Goose Books, autographed Newbery and Caldecott winners, books important in the history of children's literature, foreign language books, and Texas books in addition to a general collection.

CHILDREN'S LITERATURE (cont.)

TX —NORTH TEXAS STATE UNIVERSITY, Libraries, NT Station Box 5188, Denton, 76203. Margaret Galloway, General Librn; Pat Stinson, Library Science Librn
Holdings: Vols 29,776
Notes: Juvenile Collection. Incl 1500 rare items located in the Rare Book Room. Card catalogs for both regular and rare collections. Rare items cover primarily 1800-1940.

TX —TEXAS WOMAN'S UNIVERSITY, Bralley Memorial Library, Box 23715, TWU Sta, Denton, 76204. Metta Nicewarner, Spec Collections Libn
Holdings: Vols 3000
Notes: D Genevieve Dixon Collection of Books for Children and Young Adults. Many autographed copies. Strong in complete works of popular writers of the early 20th century.

TX —FORT WORTH PUBLIC LIBRARY, 300 Taylor St, Fort Worth, 76102. Camille Connor, Children's Materials Coordinator
Holdings: Vols (300) Cat
Budget: $500
Notes: Professional Reference Collection/ Children's Literature. Some 300 titles incl books, pamphlets, bibliographies and photocopied articles used primarily as reference tools or sources by librarians, students of children's literature and other adults working with children in the areas of children's literature and library programming for children. Collection is cataloged with access through the general catalog.

TX —TRINITY UNIVERSITY, Elizabeth Coates Maddux Library, 715 Stadium Dr, San Antonio, 78284. Richard Hume Werking, Library Dir; Craig Likness, Head Bibliographer
Notes: General reference.

VA —ARLINGTON COUNTY LIBRARIES, Children's Room, Central Room, 1015 N Quincy St, Arlington, 22201. Caroline Parr, Head
Holdings: Vols (305) Cat
Notes: The Francis and Elizabeth Booth Silver illustrator's collection; outstanding examples of illustration in children's books. Collection was begun in 1962. Incl framed original illustrations by contemporary illustrators. Anniversary brochure listing holdings was published in 1972. Collection incl early 19th century and contemporary illustrators. Books not available for interlibrary loan. No photocopying.

WA —UNIVERSITY OF WASHINGTON LIBRARIES, Suzzallo Library, Curriculum Materials Section, FM-25, Seattle, 98195. Jean Belch, Head
Holdings: Vols 22,500 Cat
Budget: ($7239)
Notes: Included are winners of all major children's literature awards in the United States and Great Britain, as well as some discontinued juvenile periodicals, notably a virtually complete set of *St Nicholas* magazine. There are approximately 7,600 books in the Children's Literature Archive, a collection acquired from libraries in the Northwest and Alaska. The basic imprint parameters are "no later than 1942, or 1946 if World War II oriented."

WI —UNIVERSITY OF WISCONSIN, MADISON, Library School Library, 600 N Park St, Madison, 53706. Sally Davis, Librn
Notes: 5000 vols of juvenile literature, incl picture books in French, German, Norwegian, Swedish, and Russian, children's classics, folk and fairy tales, juvenile illustrators and current writing, maintained at the UW Library School Library. Children's literature does not circulate outside University.

WI —UNIVERSITY OF WISCONSIN, MADISON, Cooperative Children's Book Center, Helen C White Hall, Rm 4290, 600 N Park St, Madison, 53706. Ginny Moore Kruse, Dir
Holdings: Vols (25,000) Cat
Notes: Incl most US trade books published for children in last 24 months; first editions of recommended US children's trade books published since 1965; over 400 alternative press books published for children in US and Canada since 1970; children's books about Wisconsin and by Wisconsin authors and illustrators; representative 19th and early 20th century American children's books; 19th century children's periodicals; first and significant editions of Newbury and Caldecott Medal books; historical and contemporary toybooks; 75 vols of Mother Goose published since 1828; 160 vols of Thorton Burgess books, many first editions; ms and original artwork for Ellen Raskin's *The Westing Game* and *The Mysterious Disappearance of Leon (I Mean Noel);* juvenile mass market and trade romance fiction.

WI —MILWAUKEE PUBLIC LIBRARY, 814 W Wisconsin Ave, Milwaukee, 53233. Donald J Sager, City Librn
Holdings: Vols 700
Notes: Includes titles indexed in *Index To Fairy Tales, Myths and Legends* by Mary Huse Eastman and supplements and in Norma Olin Ireland's *Index to Fairy Tales 1949-1972.*

WI —UNIVERSITY OF WISCONSIN, MILWAUKEE, Library, Box 604, Milwaukee, 53201. William C Roselle, Dir
Holdings: Vols (25,945) Cat Pix Slides Phonorecords Audiotapes Filmstrips
Notes: A card catalog of all items except textbooks is available in the department. The collection includes 14,200 children's literature books for grades kindergarten through ninth with emphasis on honor and notable book titles; a textbook collection for grades 1-12 including some programmed texts; a curriculum guide and resource unit file of 3000 items.

BC —UNIVERSITY OF BRITISH COLUMBIA, Library, Special Collections Div, 1956 Main Mall, Vancouver, V6T 1Y3, Can. Anne Yandle, Head
Holdings: Vols 1000 Cat Mss
Notes: Collection consists of English and American children's literature of 19th and 20th century up to the 1940s.

BC —VANCOUVER PUBLIC LIBRARY, Boys & Girls Div, 750 Burrard St, Vancouver, V6Z 1X5, Can.
Holdings: Vols 839 Cat
Notes: The Marion Thompson Collection. Books dating from 1726-1910 which have been read by children over the years. Access to the collection is provided through author/ title/subject and chronological indexes.

MB —UNIVERSITY OF WINNIPEG, Department of English, 515 Portage Ave, Winnipeg, R3B 2E9, Can. Perry Nodelman, Cur
Holdings: Vols 1000 Cat
Notes: This collection represents the kind of material children read during the 19th and early 20th century on the Canadian Prairies, not necessarily "Children's Literature."

ON —QUEEN'S UNIVERSITY, Douglas Library, Kingston, K7L 5C4, Can. William F E Morley, Cur, Special Collections
Holdings: Vols 2100 Uncat Pix
Notes: World classics and little known titles in English (mostly). Small reference collection. Incl school books, mainly Canadian.

†ON —UNIVERSITY OF WESTERN ONTARIO, School of Library and Information Science, Special Collections Room, London, N6A 5B9, Can.
Holdings: Vols 5500 Cat
Notes: The collection of children's books incl the 2855 volume Children's History collection, 1583-1950. Complimented by reference works in the School's main library.

ON —NATIONAL LIBRARY OF CANADA, 395 Wellington St, Ottawa, K1A 0N4, Can. Andre Preibish, Dir
Holdings: Vols 12,000
Notes: Canadian children's books in English, French and other languages, supported by a collection of professional literature and supplemented by major award-winning books from other countries and selected major works on special themes such as folklore.

ON —TORONTO PUBLIC LIBRARY, Osborne Collection of Early Children's Books, 40 St George St, Toronto, M5S 2E4, Can. Margaret Crawford Maloney, Special Collections Librn
Holdings: Vols 21,500 Cat Mss Pix Slides
Notes: *Osborne Collection of Early Children's Books: A Catalogue,* 2 vols, published by the Toronto Public Library, 1958; 1975. The Osborne Collection is chiefly books published in England from the fourteenth century through 1910, with first or early editions in the original languages of books adopted by English-speaking children. The Lillian H Smith Collection comprises distinguished children's books in English published since 1910, selected for both literary and artistic qualities. The Canadiana Collection consists of 3500 children's books in English by Canadians, about Canada or published in Canada. Friends of the Osborne and Lillian H Smith Collections organized in 1966. Worldwide membership (over 600 in 1983). Publishes an annual gift-book for members (16 titles to date).

ON —UNIVERSITY OF WINDSOR, Faculty of Education, 600 Third Concession, Windsor, N9E 1A5, Can. T J Robinson, Librn
Holdings: Vols 400 Cat
Notes: History of children's literature. No photocopying. ERIC research reports collection and ONTERIS research reports collection on microfiche.

CHILDREN'S LITERATURE—JUVENILE SERIES

CT —YALE UNIVERSITY, Box 1603A, Yale Station, New Haven, 06520.
Notes: Incl the Gimbel Collection of Science Fiction Dime Novels, the Frank Reade and Jack Wright "boy inventor" dime novels published before 1900, and the Bryher Collection of boys' books.

DC —LIBRARY OF CONGRESS, Children's Literature Center, Washington, 20540. Sybille Jagusch, Chief
Holdings: Cat
Notes: Extensive holdings of works by Jacob Abbott, Oliver Optic (Adams, William T), Alden (Pansy), Samuel G Goodrich (Peter Parley), many in Rare Book and Special Collections Division.

FL —UNIVERSITY OF SOUTH FLORIDA, Library, Tampa, 33620. J B Dobkin, Special Collections Librn
Holdings: Vols 7000 Cat
Budget: ($7500)
Notes: The Harry K Hudson Collection of American Juvenile Series Books of boys' and girls' fiction issued in series in the 19th and first part of the 20th century. Comprehensive coverage of boys' series books, incl many specimens in original dust jackets (approximately 5000 volumes). Books arranged by series with in-house finding aids rather than card catalog access. Collection contains book material only.

MA —BRANDEIS UNIVERSITY, Goldfarb Library, 415 South St, Waltham, 02154. Bessie Hahn, Dir
Notes: Dime Novel and Juvenile Literature Collection. Over 1000 dime novels, an extensive collection of the works of Horatio Alger, Harry Castlemon, Oliver Optic and other boys and girls literature of the 19th and early 20th century. Access to this collection is through the card catalog in Special Collections.

MI —MICHIGAN STATE UNIVERSITY, Libraries, Special Collections Div, East Lansing, 48824. Jannette Fiore, Librn
Holdings: Vols 5000 Mss Pix
Notes: The Russel B Nye Popular Culture Collection in the Michigan State Univ Libraries incl over (45,000) items. Most of the collection is organized into 4 categories: comic art, popular fiction, popular information materials and materials relating to the popular performing arts. Juvenile Fiction: about 4000 vols. Emphasis is on juvenile series fiction of the 19th and 20th centuries, with nearly 200 girls and over 300 boys series represented. 19th century "Sunday School" books and both fiction and non-fiction scouting books are also included.

MN —UNIVERSITY OF MINNESOTA, Libraries, Children's Literature Research

CHILDREN'S LITERATURE—JUVENILE SERIES (cont.)

Collections, 109 Walter Library, Minneapolis, 55455. Karen Nelson Hoyle, Cur
Holdings: Vols 6600 Cat
Notes: Bibliography of Girls Series Books (1900-1950) in progress. Kerlan Collection.

NC —UNIVERSITY OF NORTH CAROLINA, CHARLOTTE, J Murrey Atkins Library, UNCC Station, Charlotte, 28223. Robert F Brabham Jr, Special Collections Librn
Holdings: Vols 500 Cat Mss
Notes: Principally American and English. Strength of the collection is US, 1800-1850. Incl 200 vols from the collection of Elizabeth Botteme Lewis. Also incl first editions of Andrew Lang's fairy books, several series of books for boys (early 20th century), and 1960s comic books. Also incl small collection of papers of and ephemera collected by Wilbur Macey Stone, collector and writer about historical children's books.

NC —UNIVERSITY OF NORTH CAROLINA, GREENSBORO, Walter Clinton Jackson Library, Special Collections Dept, 1000 Spring Garden St, Greensboro, 27412. Emilie W Mills, Librn
Holdings: Vols 500 Cat
Notes: American series books for girls incl the Bobbsey Twins, Campfire Girls, Elsie Books, Honey Bunch, Pollyanna and many other series turned ouyt by the Stratemeyer Syndicate. Emphasis is on late 19th century to the mid-20th century. A part of the larger collection of early children's literature.

PA —FREE LIBRARY OF PHILADELPHIA, Central Children's Dept, Logan Sq, Philadelphia, 19103. Ellen Whitney, Head
Holdings: Vols (30,382) Cat Mss Pix
Notes: Special collections of children's literature dating from 1837 to the present are maintained by the Central Children's Department. These collections include Historical Bibliography, the Kathrine M McAlarney Collection of Illustrated Children's Books, the Folklore Collection, the Historical Collection which includes children's periodicals and the Series Collection. Featured in these non-circulating research collections are works of outstanding illustrators in the field of children's books, books by Philadelphia and Pennsylvania authors, books about Philadelphia and Pennsylvania people and places, and books published in Philadelphia and Pennsylvania. Included also are framed originals as well as manuscripts and typescripts by Evaline Ness, material for Lloyd Alexander books, Virginia Lee Burton, Marguerite (Lofft) deAngeli, Beatrice Schenk (Freedman) DeRegniers, EulalieOsgood Grover, Carolyn Haywood, Elizabeth Hoffman Honness, Kristin (Eggleston) Hunter [on loan to Free Library], Margaret Oldroyd Hyde, Katherine Milhous, Scott O'Dell, Lucy Fitch Perkins, Elizabeth Blake Ripley, Tomi Ungerer, Hendrik Willem Van Loon and Lucille Wallower. *The Checklist of Children's* Books, 1837-1876, published in 1975 and available in limited supply in book form, but also available in microform from the Office of Work with Children, Free Library of Philadelphia, lists all books in Special Collections during this period at date of publication. These special collections supplement the Rosenbach Collection of Early American Children's Books, the American Sunday School Union Collection, the Elisabeth Ball Collection of Hornbooks, and other children's books published prior to 1837, all of which are housed in the Rare Book Department of the Free Library ofPhiladelphia.

TX —TEXAS WOMAN'S UNIVERSITY, Bralley Memorial Library, Box 23715, TWU Sta, Denton, 76204. Metta Nicewarner, Spec Collections Libn
Holdings: Vols 3000 Cat
Notes: D Genevieve Dixon Collection of Books for Children and Young Adults. Many autographed copies. Strong in complete works of popular writers of the early 20th century.

WI —MILWAUKEE PUBLIC LIBRARY, 814 W Wisconsin Ave, Milwaukee, 53233. Donald J Sager, City Librn
Holdings: Vols 7200 Cat
Notes: Dates of publication between 1850-1940 incl many of the old series books and textbooks.

CHILDREN'S LITERATURE, AFRICAN

NY —AFRICAN-AMERICAN INSTITUTE, Educational Materials Center Library, 833 United Nation Plaza, New York, 10017.
Holdings: Vols 1300 Cat Maps Pix
Notes: The collection is general but does incl all the major reference materials in the field; also 300 journals. There is a special section on African published books for children plus one on African literature.

CHILDREN'S LITERATURE, AMERICAN see Children's Literature

CHILDREN'S LITERATURE, BLACK

NY —NEW YORK PUBLIC LIBRARY, Schomburg Center for Research in Black Culture, 515 Lenox Ave, New York, 10037. Catherine J Lenix Hooker, Interim Administrator
Notes: Research collection of children's books relating to Blacks, by or about Blacks and Black illustrators. Transferred from the James Weldon Johnson Memorial Collection, formerly the Countee Cullen Regional Branch Library.

CHILDREN'S LITERATURE, CZECH

PA —PENNSYLVANIA STATE UNIVERSITY, Fred Lewis Pattee Library, Slavic Library Program, University Park, 16802. Wasyl O Luciw, Head
Holdings: Vols (75,000) Cat Mss Pix
Budget: ($18,000)
Notes: The collection covers a wide range of languages Slavic and East European but its principal strengths are in Russian and Ukrainian. A special collection of 1576 volumes includes pre-revolutionary Russian, fine press publications, in our rare collection and children's literature. Besides book volumes, we have quite a large collection of manuscripts, documents, photographs and many periodicals, also including out of print books on microforms.

CHILDREN'S LITERATURE, EARLY

AL —BIRMINGHAM PUBLIC LIBRARY, Youth Dept, Grace Hardie Collection, 2020 Seventh Ave N, Birmingham, 35203. Patricia N Kyser, Head
Holdings: Vols 403 Cat
Notes: Pre-20th century. Limited photocopying.

CA —CLAREMONT COLLEGES, Ella Strong Denison Library, Scripps College, Claremont, 91711. Judy Harvey Sahak, Librn
Holdings: 425 Cat 150 Uncat
Notes: Early books for children published 1790 to early 20th century. Emphasis on moralistic and didactic literature of 1790's-1840's, tracts, alphabet books, school books, readers, chap books, horn books, verse and riddles.

CA —UNIVERSITY OF CALIFORNIA, LOS ANGELES, Research Library, Dept of Special Collections, 405 Hilgard Ave, Los Angeles, 90024. Edward Shreeves, Chairman, Bibliographers Group; David S Zeidberg, Head
Holdings: Vols 12,000 Cat
Notes: 12,000 volumes, principally British and American, with emphasis on ca 1775-1840, incl a collection of Harris and Newbery imprints.

CA —SAN DIEGO PUBLIC LIBRARY, Children's Room, 820 E St, San Diego, 92101.
Notes: Subject strengths: Children's Collection; Children's Literature, study and teaching; and Picture Books. Special catalog, indexes and files incl works of illustrator Arthur Rackham; children's books, 19th century; children's books in foreign languages; works of Dr Seuss; encyclopedia for children; local authors' works; Mother Goose works; Newbery and Caldecott award winning books; performer files; children's author-illustrator files (biographical information); and children's book reviews. Book lists, summer reading lists. Library also has pre-school story hour, puppet shows, tours for schools and children's groups, summer reading program. Spanish-speaking: Spanish language collection (350 vols).

CA —SAN DIEGO STATE UNIVERSITY, Malcolm A Love Library, 5300 Campanile Dr, San Diego, 92182. D Dickinson, Univ Librn; Don L Bosseau, Dir
Holdings:
Notes: Mary Marston Collection of Early Children's Books. Includes miniature books, fold-out books, pop-up books, children's classics dating from the 17th to he 18th centuries. (160 items)

DC —LIBRARY OF CONGRESS, Children's Literature Center, Washington, 20540. Sybille Jagusch, Chief
Holdings: Vols 117,809 Cat Microforms
Notes: English language children's books.

IL —CHICAGO PUBLIC LIBRARY, Thomas Hughes Children's Library, 78 E Washington St, Chicago, 60602. Lillian R New, Head
Holdings: Vols 3000 Cat
Notes: This special collection was developed at the Central Library to answer reference and information requests from both adults and children who were unable to find obscure materials related to children's books in the neighborhood branch library collections. Limited in its inclusion of rare children's books, but it has a good representation of out-of-print titles, series books of the 1910's like the *Hardy Boys* stories, early ethnic books for children of the 1930s and 40s, and illustrated editions of children's classics, incl those of Mother Goose, Hans Christian Andersen, and the Grimm brothers.

IN —INDIANA UNIVERSITY, Lilly Library, Seventh St, Bloomington, 47405. William R Cagle, Librn
Holdings: Uncat Mss
Notes: The Elisabeth Ball Collection consists of more than 7,000 books and many manuscripts from the late seventeenth to the early twentieth centuries. Strengths include Newbery and other early imprints, chapbooks, horn books, harlequinades, street cries, and miniature books.

IN —INDIANAPOLIS-MARION COUNTY PUBLIC LIBRARY, Riley Room for Young People, PO Box 211, Indianapolis, 46206. Margaret Barks, Head
Holdings: Vols 760 Uncat
Notes: Mostly 1800-1900.

KS —EMPORIA STATE UNIVERSITY, William Allen White Library, Emporia, 66801. Mary E Bogan, Special Collections Librn
Holdings: Vols (504) Cat
Notes: The Historical Children's Literature Collection includes books as well as periodicals important in the history of Children's Literature in the English language in the 19th and 20th centuries. There are also examples of original art work by such distinguished 20th century illustrators as Kurt Wiese, Marguerite De Angeli, Clare Newberry and Helen Sewell.

MA —JONES LIBRARY, 43 Amity St, Amherst, 01002. Daniel J Lombardo, Cur of Special Collections
Holdings: Vols (1400) Cat
Notes: The Clifton Johnson Collection of textbooks and children's literature. Books of the 18th and 19th centuries, for use within the library. Does not circulate.

MA —AUBURN PUBLIC LIBRARY, Court & Spring Sts, Auburn, 04210. Nann Blaine Hilyard, Dir; Lois C Wagner, Ref Librn
Holdings: Vols (200) Cat

MA —SMITH COLLEGE, Library, Northampton, 01063. Ruth Mortimer, Cur of Rare Books
Holdings: Vols 529 Cat
Notes: Published in America and England,

CHILDREN'S LITERATURE, EARLY (cont.)

1720-date, the majority being duplicates from the Rosenbach Collection. No photocopying.

MA —OLD STURBRIDGE VILLAGE, Research Library, Sturbridge, 01566. Theresa Rini Percy, Librn
Holdings: Cat
Notes: Northeastern US to 1860.

MA —AMERICAN ANTIQUARIAN SOCIETY LIBRARY, 185 Salisbury St, Worcester, 01609. Marcus A McCorison, Dir & Librn
Holdings: Cat
Notes: Incl the d'Alte A Welch collection of 1265 early American children's books, of which 280 were printed in this country before 1821. The Society's collection of pre-1821 American imprints of children's books now number 2800, more than two-thirds of the total known to have been printed. Also incl McLaughlin Brothers imprints.

MI —DETROIT PUBLIC LIBRARY, Rare Books Department, 5201 Woodward Ave, Detroit, 48202.
Holdings: Vols 1800 Cat Mss Pix
Notes: Chiefly English and American. Approximately half of the titles in the collection published before 1850. Other historical children's books in the Language Literature Department. Restricted use. Reference collection.

MI —WAYNE STATE UNIVERSITY, Kresge Library (Education), Detroit, 48202. Theodore Manheim, Librn
Holdings: Vols (65,000) Cat Mss Microforms
Budget: ($2000)
Notes: The Eloise Ramsey Collection (10, 000 vols). See, *The Eloise Ramsey Collection of Literature for Young People: A Catalogue;* compiled by Joan Cusenza (Detroit: Wayne State University Libraries, 1967). Besides the Ramsey Collection, which is housed separately and does not circulate, the Education Library has approx 55,000 volumes of children's and young adults' literature, with a very large picture-book collection, a large poetry collection; all with special emphasis on urban and ethnic materials.

MO —SAINT LOUIS PUBLIC LIBRARY, Gardner Rare Book Room, 1301 Olive St, Saint Louis, 63103. Julanne M Good, Supervisor; Martha Riley, Rare Books Librn
Holdings: Vols 200 // Cat
Notes: Collection incl 150 miniature chapbooks printed in the U S and in Great Britain between ca 1790 and 1880, and 2 pre-1550 printed broadsides. Noncirculating.

NH —UNIVERSITY OF NEW HAMPSHIRE, Dimond Library, Durham, 03824. Barbara A White, Special Collections Librn
Holdings: Vols 1200 Cat
Notes: Historical, mainly 19th century imprints.

NJ —RUTGERS, THE STATE UNIVERSITY OF NEW JERSEY, Alexander Library, Special Collections and Archives, College Ave & Huntington St, New Brunswick, 08903. Ronald L Becker, Cur of Manuscripts and Rare Books
Holdings: Vols 1000 Cat
Notes: Largely 19th-century American material, with departmental finding card. A large group of later juveniles, part uncataloged, is also among the general holdings of the Alexander Library.

NY —STATE UNIVERSITY OF NEW YORK, COLLEGE AT BUFFALO, E H Butler Library, 1300 Elmwood Ave, Buffalo, 14222. Marilyn C Kihl, Librn
Holdings: Vols 200 Cat
Notes: The Hertha Ganey Historical Children's Book Collection. Named in honor of former professor of children's literature with some of the material donated by her; contains various editions of better known classics in children's literature, affording comparisons with current editions. Most in English.

NY —EASTCHESTER HISTORICAL SOCIETY LIBRARY, Box 37, Eastchester, 10709. Madeline D Schaeffer, Librn
Holdings: Vols (6000) Cat Mss Maps Pix Slides
Notes: New York State history with emphasis on Westchester County and local area. Also children's literture, 1750-1910, and juvenile textbooks, 1790-1910. No photocopying.

NY —UNIVERSITY OF ROCHESTER, Rush Rhees Library, Department of Rare Books and Special Collections, Rochester, 14627. Peter Dzwonkoski, Librn
Holdings: Vols 3000 Cat
Notes: Principal strength is late eighteenth and early nineteenth century American imprints.
See also entry under Textbooks - Collections.

NC —APPALACHIAN STATE UNIVERSITY, Belk Library, Instructional Materials Center, Boone, 28608. Selma P Farthing, Librn
Holdings: Vols (20,000) Cat Pix
Notes: The collection is especially strong in poetry and folklore, chosen for the use of classes in children's literature. It also includes many old children's books, used in Critical History courses.

OH —HIRAM COLLEGE, Teachout-Price Memorial Library, Hiram, 44234. Joanne M Sawyer, Archivist; Marjorie M Adams, Music Librn
Holdings: Vols 200 Cat
Notes: There is a separate catalog for this collection. Earliest edition is 1834.

OH —MIAMI UNIVERSITY, King Library, Walter Havighurst Special Collections Library, Oxford, 45056. Helen Ball, Cur of Special Collections
Holdings: Vols 8000 Cat
Notes: A chronologically arranged collection of children's books dating from 1629. Mostly in English; some in French and other languages. Includes periodicals, related collection of 19th century American textbooks (3500), and McGuffey Collection (300).

PA —FREE LIBRARY OF PHILADELPHIA, Rare Book Dept, Logan Sq, Philadelphia, 19103. Marie E Korey, Rare Book Librn
Holdings: Vols 10,000 Cat Microforms
Notes: The A S W Rosenbach Collection of childrens's books, 1682-1836, with additions through 1840. Incl the Emerson Greenaway Collection, almost all published before the American Civil War.

PA —CARNEGIE LIBRARY OF PITTSBURGH, Children's Dept, 4400 Forbes Ave, Pittsburgh, 15213. Amy Kellman, Head
Holdings: Vols 2000 Cat
Notes: Historical children's books. Strong in folk tales.

†PA —UNIVERSITY OF PITTSBURGH, Graduate School of Library & Information Sciences Library, L I S Bldg, Third Fl, Pittsburgh, 15260. Jean Kindlin, Librn
Notes: History collection of children's literature, 5000 volumes. Archives of Mr Rogers Neighborhood television series.

TX —WEST TEXAS STATE UNIVERSITY, Cornette Library, PO Box 748 WT Sta, Canyon, 79016. Alan D Gabehart, Circulation Librn
Holdings: Vols 6400 Cat Microforms
Notes: Includes microform collections.

TX —FORT WORTH PUBLIC LIBRARY, 300 Taylor St, Fort Worth, 76102. Camille Connor, Children's Materials Coordinator
Holdings: Vols 500 Uncat //
Notes: A collection of old and rare children's books including American and European imprints, the 500 volumes published in the 1800s and early 1900s are early or out of print editions. The books are not cataloged but are periodically housed in display cases and available for examination. *Little Truths Better than Great Fables: A Collection of Old and Rare Books for Children in the Fort Worth Public Library* (Branch-Smith, 1976).

WA —SEATTLE PUBLIC LIBRARY, Central Children's Library, 1000 Fourth Ave, Seattle, 98104. Margery Loucks, Managing Librn
Holdings: Vols 2000
Notes: Exemplifying the development of children's literature from the mid-1700s to the early 1900s, the Collection primarily contains early English and American books. Cataloged and uncataloged vols. Budget acquired primarily by donation.

WI —UNIVERSITY OF WISCONSIN, MADISON, Cooperative Children's Book Center, Helen C White Hall, Rm 4290, 600 N Park St, Madison, 53706. Ginny Moore Kruse, Dir
Holdings: Vols (25,000) Cat
Notes: Incl most US trade books published for children in last 24 months; first editions of recommended US children's trade books published since 1965; over 400 alternative press books published for children in US and Canada since 1970; children's books about Wisconsin and by Wisconsin authors and illustrators; representative 19th and early 20th century American children's books; 19th century children's periodicals; first and significant editions of Newbury and Caldecott Medal books; historical and contemporary toybooks; 75 vols of Mother Goose published since 1828; 160 vols of Thorton Burgess books, many first editions; ms and original artwork for Ellen Raskin's *The Westing Game* and *The Mysterious Disappearance of Leon (I Mean Noel);* juvenile mass market and trade romance fiction.

WI —MILWAUKEE PUBLIC LIBRARY, 814 W Wisconsin Ave, Milwaukee, 53233. Donald J Sager, City Librn
Holdings: Vols 7200 Cat
Notes: Dates of publication between 1850-1940 incl many of the old series books and textbooks.

CHILDREN'S LITERATURE, ENGLISH

IN —INDIANA UNIVERSITY, Lilly Library, Seventh St, Bloomington, 47405. William R Cagle, Librn
Holdings: Uncat Mss
Notes: The Elisabeth Ball Collection consists of more than 7,000 books and many manuscripts from the late seventeenth to the early twentieth centuries. Strengths include Newbery and other early imprints, chapbooks, horn books, harlequinades, street cries, and miniature books.

NY —COLUMBIA UNIVERSITY LIBRARIES, Teachers College, Milbank Memorial Library, 525 W 120 St, New York, 10027. Jane P Franck, Dir
Holdings: Vols 1000 // Cat
Notes: The Harvey Darton Collection of English Children's Books up to 1850. Book catalog (unpublished).

CHILDREN'S LITERATURE, FOREIGN

CA —LOS ANGELES PUBLIC LIBRARY, Children's Literature Dept, 630 W 5th St, Los Angeles, 90071. Serenna Day, Sr Librn
Holdings: Vols (4500) Cat
Notes: A rich collection of over 4500 titles representing books from 40 countries around the world. Included are Argentina, Chile, Israel, Czechoslovakia, Bulgaria, and the Afrikaans language, to name a few. Especially notable are many imprints from the turn of the century, the 1920s and 1930s. Some are quite rare. Besides picture books with beautiful color illustrations, there are song books, fairy tales (familiar and obscure), and stories dealing with manners and good example. The Children's Room has a separate file where these are arranged by country.

DC —LIBRARY OF CONGRESS, Children's Literature Center, Washington, 20540. Sybille Jagusch, Chief
Holdings: Vols 50,005 Cat Phonorecords Audiotapes 16mm Films Filmstrips Microforms
Notes: In addition to this collection of children's foreign-language books, the Orientalia Division has over 2676 volumes. There is also a collection of some 60 vols from Nazi Germany (partially cat).

IL —NORTHERN ILLINOIS UNIVERSITY, Founders Memorial Library, Southeast Asia Collection, Normal Rd, De Kalb, 60115. Lee S Dutton Dr, Cur
Holdings: Vols (34,000) Cat Mss Maps

CHILDREN'S LITERATURE, FOREIGN (cont.)

Microforms
Notes: An extensive collection of books, periodicals, newspapers, maps, and microforms from or about Southeast Asia. Areas of concentration incl Thailand, Malaysia, Indonesia, Singapore, Brunei, Philippines, Laos, and Burma. Holdings (except rare books, maps, and microforms) are housed in a separate area collection within the Founders Library. A departmental card catalog and specialized reference collection support reference services. A Thai collection of several thousand vols is the largest vernacular component. Extensive Malaysia, Indonesia, Singapore, and Brunei holdings have been acquired through the NPAC program. A collection of Filipino-American newspapers, and a growing collection of children's literature in common and uncommon Southeast Asian languages are available. Resources are accessible to borrowers through OCLC.

IN —INDIANA UNIVERSITY, Lilly Library, Seventh St, Bloomington, 47405. William R Cagle, Librn
Holdings: Uncat Mss
Notes: The Elisabeth Ball Collection consists of more than 7,000 books and many manuscripts from the late seventeenth to the early twentieth centuries. Strengths include Newbery and other early imprints, chapbooks, horn books, harlequinades, street cries, and miniature books.

MA —HARVARD UNIVERSITY LIBRARY, Widener Library, Modern Greek Collection, Cambridge, 02138. Evangelie Flessas, Librn
Holdings: Vols (80,000) Cat Mss Microforms
Notes: Collection in Greek language.

MI —WAYNE STATE UNIVERSITY, Kresge Library (Education), Detroit, 48202. Theodore Manheim, Librn
Holdings: Vols (65,000) Cat Mss Microforms
Budget: ($2000)
Notes: The Eloise Ramsey Collection (10, 000 vols). See, *The Eloise Ramsey Collection of Literature for Young People: A Catalogue;* compiled by Joan Cusenza (Detroit: Wayne State University Libraries, 1967). Besides the Ramsey Collection, which is housed separately and does not circulate, the Education Library has approx 55,000 volumes of children's and young adults' literature, with a very large picture-book collection, a large poetry collection; all with special emphasis on urban and ethnic materials.

MN —UNIVERSITY OF MINNESOTA, Libraries, Children's Literature Research Collections, 109 Walter Library, Minneapolis, 55455. Karen Nelson Hoyle, Cur
Holdings: Vols 3600 Cat
Notes: 46 languages, incl Danish (217), French (504), and German (807), Icelandic (300), Russian (641), and Swedish (373). No photocopying. Kerlan Collection.

MN —SAINT PAUL PUBLIC LIBRARY, 90 W Fourth St, Saint Paul, 55102. Shirley Brady, Librn Youth Servs
Holdings: Vols 800 Cat
Budget: ($10,745)
Notes: Strong collection of Spanish, French, and German titles. Some Russian, Japanese, Swedish, Italian, Bohemian, Danish, Norwegian, Chinese, and Hebrew.

NY —HEMPSTEAD PUBLIC LIBRARY, Foreign Language Center for Children, 115 Nichols Court, Hempstead, 11550. Rosalie Zacharias, Coord
Holdings: Vols 1600 Cat Phonorecords
Notes: 1200 volumes cataloged and 400 uncataloged, periodicals and phonorecords in 28 foreign languages for children of pre-school age through high school. Major emphasis on French, German, Greek, Italian, Polish, Portuguese and Spanish; additional holdings in other European and Asian languages. Annotated bibliography available on request; revised and enlarged edition planned. Collection described in *Top of the News*, January, 1972.

PA —FREE LIBRARY OF PHILADELPHIA, Central Children's Dept, Logan Sq, Philadelphia, 19103. Ellen Whitney, Head
Holdings: Vols 7000 Uncat
Notes: 58 languages are represented, with extensive holdings in Spanish, French, German, Swedish and Japanese.

RI —PROVIDENCE PUBLIC LIBRARY, 150 Empire St, Providence, 02903. Lance J Bauer, Special Collections Librn
Holdings: Vols 2000 Mss Pix
Notes: The Edith Wetmore Collection of Books for Children. Collection spans 400 years in 20 languages, incl Japanese and Arabic, with primary emphasis on 19th and 20th century books in English. First editions of many important children's writers with many important children's illustrators represented. In addition, this collection is rich in scarce ephemeral material such as chapbooks, toybooks, peepshows, nursery rhymes and London street cries. Material must be used in-house. Photocopying when condition of material allows.

TX —SAINT EDWARD'S UNIVERSITY, Curriculum Materials Collection, 3001 S Congress, Austin, 78704. Joseph Sprug, Director
Holdings: Vols 1000 Cat
Notes: Collection consists of French, German, Spanish (300 titles), and other languages.

WI —UNIVERSITY OF WISCONSIN, MADISON, Library School Library, 600 N Park St, Madison, 53706. Sally Davis, Librn
Notes: 5000 vols of juvenile literature, incl picture books in French, German, Norwegian, Swedish, and Russian, children's classics, folk and fairy tales, juvenile illustrators and current writing, maintained at the UW Library School Library. Children's literature does not circulate outside University.

CHILDREN'S LITERATURE, FRENCH

MN —SAINT PAUL PUBLIC LIBRARY, 90 W Fourth St, Saint Paul, 55102. Shirley Brady, Librn Youth Servs
Holdings: Vols (800) Cat
Budget: ($10,745)
Notes: Strong collection of Spanish, French, and German titles. Some Russian, Japanese, Swedish, Italian, Bohemian, Danish, Norwegian, Chinese, and Hebrew.

NY —FRENCH INSTITUTE-ALLIANCE FRANCAISE, Library, 22 E 60 St, New York, 10022. Fred J Gitner, Librn
Holdings: Vols (40,000) Cat Phonorecords Audiotapes
Budget: ($23,000)
Notes: Growing collection of current children's books in the French language.

ON —NATIONAL LIBRARY OF CANADA, 395 Wellington St, Ottawa, K1A 0N4, Can. Andre Preibish, Dir
Holdings: Vols 12,000
Notes: Canadian children's books in English, French and other languages, supported by a collection of professional literature and supplemented by major award-winning books from other countries and selected major works on special themes such as folklore.

CHILDREN'S LITERATURE, GERMAN

MN —SAINT PAUL PUBLIC LIBRARY, 90 W Fourth St, Saint Paul, 55102. Shirley Brady, Librn Youth Servs
Holdings: Vols (800) Cat
Budget: ($10,745)
Notes: Strong collection of Spanish, French, and German titles. Some Russian, Japanese, Swedish, Italian, Bohemian, Danish, Norwegian, Chinese, and Hebrew.

CHILDREN'S LITERATURE, JAPANESE

NJ —FORT LEE PUBLIC LIBRARY, 320 Main St, Fort Lee, 07024. Nancy V Gallo, Dir
Holdings: Vols (1004) Cat
Notes: The greater part of this collection is juvenile literature. The adult collection is mostly fiction.

CHILDREN'S LITERATURE, JEWISH

†MA —HARVARD UNIVERSITY LIBRARY, Judaica Dept, Cambridge, 02138. Charles Berlin, Librn
Notes: Harvard's Judaica Collections have been helped by a special grant from the S H and Helen R Scheuer Family Foundation (NY) to develop its Jewish children's literature collection to encourage research in literature for and about Jewish children.

CHILDREN'S LITERATURE, OLD

RI —PROVIDENCE ATHENAEUM, 251 Benefit St, Providence, 02903. Sally Duplaix, Dir
Holdings: Vols 12,000 Cat
Budget: $5000
Notes: Incl large colleciton of early children's books, late 19th and 20th century.

CHILDREN'S LITERATURE, POLISH

IL —POLISH MUSEUM OF AMERICA, Library, 984 N Milwaukee Ave, Chicago, 60622. Donald Bilinski, OFM, Cur/Librn
Holdings: Vols (25,000) Cat Mss Maps Pix Slides Phonorecords 16mm Films Filmstrips Microforms
Notes: Material on Poland and Polish-Americans; works written by Polish-Americans, regardless of subject. About 80 percent of the works are in Polish. Extensive juvenile section in Polish for youngsters. The collection contains books not only of Poles in US but Poles beyond the borders of Poland. It contains Polish literature, incl translations into English.

PA —PENNSYLVANIA STATE UNIVERSITY, Fred Lewis Pattee Library, Slavic Library Program, University Park, 16802. Wasyl O Luciw, Head
Holdings: Vols (75,000) Cat Mss Pix
Budget: ($18,000)
Notes: The collection covers a wide range of languages Slavic and East European but its principal strengths are in Russian and Ukrainian. A special collection of 1576 volumes includes pre-revolutionary Russian, fine press publications, in our rare collection and children's literature. Besides book volumes, we have quite a large collection of manuscripts, documents, photographs and many periodicals, also including out of print books on microforms.

CHILDREN'S LITERATURE, RUSSIAN

PA —PENNSYLVANIA STATE UNIVERSITY, Fred Lewis Pattee Library, Slavic Library Program, University Park, 16802. Wasyl O Luciw, Head
Holdings: Vols (75,000) Cat Mss Pix
Budget: ($18,000)
Notes: The collection covers a wide range of languages Slavic and East European but its principal strengths are in Russian and Ukrainian. A special collection of 1576 volumes includes pre-revolutionary Russian, fine press publications, in our rare collection and children's literature. Besides book volumes, we have quite a large collection of manuscripts, documents, photographs and many periodicals, also including out of print books on microforms.

CHILDREN'S LITERATURE, SLAVIC

PA —PENNSYLVANIA STATE UNIVERSITY, Fred Lewis Pattee Library, Slavic Library Program, University Park, 16802. Wasyl O Luciw, Head
Holdings: Vols (75,000) Cat Mss Pix
Budget: ($18,000)
Notes: The collection covers a wide range of languages Slavic and East European but its principal strengths are in Russian and Ukrainian. A special collection of 1576 volumes includes pre-revolutionary Russian, fine press publications, in our rare collection and children's literature. Besides book volumes, we have quite a large collection of manuscripts, documents, photographs and many periodicals, also including out of print books on microforms.

CHILDREN'S LITERATURE, SOUTHEAST ASIAN

IL —NORTHERN ILLINOIS UNIVERSITY, Founders Memorial Library, Southeast Asia

CHILDREN'S LITERATURE, SOUTHEAST ASIAN (cont.)

Collection, Normal Rd, De Kalb, 60115. Lee S Dutton Dr, Cur
Holdings: Vols (34,000) Cat Maps Microforms
Notes: An extensive collection of books, periodicals, newspapers, maps, and microforms from or about Southeast Asia. Areas of concentration incl Thailand, Malaysia, Indonesia, Singapore, Brunei, Philippines, Laos, and Burma. Holdings (except rare books, maps, and microforms) are housed in a separate area collection within the Founders Library. A departmental card catalog and specialized reference collection support reference services. A Thai collection of several thousand vols is the largest vernacular component. Extensive Malaysia, Indonesia, Singapore, and Brunei holdings have been acquired through the NPAC program. A collection of Filipino-American newspapers, and a growing collection of children's literature in common and uncommon Southeast Asian languages are available. Resources are accessible to borrowers through OCLC.

CHILDREN'S LITERATURE, SPANISH

MN —SAINT PAUL PUBLIC LIBRARY, 90 W Fourth St, Saint Paul, 55102. Shirley Brady, Librn Youth Servs
Holdings: Vols (800) Cat
Budget: ($10,745)
Notes: Strong collection of Spanish, French, and German titles. Some Russian, Japanese, Swedish, Italian, Bohemian, Danish, Norwegian, Chinese, and Hebrew.

TX —FORT WORTH PUBLIC LIBRARY, North Branch, 601 Park St, Fort Worth, 76106. Betty M Hennington, Branch Head
Holdings: Vols (2000) Cat Phonorecords Audiotapes Videotapes Filmstrips
Notes: There is a separate catalog in North Branch for Spanish-language materials. The collection incl books in all areas.

CHILDREN'S MUSEUMS

MA —CHILDREN'S MUSEUM, Resource Center, Museum Wharf, 300 Congress St, Boston, 02210. Marie Ariel, Librn; Maria Russell, Resource Services Mgr
Holdings: Vols 150 Cat Mss Slides Audiotapes
Notes: All aspects covered. Extensive collection of current museum brochures and serials; exhibit and program documentation. Subject-related programs and services offered by Museum staff.

CHILDREN'S PERIODICALS see Periodicals, Children's

CHILDREN'S PLAYS

KY —HOPKINSVILLE COMMUNITY COLLEGE, Library, North Dr, Hopkinsville, 42240. Marjanna J Frising, Librn
Holdings: Vols (500) Cat Phonorecords Audiotapes Filmstrips
Notes: Incl most notable Broadway plays, both musical and non-musical, with soundtracks available for most. Also a large collection of children's and one-act plays, incl comedy and mystery plays.

BC —UNIVERSITY OF VICTORIA, McPherson Library, Victoria, V8W 3H5, Can.
Notes: The H C Sage Collection of English Juvenile Drama. Representative material on pantomime figures, etc, by the early 20th-century publisher, George Conetta.

CHILDREN'S POETRY

FL —FLORIDA STATE UNIVERSITY, Robert Manning Strozier Library, Childhood in Poetry Collection, Tallahassee, 32306. Frederick Korn, Cur
Holdings: Vols (25,000) Cat
Notes: The Childhood in Poetry Collection consists of the books of all the great poets and hundreds of minor poets of all periods, in first or other early and illustrated editions, in children's periodicals and "juveniles." There are more than 300 hymnals, incl the personal collection of Dr Robert Lowry, author of "Shall We Gather at the River" and other popular hymns. There are also nearly 500 annuals and gift books. The Collection is strong, as well, in works of criticism, biography and reference. An eleven-volume, illustrated catalog (1967-1980) is available from Gale Research. Over 200,000 poems are listed in a key-word index, keyed to the books in which they appear. The nucleus of the Collection was assembled as the lifetime leisure activity of the donor, John Mackay Shaw, who now serves as curator emeritus. His object has been to gather in one place the books inwhich poems relating to childhood first appeared.

RI —BROWN UNIVERSITY, John Hay Library, Harris Collection, Prospect St, Providence, 02912. Rosemary L Cullen, Cur
Holdings: Vols (200,000) Cat Mss Pix Phonorecords Microforms
Budget: ($15,000)
Notes: The Harris Collection of American Poetry and Plays is principally composed of American and Canadian poetry and plays from the 17th century to the present. Extensive holdings in juvenile poetry incl Mother Goose and *The Night Before* Christmas in many editions. See *Dictionary Catalog of The Harris Collection of American Poetry and Plays* (Boston: G K Hall, 1972), 13 vols; *Supplement* (1977), 3 vols. Separate catalog.

WI —MILWAUKEE PUBLIC LIBRARY, 814 W Wisconsin Ave, Milwaukee, 53233. Donald J Sager, City Librn
Holdings: Vols 400
Notes: Includes titles indexed in *Index To Children's Poetry* and supplements by John and Sara Brewton.

CHILDREN'S READING

MB —UNIVERSITY OF WINNIPEG, Department of English, 515 Portage Ave, Winnipeg, R3B 2E9, Can. Perry Nodelman, Cur
Holdings: Vols 1000 Cat
Notes: This Collection represents the kind of material children read during the 19th and early 20th century on the Canadian Prairies, not necessarily "Children's Literature."

CHILDREN'S THEATRE

AZ —ARIZONA STATE UNIVERSITY, Library, Tempe, 85287. Marilyn Wurzburger, Special Collections Librn
Holdings: Vols (108) Pix
Notes: Collection covers various aspects of Children's Theatre from 1944 through the present. Areas of emphasis incl International and National Child Drama Associations, award-winning theatres, educational programs, regional groups and prominent figures in Children's Theatre incl: Irene Vickers Baker, Isabel Burger, Virginia Lee Comer, Rita Criste, Moses Goldberg, Kenneth Graham, Aurand Harris, Paul Kozelka, George Latshaw, Rosemary Musil, Sara Spencer, Winifred Ward, Susan Zeder and Lin Wright. Publications incl newsletters, research papers, bibliographies and records of the proceedings of the Children's Theatre Association of America. 80 linear feet of scripts, documents, publications, films, tapes (oral history) programs, correspondence, photographs, working papers and clippings. Partially indexed; finding guides available.

NY —NEW YORK PUBLIC LIBRARY, Performing Arts Research Center, Billy Rose Theatre Collection, 111 Amsterdam Ave, New York, 10023. Dorothy L Swerdlove, Cur
Holdings: Cat
Notes: Includes material on Children's Theatre Conference, Children's Theatre Association of America, etc.

WA —UNIVERSITY OF WASHINGTON LIBRARIES, Drama Library, BH-20, Seattle, 98195. Liz Fugate, Drama Librn
Holdings: Vols
Budget: ($13,182)
Notes: Collection incl history; criticism; costume; make-up; scene design; lighting; creative dramatics; children's theatre; directing; playwriting; acting. Special Collections include 19th century acting editions, contemporary acting editions and local theatre posters. 17,731 items cataloged, 24,255 uncataloged.

CHILDS, J. RIVES

VA —UNIVERSITY OF VIRGINIA, Alderman Library, Manuscripts Dept, Charlottesville, 22901. Edmund Berkeley Jr, Cur
Holdings: Vols 200 Cat Mss Pix Phonorecords
Notes: Papers of J Rives Childs, author and diplomat; incl research material from his work on Casanova, about 7600 items. Published description of collection in *Collector's Quest: The Correspondence of Henry Miller and J Rives Childs, 1947-1965* (University Press of Virginia, 1968, for Randolph-Macon College).

CHILE

CA —UNIVERSITY OF CALIFORNIA, BERKELEY, University Library, Hispanic Collections, Berkeley, 94720. Gaston Somoshegyi-Szokol, Librn
Holdings: Vols (15,000)
Notes: General research collection in the humanities and social sciences, with particular emphasis on history, literature, economics, and political developments. Main Library holdings are supplemented by subject coverage in branch libraries. Extensive government holdings are maintained in the Government Documents Department.

CT —YALE UNIVERSITY, Sterling Memorial Library, Latin American Collections, New Haven, 06520. Lee H Williams Jr, Cur
Holdings: Vols (300,000) Cat Maps Pix Slides Phonorecords 16mm Films Filmstrips
See also entry under Latin America

NY —COLUMBIA UNIVERSITY LIBRARIES, Rare Book & Manuscript Library, 801 Butler Library, 535 W 114 St, New York, 10027. Kenneth A Lohf, Librn
Notes: More than 32,000 items documenting the rise of William Russell Grace's shipping business and other materials relating to his career as mayor of New York. Incl records and correspondence relating to all aspects of the shipping business in New York and South America, mining interest in Peru and Chile, and transportation in Costa Rica and Nicaragua. Family memorabilia and photographs, materials concerning New York Politics, banking and insurance, real estate interests and Catholic charities, and letters from Chester A Arthur, John Jacob Astor, Andrew Carnegie, Grover Cleveland, Hamilton Fish, John Hay and J Pierpont Morgan. Restricted use.

CHILE—HISTORY

AZ —UNIVERSITY OF ARIZONA, Library, Tucson, 85721. W David Laird, Librn
Notes: Latin American materials in the University of Arizona Library system may be found in all of the campus libraries. The largest collection is located in the Main Library and concentrates primarily on the history, literature, political science and economics of Mexico, Panama, Colombia, Argentina, Brazil and Chile. Special Collections specializes in the colonial period in the areas of law, religion, and economics. They also incl numerous manuscript collections, photographs, and 4000 broadsides from Mexico covering the late 18th century through the 20th century revolutionary period. There are also strong map, music and phonorecord collections primarily on Mexico. The greatest collecting effort is current materials on contemporary Latin America. Materials are fully accessible through the main card catalog as there is no separate catalog of the collection.

CHILE—HISTORY (cont.)

CA —UNIVERSITY OF CALIFORNIA, BERKELEY, University Library, Hispanic Collections, Berkeley, 94720. Gaston Somoshegyi-Szokol, Librn
Holdings: Vols (4000)
Notes: Research collection with emphasis on recent economic history, history of the Allende-period, the attempted reconquest of Chile and Peru by Spain, the War of the Pacific, and the Tacna-Arica dispute.

CT —YALE UNIVERSITY, Sterling Memorial Library, Latin American Collections, New Haven, 06520. Lee H Williams Jr, Cur
Holdings: Vols (300,000) Cat Maps Pix Slides Phonorecords 16mm Films Filmstrips
See also entry under Latin America

CT —UNIVERSITY OF CONNECTICUT, Library, Storrs, 06268. R H Schimmelpfeng, Dir of Special Collections
Holdings: Vols (2800) Cat

IN —INDIANA UNIVERSITY, Lilly Library, Seventh St, Bloomington, 47405. William R Cagle, Librn
Holdings: // Mss Pix
Notes: Papers of Claude G Bowers, newspaperman, author, ambassador to Spain, 1933-1936, and ambassador to Chile, 1939-1953. Collection incl diaries, materials relating to both ambassadorships, particularly important for Spanish Civil War period; speeches; some original political cartoons; awards, medals, etc; newspaper clippings, etc, 1868-1972. 18,386 items.

NY —STATE UNIVERSITY OF NEW YORK, STONY BROOK, Melville Library, Stony Brook, 11794. John B Smith, Dir
Holdings: Vols 30,000 Cat
Notes: Part of the general research collection. Although the collection incl most Latin American countries, it has special strengths in Chilean materials, incl government documents of the 19th century.

TX —UNIVERSITY OF TEXAS LIBRARIES, Nettie Lee Benson Latin American Collection, Sid Richardson Hall 1.109, Austin, 78712. Laura Gutierrez-Witt, Head Librn
Holdings: Vols (450,000) Cat Mss Maps Pix Microforms
Notes: Private collection of Diego Munoz relating to Chile, Bolivia, Peru and Ecuador. Incl extensive coverage of the laws of Chile and of the Congress of Chile during the 19th century; also, 200 volumes of works of Jose Toribio Medina.
See also entry under Latin America.

CHILEAN NEWSPAPERS see Newspapers, Chilean

CHILLS AND FEVER see Malarial Fever

CHIMES

MI —GUILD OF CARILLONNEURS IN NORTH AMERICA, Archives, 900 Burton Tower, University of Michigan, Ann Arbor, 48109. William De Turk, Archivist
Holdings: Mss Pix Phonorecords
Notes: Emphasis is on carillons.

CHIMING see Change Ringing

CHIMPANZEES

OR —OREGON REGIONAL PRIMATE RESEARCH CENTER, Library, 505 NW 185 Ave, Beaverton, 97006. Isabel McDonald, Librn
Holdings: Vols (765) Cat Audiotapes 16mm Films Microforms
Notes: Incl small collection of dissertations and theses.

CHINA

CA —UNIVERSITY OF CALIFORNIA, BERKELEY, University Library, East Asiatic Library, Room 208, Durant Hall, Berkeley, 94720. Donald Shively, Head
Holdings: Vols (500,000) Cat Mss Maps Pix Microforms
Notes: Library materials are mainly on humanities and social sciences covering the ancient and the modern periods and selectively in natural sciences; substantial in various fields but particularly notable in literary works, fine arts, rare books, folklore, wood-block printed editions, Chinese stone rubbings, Japanese old maps, first editions of Meiji literature, Buddhist texts, and Tibetan xylographs. Estimated 245,000 vols in Chinese, 215,000 vols in Japanese, 30,000 vols in Korean, 5000 in Manchu, Mongol or Tibetan.

CA —CLAREMONT COLLEGES, Honnold Library, Asian Studies Collection, Ninth & Dartmouth, Claremont, 91711. Frances D Wang, Cur
Holdings: Vols (69,658) Cat Mss Maps Pix Microforms
Budget: ($50,000)
Notes: Incl 62,476 vols in Chinese and Japanese; 6276 in Western languages. About 13,000 uncataloged. Collection incl artifacts, original mss, rare, original editions of Chinese, Japanese, Korean and Western language and literature, history, and archaeology, which are today totally unavailable to acquire. The most distinguished work is the collection of some 200 Chinese gazetteers (fang-chih) which is one of the best in the US. Another valuable collection is the Frederick McCormick Collection of 214 titles in 896 vols of movable-type editions of Korean printed books, 15th-19th centuries. The Western-language collection on the Far East is probably one of the strongest in the US. Recently added was a collection of Japanese books on Shinto (125 titles), periodicals, and artifacts. Separate catalog.

†CA —AMERICAN ACADEMY OF ASIAN STUDIES LIBRARY, 134-140 Church St, San Francisco, 94114.

†CA —ASIA FOUNDATION LIBRARY, 550 Kearny St, San Francisco, 94114.

CA —HOOVER INSTITUTION ON WAR, REVOLUTION & PEACE, Stanford University, Stanford, 94305. Milorad M Drachkovitch, Archivist
Holdings: Mss Pix
Notes: Papers of Ernest B Price, 1914-1950, incl correspondence, diary, dispatches, manuscripts, lecture material, photographs, and printed matter relating to Japanese military intervention in China and Manchuria, 1931-1945; political and economic development in China, 1914-1929; and E B Price's career in the U S Foreign Service in China, 1914-1929, in business, and in education. 13 ms boxes.

CA —HOOVER INSTITUTION ON WAR, REVOLUTION & PEACE, East Asian Collection, Stanford University, Stanford, 94305. Ramon H Myers, Cur
Holdings: Vols 169,753 Cat Microforms
Notes: The emphasis of this Chinese collection is on social science subjects related to 20th century China. *Catalog of the Chinese Collection, The Library Catalogs of the Hoover Institution on War, Revolution, and Peace, Stanford University* was published by G K Hall Co in 1969 (13 vols). Its first supplement was published in 1972 (2 vols), and the second supplement in 1977 (2 vols).

CT —TRINITY COLLEGE LIBRARY, 300 Summit St, Hartford, 06106. Ralph S Emerick, Librn
Holdings: Cat
Notes: Moore Collection of the Far East.

CT —YALE UNIVERSITY LIBRARY, East Asian Collection, 120 High St, New Haven, 06520. Hideo Kaneko, Cur
Holdings: Vols 240,000 Cat Maps Pix

†DC —CENTER FOR CHINESE RESEARCH MATERIALS, 1527 New Hampshire Ave, NW, Washington, 20036.

DC —HOWARD UNIVERSITY, Founders Library, Bernard B Fall Collection (Southeast Asia Collection), Washington, 20059. Steven Ilsang Yoon, Cur
Holdings: Vols (6000) Cat Microforms
Budget: $15,000
Notes: The Bernard B Fall Collection has more than 6000 books, incl 1200 books purchased from the Kendric N Marshall Estate, 3000 items in vertical files, 300 pamphlets, and 800 microfilms, about Southeastern Asia and China. In addition, there are nearly 100 current periodicals and another 100 older periodicals about Indochina in the Collection.

DC —LIBRARY OF CONGRESS, African and Middle Eastern Division, Washington, 20540.
Holdings: Cat Mss Microforms
Notes: Orientalia: the Orientalia Division contains 1,400,000 vols in Oriental languages. Chinese: more than 422,000 vols, espec strong in local histories and Ch'ing (1644-1911) period material. Japanese: over 574,000 vols, espec strong in economics, statistics, history, literature; 12,000 government, learned society, and university periodical titles, particularly science, technology, and social sciences. Korean: 56, 000 vols, espec strong in social sciences and modern history.

HI —UNIVERSITY OF HAWAII, Library, 2550 The Mall, Honolulu, 96822. Joyce Wright, Head, Asia Collection; Masato Matsu, Head, East Asia Vernacular Collection
Holdings: Vols 60,394 Cat Microforms
Notes: The Asian Collection includes materials from and about China (People's Republic, Taiwan, Hong Kong) in all languages. No figures are available for western language materials relating to China, which are supplemented by retrospective materials in the main library collection. Scope: social sciences and the humanities, traditional and contemporary.

IL —SOUTHERN ILLINOIS UNIVERSITY, CARBONDALE, Delyte W Morris Library, Carbondale, 62901.
Holdings: Vols (4100) Cat Maps Audiotapes Microforms
Notes: The Vietnamese collection has been transferred to the general library. It incl 1200 cataloged titles in the Vietnamese language, plus 56 Vietnamese language microfilms. A profile of the area emphasis on the collection appears from the following distribution of the 2987 titles entered in the holdings and accessions lists published by the Southern Illinois University Center for Vietnamese Studies: Vietnam, 1965; Cambodia and Laos, 63; Other Southeast Asia (incl Indonesia), 916; East Asia (mostly China), 246; General (reference works, bibliographies, etc), 197. Also over 1000 maps.

IL —CENTER FOR RESEARCH LIBRARIES, 6050 S Kenwood Ave, Chicago, 60637. Donald B Simpson, Dir; Esther Smith, Collection Development Librn
Holdings: Microforms
Notes: Mainland China newspapers, periodicals and clippings, early western language newspapers in China, Hong Kong newspapers in English, British Foreign Office and US State Dept records relating to China, Dunhuang manuscripts, missionary periodicals. Microfilm and reprints of newspapers, serials and monographs from Center for Chinese Research Materials. Hunter collection of Chinese communist propaganda (ca 1000 vols). Microfilm and originals of Maritime Customs publications. Microfilm of press summaries prepared by US Consulate, Hong Kong, archives of missionary organizations, Chinese folk literature, etc. Descriptive pamphlet available.

IL —QUINCY COLLEGE LIBRARY, Quincy, 62301. Victor Kingery, OFM, Librn
Notes: In general collection.

IL —NATIONAL COUNCIL OF THE YMCAS, YMCA Historical Library, 6400 Shafer Ct, Rosemont, 60018. Eleanor R Murphy, Librn
Holdings: Vols (15,000) Cat Mss Pix Slides Correspondence
Notes: YMCA work in China, 1895-1950. No separate catalog or index. Incl both Chinese and English-language material. Collection described in Shirley Garrett, *Social Reformers in Urban China* (Cambridge, Mass: Harvard University Press, 1970). Some primary material is restricted. Application should be made to librarian for permission.

CHINA (cont.)

MA —CHILDREN'S MUSEUM, Resource Center, Museum Wharf, 300 Congress St, Boston, 02210. Marie Ariel, Librn; Maria Russell, Resource Services Mgr
Holdings: Vols 200 Cat Mss Slides Audiotapes Phonorecords Filmstrips
Notes: Curriculum materials and materials for children and adults. Available for reference use by the public; borrowing privileges for Museum members; activity and curriculum kits available to public, schools and community groups for rental fee. Subject-related programs and services offered by Museum staff.

MI —UNIVERSITY OF MICHIGAN, Asia Library, Ann Arbor, 48109. Wei-Ying Wan, Head
Holdings: Vols (201,000) Cat Microforms
Notes: Strong collection on all aspects of China and Chinese culture, comprehensive Contemporary China Reference Collection with Chinese, Japanese, and Western-language publications on post-1949 China. Special collections incl Union Research Institute Classified Files on China, over 20,000 pieces of the Red Guards Materials, the Classified Files on the Great Cultural Revolution compiled by the Contemporary China Research Institute, National Peking Library Rare Books Microfilms, rare editions of Chinese fiction microfilmed from several Japanese collections. National Central Library Rare Book Microfilms, Ming literary collections photo-reprinted from Japanese collections, British Public Record Office Files on China, outstanding collection of Japanese works on China. Incl 15,600 reels of microfilm and 12,300 microfiche.

NJ —PRINCETON UNIVERSITY, Library, Gest Oriental Library & East Asian Collections, 317 Palmer Hall, Princeton, 08544. D E Perushek, Cur
Holdings: Vols (267,000) Cat Mss Maps Pix Microforms
Notes: Mostly in Chinese. Subject areas incl. Chinese civilization, language, literature, philosophy, religion, history, geography, traditional medicine and materia medica, history of books and printing, sociology, economics, politics, and other social sciences. With regard to Chinese art and archaeology, only works of a general or cultural nature and primary textual sources are collected. For works on Chinese population only the historical and economic aspects are acquired. Subject areas in science and technology, except those materials dealing with indigenous developments and historical aspects, are excluded. No historical period is excluded. The collection is particularly noted for its strength in pre-20th century works on traditional Chinese medicine in all areas, and in works on the Ming period. Some Western-language reference works as well as Western-language works on Chinese literature, language, and linguistics. Emphasis is on current publications. Separate card catalog. Publications on collection: Ch'u Wan-li, A Catalogue of the Chinese Rare Books in the Gest collection of the Princeton University Library (Taiperi: Yee Wen Publishing Co., 1974). (In Chinese): Gillis, I. V. & Pai Ping-ch'i, Title Index to the Catalogue of the Gest Oriental Library (Peking Kwei LI Press, 1941). (In Chinese): Hu, Shih, "The Gest Oriental Library at Princeton University," Princeton University Chronicle, vol. xv (Spring 1954), 113-141; Rice, Howard C., Jr., Shih-kang Tung & Frederick W. Mote, East and West, Europe's Discovery of China and China's Response to Europe, 1511-1839: A Check-list of the Exhibition in the Princeton University Library, February 15-April 30, 1957 (Princeton: Princeton University Library, 1957); and Tung, Shih-kang, Chinese Microfilms in Princeton University: A Checklist of the Gest Oriental Library (Washington, Center for Chinese Research Materials, Association of Research Libraries, 1969).

NY —CORNELL UNIVERSITY LIBRARIES, John M Olin Library, Wason Collection of China & the Chinese, Ithaca, 14853. James Cole, Cur; Paul P W Cheng, East Asia Librn
Holdings: Vols (330,000) Cat Mss Maps Pix Microforms
Notes: The collection has three major components: Western language collection; Chinese language collection; and the Japanese language collection. Volumes: Western, 40,000; Chinese 207,000; and Japanese, 35,000. The scope of the collection incl materials on all disciplines in the humanities and social sciences. Materials on the natural sciences are generally not included. A complete main entry catalog for the Wason Collection is in the Wason Reading Room. Author, title, and subject cards for all books are interfiled in the Cornell University Library Catalog. For description see: Cornell University Libraries. *The Wason Collection* (Ithaca, N Y, 1969), 8 pp, illus. (Its *Special Collection,* No 1); and *Cornell University Libraries Bulletin,* No 193 (Jan/Feb 1975), pp 36-43.

NJ —MONTCLAIR STATE COLLEGE, Harry A Sprague Library, Upper Montclair, 07043.
Holdings: Vols 636 // Cat
Notes: Formerly the library of the China Institute of New Jersey.

†NY —ASIA SOCIETY LIBRARY, 725 Park Ave, New York, 10021.

NY —COLUMBIA UNIVERSITY LIBRARIES, Lehman Library, China Documentation Center, 420 W 118 St, New York, 10027. Lawrence C Reardon, Librn
Holdings: Cat Mss Microforms
Notes: The China Documentation Center specializes in the collection of "fugitive" materials which cannot be easily cataloged or maintained in a conventional library collection. These materials incl unpublished reports and conference papers, interview protocols, visitors' reports. This collection has recently been reduced and primary documents are now located at the C V Starr and Lehman Libraries of Columbia University. Access to the library is by appointment only.

NY —NEW YORK PUBLIC LIBRARY, Oriental Div, Fifth Ave & 42 St, New York, 10018. E Christian Filstrup, Chief
Holdings: Cat Mss Microforms
Budget: ($56,455)
Notes: Described in *Dictionary Catalog of the Oriental Collection,* The Research Libraries of the New York Public Library, 1960, 16 vols, and *First Supplement,* 1976, 8 vols (144,000 cards). This catalog incl 318,000 entries for works in about 100 languages of the East, and all works in Western languages on Oriental subjects. The Oriental Collection numbers about 120,000 vols; its Arabic and Indic holdings and those on ancient Egypt and the ancient Near East are among the largest in the US. There is also a collection of 30,000 vols of PL 480 material from Egypt, Pakistan, and India to which there is main entry access, but which is not incorporated into the dictionary catalog. Other outstanding features of the Oriental Collection incl extensive holdings of Japanese technical and scientific periodicals; a unique collection of linguistic works, grammars, anddictionaries; and unusually good coverage of the field of Oriental religions and philosophies. The catalog contains numerous subject references to periodical articles in all languages. All entries are arranged alphabetically according to the Roman alphabet.

NC —DUKE UNIVERSITY, William R Perkins Library, Durham, 27706. Elvin E Strowd, University Librn
Notes: The Thomas collection relating to China and the Far East contains more than 1500 items. It is a comprehensive body of books, newspapers, prints and other materials dealing with many phases of the culture of the Orient. Additions are ongoing.

TX —UNIVERSITY OF TEXAS LIBRARIES, Asian Collection, PO Box P, Austin, 78712. Kevin Lin, Asian Librn; Merry Burlingham, South Asian Librn
Holdings: Vols 24,000 Cat Microforms
Notes: Anthropology, economics, government, history, and language and literature of China. Incl 250 periodical titles.

CHINA (PORCELAIN) see Porcelain

CHINA—ANTIQUITIES

CA —UNIVERSITY OF CALIFORNIA, BERKELEY, University Library, East Asiatic Library, Room 208, Durant Hall, Berkeley, 94720. Donald Shively, Head
Holdings: Vols 245,000 Cat Mss Maps Pix Microforms
Notes: Research

CHINA—CIVILIZATION AND CULTURE

CA —UNIVERSITY OF CALIFORNIA, BERKELEY, University Library, East Asiatic Library, Room 208, Durant Hall, Berkeley, 94720. Donald Shively, Head
Holdings: Vols 245,000 Cat Mss Maps Pix Microforms
Notes: Research

IL —CENTER FOR RESEARCH LIBRARIES, 6050 S Kenwood Ave, Chicago, 60637. Donald B Simpson, Dir; Esther Smith, Collection Development Librn
Holdings: Vols Cat Microforms
Notes: Mainland China newspapers, periodicals and clippings, early western language newspapers in China, Hong Kong newspapers in English, British Foreign Office and US State Dept records relating to China, Dunhuang manuscripts, missionary periodicals. Microfilm and reprints of newspapers, serials and monographs from Center for Chinese Research Materials. Hunter collection of Chinese communist propaganda (ca 1000 vols). Microfilm and originals of Maritime Customs publications. Microfilm of press summaries prepared by US Consulate, Hong Kong, archives of missionary organizations, Chinese folk literature, etc. Descriptive pamphlet available.

IL —FIELD MUSEUM OF NATURAL HISTORY, The Berthold Laufer Library, Roosevelt Rd & Lake Shore Dr, Chicago, 60605. W Peyton Fawcett, Librn
Holdings: Vols (12,000) // Cat Mss Maps
Notes: The part of the museum's collection of Berthold Laufer (1874-1934), Curator of Anthropology, dealing with the peoples of the pre-19th century Chinese Empire (incl Manchuria, Mongolia, Sinkiang and Tibet); their anthropology, art and religion; influences upon their cultures by those of India, Siberia, Japan, Indonesia, and Oceania--and vice versa. Incl about 500 books in Tibetan. About 2/3 of the collection is cataloged.

KS —UNIVERSITY OF KANSAS, Watson Library, East Asian Library, Lawrence, 66045. Eugene Carvalho, Librn
Holdings: Vols 50,000 Cat
Notes: Chinese language materials with special emphasis on political science, history, anthropology, sociology and economics, with

CHINA—CIVILIZATION AND CULTURE (cont.)

added emphasis on classical Chinese literature, history of art.

MA —HARVARD UNIVERSITY LIBRARY, Harvard-Yenching Library, 2 Divinity Ave, Cambridge, 02138. Eugene W Wu, Librn
Notes: Strong in languages and literature.

MA —ESSEX INSTITUTE, James Duncan Phillips Library, 132-34 Essex St, Salem, 01970. Prudence K Backman, Manuscript Librn
Holdings: Vols
Notes: Over 10,000 books, pamphlets, broadsides, periodicals, photographs and maps comprising the Frederick Townsend Ward Collection. Collection depicts the history and culture of China and interaction of China with the West from the era of Marco Polo to the early 20th Century.

MA —PEABODY MUSEUM OF SALEM, Phillips Library, E India Sq, Salem, 01970. Gregor Trinkaus-Randall, Librn
Holdings: Vols (100,000) Cat Mss Pix
Notes: Ethnology of Non-European Peoples Collection. Composed of separate divisions relating to the Pacific Islands, China, Japan, and the American Indian. No published indexes.

MI —UNIVERSITY OF MICHIGAN, Asia Library, Ann Arbor, 48109. Wei-Ying Wan, Head
Holdings: Vols (201,000) Cat Microforms
Notes: Strong collection on all aspects of China and Chinese culture, comprehensive Contemporary China Reference Collection with Chinese, Japanese, and Western-language publications on post-1949 China. Special collections incl Union Research Institute Classified Files on China, over 20, 000 pieces of the Red Guards Materials, the Classified Files on the Great Culture Revolution compiled by the Contemporary China Research Institute, National Peking Library Rare Books Microfilms, rare editions of Chinese fiction microfilmed from several Japanese collections, National Central Library Rare Book Microfilms, Ming literary collections photo-reprinted from Japanese collections, British Public Record Office Files on China, outstanding collection of Japanese works on China. Incl 15,000 reels of microfilm and 12,300 microfiche.

NY —CORNELL UNIVERSITY LIBRARIES, John M Olin Library, Wason Collection of China & the Chinese, Ithaca, 14853. James Cole, Cur; Paul P W Cheng, East Asia Librn
Holdings: Vols (330,000) Cat Mss Maps Pix Microforms
See also entry under China

NC —NORTH CAROLINA STATE UNIVERSITY, School of Education, Curriculum Materials Center, 400 Poe, Box 7801, Raleigh, 27695. James Jarrell, Coordr
Holdings: Vols (80) Cat Slides Phonorecords Audiotapes Videotapes 16mm Films Filmstrips
Notes: *SASASAAS Review,* v 2, no 2, Spring 1977. Incl curriculum guides and teachers' kits. Distributor for a 14-part TV course: *Japan, Pt I: The Living Tradition.*

OH —OHIO UNIVERSITY, Vernon R Alden Library, Athens, 45701. Kent Mulliner, Africana Specialist
Notes: A collection of 634 vols of Chinese books covering a wide range of subjects incl art, culture, economics, geography, history, language, literature, martial arts, medical science, philosophy, and technology.

OH —HEBREW UNION COLLEGE-JEWISH INSTITUTE OF RELIGION, Klau Library, 3101 Clifton Ave, Cincinnati, 45220. David J Gilner, Reference Librn
Holdings: Vols 59 // Cat Mss
Notes: Only Chinese Hebrew ms collection extant. Incl community roster of Kai-Feng-fu in Hebrew and Chinese, and many mss in fanfold form.

OH —CLEVELAND PUBLIC LIBRARY, Fine Arts and Special Collections Department, 325 Superior Ave, Cleveland, 44114. Alice N Loranth, Head
Holdings: Vols 3500 Cat Mss
Notes: Emphasis is on Western editions and translations of classic literary and religious texts prior to the impact of European influence. Additional material on antiquities, early description and travel and early history. 2400 vols are in Chinese. Separatge catalog of author entries for titles in Chinese is maintained.
See also entry under East (Far East)

WI —UNIVERSITY OF WISCONSIN, MADISON, Memorial Library, Rare Books Collection, 728 State St, Madison, 53706. Gretchen Lagana, Cur
Holdings: Vols (120,000) Cat Mss Maps Pix Slides Filmstrips Microforms
Budget: ($20,000)

CHINA—COMMERCE—U.S.

†CA —FAR EAST MERCHANTS ASSOCIATION, Femas Trade Library, 1597 Curtis St, Berkeley, 94702.
Notes: Trade with Far Eastern countries, esp China, Japan, Philippine Islands and Singapore.

CA —HOOVER INSTITUTION ON WAR, REVOLUTION & PEACE, Stanford University, Stanford, 94305. Milorad M Drachkovitch, Archivist
Notes: Papers of Julean Herbert Arnold, 1905-1946, incl diary, correspondence, speeches and writings, reports, dispatches, instructions, memoranda, and other material relating to Arnold's service in the U S. Consular Service in China and as U S Commercial Attache in China, to economic and political developments in China, and to American commercial and foreign policy interest in the Far East. 14 ms boxes.

MA —HARVARD UNIVERSITY, Graduate School of Business Administration, Baker Library, Soldiers Field, Boston, 02163. Mary V Chatfield, Librn; Florence Bartoshesky, Cur of Manuscripts and Archives
Holdings: Vols (75,000) Cat Mss Pix
Notes: Baker Library strong in historical aspects of business and economics incl original company records, company histories, business biographies, histories of industries, foreign trade, China trade, etc. See Robert W Lovett and Eleanor C Bishop, compilers, *Manuscripts in Baker Library* (Boston: The Library, 1978), 382 pp. Mss are described in the *National Union Catalog of Manuscript Collections and in Hamer's A Guide to Archives and Manuscripts in the United* States. Restricted use: Manuscripts noncirculating. Downs: 1636, 2122, 2616, 2675, 2677, 2698, 2700, 2701, 2702, 2706, 2708, 2711, 2713-15, 2716, 2717-18, 2721-26, 2734, 2737, 2774, 2814, 4300, 5162: Supplement 964, 965, 968, 998.

MA —CHINA TRADE MUSEUM, Library, 215 Adams St, Milton, 02186. Lisa L Gwirtzman, Librn
Holdings: Uncat Mss Maps Pix
Notes: A museum collection, archive and library devoted to a history of the China Trade to Boston, (1784-1900). Incl 30,000 papers of Captain Robert Bennet Forbes; 75, 000 other China Trade documents; and 3500 period photographs.

CHINA—CURRENT EVENTS

DC —LIBRARY OF CONGRESS, General Reading Rooms Division, Microform Reading Room, Washington, 20540.
Holdings: Cat Mss Maps Pix Microforms
Notes: Microform materials only in this LC Division. Works of individual authors; holdings of collections; archival records, etc, press releases and translations, etc.

CHINA—DESCRIPTION AND TRAVEL—VIEWS

NM —MUSEUM OF NEW MEXICO, Photo Archives, Box 2087, Santa Fe, 87503. Arthur L Olivas, Cur; Richard Rudisill, Photo Historian
Holdings: Cat Pix Slides
Notes: Extensive picture collections of Australia, New Zealand, China, India and the East taken in the 19th century. The Photo Archives contain approx 250,000 items, of which 200,000 are cataloged. The primary function of the archives is preserving significant historical material, and these pictures are mainly for research rather than for general browsing.

CHINA—ECONOMIC CONDITIONS

CA —HOOVER INSTITUTION ON WAR, REVOLUTION & PEACE, Stanford University, Stanford, 94305. Milorad M Drachkovitch, Archivist
Holdings: Mss Pix
Notes: Papers of Oliver J Todd, incl diaries, correspondence, reports, memoranda, photographs, and other material, relating to his service as an engineer for the International Famine Commission in China and the United Nations Relief and Rehabilitation Agency as well as to social, economic, and political conditions in China, 1919-1949. 40 ms boxes.

OH —OHIO UNIVERSITY, Vernon R Alden Library, Athens, 45701. Kent Mulliner, Africana Specialist
Notes: A collection of 634 vols of Chinese books covering a wide range of subjects incl art, culture, economics, geography, history, language, literature, martial arts, medical science, philosophy, and technology.

CHINA—HISTORY

AZ —ARIZONA STATE UNIVERSITY, Library, Tempe, 85287. Marilyn Wurzburger, Special Collections Librn
Notes: The A T Steele Collection is a unique compilation of articles and documents dealing with events in China from 1932-49. The collection is divided into five parts: dispatches, newspaper clippings, pamphlets and books, original documents of the Communist Party (ca 1945) and memorabilia, written and/or collected by American journalist A T Steele. Dispatches cover events in China from 1940-49 land are mostly first-hand experiences of Steele. These dispatches, not all of which were published, often contain details absent in the final copy. Post-war topics incl truce negotiations between the Nationalists and Chinese Communists and the "Manchurian Question." Index available. 12 linear feet of materials.

CA —UNIVERSITY OF CALIFORNIA, BERKELEY, University Library, East Asiatic Library, Room 208, Durant Hall, Berkeley, 94720. Donald Shively, Head
Holdings: Vols 245,000 Cat Mss Maps Pix Microforms
Notes: Research

†CA —LOS ANGELES PUBLIC LIBRARY, Chinatown Branch, 536 W College St, Los Angeles, 90012.
Notes: Chinese history and culture, Chinese Americans.

CA —UNIVERSITY OF CALIFORNIA, LOS ANGELES, Oriental Library, 405 Hilgard Ave, Los Angeles, 90024. Ik-Sam Kim, Head
Holdings: Vols 30,000 Cat

†CA —CHINESE CULTURE FOUNDATION OF, San Francisco Library, 750 Kearny St, San Francisco, 94108.
Notes: Chinese-American history and culture.

CA —HOOVER INSTITUTION ON WAR, REVOLUTION & PEACE, Stanford University, Stanford, 94305. Milorad M Drachkovitch, Archivist
Holdings: // Mss
Notes: Five collections: (1) The J Calvin Huston Collection. Handwritten papers, pamphlets, placards, leaflets, and newspaper clippings, chiefly in English and Russian, dealing with cultural, political, and economic conditions in China, with special reference to communism and the influence of Soviet Russia, 1917-1931. 14 boxes. Unpublished register is available in repository. (2) Papers of Paul W Frillmann, chaplain of the American Volunteer Group ("Flying Tigers"), 1941-45, and US consular offical in China and Hong Kong, 1946-50, incl correspondence, memoranda, orders, notes and photos, 1941-69, relating to activities of the American Volunteer Group in China

CHINA—HISTORY (cont.)

during World War II, US foreign relations with China, 1946-50, and conditions in China during the civil war. 3 ms boxes, 3 framed certificates. (3) Papers of Victor Chi-tsai Hoo, Nationalist Chinesediplomat and statesman, 1919-1945, and United Nations official, 1945-1972, incl diaries, correspondence, clippings, reports, memoranda, photographs, and other material, 1930-1972, relating to his government service for China, Chinese political events and foreign relations, Sino-Soviet relations, and his career with the United Nations. 7 1/2 ms boxes. (4) Papers of Robert Norton, US attorney and journalist (editor of *China Today*), incl correspondence, speeches and writings, clippings, printed matter, photographs, and other materials, 1935-1948, relating to US relations with China and Japan, India's independence from Great Britain, Japanese military incursions into China, and United Nations assistance to China. 3 1/2 boxes. (5) Papers of Wilbur J Peterkin, executive and commanding officer of the US Observer Mission to the Chinese Communists,1944-1945, incl diary transcripts, reports, maps, 16mm film, and other material, 1944-1945, relating to Chinese communist forces and the Japanese occupation of China during World War II. Also incl are rifle, bayonet, pistol, and hand grenade used by the Chinese communists during the Sino-Japanese Conflict. 1 1/2 ms boxes.

CT —YALE UNIVERSITY, Box 1603A, Yale Station, New Haven, 06520.

†DC —CENTER FOR CHINESE RESEARCH MATERIALS, 1527 New Hampshire Ave, NW, Washington, 20036.

†HI —HAWAII CHINESE HISTORY CENTER, 111 North King St, No 410, Honolulu, 96817.
Notes: Chinese in Hawaii and mainland US.

IL —CENTER FOR RESEARCH LIBRARIES, 6050 S Kenwood Ave, Chicago, 60637. Donald B Simpson, Dir; Esther Smith, Collection Development Librn
Holdings: Cat Microforms
Notes: Mainland China newspapers, periodicals and clippings, early western language newspapers in China, Hong Kong newspapers in English, British Foreign Office and US State Dept records relating to China, Dunhuang manuscripts, missionary periodicals. Microfilm and reprints of newspapers, serials and monographs from Center for Chinese Research Materials. Hunter collection of Chinese communist propaganda (ca 1000 vols). Microfilm and originals of Maritime Customs publications. Microfilm of press summaries prepared by US Consulate, Hong Kong, archives of missionary organizations, Chinese folk literature, etc. Descriptive pamphlet available.

†IL —CHICAGO PUBLIC LIBRARY, Chinatown Branch, 3214 S Wentworth Ave, Chicago, 60616.
Notes: Chinese interest and history, Chinese Americans.

IN —INDIANA UNIVERSITY, Lilly Library, Seventh St, Bloomington, 47405. William R Cagle, Librn
Holdings: Vols (2000) // Cat
Notes: The core of the collection is the specialized library of Charles R Boxer (1000 titles) dealing with the history of the Iberians in the East, 16th-18th century. Mainly incl works on China, Japan and the Philippines during the period of their early intercourse with the West through 1800, as well as materials on the English and Dutch East India Companies, and the 17th century Anglo-Dutch naval wars. Special mention should be made of the valuable letters from missions by the Jesuits, and the works in this area by the Augustinians, Franciscans, and Dominicans, from the time of the arrival of the Iberians in Asia. The collection is a valubable source of information for the study of the European expansion into the area, including Southeast Asia.

MD —UNIVERSITY OF MARYLAND, Library, East Asia Collection, College Park, 20742. Frank Joseph Shulman, Curator and Head
Holdings: Vols (90,000) // Mss
Notes: Japanese books, newspapers, periodicals, etc, of the Allied Occupation period (1945-1952), including files of censored publications. Books number 40,000; periodical titles, 13,000; newspaper titles, ca 16,500. The special collection relating to the Occupation period is supplemented by a growing collection (now ca 50,000 vols) of Chinese, Japanese, and Korean publications which form the basis of the University's general collection in East Asian language materials.

MA —HARVARD UNIVERSITY, Fairbank Center for East Asian Research, Library, 1737 Cambridge St, Cambridge, 02138. Nancy Hearst, Librn
Holdings: Vols (10,000) Mss Maps
Notes: Post-1949 China, particularly political and sociological developments. Also, post-1952 Japan. Partially cataloged.

MA —CHINA TRADE MUSEUM, Library, 215 Adams St, Milton, 02186. Lisa L Gwirtzman, Librn
Notes: Incl an indexed masterpiece collection of photographs of China.

MA —ESSEX INSTITUTE, James Duncan Phillips Library, 132-34 Essex St, Salem, 01970. Prudence K Backman, Manuscript Librn
Holdings: Vols
Notes: Over 10,000 books, pamphlets, broadsides, periodicals, photographs and maps comprising the Frederick Townsend Ward Collection. Collection depicts the history and culture of China and interaction of China with the West from the era of Marco Polo to the early 20th Century.

MI —UNIVERSITY OF MICHIGAN, Asia Library, Ann Arbor, 48109. Wei-Ying Wan, Head
Holdings: Vols (201,000) Cat Microforms
Notes: Strong collection on all apsects of China and Chinese culture, comprehensive Contemporary China Reference Collection with Chinese, Japanese, and Western-language publications on post-1949 China. Special collections incl Union Research Institute Classified Files on China, over 20, 000 pieces of the Red Guards Materials, the Classified Files on the Great Cultural Revolution compiled by the Contemporary China Research Institute, National Peking Library Rare Books, Microfilms, rare editions of Chinese fiction microfilmed from several Japanese collections. National Central Library Rare Book Microfilms. Ming literary collections photo-reprinted from Japanese collections. British Public Record Office Files on China, outstanding collection of Japanese works on China. Incl 15,600 reels of microfilm and 12,300 microfiche.

MI —MICHIGAN STATE UNIVERSITY, International Library, East Asia Collection, East Lansing, 48824. Eugene deBenko, Librn
Holdings: Vols (34,000) Cat Mss Maps Phonorecords Audiotapes Microforms
Budget: ($11,000)
Notes: Priority given to East Asian publications on contemporary China, Japan and Korea. Principal subject emphasis on language, literature and history. Important resources also on politics and government, economics, anthropology, sociology, geography and agriculture.

NJ —PRINCETON UNIVERSITY, Library, Manuscript Collection, Nassau St, Princeton, 08540. Jean F Preston, Cur
Holdings: // Cat Mss Pix
Notes: Archives of the United China Relief, Inc, and United Service to China, Inc. Incl 100 boxes of papers. The archive covers the period, 1941 to 1966. An unpublished typescript guide (36 p) is available in the Library.

NY —STATE UNIVERSITY OF NEW YORK AT ALBANY, Library, Special Collections Dept, 1400 Washington Ave, Albany, 12222. Marion P Munzer, Coordr
Notes: Fred R Brown's correspondence, mss, photographs, and maps. He was a Methodist missionary to China from 1910-31 (6 linear feet). Part of the Library's German Exile Collection.
See also entries under Brown, Fred R; Missions-China; Missionaries

NY —CORNELL UNIVERSITY LIBRARIES, John M Olin Library, Wason Collection of China & the Chinese, Ithaca, 14853. James Cole, Cur; Paul P W Cheng, East Asia Librn
Holdings: Vols (330,000) Cat Mss Maps Pix Microforms
See also entry under China

†NY —COLUMBIA UNIVERSITY LIBRARIES, Butler Library, Rare Book and Manuscript Library, 535 W 114 St, New York, 10027.
Notes: Papers of the American Bureau for Medical Aid to China, incl correspondence, memoranda, reports, minutes, membership and financial records, photographs, posters and printed material. Approx 45,000 pieces. Also, some 6000 photographs of Chinese medical colleges, hospitals, laboratories, and personnel.

†NY —NEW YORK PUBLIC LIBRARY, Chatham Square Branch, 33 E Broadway, New York, 10002.
Notes: New York's Chinatown, Chinese in the US, local Chinese newspapers.

NY —UNIVERSITY OF ROCHESTER, Rush Rhees Library, Rochester, 14627. Datta S Kharbas, Head
Holdings: Vols 100,000 Cat Maps Microforms
Notes: Area studies collection on East Asia and South Asia. Major emphasis is on social sciences and humanities. Over 57,000 volumes on East Asia, out of which 29,000 volumes are in Chinese and 15,000 in Japanese. Extensive holdings on Chinese and Japanese histories. Catalog of East Asian consisting of Chinese and Japanese language holdings published in 1968, with two subsequent supplements. Over 33,000 volumes on South Asia. Considerable depth in social sciences, history, politics and anthropology. Extensive holdings in Sanskrit, Hindi, and Marathi.

NY —US MILITARY ACADEMY LIBRARY, Special Collections Division, West Point, 10996. Angela H Kao, Orientalia Librn
Holdings: Vols 4000 Cat Mss Maps Microforms
Budget: $600
Notes: Primarily military and general history of China, incl biographies of Chinese military leaders of different political backgrounds from the early years of the Chinese Republic to recent times. Books as well as periodicals are mostly in Chinese with a few additional works in English and Japanese. Described in *Catalog of the Orientalia Collection of the USMA Library, West Point, 1978.*

OH —OHIO UNIVERSITY, Vernon R Alden Library, Athens, 45701. Kent Mulliner, Africana Specialist
Notes: A collection of 634 vols of Chinese books covering a wide range of subjects incl art, culture, economics, geography, history, language, literature, martial arts, medical science, philosophy, and technology.

†OH —CHINESE AMERICAN CULTURAL ASSOCIATION LIBRARY, 8122 Mayfield, Chesterland, 44026.
Notes: Chinese-American heritage and history.

OH —HEBREW UNION COLLEGE-JEWISH INSTITUTE OF RELIGION, Klau Library, 3101 Clifton Ave, Cincinnati, 45220. David J Gilner, Reference Librn
Holdings: Vols 59 // Cat Mss
Notes: Only Chinese Hebrew ms collection extant. Incl community roster of Kai-Feng-fu Hebrew and Chinese, and many mss in fanfold form.

PA —UNIVERSITY OF PITTSBURGH, East Asian Library, 234 Hillman Library, Pittsburgh, 15260. Thomas C Kuo, Cur
Holdings: Vols (118,000) Microforms
Budget: ($210,000)
Notes: Contains Chinese and Japanese language publications on all social sciences and humanities, with special emphasis on history and source materials on both traditional and modern China, as well as research materials on language, literature, history, anthropology, economics and sociology of modern Japan. Catalogs of Chinese local history, East Asian periodicals and serials, and microforms in the collection

CHINA—HISTORY (cont.)

have been published by the library. Also, *A Brief Guide to the Use of the East Asian Library* (1983). Incl 1600 periodicals and 2900 reels of microfilms.

RI —BROWN UNIVERSITY, John Hay Library, 20 Prospect St, Providence, 02912. Mark N Brown, Cur Mss
Holdings: Vols (74,000) Cat Microforms
Budget: ($10,000)
Notes: East Asia Collection. The primary focus is on Chinese studies with a small segment of approx 700 vols devoted to Japanese studies. Major subject areas, in descending order of strength, are: literature (incl classics), history, geography, social sciences, philosophy and religion, fine arts, science and technology. This incl the personal collection (20,000 vols) formed by Harvard University Sinologist Dr Charles Sidney Gardner, which is especially rich in materials relating to the Ch'ing Dynasty (1644-1912). In addition to books, there are 500 reels of microfilm, plus runs of 8 Chinese newspapers and 26 current Chinese periodicals.

TX —UNIVERSITY OF TEXAS LIBRARIES, Asian Collection, PO Box P, Austin, 78712. Kevin Lin, Asian Librn; Merry Burlingham, South Asian Librn
Holdings: Vols 24,000 Cat Microforms
Notes: Anthropology, economics, government, history, and language and literature of China. Incl 250 periodical titles.

WA —UNIVERSITY OF WASHINGTON LIBRARIES, East Asia Library, DO-27, Seattle, 98195. Karl Lo, Head
Holdings: Vols (300,000) Cat Microforms
Budget: ($200,000)
Notes: Southwest China: Joseph Rock Collection, ca 2000 vols; modern Chinese poetry, 1919 to date: ca 700 titles; Asian art, esp. Japanese painting: 4097 vols; Tiao-yu-t'ai movement in the U S: ca 400 items of periodicals and pamphlets; modern Korean poetry, ancient and modern: ca 1000 titles; My-yu-shu folk literature: ca 1000 items.

WI —UNIVERSITY OF WISCONSIN, MADISON, Memorial Library, Rare Books Collection, 728 State St, Madison, 53706. Gretchen Lagana, Cur
Holdings: Vols (120,000) Cat Mss Maps Pix Slides Filmstrips Microforms
Budget: ($20,000)

BC —UNIVERSITY OF VICTORIA, McPherson Library, Victoria, V8W 3H5, Can.
Notes: Incl 11 pages, 1937; ms description of the Fall of Nanking.

CHINA—HISTORY—OPIUM WARS see China—History_War of 1840-1842

CHINA—HISTORY—WAR OF 1840-1842

CA —FITZ HUGH LUDLOW MEMORIAL LIBRARY, PO Box 99346, San Francisco, 94109. Michael R Aldrich, Exec Cur
Holdings: Vols (100)
Notes: Collection stored. Important mail inquiries only. No interlibrary lending or telephone queries. This collections emphasis historical and literary works about opium and its derivatives, mostly in English, going back to the 17th century but mostly from the 19th and early 20th centuries. Excellent collection of De Quincey in different editions. Many books, pamphlets, and art relating to the 19th century international opium trade, the Chinese Opium Wars, clipper ships, and resulting international legal action in the early 20th century. Outstanding collection of the English, French, and American opium-addict confessional literature. Also incl many volumes and offprints relevant to narcotic drug prevention, treatment, and education.

CHINA—HISTORY, MILITARY

CA —HOOVER INSTITUTION ON WAR, REVOLUTION & PEACE, Stanford University, Stanford, 94305. Milorad M Drachkovitch, Archivist
Holdings: Mss
Notes: Papers of Maj Gen Haydon L Boatner, USA, 1941-1979, incl correspondence, memoranda, reports, studies, orders, maps, notes and printed matter relating to military policy and operations in the China-Burma-India Theatre during World War II. 5 ms boxes.

NY —US MILITARY ACADEMY LIBRARY, Special Collections Division, West Point, 10996. Angela H Kao, Orientalia Librn
Holdings: Vols 4000 Cat Mss Maps Microforms
Budget: $600
Notes: Primarily military and general history of China, incl biographies of Chinese military leaders of different political backgrounds from the early years of the Chinese Republic to recent times. Books as well as periodicals are mostly in Chinese with a few additional works in English and Japanese. Described in *Catalog of the Orientalia Collection of the USMA Library, West Point, 1978.*

CHINA—HOSPITALS

†NY —COLUMBIA UNIVERSITY LIBRARIES, Butler Library, Rare Book and Manuscript Library, 535 W 114 St, New York, 10027.
Notes: Papers of the American Bureau for Medical Aid to China, incl correspondence, memoranda, reports, minutes, membership and financial records, photographs, posters and printed material. Approx 45,000 pieces. Also, some 6000 photographs of Chinese medical colleges, hospitals, laboratories, and personnel.

CHINA—IMPRINTS

OH —OHIO UNIVERSITY, Vernon R Alden Library, Athens, 45701. Kent Mulliner, Africana Specialist
Notes: A collection of 634 vols of Chinese books covering a wide range of subjects incl art, culture, economics, geography, history, language, literature, martial arts, medical science, philosophy, and technology.

CHINA—MAPS

DC —LIBRARY OF CONGRESS, Geography and Map Division, Washington, 20540. John A Wolter, Chief
Holdings: Cat Mss Maps Pix Slides Microforms
Notes: *Cartographic Materials.* One of the largest cartographic collections in the world, all-inclusive in coverage. Early original manuscript maps, navigation charts by Italian, Portuguese, and Spanish 15th, 16th, and 17th-century cartographers; the Hummel & Warner Collections of rare manuscript and printed maps and atlases of China and Korea from the 17th, 18th, and 19th centuries; manuscript and printed maps of colonial America, the Revolutionary War, the War of 1812, the Civil War, and wars of the 20th century; individual sheets of large and medium-scale set maps and charts published in the 19th and 20th centuries, including official topographic, geologic, soil, mineral, and resource maps, and nautical and aeronautical charts for most countries of the world; special subject maps of the world and its various political entities; maps of the United States and the separateStates; county maps and plans of cities and towns, and the Sanborn Fire Insurance Maps, dating back to 1866 for some 13,000 cities in the United States. Atlases include earliest printed editions of Ptolemy's Geography (1482), and representative volumes of leading atlas publishers of the last five centuries covering individual continents, countries, states, counties, cities, and the world. Total: 3,800, 000 maps, 49,000 atlases, 400 globes and 2000 relief models. See *The Geography and Map Division: A Guide to Its Collections and Services,* rev ed, 1975 (LC 5.2:SE6/975).

CHINA—MISSIONS see Missions—China

CHINA—PICTURES, ILLUSTRATIONS, ETC.

MA —CHINA TRADE MUSEUM, Library, 215 Adams St, Milton, 02186. Lisa L Gwirtzman, Librn
Notes: Incl an indexed masterpiece collection of photographs of China.

CHINA—POLITICS AND GOVERNMENT

†DC —CENTER FOR CHINESE RESEARCH MATERIALS, 1527 New Hampshire Ave, NW, Washington, 20036.

NY —UNIVERSITY OF ROCHESTER, Rush Rhees Library, Rochester, 14627. Datta S Kharbas, Head
Holdings: Vols 100,000 Cat Maps Microforms
Notes: Area studies collection on East Asia and South Asia. Major emphasis is on social sciences and humanities. Over 57,000 volumes on East Asia, out of which 29,000 volumes are in Chinese and 15,000 in Japanese. Extensive holdings on Chinese and Japanese histories. Catalog of East Asian collection consisting of Chinese and Japanese language holdings published in 1968, with two subsequent supplements. Over 33,000 volumes on South Asia. Considerable depth in social sciences, history, politics and anthropology. Extensive holdings in Sanskrit, Hindi, and Marathi.

SK —UNIVERSITY OF SASKATCHEWAN, Library, Saskatoon, S7N 0W0, Can. S Perkins, Librn
Notes: *Documents on Contemporary China,* 1949-1975, 525 microfiches; material from a wide variety of sources. Much on Red Guard and the Cultural Revolution. The Library also holds the *Survey of China Mainland* Press.

CHINA—RELIGION

NY —INSTITUTE FOR ADVANCED STUDIES OF WORLD RELIGIONS (IASWR), Melville Memorial Library, State University of New York, Stony Brook, 11794. C T Shen, Dir
Holdings: Vols 25,000 Cat Periodicals Mss Maps Microforms
Notes: Incl works on Buddhism and related subjects in history, art, etc in English, European and Asian languages. Buddhist Canon: Chinese version in Chinese, Japanese and Korean editions; some rare editions of Chinese canonical texts. Ref works, monastic biographies, collected writings of Buddhist monks and scholars. Tibetan Buddhism, Taoism, Islam, and others. Microforms: Chinese mss from Tun-huang in the British Museum and Bibliotheque Nationale. Sung-chi-sha Tsang. Refer inquiries to H G Robinson or Ms L Yang.

OH —CLEVELAND PUBLIC LIBRARY, Fine Arts and Special Collections Department, 325 Superior Ave, Cleveland, 44114. Alice N Loranth, Head
Holdings: Vols (7000) Cat Mss
Notes: Part of the Oriental Religion and the Islam in China Collections. Classic texts in their original languages and Western translations are emphasized. Important serial publications in Western languages are well represented. Special emphasis is on Buddhism, and on Islam in China.
See also entries under Religion, Oriental; Islam in China.

CHINA TRADE

CA —FITZ HUGH LUDLOW MEMORIAL LIBRARY, PO Box 99346, San Francisco, 94109. Michael R Aldrich, Exec Cur
Holdings: Vols 100
Notes: Collection stored. Important mail inquiries only. No interlibrary lending or telephone queries. This collections emphasis historical and literary works about opium and its derivatives, mostly in English, going back to the 17th century but mostly from the 19th and early 20th centuries. Excellent collection of De Quincey in different editions. Many books, pamphlets, and art relating to the 19th century international opium trade, the Chinese Opium Wars, clipper ships, and resulting international legal action in the early 20th century.

CHINA TRADE (cont.)

Outstanding collection of the English, French, and American opium-addict confessional literature. Also incl many volumes and offprints relevant to narcotic drug prevention, treatment, and education.

MA —HARVARD UNIVERSITY, Graduate School of Business Administration, Baker Library, Soldiers Field, Boston, 02163. Mary V Chatfield, Librn; Florence Bartoshesky, Cur of Manuscripts and Archives
Holdings: Vols (75,000) Cat Mss Pix
Notes: Baker Library strong in historical aspects of business and economics incl original company records, company histories, business biographies, histories of industries, foreign trade, China trade, etc. See Robert W Lovett and Eleanor C Bishop, compilers, *Manuscripts in Baker Library* (Boston: The Library, 1978), 382 pp. Mss are described in the *National Union Catalog of Manuscripts in the United States.* Restricted use: Manuscripts noncirculating. Downs: 1636, 2122, 2616, 2675, 2677, 2698, 2700, 2701, 2702, 2706, 2708, 2711, 2713-15, 2716, 2717-18, 2721-26, 2734, 2737, 2774, 2814, 4300, 5162: Supplement 964, 965, 968, 998.

MA —CHINA TRADE MUSEUM, Library, 215 Adams St, Milton, 02186. Lisa L Gwirtzman, Librn
Holdings: Uncat Mss Maps Pix
Notes: A museum collection, archive and library devoted to a history of the China Trade to Boston, (1784-1900). Incl 30,000 papers of Captain Robert Bennet Forbes; 75, 000 other China Trade documents; and 3500 period photographs.

CHINAWARE see Porcelain; Pottery

CHINESE AMERICAN NEWSPAPERS see Newspapers, Chinese American

CHINESE-AMERICAN RELATIONS

MA —HARVARD UNIVERSITY LIBRARY, Widener Library, Cambridge, 02138.
Holdings: Cat
Notes: Surveys of collections by Robert L Irick and Valentin H Rabe published by Harvard University Press, 1960 (*Research Aids for American Far Eastern Policy* Studies, 1 and 3).

CHINESE ART see Art, Chinese

CHINESE CALLIGRAPHY see Calligraphy and Calligraphers, Chinese

CHINESE CERAMICS see Ceramics, Chinese

CHINESE CHESS

NY —US MILITARY ACADEMY LIBRARY, West Point, 10996. Elaine B Eatroff, Rare Book Cur
Holdings: Vols 550 Cat Mss Pix
Notes: European imprints, beginning from the early 16th century, British, and American, incl: Hagedorn No 1, early chess periodicals. Incl: bibliography, collection of games, end games, history, openings, problems, and tournaments. Also, Chinese chess. Go, backgammon, and checkers. Chess sets, ephemera, etc.

CHINESE CONSOLIDATED BENEVOLENT ASSOCIATION

BC —UNIVERSITY OF VICTORIA, McPherson Library, Victoria, V8W 3H5, Can.
Notes: Victoria, BC. Incl 170 cm, 1884-1923; 1932; correspondence (1884-1922); founding of the Association (1884); records of protest against racial discrimination (1886-1894); segregation of Chinese children in public schools in Victoria (1907-1923); record of the Association as mediator (1886-1900); ecomonic aspects (1884-1922); record of contributions of the Association (1884-97); exemption letters; history of Chinese hospitals (1888-1922). Lists: Chinese deceased, 1937; leave permits; receipts: donations to the Republic of China, 1912; donations to the CCBA 1884-85; national subscription records, Kuang-hsu 11th and 12th year; income and expenditure records; freeminers certificates and records; national bond records; population data; original mss: 75th Anniversary of CCBA Special Issue. Restrictions: requests for permission must be made tothe Chairman or other designated representative of the Association. The Collection is entirely in Chinese.

CHINESE DRAMA

MI —UNIVERSITY OF MICHIGAN, Asia Library, Ann Arbor, 48109. Wei-Ying Wan, Head
Holdings: Vols (201,000) Cat Microforms
Notes: Strong collection on all aspects of China and Chinese culture, comprehensive Contemporary China Reference Collection with Chinese, Japanese, and Western-language publications on post-1949 China. Special collections incl Union Research Institute Classified Files on China, over 20, 000 pieces of the Red Guards Materials, the Classified Files on the Great Cultural Revolution compiled by the Contemporary China Research Institute, National Peking Library Rare Books Microfilms, rare editions of Chinese fiction microfilmed from several Japanese collections, National Central Library Rare Book Microfilms, Ming literary collections photo-reprinted from several Japanese collections, British Public Record Office Files on China, outstanding collection of Japanese works on China. Incl 15,600 reels of microfilm and 12,300 microfiche.

CHINESE IN CALIFORNIA

LA —AMISTAD RESEARCH CENTER, 400 Esplanade Ave, New Orleans, 70116. Clifton H Johnson, Exec Dir; Florence E Borders, Senior Archivist
Budget: ($315,000)
Notes: Originally established at Fisk University, in Nashville, by the American Missionary Association (AMA), this research center on Black American History consists of mss, photographs, clippings, books, pamphlets, taped speeches and interviews; also, the papers of such leaders as W E B DuBois, Countee Cullen, and Mary McLeod Bethune. Also materials on other American minorities, such as Native Americans, Asian Americans, Hispanics, etc.

CHINESE IN CANADA

BC —UNIVERSITY OF VICTORIA, McPherson Library, Victoria, V8W 3H5, Can.
Notes: Victoria, BC. Incl 170 cm, 1884-1923; 1932; correspondence (1884-1922); founding of the Association (1884); records of protest against racial discrimination (1886-1894); segregation of Chinese children in public schools in Victoria (1907-1923); record of the Association as mediator (1886-1900); ecomonic aspects (1884-1922); record of contributions of the Association (1884-97); exemption letters; history of Chinese hospitals (1888-1922). Lists: Chinese deceased, 1937; leave permits; receipts: donations to the Republic of China, 1912; donations to the CCBA 1884-85; national subscription records, Kuang-hsu 11th and 12th year; income and expenditure records; freeminers certificates and records; national bond records; population data; original mss: 75th Anniversary of CCBA Special Issue. Restrictions: requests for permission must be made tothe Chairman or other designated representative of the Association. The Collection is entirely in Chinese.

CHINESE IN HAWAII

†HI —HAWAII CHINESE HISTORY CENTER, 111 North King St, No 410, Honolulu, 96817.
Notes: Chinese in Hawaii and mainland US.

CHINESE IN THE U.S.

CA —LOS ANGELES PUBLIC LIBRARY, Social Sciences Dept, 630 W Fifth St, Los Angeles, 90071. Marilyn C Wherley, Principal Librn
Holdings: Vols 400 Microforms
Budget: ($150,000)
Notes: Emphasis on minorities; immigration policies, background and social problems of ethnic minorities in the US and the Southwest in particular. Incl periodicals, government publications and documents, popular and scholarly works on Blacks, Hispanics and Asians predominantly.

†CA —LOS ANGELES PUBLIC LIBRARY, Chinatown Branch, 536 W College St, Los Angeles, 90012.
Notes: Chinese history and culture, Chinese Americans.

CA —UNIVERSITY OF CALIFORNIA, LOS ANGELES, Research Library, Dept of Special Collections, 405 Hilgard Ave, Los Angeles, 90024. Edward Shreeves, Chairman, Bibliographers Group; David S Zeidberg, Head
Notes: 150 photographs of San Francisco Chinatown by Louis J Stellman.

†CA —CHINESE CULTURE FOUNDATION OF, San Francisco Library, 750 Kearny St, San Francisco, 94108.
Notes: Chinese-American history and culture.

CA —HOOVER INSTITUTION ON WAR, REVOLUTION & PEACE, Stanford University, Stanford, 94305. Milorad M Drachkovitch, Archivist
Holdings: Mss
Notes: Records of Aid Refugee Chinese Intellectuals (ARCI), a private U S relief organization, incl correspondence, reports, minutes of meetings, financial records and photographs, 1952-1970, relating to ARCI relief work for Chinese refugees. 44 ms boxes, 3 albums.

DC —LIBRARY OF CONGRESS, Prints & Photographs Div, Washington, 20540.
Notes: The John C H Grabill collection of photographs of frontier life in Colorado, South Dakota, and Wyoming, late 19th century, incl views of hunters, prospectors, cowboys, Chinese immigrants, and US Army personnel.

†HI —HAWAII CHINESE HISTORY CENTER, 111 North King St, No 410, Honolulu, 96817.
Notes: Chinese in Hawaii and mainland US.

†IL —CHICAGO PUBLIC LIBRARY, Chinatown Branch, 3214 S Wentworth Ave, Chicago, 60616.
Notes: Chinese interest and history, Chinese Americans.

MA —CHILDREN'S MUSEUM, Resource Center, Museum Wharf, 300 Congress St, Boston, 02210. Marie Ariel, Librn; Maria Russell, Resource Services Mgr
Holdings: Vols 200 Cat Mss Slides Audiotapes Phonorecords Filmstrips
Notes: Curriculum materials and materials for children and adults. Available for reference use by the public; borrowing privileges for Museum members; activity and curriculum kits available to public, schools and community groups for rental fee. Subject-related programs and services offered by Museum staff.

†NY —CHINESE INSTITUTE IN AMERICA LIBRARY, 125 East 65 St, New York, 10021.
Notes: Chinese immigration, heritage and contribution to America.

†NY —NEW YORK PUBLIC LIBRARY, Chatham Square Branch, 33 E Broadway, New York, 10002.
Notes: New York's Chinatown, Chinese in the US, local Chinese newspapers.

†OH —CHINESE AMERICAN CULTURAL ASSOCIATION LIBRARY, 8122 Mayfield, Chesterland, 44026.
Notes: Chinese-American heritage and history.

PA —BALCH INSTITUTE FOR ETHNIC STUDIES, Library, 18 S Seventh St, Philadelphia, 19106. R Joseph Anderson, Library Dir
Holdings: Vols 300 Cat Mss Pix Microforms

WA —UNIVERSITY OF WASHINGTON LIBRARIES, East Asia Library, DO-27, Seattle, 98195. Karl Lo, Head
Holdings: Vols (300,000) Cat Microforms
Budget: ($200,000)
Notes: Southwest China: Joseph Rock

CHINESE IN THE U.S. (cont.)

Collection, ca 2000 vols; modern Chinese poetry, 1919 to date: ca 700 titles; Asian art, esp Japanese painting: 4097 vols; Tiao-yu-t'ai movement in the US: ca 400 items of periodicals and pamphlets; modern Korean poetry, ancient and modern: ca 1000 titles; Mu-yu-shu folk literature: ca 1000 items.

CHINESE JEWS see Jews, Chinese

CHINESE LANGUAGE AND LITERATURE

AZ —UNIVERSITY OF ARIZONA, Library, Oriental Studies Collection, Tucson, 85721. Mary J McWhorter, Actg Head Librn
Holdings: Vols (95,000) Cat Microforms
Budget: ($30,000)
See also entry under Oriental Languages and Literatures

CA —UNIVERSITY OF CALIFORNIA, BERKELEY, University Library, East Asiatic Library, Room 208, Durant Hall, Berkeley, 94720. Donald Shively, Head
Holdings: Vols 245,000 Cat Mss Maps Pix Microforms
Notes: Research

CA —CLAREMONT COLLEGES, Honnold Library, Asian Studies Collection, Ninth & Dartmouth, Claremont, 91711. Frances D Wang, Cur
Holdings: Vols (69,658) Cat Mss Maps Pix Microforms
Budget: ($50,000)
Notes: Incl 62,476 vols in Chinese and Japanese; 6276 in Western languages. About 13,000 uncataloged. Collection incl artifacts, original mss, rare, original editions of Chinese, Japanese, Korean and Western language and literature, history, and archaeology, which are today totally unavailable to acquire. The most distinguished work is the collection of some 200 Chinese gazetteers (fang-chih) which is one of the best in the US. Another valuable collection is the Frederick McCormick Collection of 214 titles in 896 vols of movable-type editions of Korean printed books, 15th-19th centuries. The Western-language collection on the Far East is probably one of the strongest in the US. Recently added was a collection of Japanese books on Shinto (125 titles), periodicals, and artifacts. Separate catalog.

CA —LOS ANGELES PUBLIC LIBRARY, Foreign Languages Dept, 630 W Fifth St, Los Angeles, 90071. Sylva Manoogian, Principal Librn
Holdings: Vols 1569 Cat
Budget: ($41,500)

CA —UNIVERSITY OF CALIFORNIA, LOS ANGELES, Oriental Library, 405 Hilgard Ave, Los Angeles, 90024. Ik-Sam Kim, Head
Holdings: Vols 40,000 Cat

CA —SAN JOSE PUBLIC LIBRARY, 180 W San Carlos St, San Jose, 95113. Homer Fletcher, Dir
Holdings: Vols 8300

CT —YALE UNIVERSITY, Box 1603A, Yale Station, New Haven, 06520.
Holdings: Cat

CT —CONNECTICUT COLLEGE, Library, Mohegan Ave, New London, 06320. Brian Rogers, College Librn
Holdings: Vols 2900 Cat
Notes: Collection supports the program of the Dept of Chinese.

DC —LIBRARY OF CONGRESS, African and Middle Eastern Division, Washington, 20540.
Holdings: Cat Mss Microforms
Notes: Orientalia: the Orientalia Division contains 1,400,000 vols in Oriental languages. Chinese: more than 422,000 vols, espec strong in local histories and Ch'ing (1644-1911) period material. Japanese: over 574,000 vols, espec strong in economics, statistic, history, literature; 12,000 government, learned society, and university periodical titles, particularly science, technology, and social sciences. Korean: 56, 000 vols, espec strong in social sciences and modern history.

HI —UNIVERSITY OF HAWAII, Library, 2550 The Mall, Honolulu, 96822. Joyce Wright, Head, Asia Collection; Masato Matsu, Head, East Asia Vernacular Collection
Holdings: Vols 60,394 Cat Microforms
Notes: The Asia Collection includes materials from and about China (People's Republic, Taiwan, Hong Kong) in all languages. No figures are available for western language materials relating to China, which are supplemented by retrospective materials in the main library collection. Scope: social sciences and the humanities, traditional and contemporary.

IL —UNIVERSITY OF ILLINOIS, URBANA/CHAMPAIGN, Asian Library, Urbana, 61801. William S Wong, Asian Librn
Holdings: Vols 130,000
Notes: East Asian Collection. Primarily a collection of Chinese, Japanese, and Korean language materials.

KS —UNIVERSITY OF KANSAS, Watson Library, East Asian Library, Lawrence, 66045. Eugene Carvalho, Librn
Holdings: Vols 50,000 Cat
Notes: Chinese language materials with special emphasis on political science, history, anthropology, sociology and economics, with added emphasis on classical Chinese literature, history of art.

MD —UNIVERSITY OF MARYLAND, Library, East Asia Collection, College Park, 20742. Frank Joseph Shulman, Curator and Head
Holdings: Vols (90,000) / / Mss
Notes: Japanese books, newspapers, periodicals, etc, of the Allied Occupation period (1945-1952), including files of censored publications. Books number 40,000; periodical titles, 13,000; newspaper titles, ca 16,500. The special collection relating to the Occupation period is supplemented by a growing collection (now ca 50,000 vols) of Chinese, Japanese, and Korean publications which form the basis of the University's general collection in East Asian language materials.

MA —BOSTON PUBLIC LIBRARY, South End Branch, Multilingual Library, 685 Tremont St, Boston, 02118. Laura H Reyes, Librn
Holdings: Cat

MA —HARVARD UNIVERSITY LIBRARY, Harvard-Yenching Library, 2 Divinity Ave, Cambridge, 02138. Eugene W Wu, Librn
Notes: Strong in philology and all literary genres. See *Harvard Library Bulletin,* X (1956), pp 73-93.

MI —UNIVERSITY OF MICHIGAN, Asia Library, Ann Arbor, 48109. Wei-Ying Wan, Head
Holdings: Cat
Notes: Strong collection on etymology, phonology, semantics, grammar, classical and modern literature, folk literature; special strength in early Chinese drama and fiction.

MI —MICHIGAN STATE UNIVERSITY, International Library, East Asia Collection, East Lansing, 48824. Eugene deBenko, Librn
Holdings: Vols (34,000) Cat Mss Maps Phonorecords Audiotapes Microforms
Budget: ($11,000)
Notes: Priority given to East Asian publications on contemporary China, Japan and Korea. Principal subject emphasis on language, literature, and history. Important resources also on politics and government, economics, anthropology, sociology, geography and agriculture.

NJ —PRINCETON UNIVERSITY, Library, Gest Oriental Library & East Asian Collections, 317 Palmer Hall, Princeton, 08544. D E Perushek, Cur
Holdings: Vols (267,000) Cat Mss Maps Pix Microforms
Notes: Mostly in Chinese. Subject areas incl. Chinese civilization, language, literature, philosophy, religion, history, geography, traditional medicine and materia medica, history of books and printing, sociology, economics, politics, and other social sciences. With regard to Chinese art and archaeology, only works of a general or cultural nature and primary textual sources are collected. For works on Chinese population only the historical and economic aspects are acquired. Subject areas in science and technology, except those materials dealing with indigenous developments and historical aspects, are excluded. No historical period is excluded. The collection is particularly noted for its strength in pre-20th century works on traditional Chinese medicine in all areas, and in works on the Ming period. Some Western-language reference works as well as Western-language works on Chinese literature, language, and linguistics. Emphasis is on current publications. Separate card catalog. Publications on collection: Ch'u Wan-li, A Catalogue of the Chinese Rare Books in the Gest collection of the Princeton University Library (Taiperi: Yee Wen Publishing Co., 1974). (In Chinese): Gillis, I. V. & Pai Ping-ch'i, Title Index to the Catalogue of the Gest Oriental Library (Peking Kwei LI Press, 1941). (In Chinese): Hu, Shih, "The Gest Oriental Library at Princeton University," Princeton University Chronicle, vol. xv (Spring 1954), 113-141; Rice, Howard C., Jr., Shih-kang Tung & Frederick W. Mote, East and West, Europe's Discovery of China and China's Response to Europe, 1511-1839: A Check-list of the Exhibition in the Princeton University Library, February 15-April 30, 1957 (Princeton: Princeton University Library, 1957); and Tung, Shih-kang, Chinese Microfilms in Princeton University: A Checklist of the Gest Oriental Library (Washington, Center for Chinese Research Materials, Association of Research Libraries, 1969).

NY —CORNELL UNIVERSITY LIBRARIES, John M Olin Library, Wason Collection of China & the Chinese, Ithaca, 14853. James Cole, Cur; Paul P W Cheng, East Asia Librn
Holdings: Vols (330,000) Cat Mss Maps Pix Microforms
See also entry under China

NY —COLUMBIA UNIVERSITY LIBRARIES, C V Starr East Asian Library, 300 Kent Hall, New York, 10027. James Reardon-Anderson, Librn
Holdings: Vols 230,996 Cat Mss Maps Pix
Notes: Publications in the major East Asian and Western languages in all subjects comprising the social sciences and humanities. Incl books, mss, maps, microforms, photographs, rubbings and realia related to the history of writing and printing in China.

NY —NEW YORK PUBLIC LIBRARY, Oriental Div, Fifth Ave & 42 St, New York, 10018. E Christian Filstrup, Chief
Holdings: Cat Mss Microforms
Budget: ($56,455)
Notes: Published catalog of holdings.

NY —NEW YORK PUBLIC LIBRARY, Donnell Foreign Language Library, 20 W 53 St, New York, 10019. Bosiljka Stevanovic, Supvr Librn
Holdings: Vols 2273 Cat
Notes: Chinese collection incl Chinese authors of Chinese expression. No separate catalog.

CHINESE LANGUAGE AND LITERATURE (cont.)

†NY —NEW YORK PUBLIC LIBRARY, Chatham Square Branch, 33 E Broadway, New York, 10002.
Notes: New York's Chinatown, Chinese in the US, local Chinese newspapers.

NY —UNIVERSITY OF ROCHESTER, Rush Rhees Library, Rochester, 14627. Datta S Kharbas, Head
Holdings: Vols 100,000 Cat Maps Microforms
Notes: Area studies collection on East Asia and South Asia. Major emphasis is on social sciences and humanities. Over 57,000 volumes on East Asia, out of which 29,000 volumes are in Chinese and 15,000 in Japanese. Extensive holdings on Chinese and Japanese histories. Catalog of East Asian collection consisting of Chinese and Japanese language holdings published in 1968, with two subsequent supplements. Over 33,000 volumes on South Asia. Considerable depth in social sciences, history, politics and anthropology. Extensive holdings in Sanskrit, Hindi, and Marathi.

NY —INSTITUTE FOR ADVANCED STUDIES OF WORLD RELIGIONS (IASWR), Melville Memorial Library, State University of New York, Stony Brook, 11794. C T Shen, Dir
Holdings: Vols 25,000 Cat Mss Maps Microforms
Notes: Incl works on Buddhism and related subjects in history, art, etc, in English, European and Asian languages. Buddhist Canon: Chinese version in Chinese, Japanese and Korean editions; some rare editions of Chinese canonical texts. Confucianism and other systems of thought, and comparative literature. Microforms: Chinese mss from Tun-huang in the British Museum and the Bibliotheque Nationale. Sung Chi-Sha Tsang. Refer inquiries to L Yang.
See also entry under China - Religion

NY —US MILITARY ACADEMY LIBRARY, Special Collections Division, West Point, 10996. Angela H Kao, Orientalia Librn
Notes: Primarily military and general history of China, incl biographies of Chinese military leaders of different political backgrounds from the early years of the Chinese Republic to recent times. Books as well as periodicals are mostly in Chinese with a few additional works in English and Japanese. Described in *Catalog of the Orientalia Collection of the USMA Library, West Point, 1978.*

NC —CUMBERLAND COUNTY PUBLIC LIBRARY, North Carolina Foreign Language Center, 328 Gillespie St, Fayetteville, 28301. Patrick M Valentine, Coordinator
Holdings: Vols (25,000) Cat Phonorecords Audiotapes
Notes: The largest book collections are, in descending order of size, German Spanish, French, Japanese, Korean and Vietnamese, with fair sized collections in Italian, Russian, Chinese, Arabic, Greek, Hungarian, Polish, Hebrew, Thai, and Hindi. The Center has several shelves each of books in Bengali, Dutch, Marathi, Portuguese, Urdu, and Yiddish. Smaller collections of one to three shelves each incl Catalan, Croatian, Czech, Danish, Finnish, Gujarati, Icelandic, Kannada, Latin, Lithuanian, Malayalam, Norwegian, Panjabi, Persian (Farsi), Romanian, Slovak, Swedish, Tagalog, Tamil, Telegu, and Ukrianian. The Center has grammars, dictionaries and occasionally other readings in languages from Afrikaans and Albanian to Welsh, Yoruba and Zulu.

OH —OHIO UNIVERSITY, Vernon R Alden Library, Athens, 45701. Kent Mulliner, Africana Specialist
Notes: A collection of 634 vols of Chinese books covering a wide range of subjects incl art, culture, economics, geography, history, language, literature, martial arts, medical science, philosophy, and technology.

OH —CLEVELAND PUBLIC LIBRARY, Fine Arts and Special Collections Department, 325 Superior Ave, Cleveland, 44114. Alice N Loranth, Head
Holdings: Vols (3500) Cat Mss
Notes: Emphasis is on Western editions and translations of literary and religious texts prior to European influence. Additional material on antiquities, early description and travel and early history. 2400 vols are in Chinese. Separate catalog of author entries for titles in Chinese is maintained.
See also entries under Oriental Languages and Literatures.

OH —CLEVELAND PUBLIC LIBRARY, Foreign Literature Dept, 325 Superior Ave, Cleveland, 44114. Natalia Bezugloff, Head
Holdings: Vols 1530 Cat
Notes: A popular circulating collection containing classics and the standard works with emphasis on belles lettres, history and biography. A variety of other subjects such as learning languages, how to do books, art, children's books, spoken phonodiscs and cassettes, periodicals, etc. Incl 1720 ephemera.
See also entry under Foreign Language Collections

OH —OBERLIN COLLEGE LIBRARY, Oberlin, 44074. William A Moffett, Dir of Libraries
Holdings: Cat

PA —UNIVERSITY OF PITTSBURGH, Hillman Library, Pittsburgh, 15260.
Notes: Incl the William Steinberg Collection of 800 musical scores, many signed by composers, and 1400 vols of English, French, German, Japanese, and Chinese literature.

PA —UNIVERSITY OF PITTSBURGH, East Asian Library, 234 Hillman Library, Pittsburgh, 15260. Thomas C Kuo, Cur
Holdings: Vols (118,000) Periodicals Microfilms
Budget: ($210,000)
Notes: Contains Chinese and Japanese language publications on all social sciences and humanities, with special emphasis on history and source materials on both traditional and modern China, as well as research materials on language, literature, history, anthropology, economics and sociology of modern Japan. Catalogs of Chinese local history, East Asian periodicals and serials, and microforms in the collection have been published by the library. Also, *A Brief Guide to the Use of the East Asian* Library (1983). Incl 1600 periodicals and 2900 reels of microfilms.

RI —BROWN UNIVERSITY, John Hay Library, 20 Prospect St, Providence, 02912. Mark N Brown, Cur Mss
Holdings: Vols (74,000) Cat Microforms
Budget: ($10,000)
Notes: East Asia Collection. The primary focus is on Chinese studies with a small segment of approx 700 vols devoted to Japanese studies. Major subject areas, in descending order of strength, are: literature (incl classics), history, geography, social sciences, philosophy and religion, fine arts, science and technology. This incl the personal collection (20,000 vols) formed by Harvard University Sinologist Dr Charles Sidney Gardner, which is especially rich in materials relating to the Ch'ing Dynasty (1644-1912). In addition to books, there are 500 reels of microfilm, plus runs of 8 Chinese newspapers and 26 current Chinese periodicals.

TX —UNIVERSITY OF TEXAS LIBRARIES, Asian Collection, PO Box P, Austin, 78712. Kevin Lin, Asian Librn; Merry Burlingham, South Asian Librn
Holdings: Vols 24,000 Cat Microforms
Notes: Anthropology, economics, government, history, and language and literature of China. Incl 250 periodical titles.

WA —UNIVERSITY OF WASHINGTON LIBRARIES, East Asia Library, DO-27, Seattle, 98195. Karl Lo, Head
Holdings: Vols (300,000) Cat Microforms
Budget: ($200,000)
Notes: Southwest China: Joseph Rock Collection, ca 2000 vols; modern Chinese poetry, 1919 to date: ca 700 titles; Asian Art, esp Japanese painting: 4097 vols; Tiao-yu-t'ai movement in the U S: ca 400 items of periodicals and pamphlets; modern Korean poetry, ancient and modern: ca 1000 titles; Mu-yu-shu folk literature: ca 1000 items.

BC —GREATER VANCOUVER LIBRARY FEDERATION, 110-6545 Bonsor, Burnaby, Z5H 1H3, Can. Colleen Smith, Coordr
Holdings: Vols (20,350) Cat
Notes: Deposit provided by the National Library's Multilingual Biblioservice on long-term loan to libraries in the Greater Vancouver Library Federation (Burnaby, New Westminster, N Vancouver City Public, N Vancouver District Public, Port Moody, Vancouver, W Vancouver).

BC —SIMON FRASER UNIVERSITY, Library, Burnaby, V5A 1S6, Can. Percilla Groves, Special Collections Librn
Holdings: Cat Mss
Notes: Incl a collection of 75 letters from Ezra Pound to Agnes Bedford and five letters to Wyndham Lewis, 1950-1959, plus 46 letters to Denis Goacher, his literary agent, and 140 pages to Sinologist Willis Hawley with carbons of Hawley's letters to Pound, also graphics for *Confucius: The Great Digest and Unwobbling Pivet,* and for *The Cantos.*

†ON —METROPOLITAN TORONTO LIBRARY BOARD, Language Dept, 789 Yonge St, Toronto, M4W 2G8, Can.
Notes: Incl sizeable donations of books from the people's Republic of Chinz Embassy in Canada.

CHINESE MANUSCRIPTS see Manuscripts, Chinese

CHINESE MATHEMATICS see Mathematics, Chinese

CHINESE MISSIONS see Missions—China

CHINESE MUSIC see Music, Chinese

CHINESE NEWSPAPERS see Newspapers, Chinese; Newspapers, Chinese American

CHINESE PERIODICALS see Periodicals, Chinese

CHINESE PHILOSOPHY see Philosophy, Chinese

CHINESE POETRY see Poetry, Chinese

CHINESE POTTERY see Pottery, Chinese

CHINESE QUESTION see China—History

CHINESE REFUGEES see Refugees, Chinese

CHINESE SONGS see Songs, Chinese

CHINGPAW LANGUAGE see Kachin Language

CHIPPEWA INDIANS

MI —LAKE SUPERIOR STATE COLLEGE, Library, College Dr, Sault Sainte Marie, 49783. Frederick A Michels, Dir
Holdings: Vols (400) Cat Maps Pix Slides
Notes: Michigan history with emphasis on Sault Ste Marie, eastern end of of Upper Peninsula, and area Indians (Chippewa or Ojibway).

MN —UNIVERSITY OF MINNESOTA, Libraries, Children's Literature Research Collections, 109 Walter Library, Minneapolis, 55455. Karen Nelson Hoyle, Cur
Holdings: Vols (40,000) Cat Mss Pix
Notes: Incl first editions, mss and illustrations for children's books. Newbery and Caldecott award books and honor books and their translations; Mildred L Batchelder Award nominees in original and US editions; Minnesota; Dakota and Ojibway Indian tribes; languages other than English;

CHIPPEWA INDIANS (cont.)

correspondence between authors and illustrators and Dr Irvin Kerlan, Kerlan Collection.

MN —COLLEGE OF SAINT CATHERINE, Library, 2004 Randolph Ave, Saint Paul, 55105. Sister Elizabeth Delmore, Library Dir
Holdings: Vols (800) Cat Mss Slides Phonorecords Audiotapes Filmstrips Microforms
Budget: ($800)
Notes: Both historical and cultural aspects. Special emphasis on Chippewa and Sioux Indian tribes.

MN —MINNESOTA HISTORICAL SOCIETY LIBRARY, 690 Cedar St, Saint Paul, 55101. Patricia C Harpole, Chief of Reference Library; Bonnie G Wilson, Head of Special Libraries

NY —HOFSTRA UNIVERSITY, Library, 1000 Fulton Ave, Hempstead, 11550. Charles R Andrews, Dean of Library Services
Notes: The personal library of Paul Radin. See description of the American Philosophical Society Library's collection of his anthropological papers under this entry (Pa).

PA —AMERICAN PHILOSOPHICAL SOCIETY, Library, 105 S Fifth St, Philadelphia, 19106. Edward C Carter II, Librn
Notes: The anthropological papers of Paul Radin in fields of ethnology, social organization, primitive religion, linguistics, and mythology. He worked mostly among the Winnebago, Ojibwa, Fox, Zapotec, Wappo, Wintun, and Huave Indian tribes; also Italian and other ethnic minorities of San Francisco.

ON —CHATHAM PUBLIC LIBRARY, 120 Queen St, Chatham, N7M 2G6, Can. Arlene Mason, Head of Reference
Holdings: Mss
Notes: Material on the Indians of Kent County, Ont, incl articles and books on the Pottawatamis and Chippewas of Walpole Island Reserve and on the Delaware Indians brought to Canada by the Moravian Missionaries in 1792 (the Fairfield Mission).

CHIPPEWAY INDIANS see Chippewa Indians

CHIRICAHUA INDIANS see Apache Indians

CHIROGRAPHY see Penmanship; Writing

CHIROPODY see Podiatry

CHIROPRACTIC AND CHIROPRACTORS

AZ —WORLD UNIVERSITY, Library, 711 E Blacklidge Dr, Tucson, 85719. Howard John Zitko, Cur
Holdings: Vols (15,000) Cat Mss Maps Audiotapes
Notes: Collection concerns the "frontier sciences." No interlibrary loan.

IL —NATIONAL COLLEGE OF CHIROPRACTIC, Sordoni-Burich Library, 200 E Roosevelt Rd, Lombard, 60148. Joyce Whitehead, Dir, Learning Resource Ctr
Holdings: Vols 1700 Cat Pix Slides Audiotapes Videotapes 16mm Films
Budget: $4000

TX —TEXAS CHIROPRACTIC COLLEGE, Mae Hilty Memorial Library, 5912 Spencer Highway, Pasadena, 77505. Michelle Larson, Librn
Holdings: Vols 700 Cat Pix Slides
Notes: Chiropractic science and practice. 200 currently received periodical titles; 250 paperbacks; 6000 vols directly related subjects; slides; no separate catalog. Archives Dept incl a collection on chiropractic history with 450 items of audiovisual material, and 3000 bound periodicals.

CHIROPTERA

NY —AMERICAN MUSEUM OF NATURAL HISTORY, Library Services Dept, Central Park W & 79th St, New York, 10024. Nina J Root, Chairwoman; Mary Genett, Asst Librn for Reference Services
Holdings: Vols (385,000) Mss Maps Pix Slides

CHIVALRY

DC —GEORGETOWN UNIVERSITY, Library, Special Collections Div, 37 & O Sts NW, Washington, 20057. George M Barringer, Special Collections Librn; Nicholas B Sheetz, Mss Librn
Holdings: Vols 800 Uncat Mss
Notes: Deals most extensively with Continental orders, both secular and ecclesiastical.

CHIVALRY—ROMANCES see Romances

CHIVERS, THOMAS HOLLEY

NC —DUKE UNIVERSITY, William R Perkins Library, Durham, 27706. Elvin E Strowd, University Librn
Notes: The Ethel Carr Peacock collection of 7000 volumes is strong in holdings of 19th century American literature.

NC —DUKE UNIVERSITY, William R Perkins Library, Manuscript Dept, Durham, 27706. Ellen Gartrell, Cur of Mss
Holdings: Cat Mss
Notes: Papers, correspondence, etc.

CHLORINE

OH —SDS BIOTECH CORP, PO Box 348, Painesville, 44077. Violet Forgach, Business Librn
Holdings: Cat Pix Microforms

CHOCOLATE

IN —HURTY-PECK LIBRARY OF BEVERAGE LITERATURE, 5650 W Raymond Street, PO Box 41167, Indianapolis, 46208. Ben Wilson, Librn
Holdings: Vols (6000) Cat //
Notes: The most comprehensive collection, in English, in the world on beverages of all types. History, manufacture, formulae, customs. Books on beer and brewing; cocoa and chocolate; coffee; liquors and spirits; soft drinks; tea; and wine.

MA —HARVARD UNIVERSITY, Graduate School of Business Administration, Baker Library, Soldiers Field, Boston, 02163. Mary V Chatfield, Librn; Florence Bartoshesky, Cur of Manuscripts and Archives
Notes: The Walter Baker Chocolate plant's papers dating from 1814. Incl journals, ledgers, cash books, payrolls, advertising, etc.

NY —WESTRECO INC, Research Library, 555 S Fourth St, Fulton, 13069. Janice Burns, Research Librn
Holdings: Vols 30 Cat Periodicals VF
Notes: Food Science and Technology collection of about (1200) books and pamphlets. Back files of periodicals retained up to 20 years.
See also entry under COCOA

CHOCTAW INDIANS

OK —OKLAHOMA HISTORICAL SOCIETY, Library, Historical Bldg, Oklahoma City, 73105. Andrea Clark, Dir, Library Resources Division
Holdings: Vols (43,000) Cat Mss Maps Pix Microforms
Notes: The Society also has the Indian Archives Collection of 2,500,000 pieces (Mary Lee Boyle, Archivist). This is an extensive collection of records, particularly of the Five Civilized Tribes. Incl tribal rolls, agency reports, manuscripts, etc.

OK —THOMAS GILCREASE INSTITUTE OF AMERICAN HISTORY & ART LIBRARY, 1400 North 25th West Ave, Tulsa, 74127. Sarah Hirsch, Librn
Holdings: Vols Cat Mss Maps Pix
Notes: Trans-Mississippi West, US, Indian and Hispanic history. The Gilcrease Library contains a total of about 40,000 mss; 10,000 imprints; 5000 photographs; 600 maps and 50,000 vols.

OK —UNIVERSITY OF TULSA, McFarlin Library, Dept of Rare Books and Special Collections, 600 S College, Tulsa, 74104. David Farmer, Dir; Toby Murray, Archivist; Caroline Swinson, Cur of Manuscripts & Art
Holdings: Cat
Notes: The Indian collection of John W Shleppey. Indian materials of some 6000 bibliographic items, excl of mss and photographs. Emphasis on Indian Territory imprints, laws, Cherokee and Choctaw tribes, etc.

CHOICE OF BOOKS see Bibliography—Best Books

CHOICE OF PROFESSION see Vocational Guidance

CHOIRS (MUSIC)

CA —SAN DIEGO PUBLIC LIBRARY, Art, Music & Recreation Sect, 820 E St, San Diego, 92101. Barbara A Tuhill, Supvr
Holdings: Cat
Notes: Collection consists of selections of 11,000 items for choirs of many voices. Indexed by voice, title and subject. Circulate on special loan for periods of three to six months or longer.

MI —DETROIT PUBLIC LIBRARY, Music & Performing Arts Dept, 5201 Woodward, Detroit, 48202. Agatha Pfeiffer Kalkanis, Chief
Holdings: Vols 19,000 Cat Mss Pix Microforms
Notes: Also incl (77,000) scores. General collection intended for practical use in performance and for scholarly research. Good working collection of bibliographies, thematic catalogs, dictionaries and encyclopedias, periodical indexes. Many sets of collected works, monumental editions, historical anthologies. Good representation of opera and operetta, art song and folk song, solo instrumental literature and chamber music in practical editions. 2575 titles of choral music, chiefly sacred, for use by choirs. 17,000 titles of popular sheet music, uncataloged but thoroughly indexed. Considerable recent holdings of books and periodicals in foreign languages. Special collections of black and local materials. 25, 000 recordings and extensive discographical literature. Collection of publishers' trade catalogs.

MI —WESTERN MICHIGAN UNIVERSITY, Dwight B Waldo Library, Institute of Cistercian Studies Library, Kalamazoo, 49008. Beatrice H Beck, Librn
Notes: The Abbot Obrecht Collection of mss, incunabula, and other books from the Cistercian Abbey of Gethsemane at Trappist, Kentucky. On indefinite loan (1976).

CHOLERA

MD —MEDICAL & CHIRURGICAL FACULTY OF THE STATE OF MARYLAND, Library, 1211 Cathedral St, Baltimore, 21201. Joseph E Jensen, Librn
Holdings: Vols (10,000) // Cat Mss Maps Pix
See also entry under Medicine - History and Historic

NY —UNIVERSITY OF ROCHESTER, School of Medicine and Dentistry, Edward G Miner Library, 601 Elmwood Ave, Rochester, 14642. Lucretia McClure, Medical Librn; Janet Brady Berk, History of Medicine Librn
Holdings: Vols 400 Cat
Notes: Strong in yellow fever, cholera, orthopedics, anatomy and original historic medical photographs.

TX —UNIVERSITY OF TEXAS, DALLAS, Health Science Center, Reference Dept & History of Health Sciences Dept, 5323 Harry Hines Blvd, Dallas, 75235. Helen Mayo, Head
Holdings: Vols (10,000) Cat Pix Slides Audiotapes Videotapes Microforms
Notes: History of Medicine collection contains ca 10,000 vols. This total is comprised of pre-1900 journals, primary

CHOLERA (cont.)

materials in the History of Medicine and the History of Science, and secondary studies in these two areas. The major strengths of this collection are in the areas of epidemics and plagues, military medicine, and collected works of famous medical pioneers. Incl in this collection are the medical journals published by the county medical societies in Texas, local publications by Dallas County medical organizations, and ephemeral material in a similar vein. The university archives contain all theses and dissertations form UTHSCD and miscellaneous institutional documents circulated by the school's administration.

CHOPIN, KATE

WI —UNIVERSITY OF WISCONSIN, MADISON, Memorial Library, British & American Language & Literature Collection, 728 State St, Madison, 53706. Yvonne Schofer, Bibliographer
Holdings: Vols 2200 Mss Microforms Documents Periodicals
Notes: A collection of primary and secondary materials for nine major American women writers: Anne Bradstreet; Louisa May Alcott, Emily Dickinson, Kate Chopin, Mary Williams Freeman, Margaret Fuller, Sarah Orne Jewett, Charlotte Perkins Gilman, Harriet Beecher Stowe. Primary materials also collected for a list of less well known authors together with manuscripts and archives of letters of special research interest. Variety of holdings: fiction, poetry, drama, biography and autobiography, letters, memoirs, diaries, travel, domestic economy and other kinds of writings by women mostly of the 19th century. Held in Dept of Rare Books and Special Collections.

CHOPUNNISH INDIANS see Nez Perce Indians

CHORAL MUSIC

CA —CLAREMONT COLLEGES, Honnold Library, Ninth & Dartmouth, Claremont, 91711. Tania Rizzo, Special Collections Dept Head
Holdings: Vols (500) // Uncat Mss Pix Slides
Notes: Joseph W Clokey Collection. 250 ms items, scores, opaques, transparencies and transcriptions of church choral music, often with orchestral and organ accompaniments; 195 printed copies of published works; 15 folders of correspondence with his publishers, miscellaneous notes and typescripts. Restricted use. No photocopies permitted. On deposit.

CA —OAKLAND PUBLIC LIBRARY, Art, Music and Recreation Section, 125 14 St, Oakland, 94612. Richard Colvig, Senior Librn
Holdings: Vols (5000) Cat Phonorecords Audiotapes
Budget: ($6700)
Notes: 10,000 scores, incl chamber music, instrumental music (piano and organ collections especially strong), miniature scores, opera scores, songs and song collections; 30,000 octavos (anthems and choral music of all kinds); 5000 books about music; 8000 phonorecords; and audiocassettes.

CA —SAN DIEGO PUBLIC LIBRARY, Art, Music & Recreation Sect, 820 E St, San Diego, 92101. Barbara A Tuhill, Supvr
Holdings: Cat
Notes: Collection consists of selections of 11,000 items for choirs of many voices. Indexed by voice, title and subject. Circulate on special loan for periods of three to six months or longer.

†DC —CATHOLIC UNIVERSITY OF AMERICA, Music Library, Washington, 20064. Betty Libbey, Head Music Library
Holdings: Cat Microforms
Notes: A large collection to support advanced degree study. Emphasis on church music, musicology, history and criticism, instrumental and vocal music, solo music for all voices, instruments, and musical forms.

IL —UNIVERSITY OF ILLINOIS, URBANA/CHAMPAIGN, Library, Music Library, Urbana, 61801. William M McClellan, Librn
Holdings: Vols (200,000) Cat Mss Slides Sound Recordings Microforms Books Scores
Budget: ($65,000)
Notes: Introductory, instructive, research and reference materials to support work at graduate level in ethnomusicology,, musicology, music education, performance areas. Special areas incl about 2500 pre-1800 music mss and editions of music on microfilm, 2400 graduate music theses on microfilm, a special collection of 30,000 titles of American vocal sheet music covering the period 1790-1970, the Rafael Joseffy Collection of about 2000 pieces of 19th century piano music (incl performer markings), the Joseph Szigeti Collection (700 items: published music, mss, recordings), mainly violin and piano music by various commposers. Also incl a special collection of 45,000 78 rpm sound recordings (uncat) of classical music and jazz; a collection of 2900 titles from Chicago radio station WGN. Incl orchestrations, a collection of 500,000 items (uncat) from stock of Hunleth Music Store, St Louis, Missouri, mainly early 20th century imprints of songs, wind music, string music, piano, sets of theatre orchestra parts, dance band orchestrations. A separate collection of choral octavos and instrumental parts is maintained, incl 135,000 pieces of choral music, 30,500 orchestral parts, and 5500 wind ensemble parts. Also, music publishers' catalogues (mainly European and American), ca 126 cubic feet, 1860s-1950s.

IN —INDIANA UNIVERSITY, Music Library, Bloomington, 47401. David E Fenske, Head
Holdings: Cat Slides Phonorecords Audiotapes Videotapes Filmstrips Microforms
Budget:
Notes: 120,000 books and scores; 185,583 choral and orchestral parts; 33,000 phonorecords; 37,000 audiotapes.

KS —SAINT MARY COLLEGE, Library, Leavenworth, 66048. Therese Deplazes, Special Collections Librn
Holdings: Cat Phonorecords

ME —PORTLAND PUBLIC LIBRARY, 5 Monument Sq, Portland, 04101. Edward V Chenevert, Library Dir
Notes: Collection incl 5000 phonorecords, 400 cassettes. Other collections within the department include sheet music, songbooks, picture file, periodicals, and choral music.

MD —PEABODY CONSERVATORY LIBRARY, 21 E Mt Vernon Place, Baltimore, 21202. Edwin A Quist, Librn
Holdings: Vols 70,000 Cat Mss Pix Phonorecords Audiotapes Videotapes Microforms
Budget: $30,000
Notes: The Peabody Conservatory Library, formerly a part of the Peabody Institute Library (now the George Peabody Library of the Johns Hopkins University) supplies the library needs of the faculty and student body of the Peabody Conservatory of Music. While the collection has numerous research capabilities, it is basically a collection of musical scores. The entire history of Western music is represented through collected editions, monumental anthologies, study scores, performing editions and a large collection of books and music periodicals. This collection is supplemented by a listening facility containing 14,000 discs and an ensembles library containing scores and parts of orchestral, band and chorus works.

MA —BOSTON PUBLIC LIBRARY, Music Division, 666 Boylston St, Box 286, Boston, 02117. Ruth Bleecker, Cur of Music
Notes: The Handel and Haydn Society officially transferred its collection to the library in 1978. The Society gave its books, scores, and archives to the Trustees of the Library to be maintained and preserved as part of the permanent research collection. Presently the collection ranges from early imprints of Handel's music and copies of the *Handel and Haydn Society Collection of Church Music* to the holographs of commissioned works. The archives incl copies off bills and disbursements dating back to 1815, printers' plates for tickets, programs from 1815-1912, membership lists, and by-laws.

MI —DETROIT PUBLIC LIBRARY, Music & Performing Arts Dept, 5201 Woodward, Detroit, 48202. Agatha Pfeiffer Kalkanis, Chief
Holdings: Vols 19,000 Cat Mss Pix Microforms
Notes: Also incl (77,000) scores. General collection intended for practical use in performance and for scholarly research. Good working collection of bibliographies, thematic catalogs, dictionaries and encyclopedias, periodical indexes. Many sets of collected works, monumental editions, historical anthologies. Good representation of opera and operetta, art song and folk song, solo instrumental literature and chamber music in practical editions. 2575 titles of choral music, chiefly sacred, for use by choirs. 17,000 titles of popular sheet music, uncataloged but thoroughly indexed. Considerable recent holdings of books and periodicals in foreign languages. Special collections of black and local materials. 25, 000 recordings and extensive discographical literature. Collection of publishers' trade catalogs.

MO —WASHINGTON UNIVERSITY, Gaylord Music Library, Saint Louis, 63130. Suzanne Bell, Music Librn
Holdings: Cat Microforms
Notes: Music books, scores, bound periodicals (65,294); recordings (discs and and tapes, 16,114); sheet music, (50,000); choral music (8000). 345 microfilm; 390 microcards.

NJ —WESTMINSTER CHOIR COLLEGE, Talbott Library, Hamilton Ave at Walnut Lane, Princeton, 08540. Sherry L Vellucci, Acting Dir
Holdings: Vols (43,500) Cat Scores Periodicals Phonorecords Audiotapes Videotapes Microforms
Budget: ($30,000)
Notes: Talbott Library support the curriculum of a music college which grants undergraduate and graduate degrees in church music, music education and music performance (voice, piano, organ and choral conducting), with an emphasis on choral music. Incl 7000 phonorecords, 3500 titles in quantity of choral music, 30,000 single copies of choral music.

OH —PUBLIC LIBRARY OF CINCINNATI & HAMILTON COUNTY, Art & Music Dept, 800 Vine St, Cincinnati, 45202. R Jayne Craven, Head
Holdings: Vols (122,185) Cat Pix
Budget: ($56,100)
Notes: Special collections: Eda Kuhn Loeb, "Artist and the Book, 1875-Date" (now shelved in Rare Book Room); music librettos (2345); exhibition catalogs (5474); large prints and posters (5051); Cincinnati artists vertical files; picture collection (673,906 clippings).

OH —CLEVELAND PUBLIC LIBRARY, Fine Arts and Special Collections Department, 325 Superior Ave, Cleveland, 44114. Alice N Loranth, Head
Holdings: Vols (10,550) Cat
Notes: Part of the Vocal Music Collection, which incl oratorios, masses, cantatas, etc, with mostly single copies, piano-vocal scores and about 200 orchestral scores.

PA —FREE LIBRARY OF PHILADELPHIA, Music Dept, Drinker Library of Choral Music, Logan Sq, Philadelphia, 19103. Frederick James Kent, Head
Holdings: Vols 348,000 Cat
Notes: The Drinker Library is primarily sacred choral works of the 16th-19th centuries in multiple copies, incl the Bach cantatas in English translation, many with orchestral parts. Loaned to subscribers of the Drinker Library. The Library of the American Choral Foundation was given to the Drinker Library in 1970 and contains many short 20th century works.

CHORAL MUSIC, DRINKER LIBRARY OF see Drinker Library of Choral Music

CHOREOGRAPHERS

NY —NEW YORK PUBLIC LIBRARY, Performing Arts Research Center, Dance

CHOREOGRAPHERS (cont.)

Collection, 111 Amsterdam Ave, New York, 10023. Genevieve Oswald, Cur
Holdings: Vols (40,000) Cat Mss Pix Audiotapes Videotapes 16mm Films Microforms
Budget: ($9,280)
Notes: Extensive biographical and visual documentation.
See also entry under Ballet; Choreography; Dancers; Modern Dance; Moving Pictures - Collections.

CHOREOGRAPHY

CA —CALIFORNIA INSTITUTE OF THE ARTS, Library, 24700 McBean Pkwy, Valencia, 91355. James Elrod, Dir
Holdings: Vols (61,000) Cat
Budget: ($2868)
Notes: Incl classical and modern dance forms.

IL —CHICAGO PUBLIC LIBRARY, Art Section, Fine Arts Division, 78 E Washington St, Chicago, 60602. Rosalinda I Hack, Fine Arts Division Chief; Yvonne S Brown, Head, Art Section
Notes: Reference and circulating collection of books, periodicals, pamphlets, and videotapes on all aspects of the dance eg ballet, social dance, square dance, jazz and folkdance. Focus of the collection is on ballet, history, biographies of dancers, and dance instruction. Subject is supplemented by a dance videotape collection, the *Folk Dance Index* a comprehensive index to descriptions of folkdances of all nations. Special Collections: Eliza Stigler Dance Collection of 200 dance books on ballet and dance history with particular emphasis on Spanish Dance. Ruth Page Archives: small collection of memorabilia documents the career of Ms Page. Reference collection of dance video tapes that document notable dance performances, from the past and present by well known dancers and dance groups. Subject concentration is that of ballet, with some examples of ethnic dance. There is alsoa collection of tapes that document Chicago area dance groups, dancers, and choreographers. A file to the contents of the tapes is available.

IL —UNIVERSITY OF ILLINOIS, URBANA/CHAMPAIGN, Library, Applied Life Studies Library, 1408 W Gregory Dr, Urbana, 61801.
Holdings: Vols (38,000) Cat Pix Microforms
Notes: Contains books on ballet, contemporary dance, folk and national dances, ethnic dance, dance history, choreography, dance notation, dance therapy. Also collected are programs of dance concerts and performances of the 20th century.

NY —NEW YORK PUBLIC LIBRARY, Performing Arts Research Center, Dance Collection, 111 Amsterdam Ave, New York, 10023. Genevieve Oswald, Cur
Holdings: Vols (40,000) Cat Mss Pix Audiotapes Videotapes 16mm Films Microforms
Budget: ($9,280)
Notes: Multi-media collection, international in scope, documenting every type of dance: ballet, modern, musical comedy, social, ethnic, folk. Collection includes historical treatises and technical manuals from the 15th century to the present day; manuals on various notation systems devised for recording dance movement such as those of Arbeau, Feuillet, Saint-Leon, Zorn, Stepanoff, Laban, Benesh, and Sutton; manuscripts, choreographers' notes, and letters; clippings, photographs, drawings and prints, and tape-recorded interviews and discussions. Over 480 dance notation scores, chiefly in Labanotation or Benesh notation, as well as 2230 motion pictures and 1650 videotapes record and preserve the choreography of specific dances. *Dictionary Catalog of the Dance Collection,* published by G K Hall, Boston,1974, 10 vols. Annual supplements: *Bibliographic Guide to Dance,* also published by G K Hall.

OH —OHIO STATE UNIVERSITY, William Oxley Thompson Memorial Library, 1858 Neil Ave Mall, Columbus, 43210. Robert A Tibbetts, Cur of Special Collections
Holdings: Cat Mss
Notes: Dance Notation Bureau collection, incl choreographic scores and papers on systems of notation. Emphasis on Labanotation.

ON —YORK UNIVERSITY, Scott Library, Downsview, M3J 2R2, Can. Hartwell Bowsfield, University Archivist
Notes: The Dance in Canada Association's Jean A Chalmers Choreographic Archives, incl videotapes of works by Canadian choreographers, with technical and performance data on each work.

ON —UNIVERSITY OF WATERLOO, Library, Waterloo, N2L 3G1, Can. Susan Bellingham, Special Collections Librn
Holdings: Vols (1000) Cat
Notes: Dance notation, choreography, ballet. Gift of Dr Henry H Crapo. Collection described in *A Catalogue of the Dance Collection in the Doris Lewis Rare Book* Room, University of Waterloo Library Bibliography #10, 1983.

CHORUSES, SACRED

CA —CLAREMONT COLLEGES, Honnold Library, Ninth & Dartmouth, Claremont, 91711. Tania Rizzo, Special Collections Dept Head
Holdings: Vols (500) // Uncat Mss Pix Slides
Notes: Joseph W Clokey Collection. 250 ms items, scores, opaques, transparencies and transcriptions of church choral music, often with orchestral and organ accompaniments; 195 printed copies of published works; 15 folders of correspondence with his publishers, miscellaneous notes and typescripts. Restricted use. No photocopies permitted. On deposit.

CHOTZINOFF, SAMUEL

MA —BOSTON UNIVERSITY, Mugar Memorial Library, Special Collections Dept, 771 Commonwealth Ave, Boston, 02215. Howard B Gotlieb, Dir
Holdings: Cat Mss Pix
Notes: Mss, correspondence, etc collected in depth; incl publications by or about.

CHOWN, (H.) BRUCE, 1893-

MB —UNIVERSITY OF MANITOBA, Elizabeth Dafoe Library, Archives and Special Collections Dept, Winnipeg, R3T 2N2, Can. Richard E Bennett, Dept Head; Corrado A Santoro, Reference Archivist
Notes: Correspondence, reports and various papers of the pediatrician. Haemolitic diseases of the newborn, especially erthroblastosis fetalis and the maternal Rh-factor. Incl correpspondence with Dr Louis Diamond of Boston.

CHRESTOMATHIES see Readers and Speakers

CHRIST see Jesus Christ

CHRISTENING see Baptism

CHRISTENSEN, WILLIAM

KS —WICHITA PUBLIC LIBRARY, Art & Music Division, 223 S Main, Wichita, 67202. Leonard Messineo, Jr, Head, Art & Music Division; Deborah Hamilton, Special Collections Librn
Holdings: Uncat Audiotapes Videotape Pix
Notes: Alice Bauman Dance Symposia Collection. Contains 300 hours of audio tapes, 1 hour-long video tape, several hundred photographs, and fugitive material of the American Dance Symposia held in Wichita from 1968-1972. The symposia covered all dance idioms-ballet, modern, jazz, folk, ethnic, dance education and therapy-and featured such notable figures such as Leonide Massine, Martha Hill, William Christensen, Alfonso Cimber, Toni Intravaia, James Clouser, Eleo Pomare, Juana de Laban, and many others. Characterized by the *Kansas City Star* as the "most distinguished faculties of fine artists ever assembled in the contemporary world of dance."

CHRISTIAN, GEORGE

TX —NORTH TEXAS STATE UNIVERSITY, Archives, NT Station Box 5188, Denton, 76203. Robert LaForte, University Archivist
Notes: Part of Oral History Collection. Interviews with journalist and former press secretary to President Lyndon B Johnson.

CHRISTIAN ANTIQUITIES

CA —PACIFIC SCHOOL OF RELIGION, Bade Institute of Biblical Archeology, 1798 Scenic Ave, Berkeley, 94709. Kay Schellhase, Cur
Holdings: Vols (2500) Cat
Budget: ($700)
Notes: Syro-Palestinian archaeology.

MD —JOHNS HOPKINS UNIVERSITY, Milton S Eisenhower Library, George Peabody Collection, 17 E Mt Vernon Place, Baltimore, 21201. Lyn Hart, Peabody Librn
Notes: Emphasis on materials published before 1950. Strength is a good collection through the 19th century.

MA —HARVARD UNIVERSITY LIBRARY, Widener Library, Cambridge, 02138.
Holdings: Cat
Notes: John Harvey Treat collection on Christian Antiquities of Rome comprises more than 1000 vols.

NC —DUKE UNIVERSITY, Divinity School Library, Durham, 27706. Donn Michael Farris, Librn

NC —SOUTHEASTERN BAPTIST THEOLOGICAL SEMINARY LIBRARY, PO Box 752, Wake Forest, 27587. H Eugene McLeod, Librn
Holdings: Cat Slides

CHRISTIAN ARCHAEOLOGY see Christian Antiquities

CHRISTIAN ART AND SYMBOLISM

CA —UNIVERSITY OF CALIFORNIA, LOS ANGELES, Art Library, Los Angeles, 90024. Max Marmor, Library Assistant
Holdings: Pix Microforms
Notes: Art; Art History; Early Christian and Byzantine Art; Medieval Art; Apostolic Age to 1400; Iconography; Photo Archive; Christian Art and Symbolism.

DC —HARVARD UNIVERSITY, Dumbarton Oaks, Research Library, 1703 32nd St NW, Washington, 20007. Irene Vaslef, Librn
Holdings: Vols (91,000) Cat Maps Pix Slides Microforms
Budget: ($219,000)
Notes: Byzantine civilization (including art, archaeology, literature, history, religion, law, music, etc). Extensive supplemental material on Classical, Hellenistic, Medieval, Islamic, Medieval Slavic cultures. 62,000 b/w photographs, 25,000 slides and transparencies, 1000 microfilms of books and manuscripts. Printed description of collection in *Harvard Library Bulletin,* vol 19, no 1 (Jan 1971), pp 25-35 and vol 19, no 2 (April 1971), pp 204-214, pp 25-35 and vol 19, no 2 (April 1971), pp 204-214.

MD —JOHNS HOPKINS UNIVERSITY, Milton S Eisenhower Library, George Peabody Collection, 17 E Mt Vernon Place, Baltimore, 21201. Lyn Hart, Peabody Librn
Notes: Noncirculating.

†MA —MELROSE PUBLIC LIBRARY, 63 W Emerson St, Melrose, 02176. Diane E Shaw, Art Librn
Holdings: Vols (8500) Cat Pix Slides Phonorecords
Budget: ($6900)
Notes: Framed and unframed art reproductions (110), slides (2773), periodicals, clippings, sound recordings (3000). Incl the Mary Livermore Collection of Sacred Art, the Odlin Collection and the Pierre Gendrot Collection of Fine Art.

CHRISTIAN ART AND SYMBOLISM (cont.)

MN —SAINT JOHN'S ABBEY & UNIVERSITY, Hill Monastic Manuscript Library, Collegeville, 56321. Julian G Plante, Dir
Holdings: Vols (70,000) Cat Mss Slides Microforms
Notes: Wherever miniatures and illuminations appear in a ms these are microfilmed in color. In addition to the usual ms catalogs of the collections, partial iconographic card catalog is available. Reasonable requests will be honored.

NY —STATE UNIVERSITY OF NEW YORK, BUFFALO, Baird Music Library, Baird Hall, Amherst, 14260. James B Coover, Dir
Holdings: Vols (104,000) Cat Mss Pix Slides Phonorecords Microforms
Notes: Nearly complete collections of *Denkmaeler and Gesamtausgaben* and other historical sets. Strong collection of dictionaries, bibliographies, biographies, facsimiles, works on the "new" music, organology and ethnomusicology. Special emphasis on operas, scores of the avant-garde, jazz and urban popular music, discography and music librarianship. Good collection of medieval and Renaissance anthologies, contemporary and avant-garde recordings. Houses Archives of the Center of the Creative and Performing Arts. Collections incl 2100 slides, 22,000 phonorecords, 46,000 scores and parts, 29, 000 books, 4900 microforms. Computerized record catalog in process.

NY —HISPANIC SOCIETY OF AMERICA, Library, 613 W 155 St, New York, 10032. Martha M de Narvaez, Cur of Mss; Irene S Frye, Asst Librn
Holdings: Vols (150,000) Cat Mss Maps Pix Slides Phonorecords Microforms
Notes: History, art, literature and general culture of the Hispanic countries (where Spanish or Portuguese is spoken). Incl (18, 000) vols printed before 1701, incl (250) incunabula; over (100,000) later vols, plus thousands of periodicals. About (200,000) mss incl ms maps. Printed atlases are in the Book Collection. Some microfilms, chiefly of our early books. Engraved and printed separate maps; reference collection of over 100,000 photographs; slides: all in Department of Iconography, not in library. Catalogs: *Catalogue of the Hispanic Society of America* (Boston: G K Hall, 1962), 10 vols; *First Supplement* (Boston, 1970), 4 vols. Early books: *Printed Books 1468-1700;* Mss: *Catalogo de los Manuscritos Poeticos* Castellanos (15th-17th centuries; 3 vols); *Medieval Manuscripts in the Library; Golden Age Drama Manuscripts*(the latter in press).
See also entry under Spain

NY —SAINT VLADIMIRS' ORTHODOX THEOLOGICAL SEMINARY, 575 Scarsdale Rd, Yonkers, 10707. Paul D Garrett, Librn
Holdings: Vols (36,000) Pix
Notes: Incl 250 periodicals. A major source of materials on Orthodox Church theology. Much on works of art.

NC —SOUTHEASTERN BAPTIST THEOLOGICAL SEMINARY LIBRARY, PO Box 752, Wake Forest, 27587. H Eugene McLeod, Librn
Holdings: Cat Slides

OH —OHIO STATE UNIVERSITY, Fine Arts Library, 1813 N High St, Columbus, 43210. Susan Wyngaard, Head, Fine Arts Library
Holdings: Vols (75,000) Cat Pix Slides Microforms
Budget: ($60,000)
Notes: Also have 1000 uncataloged exhibition catalogs. Book collection strong in history of art especially in area of medieval & Northern Renaissance art. Good collection of portfolios. Photographic collections on microfiche. Receive Slavic titles, many on Byzantine frescoes. Online catalog. Decimal Index of the Art of the Low Countries, as well as Marburger Index; Index Photographique de i' Arten France; Alinari Archives on microfiche and other major microform collections in art.

PA —BRYN MAWR COLLEGE, Canaday Library, Bryn Mawr, 19010. James Tanis, Dir
Notes: Baroque and Italian Renaissance painting and architecture; late antique and early Christian art; Flemish and Dutch painting 15th-17th centuries; French painting 18th-19th centuries. In Art and Archaeology Library.

PA —WILLET STAINED GLASS STUDIO, Library, 10 E Moreland Ave, Philadelphia, 19118. Helene H Weis, Librn
Holdings: Vols 1000 Cat Pix Slides Films
Notes: Stained glass and related subjects; leaded stained glass; historic and contemporary stained glass; new techniques (faceted, laminated, etc); original art work. The studio is the largest atelier making stained glass windows. Collection contains picture file of clippings, files of original designs, etc.

PA —UNIVERSITY OF PITTSBURGH, Henry Clay Frick Fine Arts Library, Pittsburgh, 15260. Anne W Gordon, Fine Arts Librn
Holdings: Vols (55,000) Cat Pix Slides Microforms
Notes: Emphasis is on the art of the Western World--architecture, sculpture, painting, minor arts, archaeology, with special strength in the Byzantine, early Christian, medieval, renaissance and modern periods. The Oriental field is represented, incl replicas of scrolls. Studio arts are also covered. Illuminated ms facsimiles. Extensive collections of slides and photographs for study of art history are available in the building but not administered by the art library.

CHRISTIAN BIOGRAPHY

NC —SOUTHEASTERN BAPTIST THEOLOGICAL SEMINARY LIBRARY, PO Box 752, Wake Forest, 27587. H Eugene McLeod, Librn
Holdings: Cat

CHRISTIAN CHURCH

MD —JOHNS HOPKINS UNIVERSITY, Milton S Eisenhower Library, George Peabody Collection, 17 E Mt Vernon Place, Baltimore, 21201. Lyn Hart, Peabody Librn
Notes: Emphasis on materials published before 1950. Strength is a good collection through the 19th century.

VA —LYNCHBURG COLLEGE, Knight-Capron Library, Lynchburg, 24501. Mary C Scudder, Dir
Holdings: Vols (84) Cat Mss
Notes: Depository for the Christian Church in Virginia (Disciples of Christ). Bibliography available upon request.

CHRISTIAN CHURCH—U.S.

MD —JOHNS HOPKINS UNIVERSITY, Milton S Eisenhower Library, George Peabody Collection, 17 E Mt Vernon Place, Baltimore, 21201. Lyn Hart, Peabody Librn
Notes: Emphasis on materials published before 1950. Strength is a good collection through the 19th century.

CHRISTIAN CHURCHES (INDEPENDENT)

CA —GRADUATE THEOLOGICAL UNION LIBRARY, New Religious Movements Research Collection, Public Services and Special Collections Dept, 2400 Ridge Road, Berkeley, 94709. Diane Choquette, Dept Head
Holdings: Vols (3000) Mss Pix
Notes: Begun in 1977, the collection focuses on religious movements new to America since 1960, and unorthodox religious movements resurgent since 1960. American forms of Hinduism, Buddhism, Sikhism, and Sufism are included along with occultism, Neo-Paganism, esoteric and alternative forms of Christianity, feminist spirituality, and human potential movements having a spiritual aspect. Legal issues, such as deprogramming, and the question of church/state relations are an important part of the collection. The Library is a depository for publications of the Unification Church in America, the Church of Scientology, and the International Society for Krishna Consciousness (America). The responses of mainstream religions and concerned citizens groups are also included. Besides 3000 monographs, the library has 400 periodical titles, 200 posters from the San FranciscoBay Area, 1965-77, 300 research papers, and 31 linear feet of ephemera.

KY —MIDWAY COLLEGE, Marrs Library, Stephens St, Midway, 40347. Kay Cordoves, Librn
Holdings: Vols (2000)// Cat
Notes: Brotherhood Collection covers history of Christian Church (Disciples of Christ) and related materials.

NE —YORK COLLEGE, Levitt Library, York, 67467. Charles Van Baucom, Dir
Holdings: Vols (1430) Cat Mss Pix Audiotapes
Notes: In the Levitt Library, The American Restoration Movement Collection currently focuses on titles related to the Churches of Christ, although titles on the Christian Churches (Independents) and the Disciples of Christ make up a fair percentage of the collection. To promote the development and the use of the Restoration History Collection, York College participates in the Christian College Librarians Conference with sister colleges David Lipscomb, Nashville, TN; Abilene Christian University, Abilene, TX; Oklahoma Christian College, Oklahoma City, OK; Harding College, Searcy, AR; Pepperdine University, Malibu, CA, and others; also, with the Disciples of Christ Historical Society, 1101 19th Ave S, Nashville, TN 37212.

TN —DISCIPLES OF CHRIST HISTORICAL SOCIETY, 1101 19th Ave S, Nashville, 37212. James M Scole, Pres
Holdings: Vols (26,000) Cat Mss Maps Pix Slides Phonorecords Audiotapes Videotapes 16mm Films Filmstrips Microforms
Budget: $184,000
Notes: The Campbell-Stone Movement--all aspects of its history, incl the Disciples of Christ, Christian Church, and Churches of Christ.

CHRISTIAN ECONOMICS see Economics, Christian

CHRISTIAN EDUCATION see Religious Education

CHRISTIAN ETHICS

CT —YALE UNIVERSITY, Beinecke Rare Book & Manuscript Library, Osborn Collection, New Haven, 06520. Stephen R Parks, Cur
Holdings: Mss

IL —JESUIT-KRAUSS-MCCORMICK LIBRARY, 1100 E 55th St, Chicago, 60615. Donald Vorp, Dir; Elvire Hilgert, Librn
Holdings: Vols (375,000) Microforms
Notes: Collections contain merger of Jesuit Library, Lutheran School of Theology of Chicago (Krauss Library), and McCormick Theological Seminary. Jesuit: Sermones Thesaurus Novi de Tempore (anonymous, Strassbourg 1486); Opera Omnia (Jean Gerson, Strassbourg 1488), 3 vols; Summa Rosella Casuum (Venice 1495); moral theology (major figures of 16th and 17th century scholasticism); early modern editions of patristics and canon law regarding procedures and organzation of the Catholic Church, incl treatises and multi-volume commentaries. Krauss: Archives of Lutheran Church in America and its predecessors; Reformation imprints; early printed versions of the Bible (L Franklin Gruber Collection); German and Scandanavian (Swedish, Danish, Finnish) theology; Lutheran Church of America document depository. McCormick: Presbyteriana; historical record of Synod of Illinois, UnitedPresbyterian

CHRISTIAN ETHICS (cont.)

Church of USA; Church Federation of Chicago archives prior to 1969; USA imprints of the Bible (Simms Collection).

NC —SOUTHEASTERN BAPTIST THEOLOGICAL SEMINARY LIBRARY, PO Box 752, Wake Forest, 27587. H Eugene McLeod, Librn
Holdings: Cat Slides Audiotapes Videotapes Microforms

OR —GEORGE FOX COLLEGE, Shambaugh Library, Newberg, 97132. F E Walls, Libr Dir
Holdings: Vols (1500) Cat
Budget: ($150)
Notes: Collection of Dr Howard Kershner, incl Christian Freedom Foundation books. Personal collection of Dr Kershner.

TX —OBLATE SCHOOL OF THEOLOGY, Library, 285 Oblate Dr, San Antonio, 78216. James Maney, Libr Dir
Holdings: Vols (22,000) Cat
Budget: ($15,500)

CHRISTIAN HOLINESS DOCTRINE

IN —FREE METHODIST CHURCH OF NORTH AMERICA, Marston Memorial Historical Center Library, 901 College Ave, Winona Lake, 46590. Evelyn L Mottweiler, Librn
Holdings: Vols (5000) Cat Mss
Budget: ($16,000)
Notes: Denominational headquarters of the Free Methodist Church in North America. Works on the Wesleyan doctrine of holiness and the Holy Spirit. Includes historical holiness classics as well as contemporary authors. Methodist and Free Methodist holdings of the Library are included in the Methodist Union Catalog: *Pre-1976* Imprints, by Kenneth E Rowe.

CHRISTIAN LIFE

CA —GRADUATE THEOLOGICAL UNION LIBRARY, New Religious Movements Research Collection, Public Services and Special Collections Dept, 2400 Ridge Road, Berkeley, 94709. Diane Choquette, Dept Head
Holdings: Vols (3000) Mss Pix
Notes: Begun in 1977, the collection focuses on religious movements new to America since 1960, and unorthodox religious movements resurgent since 1960. American forms of Hinduism, Buddhism, Sikhism, and Sufism are included along with occultism, Neo-Paganism, esoteric and alternative forms of Christianity, feminist spirituality, and human potential movements having a spiritual aspect.

CA —WESTMONT COLLEGE, Roger John Voskuyl Library, Santa Barbara, 93108. John D Murray, Librn
Holdings: Cat Microforms
Notes: The Christ and Culture Collection contains materials which express and illustrate the interaction between the Christian faith (as both faith and life, doctrine and practice) and the liberal arts and sciences.

NC —SOUTHEASTERN BAPTIST THEOLOGICAL SEMINARY LIBRARY, PO Box 752, Wake Forest, 27587. H Eugene McLeod, Librn
Holdings: Cat Slides Audiotapes Videotapes Microforms

OK —MIDWEST CHRISTIAN COLLEGE, Library, 6600 N Kelley Ave, Oklahoma City, 73111. Jean Cavett, Dir
Holdings: Vols (7000) Cat Pix Phonorecords Audiotapes Filmstrips Microforms
Notes: The Restoration Movement (Independent Christian Church) to restore the Church to its New Testament form. Incl churches called "Christian Churches," "Churches of Christ," "Disciples of Christ," and a few called just "Christ's Church."

CHRISTIAN LITERATURE, EARLY

MN —SAINT JOHN'S ABBEY & UNIVERSITY, Hill Monastic Manuscript Library, Collegeville, 56321. Julian G Plante, Dir
Holdings: Vols (61,000) Microfilms
Notes: Films of 61,000 mss. The total number of codices or bound handwritten mss represents the holdings of several hundred libraries in Europe, mostly Austria, Spain, Ethiopia, West Germany, Portugal, and also Italy, Hungary, Poland, Great Britain, Belgium, Yugoslavia, France, Switzerland, and the Netherlands.

MO —SAINT LOUIS UNIVERSITY, Pius XII Memorial Library, 3655 W Pine Blvd, Saint Louis, 63108. William Cole, Dir
Holdings: Slides Microforms
Notes: Collection covers all areas of learning and European history from Classical Antiquity to early modern period. Researchers using collection receive assistance in paleography, bibliography and reference search. Approx 10,000 1000-foot reels of microfilm (not counting master negatives) reproducing Vatican Library's Latin, Greek, Hebrew, Arabic and Ethiopic mss. Some 8000 100-foot reels of microfilm (again not counting master negative) reproducing rare and out of print books relating to subject areas in the mss. Over 50, 000 color slides of medieval and Renaissance mss illuminations. A reference collection of modern materials relating to ms research.

NC —SOUTHEASTERN BAPTIST THEOLOGICAL SEMINARY LIBRARY, PO Box 752, Wake Forest, 27587. H Eugene McLeod, Librn
Holdings: Cat

PA —LUTHERAN THEOLOGICAL SEMINARY, Krauth Memorial Library, 7301 Germantown Ave, Philadelphia, 19119. Rev David J Wartluft, Dir Libr
Notes: Major scholarly collections of patristics including, Migne, Corpus Christianorum, ACW, Fathers of the Church; Nicene and ante-Nicene Fathers.

CHRISTIAN NAMES see Names, Personal

CHRISTIAN SCIENCE

AZ —WORLD UNIVERSITY, Library, 711 E Blacklidge Dr, Tucson, 85719. Howard John Zitko, Cur
Holdings: Vols (15,000) Cat Mss Maps Audiotapes
Notes: Collection concerns the "frontier sciences". No interlibrary loan.

NY —NEW YORK PUBLIC LIBRARY, Research Libraries, General Research Division, Fifth Ave & 42 St, New York, 10018. Rodney Phillips, Chief
Holdings: Vols (2,225,000) Cat Maps Pix Microforms
Budget: ($775,718)

CHRISTIAN SYMBOLISM see Christian Art and Symbolism

CHRISTIAN UNION

NC —SOUTHEASTERN BAPTIST THEOLOGICAL SEMINARY LIBRARY, PO Box 752, Wake Forest, 27587. H Eugene McLeod, Librn
Holdings: Cat Microforms
Notes: Incl official publications of the Faith and Order Commission of the World Council of Churches from 1910 to 1970, periodicals from many countries and religious bodies, and publications of the evangelical academies and lay training centers of Europe and Great Britain.

CHRISTIANITY

CA —GRADUATE THEOLOGICAL UNION LIBRARY, New Religious Movements Research Collection, Public Services and Special Collections Dept, 2400 Ridge Road, Berkeley, 94709. Diane Choquette, Dept Head
Holdings: Vols (3000) Mss Pix
Notes: Begun in 1977, the collection focuses on religious movements new to America since 1960, and unorthodox religious movements resurgent since 1960. American forms of Hinduism, Buddhism, Sikhism, and Sufism are included along with occultism, Neo-Paganism, esoteric and alternative forms of Christianity, feminist spirituality, and human potential movements having a spiritual aspect. Legal issues, such as deprogramming, and the question of church/state relations are an important part of the collection. The Library is a depository for publications of the Unification Church in America, the Church of Scientology, and the International Society for Krishna Consciousness (America). The responses of mainstream religions and concerned citizens groups are also included. Besides 3000 monographs, the library has 400 periodical titles, 200 posters from the San FranciscoBay Area, 1965-77, 300 research papers, and 31 linear feet of ephemera.

CA —LOS ANGELES PUBLIC LIBRARY, Philosophy & Religion Dept, 630 W Fifth St, Los Angeles, 90071. Marilyn C Wherley, Librn
Holdings: Vols 2050 Cat Long runs of major Catholic and Protestant periodicals, many on microfilm
Budget: ($60,000)
Notes: Popular and scholarly works on history, theology, biography, missions, inspirational literature, cults and sects. Includes pamphlets, special indexes, serials and periodicals.

CA —WESTMONT COLLEGE, Roger John Voskuyl Library, Santa Barbara, 93108. John D Murray, Librn
Holdings: Cat Microforms
Notes: The Christ and Culture Collection contains materials which express and illustrate the interaction between the Christian faith (as both faith and life, doctrine and practice) and the liberal arts and sciences.

MD —JOHNS HOPKINS UNIVERSITY, Milton S Eisenhower Library, George Peabody Collection, 17 E Mt Vernon Place, Baltimore, 21201. Lyn Hart, Peabody Librn
Notes: Emphasis on materials published before 1950. Strength is a good collection through the 19th century.

NC —SOUTHEASTERN BAPTIST THEOLOGICAL SEMINARY LIBRARY, PO Box 752, Wake Forest, 27587. H Eugene McLeod, Librn
Holdings: Cat Slides Microforms

OK —MIDWEST CHRISTIAN COLLEGE, Library, 6600 N Kelley Ave, Oklahoma City, 73111. Jean Cavett, Dir
Holdings: Vols (7000) Cat Pix Phonorecords Audiotapes Filmstrips Microforms
Notes: The Restoration Movement (Independent Christian Church) to restore the Church to its New Testament form. Incl churches called "Christian Churches," "Churches of Christ," "Disciples of Christ," and a few called just "Christ's Church."

TX —OBLATE SCHOOL OF THEOLOGY, Library, 285 Oblate Dr, San Antonio, 78216. James Maney, Libr Dir
Holdings: Vols (22,000) Cat
Budget: ($15,500)

VA —ASSOCIATION FOR RESEARCH & ENLIGHTENMENT, Library, 67 & Atlantic Avenue, PO Box 595, Virginia Beach, 23451. Stephen Jordan, Library Mgr
Holdings: Vols (3000) Cat
Notes: Emphasis on Christian, Buddhist, Hindu religions, mysticism, comparative religion, psychological approach to biofeedback, autogenics, etc.

CHRISTIANITY—HISTORY see Church History

CHRISTIANITY—UNION BETWEEN CHURCHES see Christian Union

CHRISTIANITY, RESTORATION OF see Restoration of the Church (Movement)

CHRISTIANITY AND OTHER RELIGIONS

NC —SOUTHEASTERN BAPTIST THEOLOGICAL SEMINARY LIBRARY,

CHRISTIANITY AND OTHER RELIGIONS (cont.)

PO Box 752, Wake Forest, 27587. H Eugene McLeod, Librn
Holdings: Cat Slides Audiotapes Microforms

CHRISTIE, AGATHA

CA —UNIVERSITY OF CALIFORNIA, SAN DIEGO, Central University Library, Mandeville Dept of Special Collections, La Jolla, 92093. Lynda Corey Claassen, Head
Notes: The Ira Wolff Collection numbers some 6000 volumes and emphasizes English-language detective fiction from the mid-19th century to the present, containing important or first editions of the works of Agatha Christie, Dorothy Sayers, Raymond Chandler, Dashiell Hammett, and Wilkie Collins.

CT —YALE UNIVERSITY, Box 1603A, Yale Station, New Haven, 06520.

CHRISTMAS

CA —ARCADIA PUBLIC LIBRARY, 20 W Duarte Rd, Arcadia, 91006. James M Domney, City Librn
Notes: Christmas books.

NY —UKRAINIAN MUSUEM, 203 Second Ave, New York, 10003. Maria Shust, Dir
Notes: Also over 1500 folk artifacts and works of art. Incl Ukrainian Easter Eggs.

CHRISTMAS BOOKS see Christmas; Literary Annuals and Giftbooks; Giftbooks (Annuals, Etc.)

CHRISTMAS CARDS

IN —INDIANA UNIVERSITY, Lilly Library, Seventh St, Bloomington, 47405. William R Cagle, Librn
Holdings: Vols 500// Cat Mss
Notes: Largely 19th century cards, with emphasis on Marcus Ward and Co.

KY —UNIVERSITY OF LOUISVILLE, Allen R Hite Art Institute, Library, Belknap Campus, Louisville, 40292. Gail Gilbert, Librn
Holdings: Vols (40,000) Cat Pix
Budget: ($29,000)
Notes: Incl books on art, architecture, landscape architecture and gardening, prints, printing, illustrated books and brass rubbings. Library subscribes to 200 periodical titles in these and other areas. Collection circulates to faculty and staff only, with same restrictions placed on interlibrary loan. Library also has collections of bookplates, posters, original prints, hand-made Christmas cards and clippings file filling 56 VF drawers.

SC —COLLEGE OF CHARLESTON LIBRARY, Special Collections Dept, Charleston, 29401.
Notes: Collection of Christmas and New Year's greeting cards cleverly designed by Robert C Aldredge, who was a high official in the US Weather Bureau in Washington, DC.

CHRISTMAS CAROLS see Carols

CHRISTMAS STORIES

CA —UNIVERSITY OF SAN FRANCISCO, Richard A Gleeson Library, The Countess Bernardine Murphy Donohue Rare Book Room, San Francisco, 94117. D Steven Corey, Special Collections Librn
Holdings: Vols 400 Pix
Notes: Emphasis is on fine printing, cheifly American, but all aspects of Christmas are covered. The entire collection is about 1500 items; much ephemera, and many pieces relating to San Francisco.

CHRISTOLOGY see Jesus Christ

CHRIST'S CHURCH

OK —MIDWEST CHRISTIAN COLLEGE, Library, 6600 N Kelley Ave, Oklahoma City, 73111. Jean Cavett, Dir
Holdings: Vols (7000) Cat Pix Phonorecords Audiotapes Filmstrips Microforms
Notes: The Restoration Movement (Independent Christian Church) to restore the Church to its New Testament form. Incl churches called "Christian Churches," "Churches of Christ," "Disciples of Christ," and a few called just "Christ's Church."

CHROMATICS see Color

CHROMATOGRAPHIC ANALYSIS

CA —BECKMAN INSTRUMENTS, Research Library, 2500 Harbor Blvd, Fullerton, 92634. Jean R Miller, Librn
Holdings: Vols (7000) Cat Slides Audiotapes Videotapes Microforms
Budget: ($9000)
Notes: Strong collection in scientific and analytic instrumentation, electrochemistry, analytical chemistry, optics and spectroscopy, chromatography, clinical chemistry and biochemistry.

CHROMOLITHOGRAPHS AND CHROMOLITHOGRAPHY

CA —UNIVERSITY OF THE PACIFIC, Library, Stockton, 95211. Hiram L Davis, Dir of Libraries
Holdings: Vols (350) Uncat Pix
Notes: A general collection of Victorian literature and life given to the University by James M Perrin in 1968-1970. The primary specialization is material by and about William Morris and the Kelmscott Press, but the collection also is rich in Victorian first editions, Pre-Raphaelites and Pre-Raphaelitism, and early colored illustrations and chromolithography.

MN —SAINT PAUL PUBLIC LIBRARY, Arts & Audiovisual Services, 90 W Fourth St, Saint Paul, 55102. Delores Sundbye, Supervising Librn
Holdings: Cat Pix
Budget: ($20,000)
Notes: Complete set of first edition of Arundel Prints, color lithographic copies of Renaissance paintings, published by the Arundel Society, 1849-1897.

PA —TEMPLE UNIVERSITY LIBRARIES, Special Collections Dept, Rare Books & Mss Section, Philadelphia, 19122. Thomas M Whitehead, Cur
Holdings: Vols (200) Cat Mss Pix
Notes: The lithography collection emphasizes the technical process rather than the artistic medium and stresses the years 1800-1835. Significant are the early manuals, the Kubilius Louis Prang Collection and the documentation of early Mexican lithography. Some holdings are listed in the 1972 publication: *Aloys Senefelder 1771-1834: A Catalogue of Early Technical Literature and Selected Lithographs.* A register of the Mexican documents is available.

CHROMOXYLOGRAPHY see Color Prints

CHRONIC DISEASES

CA —UNIVERSITY OF CALIFORNIA, BERKELEY, Life Sciences Libraries, Public Health Library, 42 Earl Warren Hall, Berkeley, 94720. Thomas J Alexander, Librn
Holdings: Vols (75,000) Cat Microforms
Notes: Research collection covering all aspects of public health. Health Department annual reports from all 50 states are acquired, as well as such reports from all California health units and from major US cities. Serial publications issued by Health Departments in the 13 western states are being received.

CHRONOGRAMS

CT —YALE UNIVERSITY, Box 1603A, Yale Station, New Haven, 06520.

NY —NEW YORK PUBLIC LIBRARY, Research Libraries, General Research Division, Fifth Ave & 42 St, New York, 10018. Rodney Phillips, Chief
Holdings: Vols (2,225,000) Cat Maps Pix Microforms
Budget: ($775,718)

OH —CLEVELAND PUBLIC LIBRARY, Fine Arts and Special Collections Department, 325 Superior Ave, Cleveland, 44114. Alice N Loranth, Head
Holdings: Vols (36,500) Cat Maps Pix Microforms Tapes
Notes: Described in Cleveland, Public Libray, White collection of folk-lore and Orientalia; *Catalog of Folklore and Folk* Songs (Boston: G K Hall, 1964), 2 vols; introduction by George J Maciuszko.

TX —ROSENBERG LIBRARY, Fox Rare Book Room, 2310 Sealy Ave, Galveston, 77550. Fernando Basilza, Rare Book Librn
Holdings: Vols (2000) Cat Mss Pix
Notes: The Col Milo Pitcher Fox and Agnes Peel Fox Rare Book Room contains 2000 vols incunabula, first printings, and modern fine printing. Incl clay tablets, horn books, parchment material, illuminated books and mss, fine printing (principally 15th-18th centuries), fine binding, fore-edge paintings, etc.

CHRONOLOGY, HISTORICAL

CA —UNIVERSITY OF CALIFORNIA, RIVERSIDE, University Library, Bio-Agricultural Library, Batchelor Hall, Riverside, 92521. Barbara Montanary, Head
Holdings: Vols (130,000) Cat Mss Maps Pix Microforms
Notes: The Bio-Agricultural Library (formerly the Library of Citrus Experiment Station of the University of California) is well known for its complete collections in the fields of the agriculture sciences. It is especially known for its emphasis on entomology, incl bio-control; botany, citriculture, plant sciences, nematology and plant pathology; arid and semi-arid lands research and subtropical agriculture. Specific areas of interest are avocados, dates, desert flora, jojoba, guayule and carob.

CHRONOMETERS

PA —FRANKLIN INSTITUTE LIBRARY, 20 & The Parkway, Philadelphia, 19103. Miriam Padusis, Dir; Charles Wilt, Readers Servs Librn
Holdings: Vols 2400 Cat Mss
Notes: One of the finest collections of horology in the world.

CHRONOMETRY, MENTAL see Time Perception

CHRONOPHOTOGRAPHY see Cinematography

CHURCH, EASTERN see Eastern Churches

CHURCH, JAMES E.

NV —UNIVERSITY OF NEVADA, RENO, University Library, Special Collections Dept, Reno, 89557. Robert E Blesse, Head
Holdings: Vols (25) Uncat Pix Mss
Notes: Papers of James E Church, founder and developer of the modern science of snow surveying. Church collection, 180 cu ft, includes his writings, papers, and over 7000 photographs of Church's snow surveying expeditions in the Sierra Nevada mountains and elsewhere in the world. Papers of the Western Snow Conference, 80 cu ft.

CHURCH, RICHARD

BC —UNIVERSITY OF VICTORIA, McPherson Library, Victoria, V8W 3H5, Can.

CHURCH AND INDUSTRY

IL —INSTITUTE ON THE CHURCH IN URBAN-INDUSTRIAL SOCIETY, Library, 5700 S Woodlawn, Chicago, 60637.
Holdings: Vols 1000 Cat Microforms
Notes: Urban-industrial involvement of the

CHURCH AND INDUSTRY (cont.)

churches world-wide, international urban literature, corporate responsibility, human factors of urbanization and industrialization. Library holdings are dorment at present.

CHURCH AND SLAVERY see Slavery and the Church

CHURCH AND SOCIAL PROBLEMS

IL —INSTITUTE ON THE CHURCH IN URBAN-INDUSTRIAL SOCIETY, Library, 5700 S Woodlawn, Chicago, 60637.
Holdings: Vols 1000 Cat Microforms
Notes: Urban-industrial involvement of the churches world-wide, international urban literature, corporate responsibility, human factors of urbanization and industrialization. Library holdings are dorment at present.

NY —SALVATION ARMY ARCHIVES AND RESEARCH CENTER, 145 West 15th St, New York, 10011. Thomas Wilstead, Archivist/Administrator; Judith Johnson, Archivist
Holdings: Vols Pix Audiotapes Microforms VF
Notes: Official files and records, minutes, correspondence and photographs. Papers of Salvation Army officers. Material published by or about the Salvation Army. Incl 2300 books and pamplets, 300 serials, 40 VF, 685 microfilm reels, 300 sound recordings, 280 sound tapes, 445 films, 14,000 photoprints and negatives, 250 slides and 1050 cubic ft of archives.

NC —DUKE UNIVERSITY, Divinity School Library, Durham, 27706. Donn Michael Farris, Librn

NC —SOUTHEASTERN BAPTIST THEOLOGICAL SEMINARY LIBRARY, PO Box 752, Wake Forest, 27587. H Eugene McLeod, Librn
Holdings: Cat Slides Audiotapes Videotapes

CHURCH AND STATE

CA —UNIVERSITY OF CALIFORNIA, BERKELEY, School of Law, Library, Berkeley, 94720. Stephan G Kuttner, Dir, Canon Law Collection
Holdings: Vols (23,000) Cat Mss Microforms
Notes: Entirely supported by the R D and S M Robbins Endowment, the Robbins Canon Law Collection emphasizes particularly Roman Catholic, Eastern and Anglican canon law. Additional subject areas being developed are ecclesiastical history and institutions, historical and contemporary church and state relations, and ecumenical studies. Library is in process of obtaining complete microfilms of all medieval canon and Roman law mss held by the Vatican Library.

NY —GENERAL THEOLOGICAL SEMINARY, Saint Marks Library, 175 Ninth Ave, New York, 10011. David Green, Dir
Holdings: Vols (200,000) Cat Mss Maps Pix Slides Microforms
Notes: Extensive collection.

NC —SOUTHEASTERN BAPTIST THEOLOGICAL SEMINARY LIBRARY, PO Box 752, Wake Forest, 27587. H Eugene McLeod, Librn
Holdings: Cat Microforms

CHURCH ANTIQUITIES see Christian Antiquities

CHURCH ARCHITECTURE

NC —DUKE UNIVERSITY, Divinity School Library, Durham, 27706. Donn Michael Farris, Librn
Holdings: Vols (225,000)
Notes: Special collections and subject emphases in this library include: Archaeology, Egyptian; Archaeology, Middle Eastern; Art, Jewish; Bible; Bible-New Testament; Bible-Symbolism; Church Architecture; Egyptology; Fathers of the Church; Society of Friends; Great Britain-Religion-Methodism and Methodist Church; Hymns and Hymnals; Jansenists and Jansenism; Judaica; Mediaeval Christian Mysticism; Methodism and Methodist Church; Methodist Episcopal Church; Methodist Episcopal Church, South; Reformation; Religion-US-History; Rural Church; Theology-Great Britain-17th Century; Theology-Great Britain-18th Century; United Methodist Church; US-Church History; John Wesley.

PA —LUTHERAN THEOLOGICAL SEMINARY, Krauth Memorial Library, 7301 Germantown Ave, Philadelphia, 19119. Rev David J Wartluft, Dir Libr
Holdings: Vols 1200 Cat Pix Slides
Notes: Pictures (1500) and slides (2000) cover church architecture chiefly in Europe and America, pre-20th century. No finding aids for pictures and slides, but they are systematically arranged.

CHURCH BELLS see Bells

CHURCH BIOGRAPHY see Christian Biography

CHURCH COSTUME see Church Vestments

CHURCH COUNCILS see Councils and Synods

CHURCH FATHERS see Fathers of the Church

CHURCH HISTORY

CA —LOS ANGELES PUBLIC LIBRARY, Philosophy & Religion Dept, 630 W Fifth St, Los Angeles, 90071. Marilyn C Wherley, Librn
Holdings: Vols 2050 Cat
Budget: ($60,000)
Notes: Popular and scholarly works on history, theology, biography, missions, inspirational literature, cults and sects. Includes pamphlets, special indexes, serials and periodicals. Long runs of major Catholic and Protestant periodicals, many on microfilm.

CA —UNIVERSITY OF CALIFORNIA, LOS ANGELES, Research Library, Medieval and Renaissance Collection, 405 Hilgard Ave, Los Angeles, 90024. Edward Shreeves, Chairman, Bibliographers Group; Frances K Zeitlin, Medievan and Renaissance Bibliographer
Notes: Incl collection of early *Consilia.*

CA —UNIVERSITY OF CALIFORNIA, LOS ANGELES, Research Library, Western European Collection, Los Angeles, 90024. Edward Shreeves, Chairman, Bibliographers Group; Mary E Greco, Western European Bibliographer
Holdings: Mss Maps Pix Microforms
Notes: Good general coverage. Special strengths in the religious history of the 17th and 18th centuries.

CT —YALE UNIVERSITY, Box 1603A, Yale Station, New Haven, 06520.

GA —EMORY UNIVERSITY, Candler School of Theology, Pitts Theology Library, Atlanta, 30322. Channing Jeschke, Librn; Anita K Delaries, Curator
Notes: The Hartford Seminary Foundation Library (partial). About 205,000 vols, pamphlets, etc.

IL —NEWBERRY LIBRARY, 60 W Walton St, Chicago, 60610. Diana Haskell, Cur of Modern Mss
Holdings: Cat
Notes: Many histories of individual churches; also diocesan and state histories especially New England, the Midwest and the West.

MD —JOHNS HOPKINS UNIVERSITY, Milton S Eisenhower Library, George Peabody Collection, 17 E Mt Vernon Place, Baltimore, 21201. Lyn Hart, Peabody Librn
Notes: Emphasis on materials published before 1950. Strength is a good collection through the 19th century.

MA —HARVARD UNIVERSITY, Harvard Divinity School, Andover-Harvard Theological Library, 45 Francis Ave, Cambridge, 02138. Maria Grossmann, Librn
Holdings: Vols (370,000) Cat

MA —HARVARD UNIVERSITY LIBRARY, Widener Library, Cambridge, 02138.
Holdings: Cat Mss
Notes: See *Harvard Library Bulletin,* V (1951), 159-180.

MN —SAINT JOHN'S ABBEY & UNIVERSITY, Hill Monastic Manuscript Library, Collegeville, 56321. Julian G Plante, Dir
Holdings: Vols (61,000) Microfilms
Notes: Films of 61,000 mss. The total number of codices or bound handwritten mss represents the holdings of several hundred libraries in Europe, mostly Austria, Spain, Ethiopia, West Germany, Portugal, and also Italy, Hungary, Poland, Great Britain, Belgium, Yugoslavia, France, Switzerland, and the Netherlands.

MO —SAINT LOUIS UNIVERSITY, Pius XII Memorial Library, Vatican Film Library Collection, 3655 W Pine Blvd, Saint Louis, 63108. Charles J Ermatinger, Librn
Holdings: Mss Slides Microforms
Notes: Vatican Film Library has 75 percent of the Greek, Latin and western European vernacular holdings in the Vatican Library, plus all the Hebrew, Arabic and Ethiopic holdings on film. Covers 5th-19th centuries. Sizable collection of western European books. In addition, has largest collection on the work of the Jesuits in Latin America, the US and the Philippines, filmed from European Jesuit archives. Excellent catalogs and guides to all collections. Also, 50,608 slides of illuminated mss; 26,470 reels of microfilm.

NE —CREIGHTON UNIVERSITY, Reinert/Alumni Library, California at 24th St, Omaha, 68178. Raymond B Means, Dir
Holdings: Vols (19,175) Cat Mss
Budget: ($14,100)
Notes: In addition to English, Latin and Greek predominate in the collection. Emphasis on Catholic religion, history and saints.

NY —GENERAL THEOLOGICAL SEMINARY, Saint Marks Library, 175 Ninth Ave, New York, 10011. David Green, Dir
Holdings: Vols (200,000) Cat
Notes: Extensive collection.

NY —NEW YORK PUBLIC LIBRARY, Research Libraries, General Research Division, Fifth Ave & 42 St, New York, 10018. Rodney Phillips, Chief
Holdings: Vols (2,225,000) Cat Maps Pix Microforms
Budget: ($775,718)

NY —UNION THEOLOGICAL SEMINARY, Library, 3041 Broadway at Reinhold Niebuhr Place, New York, 10027. Richard D Spoor, Dir
Holdings: Vols (580,000) Cat Mss Microforms
Budget: ($750,000)

NY —SUFFOLK COUNTY HISTORICAL SOCIETY, Library, 300 W Main St, Riverhead, 11901. Betty Carpenter, Librn
Holdings: Vols (15,000) Cat Mss Maps Pix

†NY —COLGATE ROCHESTER DIVINITY SCHOOL, Ambrose Swasey Library, 1100 S Goodman St, Rochester, 14620.
Notes: All periods of Christian history incl, but a heavy concentration of unusual imprints from the 16th century.

NC —DUKE UNIVERSITY, William R Perkins Library, Durham, 27706. Elvin E Strowd, University Librn
Notes: The Karl Holl collection contains 8000 titles in European church history through the Reformation.

NC —DUKE UNIVERSITY, William R Perkins Library, Rare Book Room, Durham, 27706. John L Sharpe, III, Cur
Notes: Liechtenstein collection. Sixteenth and 17th century German theology and church history.

NC —SOUTHEASTERN BAPTIST THEOLOGICAL SEMINARY LIBRARY, PO Box 752, Wake Forest, 27587. H Eugene McLeod, Librn
Holdings: Cat Microforms
Notes: Incl early American sources in Readex Microprint edition of materials listed

CHURCH HISTORY (cont.)

in Evan's *American Bibliography* and in Shaw and Shoemaker's *American Bibliography: a Preliminary Checklist.*

OH —PUBLIC LIBRARY OF CINCINNATI & HAMILTON COUNTY, Education & Religion Dept, 800 Vine St, Cincinnati, 45202. Susan F Hettinger, Head
Holdings: Vols (45,000) Cat
Budget: ($10,000)
Notes: Theological and religious collection: religion, church history, theology, 18th and 19th century. Protestant writings and sermons.

OK —MIDWEST CHRISTIAN COLLEGE, Library, 6600 N Kelley Ave, Oklahoma City, 73111. Jean Cavett, Dir
Holdings: Vols (7000) Cat Pix Phonorecords Audiotapes Filmstrips Microforms
Notes: The Restoration Movement (Independent Christian Church) to restore the Church to its New Testament form. Incl churches called "Christian Churches," "Churches of Christ," "Disciples of Christ," and a few called just "Christ's Church."

OR —UNIVERSITY OF PORTLAND, Wilson W Clark Memorial Library, 5000 N Willamette Blvd, PO Box 03017, Portland, 97203. Rev Joseph P Browne, CSC, Dir
Holdings: Vols (12,000) Cat
Budget: $6000
Notes: Emphasis on Catholic theology.

PA —BALCH INSTITUTE FOR ETHNIC STUDIES, Library, 18 S Seventh St, Philadelphia, 19106. R Joseph Anderson, Library Dir

PA —TEMPLE UNIVERSITY LIBRARIES, Special Collections Dept, Conwellana-Templana Collection, 13 & Berks St, Philadelphia, 19122. Miriam I Crawford, Cur
Holdings: Vols (2200) Cat Mss Pix Slides Phonorecords Audiotapes 16mm Films
Budget: ($30,000)
Notes: The Conwellana Collection is a memorial to Dr Russell H Conwell, founder of Temple University and pastor of the Baptist Temple (Grace Baptists Church) of Philadelphia from 1882 to his death in 1925. The Collection contains almost all of his published works; his personal library of almost 2000 books, emphasizing Biblical and religious thoughts; mss both by Conwell and about his development of the institutional church; letters, including a large number written to his assistant pastor, Arthur E Harris; a near-complete bound set of his sermons and of the *Temple Review* of the Baptist Temple in which they appeared over a 36-year period; and an extensive file of articles, photographs and information on his activities. Card catalog of the Conwellana-Templana Collection incl books by and about Russell Conwell. Separate card files index his sermons, quotationsfrom his sermons, and items in the *Temple Review. Russell Herman Conwell, 1843-1925, A* Bibliography, by Maurice F Tauber (Philadelphia Temple University Library, 1935. 40 leaves mimeographed). *Russell Herman Conwell: The Individual and His Influence: Catalog of an Exhibition,* by Miriam I Crawford (Temple University General Alumni Association, 1977; unpaged).

†PA —TEMPLE UNIVERSITY LIBRARIES, Special Collections Dept, Contemporary Culture Collection, Philadelphia, 19122. Patricia J Case, Cur
Holdings: Uncat
Notes: Extensive collection (2 file drawers) of ephemeral material relating to the position of women in the hierarchy of the established church; newsletters, clippings, programs, articles, press releases, etc.

PA —UNIVERSITY OF PENNSYLVANIA, Lea Library, 3420 Walnut St, Philadelphia, 19104. Daniel Traister, Special Collections Librn
Notes: Medieval church history, particularly strong in canon law. See Downs 4234, 4241.

RI —BROWN UNIVERSITY, John Hay Library, 20 Prospect St, Providence, 02912. Mark N Brown, Cur Mss
Holdings: Vols (2000) Cat Mss
Notes: Several collections of religious history strong in material on Baptist, Congregational, and Unitarian Churches in the 19th century, incl the ms records some Rhode Island congregations plus the papers of Isaac Backus, Brown University presidents and faculty, Jones Very, Mary Ann Atwood, Thomas Ustick, and Charles King Newcomb; incl numerous ephemeral and pamphlet publications that relate to Baptist Church history, creed, biography, Sunday School literature and missions.

RI —BROWN UNIVERSITY, John Hay Library, 20 Prospect St, Providence, 02912. Mark N Brown, Cur Mss
Holdings: Vols (900) // Mss
Notes: John William Graham Collection of Literature of Psychic Science; 350 predominantly late 19th and early 20th century books dealing with alchemy, black magic, dreams, demonology, church history, mysticism, mediumship, physical and somatic types of psychic experience. Collection described in *Index to Psychic* Science compiled by S R Morgan (Swarthmore, 1950). Also, the Damon Collection of Occult and Visionary Literature; 550 vols devoted to the development of western mysticism with particular emphasis on American and British thought, incl texts on alchemy, black magic, esoteric church history, dream interpretations, mysticism, witchcraft, the Kabbalah, and visionary testaments and manifestations of all types printed during the 16th to 20th centuries; and the Samuel Wyllys Papers; 125 mss, transcripts, and photocopies of legal and government papers relating to Indianaffairs, colonial wars, civil and criminal cases, and the witchcraft trials of 1692-1693. Partially cataloged.

SC —UNIVERSITY OF SOUTH CAROLINA, Thomas Cooper Library, Columbia, 29208. Kenneth E Toombs, Dir of Libraries; Roger Mortimer, Rare Book Librn
Holdings: Vols (1000) Cat
Notes: Particularly strong in titles printed in the 16th, 17th and 18th centuries.

TX —ABILENE CHRISTIAN UNIVERSITY, Margaret & Herman Brown Library, ACU Sta, Abilene, 79601. Callie Faye Milliken, Assoc Dir
Holdings: Vols (30,000) Cat Mss Slides Audiotapes Filmstrips Microforms

TX —SOUTHWESTERN BAPTIST THEOLOGICAL SEMINARY, Roberts Library, 2001 W Seminary Dr, PO Box 22000-2E, Fort Worth, 76122. Keith C Wills, Dir
Holdings: Vols 40,000 Cat Mss Maps Pix Slides Audiotapes 16mm Films Filmstrips Microforms
Budget: $15,000

TX —OBLATE SCHOOL OF THEOLOGY, Library, 285 Oblate Dr, San Antonio, 78216. James Maney, Libr Dir
Holdings: Vols (22,000) Cat
Budget: ($15,500)

AB —CANADIAN UNION COLLEGE, Library, Box 460, College Heights, T0C 0Z0, Can. Keith Clouten, Library Services Dir
Holdings: Vols (5000) Cat Audiotapes 16mm Films Microforms
Notes: Largely theology, comparative religion, church history, especially of Seventh-day Adventists.

ON —HURON COLLEGE, Silcox Memorial Library, 1349 Western Rd, London, N6G 1H3, Can. Pamela MacKay, Chief Librn
Holdings: Vols (28,000) Cat
Budget: ($24,710)
Notes: Covers Bible, church history, church music, liturgics, pastoralia, religious education, philosophy of religion, religious studies, systematics. 95 periodical subscriptions including foreign language materials. Rare books collection of 750 volumes, including collections of sermons, commentaries, particularly rare bibles, many in foreign languages.

ON —TORONTO SCHOOL OF THEOLOGY, Consortium of Libraries, University of Toronto, Toronto, M5S 1A5, Can. R Grane Bracewell, Library Coordr
Holdings: Cat
Notes: A consortium of 7 theological college and faculty libraries at the University of Tornoto.

ON —VICTORIA UNIVERSITY, Library, Centre for Reformation and Renaissance Studies, 71 Queen's Park Crescent, Toronto, M5S 1K7, Can. Robert C Brandeis, Chief Librn; James Estes, Dir
Holdings: Vols (15,000) Cat Slides Microforms
Budget: ($9000)
Notes: The CRRS concentrates on the northern European countries and France; its chief strengths are Erasmus, 650 vols; early printed books, especially 16th century editions of Latin classics; bibliography and the history of printing. The Erasmus holdings are cataloged in W T McCready et al, "The Erasmus Collection in the Centre for Reformation and Renaissance Studies...A Catalogue"...*Reformation and Renaissance* 7 (1971), 32-76 and "A Supplementary *List"...Reformation and Renaissance,* 10 (1974), 116-119. Published catalogs. Humanist Editions of the Classics at CRRS, Toronto, 1979; Humanist Editions of Statutes and History at CRRS, Toronto, 1980; Bibles, Theological Treatises and Other Religious Literature 1491-1700 at CRRS, Toronto, 1981.

ON —WYCLIFFE COLLEGE, Leonard Library, 5 Hoskin Ave, Toronto, M5S 1H7, Can. Adrienne Taylor, Librn; Gayle Ford, Library Technician
Holdings: Vols (47,000) Cat Microforms
Budget: ($11,000)
Notes: Collection of early and rare books of prayer books, sermons, Bibles. Basic reference collection of standard theological dictionaries, encyclopedias, commentaries. Homiletics collection including 19th century works. Strong in church history, Evangelical Anglicanism, English Reformation, Wycliffe studies.

PQ —BISHOP'S UNIVERSITY, John Bassett Memorial Library, Laurie Allison Room for Special Collections, Lennoxville, J1M 1Z7, Can. Germain Belisle, Chief Librn
Holdings: Vols 10,000
Notes: Partially cataloged. Relates to ecclesiastical subjects, dating from as early as the 16th century, largely concerned with the history of the Church of England in Canada and elsewhere.

CHURCH HISTORY—MIDDLE AGES

IL —NEWBERRY LIBRARY, 60 W Walton St, Chicago, 60610. Diana Haskell, Cur of Modern Mss
Holdings: Cat Mss
Notes: A collection of mss photoduplicated from libraries all over the world dealing with the Roman Inquisition, 16th and 17th centuries.

CHURCH HISTORY—REFORMATION see Reformation and Counter-Reformation

CHURCH HISTORY, ESOTERIC see Esoteric Church History

CHURCH LAW see Ecclesiastical Law

CHURCH MUSIC

CA —CLAREMONT COLLEGES, Honnold Library, Ninth & Dartmouth, Claremont, 91711. Tania Rizzo, Special Collections Dept Head
Holdings: Vols (500) // Uncat Mss Pix Slides
Notes: Joseph W Clokey Collection. 250 ms items, scores, opaques, transparencies and transcriptions of church choral music, often with orchestral and organ accompaniments; 195 printed copies of published works; 15 folders of correspondence with his publishers, miscellaneous notes and typescripts. Restricted use. No photocopies permitted. On deposit.

CA —OAKLAND PUBLIC LIBRARY, Art, Music and Recreation Section, 125 14 St, Oakland, 94612. Richard Colvig, Senior Librn
Holdings: Vols (5000) Cat Phonorecords Audiotapes
Budget: ($6700)
Notes: 10,000 scores, incl chamber music,

CHURCH MUSIC (cont.)

instrumental music (piano and organ collections especially strong), miniature scores, opera scores, songs and song collections; 30,000 octavos (anthems and choral music of all kinds); 5000 books about music; 8000 phonorecords; and audiocassettes.

CA —SAN DIEGO PUBLIC LIBRARY, Art, Music & Recreation Sect, 820 E St, San Diego, 92101. Barbara A Tuhill, Supvr
Holdings: Cat
Notes: Score collection of 17,000 pieces covers all types of music incl religious works, opera scores, musical plays, miniature scores. Complete works of Bach, Berlioz, Beethoven, Mozart, and others are added as published in German reprint. Also, thematic indexes, and study and instructions for playing various musical instruments. General circulation.

CA —STANFORD UNIVERSITY LIBRARIES, Cecil H Green Library, Stanford, 94305. Michael T Ryan, Cur
Notes: Large archive. To be incl in the Stanford University international Lully Archive of microfilm of primary Lully sources. The first of 64 vols (Sacred Music) scheduled for 1984 publication.

†DC —CATHOLIC UNIVERSITY OF AMERICA, Music Library, Washington, 20064. Betty Libbey, Head Music Library
Holdings: Cat Microforms
Notes: A large collection to support advanced degree study. Emphasis on church music, musicology, history and critiscism, instrumental and vocal music, solo music for all voices, instruems, and musical forms.

IL —NEWBERRY LIBRARY, 60 W Walton St, Chicago, 60610. Diana Haskell, Cur of Modern Mss
Holdings: Cat Mss
Notes: Entry also under Newberry Library. *See also* entry under Music

LA —NEW ORLEANS BAPTIST THEOLOGICAL SEMINARY, Martin Music Library, 4110 Seminary Place, New Orleans, 70126. Douglas G Broomoe, Music Librn
Holdings: Vols 38,000 Cat Mss Microforms
Budget: ($10,000)
Notes: Martin Music Library serves the Division of Church Music Ministries of the New Orleans Baptist Theological Seminary. As such, its holdings lean toward church music: books (7500); scores (11,000); anthems (15,000); records (4500). Martin Music Library is maintained as a separate division of the Seminary's library and is housed in the main library. Separate catalog.

MA —BOSTON PUBLIC LIBRARY, Music Division, 666 Boylston St, Box 286, Boston, 02117. Ruth Bleecker, Cur of Music
Notes: The Handel and Haydn Society officially transferred its collection to the library in 1978. The Society gave its books, scores, and archives to the Trustees of the Library to be maintained and preserved as part of the permanent research collection. Presently the collection ranges from early imprints of Handel's music and copies of the *Handel and Haydn Society Collection of Church Music* to the holographs of commissioned works. The archives incl copies off bills and disbursements dating back to 1815, printers' plates for tickets, programs from 1815-1912, membership lists, and by-laws.

MA —OLD STURBRIDGE VILLAGE, Research Library, Sturbridge, 01566. Theresa Rini Percy, Librn
Holdings: Cat Mss
Notes: New England, 1790-1850.

MI —DETROIT PUBLIC LIBRARY, Music & Performing Arts Dept, 5201 Woodward, Detroit, 48202. Agatha Pfeiffer Kalkanis, Chief
Holdings: Vols 19,000 Cat Mss Pix Microforms
Notes: Also incl (77,000) scores. General collection intended for practical use in performance and for scholarly research. Good working collection of bibliographies, thematic catalogs, dictionaries and encyclopedias, periodical indexes. Many sets of collected works, monumental editions, historical anthologies. Good representation of opera and operetta, art song and folk song, solo instrumental literature and chamber music in practical editions. 2575 titles of choral music, chiefly sacred, for use by choirs. 17,000 titles of popular sheet music, uncataloged but thoroughly indexed. Considerable recent holdings of books and periodicals in foreign languages. Special collections of black and local materials. 25, 000 recordings and extensive discographical literature. Collection of publishers' trade catalogs.

NJ —WESTMINSTER CHOIR COLLEGE, Talbott Library, Hamilton Ave at Walnut Lane, Princeton, 08540. Sherry L Vellucci, Acting Dir
Holdings: Vols (43,500) Cat Scores Phonorecords Audiotapes Videotapes Microforms
Budget: ($30,000)
Notes: Talbott Library supports the curriculum of a music college which grants undergraduate and graduate degrees in church music, music education and music performance (voice, piano, organ and choral conducting), with an emphasis on choral music. Incl 7000 phonorecords, 3500 titles in quantity of choral music, 30,000 single copies of choral music.

NY —BUFFALO & ERIE COUNTY PUBLIC LIBRARY, Music Dept, Lafayette Sq, Buffalo, 14203. Norma Jean Lamb, Head
Holdings: Cat
Notes: 76,400 bound vols of music and music literature. Complete works of the great composers, and historical editions. Orchestral scores and parts.

NY —COLUMBIA UNIVERSITY LIBRARIES, Center for Studies in Ethnomusicology Library, Music Dept, 417 Dodge, New York, 10027. Dieter Christensen, Cur
Holdings: Cat
Notes: A particularly strong collection of recorded church music.

NY —UNION THEOLOGICAL SEMINARY, Library, 3041 Broadway at Reinhold Niebuhr Place, New York, 10027. Richard D Spoor, Dir
Holdings: Vols (580,000) Cat Mss Microforms
Budget: ($750,000)

NY —SYRACUSE UNIVERSITY LIBRARIES, Music Collection, 222 Waverly Ave, Syracuse, 13210. Donald Seibert, Librn
Holdings: // Cat Microforms
Notes: Nearly 1000 compositions survive in this collection of 17th century music deriving from the reign of Karl Liechtenstein-Castelcorn as Prince-Bishop of Olomouc. The music is preserved on microfilm in the George Arents Research Library at Syracuse University. Contents range from complete settings of masses, vesperae and litaniae to ensemble sonatas and balletti. The collection contains works by over 100 identified composers, including many who were associated with the Imperial court of Leopold I in Vienna, as well as numerous anonymous compositions. A large portion of the music remains unpublished. A catalog of the collection has been published by the Syracuse University Libraries, viz: Otto, Craig A, comp, *Seventeenth Century Music from Kromeriz, Czechoslovakia: A Catalog of the Liechtenstein Music Collection on Microfilm at Syracuse* University(duplicated typescript; 209 pp).

NC —SOUTHEASTERN BAPTIST THEOLOGICAL SEMINARY LIBRARY, PO Box 752, Wake Forest, 27587. H Eugene McLeod, Librn
Holdings: Cat Phonorecords Audiotapes

NC —MORAVIAN MUSIC FOUNDATION, Peter Memorial Library, 20 Cascade Ave, Winston-Salem, 27107. James Boeringer, Dir
Holdings: Vols (6000)
Budget: ($2500)
Notes: Emphasis on 18th and 19th century music, incl hymns, Moravian music, etc.

OH —CLEVELAND PUBLIC LIBRARY, Fine Arts and Special Collections Department, 325 Superior Ave, Cleveland, 44114. Alice N Loranth, Head
Holdings: Vols (10,550) Cat
Notes: Part of the Vocal Music Collection, which incl oratorios, masses, cantatas, etc, with mostly single copies, piano-vocal scores and about 200 orchestral scores.

PA —FREE LIBRARY OF PHILADELPHIA, Music Dept, Logan Sq, Philadelphia, 19103. Frederick James Kent, Head
Holdings: Vols 2000
Notes: The American Hymnody Collection incl early psalters, hymn books and anthologies of sacred music published in the 18th and 19th centuries. Examples of holdings are Lyon's *Urania* (1761), Billings' *Singing Master's Assistant* (1778), and Wyeth's *Repository of Sacred Music.* Arrangements to use the collection should be made in advance.

PA —LUTHERAN THEOLOGICAL SEMINARY, Krauth Memorial Library, 7301 Germantown Ave, Philadelphia, 19119. Rev David J Wartluft, Dir Libr
Holdings: Vols (2800) Cat
Notes: Lutheran, of all countries. American publications of many denominations also represented. Incl the Luther D Reed collection of Lutheran hymnals.

RI —BROWN UNIVERSITY, John Hay Library, Harris Collection, Prospect St, Providence, 02912. Rosemary L Cullen, Cur
Holdings: Vols (200,000) Cat Mss Pix Phonorecords
Budget: ($15,000)
Notes: The Harris Collection of American Poetry and Plays is principally composed of American and Canadian poetry and plays from the 17th century to the present. Extensive holdings in songsters, sheet music with lyrics (170,000 pieces), and broadsides (30,000 pieces). Incl large collection of Stephen Foster sheet music and music by Rhode Island composers and lyricists. See *Dictionary Catalog of the Harris Collection of American Poetry and Plays* (Boston: G K Hall, 1972), 13 vols: Supplement (1977), 3 vols. Separate catalog.

TX —SOUTHWESTERN BAPTIST THEOLOGICAL SEMINARY, Roberts Library, 2001 W Seminary Dr, PO Box 22000-2E, Fort Worth, 76122. Keith C Wills, Dir
Holdings: Vols 39,000 Cat Mss Phonorecords Audiotapes Microforms
Budget: $34,000

VA —UNIVERSITY OF VIRGINIA, Alderman Library, Music Collection, Charlottesville, 22901. Evan Bonds, Music Librn
Holdings: // Cat Mss Pix
Notes: Scores, books, correspondence of the Russian music historian Alfred J Swan, related to his study of Soviet music (particularly Russian church music and folk songs) and musicians. Published description: Velimirovic, Milos, "The Swan Music Collection," *Chapter & Verse* (journal of the Associates of the Univ of Va Library), Nov 1977, pp 20-21.

VA —CBN UNIVERSITY, Virginia Beach, 23463. Jack L Ralston, Fine Arts Librn
Holdings: Vols 9000
Notes: The Keith C Clark Collection of hymnology; hymnals, psazlters, oblong tune-books, hymnody, church music, composers, early sermons on church music, and journals. See Clark's *Selective Bibliography for the Study of Hymns* (1980).

ON —HURON COLLEGE, Silcox Memorial Library, 1349 Western Rd, London, N6G 1H3, Can. Pamela MacKay, Chief Librn
Holdings: Vols (28,000) Cat
Notes: Covers Bible, church history, church music, liturgics, pastoralia, religious education, philosophy of religion, religious studies, systematics, 95 periodical subscriptions including foreign language materials. Rare books collection of 750 volumes, including collections of sermons, commentaires, particularly rare bibles, many in foreign languages.

CHURCH OF CHRIST see Churches of Christ

CHURCH OF CHRIST OF LATTER-DAY SAINTS see Mormons and Mormonism

CHURCH OF ENGLAND

MD —JOHNS HOPKINS UNIVERSITY, Milton S Eisenhower Library, George

CHURCH OF ENGLAND (cont.)

Peabody Collection, 17 E Mt Vernon Place, Baltimore, 21201. Lyn Hart, Peabody Librn
Notes: Emphasis on materials published before 1950. Strength is a good collection through the 19th century.

NJ —DREW UNIVERSITY, Library, Madison, 07940. Caroline Coughlin, Assoc Dir
Notes: The Maser Collection of the *Book of Common Prayer.* Incl 152 versions, ranging from a 1522 *Psalter and Hymnal of the Sarum Use* to the 1977 version of the prayer book of the Protestant Episcopal Church of the USA.

NY —GENERAL THEOLOGICAL SEMINARY, Saint Marks Library, 175 Ninth Ave, New York, 10011. David Green, Dir
Holdings: Vols (200,000) Cat

MB —UNIVERSITY OF MANITOBA, Saint John's College, Library, 400 Dysart Rd, Winnipeg, R3T 2M5, Can. Patrick D Wright, Head
Holdings: Vols (45,600) Cat

ON —MCMASTER UNIVERSITY, Mills Memorial Library, Div of Archives & Research Collections, Hamilton, L8S 4L6, Can. G R Hill, Univ Librn
Holdings: Mss
Notes: Parish statistical and financial records for various parishes in the Diocese of Niagara.

ON —HURON COLLEGE, Silcox Memorial Library, 1349 Western Rd, London, N6G 1H3, Can. Pamela MacKay, Chief Librn
Notes: This collection is in the Charles Addington Archives. Archives of the Anglican Dioese of Huron. Records date back to before the creation of the diocese including parish registers, account books, synod reports. Records from 1840 to the present. Collection open by appointment for Scholarly research only.

†ON —METROPOLITAN TORONTO LIBRARY, Social Sciences Dept, 789 Yonge St, Toronto, M4W 2G8, Can. Abdus Salam, Head
Holdings: Vols Cat Maps Phonorecords Audiotapes 16mm Films Microforms
Notes: The collection is strong in the history and philosophy of religion and comparative religions; literature of all the major religions of the world; works on the devotional and practical aspects of religion; and books on such sacred scripture as the Bible. In additions, our holdings contain many denominational studies on religion in Canada, as well as more than 300 congregational histories, particularly Ontario churches and synagogues.

CHURCH OF ENGLAND (CANADA)

ON —HURON COLLEGE, Silcox Memorial Library, 1349 Western Rd, London, N6G 1H3, Can. Pamela MacKay, Chief Librn
Holdings: Uncat Mss Maps Pix
Notes: Archives of the Anglican Diocese of Huron. We advise any interested party to write ahead. Records date back to before the creation of the diocese including parish registers, account books, synod reports.

CHURCH OF ENGLAND—EVANGELICAL PARTY see Evangelicalism—Church of England

CHURCH OF GOD

CA —AZUSA PACIFIC COLLEGE, Marshburn Memorial Library, Citrus & Alosta, Azusa, 91702. Edward Peterman, Librn
Holdings: Vols 1000 Cat Maps
Notes: Completely cataloged with special designation. Indexed in regular card catalog.

CHURCH OF GOD (CLEVELAND, TN)

TN —LEE COLLEGE, Library, Ocoee St, Cleveland, 37311. Frances Arrington, Head Librn; JoAnne Sparks, Religion Librn
Holdings: Vols 2006 Cat Slides Phonorecords Audiotapes Filmstrips
Notes: Collection houses artifacts, books, periodicals, information files about the denomination.

CHURCH OF GOD, SEVENTH DAY

†WI —SEVENTH DAY BAPTIST HISTORICAL SOCIETY, Library, 3120 Kennedy St, PO Box 1678, Janesville, 53547.
Holdings: Vols (500) Cat Mss
Notes: Sabbatarianism began in England in the 17th century and was brought to the US by English- and German-speaking Seventh Day Baptists, from whom the Seventh-day Adventist movement emerged after 1844. The doctrine of both denominations and of the Church of God-Seventh Day are set in this collection, 1653 to date.

CHURCH OF THE BRETHREN

IN —MANCHESTER COLLEGE, Funderburg Library, North Manchester, 46962. J Allen Willmert, Librn
Holdings: Vols 1747 Cat Mss Pix
Notes: Materials about Church of the Brethren affairs, concerns, districts, and congregations. Books by and about Brethren persons. Much material on conscientious objectors, esp during World War II. Incl 200 boxes of ms materials.

NY —COLUMBIA UNIVERSITY LIBRARIES, Rare Book & Manuscript Library, 801 Butler Library, 535 W 114 St, New York, 10027. Kenneth A Lohf, Librn
Holdings: Cat Mss
Notes: Consisting of music mss of the Ephrata Community, by the founder of the community, Conrad Beissel. Restricted use.

PA —ELIZABETHTOWN COLLEGE, Zug Memorial Library, Elizabethtown, 17022. Ann M Carper, Dir
Holdings: Vols 3193 Cat Mss Maps Pix Slides Phonorecords Audiotapes Filmstrips Microforms
Budget: ($125,300)
Notes: Brethren Heritage collection incl materials about the Church of the Brethren, 1713-date, as well as publications authored by Church members.

CHURCH OF THE NAZARENE

CA —POINT LOMA NAZARENE COLLEGE, Ryan Library, 3900 Lomaland Dr, San Diego, 92106. Esther Schandorff, Librn
Holdings: Vols 1600 Cat Mss Pix Slides
Notes: Historical and other materials; ephemera, etc.

CHURCH OF THE NEW JERUSALEM see New Jerusalem Church

CHURCH OF SCIENTOLOGY see Scientology

CHURCH RECORDS AND REGISTERS

IL —NORTHWESTERN UNIVERSITY, Library, Special Collections Dept, 1937 Sheridan Rd, Evanston, 60201. R Russell Maylone, Cur
Holdings: Vols 2500 Cat //
Notes: County histories, record surveys, visitations, family histories, biographies, atlases, census records, church histories and records, civil surveys and microfilms.

KS —CENTER FOR MENNONITE BRETHREN STUDIES, Tabor College Library, 401 S Jefferson, Hillsboro, 67063. Wesley J Prieb, Dir
Holdings: Uncat Mss Maps Pix Slides Phonorecords Audiotapes 16mm Films Filmstrips Microforms
Notes: Historical materials relating to Mennonite Brethern Conference of churches and its activities. Focus on US Conference of Mennonites, incl minutes and correspondence. Keeps all data for districts, except the Pacific. Collects all data on birth of Mennonites incl local church histories, family records, and genealogy. Anabaptists classics and picture collection. Periodicals and papers incl; collection partly cataloged.

MA —NEW ENGLAND HISTORIC GENEALOGICAL SOCIETY, Library, 101 Newbury St, Boston, 02116. Ralph J Crandell, Dir
Notes: Large collection of printed British and American parish registers; some American ms parish records. Strong collection of early censuses, incl the Massachusetts Direct Tax Record of 1798, actually a census of Maine and Massachusetts and more informative than the Federal decennial record of early national censuses. Earlier similarly useful records incl the Accounts of Pay for King Philip's War (1675-1676) kept by John Hull, War Treasurer.

MI —SUOMI COLLEGE, Finnish-American Historical Archives, Hancock, 49930. Kenneth Niemi, Archives Librn
Notes: Collection incl 8000 vols, 152,000 mss, 2000 photographs, 760 audiotapes; microforms and maps; 14,000 holdings are cataloged. Subject interests: coop movement, labor, pioneer library of rare books and church records, socialist and communist movements, temperance societies. Special Collections: Finnish language newspapers (includes 100 titles from 1876-present); Suomi Synod Archives; Finnish-American Oral History.

NY —CORNELL UNIVERSITY LIBRARIES, Collection of Regional History, Dept of Manuscripts and Univ Archives, Ithaca, 14853.
Notes: Incl records and registers of Baptist, Congregational, Dutch Reformed, Episcopal, Methodist, Presbyterian, Roman Catholic and United Brethren churches.

SC —COLLEGE OF CHARLESTON LIBRARY, Special Collections Dept, Charleston, 29401.
Notes: St John's German Lutheran Church, Charleston, SC, papers, 1786-1931 incl birth, baptism, confirmation, marriage and death records (1743-1917); lists of pewholders (1812-1844). Also St Andrews Society, Charleston, SC, papers, 1730-1939.

ON —HURON COLLEGE, Silcox Memorial Library, 1349 Western Rd, London, N6G 1H3, Can. Pamela MacKay, Chief Librn
Notes: This collection is in the Charles Addington Archives. Archives of the Anglican Dioese of Huron. Records date back to before the creation of the diocese including parish registers, account books, synod reports. Records from 1840 to the present. Collection open by appointment for Scholarly research only.

CHURCH REGISTERS see Church Records and Registers; Registers of Births, Etc.

CHURCH SETTLEMENTS see Social Settlements

CHURCH SLAVIC LANGUAGES AND LITERATURE

WI —SAINT SAVA SERBIAN ORTHODOX CATHEDRAL LIBRARY, 3201 S 51 St, Milwaukee, 53219. Dijo Radisich, Librn
Holdings: 1500 Vols

MB —UNIVERSITY OF MANITOBA, Elizabeth Dafoe Library, Slavic Collection, Winnipeg, R3T 2N2, Can. John S Muchin, Librn
Holdings: Vols (33,000) Cat Mss Microforms
Budget: ($5000)
Notes: Material in all Slavic languages, mostly in Russian (approx 15,000 vols), Ukrainian (approx 15,000 vols), Polish, Old Church Slavic; mainly literature, language, history, art, geography, economics, statistics, political science; newspapers and periodicals; over 20,000 vols of microforms. Cited in *Slavic Collection of the University of Manitoba Libraries,* John S Muchin (Winnipeg: University of Manitoba Libraries and UVAN, 1970).

CHURCH UNITY see Christian Union

CHURCH VESTMENTS

CA —WESTERN COSTUME COMPANY, Research Library, 5335 Melrose Ave,

CHURCH VESTMENTS (cont.)

Hollywood, 90038. Nancy S Kinney, Dir of Research
Holdings: Vols 1000
Notes: Incl 9 vertical file drawers of photographs, 65 binders of current police uniforms incl sheriffs, state police, etc. 6 periodical subs on police profession. Card file index on selected uniform pictures from periodicals holdings. Collection can be used only by the customers of Western Costume Company. All other use is on a fee basis. Collection is non-circulating. Photocopying available.

WA —UNIVERSITY OF WASHINGTON LIBRARIES, Costume and Textile Collection, FM-25, Seattle, 98195. Krista Jensen Turnbull, Cur
Holdings: Vols (1500) Cat Pix Slides
Notes: Incl the Elizabeth Bayley Willis Collection of more than 1000 textiles from India, and the Seattle Weavers' Guild Collection of Guatemalan textiles. Coptic textiles are on loan from Yale University, and the Boston Museum of Fine Arts gave the Choate Collection of lace. There are also good collections of ecclasiastical vestments and embroideries from many nations, ranging from 1500 BC to the present.

CHURCH WORK

NC —SOUTHEASTERN BAPTIST THEOLOGICAL SEMINARY LIBRARY, PO Box 752, Wake Forest, 27587. H Eugene McLeod, Librn
Holdings: Cat Slides Audiotapes Videotapes Microforms

PA —TEMPLE UNIVERSITY LIBRARIES, Special Collections Dept, Conwellana-Templana Collection, 13 & Berks St, Philadelphia, 19122. Miriam I Crawford, Cur
Holdings: Vols (2200) Cat Mss Pix Slides Phonorecords Audiotapes 16mm Films
Budget: ($30,000)
Notes: The Conwellana Collection is a memorial to Dr Russell H Conwell, founder of Temple University and pastor of the Baptist Temple (Grace Baptists Church) of Philadelphia from 1882 to his death in 1925. The Collection contains almost all of his published works; his personal library of almost 2000 books, emphasizing Biblical and religious thoughts; mss both by Conwell and about his development of the institutional church; letters, including a large number written to his assistant pastor, Arthur E Harris; a near-complete bound set of his sermons and of the *Temple Review* of the Baptist Temple in which they appeared over a 36-year period; and an extensive file of articles, photographs and information on his activities. Card catalog of the Conwellana-Templana Collection incl books by and about Russell Conwell. Separate card files index his sermons, quotationsfrom his sermons, and items in the *Temple Review*. *Russell Herman Conwell, 1843-1925, A* Bibliography, by Maurice F Tauber (Philadelphia Temple University Library, 1935. 40 leaves mimeographed). *Russell Herman Conwell: The Individual and His Influence: Catalog of an Exhibition,* by Miriam I Crawford (Temple University General Alumni Association, 1977; unpaged).

CHURCHES, EASTERN see Eastern Churches

CHURCHES OF CHRIST

CA —PEPPERDINE UNIVERSITY, Payson Library, Malibu, 90265. Virginia Randolph, Special Collections Librn
Holdings: Vols 1000 Audiotapes Microforms
Notes: Religious history of the Church of Christ. A substantial part of collection is rare and its use is restricted.

NE —YORK COLLEGE, Levitt Library, York, 67467. Charles Van Baucom, Dir
Holdings: Vols (1430) Cat Mss Pix Audiotapes
Notes: In the Levitt Library, The American Restoration Movement Collection currently focuses on titles related to the Churches of Christ, although titles on the Christian Churches (Independents) and the Disciples of Christ make up a fair percentage of the collection. To promote the development and the use of the Restoration History Collection, York College participates in the Christian College Librarians Conference with sister colleges David Lipscomb, Nashville, TN; Abilene Christian University, Abilene, TX; Oklahoma Christian College, Oklahoma City, OK; Harding College, Searcy, AR; Pepperdine University, Malibu, CA, and others; also, with the Disciples of Christ Historical Society, 1101 19th Ave S, Nashville, TN 37212.

OK —MIDWEST CHRISTIAN COLLEGE, Library, 6600 N Kelley Ave, Oklahoma City, 73111. Jean Cavett, Dir
Holdings: Vols (7000) Cat Pix Phonorecords Audiotapes Filmstrips Microforms
Notes: The Restoration Movement (Independent Christian Church) to restore the Church to its New Testament form. Incl churches called "Christian Churches," "Churches of Christ," "Disciples of Christ," and a few called just "Christ's Church."

TN —JOHNSON BIBLE COLLEGE, Glass Memorial Library, Knoxville, 37998. Helen Lemmon, Librn
Holdings: Vols (700) // Cat
Notes: History of Churches of Christ and Disciples of Christ.

TN —DISCIPLES OF CHRIST HISTORICAL SOCIETY, 1101 19th Ave S, Nashville, 37212. James M Scole, Pres
Holdings: Vols (26,000) Cat Mss Maps Pix Slides Phonorecords Audiotapes Videotapes 16mm Films Filmstrips Microforms
Budget: $184,000
Notes: The Campbell-Stone Movement--all aspects of its history, incl the Disciples of Christ, Christian Church, and Churches of Christ.

TX —ABILENE CHRISTIAN UNIVERSITY, Margaret & Herman Brown Library, ACU Sta, Abilene, 79601. Callie Faye Milliken, Assoc Dir
Holdings: Vols 6000 Cat Mss Audiotapes Microforms

TX —TEXAS CHRISTIAN UNIVERSITY, Mary Couts Burnett Library, Fort Worth, 76129.
Notes: Disciples of Christ.

TX —LUBBOCK CHRISTIAN COLLEGE, Moody Library, 5601 W 19, Lubbock, 79407. Becky Vickers, Librn
Holdings: Vols (9000) Cat Microforms
Budget: ($6000)
Notes: Emphasis on materials related to Church of Christ. No separate catalog.

CHURCHILL, ALLEN

MA —BOSTON UNIVERSITY, Mugar Memorial Library, Special Collections Dept, 771 Commonwealth Ave, Boston, 02215. Howard B Gotlieb, Dir
Holdings: Cat Mss
Notes: Mss, correspondence, etc collected in depth; incl publications by or about.

CHURCHILL, WINSTON (AMERICAN NOVELIST), 1871-1947

CA —CLAREMONT COLLEGES, Honnold Library, Ninth & Dartmouth, Claremont, 91711. Tania Rizzo, Special Collections Dept Head
Holdings: Vols 250// Uncat Mss
Notes: Papers of Elbert A Wickes, 1884-1975, theatrical and lecture tour manager. Among his clients were Winston Churchill, William Butler Yeats, Houdini, Lowell Thomas, Vilhjalmur Stefansson, and Roy Chapman Andrews.

NH —DARTMOUTH COLLEGE, Baker Memorial Library, Hanover, 03755.
Holdings: Cat Mss Microforms
Notes: His personal papers; scrapbooks (microfilm).

CHURCHILL, SIR WINSTON LEONARD SPENCER

CT —YALE UNIVERSITY, Box 1603A, Yale Station, New Haven, 06520.
Notes: Incl the Stuart H Johnson bequest of books by and about Churchill.

DC —GEORGETOWN UNIVERSITY, Library, Special Collections Div, 37 & O Sts NW, Washington, 20057. George M Barringer, Special Collections Librn; Nicholas B Sheetz, Mss Librn
Holdings: Mss Cat Pix
Notes: The papers of the Irish man-of-letters Sir Shane Leslie (1885-1971) containing letters, mss, diaries, notebooks, clippings, and photographs. Extensive correspondence by Margot Asquith, countess of Oxford and Asquith; Lady Violet Bonham-Carter; Burke Cochran; Lord Alfred Douglas; Moreton Frewen; Cardinal Gasquet; Vyvyan Holland; Lady Leonie Leslie; Sir Wilfrid Meynell; Sir Horace Plunkett; John Quinn; Frederick Rolfe (Baron Corvo); and Elizabeth Russell, among others. Also incl are research files on Sir Winston Churchill (Leslie's first cousin); Leonard Jerome; Maria Anne Fitzherbet (wife of King George IV); Ghosts and Ghost stories; and Eton College.

IL —UNIVERSITY OF ILLINOIS, URBANA/CHAMPAIGN, Library, Rare Book Room, 346 Library, Urbana, 61801. Norman B Brown, Asst Dir for Special Collections; N Frederick Nash, Librn
Holdings: Cat Mss Maps Pix Slides Microforms
Notes: Extensive collection, described in: *Catalog of the Rare Book Room,* (Boston: G K Hall, 1972). Supplement (1978).

MO —WINSTON CHURCHILL MEMORIAL AND LIBRARY, Westminster College, Seventh and Westminster Ave, Fulton, 65251.
Holdings: Vols 800 Cat

NY —COLUMBIA UNIVERSITY LIBRARIES, Rare Book & Manuscript Library, 801 Butler Library, 535 W 114 St, New York, 10027. Kenneth A Lohf, Librn
Holdings: Mss
Notes: Incl 2000 items.

NY —UNION COLLEGE, Schaffer Library, Schenectady, 12308. Ann Seemann, Librn; Ellen Fladger, Archivist
Holdings: Cat
Notes: First editions, incl 48 vols, 30 pamphlets, etc.

CHUVAK LANGUAGE see Chuvashian Language

CHUVASHIAN LANGUAGE

NY —NEW YORK PUBLIC LIBRARY, Oriental Div, Fifth Ave & 42 St, New York, 10018. E Christian Filstrup, Chief
Holdings: Cat Mss Microforms
Budget: ($56,455)
Notes: Published catalog of holdings.

CICERO

NC —DUKE UNIVERSITY, William R Perkins Library, Rare Book Room, Durham, 27706. John L Sharpe, III, Cur
Notes: Berthold Louis Ullmann collection. Classical manuscripts - "17 substantial codices, two fragmentary manuscripts and 30 of only a few pages each, a total of 49 written between 9th and 16th centuries. Among them are four of the works of Cicero in the hand of noted 15th century scribes and two 9th century fragments of a French Sacramentary - and early Roman Catholic Service book for the Mass." In addition, Greek mss, 87 in number, dating from the 10th to the 12th centuries, incl 24 New Testament mss.

PA —UNIVERSITY OF PITTSBURGH, Hillman Library, Pittsburgh, 15260. Glenora E Rossell, Head
Holdings: Vols (11,550) Cat
Notes: The classics collection is particularly strong in Greek and Latin literature. Greek and Roman history. Greek philosophy. Greek and Latin language, and Greek epigraphy. In combination with the Frick Fine Arts collection it has a good collection in Greek and Roman art and archaeology. The collection of journals is also quite strong in these areas. There has been an emphasis in collecting books by and about Homer, Aristotles, Euripides, Vergil, Cicero and

CICERO (cont.)

Petronius. It has a unique collection of unpublished PhD dissertations and Master's theses on Petronius. It has a basic collection on Greek and Latin paleography and papyrology.

CIGARETTE CARDS

NY —NEW YORK PUBLIC LIBRARY, Rare Books and Manuscripts Div, Fifth Ave & 42 St, New York, 10018. William L Joyce, Asst Dir; Bernard McTigue, Cur, Arents Collection
Notes: Arents Tobacco Collection; incl over 81,000 cigarette cards.

CIGARETTE HABIT

MD —OFFICE ON SMOKING AND HEALTH, Park Bldg, Rm 116, 5600 Fishers Lane, Rockville, 20857. Donald R Shopland, Technical Information Officer
Notes: Smoking, tobacco and nicotine as related to health. Approx 40,000 reprints. The technical information center of the clearinghouse issues at irregular intervals (about 6 times per year) the *Smoking and Health Bulletin*. The *Bulletin* contains those items added to the collection from the world-wide literature on smoking. Bibliographic and reference services can be obtained by writing or calling the Clearinghouse. Over 10,000 records, 1970-present, are stored in an automated file and are capable of search and retrieval. Printout information corresponds to that found in the *Smoking and Health Bulletin*. The Clearinghouse has been named the "Collaborating Center for Smoking and Health" by the World Health Organization.

CIGARETTES see Cigarette Habit

CIGARMAKERS UNION

PA —PENNSYLVANIA STATE UNIVERSITY, Fred Lewis Pattee Library, Labor History Collection, University Park, 16802. Peter Gottlieb, Archivist
Holdings: Cat Mss
Notes: Trade union's archives, etc.

CIMBER, ALFONSO

KS —WICHITA PUBLIC LIBRARY, Art & Music Division, 223 S Main, Wichita, 67202. Leonard Messineo, Jr, Head, Art & Music Division; Deborah Hamilton, Special Collections Librn
Holdings: Uncat Audiotapes Videotape Pix
Notes: Alice Bauman Dance Symposia Collection. Contains 300 hours of audio tapes, 1 hour-long video tape, several hundred photographs, and fugitive material of the American Dance Symposia held in Wichita from 1968-1972. The symposia covered all dance idioms-ballet, modern, jazz, folk, ethnic, dance education and therapy-and featured such notable figures such as Leonide Massine, Martha Hill, William Christensen, Alfonso Cimber, Toni Intravaia, James Clouser, Eleo Pomare, Juana de Laban, and many others. Characterized by the *Kansas City Star* as the "most distinguished faculties of fine artists ever assembled in the contemporary world of dance."

CINCINNATI—HISTORY

OH —PUBLIC LIBRARY OF CINCINNATI & HAMILTON COUNTY, Films and Recordings Center, 800 Vine St, Cincinnati, 45202. Robert Hudzik, Head
Holdings: Vols 2500 Cat Maps Pix Slides
Notes: There is a card catalog index and a printed subject index to the entire slide collection. Printed catalog does not break down Cincinnati History Collection. 2,000 of the Cincinnati History Slides were originally on 3x4 glass slides and transferred to the more standard 2x2 size. Original slides are still in the collection. Use restricted to Cincinnati & Hamilton County and Fee Card Borrowers.

CINCINNATI NEWSPAPERS see Newspapers, Cincinnati

CINEMA see Moving Pictures

CINEMASCOPE see Wide Screen Processes (Cinematography)

CINEMATOGRAPHY

CA —BURBANK PUBLIC LIBRARY, 110 N Glenoaks Blvd, Burbank, 91502. Mary Ann Grasso, Coordr; Barbara Stones, Coordr, Media Project
Holdings: Vols (500) Videotapes Audiotapes
Notes: This collection (including technical manuals, production directories, scripts, production lectures, seminars, and university classes), is a free public clearinghouse of industry trends, job skills information, technical advances and management practices required for film and video production. Information covers such technical categories as cinematography, editing, sound recording, lighting, and special effects. Craft areas include directing, scriptwriting, art direction and costume design. Management information covers producing, programming, financing, budgets and distribution for theatrical, broadcast, and non-broadcast markets. Bulk of collection circulates. Reference texts and some other restricted material available for in-library study only. List of holdings available on request.
See also entries under Moving Pictures - Production and Direction; Television

CA —UNIVERSITY OF CALIFORNIA, LOS ANGELES, Research Library, Dept of Special Collections, 405 Hilgard Ave, Los Angeles, 90024. Edward Shreeves, Chairman, Bibliographers Group; David S Zeidberg, Head
Holdings: Cat Mss Pix Slides
Notes: 23 linear feet of correspondence, ephemera, slides, etc, concerning Walter Beyer's work as an engineer at Paramount Pictures, the development of VistaVision, the Motion Picture Research Council, and Universal Pictures.

CA —UNIVERSITY OF CALIFORNIA, LOS ANGELES, Theater Arts Library, Los Angeles, 90024. Edward Shreeves, Chairman, Bibliographers Group; Audree Malkin, Head, Theater Arts Library
Holdings: Cat Mss Pix Slides
Notes: Archival collections: (1) Star Trek Archive: Gene Roddenberry's complete files for 3 years of production of the *Star Trek* television series (1966-1969). Incl are scripts, business records and correspondence, and production materials. (2) Subject file: an extensive collection of articles, pamphlets, clippings, program notes, reviews, and other ephemera about personalities, films, and subjects relating to all aspects of film, radio and television. (3) Harold Leonard Collection: A large collection of clippings and photographs related to the film industry for the period 1930-1960. (4) Film Posters and Programs: A diverse collection of rare and early film posters, programs, and advertising campaign books for American films dating from 1915. Posters and programs for Polish and Czechoslovakian productions are alsorepresented. (5) Walter Beyer Papers, incl material on wide screen processes, traveling matte process photography, the blue screen system, and film processing.

CINEMATOGRAPHY, HIGH SPEED

NM —UNIVERSITY OF CALIFORNIA, Los Alamos National Laboratory, Libraries, PO Box 1663, MSP 362, Los Alamos, 87545. J Arthur Freed, Head Librn
Holdings: Vols (800,000) Cat Films Microforms
Budget: ($700,000)
Notes: Incl 500,000 classified and unclassified reports. There are 25 branch libraries and a central collection.

CINEMATOGRAPHY, WIDE SCREEN see Wide Screen Processes (Cinematography)

CINERAMA see Wide Screen Processes (Cinematography)

CIPHERS AND CODES see Cryptography

CIRCUITS, ELECTRIC see Electric Circuits

CIRCULATION OF THE BLOOD see Blood—Circulation; Cardiovascular System

CIRCULATORY SYSTEM see Blood—Circulation; Cardiovascular System

CIRCUMNAVIGATION see Voyages and Travels

CIRCUS

CA —UNIVERSITY OF CALIFORNIA, SANTA BARBARA, Library, Dept of Special Collections, Santa Barbara, 93106. Christian F Brun, Head
Holdings: Cat Mss Pix

FL —RINGLING MUSEUM OF THE CIRCUS, Library, PO Box 1838, Sarasota, 33578. Nan Fisher, Visitor Services Specialist
Holdings: Vols (350) Cat
Notes: Collection also incl long runs (and indexes) of circus periodicals.

IL —ILLINOIS STATE UNIVERSITY, Milner Library, Dept of Special Collections, Normal, 61761. Robert Sokan, Librn
Holdings: Vols (6200) Cat Mss Pix Slides
Notes: Circus and related arts collection consists of approx 6200 book items and approx 250,000 nonbook items. The books date from the 16th century to the present, and incl vols specifically concerned with the circus past and present, vaudeville, music halls and variety theaters, theatrical and animal history, biographies, autobiographies and memoirs, novels, poetry, drama, juvenalia and other subjects relating to the circus. Many of the books are limited editions, presentation copies or autographed copies. Incl archives of the Dobritch International Circus (20,000 items).

MA —HARVARD UNIVERSITY LIBRARY, Theatre Collection, Cambridge, 02138. Jeanne T Newlin, Cur
Holdings: Cat Mss Pix Slides Microforms
Notes: One of the largest existing collections of playbills, programs, prints, photographs, promptbooks, and other materials relating to the performing arts, the scope is worldwide; resources on the English-speaking stage of the 18th and 19th centuries are unequalled. Incl materials on ballet and modern dance, the circus, magic, minstrel shows, cinema, and pantomime. For description, see *Harvard Library Bulletin*, VI (1925): pp 281-301.

NY —NEW YORK PUBLIC LIBRARY, Performing Arts Research Center, Billy Rose Theatre Collection, 111 Amsterdam Ave, New York, 10023. Dorothy L Swerdlove, Cur
Holdings: Cat
Notes: The collection incl the Townsend Walsh Collection, a rare assembling of 19th and early 20th century circus material--route books, programs, posters--mostly on the circus in the US and Great Britain, but with extensive material on European circus--19th-20th centuries.

†NY —NEW YORK SCHOOL FOR CIRCUS ARTS (BIG APPLE CIRCUS), 1230 Fifth Ave, New York, 10029.

PA —FREE LIBRARY OF PHILADELPHIA, Theatre Collection, Logan Sq, Philadelphia, 19103. Geraldine Duclow, Librn-in-Charge
Holdings: Vols (1,250,000) Uncat Pix
Notes: The Theatre Collection contains books, magazines, playbills, broadsides, posters, photographs, and other memorabilia covering theatre, motion pictures, minstrels, vaudeville, circus, radio and television. The

CIRCUS (cont.)

Library's Philadelphia Theatre Index lists the major productions here since 1855, and partially indexes the collection of local playbills which date back to 1803. There are also programs from many other cities, incl New York; some from London date back to 1800. Early film companies as well as the present movie industry are represented by advertising materials and over 30,000 film stills. The Lubin Film Co (1910-1916) Archive has been established with over 600 photographs and related items. Circus programs and route books date back to 1900. There are minstrel programs as early as 1865. Most significant are the mss from Philadelphia's Dumont Minstrels. Variousfiles contain autographs, photographs, newspaper articles and reviews in all pertinent subject areas. Noncirculating.

TN —MEMPHIS STATE UNIVERSITY, John Willard Brister Library, Memphis, 38152. John Terreo, Special Collections Librn
Notes: Dyer Marion "Ichabod" Reynolds Circus Collection, 1878-1980. A multi-formated collection of photographic negatives and prints, letters, newspaper and periodical clippings, scrapbooks, albums, handbills, posters, route cards, couriers, lithographs, and small artifacts documenting in general details the zenith and gradual decline of the American Circus as the dominant form of entertainment in the US. Correspondence incl letters from the Reynolds family to Reynolds and from Reynolds to circus performers and employees concerning various topics about the circus. Unpublished finding aid to the collection can be found in the Mississippi Valley Collection.

TX —DALLAS PUBLIC LIBRARY, Fine Arts Div, 1515 Young St, Dallas, 75201. Richard L Waters, Acting Dir; Jane Holahan, Manager
Notes: 18th-20th century.

TX —SOUTHERN METHODIST UNIVERSITY, Fondren Library, McCord Theater Collection, Room 301, Dallas, 75275. Edyth Renshaw, Cur; Linda Sellers, Pub Serv
Holdings: Vols (2000) Uncat Mss Pix Slides Phonorecords
Notes: See *Theatre Collections in Libraries and Museums*, Gilder and Freedley (Theatre Arts, 1936). The McCord Theatre Collection encompasses the entire spectrum of the performing arts. The central purpose is to gather records of our regional theater before such ephemeral material is lost. Records of over two hundred early Texas theaters, some fragmentary and some relatively complete, are in the files. These records incl photographs of buildings, stagehands, orchestras, and performers. Local theatre history incl the once famous Dallas Little Theatre and the Margo Jones Theatre. The national theatre, opera, ballet, and circus archives incl pictures (some autographed), programs, posters, throw-aways, tear sheets, clippings, and letters. Our international archives are small, but we have some excellent material, eg, artifacts from Max Reinhardt's production of"The Miracle" which happened to go bankrupt in Dallas. After a few years the items were given to us. There are posters, tear sheets, souvenir programs, and other colorful items from Morris Gest and the Artef Collection. We have about 200 19th century English playbills and a few from the 18th century. There is a collection of modern English, French, and other European programs, many of them illustrated souvenir programs. Also, magazines on theater, cinema, and television (1800). Scrapbooks covering both southwest and Dallas theater, 1890s-1950s. Special Collections: artifacts and documents on puppets; masks; costume design; circus; and ballet and dance. The Harriet Bacon MacDonald Collection of over 200 photographs of musicians appearing in Dallas during the first three decades of the 20th century. Many autographed. Affiliated with Meadow Theatre of the Arts.

VA —GEORGE MASON UNIVERSITY, Fenwick Library, Special Collections Dept, 4400 University Drive, Fairfax, 22030. Ruth Kerns, Public Services Librn
Notes: The Federal Theatre Project (FTP) was established in August 1935 as a part of the arts program of the Works Progress Administration (renamed Work Projects Administration in 1939). Supporting 150 separate units throughout the United States, the FTP produced over 830 major stage plays, 6000 radio programs, and innumerable marionette plays, vaudeville shows, outdoor pageants, and circuses. At the conclusion of the project in June 1939, the "product materials" generated by the FTP were sent to the Library of Congress, and the administrative records to the National Archives. The Library's Federal Theatre Project collection was placed on deposit at George Mason University in Fairfax, Virginia, in 1974.

WV —SALEM COLLEGE, Library, Salem, 26426. Myron J Smith, Jr, Librn
Notes: Collection supports "the most complete equestrian studies program available anywhere". *Myron J Smith, Equestrian Studies:* the Salem College [Bibliographical] Guide to Sources in English, 1950-1980. Metuchen, NJ: Scarecrow Press, 1981; 4645 entries.

WI —CIRCUS WORLD MUSEUM LIBRARY, 415 Lynn St, Baraboo, 53913. Robert L Parkinson, Research Center Dir
Holdings: Vols (1800) Cat Mss Pix Slides Phonorecords 16mm Films
Notes: Circus and "Wild West" shows. Owned by State Historical Society of Wisconsin. Incl 1800 books on circus subject; 400 route books; 1200 programs, 8000 circus lithographs, 20,000 photo negatives, 50,000 photo prints, heralds, couriers, tickets, letterheads, route cards, original circus artwork, records and documents of circus business, movies, newspaper ads, circus band music and periodicals of show business such as *Billboard, New York Clipper, White Tops,* Bandwagon, etc. Partially cataloged.

ON —METROPOLITAN TORONTO LIBRARY, Theatre Dept, 789 Yonge St, Toronto, M4W 2G8, Can. Heather McCallum, Head
Holdings: Vols (30,500) Mss Pix Slides Phonorecords Microforms
Notes: Book and nonbook materials in all areas of the performing arts except music: theatre and drama, moving pictures, dance, television and radio programming, and varieties of popular entertainment such as circus, music hall, vaudeville, puppetry and pantomime. Special collections relating to the history of the performing arts in Canada. Access to the book and periodical collection is provided through a divided dictionary COM catalog on microfiche. In addition, extensive card indexes are available. Published descriptions of the collection: Heather McCallum. Research Collections in Canadian Libraries, Part II. Special Studies no I. *Theatre resources in Canadian* collections (Ottawa: National Library of Canada, 1973); Heather McCallum. "The Theatre Department of the Metropolitan Toronto Library" in *Special Collections,* vol 1 (1), fall 1981.

CIRCUS BAND MUSIC see Band Music, Circus

CIRCUS IN ART

WI —CIRCUS WORLD MUSEUM LIBRARY, 415 Lynn St, Baraboo, 53913. Robert L Parkinson, Research Center Dir
Holdings: Vols (1800) Cat Mss Pix Slides Phonorecords 16mm Films
Notes: Circus and "Wild West" shows. Owned by State Historical Society of Wisconsin. Incl 1800 books on circus subject; 400 route books; 1200 programs, 8000 circus lithographs, 20,000 photo negatives, 50,000 photo prints, heralds, couriers, tickets, letterheads, route cards, original circus artwork, records and documents of circus business, movies, newspaper ads, circus band music and periodicals of show business such as *Billboard, New York Clipper, White Tops,* Bandwagon, etc. Partially cataloged.

CIRCUS PROGRAMS see Programs, Circus

CISTERCIANS

MI —WESTERN MICHIGAN UNIVERSITY, Dwight B Waldo Library, Institute of Cistercian Studies Library, Kalamazoo, 49008. Beatrice H Beck, Librn
Notes: Collection contains mss and early editions of Cisstercian liturgy and authors, especially Bernard of Clairvaux. Ms sources of Cistercian documentary history, abbey histories and charters. Incl the Abbot Obrecht Collection of mss, incunabula, and other books from the Cistercian Abbey of Gethsemane at Trappist, Kentucky. On indefinite loan (1976).

CISPLATIN

MD —NATIONAL LIBRARY OF MEDICINE, 8600 Rockville Pike, Bethesda, 20209. Harold M Schoolinam, Actg Dir
Budget: ($46,400)

CITIES, IMAGINARY see Geographical Myths

CITIES AND TOWNS

AL —BIRMINGHAM PUBLIC LIBRARY, Dept of Archives & Mss, 2020 Seventh Ave N, Birmingham, 35203. Marvin Y Whiting, Archivist & Cur
Holdings: Cat Docs Mss / /
Notes: Collected papers, 1963-1967 for Albert Boutwell, first mayor of Birmingham, Alabama under the mayor-council form of government. His administration was dominated by several concerns: the Civil Rights Movement, the growth of police surveillance powers within the community, the effort to revitalize the inner city, and stimulate economic growth. Correspondence, memoranda, reports, and other documents are organized by subject categories. Collection of correspondence, reports, memoranda, scrapbooks, other documents, and photographs of Cooper Green, Mayor, Birmingham, Alabama from 1940 to 1953. The papers reflect changes in the city during World War II, post war business expansion, and concern over growing civil rights efforts by blacks.

DC —NATIONAL LEAGUE OF CITIES, Municipal Reference Service, 1301 Pennsylvania Ave NW, Washington, 20004. Olivia Kredel, Mgr
Holdings: Vols (20,000)
Notes: City reports and plans, financial reports, budgets, commission reports, plans, etc. Federal legislation on urban affairs, etc.

NY —ROCKEFELLER UNIVERSITY, Rockefeller Archive Center, Hillcrest, Pocantico Hills, North Tarrytown, 10591. Joseph W Ernst, Dir; J William Hess, Assoc Dir
Notes: The Rockefeller Archive Center, a division of The Rockefeller University, preserves and makes available to scholars the records of the University, the Rockefeller Foundation, the Rockefeller Brothers Fund, members of the family, and those of other individuals and organizations associated with their endeavors. Collections at the Center document a century of philanthropy by legions of associated social and scientific pioneers, providing a unique window into the past.

CITIES AND TOWNS—DIRECTORIES

DC —LIBRARY OF CONGRESS, Washington, 20540.
Holdings: Vols (25,000) Cat
Notes: Local History and Genealogy Room has reference collection of 5000 volumes (1800 on genealogy). General collections

CITIES AND TOWNS—DIRECTORIES (cont.)

contain 25,000 volumes on US and European genealogy. Additional large collection of American telephone and city directories. Card files in LH&G Room include: Family Name Index; Analytical Surname Index; US Biographical Index; Key to Rider's American Genealogical--Biographical Index; Author Catalog of Genealogy, Heraldry, and Local History. Family Name Index was published in two volumes in 1972 by Magna Carta Book Company as *Genealogies in the Library of Congress, A Bibliography*; 1977 supplement covers 3000 additional titles through July 1976.

NC —DUKE UNIVERSITY, William R Perkins Library, Durham, 27706. Elvin E Strowd, University Librn
Notes: The Perkins Library collection of American city directories includes more than 2000 items, in paper copy and on microfiche (pre-1900). It is especially strong in holdings for the southern states.

CITIES AND TOWNS—MAPS

DC —LIBRARY OF CONGRESS, Geography and Map Division, Washington, 20540. John A Wolter, Chief
Holdings: Cat Mss Maps Pix Slides Microforms
Notes: County maps and plans of cities and towns, and the Sanborn Fire Insurance Maps, dating back to 1866 for some 13,000 cities in the US. Also, the American Map Collection incl *A Plan of the City of* Philadelphia (1776) by Benjamin Easburn. *See also* entry under Maps and Atlases - Collections

CITIES AND TOWNS—PLANNING

AZ —ARIZONA STATE UNIVERSITY, Howe Architecture Library, Tempe, 85281.
Holdings: Vols 17,000 Cat Microforms

AZ —TUCSON PUBLIC LIBRARY, Governmental Reference Library, PO Box 27210, City Hall, Tucson, 85726. Ann Strickland, Librn
Holdings: Vols (4000) Cat Maps Audiotapes Microforms
Notes: Special emphasis on public administration, including public finance, public personnel management, social services, urban planning, public transportation, public works, water management, solid waste management, public recreation and government of growing southwestern US cities in 200,000 to 500, 000 population range.

CA —UNIVERSITY OF CALIFORNIA, BERKELEY, Institute of Transportation Studies Library, Library, 412 McLaughlin Hall, Berkeley, 94720.
Holdings: Vols (82,000)
Budget: ($215,000)
Notes: US Department of Transportation depository through NTIS.

CA —UNIVERSITY OF CALIFORNIA, BERKELEY, Environmental Design Library, (The General Library), 210 Wurster Hall, Berkeley, 94720. Arthur B Waugh, Head
Holdings: Vols 50,000 Cat Microforms
Budget: $5800
Notes: Research collection, emphasizing planning theory, housing, zoning, urban renewal, urban design, and open space. Urban social problems, as well as city planning as a profession, are covered in lesser depth. Especially strong in literature on local and metropolitan planning studies from around the world. Approximately 800 serials (including government documents) are maintained in the field of planning. Incl 16,000 pamphlets, 6000 HUD urban planning depository reports.

CA —UNIVERSITY OF CALIFORNIA, LOS ANGELES, Architecture & Urban Planning Library, 1302 Architecture Bldg, Los Angeles, 90024. Jon S Greene, Librn
Holdings: Vols (18,000) Cat
Budget: ($30,000)

CA —UNIVERSITY OF CALIFORNIA, LOS ANGELES, Map Library, Los Angeles, 90024. Carlos B Hagen, Head
Holdings: Vols (5566) Cat Maps Pix
Notes: The Library is a depository for the publications of many world-wide mapping agencies. The collection incl 507,097 maps of all areas of the world (subject and topographic maps, nautical and aeronautical charts, historical maps, and city plans), gazetteers, atlases, aerial photographs, periodicals and other basic cartographic reference tools. Incl 2550 atlases; 10,424 aerial maps; 1035 technical reports; and 311 (titles) serials subscriptions.

CA —ALAMEDA COUNTY LIBRARY SYSTEM, Business & Government Library, 2201 Broadway, Oakland, 94612. David Lewallen, Manager
Holdings: Vols (10,000) Cat Maps Microforms
Budget: ($50,000)

CA —ASSOCIATION OF BAY AREA GOVERNMENTS, MTC/ABAG Library, 101 Eighth St, Oakland, 94607. Diane Gillman, Information Coord
Notes: Concentrates heavily on the nine-county Bay Area region. About 10,000 monographs and serials. Title catalog, OCLC/ATS. Central collection of documents for six transit properties in Bay Area.

CA —UNIVERSITY OF CALIFORNIA, SANTA BARBARA, Library, Dept of Special Collections, Santa Barbara, 93106. Christian F Brun, Head
Holdings: Vols (95,980) Cat Mss
Notes: The Pearl Chase Collections of Community Development and Conservation. Papers of outstanding California leaders in conservation, community planning, Indian affairs, national parks.

CA —UNIVERSITY OF CALIFORNIA, SANTA BARBARA, Map and Imagery Laboratory, Santa Barbara, 93106. Larry Carver, Dept Head
Notes: Worldwide coverage of Landsat imagery donated by US Dept of Agriculture Aerial Photography Field Office. Consists of 153,000 scenes, covering most of the earth's surface between the years 1975 and 1980. Incl 300,000 maps, 1800 atlases, 9 globes, 300 relief models, 1,500,000 satellite imagery and aerial photographs, 700 reference books and gazetteers, 25 serials (titles received), and 21,000 microforms.

CT —YALE UNIVERSITY, Art Library, 180 York St, New Haven, 06520. Nancy S Lambert, Art Librn
Notes: The Art Library is primarily for the use of the undergraduates and graduate students of the school of Art and Architecture. There is a vertical file of urban planning material and the collection contains some materials in this field.

DC —CONSERVATION FOUNDATION, Library, 1717 Massachusetts Ave NW, Washington, 20036. Barbara K Rodes, Librn
Holdings: Vols (8000) Cat Maps
Notes: Collection incl natural resources, ecology, city and regional planning, land use, recreation, energy conservation, environmental economics, pollution control, water resources.

DC —METROPOLITAN WASHINGTON COUNCIL OF GOVERNMENTS, Research Library, 1875 Eye St NW, Suite 200, Washington, 20006. Suan Kalish, Librn
Holdings: Vols (3000) Cat Microforms
Notes: Contains (on 75 reels of microfilm) archives of Maryland-National Park and Planning Commission, archives of the Council of Governments, and audits and financial reports of local governments (1950-date). Also incl annual reports, planning reports and budgets from each jurisdiction (1973-date).

DC —NATIONAL RESEARCH COUNCIL, Transportation Research Board Library, 2101 Constitution Ave NW, Washington, 20418. Lisbeth L Luke, Librn
Holdings: Vols (17,000) Cat Microforms VF
Notes: Photocopying available.

DC —URBAN LAND INSTITUTE, Library, 1090 Vermont Ave, Washington, 20005. Ann Benson, Librn
Holdings: Vols (9000) Cat
Budget: ($6000)
Notes: Incl 200 serials.

DC —US DEPT OF HOUSING & URBAN DEVELOPMENT, HUD Library, 451 Seventh St SW Room 8141, Washington, 20410. Carol A Johnson, Project Manager
Holdings: Vols Cat Documents Microforms
Notes: 600,000 pieces. Strong in all phases of community planning. Extensive coverage of the production and financing of housing. Emphasis on federal legislation.

IL —CHICAGO PUBLIC LIBRARY, Business/Science/Technology Div, Science/Technology Information Center, 425 North Michigan Ave, Chicago, 60611. Lynda Sanford, Head; John R Moore, Environment Collection Coordinator & Engineering Librn
Holdings: Vols 1400 Cat Maps Films Slides Phonorecords Audiotapes Microforms
Budget: $4800
Notes: Incl Aaron Montgomery Ward Collection.

IL —BARTON-ASCHMAN ASSOCIATES, Library, 820 Davis St, Evanston, 60204.
Holdings: Vols (9000) Cat Mss Microforms

IL —LAKE FOREST COLLEGE, Donnelley Library, Lake Forest, 60045. Arthur H Miller Jr, College Librn
Holdings: Vols (500) Cat Maps
Budget: ($1200)
Notes: Focus on development of suburban fringe areas, particularly Lake Co, Ill, and Chicago region: local documents (plans, transit, zoning maps, etc), US documents, and special studies of suburban issues, such as historic preservation and land use.

IL —NORTHBROOK PUBLIC LIBRARY, 1201 Cedar Lane, Northbrook, 60062. Donna Hicks, Librn
Holdings: Vols (3500) Cat Slides
Notes: Maintained as architecture subject center under the North Suburban Library System's Coordinated Acquisitions Program through 1977. Library will attempt to maintain collection through its own budget.

IL —UNIVERSITY OF ILLINOIS, URBANA/CHAMPAIGN, Library, City Planning & Landscape Architecture Library, 203 Mumford Hall, 1301 West Gregory Drive, Urbana, 61801. Mary D Ravenhall, Librn
Holdings: Vols (20,000) Cat
Budget: ($11,000)
Notes: Urban and regional planning; landscape architecture.

IN —INDIANA STATE LIBRARY, Indiana Div, 140 N Senate Ave, Indianapolis, 46204. Robert Logsdon, Acting Head
Holdings: Vols (60,541)
Budget: ($242,431)
Notes: Incl books, pamphlets (50,564), mss (3,000,000), microfilm (1641 reels), photographs (5000), records (37), audiotapes (22), films (107), slides (55 sets), maps (10, 160), VF (37), broadsides (920), newspapers (10,000 bound and wrapped files and 43,000 reels of microfilm). Collects information and materials both current and historical, about Indiana. Separate catalog for printed materials, separate indexes for mss, Indianapolis newspapers and pictures. Other indexes for smaller collections and special subjects.

IN —BALL STATE UNIVERSITY, College of Architecture & Planning, Architecture

CITIES AND TOWNS—PLANNING (cont.)

Library, Muncie, 47306. Marjorie Hake Joyner, Librn
Holdings: Vols (25,000) Cat Maps Slides Microforms
Budget: ($17,360)
Notes: Strong emphasis on history of all aspects of architecture. Also, for other major areas, architecture and landscape architecture and planning 50,000 35 mm color slides, over half cataloged.

LA —LOUISIANA STATE UNIVERSITY, College of Design, Design Resource Center, 102 College of Design Bldg, Baton Rouge, 70803. Doris A Wheeler, Librn
Holdings: Vols 8500 Cat Maps Slides VF
Budget: $6000
Notes: Architecture, interior design, city planning, landscape architecture.

MD —MARYLAND DEPT OF STATE PLANNING, Library, 301 W Preston St Rm 1101, Baltimore, 21201. Helene W Jeng, Librn; John Somers, Asst Librn
Holdings: Vols (11,100) Cat
Notes: Includes depository of plans relating to Maryland.

MD —HOWARD COUNTY LIBRARY, 10375 Little Patuxemt Parkway, Columbia, 21044. Joyce Demmitt, Adult Services Coordr
Holdings: Vols (435) Cat Mss Maps Pix
Notes: New Towns, with emphasis on Columbia, Maryland.

MD —MARYLAND-NATIONAL CAPITAL PARK & PLANNING COMMISSION, Montgomery County Planning Department Library, 8787 Georgia Ave, Silver Spring, 20907. Janice C Holt, Librn
Holdings: Vols (5000) Cat Slides Microforms
Notes: Specific subject areas include: community facilities, conservation, economics, flood control, highways, housing, human and natural resources. landscape architecture, open space, parks, pollution, population, recreation, transportation, urban renewal, and zoning. Commission's publications are maintained by Records Management (not Library).

MA —HARVARD UNIVERSITY, Graduate School of Design, Frances Loeb Library, Gund Hall, Cambridge, 02138. James Hodgson, Librn
Holdings: Vols (225,000) Cat Mss Pix Slides Microforms
Budget: ($500,000)
Notes: Covers architecture, landscape architecture, city and regional planning, and urban design. Catalog, in 44 volumes, published in 1968, with 2-volume supplement in 1970, 5-volume supplement in 1974, and 3-volume supplement in 1979. It also analyzes periodical articles. Architecture collection described in *Harvard Library* Bulletin, VI (1952): pp 263-269. Noteworthy holdings incl those on Abbey of Cluny, Le Corbusier, amd Henry Hobson Richardson. City Planning collection described in *Harvard Library Bulletin,* VII (1953), 188-195. Incl professional library and papers of Charles Mulford Robinson.

MA —MASSACHUSETTS INSTITUTE OF TECHNOLOGY, Institute Archives, Special Collections, Cambridge, 02139.
Notes: Papers of Howe, Manning and Almy, an architectural firm that started in 1913 as Lois Lilley Howe and Manning, was an unusual and successful partnership of women architects. The collection incl correspondence, financial data, reports, specifications, photographs, blueprints, drawings, and research material from the firm. Housing projects incl Mariemont, Ohio, as well as designs and renovations for New England especially in the Colonial Revival style.

MI —UNIVERSITY OF MICHIGAN, Art and Architecture Library, 2106 Art and Architecture Bldg, Ann Arbor, 48109. Peggy Ann Kusnerz, Librn; Dot Shields, Asst Librn
Holdings: Vols (45,000)
Notes: Incl 200 maps, 35,000 slides, vertical file, videocassettes, blueprints, Jens Jensen Landscape drawings, oral history, and 400 serial titles.

MI —UNIVERSITY OF DETROIT, Main Library, 4001 W McNichols Rd, Detroit, 48221.
Notes: Architecture Library was closed in 1981. Collection consolidated in main library.

MI —MICHIGAN STATE UNIVERSITY, Urban Policy & Planning Library, East Lansing, 48824. Dale E Casper, Librn
Holdings: Vols (12,800) Cat
Budget: ($35,000)
Notes: Serves the curricular and research needs of faculty and students involved in urban and regional policy analysis and community planning.

MI —OAKLAND COUNTY REFERENCE LIBRARY, 1200 N Telegraph Rd, Pontiac, 48053. Phyllis Jose, Library Dir
Holdings: Vols (11,000) Cat
Budget: ($34,000)

MN —UNIVERSITY OF MINNESOTA, Architecture Library, 89 Church St, Minneapolis, 55455. A Kristine Johnson, Librn
Holdings: Vols (27,000) Cat Mss
Budget: ($20,000)
Notes: Incl architecture, architectural history, landscape architecture, design methodology, housing, urban sociology, interior design, etc.

MO —WASHINGTON UNIVERSITY, John M Olin Library, Saint Louis, 63130. B J Johnston, Urban and Regional Studies Bibliographer
Holdings: Vols 53,000 Cat Microforms
Notes: 19,000 Microforms; publications, reports, documents.

MO —WASHINGTON UNIVERSITY, Libraries, Special Collections Dept, Campus Box 1061, St Louis, 63130.
Notes: Papers of Joseph R Badarraco, espec files from his term as St Louis' president of the Board of Aldermen, 1972-75. Rich in City Plan Commission reports, etc, particularly redevelopment proposals and projects. Also records of Harland Bartholomew and Associates, early city planning firm active in St Louis and other cities.

NJ —MIDDLESEX COUNTY PLANNING BOARD, Library, 40 Livingston Ave, New Brunswick, 08901. Lou Mattei, Planning Supervisor, Data Mgt
Holdings: Vols (3500) Cat
Budget: ($500)

NJ —RUTGERS, THE STATE UNIVERSITY OF NEW JERSEY, Center for Urban Policy Research Library, Bldg 4051-Kilmer, New Brunswick, 08903. Edward E Duensing, Jr
Holdings: Vols 3500 Cat Periodicals VF
Budget: ($4000)
Notes: Collection focuses on the subjects of housing, municipal finance, and planning in American cities. The emphasis is on current material. Incl 5000 cataloged vertical files, 157 periodical subscriptions.

NJ —PRINCETON UNIVERSITY, Architecture Library, School of Architecture, Princeton, 08544. Frances Chen, Librn

NY —CORNELL UNIVERSITY LIBRARIES, Fine Arts Library, Sibley Hall, Ithaca, 14853. Judith Holliday, Librn

NY —CITY UNIVERSITY OF NEW YORK, City College, Architecture Library, 3300 Broadway, New York, 10031. Sylvia Wright, Assoc Prof
Holdings: Vols (15,000) Cat Pix Microforms
Budget: ($15,000)
Notes: Architecture, landscape architecture, urban planning and other related areas. 11, 000 pamphlets.

NY —COLUMBIA UNIVERSITY LIBRARIES, Avery Architectural and Fine Arts Library, 201 Avery Hall, New York, 10027. Angela Giral, Librn
Holdings: Vols 20,000 Cat
Notes: Restricted use: noncirculating.

NY —ELECTRIC RAILROADERS ASSOCIATION, Frank J Sprague Memorial Library, 89 E 42nd St, New York, 10018. Hugh A Dunne, First VP
Notes: Private library. Incl all forms of railroads operated by electricity. Forms of electric railroads included: street railways, subways & elevated lines, high-speed interurbans, suburban commuter lines, electrified trunk lines, monorails, mountain climbing inclines, etc. Also railroad timetables.

NY —LANDMARK SOCIETY OF WESTERN NEW YORK, Wenrich Memorial Library, 130 Spring Rd, Rochester, 14608.
Holdings: Vols (2000) Cat Maps Pix Slides
Budget: ($500)
Notes: Paintings, slides, drawings, as well as the Society's archives of local architecture and information on preservation and restoration techniques. Much on preservation ordinances; legal, physical and financial aspects of building preservation; local and regional history, especially of Rochester and Monroe County.

OH —CLEVELAND PUBLIC LIBRARY, Public Administration Library, City Hall, 601 Lakeside Ave NE Rm 100, Cleveland, 44114. Janice Ryan Novak, Head
Holdings: Vols 6000 Cat

OH —OHIO DEPT DEVELOPMENT, Library, 30 E Broad St, PO Box 1001, Columbus, 43216. Jean Fisher, Librn
Holdings: Vols (5000)
Notes: Economic data and census data.

OH —OHIO STATE UNIVERSITY, Engineering Library, 2024 Neil Ave, Columbus, 43210. Mary Jo V Arnold, Librn
Holdings: Vols (132,000) Cat Microforms
Budget: ($110,000)

OK —HTB TECHNICAL INFORMATION CENTER, PO Box 1845, Oklahoma City, 73101. Retha Robertson, Librn
Holdings: Vols (100) Cat Documents Pix Slides Audiotapes 16mm Films Filmstrips VF
Notes: Architecture and engineering of the US, especially. Extensive photograph collection, incl 3000 slides.

OK —TULSA METROPOLITAN AREA PLANNING COMMISSION LIBRARY, 200 Civic Center, Tulsa, 74103. Mary R Moss, Head Librn
Holdings: Vols 175 Cat
Notes: Present and past reports of TMAPC on subjects concerning the growth of our city and metropolitan areas. Newspaper clippings from 1969 to present of new developments in Tulsa and metropolitan area.

OR —UNIVERSITY OF OREGON, Bureau of Governmental Research Library, Box 3177, Eugene, 97403. Katherine G Eaton, Head Librn
Holdings: Vols (25,000) Cat Microforms
Budget: ($5000)
Notes: Separate catalog and classification system.

PA —DELAWARE COUNTY PLANNING DEPT, Library, Third & Orange St, Media, 19063. Jane Taggart Quin, Librn
Holdings: Vols 4800 Cat
Budget: $1500

PA —MONTGOMERY COUNTY PLANNING COMMISSION, Library, Court House, Norristown, 19404. Robin McLean, Librn
Holdings: Vols (5000) Cat Slides Microfilms
Notes: Emphasis on Montgomery County land use, transportation, and planning.

PA —TEMPLE UNIVERSITY, Samuel Paley Library, Berks & 13 Sts, Philadelphia, 19122.
Notes: 150 oral history interviews of individuals prominently associated with the Philadelphia Renaissance era from the 1940s to the early 1970s.

†PA —TEMPLE UNIVERSITY LIBRARIES, Special Collections Dept, Urban Archives Center, Philadelphia, 19122. Thomas Whitehead, Cur of Mss
Holdings: Mss
Notes: Ms collection focusing on urban life and development and drawing on the Philadelphia metropolitan area since the Civil War. Incl the papers of several private organizations, such as the Philadelphia Housing Association (1909-1972); Delaware Valley Regional Planning Commission (1965-1972); Greater Philadelphia Movement (1949-1976); YWCA of Philadelphia (1870-1960); YMCA of Philadelphia (1854-1970); Health and Welfare Council of Philadelphia (1922-1969); United Fund of Philadelphia and

CITIES AND TOWNS—PLANNING (cont.)

Vicinity (1920-1975); Philadelphia Urban League (1935-1967); ACLU-Philadelphia Chapter (1948-1975); Legal Aid Society of Philadelphia (1933-1976); etc.

PA —UNIVERSITY OF PITTSBURGH, Library, Graduate School of Public and International Affairs, Forbes Quadrangle, 1st floor West, Pittsburgh, 15260. Nicholas C Caruso, Librn
Holdings: Vols (80,000) Cat
Budget: ($150,000)
Notes: The library attempts to collect as many national economic and social development plans as possible from the developing countries of the world. It also holds city, regional and state plans for Pennsylvania, particularly, the 9 southwestern counties of Pennsylvania.

SC —CLEMSON UNIVERSITY, Emery A Gunnin Architectural Library, Lee Hall, Clemson, 29631. Leslie Abrams, Librn
Holdings: Vols (14,778) Cat Slides
Notes: Incl 2000 South Carolina planning documents. 56,000 slides.

TN —TENNESSEE STATE PLANNING OFFICE, Library, 301 Seventh Ave N, Nashville, 37219. Eleanor J Burt, Librn
Holdings: Vols (19,616) Cat Maps Slides 16mm Films Microforms
Budget: (#8500)
Notes: Comprehensive planning reference materials; materials about Tennessee for planning at local, regional, and state levels. Incl 200 maps and 1350 slides.

TX —UNIVERSITY OF TEXAS LIBRARIES, Architecture & Planning Library, PO Box P, Austin, 78712. Eloise F McDonald, Librn
Holdings: Vols (24,000) Cat

VA —VIRGINIA POLYTECHNIC INSTITUTE & STATE UNIVERSITY, Architecture Library, Blacksburg, 24061. Robert E Stephenson, Architecture Librn
Holdings: Vols (46,000) Cat Audiotapes Microforms VF
Budget: ($57,700)
Notes: Incl over 2000 planning reports.

WA —SEATTLE PUBLIC LIBRARY, Governmental Research Assistance Library, 307 Municipal Bldg, Seattle, 98104. Barbara J Guptill, Librn
Holdings: Vols (18,000) Cat Mss Maps
Budget: ($16,700)
Notes: Includes pamphlets and clippings on municipal affairs, especially Seattle. Emphasis on urban planning, criminal investigation, policy analysis, finance.

WA —UNIVERSITY OF WASHINGTON LIBRARIES, Pacific Northwest Collection, Seattle, 98195. Andrew F Johnson, Librn
Holdings: Vols (50,000) Cat Maps Pix
Budget: ($12,000)
Notes: The Pacific Northwest Collection contains printed materials documenting the historic and contemporary life and culture of the region in a broad range of subject areas. The Pacific Northwest is defined as the geographic region including Washington, Oregon, Idaho, Montana, British Columbia, Yukon Territory, and Alaska. Printed materials including books, periodicals, government documents, maps, weekly and local regional newspapers, theses and dissertations, as well as photographs and architectural drawings are included in the Pacific Northwest Collection. Photographic works of over 200 photographers active in the Pacific Northwest, Alaska, and the Yukon Territory (Canada) during the period 1860-1930, including Asahel and Edward S Curtis, Eric Hegg, and Clark Kinsey, are represented in a print collection of more than 300,000 images. The architecturaldrawings collection includes over 19,000 original plans, drawings, sketches, renderings and blue prints pertaining to the history of architecture and urban planning and landscape gardening in the Pacific Northwest ca 1880-1940. Areas of particular strength are the holdings of over 1100 published journals of Pacific Northwest exploration expeditions, photographs of Northwest Coast Native Americans and of historic Seattle, newspapers issued within the Japanese-American relocation camps, 1942-1945, materials relating to the 1980 eruption of Mt St Helens, and Sanborne fire insurance maps for Washington. A unique feature of the Collection is the subject index to regional periodicals and local newspapers maintained by the PNW Collection staff; over 100 titles are currently indexed. G K Hall Company published a books catalog of the Pacific Northwest Collectionin 1973.

WI —MILWAUKEE PUBLIC LIBRARY, 814 W Wisconsin Ave, Milwaukee, 53233. Donald J Sager, City Librn
Holdings: Vols Cat Pix
Notes: All periods of architecture with emphasis on American. Strength in Frank Lloyd Wright and Prairie School. Wisconsin Architectural Archive collections.

BC —VANCOUVER PUBLIC LIBRARY, Art Div, 750 Burrard St, Vancouver, V6Z 1X5, Can.
Holdings: Cat Pix
Notes: Book and pamphlet collection. Also, (1) Newspaper Clippings File: 31 drawers of relevant clippings from major newspapers, incl the *Sun, Province, Toronto Globe and Mail, Christian Science Monitor, New York* Times, etc on arts, music, architecture; incl biographical material (16 drawers). (2) Picture File about 500,000 pictures in 150 cabinet drawers, strong in architecture, costume, interior decoration, painting, sculpture, also portraits. (3) Exhibition Catalogs File: British Columbia and elsewhere. (4) Association and Organization File: organizations in the Lower Mainland in arts, music, city planning, etc, begun in 1940s; (5) Canadian Artists Index: begun in 1964, alphabetically by artist, with about 300,000 citationsto reproductions of work and biographical material on Canadian artist from the division's books and other sources; (6) Miscellaneous Index: material not covered in other special or published indexes, primarily of Canadian and local cultural events, hard-to-find informations, etc. Local newspapers, special Canadian publications and British film journals are the most regularly indexed items. (7) Song Index started in the 1930s. (8) Title Index to song collections and sheet music in the VPL collection, approx 100,000 entries.

MB —UNIVERSITY OF MANITOBA, Architecture & Fine Arts Library, Winnipeg, R3T 2N2, Can. Peter Anthony, Head
Holdings: Vols (50,000) Maps Microforms

ON —CANADIAN HOUSING INFORMATION CENTER, Canada Mortgage and Housing Corp, CMHC Annex Bldg Ground Floor, Montreal Rd, Ottawa, K1A 0P7, Can. Leslie Jones, Mgr
Holdings: Cat
Notes: Community service and development.

ON —METROPOLITAN TORONTO LIBRARY, Municipal Reference Library, City Hall, Toronto, M5H 2N1, Can. Margot Hewings, Head
Holdings: Vols (60,000) Cat Maps Pix Microforms Slides VF
Budget: ($112,600)
Notes: Community development; municipal finance; local municipal government; housing; urban pollution; urban transportation; urban affairs; urban geography.

ON —ONTARIO MINISTRY OF TREASURY & ECONOMICS, Library Services, Frost Bldg N, Queen's Park, Toronto, M7A 1Y8, Can. Barbara Weatherhead, Head Librn
Holdings: Vols (100,000) Cat Microforms
Budget: ($76,500)
Notes: Index to Ontario regulations.

ON —RYERSON POLYTECHNICAL INSTITUTE LIBRARY, 50 Gould St, Toronto, M5B 1E8, Can. J North, Dir
Holdings: Vols 100,000 Cat Mss

ON —UNIVERSITY OF TORONTO, Faculty of Architecture, Landscape Architecture Library, 230 College St, Toronto, M5S 1A1, Can. Pamela Manson-Smith, Librn
Holdings: Vols (14,401) Cat Slides
Notes: Incl architecture and landscape architecture.

CITIES AND TOWNS—PLANNING—ZONE SYSTEM see Zoning

CITIES AND TOWNS—STUDY AND TEACHING

NY —NEW YORK BOTANICAL GARDEN LIBRARY, Bronx, 10458. Charles R Long, Asst Vice Pres & Dir
Holdings: Vols 1500 Cat VF
Budget: ($356,000)
Notes: Over 900,000 items, incl books, serials, pamphlets, archives and manuscripts, vertical files, microfiche and microfilm, nursery and seed catalogs, photographs, paintings, prints, drawings and engravings. Covering all areas of botanical sciences.

CITIES AND TOWNS—SURVEYING see Surveying

CITIES AND TOWNS, AMERICAN—VIEWS

IL —CHICAGO HISTORICAL SOCIETY, Library, Clark St at North Ave, Chicago, 60614. Robert L Brubaker, Librn
Holdings: Maps Pix Slides
Notes: American city prints, historical.

CITIZEN PARTICIPATION

OR —UNIVERSITY OF OREGON, Bureau of Governmental Research Library, Box 3177, Eugene, 97403. Katherine G Eaton, Head Librn
Holdings: Vols (25,000) Cat Microforms
Budget: ($5000)
Notes: Separate catalog and classification system.

CITIZENS' COMMITTEE FOR A FREE CUBA

CA —HOOVER INSTITUTION ON WAR, REVOLUTION & PEACE, Stanford University, Stanford, 94305. Milorad M Drachkovitch, Archivist
Notes: Records of the Citizens Committee for a Free Cuba, Inc, an anti-communist organization founded in the US in 1963 to disseminate information about communism in Cuba and other Latin American countries, incl clipplings, newsletters, press releases, reports, conference papers, speeches, and printed matter, 1962-74, relating primarily to the political, economic, and social effects of communism in Cuba, communist subversion in Latin America, US foreign policy toward Cuba, and activities of the Cuban emigre community. 58 ms boxes.

CITIZEN'S COMMITTEE FOR THE PROTECTION OF THE ENVIRONMENT

†NY —COLUMBIA UNIVERSITY LIBRARIES, Butler Library, Rare Book and Manuscript Library, 535 W 114 St, New York, 10027.
Notes: Papers of the Citizen's Committee for the Protection of the Environment, Ossining, NY, whose activities are centered on the environmental hazards of Consolidated Edison's Indian Point nuclear power plants.

CITIZEN'S CRUSADE AGAINST POVERTY

MI —WAYNE STATE UNIVERSITY, Walter P Reuther Library, Archives of Labor & Urban Affairs, Detroit, 48202. Philip Mason, Dir
Notes: Insights into national problems of discrimination and poverty can ve found in the records and papers of the United Farm Workers Organizing Committee and its Director, Cesar Chavez; the California Migrant Ministry; and the Citizen's Crusade Against Poverty, now preserved in the Archives.

CITIZEN'S LEAGUE AGAINST THE SONIC BOOM

MA —MASSACHUSETTS INSTITUTE OF TECHNOLOGY, Institute Archives, Special Collections, Cambridge, 02139.
Notes: Correspondence, newsletters, fact-sheets, newspaper and magazine articles, books and reports of the Citizens' League Against the Sonic Boom, established in 1967 by William Shurcliff to oppose the sonic boom, stop commercial supersonic transport production, and influence public opinion and policy decisions on the SST. Major correspondents incl Bo Lundberg, Richard Wiggs, several US congressmen, and CLASB members.

CITIZENS SCHOOLS COMMITTEE

IL —CHICAGO HISTORICAL SOCIETY, Library, Clark St at North Ave, Chicago, 60614. Archie Motley, Manuscript Librn
Notes: Papers.
See also entry under Education-Illinois.

CITRUS FRUIT INDUSTRY

CA —AZUSA PACIFIC COLLEGE, Marshburn Memorial Library, Citrus & Alosta, Azusa, 91702. Edward Peterman, Librn
Holdings: Vols 5000// Maps Pix
Notes: Azusa Foothill Citrus and Local History collection is related to the genesis of Azusa, the citrus industry, the Slauson and Macneil families, and such companies as the Azusa Land and Water Company. Azusa Electric Lighting and Power Company, Azusa Foothill Citrus Association, Azusa Agricultural Water Company, and the Azusa Foothill Citrus Company. Includes letters, ledgers, etc.

CA —UNIVERSITY OF CALIFORNIA, DAVIS, Shields Library, Dept of Special Collections, Davis, 95616. Donald Kunitz, Head; C Danial Elliott, Asst Head
Notes: Graphic collection of 1500 fruit box labels used by California citrus growers in marketing their produce.

CA —UNIVERSITY OF CALIFORNIA, LOS ANGELES, Research Library, Dept of Special Collections, 405 Hilgard Ave, Los Angeles, 90024. Edward Shreeves, Chairman, Bibliographers Group; David S Zeidberg, Head
Holdings: Cat Mss Pix
Notes: 40 linear feet of various collections mostly relating to Southern California.

CA —SUNKIST GROWERS, Research Library, 760 E Sunkist St, Ontario, 91761. Martha C Nemeth, Librn
Holdings: Vols (1500) Cat
Budget: ($10,000)
Notes: Technology of citrus fruit and citrus fruit products, primarily Californian. Strong in organic and food chemistry, with additional coverage of food technology, essential oils, microbiology and environmental protection.

CA —POMONA PUBLIC LIBRARY, Special Collections, 625 S Garey Ave, PO Box 2271, Pomona, 91766. David Streeter, Librn
Holdings: Cat Mss Pix Slides Audiotapes
Notes: 4000 citrus box labels (world wide) indexed by brand name and packing house; 42 linear feet of uncataloged records of 28 California citrus companies; 200 color 35mm transparencies of citrus labels; 100 photographs of citrus industry scenes.

CA —A K SMILEY PUBLIC LIBRARY, 125 W Vine St, Redlands, 92373. Larry E Burgess, Archivist
Holdings: Vols (3500) Mss Maps Pix Phonorecords Microforms
Budget: ($45,000)
Notes: Emphasis on San Bernadino County and the Redlands area. Especially prized is *The Citrograph*, 1887-1908 (bound vols and microfilm) edited by Scipio Craig, prominent in state, national, and newspaper circles. The ms collection (250,000 pieces) incl the Smiley Family papers, much on water development, and on the citrus industry. The photograph collection (over 5000) covers the history of the area; there are many stereographs and glass slides. The collection on Indians of California and the Southwest was begun from a special gift by Andrew Carnegie honoring his friend, Albert K Smiley.

CA —THE HAGGIN MUSEUM, Petzinger Library of Californiana, 1201 N Pershing Ave, Stockton, 95203. Diane Freggiaro, Librn/Archivist
Holdings: Vols (7000) Cat Mss Maps Pix Slides Audiotapes 16mm Films
Notes: The Petzinger Library is open by appointment only. Special emphasis on Stockton and San Joaquin County and Valley area, local biography, agriculture, agricultural history, industrial history, farm machinery (especially Holt Manufacturing Co, Stockton). There is a photograph collection of 8500 pictures, and extensive manuscript holdings (about 17,000 pieces).

CITRUS FRUITS

CA —UNIVERSITY OF CALIFORNIA, RIVERSIDE, University Library, Bio-Agricultural Library, Batchelor Hall, Riverside, 92521. Barbara Montanary, Head
Holdings: Vols (130,000) Cat Mss Maps Pix Microforms
Notes: The Bio-Agricultural Library (formerly the Library of Citrus Experiment Station of the University of California) is well known for its complete collections in the fields of the agriculture sciences. It is especially known for its emphasis on entomology, incl bio-control; botany, citriculture, plant sciences, nematology and plant pathology; arid and semi-arid lands research and subtropical agriculture. Specific areas of interest are avocados, dates, desert flora, jojoba, guayule and carob.

CITRUS INDUSTRY see Citrus Fruit Industry

CITY CENTER OF MUSIC AND DRAMA, NEW YORK CITY

NY —NEW YORK PUBLIC LIBRARY, Performing Arts Research Center, Billy Rose Theatre Collection, 111 Amsterdam Ave, New York, 10023. Dorothy L Swerdlove, Cur
Holdings: Cat Mss Pix
Notes: Papers, scrapbooks, mss, photographs, memorabilia, etc.

CITY CLUB OF CHICAGO

IL —CHICAGO HISTORICAL SOCIETY, Library, Clark St at North Ave, Chicago, 60614. Robert L Brubaker, Librn
Holdings: Vols (150,000) Cat Mss Maps Pix Broadsides Microfilm
Notes: Early municipal documents, incl some not in the Municipal Reference Library, and selected later documents; archives of the City Club of Chicago, the Illinois League of Women Voters, Independent Voters of Illinois, and other organizations; papers of Chicago aldermen and other political leaders from Chicago; broadsides concerning political campaigns; ward maps; and other publications.

CITY GOVERNMENT see Municipal Government

CITY LIGHTS (PUBLICATION)

CA —UNIVERSITY OF CALIFORNIA, BERKELEY, Bancroft Library, Manuscripts Division, Berkeley, 94720. James D Hart, Dir
Holdings: Vols 2000 Cat Mss
Notes: The Contemporary Poetry Collection covers the San Francisco publishing scene, from the period of the Beat Movement through the present day. In addition to printed materials. The Bancroft Library contains the important printer/publisher/bookseller archives of the Untide Press, City Lights, and the Auerhahn Press.

CITY PLANNING see Cities and Towns—Planning

CITY SURVEYING see Surveying

CITY TRANSIT see Local Transit

CIVIC REPERTORY THEATRE

CT —YALE UNIVERSITY, Box 1603A, Yale Station, New Haven, 06520.
Notes: Press books, scripts, photographs and financial records. Gift of Eva Le Gallienne.

NY —NEW YORK PUBLIC LIBRARY, Performing Arts Research Center, Billy Rose Theatre Collection, 111 Amsterdam Ave, New York, 10023. Dorothy L Swerdlove, Cur
Holdings: Cat Mss Pix
Notes: Papers, scrapbooks, mss, photographs, memorabilia, etc.

CIVIL ENGINEERING

CA —UNIVERSITY OF CALIFORNIA, DAVIS, Physical Sciences Library, Davis, 95616. Scott Kennedy, Head
Holdings: Vols (170,000) Cat VF
Notes: Collection covers aeronautical, agricultural, chemical, civil, electrical, mechanical, water science, hydrology, nuclear reactor, extensive cold regions collection in vertical file drawers, and computer science engineering academic programs. Good strength in journal runs.

CA —CALIFORNIA STATE POLYTECHNIC UNIVERSITY, POMONA, University Library, 3801 W Temple Ave, Pomona, 91768. Harold Schleiser, Actg Dir
Notes: General reference materials on aerospace, chemical, civil, electrical, electronics, industrial, mechanical and manufacturing engineering.

GA —GEORGIA INSTITUTE OF TECHNOLOGY, Price Gilbert Memorial Library, 225 North Ave, Atlanta, 30332. Edward Graham Roberts, Dir
Holdings: Vols (1,661,559) Cat Maps Slides Microforms
Budget: ($1,383,302)
Notes: Incl (4,307,996) patents and (568, 490) government documents.

IL —CHICAGO BRIDGE & IRON CO, Technical Library, 800 Jorie Blvd, Oak Brook, 60521. Susan Beatty, Librn
Holdings: Vols (7500) Cat
Budget: ($39,000)

IL —UNIVERSITY OF ILLINOIS, URBANA/CHAMPAIGN, Library, 221 Engineering Hall, Urbana, 61801. William Mischo, Librn
Holdings: Vols (175,000) Cat Slides Microforms
Notes: Incl 3500 periodicals. Collection designed to serve teaching and research programs. Supports instructional faculty research. Also, 470 microfilm reels and 6000 microfiche sheets.

IN —PURDUE UNIVERSITY LIBRARIES, Engineering Library, A A Potter Engineering Center, West Lafayette, 47907. Edwin D Posey, Engineering Librn
Holdings: Vols (225,178) Cat Maps Audiotapes Microforms
Budget: ($300,000)

IA —IOWA STATE UNIVERSITY, Library, Ames, 50011. Warren B Kuhn, Dean of Library Services
Holdings: Cat
Notes: Extensive serial holdings

KY —UNIVERSITY OF KENTUCKY, Robert E Shaver Library of Engineering, 355 Anderson Hall, Lexington, 40506. Russell H Powell, Engineering Librn
Holdings: Vols (48,000) Cat Microforms

MA —UNIVERSITY OF MASSACHUSETTS AT AMHERST, Physical Sciences Library, Amherst, 01003. Siegfried Feller, Assoc Dir for Collection Development
Holdings: Vols Cat Microforms
Notes: Extensive journal holdings, publications of professional societies and congressional proceedings.

MA —STONE & WEBSTER ENGINEERING CORP, Technical Information Center,

CIVIL ENGINEERING (cont.)

Library, 245 Summer St, PO Box 2325, Boston, 02107. Nancy M Pellini, Mgr
Holdings: Vols (10,000) Cat Pix Microforms
Notes: Also over 1200 periodicals. Extensive vertical file collection, and 5 on-line system for search.

MA —NORTH ADAMS PUBLIC LIBRARY, Houghton Memorial Bldg, Church & Main Sts, North Adams, 01247. Constance Griffin, Librn
Holdings: Vols (57)// Cat Mss Pix Microforms
Notes: Books on the building of the Hoosac Tunnel; reports made during the construction; ledgers kept by men working on the tunnel; pictures of the construction (both photographs and lithographs); and a partial collection of the original plans of the tunnel. No separate catalog.

MI —UNIVERSITY OF MICHIGAN, Engineering-Transportation Library, 312 Undergraduate Library, Ann Arbor, 48109. Maurita Holland, Librn
Holdings: Vols (400,000) Cat Microforms
Budget: ($225,000)

NY —COLUMBIA UNIVERSITY LIBRARIES, Engineering Library, 422 Mudd Bldg, New York, 10027.
Holdings: Vols (177,000) Cat
Notes: All aspects of engineering--aeronautical, industrial mining, civil, chemical, mechanical, electrical, nuclear. Incl applied mathematics and applied physical sciences. Over (1,000,000) technical reports.

NY —ENGINEERING SOCIETIES LIBRARY, 345 E 47 St, New York, 10017. S Kirk Cabeen, Dir
Holdings: Vols 250,000 Cat Maps 16mm Films Microforms
Notes: One of the largest, most comprehensive engineering libraries in the world. Covers all engineering disciplines; particularly strong in electrical and electronic, mechanical, mining, air conditioning and refrigeration engineering. Incl Wheeler Collection of early materials on magnetism and electricity. 125,000 bound periodical volumes; 10,000 maps; 5000 serial subscriptions (many foreign-language). Virtually all materials abstracted in *Engineering Index* (1884-date) are incl in Library. Noncirculating, except to members of professional engineering societies which support the Library. See *Engineering Societies Library, New York, Classed Subject Catalog and Index* (Boston: G K Hall, 1963); and *Supplements*, 1-10, 1964-1973.

NY —NEW YORK PUBLIC LIBRARY, Research Libraries, Science and Technology Research Center, Fifth Ave & 42 St, New York, 10018.
Holdings: Vols (1,100,000) Cat Microforms
Budget: ($647,259)

NY —EASTMAN KODAK COMPANY, Kodak Park Div, Engineering Library, Bldg 23, Rochester, 14650. Raymond Curtin, Librn
Holdings: Vols (14,000) Uncat Microforms
Notes: The library is not open to the public. Use of the library for reference purposes may be requested and appointments may be obtained through the librarian.

NC —DUKE UNIVERSITY, School of Engineering, Library, Durham, 27706. Eric J Smith, Librn
Holdings: Vols (72,000) Cat Microforms
Budget: ($110,000)

NC —NORTH CAROLINA STATE UNIVERSITY, D H Hill Library, Box 7111, Raleigh, 27695. I T Littleton, Dir
Holdings: Vols 22,100 Cat Monographs
Budget: $40,000

OH —UNIVERSITY OF CINCINNATI, Engineering Library, 880 Baldwin Hall, Cincinnati, 45221. Dorothy Furber Byers, Head
Holdings: Vols (50,000) Cat Videotapes Microforms
Budget: ($100,000)
Notes: Have NASA and DOE microfiche collections.

OH —CLEVELAND PUBLIC LIBRARY, Science & Technology Dept, 325 Superior Ave, Cleveland, 44114. Jean Z Piety, Head
Holdings: Cat
Notes: Extensive collection.

OH —OHIO STATE UNIVERSITY, Engineering Library, 2024 Neil Ave, Columbus, 43210. Mary Jo V Arnold, Librn
Holdings: Vols (132,000) Cat Microforms
Budget: ($110,000)

PA —FRANKLIN INSTITUTE LIBRARY, 20 & The Parkway, Philadelphia, 19103. Miriam Padusis, Dir; Charles Wilt, Readers Servs Librn
Holdings: Vols (300,000) Cat Maps Pix Microforms

PA —UNIVERSITY OF PENNSYLVANIA, Towne Scientific Library, 220 S 33 St, Philadelphia, 19104. Charles Meyers, Librn
Holdings: Vols (65,000) Cat

PA —CARNEGIE LIBRARY OF PITTSBURGH, Science & Technology Dept, 4400 Forbes Ave, Pittsburgh, 15213. Catherine M Brosky, Dept Head
Holdings: Vols (380,000) Cat Maps Microforms
Budget: ($240,000)
See also entry under Engineering.

PA —PENNSYLVANIA STATE UNIVERSITY, Engineering Library, 325 Hammond St, University Park, 16802. Tom Conkling, Librn
Notes: This collection includes substantial microform holdings and extensive runs of periodicals.

SC —HORRY GEORGETOWN TECHNICAL COLLEGE, Library, Hwy 501, Box 1966, Conway, 29526. Barbara Brittain, Librn
Holdings: Vols (20,000) Cat Maps Slides Microforms

†SD —SOUTH DAKOTA SCHOOL OF MINES & TECHNOLOGY, Devereaux Library, Rapid City, 57701.
Holdings: Vols (166,200) Cat Maps Audiotapes Filmstrips Microforms
Budget: ($70,000)
Notes: Supportive collection incl an almost complete set of US Geological Survey materials (incl early Territorial Surveys); a microfilm copy (complete set) of the US Bureau of Mines "Mine Map Depository (Denver)" material; periodicals and technical reports (NASA, ACRL, JPL, etc) in engineering and geology; extensive government document materials (NBS, Bureau of Mines, etc).

TN —TENNESSEE VALLEY AUTHORITY (TVA), Technical Library, 400 W Summit Hill Dr, E2 B7, Knoxville, 37902. Jesse C Mills, Chief Librn
Holdings: Vols (106,900) Cat Mss Maps Pix Audiotapes Microforms
Budget: ($2,025,000)
Notes: The Technical Library Headquarters Staff (order, cataloging, information, and administration) is located in Knoxville, Tenn. In addition there are branch libraries in Knoxville, Norris, and Chattanooga, Tennessee, and Muscle Shoals, Alabama.

TX —UNIVERSITY OF TEXAS LIBRARIES, Richard W McKinney Engineering Library, 1.3 ECJ, Austin, 78712. Susan B Ardis, Librn
Holdings: Vols (83,548) Cat Microforms
Notes: Highway (transportation) engineering.

TX —RICE UNIVERSITY, Fondren Library, 6100 S Main St, PO Box 1892, Houston, 77251. Dr Samuel M Carrington, Jr, University Librn
Holdings: Vols 5860 Cat
Budget: $15,550
Notes: Each serial title counted once.

VT —VERMONT TECHNICAL COLLEGE, Hartness Library, Randolph Center, 05061. Dewey Patterson, Library Dir
Holdings: Vols 6900 Cat
Budget: ($15,000)

AB —SOUTHERN ALBERTA INSTITUTE OF TECHNOLOGY, Learning Resources Centre, 1301 16 Ave NW, Calgary, T2M 0L4, Can. Tom Skinner, Historian
Holdings: Vols (40,000) Cat Maps Pix Slides Films Videotapes Microforms
Budget: ($50,000)
Notes: Wide range of current technical information about electronics and engineering (mechanical, electrical, chemical); emphasis on vocational-technical material. Incl (50,000) slides, (300) videotapes, and (500) films.

MB —UNIVERSITY OF MANITOBA, Engineering Library, Winnipeg, R3T 2N2, Can. Y Cho, Head
Holdings: Vols (28,000) Cat Videotapes Microforms
Notes: The Engineering Library serves four academic departments: Agricultural, Civil, Electrical and Mechanical Engineering.

CIVIL GOVERNMENT see Political Science

CIVIL LAW

DC —LIBRARY OF CONGRESS, Law Library, 101 Independence Ave, SE, Washington, 20540. Carleton W Kenyon, Dir
Holdings: Vols 1,800,000 Cat Mss Microforms
Notes: The collection, comprising the legal sources and literature of the US and all foreign nations, covers all legal systems incl common, civil, international, religious, and historic law.

KS —UNIVERSITY OF KANSAS, Kenneth Spencer Research Library, Special Collections Dept, Lawrence, 66045. Alexandra Mason, Librn
Holdings: Vols 1400 Cat Mss
Notes: Especially strong in 16th century French and Italian juris consults, consilia, and commentaries on the C I C. Noncirculating.

LA —LOUISIANA STATE UNIVERSITY, Law Library, Baton Rouge, 70803. Lance E Dickson, Dir
Holdings: Vols (302,659) Cat Microforms
Notes: 358,886 microforms. Strong in civil law materials. Official depository for records and briefs of Louisiana Supreme Court and the five circuit courts of appeal for Louisiana.

PA —PENNSYLVANIA STATE UNIVERSITY, Fred Lewis Pattee Library, Special Collections Dept, University Park, 16802. Charles Mann, Chief, Special Collections
Holdings: Vols (1976) Cat Mss Pix Slides
Budget: ($37,000)
Notes: Includes The Beaver Collection (576 vols) in honor of James Beaver, Governor of Pennsylvania, mostly county histories, atlases and Regimental Civil War histories; John M Read Pamphlets (1400 titles), 1830-1890, relating to canals, railroads and civil law. No photocopying.

AB —ALBERTA ATTORNEY GENERAL, Law Library, Fourth Floor North Wing, Bowker Bldg 9833-109 St, Edmonton, T5K 2E8, Can. Andrew Balazs, Departmental Librn
Holdings: Vols (13,000) Cat Audiotapes
Budget: ($121,620)
Notes: Emphasis is on Canadian law. But if the solicitors can not find a Canadian precedent, they consult English law. If there is no precedent in English law they consult Commonwealth law, and if there is no precedent there either, then they consult American law. Therefore, the Library does have all the basic Canadian and certain basic English Commonwealth, and a very small number of American texts, as well as the basic Canadian and English law reports. There is one Australian law report. Besides texts (monographs), the Library subscribes to Albertan and Canadian legislative publications like bills, orders, votes and proceedings, Hansard, and Debates of the House of Commons. Assistance is available to users' from the simplest to the most complex legal research questions.

CIVIL LAW (JEWISH LAW) see Jewish Law

CIVIL LAW (ROMAN LAW) see Roman Law

CIVIL LIBERTIES see Civil Rights

CIVIL LIBERTIES UNION, AMERICAN see American Civil Liberties Union (ACLU)

CIVIL RIGHTS

AL —BIRMINGHAM PUBLIC LIBRARY, Dept of Archives & Mss, 2020 Seventh Ave

CIVIL RIGHTS (cont.)

N, Birmingham, 35203. Marvin Y Whiting, Archivist & Cur
Holdings: Cat Docs Mss //
Notes: Collected

CA —MEIKELJOHN CIVIL LIBERTIES INSTITUTE, 1715 Francisco St, Berkeley, 94703. David Christiano, Librn
Holdings: Mss Microforms Audiotapes Videotapes VF
Notes: All aspects of civil liberties, from cases of academic freedom to wiretapping.

CA —UNIVERSITY OF CALIFORNIA, DAVIS, Shields Library, Dept of Special Collections, Davis, 95616. Donald Kunitz, Head; C Danial Elliott, Asst Head
Notes: Overview of American political movements from the 1890s to the present: socialism, communism, labor, to ecology and women's liberation.

CA —HOMOSEXUAL INFORMATION CENTER, Library, 6758 Hollywood Blvd Rm 208, Los Angeles, 90028. Don Slater, Librn
Holdings: Vols Periodicals Unpublished Mss Pix Phonorecords Clippings
Budget: $3000
Notes: Contains over 5000 mss, periodicals, and pamphlets on the homosexual movement, from 1948, and records the movement's organizational, social, and political history. Incl are periodicals in Japanese, French, German, Dutch, and other European languages, and newsletters, records, and reports of homosexual organizations probably not to be found in any other archive. The Library publishes bibliographies, selected reading lists, a directory of homosexual movement organizations and publications, and a newsletter. It participates in an ILL network.

CA —LOS ANGELES PUBLIC LIBRARY, Social Sciences Dept, 630 W Fifth St, Los Angeles, 90071. Marilyn C Wherley, Principal Librn
Holdings: Vols 5000 Cat Microforms
Budget: ($150,000)
Notes: Black Studies Collection. Pamphlets, bibliographies, indexes, periodicals, with some historical runs on microfilm, strong collection on slavery and anti-slavery, abolition, civil rights movements, with emphasis on the black experience in the United States. No separate catalog.

CA —UNIVERSITY OF CALIFORNIA, LOS ANGELES, Research Library, Dept of Special Collections, 405 Hilgard Ave, Los Angeles, 90024. Edward Shreeves, Chairman, Bibliographers Group; David S Zeidberg, Head
Holdings: Cat Mss Pix
Notes: Civil Rights Movement in the US Collection. 6 linear feet of ms, printed, and ephemeral materials documenting the Civil Rights struggle from the 1950s to the present, with emphasis on the Black struggle in the southern United States. Also various collections, incl American Civil Liberties Union of Southern California Archive; Japanese American Research Project; Carey McWilliams; US Relocation Center (Manzanar, California) collections. The Carey McWilliams Collection incl personal papers, clippings and reports relating to migrant farm labor and the problems of the Mexican American, 1930-1940, incl material on the Zoot-Suit Riots (3 linear feet of mss with index). Stanley Fleishman Collection incl 270 feet of papers and printed material of the attorney active in cases involving civil liberties,obscenity, and rights of the disabled.

CA —HOOVER INSTITUTION ON WAR, REVOLUTION & PEACE, Stanford University, Stanford, 94305. Milorad M Drachkovitch, Archivist
Notes: Three collections: (1) The New Left Politics Collection consists of monographs and serials on the New Left that are cataloged. In addition, the collection subscribes to numerous underground newspapers and has obtained special subject collections such as the Free Speech Movement at Berkeley 1964-1965, SNCC and Mississippi Summer 1964, and the insurrectin at San Francisco State College in 1968-1969. There is also a good collection on the French student revolts of 1968. The collection is a supervised one and not open to browsers. Interested students and scholars are welcome. Only limited photocopying is permitted. (2) Papers of Kurt R Grossman, 1926-73, incl mss of writings, correspondence, clippings, and serial issues, relating to Jewish refugees from Nazi Germany, postwar German and Austrian restitution payments to Jewish war victims, German-Israeli relations,the condition of Jews throughout the world, and civil liberties in the US and Germany. 53 ms boxes, 8 scrapbooks. (3) Papers of Alice Park, 1883-1957, incl diaries, correspondence, pamphlets, clippings, and leaflets, relating to Pacifism and the peace movement, the Ford Peace Ship Expedition of 1915-1916, feminsim, socialism, the labor movement, prison reform, child labor legislation, civil liberties, and a variety of other reform movements in the US. 30 ms boxes, 3 envelopes.

DC —HOWARD UNIVERSITY, Moorland-Spingarn Research Center, 500 Howard Place NW, Washington, 20059. Clifford L Muse, Jr, Acting Dir

DC —LIBRARY OF CONGRESS, Manuscript Division, Washington, 20540. John C Broderick, Chief
Notes: Papers of Maud Wood Park (1871-1955), first president of the League of Women Voters. 3500 items, incl personal and professional correspondence, family papers, speeches and lectures, reports, photographs, and an autograph collection, documenting the women's rights movement in the US, particularly in the first half of the 20th century. In addition the papers of Roy Wilkins.

DC —LIBRARY OF CONGRESS, Washington, 20540.
Notes: Some 4500 pamphlets and sheets dealing primarily with subversive and radical activities in the US from 1900 to 1950. Incl tracts and campaign literture of the Communist and Socialist Parties in the US and works by party leaders; materials on the economic, political, and human rights issues of the pre-World War II, World War II, and early civil rights campaign periods; and pamphlets by various anti-war and anti-draft organizations, material on Russia, and materials on the communist movement in other countries.

DC —LIBRARY OF CONGRESS, European Division, Washington, 20540.
Notes: The Library of Congress collection of "Solidarity" and other uncensored Polish materials incl books, periodicals, documents, bulletins, cartoons, and posters, most of which are photocopies of originals held by other libraries.

DC —US COMMISSION ON CIVIL RIGHTS, National Clearinghouse Library, 1121 Vermont Ave NW, Washington, 20005. Lenora McMillan, Chief Librn
Holdings: Vols (50,000) Cat Slides Microforms
Notes: The National Clearinghouse Library has a special collection of the US Commission on Civil Rights publications from its inception (1957) to present date.

GA —MARTIN LUTHER KING, JR, CENTER FOR NONVIOLENT SOCIAL CHANGE, INC, King Library and Archives, 449 Auburn Ave, Atlanta, 30312. D Louise Cook, Dir of Library and Archives
Holdings: Vols 4000 Cat Mss Audiotapes Microforms
Notes: The philosophy of Martin Luther King and the movement he led. Emphasis on obscure information and ephemeral pieces. Oral history project has over 500 tapes. Incl collection of mss of various civil rights organizations of the 1950s and 1960s. All materials are noncirculating.

IL —SOUTHERN ILLINOIS UNIVERSITY, CARBONDALE, Delyte W Morris Library, Special Collections Dept, Carbondale, 62901. David V Koch, Cur of Special Collections; Louisa Bowen, Cur of Manuscripts
Holdings: Cat Mss
Notes: Papers and correspondence of Theodore A Schroeder, constitutional lawyer and founder, with Lincoln Steffens, of the Free Speech League, a forerunner of the American Civil Liberties Union. Contains extensive correspondence with Comstock, Gompers, Debs, H Ellis, Sanger, Sinclair, John Dewey, Darrow, Mencken, A G Hays, Emma Goldman, W E B Dubois, etc. Incl several thousand letters; notes and mss, records of legal cases and extensive files relating to the early history of psychiatry.

IL —CHICAGO HISTORICAL SOCIETY, Library, Clark St at North Ave, Chicago, 60614. Archie Motley, Manuscript Librn
Notes: Civil liberties and radical history holdings incl these papers: Alliance to End Repression, Chicago; Chicago Committee to Defend the Bill of Rights; Polly Connellly (Marxist activist in political, social, labor, and women's affairs); Sidney Lens (author, Marxist, international peace movement, political and social activist; trade union official); Midwest Committee for Protection of Foreign Born (an affiliate of the American Committee for Protection of Foreign Born).

IL —INSTITUTE ON THE CHURCH IN URBAN-INDUSTRIAL SOCIETY, Library, 5700 S Woodlawn, Chicago, 60637.
Holdings: Vols 1000 Cat Microforms
Notes: Urban-industrial involvement of the churches world-wide, international urban literature, corporate responsibility, human factors of urbanization and industrialization. Library holdings are dorment at present.

IL —ILLINOIS STATE UNIVERSITY, Milner Library, Dept of Special Collections, Normal, 61761. Robert Sokan, Librn
Holdings: Vols 2100 Uncat
Notes: Sigmund Livingston Collection on Intergroup Relations, 1944 to the present. The material is divided into subject headings which contain pamphlets, newsletters and commission reports.

MD —UNIVERSITY OF MARYLAND, BALTIMORE COUNTY, Albin O Kuhn Library and Gallery, 5401 Wilkens Ave, Baltimore, 21228. Ann Copeland, Special Collections Librn
Holdings: Vols 600// Uncat Mss
Notes: Major itmes in the Hugh Davis Graham papers on southern history include *Southern School News*, Southern Regional Council publications, and reports on civil rights and integration in the 1950s and 1960s.

MA —BOSTON UNIVERSITY, Mugar Memorial Library, Special Collections Dept, 771 Commonwealth Ave, Boston, 02215. Howard B Gotlieb, Dir
Notes: Personal papers of Martin Luther King, Jr.

†MA —JOHN F KENNEDY LIBRARY, Columbia Point, Boston, 02125. Dan H Fenn Jr, Dir
Holdings: Cat Mss
Notes: Papers of JFK and White House aides Lee White and Harris Wofford and RFK and Justice Department aide Burke Marshall, dealing with civil rights, 1961-1964. 42 linear ft of mss. Holdings are described in "Historical Materials in the John F Kennedy Library." Copies may be obtained by writing the Research Archivist.

MA —JOHN F KENNEDY LIBRARY, Columbia Point, Boston, 02125. Henry J Gwiazda II, Cur
Notes: The Burke Marshall papers, 50 archives boxes re civil rights, 1961-1964 and the Bedford-Stuyvesant Development and Restoration Corporations; the Joseph Dolan papers, 1 box; the Thomas Johnston papers, 3 boxes; the James Mc Shane papers, 2 boxes; the Frank Mankiewicz papers, 15 boxes; and the Scott Rafferty papers, 4 boxes. Robert F Kennedy Journalism Awards Collections: newspaper and magazine articles, and radio and television programs on the disadvantaged in American society, 1969-present; 21 microfilms for the newsprint and magazine entries, 1969-1977; 50 archives boxes of radio tapes and scripts, 1969-1981.

MA —HARVARD UNIVERSITY LIBRARY, Law School Library, Langdell Hall, Cambridge, 02138. Harry S Martin III, Librn
Notes: Personal and legal papers of William

CIVIL RIGHTS (cont.)

Henry Hastic, Governor of the Virgin Islands, Judge of the US Court of Appeals, Third Circuit, who died in April 1976. Much on his involvement in civic and antidiscrimination cases.

MI —UNIVERSITY OF MICHIGAN, Dept of Rare Books & Special Collections, Ann Arbor, 48109. Edward C Weber, Head, Labadie Collection
Holdings: Vols (40,000) Cat Mss Pix Microforms
Notes: Famous cases covered in detail are Sacco-Vanzetti and Tom Mooney. There is much material on the struggle in the South during the 1960s. We have the papers of the American Society for Protection of Foreign Born and the William Reuben papers on the Trenton Six case. Includes records and tapes. In addition, the Labadie Collection of radical materials, containing papers, tracts, handbills, and publications of minority political and social reform organizations from the mid-1800s to the present, incl 8000 serial titles and 20,000 uncataloged pamphlets. Also ms collections of the papers of Mary Hayes Weik, William A Reuben, and the American Committee for the Protection of the Foreign Born.

MI —DETROIT PUBLIC LIBRARY, Burton Historical Collection, 5201 Woodward Ave, Detroit, 48202. Alice Dalligan, Chief
Holdings: Vols Cat Pix VF
Notes: Collection on the race riots of the week of 23 July 1967.

MS —TOUGALOO COLLEGE, L Zenobia Coleman Library, Tougaloo, 39174. Virgia Brocks-Shedd, Acting Dir
Holdings: Uncat Mss Maps Pix
Budget: ($142,650)
Notes: Civil rights cases and legal papers; lawsuits; Mississippi, 1960-1968. Local attorneys have donated papers of cases they have handled, espec attorneys of two government-funded legal services offices. Individual collections: Papers of Aaron Henry, Rev Robert L T Smith, Sr, Annie B Rankin and the Howard Kester Papers. Incl VF holdings of articles from 1930 and on.

NJ —PRINCETON UNIVERSITY, Firestone Library, Afro-American Studies Collection, Princeton, 08540. William Wellburn, Cur
Holdings: Vols (2000) Cat Pix Phonorecords Audiotapes Microforms
Notes: Our emphasis is primarily Afro-American: catalogs of other collections, biographical and vertical files, reference materials, indexes, bibliographies and serials.

NJ —PRINCETON UNIVERSITY, Library, Manuscript Collection, Nassau St, Princeton, 08540. Jean F Preston, Cur
Holdings: Cat Mss
Notes: ACLU Archives and other papers; 1861 albums; as of 1983, 935 cartons. The Archives cover the period 1912 to date. Indexes for 1917 to date are available.

NM —UNIVERSITY OF NEW MEXICO, School of Law Library, 1117 Stanford Dr NE, Albuquerque, 87131. Myron Fink, Law Librn
Holdings: Vols (3000) Cat Mss
Notes: Collection supports the work of the American Indian Law Center, established by the law school. Has separate catalog with extensive subject analysis. Incl papers of William Zimmerman, Asst Commissioner of Indian Affairs, 1934-1950. Emphasis is on government relations, tribal government (especially tribal codes for all Indian tribes in US). Incl materials on indigenous peoples world-wide. Periodical literature is subject indexed. Bibliography: Sabatini, Joseph D, *American Indian Law: A Bibliography of Books, Law Review Articles and Indian* Periodicals. (Albuquerque, 1973), Supplement, 1975.

NY —CORNELL UNIVERSITY LIBRARIES, Collection of Regional History, Dept of Manuscripts and Univ Archives, Ithaca, 14853.
Notes: Records, 1976-77, of Coalition of Veterans for Human Rights; .1 ft.

NY —COLUMBIA UNIVERSITY LIBRARIES, Rare Book & Manuscript Library, 801 Butler Library, 535 W 114 St, New York, 10027. Kenneth A Lohf, Librn
Holdings: Mss
Notes: Papers of Whitney M Young, civil rights leader. 106,000 items. Restricted use.

†NY —COLUMBIA UNIVERSITY LIBRARIES, Butler Library, Rare Book and Manuscript Library, 535 W 114 St, New York, 10027.
Notes: Papers of Dr Ivan Morris, American Section chairman of Amnesty International, his researches into Japanese literature and culture, and his books on puzzles.

NY —NEW YORK STATE DIVISION OF HUMAN RIGHTS, Reference Library, Two World Trade Center, Rm 5356, New York, 10047. Rosalind Spriggs, Librn
Holdings: Vols 2000 Cat
Notes: Human rights and intergroup relations. This special collection covers the materials on civil rights and civil liberties. Intergroups relations and ethnic organizations. Minority and religious groups. Discriminations in education, employment and housing, especially, after the year 1971. *Bibliography on Human Rights and Intergroup Relations,* Special Collections no 4, 1977. This special collection contains about 2000 itmes; books, studies, journals, pamphlets, reprints, research data and reports of state and city commissions against discrimination.

NC —UNIVERSITY OF NORTH CAROLINA, CHAPEL HILL, Louis Round Wilson Academic Affairs Library, Southern Historical Collection, Chapel Hill, 27514. Carolyn Wallace, Librn
Notes: The papers of Algernon Lee Butler, former judge of the United States Court for the Eastern District of North Carolina (1959-1975).

NC —UNIVERSITY OF NORTH CAROLINA, CHARLOTTE, J Murrey Atkins Library, UNCC Station, Charlotte, 28223. Robert F Brabham Jr, Special Collections Librn
Holdings: Cat Mss Pix
Notes: Papers of Harry Golden, editor of the *Carolina Israelite;* of Julius Chambers relating to the Swann v Charlotte/Mecklenburg Board of Education case, which established the constitutionality of busing to achieve racial integration of the public schools; of Frederick Douglas Alexander, first black city councilman in Charlotte, NC in the 20th century; and of T J Reddy, a member of the Charlotte 3, a group of black men accused of burning a riding stable and killing horses.

NC —DUKE UNIVERSITY, William R Perkins Library, Durham, 27706. Elvin E Strowd, University Librn
Notes: The Race and Race Relations collection contains books, pamphlets, letters, and manuscripts dealing with Southern problems with the Negro and the subject of race generally.

NC —GREENSBORO PUBLIC LIBRARY, Oral History Program Library, Drawer X-4, Greensboro, 27402. Eugene Edwin Pfaff, Jr, Librn
Holdings: Videotapes Audiotapes
Notes: Oral history on the cultural, social, and economic development of Greensboro and Guilford County; the program is expanding to incl prominent North Carolinians throughout the State. Collection consists of 42 videotapes and 93 audiotapes which are uncataloged.

PA —TEMPLE UNIVERSITY LIBRARIES, Special Collections Dept, Contemporary Culture Collection, Philadelphia, 19122. Patricia J Case, Cur
Notes: The Contemporary Culture Collection. See full entry under US-Social Life and Customs.

†PA —TEMPLE UNIVERSITY LIBRARIES, Special Collections Dept, Urban Archives Center, Philadelphia, 19122. Thomas Whitehead, Cur of Mss
Holdings: Cat
Notes: Incl the records of several separate collections which are deposited in the Urban Archives Center. Many collections contain photographs, maps and pamphlets, in addition to manuscripts. All collections in the Urban Archives are separately cataloged.

PA —CARLOW COLLEGE, Grace Library, Fifth Ave, Pittsburgh, 15213. Joan M Mitchell, Dir of Library Services
Holdings: Vols (977) Cat Pamphlets
Budget: ($300)
Notes: The Peace Studies Collection is a collection of books which deals with the search for peace in the modern world from the perspective of the Judeo-Christian tradition. It is especially strong in the area of social justice, civil rights and world politics.

RI —PROVIDENCE PUBLIC LIBRARY, 150 Empire St, Providence, 02903. Lance J Bauer, Special Collections Librn
Notes: The Edna Frazier Memorial Collection (South Providence Branch) is the largest public library collection in Rhode Island dedicated to Black Studies. Since 1969, the Collection has served the people of this area. Adults and children concerned with the heritage of Black people in America, their roles, culture, and accomplishments, have found a wealth of information here. From its initial 900 volumes, the Collection has grown to several thousand volumes incl noted works by Black authors, reference materials, sociological studies, poetry, music, sports, biographies, and titles no longer in print. The time span covered by the Collection is 1619 to the present. It contains materials on the Black Renaissance and the early Civil Rights movements of the '30s, '40s and '50s, in addition to the more well-known movements of the '60s and '70s. A unique feature of thiscollection is the large number of children's books it contains; these reflect the same concerns and interests as the larger adult collection. Another unique feature of this collection is that it does circulate. It is available to any resident of the state as a result of the Providence Public Library's role as Rhode Island's Principal Public Library.

TN —MEMPHIS STATE UNIVERSITY, John Willard Brister Library, Memphis, 38152. John Terreo, Special Collections Librn
Notes: 1968 Memphis Sanitation Workers Strike. A collection of audiotape interviews with Memphis governmental offícals and administrators, strikers, union leaders, religious leaders, and other significant persons involved in the strike, during which civil rights leader Dr Martin Luther King, Jr was assassinated. Also incl are photographic prints and negatives and the news outakes from the news departments of the three Memphis television stations as well as clippings from newspapers and periodicals. Published finding aid can be found in the Mississippi Valley Collection.

TN —FISK UNIVERSITY, Library, Special Collections, 17 & Jackson St, Nashville, 37203. Ann Allen Shockley, Assoc Librn
Holdings: Cat Mss Pix
Notes: Papers of the late Slater King, leader of the Albany, Georgia, Civil Rights Movement. Incl interviews with Civil Rights leaders.

VA —UNIVERSITY OF VIRGINIA, Alderman Library, Manuscripts Dept, Charlottesville, 22901. Edmund Berkeley Jr, Cur
Holdings: Cat Mss
Notes: Papers of the American Civil Liberties Union (ACLU) of Virginia (partially restricted) and the Virginia Council of Human Relations focus chiefly on desegregation but contain material on the civil liberties of a variety of minority groups, incl students, prisoners, and the mentally ill, and causes such as fair housing, fair employment, gun control, capitol punishment, draft resistance and personal liberty.

VA —UNIVERSITY OF VIRGINIA, Alderman Library, Manuscripts Dept, Charlottesville, 22901. Edmund Berkeley Jr, Cur
Holdings: Cat Mss Pix
Notes: Material in over 420 collections documents the history and culture of Afro-Americans incl letters and narratives by slaves and masters, plantation accounts, letters from Liberian immigrants, folklore, literature, the desegregation movement in Virginia in the 1960s and 1970s and the

CIVIL RIGHTS (cont.)

"massive resistance" of Virginia political leaders. Michael F Plunkett (ed) *A Guide to Materials on the History, Literature, and Culture of Afro-Americans in the Manuscripts Department, University of Virginia Library.*

WI —STATE HISTORICAL SOCIETY OF WISCONSIN, Archives, 816 State St, Madison, 53706. Harold L Miller, Reference Archivist
Holdings: Mss Pix Microforms Audiotapes
Notes: Records and papers of organizations and individuals engages in social and political reform activities. Major focus areas are civil rights, 1950s to the present, and anti-Vietnam war and other protest movements of the 1960s to the present. Also covered are other reform movements, socialism, and communism from the 1930s to the present. Collections are described in *Social Action Collection at the State Historical Society of Wisconsin: A Guide,* (1983) and in current accession notes in the *Wisconsin Magazine of History.* Major collections are also listed in Hamer, *Guide to Manuscripts and Archives in the United States,* (1961) and in the *National Union Catalog of Manuscript Collections,* (1959-date).

ON —ONTARIO MINISTRY OF LABOUR, Library, 400 University Ave, Toronto, M7A 1T7, Can. Jean Collins-Williams, Librn
Holdings: Vols (80,000) Microforms Films

CIVIL RIGHTS—HISTORY

IN —PURDUE UNIVERSITY LIBRARIES, Graduate School of Management, Krannert Library, West Lafayette, 47907. Gordon Law, Librn
Notes: An important resource at the Krannert Library is its Special Collection of Business and Economics, consisting of some 8000 rare pre-20th century strengths in books, journals, tracts and pamphlets covering primarily the early literature of economic thought and business practices in America and abroad, 1500-1870. A catalog was issued in 1979.

SC —COLLEGE OF CHARLESTON LIBRARY, Special Collections Dept, Charleston, 29401.
Notes: Contains personal papers, recorded interviews and discussions, numerous writings for speeches and/or publications, various honorary degrees and awards, and materials reflecting Clark's activities as educator and civil rights activist. Among them papers from Alpha Kappa Sorority, Benedict College, Black Women's Community, Charleston County Public School Board Trustees, Hampton Institute, Highlander Center, League of Women Voters of Charleston County, NAACP, National Association of College Women, National Association of Negro Women, Neighborhood Legal Assistance Program, Old Bethel United Methodist Church, Penn Community Services, Southern Christian Leadership Conference, United Methodist Women, United States Commission on Civil Rights, and The Young Women's Christian Association of Greater Charleston. Correspondents include Ralph Abernathy, Algernon Black, Gerald Ford, Myles Horton, Hubert Humphrey, Coretta Scott King, Martin Luther King, Jr., Allard Lowenstein, Justine Wise Polier, Dick Riley, Jr., Theodore Stern, and Strom Thurmond. Also includes material relating to Martin Luther King, Jr., Esau Jenkins, and Rosa Parks. The collection contains, among others, photographs of Ralph Abernathy, Jesse Jackson, Esau Jenkins, Coretta Scott King, Martin Luther King, Jr., Poinsette family, Bernice Robinson, Hosea Williams, and Andrew Young.

CIVIL SERVICE

CA —UNIVERSITY OF CALIFORNIA, BERKELEY, Institute of Governmental Studies Library, 109 Moses Hall, Berkeley, 94720. Jack Leister, Head Librn
Holdings: Vols (350,000) Cat Mss Maps Microforms
Budget: ($160,000)
Notes: The library collects primarily pamphlets. Incl in the library's holdings are documents from all levels of government, as well as publications issued by professional associations and special interest groups. A G K Hall catalog covering the Institute's Library holdings is available. Since 1937, Library has been depository for all California local documents (city, county & special district). Formerly: Bureau of Public Administration.

DC —US OFFICE OF PERSONNEL MANAGEMENT, Library, 1900 E St NW, Washington, 20415. Betty B Guerin, Supv Librn
Holdings: Vols 10,000 Cat Pix Microforms Memorabilia
Notes: US Civil Service Commission terminated by Act of Congress, 10/78. US Office of Personnel Management created and effective 1/79. Library houses a comprehensive collection of civil service documents, newspaper clippings, legislative histories of all major legislation relating to civil service incl microfilms of dissertations, mss, rare items and a complete collection of agency issuances.

NY —CORNELL UNIVERSITY LIBRARIES, Collection of Regional History, Dept of Manuscripts and Univ Archives, Ithaca, 14853.
Notes: Records, 1882, 1884, of the Civil Service Reform League of Ithaca, NY.

CIVIL WAR—GREAT BRITAIN see Great Britain—History Civil War, 1642-1649

CIVIL WAR—U.S. see U.s. —History Civil War

CIVILIAN CONSERVATION CORPS (CCC)

IL —CENTER FOR RESEARCH LIBRARIES, 6050 S Kenwood Ave, Chicago, 60637. Donald B Simpson, Dir; Esther Smith, Collection Development Librn
Holdings: Vols 1120// Uncat
Notes: CCC camp newspapers, collections formed by University of Illinois, Urbana, and US Dept of the Interior. Checklist of Illinois collection: Wayne Stewart Yenawine, *Civilian Conservation Corps Camp Papers,* MALA thesis, U of Illinois, 1938.

CIVILIZATION, AFRICAN

MA —HARVARD UNIVERSITY, Center for Middle Eastern Studies, Library, Coolidge Hall, 1737 Cambridge St, Cambridge, 02138. Barbara Mitchell, Librn
Holdings: Vols (5000) Periodicals
Notes: Some history of countries of the Middle East; increasingly emphasizes culture and politics of the current Middle Eastern area. Special collection of Energy Economics Research. Library currently receives 15 periodical titles.

CIVILIZATION, AMERICAN see U.s. —Civilization

CIVILIZATION, ARAB

DC —HARVARD UNIVERSITY, Dumbarton Oaks, Research Library, 1703 32nd St NW, Washington, 20007. Irene Vaslef, Librn
Holdings: Vols (91,000) Cat Maps Pix Slides Microforms
Budget: ($219,000)
Notes: Byzantine civilization (including art, archaeology, literature, history, religion, law, music, etc). Extensive supplemental material on Classical, Hellenistic, Medieval, Islamic, Medieval Slavic cultures. 62,000 b/w photographs, 25,000 slides and transparencies, 1000 microfilms of books and manuscripts. Printed description of collection in *Harvard Library Bulletin,* vol 19, no 1 (Jan 1971), pp 25-35 and vol 19, no 2 (April 1971), pp 204-214, pp 25-35 and vol 19, no 2 (April 1971), pp 204-214.

MA —HARVARD UNIVERSITY, Center for Middle Eastern Studies, Library, Coolidge Hall, 1737 Cambridge St, Cambridge, 02138. Barbara Mitchell, Librn
Holdings: Vols (5000) Periodicals
Notes: Some history of countries of the Middle East; increasingly emphasizes culture and politics of the current Middle Eastern area. Special collection of Energy Economics Research. Library currently receives 15 periodical titles.

MI —UNIVERSITY OF MICHIGAN, Graduate Library, Near East Dept, Ann Arbor, 48109. John A Eilts, Bibliographer
Holdings: Vols (150,000) Cat Mss Maps Microforms
Notes: Excludes Islam in the Far East, Judaism in general, though it does incl specifically Near Eastern Judaism. Incl Bahaism and Arab philosophy, fields of study connected with Islamic or Arabic studies, Turkish language and literature.

TX —UNIVERSITY OF TEXAS LIBRARIES, Middle East Collection, PO Box P, Austin, 78712. Abazar Sepehri, Librn
Holdings: Vols (45,000) Cat Microforms
Notes: Arabic, Persian and Turkish materials in the humanities and social sciences. Incl 350 periodical and 45 newspaper titles from most of the countries of the Arab League, Turkey, Iran and Afghanistan.

CIVILIZATION, BYZANTINE

DC —HARVARD UNIVERSITY, Dumbarton Oaks, Research Library, 1703 32nd St NW, Washington, 20007. Irene Vaslef, Librn
Holdings: Vols (91,000) Cat Maps Pix Slides Microforms
Budget: ($219,000)
Notes: Byzantine civilization (including art, archaeology, literature, history, religion, law, music, etc). Extensive supplemental material on Classical, Hellenistic, Medieval, Islamic, Medieval Slavic cultures. 62,000 b/w photographs, 25,000 slides and transparencies, 1000 microfilms of books and manuscripts. Printed description of collection in *Harvard Library Bulletin,* vol 19, no 1 (Jan 1971), pp 25-35 and vol 19, no 2 (April 1971), pp 204-214, pp 25-35 and vol 19, no 2 (April 1971), pp 204-214.

CIVILIZATION, GREEK

DC —HARVARD UNIVERSITY, Dumbarton Oaks, Research Library, 1703 32nd St NW, Washington, 20007. Irene Vaslef, Librn
Holdings: Vols (91,000) Cat Maps Pix Slides Microforms
Budget: ($219,000)
Notes: Byzantine civilization (including art, archaeology, literature, history, religion, law, music, etc). Extensive supplemental material on Classical, Hellenistic, Medieval, Islamic, Medieval Slavic cultures. 62,000 b/w photographs, 25,000 slides and transparencies, 1000 microfilms of books and manuscripts. Printed description of collection in *Harvard Library Bulletin,* vol 19, no 1 (Jan 1971), pp 25-35 and vol 19, no 2 (April 1971), pp 204-214, pp 25-35 and vol 19, no 2 (April 1971), pp 204-214.

DC —HARVARD UNIVERSITY, Center for Hellenic Studies Library, 3100 Whitehaven St NW, Washington, 20008. Jeno Platthy, Librn
Holdings: Vols 42,000 Cat Microforms
Budget: ($76,824)
Notes: Greek civilization, to 200 AD.

CIVILIZATION, GREEK (cont.)

Described in *Harvard Library Bulletin,* XIX (1971): pp 244-249.

CIVILIZATION, HISPANIC

CA —UNIVERSITY OF CALIFORNIA, SAN DIEGO, Central University Library, Mandeville Dept of Special Collections, La Jolla, 92093. Lynda Corey Claassen, Head
Notes: Hispanic Collection: Approx 6000 vols describe cultures of Spain, Portugal, Mexico, Latin America, and South America. Works of literature, history, philosophy and art date from the 15th to the mid-19th century. Highlights of the collection include rare 18th century Spanish provincial dramas and works on the history of Seville and Andalusia.

NY —HISPANIC SOCIETY OF AMERICA, Library, 613 W 155 St, New York, 10032. Martha M de Narvaez, Cur of Mss; Irene S Frye, Asst Librn
Holdings: Vols (150,000) Cat Mss Maps Pix Slides Phonorecords Microforms
Notes: History, art, literature and general culture of the Hispanic countries (where Spanish or Portuguese is spoken). Incl (18, 000) vols printed before 1701, incl (250) incunabula; over (100,000) later vols, plus thousands of periodicals. About (200,000) mss incl ms maps. Printed atlases are in the Book Collection. Some microfilms, chiefly of our early books. Engraved and printed separate maps; reference collection of over 100,000 photographs; slides: all in Department of Iconography, not in library. Catalogs: *Catalogue of the Hispanic Society of America* (Boston: G K Hall, 1962), 10 vols; *First Supplement* (Boston, 1970), 4 vols. Early books: *Printed Books 1468-1700;* Mss: *Catalogo de los Manuscritos Poeticos* Castellanos (15th-17th centuries; 3 vols); *Medieval Manuscripts in the Library; Golden Age Drama Manuscripts*(the latter in press).

CIVILIZATION, ISLAMIC

†CO —AMERICAN INSTITUTE OF ISLAMIC STUDIES, Muslim Bibliographic Center, Box 10398, Denver, 80210.

DC —HARVARD UNIVERSITY, Dumbarton Oaks, Research Library, 1703 32nd St NW, Washington, 20007. Irene Vaslef, Librn
Holdings: Vols (91,000) Cat Maps Pix Slides Microforms
Budget: ($219,000)
Notes: Byzantine civilization (including art, archaeology, literature, history, religion, law, music, etc). Extensive supplemental material on Classical, Hellenistic, Medieval, Islamic, Medieval Slavic cultures. 62,000 b/w photographs, 25,000 slides and transparencies, 1000 microfilms of books and manuscripts. Printed description of collection in *Harvard Library Bulletin,* vol 19, no 1 (Jan 1971), pp 25-35 and vol 19, no 2 (April 1971), pp 204-214, pp 25-35 and vol 19, no 2 (April 1971), pp 204-214.

MI —UNIVERSITY OF MICHIGAN, Graduate Library, Near East Dept, Ann Arbor, 48109. John A Eilts, Bibliographer
Holdings: Vols (150,000) Cat Mss Maps Microforms
Notes: Excludes Islam in the Far East, Judaism in general, though it does incl specifically Near Eastern Judaism. Incl Bahaism and Arab philosophy, fields of study connected with Islamic or Arabic studies, Turkish language and literature.

NY —ISLAMIC CENTER OF NEW YORK LIBRARY, 1 Riverside Dr, New York, 10023. Elsayed M I Elkasaby,Dir
Holdings: Vols (8000) Cat
Notes: Islamic life and culture.

†PA —DROPSIE UNIVERSITY, Library, Broad & York Sts, Philadelphia, 19132.

CIVILIZATION, MEDIEVAL

DC —HARVARD UNIVERSITY, Dumbarton Oaks, Research Library, 1703 32nd St NW, Washington, 20007. Irene Vaslef, Librn
Holdings: Vols (91,000) Cat Maps Pix Slides Microforms
Budget: ($219,000)
Notes: Byzantine civilization (including art, archaeology, literature, history, religion, law, music, etc). Extensive supplemental material on Classical, Hellenistic, Medieval, Islamic, Medieval Slavic cultures. 62,000 b/w photographs, 25,000 slides and transparencies, 1000 microfilms of books and manuscripts. Printed description of collection in *Harvard Library Bulletin,* vol 19, no 1 (Jan 1971), pp 25-35 and vol 19, no 2 (April 1971), pp 204-214, pp 25-35 and vol 19, no 2 (April 1971), pp 204-214.

†IN —UNIVERSITY OF NOTRE DAME, Library, 221 Memorial Library, Notre Dame, 46556.
Notes: The Astrik L Gabriel Collection of incunabula.

MN —SAINT JOHN'S ABBEY & UNIVERSITY, Hill Monastic Manuscript Library, Collegeville, 56321. Julian G Plante, Dir
Holdings: Vols (61,000) Microfilms
Notes: Films of 61,000 mss. The total number of codices or bound handwritten mss represents the holdings of several hundred libraries in Europe, mostly Austria, Spain, Ethiopia, West Germany, Portugal, and also Italy, Hungary, Poland, Great Britain, Belgium, Yugoslavia, France, Switzerland, and the Netherlands.

NY —THE CLOISTERS, Metropolitan Museum of Art (Branch), Fort Tryon Park, New York, 10040. Suse C Childs, Librn
Holdings: Vols (5000) Cat Mss Pix Slides
Notes: A branch of the Metropolitan Museum of Art devoted solely to the literature of medieval art. Incl 16,000 slides and 5000 photographs with unique strengths in certain aspects of medieval art.

WI —UNIVERSITY OF WISCONSIN, MADISON, Seminary of Medieval Spanish Studies, 1130 Van Hise Hall, Madison, 53706. Lloyd A Kasten, Emeritus Prof of Spanish
Holdings: Vols (7500)// Cat Mss Pix Slides Microforms
Notes: Medieval materials and subjects. 100 reels of microfilm, 2500 pamphlets and reprints. Incl a 300-volume collection of 13th century Spanish law. Other emphases: language studies (incl 616,247 vocabulary cards), dictionaries, bibliographies, periodicals. The nucleus of the collection is photostats of the mss of unpublished works on Alfonso X Restricted circulation.

CIVILIZATION, MOHAMMEDAN see Civilization, Islamic

CIVILIZATION, MOSLEM see Civilization, Islamic

CIVILIZATION, OCCIDENTAL—ORIENTAL INFLUENCES see East and West

CIVILIZATION, ORIENTAL—OCCIDENTAL INFLUENCES see East and West

CIVILIZATION, PAGAN

NY —STATE UNIVERSITY OF NEW YORK, COLLEGE AT BUFFALO, Lockwood Memorial Library, Main St, Buffalo, 14260. Stanton F Biddle, Assoc Dir
Holdings: Vols 20,000 Cat Pix
Notes: About half of the collection donated by the Orthodox Catholic Alliance of Buffalo, New York. The collection is devoted chiefly to the world of Byzantium in both its secular and religious phases; Greek Patristic literature and its interpretation; and the tradition of the Greek Bible and its antecedents. As support for these subjects the pagan literature of late antiquity is strongly represented, as well as the Hellenistic and Roman background of the East Christian world and its relations with its neighbors in the Near East, in Eastern Europe, and in the Latin West.

CIVILIZATION, RENAISSANCE

ON —VICTORIA UNIVERSITY, Library, Centre for Reformation and Renaissance Studies, 71 Queen's Park Crescent, Toronto, M5S 1K7, Can. Robert C Brandeis, Chief Librn; James Estes, Dir
Holdings: Vols (15,000) Cat Slides
Notes: The CRRS concentrates on the northern European countries and France; its chief strengths are Erasmus, 650 vols; early printed books, especially 16th century editions of Latin classics; bibliography and the history of printing. The Erasmus holdings are cataloged in W T McCready et al, "The Erasmus Collection in the Centre for Reformation and Renaissance Studies...A Catalogue"...*Reformation and Renaissance* 7 (1971), 32-76 and "A Supplementary *List"...Reformation and Renaissance,* 10 (1974), 116-119. Published catalogs. Humanist Editions of the Classics at CRRS, Toronto, 1979; Humanist Editions of Statutes and History at CRRS, Toronto, 1980; Bibles, Theological Treatises and Other Religious Literature 1491-1700 at CRRS, Toronto, 1981.

CIVILIZATION, SLAVIC

CA —UNIVERSITY OF CALIFORNIA, LOS ANGELES, Library, Slavic Collection, 405 Hilgard Ave, Los Angeles, 90024. Edward Shreeves, Chairman, Bibliographers Group; Leon Ferder, Slavic Bibliographer
Holdings: Vols (250,000) Cat Mss Maps
Notes: The entire range of humanities, social sciences, and the arts. One of the most comprehensive US collections for material not only on Russia and the Soviet Union, but also on Bulgaria, Czechoslovakia, Poland, Yugoslavia, the non-Slavic countries of Eastern Europe (Romania, Hungary, Albania) and Soviet Central Asia. Holdings in Russian and Slavic linguistics, Russian literature, and Russian history are particularly strong, covering all periods. The collections are described in some detail in Paul Horecky's book on US Slavic collections.

DC —HARVARD UNIVERSITY, Dumbarton Oaks, Research Library, 1703 32nd St NW, Washington, 20007. Irene Vaslef, Librn
Holdings: Vols (91,000) Cat Maps Pix Slides Microforms
Budget: ($219,000)
Notes: Byzantine civilization (including art, archaeology, literature, history, religion, law, music, etc). Extensive supplemental material on Classical, Hellenistic, Medieval, Islamic, Medieval Slavic cultures. 62,000 b/w photographs, 25,000 slides and transparencies, 1000 microfilms of books and manuscripts. Printed description of collection in *Harvard Library Bulletin,* vol 19, no 1 (Jan 1971), pp 25-35 and vol 19, no 2 (April 1971), pp 204-214, pp 25-35 and vol 19, no 2 (April 1971), pp 204-214.

CIVILIZATION, SPANISH see Civilization, Hispanic; Spain—Civilization and Culture

CLADEL, JUDITH JEANNE

IN —INDIANA UNIVERSITY, Lilly Library, Seventh St, Bloomington, 47405. William R Cagle, Librn
Holdings: // Mss Pix
Notes: Literary papers and correspondence of French writer Judith Jeanne Cladel. Much of the collection relates to French sculptor Auguste Rodin, whom Cladel much admired and about whom she wrote several articles. Also incl copies of Rodin's correspondence, ca 1879-1917, and several photographs of Rodin and of his studio. 1589 items.

CLAFLIN, GOV. WILLIAM

CA —WHITTIER COLLEGE, Wardman Library, Whittier, 90608. Christine Erdmann, Special Collections Librn
Notes: The Frederick M Meek Collection of 7000 items by and about John Greenleaf Whittier, incl copies of limited editions and association copies, virtually all of his published works in all states, issues and editions, runs of newspapers to which

CLAFLIN, GOV. WILLIAM (cont.)

Whittier contributed, magazine articles, broadsides, handbills, pamphlets, and correspondence, incl much with Mass Gov Claflin on contemporary politics.

CLAFLIN, WILLIAM AND MARY B.

OH —RUTHERFORD B HAYES LIBRARY, 1337 Hayes Ave, Fremont, 43420. Watt P Marchman, Dir
Holdings: Cat Mss Pix
Notes: Henry Wilson and William and Mary B Claflin of Massachusetts. Mainly correspondence. Index to about 9000 items in the collection. 12 linear ft. Listed in *Guide to Manuscripts of the Ohio Historical Society*, 71.

CLAIBORNE, CRAIG

MA —BOSTON UNIVERSITY, Mugar Memorial Library, Special Collections Dept, 771 Commonwealth Ave, Boston, 02215. Howard B Gotlieb, Dir
Holdings: Mss

CLAIMANT, TICHBORNE

DC —GEORGETOWN UNIVERSITY, Library, Special Collections Div, 37 & O Sts NW, Washington, 20057. George M Barringer, Special Collections Librn; Nicholas B Sheetz, Mss Librn
Holdings: Cat Mss
Notes: The papers of the English author, journalist, and historian Douglas Woodruff (1897-1978), containing correspondence, mss, and photographs. Incl is considerable material concerning his years at Oxford University; his editorship for many years of The "Tablet"; English Catholic society in general and English Catholic literature in particular. Also present are research files on the Tichborne Claimant, one of the most famous cases of impersonation in English legal history. There is extensive correspondence from such figures as: Hilaire Belloc; Tom Burns; Rev Martin D'Arcy, SJ; Christopher Dawson; Sir Roy Harrod; Christopher Hollis; Msgr Ronald Knox; Sir Shane Leslie; Sir Arnold Lunn; Rebecca West; and Evelyn Waugh.

CLAIRMONT, CLAIRE

NC —DUKE UNIVERSITY, William R Perkins Library, Durham, 27706. Elvin E Strowd, University Librn
Notes: The Shelley-Goodwin Collection of Lord Abinger is a microfilm copy of the Shelley and Godwin collection. Lord Abinger's entire manuscript collection, representing the last portion of the papers of Sir Percy Florence Shelley which is still in private hands, has been reproduced on 16 reels of film. The Bodleian Library is the only other location for this film.

CLAIROBSCUR see Chiaroscuro

CLAN NA GAOL

†PA —BALCH INSTITUTE FOR ETHNIC STUDIES, Library, 18 S Seventh St, Philadelphia, 19106.
Notes: Papers of Dennis Clark, incl copies of minute books of two organizations, Clan na Gaol and the Irish American Club (c 1886-1923).

CLANDESTINE LITERATURE see Underground Literature

CLANS AND CLAN SYSTEMS

ON —QUEEN'S UNIVERSITY, Douglas Library, Kingston, K7L 5C4, Can. William F E Morley, Cur, Special Collections
Holdings: Vols 100 Uncat
Notes: The MacGillivray Collection. Scottish books, especially those dealing with clans, tartans and heraldry. Also the Buchan Collection (library of John Buchan, Lord Tweedsmuir), rich in Scottish books, ca 5000 vols.

CLAPP, VERNER WARREN

DC —LIBRARY OF CONGRESS, Manuscript Division, Washington, 20540. John C Broderick, Chief
Notes: Papers of Verner Warren Clapp, Chief Asst Librn of Congress, President of the Council on Library Resources, etc.

CLARINET MUSIC

CT —UNIVERSITY OF HARTFORD, Hartt School of Music, Allen Memorial Library, 200 Bloomfield Ave, West Hartford, 06117. Ethel Bacon, Music Librn
Holdings: Vols 350 Cat
Budget: ($14,500)
Notes: Kalmen Opperman Collection: 350 vols of clarinet music, solo through ensemble.

CLARK, DENNIS

†PA —BALCH INSTITUTE FOR ETHNIC STUDIES, Library, 18 S Seventh St, Philadelphia, 19106.
Notes: Papers of Dennis Clark, incl copies of minute books of two organizations, Clan na Gaol and the Irish American Club (c 1886-1923).

CLARK, DISMAS

MO —UNIVERSITY OF MISSOURI-SAINT LOUIS, Thomas Jefferson Library, Manuscript and Historical Society Collection, 8001 Natural Bridge Rd, Saint Louis, 63121.

CLARK, FRANCES ELLIOTT

†MD —UNIVERSITY OF MARYLAND, Library, Music Educators National Conference Historical Center, College Park, 20742. Bruce Wilson, Cur
Holdings: Cat Mss Pix Audiotapes
Notes: The official archive of the Music Educators' National Conference (MENC), and a repository for the documentation of music education. Incl the papers of the MENC, state units, and associated organizations and committees; personal papers and association items (notably, relating to Frances Elliott Clark, Lowell Mason, and Luther Whiting Mason); published proceedings of MENC and other groups; oral histories, numerous school music textbooks, and the archive of the Contemporary Music Project.

CLARK, GEORGE ROGERS

DC —SOCIETY OF THE CINCINNATI, Library, 2118 Massachusetts Ave NW, Washington, 20008. John D Kilbourne, Dir of Museum & Library
Holdings: Vols (12,000) Cat Mss Maps Pix Slides Microforms
Budget: ($65,000)
Notes: Because of the French connections of the Society of the Cincinnati, a particular effort is made to incl information about the French contribution to the American Revolution. The collection is also rich in biographical materials concerning the officer personnel of the American and French armies of the American Revolution. There are two significant sub-sections of this collection: The George Rogers Clark Collection concerning the history of the Old Northwest (to 1820); and the Member-Author collection, writings of members of the Society of the Cincinnati in various fields. It is advisable to make an appointment for use of the collections.

CLARK, GRENVILLE

NH —DARTMOUTH COLLEGE, Baker Memorial Library, Hanover, 03755.
Holdings: Cat Mss
Notes: Personal papers.

CLARK, REV. JAMES, S.J., 1809-1885

DC —GEORGETOWN UNIVERSITY, Library, Special Collections Div, 37 & O Sts NW, Washington, 20057. George M Barringer, Special Collections Librn; Nicholas B Sheetz, Mss Librn
Holdings: Mss Cat
Notes: The papers of Rev James Clark, SJ (1809-1885), a graduate of West Point who converted to Catholicism and entered the Society of Jesus in 1844. He spent a number of years at Georgetown College where he acted as first prefect, professor of mathematics and then as treasurer of the College. He subsequently served as president of Holy Cross and Gonzaga Colleges. The papers incl correspondence conerning his family, his West Point and army carreers, and his life as a Jesuit. Also incl are mss of sermons and various documents such as his West Point diploma (1829) and registers of officers and cadets at West Point (1827-28).

CLARK, JAMES L.

NY —AMERICAN MUSEUM OF NATURAL HISTORY, Library Services Dept, Central Park W & 79th St, New York, 10024. Nina J Root, Chairwoman; Mary Genett, Asst Librn for Reference Services
Holdings: Cat Mss Maps Pix Slides 16mm Films
Notes: Manuscripts, diaries, correspondence, artifacts, some art work, and collected materials. Not all cataloged as of 1983.

CLARK, KENNETH BANCROFT

DC —LIBRARY OF CONGRESS, Manuscript Division, Washington, 20540. John C Broderick, Chief
Holdings: 220,000 Items
Notes: Correspondence, student and financial records, subject files, articles, speeches, reports, notes, outlines, printed material, computer printouts, tape recordings, and microfilm.

CLARK, LAURA JANE STRICKLAND

GA —GEORGIA COLLEGE, Ina Dillard Russell Library, Special Collections Dept, Milledgeville, 31061. Janice C Fennell, Dir of Libraries; Nancy Davis, Special Collections Assoc
Holdings: Uncat Mss
Notes: 18 photographs, misc letters to and from friends, and programs of Georgia Normal and Industrial College. Covers the period 1892-1924 (47 items).

CLARK, LAVERNE HARRELL

TX —TEXAS WOMAN'S UNIVERSITY, Bralley Memorial Library, Box 23715, TWU Sta, Denton, 76204. Metta Nicewarner, Spec Collections Libn
Holdings: Uncat Mss Pix Audiotapes
Notes: The Laverne Harrell Clark Collection (1500 pieces). Photographer, folklorist, writer. Also incl materials by and about her husband, Dr L D Clark (University of Arizona), D H Lawrence scholar.

CLARK, LEONARD

†ON —MCMASTER UNIVERSITY, Library, Hamilton, L8S 4L6, Can.
Notes: Letters, postcards, and correspondence cards, primarily addressed to Leonard Clark from Albert Mansbridge.

CLARK, SEPTIMA POINSETTE, 1898-

SC —COLLEGE OF CHARLESTON LIBRARY, Special Collections Dept, Charleston, 29401.

CLARK, SEPTIMA POINSETTE, 1898- (cont.)

Notes: Contains personal papers, recorded interviews and discussions, numerous writings for speeches and/or publications, various honorary degrees and awards, and materials reflecting Clark's activities as educator and civil rights activist. Among them papers from Alpha Kappa Sorority, Benedict College, Black Women's Community, Charleston County Public School Board Trustees, Hampton Institute, Highlander Center, League of Women Voters of Charleston County, NAACP, National Association of College Women, National Association of Negro Women, Neighborhood Legal Assistance Program, Old Bethel United Methodist Church, Penn Community Services, Southern Christian Leadership Conference, United Methodist Women, United States Commission on Civil Rights, and The Young Women's Christian Association of Greater Charleston. Correspondents include Ralph Abernathy, Algernon Black, Gerald Ford, Myles Horton, Hubert Humphrey, Coretta Scott King, Martin Luther King, Jr., Allard Lowenstein, Justine Wise Polier, Dick Riley, Jr., Theodore Stern, and Strom Thurmond. Also includes material relating to Martin Luther King, Jr., Esau Jenkins, and Rosa Parks. The collection contains, among others, photographs of Ralph Abernathy, Jesse Jackson, Esau Jenkins, Coretta Scott King, Martin Luther King, Jr., Poinsette family, Bernice Robinson, Hosea Williams, and Andrew Young.

CLARK, SIDNEY

OK —UNIVERSITY OF OKLAHOMA, Bizzell Memorial Library, Western History Collections, 401 W Brooks, Norman, 73069. John Ezell, Cur
Holdings: Vols Mss Maps Newspapers Documents
Notes: US Representative. His papers. Guide available (1985).

CLARK, THOMAS CURTIS, 1877-1954

IN —INDIANA UNIVERSITY, Lilly Library, Seventh St, Bloomington, 47405. William R Cagle, Librn
Holdings: / / Mss
Notes: Letters and writings by Thomas Curtis Clark, 1909-1954; autographs collected by him; poems written by other authors. Writings by other authors present incl pieces by W H Auden, Witter Bynner, Harry Kemp, Vachel Lindsay, Edgar Lee Masters, Carl Sandburg, and Sara Teasdale. 761 items.

CLARK, TOM, 1941-

CA —UNIVERSITY OF CALIFORNIA, LOS ANGELES, Research Library, Dept of Special Collections, 405 Hilgard Ave, Los Angeles, 90024. Edward Shreeves, Chairman, Bibliographers Group; David S Zeidberg, Head
Notes: 3.5 linear feet of mss, drawings, and correspondence with other poets.

CT —UNIVERSITY OF CONNECTICUT, Library, Storrs, 06268. George F Butterick, Cur of Literary Archives
Holdings: Mss

MO —WASHINGTON UNIVERSITY, Libraries, Special Collections Dept, Campus Box 1061, St Louis, 63130.
Notes: A major collection, incl books, mss, correspondence, literary papers, photographs, etc. Described in *Special Collections: an Annotated Guide to the Holdings of the Manuscript Division and the University Archives and Research Collection.*

CLARK, WALTER VAN TILBURG

NV —UNIVERSITY OF NEVADA, RENO, University Library, Special Collections Dept, Reno, 89557. Robert E Blesse, Head
Holdings: Vols (93) Cat Mss Pix
Notes: Includes individual works by author in all editions including translations; also prefaces, introductions, published correspondence, appearances in anthologies, periodicals, etc. Bibliographical research collection, part of Modern Authors Collection. Author's manuscript repository. Literary manuscripts, personal papers, correspondence. Other appearances 70 cat.

CLARK, WILLIAM G.

DC —LIBRARY OF CONGRESS, Geography and Map Division, Washington, 20540. John A Wolter, Chief
Notes: Maps thought to have belonged to William Clark.

CLARKE, ANNA

MA —BOSTON UNIVERSITY, Mugar Memorial Library, Special Collections Dept, 771 Commonwealth Ave, Boston, 02215. Howard B Gotlieb, Dir
Holdings: Cat Mss

CLARKE, ARTHUR C.

MA —BOSTON UNIVERSITY, Mugar Memorial Library, Special Collections Dept, 771 Commonwealth Ave, Boston, 02215. Howard B Gotlieb, Dir
Holdings: Cat Mss
Notes: Mss, correspondence, etc collected in depth; incl publications by or about.

CLARKE, BRUCE

PA —US ARMY MILITARY HISTORY INSTITUTE, Carlisle Barracks, 17013. Richard J Sommers, Chief Archivist-Historian
Holdings: Mss Cat
Notes: TheKorean War collection, personal correspondence, daily logs, recollections, and official papers of US officers and soldiers serving in the Korean War, incl Generals Edward Almond, George Barth Bruce Clarke, Matthew Ridgway, and Arthur Trudeau.

CLARKE, J. C.

AZ —NORTHERN ARIZONA UNIVERSITY, Special Collection Library, CU Box 6022, Flagstaff, 86011. Peter M Whiteley, Coordr/Archivist; William Mullane, Librn
Notes: J C Clarke Collection; correspondence between the Department of the Interior and Clarke when he was custodian of Wupatki National Monument near Flagstaff, Ariz. Incl letters from Frank Pinkley, who was the Superintendant of Southwestern Monuments, National Park Service, 1924-1926, 1932.

CLARKE, MARY STETSON

MA —BOSTON UNIVERSITY, Mugar Memorial Library, Special Collections Dept, 771 Commonwealth Ave, Boston, 02215. Howard B Gotlieb, Dir
Holdings: Cat Mss

CLASSICAL ANTIQUITIES

CA —UNIVERSITY OF CALIFORNIA, IRVINE, Library, Irvine, 92664. Roger Berry, Dept Head
Notes: Incl the library of Professor Paul Friedlander (3000 vols).

CA —J PAUL GETTY MUSEUM, Research Library, 17985 Pacific Coast Highway, Malibu, 90265. Anne-Mieke Halbrook, Head Librn
Holdings: Vols (140,000) Cat

CA —SAN FRANCISCO STATE UNIVERSITY, Frank V de Bellis Collection, 1630 Holloway Ave, San Francisco, 94132. Serena de Bellis, Cur
Holdings: / / Cat
Notes: Catalog: Becker-Colonna, Andreina, *Etruscan, Greek and Roman Artifacts in the Frank V de Bellis Collection of the California State University,* rev and ed by Rosefannie Grabstein (San Francisco State University, 1976).

CT —YALE UNIVERSITY, Box 1603A, Yale Station, New Haven, 06520.

DC —HARVARD UNIVERSITY, Dumbarton Oaks, Research Library, 1703 32nd St NW, Washington, 20007. Irene Vaslef, Librn
Holdings: Vols (91,000) Cat Maps Pix Slides Microforms
Budget: ($219,000)
Notes: Byzantine civilization (including art, archaeology, literature, history, religion, law, music, etc). Extensive supplemental material on Classical, Hellenistic, Medieval, Islamic, Medieval Slavic cultures. 62,000 b/w photographs, 25,000 slides and transparencies, 1000 microfilms of books and manuscripts. Printed description of collection in *Harvard Library Bulletin,* vol 19, no 1 (Jan 1971), pp 25-35 and vol 19, no 2 (April 1971), pp 204-214, pp 25-35 and vol 19, no 2 (April 1971), pp 204-214.

DC —HARVARD UNIVERSITY, Center for Hellenic Studies Library, 3100 Whitehaven St NW, Washington, 20008. Jeno Platthy, Librn
Holdings: Vols (42,000) Cat Microforms
Budget: ($76,824)
Notes: Emphasis on Greek text editions, epigraphy, literature and linguistics; more than 200 periodicals devoted to classical scholarship.

IL —UNIVERSITY OF ILLINOIS, URBANA/CHAMPAIGN, Library, Classics Library, 419A Main Library, Urbana, 61801. Suzanne N Griffiths, Librn
Holdings: Vols (10,000) Cat
Notes: Ancient history section of Classics Library is strong in numismatics and in inscription materials; also incl ancient archaeology.

LA —TULANE UNIVERSITY, Howard-Tilton Memorial Library, Special Collections Div, 7001 Freret St, New Orleans, 70118. Wilbur E Meneray, Librn
Notes: The Margarete Bieber Collection.

†MA —UNIVERSITY OF MASSACHUSETTS AT AMHERST, Library, Amherst, 01003.
Notes: Classical art and archaeology. Special emphasis: Aegean area.

MA —WELLESLEY COLLEGE, Art Library, Wellesley, 02181. Katherine D Finkelpearl, Art Librn
Holdings: Vols (30,000) Cat Pix Slides
Budget: ($22,000)
Notes: Primarily the art and architecture of Western Europe, the Far East, and classical antiquity. However, efforts are being made to expand the collection in the areas of photography, primitive art, and ancient (non-classical) art. The Art Department maintains a separate collection of 62,500 mounted pictures and 90,000 slides.

NY —CORNELL UNIVERSITY LIBRARIES, Collection of Regional History, Dept of Manuscripts and Univ Archives, Ithaca, 14853.
Notes: Prints of casts of Greek and Roman sculture in the Museum in Goldwin Smith Hall at Cornell University, NY.

NY —NEW YORK PUBLIC LIBRARY, Research Libraries, General Research Division, Fifth Ave & 42 St, New York, 10018. Rodney Phillips, Chief
Holdings: Vols (2,225,000) Cat Maps Pix Microforms
Budget: ($775,718)

NC —DUKE UNIVERSITY, William R Perkins Library, Durham, 27706. Elvin E Strowd, University Librn

NC —SOUTHEASTERN BAPTIST THEOLOGICAL SEMINARY LIBRARY, PO Box 752, Wake Forest, 27587. H Eugene McLeod, Librn
Holdings: Cat Maps Slides
Notes: Near Eastern archaeology related to biblical studies.

OH —UNIVERSITY OF CINCINNATI, Classics Library, 320 Blegen, Cincinnati,

CLASSICAL ANTIQUITIES (cont.)

45221. Jean Susorney Wellington, Classics Librn; Eugenia Foster, Modern Greek Cur
Holdings: Vols (110,000) Cat Mss Maps Microforms

PA —BRYN MAWR COLLEGE, Canaday Library, Bryn Mawr, 19010. James Tanis, Dir
Notes: Greek architecture and sculpture; Anatolian and Aegean Archaeology. In Art and Archaeology Library.

PA —UNIVERSITY OF PENNSYLVANIA, University Museum Library, 33 & Spruce Sts, Philadelphia, 19104. Jean S Adelman, Librn
Holdings: Vols (80,000) Cat
Notes: World archaeology, with special emphasis on North and Central America, Egyptology, Sumerology, and the classical world. All holdings are listed in museum library catalog and are also listed in University of Pennsylvania main library (union) catalog.

PA —UNIVERSITY OF PITTSBURGH, Hillman Library, Pittsburgh, 15260. Glenora E Rossell, Head
Holdings: Vols (11,550) Cat
Notes: The classics collection is particularly strong in Greek and Latin literature, Greek and Roman history. Greek philosophy, Greek and Latin language, and Greek epigraphy. In combination with the Frick Fine Arts collection it has a good collection in Greek and Roman art and archaeology. The collection of journals is also quite strong in these areas. There has been an emphasis in collecting books by and about Homer, Arstotles, Euripides, Vergil, Cicero and Petronius. It has a unique collection of unpublished PhD dissertations and Master's theses on Petronius. It has a basic collection on Greek and Latin paleography and papyrology.

TX —RICE UNIVERSITY, Art Library, 6100 S Main St, PO Box 1892, Houston, 77001. Jet Marie Prendeville, Librn
Holdings: Vols 7,040 Cat
Budget: ($28,100)
Notes: The Art Library collection covers all periods of Western Art with particular emphasis upon Classical Archaelogy, Medieval, Renaissance, and Modern Art and Architecture. The collection also offers representative coverage of film, photography, and Oriental art.

ON —ROYAL ONTARIO MUSEUM, Main Library and Archives, 100 Queen's Park, Toronto, M5S 2C6, Can. Julia Matthews, Head Librn
Holdings: Vols (85,000) Cat
Notes: Since January 1977, acquisitions have been entered in UTLAS.

CLASSICAL ART see Art, Classical

CLASSICAL AUTHORS

CA —CLAREMONT COLLEGES, Ella Strong Denison Library, Scripps College, Claremont, 91711. Judy Harvey Sahak, Librn
Holdings: 300 Vols Uncat
Notes: Alexander Pogo Collection of 16th-20th century texts of classical authors, with majority printed before 1800.

CA —UNIVERSITY OF CALIFORNIA, SAN DIEGO, Central University Library, Mandeville Dept of Special Collections, La Jolla, 92093. Lynda Corey Claassen, Head
Holdings: Vols 550 // Uncat
Notes: T W Baldwin Collection of 16th, 17th, and 18th century texts of classical authors.

CLASSICAL LANGUAGES AND LITERATURES

CA —UNIVERSITY OF CALIFORNIA, BERKELEY, University Library, Berkeley, 94720. Donald G Williams, Classics Librn
Notes: Research collections, incl a wide array of periodicals, critical editions, works of textual criticism, history, and epigraphy. Extensive coverage of 18th and 19th century classical scholarship. German and Italian research publications are particularly well represented. Main Library holdings are supplemented by significant works in the Bancroft Library: mss, incunabula, and other rare editions; especially noteworthy are the Horace Collection and the Tebtunis papyri.

CA —CLAREMONT COLLEGES, Ella Strong Denison Library, Scripps College, Claremont, 91711. Judy Harvey Sahak, Librn
Holdings: Vols 3000 Uncat
Notes: Alexander Pogo Collection of 16th-20th century texts of classical authors, with majority printed before 1800.

CA —UNIVERSITY OF CALIFORNIA, IRVINE, Library, Irvine, 92664. Roger Berry, Dept Head
Notes: Incl the library of Professor Paul Friedlander (3000 vols). Located in general circulation collection.

CA —UNIVERSITY OF CALIFORNIA, SAN DIEGO, Central University Library, Mandeville Dept of Special Collections, La Jolla, 92093. Lynda Corey Claassen, Head
Holdings: Vols (9000) Cat Mss Maps Pix Slides
Notes: Incl the Miguel Romero Martinez Collection, especially strong in classical works printed in the 16th and 17th centuries by leading printers of the period. Also, the Renaissance Library of Don Cameron Allen, incl classical authors in 16th and 17th century editions.

CA —STANFORD UNIVERSITY LIBRARIES, Cecil H Green Library, Stanford, 94305. Michael T Ryan, Cur
Holdings: Vols Cat
Notes: An emphasis in the Rare Book Collection.

CT —YALE UNIVERSITY, Box 1603A, Yale Station, New Haven, 06520.
Holdings: Cat Mss

DC —HARVARD UNIVERSITY, Center for Hellenic Studies Library, 3100 Whitehaven St NW, Washington, 20008. Jeno Platthy, Librn
Holdings: Vols (42,000) Cat Maps
Budget: ($76,824)
Notes: Emphasis on Greek text editions, epigraphy, literature and linguistics; more than 200 periodicals devoted to classical scholarship.

IL —UNIVERSITY OF ILLINOIS, URBANA/CHAMPAIGN, Library, 1408 W Gregory Drive, Urbana, 61801. Norman B Brown, Asst Dir for Special Collections
Holdings: Vols (5900)
Notes: Rare Book Room collection of Shakespeariana, incl vols of 16th, 17th, and 18th century texts of classical authors with commentaries. Bibles and prayer books, rhetorics and histories, in addition to 16th to 20th century editions of Shakespeare.

MD —JOHNS HOPKINS UNIVERSITY, Milton S Eisenhower Library, Charles & 34 Sts, Baltimore, 21218. Ann S Gwyn, Assistant Dir for Special Collections
Holdings: Vols 21,500 Cat
Notes: Outstanding feature is exceptionally complete collection of 19th century commentaries, mostly in German, which are generally unavailable in Europe since World War II. Many are the only copies now in existence.

MA —HARVARD UNIVERSITY LIBRARY, Widener Library, Cambridge, 02138.
Holdings: Cat
Notes: Strong collection, particularly noteworthy for holdings on Aristophanes, Horace, and Persius.

†MA —CLARK UNIVERSITY, Robert Hutchings Goddard Library, Worcester, 01610. Dorothy Mosa Kowski, Rare Books Librn
Holdings: Cat
Notes: Hundreds of vols of Greek and Latin classics in English translation (the Haven Darling Brackett Collection).

MI —UNIVERSITY OF MICHIGAN, Library, Dept of Rare Books & Special Collections, Ann Arbor, 48109. Robert J Starring, Head
Holdings: Cat Mss Microforms
Notes: Greek and Latin classics; classical studies periodicals.

MI —COLOMBIERE COLLEGE, Dinan Library, 9075 Big Lake Rd, Clarkston, 48016. Stephen A Meder, SJ, Librn
Holdings: Vols 2500// Cat

MN —SAINT JOHN'S ABBEY & UNIVERSITY, Hill Monastic Manuscript Library, Collegeville, 56321. Julian G Plante, Dir
Holdings: Vols (61,000) Microforms
Notes: Films of 61,000 mss. The total number of codices or bound handwritten mss represents the holdings of several hundred libraries in Europe, mostly Austria, Spain, Ethiopia, West Germany, Portugal, and also Italy, Hungary, Poland, Great Britain, Belgium, Yugoslavia, France, Switzerland, and the Netherlands.

MO —SAINT LOUIS UNIVERSITY, Pius XII Memorial Library, Vatican Film Library Collection, 3655 W Pine Blvd, Saint Louis, 63108. Charles J Ermatinger, Librn
Holdings: Mss Slides Microforms
Notes: Vatican Film Library has 75 percent of the Greek, Latin and western European vernacular holdings in the Vatican Library, plus all the Hebrew, Arabic and Ethiopic holdings on film. Covers 5th-19th centuries. Sizable collection of western European books. In addition, has largest collection on the work of the Jesuits in Latin America, the US and the Philippines, filmed from European Jesuit archives. Excellent catalogs and guides to all collections. Also, 50,608 slides of illuminated mss; 26,470 reels of microfilm.

NJ —PRINCETON UNIVERSITY, Library, Rare Books Dept, Princeton, 08544. Stephen Ferguson, Cur
Holdings: Cat

NY —COLUMBIA UNIVERSITY LIBRARIES, Rare Book & Manuscript Library, 801 Butler Library, 535 W 114 St, New York, 10027. Kenneth A Lohf, Librn
Holdings: Vols 2000 Cat Mss
Notes: Emphasis on early texts. Restricted use: noncirculating

NY —NEW YORK PUBLIC LIBRARY, Research Libraries, General Research Division, Fifth Ave & 42 St, New York, 10018. Rodney Phillips, Chief
Holdings: Vols (2,225,000) Cat Maps Pix Microforms
Budget: ($775,718)

NC —DUKE UNIVERSITY, William R Perkins Library, Durham, 27706. Elvin E Strowd, University Librn
Notes: The Spranger Collection of classical studies contains 2500 items. The principal dramatists, Euripides, Aeschylus, Aristophanes and Sophocles are fairly comprehensively covered by way of critical texts and studies up to 1968. Practically all the texts are represented by Loeb and Bude translations, and also Didot's 19th century series. Reference books includes a complete Pauly-Wissowa, Briquet, long runs of the Classical Review and Quarterly, the O E D and some 30 to 40 volumes of codex facsimiles of Euripides and others.

OH —MOUNT UNION COLLEGE, Library, Alliance, 44601. Yost Osborne, Librn
Holdings: Vols 547 Cat
Notes: The Charles Sutherin Collection. No photocopying.

OH —UNIVERSITY OF CINCINNATI, Classics Library, 320 Blegen, Cincinnati, 45221. Jean Susorney Wellington, Classics Librn; Eugenia Foster, Modern Greek Cur
Holdings: Vols (110,000) Cat Mss Maps Microforms

PA —BRYN MAWR COLLEGE, Canaday Library, Bryn Mawr, 19010. James Tanis, Dir
Notes: Incl the Sauppe Collection, with early printed editions.

PA —HAVERFORD COLLEGE, Magill Library, Quaker Collection, Haverford, 19041. Edwin B Bonner, Librn & Cur
Holdings: Vols 3250 //
Notes: Works from the 15th through the 19th centuries by and about the humanistic Latin writers of the 14th and 15th centuries.

PA —UNIVERSITY OF PITTSBURGH, Hillman Library, Pittsburgh, 15260. Glenora E Rossell, Head
Holdings: Vols (11,550) Cat
Notes: The classics collection is particularly strong in Greek and Latin literature, Greek

CLASSICAL LANGUAGES AND LITERATURES (cont.)

and Roman history, Greek philosophy, Greek and Latin language, and Greek epigraphy. In combination with the Frick Fine Arts collection it has a good collection in Greek and Roman art and archaeology. The collection of journals is also quite strong in these areas. There has been an emphasis in collecting books by and about Homer, Aristotles, Euripides, Vergil, Cicero and Petronius. It has a unique collection of unpublished PhD dissertations and Master's theses on Petronius. It has a basic collection on Greek and Latin paleography and papyrology.

TX —UNIVERSITY OF TEXAS LIBRARIES, General Libraries, PO Box P, Austin, 78713. Carolyn Bucknell, Asst Dir for Collection Development
Holdings: Cat Microforms

WI —UNIVERSITY OF WISCONSIN, MADISON, Memorial Library, Rare Books Collection, 728 State St, Madison, 53706. Gretchen Lagana, Cur
Holdings: Vols 120// Cat
Notes: Giolito Collection. Approximately 120 titles of 16th century Italian imprints of Greek and Latin classics. Restricted use: Rare Book Department.

ON —VICTORIA UNIVERSITY, Library, Centre for Reformation and Renaissance Studies, 71 Queen's Park Crescent, Toronto, M5S 1K7, Can. Robert C Brandeis, Chief Librn; James Estes, Dir
Holdings: Vols (15,000) Cat Slides
Notes: The CRRS concentrates on the northern European countries and France; its chief strengths are Erasmus, 650 vols; early printed books, especially 16th century editions of Latin classics; bibliography and the history of printing. The Erasmus holdings are cataloged in W T McCready et al, "The Erasmus Collection in the Centre for Reformation and Renaissance Studies...A Catalogue"...*Reformation and Renaissance* 7 (1971), 32-76 and "A Supplementary List"...*Reformation and Renaissance,* 10 (1974), 116-119. Published catalogs. Humanist Editions of the Classics at CRRS, Toronto, 1979; Humanist Editions of Statutes and History at CRRS, Toronto, 1980; Bibles, Theological Treatises and Other Religious Literature 1491-1700 at CRRS, Toronto, 1981.

PQ —MCGILL UNIVERSITY, McLennan Library, Rare Books and Special Collections Dept, 3459 McTavish St, Montreal, H3A 1Y1, Can.
Notes: 5600 pamphlets, located in the Ribbeck Collection. Pamphlets, mostly in German, on Greek and Latin literature and philology.

CLASSICAL MUSIC see Music, Classical

CLASSICAL PHILOLOGY

MD —JOHNS HOPKINS UNIVERSITY, Milton S Eisenhower Library, Charles & 34 Sts, Baltimore, 21218. Ann S Gwyn, Assistant Dir for Special Collections
Holdings: Vols 12,500 Cat
Notes: Outstanding feature is exceptionally complete collection of 19th century commentaries, mostly in German, which are generally unavailable in Europe since World War II. Many are the only copies now in existence.

PA —BRYN MAWR COLLEGE, Canaday Library, Bryn Mawr, 19010. James Tanis, Dir
Notes: Collection on classical languages and literatures.

VA —UNIVERSITY OF VIRGINIA, Alderman Library, Manuscripts Dept, Charlottesville, 22901. Edmund Berkeley Jr, Cur
Notes: The Martin Julius Hertz (1818-1895) Collection of some 13,000 vols and pamphlets, some carefully annotated by him and other classical philologists. Incl a substantial archive of 19th century German classical dissertations (awaiting a volunteer cataloger), now organized in boxes by subject.

CLASSICAL STUDIES

DC —HARVARD UNIVERSITY, Dumbarton Oaks, Research Library, 1703 32nd St NW, Washington, 20007. Irene Vaslef, Librn
Holdings: Vols (91,000) Cat Maps Pix Slides Microforms
Budget: ($219,000)
Notes: Byzantine civilization (including art, archaeology, literature, history, religion, law, music, etc). Extensive supplemental material on Classical, Hellenistic, Medieval, Islamic, Medieval Slavic cultures. 62,000 b/w photographs, 25,000 slides and transparencies, 1000 microfilms of books and manuscripts. Printed description of collection in *Harvard Library Bulletin,* vol 19, no 1 (Jan 1971), pp 25-35 and vol 19, no 2 (April 1971), pp 204-214, pp 25-35 and vol 19, no 2 (April 1971), pp 204-214.

DC —HARVARD UNIVERSITY, Center for Hellenic Studies Library, 3100 Whitehaven St NW, Washington, 20008. Jeno Platthy, Librn
Holdings: Vols 25,000 Cat
Notes: Emphasis on Greek text editions, epigraphy, literature and linguistics; more than 200 periodicals devoted to classical scholarship.

IL —UNIVERSITY OF ILLINOIS, URBANA/CHAMPAIGN, Library, Classics Library, 419A Main Library, Urbana, 61801. Suzanne N Griffiths, Librn
Holdings: Vols 41,569 Cat Maps Pix
Budget: $5600
Notes: Collection is strong in 19th century German inaugural dissertations. The above figures do not include 17,000 uncataloged pamphlets (alphabetical file lists these).

LA —TULANE UNIVERSITY, Howard-Tilton Memorial Library, Special Collections Div, 7001 Freret St, New Orleans, 70118. Wilbur E Meneray, Librn
Notes: The Margarete Bieber Collection.

NY —STATE UNIVERSITY OF NEW YORK, COLLEGE AT BUFFALO, Lockwood Memorial Library, Main St, Buffalo, 14260. Stanton F Biddle, Assoc Dir
Holdings: Vols 20,000 Cat Pix
Notes: About half of the collection donated by the Orthodox Catholic Alliance of Buffalo, New York. The collection is devoted chiefly to the world of Byzantium in both its secular and religious phases; Greek Patristic literature and its interpretation; and the tradition of the Greek Bible and its antecedents. As support for these subjects the pagan literature of late antiquity is strongly represented, as well as the Hellenistic and Roman background of the East Christian world and its relations with its neighbors in the Near East, in Eastern Europe, and in the Latin West.

†NY —COLUMBIA UNIVERSITY LIBRARIES, Butler Library, Rare Book and Manuscript Library, 535 W 114 St, New York, 10027.
Notes: Papers, mss, correspondence, etc of Prof Gilbert Highet.

NC —DUKE UNIVERSITY, William R Perkins Library, Durham, 27706. Elvin E Strowd, University Librn
Notes: The Spranger Collection of classical studies contains 2500 items. The principal dramatists, Euripides, Aeschylus, Aristophanes and Sophocles are fairly comprehensively covered by way of critical texts and studies up to 1968. Practically all the texts are represented by Loeb and Bude translations, and also Didot's 19th century series. Reference books includes a complete Pauly-Wissowa, Briquet, long runs of the Classical Review and Quarterly, the O E D and some 30 to 40 volumes of codex facsimiles of Euripides and others.

OH —SAINT THOMAS INSTITUTE, Library, 1842 Madison Rd, Cincinnati, 45206. Sister M Virgil Ghering, O P Librn
Holdings: Vols 900 // Cat
Budget: ($39,878)

TX —SOUTHERN METHODIST UNIVERSITY, Fondren Library, Dallas, 75275. Curt Holleman, Librn for Collection Development

WI —UNIVERSITY OF WISCONSIN, MADISON, Memorial Library, Rare Books Collection, 728 State St, Madison, 53706. Gretchen Lagana, Cur
Notes: Incl Giolito Collection, 120 titles of 16th century Italian imprints of Greek and Latin classics; Pitman Library, 2500 vols donated by Greek and Latin professor Annie M Pitman; Moses S Slaughter Collection, 48 titles of Latin classical literature; and the Woodward Collection, over 400 vols.

ON —UNIVERSITY OF OTTAWA, Morisset Library, 65 Hastey St, Ottawa, K1N 9A5, Can. Yvon Richer, University Chief Librn
Holdings: Vols (17,000)
Notes: Incl monographs and 173 cataloged sets of periodicals. Only a small portion of this material is housed in Special Collections, but it is one of the strongest elements of our regular collection. Additional support, particularly in archaeology, philosophy and religion is also available at the affiliated St Paul University, 223 Main Street, Ottawa.

CLASSIFICATION—BOOKS

OH —CASE WESTERN RESERVE UNIVERSITY, M A Baxter School of Information and Library Science, 10900 Euclid Ave, Cleveland, 44106. Bettina MacAyeal, Librn; Gretchen Larson, Librn
Holdings: Vols (15,000) Cat

ON —UNIVERSITY OF TORONTO, Faculty of Library and Information Science Library, Subject Analysis Systems, Room 404, 140 St George St, Toronto, M5S 1A1, Can. Diane Henderson, Librn
Holdings: Vols (2000) Cat Microforms
Notes: The Subject Analysis Systems Collection is the major North American collection of classification schemes, thesauri, and subject heading lists, and it is the major world collection in the English language. Incl Bibliographic Systems Center Collection, transferred from Case Western Reserve, Cleveland.

CLASSIFICATION—BOTANY see Botany—Classification

CLASSIFICATION—PLANTS see Botany—Classification

CLASSIFICATION OF SPECIES see Biology—Classification

CLAUDEL, PAUL

IL —LOYOLA UNIVERSITY OF CHICAGO, E M Cudahy Memorial Library, 6525 N Sheridan Rd, Chicago, 60626.
Holdings: 300 Vols
Notes: A collection of Paul Claudel's works.

CLAVELL, JAMES

CA —SAN DIEGO STATE UNIVERSITY, Malcolm A Love Library, 5300 Campanile Dr, San Diego, 92182. D Dickinson, Univ Librn; Don L Bosseau, Dir
Notes: Collected works in first edition of certain prominent authors, as H G Wells, Somerset Maugham, William Dean Howells, Gertrude Atherton, Tom Stoppard, James Clavell, G A Henty, Henry Raup Wagner.

MA —BOSTON UNIVERSITY, Mugar Memorial Library, Special Collections Dept, 771 Commonwealth Ave, Boston, 02215. Howard B Gotlieb, Dir
Holdings: Cat Mss
Notes: Mss, correspondence, etc, collected in depth; incl publications by or about.

CLAY, C. C.

NC —DUKE UNIVERSITY, William R Perkins Library, Manuscript Dept, Durham, 27706. Ellen Gartrell, Cur of Mss
Holdings: Cat Mss
Notes: Papers, etc.

CLAY, HENRY

IN —INDIANA UNIVERSITY, Lilly Library, Seventh St, Bloomington, 47405. William R Cagle, Librn
Holdings: // Mss
Notes: A collection of political letters of

CLAY, HENRY (cont.)

statesman Henry Clay, 1812-1849. Incl a group of printed notices of meetings, circulars, etc of various New York City Clay organizations, 1841-1859. 292 items. Some contemporary printed material by and about Clay.

KY —UNIVERSITY OF KENTUCKY, Margaret I King Library, Dept of Special Collections, Lexington, 40506. William Marshall, Head
Holdings: Cat Mss
Notes: Holograph letters and documents. 176 pieces.

NY —NEW YORK HISTORICAL SOCIETY, Library, 170 Central Park W, New York, 10024. James Gregory, Librn
Notes: Miscellaneous papers, correspondence, etc.

NC —DUKE UNIVERSITY, William R Perkins Library, Manuscript Dept, Durham, 27706. Ellen Gartrell, Cur of Mss
Holdings: Cat Mss
Notes: Papers, etc.

CLAY, LAURA

KY —UNIVERSITY OF KENTUCKY, Margaret I King Library, Dept of Special Collections, Lexington, 40506. William Marshall, Head
Holdings: // Cat Mss
Notes: Women's suffrage. About 6000 pieces; correspondence, etc.

CLAYTON, BILL

TX —TEXAS A&M UNIVERSITY, Sterling C Evans Library, University Archives, College Station, 77843. Charles R Schultz, University Archivist
Notes: The Archives of Modern Politics: Texas Legislator Bill Clayton, 1961-1983.

TX —NORTH TEXAS STATE UNIVERSITY, Archives, NT Station Box 5188, Denton, 76203. Robert LaForte, University Archivist
Notes: Part of Oral History Collection. Interviews 1975-1979 with farmer, rancher, businessman and Speaker of the Texas House of Representatives. Closed until after he leaves public office.

CLAYTON, NICHOLAS J.

TX —ROSENBERG LIBRARY, Galveston and Texas History Center, 2310 Sealy Ave, Galveston, 77550. Jane Kenamore, Archivist
Holdings: Cat Mss
Notes: Nicholas J Clayton, 1849-1916, was the first professional architect in Texas. Collection consists of 350 of his architectural drawings.

CLAYTOR, W. GRAHAM

VA —VIRGINIA POLYTECHNIC INSTITUTE AND STATE UNIVERSITY LIBRARY, Blacksburg, 24061. Glenn L McMullen, Special Collections Librn
Holdings: Vols (2000) Cat Mss Maps Pix Audiotapes
Notes: Primarily Southwest Virginia materials. Collection incl ca 200 mss, account books and other archival records of nineteenth century area businesses and other mining operations; the extant archival records of several Southwest Virginia railroads, incl the Virginia and Tennessee Railroad and the Norfolk and Western Railroad; and papers of historically prominent Southwest Virginians, incl John Apperson, Dr Harvy Black, James P Charlton, W Graham Claytor, Henley Fugate, Clement D Johnston, Germanicus Kent, William Preston, J Hoge Tyler, and William C Wampler. Several oral history collections incl material on Appalachian customs and folklore, particularly in Patrick County.

CLEARIHUE, JOSEPH B., 1887-1976

BC —UNIVERSITY OF VICTORIA, McPherson Library, Victoria, V8W 3H5, Can.
Notes: Judge, chancellor of the University of Victoria.

CLEANLINESS see Baths; Hygiene, Public; Sanitation

CLEAVELAND, PARKER, 1780-1858

ME —BOWDOIN COLLEGE, Library, Brunswick, 04011. Dianne M Gutscher, Cur of Special Collections
Holdings: Cat Mss
Notes: The Parker Cleaveland Papers cover the period 1795-1858 and number about 1600 items. They are principally concerned with his tenure as professor of chemistry, mineralogy, and natural philosophy at Bowdoin. They incl personal correspondence, lecture notes, and writings on scientific subjects, incl his mss of the first American work on mineralogy and geology.

CLEEVE, BRIAN

MA —BOSTON UNIVERSITY, Mugar Memorial Library, Special Collections Dept, 771 Commonwealth Ave, Boston, 02215. Howard B Gotlieb, Dir
Holdings: Cat Mss Pix
Notes: Mss, correspondence, etc collected in depth; incl publications by or about.

CLELAND, RALPH ERSKINE, 1892-1971

IN —INDIANA UNIVERSITY, Lilly Library, Seventh St, Bloomington, 47405. William R Cagle, Librn
Holdings: // Mss Pix
Notes: Collections incl papers of geneticists and biologists, most notably those of Nobel Prize winner Hermann Joseph Muller, 1890-1967 and Tracy Morton Sonneborn, 1905-1981. Also papers of plant geneticists Ralph Cleland, 1892-1971, and Paul Weatherwax, 1888-1976.

CLEMENS, CYRIL

NY —COLUMBIA UNIVERSITY LIBRARIES, Rare Book & Manuscript Library, 801 Butler Library, 535 W 114 St, New York, 10027. Kenneth A Lohf, Librn
Holdings: Mss
Notes: A E Housman letters to Cyril Clemens, who planned a biography of A E Housman; also a few other Housman letters. Restricted use.

CLEMENS, SAMUEL LANGHORNE, 1835-1910 see Twain, Mark

CLEMENTS, EARLE C.

KY —UNIVERSITY OF KENTUCKY, Margaret I King Library, Dept of Special Collections, Lexington, 40506. William Marshall, Head
Holdings: Cat Mss Pix Audiotapes Films
Notes: Incl 392 boxes; papers relating to his career as US Rep from Kentucky, Gov of Kentucky and US Sen from Kentucky. Period covered: 1945-59. Unpublished inventory.

CLEMSON, THOMAS G., 1807-1888

SC —CLEMSON UNIVERSITY, Libraries, Clemson, 29631. Michael F Kohl, Head of Special Collections
Holdings: // Cat Mss
Notes: Papers of Thomas G Clemson, chemist, diplomat, proponent of scientific agriculture, and son-in-law of John C Calhoun. Clemson's bequest made possible the establishment of Clemson College. There is an unpublished register.

CLERGUE, LUCIEN

MD —UNIVERSITY OF MARYLAND, BALTIMORE COUNTY, Albin O Kuhn Library and Gallery, Edward L Bafford Photography Collection, 5401 Wilkens Ave, Baltimore, 21228. Tom Beck, Cur
Holdings: Vols Pix
Notes: The Edward L Bafford Photography Collection contains more than 200,000 images, negatives, cameras and books representing the entire history and aesthetics of photography. Incl is a large collection of the work of photographer Lucien Clergue.

CLERGYWOMEN see Women in Religion

CLERICAL OCCUPATIONS

SC —HORRY GEORGETOWN TECHNICAL COLLEGE, Library, Hwy 501, Box 1966, Conway, 29526. Barbara Brittain, Librn
Holdings: Vols (20,000) Cat Slides Microforms

CLERICAL PSYCHOLOGY see Pastoral Psychology

CLERKS—VOCATIONAL GUIDANCE see Clerical Occupations

CLEVELAND, GROVER

DC —LIBRARY OF CONGRESS, Manuscript Division, Washington, 20540. John C Broderick, Chief
Notes: The Presidential Papers collection incl the papers, etc, of numerous Presidents.

NY —COLUMBIA UNIVERSITY LIBRARIES, Rare Book & Manuscript Library, 801 Butler Library, 535 W 114 St, New York, 10027. Kenneth A Lohf, Librn
Notes: More than 32,000 items documenting the rise of William Russell Grace's shipping business and other materials relating to his career as mayor of New York. Incl records and correspondence relating to all aspects of the shipping business in New York and South America, mining interest in Peru and Chile, and transportation in Costa Rica and Nicaragua. Family memorabilia and photographs, materials concerning New York Politics, banking and insurance, real estate interests and Catholic charities, and letters from Chester A Arthur, John Jacob Astor, Andrew Carnegie, Grover Cleveland, Hamilton Fish, John Hay and J Pierpont Morgan. Restricted use.

CLEVELAND, OHIO

OH —CLEVELAND PUBLIC LIBRARY, Public Administration Library, City Hall, 601 Lakeside Ave NE Rm 100, Cleveland, 44114. Janice Ryan Novak, Head
Holdings: Vols 4000 Cat Mss Maps Pix
Notes: The Cleveland Archives incl all official reports of the city of Cleveland; special studies and surveys; materials by and about the city of Cleveland.

CLEVELAND, OHIO—DESCRIPTION—VIEWS

OH —CLEVELAND PUBLIC LIBRARY, History and Geography Department, 325 Superior Ave, Cleveland, 44114. JoAnn Petrello, Head
Holdings: Cat Pix
Notes: Cleveland Picture Collection: 13,500 pictures incl the Standiford Portrait Collection (500 pictures); the Edmondson Portrait Collection of Clevelanders (2425 glass plates and prints). The Ohio Collection (430 pictures); the Ketteringham Collection (250 glass plates and prints). Cleveland Picture Collection is now on microfiche. Reproduction of the photos may be arranged.

CLEVELAND, WILLIAM H., JR.

NY —NEW YORK PUBLIC LIBRARY, Performing Arts Research Center, Billy Rose Theatre Collection, 111 Amsterdam Ave, New York, 10023. Dorothy L Swerdlove, Cur
Holdings: Cat
Notes: The Theatre Collection maintains current clipping files about activity in the

CLEVELAND, WILLIAM H., JR. (cont.)

field and acquires photographs and programs of marionette theatre productions. Files are kept on organizations, on individual puppeteers and on associations and organizations in this area of entertainment--professional and amateur, domestic and foreign. The reviews of such productions in New York are entered in the review collection kept seasonally. The collection has been enriched by the gift of books and papers of the late William H Cleveland, Jr.

CLEVERDON, DOUGLAS

IN —INDIANA UNIVERSITY, Lilly Library, Seventh St, Bloomington, 47405. William R Cagle, Librn
Holdings: Cat Mss
Notes: Extensive collection of BBC radio scripts chiefly for the Third Programme. Ms holdings incl the correspondence of Douglas Cleverdon, producer.
See also entry under Eliot, Thomas Stearns

CLIFTON, VIOLET

DC —GEORGETOWN UNIVERSITY, Library, Special Collections Div, 37 & O Sts NW, Washington, 20057. George M Barringer, Special Collections Librn; Nicholas B Sheetz, Mss Librn
Holdings: Mss Cat
Notes: The literary papers of author and art curator, James Laver (1899-1975), and those of his wife, the actress Veronica Turleigh; consisting of letters, with a considerable number written by Lady Cnythia Asquith; Clifford Box; Enid Bagnold; Nicholas Bentley; Violet Clifton; Desmond MacCarthy; Sir Edward Marsh; Sir Francis Meynell; Kate O'Brien; Dorothy L Sayers; Andre Simon; Enid Starkie; A J A Symons; Angela Thirkell; and Alec Waugh.

CLIMATE see Climatology

CLIMATOLOGY

CT —YALE UNIVERSITY, Geology Library, 210 Whitney Ave, PO Box 6666, New Haven, 06511. Harry Scammell, Librn
Holdings: Vols (100,000) Cat Maps Pix Microforms
Budget: ($115,000)
Notes: The O C Marsh Collection (vertebrate paleontology) is also here.

IA —IOWA STATE UNIVERSITY, Library, Ames, 50011. Warren B Kuhn, Dean of Library Services
Holdings: Cat
Notes: Incl agricultural climatology, meteorology. Extensive serial holdings.

MD —NATIONAL OCEANIC & ATMOSPHERIC ADMINISTRATION, Library & Information Sciences Division, Central Library & Information Sciences Bldg, 6009 Executive Blvd, Rockville, 20852. Elizabeth J Yeates, Chief
Holdings: Vols (175,000) Cat Maps Microforms

MA —HARVARD UNIVERSITY LIBRARY, Gordon McKay Library, Division of Applied Sciences, Pierce Hall, Oxford St, Cambridge, 02138. Julie Sandall Barlas, Librn
Notes: Incl original weather records of Blue Hill and Mt Washington Observatories.

NV —UNIVERSITY OF NEVADA, RENO, Desert Research Institute, PO Box 60220, Reno, 89557. Roberta Kiefer Orcutt, Librn
Holdings: Vols (10,480) Cat Maps Microforms
Notes: Incl materials in atmospheric physics, meteorology, climatology, weather modification, antarctic studies and related materials in basic sciences. Over 3000 microforms; also 1300 technical reports and 18,000 government publications.

NY —AMERICAN MUSEUM OF NATURAL HISTORY, Library Services Dept, Central Park W & 79th St, New York, 10024. Nina J Root, Chairwoman; Mary Genett, Asst Librn for Reference Services

PA —CARNEGIE LIBRARY OF PITTSBURGH, Science & Technology Dept, 4400 Forbes Ave, Pittsburgh, 15213. Catherine M Brosky, Dept Head
Holdings: Vols (380,000) Cat Maps Microforms
Budget: ($240,000)
Notes: Complete sets of US topographic maps and geologic folios, US climatological data, water supply papers and soil surveys available.

PA —UNIVERSITY OF PITTSBURGH, Hillman Library, Pittsburgh, 15260.
Holdings: Vols (6000) Cat Maps Pix Slides Microforms
Notes: The Geography collection is strengthened by US Geological Survey depository collection; US Army Map Service depository collection; US government publications depository collection; Canadian government publications; and UN depository (partial) collection.

TX —HOUSTON ACADEMY OF MEDICINE-TEXAS MEDICAL CENTER, Library, Jesse H Jones Library Bldg, Houston, 77030. Elizabeth Borst White, Special Collections Librn
Holdings: Vols (900) Cat
Notes: Mading Collection on Public Health. English-language materials dealing with American public health conditions before 1925. Emphasis is on epidemiology and infectious diseases (excluding venereal disease), incl material on sanitation and climatology. Federal, state or municipal reports on health, mortality and sanitation are included. Also 500 pamphlets.

WI —UNIVERSITY OF WISCONSIN, MADISON, Geography Library, 280 Science Hall, Madison, 53706. Miriam E Kerndt, Librn
Holdings: Vols (40,000) Cat Microforms
Budget: ($35,000)
Notes: Geography Library collects books, journals, and atlases in all fields of regional and systematic geography to support research and university teaching. Popular works, travel accounts, and tourist literature are not collected. Maps are collected in a separate Map and Air Photo Library in the same building.

WI —MILWAUKEE PUBLIC LIBRARY, 814 W Wisconsin Ave, Milwaukee, 53233. Donald J Sager, City Librn
Holdings: Cat Maps
Notes: Emphasis on Wisconsin geology, incl climatological data.
See also entry under Geology

NS —ENVIRONMENT CANADA, Dept of Environment Regional Library, 1497 Bedford Hwy, Bedford, E4A 1E5, Can. Fraizer Macniel, Special Collections Librn
Holdings: Vols 500 Maps Microforms
Notes: Reference collection for a regional weather analysis and forecasting center and to a small staff of professionals involved in consultation and applications. Principal meteorological and related journals are purchased. Library also houses regional climatological data base. Partially cataloged.

CLIMATOLOGY—MAPS

†CA —UNIVERSITY OF CALIFORNIA, DAVIS, Peter J Shields Memorial Library, Map Collection, Davis, 95616.

CLIMATOLOGY, AGRICULTURAL see Crops and Climate

CLINE, PLATT

AZ —NORTHERN ARIZONA UNIVERSITY, Special Collection Library, CU Box 6022, Flagstaff, 86011. Peter M Whiteley, Coordr/Archivist; William Mullane, Librn
Notes: Collection of Cline Platt, president of the *Arizona Daily Sun,* Flagstaff, local historian. Historical files concerning Flagstaff and Coconino County, Incl pioneer reminiscences of Black Family, Babbitt Brothers Trading Company records, correspondence and business papers of J Gutherie Savage, 1880's-1890's, Flagstaff attorney; and Ammon Hennacy, correspondence and subject files, 1950's-1960's. Hennacy (Phoenix, Arizona, and Salt Lake City, Utah) was a noted Christian anarchist.

CLINICAL ASSISTANTS see Physicians' Assistants

CLINICAL MEDICINE see Medicine, Clinical

CLINICAL PSYCHOLOGY

CA —REISS-DAVIS CHILD STUDY CENTER, Research Library, 3200 Motor Ave, Los Angeles, 90034. Lee Freehling, Librn
Holdings: Vols (12,000) cat
Notes: Child study, child psychiatry, psychoanalysis, clinical psychology, psychiatric social work. Incl 500 audiotapes; 25 16mm Films.

CA —UNIVERSITY OF CALIFORNIA, LOS ANGELES, Biomedical Library, Center for Health Sciences, Los Angeles, 90024. Louise Darling, Biomedical Librn

CA —LANGLEY PORTER PSYCHIATRIC INSTITUTE LIBRARY, University of California, 401 Parnassus Ave Box 13-B, San Francisco, 94143. Lisa M Dunkel, Librn
Holdings: Vols (11,700) Cat
Notes: Attempt to cover, selectively, literature in psychiatry, psychoanalysis, clinical psychology, and allied fields for an institute which is involved in clinical work, training and research.

KS —MENNINGER FOUNDATION, Archives, 5600 W Sixth St, Box 829, Topeka, 66601. Alice Brand, Librn; Mark West, Archivist
Notes: Incl journals. Literature searches and document delivery available for a fee.

MD —CROWNSVILLE HOSPITAL CENTER, Medical Staff Library, Crownsville, 21032. Joyce E Munsey, Librn
Holdings: Vols (1500) Cat
Budget: $2000
Notes: Behavior therapy, clinical psychology, and family therapy.

CLINICAL RADIOLOGY see Radiology

CLINICS

†CT —YALE UNIVERSITY, Medical Library, 333 Cedar St, New Haven, 06520.
Notes: Hospital, clinic, and dispensary collection of extensive, uncatalogued materials, descriptive pamphlets, annual reports, etc. This is a large collection with much on institutional histories of European and American hospitals.

CLINTON, CLIFFORD E., 1900-1969

CA —UNIVERSITY OF CALIFORNIA, LOS ANGELES, Research Library, Dept of Special Collections, 405 Hilgard Ave, Los Angeles, 90024. Edward Shreeves, Chairman, Bibliographers Group; David S Zeidberg, Head
Holdings: // Uncat Mss
Notes: 3 linear feet of mss and clippings from the collection of the owner of Clinton's Cafeteria, Los Angeles.

CLINTON, SIR HENRY

MI —UNIVERSITY OF MICHIGAN, William L Clements Library, Ann Arbor, 48109. John C Dann, Dir
Notes: The

CLINTON, DE WITT

NY —NEW YORK HISTORICAL SOCIETY, Library, 170 Central Park W, New York, 10024. James Gregory, Librn
Notes: Miscellaneous papers, correspondence, etc.

CLIPPER SHIPS

CA —FITZ HUGH LUDLOW MEMORIAL LIBRARY, PO Box 99346, San Francisco, 94109. Michael R Aldrich, Exec Cur
Notes: Collection stored. Important mail

CLIPPER SHIPS (cont.)

inquiries only. No interlibrary lending or telephone queries. This collections emphasis historical and literary works about opium and its derivatives, mostly in English, going back to the 17th century but mostly from the 19th and early 20th centuries. Excellent collection of De Quincey in different editions. Many books, pamphlets, and art relating to the 19th century international opium trade, the Chinese Opium Wars, clipper ships, and resulting international legal action in the early 20th century. Outstanding collection of the English, French, and American opium-addict confessional literature. Also incl many volumes and offprints relevant to narcotic drug prevention, treatment, and education.

CLOCKS, ASTRONOMICAL see Astronomical Clocks

CLOCKS AND WATCHES

CT —TRINITY COLLEGE LIBRARY, Watkinson Library, 300 Summit St, Hartford, 06106. Jeffrey Kaimowitz, Cur
Holdings: Cat
Notes: The Karl Vogel Collection of Horology.

MA —OLD STURBRIDGE VILLAGE, Research Library, Sturbridge, 01566. Theresa Rini Percy, Librn
Holdings: Cat Pix
Notes: New England clockmasters in 1860.

NY —NEW YORK PUBLIC LIBRARY, Research Libraries, Science and Technology Research Center, Fifth Ave & 42 St, New York, 10018.
Holdings: Vols (1,100,000) Cat Microforms
Budget: ($647,259)

PA —FRANKLIN INSTITUTE LIBRARY, 20 & The Parkway, Philadelphia, 19103. Miriam Padusis, Dir; Charles Wilt, Readers Servs Librn
Holdings: Vols 2400 Cat Mss
Notes: One of the finest collections of horology in the world.

PA —CARNEGIE LIBRARY OF PITTSBURGH, Science & Technology Dept, 4400 Forbes Ave, Pittsburgh, 15213. Catherine M Brosky, Dept Head
Notes: Incl much of the material in *Index to* Handicrafts. Books for the home owner, repairman and craftsman and the general builder and mechanics are emphasized. Information on the use of tools and materials especially for woodworking and metal crafts; also optical instruments, clocks, and other mechanic trades.
See also entry under Science

CLOETE, STUART

MA —BOSTON UNIVERSITY, Mugar Memorial Library, Special Collections Dept, 771 Commonwealth Ave, Boston, 02215. Howard B Gotlieb, Dir
Holdings: Cat Mss Pix
Notes: Mss, correspondence, etc collected in depth; incl publications by or about.

CLOKEY, JOSEPH W., 1890-1960

CA —CLAREMONT COLLEGES, Honnold Library, Ninth & Dartmouth, Claremont, 91711. Tania Rizzo, Special Collections Dept Head
Holdings: Vols (500) // Uncat Mss Pix Slides
Notes: Joseph W Clokey Collection. 250 ms items, scores, opaques, transparencies and transcriptions of church choral music, often with orchestral and organ accompaniments; 195 printed copies of published works; 15 folders of correspondence with his publishers, miscellaneous notes and typescripts. Restricted use. No photocopies permitted. On deposit.

CLOTH see Textile Industry and Fabrics

CLOTHIER, FLORENCE, 1903-

MA —RADCLIFFE COLLEGE, Arthur & Elizabeth Schlesinger Library on the History of Women in America, 3 James St, Cambridge, 02138. Patricia Miller King, Dir; Eva Moseley, Cur of Mss
Notes: Books, pamphlets, clippings; also oral history interviews in the Family Planning Oral History Project, and numerous mss collections, espec those of the Birth Control League of Massachusetts, Mary (Steichen) Calderone, MD (1904-), Edna (Rankin) McKinnon (1893-1978), and Florence Clothier, MD (1903-).

CLOTHIERS see Clothing Trade

CLOTHING AND DRESS

CA —CARLSBAD CITY LIBRARY, 1250 Elm Ave, Carlsbad, 92008. Clifford E Lange, Library Dir
Holdings: Vols (2595) Cat
Notes: Collection of sewing patterns. Catalogs of the patterns have been made up with complete information on size, etc, and have been divided into subject areas, such as gift ideas, toys, dolls, women's clothes, men's clothes, children's clothes, etc. Also patterns for knitted and crocheted wearing apparel. Incl patterns for children's costumes, historical fashions and antique dolls.

IL —UNIVERSITY OF ILLINOIS, URBANA/CHAMPAIGN, Library, Home Economics Library, 314 Bevier Hall, Champaign, 61820. Barbara C Swain, Librn
Holdings: Vols Cat
Notes: Textiles, clothing and interior design.
See also entry under Costume.

MA —OLD STURBRIDGE VILLAGE, Research Library, Sturbridge, 01566. Theresa Rini Percy, Librn
Holdings: Cat Pix
Notes: Northeastern US, 1790-1850; some English sources.

NY —METROPOLITAN MUSEUM OF ART, Costume Institute, Fifth Ave & 82 St, New York, 10028.
Holdings:
Notes: Rich resources for reference and research. Incl almost 45,000 articles of dress, international in scope, spanning four centuries and five continents. Irene Lewisohn Costume Reference Library also has unique collection of books, periodicals, fashion plates and sketches, pattern books, and fabric swatches. Professional designers of theatre costume and fashion, students, writers, etc use the facilities.

OH —OHIO STATE UNIVERSITY, Home Economics Library, Campbell Hall Rm 325, 1787 Neil Ave, Columbus, 43210. Neosha Mackey, Librn
Holdings: Vols (14,000) Cat Microforms
Notes: Separate catalog. Also, book catalog: *Catalog of the Home Economics Library* (Boston: G K Hall, 1976), 3 vols.

PA —DREXEL UNIVERSITY LIBRARIES, General Division, 32 & Chestnut Sts, Philadelphia, 19104. Tung Chu Chen, General Division Librn
Holdings: Vols 1485 Cat Slides
Budget: ($2400)
Notes: Emphasis on clothing, dress, fashion; historic and contemporary.

WI —UNIVERSITY OF WISCONSIN-STOUT, Library Learning Center, Menomonie, 54751. Philip Sawin Jr, Coll Develop Librn
Notes: The School of Home Economics has developed a Museum of Costumes. This collection supports the museum and its programs. University of Wisconsin-Stout has been offering courses in Costumes since 1918.

CLOTHING TRADE

OR —BASSIST COLLEGE LIBRARY, 2000 SW Fifth Ave, Portland, 97201. Norma Bassist, Librn
Holdings: Vols (4100) Cat Mss Pix Slides
Notes: Some material on the history of the subject also.

CLOUD SEEDING see Rainmaking; Weather Control

CLOUDS

CO —COLORADO STATE UNIVERSITY, Libraries, Fort Collins, 80523. Marjorie Rhoades, Engineering Sciences Librn
Holdings: Vols (8000) Cat
Budget: ($6000)
Notes: Atmosphere; upper atmosphere; atmospheric chemistry; atmospheric circulation; atmospheric radiation; atmospheric research; atmospheric thermodynamics; cloud physics; and clouds.

CLOUGH, GEORGE

MA —SOCIETY FOR THE PRESERVATION OF NEW ENGLAND ANTIQUITIES, Library, 141 Cambridge St, Boston, 02114. Ellie Reichlin, Librn & Cur of Photographic Collections
Notes: Project drawings for 20 public and residential commissions, incl schools, residences, banks, and libraries both in southeastern Massachusetts and Maine done as part of Clough's private practice; also the plans for his most important Boston municipal commission, the English High School. Stored off-site in 20 rolls; catalog in process.

CLOUGH-LEIGHTER, HENRY

DC —LIBRARY OF CONGRESS, Music Division, Washington, 20540.
Notes: The business papers and music mss of the Arthur P Schmidt Company. Numerous works by important composers.

CLOUSER, JAMES

KS —WICHITA PUBLIC LIBRARY, Art & Music Division, 223 S Main, Wichita, 67202. Leonard Messineo, Jr, Head, Art & Music Division; Deborah Hamilton, Special Collections Librn
Holdings: Uncat Audiotapes Videotape Pix
Notes: Alice Bauman Dance Symposia Collection. Contains 300 hours of audio tapes, 1 hour-long video tape, several hundred photographs, and fugitive material of the American Dance Symposia held in Wichita from 1968-1972. The symposia covered all dance idioms-ballet, modern, jazz, folk, ethnic, dance education and therapy-and featured such notable figures such as Leonide Massine, Martha Hill, William Christensen, Alfonso Cimber, Toni Intravaia, James Clouser, Eleo Pomare, Juana de Laban, and many others. Characterized by the *Kansas City Star* as the "most distinguished faculties of fine artists ever assembled in the contemporary world of dance."

CLOWNS AND CLOWNING

NY —NEW YORK PUBLIC LIBRARY, Performing Arts Research Center, Billy Rose Theatre Collection, 111 Amsterdam Ave, New York, 10023. Dorothy L Swerdlove, Cur
Holdings: Cat
Notes: The collection incl the Townsend Walsh Collection, a rare assembling of 19th and early 20th century circus material--route books, programs, posters--mostly on the circus in the US and Great Britain, but with extensive material on European circus--19th-20th centuries.

†NY —NEW YORK SCHOOL FOR CIRCUS ARTS (BIG APPLE CIRCUS), 1230 Fifth Ave, New York, 10029.

WI —CIRCUS WORLD MUSEUM LIBRARY, 415 Lynn St, Baraboo, 53913. Robert L Parkinson, Research Center Dir
Holdings: Vols (1800) Cat Mss Pix Slides Phonorecords 16mm Films
Notes: Circus and "Wild West" shows. Owned by State Historical Society of Wisconsin. Incl 1800 books on circus subject; 400 route books; 1200 programs, 8000 circus lithographs, 20,000 photo negatives, 50,000 photo prints, heralds, couriers, tickets, letterheads, route cards, original circus artwork, records and documents of circus business, movies, newspaper ads, cirucs band music and periodicals of show business such as *Billboard, New York Clipper, White Tops,* Bandwagon, etc. Partially cataloged.

CLUBS AND CLUB LIFE

NY —UNIVERSITY CLUB, Library, One W 54 St, New York, 10019. Guy St Clair, Library Dir
Holdings: Vols (100,000) Cat Mss Maps Pix
Notes: A private library for the members of the University Club, their guests, and serious scholars upon written application to the Library Director. Holds extensive files on club history, incl the University Club archives.

CLUNIAC ARCHITECTURE see Architecture, Cluniac

CLUNIAC ART see Art, Cluniac

CLUNY, ABBEY OF

MA —HARVARD UNIVERSITY, Graduate School of Design, Frances Loeb Library, Gund Hall, Cambridge, 02138. James Hodgson, Librn
Holdings: Cat Mss Pix
Notes: Materials deposited by Professor Kenneth J Conant, who was in charge of archaeological excavations at Cluny.

COACH HOUSE PRESS

AB —UNIVERSITY OF CALGARY, Libraries, Special Collections Div, 2500 University Dr, Calgary, T2N 1N4, Can.
Holdings: Mss
Notes: Photolithographic production materials, postcards, posters, mss (40 meters), correspondence and administrative records. Incl correspondence of Stan Bevington and Victor Coleman, 1965-75.

COACHES see Carriages and Carts

COAL

DE —HAGLEY MUSEUM AND LIBRARY, Eleutherian Mills-Hagley Foundation Inc, PO Box 3630, Greenville, 19807. Richmond D Williams, Dir; Heddy A Richter, Imprints Librn
Notes: Westmoreland Coal Company records (1854-1982; 350 cubic feet) document the history of the nation's oldest bituminous coal mining company which operated in the Connellsville, Pa area (1880-89) and southern West Virginia (1906-56). Penn Virginia Corporation records (1864-1970; 120 cubic feet) document the history of one of Virginia's most significant coal mining companies. Also, Saint Clair Coal Company (1895-1930; 15 cubic feet). Records document the history of an important Schuylkill County, Pa anthracite coal producer. The colleciton incl minute books, financial records and photographs.

DC —COMMISSION OF THE EUROPEAN COMMUNITIES, European Community Information Service Library, 2100 M St NW Suite 707, Washington, 20037. Barbara Sloan, Head of Public Inquiries
Holdings: Vols (35,000) Cat Maps Pix Microforms
Notes: Library contains all of the official documents and occasional publications of the Institutions of the European Communities: ie, European Economic Community (Common Market), European Atomic Energy Community (Euratom), European Coal and Steel Community (ECSC). It collects non-Community publications about European integration, international trade and monetary affairs. Also has the publications of the General Agreements for Tariffs and Trade (GATT), Western European Union, and Council of Europe. Also, 1000 vertical files.

IL —ARGONNE NATIONAL LABORATORY, Chemical Engineering Branch Library, 9700 S Cass Ave, Argonne, 60439. John P Frazier III, Librn
Notes: Coal utilization. Incl 9000 vols monographs, 115 current journals, substantial collection of scientific and technical reports. Materials may be used by the public in the library by prior arrangement. Photocopies may be supplied for interlibrary loan, for which a processing and handling charge is made.

IL —ILLINOIS STATE GEOLOGICAL SURVEY, Library, 615 E Peabody, Champaign, 61820. Mary Krick, Geological Librn

KY —UNIVERSITY OF KENTUCKY COMMUNITY COLLEGES, Southeast Community College, Library, Learning Resource Center, Cumberland, 40823. Parker Boggs, Dir
Holdings: Vols (500) Cat Mss Maps Pix Slides Audiotapes Videotapes 16mm Films Filmstrips Microforms
Notes: Coal, coal mining and processing (not limited to southern Appalachia).

†PA —GILBERT ASSOCIATES, Library Information Services, PO Box 1498, Reading, 19603. Debra Bosler, Supervisor
Notes: Energy conversion technology. Many government technical reports are received regularly, particularly those on fossil fuel technology.

PA —PENNSYLVANIA STATE UNIVERSITY, Earth & Mineral Sciences Library, 105 Deike Bldg, University Park, 16802. Emilie McWilliams, Head Librn
Holdings: Vols (58,000) Cat Maps Microforms
Budget: ($49,750)
Notes: This collection includes substantial numbers of geological maps, and strong periodical holdings including microform.

VA —UNIVERSITY OF VIRGINIA, Alderman Library, Manuscripts Dept, Charlottesville, 22901. Edmund Berkeley Jr, Cur
Holdings: Cat Mss
Notes: Papers, 1901-1934, of the Borderland Coal Company, a Mingo County, West Virginia and Pike County, Kentucky bituminous porducer.

COAL—COMBUSTION see Combustion

COAL—HISTORY

DE —HAGLEY MUSEUM AND LIBRARY, Eleutherian Mills-Hagley Foundation Inc, PO Box 3630, Greenville, 19807. Richmond D Williams, Dir; Heddy A Richter, Imprints Librn
Notes: Westmoreland Coal Company records (1854-1982; 350 cubic feet) document the history of the nation's oldest bituminous coal mining company which operated in the Connellsville, Pa area (1880-89) and southern West Virginia (1906-56). Penn Virginia Corporation records (1864-1970; 120 cubic feet) document the history of one of Virginia's most significant coal mining companies. Also, Saint Clair Coal Company (1895-1930; 15 cubic feet). Records document the history of an important Schuylkill County, Pa anthracite coal producer. The colleciton incl minute books, financial records and photographs.

IN —PURDUE UNIVERSITY LIBRARIES, Graduate School of Management, Krannert Library, West Lafayette, 47907. Gordon Law, Librn
Notes: An important resource at the Krannert Library is its Special Collection of Business and Economics, consisting of some 8000 rare pre-20th century strengths in books, journals, tracts and pamphlets covering primarily the early literature of economic thought and business practices in America and abroad, 1500-1870. A catalog was issued in 1979.

COAL—TECHNOLOGY

IL —ARGONNE NATIONAL LABORATORY, Chemical Engineering Branch Library, 9700 S Cass Ave, Argonne, 60439. John P Frazier III, Librn
Notes: Coal utilization. Incl 9000 vols monographs, 115 current journals, substantial collection of scientific and technical reports. Materials may be used by the public in the library by prior arrangement. Photocopies may be supplied for interlibrary loan, for which a processing and handling charge is made.

TX —FLUOR ENGINEERS INC, Houston Library, 4620 N Braeswood, PO Box 35000, Houston, 77235. R S Holab-Abelman, Librn
Holdings: Vols (2500) Cat Maps
Budget: ($10,000)
Notes: Construction, environmental and chemical engineering, coal technology. Incl 2000 job books covering all areas of company interests.

COAL, ANTHRACITE

PA —SCRANTON PUBLIC LIBRARY, Local History & Genealogical Section, Vine St & Washington Ave, Scranton, 18503. Bettina Manzo, Librn
Holdings: Vols (2000) Cat Mss Maps Pix Microforms
Notes: Emphasis on northeastern Pennsylvania. Also, historical materials about local churches, schools, businesses, architecture, clubs and organizations, demographics, geography and geology, and biographies.

COAL, BITUMINOUS see Coal

COAL GASIFICATION

TX —MCDERMOTT HUDSON ENGINEERING, Library, 5900 Hillcroft, Houston, 77036. Chris Ramirez, Librn
Holdings: Vols (750) Uncat Microforms
Notes: Emphasis is on all forms of alternative energy sources and energy conversion.

COAL MINES AND MINING

AL —BIRMINGHAM PUBLIC LIBRARY, Dept of Archives & Mss, 2020 Seventh Ave N, Birmingham, 35203. Marvin Y Whiting, Archivist & Cur
Holdings: Cat Docs Mss //
Notes: Business and personal papers of Harry Welles Coffin covering the period from 1878 to 1938 in Birmingham, Alabama. Coffin was a vice president of The Alabama Company, a coal mining and iron products manufacturing firm. The business records incl correspondence, reports, financial records, and other documents relating to iron, steel, and coal industries in North Central Alabama. The personal papers mainly consist of love letters from Coffin to Minnie Everist Smith. These and other letters describe life on Birmingham's Southside area from 1885-1938. Papers of Joseph Squire, a mining engineer and geologist active in Shelby and Jefferson counties in Alabama from 1859 until his death in 1911. Though the collection spans the years 1873-1898, its bulk is business correspondence, 1888-1889, concerning purchase of coal lands for businessmen in Shelby County.

IN —INDIANA UNIVERSITY, Lilly Library, Seventh St, Bloomington, 47405. William R Cagle, Librn
Holdings: // Mss
Notes: Business papers and records of Indiana Cotton Mills, 1850-1947. Incl letterpress books, journals, consignment records, financial records, stock ledgers, as well as some records for the Cannelton Cotton Manufacturing Co, 1865-1867, and for D Newcomb & Co, a coal mining firm in Newburgh, Indiana, 1870-1875. 18,360 items. A related collection is that of Hamilton Smith's papers, 1823-1874. Smith (1804-1875) was a Louisville, Kentucky, lawyer and businessman involved in the organization and operation of the Cannelton Cotton Mill in 1848 until its sale to Indiana Cotton Mills in 1853.

KY —UNIVERSITY OF KENTUCKY COMMUNITY COLLEGES, Southeast Community College, Library, Learning Resource Center, Cumberland, 40823. Parker Boggs, Dir
Holdings: Vols (500) Cat Mss Maps Pix Slides Audiotapes Videotapes 16mm Films Filmstrips Microforms
Notes: Coal, coal mining and processing (not limited to southern Appalachia).

MI —MUSEUM OF THE GREAT LAKES, Bay County Historical Society, Library, 1700

COAL MINES AND MINING (cont.)

Center Ave, Bay City, 48706. Eurdine Ringwelski, Librn
Holdings: Vols (800) Cat Mss Maps Pix Slides 16mm Films
Notes: Focuses on man's relationship to his environment in the Great Lakes region in an historical perspective. Incl books, mss, photos, maps, vertical files, and scrapbooks on the history of Bay County and the Saginaw Valley, Michigan.

PA —SCRANTON PUBLIC LIBRARY, Local History & Genealogical Section, Vine St & Washington Ave, Scranton, 18503. Bettina Manzo, Librn
Holdings: Vols (2000) Cat Mss Maps Pix Microforms
Notes: Emphasis on northeastern Pennsylvania. Also, historical materials about local churches, schools, businesses, architecture, clubs and organizations, demographics, geography and geology, and biographies.

VA —UNIVERSITY OF VIRGINIA, Alderman Library, Manuscripts Dept, Charlottesville, 22901. Edmund Berkeley Jr, Cur
Holdings: Cat Mss
Notes: Papers, 1901-1934, of the Borderland Coal Company, a Mingo County, West Virginia and Pike County, Kentucky bituminous porducer.

WA —WESTERN WASHINGTON UNIVERSITY, Center for Pacific Northwest Studies, High St, Bellingham, 98225. James W Scott, Dir
Holdings: Mss Pix Videotapes
Notes: The Galen A Biery Collection. One of the historians. Incl in the collection are the copy books of the Sehome Coal Co which flourished in the 1870s and 1880s, and a variety of business records of the Pacific American Fisheries Co.
See also entry under Archie W Shiels

COAL OIL see Petroleum

COAL TAR INDUSTRY

PA —CARNEGIE LIBRARY OF PITTSBURGH, Science & Technology Dept, 4400 Forbes Ave, Pittsburgh, 15213. Catherine M Brosky, Dept Head
Notes: General information acquired in various subject areas especially those relating to iron and steel and other metals, rubber, leather, pulp and paper, textiles, glass, petroleum and coal tar by-products, lumber, plastics, etc.
See also entry under Science

COALITION AGAINST THE SST

MA —MASSACHUSETTS INSTITUTE OF TECHNOLOGY, Institute Archives, Special Collections, Cambridge, 02139.
Notes: Correspondence, newsletters, fact-sheets, newspaper and magazine articles, books and reports of the Citizens' League Against the Sonic Boom, established in 1967 by William Shurcliff to oppose the sonic boom, stop commercial supersonic transport production, and influence public opinion and policy decisions on the SST. Major correspondents incl Bo Lundberg, Richard Wiggs, several US congressmen, and CLASB members.

COAN, CARL, 1911-1976

DC —GEORGETOWN UNIVERSITY, Library, Special Collections Div, 37 & O Sts NW, Washington, 20057. George M Barringer, Special Collections Librn; Nicholas B Sheetz, Mss Librn
Holdings: Mss Pix
Notes: Collection of personal and professional papers, mss, and related items concerning housing and urban affairs. Carl Coan (1911-1976) served as staff director of the Senate Subcommittee on Housing and Urban Affairs from 1961-1976. Supplemented by related documents received since 1977.

COAST CHANGES

FL —UNIVERSITY OF FLORIDA, Coastal Engineering Archives, 433 Weil Hall, Gainesville, 32611. Lucile Lehmann, Librn
Holdings: Cat Maps Pix Slides
Budget: ($4000)
Notes: 7000 technical reports, in addition to maps, pictures, aerial photographs, 400 hydrographic surveys, etc. The Archives is not part of the University library system but is a special collection of the Coastal and Oceanographic Engineering Dept.

COAST DEFENSES

MD —US NAVAL ACADEMY, Nimitz Library, Annapolis, 21402. Alice S Creighton, Assistant Librn for Special Collections
Holdings: Mss
Notes: The William Adger Moffett Papers are a collection of official and personal letters, speeches, news releases, communications, memoranda, notes, news clippings, etc, by and about Rear Admiral William Adger Moffett, first Chief of the Bureau of Aeronautics, US Navy. The collection is a primary source for any research regarding the early history of naval aviation. Papers relate to numerous topics, including the London Naval Treaty and its ramifications, military airships, United Air Service controversy, coastal defense, carriers, etc. Index available in Special Collections Department.

OR —ASTORIA PUBLIC LIBRARY, Astor Library, 450 Tenth St, Astoria, 97103. Bruce Berney, Dir
Holdings: Vols 500 Cat Pix Audiotapes Microforms Newspapers
Budget: $300
Notes: History of Lower Columbia River area. Incl file of local newspapers, 1873 to date. 1,000 photographs of Fort Stevens and other coastal defense facilities.

COAST PROTECTION see Shore Protection

COASTAL ENGINEERING

MS —US ARMY ENGINEER WATERWAYS EXPERIMENT STATION, Library Branch, PO Box 631, Vicksburg, 39180. Bernice Black, Chief Librn
Holdings: Vols (350,000) Cat Mss Maps Microforms

ON —NATIONAL RESEARCH COUNCIL OF CANADA, Aeronautical/Mechanical Engineering Branch Library, Montreal Rd, Ottawa, K1A 0R6, Can. Louise Fletcher, Head
Notes: This branch library of the Canada Institute for Scientific and Technical Information (CISTI) of the National Research Council of Canada, Ottawa, has a collection strong in aeronautical engineering, automatic control, CAD/CAM, robotics, ocean, wind, and solar energy power, hydraulic and coastal engineering, icing, low temperature research, naval engineering, metals and metallurgy, incl composites, tribology, and air, railroad, marine transportation. Library supported the Council contribution to the development of the remote manipular Canadarm for NASA's Space Shuttle Orbiters and more recently, the Canadian Astronaut Program which will contribute payload specialists to NASA's Space Shuttle Program in 1984. 35, 000 monographs, 1200 serials. Report collection: over 500,000 items.

COASTS

CA —ASSOCIATION OF BAY AREA GOVERNMENTS, MTC/ABAG Library, 101 Eighth St, Oakland, 94607. Diane Gillman, Information Coord
Notes: Concentrates heavily on the nine-county Bay Area region. About 10,000 monographs and serials. Title catalog, OCLC/ATS. Central collection of documents for six transit properties in Bay Area.

FL —UNIVERSITY OF FLORIDA, Coastal Engineering Archives, 433 Weil Hall, Gainesville, 32611. Lucile Lehmann, Librn
Holdings: Cat Maps Pix Slides
Budget: ($4000)
Notes: 7000 technical reports, in addition to maps, pictures, aerial photographs, 400 hydrographic surveys, etc. The Archives is not part of the University library system but is a special collection of the Coastal and Oceanographic Engineering Dept.

FL —US NAVAL COASTAL SYSTEMS CENTER, Technical Information Service Branch, Panama City, 32407. Myrtle J Rhodes, Librn
Holdings: Vols (30,000) Cat
Notes: Coastal and ocean technology, inshore undersea warfare, mine countermeasures, torpedo defense, underwater sound.

ME —BIGELOW LABORATORY FOR OCEAN SCIENCES & MAINE DEPT OF MARINE RESOURCES, Library, McKown Point, West Boothbay Harbor, 04575. Pamela Shephard-Lupo, Librn
Holdings: Vols Cat Periodicals
Budget: ($55,000)
Notes: This library presently serves two institutions. The Maine Dept of Marine Resources has maintained the library since 1957 and thus the majority of our holdings are geared to their needs, ie fish biology and stock assessment on a local, national and international level. In 1973 Bigelow Laboratory for Ocean Sciences came to West Boothbay Harbor and began to contribute to the library with a very specialized collection on the Gulf of Maine marine chemistry, phytoplankton and nutrient cycles.

NY —NEW YORK STATE DEPT OF STATE, Community Affairs Library, 162 Washington Ave, Albany, 12231. M L Johnson, Librn
Holdings: Vols (14,640) Cat
Notes: Local government. Serves as research arm for official activities. 16,000 items in vertical files; 150 periodicals. Unique Community File collection of about 1600 local governments arranged by counties in the state.

NS —CANADIAN COAST GUARD COLLEGE, Library, PO Box 4500, Sydney, B1P 6L1, Can. David MacSween, Librn
Notes: Navigation.

ON —INTERNATIONAL JOINT COMMISSION LIBRARY, 100 Ouellette Ave, Seventh Floor, Windsor, N9A 6T3, Can. Pat Murrary, Librn
Notes: Emphasis on water resources, water quality, land use, coastal zones, Great Lakes. Library includes 40,000 government reports from federal, provincial and state governments; 5000 monographs to support Great Lakes Water Quality Agreement Community. Collection also includes 243 periodicals, 1700 microfiche, 800 slides & vertical files.

COAT OF ARMS see Heraldry

COATING COMPOSITIONS see Protective Coatings

COATINGS

SC —SONOCO PRODUCTS CO, Research Laboratory, Technical Information Center, One N Second St, Hartsville, 29550. Ken Chavis, Dir
Holdings: Vols (4000) Cat Mss Slides Microforms
Notes: Restricted to Sonoco employees. No photocopying.

COATINGS, PROTECTIVE see Protective Coatings

COATSWORTH, ELIZABETH JANE, 1893-

ME —BOWDOIN COLLEGE, Library, Brunswick, 04011. Dianne M Gutscher, Cur of Special Collections
Holdings: Vols 150 Cat Mss Pix
Notes: Beston Family Papers. The Beston

COATSWORTH, ELIZABETH JANE, 1893- (cont.)

Collection contains printed works, mss (10, 000), correspondence and ephemera relating to the late Henry Beston and his wife Elizabeth Coatsworth Beston of Chimney Farm, Nobleboro, Maine. Mrs Beston is a widely known author of children's books.

COBBETT, WILLIAM, 1763-1835

CT —TRINITY COLLEGE LIBRARY, Watkinson Library, 300 Summit St, Hartford, 06106. Jeffrey Kaimowitz, Cur
Holdings: // Cat

NY —FORDHAM UNIVERSITY LIBRARY, Bronx, 10458. Joseph A LoSchiavo, Reference Librn
Holdings: Vols 81 Cat Mss
Notes: The collection covers the years 1763-1835. No photocopying.

NY —ADELPHI UNIVERSITY, Library, Garden City, 11530. Jerome Yavarkovsky, Dean of Libraries
Holdings: Vols 400 Cat Mss Maps Pix
Notes: Incl Cobbett-Hunt correspondence. Bibliography: The William Cobbett Collection at Adelphi University by Donald V L Kelly, (Garden City, NY: Adelphi University Libraries, 1982).

COBLENTZ, STANTON

MA —BOSTON UNIVERSITY, Mugar Memorial Library, Special Collections Dept, 771 Commonwealth Ave, Boston, 02215. Howard B Gotlieb, Dir
Holdings: Cat Mss
Notes: Mss, correspondence, etc collected in depth; incl publications by or about.

COBURN, CHARLES

GA —UNIVERSITY OF GEORGIA, Libraries, Special Collections Division, Athens, 30602. Vesta Lee Gordon, Asst Dir for Special Collections
Notes: Theater Collection contains the Paris Music Hall set and costume designs with original drawings by Erte, Barbier, Zig and others; British Music Hall Papers; European toy theater collection; Charles Coburn papers; television script collection; Tennessee Williams papers. Collection contains 16,000 pieces.

COBURN, WALT

AZ —UNIVERSITY OF ARIZONA, Library, Tucson, 85721. W David Laird, Librn
Notes: The Walt Coburn Collection, incl the author's published stories and books, notebooks, correspondence, photographs, scrapbooks, and ephemera. Coburn was known as "King of the Western Pulps" who wrote from 1922 to 1973.

COCAINE AND COCA

CA —FITZ HUGH LUDLOW MEMORIAL LIBRARY, PO Box 99346, San Francisco, 94109. Michael R Aldrich, Exec Cur
Holdings: Vols (200)
Notes: Collection stored. Important mail inquiries only. No interlibrary lending or telephone queries. In addition to about 200 vols, we have a large collection of offprints and photocopies of articles about Coca and Cocaine. Many illustrations and art work.

COCCIA, JOE

TX —NORTH TEXAS STATE UNIVERSITY, Audio Center, Box 5188, NT Station, Denton, 76203. Morris Martin, Music Librn
Notes: More than 1600 manuscript jazz compositions, (incl scores and parts, alternate versions, expanded arrangements) by Stan Kenton, Johnny Richards, Joe Coccia, Lennie Niehaus, Pete Rugolo, Willie Maiden, Bob Curnow, Ken Hanna, Gene Rowland, Bob Graettinger and others, used by the Stan Kenton Band and given to North Texas State University in 1962 and at Kenton's death in 1979. Unpublished catalog: Breeden, Leon, *Stan Kenton Music in the NTSU Jazz Studies Library and the NTSU Music Library*, Denton, 1983 (99 pages).

COCHLEUS, JOHANN

CA —STANFORD UNIVERSITY LIBRARIES, Cecil H Green Library, Stanford, 94305. Peter R Frank, Cur, CDP-Germanic Collection
Notes: Extensive holdings in the field of Reformation and Counter-Reformation. First and early editions by Luther, Melanchthon, Bugenhagen, Cochleus, Eck, Hutten, Reuchlin, and minor figures in Special Collections.

COCHRAN, BURKE

DC —GEORGETOWN UNIVERSITY, Library, Special Collections Div, 37 & O Sts NW, Washington, 20057. George M Barringer, Special Collections Librn; Nicholas B Sheetz, Mss Librn
Holdings: Mss Cat Pix
Notes: The papers of the Irish man-of-letters Sir Shane Leslie (1885-1971) containing letters, mss, diaries, notebooks, clippings, and photographs. Extensive correspondence by Margot Asquith, countess of Oxford and Asquith; Lady Violet Bonham-Carter; Burke Cochran; Lord Alfred Douglas; Moreton Frewen; Cardinal Gasquet; Vyvyan Holland; Lady Leonie Leslie; Sir Wilfrid Meynell; Sir Horace Plunkett; John Quinn; Frederick Rolfe (Baron Corvo); and Elizabeth Russell, among others. Also incl are research files on Sir Winston Churchill (Leslie's first cousin); Leonard Jerome; Maria Anne Fitzherbet (wife of King George IV); Ghosts and Ghost stories; and Eton College.

COCKE FAMILY

VA —UNIVERSITY OF VIRGINIA, Alderman Library, Manuscripts Dept, Charlottesville, 22901. Edmund Berkeley Jr, Cur
Holdings: Cat Mss Maps Pix
Notes: 19th century Virginia Family Papers Collections enable a researcher to obtain an excellent picture of the economic and social interactions on large plantations in Virginia during the 19th century. They are invaluable as research sources in the study of slavery, women's history, economic history, agrarian and political history.

COCKERELL, DOUGLAS

NS —DALHOUSIE UNIVERSITY LIBRARY, Halifax, B3H 4H8, Can.
Notes: The Cockerell Collection of Fine Bindings is a representative collection of fine bindings from the 15th to 19th century assembled by Douglas Cockerell, famous English bookbinder. Most of the bindings are done in calf, but there are also examples of morroco, pigskin, sheepskin, vellum and fishskin. English, Scottish, French and Italian designs are represented; ornamentation is by blind and gold tooling, and with wrought silver or brass clasps and decorations. Restricted to reference use.

COCKTAIL LOUNGES see Hotels, Taverns, Etc.; Restaurants, Lunch Rooms, Bars, Etc.

COCOA

IN —HURTY-PECK LIBRARY OF BEVERAGE LITERATURE, 5650 W Raymond Street, PO Box 41167, Indianapolis, 46208. Ben Wilson, Librn
Holdings: Vols (6000) Cat //
Notes: The most comprehensive collection, in English, in the world on beverages of all types. History, manufacture, formulae, customs. Books on beer and brewing; cocoa and chocolate; coffee; liquors and spirits; soft drinks; tea; and wine.

NY —WESTRECO INC, Research Library, 555 S Fourth St, Fulton, 13069. Janice Burns, Research Librn
Holdings: Vols 30 Cat Periodicals VF
Notes: Food Science and Technology collection of about (1200) books and pamphlets. Back files of periodicals retained up to 20 years.
See also entry under CHOCOLATE

COCTEAU, JEAN

NY —COLUMBIA UNIVERSITY LIBRARIES, Rare Book & Manuscript Library, 801 Butler Library, 535 W 114 St, New York, 10027. Kenneth A Lohf, Librn
Holdings: Mss
Notes: Mss, letters, reviews, etc. Restricted use.

CODES, MUNICIPAL see Municipal Codes

CODES AND CIPHERS see Cryptography

CODICES see Manuscripts

CODMAN, OGDEN, JR.

MA —SOCIETY FOR THE PRESERVATION OF NEW ENGLAND ANTIQUITIES, Library, 141 Cambridge St, Boston, 02114. Ellie Reichlin, Librn & Cur of Photographic Collections
Notes: Drawings for his personal commissions which were mainly residential, and measured drawings of historic houses and their restoration in Massachusetts, Rhode Island, New York, and New Jersey. Strong back-up collection of Codman family papers and photographs. 2000 pieces.

CODMAN FAMILY

MA —SOCIETY FOR THE PRESERVATION OF NEW ENGLAND ANTIQUITIES, Library, 141 Cambridge St, Boston, 02114. Ellie Reichlin, Librn & Cur of Photographic Collections
Holdings: Vols (3000) Cat Pix Microforms
Budget: ($75,000)
Notes: Incl two types of mss: (1) Family papers relating to historic properties administered by SPNEA. Ca 125 linear feet, incl the Codman family archive, 1700s-1960s, with associated family photograph collection. (2) Misc mss with emphasis on topics relating to building, interior designs, material culture (ca 3500 items, cataloged). For further information, an *Annotated Checklist to Special Collections of SPNEA* Library is available. See also entry in *Architectural Records in Boston: A Guide to Architectural Research* (1983, Garland Publishing Co, New York). Additional collections incl prints, original artwork (largely by NE artists, engravers) relating to architectural subjects; maps; architectural periodicals (19th century).

CODY, 'BUFFALO BILL'

CO —DENVER PUBLIC LIBRARY, Western History Department, 1357 Broadway, Denver, 80203. Eleanor M Gehres, Head
Holdings: Cat Mss
Notes: Correspondence, scrapbooks, photographs, show posters, programs, route cards, and other Buffalo Bill's Wild West memorabilia.

COFFEE

IN —HURTY-PECK LIBRARY OF BEVERAGE LITERATURE, 5650 W Raymond Street, PO Box 41167, Indianapolis, 46208. Ben Wilson, Librn
Holdings: Vols (6000) Cat //
Notes: The most comprehensive collection, in English, in the world on beverages of all types. History, manufacture, formulae, customs. Books on beer and brewing; cocoa and chocolate; coffee; liquors and spirits; soft drinks; tea; and wine.

COFFIN, GEORGE Y.

DC —GEORGE WASHINGTON UNIVERSITY, Gelman Library, 2130 H St

COFFIN, GEORGE Y. (cont.)

NW, Washington, 20052.
Holdings: // Uncat Mss Pix
Notes: Original drawings of editorial and political cartoons by George Y Coffin, covering the period of ca 1884-1896. Coffin drew for *Puck, Harper's Weekly*, and other periodicals and was staff cartoonist for the Washington Post until 1895. The collection also includes Coffin's diaries, scrapbooks, and notebooks. Library also holds cartoons by Clifford Berryman (qv).

COFFIN, HARRY WELLES

AL —BIRMINGHAM PUBLIC LIBRARY, Dept of Archives & Mss, 2020 Seventh Ave N, Birmingham, 35203. Marvin Y Whiting, Archivist & Cur
Holdings: Cat Docs Mss //
Notes: Business and personal papers of Harry Welles Coffin covering the period from 1878 to 1938 in Birmingham, Alabama. Coffin was a vice president of The Alabama Company, a coal mining and iron products manufacturing firm. The business records incl correspondence, reports, financial records, and other documents relating to iron, steel, and coal industries in North Central Alabama. The personal papers mainly consist of love letters from Coffin to Minnie Everist Smith. These and other letters describe life on Birmingham's Southside area from 1885-1938.

COFFIN, ROBERT PETER TRISTRAM, 1892-1955

ME —BOWDOIN COLLEGE, Library, Brunswick, 04011. Dianne M Gutscher, Cur of Special Collections
Holdings: Vols Cat Mss Pix
Notes: The collection contains copies of most of Coffin's printed work, incl many presentation copies. A large group of manuscripts encompassing correspondence, first and early drafts, many of them heavily corrected, of his published writings, lecture notes on English courses. About 1100 items.

TX —TEXAS WOMAN'S UNIVERSITY, Bralley Memorial Library, Box 23715, TWU Sta, Denton, 76204. Metta Nicewarner, Spec Collections Libn
Notes: Autographs, inscriptions, and pen-and-ink drawings by Coffin.

COFFMAN, HAL

TX —FORT WORTH PUBLIC LIBRARY, Arts Division, 300 Taylor St, Fort Worth, 76102. Heather Gobel, Head
Holdings: Uncat
Notes: Original cartoon art. Emphasis is on editorial, political, historical events cartoons. Nucleus collection comprised of original Hal Coffman cartoons rendered for the editorial pages of the *Fort Worth Star-Telegram* from October 10, 1939, until his death on August 31, 1958. 4575 pieces.

COHALAN, DANIEL F.

NY —AMERICAN IRISH HISTORICAL SOCIETY, Library, 991 Fifth Ave, New York, 10028. Lisa M Hottin, Cur; William D Griffin, Libn
Holdings: Vols (20,000) Cat Maps Pix Slides
Notes: Archives and Manuscripts: The documents and papers of Friends of Irish Freedom, The Land League, the Society of the Friendly Sons of St Patrick, the Catholic Club, and the Guild of Catholic Lawyers. The papers of New York State Supreme Court Justice Daniel F Cohalan. This is the largest and most complete collection of over 20,000 American Irish and Irish history, biography and literature in the United States. Incl American-Irish Newspaper collections dating from 1811, the most comprehensive in the US; 1000 rare books and special editions. Special collections incl regular exhibits of Irish or American Irish interest incl mss, letters, books, photographs and memorabilia. Permanent collection of representative works of Irish painters.

COHAN, GEORGE M.

NY —HAMPDEN-BOOTH THEATRE LIBRARY AT THE PLAYERS, 16 Gramercy Park, New York, 10003. Louis A Rachow, Librn/Cur
Holdings: Cat Mss Pix
Notes: The George M Cohan Collection, incl 16 bound typescripts, etc.

NY —NEW YORK PUBLIC LIBRARY, Performing Arts Research Center, Billy Rose Theatre Collection, 111 Amsterdam Ave, New York, 10023. Dorothy L Swerdlove, Cur
Holdings: Cat Mss Pix
Notes: Papers, scrapbooks, mss, photographs, memorabilia, etc.

COHELAN, JEFFERY

OK —UNIVERSITY OF OKLAHOMA, Bizzell Memorial Library, Western History Collections, 401 W Brooks, Norman, 73069. John Ezell, Cur
Holdings: Mss Documents Pix
Notes: US Representative. His papers.

COHEN, ALEXANDER H.

NY —NEW YORK PUBLIC LIBRARY, Performing Arts Research Center, Billy Rose Theatre Collection, 111 Amsterdam Ave, New York, 10023. Dorothy L Swerdlove, Cur
Holdings: Cat Mss Pix
Notes: Papers, scrapbooks, mss, photographs, memorabilia, etc.

COHEN, HETTIE

IN —INDIANA UNIVERSITY, Lilly Library, Seventh St, Bloomington, 47405. William R Cagle, Librn
Holdings: // Cat Mss
Notes: Editorial office records for *Yugen*, 1958-1961, and for *The Floating Bear*, 1961. Incl correspondence of Leroi Jones, Hettie Cohen and Diane DiPrima with various authors and some mss and proofs of items published by Totem Press. Also typescripts with autograph changes and corrections of Jones' *The Baptism* and *Dutchman*, as well as galleys and manuscript for his *Preface to a Twenty Volume Suicide Note*. 572 items. Incl first editions of Jones and most issues of *Yugen* and *Floating Bear*.

COHEN, JERRY

CA —UNIVERSITY OF CALIFORNIA, LOS ANGELES, Theater Arts Library, Los Angeles, 90024. Edward Shreeves, Chairman, Bibliographers Group; Audree Malkin, Head, Theater Arts Library
Notes: Jerry Cohen Collection: several hundred portraits, scrapbooks, and clippings from the stage and silent films; primarily of the 1920's and 1930's.

COHEN, MATT, 1942-

ON —MCMASTER UNIVERSITY, Mills Memorial Library, Div of Archives & Research Collections, Hamilton, L8S 4L6, Can. G R Hill, Univ Librn
Holdings: // Mss
Notes: Ms drafts, proof copies, and correspondence relating to books of poetry and prose.

COHEN, ROBERT

MO —WASHINGTON UNIVERSITY, Libraries, Special Collections Dept, Campus Box 1061, St Louis, 63130.
Notes: A small but significant collection.

COHOS EVAMY AND PARTNERS

AB —UNIVERSITY OF CALGARY, Libraries, Special Collections Div, 2500 University Dr, Calgary, T2N 1N4, Can.
Holdings: Cat Pix
Notes: 12,366 pictures. Collection consists of original drawings for projects in the Calgary-Southern Alberta region; predominantly apartment buildings, but also representative of all other building types. Examples are: St Luke's Roman Catholic Church, Brenwood Junior High School, Happy Valley Ski Lodge, Father Lacombe Nursing Home, Banff School of Fine Arts residences, and the University of Calgary's Nickle Arts Museum. Inventories and Quick Lists are available.

COINS

CO —AMERICAN NUMISMATIC ASSOCIATION LIBRARY, 818 N Cascade Ave, Colorado Springs, 80903. Nancy W Green, Librn
Holdings: Vols (20,000) Cat Slides
Notes: One of the largest numismatic libraries, the collection incl books, periodicals and auction catalogs on coins and coin collecting, medals, tokens, military orders and decorations, paper money, primitive money, banks and banking, seals and scarabs. ANA publishes a classified subject catalog of its collection and is open to the public for research and reference services. Only members may check books out.

CT —YALE UNIVERSITY, Beinecke Rare Book & Manuscript Library, Osborn Collection, New Haven, 06520. Stephen R Parks, Cur
Holdings: Mss

NY —AMERICAN NUMISMATIC SOCIETY LIBRARY, Broadway between 155 & 156 Sts, New York, 10032. Francis D Campbell Jr, Chief Librn
Holdings: Vols (50,000) Cat Mss Maps Pix Slides 16mm Films Microforms
Budget: ($6000)
Notes: Incl materials devoted to coins, medals, decorations, orders, tokens, paper money, seals, heraldry. Aids materials incl history, economic history, art history, archaeology, inscriptions and a number of encyclopedias and biographical dictionaries. Dictionary card catalog provides access to the materials: *Dictionary Catalogue of the Library of the American Numismatic* Society. (Boston: G K Hall, 1962). 6 vols and vol listing the auction catalogs in our collection; *First Supplement: 1962-1967; Second Supplement: 1968-1972; Third Supplement: 1973-1977* (Boston: G K Hall, 1967, 1973, 1978). Noncirculating.

COKER, WILLIAM C.

†NC —UNIVERSITY OF NORTH CAROLINA, CHAPEL HILL, Department of Botany Library, 301 Coker Hall 010-A, Chapel Hill, 27514. William R Burk, Botany Librn
Notes: The mycology collection incl some 6000 pamphlets. It contains papers of the following scientists: William C Coker, John N Couch, Lindsay F Olive, mycologists; also, Victor A Greulach, plant pathologist. The mycology catalog is in preparation (1983), and will provide author, title, and subject access.

COLBERT, RICHARD G.

RI —US NAVAL WAR COLLEGE, Historical Collection & Museum, Newport, 02841. Anthony S Nicolosi, Dir; Evelyn Cherpak, Cur
Holdings: Mss
Notes: The Richard G Colbert collection consists of official, personal and foreign officer correspondence, speeches and writings and subject files on various naval and international topics. Adm Colbert was president of the Naval War College, 1968-1971 and Commander in Chief of the Allied Forces, Southern Europe, 1972. The collection is valuable to researchers for materials on NATO, the Naval War College and cooperation with allied and friendly navies.

COLD

CA —UNIVERSITY OF CALIFORNIA, DAVIS, Physical Sciences Library, Davis,

COLD (cont.)

95616. Scott Kennedy, Head
Holdings: Vols (170,000) Cat VF
Notes: Collection covers aeronautical, agricultural, chemical, civil, electrical, mechanical, water science, hydrology, nuclear reactor, extensive cold regions collection in vertical file drawers, and computer science engineering academic programs. Good strength in journal runs.

NH —US ARMY COLD REGIONS RESEARCH AND ENGINEERING LABORATORY, 72 Lyme Road, Hanover, 03755. Nancy Liston, Librn
Holdings: Cat Maps Microforms
Notes: The primary material consists of reports, documents, journal articles, cited in the library's "Bibliography on Cold Regions Science and Technology." About one third of the items cited in vols 1-22 are on microfilm or in report or reprint form; beginning with vol 23, all items are microfiched and sent to the library, which now has over 55,000 items on microfiche. These are indexed by author and subject in the annual volume of the Bibliography.

COLE, JOSEPHINE

CO —UNIVERSITY OF COLORADO, Libraries, Special Collections, Boulder, 80309. Nora J Quinlan, Head
Holdings: Cat Mss
Notes: Incl 78 Anne Ellis letters, 31 Josephine Cole letters, 9 miscellaneous letters and 6 Anne Ellis mss.

COLE, STERLING, 1904-

NY —CORNELL UNIVERSITY LIBRARIES, Collection of Regional History, Dept of Manuscripts and Univ Archives, Ithaca, 14853.
Notes: NY Congressman, 1935-52. Incl papers, ca 1935- ca 1957; letters from constituents, newspaper clippings, pamphlets, campaign materials, voters' lists, newsletters and farm accounts.

COLE, TOBY

CA —UNIVERSITY OF CALIFORNIA, DAVIS, Shields Library, Dept of Special Collections, Davis, 95616. Donald Kunitz, Head; C Danial Elliott, Asst Head
Holdings: Vols Uncat Mss Pix
Notes: Business papers of off-Broadway literary and theatrical agent, Toby Cole, for the years 1957-73. Incl mss by Saul Bellow and Sam Shepherd, among others. 4000 pix.

COLE FAMILY

CA —UNIVERSITY OF CALIFORNIA, LOS ANGELES, Research Library, Dept of Special Collections, 405 Hilgard Ave, Los Angeles, 90024. Edward Shreeves, Chairman, Bibliographers Group; David S Zeidberg, Head
Holdings: Cat Mss Pix
Notes: 28 linear feet of mss, correspondence, diaries, and ephemera concerning the public life of Senator Cornelius Cole (Calif) and members of his family.

COLEMAN, A. P.

ON —VICTORIA UNIVERSITY, Library, 71 Queen's Park Crescent, Toronto, M5S 1K7, Can. Robert C Brandeis, Chief Librn
Holdings: Vols 10 Cat Mss Pix
Notes: Field notebooks, diaries, mss, photographs, and watercolors of noted Canadian geologist Dr A P Coleman.

COLEMAN, ELLIOTT

MO —WASHINGTON UNIVERSITY, Libraries, Special Collections Dept, Campus Box 1061, St Louis, 63130.
Notes: A small but significant collection.

COLEMAN, FREDERICK W. B.

CA —HOOVER INSTITUTION ON WAR, REVOLUTION & PEACE, Stanford University, Stanford, 94305. Milorad M Drachkovitch, Archivist
Notes: Diaries (handwritten), 1909-1938, by Frederick W B Coleman, US diplomat, documenting his service in the US Army, 1917-19, and his diplomatic service as US Minister to Estonia, Latvia, and Lithuania, 1922-1931, and US Minister to Denmark, 1931-33. 1/2 ms box.

COLEMAN, HELENA

ON —VICTORIA UNIVERSITY, Library, 71 Queen's Park Crescent, Toronto, M5S 1K7, Can. Robert C Brandeis, Chief Librn
Notes: The collection is very strong in 19th-20th century poetry, drama and fiction; it contains gazetteers, travel books, biographies, and works on history and geography. Nucleus of collection listed in James, C C, *A Bibliography of Canadian Poetry (English)* (Victoria University Library Publication No 1, Toronto, 1899); and Horning, L E and Burpee, L J, *A Bibliography of Canadian Fiction (English)* (Victoria University Library Publication No 2, Toronto, 1904). Collection incl mss and vols by Canadian writers Helena Coleman, Raymond Knister, and Marjorie L C Pickthall and letters of Bliss Carman, and Duncan Campbell Scott.

COLEMAN, LONNIE

GA —UNIVERSITY OF GEORGIA, Libraries, Athens, 30602. Arlene E Luchsinger, Asst Dir Branch Libraries
Notes: His personal archive, incl mss, diaries, journals, correspondence, etc. Also, editions of his books and several foreign editions.

COLEMAN, RUFUS A., 1886-1975

BC —UNIVERSITY OF VICTORIA, McPherson Library, Victoria, V8W 3H5, Can.
Notes: Transcripts; doctoral dissertation (Boston University, 1937) John Townsend Trowbridge and research materials on Trowbridge incl photostats of correspondence from the Folger, Yale, Boston Public and Huntingdon Libraries, 1860-1907; correspondence, Trowbridge to Burroughs, 1874-1915; correspondence, Coleman to John Moore 1939-53 concerning Trowbridge; notebook, transcripts of publications; offprints of articles by Trowbridge 1939-1953; sketch of John Howard Payne from Macbeth production; playbills of Trowbridge's productions.

COLEMAN FAMILY

VA —COLLEGE OF WILLIAM AND MARY, Earl Gregg Swem Library, Williamsburg, 23185. Margaret C Cook, Cur of Manuscripts & Rare Books
Holdings: Vols 1500 Mss
Notes: Tucker-Coleman Papers (1675-1956): Family, literary, and business papers of the Tucker Family, particularly St George Tucker (1752-1827) and Nathaniel Beverley Tucker (1784-1851). This collection, which incl 600 Jefferson items, is particularly important for the study of Virginia social, economic, and political history during the period. Also, 30,000 ms items.

COLEOPTERA see Beetles

COLERIDGE, SAMUEL TAYLOR, 1772-1834

CA —CLAREMONT COLLEGES, Honnold Library, Ninth & Dartmouth, Claremont, 91711. Tania Rizzo, Special Collections Dept Head
Holdings: Vols 215 // Uncat
Notes: The Homer D Crotty Collection of first, limited, and special editions of books by and about Coleridge. Checklisted.

CT —YALE UNIVERSITY, Beinecke Rare Book & Manuscript Library, Osborn Collection, New Haven, 06520. Stephen R Parks, Cur
Holdings: Mss

IN —INDIANA UNIVERSITY, Lilly Library, Seventh St, Bloomington, 47405. William R Cagle, Librn
Holdings: Vols 330 Cat Mss
Notes: First editions, etc. Incl works about Coleridge.

IN —SAINT MARY-OF-THE-WOODS COLLEGE, College Library, Saint Mary-of-the-Woods, 47876. Sister Emily Walsh, SP, Administrator
Holdings: Vols 1000 Cat
Notes: Mainly first editions, critical works.

KY —UNIVERSITY OF KENTUCKY, Margaret I King Library, Dept of Special Collections, Lexington, 40506. William Marshall, Head
Holdings: Vols (8000) Cat Mss
Notes: W Hugh Peal Collection of mss and books chiefly relating to British and American literature. Particularly strong in Lamb, Wordsworth, Coleridge and Southey. Incl 4 cubic feet of mss. Incl 16th-20th centuries.

MA —HARVARD UNIVERSITY LIBRARY, Widener Library, Cambridge, 02138.
Holdings: Cat Mss
Notes: See *Harvard Library Notes, III* (1936), 132-135.

NC —DUKE UNIVERSITY, William R Perkins Library, Durham, 27706. Elvin E Strowd, University Librn
Notes: The Shelley-Goodwin Collection of Lord Abinger is a microfilm copy of the Shelley and Godwin collection. Lord Abinger's entire manuscript collection, representing the last portion of the papers of Sir Percy Florence Shelley which is still in private hands, has been reproduced on 16 reels of film. The Bodleian Library is the only other location for this film.

NC —DUKE UNIVERSITY, William R Perkins Library, Rare Book Room, Durham, 27706. John L Sharpe, III, Cur
Notes: Thomas J Wise collection. Many rare pieces, including works of Byron, Coleridge, Dryden, Pope and Hardy. 135 political and religious broadsides, mostly of the 17th century.

OH —OHIO UNIVERSITY, Vernon R Alden Library, Department of Archives and Special Collections, Athens, 45701. Gary A Hunt, Head
Holdings: Vols (10,191) Uncat Mss
Notes: The Edmund Blunden Collection of Romantic and Modern Literature, being the private library assembled by Blunden during 6 decades of active collecting. The bulk of the collection (6,264 titles) consists of English imprints from the period 1750-1850, concentrating on literature but also incl contemporary works on art, natural history, philosophy and other subjects important for understanding the background of English Romanticism. Among the authors most heavily represented by first and other early editions are: Allington, Barnes, Bloomfield, Byron, Clare, Coleridge, Cowper, Dyer, Edgeworth, Goldsmith, Hazlitt, Hunt, Lamb, Landor, Scott, Thompson and Wordsworth. Books written by Blunden himself, together with his Georgian contemporaries (particularly W H Davies, Walter De la Mare, and Sigfried Sassoon) form a second major area of strength. Many ofthe modern books are inscribed to Blunden, and nearly all the volumes in the collection bear his annotations.

WI —UNIVERSITY OF WISCONSIN, MADISON, Memorial Library, British & American Language & Literature Collection, 728 State St, Madison, 53706. Yvonne Schofer, Bibliographer
Holdings: Vols (1000)// Cat
Notes: Arthur Beatty Collection. Consists of over 1000 volumes, principally in the English poetry of the Romantic period, strong in Coleridge, Tennyson, Swinburne, the prose of De Quincy and the folk poetry and balladry of Great Britain and Europe. Outstanding for its first and other editions of Wordsworth. About 200 titles in the Department of Rare Books and Special Collections; the rest is in stacks.

ON —VICTORIA UNIVERSITY, Library, 71 Queen's Park Crescent, Toronto, M5S 1K7, Can. Robert C Brandeis, Chief Librn
Holdings: Vols 1100 Cat Mss
Notes: A significant collection (second only

COLERIDGE, SAMUEL TAYLOR, 1772-1834 (cont.)

to the British Museum) of books, mss, notebooks, correspondence, etc of Samuel Taylor Coleridge and his circle and family, including letters and mss of Wordsworth, Lamb and Southey. Catalog of collection by H O Dendurent in *The Wordsworth Circle* (Temple University, Philadelphia, Pa) 5:4 (Autumn 1974).

COLES, EDWARD

IL —CHICAGO HISTORICAL SOCIETY, Library, Clark St at North Ave, Chicago, 60614. Archie Motley, Manuscript Librn
Notes: Papers of Ninian Edwards and Edward Coles (Illinois Governors); Mason Brayman, attorney and Union Army officer.

COLETO, BATTLE OF, 19 MARCH 1836

TX —UNIVERSITY OF TEXAS LIBRARIES, General Libraries, Barker Texas History Center, PO Box P, Austin, 78712. Don Carleton, Dir
Notes: Papers of Dr Joseph Henry Barnard (1804-1861), surgeon in the 1836 Texas Revolution. Incl names and statistics relative to the Battle of Coleto, 19 March 1836; also other professional and financial papers.

COLLAMORE, H. B.

IN —INDIANA UNIVERSITY, Lilly Library, Seventh St, Bloomington, 47405. William R Cagle, Librn
Notes: Three A E Housman collections; (1) Housman Mss I is ex-libris H B Collamore in the main, with about 100 autograph letters; (2) Housman Mss II has about 20 AEH letters with a good number of letters about Housman's verse from G B A Fletcher; (3) Housman Mss III is the John Carter Collection of letters to him about AEH. The Library has about 30 volumes from Housman's library, and a strong collection of editions of his works.

COLLECTING see Collectors and Collecting

COLLECTIVE BARGAINING

DC —US DEPT OF LABOR, Library, 200 Constitution Ave NW, Washington, 20210. Sabina Jacobson, Dir
Holdings: Vols (550,000) Cat

IL —UNIVERSITY OF ILLINOIS, URBANA/CHAMPAIGN, Institute of Labor and Industrial Relations, Library, 504 E Armory, Champaign, 61820. Margaret A Chaplan, Librn
Holdings: Vols (11,597) Cat Audiotapes Microforms
Budget: ($7500)
Notes: Collection incl four subject areas within industrial relations: collective bargaining and labor-management relations; manpower and labor economics; international and comparative labor movements; and organizational behavior. There is an extensive vertical file containing information on individual labor unions. The resources of the library which are relevant to the study of labor history are described in "Labor History Resources of the University of Illinois," by Patricia Wilson Onsi, *Labor History*, vol 7, Spring 1966, pp 209-215.

MI —MICHIGAN STATE UNIVERSITY, Labor and Industrial Relations Library, East Lansing, 48824. Martha Jane Soltow, Librn
Holdings: Vols (55,000) Cat Microforms
Notes: All aspects of employer/employee relations.

NY —CORNELL UNIVERSITY, New York State School of Industrial & Labor Relations, Martin P Catherwood Library, Ives Hall, Ithaca, 14853. Shirley F Harper, Dir
Holdings: Vols (10,000) Cat Mss Pix Films Audiotapes Microforms
Notes: Incl periodicals and oral history tapes.

†NY —CORNELL UNIVERSITY LIBRARIES, Ithaca, 14853.
Notes: Papers of Sidney Hillman, Amalgamated Clothing and Textile Workers Union.

NY —AMALGAMATED CLOTHING & TEXTILE WORKERS UNION, Research Dept Library, 15 Union Sq, New York, 10003. Mohammad Homayon Pour, Librn
Holdings: Vols (3200) Cat Pix
Notes: Collective bargaining and economic conditions in the men's and boys' apparel industries and the textile industry.

ON —CANADA DEPT OF LABOUR, Library, Ottawa, K1A 0J2, Can. Monique Marchand, Chief Librn
Holdings: Vols (100,000) Cat Microforms

COLLECTIVE SECURITY see Security, International

COLLECTIVE SETTLEMENTS

IL —NEWBERRY LIBRARY, 60 W Walton St, Chicago, 60610. Diana Haskell, Cur of Modern Mss
Holdings: Cat
Notes: American cooperative communities.

IN —INDIANA UNIVERSITY, Lilly Library, Seventh St, Bloomington, 47405. William R Cagle, Librn
Holdings: / / Cat Mss
Notes: First and early printings of the Icarian communities (1840-1880) and of works by Rappites and the Owenites; also New Harmony, Indiana. Mss relating to the Shaker community in Kentucky (1826-1828) in the Charles Willing Byrd collection.

IN —INDIANA STATE UNIVERSITY, EVANSVILLE, Library, 8600 University Blvd, Evansville, 47712. Gina R Walker, Acting Archivist
Holdings: Vols (250) Cat Mss Pix Audiotapes
Notes: Communal societies, past and present. Secondary sources on historic communes; correspondence with, and brochures and newsletters concerning, contemporary communes.

NY —SYRACUSE UNIVERSITY LIBRARIES, Ernest S Bird Library, George Arents Research Library for Special Collections, Syracuse, 13210. Carolyn A Davis, Manuscripts Librn; Amy S Doherty, University Archivist; Mark F Weimer, Rare Book Librn
Holdings: Vols 225 Cat Pix
Notes: A collection of publications by and about the Hopedale and Oneida communities and their forerunners; supplemented by reference works dealing with Communistic societies in general. Contains ephemeral handbooks, annual reports and periodicals; particularly relating to John Humphrey Noyes.

OH —MASSILLON PUBLIC LIBRARY, 208 Lincoln Way E, Massillon, 44646. Camille Leslie, Dir
Holdings: Vols 73 Cat Mss
Budget: $100
Notes: Collection is limited to historical studies; nothing on modern communes. Special emphasis on Shakers and Zoarites. No separate catalog.

PA —TEMPLE UNIVERSITY LIBRARIES, Special Collections Dept, Contemporary Culture Collection, Philadelphia, 19122. Patricia J Case, Cur
Notes: The Contemporary Culture Collection. See full entry under US-Social Life and Customs.

VA —UNIVERSITY OF VIRGINIA, Alderman Library, Manuscripts Dept, Charlottesville, 22901. Edmund Berkeley Jr, Cur
Holdings: Cat Mss
Notes: Papers of the Twin Oaks Community, Louisa County, Va, an intentional community based on Walden Two, 1967- incl administrative and financial records, correspondence, and files on other alternative communities.

COLLECTORS AND COLLECTING

LA —R W NORTON ART GALLERY, Library, 4747 Creswell Ave, Shreveport, 71106. Jerry M Bloomer, Librn
Holdings: Vols 489 Cat

MO —SAINT LOUIS ART MUSEUM, Richardson Memorial Library, Saint Louis, 63110. Ann B Abid, Librn
Holdings: Vols (30,000) Cat Pix Slides Microforms
Notes: Art history, incl decorative arts, catalogs, exhibitions, etc.

COLLEGE ATHLETICS see Athletes and Athletics

COLLEGE BUILDINGS see Universities and Colleges—Buildings

COLLEGE CATALOGS see Catalogs, College

COLLEGE LIBRARIES see Libraries, University and College

COLLEGE LIFE see Students

COLLEGE PRESSES see University Presses

COLLEGE SONGS see Students' Songs

COLLEGE SPORTS

CA —FIRST INTERSTATE BANK, Athletic Foundation, 2141 W Adams, Los Angeles, 90018. W R Schroeder, Managing Dir
Notes: One of the most extensive library and museum collections relating to sports, the Olympic Games, etc. Bound vols of sports sections from several newspapers. Large collection of college and university annuals and yearbooks; souvenir publications from amateur, college, and professional sporting events. Also, large museum collection of sports memorabilia, ledger of halls of fame with thousands of names of outstanding athletes in all sports. Repository for the Association of Sports Museums and Halls of Fame. Noncirculating.

COLLEGE STUDENTS see Students

COLLEGES see Universities and Colleges

COLLIER, JOHN AND PHYLLIS

CT —YALE UNIVERSITY, Beinecke Rare Book & Manuscript Library, Osborn Collection, New Haven, 06520. Stephen R Parks, Cur
Holdings: Mss

MI —WAYNE STATE UNIVERSITY, Walter P Reuther Library, Archives of Labor & Urban Affairs, Detroit, 48202. Philip Mason, Dir
Notes: Insights into the political and social climate of early 20th century America can be gained from the papers of John and Phyllis Collier, writers, poets, and social activists associated with Upton Sinclair's "End Poverty in California" campaigns and the American Labor Party.

COLLINGWOOD, HARRIS

AZ —NORTHERN ARIZONA UNIVERSITY, Special Collection Library, CU Box 6022, Flagstaff, 86011. Peter M Whiteley, Coordr/Archivist; William Mullane, Librn
Notes: Collection of Harris Collingwood, forest ranger, Clifton Ranger District, Apache National Forest, Ariz; correspondence between Collingwood and family members in Michigan, 1910-1915, regarding life and work in Arizona. The collection is photocopied from the originals belonging to the Forest History Society. Inventory available.

COLLINS, PATRICK ANDREW

MA —BOSTON COLLEGE LIBRARIES, Thomas P O'Neill Library, Irish Collection, Chestnut Hill, 02167. Ralph Coffman, Cur
Holdings: Vols (10,000) Cat Mss Maps Pix
Notes: Nearly every aspect of Irish history and literature are covered in this collection. Items of special interest are the many papers of Patrick Andrew Collins, president of the

COLLINS, PATRICK ANDREW (cont.)

Irish Land League, and letters of Jeremiah O'Donovan Rossa, poet, editor and leader in the Fenian and related organizations. Holdings also incl a facsimile of the famous illuminated ms of the Gospels, the *Book of* Kells; a complete vol of *Malton's Views of Dublin, 1799; The Ordinance Surveys;* a complete set of the *Irish Bulletin;* and Colgan's *Acta Sanctorum Hiberniae* describing the lives of the Irish saints.

COLLINS, WILKIE, 1824-1889

CA —UNIVERSITY OF CALIFORNIA, LOS ANGELES, Research Library, Dept of Special Collections, 405 Hilgard Ave, Los Angeles, 90024. Edward Shreeves, Chairman, Bibliographers Group; David S Zeidberg, Head
Holdings: Vols 75 Cat Mss
Notes: 75 first and other editions of his books; 20 letters.

MA —HARVARD UNIVERSITY LIBRARY, Houghton Library, Cambridge, 02138. Rodney G Dennis, Cur of Manuscripts
Holdings: Cat Mss

NJ —PRINCETON UNIVERSITY, Library, Morris L Parrish Collection, Princeton, 08540. Alexander D Wainwright, Cur
Notes: Refer to: Robert P Ashley, "The Wilkie Collins Collection" in the *Chronicle* XVII, 2 (winter, 1956), pp 81-84. Containing the first English edition of every novel Collins wrote, as well as authorized American first editions. (Pirated American editions are lacking in some cases.) Also rich in posters, cartoons, clippings, pamphlets and offprints. About 250 vols.

NY —NEW YORK PUBLIC LIBRARY, Rare Books and Manuscripts Div, Fifth Ave & 42 St, New York, 10018. William L Joyce, Asst Dir; Bernard McTigue, Cur, Arents Collection

COLLISIONS, AUTOMOBILE see Traffic Accidents

COLLISIONS AT SEA

IL —CHICAGO HISTORICAL SOCIETY, Library, Clark St at North Ave, Chicago, 60614. Robert L Brubaker, Librn
Holdings: Cat
Notes: The J Norman Jensen Collection of Lake and River Disasters, 1679-1947. 8500 card entries.

COLLOIDS

MI —ACHESON COLLOIDS, Library, 511 Port St, Port Huron, 48060. Myles T Musgrave, Librn
Holdings: Vols (5000) Cat Mss Microforms
Notes: General data on industrial manufacture and industrial uses of colloids and colloidal materials. Incl patents.

PA —FRANKLIN INSTITUTE LIBRARY, 20 & The Parkway, Philadelphia, 19103. Miriam Padusis, Dir; Charles Wilt, Readers Servs Librn
Holdings: Vols (300,000) Cat Maps Pix Microforms

COLLOQUIES, RELIGIOUS see Disputations, Religious

COLMER, WILLIAM M.

MS —UNIVERSITY OF SOUTHERN MISSISSIPPI, William David McCain Graduate Library, Box 5148, Southern Sta, Hattiesburg, 39406.
Holdings: Cat Mss Pix
Notes: Papers, 1933-73. 365 linear feet, incl correspondence, legislative files, newsletters, speeches, photographs, scrapbooks and artifacts. Colmer served as a United States Representative from Mississippi from 1933 to 1973. Of special interest are the records of the House Special Committee on Postwar Economic Policy and Planning, of which Colmer was chairman.

COLOMBIA

AZ —UNIVERSITY OF ARIZONA, Library, Tucson, 85721. W David Laird, Librn
Notes: Farmington Plan assignment.

CT —YALE UNIVERSITY, Sterling Memorial Library, Latin American Collections, New Haven, 06520. Lee H Williams Jr, Cur
Holdings: Vols (300,000) Cat Maps Pix Slides Phonorecords 16mm Films Filmstrips
See also entry under Latin America

NY —STATE UNIVERSITY OF NEW YORK, COLLEGE AT BUFFALO, Poetry/ Rare Books Collection, 420 Capen Hall, Buffalo, 14260. Robert J Bertholf, Cur
Holdings: Vols 4200 Cat Mss Maps Pix
Notes: Materials incl books, mss, official gazettes, and periodicals for research on the short-lived political entity known as Gran Colombia (the present-day countries of Colombia, Venezuela, and Ecuador); special emphasis is on the first half of the 19th century but earlier and later periods are incl.

NY —AMERICAN MUSEUM OF NATURAL HISTORY, Library Services Dept, Central Park W & 79th St, New York, 10024. Nina J Root, Chairwoman; Mary Genett, Asst Librn for Reference Services

NC —DUKE UNIVERSITY, William R Perkins Library, Durham, 27706. Elvin E Strowd, University Librn

COLOMBIA—HISTORY

AZ —UNIVERSITY OF ARIZONA, Library, Tucson, 85721. W David Laird, Librn
Notes: Latin American materials in the University of Arizona Library system may be found in all of the campus libraries. The largest collection is located in the Main Library and concentrates primarily on the history, literature, political science and economics of Mexico, Panama, Colombia, Argentina, Brazil and Chile. Special Collections specializes in the colonial period in the areas of law, religion, and economics. They also incl numerous manuscript collections, photographs, and 4000 broadsides from Mexico covering the late 18th century through the 20th century revolutionary period. There are also strong map, music and phonorecord collections primarily on Mexico. The greatest collecting effort is current materials on contemporary Latin America. Materials are fully accessible through the main card catalog as there is no separate catalog of the collection.

FL —UNIVERSITY OF MIAMI, Otto G Richter Library, PO Box 248214, Coral Gables, 33124. Frank Rodgers, Dir of Libraries
Notes: Very good research collection in history, economics, political science, and literature of Colombia. Incl early travels, botany. Contains the collection of the late Phanor J Eder (2000 volumes), as well as materials purchased during participation in LACAP. See *Catalog of the Cuban and Caribbean Library, University of Miami* (Boston: G K Hall, 1977). Periodicals, US government publications, and those of quasi-governmental bodies, eg, UNESCO, United Nations, are incl. The Eder collection also incl correspondence, mss, maps, films, and pamphlets; about 13,300 items.

OH —HEBREW UNION COLLEGE-JEWISH INSTITUTE OF RELIGION, Klau Library, 3101 Clifton Ave, Cincinnati, 45220. David J Gilner, Reference Librn
Holdings: Cat Mss
Notes: Incl papal bulls, edicts of inquisitions, royal letters, inquisitorial instructions, sermons preached at the autos-da-fe held by the Portuguese Inquisition at Lisbon, Colombia, etc. Early and late histories.

TX —UNIVERSITY OF TEXAS LIBRARIES, Nettie Lee Benson Latin American Collection, Sid Richardson Hall 1.109, Austin, 78712. Laura Gutierrez-Witt, Head Librn
Holdings: Vols (450,000) Cat Mss Maps Pix Phonorecords Filmstrips Microforms
See also entry under Latin America

COLOMBIAN LITERATURE

CA —UNIVERSITY OF CALIFORNIA, SANTA BARBARA, Library, Dept of Special Collections, Santa Barbara, 93106. Christian F Brun, Head
Holdings: Vols 880 Cat
Notes: Colombian language and literature; books published in Colombia.

FL —UNIVERSITY OF MIAMI, Otto G Richter Library, PO Box 248214, Coral Gables, 33124. Frank Rodgers, Dir of Libraries
Notes: Very good research collection in history, economics, political science, and literature of Colombia. Incl early travels, botany. Contains the collection of the late Phanor J Eder (2000 volumes), as well as materials purchased during participation in LACAP. See *Catalog of the Cuban and Caribbean Library, University of Miami* (Boston: G K Hall, 1977). Periodicals, US government publications, and those of quasi-governmental bodies, eg, UNESCO, United Nations, are incl. The Eder collection also incl correspondence, mss, maps, films, and pamphlets; about 13,300 items.

COLOMBO, JOHN ROBERT, 1936-

ON —MCMASTER UNIVERSITY, Mills Memorial Library, Div of Archives & Research Collections, Hamilton, L8S 4L6, Can. G R Hill, Univ Librn
Holdings: // Mss
Notes: Personal correspondence with Canadian literary figures, mss of poetry and prose. Collection partially described in *McMaster University Library Research* News, vol 1, no 5, February 1971.

COLONIAL WARS see U.S. —History—Colonial Period

COLONIAL WILLIAMSBURG (1926-1961)

NY —ROCKEFELLER UNIVERSITY, Rockefeller Archive Center, Hillcrest, Pocantico Hills, North Tarrytown, 10591. Joseph W Ernst, Dir; J William Hess, Assoc Dir
Notes: Papers relative to the Rockefeller Family, Foundations, University, and other specific enterprises and contributions to particular areas of social, physical, educational, and historic reform, preservation, conservation, or development. Extensive records of administrative, financial, physical, or intellectual relationships.

COLONIALISM see Colonies, Colonialism, and Colonization; World Politics

COLONIES, AGRICULTURAL see Agricultural Colonies

COLONIES, COLONIALISM, AND COLONIZATION

DC —HOWARD UNIVERSITY, Moorland-Spingarn Research Center, 500 Howard Place NW, Washington, 20059. Clifford L Muse, Jr, Acting Dir
Holdings: Vols (106,086) Mss Maps Pix Slides Phonorecords Audiotapes 16mm Films Filmstrips Microforms
Budget: ($854,753)
See also entry under Blacks

IL —NEWBERRY LIBRARY, 60 W Walton St, Chicago, 60610. Diana Haskell, Cur of Modern Mss
Holdings: Cat
Notes: The Greenlee Collection of materials on discovery, exploration and colonization by the Portuguese.

MA —HARVARD UNIVERSITY LIBRARY, Cambridge, 02138.
Holdings: Cat

MI —UNIVERSITY OF MICHIGAN, Dept of Rare Books & Special Collections, Ann Arbor, 48109. Edward C Weber, Head, Labadie Collection
Holdings: Vols (40,000) Cat Microforms
Notes: 20th-century protest against colonial governments. Incl records, tapes, and posters.

MN —UNIVERSITY OF MINNESOTA, James Ford Bell Library, 309 19th Ave S, Minneapolis, 55455. John Parker, Cur
Holdings: Vols (11,000) Cat Mss Maps
Notes: Collection of original materials relating to European expansion, 1400-1800.

COLONIES, COLONIALISM, AND COLONIZATION (cont.)

NY —STATE UNIVERSITY OF NEW YORK, STONY BROOK, Melville Library, Dept of Special Collections, Stony Brook, 11794. Evert Volkersz, Head
Holdings: Vols 95 Cat
Notes: Spanish-American colonial trade. 101 documents of the 16th and 17th centuries presenting information about trade and administration of the Spanish-American colonies and important for linking political and financial connections. A listing of the materials is available.

RI —BROWN UNIVERSITY, John Carter Brown Library, Providence, 02912. Norman Fiering, Librn; Everett C Wilkie Jr, Bibliographer; Susan Danforth, Cur Maps & Prints
Holdings: Vols (40,000)
Notes: Extensive collection of political, economic, and social writings on European colonies in the Americas and their impact on Europe.

COLONIZATION, AFRICAN see Africa—Colonization

COLONIZATION, ASIAN see Asia—Colonization

COLOPHONS

IL —NEWBERRY LIBRARY, John M Wing Foundation on the History of Printing, 60 W Walton St, Chicago, 60610. Diana Haskell, Cur of Modern Mss
Holdings: Vols (30,000) Cat Ms
Budget: ($50,000)
Notes: The collection covers printing and printing history of Western Europe and the Americas from its invention to the present. It is particularly rich in incunabula (about 2000); the works of the great printers, among others Aldus, Bodoni, Baskerville, and Rogers. Printed catalog: *A Dictionary* Catalogue. (Boston: G K Hall, 1961); *Supplements* (1981). Brief descriptions: James M Wells, "The John M Wing Foundation of the Newberry Library," *The Book Collector, VIII,* 2 (Summer 1959), pp 157-162; Lawrece W Towner, *An Uncommon Collection of Uncommon* Collections (Chicago: The Newberry Library, 1977), pp 25-26.

COLOR

NY —ROCHESTER INSTITUTE OF TECHNOLOGY, Technical & Education Center of the Graphic Arts, Graphic Arts Information Service, One Lomb Memorial Dr, Rochester, 14623. Susan Clark, Technical Librn

NY —VISUAL STUDIES WORKSHOP, Research Center, 31 Prince St, Rochester, 14607. Linn Underhill, Coordr; Robert Bretz, Librn
Holdings: Vols (8000) Cat Pix Slides Audiotapes Videotapes
Notes: Strong emphasis on photography (over 1,000,000 pictures) and the photographic arts in many subject areas incl in the volume. Heavy emphasis on early photographic processes and collections of examples of them. Also collections of individual photographers' works.

PA —FRANKLIN INSTITUTE LIBRARY, 20 & The Parkway, Philadelphia, 19103. Miriam Padusis, Dir; Charles Wilt, Readers Servs Librn
Holdings: Vols (300,000) Cat Maps Pix Microforms

COLOR ETCHINGS see Color Prints

COLOR PLATES

CA —SAINT JOHN'S SEMINARY, Edward Laurence Doheny Memorial Library, The Estelle Doheny Collection, 5012 E Seminary Rd, Camarillo, 93010. Rita S Faulders, Cur

CA —LOS ANGELES PUBLIC LIBRARY, Children's Literature Dept, 630 W 5th St, Los Angeles, 90071. Serenna Day, Sr Librn
Holdings: Vols (4500) Cat
Notes: A rich collection of over 4500 titles representing books from 40 countries around the world. Included are Argentina, Chile, Israel, Czechoslovakia, Bulgaria, and the Afrikaans language, to name a few. Especially notable are many imprints from the turn of the century, the 1920s and 1930s. Some are quite rare. Besides picture books with beautiful color illustrations, there are stories dealing with manners and good example. The Children's Room has a separate file where these are arranged by country.

CT —YALE UNIVERSITY, Beinecke Rare Book & Manuscript Library, Osborn Collection, New Haven, 06520. Stephen R Parks, Cur

MD —US NAVAL ACADEMY, Nimitz Library, Annapolis, 21402. Alice S Creighton, Assistant Librn for Special Collections
Holdings: Vols (900)/ / Uncat
Notes: Wiedorn Collection of illustrated books, chiefly of the 19th century.

MA —BOSTON PUBLIC LIBRARY, Print Collection, Dartmouth St at Copley Sq, Boston, 02117. Sinclair H Hitchings, Keeper of Prints
Holdings: Vols (500) Cat
Notes: Fine illustrated books, mainly English, of the 18th, 19th and 20th centuries, containing original prints or photographs. Also 250 books with fore-edge paintings and books with fine bindings. No photocopying.

NY —MUSEUM OF MODERN ART, Library, 11 W 53 St, New York, 10019. Clive Phillpot, Library Dir
Notes: Art of the 20th and latter half of the 19th century (painting, sculpture, drawings and prints, architecture, photography, film).

PA —HUNT INSTITUTE FOR BOTANICAL DOCUMENTATION, Hunt Botanical Library, Carnegie-Mellon University, Pittsburgh, 15213. Bernadette G Callery, Librn
Holdings: Vols (23,000) Cat Pix
Notes: Collection of primarily historical botany and plant taxonomy, especially 1730-1840. Includes approximately 500 15th through 17th century herbals, extensive collection of 18th and 19th century color-plate works, floras and monographic works, and other works on natural history, early gardening and horticulture, and travel, particularly that dealing with plant exploration and introduction. Extensive biogrpahical materials, on people in the plant sciences. Reference collection and extensive documentation in botanical bibliography, especially concerning books published before 1850. Includes as separate collections, the Strandell Collection of Linnaeana and the Michel Adanson Library. Over 800 items described in *Catalogue of Botanical Books in the Collection of Rachel McMasters Miller Hunt, 1477-1800* (Pittsburgh, 1958-1960).

PA —PENNSYLVANIA STATE UNIVERSITY, Fred Lewis Pattee Library, Special Collections Dept, University Park, 16802. Charles Mann, Chief, Special Collections
Holdings: Vols (122,533) Cat Mss Maps Pix Slides Phonorecords Audiotapes Videotapes 16mm Films Microforms
Budget: ($37,000)
Notes: Special Collections and Rare Books includes several collections described separately. The holdings are particularly strong in literature, the 18th century, aeronautics, facsimiles, atlases, 19th century illustrated works on birds, botany and traveller's views. Special strengths are Emblem Books, Utopias, Fantastic Fiction, Australiana, Fine Presses, Labor Archives, Landscape Architecture, Pennsylvaniana. These collections are strengthened by parallel holdings in the open stacks. It also includes the collections of the Penn State Room. Several mimeographed lists are available. Audiotapes are listed in *Voices and Events, A Catalog of Audio Tapes* (Pennsylvania State University Libraries, 1975), 45 pp.

COLOR PLATES—BIRD BOOKS

MD —JOHNS HOPKINS UNIVERSITY, Milton S Eisenhower Library, Special Collections, John Work Garrett Library, 4545 N Charles St, Baltimore, 21210. Jane Katz, Garrett Librn

†MA —WILLIAMS COLLEGE, Chapin Library of Rare Books, PO Box 426, Williamstown, 01267. Robert L Volz, Custodian
Holdings: Vols 250 Cat
Notes: Color plate bird books. No material available on interlibrary loan.

PA —PENNSYLVANIA STATE UNIVERSITY, Fred Lewis Pattee Library, Special Collections Dept, University Park, 16802. Charles Mann, Chief, Special Collections
Holdings: Vols (122,533) Cat Mss Maps Pix Slides Phonorecords Audiotapes Videotapes 16mm Films Microforms
Budget: ($37,000)
Notes: Special Collections and Rare Books includes several collections described separately. The holdings are particularly strong in literature, the 18th century, aeronautics, facsimiles, atlases, 19th century illustrated works on birds, botany and traveller's views. Special strengths are Emblem Books, Utopias, Fantastic Fiction, Australiana, Fine Presses, Labor Archives, Landscape Architecture, Pennsylvaniana. These collections are strengthened by parallel holdings in the open stacks. It also includes the collections of the Penn State Room. Several mimeographed lists are available. Audiotapes are listed in *Voices and Events, A Catalog of Audio Tapes* (Pennsylvania State University Libraries, 1975), 45 pp.

RI —BROWN UNIVERSITY, John Hay Library, 20 Prospect St, Providence, 02912. Mark N Brown, Cur Mss
Holdings: Vols (50) Cat
Notes: History of Science Collection incl John James Audubon's published works on birds and quadrupeds of America, incl the elephant folio edition of *Birds of America* (Edinburgh and London: 1827-1838) plus some manuscript material.

WI —MILWAUKEE PUBLIC LIBRARY, 814 W Wisconsin Ave, Milwaukee, 53233. Donald J Sager, City Librn
Holdings: Vols 5000 Cat
Notes: A set of Audubon prints; also Gould's *Birds of Australia,* Catesby, Selby, Wilson, Edwards, and Brasher.

COLOR PLATES, BOTANICAL

†CA —HUNTINGTON BOTANICAL GARDENS LIBRARY, 1151 Oxford Rd, San Marino, 91108. Ann Ravenscroft, Secretary
Holdings: Vols (8000)
Notes: Emphases on history of botanical science; papers and notes of American botanists and naturalists of The West; botanical illustration, etc. Subtropical horticulture, incl cacti and succulents of Australia, South Africa, and Mexico.

†CO —DENVER BOTANIC GARDENS, Helen Fowler Library, 909 York St, Denver, 80206. Solange G Gignac, Librn
Notes: Emphasis on Bromeliada Literature; horticulture; Colorado, Oregon, and Rocky Mountains Region botany; landscape architecture; juvenile horticultural and botanical literature. Incl over 5000 pamphlets on botany and horticulture; also, 197 watercolors of Colorado wildflowers by Emma Irvine, and 250 of Oregon by Lillian Hallock.

NY —NEW YORK BOTANICAL GARDEN LIBRARY, Bronx, 10458. Charles R Long, Asst Vice Pres & Dir
Notes: One of the largest botanical collections in the world. Over 900,000 items. Covers botany (150,000 vols), botanists (3000), horticulture (45,000) plant diseases (25,000), plant physiology (15,000), history of botany (1500), conservation of natural resources (15,000), gardening (13,000), paleobotany (7000), ecology (20,000),

COLOR PLATES, BOTANICAL (cont.)

forestry (5000) medical botany (3000), agriculture (9000) and biology (20,000). Reference library; materials do not circulate, except for member circulating collection (1200) and standard inter-library loan. About 5000 vols uncataloged. Incl art, books, serials, pamphlets, archives and manuscripts, vertical files, microfiche and microfilm, nursery and seed catalogs, photographs, paintings, prints, drawings and engravings. Covers all areas of botanical sciences. This is an OCLC library with fullresource services incl photocopying and photography.

OH —GARDEN CENTER OF GREATER CLEVELAND, Eleanor Squire Library, 11030 East Blvd, Cleveland, 44106. Richard T Isaacson, Librn
Notes: The Warren C Corning Collection of Horticultural Classics. The Flowering Plant Index of Illustration and Information.

PA —HUNT INSTITUTE FOR BOTANICAL DOCUMENTATION, Hunt Botanical Library, Carnegie-Mellon University, Pittsburgh, 15213. Bernadette G Callery, Librn
Holdings: Vols 23,000 Cat Pix
Notes: Collection of primarily historical botany and plant taxonomy, especially 1730-1840. Includes approximately 500 15th through 17th century herbals, extensive collection of 18th and 19th century color-plate works, floras and monographic works, and other works on natural history, early gardening and horticulture, and travel, particularly that dealing with plant exploration and introduction. Extensive biographical materials, on people in plant sciences. Reference collection and extensive documentation in botanical bibliography, especially concerning books published before 1850. Includes as separate collections, the Strandell Collection of Linnaeana and the Michel Adanson Library. Over 800 items described in *Catalogue of Botanical Books in the Collection of Rachel McMasters Miller Hunt, 1477-1800* (Pittsburgh, 1958-1960).

COLOR PRINTING

CA —UNIVERSITY OF CALIFORNIA, LOS ANGELES, Research Library, Dept of Special Collections, 405 Hilgard Ave, Los Angeles, 90024. Edward Shreeves, Chairman, Bibliographers Group; David S Zeidberg, Head
Holdings: Vols 100 Cat Pix
Notes: 100 books with color illustrations, and 100 color prints, printed by George Baxter.

CT —YALE UNIVERSITY, Beinecke Rare Book & Manuscript Library, Osborn Collection, New Haven, 06520. Stephen R Parks, Cur
Holdings: Mss

NY —ROCHESTER INSTITUTE OF TECHNOLOGY, Technical & Education Center of the Graphic Arts, Graphic Arts Information Service, One Lomb Memorial Dr, Rochester, 14623. Susan Clark, Technical Librn

PA —GRAPHIC ARTS TECHNICAL FOUNDATION, Edward H Wadewitz Memorial Library, 4615 Forbes Ave, Pittsburgh, 15213. Janice L Lloyd, Librn
Holdings: Vols (3500) Cat Slides Microforms
Notes: All printing processes. Also, books, and periodicals on paper, ink, photography, optics, color theory, environmental control. Approximately 250 periodical titles and 35, 000 classified abstracts of selected periodical articles. Approximately 15,000 slides within the organization. Research reports from foreign graphic arts research institutes.

ON —UNIVERSITY OF TORONTO, Massey College, Robertson Davies Library, 4 Devonshire Place, Toronto, M5S 2E1, Can. Desmond G Neill, Librn
Holdings: Vols (12,000) Cat Mss Microforms
Notes: Library contains Bibliography Room (11 hand presses, type and equipment) and Papermaking Room. Book collections incl Ruari McLean Collection of 19th-century books on, and representative of, color printing (approx 4300 items).

PQ —MCGILL UNIVERSITY, McLennan Library, Rare Books and Special Collections Dept, 3459 McTavish St, Montreal, H3A 1Y1, Can.
Holdings: Vols 13,569
Notes: 13,159 volumes and 47,604 items of printed ephemera. Incl early printing manuals, type specimens, books on the history of printing, particularly colour printing, paper, and examples of modern fine printing. Located in the William Colgate History of Printing Collection.

COLOR PRINTS

CA —UNIVERSITY OF CALIFORNIA, LOS ANGELES, Research Library, Dept of Special Collections, 405 Hilgard Ave, Los Angeles, 90024. Edward Shreeves, Chairman, Bibliographers Group; David S Zeidberg, Head
Holdings: Vols 100 Cat Pix
Notes: 100 books with color illustrations, and 100 color prints, printed by George Baxter.

CA —UNIVERSITY OF THE PACIFIC, Library, Stockton, 95211. Hiram L Davis, Dir of Libraries
Holdings: Vols (350) Uncat Pix
Notes: A general collection of Victorian literature and life given to the University by James M Perrin in 1968-1970. The primary specialization is material by and about William Morris and the Kelmscott Press, but the collection also is rich in Victorian first editions, Pre-Raphaelites and Pre-Raphaelitism, and early colored illustrations and chromolithography.

KS —UNIVERSITY OF KANSAS, Kenneth Spencer Research Library, Special Collections Dept, Lawrence, 66045. Alexandra Mason, Librn
Holdings: Vols 5000 Cat Mss Pix
Notes: Ralph Ellis Collection. Special strengths: John Gould, Thomas Bewick. Many color plate books, Gould and other drawings, prints. 15th century to 1945, especially 19th century. Noncirculating. See Mengel, Robert M, comp *A Catalogue of the Ellis Collection of Ornithological Books in the University of Kansas Libraries*, Lawrence, Kansas. Volume 1, A-B, 1972. (University of Kansas Publications. Library series, 33) xxix, 259pp.; v. 2, C-D, 1983. (Univ of Kansas Publications, Libr Series, 48) 176 pp.

MD —JOHNS HOPKINS UNIVERSITY, Milton S Eisenhower Library, Special Collections, John Work Garrett Library, 4545 N Charles St, Baltimore, 21210. Jane Katz, Garrett Librn

NJ —NEWARK PUBLIC LIBRARY, Art & Music Dept, 5 Washington St, Newark, 07101. William J Dane, Supv
Holdings: Vols (15,000) Cat
Notes: Original prints and fine facsimiles in all major media from 16th century to contemporary times. Study and special exhibition collection of the traditional and current techniques of graphic art with emphasis on late 19th and 20th century artists; ancillary collections of Japanese prints and printed books, trade cards, music covers, greeting cards, bank notes and historic maps.

NY —MUSEUM OF MODERN ART, Library, 11 W 53 St, New York, 10019. Clive Phillpot, Library Dir
Notes: Art of the 20th and latter half of the 19th century (painting, sculpture, drawings and prints, architecture, photography, film).

COLOR PRINTS, JAPANESE

DC —AMERICAN UNIVERSITY LIBRARY, Bender Library, 4400 Massachusetts Ave NW, Washington, 20016.
Holdings: Vols 1200 Cat Mss Maps Pix
Notes: The Charles Nelson Spinks Library was donated to the University Library. The collection, many items beautifully hand-bound, is devoted chiefly to the field of Japanese local history, ukiyoe (Japanese color prints), and the civilization of the Tokugawa Period. A selected annotated bibliography for this collection is in progress. A complete shelflist is available at the American University Library.

MA —BOSTON COLLEGE LIBRARIES, Thomas P O'Neill Library, Chestnut Hill, 02167. Frank J Seegraber, Special Collections Librn
Holdings: Vols 66 // Cat
Notes: The James W Morrissey Memorial Collection of Japanese Prints is composed of over 100 original prints and reproductions of Japanese artists of the 18th and 19th centuries, with others from the contemporary period. Available by appointment only.

NJ —NEWARK PUBLIC LIBRARY, Art & Music Dept, 5 Washington St, Newark, 07101. William J Dane, Supv
Holdings: Vols (15,000) Cat
Notes: Original prints and fine facsimiles in all major media from 16th century to contemporary times. Study and special exhibition collection of the traditional and current techniques of graphic art with emphasis on late 19th and 20th century artists; ancillary collections of Japanese prints and printed books, trade cards, music covers, greeting cards, bank notes and historic maps.

COLOR SENSE

NY —STATE UNIVERSITY OF NEW YORK, State College of Optometry, Harold Kohn Vision Science Library, 100 E 24 St, New York, 10010. Margaret S Lewis, Librn
Holdings: Vols (23,000) Cat Audiotapes Microforms
Notes: All subjects related to visual disabilities; much on vision disorders among children.

COLORADO

CO —UNIVERSITY OF COLORADO, Libraries, Western Historical Collections, Boulder, 80309.
Holdings: Cat Mss Maps Pix Newspapers
Notes: This repository of Colorado economic development, political and social action holds more than 500 ms collections ranging in size from more than 700 boxes to a few pieces and occupies approx 20,000 shelf feet. It also maintains the University Archive incl printed and manuscript materials. The most useful collections in this category incl the following: (1) Hardrock mining industry at Aspen, Central City, Leadville: D R C Brown Papers (1880-1920); Henry M Teller (1861-1877); Harper M Orahood; (1880s and 1890s) J J Blow, Henry Moody, W W Old, and Henry R Pendry; (2) Union (Greeley, Colorado) Colony and the Chicago-Colorado (Longmont, Colorado) Colony Papers-both successful agricultural experiments of the 1870s; (3) James P Maxwell Papers, pioneer Colorado businessman and developer; (4) David H Nichols Papers, pioneer Colorado military and political figure; (5) Jesse SRandall Papers, pioneer Georgetown, Colorado, newspaper publisher and civic leader; (6) Thomas J O'Donnell Papers (1880s-1924), prominent Denver attorney and Democratic party leader; (7) Hal Sayre Papers (1860s-1920), pioneer mining engineer and developer; (8) John C Bell Papers, western Colorado congressman and Populist leader; (9) Warren F Bleecker Papers, Colorado mining promoter and political leader in the 1920s; (10) J Sidney Brown and Brothers Papers, records of a large mercantile chain with branches throughout Colorado, New Mexico, and Wyoming; (11) George Bull Papers, civil engineer and water problem consultant in the West; (12) Samuel W DeBusk Papers, southern Colorado pioneer and business leader; (13) Leopold H Guldman Papers, Denver department store owner and operator; (14) James A Ownbey Papers, southern Colorado mining promoter; (15) A R Wilfley Papers, miningequipment inventor and manufacturer; (16) Edgar Chenoweth Papers, (1937-1964), concerning the activities of that US Congressman on behalf of his constituents in southeastern and southern Colorado; (17) Edward Keating

COLORADO (cont.)

papers (1910-1960), containing informed comments on national events by that former US Congressman (1913-1918) and later editor of the Labor newspaper; (19) Robert Rockwell Papers (1915-1950), relating to that former US Congressman's (1941-1949) business and political career representing Colorado's Western Slope and its range cattle industry. Typescript inventories or published guides available for each of the named collections.

CO —COLORADO GEOLOGICAL SURVEY, Library, 1313 Sherman St Rm 715, Denver, 80203. Louise Slade, Librn
Holdings: Vols (3000) Uncat Mss Maps Pix Microforms
Notes: Mineral resources of Colorado.

UT —UNIVERSITY OF UTAH, Marriott Library, Special Collections, Salt Lake City, 84112. Gregory C Thompson, Cur

COLORADO—DESCRIPTION AND TRAVEL—VIEWS

CA —POMONA PUBLIC LIBRARY, Special Collections, 625 S Garey Ave, PO Box 2271, Pomona, 91766. David Streeter, Librn
Holdings: Uncat Slides
Notes: Contains 550 lantern slides (mostly of California) and 4200 color 35mm transparencies of world travel, 1960s. Also, the Burton Frasher Postal Card Collection of 60,000 negatives and prints of California, Arizona, Colorado, New Mexico, Nevada, and Utah; 30,000 world views; 8000 California views. There are also world views in nearly 1000 stereophotographs.

CO —COLORADO HISTORICAL SOCIETY, Research Collections, 1300 Broadway, Denver, 80203. Catherine Kane, Head Public Service and Access
Holdings: Cat Pix Slides
Budget:
Notes: 250,000 photographs of western and Colorado subjects incl gold rush, mining, Indians, natural features, transportation, cities and towns, portraits. William Henry Jackson photographs of area west of Mississippi.

COLORADO—ECONOMIC CONDITIONS

CO —DENVER PUBLIC LIBRARY, Conservation Library Center, 1357 Broadway, Denver, 80203.
Holdings: Vols (10,330) Cat
Notes: Historical, sociological, and economic aspects, but not scientific, except for Colorado research reports. Also, fish and wildlife reports of all states.

COLORADO—GOVERNMENT PUBLICATIONS

CO —COLORADO STATE LIBRARY, State Publications Depository & Distribution Center, 1362 Lincoln St, Denver, 80203. Tom Reynolds, Consultant
Holdings: Vols 10,000 Cat Maps Microforms
Budget: ($81,000)
Notes: Publications of Colorado state agencies.

COLORADO—HISTORY

AZ —COLORADO RIVER INDIAN TRIBES MUSEUM/LIBRARY, Rte One, Box 23-B, Parker, 85344. Priscilla Johnson, Librn
Holdings: Cat Mss Maps Pix Slides Audiotapes Microforms
Notes: Library deals with the four tribes of the Colorado River Indian Reservation: Mojave, Chemehuevi, Navajo, and Hopi. Emphasis is also given to the prehistoric cultures of this area; Patayan and Hohokam. Library collections include original manuscripts and other documents, photographs, oral history tape recordings, cultural items and artifacts. Copies of many documents relating to the reservation are in bound volumes, microfilm, and photocopies. Photos relative to the reservation from various other collections are copied in our collection. Of particular interest is the museum basket collection which incl about 1000 Chemehuevi baskets--the largest Chemehuevi basket collection. Other artifacts give special emphasis to the Mojave culture.

CO —UNIVERSITY OF COLORADO, Libraries, Western Historical Collections, Boulder, 80309.
Holdings: // Cat Mss Pix
Notes: Papers of Edward P Costigan, the founder of Colorado's Progressive (Bull Moose) Party. He became nationally known for his defense of union miners accused of murder. From 1917-1928 he served on the US Tariff Commission. In 1930 he was elected to the US Senate; during his term he supported New Deal legislation. The collection contains 43 boxes of sorted personal and legislative materials, two boxes of unsorted clippings, and a sizable personal library; it covers the period from 1897 to 1937. A published guide is available.

CO —COLORADO HISTORICAL SOCIETY, Research Collections, 1300 Broadway, Denver, 80203. Catherine Kane, Head Public Service and Access
Holdings: Cat Mss Maps Pix Microforms
Budget:
Notes: Strong collection of Colorado and western history totaling over 8,000,000 pieces. Special emphases incl people, places, land and cattle, railroads, business history, minority cultures. Colorado newspaper collection, mss, photographs.

CO —DURANGO PUBLIC LIBRARY, 1188 Second Ave, Durango, 81301. Daniel P Brassell, Dir
Holdings: Vols 3025 Cat Mss Maps
Budget: $1000
Notes: Especially southwest Colorado history. Collection cataloged separately.

CO —FORT COLLINS PUBLIC LIBRARY, 201 Peterson, Fort Collins, 80524. Jane B Davis, Library Dir
Holdings: Vols 1600 Cat Mss Maps Pix Audiotapes
Budget: $14,273
Notes: Local history collection, primarily Fort Collins and Larimer County. Incl local newspapers (1874-date; some on microform; partially indexed); clipping file; and 130,000 old photographs. Incl 75 mss, 25 maps, and 350 audiotapes (oral history).

CO —FORT MORGAN PUBLIC LIBRARY, 414 Main, Fort Morgan, 80701. Jo Ann Kruglet, Dir
Holdings: Vols 500
Notes: Lute Johnson Collection contains books about Colorado by Colorado authors, many autographed, written at the turn of the century. Noncirculating. No photocopying. Also, 40 oral history tapes, collected during the Bicentennial, predominately about the history of Fort Morgan and Morgan County, Colorado.

CO —COLORADO RAILROAD MUSEUM, Golden, 80401. R W Richardson, Exec Dir
Holdings: Vols 1000 Uncat Mss Maps Pix
Notes: Western railroads; mountain narrowgauge. Collections incl, in addition to railroad books, the papers and files of operating lines in Colorado, collected over past 30 years: letter files, records and record books, day to day operations, telegrams and other forms recording the day, week and month.

CO —LOVELAND PUBLIC LIBRARY, 205 E Sixth, Loveland, 80537. Elaine A Puls, Library Dir
Holdings: Vols 800 Cat

CO —PUEBLO REGIONAL LIBRARY DISTRICT, 100 E Abriendo Ave, Pueblo, 81004. Charles E Bates, Library Dir
Holdings: Vols 12,552 Cat Mss Maps Pix Microforms VF
Notes: Materials are noncirculating.

DC —LIBRARY OF CONGRESS, Prints & Photographs Div, Washington, 20540.
Notes: The John C H Grabill collection of photographs of frontier life in Colorado, South Dakota, and Wyoming, late 19th century, incl views of hunters, prospectors, cowboys, Chinese immigrants, and US Army personnel.

IL —NORTHERN ILLINOIS UNIVERSITY, Founders Memorial Library, Rare Books and Special Collections Dept, De Kalb, 60115. William R DuBois, Dept Head
Holdings: Vols (1200) Cat Maps Pix
Notes: Collection deals with all aspects of Colorado: early travel narratives, history, literature, geology, ecology, maps and some bibliography.

NM —ROSWELL PUBLIC LIBRARY, 301 N Pennsylvania Ave, Roswell, 88201. Sarah Beth Galloway, Library Dir
Holdings: Vols (2000) Cat Maps
Budget: $1000
Notes: Covers literature (fiction and nonfiction), history, biography, geography, of Oklahoma, Texas, Colorado, New Mexico and Arizona.

NY —STATE UNIVERSITY OF NEW YORK, BINGHAMTON, Glenn G Bartle Library, Binghamton, 13901. Marion Hanscom, Special Collections Librn
Notes: Papers, correspondence, etc of the former aide to the Rockefeller enterprises. Incl much on the Colorado mine strikes.

COLORADO—MAPS

OK —TULSA CITY-COUNTY LIBRARY, Business & Technology Dept, 400 Civic Center, Tulsa, 74103. Craig Buthod, Head
Notes: Original General Land Office survey maps for the states of Arizona, Arkansas, Colorado, Illinois, Indiana, Idaho, Kansas, Michigan, Missouri, Montana, Nebraska, Nevada, New Mexico, North Dakota, Ohio, Oklahoma, South Dakota, Utah and Wyoming. Incomplete coverage of each state.

COLORADO—MINORITIES

CO —UNIVERSITY OF SOUTHERN COLORADO, Library, 2200 Bonforte Blvd, Pueblo, 81001.
Holdings: Vols (4000) Cat Mss Maps Pix Phonorecords Audiotapes Sheet Music
Budget: ($10,000)
Notes: Yugoslavian; especially Slovenian history and culture. The collection was inaugurated in 1969. Besides published titles, 2800 in English, and 900 in Slavic languages, there are memorabilia, organizational records, and newspapers, magazines, and music. There is a separate card catalog of items in the collection. Colorado has had a number of Slavic colonies and this collection attempts to recapture the history of these early settlers. Incl sheet music and phonorecords.

COLORADO—PICTURES, ILLUSTRATIONS, ETC.

CO —UNIVERSITY OF COLORADO, Libraries, Western Historical Collections, Boulder, 80309.
Holdings: // Cat Pix
Notes: The Charles Snow (1910-1968) Collection consists of negatives and positive prints of portraits of Boulder and state residents, University of Colorado, and various sites in Colorado. Snow was an early Boulder photographer. An index is available to the material stored in 100 boxes.

COLORADO—POLITICS AND GOVERNMENT

CO —UNIVERSITY OF COLORADO, Libraries, Western Historical Collections, Boulder, 80309.
Holdings: Mss
Notes: After serving in the Civil War, Thomas M Patterson (1840-1916) studied law and in 1872 came to Colorado. He quickly became involved in Democratic politics, serving as Territorial Delegate to Congress (1874-1876), US Representative (1876-1878) and Senator (1901-1906). During this period he also maintained a successful law practice, invested in real estate and mining properties, and published the *Rocky Mountain News* (1892-1912). This collection, while containing much

COLORADO—POLITICS AND GOVERNMENT (cont.)

material on Patterson's business and political affairs, deals primarily with his personal and family life. Included are accounts of Denver social life, money and health worries, and the Patterson children's education in Europe and the United States. 8 boxes, 1865-1925. A published guide is available.

COLORADO AUTHORS see Authors, Colorado

COLORADO COUNCIL OF CHURCHES

CO —UNIVERSITY OF COLORADO, Libraries, Western Historical Collections, Boulder, 80309.
Holdings: Cat Mss Pix Newspapers
Notes: The collection consists of the records of the Colorado Council of Churches and affiliated associations for the period 1924-1968. The principal concern of the Council is Christian education, but it is also involved in social education and action and serves as a liaison between various elements of the community concerned with problems such as public welfare, civic development, and law enforcement. The collection concerns social, political, and church activities on the regional, national and international levels. A typescript inventory to the collection is available.

COLORADO NEWSPAPERS see Newspapers, Colorado

COLORADO PIONEER SOCIETY

CO —DENVER PUBLIC LIBRARY, Western History Department, 1357 Broadway, Denver, 80203. Eleanor M Gehres, Head
Holdings: Vols (50,000) Cat Mss Maps Pix Audiotapes Microforms
Notes: Western US History. The department has a separate catalog, published in 1970 in 7 vols by G K Hall Co. First supplement published in 1975 in 1 vol. There is a subject index of some 3 million entries to newspapers and magazines of the Rocky Mountain region, added to daily. The Western Newspaper Microfilm Center contains approx 7000 reels of Western US newspapers. Collection has ca 275,000 negatives and prints of Western life; and ca 2500 maps, cataloged and classified.

COLORADO PROGRESSIVE (BULL MOOSE) PARTY

CO —UNIVERSITY OF COLORADO, Libraries, Western Historical Collections, Boulder, 80309.
Holdings: // Cat Mss Pix
Notes: Papers of Edward P Costigan, the founder of Colorado's Progressive (Bull Moose) Party. He became nationally known for his defense of union miners accused of murder. From 1917-1928 he served on the US Tariff Commission. In 1930 he was elected to the US Senate; during his term he supported New Deal legislation. The collection contains 43 boxes of sorted personal and legislative materials, two boxes of unsorted clippings, and a sizable personal library; it covers the period from 1897 to 1937. A published guide is available.

COLORADO RIVER

AZ —NORTHERN ARIZONA UNIVERSITY, Special Collection Library, CU Box 6022, Flagstaff, 86011. Peter M Whiteley, Coordr/Archivist; William Mullane, Librn
Notes: Newspaper articles, mainly from the *Arizona Republic,* about the Colorado River Commission which was involved with the rights of individual states in their use of the water in the Colorado River. Many of the articles are about W S Norviel, the Arizona State Water Commissioner at the time, 1921-1923. Also, Emery Kolb Collection; incl first motion picture film of the running of the Colorado River Rapids. This collection is subject to restrictions pending the cataloging of the collection.

AZ —COLORADO RIVER INDIAN TRIBES MUSEUM/LIBRARY, Rte One, Box 23-B, Parker, 85344. Priscilla Johnson, Librn
Holdings: Cat Mss Maps Pix Slides Audiotapes Microforms
Notes: Library deals with the four tribes of the Colorado River Indian Reservation: Mojave, Chemehuevi, Navajo, and Hopi. Emphasis is also given to the prehistoric cultures of this area; Patayan and Hohokam. Library collections include original manuscripts and other documents, photographs, oral history tape recordings, cultural items and artifacts. Copies of many documents relating to the reservation are in bound volumes, microfilm, and photocopies. Photos relative to the reservation from various other collections are copied in our collection. Of particular interest is the museum basket collection which incl about 1000 Chemehuevi baskets--the largest Chemehuevi basket collection. Other artifacts give special emphasis to the Mojave culture.

CA —AZUSA PACIFIC COLLEGE, Marshburn Memorial Library, Citrus & Alosta, Azusa, 91702. Edward Peterman, Librn
Holdings: Vols (6000) Uncat
Budget: ($30,000)
Notes: Significant holdings in the George E Fullerton Library of Californiana and Western Americana.

CA —POMONA PUBLIC LIBRARY, Special Collections, 625 S Garey Ave, PO Box 2271, Pomona, 91766. David Streeter, Librn
Holdings: // Uncat Pix
Notes: Some 600 photographs taken during the construction of Hoover Dam, also known as Boulder Dam.

CA —HUNTINGTON LIBRARY, Art Gallery & Botanical Gardens, 1151 Oxford Rd, San Marino, 91108. Robert L Middlekauff, Dir; Daniel H Woodward, Librn
Notes: An extensive collection.

COLORADO STATE FEDERATION OF LABOR

CO —UNIVERSITY OF COLORADO, Libraries, Western Historical Collections, Boulder, 80309.
Holdings: Cat Mss Pix
Notes: The Archive of the Colorado State Federation of Labor for the period 1896-1955, incl correspondence, reports, publications, photographs, totaling approx 40 shelf feet. These papers deal with a wide range of labor subjects and extensively document the Federation's legal, social and political activities since the 1890s. A typescript inventory is available.

COLORADO WOMEN'S TEMPERANCE UNION

CO —UNIVERSITY OF COLORADO, Libraries, Western Historical Collections, Boulder, 80309.
Holdings: Mss
Notes: The Colorado WCTU was organized in Longmont in 1880, two years after the formation of the first three locals in Greeley, Evans and Longmont. The Colorado WCTU was active in woman's suffrage, prison reform, homes for unwed mothers, day nurseries, 8-hour laws, and other reforms in addition to their primary concern of prohibition. The collection contains minutes of the Boulder Chapter (1881-1950) plus minutes of other Colorado local chapters for shorter periods of time. In addition there are state convention proceedings (1882-1969), state officers' minutes and reports, and many pamphlets and publications. 13 boxes and 12 oversize folders, 1878-1975. A published guide is available.

COLORED FLOWER PLATES

†CA —HUNTINGTON BOTANICAL GARDENS LIBRARY, 1151 Oxford Rd, San Marino, 91108. Ann Ravenscroft, Secretary
Holdings: Vols (8000)
Notes: Emphases on history of botanical science; papers and notes of American botanists and naturalists of The West; botanical illustration, etc. Subtropical horticulture, incl cacti and succulents of Australia, South Africa, and Mexico.

†CO —DENVER BOTANIC GARDENS, Helen Fowler Library, 909 York St, Denver, 80206. Solange G Gignac, Librn
Notes: Emphasis on Bromeliada Literature; horticulture; Colorado, Oregon, and Rocky Mountains Region botany; landscape architecture; juvenile horticultural and botanical literature. Incl over 5000 pamphlets on botany and horticulture; also, 197 watercolors of Colorado wildflowers by Emma Irvine, and 250 of Oregon by Lillian Hallock.

OH —GARDEN CENTER OF GREATER CLEVELAND, Eleanor Squire Library, 11030 East Blvd, Cleveland, 44106. Richard T Isaacson, Librn
Notes: The Warren C Corning Collection of Horticultural Classics. The Flowering Plant Index of Illustration and Information.

COLORED PEOPLE (U.S.) see Blacks

COLORIMETRY

IN —INDIANA UNIVERSITY, Optometry Branch Library, Bloomington, 47405. Roger Deckman, Head; Elizabeth Egan, Branch Librn
Holdings: Vols (11,000) Cat Slides Microforms
Budget:
Notes: Incl all aspects of vision: anatomy, physiology, pathology of the eye, neurophysiology, perception, colorimetry, illumination, safety, etc. Interlibrary loans through Main Library, Indiana University, Bloomington.

NY —ROCHESTER INSTITUTE OF TECHNOLOGY, Technical & Education Center of the Graphic Arts, Graphic Arts Information Service, One Lomb Memorial Dr, Rochester, 14623. Susan Clark, Technical Librn

COLORS (FLAGS) see Flags (Vexillology)

COLSTEN, LEVIN J.

MD —UNIVERSITY OF BALTIMORE, Langsdale Library, 1420 Maryland Ave, Baltimore, 21201. Gerry Watkins, Head of Special Collections Dept
Notes: Receipts, other financial records of Levin J Colsten (1883-1903); manifests, correspondence, cargo lists, orders (0.5 cubic feet).

COLUBRINAE see Snakes

COLUM, PADRAIC

DC —GEORGETOWN UNIVERSITY, Library, Special Collections Div, 37 & O Sts NW, Washington, 20057. George M Barringer, Special Collections Librn; Nicholas B Sheetz, Mss Librn
Holdings: Mss
Notes: The Archives of the Gallery of Living Catholic Authors was founded in 1932 by Sister Mary Joseph of the Sisters of Loretto to focus attention on modern Catholic literature, and to provide a depository for manuscripts, letters, photographs, and books by contemporary Catholic writers. Contains material by hundreds of writers, incl Hilaire Belloc, Roy Campbell, Padraic Colum, Eric Gill, Paul Horgan, Mary Lavin, Marie Belloc Lowndes, Kathleen Norris, Alred Noyes, Sheila Kaye-Smith, Sigrid Undset, and Evelyn Waugh, to name only a few.

NY —STATE UNIVERSITY OF NEW YORK, BINGHAMTON, Glenn G Bartle Library, Binghamton, 13901. Marion Hanscom, Special Collections Librn
Notes: The Colum Collection, consisting of the notebooks, mss, galley proofs of Padraic Colum, and letters to both Padraic and Mary

COLUM, PADRAIC (cont.)

Colum. Books by the Colums [in variant editions], and about them.
BC —UNIVERSITY OF VICTORIA, McPherson Library, Victoria, V8W 3H5, Can.
Notes: Incl mss of poem "The Honeyseller for Marshall E Beam."

COLUMBIA BROADCASTING SYSTEM (CBS)

DC —LIBRARY OF CONGRESS, Motion Pictures, Broadcasting and Recorded Sound Div, Washington, 20540.
Notes: A F R Lawrence Collection incl radio broadcasts represented by commercials probably made between 1926 and 1932 for CBS stations and excerpts from programs featuring Jack Benny, Ed Wynn, and other leading performers. While the greater portion of Dr Lawrence's historical speech collection was acquired by the New York Public Library, many important published and unpublished items were part of the 1974 purchase, incl a number of voice transcriptions of political figures made for the Columbia Graphophone Company series "Nation's Forum."

COLUMBIA CONSERVE COMPANY, INDIANAPOLIS

IN —INDIANA UNIVERSITY, Lilly Library, Seventh St, Bloomington, 47405. William R Cagle, Librn
Holdings: // Mss
Notes: Papers of an Indianapolis cannery, the Columbia Conserve Company, 1903-1953. Incl correspondence; minutes of the Council, annual meetings, and stockholders; stock certificate books; account books and general ledgers; sales reports; production records; and some printed matter about the company. 56,321 items.

COLUMBIA RIVER, OREGON

OR —ASTORIA PUBLIC LIBRARY, Astor Library, 450 Tenth St, Astoria, 97103. Bruce Berney, Dir
Holdings: Vols 500 Cat Pix Audiotapes Microforms Newspapers
Budget: $300
Notes: History of Lower Columbia River area. Incl file of local newspapers, 1873 to date. 1,000 photographs of Fort Stevens and other coastal defense facilities.

COLUMBIA RIVER BASIN

†WA —WASHINGTON STATE UNIVERSITY, Library, Manuscripts, Archives & Special Collections, Pullman, 99164. John F Guido, Head
Holdings: Cat Mss Maps Pix
Notes: The manuscript collection incl business and financial records of banks, breweries, fisheries, insurance, land, lumber and livestock companies, trade and commodity associations; as well as the personal and professional papers of authors, aviators, educators, engineers, farmers, historians, pioneers, politicians and scientists; especially rich in documents relating to the exploration, settlement and development of the Palouse Country, the Inland Empire, the Columbia Basin and the Pacific Northwest. Described in *Selected Manuscript Resources in the Washington State University Library* (Pullman, 1974); and other published and unpublished inventories and registers.

COLUMBIA UNIVERSITY OFFICE OF RADIO RESEARCH (1940-)

NY —ROCKEFELLER UNIVERSITY, Rockefeller Archive Center, Hillcrest, Pocantico Hills, North Tarrytown, 10591. Joseph W Ernst, Dir; J William Hess, Assoc Dir
Notes: Papers relative to the Rockefeller Family, Foundations, University, and other specific enterprises and contributions to particular areas of social, physical, educational, and historic reform, preservation, conservation, or development. Extensive records of administrative, financial, physical, or intellectual relationships.

COLUMBIAN EXPOSITION, CHICAGO, 1893 see World'S Columbian Exposition, Chicago, 1893

COLUMBUS, CHRISTOPHER

CT —YALE UNIVERSITY, Sterling Memorial Library, Latin American Collections, New Haven, 06520. Lee H Williams Jr, Cur
Holdings: Vols (300,000) Cat Mss
Notes: The Columbus Collection, containing briefs, documents and mss covering the lawsuit initiated by Columbus's descendants to determine who was entitled to his estate.
DC —LIBRARY OF CONGRESS, Rare Book & Special Collections Div, Washington, 20540. William Matheson, Chief
Notes: John Boyd Thacher Collection of Books, Pamphlets, Broadsides, and Manuscripts, which incl Early Americana and works regarding Christopher Columbus. The Henry Harrisse Collection of 213 volumes, cataloged, comprises works and bibliographies relating to Americana, incl the author's own interleaved and profusely annotated copies of his writings on the Columbus period, together with volumes containing his correspondence with bibliographers and collectors of the latter part of the 19th century.
See also entry under Incunabula
IL —NEWBERRY LIBRARY, 60 W Walton St, Chicago, 60610. Diana Haskell, Cur of Modern Mss
Holdings: Cat Maps
Notes: Restricted use: noncirculating.
MA —BRANDEIS UNIVERSITY, Goldfarb Library, 415 South St, Waltham, 02154. Bessie Hahn, Dir
Notes: McKew-Parr Collection on Magellan and the Age of Discovery. Approx 4000 books relating to Magellan and Columbus and other voyagers of the 15th and early 16th century. A card catalog to the collection is located in Special Collections.
MI —UNIVERSITY OF MICHIGAN, William L Clements Library, Ann Arbor, 48109. John C Dann, Dir
Notes: The William L. Clements Library of Americana is a non-circulating rare book library of original source material, printed and manuscript, dealing with America, from the discovery period into the late nineteenth century. The collection includes approximately 55,000 books and pamphlets, 550 linear feet of manuscripts, 4,100 volumes of newspapers, 36,000 maps, 40,000 pieces of sheet music, and 1,000 prints. The collection is strongest for the period of the American Revolution, and includes the papers of Thomas Gage, Sir Henry Clinton, and the Earl of Shelburne. Other areas of strength include antislavery, cartography and geography, discovery and exploration, American Indians, The Civil War, tune-books, sermons and orations, and the War of 1812. There are selective research collections dealing with Christopher Columbus, Thomas Paine, Benjamin Franklin, George Washington, Thomas Jefferson, and the Federalist Papers. Publications describing the collections of the library are: Author/Title catalog of Americana 1493-1860 in the William L. Clements Library... 7 volumes, Boston, G. K. Hall, 1970; Guide to the manuscript collections of the William L. Clements Library, by Arlene P. Shy 3d edition, Boston, G. K. Hall, 1978; Guide to the manuscript maps in the William L. Clements Library, compiled by Christian Burn, Ann Arbor, U. of Michigan, 1959; and Research catalog of maps of America, to 1860 in the William L. Clements Library...,edited by Douglas W. Marshall, 4 volumes, Boston, G. K. Hall, 1972.
NY —NEW YORK PUBLIC LIBRARY, Rare Books and Manuscripts Div, Fifth Ave & 42 St, New York, 10018. William L Joyce, Asst Dir; Francis O Mattson, Curator
Holdings: Cat
Budget: ($7161)
Notes: Most editions of Columbus' "Letter."
PA —PENNSYLVANIA STATE UNIVERSITY, Fred Lewis Pattee Library, Special Collections Dept, University Park, 16802. Charles Mann, Chief, Special Collections
Holdings: // Mss Microforms
Notes: Papers from the Columbus family--116 microfilm reels; Boal family papers--94.5 feet. Principally 1700-date. Listed in *Columbus and Related Family Papers, 1451-1902; An Inventory of the Boal Collection*, by D C Henderson and R L Garner. (Pennsylvania State University Press, 1974), 94 pp. No photocopying.

COLVILLE INDIANS

†WA —WASHINGTON STATE UNIVERSITY, Library, Manuscripts, Archives & Special Collections, Pullman, 99164. John F Guido, Head
Holdings: Cat Mss Maps Pix
Notes: The collection is especially rich in documents relating to the exploration, settlement and development of the Palouse Country, the Inland Empire, the Columbia Basin and the Pacific Northwest. Described in *Selected Manuscript Resources in the Washington State University Library* (Pullman, 1974); and other published and unpublished inventories and registers.

COMANCHE INDIANS

OK —US ARMY FIELD ARTILLERY SCHOOL LIBRARY, Morris Swett Library, Snow Hall, Fort Sill, 73503. Lester L Miller Jr, Chief Librn
Notes: Incl data on Fort Sill, Indian Territory, settlement of Kiowa, Apache and Commanche tribes, imprisonment of Geronimo, Oklahoma territory, settlement of Lawton. Unit histories, incl 10th Cavalry (Buffalo Soldiers, a black unit that built Fort Sill); working papers of Sheridan, Grierson and other commanders; Field Artillery School. Photographs on army subjects, Fort Sill, Indians, Indian Territory, settlement of Southwest Oklahoma.

COMBE, WILLIAM

OH —OHIO UNIVERSITY, Vernon R Alden Library, Department of Archives and Special Collections, Athens, 45701. Gary A Hunt, Head
Holdings: Vols 65 Cat Mss
Notes: The collection of Dr Harlan Hamilton, Combe's biographer, augmented by later additions.

COMBINES

CA —UNIVERSITY OF CALIFORNIA, DAVIS, Shields Library, Dept of Special Collections, Davis, 95616. Donald Kunitz, Head; C Danial Elliott, Asst Head
Holdings: Uncat Mss Pix Slides
Notes: Manufacturer's catalogs, manuals, parts lists, ephemera, and literature pertaining to historical as well as current data on such items as tractors, engines,

COMBINES (cont.)

combines, hay equipment, etc. Described in "The Higgins Library: A Source for the Study of Agricultural History," Don Kunitz, *Agricultural History,* vol 49, 1975, pp 89-91. 13,000 VF, cataloged.

COMBUSTION

PA —FRANKLIN INSTITUTE LIBRARY, 20 & The Parkway, Philadelphia, 19103. Miriam Padusis, Dir; Charles Wilt, Readers Servs Librn
Holdings: Vols (300,000) Cat Maps Pix Microforms

COMBUSTORS

IA —DELEVAN DIVISION OF COLT INDUSTRIES INC, Engineering Library, 811 Fourth St, PO Box 100, West Des Moines, 50265. G A Hartman, Librn
Holdings: Vols 2000 Cat Mss Slides Microforms
Budget: $400
Notes: Incl liquid atomization, droplet size measurement and representation, fuel nozzles for combustors, and spray nozzles for industrial and agricultural applications.

COMEDIAS SUELTA

MI —WAYNE STATE UNIVERSITY, G Flint Purdy Library, Detroit, 48202. K L Kaul, Asst Dir & Head
Notes: Materials noted in *A Descriptive Catalogue of the Spanish Comedias Suelta* and the Private Library of Professor B B Ashcom (1965).

COMEDY

KY —HOPKINSVILLE COMMUNITY COLLEGE, Library, North Dr, Hopkinsville, 42240. Marjanna J Frising, Librn
Holdings: Vols (500) Cat Phonorecords Audiotapes Filmstrips
Notes: Incl most notable Broadway plays, both musical and non-musical, with sound-tracks available for most. Also a large collection of children's and one-act plays as well as non-musical but best known 3-act plays, incl comedy and mystery plays.

†MD —MARYLAND HISTORICAL SOCIETY, Library, 201 W Monument St, Baltimore, 21201.
Notes: Eubie Blake's personal and professional archive. Incl the Baltimore-born pianist, composer, and songwriter's collection of songs and instrumental pieces in mss, extensive documentation of his collaboration with Noble Sissle, Flournog Miller, Milton Reddie, and others. The Broadway musical comedy, Shuffle Along, is represented in box office records, programs, scores and parts, photographs, and sheet music. Blake's involvement with other productions is similarly documented.

NY —NEW YORK PUBLIC LIBRARY, Performing Arts Research Center, Billy Rose Theatre Collection, 111 Amsterdam Ave, New York, 10023. Dorothy L Swerdlove, Cur
Holdings: Cat Videotapes 16mm Films

NC —UNIVERSITY OF NORTH CAROLINA, CHARLOTTE, J Murrey Atkins Library, UNCC Station, Charlotte, 28223. Robert F Brabham Jr, Special Collections Librn
Holdings: Cat
Notes: Most of the plays (842 in 110 vols) were originally collected by Augusta Sophia, a daughter of George III. At her death, they passed to her brother Ernst August, Elector of Hanover, and became part of the Knigliche Ernst-August-Fideicommiss-Bibliothek, which was dispersed at auction in 1970-1971. Period covered is 1618-1826.

COMEDY, SPANISH

MI —WAYNE STATE UNIVERSITY, G Flint Purdy Library, Detroit, 48202. K L Kaul, Asst Dir & Head
Notes: Materials noted in *A Descriptive Catalogue of the Spanish Comedias Suelta* and the Private Library of Professor B B Ashcom (1965).

COMENIUS, JOHANNES AMOS

MA —HARVARD UNIVERSITY LIBRARY, Widener Library, Cambridge, 02138.
Holdings: Cat
Notes: See *Harvard Library Bulletin, XIX* (1971), 412-415.

COMER, DONALD

AL —BIRMINGHAM PUBLIC LIBRARY, Dept of Archives & Mss, 2020 Seventh Ave N, Birmingham, 35203. Marvin Y Whiting, Archivist & Cur
Holdings: Mss Pix Slides Audiotapes Microforms
Notes: Especially Birmingham history. Largest available collections are the Robert Jemison, Jr Papers (ca 1.2 million items) and the Donald Comer Papers (ca 390,000 items). Photographs incl ca one million negatives from the collection of Birmingham photographer Charles Preston.

COMER, VIRGINIA LEE

AZ —ARIZONA STATE UNIVERSITY, Library, Tempe, 85287. Marilyn Wurzburger, Special Collections Librn
Holdings: Vols (108) Pix
Notes: Collection covers various aspects of Children's Theatre from 1944 through the present. Areas of emphasis incl International and National Child Drama Associations, award-winning theatres, educational programs, regional groups and prominent figures in Children's Theatre incl: Irene Vickers Baker, Isabel Burger, Virginia Lee Comer, Rita Criste, Moses Goldberg, Kenneth Graham, Aurand Harris, Paul Kozelka, George Latshaw, Rosemary Musil, Sara Spencer, Winifred Ward, Susan Zeder and Lin Wright. Publications incl newsletters, research papers, bibliographies and records of the proceedings of the Children's Theatre Association of America. 80 linear feet of scripts, documents, publications, films, tapes (oral history) programs, correspondence, photographs, working papers and clippings. Partially indexed; finding guides available.

COMFORT, WILL LIVINGSTON, 1878-1932

CA —UNIVERSITY OF CALIFORNIA, LOS ANGELES, Research Library, Dept of Special Collections, 405 Hilgard Ave, Los Angeles, 90024. Edward Shreeves, Chairman, Bibliographers Group; David S Zeidberg, Head
Holdings: Vols 20 Cat Mss Pix
Notes: 20 first and other editions of his books; 2.5 linear feet of correspondence.

COMIC BOOKS, STRIPS, ETC.

CA —CALIFORNIA STATE UNIVERSITY, FULLERTON, Library, Box 4150, Fullerton, 92634. Kathy Morris, Archivist
Notes: 2000 comic books. All Star Trek scripts. Some fanzines and undergrounds.

CA —UNIVERSITY OF CALIFORNIA, LOS ANGELES, Research Library, Dept of Special Collections, 405 Hilgard Ave, Los Angeles, 90024. Edward Shreeves, Chairman, Bibliographers Group; David S Zeidberg, Head
Notes: 32 linear feet of comic books, mostly US, 1940s-1960s.

CA —UNIVERSITY OF CALIFORNIA, LOS ANGELES, Theater Arts Library, Los Angeles, 90024. Edward Shreeves, Chairman, Bibliographers Group; Audree Malkin, Head, Theater Arts Library
Notes: A collection of original comic books, color comic books, storyboards, and posters illustrated by Clyde Geronimi.

CA —FITZ HUGH LUDLOW MEMORIAL LIBRARY, PO Box 99346, San Francisco, 94109. Michael R Aldrich, Exec Cur
Notes: Collection stored. Important mail inquiries only. No interlibrary lending or telephone queries. Collection incl comic books relating to psychoactive drug use and abuse.

CA —SAN FRANCISCO ACADEMY OF COMIC ART, Library, 2850 Ulloa, San Francisco, 94116.
Notes: Incl largest collection of pulp magazines in US. Paper copies of all major American newspapers, emphasis on Hearst papers. Extensive collection of Sherlockiana and a member of the National Sherlockiana Society. Also extensive collection of early motion picture tapes, books, magazines and posters. 19th and early 20th century children's books also in the holdings. Collection incl 1,000,000 comic strips, 22,000 comic books, 12,500 hard cover mystery books, 8000 hard cover science fiction books and copies of all science fiction pulp magazines.

DC —LIBRARY OF CONGRESS, Serial and Government Publications Division, Washington, 20540.
Notes: Over 2300 titles in over 47,000 pieces. Grows by ca 200 issues per month. Scattered issues date to the 1930s. Most comprehensive from 1950 to the present. Faily complete runs of *Action Comics, Archie, Detective Comics, Tarzan* and *Wonder Woman.* Use restricted to serious cholarly research.

IL —CENTER FOR RESEARCH LIBRARIES, 6050 S Kenwood Ave, Chicago, 60637. Donald B Simpson, Dir; Esther Smith, Collection Development Librn
Holdings: Vols 5000 Uncat
Notes: A random sample of representative comic books and popular magazines, 1950-1983.

IL —SOUTHERN ILLINOIS UNIVERSITY, Lovejoy Library, Catalog Dept, Edwardsville, 62026. Milton C Moore, Librn
Notes: Comic books, 1500.

IL —NORTHWESTERN UNIVERSITY, Library, Special Collections Dept, 1937 Sheridan Rd, Evanston, 60201. R Russell Maylone, Cur
Holdings: Vols 9500 Cat
Notes: Collection of historical comics, underground comics and fan magazines.

IN —INDIANA UNIVERSITY, Lilly Library, Seventh St, Bloomington, 47405. William R Cagle, Librn
Holdings: Cat Mss
Notes: 1500 issues of Marvel Comics. Mss incl illustrations for Toonerville Trolley and Brenda Starr; also a growing collection of individual pieces representative of comic strip art and animation.

KY —UNIVERSITY OF LOUISVILLE, Ekstrom Library, Rare Books & Special Collections, 2301 S Third St, Louisville, 40208. George T McWhorter, Cur; Delinda Stephens Buie, Asst Cur
Holdings: Vols 5000 // Mss Pix
Notes: Mint first editions of Edgar Rice Burroughs and subsequent editions of all his works; foreign editions in 35 languages; serial publications; comics and Sunday "fulls"; big-little books; fan magazines; posters; bibliographies and related materials.

†MD —UNIVERSITY OF MARYLAND, BALTIMORE COUNTY, Library, Baltimore, 21228. Maureen Dwyer-Hirten, Librn
Notes: 1000 comic books with some Air Fighters and extensive undergrounds.

MI —MICHIGAN STATE UNIVERSITY, Libraries, Special Collections Div, East Lansing, 48824. Jannette Fiore, Librn
Holdings: Vols 23,500 Cat
Notes: The Russel B Nye Popular Culture Collection in the Michigan State Univ Libraries incl over (45,000) items. Most of the collection is organized into 4 categories: comic art, popular fiction, popular information materials and materials relating to the popular performing arts. The Comic Art Collection incl approx 20,000 comic books and another 1000 books, magazines and fanzines about comics. Best-represented are the super-hero comics of the 1960s--over 90 percent of those published can be found

COMIC BOOKS, STRIPS, ETC. (cont.)

in the collection. Samples, and sometimes substantial runs, of comics in other genres (eg, war comics, funny animal comics, underground comics) are also maintained and there are over 1000 issues from the 1940s. Also the James Haynes Collection of "Golden Age" comics incl 21,000 items.The comics are cataloged, with author-title and subject access and a checklist of holdings. Several hundred pages of indexes to comic books are added to the collection by the Amateur Press Alliance for Indexing each year,and an annual index to these is available. A quarterly newsletter of news about the MSU collection and other public comics collections is also published.

NJ —FAIRLEIGH DICKINSON UNIVERSITY, Friendship Library, 285 Madison Ave, Madison, 07940. James Fraser, Library Dir; Renee Weber, Cur
Holdings: Vols 1200 Cat Mss
Budget: $7500
Notes: Harry A Chesler Collection, incl 4000 original drawings and paintings of comic strips, covers, and magazine illustrations. No photocopying.

NY —COMICS MAGAZINE ASSOCIATION OF AMERICA, Library, 60 E 42 St, New York, 10165. J Dudley Waldner, Librn
Holdings: Vols 2000 Cat Pix Microforms
Budget: $200
Notes: Primary material incl comic books from 1979 through present; books and magazine articles relating to comics, and newspaper clippings relating to comics.

NY —MUSEUM OF CARTOON ART LIBRARY, Comly Avenue, Rye Brook, 10573.
Notes: Original comics and cartoon art, 60, 000 pieces. 800 animated cartoons. Disney collection extensive. Samples of Big-Little Books, foreign comics, fanzines, cartoon related games, posters, pulps, undergrounds. Hal Foster, Walt Kelly, Gene Byrns, Tad Dorgan, Chester Gould extensive original art collections.

†NY —SYRACUSE UNIVERSITY LIBRARIES, E S Bird Library, George Arents Research Library, Rm 600, Syracuse, 13210. Mr Sidney Huttner, Librn
Notes: Samples or selections of cartoon art, comic strips, Disney, fantasy, fanzines, horror (Ackerman mss), mystery pulps, series books and westerns.

NC —UNIVERSITY OF NORTH CAROLINA, CHARLOTTE, J Murrey Atkins Library, UNCC Station, Charlotte, 28223. Robert F Brabham Jr, Special Collections Librn
Holdings: Vols 500 Cat Mss
Notes: Principally American and English. Strength of the collection is US, 1800-1850. Incl 200 vols from the collection of Elizabeth Botteme Lewis. Also incl first editions of Andrew Lang's fairy books, several series of books for boys (early 20th century), and 1960s comic books. Also incl small collection of papers of and ephemera collected by Wilbur Macey Stone, collector and writer about historical children's books.

OH —BOWLING GREEN STATE UNIVERSITY, Library, Popular Culture Library, Bowling Green, 43403.
Notes: Extensive holdings of Big-Little books, comic books, matchbook covers, picture postcards, personal scrapbooks, trading cards, posters, magazines, film pressbooks, juvenile series novels and popular literature.

OH —OHIO STATE UNIVERSITY, Library for Communication and Graphic Arts, 242 W 18th St, Columbus, 43210. Lucy S Caswell, Curator
Notes: Original comic art of Caniff, Foster, Dunn, Dudley T Fisher. Extensive original cartoon art. Shel Dorf Collection of comic strips and related material. A small but growing collection of comic books especially those featuring *Katy Keene*, is available in the Library. Movie posters and stills, 110, 000. Incl Milton Caniff Research Room.

†PA —UNIVERSITY OF PITTSBURGH, Hillman Library, 363 Hillman Library, Pittsburgh, 15260. Charles E Aston, Jr, Coordr
Notes: 8000 issues.

BC —COMIC RESEARCH LIBRARY, Cassidy, V0R 1H0, Can. Doug Kendig, Librn
Notes: Newspaper strips and related material. A private library with approx 180, 000 newspaper strips and 1000 vols of related material in books. The strips are clipped and organized and mounted in books for the titles beginning A-F, covering the 1920s through the 1950s. Open to the public by appointment.

COMIC BOOKS, STRIPS, ETC., FOREIGN

†MI —MICHIGAN STATE UNIVERSITY, Libraries, East Lansing, 48824. Jannette Flore, Librn
Notes: Good samples of Big-Little Books, foreign comics, dime novels, pulps, TV scripts, underground comics. SFWA and Clarion depository.

NY —MUSEUM OF CARTOON ART LIBRARY, Comly Avenue, Rye Brook, 10573.
Notes: Original comics and cartoon art, 60, 000 pieces. 800 animated cartoons. Disney collection extensive. Samples of Big-Little Books, foreign comics, fanzines, cartoon related games, posters, pulps, undergrounds. Hal Foster, Walt Kelly, Gene Byrns, Tad Dorgan, Chester Gould extensive original art collections.

†OH —BOWLING GREEN STATE UNIVERSITY, Libraries, Bowling Green, 43403. Nancy White Lee, Librn
Notes: Extensive miscellaneous incl Sunday strips, Big-Little Books, fanzines, foreign comics, pulps, gum cards, undergrounds, and movie posters.

COMIC BOOKS, STRIPS, ETC., UNDERGROUND

†CA —UNIVERSITY OF CALIFORNIA, BERKELEY, Bancroft Library, Berkeley, 94720. James D Hart, Director
Notes: Underground comics, 500. Max Brand and H Rider Haggard Collections.

†CT —UNIVERSITY OF CONNECTICUT LIBRARY, Storrs, 06268.
Notes: Ca 150 underground comics. Part of the Alternative Press Collection.

†IA —IOWA STATE UNIVERSITY, Library, Dept of Special Collections, Ames, 50011. Stanley Yates, Librn
Notes: Underground comics, 1000. EC, 84 items.

†MI —MICHIGAN STATE UNIVERSITY, Libraries, East Lansing, 48824. Jannette Flore, Librn
Notes: Good samples of Big-Little Books, foreign comics, dime novels, pulps, TV scripts, underground comics. SFWA and Clarion depository.

†PA —TEMPLE UNIVERSITY LIBRARY, Philadelphia, 19122. Thomas M Whitehead, Librn
Notes: 500 underground comics.

†WI —STATE HISTORICAL SOCIETY OF WISCONSIN, Mass Communications History Center, 816 State Street, Madison, 53706.
Notes: *Kitchen Sink* underground comics standing order. August Derleth's comics collection. Microfilm of comic strips and pulp magazines.

COMIC LITERATURE see Comedy

COMIC OPERAS AND OPERETTAS see Opera, Comic, and Operetta

COMIC STRIPS see Comic Books, Strips, Etc.

COMICS see Comic Books, Strips, Etc.

COMICS, FOREIGN see Comic Books, Strips, Etc., Foreign

COMICS, UNDERGROUND see Comic Books, Strips, Etc., Underground

COMMEMORATIVE VOLUMES see Festschriften

COMMENTARIES, BIBLICAL see Bible—Commentaries

COMMENTATORS see Journalists

COMMERCE

CA —UNIVERSITY OF CALIFORNIA, DAVIS, Shields Library, Dept of Special Collections, Davis, 95616. Donald Kunitz, Head; C Danial Elliott, Asst Head
Holdings: Uncat Mss Pix Pamphlets
Notes: The Cebis Wine Collection (2500 items) incl brochures, wine lists and labels from Eastern Europe, clippings and brochures on wine by subject. The California Wineries Records (24,000 items) incl correspondence, inspection reports with emphasis on wine production, the physical nature of specific wineries, import/export involvement. These records, filed with the Federal Bureau of Alcohol, Tobacco and Firearms, cover 1922-53. Wine bottle labels for wines and liquors imported into the United States or bottled here which were submitted of the Alcohol and Tobacco Tax Division of the Internal Revenue Service for approval, 1963-68, are held in the Wine Bottle Label Collection (21,000 items).

CA —GOLDEN GATE UNIVERSITY, One Embarcadero Center, No 216, San Francisco, 94111. Jeanne Nichols, Librn
Notes: World Trade Libraries and archives.

DC —EXPORT-IMPORT BANK OF THE UNITED STATES, EXIMBANK Library, 811 Vermont Ave NW, Washington, 20571. Theodora McGill, Librn; John Posniak, Asst Librn
Holdings: Vols (15,000) Maps Audiotapes
Notes: The library has almost a complete set of the Economist Intelligence unit of London's *Quarterly Economic Reviews*; various types of materials with general, economics and statistical data on virtually every country of the world; incl foreign government publications, publications of various international organizations, and US Government documents.

DC —GEORGETOWN UNIVERSITY, Library, Special Collections Div, 37 & O Sts NW, Washington, 20057. George M Barringer, Special Collections Librn; Nicholas B Sheetz, Mss Librn
Notes: Incl the Heinrich Kronstein Memorial Collection of International and Foreign Trade Law.

DC —INTERNATIONAL MONETARY FUND AND WORLD BANK, Joint Bank-Fund Library, Washington, 20431. Maureen M Moore, Librn
Holdings: Vols Cat Films Microforms
Notes: Incl foreign trade and statistical bulletins and yearbooks, central bank reports and bulletins, budget papers, security yearbooks, economic development plans and reports on economic conditions from the 132 member countries. An index of periodical material compiled by the Library staff has been published as: *Economics and Finance; Index to Periodical Articles, 1947-1971;* First Supplement, 1972, 1973, 1974 (Second Supplement, 1975, 1976, 1977, in preparation), 5 vols. (Boston: G K Hall, 1972, 1975). Also, The Developing Areas: *A Classed Bibliography of the Joint Bank-Fund Library,* Vol 1: *Latin America and the* Caribbean; Vol 2: *Africa and the Middle* East; Vol 3: *Asia and Oceania* (Boston: G K Hall, 1976).

FL —FLORIDA DEPT OF COMMERCE, Research Library, 408 Fletcher Bldg, Tallahassee, 32301. Dennis Hitchens, Librn
Holdings: Vols (3000) Cat Mss Maps VF
Budget: ($6000)
Notes: Collect materials related to the 2 divisions of the Florida Dept of Commerce: Economic Development and Tourism, incl titles on Florida (historical and current), international trade, transportation, education, employment, management, industrial development and business. The Florida and US documents collection covers population, manufacturing, employment, agriculture, retail trade, wholesale trade and labor. VF incl files on every city and county, especially local economic data, SIC coded material, out-of-state information, county files, Florida specific material and general subject material. 100 VF drawers.

HI —BANK OF HAWAII, Information Ctr, PO Box 2900, Honolulu, 96846. Sally Campbell, Information Mgr
Holdings: Vols 4000 Cat Maps VF
Notes: Economics research in developing areas of Hawaii, US Pacific Islands, Asian

COMMERCE (cont.)

and other foreign countries. Emphasis on economics, business statistics, demography, finance, banking, tourist industry, construction, domestic and foreign trade. Incl 1000 serial titles.

IL —CENTER FOR RESEARCH LIBRARIES, 6050 S Kenwood Ave, Chicago, 60637. Donald B Simpson, Dir; Esther Smith, Collection Development Librn
Holdings: Vols Cat
Notes: Very extensive holdings of older scientific journals, especially in medicine, applied science, technology, industry and trade. Currently 5,000 titles.

MA —HARVARD UNIVERSITY, Graduate School of Business Administration, Baker Library, Soldiers Field, Boston, 02163. Mary V Chatfield, Librn; Florence Bartoshesky, Cur of Manuscripts and Archives
Holdings: Vols (470,805) Cat Mss Microforms
Notes: Catalog (32 volumes) published in 1971 by G K Hall; 3-volume supplement published in 1974 (out of print).

NY —NEW YORK PUBLIC LIBRARY, Research Libraries, Economic & Public Affairs Div, Fifth Ave & 42 St, New York, 10018. Edward DiRoma, Chief
Holdings: Vols (1,500,000) Cat Microforms

NC —GREENSBORO PUBLIC LIBRARY, Oral History Program Library, Drawer X-4, Greensboro, 27402. Eugene Edwin Pfaff, Jr, Librn
Holdings: Videotapes Audiotapes
Notes: Oral history on the cultural, social, and economic development of Greensboro and Guilford County; the program is expanding to incl prominent North Carolinians throughout the state. Collection consists of 42 videotapes and 93 audiotapes which are uncataloged.

PA —UNIVERSITY OF PENNSYLVANIA, Lippincott Library of the Wharton School, Philadelphia, 19104. Michael Halperin, Librn
Holdings: Cat
Notes: Long files of statistical data on the foreign trade of the US and many foreign countries. Extensive materials on foreign taxation and regulation of US enterprises abroad.

PA —SCRANTON PUBLIC LIBRARY, Vine & N Washington Sts, Scranton, 18503. Thomas McHale, Dir
Holdings: Vols (192) Cat
Budget: ($7000)
Notes: Foreign trade information service.

TX —EAST TEXAS STATE UNIVERSITY, James G Gee Library, Special Collections Dept, East Texas Station, Commerce, 75428. James Conrad, Dept Head
Holdings: Vols (3500) Cat Mss Pix Slides
Notes: The books on Black Literature (with the exception of those on Texas folklore) and Slavery in the US have been transferred to the general stack area of the library; however, our collection of county histories of Texas, which is still housed in the Special Collections, continues to grow. In addition, we have acquired sizable collections of books on Texas folklore and Texas placenames; and World War II posters. Another new area is printing arts in Texas. There is a separate dictionary card catalog for the book collection in the Special Collections Department.

TX —ECTOR COUNTY LIBRARY, Department of Business and Technology, 321 W 5th St, Odessa, 79760. Pat Jones, Dept Head
Holdings: Vols 100 Cat VF

PR —CARIBBEAN REGIONAL LIBRARY, General Library, University of Puerto Rico, Rio Piedras, (Mailing add: PO Box 21917, University Station, San Juan, 00931). Carmen M Costa de Ramos, Librn
Holdings: Vols (115,605) Cat Maps Pix Microforms
Notes: Collection is specialized in the Caribbean with emphasis in the areas of interest to developing countries: social sciences, politics, economics, labor, education, commerce, tourism, literature, etc. The *Current Caribbean Bibliography* is compiled at the Caribbean Regional Library, with card contributions from all countries of the Caribbean; it also lists all the new additions to the library.

COMMERCE—HISTORY

IN —PURDUE UNIVERSITY LIBRARIES, Graduate School of Management, Krannert Library, West Lafayette, 47907. Gordon Law, Librn
Holdings: Vols (7000) Cat Mss Maps Pix Microforms
Notes: The collection consists of books, journals and pamphlets dating from the early 16th to late 19th century, covering to a large degree the early literature in economic thought and business practices both here and abroad. No photocopying.

MA —HARVARD UNIVERSITY, Graduate School of Business Administration, Baker Library, Soldiers Field, Boston, 02163. Mary V Chatfield, Librn; Florence Bartoshesky, Cur of Manuscripts and Archives
Holdings: Vols (75,000) Cat Mss Pix
Notes: Baker Library strong in historical aspects of business and economics incl original company records, company histories, business biographies, histories of industries, etc; 16,000 pictures. Ms collection of more than 75,000 incl original records of business firms from 1400 (Medici Collection) to present; especially strong in 19th century. New England enterprises, textile firms, international trade, China trade, railroads, papers of several Northeast merchant families, 19th century small business. Also incl pictures, trade cards, clipper ship cards, money, trade catalogs, business cartoons, prices current and exhibit items. See Robert W Lovett and Eleanor C Bishop, compilers, *Business Manuscripts in Baker Library* (Boston: The Library, 1978), 382 pp. Mss are described in the*National Union Catlog of Manuscript Collections* and in Hamer's *A Guide to Archives and Manuscripts in the United States.* Restricted use: Manuscripts noncirculating. Downs: 1636, 2122, 2616, 2675, 2677, 2698, 2700, 2701, 2702, 2706, 2708, 2711, 2713-15, 2716, 2717-18, 2721-26, 2734, 2737, 2774, 2814, 4300, 5162: Supplement 964, 965, 968, 998.

MN —UNIVERSITY OF MINNESOTA, James Ford Bell Library, 309 19th Ave S, Minneapolis, 55455. John Parker, Cur
Holdings: Vols (11,000) Cat Mss Maps
Notes: Collection of original materials relating to European expansion, 1400-1800.

NY —STATE UNIVERSITY OF NEW YORK, STONY BROOK, Melville Library, Dept of Special Collections, Stony Brook, 11794. Evert Volkersz, Head
Holdings: Vols 95 Cat
Notes: Spanish-American colonial trade. 101 documents of the 16th and 17th centuries presenting information about trade and administration of the Spanish-American colonies and important for linking political and financial connections. A listing of the materials is available.

COMMERCE—STATISTICS

DC —US BUREAU OF THE CENSUS, Library, Federal Office Bldg 3, Rm 2451, Washington, 20233. Betty Baxtresser, Chief, ASD Library Branch
Holdings: Vols (274,863) Cat Microforms
Notes: Emphases on statistics of agriculture, business, construction, economics, foreign trade, governments, housing, industry, population, transportation, statistical methodology, and data processing. Library holdings are largely current materials covering the Bureau's programs. Outdated materials are withdrawn regularly.

COMMERCIAL AERONAUTICS see Aeronautics, Commercial

COMMERCIAL ART

CA —POMONA PUBLIC LIBRARY, Special Collections, 625 S Garey Ave, PO Box 2271, Pomona, 91766. David Streeter, Librn
Holdings: Cat
Notes: 4000 citrus box labels (world wide) indexed by brand name and packing house; 6000 California wine labels indexed by winery.

CT —YALE UNIVERSITY, Box 1603A, Yale Station, New Haven, 06520.
Holdings: Cat Mss Pix

MI —GOGEBIC COMMUNITY COLLEGE, Alex D Chisholm Learning Resources Center, Greenbush & Jackson Rd, Ironwood, 49938. Charles Tetzlaff, Dir of Learning Resources
Holdings: Vols (20,000)

MI —CAMPBELL-EWALD CO, Reference Center, 30400 Van Dyke, Warren, 48093. Susan Stepek, Mgr
Holdings: Vols 375 Cat Maps Pix
Notes: Collection intended for advertising agency personnel. Incl bound vols of periodicals, 36 vertical file drawers of pictures by subject, commercial art and photography annuals and current periodicals.

NY —PRATT INSTITUTE LIBRARY, Art & Architecture Dept, 200 Willoughby Ave, Brooklyn, 11205. Sydney Star Keaveney, Prof
Holdings: Vols (30,000) Cat Pix Slides
Budget: ($50,000)
Notes: Art and architecture, incl sculpture, photography, painting, design, costume, and commercial art. Incl 60,000 art slides. Use restricted to Pratt faculty and students.

NY —NEW YORK PUBLIC LIBRARY, Art, Prints, and Photographs Div, Fifth Ave & 42 St, New York, 10018. Donald Anderle, Chief
Holdings: Vols (150,000) Cat Mss Pix Microforms
Notes: History and design in the fine and applied arts. Architecture, painting, drawing, sculpture, costume, furniture, advertising art, prints, photography, crafts, and jewelry are among the subjects covered from ancient times to the present. See: New York Public Library *Dictionary Catalog of the Art and Architecture Division* (Boston, G K Hall, 1975), 30 vols. Holdings after that time are incl in the *Dictionary Catalog of the Research Libraries.* African Art and Afro-American Art are collected by the Schomburg Center for Research in Black Culture.

NY —ROCHESTER INSTITUTE OF TECHNOLOGY, Melbert B Cary Jr Graphic Arts Collection, School of Printing, One Lomb Memorial Drive, Rochester, 14623. David Pankow, Cur
Holdings: Vols (11,000) Cat
Notes: An extensive collection of the work of typographic artist Albert Schiller. Incl type pictures, their type forms, correspondence, sketches, books, proofs, and ephemera.

NC —TECHNICAL INSTITUTE OF ALAMANCE, Learning Resources Center, Jimmy Kerr Rd, PO Box 623, Haw River, 27258. Ron Plummer, Coordr
Holdings: Vols (465) Cat Slides Filmstrips Microforms
Notes: Commercial art and advertising design--technical illustration.

NC —NORTH CAROLINA STATE UNIVERSITY, Harry B Lyons Design Library, P. O. Box 7701, Raleigh, 27607. Maryellen LoPresti, Librn
Notes: Collection covers architecture, landscape architecture, design and related professions. Additional materials maybe found on art, painting sculpture photography and solar energy design. The library presently houses a total of 28,000 books, periodical and serial volumes to support the curriculum. A product and trade literature file and a vertical file of pamplets are also locally cataloged in the library representing an additional 3000 items of materials available for use. A significant collections of over 50,000 cataloged slides primarily representing the areas of art and architectural history are also contained in the library facility. See *Directory of Special Libraries and Information Centers.*

OH —CINCINNATI ART MUSEUM, Library, Eden Park, Cincinnati, 45202. Patrician P Rutledge, Librn
Holdings: Vols (45,850) Cat Microforms
Notes: Art library containing all subjects on

COMMERCIAL ART (cont.)

art-history, graphic arts, advertising art, etc; special strength in prints, ie engravings, etc. Near Eastern art and decorative arts are also strong. At least 90,000 art exhibition catalogs. Emphasis on artists of Cincinnati and vicinity in vertical file material.

RI —RHODE ISLAND SCHOOL OF DESIGN, Library, Two College St, Providence, 02903. James A Findlay, Dir
Holdings: Vols (70,000) Cat
Budget: ($50,000)

AB —SOUTHERN ALBERTA INSTITUTE OF TECHNOLOGY, Learning Resources Centre, 1301 16 Ave NW, Calgary, T2M 0L4, Can. Tom Skinner, Historian
Holdings: Vols (5000) Cat Pix Slides Films Audiotapes Filmstrips Videotapes
Notes: Serves Alberta College of Art (4-year professional course).

COMMERCIAL AVIATION see Aeronautics, Commercial

COMMERCIAL CATALOGS see Catalogs, Commercial

COMMERCIAL CORNERS see Speculation; Stock Exchanges

COMMERCIAL CRISES see Depressions—1929—U.S.

COMMERCIAL DESIGN see Commercial Art

COMMERCIAL EDUCATION see Business Education

COMMERCIAL LAW see Business Law

COMMERCIAL PRODUCTS—STANDARDS

ON —CANADIAN STANDARDS ASSOCIATION, Information Centre, 178 Rexdale Blvd, Rexdale, M9W 1R3, Can. Cameron D Mcdonald, Head Librn
Holdings: Vols 2000 Books; Cat Slides
Notes: 50,000 engineering and product standards; national and international. A supporting collection of books, periodicals and technical information files supports the standards collection. No photocopying.

COMMERCIAL SCHOOLS see Business Education

COMMERCIAL TEACHERS see Business Teachers

COMMERCIALS, RADIO see Radio Advertising

COMMERCIALS, TELEVISION see Television Advertising

COMMISSION FOR RELIEF IN BELGIUM, 1914-1924

CA —HOOVER INSTITUTION ON WAR, REVOLUTION & PEACE, Stanford University, Stanford, 94305. Milorad M Drachkovitch, Archivist
Holdings: Mss Pix
Notes: Records of the Commission for Relief in Belgium, organized in 1914 under the chairmanship of Herbert Hoover, incl correspondence, reports, memoranda, accounts, pamphlets, bulletins and photographs, 1914-1924, relating to procurement of food and other supplies in the US and their distribution in German-occupied Belgium and northern France during and immediately after World War I. 265 ft.

COMMITTEE FOR A SANE NUCLEAR POLICY (SANE)

PA —SWARTHMORE COLLEGE, Peace Collection, Swarthmore, 19081. Jean R Soderlund, Cur of Peace Collection
Holdings: Vols (10,000) Cat Mss Pix Microforms
Notes: The history of pacifism has been one of the major subject emphases of the Peace Collection since its inception in 1930. In addition to books, pamphlets, and current materials of all kinds on the subject, the Peace Collection is the official depository for many 20th century pacifist organizations and papers of individual peace leaders. These incl Women's International League for Peace and Freedom; War Resisters League; Fellowship of Reconciliation; SANE, A Committee for a Sane Nuclear Policy; Friends Committee on National Legislation; CCCO1 An Agency for Military and Draft Counseling; National Interreligious Service Board for Conscientious Objectors; A J Muste (1885-1967); and Devere Allen (1891-1955). Other materials collected incl records and memorabilia of 19th and early 20th century peace leaders and organizations, such as the American Peace Society and itsbranches, Jane Addams (1860-1935), the Wisbech Local Peace Association (England), Emily Greene Blach (1867-1961), English and American Friends' Peace Societies, the Universal Peace Union, William Ladd (1778-1841), Elihu Burritt (1810-1879), and Benjamin F Trueblood (1847-1916). The Peace Collection has been described in Downs 972, 978, 4633, and in Downs 1950-1961 Supplement 507 and 916. For descriptions of major document groups, see the *Guide to the Swarthmore College Peace Collection,* 2nd ed (1981).

COMMITTEE OF SMALL MAGAZINE EDITORS AND PUBLISHERS (COSMEP)

PA —TEMPLE UNIVERSITY LIBRARIES, Special Collections Dept, Contemporary Culture Collection, Philadelphia, 19122. Patricia J Case, Cur
Notes: The Contemporary Culture Collection. See full entry under US-Social Life and Customs.

COMMITTEE ON FAIR EMPLOYMENT PRACTICES

MI —MICHIGAN STATE UNIVERSITY, Labor and Industrial Relations Library, East Lansing, 48824. Martha Jane Soltow, Librn
Holdings: Cat Microforms
Notes: This material is composed primarily of special collections of papers on microfilm or microfiche.

COMMITTEE TO DEFEND AMERICA BY AIDING THE ALLIES

NJ —PRINCETON UNIVERSITY, Library, Manuscript Collection, Nassau St, Princeton, 08540. Jean F Preston, Cur
Holdings: // Cat Mss
Notes: Incl 96 cartons, 30 card-tray files. The archive of the Committee to Defend America by Aiding the Allies covers the period May 1940 to January 1942.

COMMODITY EXCHANGES

IL —CHICAGO BOARD OF TRADE, Library, 141 W Jackson Blvd, Chicago, 60604. Darlene Appleman, Librn
Holdings: Vols (4000) Cat Microforms
Notes: Incl materials on commodity exchanges, commodities that are traded on futures exchanges, finance, and agricultural economics. *Commodity Futures Trading, A* Bibliography is published annually. The archives of the Chicago Board of Trade are located in the Manuscript Collection at the University of Illinois at Chicago Circle Campus. A published catalog, *The Archives of the Chicago Board of Trade, 1859-1925,* is available from the Chicago Board of Trade.

NY —HUDSON INSTITUTE, Library, Quaker Ridge Rd, Croton-on-Hudson, 10520. Mildred Schneck, Librn
Holdings: Vols (10,000) Cat
Budget: ($40,000)
Notes: Social sciences and world futures. About 30 percent of the collection emphasizes materials useful to our ongoing program of examining possible world futures: social and economic indicators, forecasts, current social problems, arms control and disarmament.

COMMON CAUSE

NJ —PRINCETON UNIVERSITY, Seeley G Mudd Manuscript Library, Public Affairs Papers Collection, Princeton, 08544. Nancy Bressler, Cur
Notes: 1968-date. Incl 130 boxes.

COMMON MARKET COUNTRIES see European Economic Communities

COMMONER, BARRY

DC —LIBRARY OF CONGRESS, Manuscript Division, Washington, 20540. John C Broderick, Chief
Notes: Papers of Barry Commoner, biologist and ecologist.

COMMONWEALTH GAMES

ON —UNIVERSITY OF WESTERN ONTARIO, Dept of Special Collections, London, N6A 5B9, Can. Beth Miller, Librn
Notes: Large and important collection on Canadian participation in pre-Olympic and other Game series. Incl minutes of annual meetings of the Athletic Union of Canada, 1884-1898, 1908-1954.

COMMONWEALTH OF ENGLAND see Great Britain—History—Commonwealth and Protectorate, 1649-1660

COMMONWEALTH OF NATIONS

NY —BOOKS-ACROSS-THE-SEA, The English-Speaking Union, 16 E 69 St, New York, 10021. Catherine Nolan, Librn
Holdings: Vols (6500) Cat
Budget: ($25,000)
Notes: Deals mainly with humanities and social sciences of Great Britain, Australia, New Zealand, and Canada; adult books. Collection started in 1942; current titles added through exchange.

NC —DUKE UNIVERSITY, William R Perkins Library, Durham, 27706. Elvin E Strowd, University Librn

COMMUNAL SETTLEMENTS see Collective Settlements

COMMUNICABLE DISEASES

CA —UNIVERSITY OF CALIFORNIA, BERKELEY, Life Sciences Libraries, Public Health Library, 42 Earl Warren Hall, Berkeley, 94720. Thomas J Alexander, Librn
Holdings: Vols (75,000) Cat Microforms
Notes: Research collection covering all aspects of public health. Health Department annual reports from all 50 states are acquired, as well as such reports from all California health units and from major US cities. Serial publications issued by Health Departments in the 13 western states are being received.

MD —MEDICAL & CHIRURGICAL FACULTY OF THE STATE OF MARYLAND, Library, 1211 Cathedral St, Baltimore, 21201. Joseph E Jensen, Librn
Holdings: Vols (10,000) // Cat Mss Maps Pix
See also entry under Medicine - History and Historic

MT —PARKER-DAVIS MEMORIAL LIBRARY, 504 S Third St, Hamilton, 59840. William L Jellison, Dir
Notes: Most of material for this library has been transferred to Science Library at Miami University, Oxford, Ohio.

NJ —SAINT MICHAEL'S MEDICAL CENTER, Aquinas Medical Library, 268 High St, Newark, 07102. Betty L Garrison, Dir; Valerie Manuel, Library Asst
Holdings: Vols (4500) Cat
Notes: Primarily bound journals, 1958-date.

COMMUNICABLE DISEASES (cont.)

OH —MIAMI UNIVERSITY, Science Library, Oxford, 45056.
Notes: Zoonoses and related diseases. Collection partially transferred from Parker-Davis Memorial Library, Hamilton, Mont.

PA —COLLEGE OF PHYSICIANS OF PHILADELPHIA, Library, 19 S 22 St, Philadelphia, 19103. Christine Ruggere, Cur, Historical Collections
Holdings: Vols (316,223) Cat Mss
Budget: ($1,096,223)
Notes: Very strong collection.
See also entry under Medicine.

RI —MIRIAM HOSPITAL MEDICAL LIBRARY, 164 Summit Ave, Providence, 02906. Ann LeClaire, Dir of Library Services
Holdings: Cat Cassettes
Notes: Special collection on the renal system with emphasis on kidney transplantation and dialysis.

TX —HOUSTON ACADEMY OF MEDICINE-TEXAS MEDICAL CENTER, Library, Jesse H Jones Library Bldg, Houston, 77030. Elizabeth Borst White, Special Collections Librn
Holdings: Vols (900) Cat
Notes: Mading Collection on Public Health. English-language materials dealing with American public health conditions before 1925. Emphasis is on epidemiology and infectious diseases (excluding venereal disease), incl material on sanitation and climatology. Federal, state or municipal reports on health, mortality and sanitation are included. Also 500 pamphlets.

COMMUNICABLE DISEASES—HISTORY

CT —YALE UNIVERSITY, Medical Historical Library, Klebs Collection, 333 Cedar St, New Haven, 06520. Ferenc A Gyorgyey, Librn
Notes: Incl the collection of Harvey Cushing, John Fulton and Arnold C Klebs, and historical collections of the Yale Medical Library.

OH —CLEVELAND MEDICAL LIBRARY ASSOCIATION/CASE WESTERN RESERVE UNIVERSITY, Cleveland Health Sciences Library, Historical Division, Allen Memorial Medical Library, 11000 Euclid Ave, Cleveland, 44106. Glen Jenkins, Rare Book Librarian & Archivist
Notes: Incl 15,000 historical vols, 6000 in the supporting collection. Incl about 1000 16th-18th century titles. Strength of collection: diseases, epidemiology, anatomy, surgery, medicine, obstetrics, gynecology, pediatrics and yellow fever. Incl also medical Americana, listed in Robert B Austin *Early American Medical Imprints,* 1668-1820 (Washington, DC, HEW, Public Health Service, 1961) and ca 7000 19th century works. Our total medical Americana collection also incl journals (not counted), mss and archives (900 linear ft) and 5000 pictures, especially of the Western Reserve. Anatomical works discussed in I Ebner and G Jenkins *Skeletons in Our Closet* (Cleveland, Cleveland Health Sciences Library, 1983)

COMMUNICATION IN TECHNOLOGY see Communication of Technical Information

COMMUNICATION RESEARCH see Communications Research

COMMUNICATION THEORY see Information Theory

COMMUNICATIONS

CA —GTE COMMUNICATIONS PRODUCT CORP, Sylvania Systems Group, Western Division Library, MC-2201, PO Box 7188, Mountain View, 94039. J B Fierro, Supervisor Library Services
Holdings: Vols (10,000) Cat
Notes: Interlibrary loan.

IL —UNIVERSITY OF ILLINOIS, URBANA/CHAMPAIGN, Library, Communications Library, 122 Gregory Hall, Urbana, 61801. Nancy Allen, Librn
Holdings: Vols (18,000) Cat
Budget: ($27,000)
Notes: Communication theory and effects.

IA —ROCKWELL INTERNATIONAL, Collins Division, Cedar Rapids Information Center, 500 Collins Rd, Cedar Rapids, 52498. Judith A Leavitt, Supvr
Holdings: Vols 10,000 Cat
Notes: Also 8000 technical reports; 10,000 military, Federal, and industrial specifications; 3000 bound periodicals (400 periodical subsriptions). Restricted use: for company use only and interlibrary loan.

MI —WASHTENAW COMMUNITY COLLEGE, Learning Resource Center, P.O. Box D-1, Ann Arbor, 48106. Adella Scott, Dir

MO —NATIONAL MUSEUM OF TRANSPORT, Reference Library, 3105 Barrett Station Rd, Saint Louis, 63122. John P Roberts, Secretary
Holdings: Vols (10,000) Cat Mss Maps Pix Slides

NJ —AT&T BELL LABORATORIES, Libraries and Information Systems Center, 600 Mountain Ave, Murray Hill, 07974. W D Penniman, Dir
Holdings: Vols (346,000) Cat Microforms
Notes: Restricted use to AT&T employees. Catalogs/*Indexes*: Bell Laboratories Library Network and Book Serial Catalogs; Bell Laboratories Translations. Bell Laboratories Library Network with New Jersey libraries located in Holmdel, Murray Hill, Piscataway, Whippany, Princeton, Short Hills, Summit, West Long Branch, Crawford Hill; libraries also in Allentown, Pennsylvania; Reading, Pennsylvania; New York, New York; Atlanta, Georgia; Columbus, Ohio; Naperville, Illinois; Indianapolis, Indiana; North Andover, Massachusetts.

NY —AMERICAN TELEPHONE & TELEGRAPH CO, Corporate Research Center, 550 Madison Ave, Fifth floor, New York, 10022. Marianne Benjamin, Chief Librn
Holdings: Vols (8000) Cat Microforms
Notes: Collection incl complete sets of AT&T periodicals and incomplete sets of other periodicals in the field of telephony; complete sets of AT&T companies' annual reports; telephone industry directories; monographs on history and economic aspects of telephony. Member of AT&T Bell Laboratories Library Network.

NY —INTERNATIONAL PAPER CO, Corporate Information Center, 77 W 45 St, New York, 10036. Elizabeth Skerritt, Corporate Librn
Holdings: Vols 65

†NY —NEIGHBORHOOD PLAYHOUSE SCHOOL OF THE THEATRE, Irene Lewisohn Library, 340 E 54 St, New York, 10022. Alice G Owen, Librn
Holdings: Vols 100

NY —NEW YORK PUBLIC LIBRARY, Research Libraries, Science and Technology Research Center, Fifth Ave & 42 St, New York, 10018.
Holdings: Vols (1,100,000) Cat Microforms
Budget: ($647,259)

NY —NEW YORK PUBLIC LIBRARY, Research Libraries, Economic & Public Affairs Div, Fifth Ave & 42 St, New York, 10018. Edward DiRoma, Chief
Holdings: Vols (1,500,000) Cat Microforms

NY —ROCKEFELLER UNIVERSITY, Rockefeller Archive Center, Hillcrest, Pocantico Hills, North Tarrytown, 10591. Joseph W Ernst, Dir; J William Hess, Assoc Dir
Notes: Papers relative to the Rockefeller Family, Foundations, University, and other specific enterprises and contributions to particular areas of social, physical, educational, and historic reform, preservation, conservation, or development. Extensive records of administrative, financial, physical, or intellectual relationships.

PA —FRANKLIN INSTITUTE LIBRARY, 20 & The Parkway, Philadelphia, 19103. Miriam Padusis, Dir; Charles Wilt, Readers Servs Librn
Holdings: Vols (300,000) Cat Maps Pix Microforms

PA —UNIVERSITY OF PENNSYLVANIA, Annenberg School of Communications Library, 3620 Walnut St, Philadelphia, 19104. Sandra B Grilikhes, Head
Holdings: Vols 20,000 Cat Microforms
Notes: Theory and research in communication, incl visual communication, via social psychology, anthropology, ethnography, and sociology. All aspects of mass media with emphasis on methodology in research. Utilizes content analysis and computer operations. Special collections: film catalogs; collection of Annenberg Faculty Publications.

†PA —UNIVERSITY OF PITTSBURGH, Graduate School of Library & Information Sciences Library, L I S Bldg, Third Fl, Pittsburgh, 15260. Jean Kindlin, Librn
Notes: Extensive collection on the historical development of school libraries, media services, and evaluation of materials for use in all types of schools. Incl 54,800 vols, 7524 bound periodicals, 630 periodical subscriptions.

TX —E-SYSTEMS, GARLAND DIV, Technical Library, PO Box 226118, Dallas, 75226. Charlene Morris, Tech Librn
Holdings: Vols (8500) Cat
Notes: Library not open to public.

VA —AMERICAN NEWSPAPER PUBLISHERS ASSOCIATION, ANPA, Library, 11600 Sunrise Valley Dr, Reston, (Mailing add: PO Box 17407, Dulles Intl AP, Washington, DC, 20041). Yvonne Egertson, Librn
Notes: Mass Communications.

WI —STATE HISTORICAL SOCIETY OF WISCONSIN, Archives, 816 State St, Madison, 53706. Harold L Miller, Reference Archivist
Holdings: Cat Mss Microforms
Notes: About 22 million pieces. Major ms emphasis is American, with special collections in the history of anti-Vietnam War, agriculture, civil rights, industry, labor, mass communications, motion pictures and theatre, and Wisconsin. There is a separate card catalog to mss. Collections are described in the *Guide to Manuscripts of the State Historical Society of Wisconsin* (3 vols, 1944, 1957, 1966), *Guide to the Wisconsin State Archives* (1966), in current accession notes in the *Wisconsin Magazine of History,* and in other special Society publications. Major collections are also listed in Hamer, *Guide to Manuscripts and Archives in the United States* (1961) and in the *National Union Catalog of Manuscript Collections* (1959-date).

ON —QUEEN'S UNIVERSITY, Douglas Library, Kingston, K7L 5C4, Can. William F E Morley, Cur, Special Collections
Holdings: Vols 802 Uncat
Notes: Riche-Covington Collection supports McNichol Collection (history of telecommunications), brings it up to date; also astrophysics, astronomy, solar radiation. Bibliography available.

ON —CANADIAN BROADCASTING CORP, Head Office Library, 1500 Bronson Ave, PO Box 8478, Ottawa, K1G 3J5, Can. Normand Deschamps, Librn
Holdings: Vols (6400) Cat
Budget: ($18,000)
Notes: Emphasis on radio and television broadcasting. No holdings on technical aspects.

ON —NATIONAL MUSEUMS OF CANADA, Library Services Directorate, Ottawa, K1A 0M8, Can. Valerie Monkhouse, Director
Holdings: Vols 15,500
Budget: $25,000
Notes: History and technology of agriculture, astronomy, aviation, chemistry, communications, computers, electrical engineering, exploration and surveying, fire prevention, forestry, industrial technology, mathematics, medicine, mining, photography, physics, printing, space and transportation. research collection, interlibrary loans available, public may use on the premises.

COMMUNICATIONS—HISTORY

†CA —SOCIETY OF WIRELESS PIONEERS (COMMUNICATIONS), PO Box 530, Santa Rosa, 95402.
Holdings: Vols (2500)
Notes: Museum of early communication memorabilia and equiptment. Compiles statistics on shipwrecks where wireless/radio was involved.

IN —PURDUE UNIVERSITY LIBRARIES, Graduate School of Management, Krannert Library, West Lafayette, 47907. Gordon Law, Librn
Notes: An important resource at the Krannert Library is its Special Collection of Business and Economics, consisting of some 8000 rare pre-20th century strengths in books, journals, tracts and pamphlets covering primarily the early literature of economic thought and business practices in America and abroad, 1500-1870. A catalog was issued in 1979.

†NY —ANTIQUE WIRELESS ASSOCIATION, Electronic Communication Museum, Main St, Holcomb, 14469. Bruce Kelley, Curator
Holdings: Vols (2000)
Notes: Books on radio and electrical material available for research for members of association. 15,000 radio, television, and electrical artifacts.

UT —UNIVERSITY OF UTAH, Marriott Library, Special Collections, Salt Lake City, 84112. Gregory C Thompson, Cur
Notes: Papers of leading figures in Utah Communications and Broadcasting.

VA —VIRGINIA POLYTECHNIC INSTITUTE AND STATE UNIVERSITY LIBRARY, Blacksburg, 24061. Glenn L McMullen, Special Collections Librn
Holdings: Vols (1500)
Notes: Collection of primarily nineteenth century imprints on transportation, communications, and agricultural technology; technological encyclopedias and compendia; books on inventions and inventors; and travel accounts dealing with industrial and technological change.

COMMUNICATIONS—LAW AND LEGISLATION

WI —UNIVERSITY OF WISCONSIN, MADISON, Journalism Reading Room (Nieman-Grant), (formerly Bleyer Memorial Reading Room, School of Journalism), Vilas Communication Hall, Rm 2130, Madison, 53706. Arthur Cran, Librn; Mary Nagel, Asst Librn
Holdings: Vols 750 Cat
Budget: ($500)
Notes: Incl international mass communication, law.

COMMUNICATIONS—METHODOLOGY

PA —UNIVERSITY OF PENNSYLVANIA, Annenberg School of Communications Library, 3620 Walnut St, Philadelphia, 19104. Sandra B Grilikhes, Head
Holdings: Vols 20,000 Cat Microforms
Notes: Theory and research in communication, incl visual communication, via social psychology, anthropology, ethnography, and sociology. All aspects of mass media with emphasis on methodology in research. Utilizes content analysis and computer operations. Special collections: film catalogs; collection of Annenberg Faculty Publications.

COMMUNICATIONS RESEARCH

GA —UNIVERSITY OF GEORGIA, Libraries, Special Collections Division, Athens, 30602. Vesta Lee Gordon, Asst Dir for Special Collections
Notes: The Arbitron Collection of television and radio program ratings, 1949-date (except past year). In-depth, statistical analyses of the listening public by age, sex, county, some ethnic groups, farm population, listening preferences, etc. 26,302 bound vols. 2 reports, 1949-81. To be added to annually.

MA —MASSACHUSETTS INSTITUTE OF TECHNOLOGY, Lincoln Laboratory, Library, 244 Wood St, Lexington, 02173. Jane H Katayama, Library Mgr
Holdings: Vols (70,000) Cat Per Maps Microforms
Notes: 250,000 technical reports, mostly on microfiche; 2000 periodical subscriptions; Lincoln Laboratory Archives collection; map collection.

MO —WASHINGTON UNIVERSITY, John M Olin Library, Campus Box 1061, St Louis, 63130.
Holdings: Vols (1300) Cat Mss
Notes: The Philip M Arnold Semeiology Collection is concerned with the study of signs and symbols. Topics incl cryptography; artificial memory; decipherment of unknown languages; universal languages; early developments in stenography, telegraphy; and communication systems for the blind, the deaf and the mute; and various forms of nonverbal communication. Limited photocopying. Noncirculating.

NJ —AT&T BELL LABORATORIES, Libraries and Information Systems Center, 600 Mountain Ave, Murray Hill, 07974. W D Penniman, Dir
Holdings: Vols (273,100) Cat Mss Audiotapes Videotapes Microforms
Budget: ($670,000)
Notes: Restricted use to AT&T employees. Catalogs/*Indexes*: Bell Laboratories Library Network and Book Serial Catalogs; Bell Laboratories Translations. Bell Laboratories Library Network with New Jersey libraries located in Holmdel, Murray Hill, Piscataway, Whippany, Princeton, Short Hills, Summit, West Long Branch, Crawford Hill; libraries also in Allentown, Pennsylvania; Reading, Pennsylvania; New York, New York; Atlanta, Georgia; Columbus, Ohio; Naperville, Illinois; Indianapolis, Indiana; North Andover, Massachusetts.
See also entry under Communications.

OH —PREFORMED LINE PRODUCTS CO, Research & Engineering Library, 660 Beta Drive, Mayfield Village, (Mailing add: PO Box 91129, Cleveland, 44101). Edwina T Barron, Librn
Holdings: Vols (11,500) Cat Mss Pix Microfiche VF
Budget: ($30,500)
Notes: Library covering research and engineering fields emphasizing this subject. Aerodynamic characteristics and electrical characteristics of power cables, communication cables (including fiber optics), cable support systems, as well as associated fittings and hardware; in service behavior of manufactured products and materials as it relates to its static and dynamic forces and environmental conditions; oceanographic cable fittings and terminations.

VA —MITRE CORPORATION, Information Services, 1820 Dolley Madison Blvd, McLean, 22102. Paula M Strain, Mgr
Holdings: Vols (10,000) Cat Microforms
Notes: Collection incl current and back files of periodicals in bound and microfilm form, approx 70,000 technical reports mostly in microfiche format and 10,000 vols, all of which are cataloged and indexed. Collection deals with systems engineering as a methodology with special emphasis on its applications in these areas: civil systems; communication systems; energy; incl alternate energy sources; environmental problems; mass and urban transportation; and aviation operation incl collision avoidance, landing systems, and traffic scheduling.

COMMUNISM AND ANTICOMMUNISM

AZ —NORTHERN ARIZONA UNIVERSITY, Special Collection Library, CU Box 6022, Flagstaff, 86011. Peter M Whiteley, Coordr/Archivist; William Mullane, Librn
Holdings: Vols 9000 Cat Mss Phonorecords Microforms
Notes: The large Allderdice Collection of thousands of books, pamphlets, periodicals, and organizational files reflects the conservative, communist, socialist, facist, anarchist, and other viewpoints, etc, during the 20th century.

CA —CALIFORNIA STATE UNIVERSITY, FULLERTON, Library, Box 4150, Fullerton, 92634. Linda Herman, Special Collections Librn
Holdings: Cat
Notes: Mostly American (some British) newspapers and journals of labor organizations, late 1800s to present. Incl official labor association publications as well as early Marxist newspapers and bulletins. Approx 800 labor and labor-related publications.

CA —SOUTHERN CALIFORNIA LIBRARY FOR SOCIAL STUDIES & RESEARCH, 6120 S Vermont Ave, Los Angeles, 90044. Sarah Cooper, Dir
Holdings: Vols (15,000) Mss Maps Pix Slides Phonorecords Audiotapes 16mm Films News Clips
Budget: ($30,000)
Notes: Marxist, non-Marxist and anti-Marxist approaches to social change. Other important functions of the library: to make available source materials to those engaged in the Marxist vs no-Marxist dialog; to aid historians, economists, sociologists, writers, students and labor organizations researching the history of grassroots social movements; and to preserve primary and secondary sources on labor, minorities, women and radicalism. Collection incl 50 mss, 75 maps, 500 pictures, 1000 slides, 100 phonorecords, 2000 audiotapes, 50 16mm films and 150, 000 newspaper clippings.

CA —UNIVERSITY OF CALIFORNIA, LOS ANGELES, Research Library, Dept of Special Collections, 405 Hilgard Ave, Los Angeles, 90024. Edward Shreeves, Chairman, Bibliographers Group; David S Zeidberg, Head
Holdings: Cat Mss Audiotapes
Notes: 11 cartons of materials, recordings, etc relating to the John Birch Society, with runs of relevant periodicals, government documents, etc; 6.5 linear feet on Loyalty Oaths incl in other collections; 6 transcribed Oral History interviews.

CA —HOOVER INSTITUTION ON WAR, REVOLUTION & PEACE, Stanford University, Stanford, 94305. Milorad M Drachkovitch, Archivist
Notes: Five collections: (1) Records of the Citizens Committee for a Free Cuba, Inc, an anti-communist organization founded in the US in 1963 to disseminate information about communism in Cuba and other Latin American countries, incl clippings, newsletters, press releases, reports, conference papers, speeches, and printed matter, 1962-74, relating primarily to the political, economic, and social effects of communism in Cuba, communist subversion in Latin America, US foreign policy toward Cuba, and activities of the Cuban emigre community. 58 ms boxes. (2) Records of Marvin Liebman Associates, Inc, a New York public relations firm incl office files, correspondence, printed matter, press releases, campaign material, photographs and reports, 1950-1969, relating to activities of Marvin Liebman Associates in lobbying for US conservative and anti-communist organizationsinvolved with Asian and African affairs. 108 ms boxes, 3 envelopes. (3) Records of *National Republic* magazine, incl newspaper clippings, printed matter, pamphlets, reports, indices, notes, bulletins, lettergrams, weekly letters, and photographs, 1905-1960, relating to pacifist, communist, fascist, and other radical movements as well as political developments in the US and Soviet Russia. 826 ms boxes. (4) Papers of Boris K Souvarine, Russian-born French communist, incl correspondence, writing, clippings, printed matter and other material, 1925-1971, relating to the French Communist Party, the Communist International, Marxism, Soviet agricultural and economic policies, and political events in 20th century Russia. The papers consist primarily of correspondence with Ekaterina

COMMUNISM AND ANTICOMMUNISM (cont.)

Kuskova, Sergei Prokopovich, Nikolai V Volsky and the Marx-Engels Institute (Moscow). (5) Papers of BertramD Wolfe, American historian and author, Hoover Institution Senior Fellow, 1949-1950 and 1965-1968, and Senior Research Fellow, 1969-1977, incl writings, correspondence, clippings, printed matter and photographs, 1913-1977, relating primarily to international communism and communism in the Soviet Union.

CT —YALE UNIVERSITY, Box 1603A, Yale Station, New Haven, 06520.

CT —UNIVERSITY OF CONNECTICUT, Library, Storrs, 06268. Ellen Embardo, Cur Special Collections
Holdings: Cat
Notes: Alternative Press Collection. Primarily periodicals and newspapers from the 1960s to today of an alternative or underground nature. Books and pamphlets are incl, representing both the left and the right-wing viewpoints. A catalog is available. Also have archives of the First Casualty Press, which was deeply involved with Vietnam veterans' experiences in Vietnam.

DC —LIBRARY OF CONGRESS, Washington, 20540.
Notes: Some 4500 pamphlets and sheets dealing primarily with subversive and radical activities in the US from 1900 to 1950. Incl tracts and campaign literture of the Communist and Socialist Parties in the US and works by party leaders; materials on the economic, political, and human rights issues of the pre-World War II, World War II, and early civil rights campaign periods; and pamphlets by various anti-war and anti-draft organizations, material on Russia, and materials on the communist movement in other countries.

DC —LIBRARY OF CONGRESS, Prints & Photographs Div, Washington, 20540.
Notes: The Gary Yonker Collection of political propaganda posters, late 1960s to present. Strongest for US materials but incl about 50 other countries' work. Over 4500 items, arranged geographically.

GA —EMORY UNIVERSITY, Robert W Woodruff Library, Atlanta, 30322. Herbert Johnson, Dir
Holdings: Mss Pix Cat
Notes: The Philip J Jaffe Papers and books about communism and the Communist Party in the US, incl copies of rare magazines, private mss, the papers of such controversial figures as Anna Louise Strong, Agnes Smedley, Norman Bethune and Koji Ariyoshi, and documentation of the growth of Chinese communism. 36 linear ft mss.

IL —LOYOLA UNIVERSITY OF CHICAGO, E M Cudahy Memorial Library, 6525 N Sheridan Rd, Chicago, 60626.
Notes: Dorr E Felt Pamphlet and Clipping Collection. Emphasizes political and economic issues, 1902-35, and documents Illinois Manufacturers Association Conference, September 8-9, 1919; Air Board of Chicago, April 16, 1921-August 1, 1930; Allied Debts to the US, May 15, 1923-September 30, 1926; Bolshevism, Communism, "Red" Russia, 1924-27; Child Labor Bill, March 30, 1915, 1914-20; Labor, March, 1902-March, 1932; Railroad Strike, August 25, 1916-August 7, 1920; The War, August, 1914-October 23, 1930; War Industries Commission, June, 1918-November 23, 1928. A pamphlet list is available for each topic.

IL —NEWBERRY LIBRARY, 60 W Walton St, Chicago, 60610. Diana Haskell, Cur of Modern Mss
Holdings: Cat
Notes: 19th century socialism and communism.

IL —NORTHERN ILLINOIS UNIVERSITY, Founders Memorial Library, Rare Books and Special Collections Dept, De Kalb, 60115. William R DuBois, Dept Head
Holdings: Vols (1350) // Cat
Notes: American, British and Soviet pamphlet publications, ca 1860-1955 by or about the radical labor movement, socialists, communists and the radical right. Some Nazi/anti-Nazi material. Collection is computer- indexed by author, title, series, publisher and date.

MD —UNIVERSITY OF MARYLAND, BALTIMORE COUNTY, Albin O Kuhn Library and Gallery, 5401 Wilkens Ave, Baltimore, 21228. Ann Copeland, Special Collections Librn
Holdings: // Uncat
Notes: The collection incl more than 1000 pamphlets and broadsides on communism, fascism, Trotskyism, socialism, etc.

MI —UNIVERSITY OF MICHIGAN, Dept of Rare Books & Special Collections, Ann Arbor, 48109. Edward C Weber, Head, Labadie Collection
Holdings: Vols (40,000) Cat Mss Pix Phonorecords Audiotapes Microforms
Notes: International in scope and have William Reuben papers on the Hiss-Chambers, Rosenberg, Sobell, and Soblen cases.

MI —MICHIGAN STATE UNIVERSITY, Libraries, Special Collections Div, East Lansing, 48824. Jannette Fiore, Librn
Holdings: Vols (10,500) Cat Mss
Notes: Published and unpublished material generated by (1) American left and right, 1900, (2) the New Left, 1969-1970, and (3) current left, right, and alternate life-style groups. (Supported by appropriate secondary material in the Research Library). Also have in microform radical pamphlet literature from the Tamiment Library (New York University), the Right Wing Collection of the University of Iowa, et al.

MO —SAINT LOUIS UNIVERSITY, Pius XII Memorial Library, 3655 W Pine Blvd, Saint Louis, 63108. William Cole, Dir
Holdings: Vols 250 Cat
Notes: Antoine Frederic Ozanam, 1813-1853, was the Catholic answer to Karl Marx. St Louis University owns almost everything by and about Ozanam, due to the kindness of the local St Vincent de Paul Society.

NY —COLUMBIA UNIVERSITY LIBRARIES, Lehman Library, Bureau of Applied Social Research Archive, 420 W 118th St, New York, 10027. David Lewis, Librn
Holdings: Uncat
Notes: Current information file of Radio Free Europe publications. There is significant coverage of the period 1956-1973. The current file incl Radio Free Europe Situation Reports, which are published for selected countries on a weekly basis, Background Reports dealing with themes of broader significance, and Media Surveys which are translations of important East European press articles. The retrospective files incl these research products arranged on a country-by-country basis.

NY —NEW YORK PUBLIC LIBRARY, Research Libraries, Economic & Public Affairs Div, Fifth Ave & 42 St, New York, 10018. Edward DiRoma, Chief
Holdings: Vols (1,500,000) Cat Microforms

NY —NEW YORK UNIVERSITY, Elmer Holmes Bobst Library, Div of Special Collections, Tamiment Library of Labor History, Washington Sq, New York, 10012. Dorothy Swanson, Librn
Holdings: Cat Mss Maps Pix Microforms
Notes: Books, pamphlets, newspapers, periodicals and mss. Large microfilm collection. Described in Daniel Bell's *The Tamiment Library* (1969), available free from the Tamiment librarian, and *Elmer Holmes Bobst Library Information Bulletin 8* (updated periodically).

OH —OHIO UNIVERSITY, Vernon R Alden Library, Department of Archives and Special Collections, Athens, 45701. Gary A Hunt, Head
Holdings: Vols 184 Cat
Notes: Incl most of the Left Book Club editions published by that organization in the 1930s and 1940s, with some of the club's flyers and leaflets.

TX —UNIVERSITY OF TEXAS LIBRARIES, General Libraries, PO Box P, Austin, 78713. Carolyn Bucknell, Asst Dir for Collection Development
Holdings: Cat Microforms

WI —UNIVERSITY OF WISCONSIN, GREEN BAY, Library/Learning Center, Green Bay, 54301. Marian A Gould, Acting Dir, Special Collections/University Archives
Holdings: Vols 700 // Cat
Notes: This represents the collection of Leon Kramer, "idealist, philosophical anarchist and bookseller." Much of the material concerns radical literature and small socialist and communist parties in the US, although there is a considerable amount of books, booklets, and pamphlets published in Germany, Italy, and other parts of Europe. Incl uncounted pamphlets.

WI —STATE HISTORICAL SOCIETY OF WISCONSIN, Archives, 816 State St, Madison, 53706. Harold L Miller, Reference Archivist
Holdings: Mss Pix Audiotapes Microforms
Notes: Records and papers of organizations and individuals engages in social and political reform activities. Major focus areas are civil rights, 1950s to the present, and anti-Vietnam war and other protest movements of the 1960s to the present. Also covered are other reform movements, socialism, and communism from the 1930s to the present. Collections are described in *Social Action Collection at the State Historical Society of Wisconsin: A Guide,* (1983) and in current accession notes in the *Wisconsin Magazine of History.* Major collections are also listed in Hamer, *Guide to Manuscripts and Archives in the United* States, (1961) and in the *National Union Catalog of Manuscript Collections,* (1959-date).

ON —UNIVERSITY OF TORONTO, Thomas Fisher Rare Book Library, 120 Saint George St, Toronto, M5S 1A5, Can. Richard G Landon, Head
Holdings: Uncat Mss
Notes: Background material on communist countries issued by Radio Free Europe. Includes extensive materials on Poland, Czechoslovakia, Hungary, Rumania, Yugoslavia. Also contains material on East Germany, Bulgaria, Albania, Sino-Soviet conflict. Chiefly covers years 1960-1976. Some earlier material from 1950s.

COMMUNISM AND ANTICOMMUNISM—AFRICA

CA —HOOVER INSTITUTION ON WAR, REVOLUTION & PEACE, Stanford University, Stanford, 94305. Milorad M Drachkovitch, Archivist
Holdings: Mss Pix
Notes: Records of Marvin Liebman Associates, Inc, a New York public relations firm incl office files, correspondence, printed matter, press releases, campaign material, photographs and reports, 1950-1969, relating to activities of Marvin Liebman Associates in lobbying for US conservative and anti-communist organizations involved with Asian and African affairs. 108 ms boxes, 3 envelopes.

COMMUNISM AND ANTICOMMUNISM—CANADA

MB —UNIVERSITY OF MANITOBA, Elizabeth Dafoe Library, Archives and Special Collections Dept, Winnipeg, R3T 2N2, Can. Richard E Bennett, Dept Head; Corrado A Santoro, Reference Archivist
Notes: Murray S Donnelly Papers, 1925-1961. Incl correspondence and reports dealing with foreign elements (fifth columns) in Canada during WW II working to sabotage the Canadian war effort, 1944. 1925 train pass to Imperial Conference held in Australia. Material relating to the life and times of J W Dafoe of the *Manitoba Free* Press from various individuals who knew him, for the purpose of writing a biography on Dafoe.

ON —UNIVERSITY OF TORONTO, Thomas Fisher Rare Book Library, 120 Saint George St, Toronto, M5S 1A5, Can. Richard G Landon, Head
Holdings: Vols 2500 Mss Pix Phonorecords
Notes: Kenny Collection named for original

COMMUNISM AND ANTICOMMUNISM—CANADA (cont.)

collector, Robert Kenny of Toronto. Chiefly material on and by the Labor Progressive Party and the Communist Party of Canada, including their constitutions, reports of national conventions, leaflets, posters, election material, ephemera. Manuscript material of A E Smith, Tim Buck and other Canadian communists.

COMMUNISM AND ANTICOMMUNISM—CHINA

AZ —ARIZONA STATE UNIVERSITY, Library, Tempe, 85287. Marilyn Wurzburger, Special Collections Librn
Notes: The A T Steele Collection is a unique compilation of articles and documents dealing with events in China from 1932-49. The collection is divided into five parts: dispatches, newspaper clippings, pamphlets and books, original documents of the Communist Party (ca 1945) and memorabilia, written and/or collected by American journalist A T Steele. Dispatches cover events in China from 1940-49 land are mostly first-hand experiences of Steele. These dispatches, not all of which were published, often contain details absent in the final copy. Post-war topics incl truce negotiations between the Nationalists and Chinese Communists and the "Manchurian Question." Index available. 12 linear feet of materials.

CA —HOOVER INSTITUTION ON WAR, REVOLUTION & PEACE, Stanford University, Stanford, 94305. Milorad M Drachkovitch, Archivist
Holdings: Mss Maps Pix
Notes: Five collections: (1) The J Calvin Huston Collection. Handwritten papers, pamphlets, placards, leaflets, and newspaper clippings, chiefly in English and Russian, dealing with cultural, political, and economic conditions in China with special reference to communism and the influence of Soviet Russia, 1917-1931. 14 boxes. Unpublished register is available in repository. (2) Records of Marvin Liebman Associates, Inc, a New York public relations firm incl office files, correspondence, printed matter, press releases, campaign material, photographs and reports, 1950-1969, relating to activities of Marvin Liebman Associates in lobbying for US conservative and anti-communist organizations involved with Asian and African affairs. 108 ms boxes, 3 envelopes. (3) Papers of Wilbur J Peterkin, Executive and commanding officer of the US Observer Mission to the Chinese Communisits,1944-1945 incl diary transcripts, reports, maps, 16mm film, and other material, 1944-1945, relating to Chinese communist forces and the Japanese occupation of China during World War II. Also incl are rifle, bayonet, pistol, and hand grenade used by the Chinese communists during the Sino-Japanese Conflict. 1 1/2 ms boxes. (4) Papers of Nym Wales (Helen Foster Snow), journalist and writer, incl personal and collected correspondence, speeches and writings, news dispatches, interviews, reports, memoranda, organizational records, and other material, 1931-1954, related primarily to her experiences in China with the Chinese communists, industrial cooperative movement, student movement, labor movement, Sian incident (1936), Sino-Japanese conflict, and art and literature. 37 ms boxes; 30 photo envelopes. (5) Papers of Ivan D Yeaton, Colonel, US Army; Military Attache in Moscow,1939-1941; Commanding Officer of the Yenan Observer Group in China, 1945-1946; incl drafts and final copy of his memoirs, reports, memoranda, correspondence, orders and citations, charts, photographs, and other material, 1919-76; relating to Soviet military strength in 1941; US-Soviet relations, 1941-49; organization of US military intelligence during World War II; lend-lease operations; US relations with the Chinese communists, 1944-46; and the inspection of US Army procurement contracts, 1952-53. 2 ms boxes, 7 envelopes.

GA —EMORY UNIVERSITY, Robert W Woodruff Library, Atlanta, 30322. Herbert Johnson, Dir
Notes: The Philip J Jaffe Papers and books about communism and the Communist Party in the US, incl copies of rare magazines, private mss, the papers of such controversial figures as Anna Louise Strong, Agnes Smedley, Norman Bethune and Koji Ariyoshi, and documentation of the growth of Chinese communism. 36 linear ft mss.

IL —CENTER FOR RESEARCH LIBRARIES, 6050 S Kenwood Ave, Chicago, 60637. Donald B Simpson, Dir; Esther Smith, Collection Development Librn
Holdings: Vols Cat Microforms
Notes: Mainland China newspapers, periodicals and clippings, early western language newspapers in China, Hong Kong newspapers in English, British Foreign Office and US State Dept records relating to China, Dunhuang manuscripts, missionary periodicals. Microfilm and reprints of newspapers, serials and monographs from Center for Chinese Research Materials. Hunter collection of Chinese communist propaganda (ca 1000 vols). Microfilm and originals of Maritime Customs publications. Microfilm of press summaries prepared by US Consulate, Hong Kong, archives of missionary organizations, Chinese folk literature, etc. Descriptive pamphlet available.

COMMUNISM AND ANTICOMMUNISM—CUBA

CA —HOOVER INSTITUTION ON WAR, REVOLUTION & PEACE, Stanford University, Stanford, 94305. Milorad M Drachkovitch, Archivist
Holdings: Vols 1600 Mss Pix Microfilm
Notes: Books on contemporary Cuba. Intensive collecting is made of political, social and economic works covering the Castro period, especially writing and speeches of Castro and Guevara. Some 30 periodical and newspaper titles are currently received from the island. A general description of the Latin American Collection and a complete listing of the serial and newspaper holdings is available in: Bingaman, Joseph W *Latin America: a Survey of Holdings at the Hoover Institution on War, Revolution and Peace.* Hoover Institution, Stanford University, Stanford, California, 1972. 96 pp.

FL —UNIVERSITY OF MIAMI, Otto G Richter Library, PO Box 248214, Coral Gables, 33124. Frank Rodgers, Dir of Libraries
Notes: The Cuban exile periodicals incl 412 titles of which 381 have been published in Miami, Florida. The archival material incl 54 cubic feet of mss, invitations, programs, broadsides, posters, postcards, prints, reports, maps, etc. This collection incl personal and corporate papers of Cubans settled in the US or in other countries. The truth about Cuban Committee Papers: 40 cubic feet. Contains records and correspondence of intellectual and professional Cuban and American leaders in the US dedicated to the course of eliminating Communism from the Western Hemisphere.

COMMUNISM AND ANTICOMMUNISM—GREAT BRITAIN

CA —HOOVER INSTITUTION ON WAR, REVOLUTION & PEACE, Stanford University, Stanford, 94305. Milorad M Drachkovitch, Archivist
Holdings: // Mss
Notes: Left-wing British material consisting of Communist Party of Great Britain material, personal papers of E W Darling, and various society and other publications, 1871-1945. ca 6 ft.

MA —BRANDEIS UNIVERSITY, Goldfarb Library, 415 South St, Waltham, 02154. Bessie Hahn, Dir
Notes: Radical pamphlet collection. Approx 5000 pamphlets from the 1920s through the 1950s dealing with socialism and communism in the US and Great Britain. There is an author-title card catalog to ca 500 of the items in the Special Collections Card Catalog.

COMMUNISM AND ANTICOMMUNISM—U.S.

CA —HOOVER INSTITUTION ON WAR, REVOLUTION & PEACE, Stanford University, Stanford, 94305. Milorad M Drachkovitch, Archivist
Holdings: Mss
Notes: Four collections: (1) Papers of Benjamin Gitlow, a leader of the Communist Party in the US and later an anti-communist, incl writings, correspondence, minutes of meetings, clippings, and printed matter, 1918-1960, relating to communism and socialism in the US and Europe. 17 ms boxes. (2) Papers of Juraj Slavik, Czechoslovakian diplomat and government official with service as Minister and Envoy to Poland, 1936-39, Minister of Interior, 1940-45, Minister of Foreign Affairs, 1945-46, and Ambassador to the US, 1946-48, incl correspondence, speeches and writings, reports, dispatches, memoranda, telegrams, clippings, and other material, 1934-1966, relating to his diplomatic and governmental career, foreign affairs of and political developments in Czechoslovakia, and Czechoslovakian emigre community, and anti-communistmovements in the US. 32 ms boxes. (3) Papers of Herbert Solow, American journalist, and editor of *Fortune*, 1945-1964, incl correspondence, speeches, drafts of writings, memoranda, depositions, clippings and other printed matter, 1924-76, relating to the communist movement in the US, the Non-Partisan Defense League, the Commission of Inquiry into the Charges Made Against Leon Trosky in the Moscow Trials, Soviet espionage in the US, Zionism, and post-World War II international business enterprises. Incl some papers of Mrs Herbert Solow, 1964-1976. 8 ms boxes. (4) Reports and transcripts of hearings (printed, mimeographed and typewritten), of the US Subversive Activities Control Board, a quasi-judicial US government agency, 1950-72, relating to communist and communist-front activities in the US. 70 ms boxes, 6 cu ft boxes.

FL —UNIVERSITY OF MIAMI, Otto G Richter Library, PO Box 248214, Coral Gables, 33124. Frank Rodgers, Dir of Libraries
Notes: The Cuban exile periodicals incl 412 titles of which 381 have been published in Miami, Florida. The archival material incl 54 cubic feet of mss, invitations, programs, broadsides, posters, postcards, prints, reports, maps, etc. This collection incl personal and corporate papers of Cubans settled in the US or in other countries. The truth about Cuban Committee Papers: 40 cubic feet. Contains records and correspondence of intellectual and professional Cuban and American leaders in the US dedicated to the course of eliminating Communism from the Western Hemisphere.

GA —EMORY UNIVERSITY, Robert W Woodruff Library, Atlanta, 30322. Herbert Johnson, Dir
Holdings: Mss Cat
Notes: A collection of materials relating to the history of the Communist Party in the US and the Communist International, gathered by author Theodore Draper. Incl periodicals, pamphlets, party documents, and books, as well as taped interviews that Draper conducted with party leaders and correspondence relating to his research. 80 linear ft mss.

HI —HAWAII PACIFIC COLLEGE, Meader Library, 1060 Bishop St, Honolulu, 96813. Barbara Burton Hoefler, Head Librn
Holdings: Vols 900 Cat
Notes: Un-American activities represented by history, biography, political science, and fiction.

KS —UNIVERSITY OF KANSAS, Kenneth Spencer Research Library, Special

COMMUNISM AND ANTICOMMUNISM—U.S. (cont.)

Collections Dept, Lawrence, 66045. Alexandra Mason, Librn
Holdings: Vols 7800 // Cat
Notes: Leon Josephson collection of pamphlets and other ephemera on modern socialism, especially Communist Party of America. Noncirculating.

MA —BRANDEIS UNIVERSITY, Goldfarb Library, 415 South St, Waltham, 02154. Bessie Hahn, Dir
Notes: Radical pamphlet collection. Approx 5000 pamphlets from the 1920s through the 1950s dealing with socialism and communism in the US and Great Britain. There is an author-title card catalog to ca 500 of the items in the Special Collections Card Catalog.

NC —UNIVERSITY OF NORTH CAROLINA, CHARLOTTE, J Murrey Atkins Library, UNCC Station, Charlotte, 28223. Robert F Brabham Jr, Special Collections Librn
Holdings: Uncat Mss
Notes: Papers of Benjamin Gitlow, a leader in the establishment of the CPUSA and later an anti-communist. Incl correspondence, speeches, writings, clippings, and printed material, 1920-1960. Bulk of the collection (1945-60) documents Gitlow's anti-communist activities.

PA —BALCH INSTITUTE FOR ETHNIC STUDIES, Library, 18 S Seventh St, Philadelphia, 19106. R Joseph Anderson, Library Dir

COMMUNISM AND DEMOCRACY

CA —UNIVERSITY OF CALIFORNIA, LOS ANGELES, Research Library, Dept of Special Collections, 405 Hilgard Ave, Los Angeles, 90024. Edward Shreeves, Chairman, Bibliographers Group; David S Zeidberg, Head
Holdings: Cat Mss Audiotapes
Notes: 11 cartons of materials, recordings, etc relating to the John Birch Society, with runs of relevant periodicals, government documents, etc; 6.5 linear feet on Loyalty Oaths incl in other collections; 6 transcribed Oral History interviews.

COMMUNIST GERMANY see German Democratic Republic—History

COMMUNIST PARTY (U.S.)

CA —HOOVER INSTITUTION ON WAR, REVOLUTION & PEACE, Stanford University, Stanford, 94305. Milorad M Drachkovitch, Archivist
Holdings: Mss
Notes: Papers of Benjamin Gitlow, a leader of the Communist Party in the US and later an anti-communist, incl writings, correspondence, minutes of meetings, clippings, and printed matter, 1918-1960, relating to communism and socialism in the US and Europe. 17 ms boxes.

DC —LIBRARY OF CONGRESS, Washington, 20540.
Notes: Some 4500 pamphlets and sheets dealing primarily with subversive and radical activities in the US from 1900 to 1950. Incl tracts and campaign literture of the Communist and Socialist Parties in the US and works by party leaders; materials on the economic, political, and human rights issues of the pre-World War II, World War II, and early civil rights campaign periods; and pamphlets by various anti-war and anti-draft organizations, material on Russia, and materials on the communist movement in other countries.

GA —EMORY UNIVERSITY, Robert W Woodruff Library, Atlanta, 30322. Herbert Johnson, Dir
Holdings: Mss Cat
Notes: The Philip J Jaffe papers and books about communism and the Communist Party in the US, incl copies of rare magazines, private mss, the papers of such controversial figures as Anna Louise Strong, Agnes Smedley, Norman Bethune and Koji Ariyoshi, and documentation of the growth of Chinese communism. 36 linear ft mss. Also a collection of materials relating to the history of the Communist Party in the US and the Communist International, gathered by author Theodore Draper. Incl periodicals, pamphlets, party documents, and books, as well as taped interviews that Draper conducted with party leaders and correspondence relating to his research. 80 linear ft mss.

NC —UNIVERSITY OF NORTH CAROLINA, CHARLOTTE, J Murrey Atkins Library, UNCC Station, Charlotte, 28223. Robert F Brabham Jr, Special Collections Librn
Holdings: Uncat Mss
Notes: Papers of Benjamin Gitlow, a leader in the establishment of the CPUSA and later an anti-communist. Incl correspondence, speeches, writings, clippings, and printed material, 1920-1960. Bulk of the collection (1945-60) documents Gitlow's anti-communist activities.

PA —BALCH INSTITUTE FOR ETHNIC STUDIES, Library, 18 S Seventh St, Philadelphia, 19106. R Joseph Anderson, Library Dir
Holdings: Vols 470 Cat

WI —STATE HISTORICAL SOCIETY OF WISCONSIN, Archives, 816 State St, Madison, 53706. Harold L Miller, Reference Archivist
Notes: Papers of Eugene and Peggy Dennis, Communist Party activists, 1926 - date. He was national head, CP, USA. Papers trace development of CIO in '30s, Farmer-Labor-Progressive Federation, and other Wisconsin and national political groups. Much on Senator Joseph McCarthy.

COMMUNISTIC SETTLEMENTS see Collective Settlements

COMMUNITARIANISM

IL —UNIVERSITY OF ILLINOIS, URBANA/CHAMPAIGN, Library, Illinois Historical Survey Library, 1408 W Gregory Dr, 1A Library, Urbana, 61801.
Holdings: Vols 50 Cat Mss Maps Pix Microforms
Notes: Communitarianism in America. The ms material, contained in 30 separate collections (10 cubic feet), concentrates on the period 1840-70. It incl correspondence, records, minutes, ledgers and diaries. Communal societies such as Bishop Hill, Brook Farm, New Harmony, the North American Phalanx and the Sodus Bay Phalanx are represented. Among the correspondents are Albert Brisbane, Parke Godwin, Sarah Grimke, Richard Owen, Robert Owen, Robert Dale Owen, and George Ripley. Numerous pictures. Guide to the collections published in 1976.

PA —PENNSYLVANIA HISTORICAL & MUSEUM COMMISSION, Ephrata Cloister, 632 W Main St, Ephrata, 17522. James Lewars, Adminr; John L Kraft, Librn
Holdings: Vols (150) Cat Mss Maps Pix Slides Phonorecords
Notes: Ephrata Cloister and early Pennsylvania imprints.

PA —PENNSYLVANIA DIV OF ARCHIVES & MANUSCRIPTS, State Archives, PO Box 1026, Harris, 17108. Roland M Baumann, Chief, History & Museums
Holdings: Vols (3000) // Uncat Mss Maps Pix
Budget: ($40,000)
Notes: The Harmony Society (1785-1905), a German communistic and spiritual community, which immigrated to the US in 1805 and established their community in Harmony, Pennsylvania, moved to New Harmony, Indiana, and returned to Pennsylvania to set up the town of Economy, 20 miles north of Pittsburgh on the Ohio River. The Harmonists had a vast impact on the economy of the areas in which they lived. They were involved in agriculture, manufacturing and investing. 300,000 cu ft.

COMMUNITY ACTION BROADCASTING SYSTEM

AZ —NORTHERN ARIZONA UNIVERSITY, Special Collection Library, CU Box 6022, Flagstaff, 86011. Peter M Whiteley, Coordr/Archivist; William Mullane, Librn
Notes: Guy Bensusan Collection; Community Action Broadcasting System, Tucson, Ariz; transcripts of radio programs relating to Arizona subjects, 1972-1973.

COMMUNITY CENTERS

†PA —TEMPLE UNIVERSITY LIBRARIES, Special Collections Dept, Urban Archives Center, Philadelphia, 19122. Thomas Whitehead, Cur of Mss
Holdings: Cat
Notes: Incl the records of several separate collections which are deposited in the Urban Archives Center. Many collections contain photographs, maps and pamphlets, in addition to manuscripts. All collections in the Urban Archives are separately cataloged.

COMMUNITY CHESTS see Federations, Financial (Social Service)

COMMUNITY DEVELOPMENT

CA —UNIVERSITY OF CALIFORNIA, SANTA BARBARA, Library, Dept of Special Collections, Santa Barbara, 93106. Christian F Brun, Head
Holdings: Vols (95,980) Cat Mss
Notes: The Pearl Chase Collections of Community Development and Conservation. Papers of outstanding California leaders in conservation, community planning, Indian affairs, national parks.

DC —NATIONAL ASSOCIATION OF HOUSING AND REDEVELOPMENT OFFICIALS, Resource Center, 2600 Virginia Ave NW, Washington, 20037. Mary L Pike, Librn
Holdings: Vols 1000
Notes: Public housing and community development, incl urban renewal and housing code enforcement.

DC —US DEPT OF HOUSING & URBAN DEVELOPMENT, HUD Library, 451 Seventh St SW Room 8141, Washington, 20410. Carol A Johnson, Project Manager
Holdings: Vols Cat Documents Microforms
Notes: 600,000 pieces. Strong in all phases of community planning. Extensive coverage of the production and financing of housing. Emphasis on federal legislation.

IL —CHICAGO HISTORICAL SOCIETY, Library, Clark St at North Ave, Chicago, 60614. Archie Motley, Manuscript Librn
Notes: Papers of Chicago community and related organizations, in addition to similar materials in collections cited elsewhere in this listing: Greater Lawndale Conservation Commission; Lake View Citizens' Council; Lawndale Community Committee; Logan Square Neighborhood Association; South Lynne Community Council; Leadership Council for Metropolitan Open Communities; Northwest Community Organization.

IL —INSTITUTE ON THE CHURCH IN URBAN-INDUSTRIAL SOCIETY, Library, 5700 S Woodlawn, Chicago, 60637.
Holdings: Vols 1000 Cat Microforms
Notes: Urban-industrial involvement of the churches world-wide, international urban literature, corporate responsibility, human factors of urbanization and industrialization. Library holdings are dorment at present.

IL —ILLINOIS STATE UNIVERSITY, Milner Library, Dept of Special Collections, Normal, 61761. Robert Sokan, Librn
Holdings: Vols 2100 // Uncat
Notes: Sigmund Livingston Collection on Intergroup Relations, 1944 to present. The material is divided into subject headings which contain pamphlets, newsletters and commission reports.

MD —UNIVERSITY OF MARYLAND, BALTIMORE, Health Sciences Library, 111

COMMUNITY DEVELOPMENT (cont.)

S Greene St, Baltimore, 21201. Cyril C H Feng, Dir
Holdings: Vols 878 Cat
Notes: Social work and community planning.

MI —MICHIGAN STATE UNIVERSITY, Urban Policy & Planning Library, East Lansing, 48824. Dale E Casper, Librn
Holdings: Vols (4900) // Cat
Budget: ($35,000)
Notes: A reference collection in the Urban Policy and Planning Library consists of indexes, abstracts, bibliographies, directories and statistical handbooks. There is a 4000 volume pamphlet collection which covers topics incl: community development block grants, revenue sharing, municipal finance, land use and many other topics as well. A topically arranged newspaper clippings collection provides retrospective and current newsworthy information on urban problems, legislation and solutions. A periodical collection consists of the current issues of about 120 urban and ethnic studies journals.

MI —OAKLAND COUNTY REFERENCE LIBRARY, 1200 N Telegraph Rd, Pontiac, 48053. Phyllis Jose, Library Dir
Holdings: Vols (11,000) Cat
Budget: ($34,000)

NY —NEW YORK STATE DEPT OF STATE, Community Affairs Library, 162 Washington Ave, Albany, 12231. M L Johnson, Librn
Holdings: Vols (14,640) Cat
Notes: Local government. Serves as research arm for official activities. 16,000 items in vertical files; 150 periodicals. Unique Community File collection of about 1600 local governments arranged by counties in the state.

†PA —TEMPLE UNIVERSITY LIBRARIES, Special Collections Dept, Urban Archives Center, Philadelphia, 19122. Thomas Whitehead, Cur of Mss
Holdings: Cat
Notes: Incl the records of several separate collections which are deposited in the Urban Archives Center. Many collections contain photographs, maps and pamphlets, in addition to manuscripts. All collections in the Urban Archives are separately cataloged.

TN —TENNESSEE VALLEY AUTHORITY (TVA), Technical Library, 400 W Summit Hill Dr, E2 B7, Knoxville, 37902. Jesse C Mills, Chief Librn
Holdings: Vols (106,900) Cat Mss Maps Pix Audiotapes Microforms
Budget: ($2,025,000)
Notes: The Technical Library Headquarters Staff (order, cataloging, information, and administration) is located in Knoxville, Tenn. In addition there are branch libraries in Knoxville, Norris, and Chattanooga, Tennessee, and Muscle Shoals, Alabama.

VA —UNITED WAY OF AMERICA INFORMATION CENTER, 701 North Fairfax St, United Way Plaza, Alexandria, 22314. Henry M Smith, Dir; Barbara L Owen, Librn
Holdings: Vols (1200) Cat Microforms
Notes: Incl 5000 reserach reports and studies on microfiche; 100 vertical file drawers. Services primarily for United Way organizations--United Funds, Community Chests, Health and Welfare Planning Councils.

ON —CANADIAN HOUSING INFORMATION CENTER, Canada Mortgage and Housing Corp, CMHC Annex Bldg Ground Floor, Montreal Rd, Ottawa, K1A 0P7, Can. Leslie Jones, Mgr
Holdings: Cat
Notes: City and town planning, all aspects, incl urban renewal, residential rehabilitation, new towns, suburban development, etc.

ON —DEPT OF REGIONAL INDUSTRIAL EXPANSION, Ottawa Library, 235 Queen St, Ottawa, K1A 0H5, Can. Steven Rush, Librn
Holdings: Vols (100,000) Cat Maps Microforms
Notes: Pertaining to Industrial Development. Contains 1500 reports of ARDA projects (Agricultural Rehabilitation and Development Agency); also NEWSTART project reports. There is a published book catalog and two supplements. 15,000 documents; 3000 periodical subscriptions.

ON —METROPOLITAN TORONTO LIBRARY, Municipal Reference Library, City Hall, Toronto, M5H 2N1, Can. Margot Hewings, Head
Holdings: Vols (60,000) Cat Maps Pix Microforms Slides VF
Budget: ($112,600)
Notes: Community development; municipal finance; local municipal government; housing; urban pollution; urban transportation; urban affairs; urban geography.

ON —WILFRID LAURIER UNIVERSITY, Library, (Formerly Waterloo Lutheran University), 75 University Ave W, Waterloo, N2L 3C5, Can. Erich R W Schultz, Librn
Holdings: Vols (20,000) Cat Microforms
Budget: ($27,000)

COMMUNITY HEALTH see Public Health

COMMUNITY HEALTH SERVICES

IN —WISHARD MEMORIAL HOSPITAL, Professional Library, 1001 W Tenth St, Indianapolis, 46202. Fran Bischoff, Library Dir; Kirsten Quam, Librn
Holdings: Vols (60) Cat

MI —UNIVERSITY OF MICHIGAN, Public Health Library, Ann Arbor, 48109. Mary Townsend, Head
Holdings: Vols (55,000) Cat Maps Pix
Budget: ($24,000)

NY —WILLARD PSYCHIATRIC CENTER, Medical Library, Willard, 14588. Helen Bunting, Chief Library Services
Holdings: Vols (2078) Cat Audiotapes

COMMUNITY LIFE

DC —NATIONAL ASSOCIATION OF HOUSING AND REDEVELOPMENT OFFICIALS, Resource Center, 2600 Virginia Ave NW, Washington, 20037. Mary L Pike, Librn
Holdings: Vols 1000
Notes: Public housing and community development, incl urban renewal and housing code enforcement.

IL —CHICAGO HISTORICAL SOCIETY, Library, Clark St at North Ave, Chicago, 60614. Archie Motley, Manuscript Librn
Notes: Papers of Chicago community and related organizations, in addition to similar materials in collections cited elsewhere in this listing: Greater Lawndale Conservation Commission; Lake View Citizens' Council; Lawndale Community Committee; Logan Square Neighborhood Association; South Lynne Community Council; Leadership Council for Metropolitan Open Communities; Northwest Community Organization.

IL —CHICAGO PUBLIC LIBRARY, Special Collections Div, Cultural Center, 78 E Washington St, Chicago, 60602. Laura Linard, Cur
Holdings: Mss Maps Pix Slides Microforms
Notes: A vast amount of material on Chicago neighborhood history is housed at several locations in The Chicago Public Library system. A centralized program for organizing, storing and accessing this material was begun by the Special Collections Division in 1977. Major neighborhood collections which have been organized and are now accessible to researchers incl: Papers of the Calumet Pioneer Historical Society, Calumet Region Community Collection, Lawndale-Crawford Community Collection, Papers of the Lawndale-Crawford Historical Association, and the Historic Pullman Collection (all of these collections are housed in the Special Collections Division). Also, the Ravenswood-Lake View Community Collection and the Papers of the Ravenswood-Lake View Historical Association are located at the Hild Regional Library and are open foruse by appointment. Several other neighborhood collections are still housed at branch libraries and are currently being organized. Principal contact person for these neighborhood collections is Robert Marshall, Archivist.

OH —ANTIOCH COLLEGE, Olive Kettering Library, Livermore St, Yellow Springs, 45387. Nina Myatt, Cur
Notes: Personal papers and correspondence (1920-1975) of Arthur E Morgan former President of Antioch (1920-1936), first director of Ohio's Miami Valley Conservancy District, and first Chairman of the Tennessee Valley Authority (TVA). Mss, film, out-takes, much on the engineering of over 50 water-control projects in this country, Africa, and India. Materials on Edward Bellamy (Morgan wrote biography of Bellamy). Incl family papers. About 175 file boxes. Papers of Morgan's organization Community Service; writings on community life and community planning.

COMMUNITY MENTAL HEALTH SERVICES

IL —ILLINOIS DEPT OF MENTAL HEALTH & DEVELOPMENTAL DISABILITIES, Adolf Meyer Mental Health Center, Professional Library, 2310 E Mound Rd, Decatur, 62526.
Holdings: Vols (1000) Cat Audiotapes Videotapes Microforms
Budget: ($4500)
Notes: Mental health, in general, incl personal mental health and community mental health, the behavioral sciences (biomedical, psychological, and social), and treatment modalities of mental illness, with primary emphasis on community mental health and treatment modalities of mental illness.

NY —CREEDMOOR PSYCHIATRIC CENTER, Health Sciences Library, Bldg 51, 80-45 Winchester Blvd, Queens Village, 11427. Susan Taubman, Dir of Library; Pushpa Bhati, Sr Librn
Holdings: Vols (12,000) Cat Slides Phonorecords Audiotapes Filmstrips Microfiche
Budget: ($50,000)
Notes: Particularly strong in the areas of neurology, pharmacology, psychoanalysis, and psychopharmacology.

COMMUNITY SERVICE SOCIETY OF NEW YORK

NY —COLUMBIA UNIVERSITY LIBRARIES, Rare Book & Manuscript Library, 801 Butler Library, 535 W 114 St, New York, 10027. Kenneth A Lohf, Librn
Holdings: Mss
Notes: Papers of the Community Service Society of New York. Incl files, books, photographs (1000) and bound volumes of periodicals and conference proceedings. Among the papers are central and district administrative records, committee correspondence and minutes, and files of programs sponsored by the organization. Also more than 1000 photographs by Jessie Tarbox Beals and Lewis W Hine depicting conditions of the poor. 276,000 items. Restricted use.

COMMUNITY SONG BOOKS see Song Books—Collections

COMMUNITY SURVEYS see Social Surveys

COMPANIES see Corporations

COMPANY LAW see Corporation Law

COMPANY OF YOUNG CANADIANS

†ON —MCMASTER UNIVERSITY, Library, Hamilton, L8S 4L6, Can.
Notes: Administrative files, correspondence, and printed material used by the Director of the Company of Young Canadians, 1966-1972.

COMPARATIVE ANATOMY see Anatomy, Comparative

COMPARATIVE GOVERNMENT

MI —UNIVERSITY OF MICHIGAN, Bureau of Government Library, 100A Rackman

COMPARATIVE GOVERNMENT (cont.)

Bldg, Ann Arbor, 48109. Barbara Landay, Technical Libr Assistant
Holdings: Vols (66,000) Cat Microforms
Budget: ($10,000)
Notes: Library was established in 1914 to serve faculty and students of the Institute of Public Policy Studies. Emphasizes federal, state and local government, though some information on foreign governments is included. Government documents are represented. Also has a pamphlet file and a newspaper clipping collection on Michigan.

COMPARATIVE JURISPRUDENCE see Comparative Law

COMPARATIVE LAW

MA —HARVARD UNIVERSITY LIBRARY, Law School Library, Langdell Hall, Cambridge, 02138. Harry S Martin III, Librn
Holdings: Cat Mss Maps Pix Slides
Notes: Downs 1687, 1763, 1774, 1776-1779, 1782-1784, 1790-1793, 1809, 1764, 1768, 1796; Downs Supplement 789. Comprehensive collection of English common law, American Law (historical and current), foreign law, comparative law, international law, Roman law and Canon law. Over a million vols.

COMPARATIVE LEGISLATION see Comparative Law

COMPARATIVE LIBRARIANSHIP

PA —UNIVERSITY OF PITTSBURGH, Graduate School of Library & Information Sciences, International Library Information Center, 135 N Bellefield Ave, Pittsburgh, 15260. Richard Krzys, Dir
Holdings: Mss Slides
Notes: Contains primary library source materials (18,000 pieces) on countries outside of the US, from Aden to Zambia. Emphasis in on Latin America and countries of the English-speaking world.

COMPARATIVE LINGUISTICS see Language and Languages

COMPARATIVE LITERATURE see Literature, Comparative

COMPARATIVE MEDICINE see Medicine, Comparative

COMPARATIVE MORPHOLOGY see Anatomy, Comparative

COMPARATIVE PHILOSOPHY see Philosophy, Comparative

COMPARATIVE RELIGION see Religion, Comparative

COMPASS

NS —CANADIAN COAST GUARD COLLEGE, Library, PO Box 4500, Sydney, B1P 6L1, Can. David MacSween, Librn
Holdings: Vols 25 Cat

COMPENSATION see Pensions

COMPETITIVE EXAMINATIONS see Examinations

COMPLEXION see Cosmetics

COMPOSERS

CA —UNIVERSITY OF CALIFORNIA, SAN DIEGO, Central University Library, Mandeville Dept of Special Collections, La Jolla, 92093. Lynda Corey Claassen, Head
Notes: Manuscript Collection incl the correspondence and writings of composer Ernst Krenek and musicologist Peter Yates.

CA —CALIFORNIA STATE UNIVERSITY, LONG BEACH, Library, Dept of Special Collections & Archives, 1250 Bellflower Blvd, Long Beach, 90840. John Ahouse, Special Collections Librn
Holdings: Mss Phonorecords Audiotapes
Notes: Almost all of the papers, recordings, etc, published and unpublished, of Gerald V Strang.

CA —UNIVERSITY OF CALIFORNIA, LOS ANGELES, Music Library, Schonberg Hall, Los Angeles, 90024. Stephen M Fry, Music Librn
Notes: Broad scholarly scope with emphasis on musicology, incl books on music; musical scores (scholarly and practical editions) incl instrumental, vocal, chamber music with parts; periodicals; 35,000 musical recordings (disc and tape); microforms; mss. Special and archival collections. Manuscripts: Ernst Toch (see below), Henry Mancini, Alex North, Eugene Zador, Rudolf Friml, George Antheil, Fannie Charles Dillon, Walter Lantz, Harry Lubin, Clarence Mader, Colin McPhee, Mary Carr Moore, Alfred Newman, Edward B Powell, Andre Previn, Joseph Rumshinsky, Lester Spencer, Henry Temianka, Ernst Toch, John Vincent, Edward Ward, Mortimer Wilson, and Eric Zeisl. Collections: guitar music, 17th-18th century Dutch song and psalm books, 17th-18th century Venetian opera librettos, 18th-19thcentury opera scores, 18th-early 19th century French and German opera librettos, folk songs and dances of the British Isles, (popular American sheet music, c 1830-present, about 750,000 items), Alfred Newman Collection of film score recordings; 40,000 other musical scores. Published descriptions of collections: Walter H Rubsamen, Unusual music holdings of libraries on the West Coast, *MLA Notes,* X, no 4 (September 1953), pp 546-554; Malcolm Cole, A Pleyel Collection at UCLA, *MLA Notes,* XXIX, no 2 (December 1972), pp 215-223. "The Music Library" *UCLA Librarian,* XXXIV no 3-4 (March-April 1978) pp 12-14.

DC —GEORGETOWN UNIVERSITY, Library, Special Collections Div, 37 & O Sts NW, Washington, 20057. George M Barringer, Special Collections Librn; Nicholas B Sheetz, Mss Librn
Holdings: Mss
Notes: Muscical mss, incl a copyist's mss of the opening two movements of Beethoven's Ninth Symphony (1825); autograph mss of Rheinberger's Fantasie-Sonate fur die Orgel (before 1872); Gloetzner's Ave Regina and organ exercises; and a printed copy of his Mass, Op 12 (1910). Anton Gloetzner, Bavarian composer and musician, taught music at Georgetown College from 1873 to 1880.

IN —INDIANA UNIVERSITY, Lilly Library, Seventh St, Bloomington, 47405. William R Cagle, Librn
Holdings: Cat Mss
Notes: Extensive holdings of American sheet music; first editions of works by great composers (operas, symphonies, chamber music, etc); sources annotated for performances conducted by Fritz Busch. Ms incl small collections of Hoagy Carmichael materials, Paul Dresser memorabilia, and Barclay Walker compositions.

†MD —MARYLAND HISTORICAL SOCIETY, Library, 201 W Monument St, Baltimore, 21201.
Notes: Eubie Blake's personal and professional archive. Incl the Baltimore-born pianist, composer, and songwriter's collection of songs and instrumental pieces in mss, extensive documentation of his collaboration with Noble Sissle, Flournog Miller, Milton Reddie, and others. The Broadway musical comedy, Shuffle Along, is represented in box office records, programs, scores and parts, photographs, and sheet music. Blake's involvement with other productions is similarly documented.

MI —UNIVERSITY OF MICHIGAN, School of Music, Music Library, Moore Bldg, Ann Arbor, 48109. Peggy Daub, Head
Holdings: Uncat // Mss Pix Slides Microforms
Notes: The Jacob Maurice Coopersmith Collection of material by and about G F Handel. Also the Women's Music Collection of compositions by women from the 18th to 20th centuries.
See also entries under Coopersmith, Jacob M.; Women Composers

MS —UNIVERSITY OF SOUTHERN MISSISSIPPI, William David McCain Graduate Library, Box 5148, Southern Sta, Hattiesburg, 39406.
Holdings: Mss
Notes: The Paul Yoder Collection (1940-1980; 30 cubic feet) contains original musical scores and published copies of band music which Yoder composed or arranged. Some of the band music was written for foreign bands, especially Japanese. Catalog in progress.

NJ —PRINCETON UNIVERSITY, Library, Rare Books Dept, Princeton, 08544. Stephen Ferguson, Cur
Notes: The James S Hall Collection (from Walmer, England). One of the major collections.

NY —BROOKLYN PUBLIC LIBRARY, Art & Music Div, Grand Army Plaza, Brooklyn, 11238. Sue H Sharma, Chief
Holdings: Vols (4500) Cat Mss
Notes: Over 50,000 items, most of which circulate to the public. The collection contains some reference materials, incl the complete works of many composers; over 3500 popular song folios with our own in-house index for locating individual songs; some rare editions and mss of local composers; and a small collection of rare sheet music beginning with the 18th century. The circulating collection incl standard vocal scores, methods, piano music, etc, and is one of the largest public library collections in the country.

NY —AMERICAN INSTITUTE FOR VERDI STUDIES, New York University, Bobst Library, Music Div, New York, 10023. Ruth B Hilton, Librn
Holdings: Mss Maps Pix Slides Microforms
Notes: Contains the archives of the Institute for Verdi Studies.

NY —NEW YORK PUBLIC LIBRARY, Performing Arts Research Center, Rodgers & Hammerstein Archives of Recorded Sound, 111 Amsterdam Ave, New York, 10023.
Holdings: // Cat Audiotapes
Notes: The Serge Koussevitzky Music Foundation at the Library of Congress established in 1958 a tape recording project devoted to documenting, for limited library distribution, the current or near-current output of contemporary composers. American and European. By the time the last tapes from the project were received in 1971, close to 300 composers were represented. Together with the Library of Congress and a small group of similar institutions, the Rodgers and Hammerstein Archives was one of the recipients of this series.

NY —NEW YORK PUBLIC LIBRARY, Music Div, 111 Amsterdam Ave, New York, 10023. Frank C Campbell, Chief
Notes: Composers' autographs on microfilm. Works of 17-20th century composers. Major holdings: Bach, Handel, Beethoven. Original music mss, association items, etc.

NY —NEW YORK PUBLIC LIBRARY, Performing Arts Research Center, Music Div, Lincoln Center, New York, 10018.
Notes: New York Pro Musica Archives, and personal papers of Noah Greenberg, founder.

NY —PIERPONT MORGAN LIBRARY, 29 E 36 St, New York, 10016. J Rigbie Turner, Cur
Holdings: Cat Mss
Notes: Musical mss, mainly of composers of the 18th-20th centuries. Incl the Mary Flagler Cary Music Collection.

NC —UNIVERSITY OF NORTH CAROLINA, GREENSBORO, Walter Clinton Jackson Library, Special Collections Dept, 1000 Spring Garden St, Greensboro, 27412. Emilie W Mills, Librn
Holdings: Cat Mss
Notes: 78 letters by the English composer Dame Ethel Mary Smyth, chiefly to Emmeline Pankhurst, written from Helouan, Egypt, 1913-1914. Other letters incl several

COMPOSERS (cont.)

from Empress Eugenie and members of her circle, and several letters to Lady Ponsonby. This group of letters mainly traces the composer's interest in the suffrage movement and the development of her musical career. No photocopying.

OH —CASE WESTERN RESERVE UNIVERSITY LIBRARIES, Cleveland, 44106. Susie Hanson, Special Collections Librn
Notes: Manuscripts of compositions and other archival materials by the American composer Donald Erb. Contains sketches and pencil scores covering the period of Erb's 30 year career, programs, reviews, newspaper clippings, and correspondence.

OR —UNIVERSITY OF OREGON LIBRARY, Special Collections Div, Eugene, 97403. Kenneth W Duckett, Curator
Holdings: Cat Mss
Notes: Ca 15 mss collections largely containing music scores and arrangements. Major collections incl the papers of Henry J Beau, Ernest Loring "Red" Nichols, and Axel Stordahl. Publication: Martin Schmitt, comp, *Catalogue of Manuscripts in the University of Oregon Library* (Eugene: University of Oregon Books, 1971).
See also entry under Music, Popular

TX —NORTH TEXAS STATE UNIVERSITY, Audio Center, Box 5188, NT Station, Denton, 76203. Morris Martin, Music Librn
Notes: Emphasis on Contemporary and Avant Garde music. More than 450 musical compositions (mostly manuscript, many multi-media). This is an archive of materials published in, or submitted for publication to, the contemporary music magazine *Source, the Music of the Avant Garde* which appeared from 1967-1977 (although bearing dates only through 1973). Composers represented are the editors (Larry Austin and Stanley Lunetta), John Cage, Steve Reich, Pauline Oliveros, Harry Partch, Morton Feldman, Lukas Foss, Barney Childs, David Cope, Peter Garland, Philip Glass, Ben Johnston, Alcides Lanza, Alvin Lucier, David Rosenboom, Dane Rudhyar, and Nicolas Slonimsky.

VA —CBN UNIVERSITY, Virginia Beach, 23463. Jack L Ralston, Fine Arts Librn
Holdings: Vols 9000
Notes: The Keith C Clark Collection of hymnology; hymnals, psazlters, oblong tune-books, hymnody, church music, composers, early sermons on church music, and journals. See Clark's *Selective Bibliography for the Study of Hymns* (1980).

WY —UNIVERSITY OF WYOMING, William Robertson Coe Library, Performing Arts Collections, Laramie, 82071. Gene M Gressley, Dir
Holdings: Mss
Notes: Collections in the Performing Arts area incl some 300 collections of outstanding music composers, arrangers, film industry directors, writers, performers, and individuals prominent in all aspects of music, theatre, radio, television and film industry.

ON —NATIONAL LIBRARY OF CANADA, 395 Wellington St, Ottawa, K1A 0N4, Can. Andre Preibish, Dir
Holdings: Vols 35,000
Notes: Includes 2000 pieces of Canadian sheet music (mostly 19th century imprints), 40,000 cylinders, discs, tapes; over 600 serials titles devoted to music; 200 archival collections of composers, musicians and conductors, eg papers of Healy Willan, eminent composer; Glen Gould, well-known pianist; Sir Ernest MacMillan, conductor, director and composer. Since 1950 the Canadian imprints have been received on legal deposit. Intensive purchases aim at a comprehensive collection of Canadian music.

COMPOSERS, AUSTRIAN-AMERICAN

DC —LIBRARY OF CONGRESS, Music Division, Washington, 20540.
Notes: A group of seven holograph musical scores by Eric Wolfgang Korngold.

COMPOSERS, CALIFORNIA

CA —CALIFORNIA STATE UNIVERSITY, LONG BEACH, Library, Dept of Special Collections & Archives, 1250 Bellflower Blvd, Long Beach, 90840. John Ahouse, Special Collections Librn
Holdings: Cat Mss Pix Audiotapes
Notes: Manuscripts, programs, ALS, articles, clippings and recordings pertaining to the musicla careers of Wesley Kuhnle, Gerald Strang, Dane Rudhyar, Richard Buhlig, Morris Ruger and other artists active in Southern California, 1930-1960. Partially cataloged.

COMPOSERS, FINNISH

IN —BUTLER UNIVERSITY, Irwin Library, Hugh Thomas Miller Rare Book Room, 4600 Sunset Ave, Indianapolis, 46208. Gisela Terrell, Rare Books Librn
Holdings: Vols Cat Music Scores Recordings
Notes: Sibelius Collection. It contains mostly the lesser-known compositions, and includes scores in print, hectograph, and manuscript, many of them unpublished and unknown in the US. Also rare secondary sources, mostly Finnish and Swedish imprints. Also a collection of mostly historical recordings, probably complete up to 1972. Placed in trust in the Rare Book Room by Dr Harold E Johnson, Sibelius scholar, 1982-1983. A preliminary checklist is availalbe. The recordings include many pieces by lesser-known Finnish composers.

COMPOSERS, FRENCH

CA —STANFORD UNIVERSITY LIBRARIES, Cecil H Green Library, Stanford, 94305. Michael T Ryan, Cur
Notes: Large archive. To be incl in the Stanford University international Lully Archive of microfilm of primary Lully sources. The first of 64 vols (Sacred Music) scheduled for 1984 publication.

†TX —UNIVERSITY OF TEXAS LIBRARIES, Austin, 78712.
Notes: Collection of 89 autographed music manuscripts by five french composers: Gabriel Faure, Maurice Ravel, Claude Debussy, Robert Roussel, Paul Dukas. About 60 percent of Roussel's entire repertory is included, as well as nearly one-half of Ravel's total musical output.

COMPOSERS, GERMAN

DC —LIBRARY OF CONGRESS, Music Division, Washington, 20540.
Notes: A large collection of letters from Brahms to Robert Keller.

COMPOSERS, IOWA

IA —PUBLIC LIBRARY OF DES MOINES, 100 Locust, Des Moines, 50309. Stephen R Brogden, Head, Fine Arts Dept; Martha Gerstenberger, Music Librn
Holdings: Vols (8300) Cat Phonorecords
Budget: ($5000)
Notes: Incl compositions about Iowa, clippings, and biographical data. Incl 25,000 scores and sheet music.

COMPOSERS, ITALIAN

CA —SAN FRANCISCO STATE UNIVERSITY, Frank V de Bellis Collection, 1630 Holloway Ave, San Francisco, 94132. Serena de Bellis, Cur
Holdings: Uncat Mss Phonorecords Audiotapes Microforms
Notes: Rare annd current materials. Music by Italian composers, medieval through contemporary (10,000 scores). Phonorecords, cylinders, tapes, etc (20,000); primarily vocal (all nationalities).

COMPOSERS, JEWISH

NY —YIVO INSTITUTE FOR JEWISH RESEARCH, Library & Archives, 1048 Fifth Ave, New York, 10028. Dina Abramowicz, Librn; Marek Web, Archivist
Holdings: Cat Mss Slides
Notes: Collections of Jewish music organizations in pre-World War I Russia, and collections of individual musicians and composers, among them the Bernstein collection from Vilna and Leo Low collection from New York. Secular, liturgical, folk music, theatrical songs in the form of sheet music is represented. Partially cataloged.

COMPOSERS, KENTUCKY

KY —UNIVERSITY OF LOUISVILLE, School of Music, Dwight Anderson Memorial Music Library, 2301 S Third St, Louisville, 40292. Marion Korda, Librn
Holdings: Uncat Mss
Notes: 7 boxes printed music; 2 boxes mss.

COMPOSERS, MAINE

ME —MAINE STATE LIBRARY, Special Collections Dept, Cultural Bldg, Station 64, Augusta, 04333. Shirley Thayer, Librn
Holdings: Mss
Notes: Sheet music by over 200 Maine composers.

ME —PORTLAND PUBLIC LIBRARY, 5 Monument Sq, Portland, 04101. Edward V Chenevert, Library Dir
Holdings: Cat Mss
Notes: The Maine Music Collection. (In cooperation with the Maine Federation of Music Clubs). Music written by Maine composers predominantly 19th and 20th centuries. Various forms. Indexed. Other materials on Maine composers and music also available. 1723 pieces of sheet music; 849 titles.

COMPOSERS, MUSIC

DC —LIBRARY OF CONGRESS, Music Division, Washington, 20540.
Notes: Mss resources, consisting chiefly of autograph scores, letters, and scrapbooks of composers and performers from the late 18th through the 20th centuries, are exceptionally rich for the modern period. Among the many 20th century figures represented by collections of music mss are Leonard Bernstein, Elliot Carter, Mario Castelnuovo-Tedesco, Aaron Copland, Henry Cowell, Roy Harris, Alan Hovhaness, Cole Porter, David Raksin, Harold Rome, William Schuman, John Phillip Sousa, and Igor Stravinsky.

IL —CHICAGO PUBLIC LIBRARY, Music Section, Fine Arts Division, 78 E Washington St, Chicago, 60602. Rosalinda I Hack, Fine Arts Division Chief; Richard C Schwegel, Head, Music Section
Notes: Sets of complete and collected works of 50 major composers.

SC —COLLEGE OF CHARLESTON LIBRARY, Special Collections Dept, Charleston, 29401.
Notes: Meltzer Music Collection incl autographed leeters and/or photographs of composers and singers; it contains correspondence from C C Chaminade, Alphonse Daudet, Claude Debussy (1907), Emory Elgar (1916), George Gershwin (1928), J Massenet (1888, 1909), Felix Mendelsohn-Bartholdy (1839), Puccini (1911), and C Wolf-Ferrari (1911). Contains also a biography of Charles Henry Meltzer and newsclippings concerning the collection. One box.

COMPOSERS, NEW YORK (STATE)

NY —ELMIRA COLLEGE, Gannett-Tripp Learning Center, Elmira, 14901. James D Gray, Dir
Holdings: Cat Mss Pix Phonorecords
Notes: Papers, recordings, music scores, of Charles Tomlinson Griffes, 1884-1920.

COMPOSERS, PENNSYLVANIA

PA —ERIE COUNTY HISTORICAL SOCIETY LIBRARY, 417 State St, Erie, 16501. Helen Andrews, Librn
Notes: Original research materials in 16 legal size drawers, including Pennsylvania Population Company papers, Old Erie Academy papers, Erie Street railway papers, Harry Burleigh (black singer & composer)

COMPOSERS, PENNSYLVANIA (cont.)

transcripts and research papers; also four letter size drawers with old account books.

PA —FREE LIBRARY OF PHILADELPHIA, Sheet Music Collection, Logan Sq, Philadelphia, 19103. Connie Jessum, Librn
Budget: ($2000)
Notes: Covers entire span of American popular expression in song and instrumental music (piano) from colonial times to the present. Incl Newland-Zeuner and Edward I Keffer Collections on loan from the Musical Fund Society. Items printed before 1825 indexed in Sonneck-Upton and Wolfe. Checklists for cover illustrations, musical shows or films and special subjects. Songs are filed by title; piano music by composer. Examples of special materials not filed in regular collection incl early Philadelphia composers and publications, national (centennial and state), patriotic ("Star-Spangled Banner"), political (Presidents), and war (1861; 1914; 1939) songs. Most of the ms materials are anonymous. Collection contains 138,360 pieces of sheet music.

COMPOSERS, POLISH

NY —POLISH SINGERS ALLIANCE OF AMERICA, 180 2nd Ave, New York, 10003.
Notes: About 2000 pieces of music. Cataloged.

COMPOSERS, RHODE ISLAND

RI —BROWN UNIVERSITY, John Hay Library, Harris Collection, Prospect St, Providence, 02912. Rosemary L Cullen, Cur
Holdings: Vols (200,000) Cat Mss Pix Phonorecords Microforms
Budget: ($15,000)
Notes: The Harris Collection of American Poetry and Plays is principally composed of American and Canadian poetry and plays from the 17th century to the present. Extensive holdings in songsters and sheet music with lyrics (170,000 pieces). Incl large collection of Stephen Foster sheet music and music by Rhode Island composers and lyricists. See *Dictionary Catalog of the Harris Collection of American Poetry and* Plays (Boston: G K Hall, 1972), 13 vols; *Supplement* (1977), 3 vols. Separate catalog.

COMPOSERS, TEXAS

TX —DALLAS PUBLIC LIBRARY, Fine Arts Div, 1515 Young St, Dallas, 75201. Richard L Waters, Acting Dir; Jane Holahan, Manager
Holdings: Uncat Mss Pix
Notes: *The Dallas Symphony Orchestra;* printed programs beginning with first concert in 1900 are bound. Subscription series indexed by composition performed and guest artists. Scrapbooks assembled by Symphony PR office and Symphony League kept on file in Division. Reviews of performances filed. Photographs of all conductors on file. Photos of Symphony on stage. *Dallas Civic Opera;* printed programs as well as reviews and other related newspaper articles; also a collection of 200 artists' renderings of set designs, costumes, etc. *The John Rosenfield* Papers: Mr Rosenfield, Amusements Editor for the *Dallas Morning News* for over 40 years, had collected letters received from persons in the Performing Arts, mostly music, over the years. There are also photographs of many of the stars who performed in Dallas and whom he met in both New York and Hollywood. The Manuscript ArchivesCommittee of the Texas Federation of Music Clubs works with the Fine Arts Division in collecting holograph mss of those Texas composers whom the Committee feels are doing the best music composition in the state. At present there are about 50 composers represented in the Archives. Holograph mss of 3 works commissioned by the Division--the composers of which are Darius Milhaud, Gunther Schuller, and Alberto Ginastera. Also mss of the two books by John Ardoin, *Callas: the Art and the Life;* and *The Callas* Legacy, are in the collection.

COMPOSERS, WOMEN see Women Composers

COMPOSERS' COLLECTIVE

DC —LIBRARY OF CONGRESS, Music Division, Washington, 20540.
Notes: Musical aspects of the revolutionary workers' movement represented in the Workers Music League's publications and activities; also, the Composers' Collective, etc.

COMPOSITION (MUSIC)

CA —CALIFORNIA INSTITUTE OF THE ARTS, Library, 24700 McBean Pkwy, Valencia, 91355. James Elrod, Dir
Holdings: Vols (61,000) Cat Phonrecords Audiotapes
Budget: ($8500)
Notes: Incl 11,656 audiotapes. Cataloged.

†DC —CATHOLIC UNIVERSITY OF AMERICA, Music Library, Washington, 20064. Betty Libbey, Head Music Library
Holdings: Cat Microforms
Notes: A large collection to support advanced degree study. Emphasis on church music, musicology, history and criticism, instrumental and vocal music, solo music for all voices, instruments, and musical forms.

MD —UNIVERSITY OF MARYLAND, BALTIMORE COUNTY, Albin O Kuhn Library and Gallery, 5401 Wilkens Ave, Baltimore, 21228. Larry Wilt, Collection Management Librn
Holdings: Vols (3000) Cat
Notes: Collection incl musical monuments, collected editions, full scores, performing editions and study scores. Particularly strong in performing editions of chamber music (classical and romantic periods). Coverage of modern period incl Igor Stravinski, John Cage, Charles Ives, Karlheinz Stockhausen, Kenneth Gabino, Mauricio Kagel, Stuart Smith, Herbert Brun. Recent collection has emphasized graphic notation in music.

NY —STATE UNIVERSITY OF NEW YORK, BUFFALO, Baird Music Library, Baird Hall, Amherst, 14260. James B Coover, Dir
Holdings: Vols (104,000) Cat Mss Pix Slides Phonorecords Microforms
Notes: Nearly complete collections of *Denkmaeler and Gesamtausgaben* and other historical sets. Strong collection of dictionaries, bibliographies, biographies, facsimiles, works on the "new" music, organology and ethnomusicology. Special emphasis on operas, scores of the avant-garde, jazz and urban popular music, discography and music librarianship. Good collection of medieval and Renaissance anthologies, contemporary and avant-garde recordings. Houses Archives of the Center of the Creative and Performing Arts. Collections incl 2100 slides, 22,000 phonorecords, 46,000 scores and parts, 29, 000 books, 4900 microforms. Computerized record catalog in process.

COMPOSITION (RHETORIC) see Rhetoric

COMPTON, ALFRED GEORGE, 1835-1913

NY —CITY UNIVERSITY OF NEW YORK, City College, Morris R Cohen Library, North Academic Center, Convent Ave & 137th St, New York, 10031. Barbara J Dunlap, Archivist
Holdings: Cat Mss Pix
Notes: Incl personal papers.

COMPTON, ARTHUR HOLLY

IA —HERBERT HOOVER PRESIDENTIAL LIBRARY, West Branch, 52358. Dale C Mayer, Archivist
Notes: Papers.

MO —WASHINGTON UNIVERSITY, John M Olin Library, Campus Box 1061, St Louis, 63130.
Holdings: Mss Pix
Notes: Arthur Holly Compton papers and working library. Incl tapes of television series on Science and Human Responsibility.

COMPTON, BARBARA

MA —BOSTON UNIVERSITY, Mugar Memorial Library, Special Collections Dept, 771 Commonwealth Ave, Boston, 02215. Howard B Gotlieb, Dir
Holdings: Cat Mss Pix
Notes: Mss, correspondence, etc collected in depth; incl publications by or about.

COMPTON, KARL T.

IA —HERBERT HOOVER PRESIDENTIAL LIBRARY, West Branch, 52358. Dale C Mayer, Archivist
Notes: Papers.

COMPTON-BURNETT, IVY

CA —UNIVERSITY OF CALIFORNIA, LOS ANGELES, Research Library, Dept of Special Collections, 405 Hilgard Ave, Los Angeles, 90024. Edward Shreeves, Chairman, Bibliographers Group; David S Zeidberg, Head
Holdings: Vols 22 Cat Mss
Notes: 22 first and other editions of her books; mss or typescripts of five novels.

DC —GEORGETOWN UNIVERSITY, Library, Special Collections Div, 37 & O Sts NW, Washington, 20057. George M Barringer, Special Collections Librn; Nicholas B Sheetz, Mss Librn
Holdings: Mss Pix
Notes: The papers of Christopher Sykes, biographer, journalist, and novelist; containing mss, letters, photographs, and drawings. With extensive correspondence from Harold Acton; Angela, Countess of Antrim; Sir John Betjeman; Ivy Compton-Burnett; Alick Dru; T S Eliot; Max Beerbohm; Graham Greene; John Hayward; Lord Patrick Kinross; Compton Mackenzie; Nancy Mitford; Anthony Powell; Dame Flora Robson; Cecil Roth; Sir John Russell; Osbert Sitwell; John Sparrow; Freya Stark; James Stern; and Evelyn Waugh, among others. Also, considerable research material about Evelyn Waugh, Adam von Trott, Robert Byron, Lady Nancy Astor; and the foundation of the state of Israel.

MO —WASHINGTON UNIVERSITY, John M Olin Library, Campus Box 1061, St Louis, 63130.
Notes: A major collection, incl mss, correspondence, literary papers, photographs, etc. Described in *Special Collections: an Annotated Guide to the Holdings of the Manuscript Division and the University Archives and Research Collection.*

NV —UNIVERSITY OF NEVADA, RENO, University Library, Special Collections Dept, Reno, 89557. Robert E Blesse, Head
Holdings: Vols (57) Cat
Notes: Includes individual works by author in all editions including translations; also prefaces, introductions, published correspondence, appearances in anthologies, periodicals, etc. Bibliographical research collection, part of Modern Authors Collection. Other apearances 25 cataloged.

COMPULSORY LABOR see Forced Labor

COMPULSORY SCHOOL ATTENDANCE see Education—Law and Legislation

COMPUTATION LABORATORIES

CA —STANFORD UNIVERSITY LIBRARIES, Mathematical & Computer Sciences Library, Stanford, 94305. Harry Llull, Branch Librn
Holdings: Vols (42,000) Cat Microforms
Notes: There is a computer-listed keyword index to technical reports (about 20,000 items).

COMPUTATIONAL SCIENCE

CA —INTERNATIONAL BUSINESS MACHINES RESEARCH LIBRARY, 5600 Cottle Rd, San Jose, 95193. Phil Grincewich, Mgr Technical Information
Holdings: Vols (13,500) Cat
Notes: Incl 21,000 vols of 770 journals. On-line search facility. Vols are divided into three libraries, Technical Research, Technical Information, and Programing. Not open to public.

CA —STANFORD UNIVERSITY LIBRARIES, Mathematical & Computer Sciences Library, Stanford, 94305. Harry Llull, Branch Librn
Holdings: Vols (42,000) Cat Microforms
Notes: There is a computer-listed keyword index to technical reports (about 20,000 items).

CT —YALE UNIVERSITY, Engineering & Applied Science Library, 15 Prospect St, New Haven, 06520. Elizabeth B Hayes, Librn
Holdings: Vols (31,808) Cat Maps Pix Microforms
Notes: Comprehensive holdings. The Library also has NASA depository materials.

MN —CONTROL DATA CORP, Corporate Library, 8100-34th Ave So, Box O, HQW O6Z, Minneapolis, 55440. Gloria T Andrew, Mgr
Holdings: Vols (24,000) Cat
Budget: ($150,000)

MB —UNIVERSITY OF MANITOBA, Science Library, Machray Hall, Winnipeg, R3T 2N2, Can. V Simosko, Head
Holdings: Vols (90,000) Cat Microforms

COMPUTER AIDED DESIGN-COMPUTER AIDED MANUFACTURING (CAD-CAM)

ON —NATIONAL RESEARCH COUNCIL OF CANADA, Aeronautical/Mechanical Engineering Branch Library, Montreal Rd, Ottawa, K1A 0R6, Can. Louise Fletcher, Head
Notes: This branch library of the Canada Institute for Scientific and Technical Information (CISTI) of the National Research Council of Canada, Ottawa, has a collection strong in aeronautical engineering, automatic control, CAD/CAM, robotics, ocean, wind, and solar energy power, hydraulic and coastal engineering, icing, low temperature research, naval engineering, metals and metallurgy, incl composites, tribology, and air, railroad, marine transportation. Library supported the Council contribution to the development of the remote manipular Canadarm for NASA's Space Shuttle Orbiters and more recently, the Canadian Astronaut Program which will contribute payload specialists to NASA's Space Shuttle Program in 1984. 35, 000 monographs, 1200 serials. Report collection: over 500,000 items.

COMPUTER CONTROL see Automation

COMPUTER ENGINEERING

IL —UNIVERSITY OF ILLINOIS, URBANA/CHAMPAIGN, Library, 221 Engineering Hall, Urbana, 61801. William Mischo, Librn
Holdings: Vols (175,000) Cat Slides Microforms
Notes: Incl 3500 periodicals. Collection designed to serve teaching and research programs. Supports instructional faculty research. Also, 470 microfilm reels and 6000 microfiche sheets.

OH —UNIVERSITY OF CINCINNATI, Engineering Library, 880 Baldwin Hall, Cincinnati, 45221. Dorothy Furber Byers, Head
Holdings: Vols (50,000) Cat Videotapes Microforms
Budget: ($100,000)
Notes: Have NASA and DOE microfiche collections.

OH —OHIO STATE UNIVERSITY, Engineering Library, 2024 Neil Ave, Columbus, 43210. Mary Jo V Arnold, Librn
Holdings: Vols (132,000) Cat Microforms
Budget: ($110,000)

WA —BOEING COMPANY, Boeing Technical Libraries, PO Box 3707, Seattle, 98124. Corrine Campbell, Mgr Technical Library
Holdings: Vols (75,000) Cat Microforms
Notes: Books are distributed between 3 libraries, Kent, Renton, and Bellevue. Also contains many periodicals and Boeing Documents Library restricted to Boeing Personnel.

WI —MILWAUKEE SCHOOL OF ENGINEERING, Library, 500 E Kilbourn Ave, PO Box 644, Milwaukee, 53201. Mary Ann Schmidt, Head Librn
Holdings: Vols (34,500) Cat
Budget: ($215,800)

COMPUTER GRAPHICS

OR —TEKTRONIX INC, Wilsonville Library, PO Box 1000, M/S 63-531, Wilsonville, 97005. Linda Appel, Branch Librn
Holdings: Vols (5000) Cat Videotapes
Budget: ($22,300)

COMPUTER LABORATORIES see Computation Laboratories

COMPUTER MEMORY SYSTEMS see Computer Storage Devices

COMPUTER MUSIC see Electronic Music

COMPUTER PROGRAM LANGUAGES see Programming Languages (Electronic Computers)

COMPUTER SCIENCES see Computers

COMPUTER STORAGE DEVICES

CA —INTERNATIONAL BUSINESS MACHINES RESEARCH LIBRARY, 5600 Cottle Rd, San Jose, 95193. Phil Grincewich, Mgr Technical Information
Holdings: Vols (13,500) Cat
Notes: Principally electronic computer storage system architecture. Incl 21,000 vols of 770 journals. On-line search facility. Vols are divided into three libraries, Technical Research, Technical Information, and Programing. Not open to public.

COMPUTERS

AZ —HONEYWELL INFORMATION SYSTEMS, Information Center, PO Box 8000, Phoenix, 85066. Vera Minkel, Tech Librn
Holdings: Vols 15,000 Cat Microforms
Notes: Dialog, Dow Jones, BRS.

CA —UNIVERSITY OF CALIFORNIA, BERKELEY, Science Libraries, Astronomy-Mathematics-Statistics-Computer Science Library, 100 Evans Hall, Berkeley, 94720. Kimiyo Hom, Head
Holdings: Vols (53,000) Cat Maps Microforms
Budget: ($117,301)
Notes: A research collection in the fields of astronomy, mathematics, statistics and computer science. The computer science holdings emphasize the mathematics and theory of the field. The Library's serial holdings are particularly rich in foreign-language materials. Some 1300 serial titles are currently being received; over 4000 pamphlets. (Holdings in the AMSCS Library are complemented by approx 15,000 additional vols in the Main Library, as well as rare book materials in The Bancroft Library).

CA —HEWLETT-PACKARD CORP, Data Systems Div, Cupertino Library, 11000 Wolfe Rd, Cupertino, 95014. Katherine Biggs, Librn
Holdings: Vols 2000 Cat

CA —UNIVERSITY OF CALIFORNIA, DAVIS, Physical Sciences Library, Davis, 95616. Scott Kennedy, Head
Holdings: Vols (170,000) Cat VF
Notes: Collection covers aeronautical, agricultural, chemical, civil, electrical, mechanical, water science, hydrology, nuclear reactor, extensive cold regions collection in vertical file drawers, and computer science engineering academic programs. Good strength in journal runs.

†CA —XEROX CORP, Technical Library, 701 S Aviation Blvd, A3-25, El Segundo, 90245. Marilyn Durkin, Librn
Notes: 450 Journal titles.

CA —UNIVERSITY OF CALIFORNIA, LIVERMORE, Lawrence Livermore National Laboratory, Library, PO Box 5500, Livermore, 94550. John B Verity, Library Mgr
Holdings: Vols (160,000) Cat 16mm Films Microforms
Budget: ($2,323,000)
Notes: The LLL library system includes a central collection in physics, chemistry, engineering, geology, mathematics, and computer science; and branch holdings in bio-medicine, environmental science, nuclear chemistry, energy research, theoretical physics, materials science, and nuclear weapons. Collections include 160,000 books, 145,000 technical reports, 530,000 reports on microfiche, and 3000 periodical subscriptions. LLL libraries are not open to the public. Unclassified materials may be borrowed on interlibrary loan.

CA —LOS ANGELES PUBLIC LIBRARY, Science & Technology Dept, 630 W Fifth St, Los Angeles, 90071. Billie M Connor, Dept Head
Holdings: Vols (12,000) Cat
Notes: Materials on the application of electronic devices, circuits and systems in various fields such as computers, automatic control, sound productions and reproduction, radio and telecommunications. Extensive holdings of materials on computers, peripherals, and software including many texts pertaining to specific programming languages. Complete collection of Howard Sams schematics for radio television, and other electronic equipment repair as well as historical sets of Rider's Radio and Television schematics.

CA —UNIVERSITY OF CALIFORNIA, LOS ANGELES, Engineering & Mathematical Sciences Library, 405 Hilgard, Los Angeles, 90024. Rosalee I Wright, Librn
Holdings: Vols (180,000) Cat Microforms
See also entry under Engineering.

CA —UNIVERSITY OF SOUTHERN CALIFORNIA, Seaver Science Library, University Park, Los Angeles, 90089. A Albert Baker, Head
Holdings: Vols (200,000) Microforms
Budget: ($700,000)
Notes: Includes technical reports (12,000), serial and periodical titles (3600).

CA —GTE COMMUNICATIONS PRODUCT CORP, Sylvania Systems Group, Western Division Library, MC-2201, PO Box 7188, Mountain View, 94039. J B Fierro, Supervisor Library Services
Holdings: Vols (10,000) Cat
Notes: Interlibrary loan.

CA —HUGHES AIRCRAFT CO, Solid State Products Library, 500 Superior Ave, Newport Beach, 92663. Barbara Squyres, Librn
Holdings: Vols (4500)
Budget: ($17,000)
Notes: Incl 2600 journal vols and 500 microforms.

CA —BURROUGHS CORP, Library, 460 Sierra Madre Villa, Pasadena, 91107. Jean Robbins, Librn
Holdings: Vols 12,000 Cat
Notes: Computer theory and technology.

CA —CUBIC CORP, Technical Library, 9333 Balboa Ave, PO Box 85587, San Diego, 92138. Maxine Moser, Mgr Tech Librn; Ann Viera, Librn
Holdings: Vols (2500) Cat Maps Microforms
Budget: ($60,000)
Notes: Incl about 20,000 microforms and 1000 bound periodicals, technical reports, technical memoranda. On-line search service for employees, including DIALOG, BRS, SDC, DTIC/DROLS, NASA/RECON, RLIN, DMS.

CA —INTERNATIONAL BUSINESS MACHINES RESEARCH LIBRARY, 5600

COMPUTERS (cont.)

Cottle Rd, San Jose, 95193. Phil Grincewich, Mgr Technical Information
Holdings: Vols (13,500) Cat
Notes: Principally electronic computer storage system architecture. Incl 21,000 vols of 770 journals. On-line search facility. Vols are divided into three libraries, Technical Research, Technical Information, and Programing. Not open to public.

CA —STANFORD UNIVERSITY LIBRARIES, Mathematical & Computer Sciences Library, Stanford, 94305. Harry Llull, Branch Librn
Holdings: Vols (42,000) Cat Microforms
Notes: There is a computer-listed keyword index to technical reports (about 20,000 items).

CO —IBM, Boulder Library, PO Box 1900, Boulder, 80302. Beverly Jorman, Library Mgr
Holdings: Vols (10,000) Cat Microforms Reports
Notes: Emphasis in chemistry, physics, computer sciences and technology.

CO —UNIVERSITY OF COLORADO, Duane Physical Laboratories G140, Mathematics-Physics Library, Boulder, 80309. Allen Wynne, Head Librn
Holdings: Vols Cat Microforms
Notes: All areas of mathematics and physics with special emphasis on astrophysics, astrogeophysics, theoretical high energy physics and theoretical computer science. Also basic astronomy. The most comprehensive general mathematics and physics collection in the Rocky Mountain area, although not having sufficient depth to allow doctoral research in some specific areas. Excellent bibliographic control for current and retrospective searching as complete runs of most major subject indexing and abstracting services are present. ILL for businesses through the Colorado Technical Reference Center in main library building.

CT —YALE UNIVERSITY, Engineering & Applied Science Library, 15 Prospect St, New Haven, 06520. Elizabeth B Hayes, Librn
Holdings: Vols (31,808) Cat Maps Pix Microforms
Notes: Comprehensive holdings. The Library also has NASA depository materials.

CT —ROGERS CORP, Lurie Library, One Technology Drive, Rogers, 06263. Myrna D Riquier, Librn; Nini S Davis, Librn
Holdings: Vols (650) Cat
Notes: Emphasis on materials science, plastics, polymers, resins.

DE —HAGLEY MUSEUM AND LIBRARY, Eleutherian Mills-Hagley Foundation Inc, PO Box 3630, Greenville, 19807. Richmond D Williams, Dir; Heddy A Richter, Imprints Librn
Notes: Records of the Sperry-Univac Company (1940-1975; 400 cubic feet) document the early development and rapid growth of the computer industry. The collection incl technical and administrative documents relating to the ENIAC, BINAC and UNIVAC computers.

DC —US BUREAU OF THE CENSUS, Library, Federal Office Bldg 3, Rm 2451, Washington, 20233. Betty Baxtresser, Chief, ASD Library Branch
Holdings: Cat Microforms
Notes: Started in 1974, this collection of computer science-micrographic books, journals, and report literature largely represents recent materials.

FL —UNIVERSITY OF FLORIDA, Engineering & Physics Library, 410 Weil Hall, Gainesville, 32611. Roger V Krumm, Librn
Holdings: Cat Microforms
Notes: Incl AEC, ERDA, DOE, NASA reports.

FL —FLORIDA INSTITUTE OF TECHNOLOGY, Library, 150 W University Blvd, PO Box 1150, Melbourne, 32901. L L Henson, Dir of Libraries
Holdings: Vols 800 Cat Microforms

GA —GEORGIA INSTITUTE OF TECHNOLOGY, Price Gilbert Memorial Library, 225 North Ave, Atlanta, 30332. Edward Graham Roberts, Dir
Holdings: Vols (1,661,559) Cat Maps Slides Microforms
Budget: ($1,383,302)
Notes: Incl (4,307,996) patents and (568, 490) government documents.

ID —EG&G, INEL Technical Library, 1776 Science Center, Idaho Falls, 83401. Brent Jacobsen, Head Librn; Heather Redding, Ref Librn
Holdings: Vols (33,000) Cat Microforms
Notes: Energy research and development included in libraries collection. Incl over 500,000 AEC, ERDA, NRC, and foreign reports. Unclassified materials may be used by the public in the library by appointment or borrowed by interlibrary loan. Incl 12,000 bound documents, 520,000 microfiche, 400 periodical subscriptions.

IL —NORTHWESTERN UNIVERSITY, Seeley G Mudd Library for Science & Engineering, 2233 Sheridan Rd, Evanston, 60201. Robert C Michaelson, Head
Holdings: Vols (200,000) Cat Microforms
Notes: Collection emphasizes graduate and research level material.

IL —UNIVERSITY OF ILLINOIS, URBANA/CHAMPAIGN, Library, 221 Engineering Hall, Urbana, 61801. William Mischo, Librn
Holdings: Vols (175,000) Cat Slides Microforms
Notes: Incl 3500 periodicals. Collection designed to serve teaching and research programs. Supports instructional faculty research. Also, 470 microfilm reels and 6000 microfiche sheets.

IN —CUMMINS ENGINE CO, Information Center, 1000 Fifth St, Columbus, 47201. W E Poor, Tech Librn
Holdings: Vols 150 Cat

IN —PURDUE UNIVERSITY LIBRARIES, Mathematical Sciences Library, West Lafayette, 47907. Richard Funkhouser, Librn
Holdings: Vols (44,005) Cat Microforms
Budget: ($67,985)

IA —IOWA STATE UNIVERSITY, Library, Ames, 50011. Warren B Kuhn, Dean of Library Services
Holdings: Cat
Notes: Extensive serial holdings.

MD —JOHNS HOPKINS UNIVERSITY, Milton S Eisenhower Library, Charles & 34 Sts, Baltimore, 21218. Ann S Gwyn, Assistant Dir for Special Collections

MA —UNIVERSITY OF MASSACHUSETTS AT AMHERST, Physical Sciences Library, Amherst, 01003. Siegfried Feller, Assoc Dir for Collection Development
Holdings: Vols Cat Microforms
Budget: ($35,000)
Notes: Computer science and technology.

MA —HARVARD UNIVERSITY LIBRARY, Gordon McKay Library, Division of Applied Sciences, Pierce Hall, Oxford St, Cambridge, 02138. Julie Sandall Barlas, Librn
Holdings: Vols (100,000)

MA —MASSACHUSETTS INSTITUTE OF TECHNOLOGY, Institute Archives, Special Collections, Cambridge, 02139.
Notes: The materials in the Magnetic Core Memory collection assembled in support of MIT during the patent litigation over the magnetic core memory. Invented in 1947 by Jay Forrester during the development of the Whirlwind Computer, magnetic core memory set the stage for the development of high-speed digital computers. Though Whirlwind was originally begun as an aircraft simulator project during World War II, the computer which resulted became the prototype for most large scale general purpose computers. The collection dates mostly from the 1940s and 1950s.

MI —UNIVERSITY OF MICHIGAN, Engineering-Transportation Library, 312 Undergraduate Library, Ann Arbor, 48109. Maurita Holland, Librn
Holdings: Vols (400,000) Cat Microforms
Budget: ($225,000)

MN —CONTROL DATA CORP, Corporate Library, 8100-34th Ave So, Box O, HQW O6Z, Minneapolis, 55440. Gloria T Andrew, Mgr

NH —DARTMOUTH COLLEGE, Baker Memorial Library, Hanover, 03755.
Holdings: 50 Boxes
Notes: The papers of George Robert Stibitz (1904-), concerning the invention and development of the digital computer (1937-1963).

NH —NEW HAMPSHIRE COLLEGE, Harry A B and Gertrude C Shapiro Library, 2500 N River Rd, Manchester, 03104. Richard Pantano, Dir
Holdings: Vols (66,000) Cat Maps Slides Audiotapes Videotapes 16mm Films Filmstrips Microforms
Budget: ($133,173)
Notes: Strong collections in management information and computer sciences.

NJ —AT&T BELL LABORATORIES, Libraries and Information Systems Center, 600 Mountain Ave, Murray Hill, 07974. W D Penniman, Dir
Holdings: Vols (346,000) Cat Microforms
Notes: Restricted use to AT&T employees. Catalogs/*Indexes*: Bell Laboratories Library Network and Book Serial Catalogs; Bell Laboratories Translations. Bell Laboratories Library Network with New Jersey libraries located in Holmdel, Murray Hill, Piscataway, Whippany, Princeton, Short Hills, Summit, West Long Branch, Crawford Hill; libraries also in Allentown, Pennsylvania; Reading, Pennsylvania; New York, New York; Atlanta, Georgia; Columbus, Ohio; Naperville, Illinois; Indianapolis, Indiana; North Andover, Massachusetts.

NJ —DATA SYSTEMS ANALYSTS, Library, 6981 North Park Dr, Pennsauken, 08109. Elise Colabrese, Librn
Holdings: Vols (2300) Cat
Budget: ($15,000)
Notes: Incl technical reports and programming manuals relating to data communications, computer programming and computer networks.

NM —UNIVERSITY OF CALIFORNIA, Los Alamos National Laboratory, Libraries, PO Box 1663, MSP 362, Los Alamos, 87545. J Arthur Freed, Head Librn
Holdings: Vols (800,000) Cat Films Microforms
Budget: ($700,000)
Notes: Incl 500,000 classified and unclassified reports. There are 25 branch libraries and a central collection.

NY —POLYTECHNIC INSTITUTE OF NEW YORK, Long Island Center Library, Route 110, Farmingdale, 11735. Lorraine Schein, Branch Librn
Holdings: Vols 550 Cat

NY —INTERNATIONAL PAPER CO, Corporate Information Center, 77 W 45 St, New York, 10036. Elizabeth Skerritt, Corporate Librn
Holdings: Vols 80
Notes: Incl computer technology, data processing, etc.

NY —NEW YORK PUBLIC LIBRARY, Research Libraries, Science and Technology Research Center, Fifth Ave & 42 St, New York, 10018.
Holdings: Vols (1,100,000) Cat Microforms
Budget: ($647,259)

NY —NEW YORK UNIVERSITY, Courant Institute of Mathematical Sciences Library, 251 Mercer St, New York, 10012. Nancy Gubman, Librn
Holdings: Vols (52,000) Cat Audiotapes Microforms
Notes: Collection covers all aspects of mathematics, theoretical computer science, and mathematical physics on the level of graduate research. Catalog is located in Courant Institute Library.

NY —IBM CORP, Information Retrieval and Library Services, Owego, 13827. Richard Duffy, Librn
Holdings: Vols 12,000 Cat Pix Microforms
Notes: Computer technology for military and space use. Also 45,000 reports, 7500 bound period vols.

NY —UNIVERSITY OF ROCHESTER, Carlson Library, Hutchison Hall, River Campus, Rochester, 14627. Michael W Poulin, Librn
Holdings: Vols (48,720) Cat Microforms
Notes: Strong collection in the field and related areas; computer science technical reports collection. See also University Engineering Library.

COMPUTERS (cont.)

NY —UNIVERSITY OF ROCHESTER, Engineering Library, Gavett Hall, River Campus, Rochester, 14627. Isabel Kaplan, Librn
Holdings: Vols (25,000) Cat
Notes: Strong collection in the field and related areas.

NY —HARRIS CORP, Government Support Systems Division, Information Center, 6801 Jericho Tpke, Syosset, 11791. Eleanor Pienitz, Librn
Holdings: Vols (578) Cat Microfiche Mss

NY —GENERAL ELECTRIC COMPANY, Information Resources Center, Electronics Park, Bldg 3, Syracuse, 13221. Connie Webb, Mgr
Holdings: Vols (7000) Cat Microforms
Budget: ($20,000)

NY —XEROX CORP, Technical Information Center, PO Box 305, Webster, 14580. Michael D Majcher, Mgr
Holdings: Vols (30,000) Cat Microforms

NC —DUKE UNIVERSITY, School of Engineering, Library, Durham, 27706. Eric J Smith, Librn
Holdings: Vols (72,000) Cat Microforms
Budget: ($110,000)

NC —NORTH CAROLINA STATE UNIVERSITY, D H Hill Library, Box 7111, Raleigh, 27695. I T Littleton, Dir
Holdings: Vols 1950 Cat
Budget: $5000
Notes: Incl monographs.

OH —UNIVERSITY OF CINCINNATI, Engineering Library, 880 Baldwin Hall, Cincinnati, 45221. Dorothy Furber Byers, Head
Holdings: Vols (50,000) Cat Videotapes Microforms
Notes: Special highway collection contains about 2000 items by Highway Research Council and other agencies. Separate catalog.

OH —GRANDVIEW HEIGHTS PUBLIC LIBRARY, 1685 W First Ave, Columbus, 43212. Kathryn M Hannon, Librn
Holdings: Vols (250) Cat

OR —TEKTRONIX INC, Wilsonville Library, PO Box 1000, M/S 63-531, Wilsonville, 97005. Linda Appel, Branch Librn
Holdings: Vols 5000 Cat Videotapes
Budget: ($22,300)

PA —FRANKLIN INSTITUTE LIBRARY, 20 & The Parkway, Philadelphia, 19103. Miriam Padusis, Dir; Charles Wilt, Readers Servs Librn
Holdings: Vols (300,000) Cat Maps Pix Microforms

PA —UNIVERSITY OF PENNSYLVANIA, Moore School of Electrical Engineering Library, 203 Moore School, 33 & Walnut Sts, Philadelphia, 19104. Charles Myers, Head Librn
Holdings: Vols (30,000) Cat Microforms

PA —PENNSYLVANIA STATE UNIVERSITY, Mathematics Library, 109 McAllister Bldg, University Park, 16802. Miriam D Pierce, Librn
Holdings: Vols (29,101) Cat
Budget: ($35,000)

RI —BRYANT COLLEGE, Edith M Hodgson Memorial Library, Rte 7, Douglas Pike, Smithfield, 02917. John P Hannon, Dir
Holdings: Vols (103,000)
Budget: ($175,000)

TN —UNIVERSITY OF TENNESSEE, Space Institute Library, Tullahoma, 37388. Helen B Mason, Librn
Holdings: Vols (14,000)

TX —E-SYSTEMS, GARLAND DIV, Technical Library, PO Box 226118, Dallas, 75226. Charlene Morris, Tech Librn
Holdings: Vols (8500) Cat
Notes: Library not open to public.

TX —TEXAS INSTRUMENTS INC, Library, PO Box 1443, Houston, 77001. Helen Manning, Librn
Holdings: Vols (800) Cat Microforms
Notes: Systems, design, and marketing of microprocessors and electronic semiconductors. Not open to the public.

WY —US AIR FORCE INSTITUTE OF TECHNOLOGY, Library, Dept 9 Bldg 831, FE, Warren AFB, 82001. Patricia A Johnson, Librn
Holdings: Vols (7000) Cat Microforms
Budget: ($9000)
Notes: The Library supports graduate programs for students (Air Force Missile-Combat Crewmen) seeking a Master of Business Administration Degree. Civilian students and other military personnel are also admitted.

AB —SOUTHERN ALBERTA INSTITUTE OF TECHNOLOGY, Learning Resources Centre, 1301 16 Ave NW, Calgary, T2M 0L4, Can. Tom Skinner, Historian
Holdings: Vols 2000 Cat Films Videotapes
Notes: Serves students in 2-year courses. Emphasis on practical applications.

MB —UNIVERSITY OF MANITOBA, Science Library, Machray Hall, Winnipeg, R3T 2N2, Can. V Simosko, Head

ON —ATOMIC ENERGY OF CANADA LIMITED, Main Library, Technical Information Branch, Chalk River Nuclear Laboratories, Chalk River, K0J 1J0, Can. Harry Greenshields, Chief Librn
Holdings: Vols (128,700) Microforms
Budget: ($662,400)
Notes: The Main Library, Atomic Energy of Canada Limited, is the Canadian repository for the literature of nuclear science and technology. Its collections reflect both fundamental and nuclear aspects of biology, chemistry, electronics, engineering, mathematics, computers, metallurgy, physics and other specific areas of science involving nuclear technology with special emphasis on heavy water reactor systems. 512,000 research reports are available in paper copy and microfiche form. Incl US DOE, INIS and other offshore nuclear research reports. 386,000 microforms.

ON —INSTITUTE OF CHARTERED ACCOUNTANTS OF ONTARIO, The Merrilees Library, 69 Bloor St E, Toronto, M4W 1B3, Can. Theresa Wolak, Librn
Holdings: Vols 153 Cat

ON —UNIVERSITY OF TORONTO, Department of Computer Science Library, 11 King's College Rd, Toronto, M5S 1A4, Can. Mrs S Johnston, Librn
Holdings: Vols 1650 Cat
Notes: Incl books, journal volumes, and technical reports; about 9000 pieces. Incl 160 subscriptions.

COMPUTERS—HISTORY

DE —HAGLEY MUSEUM AND LIBRARY, Eleutherian Mills-Hagley Foundation Inc, PO Box 3630, Greenville, 19807. Richmond D Williams, Dir; Heddy A Richter, Imprints Librn
Notes: Records of the Sperry-Univac Company (1940-1975; 400 cubic feet) document the early development and rapid growth of the computer industry. The collection incl technical and administrative documents relating to the ENIAC, BINAC and UNIVAC computers.

MA —MASSACHUSETTS INSTITUTE OF TECHNOLOGY, Institute Archives, Special Collections, Cambridge, 02139.
Notes: Papers of Norbert Wiener, renowned mathematician, who was instrumental in the development of communication and control theories. He coined the word "cybernetics" to describe this new science. Professional papers document the development of this theory, his development as a mathematician, and his effective collaboration with students and colleagues including Vannevar Bush and John von Neumann. Unpublished finding aid with correspondent index is available in the Institute Archives.

COMPUTERS—MEMORY SYSTEMS see Computer Storage Devices

COMPUTERS—STORAGE DEVICES see Computer Storage Devices

COMPUTERS, ANALOG see Computers

COMPUTERS, DIGITAL see Computers

COMPUTERS, ELECTRONIC see Computers

COMPUTERS—DESIGN AND CONSTRUCTION see Computer Engineering

COMPUTING LABORATORIES see Computation Laboratories

COMPUTING MACHINES see Calculating Machines

COMPUTING MACHINES (COMPUTERS) see Computers

COMSTOCK, ANTHONY

IL —SOUTHERN ILLINOIS UNIVERSITY, CARBONDALE, Delyte W Morris Library, Special Collections Dept, Carbondale, 62901. David V Koch, Cur of Special Collections; Louisa Bowen, Cur of Manuscripts
Holdings: Cat Mss
Notes: Papers and correspondence of Theodore A Schroeder, constitutional lawyer and founder, with Lincoln Steffens, of the Free Speech League, a forerunner of the American Civil Liberties Union. Contains extensive correspondence with Comstock, Gompers, Debs, H Ellis, Sanger, Sinclair, John Dewey, Darrow, Mencken, A G Hays, Emma Goldman, W E B Dubois, etc. Incl several thousand letters; notes and mss, records of legal cases and extensive files relating to the early history of psychiatry.

COMSTOCK, GEORGE C., 1855-1934

WI —UNIVERSITY OF WISCONSIN, MADISON, Memorial Library, Division of Archives, 728 State St, Madison, 53706. Jay Frank Cook, Librn
Holdings: Mss
Notes: Personal and professional correspondence, papers from 1902-1948. 1.3 cu ft of records.

COMSTOCK LODE

NV —UNIVERSITY OF NEVADA, RENO, University Library, Special Collections Dept, Reno, 89557. Robert E Blesse, Head
Holdings: Vols 400 Cat Pix Mss
Notes: An extensive collection of books, 2000 photographs, mss, published reports, government publications dealing with mining in Nevada from the mid-19th century to the present. Primary emphasis is on the Comstock Lode, Virginia City, Nevada but material is available on mining in all geographic areas of the state. The 105 mss collections incl business papers and records of mining companies, and papers of firms which provided materials and equipment to the mining industry.

CONABLE, BARBER B., JR., 1922-

NY —CORNELL UNIVERSITY LIBRARIES, Collection of Regional History, Dept of Manuscripts and Univ Archives, Ithaca, 14853.
Notes: Attorney, NY State Senator, Congressman. Papers, 1963-70; 160 ft.

CONCEPTUAL ART see Art, Conceptual

CONCERT HALLS see Music Halls (Variety Theatres, Cabarets, Night Clubs, Etc.)

CONCERTS—PROGRAMS

CA —UNIVERSITY OF CALIFORNIA, LOS ANGELES, Music Library, Schonberg Hall, Los Angeles, 90024. Stephen M Fry, Music Librn
Notes: The Philip Kahgan Collection of music films, letters, programs, and photographs important to the Southern California classical music scene. Incl 16mm "home movies" of more than thirty renowned conductors and performers during Hollywood Bowl rehearsals in the late 1930s. Incl Kahgan correspondence, memorabilia, 35 scrapbooks, etc.

CONCHOLOGY see Mollusks; Shells

CONCILIAR THEORY AND MOVEMENT

CO —UNIVERSITY OF COLORADO, Libraries, Special Collections, Boulder, 80309. Nora J Quinlan, Head
Holdings: Vols 800
Notes: The Mandell Creighton Library. Renaissance papacy, Protestant reform and the Conciliar movement. Separate catalog.

CONCRETE

IA —IOWA STATE UNIVERSITY, Library, Ames, 50011. Warren B Kuhn, Dean of

CONCRETE (cont.)

Library Services
Holdings: Cat
Notes: Extensive serial holdings.

MS —US ARMY ENGINEER WATERWAYS EXPERIMENT STATION, Library Branch, PO Box 631, Vicksburg, 39180. Bernice Black, Chief Librn
Holdings: Vols (350,000) Cat Mss Maps Microforms

PQ —WARNOCK HERSEY PROFESSIONAL SERVICES, 128 Elmslie St, La Salle, H8R 1V8, Can.
Holdings: Vosl (3090) Cat
Budget: ($6000)

CONCRETE ART see Art, Concrete

CONCRETE MUSIC

CA —CALIFORNIA INSTITUTE OF THE ARTS, Library, 24700 McBean Pkwy, Valencia, 91355. James Elrod, Dir
Holdings: Vols (61,000) Cat Phonorecords Audiotapes
Budget: ($8500)
Notes: Incl 11,656 audiotapes. Cataloged.

CONCRETE POETRY

CA —UNIVERSITY OF CALIFORNIA, DAVIS, Shields Library, Dept of Special Collections, Davis, 95616. Donald Kunitz, Head; C Danial Elliott, Asst Head
Notes: Ephemeral and rare post-1946 titles which are experimental or innovative in nature. Incl Bukowski, Dorn, Everson, Ferlinghetti, Ashbery, DiPrima, Snyder, etc.

IN —INDIANA UNIVERSITY, Lilly Library, Seventh St, Bloomington, 47405. William R Cagle, Librn
Holdings: Cat Mss
Notes: Correspondence and writings of concrete poet Ian Hamilton Finlay, 1953-1973. 5091 items. Holdings incl extensive collection of printed/ published Finlay material.

NY —RUSSELL SAGE COLLEGE LIBRARY, James Wheelock Clark Library, Ferry St, Troy, 12180. Joseph Menditto, Dir of Tech Services
Holdings: Vols (8000) Cat Mss Phonorecords
Notes: Incl 20th-century traditional and avant-garde poetry in first editions. Also, the Hamilton Finlay Collection of Concrete Poetry archives.

RI —BROWN UNIVERSITY, John Hay Library, Harris Collection, Prospect St, Providence, 02912. Rosemary L Cullen, Cur
Holdings: Vols (200,000) Cat Mss Pix Phonorecords Microforms
Budget: ($15,000)
Notes: The Harris Collection of American Poetry and Plays is principally composed of American and Canadian poetry and plays, 17th century-date. Extensive holdings in songsters, gift books and annuals, hymnals, pageants, broadside verse, carriers' addresses, women poets, juvenile poetry, (incl Mother Goose and *The Night Before* Christmas), sheet music with lyrics, small press publications, fine printing, black poets, "little magazines," Yiddish-American literature. All movements or schools of American poetry are represented. Incl first editions of most American poets and playwrights, notably Whitman, Poe, Wallace Stevens, Eugene O'Neill, Edward Albee, Ezra Pound, T S Eliot, William Carlos Williams, Amy Lowell, Phyllis Wheatley, Robert Frost, Allen Ginsberg, Bliss Carman, and Stephen Foster sheet music. Also incl the Saunders Walt Whitman Collection (1300 vols); the LangdonCollection of Pageants (250 vols); the Asa Cushman Collection of plays in ms and prompt copies; the MacDougall Collection of Psalters and Hymnals; 4000 plays issued by Walter H Baker Co, Boston (1890-1957); the Vaxer Collection of Yiddish Poetry, Plays and Music (1700 vols). Collections incl 200,000 vols, 30,000 broadsides, 55,000 mss, 170,000 pieces of sheet music, 450 phonorecords, and 375 microfilm reels. See *Dictionary Catalog of the Harris Collection of American Poetry and Plays* (Boston: G K Hall, 1972), 13 vols; *Supplement* (1977), 3 vols. See also, *American Poetry*, 1609-1900, *A Collection on Microfilm, Segment I* (1609-1820); *Segment II* (1821-1850); *Segment III* (1851-1870) (Woodbridge, Conn: Research Publications). Separate catalog.

CONDENSATION CONTROL IN BUILDINGS see Dampness in Buildings

CONDOLENCE, ETIQUETTE OF see Etiquette

CONDUCTORS (MUSIC) see Conductors and Conducting

CONDON, RICHARD

MA —BOSTON UNIVERSITY, Mugar Memorial Library, Special Collections Dept, 771 Commonwealth Ave, Boston, 02215. Howard B Gotlieb, Dir
Holdings: Cat Mss Pix
Notes: Mss, correspondence, etc collected in depth; incl publications by or about.

CONDUCTING see Conductors and Conducting

CONDUCTORS AND CONDUCTING

CA —UNIVERSITY OF CALIFORNIA, LOS ANGELES, Music Library, Schonberg Hall, Los Angeles, 90024. Stephen M Fry, Music Librn
Notes: The Philip Kahgan Collection of music films, letters, programs, and photographs important to the Southern California classical music scene. Incl 16mm "home movies" of more than thirty renowned conductors and performers during Hollywood Bowl rehearsals in the late 1930s. Incl Kahgan correspondence, memorabilia, 35 scrapbooks, etc.

IN —INDIANA UNIVERSITY, Lilly Library, Seventh St, Bloomington, 47405. William R Cagle, Librn
Notes: Library of the conductor Fritz Busch, largely orchestral scores and parts. Many scores have ms annotations in the hand of the conductor. Many non-annotated printings of scores and tape copies of recordings by Fritz Busch are in the Indiana University School of Music Library.

†MD —UNIVERSITY OF MARYLAND, Library, American Bandmasters Association Research Center, College Park, 20742. Pearl Z Tubiash, Supvr
Holdings: Cat Pix Phonorecords Audiotapes
Notes: Materials on bands and band music; organizational and personal papers, with sizable collections relating to the careers of distinguished bandmasters, notably Edwin Franko Goldman.

MA —BOSTON UNIVERSITY, Mugar Memorial Library, Special Collections Dept, 771 Commonwealth Ave, Boston, 02215. Howard B Gotlieb, Dir
Notes: Personal collection of Arthur Fiedler, incl 6000 scores and sound recordings, manuscripts, photographs, memorabilia, library, and test pressings of Fiedler's performances.

CONE, BONNIE ETHEL

NC —UNIVERSITY OF NORTH CAROLINA, CHARLOTTE, J Murrey Atkins Library, UNCC Station, Charlotte, 28223. Robert F Brabham Jr, Special Collections Librn
Holdings: Vols Cat Mss Pix
Notes: Files of Bonnie Ethel Cone as first president of Charlotte College and vice chancellor of the University of North Carolina at Charlotte; papers of Charlotte area women's organizations, eg AAUW and DAR; archives of Charlotte Unitarian Church; papers of novelist and short story writer Marian Sims; collections of family papers from North and South Carolina; and first editions of 18th and early 20th century American women novelists.

CONE, ETTA

NC —UNIVERSITY OF NORTH CAROLINA, GREENSBORO, Walter Clinton Jackson Library, Special Collections Dept, 1000 Spring Garden St, Greensboro, 27412. Emilie W Mills, Librn
Holdings: Cat Mss
Notes: Letters by Etta Cone to her cousin Richard Guggenheimer, written from Baltimore and Europe, 1927-1935, and two letters by Richard to Etta, one of which is dated 24 August 1949 and relays the news of Nina Stein's death. Etta never received the letter, dying herself just one week later. There are four letters to Richard from other members of the Cone family written from Baltimore, North Carolina, and Europe. Etta's letters to Richard are concerned chiefly with his progress as a painter.

CONE, SPENCER HOUGHTON

†GA —GEORGIA SOUTHERN COLLEGE, Library, Landrum Box 8074, Statesboro, 30460.
Notes: Over 200 letters describing military and civilian activities of Spencer Houghton Cone and Spencer Wallace Cone. Spencer Houghton Cone, prominent 19th century Baptist minister who helped reconcile Northern and Southern church actions after the Civil War. His son, Spencer Wallace Cone's letters cover military tactics, etc.

CONE, SPENCER WALLACE

†GA —GEORGIA SOUTHERN COLLEGE, Library, Landrum Box 8074, Statesboro, 30460.
Notes: Over 200 letters describing military and civilian activities of Spencer Houghton Cone and Spencer Wallace Cone. Spencer Houghton Cone, prominent 19th century Baptist minister who helped reconcile Northern and Southern church actions after the Civil War. His son, Spencer Wallace Cone's letters cover military tactics, etc.

CONETTA, GEORGE

BC —UNIVERSITY OF VICTORIA, McPherson Library, Victoria, V8W 3H5, Can.
Notes: The H C Sage Collection of English Juvenile Drama. Representative material on pantomime figures, etc, by the early 20th-century publisher, George Conetta.

CONFECTIONERY

NY —WESTRECO INC, Research Library, 555 S Fourth St, Fulton, 13069. Janice Burns, Research Librn
Holdings: Vols 38 Cat Periodicals VF
Notes: Food Science and Technology collection of about (1200) books and pamphlets. Back files of periodicals retained up to 20 years.

CONFEDERATE HOME COLLEGE

SC —COLLEGE OF CHARLESTON LIBRARY, Special Collections Dept, Charleston, 29401.
Notes: Mahala Varie Folk Collection. Papers, 1911.

CONFEDERATE STATES NEWSPAPERS see Newspapers, Confederate States

CONFEDERATE STATES OF AMERICA

AL —BIRMINGHAM PUBLIC LIBRARY, Dept of Archives & Mss, 2020 Seventh Ave N, Birmingham, 35203. Marvin Y Whiting, Archivist & Cur
Holdings: Mss
Notes: Antebellum period, although some Civil War materials are also represented in the collection. 15,000 ms pieces.

AL —MOBILE PUBLIC LIBRARY, Special Collections Div, 701 Government St,

CONFEDERATE STATES OF AMERICA (cont.)

Mobile, 36602.
Notes: Personal papers, documents, etc, of Daniel Geary, Director of Defenses of Mobile, 1861-.

†AL —MUSEUMS OF THE CITY OF MOBILE, Reference Library, 355 Government St, Mobile, 36602. Caldwell Delaney, Adminr

†AL —UNIVERSITY OF ALABAMA, Amelia Gayle Gorgas Library, PO Box S, University, 35486.
Notes: The Confederate States of America collection; incl a collection of Jefferson Davis papers. Separate catalog. Published bibliography. *Confederate Imprints in the University of Alabama Library,* comp by Sara Elizabeth Mason (University: University of Alabama Press, 1961).

CA —UNIVERSITY OF CALIFORNIA, SANTA BARBARA, Library, Dept of Special Collections, Santa Barbara, 93106. Christian F Brun, Head
Holdings: Cat Mss Maps Pix
Notes: William Wyles Collection.

DC —LIBRARY OF CONGRESS, Rare Book & Special Collections Div, Washington, 20540. William Matheson, Chief
Holdings: Vols 1812 Cat
Notes: The collection contains material printed in the South between 1861 and 1865, particularly strong in official publications issued by the Congress and the various departments of the Confederate States government.

GA —CARNEGIE LIBRARY, Henderson Room, 607 Broad St, Rome, 30161. Beatrice Millican, Librn
Holdings: Vols (450) Cat Maps
Budget: ($2700)

IL —CHICAGO PUBLIC LIBRARY, Special Collections Div, Cultural Center, 78 E Washington St, Chicago, 60602. Laura Linard, Cur
Holdings: Vols (7000) Cat Mss Maps Pix
Notes: The Civil War and American History Research Collection at The Chicago Public Library is our largest collection. It spans the pre-war sectional crisis as well as Reconstruction. Scarce slavery pamphlets; large collection of regimental histories; manuscripts of US Grant, Sherman, Breckinridge; letters and diaries of soldiers and other officers; original photographs of individuals and field shots; Confederate Battle Plan for the Battle of Shiloh (original); swords, rifles, uniforms, flags and other military accessories. A substantial part of this collection has been cataloged. The museum objects are inventoried (Grand Army Hall and Memorial Association of Illinois Collection). See *Treasures of the Chicago Public Library,* comp by Thomas A Orlando and Marie Gecik, 1977, pp36-79.

LA —TULANE UNIVERSITY, Howard-Tilton Memorial Library, Special Collections Div, 7001 Freret St, New Orleans, 70118. Wilbur E Meneray, Librn
Holdings: Mss
Notes: Official and personal correspondence (in part copies) of Jefferson Davis and a section of his library. The majority is part of the Louisiana Historical Association Collection. See *Calendar of the Jefferson Davis Postwar Manuscripts* (New Orleans, 1943).

MA —AMERICAN ANTIQUARIAN SOCIETY LIBRARY, 185 Salisbury St, Worcester, 01609. Marcus A McCorison, Dir & Librn
Notes: Colonial American currency; also Confederate money, and State Bank notes.

MS —UNIVERSITY OF SOUTHERN MISSISSIPPI, William David McCain Graduate Library, Box 5148, Southern Sta, Hattiesburg, 39406.
Holdings: Vols (5000)
Notes: The Ernest A Walen Collection on the history of the Confederate States of America. Incl over 600 Confederate imprints. Catalog in progress.

NC —DUKE UNIVERSITY, William R Perkins Library, Durham, 27706. Elvin E Strowd, University Librn
Notes: The Flowers Collection of Southern Americana currently consists of 4,300,500 items. Additions are ongoing. Included in this collection are several types of materials, which are housed in appropriate sections of the library. The various types of materials are: manuscripts, books, pamphlets, maps, music, broadsides, newspapers, photographs, engravings, prints and memorabilia.

NC —DUKE UNIVERSITY, William R Perkins Library, Manuscript Dept, Durham, 27706. Ellen Gartrell, Cur of Mss
Holdings: Cat Mss
Notes: Strong collection incl papers of many officers (eg Robert E Lee, P G T Beauregard), Confederate governments, and leaders (eg Jefferson Davis), thousands of letters and diaries from Union and Confederate soldiers and homefront.

†NC —WAKE FOREST UNIVERSITY, Z Smith Reynolds Library, Box 7777, Reynold Sta, Winston-Salem, 27109. Richard J Murdoch, Rare Book Librn
Holdings: Vols 165 Cat
Notes: Confederate broadside verse; 200 items.

RI —PROVIDENCE PUBLIC LIBRARY, 150 Empire St, Providence, 02903. Lance J Bauer, Special Collections Librn
Holdings: Vols 5000 Cat Mss Maps Pix
Notes: The Harris Collection on the American Civil War and Slavery. Incl 18th and 19th century books, rare pamphlets, and periodicals concerning slavery and the slave trade, and origins, progress and results of the Civil Civil War; also regimental histories; military and naval tactics; personal narratives; women's accounts of the Civil War; works on abolition; sheet music; Union and Confederate broadside ballads; Confederate imprints; *The Liberator* from 1843 through the Civil War; and over 85 editions of *Uncle Tom's Cabin* in 14 languages. Excellent primary and secondary sources for the study of the Civil War and slavery. Material must be used in-house. Photocopying when condition of material allows.

SC —COLLEGE OF CHARLESTON LIBRARY, Special Collections Dept, Charleston, 29401.
Notes: Contains a two dollar bill with an engraving of Judah P Benjamin and a *Charleston Mercury* broadside, "The Union is Dissolved." Also incl a request by two Charleston women (Mrs Minis and Miss Rosalie Cohen) for a pass to travel to New York, approved by Generals Gillmore, Hazen, and Hatch (May 3-10, 1865). In addition, papers of numerous individuals and families incl references to the Civil War Period.

TN —UNIVERSITY OF TENNESSEE, CHATTANOOGA, Library, Chattanooga, 37401. Joseph A Jackson, Dir of Libraries
Holdings: Vols 6000 Cat Maps
Notes: The Civil War Collection, a gift of about 3500 vols for the Charles R and Anne Bachman Hyde Collection from Mrs Hyde, who spent a lifetime collecting Southern Americana with particular emphasis on the Confederate viewpoint. Also incl the Wilder Collection, from the Federal point of view. Established as a memorial to Gen John T Wilder. Restricted use: reference only.

TN —UNIVERSITY OF TENNESSEE, KNOXVILLE, Library, Knoxville, 37996. John Dobson, Special Collections Librn
Notes: Tennessee history.

TN —MEMPHIS STATE UNIVERSITY, John Willard Brister Library, Memphis, 38152. John Terreo, Special Collections Librn
Notes: Jefferson Davis-Joel Addison Family papers, 1864-1889. President of the Confederacy. Personal and business correspondence, receipts, notes, cancelled checks, and other papers, of Davis, following the Civil War (primarily 1877-1889) and his son-in-law, Joel Addison Hayes (1848-1919), banker of Memphis, TN, relating chiefly to management of Davis' plantation, Brierfield, near Vicksburg, MS, stocks and mining investments, and land sales. Incl correspondence between Davis' wife Varina (Howell) Davis and her daughter Margaret Howell (Davis) (1848-1908), and between Addison Hayes and members of his family.

TX —UNIVERSITY OF TEXAS LIBRARIES, General Libraries, Barker Texas History Center, PO Box P, Austin, 78712. Don Carleton, Dir

TX —SAM HOUSTON STATE UNIVERSITY, Library, PO Box 2179, Huntsville, 77340. Chas Dwyer, Librn
Holdings: Vols 2880 Cat Mss Pix Microforms
Notes: The Porter Confederate Collection is particularly rich in rare material relating to Texas in the Confederacy.

VA —WASHINGTON AND LEE UNIVERSITY, Library, Lexington, 24450. Maurice Leach, Dir; Richard Oram, Asst Special Collections Librn
Holdings: Vols (25,000) Cat Mss Maps Pix
Notes: Incl over 10,000 ms pieces, the collection emphasizes the life of General Robert E Lee, Virginia, and the Civil War, etc. Pictures from 1870-1930; 8000 glass photographs by Miley.

VA —PORTSMOUTH PUBLIC LIBRARY, 601 Court St, Portsmouth, 23704. Dean Burgess, Library Dir
Holdings: Vols 1300 Cat
Notes: Although particularly interested in Tidewater and Lower Tidewater history, we buy most books we can locate on Virginia as well. In 1972 we were given the distinguished collection of Judge White of Lynnhaven.

VA —VIRGINIA STATE LIBRARY, 12 & Capitol Sts, Richmond, 23219.
Holdings: Vols 4760 Cat Maps

WI —UNIVERSITY OF WISCONSIN, MILWAUKEE, Library, Box 604, Milwaukee, 53201. William C Roselle, Dir
Holdings: Vols 800 Cat Mss Maps
Notes: Allen M Slichter Collection, reflecting Confederate point of view. Restricted use. Noncirculating.

CONFEDERATE STATES OF AMERICA—IMPRINTS

AL —SAMFORD UNIVERSITY, Special Collections Library, 800 Lakeshore Dr, Birmingham, 35229. Annie Ford Wheeler, Acting Head Librn
Holdings: Uncat Mss Maps Pix Microforms
Notes: The William H Brantley Collection is in superb condition, consisting of early works on travels, Indians, and law in the southeast, plus scarce imprints of Alabama.

FL —FLORIDA STATE UNIVERSITY, Robert Manning Strozier Library, Special Collections Dept, Tallahassee, 32306. Opal M Free, Head, Special Collections
Holdings: Vols 36 Cat Mss Maps
Notes: Noncirculating. No photocopying.

GA —UNIVERSITY OF GEORGIA, Libraries, Special Collections Division, Athens, 30602. Vesta Lee Gordon, Asst Dir for Special Collections
Holdings: Vols 7300 Maps
Notes: The Confederate Imprints Collection, arranged by Crandell numbers, also incl 500 sheets of music, approx 350 broadsides and approx 1600 newspapers.

GA —EMORY UNIVERSITY, Robert W Woodruff Library, Special Collections Dept, Atlanta, 30322. Linda M Matthews, Head Special Collections; Virginia J H Cain, Processing Archivist; Richard H F Lindemann, Reference Archivist
Holdings: Vols (16,000) Cat Mss Maps Pix Microforms

MS —UNIVERSITY OF SOUTHERN MISSISSIPPI, William David McCain Graduate Library, Box 5148, Southern Sta, Hattiesburg, 39406.
Holdings: Vols (5000)
Notes: The Ernest A Walen Collection on the history of the Confederate States of America. Incl over 600 Confederate imprints. Catalog in progress.

NC —UNIVERSITY OF NORTH CAROLINA, CHAPEL HILL, Wilson Library, Rare Book Collection, Chapel Hill, 27514. Paul S Koda, Cur of Rare Books
Holdings: // Cat
Notes: Over 1000 books, pamphlets,

CONFEDERATE STATES OF AMERICA—IMPRINTS (cont.)

periodicals, and newspapers printed in the Confederate States of America, 1861-1865, covering a wide range of subjects.

NC —DUKE UNIVERSITY, William R Perkins Library, Rare Book Room, Durham, 27706. John L Sharpe, III, Cur
Notes: Collection of more than 3500 titles of Confederate imprints. Possibly the largest such collection in the country, it includes broadsides, maps, music, newspapers, Union and Confederate regimental histories, and sheet music. Also Broadside collection of approximately 8500 items. Primarily 19th century American imprints ranging from auction lists to military orders.

PA —FREE LIBRARY OF PHILADELPHIA, Social Science and History Dept, Logan Sq, Philadelphia, 19103. William Handley, Head
Holdings: Vols 300 Cat
Notes: The Simon Gratz Collection.

RI —PROVIDENCE PUBLIC LIBRARY, 150 Empire St, Providence, 02903. Lance J Bauer, Special Collections Librn
Holdings: Vols 5000 Cat Mss Maps Pix
Notes: The Harris Collection on the American Civil War and Slavery. Incl 18th and 19th century books, rare pamphlets, and periodicals concerning slavery and the slave trade, and origins, progress and results of the Civil Civil War; also regimental histories; military and naval tactics; personal narratives; women's accounts of the Civil War; works on abolition; sheet music; Union and Confederate broadside ballads; Confederate imprints; *The Liberator* from 1843 through the Civil War; and over 85 editions of *Uncle Tom's Cabin* in 14 languages. Excellent primary and secondary sources for the study of the Civil War and slavery. Material must be used in-house. Photocopying when condition of material allows.

TX —UNIVERSITY OF TEXAS LIBRARIES, General Libraries, Barker Texas History Center, PO Box P, Austin, 78712. Don Carleton, Dir
Holdings: Vols (132,000) Cat Mss Maps Pix Slides Phonorecords Audiotapes Microforms
Notes: Materials pertaining to the historical, social, economic, scientific, humanistic and literary development of Texas. Rich in early state imprints, as well as the period of the Republic. Texas archival and ms holdings number over 18,000,000 items. Texas history prior to the Republic is covered by the Bexar Archives.

TX —RICE UNIVERSITY, Fondren Library, Woodson Research Center, 6100 S Main St, PO Box 1892, Houston, 77251. Nancy Parker, Dir Woodson Research Center
Holdings: Vols 2500
Notes: Cataloged and shelved by Crandall and Harwell number. Incl some Confederate imprints not in Crandall and Harwell, plus other Civil War imprints.

VA —VIRGINIA STATE LIBRARY, 12 & Capitol Sts, Richmond, 23219.
Holdings: Vols 2200 Cat Maps

CONFEDERATE STATES OF AMERICA—NAVY

AL —MOBILE PUBLIC LIBRARY, Special Collections Div, 701 Government St, Mobile, 36602.
Notes: Hunley Collection: Papers, illustrations, etc concerning the building and history of CSS Hunley, first submarine, 1861-1865.

VA —UNIVERSITY OF VIRGINIA, Alderman Library, Manuscripts Dept, Charlottesville, 22901. Edmund Berkeley Jr, Cur
Holdings: Cat Mss Maps Pix
Notes: Personal and official papers of Sir Andrew Snape Hamond and Graham Eden Hamond concern British naval operations during the American Revolution and in the Mediterranean during the Napoleonic Wars. Paul P Hoffman (ed) *Guide to the Naval Papers of Sir Andrew Snape Hamond . . . and Sir Graham Eden Hamond . . .* (Charlottesville, Va: Microfilm Publications, University of Virginia, 1966). Papers of US and Confederate naval officer Samuel Barron; US fleet surgeon and Brooklyn Navy Yard surgeon Gustavus R B Horner; US naval surgeon John S Whittle on a scientific expedition to the Pacific, 1838-1841; and US naval officer William Conway Whittle on West Indies and Mediterranean cruises, 1823-1831.

CONFEDERATE STATES OF AMERICA—PICTURES, ILLUSTRATIONS, ETC.

DC —LIBRARY OF CONGRESS, Prints & Photographs Div, Washington, 20540.
Notes: Civil War Photograph Collection incl photographs commissioned by Mathew Brady and others. Brady employed 20 photographers at the height of his operations. His staff incl Alexander and James Gardner, James F Gibson, and Thomas C Roche.

NC —DUKE UNIVERSITY, William R Perkins Library, Durham, 27706. Elvin E Strowd, University Librn

VA —VIRGINIA STATE LIBRARY, 12 & Capitol Sts, Richmond, 23219.
Holdings: Cat Pix
Notes: Incl 86,960 prints, photographs, etc, chiefly of Virginia, the Civil War, and the Confederacy.

CONFEDERATE VETERANS see Veterans, Confederate

CONFESSIONAL LITERATURE

CA —FITZ HUGH LUDLOW MEMORIAL LIBRARY, PO Box 99346, San Francisco, 94109. Michael R Aldrich, Exec Cur
Holdings: Vols 50 Cat Mss Maps Pix Slides Phonorecords Audiotapes Videotapes
Notes: Collection stored. Important mail inquiries only. No interlibrary lending or telephone queries. This collections emphasis historical and literary works about opium and its derivatives, mostly in English, going back to the 17th century but mostly from the 19th and early 20th centuries. Excellent collection of De Quincey in different editions. Many books, pamphlets, and art relating to the 19th century international opium trade, the Chinese Opium Wars, clipper ships, and resulting international legal action in the early 20th century. Outstanding collection of the English, French, and American opium-addict confessional literature. Also incl many volumes and offprints relevant to narcotic drug prevention, treatment, and education.

CONFLAGRATIONS see Fires

CONFORMITY (RELIGION) see Dissenters, Religious

CONFUCIUS AND CONFUCIANISM

NY —NEW YORK PUBLIC LIBRARY, Oriental Div, Fifth Ave & 42 St, New York, 10018. E Christian Filstrup, Chief
Holdings: Cat Mss Microforms
Budget: ($56,455)
Notes: Described in *Dictionary Catalog of the Oriental Collection,* The Research Libraries of the New York Public Library, 1960, 16 vols, and *First Supplement,* 1976, 8 vols (144,000 cards). This catalog incl 318, 000 entries for works in about 100 languages of the East, and all works in Western languages on Oriental subjects. The Oriental Collection numbers about 120,000 vols; its Arabic and Indic holdings and those on ancient Egypt and the ancient Near East are among the largest in the US. There is also a collection of 30,000 vols of PL 480 material from Egypt, Pakistan, and India to which there is main entry access, but which is not incorporated into the dictionary catalog. Other outstanding features of the Oriental Collection incl extensive holdings of Japanese technical and scientific periodicals; a unique collection of linguistic works, grammars, anddictionaries; and unusually good coverage of the field of Oriental religions and philosophies. The catalog contains numerous subject references to periodical articles in all languages. All entries are arranged alphabetically according to the Roman alphabet.

CONGER, ARTHUR L.

OH —RUTHERFORD B HAYES LIBRARY, 1337 Hayes Ave, Fremont, 43420. Watt P Marchman, Dir
Holdings: Cat Mss
Notes: Personal, business and political correspondence; receipts and other papers. Letterbooks of A L Conger and business papers of the Zanesville Street Railway.

CONGO, BELGIAN see Zaire

CONGREGATIONALISM

CT —YALE UNIVERSITY, Box 1603A, Yale Station, New Haven, 06520.

HI —HAWAIIAN MISSION CHILDREN'S SOCIETY LIBRARY, 553 S King St, Honolulu, 96813. Mary Jane Knight, Librn
Holdings: Vols 15,000 Cat Mss Pix
Notes: Missionary period of Hawaiian history, 1819-1864, plus family and Congregational Church in Hawaii to 1947, incl a general collection of Hawaiian history and travel, an outstanding collection of early voyages to the Pacific, and an almost complete collection of early Hawaiian imprints, ie, publications in the Hawaiian language during the 19th century. Ms material incl letters, journals and reports of the Protestant missionaries who came to Hawaii (the Sandwich Islands) under the auspices of the American Board of Commissioners for Foreign Missions. The material is for research only; the stacks are closed. Unpublished papers may be examined by qualified researchers on application to the librarian. Published material is cataloged. Hawaiian imprints are cataloged,except for the Dewey classification 300's which are mainly government documents. Ms collections are cataloged or in the process of being completely arranged and cataloged.

MA —HARVARD UNIVERSITY, Harvard Divinity School, Andover-Harvard Theological Library, 45 Francis Ave, Cambridge, 02138. Maria Grossmann, Librn
Holdings: Vols (370,000) Cat

MT —ROCKY MOUNTAIN COLLEGE, Paul M Adams Memorial Library, 1511 Poly Dr, Billings, 59102. Sue Walker, Dir
Holdings: Vols (30,000) Cat Maps
Notes: Large collection on geology. Also, deposit of the Billings Archaeological Society, the Montana Methodist Historical Library (incl papers of Brother Van Oursdale, pioneer circuit rider) and the Montana Congregational Archives.

ON —TORONTO SCHOOL OF THEOLOGY, Consortium of Libraries, University of Toronto, Toronto, M5S 1A5, Can. R Grane Bracewell, Library Coordr
Holdings: Cat
Notes: A consortium of 7 theological college and faculty libraries at the University of Toronto.

CONGRESS OF INDUSTRIAL ORGANIZATIONS (CIO)

NC —DUKE UNIVERSITY, William R Perkins Library, Manuscript Dept, Durham, 27706. Ellen Gartrell, Cur of Mss
Holdings: Cat Mss
Notes: Emphasis on US South, especially CIO Organizing Committee papers, 1946-53 (ca 143,00 items). Large percentage have been commercially microfilmed under title "Operation Dixie." Also papers of Lucy Randolph Mason, Frank deVyver, Frank Morrison.

WI —STATE HISTORICAL SOCIETY OF WISCONSIN, Archives, 816 State St, Madison, 53706. Harold L Miller, Reference Archivist
Notes: Papers of Eugene and Peggy Dennis, Communist Party activists, 1926 - date. He was national head, CP, USA. Papers trace

CONGRESS OF INDUSTRIAL ORGANIZATIONS (CIO),(cont.)

development of CIO in '30s, Farmer-Labor-Progressive Federation, and other Wisconsin and national political groups. Much on Senator Joseph McCarthy.

CONGRESS OF INDUSTRIAL ORGANIZATIONS (CIO), WASHINGTON OFFICE

MI —WAYNE STATE UNIVERSITY, Walter P Reuther Library, Archives of Labor & Urban Affairs, Detroit, 48202. Philip Mason, Dir
Holdings: Mss
Notes: Papers, correspondence, etc.

CONGRESSMEN AND CONGRESSWOMEN see Legislators—U. S.

CONGREVE, WILLIAM, 1670-1729

CA —UNIVERSITY OF CALIFORNIA, LOS ANGELES, William Andrews Clark Memorial Library, 2520 Cimarron St, Los Angeles, 90018.
Holdings: Cat
Notes: Extensive collection, first editions, etc.

MA —HARVARD UNIVERSITY LIBRARY, Cambridge, 02138.

TN —UNIVERSITY OF TENNESSEE, KNOXVILLE, Library, Knoxville, 37996. John Dobson, Special Collections Librn
Holdings: Cat
Notes: The John C Hodges Collection, incl about 150 original editions of Congreve's works and a large collection of books about him, English drama, and the theater of the 16th and 17th centuries; also material by and about other dramatists of the period. Described in *The John C Hodges Collection of William Congreve in the University of Tennessee Library: A Bibliographical* Catalog, by Albert M Lyles and John Dobson (Knoxville: Univ of Tennessee Libraries, 1970), 135pp.

CONJOINED TWINS see Siamese Twins

CONNECTICUT

CT —YALE UNIVERSITY, Box 1603A, Yale Station, New Haven, 06520.
Holdings: Mss

CT —EASTERN CONNECTICUT STATE UNIVERSITY, Center for Connecticut Studies, J Eugene Smith Library, Willimantic, 06226. David M Roth, Librn
Holdings: Vols (2500) Cat Maps Pix Audiotapes
Budget: ($1500)
Notes: Materials related to Connecticut, past and present. Incl VF of ephemeral material; state documents; genealogies; town histories and annual reports; and PhD theses on Connecticut. Separate catalog.

CONNECTICUT—GENEALOGY

CT —GREENWICH LIBRARY, 101 W Putnam Ave, Greenwich, 06830. Louise M Gudelis, Ref Librn
Holdings: Vols 1112 Cat Maps Pix Microforms
Notes: History and genealogy of Greenwich, Conn area.

CT —CONNECTICUT HISTORICAL SOCIETY, One Elizabeth St, Hartford, 06105. Christopher Bickford, Dir
Notes: Over 70,000 books and periodicals, 3500 bound vols of newspapers, and thousands of broadsides, maps, prints, and photographs pertaining to Connecticut. Also, more than 1 1/2 million historical mss; incl personal correspondence, diaries, account books, business records, and town materials dating from the earliest settlement. Extensive genealogical holdings, incl nearly 4000 printed genealogies and New England town and county histories.

CT —CONNECTICUT STATE LIBRARY, 231 Capitol Ave, Hartford, 06106. Mark H Jones, Archivist; T O Wohlsen, Jr, Head Archives, Hist & Genealogy Unit; Ann Barry, Ref Librn
Holdings: Cat Mss Maps
Notes: Books, maps, mss, archives pertaining to Connecticut state and local history and to the history of New England, etc. Archival collections incl state and local government records and papers of institutions and organizations in Connecticut. There are separate catalogs for archives maps, and genealogical works.

CT —CONNECTICUT STATE LIBRARY, Readers Service Div, 231 Capitol Ave, Hartford, 06106. Ablene Bielefield, Head
Holdings: Cat
Budget: ($600,000)
Notes: Contains material of Connecticut legislative and legal sources, incl legislative histories, Connecticut Supreme Court Records and Briefs, and other sources.

CT —NEW HAVEN COLONY HISTORICAL SOCIETY, Whitney Library, 114 Whitney Ave, New Haven, 06510. M Ottilia Koel, Librn & Cur of Mss
Holdings: Vols (25,000) Cat Mss Maps Pix Microforms
Notes: 25,000 printed books and pamphlets; ca 15,000 linear feet of manuscript material including historic manuscripts, records of education, maritime and harbor industry, private papers, business and family records; 40,000 photographic images; maps and microforms relating to the early settlement and subsequent history of New Haven and vicinity.

CT —ROCKY HILL HISTORICAL SOCIETY, Library, 785 Old Main St, PO Box 185, Rocky Hill, 06067. Mrs Dudley Cooke, Librn
Holdings: Vols 600 Cat Mss Maps Pix
Notes: This is a very small collection of assorted material, local, regional and general plus a few collections of letters etc. No photocopying.

CT —STAMFORD GENEALOGICAL SOCIETY INC, 96 Broad St, PO Box 249, Stamford, 06904. Thomas J Kemp, Society Librn
Holdings: Vols 10,000 Cat Periodicals Mss Maps Pix Microforms
Notes: Current acquisitions are listed in *Connecticut Ancestry,* the Society's quarterly journal. *Connecticut Ancestry* is indexed in the *Connecticut Periodical Index* and the *Genealogical Periodical Annual* Index. Published guide to the collection: *Genealogies in the Ferguson Library,* by Thomas J Kemp; Stamford, Ct, 1982.

CT —STAMFORD'S PUBLIC LIBRARY, Ferguson Library, Adult Services Dept, 96 Broad St, Stamford, 06901. Ernest A DiMattia Jr, Dir; Doris Goodlett, Head Adult Servs
Holdings: Vols 4200 Cat Pix Microforms
Notes: Collection specializes in the genealogy of New England states and incl a comprehensive collection of local history. Also subscribes to many periodicals through the Stamford Genealogical Society. The Barbour Collection (Vital Record of Connecticut) is on microfilm and indexed by towns and by families. Library owns vols 1-165 of the DAR lineage books.

CT —SILAS BRONSON LIBRARY, 267 Grand St, Waterbury, 06702. Patricia L Joy, Reference Dept Head
Holdings: Vols 1500 Cat
Budget: $200
Notes: Incl are genealogies of families particularly from Connecticut and the other New England states.

CT —EASTERN CONNECTICUT STATE UNIVERSITY, Center for Connecticut Studies, J Eugene Smith Library, Willimantic, 06226. David M Roth, Librn
Holdings: Vols (2500) Cat Maps Pix Audiotapes
Budget: ($1500)
Notes: Materials related to Connecticut, past and present. Incl VF of ephemeral material; state documents; genealogies; town histories and annual reports; and PhD theses on Connecticut. Separate catalog.

CONNECTICUT—HISTORY

CT —LEE ASH, (personal collection), 66 Humiston Dr, Bethany, 06525.
Notes: Anything about, or that refers to Bethany or Collinsville, Conn.

CT —GREENWICH LIBRARY, 101 W Putnam Ave, Greenwich, 06830. Louise M Gudelis, Ref Librn
Holdings: Vols 1112 Cat Maps Pix Microforms
Notes: History and genealogy of Greenwich, Conn area.

CT —CONNECTICUT HISTORICAL SOCIETY, One Elizabeth St, Hartford, 06105. Christopher Bickford, Dir
Notes: Over 70,000 books and periodicals, 3500 bound vols of newspapers, and thousands of broadsides, maps, prints, and photographs pertaining to Connecticut. Also, more than 1 1/2 million historical mss; incl personal correspondence, diaries, account books, business records, and town materials dating from the earliest settlement. Extensive genealogical holdings, incl nearly 4000 printed genealogies and New England town and county histories.

CT —CONNECTICUT STATE LIBRARY, 231 Capitol Ave, Hartford, 06106. Mark H Jones, Archivist; T O Wohlsen, Jr, Head Archives, Hist & Genealogy Unit; Ann Barry, Ref Librn
Holdings: Cat Mss Maps
Notes: Books, maps, mss, archives pertaining to Connecticut state and local history and to the history of New England, etc. Archival collections incl state and local government records and papers of institutions and organizations in Connecticut. There are separate catalogs for archives maps, and genealogical works.

CT —CONNECTICUT STATE LIBRARY, Readers Service Div, 231 Capitol Ave, Hartford, 06106. Ablene Bielefield, Head
Holdings: Cat
Budget: ($600,000)
Notes: Contains material of Connecticut legislative and legal sources, incl legislative histories, Connecticut Supreme Court Records and Briefs, and other sources.

CT —HARTFORD PUBLIC LIBRARY, Reference & General Reading Dept, 500 Main St, Hartford, 06103. Beverly A Loughlin, Admin Asst
Holdings: Vols (3000) Cat Mss Maps Pix Slides Phonorecords Audiotapes Videotapes 16mm Films
Notes: The Hartford Collection is a noncirculating multimedia collection encompassing Hartford: histories of businesses, churches, schools, and organizations; Hartford authors; and Hartford imprints. Separate catalog.

CT —NEW HAVEN COLONY HISTORICAL SOCIETY, Whitney Library, 114 Whitney Ave, New Haven, 06510. M Ottilia Koel, Librn & Cur of Mss
Holdings: Vols (25,000) Cat Mss Maps Microforms
Notes: 25,000 printed books and pamphlets; ca 15,000 linear feet of manuscript material including historic manuscripts, records of education, maritime and harbor industry, private papers, business and family records; 40,000 photographic images; maps and microforms relating to the early settlement and subsequent history of New Haven and vicinity.

CT —YALE UNIVERSITY, Box 1603A, Yale Station, New Haven, 06520.

CT —CONNECTICUT COLLEGE, Library, Mohegan Ave, New London, 06320. Brian Rogers, College Librn
Holdings: Vols (382,000) Cat Mss Maps Pix
Notes: Collection includes material relating to New London and surrounding communities, including Groton, Norwich and Stonington. Includes pamphlets and broadsides printed in New London by the Greens during the Revolutionary period. Also "Atlantic Neptune" facsimiles.

CT —ROCKY HILL HISTORICAL SOCIETY, Library, 785 Old Main St, PO Box 185, Rocky Hill, 06067. Mrs Dudley Cooke, Librn
Holdings: Vols 600 Cat Mss Maps Pix
Notes: This is a very small collection of

CONNECTICUT—HISTORY (cont.)

assorted material, local, regional and general plus a few collections of letters etc. No photocopying.

CT —STAMFORD HISTORICAL SOCIETY, Library, 713 Bedford St, Stamford, 06901. Ronald Marcus, Librn
Holdings: Vols (1200) Cat Mss Maps Pix Slides
Notes: Connecticut history, with emphasis on Fairfield County area and Stamford. Over 3000 Stamford pictures. Numerous manuscript business records and archives.

CT —STAMFORD'S PUBLIC LIBRARY, Ferguson Library, Adult Services Dept, 96 Broad St, Stamford, 06901. Ernest A DiMattia Jr, Dir; Doris Goodlett, Head Adult Servs
Holdings: Vols 4200 Cat Pix Microforms
Notes: Collection specializes in the genealogy of New England states and incl a comprehensive collection of local history. Also subscribes to many periodicals through the Stamford Genealogical Society. The Barbour Collection (Vital Record of Connecticut) is on microfilm and indexed by towns and by families. Library owns vols 1-165 of the DAR lineage books.

CT —THOMPSON LIBRARY, Rte 193, Box 188, Thompson, 06277. Ted Perch, Librn
Holdings: Audiotapes
Notes: Information on French Canadians in Connecticut. Part of the Library's oral history project of the Quinebaug River Valley.

CT —TORRINGTON HISTORICAL SOCIETY, Library, 61 Main St, Torrington, 06790. Catherine C Calhoun, Executive Dir
Holdings: Vols 1740 Cat Mss Maps Pix Slides Microforms
Notes: Especially the Torrington area.

CT —SILAS BRONSON LIBRARY, 267 Grand St, Waterbury, 06702. Patricia L Joy, Reference Dept Head
Holdings: Vols 500 Cat
Budget: $200
Notes: Incl histories of individual towns, cities, and counties.

CT —EASTERN CONNECTICUT STATE UNIVERSITY, Center for Connecticut Studies, J Eugene Smith Library, Willimantic, 06226. David M Roth, Librn
Holdings: Vols (2500) Cat Maps Pix Audiotapes
Budget: ($1500)
Notes: Materials related to Connecticut, past and present. Incl VF of ephemeral material; state documents; genealogies; town histories and annual reports; and PhD theses on Connecticut. Separate catalog.

MA —OLD STURBRIDGE VILLAGE, Research Library, Sturbridge, 01566. Theresa Rini Percy, Librn
Holdings: Cat Maps Microforms
Notes: To 1900.

NY —RYE HISTORICAL SOCIETY, Library, One Purchase St, Box 155, Rye, 10580. Susan A Morison, Dir
Holdings: Vols (1000) Mss Maps Pix Slides Audiotapes
Notes: History of Rye, NY. About 125 books on colonial arts and crafts. Partially cataloged.

RI —BROWN UNIVERSITY, John Hay Library, 20 Prospect St, Providence, 02912. Mark N Brown, Cur Mss
Holdings: // Mss
Notes: Papers of Samuel Wyllys, 1632-1709, Colonial magistrate of Connecticut. A collection of 125 mss, transcripts, and photocopies of legal and government papers relating to Indian affairs, colonial wars, civil and criminal cases, and trials for witchcraft. The witchcraft trials of 1692-1693 are of particular interest as revealed in the Oyer and Terminer Court Records of the witnesses. The Library has one-half (1622-1693) of the original collection which Anmary Brown inherited from her father; the other half (1694-1696) is in the Connecticut State Library.

RI —WESTERLY PUBLIC LIBRARY, Broad St, Westerly, 02891. David J Panciera, Library Dir
Holdings: Vols (3000) Cat Mss Maps Pix Audiotapes Microforms
Notes: Extensive coverage of history of Westerly and surrounding area; also general material on Rhode Island and Connecticut. Books, clippings, mss, etc. Many unique family genealogies; local photographs; postcards. Special materials on Seventh-Day Baptist Church; Westerly granite industry; Wilcox Park; Watch Hill. Separate catalog.

CONNECTICUT—IMPRINTS

CT —HARTFORD PUBLIC LIBRARY, Reference & General Reading Dept, 500 Main St, Hartford, 06103. Beverly A Loughlin, Admin Asst
Holdings: Vols (3000) Cat Mss Maps Pix Slides Phonorecords Audiotapes Videotapes 16mm Films
Notes: The Hartford Collection is a noncirculating multimedia collection encompassing Hartford: histories of businesses, churches, schools, and organizations; Hartford authors; and Hartford imprints. Separate catalog.

CT —YALE UNIVERSITY, Box 1603A, Yale Station, New Haven, 06520.
Notes: Especially before 1851.

CONNECTICUT—MAPS

CT —CONNECTICUT HISTORICAL SOCIETY, One Elizabeth St, Hartford, 06105. Christopher Bickford, Dir
Notes: Over 70,000 books and periodicals, 3500 bound vols of newspapers, and thousands of broadsides, maps, prints, and photographs pertaining to Connecticut. Also, more than 1 1/2 million historical mss; incl personal correspondence, diaries, account books, business records, and town materials dating from the earliest settlement. Extensive New England town and county histories.

CT —CONNECTICUT STATE LIBRARY, 231 Capitol Ave, Hartford, 06106. Mark H Jones, Archivist; T O Wohlsen, Jr, Head Archives, Hist & Genealogy Unit; Ann Barry, Ref Librn
Notes: Books, maps, mss, archives pertaining to Connecticut state and local history and to the history of New England, etc. Archival collections incl state and local government records and papers of institutions and organizations in Connecticut. There are separate catalogs for archives maps, and genealogical works.

CONNECTICUT—POLITICS AND GOVERNMENT

CT —CONNECTICUT STATE LIBRARY, 231 Capitol Ave, Hartford, 06106.
Notes: Papers of many Connecticut governors, senators and congressmen.

CT —TRINITY COLLEGE LIBRARY, 300 Summit St, Hartford, 06106. Peter J Knapp, Archivist
Holdings: Uncat // Mss Pix
Notes: Late 18th and 19th century mss, letter, diaries, etc of the Curtis Family of Connecticut and New York, with emphasis on: William Edmond (1755-1838), US Congressman from Conn; Holbrook Curtis (1787-1858); William Edmond Curtis (1823-1880), Chief Justice of Superior Court of New York; Mary Ann Scovill Curtis (1831-1908); and William Edmond Curtis Jr, (1855-1923), US Asst Secy of the Treasury. Incl on basis of relation through marriage are late 18th and 19th century mss, letters and diaries of the Hiester, McLanahan and Muhlenberg Families of Pennsylvania, with emphasis on Joseph Hiester (1752-1832), US Congressman and Governor of Pennsylvania; and Andrew Gregg (1755-1835), US Congressman and Senator from Pennsylvania. 12 linear feet.

CT —UNIVERSITY OF CONNECTICUT, Library, Storrs, 06268. R H Schimmelpfeng, Dir of Special Collections
Notes: Congressman Robert N Giaimo's papers. Closed for research until 1986.

DC —LIBRARY OF CONGRESS, Manuscript Division, Washington, 20540. John C Broderick, Chief
Notes: Senatorial and other papers of Abraham Ribicoff.

DC —LIBRARY OF CONGRESS, Washington, 20540.
Notes: Papers of Senator Abraham Ribicoff. His gubernatorial and some other papers are at the Connecticut State Library.

CONNECTICUT NEWSPAPERS see Newspapers, Connecticut

CONNECTICUT RIVER VALLEY

MA —HISTORIC DEERFIELD-POCUMTUCK VALLEY MEMORIAL ASSOCIATION, Libraries, Memorial St, Box 53, Deerfield, 01342. David R Proper, Librn
Holdings: Vols (17,000) Cat Mss Maps Pix Microforms
Notes: Local and regional history, especially western Massachusetts. Also, remnants of several collection of books available to early Deerfield and Greenfield residents. Strong ms collection dealing with the region's families, businesses, etc. These consist of sermons, diaries, town and church records, voluntary societies' archives, etc. Extensive collection of photographs of the people and buildings of Deerfield and its environs, and travels in Maine, California, and England (1880s to 1920s). Also, large collection of glassplate negatives. Houses the Connecticut Valley Bibliography, a comprehensive card file on the history and culture of the Connecticut Valley of Massachusetts.

CONNELL, EVAN

MA —BOSTON UNIVERSITY, Mugar Memorial Library, Special Collections Dept, 771 Commonwealth Ave, Boston, 02215. Howard B Gotlieb, Dir
Holdings: Cat Mss
Notes: Mss, correspondence, etc collected in depth; incl publications by or about.

CONNELL, WILL

CA —UNIVERSITY OF CALIFORNIA, LOS ANGELES, Research Library, Dept of Special Collections, 405 Hilgard Ave, Los Angeles, 90024. Edward Shreeves, Chairman, Bibliographers Group; David S Zeidberg, Head
Notes: Large collection of California photographers' works, incl Will Connell, Ernest Pratt, and 136 pictures of Los Angeles architect Mark Daniels' work.

CONNOLLY, CYRIL

OK —UNIVERSITY OF TULSA, McFarlin Library, Dept of Rare Books and Special Collections, 600 S College, Tulsa, 74104. David Farmer, Dir; Toby Murray, Archivist; Caroline Swinson, Cur of Manuscripts & Art
Holdings: Vols Mss Pix Phonorecords
Notes: The personal library (8000 vols) of Cyril Connolly. Mostly modern literature; many presentation copies; in addition, there is a major holding of Connolly mss, diaries, and correspondence.

BC —UNIVERSITY OF VICTORIA, McPherson Library, Victoria, V8W 3H5, Can.
Notes: Essayist. Reviews of books by Peter Porter, Douglas Livingstone, Zulfikar Ghose, Gavin Ewart, Nathaniel Tarn and Patric Dickinson.

CONNOLLY, JAMES BRENAN

MA —BOSTON COLLEGE LIBRARIES, Chestnut Hill, 02167.

CONNOR, EDWARD

MI —WAYNE STATE UNIVERSITY, Walter P Reuther Library, Archives of Labor & Urban Affairs, Detroit, 48202. Philip Mason, Dir
Notes: Many personal ms collections in the Archives document individual strivings,

CONNOR, EDWARD (cont.)

accomplishments, and frustrations in developing a higher quality of urban life. The papers of Jerome Cavanagh, former Mayor of Detroit; George Edwards, former Detroit Housing Commissioner, Detroit Police Commissioner, and Michigan Supreme Court Justice; and Edward Connor, former Director of the Citizen's Housing and Planning Council of Detroit, are just 3 important collections concerning governmental, law enforcement, and social problems in a major metropolitan area of the country.

CONNOR, JOHN ANTHONY

BC —UNIVERSITY OF VICTORIA, McPherson Library, Victoria, V8W 3H5, Can.
Notes: Poet, playwright. Incl mss, worksheets, workbooks.

CONNOR, RALPH

MB —UNIVERSITY OF MANITOBA, Elizabeth Dafoe Library, Archives and Special Collections Dept, Winnipeg, R3T 2N2, Can. Richard E Bennett, Dept Head; Corrado A Santoro, Reference Archivist
Holdings: // Cat Mss
Notes: The "Ralph Connor" (C W Gordon) Collection, incl the mss and working papers of 19 published and 2 unpublished works. Typed catalog only.

CONNORS, CHUCK

CA —UNIVERSITY OF SOUTHERN CALIFORNIA, Edward L Doheny Memorial Library, Archives of Performing Arts, University Park, Los Angeles, 90089. Robert Knutson, Librn
Holdings: Mss Pix
Notes: Personal collection of papers, pictures, etc.

CONQUISTADORES see Spain—Exploring Expeditions

CONRAD, JOSEPH

CT —YALE UNIVERSITY, Box 1603A, Yale Station, New Haven, 06520.
Holdings: Cat Mss
Notes: Published catalog: *A Conrad Memorial Library, The Collection of George T Keating* (Garden City, NY: Doubleday, 1929).

IL —NEWBERRY LIBRARY, 60 W Walton St, Chicago, 60610. Diana Haskell, Cur of Modern Mss
Holdings: Cat

IN —INDIANA UNIVERSITY, Lilly Library, Seventh St, Bloomington, 47405. William R Cagle, Librn
Holdings: Vols 800 Cat Mss
Notes: First English and American editions, colonial issues and other printings showing bibliographical variations.

MA —BRANDEIS UNIVERSITY, Goldfarb Library, 415 South St, Waltham, 02154. Bessie Hahn, Dir
Notes: John Galsworthy Collection. Approx 175 letters written to Joseph Conrad, Sir Edmund Gosse and others and 15 linear ft of books consisting of first editions and books about John Galsworthy. Access to the collection of books is through the Main Card Catalog and Special Collections Catalog. A finding list to the correspondence is in Special Collections.

NH —DARTMOUTH COLLEGE, Baker Memorial Library, Hanover, 03755.
Holdings: Vols 240 Cat Mss
Notes: First editions, mss, etc. Noncirculating.

NY —COLGATE UNIVERSITY, Everett Needham Case Library, Hamilton, 13346. Bruce M Brown, Collections Librn
Holdings: Vols 285 Uncat Mss
Notes: Basically a collection of first editions, proof copies and some supporting material. Also, 23 manuscripts and 118 letters. Description in *Philobiblon: The Journal of the Friends of the Colgate University* Library, no 9, Spring 1972; no 10, Summer 1974. A major collection.

NY —HOFSTRA UNIVERSITY, Library, 1000 Fulton Ave, Hempstead, 11550. Charles R Andrews, Dean of Library Services
Notes: Incl first editions and six important letters from World War I.

NC —UNIVERSITY OF NORTH CAROLINA, CHAPEL HILL, Wilson Library, Rare Book Collection, Chapel Hill, 27514. Paul S Koda, Cur of Rare Books
Holdings: Cat
Notes: Fully representative collection.

†NC —WAKE FOREST UNIVERSITY, Z Smith Reynolds Library, Box 7777, Reynold Sta, Winston-Salem, 27109. Richard J Murdoch, Rare Book Librn
Holdings: Vols 275 Cat
Notes: A significant collection.

PA —BRYN MAWR COLLEGE, Canaday Library, Bryn Mawr, 19010. James Tanis, Dir
Notes: Rare books in the Adelman Collection.

PA —TEMPLE UNIVERSITY LIBRARIES, Special Collections Dept, Rare Books & Mss Section, Philadelphia, 19122. Thomas M Whitehead, Cur
Holdings: Vols 135 Cat Mss Pix
Notes: Incl the collection of the Rev Dr Frederick E Maser; first and limited editions, inscribed copies, foreign translations, books from his library; incl corrected typescript of his play *One Day More (Tomorrow)*. Catalog of Maser Collection available, issued as vol 2, number 2 (1957) of the *Temple University Library Bulletin*.

TX —TEXAS TECH UNIVERSITY, Library, Lubbock, 79409. David J Murrah, Assoc Dir for Special Collections

CONRAD, PAUL

CA —UNIVERSITY OF CALIFORNIA, SAN DIEGO, Central University Library, Mandeville Dept of Special Collections, La Jolla, 92093. Lynda Corey Claassen, Head
Holdings: Vols 301 // Uncat Mss Pix
Notes: The Paul F Conrad collection of political cartoons. He is the Pulitzer Prize-winning cartoonist of the Los Angeles *Times* (1964 and 1971).

CONSCIENTIOUS OBJECTORS

AZ —WORLD UNIVERSITY, Library, 711 E Blacklidge Dr, Tucson, 85719. Howard John Zitko, Cur
Holdings: Vols (15,000) Cat Mss Maps Audiotapes
Notes: Collection concerns the "frontier sciences." No interlibrary loan.

IN —MANCHESTER COLLEGE, Funderburg Library, North Manchester, 46962. J Allen Willmert, Librn
Holdings: Vols 1747 Cat Mss Pix
Notes: Materials about Church of the Brethren affairs, concerns, districts, and congregations. Books by and about Brethren persons. Much material on conscientious objectors, esp during World War II. Incl 200 boxes of ms materials.

NY —CORNELL UNIVERSITY LIBRARIES, Collection of Regional History, Dept of Manuscripts and Univ Archives, Ithaca, 14853.
Notes: Selective Service Papers, 1968-69; 37 items. Restricted in part.

PA —SWARTHMORE COLLEGE, Peace Collection, Swarthmore, 19081. Jean R Soderlund, Cur of Peace Collection
Holdings: Vols (10,000) Cat Mss Pix Microforms
Notes: The history of pacifism has been one of the major subject emphases of the Peace Collection since its inception in 1930. In addition to books, pamphlets, and current materials of all kinds on the subject, the Peace Collection is the official depository for many 20th century pacifist organizations and papers of individual peace leaders. These incl Women's International League for Peace and Freedom; War Resisters League; Fellowship of Reconciliation; SANE, A Committee for a Sane Nuclear Policy; Friends Committee on National Legislation; CCCO1 An Agency for Military and Draft Counseling; National Interreligious Service Board for Conscientious Objectors; A J Muste (1885-1967); and Devere Allen (1891-1955). Other materials collected incl records and memorabilia of 19th and early 20th century peace leaders and organizations, such as the American Peace Society and itsbranches, Jane Addams (1860-1935), the Wisbech Local Peace Association (England), Emily Greene Balch (1867-1961), English and American Friends' Peace Societies, the Universal Peace Union, William Ladd (1778-1841), Elihu Burritt (1810-1879), and Benjamin F Trueblood (1847-1916). The Peace Collection has been described in Downs 972, 978, 4633, and in Downs 1950-1961 Supplement 507 and 916. For descriptions of major document groups, see the *Guide to the Swarthmore College Peace Collection*, 2nd ed (1981).

CONSCIOUSNESS, MULTIPLE see Personality, Disorders of

CONSCRIPT LABOR see Forced Labor

CONSENT, INFORMED see Informed Consent (Medical Law)

CONSENT TO TREATMENT see Informed Consent (Medical Law)

CONSERVATION, MUSEUM (MATERIALS CONSERVATION)

CA —CRAFT AND FOLK ART MUSEUM, Library, 5814 Wilshire Blvd, Los Angeles, 90036. Joan M Benedetti, Museum Librn
Holdings: Vols (2000) Slides VF
Notes: Incl 2000 books; 70 journal subscriptions; artists' biographical files: 6 file drawers; clipping files: 8 file drawers; 20,000 slides. Representation of the material culture of all people, traditional and contemporary expressions. Incl visual and printed information on ethnic, traditional, popular, decorative, idiosyncratic, and contemporary crafts as well as vernacular architecture, handmade houses, and design. Information about and for professional artists on health hazards, conservation, and career management. Anthropological and art historical works; exhibition catalogues; slides, photographs, audiocassettes; clipping and pamphlet files. Contemporary Slide Registry of Craftspeople and extensive biographical files of contemporary craft artists. Information and referral files of craft related galleries, shops, festivals, organizations, etc.

MA —OLD STURBRIDGE VILLAGE, Research Library, Sturbridge, 01566. Theresa Rini Percy, Librn
Holdings: Vols (23,000) Cat
Notes: Preservation of books, papers, fabrics, artifacts of every description, and of buildings.

ON —NATIONAL MUSEUMS OF CANADA, Library Services Directorate, Ottawa, K1A 0M8, Can. Valerie Monkhouse, Director
Holdings: Vols 40,000 Cat
Budget: $43,000
Notes: Chiefly publications issued by museums (throughout the world), many acquired through publications exchange programs, and also general works on museology, conservation of museum objects, architecture, display and other related subjects.

CONSERVATION OF ART OBJECTS see Art Objects—Conservation and Restoration

CONSERVATION OF BOOKS see Books—Conservation and Restoration

CONSERVATION OF BUILDINGS see Architecture—Conservation and Restoration

CONSERVATION OF CULTURAL RESOURCES IN WARTIME

NY —COLUMBIA UNIVERSITY LIBRARIES, Rare Book & Manuscript

CONSERVATION OF CULTURAL RESOURCES IN WARTIME (cont.)

Library, 801 Butler Library, 535 W 114 St, New York, 10027. Kenneth A Lohf, Librn
Holdings: Mss
Notes: The Calvin S Hathaway Collection on the protection and salvaging of artisic and historic documents and art objects during and after two world wars. 6500 items. Restricted use.

CONSERVATION OF ENERGY see Force and Energy

CONSERVATION OF ENERGY RESOURCES see Energy Conservation

CONSERVATION OF FUEL see Fuel Economy and Conservation

CONSERVATION OF MANUSCRIPTS see Manuscripts—Conservation and Restoration

CONSERVATION OF NATURAL RESOURCES

CA —UNIVERSITY OF CALIFORNIA, BERKELEY, Life Sciences Libraries, Forestry Library, 260 Mulford Hall, Berkeley, 94720. Esther Johnson, Librn; Pete Evans, Ref Librn
Notes: Areas of particular strength are forestry, conservation, and wildlife management. The collection is rich in pamphlet material and serials, especially foreign publications. Although holdings are world-wide in scope, coverage of the western USA is given the highest priority. Dissertation and thesis collection also. Forestry Library holdings are complemented by a 6000-vol specialized collection at the Forest Products Laboratory in Richmond, California.

FL —MAITLAND LIBRARY, Florida Audubon Society, 501 S Maitland Ave, Maitland, 32751. Mary Kinney, Librn
Notes: General and technical literature on many aspects of conservation and environmental topics, indexed by subject and source. Coverage is local, statewide and national. Most materials on microfilm and microfiche.

MA —RAYTHEON SERVICE CO, Library, Spencer Laboratory, 2 Wayside Rd, Burlington, 01803. Jean C Cameron, Librn
Notes: Collection emphasizes resource recovery, recycling waste, etc.

NY —NEW YORK BOTANICAL GARDEN LIBRARY, Bronx, 10458. Charles R Long, Asst Vice Pres & Dir
Notes: One of the largest botanical collections in the world. Covers botany (150, 000 vols), botanists (3000), horticulture (45, 000), plant diseases (25,000), plant physiology (15,000), history of botany (1500), conservation of natural resources (15,000), gardening (13,000), paleobotany (7000), ecology (20,000), forestry (5000), medical botany (3000), agriculture (9000) and biology (20,000). Reference library; materials do not circulate, except via standard inter-library loan. About 5000 vols uncataloged. Incl archives, art and vertical files. An OCLC library.

WI —UNIVERSITY OF WISCONSIN, MADISON, Law Library, Law Building, Madison, 53706. Anita Morse, Dir Law Library
Holdings: Cat Microforms
Notes: Stressing environmental law. Subject cataloging only.

CONSERVATION OF NATURAL RESOURCES—STUDY AND TRAINING

CO —COLORADO SCHOOL OF MINES, Arthur Lakes Library, 14 & Illinois Sts, Golden, 80401. Hartley K Phinney, Jr, Head Librn
Holdings: Vols (270,557) Cat Mss Maps Microforms

†MD —SMITHSONIAN INSTITUTION LIBRARIES, Smithsonian Environmental Research Center, Branch Library, PO Box 28, Edgewater, 21037.
Holdings: Vols (1100)

NY —NEW YORK BOTANICAL GARDEN LIBRARY, Bronx, 10458. Charles R Long, Asst Vice Pres & Dir
Notes: One of the largest botanical collections in the world. Over 900,000 items. Covers botany (150,000 vols), botanists (3000), horticulture (45,000) plant diseases (25,000), plant physiology (15,000), history of botany (1500), conservation of natural resources (15,000), gardening (13,000), paleobotany (7000), ecology (20,000), forestry (5000) medical botany (3000), agriculture (9000) and biology (20,000). Reference library; materials do not circulate, except for member circulating collection (1200) and standard inter-library loan. About 5000 vols uncataloged. Incl art, books, serials, pamphlets, archives and manuscripts, vertical files, microfiche and microfilm, nursery and seed catalogs, photographs, paintings, prints, drawings and engravings. Covers all areas of botanical sciences. This is an OCLC library with fullresource services incl photocopying and photography.

OH —WARREN H CORNING LIBRARY, 9500 Sperry Rd, Mentor, 44060. Paul C Spector, Dir of Education
Holdings: Vols (5400) Cat VF
Notes: 1500 vols of Warren H Corning Horticulture Classics. Also 80 periodicals and 10 vertical files.

NS —BEDFORD INSTITUTE OF OCEANOGRAPHY, Library, PO Box 1006, Dartmouth, B2Y 4A2, Can. J Elizabeth Sutherland, Librn Services
Holdings: Vols 1000
Notes: Arctic and Eastern Canadian projects.

CONSERVATION OF NATURE see Nature Conservation

CONSERVATION OF POWER RESOURCES see Energy Conservation

CONSERVATION OF RESOURCES see Conservation of Natural Resources

CONSERVATION OF THE SOIL see Soil Conservation

CONSERVATION OF WATER see Water Conservation

CONSERVATION OF WILDLIFE see Wildlife Conservation

CONSERVATISM

CA —CALIFORNIA STATE UNIVERSITY, FULLERTON, Library, 800 N State College Blvd, Fullerton, 92634. Lynn M Coppel, Librn
Holdings: Pamphlets Serials Ephemera
Notes: Freedom Center of Polemic Political Ephemera incl 8000 pamphlets and over 4000 periodical titles. Strongest in right wing American politics and British socialism. Separate card catalogs for the pamphlets and folders. Periodicals are listed in the CSUF periodicals printout and the *California State University and Colleges Union List of* Periodicals.

CA —UNIVERSITY OF CALIFORNIA, LOS ANGELES, Research Library, Dept of Special Collections, 405 Hilgard Ave, Los Angeles, 90024. Edward Shreeves, Chairman, Bibliographers Group; David S Zeidberg, Head
Holdings: Cat Mss Pix
Notes: 11 cartons of materials, recordings, etc, relating to the John Birch Society, with runs of many relevant periodicals, government documents, etc.

CA —HOOVER INSTITUTION ON WAR, REVOLUTION & PEACE, Stanford University, Stanford, 94305. Milorad M Drachkovitch, Archivist
Holdings: Mss Pix
Notes: Records of Marvin Liebman Associates, Inc, a New York public relations firm incl office files, correspondence, printed matter, press releases, campaign material, photographs and reports, 1950-1969, relating to activities of Marvin Liebman Associates in lobbying for US conservative and anti-communist organizations involved with Asian and African affairs. 108 ms boxes, 3 envelopes.

CT —UNIVERSITY OF CONNECTICUT, Library, Storrs, 06268. Ellen Embardo, Cur Special Collections
Holdings: Cat
Notes: Alternative Press Collection. Primarily periodicals and newspapers from the 1960s to today of an alternative or underground nature. Books and pamphlets are incl, representing both the left and the right-wing viewpoints. A catalog is available. Also have archives of the First Casualty Press, which was deeply involved with Vietnam veterans' experiences in Vietnam.

KS —UNIVERSITY OF KANSAS, Kenneth Spencer Research Library, Kansas Collection, Lawrence, 66045. Sheryl K Williams, Cur
Holdings: Vols 6000 Cat Mss Audiotapes
Notes: The Wilcox Collection of Contemporary Political Movements containing American extremist literature from the 1950s to the present, and incl appox 4000 serials, 5000 books and pamplets, 400 audiotapes, and 50,000 pieces of ephemera. Approximately 7000 right and left wing organizations are represented by this material as well as the views of many leaders or prime movers within these organizations. The collection is partially cataloged.

NJ —PRINCETON UNIVERSITY, Library, Rare Books Dept, Princeton, 08544. Stephen Ferguson, Cur
Holdings: Vols 100 Cat
Notes: Right Wing literature, incl material on organizations.

OR —UNIVERSITY OF OREGON LIBRARY, Special Collections Div, Eugene, 97403. Kenneth W Duckett, Curator
Holdings: Cat Mss
Notes: 50 mss collections dating from the 1930's to the 1950's. Papers reflect a concern for political, economic, religious, and social issues. Incl files of individuals who were active in such organizations as the John Birch Society, the Foundation for Economic Education, Spiritual Mobilization, and the Liberty Amendment Committee. In addition, over 100 linear feet of supporting pamphlets, serials, and ephemeral literature. Publication: Martin Schmitt, comp. *Catalogue of Manuscripts in the University of Oregon Library.* Eugene: University of Oregon Books, 1971.

SD —NATIONAL COLLEGE OF BUSINESS, Thomas Jefferson Learning Resource Center, 321 Kansas City St, Rapid City, 57701. Linda Watson, Library Dir
Holdings: Vols (26,000) Cat
Notes: Analyses (Index) of national and international issues. Published at irregular, frequent intervals, produced by the American Enterprise Institute for Public Policy Research.

CONSERVATISM—U.S.

AZ —NORTHERN ARIZONA UNIVERSITY, Special Collection Library, CU Box 6022, Flagstaff, 86011. Peter M Whiteley, Coordr/Archivist; William Mullane, Librn
Holdings: Vols 9000 Cat Mss Phonorecords Microforms
Notes: The large Allderdice Collection of thousands of books, pamphlets, periodicals, and organizational files reflects the conservative, communist, socialist, facist, anarchist, and other viewpoints, etc, during the 20th century. Also, L D Sprague Collection; correspondence, subject files, 1950's-1960's relating to conservative movements and issues in America. Incl the files of "For American, Pima County Branch" organization. Inventory available.

IA —UNIVERSITY OF IOWA, University Libraries, Iowa City, 52242. Frank Paluka,

CONSERVATISM—U.S. (cont.)

Head, Special Collections Dept
Holdings: Cat Mss
Notes: Collection 441 linear feet of publications (with some ms material) dealing with right-wing groups in the US from 1950. A large portion of the collection is now available on microfilm ("The Right Wing Collection of the University of Iowa Libraries," Microfilming Corporation of America, 170 reels and guide).

MI —UNIVERSITY OF MICHIGAN, Dept of Rare Books & Special Collections, Ann Arbor, 48109. Edward C Weber, Head, Labadie Collection
Holdings: Vols (40,000) Cat Microforms
Notes: Emphasis is on the Radical Right in the US. Incl records, tapes.

MS —UNIVERSITY OF SOUTHERN MISSISSIPPI, William David McCain Graduate Library, Box 5148, Southern Sta, Hattiesburg, 39406.
Holdings: Cat Mss Pix
Notes: Papers, 1915-73. Approx 965 linear feet, incl the correspondence, subject files, clippings, photographs, and memorabilia of Theodore G Bilbo, who served two terms as Governor of Mississippi (1916-1920, 1928-1932) and was a United States Senator from 1935 until his death in 1947. The papers of US Representative William M Colmer incl correspondence, legislative files, newsletters, speeches, scrapbooks and artifacts documenting his forty years of service in Congress (1933-1973).

PA —BALCH INSTITUTE FOR ETHNIC STUDIES, Library, 18 S Seventh St, Philadelphia, 19106. R Joseph Anderson, Library Dir

WI —UNIVERSITY OF WISCONSIN, MILWAUKEE, Library, Box 604, Milwaukee, 53201. William C Roselle, Dir
Holdings: Vols 2500 Cat Mss Pix
Notes: Fromkin Memorial Collection, emphasizing third party forces in American politics. Restricted use: noncirculating. Special subject catalog of pamphlet material.

CONSIDERANT, VICTOR PROSPER

TX —UNIVERSITY OF TEXAS, ARLINGTON, Library, Arlington, 76019. Charles A Colley, Dir of Special Collections; Robert A Gamble, Head of Archives
Holdings: / / Mss
Notes: Santerre Collection. This is the library of the Santerre family who emigrated from France, Belgium, and Switzerland in 1855 to join the Utopian Socialist colony of Victor Prosper Considerant in what is now Dallas, Texas. Typical selection of books of a middle-class, well-educated family of the period. Some title deeds, legal papers, family letters, first Paris editions of works of Considerant, Charles Fourier; French translations of English classics, devotional works. See George H Santerre, *White Cliffs of Dallas* (Dallas, Texas: Book Craft, 1955).

CONSISTOIRE CENTRAL DES ISRAELITES

MA —BRANDEIS UNIVERSITY, Goldfarb Library, 415 South St, Waltham, 02154. Bessie Hahn, Dir
Notes: Consistoire Israelite Archives. Contains 12 linear ft of original documents relating to the French-Jewish community from the 18th to 20th century. A finding list of the documents is in Special Collections. Also, the Alfred Dreyfus Trial Collection: approx 1000 books, pamphlets, newspapers and photographs as well as some correspondence of French notables dealing with the Alfred Dreyfus trial at the turn of the century. An author-title card catalog can be found in the Special Collections Card Catalog.

CONSTABLE AND COMPANY, PUBLISHERS

PA —TEMPLE UNIVERSITY LIBRARIES, Special Collections Dept, Rare Books & Mss Section, Philadelphia, 19122. Thomas M Whitehead, Cur
Holdings: Cat Mss
Notes: Letters and documents (15,000 items) of the archives of the London publishers, Constable and Company. Correspondence with close to 400 authors, most of it with Otto Kyllmann and Michael Sadlier, directors. Archives of Thomas Nelson & Sons (USA) and of various Philadelphia publishers.

CONSTANT, ALEX

ON —NATIONAL LIBRARY OF CANADA, 395 Wellington St, Ottawa, K1A 0N4, Can. Andre Preibish, Dir
Notes: Papers and recordings of Canadian composer Alex Constant. Catalogue available.

CONSTITUTION see U.S. Constitution

CONSTITUTIONAL CONVENTIONS

NY —NEW YORK STATE LIBRARY, Law Library, Cultural Education Center, Empire State Plaza, Albany, 12230. Stephanie Welden, State Law Librn
Notes: Material on the constitutional conventions of the several states.

CONSTITUTIONAL LAW

DC —LIBRARY OF CONGRESS, Law Library, 101 Independence Ave, SE, Washington, 20540. Carleton W Kenyon, Dir
Holdings: Vols 1,800,000 Cat Mss Microforms
Notes: The collection, comprising the legal sources and literature of the US and all foreign nations, covers all legal systems incl common, civil, international, religious, and historic law.

AB —ALBERTA ATTORNEY GENERAL, Law Library, Fourth Floor North Wing, Bowker Bldg 9833-109 St, Edmonton, T5K 2E8, Can. Andrew Balazs, Departmental Librn
Holdings: Vols (13,000) Cat Audiotapes
Budget: ($121,620)
Notes: Emphasis is on Canadian law. But if the solicitors can not find a Canadian precedent, they consult English law. If there is no precedent in English law they consult Commonwealth law, and if there is no precedent there either, then they consult American law. Therefore, the Library does have all the basic Canadian and certain basic English Commonwealth, and a very small number of American texts, as well as the basic Canadian and English law reports. There is one Australian law report. Besides texts (monographs), the Library subscribes to Albertan and Canadian legislative publications like bills, orders, votes and proceedings, Hansard, and Debates of the House of Commons. Assistance is available to users' from the simplest to the most complex legal research questions.

CONSTITUTIONAL LIMITATIONS see Constitutional Law

CONSTITUTIONS

PA —PENNSYLVANIA ECONOMY LEAGUE, Eastern Div Library, 215 S Broad St, Philadelphia, 19107. Ellen Brennan, Librn
Holdings: Vols (15,000) Cat Maps
Notes: Public finance, charters, constitutions, public education.

CONSTITUTIONS, STATE

IL —NEWBERRY LIBRARY, 60 W Walton St, Chicago, 60610. Diana Haskell, Cur of Modern Mss
Holdings: Cat
Notes: Many important first American constitutions, particularly the eastern and western states.

PA —PENNSYLVANIA ECONOMY LEAGUE, Eastern Div Library, 215 S Broad St, Philadelphia, 19107. Ellen Brennan, Librn
Holdings: Vols (15,000) Cat Maps
Notes: Public finance, charters, constitutions, public education.

CONSTRUCTION see Architecture; Building; Construction Industry; Engineering

CONSTRUCTION INDUSTRY

CA —HOOVER INSTITUTION ON WAR, REVOLUTION & PEACE, Stanford University, Stanford, 94305. Milorad M Drachkovitch, Archivist
Holdings: Mss
Notes: Records of the President's Conference on Home Building and Home Ownership, established by President Hoover as a fact-finding conference on housing incl memoranda, reports, correspondence, pamphlets, clippings, press releases and expense statements, 1929-33, relating to housing conditions in the US and to proposals for improving them. 40 ms boxes, 3 ledgers, oversize report.

NY —NEW YORK PUBLIC LIBRARY, Mid-Manhattan Library, Science & Business Dept, 455 Fifth Ave, New York, 10016. Frederick E Dusold, Sr Principal Librn
Holdings: Vols (110,000) Cat Microforms
Budget: ($134,000)
Notes: All works are in English. Material is current; policy precludes archival collecting. Collection is geared toward the undergraduate college student, with consideration given to the professional, the lay reader and the beginning graduate student. Collection incl monographs, texts, treatises, standard reference works and periodicals in agriculture, horticulture, home economics, crafts, engineering, industrial chemistry, construction and other technologies. Books are available for circulation in addition to an extensive reference collection.

PA —CARNEGIE LIBRARY OF PITTSBURGH, Science & Technology Dept, 4400 Forbes Ave, Pittsburgh, 15213. Catherine M Brosky, Dept Head
Notes: Collection incl material on general construction, carpentry, masonry, plumbing, heating, air conditioning, corrosion and painting and numerous other building trades. Sweets Architectural File complete except for a few years. *Car Builders Encyclopedia of American Practice*, most editions since 1879.

TX —FLUOR ENGINEERS INC, Houston Library, 4620 N Braeswood, PO Box 35000, Houston, 77235. R S Holab-Abelman, Librn
Holdings: Vols (2500) Cat Maps
Budget: ($10,000)
Notes: Construction, environmental and chemical engineering, coal technology. Incl 2000 job books covering all areas of company interests.

VA —VIRGINIA POLYTECHNIC INSTITUTE & STATE UNIVERSITY, Architecture Library, Blacksburg, 24061. Robert E Stephenson, Architecture Librn
Holdings: Vols (46,000) Cat Microforms Cassettes Slides VF
Budget: ($57,700)

CONSTRUCTION INDUSTRY—STATISTICS

DC —US BUREAU OF THE CENSUS, Library, Federal Office Bldg 3, Rm 2451, Washington, 20233. Betty Baxtresser, Chief, ASD Library Branch
Holdings: Cat Microforms
Notes: Emphases on statistics of agriculture, business, construction, economics, foreign trade, governments, housing, industry, population, transportation, statistical methodology, and data processing. Library holdings are largely current materials covering the Bureau's programs. Outdated materials are withdrawn regularly.

CONSTRUCTION OF ROADS see Road Construction

CONSTRUCTIVISM (ART)

NY —STATE UNIVERSITY OF NEW YORK, COLLEGE AT PURCHASE,

CONSTRUCTIVISM (ART) (cont.)

Library, Lincoln Ave, Purchase, 10577. Robert W Evans, Dir
Holdings: Uncat Mss Pix
Notes: Gift of the artist, George Rickey, and his wife, whose collection of constructivist art works has also been given to the Neuberger Museum at the College at Purchase. The collection consists largely of over 1000 announcements and catalogs of exhibitions of constructivist works and material about the artists.

CONSTRUCTIVISM (RUSSIAN LITERATURE)

IL —UNIVERSITY OF ILLINOIS, URBANA/CHAMPAIGN, Slavic and East European Library, Urbana, 61801. Marianna Tax Choldin, Head
Holdings: Cat Microforms
Notes: IDC microfiche collection. (959) titles of symbolism, futurism, constructivism, acmeism, imagism, and zemstvo publications.

CONSUMER ADVERTISING see Advertising

CONSUMER BEHAVIOR

IL —J WALTER THOMPSON CO, Information Center, 875 N Michigan Ave, Chicago, 60611. Edward G Strable, Dir
Holdings: Vols 300 Cat Microforms
Notes: Emphasis is on Americans as consumers. Most important recent monographs, plus 20 file drawers of reports, studies, clippings, articles, releases. Indexing and organization make for rapid access.

NJ —RUTGERS, THE STATE UNIVERSITY OF NEW JERSEY, Alexander Library, Special Collections and Archives, College Ave & Huntington St, New Brunswick, 08903. Ronald L Becker, Cur of Manuscripts and Rare Books
Notes: Papers of the Consumers League of New Jersey, Consumer Research Inc, and consumer advocate Sidney Margolius.

ON —UNIVERSITY OF GUELPH, Library, Guelph, N1G 2W1, Can. Margaret Beckman, Chief Librn; Ellen Pearson, Ref Librn
Holdings: Vols 4500 Cat Audiotapes Videotapes 16mm Films
Notes: 32 periodical titles currently received. Collection supports work of the Gerontology Research Centre, as well as the undergraduate and graduate teaching program of the College of Family and Consumer Studies and the College of Social Sciences. Also 200 periodical titles. Collection as a whole concentrates on behavior, clothing and textiles, foods, housing, marketing, law.

CONSUMER EDUCATION

CA —LOS ANGELES PUBLIC LIBRARY, Science & Technology Dept, 630 W Fifth St, Los Angeles, 90071. Billie M Connor, Dept Head
Holdings: Vols (7500)
Notes: A well-rounded collection of materials related to consumer health, medicine and drugs as well as materials for the allied health and medical professions. Includes a sound representative selection of basic texts covering various aspects of medical treatment, drugs, diseases and syndromes. Indexes are collected as well as a basic collection of journals. The directories collection is strong. The broadest possible collection of books oriented toward consumer health, medicine, diets and nutrition is maintained, both traditional and alternative. Texts and examination study books are collected for nurses, laboratory technicians, physcial therapists, speech therapists, paramedics and other allied health professions.

IL —UNIVERSITY OF ILLINOIS, URBANA/CHAMPAIGN, Library, Home Economics Library, 314 Bevier Hall, Champaign, 61820. Barbara C Swain, Librn
Notes: Family and consumer economics.

IN —PURDUE UNIVERSITY LIBRARIES, Consumer & Family Sciences Library, Stone Hall W, West Lafayette, 47907. Emily Alward, Librn
Holdings: Vols (14,000) Cat

PA —DREXEL UNIVERSITY LIBRARIES, General Division, 32 & Chestnut Sts, Philadelphia, 19104. Tung Chu Chen, General Division Librn
Holdings: Vols (1226) Cat
Notes: Emphasis on home economics study and teaching, consumer education, and early childhood education.

BC —VANCOUVER PUBLIC LIBRARY, Science & Technology Div, 750 Burrard St, Vancouver, V6Z 1X5, Can. P Haffenden, Head, Science & Technology Div
Holdings: Pamphlets Periodicals
Notes: Plus special indexes, incl Organization and Association File (primarily local, British Columbian, and Canadian), begun in 1950s, expanded since 1960s; Government Documents File; Chart File; Ship Index (a source of pictures, historical and current information; engineering data, plans, etc); Boat Plans Index.

ON —UNIVERSITY OF GUELPH, Library, Guelph, N1G 2W1, Can. Margaret Beckman, Chief Librn; Ellen Pearson, Ref Librn
Holdings: Vols 4500 Cat Audiotapes Videotapes 16mm Films
Notes: 32 periodical titles currently received. Collection supports work of the Gerontology Research Centre, as well as the undergraduate and graduate teaching program of the College of Family and Consumer Studies and the College of Social Sciences. Also 200 periodical titles. Collection as a whole concentrates on behavior, clothing and textiles, foods, housing, marketing, law.

ON —ONTARIO MINISTRY OF CONSUMER & COMMERCIAL RELATIONS, Consumer Information Centre, 555 Yonge St, Toronto, M7A 2H6, Can. Sarah Coombs, Asst Dir of Communications
Notes: A collection of consumer resource materials, incl product test results, government reports, books, kits, periodicals and films. For English and French-speaking Ontarians.

CONSUMER LOANS see Loans, Personal

CONSUMER PROTECTION

NJ —RUTGERS, THE STATE UNIVERSITY OF NEW JERSEY, Alexander Library, Special Collections and Archives, College Ave & Huntington St, New Brunswick, 08903. Ronald L Becker, Cur of Manuscripts and Rare Books
Notes: Papers of the Consumers League of New Jersey, Consumer Research Inc, and consumer advocate Sidney Margolius.

NC —GREENSBORO PUBLIC LIBRARY, Business Library, 201 Greene St, Drawer X-4, Greensboro, 27402. Lebby B Lamb, Business Librn
Holdings: Vols (6000) Cat Microforms
Budget: ($12,000)

ON —UNIVERSITY OF GUELPH, Library, Guelph, N1G 2W1, Can. Margaret Beckman, Chief Librn; Ellen Pearson, Ref Librn
Holdings: Vols 4500 Cat Audiotapes Videotapes 16mm Films
Notes: 32 periodical titles currently received. Collection supports work of the Gerontology Research Centre, as well as the undergraduate and graduate teaching program of the College of Family and Consumer Studies and the College of Social Sciences. Also 200 periodical titles. Collection as a whole concentrates on behavior, clothing and textiles, foods, housing, marketing, law.

CONSUMERS

CA —CLAREMONT COLLEGES, Honnold Library, Ninth & Dartmouth, Claremont, 91711. Tania Rizzo, Special Collections Dept Head
Holdings: Vols 200 Cat Mss Pix
Notes: The papers of former Democratic Congressman Jerry Voorhis, from the 1930s to present, occupying nearly 100 document boxes. The papers reflect his life and career, incl biographical material, the history of the Voorhis School for Boys, his involvement in the Dies Committee, and his wide-ranging interests in American economic and social issues, such as cooperatives, monopolies and cartels, Latin American relations, consumers, and senior citizens. Books by and about him, with research files. Correspondence with political leaders. Inventory available. Restricted use.

IL —J WALTER THOMPSON CO, Information Center, 875 N Michigan Ave, Chicago, 60611. Edward G Strable, Dir
Holdings: Vols 500 Cat Microforms Data files
Notes: Books are not an important part of this collection. Data files of ephemeral material-clippings, studies, reports, releases-of approx 25 drawers are what make this a special collection. In addition, collection of print advertisements from past 18 years (1, 000,000 items) but some as early as 1902, with emphasis on consumer products. Indexing and organization make for immediate access.

MA —RADCLIFFE COLLEGE, Arthur & Elizabeth Schlesinger Library on the History of Women in America, 3 James St, Cambridge, 02138. Patricia Miller King, Dir; Eva Moseley, Cur of Mss
Holdings: Mss Pix
Notes: Correspondence of Esther (Eggertsen) Peterson with family and friends; correspondence and printed material re work in Industrial Union Dept of AFL-CIO (1958-1961); ILO; International Confederation of Free Trade Unions; Democratic political campaigns (1960-); National Committee on Household Employment; National Women's Committee on Civil Rights. Correspondence, speeches, and printed material re work as Dir, US Women's Bureau (1961-1964); Asst Sec of Labor (1962-1969); Special Asst to the Pres for Consumer Affairs (1964-1967, 1977-1981); Exec Vice Chmn of President's Commission on the Status of Women (1961-1963); Consumer Advisor to Giant Food (1970-1976). Other papers re Peterson's re Peterson's work for rights of women, minorities, labor, consumers.

WI —UNIVERSITY OF WISCONSIN, MADISON, College of Agricultural & Life Sciences, Steenbock Memorial Library, 550 Babcock Dr, Madison, 53706. Jan Kennedy, Dir
Holdings: Vols (186,312) Cat Docs Microforms
Notes: USDA, experiment station and state publications.

CONSUMERS' ASSOCIATION OF CANADA

MB —UNIVERSITY OF MANITOBA, Elizabeth Dafoe Library, Archives and Special Collections Dept, Winnipeg, R3T 2N2, Can. Richard E Bennett, Dept Head; Corrado A Santoro, Reference Archivist
Notes: Papers, minutes, membership lists, etc. of Consumers' Association of Canada (Manitoba). Also materials on Winnipeg and Ft Garry branches.

CONSUMERS' GOODS see Manufactures

CONSUMERS' LEAGUES

MD —PRINCE GEORGE'S COUNTY MEMORIAL LIBRARY SYSTEM, Greenbelt Branch Library, 11 Crescent Rd, Greenbelt, 20770. Harriet Ying, Branch Librn
Holdings: Vols (120) Cat Mss Maps Pix Microforms

CONTACT LENSES see Ophthalmic Lenses

CONTACT VERNACULARS see Languages, Mixed

CONTAGION AND CONTAGIOUS DISEASES see Communicable Diseases

CONTAINERS

IL —NORTHWESTERN UNIVERSITY, Transportation Center Library, Evanston,

CONTAINERS (cont.)

60201. Mary Roy, Librn
Holdings: Vols (116,000) Cat
Notes: The emphasis in this collection is on current developments in transportation operations and socioeconomics--management, planning, impact and regulation. All modes of transportation and containerization are incl; the geographic scope covers domestic and foreign activity at the urban, intercity and international levels. Publications on new systems developments and the application of analytic techniques to operations are well represented. Incl 19,000 pamphlets; 9000 company reports. *Services are offered on research conducted outside Northwestern. A fee schedule is available on request.* Publications: *Current Literature in Traffic and Transportation* (bi-monthly accessions bulletin citing 625 books, reports and periodical articles per issue).

CONTAMINATED FOOD see Food Contamination

CONTEMPORARY ARTISTS see Artists, Contemporary

CONTEMPORARY MUSIC PROJECT

†MD —UNIVERSITY OF MARYLAND, Library, Music Educators National Conference Historical Center, College Park, 20742. Bruce Wilson, Cur
Holdings: Cat Mss Pix Audiotapes
Notes: The official archive of the Music Educators' National Conference (MENC), and a repository for the documentation of music education. Incl the papers of the MENC, state units, and associated organizations and committees; personal papers and association items (notably, relating to Francis Elliott Clark, Lowell Mason, and Luther Whiting Mason); published proceedings of MENC and other groups; oral histories, numerous school music textbooks, and the archive of the Contemporary Music Project.

CONTEMPORARY PAINTING see Painting, Modern—20th Century

CONTEMPT OF THE WORLD see Asceticism

CONTESTED ELECTIONS

NY —NEW YORK STATE LIBRARY, State Education Bldg Annex, Washington Ave, Albany, 12224.
Notes: Books and other materials on contested American elections.

CONTINENTAL CONGRESS see U.S. Continental Congress

CONTINENTAL SHELF

AK —NATIONAL OCEANIC AND ATMOSPHERIC ADMINISTRATION, National Marine Fisheries Service, Fisheries Laboratory Research Library, PO Box 155, Auke Bay, 99821. Paula Johnson, Librn
Holdings: Vols (21,000) Cat Mss Maps Slides Microforms
Budget: ($20,000)
Notes: Much on the outer continental shelf, marine flora and fauna, fisheries.

TX —UNIVERSITY OF TEXAS, Marine Science Institute Library, Port Aransas, 78373. Ruth Grundy, Librn
Holdings: Vols (45,000) Cat Maps Pix
Budget: ($70,000)
Notes: Current researches in marine science, especially concerning the Gulf of Mexico, the Texas Coastal Zone, and the Continental Shelf. Incl journals.

CONTRACEPTION see Birth Control

CONTRACTIONS see Paleography

CONTROL, PRODUCTION see Production Control

CONTROL OF INDUSTRIAL PROCESSES see Process Control

CONUNDRUMS see Riddles

CONVENTIONS, CONSTITUTIONAL see Constitutional Conventions

CONVERT MAKING see Evangelistic Work

CONVERTER REACTORS see Breeder Reactors

CONVERTS FROM JUDAISM

CA —BIOLA UNIVERSITY, Rose Memorial Library, 13800 Biola Ave, La Mirada, 90639. A Lawrence Marshburn
Holdings: Vols (178,000) Cat Maps Pix Microforms
Budget: ($430,000)
Notes: Biblical and evangelical materials.

CONWAY, JAMES F.

MO —WASHINGTON UNIVERSITY, Libraries, Special Collections Dept, Campus Box 1061, St Louis, 63130.
Notes: St Louis Mayoral Papers Collection: Papers of Aloys P Kaufmann, 1944-49; Raymond R Tucker, 1953-65; Alphonso J Cervantes, 1965-73; John H Poelker, 1973-77; James F Conway, 1977-81.

CONWELL, RUSSELL H.

PA —TEMPLE UNIVERSITY LIBRARIES, Special Collections Dept, Conwellana-Templana Collection, 13 & Berks St, Philadelphia, 19122. Miriam I Crawford, Cur
Holdings: Vols (2200) Cat Mss Pix Slides Phonorecords Audiotapes 16mm Films Microforms
Notes: The Conwellana Collection is a memorial to Dr Russell H Conwell, founder of Temple University and pastor of the Baptist Temple (Grace Baptists Church) of Philadelphia from 1882 to his death in 1925. The Collection contains almost all of his published works; his personal library of almost 2000 books, emphasizing Biblical and religious thoughts; mss both by Conwell and about his development of the institutional church; letters, including a large number written to his assistant pastor, Arthur E Harris; a near-complete bound set of his sermons and of the *Temple Review* of the Baptist Temple in which they appeared over a 36-year period; and an extensive file of articles, photographs and information on his activities. Card catalog of the Conwellana-Templana Collection incl books by and about Russell Conwell. Separate card files index his sermons, quotationsfrom his sermons, and items in the *Temple Review*. *Russell Herman Conwell, 1843-1925, A* Bibliography, by Maurice F Tauber (Philadelphia Temple University Library, 1935. 40 leaves mimeographed). *Russell Herman Conwell: The Individual and His Influence: Catalog of an Exhibition,* by Miriam I Crawford (Temple University General Alumni Association, 1977; unpaged). Also, *The "Acres of Diamonds" Man, A Memorial Archive of Russell H Conwell, a truly unique institutional creator,* by Joseph C Carter, (Philadelphia Privately Printed at Temple University, 1981; 3 vols).

COOK, ALTON F.

MA —BOSTON UNIVERSITY, Mugar Memorial Library, Special Collections Dept, 771 Commonwealth Ave, Boston, 02215. Howard B Gotlieb, Dir
Holdings: Cat Mss
Notes: Mss, correspondence, etc collected in depth; incl publications by or about.

COOK, FREDERICK A.

NY —EXPLORERS CLUB, James B Ford Memorial Library, 46 E 70 St, New York, 10021. Janet Baldwin, Librn
Holdings: Vols (24,000) Cat Maps
Notes: Additions to the collection depend upon gifts. Access by appointment only.

VA —UNIVERSITY OF VIRGINIA, Alderman Library, Manuscripts Dept, Charlottesville, 22901. Edmund Berkeley Jr, Cur
Holdings: Cat Mss Pix
Notes: Papers of Edwin Swift Balch, author of *The North Pole* and *Bradley Land*, and *Antarctica*, and authority on the Cook-Peary controversy incl scrapbooks and correspondence.

COOK, GEORGE H., 1818-1889

NJ —RUTGERS, THE STATE UNIVERSITY OF NEW JERSEY, Alexander Library, Special Collections and Archives, College Ave & Huntington St, New Brunswick, 08903. Ronald L Becker, Cur of Manuscripts and Rare Books
Holdings: / / Mss
Notes: Papers, etc (15 linear feet).

COOK, JAMES, 1728-1779

CA —UNIVERSITY OF CALIFORNIA, LOS ANGELES, Research Library, Dept of Special Collections, 405 Hilgard Ave, Los Angeles, 90024. Edward Shreeves, Chairman, Bibliographers Group; David S Zeidberg, Head
Holdings: Vols 350 Cat Mss Maps Pix
Notes: Based on the Maurice Holmes Collection, the collection now incl 350 books by and about Captain Cook as well as mss, maps, pictures, and ephemera.

CA —UNIVERSITY OF CALIFORNIA, LOS ANGELES, Research Library, Indo/Pacific Collection, 405 Hilgard Ave, Los Angeles, 90024. Edward Shreeves, Chairman, Bibliographers Group; Charlotte Spence, Indo/Pacific Bibliographer
Holdings: Vols Cat Mss Maps Pix Microforms
Notes: The Pacific area collection has been developed on a combination of the research and teaching levels. It focuses on the cultural, economic, political and social history of Australia, New Zealand and the various island groups. The accounts of the early European voyagers are well represented, with the highlight being the Captain Cook collection. An effort has also been made to collect the novels, poetry, drama, etc, of Australian and New Zealand authors.

HI —UNIVERSITY OF HAWAII, Library, 2550 The Mall, Honolulu, 96822. David Kittelson, Hawaiian Cur
Holdings: Vols (65,000) Cat Microforms
Budget: ($2000)
Notes: This is a comprehensive collection of material published in and about Hawaii, including especially 20th century publications, and University of Hawaii publications and theses. The Collection publishes *Current Hawaiiana*, a quarterly bibliography of recently available publications. There is a separate Hawaiian Collection card catalog; it was published in 1963 by G K Hall as a 4 volume set.

IN —INDIANA STATE UNIVERSITY, Cunningham Memorial Library, Dept of Rare Books & Special Collections, Terre Haute, 47809. Lawrence J McCrank, Head
Holdings: Vols 400 Uncat Maps
Notes: Nature of this material essentially that of the books listed in E G Cox, *A Reference Guide to the Literature of Travel.* Books range from the 16th century to early 1960s, in English, French, German, Latin, Italian, and Dutch. Strong in Cook materials (ie, original editions of first 3 voyages, in English and French and some Dutch).

PA —PENNSYLVANIA STATE UNIVERSITY, Fred Lewis Pattee Library, University Park, 16802. Stuart Forth, Dean of Libraries
Holdings: Vols Cat Maps
Notes: Based primarily on an interest in Australia and the Pacific Ocean, the Pennsylvania State University Libraries have developed a strong collection of voyages, including many 17th and 18th century editions of specific voyages, eg, Cook, La Perouse, Vancouver, collected editions both French and English, together with related publications, eg, De Brosses, Dalrymple. The collections include both exploration and scientific voyages in original editions and reprints.

TX —UNIVERSITY OF TEXAS LIBRARIES, Nettie Lee Benson Latin American Collection, Sid Richardson Hall 1.109, Austin, 78712. Laura Gutierrez-Witt, Head Librn
Holdings: Vols (450,000) Cat Mss Maps Pix Phonorecords Filmstrips Microforms
See also entry under Latin America

COOK, MICHAEL, 1933-

AB —UNIVERSITY OF CALGARY, Libraries, Special Collections Div, 2500

COOK, MICHAEL, 1933- (cont.)

University Dr, Calgary, T2N 1N4, Can.
Holdings: Mss
Notes: The papers of Michael Cook, Canadian playwright, include drafts of plays for stage, radio, and television, as well as mss for newspaper columns, articles, and speeches. Correspondence covers the years 1968-1977.

COOK, ROBIN

MA —BOSTON UNIVERSITY, Mugar Memorial Library, Special Collections Dept, 771 Commonwealth Ave, Boston, 02215. Howard B Gotlieb, Dir
Holdings: Cat Mss Pix

COOK FAMILY

MA —NEW ENGLAND HISTORIC GENEALOGICAL SOCIETY, Library, 101 Newbury St, Boston, 02116. Ralph J Crandell, Dir
Notes: Family papers, likely to incl personal correspondence, diaries, business records, etc.

COOKBOOKS see Cookery and Cook Books

COOKE, ALISTAIR

MA —BOSTON UNIVERSITY, Mugar Memorial Library, Special Collections Dept, 771 Commonwealth Ave, Boston, 02215. Howard B Gotlieb, Dir
Holdings: Cat Mss
Notes: Mss, correspondence, etc collected in depth; incl publications by or about.

COOKE, JOHN ESTEN

VA —UNIVERSITY OF VIRGINIA, Alderman Library, Clifton Waller Barrett Collection, Charlottesville, 22901. Joan St C Crane, Cur of American Literature Collections
Holdings: Cat Mss Pix
Notes: Extensive collection of mss and printed materials.

COOKERY AND COOK BOOKS

AL —SAMFORD UNIVERSITY, Special Collections Library, 800 Lakeshore Dr, Birmingham, 35229. Annie Ford Wheeler, Acting Head Librn
Holdings: Vols 100 Cat
Notes: Nucleus is the Gottlieb Cookbook Collection, mostly early 20th century publications.

CA —LOS ANGELES PUBLIC LIBRARY, Science & Technology Dept, 630 W Fifth St, Los Angeles, 90071. Billie M Connor, Dept Head
Holdings: Vols 3500 Cat
Notes: Books on the cookery of all nationalities and ethnic groups. Strong collection of California cookery. Some early works in Spanish. Additional materials on wines and other beverages, quantity and institutional cookery, food technology, and special diets. Menu collection of approximately 1000 concentrates on Southern California.

CA —UNIVERSITY OF CALIFORNIA, LOS ANGELES, Research Library, Dept of Special Collections, 405 Hilgard Ave, Los Angeles, 90024. Edward Shreeves, Chairman, Bibliographers Group; David S Zeidberg, Head
Holdings: Vols 750 Cat
Notes: 750 cook books with California imprints.

CA —SAN DIEGO PUBLIC LIBRARY, Science & Industry Section, 820 E St, San Diego, 92101. Joanne Anderson, Senior Librn
Budget: ($33,000)

CA —CITY COLLEGE OF SAN FRANCISCO, Alice Statler Library, Hotel & Restaurant Dept, 50 Phelan Ave, San Francisco, 94112. Mary B Smyth, Librn
Holdings: Vols (7300) Cat Slides 16mm Films Filmstrips Microforms
Budget: ($5000)
Notes: The collection covers all aspects of the public hospitality industry. In addition to the book collection, it has 6000 cataloged pamphlets, 1500 menus. It also has bound hotel and restaurant magazines dating back to the 19th century. Receives 85 current periodicals in hospitality industry.

CA —FITZ HUGH LUDLOW MEMORIAL LIBRARY, PO Box 99346, San Francisco, 94109. Michael R Aldrich, Exec Cur
Holdings: Vols 20
Notes: Collection stored. Important mail inquiries only. No interlibrary lending or telephone inquiries. The heart of this special collection of psychoactive drug literature is about 400 vols of memoirs or lightly-disguised fiction concerning psychoactive drugs. Incl several hundred vols related to drug slang, drugs and music, drug art, drug cuisine, cooking with pot, etc.

†CO —UNIVERSITY OF DENVER, Penrose Library, 2150 E Evans, Denver, 80208.
Notes: Husted Culinary Collection.

DE —UNIVERSITY OF DELAWARE, Hugh M Morris Library, S College Ave, Newark, 19711. T Stuart Dick, Special Collections
Holdings: Vols 1400 Cat
Notes: The cookbook collection is composed almost entirely of original American works from the 18th century.

DE —WIDENER UNIVERSITY, Delaware Campus Library, Box 7139, Concord Pike, Wilmington, 19803. Jane E Hukill, Library Dir
Holdings: Vols (48,000) Microforms
Notes: Incl food service, restaurants, motels, volume feeding, cookery.

DC —LIBRARY OF CONGRESS, Rare Book & Special Collections Div, Washington, 20540. William Matheson, Chief
Notes: The Katherine Golden Bitting Gastronomic Library. The collection comprises materials on the sources, preparation and consumption of foods from the earliest times to the present day, embracing the whole range of human interest in food. Incl an important 15th century Italian ms, a large number of early French, Italian, English and German works (incl incunabula) and a range of early American cookbooks and works on domestic science. Regional cookbooks and works on the chemistry, bacteriology and preservation of food are strongly represented among titles of more recent date. The majority of the volumes in the collection are described in Mrs Bitting's *Gastronomic Bibliography* (San Francisco, 1939). Also, personal library of Elizabeth Robins Pennell, magazine journalist and wife of artist Joseph Pennell, incl ca 430 cookbooks in English, French and German,16th to 18th century, described in Mrs. Pennell's *My Cookery Books* (Boston, Houghton-Mifflin, 1903).

GA —GEORGIA COLLEGE, Ina Dillard Russell Library, Special Collections Dept, Milledgeville, 31061. Janice C Fennell, Dir of Libraries; Nancy Davis, Special Collections Assoc
Holdings: Vols 700 Cat

IL —GLENVIEW PUBLIC LIBRARY, 1930 Glenview Rd, Glenview, 60025. Peter Bury, Librn
Holdings: Vols (4100) Cat Filmstrips Audiotapes
Notes: Maintained as health and domestic science subject center. Incl 1840 cookbooks.

IN —INDIANA UNIVERSITY, Lilly Library, Seventh St, Bloomington, 47405. William R Cagle, Librn
Holdings: Vols 350 Cat Mss
Notes: Gernon Collection of Eighteenth and Nineteenth Century American Cookbooks. Ms consist of several receipt books, British and American, dating 1660-1917.

IN —INDIANAPOLIS-MARION COUNTY PUBLIC LIBRARY, Business, Science & Technology Div, 40 E Saint Clair St, Indianapolis, 46204. Mark Leggett, Head
Holdings: Vols 400 Cat
Notes: The Wright Marble Collection of Cookbooks and Menus. Menus uncataloged. Restricted use. No photocopying.

IN —MORRISSON-REEVES LIBRARY, 80 N Sixth St, Richmond, 47374. Harriet E Bard, Librn
Holdings: Vols 1100 Cat

KS —KANSAS STATE UNIVERSITY, Library, Special Collections & University Archives, Manhattan, 66506. Antonia Q Pigno, Coordr; John J Vander Velde, Librn; Anthony R Crawford, Univ Archivist
Holdings: Vols 4500 Cat Mss
Budget: ($10,000)
Notes: Cookbooks and related items on home economics, nutrition and domestic economy. Nucleus of the collection is from the Abby Lillian Marlatt collection augmented by a sizable bequest from the estate of Clementine Paddleford. Includes about 600 volumes of rare cookbooks from the 16th, 17th, and 18th centuries as well as unprocessed papers (scrapbooks, recipe files and correspondence of Clementine Paddleford). A chronological bibliography is available for the pre-1900 portion of the collection: *The Kansas State University Receipt Book and Household Manual* (1968) by G A Rudolph.

KY —LOUISVILLE FREE PUBLIC LIBRARY, Fourth & York Sts, Louisville, 40203. Barbara L Pickett, Mgr Reference & Adult Servs
Holdings: Vols 3000 Cat
Notes: Most circulating; some reference.

MD —JOHNS HOPKINS UNIVERSITY, Milton S Eisenhower Library, George Peabody Collection, 17 E Mt Vernon Place, Baltimore, 21201. Lyn Hart, Peabody Librn

MA —RADCLIFFE COLLEGE, Arthur & Elizabeth Schlesinger Library on the History of Women in America, 3 James St, Cambridge, 02138. Patricia Miller King, Dir; Eva Moseley, Cur of Mss
Holdings: Vols 3500 Cat Microforms
Notes: Incl the Samuel and Narcissa Chamberlain Collection; especially strong in US, French, and English cookery, 18th to 20th century. Incl 800 microforms.

MA —OLD STURBRIDGE VILLAGE, Research Library, Sturbridge, 01566. Theresa Rini Percy, Librn
Holdings: Cat Mss
Notes: Northeastern US, some English, mainly 1790-1850.

MA —AMERICAN ANTIQUARIAN SOCIETY LIBRARY, 185 Salisbury St, Worcester, 01609. Marcus A McCorison, Dir & Librn
Holdings: Cat
Notes: The largest collection of American cookbooks to 1860.

MI —DETROIT PUBLIC LIBRARY, Rare Books Department, 5201 Woodward Ave, Detroit, 48202.
Holdings: Vols 3500 Cat
Notes: Emphasis on early English and American cookery. Incl the Fred Sanders Collection. Restricted use. Reference collection.

MI —MICHIGAN STATE UNIVERSITY, Libraries, Special Collections Div, East Lansing, 48824. Jannette Fiore, Librn
Holdings: Vols 1100 Cat
Notes: Works on cookery in English before 1900, including the library of Mary Ross Reynolds, supported by a general collection of current cookery works.

MO —PET INCORPORTED, Information Center, 400 S Fourth St, PO Box 392, Saint Louis, 63166. L R Walton, Corporate Librn
Holdings: Vols 1500 Cat
Notes: Cookery books collection. Many rare items from the 1700s and 1800s. Approx 500 items pre-1920.

NM —THOMAS BRANIGAN MEMORIAL LIBRARY, 200 E Picacho Ave, Las Cruces, 88001. Don Dresp, Dir
Holdings: Cat
Notes: Louise Garrett Collection.

NY —NEW YORK STATE LIBRARY, State Education Bldg Annex, Washington Ave, Albany, 12224.
Notes: Extensive collection of cookbooks representing foreign as well as domestic cookery.

NY —BUFFALO & ERIE COUNTY PUBLIC LIBRARY, Fiction Dept, Lafayette Sq, Buffalo, 14203. Irene Dwigans, Head
Holdings: Vols 4000 Cat
Notes: Comprehensive collection, especially American 19th and 20th century and foreign.

COOKERY AND COOK BOOKS (cont.)

†NY —NEW YORK STATE HISTORICAL ASSOCIATION, Library, Cooperstown, 13326.
Notes: Incl New York Folk Life Archives and the Beaumont Culinary Arts Collection. Noncirculating.

NY —CULINARY INSTITUTE OF AMERICA, Katharine Angell Library, North Rd, Hyde Park, 12538. Gertrude Trani, Asst Librn
Holdings: Vols (23,000) Cat Slides Videotapes 16mm Films Filmstrips
Notes: Culinary arts, incl cookery, beverages, and food service management. AV materials housed in separate Learning Resources Center. Henry Woods, Dir.

NY —CORNELL UNIVERSITY LIBRARIES, Hotel Administration Library, Statler Hall, Ithaca, 14853. Margaret J Oaksford, Librn
Holdings: Vols (25,000) Cat Mss Maps
Budget: ($60,000)
Notes: Extensive collections on management, travel, hotels, food and beverage, wine, real estate and tourism. Incl menu collection.

NY —COLUMBIA UNIVERSITY LIBRARIES, Teachers College, Milbank Memorial Library, 525 W 120 St, New York, 10027. Jane P Franck, Dir
Holdings: Vols 500 Cat
Notes: 18th, 19th and early 20th centuries. Part of Mrs Talcott Williams' private collection.

NY —NEW YORK ACADEMY OF MEDICINE, Library, 2 E 103 St, New York, 10029. Brett A Kirkpatrick, Librn
Holdings: Vols 4000 Cat
Notes: Collection of Margaret Barclay Wilson, MD; one of largest collections on the subject; rare and historical items. Added to selectively incl copy of 9th century mss, De re Culinaria. Also incl 3000 uncat pamphlets, 500 menus, 50 Italian broadsides, 17th-19th centuries food regulations.

NY —NEW YORK PUBLIC LIBRARY, Research Libraries, Science and Technology Research Center, Fifth Ave & 42 St, New York, 10018.
Holdings: Vols (1,100,000) Cat Microforms
Budget: ($647,259)

NY —PAUL SMITHS COLLEGE, Frank L Cubley Library, Paul Smiths, 12970. Theodore Mack, Librn
Holdings: Vols (1000) Cat

NC —UNIVERSITY OF NORTH CAROLINA, GREENSBORO, Walter Clinton Jackson Library, Special Collections Dept, 1000 Spring Garden St, Greensboro, 27412. Emilie W Mills, Librn
Holdings: Vols 120 Cat
Notes: Special emphasis on North Carolina and southern cookery, mostly 19th century.

NC —TECHNICAL INSTITUTE OF ALAMANCE, Learning Resources Center, Jimmy Kerr Rd, PO Box 623, Haw River, 27258. Ron Plummer, Coordr
Holdings: Vols 205 Cat Audiotapes Filmstrips Microforms
Notes: Food preparation specialist training.

OH —AKRON-SUMMIT COUNTY PUBLIC LIBRARY, Science & Technology Div, 55 S Main St, Akron, 44326. Joyce McKnight, Head
Holdings: Vols 2300 Cat
Budget: ($24,000)

OH —PUBLIC LIBRARY OF CINCINNATI & HAMILTON COUNTY, Science & Technology Dept, 800 Vine St, Cincinnati, 45202. Rosemary Gaiser, Head
Holdings: Vols 9000 Cat
Notes: American and foreign cookbooks; specialty cooking.

OH —CASE WESTERN RESERVE UNIVERSITY LIBRARIES, Cleveland, 44106. Susie Hanson, Special Collections Librn
Holdings: Vols 340 Cat
Notes: The Frank Hadley Ginn Collection, a gift of Dr and Mrs W Powell Jones.

OH —CLEVELAND PUBLIC LIBRARY, Science & Technology Dept, 325 Superior Ave, Cleveland, 44114. Jean Z Piety, Head
Holdings: Vols 9000 Cat
Notes: American, regional, and foreign cookbooks; historical material, gastronomy.

OH —GRANDVIEW HEIGHTS PUBLIC LIBRARY, 1685 W First Ave, Columbus, 43212. Kathryn M Hannon, Librn
Holdings: Vols (1809) Cat

OH —OHIO STATE UNIVERSITY, Home Economics Library, Campbell Hall Rm 325, 1787 Neil Ave, Columbus, 43210. Neosha Mackey, Librn
Holdings: Vols (14,000) Cat Microforms
Notes: Separate catalog. Also, book catalog: *Catalog of the Home Economics Library* (Boston: G K Hall, 1976), 3 vols.

OK —TULSA CITY-COUNTY LIBRARY, Business & Technology Dept, 400 Civic Center, Tulsa, 74103. Craig Buthod, Head
Holdings: Vols 175 Cat

PA —DREXEL UNIVERSITY LIBRARIES, W W Hagerty Library, 32 & Chestnut Sts, Philadelphia, 19104. R L Snyder, Dir
Holdings: Vols (5000) Cat
Budget: ($9000)
Notes: Food technology and management with emphasis on nutrition. Also incl collection of cookbooks which stress cultural differences and the best in sound American cooking.

RI —JOHNSON AND WALES COLLEGE, Hospitality Center, 1150 Narragansett Blvd, Cranston, 02905. Margaret A Thomas, Librn
Holdings: Vols (8000) / /
Budget: ($15,000)
Notes: The Paul Fritzsche Cookbook Collection, incl more than 8000 cookbooks, with some rare and valuable items. Many 19th and early 20th century items; particularly strong in fund raising cookbooks. Collection is partially cataloged.

TX —ABILENE CHRISTIAN UNIVERSITY, Margaret & Herman Brown Library, ACU Sta, Abilene, 79601. Callie Faye Milliken, Assoc Dir
Notes: The Burnya Mae Moore Cookbook Collection.

TX —TEXAS WOMAN'S UNIVERSITY, Bralley Memorial Library, Box 23715, TWU Sta, Denton, 76204. Metta Nicewarner, Spec Collections Libn
Holdings: Vols 10,000 Cat
Notes: Incl Mrs Thomas M Scruggs and Margaret Cook Cookery and Gastronomy Library (75 percent); Marion S Church Collection of Cookbooks and Menus; materials on general American cookery, foreign ethnic, and regional cookery; and cookbooks from Italy and Germany.

WI —UNIVERSITY OF WISCONSIN, MADISON, College of Agricultural & Life Sciences, Steenbock Memorial Library, 550 Babcock Dr, Madison, 53706. Jan Kennedy, Dir
Holdings: Vols (186,312) Cat Docs
Notes: Collection supports the School of Family Resources and Consumer Sciences in areas of textiles and fashion design, interior decorating, consumer science, and nutrition; USDA documents and experiment station publications. Incl the Levitan Cookbook Collection, one of the 10 largest cookbook collections in the US, containing some 2615 volumes (given to the library in 1965 by Mortimer Levitan).

WI —UNIVERSITY OF WISCONSIN-STOUT, Library Learning Center, Menomonie, 54751. Philip Sawin Jr, Coll Develop Librn
Notes: Extensive collection in Cookery. This is one of the first collections to be developed to support the Institute of Domestic Science in 1883. In 1960 the University offered a graduate degree in Food Science and Nutrition. University of Wisconsin-Stout School of Home Economics currently has the largest enrollment in the United States.

WI —MILWAUKEE PUBLIC LIBRARY, 814 W Wisconsin Ave, Milwaukee, 53233. Donald J Sager, City Librn
Holdings: Vols 13,000 Cat
Notes: Extensive collection with wide scope, international & American cookery; organic, vegetable, fish, beer, etc, cookery; cookery for institutions; recipe, clippings and pamphlet files. Also, Breta Griem Culinary Arts Collection, 1573 vols, emphasis on American Regional Cookery. Reference only, 1673 vols.

ON —METROPOLITAN TORONTO LIBRARY, Science & Technology Dept, 789 Yonge St, Toronto, M4W 2G8, Can. Margaret Walshe, Head
Holdings: Vols (120,000) Cat VF
Notes: All aspects of technology for the specialist, the student, and the general public. The department gives high priority to Canadian material, but houses a collection of international materials.

COOKINGHAM, PERRY

MO —UNIVERSITY OF MISSOURI-KANSAS CITY, General Library, State Historical Society of Missouri Manuscripts, 5100 Rockhill Road, Kansas City, 64110. Kenneth J LaBudde, Dir; Gordon Hendrickson, Assoc Dir
Holdings: Mss
Notes: Western Historical Manuscript Collection incl papers of Charles B Wheeler, Jr, Charles N Kimball, Arthur Mag, Oscar D Nelson, Lou B Holland, J C Nichols, Perry Cookingham, Blevins Davis, Daniel MacMorris, and the records of the Kansas City Board of Trade.

COOKSON, CATHERINE

MA —BOSTON UNIVERSITY, Mugar Memorial Library, Special Collections Dept, 771 Commonwealth Ave, Boston, 02215. Howard B Gotlieb, Dir
Holdings: Cat Mss
Notes: Mss, correspondence, etc collected in depth; incl publications by or about.

COOLIDGE, BALDWIN

MA —SOCIETY FOR THE PRESERVATION OF NEW ENGLAND ANTIQUITIES, Library, 141 Cambridge St, Boston, 02114. Ellie Reichlin, Librn & Cur of Photographic Collections
Holdings: Cat Pix

COOLIDGE, CALVIN

DC —LIBRARY OF CONGRESS, Manuscript Division, Washington, 20540. John C Broderick, Chief
Notes: The Presidential Papers collection incl the papers, etc, of numerous Presidents.

MA —STATE LIBRARY OF MASSACHUSETTS, 341 State House, Boston, 02133. Gaspar Caso, State Librn
Holdings: Vols (750) Cat Mss Pix

MA —FORBES LIBRARY, 20 West St, Northampton, 01060. Lawrence E Wikander, Cur
Holdings: Vols 4000 Cat Mss Maps Pix Slides Microforms
Budget: $200
Notes: Collection incl portraits, cartoons, furniture, Indian gear, and other memorabilia.

MA —COLLEGE OF THE HOLY CROSS, Dinand Library, College St, Worcester, 01610. James M Mahoney, Cur of Special Collection
Notes: Frank W Stearns, Boston merchant, political advisor to Calvin Coolidge. Collection contains correspondence (282 letters), during period 1919-1923. Also (36) letters from Calvin Coolidge to him; scrapbooks. Restricted use; noncirculating.

COOLIDGE, CLARK, 1939-

CA —UNIVERSITY OF CALIFORNIA, LOS ANGELES, Research Library, Dept of Special Collections, 405 Hilgard Ave, Los Angeles, 90024. Edward Shreeves, Chairman, Bibliographers Group; David S Zeidberg, Head
Notes: 1.5 linear feet of correspondence with other poets and writers.

COOLIDGE, ELIZABETH SPRAGUE

DC —LIBRARY OF CONGRESS, Music Division, Washington, 20540.
Notes: Elizabeth Sprague Coolidge Foundation Collection incl music mss of 20th century chamber music and her papers and photographs.

COOLING APPLIANCES see Refrigeration and Refrigerating Machinery

COOPER, ASHLEY, 1621-1683

SC —COLLEGE OF CHARLESTON LIBRARY, Special Collections Dept,

COOPER, ASHLEY, 1621-1683 (cont.)

Charleston, 29401.
Notes: Papers, 1667, contains a receipt for money paid to a diocese in England, and an order by Ashley Cooper to pay a pension to the Duke of York.

COOPER, JAMES FENIMORE

CT —YALE UNIVERSITY, Box 1603A, Yale Station, New Haven, 06520.
Holdings: Cat Mss

MA —AMERICAN ANTIQUARIAN SOCIETY LIBRARY, 185 Salisbury St, Worcester, 01609. Marcus A McCorison, Dir & Librn
Notes: One of the best Cooper collections, and cosponsor of a project to produce a definitive edition of his works.

NY —BUFFALO & ERIE COUNTY PUBLIC LIBRARY, Rare Book Room, Lafayette Sq, Buffalo, 14203. William H Loos, Cur
Notes: First editions.

VA —UNIVERSITY OF VIRGINIA, Alderman Library, Clifton Waller Barrett Collection, Charlottesville, 22901. Joan St C Crane, Cur of American Literature Collections
Holdings: Vols 333 Cat Mss
Notes: Most of his mss, original mss "The Pathfinder", original mss "Two Admirals", fragment of original mss "A Float and Ashore", English, French, Dutch and American editions of original mss "Mercedes of Castile", fragment of original mss "Water Witch".

COOPER, JAMIE LEE

MA —BOSTON UNIVERSITY, Mugar Memorial Library, Special Collections Dept, 771 Commonwealth Ave, Boston, 02215. Howard B Gotlieb, Dir
Holdings: Cat Mss

COOPER, JOHN SHERMAN

KY —UNIVERSITY OF KENTUCKY, Margaret I King Library, Dept of Special Collections, Lexington, 40506. William Marshall, Head
Holdings: Cat Mss Pix Audiotapes Films
Notes: Incl 997 boxes. Cooper served as Pulaski County, Ky. judge during the Depression and in 1946 won his first race for the US Senate. In 1955, he was appointed ambassador to India and Nepal by President Eisenhower, but returned to the US to run for the Senate in 1956. The papers deal almost exclusively with Cooper's Senate career. Period covered: 1944-77. Unpublished inventory.

COOPER, LOYD

CA —POMONA PUBLIC LIBRARY, Special Collections, 625 S Garey Ave, PO Box 2271, Pomona, 91766. David Streeter, Librn
Holdings: Cat
Notes: Together, about 100,000 photographs. Burton Frasher collection, 60,000 negatives and prints of California, Arizona, New Mexico, Colorado, Utah, and Nevada, 1920-1940; Loyd Cooper collection, 20,000 negatives and prints of California, 1920-1940; Brooking Tatum, 125 color prints, 50 color 35mm transparencies of California flora; Percy Everett, 4000 color 35mm transparencies of world travels, 1960s.

COOPERAGE see Coopers and Cooperage

COOPERATION, AGRICULTURAL see Agriculture, Cooperative

COOPERATION, INTERNATIONAL see International Cooperation

COOPERATION, MEDICAL see Medical Cooperation

COOPERATIVE AGRICULTURE see Agriculture, Cooperative

COOPERATIVE ASSOCIATIONS see Cooperative Societies

CO-OPERATIVE COMMONWEALTH FEDERATION, ONTARIO (CCF)

ON —UNIVERSITY OF TORONTO, Thomas Fisher Rare Book Library, 120 Saint George St, Toronto, M5S 1A5, Can. Richard G Landon, Head
Holdings: Vols 700 Cat Mss Audiotapes
Notes: Woodsworth Collection fo books, pamphlets, and broadsides relating to the history of socialist and labour movements in Canada with particular emphasis on the CCF party in Ontario. Presented by the Ontario Woodsworth Memorial Foundation and designated as part of its official archives. Ms material from the files of the Ontario Woodsworth House in Toronto, and from former party members. Incl some private papers.

COOPERATIVE DISTRIBUTION see Cooperative Societies

COOPERATIVE PRODUCTION see Cooperative Societies

COOPERATIVE SOCIETIES

CA —CLAREMONT COLLEGES, Honnold Library, Ninth & Dartmouth, Claremont, 91711. Tania Rizzo, Special Collections Dept Head
Holdings: Vols 200 Cat Mss Pix
Notes: The papers of former Democratic Congressman Jerry Voorhis, from the 1930s to present, occupying nearly 100 document boxes. The papers reflect his life and career, incl biographical material, the history of the Voorhis School for Boys, his involvement in the Dies Committee, and his wide-ranging interests in American economic and social issues, such as cooperatives, monopolies and cartels, Latin American relations, consumers, and senior citizens. Books by and about him, with research files. Correspondence with political leaders. Inventory available. Restricted use.

IL —NEWBERRY LIBRARY, 60 W Walton St, Chicago, 60610. Diana Haskell, Cur of Modern Mss
Holdings: Cat
Notes: American cooperative communities.

IL —UNIVERSITY OF ILLINOIS, URBANA/CHAMPAIGN, Library, Illinois Historical Survey Library, 1408 W Gregory Dr, 1A Library, Urbana, 61801.
Holdings: Vols 50 Cat Mss Maps Pix Microforms
Notes: Communitarianism in America. The ms material, contained in 30 separate collections (10 cubic feet), concentrates on the period 1840-70. It incl correspondence, records, minutes, ledgers and diaries. Communal societies such as Bishop Hill, Brook Farm, New Harmony, the North American Phalanx and the Sodus Bay Phalanx are represented. Among the correspondents are Albert Brisbane, Parke Godwin, Sarah Grimke, Richard Owen, Robert Owen, Robert Dale Owen, and George Ripley. Numerous pictures. Guide to the collections published in 1976.

MD —PRINCE GEORGE'S COUNTY MEMORIAL LIBRARY SYSTEM, Greenbelt Branch Library, 11 Crescent Rd, Greenbelt, 20770. Harriet Ying, Branch Librn
Holdings: Vols (120) Cat Mss Maps Pix Microforms

MI —UNIVERSITY OF MICHIGAN, Dept of Rare Books & Special Collections, Ann Arbor, 48109. Edward C Weber, Head, Labadie Collection
Holdings: Vols (40,000) Cat Mss Microforms
Notes: Largely confined to US communities after the middle of the 19th century.

MI —SUOMI COLLEGE, Finnish-American Historical Archives, Hancock, 49930. Kenneth Niemi, Archives Librn
Notes: Collection incl 8000 vols, 152,000 mss, 2000 photographs, 760 audiotapes; microforms and maps; 14,000 holdings are cataloged. Subject interests: coop movement, labor, pioneer library of rare books and church records, socialist and communist movements, temperance societies. Special Collections: Finnish language newspapers (includes 100 titles from 1876-present); Suomi Synod Archives; Finnish-American Oral History.

PA —TEMPLE UNIVERSITY LIBRARIES, Special Collections Dept, Contemporary Culture Collection, Philadelphia, 19122. Patricia J Case, Cur
Notes: The Contemporary Culture Collection. See full entry under US-Social Life and Customs.

WI —UNIVERSITY OF WISCONSIN, GREEN BAY, Library/Learning Center, Green Bay, 54301. Marian A Gould, Acting Dir, Special Collections/University Archives
Holdings: Vols 700 // Cat
Notes: This represents the collection of Leon Kramer, "idealist, philosophical anarchist and bookseller." Much of the material concerns radical literature and small socialist and communist parties in the US, although there is a considerable amount of books, booklets, and pamphlets published in Germany, Italy, and other parts of Europe. Incl uncounted pamphlets.

WI —UNIVERSITY OF WISCONSIN, MADISON, College of Agricultural & Life Sciences, Steenbock Memorial Library, 550 Babcock Dr, Madison, 53706. Jan Kennedy, Dir
Holdings: Vols (186,312) Cat Docs
Notes: Major collection of farm and herrd management, production and marketing.

COOPERATIVE SOCIETIES, AGRICULTURAL see Agriculture, Cooperative

COOPERATIVE STORES see Cooperative Societies

COOPERS AND COOPERAGE

MA —OLD STURBRIDGE VILLAGE, Research Library, Sturbridge, 01566. Theresa Rini Percy, Librn
Holdings: Cat Mss
Notes: New England, to 1860.

COOPERSMITH, JACOB M.

†MD —UNIVERSITY OF MARYLAND, Library, Coopersmith Collection, College Park, 20742. Frederic A Heutte, Head, Music Room
Holdings: Vols 2000 Cat
Notes: The working library of the late Jacob Coopersmith, a specialist in the music of Handel.

MI —UNIVERSITY OF MICHIGAN, School of Music, Music Library, Moore Bldg, Ann Arbor, 48109. Peggy Daub, Head
Holdings: // Uncat Mss Pix Slides Microforms
Notes: The Coopersmith Handel Collection. A unique collection of the late J M Coopersmith containing music, facsimiles, photostats, letters, microfilms, slides, and extensive bibliographic records relating to Dr Coopersmith's Handelian scholarship. Included in the collection are records of his investigation of Leclair.

COPE, EDWARD DRINKER

NY —AMERICAN MUSEUM OF NATURAL HISTORY, Library Services Dept, Central Park W & 79th St, New York, 10024. Nina J Root, Chairwoman; Mary Genett, Asst Librn for Reference Services
Holdings: Cat Mss Maps Pix Slides 16mm Films
Notes: Manuscripts, diaries, correspondence, artifacts, some art work, and collected materials. Not all cataloged as of 1983.

COPE, ELMER F.

OH —OHIO HISTORICAL SOCIETY, Archives Library Division, 1982 Velma Ave, Columbus, 43211. Dennis East, Division Chief
Notes: His papers.

COPE, THOMAS DARLINGTON, 1880-1964

PA —UNIVERSITY OF PENNSYLVANIA, University Archives, North Arcade Franklin

COPE, THOMAS DARLINGTON, 1880-1964 (cont.)

Field E-6, Philadelphia, 19104. Francis James Dallett, University Archivist
Holdings: 3 Boxes
Notes: His papers (1926-1960).

COPEAU, JACQUES

ON —MCMASTER UNIVERSITY, Mills Memorial Library, Div of Archives & Research Collections, Hamilton, L8S 4L6, Can. G R Hill, Univ Librn
Holdings: // Mss
Notes: Correspondence between Jacques Copeau and Andre Obey concerning the French theatre, 1924-1945.

COPEPODA

DC —SMITHSONIAN INSTITUTION LIBRARIES, Natural History Branch, Washington, 20560. Sylvia Churgin, Chief Librn
Holdings: Cat Mss Maps Pix Slides Microforms
Notes: Invertebrate zoology, Systematics. Incl crustacea, echinoderms, mollusks, worms, Cushman collection of foraminifera; Springer collection on crinoids; Wilson collection on copepoda.

COPERNICUS

ON —UNIVERSITY OF TORONTO, Thomas Fisher Rare Book Library, 120 Saint George St, Toronto, M5S 1A5, Can. Richard G Landon, Head
Holdings: Vols 300 Cat
Notes: Stillman Drake Galileo Collection. Comprises early editions of Galileo, of his precursors (Ptolemy and Copernicus) and of his contemporaries in the fields of astronomy and physical science. Also, the Science Collection is especially rich in works on Renaissance astronomy, physics and mechanics and has noteworthy holdings of works of English experimental scientists in the 17th and 18th centuries with excellent collections for the works of Robert Boyle, Robert Hooke, and Sir Isaac Newton. Includes virtually all important early editions of Euclid; alchemical works of the 18th century chemists like Lavoisier and Priestly; works on agriculture with special emphasis on British agriculture in the 18th century; and a variety of other worksimportant in the history of science in all its branches. In addition the Fisher Library has many other specialized scientific collections which are listed separately.

COPIERS see Photocopiers

COPLAND, AARON

DC —LIBRARY OF CONGRESS, Music Division, Washington, 20540.
Notes: Mss in Koussevitzky Archives.

COPPARD, ALFRED EDGAR

IL —ILLINOIS STATE UNIVERSITY, Milner Library, Dept of Special Collections, Normal, 61761. Robert Sokan, Librn
Notes: First editions, limited editions, ephemera, etc.

COPPEL, ALFRED

MA —BOSTON UNIVERSITY, Mugar Memorial Library, Special Collections Dept, 771 Commonwealth Ave, Boston, 02215. Howard B Gotlieb, Dir
Holdings: Cat Mss

COPPER

ON —RIO ALGOM LIMITED, Library, 120 Adelaide St W, Toronto, M5H 1W5, Can. Penny Lipman, Librn
Holdings: Vols (1500) Cat
Budget: ($7000)
Notes: Espec mining of uranium and copper; geology; mining methods; nuclear energy.

COPPER ENGRAVING see Engravers, Engraving and Engravings

COPPER INDUSTRY AND TRADE—HISTORY

NY —NEW YORK HISTORICAL SOCIETY, Library, 170 Central Park W, New York, 10024. James Gregory, Librn
Holdings: Cat Mss
Notes: The Hendricks Collection traces the development of the copper industry in the US, and reflects the life of an old and prominent Sephardic family.

COPPER MINES AND MINING

AZ —NORTHERN ARIZONA UNIVERSITY, Special Collection Library, CU Box 6022, Flagstaff, 86011. Peter M Whiteley, Coordr/Archivist; William Mullane, Librn
Holdings: Uncat Mss
Notes: United Verde Copper Company (190 feet) and Phelps Dodge mining record books and files of day-to-day mining operations, 1900-1952. Also, Samuel Hill Collection incl receipts of the United Verde Copper Company from Samuel Hill Hardware, Prescott, Ariz, 1891.

MI —MICHIGAN TECHNOLOGICAL UNIVERSITY, Archives, Copper County Historical Collections, Houghton, 49931. Theresa Sanderson Spence, University Archivist
Holdings: Vols (1500) Cat Mss Maps Pix Slides Microforms
Notes: Michigan-Copper Country. Description of collection in *Michigan* Chronicle, 1st quarter, 1973. Accession lists are available for some of the collections. The collecting program embraces the university and all areas of the economic, cultural and social life of the people and institutions of the Copper Country (Baraga, Houghton, Keweenaw, and Ontonogan Counties). Special strength is in the mining history and mining company reports. Personal and business records, maps and photographs, broadsides, family histories, newspapers and oral materials as well as slides and film have been collected. Extensive holdings in area newspapers. As a regional depository for the state archives, provides access to a variety of research materials covering the Western Upper Peninsula. Also, Kenweenaw Historical Society Collection, see *Michigan History Magazine*, vol 1(1917), 129-155.

COPTIC CHURCH

DC —CATHOLIC UNIVERSITY OF AMERICA, Mullen Library, ICOR/Semitics Library, Room 20, Washington, 20064. Monica J Blanchard, Librn
Notes: The bulk of the ICOR/Semitics Library collection belongs to the Institute of Christian Oriental Research which supports the work of the Corpus Scriptorum Christianorum Orientalium. The holdings are chiefly concerned with Christian Egypt and the Coptic Church, Syriac and Syrian patristic studies, and the Syriac and Arabic speaking eastern churches. There are less extensive holdings of Ethiopic, Armenian and Georgian material. ICOR titles are cataloged by the ICOR/Semitic Library, and ICOR holdings do not appear in the general catalogue of the University Library.

COPTIC LANGUAGE AND LITERATURE

NY —NEW YORK PUBLIC LIBRARY, Oriental Div, Fifth Ave & 42 St, New York, 10018. E Christian Filstrup, Chief
Holdings: Cat Mss Microforms
Budget: ($56,455)
Notes: Published catalog of holdings.

COPTIC MAGIC see Magic, Coptic

COPYBOOKS see Penmanship; Writing

COPYING PROCESSES see Photocopying Processes

COPYRIGHT

DC —LIBRARY OF CONGRESS, Rare Book & Special Collections Div, Washington, 20540. William Matheson, Chief
Notes: The state district court ledgers recorded copyright claims for books, maps, prints, and photographs from 1790-1870. The date of registration, claimant and title are given for each entry. The title pages were deposited during the same period by authors and publishers as evidence of their intent to publish the registered work. See G Thomas Tanselle's "Copyright Records and the Bibliographer" in vol 22 of *Studies in* Bibliography.

NY —COLUMBIA UNIVERSITY LIBRARIES, Law School Library, Law Building, 435 W 116 St, New York, 10027. James L Hoover, Librn
Holdings: Vols (735,000) Cat
Notes: Incl substantial special collections in foreign and international law; also copyright law, ecclesiastical and medieval law; Roman law.

OH —PUBLIC LIBRARY OF CINCINNATI & HAMILTON COUNTY, Science & Technology Dept, 800 Vine St, Cincinnati, 45202. Rosemary Gaiser, Head
Notes: Depository for US Copyright Office publications. Noncirculating.

CORBETT, ELIZABETH

MA —BOSTON UNIVERSITY, Mugar Memorial Library, Special Collections Dept, 771 Commonwealth Ave, Boston, 02215. Howard B Gotlieb, Dir
Holdings: // Cat Mss Pix
Notes: Mss, correspondence, etc collected in depth; incl publications by or about.

CORBIN, EDYTHE PATTEN

DC —GEORGETOWN UNIVERSITY, Library, Special Collections Div, 37 & O Sts NW, Washington, 20057. George M Barringer, Special Collections Librn; Nicholas B Sheetz, Mss Librn
Holdings: Mss Cat
Notes: Correspondence written to Edythe Patten Corbin, prominent Washington socialite and wife of General Henry Clark Corbin. Extensive correspondence, spanning numerous years, is incl from William Howard Taft, Philip Bunau-Varilla, Myron T Herrick, General John Pershing, and Elihu Root, among others. The correspondence contains extensive discussions of national and international affairs.

LE CORBUSIER (CHARLES EDOUARD JEANNERET-GRIS)

MA —HARVARD UNIVERSITY, Graduate School of Design, Frances Loeb Library, Gund Hall, Cambridge, 02138. James Hodgson, Librn
Holdings: Cat Mss Pix Slides Microforms
Notes: Complete documentation of the architect is attempted.

CORDES, MR. AND MRS. HENRY E.

AZ —NORTHERN ARIZONA UNIVERSITY, Special Collection Library, CU Box 6022, Flagstaff, 86011. Peter M Whiteley, Coordr/Archivist; William Mullane, Librn
Notes: Cordes, Ariz, postal records, 1887-1916. Sterling Gold Mining Corporation, financial records, 1930's, family photos.

CORDES, JOHN

SC —COLLEGE OF CHARLESTON LIBRARY, Special Collections Dept, Charleston, 29401.
Notes: Contains the account book of the John Cordes estate, 1764-1798. Incl within is a family history for the years 1695-1728.

CORE CURRICULUM see Education—Curricula

CORELLI, MARIE, 1855-1924

CA —CLAREMONT COLLEGES, Ella Strong Denison Library, Scripps College,

CORELLI, MARIE, 1855-1924 (cont.)

Claremont, 91711. Judy Harvey Sahak, Librn
Holdings: Vols 27 Cat Mss
Notes: In addition to books, the Corelli Collection includes approximately 100 ALS, pamphlets with presentation inscriptions, autographed typescripts, photographs, many letters to her editors, telegrams, and corrected proofs of articles.

CA —UNIVERSITY OF CALIFORNIA, LOS ANGELES, Research Library, Dept of Special Collections, 405 Hilgard Ave, Los Angeles, 90024. Edward Shreeves, Chairman, Bibliographers Group; David S Zeidberg, Head
Holdings: Vols 50 Cat Mss Pix
Notes: 50 first and other editions of her books; 1 linear foot of her letters to various persons.

CORLE, EDWIN, 1906-1956

CA —FRANCIS BACON LIBRARY, 655 N Dartmouth Ave, Claremont, 91711. Elizabeth S Wrigley, Dir
Holdings: Mss Pix
Notes: Arensberg's miscellaneous correspondence with American literary figures (1920's-50's) including Bruce Bliven, Catherine Drinker Bowen, Kay Boyle, Witter Bynner, Edwin Corle, Helen A Keller, Lysander Kemp, Kenneth Macgowan, John Macy, Henry Miller, Lewis Mumford, Clifford Odets, Kenneth Patchen, Irving Stone, and William Carlos Williams.

CA —UNIVERSITY OF CALIFORNIA, LOS ANGELES, Research Library, Dept of Special Collections, 405 Hilgard Ave, Los Angeles, 90024. Edward Shreeves, Chairman, Bibliographers Group; David S Zeidberg, Head
Notes: 2.5 linear feet of mss and books; correspondence with various writers.

CORLISS, GEORGE HENRY, 1817-1888

RI —BROWN UNIVERSITY, John Hay Library, 20 Prospect St, Providence, 02912. Mark N Brown, Cur Mss
Holdings: // Mss Pix
Notes: 500 mss and typescripts, 1838 to 1880, of George Henry Corliss, mechanical engineer, inventor, and manufacturer of the Corliss Steam Engine. Incl professional and business correspondence, patent specifications, and contracts relating to the engineering firms with which he was associated. The original collection was a gift of Mr K Brooke Anderson in 1946 and was supplemented by a deposit from the Baker Library. Harvard University.

CORMAN, CID

IN —INDIANA UNIVERSITY, Lilly Library, Seventh St, Bloomington, 47405. William R Cagle, Librn
Holdings: // Cat Mss
Notes: Letters to Cid Corman from Robert Creeley, 1949-1955. 300 items. Also editorial office records of *Origin*, second series, no 1-12, 1960-1962.

MA —BOSTON UNIVERSITY, Mugar Memorial Library, Special Collections Dept, 771 Commonwealth Ave, Boston, 02215. Howard B Gotlieb, Dir
Holdings: Cat Mss

MO —WASHINGTON UNIVERSITY, Libraries, Special Collections Dept, Campus Box 1061, St Louis, 63130.
Notes: A small but significant collection.

BC —SIMON FRASER UNIVERSITY, Library, Burnaby, V5A 1S6, Can. Percilla Groves, Special Collections Librn
Holdings: Cat Mss
Notes: Eighty-three letters and 58 postcards from the poet Louis Zukofsky to poet and editor Cid Corman, with Corman's marginal notes on some pieces.

CORN

IL —ILLINOIS FARM BUREAU LIBRARY, 1701 Towanda Ave, PO Box 1901, Bloomington, 61701. Rue E Olson, Librn
Holdings: Vols (24,000) Cat Microforms
Budget: ($25,000)
Notes: Emphasis on Illinois.

IA —IOWA STATE UNIVERSITY, Library, Dept of Special Collections, Ames, 50011. Stanley M Yates, Head
Notes: Papers of Roswell Garst, Iowa's most famous farmer. Initiator of experimental feeding of corncobs to produce beef, use of hybrid seedcorn, and commercial fertilizers. Credited with opening of agricultural sales and exchanges with Russia in the 1950s.

MI —MICHIGAN STATE UNIVERSITY, Libraries, Special Collections Div, East Lansing, 48824. Jannette Fiore, Librn
Holdings: // Mss Pix
Notes: Publications, mss, personal correspondence and scrapbooks of Perry G Holden, relating to the development of hybrid corn.

OH —OHIO AGRICULTURAL RESEARCH & DEVELOPMENT CENTER, Dept of Plant Pathology, Madison Ave, Wooster, 44691. Richard M Ritter
Holdings: Vols 2000 Papers Journal Reprints
Notes: Maize viruses and corn stunt. The Maize Virus Information Service (Mavis) was started in 1971 and aims to become the world center for this literature. The collection aims to be exhaustive for all true virus diseases affecting the maize plant (corn) and for corn stunt, which is caused by a mycoplasma, but was once thought to be caused by a virus. A preliminary list (500 refs) was published in 1971, with yearly supplements.

CORN—DISEASES see Corn Stunt; Grain—Diseases and Pests

CORN LAWS (GREAT BRITAIN)

IN —PURDUE UNIVERSITY LIBRARIES, Graduate School of Management, Krannert Library, West Lafayette, 47907. Gordon Law, Librn
Notes: An important resource at the Krannert Library is its Special Collection of Business and Economics, consisting of some 8000 rare pre-20th century strengths in books, journals, tracts and pamphlets covering primarily the early literature of economic thought and business practices in America and abroad, 1500-1870. A catalog was issued in 1979.

MA —HARVARD UNIVERSITY LIBRARY, Cambridge, 02138.
Holdings: Cat

CORN STUNT

OH —OHIO AGRICULTURAL RESEARCH & DEVELOPMENT CENTER, Dept of Plant Pathology, Madison Ave, Wooster, 44691. Richard M Ritter
Holdings: Vols 2000 Papers Journal Reprints
Notes: Maize viruses and corn stunt. The Maize Virus Information Service (Mavis) was started in 1971 and aims to become the world center for this literature. The collection aims to be exhaustive for all true virus diseases affecting the maize plant (corn) and for corn stunt, which is caused by a mycoplasma, but was once thought to be caused by a virus. A preliminary list (500 refs) was published in 1971, with yearly supplements.

CORNEILLE, PIERRE

CA —UNIVERSITY OF CALIFORNIA, LOS ANGELES, William Andrews Clark Memorial Library, 2520 Cimarron St, Los Angeles, 90018.
Holdings: Cat
Notes: Original editions.

CORNELL, JOSEPH

DC —SMITHSONIAN INSTITUTION, National Museum of American Art & the National Portrait Gallery Library, Eighth & F Sts, NW, Washington, 20560. Cecilia Chin, Librn

CORNELL, KATHARINE

NY —NEW YORK PUBLIC LIBRARY, Performing Arts Research Center, Billy Rose Theatre Collection, 111 Amsterdam Ave, New York, 10023. Dorothy L Swerdlove, Cur
Holdings: Cat Mss Pix
Notes: Papers, scrapbooks, mss, photographs, memorabilia, etc.

CORNERS, COMMERCIAL see Speculation; Stock Exchanges

CORNET MUSIC

NH —MANCHESTER HISTORIC ASSOCIATION, Library, 129 Amherst St, Manchester, 03104. Elizabeth Lessard, Librn
Holdings: Vols 45// Cat
Notes: 45 band instrument books used by members of cornet band. The band books are part of the Walter Dignam Collection of Music. Dignam was a noted band leader of the 1840s and 1850s and his band accompanied the 4th New Hampshire Volunteer Regiment to the Civil War in 1863.

WI —UNIVERSITY OF WISCONSIN, MADISON, Memorial Library, Rare Books Collection, 728 State St, Madison, 53706. Gretchen Lagana, Cur
Holdings: Vols (12)// Mss Pix
Notes: Mss, part books, and photographs of the Brodhead Wisconsin Silver Cornet Band which, during the latter parts of the Civil War, formed the band of the 1st Brigade, 3rd Division, 15th Army Corp, which marched across Georgia with General Sherman.
Restricted use: Dept of Rare Books and Special Collections.

CORNISH LANGUAGE AND LITERATURE

IL —NEWBERRY LIBRARY, 60 W Walton St, Chicago, 60610. Diana Haskell, Cur of Modern Mss
Holdings: Cat Maps
Notes: The bulk of the collection (about 15, 000 vols) is in the Prince Lucien Bonaparte group, which deals with western European linguistics. In this group the major rare categories are Etruscan and Basque linguistic studies, although the bulk of the group treats the major European languages and their dialects, ie French, German, English, Spanish, Italian and Russian. There is also strong representation in Gaelic linguistics, particularly Irish, Cornish, Welsh and Manx. In other collections of the library, there are major groups of books and mss dealing with American Indian languages and Philippine languages (about 4500 books and mss).

CORNPLANTER AND JESSE CORNPLANTER

NY —NEW YORK STATE LIBRARY, State Education Bldg Annex, Washington Ave, Albany, 12224.
Holdings: Vols 110,500 Cat
Notes: Strong collection emphasis on North American Indians, especially Indians of New York. Incl books and pamphlets on Indian captivities, treaties, conferences, lives of noted Indians, laws. Bibles and catechisms, prayerbooks, grammars, etc in native languages. Outstanding collection on Iroquois Indians. Incl original treaties between the State of New York and the Iroquois, drawings by Jesse Cornplanter.

CORONA, BERT

CA —STANFORD UNIVERSITY LIBRARIES, Cecil H Green Library, Stanford, 94305. Michael T Ryan, Cur
Notes: Papers of Ernesto Galarza, Bert Corona, Manuel Ruiz, Jr, Eduardo Queredo, Edward Valenzuela.

CORONA DISCHARGE PHOTOGRAPHY see Kirlian Photography

CORONADO, FRANCISCO VAZQUEZ DE

TX —PANHANDLE-PLAINS HISTORICAL MUSEUM, Research Center, Box 967, WT

CORONADO, FRANCISCO VAZQUEZ DE (cont.)

Sta, Canyon, 79016. Claire R Kuehn, Archivist-Librn
Notes: History of the Spanish Southwest Collection. 23 reels of microfilm (100 ft each). Microfilm copies of correspondence, reports and miscellaneous documents and maps from the Archivo General de Indias, Seville, Spain, Museo Naval, Madrid, archives in Mexico and other Latin American countries, dealing with the expedition of Francisco Vazquez de Coronado.

CORONATIONS

RI —BROWN UNIVERSITY, John Hay Library, Anne S K Brown Military Collection, 20 Prospect St, Providence, 02912. Richard B Harrington, Cur
Holdings: Vols (40,000) Cat Mss Pix
Notes: The Anne S K Brown Military Collection has been formed over the past forty or more years by Mrs John Nicholas Brown, now of Newport, and contains approximately 40,000 volumes and 60,000 prints, drawings and watercolors as well as a number of oil paintings and about 5000 miniature model soldiers. At its beginning (and still today) the emphasis or focus of this collection has been upon the history of, and the accurate contemporary illustration of, military and naval uniforms of all nations from the early XVII century to the present. In the course of time, however, the collection has come to incl also a vast and related amount of material on military and naval history, military and naval arts and tactics, wars, campaigns, ceremonies, biography, portraits and caricatures of this and earlier periods. It has been probably the largest private collection of such a nature inthe world, and it contains much ms and graphic documentation which is unique. It has been useful to numerous scholars and historians, editors, filmmakers and publishers for research and for illustrative material and has also contributed to many museum exhibitions. In 1982 the entire collection, with its complete card catalog and subject index, has been presented to Brown University, where it is located in the John Hay Library. Special requests are taken care of by phone, mail and appointments with the curator.

CORPORATION LAW

CA —HELLER, EHRMAN, WHITE & MCAULIFFE, Library, 44 Montgomery St, San Francisco, 94104. Loretta Mak, Librn
Holdings: Vols (22,500) Cat Audiotapes
Notes: A private library serving 150 attorneys. Emphasis on the areas of taxation, trial practice and corporation laws.

OH —MARATHON OIL CO, Law Library, 539 S Main St, Room 854-M, Findlay, 45840. Durand S Dudley, Sr Law Librn
Holdings: Vols (18,000) Cat
Budget: ($100,000)
Notes: Library serves the informational needs of the staff attorneys of a major oil company operating in both domestic and foreign areas. Includes all of the domestic law reports and digests. Includes statutes of 25 states. Particular emphasis is given to the acquisition of mineral (petroleum) law and energy legislation and regulation. Library open to the public by permission.

CORPORATIONS

AL —UNIVERSITY OF ALABAMA, Business Library, Box 2937, University, 35486. Dorothy Eady Brown, Librn; Linda Suttle Harris, Ref Librn and Data Base Searcher
Holdings: Vols (105,000) Cat Microforms
Budget: ($60,000)
Notes: Incl 90,000 corporation reports and 38,500 microforms.

CA —COOPERS & LYBRAND, Library, 1000 W Sixth St, Los Angeles, 90017. Joan Schlimgen, Librn; Paula Edwalds, Technical Library Asst
Holdings: Cat
Notes: Corporate report files incl annual reports, interim reports and proxy statements for the current 3 years.

CA —LOS ANGELES PUBLIC LIBRARY, Business & Economic Dept, 630 W 5th St, Los Angeles, 90071. Joan Bartel, Principal Librn
Notes: Annual reports in hard copy of corporations traded on the New York, American, OTC, and Pacific Exchanges, are received on a current basis. All are retained for 5 years; S&P 500 companies and some western companies indefinitely. Annual reports and 10-Ks for New York American Stock Exchange corporations are available in microfiche, 1970-1976. Beginning with 1977, 10-K reports for all US publicly traded corporations are collected. Beginning in 1980, annual reports for all US publicly traded companies are collected on microfiche. Standard sources of information on corporations are available, current and retrospective.

CA —UNIVERSITY OF CALIFORNIA, LOS ANGELES, Graduate School of Management Library, UCLA Campus, Los Angeles, 90024. Robert Bellanti, Head Librn
Holdings: Vols (128,000) Cat Mss Microforms
Notes: The

CA —UNIVERSITY OF SOUTHERN CALIFORNIA, Crocker Business Library, Hoffman Hall, University Park, Los Angeles, 90007. Judith A Truelson, Head Librn
Holdings: Vols (100,000) Cat Microforms
Notes: The Roy P Crocker Library of Business Administration, located in Hoffman Hall, houses more than 100,000 volumes and regularly receives approximately 1500 trade, financial, economics, labor, and general business periodicals and newspapers. The areas of subject concentration include business economics, finance and investments, general management/management theory, international business, finance and management, marketing/food marketing, and quantitative business analysis.

CA —PASADENA PUBLIC LIBRARY, Business-Technology Division, 285 E Walnut St, Pasadena, 91101. Anne Cain, Librn for Reference Services
Holdings: Vols (19,000) Cat Microforms
Budget: ($35,000)
Notes: Investment and financial services (current and historical); trade and industrial directories; corporate annual reports; current economic statistics in business services and in state and federal government publications. Special index to directory collection.

CA —CONTRA COSTA COUNTY LIBRARY, 1750 Oak Park Blvd, Pleasant Hill, 94523. Lyn Talme, Business Specialist
Holdings: Vols (7000)
Notes: Incl 76 periodicals, 1000 corporate annual reports, and 316 telephone directories.

CA —SACRAMENTO PUBLIC LIBRARY, 828 I St, Sacramento, 95814. Dorothy Harvey, Librn, Special Collections
Holdings: Vols (8000) Cat
Notes: Incl 800 periodicals and services. Emphasis is on business subjects and economics and labor. Technology not incl. Incl about 1000 corporation reports.

CA —GOLDEN GATE UNIVERSITY, One Embarcadero Center, No 216, San Francisco, 94111. Jeanne Nichols, Librn
Notes: World Trade Libraries and archives.

DC —AMERICAN SOCIETY OF ASSOCIATION EXECUTIVES, Information Central, 1575 Eye St NW, Washington, 20005. Cathy L Lalush, Mgr of Research and Info
Notes: Information regarding association management. Resources are designed to provide the association executive with the background knowledge for management decisions through case studies, research and statistical reports, bibliographies, and articles.

FL —MIAMI-DADE PUBLIC LIBRARY SYSTEM, Miami Public Library, One Biscayne Blvd, Miami, 33132. Edward Oswald, Business Librn
Holdings: Vols 12,000 Cat
Notes: Incl 300 journals, annual reports on microfiche, extensive collection of US and foreign trade directories.

GA —ATLANTA PUBLIC LIBRARY, Ivan Allen Jr Dept of Science, Industry & Government, One Margaret Mitchell Square, Atlanta, 30303. William D Munro, Head
Holdings: Vols (1600) Cat Microforms
Budget: ($180,000)
Notes: This separately housed collection incl 450 corporate, international, foreign, product, service, association, and professional directories. Also manufacturing directories for all states and some foreign countries.

HI —HAWAII PACIFIC COLLEGE, Meader Library, 1060 Bishop St, Honolulu, 96813. Barbara Burton Hoefler, Head Librn
Holdings: Vols 35 Cat
Notes: The Hawaii Society of Corporate Planners concluded negotiations (1978) to provide a special collection. Presently acquisitions inactive.

IL —CHICAGO PUBLIC LIBRARY, Business/Science/Technology Div, Science/Technology Information Center, 425 North Michigan Ave, Chicago, 60611. Lynda Sanford, Head; John R Moore, Environment Collection Coordinator & Engineering Librn
Holdings: Uncat Microforms
Budget: $35,000
Notes: Reports on publicly-traded corporations. 10-K's and Prospectuses for all corporations from 1970, Proxies for all corporations from 1978, 8-K's for all corporations traded on New York and American exchanges from 1976, and Annual reports for all corporations from 1980. Standard sources of information on corporations are also available current and retrospective.

IL —INSTITUTE ON THE CHURCH IN URBAN-INDUSTRIAL SOCIETY, Library, 5700 S Woodlawn, Chicago, 60637.
Holdings: Vols 1000 Cat Microforms
Notes: Urban-industrial involvement of the churches world-wide, international urban literature, corporate responsibility, human factors of urbanization and industrialization. Library holdings are dorment at present.

IL —NORTHWESTERN UNIVERSITY, Library, 1935 Sheridan Rd, Evanston, 60201. Patricia Bush, Management Librn
Holdings: Vols (43,900) Cat Microforms
Notes: Library has a current and historical collection of 5600 bound vols of corporation annual reports representing coverage of 2500 corporations, primarily industrials. Many date to beginning of the 20th century. Annual reports for 1200 corporations are currently received. Also available since 1973 is a microfiche collection of annual reports to shareholders and 10-K reports of corporations listed on the New York Stock Exchange.

IN —PURDUE UNIVERSITY LIBRARIES, Graduate School of Management, Krannert Library, West Lafayette, 47907. Gordon Law, Librn
Holdings: Cat
Notes: Corporate records and entrepreneurial history. Annual reports of foreign and domestic companies currently received; 115,000 corporate reports; 2600 company histories. Also contains some 1600 unpublished original studies and analyses on various companies as well as valuations of corporate securities, etc, prepared by the Wall Street brokerage firm from the 1920s through the early 1950s. Also, numerous files of newspaper clippings and over 25,000 pieces of miscellaneous information housed in 110 filing cabinets.

KS —UNIVERSITY OF KANSAS, Kenneth Spencer Research Library, Kansas Collection, Lawrence, 66045. Sheryl K Williams, Cur
Holdings: Vols (92,000) Cat Mss Maps Pix
Notes: Inventories of mss and photographs maintained with card catalog index. Papers of Kansas banking firms and local businees collected. Depository of official Kansas state publications since 1978; actual holdings extend into territorial period (1854-1861) with only occasional missing titles or vols. 4000 linear feet.

MA —BANK OF NEW ENGLAND, 1 Washington Mall, Boston, 02108. Helen

CORPORATIONS (cont.)

Mavareaf, Librn
Holdings: Vols (4500) Cat Microforms
Budget: ($18,000)
Notes: Annual reports of largest US banks; corporate financial reports on microfiche; Banking School theses from Stonier and Pacific Coast; industry studies.

MA —HARVARD UNIVERSITY, Graduate School of Business Administration, Baker Library, Soldiers Field, Boston, 02163. Mary V Chatfield, Librn; Florence Bartoshesky, Cur of Manuscripts and Archives
Holdings: Vols (75,000) Cat Mss Pix
Notes: Baker Library strong in historical aspects of business and economics incl original company records, company histories, business biographies, histories of industries, etc; 16,000 pictures. Ms collection of more than 75,000 incl original records of business firms from 1400 (Medici Collection) to present; especially strong in 19th century. New England enterprises, textile firms, international trade, China trade, railroads, papers of several Northeast merchant families, 19th century small business. Also incl pictures, trade cards, clipper ship cards, money, trade catalogs, business cartoons, prices current and exhibit items. See Robert W Lovett and Eleanor C Bishop, compilers, *Business Manuscripts in Baker Library* (Boston: The Library, 1978), 382 pp. Mss are described in the*National Union Catlog of Manuscript Collections* and in Hamer's *A Guide to Archives and Manuscripts in the United States.* Restricted use: Manuscripts noncirculating. Downs: 1636, 2122, 2616, 2675, 2677, 2698, 2700, 2701, 2702, 2706, 2708, 2711, 2713-15, 2716, 2717-18, 2721-26, 2734, 2737, 2774, 2814, 4300, 5162: Supplement 964, 965, 968, 998.

MA —BOSTON COLLEGE LIBRARIES, Thomas P O'Neill Library, Chestnut Hill, 02167. John D J Slinn, Librn of the Central Library
Holdings: Vols 62,000 Cat Maps Audiotapes Filmstrips Microforms
Budget: ($120,000)

MI —GALE RESEARCH CO, Book Tower, Detroit, 48226. Annie Brewer, Librn
Holdings: Vols (65,000) Cat
Notes: Large collection of reference materials, incl computerized files used in the preparation of familiar contemporary reference books and guides to special fields.

MI —WESTERN MICHIGAN UNIVERSITY, Business Library, N Hall, Kalamazoo, 49008. David H McKee, Head
Holdings: Vols (71,977) Cat Phonorecords Microforms
Notes: Incl 14,570 vols of bound periodicals, 33,041 monographs, 14,605 government documents, 1796 microfilm and 7u965 microfiche/microcards. Large collection of corporate annual reports is separate.

MN —MANKATO STATE UNIVERSITY, Library, Mankato, 56001. Marilyn Montgomery, Reference Librn
Holdings: Uncat
Notes: Especially Midwestern corporations' reports (incl annual reports), as well as top 500 in nation.

MN —MINNEAPOLIS PUBLIC LIBRARY & INFORMATION CENTER, Business & Economics Dept, 300 Nicollet Mall, Minneapolis, 55401. Mary Lawson, Librn
Notes: Separate card catalog, telephone reference service, and directory service. Incl periodical titles; large files of corporation annual reports; VF of local company histories and annual reports; domestic and foreign telephone directories; historical US stock quotations, 1891-date; local OTC quotations, 1933-date; indexes and abstracting services; looseleaf reference services.

NJ —PRINCETON UNIVERSITY, Library, Pliny Fisk Library of Economics and Finance, Princeton, 08544. Louise Tompkins, Librn
Notes: The American railroad corporations collection is strongest for the period 1865-1915. Incl books, pamphlets, broker's circulars, newspaper clippings, annual reports and mortgages. There is a separate catalog which indexes the material by name of corporation. A good description of the collection is contained in: Brayer, Herbert O "The Pliny Fisk Collection of Railroad and Corporation Finance," *The Princeton University Chronicle*, vol 6, no 4 (1944-1945), pp 171-178.

NJ —TRENTON FREE PUBLIC LIBRARY, Business & Technology Dept, 120 Academy St, Trenton, 08608. Richard D Rebecca, Principal Librn
Holdings: Vols (9000) Cat Microforms
Notes: Financial information from Moody's, Standard & Poor's, Dun and Bradstreet, Thomas Publishing Co, various financial newspapers and financial services. Incl 400 telephone directories. Interlibrary Loan (photocopies) available.

NY —NEW YORK STATE LIBRARY, State Education Bldg Annex, Washington Ave, Albany, 12224.
Holdings: Uncat Microforms
Notes: Microform: Annual reports of all companies listed on the American and the New York State Exchanges from 1952 to date in microform.

NY —BROOKLYN PUBLIC LIBRARY, Business Library, 280 Cadman Plaza W, Brooklyn, 11201. Sylvia Mechanic, Business Librn
Holdings: Vols (107,000) Cat
Notes: Library received about 1800 periodicals, 3000 serials, 2700 directories, 1600 telephone books from all over the world with a complete back file on microfilm for greater New York. Library is a selective US Government Documents depository. Subscribes to microfiche SEC 10K reports for AMEX, NYSE and OTC from 1976 to date; annual reports for earlier years. Transnational annual reports, on fiche from 1982-to date. 78 vertical file trays; Sanborn maps for Brooklyn, special collection of corporation histories. Publish monthly newsletter, *Service to Business and Industry* with our Science Division.

NY —BUFFALO & ERIE COUNTY PUBLIC LIBRARY, Business and Labor Dept, Lafayette Sq, Buffalo, 14203. Joyce Davoli, Dept Head
Holdings: Vols (62,000) Cat
Notes: Incl bound periodicals; 41 drawers VF materials; US government depository, active microfiche collection of annual reports of companies listed on the American and New York Stock Exchanges. Also, New York State Data Center Affiliate for US Census; depository for mortgage disclosure statistics for Erie and Niagara Counties.

NY —CORNELL UNIVERSITY LIBRARIES, Graduate School of Management, Malott Hall, Ithaca, 14853. Betsy Ann Olive, Librn
Holdings: Vols (135,000) Cat Microforms
Budget: ($130,000)

NY —AMERICAN STOCK EXCHANGE, Martin J Keena Memorial Library, 86 Trinity Place, New York, 10006. Margaret A Balogh, Supvr
Holdings: Vols 600 Microforms
Notes: Reference Books such as Moody's Standard & Poors, Dunn & Bradstreet, Financial Stock Guide Service, fiche on all Amex companies, over 13,000 microfilm and 500 VF, and bound periodicals.

NY —COLUMBIA UNIVERSITY LIBRARIES, Thomas J Watson Library of Business & Economics, Box 130, Uris Hall, New York, 10027. Jane E Winland, Librn
Holdings: Vols 340,000 Microforms
Notes: The Marvin Scudder Financial Collection (corporation reports). Research material and documents pertaining to the financial histories of over one-half million corporations, domestic and foreign, for a period from 1821 to date. Incl annual reports, proxy statements, prospectuses, listing statements, brokerage house reports. Special catalog for the collection is by name of corporation only. Annual reports of listed corporations are in microform from 1951 or year of listing (if later) to the present. This collection is not open to the public unless they apply for library privileges through the Information Office in Butler Library, Room 234.

NY —CONFERENCE BOARD, Information Service Library, 845 Third Ave, New York, 10022. Tamsen M Hernandez, Dir
Holdings: Vols 25,000 Cat Microforms
Notes: Heavily directed to collection of government materials and corporate data.

NY —GEORGESON & CO, Library, Wall Street Plaza, New York, 10005. Aileen Burnes, Chief Librn
Holdings: Cat
Budget: ($65,000)
Notes: Collection incl corporate documents of all companies listed on the New York and American stock exchanges, plus all regularly traded NASDAQ O-T-C companies. The collection dates from 1939. Only 1978 to the present is available to SLA members by appointment.

NY —MERRILL LYNCH, CAPITAL MARKETS, Securities Research Library, One Liberty Plaza (165 Broadway), New York, 10006. Rita A Hughes, Chief Librn
Holdings: Vols 10,000 Cat Microforms
Notes: Subject files by industry; corporate files; all NYSE and AMEX companies on DISCLOSURE microfiches plus approx 1000 OTC companies. *Wall Street Journal* quotation pages on microfiche or microfilm from 1928 to present. as well as *Toronto Globe & Mail* and *Financial Post* Quotations. *Moody's* and *Standard & Poor's Manual* from 1916 to present. Incl 800,000 microfiche.

NY —NEW YORK PUBLIC LIBRARY, Research Libraries, Economic & Public Affairs Div, Fifth Ave & 42 St, New York, 10018. Edward DiRoma, Chief
Holdings: Vols (1,500,000) Cat Microforms

NY —SALOMON BROTHERS, Library, One New York Plaza, 46th Floor, New York, 10004. Lydia P Davies, Library Mgr
Holdings: Vols (4750) Cat
Notes: Library contains a collection of reference sources relating to corporate finance, investment banking and international finance. Extensive domestic and international corporate documents on microfiche. 11,000 corporate document files; 406,700 microforms.

NY —STANDARD & POOR'S CORP, Library, 25 Broadway, New York, 10004. Walter Nixon, Ref Librn
Holdings: Vols (22,000) Cat Microforms
Notes: Library has 800,000 microforms.

NY —UNIVERSITY OF ROCHESTER, Graduate School of Management Library, Rush Rhees Library, Rochester, 14627. Edward Wass; Janet Prentice; Datta Kharbas
Holdings: Vols (108,000) Cat Microforms
Budget: ($84,500)
Notes: Incl a reference collection, a geographical file on economic conditions, an industry file of statistics and trends, research reports and working papers, more than 2600 hardcopy annual reports. Several microfiche or microcard Collections of Corporate reports dating from the 1950s to the present and over 900 management and economics periodicals.

NY —YONKERS PUBLIC LIBRARY, Information Services, 7 Main St, Yonkers, 10701. Martita Schwarz, Dept Head
Holdings: Vols (21,500) Cat Maps Microforms
Budget: ($30,000)

NC —DUKE UNIVERSITY, William R Perkins Library, Durham, 27706. Elvin E Strowd, University Librn
Notes: The Railroad Corporation Reports collection is made up of 8000 items, issued primarily since 1900, though many go back as far as the middle of the 19th century for main trunk lines in the United States.

OH —AKRON-SUMMIT COUNTY PUBLIC LIBRARY, Business, Labor & Government Div, 55 S Main St, Akron, 44326. William G Johnson, Head
Holdings: Vols (10,000) Cat Microforms
Budget: ($20,000)

OH —CLEVELAND PUBLIC LIBRARY, Business, Economics and Labor Department, 325 Superior Ave, Cleveland, 44114. Joan Sorger, Head
Holdings: Cat
Notes: Currently receiving over 1700 periodicals and 1300 serial titles; 1000

CORPORATIONS (cont.)

individual trade, industrial and professional directories, worldwide; 324 file drawers annual reports of old companies, many local; 24 drawers historical information on Cleveland companies. Annual reports, 10-K's, Proxy Statements (disclosure SEC filings on fiche); over 200 loose-leaf services; 1700 current telephone and city directories. Emphasis on current material. Areas of special strength are banking, investments, marketing and management. Also strong insurance, accounting, real estate and transportation collections. Computerized sources available incl Dow Jones News Service and a variety of Dialog business-related databases.

PA —UNIVERSITY OF PENNSYLVANIA, Lippincott Library of the Wharton School, Philadelphia, 19104. Michael Halperin, Librn
Holdings: Cat Microforms
Notes: Approx 1000 corporation histories in book form. Annual reports from 3000 US and foreign corporations; incl total of 58,000 separate reports, 11,000 misc corporation publications, with many files going back to mid-19th century. Annual reports, (1956 to date) for all firms listed on NY and American Stock Exchanges on microfiche. Securities and Exchange Commission Forms 10-K (on microfiche) for all firms on American and NY Stock Exchanges, 1976-date; for firms incl in *Fortune* list of 500 largest industrials, 1969-date, 1982-date.

PA —CARNEGIE LIBRARY OF PITTSBURGH, Science & Technology Dept, 4400 Forbes Ave, Pittsburgh, 15213. Catherine M Brosky, Dept Head
Notes: This department serves as the Resource Library for Science and Technology in the Commonwealth of Pennsylvania. Agreements with other Resource Libraries in the Commonwealth and with certain institutions in Pittsburgh for sharing resources, cooperative acquisition of materials, provision of services and information. Collections described in *Guide to the Regional Library Resource Centers of* Pennsylvania, compiled by Ralph W McComb, 1967.

TX —DALLAS PUBLIC LIBRARY, Central Research Library, Business & Technology Div, 1515 Young St, Dallas, 75201. Sarabeth Allen, Mgr
Holdings: Vols 6000 Cat
Budget: $2500
Notes: *Business History Collection; a* Checklist. Dallas, Texas: Business and Technology Div, Dallas Public Library, 1974. Published to serve as a subject (by corporate name) catalog. Interlibrary loans are invited.

WA —UNIVERSITY OF WASHINGTON LIBRARIES, Business Administration Library, DJ-10, Seattle, 98195. Anne B Passarelli, Head
Holdings: Vols (10,000) Microforms
Notes: Includes reports of US and foreign corporations.

WI —MILWAUKEE PUBLIC LIBRARY, 814 W Wisconsin Ave, Milwaukee, 53233. Donald J Sager, City Librn
Holdings: Uncat
Notes: An inventory index is maintained for annual reports of 1100 corporation. Some 1981 microfiche copies of the Annual Reports of the companies listed on the New York and American Stock Exchange.

BC —VANCOUVER PUBLIC LIBRARY, Business and Economics Div, 750 Burrard St, Vancouver, V6Z 1X5, Can. Barbara Bell, Librn
Notes: Incl numerous special files for *Quick Reference, Subject Clippings, Companies* (information of major Canadian, US and international corporations; index to new British Columbia and Canadian company corporations, 1951 to 1978; 160,000 cards); company file, *Province Index* and *Association File* (particulars of Canadian trade and professional associations). *International Collection of Trade* directories and telephone books.

ON —QUEEN'S UNIVERSITY, Douglas Library, Kingston, K7L 5C4, Can. William F E Morley, Cur, Special Collections
Holdings: Mss Maps Pix
Notes: About 3500 linear feet of mss material with special emphasis on families and businesses of eastern Ontario; Presbyterian Church; Canadian politics and public affairs, university and city of Kingston records, literary figures.

ON —MACLEAN HUNTER LIBRARY, Maclean Hunter Bldg, 777 Day St, Toronto, M5W 1A7, Can. Theresa Butcher, Librn
Holdings: Vols 1500 Cat Pix
Notes: Mainly a resource for the journalists of the *Financial Post,* Canada's foremeost financial paper. The library is basically made up of vertical files divided into (1) general subject files, (2) Canadian public companies, (3) biographical (mainly photographic). The *Financial Post* (weekly) is completely clipped. The Toronto *Globe and Mail* (daily) and other Canadian publications are selectively clipped. In addition, the library houses all Maclean- Hunter publications (over 80 and constantly growing). The *Financial Post* is indexed by the library staff.

ON —METROPOLITAN TORONTO LIBRARY, Business Dept, 789 Yonge St, Toronto, M4W 2G8, Can. Patricia Dye, Head
Holdings: Vols (63,682) Cat Microforms
Budget: ($508,800)
Notes: Extensive current and historical information with emphasis on Canadian companies incl annual reports, clippings and pamphlets files, and a collection of business and trade directories. Also international directories. Approximately 1000 current periodicals, and up-dating services giving corporation information.

CORPORATIONS—LAWS AND LEGISLATION see Corporation Law

CORPORATIONS—REPORTS

MA —HARVARD UNIVERSITY, Graduate School of Business Administration, Baker Library, Soldiers Field, Boston, 02163. Mary V Chatfield, Librn; Florence Bartoshesky, Cur of Manuscripts and Archives
Notes: Corporate reports; company annual reports, both domestic and foreign; SEC filings; material dates from 19th century forward.

MI —WESTERN MICHIGAN UNIVERSITY, Business Library, N Hall, Kalamazoo, 49008. David H McKee, Head
Notes: 450 linear feet of corporation annual reports.

MI —MONROE COUNTY LIBRARY SYSTEM, Ellis Reference and Information Center, Dorsch Memorial Branch, 18 E First St, Monroe, 48161. Mary Jo Garmire, Head, Dorsch Memorial Branch
Holdings: Vols Periodicals Microforms
Budget: $25,000
Notes: Collection contains 1200 circulating volumes, 200 reference volumes, 95 business periodical and newspaper subscriptions, 710 microfilms and 10,725 microfiche. Annual Reports and 10K Reports for Fortune 500 corporations and local firms as available are included in 18 drawers of vertical file materials on corporations and business related topics. The collection concentrates on investments, finance, small business, mutual funds, stock market information, management, insurance and marketing. *Business Index COM* and *Business Periodicals Index* aid in access to the collection. The library publishes a quarterly newsletter included with the Monroe County Chamber of Commerce mailings to all members highlighting additions to the collection and programs of interest to the local business community. Regularly scheduled speakers, exhibits and other programsrelating to business collection topics encourage use of the collection. MCLS also publishes the Monroe County Industrial Directory in cooperation with the Monroe County Chamber of Commerce.

SK —UNIVERSITY OF SASKATCHEWAN, Library, Saskatoon, S7N 0W0, Can. S Perkins, Librn
Notes: Extensive microfiche collection of annual reports of Ontario-registered (1967-) and federally-registered companies. Some pre-1967 annual reports (papercopy). Complete set of *Annual Financial Review* Canadian, Houstons Standard Publications, 1901-1941.

CORPORATIONS, BUSINESS see Corporations

CORPORATIONS, FOREIGN

CA —UNIVERSITY OF SOUTHERN CALIFORNIA, Crocker Business Library, Hoffman Hall, University Park, Los Angeles, 90007. Judith A Truelson, Head Librn
Holdings: Vols (100,000) Cat Microforms
Notes: The Roy P Crocker Library of Business Administration, located in Hoffman Hall, houses more than 100,000 volumes and regularly receives approximately 1500 trade, financial, economics, labor, and general business periodicals and newspapers. The areas of subject concentration include business economics, finance and investments, general management/management theory, international business, finance and management, marketing/food marketing, and quantitative business analysis.

MI —UNIVERSITY OF MICHIGAN, Graduate School of Business Administration, Business Administration Library, Institute for International Commerce Reading Rm, Ann Arbor, 48109. Carol Holbrook, Dir
Holdings: Cat
Notes: International business.

OH —MARATHON OIL CO, Law Library, 539 S Main St, Room 854-M, Findlay, 45840. Durand S Dudley, Sr Law Librn
Holdings: Vols (18,000) Cat
Budget: ($100,000)
Notes: Library serves the informational needs of the staff attorneys of a major oil company operating in both domestic and foreign areas. Includes all of the domestic law reports and digests. Includes statutes of 25 states. Particular emphasis is given to the acquisition of mineral (petroleum) law and energy legislation and regulation. Library open to the public by permission.

PA —UNIVERSITY OF PENNSYLVANIA, Lippincott Library of the Wharton School, Philadelphia, 19104. Michael Halperin, Librn
Holdings: Cat
Notes: Long files of statistical data on the foreign trade of the US and many foreign countries. Extensive materials on foreign taxation and regulation of US enterprises abroad.

WA —UNIVERSITY OF WASHINGTON LIBRARIES, Business Administration Library, DJ-10, Seattle, 98195. Anne B Passarelli, Head
Holdings: Vols 10,000 Microforms
Notes: Includes reports of US and foreign corporations.

CORRECTIONAL PERSONNEL

NC —TECHNICAL INSTITUTE OF ALAMANCE, Learning Resources Center, Jimmy Kerr Rd, PO Box 623, Haw River, 27258. Ron Plummer, Coordr
Holdings: Vols (350) Cat Filmstrips Microforms
Notes: Criminal justice and corrections technology.

CORRECTIONAL SERVICES see Corrections

CORRECTIONS

IN —INDIANA LAW ENFORCEMENT ACADEMY, David F Allen Memorial Learning Resources Center, Rd 700 E, PO Box 313, Plainfield, 46168. Donna K Zimmerman, Librn
Holdings: Vols (4500) Cat Slides 16mm Films
Budget: ($8500)
Notes: Concentrated in the areas of police science, criminology, and law.

IN —WESTVILLE CORRECTIONAL CENTER, Library Services, PO Box 473,

CORRECTIONS (cont.)

Westville, 46391. Catherine M Mohlke, Dir of Library Services
Holdings: Vols 1000 Cat

NC —DUKE UNIVERSITY, William R Perkins Library, Durham, 27706. Elvin E Strowd, University Librn
Holdings: None
Notes: The Bruno Lasker collection contains 51 portfolios; the Perkins Library general collection and other collections contain a significant amount of material on the subject of slavery and antislavery.

WI —UNIVERSITY OF WISCONSIN, MADISON, Law School Library, Criminal Justice Reference & Information Center, Madison, 53706. Sue Center, Librn
Holdings: Vols (29,000) Cat
Budget: ($45,000)
Notes: In-depth subject access is provided to collection by our own cataloging and classification systems. Incl are periodical articles which are selectively cataloged to supplement the collection. Special items in collection incl penal press (prisoner newspapers); annual and statistical reports from criminal justice agencies throughout the US and Canada; theses and dissertations; and 280 periodical titles in the field of criminal justice.

ON —UNIVERSITY OF TORONTO, Centre of Criminology, Library, 130 St George St, Rm 8001, Toronto, M5S 1A5, Can. Catherine J Matthews, Librn
Holdings: Vols (20,000) Cat
Notes: Over 4500 research reports, article reprints, theses, etc. Extensive newspaper clippings file from 1963 to present indexed under 350 subject headings. The collection covers criminology, law enforcement and policing, delinquency, criminal justice system, penology and corrections. Acquisitions list published three times a year; subscription.

CORRECTIONS EMPLOYEES see Correctional Personnel

CORRELATION OF FORCES see Force and Energy

CORROSION AND ANTICORROSIVES

IN —UNION CARBIDE CORP, Coatings Service Dept, Technical Library, 1500 Polco St, PO Box 24166, Indianapolis, 46224. Mary Ann Brady, Librn
Holdings: Vols (6000) Cat
Notes: Corrosion and anticorrosives; high temperature materials and technology. Restricted use: corporate personnel.

KY —UNIVERSITY OF KENTUCKY, Robert E Shaver Library of Engineering, 355 Anderson Hall, Lexington, 40506. Russell H Powell, Engineering Librn
Holdings: Vols (29,660) Cat Microforms

MD —US BUREAU OF MINES, Avondale Metallurgy Research Center, Library, 4900 La Salle Rd, Avondale, 20782. Paul F Moran, Librn
Holdings: Vols (11,000) Cat
Budget: ($35,000)
Notes: Incl corrosion, flotation, particulate mineralogy.

MI —CONSTRUCTION CONSULTANTS, 900 Pallister, Detroit, 48202. Joan M Boram, Librn
Holdings: Vols (500) Cat Microforms
Notes: The only library in the country devoted entirely to the subject of roofing and waterproofing. Incl books and vinyl binders containing articles culled from various journals, papers from manufacturers and independent testing and laboratory facilities pertinent government documents, and in-house papers, arranged according to subject matter and indexed. When necessary, papers are cross-referenced. Also, an extensive collection of legal materials relating to roofing and waterproofing failures. Lawyers from all parts of the country avail themselves of these materials.

PA —CARNEGIE LIBRARY OF PITTSBURGH, Science & Technology Dept, 4400 Forbes Ave, Pittsburgh, 15213. Catherine M Brosky, Dept Head
Holdings: Vols (380,000) Cat Maps Microforms
Budget: ($240,000)
Notes: Collection incl material on metallurgy, chemistry, masonry, plumbing, materials science, and painting.

CORROSION RESISTANT MATERIALS

IN —UNION CARBIDE CORP, Coatings Service Dept, Technical Library, 1500 Polco St, PO Box 24166, Indianapolis, 46224. Mary Ann Brady, Librn
Holdings: Vols 6000 Cat
Notes: Advanced materials incl those for use in extreme temperatures, materials with superior wear and anti-corrosion properties, and composites.

CORSAIRS see Pirates and Piracy

CORSO, GREGORY, 1930-

NY —STATE UNIVERSITY OF NEW YORK, STONY BROOK, Melville Library, Dept of Special Collections, Stony Brook, 11794. Evert Volkersz, Head
Holdings: Vols 20 Cat Mss

BC —SIMON FRASER UNIVERSITY, Library, Burnaby, V5A 1S6, Can. Percilla Groves, Special Collections Librn
Holdings: Cat Mss
Notes: Letters written to Eshleman by Allen Ginsberg (8 pp), William Carlos Williams and Florence Williams (5 pp), Robert Duncan (4 pp), and Edward Dorn (5 pp), while Eshleman was editor of *Folio* (1959-1961). Tss from Gregory Corso (2 pp), Louis Zukofsky (8 pp), Michael Rumaker (3 pp).

CORTHELL, ELMER LAWRENCE, 1840-1916

RI —BROWN UNIVERSITY, John Hay Library, 20 Prospect St, Providence, 02912. Mark N Brown, Cur Mss
Holdings: // Mss
Notes: 45 linear feet, 1867-1916, incl journals, speeches, biographical material, business and personal correspondence, invoices and receipts, college notebooks, essays, sermons, reports, estimates, accounts, plans, charts, clippings, pamphlets, broadsides, and photographs of of Elmer Lawrence Corthell, civil engineer relating to projects in the US, Latin America, and Europe. Also material relating to international societies and engineering education.

CORTOT, ALFRED

IL —NEWBERRY LIBRARY, 60 W Walton St, Chicago, 60610. Diana Haskell, Cur of Modern Mss
Holdings: Vols 400 Cat
Notes: Music theory books, 1500-1800, from the private library of Alfred Cortot.

CORVO, BARON see Rolfe, Frederick William (Baron Corvo)

CORWIN, EDWARD SAMUEL, 1878-1963

NJ —PRINCETON UNIVERSITY, Library, Manuscript Collection, Nassau St, Princeton, 08540. Jean F Preston, Cur
Holdings: // Cat
Notes: Incl 4 boxes; 26 cartons of papers. An unpublished typescript guide (28 p) is available in the library.

CORWIN, HUGH D.

OK —UNIVERSITY OF SCIENCE & ARTS OF OKLAHOMA, Nash Library, Chickasha, 73018. William A Martin, Jr, Librn
Holdings: // Uncat Mss Pix Audiotapes
Notes: Papers of Hugh D Corwin, writer on Indian life and history, incl converstions with elderly Kiowa Indians, with audiotapes, some pictures and mss; also reprints of Corwin's historical articles from local newspapers.

CORWIN, NORMAN

MA —BOSTON UNIVERSITY, Mugar Memorial Library, Special Collections Dept, 771 Commonwealth Ave, Boston, 02215. Howard B Gotlieb, Dir
Holdings: Cat Mss
Notes: Mss, correspondence, etc collected in depth; incl publications by or about.

COSMEP see Committee of Small Magazine Editors and Publishers (COSMEP)

COSMETICS

IL —J WALTER THOMPSON CO, Information Center, 875 N Michigan Ave, Chicago, 60611. Edward G Strable, Dir
Holdings: Vols 50 Cat Microforms
Notes: Basis of collection is fugitive materials (reports, studies, clippings, articles, releases) on consumer markets and use patterns of health and beauty aids-about 20 file drawers. Indexing and organization make for immediate access.

IN —INDIANA HISTORICAL SOCIETY, Library, 315 W Ohio St, Indianapolis, 46202. Robert K O'Neill, Dir
Holdings: Vols Cat Mss Pix
Notes: Materials on blacks in Indiana, from statehood to the present day. Incl books; letters; church and organization records; photographs. Incl records of the Madam C J Walker Company, a black cosmetics firm in Indianapolis.

MI —GOGEBIC COMMUNITY COLLEGE, Alex D Chisholm Learning Resources Center, Greenbush & Jackson Rd, Ironwood, 49938. Charles Tetzlaff, Dir of Learning Resources
Holdings: Vols (20,000)

NY —REVLON RESEARCH CENTER, Research Bldg Library, 945 Zerega Ave, Bronx, 08818. Lee J Tanen, Library Services Mgr
Holdings: Vols 200 Cat

PA —FRANKLIN INSTITUTE LIBRARY, 20 & The Parkway, Philadelphia, 19103. Miriam Padusis, Dir; Charles Wilt, Readers Servs Librn
Holdings: Vols (300,000) Cat Maps Pix Microforms

WA —UNIVERSITY OF WASHINGTON LIBRARIES, Drama Library, BH-20, Seattle, 98195. Liz Fugate, Drama Librn
Holdings: Vols
Budget: ($13,182)
Notes: Collection incl history; criticism; costume; make-up; scene design; lighting; creative dramatics; children's theatre; directing; playwriting; acting. Special Collections include 19th century acting editions, contemporary acting editions and local theatre posters. 17,731 items cataloged, 24,255 uncataloged.

COSMETOLOGY see Beauty Culture

COSMOGONY, BIBLICAL see Creation

COSMOGRAPHY

IL —NEWBERRY LIBRARY, 60 W Walton St, Chicago, 60610. Robert W Karrow, Jr, Cur of Maps
Holdings: Vols 650 Cat Mss
Notes: Not incl of maps and atlases.

COSMOLOGY

CA —CALIFORNIA INSTITUTE OF TECHNOLOGY, Robert A Millikan Memorial Library, Archives, 1201 E California Blvd, Pasadena, 91125. Judith R Goodstein, Archivist
Holdings: Vols (3000) Cat Mss Maps Pix Slides Phonorecords Audiotapes Videotapes 16mm Films Microforms
Notes: Ms sources for the history of astrophysics, cosmology, mathematical physics, experimental physics, radio astronomy, geophysics and biophysics.

COSMOLOGY (cont.)

Collections incl the papers of: George Ellery Hale, Jesse Greenstein, H P Robertson, Richard Feynman, Paul Epstein, Max Delbruck, and Beno Gutenberg. Candid photos of physicists at meetings; etchings and photographs of Einstein; scientific medals; selected pieces of scientific apparatus (including the oil-drop machine constructed by Millikan at Caltech in the early 1920s); the reprint collection of Paul Epstein; over 3000 landmark books in the history of 20th century physics and mathematics. Printed publications include: Daniel Kevles, *Guide to the Microfilm Edition of the George Ellery Hale Papers* (Pasadena, Carnegie Institute of Washington and Caltech), 1968; Judith R Goodstein,*The Robert Andrews Millikan Collection at the California Institute of Technology: Guide to a Microfilm Edition* (Pasadena, Caltech), 1977; Judith R Goodstein and Carolyn Kopp, *The Theodore von Karman Collections at the California Institute of* Technology (Pasadena, Archives), 1981.

IL —UNIVERSITY OF ILLINOIS, URBANA/CHAMPAIGN, Library, Geology Library, 223 Natural History Bldg, Urbana, 61801. Dederick Ward, Librn
Holdings: Vols (105,186) Cat Maps Microforms

IN —PURDUE UNIVERSITY LIBRARIES, Geosciences Library, West Lafayette, 47907. Carolyn Lassoon, Librn
Holdings: Vols (15,000)
Notes: Geosciences.

PA —UNIVERSITY OF PITTSBURGH, Hillman Library, Pittsburgh, 15260. Glenora E Rossell, Head
Holdings: Vols (16,100) Cat Microforms
Notes: This History and Philosophy of Science collection is rapidly growing to support research interests in a very new synoptic approach in the integration of history of science, philosophy of science, and history of philosophy, and the intensive new program of instruction. The trend of collection is to include works in philosophical foundations of contemporary physics and cosmology, the philosophical problems of the social sciences, science and theology in the 17th century, the relation between science and epistemology in the 18th and 19th centuries; problems of microphysics, history of molecular biology, theories of scientific explanation, and relation between science and metaphysics.

COSMOLOGY, BIBLICAL see Creation

COSSACKS

WI —UNIVERSITY OF WISCONSIN, MADISON, Memorial Library, Slavic Studies Collection, 728 State St, Madison, 53706. Aleksander Rolich, Bibliographer for Slavic Studies; Robert P Gakovich, Slavic Cataloger; Valdis J Zeps, Baltic Studies Center
Holdings: Cat
Notes: Cossack Collection. Based on the private libraries of Kh I and P Kh Popov and S G Svatikov and is representative of the publications issued by the Cossacks between 1919 and 1939 in Rostov on Don, Paris and Prague relating to different aspects of Cossack life, military history and life in emigration. Description and listing available. Restricted use: Rare Book Department.

COST CONTROL see Value Analysis (Cost Control)

COST OF LIVING

CA —UNIVERSITY OF CALIFORNIA, BERKELEY, Giannini Foundation of Agricultural Economics, Library, 248 Giannini Hall, Berkeley, 94720. Grace Dote, Librn
Holdings: Vols (18,000) Cat Mss Maps Microforms
Notes: Noncirculating collection. No interlibrary loans. Also about 124,000 unbound vols. Open to graduate students and faculties of universities and colleges, research workers and interested public. Mostly English language materials, primarily 1900 to date. Card catalog published by G K Hall Co *Dictionary Catalog of the Giannini Foundation of Agricultural Economics Library, Univ of California*, 12 vols (Holdings thru 7/71).

COSTA, JOSEPH

NY —SYRACUSE UNIVERSITY LIBRARIES, Ernest S Bird Library, George Arents Research Library for Special Collections, Syracuse, 13210. Carolyn A Davis, Manuscripts Librn; Amy S Doherty, University Archivist; Mark F Weimer, Rare Book Librn
Notes: The George Arents Research Library for Special Collections at Syracuse University contains the papers of Margaret Bourke-White, Clara Sipprell, Gerda Peterich, Edward John Wall, Louis Fabian Bachrach, Joseph Costa (National Press Photographers Association), the University Archives Photographic Collection, and other misc photographs.

COSTA RICA

CA —UNIVERSITY OF CALIFORNIA, LOS ANGELES, Research Library, Dept of Special Collections, 405 Hilgard Ave, Los Angeles, 90024. Edward Shreeves, Chairman, Bibliographers Group; David S Zeidberg, Head
Holdings: Cat Mss Pix
Notes: Incl 4 linear feet of correspondence, 19th and 20th century documents, pamphlets, and ephemera from the collections of Mario Alberto Jimenez Quesada (700 volumes are in the main stacks); 1/2 linear foot of photographs.

CT —YALE UNIVERSITY, Sterling Memorial Library, Latin American Collections, New Haven, 06520. Lee H Williams Jr, Cur
Holdings: Vols (300,000) Caat Maps Pix Slides Phonorecords 16mm Films Filmstrips
Notes: See entry for Yale University under Latin America.

DC —GEORGETOWN UNIVERSITY, Library, Special Collections Div, 37 & O Sts NW, Washington, 20057. George M Barringer, Special Collections Librn; Nicholas B Sheetz, Mss Librn
Holdings: Mss Pix
Notes: Correspondence, documents, journals, diaries, financial accounts, mss, photographs, and art work comprising the personal and professional papers of McCeney Werlich, diplomat, as well as those of his wife, Gladys Hinckley Werlich; Thomas Hinckley, and Robert 0'Donnel Hinckley, both diplomats; papers of Eleanor O'Donnell Hinckley, mother of Gladys Werlich, and her husband Robert Hinckley, noted portrait painter. The papers incl: State Department correspondence and other material relating to McCeney Werlich's posts in Latvia (1926-1927), Poland (1927-1931), Costa Rica (1931-1932), Liberia (1932-1933), and France (1934-1936); correspondence from Robert O'Donnell Hinckley from his travels in the Orient, 1919; correspondence from Thomas Hinckley, incl accounts of the Austro-Hungarian empire, 1914-1915; as well as numerous journalsand diaries kept by Gladys Werlich regarding her extensive travels and variety of experiences.

DC —LIBRARY OF CONGRESS, Collections Management Division, Washington, 20540.
Notes: The Luis Dobles Segrada Collection of publications pertaining to Costa Rica. Contains over 5600 books and pamphlets issued between 1831 and the 1930s.

KS —UNIVERSITY OF KANSAS, Watson Library, Lawrence, 66045. George Jerkovich, Cur Slavic Collections
Notes: Over 6000 valuable Central American titles, of which fewer than half in a random sample are presently located in OCLC, and over half not incl in published holdings of the University of Texas or Tulane University. A special grant is supporting cataloging of the collection.

MA —PAN AMERICAN SOCIETY OF NEW ENGLAND, Shattuck Library, 152 North Street, Boston, 02109. Vivian Ingrao, Dir
Holdings: Vols (10,000) Cat Slides Phonorecords
Notes: Books on art, literature, history, and economy of Pan American countries.

NY —COLUMBIA UNIVERSITY LIBRARIES, Rare Book & Manuscript Library, 801 Butler Library, 535 W 114 St, New York, 10027. Kenneth A Lohf, Librn
Notes: More than 32,000 items documenting the rise of William Russell Grace's shipping business and other materials relating to his career as mayor of New York. Incl records and correspondence relating to all aspects of the shipping business in New York and South America, mining interest in Peru and Chile, and transportation in Costa Rica and Nicaragua. Family memorabilia and photographs, materials concerning New York Politics, banking and insurance, real estate interests and Catholic charities, and letters from Chester A Arthur, John Jacob Astor, Andrew Carnegie, Grover Cleveland, Hamilton Fish, John Hay and J Pierpont Morgan. Restricted use.

COSTAIN, THOMAS

BC —UNIVERSITY OF VICTORIA, McPherson Library, Victoria, V8W 3H5, Can.

COSTIGAN, EDWARD P.

CO —UNIVERSITY OF COLORADO, Libraries, Western Historical Collections, Boulder, 80309.
Holdings: // Cat Mss Pix
Notes: Papers of Edward P Costigan, the founder of Colorado's Progressive (Bull Moose) Party. He became nationally known for his defense of union miners accused of murder. From 1917-1928 he served on the US Tariff Commission. In 1930 he was elected to the US Senate; during his term he supported New Deal legislation. The collection contains 43 boxes of sorted personal and legislative materials, two boxes of unsorted clippings, and a sizable personal library; it covers the period from 1897 to 1937. A published guide is available.

COSTUME

AL —MOBILE PUBLIC LIBRARY, Special Collections Div, 701 Government St, Mobile, 36602.
Holdings: Vols 500 Cat
Notes: The Harris Collection.

CA —BURBANK PUBLIC LIBRARY, 110 N Glenoaks Blvd, Burbank, 91502. Mary Ann Grasso, Coordr; Barbara Stones, Coordr, Media Project
Holdings: Vols (32,000) Cat Clippings Pix VF

Notes: The Warner Research Collection is a full service research division designed to serve the production needs of the motion picture, television, theatrical, and creative arts communities. This is a see-based service available by appointment only. Subject specialties include costumes, U.S. military, crime and criminals, transportation, license plates, and Sears catalogues.

†CA —WED ENTERPRISES, Research Library, 1401 Flower St, Glendale, 91201.
Notes: A subject emphasis.

CA —WESTERN COSTUME COMPANY, Research Library, 5335 Melrose Ave, Hollywood, 90038. Nancy S Kinney, Dir of Research
Holdings: Vols 6000 Pix VF
Notes: Incl 70 vertical file drawers of photographs, 200 bound periodicals, 80 mail order catalogs (Sears, etc). Wardrobe stills. 5 periodical subscriptions. Collection can be

COSTUME (cont.)

used only by the customers of Western Costume Company. All other use is on a fee basis. Collection is non-circulating. Photocopying available.

CA —LOS ANGELES PUBLIC LIBRARY, Frances Howard Goldwyn Hollywood Regional Library, 1623 Ivar Ave, Los Angeles, 90028. Sally Dumaux, Librn
Holdings: Vols (100,000) Cat Mss Pix VF
Budget: ($60,000)
Notes: A general and a research collection on theatre history, US and foreign, with special emphasis on Los Angeles, Chicago, and New York theatre from the late 1800s to the present. Other aspects of the collection include theatre design, make-up, costume, and acting and directing techniques. Also includes biographies of actors and actresses (many signed). The play collection of over 15,000 titles covers mainly English and American plays of the 19th and 20th century. There are over 5000 playbills, scrapbooks, posters, and programs. Special Collections: "Hellzapoppin," NY, 1938-40. Includes photographs, clippings, and programs.

CA —UNIVERSITY OF CALIFORNIA, LOS ANGELES, Research Library, Dept of Special Collections, 405 Hilgard Ave, Los Angeles, 90024. Edward Shreeves, Chairman, Bibliographers Group; David S Zeidberg, Head
Holdings: Cat Pix
Notes: 13 linear feet of ephemera, commercial catalogs, theater photographs, and art on the history of clothing and dress in the US and Europe, incl original work by Paul Rotha, Edward Gordon Craig, and Claud Lovat Fraser.

CA —PASADENA PUBLIC LIBRARY, Fine Arts Division, Reference Services, 285 E Walnut St, Pasadena, 91101. Anne Cain, Principal Librn
Holdings: Vols (10,000) Cat Pix Films
Notes: Library has 55 vertical drawers of pictures and clippings, constantly revised and added to. Incl over 130,000 pictures, 64 films.

CA —THE POLISH ARTS AND CULTURE FOUNDATION, 1290 Sutter St, San Francisco, 94109. Wanda Tomczykowska, President
Holdings: Pix
Notes: Portraits of Polish personalities in art and culture, photographs of costumes, dances, observance of traditions, historical events. Color photographs of California.

CT —YALE UNIVERSITY, Drama Library, 222 York St, Box 1903A, Yale Station, New Haven, 06520. Pamela C Jordan, Librn
Holdings: Vols (24,000) Cat Pix Slides Audiotapes
Budget: ($6000)
Notes: Book collection covers all phases of the dramatic arts: theatre, film, opera, dance, etc, with an emphasis on 20th century theatre. Incl audiotapes of Yale Drama School and Repertory Theatre productions, other plays and dramatic readings, and dialect tapes. Incl 1200 slides on costume design and 2000 slides on architecture, interiors, and furniture. Also incl more than 80,000 pictures on set and costume design.

DE —WIDENER UNIVERSITY, Delaware Campus Library, Box 7139, Concord Pike, Wilmington, 19803. Jane E Hukill, Library Dir
Holdings: Vols (48,000) Audiotapes Videotapes Microforms
Notes: Incl fashion design, history of costume, textiles.

GA —UNIVERSITY OF GEORGIA, Libraries, Special Collections Division, Athens, 30602. Vesta Lee Gordon, Asst Dir for Special Collections
Notes: Theater Collection contains the Paris Music Hall set and costume designs with original drawings by Erte, Barbier, Zig and others; British Music Hall Papers; European toy theater collection; Charles Coburn papers; television script collection; Tennessee Williams papers. Collection contains 16,000 pieces.

IL —UNIVERSITY OF ILLINOIS, URBANA/CHAMPAIGN, Library, Home Economics Library, 314 Bevier Hall, Champaign, 61820. Barbara C Swain, Librn
Holdings: Vols Cat
Notes: Textiles, clothing and interior design.

IL —CHICAGO PUBLIC LIBRARY, Art Section, Fine Arts Division, 78 E Washington St, Chicago, 60602. Rosalinda I Hack, Fine Arts Division Chief; Yvonne S Brown, Head, Art Section
Holdings: Vols 1200
Notes: Well balanced collection of historical and national costume. With special emphasis on Western costume. Large part of the collection consists of rare 19th century folio imprints. Collection is supplemented by the costume visuals from the section's picture collection, and the colored microfiche collection of the *Index of American Design*.

IL —UNIVERSITY OF ILLINOIS, URBANA/CHAMPAIGN, Library, 1408 W Gregory Drive, Urbana, 61801. Norman B Brown, Asst Dir for Special Collections
Notes: More than 3000 costume sketches from Motley, designers, of New York and London, a firm whose influence covered 50 years of the London and New York stages, particularly Shakespeare productions. Incl story boards and fabric swatches from 160 productions. Part of the Rare Book Room.

IN —ALLEN COUNTY PUBLIC LIBRARY, 900 Webster St, Fort Wayne, 46802. Paul Deane, Reader Services Dept Head; Kay Lynn Isca, Art Music & AV Dept Head
Holdings: Vols 858 Cat Pix
Notes: Incl many uniform plates in color.

IA —IOWA STATE UNIVERSITY, Library, Ames, 50011. Warren B Kuhn, Dean of Library Services
Holdings: Cat Microforms
Notes: Specific strength: costume history.

KY —HOPKINSVILLE COMMUNITY COLLEGE, Library, North Dr, Hopkinsville, 42240. Marjanna J Frising, Librn
Holdings: Vols (500) Cat Phonorecords Audiotapes Filmstrips
Notes: Incl most notable Broadway plays, both musical and non-musical, with soundtracks available for most. Also a large collection of children's and one-act plays as well as non-musical but best known 3-act plays, incl comedy and mystery plays.

LA —NEW ORLEANS PUBLIC LIBRARY, Louisiana Div & City Archives Dept, Louisiana History Collection, 219 Loyola Ave, New Orleans, 70140. Collin B Hamer Jr, Head
Holdings: Cat Mss Pix
Notes: The Carnival Collection incl 11,000 programs, costume designs and memorabilia relative to annual Mardi Gras festivities, 1852-date. Use is restricted to on-site research by adults.

MA —HARVARD UNIVERSITY LIBRARY, Widener Library, Harry Elkins Widener Collection, Cambridge, 02138. F Thomas Noonan, Cur
Holdings: // Cat Pix
Notes: Illustrated books depicting historical costumes.

MA —OLD STURBRIDGE VILLAGE, Research Library, Sturbridge, 01566. Theresa Rini Percy, Librn
Holdings: Cat Pix
Notes: Northeastern US, 1790-1850; some English sources.

MI —UNIVERSITY OF MICHIGAN, Library, Dept of Rare Books & Special Collections, Ann Arbor, 48109. Robert J Starring, Head
Holdings: Cat Mss Pix
Notes: Extensive holdings of books on the theatre. In the Ellen Van Volkenburg-Maurice Browne Collection, about 4000 photographs of stage productions and friends and associates, as well as about 200 original stage and costume designs, promptbooks, and play manuscripts, representing the American and British careers of this husband-wife team from 1912 to about 1940.

MI —DETROIT PUBLIC LIBRARY, Fine Arts Department, 5201 Woodward Ave, Detroit, 48202. Shirley Solvick, Chief
Holdings: Vols 60,000 Cat Pix
Budget: ($20,000)
Notes: Downs number 2882, 2923, 2938. Book collection covers all phases of art. Picture collection of over 500,000 items covers all subjects; especially strong in the fine and decorative arts, portraits, costume, and Detroit.

MN —MINNEAPOLIS COLLEGE OF ART & DESIGN, Library, 200 E 25 St, Minneapolis, 55404. Richard Kronstedt, Head Librn

MN —SAINT PAUL PUBLIC LIBRARY, 90 W Fourth St, Saint Paul, 55102. Judith Devine, Supervisor
Holdings: Vols 250 Cat Pix
Notes: Costume history, folk and national costume, incl many rare portfolios of color plates. No photocopying.

MO —SAINT LOUIS PUBLIC LIBRARY, Art Dept, 1301 Olive St, Saint Louis, 63103. Martha Hilligoss, Librn
Holdings: Vols 600 Cat

NM —MUSEUM OF NEW MEXICO, Museum of International Folk Art Library, 706 Camino Lejo, Santa Fe, 87501. Judith Sellars, Librn
Holdings: Vols (8000) Cat
Notes: Folk art of all countries, incl such subjects as costume, ceramics, textiles, furniture. Restricted use; noncirculating.

NY —BROOKLYN MUSEUM, Art Reference Library, 188 Eastern Parkway, Brooklyn, 11238.
Holdings: Vols (130,000)

NY —BROOKLYN PUBLIC LIBRARY, Art & Music Div, Grand Army Plaza, Brooklyn, 11238. Sue H Sharma, Chief
Holdings: Vols (4500) Cat Mss
Notes: Approx 2000 titles on the history of costume, including periodicals and books in many languages, as well as separate plates in folios. Collection contains a number of rare items not easily available elsewhere.

NY —PRATT INSTITUTE LIBRARY, Art & Architecture Dept, 200 Willoughby Ave, Brooklyn, 11205. Sydney Star Keaveney, Prof
Holdings: Vols (30,000) Cat Pix Slides
Budget: ($50,000)
Notes: Art and architecture, incl sculpture, photography, painting, design, costume, and commercial art. Incl 60,000 art slides. Use restricted to Pratt faculty and students.

NY —BUFFALO & ERIE COUNTY PUBLIC LIBRARY, Fiction Dept, Lafayette Sq, Buffalo, 14203. Irene Dwigans, Head
Holdings: Vols 2000 Cat

NY —NEW ROCHELLE PUBLIC LIBRARY, Fine Arts Dept, Library Plaza, New Rochelle, 10801. Eugene L Mittelgluck, Library Dir
Holdings: Vols (13,000) Cat Pix Slides
Budget: ($10,000)
Notes: Incl (430,000) pictures and (6300) slides.
See also entries under Art; Ballet and the Dance; Music.

NY —COLUMBIA UNIVERSITY LIBRARIES, Avery Architectural and Fine Arts Library, 201 Avery Hall, New York, 10027. Angela Giral, Librn
Holdings: Vols 700 Cat
Notes: Restricted use: noncirculating.

NY —FASHION INSTITUTE OF TECHNOLOGY, Special Collections Library, 227 W 27 St, New York, 10001. Barbara Jones, Dir; Janette Rozene, Librn
Notes: Incl 61 uncataloged collections of designer sketches, 30 uncataloged collections fashion designer or firm scrapbooks, 245 volumes WPA scrapbooks, and 50 oral history transcripts. Highlights: 19th century fashion plate periodicals; original fashion sketches from late 1800s, incl designs by Lady Duff Gordon, Muriel King, Berley Studios; scrapbooks compiled by Claire McCardell, Mainbocher.

NY —FASHION INSTITUTE OF TECHNOLOGY, Edward C Blum Design Laboratory, 227 W 27 St, New York, 10001. Laura Sinderbrand, Dir
Holdings: Cat Pix Slides
Notes: The largest resource of its kind consisting of 4 million indexed swatches and 300 swatch books, jacquard point paper, croquis, quilts, rug samples, laces, embroideries, and color swatch cards. A collection of international scope incl antique

COSTUME (cont.)

and contemporary textiles; woven and printed patterns created for apparel and home furnishings which may be adapted to china, giftware, floor covering, wallpaper, and package design. A comprehensive research facility comprised of over one million articles of dress dating from the 17th century to the present, incl men's, women's, children's clothes, furs, foundation garments and lingerie, as well as an outstanding grouping of 19th and 20th century designer clothing. Accessories as diverse as hats, handbags, gloves, hosiery, shoes, shawls, and costume jewelry offer an additional resource to this international collection.

NY —METROPOLITAN MUSEUM OF ART, Irene Lewisohn Costume Reference Library, Fifth Ave at 82 St, New York, 10028. K Gordon Stone, Librn
Notes: History of costume and fashion. The Irene Lewisohn Costume Reference Library is part of the Costume Institute, at the Metropolitan Museum of Art. The new quarters of the library opened with the institute in October 1971. The holdings incl books, bound periodicals, costume plates, fashion sketches, swatch books, vertical file material, and photographs. The library is mainly a research adjunct to the large collection of costumes at the museum. Professional designers of theatre costume and fashion, students, writers, etc, use the facilities. 55,000 items.

NY —MUSEUM OF THE CITY OF NEW YORK, Photo Archives, Fifth Ave & 103 St, New York, 10029. Esther Brumberg, Librn
Holdings: Mss Maps Pix
Notes: All aspects of New York City--history, costume, social life and customs, etc. Also, Byron Collection--about 10,000 prints, 1880-1930, of views of New York, commercial interiors, interiors and exteriors of private residences, social events, shipping, immigration; Wurts Collection--15,000 glass negatives, 1890-1940, mostly architectural; 100,000 Wurts Architectural Photographs, to be cataloged. Underhill Collection--about 900 glass negatives, mostly architectural, 1896-1936; McKim, Mead & White Collection--1000 glass negatives of the work of the firm, 1880-1915; and Berenice Abbott Collection, Changing New York--about 350 negatives taken by Miss Abbott for the Federal Arts Project, 1930s. Other FAP photographs incl a series on Coney Island, one on Harlem, Sewing Project, and Sabbath Studies.

†NY —NEIGHBORHOOD PLAYHOUSE SCHOOL OF THE THEATRE, Irene Lewisohn Library, 340 E 54 St, New York, 10022. Alice G Owen, Librn
Holdings: Vols (5385) Cat Mss Pix
See also entry under Theatre - History.

NY —NEW YORK PUBLIC LIBRARY, Art, Prints, and Photographs Div, Fifth Ave & 42 St, New York, 10018. Donald Anderle, Chief
Holdings: Cat Mss Pix

†NY —SHUBERT ARCHIVE, Lyceum Theatre, 149 W 45th St, New York, 10036. Brigitte Kueppers, Archivist
Notes: The vast Shubert Archive, mostly unexplored is the largest collection in the world representative of the "business" of the theatre. It includes almost all of the Shubert empire's correspondence from the turn of the century to the 1950s, road company records, thousands of playscripts (American and European), set and costume designs, music scores for Shubert productions, business, financial, and legal records, actors' contracts, etc.

NY —TRAPHAGEN SCHOOL OF FASHION LIBRARY, 257 Park Ave S, New York, 10010. Allyn Bloeme, Librn
Holdings: Vols (17,000) Cat Pix Slides
Notes: Costume history, design, construction and illustration. Collection incl old and rare bound fashion periodicals: French, English and American, also continuing run of *Vogue* and *Harper's Bazaar*. No photocopying.
See also entries under Fashion; Interior Decoration.

NC —UNIVERSITY OF NORTH CAROLINA, CHAPEL HILL, Wilson Library, Rare Book Collection, Chapel Hill, 27514. Paul S Koda, Cur of Rare Books
Holdings: Vols 50// Cat
Notes: The Whitaker Collection of Costume Plates in Color contains fifty books and portfolios of costume plates viewed from both a historical and geographical perspective.

OH —PUBLIC LIBRARY OF CINCINNATI & HAMILTON COUNTY, Art & Music Dept, 800 Vine St, Cincinnati, 45202. R Jayne Craven, Head
Holdings: Vols (122,185) Cat Pix
Budget: ($56,100)
Notes: Special collections: Eda Kuhn Loeb, "Artist and the Book, 1875-Date" (now shelved in Rare Book Room); music librettos (2345); exhibition catalogs (5474); large prints and posters (5051); Cincinnati artists vertical files; picture collection (673,906 clippings).

OH —CLEVELAND PUBLIC LIBRARY, Social Sciences Department, 325 Superior Ave, Cleveland, 44114. Thelma Morris, Head
Holdings: Cat Pix
Notes: Costumes of all periods and countries, incl illustrated editions and description of accessories.

OR —OREGON STATE UNIVERSITY, Library, Corvallis, 97331. Melvin George, Dir
Holdings: Vols (980,000) Cat Pix

OR —BASSIST COLLEGE LIBRARY, 2000 SW Fifth Ave, Portland, 97201. Norma Bassist, Librn
Holdings: Vols 375 Cat Mss Pix Slides
Notes: Very complete in general history, specific types of clothing history and in geographical areas.

PA —DREXEL UNIVERSITY LIBRARIES, General Division, 32 & Chestnut Sts, Philadelphia, 19104. Tung Chu Chen, General Division Librn
Holdings: Vols 1485 Cat Slides
Budget: ($2400)
Notes: Emphasis on clothing, dress, fashion, historic and contemporary.

PA —CARNEGIE LIBRARY OF PITTSBURGH, Music and Art Dept, 4400 Forbes Ave, Pittsburgh, 15213. Ida Reed, Dept Head
Holdings: Vols 900 Cat Pix Slides

RI —RHODE ISLAND SCHOOL OF DESIGN, Library, Two College St, Providence, 02903. James A Findlay, Dir
Holdings: Vols (70,000) Cat Pix Slides
Budget: ($50,000)

TX —PANHANDLE-PLAINS HISTORICAL MUSEUM, Research Center, Box 967, WT Sta, Canyon, 79016. Claire R Kuehn, Archivist-Librn
Holdings: Vols 50 Cat
Budget: $500
Notes: Collection supplements historic costume and textile collection of the Museum. Scope: 1850-1950. This is a new collection and is building rapidly. Incl periodicals and catalogs.

WA —UNIVERSITY OF WASHINGTON LIBRARIES, Drama Library, BH-20, Seattle, 98195. Liz Fugate, Drama Librn
Holdings: Vols
Budget: ($13,182)
Notes: Collection incl history; criticism; costume; make-up; scene design; lighting; creative dramatics; children's theatre; directing; playwriting; acting. Special Collections include 19th century acting editions, contemporary acting editions and local theatre posters. 17,731 items cataloged, 24,255 uncataloged.

WA —UNIVERSITY OF WASHINGTON LIBRARIES, Costume and Textile Collection, FM-25, Seattle, 98195. Krista Jensen Turnbull, Cur
Holdings: Vols (1500) Cat Pix Slides
Notes: Incl the Elizabeth Bayley Willis Collection of more that 1000 textiles from India, and the Seattle Weavers' Guild Collection of Guatemalan textiles. Coptic textiles are on loan from Yale University, and the Boston Museum of Fine Arts gave the Choate Collection of lace. There are also good collections of ecclesiastical vestments and embroideries from many nations, ranging from 1500 BC to the present.

WI —UNIVERSITY OF WISCONSIN-STOUT, Library Learning Center, Menomonie, 54751. Philip Sawin Jr, Coll Develop Librn
Notes: The School of Home Economics has developed a Museum of Costumes. This collection supports the museum and its programs. University of Wisconsin-Stout has been offering courses in Costumes since 1918.

BC —VANCOUVER PUBLIC LIBRARY, Art Div, 750 Burrard St, Vancouver, V6Z 1X5, Can.
Holdings: Cat Pix
Notes: Book and pamphlet collection. Also, (1) Newspaper Clippings File: 31 drawers of relevant clippings from major newspapers, incl the *Sun, Province, Toronto Globe and Mail, Christian Science Monitor, New York* Times, etc on arts, music, architecture; incl biographical material (16 drawers). (2) Picture File about 500,000 pictures in 150 cabinet drawers, strong in architecture, costume, interior decoration, painting, sculpture, also portraits. (3) Exhibition Catalogs File: British Columbia and elsewhere. (4) Association and Organization File: organizations in the Lower Mainland in arts, music, city planning, etc, begun in 1940s; (5) Canadian Artists Index: begun in 1964, alphabetically by artist, with about 300,000 citationsto reproductions of work and biographical material on Canadian artist from the division's books and other sources; (6) Miscellaneous Index: material not covered in other special or published indexes, primarily of Canadian and local cultural events, hard-to-find informations, etc. Local newspapers, special Canadian publications and British film journals are the most regularly indexed items. (7) Song Index started in the 1930s. (8) Title Index to song collections and sheet music in the VPL collection, approx 100,000 entries.

ON —QUEEN'S UNIVERSITY, Douglas Library, Kingston, K7L 5C4, Can. William F E Morley, Cur, Special Collections
Holdings: Vols 100 Uncat
Notes: The MacGillivray Collection. Scottish books, especially those dealing with clans, tartans, and heraldry.

ON —NATIONAL LIBRARY OF CANADA, 395 Wellington St, Ottawa, K1A 0N4, Can. Andre Preibish, Dir
Holdings: Vols 8000
Notes: Includes 100 serial titles, also programs, play bills etc on microfilm. Performing arts collection consists of Canadian titles received on legal deposit and purchased. Areas of concentration: Canadian theatre and dance; European and American performing arts tradition; theatre architecture; stage craft; costume history, dance history and notation etc.

ON —METROPOLITAN TORONTO LIBRARY, Fine Arts Dept, 789 Yonge St, Toronto, M4W 2G8, Can. Alan Suddon, Head
Holdings: Vols (42,000) Cat Pix Microforms
Notes: Extensive collection.

ON —UNIVERSITY OF TORONTO, Thomas Fisher Rare Book Library, 120 Saint George St, Toronto, M5S 1A5, Can. Richard G Landon, Head
Notes: Juvenile Drama Collection of engravings and lithographs of costumed characters and sets for juvenile dramas to be cut out and mounted for use in children's toy theatre productions. Play booklets. Model stages. Primarily English. Some European material. Covers period from 1810 to 1940. Basis of the collection formed by Mr Seaton Reid. Includes 6000 sheets and 150 pamphlets.

COSTUME—PATTERNS

CA —CARLSBAD CITY LIBRARY, 1250 Elm Ave, Carlsbad, 92008. Clifford E Lange, Library Dir
Holdings: Vols (2297) Cat
Notes: Collection of sewing patterns. Catalogs of the patterns have been made up

COSTUME—PATTERNS (cont.)

with complete information on size, etc, and have been divided into subject areas, such as gift ideas, toys, dolls, women's clothes, men's clothes, children's clothes, etc. Also patterns for knitted and crocheted wearing apparel. Incl patterns for children's costumes, historical fashions and antique dolls.

WI —UNIVERSITY OF WISCONSIN-STOUT, Library Learning Center, Menomonie, 54751. Philip Sawin Jr, Coll Develop Librn
Notes: The School of Home Economics has developed a Museum of Costumes. This collection supports the museum and its programs. University of Wisconsin-Stout has been offering courses in Costumes since 1918.

COSTUME, MILITARY see Uniforms, Military and Naval

COSTUME, SLOVAK

PA —THE SLOVAK MUSEUM AND ARCHIVES AT JEDNOTA ESTATES, Rosedale & Jednota Sts, PO Box 150, Middletown, 17057. Edward A Tuleya, Cur & Archivist
Notes: Slavic Studies Collection incl artifacts; Slovak national costumes; looms and tools; lace, embroidery, ribbons; prayer books; documents; ceramics.

COSTUME, THEATRICAL see Costume

COSTUME DESIGN

CA —BURBANK PUBLIC LIBRARY, 110 N Glenoaks Blvd, Burbank, 91502. Mary Ann Grasso, Coordr; Barbara Stones, Coordr, Media Project
Holdings: Vols (500) Manuals Videocassettes Audiocassettes
Notes: This collection (including technical manuals, production directories, scripts, production lectures, seminars, and university classes), is a free public clearinghouse of industry trends, job skills information, technical advances and management practices required for film and video production. Information covers such technical categories as cinematography, editing, sound recording, lighting, and special effects. Craft areas include directing, scriptwriting, art direction and costume design. Management information covers producing, programming, financing, budgets and distribution for theatrical, broadcast, and non-broadcast markets. Bulk of collection circulates. Reference texts and some other restricted material available for in-library study only. List of holdings available on request.
See also entries under Moving Pictures - Production and Direction; Television

IL —UNIVERSITY OF ILLINOIS, URBANA/CHAMPAIGN, Library, 1408 W Gregory Drive, Urbana, 61801. Norman B Brown, Asst Dir for Special Collections
Notes: More than 3000 costume sketches, story boards, and fabric swatches from 160 productions designed by *Motley* Designers.

VA —GEORGE MASON UNIVERSITY, Fenwick Library, Special Collections Dept, 4400 University Drive, Fairfax, 22030. Ruth Kerns, Public Services Librn
Notes: The Federal Theatre Project Collection includes 5000 playscripts, 2500 radio scripts, 25,000 photographs, 40 blueprints, 1000 posters, over 1600 costume designs, 350 scene designs, 750 production notebooks, 1700 programs and heralds, 26 musical scores and 18 cubic feet of research materials and play readers reports.

WI —UNIVERSITY OF WISCONSIN-STOUT, Library Learning Center, Menomonie, 54751. Philip Sawin Jr, Coll Develop Librn
Notes: The School of Home Economics has developed a Museum of Costumes. This collection supports the museum and its programs. University of Wisconsin-Stout has been offering courses in Costumes since 1918.

COTTEN, JOSEPH

CA —UNIVERSITY OF SOUTHERN CALIFORNIA, Edward L Doheny Memorial Library, Archives of Performing Arts, University Park, Los Angeles, 90089. Robert Knutson, Librn
Holdings: Mss Pix
Notes: Personal collection of papers, pictures, etc.

COTTER, JOSEPH S.

KY —LOUISVILLE FREE PUBLIC LIBRARY, Western Branch, Fourth and York Sts, Louisville, 40203. Larry Rees, Mgr of Extension Services
Holdings: Vols 5000 Cat Mss Maps Pix
Notes: Includes some Joseph S Cotter ms items; also clippings.

COTTON

CA —UNIVERSITY OF CALIFORNIA, BERKELEY, Science Libraries, Natural Resources Library, 40 Giannini Hall, Berkeley, 94720. Norma Kobzina, Head Librn
Holdings: Vols (100,000) Cat Maps Microforms
Budget: ($40,000)
Notes: Subject emphasis is on basic agricultural and pest management research, particularly in the areas of tropical and subtropical agriculture and plantation crops, ie, cotton, rice, tobacco, and sugar. Materials in agricultural engineering, farm machinery, and veterinary medicine are not acquired for the Berkeley campus. Serials, especially the extensive holdings of foreign titles, constitute the collection's major strength. Over 5700 serials are being received currently.

IN —INDIANA UNIVERSITY, Lilly Library, Seventh St, Bloomington, 47405. William R Cagle, Librn
Holdings: / / Mss
Notes: Business papers and records of Indiana Cotton Mills, 1850-1947. Incl letterpress books, journals, consignment records, financial records, stock ledgers, as well as some records for the Cannelton Cotton Manufacturing Co, 1865-1867, and for D Newcomb & Co, a coal mining firm in Newburgh, Indiana, 1870-1875. 18,360 items. A related collection is that of Hamilton Smith's papers, 1823-1874. Smith (1804-1875) was a Louisville, Kentucky, lawyer and businessman involved in the organization and operation of the Cannelton Cotton Mill in 1848 until its sale to Indiana Cotton Mills in 1853.

MS —UNIVERSITY OF SOUTHERN MISSISSIPPI, William David McCain Graduate Library, Box 5148, Southern Sta, Hattiesburg, 39406.
Holdings: Vols 35 Cat
Notes: Oral history interviews with 35 individuals associated with the National Cotton Council of America (ca 1940-1980). Subject matter deals with the history of the Council and all aspects of the cotton industry, incl producers, ginners, warehouses, seed crushers, merchants, cooperatives and spinners.

COTTON, JOHN

MI —NORTHERN MICHIGAN UNIVERSITY, Lydia M Olson Library, Elizabeth L Harden Drive, Marquette, 49855. Stephen H Peters, Cataloger
Notes: A section of the personal library of Moses Coit Tyler, incl works by Thomas Hooker, John Cotton, Cotton Mather, and Jonathan Edwards.

PA —TEMPLE UNIVERSITY LIBRARIES, Special Collections Dept, Rare Books & Mss Section, Philadelphia, 19122. Thomas M Whitehead, Cur
Holdings: Vols Cat Mss
Notes: Seventeenth and 18th century books and pamphlets on political, religious, social and intellectual life and history of England. Strong holdings of John Cotton, Gilbert Burnet, Richard Overton, John Lilburne; Civil War pamphlets, ranters and levellers. The Nordell and Simpson Collections.

COTTON INDUSTRY

MS —MISSISSIPPI STATE UNIVERSITY, Mitchell Memorial Library, Box 5408, Mississippi State, 39762. Frances N Coleman, Head, Special Collections
Holdings: Mss
Notes: Papers of the Delta and Pine Land Co, 1886-1980, once the largest cotton plantation in the world.

COTTON PLANTERS LOAN ASSOCIATION

SC —COLLEGE OF CHARLESTON LIBRARY, Special Collections Dept, Charleston, 29401.
Notes: Papers of the Cotton Planters Loan Association, 1862.

COUCH, JOHN N.

†NC —UNIVERSITY OF NORTH CAROLINA, CHAPEL HILL, Department of Botany Library, 301 Coker Hall 010-A, Chapel Hill, 27514. William R Burk, Botany Librn
Notes: The mycology collection incl some 6000 pamphlets. It contains papers of the following scientists: William C Coker, John N Couch, Lindsay F Olive, mycologists; also, Victor A Greulach, plant pathologist. The mycology catalog is in preparation (1983), and will provide author, title, and subject access.

COUGHLIN, CHARLES EDWARD

NC —DUKE UNIVERSITY, William R Perkins Library, Durham, 27706. Elvin E Strowd, University Librn
Notes: The (Quasi)-Nazi collection consists of approximately 7000 items, primarily pamphlets published in the United States by and about Nazi sympathizers Gerald K Smith, Father Coughlin, etc and organizations with Nazi leanings.

COULTER, JOHN WILLIAM, 1888-1980

ON —MCMASTER UNIVERSITY, Mills Memorial Library, Div of Archives & Research Collections, Hamilton, L8S 4L6, Can. G R Hill, Univ Librn
Holdings: Mss
Notes: Extensive correspondence with theatrical figures, such as Tyrone Guthrie and Jean Gascon, authors' scripts for stage plays, television, and radio work, prose works, and research notes on creative interests, and also on Artists Brief to Turgeon Committee which led to Canada Council. Collection described in *Library Research News*, vol 6, no 2, Fall 1982 and vol 7, no 1, Spring 1983.

COUNCIL OF EUROPE

CA —UNIVERSITY OF CALIFORNIA, BERKELEY, University Library, Government Documents Department, 350 Library Annex, Berkeley, 94720. Suzanne Gold, Collection Dept Librn
Holdings: Vols (314,000) Cat Microforms
Budget: ($85,115)
Notes: General collection of government documents, historical and current, on the federal and state levels; as well as international and foreign documents. The Library's holdings are particularly strong in foreign statistics and censuses, and US Congress. The Government Documents Department serves as a full depository for GPO, NASA, State of California, EEC, GATT, IAEA, United Nations, UNESCO, Rand Corporation (non-classified), IBRD, OECD, ILO, UNITAR, ITC, and CE. Selective depository, PL-480 Programs, or gift or exchange arrangements obtain for the states of Michigan and Washington and for Canada, India, Pakistan and Indonesia. Incl microfilm and 300,000 fiche, cards, and prints.

COUNCIL ON FOREIGN RELATIONS

MD —JOHNS HOPKINS UNIVERSITY, Milton S Eisenhower Library, Charles & 34 Sts, Baltimore, 21218. Ann S Gwyn, Assistant Dir for Special Collections
Holdings: Cat Mss
Notes: Collected papers, 1904-1948. Correspondence incl council on Foreign Relations, 1931-1949, and American Geographical Society, 1915-1950. Together about 10,000 ms pieces. Restricted access; apply in advance.

COUNCIL ON GOVERNMENTS

DC —METROPOLITAN WASHINGTON COUNCIL OF GOVERNMENTS, Research Library, 1875 Eye St NW, Suite 200, Washington, 20006. Suan Kalish, Librn
Holdings: Vols (3000) Cat Microforms
Notes: Contains (on 75 reels of microfilm) archives of Maryland-National Park and Planning Commission, archives of the Council of Governments, and audits and financial reports of local governments (1950-date). Also incl annual reports, planning reports and budgets from each jurisdiction (1973-date).

COUNCIL ON LIBRARY RESOURCES

DC —LIBRARY OF CONGRESS, Manuscript Division, Washington, 20540. John C Broderick, Chief
Notes: Papers of Verner Warren Clapp, Chief Asst Librn of Congress, President of the Council on Library Resources, etc.

COUNCILS AND SYNODS

CA —STANFORD UNIVERSITY LIBRARIES, Cecil H Green Library, Stanford, 94305. Michael T Ryan, Cur
Holdings: Vols Cat
Notes: An emphasis in the Rare Book Collection.

CO —UNIVERSITY OF COLORADO, Libraries, Special Collections, Boulder, 80309. Nora J Quinlan, Head
Holdings: Vols 800
Notes: The Mandell Creighton Library. Renaissance papacy, Protestant reform and the Conciliar movement. Separate catalog.

MI —SUOMI COLLEGE, Finnish-American Historical Archives, Hancock, 49930. Kenneth Niemi, Archives Librn
Notes: Collection incl 8000 vols, 152,000 mss, 2000 photographs, 760 audiotapes; microforms and maps; 14,000 holdings are cataloged. Subject interests: coop movement, labor, pioneer library of rare books and church records, socialist and communist movements, temperance societies. Special Collections: Finnish language newspapers (includes 100 titles from 1876-present); Suomi Synod Archives; Finnish-American Oral History.

ON —HURON COLLEGE, Silcox Memorial Library, 1349 Western Rd, London, N6G 1H3, Can. Pamela MacKay, Chief Librn
Notes: Archives collection includes synod of the diocese of Huron and personal records of the Bishops.

COUNCILS AND SYNODS, ECUMENICAL—VATICAN II

NY —GENERAL THEOLOGICAL SEMINARY, Saint Marks Library, 175 Ninth Ave, New York, 10011. David Green, Dir
Holdings: Vols (200,000) Cat Mss Maps Pix Slides Microforms

COUNSELING

CA —CALIFORNIA INSTITUTE OF INTEGRAL STUDIES, Library, 3494 21st St, San Francisco, 94110. Vern Haddick, Library Dir
Holdings: Vols (23,000) Cat Maps Phonorecords Audiotapes
Budget: ($10,000)
Notes: Comparative philosophy, psychology and counseling and comparative religions of East and West. Incl 550 audiotapes.

MA —MASSACHUSETTS REHABILITATION COMMISSION, Library, 20 Park Plaza, Boston, 02116. June C Holt, Librn
Holdings: Vols (15,000) Cat Audiotapes 16mm Films Microforms
Budget: ($18,000)
Notes: For staff and community interested in rehabilitation literature, defined as publications which deal with impairments resulting in disabling conditions; mental and behavioral disorders; employment of the handicapped; counseling techniques with handicapped populations; sheltered workshops, rehabilitation facilities; halfway houses and independent living arrangements; psychological aspects of disability; attitudes toward the handicapped; and other material on services for the handicapped. Library subscribes to 70 journals relating to disability and rehabilitation.

NH —NEW HAMPSHIRE TECHNICAL INSTITUTE, Paul E Farnum Library, 5 Fan Rd, Concord, 03301. Wm John Hare, Librn
Notes: Collection incl mental health, alcoholism and counseling.

NY —FEDERATION EMPLOYMENT & GUIDANCE SERVICE, Richard J Bernhard Memorial Library, 510 Sixth Ave, 4th Floor, New York, 10011. Otto Kanocz, Chief Librn
Holdings: Vols (4000) Cat Microforms Videotapes Audiotapes VF
Notes: Occupational information, guidance and counseling, vocational rehabilitation. Incl 30,000 pamphlets; 200 periodical titles. Also incl 50 vertical files and microfiche. Open to the public.

NY —INSTITUTES OF RELIGION AND HEALTH LIBRARY, 3 W 29 St, New York, 10001. Frank P DeGeorges, Librn
Holdings: Vols 4000 Cat
Budget: $1000
Notes: Library not open to the general public. Incl 50 journals.

WI —UNIVERSITY OF WISCONSIN-STOUT, Library Learning Center, Menomonie, 54751. Philip Sawin Jr, Coll Develop Librn
Notes: One of eleven graduate programs in Marriage and Family Therapy in the United States. The program was begun in 1975. This special collection also includes video tapes of outstanding therapists and a specialized 16mm film collection.

COUNSELING, PASTORAL see Pastoral Counseling

COUNSELING AND PSYCHOLOGY see Psychology and Counseling

COUNTER-REFORMATION see Reformation and Counter-Reformation

COUNTIES—U.S.

IL —NEWBERRY LIBRARY, 60 W Walton St, Chicago, 60610. Diana Haskell, Cur of Modern Mss
Notes: Collections concerned with US historical county boundary data file, 1790-1970.

COUNTRY ARCHITECTURE see Architecture, Domestic

COUNTRY MUSIC see Music, Country

COUNTS, GEORGE S.

IL —SOUTHERN ILLINOIS UNIVERSITY, CARBONDALE, Delyte W Morris Library, Carbondale, 62901.
Holdings: Cat Mss Pix
Notes: The papers and library of John Dewey, incl letters, mss, photographs, etc. Also the library and papers of Dewey's colleague, George S Counts, authority on education in Russia; incl much correspondence with Charles and Mary Beard.

COUNTS OF REGLA see Regla, Counts of

COUNTY DOCUMENTS

CA —UNIVERSITY OF CALIFORNIA, LOS ANGELES, Research Library, Public Affairs Service, 405 Hilgard Ave, Los Angeles, 90024. Edward Shreeves, Chairman, Bibliographers Group; Eugenia Eaton, Head, Public Affairs Service
Holdings: Microforms
Notes: Depository for the official publications of California cities and counties, the state of California, the United States government, the United Nations and some of its specialized agencies (including the Food and Agricultural Organization and UNESCO), and such regional organizations as the European Communities and Organization of American States. Selected publications of other American cities and counties, of the other states and possessions of the United States, of interstate organizations, and of foreign governments (with emphasis on major world powers, Africa, Latin America and the Near and Middle East) and intergovernmental organizations.

DC —LIBRARY OF CONGRESS, Serial and Government Publications Division, Washington, 20540.
Notes: Serials. One of the largest and most extensive collections in the world, incl periodicals; scientific and learned journals in all languages and in all fields except agriculture and medicine; US Government serials (Federal, State, County, and Municipal); national foreign government serials from all countries; provincial serials from provinces possessing autonomy; municipal serials from principal cities; newspapers (850,000 unbound issues, 75,000 bound vols, 270,000 microfilm reels), 12,000 microprint cards of early American newspapers, 1704-1820, incl 1500 titles currently received, 500 of these being representative titles from all States of the Union and 1000 from all foreign countries.

DC —US BUREAU OF THE CENSUS, Library, Federal Office Bldg 3, Rm 2451, Washington, 20233. Betty Baxtresser, Chief, ASD Library Branch
Holdings: Vols (64,000) Cat
Notes: Periodic reports from the governments of the states, counties, cities with populations of over 10,000 and selected special districts of the US. Emphasis is on the financial aspects of governments. Reports are listed in a computer print-out comprising a volume of the printed *Catalogs of the Bureau of the Census Library*.

COUNTY GOVERNMENT

CA —ALAMEDA COUNTY LIBRARY SYSTEM, Business & Government Library, 2201 Broadway, Oakland, 94612. David Lewallen, Manager
Holdings: Vols (10,000) Cat Maps Microforms
Budget: ($50,000)

CA —SACRAMENTO PUBLIC LIBRARY, 828 I St, Sacramento, 95814. Dorothy Harvey, Librn, Special Collections
Holdings: Vols (4000) Cat
Notes: Incl books on public administration and police science, local government (city and county). Have over 4000 Sacramento city and county documents.

NC —GREENSBORO PUBLIC LIBRARY, Oral History Program Library, Drawer X-4, Greensboro, 27402. Eugene Edwin Pfaff, Jr, Librn
Holdings: Videotape Audiotape
Notes: Oral history on the cultural, social, and economic development of Greensboro and Guilford County; the program is expanding to incl prominent North Carolinians throughout the State. Collection consists of 42 videotapes and 93 audiotapes which are uncataloged.

COURLANDER, HAROLD

MA —BOSTON UNIVERSITY, Mugar Memorial Library, Special Collections Dept, 771 Commonwealth Ave, Boston, 02215. Howard B Gotlieb, Dir
Holdings: Mss Cat
Notes: Mss, correspondence, etc collected in depth; incl publications by or about.

COURSES OF STUDY see Education—Curricula

COURSING (RACING) see Dog Racing

COURTESY BOOKS

IL —NEWBERRY LIBRARY, 60 W Walton St, Chicago, 60610. Diana Haskell, Cur of

COURTESY BOOKS (cont.)

Modern Mss
Holdings: Vols 1550 Cat
Notes: See: Virgil Heltzel's *A Checklist of Courtesy Books in the Newberry Library,* 1942; and, Bell and Howell's microfilm package of *English Courtesy Books,* 1571-1773.

COURTLAND, IDA VAN

ON —METROPOLITAN TORONTO LIBRARY, Theatre Dept, 789 Yonge St, Toronto, M4W 2G8, Can. Heather McCallum, Head
Notes: Records of the Taverner touring company (scripts, prompt books, music correspondence, account books, photographs, clippings and programs) document the career of Albert Taverner and Ida van Courtland who toured Canada and the eastern United States in the late 19th century.

COURTS

NJ —RUTGERS, THE STATE UNIVERSITY OF NEW JERSEY, John Cotton Dana Library, 185 University Ave, Newark, 07102. Phyllis Schultze, Librn
Holdings: Vols 40,000 Cat
Notes: National Council on Crime and Delinquency. Criminology, as applied, means all phases of crime and delinquency prevention, control and treatment, ie, the whole "criminal justice" gamut: police, courts, probation and parole, prisons, community rehabilitation centers, etc. In short, everything except police laboratory materials. Collection completely cataloged; all criminological and correctional journals indexed. Incl many reports of correctional agencies, research reports, unpublished monographs, publications in the field by all government agencies, federal, state, county and local. Information file contains over 40, 000 such items, as well as about 10,000 uncataloged clippings and other pieces of information stored by specific subjects.

COURTS—U.S.

DC —LIBRARY OF CONGRESS, Law Library, 101 Independence Ave, SE, Washington, 20540. Carleton W Kenyon, Dir
Notes: US Supreme Court records and briefs. Microfilm 1832-1915 (records from January term 1832; briefs from January term 1854); microfiche 1934-date. Also, US Appellate Courts all circuits, but holdings vary for each circuit.

ME —BOWDOIN COLLEGE, Library, Brunswick, 04011. Dianne M Gutscher, Cur of Special Collections
Notes: The Harold Hitz Burton Supreme Court Collection contains about 175 volumes, incl presentation copies from Felix Frankfurter, Hugo Black, and others of that stature, and Supreme Court procedural rules and legal texts with the Justice's annotations. Also part of the collection are about 100 letters, many speeches, and autographed presentation photographs of fellow Justices.

COURTS, INTERNATIONAL see International Courts

COVARRUBIAS, MIGUEL

DC —LIBRARY OF CONGRESS, Prints & Photographs Div, Washington, 20540.
Notes: Swann Collection is strong in the work of contemporary cartoonists. Among the 400 artists represented are Peter Arno, Bil Canfield, Al Capp, Miguel Covarrubias, Louis Dalrymple, Whitney Darrow, Rube Goldberg, Thomas Nast, Jose Guadalupe Posada, Edward Sorel, and John Tenniel.

COVELL, WILLIAM EDWARD RAAB

CA —HOOVER INSTITUTION ON WAR, REVOLUTION & PEACE, Stanford University, Stanford, 94305. Milorad M Drachkovitch, Archivist
Holdings: // Mss
Notes: Papers, 1918-1968, of William Edward Raab Covell, Army officer. Official and general correspondence, diaries, documents, certificates, photos, yearbooks, clippings, memorabilia and other papers, relating to Maj Gen Covell's career. Incl material relating to his service as an Army engineer for the Caribbean Division (1942-1943) and as commanding general of the Services of Supply for China, Burma, and India (1943-1945). 4 boxes. Unpublished preliminary inventory in repository.

COVELLO, LEONARD

PA —BALCH INSTITUTE FOR ETHNIC STUDIES, Library, 18 S Seventh St, Philadelphia, 19106. R Joseph Anderson, Library Dir
Holdings: Mss Cat Pix
Notes: The Leonard Covello Papers span the years 1907-1974 and cover in detail almost every aspect of his life and activities. Incl in the papers are correspondence, biographical material, speeches, writings, teaching and administrative records, subject files, printed materials, organizational minutes and proceedings, reports and studies and news clippings. The collection also contains photographs and pamphlets as well as several reel recording tapes and two motion picture films.

COVENANT CHURCH OF AMERICA see Evangelical Covenant Church of America

COVENTRY, ENGLAND

†WA —WASHINGTON STATE UNIVERSITY, Library, Manuscripts, Archives & Special Collections, Pullman, 99164. John F Guido, Head
Holdings: Vols Cat Mss
Notes: Among the significant holdings are the William George Fretton papers relating to Coventry, England. A short-title catalog of English books prior to 1700 is cited in Down's *American Literary Resources*: p 664.

COVERED BRIDGES

IN —INDIANA HISTORICAL SOCIETY, Library, 315 W Ohio St, Indianapolis, 46202. Robert K O'Neill, Dir
Holdings: Cat Mss Maps Pix Slides

COVERLETS

NC —APPALACHIAN STATE UNIVERSITY, Belk Library, Appalachian Collection, Boone, 28608. Eric J Olson, Librn
Holdings: Vols (12,000) Cat Mss Maps Pix Slides Phonorecords Audiotapes
Budget: ($4000)
Notes: The Appalachian Collection incl the Fry Collectin of handmade quilts and coverlets; the York Collection of folk songs and ballads, plus tapes; the I G Greer Collection of Folk Songs and Ballads; the Amos Abrams ballad collection; artifacts, incl the Tatum Collection of household items, furniture, and farm implements; Daniel Boone loom; oral history tapes; the Jack Guy Collection of tapes of area music and photographs; and regional genealogy. This is a very comprehensive study on the Southern Appalachian Region. Separate catalog for the collection.

COVERS (PHILATELY)

CA —LINCOLN MEMORIAL SHRINE, A K Smiley Public Library, 125 W Vine St, Redlands, 92373. Larry E Burgess, Archivist
Holdings: Vols (3000) Cat Mss Maps Pix Slides Phonorecords 16mm Films Microforms
Budget: ($18,000)
Notes: One of the larger collections on Lincoln and his times. Incl broadsides, letters, prints, campaign badges, stamps, coins, medals; bust, by George Grey Bernard. Endowment of Watchorn Lincoln Memorial Association. There is an additional pamphlet collection of more than 3000 pieces; an extensive philately collection incl first-day covers, commemorative and foreign issues, and Civil War envelopes.

†PA —WAR COVER CLUB, American Philatelic Research Library, Library, PO Box 338, State College, 16801.
Holdings: Vols 300 Uncat Mss Maps Pix
Notes: Postal history of covers (envelopes) used by soldiers in all wars. Was cover collecting is a specialty within the general hobby of philately. It emphasizes the postal history of all wars.

ON —NATIONAL POSTAL MUSEUM, Philatelic Library, Ottawa, K1A 0B1, Can. Cimon Morin, Librn
Holdings: Vols 6000 Cat Maps Pix Slides Audiotapes Videotapes Microforms
Notes: Philatelic and postal history materials.

COVERT, JOHN

CA —FRANCIS BACON LIBRARY, 655 N Dartmouth Ave, Claremont, 91711. Elizabeth S Wrigley, Dir
Holdings: Mss Pix
Notes: Correspondence of Walter Arensberg with artists John Covert, Marcel Duchamp, Francis Picabia and his wife Gabrielle Buffet Picabia, and psychiatrist Elmer Ernest Southard, 1876-1920.

COVEY, ARTHUR

KS —SOUTHWESTERN COLLEGE, Memorial Library, 100 College St, Winfield, 67156. Daniel L Nutter, Librn
Holdings: Vols 200 // Cat Pix
Notes: The Arthur Covey Art Collection. Arthur Covey was a noted American artist from the 1920s until his death in 1960 and was a graduate of Southwestern. His wife, Lois Lenski, noted author and illustrator of children's books, gave all of his paintings, materials, and library to the college in 1960.

COVIN, KELLY

BC —UNIVERSITY OF VICTORIA, McPherson Library, Victoria, V8W 3H5, Can.
Notes: Mss of novels: *Hear That Train Blow; a Novel of the Scottsboro Case* (1970) and *Many Broken Hammers* (1971); mss of screenplays; TV scripts; correspondence; contracts (1966-1970).

COW COUNTRY see Cattle Country

COWAN, ROBERT ERNEST, 1862-1942

CA —UNIVERSITY OF CALIFORNIA, LOS ANGELES, Research Library, Dept of Special Collections, 405 Hilgard Ave, Los Angeles, 90024. Edward Shreeves, Chairman, Bibliographers Group; David S Zeidberg, Head
Holdings: Vols 45 Cat Mss Pix
Notes: Most books from his bibliography; 20 linear feet of correspondence and unprocessed mss (primarily Californiana).

COWBOYS

AZ —ARIZONA HERITAGE CENTER, Library, 949 E Second St, Tucson, 85719. Michael Weber, Dir
Notes: Espec with reference to Arizona, the West, and the Southwest.

CO —COLORADO HISTORICAL SOCIETY, Research Collections, 1300 Broadway, Denver, 80203. Catherine Kane, Head Public Service and Access
Holdings: Cat Mss Pix Microforms
Budget:
Notes: Correspondence and business records of cattle companies and cattlemen and railroads gathered as part of the Western Range Cattle Industry Study. Also, correspondence and records of companies,

COWBOYS (cont.)

organizations and related materials arranged by state (1850-1945). About 50,000 items.

CO —COLORADO STATE UNIVERSITY, Libraries, Fort Collins, 80523. John Newman, Special Collections Librn
Holdings: Vols (11,000) Cat Mss Pix
Budget: ($7000)
Notes: The Western American Literature Collection incl fiction, poetry, pictures, art, and other works of the imagination set in the American Frontier West and modern rural West, especially the Rocky Mountain Area. There is also a collection of some 500 pulp magazines, "Westerns" mostly.

DC —LIBRARY OF CONGRESS, Prints & Photographs Div, Washington, 20540.
Notes: The John C H Grabill collection of photographs of frontier life in Colorado, South Dakota, and Wyoming, late 19th century, incl views of hunters, prospectors, cowboys, Chinese immigrants, and US Army personnel. The Erwin E Smith Collection of cowboy and ranch life. Gift of 1776 original glass and nitrate film negatives of pictures taken by him. Gift of his sister, Mrs L McC Pettis in 1949.

IL —NEWBERRY LIBRARY, 60 W Walton St, Chicago, 60610. Diana Haskell, Cur of Modern Mss
Holdings: Vols 300 Cat Mss
Notes: Books incl brand books, accounts of cowboy life in late 19th, early 20th century America, biographies, Indian-White relations. Material kept in Ayer and Graff Collections; incl newspaper clippings.

MT —MONTANA HISTORICAL SOCIETY LIBRARY, 225 N Roberts St, Helena, 59601. Robert M Clark, Librn; Brian Cockhill, State Archivist
Holdings: Vols 3000 Cat
Budget: ($2500)
Notes: The Ames and Margaret Booth Teakel Range Life Memorial Collection (cowboy and cattle range subjects). The scope of this collection includes the entire West, not just Montana and contiguous states. Also, L A Huffman Collection; incl 1100 photographs.

NE —UNIVERSITY OF NEBRASKA-LINCOLN, Don L Love Library, University Archives and Special Collections, Lincoln, 68588. Joseph G Svoboda, University Archivist
Holdings: Pix Slides
Notes: R D Warden Collection of Charles Marion Russell. "Largest private collection of literature on Russell, 'The Cowboy Artist.'" 7000 items, incl first editions of every book and pamphlet by Russell and over 1000 periodical appearances of his art; 900 color prints; 142 drawings; color slides; scrapbooks about Russell and his family, from 1889.

OK —WILL ROGERS MEMORIAL LIBRARY, W Will Rogers Blvd, Box 157, Claremore, 74017. Reba N Collins, Dir
Holdings: Vols (2800) Cat Slides Phonorecords Audiotapes Videotapes 16mm Films Microforms
Notes: Thousands of original manuscripts, letters, photographs, plus many other personal items, all by or about Will Rogers. Library is available by appointment or special permission.

OK —NATIONAL COWBOY HALL OF FAME AND WESTERN HERITAGE, Library, 1700 NE 63 St, Oklahoma City, 73111. Esther Long, Librn
Holdings: Vols (8000) Uncat
Notes: Art of the American West. Covers western art and artists; rodeo and its history; cowboys; the cattle industry; and biographies on prominent westerners. Personal collection of Walter Brennen; collections of artists, Carl Link and James Earl Frazier.

OK —THOMAS GILCREASE INSTITUTE OF AMERICAN HISTORY & ART LIBRARY, 1400 North 25th West Ave, Tulsa, 74127. Sarah Hirsch, Librn
Holdings: Vols Cat Mss Maps Pix
Notes: Trans-Mississippi West, US, Indian and Hispanic history. The Gilcrease Library contains a total of about 40,000 mss; 10,000 imprints; 5000 photographs; 600 maps and 50,000 vols.

TX —AMARILLO PUBLIC LIBRARY, 413 E Fourth, Amarillo, 79101. Mary Kay Snell, Librn
Holdings: Vols Cat Mss Maps Pix
Notes: The southwest collections incl materials on the history of Texas, Louisiana, New Mexico, Arkansas, Missouri and Kansas. General subjects covered incl overland journeys, early narratives, early biographies, Indian captivities, outlaws, US government reports, Mississippi and Ohio Rivers, the Mexican War, reports of Catholic missionaries, Niles Register, early publications, fur trade, western trails, Texas Rangers, sheriffs and Texas as a sovereign state, buffalo hunting, Indian wars, cowboys, the arrival of farmers, fences, and towns. Over 1600 items which incl books, documents, maps, mss, pamphlets, unpublished theses, interviews and photographs. The three major collections are the William Henry Bush Collection, the Laurence J Fitzsimon Collection and the Calendar of John L McCarty.

TX —UNIVERSITY OF TEXAS LIBRARIES, General Libraries, Barker Texas History Center, PO Box P, Austin, 78712. Don Carleton, Dir
Holdings: Vols (132,000) Cat Mss Maps Pix Slides Phonorecords Audiotapes Microforms
Notes: See description of collection under Texas-History.

TX —PANHANDLE-PLAINS HISTORICAL MUSEUM, Research Center, Box 967, WT Sta, Canyon, 79016. Claire R Kuehn, Archivist-Librn
Holdings: Vols 8000 Cat Mss Maps Pix Microforms
Budget: $2000
Notes: History of the Texas Panhandle. Incl interviews with early settlers taken over a 50-year period, ranch records, and business records relating to the Texas Panhandle and surrounding states.

TX —TEXAS A&M UNIVERSITY, Sterling C Evans Library, Special Collections Div, College Station, 77843. Donald H Dyal, Librn
Holdings: Vols (16,000) Mss Pix
Notes: Jeff Dykes Range Livestock Collection (incl a 600-item collection of J Frank Dobie works). Part of the Dobie Collection is described in Dykes, Jeff C *My Dobie Collection* (College Station, Tex: Friends of the Texas A & M University Library).

TX —AMON CARTER MUSEUM, Library, 3510 Camp Bowie Blvd, PO Box 2365, Fort Worth, 76113. Nancy G Wynne, Librn
Holdings: Vols (25,000) Cat Mss Pix
Notes: The book collection, microfilm and photo archives have been built toward the goal of the interpretation of American history through art. At present, the greatest strengths are in Americana, Western Canadiana, bibliography, American exhibition catalogs and history of photography. Substantial books and files on American artists of the 19th and early 20th century, and particularly of Charles M Russell and Frederic Remington. Incl 25,000 pictures; 13,000 slides.

See also entries under Newspapers, American and Pictures-Collections

UT —UTAH STATE UNIVERSITY, Merrill Library, Department of Special Collections & Archives, Logan, 84322. A J Simmonds, Curator; Jeanie F Simmonds, Archivist; Bradford R Cole, Mss Librn
Holdings: Vols 110 Uncat Mss Pix Slides
Notes: The Austin E and Alla S Fife folklore archive of western, cowboy, and folksong materials. Over 300 pictures; 4200 slides; 800 field recordings; 75 ft of ms items. Complete card index to folklore themes in the collection. See Catalog of recordings in "A Bibiliography of the Archives of the Utah Humanities Research Foundation," *Bulletin of the University of Utah*, vol XXXVIII, no 9 (Dec 1947): pp 26-35; description of Fife Mormon collection in *Western Folklore* Quarterly, vol VII, no 3 (July 1948): pp 299-301; description of "Fife Collection of Western American Folksong and Folklore" in *The Folklore and Folk Music Archivist*, vol VII, no 2 (Spring 1964): pp 41-44.

VA —VIRGINIA POLYTECHNIC INSTITUTE AND STATE UNIVERSITY LIBRARY, Blacksburg, 24061. Glenn L McMullen, Special Collections Librn
Holdings: Vols (4000)
Notes: Collection largely consists of nineteenth century and early twentieth century imprints, emphasizing the role of native Virginians in the development of the trans-Mississippi West, particularly Texas; cowboys and the cattle industry; outlaws and lawlessness; and emigrants' guidebooks to states, cities, and regions in the West.

WV —SALEM COLLEGE, Library, Salem, 26426. Myron J Smith, Jr, Librn
Notes: Collection supports "the most complete equestrian studies program available anywhere". *Myron J Smith, Equestrian Studies:* the Salem College [Bibliographical] Guide to Sources in English, 1950-1980. Metuchen, NJ: Scarecrow Press, 1981; 4645 entries.

COWDRY, EDMUND V.

MO —WASHINGTON UNIVERSITY, School of Medicine, Archives, 660 S Euclid Ave, Saint Louis, 63110. Paul G Anderson, Archivist
Holdings: Mss Pix Audiotapes
Budget: ($38,000)
Notes: Institutional records and papers of faculty of Washington University School of Medicine and its predecessors and associated hospitals. Contains records of St Louis Medical College, Missouri Medical Barnard Free Skin and Cancer Hospital, Barnes Hospital, St Louis Children's Hospital and Jewish Hospital of St Louis. Incl papers of William Beaumont, Joseph Erlanger, Leo Loeb, Evarts Graham, Edmund V Cowdry, Helen Graham, Carl V Moore, Margaret Smith and others. Oral history program. See also: Anderson, Paul G and Hoolihan, Christopher, eds. *Special Collections* (St Louis: Washington University School of Medicine, 1981). 960 linear feet.

COWELL, SIDNEY ROBERTSON

DC —LIBRARY OF CONGRESS, American Folklife Center, Archive of Folk Culture, Washington, 20540.
Notes: The Sidney Robertson Cowell Collection of her folk music recordings, 1937 to 1957. Incl very unusual contributions by the Molokan community in the Potrero Hill neighborhood of San Francisco, a breakaway sect from the Russian Orthodox Church.

COWLES, BETSY MIX

OH —KENT STATE UNIVERSITY, University Archives, Kent, 44242. Stephen C Morton, University Archivist
Holdings: Uncat Mss
Notes: One cubic foot of manuscripts and printed materials of Betsy Mix Cowles, abolitionist, educator and women's rights advocate. Ms Cowles chaired the Women's Rights Convention at Salem, Ohio in 1850. The Collection contains correspondence dating from 1832, diaries, financial records, anti-slavery tracts, addresses, poems, pamphlets, and materials about Ms Cowles.

COWLES, REV. GILES HOOKER

OH —KENT STATE UNIVERSITY, University Archives, Kent, 44242. Stephen C Morton, University Archivist
Holdings: Uncat Mss
Notes: The ms material contained in 6 boxes (5 1/2 cubic feet). The collection comprises correspondence, journals, account books, sermons and miscellaneous material. From 1811 to 1834 Rev Cowles' journals provide an almost unbroken account of his activities as minister and missionary in the Western Reserve region of Ohio. There is also a sizable collection of material on the Fuller Family of Austinburg, Ohio (qv).

COWLEY, JOY

MA —BOSTON UNIVERSITY, Mugar Memorial Library, Special Collections Dept,

COWLEY, JOY (cont.)

771 Commonwealth Ave, Boston, 02215. Howard B Gotlieb, Dir
Holdings: Cat Mss Correspondence

COWLEY, MALCOLM

IL —NEWBERRY LIBRARY, 60 W Walton St, Chicago, 60610. Diana Haskell, Cur of Modern Mss
Holdings: Cat Mss
Notes: Primary repository of about 5000 ms pieces. Restricted use: noncirculating.

COWPER, WILLIAM

IN —INDIANA UNIVERSITY, Lilly Library, Seventh St, Bloomington, 47405. William R Cagle, Librn
Holdings: Vols 100// Cat
Notes: First and early editions of works by Cowper plus 43 vols from Cowper's own library.

OH —OHIO UNIVERSITY, Vernon R Alden Library, Department of Archives and Special Collections, Athens, 45701. Gary A Hunt, Head
Holdings: Vols 68 Cat
Notes: The bulk of the collection consists of early editions of Cowper's works; half the collection is dated 1820 or earlier.

PA —FREE LIBRARY OF PHILADELPHIA, Rare Book Dept, Logan Sq, Philadelphia, 19103. Marie E Korey, Rare Book Librn
Holdings: Vols 35 Cat Pix
Notes: The C Barton Brewster Collection of various editions of "John Gilpin's Ride."

COX, EARNEST S.

NC —DUKE UNIVERSITY, William R Perkins Library, Manuscript Dept, Durham, 27706. Ellen Gartrell, Cur of Mss
Holdings: Cat Mss
Notes: Papers of Robert S Rankin, member US Civil Right Commission 1960-69 and North Carolina Advisory Committee to US Commission; Boyte Family Papers; NCCLU Papers; Earnest S Cox Papers on 20th century Negro migration to Africa; papers of US senators, congressmen, others.

COX, JAMES M.

OH —WRIGHT STATE UNIVERSITY, Greater Miami Valley Research Center, University Library, Dayton, 45431. Patrick B Nolan, Head of Archives
Holdings: Mss
Notes: Correspondence, speeches, writings of Cox, 1920 Presidential Candiate. Incl 30 linear ft of manuscripts.

COX, PALMER, 1840-1924

CA —UNIVERSITY OF CALIFORNIA, LOS ANGELES, Research Library, Dept of Special Collections, 405 Hilgard Ave, Los Angeles, 90024. Edward Shreeves, Chairman, Bibliographers Group; David S Zeidberg, Head
Notes: 50 original drawings, mostly of Brownies; ephemera.

PA —FREE LIBRARY OF PHILADELPHIA, Rare Book Dept, Logan Sq, Philadelphia, 19103. Marie E Korey, Rare Book Librn
Holdings: Uncat Mss Pix
Notes: A collection of 90 pieces of original art and autograph letters.

COX, SAMUEL SULLIVAN, 1824-1889

RI —BROWN UNIVERSITY, John Hay Library, 20 Prospect St, Providence, 02912. Mark N Brown, Cur Mss
Holdings: // Mss
Notes: Samuel Sullivan Cox, lawyer, diplomat, and Congressman from Ohio and New York. About 1200 letters to Cox dealing chiefly with his role in politics. They cover the period 1852 to 1887 but are concentrated during 1861-1863 and 1883-1886. Correspondents incl his constituents, journalists, members of the Democratic Party. There are references to Salmon P Chase, General Hugh McClellan, C L Vallandigham, national elections, and abolitionists.

COYOTE'S JOURNAL ARCHIVE

BC —SIMON FRASER UNIVERSITY, Library, Burnaby, V5A 1S6, Can. Percilla Groves, Special Collections Librn
Holdings: Uncat Mss
Notes: *Coyote's Journal* Archive incl mss, correspondence and layout sheets of this little magazine, issues 5/6, 8, 9, and 10, 1966-1974.

COZACKS see Cossacks

COZZENS, JAMES GOULD

NV —UNIVERSITY OF NEVADA, RENO, University Library, Special Collections Dept, Reno, 89557. Robert E Blesse, Head
Holdings: Vols (47) Cat
Notes: Includes individual works by author in all editions including translations; also prefaces, introductions, published correspondence, appearances in anthologies, periodicals, etc. Bibliographical research collection, part of Modern Authors Collection. Other appearances 30 cataloged.

CRABB, JOHN, 1870-1961

KS —MENNINGER FOUNDATION, Archives, 5600 W Sixth St, Box 829, Topeka, 66601. Alice Brand, Librn; Mark West, Archivist
Notes: 6 boxes, 1919-55. Papers incl mss, reprints, and correspondence. Much of the collection pertains to his scientific research on peptic ulcers.

CRABBE, GEORGE, 1754-1832

CT —YALE UNIVERSITY, Box 1603A, Yale Station, New Haven, 06520.

OH —OHIO UNIVERSITY, Vernon R Alden Library, Department of Archives and Special Collections, Athens, 45701. Gary A Hunt, Head
Holdings: Vols 25 Cat
Notes: A representative collection of first and other early editions.

CRAFTS (HANDICRAFTS) see Handicrafts

CRAFTS, GEORGE INGLES

SC —COLLEGE OF CHARLESTON LIBRARY, Special Collections Dept, Charleston, 29401.
Notes: Papers, 1846-1847, incl correspondence between G I Crafts, while on a Near Eastern European tour, and his cousin, Maria Campbell, in Charleston, SC.

CRAFTSPEOPLE—BIOGRAPHY

CA —CRAFT AND FOLK ART MUSEUM, Library, 5814 Wilshire Blvd, Los Angeles, 90036. Joan M Benedetti, Museum Librn
Holdings: Vols (2000) Slides VF
Notes: Incl 2000 books; 70 journal subscriptions; artists' biographical files: 6 file drawers; clipping files: 8 file drawers; 20,000 slides. Representation of the material culture of all people, traditional and contemporary expressions. Incl visual and printed information on ethnic, traditional, popular, decorative, idiosyncratic, and contemporary crafts as well as vernacular architecture, handmade houses, and design. Information about and for professional artists on health hazards, conservation, and career management. Anthropological and art historical works; exhibition catalogues; slides, photographs, audiocassettes; clipping and pamphlet files. Contemporary Slide Registry of Craftspeople and extensive biographical files of contemporary craft artists. Information and referral files of craft related galleries, shops, festivals, organizations, etc.

MA —CHILDREN'S MUSEUM, Resource Center, Museum Wharf, 300 Congress St, Boston, 02210. Marie Ariel, Librn; Maria Russell, Resource Services Mgr
Notes: Curriculum materials and materials for children and adults. Available for reference use by the public; borrowing privileges for Museum members; activity and curriculum kits available to public, schools and community groups for rental fee. Collection of Northeast Indian objects housed in Study Storage facility for use by appointment with Curator; incl is a Folk Arts collection of oral history interviews with 40 Native American craftspeople, with supporting audio-visual materials. Subject-related programs and services offered by Museum staff.

NY —AMERICAN CRAFT COUNCIL, Library and Artists Registry, 44 W 53 St, New York, 10019. Joanne Polster, Librn
Holdings: Vols 3300 Cat Pix Slides Films
Notes: Crafts and craft-related subjects, incl portfolios for approx 2000 contemporary American craftspeople consisting of biographical material and photographs, indexed by media, geographic location, and a visual index. Over 1500 exhibition catalogs. The collection incl 35mm slide kits available for purchase. Catagories covered are: exhibitions of ACC's American Craft Museum from 1958 to date; kits in all media: fiber, metal, wood, clay, glass and multimedia; kits covering crafts processes. The Library also holds catalogs of craft school and art centers offering craft courses; newsletters, by-laws, and other materials of craft organizations and groups; the Archives and Photo-Archives of the American Craft Museum. No photocopying.

CRAHAN, MARCUS

CA —UNIVERSITY OF CALIFORNIA, LOS ANGELES, Research Library, Dept of Special Collections, 405 Hilgard Ave, Los Angeles, 90024. Edward Shreeves, Chairman, Bibliographers Group; David S Zeidberg, Head
Notes: 73 linear feet of medical files relating to Los Angeles County court cases. Closed to access until 2004 AD.

CRAIG, EDWARD GORDON, 1872-1966

CA —UNIVERSITY OF CALIFORNIA, DAVIS, Shields Library, Dept of Special Collections, Davis, 95616. Donald Kunitz, Head; C Danial Elliott, Asst Head
Holdings: Vols (35) Cat Phonorecords
Notes: Articles by and about Craig, catalogs of exhibitions of his drawings and models, recordings of Craig's Radio Talks, patent certificate of his "Improvements in Stage Scenery," and a photograph of a stage model showing the use of Craig's Screens.

CA —UNIVERSITY OF CALIFORNIA, LOS ANGELES, Research Library, Dept of Special Collections, 405 Hilgard Ave, Los Angeles, 90024. Edward Shreeves, Chairman, Bibliographers Group; David S Zeidberg, Head
Holdings: Vols (50) Cat Mss Pix
Notes: 50 books by and about Craig; 15 linear feet of correspondence, notebooks, prints, drawings, and models (incl the papers of his mother, Ellen Terry).

IL —NORTHWESTERN UNIVERSITY, Library, Special Collections Dept, 1937 Sheridan Rd, Evanston, 60201. R Russell Maylone, Cur
Holdings: Vols 210 Cat Mss Pix Phonorecords
Notes: Collection is being cataloged according to the Craig bibliography of Fletcher & Rood. Collection incl material about Ellen Terry and Henry Irving, as well as original art work by Craig, stage designs and other ephemera. Collection created by J Wesley Swanson and given to Northwestern Universtiy Library by his sister.

NY —NEW YORK PUBLIC LIBRARY, Performing Arts Research Center, Dance Collection, 111 Amsterdam Ave, New York, 10023. Genevieve Oswald, Cur
Holdings: Mss Pix
Budget: ($9,280)
Notes: Extensive written and visual

CRAIG, EDWARD GORDON, 1872-1966 (cont.)

documentation including many of the artist's published writings, as well as manuscript material relating to Isadora Duncan.
See also entry under Duncan, Isadora, 1877-1927

TN —MEMPHIS STATE UNIVERSITY, John Willard Brister Library, Memphis, 38152. John Terreo, Special Collections Librn
Notes: Theatre Collection, 1789-1972. Correspondence, scripts, programs, handbills, musical scores, clippings, drawings, sketches, and photographs, documenting careers of artists, production of plays, ballett and theatre companies, and theaters and opera houses centering in New York and London, England. Incl drawings, prints, publications, and other personal papers of British producer and designer Edward Gordon Craig (1872-1966), relating to his career, radio talks (1951-1961) for the BBC, acting school in Florence, Italy, and his mother, actress Ellen Terry; and correspondence, scripts, programs, reviews, scrapbooks, photos, and other materials, of American producer Jed Harris (?)-1979, relating to his stage productions (1926-1945).

BC —UNIVERSITY OF VICTORIA, McPherson Library, Victoria, V8W 3H5, Can.

CRAIG, EUGENE

OH —OHIO STATE UNIVERSITY, Library for Communication and Graphic Arts, 242 W 18th St, Columbus, 43210. Lucy S Caswell, Curator
Notes: The original works of editorial cartoonists Art Poinier, Scott Willis, Brian Basset, Billy Ireland, Frank Williams, Charles Werner, Ned Beard, L D Warren, Edward D Kuekes, Ray Osrin, Mike Peters, Draper Hill, Eugene Craig and Bert Whitman.

CRAIK, DINAH MARIA MULOCK, 1826-1887

CA —UNIVERSITY OF CALIFORNIA, LOS ANGELES, Research Library, Dept of Special Collections, 405 Hilgard Ave, Los Angeles, 90024. Edward Shreeves, Chairman, Bibliographers Group; David S Zeidberg, Head
Holdings: Vols 50 Cat Mss
Notes: 50 first and other editions of her books; 525 items of correspondence, mss, etc, relating to Craik, her family, her husband's family, and her friends.

NJ —PRINCETON UNIVERSITY, Library, Morris L Parrish Collection, Princeton, 08540. Alexander D Wainwright, Cur
Holdings: Vols 139
Notes: The collection contains over 6500 vols, as well as many theatre programs, playbills, photographs, clippings and other miscellanea. Parrish's goal was to assemble in both the English and the American first editions, in the original condition as issued, everything that a given author published. He was also interested in a high standard of condition for his books. Many additions have been acquired since the Parrish collection came to the Library as a bequest in 1944. The collection is an assemblage of author collections, consisting of books by: William Harrison Ainsworth, James Matthew Barrie, William Black, The Brontes, William Wilkie Collins, Dinah Mulock Craik, Marie de la Ramee ("Ouida"), Benjamin Disraeli, Charles Dickens, Charles Dodgson, George du Maurier, George Eliot (ie Mary Ann Evans), Elizabeth Gaskell, Thomas Hardy, Thomas Hughes,Charles Kingsley, Charles Lever, Edward George Earle Bulwer-Lytton, Mary Maxwell, George Meredith, Charles Reade, Walter Scott, Robert Louis Stevenson, William Makepeace Thackeray, Trollope Family, Ellen Wood, and Charlotte Yonge.

CRANACH, LUCAS

DC —FOLGER SHAKESPEARE LIBRARY, 201 E Capitol St, Washington, 20003. Philip A Knachel, Acting Dir
Notes: A major collection.
See also entry under Reformation.

CRANDALL, ELLA PHILLIPS

MA —SIMMONS COLLEGE ARCHIVES, 300 The Fenway, Boston, 02115. Megan Sniffin-Marinoff, College Archivist
Notes: Archives of the Simmons College School of Public Health Nursing (later reorganized into the School of Nursing) cover the years 1902-1970. Important correspondents in the collection incl M Adelaide Nutting, Mary Beard, Isabel Stewart, and Anne Hervey Strong, etc. Incl Strong's records of activity with regard to nursing education in the National Organization for Public Health Nursing, 1918-22. 1000 linear feet in institution, incl special collections nursing and photographs, nursing.

CRANDALL, PRUDENCE, 1803-1890

CT —CONNECTICUT COLLEGE, Library, Mohegan Ave, New London, 06320. Brian Rogers, College Librn
Holdings: Cat Mss
Notes: Prudence Crandall's married name is Philleo. Known generally as Prudence Crandall.

CRANE, GUY W.

AZ —NORTHERN ARIZONA UNIVERSITY, Special Collection Library, CU Box 6022, Flagstaff, 86011. Peter M Whiteley, Coordr/Archivist; William Mullane, Librn
Notes: Guy W Crane Collection; report by Crane, a mining geologist, entitled "Allison Mine, Pima County, Arizona," containing information on the mine's history, geology, production, and prospective development, 1940.

CRANE, HART

KY —UNIVERSITY OF LOUISVILLE, Ekstrom Library, Rare Books & Special Collections, 2301 S Third St, Louisville, 40208. George T McWhorter, Cur; Delinda Stephens Buie, Asst Cur

NV —UNIVERSITY OF NEVADA, RENO, University Library, Special Collections Dept, Reno, 89557. Robert E Blesse, Head
Holdings: // Vols (27) Cat Other appearances 475 Cat
Notes: Includes individual works by author in all editions including translations; also prefaces, introductions, published correspondence, appearances in anthologies, periodicals, etc. Bibliographical research collection, part of Modern Authors Collection.

NY —COLUMBIA UNIVERSITY LIBRARIES, Rare Book & Manuscript Library, 801 Butler Library, 535 W 114 St, New York, 10027. Kenneth A Lohf, Librn
Notes: Approx 800 ms items. Also have the Jethro Robinson collection. Restricted use.

OH —OHIO STATE UNIVERSITY, William Oxley Thompson Memorial Library, 1858 Neil Ave Mall, Columbus, 43210. Robert A Tibbetts, Cur of Special Collections
Holdings: Cat Mss
Notes: Incl 148 letters.

OH —KENT STATE UNIVERSITY, Libraries, Dept of Special Collections, Kent, 44242. Dean H Keller, Cur
Holdings: Vols 30 Cat Mss

VA —UNIVERSITY OF VIRGINIA, Alderman Library, Clifton Waller Barrett Collection, Charlottesville, 22901. Joan St C Crane, Cur of American Literature Collections
Notes: Papers.

CRANE, RICHARD T., 1882-1938

DC —GEORGETOWN UNIVERSITY, Library, Special Collections Div, 37 & O Sts NW, Washington, 20057. George M Barringer, Special Collections Librn; Nicholas B Sheetz, Mss Librn
Holdings: Mss Cat Pix
Notes: The personal papers of Richard T Crane (1882-1938), private secretary to Robert Lansing, 1915-1919; first American ambassador to Czechoslovakia, 1919-1921; and owner of the Westover Plantation in Virginia, 1921-1938. The papers - divided into three series, State Department, Prague and Westover - contain correspondence, memoranda, reports, diaries, documents, mss, printed material, and newspaper clippings. Correspondence incl letters from Robert Lansing, Charles Crane, Woodrow Wilson, Franklin Roosevelt, T G Masaryk, Jan Masaryk, Eduard Benes, Edward House, Herbert Hoover, Hugh Gibson, Joseph C Grew, Allan Dulles, and John Foster Dulles, among others.

CRANE, STEPHEN, 1871-1900

†CT —UNIVERSITY OF CONNECTICUT LIBRARY, Special Collections Dept, Storrs, 06268. Richard H Schimmelpfeng, Dir of Special Collections
Notes: Good and unusual collection.

IN —INDIANA UNIVERSITY, Lilly Library, Seventh St, Bloomington, 47405. William R Cagle, Librn
Holdings: Vols 74 Cat
Notes: First editions.

NH —DARTMOUTH COLLEGE, Baker Memorial Library, Hanover, 03755.
Holdings: Cat Mss Pix
Notes: First editions, ephemera, etc. Noncirculating.

NY —COLUMBIA UNIVERSITY LIBRARIES, Rare Book & Manuscript Library, 801 Butler Library, 535 W 114 St, New York, 10027. Kenneth A Lohf, Librn
Holdings: Mss Pix
Notes: 1200 ms items, chiefly letters. Restricted use.

NY —SYRACUSE UNIVERSITY LIBRARIES, Ernest S Bird Library, George Arents Research Library for Special Collections, Syracuse, 13210. Carolyn A Davis, Manuscripts Librn; Amy S Doherty, University Archivist; Mark F Weimer, Rare Book Librn
Holdings: Vols 600 Cat
Notes: Substantially the George Arents Collection of Stephen Crane incl first and subsequent editions of Crane works; first separate appearances of Crane stories; copies of Crane's journalistic writings, much secondary material of both a biographical and critical nature; association items.

OK —UNIVERSITY OF TULSA, McFarlin Library, Dept of Rare Books and Special Collections, 600 S College, Tulsa, 74104. David Farmer, Dir; Toby Murray, Archivist; Caroline Swinson, Cur of Manuscripts & Art
Holdings: Cat Mss Pix
Notes: The John Bennett Shaw Collection, incl 235 items by or about Crane.

PA —BRYN MAWR COLLEGE, Canaday Library, Bryn Mawr, 19010. James Tanis, Dir
Notes: Rare books and manuscripts.

PA —LAFAYETTE COLLEGE, David Bishop Skillman Library, Easton, 18042. Dorothy Cieslicki, Librn
Holdings: Vols 375 Cat
Notes: Collection of works by and about Crane. First editions and special editions only.

TX —UNIVERSITY OF HOUSTON, M D Anderson Memorial Library, University Park, Houston, 77004. David Farmer, Cur, Special Collections; Jean Jackson, Assistant Cur
Holdings: Vols 75 Cat
Notes: No published catalog. The emphasis is on textual studies, and variants, reprints, and periodical appearances are actively sought.

VA —UNIVERSITY OF VIRGINIA, Alderman Library, Clifton Waller Barrett Collection, Charlottesville, 22901. Joan St C Crane, Cur of American Literature Collections
Holdings: Vols 200 Cat Mss Pix
Notes: Includes ms of *The Red Badge of* Courage and minor works; Cora Crane's scrapbook; periodical appearances, etc: critical works.

WA —UNIVERSITY OF WASHINGTON LIBRARIES, Suzzallo Library, Special

CRANE, STEPHEN, 1871-1900 (cont.)

Collections Division, Rare Book Collection, FM-25, Seattle, 98195. Gary Menges, Coordinator for Special Collections
Notes: Printing history, including early printed books and modern fine printing; book arts, including papermaking, decorated papers, bookbinding, book design, and artist's books; American literature, 19th century includes: Stephen Crane, Ralph Waldo Emerson, Nathaniel Hawthorne, Henry James, Henry Wadsworth Longfellow, Herman Melville, Frank Norris, Harriet Beecher Stowe and Walt Whitman and 20th century includes: Theodore Roethke; illustrated books, including emblem books, historical children's illustration, books illustrated with prints, and artist's books; costume history; voyages and travels; preservation of library materials.

CRANE, WALTER, 1845-1915

CA —UNIVERSITY OF CALIFORNIA, LOS ANGELES, Research Library, Dept of Special Collections, 405 Hilgard Ave, Los Angeles, 90024. Edward Shreeves, Chairman, Bibliographers Group; David S Zeidberg, Head
Holdings: Vols 100 Cat Mss Pix
Notes: 100 books; original water colors for *Flora's Feast* and *Lionel's Latitudes;* text and original ink drawings for *Lionel's* Travels (unpublished).

MA —HARVARD UNIVERSITY LIBRARY, Widener Library, Cambridge, 02138.
Holdings: Vols 225 Cat Mss
Notes: Incl original drawings.

OH —CASE WESTERN RESERVE UNIVERSITY, M A Baxter School of Information and Library Science, 10900 Euclid Ave, Cleveland, 44106. Bettina MacAyeal, Librn; Gretchen Larson, Librn
Holdings: Vols (1100)
Notes: Incl collection of 1100 historical children's books and periodicals, housed in the Special Collections Dept of Freiberger Library, and can be used by the public. Incl *The Holy Bible Abridged* published by Isaiah Thomas in 1786, *The Life and Strange Surprising Adventures of Robinson Crusoe* of 1790, and a *Cinderella* dated 1809. There are examples of the work of illustrators Walter Crane, Randolph Caldecott, Kate Greenaway and Maurice Boutet de Monvel. The periodical collection incl a complete run of St. Nicholas Magazine.

CRANES, DERRICKS, ETC.

NC —WILSON COUNTY TECHNICAL INSTITUTE, Library, 902 Herring Ave, PO Box 4305, Wilson, 27893. Shirley Gregory, Librn
Holdings: Vols (150) Cat Slides Phonorecords Audiotapes 16mm Films Filmstrips
Notes: Emphasis on operation, maintenance, and safety for operators of earthmoving equipment and cranes. Incl 50 operator's manuals and 80 audiovisual programs.

CRANMER, THOMAS

IL —LOYOLA UNIVERSITY OF CHICAGO, E M Cudahy Memorial Library, 6525 N Sheridan Rd, Chicago, 60626.
Notes: Thomas Cranmer's working library and papers, incl ms of a critical edition of Thomas Cranmer's *Censurae* that Fr Surtz was working on at the time of his death.

CRANSON FAMILY

NY —CORNELL UNIVERSITY LIBRARIES, Collection of Regional History, Dept of Manuscripts and Univ Archives, Ithaca, 14853.
Notes: Incl 16 pieces. Papers, 1830-1886; letters, chiefly concerned with farm prices and production, and legal agreements, bills, receipts, and other papers of related families.

CRAPSEY, ADELAIDE

NY —UNIVERSITY OF ROCHESTER, Rush Rhees Library, Department of Rare Books and Special Collections, Rochester, 14627. Peter Dzwonkoski, Librn
Holdings: Vols Cat Mss Pix
Notes: Complete extant archive, including notes, drafts, and manuscripts of poems, correspondence and ephemera.

CRATER, FLORA

VA —UNIVERSITY OF VIRGINIA, Alderman Library, Manuscripts Dept, Charlottesville, 22901. Edmund Berkeley Jr, Cur
See also entry under Virginia History

CRAVEN, THOMAS TINGEY, 1808-1887

DC —GEORGETOWN UNIVERSITY, Library, Special Collections Div, 37 & O Sts NW, Washington, 20057. George M Barringer, Special Collections Librn; Nicholas B Sheetz, Mss Librn
Holdings: Mss Cat
Notes: Correspondence, mss, and documents from the naval career of Rear-Admiral Thomas Tingey Craven (1808-1887). The papers principally concern Craven's command of the US Frigate "Congress" in the Mediterranean squadron, 1856-58, as well as his duties as commander of the US practice ship "Plymouth" at Annapolis from 1860-61. Craven's long naval career incl participation in the Wilkes Expedition (1838-39), assisting Commodore Perry in the suppression of slave trade (1843), command of the "Brooklyn" in Farragut's squadron (1861-62), and the capture of the Confederate steamer "Georgia" (1864).

CRAVENS, JAMES ADDISON, 1818-1893

IN —INDIANA UNIVERSITY, Lilly Library, Seventh St, Bloomington, 47405. William R Cagle, Librn
Holdings: // Mss
Notes: Correspondence and papers of Indiana legislator and US Congressman James Addison Cravens, 1850-1872; member, Indiana House of Representatives, 1848-1849; Indiana State Senate, 1850-1853; US Congress, 1861-1865; served as delegate to Democratic national conventions in 1868, 1876, 1880, 1884. Most of papers concern his congressional years and relate to national and Indiana state politics, the progress of the war, appointments, speaking engagements, prisoners of war, etc. 78 items.

CRAWFORD, BILL

OH —OHIO STATE UNIVERSITY, Library for Communication and Graphic Arts, 242 W 18th St, Columbus, 43210. Lucy S Caswell, Curator
Notes: Original cartoons by Winsor McCay, John T McCutcheon, Dick Moores, Ned White, Walter Berndt, Jim Larrick, Carl Rose and Bill Crawford.

CRAWFORD, CHERYL

NY —NEW YORK PUBLIC LIBRARY, Performing Arts Research Center, Billy Rose Theatre Collection, 111 Amsterdam Ave, New York, 10023. Dorothy L Swerdlove, Cur
Holdings: Cat Mss Pix
Notes: Papers, scrapbooks, mss, photographs, memorabilia, etc.

TX —UNIVERSITY OF HOUSTON, M D Anderson Memorial Library, University Park, Houston, 77004. David Farmer, Cur, Special Collections; Jean Jackson, Assistant Cur
Notes: Cheryl Crawford Collection of theater books, posters, correspondence, original cast show recordings, tapes of discussions by noted theater artists, sheet music, playbills, first drafts of scripts and documents from the Actors Studio.

CRAWFORD, EDWARD F., JR.

NY —STATE UNIVERSITY OF NEW YORK, COLLEGE AT OSWEGO, Penfield Library, Oswego, 13126. Anne Commerton, Dir
Holdings: // Cat Mss Maps Pix
Notes: Collection documents Edward F Crawford's public life and political career while serving as Republican Assemblyman from Oswego County, 1956-1973 and Supreme Court Judge, 1973-1975. Incl are correspondence, scrapbooks, photographs, official property surveys, and maps. 14 ft of mss.

CRAWFORD, F. MARION

TN —F MARION CRAWFORD MEMORIAL SOCIETY, Saracinesca House, 3610 Meadowbrook Ave, Nashville, 37205. John C Moran, Dir
Notes: Almost complete collection of American first editions, etc. Reports other major collections at Harvard, The Gardner Museum (Boston), Huntington Library, Yale, Boston Public Library, Library of Congress, NYPL, etc.

CRAWFORD, JACK

CO —DENVER PUBLIC LIBRARY, 1357 Broadway, Denver, 80203.
Notes: Correspondence, papers, pictures, diaries, etc.

CRAWFORD, JOANNA

MA —BOSTON UNIVERSITY, Mugar Memorial Library, Special Collections Dept, 771 Commonwealth Ave, Boston, 02215. Howard B Gotlieb, Dir
Holdings: Cat Mss

CRAWFORD, MARTHA FOSTER

NC —DUKE UNIVERSITY, William R Perkins Library, Manuscript Dept, Durham, 27706. Ellen Gartrell, Cur of Mss
Holdings: Cat Mss
Notes: Methodist Church Papers (records of local and regional units) also many personal and professional papers of clergy, missionaries and laymen, 19th-20th centuries, eg Methodist John Lakin Brasher (holiness movement leader), Carlyle Marney (Southern Baptist minister), Methodist Bishop James Cannon, missionary Martha Foster Crawford.

CRAWFORD, MERRITT

NY —MUSEUM OF MODERN ART, Dept of Film, 11 W 53 St, New York, 10019. Eileen Bowser, Cur
Holdings: Mss Pix
Notes: Papers, correspondence, scrapbooks, pictures, etc. Partially cataloged.

CRAWFORD FAMILY

DC —GEORGETOWN UNIVERSITY, Library, Special Collections Div, 37 & O Sts NW, Washington, 20057. George M Barringer, Special Collections Librn; Nicholas B Sheetz, Mss Librn
Holdings: Mss Cat
Notes: Correspondence and documents to, from, and concerning the Crawford family of Georgetown, DC. Incl are numerous documents of a local civic nature, especially in reference to the activities of Richard R Crawford who served as mayor of Georgetown from 1857-1861, and served periodically as Justice of Peace. Among items of particular interest are a record book from the Board of Aldermen (1857-1858) and a letter from Emma D E N Southworth, noted authoress.

CRAY, ED

CA —UNIVERSITY OF CALIFORNIA, LOS ANGELES, Research Library, Dept of Special Collections, 405 Hilgard Ave, Los Angeles, 90024. Edward Shreeves, Chairman, Bibliographers Group; David S Zeidberg, Head
Notes: 21 linear feet of mss and files related to his research on General Motors and his involvement in ACLU.

CREATION

MI —ANDREWS UNIVERSITY, James White Library, Berrien Springs, 49104. Marley H Soper, Dir
Holdings: Cat Mss
Notes: The George McCready Price Collection on the theory of Creation, geology, etc. Much of this material was gathered by this author and educator in preparation for numerous books and pamphlets. He is described as an ardent creationist and a vigorous opponent of the theory of evolution. Over 900 items. Not available by interlibrary loan, but may by used at this library.

CREATIVE THINKING (EDUCATION)

NY —STATE UNIVERSITY OF NEW YORK, COLLEGE AT BUFFALO, E H Butler Library, 1300 Elmwood Ave, Buffalo, 14222. Susan M Stievater, Creative Studies Librn
Holdings: Vols 5000 Cat Mss
Budget: $2000
Notes: The Creative Studies Library is considered by the staff of The Creative Education Foundation (Dr Sidney J Parnes, President, 1300 Elmwood Avenue, Buffalo, New York, 14222) to be one of the most comprehensive collections on creativity in the world. The world-renowned annual Creative Problem Solving Institute is held on the campus and this collection is a major emphasis of the Institute. Of special significance are 2000 cataloged doctoral dissertations in microform and numerous cataloged printed material not easily found elsewhere, as well as more than 1000 unpublished papers, and miscellanea. The collection is supplemented by the College Library periodical holdings.

CREDIT, AGRICULTURAL see Agricultural Credit

CREDIT FONCIER

CA —CALIFORNIA STATE UNIVERSITY, FRESNO, Henry Madden Library, Dept of Special Collections, Fresno, 93740. Ronald J Mahoney, Head
Holdings: Vols 130 Cat Mss Maps Pix
Notes: Archives of Albert Kimsey Owen, founder of the utopian colony at Topolobampo, Sinaloa, Mexico. Over 10,000 letters, maps, documents, pictures, newspapers, pamphlets, and plans, relating to the colony and the Credit Froncier Company already represented in the Library by the Viola Gabriel Collection of about 800 similiar items and nearly 500 photographs. See *Cat's Paw Utopia*, by Ray Reynolds (El Cajon, Calif, 1971). Incl 20 linear feet of ms material. Partially cataloged.

CA —UNIVERSITY OF CALIFORNIA, SAN DIEGO, Central University Library, Mandeville Dept of Special Collections, La Jolla, 92093. Lynda Corey Claassen, Head
Holdings: Vols 15 // Uncat Mss Maps Pix
Notes: Largely manuscript materials, pamphlets, newspapers.

OH —OHIO STATE UNIVERSITY, Agriculture Library, 2120 Fyffe Rd, Agricultural Administration Bldg, Columbus, 43210. Mary P Key, Head
Holdings: Vols (12,000) Cat Mss Maps Pix
Notes: The Arnold Agricultural Credit Collection. There is a special catalog which is not being kept up-to-date. Much of the material is in a pamphlet file arranged by country or other geographical unit. All interlibrary loan requests are handled through the interlibrary loan department of our main library. Address: Interlibrary Loan; Main Library, Ohio State University, 1858 Neil Ave, Columbus, Ohio 43210.

CREE INDIANS

ON —VICTORIA UNIVERSITY, Library, 71 Queen's Park Crescent, Toronto, M5S 1K7, Can. Robert C Brandeis, Chief Librn
Holdings: Vols (1000)// Cat Mss Maps Pix
Notes: Collection consists of books, pamphlets, and government reports mainly dealing with North American Indians and western explorations and missionary enterprises among the Indian tribes in Canada. Incl Indian Bibles and hymnbooks, and mss and vols by Peter Jones (an Indian missionary) and James Evans (inventor of the Cree syllabic alphabet).

CREEK INDIANS

OK —OKLAHOMA HISTORICAL SOCIETY, Library, Historical Bldg, Oklahoma City, 73105. Andrea Clark, Dir, Library Resources Division
Holdings: Vols (43,000) Cat Mss Maps Pix Microforms
Notes: The Society also has the Indian Archives Collection of 2,500,000 pieces (Mary Lee Boyle, Archivist). This is an extensive collection of records, particularly of the Five Civilized Tribes. Incl tribal rolls, agency reports, manuscripts, etc.

OK —THOMAS GILCREASE INSTITUTE OF AMERICAN HISTORY & ART LIBRARY, 1400 North 25th West Ave, Tulsa, 74127. Sarah Hirsch, Librn
Holdings: Vols Cat Mss Maps Pix
Notes: Trans-Mississippi West, US, Indian and Hispanic history. The Gilcrease Library contains a total of about 40,000 mss; 10,000 imprints; 5000 photographs; 600 maps and 50,000 vols.

CREEKMORE, HUBERT

MA —BOSTON UNIVERSITY, Mugar Memorial Library, Special Collections Dept, 771 Commonwealth Ave, Boston, 02215. Howard B Gotlieb, Dir
Holdings: Cat Mss
Notes: Mss, correspondence, etc collected in depth; incl publications by or about.

CREEL, LORENZO D.

NV —UNIVERSITY OF NEVADA, RENO, University Library, Special Collections Dept, Reno, 89557. Robert E Blesse, Head
Holdings: Vols (1100) Mss Pix
Notes: Includes over 5000 photographs, government documents, periodicals, 80 cu ft manuscripts, and audiotapes. The Great Basin Indian Collection contains materials on the anthropology, archeology, and ethnohistory of the Great Basin region. Materials are collected for a defined group of 65 tribes including Washo, Shoshone, Northern and Southern Paiute, the major tribes of the region. Collections of importance include the Sven Liljeblad Collection, linguistics and ethnography; papers of US Indian agent Lorenzo D Creel, 1902-1922; Robert Leland Collection, Indian water rights.

CREELEY, ROBERT, 1926-

CT —UNIVERSITY OF CONNECTICUT, Library, Storrs, 06268. George F Butterick, Cur of Literary Archives
Holdings: Mss Pix Audiotapes
Notes: American poet. Collected in depth; incl publications by and about him.

IN —INDIANA UNIVERSITY, Lilly Library, Seventh St, Bloomington, 47405. William R Cagle, Librn
Holdings: // Cat Mss
Notes: Mss and letters of Robert Creeley, 1949-1961. Incl a journal; drafts of stories and poems; letters, 1950-1954. 66 items. Letters to Cid Corman from Creeley, 1949-1955. 300 items. Library's holdings incl first editions of Creeley's published works.

MO —WASHINGTON UNIVERSITY, John M Olin Library, Campus Box 1061, St Louis, 63130.
Notes: A major collection, incl mss, correspondence, literary papers, photographs, etc. Described in *Special Collections: an Annotated Guide to the Holdings of the Manuscript Division and the University Archives and Research Collection.*

NV —UNIVERSITY OF NEVADA, RENO, University Library, Special Collections Dept, Reno, 89557. Robert E Blesse, Head
Holdings: // Vols (123) Cat Other appearances 525 Cat
Notes: Includes individual works by author in all editions including translations; also prefaces, introductions, published correspondence, appearances in anthologies, periodicals, etc. Bibliographical research collection, part of Modern Authors Collection.

NY —STATE UNIVERSITY OF NEW YORK, STONY BROOK, Melville Library, Dept of Special Collections, Stony Brook, 11794. Evert Volkersz, Head
Holdings: Vols 110 Cat Mss
Notes: Publications and ms materials of poets who studied with Charles Olson at Black Mountain College, incl Robert Creeley, who also edited *Black Mountain* Review, and those associated with that generation of writers. In addition, authors and poets associated with The Perishable Press Ltd of Wisconsin, which started publication in 1966 and has published Paul Blackburn, David Kherdian, Galway Kinnell, Toby Olson, Joel Oppenheimer, W D Snodgrass, William Stafford, Diane Wakoski, Keith and Mary Waldrop, and Perishable Press owners Walter and Mary Hamady.

BC —SIMON FRASER UNIVERSITY, Library, Burnaby, V5A 1S6, Can. Percilla Groves, Special Collections Librn
Holdings: Cat Mss
Notes: Sixty-three letters and one postcard, 1950-1954, to Richard Wirtz Emerson, editor of *Golden Goose;* together with tss of poems, stories and essays sent with the letters; incl typescript of *Le Fou,* "Mr Blue," "The Party," "Three Fate Tales," and "The Grace."

CREIGHTON, TOM

TX —TEXAS A&M UNIVERSITY, Sterling C Evans Library, University Archives, College Station, 77843. Charles R Schultz, University Archivist
Notes: The Archives of Modern Politics: Texas Legislator Tom Creighton, 1961-1980.

TX —NORTH TEXAS STATE UNIVERSITY, Archives, NT Station Box 5188, Denton, 76203. Robert LaForte, University Archivist
Notes: Part of Oral History Collection. Interviews with member of Texas legislature.

CREOLE DIALECTS

MA —HARVARD UNIVERSITY LIBRARY, Cambridge, 02138.
Holdings: Cat

CRESSEY, GEORGE BABCOCK

NY —SYRACUSE UNIVERSITY LIBRARIES, Ernest S Bird Library, George Arents Research Library for Special Collections, Syracuse, 13210. Carolyn A Davis, Manuscripts Librn; Amy S Doherty, University Archivist; Mark F Weimer, Rare Book Librn
Notes: The George Arents Research Library for Special Collections at Syracuse University contains the papers of George Babcock Cressey and Preston E James.

CRESSY, HUGH PAULIN

†CA —UNIVERSITY OF SAN FRANCISCO, Richard A Gleeson Library, The Countess Bernardine Murphy Donohue Rare Book Room, San Francisco, 94117. D Steven Corey, Special Collections Librn
Holdings: Vols (300) Cat
Notes: Largely from the Virtue-Cahill library in England, and the collection of Charles A Fracchia. Incl important works of Bayly, Cressy, Sergeant, and Worsley. Incl a contemporary manuscript of the trial of Father Garnet, accused of complicity in the Gunpowder Plot.

CREST THEATRE, TORONTO

ON —METROPOLITAN TORONTO LIBRARY, Theatre Dept, 789 Yonge St, Toronto, M4W 2G8, Can. Heather McCallum, Head
Notes: Special collections relating to the

CREST THEATRE, TORONTO (cont.)

history of the performing arts in Canada incl the records of the Taverner Company which played Eastern Canada and the United States in the late 19th century, Toronto's Grand Opera House, the Marks Brothers touring company, film actor Ned Sparks, the Canadian-born actress Judith Evelyn, Crest Theatre (Toronto), the Canadian Players, Montreal Repertory Theatre, dancer/teacher Boris Volkoff, The Dumbells, the Canadian all-soldier concert party which originated in France in 1917, and vaudeville performer Charles Manny.

CRETE

†VA —GEORGE C MARSHALL RESEARCH FOUNDATION AND LIBRARY, Drawer 920, Lexington, 24450. Royster Lyle Jr, Cur Collections
Holdings: Vols Uncat Mss
Notes: Examples of ancient writings of Europe, Crete, and Easter Island, and material on the Aztecs, Incas, and particularly the Mayans.

CREWS, JUDSON C., 1918-

CA —UNIVERSITY OF CALIFORNIA, LOS ANGELES, Research Library, Dept of Special Collections, 405 Hilgard Ave, Los Angeles, 90024. Edward Shreeves, Chairman, Bibliographers Group; David S Zeidberg, Head
Notes: 2 linear feet correspondence, mss, and ephemera reflecting Crews' work as poet and editor of poetry magazines.

CT —YALE UNIVERSITY, Box 1603A, Yale Station, New Haven, 06520.

CREYTON, PAUL see Trowbridge, John Townsend (Paul Creyton)

CRICKET

PA —HAVERFORD COLLEGE, Magill Library, Special Collections Dept, Haverford, 19041. Diana Alteu, Manuscripts Librn; E Rotau Sargent, Cricket Collection Librn
Holdings: Vols 1125 Mss Pix
Notes: The C C Morris Cricket Library Association Collection. Perhaps the largest cricket collection in the Western Hemisphere. Incl books, periodicals, photographs, both foreign and American. Much on cricket in the Philadelphia area.

ON —RIDLEY COLLEGE LIBRARY, PO Box 3013, Saint Catharines, L2R 7C3, Can.
Notes: The Karl Andre Auty Collection of over 3000 books on cricket, kept current by endowed funds. Incl the scrapbooks of Sir C Aubrey Smith's career in cricket, from the 19th century.

CRIME AND CRIMINALS

CA —UNIVERSITY OF CALIFORNIA, BERKELEY, Institute of Governmental Studies Library, 109 Moses Hall, Berkeley, 94720. Jack Leister, Head Librn
Holdings: Vols (350,000) Cat Mss Maps Microforms
Budget: ($160,000)
Notes: The library collects primarily pamphlets. Incl in the library's holdings are documents from all levels of government, as well as publications issued by professional associations and special interest groups. A G K Hall catalog covering the Institute's Library holdings is available. Since 1937, Library has been depository for all California local documents (city, county & special district). Formerly: Bureau of Public Administration.
Notes: The Warner Research Collection is a full service research division designed to serve the production needs of the motion picture, television, theatrical, and creative arts communities. This is a see-based service available by appointment only. Subject specialties include costumes, U.S. military, crime and criminals, transportation, license plates, and Sears catalogues.

CA —BURBANK PUBLIC LIBRARY, 110 N Glenoaks Blvd, Burbank, 91502. Mary Ann Grasso, Coordr; Barbara Stones, Coordr, Media Project
Holdings: Vols (32,000) Cat Clippings Pix VF

CA —LOS ANGELES PUBLIC LIBRARY, Social Sciences Dept, 630 W Fifth St, Los Angeles, 90071. Marilyn C Wherley, Principal Librn
Holdings: Vols 10,000 Cat
Budget: ($150,000)
Notes: Pamphlets, periodicals, government documents, legislation, statistics. Incl Crime File, and index of over 10,000 clippings and analytics of crime and criminals throughout the world.

CA —HOOVER INSTITUTION ON WAR, REVOLUTION & PEACE, Stanford University, Stanford, 94305. Milorad M Drachkovitch, Archivist
Holdings: Mss
Notes: Papers of Rusztem Vambery, Hungarian author, lawyer, and Minister to the US, 1947-48, incl correspondence, speeches and writings, reports, printed matter, and other material, 1905-48, relating to his legal and political careers, to criminology, and to Hungarian domestic and foreign affairs. 9 ms boxes.

DC —FEDERAL BUREAU OF PRISONS, Library, 320 First St NW, Washington, 20001. Lloyd W Hooker, Librn
Holdings: Vols (2500) Cat
Budget: ($20,000)

DC —US DEPT OF JUSTICE, Drug Enforcement Administration, Library, 1405 I St NW, Washington, 20537. Morton S Goren, Librn
Holdings: Vols (10,000) Cat Microforms
Notes: Narcotics and dangerous drugs control.

FL —UNION CORRECTIONAL INSTITUTION LIBRARY, PO Box 221, Raiford, 32083. Harry Rabe, Librn
Holdings: Vols 16,000 Cat Mss Maps

IL —NORTHWESTERN UNIVERSTIY, School of Law, Library, 357 E Chicago Ave, Chicago, 60611. George S Grossman, Dir
Holdings: Cat
Notes: Comprehensive collections of Anglo-American and foreign (especially European) law; Roman and Canon law (selective); international law; European Common Market; Williams Collection of Legal Instruments (AD 1300-1700); George W Shaw Collection of Early European Law. Incl 500 ms legal documents.

IN —INDIANA UNIVERSITY, Lilly Library, Seventh St, Bloomington, 47405. William R Cagle, Librn
Holdings: // Cat
Notes: Largely 19th century materials on London crime and criminals.
See also entry under Pearson, Edmund Lester

IN —INDIANA LAW ENFORCEMENT ACADEMY, David F Allen Memorial Learning Resources Center, Rd 700 E, PO Box 313, Plainfield, 46168. Donna K Zimmerman, Librn
Holdings: Vols (4500) Cat Slides 16mm Films
Budget: ($8500)
Notes: Concentrated in the areas of police science, criminology, and law.

IA —IOWA STATE UNIVERSITY, Library, Dept of Special Collections, Ames, 50011. Stanley M Yates, Head
Holdings: Mss Pix
Notes: Iowa Bankers Association Records (1910-1973). Collection contains correspondence, printed matter, minutes, reports, financial records, photographs and newspaper clippings relating to financial and economic conditions. Also contains files and photographs relating to crimes against Iowa banks. About 700 linear feet. Finding aid available.

MD —INTERNATIONAL ASSOCIATION OF CHIEFS OF POLICE, 13 Firstfield Rd, PO Box 6010, Gaithersburg, 20760.
Holdings: Vols (6000) Cat Mss
Notes: Collection heavy in criminal investigation, crime prevention, police administration and management. Collecting in public sector labor relations, family violence, terrorism.

MA —BOSTON UNIVERSITY, Mugar Memorial Library, Special Collections Dept, 771 Commonwealth Ave, Boston, 02215. Howard B Gotlieb, Dir
Holdings: Cat Mss Pix
Notes: Mss and books by collected in depth. See also names of individual mystery writers.

MA —HARVARD UNIVERSITY LIBRARY, Law School Library, Langdell Hall, Cambridge, 02138. Harry S Martin III, Librn
Holdings: Cat Mss Maps Pix Slides
Notes: Downs 1687, 1763, 1774, 1776-1779, 1782-1784, 1790-1793, 1809, 1764, 1768, 1796; Downs Supplement 789. Comprehensive collection of English common law, American law (historical and current), foreign law, comparative law, international law, Roman law and Canon law. Over a million vols.

MI —WAYNE STATE UNIVERSITY, Arthur Neef Law Library, Detroit, 48202. Georgia Clark, Law Librn
Holdings: Vols (165,587) Cat Microforms

MI —MICHIGAN STATE UNIVERSITY, Libraries, Special Collections Div, East Lansing, 48824. Jannette Fiore, Librn
Holdings: Vols 1440 // Uncat Mss
Notes: Works from 15th to 19th centuries on criminology, criminal law and jurisprudence, including witchcraft, demonology, et al, chiefly in German and Latin.

MO —UNIVERSITY OF MISSOURI-COLUMBIA, Law Library, Tate Hall, Columbia, 65211. Susan D Csaky, Law Librn
Holdings: Vols 2200 // Cat Microfiche 150
Notes: 19th century crimes and criminal trials. Some of the material is reproduced on microfiche and published by Fred B Rothman & Co as *A Collection of Trials on* Microfiche, comp and indexed by Susan D Csaky.

MO —SAINT LOUIS POLICE LIBRARY, 315 S Tucker Blvd, Saint Louis, 63102. Cathy Reilly, Librn
Holdings: Vols (21,000) Cat Mss Pix Microforms
Budget: ($18,400)
Notes: Library on all subjects of police work is open to the public for general reference use.

MO —CENTRAL MISSOURI STATE UNIVERSITY, Ward Edwards Library, Warrensburg, 64093. Nancy E Littlejohn, Social Sciences Librn
Holdings: Vols (8000) Cat Microforms
Budget: ($7500)
Notes: Extensive criminal justice and law collection. In addition, a 7593 title microfiche collection of criminal justice and juvenile delinquency.

NJ —RUTGERS, THE STATE UNIVERSITY OF NEW JERSEY, John Cotton Dana Library, 185 University Ave, Newark, 07102. Phyllis Schultze, Librn
Holdings: Vols 40,000 Cat
Notes: National Council on Crime and Delinquency. Criminology, as applied, means all phases of crime and delinquency prevention, control and treatment, ie, the whole "criminal justice" gamut: police, courts, probation and parole, prisons, community rehabilitation centers, etc. In short, everything except police laboratory materials. Collection completely cataloged; all criminological and correctional journals indexed. Incl many reports of correctional agencies, research reports, unpublished monographs, publications in the field by all government agencies, federal, state, county and local. Information file contains over 40, 000 such items, as well as about 10,000 uncataloged clippings and other pieces of information stored by specific subjects.

NY —FORDHAM UNIVERSITY LIBRARY, Bronx, 10458. Joseph A LoSchiavo, Reference Librn
Holdings: Vols 1000 // Uncat
Notes: The McGarry Collection. No photocopying.

CRIME AND CRIMINALS (cont.)

NY —NEW YORK STATE HISTORICAL ASSOCIATION, Library, Lake Rd, Cooperstown, 13326. Amy Barnum, Librn
Holdings: Vols 400 Cat
Notes: At the present time a marked copy of T M McDade's *Annals of Murder* (1961), with additions, serves as a finding aide. Essentially collection consists of 18th-19th century American murder pamphlets. Noncirculating.

†NY —COLUMBIA UNIVERSITY LIBRARIES, Butler Library, Rare Book and Manuscript Library, 535 W 114 St, New York, 10027.
Notes: The Papers of Dr David Abrahamsen, incl letters and mss. Contains letters from and interviews with family and friends of Richard M Nixon and 167 typed and handwritten letters sent by David Berkowitz to Dr Abrahamsen from Attica Prison during 1979-81.

NY —MILTON HELPERN LIBRARY OF LEGAL MEDICINE, 520 First Ave, New York, 10016. Barry W Seaver, Librn
Holdings: Vols (2480) Cat Pix Slides Microforms
Notes: Forensic (legal) medicine (incl forensic pathology, serology, toxicology and criminalistics).

NY —NEW YORK ACADEMY OF MEDICINE, Library, 2 E 103 St, New York, 10029. Brett A Kirkpatrick, Librn
Holdings: Vols Cat
Notes: The Fenwick Beekman Collection on the criminals of 1829.

NY —NEW YORK HISTORICAL SOCIETY, Library, 170 Central Park W, New York, 10024. James Gregory, Librn
Notes: Books and pamphlets devoted to homicide and murder.

NY —NEW YORK PUBLIC LIBRARY, Research Libraries, Economic & Public Affairs Div, Fifth Ave & 42 St, New York, 10018. Edward DiRoma, Chief
Holdings: Vols (1,500,000) Cat Microforms

OH —CLEVELAND PUBLIC LIBRARY, Public Administration Library, City Hall, 601 Lakeside Ave NE Rm 100, Cleveland, 44114. Janice Ryan Novak, Head
Holdings: Vols 500 Cat
Notes: Emphasize practical police work and law enforcement as well as aspects of criminology.

OH —OHIO STATE UNIVERSITY, Social Work Library, 1947 N College Rd, Columbus, 43210. Toyo S Kawakami, Librn
Holdings: Vols (46,410) Cat
Budget: ($11,960)
Notes: VF incl approx 4500 pamphlets, arranged by LC subject headings. 278 serial titles on social work, social and public service, crime and delinquency, corrections, criminal justice, marriage and the family, probation, and related topics, are received.

PA —BALCH INSTITUTE FOR ETHNIC STUDIES, Library, 18 S Seventh St, Philadelphia, 19106. R Joseph Anderson, Library Dir

PA —TEMPLE UNIVERSITY LIBRARIES, Special Collections Dept, Conwellana-Templana Collection, 13 & Berks St, Philadelphia, 19122. Miriam I Crawford, Cur
Holdings: Vols (22) // Cat Mss Pix Newsclippings
Budget: ($30,000)
Notes: Personal papers of Negley K Teeters. The published writings, manuscripts, correspondence, and research materials of Teeters, criminologist and faculty member of Temple University, covering the years 1927-1971. Contains extended correspondence with his co-author, Harry Elmer Barnes, from 1940 to 1968, and materials dealing with their investigation of the murder trial of Caryl Chessman, which failed to halt his execution in California in 1960. Incl copies of letters from Teeters to Barnes, originals of which are in the Western History Research Center of the University of Wyoming, and incl the Index to the Barnes Papers in that collection. *Descriptive Inventory of the Personal Papers of Negley K Teeters* (1896-1971), (Conwellana-Templana Collection, Temple University, 1971, addenda 1972 and 1974; 6 leaves; unpublished typescript).

PA —UNIVERSITY OF PITTSBURGH, Hillman Library, Pittsburgh, 15260. Glenora E Rossell, Head
Holdings: Vols (18,600) Cat
Notes: Especially strong in social theory, social history, social groups, criminology and urban sociology. Emphasis is currently being given to administration of justice, sociology of the child, sociology of the aged, sociology of education and sociology of religion.

RI —BROWN UNIVERSITY, John Hay Library, 20 Prospect St, Providence, 02912. Mark N Brown, Cur Mss
Holdings: // Mss
Notes: Papers of Samuel Wyllys, 1632-1709, Colonial magistrate of Connecticut. A collection of 125 mss, transcripts, and photocopies of legal and government papers relating to Indian affairs, colonial wars, civil and criminal cases, and trials for witchcraft. The witchcraft trials of 1692-1693 are of particular interest as revealed in the Oyer and Terminer Court Records of the witnesses. The Library has one-half (1622-1693) of the original collection which Anmary Brown inherited from her father; the other half (1694-1696) is in the Connecticut State Library.

TX —WEST TEXAS STATE UNIVERSITY, Cornette Library, PO Box 748 WT Sta, Canyon, 79016. Faye Hendrickson, Special Collections Asst
Holdings: Vols (451,253) Uncat Microforms
Notes: Includes microform collection.

TX —SAM HOUSTON STATE UNIVERSITY, Library, PO Box 2179, Huntsville, 77340. Chas Dwyer, Librn
Holdings: Vols 2000
Notes: Incl the collection of Sanford Bates, head of the Federal Bureau of Prisons, 1930-1937.

WY —UNIVERSITY OF WYOMING, William Robertson Coe Library, Archives - American Heritage Center, PO Box 3412, Laramie, 82071.

BC —VANCOUVER PUBLIC LIBRARY, Sociology Div, 750 Burrard St, Vancouver, V6Z 1X5, Can.
Holdings: Cat
Notes: Incl special files of pamphlets, clippings, etc.

ON —ONTARIO MINISTRY OF CORRECTIONAL SERVICES, Library, 2001 Eglinton Ave E, Scarborough, M1L 4P1, Can. T J B Anderson, Chief Librn
Holdings: Vols (3676) Cat VF
Budget: ($16,000)
Notes: Approx 135 periodicals received. Library services also provided in approx 50 jails and adult institutions.

†ON —METROPOLITAN TORONTO LIBRARY, Social Sciences Dept, 789 Yonge St, Toronto, M4W 2G8, Can. Abdus Salam, Head
Holdings: Vols Cat Maps Phonorecords Audiotapes 16mm Films Microforms
Notes: The criminology collection includes contemporary and historical material on theories of criminality, police work, criminal law, corrections, and the rehabilitation of offenders.

ON —UNIVERSITY OF TORONTO, Centre of Criminology, Library, 130 St George St, Rm 8001, Toronto, M5S 1A5, Can. Catherine J Matthews, Librn
Holdings: Vols (20,000) Cat
Notes: Over 4500 research reports, article reprints, theses, etc. Extensive newspaper clippings file from 1963 to present indexed under 350 subject headings. The collection covers criminology, law enforcement and policing, delinquency, criminal justice system, penology and corrections. Acquisitions list published three times a year; subscription.

CRIME AND CRIMINALS—LANGUAGE see Cant

CRIME PHOTOGRAPHY see Photography, Legal

CRIMEAN WAR, 1853-1856

KS —UNIVERSITY OF KANSAS MEDICAL CENTER, College of Health Sciences & Hospital, Clendening History of Medicine Library, Rainbow Blvd at 39th, Kansas City, 66103. Robert P Hudson, Chmn/Cur
Notes: Crimean War papers, 1854-60. 32 letters written from London or the Crimea during the Crimean War; and clippings, photos and other papers relating to the war. Persons represented incl C H Bracebridge, J F Burgoyne, W E Gladstone, G R Gleig, Lord Paglan, A Tremayne and H P Wright.

CRIMEAN WAR, 1853-1856—PICTURES, ILLUSTRATIONS, ETC.

DC —LIBRARY OF CONGRESS, Prints & Photographs Div, Washington, 20540.
Notes: 265 original Crimean War photoprints by Roger Fenton of battlefields, the harbor at Balaklava, leading British, French, and Turkish commanders, and men in the ranks.

CRIMES AND MISDEMEANORS see Criminal Law

CRIMINAL ASSAULT AGAINST WOMEN see Rape

CRIMINAL INVESTIGATION

DC —GEORGETOWN UNIVERSITY, Library, Special Collections Div, 37 & O Sts NW, Washington, 20057. George M Barringer, Special Collections Librn; Nicholas B Sheetz, Mss Librn
Holdings: Cat Mss Pix
Notes: Political assassinations, espec materials pertaining to the assassinations of John F Kennedy and Robert F Kennedy and the investigations thereof.

MD —INTERNATIONAL ASSOCIATION OF CHIEFS OF POLICE, 13 Firstfield Rd, PO Box 6010, Gaithersburg, 20760.
Holdings: Vols (6000) Cat Mss
Notes: Collection heavy in criminal investigation, crime prevention, police administration and management. Collecting in public sector labor relations, family violence, terrorism.

WA —SEATTLE PUBLIC LIBRARY, Governmental Research Assistance Library, 307 Municipal Bldg, Seattle, 98104. Barbara J Guptill, Librn
Holdings: Vols (18,000) Cat Mss Maps
Budget: ($16,700)
Notes: Includes pamphlets and clippings on municipal affairs, especially Seattle. Emphasis on urban planning, criminal investigation, policy analysis, finance.

CRIMINAL JUSTICE, ADMINISTRATION OF

IL —NORTHWESTERN UNIVERSTIY, School of Law, Library, 357 E Chicago Ave, Chicago, 60611. George S Grossman, Dir
Holdings: Cat
Notes: Comprehensive collections of Anglo-American and foreign (especially European) law; Roman and Canon law (selective); international law; European Common Market; Williams Collection of Legal Instruments (AD 1300-1700); George W Shaw Collection of Early European Law. Incl 500 ms legal documents.

IN —INDIANA LAW ENFORCEMENT ACADEMY, David F Allen Memorial Learning Resources Center, Rd 700 E, PO Box 313, Plainfield, 46168. Donna K Zimmerman, Librn
Holdings: Vols (4500) Cat Slides 16mm Films
Budget: ($8500)
Notes: Concentrated in the areas of police science, criminology, and law.

MD —INTERNATIONAL ASSOCIATION OF CHIEFS OF POLICE, 13 Firstfield Rd, PO Box 6010, Gaithersburg, 20760.
Holdings: Vols (6000) Cat Mss
Notes: Collection heavy in criminal investigation, crime prevention, police administration and management. Collecting in public sector labor relations, family violence, terrorism.

CRIMINAL JUSTICE, ADMINISTRATION OF (cont.)

MO —CENTRAL MISSOURI STATE UNIVERSITY, Ward Edwards Library, Warrensburg, 64093. Nancy E Littlejohn, Social Sciences Librn
Holdings: Vols (8000) Cat Microforms
Budget: ($7500)
Notes: Extensive criminal justice and law collection. In addition, a 7593 title microfiche collection of criminal justice and juvenile delinquency.

NJ —RUTGERS, THE STATE UNIVERSITY OF NEW JERSEY, John Cotton Dana Library, 185 University Ave, Newark, 07102. Phyllis Schultze, Librn
Holdings: Vols 40,000 Cat
Notes: National Council on Crime and Delinquency. Criminology, as applied, means all phases of crime and delinquency prevention, control and treatment, ie, the whole "criminal justice" gamut: police, courts, probation and parole, prisons, community rehabilitation centers, etc. In short, everything except police laboratory materials. Collection completely cataloged; all criminological and correctional journals indexed. Incl many reports of correctional agencies, research reports, unpublished monographs, publications in the field by all government agencies, federal, state, county and local. Information file contains over 40, 000 such items, as well as about 10,000 uncataloged clippings and other pieces of information stored by specific subjects.

NY —STATE UNIVERSITY OF NEW YORK AT ALBANY, Library, Special Collections Dept, 1400 Washington Ave, Albany, 12222. Marion P Munzer, Coordr
Notes: Eliot Howland Lumbard's research files, reports, correspondence, mss, and clippings on crime and law enforcement (19 linear feet). Part of the Library's German Exile Collection.
See also entries under Law Enforcement; Lumbard, Eliot Howland

NC —TECHNICAL INSTITUTE OF ALAMANCE, Learning Resources Center, Jimmy Kerr Rd, PO Box 623, Haw River, 27258. Ron Plummer, Coordr
Holdings: Vols (350) Cat Filmstrips Microforms
Notes: Criminal justice and corrections technology.

OH —OHIO STATE UNIVERSITY, Social Work Library, 1947 N College Rd, Columbus, 43210. Toyo S Kawakami, Librn
Holdings: Vols (46,410) Cat
Budget: ($11,960)
Notes: VF incl approx 4500 pamphlets, arranged by LC subject headings. 278 serial titles on social work, social and public service, crime and delinquency, corrections, criminal justice, marriage and the family, probation, and related topics, are received.

PA —LUZERNE COUNTY COMMUNITY COLLEGE, Library, Prospect St & Middle Rd, Nanticoke, 18634. Robert N Cohee, Library Dir
Holdings: Vols 1000 Cat Slides Audiotapes 16mm Films
Budget: ($26,000)

†PA —TEMPLE UNIVERSITY LIBRARIES, Special Collections Dept, Urban Archives Center, Philadelphia, 19122. Thomas Whitehead, Cur of Mss
Holdings: Cat
Notes: Incl the records of several separate collections which are deposited in the Urban Archives Center. Many collections contain photographs, maps and pamphlets, in addition to manuscripts. All collections in the Urban Archives are separately cataloged.

WI —UNIVERSITY OF WISCONSIN, MADISON, Law School Library, Criminal Justice Reference & Information Center, Madison, 53706. Sue Center, Librn
Holdings: Vols (29,000) Cat Mss
Budget: ($45,000)
Notes: In-depth subject access is provided to collection by our own cataloging and classification systems. Incl are periodical articles which are selectively cataloged to supplement the collection. Special items in collection incl penal press (prisoner newspapers); annual and statistical reports from criminal justice agencies throughout the US and Canada; theses and dissertations; and 280 periodical titles in the field of criminal justice.

†ON —METROPOLITAN TORONTO LIBRARY, Social Sciences Dept, 789 Yonge St, Toronto, M4W 2G8, Can. Abdus Salam, Head
Holdings: Vols Cat Maps Phonorecords Audiotapes 16mm Films Microforms
Notes: The criminology collection includes contemporary and historical material on theories of criminality, police work, criminal law, corrections, and the rehabilitation of offenders.

ON —UNIVERSITY OF TORONTO, Centre of Criminology, Library, 130 St George St, Rm 8001, Toronto, M5S 1A5, Can. Catherine J Matthews, Librn
Holdings: Vols (20,000) Cat
Notes: Over 4500 research reports, article reprints, theses, etc. Extensive newspaper clippings file from 1963 to present indexed under 350 subject headings. The collection covers criminology, law enforcement and policing, delinquency, criminal justice system, penology and corrections. Acquisitions list published three times a year; subscription.

CRIMINAL LAW

CA —UNIVERSITY OF CALIFORNIA, DAVIS, Law Library, Davis, 95616. Mortimer D Schwartz, Librn
Holdings: Vols (225,000) Cat
Budget: ($211,177)

MO —SAINT LOUIS POLICE LIBRARY, 315 S Tucker Blvd, Saint Louis, 63102. Cathy Reilly, Librn
Holdings: Vols (21,000) Cat Mss Pix Microforms
Budget: ($18,400)
Notes: Library on all subjects of police work is open to the public for general reference use.

NJ —RUTGERS, THE STATE UNIVERSITY OF NEW JERSEY, John Cotton Dana Library, 185 University Ave, Newark, 07102. Phyllis Schultze, Librn
Holdings: Vols 40,000 Cat
Notes: National Council on Crime and Delinquency. Criminology, as applied, means all phases of crime and delinquency prevention, control and treatment, ie, the whole "criminal justice" gamut: police, courts, probation and parole, prisons, community rehabilitation centers, etc. In short, everything except police laboratory materials. Collection completely cataloged; all criminological and correctional journals indexed. Incl many reports of correctional agencies, research reports, unpublished monographs, publications in the field by all government agencies, federal, state, county and local. Information file contains over 40, 000 such items, as well as about 10,000 uncataloged clippings and other pieces of information stored by specific subjects.

WI —UNIVERSITY OF WISCONSIN, MADISON, Law School Library, Criminal Justice Reference & Information Center, Madison, 53706. Sue Center, Librn
Notes: In-depth subject access is provided to collection by our own cataloging and classification systems. Incl are periodical articles which are selectively cataloged to supplement the collection. Special items in collection incl penal press (prisoner newspapers); annual and statistical reports from criminal justice agencies throughout the US and Canada; theses and dissertations; and 280 periodical titles in the field of criminal justice.

AB —ALBERTA ATTORNEY GENERAL, Law Library, Fourth Floor North Wing, Bowker Bldg 9833-109 St, Edmonton, T5K 2E8, Can. Andrew Balazs, Departmental Librn
Holdings: Vols (13,000) Cat Audiotapes
Budget: ($121,620)
Notes: Emphasis is on Canadian law. But if the solicitors can not find a Canadian precedent, they consult English law. If there is no precedent in English law they consult Commonwealth law, and if there is no precedent there either, then they consult American law. Therefore, the Library does have all the basic Canadian and certain basic English Commonwealth, and a very small number of American texts, as well as the basic Canadian and English law reports. There is one Australian law report. Besides texts (monographs), the Library subscribes to Albertan and Canadian legislative publications like bills, orders, votes and proceedings, Hansard, and Debates of the House of Commons. Assistance is available to users' from the simplest to the most complex legal research questions.

CRIMINAL PATHOLOGY

†NY —COLUMBIA UNIVERSITY LIBRARIES, Butler Library, Rare Book and Manuscript Library, 535 W 114 St, New York, 10027.
Notes: The Papers of Dr David Abrahamsen, incl letters and mss. Contains letters from and interviews with family and friends of Richard M Nixon and 167 typed and handwritten letters sent by David Berkowitz to Dr Abrahamsen from Attica Prison during 1979-81.

CRIMINALS see Crime and Criminals

CRIMINALS, REHABILITATION OF see Rehabilitation of Criminals

CRIMINOLOGY

IN —WESTVILLE CORRECTIONAL CENTER, Library Services, PO Box 473, Westville, 46391. Catherine M Mohlke, Dir of Library Services
Holdings: Vols 1000 Cat

CRIMMINS, JOHN D., 1844-1917

DC —GEORGETOWN UNIVERSITY, Library, Special Collections Div, 37 & O Sts NW, Washington, 20057. George M Barringer, Special Collections Librn; Nicholas B Sheetz, Mss Librn
Holdings: Mss
Notes: Correspondence and printed ephemera from the papers of John D Crimmins (1844-1917), New York financier and philanthropist. The correspondence incl letters from Henry Gabriels (1844-1917), James Cardinal Gibbons (1834-1921), General Winfield Scott Hancock (1824-1886), and Patrick J Ryan (1831-1911), Archbishop of Philadelphia. The printed material primarily concerns Irish-American organizations and activities.

CRINOIDEA

DC —SMITHSONIAN INSTITUTION LIBRARIES, Natural History Branch, Washington, 20560. Sylvia Churgin, Chief Librn
Holdings: Cat Mss Maps Pix Slides Microforms
Notes: Invertebrate zoology, Systematics. Incl crustacea, echinoderms, mollusks, worms, Cushman collection of foraminifera; Springer collection on crinoids; Wilson collection on copepoda.

CRIPPLES see Physically Handicapped

CRISES, COMMERCIAL see Depressions—1929—U.S.

CRISIS INTERVENTION (PSYCHIATRY)

NY —CREEDMOOR PSYCHIATRIC CENTER, Health Sciences Library, Bldg 51, 80-45 Winchester Blvd, Queens Village, 11427. Susan Taubman, Dir of Library; Pushpa Bhati, Sr Librn
Holdings: Vols (12,000) Cat Slides

CRISIS INTERVENTION (PSYCHIATRY) (cont.)

Phonorecords Audiotapes Filmstrips Microfiche
Budget: ($50,000)
Notes: Particularly strong in the areas of neurology, pharmacology, psychoanalysis, and psychopharmacology.

CRISTE, RITA

AZ —ARIZONA STATE UNIVERSITY, Library, Tempe, 85287. Marilyn Wurzburger, Special Collections Librn
Holdings: Vols (108) Pix
Notes: Collection covers various aspects of Children's Theatre from 1944 through the present. Areas of emphasis incl International and National Child Drama Associations, award-winning theatres, educational programs, regional groups and prominent figures in Children's Theatre incl: Irene Vickers Baker, Isabel Burger, Virginia Lee Comer, Rita Criste, Moses Goldberg, Kenneth Graham, Aurand Harris, Paul Kozelka, George Latshaw, Rosemary Musil, Sara Spencer, Winifred Ward, Susan Zeder and Lin Wright. Publications incl newsletters, research papers, bibliographies and records of the proceedings of the Children's Theatre Association of America. 80 linear feet of scripts, documents, publications, films, tapes (oral history) programs, correspondence, photographs, working papers and clippings. Partially indexed; finding guides available.

CROATIA—HISTORY

CA —CROATIAN-SERBIAN-SLOVENE GENEALOGICAL SOCIETY, 2527 San Carlos Ave, San Carlos, 94070. Adam S Eterovich, Dir
Holdings: Vols (1000) Mss
Notes: Incl index of names of 130,000 Croatians and Serbs in the United States before 1905. Dir operates Ragusan Press.

CA —STANFORD UNIVERSITY LIBRARIES, Cecil H Green Library, Stanford, 94305. Wojciech Zalewski, Cur, Russian & East European Collection
Holdings: Vols (200,000) Cat Maps Microforms
Budget: ($90,000)
Notes: Strong collection prior to 20th century, but Stanford University Libraries' collecting effort is coordinated with Hoover Institution, Stanford, and holdings are not duplicated. Collection descriptions: Wojciech Zalewski, *Russian Materials in the Main Library of Stanford University, A Collection* Survey (Stanford: Stanford University Libraries, 1974). Wojciech Zalerski, "Stanford University" in P L Horecky, ed, *East Central and Southeast Europe, A Handbook of Library and Archival Resources in North America* (Santa Barbara: Clio Press, 1976).

IL —CROATIAN ETHNIC INSTITUTE, INC, 4851 S Drexel Blvd, Chicago, 60615.
Holdings: 3500 Vols Mss
Notes: Incl over 200 linear ft of archives. Oral history program.

PA —CROATIAN FRATERNAL UNION, 100 Delaney Drive, Pittsburgh, 15235. Bernard Luketich, Pres
Holdings: Vols 2000
Notes: Works promoting independent state of Croatia. Private library.

CROATIAN LANGUAGE AND LITERATURE see Serbo-Croatian Language and Literature

CROATIANS see Croats

CROATS

NY —NEW YORK PUBLIC LIBRARY, Slavonic Div, Fifth Ave & 42 St, New York, 10018. Edward Kasinec, Chief
Holdings: Cat Microforms
Notes: See: New York Public Library, Slavonic Div, *Dictionary Catalog of the Slavonic Collection*, 2nd ed, rev and enl (Boston: G K Hall, 1974), 44 vols; and New York Public Library, *Dictionary Catalog of the Research Libraries* (New York, 1972-).

CROATS IN CANADA

PA —BALCH INSTITUTE FOR ETHNIC STUDIES, Library, 18 S Seventh St, Philadelphia, 19106. R Joseph Anderson, Library Dir
Notes: Ethnic Heritage Collection.

CROATS IN THE U.S.

CA —CROATIAN-SERBIAN-SLOVENE GENEALOGICAL SOCIETY, 2527 San Carlos Ave, San Carlos, 94070. Adam S Eterovich, Dir
Holdings: Vols (1000) Mss
Notes: Incl index of names of 130,000 Croatians and Serbs in the United States before 1905. Dir operates Ragusan Press.

MN —UNIVERSITY OF MINNESOTA, Immigration History Research Center, 826 Berry St, Saint Paul, 55114. Susan Griegs, Cur
Holdings: Vols (35,000) Mss Maps Pix Phonorecords Audiotapes 16 mm Films Microforms
See also entry under Emigration and Immigration

PA —BALCH INSTITUTE FOR ETHNIC STUDIES, Library, 18 S Seventh St, Philadelphia, 19106. R Joseph Anderson, Library Dir
Holdings: Cat Microforms

PA —UNIVERSITY OF PITTSBURGH, Hillman Library, Archives of Industrial Society, 363 Hillman Library, Pittsburgh, 15260. Frank A Zabrosky, Cur
Holdings: Mss Maps Phonorecords Audiotapes Microforms
Notes: Records of Croat Catholic churches and organizations/societies.

CROCCHIOLA, STANLEY FRANCIS LOUIS

NM —EASTERN NEW MEXICO UNIVERSITY, Golden Library, Special Collections, Portales, 88130. Mary Jo Walker, Special Collections Librn
Holdings: Vols Cat Periodicals Mss Correspondence Pix Audiotapes
Notes: Incl 176 cataloged books by F Stanley (pseudonym of Catholic priest and historian Stanley Francis Louis Crocchiola), plus his collection of periodicals and books by other writers pertaining to southwestern history (particularly New Mexico and the Texas panhandle); 22.25 cubic ft of mss, correspondence files, photographs of F Stanley and others, and two oral history interviews with F Stanley. Unpublished register of collection available. Bio/bibliography of F Stanley in preparation.

CROCHETING

VT —SHELBURNE MUSEUM, Library, Shelburne, 05482. Barbara Reenstierna, Librn
Holdings: Vols (275) Cat Slides

CROCHETING—PATTERNS

CA —CARLSBAD CITY LIBRARY, 1250 Elm Ave, Carlsbad, 92008. Clifford E Lange, Library Dir
Holdings: Vols (2297) Cat
Notes: Collection of sewing patterns. Catalogs of the patterns have been made up with complete information on size, etc, and have been divided into subject areas, such as gift ideas, toys, dolls, women's clothes, men's clothes, children's clothes, etc. Also patterns for knitted and crocheted wearing apparel. Incl patterns for children's costumes, historical fashions and antique dolls.

CROCKERY see Pottery

CROCKET, GEORGE L.

TX —STEPHEN F AUSTIN STATE UNIVERSITY, Ralph W Steen Library, Special Collections Dept, Box 13055, SFA Sta, Nacogdoches, 75962. Linda Cheves Nicklas, Special Collections Librn
Holdings: Mss Maps Pix
Budget: ($5000)
Notes: Incl personal and business papers, letters, diaries, and other records of East Texans and East Texas institutions and businesses. Major collections incl papers of Karl Wilson Baker, George L Crocket, Bennett Blake, McFarland-Russell family, Orton family, Samuel E Asbury; and records of Nacogdoches University, East Texas Historical Association, Kelly Plow Company and many local organizations; 60 Thomas J Rusk letters. Indexes, calendars and inventories are available. Description: SFASU, *A Guide to Special Collections*, 1980.

CROFT-COOKE, RUPERT

†WA —WASHINGTON STATE UNIVERSITY, Library, Manuscripts, Archives & Special Collections, Pullman, 99164. John F Guido, Head
Holdings: Vols Mss Pix
Notes: Other 20th century English authors significantly represented by printed and/or ms material in the Virginia Woolf Collection incl the Sitwells, Margaret Sackville, Rose Macaulay, D H Lawrence, John Masefield, Rupert Croft-Cooke, & Charles Williams. Partially cataloged.

CROKER, JOHN WILSON

NC —DUKE UNIVERSITY, William R Perkins Library, Manuscript Dept, Durham, 27706. Ellen Gartrell, Cur of Mss
Holdings: Cat Mss
Notes: Incl 50,000 items, 18th-20th centuries, representing the political, diplomatic, military, ecclesiastical, and economic affairs of Great Britain and the British Empire. Incl papers of William Wilberforce, William Smith, John Wilson Croker, John Backhouse, Malet Family, etc.

CROMER, GABRIEL

NY —INTERNATIONAL MUSEUM OF PHOTOGRAPHY AT GEORGE EASTMAN HOUSE, Archives, 900 East Ave, Rochester, 14607. Rachel Stuhlman, Head Librn
Holdings: Vols (30,000) Cat Mss Microforms
Budget: ($104,000)
Notes: History, aesthetics and technology of photography and cinematography, incl the Gabriel Cromer, Josef Maria Eder, Alden Scott Boyer, Louis Walton Sipley/3M Collections, and the James Card Collection from 1893. Covers photographic, especially cinematographic history; also hundreds of negatives of Edward Muybridge as well as his notebooks. Incl 450,000 pictures and slides. Also the Lewis Hine Collection of social documentary photography.

CROMWELL, OLIVER

IL —UNIVERSITY OF CHICAGO LIBRARY, Dept of Special Collections, 1100 E 57 St, Chicago, 60637.
Notes: George Morris Eckels Collection of Cromwelliana.

IN —INDIANA UNIVERSITY, Lilly Library, Seventh St, Bloomington, 47405. William R Cagle, Librn
Holdings: Vols 1200 // Cat
Notes: Mostly contemporary vols dealing with Great Britian during Oliver Cromwell's era. Many governmental pieces.

MA —HARVARD UNIVERSITY LIBRARY, Widener Library, Cambridge, 02138.
Holdings: Cat

CROP BREEDING

DE —UNIVERSITY OF DELAWARE, Agriculture Library, 2 Townsend Hall, Newark, 19717. Frederick Getze, Assoc Librn
Holdings: Vols (32,500)
Notes: Strong in entomology and ornamental

CROP BREEDING (cont.)

horticulture. Extensive collection of state agriculture documents for each US state and Puerto Rico. Library subscribes to 500 serials (English and foreign).

IA —IOWA STATE UNIVERSITY, Library, Ames, 50011. Warren B Kuhn, Dean of Library Services
Holdings: Cat
Notes: Extensive serial holdings.

MD —US DEPT OF AGRICULTURE, National Agricultural Library, 10301 Baltimore Blvd, Beltsville, 20705. Joseph H Howard, Director
Holdings: Vols (2,000,000) Cat Mss Maps Pix Slides Microforms
Notes: Crop Fiber Collection. A special collection of approximately 50,000 reference cards, thousands of reprints, manuscript materials, photographs, and specimens relating to more than 300 genera of plants. Contains the most complete record of information in the country, if not the world, on fiber crops of the world. The collection is particularly vital to research interests and projects involving the use of natural fibers (i. e. rubber, guayule).

CROP ECOLOGY

DE —UNIVERSITY OF DELAWARE, Agriculture Library, 2 Townsend Hall, Newark, 19717. Frederick Getze, Assoc Librn
Holdings: Vols (32,500)
Notes: Strong in entomology and ornamental horticulture. Extensive collection of state agriculture documents for each US state and Puerto Rico. Library subscribes to 500 serials (English and foreign).

MD —US DEPT OF AGRICULTURE, National Agricultural Library, 10301 Baltimore Blvd, Beltsville, 20705. Joseph H Howard, Director
Holdings: Vols (2,000,000) Cat Mss Maps Pix Slides Microforms
Notes: Crop ecology, agro-climatic analogs; air pollution effects. Agronomy: agriculture and tropical and desert agriculture. For use by the staff of the Institute. Incl 5000 pamphlet items. Former collection of American Institute of Crop Ecology.

CROP STATISTICS see Agriculture—Statistics

CROPS, TROPICAL see Tropical Crops

CROPS AND CLIMATE

CO —COLORADO STATE UNIVERSITY, Libraries, Fort Collins, 80523. Marjorie Rhoades, Engineering Sciences Librn
Holdings: Vols (6000) Cat
Budget: ($5000)
Notes: Water and Soil in Arid Regions (WASAR) is an index and guide to books, conference papers, journal articles, government documents and technical reports, mostly in English, within the appropriate subject areas and held by Colorado State University Libraries. The bibliographical citations are of selected items dealing with soils, water, arid lands, crops, foods and nutrition with certain economic, political, ecological and historical parameters also included. The information needs of developing countries and of those who serve them are the prime criteria for inclusion.

MD —US DEPT OF AGRICULTURE, National Agricultural Library, 10301 Baltimore Blvd, Beltsville, 20705. Joseph H Howard, Director
Holdings: Vols (2,000,000) Cat Mss Maps Pix Slides Microforms
Notes: Crop ecology, agro-climatic analogs; air pollution effects. Agronomy: agriculture and tropical and desert agriculture. For use by the staff of the Institute. Incl 5000 pamphlet items. Former collection of American Institute of Crop Ecology.

CROQUIS

NY —FASHION INSTITUTE OF TECHNOLOGY, Edward C Blum Design Laboratory, 227 W 27 St, New York, 10001. Laura Sinderbrand, Dir
Holdings: Cat Pix Slides
Notes: The largest resource of it kind consisting of 4 million indexed swatches and 300 swatch books, jacquard point paper, croquis, quilts, rug samples, laces, embroideries, and color swatch cards. A collection of international scope incl antique and contemporary textiles; woven and printed patterns created for apparel and home furnishings which may be adapted to china, giftware, floor covering, wallpaper, and package design. A comprehensive research facility comprised of over one million articles of dress dating from the 17th Century to the present, incl men's, women's, children's clothes, furs, foundation garments and lingerie, as well as an outstanding grouping of 19th and 20th century designer clothing. Accessories as diverse as hats, handbags, gloves, hosiery, shoes, shawls, and costume jewelry offer an additonal resource to this international collection.

CROSBY, BING see Crosby, Harry Lillis 'Bing'

CROSBY, HARRY AND CARESSE

RI —BROWN UNIVERSITY, John Hay Library, 20 Prospect St, Providence, 02912. Mark N Brown, Cur Mss
Holdings: // Mss
Notes: Harry Crosby, American poet and founder with Caresse Crosby of the Black Sun Press in Paris. 13 portfolios containing proofs of *Chariot of the Sun* and *Shadows of the Sun*; typescripts of poems; 10 diaries and notebooks, 1926 to 1929; biographical notes by Caresse Crosby; 9 letters about Harry Crosby and the Black Sun Press; and a copy of Crosby's will. Also a sizable collection of the imprints of the Press. See "The Black Sun Press: 1927 to the present," by Millicent Bell, in *Books at Brown*, vols XVII, no 1-2, (January 1955), pp 1-24; and "Harry Crosby: A Heliograph," by Hugh Fox, in *Books at* Brown, vols XXIII (1969), pp 95-100.

CROSBY, HARRY LILLIS 'BING'

WA —GONZAGA UNIVERSITY, Crosby Library, East 502 Boone Ave, Spokane, 99258. Robert Burr, Dir
Notes: Books, records, memorabilia and papers, incl Jack Benny Radio Show scripts.

CROSS, ASA BEEBE

MO —UNIVERSITY OF MISSOURI-KANSAS CITY, General Library, State Historical Society of Missouri Manuscripts, 5100 Rockhill Road, Kansas City, 64110. Kenneth J LaBudde, Dir; Gordon Hendrickson, Assoc Dir
Holdings: Mss
Notes: Joint Collection Western Historical Manuscript Collection and the State Historical of Missouri Manuscripts, University of Missouri-Kansas City General Library, 5100 Rockhill Road, Kansas City, MO 64110. Ca 2,500 linear feet of manuscripts, blueprints and oral history tapes.
Notes: The manuscript collection includes material which documents the history, growth and development of Missouri, especially the Greater Kansas City area. The personal papers of business, civic, cultural, political and community leaders; local historians and other individuals of families from the area are within the collection as are the records of associations, organizations and institutions which reflect the history of the area. Prominent among the collections are the papers of Charles B. Wheeler, Jr., Charles N. Kimball, Arthur Mag, Oscar D. Nelson, Lou B. Holland, J. C. Nichols, Perry Cookingham, Blevins Davis and Daniel Macmorris and the records of the Kansas City Board of Trade. Architectural designs and plans for approximately 3,500 Kansas City buildings and the records of the Hoit, Price and Barnes architectural firm and the papers of Asa Beebe Cross, early Kansas City architect as well as a number of oral histories with Kansas City Jazz figures are in the collection.

CROSS, RICHARD

CA —CALIFORNIA STATE UNIVERSITY, LONG BEACH, Library, Dept of Special Collections & Archives, 1250 Bellflower Blvd, Long Beach, 90840. John Ahouse, Special Collections Librn
Holdings: Vols 600
Notes: Libraries of Dr Fred Modern and photojournalist Richard Cross, and incl signed books and photographs of photographer Ansel Adams.

CROSS-DRESSING see Transvestism and Transvestites

CROSSEN, KENDALL FOSTER

MA —BOSTON UNIVERSITY, Mugar Memorial Library, Special Collections Dept, 771 Commonwealth Ave, Boston, 02215. Howard B Gotlieb, Dir
Holdings: Cat Mss Correspondence

CROTON AQUEDUCT

NY —JERVIS PUBLIC LIBRARY, 613 N Washington St, Rome, 13440. William A Dillon, Dir
Holdings: Vols (1500) // Cat Mss Maps Slides
Notes: John Bloomfield Jervis Collection contains personal library (1500 vols) and papers (1300 items) of chief engineer of Croton aqueduct and other waterworks, canals, and railroads circa 1825-1860. Papers available on microfilm; indexes to papers available from Jervis Public Library.

CROUSE, RUSSEL, 1893-1966

†WI —STATE HISTORICAL SOCIETY OF WISCONSIN, Library, 816 State St, Madison, 53706.
Notes: Scripts, notes, correspondence and other items concerning the collaboration of Howard Lindsay and Russel Crouse for the theater, motion pictures and television, as well as the work of each with other collaborators and individually.

CROW INDIANS

MT —MONTANA STATE UNIVERSITY, Library, Bozeman, 59717. Minnie Ellen Paugh, Special Collections Librn
Holdings: Vols (7000) // Mss Maps Pix
Notes: Leggat-Donahoe Collection. Collection of Alexander Leggat of Butte, whose father was active in opening the mines. Mr Leggat's interests were mining, exploration, and the fur trade. There are excellent Indian materials in the collection. Also the manuscript and picture collections of James Willard Schultz, Harry James (about James Willard Schultz), and Olga Ross Hannon on Blackfeet Indian tepees. Land claim clase files and manuscripts about Blackfeet, Gros Ventre, Assiniboine and Crow Indians collected by Dr Thomas R Wessell, Edward E Barry and Dr Merrill G Burlingame.

CROWE, CECILY

MA —BOSTON UNIVERSITY, Mugar Memorial Library, Special Collections Dept,

CROWE, CECILY (cont.)

771 Commonwealth Ave, Boston, 02215. Howard B Gotlieb, Dir
Holdings: Cat Mss

CROWLEY, ROBERT T.

MA —BOSTON UNIVERSITY, Mugar Memorial Library, Special Collections Dept, 771 Commonwealth Ave, Boston, 02215. Howard B Gotlieb, Dir
Holdings: Cat Mss

CROWNE, JOHN

MA —HARVARD UNIVERSITY LIBRARY, Houghton Library, Cambridge, 02138. F Thomas Noonan, Cur, Reading Room; Lawrence Dowler, Associate Librn
Holdings: Cat

CROZIER, ANDREW

MO —WASHINGTON UNIVERSITY, Libraries, Special Collections Dept, Campus Box 1061, St Louis, 63130.
Notes: A small but significant collection.

BC —SIMON FRASER UNIVERSITY, Library, Burnaby, V5A 1S6, Can. Percilla Groves, Special Collections Librn
Holdings: Cat Mss
Notes: Letters of Charles Olson to Robin Blaser, Andrew Crozier, Barry Hall, Le Roi Jones (Amiri Baraka), Ed Sanders. Typescript and galleys for *Maximus IV, V, VI*, mss published in *Pacific Nation* and *Wivenhoe Park Review*. See *Line*, vol 1, no 1, spring 1983, for a complete list of Olson mss at SFU.

CRUCIBLES

PA —COLT INDUSTRIES, Crucible Research Center Library, Box 88, Pittsburgh, 15230. Patricia J Aducci, Technical Librn

CRUELTY

NJ —NEW JERSEY HISTORICAL SOCIETY, Library and Museum, 230 Broadway, Newark, 07104. Joan C Hull, Exec Dir; Barbara S Irwin, Library Dir; Alan R Fraser, Cur
Budget: ($100,000)
Notes: Records of eight Newark orphanages and child service organizations dating back to 1847. Incl records, casebooks, registers, adoption contracts, minutes of meetings, financial and administrative records, case studies by student interns in social work, and related printed materials.

CRUELTY TO CHILDREN see Cruelty

CRUIKSHANK, GEORGE, 1792-1878

CA —UNIVERSITY OF CALIFORNIA, LOS ANGELES, William Andrews Clark Memorial Library, 2520 Cimarron St, Los Angeles, 90018.
Holdings: Cat Pix
Notes: Collection partially described in the Library's *Cruikshank and Dickens* (1921), 2 volumes.

CA —CALIFORNIA STATE UNIVERSITY, NORTHRIDGE, Delmar T Oviatt & South Libraries, 1811 Nordhoff St, Northridge, 91330. Donald L Read, Special Collections Dept
Notes: Although not maintained as a separate collection, there is a strong representative collection of Cruikshank materials in the Department. This is due, in great part, to the efforts of a faculty member who is a well-known Cruikshak scholar. Material is fully cataloged with an index maintained in Special Collections.

CT —TRINITY COLLEGE LIBRARY, Watkinson Library, 300 Summit St, Hartford, 06106. Jeffrey Kaimowitz, Cur
Holdings: Cat Pix
Notes: The Sherman P Haight Collections of Cruikshank and Dickens.

CT —YALE UNIVERSITY, Box 1603A, Yale Station, New Haven, 06520.
Holdings: Cat Pix
Notes: An extensive collection on the first and later editions of books illus by George Cruikshank, together with original drawings, letters, engravings and other material by and about him.

DC —LIBRARY OF CONGRESS, Prints & Photographs Div, Washington, 20540.
Notes: The British Cartoon collection contains 10,000 British political caricatures and satires dating from the 17th through mid 19th centuries. Incl the work of Henry Bunbury, George Cruikshank, Issac Cruikshank, Matthew Darly, James Gillray, and Thomas Rowlandson.

IN —INDIANA UNIVERSITY, Lilly Library, Seventh St, Bloomington, 47405. William R Cagle, Librn
Holdings: Vols 400 Cat Mss
Notes: The Kenyon Starling Cruikshank Collection consists of first and special editions of books illustrated by George Cruikshank, including presentation copies and original drawings.

MD —UNIVERSITY OF MARYLAND, BALTIMORE COUNTY, Albin O Kuhn Library and Gallery, 5401 Wilkens Ave, Baltimore, 21228. Ann Copeland, Special Collections Librn
Holdings: Vols (800) // Cat Pix
Notes: The Edgar and Kathleen Merkle Collection of 19th-century English graphic satire centers around the work of George E Cruikshank. Other artists represented incl Rowlandson, Gillray, Hogarth, and "Phiz." Rare items incl Cruikshank's lavish hand-colored film *Scraps and Sketches* (1828).

MA —BOSTON UNIVERSITY, Mugar Memorial Library, Special Collections Dept, 771 Commonwealth Ave, Boston, 02215. Howard B Gotlieb, Dir
Holdings: Cat Mss
Notes: Mss, correspondence, incl publications by.

MA —HARVARD UNIVERSITY LIBRARY, Widener Library, Harry Elkins Widener Collection, Cambridge, 02138. F Thomas Noonan, Cur
Holdings: // Cat Mss Pix
Notes: Privately printed catalog (279 p) issued 1918.

NJ —PRINCETON UNIVERSITY, Library, Rare Books Dept, Princeton, 08544. Stephen Ferguson, Cur
Notes: Richard W Meirs Collection of George Cruikshank. About 1000 vols, as well as many separate prints. The collection also incl drawings, finished oil paintings, oil sketches, "panorama" prints on rollers for viewing in special boxes, etched plates, broadsides, bound mss, autograph letters, and Cruikshank correspondence. The materials are divided according to form among the follwing: General Rare Books, Graphic Arts, and Manuscripts. One of the finest Cruikshank collections in America, and deposited at Princeton in 1913. A complete list of Library holdings as of 1920 appears in the *Princeton University Classed* List, (Special Collections) vol 6 (Princeton, 1920) pp 3565-3583 (ExB) 0639.7373.5, published after the major deposit of Cruikshank material by Mr Meirs. See also: E D H Johnson. *George Cruikshank: the Collection at Princeton* (Princeton, 1973) (Cruik)747 which is the offprint of: E D H Johnson, "The George Cruikshank Collection at Princeton" in *Princeton University Library Chronicle* XXXV, 1 (autumn and winter, 1973-74) pp 1-33 as well as: Frank Jewett Mather, "A Statistical Survey of the Meirs Cruikshank Collection" in the *Princeton University Library Chronicle* IV, 2-3 (February-April, 1943) pp 50-52.

NY —NEW YORK PUBLIC LIBRARY, Rare Books and Manuscripts Div, Fifth Ave & 42 St, New York, 10018. William L Joyce, Asst Dir; Bernard McTigue, Cur, Arents Collection

NC —UNIVERSITY OF NORTH CAROLINA, CHAPEL HILL, Wilson Library, Rare Book Collection, Chapel Hill, 27514. Paul S Koda, Cur of Rare Books
Holdings: Vols 100 Cat
Notes: The Whitaker Collection of George Cruikshank consists of over 100 first and special editions of books illustrated by George Cruikshank. Work by Isaac and Robert Cruikshank is also part of the Collection.

RI —BROWN UNIVERSITY, John Hay Library, 20 Prospect St, Providence, 02912. Mark N Brown, Cur Mss
Holdings: Uncat Mss Pix
Notes: Paul Revere Bullard Collection of 185 19th century caricatures by English, French, German, Russian, and Spanish cartoonists who lampooned Napoleon throughout his career, plus 220 similar caricatures from other sources. The major English artists represented are: James Gillray, George and Isaac Cruikshank, Thomas Rowlandson, and George Woodward. Some items also part of Anne S K Brown Military Collection at Brown University.

BC —UNIVERSITY OF VICTORIA, McPherson Library, Victoria, V8W 3H5, Can.

CRUIKSHANK, ISAAC, 1756?-1811?

DC —LIBRARY OF CONGRESS, Prints & Photographs Div, Washington, 20540.
Notes: The British Cartoon collection contains 10,000 British political caricatures and satires dating from the 17th through mid 19th centuries. Incl the work of Henry Bunbury, George Cruikshank, Issac Cruikshank, Matthew Darly, James Gillray, and Thomas Rowlandson.

CRUMB, GEORGE

DC —LIBRARY OF CONGRESS, Music Division, Washington, 20540.
Notes: Mss in Koussevitzky Archives.

CRUMBINE, SAMUEL J., 1862-1954

KS —UNIVERSITY OF KANSAS MEDICAL CENTER, College of Health Sciences & Hospital, Clendening History of Medicine Library, Rainbow Blvd at 39th, Kansas City, 66103. Robert P Hudson, Chmn/Cur
Holdings: Vols (15,725) Cat Mss
Notes: Strong in all fields of medical history. Incl incunabula and serials. Mss incl Jakob Henle, 1809-1885, papers (ca 4050 items); Howard Atwood Kelly, 1858-1943, correspondence (ca 90 items); Joseph Lister, 1827-1912, letters (7); Florence Nightingale, 1820-1910, letters (20); and Samuel Jay Crumbine, 1862-1954, papers (ca 2365 items).

CRUSADES

MA —HARVARD UNIVERSITY LIBRARY, Widener Library, Cambridge, 02138.
Holdings: Cat
Notes: *Widener Library Shelflist* volume for General European and World History (No 32) lists 1454 volumes on the Crusades.

PA —UNIVERSITY OF PENNSYLVANIA, Lea Library, 3420 Walnut St, Philadelphia, 19104. Daniel Traister, Special Collections Librn
Holdings: Vols (20,000) Cat Mss
Notes: Collection incl works on Church history, the history of jurisprudence political theory, Byzantine history, the Crusades and medieval urban history. See Downs 4241, 4234.

CRUSTACEA

DC —SMITHSONIAN INSTITUTION LIBRARIES, Natural History Branch, Washington, 20560. Sylvia Churgin, Chief Librn
Holdings: Cat Mss Maps Pix Slides Microforms
Notes: Invertebrate zoology, Systematics. Incl crustacea, echinoderms, mollusks, worms, Cushman collection of foraminifera; Springer collection on crinoids; Wilson collection on copepoda.

PQ —MCGILL UNIVERSITY, Institute of Oceanography, Oceanography Library, 3620 University St, Montreal, H3A 2B2, Can. Yvonne Mahocks, Librn
Holdings: Vols (10,848) Cat Mss Maps Pix Microforms
Budget: ($1200)
Notes: Extensive periodical collection. 12,

CRUSTACEA (cont.)

332 government documents, , 322 microtech, 321 microfiche, 25,000 reprints.

CRYOGENICS see Materials at Low Temperatures; Refrigeration and Refrigerating Machinery

CRYPTANALYSIS see Cryptography

CRYPTESTHESIA see Extrasensory Perception (Esp)

CRYPTOGAMS

MA —HARVARD UNIVERSITY LIBRARY, Farlow Reference Library, 20 Divinity Ave, Cambridge, 02138. Geraldine C Kaye, Librn
Holdings: Vols (60,000) Cat Mss Serials Pix Microforms
Notes: The Farlow Reference Library provides complete coverage of the systematic literature on algae, bryophytes, fungi, and lichens. Established by bequest of Professor William G Farlow, it is one of the most extensive cryptogamic botany libraries in the US. Books do not circulate.

CRYPTOGRAPHY

CA —FRANCIS BACON LIBRARY, 655 N Dartmouth Ave, Claremont, 91711. Elizabeth S Wrigley, Dir
Holdings: Vols 350 Cat
Notes: Collection ranges from earliest printed book on cryptography to current vols. Incl clippings, articles and periodicals concernend with cryptography. Approx 1/3 of the collection composed of 16th and 17th century vols. Also cipher aids, St Cyr slides, etc.

CA —HARVEY G WOLFE LIBRARY, PO Box 3514, Grand Central Sta, Glendale, 91201. Douglas L Evans, Librn
Holdings: Vols (6580) Mss Maps Pix
Budget: ($4500)
Notes: Main emphasis on espionage, military intelligence, and sabotage.

DC —LIBRARY OF CONGRESS, Rare Book & Special Collections Div, Washington, 20540. William Matheson, Chief
Holdings: Vols 1096 Uncat
Notes: The collection, formed by Col George Fabyan, consists of 1096 volumes, 269 pamphlets and 33 periodicals, all devoted, apart from a small number of works on general subjects, to two major areas of interest: cryptography and the Bacon-Shakespeare controversy. The former includes two copies of the first edition of Trithemius' *Polygraphia* (1518), plus five editions of the *Steganographia.* The volumes of the Bacon-Shakespeare controversy consist of the original collection of John Dane of Boston together with Col Fabyan's additions. No less than 33 of the 69 distinct editions of Bacon printed before 1640 (as listed in the STC) are found in the collection.

MO —WASHINGTON UNIVERSITY, John M Olin Library, Campus Box 1061, St Louis, 63130.
Holdings: Vols (1300) Cat Mss
Notes: The Philip M Arnold Semeiology Collection is concerned with the study of signs and symbols. Topics incl cryptography; artificial memory; decipherment of unknown languages; universal languages; early developments in stenography, telegraphy; and communication systems for the blind, the deaf and the mute; and various forms of nonverbal communication. Limited photocopying. Noncirculating.

OH —KENT STATE UNIVERSITY, Libraries, Dept of Special Collections, Kent, 44242. Dean H Keller, Cur
Holdings: Vols 150 Cat Mss
Notes: This is the library of the American Cryptogram Association.

†VA —GEORGE C MARSHALL RESEARCH FOUNDATION AND LIBRARY, Drawer 920, Lexington, 24450. Royster Lyle Jr, Cur Collections
Holdings: Vols Uncat Mss Slides Microforms
Notes: The William F. Friedman Collection. Separate catalog. Incl. papers and correspondence relating to William and Elizabeth S. Friedman's personal interests and U.S. government assignments: books, pamphlets, technical papers, periodicals, microfilm, slides and newspaper clippings dealing with cryptology. Items on secret writing and signaling, radar, telephony and telegraphy, and the study of the Shakespeare-Bacon authorship controversy, Vols. of fiction relating to spies and codes, cryptographic game books for children, Civil War code items. Examples of ancient writings of Europe, Crete, and Easter Island, and material on the Aztecs, Incas, and particularly the Mayans. Also a copy of the Voynich mss., an undeciphered work, and other rare vols. on the subject dating from the 17th century. The library also has a separate collection of diaries kept by Gilbert Sandford Vernam, cryptographer and inventor. The diary is an almost day-by-day record, 1918-1926, of Vernam's inventions and development of his outstanding contributions to cryptography including techniques widely adopted by the armed forces for enciphering and deciphering coded messages. There is a typed index to this collection. No photocopying.

CRYPTOLOGY see Cryptography

CRYSTALLOGRAPHY

IL —ARGONNE NATIONAL LABORATORY, Chemistry Branch Library, 9700 S Cass Ave, Argonne, 60439. Betty Guttman, Librn
Notes: Incl 20,000 vols monographs, 190 current journals. Materials may be used by the public in the library by prior arrangement. Photocopies may be supplied for interlibrary loan, for which a processing and handling charge is made.

IL —UNIVERSITY OF ILLINOIS, URBANA/CHAMPAIGN, Library, Geology Library, 223 Natural History Bldg, Urbana, 61801. Dederick Ward, Librn
Holdings: Vols (105,186) Cat Maps Microforms

IN —INDIANA UNIVERSITY, Chemistry Library, Chemistry Bldg, Rm One, Bloomington, 47405. Gary Wiggins, Head Librn
Holdings: Vols (55,000) Cat Slides Microforms
Budget: ($157,000)

KY —UNIVERSITY OF KENTUCKY, Robert E Shaver Library of Engineering, 355 Anderson Hall, Lexington, 40506. Russell H Powell, Engineering Librn
Holdings: Vols (48,000) Cat Microforms

MA —HARVARD UNIVERSITY LIBRARY, Geological Sciences Library, 24 Oxford St, Cambridge, 02138. Constance Wick, Librn
Holdings: Vols (51,000) Cat Mss Maps Pix 16mm Films Microforms
Notes: The Geological Sciences Library supports the research efforts of faculty, graduate students, and upper-level undergraduate and graduate instruction in the geological sciences. Subjects collected deal with the earth sciences in general, mineralogy, petrology, geochemistry, geophysics, crystallography, structural geology, regional geology, economic geology, some geomorphology, and some gemology. The collection incl 850 serial publications and 15,000 maps.

MA —SMITH COLLEGE, Sophia Smith Collection, Women's History Archive, Northampton, 01063. M E Murdock, Dir
Holdings: Mss
Notes: Papers of Dorothy Wrinch, crystallographer.

NY —UNIVERSITY OF ROCHESTER, Carlson Library, Hutchison Hall, River Campus, Rochester, 14627. Michael W Poulin, Librn
Holdings: Vols (12,424) Cat Maps
Notes: Strong collection in the field and related areas.

PA —FRANKLIN INSTITUTE LIBRARY, 20 & The Parkway, Philadelphia, 19103. Miriam Padusis, Dir; Charles Wilt, Readers Servs Librn
Holdings: Vols (300,000) Cat Maps Pix Microforms
Budget: ($180,000)

PA —CARNEGIE LIBRARY OF PITTSBURGH, Science & Technology Dept, 4400 Forbes Ave, Pittsburgh, 15213. Catherine M Brosky, Dept Head
Holdings: Vols (380,000) Cat Maps Microforms
Budget: ($240,000)
Notes: Long runs of journals, reports of geological surveys and society publications. Incl abstracts, indexes, bibliographies, literature guides, dictionaries, handbooks, manuals, compilations of data.

PA —UNIVERSITY OF PITTSBURGH, Physics Library, 208 Engineering Hall, Pittsburgh, 15260. Paul J Kobulnicky, Physical Sciences Librn
Holdings: Vols (25,000) Cat Microforms
Budget: ($100,000)
Notes: The Physics Library collection is both a graduate student research-level collection in basic experimental and theoretical physics with emphasis on solid-state, nuclear, upper-atmosphere, space, and crystallography, and also a collection in the earth and planetary sciences, serving both graduate and undergraduate students. The collection is cataloged in both the University of Pittsburgh, Hillman Library union catalog and in a separate catalog in the Physics Library.

CSS HUNLEY

AL —MOBILE PUBLIC LIBRARY, Special Collections Div, 701 Government St, Mobile, 36602.
Notes: Hunley Collection: Papers, illustrations, etc concerning the building and history of CSS Hunley, first submarine, 1861-1865.

CUBA

CT —YALE UNIVERSITY, Sterling Memorial Library, Latin American Collections, New Haven, 06520. Lee H Williams Jr, Cur
Holdings: Vols (300,000) Cat Maps Pix Slides Phonorecords 16mm Films Filmstrips
Notes: Unusual strength based on partial acquisition of the Domingo del Monte Collection. Incl only known complete set of Varela's *El Habanero.* Also strong in revolutionary Cuba, with 9000 photographs of Castro's activities in the Oriente Mountains before he came to power, movie footage (24 hours), mss, et al.
See also entry under Latin America

FL —UNIVERSITY OF MIAMI, Otto G Richter Library, PO Box 248214, Coral Gables, 33124. Frank Rodgers, Dir of Libraries
Notes: The University of Miami collects on a comprehensive level materials published inside and outside of Cuba that pertain to all aspects of Cuban culture and history. In addition to a substantial circulating collection, the library also contains extensive periodical holdings, rare books, lithographs, mss, broadsides, posters, maps, correspondence, postcards and other ephemera. Collections pertaining to Cubans in the US are especially strong and unique. The library attempts to obtain all dissertations written about Cuba and Cubans. See *Catalog of the Cuban and Caribbean Library, University of Miami,* (Boston: G K Hall, 1977).

FL —MIAMI-DADE PUBLIC LIBRARY SYSTEM, 1 Biscayne Blvd, Miami, 33132.

CUBA (cont.)

Alicia Godoy, Foreign Language Librn
Holdings: Vols 32,000 Cat Maps Microforms Phonorecords Audiotapes VF
Notes: Incl books in 17 languages, mainly Spanish; fiction, technical, biography, travel, history, mysteries, westerns, science-fiction and grammar; 200 language records, 100 language cassettes, 3 vertical files of clippings related to Latin America, Spain, Miami, etc; 35 magazines, 10 newspapers (daily local paper: Diario las Americas, El Miami Herald-El Mundo Puerto Rico); Sunday editions of Latin American newspapers from Argentina, Colombia, Chile, Mexico and Brazil; 1 Yiddish and 1 German newspaper.

MO —WASHINGTON UNIVERSITY, John M Olin Library, Campus Box 1061, St Louis, 63130.
Holdings: Vols (50,000) Cat
Notes: Strong collection. Much unusual material.

NY —NEW YORK PUBLIC LIBRARY, Donnell Foreign Language Library, 20 W 53 St, New York, 10019. Bosiljka Stevanovic, Supvr Librn
Notes: A circulating collection of books written in about 80 languages. The collections are general and popular in character - current topics, travel, histories, biography, etc, emphasizing the literature of the country - fiction, drama, poetry, literary criticism. The collections are primarily intended for use of readers whose first language is other than English. Separate catalogs for each language. Collections containing less than 100 volumes are not listed. Translations are moderately included.

PA —UNIVERSITY OF PITTSBURGH, Hillman Library, Pittsburgh, 15260. Glenora E Rossell, Head
Holdings: Vols (172,000) Cat Microforms
Notes: The collection contains Cuban books and periodicals with strong emphasis on material published in Cuba from 1959 to date, and material published outside Cuba concerning Revolutionary Cuba. It is intended to be exhaustive (books, pamphlets, and periodicals on all subjects), and includes complete or fairly complete collections of periodicals (175 titles; 139 published during 1959-1972).

TX —UNIVERSITY OF TEXAS LIBRARIES, Nettie Lee Benson Latin American Collection, Sid Richardson Hall 1.109, Austin, 78712. Laura Gutierrez-Witt, Head Librn
Holdings: Vols (450,000) Cat Mss Maps Pix Phonorecords Filmstrips Microforms
See also entry under Latin America.

CUBA—HISTORY

CA —HOOVER INSTITUTION ON WAR, REVOLUTION & PEACE, Stanford University, Stanford, 94305. Milorad M Drachkovitch, Archivist
Holdings: Vols (1600) Mss Pix Microfilm
Notes: About 1600 titles on contemporary Cuba. Intensive collecting of political, social and economic works covering the Castro period, especially writings and speeches of Castro and Guevara. Some 30 periodical and newspaper titles currently received from the island. General description of the Latin American Collection and complete listing of the serial and newspaper holdings available in: Joseph W Bingaman, *Latin America: a Survey of Holdings at the Hoover Institution on War, Revolution and Peace*. Stanford, Califorinia: Hoover Institution, Stanford University, 1972. 96 pp.

CT —YALE UNIVERSITY, Sterling Memorial Library, Latin American Collections, New Haven, 06520. Lee H Williams Jr, Cur
Holdings: Vols (300,000) Cat Maps Pix Slides Phonorecords 16mm Films Filmstrips
See also entry under Latin America

FL —UNIVERSITY OF MIAMI, Otto G Richter Library, PO Box 248214, Coral Gables, 33124. Frank Rodgers, Dir of Libraries

NY —COLUMBIA UNIVERSITY LIBRARIES, Rare Book & Manuscript Library, 801 Butler Library, 535 W 114 St, New York, 10027. Kenneth A Lohf, Librn
Holdings: Cat Mss
Notes: Materials on Castro's Cuba in the Herbert Matthews and Lee Lockwood papers. Restricted use.

CUBA—POLITICS AND GOVERNMENT

CA —HOOVER INSTITUTION ON WAR, REVOLUTION & PEACE, Stanford University, Stanford, 94305. Milorad M Drachkovitch, Archivist
Holdings: Vols (1600) Mss Pix Microfilm
Notes: Three collections: (1) Books on contemporary Cuba comprise about 1600 titles. Intensive collecting is made of political, social and economic works covering the Castro period, especially writings and speeches of Castro and Guevara. Some 30 periodical and newspaper titles are currently received from the island. A general description of the Latin American Collection and a complete listing of the serial and newspaper holdings is available in: Bingaman, Joseph W *Latin America: a Survey of Holdings at the Hoover Institution on War, Revolution and Peace*. Hoover Institution, Stanford University, Stanford, California, 1972. 96 pp. (2) Records of the Citizens Committee for a Free Cuba, Inc, an anti-communist organization founded in the US in 1963 to disseminate information about communism in Cuba and other Latin American countries, incl clippings, newsletters, press releases, reports, conference papers, speeches, and printed matter, 1962-74, relating primarily to the political, economic, and social effects of communism in Cuba, communist subversion in Latin America, US foreign policy toward Cuba, and activities of the Cuban emigre community. 58 ms boxes. (3) Papers of Theodore Draper, 1948-1966, incl correspondence, clippings, pamphlets, newspaper issues, and congressional hearings, relating to the revolution led by Fidel Castro in Cuba, political, social, and economic conditions in Cuba, and the 1965 crisis and US intervention in the Dominican Republic. 22 ms boxes.

CUBAN AUTHORS see Authors, Cuban

CUBAN LITERATURE

NY —NEW YORK PUBLIC LIBRARY, Donnell Foreign Language Library, 20 W 53 St, New York, 10019. Bosiljka Stevanovic, Supvr Librn
Notes: Cuban collection incl Cuban authors of Cuban expression. No separate catalogs.

OH —KENT STATE UNIVERSITY, Libraries, Dept of Special Collections, Kent, 44242. Dean H Keller, Cur
Holdings: Vols 1800 / / Cat
Notes: Private library of Dr Andres de Piedra-Bueno incl most of his own works.

PA —UNIVERSITY OF PITTSBURGH, Hillman Library, Pittsburgh, 15260. Glenora E Rossell, Head
Holdings: Vols (172,000) Cat Microforms
Notes: A general collection of Latin American literature, with emphasis on Cuba, Mexico, Chile, Guatemala, Ecuador, Peru, Bolivia, and Argentina. The holdings on Bolivian, Ecuadorian, and Cuban literature are extremely good. Very strong in contemporary literature of the whole area.

CUBANS IN FLORIDA

FL —FLORIDA DEPT OF COMMERCE, Research Library, 408 Fletcher Bldg, Tallahassee, 32301. Dennis Hitchens, Librn
Holdings: Vols (3000) Cat Mss Maps VF
Budget: ($6000)
Notes: Collect materials related to the 2 divisions of the Florida Dept of Commerce: Economic Development and Tourism, incl titles on Florida (historical and current), international trade, transportation, education, employment, management, industrial development and business. The Florida and US documents collection covers population, manufacturing, employment, agriculture, retail trade, wholesale trade and labor. VF incl files on every city and county, especially local economic data, SIC coded material, out-of-state information, county files, Florida specific material and general subject material. 100 VF drawers.

CUBANS IN THE U.S.

CA —HOOVER INSTITUTION ON WAR, REVOLUTION & PEACE, Stanford University, Stanford, 94305. Milorad M Drachkovitch, Archivist
Notes: Records of the Citizens Committee for a Free Cuba, Inc, an anti-communist organization founded in the US in 1963 to disseminate information about communism in Cuba and other Latin American countries, incl clippings, newsletters, press releases, reports, conference papers, speeches, and printed matter, 1962-74, relating primarily to the political, economic, and social effects of communism in Cuba, communist subversion in Latin America, US foreign policy toward Cuba, and activities of the Cuban emigre community. 58 ms boxes.

FL —UNIVERSITY OF MIAMI, Otto G Richter Library, PO Box 248214, Coral Gables, 33124. Frank Rodgers, Dir of Libraries
Notes: The Cuban exile periodicals incl 412 titles of which 381 have been published in Miami, Florida. The archival material incl 54 cubic ft of mss, invitations, programs, braodsides, posters, postcards, prints, reports, maps, etc. This collection incl personal and corporate papers of Cubans settled in the US or in other countries. The truth about Cuban Committee Papers. 40 cubic ft. Contains records and correspondence of intellectual and professional Cuban and American leaders in the US dedicated to the course of eliminating Communism from the Western Hemisphere.

PA —BALCH INSTITUTE FOR ETHNIC STUDIES, Library, 18 S Seventh St, Philadelphia, 19106. R Joseph Anderson, Library Dir
Holdings: Cat Microforms

TX —UNIVERSITY OF TEXAS LIBRARIES, Nettie Lee Benson Latin American Collection, Sid Richardson Hall 1.109, Austin, 78712. Laura Gutierrez-Witt, Head Librn
Holdings: Vols (450,000) Cat Slides 16mm Films Microforms
Notes: The Mexican American Library Project has, since 1974, collected materials relating to all aspects of Spanish-speaking people in the US, with emphasis on Mexican Americans.
See also entry under Latin America.

CUDLIP, ANNIE HALL (THOMAS), 1838-1918

CA —UNIVERSITY OF CALIFORNIA, LOS ANGELES, Research Library, Dept of Special Collections, 405 Hilgard Ave, Los Angeles, 90024. Edward Shreeves, Chairman, Bibliographers Group; David S Zeidberg, Head
Notes: 500 letters from various people.

CUELLAR, FRANK, SR.

TX —NORTH TEXAS STATE UNIVERSITY, Archives, NT Station Box 5188, Denton, 76203. Robert LaForte, University Archivist
Notes: Part of Business Archive Project. Interviews with founder of El Chico Corporation.

CUKOR, GEORGE

CA —ACADEMY OF MOTION PICTURE ARTS & SCIENCES, Margaret Herrick Library, 8949 Wilshire Blvd, Beverly Hills, 90211. Linda Harris Mehr, Library Administrator
Notes: Papers.
See also entry under Moving Pictures.

CULLEN, COUNTEE

LA —AMISTAD RESEARCH CENTER, 400 Esplanade Ave, New Orleans, 70116. Clifton

CULLEN, COUNTEE (cont.)

H Johnson, Exec Dir; Florence E Borders, Senior Archivist
Holdings: Vols (10,000) Cat Mss Pix Audiotapes Microforms
Budget: ($315,000)
Notes: In addition 8,000,000 ms pieces, 10, 000 pictures, 3500 microforms, and 500 audiotapes. Amistad Research Center is an historical research library. Originally established at Fisk University, in Nashville, by the American Missionary Association (AMA), this research center on Black American History consists of mss, photographs, clippings, books, pamphlets, taped speeches, and interviews; also, the papers of such leaders as W E B DuBois, Countee Cullen, and Mary McLeod Bethune. Also materials on other American minorities, such as Native Americans, Asian Americans, Hispanics, etc.

CULLMAN, MARGUERITE

MA —BOSTON UNIVERSITY, Mugar Memorial Library, Special Collections Dept, 771 Commonwealth Ave, Boston, 02215. Howard B Gotlieb, Dir
Holdings: Cat Mss

CULLUM, GEORGE WASHINGTON

PA —ALLEGHENY COLLEGE, Lawrence Lee Pelletier Library, Meadville, 16335. Margaret L Moser, Librn
Holdings: Uncat Mss
Notes: About 800 ms pieces. Indexed.

CULP, JOHN H.

MA —BOSTON UNIVERSITY, Mugar Memorial Library, Special Collections Dept, 771 Commonwealth Ave, Boston, 02215. Howard B Gotlieb, Dir
Holdings: Cat Mss
Notes: Mss, correspondence, etc collected in depth; incl publications by or about.

CULPEPER, NICHOLAS

CA —UNIVERSITY OF CALIFORNIA, LOS ANGELES, Biomedical Library, Center for the Health Sciences, Los Angeles, 90024. Alison Bunting, Acting Biomedical Librn; Victoria Steele, Head, History & Special Collections Div
Holdings: Cat
Notes: Incl the C D O'Malley Collection of 28 editions of his works.

CULTIVATION OF SOILS see Tillage

CULTS AND SECTS see Sects

CULTURAL ANTHROPOLOGY see Ethnology

CULTURAL GEOGRAPHY see Geography, Cultural

CULVER, JOHN C.

†IA —UNIVERSITY OF IOWA, Libraries, Iowa City, 52242.
Notes: Papers, etc.

CUMBERLAND PRESBYTERIAN CHURCH

GA —AGNES SCOTT COLLEGE, McCain Library, E College Ave, Decatur, 30030. Judith Bourgeois Jensen, Librn
Holdings: Vols (945) Uncat
Budget: $300
Notes: The Frontier Religion Collection, which was given by Prof Walter Brownlow Posey, traces the effects of slavery on religion in the Old South Frontier prior to 1860. A catalog file (by author entry only) accompanies the collection at present. Noncirculating.

CUMBERLAND ROAD PAPERS

OH —WESTERN RESERVE HISTORICAL SOCIETY, History Library, William P Palmer Civil War Collection, 10825 East Blvd, Cleveland, 44106. Kermit J Pike, Dir
Holdings: Mss
Notes: The William P Palmer Civil War Collection. "The Cumberland Road Papers," of David Shriver, Jr, Superintendent. Papers range 1810-1852. Incl pamphlets, broadsides and sheet music.

CUMMINGS, E. E. (EDWARD ESTLIN)

MA —HARVARD UNIVERSITY LIBRARY, Houghton Library, Cambridge, 02138. Rodney G Dennis, Cur of Manuscripts
Holdings: Cat Mss

NV —UNIVERSITY OF NEVADA, RENO, University Library, Special Collections Dept, Reno, 89557. Robert E Blesse, Head
Holdings: Vols (95) // Cat
Notes: Includes individual works by author in all editions including translations; also prefaces, introductions, published correspondence, appearances in anthologies, periodicals, etc. Bibliographical research collection, part of Modern Authors Collection. Other appearances, 1250 cataloged.

NY —VASSAR COLLEGE, Library, Rare Books & Manuscripts Collection, Box 20, Poughkeepsie, 12601. Lisa Browar, Cur
Notes: An extensive collection of Elizabeth Bishop's papers, incl notebooks, mss, drafts, galleys, etc, as well as correspondence and business files, with files of letters from Cummings, Toklas, Dylan Thomas, and Eudora Welty.

VA —UNIVERSITY OF VIRGINIA, Alderman Library, Clifton Waller Barrett Collection, Charlottesville, 22901. Joan St C Crane, Cur of American Literature Collections
Notes: Papers.

BC —UNIVERSITY OF VICTORIA, McPherson Library, Victoria, V8W 3H5, Can.
Notes: Incl letters; postcards; Christmas cards; short note (to Mrs Ellen Stevenson); 1 TLS to Peter Russell.

CUMMINGS, HOMER STILLE

VA —UNIVERSITY OF VIRGINIA, Alderman Library, Manuscripts Dept, Charlottesville, 22901. Edmund Berkeley Jr, Cur
Holdings: Cat Mss Pix Phonorecords 16mm Films
Notes: Personal, political, and business papers.

CUMMINGS, MALCOLM

AZ —NORTHERN ARIZONA UNIVERSITY, Special Collection Library, CU Box 6022, Flagstaff, 86011. Peter M Whiteley, Coordr/Archivist; William Mullane, Librn
Notes: Papers.

CUNEIFORM INSCRIPTIONS

CA —SAN DIEGO PUBLIC LIBRARY, Wangenheim Rm, 820 E St, San Diego, 92101. Eileen Boyle, Librn
Holdings: Vols (7500) Cat
Notes: A collection on the history of the book and the development of printing with specimens ranging from Babylonian tablets to cassettes.

CT —YALE UNIVERSITY, Sterling Memorial Library, Babylonian Collection, 120 High St, New Haven, 06520. William W Hallo, Cur
Holdings: Vols (12,000) Cat Mss Pix
Budget: $2500
Notes: 30,000 mss in form of Babylonian tablets; 6000 seals and other art objects from Mesopotamia and the rest of the Ancient Near East.

FL —FLORIDA STATE UNIVERSITY, Robert Manning Strozier Library, Special Collections Dept, Tallahassee, 32306. Opal M Free, Head, Special Collections
Holdings: Vols 83 // Uncat
Notes: Babylonian clay tablets (2100-2300 BC), 25 items. Papyri, 26 fragments, with Greek text. Ostraka, 32 items, 29 in Greek text, 3 in Latin text. Noncirculating.

MO —SAINT LOUIS PUBLIC LIBRARY, Gardner Rare Book Room, 1301 Olive St, Saint Louis, 63103. Julanne M Good, Supervisor; Martha Riley, Rare Books Librn
Holdings: Vols 14// Cat
Notes: Mainly fiscal documents dating from 2375-394 BC--5 Sumerian; 1 Old Babylonian/Sumerian; 4 Old Babylonian; 4 Neo-Babylonian. Catalog gives transcription and translation. Publication rights assigned to Dr John Brinkman, Director, Oriental Institute, University of Chicago. No photocopying.

NY —COLUMBIA UNIVERSITY LIBRARIES, Rare Book & Manuscript Library, 801 Butler Library, 535 W 114 St, New York, 10027. Kenneth A Lohf, Librn
Holdings: // Cat
Notes: 650 tablets. Restricted use: noncirculating.

NY —NEW YORK PUBLIC LIBRARY, Oriental Div, Fifth Ave & 42 St, New York, 10018. E Christian Filstrup, Chief
Holdings: Cat Mss Microforms
Budget: ($56,455)
Notes: Published catalog of holdings.

NC —UNIVERSITY OF NORTH CAROLINA, CHAPEL HILL, Wilson Library, Rare Book Collection, Chapel Hill, 27514. Paul S Koda, Cur of Rare Books
Holdings: Vols 1000 Cat Mss
Notes: The Hanes Collection of the History of the Book consists of Sumerian and Babylonian clay tablets, papyri in Egyptian and in Greek, stone inscriptions, 24 olas, manuscripts, and 600 items of 16th, 17th and 18th century printing, incl many landmarks in the history of printing. It also contains many books about books, incl some rare bibliographies, histories of presses and technology, and books on collecting.

OH —CLEVELAND PUBLIC LIBRARY, Fine Arts and Special Collections Department, 325 Superior Ave, Cleveland, 44114. Alice N Loranth, Head
Holdings: Vols (54,000) Cat Mss
Notes: A small collection of cuneiform tablets, and a sizeable collection of facsimile reproductions, text editions and their translations are part of the Orientalia Collection.
See also entry under Oriental Languages and Literatures.

PA —FREE LIBRARY OF PHILADELPHIA, Rare Book Dept, Logan Sq, Philadelphia, 19103. Marie E Korey, Rare Book Librn
Holdings: Cat
Notes: The John Frederick Lewis Collection of Cuneiform Tablets. 2800 stone and clay tablets, Summerian, Babylonian, and Neo-Babylonian.

TX —ROSENBERG LIBRARY, Fox Rare Book Room, 2310 Sealy Ave, Galveston, 77550. Fernando Basilza, Rare Book Librn
Holdings: Vols (2000) Cat Mss Pix
Notes: The Col Milo Pitcher Fox and Agnes Peel Fox Rare Book Room contains 2000 vols incunabula, first printings, and modern fine printing. Incl clay tablets, horn books, parchment material, illuminated books and mss, fine printing (principally 15th-18th centuries), fine binding, fore-edge paintings, etc.

CUNEIFORM WRITING

CT —YALE UNIVERSITY, Box 1603A, Yale Station, New Haven, 06520.
Holdings: Cat Mss Pix
Notes: Correspondence of Professor Albrecht Goetze, 1932-1971, incl materials relating to his work as editor of the *Journal of Cuneiform Studies*, 1947-1971.

CUNNINGHAM, EILEEN ROACH

TN —VANDERBILT UNIVERSITY, Medical Center Library, Nashville, 37232. Mary H Teloh, Special Collections Librn
Holdings: Cat Mss Pix
Notes: Personal papers of Eileen Roach Cunningham, leader in the field of medical librarianship. Material covers the period 1925-1965. Collection contains correspondence, speeches, notes, travel diaries and photographs. 10 linear ft of mss.

CUNNINGHAM, WINFIELD SCOTT

MA —BOSTON UNIVERSITY, Mugar Memorial Library, Special Collections Dept, 771 Commonwealth Ave, Boston, 02215. Howard B Gotlieb, Dir
Holdings: Cat Mss Maps Pix
Notes: Mss correspondence, etc collected in depth; incl publications by or about.

CUNNINGHAM FAMILY

BC —UNIVERSITY OF VICTORIA, McPherson Library, Victoria, V8W 3H5, Can.
Notes: Incl 65 cm, 1850-1918; holograph testimonials and letters of Dr J P Cunningham and his son, Dr H H B Cunningham; British Army (42 Div) orders to Dr H H B Cunningham 1915-20; army payslips 1917-21; personal account books 1900-22; army reports 1916-20; memorabilia 1893-1931.

CUNNINGHAME GRAHAM, ROBERT BONTINE see Graham, Robert Bontine Cunninghame

CUOMO, GEORGE

BC —UNIVERSITY OF VICTORIA, McPherson Library, Victoria, V8W 3H5, Can.
Notes: Incl 660 cm, 1958-73; mss, tss and proofs of published novels: *Jack be nimble* (1963), *Bright day dark runner* (1964), *Among thieves* (1964), *A hero's great, great, great, great, great grandson* (1971); unpublished novel, *Bomb* (1973); short stories: *Sing choir of angels* (1969); miscellaneous short stories; poetry; essays and criticism; reviews; articles; plays; miscellaneous work timetables and ephemera.

CUPS AND SAUCERS see Porcelain; Pottery

CURACAO

CT —YALE UNIVERSITY, Sterling Memorial Library, Latin American Collections, New Haven, 06520. Lee H Williams Jr, Cur
Holdings: Vols (300,000) Cat Maps Pix Slides Phonorecords 16mm Films Filmstrips
See also entry under Latin America

CURIE, PIERRE

†MA —FRANCIS A COUNTWAY LIBRARY OF MEDICINE, Boston, 02115.

CURIOSA

IN —INDIANA UNIVERSITY, Institute for Sex Research Library, 416 Morrison Hall, Bloomington, 47401. Douglas Freeman, Collections and Services Librn; Joan Brewer, Information Services Librn
Holdings: Vols (62,000) Cat Mss Pix Phonorecords Audiotapes Slides Films Microforms
Budget: ($20,000)
Notes: One of the greatest and most extensive collections on sexual behavior, the library collects materials on all aspects of sex activity, with special emphasis on behavioral and social aspects. Also collects erotic literature and sexual ephemera. Incl 105 audiotapes, 23 vertical file drawers, 108 phonorecords, 55,000 pictures, 5000 slides, and 1700 films. Rich in French, German and American sources; also much Oriental. Semitraditional erotic poetry and song of 17th-18th century England. Bawdy limericks, double-entendre, puns, slang, erotic literature, graffiti, slang and special dictionaries, proverbs and saying, epigrams and research materials of the Kinsey Studies, etc. Contact Information Service for: literature searching, preparation of bibliographies, permission to use collection. Limited photocopying.

MN —SAINT PAUL PUBLIC LIBRARY, 90 W Fourth St, Saint Paul, 55102. Judith Devine, Supervisor
Notes: The Johnson Collection. No photocopying.

CURLEY, JAMES M., 1874-1958

MA —BOSTON COLLEGE LIBRARIES, Thomas P O'Neill Library, Brehaut Bostonian Collection, Chestnut Hill, 02167. Frank J Seegraber, Special Collections Librn
Holdings: Cat Mss Maps Pix
Notes: Over 5000 items, incl 85 scrapbooks, and 100 maps of Boston and vicinity, 1850-1900. Emphasis on political history, incl the Boston fire, 1872; Boston police strike, 1919; development of the Boston transit system; career of James Michael Curley. For reference use only, by arrangement with librarian.

MA —COLLEGE OF THE HOLY CROSS, Dinand Library, College St, Worcester, 01610. James M Mahoney, Cur of Special Collection
Holdings: Uncat Pix Microforms
Notes: Mayor of Boston, Governor of Massachusetts. Collection consists mainly of newspaper clippings (675 vols), scrapbooks, recordings of speeches (9 reels) and pictures. There is no correspondence.

CURLL, EDMUND

KS —UNIVERSITY OF KANSAS, Kenneth Spencer Research Library, Special Collections Dept, Lawrence, 66045. Alexandra Mason, Librn
Holdings: Vols 850 Cat
Notes: Publications of The Unspeakable Curll. Based on the private collection of Peter Murray Hill. Noncirculating.

TX —SAN ANTONIO COLLEGE, Library, 1001 Howard St, San Antonio, 78284. James O Wallace, Dir
Holdings: Vols 2500 Cat Microforms
Notes: The Morrison Collection of Eighteenth Century British Literature. Partially described in: Hennington, Betty M, Lois G Morrison Collection of Eighteenth Century English Literature: a Checklist (unpublished MLS thesis) Texas Woman's University, 1968. Also see The Morrison Collection *Scriblerian,* vol 1, pp 32-33 (Spring 1969). Especially strong in material relating to Eustace Budgell; A Moore, W Webb and Edmund Curll imprints. A separate catalog is maintained for the collection with entries for author, title, personal subjects, printers and booksellers, date of publication, engravers and association copies.

CURNOW, BOB

TX —NORTH TEXAS STATE UNIVERSITY, Audio Center, Box 5188, NT Station, Denton, 76203. Morris Martin, Music Librn
Notes: More than 1600 manuscript jazz compositions, (incl scores and parts, alternate versions, expanded arrangements) by Stan Kenton, Johnny Richards, Joe Coccia, Lennie Niehaus, Pete Rugolo, Willie Maiden, Bob Curnow, Ken Hanna, Gene Rowland, Bob Graettinger and others, used by the Stan Kenton Band and given to North Texas State University in 1962 and at Kenton's death in 1979. Unpublished catalog: Breeden, Leon, *Stan Kenton Music in the NTSU Jazz Studies Library and the NTSU Music Library,* Denton, 1983 (99 pages).

CURRENCY see Coins; Money; Numismatics

CURRENT EVENTS

DC —LIBRARY OF CONGRESS, Motion Pictures, Broadcasting and Recorded Sound Div, Washington, 20540.
Notes: Recordings of speeches given at the National Press Club, Washington, D.C., 1952-present.

CURRENTS

FL —UNIVERSITY OF MIAMI, Otto G Richter Library, PO Box 248214, Coral Gables, 33124. Frank Rodgers, Dir of Libraries
Holdings: Vols Microforms
Notes: The Rosenstiel School of Marine and Atmospheric Sciences Library is one of the major marine science collections in the United States and is especially strong in the literature of tropical oceanography. Special collections in the library incl 200 oceanographic atlases and more than 50 sets of the world's major expedition reports. The library also maintains a nautical chart collection. 3000 microforms; 1000 current subscriptions.

CURRICULA (COURSES OF STUDY) see Education—Curricula

CURRIER, CHARLES HENRY, 1851-1938

DC —LIBRARY OF CONGRESS, Prints & Photographs Div, Washington, 20540.
Notes: The Charles Henry Currier Collection of photographs of homes, offices, factories, charitable institutions, and recreational organizations in the Boston area, 1890s-1910s.

CURRIER AND IVES

RI —BROWN UNIVERSITY, John Hay Library, McLellan Lincoln Collection, 20 Prospect St, Providence, 02912. Jennifer B Lee, Special Collections Librn
Holdings: Vols (15,00) Cat Mss Pix Phonorecords
Notes: Prints, arranged according to Meserve numbers, contain most of the known photographs of Lincoln, rare engravings, caricatures, Currier and Ives prints, and original oil portraits done by artists of Lincoln's day, as well as original paintings of Lincoln's deathbed by Alonzo Chappel and Alexander Ritchie; some original drawings, as well as a scrapbook of Thomas Nast's Civil War sketches.

TX —AMON CARTER MUSEUM, 3501 Camp Bowie Blvd, PO Box 2365, Fort Worth, 76113. Jan K Muhlert, Dir; Marni Sandweiss, Cur of Photographs
Holdings: Cat Pix
Notes: Emphasis of American prints dating from the sixteenth century through the twentieth century. Includes book illustrations, documentary records of important scientific explorations, renderings of landscape and city views, and fine art prints produced by artists seeking to exploit the expressive qualities inherent in the materials and techniques of the medium. Large collections of Audubon, Currier and Ives, nineteenth century city views, and early American modern fine art prints.

CURTIS, ASAHEL

WA —WASHINGTON STATE HISTORICAL SOCIETY LIBRARY, 315 N Stadium Way, Tacoma, 98403. Frank L Green, Librn
Holdings: Vols 15,000 Cat Mss Maps Pix Microforms
Notes: Curtis Collection Frederick and Engerman, *Asahel Curtis: Photographs of the Great Northwest* pub 1983. Scope is entire Pacific Northwest, with emphasis on Washington.

CURTIS, EDWARD

DC —LIBRARY OF CONGRESS, Prints & Photographs Div, Washington, 20540.
Notes: The Edward S Curtis collection of photographs of North American Indians, early 20th century. About 1600 photoprints.

MD —UNIVERSITY OF MARYLAND, BALTIMORE COUNTY, Albin O Kuhn Library and Gallery, Edward L Bafford Photography Collection, 5401 Wilkens Ave, Baltimore, 21228. Tom Beck, Cur
Holdings: Pix
Notes: The Edward L Bafford Photography Collection contains more than 200,000 images, negatives, cameras and books representing the entire history and aesthetics

CURTIS, EDWARD (cont.)

of photography. There are a large number of photographs by both 19th and 20th century photographers, such as Edward Curtis, Eadweard Muybridge, Alfred Stieglitz, Diane Arbus, Lotte Jacobi, and many others. *See also* entry under Photographs - Collections.

NM —MUSEUM OF NEW MEXICO, Photo Archives, Box 2087, Santa Fe, 87503. Arthur L Olivas, Cur; Richard Rudisill, Photo Historian
Holdings: Cat Pix Slides
Notes: Extensive collection of his work.

UT —UNIVERSITY OF UTAH, Marriott Library, Special Collections, Salt Lake City, 84112. Gregory C Thompson, Cur
Notes: A majority of the books listed in H R Wagner's *The Plains and Rockies* are found in Rare Books as are the works of George Catlin, Karl Bodmer, Edward Curtis, and McKenny and Hall. Some of these are so rare that they must be used under restricted conditions.

CURTIS, GEORGE WILLIAM, 1824-1892

NY —CORNELL UNIVERSITY LIBRARIES, Collection of Regional History, Dept of Manuscripts and Univ Archives, Ithaca, 14853.
Notes: Author, orator. One ms address by Curtis at the dedication of the Sage College of Cornell University, NY.

OH —RUTHERFORD B HAYES LIBRARY, 1337 Hayes Ave, Fremont, 43420. Watt P Marchman, Dir
Holdings: Cat Mss
Notes: Mss incl largely his correspondence on various subjects; a segment as editor of *Harper's Weekly* and other literary papers.

RI —BROWN UNIVERSITY, John Hay Library, 20 Prospect St, Providence, 02912. Mark N Brown, Cur Mss
Holdings: // Mss
Notes: Author, orator, and editor of *Harper's Weekly*. Incl in the 100 items, 1852 to 1887, are correspondence, a ledger, an agreement with Harper Brothers, copyrights, and personal papers. Correspondents incl Samuel Eastman, John Hay, and William O'Connor.

CURTIS, HOLBROOK

CT —TRINITY COLLEGE LIBRARY, 300 Summit St, Hartford, 06106. Peter J Knapp, Archivist
Holdings: Uncat // Mss Pix
Notes: Late 18th and 19th century mss, letter, diaries, etc of the Curtis Family of Connecticut and New York, with emphasis on: William Edmond (1755-1838), US Congressman from Conn; Holbrook Curtis (1787-1858); William Edmond Curtis (1823-1880), Chief Justice of Superior Court of New York; Mary Ann Scovill Curtis (1831-1908); and William Edmond Curtis Jr, (1855-1923), US Asst Secy of the Treasury. Incl on basis of relation through marriage are late 18th and 19th century mss, letters and diaries of the Hiester, McLanahan and Muhlenberg Families of Pennsylvania, with emphasis on Joseph Hiester (1752-1832), US Congressman and Governor of Pennsylvania; and Andrew Gregg (1755-1835), US Congressman and Senator from Pennsylvania. 12 linear feet.

CURTIS, MARY ANN SCOVILL

CT —TRINITY COLLEGE LIBRARY, 300 Summit St, Hartford, 06106. Peter J Knapp, Archivist
Holdings: Uncat // Mss Pix
Notes: Late 18th and 19th century mss, letter, diaries, etc of the Curtis Family of Connecticut and New York, with emphasis on: William Edmond (1755-1838), US Congressman from Conn; Holbrook Curtis (1787-1858); William Edmond Curtis (1823-1880), Chief Justice of Superior Court of New York; Mary Ann Scovill Curtis (1831-1908); and William Edmond Curtis Jr, (1855-1923), US Asst Secy of the Treasury. Incl on basis of relation through marriage are late 18th and 19th century mss, letters and diaries of the Hiester, McLanahan and Muhlenberg Families of Pennsylvania, with emphasis on Joseph Hiester (1752-1832), US Congressman and Governor of Pennsylvania; and Andrew Gregg (1755-1835), US Congressman and Senator from Pennsylvania. 12 linear feet.

CURTIS, TONY

CA —UNIVERSITY OF CALIFORNIA, LOS ANGELES, Research Library, Dept of Special Collections, 405 Hilgard Ave, Los Angeles, 90024. Edward Shreeves, Chairman, Bibliographers Group; David S Zeidberg, Head
Holdings: Mss Pix
Notes: 10 linear feet of scripts and related materials of Tony Curtis (1925-).

CURTIS, WILLIAM EDMOND

CT —TRINITY COLLEGE LIBRARY, 300 Summit St, Hartford, 06106. Peter J Knapp, Archivist
Holdings: Uncat // Mss Pix
Notes: Late 18th and 19th century mss, letter, diaries, etc of the Curtis Family of Connecticut and New York, with emphasis on: William Edmond (1755-1838), US Congressman from Conn; Holbrook Curtis (1787-1858); William Edmond Curtis (1823-1880), Chief Justice of Superior Court of New York; Mary Ann Scovill Curtis (1831-1908); and William Edmond Curtis Jr, (1855-1923), US Asst Secy of the Treasury. Incl on basis of relation through marriage are late 18th and 19th century mss, letters and diaries of the Hiester, McLanahan and Muhlenberg Families of Pennsylvania, with emphasis on Joseph Hiester (1752-1832), US Congressman and Governor of Pennsylvania; and Andrew Gregg (1755-1835), US Congressman and Senator from Pennsylvania. 12 linear feet.

CURTIS, WILLIAM EDMOND, JR.

CT —TRINITY COLLEGE LIBRARY, 300 Summit St, Hartford, 06106. Peter J Knapp, Archivist
Holdings: Uncat // Mss Pix
Notes: Late 18th and 19th century mss, letter, diaries, etc of the Curtis Family of Connecticut and New York, with emphasis on: William Edmond (1755-1838), US Congressman from Conn; Holbrook Curtis (1787-1858); William Edmond Curtis (1823-1880), Chief Justice of Superior Court of New York; Mary Ann Scovill Curtis (1831-1908); and William Edmond Curtis Jr, (1855-1923), US Asst Secy of the Treasury. Incl on basis of relation through marriage are late 18th and 19th century mss, letters and diaries of the Hiester, McLanahan and Muhlenberg Families of Pennsylvania, with emphasis on Joseph Hiester (1752-1832), US Congressman and Governor of Pennsylvania; and Andrew Gregg (1755-1835), US Congressman and Senator from Pennsylvania. 12 linear feet.

CURTIS, WILLIAM ELEROY, 1850-1911

NJ —PRINCETON UNIVERSITY, Library, Manuscript Collection, Nassau St, Princeton, 08540. Jean F Preston, Cur
Holdings: // Cat Mss
Notes: 224 scrapbook volumes.

CURTIS BROWN LTD.

†NY —COLUMBIA UNIVERSITY LIBRARIES, Butler Library, Rare Book and Manuscript Library, 535 W 114 St, New York, 10027.
Notes: Archive of the literary agency Curtis Brown Ltd.

CURTIS FAMILY

CT —TRINITY COLLEGE LIBRARY, 300 Summit St, Hartford, 06106. Peter J Knapp, Archivist
Holdings: Uncat Mss Pix
Notes: Incl ms letters, diaries, etc, of 18th and early 19th century congressmen and their families, especially the Heister and Curtis families. 12 linear ft.

CT —YALE UNIVERSITY, Box 1603A, Yale Station, New Haven, 06520.
Holdings: Mss
Notes: Private and business papers of the Beers and Curtis Families, 1780-1909.

NY —CORNELL UNIVERSITY LIBRARIES, Collection of Regional History, Dept of Manuscripts and Univ Archives, Ithaca, 14853.
Notes: School notebooks and poems, 1829-39; .1 ft.

CURTISS, GLENN H.

NY —GLENN H CURTISS MUSEUM OF LOCAL HISTORY, Lake & Main Sts, Hammondsport, 14840. Merrill Stickler, Cur
Holdings: Vols 500 Uncat Mss Maps Pix Slides Audiotapes 16mm Films Microforms
Budget: $1000
Notes: The library may only be used by appointment by serious researchers. Some copying is allowed under special circumstances. Collection is basically concerned with Glenn H Curtiss and his accomplishments in early aviation. Also collecting material about his contemporaries.

NY —CORNELL UNIVERSITY LIBRARIES, Collection of Regional History, Dept of Manuscripts and Univ Archives, Ithaca, 14853.
Notes: Aviator. Scrapbook of Albany to New York flight, May 29,1910; 1 vol.

CURTISS, URSULA

MA —BOSTON UNIVERSITY, Mugar Memorial Library, Special Collections Dept, 771 Commonwealth Ave, Boston, 02215. Howard B Gotlieb, Dir
Holdings: Cat Mss
Notes: Mss, correspondence, etc collected in depth; incl publications by or about.

CURTIUS, ERNST, 1814-1896

CT —YALE UNIVERSITY, Box 1603A, Yale Station, New Haven, 06520.
Holdings: Vols 3500

CURWOOD, JAMES OLIVER

MI —OWOSSO PUBLIC LIBRARY, 502 W Main St, Owosso, 48867. Margaret A Bentley, Librn
Holdings: Vols 37 Cat Mss Pix
Notes: The library has accumulated as many titles as possible by James O Curwood. In conjunction with the area historical society, personnel have developed exhibits at the author's former studio, a rustic castle on the Shiawassee River. Since 1978, the anniversary of his birth has been celebrated annually by this community, with festivities and commemorations planned.

CUSHING, CALEB

DC —LIBRARY OF CONGRESS, Manuscript Division, Washington, 20540. John C Broderick, Chief
Holdings: Cat Mss Pix
Notes: Mss, papers, records, etc.

CUSHING, DANIEL

MA —HINGHAM PUBLIC LIBRARY, 66 Leavitt St, Hingham, 02043. Walter T Dziura, Dir
Holdings: Cat Mss Maps Pix Slides Microforms
Notes: A collection of about 2000 items relating to the history of the town from the 1600's to the present. Incl correspondence, legal documents, diaries and day books, account books, broadsides, pictures. Items of special importance incl papers of town clerk Daniel Cushing, from the 1600's. Catalog of the collection is available through interlibrary loan. Most of the collection is on

CUSHING, DANIEL (cont.)

microfilm and may be borrowed through interlibrary loan.

CUSHING, HARVEY WILLIAM, 1869-1939

CT —YALE UNIVERSITY, Medical Historical Library, 333 Cedar St, New Haven, 06510. Ferenc A Gyorgyey, Librn
Holdings: Mss Pix
Notes: Materials by and about; 75 vols, 24 file drawers. Incl correspondence with Sir William Osler.

KY —UNIVERSITY OF LOUISVILLE, Kornhauser Health Sciences Library, 520 S Preston St, PO Box 35260, Louisville, 40292. Leonard M Eddy, Dir; Sherrill R McConnell, Archivist
Holdings: Vols 30 Mss Reprints

†NY —NEW YORK ACADEMY OF MEDICINE, Library, 2 E 103 ST, New York, 10029.
Notes: Papers of Walter Timme, MD (1874-1956). Timme was a pioneer endocrinologist; described pluriglandular disease, "Timme's Syndrome." Incl correspondence from Harvey Cushing, Paul Dudley White, Charles A Elsberg, Louis I Dublin, Ely Smith Jelliffe, John F Fulton, Edna St Vincent Millay, Eva Le Gallienne, and Irving Ramsey Wiles.

CUSHING, RICHARD CARDINAL

MA —BOSTON UNIVERSITY, Mugar Memorial Library, Special Collections Dept, 771 Commonwealth Ave, Boston, 02215. Howard B Gotlieb, Dir
Holdings: Cat Correspondence

CUSHMAN, CHARLOTTE S.

DC —LIBRARY OF CONGRESS, Manuscript Division, Washington, 20540. John C Broderick, Chief
Holdings: Cat Mss Pix
Notes: Mss, papers, records, etc.

CUSHMAN, EDWARD L.

MI —WAYNE STATE UNIVERSITY, Walter P Reuther Library, Archives of Labor & Urban Affairs, Detroit, 48202. Philip Mason, Dir
Notes: Papers, etc of Edward L Cushman, assistant to the Secretary of Labor, labor arbitrator, and Vice-President of American Motors Corporation.

CUSHMAN, JOHN ASSOCIATES, INC.

†NY —COLUMBIA UNIVERSITY LIBRARIES, Butler Library, Rare Book and Manuscript Library, 535 W 114 St, New York, 10027.
Notes: The papers of the literary agency of James Oliver Brown, as well as those of John Cushman Associates, Inc, the firm he acquired in 1978.

CUSTER, GEORGE ARMSTRONG, 1839-1876

CA —AZUSA PACIFIC COLLEGE, Marshburn Memorial Library, Citrus & Alosta, Azusa, 91702. Edward Peterman, Librn
Holdings: Vols (6000) Uncat
Budget: ($30,000)
Notes: Significan holdings in the George E Fullerton Library of Californiana and Western Americana.

MI —MONROE COUNTY LIBRARY SYSTEM, Ellis Reference and Information Center, 3700 S Custer Rd, Monroe, 48161. Marie D Chulski, Head of Reference Services
Holdings: Vols (35,000) Cat
Budget: $15,000
Notes: The George Armstrong Custer Collection is a burgeoning archive of materials on General Custer and the events surrounding and shaping his life. This incl the Lawrence A Frost Collection of Custerania acquired by the library system in 1977. The Custer Monograph Series is produced by the Monroe County Library System. Publications are printed in limited numbered editions, aimed at providing insight into the life and times of General George Armstrong Custer. The continuing series consists of reprints of significant publications and original items.

MI —CENTRAL MICHIGAN UNIVERSITY, Clarke Historical Library, Mount Pleasant, 48859. William H Mulligan, Jr, Dir; William Miles, Biography Collections Librn
Holdings: Vols 1200 Mss Pix
Notes: Incl material on life and times of Gen George Custer and general subject of Indian-Army relations.

MT —EASTERN MONTANA COLLEGE, Library, 1500 N 30 St, Billings, 59101. Edward Neroda, Dir
Holdings: Mss
Notes: Incl Custer's personal and military papers and those of his widow relating to his career. Also, incomplete 7th Cavalry records and papers of the Battle of Little Big Horn. Many Civil War papers. Collection formerly at the Custer Battlefield National Monument.

†SD —SOUTH DAKOTA SCHOOL OF MINES & TECHNOLOGY, Devereaux Library, Rapid City, 57701.
Holdings: Vols 153 Cat
Notes: Indians of North America with emphasis on the Sioux Indians. Some of the books concern wars and battles with Indians, especially the Custer Massacre.

CUSTOMARY LAW

DC —LIBRARY OF CONGRESS, Law Library, 101 Independence Ave, SE, Washington, 20540. Carleton W Kenyon, Dir
Notes: Books and mss relating to European customary law.

CUSTOMARY LAW—EUROPE

DC —LIBRARY OF CONGRESS, Law Library, 101 Independence Ave, SE, Washington, 20540. Carleton W Kenyon, Dir
Notes: Books and mss relating to European customary law.

CUSTOMARY LAW—FRANCE

DC —LIBRARY OF CONGRESS, Law Library, 101 Independence Ave, SE, Washington, 20540. Carleton W Kenyon, Dir
Notes: Books and mss relating to European customary law.

CUSTOMS (LAW) see Customary Law

CUT GLASS

NY —CORNING MUSEUM OF GLASS LIBRARY, Corning, 14831. Norma P H Jenkins, Librn
Holdings: Vols (30,000) Cat Slides Videotapes Microforms
Notes: Extensive and comprehensive coverage of the art, archaeology, history and early manufacture of glass, with supporting materials in art, archaeology, and the decorative arts. Collection incl some 1800 manufacturers' trade catalogs on microfiche, 10,000 periodical vols and documents. 130 videotapes, 1000 microforms. Some incumabula. Research library primarily for use on the premises.

OH —TOLEDO-LUCAS COUNTY PUBLIC LIBRARY, 325 Michigan St, Toledo, 43624. Ardath Danford, Dir
Holdings: Vols (2000) Cat Pix Pamphlets
Notes: As complete as possible in fields of history, manufacture and technology. Antique and art glass collections are in Art Division.

WV —HUNTINGTON ART GALLERIES, Library, Art Reference Library, Park Hills, Huntington, 25701. Mary McKernon, Librn
Holdings: Vols (3500) Cat Pix Slides
Notes: Large collection of pamphlets on glass and glass memorabilia. Includes literature on venetian, pressed, patterned, carnival, victorian, and depression glasses.

CUTHBERT FAMILY

SC —COLLEGE OF CHARLESTON LIBRARY, Special Collections Dept, Charleston, 29401.
Notes: This collection, possibly gathered in 1851 by William Henry Trescott for his history of the Cuthbert family, consists of papers dealing with property owned by the family in Beaufort County, SC. The deeds, etc, do not all involve Cuthbert family members, but do pertain to property held by one or more of the family at some time. Among those landowners not of the Cuthbert family were Hugh Bryan, Thomas Corbett, Henry William De Saussure, Charles Heyward, Charles Palmer, Thomas Rutledge, and William Stoutenburg. These documents may come from Beaufort district and county judgment roles.

CUTLER, JOHN HENRY

MA —BOSTON UNIVERSITY, Mugar Memorial Library, Special Collections Dept, 771 Commonwealth Ave, Boston, 02215. Howard B Gotlieb, Dir
Holdings: Cat Mss Pix

CUTLER, MANASSEH

IL —NORTHWESTERN UNIVERSITY, Library, Special Collections Dept, 1937 Sheridan Rd, Evanston, 60201. R Russell Maylone, Cur
Holdings: Mss
Notes: The Charles G Dawes' gift of 4000 pieces incl personal papers, correspondence, Scioto Co papers, journals, diaries and sermons. Literature: Pollak, *Illinois Libraries,* April 1958, pp 322-324.

OH —OHIO UNIVERSITY, Vernon R Alden Library, Department of Archives and Special Collections, Athens, 45701. Gary A Hunt, Head
Holdings: Mss
Notes: Botanical notebooks, mss and printed documents, dating from 1776-1822.

CUTTING MACHINES AND CUTTING TOOLS

MI —GENERAL ELECTRIC COMPANY, Carboloy Systems Department, Library, Box 237, GPO, Detroit, 48232.
Holdings: Vols (4500) Cat Maps Slides 16mm Films Filmstrips Microforms
Budget: ($5000)
Notes: Collection covers cemented carbide cutting tools, powder metallurgy, metal cutting, metalworking, machining, and related subjects. Also numerical control, statistics (related to the cutting tool industry) and general management. Incl 500 maps, 4000 slides, 61 films, 261 filmstrips, 700 microfiche, 7000 patents, and 300 periodical titles.

CUTTING OF METALS see Metal Cutting

CUTTS FAMILY

KS —SAINT MARY COLLEGE, Library, Leavenworth, 66048. Therese Deplazes, Special Collections Librn
Notes: Holographs of American personalities, mostly of Colonial, Revolutionary, Confederacy periods, and 19th Century. Incl ms letters, deeds, petitions, wills, slave papers. Holographs of Col Philip Marsteller (one of George Washington's pall bearers), family papers of Richard, Mary and Edward Cutts; love letters to Mary "Polly" Carter, Frank Ellery (grandson of William Ellery, signer of the Declaration of Independence), letters of Connie Mack and Babe Ruth, of some American authors.

CYBERNETICS

MA —MASSACHUSETTS INSTITUTE OF TECHNOLOGY, Institute Archives, Special

CYBERNETICS (cont.)

Collections, Cambridge, 02139.
Notes: Papers of Norbert Wiener, renowned mathematician, was instrumental in the development of communication and control theories. He coined the word "cybernetics" to describe this new science. Professional papers document the development of this theory, his development as a mathematician, and his effective collaboration with students and colleagues including Vannevar Bush and John von Neumann. Unpublished finding aid with correspondent index is available in the Institute Archives.

NY —MORRIS N & CHESLEY V YOUNG LIBRARY OF MNEMONICS, 270 Riverside Dr, New York, 10025. Morris N Young, Cur
Holdings: Cat Mss Maps Pix Phonorecords Audiotapes 16mm Films Microforms
Notes: Collection of 5000 books, pamphlets, pictures, memorabilia, etc incl medieval art of memory; psychology of memory, forgetting and reading; medical aspects of memory, amnesia, dyslexia; biomedical aspects of learning and memory; information storage, retrieval and cybernetics; memory prodigies, lightning calculators, calendars; remembrance cups and memory mementos. All languages. Memorabilia incl engravings, posters, programs, advertisements, birthday cards, teaching cards, ASLs, and Mark Twain's Memory Builder game and other games. Items range from 1410 to 1980s.

PA —FRANKLIN INSTITUTE LIBRARY, 20 & The Parkway, Philadelphia, 19103. Miriam Padusis, Dir; Charles Wilt, Readers Servs Librn
Holdings: Vols (300,000) Cat Maps Pix Microforms

CYCLES, MOTOR see Motorcycles

CYCLIC AMP

NJ —PRINCETON UNIVERSITY, Biology Library, Guyot Hall, Princeton, 08540. Helen Zimmerberg, Librn
Notes: Papers used in preparing cyclic AMP. A bibliography, 1959-date, 9 vols.

CYCLING

DC —SMITHSONIAN INSTITUTION LIBRARIES, National Museum of American History Branch, Washington, 20560. Rhoda S Ratner, Branch Librn
Notes: Emphasis on history of American sports and recreation. Incl some 2000 baseball cards from cigarette and chewing-gum packets; 103 scrapbooks and other memorabilia about Joe Louis; much on bicycling and skating.

CYCLOPEDIAS see Encyclopedias and Dictionaries

CYCLOTRON

CA —UNIVERSITY OF CALIFORNIA, BERKELEY, Bancroft Library, Manuscripts Division, Berkeley, 94720. James D Hart, Dir
Holdings: // Cat Mss
Notes: The papers and correspondence of E O Lawrence, the eminent nuclear physicist, who was a central figure in the founding of the Berkeley Radiation Laboratory and the creation of the cyclotron. Approximately 50 cartons of mss.

CYLINDER SEALS

CT —YALE UNIVERSITY, Box 1603A, Yale Station, New Haven, 06520.
Notes: Part of the Newell Collection of Western Asiatic Seals. Contains 472 cylindrical-shaped roll seals.

CYMRIC LANGUAGE see Welsh Language and Literature

CYPRIOT LANGUAGE AND LITERATURE

DC —LIBRARY OF CONGRESS, Washington, 20540.
Holdings: Cat

CYPRUS

CA —HOOVER INSTITUTION ON WAR, REVOLUTION & PEACE, Stanford University, Stanford, 94305. Peter Duignan, Cur; Karen Fung, Deputy Cur
Holdings: Vols (100,000)
Notes: For full description of collection, see Hoover Institution entry under Near East.

CYPRUS—POLITICS AND GOVERNMENT

CA —HOOVER INSTITUTION ON WAR, REVOLUTION & PEACE, Stanford University, Stanford, 94305. Milorad M Drachkovitch, Archivist
Notes: Research files of Professor L S Stavrianos, incl reports, press releases, newspaper clippings, pamphlets, and other ephemeral publications relating to political developments in Greece and Cyprus, 1946-1960. 3 ms boxes.

CYRIL, ST.

PA —SLOVAK EASTERN CATHOLIC SYNOD OF AMERICA, 515 W Main, Monongahela, 15063.
Holdings: 1500 Vols
Notes: Promotes use of the Byzantine Rite among Slovak-Americans. Special interest in Sts Cyril and Methodius.

CYTOLOGY

MA —UNIVERSITY OF MASSACHUSETTS AT AMHERST, Library, Amherst, 01003. Siegfried Feller, Assoc Dir for Collection Development
Holdings: Cat
Notes: Special emphasis on cellular, developmental and physiological zoology.

MA —HARVARD UNIVERSITY LIBRARY, Biological Laboratories Library, 16 Divinity Ave, Cambridge, 02138. Dorothy Solbrig, Librn
Holdings: Vols (20,000) Cat Films
Notes: Materials in all areas of biology, emphasizing biochemistry and cellular and developmental biology. There is little in systematic biology and morphology.

NC —UNIVERSITY OF NORTH CAROLINA, CHAPEL HILL, Zoology Dept Library, Wilson Hall 046A, Chapel Hill, 27514. John B Darling, Librn
Holdings: Vols (31,000) Cat
Notes: Collection incl theses and dissertations.

PA —CARNEGIE LIBRARY OF PITTSBURGH, Science & Technology Dept, 4400 Forbes Ave, Pittsburgh, 15213. Catherine M Brosky, Dept Head
Notes: Of secondary interest in acquisitions because of the department's role in cooperating with Pittsburgh institutions and others across the Commonwealth in sharing resources, the cooperative acquisition of materials, and the provision of services and information. However, some aspects of the subject are incl. There are separate entries for each of these specialties in this vol.

TX —UNIVERSITY OF TEXAS, M D Anderson Hospital and Tumor Institute, Research Medical Library, Texas Medical Center, Houston, 77030. Marie Harvin, Research Medical Librn
Holdings: Vols (48,000) Cat
Notes: Library attempts to collect every publication in all languages related to clinical cancer (or oncology). Aim is an exhaustive collection in this field. Collect heavily (research level) in pathology, radiology, nuclear medicine, genetics and cell biology.

ON —AGRICULTURE CANADA, Research Branch, Neatby Library, Rm 3032, K W Neatby Bldg, CEF, Ottawa, K1A 0C6, Can. Marcel Charette, Library Technician
Holdings: Vols 1500 Cat
Notes: Nitrogen Fixation. All phases of cell biology.

CZECH ACADEMY OF SCIENCES PUBLICATIONS

IL —UNIVERSITY OF ILLINOIS, URBANA/CHAMPAIGN, Slavic and East European Library, Urbana, 61801. Marianna Tax Choldin, Head
Holdings: Vols (35,000) Cat
Notes: Extensive coverage.

CZECH AMERICAN NEWSPAPERS see Newspapers, Czech American

CZECH ART see Art, Czech

CZECH BOOK DESIGN see Book Design, Czech

CZECH FOLK DANCING see Folk Dancing, Czech

CZECH LANGUAGE AND LITERATURE

CA —LOS ANGELES PUBLIC LIBRARY, Foreign Languages Dept, 630 W Fifth St, Los Angeles, 90071. Sylva Manoogian, Principal Librn
Holdings: Vols 2344 Cat
Budget: ($41,500)

CA —UNIVERSITY OF CALIFORNIA, LOS ANGELES, Library, Slavic Collection, 405 Hilgard Ave, Los Angeles, 90024. Edward Shreeves, Chairman, Bibliographers Group; Leon Ferder, Slavic Bibliographer
Holdings: Vols (250,000) Cat
Notes: The Slavic Collection at UCLA consists of materials from and relating to Russia and the Soviet Union, Poland, Czechoslovakia, Yugoslavia, Bulgaria, the Sorbians in East Germany, and works by Slavic emigres. The collection contains nearly 250,000 vols, and is particularly strong in linguistics, literature, history and social sciences, and reference materials. Slavic materials are collected in hard copy and microform, and incl monographs, serials (incl newspapers), reference works, proceedings of Slavistic congresses and symposia, and also *Festschriften* and dissertations.

CA —STANFORD UNIVERSITY LIBRARIES, Cecil H Green Library, Stanford, 94305. Wojciech Zalewski, Cur, Russian & East European Collection
Holdings: Vols (200,000) Cat Maps Microforms
Budget: ($90,000)
Notes: Strong collection prior to 20th century, but Stanford University Libraries' collecting effort is coordinated with Hoover Institution, Stanford, and holdings are not duplicated. Collection descriptions: Wojciech Zalewski, *Russian Materials in the Main Library of Stanford University, A Collection* Survey (Stanford: Stanford University Libraries, 1974). Wojciech Zalerski, "Stanford University" in P L Horecky, ed, *East Central and Southeast Europe, A Handbook of Library and Archival Resources in North America* (Santa Barbara: Clio Press, 1976).

CT —YALE UNIVERSITY, Box 1603A, Yale Station, New Haven, 06520.

IL —CZECHOSLOVAK HERITAGE MUSEUM AND LIBRARY, 2701 S Harlem Ave, Berwyn, 60402.
Holdings: Vols 500
Notes: Incl 500 periodicals.

IL —UNIVERSITY OF ILLINOIS, URBANA/CHAMPAIGN, Slavic and East European Library, Urbana, 61801. Marianna Tax Choldin, Head
Holdings: Vols (35,000) Cat
Notes: Extensive coverage.

IN —INDIANA UNIVERSITY, Lilly Library, Seventh St, Bloomington, 47405. William R Cagle, Librn
Holdings: Vols (400) // Cat Mss
Notes: First editions and later printings of Karel H Macha (100 vols) and Vladimir Vasek (300 vols).

MA —HARVARD UNIVERSITY LIBRARY, Widener Library, Slavic Collections, Cambridge, 02138. Hugh M Olmsted, Slavic Dept Head
Holdings: Cat Microforms
Notes: Czech and Slovak literature shelflist through June, 1976 lists 7632 titles (earlier version was incl in *Widener Library Shelflist,*

CZECH LANGUAGE AND LITERATURE (cont.)

volumes 28-31, 1971). The language and literature collections continue to be developed actively, and are strong both in current and in antiquarian materials. The Jakub Deml collection is outstanding. See also *Harvard Library Bulletin,* XVII (1969), pp 425-433, and *East Central and Southeast Europe; A Handbook of Library and Archival Resources in North America,* edited by P L Horecky and D H Kraus, 1976, pp 119-122.

NE —UNIVERSITY OF NEBRASKA-LINCOLN, Don L Love Library, Czech Heritage Collection, Lincoln, 68588. Joseph G Svoboda, University Archivist
Holdings: Vols (3000) Cat Mss Pix Audiotapes Microforms
Notes: The Czech Heritage Collection.

NY —NEW YORK PUBLIC LIBRARY, Donnell Foreign Language Library, 20 W 53 St, New York, 10019. Bosiljka Stevanovic, Supvr Librn
Holdings: Vols 649 Cat
Notes: Czech collection incl Czech authors of Czech expression. No separate catalog.

NY —NEW YORK PUBLIC LIBRARY, Slavonic Div, Fifth Ave & 42 St, New York, 10018. Edward Kasinec, Chief
Holdings: Vols (28,000) Cat Microforms
Notes: Emphasis is on the humanities and social sciences, but government documents and publications of learned societies are also well represented. Materials in both languages, ie, Czech and Slovak, are collected. See New York Public Library, *Dictionary Catalog of the Slavonic* Collection (Boston: G K Hall, 1974), 44 vols.

OH —CLEVELAND PUBLIC LIBRARY, Foreign Literature Dept, 325 Superior Ave, Cleveland, 44114. Natalia Bezugloff, Head
Holdings: Vols 7140 Cat
Notes: A popular circulating collection containing classics and the standard works with emphasis on belles lettres, history and biography. A variety of other subjects such as learning languages, how to do books, art, children's books, spoken phonodiscs and cassettes, periodicals, etc. Incl 70 ephemera. *See also* entry under Foreign Language Collections

OH —KENT STATE UNIVERSITY, Libraries, Ethnic Collections, Kent, 44242.
Holdings: Vols 700 Cat
See also entry under Foreign Language Collections

PA —PENNSYLVANIA STATE UNIVERSITY, Fred Lewis Pattee Library, Slavic Library Program, University Park, 16802. Wasyl O Luciw, Head
Holdings: Vols (75,000) Cat Mss Pix
Budget: ($18,000)
Notes: The collection covers a wide range of languages Slavic and East European but its principal strengths are in Russian and Ukrainian. A special collection of 1576 volumes includes pre-revolutionary Russian, fine press publications, in our rare collection and children's literature. Besides book volumes, we have quite a large collection of manuscripts, documents, photographs and many periodicals, also including out of print books on microforms.

TX —SLOVANSKA PODPORUJICI JEDNOTA STATU TEXAS, Slavonic Benevolent Order of the State of Texas, SPJST Library, Archives, Museum, 520 N Main St, Temple, 76501. Otto Hanus, Cur-Librn; Thelma Bartosh, Asst Cur-Librn
Holdings: Vols 13,500 Cat Mss Pix Audiotapes Filmstrips
Notes: This collection consists of fiction, history, education, religion, music, medicine and agriculture.

ON —UNIVERSITY OF TORONTO, Thomas Fisher Rare Book Library, 120 Saint George St, Toronto, M5S 1A5, Can. Richard G Landon, Head
Holdings: Vols 200 Cat
Notes: Petlice Collection of typewritten copies of works by Czechoslovakian authors which cannot be published in Czechoslovakia. Includes poetry, fiction, political and philosophical works. A growing collection.

CZECH PERIODICALS see Periodicals, Czech

CZECHOSLOVAKIA

DC —GEORGETOWN UNIVERSITY, Library, Special Collections Div, 37 & O Sts NW, Washington, 20057. George M Barringer, Special Collections Librn; Nicholas B Sheetz, Mss Librn
Holdings: Mss Cat Pix
Notes: The personal papers of Richard T Crane (1882-1938), private secretary to Robert Lansing, 1915-1919; first American ambassador to Czechoslovakia, 1919-1921; and owner of the Westover Plantation in Virginia, 1921-1938. The papers - divided into three series, State Department, Prague and Westover - contain correspondence, memoranda, reports, diaries, documents, mss, printed material, and newspaper clippings. Correspondence incl letters from Robert Lansing, Charles Crane, Woodrow Wilson, Franklin Roosevelt, T G Masaryk, Jan Masaryk, Eduard Benes, Edward House, Herbert Hoover, Hugh Gibson, Joseph C Grew, Allan Dulles, and John Foster Dulles, among others.

IL —UNIVERSITY OF ILLINOIS, URBANA/CHAMPAIGN, Slavic and East European Library, Urbana, 61801. Marianna Tax Choldin, Head
Holdings: Vols (35,000) Cat
Notes: Extensive coverage.

UT —UTAH STATE UNIVERSITY, Merrill Library, Department of Special Collections & Archives, Logan, 84322. A J Simmonds, Curator; Jeanie F Simmonds, Archivist; Bradford R Cole, Mss Librn
Holdings: Vols 1000 Uncat
Notes: Books and pamphlets on Thomas G. Masaryk and the Czechoslovak Republic, 1890-1949. Languages represented: Czech, Slovak, German, French, Russian, English.

CZECHOSLOVAKIA—HISTORY

CA —UNIVERSITY OF CALIFORNIA, BERKELEY, University Library, Slavic Collections, Berkeley, 94720. Edward Kasinec, Librn
Holdings: Vols 1917 Cat Pix
Notes: The Masaryk-Benes Library is a rich resource for the study of Czechoslovak and European history, especially for the period 1918-1939. It contains Masaryk's own works in original and later editions, as well as in translation (231 volumes), and books about Tomas and Jan Masaryk and family (573). Benes is represented by his own writings (100) and items about him and his family (69). Miscellaneous titles (335) on Slavic problems, and on the history of Czechoslovakia, complete the monograph collection. The balance consists of periodical articles, reprints, and newspaper clippings. Publication dates range from 1883 to 1945, with the bulk of the material published during 1920-1940.

CA —UNIVERSITY OF CALIFORNIA, LOS ANGELES, Library, Slavic Collection, 405 Hilgard Ave, Los Angeles, 90024. Edward Shreeves, Chairman, Bibliographers Group; Leon Ferder, Slavic Bibliographer
Holdings: Vols (250,000) Cat Maps Microforms
Notes: The entire range of humanities, social sciences, and the arts. One of the most comprehensive US collections for material not only on Russia and the Soviet Union, but also on Bulgaria, Czechoslovakia, Poland, Yugoslavia, the non-Slavic countries of Eastern Europe (Romania, Hungary, Albania) and Soviet Central Asia. Holdings in Russian and Slavic linguistics, Russian literature, and Russian history are particularly strong, covering all periods. The collections are described in some detail in Paul Horecky's book on US Slavic collections.

CA —HOOVER INSTITUTION ON WAR, REVOLUTION & PEACE, Stanford University, Stanford, 94305. Milorad M Drachkovitch, Archivist
Holdings: Mss Pix
Notes: Papers

CA —STANFORD UNIVERSITY LIBRARIES, Cecil H Green Library, Stanford, 94305. Wojciech Zalewski, Cur, Russian & East European Collection
Holdings: Vols (200,000) Cat Maps Microforms
Budget: ($90,000)
Notes: Strong collection prior to 20th century, but Stanford University Libraries' collecting effort is coordinated with Hoover Institution, Stanford, and holdings are not duplicated. Collection descriptions: Wojciech Zalewski, *Russian Materials in the Main Library of Stanford University, A Collection* Survey (Stanford: Stanford University Libraries, 1974). Wojciech Zalerski, "Stanford University" in P L Horecky, ed, *East Central and Southeast Europe, A Handbook of Library and Archival Resources in North America* (Santa Barbara: Clio Press, 1976).

CT —YALE UNIVERSITY, Box 1603A, Yale Station, New Haven, 06520.

IL —AMERICAN SOKOL EDUCATIONAL AND PHYSICAL CULTURE, 6424 W Cermak Road, Berwyn, 60402. Annette Schabowski, Librn
Holdings: Vols 2000 Pix
Notes: Incl theses and dissertations on Czech life, folk dancing, gymnastics, etc.

IL —CZECHOSLOVAK HERITAGE MUSEUM AND LIBRARY, 2701 S Harlem Ave, Berwyn, 60402.
Holdings: 2500 Vols
Notes: Incl 1500 periodicals, 1000 artifacts, 500 art works. A major resource for American-Czech and Slovak history. Much on Chicago's Czech community. Also collection of books written in "Schwabach."

IN —INDIANA UNIVERSITY, University Libraries, Bloomington, 47401. Murlin Croucher, Librn for Slavic Studies
Holdings: Vols (300,000) Cat Maps Microforms
Budget: ($63,000)
Notes: The collection, established after World War 11, covers material of, and on, the Soviet Union (55 percent) and Eastern Europe (45 percent) in the languages of the area and in western European languages as well. Material is chiefly in the fields of humanities and social sciences. Many other Slavic and East European books are located in the Lilly Library (rare book Library).

IA —CZECH MUSEUM AND LIBRARY, 10 16th Ave SW, Cedar Rapids, 52404. Jana Fast, Curator
Holdings: 4000 Vols Mss
Notes: Czechoslovak history.

MA —HARVARD UNIVERSITY LIBRARY, Widener Library, Slavic Collections, Cambridge, 02138. Hugh M Olmsted, Slavic Dept Head
Holdings: Cat Microforms
Notes: Czechoslovakian history literature shelflist through June, 1976 lists 6205 titles (earlier version was incl in *Widener Library* Shelflist, volumes 28-31, 1971). The collections continue to be developed actively, and are strong both in current and in antiquarian materials. Holdings on Jan Hus, Eduard Benes, and Thomas Masaryk are particularly noteworthy.

NE —UNIVERSITY OF NEBRASKA-LINCOLN, Don L Love Library, Czech Heritage Collection, Lincoln, 68588. Joseph G Svoboda, University Archivist
Holdings: Vols (3000) Cat Mss Pix Audiotapes Microforms
Notes: The Czech Heritage Collection.

NY —NEW YORK PUBLIC LIBRARY, Slavonic Div, Fifth Ave & 42 St, New York, 10018. Edward Kasinec, Chief
Holdings: Vols (28,000) Cat Microforms
Notes: Emphasis is on the humanities and social sciences, but government documents and publications of learned societies are also well represented. Materials in both languages, ie, Czech and Slovak, are collected. See New York Public Library, *Dictionary Catalog of the Slavonic* Collection (Boston: G K Hall, 1974), 44 vols.

CZECHOSLOVAKIA—HISTORY (cont.)

NY —NEW YORK PUBLIC LIBRARY, Slavonic Div, Fifth Ave & 42 St, New York, 10018. Edward Kasinec, Chief
Holdings: Vols 180// Cat Mss
Notes: The Ukrainian archive of Mykyta Shapoval consists mainly of the correspondence of General Mykola Shapoval (Army of the Ukrainian National Republic, 1917-1920) and of his family. Document, mss, diaries relating to the activities and events of Ukrainians in Czechoslovakia and France are included. The material covers the period of the 1920s through 1950s.

†PA —BALCH INSTITUTE FOR ETHNIC STUDIES, Library, 18 S Seventh St, Philadelphia, 19106.
Notes: Papers of Vladimir Hurban, Czechoslovak ambassador to the United States.

PA —TEMPLE UNIVERSITY LIBRARIES, Special Collections Dept, Conwellana-Templana Collection, 13 & Berks St, Philadelphia, 19122. Miriam I Crawford, Cur
Holdings: Vols 3 // Cat Mss Maps Pix Newsclippings
Notes: Correspondence, manuscripts, published writings, and newspaper clippings of Herbert Adolphus Miller, from 1918 to 1951, sociologist, college teacher, active protagonist of the early Czechoslovak nation, and in the fight against racism. 25 letters, 10 manuscripts and about 50 news items, journal articles and pamphlets. Incl draft of a book by Miller on Czechoslovakia.

†PA —UNIVERSITY OF PITTSBURGH, Hillman Library, Pittsburgh, 15260.
Notes: Unpublished drafts of letters, memoranda, and messages in either English of Czech from Thomas Garrigue Masaryk to American and European Statesmen during the final phase of WWI and in the early period of Czechoslovakia's independence.

TX —SLOVANSKA PODPORUJICI JEDNOTA STATU TEXAS, Slavonic Benevolent Order of the State of Texas, SPJST Library, Archives, Museum, 520 N Main St, Temple, 76501. Otto Hanus, Cur-Librn; Thelma Bartosh, Asst Cur-Librn
Holdings: 15,000 Vols Mss Pix
Notes: 2000 periodicals; 1500 artifacts.

ON —UNIVERSITY OF TORONTO, Thomas Fisher Rare Book Library, 120 Saint George St, Toronto, M5S 1A5, Can. Richard G Landon, Head
Holdings: Vols 2500 Uncat Mss
Notes: Czechoslovakia 1968 Collection consists of books, pamphlets, journals, newspapers documenting the uprising in 1968, also mss material. Supplemented by a collection covering the political developments of Czechoslovakia from the 1930's to the uprising and by documents relating to Charter 77.

CZECHOSLOVAKIA—SOCIAL LIFE AND CUSTOMS

IL —AMERICAN SOKOL EDUCATIONAL AND PHYSICAL CULTURE, 6424 W Cermak Road, Berwyn, 60402. Annette Schabowski, Librn
Holdings: Vols 2000 Pix
Notes: Incl theses and dissertations on Czech life, folk dancing, gymnastics, etc.

CZECHS IN THE U.S.

IL —CHICAGO PUBLIC LIBRARY, Special Collections Div, Cultural Center, 78 E Washington St, Chicago, 60602. Laura Linard, Cur
Holdings: Vols 400 Cat Mss Pix
Notes: Works by, biographies and critical studies of, T G Masaryk, first President of Czechoslovakia. Contains works on Czechoslovakia, 1918-38. See *Collection Masaryk: A Catalog of the Books by and about Thomas Garrigue Masaryk, Presented by the Honorable John Toman to John Toman Branch of The Chicago Public* Library, 1939. This collection was permanently transferred from Toman Branch to the Special Collections Division in 1975.

MN —UNIVERSITY OF MINNESOTA, Immigration History Research Center, 826 Berry St, Saint Paul, 55114. Susan Griegs, Cur
Holdings: Vols (35,000) Mss Maps Pix Phonorecords Audiotapes 16mm Films Microforms
See also entry under US - Emigration and Immigration

NE —UNIVERSITY OF NEBRASKA-LINCOLN, Don L Love Library, Lincoln, 68588. Joseph G Svoboda, University Archivist
Holdings: Vols (3000) Cat Mss Pix Audiotapes Microforms
Notes: The Czech Heritage Collection.

†PA —BALCH INSTITUTE FOR ETHNIC STUDIES, Library, 18 S Seventh St, Philadelphia, 19106.
Notes: Papers of Vladimir Hurban, Czechoslovak ambassador to the United States.

D

DABNEY, VIRGINIUS

VA —UNIVERSITY OF VIRGINIA, Alderman Library, Manuscripts Dept, Charlottesville, 22901. Edmund Berkeley Jr, Cur
Holdings: Cat Mss Pix
Notes: Extensive collection of mss and printed materials.

DACTYLOGRAPHY see Fingerprints

DACTYLOSCOPY see Fingerprints

DADAISM

CA —CALIFORNIA INSTITUTE OF THE ARTS, Library, 24700 McBean Pkwy, Valencia, 91355. James Elrod, Dir
Holdings: Vols (61,000) Cat Slides
Budget: ($11,000)
Notes: Modern art, incl abstract, conceptual, concrete, environment, minimal, and pop art; art; dadaism; surrealism; happenings; and caricatures and cartoons. Slides (61,683).

CT —YALE UNIVERSITY, Beinecke Rare Book & Manuscript Library, Osborn Collection, New Haven, 06520. Stephen R Parks, Cur
Holdings: Mss

IL —NORTHWESTERN UNIVERSITY, Library, Special Collections Dept, 1937 Sheridan Rd, Evanston, 60201. R Russell Maylone, Cur
Holdings: Cat Pix
Notes: Books, periodicals, pamphlets, catalogs, ephemera.
See also entry under Surrealism; Futurism; Expressionism

NY —MUSEUM OF MODERN ART, Library, 11 W 53 St, New York, 10019. Clive Phillpot, Library Dir
Holdings: Vols (80,000) Cat Mss Audiotapes Microforms VF
Notes: See *Catalog of the Library of the Museum of Modern Art, New York City* (Boston: G K Hall, 1976), 14 vols. Collection incl exhibition catalogs.

DA FOE, JOHN WESLEY, 1866-1944

MB —UNIVERSITY OF MANITOBA, Elizabeth Dafoe Library, Archives and Special Collections Dept, Winnipeg, R3T 2N2, Can. Richard E Bennett, Dept Head; Corrado A Santoro, Reference Archivist
Notes: Diaries, personal correspondence, speeches, published writings, etc. Misc materials relating to his death. Also, 7 photographs of Dafoe and of sittings of the Rowell-Sirois Commission. In the Murry S Donnelly Papers, there is material relating to the life and times of J W Dafoe from various people who knew him, collected for the purpose of writing a biography on Dafoe.

DAGDEVIREN, HIDAYET

CA —HOOVER INSTITUTION ON WAR, REVOLUTION & PEACE, Stanford University, Stanford, 94305. Milorad M Drachkovitch, Archivist
Holdings: Mss
Notes: Letters, manuscripts, clippings, and unique documents from the library of Mr Hidayet Dagdeviren, Istanbul, Turkey. The collection covers the last years of the Ottoman Empire and the first years of the Republic as well as special problems on social organization and minorities. 28 ms boxes, 22 vols.

DAGUERREOTYPES

KY —UNIVERSITY OF LOUISVILLE, Ekstrom Library, Photographic Archives, Louisville, 40292. J C Anderson, Cur; David G Horvath, Asst Cur
Holdings: Vols (750,000) Cat Pix Slides
Budget: ($60,000)
Notes: Photographs in three broad areas: works of outstanding photographers; examples of major developments in the art and technology of photography; photographs important as sociological, historical, or behavioral documents. Actors and actresses, Louisville's Macauley Theatre. Standard Oil of New Jersey Collection, 85,000 pictures of oil industry's effect on life in the 20th century (1943-1950, directed by Roy Stryker); Stryker's collection from Farm Security Administration series on rural conditions, 1934-1972. Caufield and Shook commercial photographs, Louisville area, 1920-1949. Jean Thomas "The Traipsin' Woman" photographs of Kentucky mountain folkways. Kate Matthews' (1870-1956) photographs incl prototypes for "Little Colonel" Series. Other collections described in unpublished brochure. Print duplication service.

DAHLBERG, EDWARD

DE —UNIVERSITY OF DELAWARE, Hugh M Morris Library, S College Ave, Newark, 19711. T Stuart Dick, Special Collections
Holdings: Cat Mss Pix
Notes: Manuscripts, etc, incl literary correspondence.

MO —WASHINGTON UNIVERSITY, John M Olin Library, Campus Box 1061, St Louis, 63130.
Notes: Extensive collection.

NV —UNIVERSITY OF NEVADA, RENO, University Library, Special Collections Dept, Reno, 89557. Robert E Blesse, Head
Holdings: Vols (33) Cat Other appearances 40 Cat
Notes: Includes individual works by author in all editions including translations; also prefaces, introductions, published correspondence, appearances in anthologies, periodicals, etc. Bibliographical research collection, part of Modern Authors Collection.

BC —UNIVERSITY OF VICTORIA, McPherson Library, Victoria, V8W 3H5, Can.
Notes: Incl letters to Miss Harriot Monroe, editor of "Poetry."

DAHOMEY see Benin

DAILEY, JANET

†IA —UNIVERSITY OF IOWA LIBRARIES, Dept of Special Collections, Iowa City, 52240. Robert A McCown, Librn
Notes: Popular fiction in all genres by Iowa authors, incl Janet Dailey.

DAILEY, JOHN LEWIS

CO —DENVER PUBLIC LIBRARY, 1357 Broadway, Denver, 80203.
Notes: Correspondence, papers, pictures, diaries, etc.

DAIRIES AND DAIRYING

IL —NATIONAL DAIRY COUNCIL, Library, 6300 N River Rd, Rosemont, 60018. Diana Culbertson, Librn
Holdings: Vols (7500) Cat Microforms
Budget: ($62,000)
Notes: Dairies and dairying, with emphasis on human nutrition in the US.

IA —IOWA STATE UNIVERSITY, Library, Ames, 50011. Warren B Kuhn, Dean of Library Services
Holdings: Cat
Notes: Incl dairy science, food science and research, food technology, institutional management, marketing and nutrition. Extensive serial holdings.

NY —BORDEN FOODS INC, Research Centre Library, 600 N Franklin St, Syracuse, 13204. Carol Lenz-Taylor, Librn
Holdings: Vols (1800) Cat
Notes: Incl 10 vertical file drawers and 6100 patents.

VT —VERMONT TECHNICAL COLLEGE, Hartness Library, Randolph Center, 05061. Dewey Patterson, Library Dir
Holdings: Vols 5730 Cat
Budget: ($15,000)

WI —UNIVERSITY OF WISCONSIN, MADISON, College of Agricultural & Life Sciences, Steenbock Memorial Library, 550 Babcock Dr, Madison, 53706. Jan Kennedy, Dir
Holdings: Vols (186,312) Cat Docs
Notes: Major collection of farm and herd management, production and marketing

DAIRS, TOM

AZ —NORTHERN ARIZONA UNIVERSITY, Special Collection Library, CU Box 6022, Flagstaff, 86011. Peter M Whiteley, Coordr/Archivist; William Mullane, Librn
Notes: Papers, incl letter written from Phoenix, Ariz, in 1906 concerning the statehood question.
See also entry under Arizona-History.

DAIRY PRODUCTS

IL —NATIONAL DAIRY COUNCIL, Library, 6300 N River Rd, Rosemont, 60018. Diana Culbertson, Librn
Holdings: Vols (7500) Cat Microforms
Budget: ($62,000)
Notes: Dairies and dairying, with emphasis on human nutrition in the US.

MO —PET INCORPORTED, Information Center, 400 S Fourth St, PO Box 392, Saint Louis, 63166. L R Walton, Corporate Librn
Holdings: Vols (21,000) Cat Microforms

NY —CORNELL UNIVERSITY LIBRARIES, Collection of Regional History, Dept of Manuscripts and Univ Archives, Ithaca, 14853.
Notes: Contains 5 alumni letters from the Cornell University Department of Dairy Industry to its alumni.

DAIRYMEN'S LEAGUE

NY —CORNELL UNIVERSITY LIBRARIES, Collection of Regional History, Dept of Manuscripts and Univ Archives, Ithaca, 14853.
Notes: Incl records, 1916-60, consisting largely of executive files relating to its operations; reports, speeches, problems, correspondence, press releases, photos, scrapbooks and phonograph records. Unpublished guide available.

DAKIN, JAMES H.

LA —NEW ORLEANS PUBLIC LIBRARY, Louisiana Div & City Archives Dept, Louisiana History Collection, 219 Loyola Ave, New Orleans, 70140. Collin B Hamer Jr, Head
Holdings: Vols Mss
Notes: Private mss collection covers the period 1795-date, incl the following separate collections: James H Dakin (architect, ca 1834-47, 217 items); Walter E Easey (engineer, 1907-79, 22 cubic feet); McDonough & Payne (merchants, 1801-04, 200 items); ERA Club (women's group, 1914-19, 2 items); Neville Levy (civic leader, ca 1891-1963, 1 cubic foot & 11 vols); and Robert Tallant (author, 1945-57, 3 cubic feet & 10 vols). 92 vols scrapbooks; 100 mss vols, 55 cubic feet.

DAKOTA AUTHORS see Authors, North Dakota; Authors, South Dakota

DAKOTA INDIANS

MN —UNIVERSITY OF MINNESOTA, Libraries, Children's Literature Research Collections, 109 Walter Library, Minneapolis, 55455. Karen Nelson Hoyle, Cur
Holdings: Vols (40,000) Cat Mss Pix
Notes: Incl material on Dakota and Ojibway Indians. Kerlan Collection.

MN —MINNESOTA HISTORICAL SOCIETY LIBRARY, 690 Cedar St, Saint Paul, 55101. Patricia C Harpole, Chief of Reference Library; Bonnie G Wilson, Head of Special Libraries

DAKOTA INDIANS—WARS, 1862-1865

MN —BROWN COUNTY HISTORICAL SOCIETY, Museum and Archives, Center St

DAKOTA INDIANS—WARS, 1862-1865 (cont.)

and Broadway, Box 116, New Ulm, 56073. Paul Klammer, Dir
Holdings: Vols (250) Mss Maps Pix Slides Phonorecords Audiotapes Videotapes 16mm Films Filmstrips Microforms
Notes: History of Brown County, Minn. Also have *Historical Files,* about 500 pieces in vertical files incl newspaper clippings, advertising, letterheads, etc, pertaining to Brown County businesses, industry, schools, governmental units, etc. *Family Files,* about 2500 pioneer families. Files incl obituaries, pictures, documents, letters, etc. Also collection on Siouan Uprising of 1862-clippings, copies of treaties, letters, etc (65 vols, 10 mss, 25 maps, 40 pix, 50 slides).

DAKOTA TERRITORY

ND —MINOT STATE COLLEGE, Memorial Library, Minot, 58701. Ronald J Rudser, Dir
Holdings: Vols 3000 Cat Maps Microforms

D'ALBERT, EUGEN

CA —UNIVERSITY OF CALIFORNIA, RIVERSIDE, University Library, 4045 Canyon Crest Dr, Box 5900, Riverside, 92517.
Notes: The Oswald Jonas Memorial Collection holds the musicological mss, letters, biographical materials, and notebooks of Heinrich Schenker and also the papers of the late Oswald Jonas, musicologist and leading authority on the life and work of Schenker. Incl Schenker's diary; correspondence with Anthony van Hoboken, Reinhard Oppel, Moriz Violin, Eugen d'Albert, and Oswald Jonas; the proofs and mss of his published works; printed editions from his library with notes, marginalia, and critical annotations; *Urlinie* tables; and miscellanea. A guide to the collection will be published by the library.

DALE CHANDLER KENNEDY ARCHITECTS

AB —UNIVERSITY OF CALGARY, Libraries, Special Collections Div, 2500 University Dr, Calgary, T2N 1N4, Can.
Holdings: Cat Mss Pix
Notes: 40 meters of mss, 10,000 pictures. Collection consists of original drawings, mostly preliminary work, as well as presentation material, mounted photographs, renderings, and plans. Office records of this Calgary firm, which began as A Dale & Associates, are incl. Major projects incl the Palliser Square development, the Glenbow Museum - Calgary Convention Centre - Four Seasons Hotel complex, the University of Calgary Laboratory School, and Hull Estates highrise apartments. Inventory available.

DALI, SALVADOR

FL —SALVADOR DALI MUSEUM, Library, 1000 Third St S, Saint Petersburg, 33701. A Reynolds Morse, Pres; Joan Kropf, Cur
Holdings: Vols 2000 Cat Mss Pix Slides
Notes: Contains all known books by, on or about Dali and Dali-related material. Whole magazines and clippings, all possible references to Dali. All books, illustrations by Dali to approved grad students and for scholarly research only. No photocopying.

DALL, WILLIAM H., 1845-1927

DC —SMITHSONIAN INSTITUTION, Archives Div, Washington, 20560. William W Moss, Archivist
Holdings: Mss Maps Pix
Notes: Papers of William H Dall (1865-1927), naturalist and paleontologist. Incl material on the Western Union Telegraph Expedition to Alaska (1865-1868), and reports on the Alaskan boundary disputes in 1885 and 1888.

DALLAS, TEXAS—HISTORY

TX —UNIVERSITY OF TEXAS, ARLINGTON, Library, Arlington, 76019. Charles A Colley, Dir of Special Collections; Robert A Gamble, Head of Archives
Holdings: / / Mss
Notes: Santerre Collection. This is the library of the Santerre family who emigrated from France, Belgium, and Switzerland in 1855 to join the Utopian Socialist colony of Victor Prosper Considerant in what is now Dallas, Texas. Typical selection of books of a middle-class, well-educated family of the period. Some title deeds, legal papers, family letters, first Paris editions of works of Considerant, Charles Fourier; French translations of English classics, devotional works. See George H Santerre, *White Cliffs of Dallas* (Dallas, Texas: Book Craft, 1955).

TX —DALLAS PUBLIC LIBRARY, Urban Information Center, 1515 Young St, Dallas, 75201. Mary Todd, Mgr
Holdings: Vols 1550 Cat Microforms
Notes: Collection is being developed to meet the information needs of local government and to serve as a depository for municipal publications. At the present time, a separate catalog does not exist.

TX —DALLAS PUBLIC LIBRARY, Texas/ Dallas History and Archives Division, 1515 Young St, Dallas, 75201. Richard L Waters, Acting Dir; Wayne Gray, Manager
Holdings: Vols (152,442) Cat Maps Pix Slides Microforms
Budget: ($38,540)
Notes: Dallas and Texas history.

TX —SOUTHERN METHODIST UNIVERSITY, Fondren Library, McCord Theater Collection, Room 301, Dallas, 75275. Edyth Renshaw, Cur; Linda Sellers, Pub Serv
Holdings: Vols (2000) Uncat Mss Pix Slides Phonorecords
Notes: See *Theatre Collections in Libraries and Museums,* Gilder and Freedley (Theatre Arts, 1936). The McCord Theatre Collection encompasses the entire spectrum of the performing arts. The central purpose is to gather records of our regional theater before such ephemeral material is lost. Records of over two hundred early Texas theaters, some fragmentary and some relatively complete, are in the files. These records incl photographs of buildings, stagehands, orchestras, and performers. Local theatre history incl the once famous Dallas Little Theatre and the Margo Jones Theatre. The national theatre, opera, ballet, and circus archives incl pictures (some autographed), programs, posters, throw-aways, tear sheets, clippings, and letters. Our international archives are small, but we have some excellent material, eg, artifacts from Max Reinhardt's production of"The Miracle" which happened to go bankrupt in Dallas. After a few years the items were given to us. There are posters, tear sheets, souvenir programs, and other colorful items from Morris Gest and the Artef Collection. We have about 200 19th century English playbills and a few from the 18th century. There is a collection of modern English, French, and other European programs, many of them illustrated souvenir programs. Also, magazines on theater, cinema, and television (1800). Scrapbooks covering both southwest and Dallas theater, 1890s-1950s. Special Collections: artifacts and documents on puppets; masks; costume design; circus; and ballet and dance. The Harriet Bacon MacDonald Collection of over 200 photographs of musicians appearing in Dallas during the first three decades of the 20th century. Many autographed. Affiliated with Meadow Theatre of the Arts.

TX —NORTH TEXAS STATE UNIVERSITY, Archives, NT Station Box 5188, Denton, 76203. Robert LaForte, University Archivist
Notes: Part of Oral History Collection. Interviews with Earle Cabell, dairyman, mayor of Dallas 1961-65, member of US House of Representatives 1965-73.

DALLAS CIVIC THEATRE

TX —DALLAS PUBLIC LIBRARY, Fine Arts Div, 1515 Young St, Dallas, 75201. Richard L Waters, Acting Dir; Jane Holahan, Manager
Holdings: / / Uncat Mss Pix
Notes: *The Margo Jones Theatre Collection* (75 linear ft) contains the office papers of this theatre: financial, business, legal records, scripts, programs, photos of productions, reviews and clippings, personal correspondence; organizational records. Gift of Dallas Civic Theatre, Inc, 1962 after theatre ceased operation. Described in L C card catalog MS 66-1622. Also *The W E Hill Theatre Collection,* 18th-20th centuries, ca 75,000 items. Contains letters, portraits, and photos of leading American, British, and European dramatists, actors, managers, and other persons associated with the stage or the performing arts, particularly music; playbills, posters of stage plays, minstrel shows, and circuses; and newspaper and magazine clippings. The bulk of the collection consists of 19th and 20th century items. Described in LC card catalog MS 66-1621. Partiallydescribed in the Fine Arts Department of the Dallas Public Library presents an exhibit of selected material from the W E Hill theatre collection on the occasion of the opening of the collection... (1966). Gift of estate of William Ely Hill, 1963. Also *The John Rosenfield Collection* consisting of ca 2000 playbills assembled by this Amusements Critic of the *Dallas Morning News,* from both his travels and local productions. Also correspondence with various important artists in the theatre. There are also photographs, telegrams, etc of these people. *The Dallas Little Theatre* Collection: consists of printed programs of this group which won the Belasco Cup three consecutive years in New York City; many clippings, photographs and other related newspaper articles. Oral histories are being assembled from persons connected with the theatre during its lifetime from1922-1944.

DALLAS LITTLE THEATER

TX —SOUTHERN METHODIST UNIVERSITY, Fondren Library, McCord Theater Collection, Room 301, Dallas, 75275. Edyth Renshaw, Cur; Linda Sellers, Pub Serv
Holdings: Vols (2000) Uncat Mss Pix Slides Phonorecords
Notes: See *Theatre Collections in Libraries and Museums,* Gilder and Freedley (Theatre Arts, 1936). The McCord Theatre Collection encompasses the entire spectrum of the performing arts. The central purpose is to gather records of our regional theater before such ephemeral material is lost. Records of over two hundred early Texas theaters, some fragmentary and some relatively complete, are in the files. These records incl photographs of buildings, stagehands, orchestras, and performers. Local theatre history incl the once famous Dallas Little Theatre and the Margo Jones Theatre. The national theatre, opera, ballet, and circus archives incl pictures (some autographed), programs, posters, throw-aways, tear sheets, clippings, and letters. Our international archives are small, but we have some excellent material, eg, artifacts from Max Reinhardt's production of"The Miracle" which happened to go bankrupt in Dallas. After a few years the items were given to us. There are posters, tear-sheets, souvenir programs, and other colorful items from Morris Gest and the Artef Collection. We have about 200 19th century English playbills and a few from the 18th century. There is a collection of modern English, French, and other European programs, many of them illustrated souvenir programs. Also, magazines on theater, cinema, and television (1800). Scrapbooks covering both southwest and Dallas theater, 1890s-1950s. Special Collections: artifacts and documents on puppets; masks; costume design; circus; and ballet and dance. The Harriet Bacon MacDonald Collection of over 200 photographs of musicians appearing in Dallas during the first three decades of the 20th century. Many autographed. Affiliated with Meadow Theatre of the Arts.

DALLIN, CYRUS

MA —ROBBINS LIBRARY, 700 Massachusetts Ave, Arlington, 02174. Peter

DALLIN, CYRUS (cont.)

L Fenton, Dir
Holdings: Cat Mss Pix
Notes: This extensive special collection is comprised of material on Cyrus Dallin, a prominent sculptor of Arlington, Massachusetts, and his work. Arranged by subject, files contain pictures, newspaper and magazine articles on particular sculptures. Also incl biograhical material, programs of exhibits, letters, honors and awards received, photographic portraits of Dallin and an autograph collection, among other material. The Smithsonian Institution has microfilmed the collection.

DALMATIAN LANGUAGE (ROMANCE) AND LITERATURE

MA —HARVARD UNIVERSITY LIBRARY, Cambridge, 02138.
Holdings: Cat

DALMATION LANGUAGE (SLAVIC) AND LITERATURE see Serbo-Croatian Language and Literature

DALRYMPLE, JEAN

NY —NEW YORK PUBLIC LIBRARY, Performing Arts Research Center, Billy Rose Theatre Collection, 111 Amsterdam Ave, New York, 10023. Dorothy L Swerdlove, Cur
Holdings: Cat Mss Pix
Notes: Papers, scrapbooks, mss, photographs, memorabilia, etc.

DALRYMPLE, LOUIS

DC —LIBRARY OF CONGRESS, Prints & Photographs Div, Washington, 20540.
Notes: Swann Collection is strong in the work of contemporary cartoonists. Among the 400 artists represented are Peter Arno, Bil Canfield, Al Capp, Miguel Covarrubias, Louis Dalrymple, Whitney Darrow, Rube Goldberg, Thomas Nast, Jose Guadalupe Posada, Edward Sorel, and John Tenniel.

DALTON, JACK

NY —COLUMBIA UNIVERSITY LIBRARIES, Rare Book & Manuscript Library, 801 Butler Library, 535 W 114 St, New York, 10027. Kenneth A Lohf, Librn
Holdings: Mss
Notes: The Jack Dalton papers (12,000 items) incl documents of his activities in American and international librarianship, before and after his deanship of the Columbia University School of Library Science. Restricted use.

DALY, AUGUSTIN

MA —AMHERST COLLEGE, Library, Amherst, 01002. John Lancaster, Special Collections Librn
Holdings: Vols (20,000) Uncat Mss
Notes: Contains Augustin Daly manuscripts and the library of Clyde Fitch. 200 mss.

DALY, REV. JAMES J., S.J.

DC —GEORGETOWN UNIVERSITY, Library, Special Collections Div, 37 & O Sts NW, Washington, 20057. George M Barringer, Special Collections Librn; Nicholas B Sheetz, Mss Librn
Holdings: Mss Cat Pix
Notes: The papers of the Kilmer family incl letters and mss by the poet Joyce Kilmer and his wife, Aline Kilmer, also a poet and essayist. The papers incl correspondence by various authors, among them Rev James J Daly, SJ and Rev Charles L O'Donnell, CSC.

DAMEN (GAME) see Checkers

DAMON, S. FOSTER, 1893-1971

RI —BROWN UNIVERSITY, John Hay Library, 20 Prospect St, Providence, 02912. Mark N Brown, Cur Mss
Holdings: Mss
Notes: Two collections relating to the occult sciences: The Mary Ann Smith Atwood Collection--English theosophist and writer (700 items); and the S Foster Damon, 1893-1971, Collection--poet, dramatist and Professor of English at Brown University, (more than 15,000 items), unprocessed.

DAMPNESS IN BUILDINGS

MI —CONSTRUCTION CONSULTANTS, 900 Pallister, Detroit, 48202. Joan M Boram, Librn
Holdings: Vols (500) Cat Microforms
Notes: The only library in the country devoted entirely to the subject of roofing and waterproofing. Incl books and vinyl binders containing articles culled from various journals, papers from manufacturers and independent testing and laboratory facilities pertinent government documents, and in-house papers, arranged according to subject matter and indexed. When necessary, papers are cross-referenced. Also, an extensive collection of legal materials relating to roofing and waterproofing failures. Lawyers from all parts of the country avail themselves of these materials.

DAMROSCH, LEOPOLD AND WALTER

DC —LIBRARY OF CONGRESS, Music Division, Washington, 20540.
Notes: The Damrosch Family Collection incl papers and music mss of the Damrosch family - Leopold (1832-1885), Frank (1859-1937), and Walter (1862-1950). Sound recordings are in the Motion Picture, Broadcasting, and Recorded Sound Division.
NY —NEW YORK PUBLIC LIBRARY, Music Div, 111 Amsterdam Ave, New York, 10023. Frank C Campbell, Chief
Holdings: Cat Mss Pix
Notes: Autographs, letters, documents.

DAMROSCH FAMILY

DC —LIBRARY OF CONGRESS, Music Division, Washington, 20540.
Notes: The Damrosch Family Collection incl papers and music mss of the Damrosch family - Leopold (1832-1885), Frank (1859-1937), and Walter (1862-1950). Sound recordings are in the Motion Picture, Broadcasting, and Recorded Sound Division.

DAMS

CA —POMONA PUBLIC LIBRARY, Special Collections, 625 S Garey Ave, PO Box 2271, Pomona, 91766. David Streeter, Librn
Holdings: // Uncat Pix
Notes: Some 600 photographs taken during the construction of Hoover Dam, also known as Boulder Dam.
MS —US ARMY ENGINEER WATERWAYS EXPERIMENT STATION, Library Branch, PO Box 631, Vicksburg, 39180. Bernice Black, Chief Librn
Holdings: Vols (350,000) Cat Mss Maps Microforms
OR —US DEPT OF ENERGY, Bonneville Power Administration Library, 1002 NE Holladay St, PO Box 3621, Portland, 97232. Karen Hadman, Chief of Library Branch
Holdings: Vols (15,000) // Cat Microforms
Budget: ($8000)
SK —CANADA PRAIRIE FARM REHABILITATION ADMINISTRATION LIBRARY, Motherwell Bldg, Regina, S4P 0R5, Can. C Kosack, Head
Holdings: Vols (10,000) Cat
Budget: ($8000)
Notes: PFRA is a Canadian federal government agency initiated to alleviate the effects of drought and water shortages on the prairies. The collection covers engineering (dams), agricultural economics, hydrology, irrigation, community pastures, and soil and water conservation.

DANA, RICHARD HENRY

VA —UNIVERSITY OF VIRGINIA, Alderman Library, Clifton Waller Barrett Collection, Charlottesville, 22901. Joan St C Crane, Cur of American Literature Collections
Notes: Papers.

THE DANCE see Ballet and the Dance

DANCE—PROGRAMS see Programs, Dance

DANCE—VIDEOTAPES

IL —CHICAGO PUBLIC LIBRARY, Art Section, Fine Arts Division, 78 E Washington St, Chicago, 60602. Rosalinda I Hack, Fine Arts Division Chief; Yvonne S Brown, Head, Art Section
Notes: Reference and circulating collection of books, periodicals, pamphlets, and videotapes on all aspects of the dance eg ballet, social dance, square dance, jazz and folkdance. Focus of the collection is on ballet, history, biographies of dancers, and dance instruction. Subject is supplemented by a dance videotape collection, the *Folk Dance Index* a comprehensive index to descriptions of folkdances of all nations. Special Collections: Eliza Stigler Dance Collection of 200 dance books on ballet and dance history with particular emphasis on Spanish Dance. Ruth Page Archives: small collection of memorabilia documents the career of Ms Page. Reference collection of 85 dance videotapes that document notable dance performances, from the past and present by well known dancers and dance groups. Subject concentration is that of ballet, with some examples of ethnic dance. There is alsoa collection of tapes that document Chicago area dance groups, dancers, and choreographers. A file to the contents of the tapes is available.

DANCE, ASIAN see Asian Dance

DANCE, JAZZ see Jazz Dance

DANCE, MODERN see Modern Dance

DANCE, ORIENTAL see Oriental Dance

DANCE, SPANISH see Spanish Dance

DANCE BANDS see Dance Orchestras

DANCE INDEX

IL —CHICAGO PUBLIC LIBRARY, Art Section, Fine Arts Division, 78 E Washington St, Chicago, 60602. Rosalinda I Hack, Fine Arts Division Chief; Yvonne S Brown, Head, Art Section
Holdings: Vols 2500
Notes: Reference and circulating collection of books, periodicals, pamphlets, and videotapes on all aspects of the dance eg ballet, social dance, square dance, jazz and folkdance. Focus of the collection is on ballet, history, biographies of dancers, and dance instruction. Subject is supplemented by a dance videotape collection, the *Folk Dance Index* a comprehensive index to descriptions of folkdances of all nations. Special Collections: Eliza Stigler Dance Collection of 200 dance books on ballet and dance history with particular emphasis on Spanish Dance. Ruth Page Archives: small collection of memorabilia documents the career of Ms Page. Reference collection of 85 dance videotapes that document notable dance performances, from the past and present by well known dancers and dance groups. Subject concentration is that of ballet, with some examples of ethnic dance. There is alsoa collection of tapes that document Chicago area dance groups, dancers, and choreographers. A file to the contents of the tapes is available.
NY —NEW YORK PUBLIC LIBRARY, Performing Arts Research Center, Dance Collection, 111 Amsterdam Ave, New York, 10023. Genevieve Oswald, Cur
Notes: The *Dance Index*, compiled by the WPA, ca 1936, consists of an annotated card index of 45 catalog drawers containing

DANCE INDEX (cont.)

approximately 90,000 index cards. Comprises bibliographical references to source material on ethnic, regional and folk dance in various works on anthropology, ehtnology, comparative religion, travel, and the arts contained in eleven institutional libraries of Greater New York City. The libraries include the New York Public Library, American Geographical Society, Cooper Union Museum, Missionary Research Library, Columbia University, Metropolitan Museum of Art, General Theological Seminary, American Museum of Natural History, and Union Theological Seminary. Especially strong representation of American Indian dance and Asian dance.

DANCE MUSIC

IN —INDIANA UNIVERSITY, Lilly Library, Seventh St, Bloomington, 47405. William R Cagle, Librn
Holdings: // Uncat
Notes: Extensive collection of American 19th-20th century dance music in the Starr Sheet Music Collection.

VT —MIDDLEBURY COLLEGE, Starr Library, Flanders Ballad Collection, Middlebury, 05753. Jennifer Post Quinn, Cur
Notes: Begun as Helen Hartness Flanders' private collection in 1930, given to Middlebury College, 1941. Incl over 9000 New England items recorded or transcribed since 1930: ballads and folk songs of British, American, French-Canadian, and Russian origin; religious songs; fiddle tunes; dance music. Incl research collection of folklore and folksong monographs, scores, tunebooks, journals. Reference: Quinn, Jennifer Post. *An Index to the Field Recordings in the Flanders Ballad Collection at Middlebury College, Middlebury, Vermont* Middlebury, VT, Middlebury College, 1983.

DANCE NOTATION

CA —CALIFORNIA INSTITUTE OF THE ARTS, Library, 24700 McBean Pkwy, Valencia, 91355. James Elrod, Dir
Holdings: Vols (61,000) Cat
Budget: ($2868)
Notes: Incl classical and modern dance forms.

IL —CHICAGO PUBLIC LIBRARY, Art Section, Fine Arts Division, 78 E Washington St, Chicago, 60602. Rosalinda I Hack, Fine Arts Division Chief; Yvonne S Brown, Head, Art Section
Notes: Reference and circulating collection of books, periodicals, pamphlets, and videotapes on all aspects of the dance eg ballet, social dance, square dance, jazz and folkdance. Focus of the collection is on ballet, history, biographies of dancers, and dance instruction. Subject is supplemented by a dance videotape collection, the *Folk Dance Index* a comprehensive index to descriptions of folkdances of all nations. Special Collections: Eliza Stigler Dance Collection of 200 dance books on ballet and dance history with particular emphasis on Spanish Dance. Ruth Page Archives: small collection of memorabilia documents the career of Ms Page. Reference collection of 85 dance videotapes that document notable dance performances, from the past and present by well known dancers and dance groups. Subject concentration is that of ballet, with some examples of ethnic dance. There is alsoa collection of tapes that document Chicago area dance groups, dancers, and choreographers. A file to the contents of the tapes is available.

IL —UNIVERSITY OF ILLINOIS, URBANA/CHAMPAIGN, Library, Applied Life Studies Library, 1408 W Gregory Dr, Urbana, 61801.
Holdings: Vols (38,000) Cat Pix Microforms
Notes: Contains books on ballet, contemporary dance, folk and national dances, ethnic dance, dance history, choreography, dance notation, dance therapy. Also collected are programs of dance concerts and performances of the 20th century.

NY —NEW YORK PUBLIC LIBRARY, Performing Arts Research Center, Dance Collection, 111 Amsterdam Ave, New York, 10023. Genevieve Oswald, Cur
Notes: Multi-media collection with full documentation on various systems devised to record dance movement. Includes historical treatises and technical manuals from the 15th century to the present; manuals describing notation systems of Arbeau, Feuillet, Saint-Leon, Zorn, Stepanov, Morris, Laban, Benesh, Eshkol-Wachmann, Sutton, and others; over 250 dance notation scores, chiefly in Laban or Benesh notation, recording the choreography of special dances--ballets, modern dance works, musical comedies, folk and social dances. Visual documentation recording and preserving the choreography of contemporary dance works is provided by 2230 motion pictures and 1650 videotapes.

ON —NATIONAL LIBRARY OF CANADA, 395 Wellington St, Ottawa, K1A 0N4, Can. Andre Preibish, Dir
Holdings: Vols 8000
Notes: Includes 100 serial titles, also programs, play bills etc on microfilm. Performing arts collection consists of Canadian titles received on legal deposit and purchased. Areas of concentration: Canadian theatre and dance; European and American performing arts tradition; theatre architecture; stage craft; costume history, dance history and notation etc.

ON —UNIVERSITY OF WATERLOO, Library, Waterloo, N2L 3G1, Can. Susan Bellingham, Special Collections Librn
Holdings: Vols (1000) Cat
Notes: Dance notation, choreography, ballet. Gift of Dr Henry H Crapo. Collection described in *A Catalogue of the Dance Collection in the Doris Lewis Rare Book* Room, University of Waterloo Library Bibliography #10, 1983.

DANCE OF DEATH

MA —HARVARD UNIVERSITY LIBRARY, Widener Library, Cambridge, 02138.
Holdings: Cat Pix Slides

NY —METROPOLITAN MUSEUM OF ART, Dept of Prints & Photographs, 82 St & Fifth Ave, New York, 10028. Colta Ives, Cur

DANCE ORCHESTRA MUSIC

IL —CHICAGO PUBLIC LIBRARY, Music Section, Fine Arts Division, 78 E Washington St, Chicago, 60602. Rosalinda I Hack, Fine Arts Division Chief; Richard C Schwegel, Head, Music Section
Holdings: Vols 6000
Notes: Balaban & Katz Orchestral collection contains dance band arrangements 1920-50 used for live performances at the Chicago Theatre. Limited access at this time.

†NY —STATE UNIVERSITY OF NEW YORK, COLLEGE AT FREDONIA, Daniel A Reed Library, Fredonia, 14063.
Holdings: Vols (8000) Cat Phonorecords Audiotapes
Budget: ($12,500)
Notes: The Music Library supports the curricular needs of a large department of music which now has programs in both music education and performance. Separate card catalogs are maintained for 26,000 scores and more than 12,000 recordings and tape cassettes. The library has a small collection of 19th century American tunebooks, some Lowell Mason materials and a collection of sheet music and dance band arrangements numbering more than 3200 pieces and covering the period from 1850 through the big band era.

DANCE ORCHESTRAS

MA —NORTHEASTERN UNIVERSITY LIBRARIES, Special Collections, 360 Huntington Ave, Boston, 02115. Nieves F Farin, Head Collection Development Librn
Notes: Glen Gray and the Casa Loma Orchestra. 2000 items, incl sheet music, programs, pictures, clippings on swing music in the 1930s.

†NY —STATE UNIVERSITY OF NEW YORK, COLLEGE AT FREDONIA, Daniel A Reed Library, Fredonia, 14063.
Holdings: Vols (8000) Cat Phonorecords Audiotapes
Budget: ($12,500)
Notes: The Music Library supports the curricular needs of a large department of music which now has programs in both music education and performance. Separate card catalogs are maintained for 26,000 scores and more than 12,000 recordings and tape cassettes. The library has a small collection of 19th century American tunebooks, some Lowell Mason materials and a collection of sheet music and dance band arrangements numbering more than 3200 pieces and covering the period from 1850 through the big band era.

DANCE THERAPY

IL —UNIVERSITY OF ILLINOIS, URBANA/CHAMPAIGN, Library, Applied Life Studies Library, 1408 W Gregory Dr, Urbana, 61801.
Holdings: Vols (38,000) Cat Pix Microforms
Notes: Contains books on ballet, contemporary dance, folk and national dances, ethnic dance, dance history, choreography, dance notation, dance therapy. Also collected are programs of dance concerts and performances of the 20th century.

KS —WICHITA PUBLIC LIBRARY, Art & Music Division, 223 S Main, Wichita, 67202. Leonard Messineo, Jr, Head, Art & Music Division; Deborah Hamilton, Special Collections Librn
Holdings: Uncat Audiotapes Videotape Pix
Notes: Alice Bauman Dance Symposia Collection. Contains 300 hours of audio tapes, 1 hour-long video tape, several hundred photographs, and fugitive material of the American Dance Symposia held in Wichita from 1968-1972. The symposia covered all dance idioms-ballet, modern, jazz, folk, ethnic, dance education and therapy-and featured such notable figures such as Leonide Massine, Martha Hill, William Christensen, Alfonso Cimber, Toni Intravaia, James Clouser, Eleo Pomare, Juana de Laban, and many others. Characterized by the *Kansas City Star* as the "most distinguished faculties of fine artists ever assembled in the contemporary world of dance."

NY —NEW YORK PUBLIC LIBRARY, Performing Arts Research Center, Dance Collection, 111 Amsterdam Ave, New York, 10023. Genevieve Oswald, Cur
Notes: Books and periodicals, including publications of the American Dance Therapy Association, clippings, and films.

ON —SIRLS, Faculty of Human Kinetics & Leisure Studies, University of Waterloo, Waterloo, N2L 3G1, Can. Betty Smith, Database Mgr
Notes: Information Retrieval System for the Sociology of Leisure and Sport (SIRLS) is a computerized online database of about 13, 000 entries (1983). Incl dance as a leisure time activity.

DANCERS

CA —CALIFORNIA INSTITUTE OF THE ARTS, Library, 24700 McBean Pkwy, Valencia, 91355. James Elrod, Dir
Holdings: Vols (61,000) Cat Videotapes 16mm Films
Budget: ($2868)
Notes: Classical and modern dance forms. Incl 776 16mm films, 320 videotapes.

IL —CHICAGO PUBLIC LIBRARY, Art Section, Fine Arts Division, 78 E Washington St, Chicago, 60602. Rosalinda I Hack, Fine Arts Division Chief; Yvonne S Brown, Head, Art Section
Holdings: Vols 2500
Notes: Reference and circulating collection of books, periodicals, pamphlets, and videotapes on all aspects of the dance eg

DANCERS (cont.)

ballet, social dance, square dance, jazz and folkdance. Focus of the collection is on ballet, history, biographies of dancers, and dance instruction. Subject is supplemented by a dance videotape collection, the *Folk Dance Index* a comprehensive index to descriptions of folkdances of all nations. Special Collections: Eliza Stigler Dance Collection of 200 dance books on ballet and dance history with particular emphasis on Spanish Dance. Ruth Page Archives: small collection of memorabilia documents the career of Ms Page. Reference collection of 85 dance videotapes that document notable dance performances, from the past and present by well known dancers and dance groups. Subject concentration is that of ballet, with some examples of ethnic dance. There is alsoa collection of tapes that document Chicago area dance groups, dancers, and choreographers. A file to the contents of the tapes is available.

NY —NEW YORK PUBLIC LIBRARY, Performing Arts Research Center, Dance Collection, 111 Amsterdam Ave, New York, 10023. Genevieve Oswald, Cur
Holdings: Vols (40,000) Cat Mss Pix Audiotapes Videotapes 16mm Films Microforms
Budget: ($9,280)
Notes: Includesmulti-media collection, international in scope, documenting every type of dance: ballet, modern, social, ethnic, folk. Dancers and choreographers of all periods and countries are represented. Extensive material on 18th-20th century ballet, especially American, English, Russian, and Italian, as well as on American modern dance and Asian dance. Strong collections on Anna Pavlova, Vaslav Nijinsky, Tamara Karsavina, Leonide Massine, Isadora Duncan, Ted Shawn, Ruth St Denis, Loie Fuller, Ruth Page, Martha Graham, Doris Humphrey, Charles Weidman, Jose Limon, Helen Tamiris, George Balanchine, Agnes de Mille, Jerome Robbins. Includes manuscripts and letters, photographs, original drawings, prints, tape-recorded oral interviews, clippings, programs, posters, scrapbooks, 2230 motion pictures, 1650 videotapes. Incl a large collection by and about Agna Enters.

OK —UNIVERSITY OF OKLAHOMA, Drama Library, 550 Parrington Oval, Norman, 73019. Jan Seifert, Dir
Holdings: Vols (6683) Mss Pix Phonorecords
Notes: Incl VF material, newspaper clippings and magazine cut-outs covering the theatre and dance. Material dates from 1900. Collection of nearly 6000 plays.

ON —METROPOLITAN TORONTO LIBRARY, Theatre Dept, 789 Yonge St, Toronto, M4W 2G8, Can. Heather McCallum, Head
Notes: Manuscript collelctions include: Boris Volkoff Collection, papers of Toronto dance teacher Bettina Byers, papers of two Canadian dance critics (Ralph Hicklin and John Fraser), and the Mary Wigman Collection, consisting of copies of letters exchanged between Miss Wigman and her Canadian pupil Judy Jarvis, and a taped conversation with Miss Wigman.

DANCING see Ballet and the Dance

DANCING—LIBRARIES AND MUSEUMS see Music Libraries

DANCING—THERAPEUTIC USE see Dance Therapy

DANCING, BALLROOM see Social Dancing

DANCING, SOCIAL see Social Dancing

DANES IN THE U.S.

†IA —GRAND VIEW COLLEGE, Archives, 1351 Grandview, Des Moines, 50316.
Notes: Danish-American church life 1871-1962, Danish-American culture, Danish literature 18th to 20th century.

NE —DANA COLLEGE, C A Dana-Life Library, Blair, 68008. Ronald D Johnson, Head Librn
Holdings: Vols (10,000) Cat Audiotapes
Notes: Strong emphasis on Danish literature although we include other Scandinavian coutries. Have an oral history tape collection with recordings of Danish emigrant to the midwest. Our book collection is strongest in the literature area with history a close second.

PA —BALCH INSTITUTE FOR ETHNIC STUDIES, Library, 18 S Seventh St, Philadelphia, 19106. R Joseph Anderson, Library Dir
Holdings: Vols 200 Cat Mss

WA —UNIVERSITY OF WASHINGTON LIBRARIES, Suzzallo Library, Scandinavian Collections, FM-25, Seattle, 98195. A Gerald Anderson, Librn
Holdings: Vols (50,000) Cat Mss Pix
Budget: ($15,546)
Notes: Research collections with emphasis on languages and literatures, and auxilliary strengths in history, political science, social science. Archival and other special materials relating to Scandinavian-Americans in the Pacific Northwest are located in other appropriate collections.

DANGEROUS DRUGS, CONTROL OF

CA —ELECTRONICS MUSEUM, Foothill College, DeForest Memorial Archives, 12345 El Monte Rd, Los Altos Hills, 94022. Leonard M Lansdowne, Cur
Holdings: Vols (570)// Cat Mss Pix
Notes: This collection of 32 diaries, scrapbooks, and pictures was donated by the widow of George Hunter White. He was an agent for the US Treasury, Narcotics Dept. Limited access. No photocopying.

DC —US DEPT OF JUSTICE, Drug Enforcement Administration, Library, 1405 I St NW, Washington, 20537. Morton S Goren, Librn
Holdings: Vols (10,000) Cat Microforms
Notes: Narcotics and dangerous drugs control.

PA —PENNSYLVANIA STATE UNIVERSITY, Fred Lewis Pattee Library, Special Collections Dept, University Park, 16802. Charles Mann, Chief, Special Collections
Holdings: // Mss
Budget: ($37,000)
Notes: The papers of Harry Anslinger, formerly US Commissioner of Narcotics. No photocopying.

DANGEROUS MATERIALS see Hazardous Substances

DANIEL, FRANZ

MI —WAYNE STATE UNIVERSITY, Walter P Reuther Library, Archives of Labor & Urban Affairs, Detroit, 48202. Philip Mason, Dir
Holdings: Mss
Notes: Papers, correspondence, etc.

DANIEL, HAWTHORNE

VA —UNIVERSITY OF VIRGINIA, Alderman Library, Manuscripts Dept, Charlottesville, 22901. Edmund Berkeley Jr, Cur
Notes: Letters of many other Virginia authors, such as Sherwood Anderson, Hawthorne Daniel, Murrell Edmunds, George Cary Eggleston, John Fox, John Pendleton Kennedy, Katie Letcher Lyle, Julian Rutherfoord Meade, Thomas Nelson Page, Virginius Dabney, Clifford Dowdey, Jane McClary, Peter Taylor, and others.

DANIEL, JOHN WARWICK

VA —UNIVERSITY OF VIRGINIA, Alderman Library, Manuscripts Dept, Charlottesville, 22901. Edmund Berkeley Jr, Cur
Holdings: Cat Mss Pix
Notes: Papers, personal and political, etc.

DANIEL, PRICE

TX —NORTH TEXAS STATE UNIVERSITY, Archives, NT Station Box 5188, Denton, 76203. Robert LaForte, University Archivist
Notes: Part of Oral History Collection. Interviews with US Senator (1953-57) and Governor of Texas (1957-63).

DANIELL, DAVID

BC —UNIVERSITY OF VICTORIA, McPherson Library, Victoria, V8W 3H5, Can.
Notes: Mss of *The Interpreter's House, a Critical Assessment of the Work of John* Buchan.

DANIELS, GUY

MA —BOSTON UNIVERSITY, Mugar Memorial Library, Special Collections Dept, 771 Commonwealth Ave, Boston, 02215. Howard B Gotlieb, Dir
Holdings: Cat Mss
Notes: Mss, correspondence, etc collected in depth; incl publications by or about.

DANIELS, JONATHAN

NC —UNIVERSITY OF NORTH CAROLINA, CHAPEL HILL, Wilson Library, Rare Book Collection, Chapel Hill, 27514. Paul S Koda, Cur of Rare Books
Holdings: Cat Mss Pix
Notes: Papers of the author and former editor of the Raleigh *News and Observer.*

DANIELS, MARK

CA —UNIVERSITY OF CALIFORNIA, LOS ANGELES, Research Library, Dept of Special Collections, 405 Hilgard Ave, Los Angeles, 90024. Edward Shreeves, Chairman, Bibliographers Group; David S Zeidberg, Head
Notes: 6000 photographs recording the work of Welton Becket; 600 photographs recording the work of Mark Daniels; the Richard J Neutra archive.

DANINOS, PIERRE

MA —BOSTON UNIVERSITY, Mugar Memorial Library, Special Collections Dept, 771 Commonwealth Ave, Boston, 02215. Howard B Gotlieb, Dir
Holdings: Cat Mss
Notes: Incl publications by or about.

DANISH LANGUAGE AND LITERATURE

CA —LOS ANGELES PUBLIC LIBRARY, Foreign Languages Dept, 630 W Fifth St, Los Angeles, 90071. Sylva Manoogian, Principal Librn
Holdings: Vols 1500 Cat
Budget: ($41,500)

IL —NORTH PARK COLLEGE LIBRARY, 5125 N Spaulding Ave, Chicago, 60625. Dorothy-Ellen Gross, Dir
Holdings: Vols (4500) Cat
Notes: Scandinavian Collection, with materials mostly Swedish, but some titles in Norwegian, Danish, Finnish and Icelandic. Separate shelf list, but also incl in union catalog. General collection with emphasis on literature and history. Other Swedish books in the field of religion available through Mellander Library on same campus.

†IA —GRAND VIEW COLLEGE, Archives, 1351 Grandview, Des Moines, 50316.
Notes: Danish-American church life 1871-1962, Danish-American culture, Danish literature 18th to 20th century.

MD —JOHNS HOPKINS UNIVERSITY, Milton S Eisenhower Library, Charles & 34 Sts, Baltimore, 21218. Ann S Gwyn, Assistant Dir for Special Collections
Holdings: Vols 3250 Cat
Notes: Incl 2000 reprints. Chiefly modern Scandinavian scholarship and literature, especially Danish. Also runology, Old

DANISH LANGUAGE AND LITERATURE (cont.)

Scandinavian, history, linguistics, and archaeology. (Incl Lis Jacobsen collection).

NE —DANA COLLEGE, C A Dana-Life Library, Blair, 68008. Ronald D Johnson, Head Librn
Holdings: Vols (10,000) Cat Audiotapes
Notes: Strong emphasis on Danish literature although we include other Scandinavian countries. Have an oral history tape collection with recordings of Danish emigrants to the midwest. Our book collection is strongest in the literature area with history a close second.

NY —NEW YORK PUBLIC LIBRARY, Donnell Foreign Language Library, 20 W 53 St, New York, 10019. Bosiljka Stevanovic, Supvr Librn
Holdings: Vols 364 Cat
Notes: Danish collection incl Danish authors of Danish expression. No separate catalog.

NC —DUKE UNIVERSITY, William R Perkins Library, Durham, 27706. Elvin E Strowd, University Librn
Notes: The Scandinavian collection of 3000 items is a collection of Scandinavian literature, primarily representing the latter half of the 18th century and early 19th century.

OH —CLEVELAND PUBLIC LIBRARY, Foreign Literature Dept, 325 Superior Ave, Cleveland, 44114. Natalia Bezugloff, Head
Holdings: Vols 1870 Cat
Notes: A popular circulating collection containing classics and the standard works with emphasis on belles lettres, history and biography. A variety of other subjects such as learning languages, how to do books, art, children's books, spoken phonodiscs and cassettes, periodicals, etc.
See also entry under Foreign Language Collections

WA —UNIVERSITY OF WASHINGTON LIBRARIES, Suzzallo Library, Scandinavian Collections, FM-25, Seattle, 98195. A Gerald Anderson, Librn
Holdings: Vols (50,000) Cat Mss Pix
Budget: ($15,546)
Notes: Research collections with emphasis on languages and literatures, and auxiliary strengths in history, political science, social science. Archival and other special materials relating to Scandinavian-Americans in the Pacific Northwest are located in other appropriate collections.

WI —UNIVERSITY OF WISCONSIN, MADISON, Memorial Library, 728 State St, Madison, 53706. Erwin K Welsch, Social Studies Bibliographer
Holdings: Vols (12,000) Cat Phonorecords
Notes: Strong collection of 19th and 20th century Danish language and and literature of all types. Incl complete collection of many major authors as well as representative collections of minor writers, literary criticism, and, for contemporary literature, recordings of authors reading their own works. The collection from the 1960s to the present incl complete holdings of many major and minor authors, experimental literature (particularly poetry and vanity press publications), works in fields of trivial literature such as mystery and science fiction, and the publications of small presses somewhat outside the mainstream of publishing. Most of the collection is cataloged, but portions are not and therefore not listed in usual finding tools such as OCLC or the NUC. Holdings of contemporary major authors are listed in the Erwin K Welsch and Mogens Knudsen, "DanishLiterature after 1945 in the Memorial Library, University of Wisconsin-Madison" (Madison, 1983) which will be updated annually.

DANISH MYTHOLOGY see Mythology, Norse

DANISH NEWSPAPERS see Newspapers, Danish

DANISH POETRY

WI —UNIVERSITY OF WISCONSIN, MADISON, Memorial Library, 728 State St, Madison, 53706. Erwin K Welsch, Social Studies Bibliographer
Holdings: Vols 1000 Cat
Notes: Contemporary experimental poetry incl vanity press publications.
See also entry under Danish Language and Literature

DANISH WEST INDIES see West Indies

DANN, JACK

†PA —TEMPLE UNIVERSITY LIBRARY, Philadelphia, 19122. Thomas M Whitehead, Librn
Notes: More than 100 cubic ft of mss, incl papers of Michael Bishop, Ben Bova, Jack Dann, Gardner Dozois, Lloyd Eshback, Tom Purdom, Pamela Sargent, John Varley, and George Zebrowski.

DANNAY, FREDERIC see Queen, Ellery

DANO-NORWEGIAN LANGUAGE see Norwegian Language and Literature

DANTE ALIGHIERI

CA —UNIVERSITY OF CALIFORNIA, BERKELEY, University Library, French and Italian Collections, Berkeley, 94720. Donald G Williams, Librn
Notes: Research collection with special strengths in early Italian literature (to 1400), and Italian literature of the Renaissance. Strong holdings for such authors as Dante, Petrarch, Boccaccio, Ariosto, Machiavelli, Tasso, and many others. The collections in the Main Library are complemented by significant incunabula, rare books and ms holdings in the Bancroft Library.

CA —FRANCIS BACON LIBRARY, 655 N Dartmouth Ave, Claremont, 91711. Elizabeth S Wrigley, Dir
Holdings: Vols 300// Cat Maps Pix
Notes: Collection ranges from early Aldine editions of the 16th century to 20th century scholarship; pictures, articles, clippings.

CT —YALE UNIVERSITY, Box 1603A, Yale Station, New Haven, 06520.

IL —NEWBERRY LIBRARY, 60 W Walton St, Chicago, 60610. Diana Haskell, Cur of Modern Mss
Holdings: Cat

IN —SAINT MARY'S COLLEGE, Cushwa-Leighton Library, Notre Dame, 46556. Sister Bernice Hollenhorst, Dir
Holdings: Vols 450 Cat

IN —UNIVERSITY OF NOTRE DAME, University Libraries, Notre Dame, 46556.
Notes: This collection (5000 items) is particularly strong in incunable editions and other rare and expensive editions. Incl are editions in every major language. The collection ranks third in size compared to the Cornell and Harvard collections.

KS —SAINT MARY COLLEGE, Library, Leavenworth, 66048. Therese Deplazes, Special Collections Librn
Holdings: Vols 200 Cat

MA —HARVARD UNIVERSITY LIBRARY, Widener Library, Cambridge, 02138. Assunta S Pisani, Specialist in Book Selection
Holdings: Cat
Notes: See Harvard University Library, *Bibliographical Contributions,* 34 (1890).

MA —MOUNT HOLYOKE COLLEGE, Williston Memorial Library, South Hadley, 01075. Anne C Edmonds, Librn
Holdings: Vols 360// Uncat
Notes: Illustrated editions of *The Divine* Comedy. Separate book catalog for the collection. Collection is available by appointment only.

MI —UNIVERSITY OF MICHIGAN, Library, Dept of Rare Books & Special Collections, Ann Arbor, 48109. Robert J Starring, Head
Holdings: Vols 800 Cat
Notes: Nucleus was the 488 vol library bequeathed by Prof Edward L Walter.

NY —CORNELL UNIVERSITY LIBRARIES, John M Olin Library, Dept of Rare Books, Ithaca, 14853. Donald D Eddy, Librn
Holdings: Vols 12,917 Cat Mss
Notes: Downs 3676.

NY —NEW YORK PUBLIC LIBRARY, Research Libraries, General Research Division, Fifth Ave & 42 St, New York, 10018. Rodney Phillips, Chief
Holdings: Vols (2,225,000) Cat Maps Pix Microforms
Budget: ($775,718)

NC —DUKE UNIVERSITY, William R Perkins Library, Durham, 27706. Elvin E Strowd, University Librn
Notes: The Henry Bellamann collection of Dante's *Divine Comedy* includes approximately 300 items, consisting of "various editions" of the Italian texts of Dante's *La Divina Commedia* and numerous translations of the poems into English, French, and German.

RI —BROWN UNIVERSITY, John Hay Library, 20 Prospect St, Providence, 02912. Mark N Brown, Cur Mss
Holdings: Vols 1700 // Cat Mss
Notes: Chambers Dante Collection formed by Dante specialist William Henry Chambers during the late 19th century. The majority of books and periodicals are 19th century although the earliest books date from the 15th century. Strengths are in scholarly and critical editions, commentaries (chiefly in Italian), and general works dealing with Dante's time. Collection is supplemented by sixteen ms notebooks of Courtney Langdon, former Professor of Romance Languages and Literature.

ON —QUEEN'S UNIVERSITY, Douglas Library, Kingston, K7L 5C4, Can. William F E Morley, Cur, Special Collections
Holdings: Vols 6980 Cat Mss Pix
Notes: Subject strength of the collections.

D'ARCY, REV. MARTIN, S.J.

DC —GEORGETOWN UNIVERSITY, Library, Special Collections Div, 37 & O Sts NW, Washington, 20057. George M Barringer, Special Collections Librn; Nicholas B Sheetz, Mss Librn
Holdings: Cat Mss
Notes: The papers of the English author, journalist, and historian Douglas Woodruff (1897-1978), containing correspondence, mss, and photographs. Incl is considerable material concerning his years at Oxford University; his editorship for many years of The "Tablet"; English Catholic society in general and English Catholic literature in particular. Also present are research files on the Tichborne Claimant, one of the most famous cases of impersonation in English legal history. There is extensive correspondence from such figures as: Hilaire Belloc; Tom Burns; Rev Martin D'Arcy, SJ; Christopher Dawson; Sir Roy Harrod; Christopher Hollis; Msgr Ronald Knox; Sir Shane Leslie; Sir Arnold Lunn; Rebecca West; and Evelyn Waugh.

DARIEN COMPANY

FL —UNIVERSITY OF MIAMI, Otto G Richter Library, PO Box 248214, Coral Gables, 33124. Frank Rodgers, Dir of Libraries
Notes: Many of the earliest account (1698-1701) of the Scots' attempt to establish a colony.
See also entry under Panama.

RI —BROWN UNIVERSITY, John Carter Brown Library, Providence, 02912. Norman Fiering, Librn; Everett C Wilkie Jr, Bibliographer; Susan Danforth, Cur Maps & Prints
Notes: A substantial part of the collection of John Scott of Edinburgh. The company was to establish a colony on the coast of Panama.
See also entry under South America - History

DARK AGES see Middle Ages—History

DARLEY FAMILY

CO —UNIVERSITY OF COLORADO, Libraries, Western Historical Collections, Boulder, 80309.
Holdings: Cat Mss Pix
Notes: George M Darley came to Colorado

DARLEY FAMILY (cont.)

in 1876 as a Presbyterian missionary. He preached in Ouray and Lake City and established the first Protestant church on the Western Slope. In 1883 he founded the Presbyterian College of the Southwest in Del Norte, Colorado. He served pastorates in many Colorado towns, and published extensively. His three sons, George S, Ward, and William M, figure importantly in Colorado history; his grandson, Ward, Jr, served as president of the University of Colorado from 1953 to 1956. The collection contains genealogical material, correspondence, personal effects, and photograhs of G M Darley, his sons, and their families. Of special interest are the pastor's registers kept by G M Darley from 1876-1916. The collection consists of seven boxes, and a published guide is available.

DARLING, E. W.

CA —HOOVER INSTITUTION ON WAR, REVOLUTION & PEACE, Stanford University, Stanford, 94305. Milorad M Drachkovitch, Archivist
Holdings: / / Mss
Notes: Left-wing British material consisting of Communist Party of Great Britain material, personal papers of E W Darling, and various society and other publication 1871-1945. ca 6 ft.

DARLING, JAY 'DING'

IA —UNIVERSITY OF IOWA, University Libraries, Iowa City, 52242. Frank Paluka, Head, Special Collections Dept
Holdings: Cat Mss Pix
Notes: Collection incl 6000 cartoons and 4 file drawers of ms material by Ding. An extensive subject index is located in the library. See The SUI Ding Darling Cartoon Collection, in the *Iowa Alumni Review,* Dec 1963.

DARLINGTON, WILLIAM, 1782-1863

KS —UNIVERSITY OF KANSAS, Kenneth Spencer Research Library, Special Collections Dept, Lawrence, 66045. Alexandra Mason, Librn
Holdings: Vols 5600 Cat Mss
Notes: About 2600 items before 1800. Espec strong in herbals, medical botany, Linnaeus, early American botanists (William Darlington, C S Rafinesque). Incl material from T J Fitzpatrick collection. Noncirculating.

PA —WEST CHESTER UNIVERSITY, Francis Harvey Green Library, West Chester, 19380. R Gerald Schoelkopf, Special Collections Librn
Holdings: Vols 1700 Cat Maps
Notes: The collection was the personal library of Dr William Darlington (1782-1863), Chester County botanist. It incl many titles of important botanical works in English and Latin published between 1800 and 1860. Also contains bound volumes of early scientific journals. A herbarium of plant specimens form an adjunt to the collection.

DARLY, MATTHEW, FL., 1754-1778

DC —LIBRARY OF CONGRESS, Prints & Photographs Div, Washington, 20540.
Notes: The British Cartoon collection contains 10,000 British political caricatures and satires dating from the 17th through mid 19th centuries. Incl the work of Henry Bunbury, George Cruikshank, Issac Cruikshank, Matthew Darly, James Gillray, and Thomas Rowlandson.

DARROW, CLARENCE

IL —NEWBERRY LIBRARY, 60 W Walton St, Chicago, 60610. Diana Haskell, Cur of Modern Mss
Holdings: Cat Mss Pix
Notes: Holdings include the Mary Field Parton correspondence and work files of biographers Arthur and Lila Weinberg.

DARROW, KARL KELCHNER

NY —AMERICAN INSTITUTE OF PHYSICS, Center for the History of Physics, Niels Bohr Library, 335 E 45 St, New York, 10017. John Aubry, Librn
Notes: Physicist Karl Kelchner Darrow's professional correspondence (1928-73), diaries (1911-75), and early undergraduate notes, as well as materials on lectures, speeches, offprints, and family correspondence. Most of Dr Darrow's career was with the Bell Telephone Laboratories, and he was Secretary of the American Physical Society for 25 years.

DARROW, WHITNEY

DC —LIBRARY OF CONGRESS, Prints & Photographs Div, Washington, 20540.
Notes: Swann Collection is strong in the work of contemporary cartoonists. Among the 400 artists represented are Peter Arno, Bil Canfield, Al Capp, Miguel Covarrubias, Louis Dalrymple, Whitney Darrow, Rube Goldberg, Thomas Nast, Jose Guadalupe Posada, Edward Sorel, and John Tenniel.

DARWIN, CHARLES ROBERT, 1809-1882

CA —UNIVERSITY OF CALIFORNIA, SANTA BARBARA, Library, Dept of Special Collections, Santa Barbara, 93106. Christian F Brun, Head
Notes: Works; first editions. Part of Evolution Collection.

NY —NEW YORK BOTANICAL GARDEN LIBRARY, Bronx, 10458. Charles R Long, Asst Vice Pres & Dir
Holdings: Vols 3500 Cat VF
Budget: ($356,000)
Notes: Over 900,000 items, incl books, serials, pamphlets, archives and manuscripts, vertical files, microfiche and microfilm, nursery and seed catalogs, photographs, paintings, prints, drawings and engravings. Covering all areas of botanical sciences.

NY —CORNELL UNIVERSITY LIBRARIES, Collection of Regional History, Dept of Manuscripts and Univ Archives, Ithaca, 14853.
Notes: Naturalist. Letter from John H Comstock (photocopy), 1880; 1 item.

NY —UNIVERSITY OF ROCHESTER, Rush Rhees Library, Department of Rare Books and Special Collections, Rochester, 14627. Peter Dzwonkoski, Librn
Holdings: Vols Cat
Notes: First editions, etc.

OH —CLEVELAND MEDICAL LIBRARY ASSOCIATION/CASE WESTERN RESERVE UNIVERSITY, Cleveland Health Sciences Library, Historical Division, Allen Memorial Medical Library, 11000 Euclid Ave, Cleveland, 44106. Glen Jenkins, Rare Book Librarian & Archivist
Holdings: Vols 570 Mss Pix
Notes: The Charles Darwin Collection contains 180 original letters written by Charles Darwin, members of his family and friends. The letters are cataloged. The collection also contains over 250 other items, such as reprints, magazine articles, pamphlets, announcements of centennial celebrations, portraits, etc.

PA —LEHIGH UNIVERSITY LIBRARIES, Linderman Library, Bethlehem, 18015.
Notes: The Honeyman Collection.

PA —AMERICAN PHILOSOPHICAL SOCIETY, Library, 105 S Fifth St, Philadelphia, 19106. Edward C Carter II, Librn
Holdings: Cat Mss Pix
Notes: Incl books and mss on evolution.

VA —UNIVERSITY OF VIRGINIA, Alderman Library, Manuscripts Dept, Charlottesville, 22901. Edmund Berkeley Jr, Cur
Notes: The Paul B Victorius Collection of books on evolution.

ON —UNIVERSITY OF TORONTO, Thomas Fisher Rare Book Library, 120 Saint George St, Toronto, M5S 1A5, Can. Richard G Landon, Head
Holdings: Vols 2000 Uncat
Notes: Darwin Collection is a comprehensive collection of editions of works by Charles Darwin, including separate issues of editions published in his lifetime which show revisions of text; works by predecessors and contemporaries on concepts of evolution and natural selection. Collection described in Landon, R G *Species of Origin* (Toronto, 1971). Holdings listed in Freeman, R B, *Charles Darwin: A Bibliographical Handlist,* 2nd ed (London, 1977).

DARWINISM see Evolution

DAS, TARAKNATH

DC —GEORGETOWN UNIVERSITY, Library, Special Collections Div, 37 & O Sts NW, Washington, 20057. George M Barringer, Special Collections Librn; Nicholas B Sheetz, Mss Librn
Holdings: Mss Cat
Notes: The papers of Taraknath Das containing correspondence, mss, and newspaper clippings. The correspondence concerns the publication of Das' *Indien in der Weltpolitik* (Munchen, 1932). Incl are acknowledgement letters from Adolf Hitler (1 TLS, 1932) and from von Hindenburg (1 TLS, 1932). Also inc in the papers are numerous mss of articles written by Das, chiefly on Indian nationalism. Das joined the nationalist movement in India in 1903. Restricted.

DATA PROCESSING see Electronic Data Processing; Information Storage and Retrieval Systems

DATA STORAGE AND RETRIEVAL SYSTEMS see Computers; Information Storage and Retrieval Systems

DATES see Chronology, Historical

DATES, BOOKS OF see Calendars

DATING OF ROCKS see Geological Time

DAUBENY, SIR PETER

MA —BOSTON UNIVERSITY, Mugar Memorial Library, Special Collections Dept, 771 Commonwealth Ave, Boston, 02215. Howard B Gotlieb, Dir
Holdings: Mss Pix Correspondence

DAUPHIN, LOST see Louis XVII of France, 1785-1795

DAVEIS, CHARLES STEWART, 1788-1865

ME —BOWDOIN COLLEGE, Library, Brunswick, 04011. Dianne M Gutscher, Cur of Special Collections
Holdings: Mss
Notes: The Charles S Daveis Papers consist of about 400 items of correspondence, addresses, and documents, 1808-1864, of this Portland, Maine, lawyer who was active in the settlement of the dispute with Great Britain over Maine's northeastern boundary.

DAVENPORT, CHARLES R.

PA —AMERICAN PHILOSOPHICAL SOCIETY, Library, 105 S Fifth St, Philadelphia, 19106. Edward C Carter II, Librn
Holdings: Cat Mss Pix
Notes: Genetics.

DAVENPORT, EDWARD LOOMIS

CA —UNIVERSITY OF CALIFORNIA, DAVIS, Shields Library, Dept of Special Collections, Davis, 95616. Donald Kunitz, Head; C Danial Elliott, Asst Head
Holdings: Cat Mss Pix
Notes: Programs, playbills, photographs,

DAVENPORT, EDWARD LOOMIS (cont.)

engravings, prompt books, and personal papers of E L Davenport and his family. 80 items. Described in: Sarlos, Robert K, The Theatre Collection at Davis, *American Society for Theatre Research Newsletter,* vol 3, no 1, Fall 1974, pp 2-3, 9-10.

DAVENPORT, EUGENE

IL —UNIVERSITY OF ILLINOIS, URBANA/CHAMPAIGN, Library, University Archives, 19 Library, 1408 W Gregory Drive, Urbana, 61801. Maynard Brichford, University Archivist
Holdings: Cat Mss Maps Pix Slides Microforms
Notes: Papers, archival records, etc.

DAVENPORT, FANNY

CA —UNIVERSITY OF CALIFORNIA, DAVIS, Shields Library, Dept of Special Collections, Davis, 95616. Donald Kunitz, Head; C Danial Elliott, Asst Head
Holdings: Uncat Mss Pix
Notes: Photographs, clippings, and correspondence of personalities of American and British theatre in the 19th and 20th centuries, such as Edwin Booth, Joseph Jefferson, Julia Marlowe, E H Sothern, Ellen Terry, Henry Irving, McKee Rankin, Fanny Davenport, and Zero Mostel.

DAVENPORT, GUY, 1891-1965

NY —CORNELL UNIVERSITY LIBRARIES, Collection of Regional History, Dept of Manuscripts and Univ Archives, Ithaca, 14853.
Notes: "Guy Davenport's Childhood Memories," edited by John Phillip Davenport, 1979; 1 item.

NC —DUKE UNIVERSITY, William R Perkins Library, Rare Book Room, Durham, 27706. John L Sharpe, III, Cur
Notes: A collection of Duke University authors, established around 1963, with the writings of the students of William Blackburn and greatly enhanced by the gift of Professor Blackburn's collection. Represented are James Applewhite, Fred Chappell, Guy Davenport, Reynolds Price, William Styron, Frances Gray Patton, and Anne Tyler. Printed works are in the Rare Book Room and manuscripts are in the Manuscript Department.

VA —UNIVERSITY OF VIRGINIA, Alderman Library, Clifton Waller Barrett Collection, Charlottesville, 22901. Joan St C Crane, Cur of American Literature Collections
Notes: Papers.

DAVENPORT, MARCIA

DC —LIBRARY OF CONGRESS, Washington, 20540.
Holdings: Mss
Notes: Her literary mss and correspondence.

DAVENPORT FAMILY

NY —CORNELL UNIVERSITY LIBRARIES, Collection of Regional History, Dept of Manuscripts and Univ Archives, Ithaca, 14853.
Holdings: Pix Maps
Notes: Incl papers, 1816-1949; correspondence, legal documents, photos and maps.

DAVEY, FRANK

BC —SIMON FRASER UNIVERSITY, Library, Burnaby, V5A 1S6, Can. Percilla Groves, Special Collections Librn
Holdings: // Cat Mss
Notes: The Frank Davey Archive incl the poet's own mss, correspondence, proofs, and literary memorabilia, as well as correspondence, mss and proofs from the periodical *Open Letter,* covering the period 1962-1975.

DAVIDMAN, JOY

IL —WHEATON COLLEGE, Library, Marion E Wade Collection, Irving & Franklin Sts, Wheaton, 60187. Lyle Dorsett, Cur; Marjorie Mead, Associate Cur
Holdings: Vols (6500) Mss Pix Audiotapes Videotapes
Notes: Extensive Marion E Wade Collection contains the literary archives of Davidman's first husband, William Lindsay Gresham, as well as the personal recollections of her son, Douglas. Numerous materials also relate to Davidman's second marriage to C S Lewis.

DAVIDSON, DONALD

TN —VANDERBILT UNIVERSITY, Library, Nashville, 37240. Marice Wolfe, Special Collections Librn
Holdings: Vols 1000 Cat Mss Pix
Notes: Collection relating to the Fugitive poets of the 1920s, the Agrarian writers of the 1930s and their subsequent careers, as a complement to extensive mss collections in this field. Chief figures incl Allen Tate, John Crowe Ransom, Robert Penn Warren, Andrew Lytle, Donald Davidson, Merrill Moore, Laura Riding, et al.

DAVIDSON, DUANE

CT —YALE UNIVERSITY, Music Library, 98 Wall St, New Haven, 06520. Harold E Samuel, Librn
Notes: Personal papers and musical mss.
See also entry under Music, American.

DAVIDSON, GEORGE

CA —UNIVERSITY OF CALIFORNIA, BERKELEY, Bancroft Library, Manuscripts Division, Berkeley, 94720. James D Hart, Dir
Holdings: Cat Mss Maps Pix Microforms
Notes: Papers, correspondence, etc.

DAVIDSON, J. B.

CA —UNIVERSITY OF SAN FRANCISCO, Richard A Gleeson Library, The Countess Bernardine Murphy Donohue Rare Book Room, San Francisco, 94117. D Steven Corey, Special Collections Librn
Holdings: Vols 33

IA —IOWA STATE UNIVERSITY, Library, Dept of Special Collections, Ames, 50011. Stanley M Yates, Head
Holdings: // Mss Pix
Notes: J B Davidson (1880-1957) was one of the organizers and first president of the American Society of Agricultural Engineers. 13 linear ft, finding aid available.

DAVIDSON, JO

DC —LIBRARY OF CONGRESS, Manuscript Division, Washington, 20540. John C Broderick, Chief
Holdings: Cat Mss Pix
Notes: Mss, papers, records, etc.

DAVIE, DONALD

NV —UNIVERSITY OF NEVADA, RENO, University Library, Special Collections Dept, Reno, 89557. Robert E Blesse, Head
Holdings: Vols (42) Cat
Notes: Includes individual works by author in all editions including translations; also prefaces, introductions, published correspondence, appearances in anthologies, periodicals, etc. Bibliographical research collection, part of Modern Authors Collection. Other appearances 430 cataloged.

DAVIES, RHYS

IL —ILLINOIS STATE UNIVERSITY, Milner Library, Dept of Special Collections, Normal, 61761. Robert Sokan, Librn
Notes: First editions, limited editions, ephemera, etc.

DAVIES, WILLIAM HENRY

IL —ILLINOIS STATE UNIVERSITY, Milner Library, Dept of Special Collections, Normal, 61761. Robert Sokan, Librn
Notes: First editions, limited editions, ephemera, etc.

MA —AMHERST COLLEGE, Library, Amherst, 01002. John Lancaster, Special Collections Librn
Holdings: Vols (500) Uncat Mss
Notes: Concentration on the Georgian poets Lascelles Abercrombie, Edmund Blunden, W H Davies, John Drinkwater, Wilfrid Gibson, Harold Monro, et al.

NY —HOFSTRA UNIVERSITY, Library, 1000 Fulton Ave, Hempstead, 11550. Charles R Andrews, Dean of Library Services

OH —OHIO UNIVERSITY, Vernon R Alden Library, Department of Archives and Special Collections, Athens, 45701. Gary A Hunt, Head
Holdings: Vols 73 Cat
Notes: A comprehensive collection of Davies' published books.

BC —UNIVERSITY OF VICTORIA, McPherson Library, Victoria, V8W 3H5, Can.

DAVIS, ANDREW JACKSON

CT —YALE UNIVERSITY, Box 1603A, Yale Station, New Haven, 06520.
Holdings: Cat Mss
Notes: Incl 165 letters of Andrew Jackson Davis to William Green Jr, concerning personal, family, and financial matters, as well as Davis's work with Spiritualism and healing, 1848-1881.

DAVIS, MRS. ARTHUR POWELL

†CA —UNIVERSITY OF SAN FRANCISCO, Richard A Gleeson Library, The Countess Bernardine Murphy Donohue Rare Book Room, San Francisco, 94117. D Steven Corey, Special Collections Librn
Holdings: // Uncat Mss
Notes: Papers and correspondence of Mary MacNaughton (Mrs Arthur Powell Davis) and Clara W MacNaughton ca 1890-1910.

DAVIS, BETTE

MA —BOSTON UNIVERSITY, Mugar Memorial Library, Special Collections Dept, 771 Commonwealth Ave, Boston, 02215. Howard B Gotlieb, Dir
Holdings: Mss Pix
Notes: The Bette Davis Collection. Incl original notebooks, engagement pads, mss of articles and speeches by her, drafts of her poetry, family documents and records, some correspondence from her colleagues, school papers, childhood scrapbooks, early programs, a vast collection of clippings concerning her career, and personal and professional photographs, stage and movie scripts.

DAVIS, BLEVINS

MO —UNIVERSITY OF MISSOURI-KANSAS CITY, General Library, State Historical Society of Missouri Manuscripts, 5100 Rockhill Road, Kansas City, 64110. Kenneth J LaBudde, Dir; Gordon Hendrickson, Assoc Dir
Holdings: Mss
Notes: Western Historical Manuscript Collection incl papers of Charles B Wheeler, Jr, Charles N Kimball, Arthur Mag, Oscar D Nelson, Lou B Holland, J C Nichols, Perry Cookingham, Blevins Davis, Daniel MacMorris, and the records of the Kansas City Board of Trade.

DAVIS, CHRISTOPHER

MA —BOSTON UNIVERSITY, Mugar Memorial Library, Special Collections Dept, 771 Commonwealth Ave, Boston, 02215. Howard B Gotlieb, Dir
Holdings: Mss Correspondeence

DAVIS, DAVID

IL —CHICAGO HISTORICAL SOCIETY, Library, Clark St at North Ave, Chicago,

DAVIS, DAVID (cont.)

60614. Archie Motley, Manuscript Librn
Notes: Supreme Court Justice David Davis, a confidant of Abraham Lincoln, and Chief Justice Melville W Fuller, both collections consisting of photostatic copies of original materials in various repositories and in private hands.

DAVIS, HALLIE (FLANAGAN)

NY —NEW YORK PUBLIC LIBRARY, Performing Arts Research Center, Billy Rose Theatre Collection, 111 Amsterdam Ave, New York, 10023. Dorothy L Swerdlove, Cur
Holdings: Cat Mss Pix
Notes: Papers, scrapbooks, mss, photographs, memorabilia, etc.

DAVIS, JEFFERSON

†AL —MUSEUMS OF THE CITY OF MOBILE, Reference Library, 355 Government St, Mobile, 36602. Caldwell Delaney, Adminr

†AL —UNIVERSITY OF ALABAMA, Amelia Gayle Gorgas Library, PO Box S, University, 35486.
Notes: The Confederate States of America collection; incl a collection of Jefferson Davis papers. Separate catalog. Published bibliography. *Confederate Imprints in the University of Alabama Library*, comp by Sara Elizabeth Mason (University: University of Alabama Press, 1961).

LA —TULANE UNIVERSITY, Howard-Tilton Memorial Library, Special Collections Div, 7001 Freret St, New Orleans, 70118. Wilbur E Meneray, Librn
Holdings: Mss
Notes: Official and personal correspondence (in part copies) of Jefferson Davis and a section of his library. The majority is part of the Louisiana Historical Assocation Collection. See *Calendar of the Jefferson Davis Postwar Manuscripts* (New Orleans, 1943).

MD —JOHNS HOPKINS UNIVERSITY, Milton S Eisenhower Library, Charles & 34 Sts, Baltimore, 21218. Ann S Gwyn, Assistant Dir for Special Collections

MS —UNIVERSITY OF SOUTHERN MISSISSIPPI, William David McCain Graduate Library, Box 5148, Southern Sta, Hattiesburg, 39406.
Holdings: Cat Mss
Notes: Jefferson Davis' Home, Beauvoir, at Biloxi, Mississippi, was used as a confederate veterans home from 1902-1957. The Jefferson Davis Soldiers' Home Records document its operations between 1920 and 1954. 2.7 cubic feet of mss.

NJ —AARON BURR ASSOCIATION LIBRARY, RD 1, RT 33, Box 429, Hightstown-Freehold Rd, Hightstown, 08520. Samuel E Burr, Jr, Librn
Holdings: Vols 100 Cat Pix Microforms
Notes: Materials concerning Col Aaron Burr, his life, his career and members of his immediate family. Incl some materials on his daughter, Mrs Theodosia Burr Alston, Jefferson Davis and Mrs Jefferson Davis (Varina Howell Davis). Open to the public by appointment only.

NC —DUKE UNIVERSITY, William R Perkins Library, Manuscript Dept, Durham, 27706. Ellen Gartrell, Cur of Mss
Holdings: Cat Mss
Notes: Strong collection incl papers of many officers (eg Robert E Lee, P G T Beauregard), Confederate governments, and leaders (eg Jefferson Davis), thousands of letters and diaries from Union and Confederate soldiers and homefront.

OH —MIAMI UNIVERSITY, King Library, Walter Havighurst Special Collections Library, Oxford, 45056. Helen Ball, Cur of Special Collections

TN —MEMPHIS STATE UNIVERSITY, John Willard Brister Library, Memphis, 38152. John Terreo, Special Collections Librn
Notes: Jefferson Davis-Joel Addison Family papers, 1864-1889. President of the Confederacy. Personal and business correspondence, receipts, notes, cancelled checks, and other papers, of Davis, following the Civil War (primarily 1877-1889) and his son-in-law, Joel Addison Hayes (1848-1919), banker of Memphis, TN, relating chiefly to management of Davis' plantation, Brierfield, near Vicksburg, MS, stocks and mining investments, and land sales. Incl correspondence between Davis' wife Varina (Howell) Davis and her daughter Margaret Howell (Davis) (1848-1908), and between Addison Hayes and members of his family.

TX —UNIVERSITY OF TEXAS LIBRARIES, General Libraries, Barker Texas History Center, PO Box P, Austin, 78712. Don Carleton, Dir
Holdings: Vols (132,000) Cat Mss Maps Pix Slides Phonorecords Audiotapes Microforms
Notes: See description of collection under Texas-History.

DAVIS, JEROME

BC —UNIVERSITY OF VICTORIA, McPherson Library, Victoria, V8W 3H5, Can.

DAVIS, JOE LEE

MI —UNIVERSITY OF MICHIGAN, Library, Dept of Rare Books & Special Collections, Ann Arbor, 48109. Robert J Starring, Head
Holdings: Vols (170) Cat Mss Audiotapes Microforms
Notes: Many first editions. There are also over 2500 manuscript items, including 7 Cabell holograph letters; the archives of the Cabell Society, chiefly comprising correspondence of donor Julius Rothman, founder of the Society and editor of *The* Cabellian, with Cabell scholars; and the papers of Joe Lee Davis, president of the Cabell Society and advisory editor of *The* Cabellian.

DAVIS, JOHN

NE —NEBRASKA STATE HISTORICAL SOCIETY, Archives, 1500 R St, Box 82554, Lincoln, 68501. James E Potter, State Archivist
Holdings: Uncat Mss
Notes: Silver and the money question; also material on the Greenback Party. Printed speeches and tracts relating to the money question, 1890-1895. Many written by prominent political figures of the day. Also, pamphlets which relate to income tax, tariffs, free trade, soldiers' pensions, railroads, election laws and public lands. Collection of John Davis, Congressman from Kansas, 1891-1895.

DAVIS, REP. JOHN W.

GA —UNIVERSITY OF GEORGIA, Libraries, Special Collections Division, Athens, 30602. Vesta Lee Gordon, Asst Dir for Special Collections
Notes: Collection contains 1394.8 linear feet of mss: papers of US Senator Richard B Russell; US Congressmen John W Davis, Maston O'Neal, Robert G Stephens Jr, John L Pilcher, Dudley M Hughes; Governors Hoke Smith, Lester Maddox, Carl Sanders.

DAVIS, JOHN WILLIAM, 1873-1955

DC —GEORGETOWN UNIVERSITY, Library, Special Collections Div, 37 & O Sts NW, Washington, 20057. George M Barringer, Special Collections Librn; Nicholas B Sheetz, Mss Librn
Holdings: Mss Cat
Notes: Correspondence from John William Davis's term as Solicitor General for the United States, 1913-1918. The major portion of the incoming correspondence contains letters of endorsement supporting Davis's bid for a Supreme Court vacancy, inquiries from citizens seeking positions with the federal government, and petitions for military commission during the war years. Also incl are Davis's carbon responses. Davis (1873-1955), lawyer and diplomat, resigned his post as Solicitor General in 1918 to accept the United States ambassadorship to Great Britain.

DAVIS, JOSEPH S.

MA —BOSTON UNIVERSITY, Mugar Memorial Library, Special Collections Dept, 771 Commonwealth Ave, Boston, 02215. Howard B Gotlieb, Dir
Holdings: Mss Pix
Notes: Mss, correspondence, etc collected in depth; incl publications by or about.

DAVIS, MARY E. P.

MA —SIMMONS COLLEGE ARCHIVES, 300 The Fenway, Boston, 02115. Megan Sniffin-Marinoff, College Archivist
Notes: Archives of the Simmons College School of Public Health Nursing (later reorganized into the School of Nursing) cover the years 1902-1970. Important correspondents in the collection incl M Adelaide Nutting, Mary Beard, Isabel Stewart, and Anne Hervey Strong, etc. Incl Strong's records of activity with regard to nursing education in the National Organization for Public Health Nursing, 1918-22. 1000 linear feet in institution, incl special collections nursing and photographs, nursing.

DAVIS, MICHAEL

NY —NEW YORK ACADEMY OF MEDICINE, Library, 2 E 103 St, New York, 10029. Brett A Kirkpatrick, Librn
Notes: The papers of Michael Davis, one of the most extensive files of correspondence, surveys, government reports, news clippings, ephemera, etc concerning the development of medical care programs in the United States and other countries. Incl 14 vertical file cabinets.

DAVIS, MILDRED

MA —BOSTON UNIVERSITY, Mugar Memorial Library, Special Collections Dept, 771 Commonwealth Ave, Boston, 02215. Howard B Gotlieb, Dir
Holdings: Cat Mss
Notes: Mss, correspondence, etc colelcted in depth; incl publications by or about.

DAVIS, PAULINA WRIGHT

NY —VASSAR COLLEGE, Library, Rare Books & Manuscripts Collection, Box 20, Poughkeepsie, 12601. Lisa Browar, Cur
Holdings: Mss Pix
Notes: Emphasis is on women in the US, women's rights, suffrage and Equal Rights Amendment. Manuscript collections incl papers of Elizabeth Cady Stanton, Paulina Wright Davis, Maria Mitchell and Alma Lutz.

DAVIS, PETER

IN —BALL STATE UNIVERSITY, University Libraries, Special Collections Dept, University Ave, Muncie, 47306. David C Tambo, Head of Special Collections
Holdings: Vols Mss Maps Pix Audiotapes Videotapes
Notes: Incl one half million feet of film. Center for Middletown Studies holdings include materials by Robert and Helen Lynd, Middletown III Project and Peter Davis' Middletown Film Project.

DAVIS, REUBEN

MS —UNIVERSITY OF SOUTHERN MISSISSIPPI, William David McCain Graduate Library, Box 5148, Southern Sta, Hattiesburg, 39406.
Holdings: Cat Mss Pix
Notes: Correspondence and records (1847-1892) relating to Alexander Melvorne Jackson's participation in the Mexican War, his service as Secretary of the State of the New Mexico Territory (1857-1861), and his participation in the Civil War on the side of

DAVIS, REUBEN (cont.)

the Confederacy. Among his correspondents were Albert Gallatin Brown, Reuben Davis, Miguel A Otero, Jacob Thompson, and John Ireland. Incl are photographs of Austin, Texas, ca 1890. 1.1 cubic feet holdings.

DAVIS, RICHARD HARDING

VA —UNIVERSITY OF VIRGINIA, Alderman Library, Clifton Waller Barrett Collection, Charlottesville, 22901. Joan St C Crane, Cur of American Literature Collections
Holdings: Vols 94 Cat Mss
Notes: First editions, etc. Over 2500 manuscript pieces. Published description: *The Barrett Library Richard Harding Davis--A Checklist of Printed and Manuscript Works of Richard Harding Davis in the Library of the University of Virginia,* compiled by Fannie Mae Elliott and Lucy Clark; Manuscripts by Marjorie D Carver (Charlottesville: University of Virginia Press, 1963).

DAVIS, STUART

MA —HARVARD UNIVERSITY, Harvard College Library, Fine Arts Library, Fogg Museum, 32 Quincy St, Cambridge, 02138. Wolfgang M Freitag, Librn
Holdings: // Cat Mss
Notes: Personal archives (more than 10,000 pages).

DAVIS, WESTMORELAND

VA —UNIVERSITY OF VIRGINIA, Alderman Library, Manuscripts Dept, Charlottesville, 22901. Edmund Berkeley Jr, Cur
Holdings: Cat Mss
See also entry under Virginia - History

DAVIS, WILLIAM HEATH, 1822-1909

CA —UNIVERSITY OF CALIFORNIA, LOS ANGELES, Research Library, Dept of Special Collections, 405 Hilgard Ave, Los Angeles, 90024. Edward Shreeves, Chairman, Bibliographers Group; David S Zeidberg, Head
Holdings: Cat Mss Microforms
Notes: 1 linear foot of letters and business records; microfilm of additional ms material located elsewhere.

DAVIS FAMILY

MA —NEW ENGLAND HISTORIC GENEALOGICAL SOCIETY, Library, 101 Newbury St, Boston, 02116. Ralph J Crandell, Dir
Notes: Family papers, likely to incl personal correspondence, diaries, business records, etc.

TN —MEMPHIS STATE UNIVERSITY, John Willard Brister Library, Memphis, 38152. John Terreo, Special Collections Librn
Notes: Jefferson Davis-Joel Addison Family papers, 1864-1889. President of the Confederacy. Personal and business correspondence, receipts, notes, cancelled checks, and other papers, of Davis, following the Civil War (primarily 1877-1889) and his son-in-law, Joel Addison Hayes (1848-1919), banker of Memphis, TN, relating chiefly to management of Davis' plantation, Brierfield, near Vicksburg, MS, stocks and mining investments, and land sales. Incl correspondence between Davis' wife Varina (Howell) Davis and her daughter Margaret Howell (Davis) (1848-1908), and between Addison Hayes and members of his family.

DAVISE, HUGO

CA —UNIVERSITY OF CALIFORNIA, LOS ANGELES, Music Library, Schonberg Hall, Los Angeles, 90024. Stephen M Fry, Music Librn
Notes: Mss

DAVISON, CLARENCE BEVERLY, 1869-1938

NY —CORNELL UNIVERSITY LIBRARIES, Collection of Regional History, Dept of Manuscripts and Univ Archives, Ithaca, 14853.
Notes: Businessman. Papers, ca 1919-74; 42 ft. Millbrook, Dutchess County.

DAWES, CHARLES G.

IL —NORTHWESTERN UNIVERSITY, Library, Special Collections Dept, 1937 Sheridan Rd, Evanston, 60201. R Russell Maylone, Cur
Holdings: Mss
Notes: 350 file boxes of mss, plus letter press books, business books and patronage correspondence, diaries, journals, arranged in chronological order. Literature: Pollak, *Illinois Libraries,* April 1958, pp 328-329; Dawes Collection, R Siefer, *A Guide to the Papers of Charles G Dawes in the Special Collections Department, Northwestern University Library* (Evanston, July, 1972).

DAWSON, CHRISTOPHER

DC —GEORGETOWN UNIVERSITY, Library, Special Collections Div, 37 & O Sts NW, Washington, 20057. George M Barringer, Special Collections Librn; Nicholas B Sheetz, Mss Librn
Holdings: Cat Mss
Notes: The papers of the English author, journalist, and historian Douglas Woodruff (1897-1978), containing correspondence, mss, and photographs. Incl is considerable material concerning his years at Oxford University; his editorship for many years of The "Tablet"; English Catholic society in general and English Catholic literature in particular. Also present are research files on the Tichborne Claimant, one of the most famous cases of impersonation in English legal history. There is extensive correspondence from such figures as: Hilaire Belloc; Tom Burns; Rev Martin D'Arcy, SJ; Christopher Dawson; Sir Roy Harrod; Christopher Hollis; Msgr Ronald Knox; Sir Shane Leslie; Sir Arnold Lunn; Rebecca West; and Evelyn Waugh.

DAWSON, FIELDING, 1930-

CT —UNIVERSITY OF CONNECTICUT, Library, Storrs, 06268. George F Butterick, Cur of Literary Archives
Holdings: Mss Pix Audiotapes
Notes: Repository for this writer's papers.

MO —WASHINGTON UNIVERSITY, Libraries, Special Collections Dept, Campus Box 1061, St Louis, 63130.
Notes: A small but significant collection.

NY —STATE UNIVERSITY OF NEW YORK, STONY BROOK, Melville Library, Dept of Special Collections, Stony Brook, 11794. Evert Volkersz, Head
Holdings: Vols 25 Cat Mss

DAWSON'S BOOKSHOP

CA —UNIVERSITY OF CALIFORNIA, LOS ANGELES, Research Library, Dept of Special Collections, 405 Hilgard Ave, Los Angeles, 90024. Edward Shreeves, Chairman, Bibliographers Group; David S Zeidberg, Head
Notes: 18 linear feet of correspondence, business records, and ephemera of Dawson's Bookshop, Booksellers, Los Angeles.

DAY, F. HOLLAND, 1864-1933

DC —LIBRARY OF CONGRESS, Prints & Photographs Div, Washington, 20540.
Notes: The F Holland Day Collection of Day's photographs. 640 photoprints.

DAY, J. EDWARD

MA —BOSTON UNIVERSITY, Mugar Memorial Library, Special Collections Dept, 771 Commonwealth Ave, Boston, 02215. Howard B Gotlieb, Dir
Holdings: Cat Mss Pix
Notes: Mss, correspondence, etc collected in depth; incl publications by or about.

DAY FAMILY

AZ —NORTHERN ARIZONA UNIVERSITY, Special Collection Library, CU Box 6022, Flagstaff, 86011. Peter M Whiteley, Coordr/Archivist; William Mullane, Librn
Notes: Day Family Collection. They were Anglo traders on the eastern Navajo reservation. Correspondence, files of trading and other activities of Sam, Anna, Charles, and Sam Day, Jr, 1880's-1930's. Incl unpublished mss on Navajo ceremonies and correspondence relating to the looting of Canyon del Muerto.

DAY NURSERIES

NY —BANK STREET COLLEGE OF EDUCATION LIBRARY, 610 W 112 St, New York, 10025. Eleanor Kule Seid, Library Dir
Holdings: Vols (90,000) Cat Microforms
Notes: Education, guidance, psychology, educational psychology, curricula, textbooks, Black Studies, etc. All subjects are integrated in one professional collection; in addition there are two separately cataloged and shelved collections: Children's and Elementary Curriculum Materials.

OH —OHIO STATE UNIVERSITY, Home Economics Library, Campbell Hall Rm 325, 1787 Neil Ave, Columbus, 43210. Neosha Mackey, Librn
Holdings: Vols (14,000) Cat Microforms
Notes: Separate catalog. Also, book catalog: *Catalog of the Home Economics Library* (Boston: G K Hall, 1976), 3 vols.

†PA —TEMPLE UNIVERSITY LIBRARIES, Special Collections Dept, Urban Archives Center, Philadelphia, 19122. Thomas Whitehead, Cur of Mss
Holdings: Cat
Notes: Incl the records of several separate collections which are deposited in the Urban Archives Center. Many collections contain photographs, maps and pamphlets, in addition to manuscripts. All collections in the Urban Archives are separately cataloged.

DAY OF JUDGMENT see Judgment Day

DAYE, PIERRE, 1872-1954

CA —HOOVER INSTITUTION ON WAR, REVOLUTION & PEACE, Stanford University, Stanford, 94305. Milorad M Drachkovitch, Archivist
Notes: Unpublished memoirs (photocopy of typewritten draft with handwritten annotations, in French), by Pierre Daye, Belgian writer, politician, and journalist, concerning his life and professional career, world history, and international affairs, 1892-1953. Chapters 60, 61, and conclusion are missing. 2 ms boxes.

DAY-LEWIS, CECIL

NV —UNIVERSITY OF NEVADA, RENO, University Library, Special Collections Dept, Reno, 89557. Robert E Blesse, Head
Holdings: Vols (108) // Cat
Notes: Includes individual works by author in all editions including translations; also prefaces, introductions, published correspondence, appearances in anthologies, periodicals, etc. Bibliographical research collection, part of Modern Authors Collection. Other appearances 450 cataloged.

BC —UNIVERSITY OF VICTORIA, McPherson Library, Victoria, V8W 3H5, Can.

DE FACTO DOCTRINE (INTERNATIONAL LAW) see Military Occupation

DEAD SEA SCROLLS

NY —ALFRED UNIVERSITY, Herrick Memorial Library, Alfred, 14802. June E Brown, Head Librn
Holdings: Vols (1200) // Cat Mss
Notes: The Bergren Collection. A comprehensive collection on Biblical Studies in the Old and New Testaments. Includes material on the Dead Sea Scrolls, Eastern religions, and Hebrew and Aramaic languages.

DEAF AND DEAFNESS

DC —ALEXANDER GRAHAM BELL ASSOCIATION FOR THE DEAF, Volta Bureau Library, 3417 Volta Place, NW, Washington, 20007.
Holdings: Vols (30,000) Cat Mss Pix Slides Audiotapes Videotapes Microforms
Budget: $16,000
Notes: Incl 350 ms pieces, 500 pictures, 150 slides, 200 audiotapes, 25 videotapes and 500 microforms. Not open to public.

DC —GALLAUDET COLLEGE, Library, 800 Florida Ave, NE, Washington, 20002. Carolyn Jones, Assoc Librn, Research & Bibl
Holdings: Vols 10,315 Cat Mss Pix Slides Videotapes 16mm Films Filmstrips Microforms
Notes: A comprehensive collection on deafness and the deaf. Materials are both historical and contemporary. It is one of the world's leading collections. *Dictionary Catalog on Deafness and the Deaf* (Boston, Mass: G K Hall, 1971), 2 vols. Incl oral history program on videotape.

MO —WASHINGTON UNIVERSITY, School of Medicine, Library, 660 South Euclid Ave, Saint Louis, 63110. Christopher Hoolihan, Rare Book Librn
Holdings: Vols 850 Cat
Budget: ($40,000)
Notes: The CID-Max A Goldstein Collection in Speech and Hearing. Incl printed books from the 16th through 19th centuries on deafness, deaf education, ear diseases, hearing, speech and speech disorders.

NY —SAINT MARY'S SCHOOL FOR THE DEAF, Professional Library, 2253 Main St, Buffalo, 14214. Collette Sangster, Librn
Holdings: Vols (8939) Cat Audiotapes Microforms
Budget: ($11,802)
Notes: Medical and educational aspects of deafness.

PA —EYE & EAR HOSPITAL OF PITTSBURGH, Blair-Lippincott Library, 230 Lothrop St, Pittsburgh, 15213. Bruce A Johnston, Medical Librn
Holdings: Vols (6000) Cat
Notes: Special emphasis on ophthalmology, otorhinolaryngology, audiology, and speech pathology.

WI —MARQUETTE UNIVERSITY, Memorial Library, 1415 W Wisconsin Ave, Milwaukee, 53233. Jay Kirk, Health Sciences Librn
Notes: Supports curriculum and research.

DEAF AND DEAFNESS—EDUCATION

MO —WASHINGTON UNIVERSITY, School of Medicine, Library, 660 South Euclid Ave, Saint Louis, 63110. Christopher Hoolihan, Rare Book Librn
Holdings: Vols 850 Cat
Budget: ($40,000)
Notes: The CID-Max A Goldstein Collection in Speech and Hearing. Incl printed books from the 16th through 19th centuries on deafness, deaf education, ear diseases, hearing, speech and speech disorders.

OK —UNIVERSITY OF SCIENCE & ARTS OF OKLAHOMA, Nash Library, Chickasha, 73018. William A Martin, Jr, Librn
Notes: One of the larger departments of our University is deaf education. Incl books, periodicals and vertical file materials. We have much material to support this work.

DEAF AND DUMB see Deaf and Deafness

DEAF BLIND see Blind Deaf

DEAF-MUTES see Deaf and Deafness

DEAL, BABS

MA —BOSTON UNIVERSITY, Mugar Memorial Library, Special Collections Dept, 771 Commonwealth Ave, Boston, 02215. Howard B Gotlieb, Dir
Holdings: Cat Mss

DEAL, BORDEN

MA —BOSTON UNIVERSITY, Mugar Memorial Library, Special Collections Dept, 771 Commonwealth Ave, Boston, 02215. Howard B Gotlieb, Dir
Holdings: Cat Mss Pix
Notes: Mss, correspondence, etc collected in depth; incl publications by or about.

DEARLE, RAYMOND C., 1890-1970

†ON —PUBLIC ARCHIVES OF CANADA, Library, 395 Wellington St, Ottawa, K1A 0N3, Can. Dawn E Monroe, Collections Dept Officer
Holdings: 2.5 Cm
Notes: His papers (1939-1942, 1949, 1957, 1966).

DEASY, MARY

MA —BOSTON UNIVERSITY, Mugar Memorial Library, Special Collections Dept, 771 Commonwealth Ave, Boston, 02215. Howard B Gotlieb, Dir
Holdings: Cat Mss Pix

DEATH—ART

MA —HARVARD UNIVERSITY LIBRARY, Widener Library, Cambridge, 02138.
Holdings: Cat Pix Slides

DEATH, DANCE OF see Dance of Death

DEATH AND DYING

DC —CENTER FOR BIOETHICS, Library, Kennedy Institute, Georgetown University, 3520 Prospect St NW, Washington, 20057. Doris Goldstein, Dir; Judith Mistichelli, Senior Librn
Holdings: Vols (8200)
Notes: Largest library of its kind. Incl 31, 000 journal articles on applied ethics. Produces computer database *Bioethicsline,* available through MEDLARS; and the printed annual *Bibliography of Bioethics.* Other library publications are: *New Titles in* Bioethics (monthly); *Scope Notes* series on current topics.

MA —NATIONAL CENTER FOR DEATH EDUCATION, New England Resource Center for Thanatology & Funeral Service, 656 Beacon St, Boston, 02215. Gail Gruner, Librn

NY —CREEDMOOR PSYCHIATRIC CENTER, Health Sciences Library, Bldg 51, 80-45 Winchester Blvd, Queens Village, 11427. Susan Taubman, Dir of Library; Pushpa Bhati, Sr Librn
Holdings: Vols (12,000) Cat Slides Phonorecords Audiotapes Filmstrips Microfiche Videotapes
Budget: ($50,000)
Notes: Particularly strong in the areas of neurology, pharmacology, psychoanalysis, and psychopharmacology.

OR —UNIVERSITY OF OREGON LIBRARY, 1607 Agate St, Eugene, 97403. Ruth M Brewer, Resource Librn
Notes: Social and psychological aspects of aging.

DEATH IN ART see Death—Art

DEATH PENALTY see Capital Punishment

DEATH RATE see Mortality; Vital Statistics

DEATH VALLEY, CALIFORNIA

CA —DEATH VALLEY NATIONAL MONUMENT, Library, Death Valley, 92328. Shirley Harding, Cur/Librn
Holdings: Vols 3000 Cat Mss Maps Pix Slides
Notes: Death Valley (History, Archeology, Geology, Natural History, etc). Reference Library only.

DEATHS, REGISTERS OF see Registers of Births, Etc.

DEBATES, RELIGIOUS see Disputations, Religious

DEBS, EUGENE V. AND THEODORE

IL —SOUTHERN ILLINOIS UNIVERSITY, CARBONDALE, Delyte W Morris Library, Special Collections Dept, Carbondale, 62901. David V Koch, Cur of Special Collections; Louisa Bowen, Cur of Manuscripts
Holdings: Cat Mss
Notes: Papers and correspondence of Theodore A Schroeder, constitutional lawyer and founder, with Lincoln Steffens, of the Free Speech League, a forerunner of the American Civil Liberties Union. Contains extensive correspondence with Comstock, Gompers, Debs, H Ellis, Sanger, Sinclair, John Dewey, Darrow, Mencken, A G Hays, Emma Goldman, W E B Dubois, etc. Incl several thousand letters; notes and mss, records of legal cases and extensive files relating to the early history of psychiatry.

IN —INDIANA STATE UNIVERSITY, Cunningham Memorial Library, Dept of Rare Books & Special Collections, Terre Haute, 47809. Lawrence J McCrank, Head
Holdings: Uncat Mss Pix
Budget: ($1350)
Notes: The Debs Collection consists of aprox 7000 pieces of correspondence between Theodore Debs (brother of E V) and other persons, such as Sinclair Lewis, Upton Sinclair, Ethel Barrymore, Emma Goldman, Robert G Ingersoll, Carl Sandburg, Norman Thomas, Sacco and Vanzetti and many others. Many of the letters are from E V Debs to his brother; a good portion of these are from the federal penitentiary at Atlanta. Entire correspondence file has been microfilmed. 750 pamphlets cover all aspects of the labor movement, socialism and radical thought from the 19th century to appprox 1950. A collection ca 200 related books is also housed in the collection. See: J Robert Constantine and Gail Malmgreen, eds, *The Papers of Eugene V Debs, 1834-1945. A Guide to the Microfilm Edition.* NY: Microfilming Corp of America, 1983 (University Microfilms is the new distributer).

NY —CORNELL UNIVERSITY LIBRARIES, Collection of Regional History, Dept of Manuscripts and Univ Archives, Ithaca, 14853.
Holdings: Film
Notes: Biographical motion picture, entitled "Debs, - Labor's Martyr." Made ca 1920's.

DE CAMP, L. SPRAGUE

IN —INDIANA UNIVERSITY, Lilly Library, Seventh St, Bloomington, 47405. William R Cagle, Librn
Notes: First editions. Ms collections incl papers of writer Fritz Leiber, Jr, 1910- , containing correspondence with many authors and manuscript notes, etc, of several Leiber writings, 1932-1974. 1500 items. Papers of reviewer and critic William Anthony Parker White (Tony Boucher) which incl sizeable correspondence files with Ray Bradbury, etc, as well as reviews and manuscripts of Boucher's own writings. Letters to editor and fantastic fiction writer Lin Carter from Lyon Sprague de Camp (ca 200 items) and from various other writers (293 items). Letters, 1966-1972, from James Blish to editors at Doubleday (30 items). Letters, 1966-1976, from Roger Zelazny to editors at Doubleday (44 items).

MA —BOSTON UNIVERSITY, Mugar Memorial Library, Special Collections Dept, 771 Commonwealth Ave, Boston, 02215. Howard B Gotlieb, Dir
Holdings: Cat Mss Pix
Notes: Mss, correspondence, etc collected in depth; incl publication by or about. Some mss by his wife Catherine Crook de Camp or co-authored with her.

DECATUR, STEPHEN

IL —MILLIKIN UNIVERSITY, Staley Library, 1184 W Main St, Decatur, 62522. Charles E Hale, Librn
Holdings: Vols 50 Cat Mss Pix
Budget: $100
Notes: The Stephen Decatur Collection. The core of this collection was given by John Valentine (1895-1955) to the Millikin University Library in 1947. Also have realia of coins, busts, etc.

DECKER, PETER

MD —UNIVERSITY OF BALTIMORE, Langsdale Library, 1420 Maryland Ave, Baltimore, 21201. Gerry Watkins, Head of Special Collections Dept
Holdings: Cat Mss Maps
Notes: Incl the entire stock (10,000 vols) of Peter Decker, New York antiquarian bookdealer (acquired in 1970); incl Peter Decker's mss of his published works and his records as a dealer in Americana.

DECLAMATION see Readers and Speakers

DECLARATION OF INDEPENDENCE see U.S.—Declaration of Independence

DECORATION, FORE-EDGE see Fore-Edge Paintings

DECORATION, INTERIOR see Interior Decoration

DECORATION AND ORNAMENT

CA —CRAFT AND FOLK ART MUSEUM, Library, 5814 Wilshire Blvd, Los Angeles, 90036. Joan M Benedetti, Museum Librn
Holdings: Vols (2000) Slides VF
Notes: Incl 2000 books; 70 journal subscriptions; artists' biographical files: 6 file drawers; clipping files: 8 file drawers; 20,000 slides. Representation of the material culture of all people, traditional and contemporary expressions. Incl visual and printed information on ethnic, traditional, popular, decorative, idiosyncratic, and contemporary crafts as well as vernacular architecture, handmade houses, and design. Information about and for professional artists on health hazards, conservation, and career management. Anthropological and art historical works; exhibition catalogues; slides, photographs, audiocassettes; clipping and pamphlet files. Contemporary Slide Registry of Craftspeople and extensive biographical files of contemporary craft artists. Information and referral files of craft related galleries, shops, festivals, organizations, etc.

CT —STOWE-DAY LIBRARY, 77 Forest St, Hartford, 06105. Diana J Royce, Librn
Holdings: Vols (15,000) Cat Mss
Notes: Incl (6000) additional pamphlets. The entire collection covers architecture, decorative arts, history, literature, woman suffrage, and Harriet Beecher Stowe, through the 19th century.

DE —HENRY F DUPONT WINTERTHUR MUSEUM LIBRARY, Winterthur, 19735. Frank H Sommer, III, Head
Holdings: Cat
Notes: Strong collections.

NY —COLUMBIA UNIVERSITY LIBRARIES, Avery Architectural and Fine Arts Library, 201 Avery Hall, New York, 10027. Angela Giral, Librn
Holdings: Vols 1700 Cat
Notes: Restricted use: noncirculating.

NY —NEW YORK PUBLIC LIBRARY, Art, Prints, and Photographs Div, Fifth Ave & 42 St, New York, 10018. Donald Anderle, Chief
Holdings: Cat Mss Pix

DECORATIONS OF HONOR

NY —AMERICAN NUMISMATIC SOCIETY LIBRARY, Broadway between 155 & 156 Sts, New York, 10032. Francis D Campbell Jr, Chief Librn
Holdings: Vols (50,000) Cat Mss Maps Pix Slides 16mm Films Microforms
Budget: ($6000)
Notes: Incl materials devoted to coins, medals, decorations, orders, tokens, paper money, seals, heraldry. Aids materials incl history, economic history, art history, archaeology, inscriptions and a number of encyclopedias and biographical dictionaries. Dictionary card catalog provides access to the materials: *Dictionary Catalogue of the Library of the American Numismatic Society.* (Boston: G K Hall, 1962). 6 vols and vol listing the auction catalogs in our collection; *First Supplement: 1962-1967; Second Supplement: 1968-1972; Third Supplement: 1973-1977* (Boston: G K Hall, 1967, 1973, 1978). Noncirculating.

DECORATORS UNION see Brotherhood of Painters, Decorators, and Paperhangers Union

DEDMON, EMMETT

IL —CHICAGO HISTORICAL SOCIETY, Library, Clark St at North Ave, Chicago, 60614. Archie Motley, Manuscript Librn
Notes: Publishing and literary collections incl these papers: *Chicago Journalism* Review; *Chicago Seed*; *The Chicagoan*; Friends of American Writers, Chicago literary group; Emmett Dedmon (Chicago newspaper executive, journalist, author); Interviews of 97 Chicago journalists conducted by students in Northwestern University's Medill School.

DEDUCTION (LOGIC) see Logic

DEE, SYLVIA

MA —BOSTON UNIVERSITY, Mugar Memorial Library, Special Collections Dept, 771 Commonwealth Ave, Boston, 02215. Howard B Gotlieb, Dir
Holdings: Cat Mss Pix
Notes: Mss, correspondence, etc collected in depth; incl publications by or about.

DEEP-SEA EXPLORATION see Marine Biology; Marine Fauna; Marine Flora

DEFECTIVE SPEECH see Speech, Disorders of

DEFEND THE ALLIES COMMITTEE see Committee to Defend America by Aiding the Allies

DEFENSE (MILITARY SCIENCE) see Attack and Defense (Military Science)

DEFENSE SYSTEMS see Weapons Systems

DEFENSES, COAST see Coast Defenses

DEFOE, DANIEL

CA —UNIVERSITY OF CALIFORNIA, SAN DIEGO, Central University Library, Mandeville Dept of Special Collections, La Jolla, 92093. Lynda Corey Claassen, Head
Notes: Rare Book Collection incl 2000 vols of 18th century English literature, with special emphasis on the works of Daniel Defoe and Samuel Johnson.

CA —UNIVERSITY OF CALIFORNIA, LOS ANGELES, William Andrews Clark Memorial Library, 2520 Cimarron St, Los Angeles, 90018.
Holdings: Cat Mss
Notes: Extensive collection, first editions, etc.

CT —YALE UNIVERSITY, Art Library, 180 York St, New Haven, 06520. Nancy S Lambert, Art Librn
Holdings: Cat
Notes: Extensive collection of all editions obtainable. *The Yale University Library* Gazette, July 1970, lists 117 items not yet in the collection, as collated against John Robert Moore's compilation of *A Checklist of the Writings of Daniel Defoe* (Bloomington, Indiana: University of Indiana Press, 1960).

IN —INDIANA UNIVERSITY, Lilly Library, Seventh St, Bloomington, 47405. William R Cagle, Librn
Holdings: Vols 550 Cat
Notes: Incl 550 first and early printings by or relating to Defoe.

MD —JOHNS HOPKINS UNIVERSITY, Milton S Eisenhower Library, Charles & 34 Sts, Baltimore, 21218. Ann S Gwyn, Assistant Dir for Special Collections
Holdings: Vols Cat Mss Microforms
Notes: The Osler Collection (Tudor and Stuart Club) contains original editions of Shelley, Milton, Keats, Donne, Defoe, Thomas Fuller, Golden Book of Marcus Aurelius (1559). A collection of his articles made by Walt Whitman. 17th and 18th century commonplace books in English and French, in ms. Most English translations of Jakob Boehme. Cards in main catalog. Also, not included in the above figure, Pollard and Redgrave's, and Wing's Early English Books on microfilm.

MI —UNIVERSITY OF MICHIGAN, Library, Dept of Rare Books & Special Collections, Ann Arbor, 48109. Robert J Starring, Head
Holdings: Vols 1600 Cat
Notes: The bulk of the holdings are editions, translations, adaptations and imitations of *Robinson Crusoe* and form part of the Hubbard Collection of Imaginary Voyages.

MI —DETROIT PUBLIC LIBRARY, Rare Books Department, 5201 Woodward Ave, Detroit, 48202.
Notes: Espec editions of *Robinson Crusoe.*

DE FORD, MIRIAM ALLEN, 1888-1975

PA —TEMPLE UNIVERSITY LIBRARIES, Special Collections Dept, Conwellana-Templana Collection, 13 & Berks St, Philadelphia, 19122. Miriam I Crawford, Cur
Holdings: Vols 30 Cat Mss Pix
Notes: Miriam Allen De Ford was a prolific writer on a variety of topics, including history, biography, social reform and crime stories. Her books, as well as a number of the 25 Little Blue Books she wrote for J H Haldeman, are in the Collection, along with correspondence, proofs, and clippings related to her writings and the typescript, page proof and galleys of her *Stone Walls.* The Socialist activities of her husband, Maynard Shipley, are detailed in *Up Hill All the Way* and in some of the correspondence.

DEFOREST, JOHN W.

CT —YALE UNIVERSITY, Box 1603A, Yale Station, New Haven, 06520.

DE FOREST, LEE

CA —ELECTRONICS MUSEUM, Foothill College, DeForest Memorial Archives, 12345 El Monte Rd, Los Altos Hills, 94022. Leonard M Lansdowne, Cur
Holdings: Vols 342 Cat Mss Pix Microforms
Notes: The collection was donated by Marie de Forest, wife of the late Dr Lee De Forest, known as the Father of Radio. Awards of Dr Lee de Forest, presented to him through the years, are in the collection. The De Forest mss and papers are cataloged and microfilmed. Several file cabinets filled with correspondence, dealing with business and personal matters are to be cataloged and microfilmed in the future.

DEFORMITIES

†NY —MEDICAL RESEARCH LIBRARY OF BROOKLYN, Academy of Medicine of Brooklyn & The State University of New York Downstate Medical Center, 450 Clarkson St, Brooklyn, 11203. Kenneth E Moody, Dir
Notes: Extensive collection of 18th-19th century material.
See also entry under Medicine.

TX —SOUTHWEST FOUNDATION FOR RESEARCH AND EDUCATION LIBRARY, Preston C Northrup Memorial Library, Baboon Information Center, W Loop 410 at Military Dr, PO Box 28147, San Antonio, 78284. Dorothy M Brooks, Baboon
Notes: Principle field of research: Birth defects, atherosclerosis, reproductive physiology, cancer, genetics, organic chemistry, parasitology, primatology and behavioral sciences and their application to

DEFORMITIES (cont.)

problems of drug abuse, alcoholism and ecology. Maintains the largest baboon colony in the world.

DEGREES OF LATITUDE AND LONGITUDE see Geodesy

DE HARTOG, JAN

TX —UNIVERSITY OF HOUSTON, M D Anderson Memorial Library, University Park, Houston, 77004. David Farmer, Cur, Special Collections; Jean Jackson, Assistant Cur
Holdings: Vols 20 // Uncat Mss Audiotapes
Notes: The collection incl copies of his books, his own journals, notes, and working drafts of some of his books.

DEHAVEN, LT. EDWIN J.

MD —US NAVAL ACADEMY, Nimitz Library, Annapolis, 21402. Alice S Creighton, Assistant Librn for Special Collections
Holdings: Mss
Notes: Papers, etc.

DE ISLA, JOSE FRANCISCO, S.J., 1703-1781

DC —GEORGETOWN UNIVERSITY, Library, Special Collections Div, 37 & O Sts NW, Washington, 20057. George M Barringer, Special Collections Librn; Nicholas B Sheetz, Mss Librn
Notes: The Isla Collection. Four 18th century mss dealing with the satire on bad preaching, *Historia del Famoso predicador Fray Gerundio de Campazas alias Zotes*, by the Jesuit priest Jose Francisco de Isla (1703-1781).

DEISM

IL —NORTHWESTERN UNIVERSITY, Library, Special Collections Dept, 1937 Sheridan Rd, Evanston, 60201. R Russell Maylone, Cur
Holdings: Vols 920 Cat

DEJA VU

NY —PARAPSYCHOLOGY SOURCES OF INFORMATION CENTER, 2 Plane Tree Lane, Dix Hills, 11746. Rhea A White, Dir
Holdings: Vols (4000)
Notes: The PSI Center includes 4000 books, 100 periodical titles, cassette tapes, and unpublished mss dealing with parapsychology and the transformation of consciousness, also 12,000 articles, reprints, etc. There is a charge for reference service and bibliographies.

DE KOVEN, REGINALD

WI —UNIVERSITY OF WISCONSIN, MADISON, Mills Music Library, 728 State St, Madison, 53706. Arne Arneson, Music Librn
Holdings: // Uncat Mss
Notes: Tams-Witmark Collection formed part of the rental collection of the firm bearing that name. Incl piano-conductor scores (some in mss); ca 65 sets of orchestral parts for operas; 70 vocal scores of works by American composers incl Herbert, Sousa, Edwards and De Koven; ca 100 sets of orchestral parts of comic operas; ca 4000 vocal scores of European operas. Restricted use.

DE LA BEDOYERE, COUNT MICHAEL

DC —GEORGETOWN UNIVERSITY, Library, Special Collections Div, 37 & O Sts NW, Washington, 20057. George M Barringer, Special Collections Librn; Nicholas B Sheetz, Mss Librn
Holdings: Mss Cat
Notes: The papers of the journalist and author, Count Michael de la Bedoyere, who edited for many years the English periodical, "The Catholic Herald." Contains for the most part correspondence from contributors and readers.

DE LA MARE, WALTER

CA —UNIVERSITY OF CALIFORNIA, LOS ANGELES, Research Library, Dept of Special Collections, 405 Hilgard Ave, Los Angeles, 90024. Edward Shreeves, Chairman, Bibliographers Group; David S Zeidberg, Head
Holdings: Vols 150 Cat Mss
Notes: 150 first and other editions of his books; 20 letters; 3 mss.

CT —TRINITY COLLEGE LIBRARY, Watkinson Library, 300 Summit St, Hartford, 06106. Jeffrey Kaimowitz, Cur
Holdings: Cat
Notes: First editions, etc.

MN —UNIVERSITY OF MINNESOTA, O Meredith Wilson Library, 309 19 Ave S, Minneapolis, 55455. Austin J McLean, Chief, Special Collections
Holdings: Vols 142 Cat
Notes: First and special editions.

NV —UNIVERSITY OF NEVADA, RENO, University Library, Special Collections Dept, Reno, 89557. Robert E Blesse, Head
Holdings: // Vols (182) Cat Other appearances 800 Cat
Notes: Includes individual works by author in all editions including translations; also prefaces, introductions, published correspondence, appearances in anthologies, periodicals, etc. Bibliographical research collection, part of Modern Authors Collection.

NY —ALFRED UNIVERSITY, Herrick Memorial Library, Alfred, 14802. June E Brown, Head Librn
Notes: The Evelyn Tennyson Openhym Collection of modern British literature and social history.

NY —HOFSTRA UNIVERSITY, Library, 1000 Fulton Ave, Hempstead, 11550. Charles R Andrews, Dean of Library Services

NC —DUKE UNIVERSITY, William R Perkins Library, Rare Book Room, Durham, 27706. John L Sharpe, III, Cur
Notes: Collection of books, manuscripts, and periodicals is virtually complete; it lacks two book titles, and only a few periodical issues are wanting.

†NC —WAKE FOREST UNIVERSITY, Z Smith Reynolds Library, Box 7777, Reynold Sta, Winston-Salem, 27109.
Notes: A significant collection.

OH —OHIO UNIVERSITY, Vernon R Alden Library, Department of Archives and Special Collections, Athens, 45701. Gary A Hunt, Head
Holdings: Vols (10,191) Uncat Mss
Notes: The Edmund Blunden Collection of Romantic and Modern Literature, being the private library assembled by Blunden during 6 decades of active collecting. The bulk of the collection (6,264 titles) consists of English imprints from the period 1750-1850, concentrating on literature but also incl contemporary works on art, natural history, philosophy and other subjects important for understanding the background of English Romanticism. Among the authors most heavily represented by first and other early editions are: Allington, Barnes, Bloomfield, Byron, Clare, Coleridge, Cowper, Dyer, Edgeworth, Goldsmith, Hazlitt, Hunt, Lamb, Landor, Scott, Thompson and Wordsworth. Books written by Blunden himself, together with his Georgian contemporaries (particularly W H Davies, Walter De la Mare, and Sigfried Sassoon) form a second major area of strength. Many ofthe modern books are inscribed to Blunden, and nearly all the volumes in the collection bear his annotations.

PA —BRYN MAWR COLLEGE, Canaday Library, Bryn Mawr, 19010. James Tanis, Dir
Notes: Rare books in the Adelman Collection.

PA —TEMPLE UNIVERSITY LIBRARIES, Special Collections Dept, Rare Books & Mss Section, Philadelphia, 19122. Thomas M Whitehead, Cur
Holdings: Vols 400 Cat Mss Pix Microforms
Notes: Extensive collection on all aspects of the life and work of the author. Collection incl the Sydney Cockerell and Walter R Bett Collections; books and letters relating to De la Mare; books from his library; first, limited and association copies. Selected catalog (exhibition) issued in 1969. Incl about 1000 letters.

DELAMBRE, JEAN-BAPTISTE-JOSEPH

MN —UNIVERSITY OF MINNESOTA, O Meredith Wilson Library, 309 19 Ave S, Minneapolis, 55455. Austin J McLean, Chief, Special Collections
Holdings: Vols (103) // Cat Mss
Notes: Basically mathematical astronomy with emphasis on eclipses. Particular strengths are the works of such authors as Delambre, Euclid, Newton, Ptolemy, and Rhaticus. Important in this respect are 6 of the 10 known printed editions of the Alphonsine Astronomical Tables.

DELANEY, MARTIN

ON —CHATHAM PUBLIC LIBRARY, 120 Queen St, Chatham, N7M 2G6, Can. Arlene Mason, Head of Reference
Holdings: Vols 20 Cat
Notes: Books, pamphlets, and articles on Henry Bibb, William King, Martin Delaney, and John Brown and their work in the Chatham, Ont region.

DELANY, SAMUEL R.

MA —BOSTON UNIVERSITY, Mugar Memorial Library, Special Collections Dept, 771 Commonwealth Ave, Boston, 02215. Howard B Gotlieb, Dir
Holdings: Cat Mss Pix
Notes: Mss, correspondence, etc collected in depth; incl publications by or about.

DE LA ROCHE, MAZO

BC —UNIVERSITY OF VICTORIA, McPherson Library, Victoria, V8W 3H5, Can.

DELAWARE

NJ —SUSSEX COUNTY LIBRARY, Rd 3, Box 76, Newton, 07860. Judith Gessel, Reference Librn
Holdings: Cat Maps Slides 16mm Films Filmstrips
Notes: The Sussex County Area Reference Library is one of several locations which were named repositories for materials related to the restudy of the Tocks Island Lake Project. The items in the repository were distributed by the Delaware River Basin Commission. Collection incl study-related hearing transcripts, public notices, press clippings, correspondence, and reports of concern to the Delaware Water Gap National Recreation Area/Tocks Island Area. The Tocks Island Regional Advisory Council, when disbanded, presented its library to the Sussex County Library in 1974. The collection incl reports, surveys, maps, slides, and other materials collected or produced by TIRAC since 1965.

DELAWARE—GENEALOGY

DE —HISTORICAL SOCIETY OF DELAWARE, Library, 505 Market St Mall, Wilmington, 19801. Barbara E Benson, Library Dir
Holdings: Vols 1000 Cat Mss Microforms
Notes: Printed works fully cataloged. Emphasis on Delaware families, but supporting material from adjacent states. Delaware census material on microfilm; 8 linear feet of manuscript genealogical notes and charts; extensive surname file (10,000 entries); good run of *New England Historical and Genealogical Register.*

FL —ORLANDO PUBLIC LIBRARY, Local History & Genealogy Dept, 100 Block of

DELAWARE—GENEALOGY (cont.)

Central Ave, Orlando, 32806. Eileen B Willis, Librn
Holdings: Vols 11,000 Cat Maps Microforms
Budget: $8000
Notes: Genealogy collection on Md, Del, W Va, NC, SC, Ala, Miss, La, Texas, Ark, Ky, Ohio, Ill, Ind, and Mich are well represented. Most other states are covered by smaller collections.
See also entry under Genealogy - Collections.

PA —BALCH INSTITUTE FOR ETHNIC STUDIES, Library, 18 S Seventh St, Philadelphia, 19106. R Joseph Anderson, Library Dir
Notes: The Amandus Johnson Collection of his papers, incl biographical material on 20th century Swedish-Americans, records from the American Swedish Historical Museum in South Philadelphia, and source documents on the early Swedish settlement of the Delaware Valley, and historical writings based on these documents.

DELAWARE—HISTORY

DE —UNIVERSITY OF DELAWARE, Hugh M Morris Library, S College Ave, Newark, 19711. T Stuart Dick, Special Collections
Holdings: Cat Mss Maps Pix
Notes: History of Delaware, its families, institutions, customs and economics. Materials pertaining to the University's history are held in a separate unit: University of Delaware Archives. Also, papers of Delaware political figures Willard Saulsbury (qv) and John Lukens (see Lukens Family).

DE —HISTORICAL SOCIETY OF DELAWARE, Library, 505 Market St Mall, Wilmington, 19801. Barbara E Benson, Library Dir
Holdings: Vols 1500 Cat Mss Maps Pix Slides Microforms
Notes: Catalog complete for secondary sources, mss indexed. Photographs: 50 linear feet plus 55 linear feet of glass plate negatives. Maps: 400. Microfilm: 300 reels. Excellent collection of Delaware. Newspapers: 1750 linear feet of Delaware and other newspapers. Manuscripts: 120 linear feet. There is no printed catlog for the ms section with the exception of a listing of ms books (130 linear feet) published in *Delaware History* Vol XI, No 1 (April, 1964), pp 65-82. The collection includes the papers of such prominent Delawareans as George Read, the Rodneys, Commodore John P Gillis. Also part of the collection are the papers of the Bank of Delaware, the Chesapeake and Delaware Canal and the New Castle and Frenchtown RR. We have Delaware census material on microfilm.

DE —WIDENER UNIVERSITY, Delaware Campus Library, Box 7139, Concord Pike, Wilmington, 19803. Jane E Hukill, Library Dir
Holdings: Vols (48,000) Cat Mss Maps
Notes: Delaware Valley history.

DE —HENRY F DUPONT WINTERTHUR MUSEUM LIBRARY, Winterthur, 19735. Frank H Sommer, III, Head
Holdings: Cat
Notes: Strong collections.

IL —AUGUSTANA COLLEGE, Swenson Swedish Immigration Research Center, Rock Island, 61201. Kermit Westerberg, Archivist
Holdings: Vols 5000 Cat Mss Maps Pix Microforms
Notes: The largest collection of Swedish-Americana in this country. Many rare books relative to the Delaware Swedes (latter half of 17th century). Most of the valuable (rare) materials are gifts. The unique Swedish-American newspaper collection (with the cooperation of the Royal Library, Stockholm) has been microfilmed. Letters and papers of pioneer pastors are especially significant. The Lars Esbjorn, Eric Norelius, T N Hasselquist and Olof Olsson (all clergymen) letters are of foremost importance. (Listed in *NUC of Manuscript* Collections).

NY —HOLLAND SOCIETY OF NEW YORK, Library, 122 E 58 St, New York, 10022. Linda Rolufs, Librn
Notes: Specializes in New Netherland (New York, New Jersey, Delaware) history during the Dutch period, materials on the Dutch Reformed Church, and Dutch-American family genealogy.

PA —PHILADELPHIA MARITIME MUSEUM, Library, 321 Chestnut St, Philadelphia, 19106. Dorothy H Mueller, Librn
Holdings: Vols (8000) Cat Mss Maps Pix Slides 16mm Films
Notes: Maritime history of Bay and River Delaware and of the port of Philadelphia. Includes shipbuilding and shipbuilders on the Delaware River, mercantile activity, recreational activity, maritime-related organizations, institutions and people, development of Philadelphia as a port, vessel registers 1878-1970s. Also, artifacts and prints.

PA —FRIENDS HISTORICAL LIBRARY OF SWARTHMORE COLLEGE, Swarthmore, 19081. J William Frost, Dir
Holdings: Vols (35,000) Cat Mss Pix Microforms
Notes: Library's collection contain information on the history and doctrine of the Society of Friends, Quaker contributions to literature, science, business, education, and government, plus their reform efforts in peace, Indian rights, women's rights, and abolition of slavery. As an official depository of the records of the Philadelphia Yearly Meeting, the library holds, either in the original manuscript or on microfilm, records of Friends meetings in Delaware. Among the over 250 mss collections are several which concern Delaware Quaker leaders and Quaker families.

RI —BROWN UNIVERSITY, John Hay Library, 20 Prospect St, Providence, 02912. Mark N Brown, Cur Mss
Holdings: / / Mss
Notes: Some papers of Thomas Rodney, a farmer, Revolutionary War officer, member of the Continental Congress, Judge of the Delaware Supreme Court, and US Judge for the Mississippi Territory. 73 letters, essays, poems, documents, notes on court cases in Mississippi and Delaware for the period 1791-1810, and a journal for 1792-1800 about personal matters and Delaware politics. Register available.

DELAWARE—INDUSTRIES

DE —HAGLEY MUSEUM AND LIBRARY, Eleutherian Mills-Hagley Foundation Inc, PO Box 3630, Greenville, 19807. Richmond D Williams, Dir; Heddy A Richter, Imprints Librn
Notes: Records of the Bancroft, Simpson and Eddystone Textile Firms in Delaware and Pennsylvania (1830-1961; 650 cubic feet). The archive incl administrative, accounting, purchasing, production, and personnel records documenting the history of this important Delaware Valley textile manufacturer.

DELAWARE INDIANS

KS —WYANDOTTE COUNTY HISTORICAL SOCIETY, Museum, Trowbridge Research Library, 631 N 126 St, Bonner Springs, 66012. Stephen J Allie, Archivist
Holdings: Vols 3000 Mss Maps Pix Slides Audiotapes Microforms
Budget: $12,500
Notes: Emphasis on Wyandotte County. Cataloged. Incl 100 maps, 4000 photographs. Also County Records 1855-1820. Cataloged.

NJ —BRIDGETON FREE PUBLIC LIBRARY, George J Woodruff Museum of Indian Artifacts, 150 E Commerce St, Bridgeton, 08302. Anthony M Butler, Library Dir
Holdings: Vols (100) Cat Mss Maps Videotapes
Notes: Among the 20,000 artifacts, the oldest items are Folsom points, other items of the Adena and Hopewell periods, with the most recent items those of the Lenni Lenape (after 900 AD) and other local Delaware Indians being represented. Supportive book colletion.

ON —CHATHAM PUBLIC LIBRARY, 120 Queen St, Chatham, N7M 2G6, Can. Arlene Mason, Head of Reference
Holdings: Mss
Notes: Material on the Indians of Kent County, Ont, incl articles and books on the Pottawatamis and Chippewas of Walpole Island Reserve and on the Delaware Indians brought to Canada by the Moravian Missionaries in 1792 (the Fairfield Mission).

DELAWARE NEWSPAPERS see Newspapers, Delaware

DELAWARE VALLEY

DE —HAGLEY MUSEUM AND LIBRARY, Eleutherian Mills-Hagley Foundation Inc, PO Box 3630, Greenville, 19807. Richmond D Williams, Dir; Heddy A Richter, Imprints Librn
Holdings: Vols (25,000)
Notes: The Library's large collection of trade catalogs are fully accessible through our card catalog with further access provided by a chronological file. The collection emphasizes the products of Delaware Valley and Chesapeake area manufacturers and distributors in the chemical, iron and steel, leather, railway and petroleum industries from 1880 to 1920.

DE —UNIVERSITY OF DELAWARE, Hugh M Morris Library, S College Ave, Newark, 19711. T Stuart Dick, Special Collections
Notes: The personal and business papers of many prominent Delaware Valley politicians, merchants, lawyers, engineers. A few of those represented are the Latimer Shipping Papers, David Lenox (qv), John Lukens (see Lukens Family entry), Samuel Meredith (qv), George Messersmith (qv), and Willard Saulsbury (qv). Among the literary papers are collections of personal correspondence, holograph manuscripts of poetry, short stories and novels. Those represented include, among others, John Malsolm Brinnin, Erskine Caldwell, Waldo Frank, Elizabeth Jennings, Robert Underwood Johnson, Donald Justice, Walter Lowenfels, Howard McCord, Arthur Mizener, Ulrick O'Connor, Ishmael Reed, Carl Sandburg, Gilbert Sorrentino, Kurt Vonnegut, Tennesse Williams, William Carlos Williams, Edmund Wilson, Louis Untermeyer, William Butler Yeats, the *Pagany* archives, *Signature* archives, and Proscenium PressPapers.

PA —HAVERFORD COLLEGE, Magill Library, Quaker Collection, Haverford, 19041. Edwin B Bonner, Librn & Cur
Holdings: Vols (32,000) Cat Mss Maps Pix Phonorecords Audiotapes Microforms
Notes: Incl material about Society of Friends from inception in England, 1650, to the present. Formats incl periodicals, diaries, documents of individual Friends, families, Quaker Meetings and institutions, incl archives of Haverford College. Emphases on American Indians, antislavery, women, minorities, the Rufus M Jones Mysticism collection, Quaker fiction, and Delaware Valley, Pennsylvania.

PA —BALCH INSTITUTE FOR ETHNIC STUDIES, Library, 18 S Seventh St, Philadelphia, 19106. R Joseph Anderson, Library Dir
Notes: The Amandus Johnson Collection of his papers, incl biographical material on 20th century Swedish-Americans, records from the American Swedish Historical Museum in South Philadelphia, and source documents on the early Swedish settlement of the Delaware Valley, and historical writings based on these documents.

PA —FREE LIBRARY OF PHILADELPHIA, Social Science and History Dept, Map Collection, Logan Sq, Philadelphia, 19103.
Holdings: Vols (30,000) Cat Mss Maps
Notes: Map collection incl atlases, maps, pamphlets, and aerial views. Incl a representative collection of early atlases (1534-1827). The collection emphasizes the Philadelphia, Pennsylvania and Delaware Valley areas in particular and the eastern

DELAWARE VALLEY (cont.)

seaboard in general. Low altitude oblique aerial photographs have been transferred to the Print and Picture Dept; high altitude vertical aerial photographs have been retained; some volumes and pamphlets reassigned within the Social Science and History Dept.

PA —PHILADELPHIA MARITIME MUSEUM, Library, 321 Chestnut St, Philadelphia, 19106. Dorothy H Mueller, Librn
Holdings: Vols (8000) Cat Mss Maps Pix Slides 16mm Films
Notes: Maritime history of Bay and River Delaware and of the port of Philadelphia. Includes shipbuilding and shipbuilders on the Delaware River, mercantile activity, recreational activity, maritime-related organizations, institutions and people, development of Philadelphia as a port, vessel registers 1878-1970s. Also, artifacts and prints.

†PA —TEMPLE UNIVERSITY LIBRARIES, Special Collections Dept, Urban Archives Center, Philadelphia, 19122. Thomas Whitehead, Cur of Mss
Holdings: Mss
Notes: Ms collection focusing on urban life and development and drawing on the Philadelphia metropolitan area since the Civil War. Incl the papers of several private organizations, such as the Philadelphia Housing Association (1909-1972); Delaware Valley Regional Planning Commission (1965-1972); Greater Philadelphia Movement (1949-1976); YWCA of Philadelphia (1870-1960); YMCA of Philadelphia (1854-1970); Health and Welfare Council of Philadelphia (1922-1969); United Fund of Philadelphia and Vicinity (1920-1975); Philadelphia Urban League (1935-1967); ACLU-Philadelphia Chapter (1948-1975); Legal Aid Society of Philadelphia (1933-1976); etc.

PA —FRIENDS HISTORICAL LIBRARY OF SWARTHMORE COLLEGE, Swarthmore, 19081. J William Frost, Dir
Holdings: Vols (35,000) Cat Mss Pix Microforms
Notes: Library's collection contain information on the history and doctrine of the Society of Friends, Quaker contributions to literature, science, business, education, and government, plus their reform efforts in peace, Indian rights, women's rights, and abolition of slavery. As an official depository for the records of Philadelphia Yearly Meeting, the library holds, either in the original manuscript or on microfilm, records of Friends meetings in the Delaware Valley. Among the more than 250 mss collections are papers of individual Quaker leaders, families, and organizations.

DELAWARE WATER GAP

NJ —SUSSEX COUNTY LIBRARY, Rd 3, Box 76, Newton, 07860. Judith Gessel, Reference Librn
Holdings: Cat Maps Slides 16mm Films Filmstrips
Notes: The Sussex County Area Reference Library is one of several locations which were named repositories for materials related to the restudy of the Tocks Island Lake Project. The items in the repository were distributed by the Delaware River Basin Commission. Collection incl study-related hearing transcripts, public notices, press clippings, correspondence, and reports of concern to the Delaware Water Gap National Recreation Area/Tocks Island Area. The Tocks Island Regional Advisory Council, when disbanded, presented its library to the Sussex County Library in 1974. The collection incl reports, surveys, maps, slides and other materials collected or produced by TIRAC since 1965.

DELBRUCK, MAX

CA —CALIFORNIA INSTITUTE OF TECHNOLOGY, Robert A Millikan Memorial Library, Archives, 1201 E California Blvd, Pasadena, 91125. Judith R Goodstein, Archivist
Holdings: Vols (3000) Cat Mss Maps Pix Slides Phonorecords Audiotapes Videotapes 16mm Films Microforms
Notes: Ms sources for the history of astrophysics, cosmology, mathematical physics, experimental physics, radio astronomy, geophysics and biophysics. Collections incl the papers of: George Ellery Hale, Jesse Greenstein, H P Robertson, Richard Feynman, Paul Epstein, Max Delbruck, and Beno Gutenberg. Candid photos of physicists at meetings; etchings and photographs of Einstein; scientific medals; selected pieces of scientific apparatus (including the oil-drop machine constructed by Millikan at Caltech in the early 1920s); the reprint collection of Paul Epstein; over 3000 landmark books in the history of 20th century physics and mathematics. Printed publications include: Daniel Kevles, *Guide to the Microfilm Edition of the George Ellery Hale Papers* (Pasadena, Carnegie Institute of Washington and Caltech), 1968; Judith R Goodstein,*The Robert Andrews Millikan Collection at the California Institute of Technology: Guide to a Microfilm Edition* (Pasadena, Caltech), 1977; Judith R Goodstein and Carolyn Kopp, *The Theodore von Karman Collections at the California Institute of* Technology (Pasadena, Archives), 1981.

DELDERFIELD, R. H.

MA —BOSTON UNIVERSITY, Mugar Memorial Library, Special Collections Dept, 771 Commonwealth Ave, Boston, 02215. Howard B Gotlieb, Dir
Holdings: Cat Mss
Notes: Mss, collected in depth; incl publications by or about.

DELFORD-KENT PAPERS

NY —STATE UNIVERSITY OF NEW YORK, COLLEGE AT PLATTSBURGH, Feinberg Library, Special Collections, 153 Hawkins Hall, Plattsburgh, 12901. Joseph G Swinyer, Librn
Holdings: Cat Mss Maps Pix
See also entry under New York (State) - History

DELINQUENCY, JUVENILE see Juvenile Delinquents and Delinquency

DELINQUENTS AND DELINQUENCY

IN —INDIANA LAW ENFORCEMENT ACADEMY, David F Allen Memorial Learning Resources Center, Rd 700 E, PO Box 313, Plainfield, 46168. Donna K Zimmerman, Librn
Holdings: Vols (4500) Cat Slides 16mm Films
Budget: ($8500)
Notes: Concentrated in the areas of police science, criminology, and law.

MO —CENTRAL MISSOURI STATE UNIVERSITY, Ward Edwards Library, Warrensburg, 64093. Nancy E Littlejohn, Social Sciences Librn
Holdings: Vols (8000) Cat Microforms
Budget: ($7500)
Notes: Extensive criminal justice and law collection. In addition, a 7593 title microfiche collection of criminal justice and juvenile delinquency.

NJ —RUTGERS, THE STATE UNIVERSITY OF NEW JERSEY, John Cotton Dana Library, 185 University Ave, Newark, 07102. Phyllis Schultze, Librn
Holdings: Vols 40,000 Cat
Notes: National Council on Crime and Delinquency. Criminology, as applied, means all phases of crime and delinquency prevention, control and treatment, ie, the whole "criminal justice" gamut: police, courts, probation and parole, prisons, community rehabilitation centers, etc. In short, everything except police laboratory materials. Collection completely cataloged; all criminological and correctional journals indexed. Incl many reports of correctional agencies, research reports, unpublished monographs, publications in the field by all government agencies, federal, state, county and local. Information file contains over 40, 000 such items, as well as about 10,000 uncataloged clippings and other pieces of information stored by specific subjects.

OH —OHIO STATE UNIVERSITY, Social Work Library, 1947 N College Rd, Columbus, 43210. Toyo S Kawakami, Librn
Holdings: Vols (46,410) Cat
Budget: ($11,960)
Notes: VF incl approx 4500 pamphlets, arranged by LC subject headings. 278 serial titles on social work, social and public service, crime and delinquency, corrections, criminal justice, marriage and the family, probation, and related topics, are received.

TX —WEST TEXAS STATE UNIVERSITY, Cornette Library, PO Box 748 WT Sta, Canyon, 79016. Faye Hendrickson, Special Collections Asst
Holdings: Vols (451,253) Uncat Microforms
Notes: Includes microform collection.

WI —UNIVERSITY OF WISCONSIN, MADISON, Law School Library, Criminal Justice Reference & Information Center, Madison, 53706. Sue Center, Librn
Holdings: Vols (29,000) Cat Mss
Budget: ($45,000)
Notes: In-depth subject access is provided to collection by our own cataloging and classification systems. Incl are periodical articles which are selectively cataloged to supplement the collection. Special items in collection incl penal press (prisoner newspapers); annual and statistical reports from criminal justice agencies throughout the US and Canada; theses and dissertations; and 280 periodical titles in the field of criminal justice.

ON —UNIVERSITY OF TORONTO, Centre of Criminology, Library, 130 St George St, Rm 8001, Toronto, M5S 1A5, Can. Catherine J Matthews, Librn
Holdings: Vols (20,000) Cat
Notes: Over 4500 research reports, article reprints, theses, etc. Extensive newspaper clippings file from 1963 to present indexed under 350 subject headings. The collection covers criminology, law enforcement and policing, delinquency, criminal justice system, penology and corrections. Acquisitions list published three times a year; subscription.

DELL, FLOYD

IL —NEWBERRY LIBRARY, 60 W Walton St, Chicago, 60610. Diana Haskell, Cur of Modern Mss
Holdings: Cat Mss Pix
Notes: Primary repository of about 4000 pieces. Restriced use; noncirculating.

DELL PUBLISHERS

DC —LIBRARY OF CONGRESS, Rare Book & Special Collections Div, Washington, 20540. William Matheson, Chief
Notes: The division has an archival set of the Dell paperback books published from 1943-76.

DEL MONTE CORPORATION

CA —STANFORD UNIVERSITY, Graduate School of Business, J Hugh Jackson Library, Stanford, 94305.
Holdings: Vols (316,994) Cat Microforms Corporate Reports
Budget: ($255,000)
Notes: Incl 590,027 microforms, 300,000 corporate reports, and 2344 periodical subscriptions. Library Publications: *Selected Additions to the J Hugh Jackson Library* (bimonthly); and *Catalog of Jackson Library Periodicals and Annuals on Standing Order* (annual).

DELMARVA POWER COMPANY

DE —HAGLEY MUSEUM AND LIBRARY, Eleutherian Mills-Hagley Foundation Inc,

DELMARVA POWER COMPANY (cont.)

PO Box 3630, Greenville, 19807. Richmond D Williams, Dir; Heddy A Richter, Imprints Librn
Notes: Records of Pennsylvania Power & Light Company (1853-1955; 1000 cubic feet). The archive consists of the records of 1050 predecessor companies that merged over a 75-year period (1880-1955) to form the present-day PP&L. The collection describes the industry's tentative beginnings using the Edison system of direct current, the technological innovations which allowed small, innercity utilities to expand beyond their original urban centers, and the consolidation movement that culminated with the formation of a great regional power network. Also, records of Delmarva Power Company (1890-1965; 60 cubic feet).

DE LONGCHAMPS, FREDERIC

NV —UNIVERSITY OF NEVADA, RENO, University Library, Special Collections Dept, Reno, 89557. Robert E Blesse, Head
Holdings: Cat Mss Pix
Notes: Approximately 15,000 drawings, along with papers and photographs of three major Nevada architects. Frederic DeLongchamps, 1882-1969, was Nevada's most important for the first half of the 20th century designing many major public buildings. Edward S Parsons, Nevada's most prolific architect, did over 725 jobs between 1935 and 1983. Hewitt Wells designed the Washoe County Library, an internationally known building. These collections constitute the major holdings of the Nevada Architectural Archives.

DELUSIONS see Superstition; Witchcraft

DEMAIO, ERNEST

IL —CHICAGO HISTORICAL SOCIETY, Library, Clark St at North Ave, Chicago, 60614. Archie Motley, Manuscript Librn
Notes: Papers of trade unions and political activists.
See also entry under Labor-History

DEMARIA, ROBERT

MA —BOSTON UNIVERSITY, Mugar Memorial Library, Special Collections Dept, 771 Commonwealth Ave, Boston, 02215. Howard B Gotlieb, Dir
Holdings: Cat Mss Correspondence

DEMENTIA PRAECOX see Schizophrenia and Schizophrenics

DEMENTIA, PRESENILE see Presenile Dementia

DE MILLE, AGNES

NY —NEW YORK PUBLIC LIBRARY, Performing Arts Research Center, Dance Collection, 111 Amsterdam Ave, New York, 10023. Genevieve Oswald, Cur
Budget: ($9,280)
Notes: Extensive biographical and visual material. Includes photographs, scrapbooks, clippings and programs, dance notation scores, original drawings, 45 films, and 20 tape-recorded interviews or speeches. The Agnes De Mille Papers, 1927 to date, contain correspondence, scenarios and choreographic notes for ballets and musical comedy productions, notebooks, holographs, and drafts of articles and books.

DE MILLE, CECIL B.

CA —ACADEMY OF MOTION PICTURE ARTS & SCIENCES, Margaret Herrick Library, 8949 Wilshire Blvd, Beverly Hills, 90211. Linda Harris Mehr, Library Administrator
Notes: Stills collection.
See also entry under Moving Pictures.

UT —BRIGHAM YOUNG UNIVERSITY, Harold B Lee Library, Unversity Hill, Provo, 84602. Sterling Albrecht, Dir
Holdings: Vols (162,000) Mss
Notes: Archives of Cecile B De Mille. 400 cubic ft.

DE MILLE, WILLIAM C.

NY —NEW YORK PUBLIC LIBRARY, Performing Arts Research Center, Billy Rose Theatre Collection, 111 Amsterdam Ave, New York, 10023. Dorothy L Swerdlove, Cur
Holdings: Cat Mss Pix
Notes: Papers, scrapbooks, mss, photographs, memorabilia, etc.

DEMING, BARBARA

MA —BOSTON UNIVERSITY, Mugar Memorial Library, Special Collections Dept, 771 Commonwealth Ave, Boston, 02215. Howard B Gotlieb, Dir
Holdings: Mss Pix
Notes: Mss, correspondence, etc collected in depth.

DEML, JAKUB

MA —HARVARD UNIVERSITY LIBRARY, Widener Library, Slavic Collections, Cambridge, 02138. Hugh M Olmsted, Slavic Dept Head
Holdings: Cat Mss
Notes: Unequalled outside Czechoslovakia.

DEMOCRACY AND COMMUNISM see Communism and Democracy

DEMOCRATIC NATIONAL COMMITTEE

DE —UNIVERSITY OF DELAWARE, Hugh M Morris Library, S College Ave, Newark, 19711. T Stuart Dick, Special Collections
Holdings: // Cat Mss
Notes: Incl business, legal, personal and politcial papers of Willard Saulsbury, spanning 1850-1927. Saulsbury was a US Senator from Delaware. Incl letters and telegrams from Woodrow Wilson relating to the work of the Democratic National Committee, party politics, etc (1912-1918).

†MA —JOHN F KENNEDY LIBRARY, Columbia Point, Boston, 02125. Dan H Fenn Jr, Dir
Holdings: // Cat Mss
Notes: Records of the DNC relating to the conventions of 1952 and 1956 and the Presidential campaigns of 1952, 1956, 1960; meetings of the Committee; and research and background papers, 1952-1963. 330 linear ft of mss. Holdings are described in Historical Materials of the John F Kennedy Library. Copies may be obtained by writing the Research Archivist.

NM —EASTERN NEW MEXICO UNIVERSITY, Golden Library, Special Collections, Portales, 88130. Mary Jo Walker, Special Collections Librn
Notes: Papers and files of the late Congressman Harold Runnels (D NMex).

NY —CORNELL UNIVERSITY LIBRARIES, Collection of Regional History, Dept of Manuscripts and Univ Archives, Ithaca, 14853.
Notes: Scrapbook, 1900, of US Presidential election campaign; .2 ft.

DEMOCRATIC STUDY GROUP, U.S. HOUSE OF REPRESENTIVES

DC —LIBRARY OF CONGRESS, Manuscript Division, Washington, 20540. John C Broderick, Chief
Holdings: 60,000 Items
Notes: Records of the Democratic Study Group of the House of Representatives.

DEMOGRAPHY

DC —POPULATION REFERENCE BUREAU, Joseph Sunnen Library, 1337 Connecticut Ave NW, Washington, 20037. Janice Beattie, Dir, Library & Information Servs
Holdings: Vols 10,000 Documents Journals
Notes: Data search-Popline, Dialog. Incl 460 journals.

GA —UNIVERSITY OF GEORGIA, Libraries, Special Collections Division, Athens, 30602. Vesta Lee Gordon, Asst Dir for Special Collections
Notes: The Arbitron Collection of television and radio program ratings, 1949-date (except past year). In-depth, statistical analyses of the listening public by age, sex, county, some ethnic groups, farm population, listening preferences, etc. 26,302 bound vols. 2 reports, 1949-81. To be added to annually.

HI —BANK OF HAWAII, Information Ctr, PO Box 2900, Honolulu, 96846. Sally Campbell, Information Mgr
Holdings: Vols 4000 Cat Maps VF
Notes: Economics research in developing areas of Hawaii, US Pacific Islands, Asian and other foreign countries. Emphasis on economics, business statistics, demography, finance, banking, tourist industry, construction, domestic and foreign trade. Incl 1000 serial titles.

†HI —EAST-WEST POPULATION INSTITUTE RESOURCE MATERIALS COLLECTION, 1777 East-West Rd, Honolulu, 96848.
Notes: Demography, population problems and policy in Hawaii, Asian countries and Pacific area, family planning programs, environment.

MA —FRANCIS A COUNTWAY LIBRARY OF MEDICINE, Boston Medical Library/ Harvard Medical Library, 10 Shattuck St, Boston, 02115. C Robin LeSueur, Librn; Richard J Wolfe, Cur, Rare Books & Manuscripts
Holdings: Cat Mss microforms

MA —HARVARD UNIVERSITY, Center for Population Studies, 665 Huntington Ave, Boston, 02115. Wilma E Winters, Librn
Holdings: Vols (20,000) Cat
Notes: Incl books and pamphlets.

NJ —PRINCETON UNIVERSITY, Office of Population Research, Library, 21 Prospect Ave, Princeton, 08540. Thomas Holzmann, Librn
Holdings: Vols (25,000) Cat Mss Maps Microforms
Notes: The library is attached to the Office of Population Research, which publishes the *Population Index.* Library is particularly strong in statistical materials, such as worldwide population censuses and vital statistics; it is less strong in the biomedical aspects of population research. Incl 10,000 reprints, pamphlets, mss, etc. ILL requests should be addressed to Princeton Universtiy Library, Interlibrary Services.

NY —NEW YORK PUBLIC LIBRARY, Research Libraries, Economic & Public Affairs Div, Fifth Ave & 42 St, New York, 10018. Edward DiRoma, Chief
Holdings: Vols (1,500,000) Cat Microforms
Notes: Very strong in national censuses.

NY —STATE UNIVERSITY OF NEW YORK, STONY BROOK, Biology Library, Stony Brook, 11794. Doris Williams, Biology Librn
Holdings: Vols 625 // Uncat
Notes: Raymond Pearl Collection. The collection contains reprints collected by Raymond Pearl, founder of the *Quarterly Review of Biology.* The reprints are indexed by author and arranged by twenty subjects relating to biology and the history of science.

NC —CAROLINA POPULATION CENTER, Library, University Sq E, Chapel Hill, 27514. Patricia Shipman, Head Librn
Holdings: Vols 20,000 Cat Mss Microforms
Budget: ($10,500)
Notes: This is the largest population library in the world (65,000 citations). Emphasis is on the socioeconomic aspects of population, particularly population dynamics, population policy, fertility, the family, formal demography, family planning, and population education. The catalog to the entire collection is on microfiche and offers 6 types of access: author, title, series, major subject term, location number. Library data base is available on database on *Dialog,* population bibliography. Selected searches are available in Library.

OK —SOCIETY FOR THE NORTH AMERICAN CULTURAL SURVEY, Dept of Geography, Oklahoma State University,

DEMOGRAPHY (cont.)

Stillwater, 74078. John Rooney, Dir; Todd Zdorkowski, Asst
Notes: Has produced a cultural atlas of North America that describes the regional variations in North America's folk and popular sub populations.

PA —UNIVERSITY OF PITTSBURGH, Economics/Center for Regional Economics Studies Library, 4956 Forbes Quad, Pittsburgh, 15260. Patricia Suozzi-Crehan, Librn
Holdings: Vols 20,000
Budget: ($25,724)
Notes: Card catalog for collection. Cards for Economics Collection are in Hillman Library catalog. Collections are working collections reflecting the research and teaching interests of the Dept of Economics faculty and graduate students. The collection covers all aspects of the field of economics and demography.

TX —UNIVERSITY OF TEXAS LIBRARIES, Population Research Center Library, 1701 Main Bldg Tower, Austin, 78712. Doreen S Goyer, Librn
Holdings: Vols (20,000) Cat Microforms
Budget: ($3000)
Notes: The International Census Collection contains population censuses of 200 nations and territories, current and retrospective. Combined holdings of several University of Texas libraries constitute 80 percent of the items cited in the *International Population Census Bibliography* (original 6 volumes with 1 supplement and other revisions and updates), with the majority of items in the Population Research Center. Other books, monographs, journals and reprints also support this subject.

ON —NATIONAL LIBRARY OF CANADA, 395 Wellington St, Ottawa, K1A 0N4, Can. Andre Preibish, Dir
Holdings: Vols 10,000
Notes: Includes 130 serial titles, theses, pamphlets, government publications relating to family and marriage. The following disciplines covered: anthropology, psychology and psychiatry, law, economics, religion, sociology, demography, education, political science and biology. Earliest title 1630.

†ON —METROPOLITAN TORONTO LIBRARY, Social Sciences Dept, 789 Yonge St, Toronto, M4W 2G8, Can. Abdus Salam, Head
Holdings: Vols Cat Maps Phonorecords Audiotapes 16mm Films Microforms
Notes: Collection includes material on the size, growth, density, distribution and ecology of human populations. Covers general theory to research materials. International in scope.

DEMOGRAPHY—HISTORY

IN —PURDUE UNIVERSITY LIBRARIES, Graduate School of Management, Krannert Library, West Lafayette, 47907. Gordon Law, Librn
Notes: An important resource at the Krannert Library is its Special Collection of Business and Economics, consisting of some 8000 rare pre-20th century strengths in books, journals, tracts and pamphlets covering primarily the early literature of economic thought and business practices in America and abroad, 1500-1870. A catalog was issued in 1979.

DEMONOLOGY

CA —GRADUATE THEOLOGICAL UNION LIBRARY, New Religious Movements Research Collection, Public Services and Special Collections Dept, 2400 Ridge Road, Berkeley, 94709. Diane Choquette, Dept Head
Holdings: (3000 Vols) Mss Pix
Notes: Begun in 1977, the collection focuses on religious movements new to America since 1960, and unorthodox religious movements resurgent since 1960. American forms of Hinduism, Buddhism, Sikhism, and Sufism are included along with occultism, New-Paganism, esoteric and alternative forms of Christianity, feminist spirituality, and human potential movements having a spiritual aspect. Legal issues, such as deprogramming, and the question of church/state relations are an important part of the collection. The Library is a depository for publications of the Unification Church in America, the Church of Scientology, and the International Society for Krishna Consciousness (America). The *responses* of mainstream religions and concerned citizens groups are also included. Besides 3000 monographs, the library has 350 periodical titles, 200 posters from the San FranciscoBay Area, 1965-77, 300 research papers, and 24 linear feet of ephemera.

CA —LOS ANGELES PUBLIC LIBRARY, Philosophy & Religion Dept, 630 W Fifth St, Los Angeles, 90071. Marilyn C Wherley, Librn
Holdings: Vols 700 Cat
Budget: ($60,000)
Notes: Comprehensive coverage of popular and scholarly works on all aspects of the occult including black magic, witchcraft, demonology, paranormal occurances, psychical research and metaphysics. Includes many serials, periodicals and special indexes.

CT —LEE ASH, (personal collection), 66 Humiston Dr, Bethany, 06525.
Notes: Incl mss, books, ephemera, prints.

CT —TRINITY COLLEGE LIBRARY, Watkinson Library, 300 Summit St, Hartford, 06106. Jeffrey Kaimowitz, Cur
Holdings: Cat

CT —YALE UNIVERSITY, Medical Historical Library, Klebs Collection, 333 Cedar St, New Haven, 06520. Ferenc A Gyorgyey, Librn
Holdings: Cat Mss Pix

IL —NEWBERRY LIBRARY, 60 W Walton St, Chicago, 60610. Diana Haskell, Cur of Modern Mss
Holdings: Cat
Notes: Renaissance and 17th century.

IL —UNIVERSITY OF ILLINOIS, URBANA/CHAMPAIGN, Library, University Archives, 19 Library, 1408 W Gregory Drive, Urbana, 61801. Maynard Brichford, University Archivist
Holdings: Vols (5000) Cat
Budget: ($7000)
Notes: The Mandeville Collection in Parapsychology and Occult Sciences. Titles in the Merten J Mandeville Collection are purchased by funds from an endowment provided specifically for the collection on its establishment in 1966 by Merten J Mandeville, Professor Emeritus of Management, who donated 400 vols from his personal library as the nucleus of the collection. There are currently about 5000 titles in the collection, supplemented by related materials in the general collection. Topics include astrology, extrasensory perception, yoga, magic, satanism, faith healing, hypnosis, Eastern religions, witchcraft, fortune telling, reincarnation, flying saucers, ghosts, dreams, numerology, graphology, and mysticism. Biographies and reference books are a part of the collection as are journals devoted to the scientific study of parapsychology.

IN —INDIANAPOLIS-MARION COUNTY PUBLIC LIBRARY, Social Sciences Div, PO Box 211, Indianapolis, 46206. Lois R Laube, Head
Holdings: Vols 358 Cat
Notes: Restricted use. No photocopying.

MI —MICHIGAN STATE UNIVERSITY, Libraries, Special Collections Div, East Lansing, 48824. Jannette Fiore, Librn
Holdings: Vols 1440// Uncat Mss
Notes: Works from 15th to 19th centuries on criminology, criminal law and jurisprudence, including witchcraft, demonology, et al, chiefly in German and Latin.

OH —CLEVELAND PUBLIC LIBRARY, Fine Arts and Special Collections Department, 325 Superior Ave, Cleveland, 44114. Alice N Loranth, Head
Holdings: Vols (1600) Cat
Notes: Part of the Witchcraft Collection, which incl witchcraft, magic, sorcery, magical manuals, devil worship, incantations, charms, talismans, amulets and spells. Contemporary urban practices are almost entirely omitted.
See also entry under Folklore; Witchcraft

RI —BROWN UNIVERSITY, John Hay Library, 20 Prospect St, Providence, 02912. Mark N Brown, Cur Mss
Holdings: Vols (900) // Mss
Notes: John William Graham Collection of Literature of Psychic Science--350 predominantly late 19th and early 20th century books dealing with alchemy, black magic, dreams, demonology, church history, mysticism, mediumship, physical and somatic types of psychic experience. Collection described in *Index to Psychic* Science compiled by S R Morgan (Swathmore, 1950). Also, the Damon Collection of Occult and Visionary Literature--550 vols devoted to the development of western mysticism with particular emphasis on American and British thought, incl texts on alchemy, black magic, esoteric church history, dream interpretations, mysticism, witchcraft, the Kabbalah, and visionary testaments and manifestations of all types printed during the 16th to 20th centuries; and the Samuel Wyllys Papers--125 mss, transcripts, and photocopies of legal and government papers relating to Indianaffairs, colonial wars, civil and criminal cases, and the witchcraft trials of 1692-1693. Partially cataloged.

ON —UNIVERSITY OF GUELPH, McLaughlin Library, Guelph, N1G 2W1, Can. Margaret Beckman, Head Librn; David Hull, Sciences Librn
Holdings: Vols 1200
Budget: $1000
Notes: Monographs. Based on the original collection of Rabbi Bernard Baskin, Hamilton, Hamilton, Ontario, now much enlarged. Especially strong in Scottish related items. Incl rare volumes.

DEMOTIC INSCRIPTIONS see Egyptian Language and Literature

DEMPSEY, DAVID

MA —BOSTON UNIVERSITY, Mugar Memorial Library, Special Collections Dept, 771 Commonwealth Ave, Boston, 02215. Howard B Gotlieb, Dir
Holdings: Cat Mss

DEMPSEY, JOHN N.

†CT —CONNECTICUT STATE LIBRARY, Hartford, 06106.
Notes: Papers of many Connecticut governors, senators and congressmen, incl John Dempsey, Abraham Ribicoff, and Thomas J Dodd.

DEMPSTER, GERMAINE

CO —UNIVERSITY OF COLORADO, Libraries, Special Collections, Boulder, 80309. Nora J Quinlan, Head
Holdings: // Cat
Notes: Incl 6 boxes of Germaine Dempster notes on Chaucer, notebooks, mss, reprints, microfilms, and correspondence.

DENDROLOGY see Trees

DENMARK

NY —DANISH INFORMATION OFFICE, Library, 280 Park Ave, New York, 10017.
Holdings: Vols 2500 Uncat Maps Pix Slides 16mm Films
Notes: Noncirculating.

DENMARK—HISTORY

CA —CLAREMONT COLLEGES, Honnold Library, Ninth & Dartmouth, Claremont, 91711. Franklin D Scott, Cur, Nordic Collection; Penelope Garris, Librn
Holdings: Vols (25,000) Cat Maps Pix Slides Audiotapes Videotapes Periodicals
Budget: ($5000)
Notes: Nordic Collections are broadly

DENMARK—HISTORY (cont.)

inclusive, but emphasize history of Scandinavia, Baltic countries, and Hanseatic cities. Nucleus of collections from gifts and endowment of Waldemar Westergaard, supplemented with relevant collections of David Bjork, John H Wuorinen, Ingolf Olsen, Henry Steele Commager, Franklin Scott and other gifts and purchases. Eight vertical file drawers of news bulletins in English or vernaculars, 1941-. See: Franklin D Scott, "The Westergaard-Bjork Collection at the Honnold Library, the Claremont Colleges," *Scandinavian Studies*, 41 (1969), 346-354. Collection incl complete publications of Nordic Council.

IL —NORTHWESTERN UNIVERSITY, Library, Special Collections Dept, 1937 Sheridan Rd, Evanston, 60201. R Russell Maylone, Cur
Holdings: Vols 400 Cat
Notes: World War II underground publications (serials and monographs). Additional 550 vols from Netherlands; 65 vols from Norway; 80 vols from misc other European countries under Nazi occupation.

NE —DANA COLLEGE, C A Dana-Life Library, Blair, 68008. Ronald D Johnson, Head Librn
Holdings: Vols (10,000) Cat Audiotapes
Notes: Strong emphasis on Danish literature although we include other Scandinavian countries. Have an oral history tape collection with recordings of Danish emigrants to the midwest. Our book collection is strongest in the literature area with history a close second.

WA —UNIVERSITY OF WASHINGTON LIBRARIES, Suzzallo Library, Scandinavian Collections, FM-25, Seattle, 98195. A Gerald Anderson, Librn
Holdings: Vols (50,000) Cat Mss Pix
Budget: ($15,546)
Notes: Research collections with emphasis on languages and literatures, and auxiliary strengths in history, political science, social science. Archival and other special materials relating to Scandinavian-Americans in the Pacific Northwest are located in other appropriate collections.

DENNEE, CHARLES

DC —LIBRARY OF CONGRESS, Music Division, Washington, 20540.
Notes: The business papers and music mss of the Arthur P Schmidt Company. Numerous works by important composers.

DENNIS, EUGENE AND PEGGY

WI —STATE HISTORICAL SOCIETY OF WISCONSIN, Archives, 816 State St, Madison, 53706. Harold L Miller, Reference Archivist
Notes: Papers of Eugene and Peggy Dennis, Communist Party activists, 1926 - date. He was national head, CP, USA. Papers trace development of CIO in '30s, Farmer-Labor-Progressive Federation, and other Wisconsin and national political groups. Much on Senator Joseph McCarthy.

DENNIS, PATRICK

MA —BOSTON UNIVERSITY, Mugar Memorial Library, Special Collections Dept, 771 Commonwealth Ave, Boston, 02215. Howard B Gotlieb, Dir
Holdings: Cat Mss

DENNISON, DAVID M.

MI —UNIVERSITY OF MICHIGAN, Libraries, Michigan Historical Collections, Ann Arbor, 48109. Mary Jo Pugh, Reference Archivist
Notes: Papers, 1927-76.

DENNISON, WILLIAM

OH —RUTHERFORD B HAYES LIBRARY, 1337 Hayes Ave, Fremont, 43420. Watt P Marchman, Dir
Notes: Correspondence in the Lyman-Lincoln Collection.

DENOMINATIONS, RELIGIOUS see Religion; Sects

DENSMORE, FRANCES

DC —LIBRARY OF CONGRESS, American Folklife Center, Archive of Folk Culture, Washington, 20540.
Notes: Frances Densmore's archive of 2500 recordings of 35 tribal groups. Also, her personal papers, annotated notebooks, etc.

DENSON, ALAN

IL —NORTHERN ILLINOIS UNIVERSITY, Founders Memorial Library, Rare Books and Special Collections Dept, De Kalb, 60115. William R DuBois, Dept Head
Holdings: Vols 30 // Cat Mss
Notes: The Alan Denson Collection. Emphasis on George Russell, "A E." Includes Denson's correspondence with many mid-20th century literary figures. Mss indexed but not cataloged.

IN —INDIANA UNIVERSITY, Lilly Library, Seventh St, Bloomington, 47405. William R Cagle, Librn
Notes: Many of the vols are from the library of A E. Mss incl both his correspondence and writings and the papers of his biographer, Alan Denson.

DENT, JOHN HORRY, 1815-1892

AL —TROY STATE UNIVERSITY, Library, Troy, 36081. Kenneth Croslin, Dir of University Libraries
Holdings: // Mss
Notes: Incl the John Horry Dent Papers, 1851-1892, 25 vols, mss, farm journals, account books, letters, legal documents, clippings and miscellaneous memorabilia of a planter, plantation owner, investor, who lived in Barbour County, Alabama from 1837 to 1867 and in Floyd County, Georgia from 1867 to 1892. Typescript from tape "Sharecropping farming in Pike County, Alabama in early 1900's" (56p). Typescript of tapes of "Source material extracted from Troy, Alabama newspapers, 1871-1935" indexed under 9 subjects by color code.

DENTAL ASSISTANTS

FL —BREVARD COMMUNITY COLLEGE, Learning Resources Center, Cocoa Campus, Clearlake Rd, Cocoa, 32922. John S French, Ref Librn
Holdings: Vols 48 Cat
Notes: This collection development new to our library; contains few periodical titles plus printed texts.

NH —NEW HAMPSHIRE TECHNICAL INSTITUTE, Paul E Farnum Library, 5 Fan Rd, Concord, 03301. Wm John Hare, Librn
Holdings: Vols 900 Cat Slides 16mm Films
Budget: $600

NC —TECHNICAL INSTITUTE OF ALAMANCE, Learning Resources Center, Jimmy Kerr Rd, PO Box 623, Haw River, 27258. Ron Plummer, Coordr
Holdings: Vols 465 Cat Slides Audiotapes Filmstrips Microforms

DENTAL HYGIENE

NH —NEW HAMPSHIRE TECHNICAL INSTITUTE, Paul E Farnum Library, 5 Fan Rd, Concord, 03301. Wm John Hare, Librn
Holdings: Vols 900 Cat Slides
Budget: $1000

DENTAL MEDICINE see Teeth—Diseases

DENTAL ORTHOPEDICS see Orthodontia

DENTAL PATHOLOGY see Teeth—Diseases

DENTISTRY

AL —UNIVERSITY OF ALABAMA, BIRMINGHAM, Lister Hill Library of the Health Sciences, University Sta, Birmingham, 35294. Richard B Fredericksen, Dir

CA —UNIVERSITY OF CALIFORNIA, LOS ANGELES, Biomedical Library, Center for the Health Sciences, Los Angeles, 90024. Alison Bunting, Acting Biomedical Librn; Victoria Steele, Head, History & Special Collections Div
Holdings: Vols (400,000) Cat Slides Phonorecords Audiotapes Videotapes 16mm Films Microforms
Notes: The UCLA Biomedical Library serves primarily the Schools of Medicine, Dentistry, Nursing, and Public Health, the UCLA Medical Center, the Departments of Microbiology and Biology in the College of Letters and Science, and related institutes in biomedicine. The collections of the Library are broad in scope, designed not only to support the teaching and research needs of its many users, but also to function as a resource for the health sciences-biological field as a whole. The outstanding feature of the collection is the strength of its periodical holdings, both current and retrospective. The Library also has an excellent reference collection, a comprehensive historical section, and gives special emphasis to the fields of neuroscience, psychiatry, ophthalmology, radiation biology, molecular biology, and vertebrate zoology. Increased emphasis is being given to the acquisition of audiovisual materials.

CA —UNIVERSITY OF SOUTHERN CALIFORNIA, School of Dentistry, Library, Den 201, University Park MC-0641, Los Angeles, 90089. Frank O Mason, Dir of Library Services
Holdings: Vols 20,700 Cat Mss Pix Slides Audiocassettes Filmstrips
Budget: $45,000
Notes: Dentistry and allied sciences.

CA —UNIVERSITY OF CALIFORNIA, SAN FRANCISCO, Library, San Francisco, 94143. David Bishop, University Librn
Holdings: Vols (502,261) Cat
Budget: ($642,604)

CT —UNIVERSITY OF CONNECTICUT HEALTH CENTER, Lyman Maynard Stowe Library, Farmington, 06032. Ralph D Arcari, Dir of Libraries
Holdings: Vols 28,950 Cat Slides Audiotapes Microforms
Budget: $96,450
Notes: Incl basic sciences supporting biomedical collection, biomedical research and clinical medicine. Separate catalog for AV materials. Library produces book catalogs of serial and audiovisuals titles.

CT —YALE MEDICAL LIBRARY, 333 Cedar St, New Haven, 06510.
Holdings: Vols (334,215) Cat Mss Pix Slides Microforms
Budget: ($361,650)
Notes: Incl films, audiotapes, artifacts, etc.

DE —US VETERANS ADMINISTRATION CENTER, Medical Library, Wilmington, 19805. Mrs Donald Passidoma, Chief Librn
Holdings: Vols (5000) Cat
Notes: Staff only.

GA —EMORY UNIVERSITY, School of Dentistry, Sheppard W Foster Library, 1462 Clifton Rd NE, Atlanta, 30322. Kathryn J Torrent, Librn
Holdings: Vols 18,210 Cat
Budget: $109,724

IL —AMERICAN DENTAL ASSOCIATION, Bureau of Library Services, 211 E Chicago Ave, Chicago, 60611. Aletha Kowitz, Librn & Dir
Holdings: Vols 35,000 Cat Microforms
Notes: Publish *Index to Dental Literature*.

DENTISTRY (cont.)

IL —NORTHWESTERN UNIVERSITY, Dental School Library, 311 E Chicago Ave, Chicago, 60611. Minnie Orfanos, Dir
Holdings: Vols 67,987 Cat Mss Pix Slides Microforms
Notes: Special collections: G V Black mss and artifacts; George Teuscher mss and artifacts; NUDS archives: anesthesia, old prints, rare books, dental proceedings. Incl 16,000 pamphlets.

†IL —NORTHWESTERN UNIVERSITY, Medical School, Archibald Church Library, 303 E Chicago Ave, Chicago, 60611. Cecile E Kramer, Librn
Holdings: Cat Mss Pix Slides
Notes: Incl about 3000 vols, 5100 pictures and 1200 slides concerning the history of medicine.

IN —INDIANA UNIVERSITY, School of Dentistry, Library, 1121 W Michigan St, Indianapolis, 46202. Marie Sparks, Librn
Holdings: Vols (50,000) Cat Mss Slides Audiotapes Films Microforms
Budget: ($41,790)
Notes: Juvenile dentistry, scanning electron microscopy, pediatrics and basic sciences.

MD —UNIVERSITY OF MARYLAND, BALTIMORE, Health Sciences Library, 111 S Greene St, Baltimore, 21201. Cyril C H Feng, Dir
Holdings: Vols 2168 Cat

MA —BOSTON UNIVERSITY, Medical Center, Alumni Medical Library, 80 E Concord St, Boston, 02118. Irene Christopher, Chief Librn
Holdings: VOls 89,448

MA —FRANCIS A COUNTWAY LIBRARY OF MEDICINE, Boston Medical Library/ Harvard Medical Library, 10 Shattuck St, Boston, 02115. C Robin LeSueur, Librn; Richard J Wolfe, Cur, Rare Books & Manuscripts
Holdings: Vols (500,000) Cat Mss Pix Microforms
Budget: ($1,160,000)
Notes: Unites holdings of Boston Medical Library, Harvard's Faculty of Medicine (incl school of Dental Medicine) and Faculty of Public Health. Rare books include 800 incunabula. In resources for medical research the collection is believed to be surpassed in the United States only by the National Library of Medicine.

MA —TUFTS UNIVERSITY, Health Sciences Library, 136 Harrison Ave, Boston, 02111. Elizabeth K Eaton, Dir
Holdings: Vols (91,252) Cat Slides Phonorecords Audiotapes Videotapes Microforms
Budget: ($220,055)
Notes: Incl 219 titles, 4 journal titles, 653 videotapes, 3104 microfilms, 7027 microcards, and 1051 serials.

MN —UNIVERSITY OF MINNESOTA, Bio-Medical Library, Diehl Hall, Minneapolis, 55455. Gertrude Foreman, Acting Dir
Holdings: Vols (263,361)
Budget: ($500,000)

MO —UNIVERSITY OF MISSOURI-KANSAS CITY, School of Dentistry Library, 650 E 25 St, Kansas City, 64108. Anne Marie Corry, Librn
Holdings: Vols 19,813 Cat Mss Pix Slides Audiotapes Videotapes 16mm Films Filmstrips
Budget: $20,000
Notes: Incl 14,269 slides, 363 audiotapes, 444 videotapes, 17 16mm films and 213 filmstrips. Also incl Dental History collection (717 vols; mss and pictures).

MO —WASHINGTON UNIVERSITY, School of Dental Medicine, Library, 4559 Scott Ave, Saint Louis, 63110. Carol Murray, Chief Librn
Holdings: Vols 18,000

NJ —FAIRLEIGH DICKINSON UNIVERSITY, School of Dentistry, Library, 110 Fuller Place, Hackensack, 07601. Ruth Schwartz, Dir
Holdings: Vols 12,759 Cat Pix Slides Audiotapes Videotapes 16mm Films Filmstrips Microforms
Notes: Incl 28,534 slides, 365 audiotapes, 493 videotapes, 82 16mm films, 9 filmstrips and 1256 microforms.

NJ —UNIVERSITY OF MEDICINE AND DENTISTRY OF NEW JERSEY, George F Smith Library of the Health Sciences, 100 Bergen St, Newark, 07103. Philip Rosenstein, Dir of Libraries
Holdings: Vols (110,000) Cat Slides Audiotapes Videotapes 8mm Films Filmstrips Microforms
Budget: ($380,880)
Notes: There is a separate a/v catalog available, arranged by main entry and incl a tracings index. Incl 70,648 slides, 19,298 microforms, 395 8mm films, 2150 audiotapes.

†NY —MEDICAL RESEARCH LIBRARY OF BROOKLYN, Academy of Medicine of Brooklyn & The State University of New York Downstate Medical Center, 450 Clarkson St, Brooklyn, 11203. Kenneth E Moody, Dir
Holdings: Vols 4000 Cat
See also entry under Medicine.

NY —STATE UNIVERSITY OF NEW YORK, COLLEGE AT BUFFALO, Health Sciences Library, Stockton Kimball Tower, Buffalo, 14214. C K Huang, Dir
Holdings: Vols (222,108) Cat
Budget: ($493,931)

NY —BOOTH MEMORIAL MEDICAL CENTER, Health Education Library, Main St at Booth Memorial Ave, Flushing, 11355. Rita Maier, Library Dir
Holdings: Vols (3000) Cat Audiotapes
Notes: Incl 7000 bound journals; software slide tape programs.

NY —SUFFOLK ACADEMY OF MEDICINE, Health Sciences Library, 850 Veterans Memorial Highway, Hauppauge, 11788. Isabel V Hathorn, Dir
Holdings: Vols (13,000) Cat Videotapes Microforms

NY —COLUMBIA UNIVERSITY LIBRARIES, Health Sciences Library, 701 W 168 St, New York, 10032. Rachael K Goldstein, Librn
Notes: Restricted.
See also entry under Medicine

NY —NEW YORK UNIVERSITY DENTAL CENTER, John and Bertha E Waldmann Memorial Library, 345 E 24th St, New York, 10010. Roy C Johnson, Librn
Notes: Incl 300 vols published before the nineteenth century. Books and other historical dental materials from the Weinberger Collection, the Blum Collection, the Mestel St Apollonia Collection, and New York University College of Dentistry Archives. Also incl 9000 monographs.

NY —UNIVERSITY OF ROCHESTER, School of Medicine and Dentistry, Edward G Miner Library, 601 Elmwood Ave, Rochester, 14642. Lucretia McClure, Medical Librn; Janet Brady Berk, History of Medicine Librn
Holdings: Vols (185,000) Cat
Notes: The Edward G Miner Library serves the School of Medicine & Dentistry, the School of Nursing, and Strong Memorial Hospital. The collection encompasses all the biomedical fields, nursing and dental research, and is designed to serve the teaching, patient care and research needs of persons in the Medical Center. The Library subscribes to more than 2900 current journals and serials, has an excellent reference collection and an extensive collection of rare and historical works in medicine and nursing.
See also entry under Medicine - History and Historic

NC —UNIVERSITY OF NORTH CAROLINA, CHAPEL HILL, Health Sciences Library, 223 H, Chapel Hill, 27514. Samuel Hitt, Dir
Holdings: Vols (200,000) Cat Slides Journals Audiotapes Videotapes Microforms
Budget: ($560,000)

OK —UNIVERSITY OF OKLAHOMA, Health Sciences Center, Library, 1000 Stanton L Young Blvd, PO Box 26901, Oklahoma City, 73190. C M Thompson, Jr, Dir
Holdings: Vols (155,434) Cat Slides Audiotapes Videotapes 16mm Films Microforms
Budget: ($374,960)

OR —OREGON HEALTH SCIENCES, University Libraries, PO Box 573, Portland, 97207. James E Morgan, Dir
Holdings: Vols (178,373) Cat Mss Pix Slides Audiotapes Videotapes Microforms
Notes: Libraries incl a medical/nursing library and a separate dental library. Medical history collection of books and artifacts emphasizes the Pacific Northwest.

OR —OREGON HEALTH SCIENCES UNIVERISTY LIBRARY, Dental Branch, 611 SW Campus Dr, Portland, 97201. Dolores Z Judkins, Librn
Holdings: Vols 16,000 Cat
Budget: $100,000

PA —COLLEGE OF PHYSICIANS OF PHILADELPHIA, Library, 19 S 22 St, Philadelphia, 19103. Anthony Aguirre, Libr Dir
Holdings: Vols (316,223) // Cat Mss Microforms
Budget: ($1,096,557)
Notes: Incl 13,515 pamphlets; 1435 mss; 326,367 reports, dissertations, and reprints. Strong historical and bibliographical collections, as well as current materials. Medical documentation service provides current alerting, incl abstracting, etc.

PA —TEMPLE UNIVERSITY, Health Sciences Center Library, Broad & Tioga Sts, Philadelphia, 19140. Ruth Diamond, Dir
Holdings: Vols (87,480) Cat Slides Microforms
Budget: ($340,950)

PA —UNIVERSITY OF PENNSYLVANIA, School of Dental Medicine, Leon Levy Library, 4001 Spruce St, Philadelphia, 19104. John M Whittock Jr, Librn
Holdings: Vols (45,000) Cat Pix Slides
Notes: Collection is comprised of 15,250 monographs, 25,250 bound periodical vols. Library currently receives about 700 dental and medical journals. Houses S S White Dental Manufacture Co collection of U S dental patents, 1797-1966, and U S and foreign dental catalogs. 1000 rare books on dentistry and oral biology. 3000 pictures and 1000 slides.

PA —UNIVERSITY OF PITTSBURGH, Falk Library of the Health Professions, History of Medicine Collection, Scaife Hall, Pittsburgh, 15261. Jonathon Erlen, Cur
Holdings: Vols (13,500) Cat Pix
Budget: ($425,269)
Notes: Medicine, dentistry, nursing, pharmacy, public health, psychiatry materials, incl some rare books and 300 pamphlets on anesthesia.

†VA —VIRGINIA COMMONWEALTH UNIVERSITY/MEDICAL COLLEGE OF VIRGINIA, Tompkins-McCaw Library, Box 667, MCV Sta, Richmond, 23298. J Craig McLean, Asst Dir of University Libraries
Holdings: Vols (155,000) Cat Mss Microforms
Budget: ($281,200)
Notes: Graduate sciences (biomedical emphasis). All newly cataloged books and journals are reported in the *Abridge Book* Catalog. Citations are limited to main entry and two subject entries. The catalog is cumulated monthly in 42x microfiche format. A cumulated Union Catalog covering 6 years and parts of 5 library collections is in preparation.

WA —UNIVERSITY OF WASHINGTON LIBRARIES, Health Sciences Library, SB-55, Seattle, 98195. Gerald J Oppenheimer, Dir

WI —MARQUETTE UNIVERSITY, Memorial Library, 1415 W Wisconsin Ave, Milwaukee, 53233. Jay Kirk, Health Sciences Librn
Notes: Supports curriculum and research.

MB —UNIVERSITY OF MANITOBA, Dental Library, 780 Bannatyne Ave, Winnipeg, R3E 0W3, Can. Doris Pritchard, Dental Librn
Holdings: Vols 16,500 Cat Slides Audiotapes Videotapes Filmstrips Microforms
Budget: $19,000

DENTISTRY—HISTORY

AL —UNIVERSITY OF ALABAMA, BIRMINGHAM, Lister Hill Library of the Health Sciences, University Sta, Birmingham, 35294. Richard B Fredericksen,

DENTISTRY—HISTORY (cont.)

Dir
Holdings: Vols 15,000 Cat Mss Pix Slides
Notes: Excellent collection of Alabama dental materials as well as monographs.

CA —UNIVERSITY OF CALIFORNIA, LOS ANGELES, Biomedical Library, Center for the Health Sciences, Los Angeles, 90024. Alison Bunting, Acting Biomedical Librn; Victoria Steele, Head, History & Special Collections Div
Holdings: Vols (21,000) Cat Mss Pix Slides Microforms
Notes: The History and Special Collections Division of the UCLA Biomedical Library owns close to 13,000 rare books comprising landmarks in biomedical history, 15th through 19th centuries. Approx 13,000 supporting monographs and serial volumes related to the history of medicine, dentistry, nursing, public health and other life sciences.

CA —UNIVERSITY OF CALIFORNIA, SAN FRANCISCO, Library, San Francisco, 94143. David Bishop, University Librn
Holdings: Vols (23,000) Cat Mss Pix
Budget: ($8500)

IL —AMERICAN DENTAL ASSOCIATION, Bureau of Library Services, 211 E Chicago Ave, Chicago, 60611. Aletha Kowitz, Librn & Dir
Holdings: Vols 35,000 Cat Microforms
Notes: Publish *Index to Dental Literature.*

IL —NORTHWESTERN UNIVERSITY, Dental School Library, 311 E Chicago Ave, Chicago, 60611. Minnie Orfanos, Dir
Holdings: Vols 67,987 Cat Mss Pix Slides Microforms
Notes: Special collections: G V Black mss and artifacts; George Teuscher mss and artifacts; NUDS archives; anesthesia, old prints, rare books, dental proceedings. Complete collection of dental school catalogs, early dental philatelγ supply catalogs. Incl 16,000 pamphlets.

IL —UNIVERSITY OF ILLINOIS AT CHICAGO, Library of the Health Sciences, 1750 W Polk St, PO Box 7509, Chicago, 60612. Robert J Adelsperger, Cur, Special Collections
Holdings: Vols 180 Cat
Notes: Published catalog: *A Catalog of the Dental Literature in the Special Collections of the Library of the Health Sciences, University Illinois at the Medical Center* (Chicago, 1972).

MD —MEDICAL & CHIRURGICAL FACULTY OF THE STATE OF MARYLAND, Library, 1211 Cathedral St, Baltimore, 21201. Joseph E Jensen, Librn
Holdings: Vols (10,000) / / Cat Mss Maps Pix
See also entry under Medicine - History and Historic

MD —UNIVERSITY OF MARYLAND, BALTIMORE, Health Sciences Library, 111 S Greene St, Baltimore, 21201. Cyril C H Feng, Dir
Holdings: Vols (1000) Cat Mss Documents Pix Art Reproductions VF
Notes: The Clarence J Grieves Dental Historical Collection is one of the strongest collections of its kind in the United States. It includes some of the most significant early dental imprints; early records of the Maryland State Dental Association; and an excellent collection of prints on early dentistry and St Apollonia.

MA —SPRINGFIELD ACADEMY OF MEDICINE, Medical Library, 1400 State St, Springfield, 01109. Margaret Stoler, Dir
Holdings: Vols (10,448) Cat
Notes: Extensive historical collection; some first editions.

MI —UNIVERSITY OF MICHIGAN, Dentistry Library, 1100 School of Dentistry, Ann Arbor, 48109. Susan I Seger, Librn
Holdings: Vols (40,250) Cat
Notes: Master theses, rare books, early minutes of the Michigan State Dental Association meetings. Research and instructional materials in dentistry.

MO —WASHINGTON UNIVERSITY, School of Dental Medicine, Library, 4559 Scott Ave, Saint Louis, 63110. Carol Murray, Chief Librn

NY —STATE UNIVERSITY OF NEW YORK, STONY BROOK, Health Sciences Library, PO Box 66, East Setauket, 11733.

NY —NEW YORK UNIVERSITY DENTAL CENTER, John and Bertha E Waldmann Memorial Library, 345 E 24th St, New York, 10010. Roy C Johnson, Librn
Notes: Incl 300 vols published before the nineteenth century. Books and other historical dental materials from the Weinberger Collection, the Blum Collection, the Mestel St Apollonia Collection, and New York University College of Dentistry Archives. Also incl 9000 monographs.

PA —UNIVERSITY OF PENNSYLVANIA, School of Dental Medicine, Leon Levy Library, 4001 Spruce St, Philadelphia, 19104. John M Whittock Jr, Librn
Holdings: Vols (45,000) Cat Pix Slides
Notes: Collection is comprised of 15,250 monographs, 25,250 bound periodical vols. Library currently receives about 700 dental and medical journals. Houses S S White Dental Manufacture Co collection of U S dental patents, 1797-1966, and U S and foreign dental catalogs. 1000 rare books on dentistry and oral biology. 3000 pictures and 1000 slides.

PA —UNIVERSITY OF PITTSBURGH, Falk Library of the Health Professions, History of Medicine Collection, Scaife Hall, Pittsburgh, 15261. Jonathon Erlen, Cur
Holdings: Vols (13,500) Cat Pix
Budget: ($425,269)
Notes: Medicine, dentistry, nursing, pharmacy, public health, psychiatry materials, incl some rare books and 300 pamphlets on anesthesia.

DENTISTRY—STUDY AND TEACHING

MI —UNIVERSITY OF MICHIGAN, Dentistry Library, 1100 School of Dentistry, Ann Arbor, 48109. Susan I Seger, Librn
Holdings: Vols (40,250) Cat
Notes: Masters theses, rare books, early minutes of the Michigan State Dental Association meetings. Research and instructional materials in dentistry.

DENTON, WINFIELD K., 1896-1972

IN —INDIANA STATE UNIVERSITY, EVANSVILLE, Library, 8600 University Blvd, Evansville, 47712. Gina R Walker, Acting Archivist
Holdings: Cat Mss
Notes: Winfield K Denton (1896-1972), Evansville attorney, legislator, congressman; correspondence and papers mainly concerning 1941 session of Indiana Legislature; also law school lecture notes and typed briefs. Covers ca 1922-1967.

DEONTOLOGY see Ethics

DEOXRIBONUCLEIC ACID see Dna

DEPARTMENT STORES

IL —CHICAGO HISTORICAL SOCIETY, Library, Clark St at North Ave, Chicago, 60614. Robert L Brubaker, Librn
Holdings: Vols (150,000) Cat
Notes: Catalogs of major mail order houses and many special industries and stores in Chicago (and some firms elsewhere) since the late 19th century.

MA —HARVARD UNIVERSITY, Graduate School of Business Administration, Baker Library, Soldiers Field, Boston, 02163. Mary V Chatfield, Librn; Florence Bartoshesky, Cur of Manuscripts and Archives
Holdings: Cat Mss
Notes: Large collection on the history of department stores. Incl the Harry E Resseguie Collection.

DEPENDENCIES see Colonies, Colonialism, and Colonization

DEPEW, CHAUNCEY MITCHELL

DC —GEORGE WASHINGTON UNIVERSITY, Gelman Library, 2130 H St NW, Washington, 20052.
Holdings: Vols (500) Cat Mss Pix
Notes: The Chauncey Mitchell Depew papers cover the period of ca 1872-1928 and include correspondence (primarily incoming), manuscript speeches and misc papers, photographs, and scrapbooks, of his Senate campaigns, travels, and obituary notices. The collection primarily reflects Depew's career as a public speaker and is cataloged as a collection with an unpublished inventory for access. The inventory includes an index of correspondents.

DEPOSITION AND SEDIMENTATION see Sedimentation and Deposition

DEPUY, WILLIAM

PA —US ARMY MILITARY HISTORY INSTITUTE, Carlisle Barracks, 17013. Richard J Sommers, Chief Archivist-Historian
Holdings: Mss Cat
Notes: 2000 boxes mss. The Viet Nam War collection, personal letters, daily logs, memoirs, speeches, and official papers of American officers and soldiers serving in Viet Nam or elsewhere in the world during the era. Almost all these papers are from Generals, incl William DePuy, Harold K Johnson, Bruce Palmer, Jonathan Seaman, and William Westmoreland.

DEPRESSIONS—1929—U.S.

CA —CALIFORNIA STATE UNIVERSITY, NORTHRIDGE, Delmar T Oviatt & South Libraries, 1811 Nordhoff St, Northridge, 91330. Donald L Read, Special Collections Dept
Notes: Three newspaper boxes. Some runs incomplete. Between 1935 and 1939, the US Government maintained camps to assist the migrant farm laborers of the Great Depression. This small collection records the activities of those camps.

IN —INDIANA STATE UNIVERSITY, EVANSVILLE, Library, 8600 University Blvd, Evansville, 47712. Gina R Walker, Acting Archivist
Holdings: Uncat Mss Pix
Notes: Visiting Nurse Association of Southwestern Indiana's scrapbooks (sometimes called "Business Diaries" and "Publicity Books") covering the activities of the Association and its staff; also clippings concerning other local social problems. 1927-1971. Unpublished guide.

TX —AMARILLO PUBLIC LIBRARY, 413 E Fourth, Amarillo, 79101. Mary Kay Snell, Librn
Holdings: Vols Cat Mss Maps Pix
Notes: The southwest collections incl materials on the history of Texas, Louisiana, New Mexico, Arkansas, Missouri and Kansas. General subjects covered incl overland journeys, early narratives, early biographies, Indian captivities, outlaws, US government reports, Mississippi and Ohio Rivers, the Mexican War, reports of Catholic missionaries, Niles Register, early publications, fur trade, western trails, Texas Rangers, sheriffs and Texas as a sovereign state, buffalo hunting, Indian wars, cowboys, the arrival of farmers, fences, and towns. Over 1600 items which incl books, documents, maps, mss, pamphlets, unpublished theses, interviews and photographs. The three major collections are the William Henry Bush Collection, the Laurence J Fitzsimon Collection and the Calendar of John L McCarty.

TX —NORTH TEXAS STATE UNIVERSITY, Archives, NT Station Box 5188, Denton, 76203. Robert LaForte, University Archivist
Notes: The NTSU Archives houses the patron's copy of oral history interviews that are part of the Oral History Collection, an independent project not part of the Archives. This collection of interviews covers, in part, the following subject areas: World War II Pearl Harbor survivors, World War II prisoners of war, Texas legislators, ex-governors of Texas, Texans employed by the

DEPRESSIONS—1929—U.S. (cont.)

administrations of FDR, Texas businessmen and businesswomen, development of the Coastal Bend area of south Texas, and Mexican-American social action activities. Cataloged. Transcriptions available. See *Oral History Collection,* North Texas State University Bulletin, April 1981.

DEPROGRAMMING (RELIGIOUS)

CA —GRADUATE THEOLOGICAL UNION LIBRARY, New Religious Movements Research Collection, Public Services and Special Collections Dept, 2400 Ridge Road, Berkeley, 94709. Diane Choquette, Dept Head
Holdings: Vols (3000) Mss Pix
Notes: Begun in 1977, the collection focuses on religious movements new to America since 1960, and unorthodox religious movements resurgent since 1960. American forms of Hinduism, Buddhism, Sikhism, and Sufism are included along with occultism, Neo-Paganism, esoteric and alternative forms of Christianity, feminist spirituality, and human potential movements having a spiritual aspect. Legal issues, such as deprogramming, and the question of church/ state relations are an important part of the collection. The Library is a depository for publications of the Unification Church in America, the Church of Scientology, and the International Society for Krishna Consciousness (America). The responses of mainstream religions and concerned citizens groups are also included. Besides 3000 monographs, the library has 400 periodical titles, 200 posters from the San FranciscoBay Area, 1965-77, 300 research papers, and 31 linear feet of ephemera.

DE QUINCEY, THOMAS

CA —FITZ HUGH LUDLOW MEMORIAL LIBRARY, PO Box 99346, San Francisco, 94109. Michael R Aldrich, Exec Cur
Holdings: Vols 50 Cat Mss Maps Pix Slides Phonorecords Audiotapes Videotapes
Notes: Collection stored. Important mail inquiries only. No interlibrary lending or telephone queries. This collections emphasis historical and literary works about opium and its derivatives, mostly in English, going back to the 17th century but mostly from the 19th and early 20th centuries. Excellent collection of De Quincey in different editions. Many books, pamphlets, and art relating to the 19th century international opium trade, the Chinese Opium Wars, clipper ships, and resulting international legal action in the early 20th century. Outstanding collection of the English, French, and American opium-addict confessional literature. Also incl many volumes and offprints relevant to narcotic drug prevention, treatment, and education.

MA —HARVARD UNIVERSITY LIBRARY, Houghton Library, Cambridge, 02138. Rodney G Dennis, Cur of Manuscripts
Holdings: Cat Mss

WI —UNIVERSITY OF WISCONSIN, MADISON, Memorial Library, British & American Language & Literature Collection, 728 State St, Madison, 53706. Yvonne Schofer, Bibliographer
Holdings: Vols (1000)// Cat
Notes: Arthur Beatty Collection. Consists of over 1000 volumes, principally in the English poetry of the Romantic period, strong in Coleridge, Tennyson, Swinburne, the prose of De Quincy and the folk poetry and balladry of Great Britain and Europe. Outstanding for its first and other editions of Wordsworth. About 200 titles in the Department of Rare Books and Special Collections; the rest is in stacks.

DEREN, MAYA

MA —BOSTON UNIVERSITY, Mugar Memorial Library, Special Collections Dept, 771 Commonwealth Ave, Boston, 02215. Howard B Gotlieb, Dir
Holdings: // Cat Mss Pix Slides
Notes: Mss, correspondence, etc collected in depth; incl publications by or about.

DERLETH, AUGUST

IN —INDIANA UNIVERSITY, Lilly Library, Seventh St, Bloomington, 47405. William R Cagle, Librn
Notes: Extensive holdings. Mss include some letters by August Derleth discussing Arkham House.

OH —KENT STATE UNIVERSITY, Libraries, Dept of Special Collections, Kent, 44242. Dean H Keller, Cur
Holdings: Vols 88 Cat Mss

WI —UNIVERSITY OF WISCONSIN, LA CROSSE, Murphy Library, 1631 Pine St, La Crosse, 54601. Edwin L Hill, Special Collections Librn
Holdings: Vols 1000 Cat
Notes: The Paul W Skeeters Collection of science fiction, fantasy, and horror literature. Complements the library's complete collection of Arkham House books, which contains many titles autographed by August Derleth, and H P Lovecraft's complete fiction and poetic works.

†WI —STATE HISTORICAL SOCIETY OF WISCONSIN, Mass Communications History Center, 816 State Street, Madison, 53706.
Notes: Kitchen Sink underground comics standing order. August Derleth's comics collection. Microfilm of comic strips and pulp magazines.

WI —UNIVERSITY OF WISCONSIN, MADISON, Memorial Library, British & American Language & Literature Collection, 728 State St, Madison, 53706. Yvonne Schofer, Bibliographer
Holdings: Vols
Notes: A collection of mystery fiction mostly of the British Golden Age of the 20s and 30s, in original and reprint form; strong holdings for H Adams, J Rhode, A Upfield, and many others. Stacks. Substantial holdings also for fantasy and science fiction, mostly in stacks; Arkham House and A Derleth materials, restricted use only.

DERMATOLOGY

CT —YALE MEDICAL LIBRARY, 333 Cedar St, New Haven, 06510.
Holdings: Vols (334,215) Cat Mss Pix Slides Microforms
Budget: ($361,650)
Notes: Incl films, audiotapes, artifacts, etc.

MN —MAYO MEDICAL LIBRARY, History of Medicine Collection, Rochester, 55905. Nancy R Hensel, Librn
Holdings: Vols (18,000) Cat Mss Maps Pix Slides
Notes: The collection consists of over 18,000 vols, 6500 of which are considered source material (rare or reprint editions of classics). 4308 items from Garrison-Morton are available in the collection. Appropriate bibliographies, biographies and histories of medicine are a part of the collection. Fields of collecting interest are anesthesiology, dermatology, cardiology, neurology, immunology and radiology. Eight medical incunabula.

PA —COLLEGE OF PHYSICIANS OF PHILADELPHIA, Library, 19 S 22 St, Philadelphia, 19103. Christine Ruggere, Cur, Historical Collections
Holdings: Vols (316,223) Cat Mss
Budget: ($1,096,557)
Notes: Very strong collection.
See also entry under Medicine

DERRICKS see Cranes, Derricks, Etc.

DESALINATION

CA —UNIVERSITY OF CALIFORNIA, BERKELEY, Giannini Foundation of Agricultural Economics, Library, 248 Giannini Hall, Berkeley, 94720. Grace Dote, Librn
Holdings: Vols (18,000) Cat Mss Maps Microforms
Notes: Noncirculating collection. No interlibrary loans. Also about 124,000 unbound vols. Open to graduate students and faculties of universities and colleges, research workers and interested public. Mostly English language materials, primarily 1900 to date. Card catalog published by G K Hall Co *Dictionary Catalog of the Giannini Foundation of Agricultural Economics Library, Univ of California,* 12 vols (Holdings thru 7/71).

MD —CHARLES COUNTY COMMUNITY COLLEGE, Learning Resource Center, PO Box 910, La Plata, 20646. J Elaine Ryan, Dean
Holdings: Vols (1500) // Uncat 16mm Films Microforms
Notes: Primarily composed of government documents, this collection emphasizes the technical aspects of waste water treatment. Additional point of emphasis is desalination.

DESAUSSURE, C. A.

SC —COLLEGE OF CHARLESTON LIBRARY, Special Collections Dept, Charleston, 29401.
Notes: Papers, 1860s, incl two memoirs entitled "The Story of My Life Up to the Beginning of the War Between the States" and "The Story of My Service in the Army of the Confederate States."

DESCANT (PERIODICAL)

AB —UNIVERSITY OF CALGARY, Libraries, Special Collections Div, 2500 University Dr, Calgary, T2N 1N4, Can.
Notes: Archives of the literary periodicals: *Tish, Imago, Ariel, Descant, Canadian Review Magazine* and *Canadian Short Story* Magazine.

DESCARTES, RENE, 1596-1650

CA —UNIVERSITY OF CALIFORNIA, LOS ANGELES, Research Library, Dept of Special Collections, 405 Hilgard Ave, Los Angeles, 90024. Edward Shreeves, Chairman, Bibliographers Group; David S Zeidberg, Head
Holdings: Vols 250 Cat
Notes: 250 first and important editions of his works as well as books about him.

IN —UNIVERSITY OF NOTRE DAME, University Libraries, Notre Dame, 46556.
Notes: The collection (600 items) is noteworthy for its many first editions of works by Descartes and many editions of the 17th and 18th centuries by famous editors and printers.

DESCENT see Heredity

DESCRIPTION AND TRAVEL see Discovery and Exploration; Travel; Voyages and Travels

DESEGREGATION see Segregation and Desegregation

DESERT AGRICULTURE

CA —UNIVERSITY OF CALIFORNIA, RIVERSIDE, University Library, Bio-Agricultural Library, Batchelor Hall, Riverside, 92521. Barbara Montanary, Head
Holdings: Vols (130,000) Cat Mss Maps Pix Microforms
Notes: The Bio-Agricultural Library (formerly the Library of Citrus Experiment Station of the University of California) is well known for its complete collections in the fields of the agriculture sciences. It is especially known for its emphasis on entomology, incl bio-control; botany, citriculture, plant sciences, nematology and plant pathology; arid and semi-arid lands research and subtropical agriculture. Specific areas of interest are avocados, dates, desert flora, jojoba, guayule and carob.

MD —US DEPT OF AGRICULTURE, National Agricultural Library, 10301 Baltimore Blvd, Beltsville, 20705. Joseph H Howard, Director
Holdings: Vols (2,000,000) Cat Mss Maps Pix Slides Microforms
Notes: Crop ecology, agro-climatic analogs; air pollution effects. Agronomy: agriculture

DESERT AGRICULTURE (cont.)

and tropical and desert agriculture. For use by the staff of the Institute. Incl 5000 pamphlet items. Former collection of American Institute of Crop Ecology.

DESERT FLORA

CA —UNIVERSITY OF CALIFORNIA, RIVERSIDE, University Library, Bio-Agricultural Library, Batchelor Hall, Riverside, 92521. Barbara Montanary, Head
Holdings: Vols (130,000) Cat Mss Maps Pix Microforms
Notes: The Bio-Agricultural Library (formerly the Library of Citrus Experiment Station of the University of California) is well known for its complete collections in the fields of the agriculture sciences. It is especially known for its emphasis on entomology, incl bio-control; botany, citriculture, plant sciences, nematology and plant pathology; arid and semi-arid lands research and subtropical agriculture. Specific areas of interest are avocados, dates, desert flora, jojoba, guayule and carob.

DESERTS

AZ —DESERT BOTANICAL GARDEN, Richter Memorial Library, 1201 North Galvin Pkwy, Phoenix, 85008. J B Cole, Librn
Holdings: Vols (4000)
Notes: Emphasis on desert and arid regions ecology and horticulture.

CA —COLLEGE OF THE DESERT, Library, 43-500 Monterey Ave, Palm Desert, 92260. Harry Walthall, Librn
Holdings: Vols 500 Cat Maps
Notes: Incl desert fauna, flora, desert literature, history, travel, etc.

NV —UNIVERSITY OF NEVADA, RENO, Desert Research Institute, PO Box 60220, Reno, 89557. Roberta Kiefer Orcutt, Librn
Holdings: Vols (10,480) Cat Maps Microforms
Notes: Incl materials in atmospheric physics, meteorology, climatology, weather modification, antarctic studies and related materials in basic sciences. Over 3000 microforms; also 1300 technical reports and 18,000 government publications.

DESHETLER, IRWIN

MI —WAYNE STATE UNIVERSITY, Walter P Reuther Library, Archives of Labor & Urban Affairs, Detroit, 48202. Philip Mason, Dir
Notes: Papers, etc of Irwin DeShetler, a prominent CIO Regional Director and National AFL-CIO Coordinator for Farm Workers.

DESIGN

DE —WIDENER UNIVERSITY, Delaware Campus Library, Box 7139, Concord Pike, Wilmington, 19803. Jane E Hukill, Library Dir
Holdings: Vols (48,000) Audiotapes Videotapes Microforms
Notes: Incl fashion design, history of costume, textiles.

IL —CHICAGO PUBLIC LIBRARY, Art Section, Fine Arts Division, 78 E Washington St, Chicago, 60602. Rosalinda I Hack, Fine Arts Division Chief; Yvonne S Brown, Head, Art Section
Holdings: Vols 42,000
Notes: Reference and circulating collection of books, periodicals, exhibition catalogs, dissertations, picture collections, and microforms on all aspects of the visual arts. Major concentration of art history, especially European, with concentration on 19th and 20th century art movements and artists. We attempt to represent the works of recognized artists past and present. The Decorative Arts are well represented especially in the areas of antiques, interior decoration, and handicrafts. The collection is supplemented by a strong periodical collection, consisting of 330 current English and Foreign subscriptions, the majority of these titles we bind, as well as strong bound retrospective collections. The visual arts is supported by a clipping File on Chicago Artists, a current exhibition catalogs collection, as well as by the microfilm collections of the*Chicago Art Institute Scrapbooks,* the *Scrapbook on Art,* Artists, and the *Index of American Design.*

IN —THE ART CENTER, Library, 120 St Joseph St, South Bend, 46601. Judy Oberhausen, Cur
Holdings: Vols (1010) Cat Slides
Notes: 500 slides. This Art Center has a specific, separate collection--"The Arts of the United States"--which has its own index and is geared toward American painting, graphics, architecture, design and decorative arts, from the 19th to the 20th century, and sculpture works on paper. Incl 32 periodical titles.

MA —HARVARD UNIVERSITY, Graduate School of Design, Frances Loeb Library, Gund Hall, Cambridge, 02138. James Hodgson, Librn
Holdings: Vols (225,000) Cat Mss Pix Slides Microforms
Budget: ($500,000)
Notes: Covers architecture, landscape architecture, city and regional planning, and urban design. Catalog, in 44 volumes, published in 1968, with 2-volume supplement in 1970, 5-volume supplement in 1974, and 3-volume supplement in 1979. It also analyzes periodical articles. Architecture collection described in *Harvard Library* Bulletin, VI (1952): pp 263-269. Noteworthy holdings incl those on Abbey of Cluny, Le Corbusier, amd Henry Hobson Richardson. Collections described in *Harvard Library* Bulletin, VI (1952), 263-269, VII (1953), 188-195, and IV (1967), 281-286.

MA —SWAIN SCHOOL OF DESIGN LIBRARY, 140 Orchard St, Sch add: 19 Hawthorn St, New Bedford, 02740. Martha Maier, Librn
Notes: Rare book collection.

MI —CRANBROOK ACADEMY OF ART, 500 Lone Pine Rd, Box 801, Bloomfield Hills, 48013. Diane Gunn, Librn
Holdings: Vols (25,000) Slides

MN —MINNEAPOLIS COLLEGE OF ART & DESIGN, Library, 200 E 25 St, Minneapolis, 55404. Richard Kronstedt, Head Librn
Holdings: Vols (50,000) Cat Slides
Notes: Incl exhibition catalogs; collection emphasis in areas of graphic design, product design, clothing design, furniture design and environmental design.

MN —UNIVERSITY OF MINNESOTA, Architecture Library, 89 Church St, Minneapolis, 55455. A Kristine Johnson, Librn
Holdings: Vols (27,000) Cat Mss
Budget: ($20,000)
Notes: Incl architecture, architectural history, landscape architecture, design methodology, housing, urban sociology, interior design, etc.

MN —WALKER ART CENTER, Staff Reference Library, Vineland Place, Minneapolis, 55403. Rosemary Furtak, Librn
Holdings: Vols 5000 Cat Pix
Notes: Incl 10,000 catalogs of individual artists; museum gallery catalogs-10,000 catalogs of major exhibitions from all over the world dating back to 1940. VF material and tapes.

NJ —NEWARK PUBLIC LIBRARY, Art & Music Dept, 5 Washington St, Newark, 07101. William J Dane, Supv
Notes: Collection of 400 contemporary shopping bags (paper) arranged by design elements such as color, overall pattern, lettering, foreign sourced, etc.

NY —PRATT INSTITUTE LIBRARY, Art & Architecture Dept, 200 Willoughby Ave, Brooklyn, 11205. Sydney Star Keaveney, Prof
Holdings: Vols (30,000) Cat Pix Slides
Budget: ($50,000)
Notes: Art and architecture, incl sculpture, photography, painting, design, costume, and commercial art. Incl 60,000 art slides. Use restricted to Pratt faculty and students.

NY —STATE UNIVERSITY OF NEW YORK, COLLEGE AT BUFFALO, Lockwood Memorial Library, Art Dept, Buffalo, 14260. Florence S DaLuiso, Cur
Holdings: Vols (38,000) Cat Microforms
Budget: ($24,735)
Notes: Collection supports curriculum of the School of Fine Art. Incl 9000 exhibition catalogs. Recent acquisitions emphasize contemporary art and environmental design. The library by reciprocal agreement contains card catalog holdings of the Albrignt-Knox Art Gallery, Buffalo, New York. Books may be obtained on interlibrary loan.

NC —NORTH CAROLINA STATE UNIVERSITY, Harry B Lyons Design Library, P. O. Box 7701, Raleigh, 27607. Maryellen LoPresti, Librn
Notes: Collection covers architecture, landscape architecture, design and related professions. Additional materials may be found on art, painting, sculpture, photography and solar energy design. The library presently houses a total of 28,000 books, periodical and serial volumes to support the curriculum. A product and trade literature file and a vertical file of pamplets are also locally cataloged in the library representing an additional 3000 items of materials available for use. A significant collection of over 50,000 cataloged slides primarily representing the areas of art and architectural history are also contained in the library facility. See *Directory of Special Libraries and Information Centers.*

AB —SOUTHERN ALBERTA INSTITUTE OF TECHNOLOGY, Learning Resources Centre, 1301 16 Ave NW, Calgary, T2M 0L4, Can. Tom Skinner, Historian
Holdings: Vols (5000) Cat Pix Slides Films Audiotapes Filmstrips Videotapes
Notes: Serves Alberta College of Art (4-year professional course).

ON —ONTARIO SCIENCE CENTRE LIBRARY, 770 Don Mills Rd, Don Mills, M3C 1T3, Can. Jeanne DuPerrault, Librn
Holdings: Pix Slides 16mm Films Videotapes
Notes: 500 films, 30,000 slides and photographs, 50 videotapes, 100 periodicals.

DESIGN—HISTORY

DC —LIBRARY OF CONGRESS, Washington, 20540.
Notes: The Charles Eames Collection of original negatives and prints of each of the 106 films he created, business correspondence from 1944 to 1978, approximately 400,000 color slides, 31,000 black-and-white photographs, production materials for exhibits, and drawings for all the major furniture designs. Acquired on a grant of $500,000 from IBM.

DESIGN, ARCHITECTURAL see Architecture—Details

DESIGN, BOOK see Book Design

DESIGN, DECORATIVE

NY —HISTORICAL SOCIETY OF EARLY AMERICAN DECORATION, 19 Dove St, Albany, 12210. Doris Fry, Dir; Laura Olf, Librn
Holdings: Cat Pix Slides
Notes: The Library is housed with the Museum Collection of the Society. Incl examples of 19th century American country painting on tin, stenciling on wood and tin, bronzing decoration on wood, English stencilled tin and wood, bronzed items, painted objects, reverse painting on glass and examples of other decorating techniques of the period. Also included is a large collection of painted recordings of designs from early articles. Many of these were done by Esther Stevens Brazer in the 1930s. Another large collection has been added since that time. The library material is related to this interest. See *The Decorator,* official publication of the Historical Society of Early American Decoration. Other publications: *The Ornamented Chair* and *The Ornamented Tray* (both ed by Zilla Rider Lea), *Antique Decorations* by Brazer.

DESIGN, DECORATIVE (cont.)

NY —LANDMARK SOCIETY OF WESTERN NEW YORK, Wenrich Memorial Library, 130 Spring Rd, Rochester, 14608.
Holdings: Vols (2000) Cat Maps Pix Slides
Budget: ($500)
Notes: Paintings, slides, drawings, as well as the Society's archives of local architecture and information on preservation and restoration techniques. Much on preservation ordinances; legal, physical and financial aspects of building preservation; local and regional history, especially of Rochester and Monroe County.

NC —NORTH CAROLINA STATE UNIVERSITY, Harry B Lyons Design Library, P. O. Box 7701, Raleigh, 27607. Maryellen LoPresti, Librn
Notes: Collection covers architecture, landscape architecture, design and related professions. Additional materials maybe found on art, painting sculpture photography and solar energy design. The library presently houses a total of 28,000 books, periodical and serial volumes to support the curriculum. A product and trade literature file and a vertical file of pamplets are also locally cataloged in the library representing an additional 3000 items of materials available for use. A significant collections of over 50,000 cataloged slides primarily representing the areas of art and architectural history are also contained in the library facility. See *Directory of Special Libraries and Information Centers.*

PA —ATHENAEUM OF PHILADELPHIA, 219 S Sixth St, Philadelphia, 19106. Roger W Moss Jr, Librn
Holdings: Vols (15,000)
Notes: Nineteenth century architecture and decorative arts.

TX —UNIVERSITY OF TEXAS LIBRARIES, Fine Arts Library, PO Box P, Austin, 78712. Carole L Cable, Fine Arts Librn
Holdings: Vols (55,000) Cat Pix

VA —UNIVERSITY OF VIRGINIA, Alderman Library, Rare Book Dept, Charlottesville, 22901. Julius P Barclay, Cur
Holdings: Vols (6500) // Mss
Notes: The Oscar Ogg Collection of Book Arts covers calligraphy, letterforms, typography, printing, and graphic arts. Contains early writing books and printed works, as well as modern manuals and other works on printing, publishing, and promotion through graphic arts. The Dept also has the Edward L Stone Collection of Printing Specimens, 3000 items. Contains materials tracing the history of printing, inks, binding styles and materials, types. Also the Tompkins Collection (2000 vols), and the Stevens Watts collection (900 vols).

ON —METROPOLITAN TORONTO LIBRARY, Fine Arts Dept, 789 Yonge St, Toronto, M4W 2G8, Can. Alan Suddon, Head
Holdings: Vols (42,000) Cat Pix Microforms
Notes: Extensive collection.

DESIGN, INDUSTRIAL

CA —CALIFORNIA COLLEGE OF ARTS & CRAFTS, Meyer Library, Broadway at College, Oakland, 94618. Robert L Harper, Head Librn
Holdings: Vols 100 Cat Pix
Notes: The Sinel Collection was given to Meyer Library after the death of Mr Sinel. It includes mock-ups and sketches for most of his industrial and graphic designs (penny weight scale; Safeway logo; various brochures; typewriters). It includes his correspondence dating from the early 1930s, when he entered the profession, until his death in 1975.

MI —GENERAL MOTORS, Design Staff Library, General Motors Technical Center, Warren, 48090. Billie Delevich, Librn
Holdings: Vols 3500
Notes: Incl 130 magazine titles, 85 drawers of automotive catalogs.

MN —MINNEAPOLIS COLLEGE OF ART & DESIGN, Library, 200 E 25 St, Minneapolis, 55404. Richard Kronstedt, Head Librn
Holdings: Vols (45,000) Cat Pix Slides

NC —NORTH CAROLINA STATE UNIVERSITY, Harry B Lyons Design Library, P. O. Box 7701, Raleigh, 27607. Maryellen LoPresti, Librn
Notes: Collection covers architecture, landscape architecture, design and related professions. Additional materials may be found on art, painting, sculpture, photography and solar energy design. The library presently houses a total of 28,000 books, periodical and serial volumes to support the curriculum. A product and trade literature file and a vertical file of pamplets are also locally cataloged in the library representing an additional 3000 items of materials available for use. A significant collection of over 50,000 cataloged slides primarily representing the areas of art and architectural history are also contained in the library facility. See *Directory of Special Libraries and Information Centers.*

ON —METROPOLITAN TORONTO LIBRARY, Fine Arts Dept, 789 Yonge St, Toronto, M4W 2G8, Can. Alan Suddon, Head
Holdings: Vols (42,000) Cat Pix Microforms
Notes: Extensive collection.

DESIGN, INTERIOR see Interior Decoration

DESIGN, STAGE see Stage Design

DESIGN, TEXTILE see Textile Design

DESIGNS, ARCHITECTURAL see Architecture—Designs and Plans

DESPRES, LEON M.

IL —CHICAGO HISTORICAL SOCIETY, Library, Clark St at North Ave, Chicago, 60614. Archie Motley, Manuscript Librn
Notes: Papers of Leon M Despres, social activist.

DESTI, MARY, 1871-1931

CA —UNIVERSITY OF CALIFORNIA, LOS ANGELES, Research Library, Dept of Special Collections, 405 Hilgard Ave, Los Angeles, 90024. Edward Shreeves, Chairman, Bibliographers Group; David S Zeidberg, Head
Notes: 3 linear feet of mss and correspondence of Mary Desti, the mother of Preston Sturges and friend of Isadora Duncan.

DESTITUTION see Poverty

DESTRUCTION OF PROPERTY see Sabotage

DESTRUCTION OF THE JEWS, 1939-1945 see Holocaust, Jewish, 1939-1945

DETAILS, ARCHITECTURAL see Architecture—Details

DETECTIVE AND MYSTERY STORIES

CA —UNIVERSITY OF CALIFORNIA, SAN DIEGO, Central University Library, Mandeville Dept of Special Collections, La Jolla, 92093. Lynda Corey Claassen, Head
Holdings: Vols (7100) Uncat Mss Pix
Notes: The Ira Wolff Collection of mystery novels and dectective fiction emphasizes English-language detective fiction from the mid-19th century to the present, containing important or first editions of the works of Agatha Christie, Dorothy L Sayers, Raymond Chandler, Dashiell Hammett, and Wilkie Collins. The Erle Stanley Gardner Collection contains 2500 volumes of this author's work, much of it in languages other than English.

CA —OCCIDENTAL COLLEGE, Library, 1600 Campus Rd, Los Angeles, 90041. Michael C Sutherland, Special Collections Librn
Holdings: Vols 16,000 Uncat Mss Pix
Notes: The outstanding Guymon Mystery and Detective Fiction Collection is being given to Occidental College by Ned Guymon of San Diego. Mr Guymon still retains much of the control over his collection, even though the bulk of it is not located at Occidental College. The collection contains first editions from 1592 to the late 1960's, both British and American. Limited photocopying is permitted under careful supervision.

†CA —UNIVERSITY OF CALIFORNIA, Library, Los Angeles, 90024.

CA —SAN DIEGO PUBLIC LIBRARY, Literature & Language Sect, 820 E St, San Diego, 92101. Alyce Archuleta, Senior Librn
Holdings: Vols 202 // Uncat
Notes: Incl mystery series from 1930s and 1940s, and early fantasy and science fiction in paperback form (will circulate). Some first editions; collections has separate author-title index (will not circulate).

CA —SAN FRANCISCO ACADEMY OF COMIC ART, Library, 2850 Ulloa, San Francisco, 94116.
Notes: Incl largest collection of pulp magazines in US. Paper copies of all major American newspapers, emphasis on Hearst papers. Extensive collection of Sherlockiana and a member of the National Sherlockiana Society. Also extensive collection of early motion picture tapes, books, magazines and posters. 19th and early 20th century children's books also in the holdings. Collection incl 1,000,000 comic strips, 22, 000 comic books, 12,500 hard cover mystery books, 8000 hard cover science fiction books and copies of all science fiction pulp magazines.

CO —UNIVERSITY OF COLORADO, Libraries, Special Collections, Boulder, 80309. Nora J Quinlan, Head
Notes: Over 1000 vols of all the works of the American mystery writer John MacDonald as well as audiocassettes of some of his more popular works. A fascinating gathering which is both an example of one of America's most successful popular writers as well as a look at the history of the paperback (most of the books are in paperback).

IL —WHEATON COLLEGE, Library, Marion E Wade Collection, Irving & Franklin Sts, Wheaton, 60187. Lyle Dorsett, Cur; Marjorie Mead, Associate Cur
Holdings: Vols (6500)
Notes: Extensive Marion E Wade Collection contains a wide variety of materials relating to the study of detection and mystery literature. Numerous materials on Dorothy L Sayers and Gilbert Keith Chesterton.

IN —INDIANA UNIVERSITY, Lilly Library, Seventh St, Bloomington, 47405. William R Cagle, Librn
Holdings: Cat Mss
Notes: Extensive collection of first editions; mss incl papers of William Anthony Parker White (Tony Boucher) and Ian Fleming's mss for 11 James Bond novels.
See also entry under Fantastic Fiction

†MD —UNIVERSITY OF MARYLAND, BALTIMORE COUNTY, Library, Baltimore, 21228. Maureen Dwyer-Hirten, Librn
Notes: 4000 detective and adventure pulps and 500 TV scripts.

MA —BOSTON UNIVERSITY, Mugar Memorial Library, Special Collections Dept, 771 Commonwealth Ave, Boston, 02215. Howard B Gotlieb, Dir
Holdings: Vols 15,000 Uncat Mss Pix
Notes: Incl literary and personal papers of more than 110 outstanding writers in the field; also first editions, translations, etc. A complete list is available.

MA —BOSTON COLLEGE LIBRARIES, Chestnut Hill, 02167.
Holdings: Vols 2400 Mss
Notes: The library and personal papers of Rex Stout, 1886-1975, creator of the Nero Wolfe detective stories. Mss incl a number of adaptations for radio and television; correspondence covers Stout's years as President of the Authors' Guild, also as

DETECTIVE AND MYSTERY STORIES (cont.)

Chairman of the Writers' War Board. For reference use only by arrangement with librarian. Incl 125 literary mss; 21 cubic ft correspondence.

MI —MICHIGAN STATE UNIVERSITY, Libraries, Special Collections Div, East Lansing, 48824. Jannette Fiore, Librn
Holdings: Vols 5500
Notes: The Russel B Nye Popular Culture Collection in the Michigan State Univ Libraries incl over (45,000) items. Most of the collection is organized into 4 categories: comic art, popular fiction, popular information materials and materials relating to the popular performing arts. Popular fiction in the collection is organized into juvenile, detective-mystery, and science fiction, westerns and women's fiction. In addition, there is a sample collection of dime novels and story papers (ca 400 issues representing nearly 100 titles). Pulp magazines which fall into none of the separate categories are housed with the dime novels and story papers. Juvenile Fiction: ca 4000 vols. Emphasis is on juvenile series fiction of the 19th and 20th centuries, with nearly 200 girls and 300 boys series represented. 19th-century "Sunday School" books andboth fiction and non-fiction scouting books are also included. Western Fiction: An exceptionally fine institutional collection, with over 3000 novels (most published between 1900 and 1950), almost all hardbound and in dust jackets, and nearly 500 pulp magazine issues representing more than fifty titles. The most important pulp runs are Street and Smith's *Western Story* Magazine and Warner Publications's *Ranch* Romances. Women's Fiction: Over 3000 novels and ca 1000 issues of romance, confession and movie magazines and pulps from the 1920s through the 1970s. Most of the novels are in the romance category, with over 2000 Harlequin novels, a good representation of other modern best-selling romances, and several dozen titles from late 19th-century romance series. Science Fiction: ca 3000 books and periodicals. MSU is a depository for the Science Fiction Writersof America, which contributes review copies of new books. The bulk of the collection is periodicals, with 71 titles represented. Most issues come from the period from the late 1940s to the present. The collection subscribes to most major science fiction magazines and holds a fanzine collection which now numbers over 2500. Detective-Mystery Fiction: ca 3500 novels, in paper and hardback, and pulps representing 28 titles from 1920-1950. Complete runs of *The London Mystery* Magazine and *Ellery Queen's Mystery* Magazine are included, along with a large sample collection of the more sensational detective and crime fiction magazines from the 1930s through the present.

†MN —UNIVERSITY OF MINNESOTA, Walter Library, Room 109, Minneapolis, 55455.
Notes: Some mystery books and mss.

†NY —STATE UNIVERSITY OF NEW YORK, COLLEGE AT ONEONTA, James M Milne Library, Special Collections, Oneonta, 13820. Martha Chambers, Librn
Notes: Popular fiction before 1920, incl some gothics, "domestic sentimentalist," mysteries and westerns.

NC —UNIVERSITY OF NORTH CAROLINA, CHAPEL HILL, Wilson Library, Rare Book Collection, Chapel Hill, 27514. Paul S Koda, Cur of Rare Books
Holdings: Vols 9000 Cat
Notes: The Jacques Barzun and Wendell Hertig Taylor Collection of Crime and Detection incl first editions of many works of important British and American authors. The Collection is notable for the excellent condition of the books, many of which have original dust jackets.

NC —UNIVERSITY OF NORTH CAROLINA, GREENSBORO, Walter Clinton Jackson Library, Special Collections Dept, 1000 Spring Garden St, Greensboro, 27412. Emilie W Mills, Librn
Holdings: Vols 200 Cat
Notes: A part of the larger Woman's Collection, inc works by women or works that feature women as detectives. Restricted to American writers of the late 19th century to the mid-20th century. Authors incl Margaret Armstrong, Anna Katherine Green, Frances and Richard Lockridge, Lillian O'Donnell and many others.

†OH —KENT STATE UNIVERSITY LIBRARY, Special Collections, Kent, 44242. Dean H Keller, Librn
Notes: 1000 vols with Raymond Chandler special collection.

PA —UNIVERSITY OF PITTSBURGH, Hillman Library, Special Collections Dept, 363 Hillman Library, Pittsburgh, 15260. Charles E Aston Jr, Coordinator
Holdings: Vols 416 Cat Mss Pix Memorabilia
Notes: See Rinehart, Mary Roberts - Collection.

RI —PROVIDENCE ATHENAEUM, 251 Benefit St, Providence, 02903. Sally Duplaix, Dir
Holdings: Vols 4000 Cat
Budget: $2000
Notes: British and American, incl foreign translations.

SC —WOFFORD COLLEGE, Sandor Teszler Library, N Church St, Spartanburg, 29301. Frank J Anderson, Librn
Holdings: Vols 1500 Cat
Notes: American novels, 1920s-1970s, incl about 1500 mystery novels. Collection incl biographical, bibliographical and critical reference works.

UT —BRIGHAM YOUNG UNIVERSITY, Harold B Lee Library, Unversity Hill, Provo, 84602. Sterling Albrecht, Dir
Notes: The Sandoe Collection.

WI —UNIVERSITY OF WISCONSIN, MADISON, Memorial Library, British & American Language & Literature Collection, 728 State St, Madison, 53706. Yvonne Schofer, Bibliographer
Holdings: Vols 4000
Notes: A collection of mystery fiction mostly of the British Golden Age of the 20s and 30s, in original and reprint form; strong holdings for H Adams, J Rhode, A Upfield, and many others. Stacks. Substantial holdings also for fantasy and science fiction, mostly in stacks; Arkham House and A Derleth materials, restricted use only.

DETERGENT CHEMISTRY see Chemistry, Detergent

DE TOLEDANO, RALPH

MA —BOSTON UNIVERSITY, Mugar Memorial Library, Special Collections Dept, 771 Commonwealth Ave, Boston, 02215. Howard B Gotlieb, Dir
Holdings: Cat Mss Pix
Notes: Mss, correspondence, etc collected in depth; incl publications by or about.

DETROIT—DESCRIPTION—VIEWS

MI —DETROIT PUBLIC LIBRARY, Fine Arts Department, 5201 Woodward Ave, Detroit, 48202. Shirley Solvick, Chief
Holdings: Vols 60,000 Cat Pix
Budget: ($20,000)
Notes: Downs number 2882, 2923, 2938. Book collection covers all phases of art. Picture collection of over 500,000 items covers all subjects; especially strong in the fine and decorative arts, portraits, costume, and Detroit.

DETROIT—HISTORY

MI —DETROIT PUBLIC LIBRARY, Burton Historical Collection, 5201 Woodward Ave, Detroit, 48202. Alice Dalligan, Chief
Holdings: Vols 250,000 Cat Mss Maps Pix Slides Microforms Pamphlets Newspapers
Notes: History of Detroit, Michigan, and the Old Northwest. Incl the Clarence Monroe Burton Collection with materials illustrating the history of Detroit.

DETROIT—PICTURES, ILLUSTRATIONS, ETC.

MI —DETROIT PUBLIC LIBRARY, Burton Historical Collection, 5201 Woodward Ave, Detroit, 48202. Alice Dalligan, Chief
Notes: Thousands of pictures of Detroit scenes and people make up the Burton picture files. Many books, magazines, and newspapers have been indexed for illustrations. A large collection of postcards shows how city and state looked to tourists of earlier days.

DETROIT—POLITICS AND GOVERNMENT

MI —DETROIT PUBLIC LIBRARY, Burton Historical Collection, 5201 Woodward Ave, Detroit, 48202. Alice Dalligan, Chief

DETROIT—RIOTS

MI —DETROIT PUBLIC LIBRARY, Burton Historical Collection, 5201 Woodward Ave, Detroit, 48202. Alice Dalligan, Chief
Holdings: Vols Cat Pix VF
Notes: Collection on the race riots of the week of 23 July 1967.

DETROIT BROADSIDE PRESS

RI —BROWN UNIVERSITY, John Hay Library, 20 Prospect St, Providence, 02912. Mary T Russo, Cur of Broadsides
Notes: A major collection of 30,000 pieces of American verse in broadside form dating from the 18th through 20th century. Ephemeral in nature and all inclusive, it covers a broad spectrum of American life. Numerous examples of early American poetry, admonishing, proclaiming, celebrating, advertising and mourning are represented. Poets range from the anonymous to major figures, incl Cummings, Eliot, Emerson, Frost, Pound and Whitman as well as contemporary authors. The Beat Movement, Black Mountain School, Concrete Poetry and Poetry of the Harlem Renaissance are represented as well as that of the young black poets published by the Detroit Broadside Press and a good selection of poetry by women. Retrospective and current pieces are added annually. Partial catalog.

DETROIT INDUSTRIAL MISSION

MI —WAYNE STATE UNIVERSITY, Walter P Reuther Library, Archives of Labor & Urban Affairs, Detroit, 48202. Philip Mason, Dir
Notes: The history of the labor movement in Detroit and Michigan. The records of the Wayne County and Michigan AFL-CIO, Association of Catholic Trade Unionists, and the Detroit Industrial Mission are housed in the Archives. The official files of August Scholle, as President of the Michigan AFL-CIO, complement the organizational records in the Archives.

DETROIT NEWSPAPER GUILD

MI —WAYNE STATE UNIVERSITY, Walter P Reuther Library, Archives of Labor & Urban Affairs, Detroit, 48202. Philip Mason, Dir
Notes: The most recent national labor union to place its records in the Archives is the American Newspaper Guild. The collection contains many personal papers and writings of Heywood Broun. The records of local Guild offices are being collected and those from the Detroit Newspaper Guild have already been obtained.

DETROIT PUBLISHING COMPANY

DC —LIBRARY OF CONGRESS, Prints & Photographs Div, Washington, 20540.
Notes: Detroit Publishing Company, publishers of postcards and souvenir views of buildings, historical sites, natural landmarks,

DETROIT PUBLISHING COMPANY (cont.)

industry, sports activities, and points of interest throughout the US and, to a lesser extent, Europe, Africa, and Asia. Over 22, 000 photoprints and nearly 18,500 original glass negatives.

DEUELL, PEGGY HULL

KS —UNIVERSITY OF KANSAS, Kenneth Spencer Research Library, Kansas Collection, Lawrence, 66045. Sheryl K Williams, Cur
Holdings: Vols (92,000) Mss Pix Audiotapes
Notes: All aspects of women's history in Kansas and the region. The collection incl personal papers, such as those of Peggy Hull Deuell (first accredited woman war correspondent), and Mary Huntoon (art therapist); diaries; and organizational records of many women's organizations, such as the Kansas League of Women Voters, the Missouri State Association of Parliamentarians and women's literary and service clubs.

DEUTERIUM

CA —UNIVERSITY OF CALIFORNIA, SAN DIEGO, Central University Library, Mandeville Dept of Special Collections, La Jolla, 92093. Lynda Corey Claassen, Head
Notes: Papers of Harold Clayton Urey (1893-1981), winner of the 1934 Nobel Prize in chemistry for his discovery of Deuterium. Incl files concerning the Emergency Committee of Atomic Scientists, 1946-49; also some material on the Rosenberg/Sobell spy cases; also on his works as science advisor to John F Kennedy (president-elect).

DEUTSCH, BABETTE

MO —SAINT LOUIS PUBLIC LIBRARY, Gardner Rare Book Room, 1301 Olive St, Saint Louis, 63103. Julanne M Good, Supervisor; Martha Riley, Rare Books Librn
Holdings: Vols (2300) Cat
Budget: ($5573)
Notes: First editions of authors having some association with William Marion Reedy and *Reedy's Mirror*, such as Sara Teasdale, Zoe Akins, Fannie Hurst, Edgar Lee Masters, Babette Deutsch, Richard LeGallienne, etc. Also first editions of selected St Louis and/ or Missouri authors such as T S Eliot, Samuel L Clemens, Theodore Dreiser and Tennessee Williams. Noncirculating.

MO —WASHINGTON UNIVERSITY, Libraries, Special Collections Dept, Campus Box 1061, St Louis, 63130.
Notes: A major collection, incl books, mss, correspondence, literary papers, photographs, etc. Described in *Special Collections: an Annotated Guide to the Holdings of the Manuscript Division and the University Archives and Research Collection.*

DEUTSCH, HELEN

MA —BOSTON UNIVERSITY, Mugar Memorial Library, Special Collections Dept, 771 Commonwealth Ave, Boston, 02215. Howard B Gotlieb, Dir
Holdings: Cat Mss Pix Correspondence

DEUTSCH, JOHN J.

ON —QUEEN'S UNIVERSITY, Douglas Library, Kingston, K7L 5C4, Can. William F E Morley, Cur, Special Collections
Holdings: Cat Mss Pix
Notes: The papers of Dr John J Deutsch, incl the correspondence, notes, memoranda and other files accumulated by him during his career.

DEUTSCHES MUSIKGESCHICHTLICHES ARCHIV—COLLECTIONS

NC —UNIVERSITY OF NORTH CAROLINA, CHAPEL HILL, Music Library, Hill Hall, Chapel Hill, 27514.
Holdings: Vols (90,000) Cat Mss Pix Slides Phonorecords Audiotapes Microforms
Budget: ($60,000)
Notes: Extensive holdings of early theoretical treatises; complete editions; performing scores; music periodicals; reference works. Microfilms from the Deutsches Musikgeschichtliches Archiv; microfilms of important European primary sources.

DEVELOPING NATIONS

CA —WOMEN'S HISTORY RESEARCH CENTER, Microfilm Library, 2325 Oak St, Berkeley, 94708. Laura X, Librn
Holdings: Mss Pix Microforms
Notes: Incl material (150 subject files) on physical and mental health and illnesses; sex roles; biology; women and the life cycle; birth/population control; sex and sexuality; black and Third World women. Collection at University of Wyoming. Archive of Contemporary History, PO Box 3334, Laramie, Wyoming 82701, c/o David Crosson. Research inquiries accepted. Microfilm of collection (14 reels and reel guides) available at many universities and through Women's History Research Center, 2325 Oak St, Berkeley, CA 94708. No collections housed at this address.

CO —COLORADO STATE UNIVERSITY, Libraries, Fort Collins, 80523. Marjorie Rhoades, Engineering Sciences Librn
Holdings: Vols (6000) Cat
Budget: ($5000)
Notes: Water and Soil in Arid Regions (WASAR) is an index and guide to books, conference papers, journal articles, government documents and technical reports, mostly in English, within the appropriate subject areas and held by Colorado State University Libraries. The bibliographical citations are of selected items dealing with soils, water, arid lands, crops, foods and nutrition with certain economic, political, ecological and historical parameters also included. The information needs of developing countries and of those who serve them are the prime criteria for inclusion.

CT —YALE UNIVERSITY, Social Science Library, Economic Growth Center Collection, 140 Prospect St, New Haven, 06520. Billie I Salter, Librn
Holdings: Vols (47,600) Cat
Notes: Economic data on national economies and their development; budgets, plans, statistical yearbooks and bulletins, censuses, national accounts, trade, monetary data, statistics, etc. The focus is primarily on less-developed countries. Mostly government documents; 3800 serials currently received. Shelf list organized by country and LC number, in addition to dictionary catalog.

DC —ACTION, Photo Library, 806 Connecticut Ave NW, Washington, 20525.
Holdings: Pix Slides
Notes: Volunteer photos for ACTION, VISTA, and older Americans programs. 15, 000 photographs.

DC —INTERNATIONAL LABOR ORGANIZATION, International Labor Office, Washington Branch Library, 1750 New York Ave NW, Rm 330, Washington, 20006. Karen J Mark, Librn
Holdings: Vols (13,500) Cat Pix 16mm Films Monographs
Notes: Wide range of titles dealing with worldwide labor and social matters. The library contains ILO publications and documentation only dating back to 1919. Also, a collection of ILO films and photos, See *Subject Guide to Publications of the ILO, 1919-1964 and ILO Catalogue of Publications in Print, 1982 (ILO).*

DC —LIBRARY OF CONGRESS, Rare Book & Special Collections Div, Washington, 20540. William Matheson, Chief
Notes: A 3000-title archival set of translations sponsored by the Franklin Book Programs, Inc between the years 1952-1978.

DC —LIBRARY OF CONGRESS, General Reading Rooms Division, Microform Reading Room, Washington, 20540.
Holdings: Cat Mss Maps Pix Microforms
Notes: Microform materials only in this LC Division. Works of individual authors; holdings of collections; archival records, etc, press releases and translations, etc.

DC —PEACE CORPS, Information Services Division, 806 Connecticut Ave NW, Room M407, Washington, 20526. Rita C Warpeha, Chief Librn
Holdings: Vols (35,000) Cat
Budget: ($10,000)
Notes: Social, political, economic and health topics related to the countries of Asia, the Pacific, Africa, Latin America and the Caribbean where Peace Corp volunteers work.

DC —US BUREAU OF THE CENSUS, Library, Federal Office Bldg 3, Rm 2451, Washington, 20233. Betty Baxtresser, Chief, ASD Library Branch
Holdings: Vols (23,000) Cat Microforms
Notes: Incl censuses, statistical yearbooks, and statistical bulletins from about 100 foreign countries printed in nearly 40 languages. The span of coverage varies, depending upon the publication program of each country and on publications exchange arrangements. Materials in this collection are arranged first by geographic unit, then by subject. Publications of the international organizations are arranged by organizational unit, then by subject.

MA —HARVARD UNIVERSITY, Graduate School of Education, Monroe C Gutman Library, 6 Appian Way, Cambridge, 02138. Susan S Baughman, Associate Librn
Notes: A specialized collection of books and periodicals on demographic, economic, political, social, and systems aspects of educational planning in developing countries and in the United States. The emphasis is on the interrelationship of these disciplines in their application to educational planning and human resource development. Incl reports of education ministries, conference papers, journals, UN documents, pamphlets, UNESCO documents.

MA —HARVARD UNIVERSITY LIBRARY, John F Kennedy School of Government Library, Manpower and Industrial Relations Collection, Littauer Library, Cambridge, 02138. James C Damaskos, Librn
Holdings: Cat
Notes: Covers international aspects as well as U S.

MI —UNIVERSITY OF MICHIGAN, Center for Research on Economic Development, Library, 240 Lorch Hall, Ann Arbor, 48109. Carol Wilson, Information/Resources Coordinator
Holdings: Vols (21,000) Cat 16mm Films Microforms
Budget: ($7000)
Notes: Publications that list library and its collection: *Directory of Third World Studies in the US* (African Studies Assn, 1981), *National Reference Center Directory* 1983 (NRC), *World Guide to Libraries* 1983 (Saur Verlag), *Research Centers Directory 1983* (Gale Research), and *A Directory of Information Resources in US* (Library of Congress, 1978). Collection's focus is Third World economic development. Other areas of interest are economic planning, developing countries, Africa (specifically francophone Africa), the Sahel, African agricultural economics, commodities production, financial statistics, development plans from less developed countries (LDC), and international development. Each part of the library's collection (working papers/ reports, periodicals and government documents) has its own catalog and cataloging system.

MI —MICHIGAN STATE UNIVERSITY, International Library, Sahel Documentation Center, East Lansing, 48824. Eugene deBenko, Librn; Learthen Dorsey, Librn
Holdings: Vols (5100) Cat Mss Maps Pix Slides Phonorecords Audiotapes Videotapes Microforms
Budget: ($8000)
Notes: See description under The Sahel.

MI —MICHIGAN STATE UNIVERSITY, International Library, South and Southeast Asia Collection, East Lansing, 48824. Clinton Lockert, Bibliographer
Holdings: Vols (6000) Cat Maps Microforms

DEVELOPING NATIONS (cont.)

Notes: Emphasis is upon South and Southeast Asia, especially Bangladesh and Vietnam (South). Attempt to collect extensively the economic and social development plans of the developing nations. Monographs and serials received on PL 480 from India, Pakistan, Sri Lanka and Nepal since 1968. Extensive holdings of Academy for Rural Development, Comilla, Bangladesh (1959-), and of the Michigan State University Vietnam Advisory Group (1955-1962).

NY —US COMMITTEE FOR UNICEF, Information Center on Children's Cultures, 331 E 38 St, New York, 10016. Melinda Greenblatt, Chief Librn
Holdings: Vols (17,500) Cat Pix Slides Films Filmstrips
Notes: Social and cultural aspects of lives of children from developing countries. Especially strong in the area of school textbooks from Near Eastern Asian, African, Latin American, Caribbean, and Pacific Area countries; holidays and celebrations related to children all over the world; children's books in English which describe child life in other countries. Especially strong collection of folklore, and folklore of children, from all regions mentioned above.

NC —CAROLINA POPULATION CENTER, Library, University Sq E, Chapel Hill, 27514. Patricia Shipman, Head Librn
Holdings: Vols (20,000) Cat
Budget: ($10,500)
Notes: This is the largest population library in the world (65,000 citations). Emphasis is on the socioeconomic aspects of population, particularly population dynamics, population policy, fertility, the family, formal demography, family planning, and population education. The catalog to the entire collection is on microfiche and offers 6 types of access: author, title, series, major subject term, location number. Library data base is available on database on *Dialog*, population bibliography. Selected searches are available in Library.

PA —UNIVERSITY OF PITTSBURGH, Library, Graduate School of Public and International Affairs, Forbes Quadrangle, 1st floor West, Pittsburgh, 15260. Nicholas C Caruso, Librn
Holdings: Vols (80,000) Cat
Budget: ($150,000)
Notes: The library attempts to collect as many national economic and social development plans as possible from the developing countries of the world. It also holds city, regional and state plans for Pennsylvania, particuarly, the 9 southwestern counties of Pennsylvania.

ON —UNIVERSITY OF GUELPH, McLaughlin Library, Guelph, N1G 2W1, Can. Margaret Beckman, Head Librn; David Hull, Sciences Librn
Holdings: Vols 60,000 Cat
Notes: Archival material includes E.S. Archibald Papers, 1929-62 (Ethiopia); Ghana-Guelph Project, 1968-79; Kenya-Canada Beekeeping Project, 1971-83; Oswald McConkey Papers, 1917-74 (China, Manchuria). Special cats can be produced for any part of the collection. Holdings incl monographs, 400 periodical titles, 150,000 documents, 40 boxes of archival material.
See also entry under Agriculture

†ON —METROPOLITAN TORONTO LIBRARY, Social Sciences Dept, 789 Yonge St, Toronto, M4W 2G8, Can. Abdus Salam, Head
Holdings: Vols Cat Maps Phonorecords Audiotapes 16mm Films Microforms
Notes: General collection of documents of international organizations with emphasis on the United Nations and UNESCO. Collection ranges from international relations to social conditions in underdeveloped countries. Selected League of Nations publications. Both current and historical in scope.

DEVELOPMENT see Embryology; Evolution; Growth

DEVELOPMENT, CHILD see Child Development

DEVELOPMENT, PERSONALITY see Personality

DEVELOPMENT, RURAL see Rural Development

DEVELOPMENTAL BIOLOGY see Biology, Developmental

DEVER, WILLIAM E.

IL —CHICAGO HISTORICAL SOCIETY, Library, Clark St at North Ave, Chicago, 60614. Archie Motley, Manuscript Librn
Notes: Papers of lawyer, judge, Chicago alderman, mayor of Chicago.

DEVEREUX, JAMES P. S.

MA —BOSTON UNIVERSITY, Mugar Memorial Library, Special Collections Dept, 771 Commonwealth Ave, Boston, 02215. Howard B Gotlieb, Dir
Holdings: Cat Mss Maps Pix
Notes: Mss, correspondence, etc collected in depth; incl publications by or about.

DEVIL WORSHIP

IN —INDIANAPOLIS-MARION COUNTY PUBLIC LIBRARY, Social Sciences Div, PO Box 211, Indianapolis, 46206. Lois R Laube, Head
Holdings: Vols 358 Cat
Notes: Restricted use. No photocopying.

OH —CLEVELAND PUBLIC LIBRARY, Fine Arts and Special Collections Department, 325 Superior Ave, Cleveland, 44114. Alice N Loranth, Head
Holdings: Vols (1600) Cat
Notes: Part of the Witchcraft Collection, which incl witchcraft, magic, sorcery, magical manuals, devil worship, incantations, charms, talismans, amulets and spells. Contemporary urban practices are almost entirely omitted.
See also entry under Folklore; Witchcraft

DEVITT, REV. EDWARD, S.J., 1841-1920

DC —GEORGETOWN UNIVERSITY, Library, Special Collections Div, 37 & O Sts NW, Washington, 20057. George M Barringer, Special Collections Librn; Nicholas B Sheetz, Mss Librn
Holdings: Mss Pix
Notes: The papers of Rev Edward Devitt, SJ (1841-1920) who, during his years in the Society, taught at Gonzaga College, Woodstock College, Holy Cross and Georgetown. He was also, at one time, rector of Boston College and editor of the *Woodstock Letters.* Fr Devitt also gained wide recognition as an historian of early Catholic history in the United States. The papers incl a series of diaries (1865-1920), a commonplace book of verse and sundry documents, in addition to numerous notes, mss and published material. Also incl in the papers is the last revision of Rev Thomas Hughes's, SJ *History of the Society of Jesus in North America* with related correspondence and miscellaneous photographs.

DEVOTIONAL LITERATURE

PA —LUTHERAN THEOLOGICAL SEMINARY, Krauth Memorial Library, 7301 Germantown Ave, Philadelphia, 19119. Rev David J Wartluft, Dir Libr
Holdings: Vols 3000 Cat
Notes: Chiefly Protestant (strongly Lutheran) devotional literature of Germany and the US. The core of the collection was the personal library of Dr John W Doberstein, compiler and translator of devotional materials.

DEVRIES, PETER

MA —BOSTON UNIVERSITY, Mugar Memorial Library, Special Collections Dept, 771 Commonwealth Ave, Boston, 02215. Howard B Gotlieb, Dir
Holdings: Cat Mss
Notes: Incl publications by.

DEVYVER, FRANK

NC —DUKE UNIVERSITY, William R Perkins Library, Manuscript Dept, Durham, 27706. Ellen Gartrell, Cur of Mss
Holdings: Cat Mss
Notes: Emphasis on US South, especially CIO Organizing Committee papers, 1946-53 (ca 143,00 items). Large percentage have been commercially microfilmed under title "Operation Dixie." Also papers of Lucy Randolph Mason, Frank deVyver, Frank Morrison.

DEWEY, JOHN

IL —SOUTHERN ILLINOIS UNIVERSITY, CARBONDALE, Delyte W Morris Library, Special Collections Dept, Carbondale, 62901. David V Koch, Cur of Special Collections; Louisa Bowen, Cur of Manuscripts
Holdings: Vols 2500 Uncat Mss Pix
Notes: Twenty collections related to 20th century American philosophy incl the papers of John Dewey, acquired from the estate of his widow, incl correspondence, mss, class lecture notes, photographs, and memorabilia, of a long and distinguished career. There are letters from such scholars as William James, William Rainey Harper, James Mark Baldwin, James Cattell and Adelbert Ames. Also in the collection are letters to his wife and children, a pictorial record of his stay in China (1919-1921), and his personal library of about 1000 books, many of the volumes heavily annotated. In addition to papers from the Dewey estate, the Library has acquired, in support of the editing and publishing of the *Collected Works of John* Dewey, extensive correspondence between Dewey and his associates-Edward Scribner Ames, Paul Schilpp, Cyrus Eaton, Myrtle McGraw, Herbert W Schneider, JamesHayden Tufts and Edwin Wilson. Publishing agreements, mss and galley proofs of Dewey's work have also been assembled. (John Dewey, *The Early Works 1882-1898,* 1969-1972; Jo Ann Boydston, ed, *Guide to the Works of John Dewey, 1970;* Jo Ann Boydston, ed, *John Dewey, A Checklist of Translations, 1969*).

†NY —COLUMBIA UNIVERSITY LIBRARIES, Butler Library, Rare Book and Manuscript Library, 535 W 114 St, New York, 10027.
Notes: Dr Corliss Lamont's correspondence with John Dewey, as well as related correspondence.

DEWEY, MELVIL

NY —COLUMBIA UNIVERSITY LIBRARIES, Rare Book & Manuscript Library, 801 Butler Library, 535 W 114 St, New York, 10027. Kenneth A Lohf, Librn
Holdings: Mss
Notes: Mss and printed materials. Incl 53, 700 items. Restricted use.

DEWEY, THOMAS B.

MA —BOSTON UNIVERSITY, Mugar Memorial Library, Special Collections Dept, 771 Commonwealth Ave, Boston, 02215. Howard B Gotlieb, Dir
Holdings: Cat Mss
Notes: Mss, correspondence, etc collected in depth; incl publications by or about.

DEWEY, THOMAS E.

NY —UNIVERSITY OF ROCHESTER, Rush Rhees Library, Department of Rare Books and Special Collections, Rochester, 14627. Peter Dzwonkoski, Librn
Holdings: Vols Cat Mss Pix Films Tapes
Notes: Official and personal records from Dewey's career as District Attorney of New York County (1938-43), Governor of New York State (1943-1955). Republican Candidate for President of the United States, 1944 and 1948.

DE WOLFE, BILLY

†CA —UNIVERSITY OF SOUTHERN CALIFORNIA, University Library, Archives of Performing Arts, Los Angeles, 90089. Robert Knutson, Librn
Holdings: Mss Pix
Notes: His personal collection of stage, screen and TV memorabilia. Also his scrapbooks and photographs, from 1925.

DEXTERITY see Motor Ability

DIAGHILEV, BALLETS RUSSES DE see Ballets Russes De Diaghilev

DIAGHILEV, SERGEI PAVLOVICH, 1872-1929

NY —NEW YORK PUBLIC LIBRARY, Performing Arts Research Center, Dance

DIAGHILEV, SERGEI PAVLOVICH, 1872-1929 (cont.)

Collection, 111 Amsterdam Ave, New York, 10023. Genevieve Oswald, Cur
Budget: ($9,280)
Notes: Extensive documentation on the Russian impresario and creator of Les Ballets Russes (1909-1929). Collection includes biographical material, manuscripts and letters, scrapbooks, clippings, photographs, posters, tape-recorded interviews with artists formerly associated with Les Ballets Russes, stage and costume designs for company productions, and a documentary film, *Diaghilev,* made in 1968 by the British Broadcasting Corporation, 112 min, black and white. Manuscripts include a holograph *Black Exercise Book,* 1909-11, by Diaghilev, and 195 letters written to Diaghilev. The Gabriel Astruc papers, 1904-25, contain ca 1300 manuscripts relating to the early activities of Diaghilev. Register published in *Bulletin of the New York Public Library,* v 75, no 8, Oct 1971.Entire collection described in: *Dictionary Catalog of the Dance Collection,* published by G K Hall, Boston, 1974, 10 vols. Annual supplements: *Bibliographic Guide to Dance,* also published by G K Hall.

DIAGNOSIS, LABORATORY

NY —NASSAU COUNTY DEPARTMENT OF HEALTH, Division of Laboratories & Research, 209 Main St, Hempstead, 11550. Madeline Burston, Librn; Beatrice R Sewald, Asst Librn
Holdings: Vols (4076) Cat Mss Slides Microforms

ON —ONTARIO MINISTRY OF HEALTH, Laboratory Services Branch, Library, Box 9000, Terminal A, Toronto, M5W 1R5, Can. Doris A Standing, Librn
Holdings: Vols (4000) Cat
Budget: ($50,000)
Notes: Medical laboratory technology and related subjects: microbiology; environmental bacteriology (limited to testing of milk, food and water for bacterial quality, etc); biological chemistry (clinical); mycology; parasitology; virology; immunology; serology; automated laboratory techniques; biohazard control.

DIAGNOSTIC PSYCHOLOGICAL TESTING see Clinical Psychology

DIALECTIC (LOGIC) see Logic

DIALECTOLOGY

NC —DUKE UNIVERSITY, William R Perkins Library, Jay B Hubbell Center for American Literary Historiography, Durham, 27706. Erma Whittington, Librn
Holdings: Mss Pix
Notes: 77,312 items, incl mss, pictures, clippings, and correspondence. "The objective of the Center is to gather the papers and materials of significant scholars and critics in American literary history." The Center is a part of the Perkins Library Manuscript Department.

DIALECTS see Creole Dialects; Language and Languages; Languages, Mixed

DIALOGUES OF THE DEAD

CA —UNIVERSITY OF CALIFORNIA, LOS ANGELES, Research Library, Dept of Special Collections, 405 Hilgard Ave, Los Angeles, 90024. Edward Shreeves, Chairman, Bibliographers Group; David S Zeidberg, Head
Holdings: Vols 150 Cat
Notes: 150 volumes, based on the Moriz Grolig Collection, mostly in German or French, incl Grolig's ms bibliography of material, 1495-1792.

DIALYSIS

RI —MIRIAM HOSPITAL MEDICAL LIBRARY, 164 Summit Ave, Providence, 02906. Ann LeClaire, Dir of Library Services
Holdings: Cat Cassettes
Notes: Special collection on the renal system with emphasis on kidney transplantation and dialysis.

DIAMOND NECKLACE AFFAIR

MA —UNIVERSITY OF MASSACHUSETTS AT AMHERST, Library, Amherst, 01003. Siegfried Feller, Assoc Dir for Collection Development
Holdings: Cat
Notes: Collection Binet. Mostly contemporary works. 1524 periodicals, and pamphlets, including a 99 vol contemporary nonce collection with quite strong Dauphine representation and pamphlets on important prerevolutionary events, viz, the Diamond Necklace affair, the Kornmann affair, etc. Some cataloged, some calendared and indexed.

DIAMOND RUSH, AFRICAN

TX —SOUTHERN METHODIST UNIVERSITY, DeGolyer Library, Box 396, SMU, Dallas, 75275. Clifton H Jones, Dir
Holdings: Vols (80,000) Cat Mss Maps Pix Slides Microforms
Notes: First editions of prominent authors; also of books in subject emphasis collections. All subjects listed in this vol are strong. Numerous collections of personal papers relating to subjects also.

DIAMOND, LOUIS, M.D.

MB —UNIVERSITY OF MANITOBA, Elizabeth Dafoe Library, Archives and Special Collections Dept, Winnipeg, R3T 2N2, Can. Richard E Bennett, Dept Head; Corrado A Santoro, Reference Archivist
Notes: Correspondence, reports and various papers of Dr Bruce H Chown. Haemolitic diseases of the newborn, especially erthroblastosis fetalis and the maternal Rh-factor. Incl correpspondence with Dr Louis Diamond of Boston. Also incl are human anthropological blood group studies of Eskimo, Indian and Canadian-Japanese communities.

DIARIES—COLLECTIONS

CA —POMONA PUBLIC LIBRARY, Special Collections, 625 S Garey Ave, PO Box 2271, Pomona, 91766. David Streeter, Librn
Holdings: Vols 43,000 Cat Mss Maps Pix Slides Audiotapes Microforms
Notes: Collections consist of printed materials; manuscripts; diaries; oral history interviews; photographs (100,000 images); societies and organizations; Pomona Valley business records. Considerable emphasis on the Pomona Valley Region (Los Angeles-San Bernardino Counties).

MA —NEW ENGLAND HISTORIC GENEALOGICAL SOCIETY, Library, 101 Newbury St, Boston, 02116. Ralph J Crandell, Dir
Holdings: Vols (250,000) Mss Maps Microforms Pix
Notes: New England genealogy. Especially strong Massachusetts, Maine, and New Hampshire, although all states are well represented, as are the relevancies of each subject listed in this volume with regard to British antecedent and contemporary history. Special strengths in local history and biography, obituaries, etc, incl parish registers, censuses, British and American. 3125 linear ft of mss.

NJ —RUTGERS, THE STATE UNIVERSITY OF NEW JERSEY, Alexander Library, Special Collections and Archives, College Ave & Huntington St, New Brunswick, 08903. Ronald L Becker, Cur of Manuscripts and Rare Books
Holdings: Vols 350
Notes: Largely American mss, 1746-1957, many of New Jersey.

NY —NEW YORK PUBLIC LIBRARY, Rare Books and Manuscripts Div, Fifth Ave & 42 St, New York, 10018. William L Joyce, Asst Dir; Susan E Davis, Cur of Mss
Holdings: Cat Mss
Budget: ($7161)
Notes: Incl diaries of interest to social historians; theatrical history; science and engineering in 19th century America.

NC —DUKE UNIVERSITY, William R Perkins Library, Manuscript Dept, Durham, 27706. Ellen Gartrell, Cur of Mss
Holdings: Cat Mss
Notes: Several hundred diaries, mainly US 19th century, of women, officers and soldiers, travelers, farmers, et al.

PA —US ARMY MILITARY HISTORY INSTITUTE, Carlisle Barracks, 17013. Richard J Sommers, Chief Archivist-Historian
Holdings: Mss Cat
Notes: 950 folders and 50 boxes of mss. The Civil War Collection, personal letters, diaries, memoirs of Federal and Confederate officers and enlisted men serving on virtually every from, 1861-1865.

PA —FRIENDS HISTORICAL LIBRARY OF SWARTHMORE COLLEGE, Swarthmore, 19081. J William Frost, Dir
Holdings: Vols (35,000) Cat Mss Pix Microfilm
Notes: The library has several hundred Quaker journals, some published, but more available either in the original mss or on microfilm. Incl are diaries, religious journals, and accounts of visits, mostly in ministry to other Quakers, to Indians, and others, from the late 17th century to the present. Many of the Quaker ministers incl in this collection were women.

BC —UNIVERSITY OF VICTORIA, McPherson Library, Victoria, V8W 3H5, Can.
Notes: Incl 50 pages, 1898; irregular diary of a young man of 25 years in the employ of the Countess of Carnarvon and tutor to Aubrey Nigel Henry Molyneux Herbert.

DIAZ, PORFIRIO

IN —INDIANA UNIVERSITY, Lilly Library, Seventh St, Bloomington, 47405. William R Cagle, Librn
Holdings: Vols (10,000) // Cat Mss
Notes: Historical pronouncements and documents by the leaders of the movement of Mexican independence. Partially cataloged. See also entry under Mexico-History.
See also entry under Mexico - History

DIAZ PEREZ, VIRIATO

CA —UNIVERSITY OF CALIFORNIA, RIVERSIDE, University Library, 4045 Canyon Crest Dr, Box 5900, Riverside, 92517.
Holdings: Vols (1,000) Cat Mss Maps Pix
Notes: General research collection in the humanities and social sciences, with special strengths in history (mainly 19th and 20th centuries), literature, folklore and economic conditions, many books from the library of Julio Cesar Chaves. The Special Collections contains the papers of Juan Silvano Godoi, statesman and historian, his diaries (1897-1903, 1905-1921), the papers and correspondence of the historians Nicolas Diaz Perez, Viriato Diaz Perez, and of Hugo Rodriguez Alcala. See Thomas L Whigham and Jerry W Cooney, *Paraguayan History: Manuscript Sources in the United States,* in *Latin American Review,* vol 18 (1983) no 1: p 104-108.

DIBDIN, THOMAS FROGNALL

MA —HARVARD UNIVERSITY LIBRARY, Houghton Library, Cambridge, 02138. F Thomas Noonan, Cur, Reading Room; Lawrence Dowler, Associate Librn
Holdings: Cat
Notes: See William A Jackson's *Annotated* List of holdings published by Library, 1965.

†ON —UNIVERSITY OF WESTERN ONTARIO, School of Library and Information Science, Special Collections Room, London, N6A 5B9, Can.
Holdings: Vols 40

DIBNER, BERN

MA —BRANDEIS UNIVERSITY, Goldfarb Library, 415 South St, Waltham, 02154. Bessie Hahn, Dir
Notes: 50 or more letters from Rockwell Kent to Dr Bern Dibner and others. A schedule of the letters is located in Special Collections.

DIBNER, MARTIN

MA —BOSTON UNIVERSITY, Mugar Memorial Library, Special Collections Dept, 771 Commonwealth Ave, Boston, 02215. Howard B Gotlieb, Dir
Holdings: Cat Mss

DICK, HUGH G., 1909-1971

CA —UNIVERSITY OF CALIFORNIA, LOS ANGELES, Research Library, Dept of Special Collections, 405 Hilgard Ave, Los Angeles, 90024. Edward Shreeves, Chairman, Bibliographers Group; David S Zeidberg, Head
Notes: 10 linear feet of UCLA English Professor's correspondence, mss, lecture notes, and some research notes.

DICK, JOHN HENRY

SC —COLLEGE OF CHARLESTON LIBRARY, Special Collections Dept, Charleston, 29401.
Notes: 42 illustrations by John Henry Dick for Marjory Bartlett Sanger's *World of the Great White Heron* (1967).

DICK, KAY

MO —WASHINGTON UNIVERSITY, Libraries, Special Collections Dept, Campus Box 1061, St Louis, 63130.
Notes: A small but significant collection.

DICK, MARCEL, 1898-

OH —CASE WESTERN RESERVE UNIVERSITY LIBRARIES, Cleveland, 44106. Susie Hanson, Special Collections Librn
Notes: Manuscripts of compositions and other archival materials by the Hungarian-born American composer, Marcel Dick. Contains sketches and pencil scores. A biography in the form of an oral history conducted by Dr Anne Trenkamp, who recorded conversations with Dr Dick and transcribed the tapes into a typewritten manuscript. Contains tapes and manuscript.

DICK, PHILIP K., 1929-1982

†CA —FULLERTON COLLEGE, William T Boyce Library, 321 E Chapman Ave, Fullerton, 92634.
Notes: Books, mss, correspondence of Philip K. Dick, science fiction writer, author of the classic *Do Androids Dream of Electric* Sheep (which was made into a movie as *Blade Runner).*

CA —UNIVERSITY OF CALIFORNIA, RIVERSIDE, University Library, 4045 Canyon Crest Dr, Box 5900, Riverside, 92517.
Holdings: Vols (30,000)
Notes: The Eaton Collection of science fiction and fantasy materials, incl 5,600 pulp magazines; also horror, supernatural, and Gothic mystery fiction; boys' books; utopian and dystopian fiction, imaginary voyages, future war and lost race fiction; large holdings in French language science fiction and fantasy; critical and scholarly works pertaining to these genres; videotapes of science fiction/fantasy films and shooting scripts. Collection covers science fiction/fantasy literature from the 16th-17th centuries to the present. Strong individual author collections of Jules Verne, H Rider Haggard, H G Wells, Edgar Rice Burroughs, and Philip K Dick. For a complete description of the collection see: George Slusser, "The J Lloyd Eaton Collection," *Special Collections,* II, 1/2, 25-38 (1983), *andDictionary Catalog of the J Lloyd Eaton Collection of Science Fiction and Fantasy* Literature (Boston: G K Hall) 1982.

DICKENS, CHARLES, 1812-1870

AZ —UNIVERSITY OF ARIZONA, University Library, Special Collections, Tucson, 85721. Louis A Hieb, Head
Holdings: Vols (7000) Cat Mss Microforms
Budget: ($30,000)
Notes: The major collection of 19th century authors are Byron, Dickens, Scott, Thackeray, Trollope, the Brownings, Stevens, Tennyson, and Wordsworth.

CA —UNIVERSITY OF CALIFORNIA, LOS ANGELES, Research Library, Dept of Special Collections, 405 Hilgard Ave, Los Angeles, 90024. Edward Shreeves, Chairman, Bibliographers Group; David S Zeidberg, Head
Holdings: Vols 250 Cat Mss Pix
Notes: 250 first and other editions of his books; 30 letters; 80 playbills; original pictures used as illustrations for his books; ms materials about him.

CA —UNIVERSITY OF CALIFORNIA, LOS ANGELES, William Andrews Clark Memorial Library, 2520 Cimarron St, Los Angeles, 90018.
Holdings: Cat Mss
Notes: Extensive collection, first editions, etc.

CO —UNIVERSITY OF COLORADO, Libraries, Special Collections, Boulder, 80309. Nora J Quinlan, Head
Holdings: Vols Uncat
Notes: George Creamer Collection. Over two thousand books on 19th century English literature (Dickens), and 19th and 20th centuries British and American book illustration. In addition, approx 250 children's illustrated books.

CT —TRINITY COLLEGE LIBRARY, Watkinson Library, 300 Summit St, Hartford, 06106. Jeffrey Kaimowitz, Cur
Holdings: Cat Pix
Notes: The Sherman P Haight Collections of Cruikshank and Dickens.

CT —YALE UNIVERSITY, Box 1603A, Yale Station, New Haven, 06520.
Holdings: Cat Mss
Notes: Incl manuscripts, memorabilia, etc.

DC —GEORGETOWN UNIVERSITY, Library, Special Collections Div, 37 & O Sts NW, Washington, 20057. George M Barringer, Special Collections Librn; Nicholas B Sheetz, Mss Librn
Holdings: Vols 1500 Uncat Mss Pix
Notes: The Arnold U Ziegler Dickens Collection; books, manuscripts, etc, by and about Dickens and members of his circle.

IL —DE PAUL UNIVERSITY, Library, 2323 N Seminary, Chicago, 60614. Kathryn De Graff, Special Collections Librn
Holdings: Vols (598) Uncat Pix
Budget: $1500
Notes: The Jack Davidson and Nathan Schwartz Collection. Numerous editions of Dickens' works in the original publishers parts, first complete editions, first American editions and special editions. Also about 300 books about Dickens incl *The Dickension,* 500 prints, posters and photographs, an interesting collection of memorabilia such as figurines, etc. The extra-illustrated volumes, with over 7000 illustrations, were prepared by Mr Bradford, the original owner of the collection, and contain the conceptions of scenes and characters in Dickens' novels by various illustrators.

IL —ILLINOIS STATE UNIVERSITY, Milner Library, Dept of Special Collections, Normal, 61761. Robert Sokan, Librn
Notes: First editions, limited editions, ephemera, etc.

IL —WHEATON COLLEGE, Buswell Memorial Library, Wheaton, 60187. Paul Snezek, Library Dir
Holdings: Vols 200 Cat
Notes: A collection of first editions.

IN —INDIANA UNIVERSITY, Lilly Library, Seventh St, Bloomington, 47405. William R Cagle, Librn
Holdings: Cat
Notes: First editions in parts and in book form.

KS —SAINT MARY COLLEGE, Library, Leavenworth, 66048. Therese Deplazes, Special Collections Librn
Holdings: Vols 300 Cat Pix
Notes: Incl original monthly parts in wrappers of *Dombey and Son,* 1848; *Litt* Dorrit, 1857; and *Our Mutual Friend,* 18 Eleven editions of *Christmas Carol,* incl facsimile of author's original ms and tape Lionel Barrymore. Rare print collection, edited by Seymour Eaton, memorabilia.

MA —HARVARD UNIVERSITY LIBRAR Widener Library, Harry Elkins Widener Collection, Cambridge, 02138. F Thomas Noonan, Cur
Holdings: // Cat Mss
Notes: Privately printed catalog (111 p) issued 1918.

MI —UNIVERSITY OF MICHIGAN, Libr Dept of Rare Books & Special Collection Ann Arbor, 48109. Robert J Starring, Hea
Holdings: Vols 400 Cat Mss Pix
Notes: Incl first editions of all the major works and most of the minor, association copies, 9 mss and 8 playbills.

MN —UNIVERSITY OF MINNESOTA, O Meredith Wilson Library, 309 19 Ave S, Minneapolis, 55455. Austin J McLean, Chief, Special Collections
Holdings: Vols 250 Cat
Notes: A special collection of publications about the mystery of Edwin Drood. Partially cataloged, but complete listing available in Division.

NJ —PRINCETON UNIVERSITY, Library, Morris L Parrish Collection, Princeton, 08540. Alexander D Wainwright, Cur
Notes: Incl 600 items. The major novels are present incl many sets of the original issues. Very rich in American editions, and also incl books about Dickens. Refer to: Gordon Hall Gerould, "The Dickens Collection" in *Chronicle* VIII, 1 (November, 1946) pp 21-23. Gerould's article gives more detail about the various editions of the works. See also: Morris L Parrish. *A List of the Writings of Charles Dickens.* Philadelphia, 1938. See also: "Charles Dickens" (first editions presented to the Library)" in the *Chronicle* XX, 3 (summer, 1959) pp 158-160.

NY —NEW YORK STATE LIBRARY, State Education Bldg Annex, Washington Ave, Albany, 12224.
Holdings: Vols 120 // Cat
Notes: Nearly complete collection of Dicken's works in first edition form, in the Gotshall Collections. Downs *Supplement,* number 292.

NY —STATE UNIVERSITY OF NEW YORK, COLLEGE AT BUFFALO, Lockwood Memorial Library, Main St, Buffalo, 14260. Stanton F Biddle, Assoc Dir
Notes: A large collection.

NY —NEW YORK PUBLIC LIBRARY, Rare Books and Manuscripts Div, Fifth Ave & 42 St, New York, 10018. William L Joyce, Asst Dir; Bernard McTigue, Cur, Arents Collection

NY —NEW YORK UNIVERSITY, Elmer Holmes Bobst Library, Div of Special Collections, Washington Sq S, New York, 10012. Frank Walker, Librn; Patrick McGuire, Asst Librn
Holdings: Vols (100,000) Cat Mss Pix
Notes: The Fales Collection of first (and other) editions of English and American novels from about 1750 to date (about 70,000 titles). Mss (30,000) pieces.

NC —UNIVERSITY OF NORTH CAROLINA, CHAPEL HILL, Wilson Library, Rare Book Collection, Chapel Hill, 27514. Paul S Koda, Cur of Rare Books
Holdings: Cat
Notes: Fully representative collection.

OH —OHIO UNIVERSITY, Vernon R Alden Library, Department of Archives and Special Collections, Athens, 45701. Gary A Hunt, Head
Holdings: Vols 67 Cat
Notes: A representative collection of first and other early editions, incl books issued in parts.

PA —FREE LIBRARY OF PHILADELPHIA, Rare Book Dept, Logan Sq, Philadelphia, 19103. Marie E Korey, Rare Book Librn
Holdings: Vols (4000) Cat Mss Pix
Notes: A collection of autograph letters

DICKENS, CHARLES, 1812-1870 (cont.)

(1050 written by Dickens, 10 received by him, 127 letters of his circle), original illustrations first and important English and American editions, biographical and critical reference works. Comprised of the William M Elkins and D Jacques Benoliel Collections, etc.

ON —QUEEN'S UNIVERSITY, Douglas Library, Kingston, K7L 5C4, Can. William F E Morley, Cur, Special Collections
Holdings: Vols 667 Uncat
Notes: First and early editions; reference works.

DICKEY, JAMES

MO —WASHINGTON UNIVERSITY, John M Olin Library, Campus Box 1061, St Louis, 63130.
Notes: A major collection, incl mss, correspondence, literary papers, photographs, etc. Described in *Special Collections: an Annotated Guide to the Holdings of the Manuscript Division and the University Archives and Research Collection.*

DICKINSON, ANNA ELIZABETH, 1842-1932

†DC —LIBRARY OF CONGRESS, Manuscript Division, Washington, 20540.
Notes: Papers, etc.

DICKINSON, EMILY

CT —TRINITY COLLEGE LIBRARY, Watkinson Library, 300 Summit St, Hartford, 06106. Jeffrey Kaimowitz, Cur
Holdings: Cat
Notes: First editions, etc.

MA —AMHERST COLLEGE, Library, Amherst, 01002. John Lancaster, Special Collections Librn
Holdings: Vols 250 Cat Mss Pix Microforms

MA —JONES LIBRARY, 43 Amity St, Amherst, 01002. Daniel J Lombardo, Cur of Special Collections
Holdings: Vols 700 Cat Mss Pix
Notes: Editions, recordings, plays, theses, clippings, periodicals, etc. Does not circulate. Unpublished guide available.

MA —HARVARD UNIVERSITY LIBRARY, Houghton Library, Cambridge, 02138. F Thomas Noonan, Cur, Reading Room; Lawrence Dowler, Associate Librn
Holdings: Cat Mss
Notes: See *Harvard Library Bulletin,* V (1951), pp 386-387.

NJ —PRINCETON UNIVERSITY, Library, Rare Books Dept, Princeton, 08544. Stephen Ferguson, Cur
Holdings: Vols 200 Cat
Notes: Books by and about the poet, incl works inspired by her poetry; material by or about "The Dickinson Circle," etc, as well as on the Amherst community. Gift of Mrs John Pershing.

†NY —SARAH LAWRENCE COLLEGE, Esther Raushenbush Library, 1 Meadway, Bronxville, 10708. Rose Ann Burstein, Librn
Notes: Emily Dickinson Collection and contemporary poetry.

NC —UNIVERSITY OF NORTH CAROLINA, GREENSBORO, Walter Clinton Jackson Library, Special Collections Dept, 1000 Spring Garden St, Greensboro, 27412. Emilie W Mills, Librn
Holdings: Vols 100 Uncat
Notes: First, variant and other editions of the poems of Emily Dickinson. Early critical works, biographies, Dickinson poems set to music and related Amherst, Mass items. Three letters from Mabel Loomis Todd and Millicent Todd Bingham.

VA —UNIVERSITY OF VIRGINIA, Alderman Library, Clifton Waller Barrett Collection, Charlottesville, 22901. Joan St C Crane, Cur of American Literature Collections
Notes: Papers.

WI —UNIVERSITY OF WISCONSIN, MADISON, Memorial Library, British & American Language & Literature Collection, 728 State St, Madison, 53706. Yvonne Schofer, Bibliographer
Holdings: Vols 2200 Mss Microforms Documents Periodicals
Notes: A collection of primary and secondary materials for nine major American women writers: Anne Bradstreet; Louisa May Alcott, Emily Dickinson, Kate Chopin, Mary Williams Freeman, Margaret Fuller, Sarah Orne Jewett, Charlotte Perkins Gilman, Harriet Beecher Stowe. Primary materials also collected for a list of less well known authors together with manuscripts and archives of letters of special research interest. Variety of holdings: fiction, poetry, drama, biography and autobiography, letters, memoirs, diaries, travel, domestic economy and other kinds of writings by women mostly of the 19th century. Held in Dept of Rare Books and Special Collections.

DICKINSON, GOLDSWORTHY LOWES

NY —HOFSTRA UNIVERSITY, Library, 1000 Fulton Ave, Hempstead, 11550. Charles R Andrews, Dean of Library Services

DICKSON, EDWARD AUGUSTUS, 1879-1956

CA —UNIVERSITY OF CALIFORNIA, LOS ANGELES, Research Library, Dept of Special Collections, 405 Hilgard Ave, Los Angeles, 90024. Edward Shreeves, Chairman, Bibliographers Group; David S Zeidberg, Head
Holdings: Cat Mss Pix
Notes: 18 linear feet of mss, correspondence, photographs, etc, relating to his career in public life and as editor of the *Los Angeles* Express.

DICKSON, GORDON

MD —UNIVERSITY OF MARYLAND, BALTIMORE COUNTY, Albin O Kuhn Library and Gallery, 5401 Wilkens Ave, Baltimore, 21228. Ann Copeland, Special Collections Librn
Holdings: Cat Mss
Notes: Science fiction mss. See entry under Science Fiction.

†MN —UNIVERSITY OF MINNESOTA, Walter Library, Room 109, Minneapolis, 55455.
Notes: Science fiction with some mss and a Gordon Dickson collection.

DICKSON, WILLIAM B.

PA —PENNSYLVANIA STATE UNIVERSITY, Fred Lewis Pattee Library, Labor History Collection, University Park, 16802. Peter Gottlieb, Archivist
Holdings: Cat Mss Pix
Notes: Personal papers.

DICTIONARIES see Encyclopedias and Dictionaries

DIEGUENO LANGUAGE

MO —UNIVERSITY OF MISSOURI-COLUMBIA, Museum of Anthropology Archives, 104 Swallow Hall, Columbia, 65201. Lawrence H Feldman, Museum Dir
Holdings: Vols (30) Cat Mss Maps Slides Microforms
Notes: Copies of Latin American and colonial mss. Many of the ms copies are of census, or census-like, documents of late colonial Verapaz; a few are from Sonsonate, El Saalvador or Chiapas, Mexico. Additional material in the archives incl an original Eskimo manuscript (ca 1930) and an original Diegueno Yuman card vocabulary (ca 1964) and the Museum archives (papers on old accession systems, etc). Uncataloged microfilm copies of colonial Otomi and other vocabularies are also part of the collection. A catalog of material in this collection will appear in the Annual Report of the Museum of Anthropology, beginning with the 1976-77 volume.

DIEHL, HARRY A.

AZ —NORTHERN ARIZONA UNIVERSITY, Special Collection Library, CU Box 6022, Flagstaff, 86011. Peter M Whiteley, Coordr/Archivist; William Mullane, Librn
Notes: Incl calendar of cases brought before the Board of Adjustment-Zoning in Phoenix, Ariz, 1940's.

DIES, MARTIN

TX —NORTH TEXAS STATE UNIVERSITY, Archives, NT Station Box 5188, Denton, 76203. Robert LaForte, University Archivist
Notes: Part of Oral History Collection. Interview with Dies, Texas politician and US Congressman (1931-46; 1950-56).

DIESEL MOTORS

IN —CUMMINS ENGINE CO, Information Center, 1000 Fifth St, Columbus, 47201. W E Poor, Tech Librn
Holdings: Vols 300 Cat Mss

WI —COLT INDUSTRIES, FM Engine Div, Library, 701 Lawton Ave, Beloit, 53511. Westley A Brill, Library Admin
Holdings: Vols 100 Cat Mss

DIESEL MOTORS—HISTORY

†NY —NEW YORK STATE LIBRARY, State Education Bldg, Annex, Washington Ave, Albany, 12224. John A Humphrey, Asst Commissioner for Libraries & State Librn
Notes: Collection of material on the history of the Diesel engine.

DIET AND DIETING

CA —LOS ANGELES PUBLIC LIBRARY, Science & Technology Dept, 630 W Fifth St, Los Angeles, 90071. Billie M Connor, Dept Head
Holdings: Vols 3500 Cat
Notes: Books on the cookery of all nationalities and ethnic groups. Strong collection of California cookery. Some early works in Spanish. Additional materials on wines and other beverages, quantity and institutional cookery, food technology, and special diets. Menu collection of approximately 1000 concentrates on Southern California.

NY —YWCA NATIONAL BOARD, Library, 726-730 Broadway, New York, 10012. Elizabeth Norris, Librn
Holdings: Vols (3000) Cat Mss
Notes: Women and their contemporary interests.

WI —UNIVERSITY OF WISCONSIN-STOUT, Library Learning Center, Menomonie, 54751. Philip Sawin Jr, Coll Develop Librn
Notes: Supports graduate program in Foods and Nutrition, which was begun in 1960. Quite specific collection with emphasis on the clinical aspects of nutrition.

DIET AND DISEASE

IL —UNIVERSITY OF ILLINOIS, URBANA/CHAMPAIGN, Library, Home Economics Library, 314 Bevier Hall, Champaign, 61820. Barbara C Swain, Librn
Holdings: Vols Cat Microforms
Notes: Foods and Nutrition.

NY —US VETERANS ADMINISTRATION HOSPITAL, Medical Library, 130 W Kingsbridge Rd, Bronx, 10468. Margaret M Kinney, Chief Librn
Holdings: Vols (23,000) Cat
Notes: No photocopying.

DIETETICS see Diet and Dieting

DIETRICH, MARLENE

CA —CLAREMONT COLLEGES, Honnold Library, Ninth & Dartmouth, Claremont, 91711. Tania Rizzo, Special Collections Dept Head
Notes: Working papers of Irving Wallace

DIETRICH, MARLENE (cont.)

and his family. Incl audio and video taped interviews with Wallace, Marlene Dietrich, Raymond Chandler, and Pablo Picasso.

DIGBY, SIR KENELM

CT —YALE UNIVERSITY, Medical Historical Library, Klebs Collection, 333 Cedar St, New Haven, 06520. Ferenc A Gyorgyey, Librn
Notes: Outstanding collection of works by and about him.

DIGGERS see Levellers

DIGGS, CHARLES

MI —WAYNE STATE UNIVERSITY, Walter P Reuther Library, Archives of Labor & Urban Affairs, Detroit, 48202. Philip Mason, Dir
Notes: The politics of 20th century America are mirrored in the collections of Patrick V McNamara, US Senator; Charles Diggs, US Representative from Michigan; Ofield Dukes, aide to Vice-President Hubert H Humphrey; and George and Grace Brewer, Socialist Party workers and assistants to Eugene V Debs.

DIGITAL CIRCUITS see Computers, Electronic; Digital Electronics

DIGITAL COMPUTERS see Computers, Electronic

DIGITAL ELECTRONICS

TX —TEXAS INSTRUMENTS INC, Library, PO Box 1443, Houston, 77001. Helen Manning, Librn
Holdings: Vols (800) Cat Microforms
Notes: Systems, design, and marketing of microprocessors and electronic semiconductors. Not open to the public.

DILLON, FANNIE CHARLES

CA —UNIVERSITY OF CALIFORNIA, LOS ANGELES, Music Library, Schonberg Hall, Los Angeles, 90024. Stephen M Fry, Music Librn
Notes: Mss.

DILLON, RICHARD HUGH, 1924-

CA —UNIVERSITY OF CALIFORNIA, LOS ANGELES, Research Library, Dept of Special Collections, 405 Hilgard Ave, Los Angeles, 90024. Edward Shreeves, Chairman, Bibliographers Group; David S Zeidberg, Head
Holdings: Vols 10 Mss
Notes: Incl 45 linear feet of mss and correspondence.

DIME NOVELS

†AR —UNIVERSITY OF ARKANSAS LIBRARY, Fayetteville, 72701. Samuel A Sizer, Librn of Special Collections
Notes: 1630 items in the Dime Novel Collection.

CA —SAN DIEGO PUBLIC LIBRARY, Wangenheim Rm, 820 E St, San Diego, 92101. Eileen Boyle, Librn
Holdings: Vols 769 Cat

CO —DENVER PUBLIC LIBRARY, Western History Department, 1357 Broadway, Denver, 80203. Eleanor M Gehres, Head
Holdings: Vols (50,000) Cat Mss Maps Pix Audiotapes Microforms
Notes: Western US History. The department has a separate catalog, published in 1970 in 7 vols by G K Hall Co. First supplement published in 1975 in 1 vol. There is a subject index of some 3 million entries to newspapers and magazines of the Rocky Mountain region, added to daily. The Western Newspaper Microfilm Center contains approx 7000 reels of Western US newspapers. Collection has ca 275,000 negatives and prints of Western life; and ca 2500 maps, cataloged and classified.

CT —YALE UNIVERSITY, Box 1603A, Yale Station, New Haven, 06520.
Notes: Incl the Gimbel Collection of Science Fiction Dime Novels, the Frank Reade and Jack Wright "boy inventor" dime novels published before 1900, and the Bryher Collection of boys' books.

DC —LIBRARY OF CONGRESS, Rare Book & Special Collections Div, Washington, 20540. William Matheson, Chief
Holdings: Vols 17,012 Uncat
Notes: An extensive collection representing such publications as the various Beadle series, Dawley's, De Witt's, Munro's, Street and Smith Publications, Tousey Series, the Seaside Library, etc, in all over 270 different series. (Note: Because of the fragile condition of much of the material, photocopying is often prohibited.)

FL —UNIVERSITY OF SOUTH FLORIDA, Library, Tampa, 33620. J B Dobkin, Special Collections Librn
Holdings: Vols 8000 Cat
Budget: ($7500)
Notes: American Dime Novel Collection. American dime novels and nickel libraries from 1860 into early 20th century. Very extensive nickel library holdings. Collection arranged by series title and issue number. In-house bibliography of holdings as guide to collection. Collection incl supplementary materials relating to history of the dime novel (bibliographies, copies of articles, etc).

IL —NORTHERN ILLINOIS UNIVERSITY, Founders Memorial Library, Rare Books and Special Collections Dept, De Kalb, 60115. William R DuBois, Dept Head
Holdings: Vols 7000
Notes: The Johannsen Collection. Probably the most extensive collection there is. Noncirculating. Partially cataloged. Limited photocopying.

IN —INDIANA UNIVERSITY, Lilly Library, Seventh St, Bloomington, 47405. William R Cagle, Librn
Holdings: Cat Mss
Notes: First editions of early and modern books plus some 18th and 19th century penny dreadfuls. Mss incl some original illustrations for 19th and 20th century books.

KY —UNIVERSITY OF KENTUCKY, Margaret I King Library, Dept of Special Collections, Lexington, 40506. William Marshall, Head
Holdings: Vols 75 Uncat
Notes: Collection confined to novels with a Kentucky background only (Indian fighting, political intrigue, adventure in the "wilds" of Kentucky); 30 other novels relating to Western adventures.

MA —BRANDEIS UNIVERSITY, Goldfarb Library, 415 South St, Waltham, 02154. Bessie Hahn, Dir
Notes: Dime Novel and Juvenile Literature Collection. Over 1000 dime novels, an extensive collection of the works of Horatio Alger, Harry Castlemon, Oliver Optic and other boys and girls literature of the 19th and early 20th century. Access to this collection is through the card catalog in Special Collections.

MI —MICHIGAN STATE UNIVERSITY, Libraries, Special Collections Div, East Lansing, 48824. Jannette Fiore, Librn
Holdings: Vols 600 Cat
Notes: The Russel B Nye Popular Culture Collection in the Michigan State Univ Libraries incl over (45,000) items. Most of the collection is organized into 4 categories: comic art, popular fiction, popular information materials and materials relating to the popular performing arts. Popular fiction in the collection is organized into juvenile, detective-mystery, and science fiction, westerns and women's fiction. In addition, there is a sample collection of dime novels and story papers (ca 400 issues representing nearly 100 titles). Pulp magazines which fall into none of the separate categories are housed with the dime novels and story papers. Juvenile Fiction: ca 4000 vols. Emphasis is on juvenile series fiction of the 19th and 20th centuries, with nearly 200 girls and 300 boys series represented. 19th-century "Sunday School" books andboth fiction and non-fiction scouting books are also included. Western Fiction: An exceptionally fine institutional collection, with over 3000 novels (most published between 1900 and 1950), almost all hardbound and in dust jackets, and nearly 500 pulp magazine issues representing more than fifty titles. The most important pulp runs are Street and Smith's *Western Story* Magazine and Warner Publications's *Ranch* Romances. Women's Fiction: Over 3000 novels and ca 1000 issues of romance, confession and movie magazines and pulps from the 1920s through the 1970s. Most of the novels are in the romance category, with over 2000 Harlequin novels, a good representation of other modern best-selling romances, and several dozen titles from late 19th-century romance series. Science Fiction: ca 3000 books and periodicals. MSU is a depository for the Science Fiction Writersof America, which contributes review copies of new books. The bulk of the collection is periodicals, with 71 titles represented. Most issues come from the period from the late 1940s to the present. The collection subscribes to most major science fiction magazines and holds a fanzine collection which now numbers over 2500. Detective-Mystery Fiction: ca 3500 novels, in paper and hardback, and pulps representing 28 titles from 1920-1950. Complete runs of *The London Mystery* Magazine and *Ellery Queen's Mystery* Magazine are included, along with a large sample collection of the more sensational detective and crime fiction magazines from the 1930s through the present.

MN —UNIVERSITY OF MINNESOTA, Libraries, Children's Literature Research Collections, 109 Walter Library, Minneapolis, 55455. Karen Nelson Hoyle, Cur
Holdings: Vols 70,000 Cat
Notes: American and British. Several published descriptions. Kerlan Collection.

NM —NEW MEXICO STATE UNIVERSITY, Library, Box 3475, Las Cruces, 88003. James Dyke, Dir
Holdings: Vols 400 // Cat
Notes: An exceptional representative collection of rare paperback American novels, including the oldest types of western novels.

NY —NEW YORK PUBLIC LIBRARY, Fifth Ave & 42 St, New York, 10018.
Notes: Remarkable collection of Beadle dime novels.

NY —NEW YORK UNIVERSITY, Elmer Holmes Bobst Library, Div of Special Collections, Washington Sq S, New York, 10012. Frank Walker, Librn; Patrick McGuire, Asst Librn
Notes: More than 8000 examples of 19th century Dime novels.

NY —UNIVERSITY OF ROCHESTER, Rush Rhees Library, Department of Rare Books and Special Collections, Rochester, 14627. Peter Dzwonkoski, Librn
Holdings: Vols 12,000 Cat

NY —STATE UNIVERSITY OF NEW YORK, STONY BROOK, Melville Library, Dept of Special Collections, Stony Brook, 11794. Evert Volkersz, Head
Holdings: Vols 101 Uncat
Notes: Collection incl first and later printings and editions.

†TX —UNIVERSITY OF TEXAS LIBRARIES, General Libraries, Humanities Research Center, PO Box 7219, Austin, 78712. John Chalmers, Librn
Notes: A notable collection of dime novels relating to Texas.

AB —UNIVERSITY OF ALBERTA, Cameron Library, The Bruce Peel Special Collections Room, Edmonton, T6G 2J8, Can. John Charles, Special Collections Librn
Holdings: Vols 220 Cat
Notes: Especially 19th century "penny dreadfuls" and Gothic literature.

DIMITRY, ALEXANDER, 1805-1883

DC —GEORGETOWN UNIVERSITY, Library, Special Collections Div, 37 & O Sts NW, Washington, 20057. George M Barringer, Special Collections Librn;

DIMITRY, ALEXANDER, 1805-1883 (cont.)

Nicholas B Sheetz, Mss Librn
Holdings: Cat Mss
Notes: The Richard X Evans Collection. The family archives of Richard X Evans, incl the papers of General John Smith (1750-1836), a member of Congress; Robert Mills (1781-1855); architect; and Alexander Dimitry (1805-1883), educator and diplomat.

DIOPHANTINE ANALYSIS

RI —BROWN UNIVERSITY, John Hay Library, 20 Prospect St, Providence, 02912. Mark N Brown, Cur Mss
Notes: The Royal Vale Heath Collection of about 200 of his designs, drawings, models, ocular, and verbal descriptions of simultaneous solutions to linear Diophantine equations in such examples as magic squares, Platonic solids, etc. These curious designs often were devised as talismans in ancient India and were first developed as mathematical problems by the Chinese.

DIOXIN (HERBICIDE CONTAMINANT) see Tetrachlorodibenzodioxin

DIPLOMACY

CT —YALE UNIVERSITY, Beinecke Rare Book & Manuscript Library, Osborn Collection, New Haven, 06520. Stephen R Parks, Cur
Holdings: Mss

DC —GEORGETOWN UNIVERSITY, Library, Special Collections Div, 37 & O Sts NW, Washington, 20057. George M Barringer, Special Collections Librn; Nicholas B Sheetz, Mss Librn
Holdings: Mss Cat
Notes: The Richard X Evans Collection. The family archives of Richard X Evans, incl the papers of General John Smith (1750-1836), a member of Congress; Robert Mills (1781-1855); architect; and Alexander Dimitry (1805-1883), educator and diplomat.

DC —GEORGETOWN UNIVERSITY, Library, Special Collections Div, 37 & O Sts NW, Washington, 20057. George M Barringer, Special Collections Librn; Nicholas B Sheetz, Mss Librn
Holdings: Mss Cat Pix
Notes: The personal papers of Richard T Crane (1882-1938), private secretary to Robert Lansing, 1915-1919; first American ambassador to Czechoslovakia, 1919-1921; and owner of the Westover Plantation in Virginia, 1921-1938. The papers - divided into three series, State Department, Prague and Westover - contain correspondence, memoranda, reports, diaries, documents, mss, printed material, and newspaper clippings. Correspondence incl letters from Robert Lansing, Charles Crane, Woodrow Wilson, Franklin Roosevelt, T G Masaryk, Jan Masaryk, Eduard Benes, Edward House, Herbert Hoover, Hugh Gibson, Joseph C Grew, Allan Dulles, and John Foster Dulles, among others.

DC —GEORGETOWN UNIVERSITY, Library, Special Collections Div, 37 & O Sts NW, Washington, 20057. George M Barringer, Special Collections Librn; Nicholas B Sheetz, Mss Librn
Holdings: Mss Pix
Notes: Correspondence, documents, journals, diaries, financial accounts, mss, photographs, and art work comprising the personal and professional papers of McCeney Werlich, diplomat, as well as those of his wife, Gladys Hinckley Werlich; Thomas Hinckley, and Robert O'Donnel Hinckley, both diplomats; papers of Eleanor O'Donnell Hinckley, mother of Gladys Werlich, and her husband Robert Hinckley, noted portrait painter. The papers incl: State Department correspondence and other material relating to McCeney Werlich's posts in Latvia (1926-1927), Poland (1927-1931), Costa Rica (1931-1932), Liberia (1932-1933), and France (1934-1936); correspondence from Robert O'Donnell Hinckley from his travels in the Orient, 1919; correspondence from Thomas Hinckley, incl accounts of the Austro-Hungarian empire, 1914-1915; as well as numerous journalsand diaries kept by Gladys Werlich regarding her extensive travels and variety of experiences.

DC —LIBRARY OF CONGRESS, Washington, 20540.
Notes: Project of a consortium to microfilm about 200,000 pp of material on Great Britain, France, Russia and Prussia, for the period 1848-1918 in the ms and documentary collections of the Austrain State Archives. The collection will incl among others, documents on the Austro-Prussian War of 1866, the treaty negotiations between France and Italy in 1868-1870, the Orient Question of 1877-1887, the persecution of Jews in Russia in 1882, the Congo Conference in Berlin, 1884-1887 and the British-Portuguese conflict in East Africa, 1889-1891. Copies are available at LC, the Center for Research Libraries, the Hampshire Inter-Library Center, and the libraries of Boston College, Yale, Harvard, Duke, Stanford and the University of Virginia.

MA —HARVARD UNIVERSITY LIBRARY, Law School Library, Langdell Hall, Cambridge, 02138. Harry S Martin III, Librn
Holdings: Cat

MA —TUFTS UNIVERSITY, Fletcher School of Law & Diplomacy, Murrow Center of Public Diplomacy, Medford, 02155. Natalie Schatz, Cur of Special Collections
Holdings: Vols (1500) // Cat Mss Pix Phonorecords Audiotapes 16mm Films
Notes: Professional papers and diaries of John Moors Cabot.

NJ —PRINCETON UNIVERSITY, Library, Rare Books Dept, Princeton, 08544. Stephen Ferguson, Cur
Holdings: Cat

RI —BROWN UNIVERSITY, John Hay Library, 20 Prospect St, Providence, 02912. Mark N Brown, Cur Mss
Holdings: Mss
Notes: Several ms collections relating to American diplomatic history: The Samuel Sullivan Cox, 1824-1889, Manuscript Collection--Ohio and New York Congressman, minor diplomat, (qv) (1200 items); the John Hay, 1838-1905, Manuscript Collection-Secretary to Lincoln, Secretary of State, (qv) (12,000); the Jonathan Russell, 1771-1832, Manuscript Collection--merchant, Massachusetts Congressman, and diplomat (qv) (8000 items); and the Henry Wheaton, 1785-1848, Manuscript Collection--jurist, and Charge d'Affaires to Denmark and Minister to Prussia, (qv) (275 items).

UT —BRIGHAM YOUNG UNIVERSITY, Harold B Lee Library, Unversity Hill, Provo, 84602. Sterling Albrecht, Dir
Holdings: Vols 35,464 Cat Mss Maps Pix Microforms

VA —UNIVERSITY OF VIRGINIA, Alderman Library, Manuscripts Dept, Charlottesville, 22901. Edmund Berkeley Jr, Cur
Holdings: Cat Mss Pix
Notes: Papers of J Rives Childs, foreign sevice officer in Saudi Arabia, Yemen, Ethiopia, and Morocco, and Casanova scholar.

DIPLOMATICS

NY —NEW YORK PUBLIC LIBRARY, Rare Books and Manuscripts Div, Fifth Ave & 42 St, New York, 10018. William L Joyce, Asst Dir; Susan E Davis, Cur of Mss
Holdings: Cat Mss

UT —BRIGHAM YOUNG UNIVERSITY, Harold B Lee Library, Unversity Hill, Provo, 84602. Sterling Albrecht, Dir
Holdings: Vols 35,464 Cat Mss Maps Pix Microforms

DI PRIMA, DIANE, 1934-

IN —INDIANA UNIVERSITY, Lilly Library, Seventh St, Bloomington, 47405. William R Cagle, Librn
Holdings: Cat Mss Pix
Notes: Correspondence and writings of Diane Di Prima, 1956-1972. Most of her letters are addressed to family members. 44 items. Other Di Prima correspondence and writings are incl in the LeRoi Jones papers. Library's holdings incl first editions of published works.

KY —UNIVERSITY OF LOUISVILLE, Ekstrom Library, Rare Books & Special Collections, 2301 S Third St, Louisville, 40208. George T McWhorter, Cur; Delinda Stephens Buie, Asst Cur
Holdings: Vols 50 Mss Pix
Budget: ($1500)
Notes: Books, plays and broadsides of the "Beat Generation" poet, in addition to correspondence and holograph notebooks.

BC —UNIVERSITY OF VICTORIA, McPherson Library, Victoria, V8W 3H5, Can.

DIPSOMANIA see Alcoholism

DIRAC, P. A. M.

†TX —UNIVERSITY OF TEXAS LIBRARIES, General Libraries, Humanities Research Center, PO Box 7219, Austin, 78712. John Chalmers, Librn
Notes: The papers of Alfred Schild (1921-1977), incl letters from PAM Dirac.

DIRECT ENERGY CONVERSION

PA —UNIVERSITY OF PENNSYLVANIA, Towne Scientific Library, 220 S 33 St, Philadelphia, 19104. Charles Meyers, Librn
Holdings: Vols (65,000) Cat

TN —TENNESSEE VALLEY AUTHORITY (TVA), Technical Library, 400 W Summit Hill Dr, E2 B7, Knoxville, 37902. Jesse C Mills, Chief Librn
Holdings: Vols (106,900) Cat Mss Maps Pix Audiotapes Microforms
Budget: ($2,025,000)
Notes: The Technical Library Headquarters Staff (order, cataloging, information, and administration) is located in Knoxville, Tenn. In addition there are branch libraries in Knoxville, Norris, and Chattanooga, Tennessee, and Muscle Shoals, Alabama.

DIRECT GENERATION OF ELECTRICITY see Direct Energy Conversion

DIRECT TAXATION see Taxation

DIRECTORIES

CA —LOS ANGELES PUBLIC LIBRARY, Business & Economic Dept, 630 W 5th St, Los Angeles, 90071. Joan Bartel, Principal Librn
Holdings: Vols 10,000 Microforms
Notes: Telephone directories for all US cities 10,000 or larger (and many smaller); some kept retrospectively. Selected collection of foreign telephone directories 1873-1942, many western cities and older for major cities. Ones from cities throughout the US (approx 2700 volumes). Social registers for southern California and some other areas. Trade and industrial directories covering the US and many foreign countries (estimated 5000 volumes). Many specialized directories for product lines, etc. Retrospective and current holdings of most standard directories. Partially cataloged.

CA —PASADENA PUBLIC LIBRARY, Business-Technology Division, 285 E Walnut St, Pasadena, 91101. Anne Cain, Librn for Reference Services
Holdings: Vols (19,000) Cat Microforms
Budget: ($35,000)
Notes: Investment and financial services (current and historical); trade and industrial directories; corporate annual reports; current economic statistics in business services and in state and federal government publications. Special index to directory collection.

CT —STAMFORD'S PUBLIC LIBRARY, Ferguson Library, Adult Services Dept, 96 Broad St, Stamford, 06901. Ernest A DiMattia Jr, Dir; Doris Goodlett, Head Adult Servs
Holdings: Vols (1,140) Cat

DIRECTORIES (cont.)

DC —AMERICAN SOCIETY OF ASSOCIATION EXECUTIVES, Information Central, 1575 Eye St NW, Washington, 20005. Cathy L Lalush, Mgr of Research and Info
Notes: Information regarding association management. Resources are designed to provide the association executive with the background knowledge for management decisions through case studies, research and statistical reports, bibliographies, and articles.

DC —DISTRICT OF COLUMBIA PUBLIC LIBRARY, Martin Luther King Memorial Library, Washingtoniana Div and Washington Star Collection, 901 G St NW, Washington, 20001. Roxanna Deane, Chief
Holdings: Vols (20,000) Cat Maps Pix Slides
Budget: ($5500)
Notes: Emphasis is on DC as a city and not on the federal government. Local papers are clipped daily; most clippings have been photocopied on archival paper. Depository for DC publications. City directories, 1822 to the present. Holdings of the division comprise the largest body of materials available documenting the history of the city. Published description of collection in *Materials for the Study of Washington,* by Perry G Fisher, 1974.

DC —LIBRARY OF CONGRESS, General Reading Rooms Division, Microform Reading Room, Washington, 20540.
Holdings: Cat Mss Maps Microforms
Notes: Microform materials only in this LC Division. Works of individual authors; holdings of collections; archival records, etc, press releases and translations, etc.

DC —LIBRARY OF CONGRESS, Collections Management Division, Washington, 20540.
Notes: The Collections Management Division maintains and services the Library's general classified book collections and telephone and city directories.

GA —ATLANTA PUBLIC LIBRARY, Ivan Allen Jr Dept of Science, Industry & Government, One Margaret Mitchell Square, Atlanta, 30303. William D Munro, Head
Holdings: Vols (1600) Cat Microforms
Budget: ($180,000)
Notes: This separately housed collection incl 450 corporate, international, foreign, product, service, association, and professional directories. Also manufacturing directories for all states and some foreign countries.

IL —CHICAGO HISTORICAL SOCIETY, Library, Clark St at North Ave, Chicago, 60614. Robert L Brubaker, Librn
Holdings: Vols (150,000) Cat Mss Maps Pix Slides Microfilm
Notes: Incl Chicago imprints, periodicals, and newspapers; Chicago city, telephone, and commercial directories; catalogs of Chicago mail order houses and special industries and stores; paper and archives of Chicago leaders and organizations (4,000, 000 items); negatives and photographs from Chicago newspaper morgues, 1900-1965 (250,000); photographs from Chicagoland-in-Pictures, a project for historical photography sponsored by the Society and the Chicago Area Camera Clubs Association since 1948 (22,000); daguerreotypes, ambrotypes, tintypes, sterographs, other photographic materials, engravings, lithographs, prints in other media (228,000); clippings from major Chicago newspapers since the 1930s (50, 000); trade and advertising cards (6000); programs of Chicago theatres (5000); early sheet music concerning Chicagoor published in Chicago (4600); fiction with a Chicago locale.

IL —NEWBERRY LIBRARY, 60 W Walton St, Chicago, 60610. Diana Haskell, Cur of Modern Mss
Holdings: Cat
Notes: Large but spotty holdings.

IN —ALLEN COUNTY PUBLIC LIBRARY, Fred J Reynolds Historical Genealogy Collection, 900 Webster St, Fort Wayne, 46802. Rick J Ashton, Dir; Michael B Clegg, Manager
Holdings: Vols 200,000 Cat Mss Maps Pix Microforms
Notes: Incl state, county, regional, town and church histories. All census schedules and port of entry records released by the federal government are in the microfilm collection of 40,000 reels. The collection contains parish registers and publications of British parish register societies. Canadian, English, Scotch, Irish and Welsh records are well represented. The heraldry collection is housed with the genealogy collection. Allen County Public Library is and has been the depository for the North American Association of Directory Publishers since 1964.

KY —BOYD COUNTY PUBLIC LIBRARY, 1740 Central Ave, Ashland, 41101. Juliette Bryson, Dir
Holdings: Cat Periodicals
Notes: Over 60 city directories and telephone books relating to the Middle Atlantic states and southern states primarily, with some materials from the northeastern states. Collection will expand to incl more areas of the US.

†MA —BOSTON PUBLIC LIBRARY, Copley Sq, Boston, 02117.
Holdings: Microforms
Notes: Microforms Publication by Research Publications; 1st Segment: City Directories of the US through 1860, 2nd Segment: City Directories of the US 1861-1881.

MA —BOSTON PUBLIC LIBRARY, Kirstein Business Branch, 20 City Hall Ave, Boston, 02108. Joseph E Walsh, Business Branch Librn
Holdings: Vols 42,900 Cat
Notes: City and telephone directories, trade directories, investment manuals and services, law reporting services, trade periodicals and newspapers, government periodicals, periodical indexes, books on all aspects of business incl accounting, advertising, banking, retail and wholesale trade, marketing, real estate, etc. No separate catalog or index to the collection.

MA —OLD STURBRIDGE VILLAGE, Research Library, Sturbridge, 01566. Theresa Rini Percy, Librn
Holdings: Cat Microforms
Notes: New England cities and towns to 1860; also the microfiche edition of Speare, *American Directories through 1860* (complete texts).

MA —AMERICAN ANTIQUARIAN SOCIETY LIBRARY, 185 Salisbury St, Worcester, 01609. Marcus A McCorison, Dir & Librn
Holdings: Vols 6900 Cat
Notes: The best collection to 1860.

MI —SAINT CLAIR COUNTY LIBRARY, 210 McMorran Blvd, Port Huron, 48060. Frances A Marshall, Local History Librn
Holdings: Vols 5116 Cat Mss Maps Pix Microforms
Notes: The

MN —JAMES JEROME HILL REFERENCE LIBRARY, Fourth St at Market St, Saint Paul, 55106. Virgil F Massman, Dir
Holdings: Vols 650 Cat
Notes: US and foreign industrial directories.

NY —NEW YORK STATE LIBRARY, State Education Bldg Annex, Washington Ave, Albany, 12224.
Holdings: Vols 10,000 Uncat
Notes: Many 18th century items; emphasis on, but not exclusively, New York and neighboring states. Also hold microform ed of entries in *Spear's Bibliography of American Directories* to 1860. Purchasing directories in microfilm of major cities, 1861-1881.

NY —CORNELL UNIVERSITY LIBRARIES, Collection of Regional History, Dept of Manuscripts and Univ Archives, Ithaca, 14853.
Notes: Rural Indexes and "Compass System" maps, Ithaca, NY, 1921-40; 1.5 ft.

NY —NEW YORK PUBLIC LIBRARY, Research Libraries, General Research Division, Fifth Ave & 42 St, New York, 10018. Rodney Phillips, Chief
Holdings: Vols (2,225,000) Cat Maps Pix Microforms
Budget: ($775,718)

NY —NEW YORK PUBLIC LIBRARY, Research Libraries, Economic & Public Affairs Div, Fifth Ave & 42 St, New York, 10018. Edward DiRoma, Chief
Holdings: Vols (1,500,000) Cat Microforms

NC —DUKE UNIVERSITY, William R Perkins Library, Durham, 27706. Elvin E Strowd, University Librn
Notes: The Perkins Library collection of American city directories includes more than 2000 items, in paper copy and on microfiche (pre-1900). It is especially strong in holdings for the southern states.

OH —CLEVELAND PUBLIC LIBRARY, Business, Economics and Labor Department, 325 Superior Ave, Cleveland, 44114. Joan Sorger, Head
Holdings: Cat
Notes: A total of 1095 trade, industrial and professional directories and 1700 telephone directories. There are 688 directories arranged by trade or industry, 176 arranged by foreign country, 113 state industrial directories, 118 city directories. Telephone directories incl 1340 United States cities and 360 foreign cities.

OH —OHIO HISTORICAL SOCIETY, Archives Library Division, 1982 Velma Ave, Columbus, 43211. Dennis East, Division Chief
Holdings: Vols (96,000) Cat Mss Maps Pix Slides Microforms
Budget: ($18,000)
Notes: This library is the primary collection for Ohio. Most purchases are on the rare and out of print market. Collection area is early American history, esp relating to exploration into the Northwest Territory. Also, Ohio archaeology, natural history, and artifacts. Major media collections are books (96,000), newspapers (25,000 vols and 22, 000 microfilm), pictures (50,000), maps (2500), manuscripts (1,500,000). Library is noncirculating except through interlibrary loan of microfilm.

WI —MILWAUKEE PUBLIC LIBRARY, 814 W Wisconsin Ave, Milwaukee, 53233. Donald J Sager, City Librn
Holdings: Cat
Notes: Strong collection of trade directories for all states, regions and many foreign countries. Large collection of product directories and annual buying guides.

†ON —METROPOLITAN TORONTO LIBRARY, Social Sciences Dept, 789 Yonge St, Toronto, M4W 2G8, Can. Abdus Salam, Head
Holdings: Vols Cat Maps Phonorecords Audiotapes 16mm Films Microforms
Notes: Extensive collection of current university and college catalogs from throughout the US and Canada, as well as selected foreign universities. Also extensive collection of educational directories and guides.

ON —METROPOLITAN TORONTO LIBRARY, Business Dept, 789 Yonge St, Toronto, M4W 2G8, Can. Patricia Dye, Head
Holdings: Vols (63,682) Cat Microforms
Budget: ($5800)
Notes: Extensive current and historical information with emphasis on Canadian companies incl annual reports, clippings and pamphlets files, and a collection of business and trade directories. Also international directories. Approximately 800 current periodicals, and up-dating services giving corporation information.

ON —METROPOLITAN TORONTO LIBRARY, Canadian History Dept, 789 Yonge St, Toronto, M4W 2G8, Can.
Notes: Bell Canada Telephone Historical Collection of 448 reels of microfilm of Ontario and Quebec telephone books from 1878 to 1979. The collection will be updated. Toronto city directories from 1868-1949 are available also.

DIRECTORY PUBLISHERS ASSOCIATION see North American Association of Directory Publishers

DIRGES see Funeral Music

DIRIGIBLES

DC —LIBRARY OF CONGRESS, Prints & Photographs Div, Washington, 20540.
Notes: Incl the great French collection of

DIRIGIBLES (cont.)

Albert and Gaston Tissandier, and the aeronautical biography files compiled by Jules Francois Dupuis-Delcourt. Ms materials are in the Manuscript Division.

OH —AKRON-SUMMIT COUNTY PUBLIC LIBRARY, Science & Technology Div, 55 S Main St, Akron, 44326. Joyce McKnight, Head
Holdings: Vols 820 Cat Pix
Notes: The Lighter-Than-Air Society book collection is in the Akron Public Library. Incl foreign language books.

TX —SOUTHERN METHODIST UNIVERSITY, DeGolyer Library, Box 396, SMU, Dallas, 75275. Clifton H Jones, Dir
Holdings: Vols (80,000) Cat Mss Maps Pix Slides Microforms
Notes: First editions of prominent authors; also of books in subject emphasis collectons. All subjects listed in the vol are strong. Numerous collections of personal papers relating to subjects also.

DIRKSEN, EVERETT MCKINLEY, 1896-1969

IL —EVERETT M DIRKSEN CONGRESSIONAL LEADERSHIP RESEARCH CENTER, Fourth & Broadway, Pekin, 61554. William C McCully Jr, Dir
Holdings: Mss Maps Pix Slides Phonorecords Audiotapes Videotapes 16mm Films
Notes: The Dirksen Collection is described in published guides to specific portions of the papers as they are processed and made available for research. The collection is particularly comprehensive from 1951 through 1969. Inquiries are welcome.

DIRLAM, ARLAND

MA —SOCIETY FOR THE PRESERVATION OF NEW ENGLAND ANTIQUITIES, Library, 141 Cambridge St, Boston, 02114. Ellie Reichlin, Librn & Cur of Photographic Collections
Holdings: Vols (3000) // Cat Pix Microforms
Budget: ($75,000)
Notes: Architecture of the Northeast. Drawings (original designs, measured drawings, plot plans, etc). Over 7500 items, incl extensive collections of original designs by Ogden Codman, Jr (1890s-early 1900s); Arthur Little and Herbert Browne (1890s-1920s); Luther Briggs (1840s-1860s); Arland Dirlam (1930s-1960s), together with important examples of the work of Asher Benjamin, Richard Upjohn, and others. Measured drawings incl extensive holdings of work undertaken by HABS (Historic American Buildings Survey) in Massachusetts in the 1930s, 1940s under director Frank Chouteau Brown. Also represented are several residential and commercial commissions by F C Brown, not connected with HABS. Collection incl architectural pattern books, builders guides, 18th-19th century. Approx 350 volumes, English and American publications.

DISABLED see Handicapped

DISALLE, MICHAEL V.

OH —OHIO HISTORICAL SOCIETY, Archives Library Division, 1982 Velma Ave, Columbus, 43211. Dennis East, Division Chief
Notes: Papers of the Democratic governor 1959-1963.

DISARMAMENT

DC —US ARMS CONTROL & DISARMAMENT AGENCY, Library, George Washington Univ Special Collections, Washington, 21 St & Virginia Ave, NW, Rm 5851, Washington, 20451. Diane Ferguson, Librn
Holdings: Vols 4500 // Cat
Notes: Arms control, disarmament and related topics.

NY —HUDSON INSTITUTE, Library, Quaker Ridge Rd, Croton-on-Hudson, 10520. Mildred Schneck, Librn
Holdings: Vols (10,000) Cat
Budget: ($40,000)
Notes: Social sciences and world futures. About 30 percent of the collection emphasizes materials useful to our ongoing program of examining possible world futures: social and economic indicators, forecasts, current social problems, arms control and disarmament.

NY —SYRACUSE UNIVERSITY LIBRARIES, Ernest S Bird Library, George Arents Research Library for Special Collections, Syracuse, 13210. Carolyn A Davis, Manuscripts Librn; Amy S Doherty, University Archivist; Mark F Weimer, Rare Book Librn
Notes: Incl correspondence of Dr Benjamin Spock (1903-) on medical subjects. Vietnam peace movement, nuclear disarmament, state and national politics, education and civil rights. Papers 1904-76 (112 linear feet).

PA —CARLOW COLLEGE, Grace Library, Fifth Ave, Pittsburgh, 15213. Joan M Mitchell, Dir of Library Services
Holdings: Vols (977) Cat Pamphlets
Budget: ($300)
Notes: The Peace Studies Collection is a collection of books which deals with the search for peace in the modern world from the perspective of the Judeo-Christian tradition. It is especially strong in the area of social justice, civil rights and world politics.

PA —SWARTHMORE COLLEGE, Peace Collection, Swarthmore, 19081. Jean R Soderlund, Cur of Peace Collection
Holdings: Vols (10,000) Cat Mss Pix Microforms
Notes: Disarmament has been on of the central subject emphases of the Peace Collection since its inception in 1930. A large proportion of the total book collection deals with this subject. In addition, major records and document collections in this area incl those of the Woman's Peace Party (1915-1919), and its successor, the Women's International League for Peace and Freedom (1919-); the War Resisters League. SANE; Women Strike for Peace; and Fellowship of Reconciliation. The Peace Collection has been described in Downs 972, 978, 4633, and in Downs 1950-1961 Supplement 507 and 916. For descriptions of major collections, see the *Guide to the Swarthmore College Peace Collection,* 2nd ed (1981). *See also* entry under Pacifism - History.

DISASTERS AND DISASTER RELIEF

DC —AMERICAN NATIONAL RED CROSS, National Headquarters Library, 17th & D St NW, Washington, 20006. Roberta F Biles, Library Director
Holdings: Vols 1500 Cat
Notes: National and International Red Cross.

DC —NATIONAL ARCHIVES AND RECORDS SERVICE, National Archives Library, Pennsylvania Ave & Eighth St NW, Washington, 20408.
Notes: American National Red Cross has transferred its archives. 1881-1946, to 900 linear ft.

DC —NATIONAL ARCHIVES AND RECORDS SERVICE, Civil Archives Division, Washington, 20408.
Notes: Records of the President's Commission on the Accident at Three Mile Island (May-December 1979).

IL —CHICAGO HISTORICAL SOCIETY, Library, Clark St at North Ave, Chicago, 60614. Robert L Brubaker, Librn
Holdings: Vols (150,000) Cat Mssd Mpas Pix
Notes: Incl the J Norman Jensen Collection, a file of approximately 8500 cards concerning ships that sank in the Great Lakes area from 1679 to 1947.

NM —MUSEUM OF NEW MEXICO, Photo Archives, Box 2087, Santa Fe, 87503. Arthur L Olivas, Cur; Richard Rudisill, Photo Historian
Notes: Photographs of disasters, incl fires, train, air and water.

†NY —COLUMBIA UNIVERSITY LIBRARIES, Butler Library, Rare Book and Manuscript Library, 535 W 114 St, New York, 10027.
Notes: Papers of the US Solicitor General, 1930-33, relating to the American Red Cross Mission to Russia, 1917-18. In addition, files relating to the American Library Association's Special Committee to Aid Italian Libraries' assistance to Italian libraries to help restore books, mss and other library materials after the 1966 floods in Florence.

OH —BOWLING GREEN STATE UNIVERSITY, Jerome Library, Institute for Great Lakes Research, Bowling Green, 43403. Richard J Wright, Dir
Holdings: Vols (2500) Cat Mss Maps Pix Slides Phonorecords Audiotapes Videotapes 16mm Films Microforms
Budget: ($8300)
Notes: About 50 major ms collections, most of them processed; several thousand minor ms items, unprocessed. 100,000 pictures, incl several thousand film and glass plate negatives. Microforms of government vessel registries, vessel passages, 1500 maps, some mss. 6000 naval architectural drawings, 600 vols of scrapbooks. 140 periodical titles, current and op. Author/title/subject catalog.

OH —GREENE COUNTY DISTRICT LIBRARY, 76 E Market St, PO Box 520, Xenia, 45385. Julie M Overton, Local History Coordr
Holdings: Uncat
Notes: 8 notebooks concerning the killer tornado which hit Xenia, Ohio on April 3, 1974, which is said to be the worst in US history. This material consists of 2 vols of photos, 2 of personal stories, 3 of newspaper clippings arranged according to subject matter, 1 of miscellaneous material from other publications, some national. Also, 10 notebooks called *Xenia Rebuilds,* clippings concerning all facets of rebuilding from June 1, 1974 to the present, arranged by subject.

MB —UNIVERSITY OF MANITOBA, Elizabeth Dafoe Library, Archives and Special Collections Dept, Winnipeg, R3T 2N2, Can. Richard E Bennett, Dept Head; Corrado A Santoro, Reference Archivist
Notes: Handwritten notes of George Black, official representative of the Manitoba government on board the steamer "Assiniboine" despatched by the government to give relief to settlers in distress owing to high water flooding. April 23, 1897.

DISCIPLES OF CHRIST

GA —AGNES SCOTT COLLEGE, McCain Library, E College Ave, Decatur, 30030. Judith Bourgeois Jensen, Librn
Holdings: Vols (945) Uncat
Budget: $300
Notes: The Frontier Religion Collection, which was given by Prof Walter Browlow Posey, traces the effects of slavery on religion in the Old South Frontier prior to 1860. A catalog file (by author entry only) accompanies the collection at present. Noncirculating.

KY —MIDWAY COLLEGE, Marrs Library, Stephens St, Midway, 40347. Kay Cordoves, Librn
Holdings: Vols (2000)// Cat
Notes: Brotherhood Collection covers history of Christian Church (Disciples of Christ) and related materials.

MO —UNIVERSITY OF MISSOURI-KANSAS CITY, General Library, Snyder Collection of Americana, 5100 Rockhill Road, Kansas City, 64110. Kenneth J LaBudde, Dir; Robert Paustian, Asst Dir
Holdings: Vols 25,000 Cat
Notes: Nucleus was Robert M Snyder, Jr Americana Collection of some 14,000 items. Contains printed materials on 19th-century American history, especially the Trans-Mississippi West. Strengths include the history of Kansas City and Jackson County, Missouri, Kansas and Missouri county and state histories, American frontier religion (esp the Mormons and Alexander Campbell's Disciples of Christ), the history of railroads and transportation, the cattle

DISCIPLES OF CHRIST (cont.)

trade, 19th-Century biography and autobiography, North American Indians and early Kansas and Missouri imprints.

NE —YORK COLLEGE, Levitt Library, York, 67467. Charles Van Baucom, Dir
Holdings: Vols (1430) Cat Mss Pix Audiotapes
Notes: In the Levitt Library, The American Restoration Movement Collection currently focuses on titles related to the Churches of Christ, although titles on the Christian Churches (Independents) and the Disciples of Christ make up a fair percentage of the collection. To promote the development and the use of the Restoration History Collection, York College participates in the Christian College Librarians Conference with sister colleges David Lipscomb, Nashville, TN; Abilene Christian University, Abilene, TX; Oklahoma Christian College, Oklahoma City, OK; Harding College, Searcy, AR; Pepperdine University, Malibu, CA, and others; also, with the Disciples of Christ Historical Society, 1101 19th Ave S, Nashville, TN 37212.

OH —HIRAM COLLEGE, Teachout-Price Memorial Library, Hiram, 44234. Joanne M Sawyer, Archivist; Marjorie M Adams, Music Librn
Holdings: Vols 88 Mss Phonorecords

OK —PHILLIPS UNIVERSITY, John Rogers Graduate Seminary Library, University Sta, Enid, 73701. John L Sayre, Dir of University Libraries
Holdings: Vols 3000 Cat Mss Maps Pix Microforms
Budget: $500
Notes: Disciples of Christ Collection.

OK —MIDWEST CHRISTIAN COLLEGE, Library, 6600 N Kelley Ave, Oklahoma City, 73111. Jean Cavett, Dir
Holdings: Vols (7000) Cat Pix Phonorecords Audiotapes Filmstrips Microforms
Notes: The Restoration Movement (Independent Christian Church) to restore the Church to its New Testament form. Incl churches called "Christian Churches," "Churches of Christ," "Disciples of Christ," and a few called just "Christ's Church."

TN —JOHNSON BIBLE COLLEGE, Glass Memorial Library, Knoxville, 37998. Helen Lemmon, Librn
Holdings: Vols (700) // Cat
Notes: History of Churches of Christ and Disciples of Christ.

TN —DISCIPLES OF CHRIST HISTORICAL SOCIETY, 1101 19th Ave S, Nashville, 37212. James M Scole, Pres
Holdings: Vols (26,000) Cat Mss Maps Pix Slides Phonorecords Audiotapes Videotapes 16mm Films Filmstrips Microforms
Budget: $184,000
Notes: The Campbell-Stone Movement--all aspects of its history, incl the Disciples of Christ, Christian Church, and Churches of Christ.

TX —TEXAS CHRISTIAN UNIVERSITY, Mary Couts Burnett Library, Fort Worth, 76129.
Notes: Assimilated into main collection of the University Library, adding special strengths but no longer maintained as a separate collection.

VA —LYNCHBURG COLLEGE, Knight-Capron Library, Lynchburg, 24501. Mary C Scudder, Dir
Holdings: Vols (84) Cat Mss
Notes: Depository for the Christian Church in Virginia (Disciples of Christ). Bibliography available upon request.

DISCLOSURE, MEDICAL see Informed Consent (Medical Law)

DISCOVERERS see Discovery and Exploration; Explorers; Voyages and Travels

DISCOVERIES, MARITIME see Discovery and Exploration

DISCOVERY AND EXPLORATION

AZ —NORTHERN ARIZONA UNIVERSITY, Special Collection Library, CU Box 6022, Flagstaff, 86011. Peter M Whiteley, Coordr/Archivist; William Mullane, Librn
Holdings: Maps
Notes: Early Travel and Exploration of the West collection incl *Wheeler Atlas* of Israel C Russell, 1870's. One of the most comprehensive collections of Wheeler Survey Maps in existence. Also, *Clarence King Survey of the 40th Parallel,* 1877.

CA —AZUSA PACIFIC COLLEGE, Marshburn Memorial Library, Citrus & Alosta, Azusa, 91702. Edward Peterman, Librn
Holdings: Vols (6000) Uncat
Budget: ($30,000)
Notes: Significant holdings in the George E Fullerton Library of Californiana and Western Americana.

CA —UNIVERSITY OF CALIFORNIA, SAN DIEGO, Central University Library, Mandeville Dept of Special Collections, La Jolla, 92093. Lynda Corey Claassen, Head
Holdings: Vols (2400) Cat Mss Maps
Notes: The Hill Collection of Pacific Voyages, including reports and commentaries of important voyages in the Pacific, from those of Magellan and Sir Francis Drake to exploration through the first half of the 19th century. Includes many rare overland accounts to the Pacific across North America, Mexico, and Panama.
Bibliography: Silveira de Braganza, Ronald, *The Hill Collection of Pacific Voyages* (La Jolla: Calif, 1974-1983).

CA —UNIVERSITY OF CALIFORNIA, LOS ANGELES, Research Library, African Studies Collection, 405 Hilgard Ave, Los Angeles, 90024. Edward Shreeves, Chairman, Bibliographers Group; Joseph J Lauer, African Studies Bibliographer
Holdings: Maps Pix Slides Phonorecords Audiotapes Microforms
Notes: General collection mainly in the humanities and social sciences, covering prehistoric times to the present. Particular strengths include: early travel and exploration, mission field, literature, vernacular languages and literatures, Portuguese Africa, slavery (have the British Foreign Office's *General Correspondence. Slave Trade* on microfilm). Extensive holdings of journals, newspapers and government publications. The collection was described in the *Handbook of American Resources for African Studies* (1967).

CA —UNIVERSITY OF SOUTHERN CALIFORNIA, Allan Hancock Foundation, Hancock Library of Biology and Oceanography, Los Angeles, 90007. Kimberly Douglas, Librn
Holdings: Vols (16,000) Cat Maps
Notes: Mostly marine, but incl some land expeditions. Covers all geographical areas. Also incl serial collection of 80,000 vols.

CA —PACIFIC GROVE PUBLIC LIBRARY, 550 Central Ave, Pacific Grove, 93950. Margaret McBride, Library Dir
Holdings: Vols (1200) // Cat
Notes: Alvin Seale South Seas Collection, incl rare and unusual items, accounts of early voyages, ships' logs and artifacts. Separate catalog. Gift of Alvin Seale, curator of Steinhart Aquarium, San Francisco, 1937.

CA —UNIVERSITY OF CALIFORNIA, SANTA CRUZ, University Library, Special Collections, Santa Cruz, 95064. Rita Bottoms, Special Collections Librn; Margaret Felts, South Pacific Collection Bibliographer
Holdings: Vols (10,000) Cat
Notes: Astronomy library. Incl all major astronomical and astrophysical journals and an extensive collection of domestic and foreign observatory publications. The book collection is particularly strong in stellar structure and evolution, stellar spectroscopy, the interstellar medium, galactic structure, external galaxies, general relativity and gravitational radiation, and high-energy astrophysics.

CT —TRINITY COLLEGE LIBRARY, Watkinson Library, 300 Summit St, Hartford, 06106. Jeffrey Kaimowitz, Cur
Holdings: Cat

CT —YALE UNIVERSITY, Beinecke Rare Book & Manuscript Library, Henry C Taylor Collection, New Haven, 06520.
Holdings: Vols 396 Cat Mss
Notes: Early navigation and Americana. See Kebabian, John S, *The Henry C Taylor* Collection (New Haven: Yale University Library, 1971).

DC —LIBRARY OF CONGRESS, Rare Book & Special Collections Div, Washington, 20540. William Matheson, Chief
Notes: The Hans P and Hann Kraus Collection of contemporary materials (maps, books, mss, medals and portraits) designed to present Sir Francis Drake as his contemporaries would have learned about him. See Kraus, Hans P, *Sir Francis Drake, a Pictorial Biography,* (Amsterdam, N Israel, 1970).

DC —LIBRARY OF CONGRESS, Manuscript Division, Washington, 20540. John C Broderick, Chief
Notes: The Hans P Kraus Collection of documents relating to colonial Spanish America, 1492-1819. Focusing on colonial Mexico, incl material on exploration, government, activities of the Inquisition, taxation and economic conditions, relations with the Indians and the French, and the impending loss of land to Anglo-American settlers. Also contains items concerning the history of Spanish Florida, Tezozomoc's chronicle on the history of the Aztecs, and mss describing the explorations of Amerigo Vespucci, Giovanni da Verrazzano, Alvar Nunez Cabeza de Vaca, Pedro de Ursua, and Lope de Aguirre.

DC —NATIONAL GEOGRAPHIC SOCIETY, Library, 1146 16th St NW, Washington, 20036. Susan Fifer Canby, Dir
Holdings: Vols (63,000) Cat Mss Maps Pix
Notes: Material concerning land, sea, and space exploration--past and present. All fields of anthropology, natural history, geography, etc.

FL —UNIVERSITY OF MIAMI, Otto G Richter Library, PO Box 248214, Coral Gables, 33124. Frank Rodgers, Dir of Libraries
Notes: The rare Floridiana collection incl a great variety of primary source materials such as mss, maps, photographs, scrapbooks, correspondence, clippings, etc. Particular subject strengths in this collection incl: Spanish exploration and colonialization of Florida, the Florida Indians, wildlife conservation, landscaping, corporate records, etc. The rare Floridiana collection is complemented by a collection of titles ranging from the oldest to the very latest published books on Florida subjects.

HI —BERNICE P BISHOP MUSEUM, Library, PO Box 19000-A, Honolulu, 96819. Cynthia Timberlake, Librn
Holdings: Vols (90,000) Cat Mss Maps Pix Slides Microforms
Budget: ($30,000)
Notes: Only American library devoted exclusively to the Pacific region. Collection reflects historical and contemporary research emphases of Bishop Museum; ie the natural and cultural history of the Pacific. Areas of concentration incl archaeology, ethnology, linguistics, voyages and explorations, history, vertebrate and invertebrate zoology, botany and museology. Strong special collections incl photographs, mss and archives, maps and art. Publications: Quarterly "Additions to the Catalog," *Dictionary Catalog of the* Library (9 vols and 2 suppl; Boston: G K Hall, 1964-69).

HI —PACIFIC SCIENTIFIC INFORMATION CENTER, Bernice P Bishop Library, Geography and Map Division, PO Box 19000A, Honolulu, 96819. Lee S Motteler, Geographer; Valerie T Higa, Asst Geographer
Holdings: Vols (2000) Cat Mss Maps Pix
Notes: Incl 20,000 maps and 70,000 aerial photos of Hawaii and the Pacific.

HI —PACIFIC SUBMARINE MUSEUM, Library, Naval Submarine Base, Pearl Harbor, 96860. Ray W de Yarmin, Cur
Holdings: Vols (1500) Cat Mss Maps Pix Slides Phonorecords 16mm Films
Budget: ($600)
Notes: Incl 3000 pictures. Extensive missile and torpedo collection; submarine models;

DISCOVERY AND EXPLORATION (cont.)

salvage/deep-sea diver exhibit; Arctic exploration by submarines Worl War II submarine components. Research program for students, authors, lecturers, etc.

IL —NEWBERRY LIBRARY, 60 W Walton St, Chicago, 60610. Robert W Karrow, Jr, Cur of Maps
Holdings: Vols 20,000 Cat
Notes: Incl material in the Ayer Collection on the discovery and exploration of the Americas and the Greenlee Collection on Portuguese discovery and exploration.

IN —INDIANA UNIVERSITY, Lilly Library, Seventh St, Bloomington, 47405. William R Cagle, Librn
Holdings: Cat
Notes: Extensive holdings for the Americas from the Mendel Collection.

IN —BUTLER UNIVERSITY, Irwin Library, Hugh Thomas Miller Rare Book Room, 4600 Sunset Ave, Indianapolis, 46208. Gisela Terrell, Rare Books Librn
Holdings: Vols 2500 Cat Maps Pix
Notes: *The William F Charters South Seas* Collection. With the additions made by Butler University since the acceptance of this collection in 1931, we are housing circa 2500 volumes pertaining to the Pacific islands and their peoples; materials range from the earliest explorers' and circumnavigators' reports to detailed studies in anthropology, history, religion, art, socio-political structures, botany and zoology.

IN —INDIANA STATE UNIVERSITY, Cunningham Memorial Library, Dept of Rare Books & Special Collections, Terre Haute, 47809. Lawrence J McCrank, Head
Holdings: Vols 400 Uncat Maps
Notes: Nature of this material essentially that of the books listed in E G Cox, *A Reference Guide to the Literature of Travel.* Books range from the 16th century to early 1960s, in English, French, German, Latin, Italian, and Dutch. Strong in Cook materials (ie, original editions of first 3 voyages, in English and French and some Dutch).

KS —UNIVERSITY OF KANSAS, Kenneth Spencer Research Library, Special Collections Dept, Lawrence, 66045. Alexandra Mason, Librn
Holdings: Cat
See also entry under Voyages and Travels

MA —PEABODY MUSEUM OF SALEM, Phillips Library, E India Sq, Salem, 01970. Gregor Trinkaus-Randall, Librn
Holdings: Vols (100,000) Cat Mss Maps Pix
Notes: Pacific and Arctic voyages.

MA —BRANDEIS UNIVERSITY, Goldfarb Library, 415 South St, Waltham, 02154. Bessie Hahn, Dir
Notes: McKew-Parr Collection on Magellan and the Age of Discovery. Approx 4000 books relating to Magellan and Columbus and other voyagers of the 15th and early 16th century. A card catalog to the collection is located in Special Collections.

MI —UNIVERSITY OF MICHIGAN, William L Clements Library, Ann Arbor, 48109. John C Dann, Dir
Notes: The William L. Clements Library of Americana is a non-circulating rare book library of original source material, printed and manuscript, dealing with America, from the discovery period into the late nineteenth century. The collection includes approximately 55,000 books and pamphlets, 550 linear feet of manuscripts, 4,100 volumes of newspapers, 36,000 maps, 40,000 pieces of sheet music, and 1,000 prints. The collection is strongest for the period of the American Revolution, and includes the papers of Thomas Gage, Sir Henry Clinton, and the Earl of Shelburne. Other areas of strength include antislavery, cartography and geography, discovery and exploration, American Indians, The Civil War, tune-books, sermons and orations, and the War of 1812. There are selective research collections dealing with Christopher Columbus, Thomas Paine, Benjamin Franklin, George Washington, Thomas Jefferson, and the Federalist Papers. Publications describing the collections of the library are: Author/Title catalog of Americana 1493-1860 in the William L. Clements Library... 7 volumes, Boston, G. K. Hall, 1970; Guide to the manuscript collections of the William L. Clements Library, by Arlene P. Shy 3d edition, Boston, G. K. Hall, 1978; Guide to the manuscript maps in the William L. Clements Library, compiled by Christian Burn, Ann Arbor, U. of Michigan, 1959; and Research catalog of maps of America, to 1860 in the William L. Clements Library...,edited by Douglas W. Marshall, 4 volumes, Boston, G. K. Hall, 1972.

MI —OLIVET COLLEGE, Burrage Library, Olivet, 49076. Chris Miko, Dir
Holdings: Vols (2000) Cat
Notes: The collection consists primarily of early printed voyages of the arctic and antarctic from the earliest times to the mid-20th century.

MN —UNIVERSITY OF MINNESOTA, DULUTH, Library & Learning Resources Service, Duluth, 55812. James V. Litha, Archivist
Holdings: Vols (1700) Cat Mss Maps Pix
Notes: The Voyageur Collection incl the Grace Lee Nute Papers. Books and materials relating to the Voyageur period (1650-1850) and the area of Northeastern Minnesota, Michigan, Wisconsin, Southern Canada. Emphasis on all subjects listed in this volume.

MN —UNIVERSITY OF MINNESOTA, James Ford Bell Library, 309 19th Ave S, Minneapolis, 55455. John Parker, Cur
Holdings: Vols (11,000) Cat Mss Maps
Notes: Collection of original materials relating to European expansion, 1400-1800.

NV —FORESTA INSTITUTE FOR OCEAN AND MOUNTAIN STUDIES, Library, 6205 Franktown Rd, Carson City, 89701. Shannon Porter, Librn
Holdings: Vols 500 Cat Mss Maps Pix Slides
Notes: Collection incl historical and contemporary accounts of Antarctic voyages; special emphasis on ecology, plant and animal life, fish, and whales. Also, about 1500 pamphlets, etc. Bibliography of whales whaling materials in library published in 1977.

NY —AMERICAN MUSEUM OF NATURAL HISTORY, Library Services Dept, Central Park W & 79th St, New York, 10024. Nina J Root, Chairwoman; Mary Genett, Asst Librn for Reference Services
Holdings: Vols (385,000) Cat Mss Maps Pix Slides Microforms
Notes: Nearly all collections are outstanding for depth of coverage and international range. Early and historic works, rare books, colored illustrations, and relevant serial publications supplement the modern scientific publications necessary to the researches of the scientific staff and the work of the educational division. Open to the public.

NY —EXPLORERS CLUB, James B Ford Memorial Library, 46 E 70 St, New York, 10021. Janet Baldwin, Librn
Holdings: Vols (24,000) Cat Maps
Notes: Additions to the collection depend upon gifts. Access by appointment only. Collections incl the Ted Banks Collection; begun by Prof Harley H Bartlett, bequeathed to American Institute for Exploration, with additions by Prof Ted Bank II, and subsequently acquired by the Explorers Club. Incl field notes, diaries, and photographs of Bank, who led more than 30 scientific expeditions to the Arctic, Aleutians, Sea of Okhotsk, Japan, Taiwan, Southeast Asia and Africa.

NY —HISPANIC SOCIETY OF AMERICA, Library, 613 W 155 St, New York, 10032. Martha M de Narvaez, Cur of Mss; Irene S Frye, Asst Librn
Holdings: Vols (150,000) Cat Mss Maps Pix Slides Phonorecords Microforms
Notes: History, art, literature and general culture of the Hispanic countries (where Spanish or Portuguese is spoken). Incl (18, 000) vols printed before 1701, incl (250) incunabula; over (100,000) later vols, plus thousands of periodicals. About (200,000) mss incl ms maps. Printed atlases are in the Book Collection. Some microfilms, chiefly of our early books. Engraved and printed separate maps; reference collection of over 100,000 photographs; slides: all in Department of Iconography, not in library. Catalogs: *Catalogue of the Hispanic Society of America* (Boston: G K Hall, 1962), 10 vols; *First Supplement* (Boston, 1970), 4 vols. Early books: *Printed Books 1468-1700;* Mss: *Catalogo de los Manuscritos Poeticos* Castellanos (15th-17th centuries; 3 vols); *Medieval Manuscripts in the Library; Golden Age Drama Manuscripts*(the latter in press).
See also entry under Spain

NY —NEW YORK PUBLIC LIBRARY, Research Libraries, General Research Division, Fifth Ave & 42 St, New York, 10018. Rodney Phillips, Chief
Holdings: Vols (2,225,000) Cat Maps Pix Microforms
Budget: ($775,718)

NY —NEW YORK PUBLIC LIBRARY, Rare Books and Manuscripts Div, Fifth Ave & 42 St, New York, 10018. William L Joyce, Asst Dir; Francis O Mattson, Curator
Holdings: Cat
Budget: ($7161)
Notes: Incl one of the most extensive collections of De Bry and Hulsius and one of the finest sets of Canadian Jesuit Relations. Most editions of Columbus' "Letter."

NY —UNIVERSITY OF ROCHESTER, Rush Rhees Library, Department of Rare Books and Special Collections, Rochester, 14627. Peter Dzwonkoski, Librn
Holdings: Vols 75 Cat
Notes: Collection incl accounts of voyages by Cook, Churchill, Pinkerton, Hawkesworth and other accounts of 18th and 19th century polar, continental, and oceanic explorations.

NC —DUKE UNIVERSITY, William R Perkins Library, Rare Book Room, Durham, 27706. John L Sharpe, III, Cur
Holdings: Vols 1000
Notes: Collection of various accounts of voyages and scientific expeditions, primarily in the 18th and 19th centuries.

OH —CLEVELAND PUBLIC LIBRARY, History and Geography Department, 325 Superior Ave, Cleveland, 44114. JoAnn Petrello, Head
Holdings: Cat Maps
Notes: Collection incl rare books, especially Americana, Canadiana, Latin Americana; 19th century European travelers; Arctic and Antarctic voyages.

PA —AMERICAN PHILOSOPHICAL SOCIETY, Library, 105 S Fifth St, Philadelphia, 19106. Edward C Carter II, Librn
Holdings: Cat Mss Maps Pix
Notes: Collection (as it was in 1970) is incl in *Catalog of Books in the American Philosophical Society Library* (Westport, Conn; Greenwood Publishing Corp, 1970) and *Catalog of Manuscripts in the American Philosophical Society library* (Westport, Conn: Greenwood Publishing Corp, 1970). Both of these catalogs are reporductions of APS Library catalog cards, incl author, subject, and title entries.

PA —ATHENAEUM OF PHILADELPHIA, 219 S Sixth St, Philadelphia, 19106. Roger W Moss Jr, Librn
Holdings: Vols 2000 Cat Mss Maps Pix
Notes: Separate catalog by date.

DISCOVERY AND EXPLORATION (cont.)

†PA —LIBRARY COMPANY OF PHILADELPHIA, 1314 Locust St, Philadelphia, 19107. Edwin Wolf II, Librn
Holdings: Vols (450,000)

PA —UNIVERSITY OF PENNSYLVANIA, Van Pelt Library, Rare Books Collection, 34 & Walnut Sts, Philadelphia, 19104. Daniel Traister, Special Collections Librn
Holdings: Vols 2500 //
Notes: Robert Dechert Collection: early exploration, 17th and 18th centuries; western Americana, 19th century; Canadiana, incl Jesuit relations.

PA —PENNSYLVANIA STATE UNIVERSITY, Fred Lewis Pattee Library, University Park, 16802. Stuart Forth, Dean of Libraries
Holdings: Vols Cat Maps
Notes: Based primarily on an interest in Australia and the Pacific Ocean, the Pennsylvania State University Libraries have developed a strong collection of voyages, including many 17th and 18th century editions of specific voyages, eg, Cook, La Perouse, Vancouver, collected editions both French and English, together with related publications, eg, De Brosses, Dalrymple. The collections include both exploration and scientific voyages in original editions and reprints.

RI —BROWN UNIVERSITY, John Carter Brown Library, Providence, 02912. Norman Fiering, Librn; Everett C Wilkie Jr, Bibliographer; Susan Danforth, Cur Maps & Prints
Holdings: Vols (40,000) Cat Mss Maps Pix
Notes: History of the Americas during the Colonial Period. See also *The John Carter Brown Library Catalogues; Opportunities for Research in the John Carter Brown Library; Reprint of the John Carter Brown Library Annual Reports and Index-1901-1966.*

RI —PROVIDENCE ATHENAEUM, 251 Benefit St, Providence, 02903. Sally Duplaix, Dir
Holdings: Vols 12,500 Cat
Notes: Concentration is on the 18th and 19th centuries, worldwide in coverage. Incl many scientific expedition accounts. Approx 3,000 may be catagorized as rare books/special collections. The library projects a Short Title Catalogue of its rarer holdings in this area within the next few years.

SC —UNIVERSITY OF SOUTH CAROLINA, Thomas Cooper Library, Columbia, 29208. Kenneth E Toombs, Dir of Libraries; Roger Mortimer, Rare Book Librn
Holdings: Vols 500 Cat
Notes: Particularly strong in landmark titles published in the 18th and 19th centuries.

SC —WOFFORD COLLEGE, Sandor Teszler Library, N Church St, Spartanburg, 29301. Frank J Anderson, Librn
Holdings: Vols 300 Uncat Maps
Notes: Material from 16th-20th century atlases. A miscellaneous collection relating to voyages, travel and description of various parts of the world. Bulk of titles are 19th century imprints. Described in: *Geography and Travels,* compiled and edited by Frank J Anderson (Wofford College Library, Special Collections Checklist no 2), Spartanburg, SC: Wofford Library Press, 1970; 54 pp, mimeo with subject index.

TX —UNIVERSITY OF TEXAS, ARLINGTON, Library, PO Box 19497, Arlington, 76019. Chas Colley, Dir Special Collections
Holdings: Uncat Maps Slides
Notes: The collection focuses on the history of cartography in general, specializing in the discovery and exploration of North America, with special emphasis on Texas and the American West. The collection consists of thousands of rare maps and atlases dating from 1493, coupled with an extensive collection of related reference works and primary works on exploration and discovery.

TX —ECTOR COUNTY LIBRARY, Department of Business and Technology, 321 W 5th St, Odessa, 79760. Pat Jones, Dept Head
Notes: Incl 100 vertical files, 25 periodicals, 250 Trade Standards. Collections concentrated on the Drilling and Production industries. Also included are Exploration methods Reservoir Development, Pipeline, Construction, Well Servicing, Well Logging, and Well Control. Complete collection of the API Specifications, and Complete Welding "library".

BC —VANDUSEN GARDENS LIBRARY, 5251 Oak St, Vancouver, V6M 4H1, Can. Mary Nickel, Librn
Holdings: Vols (2100)

ON —METROPOLITAN TORONTO LIBRARY, History Dept, 789 Yonge St, Toronto, M4W 2G8, Can. Michael Pearson, Head
Holdings: Vols (2500) Cat
Notes: The collection includes reports, diaries and personal narratives of travels and voyages of exploration and discovery from the Renaissance to the present day. Areas of emphasis are the exploration of the interior of North America, early oceanic voyages of discovery and acounts of travellers to Russia. The collection also includes a number of early editions, standard collected works such as the publications of the Hakluyt Society, accounts of shipwrecks as well as a representative collection of guide books from the 18th century to the present.

ON —UNIVERSITY OF TORONTO, Thomas Fisher Rare Book Library, 120 Saint George St, Toronto, M5S 1A5, Can. Richard G Landon, Head
Holdings: Vols 30,000 Mss Maps Pix
Notes: Great variety of material relating to early exploration and settlement of Canada, including the search for the Northwest Passage and the subsequent exploration of the Arctic. Manuscript and printed material pertaining to the overland exploration of northwestern Canada and the Barren Lands. Manuscript and printed material documenting early emigration schemes and colonization attempts, including Selkirk's Red River settlement.

ON —VICTORIA UNIVERSITY, Library, 71 Queen's Park Crescent, Toronto, M5S 1K7, Can. Robert C Brandeis, Chief Librn
Holdings: Vols (1000)// Cat Mss Maps Pix
Notes: Collection consists of books, pamphlets, and government reports mainly dealing with North American Indians and western explorations and missionary enterprises amoung the Indian tribes in Canada. Incl Indian Bibles and hynmbooks, and mss and vols by Peter Jones (an Indian missionary) and James Evans (inventor of the Cree syllabic alphabet).

DISCRIMINATION

DC —HOWARD UNIVERSITY, Moorland-Spingarn Research Center, 500 Howard Place NW, Washington, 20059. Clifford L Muse, Jr, Acting Dir
Holdings: Vols (106,086) Mss Maps Pix Slides Phonorecords Audiotapes 16mm Films Microforms
Budget: ($854,753)
See also entry under Blacks

DC —US COMMISSION ON CIVIL RIGHTS, National Clearinghouse Library, 1121 Vermont Ave NW, Washington, 20005. Lenora McMillan, Chief Librn
Holdings: Vols (10,200) Cat Slides Microforms
Notes: The National Clearinghouse Library has a special collection of the US Commision on Civil Rights publications from its inception (1957) to present date.

DISCRIMINATION, RACIAL see Race Discrimination

DISCRIMINATION, SEX see Sex Discrimination

DISCRIMINATION IN EMPLOYMENT

CA —WOMEN'S HISTORY RESEARCH CENTER, Microfilm Library, 2325 Oak St, Berkeley, 94708. Laura X, Librn
Holdings: Microforms
Notes: Incl 500 subject files of material on Women and Law (General); Politics; Employment; Education; Rape/Prison/Prostitution; Black and Third World women. Collection at University of Wyoming, Archive of Contemporary History, PO Box 3334, Laramie, Wyoming 82071, c/o David Crosson. Reasearch inquiries accepted. Microfilm of collection (40 reels & reel guides) available through Women's History Research Center, 2325 Oak St, Berkeley, CA 94708. No collections housed at this address.

DC —HOWARD UNIVERSITY, Moorland-Spingarn Research Center, 500 Howard Place NW, Washington, 20059. Clifford L Muse, Jr, Acting Dir
Holdings: Vols (106,086) Mss Maps Pix Slides Phonorecords Audiotapes 16mm Films Filmstrips Microforms
Budget: ($854,753)
See also entry under Blacks

DC —INTERNATIONAL LABOR ORGANIZATION, International Labor Office, Washington Branch Library, 1750 New York Ave NW, Rm 330, Washington, 20006. Karen J Mark, Librn
Holdings: Vols (13,500) Cat Pix 16mm Films Monographs
Notes: Wide range of titles dealing with worldwide labor and social matters. The library contains ILO publications and documentation only, dating back to 1919. Also, a collection of ILO films and photos. See *Subject Guide to Publications of the ILO, 1919-1964* and *ILO Catalogue of Publications in Print, 1982* (ILO).

DC —US COMMISSION ON CIVIL RIGHTS, National Clearinghouse Library, 1121 Vermont Ave NW, Washington, 20005. Lenora McMillan, Chief Librn
Holdings: Vols (10,200) Cat Slides Microforms
Notes: The National Clearinghouse Library has a special collection of the US Commission on Civil Rights publications from its inception (1957) to present date.

DC —US DEPT OF LABOR, Library, 200 Constitution Ave NW, Washington, 20210. Sabina Jacobson, Dir
Holdings: Vols (550,000) Cat

MA —RADCLIFFE COLLEGE, Arthur & Elizabeth Schlesinger Library on the History of Women in America, 3 James St, Cambridge, 02138. Patricia Miller King, Dir; Eva Moseley, Cur of Mss
Notes: The papers of the 1974 class action suit against *The New York Times* that charged the newspaper with "a pattern and practice of discrimination in employment on the basis of sex." The *Times* agreed to an affirmative action plan, and the suit was resolved in 1978.

NY —NEW YORK STATE DIVISION OF HUMAN RIGHTS, Reference Library, Two World Trade Center, Rm 5356, New York, 10047. Rosalind Spriggs, Librn
Holdings: Vols 1500 Cat
Notes: Emphasis on materials related to discrimination in employment, aged people, and antipoverty efforts. See: Simon Fediuk, *Bibliography on Employment and Related* Subjects. Special Collection No 3 of a Series. 190 pp. This special collection contains about 1500 items: books, studies, journals, pamphlets, reprints and research data.

ON —CANADA DEPT OF LABOUR, Library, Ottawa, K1A 0J2, Can. Monique Marchand, Chief Librn
Holdings: Vols (100,000) Cat Microforms

DISCRIMINATION IN HOUSING

NY —NEW YORK STATE DIVISION OF HUMAN RIGHTS, Reference Library, Two World Trade Center, Rm 5356, New York, 10047. Rosalind Spriggs, Librn
Holdings: Vols 1200// Cat
Notes: Emphasis on materials which deal with the problems of discrimination in housing, the development of cities, and urban unrest. See *Bibliography on Housing and Urban Renewal* by Simon Fediuk. Special Collection, No 1 of a Series, 2nd printing, New York, 1972. 92 pp. This special collection contains about 1200 items: books, studies, journals, pamphlets, reports, reprints, and research data.

DISEASE (PATHOLOGY) see Pathology

DISEASE AND DIET see Diet and Disease

DISEASES—ENVIRONMENTAL ASPECTS see Environmentally Induced Diseases

DISEASES, ANIMAL see Veterinary Medicine

DISEASES, CHILDREN'S see Children—Diseases

DISEASES, CHRONIC see Chronic Diseases

DISEASES, CONTAGIOUS see Communicable Diseases

DISEASES, INFECTIOUS see Communicable Diseases

DISEASES, MENTAL see Mental Illness

DISEASES, OCCUPATIONAL see Occupational Diseases

DISEASES, PLANT see Plant Diseases

DISEASES, RHEUMATIC see Rheumatic Diseases

DISNEY STUDIOS

WY —UNIVERSITY OF WYOMING, William Robertson Coe Library, Archives - American Heritage Center, PO Box 3412, Laramie, 82071.
Notes: Music manuscripts of Carl W Stalling, writer of music for such cartoons as "Mickey Mouse," "Silly Symphonies," "Three Little Pigs," "Bugs Bunny," "Looney Tunes," and other productions of Walt Disney and Warner Brothers. Incl 1300 complete original scores, more than 2000 sheets of other music, and many other materials.

DISNEY, DORIS MILES

MA —BOSTON UNIVERSITY, Mugar Memorial Library, Special Collections Dept, 771 Commonwealth Ave, Boston, 02215. Howard B Gotlieb, Dir
Holdings: Cat Mss Pix
Notes: Mss, correspondence, etc collected in depth; incl publications by or about.

DISNEY, WALT, AND DISNEYLAND

CA —ANAHEIM PUBLIC LIBRARY, 500 W Broadway, Anaheim, 92805.
Holdings: Vols (2000) Cat Mss Maps Pix Microforms
Notes: Our specialty is local history, especially that of Anaheim and Orange County. In addition to many books on California, we have photographs, maps, directories, organization histories, ephemera, journals; books published by The Fine Arts Press, Santa Ana; periodicals, original minute books and records of the Los Angeles Vineyard Society. The Walt Disney Archives has designated the library as an official depository of material on Walt Disney, with an emphasis on Disneyland. This collection incl Disney books, Disney periodicals, press releases, operating manuals, guide-books, posters, photographs, Disney character merchandise and examples of ephemeral materials such as tickets, hand-bills, and advertising matter.

CA —UNIVERSITY OF CALIFORNIA, LOS ANGELES, Theater Arts Library, Los Angeles, 90024. Edward Shreeves, Chairman, Bibliographers Group; Audree Malkin, Head, Theater Arts Library
Holdings: Cat Mss Pix
Notes: Incl a Walt Disney Collection.

†NY —SYRACUSE UNIVERSITY LIBRARIES, E S Bird Library, George Arents Research Library, Rm 600, Syracuse, 13210. Mr Sidney Huttner, Librn
Notes: Samples or selections of cartoon art, comic strips, Disney, fantasy, fanzines, horror (Ackerman mss), mystery pulps, series books and westerns.

DISORDERS OF PERSONALITY see Personality, Disorders of

DISORDERS OF SPEECH see Speech, Disorders of

DISPENSARIES

†CT —YALE UNIVERSITY, Medical Library, 333 Cedar St, New Haven, 06520.
Notes: Hospital, clinic, and dispensary collection of extensive, uncatalogued materials, descriptive pamphlets, annual reports, etc. This is a large collection with much on institutional histories of European and American hospitals.

DISPERSOIDS see Colloids

DISPLAY OF MERCHANDISE

OR —BASSIST COLLEGE LIBRARY, 2000 SW Fifth Ave, Portland, 97201. Norma Bassist, Librn
Holdings: Vols 49 Cat

DISPOSAL OF REFUSE see Refuse and Refuse Disposal

DISPUTATIONS, RELIGIOUS

GA —EMORY UNIVERSITY, Candler School of Theology, Pitts Theology Library, Atlanta, 30322. Channing Jeschke, Librn; Anita K Delaries, Curator
Holdings: Vols 6251 Cat
Notes: Theological disputations in Latin defended primarily at German universities between 1650 and 1750.

DISRAELI, BENJAMIN

MA —BRANDEIS UNIVERSITY, Goldfarb Library, 415 South St, Waltham, 02154. Bessie Hahn, Dir
Notes: Approx 80 letters and other ephemeral items of Benjamin Disraeli, Lord Beaconsfield. A finding list is available in Special Collections.

NJ —PRINCETON UNIVERSITY, Library, Morris L Parrish Collection, Princeton, 08540. Alexander D Wainwright, Cur
Holdings: Vols 70
Notes: The collection contains over 6500 vols, as well as many theatre programs, playbills, photographs, clippings and other miscellanea. Parrish's goal was to assemble in both the English and the American first editions, in the original condition as issued, everything that a given author published. He was also interested in a high standard of condition for his books. Many additions have been acquired since the Parrish collection came to the Library as a bequest in 1944. The collection is an assemblage of author collections, consisting of books by: William Harrison Ainsworth, James Matthew Barrie, William Black, The Brontes, William Wilkie Collins, Dinah Mulock Craik, Marie de la Ramee ("Ouida"), Benjamin Disraeli, Charles Dickens, Charles Dodgson, George du Maurier, George Eliot (ie Mary Ann Evans), Elizabeth Gaskell, Thomas Hardy, Thomas Hughes,Charles Kingsley, Charles Lever, Edward George Earle Bulwer-Lytton, Mary Maxwell, George Meredith, Charles Reade, Walter Scott, Robert Louis Stevenson, William Makepeace Thackeray, Trollope Family, Ellen Wood, and Charlotte Yonge.

†NY —COLUMBIA UNIVERSITY LIBRARIES, Butler Library, Rare Book and Manuscript Library, 535 W 114 St, New York, 10027.
Notes: The William B Liebmann Benjamin Disraeli Collection. Incl first editions, writings about him, letters, memorabilia, photographs, engravings, cartoons, sheet music and works about the Victorian era.

NY —UNIVERSITY OF ROCHESTER, Rush Rhees Library, Department of Rare Books and Special Collections, Rochester, 14627. Peter Dzwonkoski, Librn
Holdings: Vols Cat Mss Pix
Notes: The Robert Metzdorf Collection about Queen Victoria, her family, and the court. With first editions by Benjamin Disraeli.

NY —SYRACUSE UNIVERSITY LIBRARIES, Ernest S Bird Library, George Arents Research Library for Special Collections, Syracuse, 13210. Carolyn A Davis, Manuscripts Librn; Amy S Doherty, University Archivist; Mark F Weimer, Rare Book Librn
Notes: Microfilm copies of Benjamin Disraeli's complete papers (200,000 frames) incl family, domestic and personal papers, copies of speeches, royal and general correspondence, papers on domestic and foreign affairs, correspondence on honors and titles, Mrs Disraeli's papers, mss of his novels and proofs and notices and correspondence about the novels. Also the papers of his father Isaac D'Israeli, of his grandfather Benjamin D'Israeli and Disraeli's biographers, Monypenny and Buckle.

OH —HEBREW UNION COLLEGE-JEWISH INSTITUTE OF RELIGION, Klau Library, 3101 Clifton Ave, Cincinnati, 45220. David J Gilner, Reference Librn
Holdings: Cat Mss
Notes: Incl early editions, political speeches, political novels, satires.

ON —QUEEN'S UNIVERSITY, Douglas Library, Kingston, K7L 5C4, Can. William F E Morley, Cur, Special Collections
Holdings: Vols 200 Cat
Notes: The "Disraeli Project".

DISSENTERS, RELIGIOUS

CA —CLAREMONT COLLEGES, Honnold Library, Ninth & Dartmouth, Claremont, 91711. Tania Rizzo, Special Collections Dept Head
Holdings: Vols 1123 Uncat Mss Pix Microforms
Notes: The combined James Mavor, Raymond Elliott, and Gregory P Tschebotarioff collections incl clippings and periodicals from the Revolutionary period, books and pictorial materials about the royal family, separatist movements, and the emigre experience. Restricted use.

†CA —UNIVERSITY OF SAN FRANCISCO, Richard A Gleeson Library, The Countess Bernardine Murphy Donohue Rare Book Room, San Francisco, 94117. D Steven Corey, Special Collections Librn
Holdings: Vols (300) Cat
Notes: Largely from the Virtue-Cahill library in England, and the collection of Charles A Fracchia. Incl important works of Bayly, Cressy, Sergeant, and Worsley. Incl a contemporary manuscript of the trial of Father Garnet, accused of complicity in the Gunpowder Plot.

WI —SEVENTH DAY BAPTIST HISTORICAL SOCIETY, Library, 3120 Kennedy Rd, PO Box 1678, Janesville, 53547. D Scott Smith, Historian
Notes: English Seventh Day Baptists Collection. These materials have to do with early and middle years of Baptist movement (1662-1920) in England, incl work of John James, Joseph Stennett, Peter Chamberlen, et al, Sabbatarians or Seventh Day Baptists. About 300 items incl record books, tracts, correspondence.

ON —UNIVERSITY OF TORONTO, Thomas Fisher Rare Book Library, 120 Saint George St, Toronto, M5S 1A5, Can. Richard G Landon, Head
Holdings: Vols 1600 // Cat Mss
Notes: Forbes Collection created by James Forbes (1629?-1712), English nonconformist minister. Kept as a separate library with few additions until present day. (Toronto, 1968). Also Heyworth, P L "Unfamiliar Libraries XVI: The Forbes Library," *The Book* Collector, Autumn 1970.

DISSERTATIONS AND THESES

AZ —NAVAJO COMMUNITY COLLEGE, Naaltsoos Ba' Hoogan, Library, Tsaile,

DISSERTATIONS AND THESES (cont.)

86556. Marvin E Pollard Jr, Dir, Library Services
Holdings: Vols (10,000) Cat Mss Maps Pix Slides Phonorecords Audiotapes Videotapes 16mm Films Filmstrips Microforms
Budget: ($15,000)
Notes: The Moses/Donner Collection emphasizes Navajos and other tribes of the Southwest; also, all Indians of North America and Mexico. All aspects of the geology, geography, sociology, archaeology, anthropology, etc, of the Four Corners region. The Collection includes a comprehensive collection of Doctoral dissertations dealing with Indians of North America and Mexico.

CA —UNIVERSITY OF CALIFORNIA, BERKELEY, Life Sciences Libraries, Forestry Library, 260 Mulford Hall, Berkeley, 94720. Esther Johnson, Librn; Pete Evans, Ref Librn
Holdings: Vols (28,000)
Budget: ($15,800)
Notes: Areas of particular strength are forestry, conservation, and wildlife management. The collection is rich in pamphlet material and serials, especially foreign publications. Although holdings are world-wide in scope, coverage of the western USA is given the highest priority. Dissertation and theses collection also. Forestry Library holdings are complemented by a 8000-vol specialized collection at the Forest Products Laboratory in Richmond, California.

CA —UNIVERSITY OF CALIFORNIA, SAN FRANCISCO, Library, San Francisco, 94143. David Bishop, University Librn
Holdings: Vols 111,253
Notes: Medical theses.

DC —DOMINICAN HOUSE OF STUDIES, Dominican College Library, 487 Michigan Ave NE, Washington, 20017. J Raymond Vandegrift, OP, Librn
Holdings: Vols (5000) Cat
Budget: ($1350)
Notes: The Dominican Order (its history, spirituality, government, liturgy), its members (directories, biographies, bibliographies, lives of saints) and works written by Dominicans: incunabula, rare books, dissertations, periodicals (2300 vols), monographs. Incl periodicals either about the Order or edited by Dominicans. Does not incl titles about the congregations of Dominican Sisters. The Library's catalog contains analytics for Dominican contributors to monographs.

DC —HOWARD UNIVERSITY, Moorland-Spingarn Research Center, 500 Howard Place NW, Washington, 20059. Clifford L Muse, Jr, Acting Dir
Notes: By and about Blacks.

GA —UNIVERSITY OF GEORGIA, Libraries, Athens, 30602. Arlene E Luchsinger, Asst Dir Branch Libraries
Holdings: Vols 19,500 Cat
Notes: The collection incl the bulk of the collection originally held by the American Mathematical Society, and purchased by the University of Georgia from Columbia University several years ago. It is strong in foreign dissertations in mathematics.

IL —CENTER FOR RESEARCH LIBRARIES, 6050 S Kenwood Ave, Chicago, 60637. Donald B Simpson, Dir; Esther Smith, Collection Development Librn
Holdings: Microforms
Budget: $65,000
Notes: Primarily western European univeristies. Incl more than 13,000 microfilms of mss and dissertations.

IL —ROOSEVELT UNIVERSITY, Murray-Green Library, 430 S Michigan Ave, Chicago, 60605. Donald Draganski, Music Librn
Holdings: Vols (28,000) Uncat Mss Pix Microforms
Notes: Subscribe to over 92 music periodicals; record collection of more than 10,000 albums; 8000 pieces of sheet music; pamphlet file; music theses on microfilm; complete file of music publishers catalogs; scores; tapes of old 78 recordings; music education; and electronic music.

IL —UNIVERSITY OF ILLINOIS, URBANA/CHAMPAIGN, Library, Classics Library, 419A Main Library, Urbana, 61801. Suzanne N Griffiths, Librn
Holdings: Vols 41,569 Cat Maps Pix
Budget: $5600
Notes: Collection is strong in 19th century German inaugural dissertations. The above figures do not include 17,000 uncataloged pamphlets (alphabetical file lists these).

MD —JOHNS HOPKINS UNIVERSITY, Milton S Eisenhower Library, Charles & 34 Sts, Baltimore, 21218. Ann S Gwyn, Assistant Dir for Special Collections
Notes: Foreign and American doctoral dissertations and reprints to 1964. Largest number in history of science, 85,000. Also biology, chemistry, geology, meteorology, psychology, physics and mathematics. Johns Hopkins not included. Incl 100,000 Western European doctoral dissertations, espec French and German; some Scandinavian. Collection is located in Gillman Storage Area accessible through Special Collection Division.

MA —FRANCIS A COUNTWAY LIBRARY OF MEDICINE, Boston Medical Library/Harvard Medical Library, 10 Shattuck St, Boston, 02115. C Robin LeSueur, Librn; Richard J Wolfe, Cur, Rare Books & Manuscripts
Holdings: Vols (500,000) Cat Mss Maps Pix Microforms
Notes: Combines resources of the Harvard Medical School and the Boston Medical Library. Strong in serials and medical history in all fields of medicine, incl incunabula, non-medical books by doctors, travel books by doctors. 300,000 medical dissertations and theses. Special strength in all medical subjects listed in this volume.

MA —HARVARD UNIVERSITY LIBRARY, Converse Memorial Library, Chemistry Library, 12 Oxford St, Cambridge, 02138. Ludmila Birladeanu, Supv
Holdings: Vols (50,000) Cat Microforms
Budget: ($110,000)
Notes: Also 13,000 bound periodical vols; 23,000 foreign chemical theses.

MI —UNIVERSITY OF MICHIGAN, Library, Dept of Rare Books & Special Collections, Ann Arbor, 48109. Robert J Starring, Head
Holdings: Cat Microforms
Notes: Incl some 90,000 uncataloged foreign dissertations with particular strength in German dissertations written between 1900 and 1939.

NM —NEW MEXICO STATE UNIVERSITY, Library, Box 3475, Las Cruces, 88003. James Dyke, Dir
Holdings: Vols 1200 Cat
Notes: Near complete collection of all astronomy PhD dissertations accepted by American universities from the early 1870s to date.

NC —CAROLINA POPULATION CENTER, Library, University Sq E, Chapel Hill, 27514. Patricia Shipman, Head Librn
Holdings: Vols 20,000 Cat Mss Microforms
Budget: ($10,500)
Notes: This is the largest population library in the world (65,000 citations). Emphasis is on the socioeconomic aspects of population, particularly population dynamics, population policy, fertility, the family, formal demography, family planning, and population education. The catalog to the entire collection is on microfiche and offers 6 types of access: author, title, series, major subject term, location number. Library data base is available on database on *Dialog*, population bibliography. Selected searches are available in Library.

PA —COLLEGE OF PHYSICIANS OF PHILADELPHIA, Library, 19 S 22 St, Philadelphia, 19103. Anthony Aguirre, Libr Dir
Holdings: Vols (316,223) Cat Mss Microforms
Budget: ($1,096,557)
Notes: Incl 13,515 pamphlets; 1435 mss; 326,367 reports, dissertations, and reprints. Strong historical and bibliographical collections, as well as current materials. Medical documentation service provides current alerting, incl abstracting, etc.

ON —NATIONAL LIBRARY OF CANADA, 395 Wellington St, Ottawa, K1A 0N4, Can. Andre Preibish, Dir
Holdings: Microforms
Notes: A collection on microfilm and microfiche of master's and doctoral theses in all subjects accepted at cooperating Canadian universities. Includes 57,000 Canadian Theses Microfiche (18,00 on microfilm). Catalogues available. Copies of theses can be obtained from NLC on ILL or purchased.

DISSERTATIONS AND THESES, MEDICAL

MA —HARVARD UNIVERSITY, Medicine and Public Health Library, Boston Medical Society Collection, Boston, 02115. Richard Wolfe, Librn
Holdings: Vols 2170

NY —CORNELL UNIVERSITY LIBRARIES, John M Olin Library, History of Science Collections, Ithaca, 14853. Lillian A Clark, Administrative Supervisor; David W Corson, History of Science Librn
Holdings: Vols (33,000)
Notes: Early printed source materials in medicine and related sciences. Published dissertations (6,500 titles) from German, Dutch, and Swiss universities dating from 1580 to 1850. Noncirculating.
See also entry under Science - History

PA —UNIVERSITY OF PENNSYLVANIA, Van Pelt Library, Rare Books Collection, 34 & Walnut Sts, Philadelphia, 19104. Daniel Traister, Special Collections Librn
Holdings: Vols 600 Cat Mss
Notes: Incl 400 Elzevier Press Leyden dissertations.

DISTRIBUTION (ECONOMICS) see Commerce; Marketing

DISTRIBUTION, COOPERATIVE see Cooperative Societies

DISTRIBUTION OF ANIMALS see Zoogeography

DISTRICT NURSES see Nurses and Nursing

DISTRICT OF COLUMBIA

DC —GEORGE WASHINGTON UNIVERSITY, Gelman Library, 2130 H St NW, Washington, 20052.
Holdings: Vols (3000) Cat Mss Maps Pix Slides Audiotapes Microforms
Notes: The W. Lloyd Wright Washingtoniana Collection, donated in 1950, contains books, manuscripts, documents, pamphlets, photographs, prints, directories, and maps about the city of Washington. Covering the period of ca 1790 to the present, it covers all aspects of Washington and its inhabitants, including the local government, physical features, social groups, important individuals, educational institutions, etc. Notable among the printed materials are early government documents on the establishment of DC as the seat of the Federal government, early Washington imprints, and ephemeral publications, such as planning reports and City Council documents. Highlights of the manuscript portion of the collection include miscellaneous correspondence by Washington individuals, a 1796 Demott ms map, the papers of the DC City Council Chairmen, 1969-74, and the US House of Representatives' DC. Committee papers of Gilbert Gude (cf Gude papers).

DISTRICT OF COLUMBIA (cont.)

DC —HOWARD UNIVERSITY, Moorland-Spingarn Research Center, 500 Howard Place NW, Washington, 20059. Clifford L Muse, Jr, Acting Dir
Holdings: Vols (106,086) Mss Maps Pix Slides Phonorecords Audiotapes 16mm Films Filmstrips Microforms
Budget: ($854,753)
See also entry under Blacks

MD —MARYLAND-NATIONAL CAPITAL PARK & PLANNING COMMISSION, Montgomery County Planning Department Library, 8787 Georgia Ave, Silver Spring, 20907. Janice C Holt, Librn
Holdings: Vols (5000) Cat
Notes: Specific subject areas include: community facilities, conservation, economics, flood control, highways, housing, human and natural resources. landscape architecture, open space, parks, pollution, population, recreation, transportation, urban renewal, and zoning. Commission's publications are maintained by Records Management (not Library).

DISTRICT OF COLUMBIA—HISTORY

DC —DISTRICT OF COLUMBIA PUBLIC LIBRARY, Martin Luther King Memorial Library, Washingtoniana Div and Washington Star Collection, 901 G St NW, Washington, 20001. Roxanna Deane, Chief
Holdings: Vols (20,000) Cat Maps Pix Slides Audiotapes Microforms
Budget: ($5500)
Notes: Emphasis is on DC as a city and not on the federal government. Local papers are clipped daily; most clippings have been photocopied on archival paper. Depository for DC publications. City directories, 1822 to the present. Holdings of the division comprise the largest body of materials available documenting the history of the city. Published description of collection in *Materials for the Study of Washington,* by Perry G Fisher, 1974.

DC —GEORGETOWN UNIVERSITY, Library, Special Collections Div, 37 & O Sts NW, Washington, 20057. George M Barringer, Special Collections Librn; Nicholas B Sheetz, Mss Librn
Holdings: Cat Mss Maps
Notes: The Eric F Menke Collection. Incl the papers of the landscape architect Eric F Menke (1901-1980), and a large collection of mss, documents, and photographs pertaining to the history of Washington, DC. Correspondence and documents to, from, and concerning the Crawford family of Georgetown, DC. Incl are numerous documents of a local civic nature, especially in reference to the activities of Richard R Crawford who served as mayor of Georgetown from 1857-1861, and served periodically as Justice of Peace. Among items of particular interest are a record book from the Board of Aldermen (1857-1858), and a letter from Emma D E N Southworth, noted authoress. Correspondence, constitutions, by-laws, agendas, minutes, reports, publications, sundry documents and printed material from the Federation of Citizen's Associations of the District of Columbia, founded in 1910. Thematerial concerns the organization, administration, and activities of the Association. Subject files outline the Association's areas of concern in the District of Columbia such as health, education, transportation, fiscal management, urban planning, public safety, youth problems, and federal legislation. Series of register books from the National Hotel in Washington, DC. The hotel, built in 1827 at the corner of Pennsylvania Avenue and 6th Street, was the first hotel in Washington approximating the dimensions of a modern hotel. Collection of photographs taken by Frank Wolfe and others which incl a photograph of General W T Sherman and staff inspecting a battery; panorama view of the Chattanooga after the Union capture; numerous views of the Washington aqueduct construction; and photographs of the Cabin John Bridge construction, outside Washington, DC. Frank Wolfe,a member of General Meigs' staff from 1838-1855, was involved in the construction of the Washington aqueduct. Also incl in the collection is correspondence from Mrs Wolfe to Georgetown University concerning her sons' education.

DC —GEORGE WASHINGTON UNIVERSITY, Gelman Library, 2130 H St NW, Washington, 20052.
Holdings: Vols (3000) Cat Mss Maps Pix Slides Audiotapes Microforms
Notes: The W. Lloyd Wright Washingtoniana Collection, donated in 1950, contains books, manuscripts, documents, pamphlets, photographs, prints, directories, and maps about the city of Washington. Covering the period of ca 1790 to the present, it covers all aspects of Washington and its inhabitants, including the local government, physical features, social groups, important individuals, educational institutions, etc. Notable among the printed materials are early government documents on the establishment of DC as the seat of the Federal government, early Washington imprints, and ephemeral publications, such as planning reports and City Council documents. Highlights of the manuscript portion of the collection include miscellaneous correspondence by Washington individuals, a 1796 Demott ms map, the papers of the DC City Council Chairmen, 1969-74, and the US House of Representatives' DC. Committee papers of Gilbert Gude (cf Gude papers).

DC —HOWARD UNIVERSITY, Moorland-Spingarn Research Center, 500 Howard Place NW, Washington, 20059. Clifford L Muse, Jr, Acting Dir
Holdings: Vols (106,086) Mss Maps Pix Slides Phonorecords Audiotapes 16mm Films Filmstrips Microforms
Budget: ($854,753)
See also entry under Blacks

†MA —JOHN F KENNEDY LIBRARY, Columbia Point, Boston, 02125. Dan H Fenn Jr, Dir
Notes: The White House staff files of Charles Horsky, advisor to President Kennedy for National Capitol Affairs, 1961-1965; the personal papers of Louis Brownlow, journalist and public administrator, relating to the District of Columbia, 1915-1920; and records of the District of Columbia, 1961-1963. 14 linear ft of mss. Holdings are described in "Historical Materials in the John F Kennedy Library." Copies may be obtained by writing the Research Archivist.

DISTRICT OF COLUMBIA—MAPS

DC —METROPOLITAN WASHINGTON COUNCIL OF GOVERNMENTS, Map Library, 1875 Eye St NW, Suite 200, Washington, 20006. Susan Kalish, Librn
Holdings: Cat Maps
Notes: 3000 current and retrospective maps covering metropolitan Washington region, incl the District of Columbia: Montgomery and Prince George's counties in Maryland; and Arlington, Fairfax, Prince William and Loudoun counties and the City of Alexandria in Virginia. Maps cover land use, community facilities, transportation, topography, statistical units, and socioeconomic information. Record of holdings on computer printout.

DISTRICT OF COLUMBIA—PICTURES, ILLUSTRATIONS, ETC.

DC —LIBRARY OF CONGRESS, Prints & Photographs Div, Washington, 20540.
Notes: The Brady-Handy Collection consists of some 10,000 negatives from the files of photographers Levin C Handy (1855?-1932) and Mathew B Brady (1823?-1896), most of which are portrait photographs and views of Washington, DC from the 19th and early 20th centuries. Incl portraits of congressmen and government leaders (1855-90). The National Photo Company Collection contains news photographs of Washington, DC, 1910s-1930s. Incl the Theodor Horydczak Collection of photographs of the Washington, DC, area, 1920s-1950s. Also, drawings by the Washington, DC architectural firm, Waggaman and Ray, early 20th century.

DISTRICTING (CITY PLANNING) see Zoning

DIVEN FAMILY

NY —CORNELL UNIVERSITY LIBRARIES, Collection of Regional History, Dept of Manuscripts and Univ Archives, Ithaca, 14853.
Notes: Mostly lawyers and businessmen. Incl papers, 1828-1936; legal papers, correspondence, notes, account books; extensive files concerning over 50 railroad lines, mostly in NY.

DIVINE HEALING see Christian Science; Faith Cure

DIVING see Scuba Diving; Swimming and Diving

DIX, DOROTHEA L., 1802-1887

KS —MENNINGER FOUNDATION, Archives, 5600 W Sixth St, Box 829, Topeka, 66601. Alice Brand, Librn; Mark West, Archivist
Notes: 2 boxes, 1826-87. Consists of correspondence and miscellaneous materials.

NY —STATE UNIVERSITY OF NEW YORK, COLLEGE AT OSWEGO, Penfield Library, Oswego, 13126. Anne Commerton, Dir
Holdings: Mss
Notes: About 10,000 Millard Fillmore letters (by and to him), incl about 80 from Dorothea Dix. See *New York Times*, 24 March 1969.

DIX, RICHARD

CA —UNIVERSITY OF CALIFORNIA, LOS ANGELES, Theater Arts Library, Los Angeles, 90024. Edward Shreeves, Chairman, Bibliographers Group; Audree Malkin, Head, Theater Arts Library
Holdings: Cat Mss Pix Slides
Notes: Incl the Richard Dix Collection of 5217 stills from Richard Dix films.

DIXIE MISSION

CA —HOOVER INSTITUTION ON WAR, REVOLUTION & PEACE, Stanford University, Stanford, 94305. Milorad M Drachkovitch, Archivist
Holdings: Mss Pix Phonorecords
Notes: Papers of David D Barrett, Colonel, US Army, chief of the US Dixie Mission to Chinese Communist forces, 1944, incl mss of writings, correspondence, printed matter, photographs and phonorecords, 1933-70, relating to the Dixie Mission and the military situation in China during World War II. 1/2 ms box, 4 envelopes, 2 phonorecords, 1 oversize box.

DIXON, JOSEPH M.

MT —UNIVERSITY OF MONTANA, Library, Missoula, 59801. Katherine

DIXON, JOSEPH M. (cont.)

Schaefer, Special Collections Librn
Holdings: Vols 6300 Cat Mss Maps Pix Slides Microforms
Notes: About 200 ms collections, measuring 5000 feet, with emphasis on Montana business and political history (papers of Senators Joseph M Dixon, James E Murray, and US Ambassador James W Gerard). Also first editions and mss of Montana authors.

DIXON, THOMAS

NC —PACK MEMORIAL PUBLIC LIBRARY, North Carolina Collection, 67 Haywood St, Asheville, 28801. John Toms, Dept Head
Notes: Collection incl early ms accounts of western North Carolina; Civil War letters; letters, diary, and mss of Horace Kephart; mss of Thomas Dixon; Thomas Wolfe Collection; contemporary North Carolina authors; North Carolina censuses, 1790-1910; rare newspapers and runs of local newspapers, and clippings from Asheville newspapers, from 1920s; early maps; information on Cherokee Indians; approx 400 vols of North Carolina genealogy and file of unpublished genealogies. Collection concentrates on western North Carolina, with some general Appalachian materials. Incl 4000 local and state photographs, separate catalog.

DIXON, WILLIAM HEPWORTH

IN —INDIANA UNIVERSITY, Lilly Library, Seventh St, Bloomington, 47405. William R Cagle, Librn
Notes: Ms collection incl editorial and correspondence files of the *Athenaeum*, Jan 1853-Aug 1869.

DJAWA see Indonesia

DNA

†CA —CALIFORNIA INSTITUTE OF TECHNOLOGY, Robert A Millikan Memorial Library, Archives, 1201 E California Blvd, Pasadena, 91125.
Notes: Papers of Robert L Sinsheimer (1920-), mainly from the period 1971-1976, some of which relate to the recombinant DNA controversy.

MA —MASSACHUSETTS INSTITUTE OF TECHNOLOGY, Institute Archives, Special Collections, Cambridge, 02139.
Notes: Collection incl over 100 oral history interviews with scientists, legislators, lobbyists, environmentalists, journalists, university administration, and citizen review board members concerned with recombinant DNA technology. Also incl are audiotapes, videotapes, and printed material collected in preparations for oral history interviews.

DOANE, JOHN WARING, 1915-1972

IN —INDIANA STATE UNIVERSITY, EVANSVILLE, Library, 8600 University Blvd, Evansville, 47712. Gina R Walker, Acting Archivist
Holdings: / / Cat Pix Slides
Notes: Collection of photographs, negatives and slides by John Waring Doane (1915-1972), Mt Vernon, Indiana, photographer. Also a group of glass negatives taken by earlier photographers; people, places, and events of Posey County and Evansville, Indiana. 1900-1972. Unpublished index.

DOBIE, JAMES FRANK, 1888-1964

CA —UNIVERSITY OF CALIFORNIA, BERKELEY, Bancroft Library, Manuscripts Division, Berkeley, 94720. James D Hart, Dir
Holdings: Cat Mss Maps Pix Microforms
Notes: Letters from Dobie, in various collections.

†NC —WAKE FOREST UNIVERSITY, Z Smith Reynolds Library, Box 7777, Reynold Sta, Winston-Salem, 27109. Richard J Murdoch, Rare Book Librn
Notes: A significant collection. 160 items.

TX —UNIVERSITY OF TEXAS LIBRARIES, General Libraries, Barker Texas History Center, PO Box P, Austin, 78712. Don Carleton, Dir
Holdings: Vols (132,000) Cat Mss Maps Pix Slides Phonorecords Audiotapes Microforms
Notes: See description of collection under Texas-History.

TX —TEXAS A&M UNIVERSITY, Sterling C Evans Library, Special Collections Div, College Station, 77843. Donald H Dyal, Librn
Holdings: Vols (16,000) Mss Pix
Notes: Jeff Dykes Range Livestock Collection (incl a 600-item collection of J Frank Dobie works). Part of the Dobie Collection is described in Dykes, Jeff C *My Dobie Collection* (College Station, Tex: Friends of the Texas A & M University Library).

TX —UNIVERSITY OF TEXAS, EL PASO, Library, Special Collections Dept, El Paso, 79968. Cesar Caballero, Dept Head
Notes: 58 items-books, pamphlets, articles by and about Dobie. First editions. Part of Carl Hertzog Collection on Books and Printing.

TX —BAYLOR UNIVERSITY, Moody Memorial Library, Texas History Collection, Waco, 76706. Kent Keeth, Librn
Notes: One of the largest collections outside his own private collection at Austin.

DOBOJINSKY, MSTISLAV

ON —METROPOLITAN TORONTO LIBRARY, Theatre Dept, 789 Yonge St, Toronto, M4W 2G8, Can. Heather McCallum, Head
Notes: The Boris Volkoff Collection documents the Russian-born dancer's 45 year career in Canada and his important contribution to the development of Canadian ballet. The collection incl scrapbooks, costume and set designs (incl original stage designs by Mstislav Dobujinsky for the Canadian ballet *Red Ear of Corn,* produced by Volkoff in 1949), photographs, programs, correspondence, choreographic notebooks, and a portrait of Boris Volkloff painted by Yulia Biriukova.

DOBSON, AUSTIN, 1840-1921

CA —UNIVERSITY OF CALIFORNIA, LOS ANGELES, Research Library, Dept of Special Collections, 405 Hilgard Ave, Los Angeles, 90024. Edward Shreeves, Chairman, Bibliographers Group; David S Zeidberg, Head
Holdings: Vols 25
Notes: 25 first and other editions of his books; 20 letters.

DOCK STREET THEATRE

SC —COLLEGE OF CHARLESTON LIBRARY, Special Collections Dept, Charleston, 29401.
Notes: Several histories of the Footlight Players, scrapbooks (1932-1964), programs (1931-1958), footnotes (1937-1970), scripts (many adapted from well known works by Emmett Robinson), photographs, and posters. Also included is material dealing with the Dock Street Theatre's history, its theatre school, and non-Footlight Player performances.

DOCTOR SEUSS see Geisel, Theodor Seuss (Dr. Seuss)

DOCTORS see Physicians

DOCTORS, WOMEN see Women Physicians

DOCUMENTARY FILMS see Moving Pictures, Documentary

DOCUMENTARY PHOTOGRAPHY see Photography, Documentary

DOCUMENTATION

†PA —UNIVERSITY OF PITTSBURGH, Graduate School of Library & Information Sciences Library, L I S Bldg, Third Fl, Pittsburgh, 15260. Jean Kindlin, Librn
Notes: Extensive collection on the historical development of school libraries, media services, and evaluation of materials for use in all types of schools. Incl 54,800 vols, 7524 bound periodicals, 630 periodical subscriptions.

DOCUMENTS see Archives; Charters; Diplomatics; Government Publications; Municipal Documents

DOCUMENTS, FOREIGN GOVERNMENT see Foreign Government Documents

DOCUMENTS, PAPAL see Papal Documents

DODD, NORRIS E., 1879-1968

CA —HOOVER INSTITUTION ON WAR, REVOLUTION & PEACE, Stanford University, Stanford, 94305. Milorad M Drachkovitch, Archivist
Holdings: Mss
Notes: Papers of Norris E Dodd, Under Secretary of Agriculture, 1946-48, and Director-General of the Food and Agricultural Organization of the United Nations, 1948-54, incl diaries, memoranda, reports, speeches and writings, audiovisual material, and memorabilia, 1900-68, relating to the United Nations Food and Agricultural Organization (FAO) and to his government service. 16 ms boxes, 3 boxes of slides, 1 bust, 4 framed citations.

DODD, THOMAS J.

†CT —CONNECTICUT STATE LIBRARY, Hartford, 06106.
Notes: Papers of many Connecticut governors, senators and congressmen, incl John Dempsey, Abraham Ribicoff, and Thomas J Dodd.

DODGE, A. C.

IA —STATE HISTORICAL SOCIETY OF IOWA LIBRARY, 402 Iowa Ave, Iowa City, 52240. Darold J Brown, Librn
Holdings: Cat
Notes: Thousands of individual items and smaller collections. Two hundred larger collections incl the papers of Cyrus C Carpenter, Jonathan P Dolliver, Gilbert Haugen, W W Waymack, Ephraim Adams, A C Dodge, Dorothy Houghton, Jesse Macy, Agnes Samuelson, Donald Johnson, Jack Miller, Ruth Sayre, Samuel Kirkwood, Thomas McKnight, Robert Lucas, Dwight McCarty, William Larrabee. Includes church, school, company and organization records, Civil War materials.

DODGE, BERTHA S.

MO —WASHINGTON UNIVERSITY, Libraries, Special Collections Dept, Campus Box 1061, St Louis, 63130.
Notes: A small but significant collection.

DODGE, GRENVILLE AND NATHAN

CO —DENVER PUBLIC LIBRARY, 1357 Broadway, Denver, 80203.
Notes: Correspondence, papers, pictures, diaries, etc.

DODGE, JOSEPH MORRELL

MI —DETROIT PUBLIC LIBRARY, Burton Historical Collection, 5201 Woodward Ave, Detroit, 48202. Alice Dalligan, Chief

DODGE, JOHN CALVIN, 1810-1890

ME —BOWDOIN COLLEGE, Library, Brunswick, 04011. Dianne M Gutscher, Cur of Special Collections
Holdings: Mss
Notes: The Dodge Papers contain material

DODGE, JOHN CALVIN, 1810-1890 (cont.)

concerning about 30 maritime cases handled by Boston lawyer, John Calvin Dodge (1810-1890), whose practice was for the most part in the departments of admiralty and marine insurance. A small collection of 24 letters of Otis Kimball, for the period 1850-64, concerns Bath, Maine, shipping. The Magoun and Clapp Papers consist of about 10,000 pieces of mss material about the vessels owned or operated by this Bath, Maine, firm from 1846-1864. Incl are letters from ships' masters, lists of ships' stores, invoices, insurance policies, etc. The Patterson Papers contain 125 pieces, 1820-1874, incl correspondence, bills, shipping documents, log book, sea journal, and photos of Actor P Patterson, shipmaster of Kennebunkport, Maine, and of Benjamin Patterson, shipmaster of Saco, Maine. The Stetson Paperscontain about 1000 items, primarily 1797-1888, of maritime and family material from Wiscasset, Maine, incl records of ships owned by Moses Carleton and Erastus Foote and three ships' logs. The Maritime Papers contain 50 items of Bibber and Randall Company material; William G Randall notebooks; and documents concerning Portland shipping; Newburyport, Mass, shipping; the steamers "Huntress" and "Kearsarge;" and a journal of a voyage on the ship "Natchez" of Brunswick. The Captain John Thomas Papers consist of 929 pieces of correspondence and ships' records, 1807-1871, of this Bowdoinham, Maine, shipmaster and his family. The Tucker Papers contain about 8000 letters and documents of this Wiscasset, Maine, shipping family for the period 1813-1860, incl a thorough documentation of the construction and voyages of eight ships belongingto the family enterprise.

DODGSON, CHARLES LUTWIDGE see Carroll, Lewis (Charles Lutwidge Dodgson), 1832-1898

DOE, EDWARD M.

AZ —NORTHERN ARIZONA UNIVERSITY, Special Collection Library, CU Box 6022, Flagstaff, 86011. Peter M Whiteley, Coordr/Archivist; William Mullane, Librn
Notes: Doe was a prominent attorney in Flagstaff from 1887 on. His law library incl in this collection was one of the first in Flagstaff. Contains law reports from California, Colorado, Kansas, Nevada, and New Mexico from the 1850's-1890's (9 feet).

DOG RACING

KS —GREYHOUND HALL OF FAME, 407 South Buckeye, Abilene, 67410. Edward Scheele, Dir
Holdings: Vols Cat Pix
Notes: Dog racing as a sport. Incl programs, magazines, memorabilia.

DOGS

OH —CLEVELAND PUBLIC LIBRARY, Science & Technology Dept, 325 Superior Ave, Cleveland, 44114. Jean Z Piety, Head
Holdings: Cat
Notes: Emphases: history of the dog; dog show catalogs; stud books of the American Kennel Club, the Canadian Kennel Club, the Kennel Club, the field dog, the foxhound, and the Irish terrier.

VA —COLLEGE OF WILLIAM AND MARY, Earl Gregg Swem Library, Williamsburg, 23185. Margaret C Cook, Cur of Manuscripts & Rare Books
Holdings: Vols 3000 Cat
Notes: The Peter Chapin collection is one of the most extensive collections of books relating to dogs in North America.

DOLAN, ELEANOR F.

IL —LOYOLA UNIVERSITY OF CHICAGO, E M Cudahy Memorial Library, 6525 N Sheridan Rd, Chicago, 60626.
Notes: Women's activist. Incl letters, reports, newspaper articles, periodicals, addresses, bibliographies, and "sample" publications relating to women. Primarily from the 1950s to the present.

DOLAN, JOSEPH

MA —JOHN F KENNEDY LIBRARY, Columbia Point, Boston, 02125. Henry J Gwiazda II, Cur
Notes: The Burke Marshall papers, 50 archives boxes re civil rights, 1961-1964 and the Bedford-Stuyvesant Development and Restoration Corporations; the Joseph Dolan papers, 1 box; the Thomas Johnston papers, 3 boxes; the James Mc Shane papers, 2 boxes; the Frank Mankiewicz papers, 15 boxes; and the Scott Rafferty papers, 4 boxes.

DOLAN, THOMAS

DC —GEORGETOWN UNIVERSITY, Library, Special Collections Div, 37 & O Sts NW, Washington, 20057. George M Barringer, Special Collections Librn; Nicholas B Sheetz, Mss Librn
Holdings: Mss Pix
Notes: Correspondence, clippings, photographs, and memorabilia incl items relating to Mr Dolan's activities in the Democratic Party in and around Chicago, his friendships with James A Farley, John W McCormack, and Fred Allen, and his student days at Georgetown University.

DOLCI, DANILO

MA —BOSTON UNIVERSITY, Mugar Memorial Library, Special Collections Dept, 771 Commonwealth Ave, Boston, 02215. Howard B Gotlieb, Dir
Holdings: Mss Pix Correspondence

DOLE AIR RACE

CA —SAN DIEGO AERO-SPACE MUSEUM, N Paul Whittier Historical Aviation Library, 2001 Pan American Plaza, Balboa Park, San Diego, 92101. B C Reynolds, Archivist
Holdings: // Uncat Microforms

DOLIM, MARY N.

MA —BOSTON UNIVERSITY, Mugar Memorial Library, Special Collections Dept, 771 Commonwealth Ave, Boston, 02215. Howard B Gotlieb, Dir
Holdings: Cat Mss Correspondence

DOLL, BILL

NY —NEW YORK PUBLIC LIBRARY, Performing Arts Research Center, Billy Rose Theatre Collection, 111 Amsterdam Ave, New York, 10023. Dorothy L Swerdlove, Cur
Holdings: Cat
See also entry under Theatre - History.

DOLLIVER, JONATHAN P.

IA —STATE HISTORICAL SOCIETY OF IOWA LIBRARY, 402 Iowa Ave, Iowa City, 52240. Darold J Brown, Librn
Holdings: Cat
Notes: Thousands of individual items and smaller collections. Two hundred larger collections incl the papers of Cyrus C Carpenter, Jonathan P Dolliver, Gilbert Haugen, W W Waymack, Ephraim Adams, A C Dodge, Dorothy Houghton, Jesse Macy, Agnes Samuelson, Donald Johnson, Jack Miller, Ruth Sayre, Samuel Kirkwood, Thomas McKnight, Robert Lucas, Dwight McCarty, William Larrabee. Includes church, school, company and organization records, Civil War materials.

DOLLS

CA —CARLSBAD CITY LIBRARY, 1250 Elm Ave, Carlsbad, 92008. Clifford E Lange, Library Dir
Holdings: Vols (2297) Cat
Notes: Collection of sewing patterns. Catalogs of the patterns have been made up with complete information on size, etc, and have been divided into subject areas, such as gift ideas, toys, dolls, women's clothes, men's clothes, children's clothes, etc. Also patterns for knitted and crocheted wearing apparel. Incl patterns for children's costumes, historical fashions and antique dolls.

CA —POMONA PUBLIC LIBRARY, Laura Ingalls Wilder Room, 625 S Garey, PO Box 2271, Pomona, 91766. Kerry Stafford, Children's Librn
Holdings: Cat
Notes: Mostly 20th century dolls dressed in national costumes; some antique dolls; also doll house furniture; cat and angel doll collections. 663 dolls.

IL —ILLINOIS STATE UNIVERSITY, Milner Library, Dept of Special Collections, Normal, 61761. Robert Sokan, Librn
Holdings: Vols (170) Uncat Mss Pix Audiotapes
Notes: Correspondence (1935-1957) to Lois Lenski concerning her doll and toy collection and her books for children; correspondence (1956-1970) from Lois Lenski to Milner Library concerning additions to the collection; bookmarks and Christmas cards designed by Miss Lenski; photograph albums; sketchbooks; scrapbooks (contain photographs, correspondence and sketches); original illustrations; handwritten mss (*Houseboat Girl*, 1957, and *Corn Farm* Boy, 1953); typewritten mss (*Coal Camp* Girl, 1959); articles, plays and speeches written by Miss Lenski; newspaper and magazine clippings; and a tape recording entitled *A Talk with Lois Lenski.*

MA —JONES LIBRARY, 43 Amity St, Amherst, 01002. Daniel J Lombardo, Cur of Special Collections
Holdings: Cat
Notes: 320 dolls of many countries; about 180 on permanent display, others exhibited from time to time.

NY —MARGARET WOODBURY STRONG MUSEUM, 1 Manhattan Square, Rochester, 14607.
Holdings: Vols (20,000) Periodicals
Notes: The Margaret Woodbury Strong Museum Library contains a collection of approx 20,000 books, periodicals and ephemera of and concerning the 19th and early 20th centuries. A large part of the library's holdings reflect the interests of Margaret Strong and her family: domestic life and literature of the 19th century and world travel, with particular emphasis on the Orient. The library's resources are available to all visitors for research. Book stacks and rare book storage are not open for browsing and do not circulate, but facilities are provided in reading room for study.

PA —CHESTER COUNTY HISTORICAL SOCIETY, 225 N High St, West Chester, 19380. Rosemary B Philips, Librn; Jack McCarthy, Archivist; Laurie Rofini, Asst Archivist
Notes: Books, photographs, mss on early art, architecture, material culture of Chester County. Espec large collection of paper dolls and paper toys (not limited to Chester County, PA).

DOLMEN MISCELLANY OF IRISH WRITING, THE

BC —UNIVERSITY OF VICTORIA, McPherson Library, Victoria, V8W 3H5, Can.
Notes: Incl 9 cm, 1962; letters and mss by John Montague, editor; Peader O'Donnell; Liam Miller, Dolmen publisher; Aidan Higgins; Pearse Hutchinson; Val Iremonger; John Jordan; Tom Kinsella; James Liddy; John McGahern; Brian Moore; Richard Murphy; James Plunkett; Richard Weber; Leslie Dakin and Thomas McIntyre; and some miscellaneous writers.

DOMESTIC ANIMALS

CA —UNIVERSITY OF CALIFORNIA, DAVIS, General Library, Davis, 95616.

DOMESTIC ANIMALS (cont.)

Bernard Kreissman, University Librn; C Danial Elliott, Asst Head, Dept Special Collections
Holdings: Vols 20,566

CA —LOS ANGELES PUBLIC LIBRARY, Science & Technology Dept, 630 W Fifth St, Los Angeles, 90071. Billie M Connor, Dept Head
Holdings: Vols (14,000) Cat Maps
Notes: Includes agricultural publications of the US Department of Agriculture, California and other state experiment station publications on all aspects of plant and animal husbandry, soil science and analysis, including Soil Surveys. Emphasis is on the Western states and semi-tropical areas.

CA —CALIFORNIA STATE POLYTECHNIC UNIVERSITY, POMONA, University Library, 3801 W Temple Ave, Pomona, 91768. Harold Schleiser, Actg Dir
Notes: General reference materials on agricultural business management, agricultural engineering, animal science, horticulture and plant and soil science.

DE —UNIVERSITY OF DELAWARE, Agriculture Library, 2 Townsend Hall, Newark, 19717. Frederick Getze, Assoc Librn
Holdings: Vols (32,500) Cat Pix Microforms
Notes: Strong in entomology and ornamental horticulture. Extensive collection of state agriculture documents for each US state and Puerto Rico. Library subscribes to 600 serials (English and foreign).

GA —UNIVERSITY OF GEORGIA, College of Agriculture, Coastal Plain Experiment Station Library, Moore Hwy, Tifton, 31793. Emory Cheek, Library Specialist
Holdings: Vols (13,500) Cat

IL —NORTHERN ILLINOIS REGIONAL HISTORY CENTER, Sven Parson Hall, Northern Illinois University, De Kalb, 60115. Glen Gildemeister, Dir
Holdings: Cat Mss Maps Pix Slides Phonorecords Audiotapes 16mm Films
Notes: "A research center for advanced research in the humanities. This northern area of Illinois (excluding Cook County) has been virtually untouched by collecting agencies and we hope to fill that void. We will be strong in agribusiness, agricultural implement business, and hybrid farming mechanics....Will be primarily a ms repository, but [have] already taken responsibility for many artifacts and books, some rare."

IN —PURDUE UNIVERSITY LIBRARIES, Life Sciences Library, Lilly Hall of Life Sciences, West Lafayette, 47907. Martha J Bailey, Librn
Holdings: Vols (73,404) Cat Microforms
Budget: ($223,445)
Notes: Incl materials in agronomy, animal sciences, botany, entomology, forestry, horticulture, biological sciences and agricultural engineering.

KY —UNIVERSITY OF KENTUCKY, Agricultural Library, Agricultural Science Center North, Lexington, 40506. Antoinette Paris Powell, Librn
Holdings: Vols (90,000) Cat Maps Microforms
Budget: ($110,385)

MA —OLD STURBRIDGE VILLAGE, Research Library, Sturbridge, 01566. Theresa Rini Percy, Librn
Holdings: Cat
Notes: Agriculture in New England, 1790-1850.

NY —NEW YORK STATE OFFICE OF PARKS & RECREATION, TACONIC REGION, Clermont State Historic Park, Library, RR 1, Box 215, Germantown, 12526. Bruce E Naramore, Historic Site Manager
Holdings: Vols (5000) Cat Mss Maps
Notes: Period editions of pre - and post-American Revolutionary War agricultural technology. Many belonged to the Chancellor Robert R Livingston (1746-1813). Incl land drainage, hybrids, fertilizers, and the introduction of Merino sheep.

OK —OKLAHOMA STATE UNIVERSITY, Library, Stillwater, 74708. Roscoe Rouse, Dir
Holdings: Vols (8000) Cat

PA —DELAWARE VALLEY COLLEGE, Joseph Krauskopf Library, Doylestown, 18901. Constance Shook, Dir

PA —TEMPLE UNIVERSITY LIBRARIES, Special Collections Dept, Rare Books & Mss Section, Philadelphia, 19122. Thomas M Whitehead, Cur
Holdings: Vols Cat Mss
Notes: Incl the Louise Bush-Brown Horticulture Collection; 15th-20th century rare herbals, animal husbandry and landscape gardening. List of majority of collection available.

PA —UNIVERSITY OF PENNSYLVANIA, Van Pelt Library, Rare Books Collection, 34 & Walnut Sts, Philadelphia, 19104. Daniel Traister, Special Collections Librn
Holdings: Vols 685 Cat Mss
Notes: Incl 18th and early 19th century English and American texts and periodicals on agriculture and animal husbandry; with mss vols of contemporary correspondence of the Philadelphia Society for Promoting Agriculture.

TN —W R GRACE & CO, Planning Services Library, 100 N Main, PO Box 277, Memphis, 38103. Carolyn A Wilhite, Librn
Holdings: Vols (6000) Cat Mss Maps Microforms
Budget: ($85,000)
Notes: Animals nutrition and production; fertilizers; weather; and agricultural statistics.

TX —TEXAS A&M UNIVERSITY, Sterling C Evans Library, Special Collections Div, College Station, 77843. Donald H Dyal, Librn
Holdings: Vols (16,000) Mss Pix
Notes: Jeff Dykes Range Livestock Collection (incl a 600-item collection of J Frank Dobie works). Part of the Dobie Collection is described in Dykes, Jeff C *My Dobie Collection* (College Station, Tex: Friends of the Texas A & M University Library).

MB —UNIVERSITY OF MANITOBA, Agriculture Library, Dafoe Rd, Winnipeg, R3T 2N2, Can. Judy Harper, Head
Holdings: Vols (9000) Cat

DOMESTIC ANIMALS—DISEASES see Veterinary Medicine

DOMESTIC ARCHITECTURE see Architecture, Domestic

DOMESTIC SCIENCE see Home Economics

DOMESTICS see Servants

DOMINICA

RI —BROWN UNIVERSITY, John Carter Brown Library, Providence, 02912. Norman Fiering, Librn; Everett C Wilkie Jr, Bibliographer; Susan Danforth, Cur Maps & Prints
Notes: Works documenting slavery and slave trade in European possessions in the New World until 1833. Particular strengths are British and French abolition movements in the early nineteenth century. (Little material on slavery in what became the United States).

DOMINICAN REPUBLIC

CA —HOOVER INSTITUTION ON WAR, REVOLUTION & PEACE, Stanford University, Stanford, 94305. Milorad M Drachkovitch, Archivist
Holdings: Mss
Notes: Papers of Theodore Draper, 1948-1966, incl correspondence, clippings, pamphlets, newspaper issues, and congressional hearings, relating to the revolution led by Fidel Castro in Cuba, political, social, and economic conditions in Cuba, and the 1965 crisis and US intervention in the Dominican Republic. 22 ms boxes.

CT —YALE UNIVERSITY, Sterling Memorial Library, Latin American Collections, New Haven, 06520. Lee H Williams Jr, Cur
Holdings: Vols (300,000) Cat Maps Pix Slides Phonorecords 16mm Films Filmstrips
See also entry under Latin America

DOMINICK, PETER

†CO —UNIVERSITY OF DENVER, Penrose Library, 2150 E Evans, Denver, 80208.
Notes: Papers of Senator Peter Dominick.

DOMINICANS

DC —DOMINICAN HOUSE OF STUDIES, Dominican College Library, 487 Michigan Ave NE, Washington, 20017. J Raymond Vandegrift, OP, Librn
Holdings: Vols (5000) Cat
Budget: ($1350)
Notes: The Dominican Order (its history, spirituality, government, liturgy), its members (directories, biographies, bibliographies, lives of saints) and works written by Dominicans: incunabula, rare books, dissertations, periodicals (2300 vols), monographs. Incl periodicals either about the Order or edited by Dominicans. Does not incl titles about the congregations of Dominican Sisters. The Library's catalog contains analytics for Dominican contributors to monographs.

DOMINIONS, BRITISH see Commonwealth of Nations

DOMPELAERS see Church of the Brethren

DON COSSACKS

WI —UNIVERSITY OF WISCONSIN, MADISON, Memorial Library, Slavic Studies Collection, 728 State St, Madison, 53706. Aleksander Rolich, Bibliographer for Slavic Studies; Robert P Gakovich, Slavic Cataloger; Valdis J Zeps, Baltic Studies Center
Notes: Cossack Collection. Based on the private libraries of Kh I and P Kh Popov and S G Svatikov and is representative of the publications issued by the Cossacks between 1919 and 1939 in Rostov on Don, Paris and Prague relating to different aspects of Cossack life, military history and life in emigration. Description and listing available. Restricted use: Rare Book Department.

DONALDSON, STEPHEN R.

OH —KENT STATE UNIVERSITY, Libraries, Dept of Special Collections, Kent, 44242. Dean H Keller, Cur
Notes: Manuscript versions of Stephen R Donaldson's fantasy trilogy, *The Chronicles of Thomas Covenant, the Unbeliever.*

DONATIONS see Charitable Uses, Trusts, and Foundations; Endowments

DONNE, JOHN

†CA —UNIVERSITY OF SAN FRANCISCO, Richard A Gleeson Library, The Countess Bernardine Murphy Donohue Rare Book Room, San Francisco, 94117. D Steven Corey, Special Collections Librn
Holdings: Vols 750 Cat
Notes: One of the most complete collections of works by and about St Thomas More. Much on John Donne, incl books with his marginalia.

MD —JOHNS HOPKINS UNIVERSITY, Milton S Eisenhower Library, Charles & 34 Sts, Baltimore, 21218. Ann S Gwyn, Assistant Dir for Special Collections
Holdings: Vols Cat Mss Microforms
Notes: The Osler Collection (Tudor and Stuart Club) contains original editions of Shelley, Milton, Keats, Donne, Defoe, Thomas Fuller, Golden Book of Marcus Aurelius (1559). A collection of his articles made by Walt Whitman. 17th and 18th century commonplace books in English and French, is ms. Most English translations of Jakob Boehme. Cards in main catalog. Also, not included in the above figure, Pollard and Redgrave's, and Wing's Early English Books on microfilm.

DONNE, JOHN (cont.)

MA —HARVARD UNIVERSITY LIBRARY, Widener Library, Cambridge, 02138.
Holdings: Cat Mss
Notes: Bibliography by Geoffrey Keynes published by Cambridge University Press, 1932.

TX —TEXAS TECH UNIVERSITY, Library, Lubbock, 79409. David J Murrah, Assoc Dir for Special Collections

DONNELLEY, R. R.

IL —LAKE FOREST COLLEGE, Donnelley Library, Lake Forest, 60045. Arthur H Miller Jr, College Librn
Holdings: Vols (500)
Notes: Limited editions, privately printed books (William Kittredge), ephemera, Lakeside Classics; examples of work from R R Donnelley extra bindery.

DONNELLY, MURRAY S., 1919-

MB —UNIVERSITY OF MANITOBA, Elizabeth Dafoe Library, Archives and Special Collections Dept, Winnipeg, R3T 2N2, Can. Richard E Bennett, Dept Head; Corrado A Santoro, Reference Archivist
Notes: Murray S Donnelly Papers, 1925-1961. Incl correspondence and reports dealing with foreign elements (fifth columns) in Canada during WW II working to sabotage the Canadian war effort, 1944. 1925 train pass to Imperial Conference held in Australia. Material relating to the life and times of J W Dafoe of the *Manitoba Free* Press from various individuals who knew him, for the purpose of writing a biography on Dafoe.

DONOSO, JOSE

IA —UNIVERSITY OF IOWA, University Libraries, Iowa City, 52242. Robert A McCown, Mss Librn
Holdings: Mss
Notes: Includes correspondence, notes for and drafts of published and unpublished novels, short stories, newspapers articles, plays, television scripts, and poems, together with notebooks, reviews, clippings, and translations. Unpublished guide available in the library. 5 ft of mss.

DONOVAN, FRANK PIERCE, JR.

MN —JAMES JEROME HILL REFERENCE LIBRARY, Fourth St at Market St, Saint Paul, 55106. Virgil F Massman, Dir
Holdings: Vols 3200 // Cat Mss Maps Pix
Notes: Railroad material collected by Frank P Donovan during his life. Books, mss, souvenirs, timetables, correspondence, travel folders, phonorecords, etc. Author catalog of books and pamphlets.

DONOVAN, RICHARD

CT —YALE UNIVERSITY, Music Library, 98 Wall St, New Haven, 06520. Harold E Samuel, Librn
Holdings: Vols (118,000) Cat Mss Pix Phonorecords Audiotapes
Notes: Personal papers and musical mss. *See also* entry under Music, American.

DONOVAN, MAJ. GEN. WILLIAM H.

NY —COLUMBIA UNIVERSITY LIBRARIES, Rare Book & Manuscript Library, 801 Butler Library, 535 W 114 St, New York, 10027. Kenneth A Lohf, Librn
Holdings: Mss
Notes: His research materials on espionage history, American Revolution and espionage. Restricted use.

DOOLEY, THOMAS A.

MO —UNIVERSITY OF MISSOURI-SAINT LOUIS, Thomas Jefferson Library, Manuscript and Historical Society Collection, 8001 Natural Bridge Rd, Saint Louis, 63121.
Holdings: Mss Pix Tapes
Notes: ca

DOOLING, JOHN F., JR., 1908-1981

MA —HARVARD UNIVERSITY LIBRARY, Law School Library, Langdell Hall, Cambridge, 02138. Erika S Chadbourn, Cur of Mss
Notes: Judicial papers. Typed inventory in repository. Inclusive dates: 1961-1980.

DOOLITTLE, HILDA

CT —YALE UNIVERSITY, Box 1603A, Yale Station, New Haven, 06520.
Holdings: Cat Mss
Notes: Incl correspondence.

PA —TEMPLE UNIVERSITY LIBRARIES, Special Collections Dept, Rare Books & Mss Section, Philadelphia, 19122. Thomas M Whitehead, Cur
Holdings: Cat Mss
Notes: First and later editions, etc mss, etc.

DOOMAN, EUGENE HOFFMAN, 1890-1969

CA —HOOVER INSTITUTION ON WAR, REVOLUTION & PEACE, Stanford University, Stanford, 94305. Milorad M Drachkovitch, Archivist
Holdings: Mss
Notes: Papers of Eugene H Dooman, US diplomat, Counsellor of Embassy at Tokyo, 1937-41, and Special Assistant to the Assistant Secretary of State for Far Eastern Affairs, 1944-45, incl mss of writings, transcripts of speeches, correspondence, diaries and printed matter, 1913-1966, relating to US foreign policy in the Far East, US-Japanese relations, the decision to drop the atomic bomb on Japan, and Allied policy regarding the occupation of Japan. 1 1/2 ms boxes.

DOOMSDAY see Judgment Day

DORF, SHEL

OH —OHIO STATE UNIVERSITY, Library for Communication and Graphic Arts, 242 W 18th St, Columbus, 43210. Lucy S Caswell, Curator
Notes: Comic strip artists Hal Foster, Dudley T Fisher, Jr, Mark Szorady, Edwina Dumm, Jim Baker have original works in the library. Also new collections of original cartoons by Windsor McCay, John T McCutcheon, Dick Moores, Ned White, Walter Berndt, Jim Larrick, Carl Rose and Bill Crawford. Also a large collection of the work of illustrator Will Rannells. The Shel Dorf Collection incl historic comic strips and related materials. A small but growing collection of comic books, especially those featuring *Katy Keene,* is available in the library.

DORIAN, MARGUERITE

MA —BOSTON UNIVERSITY, Mugar Memorial Library, Special Collections Dept, 771 Commonwealth Ave, Boston, 02215. Howard B Gotlieb, Dir
Holdings: Cat Mss
Notes: Mss, correspindence, incl publications by or about.

DORMAN, H. H.

NM —MUSEUM OF NEW MEXICO, Photo Archives, Box 2087, Santa Fe, 87503. Arthur L Olivas, Cur; Richard Rudisill, Photo Historian
Holdings: Cat Pix Slides
Notes: Extensive collection of his work.

DORN, EDWARD, 1939-

CT —UNIVERSITY OF CONNECTICUT, Library, Storrs, 06268. George F Butterick, Cur of Literary Archives
Holdings: Mss
Notes: Repository for this poet's papers.

BC —SIMON FRASER UNIVERSITY, Library, Burnaby, V5A 1S6, Can. Percilla Groves, Special Collections Librn
Holdings: Cat Mss
Notes: Letters written to Eshleman by Allen Ginsberg (8 pp), William Carlos Williams and Florence Williams (5 pp), Robert Duncan (4 pp), and Edward Dorn (5 pp), while Eshleman was editor of *Folio* (1959-1961). Tss from Gregory Corso (2 pp), Louis Zukofsky (8 pp), Michael Rumaker (3 pp).

BC —UNIVERSITY OF VICTORIA, McPherson Library, Victoria, V8W 3H5, Can.

DORN, WALTER LEWIS

†NY —COLUMBIA UNIVERSITY LIBRARIES, Butler Library, Rare Book and Manuscript Library, 535 W 114 St, New York, 10027.
Notes: Papers relating to Prof Walter Lewis Dorn's work as special advisor to Gen Lucius D Clay on denazification of Germany.

DORR REBELLION, 1842

RI —BROWN UNIVERSITY, John Hay Library, 20 Prospect St, Providence, 02912. Mark N Brown, Cur Mss
Holdings: Vols (15,000) // Cat Mss Maps Pix
Notes: Sidney S Rider Collection of 5000 books, 10,000 pamphlets and 8000 mss formed in the 19th century by a Providence antiquarian bookseller. The primary focus is on all aspects of Rhode Island: social, political, and economic history from the 17th to the mid-19th century, with some attention given to general New England history. The most significant group of primary materials within the collection relates to Thomas Wilson Dorr and the political movements in Rhode Island ca 1840-1850, especially the Dorr Rebellion over the issue of suffrage.

DORSON, RICHARD M.

IN —INDIANA UNIVERSITY, Lilly Library, Seventh St, Bloomington, 47405. William R Cagle, Librn
Holdings: // Cat Mss
Notes: Collections incl papers of folklorist and Indiana University professor Richard M Dorson, 1916-1981.

DOS PASSOS, JOHN

NV —UNIVERSITY OF NEVADA, RENO, University Library, Special Collections Dept, Reno, 89557. Robert E Blesse, Head
Holdings: // Vols (112) Cat Other appearances 235 Cat
Notes: Includes individual works by author in all editions including translations; also prefaces, introductions, published correspondence, appearances in anthologies, periodicals, etc. Bibliographical research collection, part of Modern Authors Collection.

VA —UNIVERSITY OF VIRGINIA, Alderman Library, Manuscripts Dept, Charlottesville, 22901. Edmund Berkeley Jr, Cur
Holdings: Cat Mss Pix
Notes: The John Dos Passos Archive is the writer's retained material from his life and literary activities. It includes drafts of his books, articles, stories, etc, research material, photographs, correspondence, working papers, etc. Also included are pictures of the author, reviews of his works, newspaper clippings, etc. Correspondents include E E Cummings, Ernest Hemingway, Dwight D Eisenhower, Robert Kennedy, Archibald MacLeish, Samuel Eliot Morrison, Walter Rumsey Marvin, and many others. A portion of the collection was presented to the University by Mr Dos Passos; other portions remain a loan, and have certain restrictions on copying. An unpublished guide to this archive is available. 70 linear ft.

DOUBLE CONSCIOUSNESS see Personality, Disorders of

DOUGLAS, A. VIBERT

ON —QUEEN'S UNIVERSITY, Douglas Library, Kingston, K7L 5C4, Can. William F

DOUGLAS, A. VIBERT (cont.)

E Morley, Cur, Special Collections
Notes: Papers (1924-1959).

DOUGLAS, LORD ALFRED

DC —GEORGETOWN UNIVERSITY, Library, Special Collections Div, 37 & O Sts NW, Washington, 20057. George M Barringer, Special Collections Librn; Nicholas B Sheetz, Mss Librn
Holdings: Mss Cat Pix
Notes: The papers of the Irish man-of-letters Sir Shane Leslie (1885-1971) containing letters, mss, diaries, notebooks, clippings, and photographs. Extensive correspondence by Margot Asquith, countess of Oxford and Asquith; Lady Violet Bonham-Carter; Burke Cochran; Lord Alfred Douglas; Moreton Frewen; Cardinal Gasquet; Vyvyan Holland; Lady Leonie Leslie; Sir Wilfrid Meynell; Sir Horace Plunkett; John Quinn; Frederick Rolfe (Baron Corvo); and Elizabeth Russell, among others. Also incl are research files on Sir Winston Churchill (Leslie's first cousin); Leonard Jerome; Maria Anne Fitzherbet (wife of King George IV); Ghosts and Ghost stories; and Eton College.

BC —UNIVERSITY OF VICTORIA, McPherson Library, Victoria, V8W 3H5, Can.

NS —DALHOUSIE UNIVERSITY LIBRARY, Halifax, B3H 4H8, Can.
Notes: The collection of numerous editions from Dr Henry Hicks, past president of Dalhousie.

DOUGLAS, HELEN GAHAGAN

OK —UNIVERSITY OF OKLAHOMA, Bizzell Memorial Library, Western History Collections, 401 W Brooks, Norman, 73069. John Ezell, Cur
Holdings: Mss Pix Maps
Notes: Stage actress, Helen Gahagan Douglas, US Representative. Her papers. Guide available.

DOUGLAS, LEWIS W.

AZ —UNIVERSITY OF ARIZONA, Library, Tucson, 85721. W David Laird, Librn
Notes: His papers.

DOUGLAS, NORMAN, 1868-1952

CA —CLAREMONT COLLEGES, Honnold Library, Ninth & Dartmouth, Claremont, 91711. Tania Rizzo, Special Collections Dept Head
Holdings: Vols 49 // Cat Mss
Notes: 9 ALsS. First and limited editions by and about.

CA —UNIVERSITY OF CALIFORNIA, LOS ANGELES, Research Library, Dept of Special Collections, 405 Hilgard Ave, Los Angeles, 90024. Edward Shreeves, Chairman, Bibliographers Group; David S Zeidberg, Head
Holdings: Vols 100 Cat Mss
Notes: 100 first and other editions of his books, many from his own library; 8 linear feet of papers, mss, etc. No photocopying.

CT —YALE UNIVERSITY, Box 1603A, Yale Station, New Haven, 06520.
Holdings: Cat Mss

IL —ILLINOIS STATE UNIVERSITY, Milner Library, Dept of Special Collections, Normal, 61761. Robert Sokan, Librn
Holdings: Vols (105) Cat Mss
Notes: First editions, limited editions, ephemera, etc.

NC —UNIVERSITY OF NORTH CAROLINA, CHARLOTTE, J Murrey Atkins Library, UNCC Station, Charlotte, 28223. Robert F Brabham Jr, Special Collections Librn
Holdings: Vols 100 Cat
Notes: Incl scholarly works on sex, classics by such writers as D H Lawrence, Frank Harris, and Norman Douglas, and about 40 novels published between 1890 and 1930.

BC —UNIVERSITY OF VICTORIA, McPherson Library, Victoria, V8W 3H5, Can.

ON —UNIVERSITY OF TORONTO, Thomas Fisher Rare Book Library, 120 Saint George St, Toronto, M5S 1A5, Can. Richard G Landon, Head
Holdings: Vols 5400 Cat Mss
Notes: Three collections. Duncan Collection is named for donor, Douglas Duncan, art dealer and collector, Toronto. Contains first and subsequent important editions of Richard Aldington, Max Beerbohm, Norman Douglas, Aldoux Huxley, and D H Lawrence. Manuscripts by Beerbohm, Aldington, Lawrence, William Sharp. Endicott Collection named in honor of Norman J Endicott, Professor of English, University of Toronto, contains first and significant later editions of over fifty British writers whose major work falls into the period from 1880 to 1930. Fisher Collection named for donor, Charles B Fisher, contains first and significant editions of Kipling, Norman Douglas, and Lord Dunsany.

DOUGLAS, SEN. PAUL H.

IL —CHICAGO HISTORICAL SOCIETY, Library, Clark St at North Ave, Chicago, 60614. Archie Motley, Manuscript Librn
Notes: Papers of economist, Chicago alderman, US Senator.

DOUGLAS, STEPHEN A.

IL —UNIVERSITY OF CHICAGO LIBRARY, Dept of Special Collections, 1100 E 57 St, Chicago, 60637.
Notes: Personal papers.

DOUGLAS, WILLIAM ORVILLE, 1898-1980

DC —LIBRARY OF CONGRESS, Manuscript Division, Washington, 20540. John C Broderick, Chief
Notes: The papers of William O Douglas, incl judicial case files from 1939 through 1952, correspondence, subject files relating to the Securities and Exchange Commission, and lecture notes he used as law professor.

DOUGLAS FIR

OR —OREGON STATE UNIVERSITY, Library, Corvallis, 97331. Melvin George, Dir
Holdings: Cat Mss Maps Pix Microforms

DOUGLASS, ANDREW E.

OH —RUTHERFORD B HAYES LIBRARY, 1337 Hayes Ave, Fremont, 43420. Watt P Marchman, Dir
Holdings: Cat Mss
Notes: The Andrew E Douglass Collection. Index in collections; listed in *Guide to Manuscripts of the Ohio Historical Society*, 131.

DOUGLASS, EARL

UT —UNIVERSITY OF UTAH, Marriott Library, Special Collections, Salt Lake City, 84112. Gregory C Thompson, Cur
Notes: Papers of Earl Douglass, discoverer of Dinosaur National Monument. (some restrictions apply to collection).

DOUGLASS, FREDERICK

DC —LIBRARY OF CONGRESS, Manuscript Division, Washington, 20540. John C Broderick, Chief
Holdings: Cat Mss
Notes: More than 5000 Frederick Douglass items, principally letters addressed to him; mss by Douglass, etc. transferred from the National Park Service collections.

NY —SAINT JOHN FISHER COLLEGE, Library, Rochester, 14618.
Notes: 1000 items, incl original newspapers.

NY —UNIVERSITY OF ROCHESTER, Rush Rhees Library, Department of Rare Books and Special Collections, Rochester, 14627. Peter Dzwonkoski, Librn
Holdings: Mss Letters
Notes: Autograph letters and other mss incl in the Amy and Issac Post family papers and other collections.
See also entry under Abolitionists.

DOUKHOBORS see Dukhobors

DOUWES DEKKER, NIELS

NY —CORNELL UNIVERSITY LIBRARIES, Collection of Regional History, Dept of Manuscripts and Univ Archives, Ithaca, 14853.
Notes: Photographer, Dutch East Indies. Papers, ca 1944-46; 6.6 ft.

DOW, NEAL

ME —BOWDOIN COLLEGE, Library, Brunswick, 04011. Dianne M Gutscher, Cur of Special Collections
Holdings: Mss
Notes: The Neal Dow Papers contain 110 letters, 1852-1887, of this temperance reformer, known as "father of the Maine Law." The Hubbard Family Papers contain more than 12,000 pieces of correspondence and other mss materials relating to the Hubbard Family, for the period 1794-1915. Of principal interest are extensive files of letters to and from John Hubbard (1794-1869), governor of Maine, who signed the "Maine Law" (prohibition law) in 1851, and was a commissioner under the Reciprocity Treaty with Great Britain.

DOWDEY, CLIFFORD

VA —UNIVERSITY OF VIRGINIA, Alderman Library, Manuscripts Dept, Charlottesville, 22901. Edmund Berkeley Jr, Cur
Holdings: Cat Mss Pix
Notes: Extensive collection of mss and printed materials.

DOWLING, DANIEL B.

KS —UNIVERSITY OF KANSAS, Kenneth Spencer Research Library, Kansas Collection, Lawrence, 66045. Sheryl K Williams, Cur
Holdings: Cat
Notes: The Albert T Reid Cartoon Collection. Nucleus of collection was Reid's personal collection of political and comic cartoons. Later cartoonists presented samples of their work. Bill Mauldin, Rollin Kirby, Daniel B Dowling, Thomas Nast, and other political cartoonists are represented. Comic strips from the late 1920s and 1930s also. The collection of cartoons is cataloged and represented in the Kansas Collection card catalog. A separate book catalog is maintained also. For description see: *Albert T Reid Cartoon Collection*. Lawrence, Kan. Published for the Journalistic Historical Center, University of Kansas by the William Allen White Foundation, University of Kansas, ca 1957. Originally maintained by the Journalistic Historical Center, William Allen White School of Journalism, the collection was transferred to the Kansas Collection, Kenneth Spencer Library in 1969.

DOWNEY, FAIRFAX

MA —BOSTON UNIVERSITY, Mugar Memorial Library, Special Collections Dept, 771 Commonwealth Ave, Boston, 02215. Howard B Gotlieb, Dir
Holdings: Cat Mss Pix
Notes: Mss, correspondence, etc colleted in depth; incl publications by or about.

DOWNEY, HARRIS

MA —BOSTON UNIVERSITY, Mugar Memorial Library, Special Collections Dept, 771 Commonwealth Ave, Boston, 02215. Howard B Gotlieb, Dir
Holdings: Mss Pix

DOWNING, WARWICK

MA —BOSTON UNIVERSITY, Mugar Memorial Library, Special Collections Dept,

DOWNING, WARWICK (cont.)

771 Commonwealth Ave, Boston, 02215. Howard B Gotlieb, Dir
Holdings: Cat Mss Pix
Notes: Mss correspondence, etc collected in depth; incl publications by or about.

DOWNUM, GARLAND

AZ —NORTHERN ARIZONA UNIVERSITY, Special Collection Library, CU Box 6022, Flagstaff, 86011. Peter M Whiteley, Coordr/Archivist; William Mullane, Librn
Notes: Papers.

DOWSON, ERNEST CHRISTOPHER, 1867-1900

BC —UNIVERSITY OF VICTORIA, McPherson Library, Victoria, V8W 3H5, Can.

DOYLE, SIR ARTHUR CONAN

IN —INDIANA UNIVERSITY, Lilly Library, Seventh St, Bloomington, 47405. William R Cagle, Librn
Holdings: Cat Mss
Notes: First editions, etc of author Sir Arthur Conan Doyle.

MN —UNIVERSITY OF MINNESOTA, O Meredith Wilson Library, 309 19 Ave S, Minneapolis, 55455. Austin J McLean, Chief, Special Collections
Holdings: Vols 1733 Uncat Pix Audiotapes Slides Memorabilia
Notes: The writings about Sherlock Holmes, critical studies and miscellaneous ephemera. Complete listing available in the Division.

ON —METROPOLITAN TORONTO LIBRARY, Literature Dept, 789 Yonge St, Toronto, M4W 2G8, Can. Katherine McCook, Head
Holdings: Vols 5000 Cat Mss Maps Pix Phonorecords Audiotapes Videotapes 16mm Films Filmstrips
Notes: Housed in a special room with furnishings of the Victorian period, this is a comprehensive collection of the writings by and about Arthur Conan Doyle and Sherlock Holmes. It includes first and other editions of the works; translations; biographies; parodies and imitations of Sherlock Holmes; publications of the Sherlock Holmes societies. *A Checklist of the Arthur Conan Doyle Collection,* by Donald A Redmond, is available from the Library. A free descriptive brochure *Sherlock Holmes Is Alive and Well at the Metropolitan Toronto Library* is also available.

DOZOIS, GARDNER

†PA —TEMPLE UNIVERSITY LIBRARY, Philadelphia, 19122. Thomas M Whitehead, Librn
Notes: More than 100 cubic ft of mss, incl papers of Michael Bishop, Ben Bova, Jack Dann, Gardner Dozois, Lloyd Eshback, Tom Purdom, Pamela Sargent, John Varley, and George Zebrowski.

DRABBLE, MARGARET

MA —BOSTON UNIVERSITY, Mugar Memorial Library, Special Collections Dept, 771 Commonwealth Ave, Boston, 02215. Howard B Gotlieb, Dir
Holdings: Cat Mss

DRAFT RESISTANCE

DC —LIBRARY OF CONGRESS, Washington, 20540.
Notes: Some 4500 pamphlets and sheets dealing primarily with subversive and radical activities in the US from 1900 to 1950. Incl tracts and campaign literture of the Communist and Socialist Parties in the US and works by party leaders; materials on the economic, political, and human rights issues of the pre-World War II, World War II, and early civil rights campaign periods; and pamphlets by various anti-war and anti-draft organizations, material on Russia, and materials on the communist movement in other countries.

DRAFTING, MECHANICAL see Mechanical Drawing

DRAGONETTE, JESSICA

NY —NEW YORK PUBLIC LIBRARY, Performing Arts Research Center, Billy Rose Theatre Collection, 111 Amsterdam Ave, New York, 10023. Dorothy L Swerdlove, Cur
Holdings: Cat Mss Pix
Notes: Papers, scrapbooks, mss, photographs, memorabilia, etc.

DRAGONETTI, DOMENICO

IL —NORTHWESTERN UNIVERSITY, Music Library, 1937 Sheridan Rd, Evanston, 60201. Don L Roberts, Head Music Librn
Holdings: Uncat Mss
Notes: Materials in the Moldenhauer Archive. 90 letters and documents.

DRAINAGE

NY —NEW YORK STATE OFFICE OF PARKS & RECREATION, TACONIC REGION, Clermont State Historic Park, Library, RR 1, Box 215, Germantown, 12526. Bruce E Naramore, Historic Site Manager
Holdings: Vols (5000) Cat Mss Maps
Notes: Period editions of pre- and post-American Revolutionary War agricultural technology. Many belonged to the Chancellor Robert R Livingston (1746-1813). Incl land drainage, hybrids, fertilizers, and the introduction of Merino sheep.

DRAKE, DANIEL, 1785-1852

KY —UNIVERSITY OF KENTUCKY, Margaret I King Library, Dept of Special Collections, Lexington, 40506. William Marshall, Head
Holdings: Vols 310 // Cat Mss Pix
Notes: Collection assembled by Dr Emmet Field Horine to document the work and writings of Daniel Drake in medicine and history and education; includes Drake's own publications. (Daniel Drake is important to Ohio and Kentucky history in particular.) Incl oil portrait and bust.

DRAKE, SIR FRANCIS

DC —LIBRARY OF CONGRESS, Rare Book & Special Collections Div, Washington, 20540. William Matheson, Chief
Notes: The Hans P and Hanni Kraus Collection of contemporary materials (maps, books, mss, medals and portraits) designed to present Sir Francis Drake as his contemporaries would have learned about him. See Kraus, Hans P, *Sir Francis Drake, a Pictorial Biography,* (Amsterdam, N Israel, 1970).

DRAKE, JAMES RODMAN

VA —UNIVERSITY OF VIRGINIA, Alderman Library, Clifton Waller Barrett Collection, Charlottesville, 22901. Joan St C Crane, Cur of American Literature Collections
Notes: Papers.

DRAMA

CA —UNIVERSITY OF CALIFORNIA, DAVIS, Shields Library, Dept of Special Collections, Davis, 95616. Donald Kunitz, Head; C Danial Elliott, Asst Head
Holdings: Vols Mss Pix Uncat
Notes: Programs, playbills, posters, designs, and scripts from 19th and 20th century American and British theatre. American materials incl the eastern United States (NYC) and California. Production groupings center in Sir Henry Irving, McKee Rankin, Sir John Martin-Harvey, E L Davenport. Clippings, photographs, and correspondence of theatre personalities; records of the Bread and Puppet Theatre, San Francisco Mime Troupe, Living Theatre, Firehouse Theatre, Squat Theatre, papers of Toby Cole. Described in: Sarlos, Robert K, "The Theatre Collection at Davis," *American Society for Theatre Research Newsletter,* vol 3, no 1, fall 1974, pp 2-3, 9-10.

CA —LOS ANGELES PUBLIC LIBRARY, Literature and Philology Dept, 630 W Fifth St, Los Angeles, 90071. Helene G Mochedlover, Dept Librn
Holdings: Vols (50,000) Cat Pix Slides Microforms
Notes: Incl theatre programs, playbills, clippings, play reviews on 19th and 20th century plays produced in or near Los Angeles. Play collection of over 30,000 vols is particularly strong in 19th and 20th centuries. Annotated subject index to plays is kept up-to-date. A file of local as well as New York and London play reviews is kept. Collection incl microprints and microcards. There are a number of long files of important dramatic periodicals.

CA —LOS ANGELES PUBLIC LIBRARY, Frances Howard Goldwyn Hollywood Regional Library, 1623 Ivar Ave, Los Angeles, 90028. Sally Dumaux, Librn
Holdings: Vols (100,000) Cat Mss Pix VF
Budget: ($60,000)
Notes: A general and a research collection on theatre history, US and foreign, with special emphasis on Los Angeles, Chicago, and New York theatre from the late 1800s to the present. Other aspects of the collection include theatre design, make-up, costume, and acting and directing techniques. Also includes biographies of actors and actresses (many signed). The play collection of over 15,000 titles covers mainly English and American plays of the 19th and 20th century. There are over 5000 playbills, scrapbooks, posters, and programs. Special Collections: "Hellzapoppin," NY, 1938-40. Includes photographs, clippings, and programs.

CA —HUNTINGTON LIBRARY, Art Gallery & Botanical Gardens, 1151 Oxford Rd, San Marino, 91108. Robert L Middlekauff, Dir; Daniel H Woodward, Librn
Notes: Incl the Larpent Collection of English manuscript plays submitted to the Lord Chamberlain for approval after the Licensing Act of 1737--the year and reason the phrase "legitimate stage" came into use. Refer to MacMillian, Dougald, *Catalogue of the Larpent Plays in the Huntington Library* (San Marino, Calif: 1939).

CT —YALE UNIVERSITY, Drama Library, 222 York St, Box 1903A, Yale Station, New Haven, 06520. Pamela C Jordan, Librn
Holdings: Vols (24,000) Cat Pix Slides Audiotapes
Budget: ($6000)
Notes: Book collection covers all phases of the dramatic arts: theatre, film, opera, dance, etc, with an emphasis on 20th century theatre. Incl audiotapes of Yale Drama School and Repertory Theatre productions, other plays and dramatic readings, and dialect tapes. Incl 1200 slides on costume design and 2000 slides on architecture, interiors, and furniture. Also incl more than 80,000 pictures on set and costume design.

DC —HOWARD UNIVERSITY, Founders Library, Channing Pollock Theatre Collection, 500 Howard Place NW, Washington, 20059. Marilyn Mahanand, Librn
Holdings: Vols (16,440) Cat Mss Maps Pix Slides Microforms

IL —NORTHERN ILLINOIS UNIVERSITY, Founders Memorial Library, Rare Books and Special Collections Dept, De Kalb, 60115. William R DuBois, Dept Head
Holdings: Vols 2500 // Cat
Notes: Nisbet-Snyder Drama Collection.

DRAMA (cont.)

Contains over 2500 prompt books and prompters' editions of plays, mostly published in England and the US from the last quarter of the 18th century to the end of the 19th century. Noncirculating.

IL —NORTHWESTERN UNIVERSITY, Library, Special Collections Dept, 1937 Sheridan Rd, Evanston, 60201. R Russell Maylone, Cur
Holdings: Vols (15,000) Cat
Notes: Spanish drama from the 18th to 20th centuries, incl Castilian, Catalan, Valencian, and Mexican. Additional material in general collection.

IN —BUTLER UNIVERSITY, Jordan College of Music, Library, 4600 Sunset, Indianapolis, 46208. Phyllis J Schoonover, Librn
Holdings: Vols (5383) Cat Phonorecords Filmstrips
Budget: ($16,500)

IN —INDIANA UNIVERSITY, SOUTH BEND, Library, 1700 Mishawaka Ave, South Bend, 46615. James L Mullins, Dir
Holdings: Vols (1490) Cat Mss Maps Pix Phonorecords
Notes: Incl design materials, scripts, theatre music, rare editions, theatre programs, playbills, clippings and periodicals from the 1850s to the 1940s.

KY —BEREA COLLEGE, Hutchins Library, Berea, 40404. Gerald F Roberts, Librn Special Collections
Notes: In the general collection.

KY —HOPKINSVILLE COMMUNITY COLLEGE, Library, North Dr, Hopkinsville, 42240. Marjanna J Frising, Librn
Holdings: Vols (500) Cat Phonorecords Audiotapes Filmstrips
Notes: Incl most notable Broadway plays, both musical and non-musical, with sound-tracks available for most. Also a large collection of children's and one-act plays, incl comedy and mystery plays.

KY —UNIVERSITY OF KENTUCKY, Margaret I King Library, Dept of Special Collections, Lexington, 40506. William Marshall, Head
Holdings: Cat
Notes: 2000 French and approximately 2000 Spanish and German plays. 18th-19th centuries.

MA —AMHERST COLLEGE, Library, Amherst, 01002. John Lancaster, Special Collections Librn
Holdings: Vols (20,000) Uncat Mss
Notes: Contains a comprehensive collection of paperbound Samuel French acting editions (15,000) and many from other publishers; also Augustin Daly manuscripts, David Warfield acting scripts, and the library of Clyde Fitch. 200 mss.

†MA —BOSTON PUBLIC LIBRARY, Copley Sq, Boston, 02117.
Holdings: Uncat Microforms
Notes: Microform Publications by Readex Micropoint Corp. Three Centuries of English and American Plays, 1500-1800; English and American Plays of the 19th Century.

MA —SMITH COLLEGE, Werner Josten Library for the Performing Arts, Northampton, 01063. Marlene M Wong, Librn
Notes: Special collection: Einstein Collection of Music of the 16th-18th centuries copied in score by Alfred Einstein; 25,982 books, also 34,131 music scores, 42,405 phonorecords, 150 microforms. No photocopying.

MI —UNIVERSITY OF MICHIGAN, Library, Dept of Rare Books & Special Collections, Ann Arbor, 48109. Robert J Starring, Head
Holdings: Cat
Notes: Strong collections of American, English, French and Spanish dramatic works before 1900.

MO —UNIVERSITY OF MISSOURI-KANSAS CITY, General Library, 5100 Rockhill Road, Kansas City, 64110. Kenneth J LaBudde, Dir; Gordon Hendrickson, Assoc Dir; Marilyn Carbonell, Ref Librn
Holdings: Vols 108,000 Cat
Notes: 4121 current serial subscriptions.

NJ —HADDON HEIGHTS PUBLIC LIBRARY, 608 Station Ave, Haddon Heights, 08035. Robert J Hunter, Librn
Holdings: Vols (1900) Cat Phonorecords

NY —CORNELL UNIVERSITY LIBRARIES, Collection of Regional History, Dept of Manuscripts and Univ Archives, Ithaca, 14853.
Notes: Incl records, 1893-1965; correspondence, clippings, photos, programs, broadsides and other printed matter relating to Cornell University drama clubs.

NY —COLUMBIA UNIVERSITY LIBRARIES, Rare Book & Manuscript Library, 801 Butler Library, 535 W 114 St, New York, 10027. Kenneth A Lohf, Librn
Holdings: Vols 5000 Mss
Notes: Brander Matthews Collection. Restricted use: noncirculating.

NY —HISPANIC SOCIETY OF AMERICA, Library, 613 W 155 St, New York, 10032. Martha M de Narvaez, Cur of Mss; Irene S Frye, Asst Librn
Holdings: Vols (150,000) Cat Mss Maps Pix Slides Phonorecords Microforms
Notes: Mss of the Golden Age of Spanish Drama. Hundreds of mss (some with stage business, notes and annotations); numerous titles of rare 17th-century and later printed books on the drama and the stage; English translations of Spanish plays and Spanish translations of international drama; letters and documents of the major and minor dramatists and performers from 1904 to the present day. Catalogs: *Catalogue of the Hispanic Society of America* (Boston: G K Hall, 1962), 10 vols; *First Supplement* (Boston, 1970), 4 vols. Early books: *Printed Books 1468-1700;* Mss: *Catalogo de los Manuscritos Poeticos Castellanos* (15th-17th centuries; 3 vols); *Medieval Manuscripts in the Library; Golden Age Drama Manuscripts* (the latter in press).

†NY —NEIGHBORHOOD PLAYHOUSE SCHOOL OF THE THEATRE, Irene Lewisohn Library, 340 E 54 St, New York, 10022. Alice G Owen, Librn
Holdings: Vols 4025 Cat Mss Pix
Notes: Theatre and drama are the primary emphases, but incl books on costume, dance, film, poetry, and general literature. Collection supports the school program and class work. 9 VF drawers of scenes, Neighborhood Playhouse-iana, pictures, music scores, sheet music, etc. A few rare vols. Scenes are indexed; music scores are cataloged. 568 typed scripts.

NY —NEW YORK PUBLIC LIBRARY, Performing Arts Research Center, Billy Rose Theatre Collection, 111 Amsterdam Ave, New York, 10023. Dorothy L Swerdlove, Cur
Holdings: Cat
Notes: Described in *Catalog of the Theatre and Drama Collections,* The Research Libraries of The New York Public Library. 1967. To be Supplemented. Part I *Drama Collection: Listing by Cultural Origin,* 6 vols (120,000 cards), $585; Part II, *Drama Collection: Author Listing,* 6 vols (115,000 cards), $790. This catalog represents the major portion of the Research Libraries' Drama Collection. Incl are more than 120, 000 plays written in Western languages. Translations of plays published in the Cyrillic, Hebrew and Oriental alphabets are also listed. Excluded are children's plays, Christmas plays, and moralities. The catalog is in two parts: a listing by author (or title, in the case of anonymous plays); and a listing by cultural origin. An analysis of this latter section reveals the Research Libraries' interest in collecting widely from the literatures of theworld: American, 20,000 entries; English, 21,000; French, 22,000; Spanish, 16,000; German, 14,000; and a strong representation of plays written in minor languages.

NY —NEW YORK PUBLIC LIBRARY, Research Libraries, General Research Division, Fifth Ave & 42 St, New York, 10018. Rodney Phillips, Chief
Holdings: Vols (2,225,000) Cat Maps Pix Microforms
Budget: ($775,718)

NY —NEW YORK PUBLIC LIBRARY, General Library of the Performing Arts, 111 Amsterdam Ave, New York, 10023. Larry Cioppa, Drama Specialist
Holdings: Vols (40,000) Cat Pnonorecords
Notes: Drama material on all aspects of the theatre. Film, radio, television and related performing arts. Incl 5000 drama recordings.

NY —THEATRE COLLECTION OF THE INTERNATIONAL THEATRE INSTITUTE OF THE UNITED STATES, INC, Library, Suite 1510, 1860 Broadway, New York, 10023. Elizabeth B Burdick, Dir
Holdings: Vols (4525) Cat Mss Pix
Budget: ($35,000)
Notes: The International Theatre Institute was founded by UNESCO to "promote the exchange of knowledge and practice in the theatre arts." In 1948, eleven nations, incl the United States, became charter members of the international organization, which today has national centers or affiliates in 64 countries. The American center is the International Theatre Institute of the United States (ITI/US). In 1970, as one of its programs to strengthen communication among theatre people, ITI/US opened a library devoted to international theatre since World War II. The Collection's main holdings have been amassed over the 35-year operation of ITI/US through its world-wide exchange of information, publications, and people. Holdings document theatre activity in 140 countries. The 4525 vols on American and foreign theatre(covering history, management, design, stagecraft, theory, criticism, biography, playscripts) represent only a small part of the total collection. Focus is on foreign theatre companies, directors, playwrights, designers, managers, actors. The emphasis is on the acquisition of material which is generally unavailable in this country: foreign yearbooks, house organs, newsletters, programs, press releases, production schedules, brochures, periodicals, monographs, articles, newspaper clippings. While these fugitive items have never been counted, they have been cataloged by country, then indexed by title, subject, or name of theatre. The library receives regularly 250 periodicals on the performing arts (cataloged by country, then indexed by title). It now owns 6417 foreign plays from 80 countries in ms or publishedmss or published editions, in collections and anthologies, and in periodicals. Each play is cataloged by author, title, and country of origin. The section on American theatre incl books, programs, reviews, over 60 periodicals, 2061 American plays. The activities of approx 700 theatres across the country are documented by annual files containing production schedules, press releases, programs, brochures for each theatrical season.

NY —MOUNT PLEASANT PUBLIC LIBRARY, 350 Bedford Rd, Pleasantville, 10570. Charlotte Miller, Dir
Holdings: Vols 3000 Cat Mss Pix
Notes: The Deane Winthrop Pratt collection of acting editions of mostly 19th-20th century British plays. Incl some 200 prompt books, most of them comprehensively marked with production notes. The collection was the product of a 19th-early 20th century proessional actor who turned to direction of suburban amateur acting groups and the prompt books reflect that activity. There are several ms plays by Mr Pratt in the collection. Theatre memorabilia mainly tipped into the various vols. The collection of John W Frost is especially strong in 17th and 18th century drama.

NC —PUBLIC LIBRARY OF CHARLOTTE & MECKLENBURG COUNTY, Literature and Drama Dept, 310 N Tryon St, Charlotte, 28202. Anne McNair, Reference Librn
Holdings: Cat
Notes: Large collection of plays in English, other languages and translations. Specialized indexes, commentaries and criticism, reviews.

NC —UNIVERSITY OF NORTH CAROLINA, CHARLOTTE, J Murrey Atkins Library, UNCC Station, Charlotte, 28223. Robert F Brabham Jr, Special

DRAMA (cont.)

Collections Librn
Notes: Most of the plays (842 in 110 vols) were originally collected by Augusta Sophia, a daughter of George III. At her death, they passed to her brother Ernst August, Elector of Hanover, and became part of the Knigliche Ernst-August-Fideicommiss-Bibliothek, which was dispersed at auction in 1970-1971. Period covered is 1618-1826.

NC —DUKE UNIVERSITY, William R Perkins Library, Durham, 27706. Elvin E Strowd, University Librn
Notes: The Mazzoni collection of approximately 23,000 books and 67,000 reprints and pamphlets is strong in, but not limited by any means to, Italian literature. A special aspect of this collection is a group of essays, studies, or small works published on the occasion of a marriage. These "per la nozze di" range from a poem published in post card form to a scientific or literary work. The manuscript catalog of the pamphlet collection has been published by the library in book form; the 23,000 volumes have been cataloged and are shelved in the library's bookstacks. Also includes Montrose J Moses' collection of books, mss, and papers, mostly concerned with men and women of the theatre, and creative writers of the first third of the century. 300 books; 22, 000 mss.

NC —NORTH CAROLINA SCHOOL OF THE ARTS, Semans Library, PO Box 12189, Winston-Salem, 27107. William D VanHoven, Head Librn
Holdings: Vols (98,000) Cat Slides Microforms Phonorecords Films
Budget: ($105,000)
Notes: Incl clippings, pictures and programs.

OH —CLEVELAND PUBLIC LIBRARY, Literature Dept, 325 Superior Ave, Cleveland, 44114. Evelyn Ward, Head
Holdings: Vols Cat Pix Microforms Phonorecords VF
Notes: History, criticism, biographies of playwrights. Texts of classical, English, American, Continental European and Oriental plays. Incl Barrett H Clark collection of acting editions, William F McDermont Memorial Collection. Microprint, incl "Three Centuries of English and American Plays." Noteworthy Shakespeare collection: editions, commentary, biography. Recordings: plays, speeches, sound effects. Theatre programs, clippings, play reviews, photographs, typescripts, etc. Reference aids: indexes to plays, theatres and actors in Cleveland, subject files.

OK —UNIVERSITY OF OKLAHOMA, Drama Library, 550 Parrington Oval, Norman, 73019. Jan Seifert, Dir
Holdings: Vols (6683) Mss Pix Phonorecords
Notes: Incl VF material, newspaper clippings and magazine cut-outs covering the theatre and dance. Material dates from 1900. Collection of nearly 6000 plays.

PA —UNIVERSITY OF PITTSBURGH, Special Collections Dept, Curtis Theatre Collection, 363 Hillman Library, Pittsburgh, 15260. Jeanette Blanco, Cur
Holdings: Vols (4000) Cat Mss Documents Microforms Pix Slides VF
Notes: The legitimate theatre of plays, musicals and vaudeville, chiefly of New York City and Pittsburgh, from 1865, and other US, community, summer, college and foreign theatre. Incl 500,000 programs, 12, 000 pictures, 300 posters, the Oliver P Merriman Scrapbooks and 300 other scrapbooks, clippings and other ephemera. Vols incl over 3000 acting editions and playscripts. Separate collections: Ralph G Allen Burlesque Skits Collection; Michael Ellis Papers; William P Halstead Theatre Collection; Kenyon Family Papers; Philip Dunning Playscripts Collection; Pittsburgh Playhouse Records; Pittsburgh Savoyards Records. Noncirculating.

RI —BROWN UNIVERSITY, John Hay Library, Harris Collection, Prospect St, Providence, 02912. Rosemary L Cullen, Cur
Holdings: Vols (200,000) Cat Mss Phonorecords Microforms
Budget: ($15,000)
Notes: The Harris Collection of American Poetry and Plays is principally composed of American and Canadian poetry and plays, 17th century-date. Extensive holdings in songsters, gift books and annuals, hymnals, pageants, broadside verse, carriers' addresses, women poets, juvenile poetry, (incl Mother Goose and *The Night Before* Christmas), sheet music with lyrics, small press publications, fine printing, black poets, "little magazines," Yiddish-American literature. All movements or schools of American poetry are represented. Incl first editions of most American poets and playwrights, notably Whitman, Poe, Wallace Stevens, Eugene O'Neill, Edward Albee, Ezra Pound, T S Eliot, William Carlos Williams, Amy Lowell, Phyllis Wheatley, Robert Frost, Allen Ginsberg, Bliss Carman, and Stephen Foster sheet music. Also incl the Saunders Walt Whitman Collection (1300 vols); the LangdonCollection of Pageants (250 vols); the Asa Cushman Collection of plays in ms and prompt copies; the MacDougall Collection of Psalters and Hymnals; 4000 plays issued by Walter H Baker Co, Boston (1890-1957); the Vaxer Collection of Yiddish Poetry, Plays and Music (1700 vols). Collections incl 200,000 vols, 30,000 broadsides, 55,000 mss, 170,000 pieces of sheet music, 450 phonorecords, and 375 microfilm reels. See *Dictionary Catalog of the Harris Collection of American Poetry and Plays* (Boston: G K Hall, 1972), 13 vols; *Supplement* (1977), 3 vols. See also, *American Poetry,* 1609-1900, *A Collection on Microfilm, Segment I* (1609-1820); *Segment II* (1821-1850); *Segment III* (1851-1870) (Woodbridge, Conn: Research Publications). Separate catalog.

TN —UNIVERSITY OF TENNESSEE, KNOXVILLE, Library, Knoxville, 37996. John Dobson, Special Collections Librn
Holdings: Cat
Notes: The John C Hodges Collection, incl about 150 original editions of Congreve's works and a large collection of books about him, English drama, and the theatre of the 16th and 17th centuries; also material by and about other dramatists of the period. Described in *The John C Hodges Collection of William Congreve in the University of Tennessee Library: A Bibliographical* Catalog, by Albert M Lyles and John Dobson (Knoxville: Univ of Tennessee Libraries, 1970), 135 pp.

TX —RICE UNIVERSITY, Fondren Library, Woodson Research Center, 6100 S Main St, PO Box 1892, Houston, 77251. Nancy Parker, Dir Woodson Research Center
Holdings: Vols 5000 Cat
Notes: The Axson Collection of 18th-century English drama. Many of the plays are represented in multiple editions or issues.

TX —UNIVERSITY OF HOUSTON, M D Anderson Memorial Library, University Park, Houston, 77004. David Farmer, Cur, Special Collections; Jean Jackson, Assistant Cur
Holdings: Vols 650 // Cat
Notes: Latin American drama. Copy-flow reproductions of most of holdings are available in public stacks area; original editions housed in the Department of Special Collections.

VA —GEORGE MASON UNIVERSITY, Fenwick Library, Special Collections Dept, 4400 University Drive, Fairfax, 22030. Ruth Kerns, Public Services Librn
Notes: The Federal Theatre Project Collection includes 5000 playscripts, 2500 radio scripts, 25,000 photographs, 40 blueprints, 1000 posters, over 1600 costume designs, 350 scene designs, 750 production notebooks, 1700 programs and heralds, 26 musical scores and 18 cubic feet of research materials and play readers reports.
See also entry under Theatre-History

WA —UNIVERSITY OF WASHINGTON LIBRARIES, Drama Library, BH-20, Seattle, 98195. Liz Fugate, Drama Librn
Holdings: Vols
Budget: ($13,182)
Notes: Collection incl history; criticism; costume; make-up; scene design; lighting; creative dramatics; children's theatre; directing; playwriting; acting. Special Collections include 19th century acting editions, contemporary acting editions and local theatre posters. 17,731 items cataloged, 24,255 uncataloged.

WI —STATE HISTORICAL SOCIETY OF WISCONSIN, Archives, 816 State St, Madison, 53706. Harold L Miller, Reference Archivist
Holdings: Mss Pix Microforms
Notes: Holdings incl records and papers of prominent organizations and individuals in the theater and motion picture industry, motion picture and television films, scripts, and still photographs, incl the archives of the United Artists Corporation. Collections are described in *Sources for Mass Communications, Film and Theater Research: A Guide,* (1982) and in current accession notes in the *Wisconsin Magazine of History.* Major collections are also in Hamer, *Guide to Manuscripts and Archives in the United States,* (1961) and in the *National Union Catalog of Manuscripts* Collections, (1959-date).

AB —UNIVERSITY OF CALGARY, Library, Calgary, T2N 1N4, Can. Apollonia Steele, Special Collections Librn
Holdings: Cat Mss Pix
Notes: Incl the books and papers of W Bridges Adams, Shakespearean actor, director and historian. Mr Bridges Adams was Director of the Stratford-upon-Avon Festival from 1919 to 1934 and was the author of two major works, *The British* Theatre and *The Irresistible Theatre.* Extensive correspondence with well-known literary and musical figures.

BC —VANCOUVER PUBLIC LIBRARY, Language & Literature Div, 750 Burrard St, Vancouver, V6Z 1X5, Can. B Kinnear, Head
Notes: Good general collection of drama and dramatic criticism, supplemented by biographical clippings and indexed critical periodical material, compiled by the staff. Incl play sets, audiotapes, books and pamphlets.

†BC —VANCOUVER PUBLIC LIBRARY, Vancouver, V6Z 1X5, Can.
Notes: Indexes to folk dances; children's songs; children's plays. No longer updated.

NB —MOUNT ALLISON UNIVERSITY, Ralph Pickard Bell Library, Sackville, E0A 3C0, Can. M Fancy, Librn
Holdings: Vols (13,372) Cat
Notes: The Mary Mellish Archibald Memorial Library incl folklore, folk music; children's literature. Incl phonorecords, with special emphasis on Canadian folklore and folk music.

ON —VICTORIA UNIVERSITY, Library, 71 Queen's Park Crescent, Toronto, M5S 1K7, Can. Robert C Brandeis, Chief Librn
Holdings: Vols (5000) Cat
See also entry under Canada - History

SK —SASKATCHEWAN TEACHERS' FEDERATION, Stewart Resources Centre, 2317 Arlington Ave, Saskatoon, S7K 3N3, Can. Susan Dyer, Librn
Holdings: Vols (18,000) Cat Slides Phonorecords Audiotapes Videotapes 16mm Films Filmstrips
Budget: ($15,000)
Notes: Professional teacher-education collection; curriculum materials; and Mary Ellen Burgess Drama Library.

DRAMA—HISTORY AND CRITICISM

IL —UNIVERSITY OF CHICAGO LIBRARY, Dept of Special Collections, 1100 E 57 St, Chicago, 60637.
Notes: William H Briggs Collection.

DRAMA—RECORDINGS

CT —YALE UNIVERSITY, Sterling Memorial Library, Yale Collection of Historical Sound Recordings, 120 High St, New Haven, 06520. Richard Warren Jr, Cur
Holdings: Mss Pix Phonorecords Audiotapes
Notes: Incl "classical music" ("concert music") of all types from Western culture, jazz, the American Musical Theatre, spoken

DRAMA—RECORDINGS (cont.)

material (literary, dramatic, documentary). The aim of the Collection is to document performance practice in the fields collected. See the article by Karol Berger in the *Journal of the Association for Recorded Sound Collections*, vol VI, no 1, pp 13-25. Partially cataloged.

DRAMA, AFRICAN see African Drama

DRAMA, CANADIAN see Canadian Drama

DRAMA, ENGLISH see English Drama

DRAMA, FOREIGN LANGUAGE see Foreign Language Drama

DRAMA, FRENCH see French Drama

DRAMA, GREEK see Greek Drama

DRAMA, ITALIAN see Italian Drama

DRAMA, JAPANESE see Japanese Drama

DRAMA, LATIN AMERICA see Latin American Drama

DRAMA, MODERN see Drama

DRAMA, NOH see Noh Dramas

DRAMA, PORTUGUESE see Portuguese Drama

DRAMA, SPANISH see Spanish Drama

DRAMATIC MUSIC see Music, Incidental; Music in Theatres; Opera

DRAMATIC WORKSHOP, NEW YORK CITY

IL —SOUTHERN ILLINOIS UNIVERSITY, CARBONDALE, Delyte W Morris Library, Carbondale, 62901.
Holdings: Cat Mss
Notes: Extensive files of Erwin Piscator's papers, incl work with the Dramatic Workshop in New York; files of scripts, playbills, photographs and business records; correspondence with actors, directors and playwrights; also family papers.

DRAMATISTS, AMERICAN see Playwrights, American

DRAMATISTS, AUSTRIAN

MA —BRANDEIS UNIVERSITY, Goldfarb Library, 415 South St, Waltham, 02154. Bessie Hahn, Dir
Notes: Frank Zwillinger Collection. Consists of 12 linear ft of drafts, revised drafts and final drafts of poetry and dramatic presentations in German by this Austrian literary figure. Incl in the collection are 3 linear ft of tape recordings of poetry readings by this author. A finding list to the collection is located in Special Collections.

DRAMATISTS, CANADIAN see Playwrights, Canadian

DRAMATISTS, IRISH see Playwrights, Irish

DRAMATISTS' GUILD

DC —LIBRARY OF CONGRESS, Manuscript Division, Washington, 20540. John C Broderick, Chief
Holdings: Cat Mss
Notes: Papers of George Middleton (Sen Robert LaFollette's son-in-law), editor of *La Follete's Weekly*, 1912-1930; associate producer at Fox Film Corporation, 1929-1931. Incl correspondence, literary mss, reports, notes, scrapbooks, photographs, etc. About 10,000 items.

NY —NEW YORK PUBLIC LIBRARY, Performing Arts Research Center, Billy Rose Theatre Collection, 111 Amsterdam Ave, New York, 10023. Dorothy L Swerdlove, Cur
Holdings: Cat
Notes: Contains working papers of the Guild's activities.

DRAMSHOPS see Hotels, Taverns, Etc.

DRAPER, LYMAN C.

WI —STATE HISTORICAL SOCIETY OF WISCONSIN, Archives, 816 State St, Madison, 53706. Harold L Miller, Reference Archivist
Holdings: Mss Maps Public Records Microforms
Notes: Incl are unpublished genealogies, records of Wisconsin cemetaries and churches, and mss, incl the Lyman C Draper Manuscripts. Also incl are Wisconsin state, county and local governmental records, incl 19th century state census records, Civil War service records and some naturalization records. Collections described in *Genealogical Research: An Introduction to the Resources of the State Historical Society of Wisconsin,* (1980).

DRAPER, THEODORE, 1912-

CA —HOOVER INSTITUTION ON WAR, REVOLUTION & PEACE, Stanford University, Stanford, 94305. Milorad M Drachkovitch, Archivist
Holdings: Mss
Notes: Papers of Theodore Draper, 1948-1966, incl correspondence, clippings, pamphlets, newspaper issues, and congressional hearings, relating to the revolution led by Fidel Castro in Cuba, political, social, and economic conditions in Cuba, and the 1965 crisis and US intervention in the Dominican Republic. 22 ms boxes.

GA —EMORY UNIVERSITY, Robert W Woodruff Library, Atlanta, 30322. Herbert Johnson, Dir
Holdings: Mss Cat
Notes: A collection of materials relating to the history of the Communist Party in the US and the Communist International, gathered by author Theodore Draper. Incl periodicals, pamphlets, party documents, and books, as well as taped interviews that Draper conducted with party leaders and correspondence relating to his research. 80 linear ft mss.

DRAUGHTS see Checkers

DRAVIDIAN LANGUAGES

NY —NEW YORK PUBLIC LIBRARY, Oriental Div, Fifth Ave & 42 St, New York, 10018. E Christian Filstrup, Chief
Holdings: Cat Mss Microforms
Budget: ($56,455)
Notes: Published catalog of holdings.

DRAW POKER see Poker

DRAWBELL, JAMES

MA —BOSTON UNIVERSITY, Mugar Memorial Library, Special Collections Dept, 771 Commonwealth Ave, Boston, 02215. Howard B Gotlieb, Dir
Holdings: Cat Mss Pix Correspondence

DRAWING

CA —CALIFORNIA COLLEGE OF ARTS & CRAFTS, Meyer Library, Broadway at College, Oakland, 94618. Robert L Harper, Head Librn
Holdings: Vols (29,000) Cat Pix
Budget: ($10,000)
Notes: All fields of arts and crafts.

MN —MINNEAPOLIS COLLEGE OF ART & DESIGN, Library, 200 E 25 St, Minneapolis, 55404. Richard Kronstedt, Head Librn
Holdings: Vols 1400 Cat Slides
Budget: ($9000)
Notes: Incl art exhibition catalogs, collection emphasis on 20th century drawing and illustration.

TX —UNIVERSITY OF TEXAS LIBRARIES, Fine Arts Library, PO Box P, Austin, 78712. Carole L Cable, Fine Arts Librn
Holdings: Vols (55,000) Cat Pix
Notes: Emphasis is on historical as well as practical aspects.

WI —UNIVERSITY OF WISCONSIN, MADISON, Kohler Art Library, 800 University Ave, Madison, 53706. William C Bunce, Chief; Louise Hunning, Ref Librn
Holdings: Vols (83,000) Cat Microforms

AB —SOUTHERN ALBERTA INSTITUTE OF TECHNOLOGY, Learning Resources Centre, 1301 16 Ave NW, Calgary, T2M 0L4, Can. Tom Skinner, Historian
Holdings: Vols (5000) Cat Pix Slides Films Audiotapes Filmstrips Videotapes
Notes: Serves Alberta College of Art (4-year professional course).

ON —METROPOLITAN TORONTO LIBRARY, Fine Arts Dept, 789 Yonge St, Toronto, M4W 2G8, Can. Alan Suddon, Head
Holdings: Vols (42,000) Cat Pix Microforms
Notes: Extensive collection.

DRAWING—HISTORY

CA —STANFORD UNIVERSITY LIBRARIES, Art & Architecture Library, 102 Cummings Art Bldg, Stanford, 94305. Alexander D Ross, Art Librarian
Holdings: Vols (110,000) Cat
Notes: Incl materials of scholarly interest on the history of the visual arts: painting, sculpture, architecture, drawing, printmaking, etc, for all regions and periods.

NY —FRICK ART REFERENCE LIBRARY, 10 E 71 St, New York, 10021. Helen Sanger, Librn
Holdings: Vols (154,384) Cat Pix Per
Notes: History of painting, drawing, sculpture and illuminated mss of US and western Europe from 4th century AD to about 1860. 54,862 art auction catalogs; 420, 507 study photographs.

DRAWING, ARCHITECTURAL see Architectural Drawings

DRAWINGS

CA —FINE ARTS MUSEUMS OF SAN FRANCISCO, Achenbach Foundation for Graphic Arts, California Palace of the Legion of Honor, Lincoln Park, San Francisco, 94118. Jane Nelson, Librn
Holdings: Vols (3500) Cat

DC —LIBRARY OF CONGRESS, Prints & Photographs Div, Washington, 20540.
Notes: The Cabinet of American Illustration contains over 4000 cartoons, cover designs, sketches for posters, and illustrations for magazines, novels, and children's books that were executed chiefly between 1880 and 1910.

†DC —SMITHSONIAN INSTITUTION LIBRARIES, Washington, 20560.
Notes: The published guide to the numerous Smithsonian Institution museums and deposits is one of the most helpful and successfully (and well-indexed) complementary vols that can be used with this edition of *Subject Collections.* Refer to Lynda Corey Claassen's *Finder's Guide to Prints and Drawings in the Smithsonian* Institution, 210 pp, (Washington: Smithsonian Institution Press, 1981), Los Angeles. An index of artists lists about 10, 000 names represented in the Smithsonian's collections in the Archives of American Art, Cooper-Hewitt Museum, Freer Gallery of Art, Hirshhorn Museum and Sculpture Garden, Museum of African Art, National Air and Space Museum, National Museum of American Art, National Museum of American History, National Museum of Natural History and National Museum of Man, National Portrait Gallery, Smithsonian Institution Archives, andSmithsonian Institution Libraries, and their subject departments, all of which are described.

IL —ART INSTITUTE OF CHICAGO, Ryerson & Burnham Libraries, Michigan Ave & Adams St, Chicago, 60603. Daphne

DRAWINGS (cont.)

C Roloff, Dir
Holdings: Vols (136,000) Cat Mss Slides Microforms
Budget: ($167,000)
Notes: Total collection incl 300,000 slides.

MD —BALTIMORE MUSEUM OF ART LIBRARY, Art Museum Dr, Baltimore, 21218. Anita Gilden, Librn
Holdings: Vols (40,000) Cat
Notes: General reference sources with emphasis on 19th and 20th century art and American decorative art. Incl prints and drawings. Photocopying.

MA —BOSTON PUBLIC LIBRARY, Print Collection, Dartmouth St at Copley Sq, Boston, 02117. Sinclair H Hitchings, Keeper of Prints
Holdings: Cat
Notes: The collection of about 70,000 prints and 4500 drawings as well as a few oil paintings. There is a small collection of Old Master prints and drawings and a large and growing collection of French, British, and American prints (as well as some drawings) especially of the 19th century, also 18th and 20th century. Some German and Spanish artists are also represented. An overview of the entire collection appears in *Artist's* Proof, Vol XI. Arrangements can be made for professional photocopying.

MA —HARVARD UNIVERSITY LIBRARY, Houghton Library, Printing and Graphic Arts Dept, Cambridge, 02138. Eleanor M Garvey, Cur
Notes: Collection incl illustrated books, fine printing, type specimens, illuminated and calligraphic manuscripts, and drawings for book illustration.

MO —THE NELSON-ATKINS MUSEUM OF ART, Kenneth & Helen Spencer Art Reference Library, 4525 Oak St, Kansas City, 64111. Stanley W Hess, Librn
Notes: Strong in area of Western art (European with some American).

MO —SAINT LOUIS ART MUSEUM, Richardson Memorial Library, Saint Louis, 63110. Ann B Abid, Librn
Holdings: Vols (30,000) Cat Pix Slides Microforms
Notes: Art history, incl decorative arts, catalogs, exhibitions, etc.

NY —METROPOLITAN MUSEUM OF ART, Dept of Prints & Photographs, 82 St & Fifth Ave, New York, 10028. Colta Ives, Cur

NY —NEW YORK PUBLIC LIBRARY, Print Collection, Fifth Ave & 42 St, New York, 10018. Robert Rainwater, Keeper
Holdings: Vols 12,000 Cat
Notes: Incl 175,000 prints and drawings. A representative collection of fine prints from the 15th century to the present, cataloged by artist, with strong holdings in 19th century French prints and Americana. See Stokes-Haskell, *American Historical Prints, Etc New York* (New York Public Library, 1933) and Weitenkampf, Frank, *The Eno Collection of New York City Views* (New York Public Library, 1925). See *Dictionary Catalog of the Prints Division* (Boston: G K Hall, 1975), 5 vols.

DRAWINGS, ARCHITECTURAL see Architecture—Designs and Plans; Architectural Drawings

DRAWINGS, ENGINEERING see Mechanical Drawing

DRAWINGS, MASTER

CT —LYMAN ALLYN MUSEUM, Library, 100 Mohegan Ave, New London, 06320. Mrs D Dinsmore, Librn
Holdings: Vols (5550) Cat Maps Pix
Budget: $2000
Notes: Books on old Master Drawings and the Decorative Arts. Noncirculating library with emphasis on scholarly historical works and museum amd exhibition catalogs. Also incl American decorative art, incl prints and drawings. No photocopying.

MD —BALTIMORE MUSEUM OF ART LIBRARY, Art Museum Dr, Baltimore, 21218. Anita Gilden, Librn
Holdings: Vols (40,000) Cat
Notes: General reference sources with emphasis on 19th and 20th century art and American decorative art. Incl prints and drawings. Photocopying.

MA —BOSTON PUBLIC LIBRARY, Print Collection, Dartmouth St at Copley Sq, Boston, 02117. Sinclair H Hitchings, Keeper of Prints
Holdings: Cat
Notes: The collection of about 70,000 prints and 4500 drawings as well as a few oil paintings. There is a small collection of Old Master prints and drawings and a large and growing collection of French, British, and American prints (as well as some drawings) especially of the 19th century, also 18th and 20th century. Some German and Spanish artists are also represented. An overview of the entire collection appears in *Artist's* Proof, Vol XI. Arrangements can be made for professional photocopying.

MA —HARVARD UNIVERSITY, Harvard College Library, Fine Arts Library, Fogg Museum, 32 Quincy St, Cambridge, 02138. Wolfgang M Freitag, Librn
Holdings: Vols (202,000) Cat Mss Pix Slides
Budget: ($176,500)
Notes: All areas of art history, with emphasis on Italian primitives, Italian Renaissance, master drawings, Romanesque sculpture, architectural history, ms materials (particulary American artists'), conservation and restoration of art objects. Incl the Berenson repertory of photographs from the Harvard Center for Italian Renaissance Studies in Florence, and the Decimal Index to the Art of the Low Countries. Separate card catalogs for books, photographs and lantern slides, registers for ms holdings which are not incl in *National Union Catalog of Manuscript Collections.* Slides total over 230,000; over 745,000 pictures. *Fine Arts Library Catalogue* (14 volumes) and *Catalogue of Auction Sales Catalogues* (1 volume) (Boston: G K Hall, 1972); *A Guide to the Fine Arts Library* (Cambridge, Mass: 1971); *Guide to the Harvard Libraries,* microfiche edition of holdingscataloged through 1981 published 1984 (Munich/New York: Saur).

NY —METROPOLITAN MUSEUM OF ART, Dept of Prints & Photographs, 82 St & Fifth Ave, New York, 10028. Colta Ives, Cur

†ON —NATIONAL GALLERY OF CANADA, Library, National Museums of Canada, Ottawa, K1A 0M8, Can.
Notes: History of art (postmedieval, Western). Public reference only. Emphasis of collection on painting, sculpture and graphic arts. Study collection of photographs and slides is in Curatorial Services Branch. See *Catalogue of the National Gallery of* Canada, 8 vols (Boston: G K Hall, 1973).

DRAWINGS, MECHANICAL see Mechanical Drawing

DRAYTON, MICHAEL

MD —JOHNS HOPKINS UNIVERSITY, Milton S Eisenhower Library, Charles & 34 Sts, Baltimore, 21218. Ann S Gwyn, Assistant Dir for Special Collections
Holdings: Vols Cat
Notes: Incl 20 first, early and very rare editions.

DRAYTON, S. M.

SC —COLLEGE OF CHARLESTON LIBRARY, Special Collections Dept, Charleston, 29401.
Notes: Letters to Samuel Prioleau regarding tenant/landlord relations, September 15, 1826, and May 12, 1829.

DRAYTON, WILLIAM A.

CA —HOOVER INSTITUTION ON WAR, REVOLUTION & PEACE, Stanford University, Stanford, 94305. Milorad M Drachkovitch, Archivist
Holdings: Mss Pix
Notes: Papers of William A Drayton, 1913-1946, incl correspondence, reports, memoranda, speeches and writings, photographs, and other materials, relating to Serbia, during and after World War I, and W A Drayton's activities as an American volunteer in the Serbian Army, member of the Serbian Delegation to Paris Peace Conference, and Inter-Allied Commissioner of Bulgarian Atrocities Commission. 2 ms boxes.

DREAMS

IL —UNIVERSITY OF ILLINOIS, URBANA/CHAMPAIGN, Library, University Archives, 19 Library, 1408 W Gregory Drive, Urbana, 61801. Maynard Brichford, University Archivist
Holdings: Vols (5000) Cat
Budget: ($7000)
Notes: The Mandeville Collection in Parapsychology and Occult Sciences. Titles in the Merten J Mandeville Collection are purchased by funds from an endowment provided specifically for the collection on its establishment in 1966 by Merten J Mandeville, Professor Emeritus of Management, who donated 400 vols from his personal library as the nucleus of the collection. There are currently about 5000 titles in the collection, supplemented by related materials in the general collection. Topics include astrology, extrasensory perception, yoga, magic, satanism, faith healing, hypnosis, Eastern religions, witchcraft, fortune telling, reincarnation, flying saucers, ghosts, dreams, numerology, graphology, and mysticism. Biographies and reference books are a part of the collection as are journals devoted to the scientific study of parapsychology.

NY —PARAPSYCHOLOGY FOUNDATION, Eileen J Garrett Library, 228 E 71st St, New York, 10021. Wayne Norman, Librn
Holdings: Vols (9300) Cat
Notes: One of the largest libraries on parapsychology. Main emphasis is on the literature of contemporary parapsychology; also a strong collection on the history of parapsychology (early spiritualism, mysticism, relevant philosophical works, etc). Rare book collection incl early rare books and periodicals on psychical research and psychical phenomena. Receives about 100 titles of periodicals and binds the more significant titles. The library maintains its own periodicals index to parapsychological literature, dating from 1966. Main emphasis literature is on experimental parapsychology, or those publications that approach the subject with an objective and/or analytic point of view.

RI —BROWN UNIVERSITY, John Hay Library, 20 Prospect St, Providence, 02912. Mark N Brown, Cur Mss
Holdings: Vols (900) // Mss
Notes: John William Graham Collection of Literature of Psychic Science; 350 predominantly late 19th and early 20th century books dealing with alchemy, black magic, dreams, demonology, church history, mysticism, mediumship, physical and somatic types of psychic experience. Collection described in *Index to Psychic* Science compiled by S R Morgan (Swathmore, 1950). Also, the Damon Collection of Occult and Visionary Literature; 550 vols devoted to the development of western mysticism with particular emphasis on American and British thought, incl texts on alchemy, black magic, esoteric church history, dream interpretations, mysticism, witchcraft, the Kabbalah, and visionary testaments and manifestations of all types printed during the 16th to 20th centuries; and the Samuel Wyllys Papers; 125 mss, transcripts, and photocopies of legal and government papers relating to Indianaffairs, colonial wars, civil and criminal cases, and the witchcraft trials of 1692-1693. Partially cataloged.

VA —ASSOCIATION FOR RESEARCH & ENLIGHTENMENT, Library, 67 & Atlantic Avenue, PO Box 595, Virginia Beach, 23451. Stephen Jordan, Library Mgr
Holdings: Vols (1100) Cat
Notes: Dreams and dream psychology.

DREIER, HANS, 1885-1966

CA —UNIVERSITY OF CALIFORNIA, LOS ANGELES, Research Library, Dept of Special Collections, 405 Hilgard Ave, Los Angeles, 90024. Edward Shreeves, Chairman, Bibliographers Group; David S Zeidberg, Head
Notes: 3 linear feet of photographs and set designs.

DREIER, KATHERINE S.

CT —YALE UNIVERSITY, Box 1603A, Yale Station, New Haven, 06520.
Holdings: Mss
Notes: Papers of the Societe Anonyme.

DREIKURS, RUDOLF

DC —LIBRARY OF CONGRESS, Washington, 20540.
Notes: The Rudolf Dreikurs papers, incl material on the behavioral sciences and psychiatry.

DREISER, THEODORE, 1871-1945

CA —UNIVERSITY OF CALIFORNIA, LOS ANGELES, Research Library, Dept of Special Collections, 405 Hilgard Ave, Los Angeles, 90024. Edward Shreeves, Chairman, Bibliographers Group; David S Zeidberg, Head
Holdings: Vols 175 Cat Mss
Notes: 175 first and other editions of his books; 2 linear feet of mss and ephemera.

IN —INDIANA UNIVERSITY, Lilly Library, Seventh St, Bloomington, 47405. William R Cagle, Librn
Holdings: Cat Mss
Notes: First editions, etc.

KY —UNIVERSITY OF LOUISVILLE, Ekstrom Library, Rare Books & Special Collections, 2301 S Third St, Louisville, 40208. George T McWhorter, Cur; Delinda Stephens Buie, Asst Cur

MO —SAINT LOUIS PUBLIC LIBRARY, Gardner Rare Book Room, 1301 Olive St, Saint Louis, 63103. Julanne M Good, Supervisor; Martha Riley, Rare Books Librn
Holdings: Vols (2300) Cat
Budget: ($5573)
Notes: First editions of authors having some association with William Marion Reedy and *Reedy's Mirror*, such as Sara Teasdale, Zoe Akins, Fannie Hurst, Edgar Lee Masters, Babette Deutsch, Richard LeGallienne, etc. Also first editions of selected St Louis and/or Missouri authors such as T S Eliot, Samuel L Clemens, Theodore Dreiser and Tennessee Williams. Noncirculating.

NV —UNIVERSITY OF NEVADA, RENO, University Library, Special Collections Dept, Reno, 89557. Robert E Blesse, Head
Holdings: // Vols (98) Cat
Notes: Includes individual works by author in all editions including translations; also prefaces, introductions, published correspondence, appearances in anthologies, periodicals, etc. Bibliographical research collection, part of Modern Authors Collection. Other appearances 175 cataloged.

PA —UNIVERSITY OF PENNSYLVANIA, Van Pelt Library, Rare Books Collection, 34 & Walnut Sts, Philadelphia, 19104. Daniel Traister, Special Collections Librn
Holdings: Vols 1500 Cat Mss Pix
Notes: The definitive collection of mss, letters, business files, personal library, and first editions. See Downs 549; (Supplement) 1686-7; (University of Pennsylvania) *Library Chronicle* Vol 25, no 1, Winter 1959 pp 55-57. "The Theodore Dreiser Collection--Addenda". Descriptive case file available in library.

VA —UNIVERSITY OF VIRGINIA, Alderman Library, Clifton Waller Barrett Collection, Charlottesville, 22901. Joan St C Crane, Cur of American Literature Collections
Notes: Papers.

DRENNER, DON

KS —KANSAS STATE UNIVERSITY, Library, Special Collections & University Archives, Manhattan, 66506. Antonia Q Pigno, Coordr; John J Vander Velde, Librn; Anthony R Crawford, Univ Archivist
Holdings: Vols 700 Mss
Notes: Collection includes books and correspondence from Don Drenner, owner and printer of the Zauberberg Press, Coffeyville, Kansas.

DRESS see Clothing and Dress; Costume; Uniforms; Uniforms, Military and Naval

DRESS ACCESSORIES

NY —METROPOLITAN MUSEUM OF ART, Costume Institute, Fifth Ave & 82 St, New York, 10028.
Holdings: Costumes and Accessories
Notes: Rich resources for reference and research. Incl almost 45,000 articles of dress, international in scope, spanning four centuries and five continents. Irene Lewisohn Costume Reference Library also has unique collection of books, periodicals, fashion plates and sketches, pattern books, and fabric swatches. Professional designers of theatre costume and fashion, students, writers, etc use the facilities.

DRESS DESIGN see Costume Design

DRESSAGE

WV —SALEM COLLEGE, Library, Salem, 26426. Myron J Smith, Jr, Librn
Notes: Collection supports "the most complete equestrian studies program available anywhere". *Myron J Smith, Equestrian Studies:* the Salem College [Bibliographical] Guide to Sources in English, 1950-1980. Metuchen, NJ: Scarecrow Press, 1981; 4645 entries.

DRESSER, DAVIS

MA —BOSTON UNIVERSITY, Mugar Memorial Library, Special Collections Dept, 771 Commonwealth Ave, Boston, 02215. Howard B Gotlieb, Dir
Holdings: Cat Mss
Notes: Mss, correspondence, etc collected in depth; incl publications by or about.

DRESSER, PAUL

IN —INDIANA UNIVERSITY, Lilly Library, Seventh St, Bloomington, 47405. William R Cagle, Librn
Notes: Extensive holdings of American sheet music; first editions of works by great composers (operas, symphonies, chamber music, etc); sources annotated for performances conducted by Fritz Busch. Ms incl small collections of Hoagy Carmichael materials, Paul Dresser memorabilia, and Barclay Walker compositions.

DRESSMAKING—PATTERN DESIGN

CA —CARLSBAD CITY LIBRARY, 1250 Elm Ave, Carlsbad, 92008. Clifford E Lange, Library Dir
Holdings: Vols (2297) Cat
Notes: Collection of sewing patterns. Catalogs of the patterns have been made up with complete information on size, etc, and have been divided into subject areas, such as gift ideas, toys, dolls, women's clothes, men's clothes, children's clothes, etc. Also patterns for knitted and crocheted wearing apparel. Incl patterns for children's costumes, historical fashions and antique dolls.

DREXEL, MOTHER KATHERINE, 1862-1955

DC —GEORGETOWN UNIVERSITY, Library, Special Collections Div, 37 & O Sts NW, Washington, 20057. George M Barringer, Special Collections Librn; Nicholas B Sheetz, Mss Librn
Holdings: Mss
Notes: Correspondence and documents, chiefly between Mother Katherine Drexel and Rev A J Emerick SJ, concerning the founding of the Church of Our Lady of the Blessed Sacrament for Colored Catholics in Philadelphia. Katherine Drexel (1862-1955), daughter of financier Francis Anthony Drexel, founded the religious order Sisters of the Blessed Sacrament for Indians and Colored People around the turn of the century.

DREYFUS CASE

MA —HARVARD UNIVERSITY LIBRARY, Widener Library, Cambridge, 02138.
Holdings: Cat Mss Pix Microforms

MA —BRANDEIS UNIVERSITY, Goldfarb Library, 415 South St, Waltham, 02154. Bessie Hahn, Dir
Notes: Alfred Dreyfus Trial Collection. Approx 1000 books, pamphlets, newspapers and photographs as well as some correspondence of French notables dealing with the Alfred Dreyfus trial at the turn of the century. An author-title card catalog can be found in the Special Collections Card Catalog.

DRINAN, REP. REV. ROBERT

MA —BOSTON COLLEGE LIBRARIES, Chestnut Hill, 02167.
Notes: Papers of Congressman the Rev Robert Drinan.

DRINKER LIBRARY OF CHORAL MUSIC

PA —FREE LIBRARY OF PHILADELPHIA, Music Dept, Drinker Library of Choral Music, Logan Sq, Philadelphia, 19103. Frederick James Kent, Head
Holdings: Vols 348,000 Cat
Notes: The Drinker Library is primarily sacred choral works of the 16th-19th centuries in multiple copies, incl the Bach cantatas in English translation, many with orchestral parts. Loaned to subscribers of the Drinker Library. The Library of the American Choral Foundation was given to the Drinker Library in 1970 and contains many short 20th century works.

DRINKING AND TRAFFIC ACCIDENTS

MI —UNIVERSITY OF MICHIGAN, Transportation Research Institute, Library, 2901 Baxter Rd, Ann Arbor, 48109. Ann C Grimm, Librn
Holdings: Vols (57,000) Cat Mss Maps
Budget: ($25,000)
Notes: Special emphasis on accident investigation and data analysis, vehicle dynamics, biomechanical aspects of trauma, vision and visibility, alcohol and driving.

DRINKS see Beer and Brewing; Beverages; Coffee; Liquors; Mineral Waters

DRINKWATER, JOHN

IL —ILLINOIS STATE UNIVERSITY, Milner Library, Dept of Special Collections, Normal, 61761. Robert Sokan, Librn
Holdings: Vols 135 Cat

MA —AMHERST COLLEGE, Library, Amherst, 01002. John Lancaster, Special Collections Librn
Holdings: Vols (500) Uncat Mss
Notes: Concentration on the Georgian poets Lascelles Abercrombie, Edmund Blunden, W H Davies, John Drinkwater, Wilfrid Gibson, Harold Monro, Edward Thomas.

NY —HOFSTRA UNIVERSITY, Library, 1000 Fulton Ave, Hempstead, 11550. Charles R Andrews, Dean of Library Services
Notes: Strong collection. Incl some mss.

DRIP IRRIGATION see Trickle Irrigation

DRISCOLL, J. FRANCIS

IL —NEWBERRY LIBRARY, 60 W Walton St, Chicago, 60610. Diana Haskell, Cur of

DRISCOLL, J. FRANCIS (cont.)

Modern Mss
Holdings: Vols 80,000
See also entry under Music, Popular.

DRIVER EDUCATION see Automobile Drivers

DRIVERS AND DRIVING, AUTOMOBILE see Automobile Drivers

DROLLERIES

MA —HARVARD UNIVERSITY LIBRARY, Houghton Library, Cambridge, 02138. F Thomas Noonan, Cur, Reading Room; Lawrence Dowler, Associate Librn
Holdings: Cat
Notes: Especially 17th century. See *Harvard Library Bulletin,* VI (1952), pp 40-51.

DROPS

IA —DELEVAN DIVISION OF COLT INDUSTRIES INC, Engineering Library, 811 Fourth St, PO Box 100, West Des Moines, 50265. G A Hartman, Librn
Holdings: Vols 2000 Cat Mss Slides Microforms
Budget: $400
Notes: Incl liquid atomization, droplet size measurement and representation, fuel nozzles for combustors, and spray nozzles for industrial and agricultural applications.

DROUGHT, JAMES

MA —BOSTON UNIVERSITY, Mugar Memorial Library, Special Collections Dept, 771 Commonwealth Ave, Boston, 02215. Howard B Gotlieb, Dir
Holdings: Cat Mss Pix
Notes: Mss, correspondence, etc collected in depth; incl publications by or about.

DROUGHTS

SK —CANADA PRAIRIE FARM REHABILITATION ADMINISTRATION LIBRARY, Motherwell Bldg, Regina, S4P 0R5, Can. C Kosack, Head
Holdings: Vols (10,000) Cat
Budget: ($8000)
Notes: PFRA is a Canadian federal government agency initiated to alleviate the effects of drought and water shortages on the prairies. The collection covers engineering (dams), agricultural economics, hydrology, irrigation, community pastures, and soil and water conservation.

DROWNE, SOLOMON, 1753-1834

RI —BROWN UNIVERSITY, John Hay Library, 20 Prospect St, Providence, 02912. Mark N Brown, Cur Mss
Holdings: // Mss
Notes: Solomon Drowne papers. He was a physician and Professor of Botany at Brown, Class of 1773. Mss incl accounts, invoices, receipts; originals and copies of prose and poetry; notes of Dr Drowne's; sketches and valentines; political, legal, and military documents; and ship's papers. Subjects inc Colonial and Revolutionary history of Rhode Island and Brown University; medicine and botany 1770-1834; the early history of Morgantown, Virginia; Union, Pennsylvania; and Marietta, Ohio; business and trade in the Colonial period; and the Continental Congress. Correspondence with most persons of importance in his time.

DROWNING

IL —CHICAGO HISTORICAL SOCIETY, Library, Clark St at North Ave, Chicago, 60614. Robert L Brubaker, Librn
Holdings: Cat
Notes: The J Norman Jensen Collection of Lake and River Disasters, 1679-1947. 8500 card entries.

DRU, ALICK

DC —GEORGETOWN UNIVERSITY, Library, Special Collections Div, 37 & O Sts NW, Washington, 20057. George M Barringer, Special Collections Librn; Nicholas B Sheetz, Mss Librn
Holdings: Mss Pix
Notes: The papers of Christopher Sykes, biographer, journalist, and novelist; containing mss, letters, photographs, and drawings. With extensive correspondence from Harold Acton; Angela, Countess of Antrim; Sir John Betjeman; Ivy Compton-Burnett; Alick Dru; T S Eliot; Max Beerbohm; Graham Greene; John Hayward; Lord Patrick Kinross; Compton Mackenzie; Nancy Mitford; Anthony Powell; Dame Flora Robson; Cecil Roth; Sir John Russell; Osbert Sitwell; John Sparrow; Freya Stark; James Stern; and Evelyn Waugh, among others. Also, considerable research material about Evelyn Waugh, Adam von Trott, Robert Byron, Lady Nancy Astor; and the foundation of the state of Israel.

DRUG ADDICTION see Drug Habit

DRUG DIRECTORIES

MN —3M COMPANY, 3M Center, Riker Laboratories, Saint Paul, 55101.
Holdings: Vols (6100) Cat
Budget: ($13,000)
Notes: Covers medical and pharmaceutical chemistry and medical botany. Incl 2600 books (175 drug directories) and 3500 bound journal vols.

DRUG HABIT

CA —UNIVERSITY OF SOUTHERN CALIFORNIA, School of Medicine, Norris Medical Library, 2025 Zonal Ave, Los Angeles, 90033. Nelson J Gilman, Librn
Holdings: Vols 1700 Cat AV
Budget: $8000
Notes: Substance abuse collection.

CA —FITZ HUGH LUDLOW MEMORIAL LIBRARY, PO Box 99346, San Francisco, 94109. Michael R Aldrich, Exec Cur
Holdings: Vols (12,000) Cat Mss Maps Pix Slides Phonorecords Audiotapes Videotapes
Notes: The Ludlow Library emphasizes psychoactive drug literature (nonfiction, fiction, poetry), history, sociology and art rather more than scientific research, though a sizable part of the collection incl pharmacology, chemistry, botany, etc. We have about 7000 books and an almost equal number of offprints, mss, records, tapes, comic books, newspapers, periodicals, art, and artifacts. Most of the books are catalogued by author. The Library is non-circulating reference collection accessible to members either in San Fransisco or by mail. Memberships for students and for Research Members. Much of the collection consists of rare books, autographed or presentation copies, hard-to-find historical research papers, and drug-related art and artifacts. Also emphasizes historical, literary aspects. Incl complete archives of the California Marijuana Initative, 1972-74, andmany documents from the international marijuana law reform movement. Also incl a sizeable collection of phonograph records, artwork, rolling papers, smoking paraphernaliaa and research artifacts relate to cannabis. Collection is currently in storage.

IL —JACKSONVILLE STATE HOSPITAL, Training & Research Library, 1201 S Main St, Jacksonville, 62650. Lois E Wells, Librn
Holdings: Vols (10,000) Cat
Notes: Concerned particularly with developmental disabilities.

IL —UNIVERSITY OF ILLINOIS, URBANA/CHAMPAIGN, Library, Applied Life Studies Library, 1408 W Gregory Dr, Urbana, 61801.
Holdings: Vols (38,000) Cat Pix Microforms
See also entry under Physical Education and Training.

IN —PURDUE UNIVERSITY LIBRARIES, Pharmacy, Nursing and Health Sciences Library, Pharmacy Bldg, West Lafayette, 47907. Theodora Andrews, Librn
Holdings: Vols 1000 Cat
Notes: There is a separate catalog to the collection. Contains research level materials as well as undergraduate.

MA —MCLEAN HOSPITAL MEDICAL LIBRARY, 115 Mill St, Belmont, 02178. Hector Bossange, Dir
Holdings: Vols 25,611 Cat
Notes: Extensive collection.

MA —MASSACHUSETTS COLLEGE OF PHARMACY AND ALLIED HEALTH SCIENCES, Sheppard Library, 179 Longwood Ave, Boston, 02115. Barbara M Hill, Librn
Holdings: Vols (56,000) Cat Mss Pix Slides Microforms
Notes: Worldwide representation.

MO —SAINT LOUIS POLICE LIBRARY, 315 S Tucker Blvd, Saint Louis, 63102. Cathy Reilly, Librn
Holdings: Vols (21,000) Cat Mss Pix Microforms
Budget: ($18,400)
Notes: Library on all subjects of police work is open to the public for general reference use.

NJ —EAST ORANGE GENERAL HOSPITAL, Library, 300 Central Ave, East Orange, 07019. Joann Mehalick, Dir of Library Services
Holdings: Vols (1500) Cat Videotapes

NY —LONG ISLAND UNIVERSITY, Brooklyn Center, Pharmacy Library Collection, University Plaza, Brooklyn, 11201. Barbara Chanton, Dir & Health Sciences Librn
Holdings: Vols (17,500) Cat Mss
Notes: Pharmacy, drug abuse, hospital pharmacy, medicinal chemistry.

TX —TEXAS DEPT OF MENTAL HEALTH & MENTAL RETARDATION, Central Office Library, 909 W 45, Box 12668, Austin, 78711. Becky Renfro, Librn
Holdings: Vols (4600) Cat

TX —SOUTHWEST FOUNDATION FOR RESEARCH AND EDUCATION LIBRARY, Preston C Northrup Memorial Library, Baboon Information Center, W Loop 410 at Military Dr, PO Box 28147, San Antonio, 78284. Dorothy M Brooks, Baboon
Notes: Principle field of research: Birth defects, atherosclerosis, reproductive physiology, cancer, genetics, organic chemistry, parasitology, primatology and behavioral sciences and their application to problems of drug abuse, alcoholism and ecology. Maintains the largest baboon colony in the world.

VT —FLETCHER FREE LIBRARY, 235 College St, Burlington, 05401. Maxie Ewins, Librn
Holdings: Vols 1200 Cat Maps Pix
Notes: Concentration on Burlington, Vermont. Complete run of Burlington City Reports, from 1860. Limited genealogies.

ON —ONTARIO MINISTRY OF CORRECTIONAL SERVICES, Library, 2001 Eglinton Ave E, Scarborough, M1L 4P1, Can. T J B Anderson, Chief Librn
Holdings: Vols (3676) VF
Notes: Approx 135 periodicals received. Library services also provided in approx 50 jails and adult institutions.

DRUG LAWS see Drugs—Laws and Legislation

DRUG-RELATED ARTIFACTS see Art and Drugs

DRUG RESEARCH see Pharmaceutical Research

DRUG TRADE

CA —FITZ HUGH LUDLOW MEMORIAL LIBRARY, PO Box 99346, San Francisco, 94109. Michael R Aldrich, Exec Cur
Holdings: Vols (1000) Cat Mss Maps Pix Slides Phonorecords Audiotapes Videotapes
Notes: Collection stored. Important mail inquiries only. No interlibrary lending or telephone queries. This collections emphasis historical and literary works about opium and its derivatives, mostly in English, going back to the 17th century but mostly from the 19th and early 20th centuries. Excellent collection of De Quincey in different

DRUG TRADE (cont.)

editions. Many books, pamphlets, and art relating to the 19th century international opium trade, the Chinese Opium Wars, clipper ships, and resulting international legal action in the early 20th century. Outstanding collection of the English, French, and American opium-addict confessional literature. Also incl many volumes and offprints relevant to narcotic drug prevention, treatment, and education.

IN —MILES LABORATORIES, Library Resources and Services, 1127 Myrtle St, PO Box 40, Elkhart, 46515. Allam Hagopian, Mgr
Holdings: Vols (16,500) Cat Audiotapes Microforms
Notes: Incl files of pharmaceutical product advertising pieces, extensive literature files on company related drugs; domestic and international marketing files. 32,000 bound periodicals.

IN —INDIANA STATE UNIVERSITY, EVANSVILLE, Library, 8600 University Blvd, Evansville, 47712. Gina R Walker, Acting Archivist
Holdings: Cat Mss Pix Slides Phonorecords 16mm Films Filmstrips
Notes: Historical documents, 1895 to the present, related to the growth and development of the Mead Johnson Company (a pharmaceutical company engaged in manufacture and research in Evansville, Indiana); papers concerning Company administration and organization; industrial and public relations; marketing and merchandising; product histories of Mead products, both past and present; research and development; Johnson family pictures; product samples and memorabilia. Unpublished guide.

IN —ELI LILLY AND COMPANY, Business Library, 307 E McCarty St, Indianapolis, 46206. Helen E Loftus, Dept Head
Holdings: Vols 8500 Cat
Notes: No photocopying.

DRUG TRADE—ADVERTISING see Advertising—Drug Trade

DRUGGISTS see Pharmacists

DRUGS

CA —LOS ANGELES PUBLIC LIBRARY, Science & Technology Dept, 630 W Fifth St, Los Angeles, 90071. Billie M Connor, Dept Head
Holdings: Vols (7500)
Notes: A well-rounded collection of materials related to consumer health, medicine and drugs as well as materials for the allied health and medical professions. Includes a sound representative selection of basic texts covering various aspects of medical treatment, drugs, diseases and syndromes. Indexes are collected as well as a basic collection of journals. The directories collection is strong. The broadest possible collection of books oriented toward consumer health, medicine, diets and nutrition is maintained, both traditional and alternative. Texts and examination study books are collected for nurses, laboratory technicians, physcial therapists, speech therapists, paramedics and other allied health professions.

members either in San Fransisco or by mail. Memberships for students and for Research Members. Much of the collection consists of rare books, autographed or presentation copies, hard-to-find historical research papers, and drug-related art and artifacts. Also emphasizes historical, literary aspects. Incl complete archives of the California Marijuana Initative, 1972-74, andmany documents from the international marijuana law reform movement. Also incl a sizeable collection of phonograph records, artwork, rolling papers, smoking paraphernaliaa and research artifacts relate to cannabis. Collection is currently in storage.

CA —FITZ HUGH LUDLOW MEMORIAL LIBRARY, PO Box 99346, San Francisco, 94109. Michael R Aldrich, Exec Cur
Holdings: Vols (1000) Cat Mss Maps Pix Slides Phonorecords Audiotapes Videotapes
Notes: Collection stored. Important mail inquiries only. No interlibrary lending or telephone queries. This collection emphasizes historical and literary works about opium and its derivatives, mostly in English, going back to the 17th century but mostly from the 19th and early 20th centuries. Excellent collection of De Quincey in different editions. Many books, pamphlets, and art relating to the 19th century international opium trade, the Chinese Opium Wars, clipper ships, and resulting international legal action in the early 20th century. Outstanding collection of the English, French, and American opium-addict confessional literature. Also incl many volumes and offprints relevant to narcotic drug prevention, treatment, and education.

DC —US DEPT OF JUSTICE, Drug Enforcement Administration, Library, 1405 I St NW, Washington, 20537. Morton S Goren, Librn
Holdings: Vols (10,000) Cat Microforms
Notes: Narcotics and dangerous drugs control.

IN —MILES LABORATORIES, Library Resources and Services, 1127 Myrtle St, PO Box 40, Elkhart, 46515. Allam Hagopian, Mgr
Holdings: Vols (16,500) Cat Audiotapes Microforms
Notes: Incl files of pharmaceutical product advertising pieces, extensive literature files on company related drugs; domestic and international marketing files. 32,000 bound periodicals.

IN —ELI LILLY AND COMPANY, Scientific Library, 307 E McCarty St, Indianapolis, 46285. Adele Hoskin, Chief Librn
Holdings: Vols (35,000) Cat Microforms
Notes: Drug product information (1.7 million cards); drug encyclopedias, foreign and domestic; foreign pharmacopoeias. Restricted use: company employees and approved outsiders.

†MA —JOHN F KENNEDY LIBRARY, Columbia Point, Boston, 02125. Dan H Fenn Jr, Dir
Holdings: / / Cat Mss
Notes: The White House staff files of Dean Markham, Executive Director, President's Advisory Commission on Narcotic and Drug Abuse, 1962-1965. 20 linear ft of mss. Holdings are described in "Historical Materials in the John F Kennedy Library." Copies may be obtained by writing the Research Archivist.

MA —MASSACHUSETTS COLLEGE OF PHARMACY AND ALLIED HEALTH SCIENCES, Sheppard Library, 179 Longwood Ave, Boston, 02115. Barbara M Hill, Librn
Holdings: Vols (56,000) Cat Mss Pix Slides Microforms
Notes: Worldwide representation.

MA —NEW ENGLAND COLLEGE OF OPTOMETRY, Library, 420 Beacon St, Boston, 02115. F Eleanor Warner, Librn
Holdings: Vols (7500) Cat Mss Slides Phonorecords Audiotapes Videotapes 16mm Films Microforms
Budget: ($30,000)
Notes: Acquisitions in optometry and ophthalmology are comprehensive; they are selective in areas of surgery and the therapeutic use of drugs. Collection incl 75 slide/tape programs; 75 videotapes; 11 VF drawers of pamphlets and reprints; 16 units of realia; 275 periodical subscriptions. Publishes periodicals holdings list, audiovisual holdings list and an acquisitions list. Open to the public for reference use.

MI —WARNER-LAMBERT/PARKE-DAVIS, Research Library, 2800 Plymouth Rd, Ann Arbor, 48106. Katherine C Owen, Mgr, Library Services
Holdings: Vols (27,977) Cat

MI —THE UPJOHN COMPANY, Corporate Technical Library, 301 Henrietta St, Kalamazoo, 49001. Lorraine Schulte, Manager
Holdings: Cat

MO —SAINT LOUIS POLICE LIBRARY, 315 S Tucker Blvd, Saint Louis, 63102. Cathy Reilly, Librn
Holdings: Vols (21,000) Cat Mss Pix Microforms
Budget: ($18,400)
Notes: Library on all subjects of police work is open to the public for general reference use.

PA —PHILADELPHIA COLLEGE OF PHARMACY & SCIENCE, Joseph W England Library, 42 St & Woodland Ave, Philadelphia, 19104. Carol H Fenichel, Dir of Library Services
Holdings: Vols (53,000) Cat Slides Phonorecords Audiotapes Videotapes 16mm Films Filmstrips Microforms
Budget: ($132,000)
Notes: Pharmacy and related subjects, incl pharmacology, international drug information history of pharmacy and toxicology. Incl 320 periodical titles, vertical files.

ON —ALCOHOLISM & DRUG ADDICTION RESEARCH FOUNDATION, Library, 33 Russell St, Toronto, M5S 2S1, Can. D Fridenberg, Manager, Library Services
Holdings: Vols 8000 Cat
Notes: All aspects of the use and misuse of psychotropic drugs. Incl temperance material.

DRUGS—LAWS AND LEGISLATION

CA —FITZ HUGH LUDLOW MEMORIAL LIBRARY, PO Box 99346, San Francisco, 94109. Michael R Aldrich, Exec Cur
Holdings: Vols (500) Cat Mss Maps Pix Slides Phonorecords Audiotapes Videotapes
Notes: Collection stored. Important mail inquiries only. No interlibrary lending or telephone queries. Emphasizes historical, literary aspects of illicit drug use, as well as sociology, chemistry, pharmacology, botany, legal aspects. Incl complete archives of the California Marijuana Initiative, 1972-74, and many documents from the international marijuana law reform movement. Also incl a sizeable collection of phonograph records, artwork, rolling papers, smoking paraphernalia and research artifacts related to cannabis.

DRUGS—PHYSIOLOGICAL EFFECTS

MI —UNIVERSITY OF MICHIGAN, Transportation Research Institute, Library, 2901 Baxter Rd, Ann Arbor, 48109. Ann C Grimm, Librn
Holdings: Vols (57,000) Cat Mss Maps Pix Slides Microforms
Budget: ($25,000)

NY —MEDICAL LETTER, Library, 56 Harrison St, New Rochelle, 10801. Donna Goodstein, Librn
Holdings: Vols (1000) Cat
Budget: $5000
Notes: No separate catalog or index. Main holdings are in medical journals. Book collection consists of standard texts in medicine, pharmacology and therapeutics, plus many on specific drugs and adverse effects and interactions of drugs. Library is maintained primarily for in-house use.

DRUGS—RESEARCH see Pharmaceutical Research

DRUGS, CONTROL OF see Dangerous Drugs, Control of

DRUGS, DANGEROUS see Dangerous Drugs, Control of

DRUGS, PROLONGED-RELEASE see Delayed-Action Preparations

DRUGS AND ART see Art and Drugs

DRUGS AND MUSIC see Music and Drugs

DRUGS AND MUSICIANS see Musicians and Drugs

DRUGS IN FOOD

CA —FITZ HUGH LUDLOW MEMORIAL LIBRARY, PO Box 99346, San Francisco,

DRUGS IN FOOD (cont.)

94109. Michael R Aldrich, Exec Cur
Holdings: Mss Maps Pix Slides Phonorecords Audiotapes Videotapes
Notes: Collection stored. Important mail inquiries only. No interlibrary lending or telephone queries. The heart of this special collection of psychoactive drug literature is about 400 vols of memoirs or lightly-disguised fiction concerning psychoactive drugs, plus about 600 vols related to Beat writers of the 1950s-60s, plus about 300 vols related to the "Hippie" movement of the 1960s, plus 600 vols (mostly paperback) of drug-related pornography, and several hundred vols related to drug slang, drugs and music, drug art, drug cuisine, etc. In addition we have many boxes of offprints, files of newspaper clippings, complete runs to underground newspapers, and many artifacts related to this area. Much of the 1950s-60s-70s literature is autographed or inscribed.

DRUGS IN LITERATURE

CA —FITZ HUGH LUDLOW MEMORIAL LIBRARY, PO Box 99346, San Francisco, 94109. Michael R Aldrich, Exec Cur
Holdings: Vols (3000) Mss Maps Pix Slides Phonorecords Audiotapes Videotapes
Notes: Collection stored. Important mail inquiries only. No interlibrary lending or telephone queries. The heart of this special collection of psychoactive drug literature is about 400 vols of memoirs or lightly-disguised fiction concerning psychoactive drugs, plus about 600 vols related to Beat writers of the 1950s-60s, plus about 300 vols related to the "Hippie" movement of the 1960s, plus 600 vols (mostly paperback) of drug-related pornography, and several hundred vols related to drug slang, drugs and music, drug art, drug cuisine, etc. In addition we have many boxes of offprints, files of newspaper clippings, complete runs to underground newspapers, and many artifacts related to this area. Much of the 1950s-60s-70s literature is autographed or inscribed.

DRUNKEN DRIVERS see Drinking and Traffic Accidents

DRUNKENNESS see Alcoholism; Temperance

DRURY, CLIFFORD MERRILL

†WA —WASHINGTON STATE UNIVERSITY, Library, Manuscripts, Archives & Special Collections, Pullman, 99164. John F Guido, Head
Holdings: Vols Cat Mss Maps Pix
Notes: Ms resources incl the papers of missionaries Henry Harmon Spalding, Elkanah Walker and Marcus Whitman; as well as the papers of their historian Clifford Merrill Drury. Unpublished container lists to these collections are in the library.

DRURY, KEN, 1893-1971

BC —UNIVERSITY OF VICTORIA, McPherson Library, Victoria, V8W 3H5, Can.
Notes: Incl 80 cm, 1917-54; clippings, pamphlets, press releases on BC politics, journalism, United Nations, war.

DRY BELLY-ACHE

RI —BROWN UNIVERSITY, John Carter Brown Library, Providence, 02912. Norman Fiering, Librn; Everett C Wilkie Jr, Bibliographer; Susan Danforth, Cur Maps & Prints

DRYDEN, HUGH L.

MD —JOHNS HOPKINS UNIVERSITY, Milton S Eisenhower Library, Charles & 34 Sts, Baltimore, 21218. Ann S Gwyn, Assistant Dir for Special Collections
Holdings: Cat Mss Pix Audiotapes //
Notes: Almost entirely a ms collection. Personal papers, etc 144 linear ft.

DRYDEN, JOHN, 1631-1700

AZ —UNIVERSITY OF ARIZONA, University Library, Special Collections, Tucson, 85721. Louis A Hieb, Head
Holdings: Vols (7000) Cat Mss Microforms
Budget: ($30,000)
Notes: Strong in Restoration and 18th century drama. Major author strengths of the 18th century are Dryden, Fielding, Pope, Richardson, and Smollett.

CA —CLAREMONT COLLEGES, Honnold Library, Ninth & Dartmouth, Claremont, 91711. Tania Rizzo, Special Collections Dept Head
Holdings: Vols 508 // Cat
Notes: McDonald's *Dryden Bibliography* checked for holdings. Incl 17th to 20th century editions, chiefly late 17th and early 18th, of collected works, individual titles, letters, his prefaces and translations, biographical and critical works, and associated contemporary titles. Purchased from the Dobell collection.

CA —UNIVERSITY OF CALIFORNIA, LOS ANGELES, Research Library, Dept of Special Collections, 405 Hilgard Ave, Los Angeles, 90024. Edward Shreeves, Chairman, Bibliographers Group; David S Zeidberg, Head
Holdings: Cat Mss Pix
Notes: Extensive collection of early editions and Drydeniana, incl nearly every item described in Hugh MacDonald's *John Dryden, A Bibliography* (1939); many in multiple copies, a few in facsimile.

CT —YALE UNIVERSITY, Box 1603A, Yale Station, New Haven, 06520.

MA —HARVARD UNIVERSITY LIBRARY, Widener Library, Cambridge, 02138.
Holdings: Cat

MI —UNIVERSITY OF MICHIGAN, Library, Dept of Rare Books & Special Collections, Ann Arbor, 48109. Robert J Starring, Head
Holdings: Cat Mss

NY —UNIVERSITY OF ROCHESTER, Rush Rhees Library, Department of Rare Books and Special Collections, Rochester, 14627. Peter Dzwonkoski, Librn
Holdings: Vols 250 Cat
Notes: Contemporary editions of the works of Dryden. No photocopying.

NC —DUKE UNIVERSITY, William R Perkins Library, Rare Book Room, Durham, 27706. John L Sharpe, III, Cur
Notes: Thomas J Wise collection. Many rare pieces, including works of Byron, Coleridge, Dryden, Pope and Hardy. 135 political and religious broadsides, mostly of the 17th century.

DUBLIN, LOUIS

†NY —NEW YORK ACADEMY OF MEDICINE, Library, 2 E 103 ST, New York, 10029.
Notes: Papers of Walter Timme, MD (1874-1956). Timme was a pioneer endocrinologist; described pluriglandular disease, "Timme's Syndrome." Incl correspondence from Harvey Cushing, Paul Dudley White, Charles A Elsberg, Louis I Dublin, Ely Smith Jelliffe, John F Fulton, Edna St Vincent Millay, Eva Le Gallienne, and Irving Ramsey Wiles.

DUBLIN GATE THEATRE

IL —NORTHWESTERN UNIVERSITY, Library, Special Collections Dept, 1937 Sheridan Rd, Evanston, 60201. R Russell Maylone, Cur
Holdings: Mss Pix
Notes: Dublin Gate Theatre Archive, incl the complete correspondence files, plays in mss, original production books and directors' notebooks, files of stage design, photographs, and press releases. Described in *Guide to the Archives of the Dublin Gate Theatre*, Tina Howe (Evanston, 1978).

NY —NEW YORK PUBLIC LIBRARY, Performing Arts Research Center, Billy Rose Theatre Collection, 111 Amsterdam Ave, New York, 10023. Dorothy L Swerdlove, Cur
Holdings: Cat
See also entry under Theatre.

DUBOIS, FRED T.

ID —IDAHO STATE UNIVERSITY, Library, Pocatello, 83209. Gary Domitz, Social Science Librn
Holdings: Uncat Mss Pix //
Notes: Papers, etc.

DU BOIS, WILLIAM EDWARD BURGHARDT, 1868-1963

CT —YALE UNIVERSITY, Box 1603A, Yale Station, New Haven, 06520.
Holdings: Cat Mss

LA —AMISTAD RESEARCH CENTER, 400 Esplanade Ave, New Orleans, 70116. Clifton H Johnson, Exec Dir; Florence E Borders, Senior Archivist
Notes: Originally established at Fisk University, in Nashville, by the American Missionary Association (AMA), this research center on Black American History consists of mss, photographs, clippings, books, pamphlets, taped speeches and interviews; also, the papers of such leaders as WEB DuBois, Countee Cullen, and Mary McLeod Bethune. Also materials on other American minorities, such as Native Americans, Asian Americans, Hispanics, etc.

MA —UNIVERSITY OF MASSACHUSETTS AT AMHERST, Library, Archives and Manuscripts, Amherst, 01003. Siegfried Feller, Assoc Dir for Collection Development
Holdings: Uncat Mss Pix Audiotapes Videotapes 16mm Films Microforms
Notes: Papers, 1877-1979. Correspondence 1877-1965; editorial files for *Crisis* magazine, 1910-1934, and other magazines; manuscripts and printed versions of speeches, articles, newspaper columns, and nonfiction books; research materials, pamphlets, leaflets, book reviews, petitions, essays, forewards, student papers, novels, plays, pageants, short stories, poetry, genealogical and financial records; photographs; memorabilia; motion pictures and video and audio tapes; and newspaper clippings. *The Papers of W E B Du Bois 1803 (1877-1963) 1979; a Guide,* by Robert W McDonnell, 1981. Collection available on microfilm (89 reels) from University Microfilms International.

DUBRIDGE, LEE A.

CA —CALIFORNIA INSTITUTE OF TECHNOLOGY, Robert A Millikan Memorial Library, Archives, 1201 E California Blvd, Pasadena, 91125. Judith R Goodstein, Archivist
Notes: The Lee A DuBridge papers, incl 228 boxes of correspondence, documents, reports, and memorabilia reflecting his tenure as head of MIT Radiation Laboratory, 1940-1946; as president of Caltech, 1946-1969; and his participation in professional and governmental organizations.

DUBUS, ANDRE

LA —MCNEESE STATE UNIVERSITY, Lether E Frazar Library, Ryan St, Lake Charles, 70609. Kathie Bordelon, Special Collections Librn
Holdings: Vols Cat Clippings
Notes: Efforts are being made to collect all works by and about this local author.

DUCA, GEORGE I.

CA —HOOVER INSTITUTION ON WAR, REVOLUTION & PEACE, Stanford University, Stanford, 94305. Milorad M Drachkovitch, Archivist
Holdings: Mss
Notes: Papers, correspondence, etc.

DUCHAMP, MARCEL

CA —FRANCIS BACON LIBRARY, 655 N Dartmouth Ave, Claremont, 91711. Elizabeth S Wrigley, Dir
Holdings: Mss Pix
Notes: Correspondence of Walter Arensberg

DUCHAMP, MARCEL (cont.)

with artists John Covert, Marcel Duchamp, Francis Picabia and his wife Gabrielle Buffet Picabia, and psychiatrist Elmer Ernest Southard, 1876-1920.

CA —UNIVERSITY OF CALIFORNIA, SANTA CRUZ, University Library, Special Collections, Santa Cruz, 95064. Rita Bottoms, Special Collections Librn; Margaret Felts, South Pacific Collection Bibliographer
Notes: The archives of Trianon Press. All major publications of the Press. Under the direction of Arnold Fawcus from the late 1940s through the 1970s, Trianon Press was noted for its replica editions of the works of early authors with special emphasis on the works of William Blake Marcel Duchamp.

DUDLEY FAMILY

MA —NEW ENGLAND HISTORIC GENEALOGICAL SOCIETY, Library, 101 Newbury St, Boston, 02116. Ralph J Crandell, Dir
Notes: Family papers, likely to incl personal correspondence, diaries, business records, etc.

DUKE, B. N.

NC —DUKE UNIVERSITY, William R Perkins Library, Manuscript Dept, Durham, 27706. Ellen Gartrell, Cur of Mss
Holdings: Cat Mss
Notes: Strongest for textile and tobacco industries in Southeastern US, 19th-20th centuries. Incl papers of B N Duke, Richard H Wright, British-American Tobacco Co; business records of textile mills and several lumber companies, Romeo Guest papers on development of Research Triangle Park, North Carolina.

DUKE, VERNON

DC —LIBRARY OF CONGRESS, Music Division, Washington, 20540.
Notes: Vernon Duke's musical manuscripts dating from 1919. Some of his earlier work was composed under his Russian name, Vladimir Dukelsky.

DUKE FAMILY

NC —DUKE UNIVERSITY, William R Perkins Library, Manuscript Dept, Durham, 27706. Ellen Gartrell, Cur of Mss
Holdings: Cat Mss
Notes: Tobacco culture, marketing, trade, especially US South, 19th-20th century, incl papers of Duke Family, Richard H Wright, British-American Tobacco Co, James A Thomas, Edward J Parrish, United Cigarette Machine Co; also tobacco advertising (trade cards, etc).

DUKELSKY, VLADIMIR

DC —LIBRARY OF CONGRESS, Music Division, Washington, 20540.
Notes: Vernon Duke's musical manuscripts dating from 1919. Some of his earlier work was composed under his Russian name, Vladimir Dukelsky.

DUKES, OFIELD

MI —WAYNE STATE UNIVERSITY, Walter P Reuther Library, Archives of Labor & Urban Affairs, Detroit, 48202. Philip Mason, Dir
Notes: The politics of 20th century America are mirrored in the collections of Patrick V McNamara, US Senator; Charles Diggs, US Representative from Michigan; Ofield Dukes, aide to Vice-President Hubert H Humphrey; and George and Grace Brewer, Socialist Party workers and assistants to Eugene V Debs.

DUKHOBORS

BC —SELKIRK COLLEGE, Library, PO Box 1200, Castlegar, V1N 3J1, Can. John Mansbridge, Dir
Holdings: Vols 1000 Cat Mss Maps Pix Microforms
Notes: The West Kootenay History Collection is particularly rich in works on the Dukhobor people. The West Kootenay area of BC is bounded on the south by the US border, on the north by the Trans-Canada Highway, on the east by Kootenay Lake, and on the west by the Okanagan Valley.

BC —UNIVERSITY OF BRITISH COLUMBIA, Library, Special Collections Div, 1956 Main Mall, Vancouver, V6T 1Y3, Can. Anne Yandle, Head
Holdings: Vols Cat Mss

†ON —PUBLIC ARCHIVES OF CANADA, Library, 395 Wellington St, Ottawa, K1A 0N3, Can. Dawn E Monroe, Collections Dept Officer

DULAC, EDMUND

CA —LOS ANGELES PUBLIC LIBRARY, Children's Literature Dept, 630 W 5th St, Los Angeles, 90071. Serenna Day, Sr Librn
Holdings: Vols (2120) Cat Phonorecordss Filmstrips
Notes: Also includes reference collection, covering some 50 years of published folklore and modern fairy tales. Includes extensive Mother Goose collection, examples of the work of such outstanding illustrators as Edmund Dulac and Arthur Rackham. Many volumes out of print. Index to titles of stories in collections.

DULLES, ALLEN W., 1893-1969

NJ —PRINCETON UNIVERSITY, Seeley G Mudd Manuscript Library, Public Affairs Papers Collection, Princeton, 08544. Nancy Bressler, Cur
Notes: Incl 310 boxes. The papers cover the period 1845-1971. An unpublished (83p) guide is available in the Library.

DULLES, JOHN FOSTER, 1888-1959

NJ —PRINCETON UNIVERSITY, Library, Manuscript Collection, Nassau St, Princeton, 08540. Jean F Preston, Cur
Holdings: Cat Mss Pix
Notes: The John Foster Dulles Collection of personal papers, 1907-1959, fills 621 boxes. Unpublished typescript guide (932 p) is available in library. Also oral history collection made 1964-1967 by Dulles' friends and colleagues. 275 typescripts. Published catalog: *Dulles Oral History Collection. A Descriptive Catlogue* (Princeton, 1967). Terms of access: each author controls his transcript, most are open, some are closed. Limited photocopying. See published catalog.

†TX —UNIVERSITY OF TEXAS LIBRARIES, General Libraries, Humanities Research Center, PO Box 7219, Austin, 78712. John Chalmers, Librn
Notes: The John W F Dulles collection of correspondence, diaries, autographs, speeches, and paintings by famous historical figures from the 17th century to the present. Much of the material is related to Mr Dulles' three relatives who served as Secretaries of State: John Foster Dulles, Robert Lansing, and John W Foster. Incl the secret diary of Lansing, Wilson's Secretary of State.

DUMAS, ALEXANDRE, 1824-1895

IN —INDIANA UNIVERSITY, Lilly Library, Seventh St, Bloomington, 47405. William R Cagle, Librn
Holdings: / / Cat Mss
Notes: Letters and telegrams from French novelist and playwright Alexandre Dumas to Princess Elise Soutzo, 1877-1890. Incl 2 photographs of Dumas and a scrapbook. 307 items. Holdings incl first editions of Dumas' published works.

DUMAS, M. O.

AZ —NORTHERN ARIZONA UNIVERSITY, Special Collection Library, CU Box 6022, Flagstaff, 86011. Peter M Whiteley, Coordr/Archivist; William Mullane, Librn
Notes: Incl photocopied typescript of "My First Roundup" (1896), by M O Dumas. Incl names of man on roundup and cattle brands represented, 1960. Also incl some historical information, ie, short summary of Martha Summerhayes' book *Vanished Arizona,* about her trip to Arizona in 1874.

DU MAURIER, GEORGE

NJ —PRINCETON UNIVERSITY, Library, Morris L Parrish Collection, Princeton, 08540. Alexander D Wainwright, Cur
Notes: The collection contains over 6500 vols, as well as many theatre programs, playbills, photographs, clippings and other miscellanea. Parrish's goal was to assemble in both the English and the American first editions, in the original condition as issued, everything that a given author published. He was also interested in a high standard of condition for his books. Many additions have been acquired since the Parrish collection came to the Library as a bequest in 1944. The collection is an assemblage of author collections, consisting of books by: William Harrison Ainsworth, James Matthew Barrie, William Black, The Brontes, William Wilkie Collins, Dinah Mulock Craik, Marie de la Ramee ("Ouida"), Benjamin Disraeli, Charles Dickens, Charles Dodgson, George du Maurier, George Eliot (ie Mary Ann Evans), Elizabeth Gaskell, Thomas Hardy, Thomas Hughes,Charles Kingsley, Charles Lever, Edward George Earle Bulwer-Lytton, Mary Maxwell, George Meredith, Charles Reade, Walter Scott, Robert Louis Stevenson, William Makepeace Thackeray, Trollope Family, Ellen Wood, and Charlotte Yonge.

DUMB (DEAF-MUTES) see Deaf and Deafness

THE DUMBELLS

ON —METROPOLITAN TORONTO LIBRARY, Theatre Dept, 789 Yonge St, Toronto, M4W 2G8, Can. Heather McCallum, Head
Notes: The collection incl programs, clippings, photographs, music, correspondence, scripts and route books for the all-soldier concert party formed in France in 1917, which toured Canada and the United States until 1929.

DUMITRIU, PETRU

MA —BOSTON UNIVERSITY, Mugar Memorial Library, Special Collections Dept, 771 Commonwealth Ave, Boston, 02215. Howard B Gotlieb, Dir
Holdings: Cat Mss

DUMM, EDWINA

OH —OHIO STATE UNIVERSITY, Library for Communication and Graphic Arts, 242 W 18th St, Columbus, 43210. Lucy S Caswell, Curator
Notes: Comic strip artists Hal Foster, Dudley T Fisher, Jr, Mark Szorady, Edwina Dumm, Jim Baker have original works in the library. Also new collections of original cartoons by Windsor McCay, John T McCutcheon, Dick Moores, Ned White, Walter Berndt, Jim Larrick, Carl Rose and Bill Crawford. Also a large collection of the work of illustrator Will Rannells. The Shel Dorf Collection incl historic comic strips and related materials. A small but growing collection of comic books, especially those featuring *Katy Keene,* is available in the library.

DUN, R. G., AND COMPANY

MA —HARVARD UNIVERSITY, Graduate School of Business Administration, Baker Library, Soldiers Field, Boston, 02163. Mary V Chatfield, Librn; Florence Bartoshesky,

DUN, R. G., AND COMPANY (cont.)

Cur of Manuscripts and Archives
Holdings: Cat Mss
Notes: Handwritten credit reports, 1840-1890. See *Historical Methods Newsletter,* VIII (1975), 128-131.

DUNCAN, ISADORA, 1877-1927

CA —UNIVERSITY OF CALIFORNIA, LOS ANGELES, Research Library, Dept of Special Collections, 405 Hilgard Ave, Los Angeles, 90024. Edward Shreeves, Chairman, Bibliographers Group; David S Zeidberg, Head
Holdings: Cat Mss Pix
Notes: In various collections, incl the Edward Gordon Craig, Mary Desti, and Arthur Todd collections.

NY —NEW YORK PUBLIC LIBRARY, Performing Arts Research Center, Dance Collection, 111 Amsterdam Ave, New York, 10023. Genevieve Oswald, Cur
Notes: Extensive written and visual documentation: biographies, the dancer's published writings, articles, clippings and reviews, scrapbooks, programs, posters; over 200 original photographs; original drawings by Jules Grandjouan, Gordon Craig, Antoine Bourdelle, Abraham Walkowitz, and Dunoyer de Segonzac; prints by Jose Clara and John Sloane; major collections of manuscripts and letters. The Gordon Craig-Isadora Duncan Collection numbers 400 items, 1901-1957, including over 200 letters and telegrams, also photographs, drawings, sketches, and programs. Published register in *Bulletin of the New York Public Library*, vol 76 (1972). The Irma Duncan Collection of 300 items contains the personal effects of Isadora Duncan left to her adopted daughter Irma Duncan and comprises correspondence with Gordon Craig, Sergei Esenin, Ellen Terry, and Anatolii Lunacharskii,clippings, and memorabilia. The Allan Ross MacDougall Collection of 250 items includes holographs, typescripts, and photos. Although no original film footage appears to exist, the Collection owns footage of dance performances by pupils of Isadora Duncan, including: Irma Duncan, Hortense Kooluris, Maria Theresa, and Julia Levien, as well as modern reconstructions of her art interpreted by such artists as Annabelle Gamson and Lynn Seymour. Cataloged items listed in published catalog: *Dictionary Catalog of the Dance Collection,* Boston, G K Hall, 1974, 10 vols.

DUNCAN, ROBERT EDWARD, 1919-

MO —WASHINGTON UNIVERSITY, John M Olin Library, Campus Box 1061, St Louis, 63130.
Notes: A major collection, incl mss, correspondence, literary papers, photographs, etc. Described in *Special Collections: an Annotated Guide to the Holdings of the Manuscript Division and the University Archives and Research Collection.*

NY NEW YORK UNIVERSITY, Elmer Holmes Bobst Library, Div of Special Collections, Washington Sq S, New York, 10012. Frank Walker, Librn; Patrick McGuire, Asst Librn
Holdings: Vols (100,000) Cat Mss Pix
Notes: The Fales Collection of first (and other) editions of English and American novels from about 1750 to date (about 70, 000 titles). Mss (30,000) pieces.

NY —STATE UNIVERSITY OF NEW YORK, STONY BROOK, Melville Library, Dept of Special Collections, Stony Brook, 11794. Evert Volkersz, Head
Holdings: Cat Mss

OH —KENT STATE UNIVERSITY, Libraries, Dept of Special Collections, Kent, 44242. Dean H Keller, Cur
Holdings: Vols 50 Cat Mss

BC —SIMON FRASER UNIVERSITY, Library, Burnaby, V5A 1S6, Can. Percilla Groves, Special Collections Librn
Holdings: Cat Mss
Notes: Letters written to Eshleman by Allen Ginsberg (8 pp), William Carlos Williams and Florence Williams (5 pp), Robert Duncan (4 pp), and Edward Dorn (5 pp), while Eshleman was editor of *Folio* (1959-1961). Tss from Gregory Corso (2 pp), Louis Zukofsky (8 pp), Michael Rumaker (3 pp).

BC —UNIVERSITY OF VICTORIA, McPherson Library, Victoria, V8W 3H5, Can.
Notes: Corrected proofs of the *The Years As Catches,* typed notes on the proofs.

DUNCAN, ROBERT L.

MA —BOSTON UNIVERSITY, Mugar Memorial Library, Special Collections Dept, 771 Commonwealth Ave, Boston, 02215. Howard B Gotlieb, Dir
Holdings: Cat Mss

DUNCAN, THOMAS W.

MA —BOSTON UNIVERSITY, Mugar Memorial Library, Special Collections Dept, 771 Commonwealth Ave, Boston, 02215. Howard B Gotlieb, Dir
Holdings: Cat Mss Pix
Notes: Mss, correspondence, etc collected in depth; incl publications by or about.

DUNDAS, WILLIAM OSWALD

DC —GEORGETOWN UNIVERSITY, Library, Special Collections Div, 37 & O Sts NW, Washington, 20057. George M Barringer, Special Collections Librn; Nicholas B Sheetz, Mss Librn
Holdings: Mss
Notes: Correspondnece of William Oswald Dundas. Outgoing letters addressed chiefly to Edward I Devitt, SJ (1841-1920), archivist and professor of history at Georgetown College and Henry J Shandelle, SJ (1848-1925), librarian and professor of English and philosophy; extensive recollections of student life at Georgetown 1856-58 and of life in Washington during the 1850's. Incoming correspondence incl letters from James Edward Calhoun (1796-1889) of South Carolina, cousin and brother-in-law of John C Calhoun and a member of Long's expedition of 1819-1820; and official letters from various public officials, incl Sen James Vardaman of Mississippi, Gov William Hodges Mann of Virginia, and Robert Bacon, all in connection with Dundas' attempts to obtain a roster of Confederate troops for Fr Devitt. Family correspondence sundry family documents and personalreminiscences complete the collection.

DUNGEONS see Printing, Practical

DUNHAM, KATHERINE

IL —SOUTHERN ILLINOIS UNIVERSITY, CARBONDALE, Delyte W Morris Library, Special Collections Dept, Carbondale, 62901. David V Koch, Cur of Special Collections; Louisa Bowen, Cur of Manuscripts
Holdings: Mss Pix
Notes: Personal papers, 1919-1965, 60 linear feet. Some portions of these papers are closed except with Miss Dunham's permission. Inventory and name index available at library.

DUNHAM, THEODORE, JR.

NY —AMERICAN INSTITUTE OF PHYSICS, Center for the History of Physics, Niels Bohr Library, 335 E 45 St, New York, 10017. John Aubry, Librn
Notes: The Sources for History of Modern Astrophysics documents the history of 20th-century astrophysics. Incl some 400 hours of oral history interviews with astronomers, such as Bart Bok, S Chandrasekhar, Martin Schwarzschild, and A E Whitford. The project also organized and cataloged the papers of Henry Norris Russell, Frank Schlesinger, Otto Struve, Ejnar Hertzsprung, Harlow Shapley, Charles Young, Robert Atkinson, Seth Chandler, Theodore Dunham, Jr, and G C McVittie.

DUNKARDS see Church of the Brethren

DUNN, GEORGE GRUNDY, 1812-1857

IN —INDIANA UNIVERSITY, Lilly Library, Seventh St, Bloomington, 47405. William R Cagle, Librn
Holdings: // Mss
Notes: Papers and correspondence of Indiana lawyer and congressman George Grundy Dunn, 1834-1850; served as US Congressman, 1847-49 and 1855-57; Indiana State Senator 1850-52. Collection contains law office correspondence from Bedford, Ind, and political and congressional office correspondence during Dunn's first term in Congress. 1398 items.

DUNN, J. D.

TX —NORTH TEXAS STATE UNIVERSITY, Archives, NT Station Box 5188, Denton, 76203. Robert LaForte, University Archivist
Notes: Labor arbitration manuscript collections incl papers of arbitrators Byron R Abernethy, J D Dunn, and Elvis Stephens. These arbitration papers cover the years 1960-1980 and emphasize cases in the southwestern United States and Puerto Rico. Published Description: J D Dunn and Elvis Stephens Collections, *The National Union Catalog of Manuscript Collections: Catalog* 1979 Washington: Library of Congress, 1980.

DUNNE, IRENE

CA —UNIVERSITY OF SOUTHERN CALIFORNIA, Edward L Doheny Memorial Library, Archives of Performing Arts, University Park, Los Angeles, 90089. Robert Knutson, Librn
Holdings: Mss Pix
Notes: Personal collection of papers, pictures, etc.

DUNNE, PHILIP

CA —UNIVERSITY OF SOUTHERN CALIFORNIA, Edward L Doheny Memorial Library, Archives of Performing Arts, University Park, Los Angeles, 90089. Robert Knutson, Librn
Holdings: Mss Pix
Notes: Personal collection of papers, pictures, etc.

DUNNING, CHARLES

AZ —NORTHERN ARIZONA UNIVERSITY, Special Collection Library, CU Box 6022, Flagstaff, 86011. Peter M Whiteley, Coordr/Archivist; William Mullane, Librn
Notes: Charles Dunning Collection: Detailed notes of Arizona mining history used in preparation for his book, *Rocks to Riches; The Story of American Mining, Past, Present, and Future, as Reflected in the Colorful History of Mining in Arizona* (Phoenix: Southwest Publishing Company, 1959).

DUNNING, PHILIP

PA —UNIVERSITY OF PITTSBURGH, Special Collections Dept, Curtis Theatre Collection, 363 Hillman Library, Pittsburgh, 15260. Jeanette Blanco, Cur
Holdings: Cat Mss Pix
Notes: Philip Dunning Playscripts Collection. Playscripts, film scripts, TV scripts: 69 titles by Dunning as sole author, co-author or adapter. Also incl associated items.

DUNPHY, JACK

MA —BOSTON UNIVERSITY, Mugar Memorial Library, Special Collections Dept, 771 Commonwealth Ave, Boston, 02215. Howard B Gotlieb, Dir
Holdings: Cat Mss

DUNSANY, EDWARD J. M. D. PLUNKETT, LORD, 1878-1957

MI —UNIVERSITY OF MICHIGAN, Library, Dept of Rare Books & Special Collections,

DUNSANY, EDWARD J. M. D. PLUNKETT, LORD, 1878-1957 (cont.)

Ann Arbor, 48109. Robert J Starring, Head
Holdings: Vols 55 Cat Mss
Notes: Includes many first editions, 2 manuscripts, and 2 ALS. Twenty volumes have poetic inscriptions in Dunsany's holograph.

NY —STATE UNIVERSITY OF NEW YORK, BINGHAMTON, Glenn G Bartle Library, Binghamton, 13901. Marion Hanscom, Special Collections Librn
Notes: Letters (253) of Mary Lavin, Irish playwright, largely correspondence with Lord Dunsany.

PA —BUCKNELL UNIVERSITY, Ellen Clarke Bertrand Library, Lewisburg, 17837. Ann de Klerk, Librn
Holdings: Cat
Notes: Includes books and letters.

ON —UNIVERSITY OF TORONTO, Thomas Fisher Rare Book Library, 120 Saint George St, Toronto, M5S 1A5, Can. Richard G Landon, Head
Holdings: Vols 5400 Cat Mss
Notes: Three collections. Duncan Collection is named for donor, Douglas Duncan, art dealer and collector,, Toronto. Contains first and subsequent important editions of Richard Aldington, Max Beerbohm, Norman Douglas, Aldoux Huxley, and D H Lawrence. Manuscripts by Beerbohm, Aldington, Lawrence, William Sharp. Endicott Collection named in honor of Norman J Endicott, Professor of English, University of Toronto, contains first and significant later editions of over fifty British writers whose major work falls into the period from 1880 to 1930. Fisher Collection named for donor, Charles B Fisher, contains first and significant editions of Kipling, Norman Douglas, and Lord Dunsany.

DUPLICATING PROCESSES see Photocopying Processes

DUPLICATING SYSTEMS

NY —XEROX CORP, Technical Information Center, PO Box 305, Webster, 14580. Michael D Majcher, Mgr
Holdings: Vols (30,000) Cat Microforms

DU PONCEAU, PIERRE ETIENNE

DC —GEORGETOWN UNIVERSITY, Library, Special Collections Div, 37 & O Sts NW, Washington, 20057. George M Barringer, Special Collections Librn; Nicholas B Sheetz, Mss Librn
Holdings: Mss Cat Pix
Notes: Collection of correspondence, journals, documents, photographs, and newspaper clippings concerning the family of Mimika Farish Frith. Incl is correspondence (9 ALS, 1779-1781) from Baron von Steuben to his aide-de-campe Pierre Etienne Du Ponceau and two letters (ALS, 1781) from Du Ponceau to von Steuben. Also incl is a bound journal kept by Du Ponceau from 1794-1820 which served as a family register, diary and account book. Also incl is correspondence and documents from the Bauduy, Farish and Sassenay families spanning the period from 1782-1932. Of particular interest is a bound volume of photographs from the Suez Canal, Ceylon, Colombo, Java, Borneo and New Guinea, taken by Frederick G Farish in 1907.

DU PONT, LAMMOT

RI —BROWN UNIVERSITY, John Hay Library, 20 Prospect St, Providence, 02912. Mark N Brown, Cur Mss
Holdings: // Mss
Notes: Papers of Walter Nickerson Hill, American chemist, incl correspondence, letters, autograph drafts of articles for scientific journals, lectures, letterpress copy books, scrapbook with inserted ALS, pamphlets, photographs, and memorabilia. The correspondence deals with personal, familial, and business matters (the latter during Hill's tenure as instructor in explosives at the US Torpedo Station in Newport, RI, and while he was chief chemist for the Rapauno Nitroglycerine Works, near Philadelphia, owned by the duPont Family). There is scientific correspondence between Hill and leading scientists, ordnance specialists, and influential figures. See also Papers of Augustus W Smith, Hill's father-in-law, also at Brown.

DU PONT DE NEMOURS, E. I., AND COMPANY

DE —HAGLEY MUSEUM AND LIBRARY, Eleutherian Mills-Hagley Foundation Inc, PO Box 3630, Greenville, 19807. Richmond D Williams, Dir; Heddy A Richter, Imprints Librn
Notes: Records of E I du Pont de Nemours & Company (1801-1958; 2500 cubic feet). The collection traces the founding of the company in Paris, its evolution into an American partnership during the early nineteenth century and its first incorporation in 1899. Details concerning the financial and business negotiations which led to the founding of the company, the selection of a site for operations, the erection of the mills, and methods of manufacturing, production, marketing and labor relations are well described. Records of Atlas Powder Company (1912-1955; 500 cubic feet) document the history of one of the United States' largest manufacturers of gun powder which was split off from the Du Pont Company as a result of a 1912 antitrust case.

DU PONT FAMILY

DE —HAGLEY MUSEUM AND LIBRARY, Eleutherian Mills-Hagley Foundation Inc, PO Box 3630, Greenville, 19807. Richmond D Williams, Dir; Heddy A Richter, Imprints Librn
Holdings: Mss
Notes: 1500 cubic feet of mss. The library holds the books and papers of Pierre Samuel du Pont de Nemours (173-1817), physiocrat and economic theorist; the papers of E I du Pont (1771-1834), powder company founder; and his brother Victor (1767-1827). The Admiral Samuel Francis du Pont (1803-1865) papers contain some 49,000 items documenting in detail his naval career and the papers of General Henry du Pont (1812-1889) illuminate Delaware's history during the Civil war. Also held are the papers of Colonel Henry A du Pont (1838-1926).

DURATION, INTUITION OF see Time Perception

DURBIN, CHARLES

MA —BOSTON UNIVERSITY, Mugar Memorial Library, Special Collections Dept, 771 Commonwealth Ave, Boston, 02215. Howard B Gotlieb, Dir
Holdings: Cat Mss Correspondence

DURER, ALBRECHT

CA —UNIVERSITY OF SAN FRANCISCO, Richard A Gleeson Library, The Countess Bernardine Murphy Donohue Rare Book Room, San Francisco, 94117. D Steven Corey, Special Collections Librn
Notes: Original wood engravings and etchings, 87 items.

NY —METROPOLITAN MUSEUM OF ART, Dept of Prints & Photographs, 82 St & Fifth Ave, New York, 10028. Colta Ives, Cur

DURHAM, MARILYN

IN —INDIANA STATE UNIVERSITY, EVANSVILLE, Library, 8600 University Blvd, Evansville, 47712. Gina R Walker, Acting Archivist
Holdings: Cat Mss
Notes: Typescripts and galleys of, and correspondence about, the novels *The Man Who Loved Cat Dancing* and *Dutch Uncle*. Restricted use: noncirculating.

DURHAM, PHILIP, 1912-1977

CA —UNIVERSITY OF CALIFORNIA, LOS ANGELES, Research Library, Dept of Special Collections, 405 Hilgard Ave, Los Angeles, 90024. Edward Shreeves, Chairman, Bibliographers Group; David S Zeidberg, Head
Notes: 8 linear feet of UCLA English professor's mss, correspondence, and ephemera.

DURRELL, LAWRENCE, 1912-

AZ —UNIVERSITY OF ARIZONA, University Library, Special Collections, Tucson, 85721. Louis A Hieb, Head
Holdings: Vols (7000) Cat Mss Microforms
Budget: ($30,000)
Notes: The 20th century collection is dominated by the works of Auden, Durrell, Conrad, Hardy, D H Lawrence, and Yeats.

CA —UNIVERSITY OF CALIFORNIA, LOS ANGELES, Research Library, Dept of Special Collections, 405 Hilgard Ave, Los Angeles, 90024. Edward Shreeves, Chairman, Bibliographers Group; David S Zeidberg, Head
Holdings: Vols 350 Cat Mss
Notes: 350 first and other editions of his books; 3 linear feet of correspondence, mss, and ephemera. No photocopying.

CA —STANFORD UNIVERSITY LIBRARIES, Cecil H Green Library, Stanford, 94305. Michael T Ryan, Cur
Holdings: Vols (23,000) Cat
Notes: The Charlotte Ashley Felton Memorial Library. Incl first editions.

IL —SOUTHERN ILLINOIS UNIVERSITY, CARBONDALE, Delyte W Morris Library, Special Collections Dept, Carbondale, 62901. David V Koch, Cur of Special Collections; Louisa Bowen, Cur of Manuscripts
Holdings: Vols 150 Cat Mss Pix
Notes: Personal papers, 1933-1971, incl 30 working notebooks, published and unpublished poetry and essays, and mss and galley proofs of novels; 2000 letters incl important correspondence with Henry Miller, T S Elliot, Dylan Thomas, Richard Aldington, and Anais Nin. Detailed inventory and name index available at library. Ian MacNiven, Annotated Catalog and Calendar of the Lawrence Durrell Papers. 1972 (PhD dissertation, SIU). 23 linear ft.

IL —NORTHWESTERN UNIVERSITY, Library, Special Collections Dept, 1937 Sheridan Rd, Evanston, 60201. R Russell Maylone, Cur
Holdings: Vols 110 Cat Mss

NV —UNIVERSITY OF NEVADA, RENO, University Library, Special Collections Dept, Reno, 89557. Robert E Blesse, Head
Holdings: // Vols (198) Cat
Notes: Includes individual works by author in all editions including translations; also prefaces, introductions, published correspondence, appearances in anthologies, periodicals, etc. Bibliographical research collection, part of Modern Authors Collection. Other appearances 450 cataloged.

BC —UNIVERSITY OF VICTORIA, McPherson Library, Victoria, V8W 3H5, Can.
Notes: Novelist. Correspondence with Alfred Perles, William Woods, John Lehmann, Peter Russell, T Tambimuttii and others; corrected proof of *Balthazar*.

DUST, RADIOACTIVE see Radioactive Fallout

DUST BOWL

TX —NORTH TEXAS STATE UNIVERSITY, Archives, NT Station Box 5188, Denton, 76203. Robert LaForte, University Archivist
Notes: The NTSU Archives houses the patron's copy of oral history interviews that are part of the Oral History Collection, an independent project not part of the Archives. This collection of interviews covers, in part, the following subject areas: World War II

DUST BOWL (cont.)

Pearl Harbor survivors, World War II prisoners of war, Texas legislators, ex-governors of Texas, Texans employed by the administrations of FDR, Texas businessmen and businesswomen, development of the Coastal Bend area of south Texas, and Mexican-American social action activities. Cataloged. Transcriptions available. See *Oral History Collection,* North Texas State University Bulletin, April 1981.

DUST JACKETS see Book Jackets

DUST STORMS

TX —AMARILLO PUBLIC LIBRARY, 413 E Fourth, Amarillo, 79101. Mary Kay Snell, Librn
Notes: John L McCarty, newspaper editor, author, artist, and businessman in Amarillo and Dalhart, Texas. Papers incl 4030 notes, interviews, photographs unpublished theses, clippings, and historical editions. A wide variety of subjects incl buffalo hunting, Indian wars, cowboys and the open range, the arrival of the farmers, fences, and and towns. His work begins around the turn of the century and ranges through the depression years, the Dust Bowl, and soil and water conservation studies.

DUTCH EAST INDIA COMPANY

IN —INDIANA UNIVERSITY, Lilly Library, Seventh St, Bloomington, 47405. William R Cagle, Librn
Holdings: Vols (2000) // Cat
Notes: The core of the collection is the specialized library of Charles R Boxer (1000) dealing with the history of the Iberians in the East, 16th-18th century. Mainly incl works on China, Japan and the Phillipines during the period of their early intercourse with the West through 1800, as well as materials on the English and Dutch East India Companies, and the 17th century Anglo-Dutch naval wars. Special mention should be made of the valuable letters from missions by the Jesuits, and the works in this area by the Augustinians, Franciscans, and Dominicans, from the time of the arrival of the Iberians in Asia. The collection is a valuable source of information for the study of the European expansion into the area, including Southeast Asia.

DUTCH EAST INDIAN PERIODICALS see Periodicals, Dutch East Indian

DUTCH EAST INDIES see Indonesia

DUTCH IN THE U.S.

†IA —NORTHWESTERN COLLEGE LIBRARY, Orange City, 51041.
Notes: Materials pertaining to Dutch Americans.

†MI —CALVIN LIBRARY, Colonial Origins Collection, Burton St SE, Grand Rapids, 49506.
Notes: Collection of books, periodicals, audiovisual materials, mss and personal papers, photographs and oral history materials pertaining to early Dutch settlers.

NY —HOLLAND SOCIETY OF NEW YORK, Library, 122 E 58 St, New York, 10022. Linda Rolufs, Librn
Notes: Specializes in New Netherland (New York, New Jersey, Delaware) history during the Dutch period, materials on the Dutch Reformed Church, and Dutch-American family genealogy.

NY —NEW YORK HISTORICAL SOCIETY, Library, 170 Central Park W, New York, 10024. James Gregory, Librn
Holdings: Mss
Notes: Incl original mss, illustrative materials, etc.

PA —BALCH INSTITUTE FOR ETHNIC STUDIES, Library, 18 S Seventh St, Philadelphia, 19106. R Joseph Anderson, Library Dir
Holdings: Vols 140 Cat Mss

DUTCH LANGUAGE AND LITERATURE

CA —LOS ANGELES PUBLIC LIBRARY, Foreign Languages Dept, 630 W Fifth St, Los Angeles, 90071. Sylva Manoogian, Principal Librn
Holdings: Vols 1744 Cat
Budget: ($41,500)

MA —HARVARD UNIVERSITY LIBRARY, Widener Library, Cambridge, 02138.
Holdings: Cat
Notes: This was a Farmington Plan responsibility. See *Distributable Union* Catalog (Harvard).

MI —UNIVERSITY OF MICHIGAN, Graduate Library, Ann Arbor, 48109. Janet White, Reference Librn
Holdings: Cat
Notes: Incl a collection of more than 200 periodicals published in the Netherlands.

†MI —HERRICK PUBLIC LIBRARY, 300 River Ave, Holland, 49423.
Notes: A collection of Dutch language and literature books.

NY —NEW YORK PUBLIC LIBRARY, Donnell Foreign Language Library, 20 W 53 St, New York, 10019. Bosiljka Stevanovic, Supvr Librn
Holdings: Vols 480 Cat
Notes: Dutch collection incl Dutch authors of Dutch expression. No separate catalog.

OH —CLEVELAND PUBLIC LIBRARY, Foreign Literature Dept, 325 Superior Ave, Cleveland, 44114. Natalia Bezugloff, Head
Holdings: Vols 2320 Cat
Notes: A popular circulating collection containing classics and the standard works with emphasis on belles lettres, history and biography. A variety of other subjects such as learning languages, how to do books, art, children's books, spoken phonodiscs and cassettes, periodicals, etc. Incl 50 ephemera. *See also* entry under Foreign Language Collections

BC —GREATER VANCOUVER LIBRARY FEDERATION, 110-6545 Bonsor, Burnaby, Z5H 1H3, Can. Colleen Smith, Coordr
Holdings: Vols (20,350) Cat
Notes: Deposit provided by the National Library's Multilingual Biblioservice on long-term loan to libraries in the Greater Vancouver Library Federation (Burnaby, New Westminster, N Vancouver City Public, N Vancouver District Public, Port Moody, Vancouver, W Vancouver).

DUTCH MUSIC see Music, Dutch

DUTCH REFORMED CHURCH—HISTORY

NY —CORNELL UNIVERSITY LIBRARIES, Collection of Regional History, Dept of Manuscripts and Univ Archives, Ithaca, 14853.
Notes: Protestant Reformed Dutch Church of Ithaca. Minutes of the Sunday School Society, 1831-43; 1 vol. Tompkins County.

NY —HOLLAND SOCIETY OF NEW YORK, Library, 122 E 58 St, New York, 10022. Linda Rolufs, Librn
Holdings: Vols (6000) Cat Mss
Notes: New York history in the Dutch Period (New Netherlands); the Dutch Reformed Church; and Dutch-American family genealogy.

DUTCH WEST INDIES see West Indies

DUTIES see Taxation

DUTILLEUX, HENRI

DC —LIBRARY OF CONGRESS, Music Division, Washington, 20540.
Notes: Mss in Koussevitzky Archives.

DUVAL, CAPT. MILES

DC —GEORGETOWN UNIVERSITY, Library, Special Collections Div, 37 & O Sts NW, Washington, 20057. George M Barringer, Special Collections Librn; Nicholas B Sheetz, Mss Librn
Holdings: Cat Mss Pix
Notes: Panama Canal, and papers of Tomas Herran, Earl Harding, Thomas E Martin, William McCan, Clark Thompson, Leonor K Sullivan, and Capt Miles Duval.

DUXBURY PLANTATION

MA —BRIDGEWATER PUBLIC LIBRARY, 15 South St, Bridgewater, 02324. Maryellen Remmert, Dir
Holdings: Cat Mss Maps Pix
Notes: Incl some genealogical material of considerable interest since Bridgewater was the first inland colony of the Plymouth (Pilgrim) Colony, being known as the Duxbury Plantation.

DUYCHINCK, EVERT AUGUSTUS

NY —NEW YORK PUBLIC LIBRARY, Rare Books and Manuscripts Div, Fifth Ave & 42 St, New York, 10018. William L Joyce, Asst Dir; Susan E Davis, Cur of Mss
Holdings: Mss
Budget: ($7161)
Notes: Incl personal and literary mss, papers etc.

DWIGGINS, WILLIAM A.

CT —YALE UNIVERSITY, Box 1603A, Yale Station, New Haven, 06520.
Notes: Books, broadsides, posters, ephemera, etc.

IL —NORTHWESTERN UNIVERSITY, Library, Special Collections Dept, 1937 Sheridan Rd, Evanston, 60201. R Russell Maylone, Cur
Holdings: Vols (2000) Cat Mss
Notes: The John J Louis Memorial Collection. Incl drawings and layouts. Works dealing with the typographic arts and extensive collections of major typographers, especially Rogers, Dwiggins, Goudy, Clelland and Kittredge. Additional materials in general collections.

MA —HINGHAM PUBLIC LIBRARY, 66 Leavitt St, Hingham, 02043. Walter T Dziura, Dir
Holdings: Vols 150// Cat
Notes: Samples of his typographic work, etc.

NY —ROCHESTER INSTITUTE OF TECHNOLOGY, Melbert B Cary Jr Graphic Arts Collection, School of Printing, One Lomb Memorial Drive, Rochester, 14623. David Pankow, Cur
Holdings: Vols (11,000) Cat Mss Pix

DWIGHT, MABEL

MD —UNIVERSITY OF BALTIMORE, Langsdale Library, 1420 Maryland Ave, Baltimore, 21201. Gerry Watkins, Head of Special Collections Dept
Holdings: Vols Mss
Notes: Correspondence, mss, books, and material of the artist Mabel Seidenberg Dwight (1917-); 8 cubic feet.

DYEING see Dyes and Dyeing

DYES AND DYEING

MA —UNIVERSITY OF LOWELL, Library, One University Ave, Lowell, 01854. Martha Mayo, Special Collections Librn
Holdings: Vols 2500 Cat Mss Pix Slides
Notes: One of the most comprehensive collections of books and periodicals on all phases of the textile industry and fabrics; all fibers and processes, dyes and dyeing, strong in historical materials also. Approx 200 vols, mostly in French, on sericulture and silk.

MA —OLD STURBRIDGE VILLAGE, Research Library, Sturbridge, 01566. Theresa Rini Percy, Librn
Holdings: Cat Mss
Notes: Craft and industry in New England, to 1850.

NY —SOCIETY OF BATIK ARTISTS LIBRARY, 395 Riverside Dr, New York, 10025. Astrith Deyrup, Librn
Notes: Library dedicated to batik sources.

NY —EASTMAN KODAK COMPANY, Research Library, Research Laboratories,

DYES AND DYEING (cont.)

Bldg 83, Rochester, 14650. E W Kraus, Head
Holdings: Vols 600 Cat Microforms
Notes: Excludes textile dyeing and dyestuffs.

NC —PUBLIC LIBRARY OF CHARLOTTE & MECKLENBURG COUNTY, 310 N Tyron St, Charlotte, 28202. Mae S Tucker, Asst Dir
Holdings: Vols (3950) Cat Slides 16mm Films Filmstrips
Notes: Weaving, chemistry, dyes and dyeing, and color are emphasized. Also, hosiery, knitting, machinery, manufacturing, directories and statistics. Have specialized dictionaries in the subject field in both English and other languages. 110 periodical titles.

PA —FRANKLIN INSTITUTE LIBRARY, 20 & The Parkway, Philadelphia, 19103. Miriam Padusis, Dir; Charles Wilt, Readers Servs Librn
Holdings: Vols (300,000) Cat Maps Pix Microforms

DYING PATIENTS see Terminal Care Facilities

DYKES, JEFF

TX —TEXAS A&M UNIVERSITY, Sterling C Evans Library, Special Collections Div, College Station, 77843. Donald H Dyal, Librn
Holdings: Vols (16,000) Mss Pix
Notes: Jeff Dykes Range Livestock Collection (incl a 600-item collection of J Frank Dobie works). Part of the Dobie Collection is described in Dykes, Jeff C *My Dobie Collection* (College Station, Tex: Friends of the Texas A & M University Library).

DYKSTRA, CLARENCE ADDISON, 1883-1950

CA —UNIVERSITY OF CALIFORNIA, LOS ANGELES, Research Library, Dept of Special Collections, 405 Hilgard Ave, Los Angeles, 90024. Edward Shreeves, Chairman, Bibliographers Group; David S Zeidberg, Head
Holdings: Cat Mss
Notes: 39 linear feet of unprocessed mss and correspondence.

DYNAMIC TENSIONS see Tensions, Static and Dynamic

DYNAMICS

†CA —CALIFORNIA INSTITUTE OF TECHNOLOGY, Robert A Millikan Memorial Library, Archives, 1201 E California Blvd, Pasadena, 91125.
Notes: Geophysicist Charles Richter's lecture notes and oral history interview. Incl notes from courses at Caltech taught by physicist Paul Epstein (1883-1966), such as higher dynamics, 1925; thermodynamics, 1925/26; quantum theory, 1926-28, 1940.

MA —UNIVERSITY OF MASSACHUSETTS AT AMHERST, Library, Amherst, 01002.
Notes: Strong collections in physcial education, sports studies, exercise, gymnastics, etc.

PA —FRANKLIN INSTITUTE LIBRARY, 20 & The Parkway, Philadelphia, 19103. Miriam Padusis, Dir; Charles Wilt, Readers Servs Librn
Holdings: Vols (300,000) Cat Maps Pix Microforms

PA —PENNSYLVANIA STATE UNIVERSITY, Fred Lewis Pattee Library, University Park, 16802.
Notes: Numerous and large collections on many sports. Also, materials supporting every aspect of the program of the Center for Women and Sport, incl research into kinetics, endocrinology, physiology, psychology, etc.

ON —SIRLS, Faculty of Human Kinetics & Leisure Studies, University of Waterloo, Waterloo, N2L 3G1, Can. Betty Smith, Database Mgr
Notes: Information Retrieval System for the Sociology of Leisure and Sport (SIRLS) is a computerized online database of about 13, 000 entries (1983). Incl dance as a leisure time activity.

DYNAMICS, CHEMICAL

CA —INTERNATIONAL BUSINESS MACHINES RESEARCH LIBRARY, 5600 Cottle Rd, San Jose, 95193. Phil Grincewich, Mgr Technical Information
Holdings: Vols (13,500) Cat
Notes: Collection includes emphasis on laser spectroscopy, organic photomaterial and chemical dynamics. Incl 21,000 vols of 770 journals. On-line search facility. Vols are divided into three libraries, Technical Research, Technical Information, and Programing. Not open to public.

DYSLEXIA

CA —MENLO PARK LIBRARY, Civic Center, 800 Alma, Menlo Park, 94025. Karen Fredrickson, Librn
Holdings: Vols 100 Cat
Notes: The Armstrong Collection on Dyslexia. Dyslexia and related learning disabilities.

ME —LEARNING INC, Library, Learning Place, Manset, 04656. A L Welles, Librn; E R Welles, Cur
Holdings: Vols (2000) Uncat Mss
Notes: Materials that will help people understand the various learning handicaps and some of the remedial methods for overcoming them. Anyone wishing to visit the collection telephone (207) 244-5015 to make arrangements.

NY —COLUMBIA UNIVERSITY LIBRARIES, Health Sciences Library, 701 W 168 St, New York, 10032. Rachael K Goldstein, Librn
Holdings: Microforms
Notes: Ca 3000 fiche. Incl the June Lyday and Samuel T Orton collection of patient records dating from 1928-77. Photocopying limited. Restricted.

NY —MORRIS N & CHESLEY V YOUNG LIBRARY OF MNEMONICS, 270 Riverside Dr, New York, 10025. Morris N Young, Cur
Holdings: Cat Mss Maps Pix Phonorecords Audiotapes 16mm Films Microforms
Notes: Collection of 5000 books, pamphlets, pictures, memorabilia, etc incl medieval art of memory; psychology of memory, forgetting and reading; medical aspects of memory, amnesia, dyslexia; biomedical aspects of learning and memory; information storage, retrieval and cybernetics; memory prodigies, lightning calculators, calendars; remembrance cups and memory mementos. All languages. Memorabilia incl engravings, posters, programs, advertisements, birthday cards, teaching cards, ASLs, and Mark Twain's Memory Builder game and other games. Items range from 1410 to 1980s.

NY —STATE UNIVERSITY OF NEW YORK, State College of Optometry, Harold Kohn Vision Science Library, 100 E 24 St, New York, 10010. Margaret S Lewis, Librn
Holdings: Vols (23,000) Cat Audiotapes Microforms
Notes: All subjects related to visual disabilities; much on vision disorders among children.

PQ —HOPITAL SAINTE-JUSTINE POUR LES ENFANTS, Centre d'Information sur la Sante de l'Enfant, 3175 Cote Sainte-Catherine, Montreal, H3T 1C5, Can. Louis LucLecompte, Librn
Holdings: Vols (7000) Cat Audiotapes Videotapes 16mm Films Microforms
Budget: ($11,000)
Notes: 40 percent of collection in French.

E

E. C. W. PRESS

AB —UNIVERSITY OF CALGARY, Libraries, Special Collections Div, 2500 University Dr, Calgary, T2N 1N4, Can.
Notes: Mss (12 meters), incl correspondence, financial records and production materials for publications of the press, incl the periodical *Essays on Canadian Writing,* 1974-81.
See also entry under Periodicals, Canadian.

EADS BRIDGE, ST. LOUIS, MO.

MO —WASHINGTON UNIVERSITY, Libraries, Special Collections Dept, Campus Box 1061, St Louis, 63130.
Notes: Terminal Railroad Association Records (1889-date), of more than 450 original tracings of the Eads Bridge (1874-date). Drawings show in fine and complete detail all the design features of this internationally known St Louis landmark.

EAMES, CHARLES, 1907-1978

DC —LIBRARY OF CONGRESS, Washington, 20540.
Notes: Papers and working materials of Charles Eames (1907-1978), American architect and designer. Incl are original negatives and prints of the 106 educational films he created, business correspondence 1944 to 1978, some 400,000 color slides, 31, 000 black and white photographs, production materials for exhibits, and drawings for all his major furniture designs. Acquired on a grant of $500,000 from IBM.

EAR—DISEASES

MO —WASHINGTON UNIVERSITY, School of Medicine, Library, 660 South Euclid Ave, Saint Louis, 63110. Christopher Hoolihan, Rare Book Librn
Holdings: Vols 850 Cat
Budget: ($40,000)
Notes: The CID-Max Goldstein Collection in Speech and Hearing. Incl printed books from the 16th through 19th centuries on deafness, deaf education, ear diseases, hearing, speech and speech disorders.

NY —COLUMBIA UNIVERSITY LIBRARIES, Rare Book & Manuscript Library, 801 Butler Library, 535 W 114 St, New York, 10027. Kenneth A Lohf, Librn
Holdings: Mss
Notes: Nearly 6000 letters, notes and mss relating to Cornelius Rea Agnew, professor of diseases of the eye and ear in Columbia's College of Physicians and Surgeons, and a founder of the Manhattan Eye and Ear Hospital. Much of the material relates to the treatment of eye diseases during the latter half of the 19th century. Restricted use.

EARHART, AMELIA, 1897-1937

IN —PURDUE UNIVERSITY LIBRARIES, Special Collections Dept, West Lafayette, 47907. Keith Dowden, Asst Dir, Special Collections
Holdings: Mss Maps Pix
Notes: Amelia Earhart Collection. Incl charts, maps, medals, certificates, letters and telegrams and other memorabilia.

MA —RADCLIFFE COLLEGE, Arthur & Elizabeth Schlesinger Library on the History of Women in America, 3 James St, Cambridge, 02138. Patricia Miller King, Dir; Eva Moseley, Cur of Mss
Holdings: // Cat Mss Pix
Notes: Correspondence and photographs of and about the aviator and her family. Inventory published by G K Hall; see Hamilton Family for citation.

EARHART, AMY OTIS

MA —RADCLIFFE COLLEGE, Arthur & Elizabeth Schlesinger Library on the History of Women in America, 3 James St, Cambridge, 02138. Patricia Miller King, Dir; Eva Moseley, Cur of Mss
Notes: Correspondence and photographs of and about the aviator Amelia Earhart (1897-1937). Also, papers of her mother, Amy Otis Earhart, including letters from Amelia Earhart and other aviators.

EARL OF SHELBURNE

MI —UNIVERSITY OF MICHIGAN, William L Clements Library, Ann Arbor, 48109. John C Dann, Dir
Notes: The William L. Clements Library of Americana is a non-circulating rare book library of original source material, printed and manuscript, dealing with America, from the discovery period into the late nineteenth century. The collection includes approximately 55,000 books and pamphlets, 550 linear feet of manuscripts, 4,100 volumes of newspapers, 36,000 maps, 40,000 pieces of sheet music, and 1,000 prints. The collection is strongest for the period of the American Revolution, and includes the papers of Thomas Gage, Sir Henry Clinton, and the Earl of Shelburne. Other areas of strength include antislavery, cartography and geography, discovery and exploration, American Indians, The Civil War, tune-books, sermons and orations, and the War of 1812. There are selective research collections dealing with Christopher Columbus, Thomas Paine, Benjamin Franklin, George Washington, Thomas Jefferson, and the Federalist Papers. Publications describing the collections of the library are: Author/Title catalog of Americana 1493-1860 in the William L. Clements Library... 7 volumes, Boston, G. K. Hall, 1970; Guide to the manuscript collections of the William L. Clements Library, by Arlene P. Shy 3d edition, Boston, G. K. Hall, 1978; Guide to the manuscript maps in the William L. Clements Library, compiled by Christian Burn, Ann Arbor, U. of Michigan, 1959; and Research catalog of maps of America, to 1860 in the William L. Clements Library...,edited by Douglas W. Marshall, 4 volumes, Boston, G. K. Hall, 1972.

EARLY, JUBAL A.

VA —UNIVERSITY OF VIRGINIA, Alderman Library, Manuscripts Dept, Charlottesville, 22901. Edmund Berkeley Jr, Cur
Holdings: Cat Mss Maps Pix
Notes: About 1500 collections have material pertaining to the Civil War and particularly to the Army of Northern Virginia and campaigns and battles in Virginia. There are letters, diaries, reminiscences, maps, and pictorial material of Confederate soldiers and civilians, as well as papers of Robert E Lee, J E B Stuart, Thomas L Rosser, Jubal A Early, John Daniel Imboden, William "Extra Billy" Smith, Henry Alexander Wise, Eppa Hunton, and John S Mosby.

EARLY BIRDS

CA —SAN DIEGO AERO-SPACE MUSEUM, N Paul Whittier Historical Aviation Library, 2001 Pan American Plaza, Balboa Park, San Diego, 92101. B C Reynolds, Archivist
Holdings: // Uncat Microforms

EARLY CHRISTIAN LITERATURE see Christian Literature, Early

EARLY MAN see Fossil Man

EARLY MEDICAL PERIODICALS see Periodicals, Medical

EARLY MUSIC see Music, Early

EARLY PRINTED BOOKS see Incunabula

EARTH

DC —LIBRARY OF CONGRESS, Geography and Map Division, Washington, 20540. John A Wolter, Chief

DC —SMITHSONIAN INSTITUTION LIBRARIES, National Air & Space Museum Branch, NASM Bldg, Sixth & Independence Ave SW, Washington, 20560. Frank A Pietropaoli, Branch Chief
Holdings: Vols (39,000) Cat Mss Maps Pix Slides Microforms
Notes: History of flight and aerospace development, incl biographical material on aviation pioneers, balloons and ballooning. Extensive photographic collection (600,000 pictures). Incl the Sherman Fairchild Collection of aeronautical photographs (transferred from the American Institute of Aeronautics and Astronautics). Also incl the Bella Landauer Aeronautical Sheet Music Collection (1500 pieces). 2000 films; 800,000 microforms; 9000 volumes bound.

PA —BUHL PLANETARIUM & INSTITUTE OF POPULAR SCIENCE, Staff Library, Allegheny Sq, Pittsburgh, 15212. Al DeSena, Dir
Holdings: Vols 1000 Cat Mss Maps Pix Slides Films
Notes: Science-oriented vols with several texts of historical value dating back to the 19th century.

EARTH—MAGNETISM see Magnetism, Terrestrial

EARTH HOUSES

NE —KEARNEY STATE COLLEGE, Calvin T Ryan Library, Kearney, 68847. John Mayeski, Dir; Anita Norman, Reference Librn
Holdings: Vols (1700) Cat Mss Maps Pix Slides Microforms
Notes: Collection attempts to cover total historical development of Nebraska. Special strengths incl overland journeys, pony express, sod houses, and the Union Pacific. Special consideration has been given to Indians of Nebraska and the cattle industry. The collection is well supported by the library's general strength of Western Americana.

EARTH-MOVING MACHINERY see Earthmoving Machinery

EARTH SATELLITES see Artificial Satellites

EARTH SCIENCES

CA —UNIVERSITY OF CALIFORNIA, SAN DIEGO, Scripps Institution of Oceanography Library, Mail Code C075C, La Jolla, 92093. William J Goff, Librn; Deborah Day, Archivist
Holdings: Vols (178,000) Cat Maps Microforms
Budget: ($308,200)
Notes: See *Catalogs of the Scripps Institution of Oceanography Library* (Boston: G K Hall, 1970-1980), 21 vols. Incl 44,000 maps, 17,000 microforms cat, 21,000 reprints, and 800 linear feet of archives.

CA —CALIFORNIA STATE UNIVERSITY, LONG BEACH, Library, Dept of Special

EARTH SCIENCES (cont.)

Collections & Archives, 1250 Bellflower Blvd, Long Beach, 90840. John Ahouse, Special Collections Librn
Holdings: Mss Maps Pix
Notes: Incl the personal files of Darrell Neighbors and Jan Law.

CA —UNIVERSITY OF CALIFORNIA, LOS ANGELES, Geology-Geophysics Library, 4697 Geology Bldg, Los Angeles, 90024. Sarah E How, Geology-Geophysics Librn
Holdings: Vols (85,000) Cat Maps Microforms
Notes: Incl theses and dissertations of UCLA Dept of Earth and Space Sciences; and (2000) serial titles.

CA —STANFORD UNIVERSITY, School of Earth Sciences, Branner Earth Sciences Library, Stanford, 94305. Charlotte Derksen, Head Librn
Holdings: Vols (70,000) Cat Maps
Notes: Incl 80,000 maps. Formerly the Branner Geological Library.

CO —COLORADO SCHOOL OF MINES, Arthur Lakes Library, 14 & Illinois Sts, Golden, 80401. Hartley K Phinney, Jr, Head Librn
Holdings: Vols (270,557) Cat Mss Maps Microforms
Notes: Incl 118,000 maps.

CO —US GEOLOGICAL SURVEY LIBRARY, Denver Library, MS 914 Box 25046, Denver Federal Center, Lakewood, 80225. Robert A Bier, Jr, Librn; Majorie E Dalechek, Photographic Librn; Deborah Rowen, Field Records Librn
Holdings: Vols 230,000 Cat Maps Pix Slides Microforms
Notes: Main Geological Survey Library is in Reston, Virginia. US Geological Library in Denver has 74,000 maps and mss field notes in addition to its other holdings. The Photographic Library has 250,000 slides and photos. The Field Records Library has 15, 000 notebooks, 2,000 folders, 2,400 maps groups and 60,000 aerial photos which are cataloged.

IL —UNIVERSITY OF ILLINOIS, URBANA/CHAMPAIGN, Library, Geology Library, 223 Natural History Bldg, Urbana, 61801. Dederick Ward, Librn
Holdings: Vols (105,186) Cat Maps Microforms

IN —PURDUE UNIVERSITY LIBRARIES, Geosciences Library, West Lafayette, 47907. Carolyn Lassoon, Librn
Holdings: Vols (15,000) Cat
Notes: Geosciences.

KS —UNIVERSITY OF KANSAS, Science Library, 6040 Malott Hall, Lawrence, 66045. Sharon R Cook, Asst Science Librn
Holdings: Vols Cat Maps Microforms
Notes: Incl US Geological Survey topographical maps.

KY —UNIVERSITY OF KENTUCKY, Geology Library, 100 Bowman Hall, Lexington, 40506. Vivian S Hall, Librn
Holdings: Vols (40,000) Cat Maps Microforms
Budget: ($30,000)
Notes: Incl comprehensive collection of maps on Kentucky; 98,900 maps in all. Also, 170 journal titles, 5000 microfiche titles.

MD —NATIONAL OCEANIC & ATMOSPHERIC ADMINISTRATION, Library & Information Sciences Division, Central Library & Information Sciences Bldg, 6009 Executive Blvd, Rockville, 20852. Elizabeth J Yeates, Chief
Holdings: Vols (175,000) Cat Microforms

MA —HARVARD UNIVERSITY LIBRARY, Geological Sciences Library, 24 Oxford St, Cambridge, 02138. Constance Wick, Librn
Holdings: Vols (51,000) Cat Mss Maps Pix 16mm Films Microforms
Notes: The Geological Sciences Library supports the research efforts of faculty, graduate students, and upper-level undergraduate and graduate instruction in the geological sciences. Subjects collected deal with the earth sciences in general, mineralogy, petrology, geochemistry, geophysics, crystallography, structural geology, regional geology, economic geology, some geomorphology, and some gemology. The collection incl 850 serial publications and 15,000 maps.

MA —SMITHSONIAN INSTITUTION LIBRARIES, Astrophysical Observatory Branch, 60 Garden St, Cambridge, 02138. Joyce Rey, Librn
Holdings: Vols (10,000) Cat Maps Pix Microforms

MA —BOSTON COLLEGE LIBRARIES, Catherine B O'Connor Geophysics Library, Weston Observatory, Weston, 02193. F Clifford McElroy, Science Librn
Holdings: Vols (10,231) Cat Maps Microforms
Budget: ($10,000)
Notes: This collection is being absorbed into the general collection.

MO —WASHINGTON UNIVERSITY, Earth and Planetary Sciences Library, Forsythe & Skinker Blvds, Saint Louis, 63130. Deborah Hartwig, Librn
Holdings: Vols (25,335) Cat Maps Pix Microforms
Notes: 10,931 unbound publications, technical reports.

NM —UNIVERSITY OF CALIFORNIA, Los Alamos National Laboratory, Libraries, PO Box 1663, MSP 362, Los Alamos, 87545. J Arthur Freed, Head Librn
Holdings: Vols (800,000) Cat Films Microforms
Budget: ($700,000)
Notes: Incl 500,000 classified and unclassified reports. There are 25 branch libraries and a central collection. The Medical Library contains about 40,000 vols in the areas of biomedical research.

NY —AMERICAN MUSEUM OF NATURAL HISTORY, Library Services Dept, Central Park W & 79th St, New York, 10024. Nina J Root, Chairwoman; Mary Genett, Asst Librn for Reference Services
Holdings: Vols (385,000) Cat Mss Maps Pix Slides Microforms
Notes: Nearly all collections are outstanding for depth of coverage and international range. Early and historic works, rare books, colored illustrations, and relevant serial publications supplement the modern scientific publications necessary to the researches of the scientific staff and the work of the educational division. Open to the public.

NC —UNIVERSITY OF NORTH CAROLINA, CHAPEL HILL, Geology Library, Mitchell Hall 029A, Chapel Hill, 27514. Miriam L Sheaves, Librn
Holdings: Vols (41,000) Cat Maps
Notes: Earth sciences, paleontology, oceanography, geology, geophysics. Incl theses and dissertations; 103,000 map sheets.

OH —UNIVERSITY OF CINCINNATI, Geology-Geography Library, 103 Old Tech Bldg ML 13, Cincinnati, 45221. Richard Spohn, Sr Library Assoc
Holdings: Vols (35,000) Cat Maps
Budget: ($30,000)
Notes: Collection covers the broad range of geoscience topics, incl a geologic field trip guidebook collection of almost 1400 volumes.

PA —CARNEGIE LIBRARY OF PITTSBURGH, Science & Technology Dept, 4400 Forbes Ave, Pittsburgh, 15213. Catherine M Brosky, Dept Head
Holdings: Vols (380,000) Cat Maps Microforms
Budget: ($240,000)
Notes: Geology, mineralogy, crystallography, petrology, etc. Handbooks, monographs, serials, periodicals, maps. State and US Geological survey materials.

TX —TEXAS STATE LIBRARY, Archives Div, 1201 Brazos, PO Box 12927, Capitol Sta, Austin, 78711. David B Gracy II, State Archivist

TX —UNIVERSITY OF TEXAS LIBRARIES, General Libraries, Geology Dept, PO Box P, Austin, 78712. Chestalene Pintozzi, Librn
Holdings: Vols (59,349) Cat Maps Microforms

TX —SOUTHERN METHODIST UNIVERSITY, Fondren Library, Dallas, 75275. Curt Holleman, Librn for Collection Development

TX —UNIVERSITY OF TEXAS, EL PASO, Library, El Paso, 79968. Fred W Hanes, Dir
Holdings: Vols (433,245) Cat Maps Microforms
Budget: ($550,667)
Notes: Selective depository for US and Texas state documents. Complete files of US Geological Survey & Bureau of Mines publications. USGS topographic maps & aerial photo maps. Also many state & regional geological societies' publications. Strong on Southwest.

TX —FORT WORTH PUBLIC LIBRARY, 300 Taylor St, Fort Worth, 76102. John R McCracken, Manager
Holdings: Vols (11,000)
Budget: ($21,000)

TX —ECTOR COUNTY LIBRARY, Department of Business and Technology, 321 W 5th St, Odessa, 79760. Pat Jones, Dept Head
Holdings: Vols 1000 Cat
Notes: Incl 50 vertical files, 20 periodicals, 250 Trade Specifications and Standards, 300 maps and charts, 2 manuscripts.

WY —NATRONA COUNTY PUBLIC LIBRARY, 307 E Second St, Casper, 82601. Kathleen Nowak, Earth Sciences/Reference Librn
Holdings: Vols (3000) Cat Maps
Notes: The earth sciences collection consists of technical literature published in energy-related fields. A map collection of topographic and geologic maps of Wyoming is maintained. State geological survey documents for the states surrounding Wyoming are collected. Also some thirty periodicals in the earth sciences.

AB —ALBERTA OIL SANDS INFORMATION CENTRE, 6th Floor, Highfield Place, 10010-106 St, Edmonton, T5J 3L8, Can. Helga Radvanyi, Mgr
Notes: "Major activity of the Centre has been preparation of the Alberta Oil Sands Index. However...scope has broadened to include the Heavy Oil/Enhanced Recovery Index," and other informative literature.

MB —UNIVERSITY OF MANITOBA, Science Library, Machray Hall, Winnipeg, R3T 2N2, Can. V Simosko, Head
Holdings: Vols (90,000) Cat Microforms

ON —GEOLOGICAL SURVEY OF CANADA, Library, Dept of Energy, Mines, & Resouces, 601 Booth St, Ottawa, K1A 0E8, Can. Annette E Bourgeois, Librn
Holdings: Vols (300,000) Cat Mss Maps Microforms
Notes: All aspects of Geology are collected and an attempt is made to collect all Canadian geology information. The library is a national resource collection in the geosciences. Incl 40,000 book titles (monographs), 4000 personals, 35,000 microfiche, 300,000 maps, 2000 translations of reports, 20 verrtical files, 300,000 vols of bound periodicals.

EARTH SCIENCES PERIODICALS see Periodicals, Earth Sciences

EARTHENWARE see Pottery

EARTHMOVING MACHINERY

AL —US DEPT OF AGRICULTURE, SCIENCE & EDUCATION ADMINISTRATION, National Tillage Machinery Laboratory, Library, PO Box 792, Auburn, 36830. William A Gill, Collaborator
Holdings: Vols (39,000) Cat Mss Maps Pix Slides 16mm Films Microforms
Budget: ($20,000)
Notes: The National Tillage Machinery Laboratory (NTML) has a special technical library comprised of highly selective engineering and physical science materials pertinent to soil-machine relations, such as tillage, earthmoving, mining, soil trafficability, and vehicle mobility. A high percentage of the library material comes from sources outside the US and outside agriculture. Particularly strong in Russian-language literature.

CA —UNIVERSITY OF CALIFORNIA, DAVIS, Shields Library, Dept of Special

EARTHMOVING MACHINERY (cont.)

Collections, Davis, 95616. Donald Kunitz, Head; C Danial Elliott, Asst Head
Notes: Manufacturers' catalogs, manuals, part lists, photos, ephemera pertaining to historical and current data on tractors, engines, combines, hay equipment, etc.

NC —WILSON COUNTY TECHNICAL INSTITUTE, Library, 902 Herring Ave, PO Box 4305, Wilson, 27893. Shirley Gregory, Librn
Holdings: Vols (150) Cat Slides Phonorecords Audiotapes 16mm Films Filmstrips
Notes: Emphasis on operation, maintenance, and safety for operators of earthmoving equipment and cranes. Incl 50 operator's manuals and 80 audiovisual programs.

EARTHQUAKE SEA WAVES see Tsunamis

EARTHQUAKES

CA —LONG BEACH PUBLIC LIBRARY, 101 Pacific Ave, Long Beach, 90802. Douglas Kermode, Librn
Holdings: Vols (700) Cat Mss Maps Pix
Notes: Records the development of Long Beach from its beginnings as a city (ca 1887). Picture file (ca 3400) and negative collection from local Winstead Bros, Photographers (ca 10,000).

CA —CALIFORNIA INSTITUTE OF TECHNOLOGY, Robert A Millikan Memorial Library, Archives, 1201 E California Blvd, Pasadena, 91125. Judith R Goodstein, Archivist
Notes: A *Guide* to the Seismology Microfiche Collection Publications is available. Incl *Bulletin of the CIT Seismological Laboratory; Provisional* Readings at Pasadena (1966-74), *Airletters* (1974-79); *Station Clock Corrections; International Seismological Summary*, 1918-42; Gutenberg-Richter Notepads, 1904-1958.

CA —POMONA PUBLIC LIBRARY, Special Collections, 625 S Garey Ave, PO Box 2271, Pomona, 91766. David Streeter, Librn
Holdings: Cat Mss Maps
Notes: Some 4000 maps. Strong for Pomona Valley area: tract maps, water company maps; depository for USGS California topographic maps; California earthquake fault maps.

CA —EARTHQUAKE ENGINEERING RESEARCH CENTER, Library, 1301 S 46th St, Richmond, 94804. Joy Svihra, Librn; Helen Tseng, Asst Librn
Holdings: Vols (20,000) Cat Maps Pix Slides 16mm Films Microforms
Notes: Unique collection on earthquake engineering is enriched by foreign documents received on an exchange basis that are generally not available elsewhere in the US. A major part of the collection circulates. Accessed through dictionary catalog and the *Abstract Journal in Earthquake Engineering.* A printed catalog was published in May, 1975 as EERC Report 75-12, listing holdings through 1974. New holdings are listed in *EERRC News* (quarterly) and the Library's *Acquisitions* Alert (bimonthly).

CA —SOCIETY OF CALIFORNIA PIONEERS, Library, 456 McAllister St, San Francisco, 94102. Grace E Baker, Librn
Holdings: Vols (12,000) Cat Mss Maps Pix Microforms
Notes: California history, especially the gold rush and the San Francisco earthquake, Sherman collection of early California music, business letterheads of early California firms, San Francisco City Directories 1850-1944, records of California Battalion 1846-47, ms material on overland diaries, ships' logs and passenger lists. Also, large photograph collection.

MA —BOSTON COLLEGE LIBRARIES, Catherine B O'Connor Geophysics Library, Weston Observatory, Weston, 02193. F Clifford McElroy, Science Librn
Holdings: Vols (10,231) Cat Maps Microforms
Budget: ($10,000)
Notes: This collection is being absorbed into the general collection.

MS —US ARMY ENGINEER WATERWAYS EXPERIMENT STATION, Library Branch, PO Box 631, Vicksburg, 39180. Bernice Black, Chief Librn
Holdings: Vols (350,000) Cat Mss Maps Microforms

NY —AMERICAN MUSEUM OF NATURAL HISTORY, Library Services Dept, Central Park W & 79th St, New York, 10024. Nina J Root, Chairwoman; Mary Genett, Asst Librn for Reference Services
Notes: Especially strong in periodical literature.

NY —COLUMBIA UNIVERSITY LIBRARIES, Geoscience Library, Lamont-Doherty Geological Observatory, Palisades, 10964. Susan Klimley, Librn
Holdings: Vols (20,000) Cat
Notes: Geosciences, incl geochemistry, marine geology, seismology and paleoclimatology.

RI —BROWN UNIVERSITY, John Carter Brown Library, Providence, 02912. Norman Fiering, Librn; Everett C Wilkie Jr, Bibliographer; Susan Danforth, Cur Maps & Prints
Holdings: Vols 150
Notes: Covers earthquakes in the New World through 1835.

SC —COLLEGE OF CHARLESTON LIBRARY, Special Collections Dept, Charleston, 29401.
Notes: Papers record numerous scientific and technological studies covering a wide range of areas, particularly astronomical observations (often accompanied by drawings or photos) made in Charleston in the 1880s, at times in consultation with Lewis Reeve Gibbes. An inventor of scientific instruments, Fisher's work incl a "Machine for Ruling Diffraction Plates" for which a detailed description and photograph are provided. Incl in-depth record of Fisher's experiences, scientific and personal, of the 1886 Earthquake, accompanied by diagrams.

ON —ENERGY, MINES & RESOURCES CANADA, Earth Physics Branch Library, Ottawa, K1A 0Y3, Can. W M Tsang, Chief Librn
Holdings: Vols (6000) Cat Maps Pix Slides Microforms
Notes: Incl an extensive collection of references called Seismological Pamphlet File incl reprints, private reports, seismograms, etc, all cataloged separately and being added to continuously.

EARTHQUAKES AND BUILDINGS

CA —UNIVERSITY OF CALIFORNIA, BERKELEY, Environmental Design Library, (The General Library), 210 Wurster Hall, Berkeley, 94720. Arthur B Waugh, Head
Holdings: Vols (90,000) Cat Pix Microforms
Budget: ($17,400)
Notes: A research collection devoted to the following aspects of the field of architecture: working details, drawing, theory, standards and professional practice; building materials, building types, earthquake resistant architecture, contemporary architecture of all countries, history of architecture, and architecture as a profession. A small rare book collection in the field of architecture is maintained. Approximately 1500 serials, incl many foreign-language titles, are currently being received. A collection of photographs (of buildings) and a slide collection are administered by the department of architecture.

CA —ASSOCIATION OF BAY AREA GOVERNMENTS, MTC/ABAG Library, 101 Eighth St, Oakland, 94607. Diane Gillman, Information Coord
Notes: Concentrates heavily on the nine-county Bay Area region. About 10,000 monographs and serials. Title catalog, OCLC/ATS. Central collection of documents for six transit properties in Bay Area. Incl material on hazardous geographic environments.

CA —EARTHQUAKE ENGINEERING RESEARCH CENTER, Library, 1301 S 46th St, Richmond, 94804. Joy Svihra, Librn; Helen Tseng, Asst Librn
Holdings: Vols (20,000) Cat Maps Pix Slides 16mm Films Microforms
Notes: Unique collection on earthquake engineering is enriched by foreign documents received on an exchange basis that are generally not available elsewhere in the US. A major part of the collection circulates. Accessed through dictionary catalog and the *Abstract Journal in Earthquake Engineering.* A printed catalog was published in May, 1975 as EERC Report 75-12, listing holdings through 1974. New holdings are listed in *EERRC News* (quarterly) and the Library's *Acquisitions* Alert (bimonthly).

MA —MASSACHUSETTS INSTITUTE OF TECHNOLOGY, Institute Archives, Special Collections, Cambridge, 02139.
Notes: Papers of John Ripley Freeman, a hydraulic engineer, President of Associated Factory Mutual Fire Insurance Companies, and a consulting engineer. Collection primarily documents his activities as a consultant on hydraulics projects in the United States, Canada, China, Columbia, Mexico and Panama. Also, his work on the hydraulics of fire prevention, safety precautions for theaters, and seismology; his promotion of the National Hydraulics Laboratory and of European engineering practices; his involvement with the Engineering Foundation, the National Bureau of Standards, and the National Research Council; and his investments in mining, manufacturing, and land speculation. Unpublished finding aid available in Archives.

EARTHS, RARE

IA —IOWA STATE UNIVERSITY, Library, Ames, 50011. Warren B Kuhn, Dean of Library Services
Holdings: Cat
Notes: Specific strengths: physical metallurgy and solid state physics of the rare-earth metals and alloys.

EASEY, WALTER E.

LA —NEW ORLEANS PUBLIC LIBRARY, Louisiana Div & City Archives Dept, Louisiana History Collection, 219 Loyola Ave, New Orleans, 70140. Collin B Hamer Jr, Head
Notes: Private mss collection covers the period 1795-date, incl the following separate collections: James H Dakin (architect, ca 1834-47, 217 items); Walter E Easey (engineer, 1907-79, 22 cubic feet); McDonough & Payne (merchants, 1801-04, 200 items); ERA Club (women's group, 1914-19, 2 items); Neville Levy (civic leader, ca 1891-1963, 1 cubic foot & 11 vols); and Robert Tallant (author, 1945-57, 3 cubic feet & 10 vols). 92 vols scrapbooks; 100 mss vols, 55 cubic feet.

EAST (FAR EAST)

CA —UNIVERSITY OF CALIFORNIA, BERKELEY, University Library, East Asiatic Library, Room 208, Durant Hall, Berkeley, 94720. Donald Shively, Head
Holdings: Vols (500,000) Cat Mss Maps Pix Microforms
Notes: Library materials are mainly on humanities and social sciences covering the ancient and the modern periods and selectively in natural sciences; substantial in various fields but particularly notable in literary works, fine arts, rare books, folklore, wood-block printed editions, Chinese stone rubbings, Japanese old maps, first editions of Meiji literature, Buddhist texts, and Tibetan xylographs. Estimated 160,000 vols in Chinese, 150,000 vols in Japanese, 14,000 vols in Korean, the remainder in Manchu, Mongol or Tibetan.

CA —HOOVER INSTITUTION ON WAR, REVOLUTION & PEACE, Stanford University, Stanford, 94305. Milorad M Drachkovitch, Archivist
Notes: Four collections: (1) Papers of Julean Herbert Arnold, 1905-1946, incl diary, correspondence, speeches and writings, reports, dispatches, instructions, memoranda,

EAST (FAR EAST) (cont.)

and other material relating to Arnold's service in the US Consular Service in China and as US Commercial Attache in China, to economic and political developments in China, and to American commercial and foreign policy interests in the Far East. 14 ms boxes. (2) Collection of correspondence, reports, memoranda, study papers, press releases, printed matter and photographs, 1925-1960, relating to the study of political, social and economic conditions in the Far East and of US foreign policy in the Far East by the American Council of the Institute of Pacific Relations, collected by Ray Lyman Wilbur. 21 ms boxes, 1 album, 1 envelope. (3) Papers of Ernest B Price, 1914-1950, inclcorrespondence, diary, dispatches, manuscripts, lecture material, photographs, and printed matter relating to Japanese military intervention in China and Manchuria, 1931-1945; political and economic development in China, 1914-1929; and E B Price's career in the US Foreign Service in China, 1914-1929, in business, and in education. 13 ms boxes. (4) The Herman Axelbank Film Collection on Russian history. Much footage dating from about 1901-21. Subjects incl Royal Family, Moscow and St Petersburg scenes, the Revolution and Civil War, espec good coverage of Leon Trotsky's role, Siberia, and the Far East. The first 28 of 266 reels have been recieved (Ap 1983).

CT —TRINITY COLLEGE LIBRARY, 300 Summit St, Hartford, 06106. Ralph S Emerick, Librn
Holdings: Cat
Notes: Incl Moore Collection.

DC —FREER GALLERY OF ART, Library, 12th & Jefferson Dr SW, Washington, 20560. Ellen A Nollman, Librn

IN —INDIANA UNIVERSITY, Lilly Library, Seventh St, Bloomington, 47405. William R Cagle, Librn
Holdings: Vols (2000) // Cat
Notes: The core of the collection is the specialized library of Charles R Boxer (1000 titles) dealing with the history of the Iberians in the East, 16th-18th century. Mainly incl works on China, Japan and the Philippines during the period of their early intercourse with the West through 1800, as well as materials on the English and Dutch East India Companies, and the 17th century Anglo-Dutch naval wars. Special mention should be made of the valuable letters from missions by the Jesuits, and the works in this area by the Augustinians, Franciscans, and Dominicans, from the time of the arrival of the Iberians in Asia. The collection is a valuable source of information for the study of the European expansion into the sea, including Southeast Asia.

IN —EARLHAM COLLEGE, Lilly Library, Richmond, 47374. Evan Ira Farber, Librn
Holdings: Vols (7000) Cat Slides Phonorecords Videotapes 16mm Films Microforms
Notes: The collection is predominately in English, but incl some material in Japanese.

MD —UNIVERSITY OF MARYLAND, Library, East Asia Collection, College Park, 20742. Frank Joseph Shulman, Curator and Head
Holdings: Vols (90,000) // Mss
Notes: Japanese books, newspapers, periodicals, etc, of the Allied Occupation period (1945-1952), including files of censored publications. Books number 40,000; periodical titles, 13,000; newspaper titles, ca 16,500. The special collection relating to the Occupation period is supplemented by a growing collection (now ca 50,000 vols) of Chinese, Japanese, and Korean publications which form the basis of the University's general collection in East Asian language materials.

MA —BOSTON UNIVERSITY, Mugar Memorial Library, Special Collections Dept, 771 Commonwealth Ave, Boston, 02215. Howard B Gotlieb, Dir
Holdings: Cat Mss Pix
Notes: Incl literary and personal papers of Far Eastern journalists John Hughes, formerly of the *Christian Science Monitor*, now US State Dept spokesman; Dennis Bloodworth of the *Observer of London*, and novelist Han Sayin.

†MA —JOHN F KENNEDY LIBRARY, Columbia Point, Boston, 02125. Dan H Fenn Jr, Dir
Holdings: // Cat Mss
Notes: Roger Hilsman and James C Thomson, Jr, papers relating to Far Eastern affairs and other foreign policy topics, 1960-1965. 21 linear ft of mss. Holdings are described in "Historical Materials in the John F Kennedy Library." Copies may be obtained by writing the Research Archivist.

MA —HARVARD UNIVERSITY, Fairbank Center for East Asian Research, Library, 1737 Cambridge St, Cambridge, 02138. Nancy Hearst, Librn
Holdings: Vols (10,000) Mss Maps
Notes: Post-1949 China, particularly political and sociological developments. Also, post-1952 Japan. Partially cataloged.

MA —HARVARD UNIVERSITY LIBRARY, Fine Arts Library, Rubel Asiatic Research Collection, Sackler Museum, 38 Quincy Street, Cambridge, 02138. Yen-Shew Lynn Chao, Librn
Holdings: Vols 12,000 Mss Serials
Notes: Rubel Asiatic Research Collection; specializes exclusively in the acquisition of Oriental language (Chinese, Japanese, and Korean) materials. Particular strengths incl the areas of Buddhist arts, Chinese bronzes and painting, Japanese painting and prints, and Chinese and Japanese ceramics.

MA —WELLESLEY COLLEGE, Art Library, Wellesley, 02181. Katherine D Finkelpearl, Art Librn
Holdings: Vols (30,000) Cat Pix Slides
Budget: ($22,000)
Notes: Primarily the art and architecture of Western Europe, the Far East, and classical antiquity. However, efforts are being made to expand the collection in the areas of photography, primitive art, and ancient (non-classical) art. The Art Department maintains a separate collection of 62,500 mounted pictures and 90,000 slides.

MI —UNIVERSITY OF MICHIGAN, Asia Library, Ann Arbor, 48109. Wei-Ying Wan, Head
Holdings: Vols 310,000 Cat Pix Microforms
Notes: Comprehensive coverage on East Asian social sciences and humanities; bibliographic, biographic and historical coverage on the sciences, technology and medicine. Mostly in Chinese, Japanese and Korean. Extensive holdings in Western languages in the Graduate Library collection. Also 21,190 microfilm reels and 17,280 microfiche.

NY —NEW YORK PUBLIC LIBRARY, Oriental Div, Fifth Ave & 42 St, New York, 10018. E Christian Filstrup, Chief
Holdings: Cat Mss Microforms
Budget: ($56,455)
Notes: Described in *Dictionary Catalog of the Oriental Collection,* The Research Libraries of the New York Public Library, 1960, 16 vols, and *First Supplement,* 1976, 8 vols (144,000 cards). This catalog incl 318, 000 entries for works in about 100 languages of the East, and all works in Western languages on Oriental subjects. The Oriental Collection numbers about 120,000 vols; its Arabic and Indic holdings and those on ancient Egypt and the ancient Near East are among the largest in the US. There is also a collection of 30,000 vols of PL 480 material from Egypt, Pakistan, and India to which there is main entry access, but which is not incorporated into the dictionary catalog. Other outstanding features of the Oriental Collection incl extensive holdings of Japanese technical and scientific periodicals; a unique collection of linguistic works, grammars, anddictionaries; and unusually good coverage of the field of Oriental religions and philosophies. The catalog contains numerous subject references to periodical articles in all languages. All entries are arranged alphabetically according to the Roman alphabet.

NY —UNIVERSITY OF ROCHESTER, Rush Rhees Library, Rochester, 14627. Datta S Kharbas, Head
Holdings: Vols 100,000 Cat Maps Microforms
Notes: Area studies collection on East Asia and South Asia. Major emphasis is on social sciences and humanities. Over 57,000 volumes on East Asia, out of which 29,000 volumes are in Chinese and 15,000 in Japanese. Extensive holdings on Chinese and Japanese histories. Catalog of East Asian collection consisting of Chinese and Japanese language holdings published in 1968, with two subsequent supplements. Over 30,000 volumes on South Asia. Considerable depth in social sciences, history, politics and anthropology. Extensive holdings in Sanskrit, Hindi, and Marathi.

NC —DUKE UNIVERSITY, William R Perkins Library, Durham, 27706. Elvin E Strowd, University Librn
Notes: The Thomas collection relating to China and the Far East contains more than 1500 items. It is a comprehensive body of books, newspapers, prints and other materials dealing with many phases of the culture of the Orient. Additions are ongoing.

OH —CLEVELAND PUBLIC LIBRARY, Fine Arts and Special Collections Department, 325 Superior Ave, Cleveland, 44114. Alice N Loranth, Head
Holdings: Vols (54,000) Cat Mss Maps
Notes: Part of the Orientalia Collection. Emphasis is on scholarly books, periodicals and serials in Western and in the literary languages of Orient. Incl all aspects of Oriental civilization: archaeology, history, language, literature, philogy, philosophy and religion prior to the impact of Western influence. Exception: History of British India, (extended to 1859). Strong holdings in scholarly editions of classic texts, their versions and translations. Incl 5200 vols in Chinese, Japanese, Tibetan and other Far Eastern languages. Some museum objects. *See also* entry under Oriental Languages and Literatures.

OR —UNIVERSITY OF OREGON LIBRARY, Social Science Dept, Eugene, 97403. Holway R Jones, Head Dept Librn
Holdings: Vols (40,000) Cat
Budget: $39,300
Notes: Materials are mainly in the humanities and social sciences covering from ancient times to the present, with special emphasis on modern period. In Chinese and Japanese. Materials in Western languages on East Asia are located in the main library collection. Most materials on East Asian art are in the Architecture and Allied Arts Library. Holdings are relatively strong in the following areas: Chinese art, modern Chinese history, Chinese language and literature, modern Japanese history, modern Japanese language and literature, modern Japanese government and politics, and Zen Buddhism. *See also* entry under Art, Oriental

EAST (NEAR EAST) see Near East

EAST, P. D.

MA —BOSTON UNIVERSITY, Mugar Memorial Library, Special Collections Dept, 771 Commonwealth Ave, Boston, 02215. Howard B Gotlieb, Dir
Holdings: Cat Mss Pix
Notes: Mss, correspondence, etc collected in depth; incl publications by or about.

EAST AND WEST

CA —CALIFORNIA INSTITUTE OF INTEGRAL STUDIES, Library, 3494 21st St, San Francisco, 94110. Vern Haddick, Library Dir
Holdings: Vols (23,000) Cat Maps Phonorecords Audiotapes
Budget: ($10,000)
Notes: Comparative philosophy, psychology and counseling and comparative religions of East and West. Incl 550 audiotapes.

EAST ANGLIA, ENGLAND

BC —VANCOUVER PUBLIC LIBRARY, History & Government Div, 750 Burrard St,

EAST ANGLIA, ENGLAND (cont.)

Vancouver, V6Z 1X5, Can.
Holdings: Vols 200 Cat Maps Pix
Notes: Antiquities, archaeology, biography, history, description, travel, etc concerning Norfolk and East Anglia in England. (Gift of the Bulwer Family; additional parts of the gift at the University of British Columbia Library.)

EAST ASIA see Asia, East

EAST ASIAN ART see Art, Asian

EAST EUROPE see Europe, Eastern—History

EAST GERMANY see German Democratic Republic—History

EAST INDIA COMPANY

IN —INDIANA UNIVERSITY, Lilly Library, Seventh St, Bloomington, 47405. William R Cagle, Librn
Holdings: Vols (2000) // Cat
Notes: The core of the collection is the specialized library of Charles R Boxer (1000 titles) dealing with the history of the Iberians in the East, 16th-18th century. Mainly incl works on China, Japan and the Philippines during the period of their early intercourse with the West through 1800, as well as materials on the English and Dutch East India Companies, and the 17th century Anglo-Dutch naval wars.

KS —UNIVERSITY OF KANSAS, Kenneth Spencer Research Library, Special Collections Dept, Lawrence, 66045. Alexandra Mason, Librn
Holdings: Vols 10,000 Cat Mss
Notes: Strong holdings in 18th and early 19th century English economics, incl books, pamphlets and mss (official and private records: Audit Office, Lottery Office, Admiralty, Wardrobe, etc, Levant Company, East India Company, Madeira merchants, various persons and estates). Noncirculating.

MA —HARVARD UNIVERSITY, Baker Library of the Graduate School of Business Administration, Kress Library of Business and Economics, Soldiers Field, Boston, 02163. Ruth E Rogers, Cur
Notes: See *Harvard Library Bulletin,* X (1956), 94-118.

OH —CLEVELAND PUBLIC LIBRARY, Fine Arts and Special Collections Department, 325 Superior Ave, Cleveland, 44114. Alice N Loranth, Head
Holdings: Vols 250 Cat Mss
Notes: Over 19,000 pages of mss records of the East India Company relating to British affairs in India and Central Asia (1741-1859). Incl documents, accounts, correspondence, and contains autographed material of Clive, Hastings, Lord Macartney, Henry Dundas, etc. A separate index to letters is maintained.
See also entry under India

EAST INDIAN ART see Art, East Indian

EAST INDIES, DUTCH see Indonesia

EAST INDIES, NETHERLANDS see Indonesia

EAST TEXAS HISTORICAL ASSOCIATION

TX —STEPHEN F AUSTIN STATE UNIVERSITY, Ralph W Steen Library, Special Collections Dept, Box 13055, SFA Sta, Nacogdoches, 75962. Linda Cheves Nicklas, Special Collections Librn
Holdings: Mss Maps Pix
Budget: ($5000)
Notes: Incl personal and business papers, letters, diaries, and other records of East Texans and East Texas institutions and businesses. Major collections incl papers of Karl Wilson Baker, George L Crocket, Bennett Blake, McFarland-Russell family, Orton family, Samuel E Asbury; and records of Nacogdoches University, East Texas Historical Association, Kelly Plow Company and many local organizations; 60 Thomas J Rusk letters. Indexes, calendars and inventories are available. Description: SFASU, *A Guide to Special Collections,* 1980.

EAST TIMOR see Indonesia

EASTER CAROLS see Carols

EASTER EGGS

CT —UKRAINIAN MUSEUM AND LIBRARY, 161 Glenbrook Rd, Stamford, 06902. Wasyl Lencyk, Dir
Holdings: Vols (20,000)
Notes: Paintings, sculpture, engravings and easter eggs. About 60 Ukrainian painters.

MI —UKRAINIAN-AMERICAN ARCHIVES AND MUSEUM, 26601 Ryan Rd, Warren, 48091.
Notes: Historical relics, several thousand books, periodicals, manuscripts, etc. Christmas and Easter handicrafts.

NY —UKRAINIAN MUSEUM, 203 Second Ave, New York, 10003. Maria Shust, Dir
Notes: Also over 1500 folk artifacts and works of art. Incl Ukrainian Easter Eggs.

EASTER ISLAND

†VA —GEORGE C MARSHALL RESEARCH FOUNDATION AND LIBRARY, Drawer 920, Lexington, 24450. Royster Lyle Jr, Cur Collections
Holdings: Vols Uncat Mss
Notes: Examples of ancient writings of Europe, Crete, and Easter Island, and material on the Aztecs, Incas, and particularly the Mayans.

EASTERN CHURCHES

DC —CATHOLIC UNIVERSITY OF AMERICA, Mullen Library, ICOR/Semitics Library, Room 20, Washington, 20064. Monica J Blanchard, Librn
Holdings: Vols 30,000
Notes: The bulk of the ICOR/Semitics Library collection belongs to the Institute of Christian Oriental Research which supports the work of the Corpus Scriptorum Christianorum Orientalium. The holdings are chiefly concerned with Christian Egypt and the Coptic Church, Syriac and Syrian patristic studies, and the Syriac and Arabic speaking eastern churches. There are less extensive holdings of Ethiopic, Armenian and Georgian material. ICOR titles are cataloged by the ICOR/Semitic Library, and ICOR holdings do not appear in the general catalogue of the University Library.

PA —SLOVAK EASTERN CATHOLIC SYNOD OF AMERICA, 515 W Main, Monongahela, 15063.
Holdings: 1500 Vols
Notes: Promotes use of the Byzantine Rite among Slovak-Americans. Special interest in Sts Cyril and Methodius.

UT —UNIVERSITY OF UTAH, Middle East Library, Salt Lake City, 84112. Ragai N Makar, Librn
Budget: ($40,000)
Notes: Mt Sinai Arabic Manuscripts collection. This incl about 800 Arabic manuscripts on microfilm. This collection is incl in the catalogue *The Arabic Manuscripts of Mt Sinai* by Professor Aziz S Atiya. Baltimore, The Johns Hopkins Press, 1955. All the mss are on the history and theology of the Eastern Christian Church. The Greek Manuscripts on microfilm collection of the Patriarchal Library of Alexandria, Egypt. This incl about 1000 mss on microfilm about the history and theology of the Greek Orthodox Church. This collection described in Studies and Documents edited by Jacob Geerlings. Vol XXVI Catalog of MSS of the Patriarchal Library of Alexandria by T D Mosconas, Salt Lake City, University of Utah Press, 1965. The Catholic Microfilm Center Syriac and Arabic Manuscript Collection. This incl about 985 Syriac and Arabic mss on microfilm all of whichis about the history and theology of the Eastern Orthodox Church.

EASTERN EUROPE see Byzantine Empire; Europe, Eastern—History

EASTERN STATES

DC —LIBRARY OF CONGRESS, Prints & Photographs Div, Washington, 20540.
Holdings: 11,427 Items
Notes: The Joseph S Allen Collection of architectural photographs. Covering the period 1945 to 1967, the collection consists of photographs of churches, colleges, government buildings, residential structures, and historic monuments in 27 eastern and mid-western states.

EASTERBY, JAMES, 1898-

SC —COLLEGE OF CHARLESTON LIBRARY, Special Collections Dept, Charleston, 29401.
Notes: Correspondence within the Lancelot Minor Harris Papers.

EASTHAM, MELVILLE, 1885-1964

DC —LIBRARY OF CONGRESS, Manuscript Division, Washington, 20540. John C Broderick, Chief

EASTMAN, GEORGE

NY —UNIVERSITY OF ROCHESTER, Rush Rhees Library, Department of Rare Books and Special Collections, Rochester, 14627. Peter Dzwonkoski, Librn
Holdings: Cat Mss
Notes: Five collections of materials relating to the life and career of George Eastman. Incl materials by Roger Butterfield and Lawrence Bachmann in preparation of proposed Eastman biographies. Eastman's correspondence, and architectural details and letters on Eastman House construction.

EASTMAN, MAX FORRESTER, 1883-1969

IN —INDIANA UNIVERSITY, Lilly Library, Seventh St, Bloomington, 47405. William R Cagle, Librn
Holdings: // Cat Mss
Notes: Correspondence and writings of Max Eastman, 1892-1968. Major portion of correspondence is concerned with Eastman's writings and the responses of various people to his articles, essays, etc. There is very little in the collection relating to *The Masses* or to *The Liberator*, or to his sister Crystal Eastman. 4096 items. Related collections incl Eastman's correspondence with Trotsky, 1922-1933; papers of Anstice Ford Eastman, Max Eastman's physician brother; and the correspondence and writings of Eliena Vassilyenva (Krylenko) Eastman, 1895-1946 (the second Mrs Eastman). Holdings also incl fairly complete file of Eastman's publications in first edition or first printed appearance.

EASTMAN, SETH

MN —JAMES JEROME HILL REFERENCE LIBRARY, Fourth St at Market St, Saint Paul, 55106. Virgil F Massman, Dir
Notes: Comprehensive collection of works about Seth Eastman incl copies of books which he illustrated; also about 70 original watercolor paintings.

EASTMAN KODAK COMPANY

NY —UNIVERSITY OF ROCHESTER, Rush Rhees Library, Department of Rare Books and Special Collections, Rochester, 14627. Peter Dzwonkoski, Librn
Holdings: Cat Mss
Notes: Five collections of materials relating to the life and career of George Eastman. Incl materials by Roger Butterfield and Lawrence Bachmann in preparation of

EASTMAN KODAK COMPANY (cont.)

proposed Eastman biographies. Eastman's correspondence, and architectural details and letters on Eastman House construction.

EASTWOOD, GEN.H.E.

VA —MACARTHUR MEMORIAL, Library & Archives, MacArthur Sq, Norfolk, 23510. Ellen E Folkama, Asst Archivist
Holdings: Vols (4000) Cat Maps Pix Slides Phonorecords Audiotapes 16mm Films Microforms
Notes: Everything relating to the life and related activities of MacArthur. The Archives of the collection consist of 600 shelf-feet of documents from Gen MacArthur's official headquarters files over the period 1941-1951. These papers pertain to all matters with which his various commands were involved: military, naval and air matters; international relations; political science; Japanese occupation, peace treaty and Constitution, etc. Each Record Group is indexed. The indexes are retained here since they are being expanded. They are available for researchers.

EATING see Gastronomy

EATON, CHARLES EDWARD

MA —BOSTON UNIVERSITY, Mugar Memorial Library, Special Collections Dept, 771 Commonwealth Ave, Boston, 02215. Howard B Gotlieb, Dir
Holdings: Cat Mss

EATON, EVELYN

MA —BOSTON UNIVERSITY, Mugar Memorial Library, Special Collections Dept, 771 Commonwealth Ave, Boston, 02215. Howard B Gotlieb, Dir
Holdings: Cat Mss Pix
Notes: Mss, correspondence, etc collected in depth; incl publications by or about.

EATON, WALTER P.

CT —YALE UNIVERSITY, Box 1603A, Yale Station, New Haven, 06520.
Holdings: Mss

EATON, WILLIAM J.

MA —BOSTON UNIVERSITY, Mugar Memorial Library, Special Collections Dept, 771 Commonwealth Ave, Boston, 02215. Howard B Gotlieb, Dir
Holdings: Mss Correspondence

EBENEZER COMMUNITY

NY —CORNELL UNIVERSITY LIBRARIES, Collection of Regional History, Dept of Manuscripts and Univ Archives, Ithaca, 14853.
Notes: Incl 12 pages of reminiscences concerning its members' organization, hardships, and dealings with the Ogden Land Company and the Seneca Indians.

EBERHART, MIGNON G.

MA —BOSTON UNIVERSITY, Mugar Memorial Library, Special Collections Dept, 771 Commonwealth Ave, Boston, 02215. Howard B Gotlieb, Dir
Holdings: Cat Mss
Notes: Mss, correspondence, etc collected in depth; incl publications by or about.

EBERHART, RICHARD

MO —WASHINGTON UNIVERSITY, Libraries, Special Collections Dept, Campus Box 1061, St Louis, 63130.
Notes: A small but significant collection.

NV —UNIVERSITY OF NEVADA, RENO, University Library, Special Collections Dept, Reno, 89557. Robert E Blesse, Head
Holdings: Vols (53) Cat Other appearances 925 Cat
Notes: Includes individual works by author in all editions including translations; also prefaces, introductions, published correspondence, appearances in anthologies, periodicals, etc. Bibliographical research collection, part of Modern Authors Collection.

NH —DARTMOUTH COLLEGE, Baker Memorial Library, Hanover, 03755.
Holdings: Cat Mss
Notes: All editions, as well as mss, periodical appearances, and books inscribed to Eberhart by contemporary poets. Noncirculating.

EBERSTADT, FERDINAND, 1890-1969

NJ —PRINCETON UNIVERSITY, Seeley G Mudd Manuscript Library, Public Affairs Papers Collection, Princeton, 08544. Nancy Bressler, Cur
Notes: Incl 276 boxes. The papers cover the period 1911-1969. An unpublished 83 p guide is available in the Library.

ECCLES, ADM. HENRY E.

RI —US NAVAL WAR COLLEGE, Historical Collection & Museum, Newport, 02841. Anthony S Nicolosi, Dir; Evelyn Cherpak, Cur
Notes: Papers of Adm Henry E Eccles, authority on naval logistics and strategy, consisting of official correspondence files, personal files of correspondence with fellow military scholars, speeches and writings, files on logistics, military education and the Naval War College. A manuscript collection register has been published.

ECCLES, MARRINER S.

UT —UNIVERSITY OF UTAH, Marriott Library, Special Collections, Salt Lake City, 84112. Gregory C Thompson, Cur
Notes: Papers of Marriner S Eccles, (80 ln ft, 1000 vols library, mss, films, tapes).

ECCLESIASTICAL ANTIQUITIES see Christian Antiquities

ECCLESIASTICAL ARCHITECTURE see Church Architecture

ECCLESIASTICAL ART see Christian Art and Symbolism

ECCLESIASTICAL BIOGRAPHY see Christian Biography

ECCLESIASTICAL COSTUME see Church Vestments

ECCLESIASTICAL HISTORY see Church History

ECCLESIASTICAL LAW

CA —UNIVERSITY OF CALIFORNIA, BERKELEY, School of Law, Library, Berkeley, 94720. Stephan G Kuttner, Dir, Canon Law Collection
Holdings: Vols (23,000) Cat Mss Microforms
Notes: Entirely supported by the R D and S M Robbins Endowment, the Robbins Canon Law Collection emphasizes particularly Roman Catholic, Eastern and Anglican canon law. Additional subject areas being developed are ecclesiastical history and institutions, historical and contemporary church and state relations, and ecumenical studies. Library is in process of obtaining complete microfilms of all medieval canon and Roman law mss held by the Vatican Library.

MA —HARVARD UNIVERSITY LIBRARY, Law School Library, Langdell Hall, Cambridge, 02138. Harry S Martin III, Librn
Holdings: Cat

NY —COLUMBIA UNIVERSITY LIBRARIES, Law School Library, Law Building, 435 W 116 St, New York, 10027. James L Hoover, Librn
Holdings: Vols (735,000) Cat
Notes: Incl substantial special collections in foreign and international law; also copyright law, ecclesiastical and medieval law; Roman law.

PA —UNIVERSITY OF PENNSYLVANIA, Lea Library, 3420 Walnut St, Philadelphia, 19104. Daniel Traister, Special Collections Librn
Holdings: Vols (20,000) Cat Mss
Notes: Incl Canon law.

PA —UNIVERSITY OF PENNSYLVANIA, Biddle Law Library, 3400 Chestnut St, Philadelphia, 19104. Elizabeth S. Kelly, Libn
Notes: Comprehensive collection of Anglo-American law. Legal materials from selected foreign countries, particularly in Common Market area. International law incl UN documents and other regional organizations. Substantial holdings in historical sources, particularly early English law and Canon law.

AB —UNIVERSITY OF ALBERTA, Cameron Library, The Bruce Peel Special Collections Room, Edmonton, T6G 2J8, Can. John Charles, Special Collections Librn
Holdings: Vols 3800
Notes: Salzburg Collections.

ECCLESIASTICAL RECORDS AND REGISTERS see Church Records and Registers

ECCLESIASTICAL RITES AND CEREMONIES see Liturgics and Liturgies

ECCLESIASTICAL VESTMENTS see Church Vestments

ECHINODERMATA

DC —SMITHSONIAN INSTITUTION, Archives Div, Washington, 20560. William W Moss, Archivist
Holdings: Cat Mss Maps Pix Slides
Notes: The Archives holds the records of the National Museum of Natural History's Dept of Invertebrate Zoology, Division of Echinoderms, Division of Marine Invertebrates, and Division of Mollusks, ca 1853-1975, as well as the personal papers of William H Dall, Paul Bartsch, Austin H Clark, and Waldo LaSalle Schmitt.

DC —SMITHSONIAN INSTITUTION LIBRARIES, Natural History Branch, Washington, 20560. Sylvia Churgin, Chief Librn
Holdings: Cat Mss Maps Pix Slides Microforms
Notes: Invertebrate zoology, Systematics. Incl crustacea, echinoderms, mollusks, worms, Cushman collection of foraminifera; Springer collection on crinoids; Wilson collection on copepoda.

ECHO RANGING see Sonar

ECK, JOHANN

CA —STANFORD UNIVERSITY LIBRARIES, Cecil H Green Library, Stanford, 94305. Peter R Frank, Cur, CDP-Germanic Collection
Notes: Extensive holdings in the field of Reformation and Counter-Reformation. First and early editions by Luther, Melanchthon, Bugenhagen, Cochleus, Eck, Hutten, Reuchlin, and minor figures in Special Collections.

ECKERT, ALLAN W.

MA —BOSTON UNIVERSITY, Mugar Memorial Library, Special Collections Dept, 771 Commonwealth Ave, Boston, 02215. Howard B Gotlieb, Dir
Holdings: Cat Mss Pix
Notes: Mss, correspondence, etc collected in depth; incl publications by or about.

ECKERT, JOHN E.

CA —UNIVERSITY OF CALIFORNIA, DAVIS, Shields Library, Dept of Special

ECKERT, JOHN E. (cont.)

Collections, Davis, 95616. Donald Kunitz, Head; C Danial Elliott, Asst Head
Holdings: Cat Mss Pix Slides
Notes: Correspondence of John E Eckert (1936-58) with apiculturalists from all over the world (43,000 items). Described in: USDA Agricultural Research SErvice, *Beekeeping in the Unted States* (Agricultural Handbook, no 335, rev ed 1977); and Johansson, Tag Sigvard Kjell, *Apicultural Literature Published in Canada and the United States* (New York, 1972).

ECLECTIC MEDICINE see Medicine, Eclectic

ECLIPSES

MN —UNIVERSITY OF MINNESOTA, O Meredith Wilson Library, 309 19 Ave S, Minneapolis, 55455. Austin J McLean, Chief, Special Collections
Holdings: Vols (103) / / Cat Mss
Notes: Basically mathematical astronomy with emphasis on eclipses. Particular strengths are the works of such authors as Delambre, Euclid, Newton, Ptolemy, and Rhaticus. Important in this respect are 6 of the 10 known printed editions of the Alphonsine Astronomical Tables.

ECOLA DO RECIFE see Recife School

ECOLOGY

AK —NATIONAL OCEANIC AND ATMOSPHERIC ADMINISTRATION, National Marine Fisheries Service, Fisheries Laboratory Research Library, PO Box 155, Auke Bay, 99821. Paula Johnson, Librn
Holdings: Vols (21,000) Cat Mss Maps Pix Microforms
Budget: ($20,000)

AZ —DESERT BOTANICAL GARDEN, Richter Memorial Library, 1201 North Galvin Pkwy, Phoenix, 85008. J B Cole, Librn
Holdings: Vols (4000)
Notes: Emphasis on desert and arid regions ecology and horticulture.

AZ —ARIZONA-SONORA DESERT MUSEUM, Library, Rte 9, Box 900, Tucson, 85743. Janice Hunter, Librn
Holdings: Vols (3000) Cat Pix Slides Videotapes 16mm Films
Notes: Ecology and natural history of the Southwest. Carr Collection on beavers. Incl 200 pictures, 5000 slides, 40 videotapes, and 6 films. Separate index of slides.

CA —UNIVERSITY OF CALIFORNIA, BERKELEY, Institute of Governmental Studies Library, 109 Moses Hall, Berkeley, 94720. Jack Leister, Head Librn
Holdings: Vols (350,000) Cat Mss Maps Microforms
Budget: ($160,000)
Notes: The library collects primarily pamphlets. Incl in the library's holdings are documents from all levels of government, as well as publications issued by professional associations and special interest groups. A G K Hall catalog covering the Institute's Library holdings is available. Since 1937, Library has been depository for all California local documents (city, county & special district). Formerly: Bureau of Public Administration.

CA —UNIVERSITY OF CALIFORNIA, DAVIS, Shields Library, Dept of Special Collections, Davis, 95616. Donald Kunitz, Head; C Danial Elliott, Asst Head
Notes: Overview of American political movements from the 1890s to the present: socialism, communism, labor, to ecology and women's liberation.

CA —CALIFORNIA STATE UNIVERSITY, FULLERTON, Library, Box 4150, Fullerton, 92634. Linda Herman, Special Collections Librn
Holdings: Cat
Notes: Dr Leonard B Schultz Ichthyology Collection of 13,000 pieces incl books, pamphlets, articles and ephemera. It is supplemented by the Ecology of Bay and Estuarine Fishes Collections.

CA —UNIVERSITY OF CALIFORNIA, LOS ANGELES, Research Library, Dept of Special Collections, 405 Hilgard Ave, Los Angeles, 90024. Edward Shreeves, Chairman, Bibliographers Group; David S Zeidberg, Head
Notes: Horace M Albright's correspondence and ephemera recording his activity as a conservationist and his directorship of the National Park Service.

CA —UNIVERSITY OF CALIFORNIA, LOS ANGELES, Biomedical Library, Center for Health Sciences, Los Angeles, 90024. Louise Darling, Biomedical Librn

CA —UNIVERSITY OF THE PACIFIC, Library, Stockton, 95211. Hiram L Davis, Dir of Libraries
Notes: The John Muir papers. Muir was the founder of the Sierra Club, a prime mover in the development of the national park systems, and a major force in the preservationist branch of the conservation movement.

CO —COLORADO STATE UNIVERSITY, Libraries, Fort Collins, 80523. Marjorie Rhoades, Engineering Sciences Librn
Holdings: Vols (6000) Cat
Budget: ($5000)
Notes: Water and Soil in Arid Regions (WASAR) is an index and guide to books, conference papers, journal articles, government documents and technical reports, mostly in English, within the appropriate subject areas and held by Colorado State University Libraries. The bibliographical citations are of selected items dealing with soils, water, arid lands, crops, foods and nutrition with certain economic, political, ecological and historical parameters also included. The information needs of developing countries and of those who serve them are the prime criteri for inclusion.

CO —COLORADO SCHOOL OF MINES, Arthur Lakes Library, 14 & Illinois Sts, Golden, 80401. Hartley K Phinney, Jr, Head Librn
Holdings: Vols (270,557) Cat Mss Maps Microforms

CT —YALE UNIVERSITY, Forestry Library, 205 Prospect St, New Haven, 06511. Joseph A Miller, Librn
Holdings: Vols (115,000) Cat Microforms
Notes: The Forestry Library is a unit of the Yale University Library, housed in and serving primarily the School of Forestry and Environmental Studies. Founded in 1900, it has become one of the largest forestry libraries in the world. Forestry is construed broadly to incl underlying or closely related social, physical, and biological sciences. The literature of North American forestry and forest products is most completely covered, though other countries and foreign languages are well represented. Environmental studies and allied fields of natural resources management have been emphasized during the past 10 years. See *Dictionary Catalog of the Yale Forestry Library*, 12 vols (Boston: G K Hall, 1962).

DE —UNIVERSITY OF DELAWARE, Agriculture Library, 2 Townsend Hall, Newark, 19717. Frederick Getze, Assoc Librn
Holdings: Vols (32,500) Cat Pix Microforms
Notes: Strong in entomology and ornamental horticulture. Extensive collection of state agriculture documents for each US state and Puerto Rico. Library subscribes to 600 serials (English and foreign).

DC —CONSERVATION FOUNDATION, Library, 1717 Massachusetts Ave NW, Washington, 20036. Barbara K Rodes, Librn
Holdings: Vols (8000) Cat Maps
Notes: Collection incl natural resources, ecology, city and regional planning, land use, recreation, energy conservation, environmental economics, pollution control, water resources.

DC —LIBRARY OF CONGRESS, Manuscript Division, Washington, 20540. John C Broderick, Chief
Notes: Papers of Barry Commoner, biologist and ecologist.

DC —SMITHSONIAN INSTITUTION, Smithsonian Tropical Research Institute, Washington, 20560. Carol Jopling, Chief Librn
Holdings: Vols (22,000) Cat Mss Maps Pix Slides 16mm Films Microforms
Budget: ($70,000)
Notes: Smithsonian Institution, Smithsonian Tropical Research Institute is located in Balboa, Panama.

DC —SMITHSONIAN INSTITUTION LIBRARIES, General Library, Washington, 20560. Mary Claire Grey, Chief Cent Ref & Loan Servs
Holdings: Vols (79,000) Cat Mss Maps Pix Slides Microforms

FL —ARCHBOLD BIOLOGICAL STATION, Library, Rt 2, Box 180, Lake Placid, 33852. Fred E Lohrer, Librn
Holdings: Cat Slides
Notes: Florida natural history. Emphasis on south central peninsular Florida. Habitats, plants, vertebrates, land use changes. About 8000 2x2 color transparencies and 35mm films.

FL —FLORIDA DEPT OF NATURAL RESOURCES BUREAU OF MARINE RESEARCH, Library, 100 Eighth Ave SE, Saint Petersburg, 33701. Keir Gray, Archivist
Holdings: Vols (3400) Cat Maps Pix Slides 16mm Films Microforms
Budget: ($59,000)
Notes: The library supports the research of approx 50 biologists and technicians, with emphasis on the marine resources of Florida and nearby areas. An archives section houses original research data, reports, publications,, etc, developed by the scientific staff. Marine biological literature is received on exchange from laboratories and libraries throughout the world. There are approx 1400 journal titles in the collection. Current titles received number approx 600. The 33,000 reprints are cataloged by author and subject. Current laboratory activities incl marine studies in aquaculture, descriptive biology, ecological studies, fisheries biology, and oceanography.

HI —BERNICE P BISHOP MUSEUM, Library, PO Box 19000-A, Honolulu, 96819. Cynthia Timberlake, Librn
Holdings: Vols (90,000) Cat Mss Maps Pix Slides Microforms
Budget: ($30,000)
Notes: Only American library devoted exclusively to the Pacific region. Collection reflects historical and contemporary research emphases of Bishop Museum; ie the natural and cultural history of the Pacific. Areas of concentration incl archaeology, ethnology, linguistics, voyages and explorations, history, vertebrate and invertebrate zoology, botany and museology. Strong special collections incl photographs, mss and archives, maps and art. Publications: Quarterly "Additions to the Catalog," *Dictionary Catalog of the* Library (9 vols and 2 suppl; Boston: G K Hall, 1964-69).

IL —UNIVERSITY OF ILLINOIS, URBANA/CHAMPAIGN, Library, Biology Library, 101 Burrill Hall, 407 S Goodwin, Urbana, 61801. Elisabeth B Davis, Librn
Holdings: Vols (115,000) Cat Microforms
Budget: ($200,000)
Notes: The Biology Library incl books, periodicals, and reference works that cover the fields of anatomy, biophysics, botany, ecology, entomology, genetics, immunology, microbiology, physiology and zoology. About three-quarters of the total collection is made up of journals and other serials representing 2000 distinctive titles. The serial list is comprehensive for the biological sciences, contains most of the major international titles and consists of complete runs for almost all titles. Additional materials (approx 90,000 vols) in the biological sciences are available in the Natural History Survey Library and the bookstacks at the Main Library on the Urbana campus. Professional assistance is available for reference service, online searching, and library instruction. Interlibrary loan service is provided. Photocopying.

IA —IOWA STATE UNIVERSITY, Library, Ames, 50011. Warren B Kuhn, Dean of

ECOLOGY (cont.)

Library Services
Holdings: Cat
Notes: Extensive serial holdings supplement this strong collection.

IA —IOWA STATE UNIVERSITY, Library, Dept of Special Collections, Ames, 50011. Stanley M Yates, Head
Holdings: / / Mss Pix
Notes: The Paul Errington (1902-1962) Papers. Professor of zoology at ISU (1932-1962) and a leading authority on vertebrate ecology and animal population dynamics. Collection incl correspondence, mss and articles. Collection is 15 linear feet.

IA —BICKELHAUPT ARBORETUM FREE LENDING LIBRARY, 340 S Fourteenth St, Clinton, 52732. Francie B Hill, Librn
Notes: Strong on indoor plants, horticulture, ecology, energy conservation, plant entomology and pathology, urban tree planting; also curriculum materials. Over 3000 slides available for lending.

KY —UNIVERSITY OF KENTUCKY COMMUNITY COLLEGES, Southeast Community College, Library, Learning Resource Center, Cumberland, 40823. Parker Boggs, Dir
Holdings: Vols (350) Cat Phonorecords Audiotapes Videotapes 16mm Films Filmstrips Microforms

ME —COLLEGE OF THE ATLANTIC, Thorndike Library, Bar Harbor, 04609. Marcie L Dworak, Libr Dir
Notes: A rebuilding, fire-destroyed library (1983).

MD —US DEPT OF AGRICULTURE, National Agricultural Library, 10301 Baltimore Blvd, Beltsville, 20705. Joseph H Howard, Director
Holdings: Vols (2,000,000) Cat Mss Maps Pix Slides Microforms
Notes: Crop ecology, agro-climatic analogs; air pollution effects. Agronomy: agriculture and tropical and desert agriculture. For use by the staff of the Institute. Incl 5000 pamphlet items. Former collection of American Institute of Crop Ecology.

MD —RACHEL CARSON COUNCIL INC, Library, 8940 Jones Mill Rd, Chevy Chase, 20815. Shirley A Briggs, Exec Dir
Notes: Bioassays of pesticides and other toxic substances for carcinogenicity by National Cancer Institute; government regulatory documents. Holdings approx 1500 books; 1000 documents and unbound reports; 40 drawers of specialized files. Also have Environmental Protection Agency Pesticide Product Information. Subscribe to 54 journals and others serials. Also publish on pesticides, toxic substances and alternatives to use of pesticides. Have index to pesticides by chemical formula, trade names and CAS number.

MA —HARVARD UNIVERSITY LIBRARY, Gray Herbarium Library, 22 Divinity Ave, Cambridge, 02138. Barbara A Callahan, Librn
Notes: Arnold Arboretum and Gray Herbarium Libraries hold one of the nation's largest collections (149,000 items).

MA —NEW ENGLAND WILD FLOWER SOCIETY, INC, Lawrence Newcomb Library, Hemenway Rd, Framingham, 01701. Mary M Walker, Librn
Holdings: Vols (2500)
Budget: ($1000)
Notes: Incl 15,000 slides (35mm) and 4 vertical files.

†MI —WESTERN MICHIGAN UNIVERSITY, Dwight B Waldo Library, Kalamazoo, 49008. Carl H Sachtleben, Dir
Notes: C C Adams Collection.

NV —FORESTA INSTITUTE FOR OCEAN AND MOUNTAIN STUDIES, Library, 6205 Franktown Rd, Carson City, 89701. Shannon Porter, Librn
Holdings: Vols (3000) Cat Mss Maps Pix Slides
Notes: Material on plant, animal, and human ecology with special emphasis on far western US and Nevada ecology and environmental problems. Also hold about 2000 reprints, pamphlets, reports, etc.

NH —DARTMOUTH COLLEGE, Dartmouth-Hitchcock Medical Center, Dana Biomedical Library, Hanover, 03756. Shirley J Grainger, Librn
Holdings: Vols (143,611) Cat Mss Phonorecords Audiotapes Videotapes Microforms
Budget: ($280,000)

NY —ADIRONDACK HISTORICAL ASSOCIATION, Museum Library, Blue Mountain Lake, 12812. Jerold Pepper, Librn
Holdings: Vols (7500) Cat Mss Maps Pix Phonorecords Audiotapes 16mm Films Microforms
Notes: Anything about the Adirondacks--history, people, economics, places, things. Strong in Adirondack art, outdoor recreation, logging, small boats. Resources incl more than 1000 maps, 40,000 pictures, 1600 microfilm reels, 576 linear ft of ms material, and 12 cabinets of VF ephemera, etc.

NY —NEW YORK BOTANICAL GARDEN LIBRARY, Bronx, 10458. Charles R Long, Asst Vice Pres & Dir
Holdings: Vols 20,000 Cat Mss Pix Slides Microforms VF
Budget: ($356,000)
Notes: One of the largest botanical collections in the world. Covers botany (150, 000 vols), botanists (3000), horticulture (45, 000), plant diseases (25,000), plant physiology (15,000), history of botany (1500), conservation of natural resources (15,000), gardening (13,000), paleobotany (7000), ecology (20,000), forestry (5000), medical botany (3000), agriculture (9000) and biology (20,000). Reference library; materials do not circulate, except via standard inter-library loan. About 5000 vols uncataloged. Incl archives, art and vertical files. An OCLC library.

NY —NEW YORK ZOOLOGICAL SOCIETY LIBRARY, Bronx Zoo, Bronx, 10460. Steven P Johnson, Archivist and Librn
Holdings: Vols (10,000) Cat Mss Pix
Budget: ($4500)
Notes: One of the very few zoo libraries in the United States. It is possibly the largest collection of books and periodicals in the United States concerning the captive management of wild animals. Primarily intended for the scientific staff, the collection is open to the public on a noncirculating basis, by appointment, (212) 220-5124.

NY —CORNELL UNIVERSITY LIBRARIES, Comstock Memorial Library of Entomology, Ithaca, 14853. Edwin Spragg, Librn
Holdings: Vols (30,000) Cat Maps Pix Audiotapes Microforms
Budget: ($13,500)
Notes: Major topics: general and applied entomology. Minor topics: parasitology, medical entomology, ecology, zoological nomenclature and allied orders of arthropods. Separate catalog to the collection, also extensive collection of reprints. Apiculture material kept at nearby A R Mann Library.

NY —CARY ARBORETUM OF THE NEW YORK BOTANICAL GARDEN, Library, Box AB, Millbrook, 12545. Fred Strum, Librn
Notes: This collection of alternative energy sources consists of publications concerned with solar energy, wind power, biofuel, methanol, small hydroelectric projects, and wood power.

NY —CARY ARBORETUM OF THE NEW YORK BOTANICAL GARDEN, Institute of Ecosystem Studies, Library, Box AB, Millbrook, 12545. Betsy Calvin, Librn
Holdings: Vols 10,000

NY —AMERICAN MUSEUM OF NATURAL HISTORY, Library Services Dept, Central Park W & 79th St, New York, 10024. Nina J Root, Chairwoman; Mary Genett, Asst Librn for Reference Services
Holdings: Cat Mss Pix Microforms
Notes: The Ernest Thompson Seton diaries. Thousands of pages of an unpublished 67-year diary record of one of the world's most famous naturalists, the gift of Joseph F Cullman III, a Trustee of the Museum. Preserved in 35 protective cases, the gift incl unpublished diaries, notebooks, and some other writings. The diary begins 12 June 1879; the last entries were written in hospital, just a month before Seton's death in 1946. Literally hundreds of examples of flora and fauna are pictured in the diaries in original pencil, pen-and-ink, and watercolor sketches, on nearly every page. Research will reveal information on the Indian sign language, the Boy Scouts of America, the Woodcraft League of America, and the wilderness of Canada, Florida, Texas, the West and Southwest, etc.

NY —STATE UNIVERSITY OF NEW YORK, COLLEGE OF ENVIRONMENTAL SCIENCE AND FORESTRY, F Franklin Moon Library, Syracuse, 13210. Donald F Webster, Librn
Holdings: Vols (86,430) Cat
Budget: ($120,000)

NC —UNIVERSITY OF NORTH CAROLINA, CHAPEL HILL, Zoology Dept Library, Wilson Hall 046A, Chapel Hill, 27514. John B Darling, Librn
Holdings: Vols (31,000) Cat
Notes: Collection incl theses and dissertations.

†NC —UNIVERSITY OF NORTH CAROLINA, CHAPEL HILL, Department of Botany Library, 301 Coker Hall 010-A, Chapel Hill, 27514. William R Burk, Botany Librn
Notes: The mycology collection incl some 6000 pamphlets. It contains papers of the following scientists: William C Coker, John N Couch, Lindsay F Olive, mycologists; also, Victor A Greulach, plant pathologist. The mycology catalog is in preparation (1983), and will provide author, title, and subject access.

ND —NORTHERN PRAIRIE WILDLIFE RESEARCH CENTER, Library, PO Box 1747, Jamestown, 58401.
Holdings: Vols (2500) Cat Pix Slides
Budget: ($10,000)
Notes: Wildlife management and research, incl avian biology, plant and animal ecology as related to wetlands and prairies, waterfowl research, and effects of predators on waterfowl.

OH —CLEVELAND PUBLIC LIBRARY, Science & Technology Dept, 325 Superior Ave, Cleveland, 44114. Jean Z Piety, Head
Holdings: Cat Pix
Notes: Special collection covers the environmental sciences concerned with the Great Lakes-St Lawrence drainage basins. Emphasis is on limnology, ecology, meteorology, hydraulics, biology, pollution of air and water, natural history and general research. Most of the material indexed has been donated by numerous agencies around the Great Lakes.

OH —OHIO STATE UNIVERSITY, Biological Sciences Library, 1735 Neil Ave, Columbus, 43210. Victoria Welborn, Librn
Holdings: Vols (85,000) Cat Mss Maps Microforms

OH —WARREN H CORNING LIBRARY, 9500 Sperry Rd, Mentor, 44060. Paul C Spector, Dir of Education
Holdings: Vols (5400) Cat VF
Notes: 1500 vols of Warren H Corning Horticulture Classics. Also 80 periodicals and 10 vertical files.

PA —ZOOLOGICAL SOCIETY OF PHILADELPHIA, Library, 34 & Girard Ave, Philadelphia, 19104. Alyssa N Scheuermann, Librn
Holdings: Vols (500) Cat
Notes: Photocopying with permission.

TN —TENNESSEE VALLEY AUTHORITY (TVA), Technical Library, 400 W Summit Hill Dr, E2 B7, Knoxville, 37902. Jesse C Mills, Chief Librn
Holdings: Vols (106,900) Cat Mss Maps Pix Audiotapes Microforms
Budget: ($2,025,000)
Notes: The Technical Library Headquarters Staff (order, cataloging, information, and administration) is located in Knoxville, Tenn. In addition there are branch libraries in Knoxville, Norris, and Chattanooga, Tennessee, and Muscle Shoals, Alabama.

TN —THE BOTANICAL GARDENS, Minnie Ritchie and Joel Owsley Cheek Memorial

ECOLOGY (cont.)

Library, Forrest Park Drive, Nashville, 37205. Richard C Page, Dir Botanical Gardens
Holdings: Vols (3500) Cat Pix Slides
Budget: $2500

TX —UNIVERSITY OF TEXAS LIBRARIES, Science Library, PO Box P, Austin, 78712. Betty White, Librn
Holdings: Vols (103,000) Cat Microforms

TX —TEXAS A&M UNIVERSITY, Sterling C Evans Library, Special Collections Div, College Station, 77843. Donald H Dyal, Librn
Holdings: Vols 400 Cat
Notes: The E J Dyksterhuis Collection on American forestry, range science, ecology and botany (compiled by Professor Emeritus E J Dyksterhuis).
See also entry under Ranch Life.

TX —UNIVERSITY OF TEXAS, Marine Science Institute Library, Port Aransas, 78373. Ruth Grundy, Librn
Holdings: Vols (45,000) Cat Maps Pix
Budget: ($70,000)
Notes: Current researches in marine science, especially concerning the Gulf of Mexico, the Texas Coastal Zone, and the Continental Shelf. Incl journals.

TX —SOUTHWEST FOUNDATION FOR RESEARCH AND EDUCATION LIBRARY, Preston C Northrup Memorial Library, Baboon Information Center, W Loop 410 at Military Dr, PO Box 28147, San Antonio, 78284. Dorothy M Brooks, Baboon
Notes: Principle field of research: Birth defects, atherosclerosis, reproductive physiology, cancer, genetics, organic chemistry, parasitology, primatology and behavioral sciences and their application to problems of drug abuse, alcoholism and ecology. Maintains the largest baboon colony in the world.

†WA —WASHINGTON STATE UNIVERSITY, Library, Manuscripts, Archives & Special Collections, Pullman, 99164. John F Guido, Head
Holdings: Cat Mss Maps Pix
Notes: The Carl Parcher Russell papers, a vast resource (24,916 items; 45 linear feet) on American Indian and Western pioneer activities and artifacts. Much on the fur trade; pioneer life; mountain men and trapping; wildlife; primitive life in detail. Also the National Park Service, parks, monuments, etc. Described in *His Scholarly and Professional Papers, 1920-1967, in the Washington State University Library* (Pullman, 1970), 149 pp.

WA —MOUNTAINEERS INC, Library, 300 3rd Ave West, Seattle, 98119. Verna M Ness, Library Cur
Holdings: Vols (3000) Cat
Notes: Collection incl some 19th century vols of Alpine information, incl the first issue of *The Alpine Journal* (1863). Bound serials of many important American climbing publications. Small sub-collections for American Alpine Club members and for The Mountaineer Foundation, the latter on conservation and ecology. In the main collection backpacking, skiing and natural history are also represented.

WI —UNIVERSITY OF WISCONSIN, MADISON, College of Agricultural & Life Sciences, Steenbock Memorial Library, 550 Babcock Dr, Madison, 53706. Jan Kennedy, Dir
Holdings: Vols (186,312) Cat Docs Microforms
Notes: Collection includes soil and water conservation, plant and animal ecology, eviromental toxicology.

WI —MILWAUKEE PUBLIC MUSEUM, Reference Library, 800 W Wells St, Milwaukee, 53233. Judith Campbell Turner, Museum Librn

BC —CANADIAN FORESTRY SERVICE, Pacific Forest Research Centre, Library, 506 West Burnside Rd, Victoria, V8Z 1M5, Can. Alice Solyma, Librn
Holdings: Vols (60,500) Cat Microforms
Notes: Incl forest meteorology and also a general meteorology collection.

MB —UNIVERSITY OF MANITOBA, Elizabeth Dafoe Library, Government Publications Section, Winnipeg, R3T 2N2, Can. June Dutka, Head
Holdings: Vols 1300 // Uncat Maps Pix
Notes: The collection, which dates from 1975, consists of written direct testimonies and responses with supporting exhibits from over 100 oil and gas companies, Indian and native associations and concerned citizen groups. The content of these documents incl construction plans, financial statements, alternate corridors, and describes the social and economic impact of the Arctic Gas Pipeline in northern Canada. The *Biological Report Series* offers vital information on soils and vegetation, movements of porcupine, caribou herds, bird distribution and fisheries research. An index listing the various company exhibits accompanies this collection.

ON —CANADA CENTRE FOR INLAND WATERS, Library, 867 Lakeshore Rd, Burlington, L7R 4A6, Can. Eve Dowie, Head Library Services
Holdings: Vols (20,000)
Budget: ($150,000)
Notes: A research collection oriented towards Canadian limnological research. Incl 312 subscriptions.

†ON —METROPOLITAN TORONTO LIBRARY, Social Sciences Dept, 789 Yonge St, Toronto, M4W 2G8, Can. Abdus Salam, Head
Holdings: Vols Cat Maps Phonorecords Audiotapes 16mm Films Microforms
Notes: Collection includes material on the size, growth, density, distribution and ecology of human populations. Covers general theory to research materials. International in scope.

ON —ONTARIO MINISTRY OF NATURAL RESOURCES, Natural Resources Library, Whitney Block 4540, Toronto, M5S 1B3, Can. Sandra Louet, Librn
Holdings: Cat

ECOLOGY, CROP see Crop Ecology

ECOLOGY, ESTUARINE see Estuarian Ecology

ECOLOGY, FRESHWATER see Freshwater Ecology

ECOLOGY, HUMAN see Human Ecology

ECOLOGY, MARINE see Marine Ecology

ECOLOGY, RADIATION see Radioecology

ECOLOGY, SOCIAL see Human Ecology

ECOLOGY, STREAM see Stream Ecology

ECONOMIC ASSISTANCE

CA —HOOVER INSTITUTION ON WAR, REVOLUTION & PEACE, Stanford University, Stanford, 94305. Milorad M Drachkovitch, Archivist
Holdings: Mss
Notes: Papers of Brig Gen Bonner F Fellers, head of the US Army Psychological Warfare Division, 1943-45, incl research studies, reports, correspondence, memoranda, operational instructions, etc, 1934-72, relating to his military and pulic service careers, US military propaganda during World War II, and US economic and foreign aid. Incl are materials pertaining to the Citizens Foreign Aid Committee and Taxpayers Committee to End Foreign Aid, of which B F Fellers was chairman. 15 ms boxes.

DC —GEORGETOWN UNIVERSITY, Library, Special Collections Div, 37 & O Sts NW, Washington, 20057. George M Barringer, Special Collections Librn; Nicholas B Sheetz, Mss Librn
Holdings: Mss Cat
Notes: The archives of the Commission on Security and Economic Assistance, chaired by Frank C Carlucci, consist of memberships correspondence files; papers generated or solicited by the Commission; minutes from Commission meetings and public hearings; and drafts of the Commission's final report.

MI —UNIVERSITY OF MICHIGAN, Center for Research on Economic Development, Library, 240 Lorch Hall, Ann Arbor, 48109. Carol Wilson, Information/Resources Coordinator
Holdings: Vols (21,000) Cat 16mm Films Microforms
Budget: ($7000)
Notes: Publications that list library and its collection: *Directory of Third World Studies in the US* (African Studies Assn, 1981), *National Reference Center Directory* 1983 (NRC), *World Guide to Libraries* 1983 (Saur Verlag), *Research Centers Directory 1983* (Gale Research), and *A Directory of Information Resources in US* (Library of Congress, 1978). Collection's focus is Third World economic development. Other areas of interest are economic planning, developing countries, Africa (specifically francophone Africa), the Sahel, African agricultural economics, commodities production, financial statistics, development plans from less developed countries (LDC), and international development. Each part of the library's collection (working papers/reports, periodicals and government documents) has its own catalog and cataloging system.

PQ —CANADIAN INTERNATIONAL DEVELOPMENT AGENCY, Development Information Centre, 200 Promenade du Portage, Hull, K1A 0G4, Can. Nicole Smith, Librn
Notes: International economic development.

ECONOMIC ASSISTANCE, AMERICAN

CA —HOOVER INSTITUTION ON WAR, REVOLUTION & PEACE, Stanford University, Stanford, 94305. Milorad M Drachkovitch, Archivist
Holdings: Mss Pix
Notes: Three collections: (1) Papers of R Allen Griffin, Deputy Chief of ECA China Aid Mission, 1948-49, and Chief of the 1950 Economic Mission to Southeast Asia, incl correspondence, reports, memoranda, speeches and writings, photographs, and printed matter, 1945-71, relating to American technical and economic assistance missions to China and Southeast Asia. 14 ms boxes. (2) Papers of John D Montgomery, political scientist and author, incl mss of writings, reports, notes, interview summaries, and printed matter, 1946-1959, relating to US aid to South Vietnam and other southeast Asian countries, economic conditions in these countries, Japanese and German public opinion regarding the purge of wartime leaders after World War II, and political, social, and economic effects of the purge on Japan and Germany. 15 ms boxes. (3) Records of the Famine Emergency Committee,an organization for the coordination of international famine relief after World War II, incl correspondence, reports, notes, and clippings, 1946-47, relating to US food conservation and to famine conditions throughout the world. Incl memoranda and diaries of Herbert Hoover, Honorary Chairman of the Committee. 30 ms boxes, 2 envelopes.

NJ —PRINCETON UNIVERSITY, Library, Manuscript Collection, Nassau St, Princeton, 08540. Jean F Preston, Cur
Holdings: // Cat Mss Pix
Notes: Archives of the United China Relief, Inc, and United Service to China, Inc. Incl 100 boxes of papers. The archive covers the period, 1941 to 1966. An unpublished typescript guide (36 p) is available in the Library. Also incl 96 cartons, 30 card-tray files of the archive of the Committee to Defend America by Aiding the Allies covers the period May 1940 to January 1942.

†VA —GEORGE C MARSHALL RESEARCH FOUNDATION AND LIBRARY, Drawer 920, Lexington, 24450. Royster Lyle Jr, Cur Collections
Holdings: Vols Cat Mss Pix Videotapes

ECONOMIC ASSISTANCE, AMERICAN (cont.)

Films Filmstrips
Notes: The Harry B Price Collection contains over 650 typed pages of inteviews with European and American officials concerning the Marshall Plan. This was in preparation for his book, *The Marshall Plan and Its Meaning*. These interviews incl such people as Averell Harriman, George Kennan, and Marshall himself. 15 countries, OEEC (Organization for European Economic Cooperation), and USRO (US Special Representative in Europe) are represented in these interviews. Also in the collection are papers and materials that Cecilia "Jackie" Martin collected as picture editor for the Marshall Plan Information Service in Europe, 1950-54.

ECONOMIC BOTANY see Botany, Economic

ECONOMIC CONDITIONS see Economics—History

ECONOMIC CYCLES see Business Cycles

ECONOMIC DEPRESSIONS see Depressions—1929—U.S.

ECONOMIC DEVELOPMENT

CA —UNIVERSITY OF CALIFORNIA, BERKELEY, Giannini Foundation of Agricultural Economics, Library, 248 Giannini Hall, Berkeley, 94720. Grace Dote, Librn
Holdings: Vols (18,000) Cat Mss Microforms
Notes: Agricultural development of developing countries.

CT —YALE UNIVERSITY, Social Science Library, Economic Growth Center Collection, 140 Prospect St, New Haven, 06520. Billie I Salter, Librn
Holdings: Vols (47,600) Cat Microforms
Notes: Economic data on national economies & their development; budgets, plans, statistical yearbooks and bulletins, censuses, national accounts trade, monetary, etc, statistics. Focus primarily on less developed countries. Shelf list organized by country and LC number, in addition to dictionary card catalog. Collection shelved by country; mostly government documents, 3800 serial titles currently received.
See also entry under Social Sciences

DC —INTERNATIONAL MONETARY FUND AND WORLD BANK, Joint Bank-Fund Library, Washington, 20431. Maureen M Moore, Librn
Holdings: Vols Cat Films Microforms
Notes: Incl foreign trade and statistical bulletins and yearbooks, central bank reports and bulletins, budget papers, security yearbooks, economic development plans and reports on economic conditions from the 132 member countries. An index of periodical material compiled by the Library staff has been published as: *Economics and Finance; Index to Periodical Articles, 1947-1971;* First Supplement, 1972, 1973, 1974 (Second Supplement, 1975, 1976, 1977, in preparation), 5 vols. (Boston: G K Hall, 1972, 1975). Also, The Developing Areas: *A Classed Bibliography of the Joint Bank-Fund Library,* Vol 1: *Latin America and the* Caribbean; Vol 2: *Africa and the Middle* East; Vol 3: *Asia and Oceania* (Boston: G K Hall, 1976).

DC —US DEPT OF STATE, Library, Rm 3239 NS, Washington, 20520. Conrad P Eaton, Librn
Holdings: Vols (750,000) Cat Microforms
Notes: Incl 7200 microfilm reels.

IA —IOWA STATE UNIVERSITY, Library, Ames, 50011. Warren B Kuhn, Dean of Library Services
Holdings: Cat
Notes: International development and planning.

LA —LOUISIANA DEPT OF COMMERCE, Office of Commerce & Industry, PO Box 44185, Baton Rouge, 70804. Anna Maria I Pinza, Research Dir
Holdings: Maps Pix Slides
Notes: Incl serial monographs and publications, some books.

MA —HARVARD UNIVERSITY, Graduate School of Education, Monroe C Gutman Library, 6 Appian Way, Cambridge, 02138. Susan S Baughman, Associate Librn
Holdings: Vols (150,000) Cat Mss Microforms
Budget: ($95,000)
Notes: A comprehensive research collection that seeks to acquire all scholarly works published in the English language in the fields of education, educational administration, educational psychology, and human development. Selective coverage in the related areas of counseling and psychology, business administration, finance, forecasting, statistical analysis and survey design, public and social policy, linguistics, demographics, and international and economic development. Incl 4000 educational and psychological tests.

MA —HARVARD UNIVERSITY, Institute for International Development, Library, Coolidge Hall, 1737 Cambridge St, Cambridge, 02138. Barbara Mitchell, Librn
Holdings: Vols (17,000)
Notes: Economic development, rural development, statistical material on selected underdeveloped countries. Incl 75 periodical titles.

MI —GREAT LAKES COMMISSION, Institute of Science and Technology Bldg, 2200 Bonisteel Blvd, Ann Arbor, 48109. Michael J Donahue, Natural Resources Specialist
Holdings: Vols (4000)
Notes: Incl directories, reports and related documents covering Great Lakes-related natural resources management, transportation and economic development issues. The library is available for limited public use upon appointment.

MI —UNIVERSITY OF MICHIGAN, Center for Research on Economic Development, Library, 240 Lorch Hall, Ann Arbor, 48109. Carol Wilson, Information/Resources Coordinator
Holdings: Vols (21,000) Cat 16mm Films Microforms
Budget: ($7000)
Notes: Publications that list library and its collection: *Directory of Third World Studies in the US* (African Studies Assn, 1981), *National Reference Center Directory* 1983 (NRC), *World Guide to Libraries* 1983 (Saur Verlag), *Research Centers Directory 1983* (Gale Research), and *A Directory of Information Resources in US* (Library of Congress, 1978). Collection's focus is Third World economic development. Other areas of interest are economic planning, developing countries, Africa (specifically francophone Africa), the Sahel, African agricultural economics, commodities production, financial statistics, development plans from less developed countries (LDC), and international development. Each part of the library's collection (working papers/ reports, periodicals and government documents) has its own catalog and cataloging system.

MI —MICHIGAN STATE UNIVERSITY, International Library, Sahel Documentation Center, East Lansing, 48824. Eugene deBenko, Librn; Learthen Dorsey, Librn
Holdings: Vols (5100) Cat Mss Maps Pix Slides Phonorecords Audiotapes Videotapes Microforms
Budget: ($8000)
Notes: See description under The Sahel.

MI —MICHIGAN STATE UNIVERSITY, International Library, South and Southeast Asia Collection, East Lansing, 48824. Clinton Lockert, Bibliographer
Holdings: Vols (6000) Cat Maps Microforms
Notes: Emphasis is upon South and Southeast Asia, especially Bangladesh and Vietnam (South). Attempt to collect extensively the economic and social development plans of the developing nations. Monographs and serials received on PL 480 from India, Pakistan, Sri Lanka and Nepal since 1968. Extensive holdings of Academy for Rural Development, Comilla, Bangladesh (1959-), and of the Michigan State University Vietnam Advisory Group (1955-1962).

NY —UNITED NATIONS, Dag Hammarskjold Library, Rm L382, New York, 10017. Vladimir Orlov, Librn
Holdings: Cat Microforms

PA —UNIVERSITY OF PITTSBURGH, Library, Graduate School of Public and International Affairs, Forbes Quadrangle, 1st floor West, Pittsburgh, 15260. Nicholas C Caruso, Librn
Holdings: Vols (80,000) Cat
Budget: ($150,000)
Notes: The library attempts to collect as many national economic and social development plans as possible from the developing countries of the world. It also holds city, regional and state plans for Pennsylvania, particularly, the 9 southwestern counties of Pennsylvania.

PR —CARIBBEAN REGIONAL LIBRARY, General Library, University of Puerto Rico, Rio Piedras, (Mailing add: PO Box 21917, University Station, San Juan, 00931). Carmen M Costa de Ramos, Librn
Holdings: Vols (115,605) Cat Maps Pix Microforms
Notes: Collection is specialized in the Caribbean with emphasis in the areas of interest to developing countries: social sciences, politics, economics, labor, education, commerce, tourism, literature, etc. The *Current Caribbean Bibliography* is compiled at the Caribbean Regional Library, with card contributions from all countries of the Caribbean; it also lists all the new additions to the library.

ON —DEPT OF REGIONAL INDUSTRIAL EXPANSION, Ottawa Library, 235 Queen St, Ottawa, K1A 0H5, Can. Steven Rush, Librn
Holdings: Vols (100,000) Cat Maps Microforms
Notes: Contains 1500 reports of ARDA projects (Agricultural Rehabilitation and Development Agency); also NEWSTART project reports. There is a published book catalog and two supplements. 15,000 documents; 3000 periodical subscriptions.

PQ —CANADIAN INTERNATIONAL DEVELOPMENT AGENCY, Development Information Centre, 200 Promenade du Portage, Hull, K1A 0G4, Can. Nicole Smith, Librn
Notes: International economic development.

ECONOMIC DEVELOPMENT—HISTORY

CA —CALIFORNIA STATE UNIVERSITY, FRESNO, Henry Madden Library, Dept of Special Collections, Fresno, 93740. Ronald J Mahoney, Head
Holdings: // Uncat Mss Maps
Notes: Promotional material and correspondence of an unsuccessful attempt by Americans to raise capital to exploit the Torontoy, or Cercada-de-San Antonio Estate in southern Peru. The estate was said to have been the source of ancient Peruvian gold. 50 ms items. Also, materials on unsuccessful American venture to exploit the agricultural and mineral resources of western Mexico, ca 1920. 65 ms pieces.

ECONOMIC DEVELOPMENT, WOMEN IN see Women in Economic Development

ECONOMIC FORECASTING

CA —UNIVERSITY OF CALIFORNIA, LOS ANGELES, Graduate School of Management Library, UCLA Campus, Los Angeles, 90024. Robert Bellanti, Head Librn
Holdings: Vols (128,000) Cat Mss Microforms
Notes: The

NY —JOINT COUNCIL ON ECONOMIC EDUCATION, Library, 2 Park Ave, New York, 10016.
Holdings: Cat

ECONOMIC GEOLOGY see Geology, Economic

ECONOMIC HISTORY see Economics—History

ECONOMIC INTEGRATION, INTERNATIONAL see International Economic Integration

ECONOMIC NATIONALISM see Economic Policy

ECONOMIC OPPORTUNITY

NY —NEW YORK STATE DEPT OF STATE, Community Affairs Library, 162 Washington Ave, Albany, 12231. M L Johnson, Librn
Holdings: Vols (14,640) Cat
Notes: Local government. Serves as research arm for official activities. 16,000 items in vertical files; 150 periodicals. Unique Community File collection of about 1600 local governments arranged by counties in the state.

NY —ROCKEFELLER UNIVERSITY, Rockefeller Archive Center, Hillcrest, Pocantico Hills, North Tarrytown, 10591. Joseph W Ernst, Dir; J William Hess, Assoc Dir
Notes: The Rockefeller Archive Center, a division of The Rockefeller University, preserves and makes available to scholars the records of the University, the Rockefeller Foundation, the Rockefeller Brothers Fund, members of the family, and those of other individuals and organizations associated with their endeavors. Collections at the Center document a century of philanthropy by legions of associated social and scientific pioneers, providing a unique window into the past.

ECONOMIC PLANNING see Economic Policy

ECONOMIC POISONS see Pesticides

ECONOMIC POLICY

MI —UNIVERSITY OF MICHIGAN, Center for Research on Economic Development, Library, 240 Lorch Hall, Ann Arbor, 48109. Carol Wilson, Information/Resources Coordinator
Holdings: Vols (21,000) Cat 16mm Films Microforms
Budget: ($7000)
Notes: Publications that list library and its collection: *Directory of Third World Studies in the US* (African Studies Assn, 1981), *National Reference Center Directory* 1983 (NRC), *World Guide to Libraries* 1983 (Saur Verlag), *Research Centers Directory 1983* (Gale Research), and *A Directory of Information Resources in US* (Library of Congress, 1978). Collection's focus is Third World economic development. Other areas of interest are economic planning, developing countries, Africa (specifically francophone Africa), the Sahel, African agricultural economics, commodities production, financial statistics, development plans from less developed countries (LDC), and international development. Each part of the library's collection (working papers/reports, periodicals and government documents) has its own catalog and cataloging system.

NY —JOINT COUNCIL ON ECONOMIC EDUCATION, Library, 2 Park Ave, New York, 10016.
Holdings: Cat

ECONOMIC POLICY, FOREIGN see International Economic Relations

ECONOMIC RELATIONS, FOREIGN see International Economic Relations

ECONOMIC REFORM

NY —ROCKEFELLER UNIVERSITY, Rockefeller Archive Center, Hillcrest, Pocantico Hills, North Tarrytown, 10591. Joseph W Ernst, Dir; J William Hess, Assoc Dir
Notes: The Rockefeller Archive Center, a division of The Rockefeller University, preserves and makes available to scholars the records of the University, the Rockefeller Foundation, the Rockefeller Brothers Fund, members of the family, and those of other individuals and organizations associated with their endeavors. Collections at the Center document a century of philanthropy by legions of associated social and scientific pioneers, providing a unique window into the past.

ECONOMIC RESEARCH

MO —FEDERAL RESERVE BANK OF KANSAS CITY, Research Library, 925 Grand Ave, Kansas City, 64198. Ellen M Johnson, Librn
Holdings: Vols 12,000

NY —JOINT COUNCIL ON ECONOMIC EDUCATION, Library, 2 Park Ave, New York, 10016.
Holdings: Cat

NY —NATIONAL ECONOMIC RESEARCH ASSOCIATES, INC, Library, 123 Main St, White Plains, 10601. Debra Gaffey, Asst Librn
Holdings: Vols (7500) Cat
Notes: Energy economics, power resources, anti-trust legislation, and public policy.

WA —BOEING COMPANY, Boeing Technical Libraries, PO Box 3707, Seattle, 98124. Corrine Campbell, Mgr Technical Library
Holdings: Vols (75,000) Cat Microforms
Notes: Books are distributed between 3 libraries, Kent, Renton, and Bellevue. Also contains many periodicals and Boeing Documents Library restricted to Boeing Personnel.

ECONOMIC SECURITY

MD —US SOCIAL SECURITY ADMINISTRATION, Library, Library Information & Graphics Services Branch, Altmeyer Bldg Rm 571, 6401 Security Blvd, Baltimore, 21235. Rowena S Sadler, Chief
Holdings: Vols Cat
Notes: All phases of social insurance incl OASI pensions, welfare health insurance and medical economics.

ECONOMIC STATISTICS see Economics—History; Statistics

ECONOMIC UNION see International Economic Integration

ECONOMICS

AL —UNIVERSITY OF ALABAMA, Business Library, Box 2937, University, 35486. Dorothy Eady Brown, Librn; Linda Suttle Harris, Ref Librn and Data Base Searcher
Holdings: Vols (105,000) Cat Microforms
Budget: ($50,000)
Notes: Incl 90,000 corporation reports and 38,500 microforms.

CA —UNIVERSITY OF SOUTHERN CALIFORNIA, Crocker Business Library, Hoffman Hall, University Park, Los Angeles, 90007. Judith A Truelson, Head Librn
Holdings: Vols (100,000) Cat Microforms
Notes: The Roy P Crocker Library of Business Administration, located in Hoffman Hall, houses more than 100,000 volumes and regularly receives approximately 1500 trade, financial, economics, labor, and general business periodicals and newspapers. The areas of subject concentration include business economics, finance and investments, general management/management theory, international business, finance and management, marketing/food marketing, and quantitative business analysis.

CA —ASSOCIATION OF BAY AREA GOVERNMENTS, MTC/ABAG Library, 101 Eighth St, Oakland, 94607. Diane Gillman, Information Coord
Notes: Concentrates heavily on the nine-county Bay Area region. About 10,000 monographs and serials. Title catalog, OCLC/ATS. Central collection of documents for six transit properties in Bay Area.

CA —PASADENA PUBLIC LIBRARY, Business-Technology Division, 285 E Walnut St, Pasadena, 91101. Anne Cain, Librn for Reference Services
Holdings: Vols (19,000) Cat Microforms
Budget: ($35,000)
Notes: Investment and financial services (current and historical); trade and industrial directories; corporate annual reports; current economic statistics in business services and in state and federal government publications. Special index to directory collection.

CA —CONTRA COSTA COUNTY LIBRARY, 1750 Oak Park Blvd, Pleasant Hill, 94523. Lyn Talme, Business Specialist
Holdings: Vols (7000)
Notes: Incl 76 periodicals, 1000 corporate annual reports, and 316 telephone directories.

CA —SACRAMENTO PUBLIC LIBRARY, 828 I St, Sacramento, 95814. Dorothy Harvey, Librn, Special Collections
Holdings: Vols (8000) Cat
Notes: Incl 800 periodicals and services. Emphasis is on business subjects and economics and labor. Technology not incl. Incl about 1000 corporation reports.

CA —RAND CORP, Library, 1700 Main St, Santa Monica, 90406. Vivian J Arterbery, Library Mgr
Holdings: Vols 2000 Uncat
Notes: Theory and applications, such as economic analysis.

CO —COLORADO SCHOOL OF MINES, Arthur Lakes Library, 14 & Illinois Sts, Golden, 80401. Hartley K Phinney, Jr, Head Librn
Holdings: Vols (250,557) Cat Mss Maps Microforms

CT —AMERICAN CAN CO, Business Information Center, American Lane, Greenwich, 06830. Estelle Adler, Mgr
Holdings: Vols (6000) Cat Microforms

CT —YALE UNIVERSITY, Social Science Library, 140 Prospect St, New Haven, 06520. Billie I Salter, Librn
Holdings: Vols (61,000) Cat Microforms
Notes: Incl the former Political Science Research Library, Sociology Department Library, Geography Library and Economic Study collections, as well as non-country sources from the Economic Growth Center Library.

CT —YALE UNIVERSITY, Social Science Library, Economic Growth Center Collection, 140 Prospect St, New Haven, 06520. Billie I Salter, Librn
Holdings: Vols (47,600) Cat Microforms
See also entry under Social Sciences

DC —EXPORT-IMPORT BANK OF THE UNITED STATES, EXIMBANK Library, 811 Vermont Ave NW, Washington, 20571. Theodora McGill, Librn; John Posniak, Asst Librn
Holdings: Vols (15,000) Maps Audiotapes
Notes: The library has almost a complete set of the Economist Intelligence unit of London's *Quarterly Economic Reviews*; various types of materials with general, economic and statistical data on virtually every country of the world; incl foreign government publications, publications of

ECONOMICS (cont.)

various international organizations, and US Government documents.

DC —INTERNATIONAL MONETARY FUND AND WORLD BANK, Joint Bank-Fund Library, Washington, 20431. Maureen M Moore, Librn
Holdings: Vols Cat Films Microforms
Notes: Incl foreign trade and statistical bulletins and yearbooks, central bank reports and bulletins, budget papers, security yearbooks, economic development plans and reports on economic conditions from the 132 member countries. An index of periodical material compiled by the Library staff has been published as: *Economics and Finance; Index to Periodical Articles, 1947-1971;* First Supplement, 1972, 1973, 1974 (Second Supplement, 1975, 1976, 1977, in preparation), 5 vols. (Boston: G K Hall, 1972, 1975). Also, The Developing Areas: *A Classed Bibliography of the Joint Bank-Fund Library,* Vol 1: *Latin America and the* Caribbean; Vol 2: *Africa and the Middle* East; Vol 3: *Asia and Oceania* (Boston: G K Hall, 1976).

DC —US COMMISSION ON CIVIL RIGHTS, National Clearinghouse Library, 1121 Vermont Ave NW, Washington, 20005. Lenora McMillan, Chief Librn
Holdings: Vols (10,200) Cat Slides Microforms
Notes: The National Clearinghouse Library has a special collection of the US Commission on Civil Rights publications from its inception (1957) to present date.

DC —US DEPT OF LABOR, Library, 200 Constitution Ave NW, Washington, 20210. Sabina Jacobson, Dir
Holdings: Vols 535,000 Cat Audiotapes Microforms
Notes: Economics, especially labor, incl much historical material. Receive 3200 current periodical titles.

GA —ATLANTA PUBLIC LIBRARY, Ivan Allen Jr Dept of Science, Industry & Government, One Margaret Mitchell Square, Atlanta, 30303. William D Munro, Head
Holdings: Vols (15,000) Cat Microforms
Budget: ($180,000)
Notes: This collection incl on microform annual reports and Securities Exchange Commission 10-K reports for some 11,000 companies from 1976 to date; current and retrospective stock quotations, stock reports, corporate and industry records and directories and supporting looseleaf services; information file on Atlanta's largest 15,000 with annual updates; and current plat maps for the five county Metro-Atlanta area. Atlanta and Georgia business history sections are being developed. Most material on this collection is noncirculating.

GA —FEDERAL RESERVE BANK OF ATLANTA, Research Library, PO Box 1731, Atlanta, 30301. Leigh Watson Healy, Information Services Coord; Cynthia Walsh-Kloss, Assoc Librn
Holdings: Vols (12,000) Cat Mss Microforms
Notes: Collection specializes in banking, finance, economics, publications of the Federal Reserve Banks and Federal Reserve Board.

HI —BANK OF HAWAII, Information Ctr, PO Box 2900, Honolulu, 96846. Sally Campbell, Information Mgr
Holdings: Vols 4000 Cat Maps
Notes: Economics research in developing areas of Hawaii, US Pacific Islands, Asian and other foreign countries. Emphasis on economics, business statistics, demography, finance, banking, tourist industry, construction, domestic and foreign trade. Incl 1000 serial titles.

IL —FEDERAL RESERVE BANK OF CHICAGO, Library, 230 S La Salle St, PO Box 834, Chicago, 60690. Dorothy Phillips, Librn
Holdings: Vols (19,000) Cat
Notes: Restricted use: noncirculating. No photocopying.

IL —NORTHERN ILLINOIS REGIONAL HISTORY CENTER, Sven Parson Hall, Northern Illinois University, De Kalb, 60115. Glen Gildemeister, Dir
Holdings: Cat Mss Maps Pix Slides Phonorecords Audiotapes 16mm Films Microforms
Notes: "A research center for advanced research in the humanities. This northern area of Illinois (excluding Cook County) has been virtually untouched by collecting agencies and we hope to fill that void. We will be strong in agribusiness, agricultural implement business, and hybrid farming mechanics....Will be primarily a ms repository, but [have] already taken responsibility for many artifacts and books, some rare."

IL —SCHAUMBURG TOWNSHIP PUBLIC LIBRARY, 32 W Library Lane, Schaumburg, 60194. Michael Madden, Librn
Holdings: Vols (20,000) Cat
Budget: ($60,000)
Notes: Maintained as business and economics subject center under the North Suburban Library System's Coordinated Acquisitions Program.

IL —UNIVERSITY OF ILLINOIS, URBANA/CHAMPAIGN, Library, 1408 W Gregory Drive, Urbana, 61801. Norman B Brown, Asst Dir for Special Collections
Holdings: Vols 2000
Notes: Russian, German, French and English publications in the field of economics.

IN —PURDUE UNIVERSITY LIBRARIES, Graduate School of Management, Krannert Library, West Lafayette, 47907. Gordon Law, Librn
Holdings: Vols (142,727) Cat Microforms
Budget: ($69,700)
Notes: There is an extensive collection of corporate reports and labor information material (some 115,000 items). Over 2500 periodicals are currently received.

KY —KENTUCKY WESLEYAN COLLEGE LIBRARY, 3000 Frederica, Owensboro, 42301. Stuart Stiffler, Dir
Notes: The Dr and Mrs M David Orrahood Collection.

MD —JOHNS HOPKINS UNIVERSITY, Milton S Eisenhower Library, Charles & 34 Sts, Baltimore, 21218. Ann S Gwyn, Assistant Dir for Special Collections
Holdings: Vols 85,000 Cat
Notes: A strong collection, with a large separate collection not incl in the above figure on economics classics and a small section on French 19th century works.

MA —HARVARD UNIVERSITY, Graduate School of Business Administration, Baker Library, Soldiers Field, Boston, 02163. Mary V Chatfield, Librn; Florence Bartoshesky, Cur of Manuscripts and Archives
Holdings: Vols (75,000) Cat Mss Pix
Notes: Baker Library strong in historical aspects of business and economics incl original company records, company histories, business biographies, histories of industries, etc; 16,000 pictures. Ms collection of more than 75,000 incl original records of business firms from 1400 (Medici Collection) to present; especially strong in 19th century. New England enterprises, textile firms, international trade, China trade, railroads, papers of several Northeast merchant families, 19th century small business. Also incl pictures, trade cards, clipper ship cards, money, trade catalogs, business cartoons, prices current and exhibit items. See Robert W Lovett and Eleanor C Bishop, compilers, *Business Manuscripts in Baker Library* (Boston: The Library, 1978), 382 pp. Mss are described in the*National Union Catlog of Manuscript Collections* and in Hamer's *A Guide to Archives and Manuscripts in the United States.* Restricted use: Manuscripts noncirculating. Downs: 1636, 2122, 2616, 2675, 2677, 2698, 2700, 2701, 2702, 2706, 2708, 2711, 2713-15, 2716, 2717-18, 2721-26, 2734, 2737, 2774, 2814, 4300, 5162: Supplement 964, 965, 968, 998.

†MA —JOHN F KENNEDY LIBRARY, Columbia Point, Boston, 02125. Dan H Fenn Jr, Dir
Holdings: // Cat Mss
Notes: Correspondence and other papers of Walter W Heller relating to national economic policy, 1940-1971; correspondence, draft manuscripts, reports and other personal and official papers of John K Galbraith, 1930-1963; and Seymour Harris's collection of books and other printed materials relating to economics and public affairs. 115 linear ft of mss. Holdings are described in "Historical Materials in the John F Kennedy Library." Copies may be obtained by writing the Research Archivist.

MA —HARVARD UNIVERSITY LIBRARY, Widener Library, Cambridge, 02138.
Holdings: Cat
Notes: *Widener Library Shelflist* Nos 23-24 (1970) lists 67,074 volumes on economics. For description of collection see *Harvard Library Bulletin,* XX (1972), 49-68.

MA —BOSTON COLLEGE LIBRARIES, Thomas P O'Neill Library, Chestnut Hill, 02167. John D J Slinn, Librn of the Central Library
Holdings: Vols 62,000 Cat Maps Audiotapes Filmstrips Microforms
Budget: ($120,000)

MI —UNIVERSITY OF MICHIGAN, Bureau of Government Library, 100A Rackman Bldg, Ann Arbor, 48109. Barbara Landay, Technical Libr Assistant
Holdings: Vols (66,000) Cat
Budget: ($10,000)
Notes: Established in 1914 to serve faculty and students of Institute of Public Policy Studies. Particularly concerned with state and local documents, but incl some federal documents. Also has a pamphlet and newspaper clipping collection on Michigan. Some information on foreign governments.

MI —NORTHWOOD INSTITUTE, Strosacker Library, 3225 Cook Rd, Midland, 48640. Catherine Chen, Head Librn
Holdings: Vols 3000 Cat Maps Microforms
Budget: $30,000
Notes: Business and management, incl economics and economic history. Audiovisual materials are located in the Griswold Communications Center.

MN —MINNEAPOLIS PUBLIC LIBRARY & INFORMATION CENTER, Business & Economics Dept, 300 Nicollet Mall, Minneapolis, 55401. Mary Lawson, Librn
Notes: Separate card catalog, telephone reference service, and directory service. Incl periodical titles; large files of corporation annual reports; VF of local company histories and annual reports; domestic and foreign telephone directories; historical US stock quotations, 1891-date; local OTC quotations, 1933-date; indexes and abstracting services; looseleaf reference services.

MN —JAMES JEROME HILL REFERENCE LIBRARY, Fourth St at Market St, Saint Paul, 55106. Virgil F Massman, Dir
Holdings: Vols (197,000) Cat
Budget: ($170,000)
Notes: A good standard collection of books by standard authors.

MO —WADDELL & REED, INC, Research Library, One Crown Center, PO Box 1343, Kansas City, 64141. Betty J Howerton, Head Librn
Holdings: Vols (30,000) Cat Periodicals Newspapers
Budget: ($65,000)
Notes: Economics and business.

NJ —PRINCETON UNIVERSITY, Library, Rare Books Dept, Princeton, 08544. Stephen Ferguson, Cur
Holdings: Cat

NY —BROOKLYN PUBLIC LIBRARY, Business Library, 280 Cadman Plaza W, Brooklyn, 11201. Sylvia Mechanic, Business Librn
Holdings: Vols (107,000) Cat
Notes: Library received about 1800 periodicals, 3000 serials, 2700 directories, 1600 telephone books from all over the world with a complete back file on microfilm for greater New York. Library is a selective US Government Documents depository. Subscribes to microfiche SEC 10K reports for AMEX, NYSE and OTC from 1976 to date; annual reports for earlier years. Transnational annual reports, on fiche from 1982-to date. 78 vertical file trays; Sanborn maps for Brooklyn, special collection of corporation histories. Publish monthly

ECONOMICS (cont.)

newsletter, *Service to Business and Industry* with our Science Division.

NY —HUDSON INSTITUTE, Library, Quaker Ridge Rd, Croton-on-Hudson, 10520. Mildred Schneck, Librn
Holdings: Vols (10,000) Cat
Budget: ($40,000)
Notes: Social sciences and world futures. About 30 percent of the collection emphasizes materials useful to our ongoing program of examining possible world futures: social and economic indicators, forecasts, current social problems, arms control and disarmament.

NY —CONFERENCE BOARD, Information Service Library, 845 Third Ave, New York, 10022. Tamsen M Hernandez, Dir
Holdings: Vols 25,000 Cat Microforms
Notes: Heavily directed to collection of government materials and corporate data.

NY —FEDERAL RESERVE BANK OF NEW YORK, Research Library, 33 Liberty St, Federal Reserve PO Sta, New York, 10045. Jean Deuss, Chief Librn
Holdings: Vols (60,000) Periodicals
Budget: ($115,000)
Notes: Collection incl (60,000 vols) and more than (1300) periodical titles.

NY —JOINT COUNCIL ON ECONOMIC EDUCATION, Library, 2 Park Ave, New York, 10016.
Holdings: Vols 2000 Cat
Notes: The Edwin G Nourse Library of Economic Education.

NY —NEW YORK PUBLIC LIBRARY, Research Libraries, Economic & Public Affairs Div, Fifth Ave & 42 St, New York, 10018. Edward DiRoma, Chief
Holdings: Vols (1,500,000) Cat Microforms

NY —NEW YORK PUBLIC LIBRARY, Mid-Manhattan Library, Science & Business Dept, 455 Fifth Ave, New York, 10016. Frederick E Dusold, Sr Principal Librn
Holdings: Vols (31,000) Cat Microforms
Budget: ($55,000)
Notes: Undergraduate level collection with duplicate reference and circulating copies of books. 80 drawers of pamphlet material. Standard business and financial services. 560 periodicals.

NY —STANDARD & POOR'S CORP, Library, 25 Broadway, New York, 10004. Walter Nixon, Ref Librn
Holdings: Vols (22,000) Cat Microforms
Notes: Library has 800,000 microforms.

NY —UNIVERSITY OF ROCHESTER, Graduate School of Management Library, Rush Rhees Library, Rochester, 14627. Edward Wass; Janet Prentice; Datta Kharbas
Holdings: Vols (92,000) Cat Microforms
Budget: ($38,000)
Notes: Incl a reference collection, a geographical file on economic conditions, an industry file of statistics and trends, research reports and working papers, more than 2400 hardcopy annual reports and 10K microfiche of the Fortune 500 companies, and over 900 management and economics periodicals.

NC —DUKE UNIVERSITY, William R Perkins Library, Durham, 27706. Elvin E Strowd, University Librn

NC —GREENSBORO PUBLIC LIBRARY, Business Library, 201 Greene St, Drawer X-4, Greensboro, 27402. Lebby B Lamb, Business Librn
Holdings: Vols (6000) Cat Microforms
Budget: ($12,000)

OH —CLEVELAND PUBLIC LIBRARY, Business, Economics and Labor Department, 325 Superior Ave, Cleveland, 44114. Joan Sorger, Head
Holdings: Vols (115,703) Cat
Notes: Currently receiving over 1700 periodicals and 1300 serial titles; 1000 individual trade, industrial and professional directories, worldwide; 324 file drawers annual reports of old companies, many local; 24 drawers historical information on Cleveland companies. Annual reports, 10-K's, Proxy Statements (disclosure SEC filings on fiche); over 200 loose-leaf services; 1700 current telephone and city directories. Emphasis on current material. Areas of special strength are banking, investments, marketing and management. Also strong insurance, accounting, real estate and transportation collections. Computerized sources available incl Dow Jones News Service and a variety of Dialog business-related databases.

OH —OHIO STATE UNIVERSITY, William Oxley Thompson Memorial Library, Hilander Room, 1858 Neil Ave Mall, Columbus, 43210. Predrag Matejic, Cur; G Koolemans Beynen, Slavic Bibliographer
Holdings: Vols (200,000) Cat Maps Microforms
Budget: ($45,000)
Notes: Area studies of Central, Southeastern and Eastern Europe. Emphasis on on Slavic literatures, languages and history. At present economics, sociology, law (Russian only) have been added. Within this framework the following priorities have been established: Material in Russian problems; then Medieval Slavic (Cyrillic); then Polish, then Serbo-Croatian, then Bulgarian, and now Romanian. Special attention is paid to serials, bibliographies, ms descriptions and dictionaries (incl biographical and encyclopedias). Apart from materials in native languages, materials in the following languages are acquired: Old Church Slavonic, Greek, English, French, German, Italian, a few in Scandinavian languages, incl Finnish, and a few in Baltic languages. The Hillandar Room holds approx 2000 Slavic mss, 1050 from Hilandar Monastery, Mount Athos, on microform and a related referencecollection.

PA —DREXEL UNIVERSITY LIBRARIES, W W Hagerty Library, 32 & Chestnut Sts, Philadelphia, 19104. R L Snyder, Dir
Holdings: Vols (66,500) Cat Microforms
Budget: ($16,000)
Notes: Incl 25,000 microforms of annual reports of companies traded on the NYSE and the ASE.

PA —UNIVERSITY OF PITTSBURGH, Economics/Center for Regional Economics Studies Library, 4956 Forbes Quad, Pittsburgh, 15260. Patricia Suozzi-Crehan, Librn
Holdings: Vols 20,000
Budget: ($25,724)
Notes: Card catalog for collection. Cards for Economics Collection are in Hillman Library catalog. Collections are working collections reflecting the research and teaching interests of the Dept of Economics faculty and graduate students. The collection covers all aspects of the field of economics and demography.

RI —BRYANT COLLEGE, Edith M Hodgson Memorial Library, Rte 7, Douglas Pike, Smithfield, 02917. John P Hannon, Dir
Holdings: Vols (103,000) Cat Phonorecords Audiotapes Videotapes 16mm Films Filmstrips Microforms
Budget: ($175,000)
Notes: Incl 6000 bound periodical vols, 250 phonorecords, 220 audiotapes, 120 videotapes, 30 16mm films, 150 filmstrips and 7500 microforms.

SD —MINUTEMAN GRADUATE CENTER LIBRARY, RR 3, Box 3050, Rapid City, 57701. Laura K Dickson, Librn
Holdings: Vols 1000 Cat Microforms
Budget: ($11,000)
Notes: Library mainly for use of Air Force officers and civilians enrolled in the Minuteman Education Program (MMEP), Ellsworth Air Force Base, SD. Limited public use. Interlibrary loans permitted.

TX —DALLAS PUBLIC LIBRARY, Central Research Library, Business & Technology Div, 1515 Young St, Dallas, 75201. Sarabeth Allen, Mgr
Holdings: Vols 6000 Cat
Budget: $2500
Notes: *Business History Collection; a* Checklist. Dallas, Texas: Business and Technology Div, Dallas Public Library, 1974. Published to serve as a subject (by corporate name) catalog. Interlibrary loans are invited.

TX —SOUTHERN METHODIST UNIVERSITY, Fondren Library, Dallas, 75275. Curt Holleman, Librn for Collection Development

TX —ECTOR COUNTY LIBRARY, Department of Business and Technology, 321 W 5th St, Odessa, 79760. Pat Jones, Dept Head
Holdings: Vols 2000 Cat
Notes: 25,000 Corporate Annual Reports microfilmed reports are complete from 1978-1983. 200 vertical files, 30 periodicals. Collection includes the subjects of Business, Management, Real Estate Accounting, Land Economics, Labor Economics, Finance, Personal Finance and Environmental Economics. Also included are stock and dividend reports, commodities and bond reports as well as business rankings. All items are referenced and cataloged.

VA —FEDERAL RESERVE BANK OF RICHMOND, Research Library, 701 E Byrd St, PO Box 27622, Richmond, 23261. Ruth M Eggleston Cannon, Librn
Holdings: Vols (20,000) Cat
Notes: Limited photocopying.

WA —SEATTLE PUBLIC LIBRARY, 1000 Fourth Ave, Seattle, 98104. Ronald A Dubberly, City Librn
Holdings: Cat

†WA —UNIVERSITY OF WASHINGTON LIBRARIES, Seattle, 98195.

WY —US AIR FORCE INSTITUTE OF TECHNOLOGY, Library, Dept 9 Bldg 831, FE, Warren AFB, 82001. Patricia A Johnson, Librn
Holdings: Vols (7000) Cat Microforms
Budget: ($9000)
Notes: The Library supports graduate programs for students (Air Force Missile-Combat Crewmen) seeking a Master of Business Administration Degree. Civilian students and other military personnel are also admitted.

BC —VANCOUVER PUBLIC LIBRARY, Business and Economics Div, 750 Burrard St, Vancouver, V6Z 1X5, Can. Barbara Bell, Librn
Notes: Incl numerous special files for *Quick Reference, Subject Clippings, Companies* (information of major Canadian, US and international corporations; index to new British Columbia and Canadian company corporations, 1951 to 1978; 160,000 cards); company file, *Province Index* and *Association File* (particulars of Canadian trade and professional associations). *International Collection of Trade* directories and telephone books.

ON —CANADIAN HOUSING INFORMATION CENTER, Canada Mortgage and Housing Corp, CMHC Annex Bldg Ground Floor, Montreal Rd, Ottawa, K1A 0P7, Can. Leslie Jones, Mgr
Holdings: Cat

ON —CANADIAN TRANSPORT COMMISSION, Library, Ottawa, K1A 0N9, Can. Marty H Lovelock, Librn
Holdings: Cat Microforms
Budget: ($50,000)
Notes: Books, documents, periodicals. Emphasis on transportation law and economics.

ON —NATIONAL LIBRARY OF CANADA, 395 Wellington St, Ottawa, K1A 0N4, Can. Andre Preibish, Dir
Holdings: Vols 10,000
Notes: Includes 130 serial titles, theses, pamphlets, government publications relating to family and marriage. The following disciplines covered: anthropology, psychology and psychiatry, law, economics, religion, sociology, demography, education, political science and biology. Earliest title 1630.

ON —CANADIAN IMPERIAL BANK OF COMMERCE, Information Centre, Commerce Court, Toronto, M5L 1A2, Can. Jane Cooney, Librn Head Office
Holdings: Vols (22,000) Cat Microforms
Notes: Basic economic texts; working papers, studies, etc, from Canadian and foreign universities; government publications.

ON —METROPOLITAN TORONTO LIBRARY, Business Dept, 789 Yonge St, Toronto, M4W 2G8, Can. Patricia Dye, Head
Holdings: Vols (63,682) Cat Microforms
Budget: ($508,800)
Notes: Extensive current and historical

ECONOMICS (cont.)

information with emphasis on Canadian companies incl annual reports, clippings and pamphlets files, and a collection of business and trade directories. Also international directories. Approximately 1000 current periodicals, and up-dating services giving corporation information. Statistics collection.

ON —ONTARIO MINISTRY OF TREASURY & ECONOMICS, Library Services, Frost Bldg N, Queen's Park, Toronto, M7A 1Y8, Can. Barbara Weatherhead, Head Librn
Holdings: Vols (100,000) Cat Microforms
Budget: ($76,500)
Notes: Index to Ontario regulations.

ON —TORONTO DOMINION BANK, Department of Economic Research, 55 King St W, Toronto, M5K 1A2, Can. Ruth P Smith, Librn
Holdings: Vols (6000) Cat

SK —SASKATCHEWAN LEGISLATIVE LIBRARY, 234 Legislative Bldg, Regina, S4S 0B3, Can. Marian Powell, Librn
Holdings: Vols 3200 Cat Microforms
Notes: Emphasis on books published in Canada.

ECONOMICS—CHINA

IL —UNIVERSITY OF ILLINOIS, URBANA/CHAMPAIGN, Library, 1408 W Gregory Drive, Urbana, 61801. Norman B Brown, Asst Dir for Special Collections
Notes: The Alfred Kaimang Chiu Collection of books on Chinese library administration (240 in Chinese; 170 in English), with pamphlets, manuscripts, etc, incl essays on Chinese economics. Chiu was the first librarian of the Harvard-Yenching Library at Harvard University, 1931-1965.

ECONOMICS—HISTORY

CA —UNIVERSITY OF CALIFORNIA, LOS ANGELES, Graduate School of Management Library, UCLA Campus, Los Angeles, 90024. Robert Bellanti, Head Librn
Holdings: Vols (128,000) Cat Mss Microforms
Notes: The

CT —YALE UNIVERSITY, Box 1603A, Yale Station, New Haven, 06520.

DE —HAGLEY MUSEUM AND LIBRARY, Eleutherian Mills-Hagley Foundation Inc, PO Box 3630, Greenville, 19807. Richmond D Williams, Dir; Heddy A Richter, Imprints Librn
Holdings: Vols 6000 Pamphlets
Notes: The French history collection is especially good in pamphlets of the Revolutionary and Napoleonic periods; French 18th Century economic theory, especially Physiocracy; and the works of or concerning P S du Pont de Nemours.

DC —INTERNATIONAL MONETARY FUND AND WORLD BANK, Joint Bank-Fund Library, Washington, 20431. Maureen M Moore, Librn
Holdings: Vols Cat Films Microforms
Notes: Incl foreign trade and statistical bulletins and yearbooks, central bank reports and bulletins, budget papers, security yearbooks, economic development plans and reports on economic conditions from the 132 member countries. An index of periodical material compiled by the Library staff has been published as: *Economics and Finance; Index to Periodical Articles, 1947-1971;* First Supplement, 1972, 1973, 1974 (Second Supplement, 1975, 1976, 1977, in preparation), 5 vols. (Boston: G K Hall, 1972, 1975). Also, The Developing Areas: *A Classed Bibliography of the Joint Bank-Fund Library,* Vol 1: *Latin America and the* Caribbean; Vol 2: *Africa and the Middle* East; Vol 3: *Asia and Oceania* (Boston: G K Hall, 1976).

DC —US DEPT OF LABOR, Library, 200 Constitution Ave NW, Washington, 20210. Sabina Jacobson, Dir
Holdings: Vols 535,000 Cat Audiotapes Microforms
Notes: Economics, especially labor, incl much historical material. Receive 3200 current periodical titles.

IL —NORTHWESTERN UNIVERSITY, Library, Special Collections Dept, 1937 Sheridan Rd, Evanston, 60201. R Russell Maylone, Cur
Holdings: Vols 1600 Cat
Notes: English pamphlets from 17th, 18th, 19th centuries.

IL —UNIVERSITY OF ILLINOIS, URBANA/CHAMPAIGN, Library, Rare Book Room, 346 Library, Urbana, 61801. Norman B Brown, Asst Dir for Special Collections; N Frederick Nash, Librn
Holdings: Cat Mss
Notes: Jacob Hollander Collection. Extensive collection, described in: *Catalog of the Rare Books Room,* (Boston G K Hall, 1972). Supplement (1978).

IN —PURDUE UNIVERSITY LIBRARIES, Graduate School of Management, Krannert Library, West Lafayette, 47907. Gordon Law, Librn
Holdings: Vols (7000) Cat Mss Maps Pix Microforms
Notes: The collection consists of books, journals and pamphlets dating from the early 16th to late 19th century, covering to a large degree the early literature in economic thought and business practices both here and abroad. No photocopying.

KS —UNIVERSITY OF KANSAS, Kenneth Spencer Research Library, Kansas Collection, Lawrence, 66045. Sheryl K Williams, Cur
Holdings: Vols (92,000) Cat Mss Maps Pix
Notes: Inventories of mss and photographs maintained with card catalog index. Papers of Kansas banking firms and local businees collected. Depository of official Kansas state publications since 1978; actual holdings extend into territorial period (1854-1861) with only occasional missing titles or vols. 4000 linear feet.

KS —UNIVERSITY OF KANSAS, Kenneth Spencer Research Library, Special Collections Dept, Lawrence, 66045. Alexandra Mason, Librn
Holdings: Vols 15,000 Cat Mss
Notes: Printed: Continental 15th-early 19th century. English 16th-early 19th. Mss: 14th-18th century. Strong holdings in 17th to mid-19th century English economics, incl books, pamphlets and mss (official and private records: Audit Office, Lottery Office, Admiralty, Wardrobe, etc, Levant Company, East India Company, Madeira merchants, various persons and estates). Earlier ms holdings incl Italian renaissance business records, English and Scottish manorial records, English Exchequer records, English and Scottish land records. Printed holdings also incl French, Italian sources for economic history, 15th-18th century and the Richard S Howey Collection in Economics and Economic History. Noncirculating.

LA —LOUISIANA STATE UNIVERSITY, Middleton Library, Dept of Archives & Manuscripts, Room 202, Baton Rouge, 70803. M Stone Miller Jr, Head
Holdings: Cat Mss Maps Pix Microforms
Notes: History of Louisiana and lower Mississippi Valley, colonial through 20th century. Scope: political, social and literary history; economic history, incl forestry, banking, agriculture, transportation and trade; national, regional, and Louisiana history; military history. About 4,500,000 items.

MD —JOHNS HOPKINS UNIVERSITY, Milton S Eisenhower Library, Charles & 34 Sts, Baltimore, 21218. Ann S Gwyn, Assistant Dir for Special Collections
Holdings: Vols Cat Mss
Notes: Chiefly original sources of English economic thought and history since Adam Smith, Chartism, trade unions, the Factory Acts, Luddites, Poor Law, Owenism, early socialism, Nauvoo Colony. Most items are rarities. J S Mill mss letters and correspondence, and original papers on the inception of the Industrial Revolution. 56 titles from library of Adam Smith. Important editions of *The Wealth of Nations.* Also many pamphlets from 16th century, and the Mercantilists. No published catalog. Cards in main catalog. Collection housed separately in Abram Hutzler Reading Room.

MA —HARVARD UNIVERSITY, Baker Library of the Graduate School of Business Administration, Kress Library of Business and Economics, Soldiers Field, Boston, 02163. Ruth E Rogers, Cur
Holdings: Vols 32,000 Cat Mss Microforms
Notes: Four volumes of catalog have been published (1940-1967). For description see *Business History Review,* XXXIV (1960), 474-494; *Harvard Library Notes,* III (1940), 316-319, and *Kress Library Publication,* No 1 (1939); also *Harvard Business School* Bulletin, Feb 1982. Scope of library is business and economics prior to 1850.

MI —UNIVERSITY OF MICHIGAN, Library, Dept of Rare Books & Special Collections, Ann Arbor, 48109. Robert J Starring, Head
Holdings: Cat Microforms
Notes: Incl the library of Professor Karl Heinrich Rau of the University of Heidelberg, acquired in 1871, containing 6076 vols especially rich in works on political economics and European statistics before 1850.

MI —NORTHWOOD INSTITUTE, Strosacker Library, 3225 Cook Rd, Midland, 48640. Catherine Chen, Head Librn
Holdings: Vols 3000 Cat Maps Microforms
Budget: $30,000
Notes: Business and management, incl economics and economic history. Audiovisual materials are located in the Griswold Communications Center.

MN —UNIVERSITY OF MINNESOTA, James Ford Bell Library, 309 19th Ave S, Minneapolis, 55455. John Parker, Cur
Holdings: Vols (11,000) Cat Mss Maps
Notes: Collection of original materials relating to European expansion, 1400-1800.

NY —COLUMBIA UNIVERSITY LIBRARIES, Rare Book & Manuscript Library, 801 Butler Library, 535 W 114 St, New York, 10027. Kenneth A Lohf, Librn
Holdings: Mss
Notes: The papers of Professor Carter Goodrich, economic historian, incl his papers as chairman of the governing body of the International Labor Office, 1939-1945; chief of the United Nations economic mission in Vietnam, 1955-1956; and special rerpresentative to Bolivia for the Secretary-General of the United Nations, 1952-1953. About 28,000 items. Restricted use.

NY —NEW YORK PUBLIC LIBRARY, Research Libraries, Economic & Public Affairs Div, Fifth Ave & 42 St, New York, 10018. Edward DiRoma, Chief
Holdings: Vols (1,500,000) Cat Microforms

NY —NEW YORK UNIVERSITY, Elmer Holmes Bobst Library, Div of Special Collections, Tamiment Library of Labor History, Washington Sq, New York, 10012. Dorothy Swanson, Librn
Holdings: Cat Mss Maps Pix Microforms
Notes: Books, pamphlets, newspapers, periodicals and mss. Large microfilm collection. Described in Daniel Bell's *The Tamiment Library* (1969), available free from the Tamiment librarian, and *Elmer Holmes Bobst Library Information Bulletin 8* (updated periodically).

NY —UNIVERSITY CLUB, Library, One W 54 St, New York, 10019. Guy St Clair, Library Dir
Holdings: Vols (100,000) Cat Mss Maps Pix
Notes: A private library for the members of the University Club, their guests, and serious scholars upon written application to the Library Director. Holds the Horace O White Collection of Books on Economic History.

NY —ROCKEFELLER UNIVERSITY, Rockefeller Archive Center, Hillcrest, Pocantico Hills, North Tarrytown, 10591. Joseph W Ernst, Dir; J William Hess, Assoc Dir
Notes: The Rockefeller Archive Center, a division of The Rockefeller University, preserves and makes available to scholars the records of the University, the Rockefeller Foundation, the Rockefeller Brothers Fund, members of the family, and those of other individuals and organizations associated with their endeavors. Collections at the Center document a century of philanthropy by

ECONOMICS—HISTORY (cont.)

legions of associated social and scientific pioneers, providing a unique window into the past.

OK —UNIVERSITY OF OKLAHOMA, University Libraries, 401 W Brooks, Norman, 73019. Duane Roller, Cur
Holdings: Vols 18,753
Notes: Bass Collection in Business and Economic History. Non-circulating collection.

PA —HISTORICAL SOCIETY OF PENNSYLVANIA, Library, 1300 Locust St, Philadelphia, 19107. David Fraser, Librn
Holdings: Vols (230,000) Mss Maps Pix Microforms
Notes: Incl over 14,000,000 ms pieces. The Library Company of Philadelphia mss are on deposit with the Historical Society of Pennsylvania. Many of the Society's rare books are on deposit with the Library Company. The Society maintains the collections of the Genealogical Society of Pennsylvania, incl some 20,000 printed genealogies, original mss, family, church, and civil records.

PA —UNIVERSITY OF PENNSYLVANIA, Van Pelt Library, Rare Books Collection, 34 & Walnut Sts, Philadelphia, 19104. Daniel Traister, Special Collections Librn
Holdings: / / Cat
Notes: Colwell collection of 9000 19th century English political economy pamphlets; and Mathew Carey collection of 230 American political economy pamphlets.

PA —UNIVERSITY OF PITTSBURGH, Hillman Library, Pittsburgh, 15260.
Notes: Economic and philosophical papers of the English scholar Frank Plumpton Ramsey (1903-1930), incl mss of published and unpublished writings, reading notes, etc. Significant because of his work in modern mathematics, logic, probability, and economics. Complementary to the Library's holdings of the papers of the logical empiricists, Rudolf Carnap and Hans Reichenback.

†WA —UNIVERSITY OF WASHINGTON LIBRARIES, Seattle, 98195.

WY —UNIVERSITY OF WYOMING, William Robertson Coe Library, Div of Rare Books & Special Collections, Laramie, 82071. Gene M Gressley, Dir, Asst to Pres
Holdings: Vols (10,000) Cat Mss Maps Pix Slides Microforms
Notes: Main efforts have been in the area of ms collecting in several subject areas, most of which can be grouped under Western Economic History.

ON —CANADA DEPT OF LABOUR, Library, Ottawa, K1A 0J2, Can. Monique Marchand, Chief Librn
Holdings: Vols (100,000) Cat Microforms

ON —DEPT OF REGIONAL INDUSTRIAL EXPANSION, Ottawa Library, 235 Queen St, Ottawa, K1A 0H5, Can. Steven Rush, Librn
Holdings: Vols (100,000) Cat Maps Microforms
Notes: Contains 1500 reports of ARDA projects (Agricultural Rehabilitation and Development Agency); also NEWSTART project reports. There is a published book catalog and two supplements. 15,000 documents; 3000 periodical subscriptions.

ECONOMICS—RESEARCH see Economic Research

ECONOMICS—STATISTICS

CT —YALE UNIVERSITY, Social Science Library, Economic Growth Center Collection, 140 Prospect St, New Haven, 06520. Billie I Salter, Librn
Holdings: Vols (47,600) Cat
Notes: Economic data on national economies and their development: budgets, plans, statistical yearbooks and bulletins, censuses, national accounts, trade, monetary data, statistics, etc. The focus is primarily on less-developed countries. Mostly government documents; 3800 serials currently received. Shelf list organized by country and LC number, in addition to dictionary catalog.

DC —US BUREAU OF THE CENSUS, Library, Federal Office Bldg 3, Rm 2451, Washington, 20233. Betty Baxtresser, Chief, ASD Library Branch
Holdings: Vols (200,863) Cat Microforms
Notes: Emphases on statistics of agriculture, business, construction, economics, foreign trade, governments, housing, industry, population, transportation, statistical methodology, and data processing. Library holdings are largely current materials covering the Bureau's programs. Outdated materials are withdrawn regularly.

NY —HOFSTRA UNIVERSITY, Library, 1000 Fulton Ave, Hempstead, 11550. Charles R Andrews, Dean of Library Services
Holdings: Vols (5000) Cat
Notes: The personal collection of Professor Shepard Clough of Columbia University. Especially strong in French and Italian modern history, Italian Fascism and European economic statistics.

ECONOMICS—STUDY AND TEACHING

MI —OLIVET COLLEGE, Barker-Cawood Library, Olivet, 49076. Chris Miko, Dir
Holdings: Vols (10,000) Cat Pix Slides Phonorecords Audiotapes 16mm Films Filmstrips Microforms
Budget: ($2000)
Notes: The collection was created to support the programs of the Economic Education Center at Olivet College. Promotes and trains teachers in the methods of teaching economics in elementary through high school.

NY —JOINT COUNCIL ON ECONOMIC EDUCATION, Library, 2 Park Ave, New York, 10016.
Holdings: Vols 2000 Cat
Notes: The Edwin G Nourse Library of Economic Education.

ECONOMICS, CHRISTIAN

OR —GEORGE FOX COLLEGE, Shambaugh Library, Newberg, 97132. F E Walls, Libr Dir
Holdings: Vols (1500) Cat
Budget: ($150)
Notes: Collection of Dr Howard Kershner, incl Christian Freedom Foundation books. Personal collection of Dr Kershner.

ECONOMICS, ENERGY see Energy Economics

ECONOMICS, INTERNATIONAL see International Economic Relations

ECONOMICS, MARXIST see Marxist Economics

ECONOMICS, MEDICAL see Medical Economics

ECONOMICS, REGIONAL

PA —UNIVERSITY OF PITTSBURGH, Economics/Center for Regional Economics Studies Library, 4956 Forbes Quad, Pittsburgh, 15260. Patricia Suozzi-Crehan, Librn
Holdings: Vols 20,000
Budget: ($25,724)
Notes: Card catalog for collection. Cards for Economics Collection are in Hillman Library catalog. Collections are working collections reflecting the research and teaching interests of the Dept of Economics faculty and graduate students. The collection covers all aspects of the field of economics and demography.

ECONOMICS IN RELIGION

OR —GEORGE FOX COLLEGE, Shambaugh Library, Newberg, 97132. F E Walls, Libr Dir
Holdings: Vols (1500) Cat
Budget: ($150)
Notes: Collection of Dr Howard Kershner, incl Christian Freedom Foundation books. Personal collection of Dr Kershner.

ECONOMISTS

NY —STATE UNIVERSITY OF NEW YORK AT ALBANY, Library, Special Collections Dept, 1400 Washington Ave, Albany, 12222. Marion P Munzer, Coordr
Notes: Papers (35 linear feet) of Hans Philip Neisser, Hans Staudinger, and Emil Lederer, German economists who came to the United States after 1933. Correspondence, lecture notes, mss, and publications. Part of the library's German Exile Collection.

NY —CORNELL UNIVERSITY LIBRARIES, Collection of Regional History, Dept of Manuscripts and Univ Archives, Ithaca, 14853.
Notes: Records, 1918-79, of NY State Association of Extension Home Economists; 4 ft.

ECONOMISTS' NATIONAL COMMITTEE ON MONETARY POLICY

NJ —PRINCETON UNIVERSITY, Library, Manuscript Collection, Nassau St, Princeton, 08540. Jean F Preston, Cur
Holdings: Cat Mss
Notes: Incl 42 file drawers; 21 boxes; 12 cartons. The archives cover the period 1933-52.

ECUADOR

CT —YALE UNIVERSITY, Sterling Memorial Library, Latin American Collections, New Haven, 06520. Lee H Williams Jr, Cur
Holdings: Vols (300,000) Cat Maps Pix Slides Phonorecords 16mm Films Filmstrips
Notes: See entry for Yale University under Latin America.

NY —STATE UNIVERSITY OF NEW YORK, COLLEGE AT BUFFALO, Rare Books Collection, 420 Capen Hall, Buffalo, 14260. Robert J Bertholf, Cur
Holdings: Vols 4200 Cat Mss Maps Pix
Notes: Materials incl books, mss, official gazettes, and periodicals for research on the short-lived political entity known as Gran Colombia (the present-day countries of Colombia, Venezuela, and Ecuador); special emphasis is on the first half of the 19th century but earlier and later periods are incl.

NC —DUKE UNIVERSITY, William R Perkins Library, Durham, 27706. Elvin E Strowd, University Librn
Notes: The Leonardo Jenaro Munoz collection of material on Ecuador consists of more than 2000 volumes (with additions continuing) primarily history, politics and economics; it contains numbers of special documents, journals, and government publications largely 19th and 20th century material.

PA —UNIVERSITY OF PITTSBURGH, Hillman Library, Pittsburgh, 15260. Glenora E Rossell, Head
Holdings: Vols (172,000) Cat Microforms
Notes: A collection of Ecuadorian material in the Humanities and the Social Sciences; it is particularly strong in history, literature and socio-political matters, and incl, primarily, books and periodicals published during the 20th century.

ECUADOR—HISTORY

IL —SOUTHERN ILLINOIS UNIVERSITY, CARBONDALE, Delyte W Morris Library, Carbondale, 62901.
Holdings: Vols 500 Cat Maps Pix
Notes: Described in Woodbridge, Hensley C, "Faculty and library collaboration in developing the Latin American collection for area studies programs at Southern Illinois University," Twelfth Seminar on the Acquisition of Latin American Library Materials, Final Report and Working Papers, vol 2, pp 99-108 (1967).

NY —CORNELL UNIVERSITY LIBRARIES, John M Olin Library, Ithaca, 14853.
Holdings: Vols (190,000) Cat Mss Maps

ECUADOR—HISTORY (cont.)

16mm Films Microforms
See also entry under South America

NC —DUKE UNIVERSITY, William R Perkins Library, Durham, 27706. Elvin E Strowd, University Librn
Notes: The Leonardo Jenaro Munoz collection of material on Ecuador consists of more than 2000 volumes (with additions continuing) primarily history, politics and economics; it contains numbers of special documents, journals, and government publications largely 19th and 20th century material.

TX —UNIVERSITY OF TEXAS LIBRARIES, Nettie Lee Benson Latin American Collection, Sid Richardson Hall 1.109, Austin, 78712. Laura Gutierrez-Witt, Head Librn
Holdings: Vols (450,000) Cat Maps Microforms
Notes: Private collection of Diego Munoz relating to Chile, Bolivia, Peru and Ecuador. Incl extensive coverage of the laws of Chile and of the Congress of Chile during the 19th century; also, 200 volumes of works of Jose Toribio Medina.
See also entry under Latin America

ECUADOR—POLITICS AND GOVERNMENT

NC —DUKE UNIVERSITY, William R Perkins Library, Durham, 27706. Elvin E Strowd, University Librn
Notes: The Leonardo Jenaro Munoz collection of material on Ecuador consists of more than 2000 volumes (with additions continuing) primarily history, politics and economics; it contains numbers of special documents, journals, and government publications largely 19th and 20th century material.

ECUADORIAN LITERATURE

IL —SOUTHERN ILLINOIS UNIVERSITY, CARBONDALE, Delyte W Morris Library, Carbondale, 62901.
Holdings: Vols (19,000) Cat
Notes: Especially strong in Ecuadorean and Mexican literature; complete or almost complete files of many important literary journals published in Spanish America. Described in Woodbridge, Hensley C, "Faculty and library collaboration in developing the Latin American collection for area studies programs at Southern Illinois University," Twelfth Seminar on the Acquisition of Latin American Library Materials, Final Report and Working Papers, vol 2, pp 99-108 (1967).

PA —UNIVERSITY OF PITTSBURGH, Hillman Library, Pittsburgh, 15260. Glenora E Rossell, Head
Holdings: Vols (172,000) Cat Microforms
Notes: A general collection of Latin American literature, with emphasis on Cuba, Mexico, Chile, Guatemala, Ecuador, Peru, Bolivia, and Argentina. The holdings on Bolivian, Ecuadorian, and Cuban literature are extremely good. Very strong in contemporary literature of the whole area.

ECUMENICAL MOVEMENT

CA —UNIVERSITY OF CALIFORNIA, BERKELEY, School of Law, Library, Berkeley, 94720. Stephan G Kuttner, Dir, Canon Law Collection
Holdings: Vols (23,000) Cat Mss Microforms
Notes: Entirely supported by the R D and S M Robbins Endowment, the Robbins Canon Law Collection emphasizes particularly Roman Catholic, Eastern and Anglican canon law. Additional subject areas being developed are ecclesiastical history and institutions, historical and contemporary church and state relations, and ecumenical studies. Library is in process of obtaining complete microfilms of all medieval canon and Roman law mss held by the Vatican Library.

NY —GENERAL THEOLOGICAL SEMINARY, Saint Marks Library, 175 Ninth Ave, New York, 10011. David Green, Dir
Holdings: Vols (200,000) Cat Mss Maps Pix Slides Microforms

NY —UNION THEOLOGICAL SEMINARY, Library, 3041 Broadway at Reinhold Niebuhr Place, New York, 10027. Richard D Spoor, Dir
Holdings: Vols (580,000) Cat Mss Microforms
Budget: ($750,000)

NC —SOUTHEASTERN BAPTIST THEOLOGICAL SEMINARY LIBRARY, PO Box 752, Wake Forest, 27587. H Eugene McLeod, Librn
Holdings: Cat Microforms
Notes: Incl official publications of the Faith and Order Commission of the World Council of Churches from 1910 to 1970, periodicals from many countries and religious bodies, and publications of the evangelical academies and lay training centers of Europe and Great Britain.

TX —TEXAS CHRISTIAN UNIVERSITY, Mary Couts Burnett Library, Fort Worth, 76129.

ECUMENISM

MD —SOVEREIGN HOSPITALLER ORDER OF SAINT JOHN, Villa Anneslie, 529 Dunkirk Road, Baltimore, 21212.
Notes: The Sovereign Hospitaller Order of Saint John is an ecumenical Christian religious Order founded in the 11th century; successor Order to the Knights of Rhodes and the Knights of Malta.

EDDINGTON, WILLIAM E., 1886-1977

IN —DEPAUW UNIVERSITY, Roy O West Library, University Archives, PO Box 137, Greencastle, 46135. Virginia C Brann, Sr Archives Asst
Notes: His papers, incl 21 books, 22 folders (ca 1901-ca 1970).

EDDISON, E. R.

CT —LEE ASH, (personal collection), 66 Humiston Dr, Bethany, 06525.
Notes: First editions, mss, ephemera, memorabilia.

EDDY, MARY BAKER

CT —YALE UNIVERSITY, Box 1603A, Yale Station, New Haven, 06520.
Holdings: Cat

EDELMAN, JOHN

MI —WAYNE STATE UNIVERSITY, Walter P Reuther Library, Archives of Labor & Urban Affairs, Detroit, 48202. Philip Mason, Dir
Notes: Papers, etc of John Edelman, labor consultant for the Council of National Defense and lobbyist for the United Textile Workers Union.

EDEN, DOROTHY

MA —BOSTON UNIVERSITY, Mugar Memorial Library, Special Collections Dept, 771 Commonwealth Ave, Boston, 02215. Howard B Gotlieb, Dir
Holdings: Cat Mss
Notes: Mss, correspondence, etc collected in depth; incl publications by or about.

EDENS, ROGER

CA —UNIVERSITY OF SOUTHERN CALIFORNIA, Edward L Doheny Memorial Library, Archives of Performing Arts, University Park, Los Angeles, 90089. Robert Knutson, Librn
Holdings: Mss Pix
Notes: Personal collection of papers, pictures, etc.

EDER, JOSEF MARIA

NY —INTERNATIONAL MUSEUM OF PHOTOGRAPHY AT GEORGE EASTMAN HOUSE, Archives, 900 East Ave, Rochester, 14607. Rachel Stuhlman, Head Librn
Holdings: Vols (30,000) Cat Mss Microforms
Budget: ($104,000)
Notes: History, aesthetics and technology of photography and cinematography, incl the Gabriel Cromer, Josef Maria Eder, Alden Scott Boyer, Louis Walton Sipley/3M Collections, and the James Card Collection from 1893. Covers photographic, especially cinematographic history; also hundreds of negatives of Edward Muybridge as well as his notebooks. Incl 450,000 pictures and slides. Also the Lewis Hine Collection of social documentary photography.

EDGAR ALLAN POE SOCIETY

MD —UNIVERSITY OF BALTIMORE, Langsdale Library, 1420 Maryland Ave, Baltimore, 21201. Gerry Watkins, Head of Special Collections Dept
Notes: Incl working files and correspondence (1969-1980); 4 cubic feet.

NC —DUKE UNIVERSITY, William R Perkins Library, Jay B Hubbell Center for American Literary Historiography, Durham, 27706. Erma Whittington, Librn
Notes: 77,312 items, including manuscripts, pictures, clippings, and correspondence. "The objective of the Center is to gather the papers and materials of significant scholars and critics in American literary history." The Center is a part of the Perkins Library Manuscripts Department.

EDGERTON, FAYE AND FAITH HILL

AZ —NORTHERN ARIZONA UNIVERSITY, Special Collection Library, CU Box 6022, Flagstaff, 86011. Peter M Whiteley, Coordr/Archivist; William Mullane, Librn
Notes: Faye and Faith Hill Edgerton Collection; mss and notes of the translation of the New Testament into the Apache and Navajo languages, 1940's-1960's.

EDGEWORTH, MARIA, 1767-1849

CA —UNIVERSITY OF CALIFORNIA, LOS ANGELES, Research Library, Dept of Special Collections, 405 Hilgard Ave, Los Angeles, 90024. Edward Shreeves, Chairman, Bibliographers Group; David S Zeidberg, Head
Holdings: Vols 300 Cat Mss Pix
Notes: 300 first and other editions of her books; 80 letters and mss.

CT —YALE UNIVERSITY, Box 1603A, Yale Station, New Haven, 06520.

OH —OHIO UNIVERSITY, Vernon R Alden Library, Department of Archives and Special Collections, Athens, 45701. Gary A Hunt, Head
Holdings: Vols (10,191) Uncat Mss
Notes: The Edmund Blunden Collection of Romantic and Modern Literature, being the private library assembled by Blunden during 5 decades of active collecting. The bulk of the collection (6,264 titles) consists of English imprints from the period 1750-1850, concentrating on literature but also incl contemporary works on art, natural history, philosophy and other subjects important for understanding the background of English Romanticism. Among the authors most heavily represented by first and other early editions are: Allington, Barnes, Bloomfield, Byron, Clare, Coleridge, Cowper, Dyer, Edgeworth, Goldsmith, Hazlitt, Hunt, Lamb, Landor, Scott, Thompson and Wordsworth. Books written by Blunden himself, together with his Georgian contemporaries (particularly W H Davies, Walter De la Mare, and Sigfried Sassoon) form a second major area of strength. Many ofthe modern books are inscribed to Blunden, and nearly all the volumes in the collection bear his annotations.

EDGEWORTH FAMILY LIBRARY

CA —UNIVERSITY OF CALIFORNIA, LOS ANGELES, Research Library, Dept of

EDGEWORTH FAMILY LIBRARY (cont.)

Special Collections, 405 Hilgard Ave, Los Angeles, 90024. Edward Shreeves, Chairman, Bibliographers Group; David S Zeidberg, Head
Holdings: Vols 1000 Cat
Notes: 1000 volumes (400 titles) from the library of Richard Lovell Edgeworth, Maria Edgeworth and others of the family. A miscellaneous "country house" collection; many have family signatures and other inscriptions.

EDISON, THOMAS ALVA, 1847-1931

DE —HAGLEY MUSEUM AND LIBRARY, Eleutherian Mills-Hagley Foundation Inc, PO Box 3630, Greenville, 19807. Richmond D Williams, Dir; Heddy A Richter, Imprints Librn
Notes: Records of Pennsylvania Power & Light Company (1853-1955; 1000 cubic feet). The archive consists of the records of 1050 predecessor companies that merged over a 75-year period (1880-1955) to form the present-day PP&L. The collection describes the industry's tentative beginnings using the Edison system of direct current, the technological innovations which allowed small, innercity utilities to expand beyond their original urban centers, and the consolidation movement that culminated with the formation of a great regional power network. Also, records of Delmarva Power Company (1890-1965; 60 cubic feet).

MD —TOWSON STATE UNIVERSITY, Fine Arts Bldg, Room 457, Towson, 21204. Edwin L Gerhardt, Curator
Notes: The Gerhardt Library of Musical Information is a segregated representative collection of music literature, phonograph and tape recordings, pictures and artifacts. It incl special sections on Thomas Alva Edison and the phonograph, John Philip Sousa and bands, old popular songs and percussion. Most of the material is out of print and hard to find. It is *not* a collection of scores or manuscripts. A detailed outline is available upon request. Direct all correspondence to the curator, Edwin L Gerhardt, 4926 Leeds Ave, Baltimore, MD 21227, (301) 242-0328.

NJ —YESTERYEAR MUSEUM, Library, Box 1890-M, Morristown, 07960. Lee R Munsick, Dir
Holdings: Vols (300) Uncat Mss Pix Slides Phonorecords Audiotapes 16mm Films Filmstrips
Budget: ($30,000)
Notes: Mechanical and automatic music; Edisonia; etc.

NJ —RUTGERS, THE STATE UNIVERSITY OF NEW JERSEY, Thomas Alva Edison Papers Office, New Brunswick, 08903. Reese V Jenkins, Dir and Editor
Notes: His papers; in preparation for publication; photocopies and microfilm copies of collected documents.

EDITING AND EDITORS

IA —IOWA STATE UNIVERSITY, Library, Dept of Special Collections, Ames, 50011. Stanley M Yates, Head
Holdings: Mss Pix
Notes: Papers of Frank Rinehart Eyerly, managing editor of the *Des Moines Register* and *Tribune* from 1946-69 (4 linear feet). Also papers of Lauren K Soth, editor from 1954-75, who won a Pulitzer Prize for his editorial writing in 1956 which helped establish agricultural exchanges with the Soviet Union. 20 linear ft, finding aid available.

MS —MISSISSIPPI STATE UNIVERSITY, Mitchell Memorial Library, Box 5408, Mississippi State, 39762. Frances N Coleman, Head, Special Collections
Holdings: Mss
Notes: Papers of Norman Bradley, editor of *The Chattanooga Post* and *The Chattanooga Times*.

NY —GRADUATE CENTER OF THE CITY UNIVERSITY OF NEW YORK, William H and Gwynne K Crouse Library for Publishing Arts, 33 W 42 St, New York, 10036. Alfred H Lane, Dir
Notes: Recently established and still growing, but intended to become the authoritative source of materials in the field, of particular value in research about the publishing industry. Open to staff members of publishing houses, students, scholars, authors, printers, and booksellers. Primarily 20th century materials, and particularly useful for research on technical, financial, and historical matters. Much on the history of individual houses, economics of authorship; marketing and distribution of books; etc.

EDITIONS, LIMITED see Bibliography—Limited Editions

EDMOND, WILLIAM

CT —TRINITY COLLEGE LIBRARY, 300 Summit St, Hartford, 06106. Peter J Knapp, Archivist
Holdings: Uncat Mss Pix
Notes: Late 18th and 19th century mss, letter, diaries, etc of the Curtis Family of Connecticut and New York, with emphasis on: William Edmond (1755-1838), US Congressman from Conn; Holbrook Curtis (1787-1858); William Edmond Curtis (1823-1880), Chief Justice of Superior Court of New York; Mary Ann Scovill Curtis (1831-1908); and William Edmond Curtis Jr, (1855-1923), US Asst Secy of the Treasury. Incl on basis of relation through marriage are late 18th and 19th century mss, letters and diaries of the Hiester, McLanahan and Muhlenberg Families of Pennsylvania, with emphasis on Joseph Hiester (1752-1832), US Congressman and Governor of Pennsylvania; and Andrew Gregg (1755-1835), US Congressman and Senator from Pennsylvania. 12 linear feet.

EDMONDSON, JAMES HOWARD

OK —UNIVERSITY OF OKLAHOMA, Bizzell Memorial Library, Western History Collections, 401 W Brooks, Norman, 73069. John Ezell, Cur
Holdings: Mss Documents Audiovideo Tapes Maps
Notes: Governor of Oklahoma; US Representative. His papers. Guide available.

EDMUNDS, MURRELL

VA —UNIVERSITY OF VIRGINIA, Alderman Library, Manuscripts Dept, Charlottesville, 22901. Edmund Berkeley Jr, Cur
Notes: Letters of many other Virginia authors, such as Sherwood Anderson, Hawthorne Daniel, Murrell Edmunds, George Cary Eggleston, John Fox, John Pendleton Kennedy, Katie Letcher Lyle, Julian Rutherfoord Meade, Thomas Nelson Page, Virginius Dabney, Clifford Dowdey, Jane McClary, Peter Taylor, and others.

EDSALL, JOHN T.

MA —MASSACHUSETTS INSTITUTE OF TECHNOLOGY, Institute Archives, Special Collections, Cambridge, 02139.
Notes: Correspondence, newsletters, fact-sheets, newspaper and magazine articles, books and reports of the Citizens' League Against the Sonic Boom, established in 1967 by William Shurcliff to oppose the sonic boom, stop commercial supersonic transport production, and influence public opinion and policy decisions on the SST. Major correspondents incl Bo Lundberg, Richard Wiggs, several US congressmen, and CLASB members.

EDSON, KATHERINE PHILIPPS

CA —UNIVERSITY OF CALIFORNIA, LOS ANGELES, Research Library, Dept of Special Collections, 405 Hilgard Ave, Los Angeles, 90024. Edward Shreeves, Chairman, Bibliographers Group; David S Zeidberg, Head
Notes: 8 linear feet of correspondence, pamphlets, and clippings concerning women's suffrage, the Progressive and Republican parties, minimum wage laws, etc.

EDUCATION

CA —UNIVERSITY OF CALIFORNIA, BERKELEY, Humanities-Social Sciences Libraries, Education-Psychology Library, 2600 Tolman Hall, Berkeley, 94720. Sonya Kaufman, Acting Head
Holdings: Vols (110,000)
Notes: General research collection in fields of education and psycology. Education collection's emphases are in the areas of administration, policy planning, higher education, science and math education, language and literacy. Serial holdings are strong. The library receives approx 2200 current serial titles in education and psychology.

CA —HUMAN RESOURCES RESEARCH ORGANIZATION (HUMRRO), Western Div Library, 27857 Berwick Dr, Carmel, 93923. Dianalee Stickler, Librn
Notes: Citations for HumRRO reports appear in *HumRRO Bibliography of* Publications, 1971 and *HumRRO Bibliography of Publications and Presentations During FY,* 1972-77. Library is inactive.

CA —CALIFORNIA STATE UNIVERSITY, LONG BEACH, Reference Center, 1250 Bellflower Blvd, Long Beach, 90840.
Holdings: Vols (84,000) Cat Pix Phonorecords Audiotapes Filmstrips Microforms
Notes: Outstanding collection among California state universities for quantity, diversity, and quality. Incl nearly 57,000 books on education, 27,000 textbooks, 17, 000 curriculum guides, over 2500 teaching aids, 4500 college catalogs, 30,000 pictures, 4500 phonorecords, 1000 audiotapes, 5500 filmstrips, 500 filmloops, and 175,000 microforms.

CA —CENTER FOR EARLY EDUCATION, Laura M Ellis Memorial Library, 563 N Alfred St, Los Angeles, 90048. Janice M Eastman, Librn
Holdings: Vols 3500
Budget: ($10,000)
Notes: Theory and classroom applications; infants through sixth grade. Special education and early childhood education are subspecialties. Incl periodicals in the field.

CA —LOS ANGELES PUBLIC LIBRARY, Social Sciences Dept, 630 W Fifth St, Los Angeles, 90071. Marilyn C Wherley, Principal Librn
Holdings: Vols 10,000 Cat Microforms
Budget: ($150,000)
Notes: Education collection. Over 500 bound periodicals. Collection also includes government publications, agency reports, statistics, yearbooks, directories, pamphlets, bibliographies, child and adolescent psychology theories and history, college catalogs on microfiche, and nearly complete collection of California catalogs.

CA —LOS ANGELES PUBLIC LIBRARY, Central Library, Audio Visual Dept, 630 W Fifth St, Los Angeles, 90071. Richard V Partlow, Principal Librn
Budget: ($71,989)
Notes: Includes 16mm film (4300), VHS video (300), audio recordings (20,000), audio cassettes (5500), picture file (220,000 estimated clippings), filmstrips (60), periodicals (65). Material on all subject areas are included.

CA —UNIVERSITY OF CALIFORNIA, LOS ANGELES, Education & Psychology Library, 390 Powell Library Bldg, Los Angeles, 90024. Barbara Duke, Librn
Holdings: Vols (133,000) Cat Audiotapes Microforms
Notes: Research collection serving graduate students and faculty in Education, Psychology, Kinesiology and Teaching English as a Second Language. Areas of emphasis incl higher education, education and work, comparative education, early

EDUCATION (cont.)

childhood development, reading, second language acquisition, cognition, perception, personality, social psychology, motor control and learning. Library has Univ of Oregon microfiche collection of unpublished research in sports, physical education, and recreation and is a depository for ERIC microfiche.

CA —MILLS COLLEGE LIBRARY, Oakland, 94613. Steven P Pandolfo, Librn
Holdings: Vols (300) Cat
Notes: Books printed from 17th-20th centuries; primarily 19th century with emphasis on education, women's suffrage, domestic economy and etiquette.

CA —SAN FRANCISCO STATE UNIVERSITY, J Paul Leonard Library, 1630 Holloway Ave, San Francisco, 94132. Susan Quinlan, Curriculum Librn
Holdings: Vols (49,246) Cat Phonorecords Audiotapes 8mm Films Microforms
Budget: ($8500)
Notes: The young people's collection or children's literature collection of 17,843 vols incl books with reading and interest levels ranging from preschool through senior high school. The Marguerite Archer collection of historical children's books contains an additional 3000 vols. Have 19,755 textbooks, 5150 curriculum guides, 1970 pamphlets. Collection emphasizes instructional materials that can be utitlized in the school classroom. Professional books and journals and other media relating to educational history, philosophy, research, theories of teaching, etc are in the main collection.

CO —SOCIAL SCIENCE EDUCATION CONSORTIUM, Resource & Demonstration Center (RDC), 855 Broadway, Boulder, 80302. Regina McCormick, Staff Assoc
Holdings: Vols (16,000) Cat Filmstrips Microforms
Notes: Contains over 15,000 elementary and secondary social studies textbooks, audiovisuals, games and simulations, professional books, and the complete ERIC microfiche collection. Staff available to travel to all parts of the US to consult on curriculum development, instructional methods, materials analysis and selection, evaluation, new materials, teaching strategies, and trends in the social studies.

CO —SOUTHEAST METROPOLITAN BOARD OF COOPERATIVE SERVICES, Professional Information Center, 3301 S Monaco St, Denver, 80222. Lynda Welborn, Manager
Holdings: Vols 2800 Cat
Budget: $10,000
Notes: Elementary and secondary levels.

CT —YALE UNIVERSITY, Box 1603A, Yale Station, New Haven, 06520.

†DC —AMERICAN COUNCIL ON EDUCATION, Library & Information Service, One Dupont Circle, Suite 640, Washington, 20036. Judith Pfeiffer, Librn
Holdings: Vols 3000 Cat
Budget: $4500
Notes: The collection reflects the needs and interests of the building tenants. All tenants are nonprofit, nongovernmental associations in the field of postsecondary eductiion. The collection is particularly strong in the areas of the economics, finance, history, management, and teaching in higher education. The library is a depository library for the Carnegie Commission on Higher Education and the Carnegie Council on Policy Studies in Higher Education. In addition, the library maintains an archival collection of the publications of the American Council on Education.

DC —NATIONAL ENDOWMENT FOR THE ARTS, Library, 1100 Pen Ave NW, Rm 213, Washington, 20506. Christine Morrison, Arts Librn
Holdings: Vols (6000) Cat
Notes: Incl arts and education and public policy in the arts.

DC —UNIVERSITY OF THE DISTRICT OF COLUMBIA, Mount Vernon Campus, Library & Media Services Div, 800 Mount Vernon Pl, NW, Washington, 20001. Lottie Wright, Librn
Holdings: Vols (2500)// Uncat
Notes: American history, incl literature, education, politics, and government.

DC —US COMMISSION ON CIVIL RIGHTS, National Clearinghouse Library, 1121 Vermont Ave NW, Washington, 20005. Lenora McMillan, Chief Librn
Holdings: Vols (10,200) Cat Slides Microforms
Notes: The National Clearinghouse Library has a special collection of the US Commission on Civil Rights publications from its inception (1957) to present date.

IL —ARLINGTON HEIGHTS MEMORIAL LIBRARY, 500 N Dunton Ave, Arlington Heights, 60004. Frank J Dempsey, Librn
Holdings: Vols 5000 Cat Microforms
Notes: Maintained as education subject center under the former North Suburban Library System's Coordinated Acquisitions Program. Collection incl history and philosophy of education; teaching methods; testing and measurement; and administration.

IL —STANDARD EDUCATIONAL CORPORATION, Editorial Library, 200 W Monroe St, Chicago, 60606. David E King, Librn
Holdings: Vols (8000) Cat Maps Pix Microforms
Notes: General reference.

IL —SCOTT, FORESMAN & CO, Editorial Library, 1900 E Lake Ave, Glenview, 60025. S Donal Robertson, Head Librn
Holdings: Vols (30,000) Phonorecords Audiotapes Microforms
Notes: A general collection, fairly heavy in the areas of education and children's literature. Study and teaching of reading is probably the largest single section of the collection.

IL —ILLINOIS STATE UNIVERSITY, Milner Library, Dept of Special Collections, Normal, 61761. Robert Sokan, Librn
Holdings: Vols 2100 // Uncat
Notes: Sigmund Livingston Collection on Intergroup Relations, 1944 to the present. The material is divided into subject headings which contain pamphlets, newsletters and commission reports.

IN —INDIANA UNIVERSITY, School of Education, Library, Bloomington, 47401. Adele Dendy, Head Librn
Holdings: Vols (35,000) Cat Pix Slides Phonorecords Audiotapes 16mm Films Filmstrips Microforms
Budget:
Notes: Library has complete ERIC collection of microfiche (277,308). 2098 non-ERIC items, 226 serials, and 22,823 nonprint items (housed in educational materials center). Emphasis on recent materials; the historic collections in education are located in the Main Library. The collection is geared to graduate level studies and research. A separate Teaching Materials Center includes 10,000 elementary and secondary textbooks. The Center also includes curriculum guides, supplementary materials and 17,823 nonprint teaching aids.

IN —BALL STATE UNIVERSITY, University Libraries, Muncie, 47306. Michael B Wood, Dean
Holdings: Vols 18,000 Cat Pix
Notes: Incl standardized tests; historical collection of textbooks, 1787-1945.

IN —INDIANA STATE UNIVERSITY, Cunningham Memorial Library, Dept of Rare Books & Special Collections, Terre Haute, 47809. Lawrence J McCrank, Head
Holdings: Vols 500 Cat
Notes: Cunningham Collection of classics in American education. Incl first editions of works (incl journals) by or edited by noted American educators such as Henry Barnard, John Dewey, Horace Mann, G Stanley Hall.

IA —AMERICAN COLLEGE TESTING PROGRAM, Library, Box 168, Iowa City, 52243. Lois Renter, Head Librn
Holdings: Vols (22,000) Cat Microforms
Budget: ($36,000)
Notes: Emphasis on students, educational testing, educational psychology, post-secondary education, psychometrics. Excludes educational history and philosophy, curricula and teaching.

KY —UNIVERSITY OF KENTUCKY, Education Library, Dickey Hall Room 205, Lexington, 40506. Larry Greenwood, Librn
Holdings: Vols 61,000 Cat Microforms
Budget: $40,000
Notes: Professional books, model children's and young people's collection, curriculum materials and guides and ERIC collection (297,000 microfiche).

KY —CUMBERLAND COLLEGE, Norma P Hagan Memorial Library, 821 Walnut St, Williamsburg, 40769. Robert B Williams, Dir
Holdings: Vols 35,000 Cat Microforms
Budget: $20,000
Notes: Incl 10,500 children's books, 5,500 texts, 19,000 education-related books; ERIC collection incl tests on microfiche, newsbank, college catalogs.

LA —LOUISIANA STATE UNIVERSITY, Troy H Middleton Library, Louisiana Room, Baton Rouge, 70803. Evangeline Mills Lynch, Head Librn; Ruth Murray, Associate Librn
Holdings: Vols (33,500) Cat Maps VF
Notes: Louisiana Collection of history, description and travel, biography, agriculture, literature, politics and government, folklore, anthropology, geography, geology, education, language, music and natural history. Especially large subject collections may be found on Louisiana, the history of the lower Mississippi Valley, Abraham Lincoln, Romance languages and literatures, sugar culture and technology, Southern history, petroleum engineering, plant pathology, micropaleontology, ornithology, and various aspects of crawfish life, biology and culture. Complete depository of Louisiana State Documents; extensive newspapers clipping files; separate card catalog; items listed in Louisiana Union Catalog; restricted use (research and reference). Incl both materials about Louisiana and by Louisianians without regard to subject. LSU Press Collection(preservation copy of each title kept for exhibit purposes only). LSU theses and dissertations from 1900-date. LSU Faculty Collection. Also, 1300 maps, 104 VF drawers, 250 boxes of uncataloged pamphlets.

LA —PUBLIC AFFAIRS RESEARCH COUNCIL OF LOUISIANA, Library, 300 Louisiana Ave, PO Box 3118, Baton Rouge, 70821. Jan Brashear, Research Librn
Holdings: Vols (7000) Cat Mss
Notes: State and local government problems with emphasis on Louisiana. Strong in the areas of education and public finance.

MD —UNIVERSITY OF BALTIMORE, Langsdale Library, 1420 Maryland Ave, Baltimore, 21201. Gerry Watkins, Head of Special Collections Dept
Holdings: Cat Mss Maps
Notes: Incl the entire stock (10,000 vols) of Peter Decker, New York antiquarian bookdealer (acquired in 1970); incl Peter Decker's mss of his published works and his records as a dealer in Americana.

†MA —BOSTON PUBLIC LIBRARY, Copley Sq, Boston, 02117.
Holdings: Uncat Microforms
Notes: Microform Publication: ERIC Documents.

MA —BOSTON SCHOOL COMMITTEE, Administration Library, 77 Ave Louis Pasteur, Boston, 02115. Polly Kaufman, Coordinating Dir; Barbara Elam, Coordinating Dir
Holdings: Vols (12,000) Cat Microfiche
Budget: ($10,000)
Notes: Collection incl file of Boston School Committee Documents, 1845-date and Minutes of Boston School Committee, 1869-date. Also, ERIC research materials, current index to journals, 100 periodicals on education.

MA —CHILDREN'S MUSEUM, Resource Center, Museum Wharf, 300 Congress St, Boston, 02210. Marie Ariel, Librn; Maria Russell, Resource Services Mgr
Holdings: Vols (200) Cat Slides Phonorecords
Notes: Multimedia collection of books, games and other teaching materials for early childhood, displayed in the Resource Center and available for reference use by public with borrowing privileges for Resource Center members; Museum-developed multimedia kits available to schools for rental fee; reference collection of games and kits developed from recycled materials;

EDUCATION (cont.)

subject-related programs and services avaiable by Museum staff. Collection emphasis on child study and early childhood education materials.

MA —HOUGHTON MIFFLIN CO, Library, One Beacon St, Boston, 02107. Guest Perry, Dir
Holdings: Vols (15,000) Cat Pix Microforms
Notes: Incl 5000 pictures.

MA —HARVARD UNIVERSITY, Graduate School of Education, Monroe C Gutman Library, 6 Appian Way, Cambridge, 02138. Susan S Baughman, Associate Librn
Holdings: Vols (150,000) Cat Mss Microforms
Budget: ($95,000)
Notes: A comprehensive research collection that seeks to acquire all scholarly works published in the English language in the fields of education, educational administration, educational psychology, and human development. Selective coverage in the related areas of counseling and psychology, business administration, finance, forecasting, statistical analysis and survey design, public and social policy, linguistics, demographics, and international and economic development. Incl 4000 educational and psychological tests. Also historical textbook collection of 35,000 volumes, primarily 19th century.

MA —BOSTON COLLEGE LIBRARIES, Chestnut Hill, 02167.
Notes: The archives of the Citywide Coordinating Council of Boston, Mass, established in 1975 to monitor the desegregation of the Boston school system and to foster public awareness in the implementation of the court's desegregation orders. Incl the collection of transcripts of School Committee meetings; the central files, reflecting the functioning of the council office; and the files of the senior staff, containing the key administrative records of the Council. Also contains 9000 elementary and secondary textbooks, 1000 curriculum guides covering the entire US, and 800 samples of professional tests. Separate catalog.

MA —SPRINGFIELD COLLEGE LIBRARY, Babson Library, Springfield, 01109. Henry Dutcher, Reference Librn
Holdings: Vols (13,000) Cat
Budget: ($65,000)

MI —WAYNE STATE UNIVERSITY, Kresge Library (Education), Detroit, 48202. Theodore Manheim, Librn
Holdings: Vols (297,000) Cat Microforms
Budget: ($105,000)
Notes: Incl complete ERIC microfiche file. 1191 current serial subscriptions. Also 35 drawers of vertical file material. Separate catalog to the collection.

MI —NORTHERN MICHIGAN UNIVERSITY, Lydia M Olson Library, Elizabeth L Harden Drive, Marquette, 49855. Stephen H Peters, Cataloger
Notes: A section of the personal library of Moses Coit Tyler containing a large number of books on the foundations of language and rhetoric.

MN —MANKATO STATE UNIVERSITY, Memorial Library, Educational Resource Center, Box 19, Mankato, 56001. E Colby, Film & Curriculum Librn
Holdings: Vols (50,000) Cat Pix Slides 16mm Films Microforms
Notes: Over 15,000 textbooks and curriculum guides, all subjects (k-8); nonprint materials, all subjects, incl 2800 26mm films (k-adult); career materials; publishers' catalogs.

MN —MINNEAPOLIS PUBLIC LIBRARY & INFORMATION CENTER, Sociology Dept, 300 Nicollet Mall, Minneapolis, 55401. Eileen Scwartzbauer, Dept Head
Holdings: Vols (90,000) Cat Phonorecords Audiotapes Microforms
Budget: ($69,890)
Notes: Special collections: Foundation Center Regional Collection; college catalogs on fiche; adult basic education collection. Separate department catalog.

MS —UNIVERSITY OF SOUTHERN MISSISSIPPI, William David McCain Graduate Library, Box 5148, Southern Sta, Hattiesburg, 39406.
Holdings: Uncat Mss
Notes: Records (1967-1975; 2 cubic feet) of the Mississippi Association of Educators concerning the merger of the predominantly Black, Mississippi Teachers Association and the predominantly White, Mississippi Education Association. The collection incl correspondence, minutes of meetings, conference hearings, resolutions, proposals and constitutions from various state education associations.

MO —UNIVERSITY OF MISSOURI-KANSAS CITY, School of Education, Instructional Materials Center, 615 E 52nd St, Kansas City, 64110. Kenneth J LaBudde, Dir; Victoria Spain, Librn
Holdings: Vols 14,190 Cat
Notes: 12 current serial subscriptions, 1056 microforms, 600 sound recordings.

MO —NORTHEAST MISSOURI STATE UNIVERSITY, Pickler Memorial Library, Kirksville, 63501. George N Hartje, Librn
Holdings: Vols 22,50 Cat Maps Slides Microforms

NH —PLYMOUTH STATE COLLEGE, Lamson Library, Plymouth, 03264. Phillip Wei, Dir of Library Services
Holdings: Cat Pix Microforms Films
Budget: ($30,000)
Notes: Incl 30,000 print and 87,000 nonprint items.

NJ —EDUCATIONAL TESTING SERVICE, Carl Campbell Brigham Library, Princeton, 08540. Janet Williams, Librn
Holdings: Vols 15,000 Cat Microforms
Budget: ($35,000)
Notes: Literature related to tests and measurements.

NJ —EDUCATIONAL TESTING SERVICE, Carl Campbell Brigham Library, Princeton, 08540. Janet Williams, Librn
Notes: Complete works and papers of Louis L Thurstone, a leading psychometrician of the 20th century.

NJ —NEW JERSEY EDUCATION ASSOCIATION, Research Library, 180 W State St, Trenton, 08608. E Lynne Van Buskirk, Associate Dir of Research
Holdings: Vols 1000 Cat
Notes: George H Reavis Reading Area of Phi Delta Kappa publications; 25 VF drawers of research reports, articles, etc; archives of NJEA; NEA depository; contracts from most NJ school districts.

NJ —MONTCLAIR STATE COLLEGE, Harry A Sprague Library, Upper Montclair, 07043.
Holdings: Vols 10,000 Cat Microforms
Notes: The library holds the complete ERIC collection of microfiche. The Curriculum Laboratory contains some 5000 textbooks and 2500 courses of study in addition to the main collection.

NY —NEW YORK STATE LIBRARY, State Education Bldg Annex, Washington Ave, Albany, 12224.
Holdings: Vols 100,000 Cat Microforms
Notes: Emphasis is on American education, particularly New York State. Strong retrospective file of college catalogs. Textbooks excluded. Microform holdings incl ERIC, Manpower Research, Pacesetters in innovation.

NY —STATE UNIVERSITY OF NEW YORK, COLLEGE AT BUFFALO, E H Butler Library, 1300 Elmwood Ave, Buffalo, 14222. George C Newman, Dir
Holdings: Vols (465,130) Cat Maps Microforms
Budget: ($466,000)
Notes: Fully cataloged collections in education, incl education of exceptional children, art education, social sciences education, etc, are strong since the College was formerly a college of education and approx 60 percent of current graduates still obtain some degree enabling them to teach. Incl Curriculum Laboratory containing courses of study, elementary and secondary textbooks, and collections for children's literature courses (MA in Children's Literature offered). Collection consists of 465,130 volumes incl 64,255 bound periodical volumes, plus 19,120 microfilm reels and 457,988 microtext pieces other than reels. Subscribe to 2263 periodicals.

NY —QUEENS BOROUGH PUBLIC LIBRARY, Social Sciences Div, 89-11 Merrick Blvd, Jamaica, 11432. Nathan Shoengold, Head; Renee Kaplan, Asst Div Head
Holdings: Vols Cat Microforms
Notes: Extensive pamphlet collection, incl New York State and New York City curriculum bulletins. Also education periodicals, some in microform. A separate catalog to the social sciences contains the education collection.

NY —BANK STREET COLLEGE OF EDUCATION LIBRARY, 610 W 112 St, New York, 10025. Eleanor Kule Seid, Library Dir
Holdings: Vols (80,000) Cat Microforms
Budget: ($29,000)
Notes: Education, guidance, psychology, educational psychology, curricula, textbooks, Black Studies, etc. All subjects are integrated in one professional collection; in addition there are two separately cataloged and shelved collections: Children's and Elementary Curriculum Materials.

NY —CITY UNIVERSITY OF NEW YORK, City College, Library, 138 St & Convent Ave, New York, 10031. Vira C Hinds, Assoc Prof
Holdings: Vols (35,000) Cat
Budget: ($9173)
Notes: Education, incl juveniles (10,437), textbooks, and ERIC collection. Separate author catalog.

NY —COLUMBIA UNIVERSITY LIBRARIES, Teachers College, Milbank Memorial Library, 525 W 120 St, New York, 10027. Jane P Franck, Dir
Notes: Behavioral sciences; education curricula; urban education. Textbook collections include current and historical works, both US and international. Mss materials include records of National Council for the Social Studies; National Kindergarten Association; Archives of the Board of Education of the City of New York.

NY —NEW YORK PUBLIC LIBRARY, Mid-Manhattan Library, History and Social Sciences Dept, 455 Fifth Ave, New York, 10016. Robert Sheehan, Sr Principal Librn
Holdings: Vols 20,000 Cat Audiotapes Microforms
Budget: $16,700
Notes: Strong undergraduate level collection with duplicate reference and circulating copies of books in many instances. Good collection of college catalogs incl some foreign catalogs. 65 vertical file drawers; 250 periodicals. ERIC index and microfiche collection form 1966.

NY —NEW YORK PUBLIC LIBRARY, Mid-Manhattan Library, Education Collection, 455 Fifth Ave, New York, 10016.
Holdings: Vols (31,000) Cat Audiotapes Microforms
Budget: ($22,550)
Notes: Strong undergraduate level collection of reference and circulating books. Good collection of current college catalogs incl some foreign catalogs. 32 vertical file drawers; 250 periodicals; ERIC index and microfiche collection from 1966.

NY —NEW YORK STATE DIVISION OF HUMAN RIGHTS, Reference Library, Two World Trade Center, Rm 5356, New York, 10047. Rosalind Spriggs, Librn
Holdings: Vols 1000// Cat
Notes: This subject emphasis contains the materials which deal with the problems of discrimination and integration in education and open enrollment in the schools. See Simon Fediuk, *Bibliography on Education*, Special Collection no 2, 1972, 60 pp. This special collection contains about one thousand items: books, studies, journals, pamphlets, reports and reprints.

NC —WAKE TECHNICAL COLLEGE, Library, Audio-Visual Dept, 9101 Fayetteville Road, Raleigh, 27603. James Gray, Librn; Horst Garloff, Audio-Visual Specialist
Holdings: Vols (32,332) Cat Maps Slides

EDUCATION (cont.)

Phonorecords Audiotapes Videotapes 16mm Films Filmstrips Microforms

NC —PUBLIC LIBRARY OF JOHNSTON COUNTY & SMITHFIELD, 305 Market St, Smithfield, 27577. Kenneth M Reading, Dir
Holdings: Vols 450 Cat
Notes: Primary and secondary education.

OH —CLEVELAND PUBLIC LIBRARY, Social Sciences Department, 325 Superior Ave, Cleveland, 44114. Thelma Morris, Head
Holdings: Cat
Notes: Strength of collection is in long runs of periodical sets spanning years from early 1800s. Majority of journals in the *Education* Index are held.

OR —UNIVERSITY OF OREGON LIBRARY, Education-Psychology Dept, Eugene, 97403. Rose Marie Service, Head Dept Librn
Holdings: Cat Pix Phonorecords Audiotapes Filmstrips Microforms
Budget: ($15,000)
Notes: Large up-to-date research collection with representation in all areas and particular emphases reflecting those of the College of Education: educational administration; special education, particularly mental retardation; elementary education, incl early childhood and counseling psychology. Strong serial collection. Curriculum Collection incl a representative selection of curriculum guides, student use textbooks and multimedia, pamphlets, and standardized tests. Complete ERIC microfiche collection.

OR —NORTHWEST REGIONAL EDUCATIONAL LABORATORY, Information Center & Library, 300 SW 6TH Ave, Portland, 97204. M Margaret Rogers, Dir of Information Services
Holdings: Vols (4000) Cat Microforms
Budget: $9600
Notes: Complete ERIC files and indexes. Incl 350 journals and newsletters and an extensive reference collection on education and related subjects. Perform computer searches of education, social sciences and humanities databases.

PA —SCHOOL DISTRICT OF PHILADELPHIA, Pedagogical Library, 21 St & Pkwy, Philadelphia, 19103. Helen E Howe, Librn; Patricia K Buck, Asst Librn
Holdings: Vols (47,000) Cat Pix Microforms
Budget: ($25,000)
Notes: Collection emphasis on public school education K-12 with the main areas including Afro-American history and culture, elementary and early childhood education, secondary education, educational administration, educational research, reading, school law, educational psychology. Special Collections: ERIC (140,000 documents), Archives of the School District of Philadelphia. Approx 500 periodical subscriptions.

PA —TEMPLE UNIVERSITY LIBRARIES, Special Collections Dept, Rare Books & Mss Section, Philadelphia, 19122. Thomas M Whitehead, Cur
Holdings: Vols 800 Cat
Budget: $500
Notes: Contains all available works by and about Jean Piaget and those of his principal associates. Incl over 500 journal articles and 70 dissertations. Collection originally developed as the research collection of the Jean Piaget Society.

PA —UNIVERSITY OF PITTSBURGH, Hillman Library, Pittsburgh, 15260. Glenora E Rossell, Head
Holdings: Vols 24,350 Cat
Notes: Especially strong in social theory, social history, social groups, criminology and urban sociology. Emphasis is currently being given to administration of justice, sociology of the child, sociology of the aged, sociology of education and sociology of religion. This collection is strengthened by the US government publications depository collection, the partial UN depository collection, the Canadian government publications collection and the collection of the Social Work Library.

RI —BROWN UNIVERSITY, John Carter Brown Library, Providence, 02912. Norman Fiering, Librn; Everett C Wilkie Jr, Bibliographer; Susan Danforth, Cur Maps & Prints
Holdings: Vols 500
Notes: Children's and pedagogical materials available in America through the colonial period (ca 1800).

SD —NORTHERN STATE COLLEGE, Beulah Williams Library, Aberdeen, 57401. Tedine Roos, Curriculum Librn
Holdings: Vols 6080 Cat
Budget: $1000
Notes: 3970 elementary and secondary school textbooks and Pitman-Fearon Microfiche guide collection. Separate catalog.

TN —VANDERBILT UNIVERSITY, George Peabody College for Teachers, Education Library, Box 325, Nashville, 37203. Mary Beth Blalock, Librn
Holdings: Vols (192,541) Cat Pix Slides Phonorecords Filmstrips Microforms
Budget: ($59,000)
Notes: The Education Library (192,541 vols) collects in all areas relating to education with special emphasis on Child Study and Exceptional Children. Special funds are available for continuing purchases in these areas. The collection is strong in curriculum materials, physical education, applied art, psychology related to education and all areas of education. Amoung special papers are over 300 papers by and about Jean Piaget and an extensive author and subject file referring to the location of these papers and books and journal articles by and about Piaget in the rest of the Education Library collection. The Education Library is a Division of the Vanderbilt University Library.

TX —ABILENE CHRISTIAN UNIVERSITY, Margaret & Herman Brown Library, ACU Sta, Abilene, 79601. Callie Faye Milliken, Assoc Dir
Notes: Pre-1900 Public School textbooks.

TX —TEXAS EDUCATION AGENCY, Resource Center Library, 201 E 11 St, Austin, 78701. Linda Kemp, Librn
Holdings: Vols 13,000 Microforms
Budget: $10,000
Notes: Elementary and secondary education. Incl over 200,000 titles on microforms. Partially cataloged.

TX —UNIVERSITY OF TEXAS LIBRARIES, General Libraries, PO Box P, Austin, 78713. Carolyn Bucknell, Asst Dir for Collection Development
Holdings: Cat Microforms

TX —FORT WORTH PUBLIC LIBRARY, North Branch, 601 Park St, Fort Worth, 76106. Betty M Hennington, Branch Head
Holdings: Vols 1000 Cat Phonorecords Audiotapes Filmstrips
Notes: Collection is entirely non-fiction. Although an effort is made to have novels by Mexican-American authors, these are not included in this collection. The criteria for the collection is anything written about Mexican Americans or books in which a large portion is devoted to the Mexican American. The history of Mexico until 1920 is included, but there are no books dealing with the history of Mexico since that time. Travel books are not included. An effort is made to obtain all current materials and to acquire retrospective materials when available, especially in the field of education and teaching.

TX —SOUTHWEST TEXAS STATE UNIVERSITY, Library, San Marcos, 78666. Bob Harris, Special Collections Librn
Holdings: / / Uncat
Notes: American textbooks to 1918. Liberal arts, education, business.

WA —SEATTLE PUBLIC LIBRARY, 1000 Fourth Ave, Seattle, 98104. Ronald A Dubberly, City Librn
Holdings: Cat

WI —UNIVERSITY OF WISCONSIN, EXTENSION, Bureau of AudioVisual Instruction, PO Box 2093, Madison, 53701. Hal Riehle, Dir
Holdings: Cat 16mm Films
Notes: 16mm educational films, 7500 titles (15,000 prints). Annotated catalog: *BAVI Film Reference Guide*. Selected titles in over 600 subject areas, pre-school through college and adult levels.

WI —WISCONSIN DEPT OF PUBLIC INSTRUCTION, Library, 125 S Webster St Room 311, PO Box 7841, Madison, 53707. Marjorie Westergard, Librn
Holdings: Vols (4000) Cat Microforms
Budget: ($16,000)
Notes: Main purpose of the library is to support the needs and programs of the Wisconsin Department of Public Instruction. No teaching materials are collected at the library; the complete ERIC Microfiche collection, as well as the book collection. Service is generally restricted to members of the Department and other state agencies.

WI —UNIVERSITY OF WISCONSIN, MILWAUKEE, Library, Box 604, Milwaukee, 53201. William C Roselle, Dir
Holdings: Cat Microforms
Notes: Wisconsin Legislative Reference Bureau Clippings File. Special strength in a collection mostly of Wisconsin emphasis. 440 reels of 16mm microfilm. A subject-chronological arrangement (approximately 1200 subjects covering the years from the 1890s through 1970) of pamphlets and a variety of fugitive materials and of clippings from national and Wiconsin newspapers, popular magazines and scholarly journals, and federal, state, and local government documents.

PR —CARIBBEAN REGIONAL LIBRARY, General Library, University of Puerto Rico, Rio Piedras, (Mailing add: PO Box 21917, University Station, San Juan, 00931). Carmen M Costa de Ramos, Librn
Holdings: Vols (115,605) Cat Maps Pix Microforms
Notes: Collection is specialized in the Caribbean with emphasis in the areas of interest to developing countries: social sciences, politics, economics, labor, education, commerce, tourism, literature, etc. The *Current Caribbean Bibliography* is compiled at the Caribbean Regional Library, with card contributions from all countries of the Caribbean; it also lists all the new additions to the library.

AB —UNIVERSITY OF ALBERTA, Herbert T Coutts Education Library, Education Building, Edmonton, T6G 2G5, Can. Madge MacGowan, Head Librn
Holdings: Vols 209,479
Notes: Incl periodical subscriptions 916, AV items 27,924, microfiche 228,287, microfilm 6214. Curriculum research collection of Alberta curriculum guides and prescribed Alberta textbooks. Pedagogical collection incl ERIC microfiche collection, William Gray Reading Collection, and is particularly strong in the areas of reading, educational administration and educational psychology.

BC —BRITISH COLUMBIA TEACHERS' FEDERATION, Resources Center, 2235 Burrand St, Vancouver, V6J 3H9, Can. T M Murphy, Librn
Holdings: Vols (9900) Cat Audiotapes Videotapes 16mm Films
Budget: $30,000
Notes: Emphasis on teachers' professional in-service training. Curriculum material excluded; audiovisual material lent to BCTF members province-wide.

BC —VANCOUVER COMMUNITY COLLEGE, King Edward Campus Library, 1155 E Broadway, PO Box 24620, Station C, Vancouver, V6B 4H2, Can. Paul Cook, Campus Librn
Holdings: Vols (25,000) Cat Maps Slides Audiotapes 16mm Films Filmstrips
Notes: Teaching English as a second language. Curriculum development.

BC —VANCOUVER PUBLIC LIBRARY, Sociology Div, 750 Burrard St, Vancouver, V6Z 1X5, Can.
Holdings: Cat
Notes: Incl special files of pamphlets, clippings, etc.

MB —MANITOBA DEPARTMENT OF EDUCATION LIBRARY, Main Floor Box 3, 1181 Portage Ave, Winnipeg, R3G 0T3, Can. John Tooth, Head Librn
Holdings: Vols 60,000 Cat Pix Slides

EDUCATION (cont.)

Phonorecords Audiotapes 16mm Films Filmstrips Microforms Videotapes
Budget: $200,000
Notes: Incl 250,000 ERIC documents on microform; 5000 pictures; 5000 slides; 2500 phonorecords; 2500 audiotapes; 12,000 films; and 4000 filmstrips.

MB —UNIVERSITY OF MANITOBA, Faculty of Education, D S Woods Education Library, Winnipeg, R3T 2N2, Can. Doreen Shanks, Head
Holdings: Vols 57,000 Phonorecords Videotapes Microforms
Notes: Also incl collection of 23,000 textbooks, 332,000 microforms, 615 phonorecords, and 225 videotapes. Also complete file of ERIC (Educational Resources Information Centre) documents on microfiche; Instructional Materials Centre.

ON —CANADA PUBLIC SERVICE COMMISSION, Library, Room 930 W Tower, Esplande Laurier, Ottawa, K1A 0M7, Can. A Campbell, Chief Librn
Holdings: Vols 7000 Cat
Budget: $20,000
Notes: Library supports the research, administrative, and instructional needs of the Commission. English and French materials.

ON —NATIONAL LIBRARY OF CANADA, 395 Wellington St, Ottawa, K1A 0N4, Can. Andre Preibish, Dir
Holdings: Vols 10,000
Notes: Includes 130 serial titles, theses, pamphlets, government publications relating to family and marriage. The following disciplines covered: anthropology, psychology and psychiatry, law, economics, religion, sociology, demography, education, political science and biology. Earliest title 1630.

SK —SASKATCHEWAN TEACHERS' FEDERATION, Stewart Resources Centre, 2317 Arlington Ave, Saskatoon, S7K 3N3, Can. Susan Dyer, Librn
Holdings: Vols (18,000) Cat Slides Phonorecords Audiotapes Videotapes 16mm Films Filmstrips
Budget: ($15,000)
Notes: Professional teacher-education collection; curriculum materials; and Mary Ellen Burgess Drama Library.

EDUCATION—CURRICULA

CA —UNIVERSITY OF CALIFORNIA, BERKELEY, Humanities-Social Sciences Libraries, Education-Psychology Library, 2600 Tolman Hall, Berkeley, 94720. Sonya Kaufman, Acting Head
Holdings: Vols (110,000)
Notes: General research collection in fields of education and psychology. Education collection's emphases are in the areas of administration, policy planning, higher education, science and math education, language and literacy. Serial holdings are strong. The library receives approx 2200 current serial titles in education and psychology.

CA —UNIVERSITY OF CALIFORNIA, BERKELEY, Science Education Library, Lawrence Hall of Science, Berkeley, 94720. Ann M Jensen, Librn
Holdings: Vols (6000)
Notes: Emphasis on innovative materials in the field of science, mathematics, and environmental education.

CA —CALIFORNIA STATE UNIVERSITY, LONG BEACH, Reference Center, 1250 Bellflower Blvd, Long Beach, 90840.
Notes: Outstanding collection for quantity, diversity, and quality. Incl nearly 54,000 books on education, 18,010 textbooks, 14, 565 curriculum guides, over 1075 teaching aids, 9000 pictures, 15,051 phonorecords, 3800 audiotapes, 4216 filmstrips, and 9240 microforms (not limited to education).

CA —SAN FRANCISCO STATE UNIVERSITY, J Paul Leonard Library, 1630 Holloway Ave, San Francisco, 94132. Susan Quinlan, Curriculum Librn
Holdings: Vols (49,246) Cat Phonorecords Audiotapes 8mm Films Microforms
Budget: ($8500)
Notes: The young people's collection or children's literature collection of 17,843 vols incl books with reading and interest levels ranging from preschool through senior high school. The Marguerite Archer collection of historical children's books contains an additional 3000 vols. Have 19,755 textbooks, 5150 curriculum guides, 1970 pamphlets. Collection emphasizes instructional materials that can be utitlized in the school classroom. Professional books and journals and other media relating to educational history, philosophy, research, theories of teaching, etc are in the main collection.

CO —SOCIAL SCIENCE EDUCATION CONSORTIUM, Resource & Demonstration Center (RDC), 855 Broadway, Boulder, 80302. Regina McCormick, Staff Assoc
Holdings: Vols (16,000) Cat Filmstrips Microforms
Notes: Contains over 15,000 elementary and secondary social studies textbooks, audiovisuals, games and simulations, professional books, and the complete ERIC microfiche collection. Staff available to travel to all parts of the US to consult on curriculum development, instructional methods, materials analysis and selection, evaluation, new materials, teaching strategies, and trends in the social studies.

IN —INDIANA UNIVERSITY, School of Education, Library, Bloomington, 47401. Adele Dendy, Head Librn
Holdings: Vols (35,000) Cat Pix Slides Phonorecords Audiotapes 16mm Films Filmstrips Microforms
Budget:
Notes: Library has complete ERIC collection of microfiche (277,308). 2098 non-ERIC items, 226 serials, and 22,823 nonprint items (housed in educational materials center). Emphasis on recent materials; the historic collections in education are located in the Main Library. The collection is geared to graduate level studies and research. A separate Teaching Materials Center includes 10,000 elementary and secondary textbooks. The Center also includes curriculum guides, supplementary materials and 17,823 nonprint teaching aids.

IN —BALL STATE UNIVERSITY, University Libraries, Muncie, 47306. Michael B Wood, Dean
Holdings: Vols 18,000 Cat Pix
Notes: Incl standardized tests; historical collection of textbooks, 1787-1945.

MN —MANKATO STATE UNIVERSITY, Memorial Library, Educational Resource Center, Box 19, Mankato, 56001. E Colby, Film & Curriculum Librn
Holdings: Vols (50,000) Cat Pix Slides 16mm Films Microforms
Notes: Over 15,000 textbooks and curriculum guides, all subjects (k-8); nonprint materials, all subjects, incl 2800 26mm films (k-adult); career materials; publishers' catalogs.

MO —EDEN-WEBSTER LIBRARIES, Eden Theological Seminary, Webster University, 475 E Lockwood, Saint Louis, 63119. Karen M Luebbert, Dir
Notes: Student and Faculty Curriculum materials for pre-school through secondary. Incl curriculum guides, projects, enrichment materials and a children's literature collection.

NJ —MONTCLAIR STATE COLLEGE, Harry A Sprague Library, Upper Montclair, 07043.
Holdings: Vols 10,000 Cat Microforms
Notes: The library holds the complete ERIC collection of microfiche. The Curriculum Laboratory contains some 5000 textbooks and 2500 courses of study in addition to the main collection.

NY —STATE UNIVERSITY OF NEW YORK, COLLEGE AT BUFFALO, E H Butler Library, 1300 Elmwood Ave, Buffalo, 14222. Marilyn C Kihl, Librn
Holdings: Cat
Notes: Curriculum Laboratory specializes in materials for elementary and secondary education, incl courses of study (2300), textbooks (7800), and children's books (18, 000). Materials circulate. Full cataloging for children's literature and courses of study are found in main catalog.

NY —C W POST CENTER OF LONG ISLAND UNIVERSITY, B Davis Schwartz Memorial Library, Greenvale, 11548. Manju Prasad-Rao, Media Librn
Holdings: Pix Slides Phonorecords Audiotapes Videotapes 16mm Films Filmstrips
Budget: ($12,500)
Notes: The Center, while originally established for schools of Education and Library Science with a k-12 text and trade book collection and media, now incl a circulating non-print collection for the entire campus. (8000) Separate card catalog. Incl children's trade books (17,000); k-12 textbooks (1562 series); and k-12 curriculum guides (3053).

NY —QUEENS BOROUGH PUBLIC LIBRARY, Social Sciences Div, 89-11 Merrick Blvd, Jamaica, 11432. Nathan Shoengold, Head; Renee Kaplan, Asst Div Head
Holdings: Vols Cat Microforms
Notes: Extensive pamphlet collection, incl New York State and New York City curriculum bulletins. Also education periodicals, some in microform. A separate catalog to the social sciences contains the education Collection.

NY —BANK STREET COLLEGE OF EDUCATION LIBRARY, 610 W 112 St, New York, 10025. Eleanor Kule Seid, Library Dir
Holdings: Vols (90,000) Cat Microforms
Notes: Education, guidance, psychology, educational psychology, curricula, textbooks, Black Studies, etc. All subjects are integrated in one professional collection; in addition there are two separately cataloged and shelved collections: Children's and Elementary Curriculum Materials.

NY —COLUMBIA UNIVERSITY LIBRARIES, Teachers College, Milbank Memorial Library, 525 W 120 St, New York, 10027. Jane P Franck, Dir
Holdings: Vols 12,200 Cat Microforms
Notes: Courses of study from 1880 to date. Early titles in hard copy, since 1970 in microfiche.

NY —SCHOLASTIC MAGAZINES, Editorial Library, 730 Broadway, New York, 10003. Lucy Evankow, Chief Librn
Notes: TV back to the 1950s; 1940s motion pictures; black and white photographs; political cartoons back to the 1940s-50s; curriculum educations; software.

NY —STATE UNIVERSITY OF NEW YORK, STONY BROOK, Melville Library, Dept of Special Collections, Stony Brook, 11794. Evert Volkersz, Head
Holdings: Mss
Notes: The Performing Arts Foundation of Huntington, NY, existed from 1964 to 1982. The partially cataloged collection incl records of the affiliated Arts in Education and the Performing Arts Curriculum Enrichment Project. No photocopying.

NC —APPALACHIAN STATE UNIVERSITY, Belk Library, Instructional Materials Center, Boone, 28608. Selma P Farthing, Librn
Holdings: Vols (31,847) Cat Pix Slides Phonorecords Audiotapes Videotapes Filmstrips Microforms 16mm Films
Budget: ($10,500)
Notes: Scope of the collection is life-long learning. Serving as a working laboratory for educators at all levels, we collect materials in every format available. The Instructional Materials Center has its own card catalog, and the holdings are also listed in the library's central catalog. Collection incl textbooks, children's literature, tests and computer software.

NC —NORTH CAROLINA STATE UNIVERSITY, School of Education, Curriculum Materials Center, 400 Poe, Box 7801, Raleigh, 27695. James Jarrell, Coordr
Holdings: Vols 5000 Cat Slides
Notes: Incl 551 transparencies, 979 filmstrips, 3191 slides, 323 videotapes, 139 films, and 1342 audiorecordings.

OR —UNIVERSITY OF OREGON LIBRARY, Education-Psychology Dept,

EDUCATION—CURRICULA (cont.)

Eugene, 97403. Rose Marie Service, Head Dept Librn
Holdings: Cat Pix Phonorecords Audiotapes Filmstrips Microforms
Budget: $1200
Notes: Incl about 12,000 items, incl textbooks and multimedia, and about 4000 curriculum guides and administrative materials relevant to the curriculum. Curriculum guides for ERIC Microfiche Collection also available.

PA —BALCH INSTITUTE FOR ETHNIC STUDIES, Library, 18 S Seventh St, Philadelphia, 19106. R Joseph Anderson, Library Dir
Notes: The Ethnic Heritage Studies Clearinghouse Collection of over 2000 reports, print and audiovisual materials, instructional kits, and scholarly monographs developed since 1974 under the federal government's Ethnic Heritage Studies Act, to encourage support of ethnic studies in public school and college curricula.

PA —SHIPPENSBURG STATE COLLEGE, Lehman Library, Media/Curricular Center, Shippensburg, 17257. Gene R Hanson, Dir
Holdings: Vols 23,700 Cat Maps Pix Slides
Budget: ($20,000)
Notes: Extensive curriculum collection.

RI —PROVIDENCE PUBLIC LIBRARY, 150 Empire St, Providence, 02903. Lance J Bauer, Special Collections Librn
Notes: Lippitt Hill Tutorial Shelf (Rochambeau Branch). A resource library for tutors and parents, centrally located and open after school; established in 1973. LHT is a non-profit school volunteer agency which provides in-school tutoring services, contributes money for the acquisition of new books for the LHT Shelf, and the Providence Public Library maintains the collection. A collection of educational materials, wich an emphasis on math and reading, for the information and use of the general public, parents, teachers, and especially, tutors. It is located near the front door of the Rochambeau Branch.

TN —VANDERBILT UNIVERSITY, George Peabody College for Teachers, Education Library, Box 325, Nashville, 37203. Mary Beth Blalock, Librn
Holdings: Vols (192,541) Cat Pix Slides Phonorecords Filmstrips Microforms
Budget: ($59,000)
Notes: The Education Library (192,541 vols) collects in all areas relating to education with special emphasis on Child Study and Exceptional Children. Special funds are available for continuing purchases in these areas. The collection is strong in curriculum materials, physical education, applied art, psychology related to education and all areas of education. Amoung special papers are over 300 papers by and about Jean Piaget and an extensive author and subject file referring to the location of these papers and books and journal articles by and about Piaget in the rest of the Education Library collection. The Education Library is a Division of the Vanderbilt University Library.

TX —SAINT EDWARD'S UNIVERSITY, Curriculum Materials Collection, 3001 S Congress, Austin, 78704. Joseph Sprug, Director
Holdings: Vols 5100 Cat

WA —UNIVERSITY OF WASHINGTON LIBRARIES, Suzzallo Library, Curriculum Materials Section, FM-25, Seattle, 98195. Jean Belch, Head
Holdings: Vols 22,376 Cat
Budget: ($7239)
Notes: Holds microfiche series of curriculum guides and courses of study. The Resource Center for Gifted Education holds books, films, tapes, slides and realia suitable for gifted students.

WI —WISCONSIN DEPT OF PUBLIC INSTRUCTION, Library, 125 S Webster St Room 311, PO Box 7841, Madison, 53707. Marjorie Westergard, Librn
Holdings: Vols (4000) Cat Microforms
Budget: ($16,000)
Notes: Main purpose of the library is to support the needs and programs of the Wisconsin Department of Public Instruction. No teaching materials are collected at the library; however, professional materials kept incl the complete ERIC Microfiche collection, as well as the book collection. Service is generally restricted to members of the Department and other state agencies.

WI —UNIVERSITY OF WISCONSIN, MILWAUKEE, Library, Box 604, Milwaukee, 53201. William C Roselle, Dir
Holdings: Vols (25,945) Cat Pix Slides Phonorecords Audiotapes Filmstrips
Notes: A card catalog of all items except textbooks is available in the department. The collection includes 14,200 children's literature books for grades kindergarten through ninth with emphasis on honor and notable book titles; a textbook collection for grades 1-12 including some programmed texts; a curriculum guide and resource unit file of 3000 items.

SK —SASKATCHEWAN TEACHERS' FEDERATION, Stewart Resources Centre, 2317 Arlington Ave, Saskatoon, S7K 3N3, Can. Susan Dyer, Librn
Holdings: Vols (18,000) Cat Slides Phonorecords Audiotapes Videotapes 16mm Films Filmstrips
Budget: ($15,000)
Notes: Professional teacher-education collection; curriculum materials; and Mary Ellen Burgess Drama Library.

EDUCATION—ECONOMIC ASPECTS

DC —INTERNATIONAL MONETARY FUND AND WORLD BANK, Joint Bank-Fund Library, Washington, 20431. Maureen M Moore, Librn
Holdings: Vols Cat Films Microforms
Notes: Incl foreign trade and statistical bulletins and yearbooks, central bank reports and bulletins, budget papers, security yearbooks, economic development plans and reports on economic conditions from the 132 member countries. An index of periodical material compiled by the Library staff has been published as: *Economics and Finance; Index to Periodical Articles, 1947-1971;* First Supplement, 1972, 1973, 1974 (Second Supplement, 1975, 1976, 1977, in preparation), 5 vols. (Boston: G K Hall, 1972, 1975). Also, The Developing Areas: *A Classed Bibliography of the Joint Bank-Fund Library,* Vol 1: *Latin America and the* Caribbean; Vol 2: *Africa and the Middle* East; Vol 3: *Asia and Oceania* (Boston: G K Hall, 1976).

EDUCATION—FINANCE

DC —COUNCIL FOR ADVANCEMENT & SUPPORT OF EDUCATION, Reference Center, Eleven Dupont Circle NW, Suite 400, Washington, 20036. Cynthia Snyder, Dir
Holdings: Vols (600) Cat Mss Audiotapes Microforms
Notes: A membership service containing in formation in educational fund raising, institutional relations, government relations, alumni administration, publications, and management techniques for higher education and independent schools. Collection, in addition, contains mss, microfiches, and tapes. Succeeds the American Alumni Council, dissolved in 1974.

MA —HARVARD UNIVERSITY, Graduate School of Education, Monroe C Gutman Library, 6 Appian Way, Cambridge, 02138. Susan S Baughman, Associate Librn
Holdings: Vols (150,000) Cat Mss Microforms
Budget: ($95,000)
Notes: A comprehensive research collection that seeks to acquire all scholarly works published in the English language in the fields of education, educational administration, educational psychology, and human development. Selective coverage in the related areas of counseling and psychology, business administration, finance, forecasting, statistical analysis and survey design, public and social policy, linguistics, demographics, and international and economic development. Incl 4000 educational and psychological tests.

EDUCATION—HISTORY

AZ —NORTHERN ARIZONA UNIVERSITY, Special Collection Library, CU Box 6022, Flagstaff, 86011. Peter M Whiteley, Coordr/Archivist; William Mullane, Librn
Notes: John Bury Collection; correspondence, mss, notes, subject files, oral history tapes, collected in writing 1975 NAU doctoral dissertation *Historical Role of Arizona's Superintendent of Public* Instruction. This collection is especially valuable for studying the history of education in Arizona. Inventory available.

CA —LOS ANGELES PUBLIC LIBRARY, Social Sciences Dept, 630 W Fifth St, Los Angeles, 90071. Marilyn C Wherley, Principal Librn
Holdings: Vols (13,000) Cat Microforms
Budget: ($150,000)
Notes: Education collection. Over 500 bound periodicals. Collection also includes government publications, agency reports, statistics, yearbooks, directories, pamphlets, bibliographies, child and adolescent psychology theories and history, college catalogs on microfiche, and nearly complete collection of California catalogs. General history of education and comparative educational systems.

CA —UNIVERSITY OF CALIFORNIA, LOS ANGELES, Research Library, Dept of Special Collections, 405 Hilgard Ave, Los Angeles, 90024. Edward Shreeves, Chairman, Bibliographers Group; David S Zeidberg, Head
Notes: Various collections, incl books, pamphlets, and ephemera by and about Georg Michael Kerschensteiner; modern pre-primers from various countries; 19th century elementary and secondary school textbooks, chiefly American; 20th century California school directories; William Nicholas Hailmann Collection on kindergarten education.

CT —YALE UNIVERSITY, Box 1603A, Yale Station, New Haven, 06520.

DC —GEORGETOWN UNIVERSITY, Library, Special Collections Div, 37 & O Sts NW, Washington, 20057. George M Barringer, Special Collections Librn; Nicholas B Sheetz, Mss Librn
Holdings: Vols (100) Uncat Mss
Notes: Includes the archives of Dag Hammarskjold College, Columbia, Md; a portion of the archives of Gonzaga College, Washington, DC; records of the Fells Point Hebrew Grammar School, Baltimore, Md, and other materials (Besides these collections, students can use the Georgetown University Archives, 1787- , and the Woodstock College Archives, 1866- , qv under Jesuits in the US.)

IL —ARLINGTON HEIGHTS MEMORIAL LIBRARY, 500 N Dunton Ave, Arlington Heights, 60004. Frank J Dempsey, Librn
Holdings: Vols 5000 Cat Microforms
Notes: Maintained as education subject center under the former North Suburban Library System's Coordinated Acquisitions Program. Collection incl history and philosophy of education; teaching methods; testing and measurement; and administration.

IL —MCLEAN COUNTY HISTORICAL SOCIETY LIBRARY & MUSEUM, 201 E Grove, Bloomington, 61701. Barbara Dunbar, Dir; Greg Koos, Archivist
Holdings: Vols (3000) Cat Mss Maps Pix
Notes: Illinois history, emphasis on McLean County. Strong in military heritage of Illinois, particularly the 33rd and 94th regiments (Ill Vol Inf) in the Civil War. Incl 150 LF archives and 1000 pictures. Photocopying.

IL —SOUTHERN ILLINOIS UNIVERSITY, CARBONDALE, Delyte W Morris Library, Special Collections Dept, Carbondale, 62901. David V Koch, Cur of Special Collections; Louisa Bowen, Cur of Manuscripts
Holdings: Vols 2500 Uncat Mss Pix
Notes: Twenty collections related to 20th

EDUCATION—HISTORY (cont.)

century American philosophy incl the papers of John Dewey, acquired from the estate of his widow, incl correspondence, mss, class lecture notes, photographs, and memorabilia, of a long and distinguished career. There are letters from such scholars as William James, William Rainey Harper, James Mark Baldwin, James Cattell and Adelbert Ames. Also in the collection are letters to his wife and children, a pictorial record of his stay in China (1919-1921), and his personal library of about 1000 books, many of the volumes heavily annotated. In addition to papers from the Dewey estate, the Library has acquired, in support of the editing and publishing of the *Collected Works of John* Dewey, extensive correspondence between Dewey and his associates-Edward Scribner Ames, Paul Schilpp, Cyrus Eaton, Myrtle McGraw, Herbert W Schneider, JamesHayden Tufts and Edwin Wilson. Publishing agreements, mss and galley proofs of Dewey's work have also been assembled. (John Dewey, *The Early Works 1882-1898,* 1969-1972; Jo Ann Boydston, ed, *Guide to the Works of John Dewey, 1970;* Jo Ann Boydston, ed, *John Dewey, A Checklist of Translations, 1969*).

IN —INDIANA UNIVERSITY, Lilly Library, Seventh St, Bloomington, 47405. William R Cagle, Librn
Holdings: // Mss Pix
Notes: Ms holdings in papers of Edward A Rumely, founder of Interlaken School in Indiana and apostle of the New School Movement in the US. 10,000 items in this nearly 100,000 item collection relate to Interlaken and to such college preparatory training as represented by Interlaken. The papers of William Wirt, educator, relate entirely to his work as superintendent of schools in Gary, Indiana, 1907-1938, where he developed the so-called "Gary system" of education. 22,232 items.

IN —INDIANA STATE UNIVERSITY, Cunningham Memorial Library, Dept of Rare Books & Special Collections, Terre Haute, 47809. Lawrence J McCrank, Head
Notes: The University Archives holds copies of all publications of the Indiana Normal School which became the Indiana State Teachers College and Indiana State University, plus collections of faculty publications and papers. The K Martin sub-collection contains 10,000 photographs relating to ISU from the 1890s to the 1950s. Incl 300 feet of mss.

IA —STATE HISTORICAL SOCIETY OF IOWA LIBRARY, 402 Iowa Ave, Iowa City, 52240. Darold J Brown, Librn
Holdings: Vols 1000 Cat Mss
Notes: 19th and 20th century materials on Iowa schools, incl catalogs, directories, histories, and records of public schools, academies and colleges,

MA —BOSTON SCHOOL COMMITTEE, Administration Library, 77 Ave Louis Pasteur, Boston, 02115. Polly Kaufman, Coordinating Dir; Barbara Elam, Coordinating Dir
Holdings: Vols (12,000) Cat Microfiche
Budget: ($10,000)
Notes: Collection incl file of Boston School Committee Documents, 1845-date and Minutes of Boston School Committee, 1869-date. Also, ERIC research materials, current index to journals, 100 periodicals on education.

MA —HARVARD UNIVERSITY LIBRARY, Cambridge, 02138.
Holdings: Cat
Notes: Downs: 1951, 1953, 1960. Especially early history and textbooks.

MA —OLD STURBRIDGE VILLAGE, Research Library, Sturbridge, 01566. Theresa Rini Percy, Librn
Holdings: Cat Mss
Notes: To 1850 in New England. School textbooks, treatises, peridicals.

MI —WAYNE STATE UNIVERSITY, Kresge Library (Education), Detroit, 48202. Theodore Manheim, Librn
Holdings: Vols (297,000) Cat Microforms
Budget: ($105,000)
Notes: Incl complete ERIC microfiche file. 1191 current serial subscriptions. Also 35 drawers of vertical file material. Separate catalog to the collection.

MS —UNIVERSITY OF SOUTHERN MISSISSIPPI, William David McCain Graduate Library, Box 5148, Southern Sta, Hattiesburg, 39406.
Holdings: Uncat Mss
Notes: Records (1967-1975; 2 cubic feet) of the Mississippi Association of Educators concerning the merger of the predominantly Black, Mississippi Teachers Association and the predominantly White, Mississippi Education Association. The collection incl correspondence, minutes of meetings, conference hearings, resolutions, proposals and constitutions from various state education associations.

MO —UNIVERSITY OF MISSOURI-SAINT LOUIS, Thomas Jefferson Library, Manuscript and Historical Society Collection, 8001 Natural Bridge Rd, Saint Louis, 63121.
Holdings: Mss Pix Tapes
Notes: ca

NY —ADELPHI UNIVERSITY, Library, Garden City, 11530. Jerome Yavarkovsky, Dean of Libraries
Holdings: // Mss
Notes: The collection includes 183 items consisting primarily of letters and some memorabilia. Mrs Maria Kraus-Boelte was one of the earliest and most influential apostles of the kindergarten in the US employing the Froebelian method. Collection contains letters to a pupil Carrie Coit Meleney and memorabilia relating to the Kraus Alumni Kindergarten Association.

NY —QUEENS BOROUGH PUBLIC LIBRARY, Social Sciences Div, 89-11 Merrick Blvd, Jamaica, 11432. Nathan Shoengold, Head; Renee Kaplan, Asst Div Head
Holdings: Vols (45,000) Cat Microforms
Notes: Extensive pamphlet collection, incl New York State and New York City curriculum bulletins. Also education periodicals, some in microform. A separate catalog to the social sciences contains the education collection.

NY —COLUMBIA UNIVERSITY LIBRARIES, Rare Book & Manuscript Library, 801 Butler Library, 535 W 114 St, New York, 10027. Kenneth A Lohf, Librn
Holdings: Vols 18,500 Cat

NY —COLUMBIA UNIVERSITY LIBRARIES, Teachers College, Milbank Memorial Library, 525 W 120 St, New York, 10027. Jane P Franck, Dir
Holdings: Vols 4200 Cat
Notes: Rare books in education from the 15th-19th centuries.

NY —ROCKEFELLER UNIVERSITY, Rockefeller Archive Center, Hillcrest, Pocantico Hills, North Tarrytown, 10591. Joseph W Ernst, Dir; J William Hess, Assoc Dir
Notes: Papers relative to the Rockefeller Family, Foundations, University, and other specific enterprises and contributions to particular areas of social, physical, educational, and historic reform, preservation, conservation, or development. Extensive records of administrative, financial, physical, or intellectual relationships.

NY —STATE UNIVERSITY OF NEW YORK, COLLEGE AT ONEONTA, James M Milne Library, Oneonta, 13820. Richard D Johnson, Librn
Holdings: Vols (427,646) Cat Mss Maps Pix Slides Phonorecords Audiotapes 16mm Films Filmstrips Microforms
Budget: ($338,299)
Notes: New York State Collection; 19th & early 20th century popular fiction; New York State Verse Collection; Early Textbook & Early Educational Theory Collection.

NC —DUKE UNIVERSITY, William R Perkins Library, Manuscript Dept, Durham, 27706. Ellen Gartrell, Cur of Mss
Holdings: Cat Mss
Notes: Especially strong for Southern states, 19th-20th centuries. Education of women and blacks, regional and national organizations, public and private schools. Papers of black educator Charles N Hunter; Alliance for the Guidance of Rural Youth; NEA official Belmont Farley, and much more.

OH —RUTHERFORD B HAYES LIBRARY, 1337 Hayes Ave, Fremont, 43420. Watt P Marchman, Dir
Holdings: Uncat Mss Pix Microforms
Notes: The Frank Ohlinger Family Collection: American religion; Chinese missionary; education. (9 linear feet). Index in collections.

PA —LIBRARY COMPANY OF PHILADELPHIA, 1314 Locust St, Philadelphia, 19107. Edwin Wolf II, Librn; Kenneth Finkel, Cur of Prints
Holdings: Vols (450,000) Cat
Notes: Significant collection of works on American education to 1860.

PA —UNIVERSITY OF PITTSBURGH, Hillman Library, Special Collections Dept, John A Nietz Textbook Collection, 363 Hillman Library, Pittsburgh, 15260. Charles E Aston, Jr, Coordr
Holdings: Vols 13,480 Cat Vols 3000 Uncat Mss
Notes: The John A Nietz Textbook Collection of primarily American textbooks in 3 areas; primary school books to 1900, secondary texts to ca 1930 and pedagogical books (1000 vols on the history and theory of education incl writings of the key figures in the field of education). Books are cataloged via an inhouse computer printout, and are accessible via name, title, subject, place, publisher and date. Late 18th and all of the 19th century are well represented. Important titles in each subject are discussed in John A Nietz's *Old Textbooks* (Pittsburgh, 1961) and in his *The Evolution of American Secondary School Textbooks* (Rutland, Vt, 1966). Collection also incl the papers (noncirculating) of Prof John A Nietz.

PA —FRIENDS HISTORICAL LIBRARY OF SWARTHMORE COLLEGE, Swarthmore, 19081. J William Frost, Dir
Holdings: Vols (35,000) Cat Mss Pix Microforms
Notes: Library's collection contain information on the history and doctrine of the Society of Friends, Quaker contributions to literature, science, business, education, and government, plus their reform efforts in peace, Indian rights, women's rights, and abolition of slavery. Several of the library's more than 250 mss collections incl school lesson books, papers of Quaker educators, and records of schools established by Quakers, some of which were founded to educate Blacks. The library also has the archives of Swarthmore College.

PA —KING'S COLLEGE, D Leonard Corgan Library, 14 W Jackson St, Wilkes-Barre, 18711. Judith Tierney, Special Collections Librn
Holdings: Uncat Mss Pix Audiotapes
Notes: Personal papers of Lillian Rifkin Blumenfeld, educator in the early progressive schools in the US, including correspondence, diaries, articles, poems, clippings, photographs and tapes, 1937-1981.

SC —COLLEGE OF CHARLESTON LIBRARY, Special Collections Dept, Charleston, 29401.
Notes: Papers of the Charleston High School (1843-1976, for white boys until recently), one of the Nation's oldest public institutions of secondary education, dating from 1839. Also papers of The Memminger School (for white girls until recently); two black schools--Avery Institute (1866-1940), and Laing School (1866-1940).

TN —TUSCULUM COLLEGE LIBRARY, Greenville, 37743.
Notes: The Charles Coffin Book Collection of nearly 2000 volumes, an important source reflecting the development of higher education in post-Revolutionary America and the westward spread of culture. The collection comprised the College's original library between 1794 and 1827.

TN —VANDERBILT UNIVERSITY, George Peabody College for Teachers, Education Library, Box 325, Nashville, 37203. Mary Beth Blalock, Librn
Holdings: Vols (192,541) Cat Pix Slides

EDUCATION—HISTORY (cont.)

Phonorecords Filmstrips Microforms
Budget: ($59,000)
Notes: The Education Library (192,541 vols) collects in all areas relating to education with special emphasis on Child Study and Exceptional Children. Special funds are available for continuing purchases in these areas. The collection is strong in curriculum materials, physical education, applied art, psychology related to education and all areas of education. Amoung special papers are over 300 papers by and about Jean Piaget and an extensive author and subject file referring to the location of these papers and books and journal articles by and about Piaget in the rest of the Education Library collection. The Education Library is a Division of the Vanderbilt University Library.

EDUCATION—HISTORY—MEDIEVAL, 500-1500 see Education, Medieval

EDUCATION—HUNGARY

OH —KENT STATE UNIVERSITY, School of Library Science Library, Kent, 44242. Robert Rogers, Dir
Notes: Kent State Library School has a student scholarship program for Hungarian candidates. (*Leads*, Winter 1979).

EDUCATION—ILLINOIS

IL —CHICAGO HISTORICAL SOCIETY, Library, Clark St at North Ave, Chicago, 60614. Archie Motley, Manuscript Librn
Notes: Papers relative to schools and educational matters: Cyrus Hall Adams III (department store executive, member of the Chicago Board of Education); American Association of University Women, Chicago Branch; Robert M Buck (Chicago newspaperman, Chicago alderman); Chicago Teachers' Federation (first teachers' union in Chicago); Chicago Teachers Union; Citizens Schools Committee (schools improvement group); Francis W Parker School (private grammar and high school).

EDUCATION—LAW AND LEGISLATION

MA —BOSTON COLLEGE LIBRARIES, Chestnut Hill, 02167.
Notes: The archives of the Citywide Coordinating Council of Boston, Mass, established in 1975 to monitor the desegregation of the Boston school system and to foster public awareness in the implementation of the court's desegregation orders. Incl the collection of transcripts of School Committee meetings; the central files, reflecting the functioning of the council office; and the files of the senior staff, containing the key administrative records of the Council.

NC —UNIVERSITY OF NORTH CAROLINA, CHAPEL HILL, Louis Round Wilson Academic Affairs Library, Southern Historical Collection, Chapel Hill, 27514. Carolyn Wallace, Librn
Notes: The papers of Algernon Lee Butler, former judge of the United States Court for the Eastern District of North Carolina (1959-1975).

PA —SCHOOL DISTRICT OF PHILADELPHIA, Pedagogical Library, 21 St & Pkwy, Philadelphia, 19103. Helen E Howe, Librn; Patricia K Buck, Asst Librn
Holdings: Vols (47,000) CAt Pix Microforms
Budget: ($25,000)
Notes: Collection emphasis on public school education K-12 with the main areas including Afro-American history and culture, elementary and early childhood education, secondary education, educational administration, educational research, reading, school law, educational psychology. Special Collections: ERIC (140,000 documents), Archives of the School District of Philadelphia. Approx 500 periodical subscriptions.

EDUCATION—MISSISSIPPI

MS —UNIVERSITY OF SOUTHERN MISSISSIPPI, William David McCain Graduate Library, Box 5148, Southern Sta, Hattiesburg, 39406.
Holdings: Uncat Mss
Notes: Records (1967-1975; 2 cubic feet) of the Mississippi Association of Educators concerning the merger of the predominantly Black, Mississippi Teachers Association and the predominantly White, Mississippi Education Association. The collection incl correspondence, minutes of meetings, conference hearings, resolutions, proposals and constitutions from various state education associations.

EDUCATION—NEW YORK (STATE)

NY —QUEENS BOROUGH PUBLIC LIBRARY, Social Sciences Div, 89-11 Merrick Blvd, Jamaica, 11432. Nathan Shoengold, Head; Renee Kaplan, Asst Div Head
Holdings: Vols (45,000) Cat Microforms
Notes: Extensive pamphlet collection, incl New York State and New York City curriculum bulletins. Also education periodicals, some in microform. A separate catalog to the social sciences contains the education collection.

EDUCATION—PSYCHOLOGY see Educational Psychology

EDUCATION—SOUTH CAROLINA

SC —COLLEGE OF CHARLESTON LIBRARY, Special Collections Dept, Charleston, 29401.
Notes: (1) Papers of the Charleston High School (1843-1976, for white boys until recently), one of the Nation's oldest public institutions of secondary education, dating from 1839. Also papers of The Memminger School (for white girls until recently); (2) Avery Institute Collection consists mostly of photocopied materials (correspondence, annual reports, financial records, etc) housed at the Amistad Research Center of Dillard University. Established and maintained through much of its history by the American Missionary Assn, this material reflects the organization's work in South Carolina beginning in the Reconstruction era. Incl also oral histories of graduates of Avery Institute. (3) The Laing School Collection consists of photocopied material from the papers of the Pennsylvania Abolition Society housed at the HistoricalSociety of Pennsylvania, dealing with the establishment (1866), maintenance and eventual relinquishing of the Laing School to the local Public School Board (1940). (4) Papers of the South Carolina Association of Colleges, 1945-1965; (5) Index with synopses of articles appearing in South Carolina newspapers regarding education in South Carolina during the years, 1767-1785, 1815-1876, 1878-1881, and 1883-1886.

EDUCATION—STUDY AND TEACHING

MA —HARVARD UNIVERSITY, Graduate School of Education, Monroe C Gutman Library, 6 Appian Way, Cambridge, 02138. Susan S Baughman, Associate Librn
Holdings: Vols (150,000) Cat Mss Microforms
Budget: ($95,000)
Notes: A comprehensive research collection that seeks to acquire all scholarly works published in the English language in the fields of education, educational administration, educational psychology, and human development. Selective coverage in the related areas of counseling and psychology, business administration, finance, forecasting, statistical analysis and survey design, public and social policy, linguistics, demographics, and international and economic development. Incl 4000 educational and psychological tests.

PA —CARLOW COLLEGE, Grace Library, Fifth Ave, Pittsburgh, 15213. Joan M Mitchell, Dir of Library Services
Holdings: Vols (1050) Cat
Budget: ($800)
Notes: Montessori Method of Education.

EDUCATION—U.S.

†PA —LIBRARY COMPANY OF PHILADELPHIA, 1314 Locust St, Philadelphia, 19107. Edwin Wolf II, Librn
Holdings: Vols (450,000)

EDUCATION—U.S.—HISTORY

MA —MOUNT HOLYOKE COLLEGE, Williston Memorial Library, South Hadley, 01075. Anne C Edmonds, Librn
Notes: Records of the College's history and extensive biographical files about its graduates, faculty, staff and trustees. Manuscripts (letters, diaries, etc) and early circulars dating from 1820, and providing information about early 19th century education for women in the United States.

TN —TUSCULUM COLLEGE LIBRARY, Greenville, 37743.
Notes: The Charles Coffin Book Collection of nearly 2000 volumes, an important source reflecting the development of higher education in post-Revolutionary America and the westward spread of culture. The collection comprised the College's original library between 1794 and 1827.

EDUCATION, ARTS see Arts in Education

EDUCATION, BUSINESS see Business Education

EDUCATION, CHRISTIAN see Religious Education

EDUCATION, CONSUMER see Consumer Education

EDUCATION, ETHICAL see Religious Education

EDUCATION, HIGHER

AZ —NORTHERN ARIZONA UNIVERSITY, Special Collection Library, CU Box 6022, Flagstaff, 86011. Peter M Whiteley, Coordr/Archivist; William Mullane, Librn
Notes: Foundation for the Higher Education of American Indians; by-laws, correspondence, minues of meetings of the Foundation, located in Flagstaff, Ariz.

CA —UNIVERSITY OF CALIFORNIA, BERKELEY, Humanities-Social Sciences Libraries, Education-Psychology Library, 2600 Tolman Hall, Berkeley, 94720. Sonya Kaufman, Acting Head
Holdings: Vols (110,000)
Notes: General research collection in fields of education and psycology. Education collection's emphases are in the areas of administration, policy planning, higher education, science and math education, language and literacy. Serial holdings are strong. The library receives approx 2200 current serial titles in education and psychology.

CA —CALIFORNIA STATE UNIVERSITY, FULLERTON, Library, Box 4150, Fullerton, 92634. Linda Herman, Special Collections Librn
Holdings: Vols 1000 Cat

CA —CALIFORNIA POSTSECONDARY EDUCATION COMMISSION, Library, 1020 12th St, Sacramento, 95814. Elizabeth Testa, Sr Librn
Holdings: Vols 15,000 Cat Microforms
Budget: $10,000
Notes: Higher education, especially in California. List of Commission's publications available; interlibrary loans and photocopying also available.

CO —WESTERN INTERSTATE COMMISSION FOR HIGHER

EDUCATION, HIGHER (cont.)

EDUCATION, Wiche Library, PO Drawer P, Boulder, 80302. Karon M Kelly, Dir Library Services
Holdings: Vols (10,000) Cat Microforms
Notes: Incl medical and nursing education, student exchange programs, minority involvement in education, management systems in higher education.

CT —SACRED HEART UNIVERSITY, Library, 5229 Park Ave, PO Box 6460, Bridgeport, 06606. Roch-Josef di Lisio, Actg Dir
Holdings: Vols 1200 Cat
Notes: The John A Rycenga Memorial Collection on American Catholic Higher Education.

DC —AMERICAN ASSOCIATION OF UNIVERSITY WOMEN EDUCATIONAL FOUNDATION LIBRARY, 2401 Virginia Ave NW, Washington, 20037. Nancy L Floyd, Library Information Asst
Holdings: Vols 4500 Cat Mss
Budget: $4800
Notes: Higher education (especially where related to women--their status and achievements). Library is primarily for professional staff use, but is open to members of the association. Facilities may be made available for use of scholars engaged in work regarding achievements and status of women, as well as those doing pre- or post-doctoral work in education and/or related subjects. Archival material made available by special permission to others than members. Incl vertical files and a complete bound set of the *ACA* (Association of Collegiate Alumni--forerunner of AAUW) *Journal*. 1898 to date.

†DC —AMERICAN COUNCIL ON EDUCATION, Library & Information Service, One Dupont Circle, Suite 640, Washington, 20036. Judith Pfeiffer, Librn
Holdings: Vols 5000 Cat
Notes: The collection reflects the need and interests of the building tenants. All tenants are nonprofit, nongovernmental associations in the field of post-secondary education. The collection is particularly strong in the areas of the economics, finance, history, management, and teaching in higher education. The library is a depository library for the Carnegie Commission on Higher Education and the Carnegie Council on Policy Studies in Higher Education. In addition, the library maintains an archival collection of the publications of the American Council on Education.

DC —CHRONICLE OF HIGHER EDUCATION, INC, 1333 New Hampshire Ave NW, Suite 500, Washington, 20036. Edith H Uunila, Sr Editor
Notes: *Chronicle of Higher Education* published weekly. Library is for editorial research. Collection incl books and clipping files.

DC —COUNCIL FOR ADVANCEMENT & SUPPORT OF EDUCATION, Reference Center, Eleven Dupont Circle NW, Suite 400, Washington, 20036. Cynthia Snyder, Dir
Holdings: Vols (600) Cat Mss Audiotapes Microforms
Notes: A membership service containing information in educational fund raising, institutional relations, government relations, alumni administration, publications, and management techniques for higher education and independent schools. Collection, in addition, contains mss, microfiches, and tapes. Succeeds the American Alumni Council, dissolved in 1974.

GA —SOUTHERN REGIONAL EDUCATION BOARD LIBRARY, 1340 Spring St NW, Atlanta, 30309. Ann H Carter, Research Asst/Librn
Holdings: Vols (5000) Cat Microforms
Budget: ($2000)
Notes: Particularly higher education in the South. No phoptcopying.

IL —UNIVERSITY OF ILLINOIS, URBANA/CHAMPAIGN, Library, University Archives, 19 Library, 1408 W Gregory Drive, Urbana, 61801. Maynard Brichford, University Archivist
Holdings: Uncat Mss Maps Pix Slides Phonorecords Microforms
Notes: In addition to the university archives and the collections of academic and administrative staff, the archives have numerous other series of institutional and personal papers. Published guide to the collections is available: *Manuscripts Guide to Collections at the University of Illinois at* Urbana-Champaign (University of Illinois Press, 1976). Control cards and ADP control on 3644 record series; 5132 pages of supplementary finding aids. Probably the largest ms collection in the state. Holdings on the history of librarianship and faculty and student life are particularly strong.

IA —AMERICAN COLLEGE TESTING PROGRAM, Library, Box 168, Iowa City, 52243. Lois Renter, Head Librn
Holdings: Vols (22,000) Cat Microforms
Budget: ($36,000)
Notes: Emphasis on students, educational testing, educational psychology, post-secondary education, psychometrics. Excludes educational history and philosophy, curricula and teaching.

MA —NORTHEASTERN UNIVERSITY LIBRARIES, Center for International Higher Education Documentation, 360 Huntington Ave, Boston, 02115. Solveig M Turner, Dir; Nieves F Farin, Head Collection Development Librn
Notes: Collection based on files of the International Encyclopedia of Higher Education. Provides documentation relating mainly to higher education. Collection emphasis: university administration, role of universities, international education, national systems of education, national and international associations. Also incl a collection of international university bulletins and calendars. Extensive subject index maintained. Publication: Center for International Higher Education Documentation (CIHED) Newsletter.

MA —HARVARD UNIVERSITY, Graduate School of Education, Monroe C Gutman Library, 6 Appian Way, Cambridge, 02138. Susan S Baughman, Associate Librn
Holdings: Vols (150,000) Cat Mss Microforms
Budget: ($95,000)
Notes: A comprehensive research collection that seeks to acquire all scholarly works published in the English language in the fields of education, educational administration, educational psychology, and human development. Selective coverage in the related areas of counseling and psychology, business administration, finance, forecasting, statistical analysis and survey design, public and social policy, linguistics, demographics, and international and economic development. Incl 4000 educational and psychological tests.

MN —MINNESOTA HISTORICAL SOCIETY LIBRARY, 690 Cedar St, Saint Paul, 55101. Patricia C Harpole, Chief of Reference Library; Bonnie G Wilson, Head of Special Libraries
Notes: Interviews with Minnesota's educational leaders, especially in the area of higher education are in this series.

MS —UNIVERSITY OF SOUTHERN MISSISSIPPI, William David McCain Graduate Library, Box 5148, Southern Sta, Hattiesburg, 39406.
Holdings: Cat Mss Pix
Notes: In addition to the records (1910-date; 2000 cubic feet) of the University Archives, holdings incl various collections of personal papers of faculty members, administrators, and other individuals and organizations associated with the university.

NY —CITY UNIVERSITY OF NEW YORK, City College, Morris R Cohen Library, North Academic Center, Convent Ave & 137th St, New York, 10031. Barbara J Dunlap, Archivist
Holdings: Vols 3700 Cat Mss Pix Slides Microforms
Notes: Incl City College archives; publications of and about City College; selected publications of alumni and faculty; alumni (biography and clippings about); faculty (private papers); student life (clubs, publications, activities); photographs and source material documenting City College's role as the pioneer of free higher education in New York; papers of Cleveland Abbe, Charles Baskerville, R R Bowker, Alfred G Compton, Townsend Harris, Lewis F Mott, Edward M Shepard, Everett Wheeler. Collection incl 78 microfilm reels, 12,580 photographs, 1450 blueprints, 100 slides, and 1959 linear ft of mss.

NY —SYRACUSE UNIVERSITY LIBRARIES, Ernest S Bird Library, George Arents Research Library for Special Collections, Syracuse, 13210. Carolyn A Davis, Manuscripts Librn; Amy S Doherty, University Archivist; Mark F Weimer, Rare Book Librn
Holdings: Mss Pix Audiotapes
Notes: Syracuse University Archives. Historic materials covering the academic and administrative growth of Syracuse University, incl administrative records, faculty papers, publications, photographs, films, tapes, etc.

SC —COLLEGE OF CHARLESTON LIBRARY, Special Collections Dept, Charleston, 29401.
Notes: Papers, 1945-1965.

VA —UNIVERSITY OF VIRGINIA, Alderman Library, Manuscripts Dept, Charlottesville, 22901. Edmund Berkeley Jr, Cur
Holdings: Cat Mss Pix Audiotapes
Notes: In addition to the University Archives the collection contain personal and academic papers of numerous professors, administrators and librarians.

WA —UNIVERSITY OF WASHINGTON LIBRARIES, Suzzallo Library, Manuscripts Section, FM-25, Seattle, 98195. Karyl Winn, Librn
Holdings: Mss
Notes: Personal papers and organizational records with emphasis on Pacific Northwest history and recent focus on twentieth century Western Washington. Holdings pertain to urban problems and policies, labor history, women's history, natural resource development, environmental politics, race relations, ethnic history, oral hsitory, and the arts. Holdings are complemented by textual records in the University Archives (7045 linear feet) and by graphic and printed holdings in the Pacific Northwest Collection. Described in *Comprehensive Guide to the Manuscripts Collection and to Personal Papers in the University Archives,* 1980 and in *Historical Records of Washington State: Records and Papers Held at Repositories,* 1981 and in unpublished inventories to most accessions. 15,981 linear feet of manuscripts.

WA —UNIVERSITY OF WASHINGTON LIBRARIES, University Archives, HO-10, Seattle, 98195. Richard C Berner, University Archivist
Notes: Universtiy records and personal papers of university faculty and administrators, covering a spectrum of subjects as wide as the academic range of the university and higher education administration per se. 7000 linear feet.
See also entry under Manuscripts - Collections

EDUCATION, HIGHER—CANADA

ON —ASSOCIATION OF UNIVERSITIES & COLLEGES OF CANADA LIBRARY, 151 Slater St, Ottawa, K1P 5N1, Can. Hazel J Roberts, Head Librn
Holdings: Vols 8000 Cat
Budget: $5000
Notes: Provides documentation relating to higher education in Canada and elsewhere, for the use of the association and its member institutions. Subjects covered incl university administration, teaching effectiveness, financing, student activities, the role of universities, international education, collective bargaining, academic freedom, etc. Coverage primarily Canadian with some supporting documentation for other countries, particularly the US, Commonwealth nations and French-language countries. Items from Canadian universities

EDUCATION, HIGHER—CANADA (cont.)

and colleges incl calendars, presidents' reports, faculty handbooks, student newspapers, press releases, newspapers issued by Information Offices and faculties, faculty bargaining agreements, published and unpublished reports from administrative units with the University. Extensive clipping file maintained.

†ON —METROPOLITAN TORONTO LIBRARY, Social Sciences Dept, 789 Yonge St, Toronto, M4W 2G8, Can. Abdus Salam, Head
Holdings: Vols Cat Maps Phonorecords Audiotapes 16mm Films Microforms
Notes: Extensive collection of current university and college catalogs from throughout the US and Canada, as well as selected foreign universities. Also extensive collection of educational directories and guides.

EDUCATION, HIGHER—HISTORY

MD —JOHNS HOPKINS UNIVERSITY, Milton S Eisenhower Library, Charles & 34 Sts, Baltimore, 21218. Ann S Gwyn, Assistant Dir for Special Collections
Holdings: Cat Mss
Notes: Chiefly important for the history of universities in the US, and for the history of science. Correspondence of academic leaders such as Andrew White, Daniel Coit Gilman and Charles W Eliot; scientific figures: Rowland and Osler. State Department correspondence of Isaiah Bowman in World War II. American statemen from Washington to Wilson; literary figures, chiefly American and German; many Hopkins professors and Maryland civic leaders. Housed in the Frieda C Thies Manuscript Room. About 75,000 mss.

NY —CITY UNIVERSITY OF NEW YORK, BROOKLYN COLLEGE, Library, Special Collections Div, Bedford Ave & Ave H, Brooklyn, 11210. Antoinette Ciolli, Chief
Holdings: // Uncat Audiotapes
Notes: The Brooklyn College Oral Archives project incl interviews with prominent Brooklyn individuals who were involved in the early development of the College. Among the tapes are interviews with Randolph E Evans, the architect who designed all the original buildings on the Brooklyn College Midwood campus; Mrs Mary S Ingraham and Mrs Pearl B Max, formerly of the New York City Board of Higher Education; Harry D Gideonse, Francis P Kilcoyne, Presidents Emeriti; and Walter Mais and Abraham S Goodhartz, Deans Emeriti. No transcripts.

NC —NORTH CAROLINA DIV OF ARCHIVES & HISTORY, 109 E Jones St, Raleigh, 27611.
Notes: Archive of administrative, student, and all other records of Black Mountain College, which was located at Black Mountain, North Carolina, 1933-1956.

RI —BROWN UNIVERSITY, John Hay Library, 20 Prospect St, Providence, 02912. Mark N Brown, Cur Mss
Holdings: Mss
Notes: The Brown University Manuscript Collection and University Archives possess numerous archival and ms collections relating to higher (university) education, incl the papers of Horace Mann, Francis Wayland, Asa Messer, Lester Frank Ward, and those of the university's faculty and students.

EDUCATION, INDUSTRIAL see Technical Education

EDUCATION, INTERNATIONAL see International Education

EDUCATION, JEWISH see Jews—Education

EDUCATION, MEDICAL see Medical Colleges; Medicine—Study and Teaching

EDUCATION, MEDIEVAL

SK —UNIVERSITY OF SASKATCHEWAN, Library, Saskatoon, S7N 0W0, Can. S Perkins, Librn
Notes: Extensive collection (in book form; some reprints) of matriculation records of English, Scottish, French, German, Italian, and other universities, dating from the Middle Ages and Renaissance.

EDUCATION, MUSICAL see Music—Instruction and Study

EDUCATION, OUTDOOR see Outdoor Education

EDUCATION, PHYSICAL see Physical Education and Training

EDUCATION, PRESCHOOL

NY —BANK STREET COLLEGE OF EDUCATION LIBRARY, 610 W 112 St, New York, 10025. Eleanor Kule Seid, Library Dir
Holdings: Vols (80,000) Cat Microforms
Budget: ($29,000)
Notes: Education, guidance, psychology, educational psychology, curricula, textbooks, Black Studies, etc. All subjects are integrated in one professional collection; in addition there are two separately cataloged and shelved collections: Children's and Elementary Curriculum Materials.

NC —TECHNICAL INSTITUTE OF ALAMANCE, Learning Resources Center, Jimmy Kerr Rd, PO Box 623, Haw River, 27258. Ron Plummer, Coordr
Holdings: Vols (796) Cat Slides Audiotapes 16mm Films Filmstrips Microforms

PA —DREXEL UNIVERSITY LIBRARIES, General Division, 32 & Chestnut Sts, Philadelphia, 19104. Tung Chu Chen, General Division Librn
Holdings: Vols (1226) Cat
Notes: Emphasis on home economics study and teaching, consumer education, and early childhood education.

PA —CARLOW COLLEGE, Grace Library, Fifth Ave, Pittsburgh, 15213. Joan M Mitchell, Dir of Library Services
Holdings: Vols (1050) Cat
Budget: ($800)

EDUCATION, PUBLIC

NY —QUEENS BOROUGH PUBLIC LIBRARY, Social Sciences Div, 89-11 Merrick Blvd, Jamaica, 11432. Nathan Shoengold, Head; Renee Kaplan, Asst Div Head
Holdings: Vols (45,000) Cat Microforms
Notes: Extensive pamphlet collection, incl New York State and New York City curriculum bulletins. Also education periodicals, some in microform. A separate catalog to the social sciences contains the education collection.

EDUCATION, RELIGIOUS see Religious Education

EDUCATION, SCIENTIFIC see Science—Study and Teaching

EDUCATION, SECONDARY

SC —COLLEGE OF CHARLESTON LIBRARY, Special Collections Dept, Charleston, 29401.
Notes: Papers of the Charleston High School (1843-1976, for white boys until recently), one of the Nation's oldest public institutions of secondary education, dating from 1839. Also papers of The Memminger School (for white girls until recently); two black schools--Avery Institute (1866-1940), and Laing School (1866-1940).

EDUCATION, SEX see Sex Education

EDUCATION, TECHNICAL see Technical Education

EDUCATION, THEOLOGICAL see Religious Education

EDUCATION, URBAN

NY —COLUMBIA UNIVERSITY LIBRARIES, Teachers College, Milbank Memorial Library, 525 W 120 St, New York, 10027. Jane P Franck, Dir
Holdings: Vols 2000
Notes: Archives of the Board of Education of the City of New York incl photographs, tape recordings, ledgers, and mss and related materials. 775 cu ft.

†PA —TEMPLE UNIVERSITY LIBRARIES, Special Collections Dept, Urban Archives Center, Philadelphia, 19122. Thomas Whitehead, Cur of Mss
Holdings: Cat
Notes: Incl the records of several separate collections which are deposited in the Urban Archives Center. Many collections contain photographs, maps and pamphlets, in addition to manuscripts. All collections in the Urban Archives are separately cataloged.

EDUCATION, VOCATIONAL see Vocational Education

EDUCATION, WOMEN IN see Women in Education

EDUCATION OF ADULTS see Adult Education

EDUCATION OF CHILDREN

DC —GEORGETOWN UNIVERSITY, Library, Special Collections Div, 37 & O Sts NW, Washington, 20057. George M Barringer, Special Collections Librn; Nicholas B Sheetz, Mss Librn
Notes: Archives of information used for compilation of *The American Heritage School Dictionary* (1972).

PA —CARLOW COLLEGE, Grace Library, Fifth Ave, Pittsburgh, 15213. Joan M Mitchell, Dir of Library Services
Holdings: Vols (1050) Cat
Budget: ($800)
Notes: Montessori Method of Education.

MB —UNIVERSITY OF WINNIPEG, Department of English, 515 Portage Ave, Winnipeg, R3B 2E9, Can. Perry Nodelman, Cur
Holdings: Vols 1000 Cat
Notes: This collection represents the kind of material children read during the 19th and early 20th century on the Canadian Prairies, not necessarily "Children's Literature."

EDUCATION OF FOREIGN NATIONALS

OH —KENT STATE UNIVERSITY, School of Library Science Library, Kent, 44242. Robert Rogers, Dir
Notes: Kent State Library School has a student scholarship program for Hungarian candidates. (*Leads*, Winter 1979).

EDUCATION OF GIRLS see Education of Women

EDUCATION OF WOMEN

CA —WOMEN'S HISTORY RESEARCH CENTER, Microfilm Library, 2325 Oak St, Berkeley, 94708. Laura X, Librn
Holdings: Microforms
Notes: Incl 500 subject files of material on Women and Law (General); Politics; Employment; Education; Rape/Prison/ Prostitution; Black and Third World women. Collection at University of Wyoming, Archive of Contemporary History, PO Box 3334, Laramie, Wyoming 82071, c/o David Crosson. Reasearch inquiries accepted. Microfilm of collection (40 reels & reel guides) available through Women's History Research Center, 2325 Oak St, Berkeley, CA 94708. No collections housed at this address.

DC —AMERICAN ASSOCIATION OF UNIVERSITY WOMEN EDUCATIONAL FOUNDATION LIBRARY, 2401 Virginia Ave NW, Washington, 20037. Nancy L Floyd, Library Information Asst
Holdings: Vols 4500 Cat Mss
Budget: $4800
Notes: Higher education (especially where related to women--their status and

EDUCATION OF WOMEN (cont.)

achievements). Library is primarily for professional staff use, but is open to members of the association. Facilities may be made available for use of scholars engaged in work regarding achievements and status of women, as well as those doing pre- or post-doctoral work in education and/or related subjects. Archival material made available by special permission to others than members. Incl vertical files and a complete bound set of the *ACA* (Association of Collegiate Alumni--forerunner of AAUW) *Journal.* 1898 to date.

DC —LIBRARY OF CONGRESS, Manuscript Division, Washington, 20540. John C Broderick, Chief
Holdings: 135,200 Items
Notes: Correspondence, reports, student and financial records, subject files, scrapbooks, clippings, photographs, printed matter, and other memorabilia of Nannie Helen Burroughs (1878-1961).

MA —BOSTON UNIVERSITY, Mugar Memorial Library, Special Collections Dept, 771 Commonwealth Ave, Boston, 02215. Howard B Gotlieb, Dir
Holdings: // Cat Mss
Notes: Incl records of the New England Female Medical College and the Massachusetts Society for the University Education of Women.

MA —MOUNT HOLYOKE COLLEGE, Williston Memorial Library, South Hadley, 01075. Anne C Edmonds, Librn
Notes: Records of the College's history and extensive biographical files about its graduates, faculty, staff and trustees. Manuscripts (letters, diaries, etc) and early circulars dating from 1820, and providing information about early 19th century education for women in the United States.

NS —MOUNT SAINT VINCENT UNIVERSITY, Library, 166 Bedford Hwy, Halifax, B3M 2J6, Can. Lucian Bianchini, University Librn
Holdings: Vols 18,000 Cat Mss Maps Pix Slides Microforms
Budget: ($125,000)
Notes: New Acquisitions have been put into the general collection, rather than keeping them separate. Emphasis has been on cultural, ethnic, sociological, historical, political, and professional aspects of womanhood, international in scope. The collection circulates.

EDUCATION OF THE DEAF see Deaf and Deafness—Education

EDUCATIONAL ADMINISTRATION see School Management and Organization

EDUCATIONAL ENDOWMENTS see Endowments

EDUCATIONAL FILM LIBRARY ASSOCIATION

NY —EDUCATIONAL FILM LIBRARY ASSOCIATION, Film Reference Library, 45 John St, New York, 10038. Nadine Covert, Exec Dir
Holdings: Vols (2600) Cat Pix 16mm Films Filmstrips
Budget: ($1500)
Notes: Primarily a print collection emphasizing the documentary and educational film areas, but also film as art, animation and independent film in general. Maintain film title file of over 60,000 cards (primarily educational film titles), incl credit information, running time, release date, summary, and distributor. File is a mixture of EFLA evaluations, LC cards, etc. Subject file also separates film flyers by subject or topic. Maintain festivals file (film festivals, educational film festivals, etc); a film library administration file; a filmmakers file (with bio, credits, clippings, program notes); and a vertical file (incl information on grants, distribution, showcases, film activities in the metropolitan area and in major film centers around the country). Membership organization providing telephone, mail and in-person reference. Open to the generalpublic. Do not publish a catalog, but publish annual Film Library Administration bibliography of current or noteworthy reference books for $2.00.

EDUCATIONAL FILMS see Moving Pictures in Education

EDUCATIONAL LAW AND LEGISLATION see Education—Law and Legislation

EDUCATIONAL MEASUREMENTS see Educational Tests and Measurements

EDUCATIONAL PERIODICALS see Periodicals, Education

EDUCATIONAL PSYCHOLOGY

IN —INDIANA UNIVERSITY, School of Education, Library, Bloomington, 47401. Adele Dendy, Head Librn
Holdings: Vols (35,000) Cat Pix Slides Phonorecords Audiotapes 16mm Films Filmstrips Microforms
Budget:
Notes: Library has complete ERIC collection of microfiche (277,308). 2098 non-ERIC items, 226 serials, and 22,823 nonprint items (housed in educational materials center). Emphasis on recent materials; the historic collections in education are located in the Main Library. The collection is geared to graduate level studies and research. A separate Teaching Materials Center includes 10,000 elementary and secondary textbooks. The Center also includes curriculum guides, supplementary materials and 17,823 nonprint teaching aids.

IA —AMERICAN COLLEGE TESTING PROGRAM, Library, Box 168, Iowa City, 52243. Lois Renter, Head Librn
Holdings: Vols (22,000) Cat Microforms
Budget: ($36,000)
Notes: Emphasis on students, educational testing, educational psychology, post-secondary education, psychometrics. Excludes educational history and philosophy, curricula and teaching.

MA —HARVARD UNIVERSITY, Graduate School of Education, Monroe C Gutman Library, 6 Appian Way, Cambridge, 02138. Susan S Baughman, Associate Librn
Holdings: Vols (150,000) Cat Mss Microforms
Budget: ($95,000)
Notes: A comprehensive research collection that seeks to acquire all scholarly works published in the English language in the fields of education, educational administration, educational psychology, and human development. Selective coverage in the related areas of counseling and psychology, business administration, finance, forecasting, statistical analysis and survey design, public and social policy, linguistics, demographics, and international and economic development. Incl 4000 educational and psychological tests.

NJ —EDUCATIONAL TESTING SERVICE, Carl Campbell Brigham Library, Princeton, 08540. Janet Williams, Librn
Notes: Complete works and papers of Louis L Thurstone, a leading psychometrician of the 20th century.

PA —SCHOOL DISTRICT OF PHILADELPHIA, Pedagogical Library, 21 St & Pkwy, Philadelphia, 19103. Helen E Howe, Librn; Patricia K Buck, Asst Librn
Holdings: Vols (47,000) Cat Pix Microforms
Budget: ($25,000)
Notes: Collection emphasis on public school education K-12 with the main areas including Afro-American history and culture, elementary and early childhood education, secondary education, educational administration, educational research, reading, school law, educational psychology. Special Collections: ERIC (140,000 documents), Archives of the School District of Philadelphia. Approx 500 periodical subscriptions.

PA —TEMPLE UNIVERSITY LIBRARIES, Special Collections Dept, Rare Books & Mss Section, Philadelphia, 19122. Thomas M Whitehead, Cur
Holdings: Vols 800 Cat
Notes: Contains all available works by and about Jean Piaget and those of his principal associates. Inc over 500 journal articles and 70 dissertations. Collection originally developed as the research collection of the Jean Piaget Society.

TN —VANDERBILT UNIVERSITY, George Peabody College for Teachers, Education Library, Box 325, Nashville, 37203. Mary Beth Blalock, Librn
Holdings: Vols (192,541) Cat Pix Slides Phonorecords Filmstrips Microforms
Budget: ($59,000)
Notes: The Education Library (192,541 vols) collects in all areas relating to education with special emphasis on Child Study and Exceptional Children. Special funds are available for continuing purchases in these areas. The collection is strong in curriculum materials, physical education, applied art, psychology related to education and all areas of education. Amoung special papers are over 300 papers by and about Jean Piaget and an extensive author and subject file referring to the location of these papers and books and journal articles by and about Piaget in the rest of the Education Library collection. The Education Library is a Division of the Vanderbilt University Library.

ON —CANADA PUBLIC SERVICE COMMISSION, Library, Room 930 W Tower, Esplande Laurier, Ottawa, K1A 0M7, Can. A Campbell, Chief Librn
Notes: Subject interests: linguistics, educational psychology, personnel management, psychology, public administration, sociology.

EDUCATIONAL TESTS AND MEASUREMENTS

IL —ARLINGTON HEIGHTS MEMORIAL LIBRARY, 500 N Dunton Ave, Arlington Heights, 60004. Frank J Dempsey, Librn
Holdings: Vols 5000 Cat Microforms
Notes: Maintained as education subject center under the former North Suburban Library System's Coordinated Acquisitions Program. Collection incl history and philosophy of education; teaching methods; testing and measurement; and administration.

IL —UNIVERSITY OF ILLINOIS, URBANA/CHAMPAIGN, Library, University Archives, 19 Library, 1408 W Gregory Drive, Urbana, 61801. Maynard Brichford, University Archivist
Holdings: Vols (6000) Cat
Budget: $1500
Notes: The Odell Test Collection contains 3150 items comprising intelligence, achievement, subject, and character and personality tests. Almost every educational and psychological test of consequence prior to the early 1950s is included. The collection is located in the Education and Social Science Library and is integrated into a comprehensive collection of current and recent standardized tests. The indexing of the collection follows the scheme created and used by Oscar K Buros in his *Mental Measurement Yearbooks* and in the predecessors to the Yearbooks which appeared in the Rutgers Studies in Education series. The collection was a gift in 1960 of Charles Watters Odell, Professor Emeritus of Education. No photocopying.

IN —INDIANA UNIVERSITY, School of Education, Library, Bloomington, 47401. Adele Dendy, Head Librn
Holdings: Vols (35,000) Cat Pix Slides Phonorecords Audiotapes 16mm Films Filmstrips Microforms
Budget:
Notes: Library has complete ERIC collection of microfiche (277,308). 2098 non-ERIC items, 226 serials, and 22,823 nonprint items (housed in educational materials center). Emphasis on recent materials; the historic

EDUCATIONAL TESTS AND MEASUREMENTS (cont.)

collections in education are located in the Main Library. The collection is geared to graduate level studies and research. A separate Teaching Materials Center includes 10,000 elementary and secondary textbooks. The Center also includes curriculum guides, supplementary materials and 17,823 nonprint teaching aids.

IA —AMERICAN COLLEGE TESTING PROGRAM, Library, Box 168, Iowa City, 52243. Lois Renter, Head Librn
Holdings: Vols (22,000) Cat Microforms
Budget: ($36,000)
Notes: Emphasis on students, educational testing, educational psychology, post-secondary education, psychometrics. Excludes educational history and philosophy, curricula and teaching.

MA —HARVARD UNIVERSITY, Graduate School of Education, Monroe C Gutman Library, 6 Appian Way, Cambridge, 02138. Susan S Baughman, Associate Librn
Holdings: Vols (150,000) Cat Mss Microforms
Budget: ($95,000)
Notes: A comprehensive research collection that seeks to acquire all scholarly works published in the English language in the fields of education, educational administration, educational psychology, and human development. Selective coverage in the related areas of counseling and psychology, business administration, finance, forecasting, statistical analysis and survey design, public and social policy, linguistics, demographics, and international and economic development. Incl 4000 educational and psychological tests.

MA —WORCESTER STATE COLLEGE, Learning Resources Center, 486 Chandler St, Worcester, 01602. William G Piekarski, Special Collections Librn
Holdings: Vols (9000) Cat Pix Microforms
Budget: ($12,000)
Notes: Collection contains 9000 elementary and secondary textbooks, 1000 curriculum guides covering the entire US, 800 samples of professional tests, kits, games software. Separate catalog.

NH —PLYMOUTH STATE COLLEGE, Lamson Library, Plymouth, 03264. Phillip Wei, Dir of Library Services
Holdings: Vols 30,000 Cat
Budget: ($30,000)

NJ —EDUCATIONAL TESTING SERVICE, Carl Campbell Brigham Library, Princeton, 08540. Janet Williams, Librn
Holdings: Vols 15,000 Cat Microforms
Budget: ($35,000)
Notes: Literature related to tests and measurements.

OR —UNIVERSITY OF OREGON LIBRARY, Education-Psychology Dept, Eugene, 97403. Rose Marie Service, Head Dept Librn
Holdings: Cat Pix Phonorecords Audiotapes Filmstrips Microforms
Budget: ($15,000)
Notes: Large up-to-date research collection with representation in all areas and particular emphases reflecting those of the College of Education: educational administration; special education, incl early childhood and counseling psychology. Strong serial collection. Curriculum Collection incl a representative selection of curriculum guides, student use textbooks and multimedia, pamphlets, and standardized tests. Complete ERIC microfiche collection.

EDUCATORS see Teachers

EDWARDS, GEORGE

MI —WAYNE STATE UNIVERSITY, Walter P Reuther Library, Archives of Labor & Urban Affairs, Detroit, 48202. Philip Mason, Dir
Notes: Many personal ms collections in the Archives document individual strivings, accomplishments, and frustrations in developing a higher quality of urban life. The papers of Jerome Cavanagh, former Mayor of Detroit; George Edwards, former Detroit Housing Commissioner, Detroit Police Commissioner, and Michigan Supreme Court Justice; and Edward Connor, former Director of the Citizen's Housing and Planning Council of Detroit, are just 3 important collections concerning governmental, law enforcement, and social problems in a major metropolitan area of the country.

EDWARDS, JONATHAN

CT —YALE UNIVERSITY, Box 1603A, Yale Station, New Haven, 06520.
Holdings: Cat Mss
Notes: Center for the publication of his *Works* (New Haven: Yale University Press, 1957-).

MI —NORTHERN MICHIGAN UNIVERSITY, Lydia M Olson Library, Elizabeth L Harden Drive, Marquette, 49855. Stephen H Peters, Cataloger
Notes: A section of the personal library of Moses Coit Tyler, incl works by Thomas Hooker, John Cotton, Cotton Mather, and Jonathan Edwards.

EDWARDS, JULIAN

WI —UNIVERSITY OF WISCONSIN, MADISON, Mills Music Library, 728 State St, Madison, 53706. Arne Arneson, Music Librn
Holdings: // Uncat Mss
Notes: Tams-Witmark Collection formed part of the rental collection of the firm bearing that name. Incl piano-conductor scores (some in mss); ca 65 sets of orchestral parts for operas; 70 vocal scores of works by American composers incl Herbert, Sousa, Edwards and De Koven; ca 100 sets of orchestral parts of comic operas; ca 100 sets of orchestral parts of comic operas; ca 4000 vocal scores of European operas. Restricted use.

EDWARDS, NINIAN

IL —CHICAGO HISTORICAL SOCIETY, Library, Clark St at North Ave, Chicago, 60614. Archie Motley, Manuscript Librn
Notes: Papers of Ninian Edwards and Edward Coles (Illinois Governors); Mason Brayman, attorney and Union Army officer.

EEG see Electroencephalography and Electroencephalograms

EFFECTS OF WEAPONS see Weapons Effects

EFFICIENCY, INDUSTRIAL

IN —PURDUE UNIVERSITY LIBRARIES, Special Collections Dept, West Lafayette, 47907. Keith Dowden, Asst Dir, Special Collections
Notes: The Gilbreth Collection. Incl motion study equipment and personal working papers and photographs of Frank B and Lillian Gilbreth's work in the development of the field of industrial management. Also, correspondence, certificates, diplomas, memorabilia, published and nonprint material.

EGG, PHILOSOPHERS' see Alchemy

EGGLESTON, GEORGE CARY

VA —UNIVERSITY OF VIRGINIA, Alderman Library, Manuscripts Dept, Charlottesville, 22901. Edmund Berkeley Jr, Cur
Holdings: Cat Mss Pix
Notes: Extensive collection of mss and printed materials.

EGGS (BIOLOGY) see Embryology

EGLETON, CLIVE

MA —BOSTON UNIVERSITY, Mugar Memorial Library, Special Collections Dept, 771 Commonwealth Ave, Boston, 02215. Howard B Gotlieb, Dir
Holdings: Cat Mss
Notes: Incl publications by or about.

EGLY, PAUL

CA —UNIVERSITY OF CALIFORNIA, LOS ANGELES, Research Library, Dept of Special Collections, 405 Hilgard Ave, Los Angeles, 90024. Edward Shreeves, Chairman, Bibliographers Group; David S Zeidberg, Head
Notes: 54 linear feet of correspondence, records, etc, related to Crawford vs Los Angeles Unified School District, 1977-1981.

EGYPT

CA —HOOVER INSTITUTION ON WAR, REVOLUTION & PEACE, Stanford University, Stanford, 94305. Peter Duignan, Cur; Karen Fung, Deputy Cur
Holdings: Vols (100,000)
Notes: For full description of collection, see Hoover Institution enrty under Near East.

DC —CATHOLIC UNIVERSITY OF AMERICA, Mullen Library, ICOR/Semitics Library, Room 20, Washington, 20064. Monica J Blanchard, Librn
Notes: The bulk of the ICOR/Semitics Library collection belongs to the Institute of Christian Oriental Research which supports the work of the Corpus Scriptorum Christianorum Orientalium. The holdings are chiefly concerned with Christian Egypt and the Coptic Church, Syriac and Syrian patristic studies, and the Syriac and Arabic speaking eastern churches. There are less extensive holdings of Ethiopic, Armenian and Georgian material. ICOR titles are cataloged by the ICOR/Semitic Library, and ICOR holdings do not appear in the general catalogue of the University Library.

DC —HOWARD UNIVERSITY, Moorland-Spingarn Research Center, 500 Howard Place NW, Washington, 20059. Clifford L Muse, Jr, Acting Dir

LA —UNIVERSITY OF NEW ORLEANS, Earl K Long Library, New Orleans, 70148. Susan LaHaye, Cataloger
Notes: Approximately 450 pieces (including monographs, pamphlets, serials, newspaper reprints). The Judge Pierre Crabites collection of Egyptology consisting mainly of late 19th and early 20th century imprints. Some signed editions.

MA —HARVARD UNIVERSITY LIBRARY, Widener Library, Middle Eastern Dept, Cambridge, 02138. David H Partington, Librn
Holdings: Cat Mss Microforms
Notes: The Library's published *Catalogue of Arabic, Persian, and Ottoman Turkish Books* (1968) lists some 30,000 vols in Arabic; see also *Harvard Library Bulletin,* XVI (1968), 313-325. Egyptian publications are received under P L 480. A six-volume catalog of the Arabic Collection was published in 1983.

MA —BOSTON COLLEGE LIBRARIES, Chestnut Hill, 02167.
Holdings: Vols 8000
Notes: A P L 480 responsibility.

NY —NEW YORK PUBLIC LIBRARY, Oriental Div, Fifth Ave & 42 St, New York, 10018. E Christian Filstrup, Chief
Holdings: Cat Mss Microforms
Budget: ($56,455)

EGYPT (cont.)

Notes: Described in *Dictionary Catalog of the Oriental Collection,* The Research Libraries of the New York Public Library, 1960, 16 vols, and *First Supplement,* 1976, 8 vols (144,000 cards). This catalog incl 318, 000 entries for works in about 100 languages of the East, and all works in Western languages on Oriental subjects. The Oriental Collection numbers about 120,000 vols; its Arabic and Indic holdings and those on ancient Egypt and the ancient Near East are among the largest in the US. There is also a collection of 30,000 vols of PL 480 material from Egypt, Pakistan, and India to which there is main entry access, but which is not incorporated into the dictionary catalog. Other outstanding features of the Oriental Collection incl extensive holdings of Japanese technical and scientific periodicals; a unique collection of linguistic works, grammars, anddictionaries; and unusually good coverage of the field of Oriental religions and philosophies. The catalog contains numerous subject references to periodical articles in all languages. All entries are arranged alphabetically according to the Roman alphabet.

NY —NEW YORK PUBLIC LIBRARY, Oriental Div, Fifth Ave & 42 St, New York, 10018. E Christian Filstrup, Chief
Holdings: Cat Mss Microforms
Budget: ($56,455)
Notes: Published catalog of holdings.

OH —CLEVELAND PUBLIC LIBRARY, Fine Arts and Special Collections Department, 325 Superior Ave, Cleveland, 44114. Alice N Loranth, Head
Holdings: Vols (5200) Cat Mss
Notes: Part of the Egyptology Collection. Extensive holdings of scholarly research material on Egyptian antiquities and studies. Strong holdings in French, British and German series, philogical excavation reports, etc.
See also entry under Egyptology; Oriental Languages and Literatures

EGYPT—ANTIQUITIES see Egyptology

EGYPTIAN ART see Art, Egyptian

EGYPTIAN HIEROGLYPHICS see Egyptian Language and Literature

EGYPTIAN LANGUAGE AND LITERATURE

LA —UNIVERSITY OF NEW ORLEANS, Earl K Long Library, New Orleans, 70148. Susan LaHaye, Cataloger
Notes: Approximately 450 pieces (including monographs, pamphlets, serials, newspaper reprints). The Judge Pierre Crabites collection of Egyptology consisting mainly of late 19th and early 20th century imprints. Some signed editions.

NY —BROOKLYN MUSEUM, Wilbour Library of Egyptology, Eastern Parkway, Brooklyn, 11238. Diane Guzman, Librn
Holdings: Vols (30,000) Cat Maps
Notes: The Wilbour Library of Egyptology ranks as one of the world's finest, most complete collections of works on all aspects of the culture of Ancient Egypt (down to the Islamic conquest). A card catalog records authors, subjects, series and titles of all books, periodicals and and 12,000 pamphlets. A description of the collection, as of 1924, may be found in: William Burt Cook, Jr, *Catalogue of the Egyptological Library and other Books from the Collection of the Late Charles Edwin Wilbour* (Brooklyn, NY: Brooklyn Museum, 1924). Middle Eastern art formerly included, now transferred to the Brooklyn Museum.

EGYPTIAN RELIGION

OH —CLEVELAND PUBLIC LIBRARY, Fine Arts and Special Collections Department, 325 Superior Ave, Cleveland, 44114. Alice N Loranth, Head
Holdings: Vols (7000) Cat Mss
Notes: Part of the Oriental Religion Collection. Emphasis is on religious texts in their original languages and Western translations. Treatises on religious beliefs and practices are also incl. Strong holdings in Buddhism, Egyptian religion, Hinduism, Judaica, Lamaistic texts, Islam, Sikhism and Zoroastrianism. Works on primitive religion cover aspects of animism, totemism, fetishism, etc. Special emphasis on Islam in China.
See also entries under Egyptology; Religion, Oriental.

EGYPTIAN STUDIES see Egyptology

EGYPTOLOGISTS see Egyptology

EGYPTOLOGY

CA —ROSICRUCIAN ORDER, AMORC, Research Library, Rosicrucian Park, San Jose, 95191. Clara Campbell, Librn
Holdings: Cat
Notes: Collection incl materials on Rosicrucians, ancient Egyptian history, parapsychology and mysticism. No interlibrary loans.

LA —UNIVERSITY OF NEW ORLEANS, Earl K Long Library, New Orleans, 70148. Susan LaHaye, Cataloger
Notes: Approximately 450 pieces (including monographs, pamphlets, serials, newspaper reprints). The Judge Pierre Crabites collection of Egyptology consisting mainly of late 19th and early 20th century imprints. Some signed editions.

MD —JOHNS HOPKINS UNIVERSITY, Milton S Eisenhower Library, Charles & 34 Sts, Baltimore, 21218. Ann S Gwyn, Assistant Dir for Special Collections
Holdings: Vols 2400 Cat Maps Pix
Notes: Very strong collection.

MI —UNIVERSITY OF MICHIGAN, Graduate Library, Near East Dept, Ann Arbor, 48109. John A Eilts, Bibliographer
Holdings: Cat
Notes: P L 480.

NJ —PRINCETON UNIVERSITY, Library, Rare Books Dept, Princeton, 08544. Stephen Ferguson, Cur
Holdings: Cat

NY —BROOKLYN MUSEUM, Wilbour Library of Egyptology, Eastern Parkway, Brooklyn, 11238. Diane Guzman, Librn
Holdings: Vols (30,000) Cat Maps
Notes: The Wilbour Library of Egyptology ranks as one of the world's finest, most complete collections of works on all aspects of the culture of Ancient Egypt (down to the Islamic conquest). A card catalog records authors, subjects, series and titles of all books, periodicals and and 12,000 pamphlets. A description of the collection, as of 1924, may be found in: William Burt Cook, Jr, *Catalogue of the Egyptological Library and other Books from the Collection of the Late Charles Edwin Wilbour* (Brooklyn, NY: Brooklyn Museum, 1924). Middle Eastern art formerly included, now transferred to the Brooklyn Museum.

NY —NEW YORK PUBLIC LIBRARY, Oriental Div, Fifth Ave & 42 St, New York, 10018. E Christian Filstrup, Chief
Holdings: Cat Mss Microforms
Budget: ($56,455)
Notes: Described in *Dictionary Catalog of the Oriental Collection,* The Research Libraries of the New York Public Library, 1960, 16 vols, and *First Supplement,* 1976, 8 vols (144,000 cards). This catalog incl 318, 000 entries for works in about 100 languages of the East, and all works in Western languages on Oriental subjects. The Oriental Collection numbers about 120,000 vols; its Arabic and Indic holdings and those on ancient Egypt and the ancient Near East are among the largest in the US. There is main entry access, but which is not incorporated into the dictionary catalog. Other outstanding features of the Oriental Collection incl extensive holdings of Japanese technical and scientific periodicals; a unique collection of linguistic works, grammars, and dictionaries; and unusually good coverage of the field of Oriental religions and philosophies.The catalog contains numerous subject references to periodical articles in all languages. All entries are arranged alphabetically according to the Roman alphabet.

NC —DUKE UNIVERSITY, Divinity School Library, Durham, 27706. Donn Michael Farris, Librn
Holdings: Vols (225,000)
Notes: Special collections and subject emphases in this library include: Archaeology, Egyptian; Archaeology, Middle Eastern; Art, Jewish; Bible; Bible-New Testament; Bible-Symbolism; Church Architecture; Egyptology; Fathers of the Church; Society of Friends; Great Britain-Religion-Methodism and Methodist Church; Hymns and Hymnals; Jansenists and Jansenism; Judaica; Mediaeval Christian Mysticism; Methodism and Methodist Church; Methodist Episcopal Church; Methodist Episcopal Church, South; Reformation; Religion-US-History; Rural Church; Theology-Great Britain-17th Century; Theology-Great Britain-18th Century; United Methodist Church; US-Church History; John Wesley.

OH —CLEVELAND PUBLIC LIBRARY, Fine Arts and Special Collections Department, 325 Superior Ave, Cleveland, 44114. Alice N Loranth, Head
Holdings: Vols 5200 Cat Mss
Notes: Extensive holdings of scholarly research material on Egyptian antiquities and philological studies. Strong holdings in French, British and German series, excavation reports, etc.

PA —UNIVERSITY OF PENNSYLVANIA, University Museum Library, 33 & Spruce Sts, Philadelphia, 19104. Jean S Adelman, Librn
Holdings: Vols (80,000) Cat
Notes: World archaeology, with special emphasis on North and Central America, Egyptology, Sumerology, and the classical world. All holdings are listed in museum library catalog and are also listed in University of Pennsylvania main library (union) catalog.

ON —ROYAL ONTARIO MUSEUM, Main Library and Archives, 100 Queen's Park, Toronto, M5S 2C6, Can. Julia Matthews, Head Librn
Holdings: Vols (85,000) Cat
Notes: Since January 1977, acquisitions have been entered in UTLAS.

EHRMANN, HERBERT BRUTUS, 1891-1970

MA —HARVARD UNIVERSITY LIBRARY, Law School Library, Langdell Hall, Cambridge, 02138. Erika S Chadbourn, Cur of Mss
Holdings: Cat Mss
Notes: Personal papers. Typed inventory in repository. Inclusive dates: 1906-1970.

EICHELBERGER, GEN. ROBERT L.

NC —DUKE UNIVERSITY, William R Perkins Library, Manuscript Dept, Durham, 27706. Ellen Gartrell, Cur of Mss
Holdings: Cat Mss
Notes: Especially strong for Civil War; also material from most wars that involved US. Notable World War II collection is papers of Gen Robert L Eichelberger (over 20,000 items).

EICHENBERG, FRITZ

CT —YALE UNIVERSITY, Sterling Memorial Library, Arts of the Book Collection, New Haven, 06520. Gay Walker, Cur
Notes: Wood blocks - engraved for 12 books, sketches, and prints.

EIGHTEENTH CENTURY

CT —LEWIS WALPOLE LIBRARY, 154 Main St, Farmington, 06032. Catherine Jestin, Librn
Holdings: Cat Mss Maps Pix Slides Microforms Memorabilia
Notes: Research center for English eighteenth-century studies. A department of Yale University Library. Scholars may visit by appointment only.

EIGNER, LARRY

RI —BROWN UNIVERSITY, John Hay Library, 20 Prospect St, Providence, 02912. Mark N Brown, Cur Mss
Holdings: Mss
Notes: Papers of Larry Eigner (1927-) consisting of his poetry and correspondence.

EIKON BASILIKE

NY —UNIVERSITY OF ROCHESTER, Rush Rhees Library, Department of Rare Books and Special Collections, Rochester, 14627. Peter Dzwonkoski, Librn
Holdings: Vols Cat
Notes: Some 20 editions of the meditation on death and duty attributed to Charles I of England. First published shortly after his execution in 1649.

EINSTEIN, ALBERT, 1879-1955

CT —BURNDY LIBRARY, Electra Square, Norwalk, 06856. Philip J Weimerskirch, Asst Dir
Holdings: Vols 250 Pix Paintings

†IL —SOUTHERN ILLINOIS UNIVERSITY, CARBONDALE, Library, Special Collections Dept, Carbondale, 62901.
Notes: Archives of the Library of Living Philosophers, a publishing project founded by Paul Arthur Schilpp in 1938 to provide a forum for contemporary philosophers to reply to their critics. Incl correspondence from John Dewey, George Santayana, Alfred North Whitehead, G E Moore, and Albert Einstein.

IA —HERBERT HOOVER PRESIDENTIAL LIBRARY, West Branch, 52358. Dale C Mayer, Archivist
Notes: Papers.

MA —BRANDEIS UNIVERSITY, Goldfarb Library, 415 South St, Waltham, 02154. Bessie Hahn, Dir
Notes: Albert Einstein Papers. Correspondence to and from Albert Einstein, family correspondence and other notes. A finding list to the collection is in Special Collections.

NJ —PRINCETON UNIVERSITY, Seeley G Mudd Manuscript Library, Public Affairs Papers Collection, Princeton, 08544. Nancy Bressler, Cur
Notes: Incl 91 boxes. The duplicate archives cover the period 1859-1955. An unpublished 50p guide and 11 vol computerized index is available.

NY —AMERICAN INSTITUTE OF PHYSICS, Center for the History of Physics, Niels Bohr Library, 335 E 45 St, New York, 10017. John Aubry, Librn
Holdings: Cat Mss Maps Pix Microforms

†TX —UNIVERSITY OF TEXAS LIBRARIES, General Libraries, Humanities Research Center, PO Box 7219, Austin, 78712. John Chalmers, Librn
Notes: Some of Albert Einstein's mathematical-physics topics, 230 pages, written by Albert Einstein during the period 1950-1955. These complement 250 pages of similar manuscripts notes from the same period already in the Einstein collection.

ON —UNIVERSITY OF TORONTO, Thomas Fisher Rare Book Library, 120 Saint George St, Toronto, M5S 1A5, Can. Richard G Landon, Head
Holdings: Vols 300 Cat
Notes: Einstein Collection of books, pamphlets and offprints by Einstein or on his theories; includes works by scientific colleagues.

EINSTEIN, ALFRED

CA —UNIVERSITY OF CALIFORNIA, BERKELEY, Humanities-Social Sciences Libraries, Music Library, 24 Morrison Hall, Berkeley, 94720. Michael A Keller, Head Librn
Holdings: Vols 3000 Cat Mss
Notes: The Alfred Einstein *Nachlass* comprises a scholar's working library in music history (ca 2000 vols), plus a special collection of research materials devoted to Mozart, and to Einstein's studies of the Italian madrigal. The collection also incl a file of music criticism by Einstein and selected correspondence.

EINSTEIN, CHARLES

MA —BOSTON UNIVERSITY, Mugar Memorial Library, Special Collections Dept, 771 Commonwealth Ave, Boston, 02215. Howard B Gotlieb, Dir
Holdings: Cat Mss

EINSTEIN, LEWIS

WY —UNIVERSITY OF WYOMING, William Robertson Coe Library, Performing Arts Collections, Laramie, 82071. Gene M Gressley, Dir
Holdings: Cat Mss Pix
Notes: The papers of Lewis Einstein, incl biographical materials.

EISENHOWER, DWIGHT DAVID, 1890-1969

KS —DWIGHT D EISENHOWER LIBRARY, 226 SE Fourth, Abilene, 67410. John E Wickman, Dir
Holdings: Vols 28,000 Cat Mss Pix Slides Microforms
Notes: His administration and materials on his contemporaries.

LA —LOUISIANA STATE UNIVERSITY, Troy H Middleton Library, Baton Rouge, 70803. Lance E Dickson, Acting Dir
Holdings: Vols (1000) Cat Mss Maps Pix Audiotapes
Notes: The Troy H Middleton Collection. Contains vols on military history and tactics. Letters, documents, photographs, and mementos belonging to Troy H Middleton, former President of LSU and distinguished military leader. Also, tape recordings by some of Gen Middleton's associates in the Army, incl Gen Eisenhower, and on civilian life and reminiscences by Gen Middleton. The Library has other materials on military history also.

OH —OHIO UNIVERSITY, Vernon R Alden Library, Department of Archives and Special Collections, Athens, 45701. Gary A Hunt, Head
Holdings: Vols 674 Cat Mss Maps Pix Audiotapes
Notes: The Cornelius Ryan Memorial Collection of World War II Papers, containing the research files, correspondence and working library assembled by Ryan in the course of writing his three major books on World War II. The research papers incl some 3,072 files for individual participants in the Normandy invasion, the battle for Berlin, and the Market-Garden operation. Also incl are 166 audio recordings of interviews conducted by Ryan, many with leading figures associated with the war, such as Eisenhower, Chuikov, Gavin, Montgomery, and Prince Bernhard of the Netherlands.

PA —GETTYSBURG NATIONAL MILITARY PARK, Gettysburg, 17325. Thomas J Harrison, Cultural Resources Specialist
Notes: Eisenhower at Gettysburg.

E. I. W. AND CO.

SC —COLLEGE OF CHARLESTON LIBRARY, Special Collections Dept, Charleston, 29401.
Notes: Charleston, SC. Papers, 1874.

EL DORADO WOOD AND FLUME COMPANY

NV —UNIVERSITY OF NEVADA, RENO, University Library, Special Collections Dept, Reno, 89557. Robert E Blesse, Head
Holdings: Vols (100) Cat Pix Mss
Notes: Books, manuscripts (115 cu ft), photographs (500), dealing with Lake Tahoe and the surrounding region. Included are papers of organizations concerned with the environmental quality of the lake, eg, the Lake Tahoe Area Council records, the Tahoe Regional Planning Association records. Records of two 19th-20th century business involved with logging and lumber production in the Tahoe region, the Carson, Tahoe Lumber and Fluming Company, and the El Dorado Wood and Flume Company. Photographs include many early 19th century views of the lake and structures surrounding it.

ELAMITE LANGUAGE

NY —NEW YORK PUBLIC LIBRARY, Oriental Div, Fifth Ave & 42 St, New York, 10018. E Christian Filstrup, Chief
Holdings: Cat Mss Microforms
Budget: ($56,455)
Notes: Published catalog of holdings.

ELDER, ARTHUR

MI —WAYNE STATE UNIVERSITY, Walter P Reuther Library, Archives of Labor & Urban Affairs, Detroit, 48202. Philip Mason, Dir
Notes: The records of the American Federation of Teachers, as well as the files of the Detroit, Toledo, East Detroit, and other Federations of Teachers, are now preserved in the Archives. The personal papers of several teacher union leaders, incl Arthur Elder, Selma M Borchardt, Henry R Linville, Mary Herrick, and others are important supplements to the national union's file.

ELDER, LONNE

MA —BOSTON UNIVERSITY, Mugar Memorial Library, Special Collections Dept, 771 Commonwealth Ave, Boston, 02215. Howard B Gotlieb, Dir
Holdings: Cat Mss
Notes: Mss, correspondence, etc collected in depth; incl publications by or about.

ELECTION SERMONS

CT —CONNECTICUT STATE LIBRARY, 231 Capitol Ave, Hartford, 06106.
Holdings: // Cat
Notes: Contains election sermons. Particularly strong for Connecticut.

MA —NEW ENGLAND HISTORIC GENEALOGICAL SOCIETY, Library, 101 Newbury St, Boston, 02116. Ralph J Crandell, Dir
Holdings: Vols (250,000) Mss Maps Microforms Pix
Notes: New England genealogy. Especially strong Massachusetts, Maine, and New Hampshire, although all states are well represented, as are the relevancies of each subject listed in this volume with regard to British antecedent and contemporary history. Special strengths in local history and biography, obituaries, etc, incl parish registers, censuses, British and American. 3125 linear ft of mss.

NY —NEW YORK STATE LIBRARY, State Education Bldg Annex, Washington Ave, Albany, 12224.
Holdings: Vols 173 Cat Microforms
Notes: Good, representative collection. Not all indexed for retrieval. In addition hold microform collection of Evans, Show-Shoemaker titles.

NY —NEW YORK HISTORICAL SOCIETY, 10024. James Gregory, Librn
Holdings: Mss
Notes: Incl original mss, illustrative materials, etc.

NY —NEW YORK PUBLIC LIBRARY, Research Libraries, General Research Division, Fifth Ave & 42 St, New York, 10018. Rodney Phillips, Chief
Holdings: Vols (2,225,000) Cat Maps Pix Microforms
Budget: ($775,718)

ELECTIONS

CA —LOS ANGELES PUBLIC LIBRARY, Social Sciences Dept, 630 W Fifth St, Los Angeles, 90071. Marilyn C Wherley, Principal Librn
Holdings: Vols 5000 Cat
Budget: ($150,000)
Notes: Pamphlets, bound periodicals, incl political parties (US and foreign), practical politics, elections statistics, extensive pamphlet file of California and Los Angeles City/County elections materials dating from the early 1900s.

CT —YALE UNIVERSITY, Social Science Library, 140 Prospect St, New Haven, 06520. Billie I Salter, Librn
Holdings: Vols (40,000) Cat Microforms
Notes: Political science.
See also entry under Social Sciences

DC —GEORGETOWN UNIVERSITY, Library, Special Collections Div, 37 & O Sts NW, Washington, 20057. George M Barringer, Special Collections Librn; Nicholas B Sheetz, Mss Librn
Holdings: Cat Mss Maps Pix Slides Phonorecords Audiotapes
Notes: Includes the papers (1912-49) of Sen Robert F Wagner, the Archives of the Fair Campaign Practices Committee, the archives (1903-) of the American Political Science Association and of its local Washington chapter; the archives of the Center for Public Financing of Elections; a collection of several hundred political cartoons of Eric Smith; and other smaller collections.

DC —GEORGETOWN UNIVERSITY, Library, Special Collections Div, 37 & O Sts NW, Washington, 20057. George M Barringer, Special Collections Librn; Nicholas B Sheetz, Mss Librn
Holdings: Mss Maps
Notes: The papers of Samuel Lubell - pollster, political analyst and author. Incl are state data files consisting of election surveys, election returns, voting statistics, precinct maps, correspondence, interviews, and clippings as well as material on such issues as race relations, urban development and management, youth opinion, and Congressional analysis. Also incl in the papers is correspondence and lecture material, as well as notes, mss and reviews pertaining to *Hidden Crisis Revolt of the Moderates, White and Black, The Future of American Politics, and The Future While It* Happened.

†MA —JOHN F KENNEDY LIBRARY, Columbia Point, Boston, 02125. Dan H Fenn Jr, Dir
Holdings: // Cat Mss
Notes: Draft mss of Theodore White's writings, especially *The Making of the* President, 1960, 1964 and *1968*, and the records of the Democratic National Committee, campaigns of 1952, 1956 and 1960. 70 linear ft of mss. Holdings are described in "Historical Materials in the

ELECTIONS, CENTER FOR PUBLIC FINANCING OF see Center for Public Financing of Elections

ELECTIONS, CONTESTED see Contested Elections

ELECTRIC APPARATUS AND APPLIANCES

MN —BAKKEN LIBRARY OF ELECTRICITY IN LIFE, 3537 Zenith Ave S, Minneapolis, 55416. John Edward Senior, Dir

ELECTRIC APPLIANCES see Electric Apparatus and Appliances

ELECTRIC ARC WELDING see Welding

ELECTRIC BATTERIES

ON —DURACELL INC, Research Library, 2333 N Sheridan Way, Sheridan Park, L5K 1A7, Can. Gail Robertson
Holdings: Vols 1500 Cat
Notes: Electrochemistry, as applied to dry batteries.

ELECTRIC BELLS

NY —SOCIETAS CAMPANARIORUM (SOCIETY OF BELL-RINGERS), Campanological Library, Riverside Church, 490 Riverside Dr, New York, 10027. James R Lawson, Librn
Holdings: Vols 1000 Cat
Notes: One of the largest collections of books, pamphlets, periodicals, etc on bells and bell music (chimes, carillons, change-ringing, handbells, electronic carillons, etc) in North America. Examined by appointment only.

ELECTRIC CIRCUITS

CA —LOS ANGELES PUBLIC LIBRARY, Science & Technology Dept, 630 W Fifth St, Los Angeles, 90071. Billie M Connor, Dept Head
Holdings: Vols (12,000) Cat
Notes: Materials on the application of electronic devices, circuits and systems in various fields such as computers, automatic control, sound productions and reproduction, radio and telecommunications. Extensive holdings of materials on computers, peripherals, and software including many texts pertaining to specific programming languages. Complete collection of Howard Sams schematics for radio television, and other electronic equipment repair as well as historical sets of Rider's Radio and Television schematics.

KY —UNIVERSITY OF KENTUCKY, Robert E Shaver Library of Engineering, 355 Anderson Hall, Lexington, 40506. Russell H Powell, Engineering Librn
Holdings: Vols (48,000) Cat Microforms

ELECTRIC ENGINEERING—APPARATUS AND APPLIANCES see Electric Apparatus and Appliances

ELECTRIC LIGHT AND POWER INDUSTRY see Electric Utilities

ELECTRIC LINES, OVERHEAD

NJ —AT&T BELL LABORATORIES, Libraries and Information Systems Center, 600 Mountain Ave, Murray Hill, 07974. W D Penniman, Dir
Holdings: (273,100) Cat Mss Audiotapes Videotapes Microforms
Budget: ($670,000)
Notes: Restricted use to AT&T employees. Catalogs/*Indexes*: Bell Laboratories Library Network and Book Serial Catalogs; Bell Laboratories Translations. Bell Laboratories Library Network with New Jersey libraries located in Holmdel, Murray Hill, Piscataway, Whippany, Princeton, Short Hills, Summit, West Long Branch, Crawford Hill; libraries also in Allentown, Pennsylvania; Reading, Pennsylvania; New York, New York; Atlanta, Georgia; Columbus, Ohio; Naperville, Illinois; Indianapolis, Indiana; North Andover, Massachusetts.

OH —PREFORMED LINE PRODUCTS CO, Research & Engineering Library, 660 Beta Drive, Mayfield Village, (Mailing add: PO Box 91129, Cleveland, 44101). Edwina T Barron, Librn
Holdings: Vols (11,500) Cat Mss Microfiche Pix VF
Budget: ($30,500)
Notes: Library covering research and engineering fields emphasizing this subject. Aerodynamic characteristics and electrical characteristics of power cables, communication cables (including fiber optics), cable support systems, as well as associated fittings and hardware; in service behavior of manufactured products and materials as it relates to its static and dynamic forces and environmental conditions; oceanographic cable fittings and terminations.

ELECTRIC MOTORS

SC —CLEMSON UNIVERSITY, Libraries, Clemson, 29631. Michael F Kohl, Head of Special Collections
Holdings: // Cat Mss
Notes: Electricity, theoretical and applied to motors. Collected by Bernard A Behrend, 1875-1932, inventor of machinery and large electrical units. About 1000 items, in English, German, and French, published from 1886 to 1932. Complete card index by author and subject. The ms portion of this collection consists of numerous notebooks containing records of Mr Behrend's work upon which, no doubt, he based his publications. 19 titles, written or edited by Mr Behrend, are cataloged. Also incl pamphlets and reprints. Cited in *Manuscripts in US Depositories Relating to the History of Electrical Science and Technology* (Div of Electricity and Nuclear Energy, Smithsonian Institution, Washington, DC 1973).

ELECTRIC POWER

DE —HAGLEY MUSEUM AND LIBRARY, Eleutherian Mills-Hagley Foundation Inc, PO Box 3630, Greenville, 19807. Richmond D Williams, Dir; Heddy A Richter, Imprints Librn
Notes: Records of Pennsylvania Power & Light Company (1853-1955; 1000 cubic feet). The archive consists of the records of 1050 predecessor companies that merged over a 75-year period (1880-1955) to form the present-day PP&L. The collection describes the industry's tentative beginnings using the Edison system of direct current, the technological innovations which allowed small, innercity utilities to expand beyond their original urban centers, and the consolidation movement that culminated with the formation of a great regional power network. Also, records of Delmarva Power Company (1890-1965; 60 cubic feet).

MA —STONE & WEBSTER ENGINEERING CORP, Technical Information Center, Library, 245 Summer St, PO Box 2325, Boston, 02107. Nancy M Pellini, Mgr
Holdings: Vols (10,000) Cat Pix Microforms
Notes: Also over 1200 periodicals. Extensive vertical file collection, and 5 on-line system for search.

MA —NEW ENGLAND ELECTRIC SYSTEM, Technical Information Center, 25 Research Dr, Westborough, 01581. William J McCall, Librn
Holdings: Vols 2350 Cat Microforms
Notes: Compile KWIC index to our special and technical reports. Also compile indexes to industry newsletters. Collection reflects R&D interests of electric utility industry.

NJ —PUBLIC SERVICE ELECTRIC & GAS CO, Library, 80 Park Place Plaza P3C, PO Box 570, Newark, 07101. Florine E Hunt, Corporate Librn
Holdings: Vols (20,000) Cat Microforms

NY —CARY ARBORETUM OF THE NEW YORK BOTANICAL GARDEN, Library, Box AB, Millbrook, 12545. Fred Strum, Librn
Notes: This collection of alternative energy sources consists of publications concerned with solar energy, wind power, biofuel, methanol, small hydroelectric projects, and wood power.

OR —PORTLAND STATE UNIVERSITY LIBRARY, 934 SW Harrison, PO Box 1151, 97207, Portland, 97201. Kenneth W Butler, Asst Dir
Holdings: Vols (669,592) Uncat Mss Maps Pix Microforms
Budget: ($1,321,288)
Notes: Northwest natural resources and electrical power development. Incl the Ivan Bloch Collection.

WA —WESTERN WASHINGTON UNIVERSITY, Center for Pacific Northwest Studies, High St, Bellingham, 98225. James W Scott, Dir
Holdings: Vols 400// Cat Mss
Notes: Puget Sound Power and Light Company Records Collection consists of the complete company records of 41 former companies, which were bought out, amalgamated with or in other ways came under the control of Puget Sound Power and Light Company. Most of the companies were concerned with transportation or the porduction of power--both gas and elecricity. Among the companies represented are street railways, interurban railways, traction companies and gas companies, all of which operated in the region west of the Cascades, especially in the Puget Sound area but with a few as far south as Vancouver, Washington. The collection has been placed in the Center for Pacific Northwest Studies by the Puget Sound Power and Light Company on a permanent loan basis.

ELECTRIC POWER INDUSTRY see Electric Utilities

ELECTRIC RAILROADS

CA —BAY AREA ELECTRIC RAILROAD ASSOCIATION, California Railway Museum, Star Rte 283, Box 150, Suisun City, 94585. Vernon J Sappers, Librn
Holdings: Vols (5000) Uncat Maps Pix Slides 16mm Films
Notes: Technical journals and publications pertaining to steam and electric railroads. In addition, there are ten cabinets of files of the following railroad companies: Key System, Southern Pacific and Associated Companies, Western Pacific Railroad, Sacramento Northern Railroad, Pacific Electric Railway, Northern Electric Railway, Oakland Antioch & Eastern Railway. These files deal with the history of each railroad.

CT —CONNECTICUT ELECTRIC RAILWAY ASSOCIATION, INC, Southern New England, PO Box 360, East Windsor, 06088. William E Wood, Dir of Museum
Holdings: Vols 1500 Uncat Maps Pix
Notes: All forms of railroads operated by electricity. Some 1500 items. The collection can be opened only on application.

NY —ELECTRIC RAILROADERS ASSOCIATION, Frank J Sprague Memorial Library, 89 E 42nd St, New York, 10018. Hugh A Dunne, First VP
Notes: Private library. Incl all forms of railroads operated by electricity. Forms of electric railroads included: street railways, subways & elevated lines, high-speed interurbans, suburban commuter lines, electrified trunk lines, monorails, mountain climbing inclines, etc. Also railroad timetables.

ELECTRIC RAILROADS—CARS

MO —WASHINGTON UNIVERSITY, Libraries, Special Collections Dept, Campus Box 1061, St Louis, 63130.
Holdings: //
Notes: Records of the St Louis Car Company, 1887-1973, incl the transportation manufacturing enterprise's files of over 20, 000 photographs and negatives of the firm's products; over 2000 original tracings of railroad and street car equipment. Also printed material about the firm, and catalogs published by the company from 1904 to 1965.

OR —OREGON ELECTRIC RAILWAY HISTORICAL SOCIETY, Library, HCR 71, Box 1318, Forest Grove, 97116. Paul V Class, Cur
Holdings: Vols (125) Uncat Pix Slides 16mm Films

ELECTRIC STREET RAILROADS see Street Railroads

ELECTRIC UTILITIES

AZ —NORTHERN ARIZONA UNIVERSITY, Special Collection Library, CU Box 6022, Flagstaff, 86011. Peter M Whiteley, Coordr/Archivist; William Mullane, Librn
Notes: Central Arizona Light and Power Company Collection, Phoenix; scrapbook of activities, 1929.

DC —EDISON ELECTRIC INSTITUTE, Library-8th Floor, 1111 19th St NW, Washington, 20036. Ethel Tiberg, Mgr, Library Services
Holdings: Vols (13,321) Cat Maps Pix Microforms
Notes: Electric Utility Industry.

MA —NEW ENGLAND ELECTRIC SYSTEM, Technical Information Center, 25 Research Dr, Westborough, 01581. William J McCall, Librn
Holdings: Vols 2350 Cat Microforms
Notes: Compile KWIC index to our special and technical reports. Also compile indexes to industry newsletters. Collection reflects R&D interests of electric utility industry.

OH —TOLEDO EDISON CO, Library, 300 Madison Ave, Toledo, 43652. Catherine Witker, Librn
Holdings: Vols (2000) Cat Audiotapes
Budget: ($10,000)

ELECTRICAL ENGINEERING

AL —TUSKEGEE INSTITUTE, School of Engineering Library, Tuskegee Institute, 36088. Frances F Davis, Librn
Holdings: Vols 601 Cat
Budget: $4000

CA —UNIVERSITY OF CALIFORNIA, DAVIS, Physical Sciences Library, Davis, 95616. Scott Kennedy, Head
Holdings: Vols (170,000) Cat VF
Notes: Collection covers aeronautical, agricultural, chemical, civil, electrical, mechanical, water science, hydrology, nuclear reactor, extensive cold regions collection in vertical file drawers, and computer science engineering academic programs. Good strength in journal runs.

†CA —XEROX CORP, Technical Library, 701 S Aviation Blvd, A3-25, El Segundo, 90245. Marilyn Durkin, Librn
Notes: 450 Journal titles.

CA —UNIVERSITY OF CALIFORNIA, LOS ANGELES, Engineering & Mathematical Sciences Library, 405 Hilgard, Los Angeles, 90024. Rosalee I Wright, Librn
Holdings: Vols (180,000) Cat Microforms
See also entry under Engineering

CA —GTE COMMUNICATIONS PRODUCT CORP, Sylvania Systems Group, Western Division Library, MC-2201, PO Box 7188, Mountain View, 94039. J B Fierro, Supervisor Library Services
Holdings: Vols (10,000) Cat
Notes: Interlibrary loan.

CA —CALIFORNIA STATE POLYTECHNIC UNIVERSITY, POMONA, University Library, 3801 W Temple Ave, Pomona, 91768. Harold Schleiser, Actg Dir
Notes: General reference materials on aerospace, chemical, civil, electrical, electronics, industrial, mechanical and manufacturing engineering.

CA —HEALD COLLEGE TECHNICAL DIVISION, Learning Resource Center Library, 150 4th Street, San Francisco, 94103. Tom Casas, Dir
Holdings: Vols (1000) Cat
Budget: $680

CT —NORTHEAST UTILITIES, PO Box 270, Hartford, 06141. Joan Terry, Librn
Holdings: Vols 2000 Cat

FL —FLORIDA INSTITUTE OF TECHNOLOGY, Library, 150 W University Blvd, PO Box 1150, Melbourne, 32901. L L Henson, Dir of Libraries
Holdings: Vols (6500) Cat Microforms

GA —GEORGIA INSTITUTE OF TECHNOLOGY, Price Gilbert Memorial Library, 225 North Ave, Atlanta, 30332. Edward Graham Roberts, Dir
Holdings: Vols (1,661,559) Cat Maps Slides Microforms
Budget: ($1,383,302)
Notes: Incl (4,307,996) patents and (568, 490) government documents.

IL —UNIVERSITY OF ILLINOIS, URBANA/CHAMPAIGN, Library, 221 Engineering Hall, Urbana, 61801. William Mischo, Librn
Holdings: Vols (175,000) Cat Slides Microforms
Notes: Incl 3500 periodicals. Collection designed to serve teaching and research programs. Supports instructional faculty research. Also, 470 microfilm reels and 6000 microfiche sheets.

IN —PURDUE UNIVERSITY LIBRARIES, Engineering Library, A A Potter Engineering Center, West Lafayette, 47907. Edwin D Posey, Engineering Librn
Holdings: Vols (225,178) Cat Maps Audiotapes Microforms
Budget: ($300,000)

IA —IOWA STATE UNIVERSITY, Library, Ames, 50011. Warren B Kuhn, Dean of Library Services
Holdings: Cat
Notes: Extensive serial holdings.

KY —UNIVERSITY OF KENTUCKY, Robert E Shaver Library of Engineering, 355 Anderson Hall, Lexington, 40506. Russell H Powell, Engineering Librn
Holdings: Vols (48,000) Cat Microforms

MA —MITRE CORPORATION, Bedford Library, PO Box 208, Bedford, 01730. Betsy Cogliano, Supvr
Holdings: Vols (65,000) Cat Audiotapes Microforms
Notes: Collection incl 127,000 documents.

MA —STONE & WEBSTER ENGINEERING CORP, Technical Information Center, Library, 245 Summer St, PO Box 2325, Boston, 02107. Nancy M Pellini, Mgr
Holdings: Vols (10,000) Cat Pix Microforms
Notes: Also over 1200 periodicals. Extensive vertical file collection, and 5 on-line system for search.

MI —UNIVERSITY OF MICHIGAN, Engineering-Transportation Library, 312 Undergraduate Library, Ann Arbor, 48109. Maurita Holland, Librn
Holdings: Vols (400,000) Cat Microforms
Budget: ($225,000)

MN —HONEYWELL, Defense Systems Div, Engineering Library, 600 Second St N, Hopkins, 55343. Lawrence Werner, Librn
Holdings: Vols (4000)
Budget: ($30,000)
Notes: Incl 100,000 microforms.

NJ —AT&T BELL LABORATORIES, Libraries and Information Systems Center, 600 Mountain Ave, Murray Hill, 07974. W D Penniman, Dir
Holdings: Vols (273,100) Cat Mss Audiotapes Videotapes Microforms
Budget: ($670,000)
Notes: Restricted use to AT&T employees. Catalogs/*Indexes*: Bell Laboratories Library Network and Book Serial Catalogs; Bell Laboratories Translations. Bell Laboratories Library Network with New Jersey libraries located in Holmdel, Murray Hill, Piscataway, Whippany, Princeton, Short Hills, Summit, West Long Branch, Crawford Hill; libraries also in Allentown, Pennsylvania; Reading, Pennsylvania; New York, New York; Atlanta, Georgia; Columbus, Ohio; Naperville, Illinois; Indianapolis, Indiana; North Andover, Massachusetts.

NY —POLYTECHNIC INSTITUTE OF NEW YORK, Long Island Center Library, Route 110, Farmingdale, 11735. Lorraine Schein, Branch Librn
Holdings: Vols 3000 Cat

NY —COLUMBIA UNIVERSITY LIBRARIES, Engineering Library, 422 Mudd Bldg, New York, 10027.
Holdings: Vols (177,000) Cat
Notes: All aspects of engineering--aeronautical, industrial mining, civil, chemical, mechanical, electrical, nuclear. Incl applied mathematics and applied physical sciences. Over (1,000,000) technical reports.

NY —ENGINEERING SOCIETIES LIBRARY, 345 E 47 St, New York, 10017. S Kirk Cabeen, Dir
Holdings: Vols 250,000 Cat Maps 16mm Films Microforms
Notes: One of the largest, most comprehensive engineering libraries in the world. Covers all engineering disciplines; particularly strong in electrical and electronic, mechanical, mining and metallurgical, petroleum, chemical, industrial, air conditioning and refrigeration engineering. Incl Wheeler Collection of early materials on magnetism and electricity. 125, 000 bound periodical volumes; 10,000 maps; 5000 serial subscriptions (many foreign-language). Virtually all materials abstracted in *Engineering Index* (1884-date) are incl in Library. Noncirculating, except to members of professional engineering societies which support the Library. See *Engineering Societies Library, New York, Classed Subject Catalog and Index* (Boston: G K Hall, 1963); and *Supplements*, 1-10, 1964-1973.

NY —NEW YORK PUBLIC LIBRARY, Research Libraries, Science and Technology Research Center, Fifth Ave & 42 St, New York, 10018.
Holdings: Vols (1,100,000) Cat Microforms
Budget: ($647,259)

NY —EASTMAN KODAK COMPANY, Kodak Park Div, Engineering Library, Bldg 23, Rochester, 14650. Raymond Curtin, Librn
Holdings: Vols (14,000) Uncat Microforms
Notes: The library is not open to the public. Use of the library for reference purposes may be requested and appointments may be obtained through the librarian.

NY —UNIVERSITY OF ROCHESTER, Engineering Library, Gavett Hall, River Campus, Rochester, 14627. Isabel Kaplan, Librn
Holdings: Vols (25,000) Cat
Notes: Strong collection in the field and related areas.

NY —GENERAL ELECTRIC CO, Main Library, One River Rd, Schenectady, 12345. Julia Hewitt, Mgr
Holdings: Vols (56,000) Cat

NC —DUKE UNIVERSITY, School of Engineering, Library, Durham, 27706. Eric J Smith, Librn
Holdings: Vols (72,000) Cat Microforms
Budget: ($110,000)

NC —NORTH CAROLINA STATE UNIVERSITY, D H Hill Library, Box 7111, Raleigh, 27695. I T Littleton, Dir
Holdings: Vols 9530 Cat
Budget: $10,000
Notes: Incl monographs.

OH —PUBLIC LIBRARY OF CINCINNATI & HAMILTON COUNTY, Science & Technology Dept, 800 Vine St, Cincinnati, 45202. Rosemary Gaiser, Head
Holdings: Vols (250,000) Cat
Notes: Pure and applied science. Inc over 1600 periodicals and serial titles and more than 100 abstracting and indexing services in major fields of science and technology.

OH —UNIVERSITY OF CINCINNATI, Engineering Library, 880 Baldwin Hall, Cincinnati, 45221. Dorothy Furber Byers, Head
Holdings: Vols (50,000) Cat Videotapes Microforms
Budget: ($100,000)
Notes: Have NASA and DOE microfiche collections.

OH —OHIO STATE UNIVERSITY, Engineering Library, 2024 Neil Ave, Columbus, 43210. Mary Jo V Arnold, Librn
Holdings: Vols (132,000) Cat Microforms
Budget: ($110,000)

OH —PREFORMED LINE PRODUCTS CO, Research & Engineering Library, 660 Beta Drive, Mayfield Village, (Mailing add: PO Box 91129, Cleveland, 44101). Edwina T Barron, Librn
Holdings: Vols (11,500) Cat Mss Microfiche Pix VF
Budget: ($30,500)
Notes: Library covering research and engineering fields emphasizing this subject. Aerodynamic characteristics and electrical characteristics of power cables, communication cables (including fiber optics), cable support systems, as well as associated fittings and hardware; in service behavior of manufactured products and materials as it relates to its static and dynamic forces and environmental conditions; oceanographic cable fittings and terminations.

OR —US DEPT OF ENERGY, Bonneville Power Administration Library, 1002 NE Holladay St, PO Box 3621, Portland, 97232. Karen Hadman, Chief of Library Branch
Holdings: Vols (15,000) // Cat Microforms
Budget: ($8,000)

PA —FRANKLIN INSTITUTE LIBRARY, 20 & The Parkway, Philadelphia, 19103. Miriam Padusis, Dir; Charles Wilt, Readers Servs Librn
Holdings: Vols (300,000) Cat Maps Pix Microforms

PA —UNIVERSITY OF PENNSYLVANIA, Moore School of Electrical Engineering Library, 203 Moore School, 33 & Walnut Sts, Philadelphia, 19104. Charles Myers, Head Librn
Holdings: Vols (30,000) Cat Microforms

PA —US NAVY, Philadelphia Naval Shipyard Technical Library, Philadelphia Naval Shipyard, Philadelphia, 19112. Alice R Murray, Dir
Holdings: Vols (12,500) Cat Pix
Notes: The Library also has (70,000) technical manuals, (35,00) research and development reports. Over (400) current periodicals.

PA —CARNEGIE LIBRARY OF PITTSBURGH, Science & Technology Dept, 4400 Forbes Ave, Pittsburgh, 15213. Catherine M Brosky, Dept Head
Holdings: Vols (380,000) Cat Maps Microforms
Budget: ($240,000)
See also entry under Engineering.

PA —ROCKWELL INTERNATIONAL, General Industries Operations, Technical Information Center, 400 N Lexington Ave, Pittsburgh, 15208. Kathleen H Witkowski, Library Coordr
Holdings: Vols Cat Microforms Mss Documents Periodicals VF
Budget: ($5100)

ELECTRICAL ENGINEERING (cont.)

PA —PENNSYLVANIA STATE UNIVERSITY, Engineering Library, 325 Hammond St, University Park, 16802. Tom Conkling, Librn
Holdings: Vols (60,000) Microforms
Notes: This collection includes substantial microform holdings and extensive runs of periodicals.

†SD —SOUTH DAKOTA SCHOOL OF MINES & TECHNOLOGY, Devereaux Library, Rapid City, 57701.
Holdings: Vols (166,200) Cat Maps Audiotapes Filmstrips Microforms
Budget: ($70,000)
Notes: Supportive collection incl an almost complete set of US Geological Survey materials (incl early Territorial Surveys); a microfilm copy (complete set) of the US Bureau of Mines "Mine Map Depository (Denver)" material; periodicals and technical reports NASA, ACRL, JPL, etc in engineering and geology; extensive government document materials (NBS, Bureau of Mines, etc).

TN —TENNESSEE VALLEY AUTHORITY (TVA), Technical Library, 400 W Summit Hill Dr, E2 B7, Knoxville, 37902. Jesse C Mills, Chief Librn
Holdings: Vols (106,900) Cat Mss Maps Pix Audiotapes Microforms
Budget: ($2,025,000)
Notes: The Technical Library Headquarters Staff (order, cataloging, information, and administration) is located in Knoxville, Tenn. In addition there are branch libraries in Knoxville, Norris, and Chattanooga, Tennessee, and Muscle Shoals, Alabama.

TX —UNIVERSITY OF TEXAS LIBRARIES, Richard W McKinney Engineering Library, 1.3 ECJ, Austin, 78712. Susan B Ardis, Librn
Holdings: Vols (83,548) Cat Microforms

TX —RICE UNIVERSITY, Fondren Library, 6100 S Main St, PO Box 1892, Houston, 77251. Dr Samuel M Carrington, Jr, University Librn
Holdings: Vols 3611 Cat
Budget: $23,000
Notes: Each serial title counted once.

VT —VERMONT TECHNICAL COLLEGE, Hartness Library, Randolph Center, 05061. Dewey Patterson, Library Dir
Holdings: Vols (40,000) Cat
Budget: ($15,000)

VA —ENSCO, INC, Technical Library, 5400 Port Royal Rd, Springfield, 22151. Sue E Littlepage, Research Librn
Holdings: Vols (2000) Uncat Mss Maps Slides
Notes: Especially railroad technology and seismology.

WI —MILWAUKEE SCHOOL OF ENGINEERING, Library, 500 E Kilbourn Ave, PO Box 644, Milwaukee, 53201. Mary Ann Schmidt, Head Librn
Holdings: Vols (34,500) Cat
Budget: ($215,800)

AB —SOUTHERN ALBERTA INSTITUTE OF TECHNOLOGY, Learning Resources Centre, 1301 16 Ave NW, Calgary, T2M 0L4, Can. Tom Skinner, Historian
Holdings: Vols (26,000) Cat Maps Pix Slides Films Videotapes Microforms
Budget: ($50,000)
Notes: Wide range of current technical information about electronics and engineering (mechanical, electrical, chemical); emphasis on vocational-technical material. Incl (50,000) slides, (300) videotapes, and (500) films.

MB —UNIVERSITY OF MANITOBA, Engineering Library, Winnipeg, R3T 2N2, Can. Y Cho, Head
Holdings: Vols (28,000) Cat Videotapes Microforms
Notes: The Engineering Library serves four academic departments: Agricultural, Civil, Electrical and Mechanical Engineering.

ON —METROPOLITAN TORONTO LIBRARY, Science & Technology Dept, 789 Yonge St, Toronto, M4W 2G8, Can. Margaret Walshe, Head
Holdings: Vols (120,000) Cat
Notes: All aspects of technology for the specialist, the student, and the general public. The department gives high priority to Canadian material.

ELECTRICAL ENGINEERING—HISTORY

MA —LASER HISTORY PROJECT, 25 Stoddard St, Woburn, 01801. Joan Lisa Bromberg, Dir
Notes: Four professional societies--the American Physical Society, The Laser Institute of America, The Optical Society of America and the Quantum Electronics and Applications Society have joined with the American Institute of Physics' Center for the History of Physics and the Institute of Electrical and Electronics Engineers' Center for the History of Electrical Engineering to initiate a project on the history of lasers. The project's central activities will be the taking of oral histories, the locating of papers, photographs, tapes, and equipment of historical significance.

NY —IEEE CENTER FOR THE HISTORY OF ELECTRICAL ENGINEERING, IEEE, 345 E 47 St, New York, 10017. Robert Friedel, Dir; Robert Casey, Asst Historian; Joyce Bedi, Photographic Cur
Holdings: Vols 350 Pix Audiotapes Microforms
Notes: Books, archives, documents, photographs. Incl 100 linear ft of documents, 2000 photographs, microfilms, audiotapes.

ELECTRICAL TECHNOLOGY see Electricity, Applied

ELECTRICAL WORKERS UNION see United Electrical, Radio, and Machine Workers

ELECTRICITY

CT —BURNDY LIBRARY, Electra Square, Norwalk, 06856. Philip J Weimerskirch, Asst Dir
Notes: Small collections of electrostatic generators, lightbulbs and electrical apparatus. No primary sources printed after 1900, with a few exceptions. 200 vols from library of Alexandro Volta.

DE —HAGLEY MUSEUM AND LIBRARY, Eleutherian Mills-Hagley Foundation Inc, PO Box 3630, Greenville, 19807. Richmond D Williams, Dir; Heddy A Richter, Imprints Librn
Notes: Records of Pennsylvania Power & Light Company (1853-1955; 1000 cubic feet). The archive consists of the records of 1050 predecessor companies that merged over a 75-year period (1880-1955) to form the present-day PP&L. The collection describes the industry's tentative beginnings using the Edison system of direct current, the technological innovations which allowed small, innercity utilities to expand beyond their original urban centers, and the consolidation movement that culminated with the formation of a great regional power network. Also, records of Delmarva Power Company (1890-1965; 60 cubic feet).

DC —EDISON ELECTRIC INSTITUTE, Library-8th Floor, 1111 19th St NW, Washington, 20036. Ethel Tiberg, Mgr, Library Services
Holdings: Vols (13,321) Cat Maps Pix Microforms

DC —SMITHSONIAN INSTITUTION LIBRARIES, National Museum of American History Branch, Washington, 20560. Rhoda S Ratner, Branch Librn
Holdings: Vols (1800) Cat Maps Pix

MA —MASSACHUSETTS INSTITUTE OF TECHNOLOGY, Institute Archives, Special Collections, Cambridge, 02139.
Notes: Vail collection incl many early works on telecommunications, electricity, ballooning, aeronautics, and animal magnetism.

MI —GOGEBIC COMMUNITY COLLEGE, Alex D Chisholm Learning Resources Center, Greenbush & Jackson Rd, Ironwood, 49938. Charles Tetzlaff, Dir of Learning Resources
Holdings: Vols (20,000)

MN —BAKKEN LIBRARY OF ELECTRICITY IN LIFE, 3537 Zenith Ave S, Minneapolis, 55416. John Edward Senior, Dir
Notes: Books (including periodicals, manuscripts, and archival materials) and instrument collection. 1500 instruments (focus-18th and 19th centuries). Relating to the history of electricity.

NH —NEW HAMPSHIRE VOCATIONAL-TECHNICAL COLLEGE, Library, Prescott Hill, Laconia, 03246. Patty Miller, Librn
Holdings: Vols 475 Cat Phonorecords Audiotapes Filmstrips Microforms
Budget: $505
Notes: Incl overhead transparencies.

NY —CONSOLIDATED EDISON CO OF NEW YORK, Technical Library, 4 Irving Place, Rm 1650-S, New York, 10003. Steven Jaffe, Librn
Holdings: Vols 35,000
Budget: $423,000
Notes: Have computer access to Electric Power Research Institute database, and various other online databases.

NY —ENGINEERING SOCIETIES LIBRARY, 345 E 47 St, New York, 10017. S Kirk Cabeen, Dir
Holdings: Vols 250,000 Cat Maps 16mm Films Microforms
Notes: One of the largest, most comprehensive engineering libraries in the world. Covers all engineering disciplines; particularly strong in electrical and electronic, mechanical, mining and metallurgical, petroleum, chemical, industrial, air conditioning and refrigeration engineering. Incl Wheeler Collection of early materials on magnetism and electricity. 125, 000 bound periodical volumes; 10,000 maps; 5000 serial subscriptions (many foreign-language). Virtually all materials abstracted in *Engineering Index* (1884-date) are incl in Library. Noncirculating, except to members of professional engineering societies which support the Library. See *Engineering Societies Library, New York, Classed Subject Catalog and Index* (Boston: G K Hall, 1963); and *Supplements*, 1-10, 1964-1973.

PA —AMERICAN PHILOSOPHICAL SOCIETY, Library, 105 S Fifth St, Philadelphia, 19106. Edward C Carter II, Librn
Holdings: Vols Cat Mss
Notes: Mainly history of electricity.

SC —CLEMSON UNIVERSITY, Libraries, Clemson, 29631. Michael F Kohl, Head of Special Collections
Holdings: / / Uncat Mss
Notes: Electricity, theoretical and applied to motors. Collected by Bernard A Behrend, 1875-1932, inventor of machinery and large electrical units. 29 cubic ft of material, in English, German, and French, dating primarily from 1886-1932. The mss portion of this collection consists of numerous notebooks containing records of Mr Behrend's work and some scattered correspondence. Also incl pamphlets. Cited in *Manuscripts in US Depositories Relating to the History of Electrical Science and* Technology (Div of Electricity and Nuclear Energy, Smithsonian Institution, Washington, DC, 1973).

SC —SUMTER TECHNICAL COLLEGE, Library, 506 Guignard Dr, Sumter, 29150. Fanny M Davis
Holdings: Vols (20,000) Cat Mss Maps Pix Slides Microforms
Budget: ($500,000)
Notes: Incl 85 books on electricity.

ELECTRICITY—APPARATUS AND APPLIANCES see Electric Apparatus and Appliances

ELECTRICITY—DISTRIBUTION see Electric Power

ELECTRICITY—HISTORY

CT —BURNDY LIBRARY, Electra Square, Norwalk, 06856. Philip J Weimerskirch, Asst Dir
Holdings: Vols 10,000
Notes: Small collections of electrostatic

ELECTRICITY—HISTORY (cont.)

generators, lightbulbs and electrical apparatus. No primary sources printed after 1900, with a few exceptions. 200 vols from library of Alexandro Volta.

DE —HAGLEY MUSEUM AND LIBRARY, Eleutherian Mills-Hagley Foundation Inc, PO Box 3630, Greenville, 19807. Richmond D Williams, Dir; Heddy A Richter, Imprints Librn
Notes: Records of Pennsylvania Power & Light Company (1853-1955; 1000 cubic feet). The archive consists of the records of 1050 predecessor companies that merged over a 75-year period (1880-1955) to form the present-day PP&L. The collection describes the industry's tentative beginnings using the Edison system of direct current, the technological innovations which allowed small, innercity utilities to expand beyond their original urban centers, and the consolidation movement that culminated with the formation of a great regional power network. Also, records of Delmarva Power Company (1890-1965; 60 cubic feet).

DC —SMITHSONIAN INSTITUTION LIBRARIES, National Museum of American History Branch, Washington, 20560. Rhoda S Ratner, Branch Librn
Holdings: Vols (1800) Cat Mss Maps Pix

MD —US NAVAL ACADEMY, Nimitz Library, Annapolis, 21402. Alice S Creighton, Assistant Librn for Special Collections
Holdings: Vols (1150) Cat
Notes: Park Benjamin Collection incl works published 1488 to 1905.

MN —BAKKEN LIBRARY OF ELECTRICITY IN LIFE, 3537 Zenith Ave S, Minneapolis, 55416. John Edward Senior, Dir

NY —IEEE CENTER FOR THE HISTORY OF ELECTRICAL ENGINEERING, IEEE, 345 E 47 St, New York, 10017. Robert Friedel, Dir; Robert Casey, Asst Historian; Joyce Bedi, Photographic Cur
Holdings: Vols 300 Pix Audiotapes Microforms
Notes: Books, archives, documents, photographs. Incl 100 linear ft of documents, 2000 photographs, microfilms, audiotapes.

ELECTRICITY—TRANSMISSION see Electric Power; Electrical Engineering

ELECTRICITY, APPLIED

CA —GTE COMMUNICATIONS PRODUCT CORP, Sylvania Systems Group, Western Division Library, MC-2201, PO Box 7188, Mountain View, 94039. J B Fierro, Supervisor Library Services
Holdings: Vols (10,000) Cat
Notes: Interlibrary loan.

DE —HAGLEY MUSEUM AND LIBRARY, Eleutherian Mills-Hagley Foundation Inc, PO Box 3630, Greenville, 19807. Richmond D Williams, Dir; Heddy A Richter, Imprints Librn
Notes: Records of Pennsylvania Power & Light Company (1853-1955; 1000 cubic feet). The archive consists of the records of 1050 predecessor companies that merged over a 75-year period (1880-1955) to form the present-day PP&L. The collection describes the industry's tentative beginnings using the Edison system of direct current, the technological innovations which allowed small, innercity utilities to expand beyond their original urban centers, and the consolidation movement that culminated with the formation of a great regional power network. Also, records of Delmarva Power Company (1890-1965; 60 cubic feet).

NY —QUEENSBOROUGH COMMUNITY COLLEGE, Library, Springfield Blvd & L I Expressway, Bayside, 11364. Carol Singer, Chief Librn
Holdings: Cat
Notes: Films (nearly 300) on electrical and mechanical techology. Incl 16mm films.

SC —CLEMSON UNIVERSITY, Libraries, Clemson, 29631. Michael F Kohl, Head of Special Collections
Holdings: / / Cat Mss
Notes: Electricity, theoretical and applied to motors. Collected by Bernard A Behrend, 1875-1932, inventor of machinery and large electrical units. About 1000 items, in English, German, and French, published from 1886 to 1932. Complete card index by author and subject. The ms portion of this collection consists of numerous notebooks containing records of Mr Behrend's work upon which, no doubt, he based his publications. 19 titles, written or edited by Mr Behrend, are cataloged. Also incl pamphlets and reprints. Cited in *Manuscripts in US Depositories Relating to the History of Electrical Science and Technology* (Div of Electricty and Nuclear Energy, Smithsonian Institution, Washington, DC, 1973).

SC —HORRY GEORGETOWN TECHNICAL COLLEGE, Library, Hwy 501, Box 1966, Conway, 29526. Barbara Brittain, Librn
Holdings: Vols (20,000) Cat Maps Slides Microforms

ELECTRICITY IN MEDICINE

MN —BAKKEN LIBRARY OF ELECTRICITY IN LIFE, 3537 Zenith Ave S, Minneapolis, 55416. John Edward Senior, Dir
Notes: Books (including periodicals, manuscripts, and archival materials) and instrument collection. 1500 instruments (focus-18th and 19th centuries). Relating to the history of medical electricity.

ELECTRIFICATION, RURAL see Rural Electrification

ELECTROCERAMICS

NY —NEW YORK STATE COLLEGE OF CERAMICS AT ALFRED UNIVERSITY, Scholes Library, Harder Hall, Alfred, 14802. Bruce E Connolly, Library Dir
Holdings: Vols (70,000) Cat Mss Slides Microforms
Budget: ($134,000)
Notes: Very specialized collection incl all phases of the arts and sciences related to ceramics. Incl 1112 subscriptions.

ELECTROCHEMISTRY

CA —BECKMAN INSTRUMENTS, Research Library, 2500 Harbor Blvd, Fullerton, 92634. Jean R Miller, Librn
Holdings: Vols (7000) Cat Slides Audiotapes Videotapes Microforms
Budget: ($9000)
Notes: Strong collections in scientific and analytic instrumentation, electrochemistry, analytical chemistry, optics and spectroscopy, chromatography, clinical chemistry and biochemistry.

IL —ARGONNE NATIONAL LABORATORY, Chemical Engineering Branch Library, 9700 S Cass Ave, Argonne, 60439. John P Frazier III, Librn
Notes: Incl 9000 vols monographs, 115 current journals, substantial collection of scientific and technical reports. Materials may be used by the public in the library by prior arrangement. Photocopies may be supplied for interlibrary loan, for which a processing and handling charge is made.

OH —SDS BIOTECH CORP, PO Box 348, Painesville, 44077. Violet Forgach, Business Librn
Holdings: Cat Pix Microforms

OH —UNION CARBIDE CORP, Battery Products Div, 25225 Detroit Rd, Westlake, 44145. C M Langkau, Librn
Holdings: Vols 8000 Cat Microforms

PA —FRANKLIN INSTITUTE LIBRARY, 20 & The Parkway, Philadelphia, 19103. Miriam Padusis, Dir; Charles Wilt, Readers Servs Librn
Holdings: Vols (300,000) Cat Maps Pix Microforms

WA —TACOMA PUBLIC LIBRARY, 1102 Tacoma Ave S, Tacoma, 98402. Kevin Hegarty, Dir

WI —RAY-O-VAC CORP, H J Mason Library, 630 Forward Dr, Madison, 53711. Carrol Saxe, Librn
Holdings: Vols (500) Cat Microforms
Budget: ($50,000)
Notes: Incl 6500 documents.

ON —DURACELL INC, Research Library, 2333 N Sheridan Way, Sheridan Park, L5K 1A7, Can. Gail Robertson
Holdings: Vols 1500 Cat
Notes: Electrochemistry, as applied to dry batteries.

ELECTROGRAPHY see Kirlian Photography

ELECTROMAGNETIC WAVES see Microwaves

ELECTROMAGNETISM

CA —UNIVERSITY OF CALIFORNIA, BERKELEY, Bancroft Library, Manuscripts Division, Berkeley, 94720. James D Hart, Dir
Holdings: Mss
Notes: Papers of Samuel Silver, specialist on applied electomagnetic, microwave, and radio astronomical problems. Much on the International Union of Radio Science. 48 linear ft.

MA —MASSACHUSETTS INSTITUTE OF TECHNOLOGY, Research Laboratory of Electronics, Document Room 36-412, Cambridge, 02139. J E Woore, Head
Holdings: Vols (15,000)
Notes: Incl World War II technical reports on radar. Current electromagnetism and electronic engineering, radar, etc.

ELECTROMECHANICAL DEVICES

NC —TECHNICAL INSTITUTE OF ALAMANCE, Learning Resources Center, Jimmy Kerr Rd, PO Box 623, Haw River, 27258. Ron Plummer, Coordr
Holdings: Vols (390) Cat Pix Microforms

ELECTROMETALLURGY

WA —TACOMA PUBLIC LIBRARY, 1102 Tacoma Ave S, Tacoma, 98402. Kevin Hegarty, Dir

ELECTRON MICROSCOPE AND MICROSCOPY

†DC —CATHOLIC UNIVERSITY OFF AMERICA, Nursing & Biology Library, Washington, 20064. N L Powell, Head
Holdings: Vols (17,000) Cat Microforms

IN —INDIANA UNIVERSITY, School of Dentistry, Library, 1121 W Michigan St, Indianapolis, 46202. Marie Sparks, Librn
Holdings: Vols (50,000) Cat Mss Slides Audiotapes Films Microforms
Budget: ($41,790)
Notes: Juvenile dentistry, scanning electron microscopy, pediatrics and basic sciences.

ELECTRON OPTICS

CA —INTERNATIONAL BUSINESS MACHINES RESEARCH LIBRARY, 5600 Cottle Rd, San Jose, 95193. Phil Grincewich, Mgr Technical Information
Holdings: Vols (13,500) Cat
Notes: Principally electronic computer storage system architecture. Incl 21,000 vols of 770 journals. On-line search facility. Vols are divided into three libraries, Technical Research, Technical Information, and Programing. Not open to public.

ELECTRONIC BRAINS see Computers

ELECTRONIC CALCULATING MACHINES see Computers

ELECTRONIC CIRCUITS

KY —UNIVERSITY OF KENTUCKY, Robert E Shaver Library of Engineering, 355 Anderson Hall, Lexington, 40506. Russell H Powell, Engineering Librn
Holdings: Vols (48,000) Cat Microforms

ELECTRONIC COMMUNICATION see Telecommunications

ELECTRONIC COMPUTER PROGRAMMING see Programming Languages (Electronic Computers)

ELECTRONIC COMPUTERS see Computers

ELECTRONIC DATA PROCESSING

CA —BURROUGHS CORP, Library, 460 Sierra Madre Villa, Pasadena, 91107. Jean

ELECTRONIC DATA PROCESSING (cont.)

Robbins, Librn
Holdings: Vols 12,000 Cat
Notes: Computer theory and technology.

CA —INTERNATIONAL BUSINESS MACHINES RESEARCH LIBRARY, 5600 Cottle Rd, San Jose, 95193. Phil Grincewich, Mgr Technical Information
Holdings: Vols (13,500) Cat
Notes: Principally electronic computer storage system architecture. Incl 21,000 vols of 770 journals. On-line search facility. Vols are divided into three libraries, Technical Research, Technical Information, and Programing. Not open to public.

CT —AETNA LIFE & CASUALTY, Corporate Data Processing Library, 151 Farmington Ave, Hartford, 06156. Kathryn Porter, Chief Librn
Holdings: Vols 500

DC —US BUREAU OF THE CENSUS, Library, Federal Office Bldg 3, Rm 2451, Washington, 20233. Betty Baxtresser, Chief, ASD Library Branch
Holdings: Vols (200,863) Cat Microforms
Notes: Emphases on statistics of agriculture, business, construction, economics, foreign trade, governments, housing, industry, population, transportation, statistical methodology, and data processing. Library holdings are largely current materials covering the Bureau's programs. Outdated materials are withdrawn regularly.

DC —US NAVAL OBSERVATORY LIBRARY, 30th & Massachusetts Ave, NW, Washington, 20016. Brenda G Corbin, Librn
Holdings: Vols (75,000) Cat Mss Maps Pix Slides Microforms
Notes: Incl 1000 journals, with monograph and serial publications in the fields of celestial mechanics, fundamental astronomy, time determination, photographic astrometry and astrophysics, data processing, mathematics.

FL —AMERICAN EXPRESS CO, Systems & Data Processing Library, Headway Office Building E, 4780 N State Rd, Fort Lauderdale, 33319. Sheila Goren, Librn
Holdings: Vols 300 Cat Microforms
Notes: Collection incl IBM hardware and software manuals, internal system documentation, manuals and catalogs from various vendors, books and periodicals, American Express Co internal procedure documents and manuals. Indexed in our card catalog. Library is restricted to American Express S&DP personnel.

NH —NEW HAMPSHIRE TECHNICAL INSTITUTE, Paul E Farnum Library, 5 Fan Rd, Concord, 03301. Wm John Hare, Librn
Holdings: Vols 975 Cat Microforms
Budget: $800

NY —NEW YORK PUBLIC LIBRARY, Research Libraries, Science and Technology Research Center, Fifth Ave & 42 St, New York, 10018.
Holdings: Vols (1,100,000) Cat Microforms
Budget: ($647,259)

PA —FRANKLIN INSTITUTE LIBRARY, 20 & The Parkway, Philadelphia, 19103. Miriam Padusis, Dir; Charles Wilt, Readers Servs Librn
Holdings: Vols (300,000) Cat Maps Pix Microforms

SC —HORRY GEORGETOWN TECHNICAL COLLEGE, Library, Hwy 501, Box 1966, Conway, 29526. Barbara Brittain, Librn
Holdings: Vols (20,000) Cat Maps Slides Microforms

ON —CANADA, DEPT OF EMPLOYMENT & IMMIGRATION LIBRARY, Ottawa, K1A 0J9, Can. P E Sunder-Raj, Dir Library Services
Holdings: Vols (15,000) // Cat

ON —INSTITUTE OF CHARTERED ACCOUNTANTS OF ONTARIO, The Merrilees Library, 69 Bloor St E, Toronto, M4W 1B3, Can. Theresa Wolak, Librn
Holdings: Vols 153 Cat

ELECTRONIC DIGITAL COMPUTERS—MEMORY SYSTEMS see Computer Storage Devices

ELECTRONIC ENGINEERING

†CA —XEROX CORP, Technical Library, 701 S Aviation Blvd, A3-25, El Segundo, 90245. Marilyn Durkin, Librn
Holdings: Vols 5000 Cat Microforms
Notes: 450 Journal titles.

CA —UNIVERSITY OF CALIFORNIA, LOS ANGELES, Engineering & Mathematical Sciences Library, 405 Hilgard, Los Angeles, 90024. Rosalee I Wright, Librn
Holdings: Vols (180,000) Cat Microforms
See also entry under Engineering

CA —HUGHES AIRCRAFT CO, Solid State Products Library, 500 Superior Ave, Newport Beach, 92663. Barbara Squyres, Librn
Holdings: Vols (5310) Cat Microforms

CA —CALIFORNIA STATE POLYTECHNIC UNIVERSITY, POMONA, University Library, 3801 W Temple Ave, Pomona, 91768. Harold Schleiser, Actg Dir
Notes: General reference materials on aerospace, chemical, civil, electrical, electronics, industrial, mechanical and manufacturing engineering.

CA —COGSWELL COLLEGE, Library, 600 Stockton St, San Francisco, 94108. Judith Carson-Croes, Dir
Holdings: Vols (12,000) Cat

CA —HEALD COLLEGE TECHNICAL DIVISION, Learning Resource Center Library, 150 4th Street, San Francisco, 94103. Tom Casas, Dir
Holdings: Vols (1000) Cat
Budget: $680

MA —UNIVERSITY OF MASSACHUSETTS AT AMHERST, Physical Sciences Library, Amherst, 01003. Siegfried Feller, Assoc Dir for Collection Development
Holdings: Vols Cat Microforms
Notes: Computer science and technology.

MA —MITRE CORPORATION, Bedford Library, PO Box 208, Bedford, 01730. Betsy Cogliano, Supvr
Holdings: Vols (65,000) Cat Audiotapes Microforms
Notes: Collection incl 127,000 documents.

MA —MASSACHUSETTS INSTITUTE OF TECHNOLOGY, Research Laboratory of Electronics, Document Room 36-412, Cambridge, 02139. J E Woore, Head
Holdings: Vols (15,000)
Notes: Incl World War II technical reports on radar. Current electromagnetism and electronic engineering radar, etc.

MN —CONTROL DATA CORP, Corporate Library, 8100-34th Ave So, Box O, HQW O6Z, Minneapolis, 55440. Gloria T Andrew, Mgr

NH —NEW HAMPSHIRE TECHNICAL INSTITUTE, Paul E Farnum Library, 5 Fan Rd, Concord, 03301. Wm John Hare, Librn
Holdings: Vols 2500
Budget: $2000
Notes: Incl electronic engineering technology.

NY —ENGINEERING SOCIETIES LIBRARY, 345 E 47 St, New York, 10017. S Kirk Cabeen, Dir
Holdings: Vols 250,000 Cat Maps 16mm Films Microforms
Notes: One of the largest, most comprehensive engineering libraries in the world. Covers all engineering disciplines; particularly strong in electrical and electronic, mechanical, mining and metallurgical, petroleum, chemical, industrial, air conditioning and refrigeration engineering. Incl Wheeler Collection of early materials on magnetism and electricity. 125, 000 bound periodical volumes; 10,000 maps; 5000 serial subscriptions (many foreign-language). Virtually all materials abstracted in *Engineering Index* (1884-date) are incl in Library. Noncirculating, except to members of professional engineering societies which support the Library. See *Engineering Societies Library, New York, Classed Subject Catalog and Index* (Boston: G K Hall, 1963); and *Supplements*, 1-10, 1964-1973.

NY —XEROX CORP, Technical Information Center, PO Box 305, Webster, 14580. Michael D Majcher, Mgr
Holdings: Vols (30,000) Cat Microforms

NC —TECHNICAL INSTITUTE OF ALAMANCE, Learning Resources Center, Jimmy Kerr Rd, PO Box 623, Haw River, 27258. Ron Plummer, Coordr
Holdings: Vols (390) Cat Pix Microforms

OH —PUBLIC LIBRARY OF CINCINNATI & HAMILTON COUNTY, Science & Technology Dept, 800 Vine St, Cincinnati, 45202. Rosemary Gaiser, Head
Holdings: Vols (250,000) Cat
Notes: Pure and applied science. Incl over 1600 periodicals and serial titles and more than 100 abstracting and indexing services in major fields of science and technology.

VT —VERMONT TECHNICAL COLLEGE, Hartness Library, Randolph Center, 05061. Dewey Patterson, Library Dir
Holdings: Vols 5300 Cat
Budget: ($15,000)

ELECTRONIC INDUSTRIES

CA —UNIVERSITY OF CALIFORNIA, BERKELEY, Bancroft Library, Manuscripts Division, Berkeley, 94720. James D Hart, Dir
Holdings: Cat Mss Maps Pix Slides Microforms
Notes: Mss consisting primarily of scientists' private papers, constitute the most significant part of the collection. Major emphasis is on the growth of the electronics industry located in the Palo Alto area, in the vicinity of Stanford University. A series of oral histories complements these holdings.

TX —GENERAL DYNAMICS/FORT WORTH DIV, Technical Library & Information Services, PO Box 748, Mail Zone 2246, Fort Worth, 76101. P Rogers de Tonnancour, Dir
Holdings: Vols 36,000 Cat Maps Slides Microforms Technical Documents
Budget: $100,000
Notes: Incl 500,000 microforms. Catalogs for books and documents are separate. Collection is strong in mathematics, nuclear physics, materials and aerodynamics. Emphasis on the mission of the division--the development and production of manned aircraft. Division also involved in electronic manufacturing (avionic components), so collection strength in this area is growing very rapidly.

ELECTRONIC INSTRUMENTS

TX —GENERAL DYNAMICS/FORT WORTH DIV, Technical Library & Information Services, PO Box 748, Mail Zone 2246, Fort Worth, 76101. P Rogers de Tonnancour, Dir
Holdings: Vols 36,000 Cat Maps Slides Microforms Technical Documents
Budget: $100,000
Notes: Incl 500,000 microforms. Catalogs for books and documents are separate. Collection is strong in mathematics, nuclear physics, materials and aerodynamics. Emphasis on the mission of the division--the development and production of manned aircraft. Division also involved in electronic manufacturing (avionic components), so collection strength in this area is growing very rapidly.

ELECTRONIC MUSIC

CA —CALIFORNIA STATE UNIVERSITY, HAYWARD, Library, Hayward, 94542. Melissa Rose, Dir
Holdings: Vols (15,896) Cat Phonorecords
Budget: ($21,000)
Notes: The score collection covers the entire range of instrumental and vocal concert music, incl collected works of various composers, and representative collections of hymnals, folk music, music comedy, and some popular music. Sound recordings range from ethnomusicological collections to electronic music. Emphasis is on concert music, but there is a large collection of jazz and a selective collection of popular music. Separate catalog.

CA —CALIFORNIA INSTITUTE OF THE ARTS, Library, 24700 McBean Pkwy, Valencia, 91355. James Elrod, Dir
Holdings: Vols (61,000) Cat Phonorecords Audiotapes
Budget: ($8500)
Notes: Incl 11,656 audiotapes. Cataloged.

IL —ROOSEVELT UNIVERSITY, Murray-Green Library, 430 S Michigan Ave,

ELECTRONIC MUSIC (cont.)

Chicago, 60605. Donald Draganski, Music Librn
Holdings: Vols (28,000) Uncat Mss Pix Microforms
Notes: Subscribe to over 92 music periodicals; record collection of more than 10,000 albums; 8000 pieces of sheet music; pamphlet file; music theses on microfilm; complete file of music publishers catalogs; scores; tapes of old 78 recordings; music education; and electronic music.

ELECTRONIC NAVIGATION see Electronics in Navigation

ELECTRONIC OPTICS see Electron Optics

ELECTRONICS

AR —UNIVERSITY OF ARKANSAS, Technology Campus Library, 1201 McAlmont St, PO Box 3017, Little Rock, 72203. Brent Nelson, Librn
Holdings: Vols (20,849) Cat Slides Microforms
Budget: ($35,000)

CA —HUGHES AIRCRAFT CO, Ground Systems Group, Technical Library, Bldg 600, MS C222, PO Box 3310, Fullerton, 92634. Don H Matsumiya, Chief Librn
Holdings: Vols (9000) Cat Maps Microforms
Notes: Primarily technical reports, many in microform. Incl 285 maps and 43,000 microforms. Visitors should be referred by their local public or academic libraries and give advance notice of their intentions to visit.

CA —ELECTRONICS MUSEUM, Foothill College, DeForest Memorial Archives, 12345 El Monte Rd, Los Altos Hills, 94022. Leonard M Lansdowne, Cur
Holdings: Vols 342 Cat Mss Pix Microforms
Notes: The collection was donated by Marie De Forest, wife of the late Dr Lee De Forest, known as the "Father of Radio." Awards of Dr Lee De Forest, presented to him through the years, are in the collection. The De Forest mss and papers are cataloged and microfilmed. Several file cabinets filled with correspondence, dealing with business and personal matters are to be cataloged and microfilmed in the future.

CA —LOS ANGELES PUBLIC LIBRARY, Science & Technology Dept, 630 W Fifth St, Los Angeles, 90071. Billie M Connor, Dept Head
Holdings: Vols (12,000) Cat
Notes: Materials on the application of electronic devices, circuits and systems in various fields such as computers, automatic control, sound productions and reproduction, radio and telecommunications. Extensive holdings of materials on computers, peripherals, and software including many texts pertaining to specific programming languages. Complete collection of Howard Sams schematics for radio television, and other electronic equipment repair as well as historical sets of Rider's Radio and Television schematics.

CA —UNIVERSITY OF CALIFORNIA, LOS ANGELES, Engineering & Mathematical Sciences Library, 405 Hilgard, Los Angeles, 90024. Rosalee I Wright, Librn
Holdings: Vols (180,000) Cat Microforms
Notes: IEEE journals, conference proceedings, standards, and miscellaneous publications (comprehensive).
See also entry under Engineering.

CA —GTE COMMUNICATIONS PRODUCT CORP, Sylvania Systems Group, Western Division Library, MC-2201, PO Box 7188, Mountain View, 94039. J B Fierro, Supervisor Library Services
Holdings: Vols (10,000) Cat
Notes: Interlibrary loan.

CA —HUGHES AIRCRAFT CO, Solid State Products Library, 500 Superior Ave, Newport Beach, 92663. Barbara Squyres, Librn
Holdings: Vols (5310) Cat Microforms

CA —CONTRA COSTA COUNTY LIBRARY, 1750 Oak Park Blvd, Pleasant Hill, 94523. Barbara Potter, Librn
Holdings: Vols (18,000)

CA —CALIFORNIA DEPT OF TRANSPORTATION, Transportation Library, 5900 Folsom Blvd, PO Box 19128, Sacramento, 95819. Eva Caro, Librn
Holdings: Vols (10,000) Cat Mss Maps Pix Slides Phonorecords Audiotapes Videotapes 16mm Films Filmstrips Microforms

CA —CUBIC CORP, Technical Library, 9333 Balboa Ave, PO Box 85587, San Diego, 92138. Maxine Moser, Mgr Tech Librn; Ann Viera, Librn
Holdings: Vols (2500) Cat Maps Microforms
Budget: ($60,000)
Notes: Incl about 20,000 microforms and 1000 bound periodicals, technical reports, technical memoranda. On-line search service for employees, including DIALOG, BRS, SDC, DTIC/DROLS, NASA/RECON, RLIN, DMS.

CA —SAN DIEGO PUBLIC LIBRARY, Science & Industry Section, 820 E St, San Diego, 92101. Joanne Anderson, Senior Librn
Budget: ($33,000)
Notes: Incl complete collection of riders manuals and SAMS photofacts.

CA —UNITED AIRLINES, Engineering Dept, Library, San Francisco International Airport, San Francisco, 94128. J J Whitney, Technical Librn
Holdings: Vols 1000 Cat
Budget: $4000

CA —ESL, SUBSIDIARY OF TRW, Research Library, 495 Java Dr, PO Box 3510, Sunnyvale, 94086. Verna Van Valzer, Head Librn
Holdings: Vols 500 Cat
Budget: $7000
Notes: Electronic Communication Systems.

CT —ROGERS CORP, Lurie Library, One Technology Drive, Rogers, 06263. Myrna D Riquier, Librn; Nini S Davis, Librn
Holdings: Vols (300) Cat
Notes: Emphasis on materials, components and computer science.

ID —EG&G, INEL Technical Library, 1776 Science Center, Idaho Falls, 83401. Brent Jacobsen, Head Librn; Heather Redding, Ref Librn
Holdings: Vols (33,000) Cat Microforms
Notes: Energy research and development included in libraries collection. Incl over 500,000 AEC, ERDA, NRC, and foreign reports. Unclassified materials may be used by the public in the library by appointment or borrowed by interlibrary loan. Incl 12,000 bound documents, 520,000 microfiche, 400 periodical subscriptions.

IL —UNIVERSITY OF ILLINOIS, URBANA/CHAMPAIGN, Library, 1408 W Gregory Drive, Urbana, 61801. Norman B Brown, Asst Dir for Special Collections
Holdings: Cat Mss Pix Tapes
Notes: The papers of Joseph T Tykociner (a pioneer in the field of wireless, electronics, sound movies and zetetics). Incl correspondence, notes, books, articles and reprints, photographs and negatives, biographical materials and sound tapes.

IA —ROCKWELL INTERNATIONAL, Collins Division, Cedar Rapids Information Center, 500 Collins Rd, Cedar Rapids, 52498. Judith A Leavitt, Supvr
Holdings: Vols 10,000 Cat
Notes: Also 8000 technical reports; 10,000 military, Federal, and industrial specifications; 3000 bound periodicals (400 periodical subsriptions). Restricted use: for company use only and interlibrary loan.

MD —CAPITOL INSTITUTE OF TECHNOLOGY, Library, 11301 Springfield Rd, Laurel, 20708. Pat Wissinger, Librn
Holdings: Vols (10,000) Cat Slides Phonorecords Microforms
Notes: Electronics, computers, telecommunications undergraduate academy.

MA —HARVARD UNIVERSITY LIBRARY, Gordon McKay Library, Division of Applied Sciences, Pierce Hall, Oxford St, Cambridge, 02138. Julie Sandall Barlas, Librn
Holdings: Vols (100,000)

MA —RAYTHEON CO, Research Div, Library, 131 Spring St, Lerington, 02193. Martha C Adamson, Head Librn
Holdings: Vols (5000) Cat
Notes: 6000 technical reports, 125 journal subscriptions.

MA —NORTON COMPANY, Library, 1 New Bond St, Worcester, 01606. Joan K Chaffey, Librn
Holdings: Cat
Notes: Abrasive industry collection

MI —GOGEBIC COMMUNITY COLLEGE, Alex D Chisholm Learning Resources Center, Greenbush & Jackson Rd, Ironwood, 49938. Charles Tetzlaff, Dir of Learning Resources
Holdings: Vols (20,000)

NH —NEW HAMPSHIRE VOCATIONAL-TECHNICAL COLLEGE, Library, Prescott Hill, Laconia, 03246. Patty Miller, Librn
Holdings: Vols 500 Cat Audiotapes Filmstrips Microforms
Budget: $525
Notes: Incl overhead transparencies.

NH —NEW HAMPSHIRE VOCATIONAL TECHNICAL COLLEGE, Library, 277 R Portsmouth Ave, Stratham, 03885. Nancy L Dodge, Librn
Budget: ($9500)

NJ —AT&T BELL LABORATORIES, Libraries and Information Systems Center, 600 Mountain Ave, Murray Hill, 07974. W D Penniman, Dir
Holdings: Vols (346,000) Cat Microforms
Notes: Restricted use to AT&T employees.
Catalogs/*Indexes*: Bell Laboratories Library Network and Book Serial Catalogs; Bell Laboratories Translations. Bell Laboratories Library Network with New Jersey libraries located in Holmdel, Murray Hill, Piscataway, Whippany, Princeton, Short Hills, Summit, West Long Branch, Crawford Hill; libraries also in Allentown, Pennsylvania; Reading, Pennsylvania; New York, New York; Atlanta, Georgia; Columbus, Ohio; Naperville, Illinois; Indianapolis, Indiana; North Andover, Massachusetts.

NJ —RCA CORP, David Sarnoff Research Center, Library, PO Box 432, Princeton, 08540. Wendy Chu, Librn
Holdings: (15,000) Cat Microforms

NM —UNIVERSITY OF CALIFORNIA, Los Alamos National Laboratory, Libraries, PO Box 1663, MSP 362, Los Alamos, 87545. J Arthur Freed, Head Librn
Holdings: Vols (800,000) Cat Films Microforms
Budget: ($700,000)
Notes: Incl 500,000 classified and unclassified reports. There are 25 branch libraries and a central collection. The Medical Library contains about 40,000 vols in the areas of biomedical research.

NY —ENGINEERING SOCIETIES LIBRARY, 345 E 47 St, New York, 10017. S Kirk Cabeen, Dir
Holdings: Vols 250,000 Cat Maps 16mm Films Microforms
Notes: One of the largest, most comprehensive engineering libraries in the world. Covers all engineering disciplines; particularly strong in electrical and electronic, mechanical, mining and metallurgical, petroleum, chemical, industrial, air conditioning and refrigeration engineering. Incl Wheeler Collection of early materials on magnetism and electricity. 125, 000 bound volumes; 10,000 maps; 5000 serial subscriptions (many foreign-language). Virtually all materials abstracted in *Engineering Index* (1884-date) are incl in Library. Noncirculating, except to members of professional engineering societies which support the Library. See *Engineering Societies Library, New York, Classed Subject Catalog and Index* (Boston: G K Hall, 1963); and *Supplements*, 1-10, 1964-1973.

NY —NEW YORK PUBLIC LIBRARY, Research Libraries, Science and Technology Research Center, Fifth Ave & 42 St, New York, 10018.
Holdings: Vols (1,100,000) Cat Microforms
Budget: ($647,259)

†NY —TECHNICAL CAREER INSTITUTE LIBRARY, 320 W 31st Street, New York, 10001. Michael Brent, Librn
Holdings: Vols (3500)

NY —HARRIS CORP, Government Support Systems Division, Information Center, 6801 Jericho Tpke, Syosset, 11791. Eleanor

ELECTRONICS (cont.)

Pienitz, Librn
Holdings: Vols (578) Cat Microfiche Mss

NY —GENERAL ELECTRIC COMPANY, Information Resources Center, Electronics Park, Bldg 3, Syracuse, 13221. Connie Webb, Mgr
Holdings: Vols (7000) Cat Microforms
Budget: ($20,000)

OR —TEKTRONIX INC, Wilsonville Library, PO Box 1000, M/S 63-531, Wilsonville, 97005. Linda Appel, Branch Librn
Holdings: Vols 5000 Cat Videotapes
Budget: ($22,300)

PA —FRANKLIN INSTITUTE LIBRARY, 20 & The Parkway, Philadelphia, 19103. Miriam Padusis, Dir; Charles Wilt, Readers Servs Librn
Holdings: Vols (300,000) Cat Maps Pix Microforms

SC —SUMTER TECHNICAL COLLEGE, Library, 506 Guignard Dr, Sumter, 29150. Fanny M Davis
Holdings: Vols (20,000) Cat Mss Maps Pix Slides Microforms
Budget: ($50,000)
Notes: Incl 79 books on electronics.

TX —E-SYSTEMS, GARLAND DIV, Technical Library, PO Box 226118, Dallas, 75226. Charlene Morris, Tech Librn
Holdings: Vols (8500) Cat
Notes: Library not open to public.

TX —TEXAS INSTRUMENTS INC, Library, PO Box 1443, Houston, 77001. Helen Manning, Librn
Holdings: Vols (800) Cat Microforms
Notes: Systems, design, and marketing of microprocessors and electronic semiconductors. Not open to the public.

WA —BOEING COMPANY, Boeing Technical Libraries, PO Box 3707, Seattle, 98124. Corrine Campbell, Mgr Technical Library
Holdings: Vols (75,000) Cat Microforms
Notes: Books are distributed between 3 libraries, Kent, Renton, and Bellevue. Also contains many periodicals and Boeing Documents Library restricted to Boeing Personnel.

WI —MADISON AREA TECHNICAL COLLEGE, Technical Center Library, 2125 Commercial Ave, Madison, 53704. J B Jeffcott, Librn
Holdings: Vols 2000 Cat Slides Phonorecords Audiotapes Videotapes 16mm Films Filmstrips Microforms

AB —SOUTHERN ALBERTA INSTITUTE OF TECHNOLOGY, Learning Resources Centre, 1301 16 Ave NW, Calgary, T2M 0L4, Can. Tom Skinner, Historian
Holdings: Vols (26,000) Cat Maps Pix Slides Films Videotapes Microforms
Budget: ($50,000)
Notes: Wide range of current technical information about electronics and engineering (mechanical, electrical, chemical); emphasis on vocational-technical material. Incl (50,000) slides, (300) videotapes, and (500) films.

ELECTRONICS—HISTORY

MA —LASER HISTORY PROJECT, 25 Stoddard St, Woburn, 01801. Joan Lisa Bromberg, Dir
Notes: Four professional societies--the American Physical Society, The Laser Institute of America, The Optical Society of America and the IEEE Quantum Electronics and Applications Society have joined with the American Institute of Physics' Center for History of Physics and the Institute of Electrical and Electronics Engineers' Center for the History of Electrical Engineering to initiate a project on the history of lasers. The project's central activities will be the taking of oral histories, and the locating of papers, photographs, tapes, and equipment of historical significance.

ELECTRONICS, DIGITAL see Digital Electronics

ELECTRONICS, SOLID STATE see Solid State Electronics

ELECTRONICS IN NAVIGATION

PA —US NAVY, Philadelphia Naval Shipyard Technical Library, Philadelphia Naval Shipyard, Philadelphia, 19112. Alice R Murray, Dir
Notes: Technical manuals and periodicals regarding ships and shipping. Restricted use.

ELECTROPHONIC MUSIC see Electronic Music

ELECTROPHOTOGRAPHY

CA —INTERNATIONAL BUSINESS MACHINES RESEARCH LIBRARY, 5600 Cottle Rd, San Jose, 95193. Phil Grincewich, Mgr Technical Information
Holdings: Vols (13,500) Cat
Notes: Incl 21,000 vols of 770 journals. On-line search facility. Vols are divided into three libraries, Technical Research, Technical Information, and Programing. Not open to public.

NY —XEROX CORP, Technical Information Center, PO Box 305, Webster, 14580. Michael D Majcher, Mgr
Holdings: Vols (30,000) Cat Microforms

ELECTROPHYSIOLOGY

†CT —YALE UNIVERSITY, Medical Library, 333 Cedar St, New Haven, 06520.

ELECTROSTATICS

NY —XEROX CORP, Technical Information Center, PO Box 305, Webster, 14580. Michael D Majcher, Mgr
Holdings: Vols (30,000) Cat Microforms

ELECTROTHERAPEUTICS

MN —BAKKEN LIBRARY OF ELECTRICITY IN LIFE, 3537 Zenith Ave S, Minneapolis, 55416. John Edward Senior, Dir
Notes: Books (including periodicals, manuscripts, and archival materials) and instrument collection. 1500 instruments (focus-18th and 19th centuries). Relating to the history of electricity.

ELECTROTOPOGRAPHY (ETG)

PA —ENSANIAN PHYSICOCHEMICAL INSTITUTE, Electrotopography Library, PO Box 98, Eldred, 16731. Elisabeth Anahid Ensanian, Chief Librn
Holdings: Vols 7 Cat Maps Slides
Budget: ($45,000)
Notes: Electrotopography is a new science (the Institute has pioneered the field and has coined the terms "electrotopograph" and "electrotopography") concerned with the mapping of electrical fields associated with metals, alloys, semiconductors, and living organisms. These fields may be natural and/or induced, and are converted into mappings which exhibit certain systems characteristics for both normal and stress states. In the field of the materials sciences electrotopography permits the mapping of the mechanical properties of metals nondestructively and in the field of diagnostic medicine it permits both the location and quantization of certain types of physical pain without the cooperation of the subject. Three publications are associated with these revolutionary developments and are available at cost:*New Standards in Steel and Metals Technologies; Electrotopographic Sciences & Technology Newsletter;* and *The Journal of Medical Electrotopography.* See extended definition under Artificial Intelligence.

ELEMENTARY PARTICLES (PHYSICS) see Particles (Nuclear Physics)

ELEMENTS, TRACE see Trace Elements

ELEPHANTS

NY —AMERICAN MUSEUM OF NATURAL HISTORY, Library Services Dept, Central Park W & 79th St, New York, 10024. Nina J Root, Chairwoman; Mary Genett, Asst Librn for Reference Services

ELEVATED RAILROADS see Railroads, Elevated

ELGIN, MARY

MA —BOSTON UNIVERSITY, Mugar Memorial Library, Special Collections Dept, 771 Commonwealth Ave, Boston, 02215. Howard B Gotlieb, Dir
Holdings: Cat Mss

ELIOT, CHARLES, 1859-1897

MA —HARVARD UNIVERSITY, Graduate School of Design, Frances Loeb Library, Gund Hall, Cambridge, 02138. James Hodgson, Librn
Holdings: Cat
Notes: Books and papers of a pioneer landscape architect.

ELIOT, D. G.

NY —AMERICAN MUSEUM OF NATURAL HISTORY, Library Services Dept, Central Park W & 79th St, New York, 10024. Nina J Root, Chairwoman; Mary Genett, Asst Librn for Reference Services
Holdings: Cat Mss Maps Pix 16mm Films
Notes: Original artwork for D G Eliot monographs.

ELIOT, GEORGE, 1819-1880

CA —CLAREMONT COLLEGES, Honnold Library, Ninth & Dartmouth, Claremont, 91711. Tania Rizzo, Special Collections Dept Head
Holdings: Vols 50 Cat Mss
Notes: Correspondence to Merle Armitage now in the George E Fullerton collection.

CT —YALE UNIVERSITY, Box 1603A, Yale Station, New Haven, 06520.
Holdings: Cat Mss

CT —YALE UNIVERSITY, Box 1603A, Yale Station, New Haven, 06520.

NJ —PRINCETON UNIVERSITY, Library, Morris L Parrish Collection, Princeton, 08540. Alexander D Wainwright, Cur
Notes: Most of the 150 vols both by and relating to George Eliot (Mary Ann Evans) are cataloged. Also see: Morris L Parrish. *Victorian Lady Novelists* (London, 1933) (Ex)04705.692.

ELIOT, MARTHA MAY, M.D.

MA —RADCLIFFE COLLEGE, Arthur & Elizabeth Schlesinger Library on the History of Women in America, 3 James St, Cambridge, 02138. Patricia Miller King, Dir; Eva Moseley, Cur of Mss
Notes: Incl the audiotapes and transcripts of the Women in the Federal Government Oral History Project, also papers of Clara M Beyer, Martha May Eliot, MD, Elizabeth Holtzman, Jeannette Rankin, Edith Nourse Rogers, and Mary Elizabeth Switzer.

ELIOT, THOMAS STEARNS, 1888-1965

CA —UNIVERSITY OF CALIFORNIA, BERKELEY, Bancroft Library, Manuscripts Division, Berkeley, 94720. James D Hart, Dir
Holdings: Uncat Mss
Notes: Letters from Eliot, in various collections.

CA —UNIVERSITY OF CALIFORNIA, LOS ANGELES, Research Library, Dept of Special Collections, 405 Hilgard Ave, Los Angeles, 90024. Edward Shreeves, Chairman, Bibliographers Group; David S Zeidberg, Head
Holdings: Vols 200 Cat Mss
Notes: 200 first and other editions of his books; 40 letters.

CA —UNIVERSITY OF CALIFORNIA, SANTA CRUZ, University Library, Special Collections, Santa Cruz, 95064. Rita Bottoms, Special Collections Librn; Margaret Felts, South Pacific Collection Bibliographer

CT —YALE UNIVERSITY, Box 1603A, Yale Station, New Haven, 06520.

DC —GEORGETOWN UNIVERSITY, Library, Special Collections Div, 37 & O Sts NW, Washington, 20057. George M Barringer, Special Collections Librn; Nicholas B Sheetz, Mss Librn
Holdings: Mss Pix
Notes: The papers of Christopher Sykes, biographer, journalist, and novelist; containing mss, letters, photographs, and

ELIOT, THOMAS STEARNS, 1888-1965 (cont.)

drawings. With extensive correspondence from Harold Acton; Angela, Countess of Antrim; Sir John Betjeman; Ivy Compton-Burnett; Alick Dru; T S Eliot; Max Beerbohm; Graham Greene; John Hayward; Lord Patrick Kinross; Compton Mackenzie; Nancy Mitford; Anthony Powell; Dame Flora Robson; Cecil Roth; Sir John Russell; Osbert Sitwell; John Sparrow; Freya Stark; James Stern; and Evelyn Waugh, among others. Also, considerable research material about Evelyn Waugh, Adam von Trott, Robert Byron, Lady Nancy Astor; and the foundation of the state of Israel.

IL —NORTHWESTERN UNIVERSITY, Library, Special Collections Dept, 1937 Sheridan Rd, Evanston, 60201. R Russell Maylone, Cur
Holdings: Vols 450 Cat Mss
Notes: Incl 137 letters from T S Eliot to Stephen Spender, and 70 letters from Eliot to John Middleton Murrary.

IN —INDIANA UNIVERSITY, Lilly Library, Seventh St, Bloomington, 47405. William R Cagle, Librn
Holdings: // Cat Mss
Notes: Collections contain T S Eliot correspondence with a number of people, such as Ezra Pound, 1919-1924 and 1945-1953, D G Bridson, 1947-1963, Henry Rago, 1945-1962; Louis Untermeyer, 1924-1950; Orlo Williams, 1924-1931. 100 items. Holdings incl first editions of published works. No photocopying.

MA —HARVARD UNIVERSITY LIBRARY, Houghton Library, Cambridge, 02138. F Thomas Noonan, Cur, Reading Room; Lawrence Dowler, Associate Librn
Holdings: Cat Mss
Notes: See *Harvard Library Bulletin,* VII (1953), 138.

†MA —WILLIAMS COLLEGE, Chapin Library of Rare Books, PO Box 426, Williamstown, 01267. Robert L Volz, Custodian
Holdings: Vols 250 Cat
Notes: The Hugh MacMullen Collection. No ILL.

MO —SAINT LOUIS PUBLIC LIBRARY, Gardner Rare Book Room, 1301 Olive St, Saint Louis, 63103. Julanne M Good, Supervisor; Martha Riley, Rare Books Librn
Holdings: Vols (2300) Cat
Budget: ($5573)
Notes: First editions of authors having some association with William Marion Reedy and *Reedy's Mirror,* such as Sara Teasdale, Zoe Akins, Fannie Hurst, Edgar Lee Masters, Babette Deutsch, Richard LeGallienne, etc. Also first editions of selected St Louis and/or Missouri authors such as T S Eliot, Samuel L Clemens, Theodore Dreiser and Tennessee Williams. Noncirculating.

NY —ALFRED UNIVERSITY, Herrick Memorial Library, Alfred, 14802. June E Brown, Head Librn
Notes: The Evelyn Tennyson Openhym Collection of modern British literature and social history. Papers, incl correspondence of authors concerned with the business aspects of authorship. Gift of Evelyn Tennyson Openhym of Wellsville, NY. Also, 5300 volumes of British literature. Collection also incl correspondence addressed to Ursula Roberts ("Susan Miles"), many pieces concerning the British peace movement of the 1930s.

NY —COLGATE UNIVERSITY, Everett Needham Case Library, Hamilton, 13346. Bruce M Brown, Collections Librn
Holdings: Vols 304 Cat Mss
Notes: Description in *Philobiblon: The Journal of the Friends of the Colgate University Library,* no 9, 1972.

†NC —WAKE FOREST UNIVERSITY, Z Smith Reynolds Library, Box 7777, Reynold Sta, Winston-Salem, 27109. Richard J Murdoch, Rare Book Librn
Holdings: Vols 116 Cat

RI —BROWN UNIVERSITY, John Hay Library, Harris Collection, Prospect St, Providence, 02912. Rosemary L Cullen, Cur
Holdings: Vols (200,000) Cat Mss Pix Phonorecords Microforms
Budget: ($15,000)
Notes: The Harris Collection of American Poetry and Plays is principally composed of American and Canadian poetry and plays, 17th century-date. Extensive holdings in songsters, gift books and annuals, hymnals, pageants, broadside verse, carriers' addresses, women poets, juvenile poetry, (incl Mother Goose and *The Night Before* Christmas), sheet music with lyrics, small press publications, fine printing, black poets, "little magazines," Yiddish-American literature. All movements or schools of American poetry are represented. Incl first editions of most American poets and playwrights, notably Whitman, Poe, Wallace Stevens, Eugene O'Neill, Edward Albee, Ezra Pound, T S Eliot, William Carlos Williams, Amy Lowell, Phyllis Wheatley, Robert Frost, Allen Ginsberg, Bliss Carman, and Stephen Foster sheet music. Also incl the Saunders Walt Whitman Collection (1300 vols); the LangdonCollection of Pageants (250 vols); the Asa Cushman Collection of plays in ms and prompt copies; the MacDougall Collection of Psalters and Hymnals; 4000 plays issued by Walter H Baker Co, Boston (1890-1957); the Vaxer Collection of Yiddish Poetry, Plays and Music (1700 vols). Collections incl 200,000 vols, 30,000 broadsides, 55,000 mss, 170,000 pieces of sheet music, 450 phonorecords, and 375 microfilm reels. See *Dictionary Catalog of the Harris Collection of American Poetry and Plays* (Boston: G K Hall, 1972), 13 vols; *Supplement* (1977), 3 vols. See also, *American Poetry,* 1609-1900, *A Collection on Microfilm, Segment I* (1609-1820); *Segment II* (1821-1850); *Segment III* (1851-1870) (Woodbridge, Conn: Research Publications). Separate catalog.

VA —UNIVERSITY OF VIRGINIA, Alderman Library, Clifton Waller Barrett Collection, Charlottesville, 22901. Joan St C Crane, Cur of American Literature Collections
Holdings: // Cat Mss
Notes: The David Schwab Collection. Many of the 380 items in this collection are virtually unobtainable, since Schwab began collecting Eliot before Eliot received international recognition. Mss, typescripts (autographed by) and letters of Eliot. Description in University of Virginia file, Reference Department, Alderman Library.

BC —UNIVERSITY OF VICTORIA, McPherson Library, Victoria, V8W 3H5, Can.
Notes: Incl 6 cm, 1934-60; correspondence to Mrs D Bussy, Miss J S Bussy, T Tambimuttii, R Thoma, M Wykes-Hoyce, H M Belgion, H Monro, J Lehmann, A Cronin; ms "From Poe to Valery."

ELKIN, BENJAMIN

MA —BOSTON UNIVERSITY, Mugar Memorial Library, Special Collections Dept, 771 Commonwealth Ave, Boston, 02215. Howard B Gotlieb, Dir
Holdings: Cat Mss

ELKIN, MENDL

NY —YIVO INSTITUTE FOR JEWISH RESEARCH, Library & Archives, 1048 Fifth Ave, New York, 10028. Dina Abramowicz, Librn; Marek Web, Archivist
Holdings: Cat Mss Pix Slides
Notes: Yiddish drama in the original and in English translation from its 19th-century beginnings to the present; the Yiddish theatre in the Soviet Union and the theatrical activities in the ghettos during the Nazi regime; special collections of Sholem Perelmuter, Mendl Elkin, Maurice Schwartz, Abraham Goldfaden, Jacob Gordin, and Mark Schweid; records of the Union of Jewish Actors in Poland between the two world wars; the Vilna YIVO Collection of posters, playbills, and photographs; recordings.

ELKIN, STANLEY

MO —WASHINGTON UNIVERSITY, Libraries, Campus Box 1061, Saint Louis, 63130.
Notes: Incl papers of the novelist.

MO —WASHINGTON UNIVERSITY, Libraries, Special Collections Dept, Campus Box 1061, St Louis, 63130.
Notes: A major collection, incl books, mss, correspondence, literary papers, photographs, etc. Described in *Special Collections: an Annotated Guide to the Holdings of the Manuscript Division and the University Archives and Research Collection.*

ELLENDER, SEN. ALLEN J.

LA —NICHOLLS STATE UNIVERSITY, Ellender Memorial Library, Thibodaux, 70310. Randall A Detro, Dir; Philip D Uzee, Archivist
Notes: Official papers of Senator Allen J Ellender (1936-1972).

ELLERY, FRANK

KS —SAINT MARY COLLEGE, Library, Leavenworth, 66048. Therese Deplazes, Special Collections Librn
Notes: Holographs of American personalities, mostly of Colonial, Revolutionary, Confederacy periods, and 19th Century. Incl ms letters, deeds, petitions, wills, slave papers. Holographs of Col Philip Marsteller (one of George Washington's pall bearers), family papers of Richard, Mary and Edward Cutts; love letters to Mary "Polly" Carter, Frank Ellery (grandson of William Ellery, signer of the Declaration of Independence), letters of Connie Mack and Babe Ruth, of some American authors.

ELLET, CHARLES, JR.

MI —UNIVERSITY OF MICHIGAN, Engineering-Transportation Library, 312 Undergraduate Library, Ann Arbor, 48109. Sharon A Balius, Assoc Librn
Holdings: Mss Memorabilia
Notes: Letters and papers of Charles Ellet, Jr, and family, especially as related to construction of railroads, canals, and bridges and to the construction and command of the Union ram fleet in the Civil War.

ELLICKSON, KATHRYN POLLAK

MI —WAYNE STATE UNIVERSITY, Walter P Reuther Library, Archives of Labor & Urban Affairs, Detroit, 48202. Philip Mason, Dir
Notes: Papers, etc of Kathryn Pollak Ellickson, a charter member and assistant director of research for the CIO.

PA —PENNSYLVANIA STATE UNIVERSITY, Fred Lewis Pattee Library, Labor History Collection, University Park, 16802. Peter Gottlieb, Archivist
Holdings: Cat Mss Pix
Notes: Personal papers. Microfilm of papers are at the National Archives.

ELLIN, STANLEY

MA —BOSTON UNIVERSITY, Mugar Memorial Library, Special Collections Dept, 771 Commonwealth Ave, Boston, 02215. Howard B Gotlieb, Dir
Holdings: Cat Mss
Notes: Mss, correspondence, etc collected in depth; incl publications by or about.

ELLINGTON, DUKE

TX —NORTH TEXAS STATE UNIVERSITY, Audio Center, Box 5188, NT Station, Denton, 76203. Morris Martin, Music Librn
Holdings: Cat Pix Phonorecords Audiotapes
Notes: Books, recordings, tapes, and discographies concerning or by Duke Ellington. Incl some 600 78 rpm records and 400 LP, 45 rpm records, transcriptions and tapes. In Music Library.

ELLIOT, ALONZO

CT —YALE UNIVERSITY, Music Library, 98 Wall St, New Haven, 06520. Harold E Samuel, Librn
Notes: Personal papers and musical mss.
See also entry under Music, American.

ELLIOTT, GEORGE P.

MO —WASHINGTON UNIVERSITY, Libraries, Modern Literature Collection, Skinker & Lindell Blvds, Saint Louis, 63130.
Holdings: Cat Mss
Notes: Books, mss, correpsondence, papers, etc.

MO —WASHINGTON UNIVERSITY, Libraries, Special Collections Dept, Campus Box 1061, St Louis, 63130.
Notes: A major collection, incl books, mss, correspondence, literary papers, photographs, etc. Described in *Special Collections: an Annotated Guide to the Holdings of the Manuscript Division and the University Archives and Research Collection.*

ELLIOTT, HARRIET WISEMAN

NC —UNIVERSITY OF NORTH CAROLINA, GREENSBORO, Walter Clinton Jackson Library, Special Collections Dept, 1000 Spring Garden St, Greensboro, 27412. Emilie W Mills, Librn
Holdings: Mss Pix
Notes: Harriet Wiseman Elliott Papers. This collection of 3500 items incl the papers of the Dean of Women at North Carolina State Normal and Industrial School from 1935-1947. She was active in major political, civic, educational and professional organizations such as the Council of National Defense (1940-41), War Finance Committee (1942-46) and UNESCO (1945). Incl personal and business correspondence with President and Mrs. Franklin D Roosevelt, Judge Florence Allen, Frank Porter Graham, Mary Denison and others.
See also entry under Women - History

ELLIOTT, SUMNER LOCKE

MA —BOSTON UNIVERSITY, Mugar Memorial Library, Special Collections Dept, 771 Commonwealth Ave, Boston, 02215. Howard B Gotlieb, Dir
Holdings: Cat Mss Pix
Notes: Mss, correspondence, etc collected in depth; incl publications by or about.

ELLIOTT, WILLIAM YANDELL, 1896-

CA —HOOVER INSTITUTION ON WAR, REVOLUTION & PEACE, Stanford University, Stanford, 94305. Milorad M Drachkovitch, Archivist
Holdings: Mss
Notes: Papers of William Y Elliott, author, university professor, staff director of the House Select Committee on Foreign Affairs, 1947-49, member of the planning board of the National Security Council, 1953-57, and consultant to the US Secretary of State, 1958-1970, incl correspondence, writings, speeches, research notes, clippings, government documents, and printed matter, 1930-1970, relating to his government service, teaching endeavors at Harvard University, US national security and defense, US politics and foreign relations, US military-industrial relations and the US national labor policy. 173 ms boxes.

ELLIOTT SOCIETY OF NATURAL HISTORY

SC —COLLEGE OF CHARLESTON LIBRARY, Special Collections Dept, Charleston, 29401.
Notes: Charleston, SC. Papers, 1853-1901. Incl papers in collection of Lewis Reeve Gibbes; mss copy of Gabriel Manigault on the black whale captured in Charleston Harbor, January, 1880.

ELLIS, ANNE, 1875-1938

CO —UNIVERSITY OF COLORADO, Libraries, Special Collections, Boulder, 80309. Nora J Quinlan, Head
Holdings: Cat Mss
Notes: Incl 78 Anne Ellis letters, 31 Josephine Cole letters, 9 miscellaneous letters and 6 Anne Ellis mss.

ELLIS, HAVELOCK

CT —YALE UNIVERSITY, Box 1603A, Yale Station, New Haven, 06520.
Holdings: Cat
Notes: Incl correspondence.

IL —SOUTHERN ILLINOIS UNIVERSITY, CARBONDALE, Delyte W Morris Library, Special Collections Dept, Carbondale, 62901. David V Koch, Cur of Special Collections; Louisa Bowen, Cur of Manuscripts
Holdings: Cat Mss
Notes: Papers and correspondence of Theodore A Schroeder, constitutional lawyer and founder, with Lincoln Steffens, of the Free Speech League, a forerunner of the American Civil Liberties Union. Contains extensive correspondence with Comstock, Gompers, Debs, H Ellis, Sanger, Sinclair, John Dewey, Darrow, Mencken, A G Hays, Emma Goldman, W E B Dubois, etc. Incl several thousand letters; notes and mss, records of legal cases and extensive files relating to the early history of psychiatry.

IN —INDIANA UNIVERSITY, Lilly Library, Seventh St, Bloomington, 47405. William R Cagle, Librn
Holdings: // Mss Pix
Notes: Letters from Havelock Ellis to Josephine L Walther, a staff member of the Detroit Institute of Arts, 1925-1935. 164 items, incl nine photographs of Ellis.

ELLIS, JOSEPH HENRY, 1890-1973

MB —UNIVERSITY OF MANITOBA, Elizabeth Dafoe Library, Archives and Special Collections Dept, Winnipeg, R3T 2N2, Can. Richard E Bennett, Dept Head; Corrado A Santoro, Reference Archivist
Notes: Soil scientist and professor of soil management. Papers, reports and photographs on land inspections, surveys, erosion studies, river reclamation projects, etc.

PQ —BISHOP'S UNIVERSITY, John Bassett Memorial Library, Laurie Allison Room for Special Collections, Lennoxville, J1M 1Z7, Can. Germain Belisle, Chief Librn
Notes: Soil scientist and professor of soil management. Incl studies on soil and land erosions, reclamation projects, field crop experiments, etc. 10 boxes.

ELLIS, MICHAEL

PA —UNIVERSITY OF PITTSBURGH, Special Collections Dept, Curtis Theatre Collection, 363 Hillman Library, Pittsburgh, 15260. Jeanette Blanco, Cur
Holdings: Mss Documents Pix
Notes: Michael Ellis Papers. Production records of Bucks County Playhouse and New York City; memorabilia. Catalog in process.

ELLIS, RICHARD W.

PA —TEMPLE UNIVERSITY LIBRARIES, Special Collections Dept, Rare Books & Mss Section, Philadelphia, 19122. Thomas M Whitehead, Cur
Holdings: Vols (5000) Mss Pix
Notes: The printing and graphic arts collections stress the technological developments within the printing industry and the achievements in fine printing in the 19th and 20th centuries. Selected additions are continually made of examples and secondary works. Holdings include the Library and archives of Richard W Ellis, typographer, archives of Philadelphia printers and photoengravers. Partially cataloged.

ELLIS BOOKSELLERS

CA —UNIVERSITY OF CALIFORNIA, LOS ANGELES, Research Library, Dept of Special Collections, 405 Hilgard Ave, Los Angeles, 90024. Edward Shreeves, Chairman, Bibliographers Group; David S Zeidberg, Head
Notes: 15 linear feet of correspondence and business records, 1860-1900, of Ellis Booksellers, London.

ELLISON, JAMES WHITFIELD

MA —BOSTON UNIVERSITY, Mugar Memorial Library, Special Collections Dept, 771 Commonwealth Ave, Boston, 02215. Howard B Gotlieb, Dir
Holdings: Cat Mss

ELLISON, RALPH

NV —UNIVERSITY OF NEVADA, RENO, University Library, Special Collections Dept, Reno, 89557. Robert E Blesse, Head
Holdings: Vols (10) Cat
Notes: Includes individual works by author in all editions including translations; also prefaces, introductions, published correspondence, appearances in anthologies, periodicals, etc. Bibliographical research collection, part of Modern Authors Collection. Other appearances 90 cataloged.

ELLISON, SAMUEL KITCHING, 1813-1877

KS —UNIVERSITY OF KANSAS MEDICAL CENTER, College of Health Sciences & Hospital, Clendening History of Medicine Library, Rainbow Blvd at 39th, Kansas City, 66103. Robert P Hudson, Chmn/Cur
Notes: Papers, 1832-43. Ca 25 items. In part, photocopies. British physician. Correspondence, certificates and other papers, chiefly while a student at London Hospital Medical School. Unpublished finding aid in the repository. Access restricted. Purchased from Mrs H K Ellison, 1958.

ELLSWORTH, EPHRAIM ELMER, 1837-1861

RI —BROWN UNIVERSITY, John Hay Library, 20 Prospect St, Providence, 02912. Mark N Brown, Cur Mss
Holdings: Mss
Notes: Materials relative to the history of the US Army.

ELLSWORTH, JAMES W.

IL —CHICAGO PUBLIC LIBRARY, Special Collections Div, Cultural Center, 78 E Washington St, Chicago, 60602. Laura Linard, Cur
Holdings: Vols (300) Cat Mss Pix Slides
Notes: The Chicago Public Library received deposit copies of World's Columbian Exposition publications from the Department of Publicity and Promotion, several of which are still uncataloged and not included in the NUC-Pre 1956 Imprints. The Papers of James W Ellsworth, prominent Chicago financier and member of the Board of Directors of the Exposition, are here; a finding aid to these papers has been prepared in 1978. Outstanding items in the World's Columbian collections are described in *Treasures of the Chicago Public Library*, compiled by Thomas A Orlando and Marie Gecik, 1977, pp 111-20.

ELMAN, MISCHA

MA —BOSTON UNIVERSITY, Mugar Memorial Library, Special Collections Dept, 771 Commonwealth Ave, Boston, 02215. Howard B Gotlieb, Dir
Holdings: // Cat Mss Pix
Notes: Mss, correspondence, etc collected in depth; incl publications by or about.

ELPHENSTONE, JOHN

WI —UNIVERSITY OF WISCONSIN, MADISON, Memorial Library, South Asian Collection, 728 State St, Madison, 53706. Jack C Wells, Bibliographer
Holdings: Cat Microforms
Notes: Public and private papers as Governor of Madras, India.

ELSBERG, CHARLES A.

†NY —NEW YORK ACADEMY OF MEDICINE, Library, 2 E 103 ST, New

ELSBERG, CHARLES A. (cont.)

York, 10029.
Notes: Papers of Walter Timme, MD (1874-1956). Timme was a pioneer endocrinologist; described pluriglandular disease, "Timme's Syndrome." Incl correspondence from Harvey Cushing, Paul Dudley White, Charles A Elsberg, Louis I Dublin, Ely Smith Jelliffe, John F Fulton, Edna St Vincent Millay, Eva Le Gallienne, and Irving Ramsey Wiles.

ELTING, MARY

CO —UNIVERSITY OF COLORADO, Libraries, Special Collections, Boulder, 80309. Nora J Quinlan, Head
Holdings: Vols Uncat Mss
Notes: Folsom Collection. Mss, correspondence, files and books by noted Colorado authors Franklin Folsom and Mary Elting. A husband and wife team which collaborated on a number of children's books. Subject emphasis are fiction, science and natural history. In addition the Folsoms worked on several books for adult audiences. 27 1/2 feet of ms material; approx 150 books in various editions.

ELVEY, CHRISTIAN THOMAS, 1899-1970

AK —UNIVERSITY OF ALASKA, Elmer E Rasmuson Library, Fairbanks, 99701. Robert H Geiman, Dir
Notes: His papers. A Guide of the Collections is available on hard copy and microfiche. About 1000 special collections, some 300 quite significant.

EMANCIPATION OF SLAVES see Emancipation Proclamation

EMANCIPATION OF WOMEN see Women—Civil Rights

EMANCIPATION PROCLAMATION

DC —HOWARD UNIVERSITY, Moorland-Spingarn Research Center, 500 Howard Place NW, Washington, 20059. Clifford L Muse, Jr, Acting Dir
Holdings: Vols (106,086) Mss Maps Pix Slides Phonorecords Audiotapes 16mm Films Filmstrips Microforms
Budget: ($854,753)
See also entry under Blacks

RI —BROWN UNIVERSITY, John Hay Library, McLellan Lincoln Collection, 20 Prospect St, Providence, 02912. Jennifer B Lee, Special Collections Librn
Holdings: Vols (15,000) Cat Mss Pix Phonorecords
Notes: The broadsides incl many song sheets, contemporary political sheets, ballots, and posters; also 27 of the 52 printed editions of the "Emancipation Proclamation" listed by Charles Eberstadt in *Lincoln's Emancipation Proclamation.* There is a selection of newspapers for the war years, 1860-1865, and an index of over 11,300 entries for Lincoln items in all existing files of the Illinois newspapers down through the Civil War.

EMBLEM BOOKS

CA —FRANCIS BACON LIBRARY, 655 N Dartmouth Ave, Claremont, 91711. Elizabeth S Wrigley, Dir
Holdings: Vols 200 Cat Pix
Notes: Incl rare vols from the 16th to 18th century.

CA —UNIVERSITY OF CALIFORNIA, LOS ANGELES, Research Library, Dept of Special Collections, 405 Hilgard Ave, Los Angeles, 90024. Edward Shreeves, Chairman, Bibliographers Group; David S Zeidberg, Head
Holdings: Vols 150 Cat

IL —NEWBERRY LIBRARY, 60 W Walton St, Chicago, 60610. Diana Haskell, Cur of Modern Mss
Holdings: Cat

IL —UNIVERSITY OF ILLINOIS, URBANA/CHAMPAIGN, Library, Rare Book Room, 346 Library, Urbana, 61801. Norman B Brown, Asst Dir for Special Collections; N Frederick Nash, Librn
Holdings: Cat Microforms
Notes: Extensive collection, described in: *Catalog of the Rare Book Room,* (Boston: G K Hall, 1972). Supplement (1978).

IA —UNIVERSITY OF IOWA, University Libraries, Iowa City, 52242. Frank Paluka, Head, Special Collections Dept
Holdings: Vols (13,170) Cat
Notes: See James Fitzmaurice, "A Gathering of Emblem Books", *Books at Iowa,* April 1971.

MA —HARVARD UNIVERSITY LIBRARY, Cambridge, 02138.
Holdings: Cat

MN —UNIVERSITY OF MINNESOTA, O Meredith Wilson Library, 309 19 Ave S, Minneapolis, 55455. Austin J McLean, Chief, Special Collections
Holdings: Vols 105 // Cat

MO —UNIVERSITY OF MISSOURI-COLUMBIA, Ellis Library, Special Collections Dept, Ninth & Lowry, Columbia, 65201. Margaret A Howell, Head, Special Collections
Holdings: Vols Cat
Notes: Includes rare volumes from the 17th and 18th century.

NJ —PRINCETON UNIVERSITY, Library, Rare Books Dept, Princeton, 08544. Stephen Ferguson, Cur
Holdings: Vols 600 Cat
Notes: References: *The Graver and the Pen. Renaissance Emblems and their Ramifications. Catalogue of the Exhibition held in the Princeton University Library.* (Princeton, 1954). (ExB) 0639.739 no 12. This catalog is in typescript form and is available in the Dulles Reading Room in Firestone Library (165 vols are listed and described). Also see: William S Heckscher, "Renaissance Emblems. Observations Suggested by Some Emblem-Books in the Princeton University Library" in the *Princeton University Library Chronicle* XV, 2 (winter, 1954) pp 55-68. William S Heckscher, "Heliotropes and Romantic Ruins. Recent Emblematic Acquisistions" in the *Chronicle* XLV, 1 (autumn, 1983) pp 33-40.

NC —DUKE UNIVERSITY, William R Perkins Library, Rare Book Room, Durham, 27706. John L Sharpe, III, Cur
Notes: Emblem book collection of 750 titles. One-half of the collection is from the Jantz Collection; the other half is from the general collection in the Rare Book Room. The collection covers the period from the first appearence of the emblem book by Alciati through the middle of the 19th century.

†TX —UNIVERSITY OF TEXAS LIBRARIES, General Libraries, Humanities Research Center, PO Box 7219, Austin, 78712. John Chalmers, Librn

WA —UNIVERSITY OF WASHINGTON LIBRARIES, Suzzallo Library, Special Collections Division, Rare Book Collection, FM-25, Seattle, 98195. Gary Menges, Coordinator for Special Collections
Holdings: Vols (12,000) Cat Maps
Notes: American, British, French, German and Italian books printed before 1800, chiefly in the fields of history and literature. Fine bindings and illustrated works are represented. Incl incunabula, emblemata, history of travel, and first editions of the works of major poets: Spenser, Blake, Whitman, Yeats, Roethke, etc.

EMBLEMS

MA —HARVARD UNIVERSITY LIBRARY, Widener Library, Cambridge, 02138.
Holdings: Cat

OH —OHIO STATE UNIVERSITY, Fine Arts Library, 1813 N High St, Columbus, 43210. Susan Wyngaard, Head, Fine Arts Library

EMBOMMA LANGUAGE see Congo Languages and Literature

EMBOSSED BOOKS

NY —NEW YORK STATE LIBRARY, Library for the Blind and Visually Handicapped, Cultural Education Center, Empire State Plaza, Albany, 12230.
Holdings: Cat
Notes: Small collection of New York Point books retained to preserve specimens of now defunct print for blind readers.

EMBROIDERY

MA —HISTORIC DEERFIELD-POCUMTUCK VALLEY MEMORIAL ASSOCIATION, Libraries, Memorial St, Box 53, Deerfield, 01342. David R Proper, Librn
Holdings: Vols (6500) Cat Mss Maps Pix Slides Microforms
Notes: American decorative arts, from colonial times to date. Also, a substantial collection of sketches, patterns, mss, printed material, and color swatches relating to needlework, embroidery and related arts.

MA —OLD STURBRIDGE VILLAGE, Research Library, Sturbridge, 01566. Theresa Rini Percy, Librn
Holdings: Cat Pix
Notes: New England, 1790-1850.

NY —EMBROIDERERS' GUILD OF AMERICA, INC, Library, 6 E 45 St, Room 1301, New York, 10017. Beverly A Grossaint, Executive Secretary
Notes: Incl a comprehensive reference library for the use of members.

WA —UNIVERSITY OF WASHINGTON LIBRARIES, Costume and Textile Collection, FM-25, Seattle, 98195. Krista Jensen Turnbull, Cur
Holdings: Vols (1500) Cat Pix Slides
Notes: Incl the Elizabeth Bayley Willis Collection of more than 1000 textiles from India, and the Seattle Weavers' Guild Collection of Guatemalan textiles. Coptic textiles are on loan from Yale University, and the Boston Museum of Fine Arts gave the Choate Collection of lace. There are also good collections of ecclasiastical vestments and embroideries from many nations, ranging from 1500 BC to the present.

EMBROIDERY—PATTERNS

CA —CARLSBAD CITY LIBRARY, 1250 Elm Ave, Carlsbad, 92008. Clifford E Lange, Library Dir
Holdings: Vols (2297) Cat
Notes: Collection of sewing patterns. Catalogs of the patterns have been made up with complete information on size, etc, and have been divided into subject areas, such as gift ideas, toys, dolls, women's clothes, men's clothes, children's clothes, etc. Also patterns for knitted and crocheted wearing apparel. Incl patterns for children's costumes, historical fashions and antique dolls.

NY —FASHION INSTITUTE OF TECHNOLOGY, Edward C Blum Design Laboratory, 227 W 27 St, New York, 10001. Laura Sinderbrand, Dir
Holdings: Cat Pix Slides
Notes: The largest resource of it kind consisting of 4 million indexed swatches and 300 swatch books, jacquard point paper, croquis, quilts, rug samples, laces, embroideries, and color swatch cards. A collection of international scope incl antique and contemporary textiles; woven and printed patterns created for apparel and home furnishings which may be adapted to china, giftware, floor covering, wallpaper, and package design. A comprehensive research facility comprised of over one million articles of dress dating from the 17th Century to the present, incl men's, women's, children's clothes, furs, foundation garments and lingerie, as well as an outstanding grouping of 19th and 20th century designer clothing. Accessories as diverse as hats, handbags, gloves, hosiery, shoes, shawls, and costume jewelry offer an additonal resource to this international collection.

EMBRYOGENY see Embryology

EMBRYOLOGY

KS —UNIVERSITY OF KANSAS, Kenneth Spencer Research Library, Special

EMBRYOLOGY (cont.)

Collections Dept, Lawrence, 66045. Alexandra Mason, Librn
Holdings: Cat Mss Maps Pix
Notes: Ellis Collection of Ornithology, natural history and voyages and travels; botanical literature from Fitzpatrick collection (especially medical botany, early American botanists, renaissance herbals, Matthioli); some early chemistry and mathematics; scientific voyages and travels; De Beer collection of offprints in embryology, endocrinology, and systematic zoology; D'Arcy Wentworth Thompson collection of separates in natural history and classics; Herrick, Coghill and Roofe collections in neurology. Noncirculating.

NC —UNIVERSITY OF NORTH CAROLINA, CHAPEL HILL, Zoology Dept Library, Wilson Hall 046A, Chapel Hill, 27514. John B Darling, Librn
Holdings: Vols (31,000) Cat
Notes: Collection incl theses and dissertations.

PA —CARNEGIE LIBRARY OF PITTSBURGH, Science & Technology Dept, 4400 Forbes Ave, Pittsburgh, 15213. Catherine M Brosky, Dept Head
Notes: This general subject is of secondary interest. Incl both modern and classic works. Kept up to date in cooperation with the Library in Carnegie Museum of Natural History. Materials available on the various phyla, classes, orders and species. Abstracts, indexes, bibliographies, taxonomic manuals and standard reference books. Many journals and society publications complete from the beginning.

EMBRYOLOGY—HISTORY

NY —CORNELL UNIVERSITY LIBRARIES, John M Olin Library, History of Science Collections, Ithaca, 14853. Lillian A Clark, Administrative Supervisor; David W Corson, History of Science Librn
Holdings: Vols (33,000) Cat
Notes: Howard B Adelmann Collection of early printed source materials in embryology, human and comparative anatomy (6,000 vols). Emphasis on 16th, 17th, and early 18th centuries in general, Malpighi and Italian anatomists in particular. Noncirculating.
See also entry under Science - History

EMERGENCIES, MEDICAL see First Aid; Marine Accidents; Traffic Accidents

EMERGENCY COMMITTEE OF ATOMIC SCIENTISTS, 1946-1949

CA —UNIVERSITY OF CALIFORNIA, SAN DIEGO, Central University Library, Mandeville Dept of Special Collections, La Jolla, 92093. Lynda Corey Claassen, Head
Notes: Papers of Harold Clayton Urey (1893-1981), winner of the 1934 Nobel Prize in chemistry for his discovery of Deuterium. Incl files concerning the Emergency Committee of Atomic Scientists, 1946-49; also some material on the Rosenberg/Sobell spy cases; also on his works as science advisor to John F Kennedy (president-elect).

EMERGENCY MEDICAL CARE see Emergency Medical Services; First Aid

EMERGENCY MEDICAL SERVICES

IN —WISHARD MEMORIAL HOSPITAL, Professional Library, 1001 W Tenth St, Indianapolis, 46202. Fran Bischoff, Library Dir; Kirsten Quam, Librn
Holdings: Vols 56 Cat

MD —UNIVERSITY OF MARYLAND, BALTIMORE COUNTY, Albin O Kuhn Library and Gallery, 5401 Wilkens Ave, Baltimore, 21228. Larry Wilt, Collection Management Librn
Holdings: Cat
Notes: In support of academic programs in Emergency Medical Services, this collection consists of books, journals, reports, mss and an archive.

MI —UNIVERSITY OF MICHIGAN, Transportation Research Institute, Library, 2901 Baxter Rd, Ann Arbor, 48109. Ann C Grimm, Librn
Holdings: Vols (57,000) Cat Mss Maps Pix Slides Microforms
Budget: ($25,000)

EMERGENCY RELIEF see Disasters and Disaster Relief

EMERGENCY RESCUE COMMITTEE

NY —STATE UNIVERSITY OF NEW YORK AT ALBANY, Library, Special Collections Dept, 1400 Washington Ave, Albany, 12222. Marion P Munzer, Coordr
Notes: Photocopies of the files of 170 individuals containing letters and bills regarding their attempts to leave Germany and to find jobs in the US (4 linear feet). Part of the Library's German Exile Collection.
See also entry under Exiles, Political

EMERSON, EDWIN, 1869-1959

DC —GEORGETOWN UNIVERSITY, Library, Special Collections Div, 37 & O Sts NW, Washington, 20057. George M Barringer, Special Collections Librn; Nicholas B Sheetz, Mss Librn
Holdings: Mss Cat Pix
Notes: Correspondence and manuscripts (incl an autobiography) of Edwin Emerson (1869-1959), journalist and miscellaneous writer, touching on his experiences in the Spanish-American, Russo-Japanese, and First World Wars. Incl photographic materials. Also present is an extensive correspondence by Emerson about the novelist Stephen Crane.

EMERSON, GEORGE H.

CA —HOOVER INSTITUTION ON WAR, REVOLUTION & PEACE, Stanford University, Stanford, 94305. Milorad M Drachkovitch, Archivist
Holdings: // Mss
Notes: Papers of George H Emerson, railway official. Correspondence, reports, maps, photos and clippings, concerning the work of the Russian Railway Service Corps and the political situation in the early revolutionary period, with special emphasis on the Czechoslovak movement in Siberia, 1918-1921. 2 boxes.

EMERSON, GLORIA

MA —BOSTON UNIVERSITY, Mugar Memorial Library, Special Collections Dept, 771 Commonwealth Ave, Boston, 02215. Howard B Gotlieb, Dir
Holdings: Mss Pix

EMERSON, RALPH WALDO, 1803-1882

CA —UNIVERSITY OF CALIFORNIA, LOS ANGELES, Research Library, Dept of Special Collections, 405 Hilgard Ave, Los Angeles, 90024. Edward Shreeves, Chairman, Bibliographers Group; David S Zeidberg, Head
Holdings: Vols 150 Cat
Notes: 150 books by and about him; 3 folders of ephemera.

CA —UNIVERSITY OF CALIFORNIA, SANTA BARBARA, Library, Dept of Special Collections, Santa Barbara, 93106. Christian F Brun, Head
Holdings: Cat Mss Pix

MA —HARVARD UNIVERSITY LIBRARY, Houghton Library, Cambridge, 02138. Rodney G Dennis, Cur of Manuscripts
Holdings: Cat
Notes: Incl 15,000 items deposited by the Ralph Waldo Emerson Memorial Association.

MA —CONCORD FREE PUBLIC LIBRARY, 129 Main St, Concord, 01742. Rose Marie Mitten, Dir
Holdings: Cat Mss Maps Pix Slides
Notes: Extensive collection.

NC —DUKE UNIVERSITY, William R Perkins Library, Rare Book Room, Durham, 27706. John L Sharpe, III, Cur
Notes: Carroll Wilson Collection of Emersoniana. Complete set of first editions, a number of autograph letters and other manuscripts, several periodical issues and association items.

VA —UNIVERSITY OF VIRGINIA, Alderman Library, Clifton Waller Barrett Collection, Charlottesville, 22901. Joan St C Crane, Cur of American Literature Collections
Notes: Papers.

WA —UNIVERSITY OF WASHINGTON LIBRARIES, Suzzallo Library, Special Collections Division, Rare Book Collection, FM-25, Seattle, 98195. Gary Menges, Coordinator for Special Collections
Notes: Printing history, including early printed books and modern fine printing; book arts, including papermaking, decorated papers, bookbinding, book design, and artist's books; American literature, 19th century includes: Stephen Crane, Ralph Waldo Emerson, Nathaniel Hawthorne, Henry James, Henry Wadsworth Longfellow, Herman Melville, Frank Norris, Harriet Beecher Stowe and Walt Whitman and 20th century includes: Theodore Roethke; illustrated books, including emblem books, historical children's illustration, books illustrated with prints, and artist's books; costume history; voyages and travels; preservation of library materials.

EMERSON, RICHARD WIRTZ

BC —SIMON FRASER UNIVERSITY, Library, Burnaby, V5A 1S6, Can. Percilla Groves, Special Collections Librn
Holdings: Cat Mss
Notes: Sixty-three letters and one postcard, 1950-1954, to Richard Wirtz Emerson, editor of *Golden Goose;* together with tss of poems, stories and essays sent with the letters; incl typescript of *Le Fou,* "Mr Blue," "The Party," "Three Fate Tales," and "The Grace."

EMIGRANTS' GUIDES

IL —CHICAGO HISTORICAL SOCIETY, Library, Clark St at North Ave, Chicago, 60614. Robert L Brubaker, Librn
Holdings: Vols (150,000) Cat Mss Maps Pix
Notes: Substantial holdings for the area east of the Mississippi, especially the Midwest, but little on the trans-Mississippi West. Early printed and ms journals and accounts by explorers and by foreign and domestic travelers; emigrants' guides; prints and photographs; 590 atlases; and about 10,000 maps (especially strong for Chicago, Illinois, the Midwest, US transportation, general maps of the US for the period to 1900, and general maps of the Americas from the 16th century to 1850).

EMIGRATION AND IMMIGRATION

CA —CLAREMONT COLLEGES, Honnold Library, Ninth & Dartmouth, Claremont, 91711. Tania Rizzo, Special Collections Dept Head
Holdings: Vols 1125 Uncat Mss Pix Microforms
Notes: The combined James Mavor, Raymond Elliott, and Gregory P Tschebotarioff collections incl clippings and periodicals from the Revolutionary period, books and pictorial materials about the royal family, separatist movements, and the emigre experience. Restricted use.

CA —LOS ANGELES PUBLIC LIBRARY, Social Sciences Dept, 630 W Fifth St, Los Angeles, 90071. Marilyn C Wherley, Principal Librn
Holdings: Vols 5000 Microforms
Budget: ($150,000)
Notes: Emphasis on minorities; immigration policies, background and social problems of ethnic minorities in the US and the Southwest in particular. Incl periodicals, government publications and documents, popular and scholarly works on Blacks, Hispanics and Asians predominantly.

EMIGRATION AND IMMIGRATION (cont.)

DC —HOWARD UNIVERSITY, Moorland-Spingarn Research Center, 500 Howard Place NW, Washington, 20059. Clifford L Muse, Jr, Acting Dir
Holdings: Vols (106,086) Mss Maps Pix Slides Phonorecords Audiotapes 16mm Films Filmstrips Microforms
Budget: ($854,753)
See also entry under Blacks

FL —UNIVERSITY OF MIAMI, Otto G Richter Library, PO Box 248214, Coral Gables, 33124. Frank Rodgers, Dir of Libraries
Notes: The Cuban exile periodicals incl 412 titles of which 381 have been published in Miami, Florida. The archival material incl 54 cubic feet of mss, invitations, programs, broadsides, posters, postcards, prints, reports, maps, etc. This collection incl personal and corporate papers of Cubans settled in the US or in other countries. The truth about Cuban Committee Papers: 40 cubic feet. Contains records and correspondence of intellectual and professional Cuban and American leaders in the US dedicated to the course of eliminating Communism from the Western Hemisphere.

HI —BERNICE P BISHOP MUSEUM, Library, PO Box 19000-A, Honolulu, 96819. Cynthia Timberlake, Librn
Holdings: Vols (90,000) Cat Mss Maps Pix Slides Microforms
Budget: ($30,000)
Notes: Only American library devoted exclusively to the Pacific region. Collection reflects historical and contemporary research emphases of Bishop Museum; ie the natural and cultural history of the Pacific. Areas of concentration incl archaeology, ethnology, linguistics, voyages and explorations, history, vertebrate and invertebrate zoology, botany and museology. Strong special collections incl photographs, mss and archives, maps and art. Publications: Quarterly "Additions to the Catalog," *Dictionary Catalog of the* Library (9 vols and 2 suppl; Boston: G K Hall, 1964-69).

IL —ILLINOIS STATE UNIVERSITY, Milner Library, Dept of Special Collections, Normal, 61761. Robert Sokan, Librn
Holdings: Vols 2100 // Uncat
Notes: Sigmund Livingston Collection on Intergroup Relations, 1944 to the present. The material is divided into subject headings which contain pamphlets, newsletters and commission reports.

IL —AUGUSTANA COLLEGE, Swenson Swedish Immigration Research Center, Rock Island, 61201. Kermit Westerberg, Archivist
Holdings: Vols 2000 Cat Mss
Notes: The John Hauberg Upper Mississippi Valley Collection. Incl strong collection of immigrant guide books for the Midwestern states. Fine collection relative to the Sauk and Fox tribes and Black Hawk in particular.

MA —BOSTON UNIVERSITY, Mugar Memorial Library, Special Collections Dept, 771 Commonwealth Ave, Boston, 02215. Howard B Gotlieb, Dir
Holdings: // Mss

MI —UNIVERSITY OF MICHIGAN, Dept of Rare Books & Special Collections, Ann Arbor, 48109. Edward C Weber, Head, Labadie Collection
Notes: The Labadie Collection of radical materials, containing papers, tracts, handbills, and publications of minority political and social reform organizations from the mid-1800s to the present, incl 8000 serial titles and 20,000 uncataloged pamphlets. Also ms collections of the papers of the American Committee for the Protection of Foreign Born.

MN —IMMIGRATION HISTORY SOCIETY, Library, 690 Cedar St, Saint Paul, 55103.
Notes: Originally inspired by the ethnic revivals of the 1960s, and devoted mostly to the historical experiences of European immigrant groups in North America, the Society has since responded to the changing sources of American immigration, the increasing interest in more diverse groups, and the deepening involvement of students and scholars in inter-disciplinary, quantitative, and comparative approaches to the study of America's ethnic groups.

MN —UNIVERSITY OF MINNESOTA, Immigration History Research Center, 826 Berry St, Saint Paul, 55114. Susan Griegs, Cur
Holdings: Vols (35,000) Mss Maps Pix Phonorecords Audiotapes 16mm Films Microforms
Notes: The Archives contain both published and ms material. Presently the imprint collections consist of nearly 25,000 vols of monographs, 3000 periodical titles, and files of more than 900 ethnic newspapers (of which ca 140 are currently received). For the most part, the printed items were published by ethnic presses in North America. Many of the extensive runs of newspapers are to be found in the Archives' microfilm collection of approx 5000 reels. The Archives' ms holdings are made up of 450 individual collections of papers, amounting to 2400 linear ft, or approx 3,000, 000 items. Incl are the records of such societies, churches and publishing companies, as well as collections of personal papers of ethnic leaders, clergymen, journalists, labor leaders, writers, poets and politicians. Partially cataloged.

NY —STATE UNIVERSITY OF NEW YORK AT ALBANY, Library, Special Collections Dept, 1400 Washington Ave, Albany, 12222. Marion P Munzer, Coordr
Notes: 370linear feet of mss; papers and personal libraries of 67 German-speaking emigres who came to the United States from 1933-1945. Collections of faculty members of the "University in Exile" of the New School for Social Research form the core. Major collections are: American Council for Emigres in the Professions, Ludwig Bachhofer, Vicki Baum, Erwin Bodky, Arnold Brecht, Emergency Rescue Committee, Helmut Hirsch, Erich Hula, Jugendbewegung, Ernst Jünger, Erich von Kahler, Emil Lederer, Hans Natonek, Hans Neisser, Fritz Neugass, Karl Otto Paetel, Yella Pessl, Richard Plant, Hans Simons, Hans Staudinger, Storm Publishers Archive, Hans Tischler, Widerstand. There are separate entries for each of these in this volume. Also correspondence and financial records of Abraham Bell and Son, New York shipping line which exported cotton and brought back Irish and English immigrants in the 1830s and 40s.

†NY —STATE UNIVERSITY OF NEW YORK, COLLEGE AT BUFFALO, Vietnamese Immigration Collection, Buffalo, 14260.
Notes: Oral history, interviews, orientation materials, and refugee camp newspapers.

†NY —CHINESE INSTITUTE IN AMERICA LIBRARY, 125 East 65 St, New York, 10021.
Notes: Chinese immigration, heritage and contribution to America.

†NY —CENTER FOR MIGRATION STUDIES LIBRARY, 209 Flagg Place, Staten Island, 10304.
Notes: Human migration and ethnic group relations, especially strong in Italian-American affairs.

PA —BALCH INSTITUTE FOR ETHNIC STUDIES, Library, 18 S Seventh St, Philadelphia, 19106. R Joseph Anderson, Library Dir
Holdings: Vols (50,000) Mss Pix Microforms
Notes: The library collection consists of nearly 5000 vols of monographs, pamphlets, almanacs, calendars, immingrant guides, sheet music and other printed items; 1200 linear feet of ms materials; 3000 periodical titles (of which 170 ethnic titles are on microfilm); more than 1000 pix, posters, slides and other visual documentation. These materials concern the experiences of more than 40 ethnic groups from the 17th century to the present. The library also has notable strengths in the areas of American nativism and the development of US immigration policy, the Amercian labor movement, and American Radicalism. Most of the collection circulates on ILL.

RI —BROWN UNIVERSITY, John Hay Library, 20 Prospect St, Providence, 02912. Mark N Brown, Cur Mss
Holdings: Mss
Notes: Papers of Eli Thayer, educator, US Congressman from Massachusetts, and organizer of the New England Emigrant Aid Company. Brown class of 1845. About 1000 letters, speeches, and articles on political subjects for the period 1841-1898; also Thayer's journal from 1853-1857.

SC —COLLEGE OF CHARLESTON LIBRARY, Special Collections Dept, Charleston, 29401.
Notes: Papers incl a petition with, affidavit of residency, for citizenship of Gertrut Schepeler, immigrant from Germany, Feb 1, 1805.

SD —AUGUSTANA COLLEGE, Mikkelsen Library & Learning Resource Center, Center for Western Studies, Sioux Falls, 57197. Ronelle Thompson, Dir Library
Notes: The Center for Western Studies, located in the Mikkelsen Library, is an archival and research agency of Augustana College. Dedicated to the history and culture of the Great Plains and the Trans-Mississippi West, the Center collects and preserves materials relating to Plains Indians, immigrant settlers, Norwegiana, Western Americana, Herbert Krause, Frederick Manfred, Donald Parker, Richard F Pettigrew, Augustana College, the Episcopal Diocese of South Dakota, the South Dakota District of the American Lutheran Church, the South Dakota Penitentiary and Minnehaha County.

TX —UNIVERSITY OF TEXAS LIBRARIES, Population Research Center Library, 1701 Main Bldg Tower, Austin, 78712. Doreen S Goyer, Librn
Holdings: Vols (20,000) Cat Microforms
Budget: ($3000)
Notes: The International Census Collection contains population censuses of 200 nations and territories, current and retrospective. Combined holdings of several University of Texas libraries constitute 80 percent of the items cited in the *International Population Census Bibliography* (6 volumes and 1 supplement), and the *IPCB, Revision and Update: 1945-1977,* with the majority of items in the Population Research Center. The *Handbook of National Population Censuses, Latin America and the Caribbean, North America, and Oceania* (1983) aids the researcher in the use of foreign censuses.

VA —VIRGINIA POLYTECHNIC INSTITUTE AND STATE UNIVERSITY LIBRARY, Blacksburg, 24061. Glenn L McMullen, Special Collections Librn
Holdings: Vols (4000)
Notes: Collection largely consists of nineteenth century and early twentieth century imprints, emphasizing the role of native Virginians in the development of the trans-Mississippi West, particularly Texas; cowboys and the cattle industry; outlaws and lawlessness; and emigrants' guidebooks to states, cities, and regions in the West.

ON —CANADA, DEPT OF EMPLOYMENT & IMMIGRATION LIBRARY, Ottawa, K1A 0J9, Can. P E Sunder-Raj, Dir Library Services
Holdings: Vols (35,000) Cat Microforms

ON —UNIVERSITY OF TORONTO, Thomas Fisher Rare Book Library, 120 Saint George St, Toronto, M5S 1A5, Can. Richard G Landon, Head
Notes: Sheldon Collection of Australiana, named for collector William Sheldon. Especially rich in 19th century accounts of the exploration of the South Pacific and the interior of the Australian continent. Includes narratives of exiled Canadians who took part in the Rebellion of 1837 in Canada. Includes works on colonization and settlement, the gold-rush of the mid 19th century, and on the life of the indigenous peoples. Includes literature written by Australians or about Australia.

EMISSION CONTROL DEVICES (MOTOR VEHICLES) see Motor Vehicles—Pollution Control Devices

EMMET, CHRISTOPHER T., 1900-1974

CA —HOOVER INSTITUTION ON WAR, REVOLUTION & PEACE, Stanford

EMMET, CHRISTOPHER T., 1900-1974 (cont.)

University, Stanford, 94305. Milorad M Drachkovitch, Archivist
Notes: Papers of Christopher T Emmet, anti-Nazi and anti-communist politcal writer, founder of the Christian Committee to Boycott Nazi Germany in 1939 and of the American Council on Germany in 1951, and a director of the International Rescue Committee, incl correspondence, reports, memoranda, speeches and writings, sound recordings of radio broadcasts, and other material, relating to the various political and humanitarian organizations in which C T Emmet participated. 123 ms boxes.

EMMET, THOMAS ADDIS

NY —NEW YORK PUBLIC LIBRARY, Rare Books and Manuscripts Div, Fifth Ave & 42 St, New York, 10018. William L Joyce, Asst Dir; Susan E Davis, Cur of Mss
Holdings: Mss
Budget: ($7161)
Notes: Collection of American Historical Documents; incl American historical documents from the Revolutionary Period.

EMPERORS see Rulers (Kings, Queens, Etc.)

EMPLOYEE-EMPLOYER RELATIONS see Industrial Relations

EMPLOYEES, TRAINING OF

NY —NEW YORK STATE DEPT OF STATE, Community Affairs Library, 162 Washington Ave, Albany, 12231. M L Johnson, Librn
Holdings: Vols (14,640)
Notes: Local government. Serves as research arm for official activities. 16,000 items in vertical files; 150 periodicals. Unique Community File collection of about 1600 local governments arranged by counties in the state.

EMPLOYER-EMPLOYEE RELATIONS see Industrial Relations

EMPLOYMENT

DC —INTERNATIONAL LABOR ORGANIZATION, International Labor Office, Washington Branch Library, 1750 New York Ave NW, Rm 330, Washington, 20006. Karen J Mark, Librn
Holdings: Vols (13,500) Cat Pix 16m Films Monographs
Notes: Wide range of titles dealing with worldwide labor and social matters. The library contains ILO publications and documentation only, dating back to 1919. Also, a collection of ILO films and photos. See *Subject Guide to Publications of the ILO, 1919-1964* and *ILO Catalogue of Publications in Print, 1982* (ILO).

NY —FEDERATION EMPLOYMENT & GUIDANCE SERVICE, Richard J Bernhard Memorial Library, 510 Sixth Ave, 4th Floor, New York, 10011. Otto Kanocz, Chief Librn
Holdings: Vols (4000) Microforms Videotapes Audiotapes VF
Notes: Occupational information, guidance and counseling, vocational rehabilitation. Incl 30,000 pamphlets; 200 periodical titles. Also incl 50 vertical files and microfiche. Open to the public.

EMPLOYMENT—STANDARDS

ON —ONTARIO MINISTRY OF LABOUR, Library, 400 University Ave, Toronto, M7A 1T7, Can. Jean Collins-Williams, Librn
Holdings: Vols (80,000) Microforms Films

EMPLOYMENT (ECONOMIC THEORY)

NY —NEW YORK STATE DIVISION OF HUMAN RIGHTS, Reference Library, Two World Trade Center, Rm 5356, New York, 10047. Rosalind Spriggs, Librn
Holdings: Vols 1500 Cat
Notes: Emphasis on materials related to discrimination in employment, aged people, and antipoverty efforts. See: Simon Fediuk, *Bibliography on Employment and Related* Subjects. Special Collection No 3 of a Series. 190 pp. This special collection contains about 1500 items; books, studies, journals, pamphlets, reprints and research data.

ON —ONTARIO MINISTRY OF LABOUR, Library, 400 University Ave, Toronto, M7A 1T7, Can. Jean Collins-Williams, Librn
Holdings: Vols (80,000) Microforms Films

EMPLOYMENT DISCRIMINATION see Discrimination in Employment

EMPLOYMENT MANAGEMENT see Personnel Management

EMPLOYMENT OF CHILDREN see Children—Employment

EMPLOYMENT OF YOUTH see Youth—Employment

EMPLOYMENT OPPORTUNITIES see Job Vacancies

EMPLOYMENT PRACTICES, COMMITTEE ON FAIR see Committee on Fair Employment Practices

EMPSON, WILLIAM

NV —UNIVERSITY OF NEVADA, RENO, University Library, Special Collections Dept, Reno, 89557. Robert E Blesse, Head
Holdings: Vols (25) Cat
Notes: Includes individual works by author in all editions including translations; also prefaces, introductions, published correspondence, appearances in anthologies, periodicals, etc. Bibliographical research collection, part of Modern Authors Collection. Other appearances 250 cataloged.

ENAMEL AND ENAMELING

NY —NEW YORK STATE COLLEGE OF CERAMICS AT ALFRED UNIVERSITY, Scholes Library, Harder Hall, Alfred, 14802. Bruce E Connolly, Library Dir
Holdings: Vols (70,000) Cat Mss Slides Microforms
Budget: ($134,000)
Notes: Very specialized collection incl all phases of the arts and sciences related to ceramics. Incl 1112 subscriptions.

ENAMEL PAINTS see Paint

ENAMELS see Enamel and Enameling

ENCYCLOPEDIAS AND DICTIONARIES

CA —CLAREMONT COLLEGES, Honnold Library, Ninth & Dartmouth, Claremont, 91711. Tania Rizzo, Special Collections Dept Head
Holdings: Vols 150 // Uncat
Notes: Grammars and dictionaries (some dual-language with French or Dutch) of mainly Malayo-Polynesian, some Sino-Tibetan, and other languages, dating from the late 19th to mid-20th centuries. Checklisted.

CA —LOS ANGELES PUBLIC LIBRARY, Literature and Philology Dept, 630 W Fifth St, Los Angeles, 90071. Helene G Mochedlover, Dept Librn
Holdings: Cat
Notes: Foreign Language Collection. Approximately 450 languages and dialects are represented, most of which are not included in Foreign Languages Department collection. Emphasis is on breadth of reference collection, which includes dictionaries, grammars, phrase books, and many important encyclopedias.

†CA —UNIVERSITY OF CALIFORNIA, Library, Los Angeles, 90024.
Notes: The Gerald E Baggett Memorial Collection.

CA —THE POLISH ARTS AND CULTURE FOUNDATION, 1290 Sutter St, San Francisco, 94109. Wanda Tomczykowska, President
Holdings: Vols (300)
Notes: Polish reference works pertaining to all aspects and subjects, plus dictionaries on most subjects.

CA —STANFORD UNIVERSITY LIBRARIES, Cecil H Green Library, Stanford, 94305. Peter R Frank, Cur, CDP-Germanic Collection
Notes: Library of Prof Rudolf Hildebran, Leipzig, the first large collection acquired by Stanford in 1895/1896, laid the foundation for an extensive German collection. Hildebrand's library is especially strong in German and Austrian philology (rare dictionaries, etc.), but also in literary works. The collection is now especially strong for the period of the Reformation and Baroque, up to the present, with many rare editions, journals, almanacs, and the like. Sizable collections of women's working class and popular literature, dissertations and Schulschriften. Rare and valuable items in the Stanford Collection of German, Austrian and Swiss Culture, Special Collections. Catalog: *Katalog der Bibliothek des Herrn Prof Dr Rudolf Hildebrand.* Description: *The German Area Collection: A Stanford* Tradition by Peter R Frank.

DC —GEORGETOWN UNIVERSITY, Library, Special Collections Div, 37 & O Sts NW, Washington, 20057. George M Barringer, Special Collections Librn; Nicholas B Sheetz, Mss Librn
Notes: Archives of information used for compilation of *The American Heritage School Dictionary* (1972).

IL —ENCYCLOPAEDIA BRITANNICA, Editorial Library, 310 S Michigan Ave, Chicago, 60604. Terry Miller, Editorial Librn
Holdings: Vols (25,000) Cat Maps Microforms
Budget: ($80,000)
Notes: This collection is not open to the general public, but photocopies of materials will be made. Collection contains all major and most minor encyclopedias and dictionaries. A large collection of atlases and statistical data on all foreign countries is maintained.

IL —STANDARD EDUCATIONAL CORPORATION, Editorial Library, 200 W Monroe St, Chicago, 60606. David E King, Librn
Holdings: Vols (8000) Cat Maps Pix Microforms VF

IN —INDIANA UNIVERSITY, Institute for Sex Research Library, 416 Morrison Hall, Bloomington, 47401. Douglas Freeman, Collections and Services Librn; Joan Brewer, Information Services Librn
Holdings: Vols (62,000) Cat Mss Pix Phonorecords Audiotapes Slides Films Microforms
Budget: ($20,000)
Notes: One of the greatest and most extensive collections on sexual behavior, the library collects materials on all aspects of sex activity, with special emphasis on behavioral and social aspects. Also collects erotic literature and sexual ephemera. Incl 105 audiotapes, 23 vertical file drawers, 108 phonorecords, 55,000 pictures, 5000 slides, and 1700 films. Rich in French, German and American sources; also much Oriental. Semitraditional erotic poetry and song of 17th-18th century England. Bawdy limericks, double-entendre, puns, slang, erotic literature, graffiti, slang and special dictionaries, proverbs and sayings, epigrams and research materials of the Kinsey Studies, etc. Contact Information Service for: literature searching, preparation of bibliographies, permission to use collection. Limited photocopying.

IN —ALLEN COUNTY PUBLIC LIBRARY, 900 Webster St, Fort Wayne, 46802. Paul Deane, Reader Services Dept Head; Kay

ENCYCLOPEDIAS AND DICTIONARIES (cont.)

Lynn Isca, Art Music & AV Dept Head
Holdings: Vols (850) Cat Microforms

IN —INDIANA STATE UNIVERSITY, Cunningham Memorial Library, Dept of Rare Books & Special Collections, Terre Haute, 47809. Lawrence J McCrank, Head
Holdings: Vols 6000 Cat Mss
Budget: $7200
Notes: The Warren and Suzanne Cordell Collection of Dictionaries represents virtually the entire spectrum of Western lexicography from the manuscript period to the present day. Though the collection incl more than 1500 post-1900 dictionaries, emphasis is placed on the collection of pre-1900 dictionaries, particularly English-language dictionaries and foreign dictionaries important in the development of English and American lexicography. Major strengths are Renaissance, classical and vernacular works; early English, eg Johnson (more than 200 different editions) and Bailey; and early American, eg Worcester and Webster. The acquisition of the papers of the distinguished lexicographer, Mitford Mathews, of Cordell himself, and the Archives of the Dictionary Society of North America (DSNA), adds a new dimension to the Collection. "It has earned international recognition as one of thefinest of its kind". A Short Title Catalogue of the Collection was published in 1975. A new catalogue, which incl collations, incl signature collations and notes, is in preparation. It is tentatively entitled *The Warren N and Suzanne B Cordell Collection of Rare and Early Dictionaries: The Manuscript Period to* 1900; vol 1, English Dictionaries, comp by Robert K O'Neill; Vol II, Foreign Language Dictionaries.

IA —UNIVERSITY OF IOWA, University Libraries, Iowa City, 52242. Frank Paluka, Head, Special Collections Dept
Holdings: Vols 51 // Uncat
Notes: Principally English-language dictionaries of the 17th and 18th centuries. The Ernest Horn Collection.

MA —OLD STURBRIDGE VILLAGE, Research Library, Sturbridge, 01566. Theresa Rini Percy, Librn
Holdings: Cat
Notes: Mainly American, some English, encyclopedias and English language dictionaries, to 1850.

MI —DETROIT PUBLIC LIBRARY, Language and Literature Dept, 5201 Woodward Ave, Detroit, 48202. Ann Rabjohns, Chief
Holdings: Vols 1300 Cat
Notes: Reference collection of approximately 1300 foreign-language dictionaries (excluding technical) in about 120 languages.

NY —AMERICAN MUSEUM OF NATURAL HISTORY, Library Services Dept, Central Park W & 79th St, New York, 10024. Nina J Root, Chairwoman; Mary Genett, Asst Librn for Reference Services
Holdings: // Cat
Notes: Mostly 19th and early 20th century items; collections not kept current since there are better resources in the area. Several esoteric languages are represented, however.

NY —NEW YORK PUBLIC LIBRARY, Research Libraries, General Research Division, Fifth Ave & 42 St, New York, 10018. Rodney Phillips, Chief
Holdings: Vols (2,225,000) Cat Maps Pix Microforms
Budget: ($775,718)

NY —NEW YORK PUBLIC LIBRARY, Mid-Manhattan Library, Literature and Language Dept, 455 Fifth Ave, New York, 10016. Eric Steele, Sr Principal Librn
Holdings: Vols (10,000) Cat Phonorecords Microforms
Budget: ($10,000)
Notes: Broad coverage for the study of over 100 languages and dialects, materials on most areas of theoretical and applied linguistics, incl philolgy, speech and the teaching of languages, especially of English as a second language. Extensive runs of major journals. Records and cassettes aid in the learning of 40 languages, in addition to English. Strong in materials on the history of American and English language and pronunciation. In Old, Middle and Early Modern English, Department has a representative collection of primary and secondary source materials in microfiche.

NC —CUMBERLAND COUNTY PUBLIC LIBRARY, North Carolina Foreign Language Center, 328 Gillespie St, Fayetteville, 28301. Patrick M Valentine, Coordinator
Notes: The largest book collections are, in descending order of size, German Spanish, French, Japanese, Korean and Vietnamese, with fair sized collections in Italian, Russian, Chinese, Arabic, Greek, Hungarian, Polish, Hebrew, Thai, and Hindi. The Center has several shelves each of books in Bengali, Dutch, Marathi, Portuguese, Urdu, and Yiddish. Smaller collections of one to three shelves each incl Catalan, Croatian, Czech, Danish, Finnish, Gujarati, Icelandic, Kannada, Latin, Lithuanian, Malayalam, Norwegian, Panjabi, Persian (Farsi), Romanian, Slovak, Swedish, Tagalog, Tamil, Telegu, and Ukrianian. The Center has grammars, dictionaries and occasionally other readings in languages from Afrikaans and Albanian to Welsh, Yoruba and Zulu.

OH —PUBLIC LIBRARY OF CINCINNATI & HAMILTON COUNTY, Dept of Rare Books & Special Collections, 800 Vine St, Library Square, Cincinnati, 45202. Yeatman Anderson III, Cur
Holdings: Cat
Notes: English language dictionaries. Published catalog of the collection available.

OH —CLEVELAND PUBLIC LIBRARY, Fine Arts and Special Collections Department, 325 Superior Ave, Cleveland, 44114. Alice N Loranth, Head
Holdings: Vols 1500 Cat
Notes: Contains many grammars, dictionaries, and works on linguistics in African, Asian and Western languages. Material is classified by an extensively expanded language classification scheme. Its special feature is the "Language File," indexing samples of over 7000 languages and dialects housed in the John G White Collection.
See also entry under Language and Languages.

WI —UNIVERSITY OF WISCONSIN, MADISON, Seminary of Medieval Spanish Studies, 1130 Van Hise Hall, Madison, 53706. Lloyd A Kasten, Emeritus Prof of Spanish
Holdings: Vols (7500) // Cat Mss Pix Slides Microforms
Notes: Medieval materials and subjects. 100 reels of 300-volume collection on 13th century Spanish law. Other emphases: language studies (incl 616,247 vocabulary cards), dictionaries, bibliographies, periodicals. The nucleus of the collection is photostats of the mss of unpublished works of Alfonso X. Restricted circulation.

BC —VANCOUVER PUBLIC LIBRARY, Language & Literature Div, 750 Burrard St, Vancouver, V6Z 1X5, Can. B Kinnear, Head
Notes: A good general collection of language dictionaries, supplemented by clippings and a word file compiled by the staff. Incl books and pamphlets.

†ON —UNIVERSITY OF WESTERN ONTARIO, School of Library and Information Science, Special Collections Room, London, N6A 5B9, Can.
Notes: Collection of pre-1800 dictionaries in all fields of knowledge dating from 1529.

†ON —UNIVERSITY OF WESTERN ONTARIO, School of Library and Information Science, Special Collections Room, London, N6A 5B9, Can.
Holdings: Vols 5200
Notes: Early encyclopedias and dictionaries. Approx one third of the collection of early language and subject dictionaries date from the period 1529-1800, and incl 67 different editions of Samuel Johnson's *A Dictionary of the English Language.* Short title catalog of the pre-1800 dictionaries are available as on-demand publications from SLIS. Recent acquisitions emphasize subject dictionaries.

ON —METROPOLITAN TORONTO LIBRARY, Science & Technology Dept, 789 Yonge St, Toronto, M4W 2G8, Can. Margaret Walshe, Head
Holdings: Vols (120,000) Cat
Notes: Scientific and technical dictionaries and encyclopedias. English and other language dictionaries in both general and specific fields.

ENCYCLOPEDISTS

CA —UNIVERSITY OF CALIFORNIA, BERKELEY, University Library, French and Italian Collections, Berkeley, 94720. Donald G Williams, Librn
Notes: General research collection. There are abundant resources for study of the 18th-century intellectual scene, especially pre-revolutionary political and philosophical writing. The Encyclopedists are well represented. (Numerous first editions and other rare imprints are housed in The Bancroft Library.) The library's collection of literary journals is extensive, particularly so in the period 1870-1920; many serial runs are complete, for instance: *Mercure de* France (1622-1965); *L'Annee litteraire* (1540-1790). Materials to support research on French drama have been acquired in depth, with emphasis on the 18th and 19th centuries.

ENDANGERED SPECIES

CO —DENVER PUBLIC LIBRARY, Conservation Library Center, 1357 Broadway, Denver, 80203.
Holdings: Vols (10,330) Cat
Notes: Historical, sociological, and economic aspects, but not scientific, except for Colorado research reports. Also, fish and wildlife reports of all states.

DC —SMITHSONIAN INSTITUTION LIBRARIES, National Zoological Park Branch, Washington, 20008. Kay Kenyon, Chief Librn
Holdings: Vols (5500) Cat
Notes: Collection incl animal nutrition, capture and care of animals in captivity, conservation and endangered species, pathology, veterinary medicine, zoology.

NY —AMERICAN MUSEUM OF NATURAL HISTORY, Library Services Dept, Central Park W & 79th St, New York, 10024. Nina J Root, Chairwoman; Mary Genett, Asst Librn for Reference Services

ENDICOTT FAMILY

MA —NEW ENGLAND HISTORIC GENEALOGICAL SOCIETY, Library, 101 Newbury St, Boston, 02116. Ralph J Crandell, Dir
Notes: Family papers, likely to incl personal correspondence, diaries, business records, etc.

ENDOCRINE THERAPY see Endocrinology

ENDOCRINES see Endocrinology

ENDOCRINOLOGY

†CT —YALE UNIVERSITY, Medical Library, 333 Cedar St, New Haven, 06520.

KS —UNIVERSITY OF KANSAS, Kenneth Spencer Research Library, Special Collections Dept, Lawrence, 66045. Alexandra Mason, Librn
Holdings: Cat Mss Maps Pix
Notes: De Beer collection of offprints in embryology, endocrinology, and systematic zoology. Noncirculating.

PA —PENNSYLVANIA STATE UNIVERSITY, Fred Lewis Pattee Library, University Park, 16802.
Notes: Numerous and large collections on many sports. Also, materials supporting every aspect of the program of the Center for Women and Sport, incl research into kinetics, endocrinology, physiology, psychology, etc.

WI —UNIVERSITY OF WISCONSIN, MADISON, Wisconsin Regional Primate

ENDOCRINOLOGY (cont.)

Research Center, Primate Center Library, 1223 Capitol Court, Madison, 53715. Lawrence Jacobsen, Librn
Holdings: Vols (15,000) Cat Pix
Notes: Research in reproductive physiology, neurosciences, and behavior. Extensive subject orientated primate reprint file, audiovisual collection on primates. Current research uses approximately 25 species of nonhuman pri..ates. Publications: *Primate Library Report*: print and non-print editions, biomonthly.

ENDOCRINOTHERAPY see Endocrinology

ENDORE, GUY

CA —UNIVERSITY OF CALIFORNIA, LOS ANGELES, Research Library, Dept of Special Collections, 405 Hilgard Ave, Los Angeles, 90024. Edward Shreeves, Chairman, Bibliographers Group; David S Zeidberg, Head
Holdings: Vols 25 Cat Mss
Notes: 25 books; 15 linear feet of mss and ephemera.

ENDOWED CHARITIES see Charitable Uses, Trusts, and Foundations

ENDOWMENTS

DC —COUNCIL FOR ADVANCEMENT & SUPPORT OF EDUCATION, Reference Center, Eleven Dupont Circle NW, Suite 400, Washington, 20036. Cynthia Snyder, Dir
Holdings: Vols (600) Cat Mss Audiotapes Microforms
Notes: A membership service containing information in educational fund raising, institutional relations, government relations, alumni administration, publications, and management techniques for higher education and independent schools. Collection, in addition, contains mss, microfiches, and tapes. Succeeds the American Alumni Council, dissolved in 1974.

NY —THE FOUNDATION CENTER, Library, 888 Seventh Ave, New York, 10106. Candace Kuhta, Coordr, Public Services
Holdings: Vols (2500) Cat Microforms
Budget: ($12,000)
Notes: 200,000 Foundation IRS returns on aperture cards; 500 annual reports. All available material on foundations, both current and historical. Private foundation tax returns; annual reports; books, pamphlets, and articles on foundations and philanthropy. Publish *The Foundation Directory, The Foundation Grants Index, Source Book Profiles, National Data Book, Foundation Grants to Individuals, Comsearch Printouts, Corporate Foundation Profiles, America's voluntary spirit.* Washington Library, 1001 Connecticut Ave, NW. Field offices: Foundation Center--Cleveland, 739 National City Bank Bldg, 629 Euclid Ave, Cleveland, Ohio 44114; Foundation Center--San Francisco, 312 Sutter St, San Francisco, Calif 94108. Over 130 regional depositories of foundation information and reports, in all states, Mexico, Puerto Rico, Canada, the Virgin Islands and England.

NY —ROCKEFELLER UNIVERSITY, Rockefeller Archive Center, Hillcrest, Pocantico Hills, North Tarrytown, 10591. Joseph W Ernst, Dir; J William Hess, Assoc Dir
Notes: The Rockefeller Archive Center, a division of The Rockefeller University, preserves and makes available to scholars the records of the University, the Rockefeller Foundation, the Rockefeller Brothers Fund, members of the family, and those of other individuals and organizations associated with their endeavors. Collections at the Center document a century of philanthropy by legions of associated social and scientific pioneers, providing a unique window into the past.

ENERGY see Force and Energy

ENERGY, BIOLOGICAL see Bioenergetics

ENERGY, SOLAR see Solar Energy

ENERGY CONSERVATION

CA —UNIVERSITY OF CALIFORNIA, BERKELEY, Giannini Foundation of Agricultural Economics, Library, 248 Giannini Hall, Berkeley, 94720. Grace Dote, Librn
Holdings: Cat Microforms
Notes: Energy resources (oil, gas, geothermal, etc). Material dates primarily from 1972.

CA —UPDATA PUBLICATIONS INC, Library, 1756 Westwood Blvd, Los Angeles, 90024. Sara Ferguson, Dir; Judith Harrington, Librn
Holdings: Vols (300) Uncat Maps Microforms
Notes: Incl 800,000 microforms, 35 periodicals.

CA —ASSOCIATION OF BAY AREA GOVERNMENTS, MTC/ABAG Library, 101 Eighth St, Oakland, 94607. Diane Gillman, Information Coord
Notes: Concentrates heavily on the nine-county Bay Area region. About 10,000 monographs and serials. Title catalog, OCLC/ATS. Central collection of documents for six transit properties in Bay Area.

DC —CONSERVATION FOUNDATION, Library, 1717 Massachusetts Ave NW, Washington, 20036. Barbara K Rodes, Librn
Holdings: Vols (8000) Cat Maps
Notes: Collection incl natural resources, ecology, city and regional planning, land use, recreation, energy conservation, environmental economics, pollution control, water resources.

IA —BICKELHAUPT ARBORETUM FREE LENDING LIBRARY, 340 S Fourteenth St, Clinton, 52732. Francie B Hill, Librn
Notes: Strong on indoor plants, horticulture, ecology, energy conservation, plant entomology and pathology, urban tree planting; also curriculum materials. Over 3000 slides available for lending.

MN —UNIVERSITY OF MINNESOTA, Architecture Library, 89 Church St, Minneapolis, 55455. A Kristine Johnson, Librn
Holdings: Vols (27,000) Cat Mss
Budget: ($20,000)
Notes: Incl architecture, architectural history, landscape architecture, design methodology, housing, urban sociology, interior design, etc.

NH —TOTAL ENVIRONMENTAL ACTION, INC. (TEA), Library of Conservation, Environmental Studies, and Renewable Energy, 7 Church Hill, Harrisville, 03450. Bruce Anderson, Pres
Holdings: 10,000 Vols
Notes: Available for sale. Library in temporary storage, summer 1983. One of the most extensive private collections. Reports, surveys, monographs, technical papers, bibliographies, and indexes to highly specialized studies.

ON —CANADIAN HOUSING INFORMATION CENTER, Canada Mortgage and Housing Corp, CMHC Annex Bldg Ground Floor, Montreal Rd, Ottawa, K1A 0P7, Can. Leslie Jones, Mgr
Holdings: Cat

PQ —SERVICE DE LA DOCUMENTATION ET DES RENSEIGNEMENTS MINISTERE DE L'ENERGIE ET DES RESSOURCES, 2000B, chemin Sainte-Foy, 7th floor, Quebec, G1R 4X7, Can. Normand Guerette, Dir
Holdings: Vols (114,800) Slides Videotapes
Notes: In 1979, the Bibliotheque du ministere des Richesses naturelles du Quebec merged with the Bibliotheque du ministere des Terres et Forets. The result of this merger was the creation of the service de la Documentation et des Renseignements du ministere de l'Energie et des Ressources. Publications: Info-Biblio Terres et Forets; Mines; Energy.

ENERGY CONVERSION, DIRECT see Direct Energy Conversion

ENERGY ECONOMICS

CA —UNIVERSITY OF CALIFORNIA, BERKELEY, Giannini Foundation of Agricultural Economics, Library, 248 Giannini Hall, Berkeley, 94720. Grace Dote, Librn
Holdings: Cat Microforms
Notes: Energy resources (oil, gas, geothermal, etc). Material dates primarily from 1972.

DC —EDISON ELECTRIC INSTITUTE, Library-8th Floor, 1111 19th St NW, Washington, 20036. Ethel Tiberg, Mgr, Library Services
Holdings: Vols (13,321) Cat Maps Pix Microforms

DC —FOSTER ASSOCIATES, Library, 1101 17th St NW, Washington, 20036. A Blandamer, Librn
Notes: The principal subject areas are public utility regulation and economics, and energy economics.

NY —NATIONAL ECONOMIC RESEARCH ASSOCIATES, INC, Library, 123 Main St, White Plains, 10601. Debra Gaffey, Asst Librn
Holdings: Vols 7500 Cat
Notes: Energy economics, power resources, anti-trust legislation, and public policy.

ON —ENERGY, MINES & RESOUCES CANADA, Headquarters, 580 Booth St, Ottawa, K1A 0E4, Can. F B Scollie, Chief Librn
Holdings: Vols (65,000) Cat Microforms
Budget: ($200,000)
Notes: EMR Libraries Network includes the Headquarters, Conservation and Non-Petroleum Branch, and Petroleum Incentives Branch. Topics incl energy and mineral economics, especially Canadian. Energy fiche dating to 1982 (EIC, New York).

ENERGY POLICY

MA —HARVARD UNIVERSITY, Center for Middle Eastern Studies, Library, Coolidge Hall, 1737 Cambridge St, Cambridge, 02138. Barbara Mitchell, Librn
Holdings: Vols (5000) Periodicals
Notes: Some history of countries of the Middle East; increasingly emphasizes culture and politics of the current Middle Eastern area. Special collection of Energy Economics Research. Library currently receives 15 periodical titles.

ENERGY RESOURCES see Power Resources

ENERGY SOURCES, RENEWABLE see Renewable Energy Sources

ENGEL, LEHMAN

CT —YALE UNIVERSITY, Music Library, 98 Wall St, New Haven, 06520. Harold E Samuel, Librn
Notes: Personal papers and musical mss. *See also* entry under Music, American.

MS —MILLSAPS COLLEGE, Millsaps-Wilson Library, Jackson, 39210. Kathy Holden, College Archivist
Holdings: Vols 25
Notes: Complete autographed collection of books by Eudora Welty, with 20 signed photographs then in Mississippi whilst working for the WPA as a publicity agent. Includes letters from Welty to Lehman Engel.

ENGELBERG ABBEY, SWITZERLAND

MO —CONCEPTION ABBEY, Library, Conception, 64433.
Holdings: Vols (2425) // Uncat Mss Microforms
Notes: Rare Roman Catholic theological

ENGELBERG ABBEY, SWITZERLAND (cont.)

books and mss, mostly 16th-19th centuries. A partial catalog of the collection exists. Basically this is a donation received in the last quarter of the 19th century from a 900-year-old Swiss abbey, Engelberg Abbey. Most of our mss are listed in De Ricci census. The incunabula are for the most part listed in Goff's census. No photocopying.

ENGELMANN, GEORGE, 1809-1884

MO —MISSOURI BOTANICAL GARDEN LIBRARY, PO Box 299, Saint Louis, 63166. M R Crosby, Dir of Research
Holdings: Cat
Notes: Sturtevant Collection of pre-Linnean (pre-1753) books and Linnean collection. Also George Engelmann's correspondence with famous botanists and 6000 letters discussing botanical species. Also 60 vols of his notes and beautifully drawn sketches from his extensive studies on Cactaceae, Coniferae, Yucca, Agave, Isoetes, etc.

MO —WASHINGTON UNIVERSITY, Libraries, Special Collections Dept, Campus Box 1061, St Louis, 63130.
Notes: Family and business correspondence.

ENGELS, JOHN

VT —UNIVERSITY OF VERMONT, Guy W Bailey/David W Howe Library, Burlington, 05405. John Buehler, Asst Dir for Special Collections
Notes: Poetic manuscripts of John Engels.

ENGINEERING

AL —TUSKEGEE INSTITUTE, School of Engineering Library, Tuskegee Institute, 36088. Frances F Davis, Librn
Holdings: Vols 549 Cat
Budget: $2500

AR —UNIVERSITY OF ARKANSAS, Technology Campus Library, 1201 McAlmont St, PO Box 3017, Little Rock, 72203. Brent Nelson, Librn
Holdings: Vols (20,849) Cat Slides Microforms
Budget: ($35,000)

CA —UNIVERSITY OF CALIFORNIA, DAVIS, Physical Sciences Library, Davis, 95616. Scott Kennedy, Head
Holdings: Vols (170,000) Cat VF
Notes: Collection covers aeronautical, agricultural, chemical, civil, electrical, mechanical, water science, hydrology, nuclear reactor, extensive cold regions collection in vertical file drawers, and computer science engineering academic programs. Good strength in journal runs.

CA —UNIVERSITY OF CALIFORNIA, LOS ANGELES, Engineering & Mathematical Sciences Library, 405 Hilgard, Los Angeles, 90024. Rosalee I Wright, Librn
Holdings: Vols (180,000) Cat Microforms
Notes: Approx (2500) journal titles are currently received. Subject emphases in engineering incl: biomedical, chemical, civil, computer, nuclear, electrical, electronic, environmental, mechanical, materials and metals; mathematical methods in engineering; control theory; computer science; systems science and engineering; aerospace engineering and astronautics; manufacturing engineering (incl robotics and CAD/CAM); engineering aspects of energy and pollution. Incl engineering handbooks and material data compilations; ASTM, IEEE, ESDU standards, DIN (English translation only) Standards, SAE Aerospace Standards, and selected ASME Codes; 1, 300,000 technical reports (mostly on microfiche). Full depository for DOE (AEC, ERDA) and NASA; partial depository for NTIS (pollution, environment, meteorology, and bioengineering) since 1970.

CA —UNIVERSITY OF SOUTHERN CALIFORNIA, Seaver Science Library, University Park, Los Angeles, 90089. A Albert Baker, Head
Holdings: Vols (200,000) Microforms
Budget: ($700,000)
Notes: Includes technical reports (12,000), serial and periodical titles (3600).

CA —NASA, Ames Research Center, Libraries, Library Br 202-3, Moffett Field, 94035. Sarah Dueker, Chief, Library Branch
Holdings: Cat Audiotapes Microforms
Notes: Main library collections cover physical sciences, engineering and mathematical fields related to research programs in aeronautics-space research. Life sciences library collections cover medical, physiological, behavioral and biological sciences related to research programs. Also emphases on remote sensing of earth resources and the search for extraterrestrial life. 950 journal titles and 85,000 monographs. Reports collection includes 60, 000 hard copy reports and 900,000 microfiche.

CA —HUGHES AIRCRAFT CO, Solid State Products Library, 500 Superior Ave, Newport Beach, 92663. Barbara Squyres, Librn
Holdings: Vols (4500)
Notes: Incl 2600 journal vols and 500 microforms.

CA —RAYMOND KAISER ENGINEERS INC, Engineering Library, 300 Lakeside Dr, PO Box 23210, Oakland, 94623. Elaine Zacher, Librn
Holdings: Vols (6000) Cat
Budget: ($10,000)

CA —CALIFORNIA INSTITUTE OF TECHNOLOGY, Engineering Library, Millikan Library, Pasadena, 91125. Duane M Helgeson, Librn
Holdings: Vols 31,812 Cat
Budget: $39,000

CA —RALPH M PARSONS CO, Central Library, 100 W Walnut St, Pasadena, 91124. Jennifer Stein, Librn
Holdings: Vols 10,000 Cat Maps Audiotapes
Notes: Incl 6000 reports, 100 maps and 10 audiotapes; organizational, federal, and military standards.

CA —CONTRA COSTA COUNTY LIBRARY, 1750 Oak Park Blvd, Pleasant Hill, 94523. Barbara Potter, Librn
Holdings: Vols (18,000)

CA —COGSWELL COLLEGE, Library, 600 Stockton St, San Francisco, 94108. Judith Carson-Croes, Dir
Holdings: Vols (12,000) Cat

CA —GARRETT CORPORATION, AiResearch Manufacturing Company, Technical Library, 2525 W 190 St, Torrance, 90509. Joanna M Sutton, Head Librn
Holdings: Vols 15,000 Cat Microforms
Notes: Incl 250,000 microforms, 130,000 reports (hard copy), 100,000 military specifications and standards, 30,000 NACA reports (hard copy).

CO —STONE & WEBSTER ENGINEERING CORP, Technical Information Center, PO Box 5406, Denver, 80217. Sue Newhams, Librn
Holdings: Vols (5000) Cat Microforms
Notes: The subject emphasis of this collection is centered around the power industry and energy resources.

CT —YALE UNIVERSITY, Engineering & Applied Science Library, 15 Prospect St, New Haven, 06520. Elizabeth B Hayes, Librn
Holdings: Vols (31,808) Cat Maps Pix Microforms
Notes: Comprehensive holdings. The Library also has NASA depository materials.

DC —EDISON ELECTRIC INSTITUTE, Library-8th Floor, 1111 19th St NW, Washington, 20036. Ethel Tiberg, Mgr, Library Services
Holdings: Vols (13,321) Cat Maps Pix Microforms

DC —SMITHSONIAN INSTITUTION LIBRARIES, National Museum of American History Branch, Washington, 20560. Rhoda S Ratner, Branch Librn
Holdings: Vols (369,650) Cat Mss Maps Pix Slides Microforms

FL —UNIVERSITY OF FLORIDA, Engineering & Physics Library, 410 Weil Hall, Gainesville, 32611. Roger V Krumm, Librn
Holdings: Cat Micrforms
Notes: Incl AEC, ERDA, DOE, NASA reports.

IL —ILLINOIS BELL TELEPHONE CO, Library, 225 W Randolph St, Chicago, 60606. Marguerite J Krynicki, Head Librn
Holdings: Vols (11,000) Cat

IL —LESTER B KNIGHT & ASSOCIATES, Library, 549 W Randolph St, Chicago, 60606. Clarita M Generao, Librn
Holdings: Vols (10,000) Cat Maps Slides
Notes: Collection is both technical and nontechnical; incl reports of the studies for our client companies, which incl European films.

IL —UNIVERSITY OF CHICAGO LIBRARIES, John Crerar Library Collections, 1100 E 57th St, Chicago, 60637. Robert Rosenthal, Special Collections Librn
Notes: The John Crerar Library's extensive science, medicine, and engineering collections have been transferred in trust to the University of Chicago Libraries. Incl rare books and special collections as listed here.

IL —NORTHWESTERN UNIVERSITY, Seeley G Mudd Library for Science & Engineering, 2233 Sheridan Rd, Evanston, 60201. Robert C Michaelson, Head
Holdings: Vols (200,000) Cat Microforms
Notes: Collection emphasizes graduate and research level material.

IL —UNIVERSITY OF ILLINOIS, URBANA/CHAMPAIGN, Library, 221 Engineering Hall, Urbana, 61801. William Mischo, Librn
Holdings: Vols (175,000) Cat Slides Microforms
Notes: Incl 3500 periodicals. Collection designed to serve teaching and research programs. Supports instructional faculty research. Also, 470 microfilm reels and 6000 microfiche sheets.

IN —CUMMINS ENGINE CO, Information Center, 1000 Fifth St, Columbus, 47201. W E Poor, Tech Librn
Holdings: Vols 3500 Cat Mss

IN —PURDUE UNIVERSITY LIBRARIES, Engineering Library, A A Potter Engineering Center, West Lafayette, 47907. Edwin D Posey, Engineering Librn
Holdings: Vols (225,178) Cat Maps Audiotapes Microforms
Budget: ($300,000)

IA —IOWA STATE UNIVERSITY, Library, Ames, 50011. Warren B Kuhn, Dean of Library Services
Holdings: Cat
Notes: Extensive serial holdings; extensive holdings of industry standards.

IA —DELEVAN DIVISION OF COLT INDUSTRIES INC, Engineering Library, 811 Fourth St, PO Box 100, West Des Moines, 50265. G A Hartman, Librn
Holdings: Vols 2000 Cat Mss Slides Microforms
Budget: $400
Notes: Incl liquid atomization, droplet size measurement and representation, fuel nozzles for combustors, and spray nozzles for industrial and agricultural applications.

KY —UNIVERSITY OF KENTUCKY, Robert E Shaver Library of Engineering, 355 Anderson Hall, Lexington, 40506. Russell H Powell, Engineering Librn
Holdings: Vols (48,000) Cat Microforms

KY —NAVAL ORDNANCE SYSTEMS COMMAND, Technical Library, Code 50122, Louisville, 40214. Libby Miles, Librn
Holdings: Vols 5500 Cat Maps Microforms
Notes: Excel in Government specifications, ordnance pamphlets, and all types of other Government documents. Large service in Industry Standard on film, some volumes.

MA —STONE & WEBSTER ENGINEERING CORP, Technical Information Center, Library, 245 Summer St, PO Box 2325, Boston, 02107. Nancy M Pellini, Mgr
Holdings: Vols (10,000) Cat Pix Microforms
Notes: Also over 1200 periodicals. Extensive vertical file collection, and 5 on-line system for search.

MA —INSTRUMENTATION LABORATORY, Library, 113 Hartwell Ave, Lexington, 02173. Jacqueline R Kates, Librn
Holdings: Vols (6000) Cat Microforms Reprints

MA —TUFTS UNIVERSITY, Engineering Library, Medford, 02155. Wayne Powell, Science-Engineering Librn
Holdings: Vols (20,000) Cat
Notes: Also 25,000 technical reports. Subject

ENGINEERING (cont.)

emphases: solid waste management, water pollution control, fluid mechanics.

MA —NEW ENGLAND ELECTRIC SYSTEM, Technical Information Center, 25 Research Dr, Westborough, 01581. William J McCall, Librn
Holdings: Vols 2000 Cat Microforms
Notes: Collection reflects R&D interests of electric utility industry. 120 periodical Subscriptions; 1500 technical reports.

MA —US DEPT OF HEALTH, EDUCATION & WELFARE, Public Health Service, FDA Winchester Engineering Analytical Center, 109 Holton St, Winchester, 01890. Lisa Leone, Librn
Holdings: Vols (3000) Mss Maps Audiotapes

MI —UNIVERSITY OF MICHIGAN, Engineering-Transportation Library, 312 Undergraduate Library, Ann Arbor, 48109. Maurita Holland, Librn
Holdings: Vols (400,000) Cat Microforms
Budget: ($225,000)

MS —US ARMY ENGINEER WATERWAYS EXPERIMENT STATION, Library Branch, PO Box 631, Vicksburg, 39180. Bernice Black, Chief Librn
Holdings: Vols (350,000) Cat Mss Maps Microforms

NH —DARTMOUTH COLLEGE, Feldberg Business & Engineering Library, Hanover, 03755. Phyllis E Jaynes, Librn
Holdings: Vols 30,000 Cat Microforms
Budget: $45,000
Notes: 1000 serial titles; NAFA microfiche; DOE microfiche collections.

NH —US ARMY COLD REGIONS RESEARCH AND ENGINEERING LABORATORY, 72 Lyme Road, Hanover, 03755. Nancy Liston, Librn
Holdings: Cat Maps Microforms
Notes: The primary material consists of reports, documents, journal articles, cited in the library's "Bibliography on Cold Regions Science and Technology." About one third of the items cited in vols 1-22 are on microfilm or in report or reprint form; beginning with vol 23, all items are microfiched and sent to the library, which now has over 55,000 items on microfiche. These are indexed by author and subject in the annual volume of the Bibliography.

NJ —NEW JERSEY INSTITUTE OF TECHNOLOGY, Robert W Van Houten Library, 323 High St, Newark, 07102. Morton Snowhite, Librn
Holdings: Vols (128,000)

NJ —RUTGERS, THE STATE UNIVERSITY OF NEW JERSEY, Library of Science & Medicine, PO Box 1029, Piscataway, 08854. Frank Polach, Dir
Holdings: Vols (275,000) Cat Maps

NJ —PRINCETON UNIVERSITY, Library, Rare Books Dept, Princeton, 08544. Stephen Ferguson, Cur
Holdings: Cat

NM —UNIVERSITY OF CALIFORNIA, Los Alamos National Laboratory, Libraries, PO Box 1663, MSP 362, Los Alamos, 87545. J Arthur Freed, Head Librn
Holdings: Vols (800,000) Cat Films Microforms
Budget: ($700,000)
Notes: Incl 500,000 classified and unclassified reports. There are 25 branch libraries and a central collection. The Medical Library contains about 40,000 vols in the areas of biomedical research.

NY —PRATT INSTITUTE LIBRARY, 200 Willoughby Ave, Brooklyn, 11205.

NY —CORNELL UNIVERSITY LIBRARIES, Collection of Regional History, Dept of Manuscripts and Univ Archives, Ithaca, 14853.
Notes: Incl scrapbooks, ca 1934-ca 1946; newspaper clippings, notes, and typescript anecdotes relating the Cornell University College of Engineering.

NY —CORNELL UNIVERSITY LIBRARIES, Engineering Library, Carpenter Hall, Ithaca, 14853. Susan Markowitz, Librn
Holdings: Vols 330,000 Microforms
Budget: $295,000
Notes: Depository for reports of the US Atomic Energy Commission (AEC); Energy Research and Development Administration (ERDA); NASA; National Technical Information Service (NTIS). Incl 620,000 microforms.

NY —COLUMBIA UNIVERSITY LIBRARIES, Engineering Library, 422 Mudd Bldg, New York, 10027.
Holdings: Vols (177,000) Cat
Notes: All aspects of engineering-- aeronautical, industrial mining, civil, chemical, mechanical, electrical, nuclear. Incl applied mathematics and applied physical sciences. Over (1,000,000) technical reports.

NY —ENGINEERING SOCIETIES LIBRARY, 345 E 47 St, New York, 10017. S Kirk Cabeen, Dir
Holdings: Vols 250,000 Cat Maps 16mm Films Microforms
Notes: One of the largest, most comprehensive engineering libraries in the world. Covers all engineering disciplines; particularly strong in electrical and electronic, mechanical, mining and metallurgical, petroleum, chemical, industrial, air conditioning and refrigeration engineering. Incl Wheeler Collection of early materials on magnetism and electricity. 125, 000 bound periodical volumes; 10,000 maps; 5000 serial subscriptions (many foreign-language). Virtually all materials abstracted in *Engineering Index* (1884-date) are incl in Library. Noncirculating, except to members of professional engineering societies which support the Library. See *Engineering Societies Library, New York, Classed Subject Catalog and Index* (Boston: G K Hall, 1963); and *Supplements*, 1-10, 1964-1973.

NY —NEW YORK PUBLIC LIBRARY, Research Libraries, Science and Technology Research Center, Fifth Ave & 42 St, New York, 10018.
Holdings: Vols (1,100,000) Cat Microforms
Budget: ($647,259)

NY —NEW YORK PUBLIC LIBRARY, Mid-Manhattan Library, Science & Business Dept, 455 Fifth Ave, New York, 10016. Frederick E Dusold, Sr Principal Librn
Holdings: Vols (110,000) Cat Microforms
Budget: ($134,000)
Notes: All works are in English. Material is current; policy precludes archival collecting. Collection is geared toward the undergraduate college student, with consideration given to the professional, the lay reader and the beginning graduate student. Collection incl monographs, texts, treatises, standard reference works and periodicals in agriculture, horticulture, home economics, crafts, engineering, industrial chemistry, construction and other technologies. Books are available for circulation in addition to an extensive reference collection.

NY —EASTMAN KODAK COMPANY, Kodak Park Div, Engineering Library, Bldg 23, Rochester, 14650. Raymond Curtin, Librn
Holdings: Vols (14,000) Uncat Microforms
Notes: The library is not open to the public. Use of the library for reference purposes may be requested and appointments may be obtained through the librarian.

NY —UNIVERSITY OF ROCHESTER, Engineering Library, Gavett Hall, River Campus, Rochester, 14627. Isabel Kaplan, Librn
Holdings: Vols (25,000) Cat
Notes: Strong collection in the field and related areas.

NY —US MILITARY ACADEMY LIBRARY, West Point, 10996. Robert E Schnare, Asst Librn, Special Collections
Holdings: Cat
Notes: Early British and American imprints from the 16th to early 20th century, incl Schley Collection of Military Engineering and the West Point Thayer collection.

NC —DUKE UNIVERSITY, School of Engineering, Library, Durham, 27706. Eric J Smith, Librn
Holdings: Vols (72,000) Cat Microforms
Budget: ($110,000)

NC —NORTH CAROLINA DEPT OF HUMAN RESOURCES, Div of Health Services, Public Health Library, PO Box 2091, Raleigh, 27602. Elnora H Turner, Librn
Holdings: Vols (15,000) Cat

NC —NORTH CAROLINA STATE UNIVERSITY, D H Hill Library, Box 7111, Raleigh, 27695. I T Littleton, Dir
Holdings: Vols 87,000 Cat
Budget: $50,000
Notes: Incl monographs.

OH —FIRESTONE TIRE & RUBBER CO, 1200 Firestone Pkwy, Akron, 44317. S Koo, Librn
Holdings: Vols (6000) Cat
Notes: Collection centered on engineering, mathematics, physics, and manufacturing (metal processing); no rubber or tires. Incl several hundred government reports. No index.

OH —CLEVELAND PUBLIC LIBRARY, Science & Technology Dept, 325 Superior Ave, Cleveland, 44114. Jean Z Piety, Head
Holdings: Cat
Notes: Primarily an engineering collection with basic sciences; strong in 19th and 20th century American, British, and Canadian technical societies' publications; comprehensive bibliography, standards and specifications; Rand Corp; 4400 periodicals and serials, extensive collections in chemistry, pamphlets (60,000). Incl collections on geology, aeronautics and agriculture.

OH —BATTELLE MEMORIAL INSTITUTE LIBRARY, 505 King Ave, Columbus, 43201. Carol Young, Librn
Holdings: Vols (150,000) Cat Maps Microforms
Notes: Large collection of Russian and Eastern European science and technology. Over 1600 current journal titles and extensive monography and serial holdings in Slavic languages.

OH —PREFORMED LINE PRODUCTS CO, Research & Engineering Library, 660 Beta Drive, Mayfield Village, (Mailing add: PO Box 91129, Cleveland, 44101). Edwina T Barron, Librn
Holdings: Vols (11,500) Cat Mss Microfiche Pix VF
Budget: ($30,500)
Notes: Library covering research and engineering fields emphasizing this subject. Aerodynamic characteristics and electrical characteristics of power cables, communication cables (including fiber optics), cable support systems, as well as associated fittings and hardware; in service behavior of manufactured products and materials as it relates to its static and dynamic forces and environmental conditions; oceanographic cable fittings and terminations.

OK —HTB TECHNICAL INFORMATION CENTER, PO Box 1845, Oklahoma City, 73101. Retha Robertson, Librn
Holdings: Vols (100) Cat Documents Pix Slides Audiotapes 16mm Films Filmstrips VF
Notes: Architecture and engineering of the US, especially. Extensive photograph collection, incl 3000 slides.

OK —OKLAHOMA STATE UNIVERSITY, Library, Stillwater, 74708. Roscoe Rouse, Dir
Holdings: Vols 91,965 Cat Microforms

OR —OREGON STATE UNIVERSITY, Library, Corvallis, 97331. Melvin George, Dir
Holdings: Vols 115,000 Cat Pix

OR —US DEPT OF ENERGY, Bonneville Power Administration Library, 1002 NE Holladay St, PO Box 3621, Portland, 97232. Karen Hadman, Chief of Library Branch
Holdings: Vols (1000) Cat
Budget: ($185,000)
Notes: Emphasis is on Federal and Pacific Northwest law and in subject areas of interest to the Departments of Energy and Interior.

PA —ENSANIAN PHYSICOCHEMICAL INSTITUTE, Library, PO Box 98, Eldred, 16731. Elisabeth Anahid Ensanian, Chief Librn
Holdings: Vols 200 Cat Mss Slides Films Microforms
Budget: $3800
Notes: The institute has pioneered the field

ENGINEERING (cont.)

of Gravitation Chemistry (term coined at the institute) and has original data and reports on this phenomenon, generated from its own research, that cannot be found elsewhere in the world. Also publishes own technical journal. This special collection, which also incl the biological effects of weightlessness, is continually being increased.

PA —DREXEL UNIVERSITY LIBRARIES, Engineering Library, 32 & Chestnut Sts, Philadelphia, 19104. Charlotte T Duvally, Librn
Holdings: Vols 70,000 Cat Microforms
Budget: $37,000
Notes: All phases of engineering. Also holds the Air Pollution Library (microfilm), issued by the Bay Area Air Pollution Control District, San Francisco.

PA —FRANKLIN INSTITUTE LIBRARY, 20 & The Parkway, Philadelphia, 19103. Miriam Padusis, Dir; Charles Wilt, Readers Servs Librn
Holdings: Vols (300,000) Cat Maps Pix Microforms

PA —LIBRARY COMPANY OF PHILADELPHIA, 1314 Locust St, Philadelphia, 19107. Edwin Wolf II, Librn; Kenneth Finkel, Cur of Prints
Holdings: Vols (400,000) Cat Maps Pix
Budget: ($25,000)
Notes: American science and industry before 1860. Books, pamphlets, etc on science incl math, pysics, astronomy, and industry, incl business and engineering. Incl many 18th century books printed in England and France but used by American colonials in their study and research. Impossible to estimate the exact size of collection since it is not separated from general collection.

PA —TEMPLE UNIVERSITY, Engineering and Architecture Library, 12 & Norris Sts, Philadelphia, 19122. Raelaine Ballou, Librn
Holdings: Vols (12,000) Cat Microforms
Budget: ($13,500)

PA —UNIVERSITY OF PENNSYLVANIA, Towne Scientific Library, 220 S 33 St, Philadelphia, 19104. Charles Meyers, Librn
Holdings: Vols (65,000) Cat

PA —CARNEGIE LIBRARY OF PITTSBURGH, Science & Technology Dept, 4400 Forbes Ave, Pittsburgh, 15213. Catherine M Brosky, Dept Head
Holdings: Vols (380,000) Cat Maps Microforms
Budget: ($240,000)
Notes: An area of primary interest except military and naval engineering. More than 100,000 vols and 800 cataloged serial sets in this field. Early engineering journals, both American and foreign, generally complete. Complete sets of standards and specifications, especially the American National Standards (ANSI), British Standards (BS); US Federal Specifications and Standards, US Department of Defense (Military) Specifications and Standards (MIL), US National Bureau of Standards publications, and those issued by some companies and numerous institutions such as ASME, AGMA, ASTM, IEE, AWS, NEMA, SAE. Engineering publications acquired from most State Engineering Experiment Stations. Incl monographs, conferences, handbooks, society publications. *See also* entry under Patents - Collections.

PA —ROCKWELL INTERNATIONAL, General Industries Operations, Technical Information Center, 400 N Lexington Ave, Pittsburgh, 15208. Kathleen H Witkowski, Library Coordr
Holdings: Vols Cat Microforms Mss Documents Periodicals VF
Budget: ($5100)

PA —PENNSYLVANIA STATE UNIVERSITY, Engineering Library, 325 Hammond St, University Park, 16802. Tom Conkling, Librn
Notes: 59,500 items.

SC —SUMTER TECHNICAL COLLEGE, Library, 506 Guignard Dr, Sumter, 29150. Fanny M Davis
Holdings: Vols (20,000) Cat Mss Maps Pix Slides Microforms
Budget: ($500,000)
Notes: Incl 385 books on engineering.

TN —TENNESSEE VALLEY AUTHORITY (TVA), Technical Library, 400 W Summit Hill Dr, E2 B7, Knoxville, 37902. Jesse C Mills, Chief Librn
Holdings: Vols (106,900) Cat Mss Maps Pix Audiotapes Microforms
Budget: ($2,025,000)
Notes: The Technical Library Headquarters Staff (order, cataloging, information, and administration) is located in Knoxville, Tenn. In addition there are branch libraries in Knoxville, Norris, and Chattanooga, Tennessee, and Muscle Shoals, Alabama.

TN —UNIVERSITY OF TENNESSEE, Space Institute Library, Tullahoma, 37388. Helen B Mason, Librn
Holdings: Vols (14,000)
Budget: ($50,000)
Notes: Incl NASA and other series of technical reports.

TX —SOUTHWESTERN PUBLIC SERVICE CO, Library, PO Box 1261, Amarillo, 79170. Gloria Branham, Librn
Holdings: Vols (2500) Cat Maps 16mm Films Microforms

TX —UNIVERSITY OF TEXAS LIBRARIES, Richard W McKinney Engineering Library, 1.3 ECJ, Austin, 78712. Susan B Ardis, Librn
Holdings: Vols (83,548) Cat Microforms

TX —SOUTHERN METHODIST UNIVERSITY, Science/Engineering Library, Dallas, 75275. Devertt D Bickston, Librn
Holdings: Vols (166,000) Cat Maps Pix Microforms
Notes: Incl 65,000 bound periodicals, 236, 000 government documents, 178,000 maps, 112,000 microforms, and 1416 periodical subscriptions.

TX —FLUOR ENGINEERS INC, Houston Library, 4620 N Braeswood, PO Box 35000, Houston, 77235. R S Holab-Abelman, Librn
Holdings: Vols (2500) Cat Maps
Budget: ($10,000)
Notes: Construction, environmental and chemical engineering, coal technology. Incl 2000 job books covering all areas of company interests.

TX —ECTOR COUNTY LIBRARY, Department of Business and Technology, 321 W 5th St, Odessa, 79760. Pat Jones, Dept Head
Holdings: Vols 2000 Cat
Notes: Incl 100 vertical files, 25 periodicals, 250 Trade Standards. Collections concentrated on the Drilling and Production industries. Also included are Exploration methods Reservoir Development, Pipeline, Construction, Well Servicing, Well Logging, and Well Control. Complete collection of the API Specifications, and Complete Welding "library".

VT —UNIVERSITY OF VERMONT, Chemistry/Physics Library, Burlington, 05405. Craig A Robertson, Librn
Holdings: Vols (23,000) Cat Microforms
Notes: The collection consists largely of periodicals, having about 12,000 bound periodical volumes. The number of periodical titles currently received is approximately 210.

WA —PUGET SOUND NAVAL SHIPYARD, Engineering Library, Code 202.5, Bremerton, 98314. Carol J Swanson, Engineering Librn
Holdings: Vols (6000) Cat

WA —BOEING COMPANY, Boeing Technical Libraries, PO Box 3707, Seattle, 98124. Corrine Campbell, Mgr Technical Library
Holdings: Vols (75,000) Cat Microforms
Notes: Books are distributed between 3 libraries, Kent, Renton, and Bellevue. Also contains many periodicals and Boeing Documents Library restricted to Boeing Personnel.

WA —UNIVERSITY OF WASHINGTON LIBRARIES, Engineering Library, FH-15, Seattle, 98195. Harold N Wiren, Engineering Librn
Holdings: Vols (108,313) Cat Microforms
Budget: ($314,409)
Notes: About a million technical reports and the US patent specifications on microfilm are strong adjuncts to the collection which covers all fields of engineering.

WI —UNIVERSITY OF WISCONSIN, MADISON, Kurt F Wendt Library, 215 N Randall Ave, Madison, 53706. LeRoy G Zweifel, Librn
Holdings: Vols (95,000) Cat Videotapes Microforms
Notes: Incl LANDSAT Remote Imagery; also, complete US patent collection.

WI —MILWAUKEE PUBLIC LIBRARY, 814 W Wisconsin Ave, Milwaukee, 53233. Donald J Sager, City Librn
Holdings: Vols (30,000) Cat
Notes: Strong collection acquired to support state interlibrary loan. Covers all the pure and applied sciences. Incl over (1600) periodicals and serial titles and more than (100) abstracting and indexing services in major fields of science and technology. Strong general reference service.

MB —UNIVERSITY OF MANITOBA, Engineering Library, Winnipeg, R3T 2N2, Can. Y Cho, Head
Holdings: Vols (28,000) Cat Videotapes Microforms
Notes: The Engineering Library serves four academic departments: Agricultural, Civil, Electrical and Mechanical Engineering.

ON —ONTARIO RESEARCH FOUNDATION, Library, Sheridan Park, Mississauga, L5K 1B3, Can. Carl K Wei, Librn
Holdings: Vols (13,000) Cat
Budget: ($14,000)

ON —UNIVERSITY OF OTTAWA, Vanier Library, 11 Somerset St East, Ottawa, K1N 9A4, Can. J David Holmes, Librn
Holdings: Vols (140,000)
Budget: ($570,700)
Notes: This collection contains teaching and research level material to support all branches of the pure sciences and engineering. Incl periodicals (3000), cataloged.

ON —METROPOLITAN TORONTO LIBRARY, Science & Technology Dept, 789 Yonge St, Toronto, M4W 2G8, Can. Margaret Walshe, Head
Holdings: Vols (120,000) Cat
Notes: All aspects of technology for the specialist, the student, and the general public. The department gives high priority to Canadian material.

PQ —ECOLE POLYTECHNIQUE BIBLIOTHEQUE, Campus de l'Universite de Montreal, PO Box 6079, Station "A", Montreal, H3C 3A7, Can. Josee Schepper, Chief of Public Services
Holdings: Vols (111,000) Cat Maps Microforms
Budget: ($330,000)
Notes: Catalog available on microfiche.

ENGINEERING—AUTHORSHIP see Technical Writing

ENGINEERING—HISTORY

CA —CLAREMONT COLLEGES, Norman F Sprague Memorial Library, 12 & Dartmouth, Claremont, 91711. David Kuhner, Librn
Holdings: Vols (1000) Cat Mss Pix VF
Notes: President Herbert Hoover's personal collection of rare technical books of the 15th-19th centuries. *Bibliotheca De Re Metallica: The Herbert Clark Hoover Collection of Mining and Metallurgy* (Claremont, 1980). Restricted use.

†CA —WED ENTERPRISES, Research Library, 1401 Flower St, Glendale, 91201.
Notes: A subject emphasis.

DE —HAGLEY MUSEUM AND LIBRARY, Eleutherian Mills-Hagley Foundation Inc, PO Box 3630, Greenville, 19807. Richmond D Williams, Dir; Heddy A Richter, Imprints Librn
Holdings: Vols 14,000
Notes: Our collection documents the history of American technology, especially the period in which mass production replaced the American system. Our holdings are strong in chemical technology, transportation, explosives, pyrotechnics, metallurgy and engineering.

DC —LIBRARY OF CONGRESS, Prints & Photographs Div, Washington, 20540.
Notes: The Historic American Engineering

ENGINEERING—HISTORY (cont.)

Record contains measured drawings, photographs, and data sheets documenting works of American engineering.

IN —PURDUE UNIVERSITY LIBRARIES, West Lafayette, 47907. Edwin Posey, Librn
Holdings: Vols (6271) Cat Mss Maps Pix Microforms
Budget: $2683
Notes: The William Freeman Myrick Goss Library of the History of Engineering with an emphasis on railroads.

MA —MASSACHUSETTS INSTITUTE OF TECHNOLOGY, Institute Archives, Special Collections, Cambridge, 02139.
Notes: Baldwin collection contains works on 19th century civil engineering.

MA —UNIVERSITY OF LOWELL, Library, One University Ave, Lowell, 01854. Martha Mayo, Special Collections Librn
Holdings: Vols 3000 Cat Mss Maps Pix
Notes: The Locks and Canals Collection consist of the 19th century engineering library of the Proprietors of the Locks and Canals on Merrimack River 1793-present. This collection also contains 5000 photographs and 8000 architectural and engineering drawings.

MA —OLD STURBRIDGE VILLAGE, Research Library, Sturbridge, 01566. Theresa Rini Percy, Librn
Holdings: Cat
Notes: Mainly American technology to 1900: building mills, water-power, printing, inventions.

MA —BRANDEIS UNIVERSITY, Goldfarb Library, 415 South St, Waltham, 02154. Bessie Hahn, Dir
Notes: Leonardo da Vinci Collection. Comprised of over 1000 vols dealing with all aspects of Leonardo Da Vinci's life, art and engineering feats. The collection is fully catalogued and access is provided by the Special Collections card catalog and the Main Card Catalog.

NY —CORNELL UNIVERSITY LIBRARIES, John M Olin Library, History of Science Collections, Ithaca, 14853. Lillian A Clark, Administrative Supervisor; David W Corson, History of Science Librn
Notes: Very extensive collection of history, biography and bibliography.
See also entry under Science - History.

NY —NEW YORK CITY MUNICIPAL ARCHIVES, Dept of Records and Information Services, 31 Chambers, New York, 10007. Idilio Gracia, Director
Notes: The Brooklyn Bridge Drawings Collection (1869-ca 1950), consisting of approximately 10,000 original plans, drawings, and notes.

NY —NEW YORK PUBLIC LIBRARY, Research Libraries, Science and Technology Research Center, Fifth Ave & 42 St, New York, 10018.
Holdings: Vols (1,100,000) Cat Microforms
Budget: ($647,259)

OH —CLEVELAND PUBLIC LIBRARY, Science & Technology Dept, 325 Superior Ave, Cleveland, 44114. Jean Z Piety, Head
Holdings: Cat
Notes: A hundred years of acquisitions for an ever changing diversified industrial community has assembled notable segments in aeronautics, automobile engineering, and most other branches of engineering.

RI —BROWN UNIVERSITY, John Hay Library, 20 Prospect St, Providence, 02912. Mark N Brown, Cur Mss
Holdings: Mss
Notes: Various ms collections relating to both the teaching and the practical applications of engineering.

SC —CLEMSON UNIVERSITY, Libraries, Clemson, 29631. Michael F Kohl, Head of Special Collections
Holdings: Vols 1500 //
Notes: Book collection initiated with gifts from Mrs Bernard Behrend. Incl early editions by Galileo, Newton, Priestly, and other great scientists. Collecting emphasis has been upon engineering.

TX —TEXAS A&M UNIVERSITY, Sterling C Evans Library, University Archives, College Station, 77843. Charles R Schultz, University Archivist
Notes: The Archives of Southwestern Technology: papers of nuclear physicist Paul C Aebersold, 1933-1965; papers of geologist and independent oil producer Michel T Halbouty, ca 1930-1983; records of the Texas Section of the American Society of Civil Engineers, ca 1914-1980; and records of the Texas Engineering Experiment Station, ca 1914-1970.

ENGINEERING—MATERIALS see Materials

ENGINEERING—STUDY AND TEACHING

MA —MASSACHUSETTS INSTITUTE OF TECHNOLOGY, Institute Archives, Special Collections, Cambridge, 02139.
Notes: Papers of Dugald Caleb Jackson, electrical engineer, important in development of American engineering education. Significant is material recording the ties between industry and engineering education and the growth of the Department of Electrical Engineering. Bulk of collection dates 1899 to 1948. Unpublished finding aid and correspondence index available in Archives.

ENGINEERING, AGRICULTURAL see Agricultural Engineering

ENGINEERING, BIOMEDICAL see Biomedical Engineering

ENGINEERING, CHEMICAL see Chemical Engineering

ENGINEERING, CIVIL see Civil Engineering

ENGINEERING, COMPUTER see Computer Engineering

ENGINEERING, ELECTRICAL see Electrical Engineering

ENGINEERING, ENVIRONMENTAL see Environmental Engineering

ENGINEERING, GEOLOGICAL see Geological Engineering

ENGINEERING, GEOTHERMAL see Geothermal Engineering

ENGINEERING, HYDRAULIC see Hydraulic Engineering

ENGINEERING, INDUSTRIAL see Industrial Engineering

ENGINEERING, MARINE see Marine Engineering

ENGINEERING, MECHANICAL see Mechanical Engineering; Mechanics, Applied

ENGINEERING, MEDICAL see Biomedical Engineering

ENGINEERING, METALLURGICAL see Metallurgical Engineering

ENGINEERING, MILITARY see Military Engineering

ENGINEERING, MINING see Mining Engineering

ENGINEERING, NUCLEAR see Nuclear Engineering

ENGINEERING, OCEANOGRAPHIC see Oceanographic Engineering

ENGINEERING, PRODUCTION see Production Engineering

ENGINEERING, RAILROAD see Railroad Engineering

ENGINEERING, RIVER see River Engineering

ENGINEERING, SANITARY see Sanitary Engineering

ENGINEERING, STRUCTURAL see Strains and Stresses; Strength of Materials; Structures, Theory of

ENGINEERING, SYSTEMS see Systems Engineering

ENGINEERING, TEXTILE see Textile Engineering

ENGINEERING, TRAFFIC see Traffic Engineering

ENGINEERING, WATER SUPPLY see Water Supply Engineering

ENGINEERING, WOMEN IN see Women in Engineering

ENGINEERING CYBERNETICS see Automation

ENGINEERING DRAWINGS

KY —UNIVERSITY OF KENTUCKY, Robert E Shaver Library of Engineering, 355 Anderson Hall, Lexington, 40506. Russell H Powell, Engineering Librn
Holdings: Vols (48,000) Cat Microforms

ENGINEERING LAW

OR —US DEPT OF ENERGY, Bonneville Power Administration Library, 1002 NE Holladay St, PO Box 3621, Portland, 97232. Karen Hadman, Chief of Library Branch
Notes: Emphasis is on Federal and Pacific Northwest law and in subject areas of interest to the Departments of Energy and Interior.

ENGINEERING MATERIALS see Materials

ENGINEERING SOCIETIES

MA —MASSACHUSETTS INSTITUTE OF TECHNOLOGY, Institute Archives, Special Collections, Cambridge, 02139.
Notes: Papers of Dugald Caleb Jackson, electrical engineer, important in development of American engineering education. Significant is material recording the ties between industry and engineering education and the growth of the Department of Electrical Engineering. Bulk of collection dates 1899 to 1948. Unpublished finding aid and correspondence index available in Archives.

ENGINEERING STANDARDS see Standards and Specifications

ENGINES

CA —UNIVERSITY OF CALIFORNIA, DAVIS, Shields Library, Dept of Special Collections, Davis, 95616. Donald Kunitz, Head; C Danial Elliott, Asst Head
Notes: Farming equipment: Manufacturer's catalogs, manuals, parts lists, ephemera, and literature pertaining to historical as well as current data on such items as tractors, engines, combines, hay equipment, etc. Described in "The Higgins Library: A Source for the Study of Agricultural History," Don Kunitz, *Agricultural History,* vol 49, 1975, pp 89-91.

IN —CUMMINS ENGINE CO, Information Center, 1000 Fifth St, Columbus, 47201. W E Poor, Tech Librn
Holdings: Vols 1000 Cat Mss
Notes: Engine technology.

MA —MASSACHUSETTS INSTITUTE OF TECHNOLOGY, Institute Archives, Special Collections, Cambridge, 02139.
Notes: Correspondence, newsletters, fact-sheets, newspaper and magazine articles, books and reports of the Citizens' League Against the Sonic Boom, established in 1967 by William Shurcliff to oppose the sonic boom, stop commercial supersonic transport production, and influence public opinion and policy decisions on the SST. Major correspondents incl Bo Lundberg, Richard Wiggs, several US congressmen, and CLASB members.

WI —COLT INDUSTRIES, FM Engine Div, Library, 701 Lawton Ave, Beloit, 53511. Westley A Brill, Library Admin
Holdings: Vols 100 Cat Mss

ENGINES, GASOLINE see Gas and Oil Engines

ENGLAND—HISTORY see Great Britain—History

ENGLAND, CHURCH OF see Church of England

ENGLISH, WILLIAM H.

IL —UNIVERSITY OF CHICAGO LIBRARY, Dept of Special Collections, 1100 E 57 St, Chicago, 60637.
Notes: Personal papers of William H English relating to Indiana history.

ENGLISH ART see Art, English

ENGLISH AS A FOREIGN LANGUAGE see English Language—Study and Teaching_Foreign Students

ENGLISH AUTHORS see Authors, English

ENGLISH CHILDREN'S LITERATURE see Children'S Literature, English

ENGLISH DRAMA

CA —CALIFORNIA STATE UNIVERSITY, LONG BEACH, Library, Dept of Special

ENGLISH DRAMA (cont.)

Collections & Archives, 1250 Bellflower Blvd, Long Beach, 90840. John Ahouse, Special Collections Librn
Holdings: Vols (5000) Cat Pix
Notes: Incl playbills, scripts, scrapbooks from the former Pasadena Playhouse, together with the former Hildebrand Collection of English and American Drama before 1830.

CA —HUNTINGTON LIBRARY, Art Gallery & Botanical Gardens, 1151 Oxford Rd, San Marino, 91108. Robert L Middlekauff, Dir; Daniel H Woodward, Librn
Notes: Incl the Larpent Collection of English manuscript plays submitted to the Lord Chamberlain for approval after the Licensing Act of 1737--the year and reason the phrase "legitimate stage" came into use. Refer to MacMillian, Dougald, *Catalogue of the Larpent Plays in the Huntington Library* (San Marino, Calif: 1939).

CT —YALE UNIVERSITY, Box 1603A, Yale Station, New Haven, 06520.

DC —LIBRARY OF CONGRESS, Rare Book & Special Collections Div, Washington, 20540. William Matheson, Chief
Holdings: Vols 326 Cat
Notes: The Francis Longe Collection of 17th and 18th century (some early 19th century) English plays, formed in England around 1815 and acquired by the Library in 1908. Among the 2269 plays included in the collection are first or early editions of Goldsmith, Sheridan, Webster, Dekker, Chapman, Beaumont, Fletcher, Charles Johnston, Dryden, et al. Also, English theatre playbills for productions in London, Birmingham, Liverpool, Newcastle, Manchester, etc between 1810 and 1880 (especially Shakespearean performances).

DC —LIBRARY OF CONGRESS, General Reading Rooms Division, Microform Reading Room, Washington, 20540.
Holdings: Cat Mss Maps Pix Microforms
Notes: Microform materials only in this LC Division. Works of individual authors; holdings of collections; archival records, etc, press releases and translations, etc.

FL —UNIVERSITY OF SOUTH FLORIDA, Library, Tampa, 33620. J B Dobkin, Special Collections Librn
Holdings: Vols 1000 Cat
Budget: ($7500)
Notes: 19th Century Play Collection. Consists of acting editions of British and American plays only (pamphlet format). Although concentration is in the area of 19th century plays, some items of 18th and early 20th century origin are also present in the collection. Some of the playscripts incl contemporary manuscript annotations, while a very few items are manuscript copies of published plays. Emphasis in the collection is given to American play scripts.

IL —NEWBERRY LIBRARY, 60 W Walton St, Chicago, 60610. Diana Haskell, Cur of Modern Mss
Holdings: Vols 6000 Cat Mss
Notes: Strong collection, used as basis for Woodward and McManaway's checklist. Tapers off in strength in early 18th century. Particularly interesting is a small collection of some 30 Covent Garden prompt-books, 1710-1824, reprinted by Micro-Photo, Inc.

IL —UNIVERSITY OF CHICAGO LIBRARY, Dept of Special Collections, 1100 E 57 St, Chicago, 60637.
Notes: Celia and Delia Austrian Collection of English Drama to 1800.

IL —LAKE FOREST COLLEGE, Donnelley Library, Lake Forest, 60045. Arthur H Miller Jr, College Librn
Holdings: Cat Mss
Notes: Coverage from 17th century to the present, about 5000 pieces, particularly American and English. Garrett Leverton Memorial Theatre Library emphasizes the American drama renaissance of the early 20th century. It includes, though, more than 1000 published playscripts, of which a significant number are 19th century.

IN —INDIANA UNIVERSITY, Lilly Library, Seventh St, Bloomington, 47405. William R Cagle, Librn
Holdings: / / Cat Mss Pix
Notes: Restoration period holdings constitute 23 percent of items cited in G Woodward & MacManaway checklist of English plays, 1641-1700. 18th century holdings, good; 19th century holdings, extensive; 20th century holdings, modest.

IN —MORRISSON-REEVES LIBRARY, 80 N Sixth St, Richmond, 47374. Harriet E Bard, Librn
Holdings: Vols 1250 Cat
Notes: 1000 titles are individual plays or plays-in-collections, largely American and British; 250 titles are history and criticism, stories, plots, etc.

MA —AMHERST COLLEGE, Library, Amherst, 01002. John Lancaster, Special Collections Librn
Holdings: Vols (20,000) Uncat Mss
Notes: Contains a comprehensive collection of paperbound Samuel French acting editions (15,000) and many from other publishers; also Augustin Daly manuscripts, David Warfield acting scripts, and the library of Clyde Fitch. 200 mss.

†MA —BOSTON PUBLIC LIBRARY, Copley Sq, Boston, 02117.
Holdings: Uncat Microforms
Notes: Microform Publications by Readex Microprint Corp. Three Centuries of English and American Plays, 1500-1800; English and American Plays of the 19th Century.

MI —UNIVERSITY OF MICHIGAN, Library, Dept of Rare Books & Special Collections, Ann Arbor, 48109. Robert J Starring, Head
Holdings: Cat
Notes: Especially strong in Restoration and 18th century plays.

MO —UNIVERSITY OF MISSOURI-COLUMBIA, Ellis Library, Language and Literature Dept, Columbia, 65201. Jeaneice Brewer, Librn
Holdings: Vols Cat
Notes: Extensive collection of Samuel French acting editions and many from other publishers. Retrospective and current publications are added regularly.

MO —WASHINGTON UNIVERSITY, John M Olin Library, Campus Box 1061, St Louis, 63130.
Holdings: Cat Microforms
Notes: English poetry of the Tudor period. 100 reels and microfilms and photostats of original mss in English and European libraries. Checklist of collection by library and collection number.

NJ —PRINCETON UNIVERSITY, Library, Rare Books Dept, Princeton, 08544. Stephen Ferguson, Cur
Holdings: Cat Microforms
Notes: Drama during the Restoration period (1641-1700) represents a turning point in English theatre. Princeton has a large collection in the field of Restoration drama. Most of the major Restoration dramatists are unusually well represented: Aphra Behn, William Congreve, John Crowne, John Dryden, Thomas Durfey, George Etherege, Nathaniel Lee, Thomas Shadwell, William Wycherley. for particulars refer to: Gerald Eades Bentley, "Restoration Plays at Princeton" in the *Princeton University Library Chronicle,* XXXIV, 2 (winter, 1973) pp 131-139 and Alfred L Bush, "The Jacobean and Caroline Stage: Quartos from Princeton Collections" in the *Chronicle* XXX, 2 (winter, 1969) pp 77-89. See also: Mary Ann Jensen, "Recent Acquisitions in Restoration Plays" in the *Princeton University Library Chronicle* XXXVII, 3 (spring, 1976) pp 245-247. A copy of Gertrude Woodward and JamesMacmanaway's *A Checklist of English Plays 1641-1700* (Chicago, 1945) has been checked against the Princeton holdings (ExB) 04704.984 and a second copy with a list of plays added during the past 20 years is in the office of the Curator of Rare Books.

†NY —STATE UNIVERSITY OF NEW YORK, COLLEGE AT BROCKPORT, Brockport, 14420.
Notes: Microfilm copy of the Lord Chamberlain's *Daybooks,* registers of plays licensed for presentation in London from 1824-1903. Originals in British Museum. Some other miscellaneous material is incl from the Lord Chamberlain's office.

NY —NEW YORK PUBLIC LIBRARY, Performing Arts Research Center, Billy Rose Theatre Collection, 111 Amsterdam Ave, New York, 10023. Dorothy L Swerdlove, Cur
Holdings: Cat

NY —NEW YORK PUBLIC LIBRARY, Research Libraries, General Research Division, Fifth Ave & 42 St, New York, 10018. Rodney Phillips, Chief
Holdings: Vols (2,225,000) Cat Maps Pix Microforms
Budget: ($775,718)

NY —MOUNT PLEASANT PUBLIC LIBRARY, 350 Bedford Rd, Pleasantville, 10570. Charlotte Miller, Dir
Holdings: Vols 175 Cat
Notes: The John W Frost collection consists almost exlusively of 17th and 18th century British drama. The few exceptions incl a first edition of the famous Jeremy Collier's *A Short View of the Immortality and Profaneness of the English Stage* (1698) which played an influential role in the closing of the English theatres; a 2-vol *Memoirs of John Bannister,* comedian (1839); and a *Manual for the Collector and Amateur of Old English Plays* (1892). The 365 titles provide a good representation of British theatre for the 17th and 18th centuries. (The only Shakespeare is a 1703 edition of *Hamlet.*) An interesting selection of lady playwrights: a 2-vol set of works of Aphra Behn (Astrea) (1682), *Plays Never Before Printed* by Margaret Cavendish, Duchess of Newcastle (1668), Mrs Hannah Cowley's *The Belle's Stratagem* (1782), Lady Wallace's*The Ton: or Follies of the* Fashion (1738) and the actress Fanny Kemble's *Star of Selville* printed in New York (1837). Revolutionary War General John Burgoyne is represented by *Lord of the Manor* (1781) and there is the oddity *The Empress of Morocco, A Tradegy with* Sculptures by Elkanah Settle (1673). Also, a very rare *The City Match,* printed at Oxford in 1659. Incl 20 first editions, from Dryden's *All for Love* (1678) to Sheridan's *A Trip to* Scarborough (1781).

NY —UNIVERSITY OF ROCHESTER, Rush Rhees Library, Department of Rare Books and Special Collections, Rochester, 14627. Peter Dzwonkoski, Librn
Holdings: Vols (300) Cat Mss Pix
Notes: 18th and 19th century English and 19th century American plays and works on theatre. Also includes manuscript collections on theatre, and papers of Clement William Scott, John Lawrence Toole, Authur Wing Pinero, Charles Kean, Lillian Russell and Leon Marks Lion, collection of 130 lithographic theatre posters, and collection of programs and playbills, chiefly Rochester, NY and New York City, 1870-1950. Unpublished guides to ms collections available in repostitory.

NC —UNIVERSITY OF NORTH CAROLINA, CHARLOTTE, J Murrey Atkins Library, UNCC Station, Charlotte, 28223. Robert F Brabham Jr, Special Collections Librn
Holdings: Cat
Notes: Most of the plays (842 in 110 vols) were originally collected by Augusta Sophia, a daughter of George III. At her death, they passed to her brother Ernst August, Elector of Hanover, and became part of the Knigliche Ernst-August-Fideicommiss-Bibliothek, which was dispersed at auction in 1970-1971. Period covered is 1618-1826.

NC —DUKE UNIVERSITY, William R Perkins Library, Rare Book Room, Durham, 27706. John L Sharpe, III, Cur
Notes: Thornton Shirley Graves collection of 1400 English plays. Plays of the 18th century. Percival F Hinton collection of 3000 plays - primarily 19th century. English Drama-19th Century.

ENGLISH DRAMA (cont.)

OH —OHIO UNIVERSITY, Vernon R Alden Library, Department of Archives and Special Collections, Athens, 45701. Gary A Hunt, Head
Holdings: Vols 800 Uncat
Notes: A collection of about 800 plays, chiefly by English authors, published in the 18th and 19th centuries.

OH —OHIO STATE UNIVERSITY, William Oxley Thompson Memorial Library, 1858 Neil Ave Mall, Columbus, 43210. Robert A Tibbetts, Cur of Special Collections
Holdings: Vols 325 Cat
Notes: Caroline to Restoration drama; 17th century editions.

PA —UNIVERSITY OF PENNSYLVANIA, Furness Memorial Library, 3420 Walnut St, Philadelphia, 19104. Georgianna Ziegler, Cur
Holdings: Vols (18,000) Cat
Notes: Particularly strong in Restoration drama. 700 editions. Downs 3370; (supplement) 1777. Separate catalog.

SC —UNIVERSITY OF SOUTH CAROLINA, Thomas Cooper Library, Columbia, 29208. Kenneth E Toombs, Dir of Libraries; Roger Mortimer, Rare Book Librn
Holdings: Vols 450 Cat
Notes: Limited mainly to editions published 1800-1825.

TN —UNIVERSITY OF TENNESSEE, KNOXVILLE, Library, Knoxville, 37996. John Dobson, Special Collections Librn
Holdings: Cat
Notes: The John C Hodges Collection, incl about 150 original editions of Congreve's works and a large collection of books about him, English drama, and the theater of the 16th and 17th centuries; also material by and about other dramatists of the period. Described in *The John C Hodges Collection of William Congreve in the University of Tennessee Library: A Bibliographical* Catalog, by Albert M Lyles and John Dobson (Knoxville: Univ of Tennessee Libraries, 1970), 135pp.

TX —RICE UNIVERSITY, Fondren Library, Woodson Research Center, 6100 S Main St, PO Box 1892, Houston, 77251. Nancy Parker, Dir Woodson Research Center
Holdings: Vols 5000 Cat
Notes: The Axson Collection of 18th-century English drama. Many of the plays are represented in multiple editions or issues.

†WA —WASHINGTON STATE UNIVERSITY, Library, Manuscripts, Archives & Special Collections, Pullman, 99164. John F Guido, Head
Holdings: // Cat Mss Pix
Notes: The Robert Cushman Butler Collection of Theatrical Illustrations contains: approx 1600 illustrations, sheet music covers, programs and playbills; approx 100 mss of actors, actresses and playwrights; and approx 200 volumes of theatrical history and reminiscences, several extra-illustrated, concentrating on 18th-19th century British and American drama. A guide to the collection is in preparation.

ENGLISH ENGRAVERS see Engravers, English

ENGLISH FACTORIES

WI —UNIVERSITY OF WISCONSIN, MADISON, Memorial Library, 728 State St, Madison, 53706. David Henige, Librn
Holdings: Cat Microforms
Notes: Collection consists of 90 microfilm reels of extant records of the Royal African Company (T7O series in the Public Record Office, London) together with several smaller collections of materials relating to the English presence on the Gold Coast in the 17th and 18th centuries. It is the most complete collection of its kind in the US. Various parts are described in David Henige, "Some Materials on the Early Guinea Coast in the United Kingdom," *African Research and Documentation,* no 11 (1976), pp 25-28. Also incl economics and social documents relating to the Belgian Congo particularly Katanga Province.

ENGLISH FICTION

GA —EMORY UNIVERSITY, Robert W Woodruff Library, Atlanta, 30322. Herbert Johnson, Dir
Holdings: Vols (650,000) Cat Mss Microforms
Notes: Strong in 18th and 19th century literature, especially 19th century prose fiction, incl first editions and "yellow backs." Also incl the Kemp Malone collection of Old English, Middle English, Anglo-Norman and supporting materials.

NY —NEW YORK PUBLIC LIBRARY, Research Libraries, General Research Division, Fifth Ave & 42 St, New York, 10018. Rodney Phillips, Chief
Holdings: Vols (2,225,000) Cat Maps Pix Microforms
Budget: ($775,718)

NY —NEW YORK UNIVERSITY, Elmer Holmes Bobst Library, Div of Special Collections, Washington Sq S, New York, 10012. Frank Walker, Librn; Patrick McGuire, Asst Librn
Holdings: Vols (100,000) Cat Mss Pix
Notes: The Fales Collection of first (and other) editions of English and American novels from about 1750 to date (about 70, 000 titles). Mss (30,000) pieces.

NC —DUKE UNIVERSITY, William R Perkins Library, Durham, 27706. Elvin E Strowd, University Librn

PA —UNIVERSITY OF PENNSYLVANIA, Van Pelt Library, Rare Books Collection, 34 & Walnut Sts, Philadelphia, 19104. Daniel Traister, Special Collections Librn
Holdings: Vols 1280 Cat
Notes: First editions of the major and minor English novelists of the 18th century. Downs 3382; (Supplement) 1781.

SC —GREENVILLE COUNTY LIBRARY, 300 College St, Greenville, 29601. Joan Sorensen, Asst Dir of Public Servs
Holdings: Vols 5000 Microforms
Notes: Microbook by Library Resources, Inc.

TX —TRINITY UNIVERSITY, Elizabeth Coates Maddux Library, 715 Stadium Dr, San Antonio, 78284. Richard Hume Werking, Library Dir; Craig Likness, Head Bibliographer
Notes: General reference.

WI —MILWAUKEE PUBLIC LIBRARY, 814 W Wisconsin Ave, Milwaukee, 53233. Donald J Sager, City Librn
Holdings: Vols (2700) Cat
Notes: Collection of definitive editions of collected works of British and American authors; incl most of the significant editions of Shakespeare starting with Rowe.

ENGLISH FICTION—BIOGRAPHY see Authors, English

ENGLISH FICTION—19TH CENTURY

CA —UNIVERSITY OF CALIFORNIA, LOS ANGELES, Research Library, Dept of Special Collections, 405 Hilgard Ave, Los Angeles, 90024. Edward Shreeves, Chairman, Bibliographers Group; David S Zeidberg, Head
Holdings: Vols 15,000 Cat
Notes: 15,000 books, incl the Michael Sadleir Collection; scattered letters and mss.

MA —BOSTON UNIVERSITY, Mugar Memorial Library, Special Collections Dept, 771 Commonwealth Ave, Boston, 02215. Howard B Gotlieb, Dir
Holdings: Vols Cat
Notes: Victorian fiction.

ENGLISH IN AFRICA

WI —UNIVERSITY OF WISCONSIN, MADISON, Memorial Library, 728 State St, Madison, 53706. David Henige, Librn
Holdings: Cat Microforms
Notes: Collection consists of 90 microfilm reels of extant records of the Royal African Company (T7O series in the Public Record Office, London) together with several smaller collections of materials relating to the English presence on the Gold Coast in the 17th and 18th centuries. It is the most complete collection of its kind in the US. Various parts are described in David Henige, "Some Materials on the Early Guinea Coast in the United Kingdom," *African Research and Documentation,* no 11 (1976), pp 25-28. Also incl economics and social documents relating to the Belgian Congo particularly Katanga Province.

ENGLISH LANGUAGE

CA —LOS ANGELES PUBLIC LIBRARY, Foreign Languages Dept, 630 W Fifth St, Los Angeles, 90071. Sylva Manoogian, Principal Librn
Holdings: Vols 969 Cat
Budget: ($41,500)

CA —UNIVERSITY OF CALIFORNIA, LOS ANGELES, Research Library, Dept of Special Collections, 405 Hilgard Ave, Los Angeles, 90024. Edward Shreeves, Chairman, Bibliographers Group; David S Zeidberg, Head
Notes: Charles Kay Ogden's mss and correspondence concerning, and collection of books by various authors published in, Basic English.

†CA —UNIVERSITY OF SAN FRANCISCO, Richard A Gleeson Library, The Countess Bernardine Murphy Donohue Rare Book Room, San Francisco, 94117. D Steven Corey, Special Collections Librn
Notes: Some highly specialized materials.

DC —FOLGER SHAKESPEARE LIBRARY, 201 E Capitol St, Washington, 20003. Philip A Knachel, Acting Dir
Holdings: Vols (223,571) Cat Mss Pix Periodicals Microfilms
Notes: Collections described in *Catalog of Printed Books of the Folger Shakespeare* Library, 28 vols; *First Supplement,* 3 vols (Boston: G K Hall, 1970, 1976); *Second* Supplement in 2 vols (Boston: G K Hall, 1981); *Catalog of Manuscripts of the Folger Shakespeare Library,* 3 vols (Boston: G K Hall, 1971); and *The Widening Circle: The Story of the Folger Library and Its* Collections (Washington, DC: Folger Shakespeare Library, 1976). Collections incl 39 vols of plays with ms annotations and stage directions by John Philip Kemble. Library use restricted to advanced research scholars.

IL —SOUTHERN ILLINOIS UNIVERSITY, CARBONDALE, Delyte W Morris Library, Special Collections Dept, Carbondale, 62901. David V Koch, Cur of Special Collections; Louisa Bowen, Cur of Manuscripts
Holdings: Vols 5000 Cat Mss
Notes: Expatriate American and British writers between World Wars I and II.

IL —NEWBERRY LIBRARY, 60 W Walton St, Chicago, 60610. Diana Haskell, Cur of Modern Mss
Holdings: Vols 100,000 Cat Mss
Budget: $10,000
Notes: Special strengths: Arthuriana; Spenser and Spenseriana; English drama, especially to 18th century; miscellanies; D H Lawrence (printed editions); Conrad (printed editions); Joyce (printed eds); Irish Renaissance. Standard English writers, many minor ones; periodicals.

IN —INDIANA STATE UNIVERSITY, Cunningham Memorial Library, Dept of Rare Books & Special Collections, Terre Haute, 47809. Lawrence J McCrank, Head
Holdings: Vols 7000
Notes: The Cordell Collection of early English and American dictionaries.

IA —UNIVERSITY OF IOWA, University Libraries, Iowa City, 52242. Frank Paluka, Head, Special Collections Dept
Holdings: Vols 51// Uncat
Notes: Principally English-language dictionaries of the 17th and 18th centuries. The Ernest Horn Collection.

KS —UNIVERSITY OF KANSAS, Kenneth Spencer Research Library, Special Collections Dept, Lawrence, 66045. Alexandra Mason, Librn
Holdings: Cat Mss
Notes: Strongest in 18th and 19th century. Old English (Clubb Collection); 18th-century

ENGLISH LANGUAGE (cont.)

plays, poems, sermons. English Poetical Miscellanies collection. Literary periodicals and newspapers (18th century). Noncirculating.

†MA —WILLIAMS COLLEGE, Chapin Library of Rare Books, PO Box 426, Williamstown, 01267. Robert L Volz, Custodian
Holdings: Vols 5500 Cat
Notes: No material available on interlibrary loan.

MI —UNIVERSITY OF MICHIGAN, Library, Dept of Rare Books & Special Collections, Ann Arbor, 48109. Robert J Starring, Head
Holdings: Cat Mss
Notes: Strong in English drama, especially Restoration and 18th-century plays, also dictionaries, treatises on shorthand, imaginary voyages, and in the following authors: Carlyle, Defoe, Dickens, Dryden, Dunsany, R B Cunninghame Graham, W H Hudson, Milton, Pater, Shakespeare, L A G Strong, Swift, Tennyson, Trollope, and Yeats.

MT —UNIVERSITY OF MONTANA, Library, Missoula, 59801. Katherine Schaefer, Special Collections Librn
Holdings: Cat
Notes: Incl small collection of mss and letters, mainly 19th century England.

NY —CITY UNIVERSITY OF NEW YORK, City College, Morris R Cohen Library, North Academic Center, Convent Ave & 137th St, New York, 10031. Barbara J Dunlap, Archivist
Holdings: Cat
Notes: First editions of English authors, late 19th and early 20th centuries (1900-1920). Restricted use.

NY —NEW YORK PUBLIC LIBRARY, Research Libraries, General Research Division, Fifth Ave & 42 St, New York, 10018. Rodney Phillips, Chief
Holdings: Vols (2,225,000) Cat Maps Pix Microforms
Budget: ($775,718)

NY —NEW YORK PUBLIC LIBRARY, Mid-Manhattan Library, Literature and Language Dept, 455 Fifth Ave, New York, 10016. Eric Steele, Sr Principal Librn
Holdings: Vols (160,000) Cat Phonorecords Microforms Audiotapes
Budget: ($92,000)
Notes: Large

NY —NEW YORK PUBLIC LIBRARY, Berg Collection of English & American Literature, Fifth Ave & 42 St, New York, 10018. Lola L Szladits, Cur
Holdings: Vols 20,000 Cat Mss
Notes: The preface to the Collection's G K Hall catalog, 1969, (5 vols), prints an outline of history and guide to the catalog: "The Berg Collection of English and American Literature is one of America's most celebrated collections of first editions, rare books, autograph letters, and mss. Among the 20,000 printed items and 50,000 mss, covering the entire range of English and American literature, there can be found rarities considered museum pieces by the book world. Irving, Hawthorne, Emerson, Thoreau, Whitman are represented in first editions as well as in mss. Mark Twain can be studied in depth by scholars who have not only correspondence but also the original mss of *A Connecticut Yankee in King Arthur's Court* and *Following the Equator,* besides many others, to consult. The policy of the Collection has been to acquire work of contemporaries. James RussellLowell's mss are next to ms poems by Robert Lowell. Gertrude Stein's printed works are followed by those of John Steinbeck. For the following 20th-century authors, the Collection is justly famous: Arnold Bennett, Joseph Conrad, George Gissing, Thomas Hardy, John Masefield, Bernard Shaw, Virginia Woolf, Lewis Carroll, Rudyard Kipling, and Robert Browning. The Irish Literary Renaissance survives in the papers of Lady Gregory."

NY —NEW YORK UNIVERSITY, Elmer Holmes Bobst Library, Div of Special Collections, Washington Sq S, New York, 10012. Frank Walker, Librn; Patrick McGuire, Asst Librn
Holdings: Vols (100,000) Cat Mss Pix
Notes: The Fales Collection of first (and other) editions of English and American novels from about 1750 to date (about 70, 000 titles). Mss (30,000) pieces.

NY —PIERPONT MORGAN LIBRARY, 29 E 36 St, New York, 10016. Herbert Cahoon, Librn
Notes: One of the largest collections, with many rarities, unique works and mss.

OH —CLEVELAND PUBLIC LIBRARY, Literature Dept, 325 Superior Ave, Cleveland, 44114. Evelyn Ward, Head
Holdings: Vols Cat
Notes: Comprehensive collection of literary texts, with a large body of literary history, criticism, and biography. Very strong in Shakespeare. Extensive material on all phases of the English language and its use. Many first editions, special editions, and rarities. Microprint. Many reference aids.

PA —TEMPLE UNIVERSITY LIBRARIES, Special Collections Dept, Rare Books & Mss Section, Philadelphia, 19122. Thomas M Whitehead, Cur
Holdings: Vols (3000) Cat Mss
Notes: Extensive holdings of modern English and American literature, late 19th, 20th centuries. First and limited editions, association copies, supported by mss holdings. Special sub-collections of Walter de la Mare, Joseph Conrad, Robert Louis Stevenson, Joel Chandler Harris, E H W Meyerstein, Thackeray, George MacDonald, W W Gibson, John Masefield, Tennyson, Sir Walter Scott.

PA —UNIVERSITY OF PENNSYLVANIA, Van Pelt Library, Rare Books Collection, 34 & Walnut Sts, Philadelphia, 19104. Daniel Traister, Special Collections Librn
Holdings: Cat Mss Microforms
Notes: Strong in Middle English.

TX —TEXAS CHRISTIAN UNIVERSITY, Mary Couts Burnett Library, Fort Worth, 76129.
Holdings: Vols 1500 Cat Mss
Notes: The William Luther Lewis Collection. Special strengths is English Romantic writers. See Kendall, Lyle H *A Descriptive Catalogue of the W L Lewis Collection: Part I, Manuscripts, Inscriptions, Art.* (Fort Worth: TCU Press, 1970).

TX —TEXAS TECH UNIVERSITY, Library, Lubbock, 79409. David J Murrah, Assoc Dir for Special Collections

UT —BRIGHAM YOUNG UNIVERSITY, Harold B Lee Library, Unversity Hill, Provo, 84602. Sterling Albrecht, Dir
Holdings: Vols 2000 Cat
Notes: A large collection covering all phases of literature and life in the Age of Queen Victoria. Incl an unusual collection of "Yellow Backs" (1750 printer's proofs for yellow-back covers of original paperbacks of the 19th century).

BC —VANCOUVER PUBLIC LIBRARY, Language & Literature Div, 750 Burrard St, Vancouver, V6Z 1X5, Can. B Kinnear, Head
Notes: A good general collection of language dictionaries, supplemented by clippings and a word file compiled by the staff. Incl books and pamphlets.

ENGLISH LANGUAGE—ANALYSIS AND PARSING see English Language—Grammar

ENGLISH LANGUAGE—CHRESTOMATHIES AND READERS see Readers and Speakers

ENGLISH LANGUAGE—DICTIONARIES

MA —OLD STURBRIDGE VILLAGE, Research Library, Sturbridge, 01566. Theresa Rini Percy, Librn
Holdings: Cat
Notes: American editions, to 1850.

MI —UNIVERSITY OF MICHIGAN, Library, Dept of Rare Books & Special Collections, Ann Arbor, 48109. Robert J Starring, Head
Holdings: Cat
Notes: Largely 18th and 19th century although earlier works also are represented. Substantial runs of Johnson's and Webster's dictionaries.

ENGLISH LANGUAGE—GRAMMAR

MI —UNIVERSITY OF MICHIGAN, English Language Institute/Linguistics Library, 1013 N University Bldg, Ann Arbor, 48109. Patricia M Aldridge, Librn
Holdings: Vols (4500) Cat Maps VF Videotapes
Notes: The collection on teaching English as a foreign language is fairly complete; in modern language study it is also quite good. Supporting subjects are linguistics and English grammar; psychology, American culture, education, foreign student adjustment, and bibliography are covered.

PA —UNIVERSITY OF PITTSBURGH, Hillman Library, Special Collections Dept, 363 Hillman Library, Pittsburgh, 15260. Charles E Aston Jr, Coordinator
Holdings: Vols (13,480) Cat Mss
Notes: The John A Nietz Textbook Collection of primarily American textbooks in 3 areas; primary school books to 1900, secondary texts to ca 1930, and pedagogical books (1000 vols on the history and theory of education incl writings of the key figures in the field of education). Books are cataloged via an in-house computer printout and are accessible via name, title, subject, place, publisher and date. Late 18th and all of the 19th centuries are well represented. Important titles in each subject are discussed in John A Nietz's *Old Textbooks* (Pittsburgh, 1961) and in his *The Evolution of American Secondary School Textbooks* (Rutland, Vt, 1966). Collection also incl the papers (noncirculating) of Prof John A Nietz.

ENGLISH LANGUAGE—MIDDLE ENGLISH (1100-1500)

GA —EMORY UNIVERSITY, Robert W Woodruff Library, Atlanta, 30322. Herbert Johnson, Dir
Holdings: Vols (650,000) Cat Mss Microforms
Notes: Strong in 18th and 19th century literature, especially 19th century prose fiction, incl first editions and "yellow backs." Also incl the Kemp Malone collection of Old English, Middle English, Anglo-Norman and supporting materials.

KS —UNIVERSITY OF KANSAS, Kenneth Spencer Research Library, Special Collections Dept, Lawrence, 66045. Alexandra Mason, Librn
Holdings: Cat Mss
Notes: Strongest in 18th and 19th century. Old English (Clubb Collection); 18th-century plays, poems, sermons. English Poetical Miscellanies collection. Literary periodicals and newspapers (18th century). Noncirculating.

NY —NEW YORK PUBLIC LIBRARY, Mid-Manhattan Library, Literature and Language Dept, 455 Fifth Ave, New York, 10016. Eric Steele, Sr Principal Librn
Holdings: Vols (160,000) Cat Phonorecords Microforms Audiotapes
Budget: ($92,000)

ENGLISH LANGUAGE—MIDDLE ENGLISH (1100-1500) (cont.)

Notes: Large number of bibliographic tools for undergraduate study of all aspects of literature. Important journals in the field with significant or complete runs of the major serials. Representative selection of American and English little magazines. Extensive collection of works, criticism and biographies of major and minor American and English writers; special attention directed towards Black American literature. Strong in works in translation and criticism of Spanish and French literature, representative in other foreign literatures. Considerable collection of criticism in Spanish and French. Department includes material on the teaching of literature, the techniques of creative writing, and the history of the theater when important to the study of dramatic literature. Collection has many facsimile and microfiche editions of primary and secondary sources with emphasis on English literature, from the Old English period to 1784. Substantial collection of recordings of prose, poetry and drama.

PA —UNIVERSITY OF PENNSYLVANIA, Van Pelt Library, Rare Books Collection, 34 & Walnut Sts, Philadelphia, 19104. Daniel Traister, Special Collections Librn
Holdings: Cat Mss Microforms
Notes: Strong in Middle English.

ENGLISH LANGUAGE—OLD ENGLISH see Anglo-Saxon Language and Literature

ENGLISH LANGUAGE—PARSING see English Language—Grammar

ENGLISH LANGUAGE—PRIMERS see Primers

ENGLISH LANGUAGE—READERS AND SPEAKERS see Readers and Speakers

ENGLISH LANGUAGE—SPELLERS see Spellers

ENGLISH LANGUAGE—STUDY AND TEACHING—FOREIGN STUDENTS

CA —UNIVERSITY OF CALIFORNIA, LOS ANGELES, Education & Psychology Library, 390 Powell Library Bldg, Los Angeles, 90024. Barbara Duke, Librn
Holdings: Vols (8000) Cat Audiotapes Microforms
Budget: $4000
Notes: An important collection emphasizing both the teaching of and learning of English as a second language.

MI —UNIVERSITY OF MICHIGAN, English Language Institute/Linguistics Library, 1013 N University Bldg, Ann Arbor, 48109. Patricia M Aldridge, Librn
Holdings: Vols 4500 Cat Microforms VF Videotapes
Notes: Second language learning, especially English as a second language.

NY —NEW YORK PUBLIC LIBRARY, Mid-Manhattan Library, Literature and Language Dept, 455 Fifth Ave, New York, 10016. Eric Steele, Sr Principal Librn
Holdings: Vols (160,000) Cat Phonorecords Microforms Audiotapes
Budget: ($92,000)
Notes: Broad coverage for the study of over 100 languages and dialects, materials on most areas of theoretical and applied linguistics. Extensive runs of major journals. 3000 records and cassettes aid in the learning of 40 languages, in addition to English.

NC —CUMBERLAND COUNTY PUBLIC LIBRARY, North Carolina Foreign Language Center, 328 Gillespie St, Fayetteville, 28301. Patrick M Valentine, Coordinator
Notes: The Center is an English as a Second Language (ESL) resource library for North Carolina. It has a selection of works on teaching ESL and foreign languages, plus vocabularies, grammars and cultural aids in English as well as many other languages. The Center carries bilingual records and tapes designed to help non-active speakers, ranging from Arabian and American to Spanish and Vietnamese, learn English.

BC —VANCOUVER COMMUNITY COLLEGE, King Edward Campus Library, 1155 E Broadway, PO Box 24620, Station C, Vancouver, V6B 4H2, Can. Paul Cook, Campus Librn
Holdings: Vols (25,000) Cat Maps Slides Audiotapes 16mm Films Filmstrips
Notes: Teaching English as a second language. Curriculum development.

ENGLISH LAW see Law, English

ENGLISH LITERATURE

AZ —UNIVERSITY OF ARIZONA, University Library, Special Collections, Tucson, 85721. Louis A Hieb, Head
Holdings: Vols (7000) Cat Mss Microforms
Budget: ($30,000)
Notes: Strong in Restoration and 18th century drama. Major author strengths of the 18th century are Dryden, Fielding, Pope, Richardson, and Smollett. The major collection of 19th century authors are Byron, Dickens, Scott, Thackeray, Trollope, the Brownings, Stevens, Tennyson, and Wordsworth. The 20th century collection is dominated by the works of Auden, Durrell, Conrad, Hardy, D H Lawrence, and Yeats.

CA —UNIVERSITY OF CALIFORNIA, DAVIS, Shields Library, Dept of Special Collections, Davis, 95616. Donald Kunitz, Head; C Danial Elliott, Asst Head

CA —UNIVERSITY OF CALIFORNIA, SAN DIEGO, Central University Library, Mandeville Dept of Special Collections, La Jolla, 92093. Lynda Corey Claassen, Head
Holdings: Vols 1355 Uncat
Notes: The Hooker Collection of 18th-century English literature.

CA —LOS ANGELES PUBLIC LIBRARY, Foreign Languages Dept, 630 W Fifth St, Los Angeles, 90071. Sylva Manoogian, Principal Librn
Holdings: Vols 969 Cat
Budget: ($41,500)

CA —OCCIDENTAL COLLEGE, Library, 1600 Campus Rd, Los Angeles, 90041. Michael C Sutherland, Special Collections Librn
Holdings: Vols (2000)// Cat
Notes: The Weller Collection of Romantic Literature was given by Earl V Weller. Primary emphasis is on John Keats, but first or other important editions of many Romantic poets of this period are also included.

CA —UNIVERSITY OF CALIFORNIA, LOS ANGELES, William Andrews Clark Memorial Library, 2520 Cimarron St, Los Angeles, 90018.
Holdings: Cat Mss Pix
Notes: Extensive collection, first editions, etc.

CA —CONTRA COSTA COUNTY LIBRARY, 1750 Oak Park Blvd, Pleasant Hill, 94523. Barbara Potter, Librn

CA —UNIVERSITY OF SAN FRANCISCO, Richard A Gleeson Library, The Countess Bernardine Murphy Donohue Rare Book Room, San Francisco, 94117. D Steven Corey, Special Collections Librn
Holdings: Vols 1000 Mss
Notes: A wide range of authros and literature of the period are collected. There are particularly developed collections of Oscar Wilde, Max Beerbohm, Arthur Symons, George Moore, Richard Le Gallienne, Laurence Housman, William Watson, John Davidson, and Norman Gale. The emphasis is on English rather than American literature.

CA —HUNTINGTON LIBRARY, Art Gallery & Botanical Gardens, 1151 Oxford Rd, San Marino, 91108. Robert L Middlekauff, Dir; Daniel H Woodward, Librn
Notes: Approx 350,000 rare books, 250,000 reference books, manuscript collection of nearly 2,500,000 pieces and between 200,000 and 300,000 prints, rare photographs and other related materials. The fullest available survey is now *Guide to Literary Manuscripts in the Huntington Library*, a 539-page handlist published by the Library in 1979. Also *Guide to British Historical Manuscripts in the Huntington Library* (1982). Our important collections of early English printed books are partially recorded in *Short Title Catalogue of Books Printed in* England,..1475-1640 (1926) and *Short Title Catalogue of Books Printed in* England,..1641-1700 (1945).

CA —STANFORD UNIVERSITY LIBRARIES, Cecil H Green Library, Stanford, 94305. Michael T Ryan, Cur
Holdings: Vols (23,000) Cat Mss
Notes: The Charlotte Ashley Felton Memorial Library. English and American literature of the 19th and 20th centuries: American literature beginning with the period of Hawthorne and his contemporaries and incl the first editions of 20th century authors such as Robert Frost, William Faulkner, and John Steinbeck. The collection of British literature begins with Jane Austen's novels and the poetry of Lord Byron, Shelley, and Keats, and incl 20th century authors such as Somerset Maugham, Lawrence Durrell, D H Lawrence and Anthony Powell.

CO —UNIVERSITY OF COLORADO, Libraries, Special Collections, Boulder, 80309. Nora J Quinlan, Head
Holdings: Vols Uncat
Notes: George Creamer Collection. Over two thousand books on 19th century English literature (Dickens), and 19th and 20th centuries British and American book illustration. In addition, approx 250 children's illustrated books.

CT —YALE UNIVERSITY, Beinecke Rare Book & Manuscript Library, Osborn Collection, New Haven, 06520. Stephen R Parks, Cur
Holdings: Mss

DC —FOLGER SHAKESPEARE LIBRARY, 201 E Capitol St, Washington, 20003. Philip A Knachel, Acting Dir
Holdings: Vols (223,571) Cat Mss Pix Periodicals Microfilms
Notes: Collections described in *Catalog of Printed Books of the Folger Shakespeare* Library, 28 vols; *First Supplement,* 3 vols (Boston: G K Hall, 1970, 1976); *Second* Supplement in 2 vols (Boston: G K Hall, 1981); *Catalog of Manuscripts of the Folger Shakespeare Library,* 3 vols (Boston: G K Hall, 1971); and *The Widening Circle: The Story of the Folger Library and Its* Collections (Washington, DC: Folger Shakespeare Library, 1976). Collections incl 39 vols of plays with ms annotations and stage directions by John Philip Kemble. Library use restricted to advanced research scholars.

GA —EMORY UNIVERSITY, Robert W Woodruff Library, Atlanta, 30322. Herbert Johnson, Dir
Holdings: Vols (650,000) Cat Microforms
Notes: Strong in 18th and 19th century literature, especially 19th century prose fiction, incl first editions and "yellow backs." Also incl the Kemp Malone collection of Old English, Middle English, Anglo-Norman and supporting materials.

IL —SOUTHERN ILLINOIS UNIVERSITY, CARBONDALE, Delyte W Morris Library, Special Collections Dept, Carbondale, 62901. David V Koch, Cur of Special Collections; Louisa Bowen, Cur of Manuscripts
Holdings: Vols 5000 Cat Mss
Notes: Expatriate American and British writers between World Wars I and II.

IL —NEWBERRY LIBRARY, 60 W Walton St, Chicago, 60610. Diana Haskell, Cur of Modern Mss
Holdings: Vols 100,000 Cat Mss
Budget: $10,000
Notes: Special strengths: Arthuriana; Spenser and Spenseriana; English drama, especially to 18th century miscellanies; D H Lawrence (printed editions); Conrad (printed editions); Joyce (printed eds); Irish Renaissance. Standard English writers, many minor ones; periodicals.

ENGLISH LITERATURE (cont.)

IL —NORTHWESTERN UNIVERSITY, Library, Special Collections Dept, 1937 Sheridan Rd, Evanston, 60201. R Russell Maylone, Cur
Holdings: (9000) Cat Mss
Notes: First, limited, special editions, letters, ephemera of major 20th century Anglo-Irish and English writers such as James Joyce, W B Yeats, T S Eliot, W H Auden and Lawrence Durrell, as well as representative minor writers. Correspondence files of James B Pinker & Sons, literary agents: 50,000 pieces, 1900-1934 inclusive.

IL —QUINCY COLLEGE LIBRARY, Quincy, 62301. Victor Kingery, OFM, Librn
Holdings: Vols 5000 Cat
Budget: $2000
Notes: 19th century English literature.

IL —AUGUSTANA COLLEGE, Library, Rock Island, 61201. Marjorie M Miller, Special Collections Librn
Holdings: Vols (5000) Cat

IL —SKOKIE PUBLIC LIBRARY, 5215 Oakton St, Skokie, 60077. Mary Radmacher, Chief Librn
Holdings: Vols (20,000) Cat Phonorecords
Budget: ($364,500)
Notes: Maintained as American and English literature and criticism subject center under the North Suburban Library System's Coordinated Acquisitions Program.

IN —INDIANA UNIVERSITY, Lilly Library, Seventh St, Bloomington, 47405. William R Cagle, Librn
Holdings: Cat Mss
Notes: Extensive holdings of first editions.

IN —INDIANA UNIVERSITY, Institute for Sex Research Library, 416 Morrison Hall, Bloomington, 47401. Douglas Freeman, Collections and Services Librn; Joan Brewer, Information Services Librn
Holdings: Vols (62,000) Cat Mss Pix Phonorecords Audiotapes Slides Films Microforms
Budget: ($20,000)
Notes: One of the greatest and most extensive collections on sexual behavior, the library collects materials on all aspects of sex activity, with special emphasis on behavioral and social aspects. Also collects erotic literature and sexual ephemera. Incl 105 audiotapes, 23 vertical file drawers, 108 phonorecords, 55,000 pictures, 5000 slides, and 1700 films. Rich in French, German and American sources; also much Oriental. Semitraditional erotic poetry and song of 17th-18th century England, Bawdy limericks, double-entendre, puns, slang, erotic literature, graffiti, slang and special dictionaries, proverbs and sayings, epigrams and research materials of the Kinsey Studies, etc. Contact Information Service for: literature searching, preparation of bibliographies, permission to use collection. Limited photocopying.

IN —UNIVERSITY OF EVANSVILLE, Clifford Memorial Library & Learning Resources, 1800 Lincoln Ave, Evansville, 47714. P Grady Morein, University Librn
Holdings: Vols 3900 // Cat Mss Pix Microforms
Notes: *The Library of English Literature*, Parts I, II, and III. Bookform catalogs and catalog cards.

KS —UNIVERSITY OF KANSAS, Kenneth Spencer Research Library, Special Collections Dept, Lawrence, 66045. Alexandra Mason, Librn
Holdings: Cat Mss
Notes: Strongest in 18th and 19th century. Old English (Clubb Collection); 18th-century plays, poems, sermons. English Poetical Miscellanies collection. Tennyson, Yeats, Joyce. Literary periodicals and newspapers (18th century). Noncirculating.

KY —UNIVERSITY OF KENTUCKY, Margaret I King Library, Dept of Special Collections, Lexington, 40506. William Marshall, Head
Holdings: Vols (8000) Cat Mss
Notes: W Hugh Peal Collection of mss and books chiefly relating to British and American literature. Particularly strong in Lamb, Wordsworth, Coleridge and Southey. Incl 4 cubic feet of mss. Incl 16th-20th centuries.

LA —R W NORTON ART GALLERY, Library, 4747 Creswell Ave, Shreveport, 71106. Jerry M Bloomer, Librn
Holdings: // Cat

MD —JOHNS HOPKINS UNIVERSITY, Milton S Eisenhower Library, Charles & 34 Sts, Baltimore, 21218. Ann S Gwyn, Assistant Dir for Special Collections
Holdings: Vols Cat Mss Microforms
Notes: The Osler Collection (Tudor and Stuart Club) contains original editions of Shelley, Milton, Keats, Donne, Defoe, Thomas Fuller, Golden Book of Marcus Aurelius (1559). A collection of his articles made by Walt Whitman. 17th and 18th century commonplace books in English and French, in ms. Most English translations of Jakob Boehme. Cards in main catalog. Also, not included in the above figure, Pollard and Redgrave's, and Wing's Early English Books on microfilm.

MA —HARVARD UNIVERSITY LIBRARY, Widener Library, Cambridge, 02138. Carolyn Fawcett, Specialist in Book Selection
Holdings: Cat
Notes: *Widener Library Shelflist* Nos 35-38 (1971) lists 133,256 volumes in English literature.

MA —WHEATON COLLEGE, Library, Norton, 02766. Sherrie S Bergman, College Librn
Holdings: Vols (2100) Cat
Notes: The Cole Collection. English and American literature and poetry based on the personal library of Dr Samuel Valentine Cole.

MA —BRANDEIS UNIVERSITY, Goldfarb Library, 415 South St, Waltham, 02154. Bessie Hahn, Dir
Notes: John Galsworthy Collection. Approx 175 letters written to Joseph Conrad, Sir Edmund Gosse and others and 15 linear ft of books consisting of first editions and books about John Galsworthy. Access to the collection of books is through the Main Card Catalog and Special Collections Catalog. A finding list to the correspondence is in Special Collections.

†MA —WILLIAMS COLLEGE, Chapin Library of Rare Books, PO Box 426, Williamstown, 01267. Robert L Volz, Custodian
Holdings: Vols 5500 Cat
Notes: No material available on interlibrary loan.

MI —UNIVERSITY OF MICHIGAN, Library, Dept of Rare Books & Special Collections, Ann Arbor, 48109. Robert J Starring, Head
Holdings: Cat Mss
Notes: Strong in English drama, especially Restoration and 18th-century plays, also dictionaries, treatises on shorthand, imaginary voyages, and in the following authors: Carlyle, Defoe, Dickens, Dryden, Dunsany, R B Cunninghame Graham, W H Hudson, Milton, Pater, Shakespeare, L A G Strong, Swift, Tennyson, Trollope, and Yeats.

MO —UNIVERSITY OF MISSOURI-KANSAS CITY, General Library, 5100 Rockhill Road, Kansas City, 64110. Kenneth J LaBudde, Dir; Gordon Hendrickson, Assoc Dir; Marilyn Carbonell, Ref Librn
Holdings: Vols 108,000 Cat
Notes: (4121 current serial subscriptions) includes an emphasis on drama and includes Thomas and Mila Baker Collection of Twentieth-Century British and American Literature.

MO —UNIVERSITY OF MISSOURI-SAINT LOUIS, Thomas Jefferson Library, 8001 Natural Bridge Rd, Saint Louis, 63121.
Notes: American and British Utopian Literature: Approximately 1000 vols of Literary Utopias. Collection is partially described and listed in Sargent, Lyman Tower *British and American Utopian Literature, 1516-1975: An Annotated* Bibliography, (G K Hall, 1979); note: a second edition is in preparation. Collection also includes galley proofs of some of the titles.

MO —WASHINGTON UNIVERSITY, John M Olin Library, Campus Box 1061, St Louis, 63130.
Holdings: Cat Mss
Notes: Particular strength in 19th and 20th century original editions. Also autographs and mss of prominent literary figures, entered under personal names elsewhere in this volume.

MT —UNIVERSITY OF MONTANA, Library, Missoula, 59801. Katherine Schaefer, Special Collections Librn
Holdings: Cat
Notes: Incl small collection of mss and letters, mainly 19th century England.

NE —KEENE MEMORIAL LIBRARY, 1030 N Broad St, Fremont, 68025. William S McDermott, Dir
Holdings: Vols (1500) Cat
Notes: Items in the collection incl scattered 18th century British first editions of novels, etc (20 vols) and books published by the Limited Editions Club (cat 50 vols).

NJ —PRINCETON UNIVERSITY, Library, Rare Books Dept, Princeton, 08544. Stephen Ferguson, Cur
Holdings: Cat

NJ —WILLIAM PATERSON COLLEGE OF NEW JERSEY, Sarah Byrd Askew Library, 300 Pompton Rd, Wayne, 07470. Robert Lopresti, Librn
Holdings: Vols (500) Cat
Notes: First editions of US and English authors. Bibliography available.

NY —ALFRED UNIVERSITY, Herrick Memorial Library, Alfred, 14802. June E Brown, Head Librn
Notes: The Evelyn Tennyson Openhym Collection of modern British literature and social history. Papers, incl correspondence of authors concerned with the business aspects of authorship. Gift of Evelyn Tennyson Openhym of Wellsville, NY. Also, 5300 volumes of British literature.

NY —CITY UNIVERSITY OF NEW YORK, City College, Morris R Cohen Library, North Academic Center, Convent Ave & 137th St, New York, 10031. Barbara J Dunlap, Archivist
Holdings: Cat
Notes: First editions of English authors, 19th and 20th centuries. Restricted use.

NY —NEW YORK PUBLIC LIBRARY, Research Libraries, General Research Division, Fifth Ave & 42 St, New York, 10018. Rodney Phillips, Chief
Holdings: Vols (2,225,000) Cat Maps Pix Microforms
Budget: ($775,718)

NY —NEW YORK PUBLIC LIBRARY, Mid-Manhattan Library, Literature and Language Dept, 455 Fifth Ave, New York, 10016. Eric Steele, Sr Principal Librn
Holdings: Vols (160,000) Cat Phonorecords Microforms Audiotapes
Budget: ($92,000)
Notes: Extensive collection of works, criticism and biographies of major and minor American writers for undergraduate study; special attention directed towards Black American literature. Collection includes material on the teaching of literature, the techniques of creative writing, and the history of the theater when relevant to the study of dramatic literature. Substantial or complete runs of the major journals. Representative collection of literary magazines. Recordings of prose, poetry and drama.

NY —NEW YORK PUBLIC LIBRARY, Berg Collection of English & American Literature, Fifth Ave & 42 St, New York, 10018. Lola L Szladits, Cur
Holdings: Vols 20,000 Cat Mss
Notes: The preface to the Collection's G K Hall catalog, 1969, (5 vols), prints an outline of history and guide to the catalog: "The Berg Collection of English and American Literature is one of America's most celebrated collections of first editions, rare books, autograph letters, and mss. Among the 20,000 printed items and 50,000 mss, covering the entire range of English and American literature, there can be found rarities considered museum pieces by the book world. Irving, Hawthorne, Emerson,

ENGLISH LITERATURE (cont.)

Thoreau, Whitman are represented in first editions as well as in mss. Mark Twain can be studied in depth by scholars who have not only correspondence but also the original mss of *A Connecticut Yankee in King Arthur's Court* and *Following the Equator,* besides many others, to consult. The policy of the Collection has been to acquire work of contemporaries. James RussellLowell's mss are next to ms poems by Robert Lowell. Gertrude Stein's printed works are followed by those of John Steinbeck. For the following 20th-century authors, the Collection is justly famous: Arnold Bennett, Joseph Conrad, George Gissing, Thomas Hardy, John Masefield, Bernard Shaw, Virginia Woolf, Lewis Carroll, Rudyard Kipling, and Robert Browning. The Irish Literary Renaissance survives in the papers of Lady Gregory."

NY —NEW YORK UNIVERSITY, Elmer Holmes Bobst Library, Div of Special Collections, Washington Sq S, New York, 10012. Frank Walker, Librn; Patrick McGuire, Asst Librn
Holdings: Vols (100,000) Cat Mss Pix
Notes: The Fales Collection of first (and other) editions of English and American novels from about 1750 to date (about 70, 000 titles). Mss (30,000) pieces.

NC —BELMONT ABBEY COLLEGE, Abbot Vincent Taylor Library, Belmont, 28012. Marjorie McDermott, Dir
Holdings: Vols (10,000) Cat Mss Pix
Notes: Patristics (incl Migne's *Patrologie*), Roman Catholic Church history, philosophy, literature (American and British), and both US and North Carolina history. A substantial number of the books date from the 15th, 16th, and 17th centuries. Most of the source material in Catholic studies particularly could not be obtained elsewhere in the Southeast.

NC —DUKE UNIVERSITY, William R Perkins Library, Durham, 27706. Elvin E Strowd, University Librn

†NC —WAKE FOREST UNIVERSITY, Z Smith Reynolds Library, Box 7777, Reynold Sta, Winston-Salem, 27109. Richard J Murdoch, Rare Book Librn
Notes: Literature collections with emphasis on a select list of English, Irish and American authors total 13,000 vols. Incl are first and significant editions, works about the authors and some ephemera. Noncirculating.

OH —OHIO UNIVERSITY, Vernon R Alden Library, Department of Archives and Special Collections, Athens, 45701. Gary A Hunt, Head
Holdings: Vols (10,191) Uncat Mss
Notes: The Edmund Blunden Collection of Romantic and Modern Literature, being the private library assembled by Blunden during 6 decades of active collecting. The bulk of the collection (6,264 titles) consists of English imprints from the period 1750-1850, concentrating on literature but also incl contemporary works on art, natural history, philosophy and other subjects important for understanding the background of English Romanticism. Among the authors most heavily represented by first and other early editions are: Allington, Barnes, Bloomfield, Byron, Clare, Coleridge, Cowper, Dyer, Edgeworth, Goldsmith, Hazlitt, Hunt, Lamb, Landor, Scott, Thompson and Wordsworth. Books written by Blunden himself, together with his Georgian contemporaries (particularly W H Davies, Walter De la Mare, and Sigfried Sassoon) form a second major area of strength. Many ofthe modern books are inscribed to Blunden, and nearly all the volumes in the collection bear his annotations.

OH —BOWLING GREEN STATE UNIVERSITY, Jerome Library, Center for Archival Collections, Bowling Green, 43403. Paul D Yon, Dir; Elaine R Ezell, Reference Archivist; Nancy Steen, Rare Books Librn
Holdings: Vols 1600 Cat Mss Letters Pix
Budget: ($3000)
Notes: The Robert Aickman Collection contains about 40 of Aickman's manuscripts of both published and unpublished works as well as the late author's personal library which is strong in the areas of English literature and theatre of the 19th and 20th centuries and in the area of the supernatural.

OH —CLEVELAND PUBLIC LIBRARY, Literature Dept, 325 Superior Ave, Cleveland, 44114. Evelyn Ward, Head
Holdings: Vols Cat Microforms Phonorecords
Notes: Comprehensive collection of literary texts, with a large body of literary history, criticism, and biography. Very strong in Shakespeare. Extensive material on all phases of the English language and its use. Many first editions, special editions, and rarities. Microprint. Many reference aids.

PA —FREE LIBRARY OF PHILADELPHIA, Rare Book Dept, Logan Sq, Philadelphia, 19103. Marie E Korey, Rare Book Librn
Holdings: Cat
Notes: A collection of 400 selected first and early editions of major English writers incl J M Barrie, George Borrow, Robert and Elizabeth Barrett Browning, John Keats, John Milton, Stephen Phillips, Arthur W Pinaro, Robert Louis Stevenson, Alfred Lord Tennyson, William Makepeace Thackeray, and Anthony Trollope.

PA —PHILIP H & A S W ROSENBACH FOUNDATION LIBRARY, 2010 DeLancey Pl, Philadelphia, 19103. Clive E Driver, Dir
Holdings: Cat Mss Maps Pix

PA —TEMPLE UNIVERSITY LIBRARIES, Special Collections Dept, Rare Books & Mss Section, Philadelphia, 19122. Thomas M Whitehead, Cur
Holdings: Vols (3000) Cat Mss
Notes: Extensive holdings of modern English and American literature, late 19th, 20th centuries. First and limited editions, association copies, supported by mss holdings. Special sub-collections of Walter de la Mare, Joseph Conrad, Robert Louis Stevenson, Joel Chandler Harris, E H W Meyerstein, Thackeray, George MacDonald, W W Gibson, John Masefield, Tennyson, Sir Walter Scott.

PA —UNIVERSITY OF PENNSYLVANIA, Van Pelt Library, Rare Books Collection, 34 & Walnut Sts, Philadelphia, 19104. Daniel Traister, Special Collections Librn
Holdings: Cat Mss Microforms
Notes: Strong in Middle English.

PA —UNIVERSITY OF PITTSBURGH, Hillman Library, Pittsburgh, 15260.
Notes: Incl the William Steinberg Collection of 800 musical scores, many signed by composers, and 1400 vols of English, French, German, Japanese, and Chinese literature.

PA —PENNSYLVANIA STATE UNIVERSITY, Fred Lewis Pattee Library, University Park, 16802. Stuart Forth, Dean of Libraries
Holdings: Vols (28,000) Cat Mss Microforms
Notes: Also a special collection of 1676 volumes for the period, 1660-1800.

SC —UNIVERSITY OF SOUTH CAROLINA, Thomas Cooper Library, Columbia, 29208. Kenneth E Toombs, Dir of Libraries; Roger Mortimer, Rare Book Librn
Holdings: Vols 3500 Cat
Notes: Very strong in the 18th, 19th and 20th centuries for American literature. First editions.
See also entries under English Drama; Bridges, Robert; Literary Annuals and Giftbooks.

TX —UNIVERSITY OF TEXAS LIBRARIES, General Libraries, PO Box P, Austin, 78713. Carolyn Bucknell, Asst Dir for Collection Development
Holdings: Cat Microforms

TX —WEST TEXAS STATE UNIVERSITY, Cornette Library, PO Box 748 WT Sta, Canyon, 79016. Faye Hendrickson, Special Collections Asst
Holdings: Vols (451,253) Uncat Microforms
Notes: Includes microform collection. No photocopying.

TX —SOUTHERN METHODIST UNIVERSITY, Fondren Library, Dallas, 75275. Curt Holleman, Librn for Collection Development

TX —TEXAS CHRISTIAN UNIVERSITY, Mary Couts Burnett Library, Fort Worth, 76129.
Holdings: Vols 1500 Cat Mss
Notes: The William Luther Lewis Collection. Special strengths is English Romantic writers. See Kendall, Lyle H *A Descriptive Catalogue of the W L Lewis Collection: Part I, Manuscripts, Inscriptions, Art.* (Fort Worth: TCU Press, 1970).

TX —TEXAS TECH UNIVERSITY, Library, Lubbock, 79409. David J Murrah, Assoc Dir for Special Collections

TX —SAN ANTONIO COLLEGE, Library, 1001 Howard St, San Antonio, 78284. James O Wallace, Dir
Holdings: Vols 2500 Cat Microforms
Notes: The Morrison Collection of Eighteenth Century British Literature. Partially described in: Hennington, Betty M "Lois G Morrison Collection of Eighteenth Century English Literature: a Checklist" (unpublished M L S thesis) Texas Woman's University, 1968, also see "The Morrison Collection." *Scriblerian,* vol 1 pp 32-33 (spring 1969). Especially strong in material relating to Eustace Budgell; A Moore, W Webb and Edmund Curll imprints. A separate catalog in maintained for the collection with entries for author, title, personal subjects, printers and booksellers, date of publication, engravers and association copies.

TX —TRINITY UNIVERSITY, Elizabeth Coates Maddux Library, 715 Stadium Dr, San Antonio, 78284. Richard Hume Werking, Library Dir; Craig Likness, Head Bibliographer
Notes: General reference.

UT —BRIGHAM YOUNG UNIVERSITY, Harold B Lee Library, Unversity Hill, Provo, 84602. Sterling Albrecht, Dir
Holdings: Vols 3000 Mss
Notes: Victorian books, autographed letters, mss and original drawings.

VA —MARY WASHINGTON COLLEGE, E Lee Trinkle Library, Fredericksburg, 22401. Ruby Y Weinbrecht, Librn
Holdings: Vols 26,000 Cat Microforms
Budget: $10,000

†WA —WASHINGTON STATE UNIVERSITY, Library, Manuscripts, Archives & Special Collections, Pullman, 99164. John F Guido, Head
Holdings: Vols Mss Pix
Notes: The library of Virginia and Leonard Woolf (from Monk's House and Victoria Sq) forms the nucleus of the collection, which incorporates the library of Sir Leslie Stephen, Virginia's father. Leonard's interests are reflected by works concerning the Labour Party, the Fabian Society, as well as Ceylon. Their interest in printing and publishing works of significance is reflected by the collection of Hogarth Press publications (1917-1941). Incl works by Virginia and Leonard Woolf, the Bloomsbury Group, as well as by other friends--eg, Elizabeth Robins, Victoria Sackville-West, Harold Nicholson, etc. Many of these unique copies, ie, of association and textual interest. Other 20th century English authors significantly represented by printed and/or manuscript material incl: the Sitwells, Margaret Sackville, Rose Macaulay, D H Lawrence, John Masefield, RupertCroft-Cooke, Charles Williams. Partially cataloged.

WA —SEATTLE PUBLIC LIBRARY, 1000 Fourth Ave, Seattle, 98104. Ronald A Dubberly, City Librn
Holdings: Cat

WI —UNIVERSITY OF WISCONSIN, MADISON, Memorial Library, British & American Language & Literature Collection, 728 State St, Madison, 53706. Yvonne Schofer, Bibliographer
Holdings: Vols 7500 Cat
Notes: Incl the Arthur Beatty Collection, over 1000 vols, principally English poetry of the Romantic period; Benjamin David Berry Collection of English Grammars; Miles L Hanley Collection of English and American Linguistics; William Stanley Marshall Collection, some 30 first and early editions of English literature; Pitman Library, 2500 vols; Frederick William Roe Collection, ca

ENGLISH LITERATURE (cont.)

25 early editions of English literary classics; Teerink Swift Collection, ca 100 vols on and about Jonathan Swift and others of his age; Thordarson Collection; Ruth C Wallerstein Collection, ca 1400 vols; and the Helen C White Collection, over 4000 vols and 6000 serial items. Also, the 20th Century Literature Collection, which incl 255 significant 20th century English and American authors.

WI —MILWAUKEE PUBLIC LIBRARY, 814 W Wisconsin Ave, Milwaukee, 53233. Donald J Sager, City Librn
Holdings: Vols (2700) Cat
Notes: Collection of definitive editions of collected works of British and American authors; incl most of the significant editions of Shakespeare starting with Rowe.

WI —UNIVERSITY OF WISCONSIN, MILWAUKEE, Library, Box 604, Milwaukee, 53201. William C Roselle, Dir
Holdings: Vols (68,000) Cat Mss Phonorecords Audiotapes
Notes: Special strengths of the literature collection include Shakespeare Research Collection (1800 volumes), 17th Century Collection (600 volumes), William Blake, James Joyce, Howard Fast (English-language translations), contemporary small press poetry publications, etc.

BC —UNIVERSITY OF BRITISH COLUMBIA, Library, 1956 Main Mall, Vancouver, V6T 1Y3, Can. Anne Yandle, Special Collections Librn
Holdings: Vols 45,000 Cat Mss
Notes: The Colbeck Collection of 19th century belles lettres English Literature, particularly Anglo-Irish. One of the largest collections in western Canada.

BC —VANCOUVER PUBLIC LIBRARY, Language & Literature Div, 750 Burrard St, Vancouver, V6Z 1X5, Can. B Kinnear, Head
Notes: General collection of poetry, drama criticism, novels, pamphlets. Index files of author biographies, poetry in periodicals, criticism in periodicals; also poetry index, both compiled by the staff to books and unindexed periodicals. Partially cataloged. Also incl audiotapes.

NS —MOUNT SAINT VINCENT UNIVERSITY, Library, 166 Bedford Hwy, Halifax, B3M 2J6, Can. Lucian Bianchini, University Librn
Holdings: Vols 7000 Cat
Budget: ($125,000)
Notes: The MacDonald Collection consists of 19th and 20th century English and American literature, fine bindings, a few examples of fore-edge painting, limited editions, first editions, and autographed copies.

ON —MCMASTER UNIVERSITY, Mills Memorial Library, Div of Archives & Research Collections, Hamilton, L8S 4L6, Can. G R Hill, Univ Librn
Holdings: Vols 26,000 Cat
Notes: This collection consists of books and pamphlets printed in the 18th century, as well as over 200 periodical titles. Parts of the collection have been detailed in *Library Research News*, vol 3, no 3 (Oct 1975) and vol 3, no 5 (May 1976).

ON —NATIONAL LIBRARY OF CANADA, 395 Wellington St, Ottawa, K1A 0N4, Can. Andre Preibish, Dir
Holdings: Vols 34,000
Notes: Includes 350 serial titles. The Library has been receiving on legal deposit all current literary works in English and French published in Canada since 1950. Intensive acquisition of earlier works and those published abroad. The collection aims to be comprehensive. In addition, the collection is supported by representative resources for English, American, French and Commonwealth Literature.

ON —UNIVERSITY OF TORONTO, Thomas Fisher Rare Book Library, 120 Saint George St, Toronto, M5S 1A5, Can. Richard G Landon, Head
Holdings: Vols 5400 Cat Mss
Notes: Three collections. Duncan Collection is named for donor, Douglas Duncan, art dealer and collector, Toronto. Contains first and subsequent important editions of Richard Aldington, Max Beerbohm, Norman Douglas, Aldoux Huxley, and D H Lawrence. Manuscripts by Beerbohm, Aldington, Lawrence, William Sharp. Endicott Collection named in honor of Norman J Endicott, Professor of English, University of Toronto, contains first and significant later editions of over fifty British writers whose major work falls into the period from 1880 to 1930. Fisher Collection named for donor, Charles B Fisher, contains first and significant editions of Kipling, Norman Douglas, and Lord Dunsany.

SK —UNIVERSITY OF REGINA, Campion College, Library, Regina, S4S 0A2, Can. Myfanwy Truscott, Librn
Holdings: Vols (50,000) Cat
Budget: ($100,000)

ENGLISH LITERATURE—BIOGRAPHY see Authors, English

ENGLISH LITERATURE—CANADA see Canadian Language and Literature

ENGLISH LITERATURE—15TH-17TH CENTURIES

NY —CARL H PFORZHEIMER LIBRARY, 41 E 42 St, New York, 10017. Mihai H Handrea, Librn
Holdings: Cat Mss Pix
Notes: English Literature from Caxton to 1700; first editions of 18th and 19th centuries, incl mss material on Shelley and his circle; fine presses (Bruce Rogers); George Gissing; women writers 1790-1840, (Mary Wollstonecraft, Mary Hays, Lady Blessington).

PA —PENNSYLVANIA STATE UNIVERSITY, Fred Lewis Pattee Library, University Park, 16802. Stuart Forth, Dean of Libraries
Holdings: Vols (28,000) Cat Mss Microforms
Notes: Also a special collection of 1676 volumes for the period, 1660-1800.

ENGLISH LITERATURE—MIDDLE ENGLISH

OH —CLEVELAND PUBLIC LIBRARY, Fine Arts and Special Collections Department, 325 Superior Ave, Cleveland, 44114. Alice N Loranth, Head
Holdings: Cat Mss
Notes: Part of the Medieval Literature Collection. Medieval texts, translations, facsimile reproductions, bibliographies and catalogs of mss, romances, epics, early chronicles and histories. Icelandic sagas, fabliaux (tales), legends, lives of the Saints are well represented. Monographs, scholarly journals and serials on philogy, linguistics and literature with special emphasis on Middle English, Old French, Middle High German, Middle Dutch and early Irish texts. *See also* entry under Folklore; Literature, Medieval

ENGLISH LITERATURE—NEW ZEALAND see New Zealand Literature

ENGLISH LITERATURE—OLD ENGLISH see Anglo-Saxon Language and Literature

ENGLISH LITERATURE—PHILIPPINE ISLANDS see Philippine Languages and Literature

ENGLISH MUSIC see Music, English

ENGLISH NEWSPAPERS see Newspapers, English

ENGLISH POETRY

CT —YALE UNIVERSITY, Beinecke Rare Book & Manuscript Library, Osborn Collection, New Haven, 06520. Stephen R Parks, Cur
Holdings: Mss
Notes: English poetry, especially 17th-18th centuries. Incl first-line index of all poems.

IL —NEWBERRY LIBRARY, 60 W Walton St, Chicago, 60610. Diana Haskell, Cur of Modern Mss
Holdings: Vols 10,000 Cat
Notes: Restricted use; Noncirculating.

KS —UNIVERSITY OF KANSAS, Kenneth Spencer Research Library, Special Collections Dept, Lawrence, 66045. Alexandra Mason, Librn
Holdings: Cat Mss
Notes: Strongest in 18th and 19th century. Old English (Clubb Collection); 18th-century plays, poems, sermons. English Poetical Miscellanies collection. Tennyson, Yeats, Joyce. Literary periodicals and newspapers (18th century). Noncirculating.

MD —JOHNS HOPKINS UNIVERSITY, Milton S Eisenhower Library, Charles & 34 Sts, Baltimore, 21218. Ann S Gwyn, Assistant Dir for Special Collections
Holdings: Vols Cat
Notes: Strong in Romantic Poets, particularly Byron (Dickey Collection). First editions.

MO —WASHINGTON UNIVERSITY, John M Olin Library, Campus Box 1061, St Louis, 63130.
Holdings: Cat Microforms
Notes: English poetry and drama of the Tudor period. 100 reels and microfilms and photostats of original mss in English and European libraries. Checklist of collection by library and collection number.

NY —STATE UNIVERSITY OF NEW YORK, COLLEGE AT BUFFALO, Lockwood Memorial Library, Main St, Buffalo, 14260. Stanton F Biddle, Assoc Dir
Notes: 20th century poetry in English.

NY —POETRY SOCIETY OF AMERICA, Van Voorhis Library, 15 Gramercy Park, New York, 10003. Jason Shinder, Dir
Holdings: Vols 5000 Cat Mss
Notes: The American poetry ranges from the turn of the century to contemporary poets. There is a separate catalog for American poetry. American and other poetry anthologies, biography, criticism, essays, and poetics. A large holograph collection and memorabilia of the Poetry Society of America are included in the Rare Book Division of the NY Public Library.

NC —DUKE UNIVERSITY, William R Perkins Library, Durham, 27706. Elvin E Strowd, University Librn

NC —DUKE UNIVERSITY, William R Perkins Library, Rare Book Room, Durham, 27706. John L Sharpe, III, Cur
Notes: Thomas J Wise collection. Many rare pieces, including works of Byron, Coleridge, Dryden, Pope and Hardy. 135 political and religious broadsides, mostly of the 17th century.

OH —CLEVELAND PUBLIC LIBRARY, Literature Dept, 325 Superior Ave, Cleveland, 44114. Evelyn Ward, Head
Holdings: Vols Cat Phonorecords
Notes: A large collection of poetry, substantial representation of English poets, early through modern. Extensive critical and biographical materials. Extensive card index to individual poems, by author, title, first line, and subject.

PA —UNIVERSITY OF PITTSBURGH, Hillman Library, Special Collections Dept, Hervey Allen Collection, Pittsburgh, 15260. Charles E Aston, Jr, Coordr
Holdings: Vols 600 Cat
Notes: Emphasis on British poetry of the 20th century with special focus on the period 1950-date. Largely small press publications.

TX —UNIVERSITY OF HOUSTON-CLEAR LAKE CITY, Neumann Library, 2700 Bay Area Blvd, Houston, 77058.
Notes: The Dee Walker Poetry Collection. A collection of poetry books by mostly American and English authors, many autographed. Collected and subsequently donated to the College by the one-time alternate poet laureate of Texas.

WI —UNIVERSITY OF WISCONSIN, MADISON, Memorial Library, British & American Language & Literature Collection, 728 State St, Madison, 53706. Yvonne Schofer, Bibliographer
Holdings: Vols (1000)// Cat
Notes: Arthur Beatty Collection. Consists of

ENGLISH POETRY (cont.)

over 1000 volumes, principally in the English poetry of the Romantic period, strong in Coleridge, Tennyson, Swinburne, the prose of De Quincy and the folk poetry and balladry of Great Britain and Europe. Outstanding for its first and other editions of Wordsworth. About 200 titles in the Department of Rare Books and Special Collections; the rest is in stacks.

ENGLISH POETS see Poets, English

ENGLUND, KEN, 1914-

CA —UNIVERSITY OF CALIFORNIA, LOS ANGELES, Research Library, Dept of Special Collections, 405 Hilgard Ave, Los Angeles, 90024. Edward Shreeves, Chairman, Bibliographers Group; David S Zeidberg, Head
Holdings: Mss Pix
Notes: 44 linear feet of screenplays, playscripts, and personal papers.

ENGRAVERS, ENGLISH

PA —FREE LIBRARY OF PHILADELPHIA, Rare Book Dept, Logan Sq, Philadelphia, 19103. Marie E Korey, Rare Book Librn
Holdings: Uncat Mss
Notes: The John Frederick Lewis Collection of 1650 autograph letters of 17th and 18th century British engravers.

ENGRAVERS, ENGRAVING AND ENGRAVINGS

CA —UNIVERSITY OF CALIFORNIA, LOS ANGELES, Research Library, Dept of Special Collections, 405 Hilgard Ave, Los Angeles, 90024. Edward Shreeves, Chairman, Bibliographers Group; David S Zeidberg, Head
Notes: 200 books about bookplates; 10,000 examples in various collections.

KY —UNIVERSITY OF LOUISVILLE, Allen R Hite Art Institute, Library, Belknap Campus, Louisville, 40292. Gail Gilbert, Librn
Holdings: Vols (40,000) Cat Pix
Budget: ($29,000)
Notes: Incl books on art, architecture, landscape architecture and gardening, prints, printing, illustrated books and brass rubbings. Library subscribes to 200 periodical titles in these and other areas. Collection circulates to faculty and staff only, with same restrictions placed on interlibrary loan. Library also has collections of bookplates, posters, original prints, hand-made Christmas cards and clippings file filling 56 VF drawers.

LA —R W NORTON ART GALLERY, Library, 4747 Creswell Ave, Shreveport, 71106. Jerry M Bloomer, Librn
Holdings: Vols 127 Cat

MA —ROBBINS LIBRARY, 700 Massachusetts Ave, Arlington, 02174. Peter L Fenton, Dir
Holdings: Cat Pix
Notes: 150,000 graphic works in all media, emphasizing portrait prints from the 15th century to the present day.

MA —AMERICAN ANTIQUARIAN SOCIETY LIBRARY, 185 Salisbury St, Worcester, 01609. Marcus A McCorison, Dir & Librn
Notes: A rare collection relating to the beginnings of the art among Anglo-Americans. Incl copies of all of Paul Revere's engravings, and nearly all of Peter Pelham's mezzotints, as well as most of the works by other early American engravers. Examples of about half the works in Stauffer and Fielding subject and engraver catalogs.

MN —MAYO MEDICAL LIBRARY, History of Medicine Collection, Rochester, 55905. Nancy R Hensel, Librn
Holdings: Pix
Notes: Over 300 bookplates of physicians and medical institutions. Listed. Collection described: Mann, Ruth J: "Of bookplates, books, and their owners." *Mayo Clin Proc* 46:358-360, May 1971.

MO —THE NELSON-ATKINS MUSEUM OF ART, Kenneth & Helen Spencer Art Reference Library, 4525 Oak St, Kansas City, 64111. Stanley W Hess, Librn
Notes: Strong in European Renaissance and Baroque, 18th and 19th century graphic arts.

NJ —NEWARK PUBLIC LIBRARY, Art & Music Dept, 5 Washington St, Newark, 07101. William J Dane, Supv
Holdings: Mss Maps Pix Slides
Notes: 1,000,000 pictures with supporting collections of postcards, 2000 portfolios of plates of design, fine and circulating print collections (incl Japanese), 1400 illustrated books, 4000 posters. The classification scheme and headings used are listed in *The Picture Collection Subject Headings* (Shoe String Press, 1968).

NJ —PRINCETON UNIVERSITY, Library, Graphic Arts Collection, Princeton, 08540. Dale Roylance, Cur
Notes: Sinclair Hamilton Collection. One of the largest collections of American Illustrated Books in the US. 2 vols published; catalog available. Also, large collection of illustrated books of all countries, for all periods.

NY —COLLECTORS CLUB, Library, 22 E 35 St, New York, 10016. Werner Elias, Librn
Holdings: Cat Mss Maps Pix Slides
Notes: Incl a special area of essays and proof which may be of interest to people desiring knowledge of art and engravers. Incl photographs of stamps. 100,000 items.

NY —METROPOLITAN MUSEUM OF ART, Dept of Prints & Photographs, 82 St & Fifth Ave, New York, 10028. Colta Ives, Cur
Holdings: Vols (10,000)
Notes: Contained in a collection of 500,000 prints from 15th to 20th century. Approx 10, 000 illustrated books; European and American. No photocopying.

OH —CINCINNATI ART MUSEUM, Library, Eden Park, Cincinnati, 45202. Patrician P Rutledge, Librn
Holdings: Vols (45,850) Cat Microforms
Notes: Art library containing all subjects on art-history, graphic arts, advertising art, etc; special strength in prints, ie engravings, etc. Near Eastern art and decorative arts are also strong. At least 90,000 art exhibition catalogs. Emphasis on artists of Cincinnati and vicinity in vertical file material.

RI —BROWN UNIVERSITY, John Carter Brown Library, Providence, 02912. Norman Fiering, Librn; Everett C Wilkie Jr, Bibliographer; Susan Danforth, Cur Maps & Prints
Holdings: Vols 1000
Notes: Separately published sheet engravings; most of these are European depictions of events in the New World, particularly British American colonies.

ON —METROPOLITAN TORONTO LIBRARY, Fine Arts Dept, 789 Yonge St, Toronto, M4W 2G8, Can. Alan Suddon, Head
Holdings: Vols(42,000) Cat Pix Microforms
Notes: Extensive collection.

ON —UNIVERSITY OF TORONTO, Thomas Fisher Rare Book Library, 120 Saint George St, Toronto, M5S 1A5, Can. Richard G Landon, Head
Holdings: Vols 100// Cat Maps Pix
Notes: Collection named for donor Sidney T Fisher. Collection includes copies of most books in which Hollar's plates were published. About 3500 loose prints include various states of many etchings; some proofs; group of 19th century forgeries by Peter Thompson; original chalk and wash sketch for Hollar's etching of John the Baptist. See: Pennington, Richard, *Catalogue of Wenceslaus Hollar's Etchings.* Manuscript to be published by the Cambridge University Press. Based in part of Fisher holdings and records these as well as other libraries' holdings in its location information.

ENHARMONIC ORGAN see Organ

ENIAC

DE —HAGLEY MUSEUM AND LIBRARY, Eleutherian Mills-Hagley Foundation Inc, PO Box 3630, Greenville, 19807. Richmond D Williams, Dir; Heddy A Richter, Imprints Librn
Notes: Records of the Sperry-Univac Company (1940-1975; 400 cubic feet) document the early development and rapid growth of the computer industry. The collection incl technical and administrative documents relating to the ENIAC, BINAC and UNIVAC computers.

ENIGMAS see Riddles

ENOLOGY

CA —CALIFORNIA STATE UNIVERSITY, FRESNO, Henry Madden Library, Dept of Special Collections, Fresno, 93740. Ronald J Mahoney, Head
Holdings: Vols (3400) Cat Maps Pix
Notes: Books and pamphlets relating to the history and development of viticulture and enology. Emphasizes pre-1920 worldwide imprints. Incl 900 merchants' catalogs, 1400 pamphlets, 200 wine lists, 750 periodical issues, and ephemera. Partially cataloged.

CA —WINE MUSEUM OF SAN FRANCISCO, Alfred Fromm Rare Wine Books Library, 633 Beach St, San Francisco, 94109. Barbara W Thompson, Cur
Holdings: Vols (700) Cat Maps Pix
Notes: The Library consists primarily of volumes on aspects of wine history, enology, and viticulture. All texts are completely cross-referenced by subject/title/author. Noncirculating. Chronological listing available at cost.

ENSIGNS see Flags (Vexillology)

ENTERS, AGNA

NY —NEW YORK PUBLIC LIBRARY, Performing Arts Research Center, Dance Collection, 111 Amsterdam Ave, New York, 10023. Genevieve Oswald, Cur
Notes: A very large collection by and about Agna Enters.

ENTERTAINERS

FL —RINGLING MUSEUM OF THE CIRCUS, Library, PO Box 1838, Sarasota, 33578. Nan Fisher, Visitor Services Specialist
Holdings: Vols (350) Cat
Notes: Collection also incl long runs (and indexes) of circus periodicals.

IN —INDIANA STATE UNIVERSITY, EVANSVILLE, Library, 8600 University Blvd, Evansville, 47712. Gina R Walker, Acting Archivist
Holdings: Vols 20 Cat Pix
Notes: Over 800 movie press kits sent to local film critics; 1955-present, plus some photos of entertainers from the early 1920s. Photos of film, opera and television entertainers.

MA —BOSTON UNIVERSITY, Mugar Memorial Library, Special Collections Dept, 771 Commonwealth Ave, Boston, 02215. Howard B Gotlieb, Dir
Holdings: Cat Mss Pix
Notes: Incl personal papers and literary productions of numerous modern actors, actresses, musicians (composers and performers) of all kinds. A complete list is available.

NY —NEW YORK PUBLIC LIBRARY, Performing Arts Research Center, Billy Rose Theatre Collection, 111 Amsterdam Ave, New York, 10023. Dorothy L Swerdlove, Cur
Holdings: Cat Pix
Notes: Clippings, photographs, reviews of acts, etc, periodicals devoted to news of activity in the field.

NY —NEW YORK PUBLIC LIBRARY, Performing Arts Research Center, Rodgers & Hammerstein Archives of Recorded Sound, 111 Amsterdam Ave, New York, 10023.
Holdings: Cat Tapes
Notes: A collection of taped interviews, representing over 400 prominent figures. Incl are voices of Richard Nixon, Billy Graham, Maurice Chevalier, Sammy Davis, Jr, Dr Albert Sabin, etc.

ENTERTAINERS (cont.)

†NY —SHUBERT ARCHIVE, Lyceum Theatre, 149 W 45th St, New York, 10036. Brigitte Kueppers, Archivist
Notes: The vast Shubert Archive, mostly unexplored is the largest collection in the world representative of the "business" of the theatre. It includes almost all of the Shubert empire's correspondence from the turn of the century to the 1950s, road company records, thousands of playscripts (American and European), set and costume designs, music scores for Shubert productions, business, financial, and legal records, actors' contracts, etc.

OK —WILL ROGERS MEMORIAL LIBRARY, W Will Rogers Blvd, Box 157, Claremore, 74017. Reba N Collins, Dir
Holdings: Vols (2800) Cat Slides Phonorecords Audiotapes Videotapes 16mm Films Microforms
Notes: Thousands of original manuscripts, letters, photographs, plus many other personal items, all by or about Will Rogers. Library is available by appointment or special permission.

TX —DALLAS PUBLIC LIBRARY, Fine Arts Div, 1515 Young St, Dallas, 75201. Richard L Waters, Acting Dir; Jane Holahan, Manager
Notes: Papers of John Rosenfield, eminent Dallas critic for 41 years. Also *The W E Hill Theatre Collection,* 18th-20th centuries, ca 75,000 items. Contains letters, portraits, and photos of leading American, British, and European dramatists, actors, managers and other persons associated with the stage of the performing arts, particularly music, playbills, posters of stage plays, minstrel shows, and circuses; and newspaper and magazine clippings. The bulk of the collection consists of 19th and 20th century items. Described in LC card catalog MS 66-1621. Partially described in the "Fine Arts Department of the Dallas Public Library presents an exhibit of selected material from the W E Hill theatre collection on the occasion of the opening of the collection..." (1966). Gift of estate of William Ely Hill, 1963.

ENTERTAINMENT INDUSTRY

GA —UNIVERSITY OF GEORGIA, Libraries, Special Collections Division, Athens, 30602. Vesta Lee Gordon, Asst Dir for Special Collections
Notes: The Arbitron Collection of television and radio program ratings, 1949-date (except past year). In-depth, statistical analyses of the listening public by age, sex, county, some ethnic groups, farm population, listening preferences, etc. 26,302 bound vols. 2 reports, 1949-81. To be added to annually.

ENTOMOLOGY

CA —UNIVERSITY OF CALIFORNIA, BERKELEY, Life Sciences Library, Entomology Library, 201 Wellman Hall, Berkeley, 94720. Nancy Axelrod, Librn
Holdings: Vols (12,000) Cat Microforms
Notes: A highly specialized collection limited to materials on insects, arachnida and animal parasites. Special emphasis is given to works on pest control, particularly on biological methods of control. The library's holdings in the field of parsasitology emphasize medical parsasitology. Incl over (17,000) pamphlets.

CA —UNIVERSITY OF CALIFORNIA, DAVIS, Environmental Toxicology Library, Davis, 95616. Ming-yu Li, Documentation Specialist
Holdings: Vols (5000) Cat
Notes: Library is open to the public for reference only. In addition to the cataloged holdings, the library also maintains a pamphlet collection of 50 file drawers on agricultural chemicals, environmental pollution, heavy metals, food toxicants, toxicology, pesticides and trace elements.

CA —UNIVERSITY OF CALIFORNIA, DAVIS, General Library, Davis, 95616. Bernard Kreissman, University Librn; C Danial Elliott, Asst Head, Dept Special Collections
Holdings: Vols (14,000) Cat Mss Maps Slides
Notes: Relatively strong in materials published from 1920 to date. Areas of entomology that are emphasized incl bees (apiculture), nematology, parsasitology and the control of insect populations. The slides and specimens in the collection are housed in the research collection of the Department of Entomology.

CA —CALIFORNIA STATE UNIVERSITY, FULLERTON, Library, Box 4150, Fullerton, 92634. Linda Herman, Special Collections Librn
Holdings: Vols 3530 Cat Mss
Notes: Capt P Markham Kerridge Angling Collection incl materials on angling, entomology, ichthyology, conservation, travel, recreation, and related areas. A computer author printout with title, imprint, and various codes is updated annually. Books and pamphlets are supplemented by 2750 periodical issues, and extensive ephemera.

CA —UNIVERSITY OF CALIFORNIA, LOS ANGELES, Biomedical Library, Center for Health Sciences, Los Angeles, 90024. Louise Darling, Biomedical Librn

CA —UNIVERSITY OF CALIFORNIA, RIVERSIDE, University Library, Bio-Agricultural Library, Batchelor Hall, Riverside, 92521. Barbara Montanary, Head
Holdings: Vols (130,000) Cat Mss Maps Pix Microforms
Notes: The Bio-Agricultural Library (formerly the Library of Citrus Experiment Station of the University of California) is well known for its complete collections in the fields of the agriculture sciences. It is especially known for its emphasis on entomology, incl bio-control; botany, citriculture, plant sciences, nematology and plant pathology; arid and semi-arid lands research and subtropical agriculture. Specific areas of interest are avocados, dates, desert flora, jojoba, guayule and carob.

CA —CALIFORNIA ACADEMY OF SCIENCES, J W Mailliard Jr Library, Golden Gate Park, San Francisco, 94118. Ray Brian, Librn
Notes: Downs No 2160.

DE —UNIVERSITY OF DELAWARE, Agriculture Library, 2 Townsend Hall, Newark, 19717. Frederick Getze, Assoc Librn
Holdings: Vols (32,500) Cat Pix Microforms
Notes: Strong in entomology and ornamental horticulture. Extensive collection of state agriculture documents for each US state and Puerto Rico. Library subscribes to 600 serials (English and foreign).

DC —SMITHSONIAN INSTITUTION, Archives Div, Washington, 20560. William W Moss, Archivist
Holdings: Cat Mss Pix
Notes: The Archives holds the records of the National Museum of Natural History's Division of Insects and the Department of Entomology, 1850-1974, as well as some papers of entomologists, incl Charles P Alexander.

DC —SMITHSONIAN INSTITUTION LIBRARIES, Entomology Branch, Washington, 20560. Jean C Smith, Asst Dir for Bureau Services
Holdings: Vols (17,000) Cat Maps Pix

FL —FLORIDA DEPARTMENT OF AGRICULTURE & CONSUMER SERVICES, Div of Plant Industry, Library, PO Box 1269, Gainesville, 32602. June B Jacobson, Librn; Alice Richards, Asst Librn
Holdings: Vols (11,455) Cat Mss Microforms
Budget: ($23,798)
Notes: Collection is primarily taxonomic. 464 periodical, current and antiquariat titles.

FL —UNIVERSITY OF FLORIDA, Institute of Food & Agricultural Sciences, Hume Library, Gainesville, 32611. Albert C Strickland, Librn
Holdings: Vols (135,000) Cat Mss Microforms
Notes: Including journals and monographs, this collection is a general agricultural one. The emphasis is on tropical agriculture, especially Latin America. Entomology is very strong. The library offers on-line information retrieval using Lockheed and SDC data bases.

HI —BERNICE P BISHOP MUSEUM, Library, PO Box 19000-A, Honolulu, 96819. Cynthia Timberlake, Librn
Holdings: Vols (90,000) Cat Mss Maps Pix Slides Microforms
Budget: ($30,000)
Notes: Only American library devoted exclusively to the Pacific region. Collection reflects historical and contemporary research emphases of Bishop Museum; ie the natural and cultural history of the Pacific. Areas of concentration incl archaeology, ethnology, linguistics, voyages and explorations, history, vertebrate and invertebrate zoology, botany and museology. Strong special collections incl photographs, mss and archives, maps and art. Publications: Quarterly "Additions to the Catalog," *Dictionary Catalog of the* Library (9 vols and 2 suppl; Boston: G K Hall, 1964-69).

IL —ILLINOIS NATURAL HISTORY SURVEY LIBRARY, 196 Natural Resources Bldg, Champaign, 61820. Carla G Heister, Librn
Holdings: Vols (36,000) Cat Microforms
Budget: ($25,500)
Notes: A Research and Science Branch of the State of Illinois, the Natural History Survey maintains a library of books, journals and reports on various aspects of natural history. Material is collected in all major languages. The library maintains its own exchange arrangements with some 600 worldwide institutions and organizations. Interlibrary loans and photocopy services are available through the University of Illinois Library. Publications issued regularly by the Survey incl *Biological Notes, The Bulletin, and Circulars.*

IL —FIELD MUSEUM OF NATURAL HISTORY, Library, Roosevelt Rd & Lake Shore Dr, Chicago, 60605. W Peyton Fawcett, Librn; Benjamin W Williams, Assoc Librn
Holdings: Vols (210,000) Cat
Budget: ($100,000)
Notes: Extensive collections--publications of learned societies and institutions and monographic works--in all fields of natural history, with emphasis on taxonomy and evolutionary biology; and on museum publications, American and foreign: anthropology, especially archaeology and ethnology of the Americas, Africa, East Asia, and Oceania; botany, particularly strong for the Americas; geology, chiefly paleontology and meteoritic studies; and zoology, worldwide (birds, fishes, insects, mammals, mollusks, reptiles and amphibians).

IL —UNIVERSITY OF ILLINOIS, URBANA/CHAMPAIGN, Library, Biology Library, 101 Burrill Hall, 407 S Goodwin, Urbana, 61801. Elisabeth B Davis, Librn
Holdings: Vols (115,000) Cat Microforms
Budget: ($200,000)
Notes: The Biology Library incl books, periodicals, and reference works that cover the fields of anatomy, biophysics, botany, ecology, entomology, genetics, immunology, microbiology, physiology and zoology. About three-quarters of the total collection is made up of journals and other serials representing 2000 distinctive titles. The serial list is comprehensive for the biological sciences, contains most of the major international titles and consists of complete runs for almost all titles. Additional materials (approx 90,000 vols) in the biological sciences are available in the Natural History Survey Library and the bookstacks at the Main Library on the Urbana campus. Professional assistance is available for reference service, online searching, and library instruction. Interlibrary loan service is provided. Photocopying.

IN —PURDUE UNIVERSITY LIBRARIES, Life Sciences Library, Lilly Hall of Life Sciences, West Lafayette, 47907. Martha J Bailey, Librn
Holdings: Vols (73,404) Cat Microforms
Budget: ($223,445)
Notes: Incl materials in agronomy, animal

ENTOMOLOGY (cont.)

sciences, botany, entomology, forestry, horticulture, biological sciences and agricultural engineering.

IA —IOWA STATE UNIVERSITY, Library, Ames, 50011. Warren B Kuhn, Dean of Library Services
Holdings: Cat
Notes: Incl: economic entomology, parasitology, pest management, systematic entomology and toxicology. Particular strengths: flies, mosquitoes and ticks. Extensive serial holdings.

IA —IOWA STATE UNIVERSITY, Library, Dept of Special Collections, Ames, 50011. Stanley M Yates, Head
Holdings: // Mss
Notes: Papers of Dwight Isley, who worked at the Bureau of Entomology at the USDA (1915-1921), then at Univ of Arkansas (1921-1951), and later as dir of an agriculture experiment station. 7 linear ft; finding aid available.

IA —BICKELHAUPT ARBORETUM FREE LENDING LIBRARY, 340 S Fourteenth St, Clinton, 52732. Francie B Hill, Librn
Notes: Strong on indoor plants, horticulture, ecology, energy conservation, plant entomology and pathology, urban tree planting; also curriculum materials. Over 3000 slides available for lending.

KY —UNIVERSITY OF KENTUCKY, Agricultural Library, Agricultural Science Center North, Lexington, 40506. Antoinette Paris Powell, Librn
Holdings: Vols (90,000) Cat Microforms
Budget: ($110,385)

LA —US FOREST SERVICE, Southern Forest Experiment Station Library, T-10210 Postal Service Bldg, 701 Loyola Ave, New Orleans, 70113. Linda A Korb, Librn
Holdings: Vols (50,000) Cat 16mm Films VF
Budget: ($100,000)
Notes: Field library of the National Agricultural Library (USDA), serving research scientists of the Southern Forest Experiment Station at headquarters in New Orleans and in seven states of the Mid-South and Puerto Rico.

MD —INSECT CONTROL & RESEARCH, Library, 1330 Dillon Heights Ave, Baltimore, 21228. Eugene J Gerberg, Librn
Holdings: Vols (3000) Uncat Slides Microforms

MA —UNIVERSITY OF MASSACHUSETTS AT AMHERST, Library, Amherst, 01003. Siegfried Feller, Assoc Dir for Collection Development
Holdings: Cat
Notes: Incl the Guy C Crampton Collection; also, extensive holdings on bees and beekeeping.

MA —HARVARD UNIVERSITY, Museum of Comparative Zoology, Library, 26 Oxford St, Cambridge, 02138. Eva S Jonas, Librn
Holdings: Cat Mss Pix Microforms

MI —UNIVERSITY OF MICHIGAN, Museums Library, Ann Arbor, 48109. Patricia B Yocum, Librn
Holdings: Vols 10,000 Cat

MI —MICHIGAN STATE UNIVERSITY, Science Library, East Lansing, 48824. Carole S Armstrong, Head
Holdings: Vols 7300 Cat

NE —UNIVERSITY OF NEBRASKA-LINCOLN, C Y Thompson Library, East Campus, Lincoln, 68583. Lyle Schreiner, Librn
Holdings: Vols (220,000) Cat
Notes: Agriculture, with major strength in entomology, agronomy, and animal science; medicine; veterinary medicine; and home economics.

NY —BOYCE THOMPSON INSTITUTE FOR PLANT RESEARCH, Library, Cornell University, Tower Rd, Ithaca, 14853. Greta Colavito, Librn
Holdings: Vols (5300) Cat
Budget: ($46,000)
Notes: Mainly plant physiology, biochemistry, entomology, air and water pollution, pesticides, and plant pathology.

NY —CORNELL UNIVERSITY LIBRARIES, Collection of Regional History, Dept of Manuscripts and Univ Archives, Ithaca, 14853.
Notes: Incl field reports, 1919-29, concerning control of insect pests and plant diseases; also, one volume of summaries of final reports. Unpublished guide available.

NY —CORNELL UNIVERSITY LIBRARIES, Comstock Memorial Library of Entomology, Ithaca, 14853. Edwin Spragg, Librn
Holdings: Vols (30,000) Cat Maps Pix Audiotapes Microforms
Budget: ($13,500)
Notes: Major topics: general and applied entomology. Minor topics: parasitology, medical entomology, ecology, zoological nomenclature and allied orders of arthropods. Separate catalog to the collection, also extensive collection of reprints. Apiculture material kept at nearby A R Mann Library.

NY —AMERICAN MUSEUM OF NATURAL HISTORY, Library Services Dept, Central Park W & 79th St, New York, 10024. Nina J Root, Chairwoman; Mary Genett, Asst Librn for Reference Services
Holdings: Vols (385,000) Cat Mss Maps Pix Slides Microforms
Notes: Nearly all collections are outstanding for depth of coverage and international range. Early and historic works, rare books, colored illustrations, and relevant serial publications supplement the modern scientific publications necessary to the researches of the scientific staff and the work of the educational division. Open to the public.

NC —UNIVERSITY OF NORTH CAROLINA, CHAPEL HILL, Zoology Dept Library, Wilson Hall 046A, Chapel Hill, 27514. John B Darling, Librn
Holdings: Vols (31,000) Cat
Notes: Collection incl theses and dissertations.

NC —NORTH CAROLINA STATE UNIVERSITY, D H Hill Library, Box 7111, Raleigh, 27695. I T Littleton, Dir
Holdings: Vols 7950 Cat
Budget: $5000
Notes: The Friedrich F Tippman Collection of 6200 volumes on entymology incl many unique and rare volumes which make the collection one of the best in the US. Incl the Z P Metcalf collection on Homoptera and Hemiptera: 1100 vols and 24 VF cabinets. Monographs.
See also entries under Hemiptera; Homoptera; Insects.

OH —OHIO STATE UNIVERSITY, Biological Sciences Library, 1735 Neil Ave, Columbus, 43210. Victoria Welborn, Librn
Holdings: Vols (85,000) Cat Mss Maps Microforms

OK —OKLAHOMA STATE UNIVERSITY, Library, Stillwater, 74708. Roscoe Rouse, Dir
Holdings: Vols 3650 Cat

OR —OREGON STATE UNIVERSITY, Library, Corvallis, 97331. Melvin George, Dir
Holdings: Vols (980,000) Cat Pix

PA —ACADEMY OF NATURAL SCIENCES LIBRARY, 19 Benjamin Franklin Parkway, Philadelphia, 19103.
Holdings: Vols (180,000) Cat Mss Maps Pix Slides microforms
Notes: Incl (250,000) mss. Described in *Academy of Natural Sciences of Philadelphia: Catalog* (Boston: G K Hall, 1972); *Guide to the Manuscript Collections in the Academy of Natural Sciences of* Philadelphia, by Venia T Phillips (Philadelphia: Academy of Natural Sciences, 1963).

PA —CARNEGIE LIBRARY OF PITTSBURGH, Science & Technology Dept, 4400 Forbes Ave, Pittsburgh, 15213. Catherine M Brosky, Dept Head
Notes: This general subject is of secondary interest. Incl both modern and classic works. Kept up to date in cooperation with the Library in Carnegie Museum of Natural History. Materials available on the various phyla, classes, orders and species. Abstracts, indexes, bibliographies, taxonomic manuals and standard reference books. Many journals and society publications complete from the beginning.

PA —PENNSYLVANIA STATE UNIVERSITY, Fred Lewis Pattee Library, Life Sciences Library, University Park, 16802. Keith Roe, Head
Holdings: Vols (195,000) Cat Microforms
Budget: ($258,000)
Notes: This collection is strong in periodical runs, particularly European learned societies and agriculture. It contains extensive collections of Experiment Station publications and has developed specialties in Mycology and Fusaria. There is also a special collection of 1105 glass slides on early Pennsylvania lumbering.

†TX —UNIVERSITY OF TEXAS LIBRARIES, General Libraries, Humanities Research Center, PO Box 7219, Austin, 78712. John Chalmers, Librn
Notes: A collection of the works of Vladimir Nabokov. Contains almost 500 items, incl his English and Russian language books, translations, periodicals and publications about him. Also incl some of his entomological writings. Nabokov was an authority on certain species of butterflies.

WI —UNIVERSITY OF WISCONSIN, MADISON, College of Agricultural & Life Sciences, Steenbock Memorial Library, 550 Babcock Dr, Madison, 53706. Jan Kennedy, Dir
Holdings: Vols (186,312) Cat Docs
Notes: Extensive journal collection.

WI —MILWAUKEE PUBLIC MUSEUM, Reference Library, 800 W Wells St, Milwaukee, 53233. Judith Campbell Turner, Museum Librn
Holdings: Vols (90,000) Cat Maps Microforms

AB —CANADIAN FORESTRY SERVICE, Northern Forest Research Centre Library, 5320 122nd, Edmonton, T6H 3S5, Can. David J S Robinson, Librn
Holdings: Vols (7000) Cat Microforms
Budget: ($25,000)
Notes: Also 23,000 government documents, 2600 research reports, 3000 pamphlets and reprints.

BC —CANADIAN FORESTRY SERVICE, Pacific Forest Research Centre, Library, 506 West Burnside Rd, Victoria, V8Z 1M5, Can. Alice Solyma, Librn
Holdings: Vols (60,500) Cat Microforms
Notes: Incl rearing, biological control, identification, dispersal, insect pest management, comprehensive collection re Mountain Pine Beetle, Western Spruce Budworm, Douglas Fir Tussack Moth.

MB —AGRICULTURE CANADA, Research Station Library, 195 Dafoe Rd, Winnipeg, R3T 2M9, Can. Mike Malyk, Librn
Notes: Cereal, Breading, and Entomology.

MB —UNIVERSITY OF MANITOBA, Agriculture Library, Dafoe Rd, Winnipeg, R3T 2N2, Can. Judy Harper, Head
Holdings: Vols (9000) Cat

NS —NOVA SCOTIA MUSEUM, Library, 1747 Summer St, Halifax, B3H 3A6, Can. M S Whiteside, Librn
Holdings: Vols 800 Cat
Notes: Emphasis on Lepidoptera.

ON —UNIVERSITY OF GUELPH, McLaughlin Library, Guelph, N1G 2W1, Can. Margaret Beckman, Head Librn; David Hull, Sciences Librn
Holdings: Vols 2500 Cat Mss Maps Pix Slides Phonorecords Audiotapes Videotapes 16mm Films Filmstrips Microforms
Budget: $4000
Notes: 1000 vols of bound journals (31 currently received); over 5000 reprints.
See also entry under Bees and Beekeeping

ON —ROYAL BOTANICAL GARDENS, Library, Box 399, Hamilton, L8N 3H8, Can. Ina Vrugtman, Librn
Holdings: Vols (4200)
Notes: Strengths in ornamental horticulture, botany, ornithology, entomology, natural history.

ON —AGRICULTURE CANADA, Entomology Research Library, K W Neatby Bldg, Ottawa, K1A 0C6, Can. J P Miska, Area Coordinator, NCR/Ontario
Holdings: Vols 26,000 Cat Mss Maps Pix Slides Microforms
Budget: $30,000
Notes: Also 41,000 pamphlets, reprints, etc.

ENTOMOLOGY (cont.)

PE —AGRICULTURE CANADA, Research Station Library, PO Box 1210, Charlottetown, C1A 7M8, Can. Barrie Stanfield, Librn
Holdings: Vols (2300) Cat
Budget: ($5000)

PQ —MCGILL UNIVERSITY, Institute of Oceanography, Oceanography Library, 3620 University St, Montreal, H3A 2B2, Can. Yvonne Mahocks, Librn
Holdings: Vols (10,848) Cat Mss Maps Pix Microforms
Budget: ($1200)
Notes: Extensive periodical collection. 12, 332 government documents, , 322 microtech, 321 microfiche, 25,000 reprints.

PQ —MCGILL UNIVERSITY, MacDonald College, Library, 21111 Lakeshore Road, Sainte Anne de Bellevue, H9X 1C0, Can. Janet Finlayson, Librn
Holdings: Vols 7300 Cat
Notes: The Lyman Collection. Incl books and serials.

ENTOZOA see Parasitology

ENVELOPES (PHILATELY) see Covers (Philately)

ENVIRONMENT

AR —JOHN BROWN UNIVERSITY, Library, Siloam Springs, 72761. Glenn E Rogers, Librn
Holdings: Vols 338 Cat Maps Pix Slides Microforms
Budget: $5000
Notes: Collection is funded by an initial grant of $5000 from the W K Kellogg Foundation under the College Resources for Environmental Studies Program. Additional money has been added.

CA —UNIVERSITY OF CALIFORNIA, BERKELEY, Institute of Transportation Studies Library, Library, 412 McLaughlin Hall, Berkeley, 94720.
Holdings: Vols (82,000)
Budget: ($215,000)
Notes: US Department of Transportation depository through NTIS.

CA —UNIVERSITY OF CALIFORNIA, BERKELEY, Science Education Library, Lawrence Hall of Science, Berkeley, 94720. Ann M Jensen, Librn
Holdings: Vols (6000)
Notes: Emphasis on innovative materials in the field of science, mathematics, and environmental education.

CA —UNIVERSITY OF CALIFORNIA, DAVIS, Environmental Toxicology Library, Davis, 95616. Ming-yu Li, Documentation Specialist
Holdings: Vols (5000) Cat
Notes: Library is open to the public for reference only. In addition to the cataloged holdings, the library also maintains a pamphlet collection of 50 file drawers on agricultural chemicals, environmental pollution, heavy metals, food toxicants, toxicology, pesticides and trace elements.

CA —UNIVERSITY OF CALIFORNIA, LIVERMORE, Lawrence Livermore National Laboratory, Library, PO Box 5500, Livermore, 94550. John B Verity, Library Mgr
Holdings: Vols (160,000) Cat 16mm Films Microforms
Budget: ($2,323,000)
Notes: The LLL library system includes a central collection in physics, chemistry, engineering, geology, mathematics, and computer science; and branch holdings in bio-medicine, environmental science, nuclear chemistry, energy research, theoretical physics, materials science, and nuclear weapons. Collections include 160,000 books, 145,000 technical reports, 530,000 reports on microfiche, and 3000 periodical subscriptions. LLL libraries are not open to the public. Unclassified materials may be borrowed on interlibrary loan.

CA —UNIVERSITY OF CALIFORNIA, LOS ANGELES, Biomedical Library, Center for Health Sciences, Los Angeles, 90024. Louise Darling, Biomedical Librn

CA —ASSOCIATION OF BAY AREA GOVERNMENTS, MTC/ABAG Library, 101 Eighth St, Oakland, 94607. Diane Gillman, Information Coord
Notes: Concentrates heavily on the nine-county Bay Area region. About 10,000 monographs and serials. Title catalog, OCLC/ATS. Central collection of documents for six transit properties in Bay Area.

CA —ENVIRONMENTAL PROTECTION AGENCY, Library, 215 Fremont St, San Francisco, 94105. Jean Circiello, Librn
Holdings: Vols 115,000 Cat Maps Microforms
Budget: $30,000
Notes: Especially strong in environmental pollution in California, Arizona, Nevada, and Hawaii.

CA —UNIVERSITY OF CALIFORNIA, SANTA CRUZ, University Library, Special Collections, Santa Cruz, 95064. Rita Bottoms, Special Collections Librn; Margaret Felts, South Pacific Collection Bibliographer

CA —HOOVER INSTITUTION ON WAR, REVOLUTION & PEACE, Stanford University, Stanford, 94305. Milorad M Drachkovitch, Archivist
Holdings: Mss
Notes: Papers of John A Busterud, US attorney and public official, Deputy Assistant Secretary of Defense for Environmental Quality, 1971-72, Chairman of the Council on Environmental Quality, Executive Office of the President, 1972-77, incl correspondence, speeches and writings, memoranda, reports, studies, printed matter, and other material, 1972-77, relating to his government service in the US, and to international and domestic energy and environmental programs. 22 ms boxes.

CT —YALE UNIVERSITY, Forestry Library, 205 Prospect St, New Haven, 06511. Joseph A Miller, Librn
Holdings: Vols (115,000) Cat Microforms
Notes: The Forestry Library is a unit of the Yale University Library, housed in and serving primarily the School of Forestry and Environmental Studies. Founded in 1900, it has become one of the largest forestry libraries in the world. Forestry is construed broadly to incl underlying or closely related social, physical, and biological sciences. The literature of North American forestry and forest products is most completely covered, though other countries and foreign languages are well represented. Environmental studies and allied fields of natural resources management have been emphasized during the past 10 years. See *Dictionary Catalog of the Yale Forestry Library*, 12 vols (Boston: G K Hall, 1962).

DC —CONSERVATION FOUNDATION, Library, 1717 Massachusetts Ave NW, Washington, 20036. Barbara K Rodes, Librn
Holdings: Vols (8000) Cat Maps
Notes: Collection incl natural resources, ecology, city and regional planning, land use, recreation, energy conservation, environmental economics, pollution control, water resources.

DC —EDISON ELECTRIC INSTITUTE, Library-8th Floor, 1111 19th St NW, Washington, 20036. Ethel Tiberg, Mgr, Library Services
Holdings: Vols (13,321) Cat Maps Pix Microforms

DC —MANUFACTURING CHEMISTS' ASSOCIATION, Library, 1825 Connecticut Ave NW, Washington, 20009. Rose Clark, Librn
Holdings: Vols 3000 Cat
Notes: Incl extensive files on the business and trade aspects of the chemical industry; also, environmental and health aspects.

DC —URBAN LAND INSTITUTE, Library, 1090 Vermont Ave, Washington, 20005. Ann Benson, Librn
Holdings: Vols (9000) Cat
Budget: ($6000)
Notes: Incl 200 serials.

DC —US ENVIRONMENTAL PROTECTION AGENCY, 401 M St SW, Washington, 20460. Sarah T Kadec, Dir Information Management & Services Division
Holdings: Vols (480,000) Cat Maps Pix Microforms

FL —MAITLAND LIBRARY, Florida Audubon Society, 501 S Maitland Ave, Maitland, 32751. Mary Kinney, Librn
Holdings: Cat Maps Pix Slides 16mm Films Microforms
Notes: General and technical literature on many aspects of conservation and environmental topics, indexed by subject and source. Coverage is local, statewide and national. Most materials on microfilm and microfiche.

FL —SOUTH FLORIDA WATER MANAGEMENT DISTRICT, Library, PO Box V, West Palm Beach, 33402. Cynthia H Plockelman, Research Librn
Holdings: Cat Slides Microforms Periodicals
Budget: ($13,000)
Notes: A state agency dealing in all aspects of water management, flood control, hydrology, changing environmental conditions, etc. Emphasis is changing from flood control to general water management.

†HI —EAST-WEST POPULATION INSTITUTE RESOURCE MATERIALS COLLECTION, 1777 East-West Rd, Honolulu, 96848.
Notes: Demography, population problems and policy in Hawaii, Asian countries and Pacific area, family planning programs, environment.

IL —ILLINOIS NATURAL HISTORY SURVEY LIBRARY, 196 Natural Resources Bldg, Champaign, 61820. Carla G Heister, Librn
Holdings: Vols (36,000) Cat Microforms
Budget: ($25,500)
Notes: A Research and Science Branch of the State of Illinois, the Natural History Survey maintains a library of books, journals and reports on various aspects of natural history. Material is collected in all major languages. The library maintains its own exchange arrangements with some 600 worldwide institutions and organizations. Interlibrary loans and photocopy services are available through the University of Illinois Library. Publications issued regularly by the Survey incl *Biological Notes, The Bulletin, and Circulars.*

IL —CHICAGO PUBLIC LIBRARY, Business/Science/Technology Div, Science/Technology Information Center, 425 North Michigan Ave, Chicago, 60611. Lynda Sanford, Head; John R Moore, Environment Collection Coordinator & Engineering Librn
Holdings: Vols 4000 Cat Maps Films Slides Phonorecords Audiotapes Microforms
Budget: $14,000
Notes: Incl Aaron Montgomery Ward Collection. Non-documentary materials located in appropriate subject divisions (Business/Science/Technology, Fine Arts, Social Science/History) and Audio-Visual Division. Federal, state and local depository documents held in Government Publications Division. Fee-based data base searching available. EIC indexes, abstracts, and full-text microfiche since 1979. 43 relevant journals, periodicals and services are currently received. 29,000 microforms.

IL —BARTON-ASCHMAN ASSOCIATES, Library, 820 Davis St, Evanston, 60204.
Holdings: Vols (9000) Cat Mss Microforms

IL —UNIVERSITY OF ILLINOIS, URBANA/CHAMPAIGN, Chemistry Library, 255 Noyes Laboratory, Urbana, 61801. Lucille M Wert, Chemistry Librn; Susan Eilering, Asst Chemistry Librn
Holdings: Vols (150,000) Cat Microforms
Budget: ($224,660)
Notes: The collection incl monographs, treatises and serials covering all aspects of environmental chemistry. It is designed to meet the instructional research needs of the School of Chemical Sciences and the University Community.

IN —INDIANA UNIVERSITY, Business-School of Public and Environmental Affairs (SPEA), Bloomington, 47405. Michael Parrish, Dir
Holdings: Vols (100,000)
Budget: ($200,000)
Notes: Collection covers all phases of business, public administration and environment.

ENVIRONMENT (cont.)

MD —RACHEL CARSON COUNCIL INC, Library, 8940 Jones Mill Rd, Chevy Chase, 20815. Shirley A Briggs, Exec Dir
Notes: Bioassays of pesticides and other toxic substances for carcinogenicity by National Cancer Institute; government regulatory documents. Holdings approx 1500 books; 1000 documents and unbound reports; 40 drawers of specialized files. Also have Environmental Protection Agency Pesticide Product Information. Subscribe to 54 journals and others serials. Also publish on pesticides, toxic substances and alternatives to use of pesticides. Have index to pesticides by chemical formula, trade names and CAS number.

MD —SMITHSONIAN ENVIRONMENTAL RESEARCH CENTER, Branch Library, 12441 Parklawn Dr, Rockville, 20852. Angela N Haggins, Chief
Holdings: Vols (3300) Cat Maps Pix Slides

MA —UNIVERSITY OF MASSACHUSETTS AT AMHERST, Physical Sciences Library, Amherst, 01003. Siegfried Feller, Assoc Dir for Collection Development
Holdings: Vols Cat Micrforms
Notes: Environmental sciences. Extensive journal holdings; incl water resources engineering and management.

MA —HABITAT INSTITUTE FOR THE ENVIRONMENT, Library, 10 Juniper Rd, Belmont, 02178. Barbara Herzstein, Librn
Holdings: Vols 3000// Cat

MA —CAMP, DRESSER & MCKEE, Herman G Dresser Library, One Center Plaza, Boston, 02108. Virginia L Carroll, Librn
Holdings: Vols (15,000) Cat Maps Slides Microforms
Notes: Air, land, and water pollution; environmental engineering; hazardous wastes; water resources; solid wastes; resource recycling.

MA —STONE & WEBSTER ENGINEERING CORP, Technical Information Center, Library, 245 Summer St, PO Box 2325, Boston, 02107. Nancy M Pellini, Mgr
Holdings: Vols (10,000) Cat Pix Microforms
Notes: Also over 1200 periodicals. Extensive vertical file collection, and 5 on-line system for search.

MA —MASSACHUSETTS AUDUBON SOCIETY, Hathaway Environmental Education Institute, Lincoln, 01773. Louise C Maglione, Librn
Holdings: Cat Maps Pix Slides Phonorecords Audiotapes 16mm Films Filmstrips
Notes: Largest and most comprehensive collection in the field of environmental education; especially good in the curriculum area. Extensive sections on animal, plants, behavioral and environmental issues, and quality of environment.

MA —ABCOR, INC, Library, 850 Main St, Wilmington, 01887. Eileen Smith, Librn
Holdings: Vols (2000) Cat
Budget: ($10,000)
Notes: Environmental technology; ultrafiltration; waste treatment processes. Incl technical reports. Extensive microfiche collection on air pollution.

MI —MUSEUM OF THE GREAT LAKES, Bay County Historical Society, Library, 1700 Center Ave, Bay City, 48706. Eurdine Ringwelski, Librn
Holdings: Vols (800) Cat Mss Maps Pix Slides 16mm Films
Notes: Focuses on man's relationship to his environment in the Great Lakes region in an historical perspective. Incl books, mss, photos, maps, vertical files, and scrapbooks on the history of Bay County and the Saginaw Valley, Michigan.

MN —ENVIRONMENTAL CONSERVATION LIBRARY OF MINNESOTA (ECOL), 300 Nicollet Mall, Minneapolis, 55401. Linda R Fritschel, Librn
Holdings: Vols 17,000 Cat Microforms Audiotapes
Budget: $18,000
Notes: Special focus on environment of Upper Midwest and impact of man upon it. Collection incl documents from state and local agencies as well as federal documents. Materials circulate, and are available to anyone in Minnesota without charge. Publication: *Minnesota Environmental Organizations: A Directory*, (Minneapolis Public Library, 1982), 301 pp; available from the Minneapolis Public Library for $5.00 plus $1.00 postage from the above address.

MS —US ARMY ENGINEER WATERWAYS EXPERIMENT STATION, Library Branch, PO Box 631, Vicksburg, 39180. Bernice Black, Chief Librn
Holdings: Vols (350,000) Cat Mss Maps Microforms

MO —US FISH & WILDLIFE SERVICE, Columbia National Fisheries Research Laboratory, Rte One, Columbia, 65201. Axie Hindman, Librn
Holdings: Vols (2000) Cat Microforms
Budget: ($7000)
Notes: Pesticides in aquatic biota; fisheries research; fresh-water ecology. Also incl collection in water pollution, acid rain, aquatic invertebrets, environment and 10,000 reprints.

MO —MISSOURI BOTANICAL GARDEN LIBRARY, PO Box 299, Saint Louis, 63166. M R Crosby, Dir of Research
Holdings: Vols 800 Uncat Maps
Notes: Incl about 800 environmental impact statements.

NV —FORESTA INSTITUTE FOR OCEAN AND MOUNTAIN STUDIES, Library, 6205 Franktown Rd, Carson City, 89701. Shannon Porter, Librn
Holdings: Vols (3000) Cat Mss Maps Pix Slides
Notes: Material on plant, animal, and human ecology with special emphasis on far western US and Nevada ecology and environmental problems. Also hold about 2000 reprints, pamphlets, reports, etc

NJ —MIDDLESEX COUNTY PLANNING BOARD, Library, 40 Livingston Ave, New Brunswick, 08901. Lou Mattei, Planning Supervisor, Data Mgt
Holdings: Vols (3500) Cat
Budget: ($500)

NJ —PRINCETON UNIVERSITY, Architecture Library, School of Architecture, Princeton, 08544. Frances Chen, Librn

NY —CARY ARBORETUM OF THE NEW YORK BOTANICAL GARDEN, Library, Box AB, Millbrook, 12545. Fred Strum, Librn
Notes: This collection of alternative energy sources consists of publications concerned with solar energy, wind power, biofuel, methanol, small hydroelectric projects, and wood power.

NY —ENGINEERING SOCIETIES LIBRARY, 345 E 47 St, New York, 10017. S Kirk Cabeen, Dir
Holdings: Vols 250,000 Cat Maps 16mm Films Microforms
Notes: One of the largest, most comprehensive engineering libraries in the world. Covers all engineering disciplines; particularly strong in electrical and electronic, mechanical, mining and metallurgical, petroleum, chemical, industrial, air conditioning and refrigeration engineering. Incl Wheeler Collection of early materials on magnetism and electricity. 125, 000 bound periodical volumes; 10,000 maps; 5000 serial subscriptions (many foreign-language). Virtually all materials abstracted in *Engineering Index* (1884-date) are incl in Library. Noncirculating, except to members of professional engineering societies which support the Library. See *Engineering Societies Library, New York, Classed Subject Catalog and Index* (Boston: G K Hall, 1963); and *Supplements*, 1-10, 1964-1973.

NY —EXPLORERS CLUB, James B Ford Memorial Library, 46 E 70 St, New York, 10021. Janet Baldwin, Librn
Holdings: Vols (24,000) Cat Maps
Notes: Additions to the collection depend upon gifts. Access by appointment only.

NY —PAUL SMITHS COLLEGE, Frank L Cubley Library, Paul Smiths, 12970. Theodore Mack, Librn
Holdings: Vols 1000 Cat Slides Audiotapes Filmstips Microforms
Notes: Undergraduate collection.

NY —STATE UNIVERSITY OF NEW YORK, STONY BROOK, Melville Library, Dept of Special Collections, Stony Brook, 11794. Evert Volkersz, Head
Holdings: Cat Mss
Notes: Printed and ms materials relating to local and regional Long Island history. Ms collections focus on women, environment, social welfare, and politics. Much on the Long Island Railroad (qv).

NY —STATE UNIVERSITY OF NEW YORK, COLLEGE OF ENVIRONMENTAL SCIENCE AND FORESTRY, F Franklin Moon Library, Syracuse, 13210. Donald F Webster, Librn
Holdings: Vols (86,430) Cat
Budget: ($120,000)

NY —NEW YORK UNIVERSITY MEDICAL CENTER, Institute of Environmental Medicine Library, Long Meadow Rd, Tuxedo, 10987. Christine M Singleton, Research Librn
Holdings: Vols 10,000 Cat Microforms //
Notes: Environmental medicine and sciences. Incl 12,000 microforms.

ND —UNIVERSITY OF NORTH DAKOTA, Chester Fritz Library, Dept of Special Collections, Grand Forks, 58202. Daniel F Rylance, Special Collections Coordr
Holdings: Vols (5500) Uncat Mss Maps Pix Microforms
Budget: ($2500)
Notes: Also the Orin G Libby Manuscript Collection (900 collections), and the Aandahl Collection of Western History on North Dakota and the Northern Great Plains. Emphasis on agriculture, politics, pioneering, Germans from Russia, etc. Guides to the collections available from the Coordinator of Special Collections.

OH —CASE WESTERN RESERVE UNIVERSITY LIBRARIES, Freiberger Library, 11161 East Blvd, Cleveland, 44106.
Notes: Extensive collection.

OH —CLEVELAND PUBLIC LIBRARY, Science & Technology Dept, 325 Superior Ave, Cleveland, 44114. Jean Z Piety, Head
Holdings: Cat Pix
Notes: Special collection covers the environmental sciences concerned with the Great Lakes-St Lawrence drainage basins. Emphasis is on limnology, ecology, meteorology, hydraulics, biology, pollution of air and water, natural history and general research. Most of the material indexed has been donated by numerous agencies around the Great Lakes.

PA —DREXEL UNIVERSITY LIBRARIES, Engineering Library, 32 & Chestnut Sts, Philadelphia, 19104. Charlotte T Duvally, Librn
Holdings: Vols 18,545 Uncat Microforms
Notes: The only library in Philadelphia area holding the Bay Area (San Francisco) air pollution control microfilm library. Access via uniterm subject cards (manual retrieval system) index, accession card file index, author card file index.

PA —UNIVERSITY OF PENNSYLVANIA, Towne Scientific Library, 220 S 33 St, Philadelphia, 19104. Charles Meyers, Librn
Holdings: Vols (65,000) Cat

SC —SONOCO PRODUCTS CO, Research Laboratory, Technical Information Center, One N Second St, Hartsville, 29550. Ken Chavis, Dir
Holdings: Vols (4000) Cat Mss Slides Microforms
Notes: Restricted to Sonoco employees. No photocopying.

SC —SUMTER TECHNICAL COLLEGE, Library, 506 Guignard Dr, Sumter, 29150. Fanny M Davis
Holdings: Vols (20,000) Cat Mss Maps Pix Slides Microforms
Budget: ($500,000)

TN —TENNESSEE VALLEY AUTHORITY (TVA), Technical Library, 400 W Summit Hill Dr, E2 B7, Knoxville, 37902. Jesse C Mills, Chief Librn
Holdings: Vols (106,900) Cat Mss Maps Pix Audiotapes Microforms
Budget: ($2,025,000)
Notes: The Technical Library Headquarters Staff (order, cataloging, information, and administration) is located in Knoxville,

ENVIRONMENT (cont.)

Tenn. In addition there are branch libraries in Knoxville, Norris, and Chattanooga, Tennessee, and Muscle Shoals, Alabama.

TN —TENNESSEE VALLEY AUTHORITY (TVA), Norris Branch Library, Norris, 37828. Debra D Mills, Librn
Holdings: Vols (8000) Cat Microforms
Budget: ($35,000)

TX —FLUOR ENGINEERS INC, Houston Library, 4620 N Braeswood, PO Box 35000, Houston, 77235. R S Holab-Abelman, Librn
Holdings: Vols (2500) Cat Maps
Budget: ($10,000)
Notes: Construction, environmental and chemical engineering, coal technology. Incl 2000 job books covering all areas of company interests.

TX —UNIVERSITY OF TEXAS, Marine Science Institute Library, Port Aransas, 78373. Ruth Grundy, Librn
Holdings: Vols (45,000) Cat Maps Pix
Budget: ($70,000)
Notes: Current researches in marine science, especially concerning the Gulf of Mexico, the Texas Coastal Zone, and the Continental Shelf. Incl journals.

VA —UNIVERSITY OF VIRGINIA, Alderman Library, Manuscripts Dept, Charlottesville, 22901. Edmund Berkeley Jr, Cur
Holdings: Cat Mss Maps Pix
Notes: Papers of the Conservation Council of Virginia, and its chairman, the Central Atlantic Environment Center, the Virginia Electric and Power Co, the US Atomic Energy Commission, State Water Control Board Chairman, and members of the Governor's Council on the Environment focus on a variety of environmental issues particularly the location of a nuclear power plant on an alleged geological fault, water pollution and the Potomac River cleanup of the 1970s and state environmental goals regarding water and air pollution, preservation, and development.

WA —UNIVERSITY OF WASHINGTON LIBRARIES, Forest Resources Library, AQ-15, Seattle, 98195. Barbara B Gordon, Head
Holdings: Vols (43,248) Cat Microforms
Budget: ($41,103)
Notes: Modern imprints only. Mostly in English, some Euripean and East Asian languages. International in scope but emphasis is on Pacific Northwest. Incl 1,236 microforms.

WA —URS ENGINEERS, Library, 2615 Fourth Ave, Seattle, 98121. Jill Phelps, Librn
Holdings: Vols (3100) Cat
Budget: ($5000)
Notes: Environmental impact assessment, hazardous materials disposal, oil spill cleanup and environmental effects of waterborne pollutants, especially with regard to California and the western environment.

WI —UNIVERSITY OF WISCONSIN, MADISON, Law Library, Law Building, Madison, 53706. Anita Morse, Dir Law Library
Holdings: Vols 230,160 Cat Microforms
Notes: Stressing environmental law. Subject cataloging only.

AB —ALBERTA DEPT OF THE ENVIRONMENT, Library, Oxbridge Place, 9820 106th St, Edmonton, T5K 2J6, Can. Marilyn Corbett, Head, Library Services Branch
Holdings: Vols (20,000) Cat Microforms

AB —ALBERTA OIL SANDS INFORMATION CENTRE, 6th Floor, Highfield Place, 10010-106 St, Edmonton, T5J 3L8, Can. Helga Radvanyi, Mgr
Notes: "Major activity of the Centre has been preparation of the Alberta Oil Sands Index. However...scope has broadened to include the Heavy Oil/Enhanced Recovery Index," and other informative literature.

AB —CANADIAN FORESTRY SERVICE, Northern Forest Research Centre Library, 5320 122nd, Edmonton, T6H 3S5, Can. David J S Robinson, Librn
Holdings: Vols (7000) Cat Microforms
Budget: ($25,000)
Notes: Also 23,000 government documents, 2600 research reports, 3000 pamphlets and reprints.

BC —CANADIAN FORESTRY SERVICE, Pacific Forest Research Centre, Library, 506 West Burnside Rd, Victoria, V8Z 1M5, Can. Alice Solyma, Librn
Holdings: Vols (60,500) Cat Microforms
Notes: Incl environmental impact statements and analyses, environmental law, environmental policy related to British Columbia and Canada.

MB —UNIVERSITY OF MANITOBA, Architecture & Fine Arts Library, Winnipeg, R3T 2N2, Can. Peter Anthony, Head
Holdings: Vols (50,000) Maps Audiotapes Microforms
Notes: Incl government publications.

ON —METROPOLITAN TORONTO LIBRARY, Science & Technology Dept, 789 Yonge St, Toronto, M4W 2G8, Can. Margaret Walshe, Head
Holdings: Vols (120,000) Cat Maps VF
Notes: All aspects of science and technology for the specialist, the student, and the general public. The department gives high priority to material.

PQ —NORANDA RESEARCH CENTRE, Library, 240 Hymus Blvd, Pointe-Claire, H9R 1G5, Can. Shirley Courtis, Librn
Holdings: Vols (7000)

ENVIRONMENT (ART)

CA —CALIFORNIA INSTITUTE OF THE ARTS, Library, 24700 McBean Pkwy, Valencia, 91355. James Elrod, Dir
Holdings: Vols (61,000) Slides
Budget: ($11,000)
Notes: Modern art, incl abstract, conceptual, concrete, environment, minimal, and pop art; dadaism; surrealism; happenings; and caricatures and cartoons.

ENVIRONMENTAL CONTROL see Environmental Engineering; Environmental Protection

ENVIRONMENTAL DEFENSE FUND

NY —STATE UNIVERSITY OF NEW YORK, STONY BROOK, Melville Library, Dept of Special Collections, Stony Brook, 11794. Evert Volkersz, Head
Holdings: Mss
Notes: The Environmental Defense Fund (EDF) is a public membership, non-profit, tax-exempt organization of scientists, lawyers, and citizens established in 1966. The collection, which is partially cataloged, incl records of the main and of some branch offices.

ENVIRONMENTAL EFFECTS see Environment; Environmental Engineering

ENVIRONMENTAL ENGINEERING

FL —SOUTH FLORIDA WATER MANAGEMENT DISTRICT, Library, PO Box V, West Palm Beach, 33402. Cynthia H Plockelman, Research Librn
Holdings: Cat Slides Microforms Periodicals
Budget: ($13,000)
Notes: A state agency dealing in all aspects of water management, flood control, hydrology, changing environmental conditions, etc. Emphasis is changing from flood control to general water management.

IL —ARGONNE NATIONAL LABORATORY, High-Energy Physics/ Environmental Sciences Branch Library, 9700 S Cass Ave, Argonne, 60439. Jean Castle, Library Assistant
Notes: Environmental sciences. Incl 9000 vols monographs, 207 current journals, a comprehensive collection of high-energy physics pre-prints. Materials may be used by the public in the library by prior arrangement. Photocopies may be supplied for interlibrary loan, for which a processing and handling charge is made.

IL —NORTHWESTERN UNIVERSITY, Transportation Center Library, Evanston, 60201. Mary Roy, Librn
Notes: Environmental impact, incl 17,000 Impact Statements most of which have been processed under National Environmental Policy Act of 1961.

MO —US FISH & WILDLIFE SERVICE, Columbia National Fisheries Research Laboratory, Rte One, Columbia, 65201. Axie Hindman, Librn
Holdings: Vols (2000) Cat Microforms
Notes: Pesticides in aquatic biota; fisheries research; fresh-water ecology. Also incl collection in water pollution, acid rain, aquatic invertebrets, environment and 10,000 reprints.

NH —TOTAL ENVIRONMENTAL ACTION, INC. (TEA), Library of Conservation, Environmental Studies, and Renewable Energy, 7 Church Hill, Harrisville, 03450. Bruce Anderson, Pres
Holdings: 10,000 Vols
Notes: Available for sale. Library in temporary storage, summer 1983. One of the most extensive private collections. Reports, surveys, monographs, technical papers, bibliographies, and indexes to highly specialized studies.

NY —EASTMAN KODAK COMPANY, Kodak Park Div, Engineering Library, Bldg 23, Rochester, 14650. Raymond Curtin, Librn
Holdings: Vols (14,000) Uncat Microforms
Notes: The library is not open to the public. Use of the library for reference purposes may be requested and appointments may be obtained through the librarian.

OH —UNIVERSITY OF CINCINNATI, Engineering Library, 880 Baldwin Hall, Cincinnati, 45221. Dorothy Furber Byers, Head
Holdings: Vols (50,000) Cat Videotapes Microforms
Budget: ($100,000)
Notes: Have NASA and DOE microfiche collections.

SC —SOUTH CAROLINA DEPT OF HEALTH & ENVIRONMENTAL CONTROL, Educational Resource Center, 2600 Bull St, Columbia, 29201. Michael Kronenfeld, Librn
Holdings: Vols 1000
Notes: Environmental regulation and control.

TX —UNIVERSITY OF TEXAS LIBRARIES, Richard W McKinney Engineering Library, 1.3 ECJ, Austin, 78712. Susan B Ardis, Librn
Holdings: Vols (83,548) Cat Microforms

AB —ALBERTA OIL SANDS INFORMATION CENTRE, 6th Floor, Highfield Place, 10010-106 St, Edmonton, T5J 3L8, Can. Helga Radvanyi, Mgr
Notes: "Major activity of the Centre has been preparation of the Alberta Oil Sands Index. However...scope has broadened to include the Heavy Oil/Enhanced Recovery Index," and other informative literature.

ENVIRONMENTAL HEALTH

CO —COLORADO STATE UNIVERSITY, Libraries, Fort Collins, 80523. K Suzanne Johnson, Biomedical Sciences, Librn
Holdings: Vols (2000) Cat Microforms
Budget: ($2000)

CT —YALE UNIVERSITY, Beinecke Rare Book & Manuscript Library, Osborn Collection, New Haven, 06520. Stephen R Parks, Cur
Holdings: Mss

IN —PURDUE UNIVERSITY LIBRARIES, Pharmacy, Nursing and Health Sciences Library, Pharmacy Bldg, West Lafayette, 47907. Theodora Andrews, Librn
Holdings: Vols 1000 Cat
Notes: There is a separate catalog to the collection. Contains research level materials as well as undergraduate.

NC —NATIONAL INSTITUTE OF ENVIRONMENTAL HEALTH SCIENCES, Library, PO Box 12233, Research Triangle Park, 27709. W Davenport Robertson, Head Librn
Holdings: Vols (9000) Cat Mss Audiotapes Microforms
Notes: The subject, "environmental health," incl toxicology, carcinogenesis, pharmacology, genetics, biophysics, and

ENVIRONMENTAL HEALTH (cont.)

biochemistry. Special emphasis is placed on cell biology. The collection does not incl works on pollution control or law. In addition to the collection there are some 2500 vols in the laboratories. The library has an automated catalog.

ON —ONTARIO MINISTRY OF LABOUR, Library, 400 University Ave, Toronto, M7A 1T7, Can. Jean Collins-Williams, Librn
Holdings: Vols (80,000) Microforms Films

ENVIRONMENTAL LAW

MA —MASSACHUSETTS INSTITUTE OF TECHNOLOGY, Institute Archives, Special Collections, Cambridge, 02139.
Notes: Correspondence, newsletters, fact-sheets, newspaper and magazine articles, books and reports of the Citizens' League Against the Sonic Boom, established in 1967 by William Shurcliff to oppose the sonic boom, stop commercial supersonic transport production, and influence public opinion and policy decisions on the SST. Major correspondents incl Bo Lundberg, Richard Wiggs, several US congressmen, and CLASB members.

WA —UNIVERSITY OF WASHINGTON LIBRARIES, Suzzallo Library, Manuscripts Section, FM-25, Seattle, 98195. Karyl Winn, Librn
Holdings: Mss
Notes: Personal papers and organizational records with emphasis on Pacific Northwest history and recent focus on twentieth century Western Washington. Holdings pertain to urban problems and policies, labor history, women's history, natural resource development, environmental politics, race relations, ethnic history, oral hsitory, and the arts. Holdings are complemented by textual records in the University Archives (7045 linear feet) and by graphic and printed holdings in the Pacific Northwest Collection. Described in *Comprehensive Guide to the Manuscripts Collection and to Personal Papers in the University Archives*, 1980 and in *Historical Records of Washington State: Records and Papers Held at Repositories*, 1981 and in unpublished inventories to most accessions. 15,981 linear feet of manuscripts.

WI —UNIVERSITY OF WISCONSIN, MADISON, Law Library, Law Building, Madison, 53706. Anita Morse, Dir Law Library
Holdings: Cat Microforms
Notes: Stressing environmental law. Subject cataloging only.

ENVIRONMENTAL MANAGEMENT see Environmental Engineering; Environmental Protection

ENVIRONMENTAL MEDICINE

NY —NEW YORK UNIVERSITY MEDICAL CENTER, Institute of Environmental Medicine Library, Long Meadow Rd, Tuxedo, 10987. Christine M Singleton, Research Librn
Holdings: Vols 10,000 Cat Microforms //
Notes: Environmental medicine and sciences. Incl 12,000 microforms.

OK —CIVIL AERO MEDICAL INSTITUTE LIBRARY (CAMI), PO Box 25082, AAC 64D1, Oklahoma City, 73125. Darrell R Goulden, Medical Librn
Holdings: Vols 8500 Cat Mss
Notes: Aviation and aerospace medicine. About 175 current periodicals.

ON —DEFENCE & CIVIL INSTITUTE OF ENVIRONMENTAL MEDICINE, Scientific Information Centre, 1133 Sheppard Ave W, PO Box 2000, Downsview, M3M 3B9, Can. Anthony Cheung, Librn
Notes: Incl 7000 reports; microfiche.

ENVIRONMENTAL PROTECTION

CA —SUNKIST GROWERS, Research Library, 760 E Sunkist St, Ontario, 91761. Martha C Nemeth, Librn
Holdings: Vols (1500) Cat
Budget: ($10,000)
Notes: Technology of citrus fruit and citrus fruit products, primarily Californian. Strong in organic and food chemistry, with additional coverage of food technology, essential oils, microbiology and environmental protection.

MA —ABCOR, INC, Library, 850 Main St, Wilmington, 01887. Eileen Smith, Librn
Holdings: Vols (2000) Cat
Budget: ($10,000)
Notes: Environmental technology; ultrafication; waste treatment processes. Incl technical reports. Extensive microfiche collection on air pollution.

MO —UNIVERSITY OF MISSOURI-SAINT LOUIS, Thomas Jefferson Library, Manuscript and Historical Society Collection, 8001 Natural Bridge Rd, Saint Louis, 63121.
Holdings: Mss Pix Tapes
Notes: ca

NM —UNIVERSITY OF CALIFORNIA, Los Alamos National Laboratory, Libraries, PO Box 1663, MSP 362, Los Alamos, 87545. J Arthur Freed, Head Librn
Holdings: Vols (800,000) Cat Films Microforms
Budget: ($700,000)
Notes: Incl 500,000 classified and unclassified reports. There are 25 branch libraries and a central collection. The Medical Library contains about 40,000 vols in the areas of biomedical research.

NY —SAGAMORE HILL NATIONAL HISTORIC SITE, Library, 304 Cove Neck Rd, Oyster Bay, 11771.
Holdings: Cat

NY —STATE UNIVERSITY OF NEW YORK, STONY BROOK, Melville Library, Dept of Special Collections, Stony Brook, 11794. Evert Volkersz, Head
Holdings: Mss
Notes: The Environmental Defense Fund (EDF) is a public membership, non-profit, tax-exempt organization of scientists, lawyers, and citizens established in 1966. The collection, which is partially cataloged, incl records of the main and of some branch offices.

ENVIRONMENTAL PSYCHOLOGY

MN —UNIVERSITY OF MINNESOTA, Architecture Library, 89 Church St, Minneapolis, 55455. A Kristine Johnson, Librn
Holdings: Vols (27,000) Cat Mss
Budget: ($20,000)
Notes: Incl architecture, architectural history, landscape architecture, design methodology, housing, urban sociology, interior design, etc.

ENVIRONMENTAL RADIOACTIVITY see Radioecology

ENVIRONMENTAL STRESSES see Environmental Engineering

ENVIRONMENTAL STUDIES

CA —UNIVERSITY OF CALIFORNIA, RIVERSIDE, Physical Sciences Library, Riverside, 92517. Richard W Vierich, Librn
Holdings: Vols (89,000) Cat Microforms
Budget: ($347,700)

ENVIRONMENTAL TOXICOLOGY see Toxicology, Environmental

ENVIRONMENTALLY INDUCED DISEASES

AR —NATIONAL CENTER FOR TOXICOLOGICAL RESEARCH, Library, Jefferson, 72079. Susan Laney-Sheehan, Supvr Librn
Holdings: Vols (15,000) Cat Mss Slides Audiotapes 16mm Films Microforms
Notes: Incl (860) journal titles, (230) current subscriptions.

ON —ONTARIO MINISTRY OF HEALTH, Laboratory Services Branch, Library, Box 9000, Terminal A, Toronto, M5W 1R5, Can. Doris A Standing, Librn
Notes: Environmental bacteriology limted to the testing of milk, food and drinking water for bacterial quality, or food poisoning.

ENVIRONMENTS, HAZARDOUS GEOGRAPHIC see Hazardous Geographic Environments

ENZYMES

CT —YALE MEDICAL LIBRARY, 333 Cedar St, New Haven, 06510.
Notes: A special subject emphasis.

MA —MASSACHUSETTS INSTITUTE OF TECHNOLOGY, Institute Archives, Special Collections, Cambridge, 02139.
Notes: Collection incl over 100 oral history interviews with scientists, legislators, lobbyists, environmentalists, journalists, university administration, and citizen review board members concerned with recombinant DNA technology. Also incl are audiotapes, videotapes, and printed material collected in preparations for oral history interviews.

EPHRATA COMMUNITY

NY —COLUMBIA UNIVERSITY LIBRARIES, Rare Book & Manuscript Library, 801 Butler Library, 535 W 114 St, New York, 10027. Kenneth A Lohf, Librn
Holdings: Cat Mss
Notes: Consisting of music mss of the Ephrata Community, by the founder of the community, Conrad Beissel. Restricted use.

PA —PENNSYLVANIA HISTORICAL & MUSEUM COMMISSION, Ephrata Cloister, 632 W Main St, Ephrata, 17522. James Lewars, Adminr; John L Kraft, Librn
Holdings: Vols (150) Cat Mss Maps Pix Slides Phonorecords
Notes: Ephrata Cloister and early Pennsylvania imprints.

WI —SEVENTH DAY BAPTIST HISTORICAL SOCIETY, Library, 3120 Kennedy Rd, PO Box 1678, Janesville, 53547. D Scott Smith, Historian
Holdings: Cat Mss Maps Pix
Notes: Julies Sachse Collection. Ephrata Community records (1729-1883). Original music mss, some illuminated; samples of early printing of Bibles and books form an important part of this collection. Some material also on Snow Hill, daughter colony, et al. About 500 items; incl artifacts. Much of this collection now in Pennsylvania State Archives, Pennsylvania Historical and Museum Commission, Philadelphia.

EPIC LITERATURE

MA —HARVARD UNIVERSITY LIBRARY, Widener Library, Milman Parry Collection of Oral Literature & the James A Notopoulos Collection, Cambridge, 02138. Albert B Lord, Cur
Holdings: Cat Mss

EPIDEMICS

TX —UNIVERSITY OF TEXAS, DALLAS, Health Science Center, Reference Dept & History of Health Sciences Dept, 5323 Harry Hines Blvd, Dallas, 75235. Helen Mayo, Head
Holdings: Vols (10,000) Cat Pix Slides Audiotapes Videotapes Microforms
Notes: History of Medicine collection contains ca 10,000 vols. This total is comprised of pre-1900 journals, primary materials in the History of Medicine and the History of Science, and secondary studies in these two areas. The major strengths of this collection are in the areas of epidemics and plagues, military medicine, and collected works of famous medical pioneers. Incl in this collection are the medical journals published by the county medical societies in Texas, local publications by Dallas County medical organizations, and ephemeral material in a similar vein. The university archives contain all theses and dissertations form UTHSCD and miscellaneous institutional documents circulated by the school's administration.

EPIDEMIOLOGY

CA —UNIVERSITY OF CALIFORNIA, BERKELEY, Life Sciences Libraries, Public

EPIDEMIOLOGY (cont.)

Health Library, 42 Earl Warren Hall, Berkeley, 94720. Thomas J Alexander, Librn
Holdings: Vols (75,000) Cat Microforms
Notes: Research collection covering all aspects of public health. Health Department annual reports from all 50 states are acquired, as well as such reports from all California health units and from major U S cities. Serial publications issued by Health Departments in the 13 western states are being received.

CT —YALE MEDICAL LIBRARY, 333 Cedar St, New Haven, 06510.
Holdings: Vols (334,215) Cat Mss Pix Slides Microforms
Budget: ($361,650)
Notes: Incl films, audiotapes, artifacts, etc.

IL —UNIVERSITY OF ILLINOIS, URBANA/CHAMPAIGN, Library, Applied Life Studies Library, 1408 W Gregory Dr, Urbana, 61801.
Holdings: Vols (38,000) Cat Microforms
See also entry under Physical Education and Training.

MI —UNIVERSITY OF MICHIGAN, Public Health Library, Ann Arbor, 48109. Mary Townsend, Head
Holdings: Vols (55,000) Cat Maps Pix
Budget: ($24,000)

NY —NEW YORK ACADEMY OF MEDICINE, Library, 2 E 103 St, New York, 10029. Brett A Kirkpatrick, Librn
Holdings: Uncat Mss Pix
Notes: Collection of personal papers of Frank George Boudreau, incl correspondence, from his birth to his early years as health officer in Ohio, through his international experience at the League of Nations, and as President of the Milbank Memorial Fund. Much on epidemiology, public health, and public medicine. Collection described in Lee Ash's "Frank George Boudreau, 18 July 1886-14 Februrary 1970, " *The Academy Bookman,* (New York Academy of Medicine, Friends of the Rare Book Room), Vol 26, No 1, 1973, pp 6-7.

OH —CLEVELAND MEDICAL LIBRARY ASSOCIATION/CASE WESTERN RESERVE UNIVERSITY, Cleveland Health Sciences Library, Historical Division, Allen Memorial Medical Library, 11000 Euclid Ave, Cleveland, 44106. Glen Jenkins, Rare Book Librarian & Archivist
Notes: Incl 15,000 historical vols, 6000 in the supporting collection. Incl about 1000 16th-18th century titles. Strength of collection: diseases, epidemiology, anatomy, surgery, medicine, obstetrics, gynecology, pediatrics and yellow fever. Incl also medical Americana, listed in Robert B Austin *Early American Medical Imprints,* 1668-1820 (Washington, DC, HEW, Public Health Service, 1961) and ca 7000 19th century works. Our total medical Americana collection also incl journals (not counted), mss and archives (900 linear ft) and 5000 pictures, especially of the Western Reserve. Anatomical works discussed in I Ebner and G Jenkins *Skeletons in Our Closet* (Cleveland, Cleveland Health Sciences Library, 1983)

TX —HOUSTON ACADEMY OF MEDICINE-TEXAS MEDICAL CENTER, Library, Jesse H Jones Library Bldg, Houston, 77030. Elizabeth Borst White, Special Collections Librn
Holdings: Vols (900) Cat
Notes: Mading Collection on Public Health. English-language materials dealing with American public health conditions before 1925. Emphasis is on epidemiology and infectious diseases (excluding venereal disease), incl material on sanitation and climatology. Federal, state or municipal reports on health, mortality and sanitation are included. Also 500 pamphlets.

PQ —UNIVERSITY OF MONTREAL, Bibliotheque Para-medicale, 2375 Chemin de la Cote Ste Catherine, Montreal, H3C 3J7, Can. Johanne Hopper, Head Librn
Holdings: Vols 1700 Cat
Budget: $6400
Notes: Social medicine, preventive medicine, epidemiology, industrial health and hygiene, and environmental factors (pollution) as related to health. Depository for World Health Organization publications.

EPIGENESIS see Biology; Embryology; Evolution; Life—Origin

EPIGRAMS see Aphorisms, Apothegms, Epigrams, Maxims and Proverbs

EPIGRAPHY see Inscriptions

EPILEPSY

KS —KANSAS NEUROLOGICAL INSTITUTE, Menninger Professional Library, 3107 W 21 St, Topeka, 66604. Richard Gray, Librn
Holdings: Vols 150
Notes: Incl development disabilities; special education; nursing care for the handicapped; programs for the mentally retarded; behavioral psychology; supervision in mental health/mental retardation; staff training in mental health/mental retardation.

MA —MASSACHUSETTS REHABILITATION COMMISSION, Library, 20 Park Plaza, Boston, 02116. June C Holt, Librn
Holdings: Vols Cat
Notes: For staff and community interested in rehabilitation literature, defined as publications which deal with impairments resulting in disabling conditions; mental and behavioral disorders; employment of the handicapped; counseling techniques with handicapped populations; sheltered workshops, rehabilitation facilities; halfway houses and independent living arrangements; psychological aspects of disability; attitudes toward the handicapped; and other material on services for the handicapped. Library subscribes to 70 journals relating to disability and rehabilitation.

MI —LAFAYETTE CLINIC LIBRARY, 951 E Lafayette, Detroit, 48207. Nancy E Ward, Librn
Holdings: Vols (7000) Cat
Notes: Special emphasis on epilepsy, movement disorders, Parkinson's Disease and the biological aspects, causes and treatment of mental illness.

EPISCOPAL CHURCH see Church of England; Protestant Episcopal Church in the U.s.a.

EPISTEMOLOGY

PA —UNIVERSITY OF PITTSBURGH, Hillman Library, Pittsburgh, 15260. Glenora E Rossell, Head
Holdings: Vols (6100) Cat Microforms
Notes: The History and Philosophy of Science collection is rapidly growing to support research interests in a very new synoptic approach in the integration of history of science, philosophy, and the intensive new program of instruction. The trend of collection is to include works in philosophical foundations of contemporary physics and cosmology, the philosophical problems of the social sciences, science and theology in the 17th century, the relation between science and epistemology in the 18th and 19th centuries; problems of microphysics, history of molecular biology, theories of scientific explanation, and relation between science and metaphysics.

WA —UNIVERSITY OF WASHINGTON LIBRARIES, Philosophy Library, 331 Savery, DK-50, Seattle, 98195. Carolyn Mateer, Acting Selector
Holdings: Vols (18,302)
Budget: ($27,516)
Notes: Collection includes materials in philosophy of language, law, mind, ethics, logic, mataphysics, religion, science, epistemology, social and political philosophy and the history of philosophy.

EPIZOA see Parasitology

EPSTEIN, EDWARD JAY

MA —BOSTON UNIVERSITY, Mugar Memorial Library, Special Collections Dept, 771 Commonwealth Ave, Boston, 02215. Howard B Gotlieb, Dir
Holdings: Cat Mss

EPSTEIN, JULIUS, 1901-1975

CA —HOOVER INSTITUTION ON WAR, REVOLUTION & PEACE, Stanford University, Stanford, 94305. Milorad M Drachkovitch, Archivist
Holdings: Mss Pix
Notes: Papers of Julius Epstein, journalists, research associate at the Hoover Institution, and author of *Operation Keelhaul: The Story of Forced Repatriation,* incl correspondence, speeches and writings, clippings, photographs, and printed matter, 1939-72, relating to his research on the events of World War II, communism, forced repatriation of Russian prisoners of the Soviet Union following World War II, Katyn forest massacres, and unreported deaths of Soviet Cosmonauts, as well as his efforts to obtain restricted government documents on these subjects. 180 ms boxes.

EPSTEIN, PAUL, 1883-1966

CA —CALIFORNIA INSTITUTE OF TECHNOLOGY, Robert A Millikan Memorial Library, Archives, 1201 E California Blvd, Pasadena, 91125. Judith R Goodstein, Archivist
Holdings: Vols (3000) Cat Mss Maps Pix Slides Phonorecords Audiotapes Videotapes 16mm Films Microforms
Notes: Ms sources for the history of astrophysics, cosmology, mathematical physics, experimental physics, radio astronomy, geophysics and biophysics. Collections incl the papers of: George Ellery Hale, Jesse Greenstein, H P Robertson, Richard Feynman, Paul Epstein, Max Delbruck, and Beno Gutenberg. Candid photos of physicists at meetings; etchings and photographs of Einstein; scientific medals; selected pieces of scientific apparatus (including the oil-drop machine constructed by Millikan at Caltech in the early 1920s); the reprint collection of Paul Epstein; over 3000 landmark books in the history of 20th century physics and mathematics. Printed publications include: Daniel Kevles, *Guide to the Microfilm Edition of the George Ellery Hale Papers* (Pasadena, Carnegie Institute of Washington and Caltech), 1968; Judith R Goodstein,*The Robert Andrews Millikan Collection at the California Institute of Technology: Guide to a Microfilm Edition* (Pasadena, Caltech), 1977; Judith R Goodstein and Carolyn Kopp, *The Theodore von Karman Collections at the California Institute of* Technology (Pasadena, Archives), 1981.

EPSTEIN, SEYMOUR

MA —BOSTON UNIVERSITY, Mugar Memorial Library, Special Collections Dept, 771 Commonwealth Ave, Boston, 02215. Howard B Gotlieb, Dir
Holdings: Cat Mss
Notes: Mss, correspondence, etc, collected in depth; incl publications by or about.

EQUAL EMPLOYMENT OPPORTUNITY see Affirmative Action Programs

EQUAL OPPORTUNITY IN EMPLOYMENT see Affirmative Action Programs

EQUAL PAY FOR EQUAL WORK

DC —US DEPT OF LABOR, Library, 200 Constitution Ave NW, Washington, 20210. Sabina Jacobson, Dir
Holdings: Vols (550,000) Cat

ON —CANADA DEPT OF LABOUR, Library, Ottawa, K1A 0J2, Can. Monique Marchand, Chief Librn
Holdings: Vols (100,000) Cat Microforms

EQUATIONS, INDETERMINATE see Diophantine Analysis

EQUESTRIANISM see Horse Breeding

EQUILIBRIUM, THERMAL see Thermodynamics

EQUITATION see Horse Breeding

EQUITY LIBRARY THEATRE

NY —NEW YORK PUBLIC LIBRARY, Performing Arts Research Center, Billy Rose

EQUITY LIBRARY THEATRE (cont.)

Theatre Collection, 111 Amsterdam Ave, New York, 10023. Dorothy L Swerdlove, Cur
Holdings: Cat
Notes: Important archival collection of most of the basic resource materials relating to the history of the ELT. Continuous additions.

ERAMERICA

DC —LIBRARY OF CONGRESS, Manuscript Division, Washington, 20540. John C Broderick, Chief
Notes: Records of ERAmerica; 120,000 pieces.

ERANIAN LANGUAGES see Iranian Languages

ERASMUS, DESIDERIUS

CT —YALE UNIVERSITY, Box 1603A, Yale Station, New Haven, 06520.

MA —HARVARD UNIVERSITY LIBRARY, Houghton Library, Cambridge, 02138. F Thomas Noonan, Cur, Reading Room; Lawrence Dowler, Associate Librn
Holdings: Cat
Notes: Exhibition catalog published by the Library, 1969.

ON —VICTORIA UNIVERSITY, Library, Centre for Reformation and Renaissance Studies, 71 Queen's Park Crescent, Toronto, M5S 1K7, Can. Robert C Brandeis, Chief Librn; James Estes, Dir
Holdings: Vols (15,000) Cat Slides
Notes: The CRRS concentrates on the northern European countries and France; its chief strengths are Erasmus, 650 vols; early printed books, especially 16th century editions of Latin classics; bibliography and the history of printing. The Erasmus holdings are cataloged in W T McCready et al, "The Erasmus Collection in the Centre for Reformation and Renaissance Studies...A Catalogue"...*Reformation and Renaissance* 7 (1971), 32-76 and "A Supplementary *List"...Reformation and Renaissance,* 10 (1974), 116-119. Published catalogs. Humanist Editions of the Classics at CRRS, Toronto, 1979; Humanist Editions of Statutes and History at CRRS, Toronto, 1980; Bibles, Theological Treatises and Other Religious Literature 1491-1700 at CRRS, Toronto, 1981.

ERB, DONALD

OH —CASE WESTERN RESERVE UNIVERSITY LIBRARIES, Cleveland, 44106. Susie Hanson, Special Collections Librn
Notes: Manuscripts of compositions and other archival materials by the American composer Donald Erb. Contains sketches and pencil scores covering the period of Erb's 30 year career, programs, reviews, newspaper clippings, and correspondence.

ERGOT

CA —FITZ HUGH LUDLOW MEMORIAL LIBRARY, PO Box 99346, San Francisco, 94109. Michael R Aldrich, Exec Cur
Holdings: Cat Mss Map Pix Slides Phonorecords Audiotapes Videotapes
Notes: Collection stored. Important mail inquiries only. No interlibrary lending or telephone inquiries. Hallucinogens as used in historical and contemporary cultures. Nearly complete collection of books and articles by or about Timothy Leary, incl manuscripts; also nearly complete collection of the writings of Aldous Huxley concerning drugs. Much autographed or inscribed material, mostly popular music from the 1960s but also incl ethnographic music. Emphasis on psychoactive drugs relative to religion, literature, art. Also an excellent collection of research papers (chemistry, pharmacology, epidemiology, sociology, ethnobotany) in this field, as well as artifacts and artwork relating to the field.

ERIC COLLECTION

CA —UNIVERSITY OF CALIFORNIA, LOS ANGELES, Education & Psychology Library, 390 Powell Library Bldg, Los Angeles, 90024. Barbara Duke, Librn
Holdings: Vols (133,000) Cat Microforms
Notes: Depository for ERIC microfiche.

CO —SOCIAL SCIENCE EDUCATION CONSORTIUM, Resource & Demonstration Center (RDC), 855 Broadway, Boulder, 80302. Regina McCormick, Staff Assoc
Holdings: Vols (16,000) Cat Filmstrips Microforms
Notes: Contains over 15,000 elementary and secondary social studies textbooks, audiovisuals, games and simulations, professional books, and the complete ERIC microfiche collection. Staff available to travel to all parts of the U S to consult on curriculum development, instructional methods, materials analysis and selection, evaluation, new materials, teaching strategies, and trends in the social studies.

DC —CENTER FOR APPLIED LINGUISTICS, ERIC Clearinghouse on Language & Linguistics, 3520 Prospect St NW, Washington, 20007. Martha Clarke, Coordr
Budget: $4500
Notes: ERIC microfiche, ED 000/001 to date.

DC —LIBRARY OF CONGRESS, General Reading Rooms Division, Microform Reading Room, Washington, 20540.
Holdings: Cat Mss Maps Pix Microforms
Notes: Microform materials only in this LC Division. Works of individual authors; holdings of collections; archival records, etc, press releases and translations, etc.

ID —IDAHO STATE UNIVERSITY, Library, Pocatello, 83209. Joseph K W Lu, Librn
Holdings: Uncat Microforms
Budget: ($10,000)
Notes: Over a million items. Partial depository for US Government publications (1,053,430 items); incl ERIC microfiche and unclassified AEC and Dept of Energy publications in microform; depository for Idaho State Government publications (16, 000 items); international government bodies (11,000 items).

IN —INDIANA UNIVERSITY, School of Education, Library, Bloomington, 47401. Adele Dendy, Head Librn
Holdings: Vols (35,000) Cat Pix Slides Phonorecords Audiotapes 16mm Films Filmstrips Microforms
Budget:
Notes: Library has complete ERIC collection of microfiche (277,308). 2098 non-ERIC items, 226 serials, and 22,823 nonprint items (housed in educational materials center). Emphasis on recent materials; the historic collections in education are located in the Main Library. The collection is geared to graduate level studies and research. A separate Teaching Materials Center includes 10,000 elementary and secondary textbooks. The Center also includes curriculum guides, supplementary materials and 17,823 nonprint teaching aids.

KY —UNIVERSITY OF KENTUCKY, Education Library, Dickey Hall Room 205, Lexington, 40506. Larry Greenwood, Librn
Holdings: Vols 297,000 Cat Microforms
Budget: $2000
Notes: Professional books, model children's and young people's collection, curriculum materials and guides and ERIC collection (297,000 microfiche).

MI —WAYNE STATE UNIVERSITY, Kresge Library (Education), Detroit, 48202. Theodore Manheim, Librn
Holdings: Vols (297,000)
Budget: ($105,000)
Notes: Incl complete ERIC microfiche file. 780 current periodical subcriptions. Also 35 drawers of vertical file material. Seperate catalog to the collection.

MN —MANKATO STATE UNIVERSITY, Memorial Library, Educational Resource Center, Box 19, Mankato, 56001. E Colby, Film & Curriculum Librn
Notes: Microfiche collection, separate from Education Resource Center materials.

NY —CITY UNIVERSITY OF NEW YORK, City College, Library, 138 St & Convent Ave, New York, 10031. Vira C Hinds, Assoc Prof
Holdings: Vols (35,000) Cat
Budget: ($9173)
Notes: Education, incl juveniles (10,437), textbooks, and ERIC collection. Separate author catalog.

NY —COLUMBIA UNIVERSITY LIBRARIES, Teachers College, Milbank Memorial Library, 525 W 120 St, New York, 10027. Jane P Franck, Dir
Notes: Collection completely indexed by ERIC reference tools, *Research in Education and Current Index for Journals in Education.* Have entire ERIC collection. 230,000 titles on microfiche.

NY —NEW YORK PUBLIC LIBRARY, Mid-Manhattan Library, Education Collection, 455 Fifth Ave, New York, 10016.
Holdings: Uncat
Notes: *Resources in Education* and *Current Index to Journals in Education.* Complete ERIC from inception in 1966; 315,000 microfiche cards.

NY —DOWLING COLLEGE, Library, Idle Hour Blvd, Oakdale, 11769. Wendell A Guy, Dir
Holdings: Uncat
Budget: $1800
Notes: Complete from inception in 1967. 173,000 microfiche.

NY —ERIC CLEARINGHOUSE ON INFORMATION RESOURCES, Syracuse University, School of Education, Syracuse, 13210. Donald P Ely, Dir; Pamela McLaughlin, User Services Coordinator
Holdings: Microforms
Notes: As of 1977, the ERIC Clearinghouse on Information Resources transferred from Stanford University to Syracuse University. Scope note cites: management operation and use of libraries; technology to improve their operation and the education, training and professional activities of librarians and information specialists; instructional developments; educational techniques involved in computer assisted and managed instruction, systems analysis and programmed instruction; the delivery of instruction via audiovisual teaching materials and technologies such as television, radio, computers, and films; and technology in society adaptable to education, incl cable television, communication satellites, microforms and public television.

OK —CENTRAL STATE UNIVERSITY, Library, 100 N University Dr, Edmond, 73034. Andrew Peters, Reference Librn
Holdings: Cat Maps Audiotapes Microforms
Notes: Microforms Research Center for newspapers and periodicals, incl ERIC, LAC, LEL, HRAF, and annual reports, etc. Vols on microfilm reels, microfiche; microcards; academic and music audiotapes; and maps.

OR —UNIVERSITY OF OREGON LIBRARY, Education-Psychology Dept, Eugene, 97403. Rose Marie Service, Head Dept Librn
Holdings: Cat Pix Phonorecords Audiotapes Filmstrips Microforms
Budget: ($15,000)
Notes: Large up-to-date research collection with representation in all areas and particular emphases reflecting those of the College of Education: educational administration; special education, particularly mental retardation; elementary education, incl early childhood and counseling psychology. Strong serial collection. Curriculum Collection incl a representative selection of curriculum guides, student use textbooks and multimedia, pamphlets, and standardized tests. Complete ERIC microfiche collection.

PA —SCHOOL DISTRICT OF PHILADELPHIA, Pedagogical Library, 21 St & Pkwy, Philadelphia, 19103. Helen E Howe, Librn; Patricia K Buck, Asst Librn
Holdings: Vols 47,000 Cat Pix Phonorecords Audiotapes Videotapes Filmstrips Microforms
Notes: The complete ERIC collection with reader/printers available. Also over 450

ERIC COLLECTION (cont.)

periodicals and a textbook examination center consisting of approx 23,000 textbooks and several thousand instructional aids reviewed for use in the school system.

TN —VANDERBILT UNIVERSITY, George Peabody College for Teachers, Education Library, Box 325, Nashville, 37203. Mary Beth Blalock, Librn
Holdings: Microforms
Budget: ($59,000)
Notes: The Education Library (192,541 vols) collects in all areas relating to education with special emphasis on Child Study and Exceptional Children. Special funds are available for continuing purchases in these areas. The collection is strong in curriculum materials, physical education, applied art, psychology related to education and all areas of education. Amoung special papers are over 300 papers by and about Jean Piaget and an extensive author and subject file referring to the location of these papers and books and journal articles by and about Piaget in the rest of the Education Library collection. The Education Library is a Division of the Vanderbilt University Library.

TX —WEST TEXAS STATE UNIVERSITY, Cornette Library, PO Box 748 WT Sta, Canyon, 79016. Faye Hendrickson, Special Collections Asst
Holdings: Vols (451,253) Uncat Microforms
Notes: Complete ERIC collection (microfiche).

WI —WISCONSIN DEPT OF PUBLIC INSTRUCTION, Library, 125 S Webster St Room 311, PO Box 7841, Madison, 53707. Marjorie Westergard, Librn
Holdings: Vols Cat Microforms
Budget: ($16,000)
Notes: Main purpose of the library is to support the needs and programs of the Winconsin Department of Public Instruction. No teaching materials are collected at the library; however, professional materials kept the complete ERIC Microfiche collection, as well as the book collection. Service is generally restricted to members of the Department and other state agencies.

MB —UNIVERSITY OF MANITOBA, Faculty of Education, D S Woods Education Library, Winnipeg, R3T 2N2, Can. Doreen Shanks, Head
Holdings: Vols (57,000) Cat Microforms Phonorecords Videotapes
Notes: Incl collection of 23,000 textbooks, 332,000 microforms, 615 phonorecords, and 225 videotapes. Also complete file of ERIC (Educational Resources Information Centre) documents on microfiche; Instructional Materials Centre.

ON —CANADA, DEPT OF EMPLOYMENT & IMMIGRATION LIBRARY, Ottawa, K1A 0J9, Can. P E Sunder-Raj, Dir Library Services
Holdings: Vols (35,000) Cat Microforms
Notes: In addition to cataloged material, library has approximately 1800 current journals and serials. We have holdings of ERIC documents on microfiche.

ERICKSON, ARTHUR CHARLES

AB —UNIVERSITY OF CALGARY, Libraries, Special Collections Div, 2500 University Dr, Calgary, T2N 1N4, Can.
Holdings: Cat Mss Pix
Notes: Collection consists of the business records, photographs, 19,757 drawings, specifications, design notes, project and office files, correspondence, architectural drawings, renderings, exhibition material, and photographs of the architectural practice of Arthur C Erickson, from 1963. Project lists are on hand. 55 meters documents.

ERIE CANAL

NY —BUFFALO & ERIE COUNTY HISTORICAL SOCIETY, 25 Nottingham Court, Buffalo, 14216. Herman Sass, Librn
Notes: Emphasis on the Erie Canal and the region. In various resources departments. No separate catalog.

NY —UNIVERSITY OF ROCHESTER, Rush Rhees Library, Department of Rare Books and Special Collections, Rochester, 14627. Peter Dzwonkoski, Librn
Notes: Drawings (20) for structures for enlarged Erie Canal after 1840.

NY —JERVIS PUBLIC LIBRARY, 613 N Washington St, Rome, 13440. William A Dillon, Dir
Holdings: // Cat Mss
See also entry under Autograph - Collections

NY —CANAL MUSEUM, Research Library, 318 Erie Blvd E, Syracuse, 13202. Todd S Weseloh, Librn & Archivist
Holdings: Vols (7000) Mss Maps Pix
Notes: Engineering and construction records of New York State Canal System (1833-1930). Enlargements of Erie Canal, construction of lateral canals, maintenance of New York canals, construction of Barge Canal System. Maps and surveys of canals and property along canals. Plans of canal structures: bridges, aqueducts, locks, waste weirs, culverts, dams, reservoirs, feeders, and others. 954 linear feet mss; 7000 mss and printed maps and plans.

ERITREA see Ethiopia

ERLANGER, JOSEPH

MO —WASHINGTON UNIVERSITY, School of Medicine, Archives, 660 S Euclid Ave, Saint Louis, 63110. Paul G Anderson, Archivist
Holdings: Mss Pix Audiotapes
Budget: ($38,000)
Notes: Institutional records and papers of faculty of Washington University School of Medicine and its predecessors and associated hospitals. Contains records of St Louis Medical College, Missouri Medical Barnard Free Skin and Cancer Hospital, Barnes Hospital, St Louis Children's Hospital and Jewish Hospital of St Louis. Incl papers of William Beaumont, Joseph Erlanger, Leo Loeb, Evarts Graham, Edmund V Cowdry, Helen Graham, Carl V Moore, Margaret Smith and others. Oral history program. See also: Anderson, Paul G and Hoolihan, Christopher, eds. *Special Collections* (St Louis: Washington University School of Medicine, 1981). 960 linear feet.

ERNO, RICHARD B.

MA —BOSTON UNIVERSITY, Mugar Memorial Library, Special Collections Dept, 771 Commonwealth Ave, Boston, 02215. Howard B Gotlieb, Dir
Holdings: Cat Mss Pix
Notes: Mss, correspondence, etc collected in depth; incl publications by or about.

ERNST, MAX, 1891-1976

CT —YALE UNIVERSITY, Beinecke Rare Book & Manuscript Library, Osborn Collection, New Haven, 06520. Stephen R Parks, Cur
Holdings: Mss

ERNST, MORRIS L.

CA —UNIVERSITY OF CALIFORNIA, SANTA BARBARA, Library, Dept of Special Collections, Santa Barbara, 93106. Christian F Brun, Head
Holdings: Vols 615 Cat
Notes: The Morris L Ernst Banned Books Collection.

EROSION, COAST see Coasts

EROSION CONTROL see Soil Conservation

EROTIC PHOTOGRAPHY see Photography, Erotic

EROTICA

†CA —INSTITUTE FOR THE ADVANCED STUDY OF HUMAN SEXUALITY, 1523 Franklin St, San Francisco, 94109.

CA —INTERNATIONAL MUSEUM OF EROTIC ART, Formerly, San Francisco, 94108.
Notes: Unfortunately this renowned collection has been dispersed and no longer (1984) exists, including the Phyllis and Eberhard Kronhausen Collection, according to the information we have been given.

IN —INDIANA UNIVERSITY, Institute for Sex Research Library, 416 Morrison Hall, Bloomington, 47401. Douglas Freeman, Collections and Services Librn; Joan Brewer, Information Services Librn
Holdings: Vols (62,000) Cat Mss Pix Phonorecords Audiotapes Slides Films Microforms
Budget: ($20,000)
Notes: One of the greatest and most extensive collections on sexual behavior, the library collects materials on all aspects of sex activity, with special ephasis on behavioral and social aspects. Also collects erotic literature and sexual ephemera. Incl 105 audiotapes, 23 vertical file drawers, 108 phonorecords, 55,000 pictures, 5000 slides, and 1700 films. Rich in French, German and American sources; also much Oriental. Semitraditional erotic poetry and song of 17th-18th century England. Bawdy limericks, double-entendre, puns, slang, erotic literature, graffity, slang and special dictionaries, proverbs and sayings, epigrams and research materials of the Kinsey Studies, etc. Contact Information Service for: literature searching, preparation of bibliographies, permission to use collection. Limited photocopying.

NC —UNIVERSITY OF NORTH CAROLINA, CHARLOTTE, J Murrey Atkins Library, UNCC Station, Charlotte, 28223. Robert F Brabham Jr, Special Collections Librn
Holdings: Vols 100 Cat
Notes: Incl scholarly works on sex, classics by such writers as D H Lawrence, Frank Harris, and Norman Douglas, and about 40 novels published between 1890 and 1930.

RI —PROVIDENCE ATHENAEUM, 251 Benefit St, Providence, 02903. Sally Duplaix, Dir
Holdings: Vols 175 Uncat
Notes: Emphasis on early 20th century German imprints, as well as many French. Recent gift, not yet cataloged.

ERP (EUROPEAN RECOVERY PROGRAM) see Reconstruction (Europe, 1945-1951)

ERRINGTON, PAUL L.

IA —IOWA STATE UNIVERSITY, Library, Dept of Special Collections, Ames, 50011. Stanley M Yates, Head
Holdings: // Mss Pix
Notes: The Paul Errington (1902-1962) Papers. Professor of zoology at ISU (1932-1962) and a leading authority on vertebrate ecology and animal population dynamics. Collection incl correspondence, mss and articles. Collection is 15 linear feet.

ERSE see Irish Language and Literature

ERSKINE, JOHN

NY —COLUMBIA UNIVERSITY LIBRARIES, Rare Book & Manuscript Library, 801 Butler Library, 535 W 114 St, New York, 10027. Kenneth A Lohf, Librn
Holdings: Mss
Notes: Papers, incl mss, letters, reviews, etc. 20,000 items. Restricted use.

ERUDITION see Learning and Scholarship

ERVIN, SAMUEL J., JR.

NC —UNIVERSITY OF NORTH CAROLINA, CHAPEL HILL, Louis Round Wilson Academic Affairs Library, Southern Historical Collection, Chapel Hill, 27514. Carolyn Wallace, Librn
Holdings: Mss
Notes: The papers of Senator Samuel J Ervin, Jr.

ESCAPOLOGY

DC —LIBRARY OF CONGRESS, Rare Book & Special Collections Div, Washington, 20540. William Matheson, Chief
Holdings: Cat
Notes: The Houdini Collection of Magic and Spiritism consists of over 4000 vols of printed works and a large number of scrapbooks containing clippings, programs, catalogs, posters, etc. The McManus-Young collection of 1076 vols, as well as mss, prints, and organized scrapbooks on Houdini, the history of magic, and related fields.

ESCOTT, JONATHAN

MA —BOSTON UNIVERSITY, Mugar Memorial Library, Special Collections Dept, 771 Commonwealth Ave, Boston, 02215. Howard B Gotlieb, Dir
Holdings: Cat Mss

ESHBACK, LLOYD

†PA —TEMPLE UNIVERSITY LIBRARY, Philadelphia, 19122. Thomas M Whitehead, Librn
Notes: More than 100 cubic ft of mss, incl papers of Michael Bishop, Ben Bova, Jack Dann, Gardner Dozois, Lloyd Eshback, Tom Purdom, Pamela Sargent, John Varley, and George Zebrowski.

ESHLEMAN, CLAYTON, 1935-

FL —UNIVERSITY OF MIAMI, Otto G Richter Library, PO Box 248214, Coral Gables, 33124. Frank Rodgers, Dir of Libraries
Holdings: Cat
Notes: Innovative and experimental writing of the 1960s and 1970s. Incl generous proportion of press books: Black Sparrow, Auerhahn, and many others; also other private publications ranging from the best to the least attractive. Format includes postcards and broadsides as well as periodical and book form. Writers incl Charles Bukowski, Diane Wakoski, Jerome Rothenberg, Clayton Eshleman, and many of their contemporaries.
See also entry under Poetry, Modern.

BC —SIMON FRASER UNIVERSITY, Library, Burnaby, V5A 1S6, Can. Percilla Groves, Special Collections Librn
Holdings: Cat Mss
Notes: Letters written to Eshleman by Allen Ginsberg (8 pp), William Carlos Williams and Florence Williams (5 pp), Robert Duncan (4 pp), and Edward Dorn (5 pp), while Eshleman was editor of *Folio* (1959-1961). Tss from Gregory Corso (2 pp), Louis Zukofsky (8 pp), Michael Rumaker (3 pp).

ESKIMAUAN INDIANS see Eskimos and Inuits

ESKIMO ART see Art, Eskimo

ESKIMO LANGUAGES

NT —NORTHWEST TERRITORIES PUBLIC LIBRARY SERVICES, Bos 1100, Hay River, X0E 0R0, Can.
Holdings: Vols (1235) Cat Maps Audiotapes
Notes: Originally intended to provide items of historical significance on the Northwest Territories. It contains a number of first editions, some of which have since become available in reprint form. Copies of material in relevant native languages and on learning languages.

ON —METROPOLITAN TORONTO LIBRARY, Languages Centre, 789 Yonge St, Toronto, M4W 2G8, Can. Barbara Gunther, Head
Notes: A unique collection of Canadian Inuit linguistics.

ESKIMOS AND INUITS

AK —UNIVERSITY OF ALASKA, Elmer E Rasmuson Library, Fairbanks, 99701. Robert H Geiman, Dir
Holdings: Vols Cat Mss Maps Pix Slides Phonorecords Audiotapes Films Microforms
Notes: The Alaska Collection is strong in all disciplines concerning Alaska. Main strengths are exploration and travel, pioneer memoirs, and materials on Alaska natives. Bulk of collection is in English with significant holdings in Russian, Native American, and European languages. Archival holdings incl 6000 cu ft of mss, 110,000 historic photographs, 2319 tape recordings, 727 films and videotapes, 200 rare maps and 1273 microfilms. Ms collection strongest in political and economic areas. A Guide to the Collections is available in hard copy and microfiche. About 1000 special collections, some 300 quite significant.

AK —ALASKA STATE LIBRARY, Alaska Historical Library Collection, Pouch G, Juneau, 99811. Phyllis Demuth, Readers Services Librn
Holdings: Vols (24,000) Cat Mss Maps Pix Slides Phonorecords Audiotapes Videotapes 16mm Films Microforms

DC —SMITHSONIAN INSTITUTION LIBRARIES, Anthropology Branch, Washington, 20560. Jean C Smith, Asst Dir for Bureau Services
Holdings: Vols (54,000) Cat Mss Maps Pix Slides Microforms
Budget: ($7041)
Notes: Physical anthropology, archaeology, ethnology, language and languages; Indians of both continents.

MN —UNIVERSITY OF MINNESOTA, DULUTH, Library & Learning Resources Service, Duluth, 55812. James V. Litha, Archivist
Holdings: Vols 1700 Cat Mss Maps Pix
Notes: The Voyageur Collection incl the Grace Lee Nute Papers. Books and materials relating to the Voyageur period (1650-1850) and the area of Northeastern Minnesota, Michigan, Wisconsin, Southern Canada. Emphasis on all subjects listed in this volume. Incl materials about Eskimo (Inuits) life.

NY —MUSEUM OF THE AMERICAN INDIAN, Library, 9 Westchester Square, Bronx, 10401. Mary B Davis, Librn
Holdings: Vols (40,000) Cat Mss Maps Pix Microforms VF
Notes: Collections cover all aspects of the Indians of the Western Hemisphere; some materials on Eskimos. For scholarly research only.

NY —AMERICAN MUSEUM OF NATURAL HISTORY, Library Services Dept, Central Park W & 79th St, New York, 10024. Nina J Root, Chairwoman; Mary Genett, Asst Librn for Reference Services
Holdings: Vols (385,000) Cat Mss Maps Pix Slides Microforms
Notes: Nearly all collections are outstanding for depth of coverage and international range. Early and historic works, rare books, colored illustrations, and relevant serial publications supplement the modern scientific publications necessary to the researches of the scientific staff and the work of the educational division. Open to the public.

NY —NEW YORK PUBLIC LIBRARY, Research Libraries, American History Div, Fifth Ave & 42 St, New York, 10018.
Holdings: Vols (10,000) Cat Maps Microforms
Notes: Archaeology, anthropology, linguistics, ethnology, and sociology of the American Indian. Comprehensive coverage. Much material on Indian languages, incl numerous syllabaries. Coverage ranges from the Eskimos to the Indians of Tierra del Fuego.

WA —UNIVERSITY OF WASHINGTON LIBRARIES, Rare Books, Special Collections Dept, Seattle, 98195. Sandra Kroupa, Librn
Notes: Part of a set of Siberian primers prepared in the early 1930s by Soviet ethnographers. Some are first attempts to transcribe Siberian languages. All are in Latin phonetic script, not in Cyrillic.

AB —GLENBOW-ALBERTA INSTITUTE, Historical Library & Archives, 130 9th Avenue SE, Calgary, T2G 0P3, Can. Leonard J Gottseleg, Chief Librn
Holdings: Vols (60,000) Cat Mss Maps Pix Microforms
Notes: Main emphasis is on Western Canadian history. Equally important emphasis is placed on the Canadian Arctic and Alaska, Northwest Coast explorations, Aboriginal peoples of the North and Canadian West, and the fur trade in the US Northwest.

MB —ESKIMO MUSEUM, Library, Box 10, Churchill, R0B 0E0, Can. Brother J Volant, Cur
Holdings: Vols (300) Cat
Notes: Books on the North, mainly northern Canada; explorers' journals; Eskimos ethnology, archaeology, and art.

MB —HUDSON'S BAY CO, Library, 77 Main St, Winnipeg, R3C 2R1, Can. Carol Preston, Librn Hudson's Bay House
Holdings: Vols (6000) Cat Mss Maps Pix Slides
Notes: Main purpose is to provide research materials for production of the historical quarterly *The Beaver,* and to answer inquiries about the Company's history. Incl 250,000 pictures and 7000 VF pieces. No published catalog, but Library maintains author/subject/title card catalog. Limited photocopying. Mss of HBC Archives held by the Manitoba Provincial Archives. Published descriptions: Dowdall, Judi, "Hudson's Bay Company Library," *Canadian Library* Journal, June 1974, p 179; Preston, Carol, "Hudson's Bay Company Library," *Manitoba Library Association Bulletin,* June 1976, pp 24-25.

MB —MANITOBA MUSEUM OF MAN & NATURE, Library, 190 Rupert Ave, Winnipeg, R3B 0N2, Can. V Hatten, Librn
Holdings: Vols (20,000) Cat Maps Slides Audiotapes Videotapes Microforms
Notes: Human and natural history of Manitoba.

MB —UNIVERSITY OF MANITOBA, Elizabeth Dafoe Library, Archives and Special Collections Dept, Winnipeg, R3T 2N2, Can. Richard E Bennett, Dept Head; Corrado A Santoro, Reference Archivist
Notes: Correspondence, reports and various papers of Dr Bruce H Chown. Haemolitic diseases of the newborn, especially erthroblastosis fetalis and the maternal Rh-factor. Incl correpspondence with Dr Louis Diamond of Boston. Also incl are human anthropological blood group studies of Eskimo, Indian and Canadian-Japanese communities.

NT —NORTHWEST TERRITORIES PUBLIC LIBRARY SERVICES, Bos 1100, Hay River, X0E 0R0, Can.
Holdings: Vols (1235) Cat Maps Audiotapes
Notes: Originally intended to provide items of historical significance on the Northwest Territories. It contains a number of first editions, some of which have since become available in reprint form. Copies of material in relevant native languages and on learning languages.

ON —NATIONAL LIBRARY OF CANADA, 395 Wellington St, Ottawa, K1A 0N4, Can. Andre Preibish, Dir
Holdings: Vols 18,000
Notes: The collection contains 42 incunabula. The core collection consists of early Canadiana (1752-1867) and 16th and 17th century books on Canada. The books printed in native languages are a very valuable part of the collection. Canadian Livres d'Artistes collection of limited editions and Canadian *livres d'artistes* received on legal deposit as well as examples of private press publications from other countries also form part of the Rare Book collection.

ON —NATIONAL MUSEUMS OF CANADA, Library Services Directorate, Ottawa, K1A 0M8, Can. Valerie Monkhouse, Director
Holdings: Vols (70,000) // Cat Mss Maps Slides Microforms
Budget: ($60,000)
Notes: Collection includes anthropology, archaeology, ethnology, folklore, history, Indians of North America, Inuit, linguistics

ESKIMOS AND INUITS (cont.)

of North American Indians, material history, military and naval history, museology. Also 13,500 periodical titles; vertical files of Canadian Association in Support of Native Peoples (microfilm); over 22,000 items covering every facet of contemporary native life. Mss, pictures and theses are held in Archives (National Musseum of Man). Research collection, interlibrary loans available, public may use on the premises.

ON —PUBLIC ARCHIVES OF CANADA, Library, 395 Wellington St, Ottawa, K1A 0N3, Can. Dawn E Monroe, Collections Development Officer
Holdings: Vols (80,000) Cat
Notes: The Public Archives Library has collected certain published documents, general works and specialized studies pertinent to the study of the historical and sociological development of native peoples. These documents incl accounts of the trips made by missionaries, explorers and others into Inuit or Amerindian territory, territory, specialized bibliographies, and ethnographic reference works incl dictionaries of native languages, studies on customs and habits, and specialized periodicals.

ON —CANADIAN ASSOCIATION IN SUPPORT OF THE NATIVE PEOPLES, Library, 277 Victoric St, Toronto, M5V 1W2, Can. Frances Davidson-Arnott, Librn
Holdings: Vols 4000 Cat Mss Maps Pix Slides Microforms
Notes: Native peoples of North America, especially of Canada.

ON —METROPOLITAN TORONTO LIBRARY, Canadian History Dept, Baldwin Room Section, 789 Yonge St, Toronto, M4W 2G8, Can. David B Kotin, Head
Holdings: Vols (52,000) Mss Pix
Notes: This collection consists of material on Canadian history, geography, travel, archaeology, genealogy, retrospective city and telephone directories, collective biographies, native peoples (excluding customs, rights and social conditions), Arctic regions, military history and theory. It is an extremely strong collection of both current and retrospective material. Particular strengths are national and local history (especially Ontario), Arctic regions, native peoples, travel (especially Ontario), and military history. Incl 78,000 historical pictures, 235 linear meters mss, 14,000 broadsides and 3800 bound newspapers.

ON —METROPOLITAN TORONTO LIBRARY, Languages Centre, 789 Yonge St, Toronto, M4W 2G8, Can. Barbara Gunther, Head
Holdings: Vols (90,000) Cat Phonorecords Audiotapes
Notes: Original literature in over 80 languages; books, records, cassettes, microfilm on language studies; newspapers and periodicals from 50 counties. Language study materials. Issue quarterly additions lists by language. Collect North American Indian and Eskimo language materials. Occasional bibliographies.

ON —ROYAL ONTARIO MUSEUM, Main Library and Archives, 100 Queen's Park, Toronto, M5S 2C6, Can. Julia Matthews, Head Librn
Holdings: Vols (85,000) Cat
Notes: Since January 1977, acquisitions have been entered in UTLAS.

†SK —UNIVERSITY OF REGINA, Library, Regina, S4S 0A2, Can. Margarett Hammond, Librn
Notes: Native peoples of North America, especially of Canada. Collection formerly held by Canadian Association in Support of the Native Peoples.

ESLER, ANTHONY

MA —BOSTON UNIVERSITY, Mugar Memorial Library, Special Collections Dept, 771 Commonwealth Ave, Boston, 02215. Howard B Gotlieb, Dir
Holdings: Mss Correspondence

ESOTERIC CHURCH HISTORY

RI —BROWN UNIVERSITY, John Hay Library, 20 Prospect St, Providence, 02912. Mark N Brown, Cur Mss
Holdings: Vols (900) // Mss
Notes: John William Graham Collection of Literature of Psychic Science--350 predominantly late 19th and early 20th century books dealing with alchemy, black magic, dreams, demonology, church history, mysticism, mediumship, physical and somatic types of psychic experience. Collection described in *Index to Psychic* Science compiled by S R Morgan (Swathmore, 1950). Also, the Damon Collection of Occult and Visionary Literature--550 vols devoted to the development of western mysticism with particular emphasis on American and British thought, incl texts on alchemy, black magic, esoteric church history, dream interpretations, mysticism, witchcraft, the Kabbalah, and visionary testaments and manifestations of all types printed during the 16th to 20th centuries; and the Samuel Wyllys Papers--125 mss, transcripts, and photocopies of legal and government papers relating to Indianaffairs, colonial wars, civil and criminal cases, and the witchcraft trials of 1692-1693. Partially cataloged.

ESP see Extrasensory Perception (Esp)

ESPERANTO

OR —UNIVERSITY OF OREGON, Library, Eugene, 97403. Kenneth W Duckett, Curator
Holdings: Vols (3000) Cat Mss
Notes: Incl 475 serial runs. The George Alan Connor Collection of Esperanto literature features local, regional, national, and international publications in Esperanto, mainly from the period 1910-1960. Catalog available. Also the Rev M Whipple Bishop papers which incl 31 vols and 27 serial titles as well as mss.

ESPIONAGE

CA —HARVEY G WOLFE LIBRARY, PO Box 3514, Grand Central Sta, Glendale, 91201. Douglas L Evans, Librn
Holdings: Vols (6580) Mss Maps Pix
Budget: ($4500)
Notes: Main emphasis on espionage, military intelligence, and sabotage.

CA —UNIVERSITY OF CALIFORNIA, LOS ANGELES, Research Library, Dept of Special Collections, 405 Hilgard Ave, Los Angeles, 90024. Edward Shreeves, Chairman, Bibliographers Group; David S Zeidberg, Head
Holdings: Mss Pix
Notes: Material on this subject is incl in the archive assembles by Roger Mennevee.

CA —HOOVER INSTITUTION ON WAR, REVOLUTION & PEACE, Stanford University, Stanford, 94305. Milorad M Drachkovitch, Archivist
Notes: Two collections: (1) Papers of Yves Godard, officer, French Army, 1932-1961; director of police in Algeria, 1958-60; and organizers of the Organisation de I'Armee Secrete (O A S) 1961-1962; incl correspondence, messages, reports, dossiers, maps, photos, news clipping, speeches and writings, and other material, 1929-74, related to military and resistance operations during World War II; to military operations during Indochinese War; and to military, police, and terrorist activities during the Algerian independence struggle. Incl records of the Armee Secrete de Haute-Savoie (Secret Army of Resistance Fighters of Haute-Savoie). 13 ms boxes; 1 oversize volume; 1 envelope. (2) Papers of Herbert Solow, American journalist, and editor of *Fortune,* 1945-1964, incl correspondence, speeches, drafts of writings, memoranda, depositions, clippings and other printedmatter, 1924-76, relating to the communist movement in the US, the Non-Partisan Defense League, the Commission of Inquiry into the Charges Made Against Leon Trotsky in the Moscow Trials, Soviet espionage in the US, Zionism, and post-World War II international business enterprises. Incl some papers of Mrs Herbert Solow, 1964-76. 8 ms boxes.

DC —GEORGETOWN UNIVERSITY, Library, Special Collections Div, 37 & O Sts NW, Washington, 20057. George M Barringer, Special Collections Librn; Nicholas B Sheetz, Mss Librn
Holdings: Cat
Notes: The Russell J Bowen Collection on Intelligence, Security, and Covert Activities. The collection extends over several hundred years, and incl early wars and conflicts in Europe, the American Revolutionary era, the Civil War in the United States, the World Wars, and other events. Intelligence and espionage activities during World War II, the Cold War, and recent events are extensively documented. See *Scholar's Guide to Intelligence Literature: Bibliography of the Russell J Bowen Collection* (1983).

NY —COLUMBIA UNIVERSITY LIBRARIES, Rare Book & Manuscript Library, 801 Butler Library, 535 W 114 St, New York, 10027. Kenneth A Lohf, Librn
Holdings: Mss
Notes: Major General William H Donovan's papers on his research materials on espionage during the American Revolution. Incl 15,000 items. Restricted use.

TX —RICE UNIVERSITY, Fondren Library, 6100 S Main St, PO Box 1892, Houston, 77251. Dr Samuel M Carrington, Jr, University Librn
Notes: The Stephen K Swift Collection, incl Austro-Hungarian and Austrian history (3600 items). Has complete British Intelligence Service reports on Austria. 1945-1955; original charter from the Austrian Empire to the Hungarian government (ca 1527), with signature of Charles V. Also a 360 vol history of the city of Vienna.

ESQUIMAU see Eskimos and Inuits

ESSENCES AND ESSENTIAL OILS

CA —SUNKIST GROWERS, Research Library, 760 E Sunkist St, Ontario, 91761. Martha C Nemeth, Librn
Holdings: Vols (1500) Cat
Budget: ($10,000)
Notes: Technology of citrus fruit and citrus fruit products, primarily Californian. Strong in organic and food chemistry, with additional coverage of food technology, essential oils, microbiology and environmental protection.

PA —FRANKLIN INSTITUTE LIBRARY, 20 & The Parkway, Philadelphia, 19103. Miriam Padusis, Dir; Charles Wilt, Readers Servs Librn
Holdings: Vols (300,000) Cat Maps Pix Microforms

ESSENES

AZ —WORLD UNIVERSITY, Library, 711 E Blacklidge Dr, Tucson, 85719. Howard John Zitko, Cur
Holdings: Vols (15,000) Cat Mss Maps Audiotapes
Notes: Collection concerns the "frontier sciences." No interlibrary loan.

OH —HEBREW UNION COLLEGE-JEWISH INSTITUTE OF RELIGION, Klau Library, 3101 Clifton Ave, Cincinnati, 45220. David J Gilner, Reference Librn
Holdings: Cat

ESSENTIAL OILS see Essences and Essential Oils

ESTATES (LAW)

NC —CAMPBELL COLLEGE, Carrie Rich Memorial Library, Box 98, Buies Creek, 27506. Helen Sistrunk, Asst to Dir
Holdings: Vols 8500 Cat Mss
Budget: $5600

ESTHETICS see Aesthetics

ESTONIA

MA —HARVARD UNIVERSITY LIBRARY, Widener Library, Cambridge, 02138.
Holdings: Cat Mss Microforms
Notes: *Widener Library Shelflist* No 40

ESTONIA (cont.)

(1972) lists some 6500 vols on the history, languages, and literatures of the Baltic states: Estonia, Latvia, Lithuania, and Livonia; about 1000 of these are on Estonia.

†NJ —ESTONIAN ARCHIVES IN THE UNITED STATES, 607 East 7 St, Lakewood, 08701.

†NY —ESTONIAN HOUSE LIBRARY, 243 East 34 St, New York, 10016.
Notes: Estonian literature, history and culture.

ESTONIAN LANGUAGE AND LITERATURE

†NY —ESTONIAN HOUSE LIBRARY, 243 East 34 St, New York, 10016.
Notes: Estonian literature, history and culture.

NY —NEW YORK PUBLIC LIBRARY, Donnell Foreign Language Library, 20 W 53 St, New York, 10019. Bosiljka Stevanovic, Supvr Librn
Holdings: Vols 186 Cat
Notes: Estonian collection incl Estonian authors of Estonian expression. No separate catalog.

OH —CLEVELAND PUBLIC LIBRARY, Foreign Literature Dept, 325 Superior Ave, Cleveland, 44114. Natalia Bezugloff, Head
Holdings: Vols 890 Cat
Notes: A popular circulating collection containing classics and the standard works with emphasis on belles lettres, history and biography. A variety of other subjects such as learning languages, children's art, etc. *See also* entry under Foreign Language Collections

OH —KENT STATE UNIVERSITY, Libraries, Ethnic Collections, Kent, 44242.
Holdings: Vols 425 Cat
Notes: See entry under Foreign Language Collections.

ESTONIANS IN THE U.S.

MN —UNIVERSITY OF MINNESOTA, Immigration History Research Center, 826 Berry St, Saint Paul, 55114. Susan Griegs, Cur
Holdings: Vols (35,000) Mss Maps Pix Phonorecords Audiotapes 16mm Films Microforms
Notes: See entry under US-Emigration and Immigration.

†NJ —ESTONIAN ARCHIVES IN THE UNITED STATES, 607 East 7 St, Lakewood, 08701.

PA —BALCH INSTITUTE FOR ETHNIC STUDIES, Library, 18 S Seventh St, Philadelphia, 19106. R Joseph Anderson, Library Dir
Holdings: Vols Cat

ESTUARIAN ECOLOGY

CA —CALIFORNIA STATE UNIVERSITY, FULLERTON, Library, Box 4150, Fullerton, 92634. Linda Herman, Special Collections Librn
Holdings: Cat
Notes: Dr Leonard B Schultz Ichthyology Collection of 13,000 pieces incl books, pamphlets, articles and ephemera. It is supplemented by the Ecology of Bay and Estuarine Fishes Collections.

†MD —SMITHSONIAN INSTITUTION LIBRARIES, Smithsonian Environmental Research Center, Branch Library, PO Box 28, Edgewater, 21037.
Holdings: Vols (1100)

ESTUARIES

ME —BIGELOW LABORATORY FOR OCEAN SCIENCES & MAINE DEPT OF MARINE RESOURCES, Library, McKown Point, West Boothbay Harbor, 04575. Pamela Shephard-Lupo, Librn
Holdings: Vols Cat Periodicals Maps
Budget: ($55,000)
Notes: This library presently serves two institutions. The Maine Dept of Marine Resources has maintained the library since 1957 and thus the majority of our holdings are geared to their needs, ie fish biology and stock assessment on a local, national and international level. In 1973 Bigelow Laboratory for Ocean Sciences came to West Boothbay Harbor and began to contribute to the library with a very specialized collection on the Gulf of Maine marine chemistry, phytoplankton and nutrient cycles.

MD —CALVERT MARINE MUSEUM, Library, PO Box 97, Solomons, 20688.
Holdings: Vols (2000) Cat Mss Maps Pix Slides Audiotapes 16mm Films
Notes: Estuarine biology and paleontology of southern Maryland. Large picture collection (1800), blueprints (358) and slides (1100).

TX —UNIVERSITY OF TEXAS, Marine Science Institute Library, Port Aransas, 78373. Ruth Grundy, Librn
Holdings: Vols (45,000) Cat Maps Pix
Budget: ($70,000)
Notes: Current researches in marine science, especially concerning the Gulf of Mexico, the Texas Coastal Zone, and the Continental Shelf. Incl journals.

ETCHING AND ETCHINGS

CO —DENVER PUBLIC LIBRARY, Western History Department, 1357 Broadway, Denver, 80203. Eleanor M Gehres, Head
Holdings: Cat Pix
Notes: Etchings, watercolors, drawings and other works of George Elbert Burr. Burr's correspondence with Cyrus Boutwell, art dealer, and other mss relating to Burr.

LA —R W NORTON ART GALLERY, Library, 4747 Creswell Ave, Shreveport, 71106. Jerry M Bloomer, Librn
Holdings: Vols 127 Cat

NY —METROPOLITAN MUSEUM OF ART, Dept of Prints & Photographs, 82 St & Fifth Ave, New York, 10028. Colta Ives, Cur
Holdings: Vols (10,000)
Notes: Contained in a collection of 500,000 prints from 15th to 20th century. Approx 10, 000 illustrated books; European and American. No photocopying.

ON —UNIVERSITY OF TORONTO, Thomas Fisher Rare Book Library, 120 Saint George St, Toronto, M5S 1A5, Can. Richard G Landon, Head
Holdings: Vols 100 Maps Pix
Notes: Fisher Collection of etchings by Wenceslaus Hollar. Collection named for donor Sidney T Fisher. Collection includes copies of most books in which Hollar's plates were published. About 3500 loose prints include various states of many etchings; some proofs; group of 19th century forgeries by Peter Thompson; original chalk and wash sketch for Hollar's etching of John the Baptist. See: Pennington, Richard, *A Descriptive Catalogue of the Etched Work of Wenceslaus Hollar, 1607-1677.* Cambridge: 1982. Based in part on Fisher holdings.

ETERNAL LIFE see Future Life

ETG see Electrotopography (ETG)

ETHANOL (GASOHOL) see Alcohol

ETHEREGE, SIR GEORGE

MA —HARVARD UNIVERSITY LIBRARY, Houghton Library, Cambridge, 02138. Rodney G Dennis, Cur of Manuscripts
Holdings: Cat Mss

ETHICAL EDUCATION see Religious Education

ETHICAL THEOLOGY see Christian Ethics

ETHICS

CA —LOS ANGELES PUBLIC LIBRARY, Philosophy & Religion Dept, 630 W Fifth St, Los Angeles, 90071. Marilyn C Wherley, Librn
Holdings: Vols 950 Cat
Budget: ($60,000)
Notes: Comprehensive coverage as an aspect of systematic philosophies of all historical periods and geographic areas. Scholarly and popular works include self improvement and conduct of life materials.

DC —CENTER FOR BIOETHICS, Library, Kennedy Institute, Georgetown University, 3520 Prospect St NW, Washington, 20057. Doris Goldstein, Dir; Judith Mistichelli, Senior Librn
Holdings: Vols (8200)
Notes: Largest library of its kind. Incl 31, 000 journal articles on applied ethics. Produces computer database *Bioethicsline,* available through MEDLARS; and the printed annual *Bibliography of Bioethics.* Other library publications are: *New Titles in* Bioethics (monthly); *Scope Notes* series on current topics.

MD —JOHNS HOPKINS UNIVERSITY, Milton S Eisenhower Library, George Peabody Collection, 17 E Mt Vernon Place, Baltimore, 21201. Lyn Hart, Peabody Librn
Notes: Emphasis on materials published before 1950. Strength is a good collection through the 19th century. Noncirculating.

MA —HARVARD UNIVERSITY, Graduate School of Business Administration, Baker Library, Soldiers Field, Boston, 02163. Mary V Chatfield, Librn; Florence Bartoshesky, Cur of Manuscripts and Archives
Holdings: Cat
Notes: List of collection (*Power & Morality,* by Benjamin M Selekman) published by Library, 1963.

OH —HEBREW UNION COLLEGE-JEWISH INSTITUTE OF RELIGION, Klau Library, 3101 Clifton Ave, Cincinnati, 45220. David J Gilner, Reference Librn
Holdings: Cat
Notes: Excellent collection of Pirke Avot.

OH —CLEVELAND PUBLIC LIBRARY, Social Sciences Department, 325 Superior Ave, Cleveland, 44114. Thelma Morris, Head
Holdings: Cat

PA —UNIVERSITY OF PITTSBURGH, Hillman Library, Pittsburgh, 15260. Glenora E Rossell, Head
Holdings: Vols (16,715) Cat Microforms
Notes: The collection covers all periods and philosophical disciplines. Its strength is in modern and contemporary philosophy. The approval program keeps the support for the collection up to date. The rare books, as part of the British philosophy to 1900, are located in Special Collections.

†RI —UNIVERSITY OF RHODE ISLAND, Library, Kingston, 02881.
Notes: Strong collection.

WA —UNIVERSITY OF WASHINGTON LIBRARIES, Philosophy Library, 331 Savery, DK-50, Seattle, 98195. Carolyn Mateer, Acting Selector
Holdings: Vols (18,302) Cat
Budget: ($27,516)
Notes: Collection includes materials in philosophy of language, law, mind, ethics, logic, mataphysics, religion, science, epistemology, social and political philosophy and the history of philosophy.

ETHICS, CHRISTIAN see Christian Ethics

ETHICS, MEDICAL see Medical Ethics

ETHICS, PRACTICAL see Ethics

ETHICS, SEXUAL see Sexual Ethics

ETHIOPIA

CA —HOOVER INSTITUTION ON WAR, REVOLUTION & PEACE, Stanford University, Stanford, 94305. Milorad M Drachkovitch, Archivist
Holdings: Mss
Notes: Papers of Ernest W Lefever, 1956-1969, incl ms drafts, correspondence, reports, interviews, notes, pamphlets, newspaper clippings, and printed matter, relating to modern politics in Zaire (Republic

ETHIOPIA (cont.)

of the Congo), Ethiopia, and other African nations. 3 ms boxes.

DC —HOWARD UNIVERSITY, Moorland-Spingarn Research Center, 500 Howard Place NW, Washington, 20059. Clifford L Muse, Jr, Acting Dir

MI —MICHIGAN STATE UNIVERSITY, International Library, Africana Collection, East Lansing, 48824. Eugene de Benko, Librn; Onuma Ezera, Bibliographer for Africana
Holdings: Vols (82,700) Cat Mss Maps Pix Slides Phonorecords Audiotapes Videotapes Filmstrips Microforms
Budget: ($78,000)
See also entry under Africa for full description.

VA —UNIVERSITY OF VIRGINIA, Alderman Library, Manuscripts Dept, Charlottesville, 22901. Edmund Berkeley Jr, Cur
Holdings: Cat Mss Pix
Notes: Papers of J Rives Childs, foreign sevice officer in Saudi Arabia, Yemen, Ethiopia, and Morocco, and Casanova scholar.

ETHIOPIAN LANGUAGES

NY —NEW YORK PUBLIC LIBRARY, Oriental Div, Fifth Ave & 42 St, New York, 10018. E Christian Filstrup, Chief
Holdings: Cat Mss Microforms
Notes: Published catalog of holdings.

ETHIOPIC LANGUAGE AND LITERATURE

MD —JOHNS HOPKINS UNIVERSITY, Milton S Eisenhower Library, Charles & 34 Sts, Baltimore, 21218. Ann S Gwyn, Assistant Dir for Special Collections
Holdings: Vols 4000 Cat
Notes: The August Dillmann Collection of Oriental Literature. Very strong and complete collection of Ethiopic until 1900. Dillmann was the greatest scholar in his field. Catalog published at Johns Hopkins. Also contains Biblical philology.

MN —SAINT JOHN'S ABBEY & UNIVERSITY, Hill Monastic Manuscript Library, Collegeville, 56321. Julian G Plante, Dir
Holdings: Vols 7500 Uncat Mss Microforms
Notes: Microforms of 7500 Amharic and Geez mss, mostly from Ethiopia. A systematic program of microfilming mss in the monasteries and churches of Ethiopia was established in 1973. To complement this body of primary source material, a larger collection of secondary source materials published in the field of Ethiopic studies is available and being added to.

ETHIOPIC MANUSCRIPTS see Manuscripts, Ethiopic

ETHIOPIC STUDIES

MA —HARVARD UNIVERSITY LIBRARY, Cambridge, 02138.
Holdings: Cat
Notes: Downs: 4366.

MN —SAINT JOHN'S ABBEY & UNIVERSITY, Hill Monastic Manuscript Library, Collegeville, 56321. Julian G Plante, Dir
Holdings: Vols (61,000) Microfilms
Notes: Films of 61,000 mss. The total number of codices or bound handwritten mss represents the holdings of several hundred libraries in Europe, mostly Austria, Spain, Ethiopia, West Germany, Portugal, and also Italy, Hungary, Poland, Great Britain, Belgium, Yugoslavia, France, Switzerland, and the Netherlands.

ETHNIC ART see Art, Ethnic

ETHNIC GROUPS

DC —HOWARD UNIVERSITY, Moorland-Spingarn Research Center, 500 Howard Place NW, Washington, 20059. Clifford L Muse, Jr, Acting Dir

MA —CHILDREN'S MUSEUM, Resource Center, Museum Wharf, 300 Congress St, Boston, 02210. Marie Ariel, Librn; Maria Russell, Resource Services Mgr
Holdings: Vols 600 Cat Mss Slides Phonorecords Audiotapes Videotapes Filmstrips
Notes: Focus is on Boston-area ethnic and minority communities and their countries of origin. Curriculum materials and materials for children and adults. Available for reference use by the public; borrowing privileges for Museum members; activity and curriculum kits available to public, schools and community groups for rental fee. Subject-related programs and services offered by Museum staff.

†NY —CENTER FOR MIGRATION STUDIES LIBRARY, 209 Flagg Place, Staten Island, 10304.
Notes: Human migration and ethnic group relations, especially strong in Italian-American affairs.

TX —COLLEGE OF THE MAINLAND, Library-Learning Resources Center, 8001 Palmer Hwy, Texas City, 77590. Robert Slaney, Dir of Library Services
Notes: Black studies, Mexican Americans and American Indians.

ON —CANADIAN ASSOCIATION IN SUPPORT OF THE NATIVE PEOPLES, Library, 277 Victoric St, Toronto, M5V 1W2, Can. Frances Davidson-Arnott, Librn
Holdings: Vols 4000 Cat Mss Maps Pix Slides Microforms
Notes: Native peoples of North America, especially of Canada.

†ON —METROPOLITAN TORONTO LIBRARY, Social Sciences Dept, 789 Yonge St, Toronto, M4W 2G8, Can. Abdus Salam, Head
Holdings: Vols Cat Maps Phonorecords Audiotapes 16mm Films Microforms
Notes: Collection is both current and historical. Strong in immigrants' guides, government reports and statistics, analyses, histories and studies of ethnic groups. Strong on the Underground Railroad.

†SK —UNIVERSITY OF REGINA, Library, Regina, S4S 0A2, Can. Margarett Hammond, Librn
Notes: Native peoples of North America, especially of Canada. Collection formerly held by Canadian Association in Support of the Native Peoples.

ETHNIC GROUPS IN THE U.S.

CA —LOS ANGELES PUBLIC LIBRARY, Social Sciences Dept, 630 W Fifth St, Los Angeles, 90071. Marilyn C Wherley, Principal Librn
Holdings: Vols 10,000 Microforms
Budget: ($150,000)
Notes: Emphasis on minorities; immigration policies, background and social problems of ethnic minorities in the US and the Southwest in particular. Incl periodicals, government publications and documents, popular and scholarly works on Blacks, Hispanics and Asians predominantly.

CA —LANEY COLLEGE, Library, 900 Fallon St, Oakland, 94607. Marita Davila, Dir
Holdings: Vols (70,000) Cat Maps Pix Slides Microforms
Budget: ($50,000)

CA —CALIFORNIA HISTORICAL SOCIETY, Schubert Hall Library, 2099 Pacific Ave, San Francisco, 94109. Bruce L Johnson, Library Dir
Holdings: Vols (50,000) Cat Mss Maps Pix
See also entry under California - History

GA —UNIVERSITY OF GEORGIA, Libraries, Special Collections Division, Athens, 30602. Vesta Lee Gordon, Asst Dir for Special Collections
Notes: The Arbitron Collection of television and radio program ratings, 1949-date (except past year). In-depth, statistical analyses of the listening public by age, sex, county, some ethnic groups, farm population, listening preferences, etc. 26,302 bound vols. 2 reports, 1949-81. To be added to annually.

IN —INDIANA HISTORICAL SOCIETY, Library, 315 W Ohio St, Indianapolis, 46202. Robert K O'Neill, Dir
Notes: Incl rare books, mss, pictures, maps, and ephemera relating to the history of Indiana and the Old Northwest. Mss dealing with the Old Northwest, incl a large collection of William Henry Harrison materials; papers of leading nineteenth-century Indiana figures; letters of Civil War soldiers; records of twentieth-century social welfare organizations. Rare books collection incl Jesuit *Relations,* early travel accounts, and early Indiana imprints. Pictures incl Indiana small-town life; Monon Railroad Colleciton; Callis Steamboat Collection, dealing with Terre Haute. Maps of Indiana; Sanborn real estate atlases for Indianapolis. Special collections in Indiana black, ethnic, and architectural history.

KS —FORT HAYS STATE UNIVERSITY, Forsyth Library, Ethnic Heritage Studies Collection, 600 Park St, Hays, 67601. Esta Lou Riley, Archivist/Special Collections Librn
Holdings: Vols 335 Microforms Pix Phonorecords Videotapes Maps
Notes: Emphasis on ethnic groups in Kansas, especially Germans from Russia. Does not circulate. Incl 1 linear foot vertical file material.

KS —UNIVERSITY OF KANSAS, Kenneth Spencer Research Library, Kansas Collection, Lawrence, 66045. Sheryl K Williams, Cur
Holdings: Cat Pix
Notes: The J J Pennell Collection. Joseph Judd Pennell (1866-1922) was a commercial photographer living and working in Junction City, Kansas from 1888 to 1922. This collection of more than 30,000 glass negatives and nearly 6000 prints is a pictorial record of Junction City, Kansas and nearby Ft Riley, has been photographed in their various business, professional, social, and cultural activities, while the army post. Fort Riley, has been documented as a cavalry and light artillery post, as well as an important military post during the First World War and after. The various ethnic groups which made up the population of Junction City, whites, blacks and Mexican-Americans are represented in the collection. Pennell's day books accompany the photographic collection.

MI —WAYNE STATE UNIVERSITY, Kresge Library (Education), Detroit, 48202. Theodore Manheim, Librn
Holdings: Vols (65,000) Cat Mss Microforms
Budget: ($2000)
Notes: The Eloise Ramsey Collection (10, 000 vols). See, *The Eloise Ramsey Collection of Literature for Young People: A Catalogue;* compiled by Joan Cusenza (Detroit: Wayne State University Libraries, 1967). Besides the Ramsey Collection, which is housed separately and does not circulate, the Education Library has approx 55,000 volumes of children's and young adults' literature, with a very large picture-book collection, a large poetry collection; all with special emphasis on urban and ethnic materials.

MN —IMMIGRATION HISTORY SOCIETY, Library, 690 Cedar St, Saint Paul, 55103.
Notes: Originally inspired by the ethnic revivals of the 1960s, and devoted mostly to the historical experiences of European immigrant groups in North America, the Society has since responded to the changing sources of American immigration, the increasing interest in more diverse groups, and the deepening involvement of students and scholars in inter-disciplinary, quantitative, and comparative approaches to the study of America's ethnic groups.

MN —MINNESOTA HISTORICAL SOCIETY LIBRARY, 690 Cedar St, Saint Paul, 55101. Patricia C Harpole, Chief of Reference Library; Bonnie G Wilson, Head of Special Libraries
Notes: Representatives of ethnic groups in Minnesota interviewed as a part of special projects include Blacks, Mexican-Americans, Finns in northern Minnesota, and Jews in Minneapolis.

MN —UNIVERSITY OF MINNESOTA, Immigration History Research Center, 826

ETHNIC GROUPS IN THE U.S. (cont.)

Berry St, Saint Paul, 55114. Susan Griegs, Cur
Holdings: Vols (35,000) Mss Maps Pix Phonorecords Audiotapes 16mm Films Microforms
Notes: The Archives contain both published and ms material. Presently the imprint collections consist of nearly 25,000 vols of monographs, 3000 periodical titles, and files of more than 900 ethnic newspapers (of which ca 140 are currently received). For the most part, the printed items were published by ethnic presses in North America. Many of the extensive runs of newspapers are to be found in the Archives microfilm collection of approx 5000 reels. The Archives' ms holdings are made up of 450 individual collections of papers, amounting to 2400 linear ft, or approx 3,000, 000 items. Incl are the records of such societies, churches and publishing companies, as well as collections of personal papers of ethnic leaders, clergymen, journalists, labor leaders, writers, poets and politicians. Partially cataloged.

NY —NEW YORK PUBLIC LIBRARY, Research Libraries, American History Div, Fifth Ave & 42 St, New York, 10018.
Notes: The collection of histories of ethnic groups in the US should be viewed in context of holdings of other units of The Research Libraries, including microforms and separately cataloged pamphlets. Outstanding collection of materials on Black history, which is now being collected for The Research Libraries by the Schomburg Center for Research in Black Culture.

PA —LUZERNE COUNTY COMMUNITY COLLEGE, Library, Prospect St & Middle Rd, Nanticoke, 18634. Robert N Cohee, Library Dir
Holdings: Vols 900 Cat Maps Phonorecords Audiotapes 16mm Films Filmstrips
Budget: ($26,000)

PA —BALCH INSTITUTE FOR ETHNIC STUDIES, Library, 18 S Seventh St, Philadelphia, 19106. R Joseph Anderson, Library Dir
Notes: Ethnic Heritage Collection.

†PA —TEMPLE UNIVERSITY LIBRARIES, Special Collections Dept, Urban Archives Center, Philadelphia, 19122. Thomas Whitehead, Cur of Mss
Holdings: Cat
Notes: Incl the records of several separate collections which are deposited in the Urban Archives Center. Many collections contain photographs, maps and pamphlets, in addition to manuscripts. All collections in the Urban Archives are separately cataloged.

TX —INSTITUTE OF TEXAN CULTURES, Library, 801 S Bowie Street, PO Box 1226, San Antonio, 78294. Deborah Large, Dir of Library Services
Holdings: Vols (4500) Cat Pix Slides
Budget: ($60,000)
Notes: Incl 88,000 pictures and 7000 slides.

ETHNIC HERITAGE COLLECTION

PA —BALCH INSTITUTE FOR ETHNIC STUDIES, Library, 18 S Seventh St, Philadelphia, 19106. R Joseph Anderson, Library Dir
Notes: The Ethnic Heritage Studies Clearinghouse Collection of over 2000 reports, print and audiovisual materials, instructional kits, and scholarly monographs developed since 1974 under the federal government's Ethnic Heritage Studies Act, to encourage support of ethnic studies in public school and college curricula.

ETHNIC MUSIC see Music, Ethnic

ETHNIC NEWSPAPERS—NORTH AMERICA

PA —BALCH INSTITUTE FOR ETHNIC STUDIES, Library, 18 S Seventh St, Philadelphia, 19106. R Joseph Anderson, Library Dir
Holdings: Vols Microforms
Notes: Microfilm holdings listed in *A Selected List of Newspapers and Manuscript Holdings.* There are approx 170 ethnic newspapers and periodical titles on microfilm. Collection contains approx 5000 reels of microfilm. Holdings described in *Newspapers on Microforms.* Only positive microfilm circulates on ILL.
See also entry under Emigration and Immigration.

ETHNOBOTANY

CA —RANCHO SANTA ANA BOTANIC GARDEN LIBRARY, 1500 N College Ave, Claremont, 91711. Beatrice M Beck, Librn
Holdings: Vols 30,000 Cat Maps Microforms
Notes: Incl emphasis on California flora, floras of the world, evolutionary biology and ethnobotany.

CA —UNIVERSITY OF SOUTHERN CALIFORNIA, School of Medicine, Norris Medical Library, 2025 Zonal Ave, Los Angeles, 90033. Nelson J Gilman, Librn
Holdings: Vols 275 Cat
Budget: $200
Notes: The Collection of American Indian Ethnopharmacology.

ETHNOGRAPHY

MA —HARVARD UNIVERSITY LIBRARY, Botanical Museum Library, Cambridge, 02138.
Holdings: Vols (2400) Mss Pix
Notes: The Tina and Gordon Wisson Ethnomycological Collection, one of the most important modern collections, acquired as an adjunct to the Museum's Economic Botany Library of Oakes Ames. From 15th to 20th century, it deals with hallucinogenic mushrooms in art, religion, and folklore; chemistry, pharmacology, linguistics, archaeological artifacts of Mexico, Guatemala, India, Japan, China, etc. Personal papers, etc.

PA —UNIVERSITY OF PENNSYLVANIA, University Museum Library, 33 & Spruce Sts, Philadelphia, 19104. Jean S Adelman, Librn
Holdings: Vols (80,000) Cat Microforms
Notes: Incl (5000) pamphlets, fully cataloged. Mss (primarily American Indian word lists) in Brinton collection.

ETHNOHISTORY

PA —BALCH INSTITUTE FOR ETHNIC STUDIES, Library, 18 S Seventh St, Philadelphia, 19106. R Joseph Anderson, Library Dir
Holdings: Vols Microforms
See also entry under Emigration and Immigration.

WA —UNIVERSITY OF WASHINGTON LIBRARIES, Suzzallo Library, Manuscripts Section, FM-25, Seattle, 98195. Karyl Winn, Librn
Holdings: Mss
Notes: Personal papers and organizational records with emphasis on Pacific Northwest history and recent focus on twentieth century Western Washington. Holdings pertain to urban problems and policies, labor history, women's history, natural resource development, environmental politics, race relations, ethnic history, oral hsitory, and the arts. Holdings are complemented by textual records in the University Archives (7045 linear feet) and by graphic and printed holdings in the Pacific Northwest Collection. `Described in *Comprehensive Guide to the Manuscripts Collection and to Personal Papers in the University Archives,* 1980 and in *Historical Records of Washington State: Records and Papers Held at Repositories,* 1981 and in unpublished inventories to most accessions. 15,981 linear feet of manuscripts.

ON —CANADIAN ASSOCIATION IN SUPPORT OF THE NATIVE PEOPLES, Library, 277 Victoric St, Toronto, M5V 1W2, Can. Frances Davidson-Arnott, Librn
Holdings: Vols 4000 Cat Mss Maps Pix Slides Microforms
Notes: Native peoples of North America, especially of Canada.

†SK —UNIVERSITY OF REGINA, Library, Regina, S4S 0A2, Can. Margarett Hammond, Librn
Notes: Native peoples of North America, especially of Canada. Collection formerly held by Canadian Association in Support of the Native Peoples.

ETHNOLOGY

AZ —FULTON-HAYDEN MEMORIAL LIBRARY, Dragoon, 85609. Mario Nick Klimiades, Librn
Holdings: Vols 17,000 Cat Mss Maps Pix Microforms
Budget: $3500
Notes: The Fulton-Hayden Memorial Library is a special collection of books about archaeology and ethnology specifically as they pertain to the western hemisphere and particularly to Mexico and the greater American Southwest.

AZ —ARIZONA STATE MUSEUM, Library, University of Arizona, Tucson, 85721. Hans R Bart, Museum Librn
Holdings: Vols (35,000) Cat Mss Maps Pix Slides Phonorecords Microforms

CA —UNIVERSITY OF CALIFORNIA, BERKELEY, Humanities-Social Sciences Libraries, Anthropology Library, 230 Kroeber Hall, Berkeley, 94720. Dorothy A Koenig, Librn
Holdings: Vols (55,000) Cat Microforms
Notes: The library maintains general research collections covering all aspects of social and physical anthropology, anthropological linguistics and archaeology (excluding classical archaeology). Serials constitute the collection's special strength.

CA —CRAFT AND FOLK ART MUSEUM, Library, 5814 Wilshire Blvd, Los Angeles, 90036. Joan M Benedetti, Museum Librn
Holdings: Vols (2000) Slides VF
Notes: Incl 2000 books; 70 journal subscriptions; artists' biographical files: 6 file drawers; clipping files: 8 file drawers; 20,000 slides. Representation of the material culture of all people, traditional and contemporary expressions. Incl visual and printed information on ethnic, traditional, popular, decorative, idiosyncratic, and contemporary crafts as well as vernacular architecture, handmade houses, and design. Information about and for professional artists on health hazards, conservation, and career management. Anthropological and art historical works; exhibition catalogues; slides, photographs, audiocassettes; clipping and pamphlet files. Contemporary Slide Registry of Craftspeople and extensive biographical files of contemporary craft artists. Information and referral files of craft related galleries, shops, festivals, organizations, etc.

CA —UNIVERSITY OF CALIFORNIA, LOS ANGELES, Music Dept, Ethnomusicology Archive, 405 Hilgard Ave, Los Angeles, 90024. Ann Briegleb, Ethnomusicology Librn
Holdings: Cat Mss Maps Pix Slides Audiotapes Phonorecords Microforms
Notes: Ethnomusicology of the non-Western world. Incl 7769 tapes and 8957 phonodisc recordings.

CA —UNIVERSITY OF CALIFORNIA, SANTA CRUZ, University Library, Special Collections, Santa Cruz, 95064. Rita Bottoms, Special Collections Librn; Margaret Felts, South Pacific Collection Bibliographer
Holdings: Vols (10,000) Cat
Notes: Monographs, rare books, serials, documents and atlases which treat of the Pacific areas of Polynesia, Melanesia, Micronesia, Australia and New Zealand, but excluding western New Guinea (Irian Jaya), the Phillippines and Southeast Asia. Approximately 10 per cent of the titles are multi-volume documents such as parliamentary papers, legislative journals, official yearbooks, statistical sourcebooks, laws and statutes. The collection includes an exhaustive selection of current journals and monographic series from and about the Pacific: early serials, South Pacific Commission publications. US Government and US Trust Territory publications, serials from museums, universities and scholarly societies. Chief emphasis has been placed on acquisition of the literature of history,

ETHNOLOGY (cont.)

description and travel, ethnology and anthropology, literature and literary criticism,political and constitutional histories. Other extensive holdings are in the fields of geography and maps, voyages, mission histories, mythology and folklore, art, linguistics, and science fields of natural history, environmental studies, biology, zoology, botany, geology and astronomy.

CT —YALE UNIVERSITY, Anthropology Library, Peabody Museum of Natural History, C-8 KBT, New Haven, 06511.
Holdings: Vols (16,000) Cat
Budget: ($11,000)

†CT —PHILIPPINE-AMERICAN RESEARCH CENTER, Library, PO Box507, Sharoni, 06069. John Silva, Dir
Holdings: Vols 200 Maps Pix
Notes: Philippine history and culture from pre-colonial times to the present, as well as under Spanish, Japanese, and American regimes, and post-independence. Mostly rare works of the late 19th and early 20th century; history and anthropology. Over 2, 500 photographs. Incl maps, posters, memorabilia. Limited copying. Visits by appointment.

DC —HOWARD UNIVERSITY, Moorland-Spingarn Research Center, 500 Howard Place NW, Washington, 20059. Clifford L Muse, Jr, Acting Dir
Holdings: Vols (106,086) Mss Maps Pix Slides Phonorecords Audiotapes 16mm Films Filmstrips Microforms
Budget: ($854,753)
See also entry under Blacks

DC —NATIONAL GEOGRAPHIC SOCIETY, Library, 1146 16th St NW, Washington, 20036. Susan Fifer Canby, Dir
Holdings: Vols (63,000) Cat Mss Maps Pix
Notes: Material concerning land, sea, and space exploration--past and present. All fields of anthropology, natural history, geography, etc.

DC —SMITHSONIAN INSTITUTION LIBRARIES, Anthropology Branch, Washington, 20560. Jean C Smith, Asst Dir for Bureau Services
Holdings: Vols (54,000) Cat Mss Maps Pix Slides Microforms
Budget: ($7041)
Notes: Physical anthropology, archaeology, ethnology, language and languages; Indians of both continents.

HI —BERNICE P BISHOP MUSEUM, Library, PO Box 19000-A, Honolulu, 96819. Cynthia Timberlake, Librn
Holdings: Vols (90,000) Cat Mss Maps Pix Slides Microforms
Budget: ($30,000)
Notes: Only American library devoted exclusively to the Pacific region. Collection reflects historical and contemporary research emphases of Bishop Museum; ie the natural and cultural history of the Pacific. Areas of concentration incl archaeology, ethnology, linguistics, voyages and explorations, history, vertebrate and invertebrate zoology, botany and museology. Strong special collections incl photographs, mss and archives, maps and art. Publications: Quarterly "Additions to the Catalog," *Dictionary Catalog of the* Library (9 vols and 2 suppl; Boston: G K Hall, 1964-1969).

HI —UNIVERSITY OF HAWAII, Library, 2550 The Mall, Honolulu, 96822. R Renee Heyum, Pacific Cur
Holdings: Vols (45,000) Cat Audiotapes Microforms
Budget: ($30,000)
Notes: There is a separate Pacific Collection card catalog, for items cataloged up to 1980, after which all additions are on the Library's microfiche catalog. This is a comprehensive collection of Pacific Islands material with special emphasis on government documents, linguistics, anthropology, economics and cultural change. An acquisitions list is issued quarterly.

IL —FIELD MUSEUM OF NATURAL HISTORY, Library, Roosevelt Rd & Lake Shore Dr, Chicago, 60605. W Peyton Fawcett, Librn; Benjamin W Williams, Assoc Librn
Holdings: Vols (210,000) Cat
Budget: ($100,000)
Notes: Extensive collections--publications of learned societies and institutions and monographic works--in all fields of natural history, with emphasis on taxonomy and evolutionary biology; and on museum publications, American and foreign: anthropology, especially archaeology and ethnology of the Americas, Africa, East Asia, and Oceania; botany, particularly strong for the Americas; geology, chiefly paleontology and meteoritic studies; and zoology, worldwide (birds, fishes, insects, mammals, mollusks, reptiles and amphibians).

IL —NORTHERN ILLINOIS UNIVERSITY, Founders Memorial Library, Southeast Asia Collection, Normal Rd, De Kalb, 60115. Lee S Dutton Dr, Cur
Holdings: Vols (34,000) Cat Maps Microforms
Notes: An extensive collection of books, periodicals, newspapers, maps, and microforms from or about Southeast Asia. Areas of concentration incl Thailand, Malaysia, Indonesia, Singapore, Brunei, Philippines, Laos, and Burma. Holdings (except rare books, maps, and microforms) are housed in a separate area collection within the Founders Library. A departmental card catalog and specialized reference collection support reference services. A Thai collection of several thousand vols is the largest vernacular component. Extensive Malaysia, Indonesia, Singapore, and Brunei holdings have been acquired through the NPAC program. A collection of Filipino-American newspapers, and a growing collection of children's literature in common and uncommon Southeast Asian languages are available. Resources are accessible to borrowers through OCLC.

LA —TULANE UNIVERSITY, Howard-Tilton Memorial Library, Special Collections Div, William Ransom Hogan Jazz Archive, 7001 Freret, New Orleans, 70118. Richard B Allen, Acting Cur; Alma D Williams, Assistant to the Cur
Holdings: Vols (100,000) Cat Mss Pix Slides Phonorecords Audiotapes Videotapes 16mm Films Microforms
Budget: ($90,000)
Notes: Jazz music and musicians. Outstanding collection, incl books, music scores, serials, catalogs and other archival material. Music, history, etc.
See also entry under Jazz

MA —HARVARD UNIVERSITY LIBRARY, Tozzer Library, 21 Divinity Ave, Cambridge, 02138. Nancy J Schmidt, Librn
Holdings: Vols (152,000) Cat Microforms
Budget: ($337,000)
Notes: (Formerly Peabody Museum Library). Believed to have the strongest collection in the United States for prehistoric archaeology generally, anthropology, and ethnology. Does not collect classical archaeology. Catalog, in 54 volumes, published in 1963, with 12-volume supplement in 1970, 5-volume supplement in 1971, 7-volume supplement in 1975, and 7-volume supplement in 1979, analyzes contents of serial publications. Quarterly journal, *Anthropological Literature, 1979-*. Described in *Harvard Library Bulletin*, III (1949): pp 94-101; J O Brew, *People and Projects of the Peabody Museum, 1866-1966* (Cambridge, Mass: The Museum, 1966), pp 57-59; and Nancy J Schmidt, Tozzer Library, Harvard University: *Special Libraries Association Boston Chapter News* Bulletin, 48, 2 (1982), pp 167-169.

MA —HARVARD UNIVERSITY LIBRARY, Botanical Museum Library, Cambridge, 02138.
Holdings: Vols (2400) Mss Pix
Notes: The Tina and Gordon Wisson Ethnomycological Collection, one of the most important modern collections, acquired as an adjunct to the Museum's Economic Botany Library of Oakes Ames. From 15th to 20th century, it deals with hallucinogenic mushrooms in art, religion, and folklore; chemistry, pharmacology, linguistics, archaeological artifacts of Mexico, Guatemala, India, Japan, China, etc. Personal papers, etc.

MA —GORDON COLLEGE, Winn Library, Vining Collection, 255 Grapevine Rd, Wenham, 01984. John Beauregard, Dir
Holdings: Vols 3000 Cat
Notes: The Vining Collection (of rare books).

MA —COLLEGE OF THE HOLY CROSS, Dinand Library, College St, Worcester, 01610. James M Mahoney, Cur of Special Collection
Holdings: / / Mss
Notes: The Joseph J Williams, SJ Collection contains 107 mss and 865 letters concerning religious practices of tribes in Africa. Collection is indexed, restricted use.

NJ —NEWARK MUSEUM LIBRARY, 49 Washington St, PO Box 540, Newark, 07101. Margaret DiSalvi, Librn
Holdings: Vols 4000 Cat Pix Slides
Notes: The Newark Museum has an outstanding collection of Tibetan religious books which are considered part of the museum's collections rather than the library's. The library's collections incl published books, pamphlets, etc, over 1000 photographs of Tibet and Tibetans, and many slides of Tibet and of the museum's collections. Have published a 5-vol catalog of our Tibetan collections. See, *Catalogue of the Tibetan Collection and other Lamaist* Articles, 5-vols (Newark Museum, Newark, NJ), prepared by Eleanor Olson, Curator Emeritus of the Oriental Collections, 1950-1971.

NY —MUSEUM OF THE AMERICAN INDIAN, Library, 9 Westchester Square, Bronx, 10401. Mary B Davis, Librn
Holdings: Cat
Notes: Incl information in Indians of North, Central, and South America; archaeology of North, Central, and South America; American Indian ethnology; anthropology, history.

NY —HOFSTRA UNIVERSITY, Library, 1000 Fulton Ave, Hempstead, 11550. Charles R Andrews, Dean of Library Services
Notes: The personal library of Paul Radin. See description of the American Philosophical Society Library's collection of his anthropological papers under this entry (Pa).

NY —AMERICAN MUSEUM OF NATURAL HISTORY, Library Services Dept, Central Park W & 79th St, New York, 10024. Nina J Root, Chairwoman; Mary Genett, Asst Librn for Reference Services
Holdings: Vols (385,000) Cat Mss Maps Pix Slides Microforms
Notes: Nearly all collections are outstanding for depth of coverage and international range. Early and historic works, rare books, colored illustrations, and relevant serial publications supplement the modern scientific publications necessary to the researches of the scientific staff and the work of the educational division. Open to the public.

NY —AUSTRALIAN CONSULATE-GENERAL, Australian Information Service, Reference Library, 636 Fifth Ave, New York, 10111. Jill Hutchison, Librn; Frank Long, Officer; Lynnette Shaw, Photo Librn & Press Asst
Holdings: Vols (9000) Cat Periodicals Mss Pix Slides 16mm Film VF
Notes: Collection incl Australian history, law, politics and government, economics, flora and fauna, geography, social conditions, arts, science, literature, and the Aboriginals.

NY —EXPLORERS CLUB, James B Ford Memorial Library, 46 E 70 St, New York, 10021. Janet Baldwin, Librn
Holdings: Vols (24,000) Cat Maps
Notes: Additions to the collection depend upon gifts. Access by appointment only.

NY —NEW YORK PUBLIC LIBRARY, Research Libraries, General Research Division, Fifth Ave & 42 St, New York, 10018. Rodney Phillips, Chief
Holdings: Vols (2,225,000) Cat Maps Pix Microforms
Budget: ($775,718)
Notes: Collections are strongest for Black

ETHNOLOGY (cont.)

Africans, American Indians, Gypsies, Australian Aborigines and those of Oceania.

NY —NEW YORK PUBLIC LIBRARY, Slavonic Div, Fifth Ave & 42 St, New York, 10018. Edward Kasinec, Chief
Holdings: Vols (8870) Cat Microforms
Notes: Subject strength is in Ukrainian literature, language, and folklore. Ethnology and history are also well represented. Holdings of periodicals and publications of learned societies are considerable. See New York Public Library, *Dictionary Catalog of the Slavonic Collection* (Boston: G K Hall, 1974), 44 vols.

PA —AMERICAN PHILOSOPHICAL SOCIETY, Library, 105 S Fifth St, Philadelphia, 19106. Edward C Carter II, Librn

PA —UNIVERSITY OF PENNSYLVANIA, Annenberg School of Communications Library, 3620 Walnut St, Philadelphia, 19104. Sandra B Grilikhes, Head
Holdings: Vols 20,000 Cat Microforms
Notes: Theory and research in communication, incl visual communication, via social psychology, anthropology, ethnography, and sociology. All aspects of mass media with emphasis on methodology in research. Utilizes content analysis and computer operations. Special collections: film catalogs; collection of Annenberg Faculty Publications.

PA —UNIVERSITY OF PENNSYLVANIA, University Museum Library, 33 & Spruce Sts, Philadelphia, 19104. Jean S Adelman, Librn
Holdings: Vols (80,000) Cat Microforms
Notes: Incl the Daniel Garrison Brinton collection of about 2000 vols, on aboriginal American linguistics and ethnology. Espec strong in Maya language materials.

PA —CARNEGIE LIBRARY OF PITTSBURGH, Science & Technology Dept, 4400 Forbes Ave, Pittsburgh, 15213. Catherine M Brosky, Dept Head
Notes: Of secondary interest in acquisitions because of the department's role in cooperating with Pittsburgh institutions and others across the Commonwealth in sharing resources, the cooperative acquisition of materials, and the provision of services and information. However, some aspects of the subject are emphasized. There are separate entries for each of these specialties in this vol.

WI —MILWAUKEE PUBLIC MUSEUM, Reference Library, 800 W Wells St, Milwaukee, 53233. Judith Campbell Turner, Museum Librn
Holdings: Vols (90,000) Cat Maps Microforms

MB —UNIVERSITY OF MANITOBA, Elizabeth Dafoe Library, Archives and Special Collections Dept, Winnipeg, R3T 2N2, Can. Richard E Bennett, Dept Head; Corrado A Santoro, Reference Archivist
Notes: Arctic and Sub-Arctic cultural anthropology.

ON —NATIONAL MUSEUMS OF CANADA, Library Services Directorate, Ottawa, K1A 0M8, Can. Valerie Monkhouse, Director
Holdings: Vols (70,000) Cat Mss Maps Pix Slides Microforms
Budget: ($60,000)
Notes: Collection includes anthropology, archaeology, ethnology, folklore, history, Indians of North America, Inuit, linguistics of North American Indians, material history, military and naval history, museology. Research collection, interlibrary loans available, public may use on the premises.

ON —ROYAL ONTARIO MUSEUM, Main Library and Archives, 100 Queen's Park, Toronto, M5S 2C6, Can. Julia Matthews, Head Librn
Holdings: Vols (85,000) Cat
Notes: Since January 1977, acquisitions have been entered in UTLAS.

ON —UNIVERSITY OF TORONTO, Thomas Fisher Rare Book Library, 120 Saint George St, Toronto, M5S 1A5, Can. Richard G Landon, Head
Notes: Sheldon Collection of Australiana, named for collector William Sheldon. Especially rich in 19th century accounts of the exploration of the South Pacific and the interior of the Australian continent. Includes narratives of exiled Canadians who took part in the Rebellion of 1837 in Canada. Includes works on colonization and settlement, the gold-rush of the mid 19th century, and on the life of the indigenous peoples. Includes literature written by Australians or about Australia.

ETHNOLOGY—ARCTIC REGIONS see Arctic Races

ETHNOLOGY—CANADA

MB —UNIVERSITY OF MANITOBA, Elizabeth Dafoe Library, Archives and Special Collections Dept, Winnipeg, R3T 2N2, Can. Richard E Bennett, Dept Head; Corrado A Santoro, Reference Archivist
Notes: Arctic and Sub-Arctic cultural anthropology.

ETHNOLOGY—CENTRAL ASIA

NY —COLUMBIA UNIVERSITY LIBRARIES, Lehman Library, Slavic and East Central European Collection, 420 W 118 St, New York, 10027. Nina Lencek, Bibliographer
Holdings: / / Uncat
Notes: The Soviet Nationalities Collection consists of published materials in the Indo-European, Uralic, Altaic, Transcaucasian, and Paleo-Siberian languages of the Soviet Union and contains more than 14,000 volumes as well as current and discontinued periodical literature. The author/title catalog for this collection is in Russian translation except for Armenian books, which are cataloged in the original. The collection is circulating and available through interlibrary loan.

ETHNOLOGY—NORTH AMERICA

CA —CRAFT AND FOLK ART MUSEUM, Library, 5814 Wilshire Blvd, Los Angeles, 90036. Joan M Benedetti, Museum Librn
Holdings: Vols (2000) Slides VF
Notes: Incl 2000 books; 70 journal subscriptions; artists' biographical files: 6 file drawers; clipping files: 8 file drawers; 20,000 slides. Representation of the material culture of all people, traditional and contemporary expressions. Incl visual and printed information on ethnic, traditional, popular, decorative, idiosyncratic, and contemporary crafts as well as vernacular architecture, handmade houses, and design. Information about and for professional artists on health hazards, conservation, and career management. Anthropological and art historical works; exhibition catalogues; slides, photographs, audiocassettes; clipping and pamphlet files. Contemporary Slide Registry of Craftspeople and extensive biographical files of contemporary craft artists. Information and referral files of craft related galleries, shops, festivals, organizations, etc.

NM —MUSEUM OF NEW MEXICO, Laboratory of Anthropology Library, PO Box 2087, Santa Fe, 87503. Laura Holt, Librn
Holdings: Vols (16,000) Cat Mss Maps
Notes: Southwestern archaeology, anthropology, ethnology. Noncirculating. Also incl the personal Library (2000 vols) of Sylvanus Morley, Meso-American archaeologist and historian. Some materials on Indians of Middle America.

ON —METROPOLITAN TORONTO LIBRARY, Languages Centre, 789 Yonge St, Toronto, M4W 2G8, Can. Barbara Gunther, Head
Holdings: Vols (90,000) Cat Phonorecords Audiotapes
Notes: Original literature in over 80 languages; books, records, cassettes, microfilm on language studies; newspapers and periodicals from 50 counties. Language study materials. Issue quarterly additions lists by language. Collect North American Indian and Eskimo language materials. Occasional bibliographies. Incl collections on Natives of both the Americas and Canada.

ETHNOLOGY—SOUTHEAST ASIA

IL —NORTHERN ILLINOIS UNIVERSITY, Founders Memorial Library, Southeast Asia Collection, Normal Rd, De Kalb, 60115. Lee S Dutton Dr, Cur
Holdings: Vols (34,000) Cat Mss Maps Microforms
Notes: An extensive collection of books, periodicals, newspapers, maps, and microforms from or about Southeast Asia. Areas of concentration incl Thailand, Malaysia, Indonesia, Singapore, Brunei, Philippines, Laos, and Burma. Holdings (except rare books, maps, and microforms) are housed in a separate area collection within the Founders Library. A departmental card catalog and specialized reference collection support reference services. A Thai collection of several thousand vols is the largest vernacular component. Extensive Malaysia, Indonesia, Singapore, and Brunei holdings have been acquired through the NPAC program. A collection of Filipino-American newspapers, and a growing collection of children's literature in common and uncommon Southeast Asian languages are available. Resources are accessible to borrowers through OCLC.

ETHNOLOGY—UNITED STATES

DC —LIBRARY OF CONGRESS, Prints & Photographs Div, Washington, 20540.
Holdings: 93 Items
Notes: The William A Barnhill Collection is a photographic study of the inhabitants of western North Carolina (1914-17) performing such daily tasks as milling, weaving, preparing food, and making baskets, shingles, and pottery.

ETHNOMUSICOLOGY

CA —CALIFORNIA STATE UNIVERSITY, HAYWARD, Library, Hayward, 94542. Melissa Rose, Dir
Holdings: Vols 15,896 Cat Phonorecords
Budget: ($21,000)
Notes: The score collection covers the entire range of instrumental and vocal concert music, incl collected works of various composers, and representative collections of hymnals, folk music, musical comedy, and some popular music. Sound recordings range from ethnomusicological collections to electronic music. Emphasis is on concert music, but there is a large collection of jazz and a selective collection of popular music. Separate catalog.

CA —UNIVERSITY OF CALIFORNIA, LOS ANGELES, Music Dept, Ethnomusicology Archive, 405 Hilgard Ave, Los Angeles, 90024. Ann Briegleb, Ethnomusicology Librn
Holdings: Cat Mss Maps Pix Slides Audiotapes Phonorecords
Notes: Ethnomusicology of the non-Western world. Incl 7769 tapes and 8957 phonodisc recordings.

DC —LIBRARY OF CONGRESS, American Folklife Center, Archive of Folk Culture, Washington, 20540.
Notes: The Sidney Robertson Cowell Collection of her folk music recordings, 1937 to 1957. Incl very unusual contributions by the Molokan community in the Potrero Hill neighborhood of San Francisco, a breakaway sect from the Russian Orthodox Church. The Laura Boulton Collection is comprised of 1312 discs and 367 tape recordings of traditional vocal and instrumental music of Canada, Africa, Southeast Asia, American Indians, and Eskimos, collected chiefly from the 1930s through the 1960s by Dr Boulton.

MD —UNIVERSITY OF MARYLAND, BALTIMORE COUNTY, Albin O Kuhn Library and Gallery, 5401 Wilkens Ave, Baltimore, 21228. Ann Copeland, Special Collections Librn
Holdings: 1200 Cat Phonorecords Audiotapes
Notes: Collection formed to serve strong

ETHNOMUSICOLOGY (cont.)

graduate program in ethnomusicology. *See also* entry under Phonorecords - Collections.

NY —STATE UNIVERSITY OF NEW YORK, BUFFALO, Baird Music Library, Baird Hall, Amherst, 14260. James B Coover, Dir
Holdings: Vols (104,000) Cat Mss Pix Slides Phonorecords Microforms
Notes: Nearly complete collections of *Denkmaeler and Gesamtausgaben* and other historical sets. Strong collection of dictionaries, bibliographies, biographies, facsimiles, works on the "new" music, organology and ethnomusicology. Special emphasis on operas, scores of the avant-garde, jazz and urban popular music, discography and music librarianship. Good collection of medieval and Renaissance anthologies, contemporary and avant-garde recordings. Houses Archives of the Center of the Creative and Performing Arts. Collections incl 2100 slides, 22,000 phonorecords, 46,000 scores and parts, 29, 000 books, 4900 microforms. Computerized record catalog in process.

NY —COLUMBIA UNIVERSITY LIBRARIES, Rare Book & Manuscript Library, 801 Butler Library, 535 W 114 St, New York, 10027. Kenneth A Lohf, Librn
Notes: Strong collection.

NY —COLUMBIA UNIVERSITY LIBRARIES, Music Library, 701 Dodge, Broadway & 116 St, New York, 10027. M Haefliger, Librn
Holdings: Vols (55,020) Cat Phonorecords Audiotapes Microforms
Notes: Extensive holdings, with particular emphasis on urban cultures. Incl many early music treatises and journals, early 20th century imprints.

ETHNOPHARMACOLOGY

CA —UNIVERSITY OF SOUTHERN CALIFORNIA, School of Medicine, Norris Medical Library, 2025 Zonal Ave, Los Angeles, 90033. Nelson J Gilman, Librn
Holdings: Vols 275 Cat
Budget: $200
Notes: The Collection of American Indian Ethnopharmacology.

MA —HARVARD UNIVERSITY LIBRARY, Botanical Museum Library, Cambridge, 02138.
Holdings: Vols (2400) Mss Pix
Notes: The Tina and Gordon Wisson Ethnomycological Collection, one of the most important modern collections, acquired as an adjunct to the Museum's Economic Botany Library of Oakes Ames. From 15th to 20th century, it deals with hallucinogenic mushrooms in art, religion, and folklore; chemistry, pharmacology, linguistics, archaeological artifacts of Mexico, Guatemala, India, Japan, China, etc. Personal papers, etc.

ETHOLOGY see Ethics

ETHYL ALCOHOL see Alcohol

ETIQUETTE

CA —LOS ANGELES PUBLIC LIBRARY, Children's Literature Dept, 630 W 5th St, Los Angeles, 90071. Serenna Day, Sr Librn
Holdings: Vols (4500) Cat
Notes: A rich collection of over 4500 titles representing books from 40 countries around the world. Included are Argentina, Chile, Iarael, Czechoslovakia, Bulgaria, and the Afrikaans language, to name a few. Especially notable are many imprints from the turn of the century, the 1920s and 1930s. Some are quite rare. Besides picture books with beautiful color illustrations, there are song books, fairy tales (familiar and obscure), and stories dealing with manners and good example. The Children's Room has a separate file where these are arranged by country.

CA —LOS ANGELES PUBLIC LIBRARY, Philosophy & Religion Dept, 630 W Fifth St, Los Angeles, 90071. Marilyn C Wherley, Librn
Holdings: Vols 200 Cat
Budget: ($60,000)
Notes: Comprehensive coverage of all aspects of etiquette. Particular strength in manners of various historical periods.

CA —MILLS COLLEGE LIBRARY, Oakland, 94613. Steven P Pandolfo, Librn
Holdings: Vols (300) Cat
Notes: Books printed from 17th-20th centuries; primarily 19th century with emphasis on education, women's suffrage, domestic economy and etiquette.

IL —NEWBERRY LIBRARY, 60 W Walton St, Chicago, 60610. Diana Haskell, Cur of Modern Mss
Holdings: Vols 1550 Cat
Notes: See: Virgil Heltzel's *A Checklist of Courtsey Books in the Newberry Library,* 1942; and, Bell and Howell's microfilm package of *English Courtesy Books,* 1571-1773.

MA —RADCLIFFE COLLEGE, Arthur & Elizabeth Schlesinger Library on the History of Women in America, 3 James St, Cambridge, 02138. Patricia Miller King, Dir; Eva Moseley, Cur of Mss
Holdings: Vols 125 Cat

MI —MICHIGAN STATE UNIVERSITY, Libraries, Special Collections Div, East Lansing, 48824. Jannette Fiore, Librn
Notes: The Russel B Nye Popular Culture Collection in the Michigan State Univ Libraries incl over (45,000) items. Most of the collection is organized into 4 categories: comic art, popular fiction, popular information materials and materials relating to the popular performing arts. About 3900 items. Almanacs, Blue Books, and works popularizing knowledge or offering self-help and how-to advice. There are ca 350 issues of 100 19th and 20th century almanacs. The Blue Books incl ca 2000 Little Blue Books, over 600 Big Blue Books and a good number of issues of the various Haldeman-Julius magazines. In addition to almanacs and Blue Books, Popular Information incl books of advice on etiquette, life and love, how-to-succeed books, popular history, science and biography, and several hundred public schooltextbooks from the 19th and early 20th centuries.

NY —MARGARET WOODBURY STRONG MUSEUM, 1 Manhattan Square, Rochester, 14607.
Holdings: Vols (20,000) Periodicals
Notes: The Margaret Woodbury Strong Museum Library contains a collection of approx 20,000 books, periodicals and ephemera of and concerning the 19th and early 20th centuries. A large part of the library's holdings reflect the interests of Margaret Strong and her family: domestic life and literature of the 19th century and world travel, with particular emphasis on the Orient. The library's resources are available to all visitors for research. Book stacks and rare book storage are not open for browsing and do not circulate, but facilities are provided in reading room for study.

RI —BROWN UNIVERSITY, John Hay Library, Anne S K Brown Military Collection, 20 Prospect St, Providence, 02912. Richard B Harrington, Cur
Notes: The Anne S K Brown Military Collection has been formed over the past forty or more years by Mrs John Nicholas Brown, now of Newport, and contains approximately 40,000 volumes and 60,000 prints, drawings and watercolors as well as a number of oil paintings and about 5000 miniature model soldiers. At its beginning (and still today) the emphasis or focus of this collection has been upon the history of, and the accurate contemporary illustration of, military and naval uniforms of all nations from the early XVII century to the present. In the course of time, however, the collection has come to incl also a vast and related amount of material on military and naval history, military and naval arts and tactics, wars, campaigns, ceremonies, biography, portraits and caricatures of this and earlier periods. It has been probably the largest private collection of such a nature inthe world, and it contains much ms and graphic documentation which is unique. It has been useful to numerous scholars and historians, editors, filmmakers and publishers for research and for illustrative material and has also contributed to many museum exhibitions. In 1982 the entire collection, with its complete card catalog and subject index, has been presented to Brown University, where it is located in the John Hay Library. Special requests are taken care of by phone, mail and appointments with the curator.

ETON COLLEGE

DC —GEORGETOWN UNIVERSITY, Library, Special Collections Div, 37 & O Sts NW, Washington, 20057. George M Barringer, Special Collections Librn; Nicholas B Sheetz, Mss Librn
Holdings: Mss Cat Pix
Notes: The papers of the Irish man-of-letters Sir Shane Leslie (1885-1971) containing letters, mss, diaries, notebooks, clippings, and photographs. Extensive correspondence by Margot Asquith, countess of Oxford and Asquith; Lady Violet Bonham-Carter; Burke Cochran; Lord Alfred Douglas; Moreton Frewen; Cardinal Gasquet; Vyvyan Holland; Lady Leonie Leslie; Sir Wilfrid Meynell; Sir Horace Plunkett; John Quinn; Frederick Rolfe (Baron Corvo); and Elizabeth Russell, among others. Also incl are research files on Sir Winston Churchill (Leslie's first cousin); Leonard Jerome; Maria Anne Fitzherbet (wife of King George IV); Ghosts and Ghost stories; and Eton College.

NC —UNIVERSITY OF NORTH CAROLINA, CHAPEL HILL, Wilson Library, Rare Book Collection, Chapel Hill, 27514. Paul S Koda, Cur of Rare Books
Holdings: Vols 200 Cat
Notes: The Eton College Collection consists of volumes of reminiscences, histories, poetry, and fiction relating to Eton College (Eton, England) and to graduates and others connected with the school.

ETRUSCAN LANGUAGE

IL —NEWBERRY LIBRARY, 60 W Walton St, Chicago, 60610. Diana Haskell, Cur of Modern Mss
Holdings: Cat Maps
Notes: The bulk of the collection (about 15, 000 vols) is in the Prince Lucien Bonaparte group, which deals with western European linguistics. In this group the major rare categories are Etruscan and Basque linguistic studies, although the bulk of the group treats the major European languages and their dialects, ie French, German, English, Spanish, Italian and Russian. There is also strong representation in Gaelic linguistics, particularly Irish, Cornish, Welsh and Manx. In other collections of the library, there are major groups of books and mss dealing with American Indian languages and Philippine languages (about 4500 books and mss).

ETYMOLOGY see Language and Languages—Etymology

EUCLID

MI —UNIVERSITY OF MICHIGAN, Library, Dept of Rare Books & Special Collections, Ann Arbor, 48109. Robert J Starring, Head
Holdings: Vols 250 Cat
Notes: Pre-1800 editions.

MN —UNIVERSITY OF MINNESOTA, O Meredith Wilson Library, 309 19 Ave S, Minneapolis, 55455. Austin J McLean, Chief, Special Collections
Holdings: Vols (103) / / Cat Mss
Notes: Basically mathematical astronomy with emphasis on eclipses. Particular

EUCLID (cont.)

strengths are the works of such authors as Delambre, Euclid, Newton, Ptolemy, and Rha06ticus. Important in this respect are 6 of the 10 known printed editions of the Alphonsine Astronomical Tables.

ON —UNIVERSITY OF TORONTO, Thomas Fisher Rare Book Library, 120 Saint George St, Toronto, M5S 1A5, Can. Richard G Landon, Head
Holdings: Vols 4000
Notes: The Science Collection is especially rich in works on Renaissance astronomy, physics and mechanics and has noteworthy holdings of works of English experimental scientists in the 17th and 18th centuries with excellent collections of the works of Robert Boyle, Robert Hooke, and Sir Isaac Newton. Includes virtually all important early editions of Euclid; alchemical works of the 16th and 17th centuries together with the works of 18th century chemists like Lavoisier and Priestly; works on agriculture with special emphasis on British agriculture in the 18th century; and a variety of other works important in the history of science in all its branches. In addition the Fisher Library has many other specialized scientific collections which are listed separately.

ON —UNIVERSITY OF WATERLOO, Library, Waterloo, N2L 3G1, Can. Susan Bellingham, Special Collections Librn
Holdings: Vols 50 Cat
Notes: Incl first and notable editions.

EUGENICS

NY —COLD SPRING HARBOR LABORATORY, Library, PO Box 100, Cold Spring Harbor, 11724. Susan Gensel, Library Dir; Genemary Falvey, Librn
Holdings: Vols 30,000
Budget: ($103,500)
Notes: The highly technical collection is comprised of 20,000 serial vols and 10,000 monographs. The library receives 500 current serial titles. Subjects covered incl molecular and cellular biology, virology, biochemistry, microbiology, oncology, neurobiology, biological risk assessment and genetic engineering/biotechnology. Special collections in eugenics and genetics are primarily historical dealing with the development of genetics in the US which had its beginnings here.

EUGENIE, EMPRESS

NC —UNIVERSITY OF NORTH CAROLINA, GREENSBORO, Walter Clinton Jackson Library, Special Collections Dept, 1000 Spring Garden St, Greensboro, 27412. Emilie W Mills, Librn
Holdings: Cat Mss
Notes: 78 letters by the English composer Dame Ethel Mary Smyth, chiefly to Emmeline Pankhurst, written from Helouan, Eqypt, 1913-1914. Other letters incl several from Empress Eugenie and members of her circle, and several letters to Lady Ponsonby. This group of letters mainly traces the composer's interest in the suffrage movement and the development of her musical career. No photocopying.

EUNSON, ROBERT

AZ —NORTHERN ARIZONA UNIVERSITY, Special Collection Library, CU Box 6022, Flagstaff, 86011. Peter M Whiteley, Coordr/Archivist; William Mullane, Librn
Notes: Collection of Robert Eunson, journalist, vice president, and assistant general manager of United Press Interational. NAU graduate. Incl correspondence, scrapbooks, subject files, photos, 1930's-1975. Eunson was a World War II correspondent. Also incl information on the Pacific and European theatres, Generals MacArthur and Eisenhower, and Arizona AP news articles from the Korean War era. Inventory available.

EUNUCHS AND EUNUCHISM

NY —NEW YORK ACADEMY OF MEDICINE, Library, 2 E 103 St, New York, 10029. Brett A Kirkpatrick, Librn
Notes: An extensive series of notebooks on all historical aspects of the subject.

EURATOM see European Atomic Energy Community (Euratom)

EUREKA AND PALISADE RAILROAD

NV —UNIVERSITY OF NEVADA, RENO, University Library, Special Collections Dept, Reno, 89557. Robert E Blesse, Head
Holdings: Vols (150) Cat Mss Pix Maps
Notes: Includes 370 cu ft manuscripts, 2000 photographs. Major collection include papers of Nevada railroad companies Virginia and Truckee, Carson and Colorado, Eureka and Palisade, and Nevada Copper Belt. Materials are collected which deal with the history and development of railroads within Nevada and those which have run through the state.

EURIPIDES

NC —DUKE UNIVERSITY, William R Perkins Library, Durham, 27706. Elvin E Strowd, University Librn
Notes: The Spranger Collection of classical studies contains 2500 items. The principal dramatists, Euripides, Aeschylus, Aristophanes and Sophocles are fairly comprehensively covered by way of critical texts and studies up to 1968. Practically all the texts are represented by Loeb and Bude translations, and also Didot's 19th century series. Reference books includes a complete Pauly-Wissowa, Briquet, long runs of the Classical Review and Quarterly, the O E D and some 30 to 40 volumes of codex facsimiles of Euripides and others.

PA —UNIVERSITY OF PITTSBURGH, Hillman Library, Pittsburgh, 15260. Glenora E Rossell, Head
Holdings: Vols (11,550) Cat
Notes: The classics collection is particularly strong in Greek and Latin literature, Greek and Roman history, Greek philosophy, Greek and Latin language, and Greek epigraphy. In combination with the Frick Fine Arts collection it has a good collection in Greek and Roman art and archaeology. The collection of journals is also quite strong in these areas. There has been an emphasis in collecting books by and about Homer, Aristotles, Euripides, Vergil, Cicero and Petronius. It has a unique collection of unpublished PhD dissertations and Master's theses on Petronius. It has a basic collection on Greek and Latin paleography and papyrology.

EUROPE—DESCRIPTION AND TRAVEL

NY —EXPLORERS CLUB, James B Ford Memorial Library, 46 E 70 St, New York, 10021. Janet Baldwin, Librn
Holdings: Vols (24,000) Cat Maps
Notes: Additions to the collection depend upon gifts. Access by appointment only.

EUROPE—HISTORY

CA —HOOVER INSTITUTION ON WAR, REVOLUTION & PEACE, Stanford University, Stanford, 94305. Milorad M Drachkovitch, Archivist
Holdings: Mss
Notes: Records of the European Technical Advisers, a private American advisory organization created to assist in European reconstruction after World War I, incl correspondence, reports, statistics, and financial records, 1919-1923, relating to railway operation, fuel production, and other aspects of economic reconstruction in Austria, Poland, Czechoslovakia and Yugoslavia. 72 ms boxes.

CA —STANFORD UNIVERSITY LIBRARIES, Cecil H Green Library, Stanford, 94305. Michael T Ryan, Cur
Holdings: Vols Cat Maps
Notes: An emphasis in the Rare Book Collection.

CO —UNIVERSITY OF SOUTHERN COLORADO, Library, 2200 Bonforte Blvd, Pueblo, 81001.
Holdings: Vols (4000) Cat Mss Maps Pix Phonorecords Audiotapes
Budget: ($10,000)
Notes: Yugoslavian; especially Slovenian history and culture. The collection was inaugurated in 1969. Besides published titles, 2800 in English, and 900 in Slavic languages, there are memorabilia, organizational records, and newspapers, magazines, and music. There is a separate card catalog of items in the collection. Colorado has had a number of Slavic colonies and this collection attempts to recapture the history of these early settlers. Incl sheet music and phonorecords.

CT —YALE UNIVERSITY, Box 1603A, Yale Station, New Haven, 06520.

DC —HOWARD UNIVERSITY, Moorland-Spingarn Research Center, 500 Howard Place NW, Washington, 20059. Clifford L Muse, Jr, Acting Dir
Holdings: Vols (106,086) Cat Mss Maps Pix Slides Phonorecords Audiotapes 16mm Films Filmstrips Microforms
Budget: ($854,753)
Notes: *The Glenn Carrington Collection: A Guide to the Books, Manuscripts, Music and Recordings* (DC MSRC, 1977). *Dictionary Catalog of the Jesse E Moorland Collection of Negro Life and History,* 9 vols and Supplement, 3 vols (Boston: G K Hall, 1970, 1977). *Dictionary Catalog of the Arthur Spingarn Collection of Negro Authors,* 2 vols (Boston: G K Hall, 1970). Guide to Processed Collections in the Manuscript Division of the Moorland-Spingarn Research Center (DC, MSRC, 1983). The Moorland-Spingran Research Center is recognized as one of the largest and most comprehensive repositories in the world for the collection, preservation and dissemination of historical materials documenting from antiquity to the present the history and culture of Black people in Africa, Europe, the Caribbean and the US. Since 1973, the Research Center has greatly expanded its facilitiesand resources and currently provides research services in all aspects of library and archival research, including manuscripts, oral history, music, prints and photographs and general library materials. The Research Center also maintains professional zerographic, micrographic, photographic and similar reproduction laboratories.

DC —LIBRARY OF CONGRESS, Washington, 20540.
Notes: Project of a consortium to microfilm about 200,000 pp of material on Great Britain, France, Russia and Prussia, for the period 1848-1918 in the ms and documentary collections of the Austrian State Archives. The collection will incl, among others, documents on the Austro-Prussia War of 1866, the treaty negotiations between France and Italy in 1868-1870, the Orient Question of 1877-1878, the persecation of Jews in Russia in 1882, the Congo Conference in Berlin, 1884-1887 and the British-Portuguese conflict in East Africa, 1889-1891. Copies are available at LC, the Center for Research Libraries, the Hampshire Inter-Library Center, and the libraries of Boston College, Yale, Harvard, Duke, Stanford and the University of Virginia.

IL —NEWBERRY LIBRARY, 60 W Walton St, Chicago, 60610. Diana Haskell, Cur of Modern Mss
Holdings: Cat
Notes: European history and literature, 1300 to 1800.

KS —UNIVERSITY OF KANSAS, Kenneth Spencer Research Library, Special Collections Dept, Lawrence, 66045. Alexandra Mason, Librn
Holdings: Cat Mss Maps
Notes: Great Britain, Italy, France, Spain,

EUROPE—HISTORY (cont.)

Eastern Europe (especially Poland), mediaeval to late 18th century. Noncirculating.

MA —HARVARD UNIVERSITY LIBRARY, Cambridge, 02138.
Holdings: Cat

MO —SAINT LOUIS UNIVERSITY, Pius XII Memorial Library, 3655 W Pine Blvd, Saint Louis, 63108. William Cole, Dir
Holdings: Slides Microforms
Notes: Collection covers all areas of learning and European history from Classical Antiquity to early modern period. Researchers using collection receive assistance in paleography, bibliography and reference search. Approx 10,000 1000-foot reels of microfilm (not counting master negatives) reproducing Vatican Library's Latin, Greek, Hebrew, Arabic and Ethiopic mss. Some 8000 100-foot reels of microfilm (again not counting master negative) reproducing rare and out of print books relating to subject areas in the mss. Over 50, 000 color slides of medieval and Renaissance mss illuminations. A reference collection of modern materials relating to ms research.

NY —NEW YORK PUBLIC LIBRARY, Research Libraries, General Research Division, Fifth Ave & 42 St, New York, 10018. Rodney Phillips, Chief
Holdings: Vols (2,225,000) Cat Maps Pix Microforms
Budget: ($775,718)

NY —SYRACUSE UNIVERSITY LIBRARIES, Ernest S Bird Library, George Arents Research Library for Special Collections, Syracuse, 13210. Carolyn A Davis, Manuscripts Librn; Amy S Doherty, University Archivist; Mark F Weimer, Rare Book Librn
Notes: Private library of Leopold von Ranke, father of modern historical scholarship, acquired in 1886. More than 17,000 volumes, 4000 pamphlets, and 430 mss, and private papers and letters. A complete catalogue of the ms collection published in 1983. Incl more than 100 dispatches (Relazioni) from Venetian ambassadors, 1500-1800, etc. Much unpublished primary source material.

NC —DUKE UNIVERSITY, William R Perkins Library, Durham, 27706. Elvin E Strowd, University Librn
Notes: The Karl Holl collection contains 8000 titles in European church history through the Reformation.

†OH —UNIVERSITY OF CINCINNATI LIBRARIES, Cincinnati, 45221.
Notes: The Miriam B Urban Memorial Fund Collection.

ON —VICTORIA UNIVERSITY, Library, Centre for Reformation and Renaissance Studies, 71 Queen's Park Crescent, Toronto, M5S 1K7, Can. Robert C Brandeis, Chief Librn; James Estes, Dir
Holdings: Vols (15,000) Cat Slides
Notes: The CRRS concentrates on the northern European countries and France; its chief strengths are Erasmus, 650 vols; early printed books, especially 16th century editions of Latin classics; bibliography and the history of printing. The Erasmus holdings are cataloged in W T McCready et al, "The Erasmus Collection in the Centre for Reformation and Renaissance Studies...A Catalogue"...*Reformation and Renaissance* 7 (1971), 32-76 and "A Supplementary List"...*Reformation and Renaissance,* 10 (1974), 116-119. Published catalogs. Humanist Editions of the Classics at CRRS, Toronto, 1979; Humanist Editions of Statutes and History at CRRS, Toronto, 1980; Bibles, Theological Treatises and Other Religious Literature 1491-1700 at CRRS, Toronto, 1981.

EUROPE—INDUSTRIES

PA —UNIVERSITY OF PITTSBURGH, Hillman Library, Pittsburgh, 15260. Glenora E Rossell, Head
Holdings: Vols (700) Cat Pix Microforms
Notes: Advanced industrial societies of Europe. At Hillman Library are cataloged the publications of political parties and interest organizations of Austria (7), Belgium (5), Denmark (8), Finland (6), France (12), Germany (9), Great Britain (6), Italy (6), Netherlands (12), Norway (4), Switzerland (10), Sweden (6). Supplementing this collection is the general political science collection which incl OECD publications, statistics, parliamentary records and government documents of these countries. This collection was developed in cooperation with the 8 university Council on European Studies.

EUROPE—MAPS

CT —YALE UNIVERSITY, Box 1603A, Yale Station, New Haven, 06520.
Notes: Maps and atlas collection.

EUROPE—POLITICS AND GOVERNMENT

CA —CLAREMONT COLLEGES, Honnold Library, Ninth & Dartmouth, Claremont, 91711. Tania Rizzo, Special Collections Dept Head
Holdings: Vols (1880) // Uncat Pamphlets
Notes: 19th century pamphlet collection, chiefly British, concerning contemporary religion, commerce, finance, politics, labor, literature, social problems. Some deal with continental problems, often in French, Italian, Portuguese, etc (indexed).

CA —UNIVERSITY OF CALIFORNIA, LOS ANGELES, Research Library, Dept of Special Collections, 405 Hilgard Ave, Los Angeles, 90024. Edward Shreeves, Chairman, Bibliographers Group; David S Zeidberg, Head
Notes: 90 linear feet in various collections pertaining to political and social activities in the US, Europe, Latin America, and the USSR.

EUROPE, CENTRAL see Central Europe

EUROPE, COUNCIL OF see Council of Europe

EUROPE, EASTERN

IL —UNIVERSITY OF ILLINOIS, URBANA/CHAMPAIGN, Slavic and East European Library, Urbana, 61801. Marianna Tax Choldin, Head
Holdings: Vols (420,000) Cat Maps Microforms
Notes: One of the largest Slavic and East European collections. Strong in Russian and Soviet materials-humanities, sciences, and social sciences; languages and literatures; periodicals, newspapers, and microforms. Ca 260,000 volumes in languages of the Soviet Union plus 20,000 Russian and Ukrainian titles on microform. Extensive coverage of Czechoslovakia (35,000 vols); Yugoslavia (31,000 vols); Bulgaria (9200 vols); Poland (34,600 vols); Romania (13,000 vols); and Hungary (18,000 vols) and the languages, literatures, and history of these countries.

†OH —OHIO NORTHERN UNIVERSITY, Heterick Memorial Library, 525 S Main St, Ada, 45810.

WA —UNIVERSITY OF WASHINGTON LIBRARIES, Suzzallo Library, Slavic & East European Section, FM-25, Seattle, 98195. Barbara A Galik, Head
Holdings: Vols (250,000) Cat Mss Maps Pix Phonorecords Audiotapes Microforms
Budget: ($85,000)
Notes: Strong research collections for Eastern Europe, especially Poland. Holdings cover all aspects of life and culture and are execellent in historical source materials, language, literature, geography, economics, the fine arts, and folklore. There are extensive holdings of the publications of academies, major universities, and principal scholarly institutions, especially of long serial runs. Sizeable Slavic language collections are also to be found in the sciences among the branch libraries of the university.

EUROPE, EASTERN—HISTORY

CT —YALE UNIVERSITY, Box 1603A, Yale Station, New Haven, 06520.
Notes: Books by and about Nikolai Lenin.

IN —INDIANA UNIVERSITY, University Libraries, Bloomington, 47401. Murlin Croucher, Librn for Slavic Studies
Holdings: Vols (300,000) Cat Maps Microforms
Budget: ($63,000)
Notes: The collection, established after World War II, covers material of, and on, the Soviet Union (55 percent) and Eastern Europe (45 percent) in the languages of the area and in western European languages as well. Material is chiefly in the fields of humanities and social sciences. Many other Slavic and East European books are located in the Lilly Library (rare book library).

NY —CORNELL UNIVERSITY LIBRARIES, John M Olin Library, Ithaca, 14853. Marilyn B Kann, Slavic Studies Librn
Holdings: Vols 50,000 Cat Microforms

NY —JOZEF PILSUDSKI INSTITUTE FOR RESEARCH IN THE MODERN HISTORY OF POLAND, INC, 381 Park Ave, South, New York, 10016.
Holdings: 12,000 Vols Mss Maps Pix Archive
Notes: Said to be the fourth largest Polish collection of documents in the world outside of Poland. Materials emphasize history since 1863. Incl 2000 periodicals.

OH —OHIO STATE UNIVERSITY, William Oxley Thompson Memorial Library, Hilander Room, 1858 Neil Ave Mall, Columbus, 43210. Predrag Matejic, Cur; G Koolemans Beynen, Slavic Bibliographer
Holdings: Vols (200,000) Cat Maps Microforms
Budget: ($45,000)
Notes: Area studies of Central, Southeastern and Eastern Europe. Emphasis on on Slavic literatures, languages and history. At present economics, sociology, law (Russian only) have been added. Within this framework the following priorities have been established: Material in Russian problems; then Medieval Slavic (Cyrillic); then Polish, then Serbo-Croatian, then Bulgarian, and now Romanian. Special attention is paid to serials, bibliographies, ms descriptions and dictionaries (incl biographical and encyclopedias). Apart from materials in native languages, materials in the following languages are acquired: Old Church Slavonic, Greek, English, French, German, Italian, a few in Scandinavian languages, incl Finnish, and a few in Baltic languages. The Hillandar Room holds approx 2000 Slavic mss, 1050 from Hilandar Monastery, Mount Athos, on microform and a related referencecollection.

WA —UNIVERSITY OF WASHINGTON LIBRARIES, Suzzallo Library, Slavic & East European Section, FM-25, Seattle, 98195. Barbara A Galik, Head
Holdings: Vols (250,000) Cat Mss Maps Pix Phonorecords Audiotapes Microforms
Budget: ($85,000)
Notes: Strong research collections for Eastern Europe, especially Poland. Holdings cover all aspects of life and culture and are execellent in historical source materials, language, literature, geography, economics, the fine arts, and folklore. There are extensive holdings of the publications of academies, major universities, and principal scholarly institutions, especially of long serial runs. Sizeable Slavic language collections are also to be found in the sciences among the branch libraries of the university.

EUROPEAN ATOMIC ENERGY COMMUNITY (EURATOM)

DC —COMMISSION OF THE EUROPEAN COMMUNITIES, European Community Information Service Library, 2100 M St NW Suite 707, Washington, 20037. Barbara Sloan, Head of Public Inquiries
Holdings: Vols (35,000) Cat Maps Pix Microforms
Notes: Library contains all of the official documents and occasional publications of the Institutions of the European Communities: ie, European Economic Community (Common Market), European Atomic Energy Community (Euratom), European

EUROPEAN ATOMIC ENERGY COMMUNITY (EURATOM) (cont.)

Coal and Steel Community (ECSC). It collects non-Community publications about European integration, international trade and monetary affairs. Also has the publications of the General Agreements for Tariffs and Trade (GATT), Western European Union, and Council of Europe. Also, 1000 vertical files.

EUROPEAN COAL AND STEEL COMMUNITY (ECSC)

DC —COMMISSION OF THE EUROPEAN COMMUNITIES, European Community Information Service Library, 2100 M St NW Suite 707, Washington, 20037. Barbara Sloan, Head of Public Inquiries
Holdings: Vols (35,000) Cat Maps Pix Microforms
Notes: Library contains all of the official documents and occasional publications of the Institutions of the European Communities: ie, European Economic Community (Common Market), European Atomic Energy Community (Euratom), European Coal and Steel Community (ECSC). It collects non-Community publications about European integration, international trade and monetary affairs. Also has the publications of the General Agreements for Tariffs and Trade (GATT), Western European Union, and Council of Europe. Also, 1000 vertical files.

EUROPEAN COMMON MARKET see European Economic Communities

EUROPEAN COMMUNITY

DC —COMMISSION OF THE EUROPEAN COMMUNITIES, European Community Information Service Library, 2100 M St NW Suite 707, Washington, 20037. Barbara Sloan, Head of Public Inquiries
Holdings: Vols (35,000) Cat Maps Pix Microforms Exhibits
Notes: Library contains all of the official documents and occasional publications of the Institutions of the European Communities: ie, European Economic Community (Common Market), European Atomic Energy Community (Euratom), European Coal and Steel Community (ECSC). It collects non-Community publications about European integration, international trade and monetary affairs. Also has the publications of the General Agreements for Tariffs and Trade (GATT), Western European Union, and Council of Europe. Also, 1000 vertical files.

DC —GEORGETOWN UNIVERSITY, Library, Special Collections Div, 37 & O Sts NW, Washington, 20057. George M Barringer, Special Collections Librn; Nicholas B Sheetz, Mss Librn
Holdings: Mss Cat Pix
Notes: Correspondence, minutes, reports, addresses, ACUE publications, photographs, and newspaper clippings from the American Committee on United Europe. Founded in 1949, the Committee was organized to promote public discussion and understanding of the issues and opportunities of European integration. The Committee was disbanded in 1960.

KY —UNIVERSITY OF KENTUCKY, Margaret I King Library, Government Publications Dept, Lexington, 40506. Sandra McAninch, Head
Holdings: Uncat
Notes: A depository since 1974. Incl papers.

NC —DUKE UNIVERSITY, William R Perkins Library, Public Documents and Maps Department, Durham, 27706. Jaia Barrett, Head
Holdings: Vols Maps Pamphlets Microforms
Notes: A selective depository for US Government publications since 1890, the Department currently holds well over 500, 000 items, plus publications of the European Community (a depository collection), the League of Nations, the UN and UN-affiliated agencies. Other international organizations, publications are acquired also, as are state government publications, especially from the Southeast, California, New York and Illinois. The Documents Department holds services the major map collections of Perkins Library. These collections include topographic, geologic, and special subject maps which are worldwide in coverage. The department is a depository for the US Defense Mapping Agency and the US Geological Survey. In addition, there are many other maps of general and specific interest, including US and foreign road maps. As appropriate, maps are also held in the Perkins Library's Rare BookRoom and Manuscript Department. Atlases are shelved in the Reference Department and in the bookstacks of Perkins Library.

OR —UNIVERSITY OF OREGON LIBRARY, Documents Section, Eugene, 97403. Tom Stave, Section Head; John Shuler, Documents Librn
Holdings: Vols 13,000
Notes: Depository for European Communities publications since 1974.

EUROPEAN ECONOMIC COMMUNITIES

CT —YALE UNIVERSITY LIBRARY, Government Documents Center, 38 Mansfield St, PO Box 2491, Yale Sta, New Haven, 06520. Sandra K Peterson, Documents Librn
Holdings: Microforms

DC —COMMISSION OF THE EUROPEAN COMMUNITIES, European Community Information Service Library, 2100 M St NW Suite 707, Washington, 20037. Barbara Sloan, Head of Public Inquiries
Holdings: Vols (35,000) Cat Maps Pix Microforms
Notes: Library contains all of the official documents and occasional publications of the Institutions of the European Communities: ie, European Economic Community (Common Market), European Atomic Energy Community (Euratom), European Coal and Steel Community (ECSC). It collects non-Community publications about European integration, international trade and monetary affairs. Also has the publications of the General Agreements for Tariffs and Trade (GATT), Western European Union, and Council of Europe. Also, 1000 vertical files.

DC —GEORGETOWN UNIVERSITY, Library, Special Collections Div, 37 & O Sts NW, Washington, 20057. George M Barringer, Special Collections Librn; Nicholas B Sheetz, Mss Librn
Holdings: Mss Cat Pix
Notes: Correspondence, minutes, reports, addresses, ACUE publications, photographs, and newspaper clippings from the American Committee on United Europe. Founded in 1949, the Committee was organized to promote public discussion and understanding of the issues and opportunities of European integration. The Committee was disbanded in 1960.

IL —UNIVERSITY OF ILLINOIS, URBANA/CHAMPAIGN, College of Law, Library, Champaign, 61820. Richard Surles, Law Librn
Holdings: Vols (425,000) Cat Mss Microforms
Notes: Plus 800 reels of microfilm; 150,000 microfiches. Research collection covering both Anglo-American and foreign law. Depository for documents of the US Government, Illinois, and European Economic Communities.

KY —UNIVERSITY OF KENTUCKY, Margaret I King Library, Government Publications Dept, Lexington, 40506. Sandra McAninch, Head
Holdings: Uncat
Notes: A depository since 1974. Incl papers.

PA —UNIVERSITY OF PENNSYLVANIA, Biddle Law Library, 3400 Chestnut St, Philadelphia, 19104. Elizabeth S. Kelly, Libn
Holdings: Vols (350,000) Cat
Notes: Comprehensive collection of Anglo-American law. Legal materials from selected foreign countries, particularly in Common Market area. International law incl U N documents and other regional organizations. Substantial holdings in historical sources particularly early English law and Canon law.

EUROPEAN ECONOMIC INTEGRATION

PA —UNIVERSITY OF PITTSBURGH, Hillman Library, Pittsburgh, 15260. Glenora E Rossell, Head
Holdings: Vols (700) Cat Pix Microforms
Notes: Advanced industrial societies of Europe. At Hillman Library are cataloged the publications of political parties and interest organizations of Austria (7), Belgium (5), Denmark (8), Finland (6), France (12), Germany (9), Great Britain (6), Italy (6), Netherlands (12), Norway (4), Switzerland (10), Sweden (6). Supplementing this collection is the general political science collection which incl OECD publications, statistics, parliamentary records and government documents of these countries. This collection was developed in cooperation with the 8 university Council on European Studies.

EUROPEAN EXPANSION

IN —INDIANA UNIVERSITY, Lilly Library, Seventh St, Bloomington, 47405. William R Cagle, Librn
Holdings: Vols (2000) // Cat
Notes: The core of the collection is the specialized library of Charles R Boxer (1000 titles) dealing with the history of the Iberians in the East, 16th-18th century. Mainly incl works on China, Japan and the Philippines during the period of their early intercourse with the West through 1800, as well as materials on the English and Dutch East India Companies, and the 17th century Anglo-Dutch naval wars. Special mention should be made of the valuable letters from missions by the Jesuits, and the works in this area by the Augustinians, Franciscans, and Dominicans, from the time of the valuable source of information for the study of the European expansion into the area, including Southeast Asia.

MN —UNIVERSITY OF MINNESOTA, James Ford Bell Library, 309 19th Ave S, Minneapolis, 55455. John Parker, Cur
Holdings: Vols (11,000) Cat Mss Maps
Notes: Collection of original materials relating to European expansion, 1400-1800.

EUROPEAN INTEGRATION

DC —COMMISSION OF THE EUROPEAN COMMUNITIES, European Community Information Service Library, 2100 M St NW Suite 707, Washington, 20037. Barbara Sloan, Head of Public Inquiries
Holdings: Vols (35,000) Cat Maps Pix Microforms
Notes: Library contains all of the official documents and occasional publications of the Institutions of the European Communities: ie, European Economic Community (Common Market), European Atomic Energy Community (Euratom), European Coal and Steel Community (ECSC). It collects non-Community publications about European integration, international trade and monetary affairs. Also has the publications of the General Agreements for Tariffs and Trade (GATT), Western European Union, and Council of Europe. Also, 1000 vertical files.

EUROPEAN JEWS see Jews in Eastern Europe

EUROPEAN LITERATURE

IL —NEWBERRY LIBRARY, 60 W Walton St, Chicago, 60610. Diana Haskell, Cur of Modern Mss
Holdings: Cat
Notes: European history and literature, 1300 to 1800.

EUROPEAN LITERATURE (cont.)

IL —UNIVERSITY OF CHICAGO LIBRARY, Dept of Special Collections, 1100 E 57 St, Chicago, 60637.
Notes: Hirsch-Bernays Collection of Continental Literature.

IL —NORTHWESTERN UNIVERSITY, Library, Special Collections Dept, 1937 Sheridan Rd, Evanston, 60201. R Russell Maylone, Cur
Holdings: Vols 6000 Cat Mss
Notes: First editions, letters, and works about major 20th-century authors. Incl books and periodicals from France and Germany and to a lesser extent from Italy, Spain, Poland, Rumania, Czechoslovakia, Sweden, Denmark, and the Netherlands. Strong in German Expressionism, Italian Futurism, Surrealism, and Dada.

NY —NEW YORK PUBLIC LIBRARY, Research Libraries, General Research Division, Fifth Ave & 42 St, New York, 10018. Rodney Phillips, Chief
Holdings: Vols (2,225,000) Cat Maps Pix Microforms
Budget: ($775,718)

EUROPEAN RAILROADS see Railroads, European

EUROPEAN RECOVERY PROGRAM see Reconstruction (Europe, 1945-1951)

EUROPEAN RIVALRY IN THE AMERICAS

RI —BROWN UNIVERSITY, John Carter Brown Library, Providence, 02912. Norman Fiering, Librn; Everett C Wilkie Jr, Bibliographer; Susan Danforth, Cur Maps & Prints
Holdings: Vols (40,000)
Notes: Comprehensive collections of European writings on the successive wars fought in the Americas (ie, French & Indian, American Revolution, etc).

EUROPEAN TECHNICAL ADVISORS, INC.

CA —HOOVER INSTITUTION ON WAR, REVOLUTION & PEACE, Stanford University, Stanford, 94305. Milorad M Drachkovitch, Archivist
Holdings: Mss
Notes: Records of the European Technical Advisers, a private American advisory organization created to assist in European reconstruction after World War I, incl correspondence, reports, statistics, and financial records, 1919-1923, relating to railway operation, fuel production, and other aspects of economic reconstruction in Austria, Poland, Czechoslovakia and Yugoslavia. 72 ms boxes.

EUROPEAN WAR, 1914-1918 see World War, 1914-1918

EUROPEAN WAR, 1939-1945 see World War, 1939-1945

EUROPEAN WAR ATROCITIES

CA —HOOVER INSTITUTION ON WAR, REVOLUTION & PEACE, Stanford University, Stanford, 94305. Milorad M Drachkovitch, Archivist
Holdings: Mss Pix
Notes: Papers of William A Drayton, 1913-1946, incl correspondence, reports, memoranda, speeches and writings, photographs, and other materials, relating to Serbia, during and after World War I, and W A Drayton's activities as an American volunteer in the Serbian Army, members of the Serbian Delegation to Paris Peace Conference, and Inter-Allied Commissioner of Bulgarian Atrocities Commission. 2 ms boxes.

EUSKARA LANGUAGE see Basque Language and Literature

EUTHANASIA

DC —CENTER FOR BIOETHICS, Library, Kennedy Institute, Georgetown University, 3520 Prospect St NW, Washington, 20057. Doris Goldstein, Dir; Judith Mistichelli, Senior Librn
Holdings: Vols (8200)
Notes: Largest library of its kind. Incl 31, 000 journal articles on applied ethics. Produces computer database *Bioethicsline,* available through MEDLARS; and the printed annual *Bibliography of Bioethics.* Other library publications are: *New Titles in* Bioethics (monthly); *Scope Notes* series on current topics.

†NC —DUKE UNIVERSITY, Archives, 341 Perkins Library, Durham, 27706.
Notes: Incl psychic phenomena, the plight of emigres and the growth of the police state in Nazi Germany, euthanasia and eugenics, behaviorism and John Watson, and such figures as Aldous Huxley and C G Jung. 1800 items and 24 vols. Correspondence with individuals significant in the fields of psychology, psychic research, and social sciences.

EUTROPHICATION

OH —CASE WESTERN RESERVE UNIVERSITY LIBRARIES, Cleveland, 44106. Susie Hanson, Special Collections Librn
Holdings: Vols 1000 Cat Maps Pix Microforms
Notes: The collection was previously titled the Lake Erie Study Collection. As its scope has increased, it has been renamed the Environmental Sciences Collection and has been fully incorporated into the collection of the Sears Library, which serves the University in the areas of science and technology, economics and management. The Environmental Sciences Collection incl government and nongovernment reports, monographs and serials.

WI —UNIVERSITY OF WISCONSIN, MADISON, Water Resources Reference Services, 1975 Willow Dr, Madison, 53706. Sarah L Calcese, Librn
Holdings: Uncat
Notes: Over 6860 reprints and reports. The university has been designated a center of competence in eutrophication by the Office of Water Research of the US Dept of the Interior. *Eutrophication: A Bimonthly Summary of Current Literature* published at the University of Wisconsin indexes the collection through 1975. These abstracts also appear in *Selected Water Resources* Abstracts and can be approached through a search of the GIPSY (General Information Processing System) data base centered at the University of Oklahoma.

EVALUATION OF LITERATURE see Bibliography—Best Books; Literature—History and Criticism

EVANGELICAL ASSOCIATION CHURCH AND EVANGELICAL CHURCH

NJ —UNITED METHODIST CHURCH, Commission on Archives and History, 36 Madison Ave, PO Box 127, Madison, 07940. Charles Yrigoyen, Jr, General Secy
Holdings: Vols 40,000 Cat Mss Maps Pix Slides Microforms
Budget: $110,000
Notes: The United Methodist Church Collection includes these churches and dates: The United Evangelical Church, 1891-1922; The Evangelical Association, 1800-1922; The Evangelical Church, 1922-1946; The United Brethren in Christ, 1800-1946; The Evangelical United Brethren Church, 1946-1968; The Methodist Episcopal Church, 1773-1939; The Methodist Episcopal Church, South, 1844-1939; The Methodist Church, 1939-1968; The United Methodist Church, 1968-date. There is no published catalog. The Depository is a specialized collection pertaining to manuscript and published material dealing with the United Methodist Church and its antecedent bodies. It is the official church depository for preservation of records-over 2 million items.

EVANGELICAL COVENANT CHURCH OF AMERICA

IL —EVANGELICAL COVENANT CHURCH, Archives and Historical Library, North Park College, 5125 N Spaulding Ave, Chicago, 60625. Sigurd F Westberg, Archivist
Holdings: Vols 4000 Cat Mss Pix Audiotapes 16mm Films Microforms Newspapers
Budget: $7000
Notes: The church archives of the Evangelical Covenant Church. This is a denominational archive though we do have a great deal of background material from Sweden. We also have some materials from closely related churches. Hold both officical and unofficial publications. Also, letters, diaries, sermons and photographs of pastors, missionaries, teachers, and lay leaders.

EVANGELICAL UNITED BRETHREN

IN —INDIANA CENTRAL UNIVERSITY, Krannert Memorial Library, 1400 E Hanna Ave, Indianapolis, 46227. Florabelle Wilson, Librn
Holdings: Vols 561 Cat
Notes: Collection of books and pamphlets which have been written by members of the United Brethren (UB), Evangelical United Bretheren (EUB) and United Methodist (UM) Church. The collection has conference yearbooks, proceedings, and annuals, as well as biographies and historical information about the origin and development of these faiths.

MI —ADRIAN COLLEGE, Shipman Library, Adrian, 49221. Ronald A Brunger, Cur
Holdings: Vols (4500) Cat Mss
Budget: ($4600)
Notes: United Methodist Church, Detroit Conference, Archives. Incl materials on the Evangelical, United Brethren, and Evangelical United Brethren Churches; materials on the Bishops; Minutes of the Annual Conferences; files of Christliche Botschafter, Evangelical Messenger, The Evangelical Herald, etc; files of Conference Committees and miscellaneous material. Archives incl materials on Methodism, Methodist Episcopal Church, Methodist Protestant Church and United Methodist Church.

NJ —UNITED METHODIST CHURCH, Commission on Archives and History, 36 Madison Ave, PO Box 127, Madison, 07940. Charles Yrigoyen, Jr, General Secy
Holdings: Vols 40,000 Cat Mss Maps Pix Slides Microforms
Budget: $110,000
Notes: The United Methodist Church Collection includes these churches and dates: The United Evangelical Church, 1891-1922; The Evangelical Association, 1800-1922; The Evangelical Church, 1922-1946; The United Brethren in Christ, 1800-1946; The Evangelical United Brethren Church, 1946-1968; The Methodist Episcopal Church, 1773-1939; The Methodist Episcopal Church, South, 1844-1939; The Methodist Church, 1939-1968; The United Methodist Church, 1968-date. There is no published catalog. The Depository is a specialized collection pertaining to manuscript and published material dealing with the United Methodist Church and its antecedent bodies. It is the official church depository for preservation of records-over 2 million items.

NY —CORNELL UNIVERSITY LIBRARIES, Collection of Regional History, Dept of Manuscripts and Univ Archives, Ithaca, 14853.
Notes: Records, 1800-47; 2 items. Milton and Scipio, NY.

EVANGELICALISM—CHURCH OF ENGLAND

ON —WYCLIFFE COLLEGE, Leonard Library, 5 Hoskin Ave, Toronto, M5S 1H7, Can. Adrienne Taylor, Librn; Gayle Ford, Library Technician
Holdings: Vols (47,000) Cat Microforms
Budget: ($11,000)
Notes: Collection of early and rare books of

EVANGELICALISM—CHURCH OF ENGLAND (cont.)

prayer books, sermons, Bibles. Basic reference collection of standard theological dictionaries, encyclopedias, commentaries. Homiletics collection including 19th century works. Strong in church history, Evangelical Anglicanism, English Reformation, Wycliffe studies.

EVANGELISM see Evangelistic Work

EVANGELISTIC WORK

IL —WHEATON COLLEGE, Billy Graham Center Library and Archives, Wheaton, 60187. Ferne Lauraine Weimer, Dir of Library; Robert Shuster, Dir of Archives
Notes: Archives of the Center.

MS —UNIVERSITY OF SOUTHERN MISSISSIPPI, William David McCain Graduate Library, Box 5148, Southern Sta, Hattiesburg, 39406.
Holdings: Cat Mss Pix
Notes: The Howard S Williams Papers (1916-1960; 1.8 cubic feet) contain correspondence, newspaper clippings, sermons, promotional material, broadsides, and photographs which document Williams' life as a traveling evangelist in the Southeastern and United States.

EVANS, ALICE CATHERINE, 1881-

NY —CORNELL UNIVERSITY LIBRARIES, Collection of Regional History, Dept of Manuscripts and Univ Archives, Ithaca, 14853.
Notes: Bacteriologist. Incl papers, 1908-65; scientific speeches, articles, reports, memoirs, clippings, photos, programs, official invitations, and much professional correspondence. Unpublished guide available.

EVANS, EDMUND, 1826-1905

CA —UNIVERSITY OF CALIFORNIA, LOS ANGELES, Research Library, Dept of Special Collections, 405 Hilgard Ave, Los Angeles, 90024. Edward Shreeves, Chairman, Bibliographers Group; David S Zeidberg, Head
Notes: 72 original illustrations; 150 letters to him.

EVANS, ELLICOTT

NY —SYRACUSE UNIVERSITY LIBRARIES, Ernest S Bird Library, George Arents Research Library for Special Collections, Syracuse, 13210. Carolyn A Davis, Manuscripts Librn; Amy S Doherty, University Archivist; Mark F Weimer, Rare Book Librn
Notes: Papers and memorabilia, incl ms writings.

EVANS, EVAN REES, 1856-1956

NY —CORNELL UNIVERSITY LIBRARIES, Collection of Regional History, Dept of Manuscripts and Univ Archives, Ithaca, 14853.
Notes: Presbyterian clergyman. Incl papers, ca 1880- ca 1920; consisting mainly of sermons, sermon outlines and some religious poetry.

EVANS, HENRY

CA —SOLANO COUNTY LIBRARY, John F Kennedy Library, Donovan J McCune Collection, 505 Santa Clara St, Vallejo, 94590.
Notes: The Donovan J McCune Collection (3000) vols //. Incl 32 folios; prints.

EVANS, JAMES

ON —VICTORIA UNIVERSITY, Library, 71 Queen's Park Crescent, Toronto, M5S 1K7, Can. Robert C Brandeis, Chief Librn
Holdings: Vols (1000)// Cat Mss Maps Pix
Notes: Collection consists of books, pamphlets, and government reports mainly dealing with North American Indians and western explorations and missionary enterprises among the Indian tribes in Canada. Incl Indian Bibles and hymnbooks, and mss and vols by Peter Jones (an Indian missionary) and James Evans (inventor of the Cree syllabic alphabet).

EVANS, LUTHER H.

TX —UNIVERSITY OF TEXAS LIBRARIES, General Libraries, Barker Texas History Center, PO Box P, Austin, 78712. Don Carleton, Dir
Notes: Papers, etc, documenting the career of Luther H Evans.

EVANS, MAURICE

NY —HAMPDEN-BOOTH THEATRE LIBRARY AT THE PLAYERS, 16 Gramercy Park, New York, 10003. Louis A Rachow, Librn/Cur
Holdings: Vols 30 Cat Mss Pix
Notes: The Maurice Evans Collection, incl mss, his correspondence, photographs, and playbills. Described in *Theatre & Performing Arts Collections* (New York: Haworth Press, 1981).

NY —NEW YORK PUBLIC LIBRARY, Performing Arts Research Center, Billy Rose Theatre Collection, 111 Amsterdam Ave, New York, 10023. Dorothy L Swerdlove, Cur
Holdings: Cat Mss Pix
Notes: Papers, scrapbooks, mss, photographs, memorabilia, etc.

EVANS, OLIVER

MI —UNIVERSITY OF MICHIGAN, Engineering-Transportation Library, 312 Undergraduate Library, Ann Arbor, 48109. Sharon A Balius, Assoc Librn
Holdings: Mss
Notes: The collection contains the papers of Oliver Evans, 1755-1819. Evans was a millwright and an inventor of the high pressure steam engine in America. The collection is made up of technical drawings, mss, published works by Evans and related secondary materials.

EVANS, RICHARD X.

DC —GEORGETOWN UNIVERSITY, Library, Special Collections Div, 37 & O Sts NW, Washington, 20057. George M Barringer, Special Collections Librn; Nicholas B Sheetz, Mss Librn
Holdings: Mss Cat
Notes: The Richard X Evans Collection. The family archives of Richard X Evans, incl the papers of General John Smith (1750-1836), a member of Congress; Robert Mills (1781-1855); architect; and Alexander Dimitry (1805-1883), educator and diplomat.

EVANS, ROBLEY

MA —MASSACHUSETTS INSTITUTE OF TECHNOLOGY, Institute Archives, Special Collections, Cambridge, 02139.
Holdings: Mss
Notes: The Robley Evans papers, etc.

EVANSVILLE, INDIANA

IN —INDIANA STATE UNIVERSITY, EVANSVILLE, Library, 8600 University Blvd, Evansville, 47712. Gina R Walker, Acting Archivist
Holdings: Cat Mss Pix
Notes: Evansville municipal documents, incl city ordinances, minutes of council sessions, court records, city treasurer's books, Board of Public Works, tax receipts, cemetery records, assessor's records, reports of special commissions. Also Vanderburgh County. Dates incl, 1842 to 1978. Restricted use: noncirculating. Oral history interviews (32 cat cassettes) of Evansville, Indiana natives. These interviews were used in a slide-tape presentation entitles, "Growing Up in Evansville."

EVELYN, JOHN

CA —UNIVERSITY OF CALIFORNIA, LOS ANGELES, William Andrews Clark Memorial Library, 2520 Cimarron St, Los Angeles, 90018.
Holdings: Cat Mss
Notes: Extensive collection; first editions, etc.

MA —HARVARD UNIVERSITY LIBRARY, Houghton Library, Cambridge, 02138. Rodney G Dennis, Cur of Manuscripts
Holdings: Cat Mss

EVELYN, JUDITH, 1913-1967

ON —METROPOLITAN TORONTO LIBRARY, Theatre Dept, 789 Yonge St, Toronto, M4W 2G8, Can. Heather McCallum, Head
Holdings: Vols (30,500) Mss Pix Slides Phonorecords Microforms
Notes: Scrapbooks compiled by the Canadian-born actress document her career (principally in New York) from 1936-61. *See also* entry under Actors and Actresses.

EVELYN, MICHAEL

MA —BOSTON UNIVERSITY, Mugar Memorial Library, Special Collections Dept, 771 Commonwealth Ave, Boston, 02215. Howard B Gotlieb, Dir
Holdings: Cat Mss
Notes: Mss, correspondence, etc collected in depth; incl publications by or about.

EVEN LANGUAGE see Lamut Language

EVENKI LANGUAGE see Tungusic Languages

EVERETT, EDWARD, 1794-1865

NY —CORNELL UNIVERSITY LIBRARIES, Collection of Regional History, Dept of Manuscripts and Univ Archives, Ithaca, 14853.
Notes: Orator, Unitarian clergyman, teacher. Letter to Henry W Longfellow, 1859; 1 item.

EVERETT, HOMER, 1813-1887

OH —RUTHERFORD B HAYES LIBRARY, 1337 Hayes Ave, Fremont, 43420. Watt P Marchman, Dir
Holdings: Vols 75// Cat
Notes: Personal library of Ohio local historian, incl Greek and Roman classics, philosophy, American history. Majority pre-1850 imprints.

EVERETT, PERCY

CA —POMONA PUBLIC LIBRARY, Special Collections, 625 S Garey Ave, PO Box 2271, Pomona, 91766. David Streeter, Librn
Holdings: Cat
Notes: Together, about 100,000 photographs. Burton Frasher collection, 60,000 negatives and prints of California, Arizona, New Mexico, Colorado, Utah, and Nevada, 1920-1940; Loyd Cooper collection, 20,000 negatives and prints of California, 1920-1940; Brooking Tatum, 125 color prints, 50 color 35mm transparencies of California flora; Percy Everett, 4000 color 35mm transparencies of world travels, 1960s.

EVERETT FAMILY

†MA —UNIVERSITY OF MASSACHUSETTS AT AMHERST, Library, Amherst, 01003.
Notes: Microform collections of materials in other American libraries.

EVERGLADES

FL —EVERGLADES NATIONAL PARK, South Florida Research Center, PO Box 279, Homestead, 33030. Gary Hendrix, Librn
Holdings: Vols (5500) Cat Microforms
Notes: Emphasis on South Florida, birds,

EVERGLADES (cont.)

water problems. This is a special reference collection maintained for the Park Staff only. Noncirculating. Estuaries. ILL available.

FL —FLORIDA DEPT OF COMMERCE, Research Library, 408 Fletcher Bldg, Tallahassee, 32301. Dennis Hitchens, Librn
Holdings: Vols (3000) Cat Mss Maps VF
Budget: ($6000)
Notes: Collect materials related to the 2 divisions of the Florida Dept of Commerce: Economic Development and Tourism, incl titles on Florida (historical and current), international trade, transportation, education, employment, management, industrial development and business. The Florida and US documents collection covers population, manufacturing, employment, agriculture, retail trade, wholesale trade and labor. VF incl files on every city and county, especially local economic data, SIC coded material, out-of-state information, county files, Florida specific material and general subject material. 100 VF drawers.

EVERSON, R. G.

BC —UNIVERSITY OF VICTORIA, McPherson Library, Victoria, V8W 3H5, Can.

EVERSON, WILLIAM, 1912-

AZ —UNIVERSITY OF ARIZONA, University Library, Special Collections, Tucson, 85721. Louis A Hieb, Head
Holdings: Vols (7000) Cat Mss Microforms
Budget: ($30,000)
Notes: In the 20th century, the major emphasis is Bukowski, Wakoski, Wilder, Reznikoff, Ginzberg, Ferlinghetti, Snyder, Whalen, Everson, Joyce Carol Oates, and Kurt Vonnegut.

CA —UNIVERSITY OF CALIFORNIA, DAVIS, Shields Library, Dept of Special Collections, Davis, 95616. Donald Kunitz, Head; C Danial Elliott, Asst Head
Notes: Ephemeral and rare post-1946 titles which are experimental or innovative in nature. Incl Bukowski, Dorn, Everson, Ferlinghetti, Ashbery, DiPrima, Snyder, etc.

MO —WASHINGTON UNIVERSITY, John M Olin Library, Campus Box 1061, St Louis, 63130.
Notes: A major collection, incl mss, correspondence, literary papers, photographs, etc. Described in *Special Collections: an Annotated Guide to the Holdings of the Manuscript Division and the University Archives and Research Collection.*

NV —UNIVERSITY OF NEVADA, RENO, University Library, Special Collections Dept, Reno, 89557. Robert E Blesse, Head
Holdings: // Vols (66) Cat Other appearances 160 Cat
Notes: Includes individual works by author in all editions including translations; also prefaces, introductions, published correspondence, appearances in anthologies, periodicals, etc. Bibliographical research collection, part of Modern Authors Collection.

NY —STATE UNIVERSITY OF NEW YORK, STONY BROOK, Melville Library, Dept of Special Collections, Stony Brook, 11794. Evert Volkersz, Head
Holdings: Cat Mss

EVIL SPIRITS see Demonology

EVOLUTION

CA —RANCHO SANTA ANA BOTANIC GARDEN LIBRARY, 1500 N College Ave, Claremont, 91711. Beatrice M Beck, Librn
Holdings: Vols 30,000 Cat Maps Microforms
Notes: Incl emphasis on California flora, floras of the world, evolutionary biology and ethnobotany.

CA —UNIVERSITY OF CALIFORNIA, DAVIS, General Library, Davis, 95616. Bernard Kreissman, University Librn; C Danial Elliott, Asst Head, Dept Special Collections
Holdings: Vols (5000) Cat
Notes: The collection emphasizes general works on genetics, evolution and variation. The collection is particularly strong in works dealing with plant and animal breeding.

CA —UNIVERSITY OF CALIFORNIA, SANTA BARBARA, Library, Dept of Special Collections, Santa Barbara, 93106. Christian F Brun, Head
Holdings: Vols 2000
Notes: History. Critical works.

CT —YALE MEDICAL LIBRARY, 333 Cedar St, New Haven, 06510.
Notes: A special subject emphasis.

FL —ARCHBOLD BIOLOGICAL STATION, Library, Rt 2, Box 180, Lake Placid, 33852. Fred E Lohrer, Librn
Holdings: Vols (2000) Cat Periodicals

IL —FIELD MUSEUM OF NATURAL HISTORY, Library, Roosevelt Rd & Lake Shore Dr, Chicago, 60605. W Peyton Fawcett, Librn; Benjamin W Williams, Assoc Librn
Holdings: Vols (210,000) Cat
Budget: ($100,000)
Notes: Extensive collections--publications of learned societies and institutions and monographic works--in all fields of natural history, with emphasis on taxonomy and evolutionary biology; and on museum publications, American and foreign: anthropology, especially archaeology and ethnology of the Americas, Africa, East Asia, and Oceania; botany, particularly strong for the Americas; geology, chiefly paleontology and meteoritic studies; and zoology, worldwide (birds, fishes, insects, mammals, mollusks, reptiles and amphibians).

MD —MEDICAL & CHIRURGICAL FACULTY OF THE STATE OF MARYLAND, Library, 1211 Cathedral St, Baltimore, 21201. Joseph E Jensen, Librn
Holdings: Vols (10,000) // Cat Mss Maps Pix
See also entry under Medicine - History and Historic

MA —HARVARD UNIVERSITY, Museum of Comparative Zoology, Library, 26 Oxford St, Cambridge, 02138. Eva S Jonas, Librn
Holdings: Vols (230,000) Cat Mss Microforms
Budget: ($336,000)
Notes: Catalog, in 8 vols, published in 1968. For description, see *Harvard Library* Bulletin, VI (1952): pp 202-218. Strong collections on ornithology and entomology, Linneana, and personal papers and archives of Louis Agassiz.

MI —ANDREWS UNIVERSITY, James White Library, Berrien Springs, 49104. Marley H Soper, Dir
Holdings: Cat Mss
Notes: The George McCready Price Collection on the theory of Creation, geology, etc. Much of this material was gathered by this author and educator in preparation for numerous books and pamphlets. He is described as an ardent creationist and a vigorous opponent of the theory of evolution. Over 900 items. Not available by interlibrary loan, but may be used at this library.

NY —NEW YORK BOTANICAL GARDEN LIBRARY, Bronx, 10458. Charles R Long, Asst Vice Pres & Dir
Holdings: Vols 3000 Cat VF
Budget: ($356,000)
Notes: Over 900,000 items, incl books, serials, pamphlets, archives and manuscripts, vertical files, microfiche and microfilm, nursery and seed catalogs, photographs, paintings, prints, drawings and engravings. Covering all areas of botanical sciences.

NY —UNIVERSITY OF ROCHESTER, Rush Rhees Library, Department of Rare Books and Special Collections, Rochester, 14627. Peter Dzwonkoski, Librn
Holdings: Vols Cat
Notes: First editions of Charles Darwin.

NY —UNIVERSITY OF ROCHESTER, Carlson Library, Hutchison Hall, River Campus, Rochester, 14627. Michael W Poulin, Librn
Holdings: Vols (48,720) Cat Microforms
Notes: Strong collection in the field and related areas.

NC —GEO-TECH INTERNATIONAL LTD, Paleontological Research Laboratory, Library, 3616 Garden Club Lane, Charlotte, 28210. Elizabeth Carson, Librn
Holdings: Maps Pix Slides
Notes: Special emphasis on paleontological collection devoted to reprints, source materials, and all current publications and journals on paleoanthropology and evolution.

OH —CLEVELAND MEDICAL LIBRARY ASSOCIATION/CASE WESTERN RESERVE UNIVERSITY, Cleveland Health Sciences Library, Historical Division, Allen Memorial Medical Library, 11000 Euclid Ave, Cleveland, 44106. Glen Jenkins, Rare Book Librarian & Archivist
Holdings: Vols 570 Mss Pix
Notes: The Charles Darwin Collection contains 180 original letters written by Charles Darwin, members of his family and friends. The letters are cataloged. The collection also contains over 250 other items, such as reprints, magazine articles, pamphlets, announcements of centennial celebrations, portraits, etc.

PA —AMERICAN PHILOSOPHICAL SOCIETY, Library, 105 S Fifth St, Philadelphia, 19106. Edward C Carter II, Librn
Holdings: Cat Mss

PA —CARNEGIE LIBRARY OF PITTSBURGH, Science & Technology Dept, 4400 Forbes Ave, Pittsburgh, 15213. Catherine M Brosky, Dept Head
Notes: Of secondary interest in acquisitions because of the department's role in cooperating with Pittsburgh institutions and others across the Commonwealth in sharing resources, the cooperative acquisition of materials, and the provision of services and information. However, some aspects of the subject are emphasized. There are separate entries for each of these specialities in this vol.

VA —UNIVERSITY OF VIRGINIA, Alderman Library, Manuscripts Dept, Charlottesville, 22901. Edmund Berkeley Jr, Cur
Notes: The Paul B Victorius Collection of books on evolution.

ON —UNIVERSITY OF TORONTO, Thomas Fisher Rare Book Library, 120 Saint George St, Toronto, M5S 1A5, Can. Richard G Landon, Head
Holdings: Vols 2000 Uncat
Notes: Darwin Collection is a comprehensive collection of editions of works by Charles Darwin, including separate issues of editions published in his lifetime which show revisions of text; works by predecessors and contemporaries on concepts of evolution and natural selection. Collection described in Landon, R G *Species of Origin* (Toronto, 1971). Holdings listed in Freeman, R B, *Charles Darwin: A Bibliographical Handlist,* 2nd ed (London, 1977).

EWING, CHARLES H.

DC —GEORGETOWN UNIVERSITY, Library, Special Collections Div, 37 & O Sts NW, Washington, 20057. George M Barringer, Special Collections Librn; Nicholas B Sheetz, Mss Librn
Holdings: Mss Cat Pix
Notes: Correspondence, manuscripts, diaries, documents, ledgers, scrapbooks, photographs, and printed material concerning the Ewing and Sherman families. Incl are 10 ALS (1859-1891) from William T Sherman to his daughter Minnie Sherman Fitch and grand-daughter, Eleanor Sherman Fitch; AMs, "Speech at West Point" (1887), written and delivered by Sherman; material from General Charles Ewing, incl leaves from a letter book (1887-1881), diary (1862, 1864); letter written to Thomas Ewing referring to the loss of government money in the retreat from Pilot's Knob; and a Ewing autograph book (1893-96). Also incl are numerous genealogical documents and notes.

EWING, J. H.

OH —OHIO UNIVERSITY, Vernon R Alden Library, Department of Archives and Special Collections, Athens, 45701. Gary A Hunt,

EWING, J. H. (cont.)

Head
Holdings: Vols (1400) Uncat
Notes: A miscellaneous collection of children's books by American and English authors, with most imprint dates in the period 1870-1930; numerous series books. Authors incl Jacob Abbott (196 v), "Oliver Optic" (84 v), Horatio Alger (89 v), J H Ewing (53 v), Martha Finley (47 v), G A Henty (46 v), Frank V Webster (38 v), and many others.

EWING, MAURICE

†NY —COLUMBIA UNIVERSITY LIBRARIES, Butler Library, Rare Book and Manuscript Library, 535 W 114 St, New York, 10027.
Notes: Sir Edward Crisp Bullard's research notes on Maurice Ewing which were the basis for Bullard's memoir. Incl correspondence, drafts, photographs and reprints of Ewing's scientific papers.

†TX —UNIVERSITY OF TEXAS LIBRARIES, General Libraries, Humanities Research Center, PO Box 7219, Austin, 78712. John Chalmers, Librn
Holdings: Mss
Notes: Papers of Maurice Ewing, geophysicist.

EX LIBRIS see Bookplates

EXAMINATIONS

IL —UNIVERSITY OF ILLINOIS, URBANA/CHAMPAIGN, Library, University Archives, 19 Library, 1408 W Gregory Drive, Urbana, 61801. Maynard Brichford, University Archivist
Holdings: Vols (6000) Cat
Budget: $1500
Notes: The Odell Test Collection contains 3150 items comprising intelligence, achievement, subject, and character and personality tests. Almost every educational and psychological test of consequence prior to the early 1950s is included. The collection is located in the Education and Social Science Library and is integrated into a comprehensive collection of current and recent standardized tests. The indexing of the collection follows the scheme created and used by Oscar K Buros in his *Mental Measurement Yearbooks* and in the predecessors to the Yearbooks which appeared in the Rutgers Studies in Education series. The collection was a gift in 1960 of Charles Watters Odell, Professor Emeritus of Education. No photocopying.

NJ —EDUCATIONAL TESTING SERVICE, Carl Campbell Brigham Library, Princeton, 08540. Janet Williams, Librn
Notes: Complete works and papers of Louis L Thurstone, a leading psychometrician of the 20th century.

NY —STATE UNIVERSITY OF NEW YORK, COLLEGE AT BUFFALO, E H Butler Library, 1300 Elmwood Ave, Buffalo, 14222. Jerome Earley, Librn
Notes: The work of J P Guilford, on microfilm, relating to his research on the Structure of the Intellect (SOI) model. 200 reels of microfilm contain the tests, answer sheets, and supporting data for his SOI theory. Corresponds to the Psychological Laboratory Reports at UCLA.

EXCAVATION (CONSTRUCTION)

MS —US ARMY ENGINEER WATERWAYS EXPERIMENT STATION, Library Branch, PO Box 631, Vicksburg, 39180. Bernice Black, Chief Librn
Holdings: Cat Mss Maps Microforms

EXCEPTIONAL CHILDREN

NY —STATE UNIVERSITY OF NEW YORK, COLLEGE AT BUFFALO, E H Butler Library, 1300 Elmwood Ave, Buffalo, 14222. George C Newman, Dir
Holdings: Vols (465,130) Cat Maps Microforms
Budget: ($466,000)
Notes: Fully cataloged collections in education, incl education of exceptional children, art education, social sciences education, etc, are strong since the College was formerly a college of education and approx 60 percent of current graduates still obtain some degree enabling them to teach. Incl Curriculum Laboratory containing courses of study, elementary and secondary textbooks, and collections for children's literature courses (MA in Children's Literature offered). Collection consists of 465,130 volumes incl 64,255 bound periodical volumes, plus 19,120 microfilm reels and 457,988 microtext pieces other than reels. Subscribe to 2263 periodicals.

PQ —HOPITAL SAINTE-JUSTINE POUR LES ENFANTS, Centre d'Information sur la Sante de l'Enfant, 3175 Cote Sainte-Catherine, Montreal, H3T 1C5, Can. Louis LucLecompte, Librn
Holdings: Vols (7000) Cat Audiotapes Videotapes 16mm Films Microforms
Budget: ($11,000)
Notes: 40 percent of collection in French.

EXCHANGE CLUB OF CHARLESTON, S.C.

SC —COLLEGE OF CHARLESTON LIBRARY, Special Collections Dept, Charleston, 29401.
Notes: Papers, incl material regarding the Coastal Carolina Fair (1971-1972).

EXCHANGES, COMMODITY see Commodity Exchanges

EXCHANGES, PRODUCE see Commodity Exchanges

EXCHANGES, STOCK see Stock Exchanges

EXECUTIVES

DC —AMERICAN SOCIETY OF ASSOCIATION EXECUTIVES, Information Central, 1575 Eye St NW, Washington, 20005. Cathy L Lalush, Mgr of Research and Info
Notes: Information regarding association management. Resources are designed to provide the association executive with the background knowledge for management decisions through case studies, research and statistical reports, bibliographies, and articles.

EXECUTIVES, WOMEN see Women in Business

EXERCISE

IL —UNIVERSITY OF ILLINOIS, URBANA/CHAMPAIGN, Library, Applied Life Studies Library, 1408 W Gregory Dr, Urbana, 61801.
Holdings: Vols (38,000) Cat Microforms
See also entry under Physical Education and Training.

PQ —UNIVERSITY OF MONTREAL, Physical Education Library, Montreal, H3C 3J7, Can. Lisa Mayrand, Dir
Holdings: Vols 15,000
Notes: Perhaps Canada's largest university library sports collection. Collection is bilingual (in English and French). 441 periodical subscriptions, 890 periodical titles, 4000 microfiche and 317 microfilms. On line with Ottawa's SIRC data base (qv).

EXERCISES, GYMNASTIC see Gymnastics

EXHAUST CONTROL DEVICES (MOTOR VEHICLES) see Motor Vehicles—Pollution Control Devices

EXHAUST GAS (AUTOMOBILE) see Automobile Exhaust Gas

EXHIBITIONISM, SEXUAL

IN —INDIANA UNIVERSITY, Institute for Sex Research Library, 416 Morrison Hall, Bloomington, 47401. Douglas Freeman, Collections and Services Librn; Joan Brewer, Information Services Librn
Holdings: Vols (62,000) Cat Mss Pix Microforms
See also entry under Sex.

EXHIBITIONS AND EXPOSITIONS

CA —CALIFORNIA STATE UNIVERSITY, FRESNO, Henry Madden Library, Dept of Special Collections, Fresno, 93740. Ronald J Mahoney, Head
Holdings: Vols 1100 Uncat Pix
Notes: Contains published works on all international expositions, 1851-1940. Incl pamphlets, scrapbooks, clippings, sheet music, ephemera and artifacts.

CA —INSTITUTE OF THE AMERICAN MUSICAL, Library, 121 N Detroit St, Los Angeles, 90036. Miles Kreuger, Cur
Holdings: Cat Mss Maps Pix Slides Phonorecords
Notes: Reference materials on the American musical theatre and motion pictures incl thousands of books on theatre, film, broadcasting, world's fairs and other allied areas of showmanship.

CA —CALIFORNIA POLYTECHNIC STATE UNIVERSITY LIBRARY, Special Collections and University Archives, San Luis Obispo, 93407. Nancy E Loe, Head Librn
Holdings: Vols 100 Cat Mss Pix Slides
Notes: The Fairs Collection incl 56,000 ms materials, pix and slides documenting the Western Fairs Association of Sacramento, Calif, and the management and growth of fairs in California and around the world (materials in rough sorting stage). Mss incl correspondence, scrapbooks, legislative opinions and memoranda. 5000 slides; 1000 photographs.

CT —YALE UNIVERSITY, Box 1603A, Yale Station, New Haven, 06520.

DC —SMITHSONIAN INSTITUTION LIBRARIES, National Museum of American History Branch, Washington, 20560. Rhoda S Ratner, Branch Librn
Holdings: Vols (369,650) Cat Mss Maps Pix Slides Microforms

IL —CHICAGO HISTORICAL SOCIETY, Library, Clark St at North Ave, Chicago, 60614. Robert L Brubaker, Librn
Holdings: Vols (150,000) Cat Mss Maps Pix Broadsides
Notes: The Society has nearly everything published about the World's Columbian Expositions, 1893, and the Century of Progress International Exposition, 1933-1934; and much concerning other expositions in Chicago.

IL —CHICAGO PUBLIC LIBRARY, Special Collections Div, Cultural Center, 78 E Washington St, Chicago, 60602. Laura Linard, Cur
Holdings: Vols (300) Cat Mss Pix Slides
Notes: The Chicago Public Library received deposit copies of World's Columbian Exposition publications from the Department of Publicity and Promotion, several of which are still uncataloged and not included in the NUC-Pre 1956 Imprints. The Papers of James W Ellsworth, prominent Chicago financier and member of the Board of Directors of the Exposition, are here; a finding aid to these papers has been prepared in 1978. Outstanding items in the World's Columbian collections are described in *Treasures of the Chicago Public Library*, compiled by Thomas A Orlando and Marie Gecik, 1977, pp 111-20.

IL —MUSEUM OF SCIENCE AND INDUSTRY, Library, 57th St and Lake Shore Dr, Chicago, 60637. Carla Hayden, Coordinator
Holdings: Vols (15,000) Cat Maps Pix Slides
Budget: ($10,000)
Notes: Occupying the site of the Fine Arts Building of Chicago's Columbian Exposition of 1893, the Museum Library has been the recipient of numerous gifts in this field, not only of materials from Chicago's Columbian Expositions, Century of Progress and Railroad Fairs but also from the New York World's Fair, St Louis, Paris Exposition

EXHIBITIONS AND EXPOSITIONS (cont.)

Universelle, San Francisco's Panama-Pacific etc. Incl blueprints of some buildings and areas. No separate catalog or index to this extensive collection.

IL —NORTHWESTERN UNIVERSITY, Library, Special Collections Dept, 1937 Sheridan Rd, Evanston, 60201. R Russell Maylone, Cur
Holdings: Vols 5300
Notes: Exhibitions catalogs and ephemera arranged by artist, period, group, or collection. Additional material cataloged for general collection.

†IN —PURDUE UNIVERSITY LIBRARIES, Krannert Library, West Lafayette, 47907.
Notes: Books, journals and pamphlets covering early literature of economic thought and business practives in America and abroad, 1500-1870.

MD —UNIVERSITY OF MARYLAND, Architecture Library, College Park, 20742. Berna E Neal, Architecture Librn
Holdings: Vols (24,000) Cat
Budget: $30,000
Notes: Incl 600 vol collection on world expositions, 1851-1937. There is a slide collection independent of the library, curated by Elizabeth Alley.

MA —HARVARD UNIVERSITY, Baker Library of the Graduate School of Business Administration, Kress Library of Business and Economics, Soldiers Field, Boston, 02163. Ruth E Rogers, Cur
Holdings: Cat Mss Microforms
Notes: See *Technology & Culture,* XIII (1972), 465-486, and *Kress Library Bulletin,* 7 (1971).

MA —HARVARD UNIVERSITY, Graduate School of Design, Frances Loeb Library, Gund Hall, Cambridge, 02138. James Hodgson, Librn
Holdings: Cat Mss Microforms
Notes: *Catalogue* of Library published 1968 (44 vols), with *Supplment,* 1970.

NY —BUFFALO & ERIE COUNTY HISTORICAL SOCIETY, 25 Nottingham Court, Buffalo, 14216. Herman Sass, Librn

NY —NEW YORK PUBLIC LIBRARY, Research Libraries, General Research Division, Fifth Ave & 42 St, New York, 10018. Rodney Phillips, Chief
Holdings: Vols (2,225,000) Cat Maps Pix Microforms
Budget: ($775,718)

NY —MARGARET WOODBURY STRONG MUSEUM, 1 Manhattan Square, Rochester, 14607.
Holdings: Vols (20,000) Periodicals
Notes: The Margaret Woodbury Strong Museum Library contains a collection of approx 20,000 books, periodicals and ephemera of and concerning the 19th and early 20th centuries. A large part of the library's holdings reflect the interests of Margaret Strong and her family: domestic life and literature of the 19th century and world travel, with particular emphasis on the Orient. The library's resources are available to all visitors for research. Book stacks and rare book storage are not open for browsing and do not circulate, but facilities are provided in reading room for study.

PA —LIBRARY COMPANY OF PHILADELPHIA, 1314 Locust St, Philadelphia, 19107. Edwin Wolf II, Librn; Kenneth Finkel, Cur of Prints
Holdings: 2500 Prints
Notes: Incl 2500 prints by Joseph J Kelly's firm, The Photo-Illustrators; with a large proportion on the Sesquicentennial and other Philadelphia views.

EXHIBITS see Exhibitions and Expositions

EXHUMATION

NY —NEW YORK ACADEMY OF MEDICINE, Library, 2 E 103 St, New York, 10029. Brett A Kirkpatrick, Librn
Holdings: Vols Cat
Notes: The Fenwick Beekman Collection on Burke and Hare, the criminals of 1829.

EXILES, POLITICAL

NY —STATE UNIVERSITY OF NEW YORK AT ALBANY, Library, Special Collections Dept, 1400 Washington Ave, Albany, 12222. Marion P Munzer, Coordr
Holdings: Mss
Notes: 370 linear feet of mss; papers and personal libraries of 67 German-speaking emigres who came to the United States from 1933-1945. Collections of faculty members of the "University in Exile" of the New School for Social Research form the core. Major collections are: American Council for Emigres in the Professions, Ludwig Bachhofer, Vicki Baum, Erwin Bodky, Arnold Brecht, Emergency Rescue Committee, Helmut Hirsch, Erich Hula, Jugendbewegung, Ernst Jünger, Erich von Kahler, Emil Lederer, Hans Natonek, Hans Neisser, Fritz Neugass, Karl Otto Paetel, Yella Pessl, Richard Plant, Hans Simons, Hans Staudinger, Storm Publishers Archive, Hans Tischler, Widerstand. There are separate entries for each of these in this volume.

EXISTENTIALISM

NY —NEW SCHOOL FOR SOCIAL RESEARCH, Raymond Fogelman Library, 65 Fifth Ave, New York, 10003. Michael Lordi, Director
Holdings: Mss
Notes: The papers, etc, of Edmund Husserl. Copies of unpublished notebooks.

EXLEY, FREDERICK

NY —UNIVERSITY OF ROCHESTER, Rush Rhees Library, Department of Rare Books and Special Collections, Rochester, 14627. Peter Dzwonkoski, Librn
Holdings: Vols Cat Mss
Notes: Complete extant archive including manuscripts, drafts, proofs and correspondence.

EXPANSION (U.S. POLITICS) see Imperialism

EXPATRIATE WRITERS, AMERICAN

IL —SOUTHERN ILLINOIS UNIVERSITY, CARBONDALE, Delyte W Morris Library, Special Collections Dept, Carbondale, 62901. David V Koch, Cur of Special Collections; Louisa Bowen, Cur of Manuscripts
Holdings: Vols (5000) Cat Mss Pix
Notes: Some 300 American and British avant-garde authors are represented in the expatriate collection: books, little magazines, letters, photographs and manuscripts. The holdings are a composite of the Philip Kaplan collection and the archives of the Black Sun Press, supplemented by other gifts and purchases. Collection incl several thousand letters from such writers as Richard Aldington, Djuna Barnes, Samuel Beckett, Maxwell Bodenheim, Kay Boyle, Bob Brown (extensive file of personal papers), Harry and Caresse Crosby, Nancy Cunard, Floyd Dell, Lawrence Durrell, James T Farrell, Robert Graves, D H Lawrence, Robert McAlmon, Henry Miller, Ezra Pound, Gertrude Stein, Dylan Thomas and William Carlos Williams. There are 75 mss and 5 diaries representing Kay Boyle, Hart Crane, Montgomery Evans, Ford Maddox Ford, Ernest Hemingway, John Dos Passos and Edmund Wilson.Additional materials of Henry Miller, Robert McAlmon and Nancy Cunard have been acquired. (Earl Tannenbaum, *D H Lawrence; an Exhibition...,* 1958).

MA —BRANDEIS UNIVERSITY, Goldfarb Library, 415 South St, Waltham, 02154. Bessie Hahn, Dir
Notes: Henry James Collection. Contains 24 linear ft of first editions of Henry James as well as books about Henry James. Access to the collection is through the Special Collections Catalog.

NY —ADELPHI UNIVERSITY, Library, Garden City, 11530. Jerome Yavarkovsky, Dean of Libraries
Holdings: Vols 149 Cat Mss
Notes: Expatriate American writers of the 1920s and 1930s, with primary emphasis on the works of Gertrude Stein and Laura Riding Jackson.

EXPATRIATE WRITERS, BRITISH

CT —LEE ASH, (personal collection), 66 Humiston Dr, Bethany, 06525.
Notes: A large collection of Baron Corvo's 1st editions, English and American, incl *Tarcissus,* and what is probably the only signed Corvo painting in the Western Hemisphere. Much ephemeral material and books, etc relating to Corvo. No mss materials.

IL —SOUTHERN ILLINOIS UNIVERSITY, CARBONDALE, Delyte W Morris Library, Special Collections Dept, Carbondale, 62901. David V Koch, Cur of Special Collections; Louisa Bowen, Cur of Manuscripts
Holdings: Vols (5000) Cat Mss Pix
Notes: Some 300 American and British avant-garde authors are represented in the expatriate collection: books, little magazines, letters, photographs and manuscripts. The holdings are a composite of the Philip Kaplan collection and the archives of the Black Sun Press, supplemented by other gifts and purchases. Collection incl several thousand letters from such writers as Richard Aldington, Djuna Barnes, Samuel Beckett, Maxwell Bodenheim, Kay Boyle, Bob Brown (extensive file of personal papers), Harry and Caresse Crosby, Nancy Cunard, Floyd Dell, Lawrence Durrell, James T Farrell, Robert Graves, D H Lawrence, Robert McAlmon, Henry Miller, Ezra Pound, Gertrude Stein, Dylan Thomas and William Carlos Williams. There are 75 mss and 5 diaries representing Kay Boyle, Hart Crane, Montgomery Evans, Ford Maddox Ford, Ernest Hemingway, John Dos Passos and Edmund Wilson.Additional materials of Henry Miller, Robert McAlmon and Nancy Cunard have been acquired. (Earl Tannenbaum, *D H Lawrence; an Exhibition...,* 1958).

EXPATRIATE WRITERS, CUBAN

FL —UNIVERSITY OF MIAMI, Otto G Richter Library, PO Box 248214, Coral Gables, 33124. Frank Rodgers, Dir of Libraries
Notes: The Cuban exile periodicals incl 412 titles of which 381 have been published in Miami, Florida. The archival material incl 54 cubic feet of mss, invitations, programs, broadsides, posters, postcards, prints, reports, maps, etc. This collection incl personal and corporate papers of Cubans settled in the US or in other countries. The truth about Cuban Committee Papers: 40 cubic feet. Contains records and correspondence of intellectual and professional Cuban and American leaders in the US dedicated to the course of eliminating Communism from the Western Hemisphere.

EXPATRIATES IN PORTUGAL

OK —UNIVERSITY OF TULSA, McFarlin Library, Dept of Rare Books and Special Collections, 600 S College, Tulsa, 74104. David Farmer, Dir; Toby Murray, Archivist; Caroline Swinson, Cur of Manuscripts & Art
Holdings: Vols 2500
Notes: The only known extant lending library from the 19th century. It was formed by British subjects in Oporto, Portugal between 1820-1890. 70 percent not in Sadlier.

EXPEDITIONS

AZ —NORTHERN ARIZONA UNIVERSITY, Special Collection Library, CU Box 6022, Flagstaff, 86011. Peter M Whiteley, Coordr/Archivist; William Mullane, Librn
Notes: (1) William J Floyd Collection: Floyd was surgeon of E F Beale's wagon road expedition from Ft Smith Arkansas to the

EXPEDITIONS (cont.)

Colorado River; incl diary, 1858-1859. Original in Henry E Huntington Library. (2) Wyant Alexander Collection; diary of Wyant's journey with photographer Tim O'Sullivan as part of the Wheeler Expedition through Northeastern Arizona and Southern Utah and New Mexico, 1873. Wyant was an artist.

NY —AMERICAN MUSEUM OF NATURAL HISTORY, Library Services Dept, Central Park W & 79th St, New York, 10024. Nina J Root, Chairwoman; Mary Genett, Asst Librn for Reference Services
Notes: The Photographic Collection consist of over 500,000 black-and-white prints and almost 50,000 color transparencies and slides in this and many other subjects. Many from Museum expeditions and fieldwork. Examples of human beings, scenery, animals, plants and minerals from all over the world, as well as visual documentation of scientific phenomena. Subject areas covered incl anthropology, archeology, astronomy, some botany, ecology, geography and travel, geology, the history of natural history, mineralogy, gemstones, paleontology, fossils, primitive art, scientists, and zoology.

EXPEDITIONS—PICTURES, ILLUSTRATIONS, ETC.

NY —AMERICAN MUSEUM OF NATURAL HISTORY, Library Services Dept, Central Park W & 79th St, New York, 10024. Nina J Root, Chairwoman; Mary Genett, Asst Librn for Reference Services
Notes: The Photographic Collection consist of over 500,000 black-and-white prints and almost 50,000 color transparencies and slides in this and many other subjects. Many from Museum expeditions and fieldwork. Examples of human beings, scenery, animals, plants and minerals from all over the world, as well as visual documentation of scientific phenomena. Subject areas covered incl anthropology, archeology, astronomy, some botany, ecology, geography and travel, geology, the history of natural history, mineralogy, gemstones, paleontology, fossils, primitive art, scientists, and zoology.

EXPEDITIONS, ANTARCTIC see Antarctic Regions

EXPEDITIONS, ARCTIC see Arctic Regions

EXPEDITIONS, SCIENTIFIC see Scientific Expeditions

EXPERIMENTAL ANIMALS see Laboratory Animals

EXPERIMENTAL MEDICINE see Medicine, Experimental

EXPERIMENTAL MOVING PICTURES see Moving Pictures, Experimental

EXPERIMENTAL PHARMACOLOGY see Pharmacology, Experimental

EXPERIMENTAL PHYSICS

CA —CALIFORNIA INSTITUTE OF TECHNOLOGY, Robert A Millikan Memorial Library, Archives, 1201 E California Blvd, Pasadena, 91125. Judith R Goodstein, Archivist
Holdings: Vols (3000) Cat Mss Maps Pix Slides Phonorecords Audiotapes Videotapes 16mm Films Microforms
Notes: Ms sources for the history of astrophysics, cosmology, mathematical physics, experimental physics, radio astronomy, geophysics and biophysics. Collections incl the papers of: George Ellery Hale, Jesse Greenstein, H P Robertson, Richard Feynman, Paul Epstein, Max Delbruck, and Beno Gutenberg. Candid photos of physicists at meetings; etchings and photographs of Einstein; scientific medals; selected pieces of scientific apparatus (including the oil-drop machine constructed by Millikan at Caltech in the early 1920s); the reprint collection of Paul Epstein; over 3000 landmark books in the history of 20th century physics and mathematics. Printed publications include: Daniel Kevles, *Guide to the Microfilm Edition of the George Ellery Hale Papers* (Pasadena, Carnegie Institute of Washington and Caltech), 1968; Judith R Goodstein,*The Robert Andrews Millikan Collection at the California Institute of Technology: Guide to a Microfilm Edition* (Pasadena, Caltech), 1977; Judith R Goodstein and Carolyn Kopp, *The Theodore von Karman Collections at the California Institute of* Technology (Pasadena, Archives), 1981.

EXPERIMENTAL POETRY

CA —UNIVERSITY OF CALIFORNIA, DAVIS, Shields Library, Dept of Special Collections, Davis, 95616. Donald Kunitz, Head; C Danial Elliott, Asst Head
Holdings: Vols 4700 Cat
Notes: Ephemeral and rare post-1946 titles which are experimental or innovative in nature. Incl Bukowski, Dorn, Everson, Ferlinghetti, Ashbery, DiPrima, Snyder, etc.

EXPERIMENTAL PSYCHOLOGY see Psychology, Physiological

EXPERIMENTAL THEATRE

CA —CALIFORNIA INSTITUTE OF THE ARTS, Library, 24700 McBean Pkwy, Valencia, 91355. James Elrod, Dir
Holdings: Vols (61,000) Cat
Budget: ($4500)

EXPLORATION AND DISCOVERY see Discovery and Exploration

EXPLORATION OF THE DEEP SEA see Marine Biology; Marine Fauna; Marine Flora

EXPLORERS

CA —UNIVERSITY OF CALIFORNIA, SAN DIEGO, Central University Library, Mandeville Dept of Special Collections, La Jolla, 92093. Lynda Corey Claassen, Head
Holdings: Vols (2400) Cat Mss Maps
Notes: The Hill Collection of Pacific Voyages, including reports and commentaries of important voyages in the Pacific, from those of Magellan and Sir Francis Drake to exploration through the first half of the 19th century. Includes many rare overland accounts to the Pacific across North America, Mexico, and Panama. Bibliography: Silveira de Braganza, Ronald, *The Hill Collection of Pacific Voyages* (La Jolla: Calif, 1974-1983).

CA —UNIVERSITY OF CALIFORNIA, LOS ANGELES, Research Library, African Studies Collection, 405 Hilgard Ave, Los Angeles, 90024. Edward Shreeves, Chairman, Bibliographers Group; Joseph J Lauer, African Studies Bibliographer
Holdings: Maps Pix Slides Phonorecords Audiotapes Microforms
Notes: General collection mainly in the humanities and social sciences, covering prehistoric times to the present. Particular strengths include: early travel and exploration, mission field, literature, vernacular languages and literatures, Portuguese Africa, slavery (have the British Foreign Office's *General Correspondence. Slave Trade* on microfilm). Extensive holdings of journals, newspapers and government publications. The collection was described in the *Handbook of American Resources for African Studies* (1967).

DC —CATHOLIC UNIVERSITY OF AMERICA, Mullen Library, ICOR/Semitics Library, Room 20, Washington, 20064. Monica J Blanchard, Librn
Notes: The bulk of the ICOR/Semitics Library collection belongs to the Institute of Christian Oriental Research which supports the work of the Corpus Scriptorum Christianorum Orientalium. The holdings are chiefly concerned with Christian Egypt and the Coptic Church, Syriac and Syrian patristic studies, and the Syriac and Arabic speaking eastern churches. There are less extensive holdings of Ethiopic, Armenian and Georgian material. ICOR titles are cataloged by the ICOR/Semitic Library, and ICOR holdings do not appear in the general catalogue of the University Library.

DC —NATIONAL GEOGRAPHIC SOCIETY, Library, 1146 16th St NW, Washington, 20036. Susan Fifer Canby, Dir
Holdings: Vols (63,000) Cat Mss Maps Pix
Notes: Material concerning land, sea, and space exploration--past and present. All fields of anthropology, natural history, geography, etc.

FL —UNIVERSITY OF MIAMI, Otto G Richter Library, PO Box 248214, Coral Gables, 33124. Frank Rodgers, Dir of Libraries
Holdings: Mss Maps Pix
Notes: The rare Floridiana collection incl a great variety of primary source materials such as mss, maps, photographs, scrapbooks, correspondence, clippings, etc. Particular subject strengths in this collection incl: Spanish exploration and colonialization of Florida, the Florida Indians, wildlife conservation, landscaping, corporate records, etc. The rare Floridiana collection is complemented by a collection of titles ranging from the oldest to the very latest published books on Florida subjects.

HI —BERNICE P BISHOP MUSEUM, Library, PO Box 19000-A, Honolulu, 96819. Cynthia Timberlake, Librn
Notes: Early voyages, natural and general history, archaeology, and ethnology of the Pacific area. Hawaiian materials incl mss, maps, 360,000 photographs dating from 1845, and Hawaiian language newspapers.

IN —INDIANA UNIVERSITY, Lilly Library, Seventh St, Bloomington, 47405. William R Cagle, Librn
Holdings: Cat
Notes: First and early printings of 15th through 17th century European voyages to the western hemisphere, incl such collections as the *Decades of Peter Martyr,* and *Grands* and *Petits Voyages* gathered by DeBry, and Hakluyt's *Principall Navigations;* travels to the Orient, incl first printed account of Marco Polo; the Portuguese in India from the time of the arrival of Vasco da Gama; 18th century voyages by Captain James Cook, Le Comte de Laperouse and others; and the great scientific expeditions of the 18th and 19th centuries.

ME —BOWDOIN COLLEGE, Library, Brunswick, 04011. Dianne M Gutscher, Cur of Special Collections
Holdings: Vols 4000 Cat Mss Maps Pix
Notes: The papers (about 15,000 items) of Robert A Bartlett, arctic explorer and shipmaster for Admirals Robert E Peary and Donald B MacMillan, contain 10,000 mss, 23,000 photographs, clippings, diaries, 300 maps, logbooks and some printed material relating to Bartlett's arctic voyages. Also, Admiral MacMillan's personal library of about 4000 books relating to arctic exploration, several volumes of clippings, numerous scrapbooks, ms diaries, logbooks, and journals, photographs, maps, and other records.

MA —BRANDEIS UNIVERSITY, Goldfarb Library, 415 South St, Waltham, 02154. Bessie Hahn, Dir
Notes: McKew-Parr Collection on Magellan and the Age of Discovery. Approx 4000 books relating to Magellan and Columbus and other voyagers of the 15th and early 16th century. A card catalog to the collection is located in Special Collections.

MI —UNIVERSITY OF MICHIGAN, Library, Dept of Rare Books & Special Collections, Ann Arbor, 48109. Robert J Starring, Head
Holdings: Cat Mss Maps Pix
Notes: Includes over 100 books, mostly autographed presentation copies from polar explorers to donor William H Hobbs, and 62 scrapbooks, notebooks albums, and made-up

EXPLORERS (cont.)

volumes of pamphlets, documents and correspondence, 11 relating to Admiral Peary. Also there are such primary records from Professor Hobbs's own expeditions as his journals, radio logs, purchase requisitions, pilot balloon ascension reports and graphs, and anemoscope records. In addition there are an estimated 3500 items of correspondence with explorers and other notables, 800 photographs, and maps.

MI —OLIVET COLLEGE, Burrage Library, Olivet, 49076. Chris Miko, Dir
Holdings: Vols (2000) Cat
Notes: The collection consists primarily of early printed voyages of the arctic and antarctic from the earliest times to the mid-20th century.

MN —UNIVERSITY OF MINNESOTA, James Ford Bell Library, 309 19th Ave S, Minneapolis, 55455. John Parker, Cur
Holdings: Vols (11,000) Cat Mss Maps
Notes: Collection of original materials relating to European expansion, 1400-1800.

NY —AMERICAN MUSEUM OF NATURAL HISTORY, Library Services Dept, Central Park W & 79th St, New York, 10024. Nina J Root, Chairwoman; Mary Genett, Asst Librn for Reference Services
Holdings: Vols (385,000) Cat Mss Maps Pix Slides Microforms
Notes: Nearly all collections are outstanding for depth of coverage and international range. Early and historic works, rare books, colored illustrations, and relevant serial publications supplement the modern scientific publications necessary to the researches of the scientific staff and the work of the educational division. Open to the public.

NY —EXPLORERS CLUB, James B Ford Memorial Library, 46 E 70 St, New York, 10021. Janet Baldwin, Librn
Holdings: Vols (24,000) Cat Maps
Notes: Additions to the collection depend upon gifts. Access by appointment only.

NY —NEW YORK SOCIETY LIBRARY, 53 E 79 St, New York, 10021. Mark Piel, Librn
Holdings: 3500 Vols
Notes: Travel and world explorers in 19th century.

NC —DUKE UNIVERSITY, William R Perkins Library, Rare Book Room, Durham, 27706. John L Sharpe, III, Cur
Holdings: Vols 1000
Notes: Collection of various accounts of voyages and scientific expeditions, primarily in the 18th and 19th centuries.

OH —CLEVELAND PUBLIC LIBRARY, History and Geography Department, 325 Superior Ave, Cleveland, 44114. JoAnn Petrello, Head
Holdings: Cat Maps
Notes: Collection incl rare books, especially Americana, Canadiana, Latin Americana; 19th century European travelers; Arctic and Antarctic voyages.

PA —PENNSYLVANIA STATE UNIVERSITY, Fred Lewis Pattee Library, University Park, 16802. Stuart Forth, Dean of Libraries
Holdings: Vols Cat Maps
Notes: Based primarily on an interest in Australia and the Pacific Ocean, the Pennsylvania State University Libraries have developed a strong collection of voyages, including many 17th and 18th century editions of specific voyages, eg, Cook, La Perouse, Vancouver, collected editions both French and English, together with related publications, eg, De Brosses, Dalrymple. The collections include both exploration and scientific voyages in original editions and reprints.

RI —PROVIDENCE ATHENAEUM, 251 Benefit St, Providence, 02903. Sally Duplaix, Dir
Holdings: Vols 12,500 cat
Notes: Concentration is on the 18th and 19th centuries, worldwide in coverage. Incl many scientific expedition accounts. Approx 3000 may be catagorized as rare books/special collections. The library projects a Short Title Catalogue of its rarer holdings in this area within the next few years.

UT —UNIVERSITY OF UTAH, Marriott Library, Special Collections, Salt Lake City, 84112. Gregory C Thompson, Cur
Notes: Exploration of the West.

VA —UNIVERSITY OF VIRGINIA, Alderman Library, Manuscripts Dept, Charlottesville, 22901. Edmund Berkeley Jr, Cur
Holdings: Cat Mss Pix
Notes: Papers of Edwin Swift Balch, author of *The North Pole* and *Bradley Land*, and *Antarctica*, and authority on the Cook-Peary controversy incl scrapbooks and correspondence.

WA —UNIVERSITY OF WASHINGTON LIBRARIES, Pacific Northwest Collection, Seattle, 98195. Andrew F Johnson, Librn
Holdings: Vols (50,000) Cat Maps Pix
Budget: ($12,000)
Notes: The Pacific Northwest Collection contains printed materials documenting the historic and contemporary life and culture of the region in a broad range of subject areas. The Pacific Northwest is defined as the geographic region including Washington, Oregon, Idaho, Montana, British Columbia, Yukon Territory, and Alaska. Printed materials including books, periodicals, government documents, maps, weekly and local regional newspapers, theses and dissertations, as well as photographs and architectural drawings are included in the Pacific Northwest Collection. Photographic works of over 200 photographers active in the Pacific Northwest, Alaska, and the Yukon Territory (Canada) during the period 1860-1930, including Asahel and Edward S Curtis, Eric Hegg, and Clark Kinsey, are represented in a print collection of more than 300,000 images. The architecturaldrawings collection includes over 19,000 original plans, drawings, sketches, renderings and blue prints pertaining to the history of architecture and urban planning and landscape gardening in the Pacific Northwest ca 1880-1940. Areas of particular strength are the holdings of over 1100 published journals of Pacific Northwest exploration expeditions, photographs of Northwest Coast Native Americans and of historic Seattle, newspapers issued within the Japanese-American relocation camps, 1942-1945, materials relating to the 1980 eruption of Mt St Helens, and Sanborne fire insurance maps for Washington. A unique feature of the Collection is the subject index to regional periodicals and local newspapers maintained by the PNW Collection staff; over 100 titles are currently indexed. G K Hall Company published a books catalog of the Pacific Northwest Collectionin 1973.

WI —UNIVERSITY OF WISCONSIN, MILWAUKEE, American Geographical Society Collection, 2311 E Hartford Ave, PO Box 399, Milwaukee, 53201. Roman Drazniowsky, Cur
Holdings: Vols (196,800)
Budget: ($270,000)
Notes: The largest special collection in the field of geography, cartography, and related fields in the Western Hemisphere. Incl 6469 atlases; 385,610 maps; 72 globes; 33,700 pamphlets; 79,000 photographs; 99,000 Landsat Images. Catalog published by G K Hall, Boston.

AB —PETER WHYTE FOUNDATION, Archives of the Canadian Rockies, Box 160, Banff, T0L 0C0, Can. Mary Andrews, ACR Librn
Holdings: Vols (4247) Cat Mss Maps Pix Slides Phonorecords Audiotapes Videotapes 16mm Films Filmstrips Microforms
Budget: ($1500)
Notes: Collect all available material which touches on the Rocky Mountains of Canada (from the US border to the Peace River in the north; from the west of Calgary on the east to the town of Revelstoke, BC on the west). This material incl history (the early explorers, Indians, construction of the railroads, mountaineering, and development of the national parks), natural history (geology, botany, wildlife) and poetry and fiction with the Rockies as a setting. Collect maps of the area, photographs, tape recordings of the pioneers. We also house on our premises the Alpine Club of Canada's library, which is one of the most comprehensive collections on the subject of mountaineering worldwide. Noncirculating.

ON —PUBLIC ARCHIVES OF CANADA, Library, 395 Wellington St, Ottawa, K1A 0N3, Can. Dawn E Monroe, Collections Development Officer
Holdings: Vols (80,000) Cat Mss Maps
Notes: The sixteenth and seventeenth centuries were times when explorers from the great European nations set out in search of new trade routes to the spices and silks of the Orient, only to fine themselves at the door of an unknown universe. This "age of discovery" was a period of progressive exploration of what later became Canada's Atlantic coast. It was a time when enterprising individuals attempted to turn this unexplored territory into a new colony where a nation could take root and grow. The attraction of this period for researchers has led to the discovery of an incredible number of scholarly works. The Public Archives Library, which has a large number of these printed documents in its collection, can also provide researchers with a number of finding aids, incl bibliographies, historical atlases, inventories of archives and lists of documents.

ON —VICTORIA UNIVERSITY, Library, 71 Queen's Park Crescent, Toronto, M5S 1K7, Can. Robert C Brandeis, Chief Librn
Holdings: Vols (1000) // Cat Mss Maps Pix
Notes: Collection consists of books, pamphlets, and government reports mainly dealing with North American Indians, western explorations and missionary enterprises among the Indian tribes in Canada. Incl Indian Bibles and hymnbooks, and mss and vols by Peter Jones (an Indian missionary) and James Evans (inventor of the Cree syllabic alphabet).

EXPLORERS—PICTURES, ILLUSTRATIONS, ETC.

NY —AMERICAN MUSEUM OF NATURAL HISTORY, Library Services Dept, Central Park W & 79th St, New York, 10024. Nina J Root, Chairwoman; Mary Genett, Asst Librn for Reference Services
Notes: The Photographic Collection consist of over 500,000 black-and-white prints and almost 50,000 color transparencies and slides in this and many other subjects. Many from Museum expeditions and fieldwork. Examples of human beings, scenery, animals, plants and minerals from all over the world, as well as visual documentation of scientific phenomena. Subject areas covered incl anthropology, archeology, astronomy, some botany, ecology, geography and travel, geology, the history of natural history, mineralogy, gemstones, paleontology, fossils, primitive art, scientists, and zoology.

EXPLORERS, AMERICAN

†WA —WASHINGTON STATE UNIVERSITY, Library, Manuscripts, Archives & Special Collections, Pullman, 99164. John F Guido, Head
Holdings: Cat Mss Maps Pix
Notes: The Carl Parcher Russell papers, a vast resource (24,916 items; 45 linear feet) on American Indian and Western pioneer activities and artifacts. Much on the fur trade; pioneer life; mountain men and trapping; wildlife; primitive life in detail. Also the National Park Service, parks, monuments, etc. Described in *Carl Parcher Russell: An Indexed Register of His Scholarly and Professional Papers, 1920-1967, in the Washington State University* Library (Pullman, 1970) 149 pp.

EXPLOSIVES

DE —HAGLEY MUSEUM AND LIBRARY, Eleutherian Mills-Hagley Foundation Inc,

EXPLOSIVES (cont.)

PO Box 3630, Greenville, 19807. Richmond D Williams, Dir; Heddy A Richter, Imprints Librn
Holdings: Vols 1200 Pamphlets
Notes: The Oscar Guttman Collection of books and pamphlets relating to explosives concentrates on early pritned works on explosives and pyrotechnics.

MS —US ARMY ENGINEER WATERWAYS EXPERIMENT STATION, Library Branch, PO Box 631, Vicksburg, 39180. Bernice Black, Chief Librn
Holdings: Vols (350,000) Cat Mss Maps Microforms

NM —UNIVERSITY OF CALIFORNIA, Los Alamos National Laboratory, Libraries, PO Box 1663, MSP 362, Los Alamos, 87545. J Arthur Freed, Head Librn
Holdings: Vols (800,000) Cat Films Microforms
Budget: ($700,000)
Notes: Incl 500,000 classified and unclassified reports. There are 25 branch libraries and a central collection. The Medical Library contains about 40,000 vols in the areas of biomedical research.

PA —FRANKLIN INSTITUTE LIBRARY, 20 & The Parkway, Philadelphia, 19103. Miriam Padusis, Dir; Charles Wilt, Readers Servs Librn
Holdings: Vols (300,000) Cat Maps Pix Microforms

EXPLOSIVES—HISTORY

DE —HAGLEY MUSEUM AND LIBRARY, Eleutherian Mills-Hagley Foundation Inc, PO Box 3630, Greenville, 19807. Richmond D Williams, Dir; Heddy A Richter, Imprints Librn
Notes: The Oscar Guttman Collection of books and pamphlets relating to explosives concentrates on early printed works on explosives and pyrotechnics.

RI —BROWN UNIVERSITY, John Hay Library, 20 Prospect St, Providence, 02912. Mark N Brown, Cur Mss
Holdings: / / Mss
Notes: Papers of Walter Nickerson Hill, American chemist, incl correspondence, letters, autograph drafts of articles for scientific journals, lectures, letterpress copy books, scrapbook with inserted ALS, pamphlets, photographs, and memorabilia. The correspondence deals with personal, familial, and business matters (the latter during Hill's tenure as instructor in explosives at the US Torpedo Station in Newport, RI, and while he was chief chemist for the Rapauno Nitroglycerine Works, near Philadelphia, owned by the duPont Family). There is scientific correspondence between Hill and leading scientists, ordnance specialists, and influential figures. See also Papers of Augustus W Smith, Hill's father-in-law, also at Brown.

EXPORTS see Commerce

EXPOSITIONS see Exhibitions and Expositions

EXPRESSIONISM see Art, Expressionistic

EXPULSION see U.S.-Emigration and Immigration

EXTEMPORIZATION (MUSIC) see Improvisation (Music)

EXTERMINATION, JEWISH, 1939-1945 see Holocaust, Jewish, 1939-1945

EXTRASENSORY PERCEPTION (ESP)

AZ —WORLD UNIVERSITY, Library, 711 E Blacklidge Dr, Tucson, 85719. Howard John Zitko, Cur
Holdings: Vols (15,000) Cat Mss Maps Audiotapes
Notes: Collection concerns what are generally called the "frontier sciences". No interlibrary loan.

IL —UNIVERSITY OF ILLINOIS, URBANA/CHAMPAIGN, Library, University Archives, 19 Library, 1408 W Gregory Drive, Urbana, 61801. Maynard Brichford, University Archivist
Holdings: Vols (5000) Cat
Budget: ($7000)
Notes: The Mandeville Collection in Parapsychology and Occult Sciences. Titles in the Merten J Mandeville Collection are purchased by funds from an endowment provided specifically for the collection on its establishment in 1966 by Merten J Mandeville, Professor Emeritus of Management, who donated 400 vols from his personal library as the nucleus of the collection. There are currently about 5000 titles in the collection, supplemented by related materials in the general collection. Topics include astrology, extrasensory perception, yoga, magic, satanism, faith healing, hypnosis, Eastern religions, witchcraft, fortune telling, reincarnation, flying saucers, ghosts, dreams, numerology, graphology, and mysticism. Biographies and reference books are a part of the collection as are journals devoted to the scientific study of parapsychology.

NY —PARAPSYCHOLOGY FOUNDATION, Eileen J Garrett Library, 228 E 71st St, New York, 10021. Wayne Norman, Librn
Holdings: Vols (9300) Cat
Notes: One of the largest libraries on parapsychology. Main emphasis is on the literature of contemporary parapsychology; also a strong collection on the history of parapsychology (early spiritualism, mysticism, relevant philosophical works, etc). Rare book collection incl early rare books and periodicals on psychical research and psychical phenomena. Receives about 100 titles of periodicals and binds the more significant titles. The library maintains its own periodicals index to parapsychological literature, dating from 1966. Main emphasis literature is on experimental parapsychology, or those publications that approach the subject with an objective and/or analytic point of view.

VA —ASSOCIATION FOR RESEARCH & ENLIGHTENMENT, Library, 67 & Atlantic Avenue, PO Box 595, Virginia Beach, 23451. Stephen Jordan, Library Mgr
Holdings: Vols (1800) Cat
Notes: A R E Library Booklist incl 6000 items in 24 subject categories. This special collection is especially strong in the following subjects: astrology, spiritualism, reincarnation, healing arts, Theosophy, Atlantis, parapsychology and transpersonal psychology.

EXTRATERRESTRIAL LIFE

CA —NASA, Ames Research Center, Libraries, Library Br 202-3, Moffett Field, 94035. Sarah Dueker, Chief, Library Branch
Holdings: Cat Audiotapes Microforms
Notes: Main library collections cover physical sciences, engineering and mathematical fields related to research programs in aeronautics-space research. Life sciences library collections cover medical, physiological, behavioral and biological sciences related to research programs. Also emphases on remote sensing of earth resources and the search for extraterrestrial life. 950 journal titles and 85,000 monographs. Reports collection includes 60, 000 hard copy reports and 900,000 microfiche.

PA —ENSANIAN PHYSICOCHEMICAL INSTITUTE, Library, PO Box 98, Eldred, 16731. Elisabeth Anahid Ensanian, Chief Librn
Holdings: Vols 200 Cat Mss Slides Films Microforms
Budget: $3800
Notes: The institute has pioneered the field of Gravitation Chemistry (term coined at the institute) and has original data and reports on this phenomenon, generated from its own research, that cannot be found elsewhere in the world. Also publishes own technical journal. This special collection, which also incl the biological effects of weightlessness, is continually being increased.

EXTREMIST LITERATURE

MA —BRANDEIS UNIVERSITY, Goldfarb Library, 415 South St, Waltham, 02154. Bessie Hahn, Dir
Notes: Hall-Hoag Archives on Extremism in the U.S. Approx 5000 pieces of Extremist literature, both Right and Left, dealing with various social, religious and political aspects of the US from the 1960s, 1970s and 1980s. A finding list is in Special Collections. Material is arranged by the name of the sponsoring organization in alphabetical order.

EYE

CA —UNIVERSITY OF CALIFORNIA, BERKELEY, General Library, Optometry Library, 490 Minor Hall, Berkeley, 94720. Alison Howard, Librn
Holdings: Vols (8000) Cat Pix Microforms
Budget: ($13,500)
Notes: Incl 350 microfiches.

IL —ILLINOIS COLLEGE OF OPTOMETRY, Carl F Shepard Memorial Library, 3241 S Michigan Ave, Chicago, 60616. Kevin K Wah, Dir of Library and Instructional Services
Holdings: Vols (13,000) Cat Slides Phonorecords Audiotapes Videotapes 16mm Films Filmstrips Microforms
Budget: ($25,000)
Notes: Research and teaching collection on every aspect of the eye and vision and their disorders, excl surgery. Incl historical and current materials; excl foreign-language materials. Library participates in Midwest Health Sciences Library Network and ILLINET.

IN —INDIANA UNIVERSITY, Optometry Branch Library, Bloomington, 47405. Roger Deckman, Head; Elizabeth Egan, Branch Librn
Holdings: Vols (11,000) Cat Slides Microforms
Budget:
Notes: Incl all aspects of vision: anatomy, physiology, pathology of the eye, neurophysiology, perception, colorimetry, illumination, safety, etc. Interlibrary loans through Main Library, Indiana University, Bloomington.

MO —INTERNATIONAL LIBRARY, ARCHIVES AND MUSEUM OF OPTOMETRY, 243 N Lindbergh, Saint Louis, 63141. Maria Dablemont, Librn
Holdings: Vols (12,000) Cat Mss Pix Slides Phonorecords Audiotapes Videotapes 16mm Films Filmstrips
Notes: Established to collect, preserve, and make available for researchers materials related to optometry and the visual sciences; the oldest special library of vision science in this country, serving the public worldwide with reference services and materials. The archives contain documents pertaining to the history of optometry and the history of the American Optometric Association. In the museum are found antique eyeglasses and optical instruments as well as artifacts from the history of the optometric profession and items associated with its leaders.

NY —STATE UNIVERSITY OF NEW YORK, State College of Optometry, Harold Kohn Vision Science Library, 100 E 24 St, New York, 10010. Margaret S Lewis, Librn
Holdings: Vols (23,000) Cat Audiotapes Microforms
Notes: All subjects related to visual disabilities; much on vision disorders among children.

EYE—DISEASES AND DEFECTS

AL —UNIVERSITY OF ALABAMA, BIRMINGHAM, Lister Hill Library of the Health Sciences, University Sta, Birmingham, 35294. Richard B Fredericksen, Dir

IL —ILLINOIS COLLEGE OF OPTOMETRY, Carl F Shepard Memorial Library, 3241 S Michigan Ave, Chicago, 60616. Kevin K Wah, Dir of Library and Instructional Services
Holdings: Vols (13,000) Cat Slides

EYE—DISEASES AND DEFECTS (cont.)

Phonorecords Audiotapes Videotapes 16mm Films Filmstrips Microforms
Budget: ($25,000)
Notes: Research and teaching collection on every aspect of the eye and vision and their disorders, excl surgery. Incl historical and current materials; excl foreign-language materials. Library participates in Midwest Health Sciences Library Network and ILLINET.

NY —COLUMBIA UNIVERSITY LIBRARIES, Rare Book & Manuscript Library, 801 Butler Library, 535 W 114 St, New York, 10027. Kenneth A Lohf, Librn
Holdings: Mss
Notes: Nearly 6000 letters, notes and mss relating to Cornelius Rea Agnew, professor of diseases of the eye and ear at Columbia's College of Physicians and Surgeons, and a founder of the Manhatan Eye and Ear Hospital. Much of the material relates to the treatment of eye diseases during the latter half of the 19th century. Restricted use.

NY —STATE UNIVERSITY OF NEW YORK, State College of Optometry, Harold Kohn Vision Science Library, 100 E 24 St, New York, 10010. Margaret S Lewis, Librn
Holdings: Vols (23,000) Cat Audiotapes Microforms
Notes: All subjects related to visual disabilities; much on vision disorders among children.

EYE—PROTECTION

IN —INDIANA UNIVERSITY, Optometry Branch Library, Bloomington, 47405. Roger Deckman, Head; Elizabeth Egan, Branch Librn
Holdings: Vols (11,000) Cat Slides Microforms
Budget:
Notes: Incl all aspects of vision: anatomy, physiology, pathology of the eye, neurophysiology, perception, colorimetry, illumination, safety, etc. Interlibrary loans through Main Library, Indiana University, Bloomington.

NY —NATIONAL SOCIETY FOR THE PREVENTION OF BLINDNESS, Conrad Berens Library, 79 Madison Ave, New York, 10016. Dede Silverston, Librn
Holdings: Vols (3000) Cat
Notes: Includes complete and up-to-date ophthalmology collection. Current vertical file of 21 drawers on phases of eye care.

EYE (PHYSIOLOGY)

CT —YALE MEDICAL LIBRARY, 333 Cedar St, New Haven, 06510.
Notes: A special subject emphasis.

EYEGLASSES

MO —INTERNATIONAL LIBRARY, ARCHIVES AND MUSEUM OF OPTOMETRY, 243 N Lindbergh, Saint Louis, 63141. Maria Dablemont, Librn
Holdings: Vols (12,000) Cat Mss Pix Slides Phonorecords Audiotapes Videotapes 16mm Films Filmstrips
Notes: Established to collect, preserve, and make available for researchers materials related to optometry and the visual sciences; the oldest special library of vision science in this country, serving the public worldwide with reference services and materials. The archives contain documents pertaining to the history of optometry and the history of the American Optometric Association. In the museum are found antique eyeglasses and optical instruments as well as artifacts from the history of the optometric profession and items associated with its leaders.

EYERLY, FRANK RINEHART

IA —IOWA STATE UNIVERSITY, Library, Dept of Special Collections, Ames, 50011. Stanley M Yates, Head
Holdings: // Mss
Notes: Eyerly was managing editor of Des Moines Resister and Tribune from 1946-1969. 4 linear ft, finding aid available.

EYES see Eye

F

FABER, FREDERICK WILLIAM, 1814-1863

DC —GEORGETOWN UNIVERSITY, Library, Special Collections Div, 37 & O Sts NW, Washington, 20057. George M Barringer, Special Collections Librn; Nicholas B Sheetz, Mss Librn
Holdings: Mss
Notes: Correspondence (1841-45, 1898-1900), documents, mss sermons, themes for class (1860-61) and diaries (1888-1904). Welch (1822-1904) graduated from Harvard College in 1840 and subsequently taught at Georgetown College. Also, present is an extensive correspondence with Frederick William Faber (1814-1863), poet and founder of the London Oratory. 1.75 linear feet.

FABIAN, BELA

NY —COLUMBIA UNIVERSITY LIBRARIES, Rare Book & Manuscript Library, 801 Butler Library, 535 W 114 St, New York, 10027. Kenneth A Lohf, Librn
Holdings: Mss
Notes: Concerns activities against Communists in Hungary. 1000 items. Restricted use.

FABIAN, HAROLD B., 1917-1960

NY —ROCKEFELLER UNIVERSITY, Rockefeller Archive Center, Hillcrest, Pocantico Hills, North Tarrytown, 10591. Joseph W Ernst, Dir; J William Hess, Assoc Dir
Notes: Papers relative to the Rockefeller Family, Foundations, University, and other specific enterprises and contributions to particular areas of social, physical, educational, and historic reform, preservation, conservation, or development. Extensive records of administrative, financial, physical or intellectual relationships.

NY —ROCKEFELLER UNIVERSITY, Rockefeller Archive Center, Hillcrest, Pocantico Hills, North Tarrytown, 10591. Joseph W Ernst, Dir; J William Hess, Assoc Dir
Notes: The Rockefeller Archive Center, a division of The Rockefeller University, preserves and makes available to scholars the records of the University, the Rockefeller Foundation, the Rockefeller Brothers Fund, members of the family, and those of other individuals and organizations associated with their endeavors. Collections at the Center document a century of philanthropy by legions of associated social and scientific pioneers, providing a unique window into the past.

FABLES

CA —CLAREMONT COLLEGES, Ella Strong Denison Library, Scripps College, Claremont, 91711. Judy Harvey Sahak, Librn
Holdings: 63 Cat
Notes: Includes 36 vols of Aesop's fables (earliest, 1544), 9 vols of Gay's fables (earliest, 1729), and 8 vols of LaFontaine (earliest, 1734).

OH —CLEVELAND PUBLIC LIBRARY, Fine Arts and Special Collections Department, 325 Superior Ave, Cleveland, 44114. Alice N Loranth, Head
Holdings: Vols 700 Cat Mss
Notes: Strong collection of Medieval European and Oriental works. Numerous rare and early editions of Reynard the Fox (200 vols), Panchatantra, Bidpai, Hitopadesa, etc. Aesop and the modern fabulists are incl only by representative editions.

FABRICS see Textile Industry and Fabrics

FABYAN, GEORGE

DC —LIBRARY OF CONGRESS, Rare Book & Special Collections Div, Washington, 20540. William Matheson, Chief
Notes: Research collection on cryptography and Shakespeare-Bacon controversy. See description of collection under Cryptography.

FACETIAE see Wit and Humor

FACOS, JAMES

MA —BOSTON UNIVERSITY, Mugar Memorial Library, Special Collections Dept, 771 Commonwealth Ave, Boston, 02215. Howard B Gotlieb, Dir
Holdings: Mss Pix
Notes: Mss, correspondence, etc collected in depth; incl publications by or about.

FACSIMILE TRANSMISSION

NY —XEROX CORP, Technical Information Center, PO Box 305, Webster, 14580. Michael D Majcher, Mgr
Holdings: Vols (30,000) Cat Microforms

FACSIMILES (BOOKS, MANUSCRIPTS, AND DOCUMENTS)

IN —INDIANA STATE UNIVERSITY, Cunningham Memorial Library, Dept of Rare Books & Special Collections, Terre Haute, 47809. Lawrence J McCrank, Head
Notes: The reference collection of the Rare Books and Special Collections Department holds bibliographies and reference works related specifically to the department's collections in lexicography, Indiana local and regional history, education, travel and discovery, etc, and on the book arts, eg, printing, typography, paper making, illustration, conservation and binding. Incl several facsimile editions of famous codices.

MI —MICHIGAN STATE UNIVERSITY, Art Library, East Lansing, 48824. Shirlee A Studt, Librn
Holdings: Vols (45,000) Cat
Notes: The Illuminated Manuscript Facsimile Collection includes examples of religious and secular works from the earliest codex to the age of printing. It has particular strengths in Carolingian, Ottonian, French Gothic and works from the British Isles. The facsimile collection is strengthened by related research materials (biographical material, critical studies, etc) The facsimile collection and related materials are part of a 45,000 volume separately housed and staffed collection on the visual and decorative arts (including photography) serving the curricular and research needs of the University community. A guide to full facsimiles in the collection is available in the Art Library and in the Special Collections division. A strong collection of architectural history.

NY —STATE UNIVERSITY OF NEW YORK, BUFFALO, Baird Music Library, Baird Hall, Amherst, 14260. James B Coover, Dir
Holdings: Vols (104,000) Cat Mss Pix Slides Phonorecords Microforms
Notes: Nearly complete collections of *Denkmaeler und Gesamtausgaben* and other historical sets. Strong collection of dictionaries, bibliographies, biographies, facsimiles, works on the "new" music, organology and ethnomusicology. Special emphasis on operas, scores of the avant-garde, jazz and urban popular music, discography and music librarianship. Good collection of medieval and Renaissance anthologies, contemporary and avant-garde recordings. Houses Archives of the Center of the Creative and Performing Arts. Collections incl 2100 slides, 22,000 phonorecords, 46,000 scores and parts, 29, 000 books, 4900 microforms. Computerized record catalog in process.

PA —PENNSYLVANIA STATE UNIVERSITY, Fred Lewis Pattee Library, Special Collections Dept, University Park, 16802. Charles Mann, Chief, Special Collections
Holdings: Vols (122,533) Cat Mss Maps Pix Slides Phonorecords Audiotapes Videotapes 16mm Films Microforms
Budget: ($37,000)
Notes: Special Collections and Rare Books includes several collections described separately. The holdings are particularly strong in literature, the 18th century, aeronautics, facsimiles, atlases, 19th century illustrated works on birds, botany and traveller's views. Special strengths are Emblem Books, Utopias, Fantastic Fiction, Australiana, Fine Presses, Labor Archives, Landscape Architecture, Pennsylvaniana. These collections are strengthened by parall holdings in the open stacks. It also includes the collections of the Penn State Room. Several mimeographed lists are available. Audiotapes are listed in *Voices and Events, A Catalog of Audio Tapes* (Pennsylvania State University Libraries, 1975), 45 pp.

ON —QUEEN'S UNIVERSITY, Douglas Library, Kingston, K7L 5C4, Can. William F E Morley, Cur, Special Collections
Holdings: Vols 6980 Cat Mss Pix
Notes: Subject strength of the collections.

FACTORIES

MA —MERRIMACK VALLEY TEXTILE MUSEUM, Library, 800 Massachusetts Ave, North Andover, 01845. Clare Sheridan, Librn; Laurence Gross, Cur
Holdings: Vols (35,000) Cat Mss Maps Pix Slides
Notes: *Checklist of Prints, Drawings and Painting in the Merrimack Valley Textile* Museum, Helena E Wright, 1972; *Checklist of Finished Textiles,* Katherine R Koob, 1980; *New City on the Merrimack: Prints of Lawrence 1845-1876,* Helena Wright, 1974; *Homespun to Factory Made: Woolen Textiles in America 1776-1876* (exhibit catalog) 1978; *Textile Technology Prints: A Checklist of Prints, Drawings and Paintings in the Merrimack Valley Textile Museum,* Helena E Wright, 1980; *All Sorts of Good Sufficient Cloth: Linen-making in New England, 1640-1860,* (exhibit catalogue) 1980; *The Merrimack Valley Textile Museum: A Guide to the Manuscript* Collections Helena E Wright, Garland Press 1983.

FACTORY AND TRADE WASTE

IL —GREELEY & HANSEN ENGINEERS, 222 S Riverside Plaza, Chicago, 60606. Marilyn Cichom, Librn
Holdings: Vols (6000) Cat Maps Slides Microforms

MA —CAMP, DRESSER & MCKEE, Herman G Dresser Library, One Center Plaza, Boston, 02108. Virginia L Carroll, Librn
Holdings: Vols (15,000) Cat Maps Slides Microforms
Notes: Air, land, and water pollution; environmental engineering; hazardous wastes; water resources; solid wastes; resource recycling.

FACULTY (EDUCATION) see Teachers

FADIMAN, CLIFTON

NY —COLUMBIA UNIVERSITY LIBRARIES, Rare Book & Manuscript Library, 801 Butler Library, 535 W 114 St, New York, 10027. Kenneth A Lohf, Librn
Holdings: Mss
Notes: Mss and letters. Restricted use.

FAGIN, LARRY

CT —UNIVERSITY OF CONNECTICUT, Library, Storrs, 06268. George F Butterick, Cur of Literary Archives
Holdings: Mss
Notes: Collection includes Adventures in Poetry archive.

FAIENCE see Pottery

FAILURE TO THRIVE (HEALTH)

MD —NATIONAL LIBRARY OF MEDICINE, 8600 Rockville Pike, Bethesda, 20209. Harold M Schoolinam, Actg Dir
Budget: ($46,400)

FAIR EMPLOYMENT PRACTICE see Discrimination in Employment

FAIRBAIRN, ANN

MA —BOSTON UNIVERSITY, Mugar Memorial Library, Special Collections Dept, 771 Commonwealth Ave, Boston, 02215. Howard B Gotlieb, Dir
Holdings: // Cat Mss Pix
Notes: Mss, correspondence, etc collected in depth; incl pulications by or about.

FAIRBAIRN, DOUGLAS

MA —BOSTON UNIVERSITY, Mugar Memorial Library, Special Collections Dept, 771 Commonwealth Ave, Boston, 02215. Howard B Gotlieb, Dir
Holdings: Cat Mss

FAIRBANKS, CHARLES WARREN

IN —INDIANA UNIVERSITY, Lilly Library, Seventh St, Bloomington, 47405. William R Cagle, Librn
Holdings: // Mss Pix
Notes: Papers of US Senator and Vice-President Charles Warren Fairbanks. Contains correspondence with prominent political figures, friends, relatives, etc; speeches; law office papers; photographs. Most of the material is from his early years of practice as a railroad attorney and his senatorial and vice-presidential years. The later papers deal with the settlement of his estate. 150,006 items.

FAIRBANKS, DOUGLAS, JR.

MA —BOSTON UNIVERSITY, Mugar Memorial Library, Special Collections Dept, 771 Commonwealth Ave, Boston, 02215. Howard B Gotlieb, Dir
Holdings: Mss Pix Correspondence

FAIRCHILD, HERMAN LE ROY

NY —UNIVERSITY OF ROCHESTER, Rush Rhees Library, Department of Rare Books and Special Collections, Rochester, 14627. Peter Dzwonkoski, Librn
Holdings: Vols Cat Mss Pix
Notes: Fairchild was a professor of Geology at the University of Rochester (1888-1920) and a founder of the Geological Society of America.

FAIRE, VIRGINIA BROWNE

CA —UNIVERSITY OF CALIFORNIA, LOS ANGELES, Theater Arts Library, Los Angeles, 90024. Edward Shreeves, Chairman, Bibliographers Group; Audree Malkin, Head, Theater Arts Library
Notes: Virginia Browne Faire Collection: portraits and production stills relating to the career of Virginia Browne Faire, actress in the late teens through mid-thirties.

FAIRFIELD, JOSEPHINE LETITIA

BC —UNIVERSITY OF VICTORIA, McPherson Library, Victoria, V8W 3H5, Can.

FAIRLIE, JOHN

IL —UNIVERSITY OF ILLINOIS, URBANA/CHAMPAIGN, Library, University Archives, 19 Library, 1408 W Gregory Drive, Urbana, 61801. Maynard Brichford, University Archivist
Holdings: Cat Mss Maps Pix Slides Microforms
Notes: Papers, archival records, etc.

FAIRS

CA —CALIFORNIA POLYTECHNIC STATE UNIVERSITY LIBRARY, Special Collections and University Archives, San Luis Obispo, 93407. Nancy E Loe, Head Librn
Holdings: Vols (100) Mss Pix Slides
Notes: The Fairs Collection incl 56,000 ms materials, pix and slides documenting the Western Fairs Association of Sacramento, Calif, and the management and growth of fairs in California and around the world (materials in rough sorting stage). Mss incl correspondence, scrapbooks, legislative opinions and memoranda. 5000 slides; 1000 photographs.

CT —YALE UNIVERSITY, Box 1603A, Yale Station, New Haven, 06520.
Notes: Incl Philadelphia Centennial Exhibition, 1876; Century of Progress Exhibiton, Chicago, 1892; World's Fair, New York, 1939-40.

IL —MUSEUM OF SCIENCE AND INDUSTRY, Library, 57th St and Lake Shore Dr, Chicago, 60637. Carla Hayden, Coordinator
Holdings: Vols Cat Maps Pix
Notes: Occupying the site of the Fine Arts Building of Chicago's Columbian Exposition of 1893, the Museum Library has been the recipient of numerous gifts in this field, not only of materials from Chicago's Columbian Expositons, Century of Progress and Railroad Fairs but also from the New York World's Fair, St Louis, Paris Exposition Universelle, San Francisco's Panama-Pacific etc. Incl blueprints of some buildings and areas. No separate catalog or index to this extensive collection.

LA —LOUISIANA STATE UNIVERSITY, SHREVEPORT, Library-Archives, 8515 Youree Dr, Shreveport, 71129. Patricia L Meador, Archivist & Asst Librn
Notes: See Louisiana - History entry for LSU Archives.

NY —NEW YORK PUBLIC LIBRARY, Performing Arts Research Center, Billy Rose Theatre Collection, 111 Amsterdam Ave, New York, 10023. Dorothy L Swerdlove, Cur
Holdings: Cat Pix
Notes: Clippings, photographs, reviews of acts, etc, periodicals devoted to news of activity in the field.

FAIRY TALES

CA —LOS ANGELES PUBLIC LIBRARY, Children's Literature Dept, 630 W 5th St, Los Angeles, 90071. Serenna Day, Sr Librn
Holdings: Vols (2120) Cat Phonorecords Filmstrips
Notes: Also includes reference collection, covering some 50 years of published folklore and modern fairy tales. Includes extensive Mother Goose collection, examples of the work of such outstanding illustrators as Edmund Dulac and Arthur Rackham. Many volumes out of print. Index to titles of stories in collections.

IN —INDIANAPOLIS-MARION COUNTY PUBLIC LIBRARY, Riley Room for Young People, PO Box 211, Indianapolis, 46206. Margaret Barks, Head
Holdings: Vols 1110 Cat
Notes: The Harding Memorial Collection. This is a resource collection of folk and fairy tales as well as other suitable materials for telling.

FAITH AND ORDER

KY —ASBURY THEOLOGICAL SEMINARY, B L Fisher Library, Wilmore, 40390. D William Faupel, Dir of Library Services
Holdings: Uncat
Notes: Official Numbered Documents, 1910-date. See *Index, 1910-1948* and *Check List, 1910-1970, Faith and Order Commission, World Council of Churches, Official Numbered Publications,* A T DeGroot (Geneva, Switzerland: WCC, 1977), 258pp.

NY —GENERAL THEOLOGICAL SEMINARY, Saint Marks Library, 175 Ninth Ave, New York, 10011. David Green, Dir
Holdings: Vols (200,000) Cat Mss Pix Slides Microforms

NY —UNION THEOLOGICAL SEMINARY, Library, 3041 Broadway at Reinhold Niebuhr Place, New York, 10027. Richard D Spoor, Dir
Holdings: Vols (580,000) Cat Mss Microforms
Budget: ($750,000)

FAITH CURE

IL —UNIVERSITY OF ILLINOIS, URBANA/CHAMPAIGN, Library, University Archives, 19 Library, 1408 W Gregory Drive, Urbana, 61801. Maynard Brichford, University Archivist
Holdings: Vols (5000) Cat
Budget: ($7000)
Notes: The Mandeville Collection in Parapsychology and Occult Sciences. Titles in the Merten J Mandeville Collection are purchased by funds from an endowment provided specifically for the collection on its establishment in 1966 by Merten J Mandeville, Professor Emeritus of Management, who donated 400 vols from his personal library as the nucleus of the collection. There are currently about 5000 titles in the collection, supplemented by related materials in the general collection. Topics include astrology, extrasensory perception, yoga, magic, satanism, faith healing, hypnosis, Eastern religions, witchcraft, fortune telling, reincarnation, flying saucers, ghosts, dreams, numerology, graphology, and mysticism. Biographies and reference books are a part of the collection as are journals devoted to the scientific study of parapsychology.

TN —LEE COLLEGE, Library, Ocoee St, Cleveland, 37311. Frances Arrington, Head Librn; JoAnne Sparks, Religion Librn
Holdings: Vols 28,204 Cat Slides Phonorecords Audiotapes Filmstrips
Budget: $27,000
Notes: General religion collection which supports undergraduate and graduate level curriculum. The Pentecostal Research Center houses two special collections: the Church of God (Cleveland, Tennessee) collection and the Pentecostal collection. The latter includes works about the movement and its history, works by Pentecostal authors, and specific subject areas (Holy Spirit, glossolalia, divine healing).

VA —ASSOCIATION FOR RESEARCH & ENLIGHTENMENT, Library, 67 & Atlantic Avenue, PO Box 595, Virginia Beach, 23451. Stephen Jordan, Library Mgr
Holdings: Vols (1800) Cat
Notes: A R E Library Booklist incl 6000 items in 24 subject categories. This special collection is especially strong in the following subjects: astrology, spiritualism, reincarnation, healing arts, Theosophy, Atlantis, parapsychology and transpersonal psychology.

FAITH HEALING see Faith Cure

FAKE MONEY see Stage Money

FALCONRY AND FALCONS

CO —US AIR FORCE ACADEMY, Library, USAF Academy, Colorado Springs, 80840. Reiner H Schaeffer, Dir
Holdings: Vols 265 Cat Pix
Notes: Air Force Academy Library Special Bibliography no 54 on falconry describes the collection.

PQ —MCGILL UNIVERSITY, Blacker-Wood Library of Zoology & Ornithology, 3459 McTavish St, Montreal, H3A 1Y1, Can. Eleanor MacLean, Librn
Notes: Incl a small collection of falconry equipment, falconry imprints spanning four centuries, incl oriental mss (mostly collected in Northern Muslim India, 1926/27), and collection of 156 17th century feather pictures.

FALK, ISADORE S.

CT —YALE UNIVERSITY, Box 1603A, Yale Station, New Haven, 06520.
Holdings: Mss Pix
Notes: The Contemporary Medical Care and Health Policy Collection. Letters, memos, records, photographs, etc of the principal strategists of the social medical movement in the US.

FALKE, UMAR

IL —NORTHWESTERN UNIVERSITY, Melville J Herskovits Library of African

FALKE, UMAR (cont.)

Studies, Evanston, 60201. Hans E Panofsky, Cur
Holdings: Vols (85,000) Mss
Budget: ($70,000)
Notes: Papers, incl Arabic and Hausa mss.
See also entry under Africa.

FALKENBURG FAMILY

NJ —GLASSBORO STATE COLLEGE, Savitz Library, Stewart Room, Glassboro, 08028. Clara Kirner, Special Collection Librn
Notes: Papers.

FALLACI, ORIANA

MA —BOSTON UNIVERSITY, Mugar Memorial Library, Special Collections Dept, 771 Commonwealth Ave, Boston, 02215. Howard B Gotlieb, Dir
Holdings: Cat Mss Pix Audiotapes
Notes: Mss, correspondence, etc collected in depth; incl publications by or about.

FALLING STARS see Meteors

FALLOUT, RADIOACTIVE see Radioactive Fallout

FAMILIES IN POLITICS

MI —NATIONAL HAMILTONIAN PARTY, Library, 3314 Dillon Rd, Flushing, 48433.
Holdings: Vols 4670
Notes: The life and writings of Alexander Hamilton. The National Hamiltonian Library is a part of the offices of the Hamiltonian National Committee, the governing body of the National Hamiltonian Party, a Neo-Federalist political movement. Incl 4835 vols. Also the Kelly Collection, a group of over 10,000 pieces of American political memorabilia covering presidents and presidential hopefuls of major and minor parties as well as special sectons on women, minorities and families in politics.

FAMILY

IL —UNIVERSITY OF ILLINOIS, URBANA/CHAMPAIGN, Library, Home Economics Library, 314 Bevier Hall, Champaign, 61820. Barbara C Swain, Librn
Holdings: Vols Cat
Notes: Human development and family ecology.

IN —PURDUE UNIVERSITY LIBRARIES, Consumer & Family Sciences Library, Stone Hall W, West Lafayette, 47907. Emily Alward, Librn
Holdings: Vols (14,000) Cat

MA —RADCLIFFE COLLEGE, Arthur & Elizabeth Schlesinger Library on the History of Women in America, 3 James St, Cambridge, 02138. Patricia Miller King, Dir; Eva Moseley, Cur of Mss
Holdings: Vols (23,000) Cat Mss Pix Audiotapes Microforms
Notes: Emphasis on women in the US; subject areas incl woman's rights, suffrage, feminism, and the women's movement; the family; women in government and politics, social welfare and reform, and the trade unions; women's education, employment, and health; mss collections incl those of the Blackwell family, the Beecher-Stowe family, Betty Friedan, Charlotte Perkins Gilman, Emma Goldman, Dr Alice Hamilton and the Hamilton family, the National Abortion Rights Action League, the National Organization for Women, Leonora O'Reilly, and the Women's Equity Action League. For description see *Harvard Library Bulletin XVI* (1968), pp 385-99; *Wilson Library Bulletin LV, 10* (1981), pp 750-55; *Special* Collections (forthcoming 1984); also the Library's *40th Anniversary Report* (1983). Formerly the Women's Archives. Incl 463 personal and family collections and 103organizational collections; also incl 40, 000 pictures, 10,000 microforms; oral history tapes and transcripts.

MN —MINNESOTA HISTORICAL SOCIETY LIBRARY, 690 Cedar St, Saint Paul, 55101. Patricia C Harpole, Chief of Reference Library; Bonnie G Wilson, Head of Special Libraries
Notes: Interviews with early builders of Minnesota on a wide range of subjects.

NY —FAMILY SERVICE, America Library, 44 E 23 St, New York, 10010. Joan Fenton, Librn
Holdings: Vols (3600) Cat
Notes: No Photocopying.

OH —CLEVELAND PUBLIC LIBRARY, Social Sciences Department, 325 Superior Ave, Cleveland, 44114. Thelma Morris, Head
Notes: Incl books and periodicals on personal relationships, the family, and sex relations.

OH —OHIO STATE UNIVERSITY, Home Economics Library, Campbell Hall Rm 325, 1787 Neil Ave, Columbus, 43210. Neosha Mackey, Librn
Holdings: Vols (14,000) Cat Microforms
Notes: Separate catalog. Also, book catalog: *Catalog of the Home Economics Library* (Boston: G K Hall, 1976), 3 vols.

OH —OHIO STATE UNIVERSITY, Social Work Library, 1947 N College Rd, Columbus, 43210. Toyo S Kawakami, Librn
Holdings: Vols (46,410) Cat
Budget: ($11,960)
Notes: VF incl approx 4500 pamphlets, arranged by LC subject headings. 278 serial titles on social work, social and public service, crime and delinquency, corrections, criminal justice, marriage and the family, probation, and related topics, are received.

WI —STATE HISTORICAL SOCIETY OF WISCONSIN, Archives, 816 State St, Madison, 53706. Harold L Miller, Reference Archivist
Holdings: Mss Maps Public Records Microforms
Notes: Incl are unpublished genealogies, records of Wisconsin cemetaries and churches, and mss, incl the Lyman C Draper Manuscripts. Also incl are Wisconsin state, county and local governmental records, incl 19th century state census records, civil war service records and some naturalization records. Collections described in *Genealogical Research: An Introduction to the Resources of the State Historical Society of Wisconsin,* (1980).

ON —NATIONAL LIBRARY OF CANADA, 395 Wellington St, Ottawa, K1A 0N4, Can. Andre Preibish, Dir
Holdings: Vols 10,000
Notes: Includes 130 serial titles, theses, pamphlets, government publications relating to family and marriage. The following disciplines covered: anthropology, psychology and psychiatry, law, economics, religion, sociology, demography, education, political science and biology. Earliest title 1630.

ON —ONTARIO MINISTRY OF COMMUNITY & SOCIAL SERVICES, Library, 880 Bay St, Rm 663, Toronto, M7A 1E9, Can. Sandra Walsh, Chief Librn
Holdings: Vols (30,000) Cat Slides Videotapes 16mm Films Microforms

ON —WILFRID LAURIER UNIVERSITY, Library, (Formerly Waterloo Lutheran University), 75 University Ave W, Waterloo, N2L 3C5, Can. Erich R W Schultz, Librn
Holdings: Vols (20,000) Cat Microforms
Budget: ($27,000)

FAMILY GROUP THERAPY see Family Psychotherapy

FAMILY PLANNING

CA —UNIVERSITY OF CALIFORNIA, BERKELEY, Life Sciences Libraries, Public Health Library, 42 Earl Warren Hall, Berkeley, 94720. Thomas J Alexander, Librn
Holdings: Vols (75,000) Cat Microforms
Notes: Research collection covering all aspects of public health. Health Department annual reports from all 50 states are acquired, as well as such reports from all California health units and from major US cities. Serial publications issued by Health Departments in the 13 western states are being received.

†HI —EAST-WEST POPULATION INSTITUTE RESOURCE MATERIALS COLLECTION, 1777 East-West Rd, Honolulu, 96848.
Notes: Demography, population problems and policy in Hawaii, Asian countries and Pacific area, family planning programs, environment.

MA —HARVARD UNIVERSITY, Center for Population Studies, 665 Huntington Ave, Boston, 02115. Wilma E Winters, Librn
Holdings: Vols (20,000) Cat
Notes: Incl books and pamphlets.

NY —MATERNITY CENTER ASSOCIATION, Library, 48 E 92 St, New York, 10028. Esther Hanchett, Acting Librn
Holdings: Vols 2000 Cat
Notes: No photocopying.

NY —PLANNED PARENTHOOD FEDERATION OF AMERICA, Katharine Dexter McCormick Library, 810 Seventh Ave, New York, 10019. Gloria A Roberts, Head Librn
Holdings: Vols (4000) Cat
Notes: Birth control, teenagers, contraception and contraceptive research, family planning, religion and birth control.

NC —CAROLINA POPULATION CENTER, Library, University Sq E, Chapel Hill, 27514. Patricia Shipman, Head Librn
Holdings: Vols (20,000) Cat
Budget: ($10,500)
Notes: Try to acquire everything published in English on population, with particular emphasis on the US and developing countries. Also acquire conference proceedings, seminar papers. These and journal articles are indexed and the analytics are incl in the catalog. Incl 13,000 reprints and other pieces of ephemera. Most extensive area files are on India, Africa, Thailand, Iran, Korea, and Latin America. Holdings are recorded on an automated data base. A microfiche catalog is available for use in the Library and for purchase. Subject access and access by geographic area are available through the Library's own thesaurus-based indexing system and a KWIC Index.

WI —PLANNED PARENTHOOD OF WISCONSIN, Maurice Ritz Resource Library & Bookstore, 1135 W State St, Milwaukee, 53233. Ann McIntyre, Librn
Holdings: Vols (2500) Cat Pix Slides Phonorecords 16mm Films Filmstrips VF
Notes: Special emphasis on family planning and reproductive health, birth control and contraception.

FAMILY PSYCHOTHERAPY

KS —MENNINGER FOUNDATION, Archives, 5600 W Sixth St, Box 829, Topeka, 66601. Alice Brand, Librn; Mark West, Archivist
Holdings: Vols (33,000) Cat Pix Audiotapes Microforms
Notes: Incl journals. Literature searches and document delivery available for a fee.

MD —CROWNSVILLE HOSPITAL CENTER, Medical Staff Library, Crownsville, 21032. Joyce E Munsey, Librn
Holdings: Vols (1500) Cat
Budget: $2000
Notes: Behavior therapy, clinical psychology, and family therapy.

FAMILY SIZE see Family Planning

FAMILY THERAPY see Family Psychotherapy

FAMILY VIOLENCE

AL —BIRMINGHAM PUBLIC LIBRARY, Southern Women's Archives, 2020 Park Place, Birmingham, 35203. Theresa A Ceravolo, Archivist
Holdings: Cat Mss
Notes: Monthly legislative reports, 1981-

FAMILY VIOLENCE (cont.)

1983, which discuss Alabama legislative and, to some extent, US Congress activities regarding abortion, domestic violence, child support, and other related issues.

MD —INTERNATIONAL ASSOCIATION OF CHIEFS OF POLICE, 13 Firstfield Rd, PO Box 6010, Gaithersburg, 20760.
Holdings: Vols (6000) Cat Mss
Notes: Collection heavy in criminal investigation, crime prevention, police administration and management. Collecting in public sector labor relations, family violence, terrorism.

MO —SAINT LOUIS POLICE LIBRARY, 315 S Tucker Blvd, Saint Louis, 63102. Cathy Reilly, Librn
Holdings: Vols (21,000) Cat Mss Pix Microforms
Budget: ($18,400)
Notes: Library on all subjects of police work is open to the public for general reference use.

ON —UNIVERSITY OF GUELPH, Library, Guelph, N1G 2W1, Can. Margaret Beckman, Chief Librn; Ellen Pearson, Ref Librn
Holdings: Vols 30,000 Cat Audiotapes Videotapes 16mm Films Microforms
Budget: ($21,500)
Notes: 320 periodical titles. Special catalogs can be produced for any part of the collection. Additional historical material in archives on early rural movements, such as the women's institutes.
See also entry under Rural Sociology

ON —ONTARIO MINISTRY OF COMMUNITY & SOCIAL SERVICES, Library, 880 Bay St, Rm 663, Toronto, M7A 1E9, Can. Sandra Walsh, Chief Librn
Holdings: Vols (30,000) Cat Slides Videotapes 16mm Films Microforms

FAMINES

CA —HOOVER INSTITUTION ON WAR, REVOLUTION & PEACE, Stanford University, Stanford, 94305. Milorad M Drachkovitch, Archivist
Holdings: Mss
Notes: Records of the Famine Emergency Committee, an organization for the coordination of international famine relief after World War II, incl correspondence, reports, notes, and clippings, 1946-47, relating to US food conservation and to famine conditions throughout the world. Incl memoranda and diaries of Herbert Hoover, Honorary Chairman of the Committee. 30 ms boxes, 2 envelopes.

FAMOUS PEOPLE see Celebrities; Notable Persons

FANCY DRESS see Costume

FANKUCHEN, ISIDOR

NY —AMERICAN INSTITUTE OF PHYSICS, Center for the History of Physics, Niels Bohr Library, 335 E 45 St, New York, 10017. John Aubry, Librn
Notes: Papers and records.

FANNIN, PAUL J.

AZ —ARIZONA STATE UNIVERSITY, Library, Arizona Collection, Tempe, 85281. Edward C Oetting, Head
Holdings: Cat Mss
Notes: Papers, etc.

FANON, FRANTZ

†MA —FRANCIS A COUNTWAY LIBRARY OF MEDICINE, Boston, 02115.

FANTASTIC FICTION

CA —UNIVERSITY OF CALIFORNIA, DAVIS, Shields Library, Dept of Special Collections, Davis, 95616. Donald Kunitz, Head; C Danial Elliott, Asst Head
Holdings: Vols 230 Cat
Notes: Unique literary form from the 1930s; incl Charlie Chan, Popeye, Tom Mix, Buck Rogers, Little Orphan Annie, the Lone Ranger, and many more.

CA —OCCIDENTAL COLLEGE, Library, 1600 Campus Rd, Los Angeles, 90041. Michael C Sutherland, Special Collections Librn
Notes: Mystery and detective fiction. Samples of fantasy, gothic romance, horror and pulps.

CA —UNIVERSITY OF CALIFORNIA, LOS ANGELES, Research Library, Dept of Special Collections, 405 Hilgard Ave, Los Angeles, 90024. Edward Shreeves, Chairman, Bibliographers Group; David S Zeidberg, Head
Holdings: Vols 7000 Cat Periodicals
Notes: Various collections, incl almanacs, comic books, commercial catalogs, fantasy fiction, pulp magazines, trade cards, and 19th century American paperbacks.

CA —UNIVERSITY OF CALIFORNIA, RIVERSIDE, University Library, 4045 Canyon Crest Dr, Box 5900, Riverside, 92517.
Holdings: Vols (30,000)
Notes: The Eaton Collection of science fiction and fantasy materials, incl 5,600 pulp magazines; also horror, supernatural, and Gothic mystery fiction; boys' books; utopian and dystopian fiction, imaginary voyages, future war and lost race fiction; large holdings in French language science fiction and fantasy; critical and scholarly works pertaining to these genres; videotapes of science fiction/fantasy films and shooting scripts. Collection covers science fiction/ fantasy literature from the 16th-17th centuries to the present. Strong individual author collections of Jules Verne, H Rider Haggard, H G Wells, Edgar Rice Burroughs, and Philip K Dick. For a complete description of the collection see: George Slusser, "The J Lloyd Eaton Collection," *Special Collections*, II, 1/2, 25-38 (1983), *andDictionary Catalog of the J Lloyd Eaton Collection of Science Fiction and Fantasy* Literature (Boston: G K Hall) 1982.

CA —SAN DIEGO PUBLIC LIBRARY, Literature & Language Sect, 820 E St, San Diego, 92101. Alyce Archuleta, Senior Librn
Holdings: Vols 202 // Uncat
Notes: Incl mystery series from 1930s and 1940s, and early fantasy and science fiction in paperback form (will circulate). Some first editions; collections has separate author-title index (will not circulate).

CA —SAN FRANCISCO PUBLIC LIBRARY, Civic Center, San Francisco, 94102. Dennis L Maness, Cur
Holdings: Vols 2000 Cat
Notes: McComas Collection of Fantasy and Science Fiction. In addition to the 2000 vols of fiction, there is incl a complete run (vol 1, no 1) of 92 fantasy and science fiction magazines, starting with *Amazing* in 1926.

IL —NORTHERN ILLINOIS UNIVERSITY, Founders Memorial Library, Rare Books and Special Collections Dept, De Kalb, 60115. William R DuBois, Dept Head
Holdings: Cat
Notes: American science fiction. Incl 2600 magazines. Noncirculating. Limited photocopying.

IL —WHEATON COLLEGE, Library, Marion E Wade Collection, Irving & Franklin Sts, Wheaton, 60187. Lyle Dorsett, Cur; Marjorie Mead, Associate Cur
Holdings: Vols (6500)
Notes: Extensive Marion E Wade Collection contains a wide variety of materials on the lives and writings of the Oxford literary circle, the Inklings. Concerns C S Lewis, Owen Barfield J R R Tolkien and Charles Williams.

IN —INDIANA UNIVERSITY, Lilly Library, Seventh St, Bloomington, 47405. William R Cagle, Librn
Holdings: Cat Mss Pix
Notes: First editions. Ms collections incl papers of writer Fritz Leiber, Jr, 1910- , containing correspondence with many authors and manuscript notes, etc, of several Leiber writings, 1932-1974. 1500 items. Papers of reviewer and critic William Anthony Parker White (Tony Boucher) which incl sizeable correspondence files with Ray Bradbury, etc, as well as reviews and manuscripts of Boucher's own writings. Letters to editor and fantastic fiction writer Lin Carter from Lyon Sprague de Camp (ca 200 items) and from various other writers (293 items). Letters, 1966-1972, from James Blish to editors at Doubleday (30 items). Letters, 1966-1976, from Roger Zelazny to editors at Doubleday (44 items).
See also entry under White, William Anthony Parker (Tony Boucher).

KS —UNIVERSITY OF KANSAS, Kenneth Spencer Research Library, Special Collections Dept, Lawrence, 66045. Alexandra Mason, Librn
Holdings: Vols 4000 Cat Mss
Notes: US and foreign science fiction incl periodicals, 1920s to date, North American repository for World SF. Mss of science fiction writers and Science Fiction Research Association, some owned, some on deposit. Incl fan literature (uncat). Noncirculating.

KY —UNIVERSITY OF LOUISVILLE, Ekstrom Library, Rare Books & Special Collections, 2301 S Third St, Louisville, 40208. George T McWhorter, Cur; Delinda Stephens Buie, Asst Cur
Holdings: Mss
Notes: Edgar Rice Burroughs Collection (7000 items) and pulp magazines (10,000), largely duplicates from UCLA.
See also entry under Burroughs, Edgar Rice.

†MO —UNIVERSITY OF MISSOURI-SAINT LOUIS, Thomas Jefferson Library, 8001 Natural Bridge Road, Saint Louis, 63121.
Notes: Utopian Literature Collection, 600 vols which incl some science fiction and fantasy.

†NY —SYRACUSE UNIVERSITY LIBRARIES, E S Bird Library, George Arents Research Library, Rm 600, Syracuse, 13210. Mr Sidney Huttner, Librn
Notes: Samples or selections of cartoon art, comic strips, Disney, fantasy, fanzines, horror (Ackerman mss), mystery pulps, series books and westerns.

OH —KENT STATE UNIVERSITY, Libraries, Dept of Special Collections, Kent, 44242. Dean H Keller, Cur
Notes: Manuscript versions of Stephen R Donaldson's fantasy trilogy, *The Chronicles of Thomas Covenant, the Unbeliever.*

OR —AMERICAN PRIVATE PRESS ASSOCIATION, 112 E Burnett St, Stayton, 97383. Martin M Horvat, Librn
Notes: The collection is divided into two primary segments: the first is the traditional one of Amateur Journalism, the second is science fiction and fantasy oriented. The collection was once at New York University Libraries but moved in 1981.

PA —TEMPLE UNIVERSITY LIBRARIES, Special Collections Dept, Rare Books & Mss Section, Philadelphia, 19122. Thomas M Whitehead, Cur
Holdings: Vols 6000 Cat Mss
Notes: The David Charles Paskow Science Fiction Collection of hardbacks and paperbacks, with additions of printed books and mss, kept as a separate unit of the Department of Special Collections. The collection is particularly good in the period 1950-1970, though dates basically from the late twenties. Books, periodicals and mss. Some fantasy, extensive fanzines. No listing or catalog available at this time. Manuscript deposits of Ben Bova, Gardner Dozois, Jack Dann, George Zebrowski, Tom Purdom, Pamela Sargent, John Varley, and others. Also, contemporary printed books (200 vols), first and later editions, of 18th and early 19th century gothic fiction. Significant strength in Matthew Gregory "Monk" Lewis books.

PA —PENNSYLVANIA STATE UNIVERSITY, Fred Lewis Pattee Library, Special Collections Dept, University Park, 16802. Charles Mann, Chief, Special Collections
Holdings: Vols 3856 Cat
Budget: ($37,000)
Notes: Fantastic Fiction of all genres. Collection also has 607 paperback volumes. There is also a substantial number of science fiction titles in the general stacks.

FANTASTIC FICTION (cont.)

RI —BROWN UNIVERSITY, John Hay Library, 20 Prospect St, Providence, 02912. Mark N Brown, Cur Mss
Holdings: Vols (600) Cat Mss Pix Phonorecords Audiotapes
Notes: Howard Phillips Lovecraft Collection of books, amateur and professional magazines, plus mss/typescripts by and about Howard Phillips Lovecraft, incl first and subsequent editions of Lovecraft's work in 12 languages; complete runs of *Weird Tales, Marvel Tales, The Californian, Driftwind, Rainbow, Leaves, and Amateur Fantasy Correspondent* plus scattered issues of 50 amateur and professional magazines; 1500 letters written by Lovecraft to more than 200 correspondents, 270 mss/typescripts of his essays fiction and poetry plus over 3000 mss/typescripts of essays, fiction, letters, and poetry written by his correspondents. Photocopying of mss is restricted. Also published and mss works of other fantastic fiction writers such as Clark Ashton Smith, August Wiiliam Derleth and a large collection of editions of Edgar Allan Poe.

TX —DALLAS PUBLIC LIBRARY, Central Library, Humanities Division, 1515 Young St, Dallas, 75201. Richard L Waters, Acting Dir; Ron Boyd, Fiction Librn
Holdings: Vols Cat Microforms
Notes: Cited in Tymn, Marshall, Roger C Schlobin, and L W Currey. *A Research Guide to Science Fiction* New York: Garland, 1977. The science fiction collection now exceeds 8000 circulating vols. In addition, the Library purchased in 1983 the personal library and archives of Brian Aldiss (which will be for reference use only). This collection consists of 350 books by Aldiss, 1900 other books by other science fiction writers, 800 issues of science fiction and fantasy periodicals, 100 vols concerning astronautics and space travel, over 1000 typescript pages of mss(incl 6 corrected mss), several sound recordings (incl BBC tapes), and a considerable amount of correspondence.

†UT —BRIGHAM YOUNG UNIVERSITY, Harold B Lee Library, Provo, 84602. Elizabeth Pope, Librn
Notes: Science Fiction-Fantasy Collection, extensive circulating collection. Arkham House near complete, non-circulating. Mysteries, westerns and gothic romances in general fiction. Edgar Rice Burroughs 1st edition collection does not circulate. Science fiction and fantasy art special collection.

WI —UNIVERSITY OF WISCONSIN, LA CROSSE, Murphy Library, 1631 Pine St, La Crosse, 54601. Edwin L Hill, Special Collections Librn
Holdings: Vols 1000 Cat
Notes: The Paul W Skeeters Collection of science fiction, fantasy, and horror literature. Complements the library's complete collection of Arkham House books, which contains many titles autographed by August Derleth, and H P Lovecraft's complete fiction and poetic works.

WI —UNIVERSITY OF WISCONSIN, MADISON, Memorial Library, British & American Language & Literature Collection, 728 State St, Madison, 53706. Yvonne Schofer, Bibliographer
Holdings: Vols
Notes: A collection of mystery fiction mostly of the British Golden Age of the 20s and 30s, in original and reprint form; strong holdings for H Adams, J Rhode, A Upfield, and many others. Stacks. Substantial holdings also for fantasy and science fiction, mostly in stacks; Arkham House and A Derleth materials, restricted use only.

NB —UNIVERSITY OF NEW BRUNSWICK, Ward Chipman Library, PO Box 5050, Saint John, E2L 4L5, Can. Dennis Abblitt, Librn
Notes: Science Fiction and Fantasy Collection, 14,000 books, 9000 magaines. Extensive fanzines. Some comics, posters, records, undergrounds in science fiction genre. Pamphlet and microfiche on magazine collection available.

ON —QUEEN'S UNIVERSITY, Douglas Library, Kingston, K7L 5C4, Can. William F E Morley, Cur, Special Collections
Holdings: Vols 2050 Cat
Notes: Incl about 200 items in the H P Lovecraft collection--books, articles and offprints. Also, 6500 pulp magazines (which are not cataloged). Checklist of holdings is available.

ON —TORONTO PUBLIC LIBRARY, Spaced Out Library, 40 Saint George St, Toronto, M5S 2E4, Can. Doris Mehegan, Librn
Holdings: Cat
Budget: ($18,000)
Notes: Part of the Toronto Public Library. Science fiction, fantasy and related non-fiction. Incl 25,000 items and 8,000 periodicals. Complete catalog and indexes.

FANZINES

CA —SAN FRANCISCO ACADEMY OF COMIC ART, Library, 2850 Ulloa, San Francisco, 94116.
Notes: Incl largest collection of pulp magazines in US. Paper copies of all major American newspapers, emphasis on Hearst papers. Extensive collection of Sherlockiana and a member of the National Sherlockiana Society. Also extensive collection of early motion picture tapes, books, magazines and posters. 19th and early 20th century children's books also in the holdings. Collection incl 1,000,000 comic strips, 22, 000 comic books, 12,500 hard cover mystery books, 8000 hard cover science fiction books and copies of all science fiction pulp magazines.

†IL —WHEATON COLLEGE, Library, Wheaton, 60187. Marjorie E Mead, Librn
Notes: The Marion E Wade Collection of papers and books of seven authors: Owen Barfield, G K Chesterton, C S Lewis, George MacDonald, Dorothy L Sayers, J R R Tolkien, and Charles Williams. Fanzines relating to same.

KS —UNIVERSITY OF KANSAS, Kenneth Spencer Research Library, Special Collections Dept, Lawrence, 66045. Alexandra Mason, Librn
Holdings: Vols Mss
Notes: US and foreign science fiction incl periodicals, 1920s to date, North American repository for World SF. Mss of science fiction writers and Science Fiction Research Association, some owned, some on deposit. Incl fan literature (uncat). Noncirculating.

†KS —UNIVERSITY OF KANSAS, Spencer Research Library, Dept of Special Collections, Lawrence, 66045. Alexandra Mason, Librn
Notes: Extensive science fiction, 6 ft of fanzines, 500 Big-Little Books, extensive series books, James E Gunn and Lloyd Biggle special collections in the Dept of Special Collections.

KY —UNIVERSITY OF LOUISVILLE, Ekstrom Library, Rare Books & Special Collections, 2301 S Third St, Louisville, 40208. George T McWhorter, Cur; Delinda Stephens Buie, Asst Cur
Holdings: Vols 5000 // Mss Pix
Notes: Mint first editions of Edgar Rice Burroughs and subsequent editions of all his works; foreign editions in 35 languages; serial publications; comics and Sunday "fulls"; big-little books; fan magazines; posters; bibliographies and related materials.

MD —UNIVERSITY OF MARYLAND, BALTIMORE COUNTY, Albin O Kuhn Library and Gallery, 5401 Wilkens Ave, Baltimore, 21228. Ann Copeland, Special Collections Librn
Holdings: Vols (10,000) Uncat //
Notes: The Azriel Rosenfeld Science Fiction Research Collection of about 20,000 items; the Walter Coslet collection of 10,000 fanzines.
See also entry under Science Fiction.

MI —MICHIGAN STATE UNIVERSITY, Libraries, Special Collections Div, East Lansing, 48824. Jannette Fiore, Librn
Notes: The Russel B Nye Popular Culture Collection in the Michigan State Univ Libraries incl over (45,000) items. Most of the collection is organized into 4 categories: comic art, popular fiction, popular information materials and materials relating to the popular performing arts. The Comic Art Collection incl approx 20,000 comic books and another 1000 books, magazines and fanzines about comics. Best-represented are the super-hero comics of the 1960s--over 90 percent of those published can be found in the collection. Samples, and sometimes substantial runs, of comics in other genres (eg, war comics, funny animal comics, underground comics) are also maintained and there are over 1000 issues from the 1940s. The comics are cataloged, with author-title and subject access and a checklist of holdings. Several hundred pages of indexesto comic books are added to the collection by the Amateur Press Alliance for Indexing each year,and an annual index to these is available. A quarterly newsletter of news about the MSU collection and other public comics collections is also published.

NY —MUSEUM OF CARTOON ART LIBRARY, Comly Avenue, Rye Brook, 10573.
Notes: Original comics and cartoon art, 60, 000 pieces. 800 animated cartoons. Disney collection extensive. Samples of Big-Little Books, foreign comics, fanzines, cartoon related games, posters, pulps, undergrounds. Hal Foster, Walt Kelly, Gene Byrns, Tad Dorgan, Chester Gould extensive original art collections.

†NY —SYRACUSE UNIVERSITY LIBRARIES, E S Bird Library, George Arents Research Library, Rm 600, Syracuse, 13210. Mr Sidney Huttner, Librn
Notes: Samples or selections of cartoon art, comic strips, Disney, fantasy, fanzines, horror (Ackerman mss), mystery pulps, series books and westerns.

†OH —BOWLING GREEN STATE UNIVERSITY, Libraries, Bowling Green, 43403. Nancy White Lee, Librn
Notes: Extensive miscellaneous incl Sunday strips, Big-Little Books, fanzines, foreign comics, pulps, gum cards, undergrounds, and movie posters.

OR —AMERICAN PRIVATE PRESS ASSOCIATION, 112 E Burnett St, Stayton, 97383. Martin M Horvat, Librn
Notes: The collection is divided into two primary segments: the first is the traditional one of Amateur Journalism, the second is science fiction and fantasy oriented. The collection was once at New York University Libraries but moved in 1981.

†TX —TEXAS A&M UNIVERSITY, Library, College Station, 77843. Donald H Dyal, Librn
Notes: 4000 fanzines.

NB —UNIVERSITY OF NEW BRUNSWICK, Ward Chipman Library, PO Box 5050, Saint John, E2L 4L5, Can. Dennis Abblitt, Librn
Notes: Science Fiction and Fantasy Collection, 14,000 books, 9000 magaines. Extensive fanzines. Some comics, posters, records, undergrounds in science fiction genre. Pamphlet and microfiche on magazine collection available.

ON —TORONTO PUBLIC LIBRARY, Spaced Out Library, 40 Saint George St, Toronto, M5S 2E4, Can. Doris Mehegan, Librn
Notes: Some fanzines, foreign langage science fiction, and some pulps on microfiche.

FAR EAST see East (Far East)

FARADIZATION see Electrotherapeutics

FARAGO, LADISLAS

MA —BOSTON UNIVERSITY, Mugar Memorial Library, Special Collections Dept, 771 Commonwealth Ave, Boston, 02215. Howard B Gotlieb, Dir
Holdings: Mss Pix

FARB, PETER

MA —BOSTON UNIVERSITY, Mugar Memorial Library, Special Collections Dept, 771 Commonwealth Ave, Boston, 02215. Howard B Gotlieb, Dir
Holdings: Mss

FARCES

NC —UNIVERSITY OF NORTH CAROLINA, CHARLOTTE, J Murrey Atkins Library, UNCC Station, Charlotte, 28223. Robert F Brabham Jr, Special Collections Librn
Holdings: Cat
Notes: Most of the plays (842 in 110 vols) were originally collected by Augusta Sophia, a daughter of George III. At her death, they passed to her brother Ernst August, Elector of Hanover, and became part of the Knigliche Ernst-August-Fideicommiss-Bibliothek, which was dispersed at auction in 1970-1971. Period covered is 1618-1826.

FARJEON, BENJAMIN L.

CA —UNIVERSITY OF CALIFORNIA, LOS ANGELES, Research Library, Dept of Special Collections, 405 Hilgard Ave, Los Angeles, 90024. Edward Shreeves, Chairman, Bibliographers Group; David S Zeidberg, Head
Holdings: Vols 50 Cat
Notes: 50 first and other editions of his books; 25 letters.

FARLEY, BELMONT

NC —DUKE UNIVERSITY, William R Perkins Library, Manuscript Dept, Durham, 27706. Ellen Gartrell, Cur of Mss
Holdings: Cat Mss
Notes: Especially strong for Southern states, 19th-20th centuries. Education of women and blacks, regional and national organizations, public and private schools. Papers of black educator Charles N Hunter; Alliance for the Guidance of Rural Youth; NEA official Belmont Farley, and much more.

FARLEY, JAMES A.

DC —GEORGETOWN UNIVERSITY, Library, Special Collections Div, 37 & O Sts NW, Washington, 20057. George M Barringer, Special Collections Librn; Nicholas B Sheetz, Mss Librn
Holdings: Mss Pix
Notes: Correspondence, clippings, photographs, and memorabilia incl items relating to Mr Dolan's activities in the Democratic Party in and around Chicago, his friendships with James A Farley, John W McCormack, and Fred Allen, and his student days at Georgetown University.

DC —LIBRARY OF CONGRESS, Manuscript Division, Washington, 20540. John C Broderick, Chief
Holdings: Cat Mss Pix
Notes: Mss, papers, records, etc.

FARLOW, W. G.

MA —HARVARD UNIVERSITY LIBRARY, Farlow Reference Library, 20 Divinity Ave, Cambridge, 02138. Geraldine C Kaye, Librn
Holdings: Vols (60,000)
Notes: The Farlow Reference Library provides complete coverage of the systematic literature on algae, bryophytes, fungi, and lichens. Established by bequest of Professor William G Farlow, it is one of the most extensive cryptogamic botany libraries in the US. Incl ms and archival collections of W G Farlow and R Thaxter. Books do not circulate.

FARM ANIMALS see Domestic Animals; Stock and Stockbreeding

FARM EQUIPMENT

AL —US DEPT OF AGRICULTURE, SCIENCE & EDUCATION ADMINISTRATION, National Tillage Machinery Laboratory, Library, PO Box 792, Auburn, 36830. William A Gill, Collaborator
Holdings: Vols (39,000) Cat Mss Maps Pix Slides 16mm Films Microforms
Budget: ($20,000)
Notes: The National Tillage Machinery Laboratory (NTML) has a special technical library comprised of highly selective engineering and physical science materials pertinent to soil-machine relations, such as tillage, earthmoving, mining, soil trafficability, and vehical mobility. A high percentage of the library material comes from sources outside the US and outside agriculture. Particularly strong in Russian-language literature.

CA —UNIVERSITY OF CALIFORNIA, DAVIS, Shields Library, Dept of Special Collections, Davis, 95616. Donald Kunitz, Head; C Danial Elliott, Asst Head
Notes: Farming equipment: Manufacturer's catalogs, manuals, parts lists, ephemera, and literature pertaining to historical as well as current data on such items as tractors, engines, combines, hay equipment, etc. Described in "The Higgins Library: A Source for the Study of Agricultural History," Don Kunitz, *Agricultural History,* vol 49, 1975, pp 89-91.

CA —THE HAGGIN MUSEUM, Petzinger Library of Californiana, 1201 N Pershing Ave, Stockton, 95203. Diane Freggiaro, Librn/Archivist
Holdings: Vols (7000) Cat Mss Maps Pix Slides Audiotapes 16mm Films
Notes: The Petzinger Library is open by appointment only. Special emphasis on Stockton and San Joaquin County and Valley area, local biography, agriculture, agricultural history, industrial history, farm machinery (especially Holt Manufacturing Co, Stockton). There is a photograph collection of 8500 pictures, and extensive manuscript holdings (about 17,000 pieces).

IL —NORTHERN ILLINOIS REGIONAL HISTORY CENTER, Sven Parson Hall, Northern Illinois University, De Kalb, 60115. Glen Gildemeister, Dir
Holdings: Cat Mss Maps Pix Slides Phonorecords Audiotapes 16mm Films Microforms
Notes: "A research center for advanced research in the humanities. This northern area of Illinois (excluding Cook County) has been virtually untouched by collecting agencies and we hope to fill that void. We will be strong in agribusiness, agricultural implement business, and hybrid farming mechanics....Will be primarily a ms repository, but [have] already taken responsibility for many artifacts and books, some rare."

NY —NEW YORK STATE OFFICE OF PARKS & RECREATION, TACONIC REGION, Clermont State Historic Park, Library, RR 1, Box 215, Germantown, 12526. Bruce E Naramore, Historic Site Manager
Holdings: Vols (5000) Cat Mss Maps
Notes: Period editions of pre - and post-American Revolutionary War agricultural technology. Many belonged to the Chancellor Robert R Livingston (1746-1813). Incl land drainage, hybrids, fertilizers, and the introduction of Merino sheep.

OH —WRIGHT STATE UNIVERSITY, Greater Miami Valley Research Center, University Library, Dayton, 45431. Patrick B Nolan, Head of Archives
Holdings: Mss
Notes: Records of OS Kelly Company of Springfield, Ohio. Incl 100 linear ft of archives and manuscript collections.

FARM LABORERS see Agricultural Laborers

FARM LIFE

AL —TROY STATE UNIVERSITY, Library, Troy, 36081. Kenneth Croslin, Dir of University Libraries
Holdings: / / Mss
Notes: Incl the John Horry Dent Papers, 1851-1892, 25 vols, mss, farm journals, account books, letters, legal documents, clippings and miscellaneous memorabilia of a planter, plantation owner, investor, who lived in Barbour County, Alabama from 1837 to 1867 and in Floyd County, Georgia from 1867 to 1892. Typescript from tape "Sharecropping farming in Pike County, Alabama in early 1900's" (56p). Typescript of tapes of "Source material extracted from Troy, Alabama newspapers, 1871-1935" indexed under 9 subjects by color code.

CA —POMONA PUBLIC LIBRARY, Special Collections, 625 S Garey Ave, PO Box 2271, Pomona, 91766. David Streeter, Librn
Holdings: Cat Audiotapes
Notes: Oral, taped interviews with Pomona Valley settlers and residents.

CA —THE HAGGIN MUSEUM, Petzinger Library of Californiana, 1201 N Pershing Ave, Stockton, 95203. Diane Freggiaro, Librn/Archivist
Holdings: Vols (7000) Cat Mss Maps Pix Slides Audiotapes 16mm Films
Notes: The Petzinger Library is open by appointment only. Special emphasis on Stockton and San Joaquin County and Valley area, local biography, agriculture, agricultural history, industrial history, farm machinery (especially Holt Manufacturing Co, Stockton). There is a photograph collection of 8500 pictures, and extensive manuscript holdings (about 17,000 pieces).

CO —COLORADO STATE UNIVERSITY, Libraries, Fort Collins, 80523. John Newman, Special Collections Librn
Holdings: Vols (11,000) Cat Mss Pix
Budget: ($7000)
Notes: The Western American Literature Collection incl fiction, poetry, pictures, art, and other works of the imagination set in the American Frontier West and modern rural West, especially the Rocky Mountain Area. There is also a collection of some 500 pulp magazines, "Westerns" mostly.

DC —LIBRARY OF CONGRESS, Prints & Photographs Div, Washington, 20540.
Notes: The Abdul-Hamid II Collection of photographs of Turkey. Formal views of military installations and personnel, naval vessels, schools, hospitals, historic monuments, fire-fighting and lifesaving equipment, major cities, palaces and stables of the Imperial Court, and other subjects of official interest.

GA —UNIVERSITY OF GEORGIA, Libraries, Special Collections Division, Athens, 30602. Vesta Lee Gordon, Asst Dir for Special Collections
Notes: The Arbitron Collection of television and radio program ratings, 1949-date (except past year). In-depth, statistical analyses of the listening public by age, sex, county, some ethnic groups, farm population, listening preferences, etc. 26,302 bound vols. 2 reports, 1949-81. To be added to annually.

IL —NORTHERN ILLINOIS REGIONAL HISTORY CENTER, Sven Parson Hall, Northern Illinois University, De Kalb, 60115. Glen Gildemeister, Dir
Holdings: Cat Mss Maps Pix Slides Phonorecords Audiotapes 16mm Films Microforms
Notes: "A research center for advanced research in the humanities. This northern area of Illinois (excluding Cook County) has been virtually untouched by collecting agencies and we hope to fill that void. We will be strong in agribusiness, agricultural implement business, and hybrid farming mechanics....Will be primarily a ms repository, but [have] already taken responsibility for many artifacts and books, some rare."

KS —UNIVERSITY OF KANSAS, Kenneth Spencer Research Library, Kansas Collection, Lawrence, 66045. Sheryl K Williams, Cur
Holdings: Vols (92,000) Cat Mss Maps Pix
Notes: All aspects of the American West and trans-Mississippi history, especially Kansas and the Plains region. Overland diaries, cartographic history, Indians, emigration and immigration, printing history, cattle industry, agriculture and farm life, conservation are some special interests, in addition to the usual political, economic, military and social interests.

NY —CORNELL UNIVERSITY LIBRARIES, Collection of Regional History, Dept of Manuscripts and Univ Archives, Ithaca, 14853.
Notes: The noncurrent records, letters,

FARM LIFE (cont.)

records of meetings and other historic data dating back to Dec 4, 1867, the date of organization of the National Grange. Also the papers of Louis I Taber, National Master of the Grange from 1923 to 1941.

NY —COLUMBIA UNIVERSITY LIBRARIES, Rare Book & Manuscript Library, 801 Butler Library, 535 W 114 St, New York, 10027. Kenneth A Lohf, Librn
Holdings: Mss
Notes: The papers of Professor Frank Tannenbaum, approx 28,000 items of correspondence and mss relating to Latin American and Mexican history, also the US Farm Security Program, 1934-1937. Professor Tannenbaum also bequeathed his research library of more than 3000 vols on all phases of Latin American history and literature to Columbia. Restricted use.

ND —NORTH DAKOTA STATE UNIVERSITY, Library, Fargo, 58105. John E Bye, Archivist
Holdings: Vols (2500) Cat Mss Maps Pix
Budget: ($14,000)
Notes: The Collection is administered by the North Dakota Institute for Regional Studies. It contains materials on North Dakota history, especially the Red River Valley, with emphasis on bonanza farming, pioneer life, agriculture, local history, literary figures, business, Fargo, ND, and some political collections, particularly of the Nonpartisan League. Also, there is an extensive photographic collection covering the pioneer to post-World War I period and includes the "Hultstrand 'History in Pictures' Collection" of sod houses, pioneer life and farming. For the small collections, there has been published, *Guide to the Small Collection Manuscripts of the North Dakota Institute for Regional Studies,* by John E Bye, 1977.

PA —FRIENDS HISTORICAL LIBRARY OF SWARTHMORE COLLEGE, Swarthmore, 19081. J William Frost, Dir
Holdings: Vols (35,000) Cat Mss Pix
Notes: Library's collection contain information on the history and doctrine of the Society of Friends, Quaker contributions to literature, science, business, education, and government, plus their reform efforts in peace, Indian rights, women's rights, and abolition of slavery. Incl in the more than 250 mss collections are farm journals, account books, and correspondence of several rural families, mostly from the 19th century.

PA —PENNSYLVANIA STATE UNIVERSITY, Fred Lewis Pattee Library, Life Sciences Library, University Park, 16802. Keith Roe, Head
Notes: This collection is strong in periodical runs, particularly European learned societies and agriculture. It contains extensive collections of Experiment Station publications and has developed specialties in Mycology and Fusaria. There is also a special collection of 1105 glass slides on early Pennsylvania lumbering.

†SD —SOUTH DAKOTA SCHOOL OF MINES & TECHNOLOGY, Devereaux Library, Rapid City, 57701.
Holdings: Vols (3786) Cat Mss Maps Pix Audiotapes Micrforms
Notes: This special collection, in general, relates to the Black Hills area of South Dakota and Wyoming, especially mining and exploration of the area; the West River area of South Dakota, primarily county histories; and South Dakota Territorial and State materials. There are also specialized areas of this collection: (1) *Marion N Bruce* Collection. Documents, correspondence, books and periodicals dealing with weather modification in South Dakota; (2) *Mildred Fielder Collection*. Mss, pictures, books and periodicals from an author whose special area was the Black Hills. Most of her work on railroads, mines, trails, etc, relates to historical aspects. Collection incl research materials, galley proofs and final copies of her various publications; (3) *Cleophas C O'Harra Collection*. Mss, pictures, books and original source materials, primarily related to the Black Hills area andexpeditions thereto. Much of the data was collected for a book on the Black Hills which was never published; and (4) *Caving* Collection. Maps of various caves in Black Hills area, being kept current and updated by members of the Paha Sapa Grotto. Also, some books and periodicals on caving in genral.

TX —AMARILLO PUBLIC LIBRARY, 413 E Fourth, Amarillo, 79101. Mary Kay Snell, Librn
Holdings: Vols Cat Mss Maps Pix
Notes: The southwest collections incl materials on the history of Texas, Louisiana, New Mexico, Arkansas, Missouri and Kansas. General subjects covered incl overland journeys, early narratives, early biographies, Indian captivities, outlaws, US government reports, Mississippi and Ohio Rivers, the Mexican War, reports of Catholic missionaries, Niles Register, early publications, fur trade, western trails, Texas Rangers, sheriffs and Texas as a sovereign state, buffalo hunting, Indian wars, cowboys, the arrival of farmers, fences, and towns. Over 1600 items which incl books, documents, maps, mss, pamphlets, unpublished theses, interviews and photographs. The three major collections are the William Henry Bush Collection, the Laurence J Fitzsimon Collection and the Calendar of John L McCarty.

TX —NORTH TEXAS STATE UNIVERSITY, Archives, NT Station Box 5188, Denton, 76203. Robert LaForte, University Archivist
Notes: The NTSU Archives houses the patron's copy of oral history interviews that are part of the Oral History Collection, an independent project not part of the Archives. This collection of interviews covers, in part, the following subject areas: World War II Pearl Harbor survivors, World War II prisoners of war, Texas legislators, ex-governors of Texas, Texans employed by the administrations of FDR, Texas businessmen and businesswomen, development of the Coastal Bend area of south Texas, and Mexican-American social action activities. Cataloged. Transcriptions available. See *Oral History Collection,* North Texas State University Bulletin, April 1981.

TX —TEXAS TECH UNIVERSITY, Library, Lubbock, 79409. David J Murrah, Assoc Dir for Special Collections

UT —UNIVERSITY OF UTAH, Marriott Library, Special Collections, Salt Lake City, 84112. Gregory C Thompson, Cur

WI —UNIVERSITY OF WISCONSIN, GREEN BAY, Library/Learning Center, Green Bay, 54301. Marian A Gould, Acting Dir, Special Collections/University Archives
Holdings: Vols 100 Cat Mss Maps Pix Slides Audiotapes Videotapes
Notes: Belgian-American Research Collection deals with the Belgian-American Settlement in Brown, Door and Kewaunee counties of northeastern Wisconsin. Emphasis is on the rural life and commerical fishing activities in the Bay of Green Bay. Bibliography, *Belgian-American Research* Materials, is available on request.

ON —UNIVERSITY OF GUELPH, Library, Guelph, N1G 2W1, Can. Margaret Beckman, Chief Librn; Ellen Pearson, Ref Librn
Notes: 15,000 monographs, 350 periodical subscriptions, 5000 documents, also maps, mss, audio/videotapes, 16mm films. Supports research activities related to planning theory, public administration, rural sociology, rural planning and development, rural and urban community studies, regional analysis, rural environment and resource use, policy design.

FARM LIFE CLUBS see Agricultural Societies

FARM MACHINERY see Agricultural Machinery

FARM MANAGEMENT

IL —NORTHERN ILLINOIS REGIONAL HISTORY CENTER, Sven Parson Hall, Northern Illinois University, De Kalb, 60115. Glen Gildemeister, Dir
Holdings: Cat Mss Maps Pix Slides Phonorecords Audiotapes 16mm Films Microforms
Notes: "A research center for advanced research in the humanities. This northern area of Illinois (excluding Cook County) has been virtually untouched by collecting agencies and we hope to fill that void. We will be strong in agribusiness, agricultural implement business, and hybrid farming mechanics....Will be primarily a ms repository, but [have] already taken responsibility for many artifacts and books, some rare."

IA —IOWA STATE UNIVERSITY, Library, Ames, 50011. Warren B Kuhn, Dean of Library Services
Holdings: Cat Mss
Notes: Incl agriculture finance and policy, agricultural marketing, farm management, land valuation, and rural development. Extensive serial holdings.

IA —IOWA STATE UNIVERSITY, Library, Dept of Special Collections, Ames, 50011. Stanley M Yates, Head
Notes: Papers of Roswell Garst, Iowa's most famous farmer. Initiator of experimental feeding of corncobs to produce beef, use of hybrid seedcorn, and commercial fertilizers. Credited with opening of agricultural sales and exchanges with Russia in the 1950s.

TX —AMARILLO PUBLIC LIBRARY, 413 E Fourth, Amarillo, 79101. Mary Kay Snell, Librn
Holdings: Vols Cat Mss Maps Pix
Notes: The southwest collections incl materials on the history of Texas, Louisiana, New Mexico, Arkansas, Missouri and Kansas. General subjects covered incl overland journeys, early narratives, early biographies, Indian captivities, outlaws, US government reports, Mississippi and Ohio Rivers, the Mexican War, reports of Catholic missionaries, Niles Register, early publications, fur trade, western trails, Texas Rangers, sheriffs and Texas as a sovereign state, buffalo hunting, Indian wars, cowboys, the arrival of farmers, fences, and towns. Over 1600 items which incl books, documents, maps, mss, pamphlets, unpublished theses, interviews and photographs. The three major collections are the William Henry Bush Collection, the Laurence J Fitzsimon Collection and the Calendar of John L McCarty.

FARM MECHANICS see Agricultural Engineering

FARM WORKERS see Agricultural Laborers

FARMER, GEORGE, 1860-1921

MO —WASHINGTON UNIVERSITY, Libraries, Special Collections Dept, Campus Box 1061, St Louis, 63130.
Notes: Farmer Family correspondence, 1840-1870.

FARMERS

CO —UNIVERSITY OF COLORADO, Libraries, Western Historical Collections, Boulder, 80309.
Holdings: Mss
Notes: Papers of James G Patton (b 1902), a native of Nucla, Colorado, who spent most of his early life in western Colorado. He became interested in the organization of farmers while promoting farmers' cooperative insurance during the early 1930s. He was successively secretary (1932) and president (1937) of the Colorado Farmers Union and an executive board member (1937) and president (1940-1966) of the National Farmers Union. After his retirement he served as an aide to the Pennsylvania Secretary of Agriculture. Throughout his life he has been deeply involved in agriculture in developing countries. The collection contains correspondence, published materials and

FARMERS (cont.)

topical files on Patton's wide-ranging agricultural, political and social interests. 30 boxes, 85 vols, 1940s-1970s. A typescript inventory is available.

GA —UNIVERSITY OF GEORGIA, Libraries, Special Collections Division, Athens, 30602. Vesta Lee Gordon, Asst Dir for Special Collections
Notes: The Arbitron Collection of television and radio program ratings, 1949-date (except past year). In-depth, statistical analyses of the listening public by age, sex, county, some ethnic groups, farm population, listening preferences, etc. 26,302 bound vols. 2 reports, 1949-81. To be added to annually.

IL —NORTHERN ILLINOIS REGIONAL HISTORY CENTER, Sven Parson Hall, Northern Illinois University, De Kalb, 60115. Glen Gildemeister, Dir
Holdings: Cat Mss Maps Pix Slides Phonorecords Audiotapes 16mm Films Microforms
Notes: "A research center for advanced research in the humanities. This northern area of Illinois (excluding Cook County) has been virtually untouched by collecting agencies and we hope to fill that void. We will be strong in agribusiness, agricultural implement business, and hybrid farming mechanics....Will be primarily a ms repository, but [have] already taken responsibility for many artifacts and books, some rare."

IA —IOWA STATE UNIVERSITY, Library, Dept of Special Collections, Ames, 50011. Stanley M Yates, Head
Notes: Papers of Roswell Garst, Iowa's most famous farmer. Initiator of experimental feeding of corncobs to produce beef, use of hybrid seedcorn, and commercial fertilizers. Credited with opening of agricultural sales and exchanges with Russia in the 1950s. Also mss of the National Farmers Process Tax Recovery Association.

NY —CORNELL UNIVERSITY LIBRARIES, Collection of Regional History, Dept of Manuscripts and Univ Archives, Ithaca, 14853.
Notes: The noncurrent records, letters, records of meetings and other historic data dating back to Dec 4, 1867, the date of organization of the National Grange. Also the papers of Louis I Taber, National Master of the Grange from 1923 to 1941.

FARMERS COOPERATIVES see Agriculture, Cooperative

FARMING see Agriculture

FARNUM, WILLIAM

CA —UNIVERSITY OF SOUTHERN CALIFORNIA, Edward L Doheny Memorial Library, Archives of Performing Arts, University Park, Los Angeles, 90089. Robert Knutson, Librn
Holdings: Mss Pix
Notes: Personal collection of papers, pictures, etc.

FAROESE LANGUAGE AND LITERATURE

WA —UNIVERSITY OF WASHINGTON LIBRARIES, Suzzallo Library, Scandinavian Collections, FM-25, Seattle, 98195. A Gerald Anderson, Librn
Holdings: Vols (50,000) Cat Mss Pix
Budget: ($15,546)
Notes: Research collections with emphasis on languages and literatures, and auxiliary strengths in history, political science, social science. Archival and other special materials relating to Scandinavian-Americans in the Pacific Northwest are located in other appropriate collections.

FARQUHAR, FRANCIS PELOUBET, 1887-1974

CA —UNIVERSITY OF CALIFORNIA, LOS ANGELES, Research Library, Dept of Special Collections, 405 Hilgard Ave, Los Angeles, 90024. Edward Shreeves, Chairman, Bibliographers Group; David S Zeidberg, Head
Notes: 2000 books in the Francis P Farquhar Collection of Mountaineering Literature.

FARQUHAR, PERCIVAL

CA —HOOVER INSTITUTION ON WAR, REVOLUTION & PEACE, Stanford University, Stanford, 94305. Milorad M Drachkovitch, Archivist
Holdings: // Mss
Notes: Papers of Percival Farquhar, 1922-1928. Telegrams, cablegrams, reports, memoranda, and other material relating to the negotiations between Farquhar and associates and the government of the USSR concernig the development of Russia's iron ore and steel resources and subsequent arbitration of the differences between the parties. 5 ft.

FARQUHAR, ROBERT D.

CA —UNIVERSITY OF CALIFORNIA, LOS ANGELES, William Andrews Clark Memorial Library, 2520 Cimarron St, Los Angeles, 90018.
Holdings: Cat Mss Maps Pix
Notes: A small collection of his architectural sketches, blueprints and albums.

FARR, FINIS

MA —BOSTON UNIVERSITY, Mugar Memorial Library, Special Collections Dept, 771 Commonwealth Ave, Boston, 02215. Howard B Gotlieb, Dir
Holdings: Cat Mss
Notes: Mss, correspondence, etc collected in depth; incl publications by or about.

FARRAGUT, DAVID G.

†AL —MUSEUMS OF THE CITY OF MOBILE, Reference Library, 355 Government St, Mobile, 36602. Caldwell Delaney, Adminr

DC —LIBRARY OF CONGRESS, Manuscript Division, Washington, 20540. John C Broderick, Chief
Notes: Papers of his pre-Civil War career.

FARRAR, GERALDINE

DC —LIBRARY OF CONGRESS, Music Division, Washington, 20540.
Notes: The Geraldine Farrar Collection incl correspondence, scripts, contracts, programs, playbills, scrapbooks, posters, and photographs. Also in the Motion Picture, Broadcasting, and Recorded Sound Division are 50 disc recordings of radio broadcast transcriptions and special pressings made by the Gramophone and Typewriter Company, Ltd.

NY —YONKERS PUBLIC LIBRARY, Grinton I Will Library, 1500 Central Park Ave, Yonkers, 10701. Joan W Stevenson, Head of Fine Arts Dept
Holdings: Vols (12,000) Cat
Budget: ($36,000)
Notes: Incl periodicals, 70 titles (ca 15 yr back issues); 27 vertical file drawers (18 on artists & musicians); 1230 slides; 2200 music scores; cat; sheet music, ca 1200 titles; 140 libretti; 13,0000 phonograph albums; cat; 1000 cassettes. Books, scores, phonograph albums, cassettes are cataloged. Rare collection of 57 test pressings of Geraldine Farrar, some of which have never been issued.

FARRELL, HENRY

MA —BOSTON UNIVERSITY, Mugar Memorial Library, Special Collections Dept, 771 Commonwealth Ave, Boston, 02215. Howard B Gotlieb, Dir
Holdings: Cat Mss

FARRELL, JAMES T.

NV —UNIVERSITY OF NEVADA, RENO, University Library, Special Collections Dept, Reno, 89557. Robert E Blesse, Head
Holdings: // Vols (93) Cat Other appearances 225 Cat
Notes: Includes individual works by author in all editions including translations; also prefaces, introductions, published correspondence, appearances in anthologies, periodicals, etc. Bibliographical research collection, part of Modern Authors Collection.

PA —UNIVERSITY OF PENNSYLVANIA, Van Pelt Library, Rare Books Collection, 34 & Walnut Sts, Philadelphia, 19104. Daniel Traister, Special Collections Librn
Holdings: Vols 250 Cat Mss Pix
Notes: The definitive collection, 1000 boxes of mss and correspondence. Descriptive case file available in library.

FARRIERY see Horses; Veterinary Medicine

FASCISM

CA —HOOVER INSTITUTION ON WAR, REVOLUTION & PEACE, Stanford University, Stanford, 94305. Milorad M Drachkovitch, Archivist
Holdings: Mss Pix
Notes: Records of *National Republic* magazine, incl newspaper clippings, printed matter, pamphlets, reports, indices, notes, bulletins, lettergrams, weekly letters, and photographs, 1905-1960, relating to pacifist, communist, fascist, and other radical movements as well as political developments in the US and Soviet Russia. 826 ms boxes.

KS —UNIVERSITY OF KANSAS, Kenneth Spencer Research Library, Kansas Collection, Lawrence, 66045. Sheryl K Williams, Cur
Holdings: Vols 6000 Cat Mss Audiotapes
Notes: The Wilcox Collection of Contemporary Political Movements containing American extremist literature from the 1950s to the present, and incl appox 4000 serials, 5000 books and pamplets, 400 audiotapes, and 50,000 pieces of ephemera. Approximately 7000 right and left wing organizations are represented by this material as well as the views of many leaders or prime movers within these organizations. The collection is partially cataloged.

TX —UNIVERSITY OF TEXAS LIBRARIES, General Libraries, PO Box P, Austin, 78713. Carolyn Bucknell, Asst Dir for Collection Development
Holdings: Cat Microforms

FASCISM—GERMANY

NY —ALFRED UNIVERSITY, Herrick Memorial Library, Alfred, 14802. June E Brown, Head Librn
Holdings: Vols (700) // Uncat Pix
Notes: The Waid Collection. Incl a number of rare titles from the Nazi period. Books in the collection, not on the "verboten list," incl the writings of Stegmann, Ganghofer, Brandi and Sealsfield.

FASCISM—ITALY

NY —HOFSTRA UNIVERSITY, Library, 1000 Fulton Ave, Hempstead, 11550. Charles R Andrews, Dean of Library Services
Holdings: Vols (5000) Cat
Notes: The personal collection of Professor Shepard Clough of Columbia University. Especially strong in French and Italian modern history, Italian Fascism and European economic statistics.

FASCISM—U.S.

PA —TEMPLE UNIVERSITY LIBRARIES, Special Collections Dept, Contemporary Culture Collection, Philadelphia, 19122. Patricia J Case, Cur
Notes: The Contemporary Culture Collection. See full entry under US-Social Life and Customs.

FASHION

CA —WESTERN COSTUME COMPANY, Research Library, 5335 Melrose Ave,

FASHION (cont.)

Hollywood, 90038. Nancy S Kinney, Dir of Research
Holdings: Vols 6000
Notes: Incl 70 vertical file drawers of photographs, 200 bound periodicals, 80 mail order catalogs (Sears, etc). Wardrobe stills. 5 periodical subscriptions. Collection can be used only by the customers of Western Costume Company. All other use is on a fee basis. Collection is non-circulating. Photocopying available.

DE —WIDENER UNIVERSITY, Delaware Campus Library, Box 7139, Concord Pike, Wilmington, 19803. Jane E Hukill, Library Dir
Holdings: Vols (48,000) Audiotapes Videotapes Microforms
Notes: Incl fashion design, history of costume, textiles.

DC —LIBRARY OF CONGRESS, Prints & Photographs Div, Washington, 20540.
Holdings: Cat Pix
Notes: Toni Frissell's entire collection of photographs and negatives. Incl fashion photography and informal portraits of prominent figures. 270,000 black and white negatives, 42,000 color transparencies, 25, 000 enlargement prints, and proof sheets dating from 1935-71.

IL —UNIVERSITY OF ILLINOIS, URBANA/CHAMPAIGN, Library, Home Economics Library, 314 Bevier Hall, Champaign, 61820. Barbara C Swain, Librn
Holdings: Vols Cat
Notes: Textiles, clothing, and interior design. *See also* entry under Retail Trade.

IN —PURDUE UNIVERSITY LIBRARIES, Consumer & Family Sciences Library, Stone Hall W, West Lafayette, 47907. Emily Alward, Librn
Holdings: Vols (14,000) Cat

MA —OLD STURBRIDGE VILLAGE, Research Library, Sturbridge, 01566. Theresa Rini Percy, Librn
Holdings: Cat Pix
Notes: Northeastern US, 1790-1850; some English sources.

MN —MINNEAPOLIS COLLEGE OF ART & DESIGN, Library, 200 E 25 St, Minneapolis, 55404. Richard Kronstedt, Head Librn

MO —SAINT LOUIS PUBLIC LIBRARY, Art Dept, 1301 Olive St, Saint Louis, 63103. Martha Hilligoss, Librn
Notes: Plus more than 10,000 slides.

MO —WASHINGTON UNIVERSITY, Art & Architecture Library, Saint Louis, 63130. Imre Meszaros, Librn
Holdings: Vols (60,413) Cat Maps Pix Microforms
Budget: ($100,000)
Notes: Art and architecture of East Asia; rare books; archaeology; fashion design.

NY —BROOKLYN MUSEUM, Art Reference Library, 188 Eastern Parkway, Brooklyn, 11238.
Holdings: Vols (130,000)
Notes: Collection incl original fashion sketches.

NY —FASHION INSTITUTE OF TECHNOLOGY, Special Collections Library, 227 W 27 St, New York, 10001. Barbara Jones, Dir; Janette Rozene, Librn
Holdings: Vols (4900) Cat Periodicals Audiotapes
Budget: ($7500)
Notes: Incl 61 uncataloged collections of designer sketches, 30 uncataloged collections fashion designer or firm scrapbooks, 245 volumes WPA scrapbooks, and 50 oral history transcripts. Highlights: 19th century fashion plate periodicals; original fashion sketches from late 1800s, incl designs by Lady Duff Gordon, Muriel King, Berley Studios; scrapbooks compiled by Claire McCardell, Mainbocher.

NY —FASHION INSTITUTE OF TECHNOLOGY, Edward C Blum Design Laboratory, 227 W 27 St, New York, 10001. Laura Sinderbrand, Dir
Holdings: Cat Pix Slides
Notes: The largest resource of it kind consisting of 4 million indexed swatches and 300 swatch books, jacquard point paper, croquis, quilts, rug samples, laces, embroideries, and color swatch cards. A collection of international scope incl antique and contemporary textiles; woven and printed patterns created for apparel and home furnishings which may be adapted to china, giftware, floor covering, wallpaper, and package design. A comprehensive research facility comprised of over one million articles of dress dating from the 17th Century to the present, incl men's, women's, children's clothes, furs, foundation garments and lingerie, as well as an outstanding grouping of 19th and 20th century designer clothing. Accessories as diverse as hats, handbags, gloves, hosiery, shoes, shawls, and costume jewelry offer an additonal resource to this international collection.

NY —METROPOLITAN MUSEUM OF ART, Irene Lewisohn Costume Reference Library, Fifth Ave at 82 St, New York, 10028. K Gordon Stone, Librn
Notes: History of costume and fashion. The Irene Lewisohn Costume Reference Library is part of the Costume Institute, at the Metropolitan Museum of Art. The new quarters of the library opened with the institute in October 1971. The holdings incl books, bound periodicals, costume plates, fashion sketches, swatch books, vertical file material, and photographs. The library is mainly a research adjunct to the large collection of costumes at the museum. Professional designers of theatre costume and fashion, students, writers, etc, use the facilities. 55,000 items.

NY —TRAPHAGEN SCHOOL OF FASHION LIBRARY, 257 Park Ave S, New York, 10010. Allyn Bloeme, Librn
Holdings: Vols (17,000) Cat Pix Slides
Notes: Costume history, design, construction and illustration. Collection incl old and rare bound fashion periodicals: French, English and American, also continuing run of *Vogue* and *Harper's Bazaar*. No photocopying.

OR —BASSIST COLLEGE LIBRARY, 2000 SW Fifth Ave, Portland, 97201. Norma Bassist, Librn
Holdings: Vols 480 Cat Mss Pix Slides

PA —DREXEL UNIVERSITY LIBRARIES, General Division, 32 & Chestnut Sts, Philadelphia, 19104. Tung Chu Chen, General Division Librn
Holdings: Vols 1485 Cat Slides
Budget: ($2400)
Notes: Emphasis on clothing, dress, fashion; historic and contemporary.

RI —RHODE ISLAND SCHOOL OF DESIGN, Library, Two College St, Providence, 02903. James A Findlay, Dir
Holdings: Vols (70,000) Cat Pix Slides
Budget: ($50,000)

TX —NORTHWOOD INSTITUTE, Library, Box 58, Cedar Hill, 75104. Jennifer Cope, Librn
Holdings: Vols (200) Cat Slides Audiotapes Filmstrips
Budget: ($1500)
Notes: Fashion merchandising and some history of fashion.

ON —METROPOLITAN TORONTO LIBRARY, Fine Arts Dept, 789 Yonge St, Toronto, M4W 2G8, Can. Alan Suddon, Head
Holdings: Vols (42,000) Cat Pix Microforms
Notes: Extensive collection.

FASHION DESIGN see Costume Design

FAST, HOWARD

WI —UNIVERSITY OF WISCONSIN, MILWAUKEE, Library, Box 604, Milwaukee, 53201. William C Roselle, Dir
Holdings: Vols (68,000) Cat Mss Phonorecords Audiotapes
Notes: Special strengths of the literature collection include Shakespeare Research Collection (1800 volumes), 17th Century Collection (600 volumes), William Blake, James Joyce, Howard Fast (English-language editions and unique collection of foreign-language translations), contemporary small press poetry publications, etc.

FAT LIBERATION MOVEMENT

CT —UNIVERSITY OF CONNECTICUT, Library, Storrs, 06268. Ellen Embardo, Cur Special Collections
Holdings: Cat
Notes: Alternative Press Collection. Primarily periodicals and newspapers from the 1960s to today of an alternative or underground nature. Books and and pamphlets are incl, representing both the left and the right-wing viewpoints. A catalog is available. Also have archives of the First Casualty Press, which was deeply involved with Vietnam veterans' experiences in Vietnam, as well as the Fat Liberation Movement.

FATHERS OF THE CHURCH

DC —GEORGETOWN UNIVERSITY, Library, Special Collections Div, 37 & O Sts NW, Washington, 20057. George M Barringer, Special Collections Librn; Nicholas B Sheetz, Mss Librn
Holdings: Cat

DC —HARVARD UNIVERSITY, Center for Hellenic Studies Library, 3100 Whitehaven St NW, Washington, 20008. Jeno Platthy, Librn
Holdings: Vols (42,000) Cat Maps
Budget: ($76,824)
Notes: In addition to a large collection of editions of ancient Greek authors, the library is well equipped to cover every aspect of ancient Greek civilization from prehistoric times to about AD 200. The subject fields covered include epigraphy, paleography, paprology, history, literature, philosophy, religion, mythology, archaeology and art. A small collection of works on Patristics as well as all important Latin authors complete the Center's holdings.

IL —JESUIT-KRAUSS-MCCORMICK LIBRARY, 1100 E 55th St, Chicago, 60615. Donald Vorp, Dir; Elvire Hilgert, Librn
Notes: Collection contains merger of Jesuit Library, Lutheran School of Theology of Chicago (Krauss Library), and McCormick Theological Seminary. Jesuit: Sermones Thesaurus Novi de Tempore (anonymous, Strassbourg 1486); Opera Omnia (Jean Gerson, Strassbourg 1488), 3 vols; Summa Rosella Casuum (Venice 1495); moral theology (major figures of 16th and 17th century scholasticism); early modern editions of patristics and canon law regarding procedures and organzation of the Catholic Church, incl treatises and multi-volume commentaries.
See also entries under Religion; Lutheran Church; Presbyterian Church

MO —SAINT LOUIS UNIVERSITY, Pius XII Memorial Library, 3655 W Pine Blvd, Saint Louis, 63108. William Cole, Dir
Holdings: Slides Microforms
Notes: Collection covers all areas of learning and European history from Classical Antiquity to early modern period. Researchers using collection receive assistance in paleography, bibliography and reference search. Approx 10,000 1000-foot reels of microfilm (not counting master negatives) reproducing Vatican Library's Latin, Greek, Hebrew, Arabic and Ethiopic mss. Some 8000 100-foot reels of microfilm (again not counting master negative) reproducing rare and out of print books relating to subject areas in the mss. Over 50, 000 color slides of medieval and Renaissance mss illuminations. A reference collection of modern materials relating to ms research.

NY —STATE UNIVERSITY OF NEW YORK, COLLEGE AT BUFFALO, Lockwood Memorial Library, Main St, Buffalo, 14260. Stanton F Biddle, Assoc Dir
Holdings: Vols 48,000 Cat Pix
Notes: About half of the collection donated by the Orthodox Catholic Alliance of Buffalo, New York. The collection is devoted chiefly to the world of Byzantium in both its secular and religious phases; Greek Patristic literature and its interpretation; and the tradition of the Greek Bible and its antecedents. As support for these subjects the pagan literature of late antiquity is strongly represented, as well as the Hellenistic and Roman background of the East Christian world and its relations with its neighbors in the Near East, in Eastern Europe, and in the Latin West.

FATHERS OF THE CHURCH (cont.)

NY —UNION THEOLOGICAL SEMINARY, Library, 3041 Broadway at Reinhold Niebuhr Place, New York, 10027. Richard D Spoor, Dir
Holdings: Vols (550,000) Cat Mss Microforms
Budget: ($350,000)

NC —BELMONT ABBEY COLLEGE, Abbot Vincent Taylor Library, Belmont, 28012. Marjorie McDermott, Dir
Holdings: Vols (10,000) Cat Mss Pix
Notes: Patristics (incl Migne's *Patrologie*), Roman Catholic Church history, philosophy, literature (American and British), and both US and North Carolina history. A substantial number of the books date from the 15th, 16th, and 17th centuries. Most of the source material in Catholic studies particularly could not be obtained elsewhere in the Southeast.

NC —DUKE UNIVERSITY, Divinity School Library, Durham, 27706. Donn Michael Farris, Librn
Holdings: Vols (225,000)
Notes: Special collections and subject emphases in this library include: Archaeology, Egyptian; Archaeology, Middle Eastern; Art, Jewish; Bible; Bible-New Testament; Bible-Symbolism; Church Architecture; Egyptology; Fathers of the Church; Society of Friends; Great Britain-Religion-Methodism and Methodist Church; Hymns and Hymnals; Jansenists and Jansenism; Judaica; Mediaeval Christian Mysticism; Methodism and Methodist Church; Methodist Episcopal Church; Methodist Episcopal Church, South; Reformation; Religion-US-History; Rural Church; Theology-Great Britain-17th Century; Theology-Great Britain-18th Century; United Methodist Church; US-Church History; John Wesley.

NC —SOUTHEASTERN BAPTIST THEOLOGICAL SEMINARY LIBRARY, PO Box 752, Wake Forest, 27587. H Eugene McLeod, Librn
Holdings: Cat

OH —CLEVELAND PUBLIC LIBRARY, Fine Arts and Special Collections Department, 325 Superior Ave, Cleveland, 44114. Alice N Loranth, Head
Holdings: Vols 400 Cat
Notes: Part of the Medieval Literature Collection. Incl are medieval texts, translations, facsimile reproductions, bibliographies, catalogs of mss and lives of the saints.

OH —CLEVELAND PUBLIC LIBRARY, Social Sciences Department, 325 Superior Ave, Cleveland, 44114. Thelma Morris, Head
Holdings: Vols (55,000) Cat
Notes: Strong collection of important editions of and books about the Bible, the Reformation, and patrology.

PA —LUTHERAN THEOLOGICAL SEMINARY, Krauth Memorial Library, 7301 Germantown Ave, Philadelphia, 19119. Rev David J Wartluft, Dir Libr
See also entry under Christian Literature, Early

SC —UNIVERSITY OF SOUTH CAROLINA, Thomas Cooper Library, Columbia, 29208. Kenneth E Toombs, Dir of Libraries; Roger Mortimer, Rare Book Librn
Holdings: Vols (1000) Cat
Notes: Particularly strong in titles printed in the 16th, 17th and 18th centuries.

TX —OBLATE SCHOOL OF THEOLOGY, Library, 285 Oblate Dr, San Antonio, 78216. James Maney, Libr Dir
Holdings: Vols (22,000) Cat
Budget: ($15,500)

WI —MARQUETTE UNIVERSITY, Memorial Library, 1415 W Wisconsin Ave, Milwaukee, 53233. Jay Kirk, Health Sciences Librn
Holdings: Vols (57,150) Cat Filmstrips
Budget: ($54,488)
Notes: The Philosophy/Theology Collection has particular strengths in the areas of ancient, patristic and medieval thought and in scholastic philosophy and theology after the Middle Ages. This Collection also has an added dimension in its classification arrangement, which brings together into one unified grouping both the works and the criticisms of an individual philosopher or theologian.

FATIGUE OF MATERIALS see Materials—Fatigue

FATIGUE TESTING see Materials—Fatigue

FATS see Oils and Fats

FATTY ACIDS see Acids, Fatty

FAULKNER, VIRGINIA

NE —UNIVERSITY OF NEBRASKA-LINCOLN, Don L Love Library, University Archives and Special Collections, Lincoln, 68588. Joseph G Svoboda, University Archivist
Notes: Virginia Faulkner was recognized as one of Nebraska's most distinguished writers and scholars. The Virginia Faulkner Collection, containing over 2000 titles, is housed in the Special Collections Department of Love Library. It is especially strong in twentieth century writers and in University of Nebraska Press publications. Of especial value to scholars are her extensive holdings of Willa Cather, Wright Morris and John Neihardt. Her correspondence with S N Behrman, E B White, Edward Wagenknecht, Donald Sutherland, Wright Morris, Louise Pound, Mari Sandoz, Hazel Barnes, Alfred A and Blanche Knopf, and others provide insight into the literary development of these figures, as well as chronicle the intellectual thought of the period. Amassed in a separate file, these letters are available to interested scholars.

FAULKNER, WILLIAM

CA —STANFORD UNIVERSITY LIBRARIES, Cecil H Green Library, Stanford, 94305. Michael T Ryan, Cur
Holdings: Vols (23,000) Cat
Notes: The Charlotte Ashley Felton Memorial Library. Incl first editions.

CT —TRINITY COLLEGE LIBRARY, Watkinson Library, 300 Summit St, Hartford, 06106. Jeffrey Kaimowitz, Cur
Holdings: Cat
Notes: First editions, etc.

CT —YALE UNIVERSITY, Box 1603A, Yale Station, New Haven, 06520.
Holdings: Cat Mss

CT —CONNECTICUT COLLEGE, Library, Mohegan Ave, New London, 06320. Brian Rogers, College Librn
Holdings: Vols (382,000) Cat
Notes: First editions.

IL —NORTHWESTERN UNIVERSITY, Library, Special Collections Dept, 1937 Sheridan Rd, Evanston, 60201. R Russell Maylone, Cur
Holdings: Vols 20,000 Cat
Notes: First, limited, special editions, works about and ephemera of the major authors of the 20th century as well as representative minor writers. Incl English, American, French and German authors and to a lesser extent Italian, Spanish and other European writers. Extensive collections of Lawrence Durrell, T S Eliot, William Faulkner, Robert Graves, Ernest Hemingway, James Joyce, Karl Kraus, D H Lawrence, Hugh MacDiarmid, Henry Miller, Anais Nin, Ezra Pound, Gertrude Stein, H G Wells, W B Yeats. 15,000 "little magazine" titles (exclusive of runs in the general library collections).

KY —UNIVERSITY OF LOUISVILLE, Ekstrom Library, Rare Books & Special Collections, 2301 S Third St, Louisville, 40208. George T McWhorter, Cur; Delinda Stephens Buie, Asst Cur

LA —TULANE UNIVERSITY, Howard-Tilton Memorial Library, Special Collections Div, 7001 Freret St, New Orleans, 70118. Wilbur E Meneray, Librn
Holdings: Vols 665 Cat Mss Pix
Notes: Published works and criticism of William Faulkner. See *William Faulkner-the William B Wisdom Collection: A Descriptive Catalogue* (New Orleans, 1980).

LA —UNIVERSITY OF NEW ORLEANS, Earl K Long Library, New Orleans, 70148. Susan LaHaye, Cataloger
Holdings: Vols 900
Notes: The Frank Von der Haar Collection, incl special signed editions, first trade editions, movie scripts, recordings, and posters.

MA —HARVARD UNIVERSITY LIBRARY, Cambridge, 02138.

†MA —WILLIAMS COLLEGE, Chapin Library of Rare Books, PO Box 426, Williamstown, 01267. Robert L Volz, Custodian
Notes: The Sprague Collection, Editions, inscribed copies, ephemerra, etc. No ILL.

MS —MISSISSIPPI STATE UNIVERSITY, Mitchell Memorial Library, Box 5408, Mississippi State, 39762. Frances N Coleman, Head, Special Collections
Holdings: Vols (15,000) Cat Mss Maps Pix Microforms
Notes: Social and political history of Mississippi, incl University Archives (now separate branch). Microfilms of Protestant Church records. There are strong collections on history of the Southern States, Mississippi authors (especially Faulkner, Williams, Carter, Welty, and Young); also the John C Stennis Collection of over 2 million items, his books, papers, photographs, etc. Incl 400 collections of mss; papers of US Rep David R Bowen 1973-1983; papers of US Rep G V Montgomery 1967-.

NV —UNIVERSITY OF NEVADA, RENO, University Library, Special Collections Dept, Reno, 89557. Robert E Blesse, Head
Holdings: / / Vols (271) Cat Other appearances 430 Cat
Notes: Includes individual works by author in all editions including translations; also prefaces, introductions, published correspondence, appearances in anthologies, periodicals, etc. Bibliographical research collection, part of Modern Authors Collection.

NY —US MILITARY ACADEMY LIBRARY, West Point, 10996. Elaine B Eatroff, Rare Book Cur
Holdings: Vols 600 Cat Microfilm Periodicals
Notes: First editions, criticism and commentary, and association materials. Full library cataloging has been accorded each imprint and over 300 periodical articles. A computer-based concordance of the novels and poems is available at West Point. Selective listing in *The William Faulkner Collection at West Point and the Faulkner* Concordances, ed by Col Jack L Capps. Separate catalog. No photocopying.

†NC —WAKE FOREST UNIVERSITY, Z Smith Reynolds Library, Box 7777, Reynold Sta, Winston-Salem, 27109.
Notes: A significant collection.

OH —PUBLIC LIBRARY OF CINCINNATI & HAMILTON COUNTY, Dept of Rare Books & Special Collections, 800 Vine St, Library Square, Cincinnati, 45202. Yeatman Anderson III, Cur
Holdings: Cat
Notes: First and special editions by and about him.

OH —KENT STATE UNIVERSITY, Libraries, Dept of Special Collections, Kent, 44242. Dean H Keller, Cur
Holdings: Vols 200 Cat
Notes: Incl Faulkner's books, periodical appearances, translations, criticism.

†TX —UNIVERSITY OF TEXAS LIBRARIES, Hoblitzelle Theatre Arts Library, Austin, 78712.
Notes: A 100,000-item collection of correspondence and documents related to the career and personal life of Gloria Swanson, one of the largest archives from 1913 to 1983. Correspondence with Mary Pickford, William Faulkner, and the Kennedy Family, the latter to remain sealed until the year 2000.

VA —UNIVERSITY OF VIRGINIA, Alderman Library, Manuscripts Dept, Charlottesville, 22901. Edmund Berkeley Jr,

FAULKNER, WILLIAM (cont.)

Cur
Holdings: Vols 3500 Cat Mss Maps Pix Slides Phonorecords Audiotapes 16mm Films Microforms
Notes: The William Faulkner collections are the most complete known. They include all available printed works by and about Faulkner. Access to the manuscripts is restricted; contact the curator of manuscripts. The manuscripts include drafts of ten novels, some unpublished; of many short stories and poetry, some unpublished; letters; movie scripts; photographs; tape recordings, etc. Linton R Massey, "*Man Working,*" *1919-1962; William Faulkner: A Catalog of the William Faulkner Collections at the University of Virginia* (Charlottesville: Bibliographical Society of the University of Virginia, and the University Press of Virginia, 1969). Partially microfilmed. An unpublished guide to the manuscripts is available at the Library. It is very important that the notice of the restriction on access be recognized. The restrictions are rigid and are enforced.*Manuscripts are restricted to doctoral candidates, established scholars, and certain other persons under exceptional* circumstances.

FAULKNOR, CHAUNCEY CLIFFORD VERNON, 1913-

AB —UNIVERSITY OF CALGARY, Libraries, Special Collections Div, 2500 University Dr, Calgary, T2N 1N4, Can.
Holdings: Cat Mss
Notes: Manuscripts, galleys, correspondence and research for Cliff Faulknor's books *The White Calf, The White Peril, The* In-Betweener, and *The Smoke Horse*, as well as articles, clippings, and a miscellany of editorial correspondence, scrapbooks, short stories, and scripts.

FAUNA see Marine Fauna; Zoology

FAUNA, PREHISTORIC see Paleontology

FAVROT FAMILY

LA —TULANE UNIVERSITY, Howard-Tilton Memorial Library, Special Collections Div, 7001 Freret St, New Orleans, 70118. Wilbur E Meneray, Librn
Holdings: Vols 1500 Cat Mss
Notes: The Favrot Library is mainly 19th century Louisiana imprints or works on Louisiana. The Favrot Family Papers consist of official and family correspondence in colonial and early ante-bellum Louisiana. Most of the correspondence is in French and Spanish. 17 volumes of transcriptions of the papers have been published.

FAWCUS, ARNOLD

CA —UNIVERSITY OF CALIFORNIA, SANTA CRUZ, University Library, Special Collections, Santa Cruz, 95064. Rita Bottoms, Special Collections Librn; Margaret Felts, South Pacific Collection Bibliographer
Notes: The archives of Trianon Press. All major publications of the Press. Under the direction of Arnold Fawcus from the late 1940s through the 1970s, Trianon Press was noted for its replica editions of the works of early authors with special emphasis on the works of William Blake Marcel Duchamp.

FAX see Facsimile Transmission

FAX, ELTON C.

MA —BOSTON UNIVERSITY, Mugar Memorial Library, Special Collections Dept, 771 Commonwealth Ave, Boston, 02215. Howard B Gotlieb, Dir
Holdings: Mss Pix
Notes: Mss, correspondence, drawings, etc collected in depth; incl publications by or about.

FAYENCE see Pottery

FEARING, KENNETH

NV —UNIVERSITY OF NEVADA, RENO, University Library, Special Collections Dept, Reno, 89557. Robert E Blesse, Head
Holdings: Vols (17) Cat
Notes: Includes individual works by author in all editions including translations; also prefaces, introductions, published correspondence, appearances in anthologies, periodicals, etc. Bibliographical research collection, part of Modern Authors Collection. Other appearances 130 cataloged.

FEDDERSON, DON, PRODUCTIONS

CA —UNIVERSITY OF CALIFORNIA, LOS ANGELES, Theater Arts Library, Los Angeles, 90024. Edward Shreeves, Chairman, Bibliographers Group; Audree Malkin, Head, Theater Arts Library
Notes: Collection of material pertaining to Producer Don Fedderson's 15 television series: scripts in various versions, production material press releases, clippings, stills, publicity photographs, negatives, color transparencies, slides. Series represented: *Family Affair, The Millionaire, The Fess Parker Show, Weekend Father, Joey, Cody's Paradise, Murdock's Gang, Luke, The Windward Wide, Hiawatha, A Day With the Angels, Do You Trust Your Wife, The Betty White Show, To Rome with Love,* and *The Smith Family.*

FEDERAL COMMUNICATIONS BAR ASSOCIATION

DC —BROADCAST PIONEERS LIBRARY, 1771 N St NW, Washington, 20036. Catharine Heinz, Dir
Holdings: Vols (6500) Uncat Pix Phonorecords Audiotapes
Notes: Special collections: Oral History (750); Havrilla (photos, radio performers); William S Hedges Collection; Elmo Neale Pickerill Collection; Joseph E Baudino Collection; Archive of Federal Communications Bar Association. Incl 20, 000 pictures, 1450 phonorecords and 1200 audiotapes.

FEDERAL GRANTS see Grants-In-Aid

FEDERAL PARTY

MI —UNIVERSITY OF MICHIGAN, William L Clements Library, Ann Arbor, 48109. John C Dann, Dir
Notes: The William L. Clements Library of Americana is a non-circulating rare book library of original source material, printed and manuscript, dealing with America, from the discovery period into the late nineteenth century. The collection includes approximately 55,000 books and pamphlets, 550 linear feet of manuscripts, 4,100 volumes of newspapers, 36,000 maps, 40,000 pieces of sheet music, and 1,000 prints. The collection is strongest for the period of the American Revolution, and includes the papers of Thomas Gage, Sir Henry Clinton, and the Earl of Shelburne. Other areas of strength include antislavery, cartography and geography, discovery and exploration, American Indians, The Civil War, tune-books, sermons and orations, and the War of 1812. There are selective research collections dealing with Christopher Columbus, Thomas Paine, Benjamin Franklin, George Washington, Thomas Jefferson, and the Federalist Papers. Publications describing the collections of the library are: Author/Title catalog of Americana 1493-1860 in the William L. Clements Library... 7 volumes, Boston, G. K. Hall, 1970; Guide to the manuscript collections of the William L. Clements Library, by Arlene P. Shy 3d edition, Boston, G. K. Hall, 1978; Guide to the manuscript maps in the William L. Clements Library, compiled by Christian Burn, Ann Arbor, U. of Michigan, 1959; and Research catalog of maps of America, to 1860 in the William L. Clements Library...,edited by Douglas W. Marshall, 4 volumes, Boston, G. K. Hall, 1972.

FEDERAL REPUBLIC OF GERMANY see Germany

FEDERAL RESERVE BANKS AND SYSTEM

DC —LIBRARY OF CONGRESS, Manuscript Division, Washington, 20540. John C Broderick, Chief
Notes: Papers of Adolph C Miller (1866-1953), economist and original appointee and member of the Federal Reserve Board of Governors (1914-36). Approx 10,000 items, incl personal and professional files.

GA —FEDERAL RESERVE BANK OF ATLANTA, Research Library, PO Box 1731, Atlanta, 30301. Leigh Watson Healy, Information Services Coord; Cynthia Walsh-Kloss, Assoc Librn
Holdings: Vols (12,000) Cat Mss Microforms
Notes: Collection specializes in banking, finance, economics, publications of the Federal Reserve Banks and Federal Reserve Board.

IL —FEDERAL RESERVE BANK OF CHICAGO, Library, 230 S La Salle St, PO Box 834, Chicago, 60690. Dorothy Phillips, Librn
Holdings: Vols (19,000) Cat
Notes: Restricted use: noncirculating. No photocopying.

NY —COLUMBIA UNIVERSITY LIBRARIES, Rare Book & Manuscript Library, 801 Butler Library, 535 W 114 St, New York, 10027. Kenneth A Lohf, Librn
Holdings: Mss
Notes: Incl the Henry Parker Willis Collection. Strong on formation of the Federal Reserve system, and papers, correspondence, about the Philippine National Bank, the Irish Banking Commission, the Banking Inquiry of 1925, the Banking Act of 1933, the New Zealand Monetary Commission, the Indian Currency Commission, and the George L Harrison papers. Incl 25,000 items. Restricted use.

PA —FEDERAL RESERVE BANK OF PHILADELPHIA, PO Box 66, Philadelphia, 19105. Aileen Boer, Librn
Holdings: Vols (10,000) Cat
Notes: Incl Philadelphia Bank Returns, 1890-date; other runs of important financial serials, etc. No photocopying.

UT —UNIVERSITY OF UTAH, Marriott Library, Special Collections, Salt Lake City, 84112. Gregory C Thompson, Cur
Notes: Papers of Marriner S Eccles, (80 ln ft, 1000 vols library, mss, films, tapes).

FEDERAL SHIPBUILDING CO.

MO —WASHINGTON UNIVERSITY, Libraries, Special Collections Dept, Campus Box 1061, St Louis, 63130.
Notes: Papers of Charles W Bryan Jr, incl correspondence, personal journals, scrapbooks, photographs, and printed material associated with the Federal Shipbuilding Company from 1917 to 1948, and as president of the Pullman Standard Car Manufacturing Company from 1950 to 1958.

FEDERAL THEATRE PROJECT (WPA)

IN —INDIANA UNIVERSITY, Lilly Library, Seventh St, Bloomington, 47405. William R

FEDERAL THEATRE PROJECT (WPA) (cont.)

Cagle, Librn
Holdings: Mss Pix Recordings
Notes: Correspondence, papers, and memorabilia, 1930-1959, of actor, producer, writer, and director Orson Welles. Includes material on the Federal Theater Project, Mercury Theatre, radio programming, film-making, RKO studios, etc. Radio scripts, screen plays, movie stills, and tape recordings of the radio shows done by Welles are all present. 19,875 items.

NY —NEW YORK PUBLIC LIBRARY, Performing Arts Research Center, Billy Rose Theatre Collection, 111 Amsterdam Ave, New York, 10023. Dorothy L Swerdlove, Cur
Holdings: Cat Mss Pix
Notes: Papers, scrapbooks, mss, photographs, memorabilia, etc.

VA —GEORGE MASON UNIVERSITY, Fenwick Library, Special Collections Dept, 4400 University Drive, Fairfax, 22030. Ruth Kerns, Public Services Librn
Notes: The Federal Theatre Project (FTP) was established in August 1935 as a part of the arts program of the Works Progress Administration (renamed Work Projects Administration in 1939). Supporting 150 separate units throughout the United States, the FTP produced over 830 major stage plays, 6000 radio programs, and innumerable marionette plays, vaudeville shows, outdoor pageants, and circuses. At the conclusion of the project in June 1939, the "product materials" generated by the FTP were sent to the Library of Congress, and the administrative records to the National Archives. The Library's Federal Theatre Project collection was placed on deposit at George Mason University in Fairfax, Virginia, in 1974. Occupying over eight hundred cubic feet of shelf space, the collection is the largest single gathering of original FTP materials and containsdocumentation for many FTP productions, particularly those which originated in the New York City, San Francisco, and Los Angeles areas. Included are 5000 playscripts, 2500 radio scripts, 25, 000 photographs, 40 blueprints, 1000 posters, over 1600 costume designs, 350 scene designs, 750 production notebooks, 1700 programs and heralds, 26 musical scores and 18 cubic feet of research materials and play readers' reports.

FEDERAL WRITERS, PROJECT (U.S.)

PA —BALCH INSTITUTE FOR ETHNIC STUDIES, Library, 18 S Seventh St, Philadelphia, 19106. R Joseph Anderson, Library Dir

FEDERALISTS (U.S.) see Federal Party

FEDERATION, INTERNATIONAL see International Organization

FEDERATIONS, FINANCIAL (SOCIAL SERVICE)

VA —UNITED WAY OF AMERICA INFORMATION CENTER, 701 North Fairfax St, United Way Plaza, Alexandria, 22314. Henry M Smith, Dir; Barbara L Owen, Librn
Holdings: Vols (1200) Cat Microforms
Notes: Incl 5000 research reports and studies on microfiche; 100 vertical file drawers. Serivces primarily for United Way organizations--United Funds, Community Chests, Health and Welfare Planning Councils.

FEDERATION OF CITIZENS' ASSOCIATIONS OF THE DISTRICT OF COLUMBIA

DC —GEORGETOWN UNIVERSITY, Library, Special Collections Div, 37 & O Sts NW, Washington, 20057. George M Barringer, Special Collections Librn; Nicholas B Sheetz, Mss Librn
Holdings: Mss Cat
Notes: Correspondence, constitutions, by-laws, agendas, minutes, reports, publications, sundry documents and printed material from the Federation of Citizens' Associations of the District of Columbia, founded in 1910. The material concerns the organization, administration, and activities of the Association. Subject files outline the Association's areas of concern in the District of Columbia such as health, education, transportation, fiscal management, urban planning, public safety, youth problems, and federal legislation.

FEDERATIONS FOR CHARITY AND PHILANTHROPY see Federations, Financial (Social Service)

FEDOR, FERENZ

NM —MUSEUM OF NEW MEXICO, Photo Archives, Box 2087, Santa Fe, 87503. Arthur L Olivas, Cur; Richard Rudisill, Photo Historian
Holdings: Cat Pix Slides
Notes: Extensive collection of his work.

FEE, JOHN G.

KY —BEREA COLLEGE, Hutchins Library, Berea, 40404. Gerald F Roberts, Librn Special Collections
Holdings: Vols 500 Cat Mss Maps Pix Microforms Phonorecords
Notes: Private papers and library of John G Fee, abolitionist and founder of Berea College. Incl papers of other 19th-century abolitionists and liberals as pertain to Berea College or interests of John Fee.

FEE SYSTEM (TAXATION) see Taxation

FEEBLE-MINDED see Mentally Handicapped

FEED see Feeds

FEED INDUSTRY AND TRADE see Flour and Feed Trade

FEEDING

DC —SMITHSONIAN INSTITUTION LIBRARIES, National Zoological Park Branch, Washington, 20008. Kay Kenyon, Chief Librn
Holdings: Vols (5500) Cat
Notes: Collection incl animal nutrition, capture and care of animals in captivity, conservation and endangered species, pathology, veterinary medicine, zoology.

MA —UNIVERSITY OF MASSACHUSETTS AT AMHERST, Library, Amherst, 01003. Siegfried Feller, Assoc Dir for Collection Development
Holdings: Cat
Notes: Veterinary medicine and animal sciences. Special emphases: reproductive physiology, poultry genetics, animal nutrition.

TN —W R GRACE & CO, Planning Services Library, 100 N Main, PO Box 277, Memphis, 38103. Carolyn A Wilhite, Librn
Holdings: Vols (6000) Cat Mss Maps Microforms
Budget: ($85,000)
Notes: Animal nutrition and production; fertilizers; weather; and agricultural statistics.

FEEDING—EQUIPMENT AND SUPPLIES

CA —UNIVERSITY OF CALIFORNIA, DAVIS, Shields Library, Dept of Special Collections, Davis, 95616. Donald Kunitz, Head; C Danial Elliott, Asst Head
Notes: 13,000 VF cataloged; mss and pictures uncataloged. Manufacturer's catalogs, manuals, parts lists, ephemera, and literature pertaining to historical as well as current data on such items as tractors, engines, combines, hay equipment, etc. Described in "The Higgins Library: A Source for the Study of Agricultural History," Don Kunitz, *Agricultural History,* vol 49, 1975, pp 89-91.

FEEDING STUFFS see Feeds

FEEDS

IA —IOWA STATE UNIVERSITY, Library, Ames, 50011. Warren B Kuhn, Dean of Library Services
Holdings: Cat
Notes: Incl animal nutrition, dietetics and food science, and research. Extensive serial holdings.

IA —IOWA STATE UNIVERSITY, Library, Dept of Special Collections, Ames, 50011. Stanley M Yates, Head
Notes: Papers of Roswell Garst, Iowa's most famous farmer. Initiator of experimental feeding of corncobs to produce beef, use of hybrid seedcorn, and commercial fertilizers. Credited with opening of agricultural sales and exchanges with Russia in the 1950s.

KY —UNIVERSITY OF KENTUCKY, Agriculture Library, Agricultural Science Center North, Lexington, 40546. Antoinette P Powell, Head Librn
Holdings: Vols (90,000) Cat Maps Microforms
Budget: ($110,582)

FEINBERG, CHARLES

DC —LIBRARY OF CONGRESS, Rare Book & Special Collections Div, Washington, 20540. William Matheson, Chief
Notes: See description of collection under Whitman, Walt. Incl mss, rare books.

FEINGLASS, ABE

IL —CHICAGO HISTORICAL SOCIETY, Library, Clark St at North Ave, Chicago, 60614. Archie Motley, Manuscript Librn
Notes: Papers of trade union leader and radical activist.

FEININGER, ANDREAS

AZ —UNIVERSITY OF ARIZONA, Center for Creative Photography, 843 E University Blvd, Tucson, 85721. James Enyeart, Dir; Terence Pitts, Cur and Librn
Notes: Center has significant collections consisting of more than 25 photographs plus other archival material such as negatives, contact sheets, work prints, correspondence, financial records, diaries, project files, etc. Inventories of the collections are available to researchers. Published guides available for some collections.

FEISS, CARL, 1907-

NY —CORNELL UNIVERSITY LIBRARIES, Collection of Regional History, Dept of Manuscripts and Univ Archives, Ithaca, 14853.
Notes: Planner. Papers, 1928-74; 60 ft.

FELD, BERNARD TAUB, 1919-

MA —MASSACHUSETTS INSTITUTE OF TECHNOLOGY, Institute Archives, Special Collections, Cambridge, 02139.
Notes: Papers of Bernard Feld, nuclear physicist at MIT and a world leader in disarmament activities. Graduate student under Leo Szilard and Enrico Fermi and continued as a physicist with the Manhattan Engineer District in Los Alamos, New Mexico. The collection incl extensive documentation of national and international arms control efforts which Feld initiated in the Cold War which followed the destruction of Hiroshima and Nagasaki. Founder and Editor-in-Chief of the Bulletin of Atomic Scientists.

FELDMAN, GEORGE

MA —BOSTON UNIVERSITY, Mugar Memorial Library, Special Collections Dept,

FELDMAN, GEORGE (cont.)

771 Commonwealth Ave, Boston, 02215. Howard B Gotlieb, Dir
Holdings: Mss Correspondence

FELDSHERS see Physicians' Assistants

FELLERS, BONNER FRANK, 1896-1973

CA —HOOVER INSTITUTION ON WAR, REVOLUTION & PEACE, Stanford University, Stanford, 94305. Milorad M Drachkovitch, Archivist
Holdings: Mss
Notes: Papers of Brig Gen Bonner F Fellers, head of the US Army Psychological Warfare Division, 1943-45, incl research studies, reports, correspondence, memoranda, operational instructions, etc, 1934-72, relating to his military and public service careers, US military propaganda during World War II, and US economic and foreign aid. Incl are materials pertaining to the Citizens Foreign Aid Committee and Taxpayers Committee to End Foreign Aid, of which B F Fellers was chairman, 15 ms boxes.

FELLS POINT HEBREW GRAMMAR SCHOOL, BALTIMORE

DC —GEORGETOWN UNIVERSITY, Library, Special Collections Div, 37 & O Sts NW, Washington, 20057. George M Barringer, Special Collections Librn; Nicholas B Sheetz, Mss Librn
Holdings: Vols (100) Uncat Mss
Notes: Includes the archives of Dag Hammarskjold College, Columbia, Md; a portion of the archives of Gonzaga College, Washington, DC; records of the Fells Point Hebrew Grammar School, Baltimore, Md, and other materials (Besides these collections, students can use the Georgetown University Archives, 1787- , and the Woodstock College Archives, 1866- , qv under Jesuits in the US.)

FELONY see Criminal Law

FEMALE STUDIES see Women's Studies

FEMINISM see Women's Liberation Movement

FEMINIST STUDIES see Women's Studies

FENCES

TX —AMARILLO PUBLIC LIBRARY, 413 E Fourth, Amarillo, 79101. Mary Kay Snell, Librn
Holdings: Vols Cat Mss Maps Pix
Notes: The southwest collections incl materials on the history of Texas, Louisiana, New Mexico, Arkansas, Missouri and Kansas. General subjects covered incl overland journeys, early narratives, early biographies, Indian captivities, outlaws, US government reports, Mississippi and Ohio Rivers, the Mexican War, reports of Catholic missionaries, Niles Register, early publications, fur trade, western trails, Texas Rangers, sheriffs and Texas as a sovereign state, buffalo hunting, Indian wars, cowboys, the arrival of farmers, fences, and towns. Over 1600 items which incl books, documents, maps, mss, pamphlets, unpublished theses, interviews and photographs. The three major collections are the William Henry Bush Collection, the Laurence J Fitzsimon Collection and the Calendar of John L McCarty.

FENCING

PA —MUHLENBERG COLLEGE, Haas Library, 2400 Chew St, Allentown, 18104. Linda Bowers
Holdings: Vols 150
Notes: Incl rare 18th and 19th century material, as well as 20th century material, in various languages.

FENN, G. MANNVILLE

MS —UNIVERSITY OF SOUTHERN MISSISSIPPI, William David McCain Graduate Library, Box 5148, Southern Sta, Hattiesburg, 39406.
Holdings: Vols 30
Notes: The Lena Y de Grummond Collection of Children's Literature. Incl the Robert L Dartt Collection of over 1800 books for boys from the late 19th and early 20th centuries. Extensive Henty (over 550 vols), Alger, Brereton, Castlemon, Fenn, Kingston, Optic, and Stratemeyer holdings. Catalog in progress.

FENOLLOSA, ERNEST F.

MA —HARVARD UNIVERSITY LIBRARY, Houghton Library, Cambridge, 02138. Rodney G Dennis, Cur of Manuscripts
Holdings: Mss

FENTON, REUBEN EATON

NY —FENTON HISTORICAL SOCIETY, Library, 67 South Washington, Jamestown, 14701. Ellen Fessenden, Co-Dir; Candy Larson, Co-Dir
Holdings: Mss

FENTON, ROGER, 1819-1869

DC —LIBRARY OF CONGRESS, Prints & Photographs Div, Washington, 20540.
Notes: The Roger Fenton Collection of 265 original Crimean War photoprints.

FENTON, WILLIAM

NY —SAINT LAWRENCE UNIVERSITY, Owen D Young Library, Canton, 13617. Mahlon Peterson, Librn
Holdings: Mss
Notes: Correspondence between Edmund Wilson and William Fenton during the years 1857-1872. The letters are concerned primarily with New York State Indians and Wilson's book *Apologies to the Iroquois.* Approx 60 items.

FENWICK, ELIZABETH

MA —BOSTON UNIVERSITY, Mugar Memorial Library, Special Collections Dept, 771 Commonwealth Ave, Boston, 02215. Howard B Gotlieb, Dir
Holdings: Cat Mss

FENWICK, MILLICENT

OK —UNIVERSITY OF OKLAHOMA, Bizzell Memorial Library, Western History Collections, 401 W Brooks, Norman, 73069. John Ezell, Cur
Holdings: Mss Documents
Notes: US Representative. Her papers.

FERBER, EDNA

WI —UNIVERSITY OF WISCONSIN, MADISON, Memorial Library, British & American Language & Literature Collection, 728 State St, Madison, 53706. Yvonne Schofer, Bibliographer
Holdings: Vols 1300 Cat
Notes: From the library of Edna Ferber, including many editions of her own works and materials used for the background of her novels. Includes many literary works inscribed to her. Held in stacks.

FERGUSON, CHARLES W.

MA —BOSTON UNIVERSITY, Mugar Memorial Library, Special Collections Dept, 771 Commonwealth Ave, Boston, 02215. Howard B Gotlieb, Dir
Holdings: Cat Mss
Notes: Mss, correspondence, etc collected in depth; incl publications by or about.

FERGUSON, JAMES EDWARD, 1911-1936

TX —UNIVERSITY OF TEXAS LIBRARIES, General Libraries, Barker Texas History Center, PO Box P, Austin, 78712. Don Carleton, Dir
Holdings: Cat Mss Pix
Notes: Personal and business papers of Texas Governor James Edward "Pa" Ferguson (1914-1917).

FERGUSON, ROBERT

DC —GEORGETOWN UNIVERSITY, Library, Special Collections Div, 37 & O Sts NW, Washington, 20057. George M Barringer, Special Collections Librn; Nicholas B Sheetz, Mss Librn
Holdings: Mss Cat
Notes: Correspondence among merchants in Maryland, the largest portion between two factors, Robert Ferguson and Alexander Hamilton. Ferguson (d 1813) was sent to Maryland as a factor for the John Glassford Company of Scotland. He left the colonies during the Revolution and returned to his native Scotland. In 1784 he came back to Maryland with power of attorney to collect debts and dispose of the company's property. He spent the remaining years of his life in America, working as a factor for numerous companies. Alexander Hamilton (d 1799), also a factor for the Glassford Company and a native of Scotland, chose to remain in this country until his death. The correspondence between these two men difficulties encountered in collecting debts after the Revolution.

FERLINGHETTI, LAWRENCE

AZ —UNIVERSITY OF ARIZONA, University Library, Special Collections, Tucson, 85721. Louis A Hieb, Head
Holdings: Vols (7000) Cat Mss Microforms
Budget: ($30,000)
Notes: In the 20th century, the major emphasis is Bukowski, Wakoski, Wilder, Reznikoff, Ginzberg, Ferlinghetti, Snyder, Whalen, Everson, Joyce Carol Oates, and Kurt Vonnegut.

VA —UNIVERSITY OF VIRGINIA, Alderman Library, Rare Book Dept, Charlottesville, 22901. Julius P Barclay, Cur
Holdings: Vols (6500) Cat
Notes: The Marvin Tatum Collection of Contemporary Prose and Poetry contains some extremely rare items (mostly paperback) of early beat poetry and prose. Some of Lawrence Ferlinghetti's earliest publications in mimeograph form are here. Posters, portfolios.

BC —UNIVERSITY OF VICTORIA, McPherson Library, Victoria, V8W 3H5, Can.

FERMENTATION

CA —UNIVERSITY OF CALIFORNIA, DAVIS, General Library, Davis, 95616. Bernard Kreissman, University Librn; C Danial Elliott, Asst Head, Dept Special Collections
Holdings: Vols 6000 Cat Pix

IN —INTERNATIONAL MINERALS & CHEMICAL CORP, R & D Library, 1331 S First St, PO Box 207, Terre Haute, 47808. Ruth Smedlund, Librn
Holdings: Vols (50,000) Cat

IA —ARCHER DANIELS MIDLAND, Research Library, PO Box 340, Clinton, 52732. Carol L Kolk, Research Librn
Holdings: Vols 2200 Cat Microforms
Notes: Card index to patent file. Keydex index to Research Experiment Reports.

PA —FRANKLIN INSTITUTE LIBRARY, 20 & The Parkway, Philadelphia, 19103. Miriam Padusis, Dir; Charles Wilt, Readers Servs Librn
Holdings: Vols (300,000) Cat Maps Pix Microforms

FERMENTS see Enzymes; Fermentation

FERMI, ENRICO

IL —UNIVERSITY OF CHICAGO LIBRARY, Dept of Special Collections, 1100 E 57 St, Chicago, 60637.
Notes: Papers.

FERNANDEZ DE LIZARDI, J. J.

MA —HARVARD UNIVERSITY LIBRARY, Widener Library, Cambridge, 02138. Ellen H Brow, Specialist in Book Selection
Holdings: Cat
Notes: See *Harvard Library Notes,* III (1935), 89-93, and *Hispanic American Historical Review* XXVI (1946), 284-291.

FERNS

IA —IOWA STATE UNIVERSITY, Library, Ames, 50011. Warren B Kuhn, Dean of Library Services
Holdings: Cat Mss
Notes: Specific strengths: botanical taxonomy, ferns, mycology and plant pathology. Extensive serial holdings.

MA —HARVARD UNIVERSITY LIBRARY, Gray Herbarium Library, 22 Divinity Ave, Cambridge, 02138. Barbara A Callahan, Librn
Holdings: Vols (61,445) Microforms
Notes: Flowering plants and ferns are emphasized. *Gray Herbarium Index,* 10 volumes (published 1968) reproduces 265, 000 cards giving names and literature citations of newly described or established vascular plants of the Western Hemisphere.

FERRAR, NICOLAS

NC —UNIVERSITY OF NORTH CAROLINA, GREENSBORO, Walter Clinton Jackson Library, Special Collections Dept, 1000 Spring Garden St, Greensboro, 27412. Emilie W Mills, Librn
Holdings: Vols (100) Cat Pix Microforms
Notes: First, early and later editions of George Herbert, 17th to 20th centuries. Early manuscripts and documents relating to Nicolas Ferrar and the Herbert family (microfilm). Also incl are early works of Edward, Lord Herbert of Cherbury, Izaak Walton and Nicolas Ferrar; items issued by the Friends of Bemerton are added as published.

FERRERO, GUGLIELMO

NY —COLUMBIA UNIVERSITY LIBRARIES, Rare Book & Manuscript Library, 801 Butler Library, 535 W 114 St, New York, 10027. Kenneth A Lohf, Librn
Holdings: Mss
Notes: Extensive correspondence, publications, etc. Incl 30,000 items. Restricted use.

FERRINI, VINCENT, 1913-

CT —UNIVERSITY OF CONNECTICUT, Library, Storrs, 06268. George F Butterick, Cur of Literary Archives
Holdings: Mss Audiotapes
Notes: Repository for his papers.

FERRIS, DEBORAH

ME —BOWDOIN COLLEGE, Library, Brunswick, 04011. Dianne M Gutscher, Cur of Special Collections
Holdings: Cat Mss
Notes: The Charles Brockden Brown Papers contain 159 letters and mss relating to America's first professional novelist. There are 54 letters from Brown to Joseph Bringhurst, and 105 letters and mss from the Bringhurst-Deborah Ferris correspondence.

FERRIS, WOODBRIDGE N.

MI —FERRIS STATE COLLEGE ARCHIVES, 901 S State St, Big Rapids, 49307. R Lawrence Martin, Coordr
Holdings: Vols 11,500 Cat Mss Pix Audiotapes
Notes: Incl 36 volumes of letters written by W N Ferris as well as numerous ms letters; also Ferris State College history. Ferris was founder of the college, Governor of Michigan (1913-1916), and a US Senator (1923-1928).

FERROELECTRICITY

CA —INTERNATIONAL BUSINESS MACHINES RESEARCH LIBRARY, 5600 Cottle Rd, San Jose, 95193. Phil Grincewich, Mgr Technical Information
Holdings: Vols (13,500) Cat
Notes: Incl 21,000 vols of 770 journals. On-line search facility. Vols are divided into three libraries, Technical Research, Technical Information, and Programing. Not open to public.

FERROTYPE see Tintypes

FERROUS METAL INDUSTRIES see Iron Industry and Trade; Steel Industry and Trade

FERRY-MORSE COMPANY

CA —UNIVERSITY OF CALIFORNIA, DAVIS, Shields Library, Dept of Special Collections, Davis, 95616. Donald Kunitz, Head; C Danial Elliott, Asst Head
Holdings: Cat Mss Pix
Notes: Records, photographs, seed posters, and scrapbooks of the Ferry-Morse Company document the success of this well-known nursery.

FERTILITY, HUMAN

DC —CENTER FOR BIOETHICS, Library, Kennedy Institute, Georgetown University, 3520 Prospect St NW, Washington, 20057. Doris Goldstein, Dir; Judith Mistichelli, Senior Librn
Holdings: Vols 8200
Notes: Largest library of its kind. Incl 31, 000 journal articles. Collects in the following subject areas: applied ethics; medical ethics; philosophy of medicine; science, technology and society; sociology of medicine; patient-physician care; sexuality; contraception; abortion; population policy; reproductive technologies; in vitro fertilization; genetic counseling and screening; genetic engineering; mental organ transplantation; death and dying; "baby doe" issues; euthanasia; suicide; use of chemical and biological weapons. Produces computer database *Bioethicsline,* available through MEDLARS; and the printed annual *Bibliography of Bioethics.* Other library publications are: *New Titles in Bioethics* (monthly); *Scope Notes* series on current topics.

NC —CAROLINA POPULATION CENTER, Library, University Sq E, Chapel Hill, 27514. Patricia Shipman, Head Librn
Holdings: Vols (20,000) Cat
Budget: ($10,500)
Notes: Try to acquire everything published in English on population, with particular emphasis on the US and developing countries. Also acquire conference proceedings, seminar papers. These and journal articles are indexed and the analytics are incl in the catalog. Incl 13,000 reprints and other pieces of ephemera. Most extensive area files are on India, Africa, Thailand, Iran, Korea, and Latin America. Holdings are recorded on an automated data base. A microfiche catalog is available for use in the Library and for purchase. Access by subject and geographic area are available through the Library's own thesaurus-based indexing systems.

TX —UNIVERSITY OF TEXAS LIBRARIES, Population Research Center Library, 1701 Main Bldg Tower, Austin, 78712. Doreen S Goyer, Librn
Notes: The library is a depository for the World Fertility Survey publications.

FERTILIZERS AND MANURES

AL —NATIONAL FERTILIZER DEVELOPMENT CENTER, Tennessee Valley Authority Technical Library, TVA National Fertilizer Development Center, Muscle Shoals, 35660. Shirley G Nichols, Librn
Holdings: Vols (32,000) Cat Mss Maps Pix Slides Microforms
Notes: One of the most complete collections of material on fertilizer as it relates to agriculture, agro-economics, chemistry, chemical engineering, etc, in the country.

IN —INTERNATIONAL MINERALS & CHEMICAL CORP, R & D Library, 1331 S First St, PO Box 207, Terre Haute, 47808. Ruth Smedlund, Librn
Holdings: Vols (50,000) Cat Maps Microforms
Notes: Phosphate and potash fertilizers.

IA —IOWA STATE UNIVERSITY, Library, Dept of Special Collections, Ames, 50011. Stanley M Yates, Head
Notes: Papers of Roswell Garst, Iowa's most famous farmer. Initiator of experimental feeding of corncobs to produce beef, use of hybrid seedcorn, and commercial fertilizers. Credited with opening of agricultural sales and exchanges with Russia in the 1950s.

KY —UNIVERSITY OF KENTUCKY, Agriculture Library, Agricultural Science Center North, Lexington, 40546. Antoinette P Powell, Head Librn
Holdings: Vols (90,000) Cat Maps Microforms
Budget: ($110,582)

NY —NEW YORK STATE OFFICE OF PARKS & RECREATION, TACONIC REGION, Clermont State Historic Park, Library, RR 1, Box 215, Germantown, 12526. Bruce E Naramore, Historic Site Manager
Holdings: Vols (5000) Cat Mss Maps
Notes: Period editions of pre - and post-American Revolutionary War agricultural technology. Many belonged to the Chancellor Robert R Livingston (1746-1813). Incl land drainage, hybrids, fertilizers, and the introduction of Merino sheep.

TN —TENNESSEE VALLEY AUTHORITY (TVA), Technical Library, 400 W Summit Hill Dr, E2 B7, Knoxville, 37902. Jesse C Mills, Chief Librn
Holdings: Vols (106,900) Cat Mss Maps Pix Audiotapes Microforms
Budget: ($2,025,000)
Notes: The Technical Library Headquarters Staff (order, cataloging, information, and administration) is located in Knoxville, Tenn. In addition there are branch libraries in Knoxville, Norris, and Chattanooga, Tennessee, and Muscle Shoals, Alabama.

TN —W R GRACE & CO, Planning Services Library, 100 N Main, PO Box 277, Memphis, 38103. Carolyn A Wilhite, Librn
Holdings: Vols (6000) Cat Mss Maps Microforms
Budget: ($85,000)
Notes: Animal nutrition and production; fertilizers; weather; and agricultural statistics.

AB —SHERRITT RESEARCH CENTRE, Library, Sherritt Gordon Mines Ltd, Fort Saskatchewan, T8L 2P2, Can. D Sim, Librn

FESSENDEN, WILLIAM PITT, 1806-1869

ME —BOWDOIN COLLEGE, Library, Brunswick, 04011. Dianne M Gutscher, Cur of Special Collections
Holdings: Mss
Notes: The Fessenden Family Papers contain 4000 mss for the period 1801-1908 and incl almost 1300 letters written by William Pitt Fessenden, US Senator from Maine, 1854-1869, and Secretary of the Treasury, 1864-65.

FESSENDEN FAMILY

ME —BOWDOIN COLLEGE, Library, Brunswick, 04011. Dianne M Gutscher, Cur of Special Collections
Holdings: Mss
Notes: The Fessenden Family Papers contain 4000 mss for the period 1801-1908 and incl almost 1300 letters written by William Pitt Fessenden, US Senator from Maine, 1854-1869, and Secretary of the Treasury, 1864-65.

FESTIVAL BOOKS

ON —METROPOLITAN TORONTO LIBRARY, Theatre Dept, 789 Yonge St, Toronto, M4W 2G8, Can. Heather McCallum, Head
Holdings: Vols (30,000) Mss Pix Slides

FESTIVAL BOOKS (cont.)

Phonorecords Microforms
Notes: Over 75 court festival books, dating from the 16th to the 19th centuries, document royal entrances, tournaments, wedding and birthday celebrations in a variety of European countries.

FESTIVALS

IL —AMERICAN SOKOL EDUCATIONAL AND PHYSICAL CULTURE, 6424 W Cermak Road, Berwyn, 60402. Annette Schabowski, Librn
Notes: SLET (Physical Fitness Festival). Library's collection incl theses and dissertations on Czech life, folk dancing, gymnastics, etc.

LA —LOUISIANA STATE UNIVERSITY, SHREVEPORT, Library-Archives, 8515 Youree Dr, Shreveport, 71129. Patricia L Meador, Archivist & Asst Librn
Notes: See Louisiana - History entry for LSU Archives.

FESTSCHRIFTEN

FL —UNIVERSITY OF FLORIDA LIBRARY, Isser and Rae Price Library of Judaica, 18 Libr East, Gainesville, 32611. Robert Singerman, Head Librn
Budget: ($30,000)
Notes: Total holdings estimated at 55,000 vols dealing with the political, social, economic and intellectual history of the Jews in the ancient, medieval and modern periods and in all geographic areas. The following areas are especially well represented by printed matter in all relevant languages: Bibliography, Festschriften, History, Bible, Judaism and Jewish theology, liturgy, responsa, rabbinical literature, Jewish law, Hebrew language and literature, Yiddish language and literature, anti-semitism, Zionism, Palestine and the *Yishuv*, and the State of Israel. German and American Judaica form a collecting emphasis with holdings for all the standard histories as well as histories of individual synagogues, institutions and local communities. Works in Hebrew and Yiddish comprise about 60 percent of the collection (estimated 30,000 vols). With few exceptions, holdingsare limited to nineteenth and twentieth century imprints, with complete sets of journals and thousands of ephemeral pamphlets, many of them commemorating anniversaries, enhancing the research value of the collection, the largest Judaica research library in the southeastern United States. Only about half of the collection is cataloged; the collection is a circulating one and vols may be borrowed on interlibrary loan. Incl the Leonard C Mishkin Collection (40,000 vols), the largest personal Judaica collection in the United States, the Shlomo Marenof Collection (3500 vols), and the inventory of Bernard Morgenstern's Lower East Side Book Store (8000 vols). Scholars should inquire in advance of their visit. *The Isser and Rae Price Library of Judaica* Report (circulation 2900 copies) is mailed gratis twice a year to all interested parties. Special catalogs:Pre-1881 Hebrew imprints recorded in a chronological card file.

NY —NEW YORK PUBLIC LIBRARY, Research Libraries, General Research Division, Fifth Ave & 42 St, New York, 10018. Rodney Phillips, Chief
Holdings: Cat
Notes: Festschriften, collections of essays written to honor an eminent scholar, cover all areas of intellectual inquiry and are rarely classified separately. The G K Hall *Guide* offers access to over 9000 festschriften. The humanities and social sciences are extensively covered. See *Guide to* Festschriften, 2 vols (Boston: G K Hall): Vol 1: *The Retrospective Festschriften Collection of NYPL: Materials Catalogued through* 1971; and Vol II: *Dictionary Catalog of Festschriften in NYPL and LC* (1968-1976).

FETHERLING, DOUGLAS, 1947-

ON —MCMASTER UNIVERSITY, Mills Memorial Library, Div of Archives & Research Collections, Hamilton, L8S 4L6, Can. G R Hill, Univ Librn
Holdings: Mss
Notes: Mss of published poems and books of poetry; also notebooks and correspondence with other Canadian writers and poets.

FETICIDE see Abortion

FETISHISM, SEXUAL

IN —INDIANA UNIVERSITY, Institute for Sex Research Library, 416 Morrison Hall, Bloomington, 47401. Douglas Freeman, Collections and Services Librn; Joan Brewer, Information Services Librn
Holdings: Vols (62,000) Cat Mss Pix Microforms
See also entry under Sex.

FEUDAL CASTLES see Castles

FEUDAL TENURE see Land Tenure

FEYNMAN, RICHARD P.

CA —CALIFORNIA INSTITUTE OF TECHNOLOGY, Robert A Millikan Memorial Library, Archives, 1201 E California Blvd, Pasadena, 91125. Judith R Goodstein, Archivist
Holdings: Vols (3000) Cat Mss Maps Pix Slides Phonorecords Audiotapes Videotapes 16mm Films Microforms
Notes: Ms sources for the history of astrophysics, cosmology, mathematical physics, experimental physics, radio astronomy, geophysics and biophysics. Collections incl the papers of: George Ellery Hale, Jesse Greenstein, H P Robertson, Richard Feynman, Paul Epstein, Max Delbruck, and Beno Gutenberg.

FIAT MONEY see Paper Money

FIBER ARTS

MI —CRANBROOK ACADEMY OF ART, 500 Lone Pine Rd, Box 801, Bloomfield Hills, 48013. Diane Gunn, Librn
Holdings: Vols 25,000
Notes: Incl 20,000 slides.

FIBER PLANTS see Fibers

FIBERS

CA —STANFORD UNIVERSITY, Food Research Institute Library, Stanford, 94305. Charles C Milford, Librn
Holdings: Vols (11,595) Cat Maps Pix Microforms
Budget: ($8046)
Notes: The economic aspects of the production, trade, disposition, and prices of food, feed, and fiber commodities throughout the world. Incl 25,000 pamphlets.

†DE —E I DUPONT DE NEMOURS & CO, Textile Fabrics Library, Experimental Station, Wilmington, 19898.

MD —US DEPT OF AGRICULTURE, National Agricultural Library, 10301 Baltimore Blvd, Beltsville, 20705. Joseph H Howard, Director
Holdings: Vols (2,000,000) Cat Mss Maps Pix Slides Microforms
Notes: Crop Fiber Collection. A special collection of approximately 50,000 reference cards, thousands of reprints, manuscript materials, photographs, and specimens relating to more than 300 genera of plants. Contains the most complete record of information in the country, if not the world, on fiber crops of the world. The collection is particularly vital to research interests and projects involving the use of natural fibers (i. e. rubber, guayule).

MA —UNIVERSITY OF LOWELL, Library, One University Ave, Lowell, 01854. Martha Mayo, Special Collections Librn
Holdings: Vols (24,000) Cat Mss Maps Pix
Notes: The Olney Collections contain books and journals on all aspects of textile technology particularly textile chemistry and textile engineering. The Flather Collection of the Boott Mill company papers 1835-1954. Photographic collections with emphasis on Lowell's textile industry.

PA —FRANKLIN INSTITUTE LIBRARY, 20 & The Parkway, Philadelphia, 19103. Miriam Padusis, Dir; Charles Wilt, Readers Servs Librn
Holdings: Vols (300,000) Cat Maps Pix Microforms

FICHTE, JOHANN GOTTLIEB

IL —NORTHWESTERN UNIVERSITY, Library, Special Collections Dept, 1937 Sheridan Rd, Evanston, 60201. R Russell Maylone, Cur
Holdings: Vols 30 Cat
Notes: Incl many first editions. Additional material in general collection.

FICKE, ARTHUR DAVISON

CT —YALE UNIVERSITY, Box 1603A, Yale Station, New Haven, 06520.
Holdings: Cat Mss
Notes: First editions, mostly with presentation inscriptions to his first wife, Evelyn Blunt, or their son, Stanhope.

FICTION

CA —LOS ANGELES PUBLIC LIBRARY, Fiction Dept, 630 W 5th St, Los Angeles, 90071. Helene G Mochedlover, Dept Librn
Holdings: Vols 215,000 Cat
Budget: $25,000
Notes: A permanent reference and circulating collection of approximately 55, 000 titles in English, representing mainly 19th and 20th century novels and short stores, including translations from 35 foreign languages. Collection is indexed by subject, as well as by author and title. Strong collections of California authors and of California in fiction.

KY —BEREA COLLEGE, Hutchins Library, Berea, 40404. Gerald F Roberts, Librn Special Collections
Holdings: Vols (10,000) Cat Mss Maps Pix
Notes: Weatherford-Hammond Appalachian Collection is strong in Appalachian fiction. A Fiction List--a bibliography of Appalachian fiction holdings--has been distributed to selected academic libraries and Friends of Hutchins Library. Collection is also strong in history, ballads, folklore and religion.

MA —HARVARD UNIVERSITY LIBRARY, Cambridge, 02138.
Holdings: Cat Mss

MI —DETROIT PUBLIC LIBRARY, Language and Literature Dept, 5201 Woodward Ave, Detroit, 48202. Ann Rabjohns, Chief
Holdings: Vols 8500 Cat
Notes: A reference collection of fiction, chiefly English and American, illustrating the history of the novel as a form, the work of individual novelists, trends and fashions in fiction. Supplements the department's historical and critical studies of the novel and novelists.

MS —UNIVERSITY OF SOUTHERN MISSISSIPPI, William David McCain Graduate Library, Box 5148, Southern Sta, Hattiesburg, 39406.
Holdings: Cat Mss
Notes: Literary mss and related correspondence (4.3 cubic feet) of Con Sellers, a best selling author of popular novels and historical romances. Sellers writes under numerous pseudonyms and has written such best sellers as *Dallas* and *Night* Shadows.

NY —NEW YORK PUBLIC LIBRARY, Research Libraries, General Research Division, Fifth Ave & 42 St, New York, 10018. Rodney Phillips, Chief
Holdings: Vols (2,225,000) Cat Maps Pix Microforms
Budget: ($775,718)

OH —BOWLING GREEN STATE UNIVERSITY, Library, Popular Culture Library, Bowling Green, 43403.
Notes: Extensive holdings of Big-Little books, comic books, matchbook covers, picture postcards, personal scrapbooks,

FICTION (cont.)

trading cards, posters, magazines, film pressbooks, juvenile series novels and popular literature.

OH —PUBLIC LIBRARY OF CINCINNATI & HAMILTON COUNTY, Fiction Dept, 800 Vine St, Cincinnati, 45202. Janet C Wiehe, Head
Holdings: Vols 110,000 Cat
Notes: Circulating collection of approx 58, 000 titles; classic and contemporary fiction with emphasis on 19th and 20th century American novels and short stories, and incl a widely representative selection of fiction translated from foreign languages.

OH —RUTHERFORD B HAYES LIBRARY, 1337 Hayes Ave, Fremont, 43420. Watt P Marchman, Dir
Holdings: Vols 700 Cat
Notes: 19th century.

OK —UNIVERSITY OF TULSA, McFarlin Library, Dept of Rare Books and Special Collections, 600 S College, Tulsa, 74104. David Farmer, Dir; Toby Murray, Archivist; Caroline Swinson, Cur of Manuscripts & Art
Holdings: Vols 2500
Notes: The only known extant lending library from the 19th century. It was formed by British subjects in Oporto, Portugal between 1820-1890. 70 percent not in Sadlier.

TX —UNIVERSITY OF TEXAS, ARLINGTON, Library, PO Box 19497, Arlington, 76019. Chas Colley, Dir Special Collections
Holdings: Vols (10,000) Cat
Notes: The Library of American Fiction includes works of American authors whose professional reputations rest primarily upon the production of fictitious prose narratives, or novels, and whose literary careers flourished during the period from 1870-1910. Writing forms other than novels are included only to the extent that they relate to the author's fiction. Reference works and studies directly supporting research in the literature of these authors are also included.

VA —UNIVERSITY OF VIRGINIA, Alderman Library, Rare Book Dept, Charlottesville, 22901. Julius P Barclay, Cur
Holdings: Vols 1200 // Cat
Notes: The Mrs Robert Coleman Taylor Collection of First Editions of American Best Sellers (Fiction). Almost without exception, these books are in mint and fine condition. Scope: 1752-1949. Incl very rare early American fiction.

FICTION, AMERICAN see American Fiction

FICTION, ARABIC

OH —OHIO STATE UNIVERSITY, Library, 1858 Neil Mall, Columbus, 43210. Dona Straley, Islamica Librn
Notes: Incl modern Arabic fiction and literature, and foreign literature in Arabic translations.

FICTION, ENGLISH see English Fiction

FICTION, FANTASTIC see Fantastic Fiction

FICTION, GOTHIC

CA —OCCIDENTAL COLLEGE, Library, 1600 Campus Rd, Los Angeles, 90041. Michael C Sutherland, Special Collections Librn
Notes: Mystery and detective fiction. Samples of fantasy, gothic romance, horror and pulps.

CA —UNIVERSITY OF CALIFORNIA, LOS ANGELES, Research Library, Dept of Special Collections, 405 Hilgard Ave, Los Angeles, 90024. Edward Shreeves, Chairman, Bibliographers Group; David S Zeidberg, Head
Holdings: Cat
Notes: Various collections, incl almanacs, comic books, commercial catalogs, fantasy fiction, pulp magazines, trade cards, and 19th century American paperbacks.

CA —UNIVERSITY OF CALIFORNIA, RIVERSIDE, University Library, 4045 Canyon Crest Dr, Box 5900, Riverside, 92517.
Holdings: Vols (30,000)
Notes: The Eaton Collection of science fiction and fantasy materials, incl 5,600 pulp magazines; also horror, supernatural, and Gothic mystery fiction; boys' books; utopian and dystopian fiction, imaginary voyages, future war and lost race fiction; large holdings in French language science fiction and fantasy; critical and scholarly works pertaining to these genres; videotapes of science fiction/fantasy films and shooting scripts. Collection covers science fiction/ fantasy literature from the 16th-17th centuries to the present. Strong individual author collections of Jules Verne, H Rider Haggard, H G Wells, Edgar Rice Burroughs, and Philip K Dick. For a complete description of the collection see: George Slusser, "The J Lloyd Eaton Collection," *Special Collections*, II, 1/2, 25-38 (1983), *andDictionary Catalog of the J Lloyd Eaton Collection of Science Fiction and Fantasy* Literature (Boston: G K Hall) 1982.

IN —INDIANA UNIVERSITY, Lilly Library, Seventh St, Bloomington, 47405. William R Cagle, Librn
Holdings: Cat Mss
Notes: First editions of early and modern books plus some 18th and 19th century penny dreadfuls. Mss incl some original illustrations for 19th and 20th century books.

MI —MICHIGAN STATE UNIVERSITY, Libraries, Special Collections Div, East Lansing, 48824. Jannette Fiore, Librn
Notes: The Russel B Nye Popular Culture Collection in the Michigan State Univ Libraries incl over (45,000) items. Most of the collection is organized into 4 categories: comic art, popular fiction, popular information materials and materials relating to the popular performing arts. Popular fiction in the collection is organized into juvenile, detective-mystery, and science fiction, westerns and women's fiction. In addition, there is a sample collection of dime novels and story papers (ca 400 issues representing nearly 100 titles). Pulp magazines which fall into none of the separate categories are housed with the dime novels and story papers. Juvenile Fiction: ca 4000 vols. Emphasis is on juvenile series fiction of the 19th and 20th centuries, with nearly 200 girls and 300 boys series represented. 19th-century "Sunday School" books andboth fiction and non-fiction scouting books are also included. Western Fiction: An exceptionally fine institutional collection, with over 3000 novels (most published between 1900 and 1950), almost all hardbound and in dust jackets, and nearly 500 pulp magazine issues representing more than fifty titles. The most important pulp runs are Street and Smith's *Western Story* Magazine and Warner Publications's *Ranch* Romances. Women's Fiction: Over 3000 novels and ca 1000 issues of romance, confession and movie magazines and pulps from the 1920s through the 1970s. Most of the novels are in the romance category, with over 2000 Harlequin novels, a good representation of other modern best-selling romances, and several dozen titles from late 19th-century romance series. Science Fiction: ca 3000 books and periodicals. MSU is a depository for the Science Fiction Writersof America, which contributes review copies of new books. The bulk of the collection is periodicals, with 71 titles represented. Most issues come from the period from the late 1940s to the present. The collection subscribes to most major science fiction magazines and holds a fanzine collection which now numbers over 2500. Detective-Mystery Fiction: ca 3500 novels, in paper and hardback, and pulps representing 28 titles from 1920-1950. Complete runs of *The London Mystery* Magazine and *Ellery Queen's Mystery* Magazine are included, along with a large sample collection of the more sensational detective and crime fiction magazines from the 1930s through the present.

†NY —STATE UNIVERSITY OF NEW YORK, COLLEGE AT ONEONTA, James M Milne Library, Special Collections, Oneonta, 13820. Martha Chambers, Librn
Notes: Popular fiction before 1920, incl some gothics, "domestic sentimentalist," mysteries and westerns.

PA —TEMPLE UNIVERSITY LIBRARIES, Special Collections Dept, Rare Books & Mss Section, Philadelphia, 19122. Thomas M Whitehead, Cur
Holdings: Vols (200) Cat
Notes: Holdings include contemporary printed books, first and later editions, of 18th and early 19th century gothic fiction. Significant strength in Matthew Gregory "Monk" Lewis books.

†UT —BRIGHAM YOUNG UNIVERSITY, Harold B Lee Library, Provo, 84602. Elizabeth Pope, Librn
Notes: Science Fiction-Fantasy Collection, extensive circulating collection. Arkham House near complete, non-circulating. Mysteries, westerns and gothic romances in general fiction. Edgar Rice Burroughs 1st edition collection does not circulate. Science fiction and fantasy art special collection.

WI —UNIVERSITY OF WISCONSIN, LA CROSSE, Murphy Library, 1631 Pine St, La Crosse, 54601. Edwin L Hill, Special Collections Librn
Holdings: Vols 1000 Cat
Notes: The Paul W Skeeters Collection of science fiction, fantasy, and horror literature. Complements the library's complete collection of Arkham House books, which contains many titles autographed by August Derleth, and H P Lovecraft's complete fiction and poetic works.

AB —UNIVERSITY OF ALBERTA, Cameron Library, The Bruce Peel Special Collections Room, Edmonton, T6G 2J8, Can. John Charles, Special Collections Librn
Holdings: Vols 220 Cat
Notes: Especially 19th century "penny dreadfuls" and Gothic literature.

†MB —UNIVERSITY OF WINNIPEG, Library, 515 Portage Avenue, Winnipeg, R3B 2E9, Can. Raymond C Wright, Librn
Notes: Edgar Rice Burroughs special collection. Extensive collection of books on film. Sample Gothic, Romance and Horror collections.

ON —QUEEN'S UNIVERSITY, Douglas Library, Kingston, K7L 5C4, Can. William F E Morley, Cur, Special Collections
Holdings: Vols (2050) Cat
Notes: Incl about 200 items in the H P Lovecraft collection--books, articles and offprints (225 vols). Also, 6500 pulp magazines (which are not cataloged. Checklist of holdings is available).

FICTION, HISTORICAL see Historical Fiction

FICTION, NEW YORK

NY —STATE UNIVERSITY OF NEW YORK, STONY BROOK, Melville Library, Dept of Special Collections, Stony Brook, 11794. Evert Volkersz, Head
Holdings: Vols Uncat
Notes: A growing collection of fiction and literature with Long Island, incl Queens and Brooklyn, as a fictional setting.

FICTION, OLD

RI —PROVIDENCE ATHENAEUM, 251 Benefit St, Providence, 02903. Sally Duplaix, Dir
Holdings: Vols 25,000 Cat
Budget: $5000
Notes: Classic and contemporary fiction with emphasis on 19th and 20th century American fiction and incl large selection translated from foreign languages.

FICTION, ROMANCE

CA —CALIFORNIA STATE UNIVERSITY, FULLERTON, Library, Box 4150, Fullerton, 92634. Kathy Morris, Archivist
Notes: 1300 vols of Romance fiction

FICTION, ROMANCE (cont.)

(Harlequins, etc). Mss of 25 sf authors with major ms holdings by Avram Davidson, Phillip K Dick, Harry Harrison, Frank Herbert and Robert Moore Williams.

CA —OCCIDENTAL COLLEGE, Library, 1600 Campus Rd, Los Angeles, 90041. Michael C Sutherland, Special Collections Librn
Notes: Mystery and detective fiction. Samples of fantasy, gothic romance, horror and pulps.

MI —MICHIGAN STATE UNIVERSITY, Libraries, Special Collections Div, East Lansing, 48824. Jannette Fiore, Librn
Notes: The Russel B Nye Popular Culture Collection in the Michigan State Univ Libraries incl over (45,000) items. Most of the collection is organized into 4 categories: comic art, popular fiction, popular information materials and materials relating to the popular performing arts. Popular fiction in the collection is organized into juvenile, detective-mystery, and science fiction, westerns and women's fiction. In addition, there is a sample collection of dime novels and story papers (ca 400 issues representing nearly 100 titles). Pulp magazines which fall into none of the separate categories are housed with the dime novels and story papers. Juvenile Fiction: ca 4000 vols. Emphasis is on juvenile series fiction of the 19th and 20th centuries, with nearly 200 girls and 300 boys series represented. 19th-century "Sunday School" books andboth fiction and non-fiction scouting books are also included. Western Fiction: An exceptionally fine institutional collection, with over 3000 novels (most published between 1900 and 1950), almost all hardbound and in dust jackets, and nearly 500 pulp magazine issues representing more than fifty titles. The most important pulp runs are Street and Smith's *Western Story* Magazine and Warner Publications's *Ranch* Romances. Women's Fiction: Over 3000 novels and ca 1000 issues of romance, confession and movie magazines and pulps from the 1920s through the 1970s. Most of the novels are in the romance category, with over 2000 Harlequin novels, a good representation of other modern best-selling romances, and several dozen titles from late 19th-century romance series. Science Fiction: ca 3000 books and periodicals. MSU is a depository for the Science Fiction Writersof America, which contributes review copies of new books. The bulk of the collection is periodicals, with 71 titles represented. Most issues come from the period from the late 1940s to the present. The collection subscribes to most major science fiction magazines and holds a fanzine collection which now numbers over 2500. Detective-Mystery Fiction: ca 3500 novels, in paper and hardback, and pulps representing 28 titles from 1920-1950. Complete runs of *The London Mystery* Magazine and *Ellery Queen's Mystery* Magazine are included, along with a large sample collection of the more sensational detective and crime fiction magazines from the 1930s through the present.

†UT —BRIGHAM YOUNG UNIVERSITY, Harold B Lee Library, Provo, 84602. Elizabeth Pope, Librn
Notes: Science Fiction-Fantasy Collection, extensive circulating collection. Arkham House near complete, non-circulating. Mysteries, westerns and gothic romances in general fiction. Edgar Rice Burroughs 1st edition collection does not circulate. Science fiction and fantasy art special collection.

WI —UNIVERSITY OF WISCONSIN, MADISON, Cooperative Children's Book Center, Helen C White Hall, Rm 4290, 600 N Park St, Madison, 53706. Ginny Moore Kruse, Dir
Holdings: Vols (25,000) Cat
Notes: Cooperative Children's Book Center collections incl most US trade books published for children in last 24 months; first editions of recommended US children's trade books published since 1965; over 400 alternative press books published for children in US and Canada since 1970; children's books about Wisconsin and by Wisconsin authors and illustrators; representative 19th and early 20th century American children's books; 19th century children's periodicals; first and significant editions of Newbury and Caldecott Medal books; historical and contemporary toybooks; 75 vols of Mother Goose published since 1828; 160 vols of Thorton Burgess books, many first editions; ms and original artwork for Ellen Raskin's *The Westing Game* and *The Mysterious Disappearance of Leon (I Mean Noel);* juvenile mass market and traderomance fiction.

†MB —UNIVERSITY OF WINNIPEG, Library, 515 Portage Avenue, Winnipeg, R3B 2E9, Can. Raymond C Wright, Librn
Notes: Edgar Rice Burroughs special collection. Extensive collection of books on film. Sample Gothic, Romance and Horror collections.

FICTION, SENTIMENTALIST

†NY —STATE UNIVERSITY OF NEW YORK, COLLEGE AT ONEONTA, James M Milne Library, Special Collections, Oneonta, 13820. Martha Chambers, Librn
Notes: Popular fiction before 1920, incl some gothics, "domestic sentimentalist," mysteries and westerns.

FICTION, 'WESTERN'

AZ —UNIVERSITY OF ARIZONA, Library, Tucson, 85721. W David Laird, Librn
Notes: The Walt Coburn Collection, incl the author's published stories and books, notebooks, correspondence, photographs, scrapbooks, and ephemera. Coburn was known as "King of the Western Pulps" who wrote from 1922 to 1973.

CO —COLORADO STATE UNIVERSITY, Libraries, Fort Collins, 80523. John Newman, Special Collections Librn
Holdings: Vols (11,000) Cat Mss Pix
Notes: The Western American Literature Collection incl fiction, poetry, pictures, art, and other works of the imagination set in the American Frontier West and modern rural West, especially the Rocky Mountain Area.

IL —NORTHERN ILLINOIS UNIVERSITY, Founders Memorial Library, Rare Books and Special Collections Dept, De Kalb, 60115. William R DuBois, Dept Head
Holdings: Cat
Notes: The Western Pulp Magazine Collection. Incl 600 magazines. Noncirculating. Limited photocopying.

MI —MICHIGAN STATE UNIVERSITY, Libraries, Special Collections Div, East Lansing, 48824. Jannette Fiore, Librn
Holdings: Vols 4000 Cat
Notes: The Russel B Nye Popular Culture Collection in the Michigan State Univ Libraries incl over (45,000) items. Most of the collection is organized into 4 categories: comic art, popular fiction, popular information materials and materials relating to the popular performing arts. Popular fiction in the collection is organized into juvenile, detective-mystery, and science fiction, westerns and women's fiction. In addition, there is a sample collection of dime novels and story papers (ca 400 issues representing nearly 100 titles). Pulp magazines which fall into none of the separate categories are housed with the dime novels and story papers. Juvenile Fiction: ca 4000 vols. Emphasis is on juvenile series fiction of the 19th and 20th centuries, with nearly 200 girls and 300 boys series represented. 19th-century "Sunday School" books andboth fiction and non-fiction scouting books are also included. Western Fiction: An exceptionally fine institutional collection, with over 3000 novels (most published between 1900 and 1950), almost all hardbound and in dust jackets, and nearly 500 pulp magazine issues representing more than fifty titles. The most important pulp runs are Street and Smith's *Western Story* Magazine and Warner Publications's *Ranch* Romances. Women's Fiction: Over 3000 novels and ca 1000 issues of romance, confession and movie magazines and pulps from the 1920s through the 1970s. Most of the novels are in the romance category, with over 2000 Harlequin novels, a good representation of other modern best-selling romances, and several dozen titles from late 19th-century romance series. Science Fiction: ca 3000 books and periodicals. MSU is a depository for the Science Fiction Writersof America, which contributes review copies of new books. The bulk of the collection is periodicals, with 71 titles represented. Most issues come from the period from the late 1940s to the present. The collection subscribes to most major science fiction magazines and holds a fanzine collection which now numbers over 2500. Detective-Mystery Fiction: ca 3500 novels, in paper and hardback, and pulps representing 28 titles from 1920-1950. Complete runs of *The London Mystery* Magazine and *Ellery Queen's Mystery* Magazine are included, along with a large sample collection of the more sensational detective and crime fiction magazines from the 1930s through the present.

NM —NEW MEXICO STATE UNIVERSITY, Library, Box 3475, Las Cruces, 88003. James Dyke, Dir
Holdings: Vols 400 // Cat
Notes: An exceptional representative collection of rare paperback American novels, including the oldest types of western novels.

NM —ROSWELL PUBLIC LIBRARY, 301 N Pennsylvania Ave, Roswell, 88201. Sarah Beth Galloway, Library Dir
Holdings: Vols (2000) Cat Maps
Budget: $1000
Notes: Covers literature (fiction and nonfiction), history, biography, geography, of Oklahoma, Texas, Colorado, New Mexico and Arizona.

†NY —STATE UNIVERSITY OF NEW YORK, COLLEGE AT ONEONTA, James M Milne Library, Special Collections, Oneonta, 13820. Martha Chambers, Librn
Notes: Popular fiction before 1920, incl some gothics, "domestic sentimentalist," mysteries and westerns.

OH —OHIO HISTORICAL SOCIETY, Archives Library Division, 1982 Velma Ave, Columbus, 43211. Dennis East, Division Chief
Holdings: Vols 2000 // Cat Mss Pix
Notes: Collection is comprised of books by Grey, magazines in which his writings appeared, mss & typescripts, and 700 items from his personal library, incl scarce items on hunting, big-game fishing, and travel. Museum objects are at the Zane Grey Museum, Zanesville, Ohio, operated by the Ohio Historical Society.

OR —UNIVERSITY OF OREGON LIBRARY, Special Collections Div, Eugene, 97403. Kenneth W Duckett, Curator
Holdings: Cat Mss
Notes: Nearly 40 mss collections of authors of Western fiction, usually containing correspondence with publishers, agents, and other writers; mss of their books, stories, TV scripts and movie scripts; and often tearsheets or publications incl their work. There are also files of literary agents, such as August Lenninger, Lurton Blassingame, and Lowell Brentano. Publication: Martin Schmitt, comp, *Catalogue of Manuscripts in the University of Oregon Library* (Eugene: University of Oregon Books, 1971).
See also entry under Pulp Magazines; Television Scripts; Haycox, Ernest, 1899-1950

TX —UNIVERSITY OF TEXAS LIBRARIES, General Libraries, Barker Texas History Center, PO Box P, Austin, 78712. Don Carleton, Dir
Holdings: Vols (132,000) Cat Mss Maps Pix Slides Phonorecords Audiotapes Microforms
Notes: See description of collection under Texas-History.

TX —UNIVERSITY OF TEXAS, EL PASO, Library, Special Collections Dept, El Paso, 79968. Cesar Caballero, Dept Head
Holdings: Vols 1680 Cat
Budget: ($5000)
Notes: Western Fiction Collection.

FICTION, 'WESTERN' (cont.)

Established with the purchase of over 1500 volumes from the private collection of Dr C L Sonnichsen, the well-known historian and Western Literature professor.

†UT —BRIGHAM YOUNG UNIVERSITY, Harold B Lee Library, Provo, 84602. Elizabeth Pope, Librn
Notes: Science Fiction-Fantasy Collection, extensive circulating collection. Arkham House near complete, non-circulating. Mysteries, westerns and gothic romances in general fiction. Edgar Rice Burroughs 1st edition collection does not circulate. Science fiction and fantasy art special collection.

FICTION, WOMEN'S

MI —MICHIGAN STATE UNIVERSITY, Libraries, Special Collections Div, East Lansing, 48824. Jannette Fiore, Librn
Notes: The Russel B Nye Popular Culture Collection in the Michigan State Univ Libraries incl over (45,000) items. Most of the collection is organized into 4 categories: comic art, popular fiction, popular information materials and materials relating to the popular performing arts. Popular fiction in the collection is organized into juvenile, detective-mystery, and science fiction, westerns and women's fiction. In addition, there is a sample collection of dime novels and story papers (ca 400 issues representing nearly 100 titles). Pulp magazines which fall into none of the separate categories are housed with the dime novels and story papers. Juvenile Fiction: ca 4000 vols. Emphasis is on juvenile series fiction of the 19th and 20th centuries, with nearly 200 girls and 300 boys series represented. 19th-century "Sunday School" books andboth fiction and non-fiction scouting books are also included. Western Fiction: An exceptionally fine institutional collection, with over 3000 novels (most published between 1900 and 1950), almost all hardbound and in dust jackets, and nearly 500 pulp magazine issues representing more than fifty titles. The most important pulp runs are Street and Smith's *Western Story* Magazine and Warner Publications's *Ranch* Romances. Women's Fiction: Over 3000 novels and ca 1000 issues of romance, confession and movie magazines and pulps from the 1920s through the 1970s. Most of the novels are in the romance category, with over 2000 Harlequin novels, a good representation of other modern best-selling romances, and several dozen titles from late 19th-century romance series. Science Fiction: ca 3000 books and periodicals. MSU is a depository for the Science Fiction Writersof America, which contributes review copies of new books. The bulk of the collection is periodicals, with 71 titles represented. Most issues come from the period from the late 1940s to the present. The collection subscribes to most major science fiction magazines and holds a fanzine collection which now numbers over 2500. Detective-Mystery Fiction: ca 3500 novels, in paper and hardback, and pulps representing 28 titles from 1920-1950. Complete runs of *The London Mystery* Magazine and *Ellery Queen's Mystery* Magazine are included, along with a large sample collection of the more sensational detective and crime fiction magazines from the 1930s through the present.

FICTITIOUS IMPRINTS (IN BOOKS) see Imprints (In Books), Fictitious

FIDDLERS AND FIDDLING

PA —PENNSYLVANIA STATE UNIVERSITY, Arts Library, 405 E Pattee Library, University Park, 16802. Daniel Zager, Music Librn
Holdings: Vols (14,000) Cat Phonorecords
Notes: The music collection supports a School of Music curriculum which is comprehensive at the undergraduate and masters degree levels. The collection includes scores (collected works and performance editions), books, periodicals, and recordings. The Special Collections area of the library includes the following music collections: the manuscripts, published scores, personal papers, and some recordings of the American composer Charles Wakefield Cadman; 18th and 19th century American tunebooks and 18th and 19th century Pennsylvania German hymnbooks and songbooks; and the Doyle Guntharp collection of field recordings of fiddler's performances and interviews from Central Pennsylvania.

VT —MIDDLEBURY COLLEGE, Starr Library, Flanders Ballad Collection, Middlebury, 05753. Jennifer Post Quinn, Cur
Notes: Begun as Helen Hartness Flanders' private collection in 1930, given to Middlebury College, 1941. Incl over 9000 New England items recorded or transcribed since 1930: ballads and folk songs of British, American, French-Canadian, and Russian origin; religious songs; fiddle tunes; dance music. Incl research collection of folklore and folksong monographs, scores, tunebooks, journals. Reference: Quinn, Jennifer Post. *An Index to the Field Recordings in the Flanders Ballad Collection at Middlebury College, Middlebury, Vermont* Middlebury, VT, Middlebury College, 1983.

FIEDLER, ARTHUR

MA —BOSTON UNIVERSITY, Mugar Memorial Library, Special Collections Dept, 771 Commonwealth Ave, Boston, 02215. Howard B Gotlieb, Dir
Notes: Personal collection of Arthur Fiedler, incl 6000 scores and sound recordings, manuscripts, photographs, memorabilia, library, and test pressings of Fiedler's performances.

FIEFS see Land Tenure

FIELD, EUGENE

CO —DENVER PUBLIC LIBRARY, Western History Department, 1357 Broadway, Denver, 80203. Eleanor M Gehres, Head
Holdings: Vols 375 Cat Mss Pix
Notes: Books by or about Eugene Field, and from his personal library. Incl 800 mss also, a small collection of the works of Roswell Field.

IL —NEWBERRY LIBRARY, 60 W Walton St, Chicago, 60610. Diana Haskell, Cur of Modern Mss
Holdings: Cat Mss Pix
Notes: Books and mss. Restricted use: noncirculating.

MA —JONES LIBRARY, 43 Amity St, Amherst, 01002. Daniel J Lombardo, Cur of Special Collections
Holdings: Vols 165 Cat Mss Pix
Notes: Editions, mss, newspaper clippings, ephemera. Does not circulate. Unpublished guide available.

MO —WASHINGTON UNIVERSITY, John M Olin Library, Campus Box 1061, St Louis, 63130.
Holdings: Cat Mss
Notes: First and variant editions of Field's works; materials from his library; mss, letters, ephemera. Large group of Field materials are with the William K Bixby papers.

VA —UNIVERSITY OF VIRGINIA, Alderman Library, Clifton Waller Barrett Collection, Charlottesville, 22901. Joan St C Crane, Cur of American Literature Collections
Notes: Papers.

FIELD, FREDERICK

MI —MICHIGAN STATE UNIVERSITY, International Library, South and Southeast Asia Collection, East Lansing, 48824. Clinton Lockert, Bibliographer
Holdings: Vols (13,500) Cat Mss Maps Pix Audiotapes Microforms
Notes: Correspondence and papers of Frederick Field, Gilbert Jonas, and Wesley Fishel.

FIELD, MICHAEL, 1915-1971

NY —CORNELL UNIVERSITY LIBRARIES, Collection of Regional History, Dept of Manuscripts and Univ Archives, Ithaca, 14853.
Notes: Papers, 1965-71; 8 ft. Gourmet chef, author.

FIELD, RICHARD HINKLEY, 1903-1978

MA —HARVARD UNIVERSITY LIBRARY, Law School Library, Langdell Hall, Cambridge, 02138. Erika S Chadbourn, Cur of Mss
Holdings: Cat Mss
Notes: Personal-professional papers. Typed inventory in repository. Inclusive dates: 1942-1978.

FIELD BORDERS see Windbreaks, Shelterbelts, Etc.

FIELD CROPS

MB —UNIVERSITY OF MANITOBA, Elizabeth Dafoe Library, Archives and Special Collections Dept, Winnipeg, R3T 2N2, Can. Richard E Bennett, Dept Head; Corrado A Santoro, Reference Archivist
Notes: Papers of soil scientist and professor Joseph Henry Ellis. Soil and land inspections, surveys and reports; stream bank erosion studies; river reclamation projects; field crop experiments; prairie rehabilitation activities; fertilizer experiments; land utilization studies; tree planting.

FIELD DOGS see Hunting Dogs

FIELD FAMILY

MA —STOCKBRIDGE LIBRARY ASSOCIATION, Main St, Box H, Stockbridge, 01262. Rosemary Schmeyer, Librn
Holdings: Vols (1200) Cat Mss Maps Pix
Notes: The Historical Room contains approximately 1200 vols of genealogical reference, ie Massachusetts Soldiers and Sailors of the Revolution, Vital Statistics for towns in Massachusetts, local history, Indian history, books by and about Stockbridge residents, and a large collection of family papers of the Sedgwick and Field families among many others. These are being cataloged with the help of a special grant.

NY —CORNELL UNIVERSITY LIBRARIES, Collection of Regional History, Dept of Manuscripts and Univ Archives, Ithaca, 14853.
Holdings: Pix
Notes: Incl 5 pieces, ca 1860-80; autographed photo of Presidential candidate James A Garfield.

FIELD HOSPITALS see Medicine, Military; Red Cross

FIELD SPORTS see Hunting; Sports

FIELDER, MILDRED

†SD —SOUTH DAKOTA SCHOOL OF MINES & TECHNOLOGY, Devereaux Library, Rapid City, 57701.
Holdings: Cat Mss
Notes: Papers, mss, etc.

FIELDING, GABRIEL, 1916-

ON —MCMASTER UNIVERSITY, Mills Memorial Library, Div of Archives & Research Collections, Hamilton, L8S 4L6, Can. G R Hill, Univ Librn
Holdings: Mss
Notes: Original typescripts of poetry, plays, and novels (published and unpublished). Also correspondence with British writers, such as Graham Greene, Evelyn Waugh, and T S Eliot.

FIELDING, HENRY

CT —YALE UNIVERSITY, Box 1603A, Yale Station, New Haven, 06520.
Holdings: Cat

FIELDING, HENRY (cont.)

IA —UNIVERSITY OF IOWA, University Libraries, Iowa City, 52242. Frank Paluka, Head, Special Collections Dept
Holdings: Vols 89 Uncat
Notes: Article O M Brack, Jr and Curt A Zimansky "The Charles B Woods Fielding Collection," in *Books at Iowa,* Nov 1971.

FIELDS, MAURICE COLFAX

KS —SAINT MARY COLLEGE, Library, Leavenworth, 66048. Therese Deplazes, Special Collections Librn

FIFE, AUSTIN AND ALTA

DC —LIBRARY OF CONGRESS, American Folklife Center, Archive of Folk Culture, Washington, 20540.
Notes: The Fife Collection of Mormon and Western folksongs; Mormon superstitions, folk cures, frontier legends, religious stories, and traditional American and Danish folksongs. 106 disc recordings.

UT —UNIVERSITY OF UTAH, Marriott Library, Special Collections, Salt Lake City, 84112. Gregory C Thompson, Cur
Notes: Mormon-Folklore. Papers of Austin and Alta Fife, catalogs, manuscripts, phonorecords, tapes.

FIFTH COLUMN see Subversive Activities

FIGHT FOR FREEDOM

NJ —PRINCETON UNIVERSITY, Library, Manuscript Collection, Nassau St, Princeton, 08540. Jean F Preston, Cur
Holdings: / / Cat Mss
Notes: Incl 200 boxes; 126 cartons. The archives cover the period April to December, 1941.

FIGHTING see Boxing; Fencing; Military Art and Science; War; Naval Art and Science

FIGUIER, LOUIS GUILLAUME

NY —CORNELL UNIVERSITY LIBRARIES, Collection of Regional History, Dept of Manuscripts and Univ Archives, Ithaca, 14853.
Notes: 19th century French scientist. Incl mss and letters from Figuier.

FIGURE SKATING see Skating

FIGURES (MUSIC) see Canons, Fugues, Etc.

FIGURINES see Bronzes; Dolls

FILICINEAE see Ferns

FILIGRAINS see Watermarks (Paper)

FILLMORE, MILLARD

NY —BUFFALO & ERIE COUNTY HISTORICAL SOCIETY, 25 Nottingham Court, Buffalo, 14216. Herman Sass, Librn
Notes: Microfilm edition of papers in preparation. Separate index. Many books and pamphlets, but mainly ms pieces.

NY —STATE UNIVERSITY OF NEW YORK, COLLEGE AT OSWEGO, Penfield Library, Oswego, 13126. Anne Commerton, Dir
Holdings: Cat Mss
Notes: President Millard Fillmore Collection. Incl about 9000 items, with legal papers relating to Fillmore's law practice; personal letters of family, relatives and friends; political correspondence during career as State legislator, Congressman, Comptroller of New York, Vice-President, President and during retirement. Among Fillmore's correspondents were his two law partners and long time political associates, Nathan K Hall and Solomon G Haven as well as Anna Ella Carroll and Dorothea Dix. Papers cover the period 1825-1889. Unpublished calendar. See *New York Times,* 24 March 1969.

FILLMORE WEST

IL —NORTHWESTERN UNIVERSITY, Library, Special Collections Dept, 1937 Sheridan Rd, Evanston, 60201. R Russell Maylone, Cur
Notes: Over 350 original posters produced at the schools of the Sorbonne, Beaux Arts and other ad hoc ateliers during the student and worker uprising, May-June Revolution, Paris, 1968. French posters from World War I; Russian posters from the 1920s and 1930s. Broadside poems produced in England and American during the 20th century. Fillmore West posters (500).

FILM CATALOGS see Moving Pictures—Catalogs

FILM FESTIVAL, AMERICAN see American Film Festival

FILM FESTIVALS see Moving Picture Festivals

FILM MUSIC see Moving Picture Music

FILMS see Moving Pictures

FILMS, TELEVISION see Television Films

FILTERS AND FILTRATION

MA —ABCOR, INC, Library, 850 Main St, Wilmington, 01887. Eileen Smith, Librn
Holdings: Vols (2000) Cat
Budget: ($10,000)
Notes: Environmental technology; ultrafiltration; waste treatment processes. Incl technical reports. Extensive microfiche collection on air pollution.

FINANCE

AL —UNIVERSITY OF ALABAMA, Business Library, Box 2937, University, 35486. Dorothy Eady Brown, Librn; Linda Suttle Harris, Ref Librn and Data Base Searcher
Holdings: Vols (105,000) Cat Microforms
Budget: ($60,000)
Notes: Incl 90,000 corporation reports and 38,500 microforms.

CA —UNIVERSITY OF CALIFORNIA, BERKELEY, Institute of Governmental Studies Library, 109 Moses Hall, Berkeley, 94720. Jack Leister, Head Librn
Holdings: Vols (350,000) Cat Mss Maps Microforms
Budget: ($160,000)
Notes: The library collects primarily pamphlets. Incl in the library holdings are documents from all levels of government, as well as publications issued by professional associations and special interest groups. A G K Hall catalog covering the Institute's Library holdings is available. Since 1937, Library has been depository for all California local documents (city, county & special district). Formerly: Bureau of Public Administration.

CA —LOS ANGELES PUBLIC LIBRARY, Business & Economic Dept, 630 W 5th St, Los Angeles, 90071. Joan Bartel, Principal Librn
Notes: Annual reports in hard copy of corporations traded on the New York, American, OTC, and Pacific Exchanges, are received on a current basis. All are retained for 5 years; S&P 500 companies and some western companies indefinitely. Annual reports and 10-Ks for New York American Stock Exchange corporations are available in microfiche, 1970-1976. Beginning with 1977, 10-K reports for all US publicly traded corporations are collected. Beginning in 1980, annual reports for all US publicly traded companies are collected on microfiche. Standard sources of information on corporations are available, current and retrospective.

CA —UNIVERSITY OF CALIFORNIA, LOS ANGELES, Graduate School of Management Library, UCLA Campus, Los Angeles, 90024. Robert Bellanti, Head Librn
Holdings: Vols (128,000) Cat Mss Microforms
Notes: The

CA —UNIVERSITY OF SOUTHERN CALIFORNIA, Crocker Business Library, Hoffman Hall, University Park, Los Angeles, 90007. Judith A Truelson, Head Librn
Holdings: Vols (100,000) Cat Microforms
Notes: The Roy P Crocker Library of Business Administration, located in Hoffman Hall, houses more than 100,000 volumes and regularly receives approximately 1500 trade, financial, economics, labor, and general business periodicals and newspapers. The areas of subject concentration include business economics, finance and investments, general management/management theory, international business, finance and management, marketing/food marketing, and quantitative business analysis.

CA —ALAMEDA COUNTY LIBRARY SYSTEM, Business & Government Library, 2201 Broadway, Oakland, 94612. David Lewallen, Manager
Holdings: Vols (10,000) Cat Maps Microforms
Budget: ($50,000)

CT —YALE UNIVERSITY, Social Science Library, 140 Prospect St, New Haven, 06520. Billie I Salter, Librn
Holdings: Vols (40,000) Cat Microforms
See also entry under Social sciences.

DC —EXPORT-IMPORT BANK OF THE UNITED STATES, EXIMBANK Library, 811 Vermont Ave NW, Washington, 20571. Theodora McGill, Librn; John Posniak, Asst Librn
Holdings: Vols (15,000) Maps Audiotapes
Notes: The library has almost a complete set of the Economist Intelligence unit of London's *Quarterly Economic Reviews*; various types of materials with general, economic and statistical data on virtually every country of the world; incl foreign government publications, publications of various international organizations, and US Government documents.

DC —US BUREAU OF THE CENSUS, Library, Federal Office Bldg 3, Rm 2451, Washington, 20233. Betty Baxtresser, Chief, ASD Library Branch
Holdings: Vols (64,000) Cat
Notes: Periodic reports from the governments of the states, counties, cities with populations of over 10,000 and selected special districts of the US. Emphasis is on the financial aspects of governments. Reports are listed in a computer print-out comprising a volume of the printed *Catalogs of the Bureau of the Census Library.*

GA —ATLANTA PUBLIC LIBRARY, Ivan Allen Jr Dept of Science, Industry & Government, One Margaret Mitchell Square, Atlanta, 30303. William D Munro, Head
Holdings: Vols (15,000) Cat Microforms
Budget: ($180,000)
Notes: This collection incl on microform annual reports and Securities Exchange Commission 10-K reports for some 11,000 companies from 1976 to date; current and retrospective stock quotations, stock reports, corporate and industry records and directories and supporting looseleaf services; information file on Atlanta's largest 15,000 with annual updates; and current plat maps for the five county Metro-Atlanta area. Atlanta and Georgia business history sections are being developed. Most material on this collection is noncirculating.

GA —FEDERAL RESERVE BANK OF ATLANTA, Research Library, PO Box 1731, Atlanta, 30301. Leigh Watson Healy, Information Services Coord; Cynthia Walsh-Kloss, Assoc Librn
Holdings: Vols (12,000) Cat Mss Microforms
Notes: Collection specializes in banking, finance, economics, publications of the Federal Reserve Banks and Federal Reserve Board.

HI —BANK OF HAWAII, Information Ctr, PO Box 2900, Honolulu, 96846. Sally Campbell, Information Mgr
Holdings: Vols 4000 Cat Maps VF
Notes: Economics research in developing

FINANCE (cont.)

areas of Hawaii, US Pacific Islands, Asian and other foreign countries. Emphasis on economics, business statistics, demography, finance, banking, tourist industry, construction, domestic and foreign trade. Incl 1000 serial titles.

HI —HAWAII PACIFIC COLLEGE, Meader Library, 1060 Bishop St, Honolulu, 96813. Barbara Burton Hoefler, Head Librn
Holdings: Vols 35 Cat
Notes: The Hawaii Society of Corporate Planners concluded negotiations (1978) to provide a special collection. Presently acquisitions inactive.

IL —CHICAGO BOARD OF TRADE, Library, 141 W Jackson Blvd, Chicago, 60604. Darlene Appleman, Librn
Holdings: Vols (3500) Cat Microforms
Notes: Incl materials on commodity exchanges, commodities that are traded on futures exchanges, finance, and agricultural economics. *Commodity Futures Trading, A Bibliography* is published annually. The archives of the Chicago Board of Trade are located in the Manuscript Collection at the University of Illinois at Chicago Circle Campus. A published catalog, *The Archives of the Chicago Board of Trade, 1859-1925,* is available from the Chicago Board of Trade.

IL —CONTINENTAL ILLINOIS NATIONAL BANK & TRUST CO OF CHICAGO, Information Services Division, 231 S LaSalle St, Chicago, 60697. Susan J Montgomery, Mgr
Holdings: Vols (27,700) Cat Microforms

IL —FEDERAL RESERVE BANK OF CHICAGO, Library, 230 S La Salle St, PO Box 834, Chicago, 60690. Dorothy Phillips, Librn
Holdings: Vols (19,000) Cat
Notes: Restricted use; noncirculating. No photocopying.

IL —MONTGOMERY WARD CORPORATE LIBRARY, One Montgomery Ward Plaza, Chicago, 60671. Barbara J Burnett, Librn
Holdings: Vols (1300) Cat Mss Pix

IL —NORTHERN TRUST COMPANY LIBRARY, 50 S LaSalle St, Chicago, 60675. Marianne Lee, Head Librn
Holdings: Vols (2500) Cat Audiotapes Microforms

IN —PURDUE UNIVERSITY LIBRARIES, Graduate School of Management, Krannert Library, West Lafayette, 47907. Gordon Law, Librn
Holdings: Vols (142,727) Cat Microforms
Budget: ($69,700)
Notes: There is an extensive collection of corporate reports and labor information material (some 115,000 items). Over 2500 periodicals are currently received.

MA —BANK OF NEW ENGLAND, 1 Washington Mall, Boston, 02108. Helen Mavareaf, Librn
Holdings: Vols (4500) Cat Micrforms
Budget: ($18,000)
Notes: Annual reports of largest US banks; corporate financial reports on microfiche; Banking School theses from Stonier and Pacific Coast; industry studies.

MA —HARVARD UNIVERSITY, Baker Library of the Graduate School of Business Administration, Kress Library of Business and Economics, Soldiers Field, Boston, 02163. Ruth E Rogers, Cur
Holdings: Cat
Notes: Covers the progress of economic thought and the evolution of economic institutions and business life, with special strength in agriculture, banking, commerce, finance, industry, money, railroads, socialism, tariff. Restricted use: noncirculating. Collection available on microfilm: *Goldsmiths'-Kress Library of Economic Literature,* published by Research Publications, Inc. Downs 1477, 2704, 2712, 2719, 2727, Supplement 962, 963.

MA —HARVARD UNIVERSITY, Graduate School of Business Administration, Baker Library, Soldiers Field, Boston, 02163. Mary V Chatfield, Librn; Florence Bartoshesky, Cur of Manuscripts and Archives
Holdings: Mss
Notes: Incl handwritten credit ledgers of R G Dun and Co (1840-1890) and papers of Thomas W Lamont and Winthrop W Aldrich. Published reports of 18,000 corporations are in Corporate Reports Division.

MA —STATE STREET BANK & TRUST CO, Library, 225 Franklin St, Boston, 02110. Debra Wahl, Librn
Holdings: Uncat

MI —UNIVERSITY OF MICHIGAN, Graduate School of Business Administration, Business Administration Library, Institute for International Commerce Reading Rm, Ann Arbor, 48109. Carol Holbrook, Dir
Holdings: Vols Cat
Notes: Incl periodicals.

MI —WESTERN MICHIGAN UNIVERSITY, Business Library, N Hall, Kalamazoo, 49008. David H McKee, Head
Holdings: Vols (71,977) Cat Phonorecords Microforms
Notes: Incl 14,570 vols of bound periodicals, 33,041 monographs, 14,605 government documents, 1796 microfilm and 7u965 microfiche/microcards. Large collection of corporate annual reports is separate.

MN —MANKATO STATE UNIVERSITY, Library, Mankato, 56001. Marilyn Montgomery, Reference Librn
Holdings: Uncat
Notes: Especially Midwestern corporations' reports, incl annual reports; as well as top 500 in nation.

NJ —PRINCETON UNIVERSITY, Library, Rare Books Dept, Princeton, 08544. Stephen Ferguson, Cur
Holdings: Vols (7807) Cat
Budget: $2000
Notes: Incl annual reports of 1600 corporations.

NY —KEY BANK N A, 60 State St, Albany, 12207. Joy Pauline Longo, Librn
Holdings: Vols 400 Cat

NY —CORNELL UNIVERSITY LIBRARIES, Graduate School of Management, Malott Hall, Ithaca, 14853. Betsy Ann Olive, Librn
Holdings: Vols (135,000) Cat Microforms
Budget: ($130,000)

NY —FEDERAL RESERVE BANK OF NEW YORK, Research Library, 33 Liberty St, Federal Reserve PO Sta, New York, 10045. Jean Deuss, Chief Librn
Holdings: Vols (60,000) Periodicals
Budget: ($115,000)
Notes: Collection incl (60,000 vols) and more than (1300) periodical titles.

NY —INTERNATIONAL PAPER CO, Corporate Information Center, 77 W 45 St, New York, 10036. Elizabeth Skerritt, Corporate Librn
Holdings: Vols 140 Cat Maps Pix Slides Microforms
Notes: Extensive statistics and VF on paper industry.

NY —MUTUAL LIFE INSURANCE CO OF NEW YORK, Corporate Library, 1740 Broadway, New York, 10028. Marion Koshar, Librn
Holdings: Vols (6000) Cat Periodicals Microforms
Notes: Incl Mutual's company history and archives; over 200 periodical titles.

NY —NEW YORK PUBLIC LIBRARY, Research Libraries, Economic & Public Affairs Div, Fifth Ave & 42 St, New York, 10018. Edward DiRoma, Chief
Holdings: Vols (1,500,000) Cat Microforms

NY —NEW YORK PUBLIC LIBRARY, Mid-Manhattan Library, Science & Business Dept, 455 Fifth Ave, New York, 10016. Frederick E Dusold, Sr Principal Librn
Holdings: Vols (31,000) Cat Microforms
Budget: ($55,000)
Notes: Undergraduate level collection with duplicate reference and circulating copies of books. 80 drawers of pamphlet material. Standard business and financial services. 560 periodicals.

NY —SALOMON BROTHERS, Library, One New York Plaza, 46th Floor, New York, 10004. Lydia P Davies, Library Mgr
Holdings: Vols (4750) Cat
Notes: Library contains a collection of reference sources relating to corporate finance, investment banking and international finance. Extensive domestic and international corporate documents on microfiche. 11,000 corporate document files; 406,700 microforms.

NY —STANDARD & POOR'S CORP, Library, 25 Broadway, New York, 10004. Walter Nixon, Ref Librn
Holdings: Vols (22,000) Cat Microforms
Notes: Library has 800,000 microforms.

NY —YONKERS PUBLIC LIBRARY, Information Services, 7 Main St, Yonkers, 10701. Martita Schwarz, Dept Head
Holdings: Vols (21,500) Cat Maps Microforms
Budget: ($30,000)

NC —TECHNICAL INSTITUTE OF ALAMANCE, Learning Resources Center, Jimmy Kerr Rd, PO Box 623, Haw River, 27258. Ron Plummer, Coordr
Holdings: Vols (1025) Cat Pix Audiotapes Filmstrips Microforms
Notes: Accounting, banking & finance, business administration.

OH —ALCAN ALUMINUM CORP, Library, 100 Erieview Plaza, Cleveland, 44114. Winifred B Bowes, Librn
Holdings: Vols 3000 Cat

OH —RUTHERFORD B HAYES LIBRARY, 1337 Hayes Ave, Fremont, 43420. Watt P Marchman, Dir
Holdings: Cat Mss
Notes: The Andrew E Douglass Collection. Index in collections; listed in *Guide to Manuscripts of the Ohio Historical Society,* 131.

PA —DREXEL UNIVERSITY LIBRARIES, W W Hagerty Library, 32 & Chestnut Sts, Philadelphia, 19104. R L Snyder, Dir
Holdings: Vols (66,500) Cat Microforms
Budget: ($18,000)
Notes: Incl 25,000 microforms of annual reports of companies traded on the NYSE and ASE.

PA —FEDERAL RESERVE BANK OF PHILADELPHIA, PO Box 66, Philadelphia, 19105. Aileen Boer, Librn
Holdings: Vols (10,000) Cat
Notes: Incl Philadelphia Bank Returns, 1890-date; other runs of important financial serials, etc. No photocopying.

PA —UNIVERSITY OF PENNSYLVANIA, Lippincott Library of the Wharton School, Philadelphia, 19104. Michael Halperin, Librn
Holdings: Cat
Notes: Complete files of financial manuals from mid-19th century; long files of many financial and investment advisory services.

RI —BRYANT COLLEGE, Edith M Hodgson Memorial Library, Rte 7, Douglas Pike, Smithfield, 02917. John P Hannon, Dir
Holdings: Vols (103,000) Cat Phonorecords Audiotapes Videotapes 16mm Films Filmstrips Microforms
Budget: ($175,000)
Notes: Incl 6000 bound periodical vols, 250 phonorecords, 220 audiotapes, 120 videotapes, 30 16mm films, 150 filmstrips and 7500 microforms.

TX —UNIVERSITY OF TEXAS LIBRARIES, General Libraries, PO Box P, Austin, 78713. Carolyn Bucknell, Asst Dir for Collection Development
Holdings: Cat Microforms

TX —ECTOR COUNTY LIBRARY, Department of Business and Technology, 321 W 5th St, Odessa, 79760. Pat Jones, Dept Head
Holdings: Vols 2000 Cat
Notes: 25,000 Corporate Annual Reports microfilmed reports are complete from 1978-1983. 200 vertical files, 30 periodicals. Collection includes the subjects of Business, Management, Real Estate Accounting, Land Economics, Labor Economics, Finance, Personal Finance and Environmental Economics. Also included are stock and dividend reports, commodities and bond reports as well as business rankings. All items are referenced and cataloged.

WY —US AIR FORCE INSTITUTE OF TECHNOLOGY, Library, Dept 9 Bldg 831, FE, Warren AFB, 82001. Patricia A Johnson, Librn
Holdings: Vols (7000) Cat Microforms
Budget: ($9000)
Notes: The Library supports graduate programs for students (Air Force Missile-

FINANCE (cont.)

Combat Crewmen) seeking a Master of Business Administration Degree. Civilian students and other military personnel are also admitted.

BC —VANCOUVER PUBLIC LIBRARY, Business and Economics Div, 750 Burrard St, Vancouver, V6Z 1X5, Can. Barbara Bell, Librn
Notes: Incl numerous special files for *Quick Reference, Subject Clippings, Companies* (information of major Canadian, US and international corporations; index to new British Columbia and Canadian company corporations, 1951 to 1978; 160,000 cards); company file, *Province Index* and *Association File* (particulars of Canadian trade and professional associations). *International Collection of Trade* directories and telephone books.

MB —UNIVERSITY OF MANITOBA, Faculty of Administrative Studies, Administrative Studies Library, Winnipeg, R3T 2N2, Can. Judith Head, Librn
Holdings: Vols (15,000) Cat Microforms
Notes: Public policy. 15,000 volumes cat, 11, 000 microfiche cat.

ON —CANADIAN HOUSING INFORMATION CENTER, Canada Mortgage and Housing Corp, CMHC Annex Bldg Ground Floor, Montreal Rd, Ottawa, K1A 0P7, Can. Leslie Jones, Mgr
Holdings: Cat

ON —DEPT OF REGIONAL INDUSTRIAL EXPANSION, Ottawa Library, 235 Queen St, Ottawa, K1A 0H5, Can. Steven Rush, Librn
Holdings: Vols (100,000) Cat Maps Microforms
Notes: Contains 1500 reports of ARDA projects (Agricultural Rehabilitation and Development Agency); also NEWSTART project reports. There is a published book catalog and two supplements. 15,000 documents; 3000 periodical subscriptions.

ON —METROPOLITAN TORONTO LIBRARY, Municipal Reference Library, City Hall, Toronto, M5H 2N1, Can. Margot Hewings, Head
Holdings: Vols (60,000) Cat Maps Pix Microforms Slides VF
Budget: ($112,600)
Notes: Community development; municipal finance; local municipal government; housing; urban pollution; urban transportation; urban affairs; urban geography.

ON —TORONTO CORPORATE INFORMATION CENTER, First Canadian Place, 15th Floor, Box 1, Toronto, L5P 1A2, Can. Rosale Kanshansky, Chief Librn
Holdings: Vols (10,000) Cat Maps
Notes: Canadian interests.

FINANCE—HISTORY

IN —PURDUE UNIVERSITY LIBRARIES, Graduate School of Management, Krannert Library, West Lafayette, 47907. Gordon Law, Librn
Holdings: Vols (7000) Cat Mss Maps Pix Micrforms
Notes: The collection consists of books, journals and pamphlets dating from the early 16th to late 19th century, covering to a large degree the early literature in economic thought and business practices both here and abroad. No photocopying.

MA —HARVARD UNIVERSITY, Baker Library of the Graduate School of Business Administration, Kress Library of Business and Economics, Soldiers Field, Boston, 02163. Ruth E Rogers, Cur
Holdings: Cat Mss Microforms

NY —COLUMBIA UNIVERSITY LIBRARIES, Rare Book & Manuscript Library, 801 Butler Library, 535 W 114 St, New York, 10027. Kenneth A Lohf, Librn
Holdings: Mss
Notes: Incl the Henry Parker Willis Collection. Strong on formation of the Federal Reserve System and papers, correspondence, about the Phillipine National Bank, the Irish Banking Commission, the Banking Inquiry of 1925, the Banking Act of 1933, the New Zealand Monetary Commission, the Indian Currency Commission, etc. 22,500 items. Restricted use.

SC —COLLEGE OF CHARLESTON LIBRARY, Special Collections Dept, Charleston, 29401.
Notes: Contains the Bank of Charleston, SC's ledgers for deposits, loans, bonds, stocks, real estate holdings, businesses' accounts, and accounts with the Bank of Liverpool and the Merchant's National Bank, 1837-1872; also contains a ledger of information regarding foreign investments.

FINANCE, INTERNATIONAL see International Finance

FINANCE, PUBLIC MUNICIPAL FINANCE see Finance, Public

FINANCE, PUBLIC

AZ —TUCSON PUBLIC LIBRARY, Governmental Reference Library, PO Box 27210, City Hall, Tucson, 85726. Ann Strickland, Librn
Holdings: Vols (4000) Cat Maps Audiotapes Microforms
Notes: Special emphasis on public administration, including public finance, public personnel management, social services, urban planning, public transportation, public works, water management, solid waste management, public recreation and government of growing southwestern US cities in 200,000 to 500, 000 population range.

DC —US TREASURY DEPT, Library, 15 & Pennsylvania Ave NW-Room 5030, Washington, 20220. Elisabeth S Knauff, Mgr Information Services Division
Holdings: Vols (50,000) Cat Microforms
Notes: Includes publications of US and foreign governments, and international organizations.

LA —PUBLIC AFFAIRS RESEARCH COUNCIL OF LOUISIANA, Library, 300 Louisiana Ave, PO Box 3118, Baton Rouge, 70821. Jan Brashear, Research Librn
Holdings: Vols (7000) Cat Mss
Notes: State and local government problems with emphasis on Louisiana. Strong in the areas of education and public finance.

MI —UNIVERSITY OF MICHIGAN, Bureau of Government Library, 100A Rackman Bldg, Ann Arbor, 48109. Barbara Landay, Technical Libr Assistant
Holdings: Vols (66,000) Cat Microforms
Budget: ($10,000)
Notes: Library was established in 1914 to serve faculty and students of the Institute of Public Policy Studies. Emphasizes federal, state and local government, though some information on foreign governments is included. Government documents are represented. Also has a pamphlet file and a newspaper clipping collection on Michigan.

NJ —RUTGERS, THE STATE UNIVERSITY OF NEW JERSEY, Center for Urban Policy Research Library, Bldg 4051-Kilmer, New Brunswick, 08903. Edward E Duensing, Jr
Holdings: Vols 3500 Cat Periodicals VF
Budget: ($4000)
Notes: Collection focuses on the subjects of housing, municipal finance, and planning in American cities. The emphasis is on current material. Incl 5000 cataloged vertical files, 157 periodical subscriptions.

NY —STATE UNIVERSITY OF NEW YORK AT ALBANY, Library, Special Collections Dept, 1400 Washington Ave, Albany, 12222. Marion P Munzer, Coordr
Notes: Howard F Miller's correspondence, lecture outlines, reports, relating to academic and administrative career in public budgeting (8.6 linear feet).
See also entries under Miller, Howard F; Budgeting

NY —NEW YORK PUBLIC LIBRARY, Research Libraries, Economic & Public Affairs Div, Fifth Ave & 42 St, New York, 10018. Edward DiRoma, Chief
Holdings: Vols (1,500,000) Cat Microforms
Notes: Strong collection of government reports.

OH —PUBLIC LIBRARY OF CINCINNATI & HAMILTON COUNTY, Government and Business Dept, 800 Vine St, Cincinnati, 45202. Paul T Hudson, Head
Holdings: Vols 2000 Cat
Notes: The Murray Seasongood Collection of Government, Law and Public Administration contains works on local government, city management, public finance and municipal law. The collection also houses the collected works of Murray Seasongood.

OR —UNIVERSITY OF OREGON, Bureau of Governmental Research Library, Box 3177, Eugene, 97403. Katherine G Eaton, Head Librn
Holdings: Vols (25,000) Cat Microforms
Budget: ($5000)
Notes: Separate catalog and classification system.

PA —PENNSYLVANIA ECONOMY LEAGUE, Eastern Div Library, 215 S Broad St, Philadelphia, 19107. Ellen Brennan, Librn
Holdings: Vols (15,000) Cat Maps
Notes: Public finance, charters, constitutions, public education.

WI —LEGISLATIVE REFERENCE BUREAU LIBRARY, City of Milwaukee, City Hall Rm 404, 200 E Wells St, Milwaukee, 53202. Ronald Leonhardt, Dir
Holdings: Vols (50,000) Cat Mss Maps Pix Microforms
Budget: ($8000)

ON —CANADIAN TAX FOUNDATION LIBRARY, 130 Adelaide St W, Toronto, M5H 3P5, Can. Marjorie Robinson, Librn
Holdings: Vols (16,500) Cat
Notes: Worldwide scope; emphasis on Canada.

FINANCIAL FEDERATIONS see Federations, Financial (Social Service)

FINANCIAL STATEMENTS

MA —HARVARD UNIVERSITY, Graduate School of Business Administration, Baker Library, Soldiers Field, Boston, 02163. Mary V Chatfield, Librn; Florence Bartoshesky, Cur of Manuscripts and Archives
Notes: Corporate reports; company annual reports, both domestic and foreign; SEC filings; material dates from 19th century forward.

NY —DUN & BRADSTREET BUSINESS LIBRARY, 99 Church St, New York, 10007. Carol Stankiewicz, Librn
Holdings: Vols (400) Cat
Budget: ($2500)
Notes: A collection of industry financial ratios (or operating ratios) showing such items as current assets, net profits, debt, fixed assets, etc--components of composite company balance sheets--not individual companies.

NY —GEORGESON & CO, Library, Wall Street Plaza, New York, 10005. Aileen Burnes, Chief Librn
Holdings: Cat
Budget: ($65,000)
Notes: Collection incl corporate documents of all companies listed on the New York and American stock exchanges, plus all regularly traded NASDAQ O-T-C companies. The collection dates from 1939. Only 1978 to the present is available to SLA members by appointment.

FINDING LISTS see Library Catalogs

FINE, IRVING, 1914-1962

DC —LIBRARY OF CONGRESS, Music Division, Washington, 20540.
Notes: Music mss, papers, photographs. Sound recordings are in the Motion Picture, Broadcasting, and Recorded Sound Division.

FINE, MORT

CA —UNIVERSITY OF CALIFORNIA, LOS ANGELES, Theater Arts Library, Los Angeles, 90024. Edward Shreeves, Chairman, Bibliographers Group; Audree

FINE, MORT (cont.)

Malkin, Head, Theater Arts Library
Notes: Mort Fine (writer) Collection: screenplays and television scripts, treatments, proproduction notes, production material, story outlines, interviews, background research (9 linear feet).

FINE ARTS see Art; Music

FINE BINDINGS see Bookbinding and Bookbinders

FINE PRINTING see Printing—History

FINERTY, JOHN F.

MI —UNIVERSITY OF MICHIGAN, Library, Dept of Rare Books & Special Collections, Ann Arbor, 48109. Robert J Starring, Head
Holdings: Uncat Mss
Notes: The Irish Papers of John F Finerty, long-time friend of President Eamon de Valera and his legal counsel in the Irish Republican bond litigation, comprise over 3 ft of records, 1921-60, documenting the struggle for the establishment of the Republic of Ireland and related Irish-American activities. Included are correspondence, legal documents, speeches, clippings, and pamphlets on a range of subjects including the Irish bond drive and litigation, the Irish Free State, civil strife, recognition of the Irish Republic, Irish neutrality in World War II, and Finerty's trips to Ireland in the 1950s.

FINGER MARKS see Fingerprints

FINGERPRINTS

†TX —UNIVERSITY OF TEXAS LIBRARIES, General Libraries, Humanities Research Center, PO Box 7219, Austin, 78712. John Chalmers, Librn
Notes: Part of the History of Science Collection. Incl papers of various members of the Herschel Family.

FINISHING, METAL see Metals—Finishing

FINKEL, DONALD

MO —WASHINGTON UNIVERSITY, John M Olin Library, Campus Box 1061, St Louis, 63130.
Notes: A major collection, incl mss, correspondence, literary papers, photographs, etc. Described in *Special Collections: an Annotated Guide to the Holdings of the Manuscript Division and the University Archives and Research Collection.*

FINLAND—CIVILIZATION AND CULTURE

†MA —FITCHBURG HISTORICAL SOCIETY LIBRARY, 50 Grove St, Box 953, Fitchburg, 01420.
Notes: Finnish Collection, cataloged and maintained to support research on Finnish history, language and culture.

MI —SUOMI COLLEGE, Library, Hancock, 49931. Janet A Dalquist, Librn
Holdings: Vols (550) Cat Maps Pix Slides Phonorecords Audiotapes Videotapes Microforms
Notes: The library is a regular junior college library for the purpose of fulfilling curriculum needs. The Finnish material is on or about Finland. Library periodically updates a typed bibliography.

FINLAND—HISTORY

CA —CLAREMONT COLLEGES, Honnold Library, Ninth & Dartmouth, Claremont, 91711. Franklin D Scott, Cur, Nordic Collection; Penelope Garris, Librn
Holdings: Vols (25,000) Books Cat Maps Pix Slides Audiotapes Videotapes Periodicals
Notes: Nordic Collections are broadly inclusive, but emphasize history of Scandinavia, Baltic countries, and Hanseatic cities. Nucleus of collections from gifts and endowment of Waldemar Westergaard, supplemented with relevant collections of David Bjork, John H Wuorinen, Ingolf Olsen, Henry Steele Commager, Franklin Scott and other gifts and purchases. Eight vertical file drawers of news bulletins in English or vernaculars, 1941-. See: Franklin D Scott, "The Westergaard-Bjork Collection at the Honnold Library, the Claremont Colleges," *Scandinavian Studies,* 41 (1969), 346-354. Collection incl complete publications of Nordic Council.

CA —HOOVER INSTITUTION ON WAR, REVOLUTION & PEACE, Stanford University, Stanford, 94305. Milorad M Drachkovitch, Archivist
Notes: Papers of David D Grimm, Professor of Law and Rector of Petersburg University, 1899-1910, Assistant Minister of Education in the Russian Provisional Government, 1917, and an emigre political activist and journalist, incl correspondence, memoranda, press reports, printed and other material, 1919-1934, relating to his service to the Russian emigre community in Finland and other parts of Europe and to the Russian Civil War. 4 ms boxes.

MA —HARVARD UNIVERSITY LIBRARY, Widener Library, Cambridge, 02138.
Holdings: Cat
Notes: *Widener Library Shelflist* No 40 (1972) lists some 3000 vols on Finnish history. See *Distributable Union Catalog* (Harvard).

†MA —FITCHBURG HISTORICAL SOCIETY LIBRARY, 50 Grove St, Box 953, Fitchburg, 01420.
Notes: Finnish Collection, cataloged and maintained to support research on Finnish history, language and culture.

MI —SUOMI COLLEGE, Library, Hancock, 49931. Janet A Dalquist, Librn
Holdings: Vols (550) Cat Maps Pix Slides Phonorecords Audiotapes Videotapes Microforms
Notes: The library is a regular junior college library for the purpose of fulfilling curriculum needs. The Finnish material is on or about Finland. Library periodically updates a typed bibliography.

MI —NORTHERN MICHIGAN UNIVERSITY, Lydia M Olson Library, Elizabeth L Harden Drive, Marquette, 49855. Stephen H Peters, Cataloger
Notes: The personal library of John Kolehmainen. Incl 500 items of research materials dealing with Finland and Finnish-American studies. Most of the literature is in Finnish and covers a wide range of subjects incl literature, language, history, geography, and ethnic studies. Uncataloged.

FINLAY, IAN HAMILTON

IN —INDIANA UNIVERSITY, Lilly Library, Seventh St, Bloomington, 47405. William R Cagle, Librn
Holdings: Cat Mss
Notes: Correspondence and writings of concrete poet Ian Hamilton Finlay, 1953-1973. 5091 items. Holdings incl extensive collection of printed/published Finlay material.

FINLEY, MARTHA

OH —OHIO UNIVERSITY, Vernon R Alden Library, Department of Archives and Special Collections, Athens, 45701. Gary A Hunt, Head
Holdings: Vols (1400) Uncat
Notes: A miscellaneous collection of children's books by American and English authors, with most imprint dates in the period 1870-1930; numerous series books. Authors incl Jacob Abbott (196 v), "Oliver Optic" (84 v), Horatio Alger (89 v), J H Ewing (53 v), Martha Finley (47 v), G A Henty (46 v), Frank V Webster (38 v), and many others.

FINLEY, SAMUEL L.

AZ —NORTHERN ARIZONA UNIVERSITY, Special Collection Library, CU Box 6022, Flagstaff, 86011. Peter M Whiteley, Coordr/Archivist; William Mullane, Librn
Notes: Collection primarily devoted to Sam Finley (1868-1943). Humorist, cartoonist, Mayor of Flagstaff, mercantile dealer in Flagstaff and Phoenix (Swaparee). Correspondence, subject files, scrapbooks, incl ms "Life and Good Times of Sam Finley, Arizona Folk Character."

FINNEGAN, RICHARD J.

IL —CHICAGO HISTORICAL SOCIETY, Library, Clark St at North Ave, Chicago, 60614. Archie Motley, Manuscript Librn
Notes: Papers of: Emmet Dedmon, newspaper editor; Richard J Finnegan, newspaper editor; Rev Andres M Greeley, sociologist and author; attorney and civil liberties activist Pearl Hart; Robert J Havighurst, educator; social activist John Kearney; Kenesaw Mountain Landis, Federal Judge and first Commissioner of Baseball; Judge David F Matchett; Ivan Molek, Slovenian language publisher in Chicago; Max R Naiman, Communist Party activist; Ralph G Newman, book and autograph dealer and manuscript appraiser; Otto L Schmidt, physician and President of the Chicago and Illinois State Historical Societites; and Dempsey Travis, black mortgage banker.

FINNEY, THEODORE M.

PA —UNIVERSITY OF PITTSBURGH, Music Library, B-31 Music Bldg, Pittsburgh, 15260. Norris L Stephens, Music Librn
Holdings: Vols 7500// Cat
Notes: The Theodore M Finney Collection of books, scores, sheet music, pamphlets, programs, etc, given to the University of Pittsburgh Libraries between 1963 and 1968. No photocopying.

FINNISH FOLK MUSIC see Folk Music, Finnish

FINNISH LANGUAGE AND LITERATURE

CA —LOS ANGELES PUBLIC LIBRARY, Foreign Languages Dept, 630 W Fifth St, Los Angeles, 90071. Sylva Manoogian, Principal Librn
Holdings: Vols 776 Cat
Budget: ($41,500)

IL —NORTH PARK COLLEGE LIBRARY, 5125 N Spaulding Ave, Chicago, 60625. Dorothy-Ellen Gross, Dir
Holdings: Vols (4500) Cat
Notes: Scandinavian Collection, with materials mostly Swedish, but some titles in Norwegian, Danish, Finnish and Icelandic. Separate shelf list, but also incl in union catalog. General collection with emphasis on literature and history. Other Swedish books in the field of religion available through Mellander Library on same campus.

MA —HARVARD UNIVERSITY LIBRARY, Widener Library, Cambridge, 02138.
Holdings: Cat
Notes: *Widener Library Shelflist* No 40 (1972) lists some 2500 vols on Finnish language and literature. See also the *Distributable Union Catalog* (Harvard).

†MA —FITCHBURG HISTORICAL SOCIETY LIBRARY, 50 Grove St, Box 953, Fitchburg, 01420.
Notes: Finnish Collection, cataloged and maintained to support research on Finnish history, language and culture.

MI —SUOMI COLLEGE, Finnish-American Historical Archives, Hancock, 49930. Kenneth Niemi, Archives Librn
Notes: Collection incl 8000 vols, 152,000 mss, 2000 photographs, 760 audiotapes; microforms and maps; 14,000 holdings are cataloged. Subject interests: coop movement, labor, pioneer library of rare books and church records, socialist and communist movements, temperance societies. Special Collections: Finnish language newspapers (includes 100 titles from 1876-present);

FINNISH LANGUAGE AND LITERATURE (cont.)

Suomi Synod Archives; Finnish-American Oral History.

MI —NORTHERN MICHIGAN UNIVERSITY, Lydia M Olson Library, Elizabeth L Harden Drive, Marquette, 49855. Stephen H Peters, Cataloger
Notes: The personal library of John Kolehmainen. Incl 500 items of research materials dealing with Finland and Finnish-American studies. Most of the literature is in Finnish and covers a wide range of subjects incl literature, language, history, geography, and ethnic studies. Uncataloged.

NY —NEW YORK PUBLIC LIBRARY, Donnell Foreign Language Library, 20 W 53 St, New York, 10019. Bosiljka Stevanovic, Supvr Librn
Holdings: Vols 274 Cat
Notes: Finnish collection incl Finnish authors of Finnish expression. No separate catalog.

OH —CLEVELAND PUBLIC LIBRARY, Foreign Literature Dept, 325 Superior Ave, Cleveland, 44114. Natalia Bezugloff, Head
Holdings: Vols 2690 Cat
Notes: A popular circulating collection containing classics and the standard works with emphasis on belles lettres, history and biography. A variety of other subjects such as learning languages, how to do books, art, children's books, spoken phonodiscs and cassettes, periodicals, etc.
See also entry under Foreign Language Collections

OH —KENT STATE UNIVERSITY, Libraries, Ethnic Collections, Kent, 44242.
Holdings: Vols 375 Cat
See also entry under Foreign Language Collections

FINNO-BALTIC LANGUAGES see Finnish Language and Literature

FINNO-HUNGARIAN LANGUAGES see Finno-Ugrian Languages and Literatures

FINNO-UGRIAN LANGUAGES AND LITERATURES

MA —HARVARD UNIVERSITY LIBRARY, Cambridge, 02138.
Holdings: Cat

NY —NEW YORK PUBLIC LIBRARY, Slavonic Div, Fifth Ave & 42 St, New York, 10018. Edward Kasinec, Chief
Holdings: Cat Microforms
Notes: See New York Public Library, *Dictionary Catalog of the Slavonic* Collection (Boston: G K Hall, 1974) 44 vols.

FINNS IN THE U.S.

MI —SUOMI COLLEGE, Finnish-American Historical Archives, Hancock, 49930. Kenneth Niemi, Archives Librn
Notes: Collection incl 8000 vols, 152,000 mss, 2000 photographs, 760 audiotapes; microforms and maps; 14,000 holdings are cataloged. Subject interests: coop movement, labor, pioneer library of rare books and church records, socialist and communist movements, temperance societies. Special Collections: Finnish language newspapers (includes 100 titles from 1876-present); Suomi Synod Archives; Finnish-American Oral History.

MI —NORTHERN MICHIGAN UNIVERSITY, Lydia M Olson Library, Elizabeth L Harden Drive, Marquette, 49855. Stephen H Peters, Cataloger
Notes: The personal library of John Kolehmainen. Incl 500 items of research materials dealing with Finland and Finnish-American studies. Most of the literature is in Finnish and covers a wide range of subjects incl literature, language, history, geography, and ethnic studies. Uncataloged.

MN —MINNESOTA HISTORICAL SOCIETY LIBRARY, 690 Cedar St, Saint Paul, 55101. Patricia C Harpole, Chief of Reference Library; Bonnie G Wilson, Head of Special Libraries
Holdings: Mss
Notes: Tape-recorded interviews with Finnish immigrants to the US.

MN —UNIVERSITY OF MINNESOTA, Immigration History Research Center, 826 Berry St, Saint Paul, 55114. Susan Griegs, Cur
Holdings: Vols (35,000) Mss Maps Pix Phonorecords Audiotapes 16mm Films Microforms
See also entry under US - Emigration and Immigration

†NM —SUOMI CONFERENCE OF THE LUTHERAN CHURCH IN AMERICA, 516 Villa Verde, Rio Rancho, 87124.
Notes: Contains mss, correspondence, dissertations, documents, pictorial material, and oral history for the use of scholars conducting research on Finnish-Americans.

PA —BALCH INSTITUTE FOR ETHNIC STUDIES, Library, 18 S Seventh St, Philadelphia, 19106. R Joseph Anderson, Library Dir
Holdings: Cat Microforms

FINOTTI, REV. JOSEPH, S.J.

DC —GEORGETOWN UNIVERSITY, Library, Special Collections Div, 37 & O Sts NW, Washington, 20057. George M Barringer, Special Collections Librn; Nicholas B Sheetz, Mss Librn
Holdings: Mss
Notes: Jesuit, author, and bibliographer of Boston. Correspondence (1847-80) relating to Finotti's publication of *Bibliographica Catholica Americana* (1872) and its projected continuation, diaries (1846-76), autobiography (1873), bibliographical notes on the Ursuline Convent and Maria Monk affairs, and scrapbooks (1877-78).

FIOTI LANGUAGE see Congo Languages and Literature

FIR

BC —CANADIAN FORESTRY SERVICE, Pacific Forest Research Centre, Library, 506 West Burnside Rd, Victoria, V8Z 1M5, Can. Alice Solyma, Librn
Holdings: Vols (60,500) Cat Microforms
Notes: Incl rearing, biological control, identification, dispersal, insect pest management, comprehensive collection re Mountain Pine Beetle, Western Spruce Budworm, Douglas Fir Tussack Moth.

FIRBANK, RONALD

NV —UNIVERSITY OF NEVADA, RENO, University Library, Special Collections Dept, Reno, 89557. Robert E Blesse, Head
Holdings: Vols (29) Cat Other appearances 20 Cat
Notes: Includes individual works by author in all editions including translations; also prefaces, introductions, published correspondence, appearances in anthologies, periodicals, etc. Bibliographical research collection, part of Modern Authors Collection.

OH —OHIO UNIVERSITY, Vernon R Alden Library, Department of Archives and Special Collections, Athens, 45701. Gary A Hunt, Head
Holdings: Vols 27 Cat
Notes: First and later editions of Firbank's books.

FIRE BALLS see Meteors

FIRE COMPANIES see Fire Departments

FIRE DEPARTMENTS

†AL —MUSEUMS OF THE CITY OF MOBILE, Reference Library, 355 Government St, Mobile, 36602. Caldwell Delaney, Adminr
Notes: Collections incl Creole Fire Co records; Torrent Fire Co records; Volunteer Fire Dept records.

NS —FIREFIGHTERS' MUSEUM OF NOVA SCOTIA, 451 Main St, Yarmouth, B5A 1G9, Can. R Bruce Hopkins, Cur
Holdings: Vols 200 Cat Pix
Budget: $300
Notes: Noncirculating.

FIRE ENGINES

†AL —MUSEUMS OF THE CITY OF MOBILE, Reference Library, 355 Government St, Mobile, 36602. Caldwell Delaney, Adminr
Notes: Collections incl Creole Fire Co records; Torrent Fire Co records; Volunteer Fire Dept records.

AZ —NATIONAL HISTORICAL FIRE FOUNDATION, Hall of Flame Museum, Richard S Fowler Library, 6101 E Van Buren, Phoenix, 85008.
Holdings: Vols (4000) Cat Pix
Notes: Covers the entire range of fire-fighting, equipment, suppression, extinguishment, and prevention education worldwide.

MD —FIRE MUSEUM OF MARYLAND, 1301 York Rd, Lutherville, 21093. Stephen Heaver, Jr, Cur
Holdings: Vols (400) Uncat Mss Maps Pix 16mm Films
Budget: ($150)
Notes: Collection in two parts: printed volumes of history, department regulations and operations; vertical files of apparatus sales and maintenance catalogs, pictures, and some mss, such as patent papers and department journals.

NS —FIREFIGHTERS' MUSEUM OF NOVA SCOTIA, 451 Main St, Yarmouth, B5A 1G9, Can. R Bruce Hopkins, Cur
Holdings: Vols 200 Cat Pix
Budget: $300
Notes: Noncirculating.

FIRE EQUIPMENT

†AL —MUSEUMS OF THE CITY OF MOBILE, Reference Library, 355 Government St, Mobile, 36602. Caldwell Delaney, Adminr
Notes: Collections incl Creole Fire Co records; Torrent Fire Co records; Volunteer Fire Dept records.

AZ —NATIONAL HISTORICAL FIRE FOUNDATION, Hall of Flame Museum, Richard S Fowler Library, 6101 E Van Buren, Phoenix, 85008.
Holdings: 4000 Vols
Notes: Collection on the history and development of fire service, equipment, etc. Collection of manuals. Sponsored by the National Historical Fire Foundation, Scottsdale, Az.

MD —FIRE MUSEUM OF MARYLAND, 1301 York Rd, Lutherville, 21093. Stephen Heaver, Jr, Cur
Holdings: Vols (400) Uncat Mss Maps Pix 16mm Films
Budget: ($150)
Notes: Collection in two parts: printed volumes of history, department regulations and operations; vertical files of apparatus sales and maintenance catalogs, pictures, and some mss, such as patent papers and department journals.

FIRE EXTINCTION

AZ —NATIONAL HISTORICAL FIRE FOUNDATION, Hall of Flame Museum, Richard S Fowler Library, 6101 E Van Buren, Phoenix, 85008.
Holdings: 4000 Vols
Notes: Collection on the history and development of fire service, equipment, etc. Collection of manuals. Sponsored by the National Historical Fire Foundation, Scottsdale, Az. Covers the entire range of fire-fighting, equipment, suppression, extinguishment, and prevention education worldwide.

FIRE FIGHTING see Fire Extinction

FIRE INSURANCE see Insurance, Fire

FIRE LOSSES see Fires; Insurance, Fire

FIRE PLATES see Fire Marks

FIRE PREVENTION

AZ —NATIONAL HISTORICAL FIRE FOUNDATION, Hall of Flame Museum,

FIRE PREVENTION (cont.)

Richard S Fowler Library, 6101 E Van Buren, Phoenix, 85008.
Holdings: Vols (4000) Cat Pix
Notes: Covers the entire range of fire-fighting, equipment, suppression, extinguishment, and prevention education worldwide.

CA —COLLEGE OF SAN MATEO, Library, 1700 W Hillsdale Blvd, San Mateo, 94402. Gregg T Atkins, Coordinator of Library Services
Holdings: Vols 400 Cat

MA —MASSACHUSETTS INSTITUTE OF TECHNOLOGY, Institute Archives, Special Collections, Cambridge, 02139.
Notes: Papers of John Ripley Freeman, a hydraulic engineer, President of Associated Factory Mutual Fire Insurance Companies, and a consulting engineer. Collection primarily documents his activities as a consultant on hydraulics projects in the United States, Canada, China, Columbia, Mexico and Panama. Also, his work on the hydraulics of fire prevention, safety precautions for theaters, and seismology; his promotion of the National Hydraulics Laboratory and of European engineering practices; his involvement with the Engineering Foundation, the National Bureau of Standards, and the National Research Council; and his investments in mining, manufacturing, and land speculation. Unpublished finding aid available in Archives.

MA —NATIONAL FIRE PROTECTION ASSOCIATION, Morgan Technical Library, Batterymarch Park, Quincy, 02269. Nancy Corrin, Mgr; Dorinda Fergason, Fire Information Specialist
Holdings: Vols 5000 Cat Per Audiotapes Microforms
Budget: $4500
Notes: Fire safety (prevention and protection). Incl 5000 books; 11,500 technical reports; 450 periodical titles; 13, 000 microforms; 276 film reels; 350 audio-cassette tapes, 45 shelf-feet of voluntary industrial standards; 200 shelf-feet of NFPA published archives; and, 108 shelf-feet of topical file literature. Some of collection classified according to LC from 1972. Books and reports prior to 1972 key-worded according to EJC concept of inverted coordinate file. Collection believed to be one of the most complete fire libraries.

NH —NEW HAMPSHIRE VOCATIONAL-TECHNICAL COLLEGE, Library, Prescott Hill, Laconia, 03246. Patty Miller, Librn
Holdings: Vols 475 Cat Slides Audiotapes 16mm Films Filmstrips Microforms
Budget: $505

NC —TECHNICAL INSTITUTE OF ALAMANCE, Learning Resources Center, Jimmy Kerr Rd, PO Box 623, Haw River, 27258. Ron Plummer, Coordr
Holdings: Vols 180 Cat Slides 16mm Films Microforms

NS —FIREFIGHTERS' MUSEUM OF NOVA SCOTIA, 451 Main St, Yarmouth, B5A 1G9, Can. R Bruce Hopkins, Cur
Holdings: Vols 221 Cat
Budget: $225
Notes: Firefighting history.

OK —OKLAHOMA STATE UNIVERSITY, Library, Stillwater, 74708. Roscoe Rouse, Dir
Holdings: Vols 850 Cat
Notes: Fire prevention and fire protection.

FIRE PREVENTION—RESEARCH

DC —NATIONAL BUREAU OF STANDARDS, Fire Research Information Services, Bldg 224, Room 1252, Washington, 20234. Nora H Jason, Project Leader
Holdings: Vols 25,000 Microforms
Notes: Incl books, reports and conference proceedings.

FIRE RESEARCH see Fire Prevention—Research

FIREARMS

CA —SAN DIEGO PUBLIC LIBRARY, Science & Industry Section, 820 E St, San Diego, 92101. Joanne Anderson, Senior Librn
Holdings: Vols 1000 Cat Pix

CO —TRINIDAD STATE JUNIOR COLLEGE, Samuel Freudenthal Memorial Library, Trinidad, 81082. Ena M Sroat, Librn
Holdings: Vols 900 Cat 16mm Films
Notes: Incl almost all gunsmithing books in print as well as many rare, out of print items. No separate catalog or index.

DC —NATIONAL RIFLE ASSOCIATION OF AMERICA, Reference Library, 1600 Rhode Island Ave, 7th Floor, Washington, 20036. Maureen Booth, Librn
Notes: Inter-library loan limited to members and libraries.

GA —US ARMY INFANTRY CENTER, National Infantry Museum, Fort Benning, 31905. Dick D Grube, Dir; Z Frank Hanner, Cur; Carol Sims, Librn
Holdings: Vols (6000) Cat Mss Maps Pix Slides
Notes: Published and unpublished works dealing with infantry history, equipment, and units, for research on the Museum's collections of artifacts. Items cannot be checked out except under unusual and compelling circumstances. The collection traces the two centuries of history of the US Infantry. Of special interest are: unpublished reports of tests conducted on US Army Infantry equipment; photographs showing the history of Fort Benning; books and periodical articles dealing with Infantry small arms, both American and foreign, especially Japanese, Soviet, Chinese, and British; US Army manuals, incl many from the early 20th and late 19th centuries; WWII battlefield maps; WWI and WWII posters; histories of WWI; US Army insignia and medals; WWII era German uniforms and insignia. Also, over 2500 weapons.

IN —INDIANA LAW ENFORCEMENT ACADEMY, David F Allen Memorial Learning Resources Center, Rd 700 E, PO Box 313, Plainfield, 46168. Donna K Zimmerman, Librn
Holdings: Vols (4978) Cat Slides 16mm Films
Budget: ($15,000)
Notes: Concentrated in the areas of police science, criminology, corrections, and law.

MA —OLD STURBRIDGE VILLAGE, Research Library, Sturbridge, 01566. Theresa Rini Percy, Librn
Holdings: Cat Pix
Notes: New England, to 1860.

MA —LUCIUS BEEBE MEMORIAL LIBRARY, Main St, Wakefield, 01880.
Holdings: Vols (350) Cat
Notes: The Keough Collection of guns and arms and armor. Also emphasis on rifles and target shooting.

MO —SCHOOL OF THE OZARKS, Lois Brownell Research Library, Ralph Foster Museum, Point Lookout, 65726. Robert Esworthy, Librn
Holdings: Vols (1300) Cat
Notes: Firearms and weapons of the world.

NE —NEBRASKA STATE HISTORICAL SOCIETY, Fort Robinson Museum, Box 304, Crawford, 69339. Vance Nelson, Cur
Holdings: Vols (1500) Cat Mss Maps Pix Slides Phonorecords Audiotapes 16mm Films Microforms
Notes: Materials related to the history of Fort Robinson, and incl the Post Medical Library, reference books on state government, etc. Western Americana: books on ranching, homesteaders, Indian wars, etc; microfilm records for Fort Robinson records, Red Cloud and Spotted Tail Indian Agency records, Crawford and Chadron Nebraska newspapers, diaries and interviews. Library incl the E Kopac Collection of books dealing with Western Americana; particularly Indian wars, transportation, guns and railroads.

NJ —PASSAIC COUNTY HISTORICAL SOCIETY, Lamhurt Castle, Valley Rd, Paterson, 07503. Helen D Hamilton, Dir
Holdings: Vols (5000) Cat Mss Maps Pix
Notes: Material on the Society for the Establishment of Useful Manufacturing (founded) by Alexander Hamilton, papers relating to John Holland, who developed the submarine, the industrial magnates of the area who were active in the manufacture of locomotives, Colt revolvers, and textiles, especially silk.

NY —REMINGTON ARMS CO, Remington Gun Museum, Catherine St, Ilion, 13357. Laurence Goodstal, Cur
Notes: Museum displays sporting and military firearms built by Remington Arms Co, ca 1825 to modern firearms of today.

NY —UNIVERSITY CLUB, Library, One W 54 St, New York, 10019. Guy St Clair, Library Dir
Holdings: Vols (100,000) Cat Mss Maps Pix
Notes: A private library for the members of the University Club, their guests, and serious scholars upon written application to the Library Director. Holds the Carroll O Bickelhaupt Collection of Books on Hunting and Firearms.

NY —FORT ONTARIO HISTORIC SITE, Oswego, 13126. Shelley B Weinreb, Historic Site Mgr
Holdings: Vols (400) Cat Mss Maps Pix Slides
Notes: Primary focus is upon military activities at the mouth of the Oswego River and the utilization of fortifications (Fort Ontario, Fort Oswego, and Fort George) at that point which served to control the outlet of the traditional Mohawk-Oneida-Oswego route to the Great Lakes. A limited number of sources on fortification design, weapons, uniforms, and military equipment are included. Also incl 4000 slides and 400 pictures.

NY —HISTORICAL SOCIETY OF THE TARRYTOWNS, Library, One Grove St, Tarrytown, 10591. Adelaide R Smith, Cur
Notes: Collection incl the Colonel Edward H Kent collection of muskets and rifles; Revolutionary War items; Civil War memorabilia, incl weapons, uniform pieces, souvenirs and papers.

NY —US MILITARY ACADEMY LIBRARY, West Point, 10996. Egon A Weiss, Librn
Holdings: Vols (100,000) Cat Mss Maps Pix Slides Phonorecords Videotapes 16mm Films Filmstrips Microforms
Notes: Described in *Subject Catalog of the Military Art and Science Collection in the Library of the US Military Academy* (Greenwood Publishing Corp., 1969).

OK —J M DAVIS GUN MUSEUM LIBRARY, Claremore, 74017. Lee T Good, Cur; Sue E Cook, Business Mgr
Holdings: Vols 1100 Cat
Notes: US and foreign firearms and associated items.

PA —CARNEGIE LIBRARY OF PITTSBURGH, Science & Technology Dept, 4400 Forbes Ave, Pittsburgh, 15213. Catherine M Brosky, Dept Head
Notes: Incl much of the material in *Index to* Handicrafts. Books for the home owner, repairman and craftsman and the general builder and mechanics are emphasized. Information on the use of tools and materials especially for woodworking and metal crafts; also optical instruments, clocks, guns, and other mechanic trades.
See also entry under Science

SC —FRANCIS MARION COLLEGE, James A Rogers Library, Florence, 29501. H Paul Dove, Dir; Roger K Hux, Special Collections Librn
Holdings: Vols (400) Cat
Notes: Includes publications of the Small Arms Technical Pub Co.

TX —PANHANDLE-PLAINS HISTORICAL MUSEUM, Research Center, Box 967, WT Sta, Canyon, 79016. Claire R Kuehn, Archivist-Librn
Holdings: Vols 150 Cat
Budget: $300
Notes: American firearms, supplementing firearms collection of approx 500 weapons in the Museum. Incl periodicals. Cataloged in the General Research Center catalog.

FIREARMS (cont.)

†WA —WASHINGTON STATE UNIVERSITY, Library, Manuscripts, Archives & Special Collections, Pullman, 99164. John F Guido, Head
Holdings: Cat Mss Maps Pix
Notes: The Carl Parcher Russell papers, a vast resource (24,916 items; 45 linear feet) on American Indian and Western pioneer activities and artifacts. Much on the fur trade; pioneer life; mountain men and trapping; wildlife; primitive life in detail. Also the National Park Service, parks, monuments, etc. Described in *Carl Parcher Russell: An Indexed Register of His Scholarly and Professional Papers, 1920-1967, in the Washington State University* Library (Pullman, 1970), 149 pp.

ON —FORT MALDEN NATIONAL HISTORIC PARK, Library, 100 Laird Ave, Box 38, Amherstburg, N9V 2Z2, Can. Sally E Snyder, Librn
Holdings: Vols (400) Cat Mss Pix Slides
Notes: British and Canadian military life, weaponry, uniforms, from about 1760 to 1860.

FIREFIGHTERS

AZ —NATIONAL HISTORICAL FIRE FOUNDATION, Hall of Flame Museum, Richard S Fowler Library, 6101 E Van Buren, Phoenix, 85008.
Holdings: 4000 Vols
Notes: Collection on the history and development of fire service, equipment, etc. Collection of manuals. Sponsored by the National Historical Fire Foundation, Scottsdale, Az.

FIREFIGHTING see Fire Extinction

FIREHOUSE THEATRE

CA —UNIVERSITY OF CALIFORNIA, DAVIS, Shields Library, Dept of Special Collections, Davis, 95616. Donald Kunitz, Head; C Danial Elliott, Asst Head
Holdings: Cat Mss Pix 16mm Films
Notes: Archives of the Firehouse Theatre (founded in Minneapolis, 1963; moved to San Francisco, 1969) incl scripts, director's notebooks, business records, correspondence, photographs, programs, and reviews. 1100 items.

FIREMARKS

OH —OHIO STATE UNIVERSITY, Commerce Library, Columbus, 43210.
Notes: 18 British, 10 American and 8 German insurance firemarks, with 23 from fifteen other countries.

FIREMEN see Firefighters

FIRES

NS —FIREFIGHTERS' MUSEUM OF NOVA SCOTIA, 451 Main St, Yarmouth, B5A 1G9, Can. R Bruce Hopkins, Cur
Holdings: Vols 200 Cat Pix
Budget: $300
Notes: Noncirculating.

FIREWOOD see Wood As Fuel

FIREWORKS

DE —HAGLEY MUSEUM AND LIBRARY, Eleutherian Mills-Hagley Foundation Inc, PO Box 3630, Greenville, 19807. Richmond D Williams, Dir; Heddy A Richter, Imprints Librn
Notes: The Oscar Guttman Collection of books and pamphlets relating to explosives concentrates on early printed works on explosives and pyrotechnics.

FIRST AID

MI —UNIVERSITY OF MICHIGAN, Transportation Research Institute, Library, 2901 Baxter Rd, Ann Arbor, 48109. Ann C Grimm, Librn
Holdings: Vols (57,000) Cat Mss Maps Pix Slides Microforms
Budget: ($25,000)

TX —US AIR FORCE, School of Aerospace Medicine, Strughold Aeromedical Library, Brooks AFB, 78235. Fred W Todd, Chief Librn
Holdings: Vols (119,188) Cat Mss Maps Pix Microforms
Budget: ($499,000)
Notes: Aviation and space medicine and physiology, including the physiological effects of altitude and decompression. Biomedical and and human engineering. Military medicine, including chemical and biological warfare. Emergency medicine in both professional and technical areas. Radiobiology, including atomic medicine, nuclear medicine, and space radiation. Material not oriented to the School of Aerospace Medicine are excluded. Incl also 45,787 microforms and 142,371 technical documents.

FIRST DAY COVERS see Covers (Philately)

FIRST EDITIONS

AL —MOBILE PUBLIC LIBRARY, Special Collections Div, 701 Government St, Mobile, 36602.
Holdings: Vols 500 Cat
Notes: The Harris Collection.

†AL —UNIVERSITY OF ALABAMA, Amelia Gayle Gorgas Library, PO Box S, University, 35486.
Notes: Incl a collection of Sir Walter Scott first editions, 41 vols; Robinson Jeffers collection of 37 vols and mss; Lafcadio Hearn Collection of 110 vols and pamphlets.

CA —SAINT JOHN'S SEMINARY, Edward Laurence Doheny Memorial Library, The Estelle Doheny Collection, 5012 E Seminary Rd, Camarillo, 93010. Rita S Faulders, Cur
Notes: English and American authors.

CA —UNIVERSITY OF CALIFORNIA, SAN DIEGO, Central University Library, Mandeville Dept of Special Collections, La Jolla, 92093. Lynda Corey Claassen, Head
Notes: Rare Book Collection incl first and/or important editions of the writings of D H Lawrence, Ernest Hemingway, William Butler Yeats, Virginia Woolf, Aldous Huxley, and Robert Southey.

CA —OCCIDENTAL COLLEGE, Library, 1600 Campus Rd, Los Angeles, 90041. Michael C Sutherland, Special Collections Librn
Holdings: Vols 16,000 Cat Mss Pix
Notes: Outstanding collection formed by E T Guymon, Jr consisting of first editions of 19th and 20th century authors.

CA —UNIVERSITY OF CALIFORNIA, LOS ANGELES, William Andrews Clark Memorial Library, 2520 Cimarron St, Los Angeles, 90018.
Holdings: Cat
Notes: Extensive collection, first editions, etc.

CA —CALIFORNIA STATE UNIVERSITY, NORTHRIDGE, Delmar T Oviatt & South Libraries, 1811 Nordhoff St, Northridge, 91330. Donald L Read, Special Collections Dept
Holdings: Vols 2500 Cat
Notes: McDermott collection of contemporary writers of American fiction and poetry, signed, first editions. Emphasis is upon both established and new contemporary writers. Collection fully cataloged.

CA —SAN DIEGO PUBLIC LIBRARY, Wangenheim Rm, 820 E St, San Diego, 92101. Eileen Boyle, Librn
Holdings: Vols (7500) Cat
Notes: A collection on the history of the book and the development of printing with specimens ranging from Babylonian tablets to cassettes.

CA —UNIVERSITY OF CALIFORNIA, SANTA BARBARA, Library, Dept of Special Collections, Santa Barbara, 93106. Christian F Brun, Head
Holdings: Vols 3000
Notes: English and American Authors, 19th and 20th centuries.

CT —TRINITY COLLEGE LIBRARY, Watkinson Library, 300 Summit St, Hartford, 06106. Jeffrey Kaimowitz, Cur
Holdings: Cat
Notes: Incl Edward Albee, Rupert Brooke, Robert Browning, Walter De la Mare, Charles Dickens, Emily Dickinson, William Faulkner, Robert Frost, H Rider Haggard, Nathaniel Hawthorne, Rudyard Kipling, John Masefield, Edna St Vincent Millay, Marianne Moore, Kenneth Roberts, Edwin Arlington Robinson, Wallace Stevens, Robert Louis Stevenson, Algernon Charles Swinburne, William Makepeace Thackeray, Elinor Wylie, and other 19th and 20th century English & American writers and poets.

FL —FLORIDA STATE UNIVERSITY, Robert Manning Strozier Library, Special Collections Dept, Tallahassee, 32306. Opal M Free, Head, Special Collections
Holdings: Vols (12,254) Cat Mss Maps
Notes: Noncirculating. No photocopying.

IL —SOUTHERN ILLINOIS UNIVERSITY, CARBONDALE, Delyte W Morris Library, Special Collections Dept, Carbondale, 62901. David V Koch, Cur of Special Collections; Louisa Bowen, Cur of Manuscripts
Holdings: Vols 3600 Cat

IL —NEWBERRY LIBRARY, 60 W Walton St, Chicago, 60610. Diana Haskell, Cur of Modern Mss
Holdings: Cat

IL —NORTHWESTERN UNIVERSITY, Library, Special Collections Dept, 1937 Sheridan Rd, Evanston, 60201. R Russell Maylone, Cur
Holdings: Vols 20,000 Cat
Notes: First, limited, special editions, works about and ephemera of the major authors of the 20th century as well as representative minor writers. Incl English, American, French and German authors and to a lesser extent Italian, Spanish and other European writers. Extensive collections of Lawrence Durrell, T S Eliot, William Faulkner, Robert Graves, Ernest Hemingway, James Joyce, Karl Kraus, D H Lawrence, Hugh MacDiarmid, Henry Miller, Anais Nin, Ezra Pound, Gertrude Stein, HG Wells, W B Yeats. 15,000 "little magazine" titles (exclusive of runs in the general library collections).

IL —AUGUSTANA COLLEGE, Library, Rock Island, 61201. Marjorie M Miller, Special Collections Librn
Holdings: Vols (5000) Cat

IA —UNIVERSITY OF NORTHERN IOWA, Library, Cedar Falls, 50613. Gerald L Peterson, Special Collections Librn
Holdings: Vols (3500) Audiotapes
Budget: ($2000)
Notes: This is a collection of work done by American novelists who began their work after 1960. First editions only. We add as these novelists continue to publish. Include galley and page proofs when possible--also movie scripts and typescripts. Cataloged.

KY —UNIVERSITY OF LOUISVILLE, Ekstrom Library, Rare Books & Special Collections, 2301 S Third St, Louisville, 40208. George T McWhorter, Cur; Delinda Stephens Buie, Asst Cur

MA —BOSTON UNIVERSITY, Mugar Memorial Library, Special Collections Dept, 771 Commonwealth Ave, Boston, 02215. Howard B Gotlieb, Dir
Holdings: Cat
Notes: Extensive collection; especially works of authors who have deposited their publications, mss and papers with the library.

MA —GORDON COLLEGE, Winn Library, Vining Collection, 255 Grapevine Rd, Wenham, 01984. John Beauregard, Dir
Holdings: Vols 2600 Cat Maps
Notes: The Vining Collection (of rare books).

†MA —WILLIAMS COLLEGE, Chapin Library of Rare Books, PO Box 426, Williamstown, 01267. Robert L Volz, Custodian
Notes: Classic and modern authors.

MA —AMERICAN ANTIQUARIAN SOCIETY LIBRARY, 185 Salisbury St, Worcester, 01609. Marcus A McCorison, Dir & Librn
Holdings: Cat Mss Maps Pix Slides

FIRST EDITIONS (cont.)

Microforms
Notes: Over half a million manuscript pieces; extensive collection of contemporary imprints before 1850 (with supplementary supporting studies); over 10,000 maps (weak for 15th-17th centuries; excellent for 18th, strongest in 19th century, especially maps of local nature). Strongest collection of American newspapers before 1821 (see entry under Newspapers, American). Also a good collection of portraits of early New Englanders; paintings, engravings, and miniatures. Further, the largest collection of regional, state, county, and local histories.

†MA —CLARK UNIVERSITY, Robert Hutchings Goddard Library, Worcester, 01610. Dorothy Mosa Kowski, Rare Books Librn
Holdings: Vols Cat Mss
Notes: Rare books, first editions, mss, incunabula (50), bindings, fore-edge paintings.

MI —DETROIT PUBLIC LIBRARY, Rare Books Department, 5201 Woodward Ave, Detroit, 48202.
Holdings: Cat
Notes: Incl bibliographies, exhibit catalogs, booksellers' catalogs, auction catalogs, books about collecting, book arts, printing history, etc. Restricted use. Reference collection.

NJ —WILLIAM PATERSON COLLEGE OF NEW JERSEY, Sarah Byrd Askew Library, 300 Pompton Rd, Wayne, 07470. Robert Lopresti, Librn
Holdings: Vols (500) Cat
Notes: First editions of US and English authors. Bibliography available.

NY —ALFRED UNIVERSITY, Herrick Memorial Library, Alfred, 14802. June E Brown, Head Librn
Notes: The Openhym Collection of modern British literature incl first editions signed by prominent writers.

NY —BUFFALO MUSEUM OF SCIENCE, Buffalo Society of Natural Sciences, Research Library, Humboldt Park, Buffalo, 14211. Marcia T Morrison, Chief Librn
Holdings: Vols 291 // Mss
Notes: First and rare editions of books in the history of science. *Milestones of Science* describes epochal books in the history of science as represented in the library of the Buffalo Society of Natural Sciences. Catalog compiled by Ruth A Sparrow. Buffalo Society of Natural Sciences. Collection Catalog no 1. Buffalo Museum of Science, Buffalo, New York, 1972. Colored frontispiece, 308 pages (of which 207 are plates). 100 limited numbered edition; 2000 regular edition. See especially no 68 Audubonia--letters, mss, autographs.

NY —CARL H PFORZHEIMER LIBRARY, 41 E 42 St, New York, 10017. Mihai H Handrea, Librn
Holdings: Cat Mss Pix
Notes: English Literature from Caxton to 1700; first editions of 18th and 19th centuries, incl mss material on Shelley and his circle; fine presses (Bruce Rogers); George Gissing; women writers 1790-1840, (Mary Wollstonecraft, Mary Hays, Lady Blessington).

NY —CITY UNIVERSITY OF NEW YORK, City College, Morris R Cohen Library, North Academic Center, Convent Ave & 137th St, New York, 10031. Barbara J Dunlap, Archivist
Holdings: Cat
Notes: First editions of English authors, 19th and 20th centuries. Restricted use.

NY —NEW YORK PUBLIC LIBRARY, Rare Books and Manuscripts Div, Fifth Ave & 42 St, New York, 10018. William L Joyce, Asst Dir; Francis O Mattson, Curator
Holdings: Cat
Budget: ($7161)
Notes: Literary first editions. Incl notable collections of Shakespeare, Milton, Walton, Bunyan and Whitman (The Oscar Lion Collection).

NY —NEW YORK UNIVERSITY, Elmer Holmes Bobst Library, Div of Special Collections, Washington Sq S, New York, 10012. Frank Walker, Librn; Patrick McGuire, Asst Librn
Holdings: Vols (100,000) Cat Mss Pix
Notes: The Fales Collection of first (and other) editions of English and American novels from about 1750 to date (about 70, 000 titles). Mss (30,000) pieces.

NY —RUSSELL SAGE COLLEGE LIBRARY, James Wheelock Clark Library, Ferry St, Troy, 12180. Joseph Menditto, Dir of Tech Services
Notes: Incl 20th-century traditional and avant-garde poetry in first editions. Also, the Hamilton Finlay Collection of Concrete Poetry archives.

OH —CLEVELAND PUBLIC LIBRARY, Fine Arts and Special Collections Department, 325 Superior Ave, Cleveland, 44114. Alice N Loranth, Head
Holdings: Cat Mss Microforms
Notes: Part of the Rare Books Collection. *See also* entries under Chess; Folklore; Rare Books; Oriental Languages and Literatures.

PA —PHILIP H & A S W ROSENBACH FOUNDATION LIBRARY, 2010 DeLancey Pl, Philadelphia, 19103. Clive E Driver, Dir
Holdings: Cat Mss Maps Pix

PA —TEMPLE UNIVERSITY LIBRARIES, Special Collections Dept, Rare Books & Mss Section, Philadelphia, 19122. Thomas M Whitehead, Cur
Holdings: Vols (3000) Cat Mss
Notes: Extensive holdings of modern English and American literature, late 19th, 20th centuries. First and limited editions, association copies, supported by mss holdings. Special sub-collectiions of Walter de la Mare, Joseph Conrad, Robert Louis Stevenson, Joel Chandler Harris, E H W Meyerstein, Thackeray, George MacDonald, W W Gibson, John Masefield, Tennyson, Sir Walter Scott.

PA —UNIVERSITY OF PITTSBURGH, Hillman Library, Special Collections Dept, 363 Hillman Library, Pittsburgh, 15260. Charles E Aston Jr, Coordinator
Holdings: Vols Cat
Notes: Limited editions of 20th-century British and US authors; also a representative collection of Limited Editions Club imprints. Incl over 5000 vols.

PA —WEST CHESTER UNIVERSITY, Francis Harvey Green Library, West Chester, 19380. R Gerald Schoelkopf, Special Collections Librn
Holdings: Uncat Mss Pix
Notes: Historical Treasures Collection contains: all four Shakespeare Folios, *Biographies of the Signers of the Declaration of Independence* by John Sanderson, illustrated by Thomas Addis Emmet. Inset in the volumes are actual autographs of the signers. Also, Anthony Wayne Letters--15 original letters comprising correspondence between General Anthony Wayne and Generals Washington, Arnold, Gates, Putnam and Schuyler, as well as others.

RI —BROWN UNIVERSITY, John Hay Library, Harris Collection, Prospect St, Providence, 02912. Rosemary L Cullen, Cur
Holdings: Vols (200,000) Cat Mss Pix Phonorecords Microforms
Budget: ($15,000)
Notes: The Harris Collection of American Poetry and Plays is principally composed of American and Canadian poetry and plays, 17th century-date. Extensive holdings in songsters, gift books and annuals, hymnals, pageants, broadside verse, carriers' addresses, women poets, juvenile poetry, (incl Mother Goose and *The Night Before* Christmas), sheet music with lyrics, small press publications, fine printing, black poets, "little magazines," Yiddish-American iiterature. All movements or schools of American poetry are represented. Incl first editions of most American poets and playwrights, notably Whitman, Poe, Wallace Stevens, Eugene O'Neill, Edward Albee, Ezra Pound, T S Eliot, William Carlos Williams, Amy Lowell, Phyllis Wheatley, Robert Frost, Allen Ginsberg, Bliss Carman, and Stephen Foster sheet music. Also incl the Saunders Walt Whitman Collection (1300 vols); the LangdonCollection of Pageants (250 vols); the Asa Cushman Collection of plays in ms and prompt copies; the MacDougall Collection of Psalters and Hymnals; 4000 plays issued by Walter H Baker Co, Boston (1890-1957); the Vaxer Collection of Yiddish Poetry, Plays and Music (1700 vols). Collections incl 200,000 vols, 30,000 broadsides, 55,000 mss, 170,000 pieces of sheet music, 450 phonorecords, and 375 microfilm reels. See *Dictionary Catalog of the Harris Collection of American Poetry and Plays* (Boston: G K Hall, 1972), 13 vols; *Supplement* (1977), 3 vols. See also, *American Poetry,* 1609-1900, *A Collection on Microfilm, Segment I* (1609-1820); *Segment II* (1821-1850); *Segment III* (1851-1870) (Woodbridge, Conn: Research Publications). Separate catalog.

RI —BROWN UNIVERSITY, John Carter Brown Library, Providence, 02912. Norman Fiering, Librn; Everett C Wilkie Jr, Bibliographer; Susan Danforth, Cur Maps & Prints
Notes: Library seeks to collect first editions of materials pertaining to the New World in the colonial period.

SC —UNIVERSITY OF SOUTH CAROLINA, Thomas Cooper Library, Columbia, 29208. Kenneth E Toombs, Dir of Libraries; Roger Mortimer, Rare Book Librn
Holdings: Vols 7000 Cat
Notes: Very strong in the 19th and 20th centuries for English and American literature.

VA —UNIVERSITY OF VIRGINIA, Alderman Library, Rare Book Dept, Charlottesville, 22901. Julius P Barclay, Cur
Holdings: Vols (1200) // Cat
Notes: The Mrs Robert Coleman Taylor Collection of First Editions of American Best Sellers (Fiction). Almost without exception, these books are in mint and fine condition. Scope: 1752-1949. Incl very rare early American fiction.

WA —UNIVERSITY OF WASHINGTON LIBRARIES, Suzzallo Library, Special Collections Division, Rare Book Collection, FM-25, Seattle, 98195. Gary Menges, Coordinator for Special Collections
Notes: Printing history, including early printed books and modern fine printing; book arts, including papermaking, decorated papers, bookbinding, book design, and artist's books; American literature, 19th century includes: Stephen Crane, Ralph Waldo Emerson, Nathaniel Hawthorne, Henry James, Henry Wadsworth Longfellow, Herman Melville, Frank Norris, Harriet Beecher Stowe and Walt Whitman and 20th century includes: Theodore Roethke; illustrated books, including emblem books, historical children's illustration, books illustrated with prints, and artist's books; costume history; voyages and travels; preservation of library materials.

WI —UNIVERSITY OF WISCONSIN, MADISON, Cooperative Children's Book Center, Helen C White Hall, Rm 4290, 600 N Park St, Madison, 53706. Ginny Moore Kruse, Dir
Holdings: Vols (25,000) Cat
Notes: Cooperative Children's Book Center collections incl most US trade books published for children in last 24 months; first editions of recommended US children's trade books published since 1965; over 400 alternative press books published for children in US and Canada since 1970; children's books about Wisconsin and by Wisconsin authors and illustrators; representative 19th and early 20th century American children's books; 19th century children's periodicals; first and significant editions of Newbury and Caldecott Medal books; historical and contemporary toybooks; 75 vols of Mother Goose published since 1828; 160 vols of Thorton Burgess books, many first editions; ms and original artwork for Ellen Raskin's *The Westing Game* and *The Mysterious Disappearance of Leon (I Mean Noel);* juvenile mass market and traderomance fiction.

NS —DALHOUSIE UNIVERSITY LIBRARY, Halifax, B3H 4H8, Can.
Holdings: Vols 150 Cat Pix
Notes: A representative collection of the

FIRST EDITIONS (cont.)

British, American and Canadian first editions and later editions of the important and popular 19th humorist and Nova Scotian historian, Thomas Chandler Haliburton. Critical works, biogrpahies of Haliburton, and prints of his major literary creation "Sam Slick" are incl in the collection.

NS —MOUNT SAINT VINCENT UNIVERSITY, Library, 166 Bedford Hwy, Halifax, B3M 2J6, Can. Lucian Bianchini, University Librn
Holdings: Vols 7000 Cat
Budget: ($125,000)
Notes: The MacDonald Collection consists of 19th and 20th century English and American literature, fine bindings, a few examples of fore-edge painting, limited editions, first editions, and autographed copies.

FIRST PENNSYLVANIA BANKING AND TRUST COMPANY

DE —HAGLEY MUSEUM AND LIBRARY, Eleutherian Mills-Hagley Foundation Inc, PO Box 3630, Greenville, 19807. Richmond D Williams, Dir; Heddy A Richter, Imprints Librn
Notes: First Pennsylvania Banking and Trust Company (1850-1925; 500 cubic feet).

FIRTH, RAYMOND

CA —UNIVERSITY OF CALIFORNIA, SANTA CRUZ, University Library, Special Collections, Santa Cruz, 95064. Rita Bottoms, Special Collections Librn; Margaret Felts, South Pacific Collection Bibliographer
Notes: South Pacific Collection. Extensive collection. Personal papers of Firth and library on South Pacific.
See also entry under Anthropology.

FISCHER, EMIL

CA —UNIVERSITY OF CALIFORNIA, BERKELEY, Bancroft Library, Manuscripts Division, Berkeley, 94720. James D Hart, Dir
Holdings: Cat Mss Pix
Notes: Correspondence and papers (37 boxes; 73 cartons) of the eminent German biochemist and Nobel Prize winner. Incl are Fischer's labor notebooks as well as notebooks of many of his students. Many of his speeches and other writings are represented. The collection also contains subject files relating to his many scientific discoveries as well as items reflecting his involvement in scientific societies.

FISCHER, LOUIS

NJ —PRINCETON UNIVERSITY, Library, Rare Books Dept, Princeton, 08544. Stephen Ferguson, Cur
Holdings: Mss
Notes: Papers of Louis Fischer, journalist and authority on the Soviet Union.

FISCHER, SAMUEL

IN —INDIANA UNIVERSITY, Lilly Library, Seventh St, Bloomington, 47405. William R Cagle, Librn
Notes: Correspondence of Gerhart Hauptmann and his wife with his publisher Samuel Fischer, 1890-1949 (686 items). Collection includes 9 Hauptmann manuscripts.

FISCHER VERLAG

IN —INDIANA UNIVERSITY, Lilly Library, Seventh St, Bloomington, 47405. William R Cagle, Librn
Holdings: Cat Mss Pix
Notes: Correspondence files of S Fischer Verlag, 1888-1975. Incl important correspondence files with such authors as Gerhardt Hauptmann, Hermann Hesse, Thomas Mann, etc. Also mss by many of the authors. 5,000 items. Incl first editions of many 19th century works, and some 20th century holdings.

FISH see Fishes

FISH—LAW see Fisheries—Laws and Legislation

FISH, BIG GAME see Game Fishing

FISH, FRESHWATER see Fishes, Freshwater

FISH, HAMILTON

NY —COLUMBIA UNIVERSITY LIBRARIES, Rare Book & Manuscript Library, 801 Butler Library, 535 W 114 St, New York, 10027. Kenneth A Lohf, Librn
Notes: More than 32,000 items documenting the rise of William Russell Grace's shipping business and other materials relating to his career as mayor of New York. Incl records and correspondence relating to all aspects of the shipping business in New York and South America, mining interest in Peru and Chile, and transportation in Costa Rica and Nicaragua. Family memorabilia and photographs, materials concerning New York Politics, banking and insurance, real estate interests and Catholic charities, and letters from Chester A Arthur, John Jacob Astor, Andrew Carnegie, Grover Cleveland, Hamilton Fish, John Hay and J Pierpont Morgan. Restricted use.

FISH, JOB

OH —OHIO HISTORICAL SOCIETY, Archives Library Division, 1982 Velma Ave, Columbus, 43211. Dennis East, Division Chief

FISH, ROBERT L.

MA —BOSTON UNIVERSITY, Mugar Memorial Library, Special Collections Dept, 771 Commonwealth Ave, Boston, 02215. Howard B Gotlieb, Dir
Holdings: Cat Mss Pix
Notes: Mss, correspondence, etc collected in depth; incl publications by or about.

FISH, STUYVESANT

IL —NEWBERRY LIBRARY, 60 W Walton St, Chicago, 60610. Diana Haskell, Cur of Modern Mss
Holdings: / / Mss Maps Posters Timetables
Notes: Collection of 350 sq feet of archival material is particularly valuable for the long series of letters from the President, Stuyvesant Fish, 1887-1906 (80 vols). The richest part of the collection runs from 1880 to 1905. There are no "working papers" dealing with railway operations or personnel for this period, but rather administrative detail at the higher levels. Carolyn Curtis Mohr, comp, *Guide to the Illinois Central Archives in the Newberry Library,* 1851-1906. Chicago: The Newberry Library, 1951.

FISH, TROPICAL see Tropical Fish

FISH CULTURE

FL —FLORIDA DEPT OF NATURAL RESOURCES BUREAU OF MARINE RESEARCH, Library, 100 Eighth Ave SE, Saint Petersburg, 33701. Keir Gray, Archivist
Notes: The library supports the research of approx 50 biologists and technicians, with emphasis on the marine resources of Florida and nearby areas. An archives section houses original research data, reports, publications,, etc, developed by the scientific staff. Marine biological literature is received on exchange from laboratories and libraries throughout the world. There are approx 1400 journal titles in the collection. Current titles received number approx 600. The 33,000 reprints are cataloged by author and subject. Current laboratory activities incl marine studies in aquaculture, descriptive biology, ecological studies, fisheries biology, and oceanography.

FISH CULTURE—PESTS see Fishes—Diseases and Pests

FISH DISEASES see Fishes—Diseases and Pests

FISH FARMING see Fish Culture

FISHBAUGH, W. A.

FL —FLORIDA DEPT OF STATE, Florida State Archives, Florida Photographic Collection, R A Gray Bldg, Tallahassee, 32301. Mrs Allen Morris, Archives Supervisor
Holdings: Maps Pix Slides Films Audiotapes
Notes: Several thousand photographs by Fishbaugh of the "boom" in Miami and Coral Gables in the 1920s.

FISHEL, WESLEY

MI —MICHIGAN STATE UNIVERSITY, International Library, South and Southeast Asia Collection, East Lansing, 48824. Clinton Lockert, Bibliographer
Holdings: Vols (13,500) Cat Mss Maps Pix Audiotapes Microforms
Notes: Correspondence and papers of Frederick Field, Gilbert Jonas, and Wesley Fishel.

FISHER, CLAY

CA —UNIVERSITY OF CALIFORNIA, LOS ANGELES, Research Library, Dept of Special Collections, 405 Hilgard Ave, Los Angeles, 90024. Edward Shreeves, Chairman, Bibliographers Group; David S Zeidberg, Head
Holdings: Mss
Notes: 25 linear feet of mss and books written by Henry Allen under the pseudonym, Clay Fisher.

FISHER, DUDLEY T.

OH —OHIO STATE UNIVERSITY, Library for Communication and Graphic Arts, 242 W 18th St, Columbus, 43210. Lucy S Caswell, Curator
Notes: Comic strip artists Hal Foster, Dudley T Fisher, Jr, Mark Szorady, Edwina Dumm, Jim Baker have original works in the library. Also new collections of original cartoons by Windsor McCay, John T McCutcheon, Dick Moores, Ned White, Walter Berndt, Jim Larrick, Carl Rose and Bill Crawford. Also a large collection of the work of illustrator Will Rannells. The Shel Dorf Collection incl historic comic strips and related materials. A small but growing collection of comic books, especially those featuring *Katy Keene,* is available in the library.

FISHER, FRANK R.

SC —COLLEGE OF CHARLESTON LIBRARY, Special Collections Dept, Charleston, 29401.
Notes: Papers record numerous scientific and technological studies covering a wide range of areas, particularly astronomical observations (often accompanied by drawings or photos) made in Charleston in the 1880s, at times in consultation with Lewis Reeve Gibbes. An inventor of scientific instruments, Fisher's work incl a "Machine for Ruling Diffraction Plates" for which a detailed description and photograph are provided. Incl in-depth record of Fisher's experiences, scientific and personal, of the 1886 Earthquake, accompanied by diagrams.

FISHER, IRVING

CT —YALE UNIVERSITY, Box 1603A, Yale Station, New Haven, 06520.
Notes: Incl his personal library.

FISHER, JAMES BOORMAN, 1833-1889

NY —CORNELL UNIVERSITY LIBRARIES, Collection of Regional History, Dept of

FISHER, JAMES BOORMAN, 1833-1889 (cont.)

Manuscripts and Univ Archives, Ithaca, 14853.
Notes: Presbyterian clergyman. Incl papers, 1831-(1858-1887)-1945; sermons, lectures and newspaper clippings.

FISHER, ST. JOHN

IL —LOYOLA UNIVERSITY OF CHICAGO, E M Cudahy Memorial Library, 6525 N Sheridan Rd, Chicago, 60626.
Notes: Thomas Cranmer's working library and papers, incl ms of a critical edition of Thomas Cranmer's *Censurae* that Fr Surtz was working on at the time of his death.

FISHER, VARDIS

CT —YALE UNIVERSITY, Box 1603A, Yale Station, New Haven, 06520.
Holdings: Cat Mss

†ID —BOISE STATE UNIVERSITY, Library, Boise, 83725.

ID —IDAHO FALLS PUBLIC LIBRARY, 457 Broadway, Idaho Falls, 83402. Craig Anderson, Head Reference Librn
Holdings: Vols 53 Cat
Notes: Incl 33 fiction titles by Fisher and 20 nonfiction titles by or about Fisher; file of his newspaper articles, 1936-1968; and miscellaneous periodical articles about him.

NV —UNIVERSITY OF NEVADA, RENO, University Library, Special Collections Dept, Reno, 89557. Robert E Blesse, Head
Holdings: Vols (46) Cat
Notes: Includes individual works by author in all editions including translations; also prefaces, introductions, published correspondence, appearances in anthologies, periodicals, etc. Bibliographical research collection, part of Modern Authors Collection.

FISHER, WELTHY HONSINGER AND FREDERICK BOHN FISHER

MA —BOSTON UNIVERSITY, Mugar Memorial Library, Special Collections Dept, 771 Commonwealth Ave, Boston, 02215. Howard B Gotlieb, Dir
Holdings: Cat Mss Pix
Notes: Mss, Correspondence, etc collected in depth; incl publications by or about Welthy and Frederick Bohn Fisher.

FISHERIES

AK —NATIONAL OCEANIC AND ATMOSPHERIC ADMINISTRATION, National Marine Fisheries Service, Fisheries Laboratory Research Library, PO Box 155, Auke Bay, 99821. Paula Johnson, Librn
Holdings: Vols (21,000) Cat Mss Maps Slides Microforms
Budget: ($20,000)
Notes: Much on the outer continental shelf, marine flora and fauna, fisheries.

AK —ALASKA STATE LIBRARY, Alaska Historical Library Collection, Pouch G, Juneau, 99811. Phyllis Demuth, Readers Services Librn
Holdings: Vols (24,000) Cat Mss Maps Pix Slides Phonorecords Audiotapes Videotapes 16mm Films Microforms
Notes: Much material added with merger of the Alaska Department of Fish and Game Library into the Alaska State Library.

CA —UPDATA PUBLICATIONS INC, Library, 1756 Westwood Blvd, Los Angeles, 90024. Sara Ferguson, Dir; Judith Harrington, Librn
Holdings: Vols (300) Uncat Maps Microforms
Notes: Incl 800,000 microforms, 35 periodicals.

DC —GEORGETOWN UNIVERSITY, Library, Special Collections Div, 37 & O Sts NW, Washington, 20057. George M Barringer, Special Collections Librn; Nicholas B Sheetz, Mss Librn
Holdings: Mss Cat
Notes: Diaries and journals kept by Hugh McCormick Smith (1865-1941) and his wife, Emma, documenting their years in Siam. In 1922 Smith resigned his position as United States Commissioner of Fisheries, accepting an invitiation from the King of Siam to serve as advisor on Siamese fisheries. When the first Siamese Department of Fisheries was created in 1926, Smith was named director, remaining in that office until his return to the United States in 1934. The diaries not only contain accounts of Smith's work in Siam, but also provide vivid descriptions of Siamese life, culture, and topography.

FL —FLORIDA DEPT OF NATURAL RESOURCES BUREAU OF MARINE RESEARCH, Library, 100 Eighth Ave SE, Saint Petersburg, 33701. Keir Gray, Archivist
Holdings: Vols (3400) Cat Maps Pix Slides 16mm Films Microforms
Budget: ($59,000)
Notes: The library supports the research of approx 50 biologists and technicians, with emphasis on the marine resources of Florida and nearby areas. An archives section houses original research data, reports, publications,, etc, developed by the scientific staff. Marine biological literature is received on exchange from laboratories and libraries throughout the world. There are approx 1400 journal titles in the collection. Current titles received number approx 600. The 33,000 reprints are cataloged by author and subject. Current laboratory activities incl marine studies in aquaculture, descriptive biology, ecological studies, fisheries biology, and oceanography.

ME —BOWDOIN COLLEGE, Library, Brunswick, 04011. Dianne M Gutscher, Cur of Special Collections
Notes: The Hubbard Family Papers incl documents and letters of John Hubbard, while he was a commissioner under the Reciprocity Treaty. The Leslie A Lee Papers contain the records of a voyage to South America in 1887-88, while he was Assistant US Fish Commissioner.

ME —BIGELOW LABORATORY FOR OCEAN SCIENCES & MAINE DEPT OF MARINE RESOURCES, Library, McKown Point, West Boothbay Harbor, 04575. Pamela Shephard-Lupo, Librn
Holdings: Vols Cat Periodicals
Budget: ($55,000)
Notes: This library presently serves two institutions. The Maine Dept of Marine Resources has maintained the library since 1957 and thus the majority of our holdings are geared to their needs, ie fish biology and stock assessment on a local, national and international level. In 1973 Bigelow Laboratory for Ocean Sciences came to West Boothbay Harbor and began to contribute to the library with a very specialized collection on the Gulf of Maine marine chemistry, phytoplankton and nutrient cycles.

MD —NATIONAL OCEANIC & ATMOSPHERIC ADMINISTRATION, Library & Information Sciences Division, Central Library & Information Sciences Bldg, 6009 Executive Blvd, Rockville, 20852. Elizabeth J Yeates, Chief
Holdings: Vols (175,000) Cat Microforms
Notes: This collection activated January 1973. Title is Georgetown Branch. Location is Rm 193, Page Bldg 2, 3300 Whitehaven St NW Washington, DC 20235.

MA —UNIVERSITY OF MASSACHUSETTS AT AMHERST, Library, Amherst, 01003. Siegfried Feller, Assoc Dir for Collection Development
Holdings: Cat

MA —US DEPT OF COMMERCE, NATIONAL OCEANIC & ATMOSPHERIC ADMINISTRATION, National Marine Fisheries Service, Northeast Fisheries Center, Woods Hole, 02543. Judith Brownlow, Librn
Holdings: Vols 30,000 Cat Mss Maps
Notes: Oldest fishery library in the US: founded 1885 with the US Commission of Fisheries, Woods Hole. Contains complete collection of US government publications on fisheries and many state and foreign publications. No photocopying.

NJ —PRINCETON UNIVERSITY, Library, Rare Books Dept, Princeton, 08544. Stephen Ferguson, Cur
Notes: (1) Kenneth H Rockey Angling Collection; about 4300 volumes, of which 350 are considered rare. Main strength is in the American and English 19th and 20th century literature of angling in fresh and salt water. (2) Otto von Kienbusch Angling Collection; incl the earliest angling book in English, Dame Juliana Berners, *A Treatysse on Fysshynge Wyth an Angle,* printed by Wynkyn de Worde, assistant to England's first printer, William Caxton, 1496. Also the unique copy of the second angling book printed in English (anonymous), *The Art of* Angling, London: Henry Middleton, 1577. For particulars refer to: *Fresh Water Angling; 50 Books and Other Materials Tracing its Development: An Exhibition.* Princeton, 1946. A more recent exhibition of sporting books also featured angling. For particulars refer to: Stephen Ferguson, "The Gentelman's Recreation:Sporting Books in the Princeton University Library" in the *Chronicle* XL, 3 (spring, 1979). A catalog of the exhibition is available.
See also entry under Fishing and Angling

NJ —GLOUCESTER COUNTY HISTORICAL SOCIETY LIBRARY, 17 Hunter St, PO Box 409, Woodbury, 08096. Edith E Hoelle, Librn
Notes: Cataloged mss pertaining to the Howell Family of Fancy Hill, Gloucester County, NJ from 1739-1890. Incl letters, bills, account books and memorabilia of the Shad Fisheries along the Delaware River and Etna Furnace at Tuckahoe, NJ, a 19th century bog iron furnace; lists of (State of) Delaware suppliers to the Continental Army, Revolutionary War, etc, as well as household memorabilia of Anna Blackwood Howell (1769-1855), ca 3800 items.

NC —NATIONAL MARINE FISHERIES SERVICE, SOUTHEAST FISHERIES CENTER, Beaufort Laboratory, Library, Beaufort, 28516. Ann Bowman Hall, Librn
Holdings: Vols (15,000) Cat

†PA —PENNSYLVANIA STATE UNIVERSITY, Du Bois Campus Library, College Place, Du Bois, 15801.
Notes: The Paul A Handwerk Collection and the David D Wanless Collection of materials in fisheries and wildlife.

RI —UNIVERSITY OF RHODE ISLAND, International Center for Marine Resource Development, Library, Main Library Building, Kingston, 02881.
Holdings: Vols (13,000) Periodicals
Notes: Devoted to the development of marine resources in third world countries. Small-scale fisheries, anthropology of fishing peoples, coastal fisheries, aquaculture program planning. Approx 13,000 documents, 200 periodicals.

WA —WESTERN WASHINGTON UNIVERSITY, Center for Pacific Northwest Studies, High St, Bellingham, 98225. James W Scott, Dir
Holdings: // Cat Mss Maps Pix
Notes: The Archie W Shiels Collection. Archie W Shiels, who died in his 95th year in 1974, was formerly Managing Dir of Pacific American Fisheries and an author of some note on Alaskan topics. A few papers of his company are incl in the collection, which is primarily focused on Alaska, particularly its history and its seal and other fisheries. See also entry for Galen A Biery.

WA —UNIVERSITY OF WASHINGTON LIBRARIES, Fisheries-Oceanography Library, WB-30, Seattle, 98195. Thomas D Moritz, Head Librn
Holdings: Vols (49,000)
Budget: ($83,000)
Notes: All aspects of fisheries science are included.

FISHERIES—LAWS AND LEGISLATION

†WA —WASHINGTON STATE UNIVERSITY, Library, Manuscripts, Archives & Special Collections, Pullman, 99164. John F Guido, Head
Holdings: Cat Mss Maps Pix
Notes: The manuscript collection incl

FISHERIES—LAWS AND LEGISLATION (cont.)

business and financial records of banks, breweries, fisheries, insurance, land, lumber and livestock companies, trade and commodity associations; as well as the personal and professional papers of authors, aviators, educators, engineers, farmers, historians, pioneers, politicians and scientists; especially rich in documents relating to the exploration, settlement and development of the Palouse Country, the Inland Empire, the Columbia Basin and the Pacific Northwest. Described in *Selected Manuscript Resources in the Washington State University Library* (Pullman, 1974); and other published and unpublished inventories and registers.

FISHERIES—RESEARCH

AR —US FISH & WILDLIFE SERVICE, Fish Farming Experimental Station, PO Box 860, Stuttgart, 72160. Joyce Cooper, Information Officer
Holdings: Vols (850)
Budget: ($2000)
See also entry under Fishes - Diseases and Pests

MO —US FISH & WILDLIFE SERVICE, Columbia National Fisheries Research Laboratory, Rte One, Columbia, 65201. Axie Hindman, Librn
Holdings: Vols (2000) Cat Microforms
Budget: ($7000)
Notes: Pesticides in aquatic biota; fisheries research; fresh-water ecology. Also incl collection in water pollution, acid rain, aquatic invertebrets, environment and 10,000 reprints.

OR —OREGON STATE UNIVERSITY, Marine Science Center, Library, Newport, 97365. Marilyn Guin, Librn
Holdings: Vols (8000) Cat Maps Microforms
Budget: ($15,000)
Notes: Collection emphasizes marine ecology, invertebrate zoology and marine ecology, invertebrate zoology and marine algae. The portion of the collection concerned with fisheries emphasizes aquaculture. Collection is divided between the Marine Science Library and the Main OSU Library.

TN —TENNESSEE VALLEY AUTHORITY (TVA), Norris Branch Library, Norris, 37828. Debra D Mills, Librn
Holdings: Vols (8000) Cat Microforms
Budget: ($35,000)

WI —WISCONSIN DEPT OF NATURAL RESOURCES, Technical Library, 3911 Fish Hatchery Rd, Madison, 53711. Rose Smith, Librn
Holdings: Vols (1200) Cat
Budget: $2000

MB —UNIVERSITY OF MANITOBA, Elizabeth Dafoe Library, Government Publications Section, Winnipeg, R3T 2N2, Can. June Dutka, Head
Holdings: Vols 1300 // Uncat Maps Pix
Notes: The collection, which dates from 1975, consists of written direct testimonies and responses with supporting exhibits from over 100 oil and gas companies, Indian and native associations and concerned citizen groups. The content of these documents incl construction plans, financial statements, alternate corridors, and describes the social and economic impact of the Arctic Gas Pipeline in northern Canada. The *Biological Report Series* offers vital information on soils and vegetation, movements of porcupine, caribou herds, bird distribution and fisheries research. An index listing the various company exhibits accompanies this collection.

FISHES

AK —NATIONAL OCEANIC AND ATMOSPHERIC ADMINISTRATION, National Marine Fisheries Service, Fisheries Laboratory Research Library, PO Box 155, Auke Bay, 99821. Paula Johnson, Librn
Holdings: Vols (21,000) Cat Mss Maps Slides Microforms
Budget: ($20,000)
Notes: Much on the outer continental shelf, marine flora and fauna, fisheries.

CA —UNIVERSITY OF CALIFORNIA, DAVIS, General Library, Davis, 95616. Bernard Kreissman, University Librn; C Danial Elliott, Asst Head, Dept Special Collections
Holdings: Vols 1600 Cat

CA —CALIFORNIA STATE UNIVERSITY, FULLERTON, Library, Box 4150, Fullerton, 92634. Linda Herman, Special Collections Librn
Holdings: Cat
Notes: Dr Leonard B Schultz Ichthyology Collection of 13,000 pieces incl books, pamphlets, articles and emphermera. It is supplemented by the Ecology of Bay and Estuarine Fishes Collections.

CA —CALIFORNIA ACADEMY OF SCIENCES, J W Mailliard Jr Library, Golden Gate Park, San Francisco, 94118. Ray Brian, Librn
Notes: Downs No 2160.

CO —DENVER PUBLIC LIBRARY, Conservation Library Center, 1357 Broadway, Denver, 80203.
Holdings: Vols (10,330) Cat
Notes: Historical, sociological, and economic aspects, but not scientific, except for Colorado research reports. Also, fish and wildlife reports of all states.

CT —YALE UNIVERSITY, Medical Historical Library, 333 Cedar St, New Haven, 06510. Ferenc A Gyorgyey, Librn
Holdings: Vols 600 Cat
Notes: The George Milton Smith Collection of early ichthyology.

DC —SMITHSONIAN INSTITUTION LIBRARIES, Natural History Branch, Washington, 20560. Sylvia Churgin, Chief Librn
Holdings: Vols 2400 Cat Maps Pix Slides

FL —ARCHBOLD BIOLOGICAL STATION, Library, Rt 2, Box 180, Lake Placid, 33852. Fred E Lohrer, Librn
Holdings: Vols (2000) Cat Periodicals

IL —FIELD MUSEUM OF NATURAL HISTORY, Library, Roosevelt Rd & Lake Shore Dr, Chicago, 60605. W Peyton Fawcett, Librn; Benjamin W Williams, Assoc Librn
Holdings: Vols (210,000) Cat
Budget: ($100,000)
Notes: Extensive collections--publications of learned societies and institutions and monographic works--in all fields of natural history, with emphasis on taxonomy and evolutionary biology; and on museum publications, American and foreign: anthropology, especially archaeology and ethnology of the Americas, Africa, East Asia, and Oceania; botany, particularly strong for the Americas; geology, chiefly paleontology and meteoritic studies; and zoology, worldwide (birds, fishes, insects, mammals, mollusks, reptiles and amphibians).

ME —BIGELOW LABORATORY FOR OCEAN SCIENCES & MAINE DEPT OF MARINE RESOURCES, Library, McKown Point, West Boothbay Harbor, 04575. Pamela Shephard-Lupo, Librn
Holdings: Vols Cat Periodicals Maps
Budget: ($55,000)
Notes: This library presently serves two institutions. The Maine Dept of Marine Resources has maintained the library since 1957 and thus the majority of our holdings are geared to their needs, ie fish biology and stock assessment on a local, national and international level. In 1973 Bigelow Laboratory for Ocean Sciences came to West Boothbay Harbor and began to contribute to the library with a very specialized collection on the Gulf of Maine marine chemistry, phytoplankton and nutrient cycles.

MD —NATIONAL AQUARIUM IN BALTIMORE, Pier 3, 501 East Pratt St, Baltimore, 21202. Lee Campbell, Librn
Notes: Staff members only.

MD —CALVERT MARINE MUSEUM, Library, PO Box 97, Solomons, 20688.
Holdings: Vols (2000) Cat Mss Maps Pix Slides Audiotapes 16mm Films
Notes: Local maritime history, estuarine biology, and paleontology of southern Maryland. Large picture collection (1800), blueprints (358) and slides (1100).

MA —UNIVERSITY OF MASSACHUSETTS AT AMHERST, Library, Amherst, 01003. Siegfried Feller, Assoc Dir for Collection Development
Holdings: Cat

MA —US DEPT OF COMMERCE, NATIONAL OCEANIC & ATMOSPHERIC ADMINISTRATION, National Marine Fisheries Service, Northeast Fisheries Center, Woods Hole, 02543. Judith Brownlow, Librn
Holdings: Vols 30,000 Cat Mss Maps
Notes: Oldest fishery library in the US: founded 1885 with the US Commission of Fisheries, Woods Hole. Contains complete collection of US government publications on fisheries and many state and foreign publications. No photocopying.

MI —UNIVERSITY OF MICHIGAN, Museums Library, Ann Arbor, 48109. Patricia B Yocum, Librn
Holdings: Vols 8000 Cat

MO —US FISH & WILDLIFE SERVICE, Columbia National Fisheries Research Laboratory, Rte One, Columbia, 65201. Axie Hindman, Librn
Holdings: Vols (2000) Cat Microforms
Budget: ($7000)
Notes: Pesticides in aquatic biota; fisheries research; fresh-water ecology. Also incl collection in water pollution, acid rain, aquatic invertebrets, environment and 10,000 reprints.

NV —FORESTA INSTITUTE FOR OCEAN AND MOUNTAIN STUDIES, Library, 6205 Franktown Rd, Carson City, 89701. Shannon Porter, Librn
Holdings: Vols 500 Cat Maps Slides
Notes: Collection is international in scope; incl material on fish of the far western US, espec Nevada from prehistoric times to the present. Also, about 1000 pamphlets, etc.

NY —AMERICAN MUSEUM OF NATURAL HISTORY, Library Services Dept, Central Park W & 79th St, New York, 10024. Nina J Root, Chairwoman; Mary Genett, Asst Librn for Reference Services
Holdings: Vols (385,000) Cat Mss Maps Pix Slides Microforms
Notes: Nearly all collections are outstanding for depth of coverage and international range. Early and historic works, rare books, colored illustrations, and relevant serial publications supplement the modern scientific publications necessary to the researches of the scientific staff and the work of the educational division. Open to the public.

NC —NATIONAL MARINE FISHERIES SERVICE, SOUTHEAST FISHERIES CENTER, Beaufort Laboratory, Library, Beaufort, 28516. Ann Bowman Hall, Librn
Holdings: Vols (15,000) Cat

OR —OREGON STATE UNIVERSITY, Library, Corvallis, 97331. Melvin George, Dir
Holdings: Vols (980,000) Cat

PA —CARNEGIE LIBRARY OF PITTSBURGH, Science & Technology Dept, 4400 Forbes Ave, Pittsburgh, 15213. Catherine M Brosky, Dept Head
Notes: Subject of secondary interest with emphasis on North America. Covers paleobotany, vertebrates and invertebrates, foraminifera, mollusks, fish, reptiles, mammals. Abstracts, indexes, catalogs, bibliographies, journals, continuations, federal, state and society publications available.

TN —TENNESSEE VALLEY AUTHORITY (TVA), Technical Library, 400 W Summit Hill Dr, E2 B7, Knoxville, 37902. Jesse C Mills, Chief Librn
Holdings: Vols (106,900) Cat Mss Maps Pix Audiotapes Microforms
Budget: ($2,025,000)
Notes: The Technical Library Headquarters Staff (order, cataloging, information, and administration) is located in Knoxville, Tenn. In addition there are branch libraries in Knoxville, Norris, and Chattanooga, Tennessee, and Muscle Shoals, Alabama.

TX —UNIVERSITY OF TEXAS, Marine Science Institute Library, Port Aransas, 78373. Ruth Grundy, Librn
Holdings: Vols (45,000) Cat Maps Pix
Budget: ($70,000)
Notes: Current researches in marine science,

FISHES (cont.)

especially concerning the Gulf of Mexico, the Texas Coastal Zone, and the Continental Shelf. Incl journals.

WI —WISCONSIN DEPT OF NATURAL RESOURCES, Technical Library, 3911 Fish Hatchery Rd, Madison, 53711. Rose Smith, Librn
Holdings: Vols (1200) Cat
Budget: $2000

ON —NATIONAL MUSEUMS OF CANADA, Library Services Directorate, Ottawa, K1A 0M8, Can. Valerie Monkhouse, Director
Holdings: Vols (90,000) Cat Mss Microforms
Budget: ($81,000)
Notes: Emphasis on Canadian and circumpolar natural history. Collection incl botany, herpetology, ichthyology, invertebrate zoology, malacology, mammology, mineralogy, ornithology, paleobiology, zooarchaeology. Exceptional collections in lichenology, bryology, malacology, ornithology. Research collection, interlibrary loans available, public may use on the premises.

ON —ONTARIO MINISTRY OF NATURAL RESOURCES, Natural Resources Library, Whitney Block 4540, Toronto, M5S 1B3, Can. Sandra Louet, Librn
Holdings: Cat

FISHES—DISEASES AND PESTS

AL —US FISH & WILDLIFE SERVICE, Southeastern Fish Cultural Laboratory, Route 3 Box 86, Marion, 36756.
Notes: This collection is cataloged as part of the Library of the US Fish and Wildlife Service, National Fisheries Center, Box 700, Kearneysville, WV 25430.

AR —US FISH & WILDLIFE SERVICE, Fish Farming Experimental Station, PO Box 860, Stuttgart, 72160. Joyce Cooper, Information Officer
Holdings: Vols (850)
Budget: ($2000)
Notes: This is mainly a research library, but it also contains many articles pertinent to fisheries management, biology, nutrition, water quality and general information for fish farmers. Incl 7500 cataloged reprints, 250 journals, periodicals, etc. We will lend with interlibrary loan request forms. Photocopy up to 35 pages.

FL —FLORIDA DEPT OF NATURAL RESOURCES BUREAU OF MARINE RESEARCH, Library, 100 Eighth Ave SE, Saint Petersburg, 33701. Keir Gray, Archivist
Holdings: Vols (3400) Cat Maps Pix Slides 16mm Films Microforms
Budget: ($59,000)
Notes: The library supports the research of approx 50 biologists and technicians, with emphasis on the marine resources of Florida and nearby areas. An archives section houses original research data, reports, publications,, etc, developed by the scientific staff. Marine biological literature is received on exchange from laboratories and libraries throughout the world. There are approx 1400 journal titles in the collection. Current titles received number approx 600. The 33,000 reprints are cataloged by author and subject. Current laboratory activities incl marine studies in aquaculture, descriptive biology, ecological studies, fisheries biology, and oceanography.

ID —US FISH & WILDLIFE SERVICE, Hagerman Field Station, Route 1, Hagerman, 83332. Ilabell Casper, Librn
Holdings: Vols 400

NY —US FISH & WILDLIFE SERVICE, Tunison Laboratory of Fish Nutrition, Cortland, 13045.

PA —US FISH & WILDLIFE SERVICE, National Fisheries Research and Development Laboratory, Wellsboro, 16901.
Notes: Approx 1050 books and 3000 reprints.

TX —UNIVERSITY OF TEXAS, Marine Science Institute Library, Port Aransas, 78373. Ruth Grundy, Librn
Holdings: Vols (45,000) Cat Maps Pix
Budget: ($70,000)
Notes: Current researches in marine science, especially concerning the Gulf of Mexico, the Texas Coastal Zone, and the Continental Shelf. Incl journals.

WV —US FISH & WILDLIFE SERVICE, National Fisheries Center, Technical Information Services, Route 3 Box 700, Kearneysville, 25430. Joyce A Mann-Grim, Librn
Holdings: Vols (22,900) Slides
Budget: $140,800
Notes: Collection topics incl fish virology, histology bacteriology, immunology, nutrition and parasitology. Publish *Fish Heath News*. Incl 20,000 reprints, 5000 slides.

FISHES, FRESHWATER

TN —TENNESSEE VALLEY AUTHORITY (TVA), Technical Library, 400 W Summit Hill Dr, E2 B7, Knoxville, 37902. Jesse C Mills, Chief Librn
Holdings: Vols (106,900) Cat Mss Maps Pix Audiotapes Microforms
Budget: ($2,025,000)
Notes: The Technical Library Headquarters Staff (order, cataloging, information, and administration) is located in Knoxville, Tenn. In addition there are branch libraries in Knoxville, Norris, and Chattanooga, Tennessee, and Muscle Shoals, Alabama.

FISHHOOKS see Flies, Artificial

FISHING, ATLANTIC SALMON see Atlantic Salmon—Fishing

FISHING, BIG GAME see Game Fishing

FISHING, SALMON see Salmon Fishing

FISHING, TROUT see Trout Fishing

FISHING AND ANGLING

CA —CALIFORNIA STATE UNIVERSITY, FULLERTON, Library, Box 4150, Fullerton, 92634. Linda Herman, Special Collections Librn
Holdings: Vols (3530) Cat Mss
Notes: Capt P Markham Kerridge Angling Collection incl materials on angling, entomology, ichthyology, conservation, travel, recreation, and related areas. A computer author printout with title, imprint, and various codes is updated annually. Books and pamphlets are supplemented by 2750 periodical issues, and extensive ephemera.

CT —TRINITY COLLEGE LIBRARY, 300 Summit St, Hartford, 06106. Ralph S Emerick, Librn
Holdings: Cat
Notes: Incl Sherman Parker Collection of most editions of Izaak Walton.

CT —YALE UNIVERSITY, Box 1603A, Yale Station, New Haven, 06520.

CT —CONNECTICUT COLLEGE, Library, Mohegan Ave, New London, 06320. Brian Rogers, College Librn
Holdings: Vols 1600 Cat
Notes: The Wilbur and Dorothy Downs Collection, including early 19th century British and American titles, 20th century limited editions, salmon and trout-fly albums, and an uncataloged collection of books on angling technique.

FL —INTERNATIONAL GAME FISH ASSOCIATION, Fort Lauderdale, 33316. E K Harry, President
Notes: Large library on freshwater and saltwater recreational angling, game fish species and related subjects. Reference library only. No books are removed from premises.

IL —AMERICAN FISHING TACKLE MANUFACTURERS ASSOCIATION, 2625 Clearhook Dr, Arlington Heights, 60005.
Notes: A newly begun library, 1983. Emphasis on fishing tackle of all kinds.

IL —DE PAUL UNIVERSITY, Library, 2323 N Seminary, Chicago, 60614. Kathryn De Graff, Special Collections Librn
Notes: About 1000 vols on British field sports. Also, 20 hand-colored sets of prints by Edward Troye (1808-1874) of American thoroughbred horses.

IL —NORTHWESTERN UNIVERSITY, Library, Special Collections Dept, 1937 Sheridan Rd, Evanston, 60201. R Russell Maylone, Cur
Holdings: Vols 250 Cat Pix
Notes: History of fly-fishing, 16th-20th centuries.

KY —UNIVERSITY OF KENTUCKY, Margaret I King Library, Dept of Special Collections, Lexington, 40506. William Marshall, Head

MA —STURGIS LIBRARY, Rte 6A, Barnstable, 02630. Susan R Klein, Chief Librn
Holdings: Vols (1000) Mss Pix
Budget: $500
Notes: Massachusetts maritime history. The Henry Crocker Kittredge Maritime History Collection contains vols, mss, documents and photographs, many of great rarity, related to the history of maritime life of Barnstable County incl its shipmasters, shipbuilding and fishing industries. Major emphasis of materials is on eighteenth, nineteenth and early 20th centuries. The core of the collection was provided through an estate gift of Henry Crocker Kittredge, Harvard scholar and maritime historian (1890-1967).

MA —HARVARD UNIVERSITY LIBRARY, Widener Library, Cambridge, 02138.
Holdings: // Cat
Notes: Extensive collection of all phases of sports. Incl the Fearing Collection on Angling and Fishing containing over 15,000 books, mss, photographs, etc. See Downs 3139-3143.

MO —CENTRAL MISSOURI STATE UNIVERSITY, Ward Edwards Library, Warrensburg, 64093. Nancy E Littlejohn, Social Sciences Librn
Holdings: Vols 200 Cat
Notes: Over 160 different editions of the *Compleat Angler* plus other related books by and about Walton.

NH —UNIVERSITY OF NEW HAMPSHIRE, Dimond Library, Durham, 03824. Barbara A White, Special Collections Librn
Holdings: Vols 2000 Cat
Notes: Special emphasis on fly-tying and trout and salmon fishing.

NJ —PRINCETON UNIVERSITY, Library, Rare Books Dept, Princeton, 08544. Stephen Ferguson, Cur
Holdings: Cat
Notes: Kenneth H Rockey Angling Collection. About 4300 vols, of which 350 are considered rare. Main strength is in the American and English 19th and 20th century literature of angling in fresh and salt water. Practical treatises on fish, fishing, tackle, angling reminiscences, fiction and poetry of angling, scientific works and government publications on fish and fisheries, publications of angling societies, etc. Incl about 150 different editions of Izaak Walton's *Compleat Angler.* Otto von Kienbusch Angling Collection. For particulars refer to: *Fresh Water Angling; 50 Books and Other Materials Tracing Its Development: An Exhibition.* Princeton, 1946. 24 pp (Ex Ki Z5975.P7 and 4222.737). A more recent exhibition of sporting books also featured angling. For particulars refer to: Stephen Ferguson, "The Gentleman's Recreation: Sporting Books in the Princeton UniversityLibrary" in the *Chronicle* XL (spring, 1979) pp 269-271. A catalog of the exhibition is available and cataloged.

NY —ADIRONDACK HISTORICAL ASSOCIATION, Museum Library, Blue Mountain Lake, 12812. Jerold Pepper, Librn
Holdings: Vols (7500) Cat Mss Maps Pix Phonorecords Audiotapes 16mm Films Microforms
Notes: Anything about the Adirondacks--history, people, economics, places, things. Strong in Adirondack art, outdoor recreation, logging, small boats. Resources incl more than 1000 maps, 40,000 pictures, 1600 microfilm reels, 576 linear ft of ms material, and 12 cabinets of VF ephemera, etc.

FISHING AND ANGLING (cont.)

NY —C W POST CENTER OF LONG ISLAND UNIVERSITY, B Davis Schwartz Memorial Library, Greenvale, 11548. Manju Prasad-Rao, Media Librn
Notes: The Franklin B Lord Collection of some 600 vols on hunting and fishing. Many 19th century.

NY —COLUMBIA UNIVERSITY LIBRARIES, Rare Book & Manuscript Library, 801 Butler Library, 535 W 114 St, New York, 10027. Kenneth A Lohf, Librn
Notes: The Elliot V Bell Collection of over 500 books on fishing and angling, from the 17th to 20th centuries; more than 20 early editions of Izaak Walton. Restricted use.

NY —RACQUET & TENNIS CLUB, Library, 370 Park Ave, New York, 10022. Gerald Belliveau, Jr, Librn
Holdings: Vols (17,500) Cat
Budget: ($6000)
Notes: Specializes in court tennis, lawn tennis, early American sport. See *Dictionary Catalogue of the Library of Sports in the Racquet and Tennis Club* (Boston: G K Hall, 1971). Also, Robert W Henderson, *Early American Sport,* 3rd ed. (Cranbury, NJ: Fairleigh Dickinson University Press, 1977).

NY —GLADDING INTERNATIONAL SPORT FISHING MUSEUM, Octagon House, South Otselic, 13155.
Notes: Important collection of old and new books on angling and related subjects.

OH —PUBLIC LIBRARY OF CINCINNATI & HAMILTON COUNTY, Dept of Rare Books & Special Collections, 800 Vine St, Library Square, Cincinnati, 45202. Yeatman Anderson III, Cur
Notes: Large hunting and fishing collection, and a nearly complete set of Derrydale Press publications.

PA —LAFAYETTE COLLEGE, David Bishop Skillman Library, Easton, 18042. Dorothy Cieslicki, Librn
Holdings: Vols (825) Cat
Notes: Robert Tinsman Angling Collection. Incl 58 editions of Walton, *Complete Angler.* Also, the Robert S Conahay, Jr, Atlantic Salmon Collection, which incl over 1000 hand-tied salmon and trout flies, many mounted and framed.

PA —FREE LIBRARY OF PHILADELPHIA, Rare Book Dept, Logan Sq, Philadelphia, 19103. Marie E Korey, Rare Book Librn
Holdings: Uncat Pix
Notes: The Evan Randolph Collection of 1300 angling prints.

PA —UNIVERSITY OF PITTSBURGH, Hillman Library, Special Collections Dept, Bernard S Horne Memorial Collection, Pittsburgh, 15260. Charles E Aston Jr, Coordinator
Holdings: Vols 375 Cat
Notes: A collection of 231 editions of Izaak Walton's *Compleat Angler,* represented by 375 different issues and states, donated to the University of Pittsburgh Libraries as a memorial to the late Bernard S Horne. One of the largest collections of the *Angler* in existence, it begins with the second edition (London, 1655) and presently ends with the Buchan Reprint (London, 1967). The collection is described in full in Bernard S Horne's *Compleat Angler, 1953-1967: a New Bibliography.* (Pittsburgh, 1970). Noncirculating.

RI —UNIVERSITY OF RHODE ISLAND, Graduate School of Oceanography, Pell Library Bldg, Narragansett, 02882. Kenneth T Morse, Chief Librn

SC —FRANCIS MARION COLLEGE, James A Rogers Library, Florence, 29501. H Paul Dove, Dir; Roger K Hux, Special Collections Librn
Holdings: Vols (400) Cat
Notes: Includes publications of the Small Arms Technical Pub Co, emphasis on hunting and fishing.

TN —TENNESSEE VALLEY AUTHORITY (TVA), Technical Library, 400 W Summit Hill Dr, E2 B7, Knoxville, 37902. Jesse C Mills, Chief Librn
Holdings: Vols (106,900) Cat Mss Maps Pix Audiotapes Microforms
Budget: ($2,025,000)
Notes: The Technical Library Headquarters Staff (order, cataloging, information, and administration) is located in Knoxville, Tenn. In addition there are branch libraries in Knoxville, Norris, and Chattanooga, Tennessee and Muscle Shoals, Alabama.

VT —THE AMERICAN MUSEUM OF FLY FISHING, PO Box 42, Manchester, 05254.
Holdings: Vols (1500)
Notes: Large collection for conservation of all fishing equipment, rods, reels, and flies.

†WA —WASHINGTON STATE UNIVERSITY, Library, Manuscripts, Archives & Special Collections, Pullman, 99164. John F Guido, Head
Holdings: Cat Mss Maps Pix
Notes: The collection is especially rich in documents relating to the exploration, settlement and development of the Palouse Country, the Inland Empire, the Columbia Basin and the Pacific Northwest. Described in *Selected Manuscript Resources in the Washington State University Library* (Pullman, 1974); and other published and unpublished inventories and registers.

WI —UNIVERSITY OF WISCONSIN, GREEN BAY, Library/Learning Center, Green Bay, 54301. Marian A Gould, Acting Dir, Special Collections/University Archives
Holdings: Vols 100 Cat Mss Maps Pix Slides Audiotapes Videotapes
Notes: Belgian-American Research Collection deals with the Belgian-American Settlement in Brown, Door and Kewaunee counties of northeastern Wisconsin. Emphasis is on the rural life and commerical fishing activities in the Bay of Green Bay. Bibliography, *Belgian-American Research* Materials, is available on request.

BC —UNIVERSITY OF BRITISH COLUMBIA, Library, 1956 Main Mall, Vancouver, V6T 1Y3, Can. Anne Yandle, Special Collections Librn
Notes: British Columbia Mountaineering Club photograph collection covering many years of activities. Incl 420 negatives, 2 albums (photos), 1 book.

FISHING EQUIPMENT

ME —BIGELOW LABORATORY FOR OCEAN SCIENCES & MAINE DEPT OF MARINE RESOURCES, Library, McKown Point, West Boothbay Harbor, 04575. Pamela Shephard-Lupo, Librn
Holdings: Vols Cat Docs
Budget: ($55,000)
Notes: This library presently serves two institutions. The Maine Dept of Marine Resources has maintained the library since 1957 and thus the majority of our holdings are geared to their needs, ie fish biology and stock assessment on a local, national and international level. In 1973 Bigelow Laboratory for Ocean Sciences came to West Boothbay Harbor and began to contribute to the library with a very specialized collection on the Gulf of Maine marine chemistry, phytoplankton and nutrient cycles.

FISHING LAW AND LEGISLATION see Fisheries—Laws and Legislation

FITCH, GEORGE

BC —UNIVERSITY OF VICTORIA, McPherson Library, Victoria, V8W 3H5, Can.
Notes: Incl 11 pages, 1937; ms description of the Fall of Nanking.

FITCH, WILLIAM CLYDE, 1865-1909

MA —AMHERST COLLEGE, Library, Amherst, 01002. John Lancaster, Special Collections Librn
Holdings: Vols 1536 Cat Mss Pix
Notes: The library of Clyde Fitch.

FITTING OUT OF BOATS see Boats and Boating—Equipment and Supplies

FITZGERALD, ELLA

MA —BOSTON UNIVERSITY, Mugar Memorial Library, Special Collections Dept, 771 Commonwealth Ave, Boston, 02215. Howard B Gotlieb, Dir
Holdings: Cat Mss
Notes: Mss, scores, correspondence, photographs, phonorecords, etc collected in depth.

FITZGERALD, F. SCOTT, 1896-1940

CT —LEE ASH, (personal collection), 66 Humiston Dr, Bethany, 06525.
Notes: First editions, mss, ephemera, memorabilia.

IN —INDIANA UNIVERSITY, Lilly Library, Seventh St, Bloomington, 47405. William R Cagle, Librn
Holdings: // Cat Mss
Notes: Correspondence of F Scott Fitzgerald with his literary agent Harold Ober, 1919-1941. Much, but not all, of this material was published in *As Ever, Scott Fitz.* (Philedelphia: Lippincott, 1972). 1191 items. Other Fitzgerald ms holdings have been reported in the *Fitzgerald Newsletter,* no 17, Spring 1962, and no 24, Winter 1964. Incl first editions of Fitzgerald's works.

MN —MINNESOTA HISTORICAL SOCIETY LIBRARY, 690 Cedar St, Saint Paul, 55101. Patricia C Harpole, Chief of Reference Library; Bonnie G Wilson, Head of Special Libraries
Holdings: Vols Pix
Notes: A unique copy of the one-sheet mock newspaper, called the *St Paul Daily Dirge,* edited and mostly written by F Scott Fitzgerald for circulation at a January 22 dance at the local University Club.

MN —SAINT PAUL PUBLIC LIBRARY, Highland Park Branch Library, Perrie Jones Memorial Rm, 1974 Ford Pkwy, Saint Paul, 55116. Elizabeth Monigal
Holdings: Vols (1850) Cat
Notes: Rare and interesting books from the 16th century to the present. Also collection of F Scott Fitzgerald and other St Paul authors.

NV —UNIVERSITY OF NEVADA, RENO, University Library, Special Collections Dept, Reno, 89557. Robert E Blesse, Head
Holdings: // Vols (114) Cat Other appearances 280 Cat
Notes: Includes individual works by author in all editions including translations; also prefaces, introductions, published correspondence, appearances in anthologies, periodicals, etc. Bibliographical research collection, part of Modern Authors Collection.

NJ —PRINCETON UNIVERSITY, Library, Manuscript Collection, Nassau St, Princeton, 08540. Jean F Preston, Cur
Holdings: Cat Mss Pix
Notes: The manuscript section occupies 85 ms boxes. See *Princeton University Library* Chronicle, v 12, p 190-95. An unpublished typescript guide (234p) is available in the Library.

FITZGERALD, FRANCES

MA —BOSTON UNIVERSITY, Mugar Memorial Library, Special Collections Dept, 771 Commonwealth Ave, Boston, 02215. Howard B Gotlieb, Dir
Holdings: Cat Mss Pix
Notes: Mss, correspondence, etc collected in depth; incl publications by or about.

FITZGERALD, JOHN

DC —GEORGETOWN UNIVERSITY, Library, Special Collections Div, 37 & O Sts NW, Washington, 20057. George M Barringer, Special Collections Librn; Nicholas B Sheetz, Mss Librn
Holdings: Mss Cat
Notes: Correspondence and documents constituting the papers of Col John Fitzgerald. Fitzgerald, a colonial merchant, served as a member of the Committee of Safety in Alexandria, Virginia, and received his military rank during the Revolution. After the war he became mayor and customs collector of Alexandria. In 1799, while serving in the latter capacity, Fitzgerald was held responsible for the sum of forty

FITZGERALD, JOHN (cont.)

thousand dollars discovered missing from the treasury. Apart from miscellaneous correspondence and deeds, the papers primarily concern this incident. Incl is correspondence from Oliver Wolcott, Secretary of the Treasury.

FITZGERALD, PERCY HEATHERINGTON

CT —LEE ASH, (personal collection), 66 Humiston Dr, Bethany, 06525.
Notes: Books, ephemera, etc, by or about.

FITZGERALD, ZELDA (SAYRE)

NJ —PRINCETON UNIVERSITY, Library, Manuscript Collection, Nassau St, Princeton, 08540. Jean F Preston, Cur
Holdings: Cat Mss Pix
Notes: The collection, which fills 6 ms boxes, is restricted. An unpublished typescript guide (48p) is available for consultation.

FITZHENRY, LOUIS

IL —ILLINOIS STATE UNIVERSITY, Milner Library, Dept of Special Collections, Normal, 61761. Robert Sokan, Librn
Holdings: Mss Pix
Notes: US Congressman from Illinois and federal judge. Correspondence, diaries, address books, deeds, certificates, receipts, business agreements, news clippings, programs for testimonial dinners, notebooks, photos, pamphlets and Congressional directories. Incl business papers of the Rankin family. The bulk of the material dates from 1883-1940. Correspondents incl Lottie Rankin Fitzhenry, Mildred Fitzhenry, Charlotte Fitzhenry, Herbert Hoover and William H Taft (as Supreme Court Justice). Incl 2060 items, which are cataloged.

FITZHERBET, MARIA ANNE

DC —GEORGETOWN UNIVERSITY, Library, Special Collections Div, 37 & O Sts NW, Washington, 20057. George M Barringer, Special Collections Librn; Nicholas B Sheetz, Mss Librn
Holdings: Mss Cat Pix
Notes: The papers of the Irish man-of-letters Sir Shane Leslie (1885-1971) containing letters, mss, diaries, notebooks, clippings, and photographs. Extensive correspondence by Margot Asquith, countess of Oxford and Asquith; Lady Violet Bonham-Carter; Burke Cochran; Lord Alfred Douglas; Moreton Frewen; Cardinal Gasquet; Vyvyan Holland; Lady Leonie Leslie; Sir Wilfrid Meynell; Sir Horace Plunkett; John Quinn; Frederick Rolfe (Baron Corvo); and Elizabeth Russell, among others. Also incl are research files on Sir Winston Churchill (Leslie's first cousin); Leonard Jerome; Maria Anne Fitzherbet (wife of King George IV); Ghosts and Ghost stories; and Eton College.

FITZPATRICK, JOHN

IL —CHICAGO HISTORICAL SOCIETY, Library, Clark St at North Ave, Chicago, 60614. Archie Motley, Manuscript Librn
Notes: Papers of labor leader.
See also entry under Labor - History.

FITZ RANDOLPH FAMILY

†WI —SEVENTH DAY BAPTIST HISTORICAL SOCIETY, Library, 3120 Kennedy St, PO Box 1678, Janesville, 53547.
Holdings: Uncat Mss Maps Pix
Notes: Largely the work of Hector Craig Fitz Randolph, these five file drawers of material were gathered over a period of years to trace some of the lines of the family in New Jersey and elsewhere. Notes and books.

FIVE CIVILIZED TRIBES

NY —NEW YORK STATE LIBRARY, State Education Bldg Annex, Washington Ave, Albany, 12224.
Notes: Strong collection emphasis on North American Indians, especially Indians of New York. Incl books and pamphlets on Indian captivities, treaties, conferences, lives of noted Indians, laws. Bibles and catechisms, prayerbooks, grammars, etc in native languages. Outstanding collection on Iroquois Indians. Incl original treaties between the State of New York and the Iroquois, papers of Cornplanter, drawings by Jesse Cornplanter.

OK —FIVE CIVILIZED TRIBES MUSEUM, Library, Agency Hill, Honor Hts Dr, Muskogee, 74401. Mrs Spencer Denton, Dir
Holdings: Maps Pix
Notes: The collection pertains to the history, culture, and traditions of the Five Civilized Tribes plus history of Indian Territory prior to statehood.

OK —OKLAHOMA HISTORICAL SOCIETY, Library, Historical Bldg, Oklahoma City, 73105. Andrea Clark, Dir, Library Resources Division
Holdings: Vols (43,000) Cat Mss Maps Pix Microforms
Notes: The Society also has the Indian Archives Collection of 2,500,000 pieces (Mary Lee Boyle, Archivist). This is an extensive collection of records, particularly of the Five Civilized Tribes. Incl tribal rolls, agency reports, manuscripts, etc.

OK —THOMAS GILCREASE INSTITUTE OF AMERICAN HISTORY & ART LIBRARY, 1400 North 25th West Ave, Tulsa, 74127. Sarah Hirsch, Librn
Holdings: Vols Cat Mss Maps Pix
Notes: Trans-Mississippi West, US, Indian and Hispanic history. The Gilcrease Library contains a total of about 40,000 mss; 10,000 imprints; 5000 photographs; 600 maps and 50,000 vols.

FIVE NATIONS see Iroquois Indians

FIVE-YEAR PLAN (RUSSIA) see Russia—Economic Policy

FLACCUS, KIMBALL

DC —GEORGETOWN UNIVERSITY, Library, Special Collections Div, 37 & O Sts NW, Washington, 20057. George M Barringer, Special Collections Librn; Nicholas B Sheetz, Mss Librn
Holdings: Vols (200) Uncat Mss Pix
Notes: Papers of Kimball Flaccus, American poet, relating to his unpublished biography of Masters; including correspondence from Masters, run of books by and about Masters.

FLAGG, MILDRED BUCHANAN

MA —BOSTON UNIVERSITY, Mugar Memorial Library, Special Collections Dept, 771 Commonwealth Ave, Boston, 02215. Howard B Gotlieb, Dir
Holdings: //Cat Mss

FLAGS (VEXILLOLOGY)

CA —LOS ANGELES PUBLIC LIBRARY, Genealogy & Local History Dept, 630 W 5th St, Los Angeles, 90071. Lucile Lipman, Sr Librn
Holdings: Vols (55,000) Cat Mss Pix
Budget: ($16,000)
Notes: Collection on national, civic and maritime flags.

NY —NEW YORK PUBLIC LIBRARY, Local History and Genealogy Div, Fifth Ave & 42 St, New York, 10018. Gunther E Pohl, Chief
Holdings: Vols (160,000) Cat Pix
Budget: ($38,548)
Notes: Civic, maritime and national. *Dictionary Catalog of the Local History and Genealogy Division,* The Research Libraries of the New York Public Library, 18 vols, $1420 (Boston: G K Hall). See also *United States Local History Catalog* (Boston: G K Hall, 1974), 2 vols, $145. Represented in the catalog is a sizeable collection on flags.

FLAGSTAD, KIRSTEN

NY —NEW YORK PUBLIC LIBRARY, Performing Arts Research Center, Rodgers & Hammerstein Archives of Recorded Sound, 111 Amsterdam Ave, New York, 10023.
Holdings: // Audiotapes
Notes: Given by Mr and Mrs Arthur V Dusenberry in 1969, the 33 audiotapes comprise private recordings made by the great Norwegian soprano in Oslo subsequent to her retirement from the operatic stage. Virtually the whole of her German and Scandinavian art-song repertoire is included.

FLAHERTY, ANTHONY

LA —NEW ORLEANS PUBLIC LIBRARY, Louisiana Div, 219 Loyola Ave, New Orleans, 70140. Collin B Hamer Jr, Head; Brenda M Osbey, Library Associate
Holdings: Cat Maps Pix
Notes: Louisiana and New Orleans Picture File Collection ranges from the late 19th century-date and incl the following separate collections: Alexander Allison (ca 1898-1951, 337 pieces); Charles Franck (ca 1920-50, 170 pieces); Leda Plauche (ca 1935-53, 220 pieces); C Milo Williams (ca 1910, 85 pieces); Wilson S Howell (ca 1890, 49 pieces); Grauman Marks (ca 1960, 268 pieces); Robert Tallant (ca 1940-50, 70 pieces); Robert E Tracy (1959, 87 pieces); Anthony J Flaherty (ca 1970-84, 83 pieces); George F Mugnier (1880-1920, 186 pieces); Color Slides (ca 1945-date, 500 pieces); 30, 000 photographs incl 500 color slides and 104 negatives. Use of the material is restricted to on-site research. Publication must be accompanied by credit cut line.

FLAHERTY, ROBERT

NY —COLUMBIA UNIVERSITY LIBRARIES, Rare Book & Manuscript Library, 801 Butler Library, 535 W 114 St, New York, 10027. Kenneth A Lohf, Librn
Holdings: Mss Pix
Notes: Papers, negatives and stills from his films. Incl 30,000 items. Restricted use.

NY —MUSEUM OF MODERN ART, Dept of Film, 11 W 53 St, New York, 10019. Eileen Bowser, Cur
Holdings: Mss Pix
Notes: Papers, correspondence, scrapbooks, pictures, etc. Partially cataloged.

FLAMMARION, NICOLAS

NY —CORNELL UNIVERSITY LIBRARIES, Collection of Regional History, Dept of Manuscripts and Univ Archives, Ithaca, 14853.
Notes: 19th century French scientist. Incl mss and letters from Flammarion.

FLANAGAN, HALLIE

NY —NEW YORK PUBLIC LIBRARY, Performing Arts Research Center, Billy Rose Theatre Collection, 111 Amsterdam Ave, New York, 10023. Dorothy L Swerdlove, Cur
Holdings: Cat Mss Pix
Notes: Papers, scrapbooks, mss, photographs, memorabilia, etc.

FLANDERS—HISTORY

IL —NORTHWESTERN UNIVERSITY, Library, Special Collections Dept, 1937 Sheridan Rd, Evanston, 60201. R Russell Maylone, Cur
Notes: Incl 2500 pamphlets dealing with the Brabant Revolution. Additional 14,000 pamphlets, legal documents, and periodical issues published in France 1787-1800.

FLANNER, JANET

DC —LIBRARY OF CONGRESS, Manuscript Division, Washington, 20540. John C Broderick, Chief
Notes: The Janet Flanner-Solita Solano Papers, containing correspondence, literary mss, printed material, photographs, and mementoes.

FLATWARE, SILVER see Silverware

FLAXMAN, TED

LA —LOUISIANA STATE UNIVERSITY, SHREVEPORT, Library-Archives, 8515

FLAXMAN, TED (cont.)

Youree Dr, Shreveport, 71129. Patricia L Meador, Archivist & Asst Librn
Notes: Archives incl catalogued manuscripts and records, 500 maps, more than 5000 photographs, 1000 architectural drawings, slides. The collection's primary emphasis is the history of North Louisiana, particularly Northwest Louisiana. The 1500 linear ft incl area plantation records and ledgers; personal papers of area pioneers, planters, legislators, politicians, educators, businessmen, and architects; papers and records of longtime (1919-1961) Caddo Parish Coroner, Willis P Butler; the Samuel G Wiener, Sr architectural records (1921-1976) with drawings and photographs; the Ted Flaxman architectural records (1919-1968); the papers (1860-1921) of architect Nathaniel S Allen; the collection of Dewey A Somdal, Shreveport architect, historian and collector, with emphasis on steamboats, travel on the Red River and Louisiana history, 1780-1972.

FLEAS

OH —MIAMI UNIVERSITY, Science Library, Oxford, 45056.
Notes: Zoonoses and related diseases. Collection partially transferred from Parker-Davis Memorial Library, Hamilton, Mont.

FLEECE see Wool

FLEISHMAN, STANLEY

CA —UNIVERSITY OF CALIFORNIA, LOS ANGELES, Research Library, Dept of Special Collections, 405 Hilgard Ave, Los Angeles, 90024. Edward Shreeves, Chairman, Bibliographers Group; David S Zeidberg, Head
Notes: 270 linear feet of papers and printed material of the attorney active in cases involving civil liberties, obscenity, and rights of the disabled.

FLEMING, IAN

IN —INDIANA UNIVERSITY, Lilly Library, Seventh St, Bloomington, 47405. William R Cagle, Librn
Holdings: Cat Mss
Notes: Extensive collection of first editions; mss incl papers of Leonard Russell and John Pearson relating to a Fleming biography and Ian Fleming's mss for 11 James Bond novels.

FLEMING, JOAN

MA —BOSTON UNIVERSITY, Mugar Memorial Library, Special Collections Dept, 771 Commonwealth Ave, Boston, 02215. Howard B Gotlieb, Dir
Holdings: Cat Mss Pix
Notes: Mss, correspondence, etc collected in depth; incl publications by or about.

FLEMING, PETER D., 1917-

KS —MENNINGER FOUNDATION, Archives, 5600 W Sixth St, Box 829, Topeka, 66601. Alice Brand, Librn; Mark West, Archivist
Notes: 7 boxes, 1955-69. Consists of correspondence and memoranda, most of which pertain to his work at the Foundation.

FLEMING, THOMAS J.

MA —BOSTON UNIVERSITY, Mugar Memorial Library, Special Collections Dept, 771 Commonwealth Ave, Boston, 02215. Howard B Gotlieb, Dir
Holdings: Cat Mss Pix
Notes: Mss, correspondence, etc collected in depth; incl publications by or about.

FLEMISH LANGUAGE AND LITERATURE

MA —HARVARD UNIVERSITY LIBRARY, Widener Library, Cambridge, 02138.
Holdings: Cat
Notes: See *Distributable Union Catalog* (Harvard).

†NY —BELGIAN CONSULATE GENERAL LIBRARY, 50 Rockefeller Plaza, New York, 10020.
Notes: Belgian history, art, cultures, and other aspects of Belgian life.

FLETCHER, ADM. FRANK F.

VA —UNIVERSITY OF VIRGINIA, Alderman Library, Manuscripts Dept, Charlottesville, 22901. Edmund Berkeley Jr, Cur
Holdings: Cat Mss Pix
Notes: 1900 items. Papers, incl correspondence, official records and reports, regarding naval inventions and innovations, official orders, the Mexican crisis, 1913-14, and the occupation of Vera Cruz, 1914.

FLETCHER, G. B. A.

IN —INDIANA UNIVERSITY, Lilly Library, Seventh St, Bloomington, 47405. William R Cagle, Librn
Notes: Three A E Housman collections; (1) Housman Mss I is ex-libris H B Collamore in the main, with about 100 autograph letters; (2) Housman Mss II has about 20 AEH letters with a good number of letters about Housman's verse from G B A Fletcher; (3) Housman Mss III is the John Carter Collection of letters to him about AEH. The Library has about 30 volumes from Housman's library, and a strong collection of editions of his works.

FLETCHER, GRACE NIES

MA —BOSTON UNIVERSITY, Mugar Memorial Library, Special Collections Dept, 771 Commonwealth Ave, Boston, 02215. Howard B Gotlieb, Dir
Holdings: Cat Mss Pix
Notes: Mss, correspondence, etc collected in depth; incl publications by or about.

FLETCHER, HARVEY, 1884-

UT —BRIGHAM YOUNG UNIVERSITY, Harold B Lee Library, Unversity Hill, Provo, 84602. Sterling Albrecht, Dir
Holdings: 40 Boxes
Notes: Papers of Harvey Fletcher, about half consisting of publications of other scientists (ca 1934-ca 1971).

FLETCHER, JAMES CHIPMAN

†UT —UNIVERSITY OF UTAH, Marriott Library, Salt Lake City, 84112.
Notes: The papers of James Chipman Fletcher, generated while director of the National Aeronautics and Space Administration, 1971-1977.

FLETCHER, JOHN GOULD

CT —YALE UNIVERSITY, Box 1603A, Yale Station, New Haven, 06520.
Holdings: Cat Mss

MO —WASHINGTON UNIVERSITY, Libraries, Campus Box 1061, Saint Louis, 63130.
Notes: A collection of primary material.

FLETCHER, THOMAS, 1787-1866

PA —ATHENAEUM OF PHILADELPHIA, 219 S Sixth St, Philadelphia, 19106. Roger W Moss Jr, Librn
Holdings: Vols (70,000) Cat Mss Pix Microforms
Notes: Part of the overall thrust of the Athenaeum's main area of concentration: 19th century social and cultural history. This collection, primarily developed in support of the Victorian Society in America whose national offices are located in the Athenaeum building, is supported by modern secondary works on 19th century architecture. Small part of holdings listed in Henry Russell Hitchcock, *American Architectural Books* (Minneapolis, Minn: University of Minnesota Press, 1962). Also contains 14 boxes of papers relating to the silversmith Thomas Fletcher, 1787-1866.

FLEXNER, SIMON

NY —ROCKEFELLER UNIVERSITY, Rockefeller Archive Center, Hillcrest, Pocantico Hills, North Tarrytown, 10591. Joseph W Ernst, Dir; J William Hess, Assoc Dir
Notes: Papers relative to the Rockefeller Family, Foundations, University, and other specific enterprises and contributions to particular areas of social, physical, educational, and historic reform, preservation, conservation, or development. Extensive records of administrative, financial, physical, or intellectual relationships.

PA —AMERICAN PHILOSOPHICAL SOCIETY, Library, 105 S Fifth St, Philadelphia, 19106. Edward C Carter II, Librn
Holdings: Cat Mss
Notes: Medical research.

FLIES

IA —IOWA STATE UNIVERSITY, Library, Ames, 50011. Warren B Kuhn, Dean of Library Services
Holdings: Cat
Notes: Specific strengths: flies, mosquitoes and ticks.

NY —AMERICAN MUSEUM OF NATURAL HISTORY, Library Services Dept, Central Park W & 79th St, New York, 10024. Nina J Root, Chairwoman; Mary Genett, Asst Librn for Reference Services
Notes: A major literature collection supplements the museum's entomology collections; perhaps the largest in the world.

FLIES, ARTIFICIAL

IL —NORTHWESTERN UNIVERSITY, Library, Special Collections Dept, 1937 Sheridan Rd, Evanston, 60201. R Russell Maylone, Cur
Holdings: Vols 250 Cat Pix
Notes: History of fly-fishing, 16th-20th centuries.

NH —UNIVERSITY OF NEW HAMPSHIRE, Dimond Library, Durham, 03824. Barbara A White, Special Collections Librn
Holdings: Vols 2000 Cat
Notes: Special emphasis on fly-tying and trout and salmon fishing.

PA —LAFAYETTE COLLEGE, David Bishop Skillman Library, Easton, 18042. Dorothy Cieslicki, Librn
Holdings: Vols (825) Cat
Notes: Robert Tinsman Angling Collection. Incl 58 editions of Walton, *Compleat Angler*. Also, the Robert S Conahay, Jr, Atlantic Salmon Collection, which incl over 1000 hand-tied salmon and trout flies, many mounted and framed.

FLIGHT

CO —US AIR FORCE ACADEMY, Library, USAF Academy, Colorado Springs, 80840. Reiner H Schaeffer, Dir
Holdings: Vols 6000 Cat Mss Maps Pix
Notes: The Colonel Richard Gimbel Aeronautical History Collection. Incl material from ancient myth to 1903 on manned flight; early scientific works on physical properties of the atmosphere, and imaginative literature on moon voyages. Collection is most complete in manned pioneer balloon ascents (1783ff). Also the Richard Upjohn Light Collection formerly at Culver Military Academy. Separate catalog, index to be published. 250 mss, 100 maps, 2000 pictures, 5000 prints, 7000 clippings.

FLIGHT—HISTORY

DC —SMITHSONIAN INSTITUTION LIBRARIES, National Air & Space Museum Branch, NASM Bldg, Sixth & Independence Ave SW, Washington, 20560. Frank A Pietropaoli, Branch Chief
Holdings: Vols (39,000) Cat Mss Maps Pix Slides Microforms
Notes: History of flight and aerospace

FLIGHT—HISTORY (cont.)

development, incl biographical material on aviation pioneers, balloons and ballooning. Extensive photographic collection (600,000 pictures). Incl the Sherman Fairchild Collection of aeronautical photographs (transferred from the American Institute of Aeronautics and Astronautics). Also incl the Bella Landauer Aeronautical Sheet Music Collection (1500 pieces). 2000 films; 800,000 microforms; 9000 volumes bound.

FL —EMBRY-RIDDLE AERONAUTICAL UNIVERSITY, Regional Airport, Daytona Beach, 32014. M Judy Luther, Dir of Learning Resources

OH —WRIGHT STATE UNIVERSITY, Greater Miami Valley Research Center, University Library, Dayton, 45431. Patrick B Nolan, Head of Archives
Holdings: Vols 2000 Mss Pix
Notes: Books, private papers and business records of aviation pioneers, companies etc. Incl 100 linear ft of manuscripts and 5000 photographs.

FLIGHT—MEDICAL ASPECTS see Aviation Medicine

FLIGHT, UNPOWERED see Gliding and Soaring

FLINT, SIR WILLIAM RUSSELL

OH —OHIO UNIVERSITY, Vernon R Alden Library, Department of Archives and Special Collections, Athens, 45701. Gary A Hunt, Head
Holdings: Vols 17 Cat
Notes: A comprehensive collection of books written or illustrated by Flint.

FLINTLOCKS see Rifles

FLIPPEN, RUTH BROOKS

CA —UNIVERSITY OF CALIFORNIA, LOS ANGELES, Theater Arts Library, Los Angeles, 90024. Edward Shreeves, Chairman, Bibliographers Group; Audree Malkin, Head, Theater Arts Library
Notes: Ruth Brooks Flippen Collection of scripts, production material, stills, publicity material, and correspondence relating to her career as a writer.

FLISCH, JULIA A., 1861-1941

GA —GEORGIA COLLEGE, Ina Dillard Russell Library, Special Collections Dept, Milledgeville, 31061. Janice C Fennell, Dir of Libraries; Nancy Davis, Special Collections Assoc
Holdings: // Uncat Mss
Notes: Incl 31 mss; 150 letters to her; memorabilia.

FLOOD, DANIEL J.

PA —KING'S COLLEGE, D Leonard Corgan Library, 14 W Jackson St, Wilkes-Barre, 18711. Judith Tierney, Special Collections Librn
Holdings: Mss Pix
Notes: Personal papers, 1945-1980, of the Representative of the 11th Congressional District of Pennsylvania, incl sound and videotapes. Photocopying limited. See Judith Tierney, comp, *Daniel J Flood: A Register of His Papers* (Wilkes-Barre, Pa, King's College Press, 1974).

FLOOD CONTROL

CA —UNIVERSITY OF CALIFORNIA, BERKELEY, Water Resources Center Archives, 410 O'Brien Hall, Berkeley, 94720. Gerald J Giefer, Librn
Holdings: Vols (83,000) Cat Mss Maps
Notes: The engineering, economic, social and legal aspects of water: water as a natural resource and its utilization; irrigation and reclamation; flood control; municipal and industrial water uses and problems; water rights; and water development projects. Particular concentration is on California and the West. Much ephemeral material. See *Dictionary Catalog of the Water Resources Center Archives, University of California* (Boston: G K Hall, 5 vols; First Supp, 1971; Second Supp, 1972; Third Supp, 1973; Fourth Supp, 1974; Fifth Supp, 1976; and Sixth Supp, 1978).

FL —SOUTH FLORIDA WATER MANAGEMENT DISTRICT, Library, PO Box V, West Palm Beach, 33402. Cynthia H Plockelman, Research Librn
Holdings: Cat Slides Microforms Periodicals
Budget: ($13,000)
Notes: A state agency dealing in all aspects of water management, flood control, hydrology, changing environmental conditions, etc. Emphasis is changing from flood control to general water management.

MD —MARYLAND-NATIONAL CAPITAL PARK & PLANNING COMMISSION, Montgomery County Planning Department Library, 8787 Georgia Ave, Silver Spring, 20907. Janice C Holt, Librn
Holdings: Vols (5000) Cat Microforms
Notes: Specific subject areas include: community facilities, conservation, economics, flood control, highways, housing, human and natural resources. landscape architecture, open space, parks, pollution, population, recreation, transportation, urban renewal, and zoning. Commission's publications are maintained by Records Management (not Library).

†NY —COLUMBIA UNIVERSITY LIBRARIES, Butler Library, Rare Book and Manuscript Library, 535 W 114 St, New York, 10027.
Notes: Files relating to the American Library Association's Special Committee to Aid Italian Libraries' assistance to Italian libraries to help restore books, mss and other library materials after the 1966 floods in Florence.

OH —WRIGHT STATE UNIVERSITY, Greater Miami Valley Research Center, University Library, Dayton, 45431. Patrick B Nolan, Head of Archives
Notes: Records of Miami Conservancy District 1913-1978. Incl 50 linear ft of archives and records.

SK —CANADA PRAIRIE FARM REHABILITATION ADMINISTRATION LIBRARY, Motherwell Bldg, Regina, S4P 0R5, Can. C Kosack, Head
Holdings: Vols (10,000) Cat
Budget: ($8000)
Notes: PFRA is a Canadian federal government agency initiated to alleviate the effects of drought and water shortages on the prairies. The collection covers engineering (dams), agricultural economics, hydrology, irrigation, community pastures, and soil and water conservation.

FLOOD PREVENTION see Flood Control

FLOODS

OH —ANTIOCH COLLEGE, Olive Kettering Library, Livermore St, Yellow Springs, 45387. Nina Myatt, Cur
Notes: Personal papers and correspondence (1920-1975) of Arthur E Morgan former President of Antioch (1920-1936), first director of Ohio's Miami Valley Conservancy District, and first Chairman of the Tennessee Valley Authority (TVA). Mss, film, out-takes, much on the engineering of over 50 water-control projects in this country, Africa, and India. Materials on Edward Bellamy (Morgan wrote biography of Bellamy). Incl family papers. About 175 file boxes.

FLOOR COVERING DESIGN

NY —FASHION INSTITUTE OF TECHNOLOGY, Edward C Blum Design Laboratory, 227 W 27 St, New York, 10001. Laura Sinderbrand, Dir
Holdings: Cat Pix Slides
Notes: The largest resource of it kind consisting of 4 million indexed swatches and 300 swatch books, jacquard point paper, croquis, quilts, rug samples, laces, embroideries, and color swatch cards. A collection of international scope incl antique and contemporary textiles; woven and printed patterns created for apparel and home furnishings which may be adapted to china, giftware, floor covering, wallpaper, and package design. A comprehensive research facility comprised of over one million articles of dress dating from the 17th Century to the present, incl men's, women's, children's clothes, furs, foundation garments and lingerie, as well as an outstanding grouping of 19th and 20th century designer clothing. Accessories as diverse as hats, handbags, gloves, hosiery, shoes, shawls, and costume jewelry offer an additonal resource to this international collection.

FLORA see Botany; Marine Flora

FLORA, ARCTIC see Botany—Arctic Regions

FLORAL DECORATION see Flower Arrangement

FLORICULTURE

CA —UNIVERSITY OF CALIFORNIA, IRVINE, Library, Irvine, 92664. Roger Berry, Dept Head
Notes: The Emma D Menninger extensive collection of 19th and 20th century information on horticulture, with special emphasis on orchids.

IL —MORTON ARBORETUM, Sterling Morton Library, Lisle, 60532. Ian MacPhail, Librn
Holdings: Vols (20,000) Cat Maps Pix
Budget: ($10,000)
Notes: The library is especially concerned with the literature of woody plants (trees and shrubs) of north temperate zones but has substantial holdings in the taxonomy and systematics of plants in general, both wild and cultivated, flora of different parts of the world, and a growing collection on plant monographs. Also about 2000 pictures. Described in *The Morton Arboretum* Quarterly, vol 9, no 4 (Winter 1973), pp 56-61.

IA —IOWA STATE UNIVERSITY, Library, Ames, 50011. Warren B Kuhn, Dean of Library Services
Holdings: Cat
Notes: Extensive serial holdings.

KY —UNIVERSITY OF KENTUCKY, Agriculture Library, Agricultural Science Center North, Lexington, 40546. Antoinette P Powell, Head Librn
Holdings: Vols (90,000) Cat Maps Microforms
Budget: ($110,582)

MA —MASSACHUSETTS HORTICULTURAL SOCIETY, 300 Massachusetts Ave, Boston, 02115. Becky Ellis, Librn
Holdings: Vols (37,000)
Notes: Garden history, pomology, flora, landscape design. Print collection of many centuries; nursery catalogues from the mid-18th century. In storage, remodeling, will be available in about a year. Open to the public.

MA —HARVARD UNIVERSITY, Arnold Arboretum, Horticultural Library, The Arborway, Jamaica Plain, 02130.
Holdings: Vols Pix Slides
Notes: Arboriculture.

OH —CLEVELAND PUBLIC LIBRARY, Science & Technology Dept, 325 Superior Ave, Cleveland, 44114. Jean Z Piety, Head
Holdings: Cat
Notes: Part of the Gardening Collection, which emphasizes the history of gardens around the world, domestic landscape planning and planting, incl flower gardening, annuals and perennials and indoor plants.

OH —MASSILLON PUBLIC LIBRARY, 208 Lincoln Way E, Massillon, 44646. Camille Leslie, Dir
Holdings: Vols 250 Cat

OH —HOLDEN ARBORETUM, Warren H Corning Library, 9500 Sperry Rd, Mentor, 44060. Paul C Spector, Dir of Education
Holdings: Vols (5500) // Cat
Notes: Extensive collection of horticultural

FLORICULTURE (cont.)

classics, floras, herbals and monographs prior to 1850. Primarily European works.

OR —OREGON STATE UNIVERSITY, Library, Corvallis, 97331. Melvin George, Dir
Holdings: Vols (980,000) Cat

TX —SLOVANSKA PODPORUJICI JEDNOTA STATU TEXAS, Slavonic Benevolent Order of the State of Texas, SPJST Library, Archives, Museum, 520 N Main St, Temple, 76501. Otto Hanus, Cur-Librn; Thelma Bartosh, Asst Cur-Librn
Holdings: Vols (400) Cat
Notes: Our agricultural section contains US Dept of Agriculture books plus many bound magazines dealng with agriculture, gardening and flower growing.

VA —NORFOLK BOTANICAL GARDENS LIBRARY, Airport Rd, Norfolk, 23518. Marian Cole, Librn
Holdings: Vols 1903 Cat Pix

ON —ROYAL BOTANICAL GARDENS, Library, Box 399, Hamilton, L8N 3H8, Can. Ina Vrugtman, Librn
Holdings: Vols (5000) Cat
Budget: ($13,000)
Notes: Botany and ornamental horticulture. Incl 10,000 slides. Periodicals are not yet union listed. Collection of nursery and seed trade catalogs; *Gray Herbarium Index;* Centre for Canadian Historical Horitcultural Studies. The library is located in the headquarters building of the Royal Botanical Gradens, 680 Plains Road West (Highway No 2) Burlington, Ontario. Phone: (416) 527-1158. Road West (Highway No 2) Burlington, Ontario. Phone: (416) 527-1158.

FLORIDA

FL —UNIVERSITY OF FLORIDA, Coastal Engineering Archives, 433 Weil Hall, Gainesville, 32611. Lucile Lehmann, Librn
Holdings: Cat Maps Pix Slides
Budget: $4000
Notes: We have a collection of reports (7000), maps (700), surveys, and aerial photos (600) documenting coastal changes in Florida. This material is arranged in a geographic classification. The Archives is not part of the University library system but is a special collection of the Coastal and Oceanographic Engineering Dept.

FL —EVERGLADES NATIONAL PARK, South Florida Research Center, PO Box 279, Homestead, 33030. Gary Hendrix, Librn
Holdings: Vols (5500) Cat Microforms
Notes: Emphasis on South Florida, birds, water problems. This is a special reference collection maintained for the Park Staff only. Noncirculating. Estuaries. ILL available.

FL —ARCHBOLD BIOLOGICAL STATION, Library, Rt 2, Box 180, Lake Placid, 33852. Fred E Lohrer, Librn
Holdings: Cat Slides
Notes: Florida natural history. Emphasis on south central peninsular Florida. Habitats, plants, vertebrates, land use changes. About 8000 2x2 color transparencies and 35mm films.

FL —UNIVERSITY OF CENTRAL FLORIDA, Library, Box 25000, Orlando, 32816.
Holdings: Vols (3000)
Notes: The William L Bryant West Indies Collection of books, documents, periodicals, paintings and artifacts either about or produced in the islands of the West Indies and Florida.

FL —FLORIDA DEPT OF NATURAL RESOURCES BUREAU OF MARINE RESEARCH, Library, 100 Eighth Ave SE, Saint Petersburg, 33701. Keir Gray, Archivist
Holdings: Vols (3400) Cat Maps Pix Slides 16mm Films Microforms
Budget: ($27,500)
Notes: The library supports the research of approx 50 biologists and technicians, with emphasis on the marine resources of Florida and nearby areas. An archives section houses original research data, reports, publications,, etc, developed by the scientific staff. Marine biological literature is received on exchange from laboratories and libraries throughout the world. There are approx 1400 journal titles in the collection. Current titles received number approx 600. The 33,000 reprints are cataloged by author and subject. Current laboratory activities incl marine studies in aquaculture, descriptive biology, ecological studies, fisheries biology, and oceanography.

FL —SAINT PETERSBURG PUBLIC LIBRARY, 3745 Ninth Ave N, Saint Petersburg, 33713. Luccille Bostforff, Reference Supvr
Holdings: Vols 2240 Cat Maps Pix Microforms
Notes: Florida document depository. Spanish land grants on microfilm. Local newspapers on microfilm. Approximately 196,000 cards indexing local newspapers and Florida magazines by subject. Incl 125 pictures, 2474 microfilm reels; 30,943 pamphlets and documents.

FL —FLORIDA DEPT OF COMMERCE, Research Library, 408 Fletcher Bldg, Tallahassee, 32301. Dennis Hitchens, Librn
Holdings: Vols (3000) Cat Mss Maps VF
Budget: ($6000)
Notes: Collect materials related to the 2 divisions of the Florida Dept of Commerce: Economic Development and Tourism, incl titles on Florida (historical and current), international trade, transportation, education, employment, management, industrial development and business. The Florida and US documents collection covers population, manufacturing, employment, agriculture, retail trade, wholesale trade and labor. VF incl files on every city and county, especially local economic data, SIC coded material, out-of-state information, county files, Florida specific material and general subject material. 100 VF drawers.

FL —FLORIDA STATE UNIVERSITY, Robert Manning Strozier Library, Special Collections Dept, Tallahassee, 32306. Opal M Free, Head, Special Collections
Holdings: Vols (12,301) Cat Microforms
Notes: Incl books by Floridians and about all aspects of Florida's development. Also fiction with Florida settings. Vertical file of 138,367 clippings and pamphlets.

FL —FLORIDA STATE UNIVERSITY, Robert Manning Strozier Library, Tallahassee, 32306. Judith Depew, Head, Documents-Maps Dept
Holdings: Vols (680,000) Uncat Microforms
Notes: A depository for Florida, GPO, NASA, UN, and UNESCO documents, with standing orders for British, ILO, OAS, IMF; selected documents are purchased from various government levels. The collection incl historical as well as current material, especially Florida, US, Great Britain. The Library's holdings are strong in congressional bills and hearings, decennial censuses, and British Sessional papers. Number of volumes incl microprint and microfiche, but not cataloged documents and microfilm.

FL —STATE LIBRARY OF FLORIDA, R A Gray Bldg, Tallahassee, 32304. Mary McRory, Florida Collection Librn
Holdings: Vols 14,197 Cat Mss Maps Videotapes 16mm Films Microforms
Budget: $5000
Notes: The Florida Collection: inclusive collection of books, pamphlets, periodicals, and ephemera pertaining to Florida; supplemented by extensive collection of Florida public documents. Separate catalog. Index of biographical sketches of Floridians.

FL —SOUTH FLORIDA WATER MANAGEMENT DISTRICT, Library, PO Box V, West Palm Beach, 33402. Cynthia H Plockelman, Research Librn
Holdings: Cat Slides Microforms Periodicals
Budget: ($13,000)
Notes: A state agency dealing in all aspects of water management, flood control, hydrology, changing environmental conditions, etc. Emphasis is changing from flood control to general water management.

FL —ROLLINS COLLEGE, Mills Memorial Library, Winter Park, 32789. Patricia J Delks, Dir of Libraries
Holdings: Vols 4000 Cat Maps Pix VF
Notes: VF drawers of pamphlets and clippings.

NY —AMERICAN MUSEUM OF NATURAL HISTORY, Library Services Dept, Central Park W & 79th St, New York, 10024. Nina J Root, Chairwoman; Mary Genett, Asst Librn for Reference Services
Holdings: Cat Mss Pix Microforms
Notes: The Ernest Thompson Seton diaries. Thousands of pages of an unpublished 67-year diary record of one of the world's most famous naturalists, the gift of Joseph F Cullman III, a Trustee of the Museum. Preserved in 35 protective cases, the gift incl unpublished diaries, notebooks, and some other writings. The diary begins 12 June 1879; the last entries were written in hospital, just a month before Seton's death in 1946. Literally hundreds of examples of flora and fauna are pictured in the diaries in original pencil, pen-and-ink, and watercolor sketches, on nearly every page. Research will reveal information on the Indian sign language, the Boy Scouts of America, the Woodcraft League of America, and the wilderness of Canada, Florida, Texas, the West and Southwest, etc.

FLORIDA—GENEALOGY

FL —POLK COUNTY HISTORICAL & GENEALOGICAL LIBRARY, 495 N Hendry Ave, Bartow, 33830. LaCona R Padgett, Librn
Holdings: Vols (9000) Cat Maps Pix Microfilms
Budget: $18,500
Notes: Collection being cataloged. When completed, will have a computer printout of catalog. Incl 200 maps and 500 pictures, 4000 reels.

FL —MIAMI-DADE PUBLIC LIBRARY SYSTEM, 1 Biscayne Blvd, Miami, 33132. Mrs Pat Warren, Cur
Holdings: Vols 6000 Cat Microforms
Notes: Incl 6691 microforms. Separate catalog. 1910 census reels for the US Census index, up to 1850.

FL —ORLANDO PUBLIC LIBRARY, Local History & Genealogy Dept, 100 Block of Central Ave, Orlando, 32806. Eileen B Willis, Librn
Holdings: Vols 11,000 Cat Maps Microforms
Budget: $8000
Notes: Strong collection in local genealogy materials on Mass, NY, Va, Ga, and Florida. Contains exceptional holdings on all New England States, Penn, and NJ.
See also entry under Genealogy - Collections.

FL —FLORIDA STATE ARCHIVES, R A Gray Bldg, Tallahassee, 32301. Richard Roberts, Supervisor, Central Reference Section
Holdings: Vols 12,000 Cat Microforms
Budget: $6000
Notes: National scope, with primary emphasis on the South and Southeast, and basic source materials of New England. Incl county and family histories, vital statistics, passenger lists, abstracts of military records, and heraldry. Catalog: *Genealogy and Local History: A Bibliography.* Incl 12,000 microforms.

FL —TAMPA-HILLSBOROUGH COUNTY PUBLIC LIBRARY, 900 N Ashley St, Tampa, 33602. Joseph Hipp, Dir
Holdings: Vols (4000) Maps Pix
Notes: Books on southern history and genealogy. Florida map collection. Incl 6000 photographs of southwestern Florida, from 1885-1950; 35 maps from 1770-1875.

FLORIDA—HISTORY

CA —HOOVER INSTITUTION ON WAR, REVOLUTION & PEACE, Stanford University, Stanford, 94305. Milorad M Drachkovitch, Archivist
Holdings: Mss Pix
Notes: Papers of G B Stockton, 1911-59, incl correspondence, dispatches, reports, clippings, and photographs, relating to activities of the Commission for Reliefin Belgium, 1915-16, and of the American Relief Administration in Austria, 1919-20; to US and Florida politics, 1924-28;to US-Austrian relations, 1930-33; and to the

FLORIDA—HISTORY (cont.)

establishment of the Jacksonville, Florida, Naval Air Base. 11 ms boxes.

DC —LIBRARY OF CONGRESS, Manuscript Division, Washington, 20540. John C Broderick, Chief
Notes: The Hans P Kraus Collection of documents relating to colonial Spanish America, 1492-1819. Focusing on colonial Mexico, incl material on exploration, government, activities of the Inquisition, taxation and economic conditions, relations with the Indians and the French, and the impending loss of land to Anglo-American settlers. Also contains items concerning the history of Spanish Florida, Tezozomoc's chronicle on the history of the Aztecs, and mss describing the explorations of Amerigo Vespucci, Giovanni da Verrazzano, Alvar Nunez Cabeza de Vaca, Pedro de Ursua, and Lope de Aguirre.

FL —POLK COUNTY HISTORICAL & GENEALOGICAL LIBRARY, 495 N Hendry Ave, Bartow, 33830. LaCona R Padgett, Librn
Holdings: Vols (9000) Cat Maps Pix Microfilms
Budget: $18,500
Notes: Collection being cataloged. When completed, will have a computer printout of catalog. Incl 200 maps and 500 pictures, 4000 reels.

FL —UNIVERSITY OF MIAMI, Otto G Richter Library, PO Box 248214, Coral Gables, 33124. Frank Rodgers, Dir of Libraries
Holdings: Vols 12,305 Cat
Notes: The rare Floridiana collection incl a great variety of primary source materials such as mss, maps, photographs, scrapbooks, correspondence, clippings, etc. Particular subject strengths in this collection incl: Spanish exploration and colonization of Florida, the Florida Indians, wildlife conservation, landscaping, corporate records, etc. The rare Floridiana collection is complemented by a collection of titles ranging from the oldest to the very latest published books on Florida subjects. Inc 445 periodical titles.

FL —FLORIDA SOUTHERN COLLEGE, Roux Library, Johnson at McDonald, Lakeland, 33802. Larry Stallings, Special Collections Librn
Holdings: Vols (5100) Cat Mss
Notes: Incl Florida church histories and minutes of District Conventions. Methodist-related books and hymnals, and many old Bibles, are also included. Separate indexes.

FL —HISTORICAL ASSOCIATION OF SOUTHERN FLORIDA, Charlton W Tebeau Library of Florida History, 101 W Flager St, Miami, 33130. Rebecca A Smith, Cur of Research Materials
Holdings: Vols (3000) Cat Mss Maps Pix Slides Audiotapes 16mm Films Microforms
Notes: History of Florida, with emphasis on southern area. Less extensively, history of the Caribbean area, especially as related to Florida. Florida materials incl anthropology, archaeology, Indians of south Florida, incl Seminole Indians, Dade County history, and a complete run of the newspaper *The American Eagle* (1906-date), printed by Koreshan Unity, Estero, Florida. Incl 300 feet of mss, 1500 maps, 75,000 pictures, 2000 slides, 125 audiotapes, 25 16mm films, 200 microforms, 50 feet of vertical files, and 7000 postcards. Work in progress on guide to ms collection and on indexing of photographs. Also incl books and journals on museum science: conservation and preservation of museum materials.

FL —MIAMI-DADE PUBLIC LIBRARY SYSTEM, 1 Biscayne Blvd, Miami, 33132. Samuel J Boldrick, Librn
Holdings: Vols (4950) Cat Mss Maps Pix Audiotapes Microforms
Notes: Also incl 40,000 state and local documents; 700,000 newspaper clippings; and 195 reels of microfilmed newspaper clippings. Separate finding aids incl the *Miami Newspapers Index*, a computer generated index to six Miami newspapers which is on an in house on-line database.

†FL —ORLANDO PUBLIC LIBRARY, Orlando, 32801.
Notes: Books by Floridians; books on Florida.

FL —UNIVERSITY OF WEST FLORIDA, John C Pace Library, Pensacola, 32514. Dean Debolt, Head, Special Collections
Holdings: Vols 1550 Cat Mss Maps Pix Slides Microforms
Notes: History of Florida before 1865; almost exclusively West Florida and Pensacola after 1865. Catalog of ms collection: *The First One Hundred* and an article describing the collection in *Manuscripts*, vol 25, no 1, Winter 1973; and *The Second One Hundred* (pamphlet, 1978). Collection incl 800,000 ms pieces, 3000 maps, 10,000 pictures (chiefly photographs of early 20th century Pensacola). Also incl speeches of early 20th century legislators.

FL —SAINT AUGUSTINE HISTORICAL SOCIETY LIBRARY, 271 Charlotte St, Saint Augustine, 32084. Jacqueline K Fretwell, Librn
Holdings: Vols 7500 Cat Mss Maps Pix Slides Phonorecords Audiotapes 16mm Films Microforms
Notes: St Augustine and early Florida history.

FL —FLORIDA STATE UNIVERSITY, Robert Manning Strozier Library, Maps Dept, Tallahassee, 32306. Marianne Donnell, Map Librn
Holdings: Vols (3314) Cat Maps Microforms
Notes: Emphasis on Florida and Florida history. Also a depository for USGS topographic maps of the entire US, National Ocean Survey nautical charts of Atlantic and Gulf Coasts, Army Topographic Command maps, and various special sets issued by National Ocean Survey. Incl 1140 vols of books, bibliographies, and periodicals; 2070 atlases; 136,000 sheet maps; 104 microfilm reels.

FL —TAMPA-HILLSBOROUGH COUNTY PUBLIC LIBRARY, 900 N Ashley St, Tampa, 33602. Joseph Hipp, Dir
Holdings: Vols (4000) Maps Pix
Notes: Books on southern history and genealogy. Florida map collection. Incl 6000 photographs of southwestern Florida, from 1885-1950; 35 maps from 1770-1875.

FL —UNIVERSITY OF SOUTH FLORIDA, Library, Tampa, 33620. J B Dobkin, Special Collections Librn
Holdings: Vols 20,000 Cat Mss Maps Pix Slides Phonorecords Audiotapes Videotapes 16mm Films Filmstrips Microforms
Budget: ($7500)
Notes: Florida

FL —ROLLINS COLLEGE, Mills Memorial Library, Winter Park, 32789. Patricia J Delks, Dir of Libraries
Holdings: Vols 1500 Cat Maps Pix

FLORIDA—PICTURES, ILLUSTRATIONS, ETC.

FL —FLORIDA DEPT OF STATE, Florida State Archives, Florida Photographic Collection, R A Gray Bldg, Tallahassee, 32301. Mrs Allen Morris, Archives Supervisor
Holdings: Maps Pix Slides Films Audiotapes
Notes: Areas of emphasis within the collection: (1) Florida government. There is a complete file of governors' photos, and many photos of legislative sessions and legislators going back to the late 1800s. (2) Stanley J Morrow. Mr Morrow learned his craft under Mathew B Brady. He worked in Florida from 1882-1887. Collection has several hundred of his glass negatives that document a period of southward expansion in Florida. (3) Alvan S Harper, Tallahassee portrait artist; 1700 glass negatives of Tallahassee people between 1885-1910. (4) W A Fishbaugh. Several thousand photographs of the "boom," Miami and Coral Gables in the 1920s. (5) Charles A Mosier, Charles Torrey Simpson and J K Small; 500 photographs of Florida flora, made by these famous naturalists, mostly in South Dade County. (6) Added March, 1983; 2200 glass and nitrate negatives by J K Small. (7) Collectionalso incl 40,000 negatives (4x5) made by Harvey Slade in Tallahassee, 1946-1975, predominantly portraits; also 15,000 news story negatives (4x5 and 2x2) relative to local and state government, 1957-1969, unprinted, from *The Tallahassee Democrat*. (8) 39,000 (4x5) negatives and contact prints deposited by the Florida Dept of Commerce, 1946-late 1970s. Subjects incl Florida cities, attractions, industries, beaches, festivals, boating, fishing, forts, gardens, hotels, highways, lighthouses, monuments, museums and recreations. (9) 25,000 (8x10, 4x5 & 35mm) negatives by Jacksonville commercial photographer Gordon Spottswood & Son, 1916-1967. Subjects incl Jacksonville people (individuals and groups), street scenes, commercial buildings, Atlantic Coast Line & Seaboard Airline Railroads, and Boy Scout Activities. (10) 15,000 (4x5) negativesfrom Seldomridge portrait studio in Tampa. Tampa people from the 1940s to the 1970s.

FLORIDA—POLITICS AND GOVERNMENT

FL —FLORIDA STATE UNIVERSITY, Robert Manning Strozier Library, Special Collections Dept, Tallahassee, 32306. Opal M Free, Head, Special Collections
Notes: The official papers, documents, photographs, recordings, and memorabilia of US Representative Claude Pepper. Incl the papers, photographs, and memorabilia of his wife, Mildred Irene Webster Pepper (706, 536 items).

FLORIDA, CUBANS IN see Cubans in Florida

FLORIDA AUTHORS see Authors, Florida

FLOTATION

MD —US BUREAU OF MINES, Avondale Metallurgy Research Center, Library, 4900 La Salle Rd, Avondale, 20782. Paul F Moran, Librn
Holdings: Vols (11,000) Cat
Budget: ($35,000)
Notes: Incl corrosion, flotation, particulate mineralogy.

FLOUR AND FEED TRADE

CA —STANFORD UNIVERSITY, Food Research Institute Library, Stanford, 94305. Charles C Milford, Librn
Holdings: Vols (11,595) Cat Maps Pix Microforms
Budget: ($8046)
Notes: The economic aspects of the production, trade, disposition, and prices of food, feed, and fiber commodities throughout the world. Incl 25,000 pamphlets.

MN —MINNESOTA HISTORICAL SOCIETY LIBRARY, 690 Cedar St, Saint Paul, 55101. Patricia C Harpole, Chief of Reference Library; Bonnie G Wilson, Head of Special Libraries

NY —BORDEN FOODS INC, Research Centre Library, 600 N Franklin St, Syracuse, 13204. Carol Lenz-Taylor, Librn
Holdings: Vols (1800) Cat
Notes: Incl 12 vertical file drawers and 10, 000 patents.

MB —CANADIAN GRAIN COMMISSION, Library, 303 Main St, Winnipeg, R3C 3G7, Can. Jim Blanchard, Librn
Holdings: Vols (7500) Cat Mss Maps Slides Microforms
Budget: ($20,000)

FLOWER, ROSWELL P.

NY —STATE UNIVERSITY OF NEW YORK, COLLEGE AT OSWEGO, Penfield Library, Oswego, 13126. Anne Commerton, Dir
Holdings: / / Uncat Mss Pix
Notes: Flower (1835-1899) was an active member of the Democratic Party and served several terms as a New York Congressman and was Governor of New York from 1892

FLOWER, ROSWELL P. (cont.)

to 1895. The collection incl correspondence, printed speeches, newspaper clippings, financial records, books, a scrapbook, and photographs. 10 linear inches. Unpublished index to correspondence.

FLOWER ARRANGEMENT

AL —BIRMINGHAM BOTANICAL GARDENS, Horace Hammond Memorial Library, 2612 Lane Park Road, Birmingham, 35223. Ida Burns, Librn
Holdings: Vols 2800 Cat Pix Films Slides VF

DE —WILMINGTON GARDEN CENTER LIBRARY, 503 Market Street Mall, Wilmington, 19801. Bonnie J Swan Day, Admin Asst; Karen Bidus, Librn
Holdings: Vols (1500)
Notes: Library open to the public, only circulates to members.

IL —JAMES MORETZ LIBRARY, 3347 N. Clark St, Chicago, 60657.
Holdings: Vols 4500 Cat
Budget: ($4000)

NY —GARDEN CENTER OF ROCHESTER INC, Library, 5 Castle Park, Rochester, 14620. Dorothea Baschnagel, Librn
Holdings: Vols (3000)
Notes: Gardening and home landscaping; plant identification; decorative use of plants; 19th century gardening. 700 bound periodicals, 30 periodical subscriptions.

OH —GARDEN CENTER OF GREATER CLEVELAND, Eleanor Squire Library, 11030 East Blvd, Cleveland, 44106. Richard T Isaacson, Librn
Notes: The Warren C Corning Collection of Horticultural Classics. The Flowering Plant Index of Illustration and Information.

OH —KINGWOOD CENTER, Library, 900 Park Ave W, Mansfield, 44906. Timothy Gardner, Horticulturist
Holdings: Vols 8500
Notes: Espec ornamental horticulture, home gardening, landscaping, and floral arrangements. Incl 12,000 35mm slides of plants.

ON —CIVIC GARDEN CENTRE LIBRARY, 777 Lawrence Ave E, Don Mills, M3C 1P2, Can. Pamela MacKenzie, Librn
Holdings: Vols (5000) Cat
Budget: ($3200)

FLOWER BOOKS, ILLUSTRATED

†CO —DENVER BOTANIC GARDENS, Helen Fowler Library, 909 York St, Denver, 80206. Solange G Gignac, Librn
Notes: Emphasis on Bromeliada Literature; horticulture; Colorado, Oregon, and Rocky Mountains Region botany; landscape architecture; juvenile horticultural and botanical literature. Incl over 5000 pamphlets on botany and horticulture; also, 197 watercolors of Colorado wildflowers by Emma Irvine, and 250 of Oregon by Lillian Hallock.

MO —MISSOURI BOTANICAL GARDEN LIBRARY, PO Box 299, Saint Louis, 63166. M R Crosby, Dir of Research

PA —HUNT INSTITUTE FOR BOTANICAL DOCUMENTATION, Hunt Botanical Library, Carnegie-Mellon University, Pittsburgh, 15213. Bernadette G Callery, Librn
Holdings: Vols 23,000 Cat Pix
Notes: Collection of primarily historical botany and plant taxonomy, especially 1730-1840. Includes approximately 500 15th through 17th century herbals, extensive collection of 18th and 19th century color-plate works, floras and monographic works, and other works on natural history, early gardening and horticulture, and travel, particularly that dealing with plant exploration and introduction. Extensive biographical materials, on people in plant sciences. Reference collection and extensive documentation in botanical bibliography, especially concerning books published before 1850. Includes as separate collections, the Strandell Collection of Linnaeana and the Michel Adanson Library. Over 800 items described in *Catalogue of Botanical Books in the Collection of Rachel McMasters Miller Hunt, 1477-1800* (Pittsburgh, 1958-1960).

FLOWER CHILDREN see Youth Movement

FLOWER LANGUAGE

IL —JAMES MORETZ LIBRARY, 3347 N. Clark St, Chicago, 60657.
Holdings: Vols 500

FLOWERS

DC —LIBRARY OF CONGRESS, Manuscript Division, Washington, 20540. John C Broderick, Chief
Notes: The papers of Luther Burbank (1849-1926), incl approximately 10,000 items range in date over much of his life span. Contains correspondence, writings, scientific notes and records, ledgers, account books, scrapbooks, photographs, and journal reprints and other printed matter.

IL —MORTON ARBORETUM, Sterling Morton Library, Lisle, 60532. Ian MacPhail, Librn
Holdings: Vols (20,000) Cat Maps Pix
Budget: ($10,000)
Notes: The library is especially concerned with the literature of woody plants (trees and shrubs) of north temperate zones but has substantial holdings in the taxonomy and systematics of plants in general, both wild and cultivated, flora of different parts of the world, and a growing collection on plant monographs. Also about 2000 pictures. Described in *The Morton Arboretum* Quarterly, vol 9, no 4 (Winter 1973), pp 56-61.

MA —NEW ENGLAND WILD FLOWER SOCIETY, INC, Lawrence Newcomb Library, Hemenway Rd, Framingham, 01701. Mary M Walker, Librn
Holdings: Vols (2500)
Budget: ($1000)
Notes: Incl 15,000 slides (35mm) and 4 vertical files.

MN —UNIVERSITY OF MINNESOTA, Landscape Arboretum, Andersen Horticultural Library, 3675 Arboretum Drive, Box 39, Chanhassen, 55317. June Rogier, Head
Holdings: Vols (8000)

NY —NEW YORK BOTANICAL GARDEN LIBRARY, Bronx, 10458. Charles R Long, Asst Vice Pres & Dir
Holdings: Vols (385,000) Cat Mss Pix Slides Microforms VF
Budget: ($356,000)
Notes: One of the largest botanical collections in the world. Covers botany (150,000 vols), botanists (3000), horticulture (45,000), plant diseases (25,000), plant physiology (15,000), history of botany (1500), conservation of natural resources (15,000), gardening (13,000), paleobotany (7000), ecology (20,000), forestry (5000), medical botany (3000), agriculture (9000) and biology (20,000). Reference library; materials do not circulate, except via standard inter-library loan. About 5000 vols uncataloged. Incl archives, art and vertical files. An OCLC library.

†NC —UNIVERSITY OF NORTH CAROLINA, CHAPEL HILL, Department of Botany Library, 301 Coker Hall 010-A, Chapel Hill, 27514. William R Burk, Botany Librn
Notes: The mycology collection incl some 6000 pamphlets. It contains papers of the following scientists: William C Coker, John N Couch, Lindsay F Olive, mycologists; also, Victor A Greulach, plant pathologist. The mycology catalog is in preparation (1983), and will provide author, title, and subject access.

OH —CLEVELAND PUBLIC LIBRARY, Science & Technology Dept, 325 Superior Ave, Cleveland, 44114. Jean Z Piety, Head
Holdings: Cat
Notes: Part of the Gardening Collection, which emphasizes the history of gardens around the world, domestic landscape planning and planting, incl flower gardening, annuals and perennials and indoor plants.

PA —LONGWOOD GARDENS, INC, Library, Kennett Square, 19348. Enola Jane N Teeter, Librn

ON —AGRICULTURE CANADA, Plant Research Library, Research Branch, Central Experimental Farm 49, Ottawa, K1A 0C6, Can. Mrs E Gavora, Librn
Holdings: Vols (10,500) Cat Maps Microforms
Notes: One of the most extensive botanical collections in Canada, especially in the taxonomy of higher plants and fungi. Contains many of the basic works from the starting point of botany in 1753 to date. Major botanical works of Linnaeus and others, covering flora of land areas of most parts of the world.

FLOWERS—ARRANGEMENT see Flower Arrangement

FLOWERS—CALIFORNIA see California—Flowers

FLOWERS—CLASSIFICATION

MI —UNIVERSITY OF MICHIGAN, Herbarium Library, University Herbarium, 2003 N University Bldg, Ann Arbor, 48109. Robert L Shaffer, Dir, Herbarium
Holdings: Vols (22,000) Cat Mss Maps Microforms
Notes: Systematic Botany including floristics, revisions and monographs in all groups of plants. Collection incl maps, mss (fieldbooks, correspondence, etc), photographs, microfiches, and approx 100,000 reprints that are not officially part of the University Library. These are indexed and are available to qualified scholars. Incl botanical libraries of Parke, Davis & Co, Harley H Bartlett, Bruce Fink (lichens), Howard A Kelly (mycology).

FLOWERS—PICTORIAL WORKS

CA —POMONA PUBLIC LIBRARY, Special Collections, 625 S Garey Ave, PO Box 2271, Pomona, 91766. David Streeter, Librn
Holdings: / / Uncat Pix Slides
Notes: Brooking Tatum collection of California Flora: 125 8x10 color prints and 50 35mm color transparencies; Estella E Howes water color paintings of local flora (98 paintings); Cyril Albritt oil painting.

FL —FLORIDA DEPT OF STATE, Florida State Archives, Florida Photographic Collection, R A Gray Bldg, Tallahassee, 32301. Mrs Allen Morris, Archives Supervisor
Holdings: Maps Pix Slides Films Audiotapes
Notes: Charles A Mosier, Charles Torrey Simpson and J K Small. 500 photographs of Florida flora, made by these famous naturalists, mostly in South Dade county. Also incl 2200 glass and nitrate negatives by J K Small.

FLOWERS, WILD see Wild Flowers

FLOYD, WILLIAM J.

AZ —NORTHERN ARIZONA UNIVERSITY, Special Collection Library, CU Box 6022, Flagstaff, 86011. Peter M Whiteley, Coordr/Archivist; William Mullane, Librn
Notes: Floyd was surgeon of E F Beale's wagon road expedition from Ft Smith Arkansas to the Colorado River; incl diary, 1858-1859. Original in Henry E Huntington Library.

FLUID MECHANICS

CA —INTERNATIONAL BUSINESS MACHINES RESEARCH LIBRARY, 5600 Cottle Rd, San Jose, 95193. Phil Grincewich, Mgr Technical Information
Holdings: Vols (13,500) Cat
Notes: Incl 21,000 vols of 770 journals. On-line search facility. Vols are divided into three libraries, Technical Research,

FLUID MECHANICS (cont.)

Technical Information, and Programing. Not open to public.
IL —ARGONNE NATIONAL LABORATORY, Reactor Science/ Engineering Branch Library, 9700 S Cass Ave, Argonne, 60439. Marion Benson, Librn
Notes: Fluid dynamics. Incl 10,000 vols monographs, 200 current journals, a comprehensive collection of AEC, ERDA, DOE, and NRC scientific and technical reports. Materials may be used by the public in the library by prior arrangement. Photocopies may be supplied for interlibrary loan, for which a processing and handling charge is made.
MA —AVCO EVERETT RESEARCH LABORATORY, INC, Library, 2385 Revere Beach Parkway, Everett, 02149. Lorraine T Nazzaro, Librn
Holdings: Vols (24,000) Cat Maps Microforms
Budget: ($150,000)
Notes: Incl 50,000 reports.
WI —MILWAUKEE SCHOOL OF ENGINEERING, Library, 500 E Kilbourn Ave, PO Box 644, Milwaukee, 53201. Mary Ann Schmidt, Head Librn
Holdings: Vols (34,500) Cat
Budget: $215,800

FLUORIDES

OH —GOODYEAR ATOMIC CORP, Technical Library, PO Box 628, Piketon, 45661. Robert Holland, Supvr
Holdings: Vols (50,000) Cat Mss Microforms
Notes: Uranium enrichment; gas flow, heat transfer, isotope analyses, uranium-fluoride chemistry.

FLUTE

DC —LIBRARY OF CONGRESS, Music Division, Washington, 20540.
Holdings: Cat Mss Maps Pix Slides Microforms
Notes: The Dayton C Miller Flute Collection, incl nearly 1600 instruments, plus music and books.

FLY TYING see Flies, Artificial

FLYING see Flight—History

FLYING CARS

CA —SAN DIEGO AERO-SPACE MUSEUM, N Paul Whittier Historical Aviation Library, 2001 Pan American Plaza, Balboa Park, San Diego, 92101. B C Reynolds, Archivist
Holdings: // Uncat Microforms

FLYING MACHINES see Aeronautics—History

FLYING SAUCERS see Unidentified Flying Objects (Ufo)

FLYING TIGERS see American Volunteer Group (Flying Tigers)

FLYING WINGS

CA —SAN DIEGO AERO-SPACE MUSEUM, N Paul Whittier Historical Aviation Library, 2001 Pan American Plaza, Balboa Park, San Diego, 92101. B C Reynolds, Archivist
Holdings: // Uncat Microforms

FLYNN, HAZEL

CA —LOS ANGELES PUBLIC LIBRARY, Frances Howard Goldwyn Hollywood Regional Library, 1623 Ivar Ave, Los Angeles, 90028. Sally Dumaux, Librn
Holdings: Vols (100,000) Cat Mss Pix VF
Budget: ($60,000)
Notes: A general and a research collection covering motion pictures, radio broadcasting, and television. Over 2000 motion picture and television scripts. Biographical information on actors and actresses. Casts, credits, and other production information on over 1500 motion pictures from the 1920s to the present. Collections also include posters, lobby cards, souvenir programs, scrapbooks, vertical files, and over 3000 publicity stills. Including the following Special Collections: Fred Archer Collection, photographs, including the Hunchback of Notre Dame (1923), and personalities of the stage and screen, 1907-1930; Gilbert A Adrian, designer, sketches and photographs; Hazel Flynn, publicist, correspondence and photographs.

FODDER see Feeds

FOERSTER, ADOLPH M.

PA —UNIVERSITY OF PITTSBURGH, Music Library, B-31 Music Bldg, Pittsburgh, 15260. Norris L Stephens, Music Librn
Holdings: Vols 290// Cat Mss
Notes: Kniseley, S Philip, "Catalogue of the manuscripts and printed music of Adolph M Foerster in the Music Library, University of Pittsburgh," 1960.

FOERSTER, NORMAN

NC —DUKE UNIVERSITY, William R Perkins Library, Jay B Hubbell Center for American Literary Historiography, Durham, 27706. Erma Whittington, Librn
Notes: 77,312 items, including manuscripts, pictures, clippings, and correspondence. "The objective of the Center is to gather the papers and materials of significant scholars and critics in American literary history." The Center is a part of the Perkins Library Manuscripts Department.

FOLEY, JOHN L.

NY —COLUMBIA UNIVERSITY LIBRARIES, Rare Book & Manuscript Library, 801 Butler Library, 535 W 114 St, New York, 10027. Kenneth A Lohf, Librn
Holdings: Pix
Notes: 163 photographs of and relating to the poet, Thomas S Jones, and his friend John L Foley. Restricted use.

FOLEY, MARTHA

MA —BOSTON UNIVERSITY, Mugar Memorial Library, Special Collections Dept, 771 Commonwealth Ave, Boston, 02215. Howard B Gotlieb, Dir
Holdings: //Cat Mss Correspondence

FOLK ART

CA —CRAFT AND FOLK ART MUSEUM, Library, 5814 Wilshire Blvd, Los Angeles, 90036. Joan M Benedetti, Museum Librn
Holdings: Vols (2000) Slides VF
Notes: Incl 2000 books; 70 journal subscriptions; artists' biographical files: 6 file drawers; clipping files: 8 file drawers; 20,000 slides. Representation of the material culture of all people, traditional and contemporary expressions. Incl visual and printed information on ethnic, traditional, popular, decorative, idiosyncratic, and contemporary crafts as well as vernacular architecture, handmade houses, and design. Information about and for professional artists on health hazards, conservation, and career management. Anthropological and art historical works; exhibition catalogues; slides, photographs, audiocassettes; clipping and pamphlet files. Contemporary Slide Registry of Craftspeople and extensive biographical files of contemporary craft artists. Information and referral files of craft related galleries, shops, festivals, organizations, etc.
CA —MONTEREY PENINSULA MUSEUM OF ART, Library, 559 Pacific St, Monterey, 93940. Rick Deragon, Asst Cur
Notes: Folk art is emphasized, although other arts are represented.
DC —LIBRARY OF CONGRESS, Prints & Photographs Div, Washington, 20540.
Holdings: 93 Items
Notes: The William A Barnhill Collection is a photographic study of the inhabitants of western North Carolina (1914-17) performing such daily tasks as milling, weaving, preparing food, and making baskets, shingles, and pottery.
MA —OLD STURBRIDGE VILLAGE, Research Library, Sturbridge, 01566. Theresa Rini Percy, Librn
Holdings: Cat Pix
Notes: New England, to 1850.
NM —MUSEUM OF NEW MEXICO, Museum of International Folk Art Library, 706 Camino Lejo, Santa Fe, 87501. Judith Sellars, Librn
Holdings: Vols (8000) Cat
Notes: Folk art of all countries, incl such subjects as costume, ceramics, textiles, furniture. Restricted use: noncirculating.
NY —HISTORICAL SOCIETY OF EARLY AMERICAN DECORATION, 19 Dove St, Albany, 12210. Doris Fry, Dir; Laura Olf, Librn
Holdings: Cat Pix Slides
Notes: The Library is housed with the Museum Collection of the Society. Incl examples of 19th century American country painting on tin, stenciling on wood and tin, bronzing decoration on wood, English stencilled tin and wood, bronzed items, painted objects, reverse painting on glass and examples of other decorating techniques of the period. Also included is a large collection of painted recordings of designs from early articles. Many of these were done by Esther Stevens Brazer in the 1930s. Another large collection has been added since that time. The library material is related to this interest. See *The Decorator*, official publication of the Historical Society of Early American Decoration. Other publications: *The Ornamented Chair* and *The Ornamented Tray* (both ed by Zilla Rider Lea), *Antique Decorations* by Brazer.
PA —JANKOLA LIBRARY AND SLOVAK ARCHIVES, Danville, 17821.
Holdings: Vols 500
VT —SHELBURNE MUSEUM, Library, Shelburne, 05482. Barbara Reenstierna, Librn
Holdings: Vols 700 Cat Pix
VA —COLONIAL WILLIAMSBURG FOUNDATION, Abby Aldrich Rockefeller Folk Art Center, PO Box C, Williamsburg, 23187. Anne E Watkins, Registrar
Holdings: Vols (5000) Cat
Notes: American folk arts and crafts. Periodicals of current art, antiques, and history. Researchers wishing to use the library are requested to call the museum for an appointment.

FOLK DANCING

CA —THE POLISH ARTS AND CULTURE FOUNDATION, 1290 Sutter St, San Francisco, 94109. Wanda Tomczykowska, President
Holdings: Pix
Notes: Portraits of Polish personalities in art and culture, photographs of costumes, dances, observance of traditions, historical events. Color photographs of California.
IL —CHICAGO PUBLIC LIBRARY, Art Section, Fine Arts Division, 78 E Washington St, Chicago, 60602. Rosalinda I Hack, Fine Arts Division Chief; Yvonne S Brown, Head, Art Section
Holdings: Vols 2500
Notes: Reference and circulating collection of books, periodicals, pamphlets, and videotapes on all aspects of the dance eg ballet, social dance, square dance, jazz and folkdance. Focus of the collection is on ballet, history, biographies of dancers, and dance instruction. Subject is supplemented by a dance videotape collection, the *Folk Dance Index* a comprehensive index to descriptions of folkdances of all nations. Special Collections: Eliza Stigler Dance Collection of 200 dance books on ballet and dance history with particular emphasis on Spanish Dance. Ruth Page Archives: small collection of memorabilia documents the career of Ms Page. Reference collection of dance video tapes that document notable dance performances, from the past and

FOLK DANCING (cont.)

present by well known dancers and dance groups. Subject concentration is that of ballet, with some examples of ethnic dance. These is alsoa collection of tapes that document Chicago area dance groups, dancers, and choreographers. A file to the contents of the tapes is available.

IL —UNIVERSITY OF ILLINOIS, URBANA/CHAMPAIGN, Library, Applied Life Studies Library, 1408 W Gregory Dr, Urbana, 61801.
Holdings: Vols (38,000) Cat Pix Microforms
Notes: Contains books on ballet, contemporary dance, folk and national dances, ethnic dance, dance history, choreography, dance notation, dance therapy. Also collected are programs of dance concerts and performances of the 20th century.

KS —WICHITA PUBLIC LIBRARY, Art & Music Division, 223 S Main, Wichita, 67202. Leonard Messineo, Jr, Head, Art & Music Division; Deborah Hamilton, Special Collections Librn
Holdings: Uncat Audiotapes Videotape Pix
Notes: Alice Bauman Dance Symposia Collection. Contains 300 hours of audio tapes, 1 hour-long video tape, several hundred photographs, and fugitive material of the American Dance Symposia held in Wichita from 1968-1972. The symposia covered all dance idioms-ballet, modern, jazz, folk, ethnic, dance education and therapy-and featured such notable figures such as Leonide Massine, Martha Hill, William Christensen, Alfonso Cimber, Toni Intravaia, James Clouser, Eleo Pomare, Juana de Laban, and many others. Characterized by the *Kansas City Star* as the "most distinguished faculties of fine artists ever assembled in the contemporary world of dance."

NY —NEW YORK PUBLIC LIBRARY, Performing Arts Research Center, Dance Collection, 111 Amsterdam Ave, New York, 10023. Genevieve Oswald, Cur
Budget: ($9,280)
Notes: Over 3000 published volumes, microfilms, as well as American and foreign periodicals, articles, newspaper clippings, photographs, prints, manuscripts, and films. Extensive coverage of American and European folk and social dance. Good representation of non-Western dance with particular emphasis on Asia. Collections containing music, directions, or descriptions of over 15,000 individual dances have been indexed for inclusion in the catalog: *Dictionary Catalog of the Dance Collection,* published by G K Hall, Boston, 1974, 10 vols. Annual supplements: *Bibliographic Guide to Dance,* also published by G K Hall.
See also entry under Asian Dance; US Works Progress Administration, New York (City); Dance Index

PA —JANKOLA LIBRARY AND SLOVAK ARCHIVES, Danville, 17821.
Holdings: Vols (800)
Notes: Folk instruments and dancing.

†BC —VANCOUVER PUBLIC LIBRARY, Vancouver, V6Z 1X5, Can.
Notes: Indexes to folk dances; children's songs; children's plays. No longer updated.

FOLK DANCING, CZECH

IL —AMERICAN SOKOL EDUCATIONAL AND PHYSICAL CULTURE, 6424 W Cermak Road, Berwyn, 60402. Annette Schabowski, Librn
Holdings: Vols 2000 Pix
Notes: Incl theses and dissertations on Czech life, folk dancing, gymnastics, etc.

FOLK MEDICINE

KS —WICHITA PUBLIC LIBRARY, Art & Music Division, 223 S Main, Wichita, 67202. Leonard Messineo, Jr, Head, Art & Music Division; Deborah Hamilton, Special Collections Librn
Notes: Joan O'Bryant Kansas Folklore Collection. Contains approximately 200 hours of folkmusic and oral histories on tape; over 27,000 note cards covering topics such as anecdotes, beliefs, customs, games, jokes, medicines and cures, proverbs, recipes, rhymes, riddles, sayings, songs, speech and dialect, etc; 102 research papers covering family histories, town and area histories, biographies, tales, recipes, etc; and well over 70 mounted quilt blocks-covering the folk history of Kansas. This material was collected by Joan O'Bryant and her students from 1947-1964, the period in which she taught Folklore and English at Wichita State University.

FOLK MUSIC

CA —CALIFORNIA STATE UNIVERSITY, HAYWARD, Library, Hayward, 94542. Melissa Rose, Dir
Holdings: Vols (15,986) Cat Phonorecords
Budget: ($21,000)
Notes: The score collection covers the entire range of instrumental and vocal concert music, incl collected works of various composers, and representative collections of hymnals, folk music, musical comedy, and some popular music. Sound recordings range from ethnomusicological collections to electronic music. Emphasis is on concert music, but there is a large collection of jazz and a selective collection of popular music. Separate catalog.

CA —SOCIETY OF CALIFORNIA PIONEERS, Library, 456 McAllister St, San Francisco, 94102. Grace E Baker, Librn
Holdings: Vols (12,000) Cat Mss Maps Pix Microforms
Notes: California history, especially the gold rush and the San Francisco earthquake, Sherman collection of early California music, business letterheads of early California firms, San Francisco City Directories 1850-1944, records of California Battalion 1846-47, ms material on overland diaries, ships' logs and passenger lists. Also, large photograph collection.

DC —LIBRARY OF CONGRESS, American Folklife Center, Archive of Folk Culture, Washington, 20540.
Notes: The Laura Boulton Collection is comprised of 1312 discs and 367 tape recordings of traditional vocal and instrumental music of Canada, Africa, Southeast Asia, American Indians, and Eskimos, collected chiefly from the 1930s through the 1960s by Dr Boulton. Recordings and papers of Woody Guthrie. Vance Randolph's papers, photographs, and field recordings of Ozark folk music, 1930s - 1960s.

IN —MORRISSON-REEVES LIBRARY, 80 N Sixth St, Richmond, 47374. Harriet E Bard, Librn
Holdings: Cat
Notes: All recordings circulate and are long playing, monaural and stereo-- 4527 adult and 392 juvenile discs. Mainly classical music but incl spoken records, musicals, folk music and historical jazz.

KY —WESTERN KENTUCKY UNIVERSITY, Kentucky Building, Folklore, Folklife & Oral History Archives, Bowling Green, 42101. Patricia M Hodges, Archivist
Holdings: Cat Mss Audiotapes Videotapes
Notes: Archive contains manuscripts of field collection projects done by students and faculty. There is a large folk song collection in manuscript and tapes of local performers of traditional songs and music. Materials generally relate to Kentucky and surrounding areas; or to country music and traditional music. 3500 tapes; 135 linear ft of manuscripts.

LA —TULANE UNIVERSITY, Howard-Tilton Memorial Library, Special Collections Div, William Ransom Hogan Jazz Archive, 7001 Freret, New Orleans, 70118. Richard B Allen, Acting Cur; Alma D Williams, Assistant to the Cur
Holdings: Vols (100,000) Cat Mss Pix Slides Phonorecords Audiotapes Videotapes 16mm Films Microforms
Budget: ($90,000)
Notes: Jazz music and musicians. Outstanding collection, incl books, music scores, serials, catalogs and other archival material. Music, history, etc.
See also entry under Jazz

MI —DETROIT PUBLIC LIBRARY, Music & Performing Arts Dept, 5201 Woodward, Detroit, 48202. Agatha Pfeiffer Kalkanis, Chief
Holdings: Cat
Notes: Over 5000 song collections of all types. Incl all collections in standard indexes (Sears, DeCharms & Breed, Leigh, etc). Printed indexes supplemented by extensive song index on cards in department. Also incl about 1000 commercial recordings of folk music.
See also entry under Songs

NE —UNIVERSITY OF NEBRASKA-LINCOLN, Don L Love Library, Lincoln, 68588. Joseph G Svoboda, University Archivist
Holdings: Vols (8000)// Uncat Mss Pix Slides Phonorecords Audiotapes Microforms
Notes: This is an extensive collection belonging to the folklorist Benjamin A Botkin, about 500 linear ft, consisting of various types of materials. Main emphasis is American folklore, although folklore of all nations is included.

NY —NEW YORK PUBLIC LIBRARY, Schomburg Center for Research in Black Culture, 515 Lenox Ave, New York, 10037. Catherine J Lenix Hooker, Interim Administrator
Notes: A repository for 10,000 phonodiscs and 2000 tapes covering African and West Indian folk music, early blues, and jazz.

NY —YIVO INSTITUTE FOR JEWISH RESEARCH, Library & Archives, 1048 Fifth Ave, New York, 10028. Dina Abramowicz, Librn; Marek Web, Archivist
Holdings: Cat Mss Slides
Notes: Collections of Jewish music organizations in pre-World War I Russia, and collections of individual musicians and composers, among them the Bernstein collection from Vilna and Leo Low collection from New York. Secular, liturgical, folk music, theatrical songs in the form of sheet music is represented. Partially cataloged.

NY —STATE UNIVERSITY OF NEW YORK, COLLEGE AT PLATTSBURGH, Feinberg Library, Special Collections, 153 Hawkins Hall, Plattsburgh, 12901. Joseph G Swinyer, Librn
Holdings: Cat Mss Maps Pix Phonorecords Scores
See also entry under New York (State) - History

NC —APPALACHIAN STATE UNIVERSITY, Belk Library, Appalachian Collection, Boone, 28608. Eric J Olson, Librn
Holdings: Vols (12,000) Cat Mss Maps Pix Slides Phonorecords Audiotapes
Budget: ($4000)
Notes: The Appalachian Collection incl the Fry Collectin of handmade quilts and coverlets; the York Collection of folk songs and ballads, plus tapes; the I G Greer Collection of Folk Songs and Ballads; the Amos Abrams ballad collection; artifacts, incl the Tatum Collection of household items, furniture, and farm implements; Daniel Boone loom; oral history tapes; the Jack Guy Collection of tapes of area music and photographs; and regional genealogy. This is a very comprehensive study on the Southern Appalachian Region. Separate catalog for the collection.

NC —CUMBERLAND COUNTY PUBLIC LIBRARY, North Carolina Foreign Language Center, 328 Gillespie St, Fayetteville, 28301. Patrick M Valentine, Coordinator
Holdings: Phonorecords
Notes: Represents language groups and countries around the world, incl 300 cataloged records.

PA —JANKOLA LIBRARY AND SLOVAK ARCHIVES, Danville, 17821.
Holdings: Vols 800
Notes: Folk instruments and Dances.

TN —COUNTRY MUSIC FOUNDATION, Library & Media Center, 4 Music Sq E, Nashville, 37203. Charlie Seemann, Dir
Holdings: Vols (6000) Mss Pix Slides

FOLK MUSIC (cont.)

Phonorecords Audiotapes Videotapes 16mm Films Microforms
Notes: The largest collection in the world dealing with American country music. Related subject areas are also included--Anglo-American folksong, popular music in general (soul, jazz, rock and roll, rhythm and blues, etc), recorded sound technology, music law.

VA —UNIVERSITY OF VIRGINIA, Alderman Library, Manuscripts Dept, Charlottesville, 22901. Edmund Berkeley Jr, Cur
Holdings: Cat Mss Pix
Notes: Virginia Folklore Collection (23,000 items) incl the following collection: Virginia WPA Folklore Files, compiled ca 1936-1943, under US Works Project Administration, ca 8000 items. Black and white folklore and folk music collected by field workers from informants throughout Virginia. Incl ms reports, phonorecords. Described in Rosenberg, Bruce A (comp), *The Folksongs of Virginia: A Checklist of the WPA Holdings in the Alderman Library, University of Virginia* (Charlottesville: University Press of Virginia, 1969); also, typescript and computer printed guides--Charles L Perdue, Jr, and others (comps), *The White Folklore of the Virginia WPA Files: A Checklist ...* (Charlottesville, 1973); Thomas Barden and others (comps), *Afro-American Folklore of the WPA Folklore Files in the Alderman Library ...* (Charlottesville, 1973).

WI —MILWAUKEE PUBLIC LIBRARY, 814 W Wisconsin Ave, Milwaukee, 53233. Donald J Sager, City Librn
Holdings: Vols Cat
Notes: An extensive general music literature collection incl classical, contemporary, jazz, and musical biographies, as well as the most significant reference works in music. Also incl 46,708 sound recordings, 73,150 historical recorded sound collection, 20,000 historic popular song collection, and WPA copied music. Local area music materials incl concert programs and newspaper clippings.

NB —MOUNT ALLISON UNIVERSITY, Ralph Pickard Bell Library, Sackville, E0A 3C0, Can. M Fancy, Librn
Holdings: Vols (13,372) Cat
Notes: The Mary Mellish Archibald Memorial Library incl folklore, folk music; children's literature. Incl phonorecords, with special emphasis on Canadian folklore and folk music.

FOLK MUSIC, ARMENIAN

DC —LIBRARY OF CONGRESS, American Folklife Center, Archive of Folk Culture, Washington, 20540.
Notes: The Sidney Robertson Cowell Collection of her folk music recordings, 1937 to 1957. Incl very unusual contributions by the Molokan community in the Potrero Hill neighborhood of San Francisco, a breakaway sect from the Russian Orthodox Church.

FOLK MUSIC, BRITISH

DC —LIBRARY OF CONGRESS, American Folklife Center, Archive of Folk Culture, Washington, 20540.
Notes: The Sidney Robertson Cowell Collection of her folk music recordings, 1937 to 1957. Incl very unusual contributions by the Molokan community in the Potrero Hill neighborhood of San Francisco, a breakaway sect from the Russian Orthodox Church.

FOLK MUSIC, GAELIC

DC —LIBRARY OF CONGRESS, American Folklife Center, Archive of Folk Culture, Washington, 20540.
Notes: The Sidney Robertson Cowell Collection of her folk music recordings, 1937 to 1957. Incl very unusual contributions by the Molokan community in the Potrero Hill neighborhood of San Francisco, a breakaway sect from the Russian Orthodox Church.

FOLK MUSIC, IRISH

DC —LIBRARY OF CONGRESS, American Folklife Center, Archive of Folk Culture, Washington, 20540.
Notes: The Sidney Robertson Cowell Collection of her folk music recordings, 1937 to 1957. Incl very unusual contributions by the Molokan community in the Potrero Hill neighborhood of San Francisco, a breakaway sect from the Russian Orthodox Church.

FOLK MUSIC, FINNISH

DC —LIBRARY OF CONGRESS, American Folklife Center, Archive of Folk Culture, Washington, 20540.
Notes: The Sidney Robertson Cowell Collection of her folk music recordings, 1937 to 1957. Incl very unusual contributions by the Molokan community in the Potrero Hill neighborhood of San Francisco, a breakaway sect from the Russian Orthodox Church.

FOLK MUSIC, MOLOKAN

DC —LIBRARY OF CONGRESS, American Folklife Center, Archive of Folk Culture, Washington, 20540.
Notes: The Sidney Robertson Cowell Collection of her folk music recordings, 1937 to 1957. Incl very unusual contributions by the Molokan community in the Potrero Hill neighborhood of San Francisco, a breakaway sect from the Russian Orthodox Church.

FOLK MUSIC, NORTH CAROLINA

DC —LIBRARY OF CONGRESS, American Folklife Center, Archive of Folk Culture, Washington, 20540.
Notes: The Frank C Brown Collection of 80 sixteen-inch disc copies predominantly of ballads and songs recorded by Brown in North Carolina, primarily in the late 1910s to early 1940s.

FOLK MUSIC, PORTUGUESE

DC —LIBRARY OF CONGRESS, American Folklife Center, Archive of Folk Culture, Washington, 20540.
Notes: The Sidney Robertson Cowell Collection of her folk music recordings, 1937 to 1957. Incl very unusual contributions by the Molokan community in the Potrero Hill neighborhood of San Francisco, a breakaway sect from the Russian Orthodox Church.

FOLK SONGS

DC —LIBRARY OF CONGRESS, American Folklife Center, Archive of Folk Culture, Washington, 20540.
Notes: The Laura Boulton Collection is comprised of 1312 discs and 367 tape recordings of traditional vocal and instrumental music of Canada, Africa, Southeast Asia, American Indians, and Eskimos, collected chiefly from the 1930s through the 1960s by Dr Boulton.

IA —UNIVERSITY OF IOWA, University Libraries, Iowa City, 52242. Frank Paluka, Head, Special Collections Dept
Holdings: // Cat
Notes: Collection incl 1050 items. See Harry Oster, "The Edwin Ford Piper Collection of Folksongs," *Books at Iowa,* Oct 1964. Also an unpublished thesis, Harold D Peterson, "Syllabus of the Ballad Collection of Edwin Ford Piper," June 1934, MA, Iowa.

MD —UNIVERSITY OF MARYLAND, Maryland Folklore Archive, College Park, 20742. Barry Pearson, Lecturer in English
Holdings: Cat Mss
Notes: Maryland folk songs and folklore. 60 file drawers of mss, held in trust for the Maryland Arts Council. Subject index in preparation.

MA —HARVARD UNIVERSITY LIBRARY, Widener Library, Cambridge, 02138. Ellen H Brow, Specialist in Book Selection
Holdings: Cat
Notes: Incl in *Widener Library Shelflist* No 41 (1972).

MI —DETROIT PUBLIC LIBRARY, Music & Performing Arts Dept, 5201 Woodward, Detroit, 48202. Agatha Pfeiffer Kalkanis, Chief
Holdings: Cat
Notes: Over 5000 song collections of all types. Incl all collections in standard indexes (Sears, DeCharms & Breed, Leigh, etc). Printed indexes supplemented by extensive song index on cards in department. Also incl about 1000 commercial recordings of folk music.
See also entry under Songs

MS —UNIVERSITY OF MISSISSIPPI, John Davis Williams Library, University, 38677.
Notes: The folklore library of Professor Kenneth S Goldstein comprises more than 12,000 vols and 4500 phonodiscs. Incl a comprehensive 3000 vol collection of editions of collected folksongs and works about the evolution of the Anglo-American folksong, as well as works treating the folklore and folk life of Britain, Ireland, Canada, and Australia. The collection contains specialized holdings on children's lore and games, Afro-American folklore, and folklore theory. The phonodisc collection is rich in examples of American, English, Scottish, and Irish revival.

MO —SPRINGFIELD-GREENE COUNTY PUBLIC LIBRARY, 397 E Central, PO Box 737, Springfield, 65801. Jewell Smith, Administrative Librn
Holdings: Cat
Notes: The Max Hunter Collection of Ozark Folksongs. Collection consists of approx 1000 folksongs collected orally in the Missouri and Arkansas Ozark region. Songs recorded on 51 cassettes and accompanied by 25 notebooks giving the words of the songs. Collection indexed by title and singer. Material collected from 1957 to present. All unpublished.

NJ —NEWARK PUBLIC LIBRARY, Art & Music Dept, 5 Washington St, Newark, 07101. William J Dane, Supv
Holdings: Vols Uncat
Notes: 2500 song sheets of popular music, with emphasis on late 19th and 20th century titles. General collection of art songs, sacred songs, folk songs, Tune Dex and standard song collections incl all of Sears. Special song indexes supplement printed indexes.

NY —NEW YORK PUBLIC LIBRARY, Music Div, 111 Amsterdam Ave, New York, 10023. Frank C Campbell, Chief
Holdings: Vols (300,000) Cat Mss Pix Microforms
Notes: Described in *Dictionary Catalog of the Music Collection, The Research Libraries of the New York Public Library,* 33 vols (532,000 cards), 1964, $2190; Supplement 1, 1 vol (17,000 cards), 1966, $100. Also, *Bibliographic Guide to Music,* 2 vols, 1975-1976, $70 ea. Literature pertaining to virtually all musical subjects, and scores covering the broadest range of musical style and history are represented in this catalog. Special strengths of the collection incl folk songs, 18th and 19th-century librettos, full scores of operas, complete works, historical editions, Beethoven, Americana, American music, periodicals, vocal music, literature on the voice, programs, record catalogs, and mss in detail; sheet music, 355,414; sound recordings, 400,000; clippings and programs, 2 million; broadsides, 1821; songsters, 375; pictures, 51,002; ms, 29,877.

OH —CLEVELAND PUBLIC LIBRARY, Fine Arts and Special Collections Department, 325 Superior Ave, Cleveland, 44114. Alice N Loranth, Head
Holdings: Vols (41,050) Cat Mss Pix Microforms Tapes
Notes: Part of the Folklore Collection. Comprehensive in scope, incl folk tales, riddles, proverbs, folk songs, ballads, fables, chapbooks, medieval romances, works on superstition, magic, witchcraft and studies of folk habits, beliefs, manners and customs. Extensive indexes for French, Provencal and Italian songs (//). Described in Cleveland, Public Library, White collection of folk-lore and Orientalia; *Catalog of Folklore, Folklife and Folk Songs.* 2nd edition (Boston: G K

FOLK SONGS (cont.)

Hall, 1978), 3 vols; introduction by Alice N Loranth.
See also entry under Ballads; Folklore.

TN —COUNTRY MUSIC FOUNDATION, Library & Media Center, 4 Music Sq E, Nashville, 37203. Charlie Seemann, Dir
Holdings: Vols (6000) Mss Pix Slides Phonorecords Audiotapes Videotapes 16mm Films Microforms
Notes: The largest collection in the world dealing with American country music. Related subject areas are also included--Anglo-American folksong, popular music in general (soul, jazz, rock and roll, rhythm and blues, etc), recorded sound technology, music law.

TX —FORT WORTH PUBLIC LIBRARY, Arts Division, 300 Taylor St, Fort Worth, 76102. Heather Gobel, Head
Holdings: Vols (21,500) Cat Mss Phonorecords
Budget: ($26,700)
Notes: Emphasis is on older popular music and musical comedies, folk songs, operas, music composed by Fort Worth and Texas composers, and music about Texas. Sheet music has a separate index.

TX —TEXAS TECH UNIVERSITY, Library, Lubbock, 79409. David J Murrah, Assoc Dir for Special Collections

VT —MIDDLEBURY COLLEGE, Starr Library, Flanders Ballad Collection, Middlebury, 05753. Jennifer Post Quinn, Cur
Holdings: Vols (3000) Cat Pix Phonorecords Audiotapes Mss
Notes: Begun as Helen Hartness Flanders' private collection in 1930, given to Middlebury College, 1941. Incl over 9000 New England items recorded or transcribed since 1930: ballads and folk songs of British, American, French-Canadian, and Russian origin; religious songs; fiddle tunes; dance music. Incl research collection of folklore and folksong monographs, scores, tunebooks, journals. Reference: Quinn, Jennifer Post. *An Index to the Field Recordings in the Flanders Ballad Collection at Middlebury College, Middlebury, Vermont* Middlebury, VT, Middlebury College, 1983.
See also entries under Ballads; Songs - Collections.

VA —UNIVERSITY OF VIRGINIA, Alderman Library, Manuscripts Dept, Charlottesville, 22901. Edmund Berkeley Jr, Cur
Holdings: Cat Mss Pix
Notes: Virginia Folklore Collection (23,000 items) incl the following collection: Virginia WPA Folklore Files, compiled ca 1936-1943, under US Works Project Administration, ca 8000 items. Black and white folklore and folk music collected by field workers from informants throughout Virginia. Incl ms reports, phonorecords. Described in Rosenberg, Bruce A (comp). *The Folksongs of Virginia: A Checklist of the WPA Holdings in the Alderman Library, University of Virginia* (Charlottesville: University Press of Virginia, 1969); also, typescript and computer printed guides--Charles L Perdue, Jr, and others (comps), *The White Folklore of the Virginia WPA Files: A Checklist ...* (Charlottesville, 1973); Thomas Barden and others (comps), *Afro-American Folklore of the WPA Folklore Files in the Alderman Library ...* (Charlottesville, 1973).

VA —UNIVERSITY OF VIRGINIA, Alderman Library, Music Collection, Charlottesville, 22901. Evan Bonds, Music Librn
Holdings: // Cat Mss Pix
Notes: Scores, books, correspondence of the Russian music historian Alfred J Swan, related to his study of Soviet music (particularly Russian church music and folk songs) and musicians. Published description: Velimirovic, Milos, "The Swan Music Collection," *Chapter & Verse* (journal of the Associates of the Univ of Va Library), Nov 1977, pp 20-21.

WI —UNIVERSITY OF WISCONSIN, MADISON, Memorial Library, British & American Language & Literature Collection, 728 State St, Madison, 53706. Yvonne Schofer, Bibliographer
Holdings: Vols (1000)// Cat
Notes: Arthur Beatty Collection. Consists of over 1000 volumes, principally in the English poetry of the Romantic period, strong in Coleridge, Tennyson, Swinburne, the prose of De Quincy and the folk poetry and balladry of Great Britain and Europe. Outstanding for its first and other editions of Wordsworth. About 200 titles in the Department of Rare Books and Special Collections; the rest is in stacks.

ON —VICTORIA UNIVERSITY, Library, 71 Queen's Park Crescent, Toronto, M5S 1K7, Can. Robert C Brandeis, Chief Librn
Holdings: Vols 350// Cat
Notes: Includes many of the major works and collections.

FOLK SONGS, AFRICAN

NY —NEW YORK PUBLIC LIBRARY, Schomburg Center for Research in Black Culture, 515 Lenox Ave, New York, 10037. Catherine J Lenix Hooker, Interim Administrator
Notes: A repository for 10,000 phonodiscs and 2000 tapes covering African and West Indian folk music, early blues, and jazz.

FOLK SONGS, AMERICAN

AR —UNIVERSITY OF ARKANSAS, Library, Special Collections Dept, Fayetteville, 72701. Michael J Dabrishus, Cur
Holdings: Vols (40,299) Cat Mss Maps Pix Phonorecords Audiotapes Microforms
Notes: Material pertaining to the political, governmental, economic, social, cultural, educational, religious, scientific and literary history of Arkansas, its people and its institutions, incl the "natural history," anthropological development, and folk traditions of the area, from prehistoric times to the present. Holdings described in: Samuel A Sizer, *A Guide to Selected Manuscript Collections in the University of Arkansas Library* (Fayetteville, Ark, 1976) and in supplementary catalogs, inventories, indexes and other unpublished finding aids in the library.

CA —SOCIETY OF CALIFORNIA PIONEERS, Library, 456 McAllister St, San Francisco, 94102. Grace E Baker, Librn
Holdings: Vols (12,000) Cat Mss Maps Pix Microforms
Notes: California history, especially the gold rush and the San Francisco earthquake, Sherman collection of early California music, business letterheads of early California firms, San Francisco City Directories 1850-1944, records of California Battalion 1846-47, ms material on overland diaries, ships' logs and passenger lists. Also, large photograph collection.

KY —WESTERN KENTUCKY UNIVERSITY, Kentucky Building, Folklore, Folklife & Oral History Archives, Bowling Green, 42101. Patricia M Hodges, Archivist
Holdings: Cat Mss Audiotapes Videotapes
Notes: Archive contains manuscripts of field collection projects done by students and faculty. There is a large folk song collection in manuscript and tapes of local performers of traditional songs and music. Materials generally relate to Kentucky and surrounding areas; or to country music and traditional music. 3500 tapes; 135 linear ft of manuscripts.

NC —APPALACHIAN STATE UNIVERSITY, Belk Library, Appalachian Collection, Boone, 28608. Eric J Olson, Librn
Holdings: Vols (12,000) Cat Mss Maps Pix Slides Phonorecords Audiotapes
Budget: ($4000)
Notes: The Appalachian Collection incl the Fry Collectin of handmade quilts and coverlets; the York Collection of folk songs and ballads, plus tapes; the I G Greer Collection of Folk Songs and Ballads; the Amos Abrams ballad collection; artifacts, incl the Tatum Collection of household items, furniture, and farm implements; Daniel Boone loom; oral history tapes; the Jack Guy Collection of tapes of area music and photographs; and regional genealogy. This is a very comprehensive study on the Southern Appalachian Region. Separate catalog for the collection.

PA —FREE LIBRARY OF PHILADELPHIA, Rare Book Dept, Logan Sq, Philadelphia, 19103. Marie E Korey, Rare Book Librn
Holdings: Uncat Mss Phonorecords
Notes: The Colonel Richard Gimble Collection of Robert L May's "Rudolph, the Red-Nosed Reindeer": 200 books and periodicals, manuscripts, musical scores, newspaper clippings, and records.

RI —BROWN UNIVERSITY, John Hay Library, 20 Prospect St, Providence, 02912. Mark N Brown, Cur Mss
Holdings: Mss
Notes: Papers of William O Fuller (1828-1910), music teacher of Providence, comprising letters 1848 from Europe, incl a letter from Franz Liszt; papers of Johann Christian Gottlieb Graupner (1767-1836) and John Rowe Parker (fl 1820s) collected by Horace Mason Reynolds, relating to the music-publishing business in Boston, 1802-1838; papers of the American folklorist Mellinger Edward Henry (1873-1946) relating to his research and publications on American folk-songs 1910-1942; papers, 1912-1948, of Providence composer Hugh Frederick MacColl (1885-1953); papers of Frances Herriot Sargent, stage manager for "Porgy" and "Porgy and Bess", relating to productions of these, 1928-1942.

RI —BROWN UNIVERSITY, John Hay Library, Harris Collection, Prospect St, Providence, 02912. Rosemary L Cullen, Cur
Holdings: Vols (200,000) Cat Mss Phonorecords Microforms
Budget: ($15,000)
Notes: The Harris Collection of American Poetry and Plays is principally composed of American and Canadian poetry and plays, 17th century-date. Extensive holdings in songsters, gift books and annuals, hymnals, pageants, broadside verse, carriers' addresses, women poets, juvenile poetry (incl Mother Goose and *The Night Before Christmas*), sheet music with lyrics, small press publications, fine printing, black poets, "little magazines", Yiddish-American literature. See *Dictionary Catalog of the Harris Collection of American Poetry and Plays* (Boston: G K Hall, 1972), 13 vols; Supplement (1977), 3 vols. Separate catalog.

UT —UTAH STATE UNIVERSITY, Merrill Library, Department of Special Collections & Archives, Logan, 84322. A J Simmonds, Curator; Jeanie F Simmonds, Archivist; Bradford R Cole, Mss Librn
Holdings: Vols 1100 Uncat Mss Pix Slides
Notes: The Austin E and Alla S Fife folklore archive of western, cowboy, and folksong materials. Over 300 pictures; 4200 slides; 800 field recordings; 75 ft of ms items. Complete card index to folklore themes in the collection. See Catalog of recordings in "A Bibiliography of the Archives of the Utah Humanities Research Foundation," *Bulletin of the University of Utah*, vol XXXVIII, no 9 (Dec 1947): pp 26-35; description of Fife Mormon collection in *Western Folklore* Quarterly, vol VII, no 3 (July 1948): pp 299-301; description of "Fife Collection of Western American Folksong and Folklore" in *The Folklore and Folk Music Archivist*, vol VII, no 2 (Spring 1964): pp 41-44.

VT —MIDDLEBURY COLLEGE, Starr Library, Flanders Ballad Collection, Middlebury, 05753. Jennifer Post Quinn, Cur
Holdings: Vols (3000) Cat Mss Pix Phonorecords Audiotapes
Notes: Begun as Helen Hartness Flanders' private collection in 1930, given to Middlebury College, 1941. Incl over 9000 New England items recorded or transcribed since 1930: ballads and folk songs of British, American, French-Canadian, and Russian origin; religious songs; fiddle tunes; dance music. Incl research collection of folklore and folksong monographs, scores, tunebooks, journals. Reference: Quinn, Jennifer Post.

FOLK SONGS, AMERICAN (cont.)

An Index to the Field Recordings in the Flanders Ballad Collection at Middlebury College, Middlebury, Vermont Middlebury, VT, Middlebury College, 1983.

WI —MILWAUKEE PUBLIC LIBRARY, 814 W Wisconsin Ave, Milwaukee, 53233. Donald J Sager, City Librn
Holdings: Vols Cat
See also entries under Music; Songs, American.

FOLK SONGS, ANGLO-AMERICAN

MS —UNIVERSITY OF MISSISSIPPI, John Davis Williams Library, University, 38677.
Notes: The folklore library of Professor Kenneth S Goldstein comprises more than 12,000 vols and 4500 phonodiscs. Incl a comprehensive 3000 vol collection of editions of collected folksongs and works about the evolution of the Anglo-American folksong, as well as works treating the folklore and folk life of Britain, Ireland, Canada, and Australia. The collection contains specialized holdings on children's lore and games, Afro-American folklore, and folklore theory. The phonodisc collection is rich in examples of American, English, Scottish, and Irish revival.

FOLK SONGS, BRITISH

MS —UNIVERSITY OF MISSISSIPPI, John Davis Williams Library, University, 38677.
Notes: The folklore library of Professor Kenneth S Goldstein comprises more than 12,000 vols and 4500 phonodiscs. Incl a comprehensive 3000 vol collection of editions of collected folksongs and works about the evolution of the Anglo-American folksong, as well as works treating the folklore and folk life of Britain, Ireland, Canada, and Australia. The collection contains specialized holdings on children's lore and games, Afro-American folklore, and folklore theory. The phonodisc collection is rich in examples of American, English, Scottish, and Irish revival.

VT —MIDDLEBURY COLLEGE, Starr Library, Flanders Ballad Collection, Middlebury, 05753. Jennifer Post Quinn, Cur
Holdings: Vols (3000) Cat Pix Phonorecords Audiotapes Mss
Notes: Begun as Helen Hartness Flanders' private collection in 1930, given to Middlebury College, 1941. Incl over 9000 New England items recorded or transcribed since 1930: ballads and folk songs of British, American, French-Canadian, and Russian origin; religious songs; fiddle tunes; dance music. Incl research collection of folklore and folksong monographs, scores, tunebooks, journals. Reference: Quinn, Jennifer Post. *An Index to the Field Recordings in the Flanders Ballad Collection at Middlebury College, Middlebury, Vermont* Middlebury, VT, Middlebury College, 1983.

FOLK SONGS, DANISH

DC —LIBRARY OF CONGRESS, American Folklife Center, Archive of Folk Culture, Washington, 20540.
Notes: The Fife Collection of Mormon and Western folksongs; Mormon superstitions, folk cures, frontier legends, religious stories, and traditional American and Danish folksongs. 106 disc recordings.

FOLK SONGS, FRENCH CANADIAN

VT —MIDDLEBURY COLLEGE, Starr Library, Flanders Ballad Collection, Middlebury, 05753. Jennifer Post Quinn, Cur
Holdings: Vols (3000) Cat Mss Pix Phonorecords Audiotapes
Notes: Begun as Helen Hartness Flanders' private collection in 1930, given to Middlebury College, 1941. Incl over 9000 New England items recorded or transcribed since 1930: ballads and folk songs of British, American, French-Canadian, and Russian origin; religious songs; fiddle tunes; dance music. Incl research collection of folklore and folksong monographs, scores, tunebooks, journals. Reference: Quinn, Jennifer Post. *An Index to the Field Recordings in the Flanders Ballad Collection at Middlebury College, Middlebury, Vermont* Middlebury, VT, Middlebury College, 1983.

FOLK SONGS, GERMAN

IL —UNIVERSITY OF CHICAGO LIBRARY, Dept of Special Collections, 1100 E 57 St, Chicago, 60637.
Notes: Wieboldt-Rosenwald Collection of Photostats of German Folksongs.

FOLK SONGS, IRISH

MS —UNIVERSITY OF MISSISSIPPI, John Davis Williams Library, University, 38677.
Notes: The folklore library of Professor Kenneth S Goldstein comprises more than 12,000 vols and 4500 phonodiscs. Incl a comprehensive 3000 vol collection of editions of collected folksongs and works about the evolution of the Anglo-American folksong, as well as works treating the folklore and folk life of Britain, Ireland, Canada, and Australia. The collection contains specialized holdings on children's lore and games, Afro-American folklore, and folklore theory. The phonodisc collection is rich in examples of American, English, Scottish, and Irish revival.

FOLK SONGS, NORTH CAROLINA

DC —LIBRARY OF CONGRESS, American Folklife Center, Archive of Folk Culture, Washington, 20540.
Notes: The Frank C Brown Collection of 80 sixteen-inch disc copies predominantly of ballads and songs recorded by Brown in North Carolina, primarily in the late 1910s to early 1940s.

FOLK SONGS, OZARK

AR —UNIVERSITY OF ARKANSAS, Library, Special Collections Dept, Fayetteville, 72701. Michael J Dabrishus, Cur
Holdings: Vols (40,299) Cat Mss Maps Pix Phonorecords Audiotapes Microforms
Notes: Material pertaining to the political, governmental, economic, social, cultural, educational, religious, scientific and literary history of Arkansas, its people and its institutions, incl the "natural history," anthropological development, and folk traditions of the area, from prehistoric times to the present. Holdings described in: Samuel A Sizer, *A Guide to Selected Manuscript Collections in the University of Arkansas Library* (Fayetteville, Ark, 1976) and in supplementary catalogs, inventories, indexes and other unpublished finding aids in the library.

DC —LIBRARY OF CONGRESS, American Folklife Center, Archive of Folk Culture, Washington, 20540.
Notes: Vance Randolph's papers, photographs, and field recordings of Ozark folk music, 1930s - 1960s.

MO —SPRINGFIELD-GREENE COUNTY PUBLIC LIBRARY, 397 E Central, PO Box 737, Springfield, 65801. Jewell Smith, Administrative Librn
Holdings: Cat
Notes: The Max Hunter Collection of Ozark Folksongs. Collection consists of approx 1000 folksongs collected orally in the Missouri and Arkansas Ozark region. Songs recorded on 51 cassettes and accompanied by 25 notebooks giving the works of the songs. Collection indexed by title and singer. Material collected from 1957 to present. All unpublished.

FOLK SONGS, RUSSIAN

VT —MIDDLEBURY COLLEGE, Starr Library, Flanders Ballad Collection, Middlebury, 05753. Jennifer Post Quinn, Cur
Holdings: Vols (3000) Cat Mss Pix Phonorecords Audiotapes
Notes: Begun as Helen Hartness Flanders' private collection in 1930, given to Middlebury College, 1941. Incl over 9000 New England items recorded or transcribed since 1930: ballads and folk songs of British, American, French-Canadian, and Russian origin; religious songs; fiddle tunes; dance music. Incl research collection of folklore and folksong monographs, scores, tunebooks, journals. Reference: Quinn, Jennifer Post. *An Index to the Field Recordings in the Flanders Ballad Collection at Middlebury College, Middlebury, Vermont* Middlebury, VT, Middlebury College, 1983.

FOLK SONGS, SCOTTISH

MS —UNIVERSITY OF MISSISSIPPI, John Davis Williams Library, University, 38677.
Notes: The folklore library of Professor Kenneth S Goldstein comprises more than 12,000 vols and 4500 phonodiscs. Incl a comprehensive 3000 vol collection of editions of collected folksongs and works about the evolution of the Anglo-American folksong, as well as works treating the folklore and folk life of Britain, Ireland, Canada, and Australia. The collection contains specialized holdings on children's lore and games, Afro-American folklore, and folklore theory. The phonodisc collection is rich in examples of American, English, Scottish, and Irish revival.

FOLK SONGS, WEST INDIAN

NY —NEW YORK PUBLIC LIBRARY, Schomburg Center for Research in Black Culture, 515 Lenox Ave, New York, 10037. Catherine J Lenix Hooker, Interim Administrator
Notes: A repository for 10,000 phonodiscs and 2000 tapes covering African and West Indian folk music, early blues, and jazz.

FOLK SONGS, WESTERN

DC —LIBRARY OF CONGRESS, American Folklife Center, Archive of Folk Culture, Washington, 20540.
Notes: The Fife Collection of Mormon and Western folksongs; Mormon superstitions, folk cures, frontier legends, religious stories, and traditional American and Danish folksongs. 106 disc recordings.

FOLK TALES see Folklore; Legends; Tales

FOLKLORE

AR —UNIVERSITY OF ARKANSAS, Library, Special Collections Dept, Fayetteville, 72701. Michael J Dabrishus, Cur
Holdings: Vols (40,299) Cat Mss Maps Pix Phonorecords Audiotapes Microforms
Notes: Material pertaining to the political, governmental, economic, social, cultural, educational, religious, scientific and literary history of Arkansas, its people and its institutions, incl the "natural history," anthropological developmen, and folk traditions of the area, from prehistoric times to the present. Holdings described in: Samuel A Sizer, *A Guide to Selected Manuscript Collections in the University of Arkansas Library* (Fayetteville, Ark, 1976) and in supplementary catalogs, inventories, indexes and other unpublished finding aids in the library.

CA —UNIVERSITY OF CALIFORNIA, BERKELEY, University Library, Slavic Collections, Berkeley, 94720. Edward Kasinec, Librn
Holdings: Vols (210,000) Cat Maps Microforms
Budget: ($40,000)
Notes: Strong research collections for Bulgaria, Czechoslovakia, Poland, Russia-USSR, and Yugoslavia. Holdings are excellent in economics, folklore, history, linguistics, and literature.

CA —CLAREMONT COLLEGES, Honnold Library, Ninth & Dartmouth, Claremont,

FOLKLORE (cont.)

91711. Franklin D Scott, Cur, Nordic Collection; Penelope Garris, Librn
Holdings: Vols (25,000) Cat Maps Pix Slides Audiotapes Videotapes
Notes: Nordic Collections are broadly inclusive, but emphasize history of Scandinavia, Baltic countries, and Hanseatic cities. Nucleus of collections from gifts and endowment of Waldemar Westergaard, supplemented with relevant collections of David Bjork, John H Wuorinen, Ingolf Olsen, Henry Steele Commager, Franklin Scott and other gifts and purchases. Eight vertical file drawers of news bulletins in English or vernaculars, 1941-. See: Franklin D Scott, "The Westergaard-Bjork Collection at the Honnold Library, the Claremont Colleges," *Scandinavian Studies,* 41 (1969), 346-354.

CA —LOS ANGELES PUBLIC LIBRARY, Children's Literature Dept, 630 W 5th St, Los Angeles, 90071. Serenna Day, Sr Librn
Holdings: Vols (2120) Cat Phonorecords Filmstrips
Notes: Also includes reference collection, covering some 50 years of published folklore and modern fairy tales. Includes extensive Mother Goose collection, examples of the work of such outstanding illustrators as Edmund Dulac and Arthur Rackham. Many volumes out of print. Index to titles of stories in collections.

CA —LOS ANGELES PUBLIC LIBRARY, Philosophy & Religion Dept, 630 W Fifth St, Los Angeles, 90071. Marilyn C Wherley, Librn
Holdings: Vols 500 Cat
Budget: ($60,000)
Notes: Comprehensive coverage of popular and scholarly works on myths, legends, superstitions and primitive religions.

CA —UNIVERSITY OF CALIFORNIA, LOS ANGELES, Research Library, Dept of Special Collections, 405 Hilgard Ave, Los Angeles, 90024. Edward Shreeves, Chairman, Bibliographers Group; David S Zeidberg, Head
Notes: 10 books, 25 mss, 50 letters, and 20 photographs of Jaime de Angulo, folklorist who spent many years with the Pit River Indians of Northern California.

CA —FITZ HUGH LUDLOW MEMORIAL LIBRARY, PO Box 99346, San Francisco, 94109. Michael R Aldrich, Exec Cur
Holdings: Cat Mss Maps Pix Slides Phonorecords Audiotapes Videotapes
Notes: Collection stored. Important mail inquiries only. No interlibrary lending or telephone inquiries. Original art works, artifacts, paraphernalia, comic books, newspaper illustrations, and drug advertisements relating to psychoactive drug use and abuse. In addition we have available many illustrations pertinent to mythology (ancient and modern) peripherally related to drug history and folklore.

CA —SAN JOSE PUBLIC LIBRARY, 180 W San Carlos St, San Jose, 95113. Homer Fletcher, Dir
Holdings: Vols 2200
Notes: A resource collection for children and storytellers. Library has 98 percent holdings in: Eastman-Index to Fairy Tales, 2nd supp; Ireland-Index to Fairy Tales; MacDonald-Storyteller's Sourcebook. Holdings for first two volumes of Eastman show approximately 50 percent. See Children's Research Collection.

CA —UNIVERSITY OF CALIFORNIA, SANTA CRUZ, University Library, Special Collections, Santa Cruz, 95064. Rita Bottoms, Special Collections Librn; Margaret Felts, South Pacific Collection Bibliographer
Holdings: Vols (10,000) Cat
Notes: Astronomy library. Incl all major astronomical and astrophysical journals and an extensive collection of domestic and foreign observatory publications. The book collection is particularly strong in stellar structure and evolution, stellar spectroscopy, the interstellar medium, galactic structure, external galaxies, general relativity and gravitational radiation, and high-energy astrophysics.

†CO —UNIVERSITY OF DENVER, Penrose Library, 2150 E Evans, Denver, 80208.
Notes: Levette J Davidson Folklore Collection.

CT —TRINITY COLLEGE LIBRARY, Watkinson Library, 300 Summit St, Hartford, 06106. Jeffrey Kaimowitz, Cur
Holdings: Cat

DC —DISTRICT OF COLUMBIA PUBLIC LIBRARY, Martin Luther King Memorial Library, Children's Div, 901 G St NW, Washington, 20001. Maria B Salvadore, Coordr, Children's Service
Holdings: Vols (13,000)
Notes: Collection incl examples of illustrated children's books from the 18th century to the present, mainly English and American, as well as general titles about illustrations and biographical information on illustrators. Collection is cited in *Subject Collections in Children's Literature,* ed by Carolyn Field (Bowker, 1969). "Source Collection" of folk literature is currently being developed to aid research. Partially cataloged. No photocopying.

DC —LIBRARY OF CONGRESS, American Folklife Center, Archive of Folk Culture, Washington, 20540.
Notes: US and foreign folk music and folklore.

IL —SOUTHERN ILLINOIS UNIVERSITY, CARBONDALE, Delyte W Morris Library, Carbondale, 62901.
Holdings: Vols 1000 Cat
Notes: The Alexander Haggerty Krappe Folklore Collection is a scholar's working library; international in scope. Strong in monographs of the 19th through mid-20th centuries. A complete set of off-prints of Dr Krappe's voluminous periodical output have been bound in 3 large vols. There is a mimeographed checklist of the collection which is not maintained as a separate collection.

IL —NEWBERRY LIBRARY, 60 W Walton St, Chicago, 60610. Diana Haskell, Cur of Modern Mss
Holdings: Cat
Notes: Good collection. Emphasis on US.

IL —UNIVERSITY OF ILLINOIS, URBANA/CHAMPAIGN, Library, University Archives, 19 Library, 1408 W Gregory Drive, Urbana, 61801. Maynard Brichford, University Archivist
Holdings: Vols 30,000 Cat
Notes: The School Collection consists of fiction and nonfiction for children and young adults. Included are children's classics, easy readers, picture books, folk literature and mythology. In addition to the Newbery and Caldecott winners, national award-winning books which encompass the areas of literature, science and the social sciences are collected. Current representative children's magazines are also part of the collection. A reference collection relevant to the study of children's literature is maintained. An exellent representation of historical children's literature dating back to 1800 is part of the School Collection. Special reprint collections are *Classics of Children's Literature 1621-1932* and the *Osborne Collection of Early Children's Books.* Children's materials from 1600-1800 are in the Rare Book Room.

IL —UNIVERSITY OF ILLINOIS, URBANA/CHAMPAIGN, Library, Rare Book Room, 346 Library, Urbana, 61801. Norman B Brown, Asst Dir for Special Collections; N Frederick Nash, Librn
Holdings: Cat Mss Maps
Notes: Meine Collection. Extensive collection, described in: *Catalog of the Rare Book Room,* (Boston: G K Hall, 1972). Supplement (1978).

IN —INDIANA UNIVERSITY, Lilly Library, Seventh St, Bloomington, 47405. William R Cagle, Librn
Holdings: // Cat Mss
Notes: Collections incl papers of folklorists Richard M Dorson, 1916-1981, and Stith Thompson, 1885-1976. Also a small collection (76 items) of Andrew Lang letters and writings, 1886-1913. Incl first and early editions of Andrew Lang and Hans Christian Andersen.

IN —INDIANA UNIVERSITY, Institute for Sex Research Library, 416 Morrison Hall, Bloomington, 47401. Douglas Freeman, Collections and Services Librn; Joan Brewer, Information Services Librn
Holdings: Vols (62,000) Cat Mss Pix Phonorecords Audiotapes Slides Films Microforms
Budget: ($20,000)
Notes: One of the greatest and most extensive collections on sexual behavior, the library collects materials on all aspects of sex activity, with special emphasis on behavioral and social aspects. Also collects erotic literature and sexual ephemera. Incl 105 audiotapes, 23 vertical file drawers, 108 phonorecords, 55,000 pictures, 5000 slides, and 1700 films. Rich in French, German and American sources; also much Oriental. Semitraditional erotic poetry and song of 17th-18th century England. Bawdy limericks, double-entendre, puns, slang, erotic literature, graffiti, slang and special dictionaries, proverbs and sayings, epigrams and research materials of the Kinsey Studies, etc. Contact Information Service for: literature searching, preparation of bibliographies, permission to use collection. Limited photocopying.

IN —INDIANA UNIVERSITY, University Libraries, Bloomington, 47405. Polly S Grimshaw, Librn
Holdings: Vols 35,000 Cat Mss Maps
Budget: $14,000
Notes: Author, title, subject and shelflist catalog provided for researchers. This is a working collection, international in scope and covering all genres. Also includes 676 different serial titles and 6000 items of the Henri Gaidoz ms collection.

IN —INDIANAPOLIS-MARION COUNTY PUBLIC LIBRARY, Riley Room for Young People, PO Box 211, Indianapolis, 46206. Margaret Barks, Head
Holdings: Vols 1100 Cat
Notes: The Harding Memorial Collection. This is a resource collection of folk and fairy tales as well as other suitable materials for telling.

KS —FORT HAYS STATE UNIVERSITY, Forsyth Library, Folklore and Oral History Collection, 600 Park St, Hays, 67601. Esta Lou Riley, Archivist/Special Collections Librn
Holdings: //
Notes: Kansas folklore, personal reminiscences (dust storms, depression, war experiences) collected by students. Consists principally of oral interviews on tape (cassettes, reels) and beliefs, superstitions, autograph verses, etc in standard folklore form. Incl (725) tapes with transcriptions; (10 linear feet) of vertical file material. Partially cataloged.

KS —WICHITA PUBLIC LIBRARY, Art & Music Division, 223 S Main, Wichita, 67202. Leonard Messineo, Jr, Head, Art & Music Division; Deborah Hamilton, Special Collections Librn
Holdings: Audiotapes
Notes: Joan O'Bryant Kansas Folklore Collection. Contains approximately 200 hours of folkmusic and oral histories on tape; over 27,000 note cards covering topics such as anecdotes, beliefs, customs, games, jokes, medicines and cures, proverbs, recipes, rhymes, riddles, sayings, songs, speech and dialect, etc; 102 research papers covering family histories, town and area histories, biographies, tales, recipes, etc; and well over 70 mounted quilt blocks-covering the folk history of Kansas. This material was collected by Joan O'Bryant and her students from 1947-1964, the period in which she taught Folklore and English at Wichita State University.

KY —WESTERN KENTUCKY UNIVERSITY, Kentucky Building, Folklore, Folklife & Oral History Archives, Bowling Green, 42101. Patricia M Hodges, Archivist
Holdings: Cat Mss Audiotapes Videotapes
Notes: Archive contains manuscripts of field collection projects done by students and faculty. There is a large folk song collection in manuscript and tapes of local performers of traditional songs and music. Materials

FOLKLORE (cont.)

generally relate to Kentucky and surrounding areas; or to country music and traditional music. 3500 tapes; 135 linear ft of manuscripts.

KY —UNIVERSITY OF KENTUCKY COMMUNITY COLLEGES, Southeast Community College, Library, Learning Resource Center, Cumberland, 40823. Parker Boggs, Dir
Holdings: Vols (700) Cat Mss Maps Pix Slides Phonorecords Audiotapes Videotapes 16mm Films Filmstrips Microforms
Notes: Literature of southern Appalachia; fiction and non-fiction.

LA —LOUISIANA STATE UNIVERSITY, Troy H Middleton Library, Louisiana Room, Baton Rouge, 70803. Evangeline Mills Lynch, Head Librn; Ruth Murray, Associate Librn
Holdings: Vols (33,500) Cat Maps VF
Notes: Louisiana Collection of history, description and travel, biography, agriculture, literature, politics and government, folklore, anthropology, geography, geology, education, language, music and natural history. Especially large subject collections may be found on Louisiana, the history of the lower Mississippi Valley, Abraham Lincoln, Romance languages and literatures, sugar culture and technology, Southern history, petroleum engineering, plant pathology, micropaleontology, ornithology, and various aspects of crawfish life, biology and culture. Complete depository of Louisiana State Documents; extensive newspapers clipping files; separate card catalog; items listed in Louisiana Union Catalog; restricted use (research and reference). Incl both materials about Louisiana and by Louisianians without regard to subject. LSU Press Collection(preservation copy of each title kept for exhibit purposes only). LSU theses and dissertations from 1900-date. LSU Faculty Collection. Also, 1300 maps, 104 VF drawers, 250 boxes of uncataloged pamphlets.

MD —UNIVERSITY OF MARYLAND, Maryland Folklore Archive, College Park, 20742. Barry Pearson, Lecturer in English
Holdings: Cat Mss
Notes: Maryland folk songs and folklore. 60 file drawers of mss, held in trust for the Maryland Arts Council. Subject index in preparation.

MA —HARVARD UNIVERSITY LIBRARY, Widener Library, Milman Parry Collection of Oral Literature & the James A Notopoulos Collection, Cambridge, 02138. Albert B Lord, Cur
Holdings: Cat Mss

MA —HARVARD UNIVERSITY LIBRARY, Botanical Museum Library, Cambridge, 02138.
Holdings: Vols (2400) Mss Pix
Notes: The Tina and Gordon Wisson Ethnomycological Collection, one of the most important modern collections, acquired as an adjunct to the Museum's Economic Botany Library of Oakes Ames. From 15th to 20th century, it deals with hallucinogenic mushrooms in art, religion, and folklore; chemistry, pharmacology, linguistics, archaeological artifacts of Mexico, Guatemala, India, Japan, China, etc. Personal papers, etc.

MA —BOSTON COLLEGE LIBRARIES, Thomas P O'Neill Library, Nicholas M Williams Ethnological Collection, Chestnut Hill, 02167. Frank J Seegraber, Special Collections Librn
Holdings: Vols 10,000 // Cat Maps
Notes: Collection emphasizes Caribbeana, especially Jamaica, to 1940. Incl discovery, exploration and natural history of the British, French and Spanish settlements; the slave question; piracy. There are over 6000 mss, 5000 of which are Anansi folk tales recorded by native school children. Also small ancillary sections of Africana and Judaica. For reference use only, by arrangement with librarian.

MI —AQUINAS COLLEGE, Learning Resource Center, 1607 Robinson Rd SE, Grand Rapids, 49506. Larry Zysk, Dir
Holdings: Vols (55)// Cat
Notes: Mother Goose in all languages. Built on a collection begun as a gift from a former Grand Rapids teacher, Miss Coye.

MI —OAKLAND UNIVERSITY, Kresge Library, Rochester, 48063. Suzanne O Frankie, Dean; Elizabeth Titus, Special Collections Librn
Holdings: Vols 750// Cat
Notes: The Thelma James Folklore Collection covering a wide variety of people and countries.

MN —MINNEAPOLIS PUBLIC LIBRARY & INFORMATION CENTER, Sociology Dept, 300 Nicollet Mall, Minneapolis, 55401. Eileen Scwartzbauer, Dept Head
Holdings: Vols (90,000) Cat Phonorecords Audiotapes Microforms
Budget: ($69,890)
Notes: Special collections: Foundation Center Regional Collection; college catalogs. Separate department catalog.

MN —UNIVERSITY OF MINNESOTA, Libraries, Children's Literature Research Collections, 109 Walter Library, Minneapolis, 55455. Karen Nelson Hoyle, Cur
Notes: A center for study and research in children's literature.

MN —COLLEGE OF SAINT CATHERINE, Library, 2004 Randolph Ave, Saint Paul, 55105. Sister Elizabeth Delmore, Library Dir
Holdings: Vols 2000 Cat Mss Pix Phonorecords Audiotapes
Budget: $500
Notes: The Ruth Sawyer Collection. Also personal letters, medals.

MS —UNIVERSITY OF MISSISSIPPI, John Davis Williams Library, University, 38677.
Notes: The folklore library of Professor Kenneth S Goldstein comprises more than 12,000 vols and 4500 phonodiscs. Incl a comprehensive 3000 vol collection of editions of collected folksongs and works about the evolution of the Anglo-American folksong, as well as works treating the folklore and folk life of Britain, Ireland, Canada, and Australia. The collection contains specialized holdings on children's lore and games, Afro-American folklore, and folklore theory. The phonodisc collection is rich in examples of American, English, Scottish, and Irish revival.

NE —NEBRASKA STATE HISTORICAL SOCIETY, Archives, 1500 R St, Box 82554, Lincoln, 68501. James E Potter, State Archivist
Holdings: // Uncat Mss
Notes: Folklore and literature. Collection and mss of Dr Louise Pound of the University of Nebraska.

NE —UNIVERSITY OF NEBRASKA-LINCOLN, Don L Love Library, Lincoln, 68588. Joseph G Svoboda, University Archivist
Holdings: Vols (8000) // Uncat Mss Pix Slides Phonorecords Audiotapes Microforms
Notes: This is an extensive collection belonging to the folklorist Benjamin A Botkin, about 500 linear ft, consisting of various types of materials. Main emphasis is American folklore, although folklore of all nations is included.

NY —NEW YORK STATE HISTORICAL ASSOCIATION, Library, Lake Rd, Cooperstown, 13326. Amy Barnum, Librn
Holdings: Vols (55,000) Cat Mss Maps Pix Slides Audiotapes
Notes: Folklore, essentially American, with European antecedents. Incl Cooperstown Graduate Program Archives which consists of ms material from the collection of Louis C Jones and Harold Thompson as well as additional materials (mss, 7800 slides, 535 tapes) generated by the American Folk Culture students in the Cooperstown Graduate Program. Noncirculating.

NY —AMERICAN MUSEUM OF NATURAL HISTORY, Library Services Dept, Central Park W & 79th St, New York, 10024. Nina J Root, Chairwoman; Mary Genett, Asst Librn for Reference Services
Holdings: Vols (385,000) Cat Mss Maps Pix Slides Microforms
Notes: Nearly all collections are outstanding for depth of coverage and international range. Early and historic works, rare books, colored illustrations, and relevant serial publications supplement the modern scientific publications necessary to the researchers of the scientific staff and the work of the educational division. Open to the public.

NY —NEW YORK PUBLIC LIBRARY, Slavonic Div, Fifth Ave & 42 St, New York, 10018. Edward Kasinec, Chief
Holdings: Vols (8870) Cat Microforms
Notes: Subject strength is in Ukrainian literature, language, and folklore. Ethnology and history are also well represented. Holdings of periodicals and publications of learned societies are considerable. See New York Public Library, *Dictionary Catalogof the Slavonic Collection* (Boston: G K Hall, 1974), 44 vols; and New York Public Library, *Dictionary Catalog of the Research* Libraries (New York, 1972-).

NY —NEW YORK PUBLIC LIBRARY, Research Libraries, American History Div, Fifth Ave & 42 St, New York, 10018.
Holdings: Vols 1000 Cat Maps Microforms
Notes: Collected comprehensively for the Western Hemisphere. Must be considered in connection with holdings of other units of The Research Libraries.

NY —US COMMITTEE FOR UNICEF, Information Center on Children's Cultures, 331 E 38 St, New York, 10016. Melinda Greenblatt, Chief Librn
Holdings: Vols (17,500) Cat Pix Slides Films Filmstrips
Notes: Social and cultural aspects of lives of children from developing countries. Especially strong in the area of school textbooks from Near Eastern Asian, African, Latin American, Caribbean, and Pacific Area countries; holidays and celebrations related to children all over the world; children's books in English which describe child life in other countries. Especially strong collection of folklore, and folklore of children, from all regions mentioned above.

NC —APPALACHIAN STATE UNIVERSITY, Belk Library, Appalachian Collection, Boone, 28608. Eric J Olson, Librn
Holdings: Vols (12,000) Cat Mss Maps Pix Slides Phonorecords Audiotapes
Budget: ($4000)
Notes: The Appalachian Collection incl the Fry Collectin of handmade quilts and coverlets; the York Collection of folk songs and ballads, plus tapes; the I G Greer Collection of Folk Songs and Ballads; the Amos Abrams ballad collection; artifacts, incl the Tatum Collection of household items, furniture, and farm implements; Daniel Boone loom; oral history tapes; the Jack Guy Collection of tapes of area music and photographs; and regional genealogy. This is a very comprehensive study on the Southern Appalachian Region. Separate catalog for the collection.

NC —APPALACHIAN STATE UNIVERSITY, Belk Library, Instructional Materials Center, Boone, 28608. Selma P Farthing, Librn
Holdings: Vols (20,000) Cat Pix
Notes: The collection is especially strong in poetry and folklore, chosen for the use of classes in children's literature. It also includes many old children's books, used in Critical History courses.

NC —DUKE UNIVERSITY, William R Perkins Library, Durham, 27706. Elvin E Strowd, University Librn

NC —MARS HILL COLLEGE, Memorial Library, Appalachian Room, Mars Hill, 28754. Richard Dillingham, Dir, Special Collections
Holdings: Vols (9600) Cat Mss Maps Pix Slides Phonorecords Audiotapes Microforms
Budget: ($4000)
Notes: Collection strong on local history, folklore, fiction. Incl Bascom Lamar Lunsford papers, books, sound recordings. Separate catalog.

OH —CLEVELAND PUBLIC LIBRARY, Fine Arts and Special Collections Department, 325 Superior Ave, Cleveland, 44114. Alice N Loranth, Head
Holdings: Vols 41,050 Cat Mss Pix

FOLKLORE (cont.)

Microforms
Notes: One of the large folklore collections in the US. Comprehensive in scope, incl folk tales, riddles, proverbs, folk songs, ballads, fables, chapbooks, medieval romances, works on superstition, magic, witchcraft and studies of folk habits beliefs, manners and customs. Archival holdings incl the "Newbell Niles Puckett Archives on Popular Beliefs and Superstitions" (19 linear ft); "Black Names in America" (10 linear ft); miscellaneous folklore papers (10 linear ft); "Religious Life of the southern Black" (6 linear ft); "Canadian Lumberjack Songs" (20 tapes); and the "M A Klipple African Folktales" (19 linear ft). Described in Cleveland Library, White collection of folklore and Orientalia. *Catalog of Folklore, Folklife and Folk Songs* 2nd edition (Boston: G K Hall, 1978). 3 vols; introduction by Alice N Loranth.
See also entry under Literature, Medieval

PA —BALCH INSTITUTE FOR ETHNIC STUDIES, Library, 18 S Seventh St, Philadelphia, 19106. R Joseph Anderson, Library Dir
Notes: Folklore of the US.

PA —FREE LIBRARY OF PHILADELPHIA, Central Children's Dept, Logan Sq, Philadelphia, 19103. Ellen Whitney, Head
Holdings: Vols (30,382) Cat Mss Pix
Notes: Special collections of children's literature dating from 1837 to the present are maintained by the Central Children's Department. These collections include Historical Bibliography, the Kathrine M McAlarney Collection of Illustrated Children's Books, the Folklore Collection, the Historical Collection which includes children's periodicals and the Series Collection. Noncirculating.

PA —UNIVERSITY OF PITTSBURGH, Hillman Library, Pittsburgh, 15260.
Holdings: Vols 500
Notes: A Rumanian collection, which deals with the country's history; racial, ethnic and religious minorities; folklore; art; literature; customs; agriculture; politics.

PA —PENNSYLVANIA STATE UNIVERSITY, Fred Lewis Pattee Library, Special Collections Dept, University Park, 16802. Charles Mann, Chief, Special Collections
Holdings: Vols (93) Cat Mss
Budget: ($37,000)
Notes: Publications and correspondence of the Pennsylvania historian and folklorist Henry W Shoemaker, 1900-1950.

PA —KING'S COLLEGE, D Leonard Corgan Library, 14 W Jackson St, Wilkes-Barre, 18711. Judith Tierney, Special Collections Librn
Holdings: Vols 850 Cat Mss Pix
Notes: The George Korson Folklore Archive. Separate catalog to books in collection. Books and periodicals relate to folklore generally; mss, 107 tapes and 70 disc recordings focus on folklore of the coal mining industry, 1918-1969. See Judith Tierney, comp. *A Description of the George Korson Folklore Archive* (Wilkes-Barre, Pa: King's College Press, 1973). Photocopying limited.

RI —PROVIDENCE PUBLIC LIBRARY, 150 Empire St, Providence, 02903. Lance J Bauer, Special Collections Librn
Holdings: Vols 122 // Cat
Notes: Works dating from 1670 on the history, lore and legends of precious stones, and the history and practice of jewelry and silversmithing. Restricted use.

TX —EAST TEXAS STATE UNIVERSITY, James G Gee Library, Special Collections Dept, East Texas Station, Commerce, 75428. James Conrad, Dept Head
Holdings: Vols (3500) Cat Mss Pix Slides
Notes: The books on Black Literature (with the exception of those on Texas folklore) and Slavery in the US have been transferred to the general stack area of the library; however, our collection of county histories of Texas, which is still housed in the Special Collections, continues to grow. In addition, we have acquired sizable collections of books on Texas folklore and Texas placenames; and World War II posters. Another new area is printing arts in Texas. There is a separate dictionary card catalog for the book collection in the Special Collections Department.

TX —TEXAS TECH UNIVERSITY, Library, Lubbock, 79409. David J Murrah, Assoc Dir for Special Collections

UT —UTAH STATE UNIVERSITY, Merrill Library, Department of Special Collections & Archives, Logan, 84322. A J Simmonds, Curator; Jeanie F Simmonds, Archivist; Bradford R Cole, Mss Librn
Holdings: Vols 1100 Uncat Mss Pix Slides
Notes: The Austin E and Alla S Fife folklore archive of western, cowboy, and folksong materials. Over 300 pictures; 4200 slides; 800 field recordings; 75 ft of ms items. Complete card index to folklore themes in the collection. See Catalog of recordings in "A Bibiliography of the Archives of the Utah Humanities Research Foundation," *Bulletin of the University of Utah*, vol XXXVIII, no 9 (Dec 1947): pp 26-35; description of Fife Mormon collection in *Western Folklore* Quarterly, vol VII, no 3 (July 1948): pp 299-301; description of "Fife Collection of Western American Folksong and Folklore" in *The Folklore and Folk Music Archivist*, vol VII, no 2 (Spring 1964): pp 41-44.

VT —MIDDLEBURY COLLEGE, Starr Library, Flanders Ballad Collection, Middlebury, 05753. Jennifer Post Quinn, Cur
Holdings: Vols (3000) Cat Mss Pix Phonorecords Audiotapes
Notes: Begun as Helen Hartness Flanders' private collection in 1930, given to Middlebury College, 1941. Incl over 9000 New England items recorded or transcribed since 1930: ballads and folk songs of British, American, French-Canadian, and Russian origin; religious songs; fiddle tunes; dance music. Incl research collection of folklore and folksong monographs, scores, tunebooks, journals. Reference: Quinn, Jennifer Post. *An Index to the Field Recordings in the Flanders Ballad Collection at Middlebury College, Middlebury, Vermont* Middlebury, VT, Middlebury College, 1983.

VA —VIRGINIA POLYTECHNIC INSTITUTE AND STATE UNIVERSITY LIBRARY, Blacksburg, 24061. Glenn L McMullen, Special Collections Librn
Holdings: Vols (2000) Cat Mss Maps Pix Audiotapes
Notes: Primarily Southwest Virginia materials. Collection incl ca 200 mss, account books and other archival records of nineteenth century area businesses and other mining operations; the extant archival records of several Southwest Virginia railroads, incl the Virginia and Tennessee Railroad and the Norfolk and Western Railroad; and papers of historically prominent Southwest Virginians, incl John Apperson, Dr Harvy Black, James P Charlton, W Graham Claytor, Henley Fugate, Clement D Johnston, Germanicus Kent, William Preston, J Hoge Tyler, and William C Wampler. Several oral history collections incl material on Appalachian customs and folklore, particularly in Patrick County.

VA —UNIVERSITY OF VIRGINIA, Alderman Library, Manuscripts Dept, Charlottesville, 22901. Edmund Berkeley Jr, Cur
Holdings: Cat Mss Pix
Notes: Virginia Folklore Collection (23,000 items) incl the following collection: Virginia WPA Folklore Files, compiled ca 1936-1943, under US Works Project Administration, ca 8000 items. Black and white folklore and folk music collected by field workers from informants throughout Virginia. Incl ms reports, phonorecords. Described in Rosenberg, Bruce A (comp), *The Folksongs of Virginia: A Checklist of the WPA Holdings in the Alderman Library, University of Virginia* (Charlottesville: University Press of Virginia, 1969); also, typescript and computer printed guides--Charles L Perdue, Jr, and others (comps), *The White Folklore of the Virginia WPA Files: A Checklist ...* (Charlottesville, 1973); Thomas Barden and others (comps), *Afro-American Folklore of the WPA Folklore Files in the Alderman Library ...* (Charlottesville, 1973).

BC —VANCOUVER PUBLIC LIBRARY, Sociology Div, 750 Burrard St, Vancouver, V6Z 1X5, Can.
Holdings: Cat
Notes: Incl special files of pamphlets, clippings, etc.

NB —MOUNT ALLISON UNIVERSITY, Ralph Pickard Bell Library, Sackville, E0A 3C0, Can. M Fancy, Librn
Holdings: Vols (13,372) Cat
Notes: The Mary Mellish Archibald Memorial Library incl folklore, folk music; children's literature. Incl phonorecords, with special emphasis on Canadian folklore and folk music.

ON —NATIONAL LIBRARY OF CANADA, 395 Wellington St, Ottawa, K1A 0N4, Can. Andre Preibish, Dir
Holdings: Vols 12,000
Notes: Canadian children's books in English, French and other languages, supported by a collection of professional literature and supplemented by major award-winning books from other countries and selected major works on special themes such as folklore.

ON —NATIONAL MUSEUMS OF CANADA, Library Services Directorate, Ottawa, K1A 0M8, Can. Valerie Monkhouse, Director
Holdings: Vols (70,000) Cat Mss Maps Pix Slides Microforms
Budget: ($60,000)
Notes: Collection includes anthropology, archaeology, ethnology, folklore, history, Indians of North America, Inuit, linguistics of North American Indians, material history, military and naval history, museology. Research collection, interlibrary loans available, public may use on the premises.

ON —VICTORIA UNIVERSITY, Library, 71 Queen's Park Crescent, Toronto, M5S 1K7, Can. Robert C Brandeis, Chief Librn
Holdings: Vols 350// Cat
Notes: Includes many of the major works and collections.

FOLKLORE, AFRICAN

DC —HOWARD UNIVERSITY, Moorland-Spingarn Research Center, 500 Howard Place NW, Washington, 20059. Clifford L Muse, Jr, Acting Dir
Holdings: Vols (106,086) Mss Maps Pix Slides Phonorecords Audiotapes 16mm Films Filmstrips Microforms
Budget: ($854,753)
See also entry under Blacks

OH —CLEVELAND PUBLIC LIBRARY, Fine Arts and Special Collections Department, 325 Superior Ave, Cleveland, 44114. Alice N Loranth, Head
Holdings: Cat Mss Microforms
Notes: Part of the Folklore Collection. Incl the "May Augusta Klipple Dissertation Archive of African Folktales with Foreign Analogues," translated form German and French sources, and from vols 1-12 of *Atlantis* (19 linear ft); Newbell Niles Puckett Archives "Black Names in America" (10 linear ft); and "Religious Life of the Southern Black" (6 linear ft).
See also entry under Africa; Folklore.

FOLKLORE, ALABAMA

AL —WHEELER BASIN REGIONAL LIBRARY, 504 Cherry St NE, PO Box 1766, Decatur, 35602. Margarete Lange, Reference Librn
Holdings: Vols 5 Cat Mss Pix Slides Audiotapes VF
Notes: Primarily oral history on North Alabama, incl history, politics, folklore.

FOLKLORE, APPALACHIAN see Appalachian Region

FOLKLORE, ARIZONA

AZ —NORTHERN ARIZONA UNIVERSITY, Special Collection Library,

FOLKLORE, ARIZONA (cont.)

CU Box 6022, Flagstaff, 86011. Peter M Whiteley, Coordr/Archivist; William Mullane, Librn
Notes: Margaret Carrigan Collection; NAU student folklore papers, 1950's-1960's. Many papers involve original research on Arizona topics.

FOLKLORE, ARMENIAN

CA —UNIVERSITY OF CALIFORNIA, LOS ANGELES, Research Library, Armenian Collection, 405 Hilgard Ave, Los Angeles, 90024. Edward Shreeves, Chairman, Bibliographers Group; Gia Aivazian, Armenian Bibliographer
Holdings: Vols (16,000)
Notes: Incl one of the largest collections in the US of publications in Armenian and relating to Armenia.

FOLKLORE, AUSTRALIAN

MS —UNIVERSITY OF MISSISSIPPI, John Davis Williams Library, University, 38677.
Notes: The folklore library of Professor Kenneth S Goldstein comprises more than 12,000 vols and 4500 phonodiscs. Incl a comprehensive 3000 vol collection of editions of collected folksongs and works about the evolution of the Anglo-American folksong, as well as works treating the folklore and folk life of Britain, Ireland, Canada, and Australia. The collection contains specialized holdings on children's lore and games, Afro-American folklore, and folklore theory. The phonodisc collection is rich in examples of American, English, Scottish, and Irish revival.

FOLKLORE, BALKAN

CA —UNIVERSITY OF CALIFORNIA, LOS ANGELES, Research Library, Dept of Special Collections, 405 Hilgard Ave, Los Angeles, 90024. Edward Shreeves, Chairman, Bibliographers Group; David S Zeidberg, Head
Holdings: Vols 10 Mss
Notes: Incl 18 linear feet of mss and letters relating to Slavic and Balkan folklore and ethnology.

FOLKLORE, BLACK

DC —HOWARD UNIVERSITY, Moorland-Spingarn Research Center, 500 Howard Place NW, Washington, 20059. Clifford L Muse, Jr, Acting Dir
Holdings: Vols (106,086) Mss Maps Pix Slides Phonorecords Audiotapes 16mm Films Filmstrips Microforms
Budget: ($854,753)
See also entry under Blacks

MS —UNIVERSITY OF MISSISSIPPI, John Davis Williams Library, University, 38677.
Notes: The folklore library of Professor Kenneth S Goldstein comprises more than 12,000 vols and 4500 phonodiscs. Incl a comprehensive 3000 vol collection of editions of collected folksongs and works about the evolution of the Anglo-American folksong, as well as works treating the folklore and folk life of Britain, Ireland, Canada, and Australia. The collection contains specialized holdings on children's lore and games, Afro-American folklore, and folklore theory. The phonodisc collection is rich in examples of American, English, Scottish, and Irish revival.

TX —UNIVERSITY OF TEXAS LIBRARIES, General Libraries, PO Box P, Austin, 78713. Carolyn Bucknell, Asst Dir for Collection Development
Holdings: Cat Microforms

VA —UNIVERSITY OF VIRGINIA, Alderman Library, Manuscripts Dept, Charlottesville, 22901. Edmund Berkeley Jr, Cur
Holdings: Cat Mss Pix
Notes: Material in over 420 collections documents the history and culture of Afro-Americans. Virginia Folklore Collection (23,000 items) incl the following collection: Virginia WPA Folklore Files, compiled ca 1936-1943, under US Works Project Administration, ca 8000 items. Black and white folklore and folk music collected by field workers from informants throughout Virginia. Incl ms reports, phonorecords. Described in Rosenberg, Bruce A (comp), *The Folksongs of Virginia: A Checklist of the WPA Holdings in the Alderman Library, University of Virginia* (Charlottesville: University Press of Virginia, 1969); also, typescript and computer printed guides-- Charles L Perdue, Jr, and others (comps), *The White Folklore of the Virginia WPA Files: A Checklist ...* (Charlottesville, 1973); Thomas Barden and others(comps), *Afro-American Folklore of the WPA Folklore Files in the Alderman Library ...* (Charlottesville, 1973). Also incl the desegration movement in Virginia in the 1960s and 1970s and the massive resistance of Virginia politcal leaders. Michael F Plunkett *A Guide to Materials on the History, Literature, and Culture of Afro-Americans in the Manuscripts Department, University of Virginia Library.*

FOLKLORE, BRAZILIAN

AZ —UNIVERSITY OF ARIZONA, Library, Tucson, 85721. W David Laird, Librn
Notes: The greatest strength of this collection is in long back-runs of periodicals.

CA —UNIVERSITY OF CALIFORNIA, RIVERSIDE, University Library, 4045 Canyon Crest Dr, Box 5900, Riverside, 92517.
Holdings: Vols 2,500
Notes: General research collection in the humanities and social sciences, with special strengths in history, literature, folklore and economic conditions, chiefly 20th century.

FOLKLORE, BRITISH

MS —UNIVERSITY OF MISSISSIPPI, John Davis Williams Library, University, 38677.
Notes: The folklore library of Professor Kenneth S Goldstein comprises more than 12,000 vols and 4500 phonodiscs. Incl a comprehensive 3000 vol collection of editions of collected folksongs and works about the evolution of the Anglo-American folksong, as well as works treating the folklore and folk life of Britain, Ireland, Canada, and Australia. The collection contains specialized holdings on children's lore and games, Afro-American folklore, and folklore theory. The phonodisc collection is rich in examples of American, English, Scottish, and Irish revival.

FOLKLORE, CANADIAN

MS —UNIVERSITY OF MISSISSIPPI, John Davis Williams Library, University, 38677.
Notes: The folklore library of Professor Kenneth S Goldstein comprises more than 12,000 vols and 4500 phonodiscs. Incl a comprehensive 3000 vol collection of editions of collected folksongs and works about the evolution of the Anglo-American folksong, as well as works treating the folklore and folk life of Britain, Ireland, Canada, and Australia. The collection contains specialized holdings on children's lore and games, Afro-American folklore, and folklore theory. The phonodisc collection is rich in examples of American, English, Scottish, and Irish revival.

FOLKLORE, CHINESE

IL —CENTER FOR RESEARCH LIBRARIES, 6050 S Kenwood Ave, Chicago, 60637. Donald B Simpson, Dir; Esther Smith, Collection Development Librn
Holdings: Vols Cat Microforms
Notes: Mainland China newspapers, periodicals and clippings, early western language newspapers in China, Hong Kong newspapers in English, British Foreign Office and US State Dept records relating to China, Dunhuang manuscripts, missionary periodicals. Microfilm and reprints of newspapers, serials and monographs from Center for Chinese Research Materials. Hunter collection of Chinese communist propaganda (ca 1000 vols). Microfilm and originals of Maritime Customs publications. Microfilm of press summaries prepared by US Consulate, Hong Kong, archives of missionary organizations, Chinese folk literature, etc. Descriptive pamphlet available.

FOLKLORE, GAELIC

MS —UNIVERSITY OF MISSISSIPPI, John Davis Williams Library, University, 38677.
Notes: The folklore library of Professor Kenneth S Goldstein comprises more than 12,000 vols and 4500 phonodiscs. Incl a comprehensive 3000 vol collection of editions of collected folksongs and works about the evolution of the Anglo-American folksong, as well as works treating the folklore and folk life of Britain, Ireland, Canada, and Australia. The collection contains specialized holdings on children's lore and games, Afro-American folklore, and folklore theory. The phonodisc collection is rich in examples of American, English, Scottish, and Irish revival.

FOLKLORE, IRISH

MS —UNIVERSITY OF MISSISSIPPI, John Davis Williams Library, University, 38677.
Notes: The folklore library of Professor Kenneth S Goldstein comprises more than 12,000 vols and 4500 phonodiscs. Incl a comprehensive 3000 vol collection of editions of collected folksongs and works about the evolution of the Anglo-American folksong, as well as works treating the folklore and folk life of Britain, Ireland, Canada, and Australia. The collection contains specialized holdings on children's lore and games, Afro-American folklore, and folklore theory. The phonodisc collection is rich in examples of American, English, Scottish, and Irish revival.

FOLKLORE, JEWISH

DC —LIBRARY OF CONGRESS, American Folklife Center, Archive of Folk Culture, Washington, 20540.
Notes: The Ruth Rubin Collection of field recordings of Jewish folklore, 1940s - 1960s.

IA —UNIVERSITY OF IOWA, University Libraries, Iowa City, 52242.
Holdings: Vols 1850 Mss
Notes: The Leo W Schwarz Collection, a valuable and rare group of books dealing with Hasidic literature, a portion on Old Testament studies and works on Jewish history, philosophy and culture, the Jews in Nazi Germany, Jewish folklore and the history of the Jews in the US. Incl about 850 books in Hebrew and 1000 in other languages, mss of several of Schwarz's books and articles, correspondence, notes, and background research relating to his publications.

NY —YIVO INSTITUTE FOR JEWISH RESEARCH, Library & Archives, 1048 Fifth Ave, New York, 10028. Dina Abramowicz, Librn; Marek Web, Archivist
Holdings: Cat Pix
Notes: Extensive collections on Yiddish folklore, incl folk songs, folk tales, art and music. Scholarship: monographs, periodicals, bibliographies in Yiddish and other languages incl.

RI —BROWN UNIVERSITY, John Hay Library, 20 Prospect St, Providence, 02912. Mark N Brown, Cur Mss
Holdings: Vols 1500 Cat
Notes: A virtually complete collection of the literature dealing with the Legend of the Wandering Jew printed from the 17th century to date. In addition to historical discussion of the legend, there are sections devoted to the appearance of Ahasuerus in drama, fiction, illustrations, poetry, song, and music.

FOLKLORE, KENTUCKY

KY —WESTERN KENTUCKY UNIVERSITY, The Kentucky Museum and

FOLKLORE, KENTUCKY (cont.)

Library, Bowling Green, 42101. Diane L Alpert, Cur of the Museum
Holdings: Vols 60 Uncat Pix Slides Audiotapes
Notes: Folklore Archives, and individual and general research files on 150,000 museum objects and regional museum collections. No photocopying.

FOLKLORE, LATVIAN

WI —UNIVERSITY OF WISCONSIN, MADISON, Memorial Library, Slavic Studies Collection, 728 State St, Madison, 53706. Aleksander Rolich, Bibliographer for Slavic Studies; Robert P Gakovich, Slavic Cataloger; Valdis J Zeps, Baltic Studies Center
Holdings: Vols 4000 Cat Microforms
Notes: Emigre literature and respectable in lingustics, history, folklore, and theatre.

FOLKLORE, NEAR EAST

TX —TEXAS TECH UNIVERSITY, Library, Lubbock, 79409. David J Murrah, Assoc Dir for Special Collections
Notes: Archive of Turkish Oral Narrative.

FOLKLORE, NORTH CAROLINA

NC —DUKE UNIVERSITY, William R Perkins Library, Manuscript Dept, Durham, 27706. Ellen Gartrell, Cur of Mss
Holdings: Cat Mss
Notes: Papers of Frank C Brown and colleagues, much of which later published in *The Frank C Brown Collection of North Carolina Folklore* (7 vols, Durham, 1952-1964). Incl correspondence, texts, recordings, clippings, quilt blocks.

FOLKLORE, ORIENTAL

IL —CENTER FOR RESEARCH LIBRARIES, 6050 S Kenwood Ave, Chicago, 60637. Donald B Simpson, Dir; Esther Smith, Collection Development Librn
Holdings: Vols Cat Microforms
Notes: Mainland China newspapers, periodicals and clippings, early western language newspapers in China, Hong Kong newspapers in English, British Foreign Office and US State Dept records relating to China, Dunhuang manuscripts, missionary periodicals. Microfilm and reprints of newspapers, serials and monographs from Center for Chinese Research Materials. Hunter collection of Chinese communist propaganda (ca 1000 vols). Microfilm and originals of Maritime Customs publications. Microfilm of press summaries prepared by US Consulate, Hong Kong, archives of missionary organizations, Chinese folk literature, etc. Descriptive pamphlet available.

WA —UNIVERSITY OF WASHINGTON LIBRARIES, East Asia Library, DO-27, Seattle, 98195. Karl Lo, Head
Holdings: Vols (300,000) Cat Microforms
Budget: ($200,000)
Notes: Southwest China: Joseph Rock Collection, ca 2000 vols; modern Chinese poetry, 1919 to date: ca 700 titles; Asian art, esp Japanese painting: 4097 vols;Tiao-yu-t'ai movement in the US: ca 400 items of periodicals and pamphlets; modern Korean poetry, ancient and modern: ca 1000 titles; Mu-yu-shu folk literature: ca 1000 items.

FOLKLORE, SLAVIC

CA —UNIVERSITY OF CALIFORNIA, LOS ANGELES, Research Library, Dept of Special Collections, 405 Hilgard Ave, Los Angeles, 90024. Edward Shreeves, Chairman, Bibliographers Group; David S Zeidberg, Head
Holdings: Vols 10 Mss
Notes: Incl 18 linear feet of mss and letters relating to Slavic and Balkan folklore and ethnology.

WA —UNIVERSITY OF WASHINGTON LIBRARIES, Suzzallo Library, Slavic & East European Section, FM-25, Seattle, 98195. Barbara A Galik, Head
Holdings: Vols (250,000) Cat Mss Maps Pix Phonorecords Audiotapes Microforms
Budget: ($85,000)
Notes: Strong research collections for Russia--USSR, including Central Asia, Eastern Europe and the Balkans especially Yugoslavia and Poland. Holdings are strongest in Russian folklore, with additional holdings in the republics of the USSR, East European and Balkan countries. There are extensive holdings of the publications of academies, major universities, and principal scholarly institutions, especially of long serial runs.

FOLKLORE, TURKISH

TX —TEXAS TECH UNIVERSITY, Library, Lubbock, 79409. David J Murrah, Assoc Dir for Special Collections

FOLKLORE, UPPER VOLTA

DC —LIBRARY OF CONGRESS, American Folklife Center, Archive of Folk Culture, Washington, 20540.
Notes: The Jim Rosellini Collection of field recordings of the folklore of the Republic of Upper Volta, 1969-75.

FOLKLORE OF ANIMALS see Animal Lore

FOLKLORE OF CATS see Cats and Catlore

FOLKLORE OF CHILDREN

MS —UNIVERSITY OF MISSISSIPPI, John Davis Williams Library, University, 38677.
Notes: The folklore library of Professor Kenneth S Goldstein comprises more than 12,000 vols and 4500 phonodiscs. Incl a comprehensive 3000 vol collection of editions of collected folksongs and works about the evolution of the Anglo-American folksong, as well as works treating the folklore and folk life of Britain, Ireland, Canada, and Australia. The collection contains specialized holdings on children's lore and games, Afro-American folklore, and folklore theory. The phonodisc collection is rich in examples of American, English, Scottish, and Irish revival.

NY —US COMMITTEE FOR UNICEF, Information Center on Children's Cultures, 331 E 38 St, New York, 10016. Melinda Greenblatt, Chief Librn
Holdings: Vols (17,500) Cat Pix Slides Films Filmstrips
Notes: Social and cultural aspects of lives of children from developing countries. Especially strong in the area of school textbooks from Near Eastern Asian, African, Latin American, Caribbean, and Pacific Area countries; holidays and celebrations related to children all over the world; children's books in English which describe child life in other countries. Especially strong collection of folklore, and folklore of children, from all regions mentioned above.

WI —UNIVERSITY OF WISCONSIN, MADISON, Library School Library, 600 N Park St, Madison, 53706. Sally Davis, Librn
Notes: 5000 vols of juvenile literature, incl picture books in French, German, Norwegian, Swedish, and Russian, children's classics, folk and fairy tales, juvenile illustrators and current writing, maintained at the UW Library School Library. Children's literature does not circulate outside University.

WI —MILWAUKEE PUBLIC LIBRARY, 814 W Wisconsin Ave, Milwaukee, 53233. Donald J Sager, City Librn
Holdings: Vols 700
Notes: Includes titles indexed in *Index To Fairy Tales, Myths and Legends* by Mary Huse Eastman and supplements and in Norma Olin Ireland's *Index to Fairy Tales 1949-1972.*

FOLKLORE OF COUNTRIES see Geographical Myths

FOLKLORE OF JEWS see Folklore, Jewish

FOLKLORE OF MINES

AZ —PHOENIX PUBLIC LIBRARY, Arizona Room, 12 E McDowell, Phoenix, 85004. Jeannette Brush, Librn
Holdings: Vols (30,000) Cat Maps Pix
Budget: ($12,000)
See also entry under Arizona - History.

CO —DENVER PUBLIC LIBRARY, Western History Department, 1357 Broadway, Denver, 80203. Eleanor M Gehres, Head
Holdings: Vols (50,000) Cat Mss Maps Pix Audiotapes Microforms
Notes: Western US History. The department has a separate catalog, published in 1970 in 7 vols by G K Hall Co. First supplement published in 1975 in 1 vol. There is a subject index of some 3 million entries to newspapers and magazines of the Rocky Mountain region, added to daily. The Western Newspaper Microfilm Center contains approx 7000 reels of Western US newspapers. Collection has ca 275,000 negatives and prints of Western life; and ca 2500 maps, cataloged and classified.

PA —KING'S COLLEGE, D Leonard Corgan Library, 14 W Jackson St, Wilkes-Barre, 18711. Judith Tierney, Special Collections Librn
Holdings: Vols 850 Cat Mss Pix
Notes: The George Korson Folklore Archive. Separate catalog to books in collection. Books and periodicals relate to folklore generally; mss, 107 tapes and 70 disc recordings focus on folklore of the coal mining industry, 1918-1969. See Judith Tierney, comp. *A Description of the George Korson Folklore Archive* (Wilkes-Barre, Pa: King's College Press, 1973). Photocopying limited.

FOLKTALES see Folklore

FOLLETT, BARBARA

NY —COLUMBIA UNIVERSITY LIBRARIES, Rare Book & Manuscript Library, 801 Butler Library, 535 W 114 St, New York, 10027. Kenneth A Lohf, Librn
Holdings: Mss
Notes: Papers, incl mss, letters, reviews, etc. Incl 2000 items. Restricted use.

FOLSOM, FRANKLIN

CO —UNIVERSITY OF COLORADO, Libraries, Special Collections, Boulder, 80309. Nora J Quinlan, Head
Holdings: Vols Uncat Mss
Notes: Folsom Collection. Mss, correspondence, files and books by noted Colorado authors Franklin Folsom and Mary Elting. A husband and wife team which collaborated on a number of children's books. Subject emphasis are fiction, science and natural history. In addition the Folsoms worked on several books for adult audiences. 27 1/2 feet of ms material; approx 150 books in various editions.

FOLSOM, JAMES C., 1921-

KS —MENNINGER FOUNDATION, Archives, 5600 W Sixth St, Box 829, Topeka, 66601. Alice Brand, Librn; Mark West, Archivist
Notes: 15 boxes, 1948-82. Incl correspondence, mss, publications, and miscellaneous materials.

FOLSOM, MARION BAYARD

NY —UNIVERSITY OF ROCHESTER, Rush Rhees Library, Department of Rare Books and Special Collections, Rochester, 14627. Peter Dzwonkoski, Librn
Holdings: Cat Mss
Notes: Material related to the creation, passage, and subsequent amendments to the Social Security Act of 1935; also correspondence, printed material, and reports related to Folsom's career as an Eastman Kodak executive, Under Secretary of the Treasury (1953-55), and Secretary of Health, Education, and Welfare (1955-58).

FOOD

CA —UNIVERSITY OF CALIFORNIA, DAVIS, General Library, Davis, 95616.

FOOD (cont.)

Bernard Kreissman, University Librn; C Danial Elliott, Asst Head, Dept Special Collections
Holdings: Vols 15,000 Cat

CA —LOS ANGELES PUBLIC LIBRARY, Science & Technology Dept, 630 W Fifth St, Los Angeles, 90071. Billie M Connor, Dept Head
Holdings: Vols 3500 Cat
Notes: Books on the cookery of all nationalities and ethnic groups. Strong collection of California cookery. Some early works in Spanish. Additional materials on wines and other beverages, quantity and institutional cookery, food technology, and special diets. Menu collection of approximately 1000 concentrates on Southern California.

CA —CITY COLLEGE OF SAN FRANCISCO, Alice Statler Library, Hotel & Restaurant Dept, 50 Phelan Ave, San Francisco, 94112. Mary B Smyth, Librn
Holdings: Vols (7300) Cat Slides 16mm Films Filmstrips Microforms
Budget: ($5000)
Notes: The collection covers all aspects of the public hospitality industry. In addition to the book collection, it has 6000 cataloged pamphlets, 1500 menus. It also has bound hotel and restaurant magazines dating back to the 19th century. Receives 85 current periodicals in hospitality industry.

CA —FITZ HUGH LUDLOW MEMORIAL LIBRARY, PO Box 99346, San Francisco, 94109. Michael R Aldrich, Exec Cur
Holdings: Mss Maps Pix Slides Phonorecords Audiotapes Videotapes
Notes: Collection stored. Important mail inquiries only. No interlibrary lending or telephoned inquiries. Collection of psychoactive drug literature, incl vols on drug cuisine.

CA —STANFORD UNIVERSITY, Food Research Institute Library, Stanford, 94305. Charles C Milford, Librn
Holdings: Vols (13,915) Cat Maps Pix Microforms
Budget: ($31,565)
Notes: The economic aspects of the production, trade, disposition, and prices of food, feed, and fiber commodities throughout the world. Incl 25,000 pamphlets.

CO —COLORADO STATE UNIVERSITY, Libraries, Fort Collins, 80523. Marjorie Rhoades, Engineering Sciences Librn
Holdings: Vols (6000) Cat
Budget: ($5000)
Notes: Water and Soil in Arid Regions (WASAR) is an index and guide to books, conference papers, journal articles, government documents and technical reports, mostly in English, within the appropriate subject areas and held by Colorado State University Libraries. The bibliographical citations are of selected items dealing with soils, water, arid lands, crops, foods and nutrition with certain economic, political, ecological and historical parameters also included. The information needs of developing countries and of those who serve them are the prime criteria for inclusion.

DC —SUGAR ASSOCIATION LIBRARY, 1511 K Street, NW, Washington, 20005.
Holdings: Vols 1000 Cat Mss Maps Pix Slides Microforms
Budget: $8000
Notes: Sugar utilization and research, public health, food technology, and sucrose chemistry.

IL —UNIVERSITY OF ILLINOIS, URBANA/CHAMPAIGN, Library, Home Economics Library, 314 Bevier Hall, Champaign, 61820. Barbara C Swain, Librn
Holdings: Vols 17,640 Cat Microforms
Budget: $20,283
Notes: Food and nutrition.
See also entries under Food Industry and Trade; Food Service.

IL —J WALTER THOMPSON CO, Information Center, 875 N Michigan Ave, Chicago, 60611. Edward G Strable, Dir
Holdings: Vols 500 Cat Microforms
Notes: Food history, customs, and use in (cookbooks) in book collection. Data files (35 drawers) emphasize food markets in reports, releases, clippings, articles, studies.

IL —ARCHER DANIELS MIDLAND CO, Library, 4666 Faries Parkway, Decatur, 62525. Richard E Wallace, Manager, Information Services; Karen E Perman, Librn
Holdings: Vols (8000) Cat Maps Slides 16mm Films Microforms
Notes: Incl all aspects of foods-processing, economics, nutrition, science, technology, statistics, research, marketing, etc. Special interest in foods derived from plant materials. Incl 100 maps, 1200 slides, 105 films, over 2000 microforms, patents, and research reports.

IN —MILES LABORATORIES, Library Resources and Services, 1127 Myrtle St, PO Box 40, Elkhart, 46515. Allam Hagopian, Mgr
Holdings: Vols (16,500) Cat Audiotapes Microforms
Notes: Incl files of pharmaceutical product advertising pieces, extensive literature files on company related drugs; domestic and international marketing files. 32,000 bound periodicals.

IN —HURTY-PECK LIBRARY OF BEVERAGE LITERATURE, 5650 W Raymond Street, PO Box 41167, Indianapolis, 46208. Ben Wilson, Librn
Holdings: Vols (6000) Cat //
Notes: The most comprehensive collection, in English, in the world on beverages of all types. History, manufacture, formulae, customs. Books on beer and brewing; cocoa and chocolate; coffee; liquors and spirits; soft drinks; tea; and wine.

IN —PURDUE UNIVERSITY LIBRARIES, Consumer & Family Sciences Library, Stone Hall W, West Lafayette, 47907. Emily Alward, Librn
Holdings: Vols (14,000) Cat

IA —IOWA STATE UNIVERSITY, Library, Ames, 50011. Warren B Kuhn, Dean of Library Services
Holdings: Cat
Notes: Incl dairy science, food science and research, food technology, institutional management, marketing and nutrition. Extensive serial holdings.

IA —ARCHER DANIELS MIDLAND, Research Library, PO Box 340, Clinton, 52732. Carol L Kolk, Research Librn
Holdings: Vols 2200 Cat Microforms
Notes: Card index to patent file. Keydex index to Research Experiment Reports.

KY —UNIVERSITY OF KENTUCKY, Agricultural Library, Agricultural Science Center North, Lexington, 40506. Antoinette Paris Powell, Librn
Holdings: Vols (90,000) Cat Microforms
Budget: ($110,385)

MD —US DEPT OF AGRICULTURE, National Agricultural Library, 10301 Baltimore Blvd, Beltsville, 20705. Joseph H Howard, Director
Notes: Worldwide coverage of all aspects of agriculture and related fields. Crop ecology, agro-climatic analogs; air pollution effects. Agronomy: agricultural and tropical and desert agriculture. For use by the staff of the USDA. Incl in the former collections of American Institute of Crop Ecology.

MA —UNIVERSITY OF MASSACHUSETTS AT AMHERST, Physical Sciences Library, Amherst, 01003. Siegfried Feller, Assoc Dir for Collection Development
Holdings: Vols Cat Microforms
Notes: Food technology.

MI —GERBER PRODUCTS COMPANY, Corporate Library, 445 State St, Fremont, 49412. Sherrie Anderson, Librn
Holdings: Vols (4270) Cat

MN —GENERAL MILLS, James Ford Bell Technical Center Library, 9000 Plymouth Ave N, Minneapolis, 55427. Curtis H Hallstrom, Mgr, Technical Information Services; Jacqueline A Angus, Suprv, Library Services
Holdings: Vols (6000) Cat Microforms
Budget: ($28,000)

MO —PET INCORPORTED, Information Center, 400 S Fourth St, PO Box 392, Saint Louis, 63166. L R Walton, Corporate Librn
Holdings: Vols (21,000) Cat Microforms

NJ —CPC INTERNATIONAL, Best Food Research & Engineering Center, Information Center, 1120 Commerce Ave, Union, 07083. Anne Troop, Mgr
Holdings: Vols (5000) Cat Slides Videotapes 16mm Films Microforms
Notes: Food science and technology.

NY —CULINARY INSTITUTE OF AMERICA, Katharine Angell Library, North Rd, Hyde Park, 12538. Gertrude Trani, Asst Librn
Holdings: Vols (23,000) Cat Slides Videotapes 16mm Films Filmstrips
Notes: Culinary arts, incl cookery, beverages, and food service management. AV materials housed in separate Learning Resources Center. Henry Woods, Dir.

NY —CORNELL UNIVERSITY LIBRARIES, Hotel Administration Library, Statler Hall, Ithaca, 14853. Margaret J Oaksford, Librn
Holdings: Vols (25,000) Cat Mss Maps
Budget: ($60,000)
Notes: Extensive collections on management, travel, hotels, food and beverage, wine, real estate and tourism. Incl menu collection.

NY —NEW YORK ACADEMY OF MEDICINE, Library, 2 E 103 St, New York, 10029. Brett A Kirkpatrick, Librn
Notes: Collection of Margaret Barclay Wilson, MD; one of largest collections on the subject; rare and historical items. Added to selectively incl copy of 9th century Ms, De re Culinaria. Also incl 3000 uncat pamphlets, 500 menus, 50 Italian broadsides, 17th-19th centuries food regulations.

NC —NORTH CAROLINA STATE UNIVERSITY, D H Hill Library, Box 7111, Raleigh, 27695. I T Littleton, Dir
Holdings: Vols 4595 Cat
Budget: $2000
Notes: Incl monographs.

NC —R J REYNOLDS TOBACCO CO, Scientific Information Services Library, Bowman Gray Technical Center, BGTC 611-12/205, Winston-Salem, 27102. Nellie W Sizemore, Librn
Holdings: Vols 500 Cat Microforms

OH —OHIO STATE UNIVERSITY, Home Economics Library, Campbell Hall Rm 325, 1787 Neil Ave, Columbus, 43210. Neosha Mackey, Librn
Holdings: Vols (14,000) Cat Microforms
Notes: Separate catalog. Also, book catalog: *Catalog of the Home Economics Library* (Boston: G K Hall, 1976), 3 vols.

PA —DREXEL UNIVERSITY LIBRARIES, W W Hagerty Library, 32 & Chestnut Sts, Philadelphia, 19104. R L Snyder, Dir
Holdings: Vols (5000) Cat
Budget: ($9000)
Notes: Food technology and management with emphasis on nutrition. Also incl collection of cookbooks which stress cultural differences and the best in sound American cooking.

PA —FRANKLIN INSTITUTE LIBRARY, 20 & The Parkway, Philadelphia, 19103. Miriam Padusis, Dir; Charles Wilt, Readers Servs Librn
Holdings: Vols (300,000) Cat Maps Pix Microforms

RI —UNIVERSITY OF RHODE ISLAND, Graduate School of Oceanography, Pell Library Bldg, Narragansett, 02882. Kenneth T Morse, Chief Librn

TX —UNIVERSITY OF TEXAS LIBRARIES, John W Mallet Chemistry Library, Welch Hall 2132, Austin, 78712. A E Skinner, Chemistry Librn
Holdings: Vols (44,000) Cat Microforms
Notes: Described in *The John W Mallet Chemistry Library (The University of Texas at Austin)* (Austin: The General Libraries, 1975).

WA —UNIVERSITY OF WASHINGTON LIBRARIES, Fisheries-Oceanography Library, WB-30, Seattle, 98195. Thomas D Moritz, Head Librn
Holdings: Vols (49,000)
Budget: ($83,000)
Notes: Includes all aspects of food science and technology with principal emphasis on seafood.

WI —UNIVERSITY OF WISCONSIN, MADISON, College of Agricultural & Life

FOOD (cont.)

Sciences, Steenbock Memorial Library, 550 Babcock Dr, Madison, 53706. Jan Kennedy, Dir
Holdings: Vols (186,312) Cat Docs
Notes: Collection incl dairy and food science, food toxicology and microbiology, and nutrition; extensive cookbook collection.

WI —UNIVERSITY OF WISCONSIN-STOUT, Library Learning Center, Menomonie, 54751. Philip Sawin Jr, Coll Develop Librn
Notes: Extensive collection in Cookery. This is one of the first collections to be developed to support the Institute of Domestic Science in 1883. In 1960 the University offered a graduate degree in Food Science and Nutrition. University of Wisconsin-Stout School of Home Economics currently has the largest enrollment in the United States.

BC —UNIVERSITY OF BRITISH COLUMBIA, Macmillan Library, 2357 Main Mall, Vancouver, V6T 2A2, Can. Mary W Macaree, Head
Holdings: Vols (35,000) Cat Maps Slides Microforms
Budget: ($8500)

MB —UNIVERSITY OF MANITOBA, Agriculture Library, Dafoe Rd, Winnipeg, R3T 2N2, Can. Judy Harper, Head
Holdings: Vols (9000) Cat

FOOD—ANALYSIS

AR —NATIONAL CENTER FOR TOXICOLOGICAL RESEARCH, Library, Jefferson, 72079. Susan Laney-Sheehan, Supvr Librn
Holdings: Vols (15,000) Cat Mss Slides Audiotapes 16mm Films Microforms
Notes: Incl (860) journal titles, (230) current subscriptions.

CA —UNIVERSITY OF CALIFORNIA, DAVIS, Shields Library, Dept of Special Collections, Davis, 95616. Donald Kunitz, Head; C Danial Elliott, Asst Head
Holdings: Uncat Mss Pix
Notes: Food technology files, 1943-1959, involving the research of Leonard Born on the irradiation of foods, cold sterilization, and algae production. Also, mss, correspondence, photographs, and clippings on various aspects of growing and processing fruit and vegetables, with an emphasis on canning. 3800 items.

CA —SUNKIST GROWERS, Research Library, 760 E Sunkist St, Ontario, 91761. Martha C Nemeth, Librn
Holdings: Vols (1500) Cat
Budget: ($10,000)
Notes: Technology of citrus fruit and citrus fruit products, primarily Californian. Strong in organic and food chemistry, with additional coverage of food technology, essential oils, microbiology and environmental protection.

FOOD—CHEMISTRY see Food—Analysis

FOOD—CONTAMINATION see Food Contamination

FOOD—HISTORY

IL —J WALTER THOMPSON CO, Information Center, 875 N Michigan Ave, Chicago, 60611. Edward G Strable, Dir
Holdings: Vols 50 Cat Microforms
Notes: Food history, customs, and use in book collection. Data files (35 drawers) emphasize food markets in reports, releases, clippings, articles, studies.

FOOD—PACKAGING

NY —WESTRECO INC, Research Library, 555 S Fourth St, Fulton, 13069. Janice Burns, Research Librn
Holdings: Vols (1200) Cat Periodicals VF
Notes: Food Science and Technology collection of about (1200) books and pamphlets. Back files of periodicals retained up to 20 years.

SC —CRYOVAC TECHNICAL LIBRARY, PO Box 464, Duncan, 29334. M M Ezell, Libn
Holdings: Vols 6000 Cat
Notes: Library supports corporate research, development, and engineering. Incl materials on chemical and mechanical engineering, polymers and polymerization, plastics, and food packaging. 175 periodical titles received. Library open by appointment or through ILL.

WI —UNIVERSITY OF WISCONSIN-STOUT, Library Learning Center, Menomonie, 54751. Philip Sawin Jr, Coll Develop Librn
Notes: Supports the Packaging concentration of the Master's Degree in Industrial Management. Concentration was authorized at the graduate level in 1974, but specialized collection since 1965.

FOOD—PRESERVATION

CA —UNIVERSITY OF CALIFORNIA, DAVIS, Shields Library, Dept of Special Collections, Davis, 95616. Donald Kunitz, Head; C Danial Elliott, Asst Head
Holdings: Uncat Mss Pix
Notes: Food technology files, 1943-1959, involving the research of Leonard Born on the irradiation of foods, cold sterilization, and algae production. Also, mss, correspondence, photographs, and clippings on various aspects of growing and processing fruit and vegetables, with an emphasis on canning. 3800 items.

CA —SUNKIST GROWERS, Research Library, 760 E Sunkist St, Ontario, 91761. Martha C Nemeth, Librn
Holdings: Vols (1500) Cat
Budget: ($10,000)
Notes: Technology of citrus fruit and citrus fruit products, primarily Californian. Strong in organic and food chemistry, with additional coverage of food technology, essential oils, microbiology and environmental protection.

NY —WESTRECO INC, Research Library, 555 S Fourth St, Fulton, 13069. Janice Burns, Research Librn
Holdings: Vols (1200) Cat Periodicals VF
Notes: Food Science and Technology collection of about (1200) books and pamphlets. Back files of periodicals retained up to 20 years.

OR —OREGON STATE UNIVERSITY, Library, Corvallis, 97331. Melvin George, Dir
Holdings: Vols (980,000) Cat

FOOD—STATISTICS

IL —ARCHER DANIELS MIDLAND CO, Library, 4666 Faries Parkway, Decatur, 62525. Richard E Wallace, Manager, Information Services; Karen E Perman, Librn
Holdings: Vols (8000) Cat Maps Slides 16mm Films Microforms
Notes: Incl all aspects of foods-processing, economics, nutrition, science, technology, statistics, research, marketing, etc. Special interest in foods derived from plant materials. Incl 100 maps, 1200 slides, 105 films, over 2000 microforms, patents, and research reports.

FOOD, CHEMISTRY OF see Food—Analysis

FOOD, DRUGS IN see Drugs in Food

FOOD CANNERIES see Canneries

FOOD CHEMISTRY see Food—Analysis

FOOD CONTAMINATION

AR —NATIONAL CENTER FOR TOXICOLOGICAL RESEARCH, Library, Jefferson, 72079. Susan Laney-Sheehan, Supvr Librn
Holdings: Vols (15,000) Cat Mss Slides Audiotapes 16mm Films Microforms
Notes: Incl (860) journal titles, (230) current subscriptions.

CA —UNIVERSITY OF CALIFORNIA, DAVIS, Environmental Toxicology Library, Davis, 95616. Ming-yu Li, Documentation Specialist
Holdings: Vols (5000) Cat
Notes: Library is open to the public for reference only. In addition to the cataloged holdings, the library also maintains a pamphlet collection of 50 file drawers on agricultural chemicals, environmental pollution, heavy metals, food toxicants, toxicology, pesticides and trace elements.

NY —NASSAU COUNTY DEPARTMENT OF HEALTH, Division of Laboratories & Research, 209 Main St, Hempstead, 11550. Madeline Burston, Librn; Beatrice R Sewald, Asst Librn
Notes: Laboratory diagnosis.

FOOD CONTROL see Food Supply

FOOD INDUSTRY AND TRADE

CA —UNIVERSITY OF CALIFORNIA, DAVIS, General Library, Davis, 95616. Bernard Kreissman, University Librn; C Danial Elliott, Asst Head, Dept Special Collections
Holdings: Vols 7600 Cat

CA —UNIVERSITY OF SOUTHERN CALIFORNIA, Crocker Business Library, Hoffman Hall, University Park, Los Angeles, 90007. Judith A Truelson, Head Librn
Holdings: Vols (100,000) Cat Microforms
Notes: The Roy P Crocker Library of Business Administration, located in Hoffman Hall, houses more than 100,000 volumes and regularly receives approximately 1500 trade, financial, economics, labor, and general business periodicals and newspapers. The areas of subject concentration include business economics, finance and investments, general management/management theory, international business, finance and management, marketing/food marketing, and quantitative business analysis.

CA —STANFORD UNIVERSITY, Food Research Institute Library, Stanford, 94305. Charles C Milford, Librn
Holdings: Vols (13,915) Cat Maps Pix Microforms
Budget: ($31,565)
Notes: The economic aspects of the production, trade, disposition, and prices of food, feed, and fiber commodities throughout the world. Incl 25,000 pamphlets.

DE —UNIVERSITY OF DELAWARE, Agriculture Library, 2 Townsend Hall, Newark, 19717. Frederick Getze, Assoc Librn
Holdings: Vols (32,500) Cat Pix Microforms
Notes: Strong in entomology and ornamental horticulture. Extensive collection of state agriculture documents for each US state and Puerto Rico. Library subscribes to 600 serials (English and foreign).

DE —WIDENER UNIVERSITY, Delaware Campus Library, Box 7139, Concord Pike, Wilmington, 19803. Jane E Hukill, Library Dir
Holdings: Vols (48,000) Microforms
Notes: Incl food service, restaurants, motels, volume feeding, cookery.

IL —UNIVERSITY OF ILLINOIS, URBANA/CHAMPAIGN, Library, Home Economics Library, 314 Bevier Hall, Champaign, 61820. Barbara C Swain, Librn
Holdings: Vols 17,640 Cat Microforms
Notes: Food and nutrition.

IL —J WALTER THOMPSON CO, Information Center, 875 N Michigan Ave, Chicago, 60611. Edward G Strable, Dir
Holdings: Vols 50 Cat Microforms
Notes: Food history, customs, and use in book collection. Data files (35 drawers) emphasize food markets in reports, releases, clippings, articles, studies.

IL —ARCHER DANIELS MIDLAND CO, Library, 4666 Faries Parkway, Decatur, 62525. Richard E Wallace, Manager, Information Services; Karen E Perman, Librn
Holdings: Vols (8000) Cat Maps Slides 16mm Films Microforms
Notes: Incl all aspects of foods-processing, economics, nutrition, science, technology, statistics, research, marketing, etc. Special interest in foods derived from plant

FOOD INDUSTRY AND TRADE (cont.)

materials. Incl 100 maps, 1200 slides, 105 films, over 2000 microforms, patents, and research reports.

IA —IOWA STATE UNIVERSITY, Library, Ames, 50011. Warren B Kuhn, Dean of Library Services
Holdings: Cat
Notes: Incl dairy science, food science and research, food technology, institutional management, marketing and nutrition. Extensive serial holdings.

IA —ARCHER DANIELS MIDLAND, Research Library, PO Box 340, Clinton, 52732. Carol L Kolk, Research Librn
Holdings: Vols 2200 Cat Microforms
Notes: Card index to patent file. Keydex index to Research Experiment Reports.

MI —UNIVERSITY OF MICHIGAN, Engineering-Transportation Library, 312 Undergraduate Library, Ann Arbor, 48109. Maurita Holland, Librn
Holdings: Vols (400,000) Cat Microforms
Budget: ($225,000)

MI —GERBER PRODUCTS COMPANY, Corporate Library, 445 State St, Fremont, 49412. Sherrie Anderson, Librn
Holdings: Vols (4270) Cat

MN —GENERAL MILLS, James Ford Bell Technical Center Library, 9000 Plymouth Ave N, Minneapolis, 55427. Curtis H Hallstrom, Mgr, Technical Information Services; Jacqueline A Angus, Suprv, Library Services
Holdings: Vols (6000) Cat Microforms
Budget: ($28,000)

NY —CORNELL UNIVERSITY LIBRARIES, Collection of Regional History, Dept of Manuscripts and Univ Archives, Ithaca, 14853.
Notes: Oral history interviews, 1964-66, dealing mainly with the canning and freezing industries from 1890 to the present, researchers and pioneers in processing techniques, success and failure in the industry, sources of raw materials, warehouse storage and distribution, and many other related subjects.

NC —TECHNICAL INSTITUTE OF ALAMANCE, Learning Resources Center, Jimmy Kerr Rd, PO Box 623, Haw River, 27258. Ron Plummer, Coordr
Holdings: Vols 205 Cat Audiotapes Filmstrips Microforms
Notes: Food preparation specialist training.

PA —DELAWARE VALLEY COLLEGE, Joseph Krauskopf Library, Doylestown, 18901. Constance Shook, Dir

PA —SAINT JOSEPH'S UNIVERSITY, Academy of Food Marketing, Campbell Library, 54 St & City Line Ave, Philadelphia, 19131. Anna Mae Penrose, Librn
Holdings: Vols (3475) Cat Microforms
Budget: ($9000)
Notes: Marketing of food from farm to table. Also food trade journal holdings from the 1940s, with some incomplete years. Incl extensive vertical files.

TX —AMARILLO PUBLIC LIBRARY, 413 E Fourth, Amarillo, 79101. Mary Kay Snell, Librn
Holdings: Vols 1210 Cat Maps Filmstrips VF
Notes: The Meat Industry Collection contains documents, periodicals, pamphlets, AV materials on the production of processing and marketing of cattle, swine, sheep, poultry and rabbits. Most of the collection circulates except for the magazines.

TX —UNIVERSITY OF TEXAS LIBRARIES, John W Mallet Chemistry Library, Welch Hall 2132, Austin, 78712. A E Skinner, Chemistry Librn
Holdings: Vols (44,000) Cat Microforms
Notes: Described in *The John W Mallet Chemistry Library (The University of Texas at Austin)* (Austin: The General Libraries, 1975).

ON —METROPOLITAN TORONTO LIBRARY, Science & Technology Dept, 789 Yonge St, Toronto, M4W 2G8, Can. Margaret Walshe, Head
Holdings: Vols (80,000) Cat
Budget: ($30,000)
Notes: All aspects of technology for the specialist, the student, and the general public. The department gives high priority to Canadian material.

FOOD POISONING

CA —UNIVERSITY OF CALIFORNIA, DAVIS, Environmental Toxicology Library, Davis, 95616. Ming-yu Li, Documentation Specialist
Holdings: Vols (5000) Cat
Notes: Library is open to the public for reference only. In addition to the cataloged holdings, the library also maintains a pamphlet collection of 50 file drawers on agricultural chemicals, environmental pollution, heavy metals, food toxicants, toxicology, pesticides and trace elements.

FOOD PRESERVATION see Food—Preservation

FOOD RELIEF

CA —HOOVER INSTITUTION ON WAR, REVOLUTION & PEACE, Stanford University, Stanford, 94305. Milorad M Drachkovitch, Archivist
Holdings: // Mss
Notes: Records of the Inter-Allied Food Council, 1918, relating to the work of the Council in Great Britain, France, Italy, and the US. 21 boxes. Unpublished register is available in repository.

FOOD STAMP PLAN see Food Relief

FOOD SUPPLY

CA —UNIVERSITY OF CALIFORNIA, BERKELEY, Giannini Foundation of Agricultural Economics, Library, 248 Giannini Hall, Berkeley, 94720. Grace Dote, Librn
Holdings: Vols (18,000) Cat Mss Maps Microforms
Notes: Noncirculating collection. No interlibrary loans. Also about 124,000 unbound vols. Open to graduate students and faculties of universities and colleges, research workers and interested public. Mostly English language materials, primarily 1900 to date. Card catalog published by G K Hall Co. *Dictionary Catalog of the Giannini Foundation of Agricultural Economics Library, Univ of California*, 12 vols (Holdings thru 7/71).

PA —SAINT JOSEPH'S UNIVERSITY, Academy of Food Marketing, Campbell Library, 54 St & City Line Ave, Philadelphia, 19131. Anna Mae Penrose, Librn
Holdings: Vols (3475) Cat Microforms
Budget: ($9000)
Notes: Marketing of food from farm to table. Also food trade journal holdings from the 1940s, with some incomplete years. Incl extensive vertical files.

FOOD TRADE see Food Industry and Trade

FOODS, CONTAMINATED see Food Contamination

FOOT

NY —UNIVERSITY OF ROCHESTER, School of Medicine and Dentistry, Edward G Miner Library, 601 Elmwood Ave, Rochester, 14642. Lucretia McClure, Medical Librn; Janet Brady Berk, History of Medicine Librn
Holdings: Slides
Notes: Very rare historical collection of some 300 glass slides, most of which relate to human gait, the foot, footwear, and myodynamics.

FOOT—DISEASES see Podiatry

FOOT-AND-MOUTH DISEASE

NY —US DEPT OF AGRICULTURE, Agriculture Research Service, Plum Island Animal Disease Laboratory, PO Box 848, Greenport, 11944. Stephen Perlman, Librn
Holdings: Vols (15,000) Cat Pix Slides Microforms
Budget: ($37,000)

FOOTLIGHT PLAYERS

SC —COLLEGE OF CHARLESTON LIBRARY, Special Collections Dept, Charleston, 29401.
Notes: Several histories of the Footlight Players, scrapbooks (1932-1964), programs (1931-1958), footnotes (1937-1970), scripts (many adapted from well known works by Emmett Robinson), photographs, and posters. Also included is material dealing with the Dock Street Theatre's history, its theatre school, and non-Footlight Player performances.

FOOT SOLDIERS see Infantry

FOOTBALL

CA —UNIVERSITY OF THE PACIFIC, Holt-Atherton Pacific Center for Western Studies, Stockton, 95211. Hiram L Davis, Dir of Libraries
Holdings: Cat Mss
Notes: Primarily correspondence and newspaper clippings from the papers of Amos Alonzo Stagg, football coach and athletic director at the University of Chicago and later at the College of the Pacific. 1 linear ft (2 document boxes).

CT —YALE UNIVERSITY, Box 1603A, Yale Station, New Haven, 06520.
Notes: Papers of Walter Camp, father of American football and foremost authority on sports and physical fitness. 48 microfilm reels; incl also over 20,000 clippings, etc on sports, providing virtual history, 1866-1925. Published guide to the collection for sale.

IN —UNIVERSITY OF NOTRE DAME, University Libraries, Notre Dame, 46556.
Notes: Very likely the largest collection of sporting materials in the world. Over 500 sports and games are represented in a half-million documents. All physical forms of records are included, and there is no geographical restriction. Major center for research into all aspects of games and sports.

NY —COLUMBIA UNIVERSITY LIBRARIES, Rare Book & Manuscript Library, 801 Butler Library, 535 W 114 St, New York, 10027. Kenneth A Lohf, Librn
Notes: The L S Alexander Gumby Collection, which incl material on Blacks in sports. Restricted use.

OH —PRO FOOTBALL HALL OF FAME, Library, 2121 Harrison Ave NW, Canton, 44708. Anne Mangus, Librn; Joe Horrigan, Cur
Holdings: Vols 1000 Cat Pix Slides Audiotapes 16mm Films
Notes: Incl materials on all aspects of professional football, with special emphasis on the 119 men enshrined in the Hall of Fame. Mainly a research library. Incl periodicals and a vast array of historical material and mementos. Incl 17,000 pictures, 1500 slides, 50 audiotapes, 1300 16mm films, 3000 game programs and and 500 team media guides.

OH —COLLEGE FOOTBALL HALL OF FAME, Library, PO Box 300, Kings Mills, 45034. Don Schumacher, Cur
Notes: College of Football History, tourist attraction. Museum of football memorabilia and publications. Library not open to public.

OH —NATIONAL FOOTBALL HALL OF FAME, Kings Island Dr, Kings Mills, 45034. Don Schumacher, Librn in Charge

ON —CANADIAN FOOTBALL HALL OF FAME, 58 Jackson St, West, Hamilton, L8P 1L4, Can. William McBride, Dir
Holdings: Bks Cat
Notes: History of Canadian football for 115 years. Incl programs, memorabilia, 200 16mm films of all Canadian championship games since 1950's. Also a museum and archives of Canadian Rugby Football Union with original minutes of meetings and photographs and artifacts.

FOOTE, ARTHUR

DC —LIBRARY OF CONGRESS, Music Division, Washington, 20540.
Notes: The business papers and music mss of

FOOTE, ARTHUR (cont.)

the Arthur P Schmidt Company. Numerous works by important composers.

FOOTE, SAMUEL, 1720-1777

OH —OHIO UNIVERSITY, Vernon R Alden Library, Department of Archives and Special Collections, Athens, 45701. Gary A Hunt, Head
Holdings: Vols 18 Cat
Notes: A collection of first and other early editions.

FORAGE PLANTS

PE —AGRICULTURE CANADA, Research Station Library, PO Box 1210, Charlottetown, C1A 7M8, Can. Barrie Stanfield, Librn
Holdings: Vols (2300) Cat
Budget: ($5000)

FORAMINIFERA

DC —SMITHSONIAN INSTITUTION LIBRARIES, Natural History Branch, Washington, 20560. Sylvia Churgin, Chief Librn
Holdings: Cat Mss Maps Pix Microforms
Notes: Invertebrate zoology, Systematics. Incl crustacea, echinoderms, mollusks, worms, Cushman collection of foraminifera; Springer collection on crinoids; Wilson collection on copepoda.

PA —CARNEGIE LIBRARY OF PITTSBURGH, Science & Technology Dept, 4400 Forbes Ave, Pittsburgh, 15213. Catherine M Brosky, Dept Head
Notes: Subject of secondary interest with emphasis on North America. Covers paleobotany, vertebrates and invertebrates, foraminifera, mollusks, fish, reptiles, mammals. Abstracts, indexes, catalogs, bibliographies, journals, continuations, federal, state and society publications available.

FORBES, BERTIE CHARLES, 1880-1954

NY —SYRACUSE UNIVERSITY LIBRARIES, Ernest S Bird Library, George Arents Research Library for Special Collections, Syracuse, 13210. Carolyn A Davis, Manuscripts Librn; Amy S Doherty, University Archivist; Mark F Weimer, Rare Book Librn
Notes: His correspondence, papers and works. Papers 1892-1964 (9 linear feet).

FORBES, DELORIS STANTON

MA —BOSTON UNIVERSITY, Mugar Memorial Library, Special Collections Dept, 771 Commonwealth Ave, Boston, 02215. Howard B Gotlieb, Dir
Holdings: Cat Mss Pix
Notes: Mss, correspondence, etc collected in depth; incl publications by or about.

FORBES, EDWIN, 1880-1959

DC —LIBRARY OF CONGRESS, Prints & Photographs Div, Washington, 20540.
Notes: The Civil War Drawings Collection consists of 1600 original eyewitness drawings by Alfred R Waud, William Waud, and Edwin Forbes.

DC —LIBRARY OF CONGRESS, Prints & Photographs Div, Washington, 20540.
Notes: The Civil War Drawings Collection consists of 1600 original eyewitness drawings by Alfred R Waud, William Waud, and Edwin Forbes.

FORBES, ESTHER, 1891-1967

†MA —CLARK UNIVERSITY, Robert Hutchings Goddard Library, Worcester, 01610. Dorothy Mosa Kowski, Rare Books Librn
Holdings: Uncat
Notes: Her papers, 1906-1967; ca 250 items, ms of an unpublished novel entitled *The Sons of Ugo*; some hundreds of pages of notes concerning the early history of Massachusetts; carbon copy of typescript of the novel *Paradise* (1937); set of uncorrected printer's proofs of the novel *The Running of the Tide* (1948); and several hundred compositions, themes, essays, and stories, written by Miss Forbes both as school assignments and on her own, from childhood through high school and college. Gift from the family of Esther Forbes.

FORBES, JAMES

ON —UNIVERSITY OF TORONTO, Thomas Fisher Rare Book Library, 120 Saint George St, Toronto, M5S 1A5, Can. Richard G Landon, Head
Holdings: Vols 1600 // Cat Mss
Notes: Forbes Collection created by James Forbes (1629?-1712), English nonconformist minister. Kept as a separate library with few additions until present day. (Toronto, 1968). Also Heyworth, P L "Unfamiliar Libraries XVI: The Forbes Library," *The Book Collector*, Autumn 1970.

FORBES, GEN. JOHN

VA —UNIVERSITY OF VIRGINIA, Alderman Library, Charlottesville, 22901.
Holdings: Mss
Notes: Papers of Gen John Forbes, 1757-1759, on operations against the French at Fort Duquesne (Pittsburgh).

FORBES, KATHRYN

MA —BOSTON UNIVERSITY, Mugar Memorial Library, Special Collections Dept, 771 Commonwealth Ave, Boston, 02215. Howard B Gotlieb, Dir
Holdings: // Cat Mss Pix
Notes: Mss, correspondence, etc collected in depth; incl publications by or about.

FORBES, CAPT. ROBERT BENNET

MA —CHINA TRADE MUSEUM, Library, 215 Adams St, Milton, 02186. Lisa L Gwirtzman, Librn
Holdings: Uncat Mss Maps Pix
Notes: A museum collection, archive and library devoted to a history of the China Trade to Boston, (1784-1900). Incl 30,000 papers of Captain Robert Bennet Forbes; 75, 000 other China Trade documents; and 3500 period photographs.

FORBES FAMILY

†MA —UNIVERSITY OF MASSACHUSETTS AT AMHERST, Library, Amherst, 01003.
Notes: Microform collections of materials in other American libraries.

FORCE AND ENERGY

CA —UNIVERSITY OF CALIFORNIA, LIVERMORE, Lawrence Livermore National Laboratory, Library, PO Box 5500, Livermore, 94550. John B Verity, Library Mgr
Holdings: Vols (160,000) Cat 16mm Films Microforms
Budget: ($2,323,000)
Notes: The LLL library system includes a central collection in physics, chemistry, engineering, geology, mathematics, and computer science; and branch holdings in bio-medicine, environmental science, nuclear chemistry, energy research, theoretical physics, materials science, and nuclear weapons. Collections include 160,000 books, 145,000 technical reports, 530,000 reports on microfiche, and 3000 periodical subscriptions. LLL libraries are not open to the public. Unclassified materials may be borrowed on interlibrary loan.

CA —UPDATA PUBLICATIONS INC, Library, 1756 Westwood Blvd, Los Angeles, 90024. Sara Ferguson, Dir; Judith Harrington, Librn
Holdings: Vols (300) Uncat Maps Microforms
Notes: Incl 800,000 microforms, 35 periodicals.

DC —EDISON ELECTRIC INSTITUTE, Library-8th Floor, 1111 19th St NW, Washington, 20036. Ethel Tiberg, Mgr, Library Services
Holdings: Vols (13,321) Cat Maps Pix Microforms

KS —WICHITA PUBLIC LIBRARY, 223 S Main, Wichita, 67202. Larry DePiesse, Head, Business & Technology Dept; Jayne F Young, Business & Technology Dept
Holdings: Vols 800 Cat
Budget: $700
Notes: 456 of our holdings are circulating books. The remaining 344 books are in a special non-circulating collection, the "Energy Collection." Includes solar, wind, nuclear, etc.

OH —CASE WESTERN RESERVE UNIVERSITY LIBRARIES, Cleveland, 44106. Susie Hanson, Special Collections Librn
Holdings: Vols 1000 Cat
Notes: The collection was previously titled the Lake Erie Study Collection. As its scope has increased, it has been renamed the Environmental Sciences Collection and has been fully incorporated into the collection of the Sears Library, which serves the University in the areas of science and technology, economics and management. The Environmental Sciences Collection incl government and nongovernment reports, monographs and serials.

PA —UNIVERSITY OF PENNSYLVANIA, Towne Scientific Library, 220 S 33 St, Philadelphia, 19104. Charles Meyers, Librn
Holdings: Vols (65,000) Cat
Notes: Energy conversion.

TX —UNIVERSITY OF TEXAS LIBRARIES, Richard W McKinney Engineering Library, 1.3 ECJ, Austin, 78712. Susan B Ardis, Librn
Holdings: Vols (83,548) Cat Microforms

WV —US DEPT OF ENERGY, Morgantown Energy Technology Center, Library, PO Box 880, Morgantown, 26505. Elaine Pasini, Librn
Holdings: Cat Maps Microforms Patents

ON —RYERSON POLYTECHNICAL INSTITUTE LIBRARY, 50 Gould St, Toronto, M5B 1E8, Can. J North, Dir
Holdings: Vols 100,000 Cat Mss

FORCED LABOR

NC —DUKE UNIVERSITY, William R Perkins Library, Durham, 27706. Elvin E Strowd, University Librn
Notes: The Bruno Lasker collection contains 51 portfolios; the Perkins Library general collection and other collections contain a significant amount of material on the subject of slavery and antislavery.

FORD, CHARLES HENRI

CT —YALE UNIVERSITY, Box 1603A, Yale Station, New Haven, 06520.
Holdings: Cat Mss

DE —UNIVERSITY OF DELAWARE, Hugh M Morris Library, S College Ave, Newark, 19711. T Stuart Dick, Special Collections
Holdings: Cat Mss Pix
Notes: Manuscripts, etc, incl literary correspondence.

MO —WASHINGTON UNIVERSITY, Libraries, Special Collections Dept, Campus Box 1061, St Louis, 63130.
Notes: A small but significant collection.

FORD, FORD MADOX

MO —WASHINGTON UNIVERSITY, John M Olin Library, Campus Box 1061, St Louis, 63130.
Notes: Extensive collection.

NV —UNIVERSITY OF NEVADA, RENO, University Library, Special Collections Dept, Reno, 89557. Robert E Blesse, Head
Holdings: // Vols (106) Cat Other appearances 140 Cat
Notes: Includes individual works by author in all editions including translations; also prefaces, introductions, published correspondence, appearances in anthologies,

FORD, FORD MADOX (cont.)

periodicals, etc. Bibliographical research collection, part of Modern Authors Collection.

NY —CORNELL UNIVERSITY LIBRARIES, John M Olin Library, Dept of Rare Books, Ithaca, 14853. Donald D Eddy, Librn
Holdings: Vols 150 Cat Mss Pix

FORD, JESSE HILL

TN —MEMPHIS STATE UNIVERSITY, John Willard Brister Library, Memphis, 38152. John Terreo, Special Collections Librn
Notes: Author and screenwriter Jesse Hill Ford, c. 1959-1970

FORD, JOHN

IN —INDIANA UNIVERSITY, Lilly Library, Seventh St, Bloomington, 47405. William R Cagle, Librn
Holdings: Mss Pix Recordings
Notes: Correspondence, papers, and memorabilia, 1906-1976, of motion picture director John Ford, 1895-1973. Includes scripts and production materials relating to most of his films, tape recordings of interviews with his friends and colleagues about his career, movie stills and photographs of family and friends. ca 7000 items.

FORD, LEMUEL

CO —DENVER PUBLIC LIBRARY, 1357 Broadway, Denver, 80203.
Notes: Correspondence, papers, pictures, diaries, etc.

FORD, PAUL LEICESTER

CT —YALE UNIVERSITY, Box 1603A, Yale Station, New Haven, 06520.
Holdings: Cat Mss

FORD AIR TOURS

CA —SAN DIEGO AERO-SPACE MUSEUM, N Paul Whittier Historical Aviation Library, 2001 Pan American Plaza, Balboa Park, San Diego, 92101. B C Reynolds, Archivist
Holdings: // Uncat Microforms

FORECASTING, ECONOMIC see Economic Forecasting

FORE-EDGE PAINTINGS

CA —SAINT JOHN'S SEMINARY, Edward Laurence Doheny Memorial Library, The Estelle Doheny Collection, 5012 E Seminary Rd, Camarillo, 93010. Rita S Faulders, Cur
Holdings: Vols 660
Notes: One of the most outstanding collections.

CA —CLAREMONT COLLEGES, Honnold Library, Ninth & Dartmouth, Claremont, 91711. Tania Rizzo, Special Collections Dept Head
Holdings: Vols (70,000) Cat VF
Notes: Books on typography, bibliography, and history of printing; incunabula; specimen books; fine press books, esp Kelmscott, Doves, Daniel, Mosher, Grabhorn, Nash, and Arion presses and many Southern California printers. A comprehensive collection of Zamorano Club publications and keepsakes, partial source for George E Fulleton, *The Zamorano Club: The First Half Century* (Los Angeles, 1978). Extensive files of ephemera. Fine bindings and fore-edge paintings. Samples of Oriental type and printing.

CA —SAN DIEGO PUBLIC LIBRARY, Wangenheim Rm, 820 E St, San Diego, 92101. Eileen Boyle, Librn
Holdings: Vols 185 Cat
Notes: Incl 36 double fore-edge paintings.

FL —FLORIDA STATE UNIVERSITY, Robert Manning Strozier Library, Special Collections Dept, Tallahassee, 32306. Opal M Free, Head, Special Collections
Holdings: Vols 29 Cat Mss Maps
Notes: Noncirculating. No photocopying.

IN —SAINT MARY-OF-THE-WOODS COLLEGE, College Library, Saint Mary-of-the-Woods, 47876. Sister Emily Walsh, SP, Administrator
Holdings: Vols 133 Cat Slides
Notes: Catalog available, denoting subject of the Library's first 92 paintings, geographical location (if of some place), binder, names of previous owners, etc. Slides of paintings.

MD —LOYOLA/NOTRE DAME LIBRARY, 200 Winston Ave, Baltimore, 21212. Jack Ray, Dir
Holdings: Vols (215,000)
Notes: "One of the most outstanding collections."

MA —BOSTON PUBLIC LIBRARY, Print Collection, Dartmouth St at Copley Sq, Boston, 02117. Sinclair H Hitchings, Keeper of Prints
Holdings: Vols (500) Cat
Notes: Fine illustrated books, mainly English, of the 18th, 19th and 20th centuries, containing original prints or photographs. Also, 250 books with fore-edge paintings and books with fine bindings. No photocopying.

†MA —CLARK UNIVERSITY, Robert Hutchings Goddard Library, Worcester, 01610. Dorothy Mosa Kowski, Rare Books Librn
Holdings: Vols Cat Mss
Notes: Rare books, first editions, mss, incunabula (50), bindings, fore-edge paintings.

NY —MARGARET WOODBURY STRONG MUSEUM, 1 Manhattan Square, Rochester, 14607.
Holdings: Vols (20,000) Periodicals
Notes: The Margaret Woodbury Strong Museum Library contains a collection of approx 20,000 books, periodicals and ephemera of and concerning the 19th and early 20th centuries. A large part of the library's holdings reflect the interests of Margaret Strong and her family: domestic life and literature of the 19th century and world travel, with particular emphasis on the Orient. The library's resources are available to all visitors for research. Book stacks and rare book storage are not open for browsing and do not circulate, but facilities are provided in reading room for study.

SC —UNIVERSITY OF SOUTH CAROLINA, Thomas Cooper Library, Columbia, 29208. Kenneth E Toombs, Dir of Libraries; Roger Mortimer, Rare Book Librn
Holdings: Vols (1000) Cat
Notes: Collection contains examples of bookmaking for the 15th-20th twentieth centuries, especially, noteworthy bindings and fore-edge paintings.

TX —UNIVERSITY OF TEXAS, EL PASO, Library, Special Collections Dept, El Paso, 79968. Cesar Caballero, Dept Head
Holdings: Vols 13// Cat

TX —ROSENBERG LIBRARY, Fox Rare Book Room, 2310 Sealy Ave, Galveston, 77550. Fernando Basilza, Rare Book Librn
Holdings: Vols (2000) Cat Mss Pix
Notes: The Col Milo Pitcher Fox and Agnes Peel Fox Rare Book Room contains 2000 vols incunabula, first printings, and modern fine printing. Incl clay tablets, horn books, parchment material, illuminated books and mss, fine printing (principally 15th-18th centuries), fine binding, fore-edge paintings, etc.

NS —MOUNT SAINT VINCENT UNIVERSITY, Library, 166 Bedford Hwy, Halifax, B3M 2J6, Can. Lucian Bianchini, University Librn
Holdings: Vols 7000 Cat
Budget: ($125,000)
Notes: The MacDonald Collection consists of 19th and 20th century English and American literature, fine bindings, a few examples of fore-edge painting, limited editions, first editions, and autographed copies.

FOREIGN AID PROGRAM see Economic Assistance

FOREIGN AND INTERNATIONAL STATISTICS see Statistics, Foreign and International

FOREIGN ANIMAL DISEASES see Veterinary Medicine

FOREIGN ARCHIVES see Archives, Foreign

FOREIGN BUSINESS ENTERPRISES see Business Enterprises, Foreign

FOREIGN CHILDREN'S LITERATURE see Children'S Literature, Foreign

FOREIGN COMICS see Comic Books, Strips, Etc., Foreign

FOREIGN CORPORATIONS see Corporations, Foreign

FOREIGN ECONOMIC RELATIONS see International Economic Relations

FOREIGN ELEMENTS IN THE U.S.

PA —BALCH INSTITUTE FOR ETHNIC STUDIES, Library, 18 S Seventh St, Philadelphia, 19106. R Joseph Anderson, Library Dir

FOREIGN GOVERNMENT DOCUMENTS

CA —UNIVERSITY OF CALIFORNIA, LOS ANGELES, Research Library, Public Affairs Service, 405 Hilgard Ave, Los Angeles, 90024. Edward Shreeves, Chairman, Bibliographers Group; Eugenia Eaton, Head, Public Affairs Service
Holdings: Microforms
Notes: Depository for the official publications of California cities and counties, the state of California, the United States government, the United Nations and some of its specialized agencies (including the Food and Agricultural Organization and UNESCO), and such regional organizations as the European Communities and Organization of American States. Selected publications of other American cities and counties, of the other states and possessions of the United States, of interstate organizations, and of foreign governments (with emphasis on major world powers, Africa, Latin America and the Near and Middle East) and intergovernmental organizations.

MA —BOSTON PUBLIC LIBRARY, Government Documents Department, Boston, 02117. V Lloyd Jameson, Cur
Notes: Foreign Government Publications: Attempt to collect major statistical series of all countries, plus other major documents such as Social and Economic Development plans. Great Britain: Extensive collection. States (other than Massachusetts): Bluebooks, statistical abstracts, and legislative research reports. Municipal documents: All are available as listed in *Index to Current Urban Documents.*

FOREIGN INVESTMENTS see Investments, Foreign

FOREIGN LANGUAGE COLLECTIONS

CA —LOS ANGELES PUBLIC LIBRARY, Foreign Languages Dept, 630 W Fifth St, Los Angeles, 90071. Sylva Manoogian, Principal Librn
Holdings: Vols 168,596 Cat
Budget: ($41,500)

CA —DEFENSE LANGUAGE INSTITUTE FOREIGN LANGUAGE CENTER, Academic Library, Presidio of Monterey, Monterey, 93944. Gary D Walter, Librn
Holdings: Vols 85,000 Cat Videotapes
Budget: $90,000
Notes: Linguistics and foreign languages. Formerly US Army Language School Technical Library, Monterey, Calif.

FL —MIAMI-DADE PUBLIC LIBRARY SYSTEM, 1 Biscayne Blvd, Miami, 33132. Alicia Godoy, Foreign Language Librn
Holdings: Vols 32,000 Cat Maps Microforms Phonorecords Audiotapes VF
Notes: Incl books in 17 languages, mainly Spanish; fiction, technical, biography, travel, history, mysteries, westerns, science-fiction and grammar; 200 language records, 100 language cassettes, 3 vertical files of clippings related to Latin America, Spain, Miami, etc; 35 magazines, 10 newspapers (daily local paper: Diario las Americas, El Miami Herald-El Mundo Puerto Rico); Sunday editions of Latin American newspapers from Argentina, Colombia, Chile, Mexico and Brazil; 1 Yiddish and 1 German newspaper.

IL —CENTER FOR RESEARCH LIBRARIES, 6050 S Kenwood Ave, Chicago, 60637. Donald B Simpson, Dir; Esther Smith, Collection Development Librn
Holdings: Vols 4000 Cat Microforms

MA —BOSTON PUBLIC LIBRARY, South End Branch, Multilingual Library, 685 Tremont St, Boston, 02118. Laura H Reyes, Librn
Holdings: Cat

MN —MINNEAPOLIS PUBLIC LIBRARY & INFORMATION CENTER, Literature & Language Dept, 300 Nicollet Mall,

FOREIGN LANGUAGE COLLECTIONS (cont.)

Minneapolis, 55401. Dorothy D Thews, Head
Holdings: Vols (210,000) Cat Microforms Phonorecords Audiotapes
Budget: ($49,124)
Notes: Foreign language collection: 30,000 vols, separate catalog. Theatre collection: 9 vertical file drawers. Books integrated with department collection.

MN —SAINT PAUL PUBLIC LIBRARY, 90 W Fourth St, Saint Paul, 55102. Ortha Robbins, Supvr of Circulation Room
Holdings: Vols 4500 Cat
Notes: Popular circulating collection with emphasis on classics and contemporary literature.

NJ —ENGLEWOOD LIBRARY, 31 Engle St, Englewood, 07631. N E Rhoades, Reference Librn
Holdings: Vols 2788 Cat
Notes: Circulating collections of books in 4 languages. Reference: foreign language dictionaries, encyclopedias. Separate catalogs for each language. 5 foreign magazines.

NY —HEMPSTEAD PUBLIC LIBRARY, Foreign Language Collection, 115 Nichols Court, Hempstead, 11550. Irene A Duszkiewicz, Dir
Holdings: Vols 10,000 Cat
Notes: Mainly French, German, Italian, Polish, Spanish, Yiddish, Hebrew. Holdings in other languages, incl Asian.

NY —NEW YORK PUBLIC LIBRARY, Oriental Div, Fifth Ave & 42 St, New York, 10018. E Christian Filstrup, Chief
Holdings: Cat Mss Microforms
Notes: Described in *Dictionary Catalog of the Oriental Collection,* The Research Libraries of the New York Public Library, 1960, 16 vols, and *First Supplement,* 1976, 8 vols (144,000 cards). This catalog incl 318, 000 entries for works in about 100 languages of the East, and all works in Western languages on Oriental subjects. The Oriental Collection numbers about 120,000 vols; its Arabic and Indic holdings and those on ancient Egypt and the ancient Near East are among the largest in the US. There is also a collection of 30,000 vols of PL 480 material from Egypt, Pakistan, and India to which there is main entry access, but which is not incorporated into the dictionary catalog. Other outstanding features of the Oriental Collection incl extensive holdings of Japanese technical and scientific periodicals; a unique collection of linguistic works, grammars, anddictionaries; and unusually good coverage of the field of Oriental religions and philosophies. The catalog contains numerous subject references to periodical articles in all languages. All entries are arranged alphabetically according to the Roman alphabet.

NY —NEW YORK PUBLIC LIBRARY, Donnell Foreign Language Library, 20 W 53 St, New York, 10019. Bosiljka Stevanovic, Supvr Librn
Holdings: Vols 62,338
Budget: $49,895
Notes: A circulating collection of books written in about 80 languages. The collections are general and popular in character - current topics, travel, histories, biography, etc, emphasizing the literature of the country - fiction, drama, poetry, literary criticism. The collections are primarily intended for use of readers whose first language is other than English. Separate catalogs for each language. Collections containing less than 100 volumes are not listed. Translations are moderately included.

NC —CUMBERLAND COUNTY PUBLIC LIBRARY, North Carolina Foreign Language Center, 328 Gillespie St, Fayetteville, 28301. Patrick M Valentine, Coordinator
Holdings: Vols (25,000) Cat Phonorecords Audiotapes
Notes: The largest book collections are, in descending order of size, German Spanish, French, Japanese, Korean and Vietnamese, with fair sized collections in Italian, Russian, Chinese, Arabic, Greek, Hungarian, Polish, Hebrew, Thai, and Hindi. The Center has several shelves each of books in Bengali, Dutch, Marathi, Portuguese, Urdu, and Yiddish. Smaller collections of one to three shelves each incl Catalan, Croatian, Czech, Danish, Finnish, Gujarati, Icelandic, Kannada, Latin, Lithuanian, Malayalam, Norwegian, Panjabi, Persian (Farsi), Romanian, Slovak, Swedish, Tagalog, Tamil, Telegu, and Ukrianian. The Center has grammars, dictionaries and occasionally other readings in languages from Afrikaans and Albanian to Welsh, Yoruba and Zulu.

OH —PUBLIC LIBRARY OF CINCINNATI & HAMILTON COUNTY, Literature Dept, 800 Vine St, Cincinnati, 45202. Donna S Monnig, Head
Holdings: Vols 12,640 Cat
Notes: Circulating collection of books in 25 languages. Emphasis is on German language fiction. Large reference collection of foreign language dictionaries.

OH —CLEVELAND PUBLIC LIBRARY, Foreign Literature Dept, 325 Superior Ave, Cleveland, 44114. Natalia Bezugloff, Head
Holdings: Vols 182,330 Cat
Notes: Popular circulating collections in 35 languages (language collections under 100 vols not listed) containing classics and the standard works with emphasis on belles lettres, history and biography. A variety of other subjects such as learning languages, hobbies, how to do books, art, children's books, books for young adults, etc. Incl titles fiction adult, 60,120; titles fiction juvenile, 2100; titles nonfiction adult, 108,510; titles nonfiction juvenile, 3200; 6380 ephemera; 4933 bound periodicals; 1850 spoken phonodiscs; 1330 spoken cassettes; 2663 vols reference (bibliographies, dictionaries, indexes, directories, encyclopedias in 24 languages, etc); subscriptions to over 120 foreign literary and popular periodicals. Incl Arabic, Armenian, Bulgarian, Byelorussian, Czech, Chinese, Serbo-Croatian, Danish, Dutch, Estonian, Finnish, French, German, Greek (Modern),Hebrew, Hungarian, Italian, Japanese, Korean, Lettish, Lithuanian, Norwegian, Polish, Portuguese, Romanian, Russina, Slovak, Slovenian, Spanish, Swahili, Swedish, Ukrainian, Vietnamese and Yiddish Language and Literature.

OH —KENT STATE UNIVERSITY, Libraries, Ethnic Collections, Kent, 44242.
Holdings: Vols 5000 Cat
Notes: Both European and US publications in Croatian, Estonian, Czech, Finnish, Hungarian, Latvian, Lithuanian, Polish, Romanian, Serbian, Slovenian, Slovac, Swedish, Ukrainian, and Welsh. Materials gathered in part to support a Critical Languages Program at Kent State and to develop a center for the study of Baltic languages, especially Lithuanian.

TX —SOUTHERN METHODIST UNIVERSITY, DeGolyer Library, Box 396, SMU, Dallas, 75275. Clifton H Jones, Dir
Holdings: Vols (15,000) Cat Mss Maps Pix
Notes: One of the largest railroad photograph collections in the world; about 230,000 prints and 70,000 negatives, all countries. Accompanied by a major collection (12,000 vols), of railroadiana; much on locomotives. All languages.

WA —SEATTLE PUBLIC LIBRARY, 1000 Fourth Ave, Seattle, 98104. Ronald A Dubberly, City Librn
Holdings: Cat

BC —GREATER VANCOUVER LIBRARY FEDERATION, 110-6545 Bonsor, Burnaby, Z5H 1H3, Can. Colleen Smith, Coordr
Holdings: Vols (20,350) Cat
Notes: Deposit provided by the National Library's Multilingual Biblioservice on long-term loan to libraries in the Greater Vancouver Library Federation (Burnaby, New Westminster, N Vancouver City Public, N Vancouver District Public, Port Moody, Vancouver, W Vancouver). Other Languages available; Spanish, Greek, Polish, Urdu, Hindi, Finnish, Italian, etc.

ON —METROPOLITAN TORONTO LIBRARY, Languages Centre, 789 Yonge St, Toronto, M4W 2G8, Can. Barbara Gunther, Head
Holdings: Vols (90,000) Cat Phonorecords Audiotapes
Notes: Original literature in over 80 languages; books, records, cassettes, microfilm on language studies; newspapers and periodicals from 50 counties. Language study materials. Issue quarterly additions lists by language. Collect North American Indian and Eskimo language materials. Occasional bibliographies.

FOREIGN LANGUAGE DRAMA

NY —THEATRE COLLECTION OF THE INTERNATIONAL THEATRE INSTITUTE OF THE UNITED STATES, INC, Library, Suite 1510, 1860 Broadway, New York, 10023. Elizabeth B Burdick, Dir
Holdings: Vols (4525) Cat Mss Pix
Budget: ($35,000)
Notes: The International Theatre Institute was founded by UNESCO to "promote the exchange of knowledge and practice in the theatre arts." In 1948, eleven nations, incl the United States, became charter members of the international organization, which today has national centers or affiliates in 64 countries. The American center is the International Theatre Institute of the United States (ITI/US). In 1970, as one of its programs to strengthen communication among theatre people, ITI/US opened a library devoted to international theatre since World War II. The Collection's main holdings have been amassed over the 35-year operation of ITI/US through its world-wide exchange of information, publications, and people. Holdings document theatre activity in 140 countries. The 4525 vols on American and foreign theatre(covering history, management, design, stagecraft, theory, criticism, biography, playscripts) represent only a small part of the total collection. Focus is on foreign theatre companies, directors, playwrights, designers, managers, actors. The emphasis is on the acquisition of material which is generally unavailable in this country: foreign yearbooks, house organs, newsletters, programs, press releases, production schedules, brochures, periodicals, monographs, articles, newspaper clippings. While these fugitive items have never been counted, they have been cataloged by country, then indexed by title, subject, or name of theatre. The library receives regularly 250 periodicals on the performing arts (cataloged by country, then indexed by title). It now owns 6417 foreign plays from 80 countries in ms or publishedmss or published editions, in collections and anthologies, and in periodicals. Each play is cataloged by author, title, and country of origin. The section on American theatre incl books, programs, reviews, over 60 periodicals, 2061 American plays. The activities of approx 700 theatres across the country are documented by annual files containing production schedules, press releases, programs, brochures for each theatrical season.

FOREIGN LANGUAGE NEWSPAPERS see Newspapers, Foreign Language

FOREIGN LANGUAGE PERIODICALS see Periodicals, Foreign

FOREIGN LANGUAGE PERIODICALS (AMERICAN) see Periodicals, Foreign Language (American)

FOREIGN LAW see Law, Foreign

FOREIGN LIBRARIES see Libraries, Foreign

FOREIGN MISSIONS see Missions, Foreign

FOREIGN MOVING PICTURES see Moving Pictures, Foreign

FOREIGN NEWSPAPERS see Newspapers, Foreign

FOREIGN PERIODICALS see Periodicals, Foreign

FOREIGN POPULATION see Emigration and Immigration; Minorities

FOREIGN RADIO BROADCASTS

IL —CENTER FOR RESEARCH LIBRARIES, 6050 S Kenwood Ave,

FOREIGN RADIO BROADCASTS (cont.)

Chicago, 60637. Donald B Simpson, Dir; Esther Smith, Collection Development Librn
Holdings: Microforms
Notes: Microfilms of: *Daily Report of Foreign Radio Broadcasts,* 1941-1974, *Foreign Broadcast Information Service,* (area editions, 1974-); *Voice of America* scripts 1953-, foreign broadcasts as monitored by CBS, Aug 1939-March 1945, BBC monitoring service reports, 1974-date, and BBC Home Service News 1939-1945.

FOREIGN RELATIONS see International Relations

FOREIGN STATISTICS see Statistics, Foreign and International

FOREIGN STUDENTS see Students, Foreign

FOREIGN TRADE see Commerce

FORENAMES see Names, Personal

FORENSIC HEMATOLOGY

NY —MILTON HELPERN LIBRARY OF LEGAL MEDICINE, 520 First Ave, New York, 10016. Barry W Seaver, Librn
Holdings: Vols (2480) Cat Pix Slides Microforms
Notes: Forensic (legal) medicine (incl forensic pathology, serology, toxicology and criminalistics).

FORENSIC MEDICINE see Medical Jurisprudence

FORENSIC PHOTOGRAPHY see Photography, Legal

FORENSIC PSYCHIATRY

KS —MENNINGER FOUNDATION, Archives, 5600 W Sixth St, Box 829, Topeka, 66601. Alice Brand, Librn; Mark West, Archivist
Notes: Incl journals. Literature searches and document delivery available for a fee.

MA —MCLEAN HOSPITAL MEDICAL LIBRARY, 115 Mill St, Belmont, 02178. Hector Bossange, Dir
Holdings: Vols 25,611 Cat
Notes: Extensive collection.

WI —MENDOTA MENTAL HEALTH INSTITUTE, Library-Media Center, 301 Troy Dr, Madison, 53704. Margaret Tiekle Grinnell, Librn
Holdings: Vols 14,800 Cat Slides Phonorecords Audiotapes Videotapes 16mm Films Filmstrips

FOREST ENTOMOLOGY see Forest Insects

FOREST FIRES

CT —YALE UNIVERSITY, Forestry Library, 205 Prospect St, New Haven, 06511. Joseph A Miller, Librn
Holdings: Vols (115,000) Cat Microforms
Notes: Environment studies and allied fields of natural resources management have been emphasized during the past 10 years. See *Dictionary Catalog of the Yale Forestry Library,* 12 vols (Boston: G K Hall, 1962).

BC —CANADIAN FORESTRY SERVICE, Pacific Forest Research Centre, Library, 506 West Burnside Rd, Victoria, V8Z 1M5, Can. Alice Solyma, Librn
Holdings: Vols (60,500) Cat Microforms
Notes: Incl detection, prevention and control, fire ecology, forecasting, research, statistics, computer programs.

FOREST FLORA see Forests and Forestry

FOREST INDUSTRIES see Wood-Using Industries

FOREST INSECTS

AB —CANADIAN FORESTRY SERVICE, Northern Forest Research Centre Library, 5320 122nd, Edmonton, T6H 3S5, Can. David J S Robinson, Librn
Holdings: Vols (7000) Cat Microforms
Budget: ($25,000)
Notes: Also 23,000 government documents, 2600 research reports, 3000 pamphlets and reprints.

BC —CANADIAN FORESTRY SERVICE, Pacific Forest Research Centre, Library, 506 West Burnside Rd, Victoria, V8Z 1M5, Can. Alice Solyma, Librn
Holdings: Vols (60,500) Cat Microforms
Notes: Incl rearing, biological control, identification, dispersal, insect pest management, comprehensive collection re Mountain Pine Beetle, Western Spruce Budworm, Douglas Fir Tussack Moth.

FOREST PLANTING see Forests and Forestry

FOREST PRODUCTS

CA —UNIVERSITY OF CALIFORNIA, BERKELEY, Life Sciences Libraries, Forestry Library, 260 Mulford Hall, Berkeley, 94720. Esther Johnson, Librn; Pete Evans, Ref Librn
Holdings: Vols (28,000) Cat Microforms
Budget: ($15,800)
Notes: Areas of particular strength are forestry, conservation, and wildlife management. The collection is rich in pamphlet material and serials, especially foreign publications. Although holdings are world-wide in scope, coverage of the western USA is given the highest priority. Dissertation and theses collection also. Forestry Library holdings are complemented by a 8000-vol specialized collection at the Forest Products Laboratory in Richmond, California.

CA —UNIVERSITY OF CALIFORNIA, RICHMOND, Forest Products Library, 1301 S 46th St, Richmond, 94804. Peter A Evans, Librn
Holdings: Vols (8000) Cat Maps Audiotapes Microforms
Notes: Areas of strength are pulp and paper, physical properties of wood, seasoning, wood preservation, wood extractives chemistry, adhesion and adhesives.

CT —YALE UNIVERSITY, Forestry Library, 205 Prospect St, New Haven, 06511. Joseph A Miller, Librn
Holdings: Vols (115,000) Cat Microforms
Notes: The Forestry Library is a unit of the Yale University Library, housed in and serving primarily the School of Forestry and Environmental Studies. Founded in 1900, it has become one of the largest forestry libraries in the world. Forestry is construed broadly to incl underlying or closely related social, physical, and biological sciences. The literature of North American forestry and forest products is most completely covered, though other countries and foreign languages are well represented. Environmental studies and allied fields of natural resources management have been emphasized during the past 10 years. See *Dictionary Catalog of the Yale Forestry Library,* 12 vols (Boston: G K Hall, 1962).

DC —NATIONAL FOREST PRODUCTS ASSOCIATION, Bemis Information Center, 1619 Massachusetts Ave NW, Washington, 20036. Barbara A Beall, Mgr
Holdings: Vols (5000) Cat Maps Pix
Notes: Plus 25,000 pamphlets.

NY —INTERNATIONAL PAPER CO, Corporate Information Center, 77 W 45 St, New York, 10036. Elizabeth Skerritt, Corporate Librn
Holdings: Vols 280 Cat Maps Pix Slides Microforms
Notes: Extensive statistics and VF on paper industry.

WA —UNIVERSITY OF WASHINGTON LIBRARIES, Forest Resources Library, AQ-15, Seattle, 98195. Barbara B Gordon, Head
Holdings: Vols (43,248) Cat Microforms
Budget: ($41,103)
Notes: Modern imprints only. Mostly in English, some East Asian languages. No geographical limits but emphasis is on Pacific Northwest. Incl 1,236 microforms.

WI —US FOREST SERVICE, Forest Products Laboratory Library, Box 5130, Madison, 53705. Roger Schurmer, Librn; Dr Regis Miller, Librn; Dr Harold H Burdsall, Jr, Librn
Holdings: Vols (136,240) Cat Microforms //
Budget: ($122,083)
Notes: Forest products utilization research. KWIC index of FPL reports; centralized title service from Forestry Bureau, Oxford, England (card and microfilm).
See also entries under Wood; Mycology.

FORESTATION see Forests and Forestry

FORESTER, C. S.

MD —US NAVAL ACADEMY, Nimitz Library, Annapolis, 21402. Alice S Creighton, Assistant Librn for Special Collections
Holdings: Vols (54) Mss
Notes: The Frances Phillips Collection of C S Forester books and manuscripts. Most of the 54 books and all 12 manuscripts are presentation copies inscribed by the author.

FORESTS AND FORESTRY

AZ —NORTHERN ARIZONA UNIVERSITY, Special Collection Library, CU Box 6022, Flagstaff, 86011. Peter M Whiteley, Coordr/Archivist; William Mullane, Librn
Notes: (1) Collection of Harris Collingwood, forest ranger, Clifton Ranger District, Apache National Forest, Ariz; correspondence between Collingwood and family members in Michigan, 1910-1915, regarding life and work in Arizona. The collection is photocopied from the originals belonging to the Forest History Society. Inventory available. (2) Charles Koch Collection; notes concerning an *Arizona Sawmill Directory* and notes for a felling and bucking study, prepared by Charles Koch, a forester. Both were published in *Arizona Land Marks,* 1978. (3) Jay Price Collection; correspondence, files, and reports pertaining to *Forestry Topics,* 1950's. Incl information on watershed and forest management for the Salt River and Central Arizona Projects as part of the Arizona Water Resource Committee files, 1956-1960;and files of the Soil Conservation Society, Arizona Chapter, 1956-1957 (2 feet).
See also entries under Lumber and Lumbering; Lumber Industry and Trade

CA —UNIVERSITY OF CALIFORNIA, BERKELEY, Life Sciences Libraries, Forestry Library, 260 Mulford Hall, Berkeley, 94720. Esther Johnson, Librn; Pete Evans, Ref Librn
Holdings: Vols (28,000) Cat Mss
Budget: ($15,800)
Notes: Areas of particular strength are forestry, conservation, and wildlife management. The collection is rich in pamphlet material and serials, especially foreign publications. Although holdings are world-wide in scope, coverage of the western USA is given the highest priority. Dissertation and theses collection also. Forestry Library holdings are complemented by a 8000-vol specialized collection at the Forest Products Laboratory in Richmond, California.

CA —FOREST HISTORY SOCIETY INC, Library, 109 Coral St, Santa Cruz, 95060. Mary E Johnson, Librn
Holdings: Vols (4000) Cat Mss Maps Pix Slides Films Audiotapes Microforms Serials
Budget: ($2000)
Notes: Incl archives of the Society of American Foresters, the American Forestry Association, the National Lumber Manufacturers Association, National Forest Products Association, and the American Forest Institute.

CO —COLORADO STATE UNIVERSITY, Libraries, Fort Collins, 80523. Curtis L Gifford, Forestry & Agricultural Sciences Librn
Holdings: Vols 17,719 Cat Maps Microforms
Budget: $9000

CT —YALE UNIVERSITY, Box 1603A, Yale Station, New Haven, 06520.

FORESTS AND FORESTRY (cont.)

CT —YALE UNIVERSITY, Forestry Library, 205 Prospect St, New Haven, 06511. Joseph A Miller, Librn
Holdings: Vols (115,000) Cat Microforms
Notes: The Forestry Library is a unit of the Yale University Library, housed in and serving primarily the School of Forestry and Environmental Studies. Founded in 1900, it has become one of the largest forestry libraries in the world. Forestry is construed broadly to incl underlying or closely related social, physical, and biological sciences. The literature of North American forestry and forest products is most completely covered, though other countries and foreign languages are well represented. Environmental studies and allied fields of natural resources management have been emphasized during the past 10 years. See *Dictionary Catalog of the Yale Forestry Library*, 12 vols (Boston: G K Hall, 1962).

DC —NATIONAL FOREST PRODUCTS ASSOCIATION, Bemis Information Center, 1619 Massachusetts Ave NW, Washington, 20036. Barbara A Beall, Mgr
Holdings: Vols (5000) Cat Maps Pix
Notes: Plus 25,000 pamphlets.

GA —UNIVERSITY OF GEORGIA, Libraries, Athens, 30602. Arlene E Luchsinger, Asst Dir Branch Libraries
Notes: Collection of over 1000 photographs on Southern forestry and the Southern logging industry, 1939-46. This gift, from the Southern Forest Institute, includes the records and files of four groups formed to solve specific problems of Southern forests. Several collections on the history of forestry in the South for the last 30 years.

†IL —UNIVERSITY OF ILLINOIS, URBANA/CHAMPAIGN, Agricultural Library, 226 Mumford Hall, 1301 W Gregory Dr, Urbana, 61801.

IN —PURDUE UNIVERSITY LIBRARIES, Life Sciences Library, Lilly Hall of Life Sciences, West Lafayette, 47907. Martha J Bailey, Librn
Holdings: Vols (73,404) Cat Microforms
Budget: ($223,445)
Notes: Incl materials in agronomy, animal sciences, botany, entomology, forestry, horticulture, biological sciences and agricultural engineering.

IA —IOWA STATE UNIVERSITY, Library, Ames, 50011. Warren B Kuhn, Dean of Library Services
Holdings: Cat
Notes: Extensive serial holdings.

IA —BICKELHAUPT ARBORETUM FREE LENDING LIBRARY, 340 S Fourteenth St, Clinton, 52732. Francie B Hill, Librn
Notes: Strong on indoor plants, horticulture, ecology, energy conservation, plant entomology and pathology, urban tree planting; also curriculum materials. Over 3000 slides available for lending.

KY —UNIVERSITY OF KENTUCKY, Agricultural Library, Agricultural Science Center North, Lexington, 40506. Antoinette Paris Powell, Librn
Holdings: Vols (90,000) Cat Microforms
Budget: ($110,385)

LA —LOUISIANA STATE UNIVERSITY, Middleton Library, Dept of Archives & Manuscripts, Room 202, Baton Rouge, 70803. M Stone Miller Jr, Head
Holdings: Cat Mss Maps Pix Microforms
Notes: History of Louisiana and lower Mississippi Valley, colonial through 20th century. Scope: political, social and literary history; economic history, incl forestry, banking, agriculture, transportation and trade; national, regional, and Louisiana history; military history. About 4,500,000 items.

LA —US FOREST SERVICE, Southern Forest Experiment Station Library, T-10210 Postal Service Bldg, 701 Loyola Ave, New Orleans, 70113. Linda A Korb, Librn
Holdings: Vols (50,000) Cat 16mm Films VF
Budget: ($100,000)
Notes: Field library of the National Agricultural Library (USDA), serving research scientists of the Southern Forest Experiment Station at headquarters in New Orleans and in seven states of the Mid-South and Puerto Rico.

MA —UNIVERSITY OF MASSACHUSETTS AT AMHERST, Library, Amherst, 01003. Siegfried Feller, Assoc Dir for Collection Development
Holdings: Cat

MA —HARVARD UNIVERSITY, Harvard Forest Library, Petersham, 01366. Catherine M Danahar, Librn
Holdings: Vols 9800 Cat Maps Microforms

MN —US DEPT OF AGRICULTURE, FOREST SERVICE, North Central Forest Experiment Station, Library, 1992 Fowell Ave, Saint Paul, 55108. Floyd L Henderson, Librn
Holdings: Vols (5000) Maps 16mm Films
Budget: ($14,000)
Notes: Forests of the North Central states.

MT —UNIVERSITY OF MONTANA, Maureen and Mike Mansfield Library, Missoula, 59801. Irene Evers, Asst Science Librn
Holdings: Vols 13,500 Cat Mss
Notes: School of Forestry, Cooperative Forest and Conservation Library was moved from the school to the Mansfield Library, and books and journals were added to the general collection. The unbound pamphlet collection has been kept intact and is called the Oxford Collection, as it is classified by the Oxford System of Decimal Classification for Forestry. It consists of about 36,600 items. It is still active. Incl 33,000 bulletins, reprints, etc on all aspects of forestry.

NY —NEW YORK BOTANICAL GARDEN LIBRARY, Bronx, 10458. Charles R Long, Asst Vice Pres & Dir
Holdings: Vols 15,000 Cat Mss Pix Slides Microforms VF
Budget: ($356,000)
Notes: One of the largest botanical collections in the world. Over 900,000 items. Covers botany (150,000 vols), botanists (3000), horticulture (45,000) plant diseases (25,000), plant physiology (15,000), history of botany (1500), conservation of natural resources (15,000), gardening (13,000), paleobotany (7000), ecology (20,000), forestry (5000) medical botany (3000), agriculture (9000) and biology (20,000). Reference library; materials do not circulate, except for member circulating collection (1200) and standard inter-library loan. About 5000 vols uncataloged. Incl art, books, serials, pamphlets, archives and manuscripts, vertical files, microfiche and microfilm, nursery and seed catalogs, photographs, paintings, prints, drawings and engravings. Covers all areas of botanical sciences. This is an OCLC library with fullresource services incl photocopying and photography.

NY —HARVARD UNIVERSITY LIBRARY, Harvard Black Rock Forest Library, Continental Rd, Cornwall, 12518. Jack J Karnig, Forest Mgr
Holdings: Vols 8962 Maps Slides Microforms
Notes: No photocopying.

NY —CARY ARBORETUM OF THE NEW YORK BOTANICAL GARDEN, Library, Box AB, Millbrook, 12545. Fred Strum, Librn
Notes: This collection of alternative energy sources consists of publications concerned iwth solar energy, wind power, biofuel, methanol, small hydroelectric projects, and wood power.

NY —CARY ARBORETUM OF THE NEW YORK BOTANICAL GARDEN, Institute of Ecosystem Studies, Library, Box AB, Millbrook, 12545. Betsy Calvin, Librn
Holdings: Vols 10,000

NY —PAUL SMITHS COLLEGE, Frank L Cubley Library, Paul Smiths, 12970. Theodore Mack, Librn
Holdings: Vols 1850 Cat Slides
Notes: 17,800 cataloged pamphlets; 1660 slides.

NY —STATE UNIVERSITY OF NEW YORK, COLLEGE OF ENVIRONMENTAL SCIENCE AND FORESTRY, F Franklin Moon Library, Syracuse, 13210. Donald F Webster, Librn
Holdings: Vols (86,430) Cat
Budget: ($120,000)

NC —DUKE UNIVERSITY, William R Perkins Library, Manuscript Dept, Durham, 27706. Ellen Gartrell, Cur of Mss
Holdings: Mss
Notes: Large collections of several lumber companies, 20th century (mostly North Carolina) plus other references.

NC —DUKE UNIVERSITY, Biology-Forestry Library, Durham, 27706. Bertha Livingstone, Librn
Holdings: Vols 143,474

NC —NORTH CAROLINA STATE UNIVERSITY, Forest Resources Library, 4012 Biltmore Hall, Raleigh, 27650. Pamela E Puryear, Head
Holdings: Vols (9000) Cat Microforms
Notes: Forestry, wood and paper sciences; recreation; remote sensing; FAO and forest service and forest products labs. Publications and audiovisual materials. Also incl 24 file drawers of Carl A Shenck, prominent American forester and founder of the Biltmore Forest School, the first school of forestry in the Western Hemisphere.

OR —OREGON STATE UNIVERSITY, Library, Corvallis, 97331. Melvin George, Dir
Holdings: Vols 10,000 Cat Maps Pix

OR —UNIVERSITY OF OREGON, Library, Eugene, 97403. Kenneth W Duckett, Curator
Notes: Papers of James C Rettie, Senior Economist of the Department of the Interior.

OR —UNIVERSITY OF PORTLAND, Wilson W Clark Memorial Library, 5000 N Willamette Blvd, PO Box 03017, Portland, 97203. Rev Joseph P Browne, CSC, Dir
Holdings: Vols 500 // Cat
Notes: This forestry collection, the Daniel D Buckley Memorial Collection, is no longer maintained as a separate collection and is not being developed or added to in any way.

OR —US DEPT OF ENERGY, Bonneville Power Administration Library, 1002 NE Holladay St, PO Box 3621, Portland, 97232. Karen Hadman, Chief of Library Branch
Holdings: Vols (2000)
Notes: Emphasis is on Federal and Pacific Northwest law and in subject areas of interest to the Departments of Energy and Interior.

PA —PENNSYLVANIA STATE UNIVERSITY, Fred Lewis Pattee Library, Life Sciences Library, University Park, 16802. Keith Roe, Head
Notes: This collection is strong in periodical runs, particularly European learned societies and agriculture. It contains extensive collections of Experiment Station publications and has developed specialties in Mycology and Fusaria. There is also a special collection of 1105 glass slides on early Pennsylvania lumbering.

TN —TENNESSEE VALLEY AUTHORITY (TVA), Technical Library, 400 W Summit Hill Dr, E2 B7, Knoxville, 37902. Jesse C Mills, Chief Librn
Holdings: Vols (106,900) Cat Mss Maps Pix Audiotapes Microforms
Budget: ($2,025,000)
Notes: The Technical Library Headquarters Staff (order, cataloging, information, and administration) is located is Knoxville, Tenn. In addition there are branch libraries in Knoxville, Norris, and Chattanooga, Tennessee, and Muscle Shoals, Alabama.

TN —TENNESSEE VALLEY AUTHORITY (TVA), Norris Branch Library, Norris, 37828. Debra D Mills, Librn
Holdings: Vols (8000) Cat Microforms
Budget: ($35,000)

TX —TEXAS A&M UNIVERSITY, Sterling C Evans Library, Special Collections Div, College Station, 77843. Donald H Dyal, Librn
Holdings: Vols 400 Cat
Notes: The E J Dyksterhuis Collection on American forestry, range science, ecology and botany (compiled by Professor Emeritus E J Dyksterhuis).

WA —UNIVERSITY OF WASHINGTON LIBRARIES, Forest Resources Library, AQ-15, Seattle, 98195. Barbara B Gordon, Head
Holdings: Vols (43,248) Cat Microforms
Budget: ($41,103)
Notes: Modern imprints only. Mostly in

FORESTS AND FORESTRY (cont.)

English, some Euripean and East Asian languages. International in scope but emphasis is on Pacific Northwest. Incl 1,236 microforms.

WI —UNIVERSITY OF WISCONSIN, MADISON, College of Agricultural & Life Sciences, Steenbock Memorial Library, 550 Babcock Dr, Madison, 53706. Jan Kennedy, Dir
Holdings: Vols (186,312) Cat Docs Maps Microforms
Notes: Supports forestry, plant pathology and horticulture programs; USDA, USDI, experiment station and state documents relating to forestry, parks, land management and natural resources.

WI —US FOREST SERVICE, Forest Products Laboratory Library, Box 5130, Madison, 53705. Roger Schurmer, Librn; Dr Regis Miller, Librn; Dr Harold H Burdsall, Jr, Librn
See also entries under Wood; Mycology.

AB —CANADIAN FORESTRY SERVICE, Northern Forest Research Centre Library, 5320 122nd, Edmonton, T6H 3S5, Can. David J S Robinson, Librn
Holdings: Vols (7000) Cat Microforms
Budget: ($25,000)
Notes: Also 23,000 government documents, 2600 research reports, 3000 pamphlets and reprints.

BC —UNIVERSITY OF BRITISH COLUMBIA, Macmillan Library, 2357 Main Mall, Vancouver, V6T 2A2, Can. Mary W Macaree, Head
Holdings: Vols (35,000) Cat Maps Slides Microforms
Budget: ($8500)

BC —CANADIAN FORESTRY SERVICE, Pacific Forest Research Centre, Library, 506 West Burnside Rd, Victoria, V8Z 1M5, Can. Alice Solyma, Librn
Holdings: Vols (60,500) Cat Microforms
Notes: Incl forest and plant pathology, entomology, silviculture, meteorology, mensuration, fire research, hydrology, environmental science and ecology, biometrics, land use and classification, soil science, and forest economics. Depository for all Canadian Forestry Service publications.

MB —UNIVERSITY OF MANITOBA, Elizabeth Dafoe Library, Archives and Special Collections Dept, Winnipeg, R3T 2N2, Can. Richard E Bennett, Dept Head; Corrado A Santoro, Reference Archivist
Notes: Churchill Forest Industry.

ON —LAURENTIAN UNIVERSITY LIBRARY, Ramsey Lake Rd, Sudbury, P3E 2C6, Can. Suzanne Brunette, Special Collection Librn; Sue Vongpeisal, Head Librn
Notes: Materials on northern Canada, incl 2200 books and pamphlets, 60,000 press clippings on northern topics 75 series of periodicals and over 1500 maps, plus photographs and thousands of samples of arctic and subarctic plants incl mosses, lichens, algae and wood sections. Much of the material is in French.

ON —ONTARIO MINISTRY OF NATURAL RESOURCES, Natural Resources Library, Whitney Block 4540, Toronto, M5S 1B3, Can. Sandra Louet, Librn
Holdings: Cat

PQ —PULP AND PAPER RESEARCH INSTITUTE OF CANADA, Library, Saint John's Rd, Pointe-Claire, H9R 3J9, Can. Alison Finnemore, Librn
Holdings: Vols (14,000) Cat Microforms
Budget: ($16,000)
Notes: Book catalog.

PQ —SERVICE DE LA DOCUMENTATION ET DES RENSEIGNEMENTS MINISTERE DE L'ENERGIE ET DES RESSOURCES, 2000B, chemin Sainte-Foy, 7th floor, Quebec, G1R 4X7, Can. Normand Guerette, Dir
Holdings: Vols (114,800) Slides Videotapes
Notes: In 1979, the Bibliotheque du ministere des Richesses naturelles du Quebec merged with the Bibliotheque du ministere des Terres et Forets. The result of this merger was the creation of the service de la Documentation et des Renseignements du ministere de l'Energie et des Ressources. Publications: Info-Biblio Terres et Forets; Mines; Energy.

PQ —CENTRE DE RECHERCHES FORESTIERES DE LAURENTIDES, Bibliotheque, CP 3800, Sainte-Foy, G1V 4C7, Can. Claudine Lussier, Librn
Holdings: Vols 4800 Cat Microforms
Budget: $30,000
Notes: Very little on forest products. Publish *Milieu.*

FORESTS AND FORESTRY—HISTORY

AZ —NORTHERN ARIZONA UNIVERSITY, Special Collection Library, CU Box 6022, Flagstaff, 86011. Peter M Whiteley, Coordr/Archivist; William Mullane, Librn
Holdings: Cat Mss Maps Pix Audiotapes
Notes: (1) Charles Koch Collection: notes concerning an *Arizona Sawmill Directory* and notes for a felling and bucking study, prepared by Charles Koch, a forester. Both were published in *Arizona Land Marks.* (2) Jay Price Collection: correspondence, files, and reports reports pertaining to *Forestry* Topics, (1950's). Incl information on watershed and forest management for the Salt River and Central Arizona Projects as part of the Arizona Water Resource Committee files, 1956-1960; also files of the Soil Conservation Society, Arizona Chapter, 1956-1957 (2 feet).

CA —CALIFORNIA STATE UNIVERSITY, FRESNO, Henry Madden Library, Dept of Special Collections, Fresno, 93740. Ronald J Mahoney, Head
Holdings: / / Uncat Pix
Notes: The Harry Pidgeon Collection of photographs of logging in the Sugar Pine area of the Sierra Nevada mountains, Madera County, California. About 600 photos, 1913-1925.

CA —FOREST HISTORY SOCIETY INC, Library, 109 Coral St, Santa Cruz, 95060. Mary E Johnson, Librn
Holdings: Vols (4000) Cat Mss Maps Pix Slides Audiotapes Microforms Serials Films VF
Budget: ($2000)
Notes: Incl archives of the Society of American Foresters, the American Forestry Association, the National Lumber Manufacturers Association, National Forest Products Association, and the American Forest Institute.

†IL —UNIVERSITY OF ILLINOIS, URBANA/CHAMPAIGN, Agricultural Library, 226 Mumford Hall, 1301 W Gregory Dr, Urbana, 61801.

OR —UNIVERSITY OF OREGON LIBRARY, Special Collections Div, Eugene, 97403. Kenneth W Duckett, Curator
Holdings: Cat Mss Pix
Notes: Over 20 mss collections of Pacific Northwest foresters containing field diaries, reminiscences, mss of books, articles, and speeches, correspondence, reports and documents. Publication: Martin Schmitt, comp, *Catalogue of Manuscripts in the University of Oregon Library* (Eugene: University of Oregon Books, 1971).
See also entry under Lumber and Lumbering

OR —GEORGIA-PACIFIC HISTORICAL MUSEUM, Library, 900 SW Fifth, Portland, 97204. Richard Thompson, Museum Dir
Holdings: Vols (300) Uncat Videotapes 16mm Films Pix
Notes: Use of collection is by written request for specific information or materials.

PA —PENNSYLVANIA STATE UNIVERSITY, Fred Lewis Pattee Library, Special Collections Dept, University Park, 16802. Charles Mann, Chief, Special Collections
Holdings: / / Slides
Budget: ($37,000)
Notes: A special collection on early Pennsylvania lumbering. The collections of the Life Science Library contain the regular collection on this subject.

TX —STEPHEN F AUSTIN STATE UNIVERSITY, Ralph W Steen Library, Special Collections Dept, Box 13055, SFA Sta, Nacogdoches, 75962. Linda Cheves Nicklas, Special Collections Librn
Holdings: Cat Mss Maps Pix
Budget: ($5000)
Notes: Forest History Collection (late 1800s-1965). Incl personal and business correspondence, contracts, timber plats, logging and hauling contracts, photos and other records of early East Texas lumber companies and logging railroads. Calendars for records of each company are available. Published description: Maxwell, R S, "Manuscript Collections at Stephen F Austin State College", American Archivist, vol 28, July, 1965; and SFASU, *A Guide to Special* Collections, 1980.

FORESTS AND FORESTRY-MOISTURE

BC —CANADIAN FORESTRY SERVICE, Pacific Forest Research Centre, Library, 506 West Burnside Rd, Victoria, V8Z 1M5, Can. Alice Solyma, Librn
Holdings: Vols (60,500) Cat Microforms
Notes: Incl soil biology, soil microbiology, soil ecology, fauna, fertility, moisture.

FORGERIES, LITERARY see Literary Forgeries and Mystifications

FORGERY OF MANUSCRIPTS

NY —NEW YORK PUBLIC LIBRARY, Rare Books and Manuscripts Div, Fifth Ave & 42 St, New York, 10018. William L Joyce, Asst Dir; Susan E Davis, Cur of Mss
Holdings: Cat Mss
Notes: The division holds over 9 million pieces, incl medieval, Renaissance, and Oriental examples. Major emphasis on American, incl exploration, discovery, Spanish expansion, US history and historical persons; political, economic, and literary materials up to the 20th century, especially post-Civil War period; diaries of interest to social historians; theatrical history; science and engineering in the 19th century America. Also the Maloney Irish Historical Collections; collections on Korean history, 1870-1948; Archives of the NY World's Fairs, 1939-1940 and 1964-1965. Autograph collections, and fraudulent signatures and documents. See *Dictionary Catalog of the Manuscript Division*. The Research Libraries of the New York Public Library, 1967. 1155 pp, 2 vols. $110.

FORGETFULNESS see Memory

FORGUE, NORMAN

IL —CHICAGO PUBLIC LIBRARY, Special Collections Div, Cultural Center, 78 E Washington St, Chicago, 60602. Laura Linard, Cur
Holdings: Vols (800) Cat
Budget: ($3000)
Notes: The Special Collections Division endeavors to collect all Chicago imprints produced before 1900, and all Chicago private press productions 1900-50. An exceptional collection of books and keepsakes designed by Norman Forgue. We actively purchase in this area. Outstanding items in the Chicago Imprints Inventory are described in the recent catalog, *Treasures of The Chicago Public Library*, compiled by Thomas A Orlando and Marie Gecik, 1977, pp 93-120.

FORMAL GARDENS see Gardens and Gardening

FORMALDEHYDE

MD —NATIONAL LIBRARY OF MEDICINE, 8600 Rockville Pike, Bethesda, 20209. Harold M Schoolinam, Actg Dir
Budget: ($46,400)

FORMALIN see Formaldehyde

FORMICIDAE see Ants

FORNAROLI, CIA, 1888-1954

NY —NEW YORK PUBLIC LIBRARY, Performing Arts Research Center, Dance

FORNAROLI, CIA, 1888-1954 (cont.)

Collection, 111 Amsterdam Ave, New York, 10023. Genevieve Oswald, Cur
Notes: The Cia Fornaroli Collection, given in 1955-71 by Dr Walter Toscanini as a memorial to his wife, the Italian ballerina Cia Fornaroli, consists of more than 4500 prints, 3300 books, 3500 librettos, 850 pieces of music, 15,000 clippings, photographs, and playbills, manuscripts, and letters. Many rare and unique items, including works of Noverre, Caroso, Vigano, Blasis, Pemberton, Angiolini, Negri, and Taubert. Particularly strong in Italian materials of the 19th century.

FORRESTAL, JAMES VINCENT, 1892-1949

NJ —PRINCETON UNIVERSITY, Library, Manuscript Collection, Nassau St, Princeton, 08540. Jean F Preston, Cur
Holdings: // Cat Mss Pix
Notes: The James Vincent Forrestal Collection, 134 boxes and 19 cartons of papers, 1940-49; and 19 vols of diaries, 1944-49. Terms of access: Diaries are mostly open; personal papers require permission of Forrestal estate, which Library staff can process. An unpublished typescript guide (362 p) is available in the Library.

FORRAWS, JOHN

SC —COLLEGE OF CHARLESTON LIBRARY, Special Collections Dept, Charleston, 29401.
Notes: Correspondence between John Forraws and Alexander Rose regarding the purchase of a vessel and the use of slaves as collateral.

FORRESTER, ALFRED HENRY, 1804-1872

CA —UNIVERSITY OF CALIFORNIA, LOS ANGELES, Research Library, Dept of Special Collections, 405 Hilgard Ave, Los Angeles, 90024. Edward Shreeves, Chairman, Bibliographers Group; David S Zeidberg, Head
Holdings: Mss Pix
Notes: 4 mss; 100 letters; 40 original drawings

FORSTER, EDWARD MORGAN, 1879-1970

CA —UNIVERSITY OF CALIFORNIA, BERKELEY, Bancroft Library, Manuscripts Division, Berkeley, 94720. James D Hart, Dir
Holdings: Uncat Mss
Notes: Letters from Forster in various collections.

CA —CLAREMONT COLLEGES, Honnold Library, Ninth & Dartmouth, Claremont, 91711. Tania Rizzo, Special Collections Dept Head
Holdings: Vols 50 Cat Mss
Notes: Correspondence to Merle Armitage now in the George E Fullerton collection.

CA —UNIVERSITY OF CALIFORNIA, LOS ANGELES, Research Library, Dept of Special Collections, 405 Hilgard Ave, Los Angeles, 90024. Edward Shreeves, Chairman, Bibliographers Group; David S Zeidberg, Head
Holdings: Vols 150 Cat
Notes: 150 first and other editions of his books; 10 letters.

IL —NORTHWESTERN UNIVERSITY, Library, Special Collections Dept, 1937 Sheridan Rd, Evanston, 60201. R Russell Maylone, Cur
Holdings: Vols 58 Cat Mss
Notes: Incl 57 letters to David and Edward Garnett from E M Forster.

NV —UNIVERSITY OF NEVADA, RENO, University Library, Special Collections Dept, Reno, 89557. Robert E Blesse, Head
Holdings: // Vols (109) Cat
Notes: Includes individual works by author in all editions including translations; also prefaces, introductions, published correspondence, appearances in anthologies, periodicals, etc. Bibliographical research collection, part of Modern Authors Collection.

NY —ALFRED UNIVERSITY, Herrick Memorial Library, Alfred, 14802. June E Brown, Head Librn
Notes: The Evelyn Tennyson Openhym Collection of modern British literature and social history. Correspondence addressed to Ursula Roberts ("Susan Miles"), many pieces concerning the British peace movement of the 1930s.

NY —HOFSTRA UNIVERSITY, Library, 1000 Fulton Ave, Hempstead, 11550. Charles R Andrews, Dean of Library Services
Notes: Strong collection. Incl some mss.

BC —UNIVERSITY OF VICTORIA, McPherson Library, Victoria, V8W 3H5, Can.
Notes: Incl 20 leaves, 1928-68; letters to Sir Alex Randall.

ON —VICTORIA UNIVERSITY, Library, 71 Queen's Park Crescent, Toronto, M5S 1K7, Can. Robert C Brandeis, Chief Librn
Holdings: Vols Cat
Notes: A collection of first editions and others of Virginia Woolf and Bloomsbury writers: Clive Bell, Roger Fry, E M Forster, V Sackville-West, K Mansfield, etc. Contains a significant collection of Hogarth Press books, and many of those handprinted by the Woolfs.

FORSYTH, W. FRANK

NC —WESTERN CAROLINA UNIVERSITY, Hunter Memorial Library, Cullowhee, 28723. James B Lloyd, Cur
Notes: The papers of former North Carolina state senators William E Breese, Jr (1875-1939), W Frank Forsyth (1913-70), and Carl Dan Killian, Sr (1903-76).

FORT APACHE, ARIZONA

AZ —NORTHERN ARIZONA UNIVERSITY, Special Collection Library, CU Box 6022, Flagstaff, 86011. Peter M Whiteley, Coordr/Archivist; William Mullane, Librn
Notes: Postal records, 1888-1919. Also, Lester Oliver Collection; Movie script of *Broken Arrow,* 1949, autographed by Jeff Chandler. Reports, correspondence, and orders of the Fort Apache Quartermaster, 1908-1921. Oliver was a former Whiteriver Apache tribal chairman and judge.

FORT BOWIE, ARIZONA

AZ —NORTHERN ARIZONA UNIVERSITY, Special Collection Library, CU Box 6022, Flagstaff, 86011. Peter M Whiteley, Coordr/Archivist; William Mullane, Librn
Notes: Letter written by J P Widney, an officer stationed at Fort Bowie, Ariz, in 1867. Also describes southern Ariz, particularly Tucson.

FORT HUACHUCA, ARIZONA

AZ —FORT HUACHUCA HISTORICAL ASSOCIATION, Fort Huachuca, 85705. James P Finley, Dir
Holdings: Cat Mss Maps Pix Slides Microforms Artifacts
Notes: Voluminous collection of documents concerning Fort Huachuca, southeastern Arizona, Indians, pioneer settlements, and military history. About 50,000 manuscript pieces and documents.

FORT MALDEN, ONTARIO

ON —FORT MALDEN NATIONAL HISTORIC PARK, Library, 100 Laird Ave, Box 38, Amherstburg, N9V 2Z2, Can. Sally E Snyder, Librn
Holdings: Vols 300 Cat Mss Maps Pix Slides Microforms
Notes: Fort Malden and its history.

FORT RILEY, KANSAS

KS —UNIVERSITY OF KANSAS, Kenneth Spencer Research Library, Kansas Collection, Lawrence, 66045. Sheryl K Williams, Cur
Holdings: Cat Pix
Notes: The J J Pennell Collection, Joseph Judd Pennell (1866-1922) was a commercial photographer living and working in Junciton City, Kansas from 1888-1922. This collection of more than 30,000 glass negatives and nearly 6000 prints is a pictorial record of Junction City, Kansas and nearby Ft Riley. The residents of Junction City have been photographed in their various business, professional, social, and cultural activities, while the army post, Fort Riley, has been documented as a calvary and light artillery post, as well as an important military post during the First World War and after. The various ethnic groups which made up the population of Junction City, whites, blacks, and Mexican-Americana are represented in the collection. Pennell's accounts books accompany the photographic collection.

FORT TUTHILL, ARIZONA

AZ —NORTHERN ARIZONA UNIVERSITY, Special Collection Library, CU Box 6022, Flagstaff, 86011. Peter M Whiteley, Coordr/Archivist; William Mullane, Librn
Notes: Arizona National Guard Collection; microfilm copies of the papers of Fort Tuthill, located near Flagstaff, Ariz, 1929-1957, 1974.

FORT UNION, NEW MEXICO

NM —NEW MEXICO HIGHLANDS UNIVERSITY, Donnelly Library, National Ave, Las Vegas, 87701. Karen Jaggers, Assoc Librn
Holdings: // Mss Maps Microforms
Notes: The outstanding collection is the Arrott Collection on Fort Union, New Mexico, 1851-1891.

FORT WORTH STOCKYARDS COMPANY

TX —NORTH TEXAS STATE UNIVERSITY, Archives, NT Station Box 5188, Denton, 76203. Robert LaForte, University Archivist
Notes: Fort Worth Stockyards Company Collection (7200 linear feet). The development of agriculture and businesses dependent on agriculture in the North Texas area is a collecting strength at the NTSU Archives. The Fort Worth Stockyards Company Collection includes correspondence, reports, and business ledgers of a major Texas stockyards from 1893-1956.

FORTIFICATIONS

IL —NEWBERRY LIBRARY, 60 W Walton St, Chicago, 60610. Diana Haskell, Cur of Modern Mss
Holdings: Cat Mss Maps
Notes: Strong collection to 1900.

MN —UNIVERSITY OF MINNESOTA, O Meredith Wilson Library, 309 19 Ave S, Minneapolis, 55455. Austin J McLean, Chief, Special Collections
Holdings: Vols (410) Cat
Notes: Fortification from the Renaissance to 1800. Related materials on attack and defense and accounts of famous sieges.

NM —NEW MEXICO HIGHLANDS UNIVERSITY, Donnelly Library, National Ave, Las Vegas, 87701. Karen Jaggers, Assoc Librn
Holdings: // Mss Maps Microforms
Notes: The outstanding collection is the Arrott Collection on Fort Union, New Mexico, 1851-1891.

NY —NEW YORK STATE LIBRARY, State Education Bldg Annex, Washington Ave, Albany, 12224.
Notes: Select collection, contemporary materials on fortification and allied subjects. Primarily European and American and before 1900. Restricted use: Most items exclusive of manuscripts, local histories and genealogies are available for loan.

FORTIFICATIONS (cont.)

NY —FORT ONTARIO HISTORIC SITE, Oswego, 13126. Shelley B Weinreb, Historic Site Mgr
Holdings: Vols (400) Cat Mss Maps Pix Slides
Notes: Primary focus is upon military activities at the mouth of the Oswego River and the utilization of fortifications (Fort Ontario, Fort Oswego, and Fort George) at that point which served to control the outlet of the traditional Mohawk-Oneida-Oswego route to the Great Lakes. A limited number of sources on fortification design, weapons, uniforms, and military equipment are included. Also incl 4000 slides and 400 pictures.

NY —US MILITARY ACADEMY LIBRARY, West Point, 10996. Robert E Schnare, Asst Librn, Special Collections
Holdings: Cat Mss Maps
Notes: Maps, mss and printed works from the 16th century to present.

VA —COLLEGE OF WILLIAM AND MARY, Earl Gregg Swem Library, Williamsburg, 23185. Margaret C Cook, Cur of Manuscripts & Rare Books
Holdings: Vols 100 // Cat Maps
Notes: The John Womack Wright Collection incl 17th and 18th century books on the campaigns of the Napoleonic wars. Also, 89 maps of theatre of war area of Napoleonic campaigns.

FORTIFICATIONS, ATTACK AND DEFENSE OF see Attack and Defense (Military Science)

FORTIFICATIONS, FRONTIER

NY —FORT ONTARIO HISTORIC SITE, Oswego, 13126. Shelley B Weinreb, Historic Site Mgr
Holdings: Vols (400) Cat Mss Maps Pix Slides
Notes: Primary focus is upon military activities at the mouth of the Oswego River and the utilization of fortifications (Fort Ontario, Fort Oswego, and Fort George) at that point which served to control the outlet of the traditional Mohawk-Oneida-Oswego route to the Great Lakes. A limited number of sources on fortification design, weapons, uniforms, and military equipment are included. Also incl 4000 slides and 400 pictures.

†WA —WASHINGTON STATE UNIVERSITY, Library, Manuscripts, Archives & Special Collections, Pullman, 99164. John F Guido, Head
Holdings: Cat Mss Maps Pix
Notes: The Carl Parcher Russell papers, a vast resource (24,916 items; 45 linear feet) on American Indian and Western pioneer activities and artifacts. Much on the fur trade; pioneer life; mountain men and trapping; wildlife; primitive life in detail. Also the National Park Service, parks, monuments, etc. Described in *Carl Parcher Russell: An Indexed Register of His Scholarly and Professional Papers, 1920-1967, in the Washington State University* Library (Pullman, 1970), 149 pp.

FORTRESS WARFARE see Attack and Defense (Military Science)

FORTS see Fortifications

FORTUNE TELLING

IL —UNIVERSITY OF ILLINOIS, URBANA/CHAMPAIGN, Library, University Archives, 19 Library, 1408 W Gregory Drive, Urbana, 61801. Maynard Brichford, University Archivist
Holdings: Vols (5000) Cat
Budget: ($7000)
Notes: The Mandeville Collection in Parapsychology and Occult Sciences. Titles in the Merten J Mandeville Collection are purchased by funds from an endowment provided specifically for the collection on its establishment in 1966 by Merten J Mandeville, Professor Emeritus of Management, who donated 400 vols from his personal library as the nucleus of the collection. There are currently about 5000 titles in the collection, supplemented by related materials in the general collection. Topics include astrology, extrasensory perception, yoga, magic, satanism, faith healing, hypnosis, Eastern religions, witchcraft, fortune telling, reincarnation, flying saucers, ghosts, dreams, numerology, graphology, and mysticism. Biographies and reference books are a part of the collection as are journals devoted to the scientific study of parapsychology.

FOSCOLO

NC —DUKE UNIVERSITY, William R Perkins Library, Durham, 27706. Elvin E Strowd, University Librn
Notes: The Mazzoni collection of approximately 23,000 books and 67,000 reprints and pamphlets is strong in, but not limited by any means to, Italian literature. A special aspect of this collection is a group of essays, studies, or small works published on the occasion of a marriage. These "per la nozze di" range from a poem published in post card form to a scientific or literary work. The manuscript catalog of the pamphlet collection has been published by the library in book form; the 23,000 volumes have been cataloged and are shelved in the library's bookstacks.

FOSDICK, CHARLES AUSTIN

DC —LIBRARY OF CONGRESS, Rare Book & Special Collections Div, Washington, 20540. William Matheson, Chief
Notes: The Juvenile Collection covers the early 18th century to the present and is particularly strong in fiction. Authors extensively represented are: Alcott, Alger, Abbott, Goodrich, Fosdick, Lothrop and McGuffey.

IN —INDIANA UNIVERSITY, Lilly Library, Seventh St, Bloomington, 47405. William R Cagle, Librn
Holdings: Vols 400 // Cat

MA —BRANDEIS UNIVERSITY, Goldfarb Library, 415 South St, Waltham, 02154. Bessie Hahn, Dir
Notes: Dime Novel and Juvenile Literature Collection. Over 1000 dime novels, an extensive collection of the works of Horatio Alger, Harry Castlemon, Oliver Optic and other boys and girls literature of the 19th and early 20th century. Access to this collection is through the card catalog in Special Collections.

MS —UNIVERSITY OF SOUTHERN MISSISSIPPI, William David McCain Graduate Library, Box 5148, Southern Sta, Hattiesburg, 39406.
Holdings: Vols 88
Notes: The Lena Y de Grummond Collection of Children's Literature. Incl the Robert L Dartt Collection of over 1800 books for boys from the late 19th and early 20th centuries. Extensive Henty (over 550 vols), Alger, Brereton, Castlemon, Fenn, Kingston, Optic, and Stratemeyer holdings. Catalog in progress.

FOSDICK, RAYMOND BLAINE, 1883-

NJ —PRINCETON UNIVERSITY, Library, Manuscript Collection, Nassau St, Princeton, 08540. Jean F Preston, Cur
Holdings: // Cat Mss
Notes: Incl 39 boxes.

FOSS, LUKAS

TX —NORTH TEXAS STATE UNIVERSITY, Audio Center, Box 5188, NT Station, Denton, 76203. Morris Martin, Music Librn
Notes: Emphasis on Contemporary and Avant Garde music. More than 450 musical compositions (mostly manuscript, many multi-media). This is an archive of materials published in, or submitted for publication to, the contemporary music magazine *Source, the Music of the Avant Garde* which appeared from 1967-1977 (although bearing dates only through 1973). Composers represented are the editors (Larry Austin and Stanley Lunetta), John Cage, Steve Reich, Pauline Oliveros, Harry Partch, Morton Feldman, Lukas Foss, Barney Childs, David Cope, Peter Garland, Philip Glass, Ben Johnston, Alcides Lanza, Alvin Lucier, David Rosenboom, Dane Rudhyar, and Nicolas Slonimsky.

FOSS FAMILY

CA —SAN DIEGO PUBLIC LIBRARY, 820 E St, San Diego, 92101. Rhoda E Kruse, Sr Librn
Notes: Extensive local history collection. Incl papers of the Kelly and Foss families.

FOSSIL BOTANY see Paleobotany

FOSSIL FUEL TECHNOLOGY

†PA —GILBERT ASSOCIATES, Library Information Services, PO Box 1498, Reading, 19603. Debra Bosler, Supervisor
Notes: Energy conversion technology. Many government technical reports are received regularly, particularly those on fossil fuel technology.

FOSSIL HUMANOIDS

NC —GEO-TECH INTERNATIONAL LTD, Paleontological Research Laboratory, Library, 3616 Garden Club Lane, Charlotte, 28210. Elizabeth Carson, Librn
Holdings: Maps Pix Slides
Notes: Special emphasis on paleoanthropological collection devoted to reprints, source materials, and all current publications and journals on paleoanthropology and evolution.

FOSSIL MAN see Fossil Humanoids

FOSSIL REDWOOD see Redwood, Fossil

FOSSIL VERTEBRATES see Vertebrates, Fossil

FOSSILS see Paleontology

FOSTER, HAL

OH —OHIO STATE UNIVERSITY, Library for Communication and Graphic Arts, 242 W 18th St, Columbus, 43210. Lucy S Caswell, Curator
Notes: Comic strip artists Hal Foster, Dudley T Fisher, Jr, Mark Szorady, Edwina Dumm, Jim Baker have original works in the library. Also new collections of original cartoons by Windsor McCay, John T McCutcheon, Dick Moores, Ned White, Walter Berndt, Jim Larrick, Carl Rose and Bill Crawford. Also a large collection of the work of illustrator Will Rannells. The Shel Dorf Collection incl historic comic strips and related materials. A small but growing collection of comic books, especially those featuring *Katy Keene,* is available in the library.

FOSTER, J. S.

PQ —MCGILL UNIVERSITY, McLennan Library, University Archives, 3459 McTavish St, Montreal, H3A 1Y1, Can. Martha Caya, Archivist
Notes: Director's files of Foster Radiation Laboratory (1922-1965). Miscellaneous administrative papers and files. Not a complete collection of his papers.

FOSTER, JOHN W.

†TX —UNIVERSITY OF TEXAS LIBRARIES, General Libraries, Humanities Research Center, PO Box 7219, Austin, 78712. John Chalmers, Librn
Notes: The John W F Dulles collection of correspondence, diaries, autographs, speeches, and paintings by famous historical figures from the 17th century to the present.

FOSTER, JOHN W. (cont.)

Much of the material is related to Mr Dulles' three relatives who served as Secretaries of State: John Foster Dulles, Robert Lansing, and John W Foster.

FOSTER, STEPHEN COLLINS, 1826-1864

IN —INDIANA UNIVERSITY, Lilly Library, Seventh St, Bloomington, 47405. William R Cagle, Librn
Holdings: // Uncat
Notes: Extensive holdings in the Starr Collection of American Sheet Music.

PA —UNIVERSITY OF PITTSBURGH, Stephen Foster Memorial, Foster Hall Collection, Pittsburgh, 15260. Deane L Root, Cur
Holdings: Vols (1000) Cat Mss Pix Phonorecords VF //
Budget: ($50,000)
Notes: Collection comprises more than 10, 000 separate American items: original mss and letters; first editions, and early modern editions of Foster's music; personal possessions of the composer; books; magazine and newspaper articles; pictures and portraits; phonograph records; broadsides; and other material.

RI —BROWN UNIVERSITY, John Hay Library, Harris Collection, Prospect St, Providence, 02912. Rosemary L Cullen, Cur
Holdings: Vols (200,000) Cat Mss Pix Phonorecords Microforms
Budget: ($15,000)
Notes: The Harris Collection of American Poetry and Plays is principally composed of American and Canadian poetry and plays from the 17th century to the present. Extensive holdings in songsters and sheet music with lyrics (170,000). Incl large collection of Stephen Foster sheet music. See *Dictionary Catalog of American Poetry and* Plays (Boston: G K Hall, 1972), 13 vols; Supplement (1977), 3 vols. Separate catalog.

FOULIS, THOMAS NOBLE

†ON —UNIVERSITY OF WESTERN ONTARIO, School of Library and Information Science, Special Collections Room, London, N6A 5B9, Can.
Holdings: Vols 560
Notes: A collection of books published by the firm T N Foulis of Edinburgh between 1903-1926.

FOUNDATIONS (ENDOWMENTS) see Charitable Uses, Trusts, and Foundations

FOUNDATIONS, RELIGIOUS see Religious Foundations

FOUNDATIONS OF ARITHMETIC see Arithmetic—Foundations

FOUNDRIES AND FOUNDRYWORKERS

IL —AMERICAN FOUNDRYMEN'S SOCIETY, Technical Information Center, Golf & Wolf Rds, Des Plaines, 60016. Ann V Duggan, Mgr Library Services
Holdings: Vols (3000) 16mm Films
Notes: Incl current awareness service.

FOUNTAIN, LEATRICE

MA —BOSTON UNIVERSITY, Mugar Memorial Library, Special Collections Dept, 771 Commonwealth Ave, Boston, 02215. Howard B Gotlieb, Dir
Holdings: Cat Mss
Notes: Mss, correspondence, etc collected in depth; incl publications by or about.

FOURIER, CHARLES

TX —UNIVERSITY OF TEXAS, ARLINGTON, Library, Arlington, 76019. Charles A Colley, Dir of Special Collections; Robert A Gamble, Head of Archives
Holdings: // Mss
Notes: Santerre Collection. This is the library of the Snterre family who emigrated from France, Belgium, and Switzerland in 1855 to join the Utopian Socialist colony of Victor Prosper Considerant in what is now Dallas, Texas. Typical selection of books of a middle-class, well-educated family of the period. Some title deeds, legal papers, family letters, first Paris editions of works of Considerant, Charles Fourier; French translations of English classics, devotional works. See George H Santerre, *White Cliffs of Dallas* (Dallas, Texas: Book Craft, 1955).

FOURTH INTERNATIONAL see International, Fourth

FOURTH OF JULY

IL —NEWBERRY LIBRARY, 60 W Walton St, Chicago, 60610. Diana Haskell, Cur of Modern Mss
Holdings: Cat
Notes: Celebrations and orations.

FOURTH OF JULY ORATIONS

IL —NEWBERRY LIBRARY, 60 W Walton St, Chicago, 60610. Diana Haskell, Cur of Modern Mss
Holdings: Cat
Notes: Celebrations and orations.

MA —NEW ENGLAND HISTORIC GENEALOGICAL SOCIETY, Library, 101 Newbury St, Boston, 02116. Ralph J Crandell, Dir
Holdings: Vols (250,000) Mss Maps Microforms Pix
Notes: New England genealogy. Especially strong Massachusetts, Maine, and New Hampshire, although all states are well represented, as are the relevancies of each subject listed in this volume with regard to British antecedent and contemporary history. Special strengths in local history and biography, obituaries, etc, incl parish registers, censuses, British and American. 3125 linear ft of mss.

NY —NEW YORK STATE LIBRARY, State Education Bldg Annex, Washington Ave, Albany, 12224.
Holdings: Cat Microforms
Notes: More than 700 Fourth of July orations, 51 being before 1800, 186 between 1800 and 1824 and 207 between 1825 and 1849. There are 432 New England orations and 159 New York State items.

NY —NEW YORK HISTORICAL SOCIETY, Library, 170 Central Park W, New York, 10024. James Gregory, Librn
Holdings: Mss
Notes: Incl original mss, illustrative materials, etc.

FOWLER, GENE, 1890-1960

CO —UNIVERSITY OF COLORADO, Libraries, Special Collections, Boulder, 80309. Nora J Quinlan, Head
Holdings: Vols 58 Uncat Mss
Notes: Incl mss, etc.

FOWLER, WILLIAM A.

CA —CALIFORNIA INSTITUTE OF TECHNOLOGY, Robert A Millikan Memorial Library, Archives, 1201 E California Blvd, Pasadena, 91125. Judith R Goodstein, Archivist
Notes: Correspondence and printed matter of William A Fowler, Nuclear Science Advisory Committee, 1977-1980; the National Academy of Science's Astronomy Survey Committee, 1979-1980; the National Science Foundation's Astronomy Advisory Committee, 1978-1979; and proceedings of the Pugwash Conference for the years 1960, 1962-1963.

FOWLES, JOHN

NV —UNIVERSITY OF NEVADA, RENO, University Library, Special Collections Dept, Reno, 89557. Robert E Blesse, Head
Holdings: Vols (55) Cat
Notes: Includes individual works by author in all editions including translations; also prefaces, introductions, published correspondence, appearances in anthologies, periodicals, etc. Bibliographical research collection, part of Modern Authors Collection. Other appearances 100 cataloged.

FOWLIE, WALLACE

MA —BOSTON UNIVERSITY, Mugar Memorial Library, Special Collections Dept, 771 Commonwealth Ave, Boston, 02215. Howard B Gotlieb, Dir
Holdings: Cat Mss Pix
Notes: Mss, correspondence, etc collected in depth; incl publications by or about.

FOWLS see Poultry

FOX, FONTANE

IN —INDIANA UNIVERSITY, Lilly Library, Seventh St, Bloomington, 47405. William R Cagle, Librn
Notes: Contemporary with and depicting Lincoln; the War of 1812 and other periods. Incl significant mss of the modern cartoonists and caricaturists Ardizzone, Beerbohm, Fontane Fox, Kin Hubbard, Charles Bacon Jackson, McCutcheon, Messick, Nast, Rothenstein, Sendak, and many miscellaneous items.

FOX, GEORGE

PA —FRIENDS HISTORICAL LIBRARY OF SWARTHMORE COLLEGE, Swarthmore, 19081. J William Frost, Dir
Holdings: Vols (31,340) Cat Mss Pix Microforms
Notes: Comprehensive collection of writings by and about the organizer of The Society of Friends (qv).

FOX, JOHN

KY —UNIVERSITY OF KENTUCKY, Margaret I King Library, Dept of Special Collections, Lexington, 40506. William Marshall, Head
Holdings: Vols 31 Cat Mss Pix
Notes: 83 pieces of ms, 12 boxes material incl various editions, original ms of novels, reviews of books, letters.

VA —UNIVERSITY OF VIRGINIA, Alderman Library, Manuscripts Dept, Charlottesville, 22901. Edmund Berkeley Jr, Cur
Holdings: Cat Mss

FOX, KATE AND MARGARET

NY —UNIVERSITY OF ROCHESTER, Rush Rhees Library, Department of Rare Books and Special Collections, Rochester, 14627. Peter Dzwonkoski, Librn
Holdings: Mss
Notes: Autograph letters and other mss incl in the Amy and Issac Post family papers. *See also* entry under Spiritualism.

FOX HUNTING

IL —DE PAUL UNIVERSITY, Library, 2323 N Seminary, Chicago, 60614. Kathryn De Graff, Special Collections Librn
Holdings: Vols (900) // Uncat
Notes: The Anita Peabody Sports Collection of approx 900 volumes, incl about 250 periodical volumes, covering such topics as foxhunting, gambling, horse racing, and breeding, along with rule books and song books. Materials cover the middle to late 19th century. A complete run of *The Sporting Magazine,* begun in 1792, is also part of the collection.

NJ —PRINCETON UNIVERSITY, Library, Rare Books Dept, Princeton, 08544. Stephen Ferguson, Cur
Notes: Laurence Roberts Carton Hunting Collection. Consists of over 1000 vols, comprising a portion of the Library's sizable Sporting Books Collection. See: William Dix, "The Hunting Library of Laurence Roberts Carton" in the *Princeton University Library* Chronicle XV, 1 (Autumn, 1953) pp 43-45.

FOX HUNTING (cont.)

The books are a discriminating and representative collection of the literature of fox hunting and related subjects, particularly in England and America. Works from the 15th century are represented by facsimiles and other modern printed versions. There are a number of first editions of notable 16th, 17th and 18th century books, especially in English. The verse and fiction of sport are extensively represented, and biographies of dozens of notable figures and histories of scores of individual packs and hunting territories can be found. Incidental to the collection is thefine collection of illustrated hunting books. It is rich in examples of the work of the major illustrators of the period who helped make, and in turn were made by, the popularity of the sporting book. Especially notable are the works of Henry Alken.

NY —MERCY COLLEGE LIBRARY, Dobbs Ferry, 10522. Larry Earle Bone, Dir
Holdings: Vols (406) Cat Pix
Notes: General collection of American and British books and periodicals on horses, hounds and hunting, with special emphasis on the Millbrook Hunt. 15 percent of the collection is rare books and periodicals. Rare photographs and paintings also incl. Many of the books are from the private libraries of members of the Millbrook Hunt. Collection formerly at Bennett College, Millbrook, New York.

NY —RACQUET & TENNIS CLUB, Library, 370 Park Ave, New York, 10022. Gerald Belliveau, Jr, Librn
Holdings: Vols (17,500) Cat
Budget: ($6000)
Notes: Specializes in court tennis, lawn tennis, early American sport. See *Dictionary Catalogue of the Library of Sports in the Racquet and Tennis Club* (Boston: G K Hall, 1971). Also, Robert W Henderson, *Early American Sport*, 3rd ed. (Cranbury, NJ: Fairleigh Dickinson University Press, 1977).

FOX INDIANS

IL —AUGUSTANA COLLEGE, Library, Rock Island, 61201. Marjorie M Miller, Special Collections Librn
Holdings: Vols 2000 Cat Mss
Notes: The John Hauberg Upper Mississippi Valley Collection. Incl strong collection of immigrant guide books for the Midwestern states. Fine collection relative to the Sauk and Fox tribes and Black Hawk in particular.

KS —UNIVERSITY OF KANSAS, Kenneth Spencer Research Library, Kansas Collection, Lawrence, 66045. Sheryl K Williams, Cur
Holdings: Vols (92,000) Cat Mss Maps Pix
Notes: Several photographic collections devoted exclusively to American Indian subjects, collections of personal papers, contemporary American Indian periodicals, 19th century tracts and treatises. Wars, missionary contracts, reservation life, etc in Kansas, Oklahoma and Nebraska. Good holdings treating Potawatomie Indians (Prairie Band), Sauk, Fox, Osage. Incl pamphlets, serials, and state publications.

NY —HOFSTRA UNIVERSITY, Library, 1000 Fulton Ave, Hempstead, 11550. Charles R Andrews, Dean of Library Services
Notes: The personal library of Paul Radin. See description of the American Philosophical Society Library's collection of his anthropological papers under this entry (Pa).

PA —AMERICAN PHILOSOPHICAL SOCIETY, Library, 105 S Fifth St, Philadelphia, 19106. Edward C Carter II, Librn
Notes: The anthropological papers of Paul Radin in fields of ethnology, social organization, primitive religion, linguistics, and mythology. He worked mostly among the Winnebago, Ojibwa, Fox, Zapotec, Wappo, Wintun, and Huave Indian tribes; also Italian and other ethnic minorities of San Francisco.

FOXALL, RAYMOND

MA —BOSTON UNIVERSITY, Mugar Memorial Library, Special Collections Dept, 771 Commonwealth Ave, Boston, 02215. Howard B Gotlieb, Dir
Holdings: Cat Mss
Notes: Mss, correspondence, etc collected in depth; incl publications by or about.

FOXCROFT, THOMAS, 1697-1769, AND FAMILY

MA —BOSTON UNIVERSITY, Mugar Memorial Library, Special Collections Dept, 771 Commonwealth Ave, Boston, 02215. Howard B Gotlieb, Dir
Holdings: // Cat Mss
Notes: Correspondence and sermons.

FOXHOUNDS

OH —CLEVELAND PUBLIC LIBRARY, Science & Technology Dept, 325 Superior Ave, Cleveland, 44114. Jean Z Piety, Head
Holdings: Cat
Notes: Emphases: history of the dog; dog show catalogs; stud books of the American Kennel Club, the Canadian Kennel Club, the Kennel Club, the field dog, the foxhound, and the Irish terrier.

FRAENKEL, MICHAEL, 1897-1957

BC —UNIVERSITY OF VICTORIA, McPherson Library, Victoria, V8W 3H5, Can.
Notes: Poet and critic. Incl 60 leaves, 1945-51; correspondence to Jasper Wood on literary matters containing many references to Henry Miller.

FRAKTUR

PA —FRANKLIN & MARSHALL COLLEGE, Library, Lancaster, 17604. Kathleen J Moretto, Library Dir
Holdings: Uncat Pix
Notes: Calligraphic art form dating generally from 1742 to 1830 and used to record important family events; "Geburtsbriefe," "Taufschein" and "Vorschiffen" are represented in the collection (ca 400 items).

PA —FREE LIBRARY OF PHILADELPHIA, Rare Book Dept, Logan Sq, Philadelphia, 19103. Marie E Korey, Rare Book Librn
Holdings: Vols (1100) Cat Mss Pix
Notes: A collection of 1100 pieces of Pennsylvania German folk art on paper in manuscript and printed form, incl birth and baptismal certificates, writing examples, and bookplates.

FRAMBOESIA see Yaws

FRANCE—CIVILIZATION AND CULTURE

†MA —FRENCH LIBRARY IN BOSTON, INC, 53 Marlborough St, Boston, 02116.
Notes: Classical and contemporary French literature incl criticism, French history, politics, social life, language and art, cinema, education, architecture, and Canadian literature.

NH —ASSOCIATION CANADO-AMERICAIN (FRATERNAL LIFE INSURANCE SOCIETY), Institute Canado-Americain, 52 Concord St, Manchester, 03101. Robert A Beaudoin, Librn
Holdings: Vols (40,000) Cat Mss Maps Pix Slides Phonorecords Audiotapes Microforms
Budget: ($2000)
Notes: Contains books, pamphlets, mss, university dissertations, newspapers, manuscripts, periodicals, and archives of various other societies (active of defunct). Subjects covered incl art, music, literature, folklore, religion, politics, sociology, history, etc of the French in France, Canada, and US (especially New England's Franco-Americans, Louisiana's Cajuns, and Quebec's French-Canadians). There is also an extensive collection of genealogical works dealing with Quebec Acadia, and New England Francophones. Articles dealing with the library are: "The Library of the Association Canado-Americaine" by Edward B Ham in *Modern Language Notes*, vol LII, no 7, November 1937 and a bilingual article "Appel d'un jeune aux jeunes en faveur de al Bibliotheque ACA" by Robert B Perreault in *Le Canado-Americain*, nouvelle serie, vol 1, no 5, julliet-aout-septembre 1975, pp 18-19.

NY —FRENCH INSTITUTE-ALLIANCE FRANCAISE, Library, 22 E 60 St, New York, 10022. Fred J Gitner, Librn
Holdings: Vols (40,000) Cat Phonorecords Audiotapes
Budget: ($23,000)
Notes: Special collections of art books, books about Paris. Rich in bibliographical, biographical and lexicographical works. Standard editions of all major French authors. Name has been changed from French Institute in the United States Library since merger with the Alliance Francaise de New York.

ON —VICTORIA UNIVERSITY, Library, 71 Queen's Park Crescent, Toronto, M5S 1K7, Can. Robert C Brandeis, Chief Librn
Holdings: Vols 2500
Notes: The Riese Collection, partially cataloged, containing presentation copies of works by modern and contemporary French authors. Strong in Surrealism.

FRANCE—COLONIES

NY —STATE UNIVERSITY OF NEW YORK, COLLEGE AT NEW PALTZ, Sojourner Truth Library, World Study Center, William J Haggerty Collection of French Colonial History, New Paltz, 12561. Corinne Nyquist, Librn
Holdings: Vols (19,153) // Uncat Mss Maps Pix
Notes: French colonial history, In 1966 this college acquired the research Library of the Comite Francais pour l'outre-mer. This library served the needs of a society in Paris whose membership incl French colonial administrators, scholars, and students. The more than 19,000 books and pamphlets and 135 sets of periodicals date from 1830, and cover the administration and development of the former colonies of France. Much of the material is economic, statistical, or agricultural, reflecting the interests of the collectors. British colonial history is well represented. Described in *Africana Library* Journal, Winter 1971.

FRANCE—FOREIGN RELATIONS—ALGERIA

CA —HOOVER INSTITUTION ON WAR, REVOLUTION & PEACE, Stanford University, Stanford, 94305. Milorad M Drachkovitch, Archivist
Notes: Papers of Yves Godard, officer, French Army, 1932-1961; director of police in Algeria, 1958-60; and organizer of the Organisation de l'Armee Secrete (OAS) 1961-62; incl correspondence, messages, reports, dossiers, maps, photos, news clippings, speeches and writings, and other material, 1929-74, related to military and resistance operations during World War II; to military operations during Indochinese War; and to military, police, and terrorist activities during the Algerian independence struggle. Incl records of the Armee Secrete de Haute-Savoie (Secret Army of Resistance Fighters of Haute-Savoie). 13 ms boxes; 1 oversize volume; 1 envelope.

FRANCE—FOREIGN RELATIONS—MEXICO

AZ —UNIVERSITY OF ARIZONA, Library, Tucson, 85721. W David Laird, Librn
Notes: Strong collection on Maximilian and Carlotta and the French intervention in Mexico, some official publications.

FRANCE—FOREIGN RELATIONS—U. S.

DC —LIBRARY OF CONGRESS, Geography and Map Division, Washington, 20540. John

FRANCE—FOREIGN RELATIONS—U.S. (cont.)

A Wolter, Chief
Notes: Pierre Ozanne Collection of maps and views of French naval operations during the American Revolution.

FRANCE—HISTORY

CA —UNIVERSITY OF CALIFORNIA, LOS ANGELES, Research Library, Dept of Special Collections, 405 Hilgard Ave, Los Angeles, 90024. Edward Shreeves, Chairman, Bibliographers Group; David S Zeidberg, Head
Holdings: Mss Pix
Notes: Material on 20th century French history is incl in the archive assembled by Roger Mennevee.

CA —UNIVERSITY OF CALIFORNIA, LOS ANGELES, Research Library, Western European Collection, Los Angeles, 90024. Edward Shreeves, Chairman, Bibliographers Group; Mary E Greco, Western European Bibliographer
Holdings: Mss Maps Pix Microforms
Notes: Early modern and modern France. Special strengths in intellectual and religious history of the 17th and 18th centuries, Jansenism in particular, and popular culture of the 19th and 20th centuries. Good coverage.

DC —LIBRARY OF CONGRESS, Washington, 20540.
Notes: Project of a consortium to microfilm about 200,000 pp of material on Great Britain, France, Russia and Prussia, for the period 1848-1918 in the ms and documentary collections of the Austrian State Archives. The collection will incl, among others, documents on the Austro-Prussian War of 1866, the treaty negotiations between France and Italy in 1868-1870, the Orient Question of 1877-1878, the persecution of Jews in Russia in 1882, the Congo Conference in Berlin, 1884-1887 and the British-Portuguese conflict in East Africa, 1889-1891. Copies are available at LC, the Center for Research Libraries, the Hampshire Inter-Library Center, and the libraries of Boston College, Yale, Harvard, Duke, Stanford and the University of Virginia.

IL —CENTER FOR RESEARCH LIBRARIES, 6050 S Kenwood Ave, Chicago, 60637. Donald B Simpson, Dir; Esther Smith, Collection Development Librn
Holdings: Microform
Notes: Journal officiel and parlimentary proceedings, collections on revolutions of 1789, 1830 and 1848. Political party proceedings. Statistical collections. Archival materials from Archives du Ministere des Affaries Etrangeres. Newspaper backfiles.

IL —DE PAUL UNIVERSITY, Library, 2323 N Seminary, Chicago, 60614. Kathryn De Graff, Special Collections Librn
Holdings: Vols (4000) Cat Maps Pix
Budget: $1500
Notes: The Lemke Napoleon Collection of approx 4000 volumes. Rich in contemporary literary works, pamphlets, broadsides, illustrations, military maps and atlases. A catalog was prepared by Mrs Virginia Goult and published in 1941, with an addendum in 1978.

IL —NEWBERRY LIBRARY, 60 W Walton St, Chicago, 60610. Diana Haskell, Cur of Modern Mss
Holdings: Cat Mss
Notes: Several thousand vols, especially 16th-18th centuries.

IL —NORTHWESTERN UNIVERSITY, Library, Special Collections Dept, 1937 Sheridan Rd, Evanston, 60201. R Russell Maylone, Cur
Notes: 14,000 French Revolution pamphlets; 1560 mazarinades; 2500 Brabant Revolution pamphlets. Large collection of material from the Siege of Paris, 1870, and the Paris Commune, 1871, incl posters, caricatures and drawings, books, pamphlets, newspapers, journals, letters and photographs. Documentation of the May-June Revolution, Paris, 1968, incl film, books, pamphlets and over 250 original posters.

IN —SAINT MARY-OF-THE-WOODS COLLEGE, College Library, Saint Mary-of-the-Woods, 47876. Sister Emily Walsh, SP, Administrator
Holdings: Vols 2500 Cat
Notes: Books published in French, 18th-19th century.

IN —INDIANA STATE UNIVERSITY, Cunningham Memorial Library, Dept of Rare Books & Special Collections, Terre Haute, 47809. Lawrence J McCrank, Head
Holdings: Cat Maps Pix

KS —UNIVERSITY OF KANSAS, Kenneth Spencer Research Library, Special Collections Dept, Lawrence, 66045. Alexandra Mason, Librn
Holdings: Cat Mss Maps
Notes: Great Britain, Italy, France, Spain, Eastern Europe (especially Poland), medieval to late 18th century. Noncirculating.

MD —UNIVERSITY OF MARYLAND, Library, Rare Book Collection, College Park, 20742. Donald Farren, Assoc Dir for Special Collections
Holdings: Vols (10,000) Cat
Notes: Ranging from incunabula to modern first editions, the Rare Book Collection is particularly strong in materials relating to the history of France and in *exempla* of interest to students of bibliography. Related collections include sizable groups of books and other items relating to the Savoy, to *Expressionismus,* and to Pompeii. Pamphlet collections include many Mazarinades, many pamphlets relating to slavery and abolition, numerous French plays, and press books.

†MA —FRENCH LIBRARY IN BOSTON, INC, 53 Marlborough St, Boston, 02116.
Notes: Classical and contemporary French literature incl criticism, French history, politics, social life, language and art, cinema, education, architecture, and Canadian literature.

MA —HARVARD UNIVERSITY LIBRARY, Widener Library, Cambridge, 02138. Assunta S Pisani, Specialist in Book Selection
Holdings: Cat Mss Maps Microforms
Notes: Strong points incl local history, medieval history, and the Revolutionary period; there are special collections on the Dreyfuss case and on Joan of Arc.

MA —BRANDEIS UNIVERSITY, Goldfarb Library, 415 South St, Waltham, 02154. Bessie Hahn, Dir
Notes: Consistoire Israelite Archives. Contains 12 linear ft of original documents relating to the French-Jewish community from the 18th to 20th century. A finding list of the documents is in Special Collections. Also, the Alfred Dreyfus Trial Collection: approx 1000 books, pamphlets, newspapers and photographs as well as some correspondence of French notables dealing with the Alfred Dreyfus trial at the turn of the century. An author-title card catalog can be found in the Special Collections Card Catalog.

MI —UNIVERSITY OF MICHIGAN, Library, Dept of Rare Books & Special Collections, Ann Arbor, 48109. Robert J Starring, Head
Holdings: Cat
Notes: Espec 16th-17th centuries. Incl about 1100 pamphlets in 878 vols, checklisted on cards. Also recorded in *French Political Pamphlets, 1547-1648,* compiled by R O Lindsay and John Neu, Madison: The University of Wisconsin Press, 1969. Also incl 68 vols of pamphlets collected by the French historian Guizot, and many French learned society publications.

MI —MICHIGAN STATE UNIVERSITY, Libraries, Special Collections Div, East Lansing, 48824. Jannette Fiore, Librn
Holdings: Vols 10,000 Uncat
Notes: A collection of monographs and pamphlets 16th through 19th centuries, all bearing to some degree on the French monarchy.

MN —UNIVERSITY OF MINNESOTA, O Meredith Wilson Library, 309 19 Ave S, Minneapolis, 55455. Austin J McLean, Chief, Special Collections
Holdings: Vols 1600 // Cat
Notes: Primarily consists of pamphlets from the Consulate 1799-1803.

NY —STATE UNIVERSITY OF NEW YORK, COLLEGE AT BUFFALO, Poetry/Rare Books Collection, 420 Capen Hall, Buffalo, 14260. Robert J Bertholf, Cur
Holdings: Vols 1145
Notes: Collection of pamphlets covering the period of 1547-1652, incl 430 Mazarinades. See also Lindsay and Neu: *French Political Pamphlets 1547-1648; a Catalog of Major Collections in American Libraries* (1969).

NY —HOFSTRA UNIVERSITY, Library, 1000 Fulton Ave, Hempstead, 11550. Charles R Andrews, Dean of Library Services
Holdings: Vols (5000) Cat
Notes: The personal collection of Professor Shepard Clough of Columbia University. Especially strong in French and Italian modern history, Italian Fascism and European economic statistics.

NY —CORNELL UNIVERSITY LIBRARIES, Manuscript and Archives Division, Ithaca, 14853. H Thomas Hickerson, Special Collections Librn

NY —FRENCH INSTITUTE-ALLIANCE FRANCAISE, Library, 22 E 60 St, New York, 10022. Fred J Gitner, Librn
Holdings: Vols (40,000) Cat Phonorecords Audiotapes
Budget: ($23,000)
Notes: Special collections of art books, books about Paris. Rich in bibliographical, biographical and lexicographical works. Standard editions of all major French authors. Name has been changed from French Institute in the United States Library since merger with the Alliance Francaise de New York.

NY —NEW YORK PUBLIC LIBRARY, Slavonic Div, Fifth Ave & 42 St, New York, 10018. Edward Kasinec, Chief
Holdings: Vols 180 // Cat mss
Notes: The Ukrainian archive of Mykyta Shapoval consists mainly of the correspondence of General Mykola Shapoval (Army of the Ukrainian National Republic, 1917-1920) and of his family. Documents, mss, diaries relating to the activities and events of Ukrainians in Czechoslovakia and France are included. The material covers the period of the 1920s through 1950s.

NY —UNIVERSITY OF ROCHESTER, Rush Rhees Library, Department of Rare Books and Special Collections, Rochester, 14627. Peter Dzwonkoski, Librn
Holdings: Vols 450 Cat
Notes: Collection of materials on 16th and 17th century European law and political theory with special emphasis on works emanating from the French Civil Wars of the late 16th century. Particularly notable are the editions of the works of Francois Hotman and the editions of the Corpus Juris Civilis printed in Lyon. No photocopying.

NC —UNIVERSITY OF NORTH CAROLINA, CHAPEL HILL, Wilson Library, Rare Book Collection, Chapel Hill, 27514. Paul S Koda, Cur of Rare Books
Holdings: Vols 6000 Cat Mss Pix
Notes: The William Henry Hoyt Collection of French History contains over 6000 volumes primarily concerned with the French Revolution and the Napoleonic era. There is also personal correspondence of Napoleon, as well as 27 boxes of pamphlets, 1650-1779.

NC —DUKE UNIVERSITY, William R Perkins Library, Durham, 27706. Elvin E Strowd, University Librn

NC —DUKE UNIVERSITY, William R Perkins Library, Rare Book Room, Durham, 27706. John L Sharpe, III, Cur
Notes: French pamphlet collection relating to the political, economic, and social life of France from the early 18th century down to 1830.

OH —CLEVELAND PUBLIC LIBRARY, History and Geography Department, 325 Superior Ave, Cleveland, 44114. JoAnn Petrello, Head
Holdings: Cat
Notes: Strong in Normandy, Britanny, Gascony. Nearly complete collection of historical memoirs (analyzed). Mazarinade collection. Contemporary political pamphlets of the period of the Fronde, 1648-1653 (about 2000 pamphlets). No photocopying.

FRANCE—HISTORY (cont.)

WI —UNIVERSITY OF WISCONSIN, MADISON, Memorial Library, 728 State St, Madison, 53706. Erwin K Welsch, Social Studies Bibliographer
Notes: Incl

ON —NATIONAL LIBRARY OF CANADA, 395 Wellington St, Ottawa, K1A 0N4, Can. Andre Preibish, Dir
Holdings: Vols 44,000 Documents
Budget: $50,000
Notes: Includes 400 serials titles. Collection aims to be comprehensive and covers all aspects of Canadian history. The library has received all Canadian titles on legal deposit since 1950; intensive acquisition of earlier works and those published abroad. In addition, the collection is supported by representative resources for American, British and French history.

ON —VICTORIA UNIVERSITY, Library, Centre for Reformation and Renaissance Studies, 71 Queen's Park Crescent, Toronto, M5S 1K7, Can. Robert C Brandeis, Chief Librn; James Estes, Dir
Holdings: Vols (15,000) Cat Slides
Notes: The CRRS concentrates on the northern European countries and France; its chief strengths are Erasmus, 650 vols; early printed books, especially 16th century editions of Latin classics; bibliography and the history of printing. The Erasmus holdings are cataloged in W T McCready et al, "The Erasmus Collection in the Centre for Reformation and Renaissance Studies...A Catalogue"...*Reformation and Renaissance* 7 (1971), 32-76 and "A Supplementary List"...*Reformation and Renaissance,* 10 (1974), 116-119. Published catalogs. Humanist Editions of the Classics at CRRS, Toronto, 1979; Humanist Editions of Statutes and History at CRRS, Toronto, 1980; Bibles, Theological Treatises and Other Religious Literature 1491-1700 at CRRS, Toronto, 1981.

FRANCE—HISTORY—REVOLUTION, 1789-1799

CA —UNIVERSITY OF CALIFORNIA, SANTA BARBARA, Library, Dept of Special Collections, Santa Barbara, 93106. Christian F Brun, Head
Holdings: Vols 1270 Uncat Microforms

CA —STANFORD UNIVERSITY LIBRARIES, Cecil H Green Library, Stanford, 94305. Michael T Ryan, Cur
Notes: Research collection.

DE —HAGLEY MUSEUM AND LIBRARY, Eleutherian Mills-Hagley Foundation Inc, PO Box 3630, Greenville, 19807. Richmond D Williams, Dir; Heddy A Richter, Imprints Librn
Holdings: Vols 6000 Pamphlets
Notes: The French history collection is especially good in pamphlets of the Revolutionary and Napoleonic periods; French 18th Century economic theory, especially Physiocracy; and the works of or concerning P S du Pont de Nemours.

DC —LIBRARY OF CONGRESS, Rare Book & Special Collections Div, Washington, 20540. William Matheson, Chief
Notes: The John Boyd Thacher Collection incl books and mss relating to the French Revolution.
See also entry under Incunabula

FL —FLORIDA STATE UNIVERSITY, Robert Manning Strozier Library, Special Collections Dept, Tallahassee, 32306. Opal M Free, Head, Special Collections
Holdings: Vols (12,616) Cat Mss Maps Pix Microforms
Notes: One of the most extensive collections in this period in the US. Several hundred volumes are held in the US only in this collection. See Donald D Horward, *The French Revolution and Napoleonic Collection at Florida State University: A Bibliographical Guide* (Tallahassee: Friends of Florida State Univ, 1973). (A second vol is expected early in 1984.) No photocopying.

GA —EMORY UNIVERSITY, Robert W Woodruff Library, Special Collections Dept, Atlanta, 30322. Linda M Matthews, Head Special Collections; Virginia J H Cain, Processing Archivist; Richard H F Lindemann, Reference Archivist
Holdings: Cat
Notes: About 2400 pamphlets of the French Revolution.

IL —NEWBERRY LIBRARY, 60 W Walton St, Chicago, 60610. Diana Haskell, Cur of Modern Mss
Holdings: Vols 35,000 Cat

IL —NORTHWESTERN UNIVERSITY, Library, Special Collections Dept, 1937 Sheridan Rd, Evanston, 60201. R Russell Maylone, Cur
Notes: Incl 14,000 pamphlets, legal documents, and periodical issues published 1787-1800. Additional 2500 pieces dealing with revolutionary events in Flanders.

IN —INDIANA UNIVERSITY, Lilly Library, Seventh St, Bloomington, 47405. William R Cagle, Librn
Holdings: Vols 4000 // Cat
Notes: Contemporary printings.

IA —UNIVERSITY OF IOWA, University Libraries, Iowa City, 52242. Frank Paluka, Head, Special Collections Dept
Holdings: // Cat
Notes: Collection incl 8000 pamphlets. See Marcia Haubold, "The French Revolution Collection", in *Books at Iowa,* Nov 1965.

KS —UNIVERSITY OF KANSAS, Kenneth Spencer Research Library, Special Collections Dept, Lawrence, 66045. Alexandra Mason, Librn
Holdings: Vols 12,000 Cat
Notes: Frank E Melvin Collection of French Revolutionary Pamphlets. Incl some periodicals. Noncirculating. See Saricks, Ambrose. *A Bibliography of the Frank E Melvin Collection,* Lawrence, Kansas, 1961. (Univ of Kansas Publications. Library series, 10). 2 vols, cover 6800 pamphlets purchased before 1960. Collection being published in NCR Microcard series of French Revolutionary pamphlets.

KY —UNIVERSITY OF KENTUCKY, Margaret I King Library, Dept of Special Collections, Lexington, 40506. William Marshall, Head
Holdings: Uncat
Notes: About 500 French Revolution pamphlets. Author checklist.

ME —BOWDOIN COLLEGE, Library, Brunswick, 04011. Dianne M Gutscher, Cur of Special Collections
Holdings: Vols
Notes: A collection of several hundred pamphlets of the French Revolution.

MA —UNIVERSITY OF MASSACHUSETTS AT AMHERST, Library, Amherst, 01003. Siegfried Feller, Assoc Dir for Collection Development
Holdings: Cat
Notes: Collection Binet. Mostly contemporary works, 1524 periodicals, and pamphlets, including a 99 vol contemporary nonce collection with quite strong Dauphine representation and pamphlets on important prerevolutionary events, viz, the Diamond Necklace affair, the Kornmann affair, etc. Some cataloged, some calendared and indexed.

MA —HARVARD UNIVERSITY LIBRARY, Widener Library, Cambridge, 02138. Assunta S Pisani, Specialist in Book Selection
Holdings: Cat Mss Maps Microforms
Notes: Strong points incl local history, medieval history, and the Revolutionary period; there are special collections on the Dreyfus case and on Joan of Arc.

NJ —PRINCETON UNIVERSITY, Library, Manuscript Collection, Nassau St, Princeton, 08540. Jean F Preston, Cur
Holdings: Vols 24 Cat Mss Maps
Notes: About 100 of the French cartographer Louis Alexandre Berthier's maps and associated papers involving French campaigns in the Revolutionary War form the manuscript section of the collection. See *Princeton University Library Chronicle,* v 1, no 1, p 3-8. An unpublished guide (25p) of the manuscripts and map section of the collection is available for consultation. See *The American Campaigns of Rochambeau's Army,* ed by Howard C Rice Jr and Anne S K Brown (Princeton, 1972).

NY —FORDHAM UNIVERSITY LIBRARY, Bronx, 10458. Joseph A LoSchiavo, Reference Librn
Holdings: Vols 5200 Cat
Notes: Joseph Givernaud Collection.

NY —CORNELL UNIVERSITY LIBRARIES, John M Olin Library, Dept of Rare Books, Ithaca, 14853. Donald D Eddy, Librn
Holdings: Vols 2845 Cat Mss
Notes: The 2,845 vols contain 12,071 titles. Described in: Cornell University Library, President White Library. *Catalogue of the Historical Library of Andrew Dickson* White, vols 1-2, 4. Ithaca, NY: University Press, 1889-1897. Vol 2, *The French* Revolution.

NY —NEW YORK PUBLIC LIBRARY, Research Libraries, General Research Division, Fifth Ave & 42 St, New York, 10018. Rodney Phillips, Chief
Holdings: Vols (2,225,000) Cat Maps Pix Microforms
Budget: ($775,718)
Notes: Especially strong and extensive collection of revolutionary pamphlets.

NY —UNIVERSITY OF ROCHESTER, Rush Rhees Library, Department of Rare Books and Special Collections, Rochester, 14627. Peter Dzwonkoski, Librn
Holdings: Vols 300 // Cat
Notes: Pamphlets relating to the Estates-General of 1789. No photocopying.

NC —UNIVERSITY OF NORTH CAROLINA, CHAPEL HILL, Wilson Library, Rare Book Collection, Chapel Hill, 27514. Paul S Koda, Cur of Rare Books
Holdings: Vols 6000 Cat Mss Pix
Notes: The William Henry Hoyt Collection of French History contains over 6000 volumes primarily concerned with the French Revolution and the Napoleonic era. There is also personal correspondence of Napoleon, as well as 27 boxes of pamphlets, 1650-1779.

NC —DUKE UNIVERSITY, William R Perkins Library, Rare Book Room, Durham, 27706. John L Sharpe, III, Cur
Notes: French Revolution pamphlets collection of 800 items.

OH —OHIO UNIVERSITY, Vernon R Alden Library, Department of Archives and Special Collections, Athens, 45701. Gary A Hunt, Head
Holdings: Vols 190 Uncat
Notes: A small collection of books and pamphlets relating to the French Revolution, from the library of Dr Beatrice Hyslop; mostly French imprints of the Revolutionary period.

PA —UNIVERSITY OF PENNSYLVANIA, Van Pelt Library, Rare Books Collection, 34 & Walnut Sts, Philadelphia, 19104. Daniel Traister, Special Collections Librn
Holdings: Cat
Notes: Incl the William S Maclure Collection of 1460 vols containing some 25, 000 pamphlets and other printed items relating to the French Revolution (deposited in 1821 with the Academy of Natural Sciences, and later held, until 1949, at the Historical Society of Pennsylvania, 1966). Described and cataloged in *The Maclure Collection of French Revolutionary Material,* ed by James D Hardy et al (Phila: University of Pennsylvania, 1966). With considerable pre-revolutionary materials.

ON —UNIVERSITY OF TORONTO, Thomas Fisher Rare Book Library, 120 Saint George St, Toronto, M5S 1A5, Can. Richard G Landon, Head
Holdings: Vols 900 Cat
Notes: Pamphlets published between 1788 and 1801 pertaining to the Revolution.

FRANCE—HISTORY—FEBRUARY REVOLUTION, 1848

IL —CENTER FOR RESEARCH LIBRARIES, 6050 S Kenwood Ave, Chicago, 60637. Donald B Simpson, Dir; Esther Smith, Collection Development Librn
Holdings: // Cat
Notes: 134 newspaper titles, 45 periodicals, 71 pamphlets and broadsides.

FRANCE—HISTORY—FEBRUARY REVOLUTION, 1848 (cont.)

IA —UNIVERSITY OF IOWA, University Libraries, Iowa City, 52242. Frank Paluka, Head, Special Collections Dept
Holdings: / / Uncat
Notes: Collection of 842 Medals, described in Alan B Spitzer, "The Mabbott Collection of Medals of the French Revolution of 1848", *Books at Iowa,* no 24 (April 1976), pp 32-33, 38-39.

FRANCE—HISTORY—CRIMEAN WAR, 1853-1856 see Crimean War, 1853-1856

FRANCE—HISTORY—THIRD REPUBLIC, 1870-1940

CA —HOOVER INSTITUTION ON WAR, REVOLUTION & PEACE, Stanford University, Stanford, 94305. Milorad M Drachkovitch, Archivist
Holdings: Mss
Notes: Papers of Gaston Bergery, French attorney, diplomat, author, journalist, politician, with service as Secretary-General for the Inter-Allied Commission for Reparations, 1918-1924, Director of the Cabinet of the Ministry of Foreign Affairs, 1924-25, and French Ambassador to Moscow, 1941, incl correspondence, telegrams, reports, memoranda, lists, speeches and writings, posters, leaflets, and other material, 1924-1973, relating to his government service in France and abroad, his literary and legal carrers, French during World War II, and his activities in the Front Populaire. Primarily in French. 28 ms boxes.

IL —NORTHWESTERN UNIVERSITY, Library, Special Collections Dept, 1937 Sheridan Rd, Evanston, 60201. R Russell Maylone, Cur
Holdings: Cat Mss Pix
Notes: Large collection of material from the Siege of Paris, 1870, and the Paris Commune, 1871, incl posters, caricatures and drawings, books, pamphlets, newspapers, journals, letters, and photographs. Literature: Pardo and Press, "Siege and Paris Commune", Special Collections Department, Northwestern University Library. 1973.

WI —UNIVERSITY OF WISCONSIN, MADISON, Memorial Library, 728 State St, Madison, 53706. Erwin K Welsch, Social Studies Bibliographer
Holdings: Vols 25,000 Microforms
Notes: French Socialism Collection, 1871-1914. Collection of pamphlets, periodicals, and monographs on French socialism and the working-class movement. Incl the reports of 81 socialist congresses held from 1876 to 1914 (original, manuscript or microfilm), manuscripts and other materials form the First International, and a very large collection (in microform) of periodicals, together with a substantial number of volumes in the original. Described in Jack A Clarke, "French Social Congresses," *Journal of Modern History,* 31 (June, 1959), pp 124-129; Robert Brecy, *Le Mouvement syndical en France 1871-1921* (Paris, 1963) can also be used as a guide since 90 per cent of the items cited are in the collection.

FRANCE—HISTORY—FOURTH REPUBLIC, 1946-1958

CA —HOOVER INSTITUTION ON WAR, REVOLUTION & PEACE, Stanford University, Stanford, 94305. Milorad M Drachkovitch, Archivist
Holdings: Mss
Notes: Papers of Gaston Bergery, French attorney, diplomat, author, journalist, politician, with service as Secretary-General for the Inter-Allied Commission for Reparations, 1918-1924, Director of the Cabinet of the Ministry of Foreign Affairs, 1924-25, and French Ambassador to Moscow, 1941, incl correspondence, telegrams, reports, memoranda, lists, speeches and writings, posters, leaflets, and other material, 1924-1973, relating to his government service in France and abroad, his literary and legal careers, France during World War II, and his activities in the Front Populaire. Primarily in French. 28 ms boxes.

FRANCE—HISTORY—FIFTH REPUBLIC, 1958-

CA —HOOVER INSTITUTION ON WAR, REVOLUTION & PEACE, Stanford University, Stanford, 94305. Milorad M Drachkovitch, Archivist
Holdings: Vols 3500 Cat Mss Microforms
Notes: History of the Fifth Republic of France. Noteworthy among ephemera is a collection of official French election propaganda for the general elections of 1958-1978. Bibliography: *The French Fifth Republic, Establishment and Consolidation (1958-1965): An Annotated Bibliography of the Holdings at the Hoover Institution* and the sequel *The French Fifth Republic, Continuity and Change (1966-1970),* Grete Heinz and Agnes F Peterson (Stanford, 1970, 1974).

FRANCE—HISTORY—STUDENT REVOLTS, 1968

CA —UNIVERSITY OF CALIFORNIA, LOS ANGELES, Research Library, Dept of Special Collections, 405 Hilgard Ave, Los Angeles, 90024. Edward Shreeves, Chairman, Bibliographers Group; David S Zeidberg, Head
Notes: 7 linear feet of correspondence, ephemera, and broadsides produced by US and European protest movements.

CA —HOOVER INSTITUTION ON WAR, REVOLUTION & PEACE, Stanford University, Stanford, 94305. Milorad M Drachkovitch, Archivist
Notes: The New Left Politics Collection consists of monographs and serials on the New Left that are cataloged. In addition, the collection subscribes to numerous underground newspapers and has obtained special subject collections such as the Free Speech Movement at Berkeley 1964-1965, SNCC and Mississippi Summer 1964, and the insurrection at San Francisco State College in 1968-1969. There is also a good collection on the French student revolts of 1968. The collection is a supervised one and not open to browsers. Interested students and scholars are welcome. Only limited photocopying is permitted.

WI —UNIVERSITY OF WISCONSIN, MADISON, Memorial Library, Rare Books Collection, 728 State St, Madison, 53706. Gretchen Lagana, Cur
Holdings: Uncat Pix Microforms
Notes: A collection of pamphlets, posters, and miscellaneous materials produced by students and other left-wing groups in France during the revolt of May-June 1968. Also included are books on the event and pictures taken by a UW student in Paris at the time. Collection partly described in *UW Library News,* vol 13 (Dec 1968), pp 1-8. Housed in the Dept of Rare Books and Special Collections.

FRANCE—INDUSTRY AND TRADE

IL —NEWBERRY LIBRARY, 60 W Walton St, Chicago, 60610. Diana Haskell, Cur of Modern Mss
Notes: John M Wing History of Printing collection. Incl some 1100 French edicts, 17th-19th century, regulating the printing and publishing industries.

WI —UNIVERSITY OF WISCONSIN, MADISON, Memorial Library, 728 State St, Madison, 53706. Erwin K Welsch, Social Studies Bibliographer
Holdings: Vols 2500 Cat Microforms
Notes: Espec strong in the publications of French trade unions and syndicalist groups for the period 1870-1940. Incl microfilms of some syndicalist and trade union periodicals rarely held in the US, eg *Le Batiment* (1907-1921), *Bulletin federale des dessinateurs de* France (1906-1912), *La Bataille Syndicaliste* (1911-1915), as well as numerous others in their original format; also memoirs of trade union leaders and secondary supporting sources.

FRANCE—POLITICS AND GOVERNMENT

CA —UNIVERSITY OF CALIFORNIA, LOS ANGELES, Research Library, Dept of Special Collections, 405 Hilgard Ave, Los Angeles, 90024. Edward Shreeves, Chairman, Bibliographers Group; David S Zeidberg, Head
Notes: Various collections, incl French Political Broadsides, Mazarinades, and the Roger Menevee Collection.

MA —BRANDEIS UNIVERSITY, Goldfarb Library, 415 South St, Waltham, 02154. Bessie Hahn, Dir
Holdings: Vols Pix
Notes: Consistoire Israelite Archives. Contains 12 linear ft of original documents relating to the French-Jewish community from the 18th to 20th century. A finding list of the documents is in Special Collections. Also, the Alfred Dreyfus Trial Collection: approx 1000 books, pamphlets, newspapers and photographs as well as some correspondence of French notables dealing with the Alfred Dreyfus trial at the turn of the century. An author-title card catalog can be found in the Special Collections Card Catalog.

NC —DUKE UNIVERSITY, William R Perkins Library, Durham, 27706. Elvin E Strowd, University Librn

WI —UNIVERSITY OF WISCONSIN, MADISON, Memorial Library, 728 State St, Madison, 53706. Erwin K Welsch, Social Studies Bibliographer
Notes: French political pamphlets from 1547 to 1648.

FRANCE—POLITICS AND GOVERNMENT—CARICATURES AND CARTOONS

DC —LIBRARY OF CONGRESS, Prints & Photographs Div, Washington, 20540.
Notes: French Political Cartoon Collection pertains chiefly to the French Revolution and the reign of Napoleon Bonaparte.

FRANCE—RELIGION

MA —BRANDEIS UNIVERSITY, Goldfarb Library, 415 South St, Waltham, 02154. Bessie Hahn, Dir
Notes: Consistoire Israelite Archives. Contains 12 linear ft of original documents relating to the French-Jewish community from the 18th to 20th century. A finding list of the documents is in Special Collections. Also, the Alfred Dreyfus Trial Collection: approx 1000 books, pamphlets, newspapers and photographs as well as some correspondence of French notables dealing with the Alfred Dreyfus trial at the turn of the century. An author-title card catalog can be found in the Special Collections Card Catalog.

FRANCE—SOCIAL LIFE AND CUSTOMS

NC —DUKE UNIVERSITY, William R Perkins Library, Rare Book Room, Durham, 27706. John L Sharpe, III, Cur
Notes: French pamphlet collection relating to the political, economic, and social life of France from the early 18th century down to 1830.

FRANCE, ANATOLO

†NY —COLUMBIA UNIVERSITY LIBRARIES, Butler Library, Rare Book and Manuscript Library, 535 W 114 St, New York, 10027.
Notes: Papers of Prof Jean-Albert Bede, with much emphasis on Francois Chateaubriand and Anatolo France.

FRANCESCHI, FRANCESCO

CA —UNIVERSITY OF CALIFORNIA, BERKELEY, Bancroft Library, Manuscripts

FRANCESCHI, FRANCESCO (cont.)

Division, Berkeley, 94720. James D Hart, Dir
Holdings: Cat Mss Maps Pix Microforms
Notes: Papers, correspondence, etc.

FRANCHISE see Elections; Suffrage

FRANCIS, ROBERT, 1901-

MA —JONES LIBRARY, 43 Amity St, Amherst, 01002. Daniel J Lombardo, Cur of Special Collections
Holdings: Vols 50 Cat Mss Pix Phonorecords Audiotapes
Notes: Unpublished guide available.

MA —UNIVERSITY OF MASSACHUSETTS AT AMHERST, Library, Amherst, 01003. Siegfried Feller, Assoc Dir for Collection Development
Holdings: Cat
Notes: Books, pamphlets, broadsides, and appearances in anthologies, school and college texts, etc, and some magazine appearances. Also works with presentation inscriptions to Francis from other authors. More than 300 items.

MA —UNIVERSITY OF MASSACHUSETTS AT AMHERST, Library, Archives and Manuscripts, Amherst, 01003. Siegfried Feller, Assoc Dir for Collection Development
Holdings: Mss Cat
Notes: The poet's correspondence, drafts, galleys, carbons of newspaper and journal articles, photocopied newspaper and journal appearances, sound recordings, photographs, student papers about, memorabilia.

FRANCIS W. PARKER SCHOOL

IL —CHICAGO HISTORICAL SOCIETY, Library, Clark St at North Ave, Chicago, 60614. Archie Motley, Manuscript Librn
Notes: Papers.
See also entry under Education-Illinois.

FRANCISCANS

MA —SAINT HYACINTH COLLEGE & SEMINARY, Kolbe Memorial Library, 66 School St, Granby, 01033. Brother Christian Katusz, OFM Conv, Librn
Notes: Franciscans and St Francis. Partially cataloged.

MI —DUNS SCOTUS, Library, 2000 W Nine Mile, Southfield, 48075. Brother Gabriel Balassone, OFM, Dir
Holdings: Vols 3200 Cat
Notes: Materials by and about Franciscans. Incl 900 bound periodical vols, uncataloged.

NY —SAINT BONAVENTURE UNIVERSITY, Friedsam Memorial Library, Saint Bonaventure, 14778. John Capozzi, OFM, Art Cur
Holdings: Vols 4000 Cat Mss
Notes: Incl union catalog of Franciscana in US and union bibliography of Franciscana.

†OH —UNIVERSITY OF DAYTON LIBRARY, Dayton, 45469.
Notes: Major part of the library of the former St Leonard's Franciscan Seminary in Centerville, Ohio. Incl some 1600 rare books, 2500 reference books, 5500 journal volumes, and about 33,000 books of theology and philosophy.

OH —WILLIAM FABER FRANCISCANA LIBRARY, 10290 Mill Rd, Dayton, 45231. Betty A O'Brien, Librn
Holdings: Vols (7000) Cat
Notes: Provincial library of the Province of St John Baptist, Order of Friars Minor contains material about St Francis and the Franciscans. This represents the special Franciscana collection formerly housed in the now defunct Saint Leonard College Library.

FRANCK, CHARLES

LA —NEW ORLEANS PUBLIC LIBRARY, Louisiana Div, 219 Loyola Ave, New Orleans, 70140. Collin B Hamer Jr, Head; Brenda M Osbey, Library Associate
Holdings: Cat Maps Pix
Notes: Louisiana and New Orleans Picture File Collection ranges from the late 19th century-date and incl the following separate collections: Alexander Allison (ca 1898-1951, 337 pieces); Charles Franck (ca 1920-50, 170 pieces); Leda Plauche (ca 1935-53, 220 pieces); C Milo Williams (ca 1910, 85 pieces); Wilson S Howell (ca 1890, 49 pieces); Grauman Marks (ca 1960, 268 pieces); Robert Tallant (ca 1940-50, 70 pieces); Robert E Tracy (1959, 87 pieces); Anthony J Flaherty (ca 1970-84, 83 pieces); George F Mugnier (1880-1920, 186 pieces); Color Slides (ca 1945-date, 500 pieces); 30, 000 photographs incl 500 color slides and 104 negatives. Use of the material is restricted to on-site research. Publication must be accompanied by credit cut line.

FRANCK, JAMES

IL —UNIVERSITY OF CHICAGO LIBRARY, Dept of Special Collections, 1100 E 57 St, Chicago, 60637.
Notes: Papers.

FRANCO, FRANCISCO

CA —UNIVERSITY OF CALIFORNIA, DAVIS, Shields Library, Dept of Special Collections, Davis, 95616. Donald Kunitz, Head; C Danial Elliott, Asst Head
Notes: Pamphlets (over 800), both pro- and anti-Franco cover the immediate causes of the Spanish Civil War, its duration and aftermath. Most are in Spanish. Also 15 posters (reproductions) from the war.

FRANCO-AMERICAN STUDIES

NH —ASSOCIATION CANADO-AMERICAIN (FRATERNAL LIFE INSURANCE SOCIETY), Institute Canado-Americain, 52 Concord St, Manchester, 03101. Robert A Beaudoin, Librn
Holdings: Vols (40,000) Cat Mss Maps Pix Slides
Budget: ($2000)
Notes: Contains books, pamphlets, mss, university dissertations, newspapers, manuscripts, periodicals, and archives of various other societies (active of defunct). Subjects covered incl art, music, literature, folklore, religion, politics, sociology, history, etc of the French in France, Canada, and US (especially New England's Franco-Americans, Louisiana's Cajuns, and Quebec's French-Canadians). There is also an extensive collection of genealogical works dealing with Quebec Acadia, and New England Francophones. Articles dealing with the library are: "The Library of the Association Canado-Americaine" by Edward B Ham in *Modern Language Notes*, vol LII, no 7, November 1937 and a bilingual article "Appel d'un jeune aux jeunes en faveur de al Bibliotheque ACA" by Robert B Perreault in *Le Canado-Americain*, nouvelle serie, vol 1, no 5, julliet-aout-septembre 1975, pp 18-19.

FRANCO-ENGLISH WAR, 1775-1763 see U.s.—History_French and Indian War, 1755-1763

FRANK, GLENN

MO —NORTHEAST MISSOURI STATE UNIVERSITY, Pickler Memorial Library, Kirksville, 63501. George N Hartje, Librn
Holdings: // Mss Pix
Notes: The Glenn Frank Colleciton, incl his papers of period of his Presidency at the University of Wisconsin. The mss (60 cubic feet) are the strength of the collection.

FRANK, LEO, 1884-1915

MA —BRANDEIS UNIVERSITY, Goldfarb Library, 415 South St, Waltham, 02154. Bessie Hahn, Dir
Notes: Leo Frank Trial Collection. Approx 60 letters, between Leo Frank and his wife and some 250 other letters from individuals interested in the case. Various scarce pamphlets and trial proceedings are also included. A finding list is available in Special Collections. Restricted use.

FRANK, LOUIS, 1901-

NC —DUKE UNIVERSITY, William R Perkins Library, Jay B Hubbell Center for American Literary Historiography, Durham, 27706. Erma Whittington, Librn
Notes: 77,312 items, including manuscripts, pictures, clippings, and correspondence. "The objective of the Center is to gather the papers and materials of significant scholars and critics in American literary history." The Center is a part of the Perkins Library Manuscripts Department.

FRANK, WALDO

DE —UNIVERSITY OF DELAWARE, Hugh M Morris Library, S College Ave, Newark, 19711. T Stuart Dick, Special Collections
Holdings: Cat Mss Pix
Notes: Manuscripts, etc, incl literary correspondence.

PA —UNIVERSITY OF PENNSYLVANIA, Van Pelt Library, Rare Books Collection, 34 & Walnut Sts, Philadelphia, 19104. Daniel Traister, Special Collections Librn
Holdings: Vols 30 Cat Mss Pix
Notes: Collection incl 100 boxes of mss and correspondence. Descriptive case file available in library.

FRANKFURTER, JUSTICE FELIX, 1882-1965

DC —LIBRARY OF CONGRESS, Manuscript Division, Washington, 20540. John C Broderick, Chief
Notes: His papers, incl a good many family letters. Over 70,000 items.

MA —HARVARD UNIVERSITY LIBRARY, Law School Library, Langdell Hall, Cambridge, 02138. Erika S Chadbourn, Cur of Mss
Holdings: Cat Mss
Notes: Judicial and personal papers. Printed inventory: *Felix Frankfurter: An Inventory of His Papers in the Harvard Law School* Library, Manuscript Division, Harvard Law School Library, 1982. Inclusive dates, 1914-1965.

FRANKLIN, BENJAMIN

CT —YALE UNIVERSITY, Box 1603A, Yale Station, New Haven, 06520.
Holdings: Cat Mss Pix
Notes: Center for publication of *The Pages of Benjamin Franklin.*

DC —LIBRARY OF CONGRESS, Rare Book & Special Collections Div, Washington, 20540. William Matheson, Chief
Holdings: Vols 850 Cat
Notes: The Benjamin Franklin Collection embraces books, pamphlets and serials written, printed and edited by Benjamin Franklin and by firms in which he has a financial interest. Also books about Franklin. Of works edited by Franklin, the outstanding item is the copy of the *Abridgement of the Book of Common Prayer* (London: 1773) with ms notes by the Baroness Le Despencer, whose nephew financed the publication. Incl one of the four known copies of *A Vindication of the New-North-Church in Boston,* printed by James Franklin when Franklin was apprenticed in his brother's shop. The collection is especially rich in early editions and translations of the *Autobiography.* The bulk of the collection was acquired *en bloc* from Henry Stevens in 1882.

DC —LIBRARY OF CONGRESS, Manuscript Division, Washington, 20540. John C Broderick, Chief
Holdings: Cat Mss Pix
Notes: Mss, papers, records, etc.

FL —ROLLINS COLLEGE, Mills Memorial Library, Winter Park, 32789. Patricia J Delks, Dir of Libraries
Holdings: Vols 96 Cat Pix
Notes: Incl memorabilia. Noncirculating.

MA —BOSTON PUBLIC LIBRARY, Print Collection, Dartmouth St at Copley Sq, Boston, 02117. Sinclair H Hitchings, Keeper

FRANKLIN, BENJAMIN (cont.)

of Prints
Holdings: Cat
Notes: The Americana collection is especially strong in the 19th century. Incl 250 prints of American views, tradesmen's calling cards, illustrated diplomas and advertisements. Also in it is the McGreevey Baseball Collection of 225 photos, photoreproductions and paintings from the period 1870 to 1914. The American portrait collection contains 300 engravings, etchings and lithographs of prominent figures of the 18th and 19th century. In addition there are 200 portraits of Benjamin Franklin. Items cataloged by subject. Prints also by artist/publisher.

MA —NEEDHAM FREE PUBLIC LIBRARY, 1139 Highland Ave, Needham Heights, 02194. Vivian D McIver, Dir
Holdings: Vols 130 Cat Pix

MI —UNIVERSITY OF MICHIGAN, William L Clements Library, Ann Arbor, 48109. John C Dann, Dir

Notes: The William L. Clements Library of Americana is a non-circulating rare book library of original source material, printed and manuscript, dealing with America, from the discovery period into the late nineteenth century. The collection includes approximately 55,000 books and pamphlets, 550 linear feet of manuscripts, 4,100 volumes of newspapers, 36,000 maps, 40,000 pieces of sheet music, and 1,000 prints. The collection is strongest for the period of the American Revolution, and includes the papers of Thomas Gage, Sir Henry Clinton, and the Earl of Shelburne. Other areas of strength include antislavery, cartography and geography, discovery and exploration, American Indians, The Civil War, tune-books, sermons and orations, and the War of 1812. There are selective research collections dealing with Christopher Columbus, Thomas Paine, Benjamin Franklin, George Washington, Thomas Jefferson, and the Federalist Papers. Publications describing the collections of the library are: Author/Title catalog of Americana 1493-1860 in the William L. Clements Library... 7 volumes, Boston, G. K. Hall, 1970; Guide to the manuscript collections of the William L. Clements Library, by Arlene P. Shy 3d edition, Boston, G. K. Hall, 1978; Guide to the manuscript maps in the William L. Clements Library, compiled by Christian Burn, Ann Arbor, U. of Michigan, 1959; and Research catalog of maps of America, to 1860 in the William L. Clements Library...,edited by Douglas W. Marshall, 4 volumes, Boston, G. K. Hall, 1972.

MI —NORTHERN MICHIGAN UNIVERSITY, Lydia M Olson Library, Elizabeth L Harden Drive, Marquette, 49855. Stephen H Peters, Cataloger
Notes: A major section of the personal library of Moses Coit Tyler. Strong in the Colonial and Early National periods. Includes biographies and published letters and writings of such figures as Benjamin Franklin, John Adams, John Jay, Thomas Jefferson, Charles Sumner.

NJ —RUTGERS, THE STATE UNIVERSITY OF NEW JERSEY, Alexander Library, Special Collections and Archives, College Ave & Huntington St, New Brunswick, 08903. Ronald L Becker, Cur of Manuscripts and Rare Books
Holdings: Pix
Notes: The pictorial collection of Special Collections, dating from the 18th century to the present, incl foreign, US, and New Jersey material: portraits, local views, historical scenes. Special groups: George Washington and Benjamin Franklin engraved portraits; photos of New Jersey localities (among these about 10,000 postal cards).

NY —NEW YORK HISTORICAL SOCIETY, Library, 170 Central Park W, New York, 10024. James Gregory, Librn
Notes: Miscellaneous papers, correspondence, etc.

PA —HARRY C TREXLER MASONIC LIBRARY, Masonic Temple, Allentown, 18102.
Holdings: Vols (5000) Mss Pix

PA —AMERICAN PHILOSOPHICAL SOCIETY, Library, 105 S Fifth St, Philadelphia, 19106. Edward C Carter II, Librn
Holdings: Vols 4000 Cat Mss Pix

PA —FRANKLIN INSTITUTE LIBRARY, 20 & The Parkway, Philadelphia, 19103. Miriam Padusis, Dir; Charles Wilt, Readers Servs Librn
Holdings: Cat
Notes: Incl over 60 Franklin imprints.

PA —HISTORICAL SOCIETY OF PENNSYLVANIA, Library, 1300 Locust St, Philadelphia, 19107. David Fraser, Librn
Holdings: Vols (230,000) Mxx Maps Pix Microforms
Notes: Incl over 14,000,000 ms pieces. The Library Company of Philadelphia mss are on deposit with the Historical Society of Pennsylvania. Many of the Society's rare books are on deposit with the Library Company. The Society maintains the collections of the Genealogical Society of Pennsylvania, incl some 20,000 printed genealogies, original mss, family, church, and civil records.

PA —UNIVERSITY OF PENNSYLVANIA, Van Pelt Library, Rare Books Collection, 34 & Walnut Sts, Philadelphia, 19104. Daniel Traister, Special Collections Librn
Holdings: Vols 250 Cat Mss
Notes: Incl Franklin Imprints and 12 boxes of correspondence. See Downs 3978 (Supplement) 2127.

FRANKLIN, BENJAMIN—IMPRINTS

CT —YALE UNIVERSITY, Box 1603A, Yale Station, New Haven, 06520.
Holdings: Cat Mss

DC —LIBRARY OF CONGRESS, Rare Book & Special Collections Div, Washington, 20540. William Matheson, Chief
Holdings: Cat
See also entry under Franklin, Benjamin

NJ —GLASSBORO STATE COLLEGE, Savitz Library, Stewart Room, Glassboro, 08028. Clara Kirner, Special Collection Librn
Holdings: Vols 15 Cat Mss

PA —AMERICAN PHILOSOPHICAL SOCIETY, Library, 105 S Fifth St, Philadelphia, 19106. Edward C Carter II, Librn
Holdings: Cat Mss Maps Pix Microforms

PA —FRANKLIN INSTITUTE LIBRARY, 20 & The Parkway, Philadelphia, 19103. Miriam Padusis, Dir; Charles Wilt, Readers Servs Librn
Holdings: Cat
Notes: Incl over 60 Franklin imprints.

PA —UNIVERSITY OF PENNSYLVANIA, Van Pelt Library, Rare Books Collection, 34 & Walnut Sts, Philadelphia, 19104. Daniel Traister, Special Collections Librn
Holdings: Vols 300 Cat
Notes: The Curtis Collection of Franklin imprints.

PA —PENNSYLVANIA STATE UNIVERSITY, Fred Lewis Pattee Library, Special Collections Dept, University Park, 16802. Charles Mann, Chief, Special Collections
Holdings: Vols 13 Cat
Budget: ($37,000)

FRANKLIN BOOK PROGRAMS, INC.

DC —LIBRARY OF CONGRESS, Rare Book & Special Collections Div, Washington, 20540. William Matheson, Chief
Notes: An archival set of translations sponsored by the Franklin Book Programs (1952-1978), incl 3000 titles translated into Arabic, Persian, Bengali and other languages.

FRANZ JOSEPH, EMPEROR

TX —RICE UNIVERSITY, Fondren Library, 6100 S Main St, PO Box 1892, Houston, 77251. Dr Samuel M Carrington, Jr, University Librn
Holdings: Vols 21,500 // Cat Maps Pix
Notes: The Austro-Hungarian Empire of Franz Josef. Historical and literary materials. Incl newspapers. Downs 2706.

FRASER, CHARLES, 1782-1860

SC —COLLEGE OF CHARLESTON LIBRARY, Special Collections Dept, Charleston, 29401.
Notes: Incl Commonplace Book, study book of law cases in South Carolina adjudicated 1736-1819, compiled mostly 1800-1807, while studying for admission to the bar, as a forms manual. Contains copies of writs for both civil and criminal actions and decisions from the Court of Chancery, Court of Pleas, and Commissions of the Peace.

FRASER, CLAUD LOVAT

CA —UNIVERSITY OF CALIFORNIA, LOS ANGELES, Research Library, Dept of Special Collections, 405 Hilgard Ave, Los Angeles, 90024. Edward Shreeves, Chairman, Bibliographers Group; David S Zeidberg, Head
Notes: 13 linear feet of ephemera, commercial catalogs, theater photographs, and art on the history of clothing and dress in the US and Europe, incl original work by Paul Rotha, Edward Gordon Craig, and Claud Lovat Fraser.

PA —BRYN MAWR COLLEGE, Canaday Library, Bryn Mawr, 19010. James Tanis, Dir
Notes: Sketches, drawings and proofs for much of his printed work, accompanied by hand-colored broadsides and books.

FRASER, DONALD M.

MN —MINNESOTA HISTORICAL SOCIETY LIBRARY, 690 Cedar St, Saint Paul, 55101. Patricia C Harpole, Chief of Reference Library; Bonnie G Wilson, Head of Special Libraries
Notes: Materials by such well-known figures as Hubert H. Humphrey, Eugene J. McCarthy, Orville L Freeman, Maurice H. Stans, Donald M Fraser, Albert H Quie, Clark MacGregor and John A Blatnik. A list of these holdings is on file in the Audio-Visual Library, the tapes are housed in the MHS Research Center, 1500 Mississippi Street, St Paul, Minn.

FRASER, JOHN

ON —METROPOLITAN TORONTO LIBRARY, Theatre Dept, 789 Yonge St, Toronto, M4W 2G8, Can. Heather McCallum, Head
Notes: Papers of John Fraser, Canadian dance critic for *Toronto Telegram*, *Globe and Mail* (1972-1975), and *Globe* (1975-1977).

FRASER, KEVIN

TX —HOUSTON ACADEMY OF MEDICINE-TEXAS MEDICAL CENTER, Library, Jesse H Jones Library Bldg, Houston, 77030. Elizabeth Borst White, Special Collections Librn
Holdings: Vols (1300) Mss Pix
Notes: Burbank Collection on Arthritis, Rheumatism and Gout. An exhaustive collection on arthritis and gout before 1957.

FRASER, KEVIN (cont.)

Largely from the 16th-19th centuries (also a medical manuscript dated about 1450). Bound volumes of German, French and American offprints complement the monograph collection. In 1983 the Kevin Fraser Addition to this Collection included 130 titles published before 1900.

FRASER FAMILY

SC —COLLEGE OF CHARLESTON LIBRARY, Special Collections Dept, Charleston, 29401.
Notes: Papers, 1826-1926, contains genealogical materials tracing the Fraser family's origins in mid-18th century Scotland, the arrival of John Fraser in 1748, in Georgetown, SC, the union with Ford family, and the descendants through 1926. Also the bill of sale for Sea Island cotton, owned by Thomas Banksdale, and sold by John Fraser, June 4, 1821.

FRASHER, BURTON

CA —POMONA PUBLIC LIBRARY, Special Collections, 625 S Garey Ave, PO Box 2271, Pomona, 91766. David Streeter, Librn
Holdings: Cat
Notes: Together, about 100,000 photographs. Burton Frasher collection, 60,000 negatives and prints of California, Arizona, New Mexico, Colorado, Utah, and Nevada, 1920-1940; Loyd Cooper collection, 20,000 negatives and prints of California, 1920-1940; Brooking Tatum, 125 color prints, 50 color 35mm transparencies of California flora; Percy Everett, 4000 color 35mm transparencies of world travels, 1960s.

FRATERNITIES see Secret Societies

FRAUDS, LITERARY see Literary Forgeries and Mystifications

FREAKS see Deformities; Monsters

FREAS, FRANK KELLY

MD —UNIVERSITY OF MARYLAND, BALTIMORE COUNTY, Albin O Kuhn Library and Gallery, 5401 Wilkens Ave, Baltimore, 21228. Ann Copeland, Special Collections Librn
Holdings: Vols (4500) Cat Mss Pix Phonorecords
Notes: The Azriel Rosenfeld Science Fiction Research Collection of about 20,000 items, incl an unusual science fiction art collection which centers around the work of illustrator Frank Kelly Freas. Unique items incl Freas' designs for NASA's Skylab I patch.

FRECHETTE, ACHILLE

NY —ALFRED UNIVERSITY, Herrick Memorial Library, Alfred, 14802. June E Brown, Head Librn
Notes: The Howells/Frechette Collection. Family documents, 7000 letters of William Cooper Howells (American consul to Quebec, later to Toronto), William Dean Howells, his sister Annie Frechette, Achille Frechette (official translator, Canadian House of Commons), and Louis Frechette (poet laureate of Canada).

FRECHETTE, ANNIE HOWELLS

NY —ALFRED UNIVERSITY, Herrick Memorial Library, Alfred, 14802. June E Brown, Head Librn
Notes: The Howells/Frechette Collection. Family documents, 7000 letters of William Cooper Howells (American consul to Quebec, later to Toronto), William Dean Howells, his sister Annie Frechette, Achille Frechette (official translator, Canadian House of Commons), and Louis Frechette (poet laureate of Canada).

FRECHETTE, LOUIS

NY —ALFRED UNIVERSITY, Herrick Memorial Library, Alfred, 14802. June E Brown, Head Librn
Notes: The Howells/Frechette Collection. Family documents, 7000 letters of William Cooper Howells (American consul to Quebec, later to Toronto), William Dean Howells, his sister Annie Frechette, Achille Frechette (official translator, Canadian House of Commons), and Louis Frechette (poet laureate of Canada).

FREDERIC, HAROLD

†NY —COLUMBIA UNIVERSITY LIBRARIES, Butler Library, Rare Book and Manuscript Library, 535 W 114 St, New York, 10027.

FREE CHURCHES see Dissenters, Religious

FREE FALL—PHYSIOLOGICAL EFFECT see Weightlessness

FREE METHODIST CHURCH

IN —FREE METHODIST CHURCH OF NORTH AMERICA, Marston Memorial Historical Center Library, 901 College Ave, Winona Lake, 46590. Evelyn L Mottweiler, Librn
Holdings: Vols (6000) Cat Mss Documents Mirofilms Pix Records Audiotapes Videotapes Films Slides Charts VF
Budget: ($16,000)
Notes: Denominational headquarters of the Free Methodist Church in North America. Official histories of the denomination, annual conferences (districts), foreign and home missions, schools and colleges; complete sets of denominational Yearbooks, Disciplines, and periodicals. Biographies and writings of prominent leaders. Methodist and Free Methodist of the Library are included in the Methodist Union Catalog: *Pre-1976* Imprints, ed by Kenneth E Rowe.

FREE SPEECH

CA —UNIVERSITY OF CALIFORNIA, LOS ANGELES, Research Library, Social Sciences Collection, 405 Hilgard Ave, Los Angeles, 90024. Edward Shreeves, Chairman, Bibliographers Group; Oscar L Sims, Social Sciences Bibliographer
Notes: A collection of over 200 underground newspapers on 26 reels of microfilm. Among the titles included are: *The Tribe, The Berkeley Barb, New York Roach, Rat,* and *Win.*

CA —HOOVER INSTITUTION ON WAR, REVOLUTION & PEACE, Stanford University, Stanford, 94305. Milorad M Drachkovitch, Archivist
Holdings: Mss Pix
Notes: Papers of Julius Epstein, journalist, research associate at the Hoover Institution, and author of *Operation Keelhaul: The Story of Forced Repatriation*, incl correspondence, speeches and writings, clippings, photographs, and printed matter, 1932-72, relating to his research on the events of World War II, Katyn forest massacres, and unreported deaths of Soviet Cosmonauts, as well as his efforts to obtain restricted government documents on these subjects. 180 ms boxes.

DC —LIBRARY OF CONGRESS, European Division, Washington, 20540.
Notes: The Library of Congress collection of "Solidarity" and other uncensored Polish materials incl books, periodicals, documents, bulletins, cartoons, and posters, most of which are photocopies of originals held by other libraries.

IL —SOUTHERN ILLINOIS UNIVERSITY, CARBONDALE, Delyte W Morris Library, Special Collections Dept, Carbondale, 62901. David V Koch, Cur of Special Collections; Louisa Bowen, Cur of Manuscripts
Holdings: Vols 430 Cat Mss Pix
Notes: Personal papers (78 linear feet) of Theodore Schroeder, 1873-1957, founder of the Free Speech League, incl archives of the League. Thousands of letters, mss, and notes, with letters from Anthony Comstock, Samuel Gompers, Eugene V Debs, Havelock Ellis, Margaret Sanger, Upton Sinclair, H L Mencken, and Emma Goldman. The archives reflect Schroeder's crusades in the areas of free speech, sex expression, religion, and psychoanalysis. Inventory and name index available at the Library. Described by Ralph E McCoy, *Theodore Schroeder, the Cold Enthusiast,* Carbondale: Southern Illinois University Libraries, 1973. (Bibliographic Contributions, No 8).

IL —NEWBERRY LIBRARY, 60 W Walton St, Chicago, 60610. Diana Haskell, Cur of Modern Mss
Notes: John M Wing History of Printing collection, Incl some 1100 French edicts, 17th-19th century, regulating the printing and publishing industries.

IL —NORTHWESTERN UNIVERSITY, Library, Special Collections Dept, 1937 Sheridan Rd, Evanston, 60201. R Russell Maylone, Cur
Holdings: Vols 180 Uncat
Notes: Periodicals, posters, leaflets, and street sheets documenting the Free Speech Movement, University of California at Berkeley, 1964.

IN —INDIANA UNIVERSITY, Lilly Library, Seventh St, Bloomington, 47405. William R Cagle, Librn
Holdings: Vols (1000) // Cat Mss
Notes: 1000 vols of contemporary printings (largely British) on Anglo-American relations leading to the American Revolution.

NY —COLUMBIA UNIVERSITY LIBRARIES, Law School Library, Law Building, 435 W 116 St, New York, 10027. James L Hoover, Librn
Notes: Collection being strengthened to support the civil liberties program under a new Corliss Lamont Chair.

FREE SPEECH LEAGUE

IL —SOUTHERN ILLINOIS UNIVERSITY, CARBONDALE, Delyte W Morris Library, Carbondale, 62901.
Holdings: Cat Mss
Notes: Papers and correspondence of Theodore A Schroeder, constitutional lawyer and founder, with Lincoln Steffens, of the Free Speech League, a forerunner of the American Civil Liberties Union. Contains extensive correspondence with Comstock, Gompers, Debs, H Ellis, Sanger, Sinclair, John Dewey, Darrow, Mencken, A G Hays, Emma Goldman, W E B Dubois, etc. Incl several thousand letters; notes and mss, records of legal cases and extensive files relating to the early history of psychiatry.

FREE THOUGHT

CA —ATHEIST ASSOCIATION, Atheist Library, 3024 Fifth Ave, PO Box 2832, San Diego, 92112. James Hervey Johnson, Librn
Notes: The Atheist Library and the building at 3024 Fifth Ave were completely destroyed by fire in October of 1981. There is no library at this time.

MA —HARVARD UNIVERSITY LIBRARY, Cambridge, 02138.
Holdings: Cat

MI —UNIVERSITY OF MICHIGAN, Dept of Rare Books & Special Collections, Ann Arbor, 48109. Edward C Weber, Head, Labadie Collection
Holdings: Vols (40,000) Cat Mss Pix Microforms Records
Notes: Mostly 19th-century US pamphlets and serials.

NE —UNIVERSITY OF NEBRASKA-LINCOLN, Don L Love Library, Czech Heritage Collection, Lincoln, 68588. Joseph G Svoboda, University Archivist
Holdings: Vols (3000) Cat Mss Pix Audiotapes Microforms
Notes: The Czech Heritage Collection.

WI —UNIVERSITY OF WISCONSIN, MADISON, Memorial Library, 728 State St, Madison, 53706. Erwin K Welsch, Social Studies Bibliographer
Holdings: Vols 1500 Cat Microforms
Notes: British Atheism and Free Thought. The collection consists largely of pamphlets

FREE THOUGHT (cont.)

published by leading advocates of the Free Thought and Atheist movements in the 19th century, incl George Holyoake, Charles Bradlaugh, Annie Besant, Thomas Scott, Charles Southwell, Charles Robert Newman, and G W Foote. Also incl numerous vols of debates between freethinkers and religious spokesmen and several important periodicals: the only complete copies of Robert Taylor's *The Philalethean by Talasophron* (1833-1834), *The Atheist and Republican* (1841), *The Blasphemer* (1842), and *The Free Inquirer in Science, Politics, and Theology* (1850), as well as others such as *The Secular Chronicle* (1872-1879), *Our Corner* (1883-1888), and *The Reformer* (1897-1898). Finally, there are representative pamphlets of the types intended to reach a "popular" or working class audience which containson occasion, scurrilous illustrations. Many items in the collection were originally owned by Hypatia Bradlaugh Bonner, daughter of a leading 19th century English politician and freethinker.

FREE TRADE AND PROTECTION

CA —HOOVER INSTITUTION ON WAR, REVOLUTION & PEACE, Stanford University, Stanford, 94305. Milorad M Drachkovitch, Archivist
Holdings: Mss
Notes: Papers of Walter Schevenels, Belgian syndicalist and international trade union official, General Secretary of the International Federation of Trade Unions, 1929-1945, and General Secretary for the European Regional Organization of the International Confederation of Free Trade Unions, 1951-1966, incl correspondence, reports, speeches, writings, telegrams, bulletins, interviews, pamphlets, clippings, and printed materials, 1930-1966, relating to syndicalism and free European trade unions, labor and laboring classes in Europe, and international labor problems. 13 ms boxes.

MA —HARVARD UNIVERSITY LIBRARY, Cambridge, 02138.
Holdings: Cat

NE —NEBRASKA STATE HISTORICAL SOCIETY, Archives, 1500 R St, Box 82554, Lincoln, 68501. James E Potter, State Archivist
Holdings: Uncat Mss
Notes: Silver and the money question; also material on the Greenback Party. Printed speeches and tracts relating to the money question, 1890-1895. Many written by prominent political figures of the day. Also, pamphlets which relate to income tax, tariffs, free trade, soldiers' pensions, railroads, election laws and public lands. Collection of John Davis, Congressman from Kansas, 1891-1895.

FREE WILL AND DETERMINISM

MA —HARVARD UNIVERSITY LIBRARY, Cambridge, 02138.
Holdings: Cat

FREEBOOTERS see Pirates and Piracy

FREEBORN, BRIAN

MA —BOSTON UNIVERSITY, Mugar Memorial Library, Special Collections Dept, 771 Commonwealth Ave, Boston, 02215. Howard B Gotlieb, Dir
Holdings: Cat Mss

FREEBORN, MALCOLM JONATHAN, 1907-

NY —CORNELL UNIVERSITY LIBRARIES, Collection of Regional History, Dept of Manuscripts and Univ Archives, Ithaca, 14853.
Notes: Educator, civic and social worker. Papers, 1929-73; 20 ft.

FREED, ARTHUR

CA —UNIVERSITY OF SOUTHERN CALIFORNIA, Edward L Doheny Memorial Library, Archives of Performing Arts, University Park, Los Angeles, 90089. Robert Knutson, Librn
Holdings: Mss Pix
Notes: Personal collection of papers, pictures, etc.

FREED, DONALD

MA —BOSTON UNIVERSITY, Mugar Memorial Library, Special Collections Dept, 771 Commonwealth Ave, Boston, 02215. Howard B Gotlieb, Dir
Holdings: Cat Mss
Notes: Mss, correspondence, etc collected in depth; incl publications by or about.

FREED SLAVES see Freedmen

FREEDMAN, BENEDICT AND NANCY

MA —BOSTON UNIVERSITY, Mugar Memorial Library, Special Collections Dept, 771 Commonwealth Ave, Boston, 02215. Howard B Gotlieb, Dir
Holdings: Cat Mss Pix
Notes: Mss, correspondence, etc collected in depth; incl publications by or about.

FREEDMEN

ME —BOWDOIN COLLEGE, Library, Brunswick, 04011. Dianne M Gutscher, Cur of Special Collections
Holdings: Mss Pix
Notes: The Oliver Otis Howard Papers consist of more than 150,000 pieces of correspondence, articles, lectures, and ephemera for the period 1843-1908, covering his services as a Civil War officer, as founder of the Freedmen's Bureau, as president of Howard University, and as superintendent of the US Military Academy at West Point.

FREEDMEN'S BUREAU

ME —BOWDOIN COLLEGE, Library, Brunswick, 04011. Dianne M Gutscher, Cur of Special Collections
Holdings: Mss Pix
Notes: The Oliver Otis Howard Papers consist of more than 150,000 pieces of correspondence, articles, lectures, and ephemera for the period 1843-1908, covering his services as a Civil War officer, as founder of the Freedmen's Bureau, as president of Howard University, and as superintendent of the US Military Academy at West Point.

FREEDOM, SEXUAL see Sexual Ethics

FREEDOM FIGHT see Fight for Freedom

FREEDOM OF RELIGION see Religious Liberty

FREEDOM OF SPEECH see Free Speech

FREEDOM OF THE PRESS see Liberty of the Press

FREEDOM OF WORSHIP see Religious Liberty

FREEHOLD see Land Tenure

FREEMAN, ARTHUR

MA —BOSTON UNIVERSITY, Mugar Memorial Library, Special Collections Dept, 771 Commonwealth Ave, Boston, 02215. Howard B Gotlieb, Dir
Holdings: Cat Mss

FREEMAN, DAVID

CA —UNIVERSITY OF CALIFORNIA, LOS ANGELES, Research Library, Dept of Special Collections, 405 Hilgard Ave, Los Angeles, 90024. Edward Shreeves, Chairman, Bibliographers Group; David S Zeidberg, Head
Notes: 5 linear feet of radio scripts.

FREEMAN, DOUGLAS SOUTHALL

MD —JOHNS HOPKINS UNIVERSITY, Milton S Eisenhower Library, Charles & 34 Sts, Baltimore, 21218. Ann S Gwyn, Assistant Dir for Special Collections
Holdings: Cat Mss
Notes: 800 letters to and from the author, cataloged in manuscript room.

VA —UNIVERSITY OF VIRGINIA, Alderman Library, Manuscripts Dept, Charlottesville, 22901. Edmund Berkeley Jr, Cur
Holdings: Cat Mss Pix
Notes: Papers, etc.

FREEMAN, JOHN RIPLEY, 1855-1932

MA —MASSACHUSETTS INSTITUTE OF TECHNOLOGY, Institute Archives, Special Collections, Cambridge, 02139.
Notes: Papers of John Ripley Freeman, a hydraulic engineer, President of Associated Factory Mutual Fire Insurance Companies, and a consulting engineer. Collection primarily documents his activities as a consultant on hydraulics projects in the United States, Canada, China, Columbia, Mexico and Panama. Also, his work on the hydraulics of fire prevention, safety precautions for theaters, and seismology; his promotion of the National Hydraulics Laboratory and of European engineering practices; his involvement with the Engineering Foundation, the National Bureau of Standards, and the National Research Council; and his investments in mining, manufacturing, and land speculation. Unpublished finding aid available in Archives.

FREEMAN, LUCY

MA —BOSTON UNIVERSITY, Mugar Memorial Library, Special Collections Dept, 771 Commonwealth Ave, Boston, 02215. Howard B Gotlieb, Dir
Holdings: Cat Mss
Notes: Mss, correspondence, etc collected in depth; incl publications by or about.

FREEMAN, MARY WILKINS

VA —UNIVERSITY OF VIRGINIA, Alderman Library, Clifton Waller Barrett Collection, Charlottesville, 22901. Joan St C Crane, Cur of American Literature Collections
Notes: Papers.

WI —UNIVERSITY OF WISCONSIN, MADISON, Memorial Library, British & American Language & Literature Collection, 728 State St, Madison, 53706. Yvonne Schofer, Bibliographer
Holdings: Vols 2200 Mss Microforms Documents Periodicals
Notes: A collection of primary and secondary materials for nine major American women writers: Anne Bradstreet; Louisa May Alcott, Emily Dickinson, Kate Chopin, Mary Williams Freeman, Margaret Fuller, Sarah Orne Jewett, Charlotte Perkins Gilman, Harriet Beecher Stowe. Primary materials also collected for a list of less well known authors together with manuscripts and archives of letters of special research interest. Variety of holdings: fiction, poetry, drama, biography and autobiography, letters, memoirs, diaries, travel, domestic economy and other kinds of writings by women mostly of the 19th century. Held in Dept of Rare Books and Special Collections.

FREEMAN, ORVILLE L.

MN —MINNESOTA HISTORICAL SOCIETY LIBRARY, 690 Cedar St, Saint Paul, 55101. Patricia C Harpole, Chief of Reference Library; Bonnie G Wilson, Head of Special Libraries
Notes: Materials by such well-known figures as Hubert H. Humphrey, Eugene J. McCarthy, Orville L Freeman, Maurice H. Stans, Donald M Fraser, Albert H Quie, Clark MacGregor and John A Blatnik. A list of these holdings is on file in the Audio-Visual Library, the tapes are housed in the MHS Research Center, 1500 Mississippi Street, St Paul, Minn.

FREEMANTLE, BRIAN

MA —BOSTON UNIVERSITY, Mugar Memorial Library, Special Collections Dept,

FREEMANTLE, BRIAN (cont.)

771 Commonwealth Ave, Boston, 02215. Howard B Gotlieb, Dir
Holdings: Cat Mss Correspondence Drawings

FREEMASONS AND FREEMASONRY

AZ —WORLD UNIVERSITY, Library, 711 E Blackldge Dr, Tucson, 85719. Howard John Zitko, Cur
Holdings: Vols (15,000) Cat Mss Maps Audiotapes
Notes: Collection concerns the "frontier sciences". No interlibrary loan.

CA —SCOTTISH RITE CATHEDRAL, 455 Elm, Long Beach, 90802. Al Ebentier, Librn
Holdings: Vols 30,000 Cat
Notes: Special collection of fraternal groups including Blue Lodge, Yorks, and Scottish Rites. Open for research with permission.

DC —SCOTTISH RITE OF FREEMASONRY, Library of the Supreme Council, 1733 16th St NW, Washington, 20009. Ingeborg R Baum, Librn and Cur
Holdings: Vols 175,000 Cat
Budget: $8000

MD —GRAND LODGE AF & AM OF MARYLAND, Masonic Museum & Library, 225 N Charles St, Baltimore, 21201. William H Gunther, Cur
Notes: The Masonic Museum and Library of the Grand Lodge of Maryland is entirely made up of Masonic information and all have been gifts to the Grand Lodge of Maryland.

MD —MASONIC SERVICE ASSOCIATION OF THE UNITED STATES, Library, 8120 Fenton St, Silver Spring, 20910. Stewart Pollard, Librn
Holdings: Vols 5000 Cat Mss

MA —GRAND LODGE OF MASONS IN MASSACHUSETTS, Library, 186 Tremont St, Boston, 20111. Roberta Hankamer, Librn
Holdings: Vols 60,000 Cat Mss Maps Pix Slides Microforms
Notes: Collection incl philosophy, religion, local history, biography, etc, as they might further Masonic research, in addition to strictly Masonic works--transactions of research lodges worldwide, lodge histories, theory, origins, Masonic jurisprudence, Masonic music, etc. Museum collection of aprons, jewels, diplomas and other artifacts is a prime research source. No estimate has been made of the depth of these holdings. John Paul Jones materials are notable. Incl scrapbooks and clipping file.

NY —NEW YORK STATE LIBRARY, State Education Bldg Annex, Washington Ave, Albany, 12224.
Holdings: Vols 72,750 Cat
Notes: Masonic and anti-Masonic literature, mainly New York State material, relating to the Morgan case and trial, and the resulting controversies. Proceedings of national, state, and local masonic bodies is considerable, incl many early imprints.

NY —NEW YORK PUBLIC LIBRARY, Research Libraries, General Research Division, Fifth Ave & 42 St, New York, 10018. Rodney Phillips, Chief
Holdings: Vols (2,225,000) Cat Maps Pix Microforms
Budget: ($775,718)
Notes: Incl special materials on Black Freemasonry.

NY —UNIVERSITY OF ROCHESTER, Rush Rhees Library, Department of Rare Books and Special Collections, Rochester, 14627. Peter Dzwonkoski, Librn
Holdings: Vols 100 Cat
Notes: Antimasonic collection. Related to this printed material are two of our manuscript collections, the William Henry Seward papers and the Thurlow Weed papers.

PA —HARRY C TREXLER MASONIC LIBRARY, Masonic Temple, Allentown, 18102.
Holdings: Vols (5000) Mss Pix

PA —PENNSYLVANIA STATE UNIVERSITY, Fred Lewis Pattee Library, Special Collections Dept, University Park, 16802. Charles Mann, Chief, Special Collections
Holdings: Vols 392
Budget: ($37,000)
Notes: Emphasis on England, 17th and 18th centuries, including *Books of Constitutions*, 1723.

TX —ABILENE CHRISTIAN UNIVERSITY, Margaret & Herman Brown Library, ACU Sta, Abilene, 79601. Callie Faye Milliken, Assoc Dir
Holdings: Vols 5000 // Cat
Notes: Donner Library of Americanism. Books, pamphlets, documents, and periodical materials dealing with American politics of the far right collected by Robert Donner during and after World War II. Also incl materials of Jews and Freemasonry.

TX —ROSENBERG LIBRARY, Galveston and Texas History Center, 2310 Sealy Ave, Galveston, 77550. Jane Kenamore, Archivist
Holdings: Vols 7368 Cat Mss Maps Pix Slides Microforms
Budget: $1000
Notes: Emphasis on upper Texas coast material; Republic of Texas period; Civil War period; Shipping; Texas Navy; Jean Laffite; Freemasonry in Texas; Texas politics, 19th-20th century; Railroads; Episcopal Church in Texas. Texas journalism, incl microfilms of Galveston newspapers, 1838-date. In addition to the 7368 cataloged volumes, collection also has approx 100,000 uncataloged pamphlets, state documents, reports, invitations, etc.

TX —GRAND LODGE OF TEXAS, AF & AM Library & Museum, 715 Columbus Ave, Box 446, Waco, 76702. Janet M Melton, Librn; Emery Stewart, Cur
Holdings: Vols 14,000 Cat Mss Pix
Budget: $1500

UT —UNIVERSITY OF UTAH, Marriott Library, Special Collections, Salt Lake City, 84112. Gregory C Thompson, Cur
Notes: The publications of Utah presses are also acquired. These presses are Olympus, Peregrine, Smith, Real Peoples, Horizon, Canticle, and Westwater. For the Rare Books collection materials from certain outside presses are also included. These presses are Northland, Allen, Grabhorn, Black Sparrow, Lime Kiln and Black Mountain. Books on Freemasonry are also collected.

ON —PUBLIC ARCHIVES OF CANADA, Library, 395 Wellington St, Ottawa, K1A 0N3, Can. Dawn E Monroe, Collections Development Officer
Notes: Milborne Masonic Collection. 1200 items. The imprints span four centuries from 1600 through 1900 and incl vols in five languages incl English, French, German, Latin and Spanish. Although the core of the collection covers North American Masonic history, it also incl British and European influences and other restrictive or secret societies. The collection contains bulletins, proceedings, reports, summonses and bylaws of the various orders and rites of Masonry. The general history of Masonry is complemented by histories of districts, grand lodges, jurisprudence, symbolism and research societies. A small number of items on Masonic drama and music, novels and poems. The papers, notes and photographs which were presented with Milborne Library are retained in the Manuscript Division.

PQ —CONCORDIA UNIVERSITY LIBRARIES, Vanier Library, 7141 Sherbrooke St SW, Montreal, H3G 1M8, Can. Martin Cohen, Collections Coordinator
Holdings: Vols 350 // Cat Mss
Notes: About 200 titles and 150 books of ritual; emphases on history, ritual, encyclopedias, biography, magic. Incl North American and European works.

FREEZE-DRYING see Lyophilization

FRELINGHUYSEN, JOSEPH S., 1869-1948

NJ —RUTGERS, THE STATE UNIVERSITY OF NEW JERSEY, Alexander Library, Special Collections and Archives, College Ave & Huntington St, New Brunswick, 08903. Ronald L Becker, Cur of Manuscripts and Rare Books
Holdings: // Mss
Notes: Papers, etc (110 linear feet).

FRELINGHUYSEN, PETER H. B.

NJ —PRINCETON UNIVERSITY, Library, Rare Books Dept, Princeton, 08544. Stephen Ferguson, Cur
Holdings: Mss
Notes: Papers of his Congressional service.

NJ —PRINCETON UNIVERSITY, Seeley G Mudd Manuscript Library, Public Affairs Papers Collection, Princeton, 08544. Nancy Bressler, Cur
Notes: Incl 241 cartons. The papers cover the period 1953-74. An unpublished 16p checklist is available in the Library.

FRENCH, ALICE (OCTAVE THANET)

IL —NEWBERRY LIBRARY, 60 W Walton St, Chicago, 60610. Diana Haskell, Cur of Modern Mss
Holdings: Vols 584 Cat Mss
Notes: Books and mss. Restricted use: noncirculating.

FRENCH, AUGUSTUS C. see French Family

FRENCH, BENJAMIN BROWN

DC —LIBRARY OF CONGRESS, Manuscript Division, Washington, 20540. John C Broderick, Chief
Holdings: Cat Mss
Notes: His papers; incl 11 of his journals, covering 1828-1870, about 3700 pp.

FRENCH, DANIEL CHESTER

DC —LIBRARY OF CONGRESS, Manuscript Division, Washington, 20540. John C Broderick, Chief
Holdings: Cat Mss Pix
Notes: Mss, papers, records, etc.

MA —CONCORD FREE PUBLIC LIBRARY, 129 Main St, Concord, 01742. Rose Marie Mitten, Dir
Holdings: Cat Mss Pix
Notes: A Concord sculptor who knew the people of the town, especially Emerson. Collection incl sculptures.

FRENCH, EDWIN DAVIS

PA —EASTERN COLLEGE, Frank Warner Memorial Library, Saint Davids, 19087. James L Sauer, Librn
Holdings: Uncat Mss Pix
Notes: The Harry C Goebel Collection. Incl Bruce Rogers printings (over 460); press books (about 350); oriental art (over 250); bookplates (with a separate collection of an almost complete set of bookplates designed by Edwin Davis French); Christmas Books; art and graphic arts (incl the French Graphic Arts Collection of Adolph DeMilly); first editions of Christopher Morley; Print Collection (1315 prints); Oriental art realia and artifacts.

FRENCH AMERICAN NEWSPAPERS see Newspapers, French American

FRENCH AND INDIAN WAR see U.s. —History_French and Indian War, 1755-1763

FRENCH ARCHITECTURE see Architecture, French

FRENCH ARTISTS see Artists, French

FRENCH AUTHORS see Authors, French

FRENCH CANADA

CT —YALE UNIVERSITY, Box 1603A, Yale Station, New Haven, 06520.

†MA —BOSTON PUBLIC LIBRARY, Copley Sq, Boston, 02117.
Notes: Archives of Wilfred Beaulieu, founder

FRENCH CANADA (cont.)

and editor of the Franco-American newspaper *Le Travailleur.*

MA —AMERICAN ANTIQUARIAN SOCIETY LIBRARY, 185 Salisbury St, Worcester, 01609. Marcus A McCorison, Dir & Librn
Holdings: Vols 1300 Cat
Notes: Incl the collection of Dr Gabriel Nadeau.

NH —ASSOCIATION CANADO-AMERICAIN (FRATERNAL LIFE INSURANCE SOCIETY), Institute Canado-Americain, 52 Concord St, Manchester, 03101. Robert A Beaudoin, Librn
Holdings: Vols (40,000) Cat Mss Maps Pix Slides Phonorecords Audiotapes Microforms
Budget: ($2000)
Notes: Contains books, pamphlets, mss, university dissertations, newspapers, manuscripts, periodicals, and archives of various other societies (active of defunct). Subjects covered incl art, music, literature, folklore, religion, politics, sociology, history, etc of the French in France, Canada, and US (especially New England's Franco-Americans, Louisiana's Cajuns, and Quebec's French-Canadians). There is also an extensive collection of genealogical works dealing with Quebec Acadia, and New England Francophones. Articles dealing with the library are: "The Library of the Association Canado-Americaine" by Edward B Ham in *Modern Language Notes*, vol LII, no 7, November 1937 and a bilingual article "Appel d'un jeune aux jeunes en faveur de al Bibliotheque ACA" by Robert B Perreault in *Le Canado-Americain*, nouvelle serie, vol 1, no 5, julliet-aout-septembre 1975, pp 18-19.

NY —UNIVERSITY OF ROCHESTER, Rush Rhees Library, Department of Rare Books and Special Collections, Rochester, 14627. Peter Dzwonkoski, Librn
Holdings: // Cat Mss
Notes: Jean Frederic Phelypeaux, Comte de Maurepas. Manuscripts relating to the French in Canada and Louisiana in the mid-18th century.

†RI —UNION SAINT-JEAN-BAPTISTE, Bibliotheque Mallet, Woonsocket, 02895.
Notes: Emphasis on genealogy, French parish histories; theses and dissertations on French Canadian topics.

ON —PUBLIC ARCHIVES OF CANADA, Library, 395 Wellington St, Ottawa, K1A 0N3, Can. Dawn E Monroe, Collections Development Officer
Holdings: Vols (80,000) Cat Mss Maps
Notes: The Public Archives Library's extensive collection covers almost all historical disciplines. Accounts of explorations and discoveries certainly represent the core of the Public Archives Library's Rare Book Collection. Indeed, the works of early explorers such as Champlain, Bacqueville de la Potherie, Lahontan, La Perouse, Le Clerq, Hakluyt, Cook, Mackenzie, Heriot, Hearne and many others can be consulted. The Library also holds both the original Swedish edition and the rare English translation of Pehr Kalm's voyages in North America: Kalm, Pehr. An important well-documented area concerns the settlement of the French in Canada, their dealings with native people, and descriptions of New France's natural environment. This early material on indigenous people is further supplemented by prayer and hymn books such as Henry Aaron Hill's translation of*A Collection of of Hymns for the Use of Native Christians of the Mohawk Language; To Which Are Added a Number of Hymns for Sabbath Schools* (New York: Printed by M'Elrath & Bangs, 1832, various pagings); Micmac, Algonquin and Iroquois dictionaries; and an illustrated reading book an illustrated reading book entitled *Indian Child's Book: A Primer in English and Cree* Languages (np, nd, 37 pp).

ON —UNIVERSITY OF OTTAWA, Morisset Library, 65 Hastey St, Ottawa, K1N 9A5, Can. Yvon Richer, University Chief Librn
Holdings: Vols (900,000) Cat Maps Slides Phonorecords 16mm Films Microforms
Notes: Holdings in French Canadian studies incl literature, history, politics, government documents, art history, law, etc. We are a bilingual university and most courses except literature are offered in both languages. Several hundred items in Special Collections support these areas. In addition, there is a valuable ms collection of the campus, the major resource of the *Centre de recherche en civilisation Canadienne Francaise.* It is presently housed in the library, but is not under our jurisdiction. It is open to scholars.

PQ —MCGILL UNIVERSITY, McLennan Library, Rare Books and Special Collections Dept, 3459 McTavish St, Montreal, H3A 1Y1, Can.
Notes: 3000 books and a large collection of newspapers. The Rodolphe Joubert Collection on French Canada includes material on economic conditions, history, politics and government of the province of Quebec. Also the department includes much material on the subject throughout its collections.

FRENCH CANADA—GENEALOGY

†RI —UNION SAINT-JEAN-BAPTISTE, Bibliotheque Mallet, Woonsocket, 02895.
Notes: Emphasis on genealogy, French parish histories; theses and dissertations on French Canadian topics.

FRENCH CANADA—HISTORY

AB —UNIVERSITY OF CALGARY, Library, Calgary, T2N 1N4, Can. Apollonia Steele, Special Collections Librn
Holdings: Cat
Notes: With a strengthened collection of materials on French Canada, incl many runs of periodicals and an extensive amount of early pamphlets, incl those of Henri Bourassa and other political figures.

FRENCH CANADA—SOCIAL LIFE AND CUSTOMS

BC —CAPILANO COLLEGE, Media Centre, 2055 Purcell Way N, Vancouver, V7J 3H5, Can. Pat Biggins, Reference Librn
Holdings: Vols 600 Cat Maps Slides Phonorecords Audiotapes 16mm Films Filmstrips
Notes: Scope is general with emphasis on arts (in French).

FRENCH CANADIAN LANGUAGE AND LITERATURE

CT —YALE UNIVERSITY, Box 1603A, Yale Station, New Haven, 06520.
Notes: French Canadiana and immigrationist material, largely books and pamphlets.

ME —LEWISTON PUBLIC LIBRARY, 118 Park St, Lewiston, 04240. Muriel P Landry, Actg Dir
Holdings: Vols 5387 Cat
Notes: This collection is added to constantly because of the demand from French-speaking people in this community. The collection contains mostly classics, light novels, romances, mysteries, biographies, etc. Loan small collections to other libraries in the area on a temporary basis. Do not attempt to collect intellectual materials in French. Description in *North Country* Libraries, March-April 1971.

†MA —FRENCH LIBRARY IN BOSTON, INC, 53 Marlborough St, Boston, 02116.
Notes: Classical and contemporary French literature incl criticism, French history, politics, social life, language and art, cinema, education, architecture, and Canadian literature.

MA —HARVARD UNIVERSITY LIBRARY, Widener Library, Cambridge, 02138. Carolyn Fawcett, Specialist in Book Selection
Holdings: Cat
Notes: 19,000 volumes on Canadian history and literature. Both French and English materials are well represented.

MI —UNIVERSITY OF MICHIGAN, Graduate Library, Ann Arbor, 48109. Janet White, Reference Librn
Holdings: Cat
Notes: Espec French Canadian aspects of Canadian civilization, language, and literature.

PA —BALCH INSTITUTE FOR ETHNIC STUDIES, Library, 18 S Seventh St, Philadelphia, 19106. R Joseph Anderson, Library Dir

RI —BROWN UNIVERSITY, John Hay Library, Harris Collection, Prospect St, Providence, 02912. Rosemary L Cullen, Cur
Holdings: Vols (200,000) Cat Mss Phonorecords Microforms
Budget: ($15,000)
Notes: The Harris Collection of American Poetry and Plays is principally composed of American and Canadian poetry and plays, 17th century-date. Extensive holdings in songsters, gift books and annuals, hymnals, pageants, broadside verse, carriers' addresses, women poets, juvenile poetry, (incl Mother Goose and *The Night Before* Christmas), sheet music with lyrics, small press publications, fine printing, black poets, "little magazines," Yiddish-American literature. All movements or schools of American poetry are represented. Incl first editions of most American poets and playwrights, notably Whitman, Poe, Wallace Stevens, Eugene O'Neill, Edward Albee, Ezra Pound, T S Eliot, William Carlos Williams, Amy Lowell, Phyllis Wheatley, Robert Frost, Allen Ginsberg, Bliss Carman, and Stephen Foster sheet music. Also incl the Saunders Walt Whitman Collection (1300 vols); the LangdonCollection of Pageants (250 vols); the Asa Cushman Collection of plays in ms and prompt copies; the MacDougall Collection of Psalters and Hymnals; 4000 plays issued by Walter H Baker Co, Boston (1890-1957); the Vaxer Collection of Yiddish Poetry, Plays and Music (1700 vols). Collections incl 200,000 vols, 30,000 broadsides, 55,000 mss, 170,000 pieces of sheet music, 450 phonorecords, and 375 microfilm reels. See *Dictionary Catalog of the Harris Collection of American Poetry and Plays* (Boston: G K Hall, 1972), 13 vols; *Supplement* (1977), 3 vols. See also, *American Poetry,* 1609-1900, *A Collection on Microfilm, Segment I* (1609-1820); *Segment II* (1821-1850); *Segment III* (1851-1870) (Woodbridge, Conn: Research Publications). Separate catalog.

AB —UNIVERSITY OF ALBERTA, Cameron Library, The Bruce Peel Special Collections Room, Edmonton, T6G 2J8, Can. John Charles, Special Collections Librn
Holdings: Vols 3000

BC —CAPILANO COLLEGE, Media Centre, 2055 Purcell Way N, Vancouver, V7J 3H5, Can. Pat Biggins, Reference Librn
Holdings: Vols 600 Cat Maps Slides Phonorecords Audiotapes 16mm Films Filmstrips
Notes: Scope is general with emphasis on arts and culture (in French).

ON —QUEEN'S UNIVERSITY, Douglas Library, Kingston, K7L 5C4, Can. William F E Morley, Cur, Special Collections
Holdings: Vols (50,000) Cat Mss Maps Pix Microforms
Budget: ($12,000)
Notes: The Edith and Lorne Pierce Collection of Canadiana. Also over 15,000 titles in Canadian Pamphlet Collection. Strong in humanities and social sciences, special strength in English and French Canadian literature; discovery and exploration narratives; Loyalists; War of 1812; opening of the West; local history, 19th century pamphlets and association items. Described in *A Catalogue of Canadian Manuscripts Collected by Lorne Pierce and Presented to Queen's University* (Toronto: Ryerson, 1946); and in *Canadiana 1698-1900 in the Possession of the Douglas* Library, comp by Janet S Porteous, foreword by Lorne Pierce (Kingston, 1932). Also later books and articles on parts of the collection.

ON —NATIONAL LIBRARY OF CANADA, 395 Wellington St, Ottawa, K1A 0N4, Can. Andre Preibish, Dir
Holdings: Vols 34,000
Notes: Includes 350 serial titles. The Library has been receiving on legal deposit all current literary works in English and French published in Canada since 1950. Intensive acquisition of earlier works and those published abroad. The collection aims to be

FRENCH CANADIAN LANGUAGE AND LITERATURE (cont.)

comprehensive. In addition, the collection is supported by representative resources for English, American, French and Commonwealth Literature.

ON —UNIVERSITY OF OTTAWA, Morisset Library, 65 Hastey St, Ottawa, K1N 9A5, Can. Yvon Richer, University Chief Librn
Holdings: Vols (900,000) Cat Maps Slides Phonorecords 16mm Films Microforms
Notes: Holdings in French Canadian studies incl literature, history, politics, government documents, art history, law, etc. We are a bilingual university and most courses except literature are offered in both languages. Several hundred items in Special Collections support these areas. In addition, there is a valuable ms collection on the campus, the major resource of the *Centre de recherche en civilisation Canadienne Francaise*. It is presently housed in the library, but it is not under our jurisdiction. It is open to scholars.

ON —UNIVERSITY OF TORONTO, Thomas Fisher Rare Book Library, 120 Saint George St, Toronto, M5S 1A5, Can. Richard G Landon, Head
Holdings: Vols (30,000) Mss
Notes: Comprehensive collection of first and as many subsequent editions as may be obtained of works of Canadian fiction, poetry, and drama. Large collections of Canadian literary papers; papers of Margaret Atwood, Earle Birney, Ernest Buckler, Leonard Cohen, Mavis Gallant, Dennis Lee, Raymond Souster, Josef Skvorecky, and many others.

ON —VICTORIA UNIVERSITY, Library, 71 Queen's Park Crescent, Toronto, M5S 1K7, Can. Robert C Brandeis, Chief Librn
Holdings: Vols 2500
Notes: The Riese Collection, partially cataloged, containing presentation copies of works by modern and contemporary French authors. Strong in Surrealism.

PQ —BIBLIOTHEQUE DE LA VILLE DE MONTREAL, Montreal City Library, Salle Gagnon Collection, 1210 Sherbrooke St E, Montreal, H2L 1L9, Can. Daniel Olivier, Dept Head
Holdings: Vols (44,055) Cat Mss Maps Slides Microforms
Budget: ($30,000)

FRENCH CANADIANS

CT —YALE UNIVERSITY, Box 1603A, Yale Station, New Haven, 06520.
Holdings: Cat Microforms
Notes: Strong collection in history and literature in Sterling Library.

CT —THOMPSON LIBRARY, Rte 193, Box 188, Thompson, 06277. Ted Perch, Librn
Holdings: Audiotapes
Notes: Information on French Canadians in Connecticut. Part of the Library's oral history project of the Quinebaug River Valley.

MA —FREE PUBLIC LIBRARY, Genealogy Room, 613 Pleasant St, Bedford, 02740. Paul A Cyr, Librn
Notes: Extensive collection on the history and genealogy of New England, with a strong emphasis on southeastern Massachusetts. Materials incl books, periodicals, mss, microfilms, and pictures of New England life. Unique features of collection incl the *Leonard Papers* ms of vital records of early Bristol County, *Repertoires des Mariages* of Province Quebec, Canada, and a collection on the Society of Friends, or Quakers.

†MA —BOSTON PUBLIC LIBRARY, Copley Sq, Boston, 02117.
Notes: Archives of Wilfred Beaulieu, founder and editor of the Franco-American newspaper *Le Travailleur.*

MA —HARVARD UNIVERSITY LIBRARY, Widener Library, Cambridge, 02138. Carolyn Fawcett, Specialist in Book Selection
Holdings: Vols 19,000 Cat
Notes: 19,000 volumes on Canadian history and literature. Both French and English materials are well represented.

MA —SPRINGFIELD CITY LIBRARY, Genealogy and Local History Dept, 220 State St, Springfield, 01103. Joseph Carvalho III, Supervisor
Holdings: Vols (17,000) Cat Mss Maps Pix Microforms VF
Budget: ($8000)
Notes: New England, Massachusetts, local history, and genealogy collections. 18,000 pictures, 3200 microforms, ca 15,000 clippings, pamphlets, etc (280 ft of vertical files).

MI —UNIVERSITY OF MICHIGAN, Graduate Library, Ann Arbor, 48109. Janet White, Reference Librn
Holdings: Cat
Notes: Espec French Canadian aspects of Canadian civilization, language, and literature.

NH —ASSOCIATION CANADO-AMERICAIN (FRATERNAL LIFE INSURANCE SOCIETY), Institute Canado-Americain, 52 Concord St, Manchester, 03101. Robert A Beaudoin, Librn
Holdings: Vols (40,000) Cat Mss Maps Pix Slides Phonorecords Audiotapes Microforms
Budget: ($2000)
Notes: Contains books, pamphlets, mss, university dissertations, newspapers, manuscripts, periodicals, and archives of various other societies (active of defunct). Subjects covered incl art, music, literature, folklore, religion, politics, sociology, history, etc of the French in France, Canada, and US (especially New England's Franco-Americans, Louisiana's Cajuns, and Quebec's French-Canadians). There is also an extensive collection of genealogical works dealing with Quebec Acadia, and New England Francophones. Articles dealing with the library are: "The Library of the Association Canado-Americaine" by Edward B Ham in *Modern Language Notes*, vol LII, no 7, November 1937 and a bilingual article "Appel d'un jeune aux jeunes en faveur de al Bibliotheque ACA" by Robert B Perreault in *Le Canado-Americain*, nouvelle serie, vol 1, no 5, julliet-aout-septembre 1975, pp 18-19.

NY —UNIVERSITY OF ROCHESTER, Rush Rhees Library, Department of Rare Books and Special Collections, Rochester, 14627. Peter Dzwonkoski, Librn
Holdings: / / Cat Mss
Notes: Jean Frederic Phelypeaux, Comte de Maurepas. Manuscripts relating to the French in Canada and Louisiana in the mid-18th century.

PA —BALCH INSTITUTE FOR ETHNIC STUDIES, Library, 18 S Seventh St, Philadelphia, 19106. R Joseph Anderson, Library Dir
Holdings: Vols 300 Cat

RI —UNION SAINT-JEAN-BAPTISTE, Bibliotheque Mallet, 1 Social St, Woonsocket, 02895. Brother Felician, SC, Librn
Holdings: Vols (4797) Cat Mss Phonorecords Microforms
Notes: French and French Canadian contributions to America.

†RI —UNION SAINT-JEAN-BAPTISTE, Bibliotheque Mallet, Woonsocket, 02895.
Notes: Emphasis on genealogy, French parish histories; theses and dissertations on French Canadian topics.

VT —SAINT MICHAEL'S COLLEGE, Durick Library, Winooski, 05404. Joseph Popecki, Dir; Henry Nadeau, Head of Archives & Special Collections
Holdings: Vols (5000) Cat
Notes: French Canadian genealogy, Irish genealogy, art, a complete set of Jesuit Relations and allied documents with a deluxe binding.

NB —MOUNT ALLISON UNIVERSITY, Ralph Pickard Bell Library, Sackville, E0A 3C0, Can. M Fancy, Librn
Holdings: Vols 6600 Cat Maps Microforms Slides VF
Notes: The Winthrop P Bell Collection on Acadian history concentrates on foreign Protestant settlements in, and history of, the area once known as Acadia. Also contains material on the French Acadians.

ON —FORT MALDEN NATIONAL HISTORIC PARK, Library, 100 Laird Ave, Box 38, Amherstburg, N9V 2Z2, Can. Sally E Snyder, Librn

ON —PUBLIC ARCHIVES OF CANADA, Library, 395 Wellington St, Ottawa, K1A 0N3, Can. Dawn E Monroe, Collections Development Officer
Holdings: Vols (80,000) Cat
Notes: The Public Archives Library's extensive collection covers almost all historical disciplines. Accounts of explorations and discoveries certainly represent the core of the Public Archives Library's Rare Book Collection. Indeed, the works of early explorers such as Champlain, Bacqueville de la Potherie, Lahontan, La Perouse, Le Clerq, Hakluyt, Cook, Mackenzie, Heriot, Hearne and many others can be consulted. The Library also holds both the original Swedish edition and the rare English translation of Pehr Kalm's voyages in North America: Kalm, Pehr. An important well-documented area concerns the settlement of the French in Canada, their dealings with native people, and descriptions of New France's natural environment. This early material on indigenous people is further supplemented by prayer and hymn books such as Henry Aaron Hill's translation of*A Collection of of Hymns for the Use of Native Christians of the Mohawk Language; To Which Are Added a Number of Hymns for Sabbath Schools* (New York: Printed by M'Elrath & Bangs, 1832, various pagings); Micmac, Algonquin and Iroquois dictionaries; and an illustrated reading book an illustrated reading book entitled *Indian Child's Book: A Primer in English and Cree* Languages (np, nd, 37 pp).

PQ —BIBLIOTHEQUE DE LA VILLE DE MONTREAL, Montreal City Library, Salle Gagnon Collection, 1210 Sherbrooke St E, Montreal, H2L 1L9, Can. Daniel Olivier, Dept Head
Holdings: Vols (44,055) Cat Mss Maps Slides Microforms
Budget: ($30,000)

PQ —CONCORDIA UNIVERSITY LIBRARIES, Vanier Library, 7141 Sherbrooke St SW, Montreal, H3G 1M8, Can. Martin Cohen, Collections Coordinator
Holdings: Uncat Mss
Notes: Dr J B Rudnyckyj was on the Royal Commission on Bilingualism and Biculturalism in Canada. His papers deal with bilingualism, multi-culturalism, minorities, languages. 400 boxes.

FRENCH CHILDREN'S LITERATURE see Children'S Literature, French

FRENCH COMPOSERS see Composers, French

FRENCH DRAMA

CA —UNIVERSITY OF CALIFORNIA, BERKELEY, University Library, French and Italian Collections, Berkeley, 94720. Donald G Williams, Librn
Notes: General research collection. There are abundant resources for study of the 18th-century intellectual scene, especially pre-revolutionary political and philosophical writing. The Encyclopedists are well represented. (Numerous first editions and other rare imprints are housed in The Bancroft Library.) The library's collection of literary journals is extensive, particularly so in the period 1870-1920; many serial runs are complete, for instance: *Mercure de* France (1622-1965); *L'Annee litteraire* (1540-1790). Materials to support research on French drama have been acquired in depth, with emphasis on the 18th and 19th centuries.

KY —UNIVERSITY OF KENTUCKY, Margaret I King Library, Dept of Special Collections, Lexington, 40506. William Marshall, Head
Holdings: Cat
Notes: 2000 French and approximately 2000 Spanish and German plays. 18th-19th centuries.

MD —JOHNS HOPKINS UNIVERSITY, Milton S Eisenhower Library, Charles & 34

FRENCH DRAMA (cont.)

Sts, Baltimore, 21218. Ann S Gwyn, Assistant Dir for Special Collections
Holdings: Vols Cat
Notes: Strongest in 18th and 19th century drama (plays) and in history and criticism.

MD —UNIVERSITY OF MARYLAND, Library, Rare Book Collection, College Park, 20742. Donald Farren, Assoc Dir for Special Collections
Holdings: Vols (10,000) Cat
Notes: Ranging from incunabula to modern first editions, the Rare Book Collection is particularly strong in materials relating to the history of France and in *exempla* of interest to students of bibliography. Related collections include sizable groups of books and other items relating to the Savoy, to *Expressionismus,* and to Pompeii. Pamphlet collections include many Mazarinades, many pamphlets relating to slavery and abolition, numerous French plays, and press books.

MI —UNIVERSITY OF MICHIGAN, Library, Dept of Rare Books & Special Collections, Ann Arbor, 48109. Robert J Starring, Head
Holdings: Cat
Notes: Over 1650 titles published in late 18th and early 19th centuries by minor French dramatists, in addition to a well-rounded general collection.

MN —CARLETON COLLEGE LIBRARY, Northfield, 55057.
Holdings: Vols 7000 Cat
Notes: Books and periodicals relating to French literature of the second half of the 19th century, incl the French symbolist and decadent writers and critical works about them. Major writers are well represented as are some of the relatively minor figures, such as Paul Adam, Rene Boylesve, Abel Hermant, Pierre Louys, and others. The collection incl 69 plays written and produced in the period.

NH —DARTMOUTH COLLEGE, Baker Memorial Library, Hanover, 03755.
Holdings: Cat
Notes: The Barrett Clark Collection.

NY —NEW YORK PUBLIC LIBRARY, Performing Arts Research Center, Billy Rose Theatre Collection, 111 Amsterdam Ave, New York, 10023. Dorothy L Swerdlove, Cur
Holdings: Cat
Notes: Described in *Catalog of the Theatre and Drama Collections,* The Research Libraries of The New York Public Library. 1967. To be Supplemented. Part 1, *Drama Collection: Listing by Cultural Origin,* 6 vols (120,000 cards), $585; Part II, *Drama Collection: Author Listing,* 6 vols (115,000 cards), $790. This catalog represents the major portion of the Research Libraries' Drama Collection. Incl are more than 120, 000 plays written in Western languages. Translations of plays published in the Cyrillic, Hebrew and Oriental alphabets are also listed. Excluded are children's plays, Christmas plays, and moralities. The catalog is in two parts: a listing by author (or title, in the case of anonymous plays); and a listing by cultural origin. An analysis of this latter section reveals the Research Libraries' interest in collecting widely from the literatures of theworld: American, 20,000 entries; English, 21,000; French, 22,000; Spanish, 16,000; German, 14,000; and a strong representation of plays written in minor languages.

NC —DUKE UNIVERSITY, William R Perkins Library, Durham, 27706. Elvin E Strowd, University Librn

FRENCH FAMILY

IL —ILLINOIS STATE HISTORICAL SOCIETY, Library, Old State Capitol, Springfield, 62706. Roger D Bridges, Head Librn
Holdings: Cat Mss Pix
Notes: The Augustus C French family papers.

FRENCH GUIANA

CT —YALE UNIVERSITY, Sterling Memorial Library, Latin American Collections, New Haven, 06520. Lee H Williams Jr, Cur
Holdings: Vols (300,000) Cat Maps Pix Slides Phonorecords 16mm Films Filmstrips
See also entry under Latin America

NY —AMERICAN MUSEUM OF NATURAL HISTORY, Library Services Dept, Central Park W & 79th St, New York, 10024. Nina J Root, Chairwoman; Mary Genett, Asst Librn for Reference Services

FRENCH IN CANADA see French Canadians

FRENCH IN TEXAS

TX —UNIVERSITY OF TEXAS, ARLINGTON, Library, Arlington, 76019. Charles A Colley, Dir of Special Collections; Robert A Gamble, Head of Archives
Holdings: // Mss
Notes: Santerre Collection. This is the library of the Santerre family who emigrated from France, Belgium, and Switzerland in 1855 to join the Utopian Socialist colony of Victor Prosper Considerant in what is now Dallas, Texas. Typical selection of books of a middle-class, well-educated family of the period. Some title deeds, legal papers, family letters, first Paris editions of works of Considerant, Charles Fourier; French translations of English classics, devotional works. See George H Santerre, *White Cliffs of Dallas* (Dallas, Texas: Book Craft, 1955).

FRENCH IN THE U.S.

DC —SOCIETY OF THE CINCINNATI, Library, 2118 Massachusetts Ave NW, Washington, 20008. John D Kilbourne, Dir of Museum & Library
Holdings: Vols (12,000) Cat Mss Maps Pix Slides Microforms
Budget: ($65,000)
Notes: Because of the French connections of the Society of the Cincinnati, a particular effort is made to incl information about the French contribution to the American Revolution. The collection is also rich in biographical materials concerning the officer personnel of the American and French armies of the American Revolution. There are two significant sub-sections of this collection: The George Rogers Clark Collection concerning the history of the Old Northwest (to 1820); and the Member-Author collection, writings of members of the Society of the Cincinnati in various fields. It is advisable to make an appointment for use of the collections.

MA —SPRINGFIELD CITY LIBRARY, Genealogy and Local History Dept, 220 State St, Springfield, 01103. Joseph Carvalho III, Supervisor
Holdings: Vols (17,000) Cat Mss Maps Pix Microforms VF
Budget: ($8000)
Notes: New England, Massachusetts, local history, and genealogy collections. 18,000 pictures, 3200 microforms, ca 15,000 clippings, pamphlets, etc (280 ft of vertical files).

NH —ASSOCIATION CANADO-AMERICAIN (FRATERNAL LIFE INSURANCE SOCIETY), Institute Canado-Americain, 52 Concord St, Manchester, 03101. Robert A Beaudoin, Librn
Holdings: Vols (40,000) Cat Mss Maps Pix Slides Phonorecords Audiotapes Microforms
Budget: ($2000)
Notes: Contains books, pamphlets, mss, university dissertations, newspapers, manuscripts, periodicals, and archives of various other societies (active of defunct). Subjects covered incl art, music, literature, folklore, religion, politics, sociology, history, etc of the French in France, Canada, and US (especially New England's Franco-Americans, Louisiana's Cajuns, and Quebec's French-Canadians). There is also an extensive collection of genealogical works dealing with Quebec Acadia, and New England Francophones. Articles dealing with the library are: "The Library of the Association Canado-Americaine" by Edward B Ham in *Modern Language Notes,* vol LII, no 7, November 1937 and a bilingual article "Appel d'un jeune aux jeunes en faveur de al Bibliotheque ACA" by Robert B Perreault in *Le Canado-Americain,* nouvelle serie, vol 1, no 5, julliet-aout-septembre 1975, pp 18-19.

†NY —HUGUENOT SOCIETY OF AMERICA LIBRARY, 122 E 58 St, New York, 10022.
Notes: French Huguenot migration to America, Huguenot history in France and elsewhere, biography, genealogy.

PA —BALCH INSTITUTE FOR ETHNIC STUDIES, Library, 18 S Seventh St, Philadelphia, 19106. R Joseph Anderson, Library Dir
Holdings: Vols 2232 Cat

RI —UNION SAINT-JEAN-BAPTISTE, Bibliotheque Mallet, 1 Social St, Woonsocket, 02895. Brother Felician, SC, Librn
Holdings: Vols (4797) Cat Mss Phonorecords Microforms
Notes: Franco-Americans in the US, especially in New England.

†RI —UNION SAINT-JEAN-BAPTISTE, Bibliotheque Mallet, Woonsocket, 02895.
Notes: Emphasis on genealogy, French parish histories; theses and dissertations on French Canadian topics.

†SC —HUGUENOT SOCIETY OF SOUTH CAROLINA LIBRARY, 25 Chalmers St, Charleston, 29401.
Notes: Genealogical data on Huguenots and allied families, especially French Huguenots.

FRENCH INDOCHINA see Indochina, French

FRENCH LANGUAGE AND LITERATURE

CA —UNIVERSITY OF CALIFORNIA, BERKELEY, University Library, French and Italian Collections, Berkeley, 94720. Donald G Williams, Librn
Budget: ($33,000)
Notes: General research collection. There are abundant resources for study of the 18th-century intellectual scene, espec of prerevolutionary political and philosophical writing. The Encyclopedists are well represented. (Numerous first editions and other rare imprints are housed in The Bancroft Library.) The library's collection of literary journals is extensive, particularly so in the period 1870-1920; many serial runs are complete, for instance: *Mercure de* France (1622-1965); *L'Annee litteraire* (1540-1790). Materials to support research on French drama have been acquired in depth, with emphasis on the 18th and 19th centuries.

CA —LOS ANGELES PUBLIC LIBRARY, Foreign Languages Dept, 630 W Fifth St, Los Angeles, 90071. Sylva Manoogian, Principal Librn
Holdings: Vols 32,074 Cat
Budget: ($41,500)

CA —UNIVERSITY OF CALIFORNIA, LOS ANGELES, William Andrews Clark Memorial Library, 2520 Cimarron St, Los Angeles, 90018.
Holdings: Cat
Notes: Original editions.

CT —YALE UNIVERSITY, Box 1603A, Yale Station, New Haven, 06520.
Holdings: Cat Mss

CT —UNIVERSITY OF CONNECTICUT, Library, Storrs, 06268. R H Schimmelpfeng, Dir of Special Collections
Notes: Belgian revolution of 1830. The collection consists of primary sources, books and pamphlets, of the period, along with secondary materials. Two-thirds of the collection is in French, the rest in Dutch. An author/title checklist is also available.

†DC —LIBRARY OF CONGRESS, Washington, 20540.
Notes: The Raymond Toinet Collection of French literary works.

IL —NORTHWESTERN UNIVERSITY, Library, Special Collections Dept, 1937 Sheridan Rd, Evanston, 60201. R Russell Maylone, Cur
Holdings: Vols 6000 Cat Mss
Notes: First editions, letteres, and works

FRENCH LANGUAGE AND LITERATURE (cont.)

about major 20th-century authors. Incl books and periodicals from Fance and Germany and to a lesser extent from Italy, Spain, Poland, Rumania, Czechoslovakia, Sweden, Denmark, and the Netherlands. Strong in German Expressionism, Italian Futurism, Surrealism, and Dada.

IN —INDIANA UNIVERSITY, Lilly Library, Seventh St, Bloomington, 47405. William R Cagle, Librn
Holdings: Cat Mss
Notes: Emphasizes 19th and 20th centuries. Ms holdings incl the papers of Judith Jeanne Cladel, 1834-1892, novelist; correspondence of Alexandre Dumas, 1824-1895, novelist and playwright; Jean Giono, 1895-1970; Henry Milon de Montherlant; 1895-1972; Romain Rolland, 1866-1944. Also many individual letters and ms pieces.

IN —SAINT MARY-OF-THE-WOODS COLLEGE, College Library, Saint Mary-of-the-Woods, 47876. Sister Emily Walsh, SP, Administrator
Holdings: Vols 2500 Cat
Notes: Books published in French, 18th-19th century.

IN —INDIANA STATE UNIVERSITY, Cunningham Memorial Library, Dept of Rare Books & Special Collections, Terre Haute, 47809. Lawrence J McCrank, Head
Holdings: Cat Maps Pix

KS —UNIVERSITY OF KANSAS, Kenneth Spencer Research Library, Special Collections Dept, Lawrence, 66045. Alexandra Mason, Librn
Holdings: Caat
Notes: 16th and 17th century French in the Summerfield collection; French Revolutionary pamphlets; 17th and 18th century political poems in ms. Noncirculating.

KY —UNIVERSITY OF KENTUCKY, Margaret I King Library, Dept of Special Collections, Lexington, 40506. William Marshall, Head
Holdings: Vols 1500 Cat
Notes: French romantic literature.

LA —LOUISIANA STATE UNIVERSITY, Library, Baton Rouge, 70803. Anna H Perrault, Humanities Bibliographer
Holdings: Vols (25,500) Cat Microforms
Budget: ($5000)

LA —UNIVERSITY OF SOUTHERN LOUISIANA, Dupre Library, Jefferson Caffery Louisiana Room, 302 East St Mary Blvd, Lafayette, 70504. Cynthia J Rice, Louisiana Room Ref Librn
Holdings: Vols 500

ME —BOWDOIN COLLEGE, Library, Brunswick, 04011. Dianne M Gutscher, Cur of Special Collections
Holdings: Vols (24,000) Cat Mss
Notes: The Charles Livingston French Autograph Collection contains about 800 letters of illustrious French personalities, primarily of the 18th and 19th centuries, incl Balzac, Diderot, Rousseau, and Voltaire; the Marguerite Yourcenar Collection contains heavily annotated and presentation copies of more than 150 novels, essays, plays, poems, and translations, as well as mss and correspondence of this noted French author and first woman to be elected to the French Academy; the general collection of the Library incl about 24,000 vols on this subject.

ME —LEWISTON PUBLIC LIBRARY, 118 Park St, Lewiston, 04240. Muriel P Landry, Actg Dir
Holdings: Vols 5387 Cat
Notes: This collection is added to constantly because of the demand from French-speaking people in this community. The collection contains mostly classics, light novels, romances, mysteries, biographies, etc. Loan small collections to other libraries in the area on a temporary basis. Do not attempt to collect intellectual materials in French. Description in *North Country* Libraries, March-April 1971.

†MA —FRENCH LIBRARY IN BOSTON, INC, 53 Marlborough St, Boston, 02116.
Notes: Classical and contemporary French literature incl criticism, French history, politics, social life, language and art, cinema, education, architecture, and Canadian literature.

MA —HARVARD UNIVERSITY LIBRARY, Widener Library, Cambridge, 02138. Assunta S Pisani, Specialist in Book Selection
Holdings: Cat Mss Microforms
Notes: *Widener Library Shelflist* nos 47-48 (1973) list some 40,00 vols on French literature, incl a good Provencal collection.

MA —PINE MANOR COLLEGE, Library, 310 Heath St, Chestnut Hill, 02167. Linda Denners, Head Librn
Holdings: Vols (500) Cat
Notes: French symbolist poets.

MI —UNIVERSITY OF MICHIGAN, Graduate Library, Ann Arbor, 48109. Janet White, Reference Librn
Holdings: Cat Microforms
Notes: Comprehensive collection of French language and literature with particular strength in dramatic works by early major and minor playwrights; currently receives about 625 periodical titles published in France.

MN —CARLETON COLLEGE LIBRARY, Northfield, 55057.
Holdings: Vols 7000 Cat
Notes: Books and periodicals relating to French literature of the second half of the 19th century, incl the French symbolist and decadent writers and critical works about them. Major writers are well represented as are some of the relatively minor figures, such as Paul Adam, Rene Boylesve, Abel Hermant, Pierre Louys, and others. The collection incl 69 plays written and produced in the period.

NY —HEMPSTEAD PUBLIC LIBRARY, Foreign Language Collection, 115 Nichols Court, Hempstead, 11550. Irene A Duszkiewicz, Dir
Notes: Mainly French, German, Italian, Spanish, Polish, Yiddish, Hebrew. Holdings in other languages, including Asian.

†NY —COLUMBIA UNIVERSITY LIBRARIES, Butler Library, Rare Book and Manuscript Library, 535 W 114 St, New York, 10027.
Notes: Lewis Galantiere's papers, etc, with much on Antoine de Saint-Exupery, French language and literature, modern French authors and their works, etc. Considerable correspondence with many of the latter as well as with American and British authors.

NY —FRENCH INSTITUTE-ALLIANCE FRANCAISE, Library, 22 E 60 St, New York, 10022. Fred J Gitner, Librn
Holdings: Vols (40,000) Cat Phonorecords Audiotapes
Budget: ($23,000)
Notes: Special collections of art books, books about Paris. Rich in bibliographical, biographical and lexicographical works. Standard editions of all major French authors. Name has been changed from French Institute in the United States Library since merger with the Alliance Francaise de New York.

NY —NEW YORK PUBLIC LIBRARY, Research Libraries, General Research Division, Fifth Ave & 42 St, New York, 10018. Rodney Phillips, Chief
Holdings: Vols (2,225,000) Cat Maps Pix Microforms
Budget: ($775,718)

NY —NEW YORK PUBLIC LIBRARY, Donnell Foreign Language Library, 20 W 53 St, New York, 10019. Bosiljka Stevanovic, Supvr Librn
Holdings: Vols 9420 Cat
Notes: French collection incl French authors of French expression. No separate catalog.

NY —NEW YORK PUBLIC LIBRARY, Mid-Manhattan Library, Literature and Language Dept, 455 Fifth Ave, New York, 10016. Eric Steele, Sr Principal Librn
Holdings: Vols (160,000) Cat Phonorecords Microforms Audiotapes
Budget: ($92,000)
Notes: College-oriented collection. Standard editions of all major authors. Emphasis on criticism in French and English. Extensive runs of most important journals in the field.

NY —STATE UNIVERSITY OF NEW YORK, STONY BROOK, Melville Library, Stony Brook, 11794. John B Smith, Dir
Holdings: Cat
Notes: This 18th century French literature collection is part of the library's general research collections. Strengths in French Romanticism.

NC —DUKE UNIVERSITY, William R Perkins Library, Durham, 27706. Elvin E Strowd, University Librn
Notes: The Gustav Lanson collection is made up of 15,000 titles. It is "rich in standard works of modern French authors and the literature of technical criticism."

NC —CUMBERLAND COUNTY PUBLIC LIBRARY, North Carolina Foreign Language Center, 328 Gillespie St, Fayetteville, 28301. Patrick M Valentine, Coordinator
Holdings: Vols 2300 Cat
Notes: The largest book collections are, in descending order of size, German Spanish, French, Japanese, Korean and Vietnamese, with fair sized collections in Italian, Russian, Chinese, Arabic, Greek, Hungarian, Polish, Hebrew, Thai, and Hindi. The Center has several shelves each of books in Bengali, Dutch, Marathi, Portuguese, Urdu, and Yiddish. Smaller collections of one to three shelves each incl Catalan, Croatian, Czech, Danish, Finnish, Gujarati, Icelandic, Kannada, Latin, Lithuanian, Malayalam, Norwegian, Panjabi, Persian (Farsi), Romanian, Slovak, Swedish, Tagalog, Tamil, Telegu, and Ukrianian. The Center has grammars, dictionaries and occasionally other readings in languages from Afrikaans and Albanian to Welsh, Yoruba and Zulu.

OH —CLEVELAND PUBLIC LIBRARY, Foreign Literature Dept, 325 Superior Ave, Cleveland, 44114. Natalia Bezugloff, Head
Holdings: Vols 23,730 Cat
Notes: A popular circulating collection containing classics and the standard works with emphasis on belles lettres, history and biography. A variety of other subjects such as learning languages, how to do books, art, children's books, spoken phonodiscs and cassettes, periodicals, etc. Incl 310 ephemera.
See also entry under Foreign Language Collections

PA —UNIVERSITY OF PENNSYLVANIA, Van Pelt Library, Rare Books Collection, 34 & Walnut Sts, Philadelphia, 19104. Daniel Traister, Special Collections Librn
Notes: Especially Old French.

PA —UNIVERSITY OF PITTSBURGH, Hillman Library, Pittsburgh, 15260. Glenora E Rossell, Head
Holdings: Vols 14,250 Cat Microforms
Notes: The collection tends to be a comprehensive one, incl complete editions of an author's works and critical editions of an author's complete works.

RI —BROWN UNIVERSITY, John Hay Library, 20 Prospect St, Providence, 02912. Mark N Brown, Cur Mss
Holdings: Mss
Notes: See the listing for the Emile Zola Manuscript Collection.

TX —UNIVERSITY OF TEXAS LIBRARIES, General Libraries, PO Box P, Austin, 78713. Carolyn Bucknell, Asst Dir for Collection Development
Holdings: Cat Microforms

WI —UNIVERSITY OF WISCONSIN, MADISON, Memorial Library, 728 State St, Madison, 53706. Erwin K Welsch, Social Studies Bibliographer
Notes: Incl the Chateaubriand Manuscripts; Rousseau Collection, 243 works by and about Rousseau and his impact on 18th century thought; and the Joseph E Tucker Bequest, ca 150 vols from the Library of Prince Nikolai Romanovskii.
See also entry under Chateaubriand, Francois Auguste Rene.

ON —NATIONAL LIBRARY OF CANADA, 395 Wellington St, Ottawa, K1A 0N4, Can. Andre Preibish, Dir
Holdings: Vols 34,000
Notes: Includes 350 serial titles. The Library has been receiving on legal deposit all current literary works in English and French

FRENCH LANGUAGE AND LITERATURE (cont.)

published in Canada since 1950. Intensive acquisition of earlier works and those published abroad. The collection aims to be comprehensive. In addition, the collection is supported by representative resources for English, American, French and Commonwealth Literature.

ON —VICTORIA UNIVERSITY, Library, 71 Queen's Park Crescent, Toronto, M5S 1K7, Can. Robert C Brandeis, Chief Librn
Holdings: Vols 5000
Notes: The Riese Collection, partially cataloged, containing presentation copies of works by modern and contemporary French authors. Strong in Surrealism.

PQ —CONCORDIA UNIVERSITY LIBRARIES, 1455 de Maisonneuve Blvd W, Montreal, H3G 1M8, Can. Martin Cohen, Special Collections Librn
Holdings: Vols 60// Cat Mss
Notes: The Maximilien Bibaud Collection contains the author's memoirs and correspondence as well as his writing on diverse subjects such as religion, theology, Canadian, European and ancient history, and the French language. 51 vols of ms materials.

FRENCH LANGUAGE AND LITERATURE—CANADA see French Canadian Language and Literature

FRENCH LANGUAGE AND LITERATURE—HAITIAN AUTHORS

NY —NEW YORK PUBLIC LIBRARY, Donnell Foreign Language Library, 20 W 53 St, New York, 10019. Bosiljka Stevanovic, Supvr Librn
Notes: Haitian materials incl in the French collection. No separate catalog.

FRENCH LANGUAGE AND LITERATURE—OLD FRENCH

OH —CLEVELAND PUBLIC LIBRARY, Fine Arts and Special Collections Department, 325 Superior Ave, Cleveland, 44114. Alice N Loranth, Head
Holdings: Cat Mss
Notes: Part of the Medieval Literature Collection. Medieval texts, translations, facsimile reproductions, bibliographies and catalogs of mss, romances, epics, early chronicles and histories. Icelandic sagas, fabliaux (tales), legends, lives of the Saints are well represented. Monographs, scholarly journals and serials on philogy, linguistics and literature with special emphasis on Middle English, Old French, Middle High German, Middle Dutch and early Irish texts. *See also* entries under Folklore; Literature, Medieval.

PA —UNIVERSITY OF PENNSYLVANIA, Van Pelt Library, Rare Books Collection, 34 & Walnut Sts, Philadelphia, 19104. Daniel Traister, Special Collections Librn
Notes: Especially Old French.

FRENCH LAW see Law, French

FRENCH LITERATURE see French Language and Literature

FRENCH MEDICINE—HISTORY see Medicine, French—History and Historic

FRENCH MONARCHY see Monarchy, French

FRENCH MUSIC see Music, French

FRENCH NEWSPAPERS see Newspapers, French

FRENCH OPERA see Opera, French

FRENCH PERIODICALS see Periodicals, French

FRENCH PHILOSOPHY see Philosophy, French

FRENCH POETRY

MA —PINE MANOR COLLEGE, Library, 310 Heath St, Chestnut Hill, 02167. Linda Denners, Head Librn
Holdings: Vols (500) Cat
Notes: French symbolist poets.

MN —CARLETON COLLEGE LIBRARY, Northfield, 55057.
Holdings: Vols 7000 Cat
Notes: Books and periodicals relating to French literature of the second half of the 19th century, incl the French symbolist and decadent writers and critical works about them. Major writers are well represented as are some of the relatively minor figures, such as Paul Adam, Rene Boylesve, Abel Hermant, Pierre Louys, and others. The collection incl 69 plays written and produced in the period.

PA —TEMPLE UNIVERSITY LIBRARIES, Special Collections Dept, Rare Books & Mss Section, Philadelphia, 19122. Thomas M Whitehead, Cur
Holdings: Vols 100 Uncat Mss Pix
Notes: Collection of French symbolist poets based on the personal papers of Charles Morice, French poet and critics; first editions and inscribed copies of Morice, Verlaine, Mallarme et al; supportive titles: *La Plume,* etc. Incl correspondence.

FRENCH POLITICAL PAMPHLETS, 1547-1648

WI —UNIVERSITY OF WISCONSIN, MADISON, Memorial Library, Rare Books Collection, 728 State St, Madison, 53706. Gretchen Lagana, Cur
Holdings: // Cat
Notes: A collection of literary, political, and satirical pamphlets covering all aspects of French life and civilization during 1547-1648. Included in Robert O Lindsay and John Neu, *French Political Pamphlets* 1547-1648 (Madison,1969). Housed in the Dept of Rare Books and Special Collections.

FRENCH PROTESTANTS see Huguenots

FRENCH RADIO see Radio, French

FRENCH REVOLUTION see France—History—Revolution, 1789-1799

FRENCH SOUDAN see Mali

FRENCH SCHOOL (MEDICINE)

MD —JOHNS HOPKINS UNIVERSITY, Institute of the History of Medicine, 1900 E Monument St, Baltimore, 21205. Doris Thibodeau, Librn
Holdings: Vols 730 Cat

FRENCH WEST INDIES see West Indies

FRENEAU, PHILIP, 1752-1832

NJ —MONMOUTH COUNTY HISTORICAL ASSOCIATION, Library, 70 Court St, Freehold, 07728. Loretta M Zwolak, Archivist & Librn
Holdings: Vols (6500) Cat Mss Maps Pix Slides Microforms
Budget: ($15,800)
Notes: Especially Monmouth County area. See *Monmouth County Historical Association Bulletin,* vol 1, no 2 July 1948, p 23-48. Allaire Papers (Howell Works); Battle of Monmouth; Mott Family Papers; North American Phalanx; Philip Freneau; Steamship Coll.

NJ —RUTGERS, THE STATE UNIVERSITY OF NEW JERSEY, Alexander Library, Special Collections and Archives, College Ave & Huntington St, New Brunswick, 08903. Ronald L Becker, Cur of Manuscripts and Rare Books
Holdings: // Mss
Notes: Papers, etc (6 linear feet).

VA —UNIVERSITY OF VIRGINIA, Alderman Library, Clifton Waller Barrett Collection, Charlottesville, 22901. Joan St C Crane, Cur of American Literature Collections
Notes: Papers.

FRESCO PAINTING see Mural Painting and Decoration

FRESHWATER BIOLOGY

IL —ILLINOIS NATURAL HISTORY SURVEY LIBRARY, 196 Natural Resources Bldg, Champaign, 61820. Carla G Heister, Librn
Holdings: Vols (36,000) Cat Microforms
Budget: ($25,500)
Notes: A Research and Science Branch of the State of Illinois, the Natural History Survey maintains a library of books, journals and reports on various aspects of natural history. Material is collected in all major languages. The library maintains its own exchange arrangements with some 600 worldwide institutions and organizations. Interlibrary loans and photocopy services are available through the University of Illinois Library. Publications issued regularly by the Survey incl *Biological Notes, The Bulletin, and Circulars.*

MI —UNIVERSITY OF MICHIGAN, North Engineering Library, 1002 I St, Ann Arbor, 48109. Maurita Holland, Librn
Holdings: Vols 2500 Cat Maps Pix
Budget: $3500
Notes: Subject emphasis is on the natural science aspects of the Great Lakes; limnology. Also 5000 reports.

MI —MICHIGAN STATE UNIVERSITY, W K Kellogg Biological Station, Walter F Morofsky Memorial Library, 3700 E Gull Lake Dr, Hickory Corners, 49060. Carolyn Hammarskjold, Librn
Holdings: Vols 8000 Cat

FRESHWATER ECOLOGY

FL —SOUTH FLORIDA WATER MANAGEMENT DISTRICT, Library, PO Box V, West Palm Beach, 33402. Cynthia H Plockelman, Research Librn
Holdings: Cat Slides Microforms Periodicals
Budget: ($13,000)
Notes: A state agency dealing in all aspects of water management, flood control, hydrology, changing environmental conditions, etc. Emphasis is changing from flood control to general water management.

MO —US FISH & WILDLIFE SERVICE, Columbia National Fisheries Research Laboratory, Rte One, Columbia, 65201. Axie Hindman, Librn
Holdings: Vols (2000) Cat Microforms
Budget: ($7000)
Notes: Pesticides in aquatic biota; fisheries research; fresh-water ecology. Also incl collection in water pollution, acid rain, aquatic invertebrets, environment and 10,000 reprints.

FRESHWATER FISHES see Fishes, Freshwater

FRETTED INSTRUMENTS

IL —NEWBERRY LIBRARY, 60 W Walton St, Chicago, 60610. Diana Haskell, Cur of Modern Mss
Holdings: Cat Mss Microforms
Notes: Incl the library of Count Pio Resse and a portion of Alfred Cortot library. Particularly strong in Italian theoretical treatises, vocal music and music for fretted instruments. Restricted use: noncirculating.

FREUD, ANNA, 1895-1982

KS —MENNINGER FOUNDATION, Archives, 5600 W Sixth St, Box 829, Topeka, 66601. Alice Brand, Librn; Mark West, Archivist
Notes: 2 boxes, 1936-69. Incl correspondence, mss, and miscellaneous materials. Much of the correspondence deals with her visits to The Menninger Foundation.

FREUD, SIGMUND, 1856-1939

CA —LOS ANGELES PSYCHOANALYTIC SOCIETY AND INSTITUTE, The Simmel-Fenichel Library, 2014 Sawtelle Blvd, Los Angeles, 90025.
Holdings: Cat Mss Pix Phonorecords
Notes: The Freudiana Special Collection (150 vols; photocopied letters, translations, etc; voice recordings), is part of the library's main collection on psychoanalysis and psychiatry.

FREUD, SIGMUND, 1856-1939 (cont.)

DC —LIBRARY OF CONGRESS, Rare Book & Special Collections Div, Washington, 20540. William Matheson, Chief
Holdings: Vols (125) Cat
Notes: The Sigmund Freud Collection of first editions, revised editions, important translations of his writings, etc was formed to complement extensive Freud manuscript holdings previously acquired by the Library. In additions to rare editions of books, eg, the author's first book *Zur Auffassung der* Aphasien (Leipzig & Vienna, 1891) and the first edition of his *Die Traumdeutung* (Leipzig & Vienna, 1900), the collection incl scarce pamphlets and offprints such as his early Uber Coca (Vienna, 1885). Associated with this collection, but separately maintained, are ca 50 books from Freud's personal library. Most are presentation copies from such authors as Havelock Ellis, Norman Douglas, Andre Breton, Paul Eluard and Morton Prince. Others which Freud acquired personally are by Pierre Janet, Friedrich Goltz, Daniel Hack Tuke, Carl Wernicke, et al.

DC —LIBRARY OF CONGRESS, Manuscript Division, Washington, 20540. John C Broderick, Chief
Holdings: Cat Mss
Notes: The Freud Archives. Also, the papers of Siegfried Bernfeld, one of Freud's pupils and associates.

IL —INSTITUTE FOR PSYCHOANALYSIS, McLean Library, 180 N Michigan Ave, Chicago, 60601. Glenn Miller, Librn
Holdings: Vols (10,000)
Budget: ($5000)

KS —MENNINGER FOUNDATION, Archives, 5600 W Sixth St, Box 829, Topeka, 66601. Alice Brand, Librn; Mark West, Archivist
Notes: 2 boxes, 1912-38. The Freud collection contians correspondence, reprints about Freud, and miscellaneous materials.

MA —BRANDEIS UNIVERSITY, Goldfarb Library, 415 South St, Waltham, 02154. Bessie Hahn, Dir
Notes: Lou Andreas-Salome Collection. 6 linear ft of mss mateial and books by and about Lou Andreas-Salome, novelist and poet, who took an active interest in psychoanalysis in the early part of the 20th century. There is a finding list to the collection in Special Collections.

†MA —CLARK UNIVERSITY, Robert Hutchings Goddard Library, Worcester, 01610. Dorothy Mosa Kowski, Rare Books Librn
Holdings: Cat Mss
Notes: Correspondence of Sigmund Freud with G Stanley Hall (first president of Clark University) over the period 1908-1923; also, copies of Freud's writings (from his first book on) in several languages.

NY —NEW YORK PSYCHOANALYTIC INSTITUE, Abraham A Brill Library, 247 E 82 St, New York, 10028. Ellen D Gilbert, Librn
Holdings: Vols (15,000) Cat Mss Pix Audiotapes
Notes: Subject catalog indexing both book and journal literature. Special collections incl Institute archives, manuscript collections, memorabilia and oral histories. Freud's writings complete in English and German and in part in at least 10 other languages. Open to members and students of Institute and other researchers and students. Photocopying.

OH —CLEVELAND MEDICAL LIBRARY ASSOCIATION/CASE WESTERN RESERVE UNIVERSITY, Cleveland Health Sciences Library, Historical Division, Allen Memorial Medical Library, 11000 Euclid Ave, Cleveland, 44106. Glen Jenkins, Rare Book Librarian & Archivist
Holdings: Vols 420 Cat
Notes: The Sigmund Freud Colletion.

FREUND, GISELE

BC —UNIVERSITY OF VICTORIA, McPherson Library, Victoria, V8W 3H5, Can.
Notes: Photographer. Incl 11 cm, 1963-66; mss, correspondence and photographs for the books: *James Joyce in Paris: His Final* Years, Gisele Freund and V B Carleton with a preface by Simone de Beauvoir (NY, Harcourt, Brace, & World, 1965).

FREWEN, MORETON

DC —GEORGETOWN UNIVERSITY, Library, Special Collections Div, 37 & O Sts NW, Washington, 20057. George M Barringer, Special Collections Librn; Nicholas B Sheetz, Mss Librn
Holdings: Mss Cat Pix
Notes: The papers of the Irish man-of-letters Sir Shane Leslie (1885-1971) containing letters, mss, diaries, notebooks, clippings, and photographs. Extensive correspondence by Margot Asquith, countess of Oxford and Asquith; Lady Violet Bonham-Carter; Burke Cochran; Lord Alfred Douglas; Moreton Frewen; Cardinal Gasquet; Vyvyan Holland; Lady Leonie Leslie; Sir Wilfrid Meynell; Sir Horace Plunkett; John Quinn; Frederick Rolfe (Baron Corvo); and Elizabeth Russell, among others. Also incl are research files on Sir Winston Churchill (Leslie's first cousin); Leonard Jerome; Maria Anne Fitzherbet (wife of King George IV); Ghosts and Ghost stories; and Eton College.

FRIARS, BLACK see Dominicans

FRIARS, GRAY see Franciscans

FRIARS MINOR see Franciscans

FRIARS PREACHERS, ORDER OF see Dominicans

FRIEDAN, BETTY (GOLDSTEIN), 1921-

MA —RADCLIFFE COLLEGE, Arthur & Elizabeth Schlesinger Library on the History of Women in America, 3 James St, Cambridge, 02138. Patricia Miller King, Dir; Eva Moseley, Cur of Mss
Holdings: Uncat Mss Pix Phonorecords Audiotapes Videotapes
Notes: Extensive collection covering all aspects of Betty Friedan's life from high school to the present. Poems and short stories written while student at Smith College; articles for labor press; drafts of *Feminine Mystique, It Changed My Life;* magazine articles; letters from readers; correspondence and printed material from the National Organization for Women, National Women's Political Caucus, National Abortion Rights Action League, and other feminist organizations; correspondence and printed material re International Women's Year, World Population Conference, etc; notes on interviews with women in government; notes for classes on sex roles; other. Restricted.

FRIEDMAN, COL. WILLIAM F.

†VA —GEORGE C MARSHALL RESEARCH FOUNDATION AND LIBRARY, Drawer 920, Lexington, 24450. Royster Lyle Jr, Cur Collections
Holdings: Cat Mss Maps Pix
Notes: The William F. Friedman Collection. Separate catalog. Incl. papers and correspondence relating to William and Elizabeth S. Friedman's personal interests and U.S. government assignments: books, pamphlets, technical papers, periodicals, microfilm, slides and newspaper clippings dealing with cryptology. Items on secret writing and signaling, radar, telephony and telegraphy, and the study of the Shakespeare-Bacon authorship controversy, Vols. of fiction relating to spies and codes, cryptographic game books for children, Civil War code items. Examples of ancient writings of Europe, Crete, and Easter Island, and material on the Aztecs, Incas, and particularly the Mayans. Also a copy of the Voynich mss., an undeciphered work, and other rare vols. on the subject dating from the 17th century. The library also has a separate collection of diaries kept by Gilbert Sandford Vernam, cryptographer and inventor. The diary is an almost day-by-day record, 1918-1926, of Vernam's inventions and development of his outstanding contributions to cryptography including techniques widely adopted by the armed forces for enciphering and deciphering coded messages. There is a typed index to this collection. No photocopying.

FRIEDMAN-ABELES PHOTO COLLECTION

NY —NEW YORK PUBLIC LIBRARY, Performing Arts Research Center, Billy Rose Theatre Collection, 111 Amsterdam Ave, New York, 10023. Dorothy L Swerdlove, Cur
Holdings: Pix
Notes: Theatre Collection received part of the Friedman-Abeles photograph archive when the partners decided to split up into separate companies.

FRIENDLY MORALIST SOCIETY

SC —COLLEGE OF CHARLESTON LIBRARY, Special Collections Dept, Charleston, 29401.
Notes: Papers, 1841-1871.

FRIENDS, SOCIETY OF

CA —WHITTIER COLLEGE, Wardman Library, Whittier, 90608. Christine Erdmann, Special Collections Librn
Holdings: Vols 1400 Cat Mss Pix

DE —UNIVERSITY OF DELAWARE, Hugh M Morris Library, S College Ave, Newark, 19711. T Stuart Dick, Special Collections
Holdings: // Mss
Notes: Personal and business letters and receipts of the Albertson family, Quaker lumber and lime merchants (1782-1862) residing in Plymouth, Montgomery Co, Pa. Included are many letters concerning the Plymouth RR and rules and regulations for its administration.

IN —EARLHAM COLLEGE, Lilly Library, Richmond, 47374.
Holdings: Vols 10,000 Cat Mss Maps Pix Microforms Audiotapes
Notes: The Quaker Collection in the archives is cataloged separately. In addition the archives incl the Earlham College Historical Collection. The Earlham Archives is the designated depository for materials relating to Young Friends organizations and activities. Its collection of materials relating to the work of Friends with the American Indians is probably the largest anywhere. Sources for Quaker genealogical research are good. See "Earlham's Quaker Collection" by Opal Thornburg, *Quaker History*, Autumn 1965, Vol 54, No 2.

KS —FRIENDS UNIVERSITY, Edmund Stanley Library, 2100 University, Wichita, 67213. Helen Wood, Cur
Holdings: Vols 3500 Cat Mss Pix Microforms

MD —JOHNS HOPKINS UNIVERSITY, Milton S Eisenhower Library, George Peabody Collection, 17 E Mt Vernon Place, Baltimore, 21201. Lyn Hart, Peabody Librn
Notes: Emphasis on materials published before 1950. Strength is a good collection through the 19th century.

MA —FREE PUBLIC LIBRARY, Genealogy Room, 613 Pleasant St, Bedford, 02740. Paul

FRIENDS, SOCIETY OF (cont.)

A Cyr, Librn
Holdings: Vols (10,000) Cat Mss Maps Pix Microforms
Budget: ($1000)
Notes: Extensive collection on the history and genealogy of New England, with a strong emphasis on southeastern Massachusetts. Materials incl books, periodicals, mss, microfilms, and pictures of New England life. Unique features of the collection incl the *Leonard Papers* ms of vital records of early Bristol County, *Repertoires des Mariages* of Province Quebec, Canada, and a collection on the Society of Friends, or Quakers.

MA —HARVARD UNIVERSITY, Harvard Divinity School, Andover-Harvard Theological Library, 45 Francis Ave, Cambridge, 02138. Maria Grossmann, Librn
Holdings: Vols (370,000) Cat Mss

MA —NEW ENGLAND QUAKER RESEARCH LIBRARY, PO Box 655, North Amherst, 01059. Francis W Holmes, Librn
Holdings: Vols (6000) Cat Mss Pix Slides Phonorecords Audiotapes Microforms
Budget: ($300)
Notes: No photocopying on premises. Subject emphases: Quakers and Quaker concerns; Pacifism; Racism; Feminism; Religion; Bible; Poverty.

NH —DOVER PUBLIC LIBRARY, 73 Locust St, Dover, 03820. Donald K Mullen, Librn
Holdings: Cat Mss Maps Pix Microforms
Notes: Collection contains a variety of New Hampshire records, clippings, town histories, genealogies. Quaker Meeting House records to the late 18th century. Local newspapers to early 19th century.

NJ —GLASSBORO STATE COLLEGE, Savitz Library, Stewart Room, Glassboro, 08028. Clara Kirner, Special Collection Librn
Holdings: Vols 86 Cat Mss
Notes: Miscellaneous mss incl marriage certificates, dismissals from Salem Monthly Meeting (33); intentions of marriage (9); manumission papers (44); Haddonfield Friends Meeting minutes, 1743-1776. Books incl: Memorials, biographies, etc, of west Jersey in 1700s and 1800s.

NJ —HISTORICAL SOCIETY OF HADDONFIELD, 343 King's Highway, E, Haddonfield, 08033. Doug Rauschenberger, Librn
Holdings: Vols 6000 Cat Mss Maps Pix Slides Audiotapes Microforms
Notes: New Jersey, especially history of the Haddonfield area, incl special material on Quakers in Haddonfield. Local newspapers on microfilm from 1920. Property deeds; local genealogies.

NY —C W POST CENTER OF LONG ISLAND UNIVERSITY, B Davis Schwartz Memorial Library, Greenvale, 11548. Jean Goldberg, Special Collections Librn
Notes: The Dudley Field Underhill Collection on Quaker history.

†NY —UNION THEOLOGICAL SEMINARY, Library, 3041 Broadway, New York, 10027.

NC —DUKE UNIVERSITY, Divinity School Library, Durham, 27706. Donn Michael Farris, Librn
Holdings: Vols (225,000)
Notes: Special collections and subject emphases in this library include: Archaeology, Egyptian; Archaeology, Middle Eastern; Art, Jewish; Bible; Bible-New Testament; Bible-Symbolism; Church Architecture; Egyptology; Fathers of the Church; Society of Friends; Great Britain-Religion-Methodism and Methodist Church; Hymns and Hymnals; Jansenists and Jansenism; Judaica; Mediaeval Christian Mysticism; Methodism and Methodist Church; Methodist Episcopal Church; Methodist Episcopal Church, South; Reformation; Religion-US-History; Rural Church; Theology-Great Britain-17th Century; Theology-Great Britain-18th Century; United Methodist Church; US-Church History; John Wesley.

OH —WESTGATE FRIENDS MEETING, Library, 3750 Sullivant Ave, Columbus, 43227. William Peters, Librn
Holdings: Vols 1500 Cat Mss Pix Audiotapes Filmstrips
Notes: Antiquarian and current imprints; regional and international items. No photocopying.

OH —MASSILLON PUBLIC LIBRARY, 208 Lincoln Way E, Massillon, 44646. Camille Leslie, Dir
Holdings: / / Mss Maps
Notes: 22 linear fr. Correspondence and business papers of Thomas Rotch and Arvine Wales who migrated in 1811 from New England of Ohio; and of Arvine C Wales, his son, lawyer and civic leader in Massillon, Ohio. Covers period ca 1780-1880; contains much Quaker and anti-slavery material, as well as material on early Ohio. Index in preparation.

OH —WILMINGTON COLLEGE, Watson Library, Quaker Collection, Pyle Center, Box #1227, Wilmington, 45177. Audrey Haines, Cur
Holdings: Vols (6000) Cat Mss Maps Pix Microforms
Notes: Collection houses Wilmington College archives, 1870-present, and serves as repository for the records of the Wilmington and Ohio Valley Yearly Meetings of the Religious Society of Friends (Quakers), ca 1800-present. Also incl 120 Quaker periodical and newsletter titles, ca 1828-present; several hundred pamphlets, tracts, and epistles; 220 genealogical works, primarily Quaker families; and 3900 vols on Quaker history, philosophy, thought, and practice, particularly peace, war, slavery, education, and biography, ca 1750-present. Incl some fiction, poetry and children's books. Rare or fragile materials, reference works, pamphlets, and genealogies do not circulate. Please notify prior to visiting.

OR —GEORGE FOX COLLEGE, Shambaugh Library, Newberg, 97132. F E Walls, Libr Dir
Holdings: Vols 3300 Cat Pix Microforms
Budget: $300
Notes: Incl periodicals, scrapbooks, pamphlets, etc and books relating to Herbert Hoover.

PA —HAVERFORD COLLEGE, Magill Library, Quaker Collection, Haverford, 19041. Edwin B Bonner, Librn & Cur
Holdings: Vols (32,000) Cat Mss Maps Pix Phonorecords Audiotapes Microforms
Notes: Incl material about Society of Friends from inception in England, 1650, to the present. Formats incl periodicals, diaries, documents of individual Friends, families, Quaker Meetings and institutions, incl archives of Haverford College. Emphases on American Indians, antislavery, women, minorities, the Rufus M Jones Mysticism collection, Quaker fiction, and Delaware Valley, Pennsylvania.

PA —HISTORICAL SOCIETY OF PENNSYLVANIA, Library, 1300 Locust St, Philadelphia, 19107. David Fraser, Librn
Holdings: Vols (230,000) Mss Maps Pix Microforms
Notes: Incl over 14,000,000 ms pieces. The Library Company of Philadelphia mss are on deposit with the Historical Society of Pennsylvania. Many of the Society's rare books are on deposit with the Library Company. The Society maintains the collections of the Genealogical Society of Pennsylvania, incl some 20,000 printed genealogies, original mss, family, church, and civil records.

PA —FRIENDS HISTORICAL LIBRARY OF SWARTHMORE COLLEGE, Swarthmore, 19081. J William Frost, Dir
Holdings: Vols (35,000) Cat Mss Maps Pix Slides Phonorecords Audiotapes Microforms
Notes: Library's collections contain information on the history and doctrine of the Society of Friends, Quaker contributions to literature, science, business, education, and government, plus their reform efforts in peace, Indian rights, women's rights, and abolition of slavery. As an official depository of the records of Philadelphia and Baltimore Yearly Meetings, the library holds either in the original mss or on microfilm the largest collection in the world of Quaker meeting archives, incl some records of Ohio and Illinois Yearly Meetings (Hicksite), and microfilm copies of minutes and registers of many meetings in New England, New York, North Carolina, Indiana, and Great Britain. Among the more than 250 mss collections are papers of individual Quaker leaders, families, and organizations.

WI —UNIVERSITY OF WISCONSIN, MADISON, Memorial Library, Western European Humanities Collection, 728 State St, Madison, 53706. Charles Szabo, Bibliographer
Notes: Tank Collection. The core of this extensive collection is its works on theology, the largest portion of which deals with Calvinsim. Practically all the printed sermons of the major Calvinist preachers of the 18th century are represented. Includes many 16th and 17th century sermons. About a third of the collection deals with Church history; not only are Calvinist histories represented but also 18th century histories of Methodists, Quakers, and Moravians. Supplements the Montauban Collection (French Protestantism) and the Chwalibog Collection (theology).

FRIENDS OF BEMERTON

NC —UNIVERSITY OF NORTH CAROLINA, GREENSBORO, Walter Clinton Jackson Library, Special Collections Dept, 1000 Spring Garden St, Greensboro, 27412. Emilie W Mills, Librn
Holdings: Vols (100) Cat Pix Microforms
Notes: Items issued by the Friends of Bemerton.

FRIENDS OF IRISH FREEDOM

NY —AMERICAN IRISH HISTORICAL SOCIETY, Library, 991 Fifth Ave, New York, 10028. Lisa M Hottin, Cur; William D Griffin, Librn
Holdings: Vols (20,000) Cat Maps Pix Slides
Notes: Archives and Manuscripts: The documents and papers of Friends of Irish Freedom, The Land League, the Society of the Friendly Sons of St Patrick, the Catholic Club, and the Guild of Catholic Lawyers. The papers of New York State Supreme Court Justice Daniel F Cohalan. This is the largest and most complete collection of over 20,000 American Irish and Irish history, biography and literature in the United States. Incl American-Irish Newspaper collections dating from 1811, the most comprehensive in the US; 1000 rare books and special editions. Special collections incl regular exhibits of Irish or American Irish interest incl mss, letters, books, photographs and memorabilia. Permanent collection of representative works of Irish painters.

FRIER, THOMAS AND DELLA

AZ —NORTHERN ARIZONA UNIVERSITY, Special Collection Library, CU Box 6022, Flagstaff, 86011. Peter M Whiteley, Coordr/Archivist; William Mullane, Librn
Notes: Scrapbooks especially good for Flagstaff and Northern Arizona history. Incl materials on the development of the Flagstaff Cemetery and an account of the 1911 Hopi Snake Dance attended by Teddy Roosevelt. The Friers were ranchers from Marshall Lake and Verde Valley, Ariz. Inventory available (3 feet).

FRIES, WALDEMAR HANS, 1889-

NY —CORNELL UNIVERSITY LIBRARIES, Collection of Regional History, Dept of Manuscripts and Univ Archives, Ithaca, 14853.
Notes: Audubon Research Papers, 1805-1974; 17 ft.

FRIESIAN LANGUAGE AND LITERATURE

CA —UNIVERSITY OF CALIFORNIA, BERKELEY, University Library, Germanic

FRIESIAN LANGUAGE AND LITERATURE (cont.)

Collections, 208 Main Library, Berkeley, 94720.
Holdings: Vols 1500 Cat Maps
Notes: Major strength in Friesian philology. Incl the significant Friesian collections of Otto Bremer and Konrad Burdach.

†CA —UNIVERSITY OF CALIFORNIA, LOS ANGELES, Research Library, Germanic Dept, 405 Hilgard Ave, Los Angeles, 90024. Edward Shreeves, Chairman, Bibliographers Group; Antonina Babb, Germanic Bibliographer

MA —HARVARD UNIVERSITY LIBRARY, Widener Library, Cambridge, 02138.
Holdings: Cat
Notes: See *Distributable Union Catalog* (Harvard).

NY —NEW YORK PUBLIC LIBRARY, Research Libraries, General Research Division, Fifth Ave & 42 St, New York, 10018. Rodney Phillips, Chief
Holdings: Vols (2,225,000) Cat Maps Pix Microforms
Budget: ($775,718)

FRIESS, HORACE

†NY —COLUMBIA UNIVERSITY LIBRARIES, Butler Library, Rare Book and Manuscript Library, 535 W 114 St, New York, 10027.
Notes: Papers, correspondence, etc.

FRILLMANN, PAUL WILLIAM, 1911-1972

CA —HOOVER INSTITUTION ON WAR, REVOLUTION & PEACE, Stanford University, Stanford, 94305. Milorad M Drachkovitch, Archivist
Notes: Papers of Paul W Frillmann, chaplain of the American Volunteer Group (Flying Tigers), 1941-45, and US Consular official in China and Hong Kong, 1946-50, incl correspondence, memoranda, orders, notes and photos, 1941-69, relating to activities of the American Volunteer Group in China during World War II, US foreign relations with China, 1946-50, and conditions in China during the civil war. 3 ms boxes, 3 framed certificates.

FRIML, RUDOLF

NY —NEW YORK PUBLIC LIBRARY, Performing Arts Research Center, Billy Rose Theatre Collection, 111 Amsterdam Ave, New York, 10023. Dorothy L Swerdlove, Cur
Holdings: Cat
Notes: Material relating to production of his operettas and musical comedies.

FRINGE BENEFITS

DC —US DEPT OF LABOR, Library, 200 Constitution Ave NW, Washington, 20210. Sabina Jacobson, Dir
Holdings: Vols (550,000) Cat

ON —CANADA DEPT OF LABOUR, Library, Ottawa, K1A 0J2, Can. Monique Marchand, Chief Librn
Holdings: Vols (100,000) Cat Microforms

FRISIAN LANGUAGE AND LITERATURE see Friesian Language and Literature

FRISSELL, TONI AND VARICK

DC —LIBRARY OF CONGRESS, Prints & Photographs Div, Washington, 20540.
Holdings: Pix
Notes: Her entire collection of photographs and negatives. Incl fashion photography and informal portraits of prominent figures. 270, 000 black and white negatives, 42,000 color transparencies, 25,000 enlargement prints, and proof sheets dating from 1935-71.

FRITZ, BERNADINE (SZOLD), ?-1982

CA —UNIVERSITY OF CALIFORNIA, LOS ANGELES, Research Library, Dept of Special Collections, 405 Hilgard Ave, Los Angeles, 90024. Edward Shreeves, Chairman, Bibliographers Group; David S Zeidberg, Head
Holdings: Mss
Notes: 3 linear feet of mss and letters from Henry Miller, Glenway Wescott, and others.

FROELICHER, HANS

MD —UNIVERSITY OF BALTIMORE, Langsdale Library, 1420 Maryland Ave, Baltimore, 21201. Gerry Watkins, Head of Special Collections Dept
Notes: Correspondence, mss, working files, news clippings of Hans Froelicher (1929-1977); 92 cubic feet.

FROESCHEL, GEORGE, 1891-1979

MA —BRANDEIS UNIVERSITY, Goldfarb Library, 415 South St, Waltham, 02154. Bessie Hahn, Dir
Notes: 27 linear ft of books and 30 linear ft of mss material, correspondence, photographs and memorabilia of this novelist and former Hollywood screen writer. The collection is unprocessed, spring 1984.

FROGMEN see Underwater Demolition Teams

FROHMAN, CHARLES E.

OH —RUTHERFORD B HAYES LIBRARY, 1337 Hayes Ave, Fremont, 43420. Watt P Marchman, Dir
Holdings: Vols 800 Cat Mss Maps Pix Microforms Newspapers
Notes: American history; northern Ohio; theatre. The collections are housed in the Hayes Index in the collections. (69 linear feet).

FROHMILLER, ANA COLLINS

AZ —NORTHERN ARIZONA UNIVERSITY, Special Collection Library, CU Box 6022, Flagstaff, 86011. Peter M Whiteley, Coordr/Archivist; William Mullane, Librn
Notes: Papers.

FROMM, BELLA

MA —BOSTON UNIVERSITY, Mugar Memorial Library, Special Collections Dept, 771 Commonwealth Ave, Boston, 02215. Howard B Gotlieb, Dir
Holdings: // Cat Mss Pix
Notes: Mss, correspondence, etc collected in depth; incl publications by or about.

FRONCZAK, FRANCIS E.

NY —STATE UNIVERSITY OF NEW YORK, COLLEGE AT BUFFALO, Library, The Francis E Fronczak Collection, Buffalo, 14222. Lucien E Palmieri, Head Collections Dept
Holdings: 1000 Vols
Notes: Collection of Buffalo's noted Polish-American, Francis E Fronczak.

FRONDE

MA —HARVARD UNIVERSITY LIBRARY, Cambridge, 02138.
Holdings: Cat

NY —NEW YORK PUBLIC LIBRARY, Research Libraries, General Research Division, Fifth Ave & 42 St, New York, 10018. Rodney Phillips, Chief
Holdings: Vols (2,225,000) Cat Maps Pix Microforms
Budget: ($775,718)

OH —CLEVELAND PUBLIC LIBRARY, History and Geography Department, 325 Superior Ave, Cleveland, 44114. JoAnn Petrello, Head
Holdings: Cat
Notes: Strong in Normandy, Britanny, Gascony. Nearly complete collection of historical memoirs (analyzed). Mazarinade collection. Contemporary political pamphlets of the period of the Fronde, 1648-1653 (about 2000 pamphlets). No photocopying.

FRONTIER AND PIONEER LIFE

AK —UNIVERSITY OF ALASKA, Elmer E Rasmuson Library, Fairbanks, 99701. Robert H Geiman, Dir
Holdings: Vols Cat Mss Maps Pix Slides Phonorecords Audiotapes Films Microforms
Notes: The Alaska Collection is strong in all disciplines concerning Alaska. Main strengths are exploration and travel, pioneer memoirs, and materials on Alaska natives. Bulk of collection is in English with significant holdings in Russian, Native American, and European languages. Archival holdings incl 6000 cu ft of mss, 110,000 historic photographs, 2319 tape recordings, 727 films and videotapes, 200 rare maps and 1273 microfilms. Ms collection strongest in political and economic areas. A Guide to the Collections is available in hard copy and microfiche. About 1000 special collections, some 300 quite significant.

AZ —NORTHERN ARIZONA UNIVERSITY, Special Collection Library, CU Box 6022, Flagstaff, 86011. Peter M Whiteley, Coordr/Archivist; William Mullane, Librn
Holdings: Cat Mss Maps Pix Slides Audiotapes Microforms
Notes: Northern Arizona history and Arizona economic history. Depository of Forest History Society of America; custodian for Northern Arizona Pioneers Historical Society Manuscript Collection. Also, Arizona newspapers and periodicals. Also, William J Floyd Collection. Floyd was surgeon of E F Beale's wagon road expedition from Ft Smith Arkansas to the Colorado River; incl diary, 1858-1859. Original in Henry E Huntington Library.

AZ —FORT HUACHUCA HISTORICAL ASSOCIATION, Fort Huachuca, 85705. James P Finley, Dir
Holdings: Cat Mss Maps Pix Slides Microforms
Notes: Voluminous collection of documents concerning Fort Huachuca, southeastern Arizona, Indians, pioneer settlements, and military history. About 50,000 manuscript pieces and documents.

AZ —ARIZONA HERITAGE CENTER, Library, 949 E Second St, Tucson, 85719. Michael Weber, Dir
Notes: Espec with reference to Arizona, the West, and the Southwest.

CA —AZUSA PACIFIC COLLEGE, Marshburn Memorial Library, Citrus & Alosta, Azusa, 91702. Edward Peterman, Librn
Holdings: Vols (6000) Uncat
Budget: ($30,000)
Notes: Significant holidngs in the George E Fullerton Library of California, and Western Americana.

CA —UNIVERSITY OF CALIFORNIA, BERKELEY, Bancroft Library, Manuscripts Division, Berkeley, 94720. James D Hart, Dir
Holdings: Vols Mss Maps Pix Slides Microforms
Notes: Approxi. twelve million pieces, with primary emphasis on California, with a lesser emphasis on the other Pacific States, incl. Alaska and the Province of British Columbia. In general, the Bancroft Library seeks to acquire historical and biographical works and primary source materials, documenting: the development of a geographic area or political unit; man and his activities, and his impact on the land and on his institutions. Methodological and theoretical work and texts in the physical and biological sciences are not collected, as a rule; exceptions here are

FRONTIER AND PIONEER LIFE (cont.)

publications essential to the study of an area's historical development and those providing general background information. Hubert Howe Bancroft's own distinguished holdings, assembled 1860-1880, constitute the core of the collection. The Bancroft Library's collections are noncirculating. A. G. K. Hall catalog has been published. The Bolton Collection (146,000 pages of archival material) contains ms. materials for the history of the Pacific Coast and the Southwest, gathered by Herbert Eugene Bolton. There is a comprehensive key to the arrangement of the collection.

CA —CLAREMONT COLLEGES, Ella Strong Denison Library, Scripps College, Claremont, 91711. Judy Harvey Sahak, Librn
Holdings: Vols (2000) Cat Mss Pix
Notes: Ida Rust Macpherson Collection centers on the humanistic accomplishments of women, suffrage and emancipation, domestic economy, and women in the Westward movement. Provides historical materials for the contemporary women's movement.

CA —UNIVERSITY OF SOUTHERN CALIFORNIA, School of Medicine, Norris Medical Library, 2025 Zonal Ave, Los Angeles, 90033. Nelson J Gilman, Librn
Notes: The Collection of American Indian Ethnopharmacology.

CO —COLORADO HISTORICAL SOCIETY, Research Collections, 1300 Broadway, Denver, 80203. Catherine Kane, Head Public Service and Access
Holdings: Cat Pix Slides
Budget:
Notes: 250,000 photographs of western and Colorado subjects incl gold rush, mining, Indians, natural features, transportation, cities and towns, portraits. William Henry Jackson photographs of area west of Mississippi.

CO —DENVER PUBLIC LIBRARY, Western History Department, 1357 Broadway, Denver, 80203. Eleanor M Gehres, Head
Holdings: Vols (50,000) Cat Mss Maps Pix Audiotapes Microforms
Notes: Western US History. The department has a separate catalog, published in 1970 in 7 vols by G K Hall Co. First supplement published in 1975 in 1 vol. There is a subject index of some 3 million entries to newspapers and magazines of the Rocky Mountain region, added to daily. The Western Newspaper Microfilm Center contains approx 7000 reels of Western US newspapers. Collection has ca 275,000 negatives and prints of Western life; and ca 2500 maps, cataloged and classified.

CO —COLORADO STATE UNIVERSITY, Libraries, Fort Collins, 80523. John Newman, Special Collections Librn
Holdings: Vols (11,000) Cat Mss Pix
Notes: The Western American Literature Collection incl fiction, poetry, pictures, art, and other works of the imagination set in the American Frontier West and modern rural West, especially the Rocky Mountain Area.

CT —YALE UNIVERSITY, Box 1603A, Yale Station, New Haven, 06520.

GA —AGNES SCOTT COLLEGE, McCain Library, E College Ave, Decatur, 30030. Judith Bourgeois Jensen, Librn
Holdings: Vols (945) Uncat
Budget: $300
Notes: The Frontier Religion Collection, which was given by Prof Walter Brownlow Posey, traces the effects of slavery on religion in the Old South Frontier prior to 1860. A Catalog file (by author entry only) accompanies the collection at present. Noncirculating.

IL —NEWBERRY LIBRARY, 60 W Walton St, Chicago, 60610. Diana Haskell, Cur of Modern Mss
Holdings: Cat
Notes: Incl the Everett D Graff Collection, the E E Ayer Collection.

IL —NORTHERN ILLINOIS UNIVERSITY, Founders Memorial Library, Rare Books and Special Collections Dept, De Kalb, 60115. William R DuBois, Dept Head
Holdings: Vols (1000) Cat Maps Pix
Notes: Collection deals with all aspects of Colorado: early travel narratives, history, literature, geology, ecology, maps and some bibliography.

IL —KNOX COLLEGE, Henry M Seymour Library, Galesburg, 61401. Douglas L Wilson, Dir
Holdings: Vols 4780 Cat Mss Maps Pix
Notes: Special emphasis on the earliest European contacts in the upper Mississippi, early settlement in Illinois.

IN —INDIANA UNIVERSITY, Lilly Library, Seventh St, Bloomington, 47405. William R Cagle, Librn
Holdings: / / Cat Mss Maps
Notes: Description and travel of the US Plains and Rockies; overland accounts; issues of California newspapers of the gold rush era, etc.

KS —UNIVERSITY OF KANSAS, Kenneth Spencer Research Library, Kansas Collection, Lawrence, 66045. Sheryl K Williams, Cur
Holdings: Vols (92,000) Cat Mss Maps Pix
Notes: All aspects of the American West and trans-Mississippi history, especially Kansas and the Plains region. Overland diaries, cartographic history, Indians, emigration and immigration, printing history, cattle industry, agriculture and farm life, conservation are some special interests, in addition to the usual political, economic, military and social interests.

KY —UNIVERSITY OF KENTUCKY, Margaret I King Library, Dept of Special Collections, Lexington, 40506. William Marshall, Head
Holdings: Cat Mss Maps Pix Microforms
Notes: Kentucky history and travel. Incl the Samuel M Wilson Library, Kentucky imprints, Kentucky authors, biography and autography, regional history (Ohio Valley), Kentucky maps. Also sheet music, clippings, etc.

MA —AMERICAN ANTIQUARIAN SOCIETY LIBRARY, 185 Salisbury St, Worcester, 01609. Marcus A McCorison, Dir & Librn
Holdings: Vols 1500 Cat
Notes: Narratives especially. Incl the Donald McKay Frost Collection.

MI —EDISON INSTITUTE, Greenfield Village and Henry Ford Museum, Archives & Research Library, PO Box 1970, Dearborn, 48121. Steve Hamp, Dir; Joan W Gartland, Librn
Holdings: Vols 400,000 Cat Mss Maps Microforms
Notes: 400,000 vols incl pamphlets. The Archives and research library supports the program of Greenfield Village and the Henry Ford Museum. Special collections incl: automotive literature, ephemera, McGuffey Readers, trade catalogs, photographs and graphics.

MN —BROWN COUNTY HISTORICAL SOCIETY, Museum and Archives, Center St and Broadway, Box 116, New Ulm, 56073. Paul Klammer, Dir
Holdings: Vols (250) Mss Maps Pix Slides Phonorecords Audiotapes Videotapes 16mm Films Filmstrips Microforms
Notes: History of Brown County, Minn. Also have *Historical Files,* about 500 pieces in vertical files incl newspaper clippings, advertising, letterheads, etc, pertaining to Brown County businesses, industry, schools, governmental units, etc. *Family Files,* about 2500 pioneer families. Files incl obituaries, pictures, documents, letters, etc. Also collection on Siouan Uprising of 1862-clippings, copies of treaties, letters, etc (65 vols, 10 mss, 25 maps, 40 pix, 50 slides).

MN —MINNESOTA HISTORICAL SOCIETY LIBRARY, 690 Cedar St, Saint Paul, 55101. Patricia C Harpole, Chief of Reference Library; Bonnie G Wilson, Head of Special Libraries
Notes: Interviews with early builders of Minnesota on a wide range of subjects.

MO —SAINT LOUIS PUBLIC LIBRARY, Gardner Rare Book Room, 1301 Olive St, Saint Louis, 63103. Julanne M Good, Supervisor; Martha Riley, Rare Books Librn
Holdings: Vols 100 Cat Maps
Budget: ($5573)
Notes: Small growing collection of travels incl St Louis or Missouri, largely transferred from the general stacks, although an occasional purchase is made. Incl early business directories of St Louis, river pilots' handbooks and maps. Noncirculating.

MO —WASHINGTON UNIVERSITY, John M Olin Library, Campus Box 1061, St Louis, 63130.
Holdings: Vols (1800) Cat Mss
Notes: Incl material from the Arthur C Hoskins, Richard S Hawes, Ernst C Krohn, George N Meissner, Stratford Lee Morton, and Edgar M Queeny collections; strong in early travel literature of the US and Latin America; accounts of exploration in the Mississippi Valley and Trans-Mississippi West; miscellaneous accounts of history, pioneer life, and travel in the Ohio Valley, Old Southwest, and California; material on the American Indian; 18th century American music; early American imprints.

MT —MONTANA HISTORICAL SOCIETY LIBRARY, 225 N Roberts St, Helena, 59601. Robert M Clark, Librn; Brian Cockhill, State Archivist
Holdings: Vols 3000 Cat
Budget: ($2500)
Notes: The Ames and Margaret Booth Teakel Range Life Memorial Collection (cowboy and cattle range subjects). The scope of this collection includes the entire West, not just Montana and contiguous states. Also, L A Huffman Collection; incl 1100 photographs.

NE —NEBRASKA STATE HISTORICAL SOCIETY, Fort Robinson Museum, Box 304, Crawford, 69339. Vance Nelson, Cur
Holdings: Vols (1500) Cat Mss Maps Pix Slides Phonorecords Audiotapes 16mm Films Microforms
Notes: Materials related to the history of Fort Robinson, and incl the Post Medical Library, reference books on state government, etc, Western Americana: books on ranching, homesteaders, Indian wars, etc; microfilm records for Fort Robinson records, Red Cloud and Spotted Tail Indian Agency records, Crawford and Chadron, Nebraska newspapers, diaries and interviews. Library incl the E Kopac Collection of books dealing with Western Americana; particularly Indian wars, transportation, guns and railroads.

NE —UNIVERSITY OF NEBRASKA-LINCOLN, Don L Love Library, University Archives and Special Collections, Lincoln, 68588. Joseph G Svoboda, University Archivist
Notes: R D Warden Collection of Charles Marion Russell: Largest private collection of literature on Russell, The Cowboy Artist. 7000 items, incl first editions of every book and pamphlet by Russell and over 1000 periodical appearances of his art; 900 color prints; 142 drawings; color slides; scrapbooks about Russell and his family, from 1889. The Mari Sandoz Collection: (1) Correspondence files, 25,000 letters in all, including letters received from 1925 on and carbon copies of letters sent. The correspondence files are a rich source of information about the author's life and career, creative writing, and Plains Indian and western American history. (2) Author's personal library of books and periodicals, many annotated.(3) Author's published works, including most of the editions foreign and domestic and some unpublished manuscripts as well. Many of the early drafts of books, copy-edited manuscripts, and galley and page proofs are also contained in this portion of the collection. (4) Author's resource files, research files, research and reading notes, clippings, and related materials. These materials fill over fifty standard letter boxes. In addition, the author prepared 45,000 index cards referring to information contained both in and out of the collection. Finding aid available.

NV —UNIVERSITY OF NEVADA, RENO, University Library, Special Collections Dept, Reno, 89557. Robert E Blesse, Head
Holdings: Vols 800 Cat
Notes: The Women in the West Collection

FRONTIER AND PIONEER LIFE (cont.)

contains materials which document experience of women in the trans-Mississippi West. Major emphasis is on first-hand experience, diaries, letters and autobiographies, but major biographies of women who were prominent or greatly influenced others are also collected. Emphasis is the 19th and 20th centuries.

NM —NEW MEXICO HIGHLANDS UNIVERSITY, Donnelly Library, National Ave, Las Vegas, 87701. Karen Jaggers, Assoc Librn
Holdings: Vols (5000) Cat Mss Maps Pix Microforms
Notes: The outstanding collection is the Arrott Collection on Fort Union, New Mexico, 1851-1891.

NY —MUSEUM OF THE AMERICAN INDIAN, Library, 9 Westchester Square, Bronx, 10401. Mary B Davis, Librn
Holdings: Vols (40,000) Cat Mss Maps Pix Microforms VF
Notes: Collections cover all aspects of the Indians of the Western Hemisphere; some materials on Eskimos. For scholarly research only.

NY —NEW YORK HISTORICAL SOCIETY, Library, 170 Central Park W, New York, 10024. James Gregory, Librn
Holdings: Mss
Notes: Incl original mss, illustrative materials, etc.

NY —NEW YORK PUBLIC LIBRARY, Research Libraries, American History Div, Fifth Ave & 42 St, New York, 10018.
Holdings: Vols (14,000) Cat
Notes: Outstanding collection of material on the Old West, incl early settlement, the lawless era, and the resulting vigilantism.

ND —NORTH DAKOTA STATE UNIVERSITY, Library, Fargo, 58105. John E Bye, Archivist
Holdings: Vols (2500) Cat Mss Maps Pix
Budget: ($14,000)
Notes: The Collection is administered by the North Dakota Institute for Regional Studies. It contains materials on North Dakota history, especially the Red River Valley, with emphasis on bonanza farming, pioneer life, agriculture, local history, literary figures, business, Fargo, ND, and some political collections, particularly of the Nonpartisan League. Also, there is an extensive photographic collection covering the pioneer to post-World War I period and includes the "Hultstrand 'History in Pictures' Collection" of sod houses, pioneer life and farming. For the small collections, there has been published, *Guide to the Small Collection Manuscripts of the North Dakota Institute for Regional Studies,* by John E Bye, 1977.

ND —UNIVERSITY OF NORTH DAKOTA, Chester Fritz Library, Dept of Special Collections, Grand Forks, 58202. Daniel F Rylance, Special Collections Coordr
Holdings: Vols (5500) Uncat Mss Maps Pix Microforms
Budget: ($2500)
Notes: Also the Orin G Libby Manuscript Collection (900 collections), and the Aandahl Collection of Western History on North Dakota and the Northern Great Plains. Emphasis on agriculture, politics, pioneering, Germans from Russia, etc. Guides to the collections available from the Coordinator of Special Collections.

ND —THEODORE ROOSEVELT NATIONAL PARK, Library, PO Box 7, Medora, 58645. Susan Snow, Librn; Miki Hellickson, Chief Naturalist
Holdings: Vols (1500) Cat Mss Maps Pix Slides Audiotapes 16mm Films
Budget: ($5000)
Notes: Theodore Roosevelt, cattle county history, natural history. Also 2400 pictures and 2200 slides.

OH —OHIO HISTORICAL SOCIETY, Archives Library Division, 1982 Velma Ave, Columbus, 43211. Dennis East, Division Chief
Holdings: Vols (96,000) Cat Mss Maps Pix Slides Microforms
Budget: ($18,000)
Notes: This library is the primary collection for Ohio. Most purchases are on the rare and op market. Collecting area is early American history, esp relating to exploration into the Northwest Territory, Major subject areas are Ohio politics and government (8 presidents) military history (good collection of regimental histories and Ohio narratives of the Civil War), economic and social history, local history, esp county histories & atlases and city directories. Also, Ohio archaeology, natural history, artifacts. Major media collections are books (96,000), newspapers (25,000 vols and 22,000 microfilm), pictures (50,000), maps (2500), manuscripts (1,500,000). Library is noncirculating except through interlibrary loan of microfilm.

OH —FLESH PUBLIC LIBRARY, 124 W Greene St, Piqua, 45356. Wallace White, Librn
Holdings: Vols (1400) // Cat Maps
Notes: The Jerome C Smiley Collection.

OK —UNIVERSITY OF OKLAHOMA, Bizzell Memorial Library, Western History Collections, 401 W Brooks, Norman, 73069. John Ezell, Cur
Holdings: Cat Mss Maps Pix Microforms

OK —OKLAHOMA DEPT OF LIBRARIES, Law Library, 109 State Capital, Oklahoma City, 73105. Robert Clark, Dir; Betty Brown, Okla Collection Librn; Virginia Collier, US Documents; Jan Blakely, State Documents; Blane Dessy, Library Science
Holdings: Vols 18,000 Cat
Notes: Noncirculating.

OK —THOMAS GILCREASE INSTITUTE OF AMERICAN HISTORY & ART LIBRARY, 1400 North 25th West Ave, Tulsa, 74127. Sarah Hirsch, Librn
Holdings: Vols Cat Mss Maps Pix
Notes: Trans-Mississippi West, US, Indian and Hispanic history. The Gilcrease Library contains a total of about 40,000 mss; 10,000 imprints; 5000 photographs; 600 maps and 50,000 vols.

OR —COLLIER STATE PARK LOGGING MUSEUM LIBRARY, PO Box 428, Klamath Falls, 97601. Alfred D Collier, Cur; Lowell N Jones, Asst Cur
Holdings: Uncat Mss Maps Pix Slides
Notes: 600 pieces of equipment showing evolution of logging. 800 pictures of logging. 15 pioneer log cabins. 500 Indian Stone artifacts. Collection of cruisers marks and sleighs.

PA —UNIVERSITY OF PENNSYLVANIA, Van Pelt Library, Rare Books Collection, 34 & Walnut Sts, Philadelphia, 19104. Daniel Traister, Special Collections Librn
Holdings: Vols 2500 //
Notes: Robert Dechert Collection: early exploration, 17th and 18th centuries; western Americana, 19th century; Canadiana, incl Jesuit relations.

PA —WASHINGTON AND JEFFERSON COLLEGE, Library, Washington, 15301. Robert E Connell, Librn
Holdings: Vols 2100 Cat Mss Maps Pix
Notes: A general subject and author card catalog has been prepared for the ms collection. Published description of the collection appears in: Pennsylvania, Historical and Museum Commission, *Historical Manuscript Depositories in* Pennsylvania (Harrisburg, 1965), compiled by Irwin Richman. Incl are materials concerning the "Westward movement"--letters, land grants, etc. Much on the Revolutionary War, the "Whiskey Rebellion" of 1794. Many other small collections of mss, some containing American Indian and Western Pennsylvania history.

RI —BROWN UNIVERSITY, John Hay Library, 20 Prospect St, Providence, 02912. Mark N Brown, Cur Mss
Holdings: Vols 350 // Uncat
Notes: Eberstadt Collection of Narratives of California Pioneers. Personal narratives written by pioneers who crossed the Plains to California after the discovery of gold in 1849. A large portion of the books were printed in late 19th and early 20th centuries and deal with: Indian contacts, captivities, frontier lore, travel routes, topography, fauna and flora, outlaws, traders and trappers, and frontier army life. Also a collection of 111 printed proclamations of treaties with various Indian tribes, primarily in Florida and the Midwest from 1833-1868.

SD —AUGUSTANA COLLEGE, Mikkelsen Library & Learning Resource Center, Center for Western Studies, Sioux Falls, 57197. Ronelle Thompson, Dir Library
Notes: The Center for Western Studies, located in the Mikkelsen Library, is an archival and research agency of Augustana College. Dedicated to the history and culture of the Great Plains and the Trans-Mississippi West, the Center collects and preserves materials relating to Plains Indians, immigrant settlers, Norwegiana, Western Americana, Herbert Krause, Frederick Manfred, Donald Parker, Richard F Pettigrew, Augustana College, the Episcopal Diocese of South Dakota, the South Dakota District of the American Lutheran Church, the South Dakota Penitentiary and Minnehaha County.

SD —W H OVER MUSEUM, 414 E Clark, University of South Dakota, Vermillion, 57069. Julia Vodicka, Dir
Holdings: Cat Pix
Notes: The Stanley J Morrow Collection of Stereographs: frontier military posts, Indians, riverboats, pioneer life in Dakota Territory. The 440 stereographs of this collection were made in Dakota Territory and the Upper Missouri region between 1868 and 1883 by Stanley J Morrow, Yankton, D T Copy photographs may be ordered. The collection is described in Wesley Hurt's *Stanley J Morrow: Pioneer Photographer.*

TX —AMARILLO PUBLIC LIBRARY, 413 E Fourth, Amarillo, 79101. Mary Kay Snell, Librn
Holdings: Vols Cat Mss Maps Pix
Notes: The southwest collections incl materials on the history of Texas, Louisiana, New Mexico, Arkansas, Missouri and Kansas. General subjects covered incl overland journeys, early narratives, early biographies, Indian captivities, outlaws, US government reports, Mississippi and Ohio Rivers, the Mexican War, reports of Catholic missionaries, Niles Register, early publications, fur trade, western trails, Texas Rangers, sheriffs and Texas as a sovereign state, buffalo hunting, Indian wars, cowboys, the arrival of farmers, fences, and towns. Over 1600 items which incl books, documents, maps, mss, pamphlets, unpublished theses, interviews and photographs. The three major collections are the William Henry Bush Collection, the Laurence J Fitzsimon Collection and the Calendar of John L McCarty.

TX —UNIVERSITY OF TEXAS LIBRARIES, General Libraries, Barker Texas History Center, PO Box P, Austin, 78712. Don Carleton, Dir
Holdings: Vols (132,000) Cat Mss Maps Pix Slides Phonorecords Audiotapes Microforms
Notes: See description of collection under Texas-History.

TX —PANHANDLE-PLAINS HISTORICAL MUSEUM, Research Center, Box 967, WT Sta, Canyon, 79016. Claire R Kuehn, Archivist-Librn
Holdings: Vols 8000 Cat Mss Maps Pix Microforms
Budget: $2000
Notes: History of the Texas Panhandle. Incl interviews with early settlers taken over a 50-year period, ranch records, and business records relating to the Texas Panhandle and surrounding states.

TX —TEXAS A&M UNIVERSITY, Sterling C Evans Library, Special Collections Div, College Station, 77843. Donald H Dyal, Librn
Holdings: Vols (16,000) Mss Pix
Notes: Jeff Dykes Range Livestock Collection (incl a 600-item collection of J Frank Dobie Works). Part of the Dobie Collection is described in Dykes, Jeff C *My Dobie Collection* (College Station, Tex: Friends of the Texas A & M University Library).

TX —SOUTHERN METHODIST UNIVERSITY, DeGolyer Library, Box 396, SMU, Dallas, 75275. Clifton H Jones, Dir
Holdings: Vols 50,000 Cat Mss Maps Pix
Notes: History of the trans-Mississippi West

FRONTIER AND PIONEER LIFE (cont.)

and Mexico, from discovery to present. Original editions of most of the important early collections of travels.

TX —LUBBOCK CITY-COUNTY LIBRARY, 1306 Ninth St, Lubbock, 79401. Marlene M Harp, Dir, Adult Services
Holdings: Vols (10,000) Mss Microforms
Notes: Emphasis on the South and the various immigration routes used by settlers or their descendents from the Virginia-Georgia coast to west Texas. Very few periodical holdings prior to 1955. Material is not available for circulation or interlibrary loan.

TX —STEPHEN F AUSTIN STATE UNIVERSITY, Ralph W Steen Library, Special Collections Dept, Box 13055, SFA Sta, Nacogdoches, 75962. Linda Cheves Nicklas, Special Collections Librn
Holdings: Vols (13,500) Cat Mss Maps Pix
Budget: ($5000)
Notes: Emphasis on local and university-related subjects, especially people, culture, events, buildings of Texas, East Texas, and historic Nacogdoches. Extensive ms collection (1200 linear ft); 344 maps; 1600 pictures. Published description: SFASU, *A Guide to Special Collections,* 1980.

TX —RAILROAD & PIONEER MUSEUM, Library, 710 Jack Baskin St, PO Box 5126, Temple, 76501. Mary Pat McLaughlin, Dir
Holdings: Uncat Mss Maps Pix Slides Phonorecords Audiotapes 16mm Films
Notes: Temple Area History.

UT —PROVO CITY PUBLIC LIBRARY, 13 N 100 E, Provo, 84601. Larry Hortin, Dir
Holdings: Vols (600) Cat
Notes: Western states history with emphasis on Utah State and Utah County.

UT —UNIVERSITY OF UTAH, Marriott Library, Special Collections, Salt Lake City, 84112. Gregory C Thompson, Cur
Notes: Exploration of the West.

WA —WESTERN WASHINGTON UNIVERSITY, Center for Pacific Northwest Studies, High St, Bellingham, 98225. James W Scott, Dir
Holdings: Cat Mss Maps Pix
Notes: The Percival R Jeffcott Collection of Local History is particularly rich in photographic materials, incl about 1800 negatives and about 1100 photographs, which deal with pioneer settlement and economic and cultural developments in Whatcom County, Washington, and a few adjacent areas, such as the Lower Mainland of British Columbia to the north and neighboring counties of Washington to the south and west. Incl also ms versions of Jeffcott's published works: *Nooksack Tales and Trails, Chechaco and Sourdough* and *Blanket Bill Jarman* and numerous unpublished papers and workbooks. A small collection of Jeffcott materials is housed in the Washington State Historical Society, Tacoma, and for this there is an unpublished inventory. An inventory of the present collection is being prepared for publication by the Center for Pacific Northwest Studies.

†WA —WASHINGTON STATE UNIVERSITY, Library, Manuscripts, Archives & Special Collections, Pullman, 99164. John F Guido, Head
Holdings: Cat Mss Maps Pix
Notes: Three collections: (1) The Carl Parcher Russell papers, a vast resource (24, 916 items; 45 linear feet) on American Indian and Western pioneer activities and artifacts. Much on the fur trade; pioneer life; mountain men and trapping; wildlife; primitive life in detail. Also the National Park Service, parks, monuments, etc. Described in *Carl Parcher Russell: An Indexed Register of His Scholarly and Professional Papers, 1920-1967, in the Washington State University Library* (Pullman, 1970), 140 pp. (2) The manuscript collection incl business and financial records of banks, breweries, fisheries, insurance, land, lumber and livestock companies, trade and commodity associations; as well as the personal and professional papers of authors, aviators, educators, engineers, farmers, historians, pioneers, politicians and scientists; especially rich indocuments relating to the exploration, settlement and development of the Palouse Country, the Inland Empire, the Columbia Basin and the Pacific Northwest. Described in *Selected Manuscuript Resources in the Washington State University Library* (Pullman, 1974); and other published and unpublished inventories and registers. (3) Papers, 1821-1873, covering Father De Smet's early sojourns at Whitemarsh and St Louis, his founding of the Rocky Mountain Missions, his long service as Procurator and Socius of the Missouri Province, and his many travels. Correspondence with his family in Belgium, mss of his published journals, 2 small maps, sketches and engravings used to illustrate his books. Incl about 100 small pencil sketches by Father Nicholas Point depicting the 1841 journey from Westport to St Mary's Mission in the Bitterroot Valley. Described in *The* Record, 30(1969) 6-40; and 32 (1971) 47-63.

AB —PETER WHYTE FOUNDATION, Archives of the Canadian Rockies, Box 160, Banff, T0L 0C0, Can. Mary Andrews, ACR Librn
Holdings: Vols (4247) Cat Mss Maps Pix Slides Phonorecords Audiotapes Videotapes 16mm Films Filmstrips Microforms
Budget: ($1500)
Notes: Collect all available material which touches on the Rocky Mountains of Canada (from the US border to the Peace River in the north; from west of Cagary on the east to the town of Revelstoke, BC on the west). This material incl history (the early explorers Indians, construction of the railroads, mountaineering, and development of the national parks), natural history (geology, botany, wildlife) and poetry and fiction with the Rockies as a setting. Collect maps of the area, photographs, tape recordings of the pioneers. We also house on our premises the Alpine Club of Canada's library, which is one of the most comprehensive collections on the subject of mountaineering worldwide. Noncirculating.

MB —UNIVERSITY OF MANITOBA, Elizabeth Dafoe Library, Archives and Special Collections Dept, Winnipeg, R3T 2N2, Can. Richard E Bennett, Dept Head; Corrado A Santoro, Reference Archivist
Notes: Photographs of western prairie Canada as collected by Heather Robertson from archives and museums across Canada for use in her book *Salt from the Earth.* Pictures are between 1880-1915, showing such things as immigrant families, farms, towns and city life on the prairies, churches, schools, railroads, homestead residences and other aspects of life in the developing Canadian West.

ON —FORT MALDEN NATIONAL HISTORIC PARK, Library, 100 Laird Ave, Box 38, Amherstburg, N9V 2Z2, Can. Sally E Snyder, Librn
Holdings: Vols 300 Cat

ON —QUEEN'S UNIVERSITY, Douglas Library, Kingston, K7L 5C4, Can. William F E Morley, Cur, Special Collections
Holdings: Vols (50,000) Cat Mss Maps Pix Microforms
Budget: ($12,000)
Notes: The Edith and Lorne Pierce Collection of Canadiana. Also over 15,000 titles in Canadian Pamphlet Collection. Strong in humanities and social sciences, special strength in English and French Canadian literature; discovery and exploration narratives; Loyalists; War of 1812; opening of the West; local history, 19th century pamphlets and association items. Described in *A Catalogue of Canadian Manuscripts Collected by Lorne Pierce and Presented to Queen's University* (Toronto: Ryerson, 1946); and in *Canadiana 1698-1900 in the Possession of the Douglas* Library, comp by Janet S Porteous, foreword by Lorne Pierce (Kingston, 1932). Also later books and articles on parts of the collection.

FRONTIER AND PIONEER LIFE—CALIFORNIA

CA —LONG BEACH PUBLIC LIBRARY, Historic Sites Section, Rancho Los Cerritos, 4600 Virginia Rd, Long Beach, 90807. Ellen Calomiris, Historical Cur
Holdings: Vols (3000) Cat Mss Maps Pix Audiotapes
Budget: $1000
Notes: Emphasis on rancho, Long Beach, and Southern California history; incl materials on the westward movement. Incl 250 maps and 3000 pictures. Additional historic site: Rancho Los Alamitos, 6400 Bixby Hill Rd, Long Beach, Calif, 90815.

FRONTIER AND PIONEER LIFE—PICTURES, ILLUSTRATIONS, ETC.

DC —LIBRARY OF CONGRESS, Prints & Photographs Div, Washington, 20540.
Notes: The John C H Grabill collection of photographs of frontier life in Colorado, South Dakota, and Wyoming, late 19th century, incl views of hunters, prospectors, cowboys, Chinese immigrants, and US Army personnel.

FRONTIER SCIENCES

AZ —WORLD UNIVERSITY, Library, 711 E Blacklidge Dr, Tucson, 85719. Howard John Zitko, Cur
Holdings: Vols (15,000) Cat Mss Maps Audiotapes
Notes: Collection concerns what are generally called the "frontier sciences". No interlibrary loan.

IL —UNIVERSITY OF ILLINOIS, URBANA/CHAMPAIGN, Library, University Archives, 19 Library, 1408 W Gregory Drive, Urbana, 61801. Maynard Brichford, University Archivist
Holdings: Vols (5000) Cat
Budget: ($7000)
Notes: The Mandeville Collection in Parapsychology and Occult Sciences. Titles in the Merten J Mandeville Collection are purchased by funds from an endowment provided specifically for the collection on its establishment in 1966 by Merten J Mandeville, Professor Emeritus of Management, who donated 400 vols from his personal library as the nucleus of the collection. There are currently about 5000 titles in the collection, supplemented by related materials in the general collection. Topics include astrology, extrasensory perception, yoga, magic, satanism, faith healing, hypnosis, Eastern religions, witchcraft, fortune telling, reincarnation, flying saucers, ghosts, dreams, numerology, graphology, and mysticism. Biographies and reference books are a part of the collection as are journals devoted to the scientific study of parapsychology.

NJ —SOCIETY FOR THE INVESTIGATION OF THE UNEXPLAINED, Library, PO Box 265, Little Silver, 07739. Robert C Warth, Pres
Holdings: Mss Maps Pix Slides Videotapes
Notes: Information file of original material, map collection, and specialized library.

NC —FOUNDATION FOR RESEARCH ON THE NATURE OF MAN (FRNM), Institute for Parapsychology, 402 Buchanan Blvd, Box 6847, College Sta, Durham, 27708. K Ramakrishna Rao, Dir
Holdings: Vols (2500) Cat Mss Pix 16mm Films
Budget: ($12,000)
Notes: There is also a large body of early "psychical research" literature as well as most of the latest books in the field of parapsychology. Since the Foundation's activities are primarily devoted to the quantitative investigation of psi phenomena, the library in general does not stock books on occult topics (magic, witchcraft, astrology, etc).

OH —CLEVELAND PUBLIC LIBRARY, Fine Arts and Special Collections Department, 325 Superior Ave, Cleveland, 44114. Alice N Loranth, Head
Holdings: Vols (2500) Cat
Notes: Part of the Occult Sciences Collection. Emphasis is on historical treatises, folklore aspects and the classic

FRONTIER SCIENCES (cont.)

texts pertaining to apparitions, ghosts, divinations, oracles, omens, witchcraft, magic and sorcery in various civilizations. Astrology, palmistry, psychical research and contemporary manifestations are almost entirely omitted.
See also entries under Folklore; Occult Sciences.

VA —ASSOCIATION FOR RESEARCH & ENLIGHTENMENT, Library, 67 & Atlantic Avenue, PO Box 595, Virginia Beach, 23451. Stephen Jordan, Library Mgr
Holdings: Vols (1800) Cat
Notes: A R E Library Booklist incl 6000 items in 24 subject categories. This special collection is especially strong in the following subjects: astrology, spiritualism, reincarnation, healing arts, Theosophy, Atlantis, parapsychology and transpersonal psychology.

FRONTIERS see Boundaries

FROST, A.B.

PA —FREE LIBRARY OF PHILADELPHIA, Rare Book Dept, Logan Sq, Philadelphia, 19103. Marie E Korey, Rare Book Librn
Holdings: Vols (250) Uncat Mss Pix
Notes: The C Barton Brewster Collection, incl books, autograph letters and original art.

FROST, RICHARD

MA —BOSTON UNIVERSITY, Mugar Memorial Library, Special Collections Dept, 771 Commonwealth Ave, Boston, 02215. Howard B Gotlieb, Dir
Holdings: Cat Mss Correspondence

FROST, ROBERT

CA —UNIVERSITY OF CALIFORNIA, SANTA BARBARA, Library, Dept of Special Collections, Santa Barbara, 93106. Christian F Brun, Head
Notes: Collections of all major works.

CA —STANFORD UNIVERSITY LIBRARIES, Cecil H Green Library, Stanford, 94305. Michael T Ryan, Cur
Holdings: Vols Cat Mss
Notes: The Charlotte Ashley Felton Memorial Library. Incl first editions.

CT —TRINITY COLLEGE LIBRARY, Watkinson Library, 300 Summit St, Hartford, 06106. Jeffrey Kaimowitz, Cur
Holdings: Cat Mss Pix
Notes: Many first editions, some mss and letters. Incl the H Bacon Collamore Collection. A bibliography of the collection published in 1974.

CT —CONNECTICUT COLLEGE, Library, Mohegan Ave, New London, 06320. Brian Rogers, College Librn
Holdings: Vols (382,000) Mss
Notes: First editions. No photocopying.

DE —UNIVERSITY OF DELAWARE, Hugh M Morris Library, S College Ave, Newark, 19711. T Stuart Dick, Special Collections
Holdings: Cat
Notes: First, English, American and variant editions.

GA —AGNES SCOTT COLLEGE, McCain Library, E College Ave, Decatur, 30030. Judith Bourgeois Jensen, Librn
Holdings: Vols 600 Cat Mss Pix Slides Audiotapes Films
Notes: The Robert Frost Collection, developed by Edna Hanley Byers, contains works by and about the poet, incl over 100 first editions (several of these works are inscribed by Frost), 323 Christmas greeting cards privately printed by the poet, mss, letters, films, separate printings, etchings, translations, phonograph recordings, clippings, brochures, and memorabilia relating to Frost's association with Agnes Scott College. Restricted use: noncirculating. There is also a separate catalog to the collection. The collection's contents are largely described in *Robert Frost at Agnes Scott College* (a bibliography) compiled by Edna Hanley Byers (Decatur: McCain Library at Agnes Scott College, 1963), 75 pp.

IA —UNIVERSITY OF IOWA, University Libraries, Iowa City, 52242. Frank Paluka, Head, Special Collections Dept
Holdings: Vols 130 Cat
Notes: Collection was formed by James M Wallace of Bryn Mawr, Pennsylvania, and includes a few presentation items from Frost to Mr Wallace.

MD —JOHNS HOPKINS UNIVERSITY, Milton S Eisenhower Library, Charles & 34 Sts, Baltimore, 21218. Ann S Gwyn, Assistant Dir for Special Collections
Holdings: Vols Cat Mss

MA —AMHERST COLLEGE, Library, Amherst, 01002. John Lancaster, Special Collections Librn
Holdings: Vols 950 Cat Mss Pix Audiotapes

MA —JONES LIBRARY, 43 Amity St, Amherst, 01002. Daniel J Lombardo, Cur of Special Collections
Holdings: Vols 1200 Cat Mss Pix
Notes: Editions, mss, clippings, ephemera, recordings. Does not circulate. Unpublished guide available.

MA —BOSTON UNIVERSITY, Mugar Memorial Library, Special Collections Dept, 771 Commonwealth Ave, Boston, 02215. Howard B Gotlieb, Dir
Holdings: Vols 750 Mss Pix
Notes: Mss, correspondence, etc collected in depth; incl publications by or about.

MA —HARVARD UNIVERSITY LIBRARY, Houghton Library, Cambridge, 02138. F Thomas Noonan, Cur, Reading Room; Lawrence Dowler, Associate Librn
Holdings: Cat Mss

MI —UNIVERSITY OF MICHIGAN, Library, Dept of Rare Books & Special Collections, Ann Arbor, 48109. Robert J Starring, Head
Holdings: Vols 83 Cat Mss Pix
Notes: Includes 20 Christmas books. There are also 38 manuscript items, chiefly letters, 26 in Frost's holograph, 11 photographs, and the Leon Makielski portrait of Frost. Also manuscript scores of musical settings by Carl E Gehring for 20 Frost poems.

NV —UNIVERSITY OF NEVADA, RENO, University Library, Special Collections Dept, Reno, 89557. Robert E Blesse, Head
Holdings: // Vols (111) Cat Other appearances 1300 Cat
Notes: Includes individual works by author in all editions including translations; also prefaces, introductions, published correspondence, appearances in anthologies, periodicals, etc. Bibliographical research collection, part of Modern Authors Collection.

NH —UNIVERSITY OF NEW HAMPSHIRE, Dimond Library, Durham, 03824. Barbara A White, Special Collections Librn
Holdings: Vols 200 Cat Mss Pix
Budget: $500
Notes: See *Robert Frost, New Hampshire,* comp by William B Ewert, Durham, NH: Friends of the Library, 1976.

NH —DARTMOUTH COLLEGE, Baker Memorial Library, Hanover, 03755.
Holdings: Cat Mss Pix
Notes: Extensive collection of first editions, mss, ephemera, and mss and correspondence files presented by his secretary and manager. Noncirculating.

NH —PLYMOUTH STATE COLLEGE, Lamson Library, Plymouth, 03264. Phillip Wei, Dir of Library Services
Holdings: Cat Mss Pix
Budget: ($30,000)
Notes: A collection of Robert Frost material, incl correspondence, prepublication typescripts of various poems by Frost, autographed first editions, unpublished photographs of him at Franconia, New Hampshire and miscellaneous other material by or about Frost.

NY —CORNELL UNIVERSITY LIBRARIES, Collection of Regional History, Dept of Manuscripts and Univ Archives, Ithaca, 14853.
Notes: Lecture, April 20, 1950; one tape recording with transcript of a lecture delivered during the Wordsworth Centenary observances at Cornell University, NY.

NY —NEW YORK UNIVERSITY, Robert Frost Library, 70 Washington Sq S, New York, 10012.
Holdings: Vols Periodicals Pix
Notes: Frost's personal library from his home in Cambridge, Mass. Incl books, periodicals, family photographs, clippings. Presentation copies of first editions.

NC —DUKE UNIVERSITY, William R Perkins Library, Rare Book Room, Durham, 27706. John L Sharpe, III, Cur
Notes: Robert Frost collection given by The Rev George Brinkmann Ehlhardt. First and limited editions, anthologies containing Frost's poetry, pamphlets and ephemeral pieces.

NC —UNIVERSITY OF NORTH CAROLINA, GREENSBORO, Walter Clinton Jackson Library, Special Collections Dept, 1000 Spring Garden St, Greensboro, 27412. Emilie W Mills, Librn
Holdings: Vols (200) Cat Mss Pix Phonorecords Audiotapes
Notes: Randall Jarrell taught at the University from 1947 until his death in 1965. Over 3000 ms items were the gift of the author and incl various drafts of poems, translations, critical works and essays. Books incl first, foreign, and variant editions, association books and many other heavily annotated by Jarrell readings, conversations (tapes) with other poets, incl John Crowe Ransom and Robert Frost. A one-hour color film made after the poet's death incl readings of his poems made from the earlier tapes, and an interview with the poet's widow, Mary Jarrell. Jarrell memorabilia is also included.

†NC —WAKE FOREST UNIVERSITY, Z Smith Reynolds Library, Box 7777, Reynold Sta, Winston-Salem, 27109. Richard J Murdoch, Rare Book Librn
Holdings: Vols 126 Cat

OH —BLUFFTON COLLEGE, Musselman Library, Bluffton, 45817. Delbert Gratz, Librn
Holdings: Vols 50 Cat Mss Pix Microforms

OH —KENT STATE UNIVERSITY, Libraries, Dept of Special Collections, Kent, 44242. Dean H Keller, Cur
Holdings: Vols 263 Cat
Notes: Incl books by and about Frost and contributions by him to books and periodicals.

OK —UNIVERSITY OF TULSA, McFarlin Library, Dept of Rare Books and Special Collections, 600 S College, Tulsa, 74104. David Farmer, Dir; Toby Murray, Archivist; Caroline Swinson, Cur of Manuscripts & Art
Notes: The Robert Frost Collection, assembled by the late John Kohn, a friend of Frost and proprietor of Seven Gables Book Shop in New York. Incl all first editions of Frost's works, his appearances in anthologies and periodicals, translations into other languages, and critical works.

PA —BRYN MAWR COLLEGE, Canaday Library, Bryn Mawr, 19010. James Tanis, Dir
Notes: Rare books and manuscripts.

RI —BROWN UNIVERSITY, John Hay Library, Harris Collection, Prospect St, Providence, 02912. Rosemary L Cullen, Cur
Holdings: Vols (200,000) Cat Mss Pix Phonorecords Microforms
Budget: ($15,000)
Notes: The Harris Collection of American Poetry and Plays is principally composed of American and Canadian poetry and plays, 17th century-date. Extensive holdings in songsters, gift books and annuals, hymnals, pageants, broadside verse, carriers' addresses, women poets, juvenile poetry, (incl Mother Goose and *The Night Before* Christmas), sheet music with lyrics, small press publications, fine printing, black poets, "little magazines," Yiddish-American literature. All movements or schools of American poetry are represented. Incl first editions of most American poets and playwrights, notably Whitman, Poe, Wallace Stevens, Eugene O'Neill, Edward Albee, Ezra Pound, T S Eliot, William Carlos Williams, Amy Lowell, Phyllis Wheatley, Robert Frost, Allen Ginsberg, Bliss Carman, and Stephen Foster sheet music. Also incl the Saunders Walt Whitman Collection (1300 vols); the LangdonCollection of Pageants (250 vols); the Asa Cushman Collection of plays in ms and prompt copies; the MacDougall Collection of Psalters and

FROST, ROBERT (cont.)

Hymnals; 4000 plays issued by Walter H Baker Co, Boston (1890-1957); the Vaxer Collection of Yiddish Poetry, Plays and Music (1700 vols). Collections incl 200,000 vols, 30,000 broadsides, 55,000 mss, 170,000 pieces of sheet music, 450 phonorecords, and 375 microfilm reels. See *Dictionary Catalog of the Harris Collection of American Poetry and Plays* (Boston: G K Hall, 1972), 13 vols; *Supplement* (1977), 3 vols. See also, *American Poetry,* 1609-1900, *A Collection on Microfilm, Segment I* (1609-1820); *Segment II* (1821-1850); *Segment III* (1851-1870) (Woodbridge, Conn: Research Publications). Separate catalog.

SC —UNIVERSITY OF SOUTH CAROLINA, Thomas Cooper Library, Columbia, 29208. Kenneth E Toombs, Dir of Libraries; Roger Mortimer, Rare Book Librn
Holdings: Vols 150 Cat
Notes: A very fine collection of first signed editions.

VA —UNIVERSITY OF VIRGINIA, Alderman Library, Clifton Waller Barrett Collection, Charlottesville, 22901. Joan St C Crane, Cur of American Literature Collections
Holdings: Vols 450 Cat Mss Pix
Notes: Most complete and important collection of Robert Frost. Includes hundreds of letters; periodical appearances; only copy of Frost's first book, *Twilight,* 1894. Published description: *Robert Frost, 1874-1963; An Exhibition of Books Manuscripts and Memorabilia, Arranged in Honor of the Poetry Society of Virginia on the Occasion of Their Meeting in* Charlottesville (Charlottesville, Va: Clifton Waller Barrett Library, 1966); *Robert Frost--A Descriptive Catalogue of Books and Manuscripts in the Clifton Waller Barrett Library, University of Virginia,* compiled by Joan St C Crane (Charlottesville: Published for the Associates of the University of Virginia Library by the University Press of Virginia, [1974]).

FROTTAGE

IN —INDIANA UNIVERSITY, Institute for Sex Research Library, 416 Morrison Hall, Bloomington, 47401. Douglas Freeman, Collections and Services Librn; Joan Brewer, Information Services Librn
Holdings: Vols (62,000) Cat Mss Pix Microforms
See also entry under Sex.

FROZEN STARS see Black Holes (Astronomy)

FRUEH, ALFRED J.

NY —NEW YORK PUBLIC LIBRARY, Performing Arts Research Center, Billy Rose Theatre Collection, 111 Amsterdam Ave, New York, 10023. Dorothy L Swerdlove, Cur
Holdings: Cat
Notes: A large collection of original caricatures, many of which appeared in the New Yorker magazine, 1925-1962. Published description: Frueh, Alfred J, *Frueh on the Theatre; Theatrical Caricatures, 1906-1962* (New York Public Library, 1972).
See also entry under Sardi's Restaurant.

FRUIT

FL —RARE FRUIT COUNCIL INTERNATIONAL, 13609 Old Cutler Rd, Miami, 33158. Fred Frazer, Pres; Louise Garavatlia, Librn
Holdings: Vols (300)
Notes: Not open to the public.

IL —MORTON ARBORETUM, Sterling Morton Library, Lisle, 60532. Ian MacPhail, Librn
Holdings: Vols (20,000) Cat Maps Pix
Budget: ($10,000)
Notes: The library is especially concerned with the literature of woody plants (trees and shrubs) of north temperate zones but has substantial holdings in the taxonomy and systematics of plants in general, both wild and cultivated, flora of different parts of the world, and a growing collection on plant monographs. Also about 2000 pictures. Described in *The Morton Arboretum* Quarterly, vol 9, no 4 (Winter 1973), pp 56-61.

MA —MASSACHUSETTS HORTICULTURAL SOCIETY, 300 Massachusetts Ave, Boston, 02115. Becky Ellis, Librn
Holdings: Vols (37,000)
Notes: Garden history, pomology, flora, landscape design. Print collection of many centuries; nursery catalogues from the mid-18th century. In storage, remodeling, will be available in about a year. Open to the public.

NY —NEW YORK BOTANICAL GARDEN LIBRARY, Bronx, 10458. Charles R Long, Asst Vice Pres & Dir
Holdings: Vols (385,000) Cat Mss Pix Slides Microforms VF
Budget: ($356,000)
Notes: One of the largest botanical collections in the world. Covers botany (150, 000 vols), botanists (3000), horticulture (45, 000), plant diseases (25,000), plant physiology (15,000), history of botany (1500), conservation of natural resources (15,000), gardening (13,000), paleobotany (7000), ecology (20,000), forestry (5000), medical botany (3000), agriculture (9000) and biology (20,000). Reference library; materials do not circulate, except via standard inter-library loan. About 5000 vols uncataloged. Incl archives, art and vertical files. An OCLC library.

FRUIT CULTURE

CA —UNIVERSITY OF CALIFORNIA, DAVIS, Shields Library, Dept of Special Collections, Davis, 95616. Donald Kunitz, Head; C Danial Elliott, Asst Head
Notes: Agricultural machinery: Manufacturer's catalogs, manuals, parts lists, ephemera, and literature pertaining to historical as well as current data on such items as tractors, engines, combines, hay equipment, etc. Described in "The Higgins Library: A Source for the Study of Agricultural History," Don Kunitz, *Agricultural History,* vol 49, 1975, pp 89-91.

MA —MASSACHUSETTS HORTICULTURAL SOCIETY, 300 Massachusetts Ave, Boston, 02115. Becky Ellis, Librn
Holdings: Vols (37,000)
Notes: Garden history, pomology, flora, landscape design. Print collection of many centuries; nursery catalogues from the mid-18th century. In storage, remodeling, will be available in about a year. Open to the public.

MA —OLD STURBRIDGE VILLAGE, Research Library, Sturbridge, 01566. Theresa Rini Percy, Librn
Holdings: Cat Mss
Notes: Northeastern US, 1790-1850.

NY —UNIVERSITY OF ROCHESTER, Rush Rhees Library, Department of Rare Books and Special Collections, Rochester, 14627. Peter Dzwonkoski, Librn
Holdings: Vols 1000 // Cat Mss
Notes: Ellwanger and Barry Horticultural Library: American and European books and pomological journals of the 19th century. Also have records of the Ellwanger and Barry Nursery of Rochester, NY.

OR —OREGON STATE UNIVERSITY, Library, Corvallis, 97331. Melvin George, Dir
Holdings: Vols (980,000) Cat

FRUIT TREES

CA —SUNKIST GROWERS, Research Library, 760 E Sunkist St, Ontario, 91761. Martha C Nemeth, Librn
Notes: Technology of citrus fruit and citrus fruit products, primarily Californian. Strong in organic and food chemistry, with additional coverage of food technology, essential oils, microbiology and environmental protection.

FRUITLANDS (UTOPIAN COMMUNITY)

MA —FRUITLANDS MUSEUMS LIBRARY, Prospect Hill, RR 2 Box 87, Harvard, 01451. Richard S Reed, Dir; John L Crispen, Admin Secy
Budget: ($21,900)
Notes: Fruitlands (utopian community), books and mss; New England Transcendentalism; and Shakers' books and mss, primarily the Harvard Shaker Society and Shirley Shaker Society. Primary source materials of a scholarly nature consisting for the most part of mss, letters, and a few journals by members or friends of the Fruitlands Community.

FRY, BENJAMIN, 1755-1840

RI —BROWN UNIVERSITY, John Hay Library, 20 Prospect St, Providence, 02912. Mark N Brown, Cur Mss
Holdings: Mss
Notes: Materials relative to the history of the US Army.

FRY, CHRISTOPHER

BC —UNIVERSITY OF VICTORIA, McPherson Library, Victoria, V8W 3H5, Can.

FRY, ELIZABETH

PA —FRIENDS HISTORICAL LIBRARY OF SWARTHMORE COLLEGE, Swarthmore, 19081. J William Frost, Dir
Holdings: Vols (31,340) Cat Mss Pix
Notes: Incl works on prison conditions, capital punishment, and works by and about Quaker prison reformers, Elizabeth Fry, John Howard, Richard Vaux, Roberts Vaux, American Friends Service Committee, and others.

FRY, ROGER

NY —HOFSTRA UNIVERSITY, Library, 1000 Fulton Ave, Hempstead, 11550. Charles R Andrews, Dean of Library Services

ON —VICTORIA UNIVERSITY, Library, 71 Queen's Park Crescent, Toronto, M5S 1K7, Can. Robert C Brandeis, Chief Librn
Holdings: Vols Cat
Notes: A collection of first editions and others of Virginia Woolf and Bloomsbury writers: Clive Bell, Roger Fry, E M Forster, V Sackville-West, K Mansfield, etc. Contains a significant collection of Hogarth Press books, and many of those handprinted by the Woolfs.

FRY, VARIAN

NY —COLUMBIA UNIVERSITY LIBRARIES, Rare Book & Manuscript Library, 801 Butler Library, 535 W 114 St, New York, 10027. Kenneth A Lohf, Librn
Holdings: Mss Pix
Notes: Papers, mss, archives, etc. Incl 3000 items.

FRYE, H. NORTHROP

ON —VICTORIA UNIVERSITY, Library, 71 Queen's Park Crescent, Toronto, M5S 1K7, Can. Robert C Brandeis, Chief Librn
Holdings: Vols (100) Cat Mss
Notes: Books and mss by noted literary critic Northrop Frye. Inc sound recordings.

FRYE, WILLIAM R.

MA —BOSTON UNIVERSITY, Mugar Memorial Library, Special Collections Dept, 771 Commonwealth Ave, Boston, 02215. Howard B Gotlieb, Dir
Holdings: Cat Mss

FRYKLUND, VERNE C., 1896-1980

WI —UNIVERSITY OF WISCONSIN-STOUT, Library Learning Center, Menomonie, 54751. Philip Sawin Jr, Coll Develop Librn
Notes: Verne C Fryklund was an educator with a national reputation in industrial and vocational education. He was the third President of the University. The library

FRYKLUND, VERNE C., 1896-1980 (cont.)

holds photos, geographical material, correspondence, speeches, blueprints and designs, miscellaneous course materials, papers of Fryklund's students, and his writings and publications.

FUCHS, THEODORE

†UT —BRIGHAM YOUNG UNIVERSITY, Harold B Lee Library, University Hill, Provo, 84602.
Notes: The Theodore Fuchs Collection of material relating to modern stage lighting and design. Incl books, theses, seminar reports, theatre brochures, commercial catalogs, class notebooks, professional publications, course material, files, slides, photographs, programs, blueprints, technical correspondence and recording discs.

FUCHS, DANIEL

MA —BOSTON UNIVERSITY, Mugar Memorial Library, Special Collections Dept, 771 Commonwealth Ave, Boston, 02215. Howard B Gotlieb, Dir
Holdings: Mss
Notes: Mss, correspondence, etc collected in depth; incl publications by or about.

FUEL

PA —FRANKLIN INSTITUTE LIBRARY, 20 & The Parkway, Philadelphia, 19103. Miriam Padusis, Dir; Charles Wilt, Readers Servs Librn
Holdings: Vols (300,000) Cat Maps Pix Microforms

PA —PENNSYLVANIA STATE UNIVERSITY, Earth & Mineral Sciences Library, 105 Deike Bldg, University Park, 16802. Emilie McWilliams, Head Librn
Holdings: Vols (58,000) Cat Maps Microforms
Budget: ($49,750)
Notes: This collection includes substantial numbers of geological maps, and strong periodical holdings including microform.

FUEL, ALTERNATE see Alternate Fuels

FUEL ECONOMY AND CONSERVATION

MI —US ENVIRONMENTAL PROTECTION AGENCY, Motor Vehicle Emission Laboratory Library, 2565 Plymouth Rd, Ann Arbor, 48105. Debra Talsma, Librn
Holdings: // Uncat Microforms
Notes: No separate catalog. Collection described in: US EPA, Library System Branch, *Guide to EPA Libraries*, July, 1977. Collection includes 9500 technical reports on air pollution from mobile sources (especially automobiles); air pollution legislation (350 vols); fuel economy and conservation (800 technical reports); automobile engineering (300 vols); emission control technology for mobile source (8000 reports and papers); use of methanol and other alternative fuels in motor vehicles (600 technical reports).

FUEL NOZZLES

IA —DELEVAN DIVISION OF COLT INDUSTRIES INC, Engineering Library, 811 Fourth St, PO Box 100, West Des Moines, 50265. G A Hartman, Librn
Holdings: Vols 2000 Cat Mss Slides Microforms
Budget: $400
Notes: Incl liquid atomization, droplet size measurement and representation, fuel nozzles for combustors, and spray nozzles for industrial and agricultural applications.

FUERTES, LOUIS AGASSIZ, 1874-1927

NY —CORNELL UNIVERSITY LIBRARIES, Collection of Regional History, Dept of Manuscripts and Univ Archives, Ithaca, 14853.
Notes: Artist-naturalist. Papers, ca 1890-ca 1927; 9.5 ft., 7 map case drawers. Restricted.

FUGATE, HENLEY

VA —VIRGINIA POLYTECHNIC INSTITUTE AND STATE UNIVERSITY LIBRARY, Blacksburg, 24061. Glenn L McMullen, Special Collections Librn
Holdings: Vols (2000) Cat Mss Maps Pix Audiotapes
Notes: Primarily Southwest Virginia materials. Collection incl ca 200 mss, account books and other archival records of nineteenth century area businesses and other mining operations; the extant archival records of several Southwest Virginia railroads, incl the Virginia and Tennessee Railroad and the Norfolk and Western Railroad; and papers of historically prominent Southwest Virginians, incl John Apperson, Dr Harvy Black, James P Charlton, W Graham Claytor, Henley Fugate, Clement D Johnston, Germanicus Kent, William Preston, J Hoge Tyler, and William C Wampler. Several oral history collections incl material on Appalachian customs and folklore, particularly in Patrick County.

FUGITIVE POETS

TN —VANDERBILT UNIVERSITY, Library, Nashville, 37240. Marice Wolfe, Special Collections Librn
Holdings: Vols 1000 Cat Mss Pix
Notes: Collection relating to the Fugitive poets of the 1920s, the Agrarian writers of the 1930s and their subsequent careers, as a complement to extensive mss collections in this field. Chief figures incl Allen Tate, John Crowe Ransom, Robert Penn Warren, Andrew Lytle, Donald Davidson, Merrill Moore, Laura Riding, et al.

FUGUES see Canons, Fugues, Etc.

FULLER, BLAIR

MA —BOSTON UNIVERSITY, Mugar Memorial Library, Special Collections Dept, 771 Commonwealth Ave, Boston, 02215. Howard B Gotlieb, Dir
Holdings: Cat Mss

FULLER, EDMUND

MA —BOSTON UNIVERSITY, Mugar Memorial Library, Special Collections Dept, 771 Commonwealth Ave, Boston, 02215. Howard B Gotlieb, Dir
Holdings: Cat Mss Pix
Notes: Mss, correspondence, etc collected in depth; incl publications by or about.

FULLER, F. BUCKMINSTER

VA —UNIVERSITY OF VIRGINIA, Alderman Library, Clifton Waller Barrett Collection, Charlottesville, 22901. Joan St C Crane, Cur of American Literature Collections
Notes: Papers.

FULLER, HENRY BLAKE

IL —NEWBERRY LIBRARY, 60 W Walton St, Chicago, 60610. Diana Haskell, Cur of Modern Mss
Holdings: Vols 1162 Cat Mss Pix
Notes: Primary repository. Restricted use: noncirculating.

FULLER, JOHN G.

MA —BOSTON UNIVERSITY, Mugar Memorial Library, Special Collections Dept, 771 Commonwealth Ave, Boston, 02215. Howard B Gotlieb, Dir
Holdings: Cat Mss Pix
Notes: Mss, correspondence, etc collected in depth; incl publications by or about.

FULLER, LOIE, 1862-1928

NY —NEW YORK PUBLIC LIBRARY, Performing Arts Research Center, Dance Collection, 111 Amsterdam Ave, New York, 10023. Genevieve Oswald, Cur
Notes: Extensive biographical and visual material. Includes photographs, silent film footage, ca 1906, clippings, programs, watercolors. The Loie Fuller Papers, 1892-1913, and Loie Fuller Collection, 1914-1928, contain about 1680 manuscript items.

FULLER, LON LUVOIS, 1902-1978

MA —HARVARD UNIVERSITY LIBRARY, Law School Library, Langdell Hall, Cambridge, 02138. Erika S Chadbourn, Cur of Mss
Holdings: Cat Mss
Notes: Professional papers. Typed inventory in repository. Inclusive dates, 1926-1977.

FULLER, MARGARET W. see Ossoli, Margaret Fuller, 1872-1959

FULLER, MELVILLE W.

IL —CHICAGO HISTORICAL SOCIETY, Library, Clark St at North Ave, Chicago, 60614. Archie Motley, Manuscript Librn
Notes: Supreme Court Justice David Davis, a confidant of Abraham Lincoln, and Chief Justice Melville W Fuller, both collections consisting of photostatic copies of original materials in various repositories and in private hands.

FULLER, THOMAS

MD —JOHNS HOPKINS UNIVERSITY, Milton S Eisenhower Library, Charles & 34 Sts, Baltimore, 21218. Ann S Gwyn, Assistant Dir for Special Collections
Holdings: Vols Cat Mss Microforms
Notes: The Osler Collection (Tudor and Stuart Club) contains original editions of Shelley, Milton, Keats, Donne, Defoe, Thomas Fuller, Golden Book of Marcus Aurelius (1559). A collection of his articles made by Walt Whitman. 17th and 18th century commonplace books in English and French, in ms. Most English translations of Jakob Boehme. Cards in main catalog. Also, not included in the above figure, Pollard and Regrave's, and Wing's Early English Books on microfilm.

FULLER, WILLIAM O.

RI —BROWN UNIVERSITY, John Hay Library, 20 Prospect St, Providence, 02912. Mark N Brown, Cur Mss
Holdings: Mss
Notes: Papers of William O Fuller (1828-1910), music teacher of Providence, comprising letters 1848 from Europe, incl a letter from Franz Liszt; papers of Johann Christian Gottlieb Graupner (1767-1836) and John Rowe Parker (fl 1820s) collected by Horace Mason Reynolds, relating to the music-publishing business in Boston, 1802-1838; papers of the American folklorist Mellinger Edward Henry (1873-1946) relating to his research and publications on American folk-songs 1910-1942; papers, 1912-1948, of Providence composer Hugh Frederick MacColl (1885-1953); papers of Frances Herriot Sargent, stage manager for "Porgy" and "Porgy and Bess", relating to productions of these, 1928-1942.

FULLER FAMILY

OH —KENT STATE UNIVERSITY, University Archives, Kent, 44242. Stephen C Morton, University Archivist
Holdings: Uncat Mss Pix
Notes: Books, periodical articles, and correspondence from various members of the Fuller Family of Austinburg, Ohio. The collection includes correspondence of Ira Fuller (1840s), his son Allen O Fuller, his wife, and their daughter Jeannette Fuller (1868-1952), a midwestern temperance lecturer and union organizer and interested correspondent in the Non-Tobacco League of America.

FULTON, GEORGE W.

TX —UNIVERSITY OF TEXAS LIBRARIES, General Libraries, Barker Texas History Center, PO Box P, Austin, 78712. Don Carleton, Dir

FULTON, JAMES C.

TX —UNIVERSITY OF TEXAS LIBRARIES, General Libraries, Barker Texas History Center, PO Box P, Austin, 78712. Don Carleton, Dir

FULTON, JOHN FARQUHAR, 1899-1960

CT —YALE UNIVERSITY, Medical Historical Library, 333 Cedar St, New Haven, 06510. Ferenc A Gyorgyey, Librn
Holdings: Uncat Mss Pix
Notes: Materials by and about; 45 vols, 38 file drawers.

†NY —NEW YORK ACADEMY OF MEDICINE, Library, 2 E 103 ST, New York, 10029.
Notes: Papers of Walter Timme, MD (1874-1956). Timme was a pioneer endocrinologist; described pluriglandular disease, "Timme's Syndrome." Incl correspondence from Harvey Cushing, Paul Dudley White, Charles A Elsberg, Louis I Dublin, Ely Smith Jelliffe, John F Fulton, Edna St Vincent Millay, Eva Le Gallienne, and Irving Ramsey Wiles.

FULTON, ROBERT, 1765-1815

DC —LIBRARY OF CONGRESS, Rare Book & Special Collections Div, Washington, 20540. William Matheson, Chief
Notes: Important holdings relating to subjects such as railroads and canals. Material by and about Robert Fulton is particularly strong. The division contains many pre-Civil War technical manuals.

NY —NEW YORK STATE OFFICE OF PARKS & RECREATION, TACONIC REGION, Clermont State Historic Park, Library, RR 1, Box 215, Germantown, 12526. Bruce E Naramore, Historic Site Manager
Holdings: Vols 200 Cat Mss Maps
Notes: Primarily correspondence from Robert Fulton to the Chancellor Robert R Livingston. Covers most aspects of the planning and building of the "Clermont," the first successful steamboat; also its navigation. Maps and diagrams of construction of the original vessel. Interesting highlights into the lives of the two partners, and their success. It is interesting to note here that the Chancellor and Robert Fulton never called the vessel the "Clermont," rather, simply the "steamboat" and the "North River Steamboat, of Clermont" (as the ship was registered). No photocopying.

NY —NEW YORK HISTORICAL SOCIETY, Library, 170 Central Park W, New York, 10024. James Gregory, Librn
Notes: Randall J LeBoeuf Jr's collection of Robert Fulton and related material, 1764-1857, consisting of correspondence, drawings, legal papers, etc, relating to steam engines and boats, canals, and torpedoes. The correspondents incl John Quincy Adams, Henry Clay, De Witt Clinton, Albert Gallatin, Benjamin H Latrobe, James Madison, James Monroe, John Livingston, Robert R Livingston, and William Thornton. Also incl are Fulton's expense and note book, 1803-1808, and Robert R Livingston's receipt book, 1808-1812. Approx 215 items, cataloged.

NY —NEW YORK PUBLIC LIBRARY, Rare Books and Manuscripts Div, Fifth Ave & 42 St, New York, 10018. William L Joyce, Asst Dir; Susan E Davis, Cur of Mss
Holdings: Mss
Budget: ($7161)
Notes: Incl personal and literary mss, papers, etc.

FUND FOR THE REPUBLIC

NJ —PRINCETON UNIVERSITY, Library, Manuscript Collection, Nassau St, Princeton, 08540. Jean F Preston, Cur
Holdings: Cat Mss
Notes: Fund for the Republic (1952-45) archives, incl 141 cartons, 121 shipping cases. Archives, 1952-65.

FUND RAISING

DC —COUNCIL FOR ADVANCEMENT & SUPPORT OF EDUCATION, Reference Center, Eleven Dupont Circle NW, Suite 400, Washington, 20036. Cynthia Snyder, Dir
Holdings: Vols (600) Cat Mss Audiotapes Microforms
Notes: A membership service containing information in educational fund raising, institutional relations, government relations, alumni administration, publications, and management techniques for higher education and independent schools. Collection, in addition, contains mss, microfiches, and tapes. Succeeds the American Alumni Council, dissolved in 1974.

NY —UNITED HOSPITAL FUND OF NEW YORK, Library, 3 E 54th St, New York, 10022. Christine Bahr, Librn
Holdings: Vols (4000) Cat Mss Maps Pix
Notes: Incl 100 journal titles.

RI —JOHNSON AND WALES COLLEGE, Hospitality Center, 1150 Narragansett Blvd, Cranston, 02905. Margaret A Thomas, Librn
Budget: ($15,000)
Notes: The Paul Fritzsche Cookbook Collection, incl more than 8000 cookbooks, with some rare and valuable items. Many 19th and early 20th century items; particularly strong in fund raising cookbooks. Collection is partially cataloged.

VA —UNITED WAY OF AMERICA INFORMATION CENTER, 701 North Fairfax St, United Way Plaza, Alexandria, 22314. Henry M Smith, Dir; Barbara L Owen, Librn
Holdings: Vols (1200) Cat Microforms
Notes: Incl 5000 research reports and studies on microfiche; 100 vertical file drawers. Services primarily for United Way organizations--United Funds, Community Chests, Health and Welfare Planning Councils.

FUNDAMENTAL EDUCATION (COMMUNITY DEVELOPMENT) see Community Development

FUNDAMENTALISM

OK —MIDWEST CHRISTIAN COLLEGE, Library, 6600 N Kelley Ave, Oklahoma City, 73111. Jean Cavett, Dir
Holdings: Vols (7000) Cat Pix Phonorecords Audiotapes Filmstrips Microforms
Notes: The Restoration Movement (Independent Christian Church) to restore the Church to its New Testament form. Incl churches called "Christian Churches," "Churches of Christ," "Disciples of Christ," and a few called just "Christ's Church."

OR —MULTNOMAH SCHOOL OF THE BIBLE, Library, 8435 NE Gilsan St, Portland, 97220. James F Scott, Dir of Library; Susan Johnson, Asst Librn
Holdings: Vols (40,686) Cat Slides Phonorecords Audiotapes Filmstrips
Budget: ($33,950)
Notes: Multnomah School of the Bible is an evangelical school that educates students through a program of instruction having the Bible as its center. It supports this centralized Bible major with several ancillary, pertinent supporting minors, ie, Christian education, pastoral, missions and New Testament Greek.

FUNDS see Finance

FUNERAL MUSIC

LA —TULANE UNIVERSITY, Howard-Tilton Memorial Library, Special Collections Div, William Ransom Hogan Jazz Archive, 7001 Freret, New Orleans, 70118. Richard B Allen, Acting Cur; Alma D Williams, Assistant to the Cur
Holdings: Vols (100,000) Cat Mss Pix Slides Phonorecords Audiotapes Videotapes 16mm Films Microforms
Budget: ($90,000)
Notes: Jazz music and musicians. Outstanding collection, incl books, music scores, serials, catalogs and other archival material. Music, history, etc.
See also entry under Jazz

FUNERAL RECORDS

AZ —NORTHERN ARIZONA UNIVERSITY, Special Collection Library, CU Box 6022, Flagstaff, 86011. Peter M Whiteley, Coordr/Archivist; William Mullane, Librn
Notes: (1) Parker Mortuary Collection; funeral registers, December 1898 to 1912. (2) Ruffner, Lester Ward, Funeral Home Collection, Prescott, Ariz; funeral records, 1901-1939.

FUNERAL SERVICE

MA —NATIONAL CENTER FOR DEATH EDUCATION, New England Resource Center for Thanatology & Funeral Service, 656 Beacon St, Boston, 02215. Gail Gruner, Librn

FUNGI

MA —UNIVERSITY OF MASSACHUSETTS AT AMHERST, Library, Amherst, 01003. Siegfried Feller, Assoc Dir for Collection Development
Holdings: Cat
Notes: Botanical taxonomy, physiology, pathology and mycology.

MA —HARVARD UNIVERSITY LIBRARY, Farlow Reference Library, 20 Divinity Ave, Cambridge, 02138. Geraldine C Kaye, Librn
Holdings: Vols (60,000) Cat Mss Serials Pix Microforms
Notes: The Farlow Reference Library provides complete coverage of the systematic literature on algae, bryophytes, fungi, and lichens. Established by bequest of Professor William G Farlow, it is one of the most extensive cryptogamic botany libraries in the US. Books do not circulate.

PA —PENNSYLVANIA STATE UNIVERSITY, Fred Lewis Pattee Library, Life Sciences Library, University Park, 16802. Keith Roe, Head
Notes: This collection is strong in periodical runs, particularly European learned societies and agriculture. It contains extensive collections of Experiment Station publications and has developed specialties in Mycology and Fusaria. There is also a special collection of 1105 glass slides on early Pennsylvania lumbering.

ON —AGRICULTURE CANADA, Plant Research Library, Research Branch, Central Experimental Farm 49, Ottawa, K1A 0C6, Can. Mrs E Gavora, Librn
Holdings: Vols (10,500) Cat Maps Microforms
Notes: One of the most extensive botanical collections in Canada, especially in the taxonomy of higher plants and fungi. Contains many of the basic works from the starting point of botany in 1753 to date. Major botanical works of Linnaeus and others, covering flora of land areas of most parts of the world.

FUNICULAR RAILROADS see Railroads, Cable Car

FUNK, CASIMIR

CT —BURNDY LIBRARY, Electra Square, Norwalk, 06856. Philip J Weimerskirch, Asst Dir
Notes: Incl many reprints, seventeen student and lab notebooks, and some correspondence.

FUNNIES see Comic Books, Strips, Etc.

FUNSTON-HASH FAMILY

AZ —NORTHERN ARIZONA UNIVERSITY, Special Collection Library, CU Box 6022, Flagstaff, 86011. Peter M Whiteley, Coordr/Archivist; William Mullane, Librn
Notes: Newspaper articles, photographs, and

FUNSTON-HASH FAMILY (cont.)

correspondence involving the Funston-Hash Family. Also incl folk material cultural items.

FUR-BEARING ANIMALS

†WA —WASHINGTON STATE UNIVERSITY, Library, Manuscripts, Archives & Special Collections, Pullman, 99164. John F Guido, Head
Holdings: Cat Mss Maps Pix
Notes: The Carl Parcher Russell papers, a vast resource (24,916 items; 45 linear feet) on American Indian and Western pioneer activities and artifacts. Much on the fur trade; pioneer life; mountain men and trapping; wildlife; primitive life in detail. Also the National Park Service, parks, monuments, etc. Described in *Carl Parcher Russell: An Indexed Register of His Scholarly and Professional Papers, 1920-1967, in the Washington State University* Library (Pullman, 1970), 149 pp.

FUR SEAL ARBITRATION see Bering Sea Controversy

FUR TRADE

CA —AZUSA PACIFIC COLLEGE, Marshburn Memorial Library, Citrus & Alosta, Azusa, 91702. Edward Peterman, Librn
Holdings: Vols (6000) Uncat
Budget: ($30,000)
Notes: Significant holdings in the George E Fullerton Library of Californiana and Western Americana.

CT —YALE UNIVERSITY, Box 1603A, Yale Station, New Haven, 06520.

MN —UNIVERSITY OF MINNESOTA, DULUTH, Library & Learning Resources Service, Duluth, 55812. James V. Litha, Archivist
Holdings: Vols (1700) Cat Mss Maps Pix
Notes: The Voyageur Collection incl the Grace Lee Nute Papers. Books and materials relating to the Voyageur period (1650-1850) and the area of Northeastern Minnesota, Michigan, Wisconsin, Southern Canada. Emphasis on all subjects listed in this volume.

MN —GRAND PORTAGE NATIONAL MONUMENT, Library, Box 666, Grand Marais, 55604.
Holdings: Vols (1000) Cat Mss Pix
Notes: Deals primarily with the Canadian fur trade, especially the activities of the North West Co and the Hudson's Bay Co.

MN —UNIVERSITY OF MINNESOTA, James Ford Bell Library, 309 19th Ave S, Minneapolis, 55455. John Parker, Cur
Holdings: Vols (11,000) Cat Mss Maps
Notes: Collection of original materials relating to European expansion, 1400-1800.

MO —MISSOURI HISTORICAL SOCIETY, Library, Jefferson Memorial Bldg, Saint Louis, 63112. Stephanie Klein, Librn-Archivist; Peter Michel, Cur of Manuscripts
Holdings: Cat Mss Maps Pix
Notes: Extensive ms holdings relating to Missouri, US history, etc. Also ms collections of many noted persons (all but subsequent additions listed in Hamer, 1961). Library holdings described in Whitehall, Walter Muir, *Independent Historical* Societies (Boston, 1962).

MT —MONTANA STATE UNIVERSITY, Library, Bozeman, 59717. Minnie Ellen Paugh, Special Collections Librn
Holdings: Vols (7000) // Mss Maps Pix
Notes: Leggat-Donahoe Collection. Collection of Alexander Leggat of Butte, whose father was active in opening the mines. Mr Leggat's interests were mining, exploration, and the fur trade. There are excellent Indian materials in the collection. Also the manuscript and picture collections of James Willard Schultz, Harry James (about James Willard Schultz), and Olga Ross Hannon on Blackfeet Indian tepees. Land claim clase files and manuscripts about Blackfeet, Gros Ventre, Assiniboine and Crow Indians collected by Dr Thomas R Wessell, Edward E Barry and Dr Merrill G Burlingame.

NY —AMERICAN MUSEUM OF NATURAL HISTORY, Library Services Dept, Central Park W & 79th St, New York, 10024. Nina J Root, Chairwoman; Mary Genett, Asst Librn for Reference Services

TX —AMARILLO PUBLIC LIBRARY, 413 E Fourth, Amarillo, 79101. Mary Kay Snell, Librn
Holdings: Vols Cat Mss Maps Pix
Notes: The southwest collections incl materials on the history of Texas, Louisiana, New Mexico, Arkansas, Missouri and Kansas. General subjects covered incl overland journeys, early narratives, early biographies, Indian captivities, outlaws, US government reports, Mississippi and Ohio Rivers, the Mexican War, reports of Catholic missionaries, Niles Register, early publications, fur trade, western trails, Texas Rangers, sheriffs and Texas as a sovereign state, buffalo hunting, Indian wars, cowboys, the arrival of farmers, fences, and towns. Over 1600 items which incl books, documents, maps, mss, pamphlets, unpublished theses, interviews and photographs. The three major collections are the William Henry Bush Collection, the Laurence J Fitzsimon Collection and the Calendar of John L McCarty.

UT —UNIVERSITY OF UTAH, Marriott Library, Special Collections, Salt Lake City, 84112. Gregory C Thompson, Cur

†WA —WASHINGTON STATE UNIVERSITY, Library, Manuscripts, Archives & Special Collections, Pullman, 99164. John F Guido, Head
Holdings: Cat Mss Maps Pix
Notes: The Carl Parcher Russell papers, a vast resource (24,916 items; 45 linear feet) on American Indian and Western pioneer activities and artifacts. Much on the fur trade; pioneer life; mountain men and trapping; wildlife; primitive life in detail. Also the National Park Service, parks, monuments, etc. Described in *Carl Parcher Russell: An Indexed Register of His Scholarly and Professional Papers, 1920-1967, in the Washington State University* Library (Pullman, 1970), 149 pp. The manuscript collection incl business and financial records of banks, breweries, fisheries, insurance, land, lumber and livestock companies, trade and commodity associations; as well as the personal and professional papers of authors, aviators, educators, engineers, farmers, historians, pioneers, politicians and scientists; especially rich in documents relating to the exploration, settlementand development of the Palouse Country, the Inland Empire, the Columbia Basin and the Pacific Northwest. Described in *Selected Manuscript Resources in the Washington State University Library* (Pullman, 1974); and other published and unpublished inventories and registers.

WA —FORT VANCOUVER NATIONAL HISTORIC SITE, E Evergreen Blvd, Vancouver, 98661. Kent Taylor, Supervisory Ranger
Holdings: Vols (600) Cat Maps Pix Slides Audiotapes Videotapes 16mm Films
Notes: Fur trade of the Northwest. Use of library is restricted.

AB —ALPINE CLUB OF CANADA LIBRARY, Archives of the Canadian Rockies, Box 160, Banff, T0L 0C0, Can. E J Hart, Head Archivist
Holdings: Vols (2429) Cat Mss Maps Pix Slides Audiotapes
Budget: ($1000)
Notes: The Archives of the Canadian Rockies is the custodian of the library and archival collection of the Alpine Club of Canada. The materials cover mountaineering technique and attempts worldwide, incl the Alps, Rockies, Himalayas, Andes, etc. Subject areas incl history, personal records, mountain rescue and medicine, alpine flora and fauna, guide books, manuals and handbooks. A large part of the archival collection is concentrated on the Canadian Rocky Mountains, as the headquarters of The Alpine Club of Canada is in Banff, Alberta.

AB —GLENBOW-ALBERTA INSTITUTE, Historical Library & Archives, 130 9th Avenue SE, Calgary, T2G 0P3, Can. Leonard J Gottseleg, Chief Librn
Holdings: Vols (60,000) Cat Mss Maps Pix Microforms
Notes: Main emphasis is on Western Canadian history. Equally important emphasis is placed on the Canadian Arctic and Alaska, Northwest Coast explorations, Aboriginal peoples of the North and Candian West, and the fur trade in the US Northwest.

MB —HUDSON'S BAY CO, Library, 77 Main St, Winnipeg, R3C 2R1, Can. Carol Preston, Librn Hudson's Bay House
Holdings: Vols (6000) Cat Mss Maps Pix Slides
Notes: Main purpose is to provide research materials for production of the historical quarterly *The Beaver,* and to answer inquiries about the Company's history. Incl 250,000 pictures and 7000 VF pieces. No published catalog, but Library maintains author/subject/title card catalog. Limited photocopying. Mss of HBC Archives held by the Manitoba Provincial Archives. Published descriptions: Dowdall, Judi, "Hudson's Bay Company Library," *Canadian Library* Journal, June 1974, p 179; Preston, Carol, "Hudson's Bay Company Library," *Manitoba Library Association Bulletin*, June 1976, pp 24-25.

MB —UNIVERSITY OF MANITOBA, Elizabeth Dafoe Library, Archives and Special Collections Dept, Winnipeg, R3T 2N2, Can. Richard E Bennett, Dept Head; Corrado A Santoro, Reference Archivist
Notes: History of fur trade in Canada.

ON —PUBLIC ARCHIVES OF CANADA, Library, 395 Wellington St, Ottawa, K1A 0N3, Can. Dawn E Monroe, Collections Development Officer
Holdings: Vols (80,000) Cat
Notes: The Library has many works, mostly thematic, on the factors which have influenced Canada's economic development. They are largely general works. The Library's collection also contains numerous printed sources on specific sectors such as agriculture, the exploitation of natural resources, commercial trade, financial transactions, industrial production and the development of transportation and communications networks. For those interested in the history of business and financial institutions, there are studies on the major commercial activities involved in fishing, the fur trade, logging and the foreign trde of manufactured goods, raw materials, energy resources and technological products.

FURBISH, KATE, 1834-1931

ME —BOWDOIN COLLEGE, Library, Brunswick, 04011. Dianne M Gutscher, Cur of Special Collections
Holdings: Mss
Notes: The Kate Furbish collection of the "Flora of Maine" consists of her watercolor sketches of specimens collected between 1870 and 1908 (16 folio volumes).

FURLONG, CHARLES WELLINGTON

CA —HOOVER INSTITUTION ON WAR, REVOLUTION & PEACE, Stanford University, Stanford, 94305. Milorad M Drachkovitch, Archivist
Holdings: // Mss
Notes: Papers of Charles W Furlong, army officer, member of the American Commission to Negotiate Peace, Paris Peace Conference, special aide to President Wilson, 1918-1919, and military observer and intelligence officer in the Balkans and Near East, 1919. Documents, clippings, reports, records, and ephemera of the voyage of the USS *George Washington* carrying Wilson and members of the American Commission to Negotiate Peace; correspondence, documents, and reports as military observer to the American mission to study the military and political conditions in the Balkans; correspondence, documents, and memoranda of the Plebiscitary Commission,

FURLONG, CHARLES WELLINGTON (cont.)

Tacna-Arica Arbitration, 1925-1926; and administrative correspondence, orders, field notebooks, and Col Furlong's "Press review" consisting of resumes of the South American press in 1926. 6 ft.

FURNITURE

IL —UNIVERSITY OF ILLINOIS, URBANA/CHAMPAIGN, Library, Home Economics Library, 314 Bevier Hall, Champaign, 61820. Barbara C Swain, Librn
Holdings: Vols Cat Microforms
Notes: Textiles, apparel and interior design.

IL —ART INSTITUTE OF CHICAGO, Ryerson & Burnham Libraries, Michigan Ave & Adams St, Chicago, 60603. Daphne C Roloff, Dir
Holdings: Vols (136,000) Cat Mss Slides Microforms
Budget: ($167,000)
Notes: Total collection incl 300,000 slides.

IN —ALLEN COUNTY PUBLIC LIBRARY, 900 Webster St, Fort Wayne, 46802. Paul Deane, Reader Services Dept Head; Kay Lynn Isca, Art Music & AV Dept Head
Holdings: Vols 1257 Cat Pix

MA —OLD STURBRIDGE VILLAGE, Research Library, Sturbridge, 01566. Theresa Rini Percy, Librn
Holdings: Cat Mss Pix
Notes: New England, to 1850.

MO —THE NELSON-ATKINS MUSEUM OF ART, Kenneth & Helen Spencer Art Reference Library, 4525 Oak St, Kansas City, 64111. Stanley W Hess, Librn

NM —MUSEUM OF NEW MEXICO, Museum of International Folk Art Library, 706 Camino Lejo, Santa Fe, 87501. Judith Sellars, Librn
Holdings: Vols (8000) Cat
Notes: Folk art of all countries, incl such subjects as costume, ceramics, textiles, furniture. Restricted use; noncirculating.

NY —GENEVA HISTORICAL SOCIETY, James Luckett Memorial Archives, 543 S Main St, Geneva, 14456. Eleanore Clise, Librn

NY —COLUMBIA UNIVERSITY LIBRARIES, Avery Architectural and Fine Arts Library, 201 Avery Hall, New York, 10027. Angela Giral, Librn
Holdings: Vols 700 Cat
Notes: Emphasis on decorative art. Restricted use: noncirculating.

NY —NEW YORK PUBLIC LIBRARY, Art, Prints, and Photographs Div, Fifth Ave & 42 St, New York, 10018. Donald Anderle, Chief
Holdings: Vols (150,000) Cat Mss Pix Microforms
Notes: History and design in the fine and applied arts. Architecture, painting, drawing, sculpture, costume, furniture, advertising art, prints, photography, crafts, and jewelry are among the subjects covered from ancient times to the present. See: New York Public Library *Dictionary Catalog of the Art and Architecture Division* (Boston, G K Hall, 1975), 30 vols. Holdings after that time are incl in the *Dictionary Catalog of the Research Libraries.* African Art and Afro-American Art are collected by the Schomburg Center for Research in Black Culture.

NC —NORTH CAROLINA STATE UNIVERSITY, D H Hill Library, Box 7111, Raleigh, 27695. I T Littleton, Dir
Holdings: Vols 454 Cat
Notes: Emphasis on manufacturing and management.

OH —OHIO STATE UNIVERSITY, Home Economics Library, Campbell Hall Rm 325, 1787 Neil Ave, Columbus, 43210. Neosha Mackey, Librn
Holdings: Vols (14,000) Cat Microforms
Notes: Separate catalog. Also, book catalog: *Catalog of the Home Economics Library* (Boston: G K Hall, 1976), 3 vols.

OR —UNIVERSITY OF OREGON LIBRARY, Architecture & Allied Arts Branch, Eugene, 97403. Reyburn R McCready, Head Librn
Holdings: Cat
Notes: Farmington Plan assignment.

OR —BASSIST COLLEGE LIBRARY, 2000 SW Fifth Ave, Portland, 97201. Norma Bassist, Librn
Holdings: Vols 250 Cat Mss Pix Slides
Notes: Significant additions in the "history of" category and modern furniture and designers.

RI —RHODE ISLAND SCHOOL OF DESIGN, Library, Two College St, Providence, 02903. James A Findlay, Dir
Holdings: Vols (70,000) Cat
Budget: ($50,000)

VT —SHELBURNE MUSEUM, Library, Shelburne, 05482. Barbara Reenstierna, Librn
Holdings: Vols 200 Cat Slides

VA —COLONIAL WILLIAMSBURG FOUNDATION, Abby Aldrich Rockefeller Folk Art Center, PO Box C, Williamsburg, 23187. Anne E Watkins, Registrar
Holdings: Vols (5000) Cat
Notes: American folk arts and crafts. Periodicals of current art, antiques, and history. Researchers wishing to use the library are requested to call the museum for an appointment.

WI —MILWAUKEE PUBLIC LIBRARY, 814 W Wisconsin Ave, Milwaukee, 53233. Donald J Sager, City Librn
Holdings: Vols Cat
Notes: Special strength.
See also entry under Art, Decorative.

FURNITURE—DESIGN see Furniture Design

FURNITURE—HISTORY

DC —LIBRARY OF CONGRESS, Washington, 20540.
Notes: The Charles Eames Collection of original negatives and prints of each of the 106 films he created, business correspondence from 1944 to 1978, approximately 400,000 color slides, 31,000 black-and-white photographs, production materials for exhibits, and drawings for all the major furniture designs. Acquired on a grant of $500,000 from IBM.

NY —NEW YORK PUBLIC LIBRARY, Art, Prints, and Photographs Div, Fifth Ave & 42 St, New York, 10018. Donald Anderle, Chief
Holdings: Vols (150,000) Cat Mss Pix Microforms
Notes: History and design in the fine and applied arts. Architecture, painting, drawing, sculpture, costume, furniture, advertising art, prints, photography, crafts, and jewelry are among the subjects covered from ancient times to the present. See: New York Public Library *Dictionary Catalog of the Art and Architecture Division* (Boston, G K Hall, 1975), 30 vols. Holdings after that time are incl in the *Dictionary Catalog of the Research Libraries.* African Art and Afro-American Art are collected by the Schomburg Center for Research in Black Culture.

FURNITURE DESIGN

DC —LIBRARY OF CONGRESS, Washington, 20540.
Notes: Papers and working materials of Charles Eames (1907-1978), American architect and designer. Incl are original negatives and prints of the 106 educational films he created, business correspondence 1944 to 1978, some 400,000 color slides, 31,000 black and white photographs, production materials for exhibits and drawings for all his major furniture designs.

FURNITURE INDUSTRY AND TRADE

NC —NORTH CAROLINA STATE UNIVERSITY, D H Hill Library, Box 7111, Raleigh, 27695. I T Littleton, Dir
Holdings: Vols 600 Cat
Budget: $1000
Notes: Emphasis on manufacturing and management. Incl monographs.
See also entry under Furniture

FUSARIA

PA —PENNSYLVANIA STATE UNIVERSITY, Fred Lewis Pattee Library, Life Sciences Library, University Park, 16802. Keith Roe, Head
Notes: This collection is strong in periodical runs, particularly European learned societies and agriculture. It contains extensive collections of Experiment Station publications and has developed specialties in Mycology and Fusaria. There is also a special collection of 1105 glass slides on early Pennsylvania lumbering.

FUTURE LIFE

NY —PARAPSYCHOLOGY FOUNDATION, Eileen J Garrett Library, 228 E 71st St, New York, 10021. Wayne Norman, Librn
Holdings: Vols (9300) Cat
Notes: One of the largest libraries on parapsychology. Main emphasis is on the literature of contemporary parapsychology; also a strong collection on the history of parapsychology (early spiritualism, mysticism, relevant philosophical works, etc). Rare book collection incl early rare books and periodicals on psychical research and psychical phenomena. Receives about 100 titles of periodicals and binds the more significant titles. The library maintains its own periodicals index to parapsychological literature, dating from 1966. Main emphasis literature is on experimental parapsychology, or those publications that approach the subject with an objective and/or analytic point of view.

FUTURES see Commodity Exchanges; Speculation

FUTURISM (ART)

CT —YALE UNIVERSITY, Beinecke Rare Book & Manuscript Library, Osborn Collection, New Haven, 06520. Stephen R Parks, Cur
Holdings: Mss

IL —NORTHWESTERN UNIVERSITY, Library, Special Collections Dept, 1937 Sheridan Rd, Evanston, 60201. R Russell Maylone, Cur
Holdings: Vols 600 Cat Mss Pix
Notes: Futurism in Italian art and literature. Books, periodicals, pamphlets, manifesti catalogs, ephemra. Incl correspondence of F T Marinetti.

FUTURISM (LITERATURE)

CA —UNIVERSITY OF CALIFORNIA, LOS ANGELES, Library, Slavic Collection, 405 Hilgard Ave, Los Angeles, 90024. Edward Shreeves, Chairman, Bibliographers Group; Leon Ferder, Slavic Bibliographer
Holdings: Vols (250,000) Cat Mss Maps
Notes: The entire range of humanities, social sciences, and the arts. One of the most comprehensive US collections for material not only on Russia and the Soviet Union, but also on Bulgaria, Czechoslovakia, Poland, Yugoslavia, the non-Slavic countries of Eastern Europe (Romania, Hungary, Albania) and Soviet Central Asia. Holdings in Russian and Slavic linguistics, Russian literature, and Russian history are particularly strong, covering all periods. The collections are described in some detail in Paul Horecky's book on US Slavic collections.

CT —YALE UNIVERSITY, Beinecke Rare Book & Manuscript Library, Osborn Collection, New Haven, 06520. Stephen R Parks, Cur
Holdings: Mss

IL —UNIVERSITY OF ILLINOIS, URBANA/CHAMPAIGN, Slavic and East European Library, Urbana, 61801. Marianna Tax Choldin, Head
Holdings: Cat Microforms
Notes: IDC microfiche collection. (959)

FUTURISM (LITERATURE) (cont.)

titles of symbolism, futurism, constructivism, acmeism, imagism, and zemstvo publications.

ON —METROPOLITAN TORONTO LIBRARY, Literature Dept, 789 Yonge St, Toronto, M4W 2G8, Can. Katherine McCook, Head
Holdings: Vols (200) Cat
Notes: Books, periodicals, pamphlets, especially on French literature. Part of a collection on other international avant-garde literary movements.

G

GABLE, CLARK

CA —UNIVERSITY OF SOUTHERN CALIFORNIA, Edward L Doheny Memorial Library, Archives of Performing Arts, University Park, Los Angeles, 90089. Robert Knutson, Librn
Holdings: Mss Pix
Notes: Personal collection of papers, pictures, etc.

GABON

DC —HOWARD UNIVERSITY, Moorland-Spingarn Research Center, 500 Howard Place NW, Washington, 20059. Clifford L Muse, Jr, Acting Dir

MA —BRANDEIS UNIVERSITY, Goldfarb Library, 415 South St, Waltham, 02154. Bessie Hahn, Dir
Notes: Albert Schweitzer Collection. This collection consists of 255 letters of correspondence to and from Dr Albert Schweitzer and other staff members of the Lambarene Hospital, Gabon, Africa. Also included in the collection are some artifacts, memorabilia and two commemorative Albert Schweitzer volumes. A guide to the collection was published in *Guide to Albert Schweitzer Collections in the United States.* New York, 1981.

GADE, NIELS WILHELM, 1877-1890

CA —UNIVERSITY OF CALIFORNIA, RIVERSIDE, University Library, 4045 Canyon Crest Dr, Box 5900, Riverside, 92517.
Holdings: Vols 600 Cat Mss
Notes: Complete collection of the printed music of the Danish composer, Niels W Gade, incl first editions, arrangements, and parts. A typescript list, "Niels W Gade (1817-1890) Bibliography; a catalog, compiled by Dan Fog" (Copenhagen, 1967) is available for consultation.

GADNEY, REG

MA —BOSTON UNIVERSITY, Mugar Memorial Library, Special Collections Dept, 771 Commonwealth Ave, Boston, 02215. Howard B Gotlieb, Dir
Holdings: Cat Mss Pix
Notes: Mss, correspondence, etc collected in depth; incl publications by or about.

GAELIC FOLK MUSIC see Folk Music, Gaelic

GAELIC FOLKLORE see Folklore, Gaelic

GAELIC LANGUAGE (IRISH) see Irish Language and Literature

GAG, WANDA, 1893-1946

MN —UNIVERSITY OF MINNESOTA, Libraries, Children's Literature Research Collections, 109 Walter Library, Minneapolis, 55455. Karen Nelson Hoyle, Cur
Holdings: Vols 22 Cat Mss Pix
Notes: Wanda Gag Collection, incl translations of her work.

GAGE, THOMAS

IL —UNIVERSITY OF ILLINOIS, URBANA/CHAMPAIGN, Library, Illinois Historical Survey Library, 1408 W Gregory Dr, 1A Library, Urbana, 61801.
Holdings: Vols 500 Cat Mss Maps Microforms
Notes: Colonial and Revolutionary Period--Midwest, particularly Illinois. Important ms collections (75 cubic feet) under this subject incl: Baynton, Wharton and Morgan, papers, 1757-1799, 6 reels of microfilm; British Archives, 1547-1958, 7000 items, 40 reels of microfilm; Cunningham Collection, 1600-1836, 40 cubic feet (typed copies from Archives in Spain and South America); French Archives, 1671-1796, 3500 items; Gage, Thomas, papers, 1759-1773, 1300 items; Morgan, George, papers, 1766-1826, 280 items, 5 reels of microfilm; Randolph County Records, 1720-1853, 91 items, 59 reels of microfilm; St Clair County Records, 1722-1809, 6 items, 5 reels of microfilm. Guide to the collections published: Maynard J Brichford, Robert M Sutton, Dennis F Walle, *Manuscripts Guide to Collections at the University of Illinois at* Urbana-Champaign(Urbana, Chicago, London: University of Illinois Press, 1976).

MI —UNIVERSITY OF MICHIGAN, William L Clements Library, Ann Arbor, 48109. John C Dann, Dir
Notes: The William L. Clements Library of Americana is a non-circulating rare book library of original source material, printed and manuscript, dealing with America, from the discovery period into the late nineteenth century. The collection includes approximately 55,000 books and pamphlets, 550 linear feet of manuscripts, 4,100 volumes of newspapers, 36,000 maps, 40,000 pieces of sheet music, and 1,000 prints. The collection is strongest for the period of the American Revolution, and includes the papers of Thomas Gage, Sir Henry Clinton, and the Earl of Shelburne. Other areas of strength include antislavery, cartography and geography, discovery and exploration, American Indians, The Civil War, tune-books, sermons and orations, and the War of 1812. There are selective research collections dealing with Christopher Columbus, Thomas Paine, Benjamin Franklin, George Washington, Thomas Jefferson, and the Federalist Papers. Publications describing the collections of the library are: Author/Title catalog of Americana 1493-1860 in the William L. Clements Library... 7 volumes, Boston, G. K. Hall, 1970; Guide to the manuscript collections of the William L. Clements Library, by Arlene P. Shy 3d edition, Boston, G. K. Hall, 1978; Guide to the manuscript maps in the William L. Clements Library, compiled by Christian Burn, Ann Arbor, U. of Michigan, 1959; and Research catalog of maps of America, to 1860 in the William L. Clements Library...,edited by Douglas W. Marshall, 4 volumes, Boston, G. K. Hall, 1972.

GAGLIARDO, RUTH GARVER

KS —EMPORIA STATE UNIVERSITY, William Allen White Library, Emporia, 66801. Mary E Bogan, Special Collections Librn
Holdings: Vols (1804) Cat
Notes: The Ruth Garver Gagliardo Collection contains books from the personal library of this noted Specialist in Children's Literature who established the William Allen White Children's Book Award as the first statewide reader's choice award program. Included are rare and valuable books, many of which were inscribed to her by the notable authors and illustrators. The collection also contains correspondence and photographs as well as writings by Ruth Gagliardo and articles about her. (Approx 4 1/2 linear feet of other materials.) Ruth Gagliardo, a former teacher and a journalist on the staff of William Allen White's *Emporia Gazette*, became known as the "Kansas Book Lady" for her work in bringing books to Kansas children.
See also entry under Children's Literature

GAIT, HUMAN

NY —UNIVERSITY OF ROCHESTER, School of Medicine and Dentistry, Edward G Miner Library, 601 Elmwood Ave, Rochester, 14642. Lucretia McClure, Medical Librn; Janet Brady Berk, History of Medicine Librn
Holdings: Slides
Notes: Very rare historical collection of some 300 glass slides, most of which relate to human gait, the foot, footwear, and myodynamics.

GALANTIERE, LEWIS

†NY —COLUMBIA UNIVERSITY LIBRARIES, Butler Library, Rare Book and Manuscript Library, 535 W 114 St, New York, 10027.
Notes: Lewis Galantiere's papers, etc, with much on Antoine de Saint-Exupery, French language and literature, modern French authors and their works, etc. Considerable correspondence with many of the latter as well as with American and British authors.

GALARZA, ERNESTO

CA —STANFORD UNIVERSITY LIBRARIES, Cecil H Green Library, Stanford, 94305. Michael T Ryan, Cur
Notes: Ms collections of individuals and organizations whose activities have influenced public policy issues pertaining to Mexican Americans. Collections incl: the Mexican American Legal Defense Educational Fund (MALDEF) archives, the Centro de Accion Social Autonomo (CASA) records, the Ernesto Galarza papers, the Bert Corona papers, the Manuel Ruiz Jr papers, the Eduardo Queredo papers and the Edward Valenzuela papers.

GALAXIES—STRUCTURE

CA —UNIVERSITY OF CALIFORNIA, SANTA CRUZ, University Library, Special Collections, Santa Cruz, 95064. Rita Bottoms, Special Collections Librn; Margaret Felts, South Pacific Collection Bibliographer
Holdings: Cat
Notes: Astronomy library. Incl all major astronomical and astrophysical journals and an extensive collection of domestic and foreign observatory publications. The book collection is particularly strong in stellar structure and evolution, stellar spectroscopy, the interstellar medium, galactic structure, external galaxies, general relativity and gravitational radiation, and high-energy astrophysics.

GALBRAITH, JOHN KENNETH, JR.

†MA —JOHN F KENNEDY LIBRARY, Columbia Point, Boston, 02125. Dan H Fenn Jr, Dir
Holdings: Cat Mss
Notes: Correspondence, draft manuscripts of books and articles, reports, and other personal and official papers, 1930-1963. 45 linear ft of mss. Holdings are described in "Historical Materials in the John F Kennedy Library." Copies may by obtained by writing the Research Archivist.

GALDOS, BENITO PEREZ

MO —WASHINGTON UNIVERSITY, John M Olin Library, Campus Box 1061, St Louis, 63130.
Holdings: Vols (15,000) Cat Microforms
Notes: Major subject concentration.

GALE, NORMAN

CA —UNIVERSITY OF SAN FRANCISCO, Richard A Gleeson Library, The Countess

GALE, NORMAN (cont.)

Bernardine Murphy Donohue Rare Book Room, San Francisco, 94117. D Steven Corey, Special Collections Librn
Holdings: Vols 20
Notes: Incl 15 ALS.

GALEN

CT —YALE UNIVERSITY, Medical Historical Library, 333 Cedar St, New Haven, 06510. Ferenc A Gyorgyey, Librn
Holdings: Vols 280 Cat
Notes: Incl numerous editions of his writings.

PA —COLLEGE OF PHYSICIANS OF PHILADELPHIA, Library, 19 S 22 St, Philadelphia, 19103. Christine Ruggere, Cur, Historical Collections
Holdings: Vols (316,223) Cat Mss
Budget: ($1,096, 223)
Notes: Very strong collection.
See also entry under Medicine.

GALENA ORE see Lead

GALES see Storms

GALICIAN LANGUAGE AND LITERATURE

DC —LIBRARY OF CONGRESS, Collections Management Division, Washington, 20540.
Notes: 8000 plays published principally in Madrid and Barcelona after 1850. Considerable number in Catalan and Galician dialects.

GALILEO GALILEI

CA —CALIFORNIA INSTITUTE OF TECHNOLOGY, Robert A Millikan Memorial Library, 1201 E California Blvd, Pasadena, 91125. Judith R Goodstein, Archivist
Holdings: Vols (2300) Cat
Notes: Emphasis on the period of Galileo and Kepler. Incl the Watson History of Science Collection and the Rocco Collection. Catalogs.

ON —UNIVERSITY OF TORONTO, Thomas Fisher Rare Book Library, 120 Saint George St, Toronto, M5S 1A5, Can. Richard G Landon, Head
Holdings: Vols 300 Cat
Notes: Stillman Drake Galileo Collection, named for collector Prof Stillman Drake, University of Toronto. Comprises early editions of Galileo, of his precursors (Ptolemy and Copernicus) and of his contemporaries in the fields of astronomy and physical science.

GALLAGHER, CORNELIUS

OK —UNIVERSITY OF OKLAHOMA, Bizzell Memorial Library, Western History Collections, 401 W Brooks, Norman, 73069. John Ezell, Cur
Holdings: Mss Documents Pix
Notes: US Representative. His papers.

GALLAGHER, SISTER MIRIAM

DC —GEORGETOWN UNIVERSITY, Library, Special Collections Div, 37 & O Sts NW, Washington, 20057. George M Barringer, Special Collections Librn; Nicholas B Sheetz, Mss Librn
Holdings: Mss Cat
Notes: Correspondence between the author and poet Sister Miriam Gallagher; and numerous authors such as Theodore Maynard, Robert Tristram Coffin, and John Hall Wheelock, among others. Of particular interest are long runs of correspondence from H L Mencken (1937-1943, 64 TLS) and Odell Shepard (1933-1945, 47 TLS and ALS).

GALLATIN, ALBERT

NY —NEW YORK HISTORICAL SOCIETY, Library, 170 Central Park W, New York, 10024. James Gregory, Librn
Notes: Miscellaneous papers, correspondence, etc.

GALLERY, ADM. DANIEL V., 1901-1977

MD —US NAVAL ACADEMY, Nimitz Library, Annapolis, 21402. Alice S Creighton, Assistant Librn for Special Collections
Holdings: Mss Pix
Notes: Rear admiral Daniel V Gallery, naval officer and author of many books. Papers fill 98 boxes and cover Gallery's naval and literary careers. Inventory available in Special Collections Department.

GALLICO, PAUL

NY —COLUMBIA UNIVERSITY LIBRARIES, Rare Book & Manuscript Library, 801 Butler Library, 535 W 114 St, New York, 10027. Kenneth A Lohf, Librn
Holdings: Mss Pix
Notes: Papers, incl mss, letters, reviews, etc. Incl 15,000 items. Restricted use.

GALLIE, MENNA

MA —BOSTON UNIVERSITY, Mugar Memorial Library, Special Collections Dept, 771 Commonwealth Ave, Boston, 02215. Howard B Gotlieb, Dir
Holdings: Cat Mss Correspondence

GALLMAN, WALDEMAR J., 1899-1980

MA —BOSTON UNIVERSITY, Mugar Memorial Library, Special Collections Dept, 771 Commonwealth Ave, Boston, 02215. Howard B Gotlieb, Dir
Holdings: // Cat Mss
Notes: Mss, correspondence, etc collected in depth; incl publications by or about.

GALLOWAY FAMILY

OH —GREENE COUNTY DISTRICT LIBRARY, 76 E Market St, PO Box 520, Xenia, 45385. Julie M Overton, Local History Coordr
Holdings: // Uncat
Notes: Galloway Collection of Ohio history is housed in a five-drawer filing cabinet, incl letters, some at the time of the Gold Rush; family letters of the Galloways, Lyons, Worthingtons and others; material about William Maxwell, editor and publisher of the first newspaper in the Northwest Territory, also legal papers concerning him; papers, some legal, concerning Galloways, incl "The Galloway Lands in 1812," and papers about the Worthingtons and Lyons; indentures; Civil War diary of Clark Galloway, MD, a surgeon in the war; pictures of families, covered bridges, mills etc; material about Tecumseh and some other Indians and their traditions; galley sheets and correspondence concerning the publishing of the New Testament in the Shawnee language; material about the railroad, OVCH (formerly OS&OS Home) Antioch College, Wilberforce University and other items about Ohiohistory; many notes, papers and correspondence acquired when William Galloway was preparing to write the book "Old Chillicothe," published posthumously in 1934.

GALSWORTHY, JOHN, 1867-1933

CA —AZUSA PACIFIC COLLEGE, Marshburn Memorial Library, Citrus & Alosta, Azusa, 91702. Edward Peterman, Librn
Holdings: Vols (150) Uncat
Notes: The Odo B Stade Collection of Literary First Editions. No photocopying.

CA —UNIVERSITY OF CALIFORNIA, LOS ANGELES, Research Library, Dept of Special Collections, 405 Hilgard Ave, Los Angeles, 90024. Edward Shreeves, Chairman, Bibliographers Group; David S Zeidberg, Head
Holdings: Vols 250 Cat
Notes: 250 first and other editions of his books; 1/2 linear foot of papers.

CA —STANFORD UNIVERSITY LIBRARIES, Cecil H Green Library, Stanford, 94305. Michael T Ryan, Cur
Holdings: Vols Cat
Notes: Also incl correspondence and literary mss.

IL —ILLINOIS STATE UNIVERSITY, Milner Library, Dept of Special Collections, Normal, 61761. Robert Sokan, Librn
Notes: First editions, limited editions, ephemera, etc.

IN —INDIANA UNIVERSITY, Lilly Library, Seventh St, Bloomington, 47405. William R Cagle, Librn
Holdings: Vols 160 // Cat Mss
Notes: First editions and 285 ms pieces.

MA —BOSTON UNIVERSITY, Mugar Memorial Library, Special Collections Dept, 771 Commonwealth Ave, Boston, 02215. Howard B Gotlieb, Dir
Holdings: Cat
Notes: Publications by, collected in depth.

MA —BRANDEIS UNIVERSITY, Goldfarb Library, 415 South St, Waltham, 02154. Bessie Hahn, Dir
Notes: John Galsworthy Collection. Approx 175 letters written to Joseph Conrad, Sir Edmund Gosse and others and 15 linear ft of books consisting of first editions and books about John Galsworthy. Access to the collection of books is through the Main Card Catalog and Special Collections Catalog. A finding list to the correspondence is in Special Collections.

MI —DETROIT PUBLIC LIBRARY, Rare Books Department, 5201 Woodward Ave, Detroit, 48202.
Holdings: Vols 180 Cat
Notes: Restricted use. Reference collection.

MN —UNIVERSITY OF MINNESOTA, O Meredith Wilson Library, 309 19 Ave S, Minneapolis, 55455. Austin J McLean, Chief, Special Collections
Holdings: Vols 120 Cat
Notes: First and special editions.

NY —ALFRED UNIVERSITY, Herrick Memorial Library, Alfred, 14802. June E Brown, Head Librn
Notes: The Evelyn Tennyson Openhym Collection of modern British literature and social history. Papers, incl correspondence of authors concerned with the business aspects of authorship. Gift of Evelyn Tennyson Openhym of Wellsville, NY. Also, 5300 volumes of British literature.

NY —HOFSTRA UNIVERSITY, Library, 1000 Fulton Ave, Hempstead, 11550. Charles R Andrews, Dean of Library Services
Notes: Strong collection. Incl some mss.

NY —UNIVERSITY OF ROCHESTER, Rush Rhees Library, Department of Rare Books and Special Collections, Rochester, 14627. Peter Dzwonkoski, Librn
Holdings: Vols 150 Cat Mss
Notes: No photocopying.

NY —UNION COLLEGE, Schaffer Library, Schenectady, 12308. Ann Seemann, Librn; Ellen Fladger, Archivist
Holdings: Vols 68 Cat
Notes: First editions.

NC —UNIVERSITY OF NORTH CAROLINA, CHAPEL HILL, Wilson Library, Rare Book Collection, Chapel Hill, 27514. Paul S Koda, Cur of Rare Books
Holdings: Cat
Notes: Fully representative collection.

OH —OHIO UNIVERSITY, Vernon R Alden Library, Department of Archives and Special Collections, Athens, 45701. Gary A Hunt, Head
Holdings: Vols 135 Cat
Notes: Incl many early works, several pamphlets, and a few American firsts.

ON —QUEEN'S UNIVERSITY, Douglas Library, Kingston, K7L 5C4, Can. William F E Morley, Cur, Special Collections
Holdings: Vols 100 Cat Mss Pix
Notes: Subject strength of the collection. Also Buchan Collection, 5000 vols.

GALT, JOHN

ON —UNIVERSITY OF GUELPH, McLaughlin Library, Guelph, N1G 2W1, Can. Margaret Beckman, Head Librn; David

GALT, JOHN (cont.)

Hull, Sciences Librn
Holdings: 200 Cat
Notes: Monographs and periodicals.
See also entries under Ontario - History; Scotland

GALVANIC BATTERIES see Electric Batteries

GALVANISM see Electricity

GALVANOPLASTY see Electrometallurgy; Electroplating

GALVESTON, TEXAS

TX —ROSENBERG LIBRARY, Galveston and Texas History Center, 2310 Sealy Ave, Galveston, 77550. Jane Kenamore, Archivist
Holdings: Vols 7368 Cat Mss Maps Pix Slides Microforms
Budget: $60,000
Notes: Emphasis on upper Texas coast material; Republic of Texas period; Civil War period; Shipping; Texas Navy; Jean Laffite; Texas politics, 19th-20th century; Railroads; Texas journalism, incl microfilms of Galveston newspapers, 1838-date.

THE GAMBIA

DC —HOWARD UNIVERSITY, Moorland-Spingarn Research Center, 500 Howard Place NW, Washington, 20059. Clifford L Muse, Jr, Acting Dir

MI —MICHIGAN STATE UNIVERSITY, International Library, Sahel Documentation Center, East Lansing, 48824. Eugene deBenko, Librn; Learthen Dorsey, Librn
Holdings: Vols (5100) Cat Mss Maps Pix Slides Phonorecords Audiotapes Videotapes Microforms
Budget: ($8000)
Notes: See description under The Sahel.

GAMBLING

IL —DE PAUL UNIVERSITY, Library, 2323 N Seminary, Chicago, 60614. Kathryn De Graff, Special Collections Librn
Holdings: Vols (900) // Uncat
Notes: The Anita Peabody Sports Collection of approx 900 volumes, incl about 250 periodical volumes, covering such topics as foxhunting, gambling, horse racing, and breeding, along with rule books and song books. Materials cover the middle to late 19th century. A complete run of *The Sporting Magazine,* begun in 1792, is also part of the collection.

LA —LOUISIANA STATE UNIVERSITY, Troy H Middleton Library, Baton Rouge, 70803. Lance E Dickson, Acting Dir
Notes: About two thirds of all the known books and other materials published on the subject of poker. Some 500 pieces. Gift of former Judge Oliver P "Ike" Carriere, of New Orleans.

NV —CLARK COUNTY LIBRARY DISTRICT, Las Vegas Library, 1726 E Charleston, Las Vegas, 89104. Jack Gardner, Librn Administrator
Holdings: Vols 400 Cat

NM —MUSEUM OF NEW MEXICO, Photo Archives, Box 2087, Santa Fe, 87503. Arthur L Olivas, Cur; Richard Rudisill, Photo Historian
Notes: Photographs of recreation, indoor and outdoor, to include games, gambling, camping, etc.

GAME AND GAME BIRDS

OR —OREGON STATE UNIVERSITY, Library, Corvallis, 97331. Melvin George, Dir

GAME FISHING

OH —OHIO HISTORICAL SOCIETY, Archives Library Division, 1982 Velma Ave, Columbus, 43211. Dennis East, Division Chief
Holdings: Vols 2000// Cat Mss Pix
Notes: Collection is comprised of books by Grey, magazines in which his writings appeared, mss & typescripts, and 700 items from his personal library, incl scarce items on hunting, big-game fishing, and travel. Museum objects are at the Zane Grey Museum, Zanesville, Ohio, operated by the Ohio Historical Society.

GAME MANAGEMENT see Wildlife Management

GAME RECORDS

NY —AMERICAN MUSEUM OF NATURAL HISTORY, Library Services Dept, Central Park W & 79th St, New York, 10024. Nina J Root, Chairwoman; Mary Genett, Asst Librn for Reference Services
Holdings: Vols (385,000) Cat Mss Maps Pix Slides Microforms
Notes: Nearly all collections are outstanding for depth of coverage and international range. Early and historic works, rare books, colored illustrations, and relevant serial publications supplement the modern scientific publications necessary to the researches of the scientific staff and the work of the educational division. Open to the public.

GAMES

CO —SOCIAL SCIENCE EDUCATION CONSORTIUM, Resource & Demonstration Center (RDC), 855 Broadway, Boulder, 80302. Regina McCormick, Staff Assoc
Holdings: Vols (16,000) Cat Filmstrips Microforms
Notes: Educational games. Contains over 15, 000 elementary and secondary social studies, textbooks, audiovisuals, games and simulations, professional books, and the complete ERIC microfiche collection. Staff available to travel to all parts of the US to consult on curriculum development, instructional methods, materials analysis and selection, evaluation, new materials, teaching strategies, and trends in the social studies.

IL —UNIVERSITY OF ILLINOIS, URBANA/CHAMPAIGN, Library, Applied Life Studies Library, 1408 W Gregory Dr, Urbana, 61801.
Holdings: Vols (38,000) Cat Microforms
Notes: Library has own card catalog and shelf list for this collection; it is also represented in the main card catalog and shelf list of the University of Illinois Library. Card indexes to games and sports are incl in books in the collection, also to folk and national dances. Try to have fairly complete coverage of books published in all aspects of the field of physical education which would be of interest to students, as well as a lot of more general books on sports. Coverage of health education and recreation is also quite complete. This is one of the few (if not only) departmental libraries in the US devoted to this field. Published catalog: *Dictionary Catalog of the Applied Life Studies Library* (formerly Physical Education Library) *University of Illinois at Urbana-Champaign* v 1-4 (Boston: G K Hall, 1977) and *First* Supplement v 1-2 (Boston: G K Hall, 1982).

IN —INDIANA UNIVERSITY, Lilly Library, Seventh St, Bloomington, 47405. William R Cagle, Librn
Holdings: Vols 140 // Cat
Notes: American card games of the late 19th century.

IN —UNIVERSITY OF NOTRE DAME, University Libraries, Notre Dame, 46556.
Notes: Very likely the largest collection of sporting materials in the world. Over 500 sports and games are represented in a half-million documents. All physical forms of records are included, and there is no geographical restriction. Major center for research into all aspects of games and sports.

KY —UNIVERSITY OF KENTUCKY, Margaret I King Library, Dept of Special Collections, Lexington, 40506. William Marshall, Head
Holdings: Vols (400) Uncat
Notes: Early physical education manuals and textbooks to 1925; 18th and 19th century sports, games.

MN —MINNEAPOLIS PUBLIC LIBRARY & INFORMATION CENTER, Sociology Dept, 300 Nicollet Mall, Minneapolis, 55401. Eileen Scwartzbauer, Dept Head
Holdings: Vols (90,000) Cat Phonorecords Audiotapes Microforms
Budget: ($69,890)
Notes: Special collections: Foundation Center Regional Collection; college catalogs on fiche; adult basic education collection. Separate department catalog.

MS —UNIVERSITY OF MISSISSIPPI, John Davis Williams Library, University, 38677.
Notes: The folklore library of Professor Kenneth S Goldstein comprises more than 12,000 vols and 4500 phonodiscs. Incl a comprehensive 3000 vol collection of editions of collected folksongs and works about the evolution of the Anglo-American folksong, as well as works treating the folklore and folk life of Britain, Ireland, Canada, and Australia. The collection contains specialized holdings on children's lore and games, Afro-American folklore, and folklore theory. The phonodisc collection is rich in examples of American, English, Scottish, and Irish revival.

NJ —PRINCETON UNIVERSITY, Library, Gest Oriental Library & East Asian Collections, 317 Palmer Hall, Princeton, 08544. D E Perushek, Cur
Holdings: Vols 500 // Cat
Notes: Gift from the American Go Association. About 500 volumes on Go; all in Japanese. Separate catalog to the collection.

NY —QUEENS BOROUGH PUBLIC LIBRARY, Art & Music Div, 89-11 Merrick Blvd, Jamaica, 11432. Dorothea Wu, Head
Holdings: Vols (85,000) Cat Maps Pix Phonorecords Audiotapes Microforms
Budget: ($44,000)
Notes: The Picture Collection, covering all subjects, consists of approximately 1,500,000 pictures, mainly reproductions and clippings from books and magazines, photographs, and postcards on all subjects; The Framed Picture Collection, approx 180 framed pictures, mostly reproductions of paintings from various periods; and The Phonorecord and Cassette Collection consists of approx 3500 reference phonorecords and 6500 circulating records as well as 1000 reference cassettes and 1500 circulating cassettes.

NY —MORRIS N & CHESLEY V YOUNG LIBRARY OF MNEMONICS, 270 Riverside Dr, New York, 10025. Morris N Young, Cur
Holdings: Cat Mss Maps Pix Phonorecords Audiotapes 16mm Films Microforms
Notes: Collection of 5000 books, pamphlets, pictures, memorabilia, etc incl medieval art of memory; psychology of memory, forgetting and reading; medical aspects of memory, amnesia, dyslexia; biomedical aspects of learning and memory; information storage, retrieval and cybernetics; memory prodigies, lightning calculators, calendars; remembrance cups and memory mementos. All languages. Memorabilia incl engravings, posters, programs, advertisements, birthday cards, teaching cards, ASLs, and Mark Twain's Memory Builder game and other games. Items range from 1410 to 1980s.

NY —NEW YORK PUBLIC LIBRARY, Research Libraries, General Research Division, Fifth Ave & 42 St, New York, 10018. Rodney Phillips, Chief
Holdings: Vols (2,225,000) Cat Maps Pix Microforms
Budget: ($775,718)

OK —SOCIETY FOR THE NORTH AMERICAN CULTURAL SURVEY, Dept of Geography, Oklahoma State University, Stillwater, 74078. John Rooney, Dir; Todd Zdorkowski, Asst
Notes: Is producing a cultural survey of North American sports and games. Includes both conventional sports (professional, college, high school) and a study of adult and children's games.

RI —PROVIDENCE ATHENAEUM, 251 Benefit St, Providence, 02903. Sally Duplaix, Dir
Holdings: (152,000) Vols
Notes: Material available on interlibrary loan under certain conditions.

GAMES (cont.)

RI —PROVIDENCE PUBLIC LIBRARY, 150 Empire St, Providence, 02903. Lance J Bauer, Special Collections Librn
Holdings: 542 Vols
Notes: The Edward B Hanes Checkers Collection. Incl scarce periodicals on draughts and imprints in many languages dating from 1694.

†ON —METROPOLITAN TORONTO LIBRARY, 789 Yonge St, Toronto, M4W 2G8, Can.
Notes: Good subject strengths.

GAMES, WAR see War Games

GAMING see Gambling

GANDHI, MOHANDAS K.

MA —HARVARD UNIVERSITY LIBRARY, Widener Library, Cambridge, 02138.
Holdings: Cat

WI —BELOIT COLLEGE LIBRARIES, Beloit, 53511. Dennis W Dickinson, Dir
Holdings: Vols 700 Cat
Notes: The Martin Luther King Jr Collection on Nonviolence. This small collection was given by H Vail Deale, Director, at the time of the assassination of Dr King in 1968. Comprises books by and about: M K Gandhi, H D Thoreau, M L King, world peace, pacifism, nonviolence, etc. Contains a 35-year bound file of *Fellowship,* the magazine of US pacifism. At present time there is only a local card index of the collection, though items are fully cataloged in the Public Card Catalog. A specially designed bookplate by local artist, O Vernon Shaffer, is used for books in this collection.

GANN, ERNEST

NY —COLGATE UNIVERSITY, Everett Needham Case Library, Hamilton, 13346. Bruce M Brown, Collections Librn
Holdings: Vols 60 Uncat Mss
Notes: 5 linear ft of mss.

GANNETT, WILLIAM CHANNING, 1840-1923

NY —UNIVERSITY OF ROCHESTER, Rush Rhees Library, Department of Rare Books and Special Collections, Rochester, 14627. Peter Dzwonkoski, Librn
Holdings: Cat Mss
Notes: Correspondence, annual reports, financial records and ephemera of congregation, 1829-1960. Church attended by Susan B Anthony and other active social reformers. Papers of ministers William Channing Gannett (1840-1923) and David Rhys Williams (1890-1970).

GANNETT NEWSPAPERS

NY —CORNELL UNIVERSITY LIBRARIES, Collection of Regional History, Dept of Manuscripts and Univ Archives, Ithaca, 14853.
Notes: "Who Runs New York," 1981; 1 item.

†OK —OKLAHOMA STATE UNIVERSITY, Library, Stillwater, 74074.
Notes: Papers of Paul Miller, chairman emeritus of the Gannett Company. Incl personal papers reflecting his career in journalism and as president of the Associated Press.

GANSEVOORT, PETER

NY —NEW YORK PUBLIC LIBRARY, Rare Books and Manuscripts Div, Fifth Ave & 42 St, New York, 10018. William L Joyce, Asst Dir; Susan E Davis, Cur of Mss
Holdings: Mss
Notes: Incl personal and literary mss, papers, etc.

GANZ, RUDOLPH

IL —NEWBERRY LIBRARY, 60 W Walton St, Chicago, 60610. Diana Haskell, Cur of Modern Mss
Holdings: Uncat Mss Pix
Notes: Correspondence, scrapbooks, ms scores and marked performing scores. Restricted use: noncirculating. A new collection (1972-1973); uncataloged.

GAOLS see Prisons and Prisoners

GARBAGE see Refuse and Refuse Disposal

GARBER, MILTON CLINE

OK —UNIVERSITY OF OKLAHOMA, Bizzell Memorial Library, Western History Collections, 401 W Brooks, Norman, 73069. John Ezell, Cur
Holdings: Mss Documents
Notes: US Representative. His papers. Guide available.

GARD, ALEX

NY —NEW YORK PUBLIC LIBRARY, Performing Arts Research Center, Billy Rose Theatre Collection, 111 Amsterdam Ave, New York, 10023. Dorothy L Swerdlove, Cur
Notes: A large collection (270) of Alex Gard's original caricatures, from Sardi's Restaurant, New York.

GARDEN ARCHITECTURE see Architecture, Domestic; Landscape Gardening

GARDENING see Gardens and Gardening

GARDENS AND GARDENING

CA —UNIVERSITY OF CALIFORNIA, BERKELEY, Environmental Design Library, (The General Library), 210 Wurster Hall, Berkeley, 94720. Arthur B Waugh, Head
Holdings: Vols (9000) Cat
Budget: ($4900)
Notes: Research collection emphasizing the following areas: Park and garden design; site planning; spatial planning; professional practice. Lesser emphasis on horticulture. The Library also includes the Beatrix Farrand Collection of rare books in the field of landscape architecture.

CT —PERROT MEMORIAL LIBRARY, 90 Sound Beach Ave, Old Greenwich, 06870. Michael F Hagan, Dir
Holdings: Vols 340 Cat Pix

IL —LAKE FOREST PUBLIC LIBRARY, 360 E Deerpath, Lake Forest, 60045. Sydney S Mellinger, Admin Librn
Holdings: Vols 1500 Cat

IL —MORTON ARBORETUM, Sterling Morton Library, Lisle, 60532. Ian MacPhail, Librn
Holdings: Vols (20,000) Cat Maps Pix
Budget: ($10,000)
Notes: The library is especially concerned with the literature of woody plants (trees and shrubs) of north temperate zones but has substantial holdings in the taxonomy and systematics of plants in general, both wild and cultivated, flora of different parts of the world, and a growing collection on plant monographs. Also about 2000 pictures. Described in *The Morton Arboretum* Quarterly, vol 9, no 4 (Winter 1973), pp 56-61.

MA —MASSACHUSETTS HORTICULTURAL SOCIETY, 300 Massachusetts Ave, Boston, 02115. Becky Ellis, Librn
Holdings: Vols (37,000)
Notes: Garden history, pomology, flora, landscape design. Print collection of many centuries; nursery catalogues from the mid-18th century. In storage, remodeling, will be available in about a year. Open to the public.

MA —NEW ENGLAND WILD FLOWER SOCIETY, INC, Lawrence Newcomb Library, Hemenway Rd, Framingham, 01701. Mary M Walker, Librn
Holdings: Vols (2500)
Notes: Incl 15,000 slides (35mm) and 4 vertical files.

MA —OLD STURBRIDGE VILLAGE, Research Library, Sturbridge, 01566. Theresa Rini Percy, Librn
Holdings: Cat
Notes: Flower and vegetable gardening in New England, to 1850.

NH —STRAWBERY BANKE, Thayer Cumings Historical Reference Library, Portsmouth, 03801. Nicole R Osborn, Librn
Holdings: Vols (2850) Cat Mss Maps Pix Microforms
Budget: ($1900)
Notes: The Library is a small, highly specialized library with holdings in American art, architecture and decorative arts. The collection is especially strong in the American decorative arts, with additional concentration in European decorative arts. In addition, the collection contains books on American painting, American architecture, archaeology, technology, maritime history and boatbuilding, landscape gardening and design, as well as books on local and regional history and social and material culture of the 17th-19th centuries. Collection of mss microfilm and documents is related to important properties and personages of Portsmouth and the surrounding area.

NY —NEW YORK BOTANICAL GARDEN LIBRARY, Bronx, 10458. Charles R Long, Asst Vice Pres & Dir
Holdings: Vols 13,000 Cat Mss Pix Slides Microforms VF
Budget: ($356,000)
Notes: One of the largest botanical collections in the world. Covers botany (150, 000 vols), botanists (3000), horticulture (45, 000), plant diseases (25,000), plant physiology (15,000), history of botany (1500), conservation of natural resources (15,000), gardening (13,000), paleobotany (7000), ecology (20,000), forestry (5000), medical botany (3000), agriculture (9000) and biology (20,000). Reference library; materials do not circulate, except via standard inter-library loan. About 5000 vols uncataloged. Incl archives, art and vertical files. An OCLC library.

NY —GARDEN CENTER OF ROCHESTER INC, Library, 5 Castle Park, Rochester, 14620. Dorothea Baschnagel, Librn
Holdings: Vols (3000)
Notes: Gardening and home landscaping; plant identification; decorative use of plants; 19th century gardening. 700 bound periodicals, 30 periodical subscriptions.

OH —CLEVELAND PUBLIC LIBRARY, Science & Technology Dept, 325 Superior Ave, Cleveland, 44114. Jean Z Piety, Head
Holdings: Cat
Notes: History of gardens around the world, domestic landscape planning and planting, incl flower gardening, annuals and perennials, and indoor plants.

OH —KINGWOOD CENTER, Library, 900 Park Ave W, Mansfield, 44906. Timothy Gardner, Horticulturist
Holdings: Vols 8500 Cat Slides
Budget: $1500

OH —MASSILLON PUBLIC LIBRARY, 208 Lincoln Way E, Massillon, 44646. Camille Leslie, Dir
Holdings: Vols 250 Cat

OH —THE DAWES ARBORETUM LIBRARY, 7770 Jacksontown Rd SE, Newark, 43055. Alan D Cook, Senior Horticulturist
Holdings: Vols 5000

OR —OREGON STATE UNIVERSITY, Library, Corvallis, 97331. Melvin George, Dir
Holdings: Vols (980,000) Cat

PA —LONGWOOD GARDENS, INC, Library, Kennett Square, 19348. Enola Jane N Teeter, Librn

RI —BLITHEWOLD GARDENS AND ARBORETUM LIBRARY, Ferry Road, Bristol, 02809. Julia L Morris, Horticulturist
Notes: American gardening, 1890-1920, is special strength. Blithewold, built in 1906; its gardens were at their prime in the 1920s.

WI —MANITOWOC PUBLIC LIBRARY, 808 Hamilton St, Manitowoc, 54220. Charles O Perdue, Dir
Holdings: Vols 620 Cat
Budget: $500
Notes: The Ruth West Library of Beauty.

GARDENS AND GARDENING (cont.)

ON —CIVIC GARDEN CENTRE LIBRARY, 777 Lawrence Ave E, Don Mills, M3C 1P2, Can. Pamela MacKenzie, Librn
Holdings: Vols (5000) Cat
Budget: ($3200)

ON —METROPOLITAN TORONTO LIBRARY, Science & Technology Dept, 789 Yonge St, Toronto, M4W 2G8, Can. Margaret Walshe, Head
Holdings: Vols (120,000) Cat VF
Notes: All aspects of technology for the specialist, the student, and the general public. The department gives high priority to Canadian material.

GARDENS AND GARDENING—CALIFORNIA

CA —RANCHO SANTA ANA BOTANIC GARDEN LIBRARY, 1500 N College Ave, Claremont, 91711. Beatrice M Beck, Librn
Notes: Incl emphasis on California flora, floras of the world, evolutionary biology and ethnobotany.

GARDENS AND GARDENING—HISTORY

AZ —NORTHERN ARIZONA UNIVERSITY, Special Collection Library, CU Box 6022, Flagstaff, 86011. Peter M Whiteley, Coordr/Archivist; William Mullane, Librn
Notes: The Alpine Garden Club (Flagstaff, Ariz) Collection; incl scrapbooks, 1948-1965, minute books, 1948-1969, and various landscaping projects.

†DC —HARVARD UNIVERSITY, Dumbarton Oaks, Garden Library, 1703 32nd Street NW, Washington, 20007. Laura Byers, Librn

MA —MASSACHUSETTS HORTICULTURAL SOCIETY, 300 Massachusetts Ave, Boston, 02115. Becky Ellis, Librn
Holdings: Vols (37,000)
Notes: Garden history, pomology, flora, landscape design. Print collection of many centuries; nursery catalogues from the mid-18th century. In storage, remodeling, will be available in about a year. Open to the public.

OH —CLEVELAND PUBLIC LIBRARY, Science & Technology Dept, 325 Superior Ave, Cleveland, 44114. Jean Z Piety, Head
Holdings: Cat
Notes: Part of the Gardening Collection, which emphasizes the history of gardens around the world, domestic landscape planning and planting, incl flower gardening, annuals and perennials and indoor plants.

PA —HUNT INSTITUTE FOR BOTANICAL DOCUMENTATION, Hunt Botanical Library, Carnegie-Mellon University, Pittsburgh, 15213. Bernadette G Callery, Librn
Holdings: Vols (23,000) Cat Pix
Notes: Collection of primarily historical botany and plant taxonomy, especially 1730-1840. Includes approximately 500 15th through 17th central herbals, extensive collection of 18th and 19th century color-plate works, floras and monographic works, and other works on natural history, early gardening and horticulture, and travel, particularly that dealing with plant exploration and introduction. Extensive biographical materials, on people in the plant sciences. Reference collection and extensive documentation in botanical bibliography, especially concerning books published before 1850. Includes as separate collections, the Strandell Collection of Linnaesana and the Michel Adanson Library. Over 800 items described in *Catalogue of Botanical Books in the Collection of Rachel McMasters Miller Hunt, 1477-1800* (Pittsburgh, 1958-1960).

VA —COLLEGE OF WILLIAM AND MARY, Earl Gregg Swem Library, Williamsburg, 23185. Margaret C Cook, Cur of Manuscripts & Rare Books
Holdings: Vols 50 // Cat
Notes: The Hetty Cary Harrison Memorial Collection. The majority of volumes in this collection are 17th-19th centuries. Also, uncataloged American seedman's catalogs, 19th-20th centuries; 7 running ft.

GARDINER, JUDY

MA —BOSTON UNIVERSITY, Mugar Memorial Library, Special Collections Dept, 771 Commonwealth Ave, Boston, 02215. Howard B Gotlieb, Dir
Holdings: Mss Pix

GARDNER, ALAN

MA —BOSTON UNIVERSITY, Mugar Memorial Library, Special Collections Dept, 771 Commonwealth Ave, Boston, 02215. Howard B Gotlieb, Dir
Holdings: Cat Mss

GARDNER, ALEXANDER AND JAMES

DC —LIBRARY OF CONGRESS, Prints & Photographs Div, Washington, 20540.
Notes: Civil War Photograph Collection incl photographs commissioned by Mathew Brady and others. Brady employed 20 photographers at the height of his operations. His staff incl Alexander and James Gardner, James F Gibson, and Thomas C Roche.

GARDNER, ERLE STANLEY

CA —UNIVERSITY OF CALIFORNIA, SAN DIEGO, Central University Library, Mandeville Dept of Special Collections, La Jolla, 92093. Lynda Corey Claassen, Head
Notes: The Erle Stanley Gardner Collection contains 2500 volumes of this author's work, much of it in languages other than English.

GARDNER, H. F., AND FAMILY

CA —UNIVERSITY OF CALIFORNIA, LOS ANGELES, Research Library, Dept of Special Collections, 405 Hilgard Ave, Los Angeles, 90024. Edward Shreeves, Chairman, Bibliographers Group; David S Zeidberg, Head
Holdings: Cat Mss Pix
Notes: 6 linear feet of their papers, incl correspondence, legal records, and ephemera relating to their business affairs.

GARDNER, ISABELLA

MO —WASHINGTON UNIVERSITY, Libraries, Campus Box 1061, Saint Louis, 63130.
Holdings: Vols 1000
Notes: Incl her papers, consisting of more than 1000 letters of substantial literary and personal content; more than 500 professional letters. Much correspondence with other modern poets. Described in *Special Collections: An Annotated Guide to the Holdings of the Manuscript Division and the University Archives and Research* Collection.

GARDNER, JAMES I.

AZ —NORTHERN ARIZONA UNIVERSITY, Special Collection Library, CU Box 6022, Flagstaff, 86011. Peter M Whiteley, Coordr/Archivist; William Mullane, Librn
Notes: James I Gardner (1857-1935) General Merchandise Store, Jerome, Ariz. Cash journals, 1888-1890. Bank book, 1890-1891. Ledger, 1888-1890.
See also entry under Jerome, Arizona.

GARDNER, JOHN

NY —UNIVERSITY OF ROCHESTER, Rush Rhees Library, Department of Rare Books and Special Collections, Rochester, 14627. Peter Dzwonkoski, Librn
Holdings: Vols Cat

GARDNER, NANCY BRUFF

MA —BOSTON UNIVERSITY, Mugar Memorial Library, Special Collections Dept, 771 Commonwealth Ave, Boston, 02215. Howard B Gotlieb, Dir
Holdings: Cat Mss Pix
Notes: Mss, correspondence, etc collected in depth; incl publications by or about.

GARDNER-TYLER FAMILY PAPERS

CT —YALE UNIVERSITY, Box 1603A, Yale Station, New Haven, 06520.
Holdings: Cat Mss

GARFIELD, JAMES A.

DC —LIBRARY OF CONGRESS, Manuscript Division, Washington, 20540. John C Broderick, Chief
Notes: The Presidential Papers collection incl the papers, etc, of numerous Presidents.

OH —HIRAM COLLEGE, Teachout-Price Memorial Library, Hiram, 44234. Joanne M Sawyer, Archivist; Marjorie M Adams, Music Librn
Holdings: Vols 80 Cat Mss Pix Microforms
Notes: Collection incl mostly published works; photographs of Garfield and his family; some mss and correspondence not in LC collection; complete microfilm of LC collection emphasizes Garfield's connection with Hiram College; restricted hours: call or write in advance.

OH —LAKE COUNTY HISTORICAL SOCIETY, Percy Kendall Smith Library, 8095 Mentor Ave, Mentor, 44060. Carl Thomas Engel, Librn
Holdings: Vols (2400) Cat Mss Pix

GARIBALDI, GIUSEPPE, 1802-1882

†NY —LIBRARY OF THE ITALIAN RISORGIMENTO, Garibaldi and Meucci Memorial Museum, John Jay Homestead, Box AH, Katonah, 10536.
Notes: History of the Italian Unification Wars and mementos of Garibaldi.

GARLAND, HAMLIN

AZ —UNIVERSITY OF ARIZONA, University Library, Special Collections, Tucson, 85721. Louis A Hieb, Head
Holdings: Vols (7000) Cat Mss Microforms
Budget: ($30,000)
Notes: Major authors collected are Twain, Garland, Hart, Irving, Melville and James.

VA —UNIVERSITY OF VIRGINIA, Alderman Library, Clifton Waller Barrett Collection, Charlottesville, 22901. Joan St C Crane, Cur of American Literature Collections
Notes: Papers.

GARN, SEN. JAKE

UT —UNIVERSITY OF UTAH, Marriott Library, Special Collections, Salt Lake City, 84112. Gregory C Thompson, Cur
Holdings: Cat Mss Microfilm Film Oral History
Notes: Papers.

GARNETT, DAVID

IL —NORTHWESTERN UNIVERSITY, Library, Special Collections Dept, 1937 Sheridan Rd, Evanston, 60201. R Russell Maylone, Cur
Holdings: Vols 58 Cat Mss
Notes: Incl 57 letters to David and Edward Garnett from E M Forster.

GARNETT, EDWARD

IL —NORTHWESTERN UNIVERSITY, Library, Special Collections Dept, 1937 Sheridan Rd, Evanston, 60201. R Russell Maylone, Cur
Holdings: Vols 58 Cat Mss
Notes: Incl 57 letters to David and Edward Garnett from E M Forster.

GARRICK, DAVID

CT —YALE UNIVERSITY, Box 1603A, Yale Station, New Haven, 06520.
Holdings: Cat Mss

GARRISON, GEORGE PRICE

TX —UNIVERSITY OF TEXAS LIBRARIES, General Libraries, Barker Texas History Center, PO Box P, Austin, 78712. Don Carleton, Dir

GARRISON, LINDLEY MILLER, 1864-1932

NJ —PRINCETON UNIVERSITY, Library, Manuscript Collection, Nassau St, Princeton, 08540. Jean F Preston, Cur
Holdings: // Cat Mss
Notes: Incl 25 boxes; 23 binders. Terms of Access: Access to the papers requires an agreement by the reader to submit for approval of the donor or his designate any manuscript based upon the papers if publication is intended. The papers cover the period, 1913-1916. An unpublished typescript guide (27p) is available in the Library.

GARRISON, WILLIAM LLOYD

KS —WICHITA STATE UNIVERSITY, Ablah Library, Box 68, Wichita, 67208. Michael T Kelly, Cur of Special Collections
Notes: The Eunice McIntosh Merrill Memorial Collection of letters and papers of the abolitionist William Lloyd Garrison.

GARST, ROSWELL

IA —IOWA STATE UNIVERSITY, Library, Dept of Special Collections, Ames, 50011. Stanley M Yates, Head
Notes: Papers of Roswell Garst, Iowa's most famous farmer. Initiator of experimental feeding of corncobs to produce beef, use of hybrid seedcorn, and commercial fertilizers. Credited with opening of agricultural sales and exchanges with Russia in the 1950s.

GARTNER, CHLOE

MA —BOSTON UNIVERSITY, Mugar Memorial Library, Special Collections Dept, 771 Commonwealth Ave, Boston, 02215. Howard B Gotlieb, Dir
Holdings: Cat Mss

GARVEY, DAN

AZ —ARIZONA STATE UNIVERSITY, Library, Arizona Collection, Tempe, 85281. Edward C Oetting, Head
Holdings: Cat Mss
Notes: Papers, etc.

GAS

PA —FRANKLIN INSTITUTE LIBRARY, 20 & The Parkway, Philadelphia, 19103. Miriam Padusis, Dir; Charles Wilt, Readers Servs Librn
Holdings: Vols (300,000) Cat Maps Pix Microforms

GAS, NATURAL

AL —SOUTHERN NATURAL GAS CO, Corporate Library, PO Box 2563, Birmingham, 35202. Regina Hinkle, Librn
Holdings: Vols 2500 Cat Mss Maps

IL —INSTITUTE OF GAS TECHNOLOGY, Technical Information Center, Library, 3424 S State St, Chicago, 60616. Anne C Roess, Mgr
Holdings: Vols 30,000 Cat Maps

IL —PEOPLES GAS, LIGHT & COKE COMPANY, Library, 122 S Michigan Ave Rm 727, Chicago, 60603. Rosann Meagher, Librn
Holdings: Vols 5000 Cat Maps
Notes: The gas industry, incl production and distribution.

NE —NORTHERN NATURAL GAS CO, 2223 Dodge St, Omaha, 68102. Marvin E Lauver, Librn
Holdings: Vols 30,000 Cat

PA —FRANKLIN INSTITUTE LIBRARY, 20 & The Parkway, Philadelphia, 19103. Miriam Padusis, Dir; Charles Wilt, Readers Servs Librn
Holdings: Vols (300,000) Cat Maps Pix Microforms

TX —SOUTHERN UNION CO, Library, Inter-First II, Suite 1800, Dallas, 75270. Charles Woodard, Research Librn
Holdings: Vols (100) Uncat
Notes: Incl periodicals (43 subscriptions), and annual reports (1500).

TX —MCDERMOTT HUDSON ENGINEERING, Library, 5900 Hillcroft, Houston, 77036. Chris Ramirez, Librn
Holdings: Vols 1000 Cat Slides 16mm Films Microforms
Notes: Design and construction of natural gas processing facilities.

TX —TRANSCONTINENTAL GAS PIPE LINE CORP, Corporate Library, PO Box 1396, Houston, 77251. Cheryl L Watson, Librn; Jane Mascher, Library Specialist
Holdings: Vols (8000) Cat

MB —UNIVERSITY OF MANITOBA, Elizabeth Dafoe Library, Government Publications Section, Winnipeg, R3T 2N2, Can. June Dutka, Head
Holdings: Uncat Maps Pix Microforms
Notes: The Canadian National Energy Board's Polar Gas Project documentation provides an extremely useful source of information describing the proposed construction of the pipeline route which would generally pass from the Arctic Islands through the Northwest Territories, northern Manitoba and into Ontario, Canada.

GAS, NATURAL—LAW AND LEGISLATION

AB —UNIVERSITY OF ALBERTA, John Weir Memorial Law Library, Law Centre, Second Floor, Edmonton, T6G 2H5, Can. Lillian MacPherson, Law Librn
Holdings: Vols (140,000) Cat Maps Audiotapes Microforms
Budget: ($400,000)
Notes: Emphases on Canadian Government Publications, oil and gas, Canadian and US, UK, Australian, New Zealand primary materials. Separate catalog.

GAS AND OIL ENGINES

NH —NEW HAMPSHIRE VOCATIONAL-TECHNICAL COLLEGE, Library, Prescott Hill, Laconia, 03246. Patty Miller, Librn
Holdings: Vols 475 Cat Phonorecords Audiotapes Filmstrips Microforms
Budget: $475

GAS DYNAMICS

TN —UNIVERSITY OF TENNESSEE, Space Institute Library, Tullahoma, 37388. Helen B Mason, Librn
Holdings: Vols (14,000) Cat Microforms
Budget: ($50,000)
Notes: Incl NASA and other series of technical reports.

GAS ENGINEERING

MA —STONE & WEBSTER ENGINEERING CORP, Technical Information Center, Library, 245 Summer St, PO Box 2325, Boston, 02107. Nancy M Pellini, Mgr
Holdings: Vols (10,000) Cat Pix Microforms
Notes: Also over 1200 periodicals. Extensive vertical file collection, and 5 on-line system for search.

NJ —PUBLIC SERVICE ELECTRIC & GAS CO, Library, 80 Park Place Plaza P3C, PO Box 570, Newark, 07101. Florine E Hunt, Corporate Librn
Holdings: Vols (20,000) Cat Microforms

PA —FRANKLIN INSTITUTE LIBRARY, 20 & The Parkway, Philadelphia, 19103. Miriam Padusis, Dir; Charles Wilt, Readers Servs Librn
Holdings: Vols (300,000) Cat Maps Pix Microforms

TX —UNIVERSITY OF TEXAS LIBRARIES, Richard W McKinney Engineering Library, 1.3 ECJ, Austin, 78712. Susan B Ardis, Librn
Holdings: Vols (83,548) Cat Microforms
Notes: All US Patents since 1977.

GAS ENGINES see Gas and Oil Engines

GAS FLOW

OH —GOODYEAR ATOMIC CORP, Technical Library, PO Box 628, Piketon, 45661. Robert Holland, Supvr
Holdings: Vols (50,000) Cat Mss Microforms
Notes: Uranium enrichment; gas flow, heat transfer, isotope analyses, uranium-fluoride chemistry.

GAS INDUSTRY

IL —PEOPLES GAS, LIGHT & COKE COMPANY, Library, 122 S Michigan Ave Rm 727, Chicago, 60603. Rosann Meagher, Librn
Holdings: Vols 5000 Cat Maps
Notes: The gas industry, incl production and distribution.

MB —UNIVERSITY OF MANITOBA, Elizabeth Dafoe Library, Government Publications Section, Winnipeg, R3T 2N2, Can. June Dutka, Head
Holdings: Vols 1300 // Uncat Maps Pix
Notes: The collection, which dates from 1975, consists of written direct testimonies and responses with supporting exhibits from over 100 oil and gas companies, Indian and native associations and concerned citizen groups. The content of these documents incl construction plans, financial statements, alternate corridors, and describes the social and economic impact of the Arctic Gas Pipeline in northern Canada. The *Biological Report Series* offers vital information on soils and vegetation, movements of porcupine, caribou herds, bird distribution and fisheries research. An index listing the various company exhibits accompanies this collection.

GAS POWER PLANTS

WA —WESTERN WASHINGTON UNIVERSITY, Center for Pacific Northwest Studies, High St, Bellingham, 98225. James W Scott, Dir
Holdings: Vols 400 // Cat Mss
Notes: Puget Sound Power and Light Company Records Collection consists of the complete company records of 41 former companiess, which were bought out, amalgamated with or in other ways came under the control of Puget Sound Power and Light Company. Most of the companies were concerned with transportation or the production of power--both gas and electricity. Among the companies represented are street railways, interurban railways, traction companies and gas companies, all of which operated in the region west of the Cascades, especially in the Puget Sound area but with a few as far south as Vancouver, Washington. The collection has been placed in the Center for Pacific Northwest Studies by the Puget Sound Power and Light Company on a permanent loan basis.

GAS TURBINES

PQ —PRATT & WHITNEY AIRCRAFT OF CANADA, Library, PO Box 10, Longueuil, J4K 4X9, Can. Joyce Chalevois, Librn
Holdings: Cat Slides 16mm Films Microforms
Notes: Gas turbine engines.

GAS TURBINES, AIRCRAFT see Aircraft Gas Turbines

GASCOYNE, DAVID

BC —UNIVERSITY OF VICTORIA, McPherson Library, Victoria, V8W 3H5, Can.
Notes: Poet, writer. Incl 5 cm, 1961-72; mss *Collection Verse Translations,* 1970. "The book of the South West's desire for a North Eastern resting place." Corrected galley and page proofs *The Sun at Midnight,* 1970.

GASEOUS DISCHARGE see Plasma (Ionized Gases)

GASEOUS PLASMA see Plasma (Ionized Gases)

GASES, FLOW OF see Gas Flow

GASIFICATION OF COAL see Coal Gasification

GASKELL, ELIZABETH, 1810-1865

NJ —PRINCETON UNIVERSITY, Library, Morris L Parrish Collection, Princeton,

GASKELL, ELIZABETH, 1810-1865 (cont.)

08540. Alexander D Wainwright, Cur
Notes: About 60 vols. For particulars refer to: Morris L Parrish, *Victorian Lady* Novelists (London, 1933) (Ex)04705.692.

GASOHOL see Alcohol

GASOLINE AUTOMOBILES see Automobiles

GASOLINE ENGINES see Gas and Oil Engines

GASQUET, CARDINAL

DC —GEORGETOWN UNIVERSITY, Library, Special Collections Div, 37 & O Sts NW, Washington, 20057. George M Barringer, Special Collections Librn; Nicholas B Sheetz, Mss Librn
Holdings: Mss Cat Pix
Notes: The papers of the Irish man-of-letters Sir Shane Leslie (1885-1971) containing letters, mss, diaries, notebooks, clippings, and photographs. Extensive correspondence by Margot Asquith, countess of Oxford and Asquith; Lady Violet Bonham-Carter; Burke Cochran; Lord Alfred Douglas; Moreton Frewen; Cardinal Gasquet; Vyvyan Holland; Lady Leonie Leslie; Sir Wilfrid Meynell; Sir Horace Plunkett; John Quinn; Frederick Rolfe (Baron Corvo); and Elizabeth Russell, among others. Also incl are research files on Sir Winston Churchill (Leslie's first cousin); Leonard Jerome; Maria Anne Fitzherbet (wife of King George IV); Ghosts and Ghost stories; and Eton College.

GASS, WILLIAM

MO —WASHINGTON UNIVERSITY, Libraries, Modern Literature Collection, Skinker & Lindell Blvds, Saint Louis, 63130.
Holdings: Cat Mss
Notes: Books, mss, correspondence, papers, etc. Described in *Special Collections: An Annotated Guide to the Holdings of the Manuscript Division and the University Archives and Research Collection.*

NV —UNIVERSITY OF NEVADA, RENO, University Library, Special Collections Dept, Reno, 89557. Robert E Blesse, Head
Holdings: Vols 20 Cat Other appearances 55 Cat
Notes: Includes individual works by author in all editions including translations; also prefaces, introductions, published correspondence, appearances in anthologies, periodicals, etc. Bibliographical research collection, part of Modern Authors Collection.

GASSAWAY, PERCY LEE

OK —UNIVERSITY OF OKLAHOMA, Bizzell Memorial Library, Western History Collections, 401 W Brooks, Norman, 73069. John Ezell, Cur
Holdings: Mss Documents
Notes: US Representative. His papers. Guide available.

GAST BANKNOTE COMPANY, 1884-1952

MO —WASHINGTON UNIVERSITY, Libraries, Special Collections Dept, Campus Box 1061, St Louis, 63130.
Holdings: //
Notes: The Gast Banknote Company's records, 1884-1952. Incl general ledgers, sales ledgers, payroll books, equipment inventories, and selected sample books of printing work of this lithography and printing firm.

GASTROENTEROLOGY

RI —MIRIAM HOSPITAL MEDICAL LIBRARY, 164 Summit Ave, Providence, 02906. Ann LeClaire, Dir of Library Services
Holdings: Cat Cassettes
Notes: Special collection on the renal system with emphasis on kidney transplantation and dialysis.

†TN —SAINT THOMAS HOSPITAL, Health Sciences Library, Box 380, Nashville, 37202. Dee Platt, Dir
Holdings: Vols (2600) Cat Slides

GASTRONOMY

DC —LIBRARY OF CONGRESS, Rare Book & Special Collections Div, Washington, 20540. William Matheson, Chief
Notes: The Katherine Golden Bitting Gastronomic Library. The collection comprises materials on the sources, preparation and consumption of foods from the earliest times to the present day, embracing the whole range of human interest in food. Incl an important 15th century Italian ms, a large number of early French, Italian, English and German works (incl incunabula) and a range of early American cookbooks and works on domestic science. Regional cookbooks and works on the chemistry, bacteriology and preservation of food are strongly represented among titles of more recent date. The majority of the volumes in the collection are described in Mrs Bitting's *Gastronomic Bibliography* (San Francisco, 1939). Also, personal library of Elizabeth Robins Pennell, magazine journalist and wife of artist Joseph Pennell, incl ca 430 cookbooks in English, French and German,16th to 18th century, described in Mrs. Pennell's *My Cookery Books* (Boston, Houghton-Mifflin, 1903).

NY —NEW YORK ACADEMY OF MEDICINE, Library, 2 E 103 St, New York, 10029. Brett A Kirkpatrick, Librn
Notes: Collection of Margaret Barclay Wilson, MD; one of largest collections on the subject; rare and historical items. Added to selectively incl copy of 9th century Ms, De re Culinaria. Also incl 3000 uncat pamphlets, 500 menus, 50 Italian broadsides, 17th-19th centuries food regulations.

OH —CLEVELAND PUBLIC LIBRARY, Science & Technology Dept, 325 Superior Ave, Cleveland, 44114. Jean Z Piety, Head
Holdings: Vols 9000 Cat
Notes: American, regional, and foreign cookbooks; historical material, gastronomy.

GATENBY, ROSEMARY

MA —BOSTON UNIVERSITY, Mugar Memorial Library, Special Collections Dept, 771 Commonwealth Ave, Boston, 02215. Howard B Gotlieb, Dir
Holdings: Cat Mss

GATES, HORATIO

NY —NEW YORK PUBLIC LIBRARY, Rare Books and Manuscripts Div, Fifth Ave & 42 St, New York, 10018. William L Joyce, Asst Dir; Susan E Davis, Cur of Mss
Holdings: Mss
Budget: ($7161)
Notes: Incl personal and literary mss, papers, etc.

GAUCHOS

MO —WASHINGTON UNIVERSITY, John M Olin Library, Campus Box 1061, St Louis, 63130.
Holdings: Vols (50,000) Cat
Notes: Strong collection. Much unusual material.

TX —UNIVERSITY OF TEXAS LIBRARIES, Nettie Lee Benson Latin American Collection, Sid Richardson Hall 1.109, Austin, 78712. Laura Gutierrez-Witt, Head Librn
Holdings: Vols (450,000) Cat Microforms
Notes: The library of Pedro Martinez Reales, emphasizing the literature of the Argentine gaucho, incl some 1500 books, pamphlets and articles, as well as 300 editions of the epic poem *Martin Fierro.*
See also entry under Latin America.

GAUSS, CHRISTIAN FREDERICK, 1878-1955

NJ —PRINCETON UNIVERSITY, Library, Manuscript Collection, Nassau St, Princeton, 08540. Jean F Preston, Cur
Holdings: // Mss
Notes: The collection occupies 67 ms boxes.

GAUTIER, EVA

NY —NEW YORK PUBLIC LIBRARY, Music Div, 111 Amsterdam Ave, New York, 10023. Frank C Campbell, Chief

GAY, EDWIN F.

CA —HOOVER INSTITUTION ON WAR, REVOLUTION & PEACE, Stanford University, Stanford, 94305. Milorad M Drachkovitch, Archivist
Holdings: // Mss
Notes: Papers, 1917-1918, of Edwin F Gay, economist with the Commercial Economy Board, Council of National Defense, War Industries Board, War Shipping Board, and War Trade Board. Correspondence, office diary, reports, charts, and memoranda. 12 ft.

GAY, JOHN

CT —YALE UNIVERSITY, Box 1603A, Yale Station, New Haven, 06520.

IN —INDIANA UNIVERSITY, Lilly Library, Seventh St, Bloomington, 47405. William R Cagle, Librn
Holdings: Vols 140 Cat
Notes: First and early editions.

MA —HARVARD UNIVERSITY LIBRARY, Houghton Library, Cambridge, 02138. Rodney G Dennis, Cur of Manuscripts
Holdings: Cat Mss

GAY, KENNETH CHARLES (KARL)

IN —INDIANA UNIVERSITY, Lilly Library, Seventh St, Bloomington, 47405. William R Cagle, Librn
Holdings: Cat Mss Pix
Notes: Correspondence of Robert Graves with Kenneth Charles (Karl) Gay, 1934-1968. 1332 letters and 14 Graves mss. Incl first editions of Graves' publications and several association or inscribed copies.

GAY LIBERATION MOVEMENT

CA —NATIONAL GAY ARCHIVES, 1654 North Hudson, Hollywood, 90028. Jim Kipner, Archivist
Notes: One of the most important collections.

CA —ONE, INCORPORATED, Blanche M Baker Memorial Library, 3340 Country Club Dr, Los Angeles, 90019. David G Moore, Dir
Holdings: Vols (7600) Cat Mss Pix Slides Phonorecords Audiotapes
Notes: Nonfiction in numerous disciplines relating to homosexuality, homophile movement, sexual minorities, and human sexuality; biography, gay and lesbian fiction, poetry, erotica; standard reference works; 200 periodicals in many languages; 65 file drawers and containers of VF materials (clippings, fliers, brochures, newsletters, correspondence, archival collections). Partially cataloged.

CA —SAN FRANCISCO STATE UNIVERSITY, Center for Homosexual Education, Evaluation, and Research (CHEER), San Francisco, 94132. Salvatore J Licata, Dir
Notes: Homosexuality in its historical and contemporary contexts; its social sex-role, and the increase of public awareness in American society.

CT —UNIVERSITY OF CONNECTICUT, Library, Storrs, 06268. Ellen Embardo, Cur Special Collections
Holdings: Cat
Notes: Alternative Press Collection. Primarily periodicals and newspapers from the 1960s to today of an alternative or underground nature. Books and pamphlets are incl, representing both the left and the right-wing viewpoints. A catalog is available. Also have archives of the First Casualty Press, which was deeply involved with Vietnam veterans' experiences in Vietnam.

FL —LESBIAN AND GAY ARCHIVES OF NAIAD PRESS, INC, PO Box 10543,

GAY LIBERATION MOVEMENT (cont.)

Tallahassee, 32302. Barbara Grier, Librn; Donna J McBride, Librn
Holdings: Vols 22,000
Budget: $2500
Notes: The Lesbian and Gay Archives of Naiad Press. A private collection of lesbian and gay literature. Open to researchers on appointment basis.

IL —NORTHWESTERN UNIVERSITY, Library, Special Collections Dept, 1937 Sheridan Rd, Evanston, 60201. R Russell Maylone, Cur
Holdings: Cat //
Notes: Newsletters, newspapers, pamphlets distributed by homophile organizations in the US, Canada, and Great Britain. Particular emphasis is on the Gay Liberation Movement, 1965 to date.

MI —UNIVERSITY OF MICHIGAN, Dept of Rare Books & Special Collections, Ann Arbor, 48109. Edward C Weber, Head, Labadie Collection
Holdings: Vols (40,000) Cat Mss Phonorecords Audiotapes
Notes: Particularly material concerned with radical Gay Liberation. Mostly serials and pamphlets, many of which represent homosexual protest before the official designation of Gay Liberation.

MI —MICHIGAN STATE UNIVERSITY, Libraries, Special Collections Div, East Lansing, 48824. Jannette Fiore, Librn
Holdings: Vols (10,500) Cat Mss
Notes: Published and unpublished material generated by (1) American left and right, 1900, (2) the New Left, 1969-1970, and (3) current left, right, and alternate life-style groups. (Supported by appropriate secondary material in the Research Library). Also have in microform radical pamphlet literature from the Tamiment Library (New York University), the Right Wing Collection of the University of Iowa, et al.

NY —GAY PEOPLE AT COLUMBIA, Library, Broadway & 116 St, New York, 10027.

NY —LESBIAN HERSTORY EDUCATIONAL FOUNDATION INC, Lesbian Herstory Archives, PO Box 1258, New York, 10116. Deborah Edel, Treasurer
Notes: Lesbian, feminist, and Gay books and periodicals on all aspects of Lesbian culture, photographs and slides of Lesbians and Lesbian art, records, tapes, graphics and crafts. Also, unpublished materials such as first drafts, term papers from Lesbian and Gay studies courses, diaries, letters, poetry, and conference notes.

PA —TEMPLE UNIVERSITY LIBRARIES, Special Collections Dept, Contemporary Culture Collection, Philadelphia, 19122. Patricia J Case, Cur
Notes: The Contemporary Culture Collection. See full entry under US-Social Life and Customs.

ON —CANADIAN GAY ARCHIVES, 54 Wolsley St, Box 639, Station A, Toronto, M5T 1A5, Can.
Notes: One of the best collections, incl memorabilia, such as buttons and other historically important material.

ON —WOMEN'S MOVEMENT ARCHIVES, PO Box 928, Station Q, Toronto, M5W 1G2, Can.
Holdings: Vols 250 Pix
Notes: Graphics, individual files, 250 periodicals and newsletters, 450 group files.

GAYS see Homosexuals and Homosexuality

GAZETTEERS see Geography—Dictionaries

GAZETTES

DC —LIBRARY OF CONGRESS, General Reading Rooms Division, Microform Reading Room, Washington, 20540.
Holdings: Cat Mss Maps Pix Microforms
Notes: Microform materials only in this LC Division. Works of individual authors; holdings of collections; archival records, etc, press releases and translations, etc.

DC —LIBRARY OF CONGRESS, Law Library, 101 Independence Ave, SE, Washington, 20540. Carleton W Kenyon, Dir
Holdings: Vols Microforms
Notes: The Law Library receives 270 national, state, provincial, regional, and municipal gazettes from 118 countries.

NY —NEW YORK PUBLIC LIBRARY, Research Libraries, Economic & Public Affairs Div, Fifth Ave & 42 St, New York, 10018. Edward DiRoma, Chief
Holdings: Vols (1,500,000) Cat Microforms
Notes: Long files of most national and some state and local gazettes. Part of joint program with Library of Congress to film all national gazettes from 1971 on.

NY —UNITED NATIONS, Dag Hammarskjold Library, Rm L382, New York, 10017. Vladimir Orlov, Librn
Holdings: Cat Microforms

GEARY, DANIEL

AL —MOBILE PUBLIC LIBRARY, Special Collections Div, 701 Government St, Mobile, 36602.
Notes: Personal papers, documents, etc, of Daniel Geary, Director of Defenses of Mobile, 1861-.

GEEZ LANGUAGE AND LITERATURE

MN —SAINT JOHN'S ABBEY & UNIVERSITY, Hill Monastic Manuscript Library, Collegeville, 56321. Julian G Plante, Dir
Holdings: Vols (61,000) Microfilms
Notes: Films of 61,000 mss. The total number of codices or bound handwritten mss represents the holdings of several hundred libraries in Europe, mostly Austria, Spain, Ethiopia, West Germany, Portugal, and also Italy, Hungary, Poland, Great Britain, Belgium, Yugoslavia, France, Switzerland, and the Netherlands.

NY —NEW YORK PUBLIC LIBRARY, Oriental Div, Fifth Ave & 42 St, New York, 10018. E Christian Filstrup, Chief
Holdings: Cat Mss Microforms
Budget: ($56,455)
Notes: Published catalog of holdings.

GEHRIG, LOU

NY —COLUMBIA UNIVERSITY LIBRARIES, Rare Book & Manuscript Library, 801 Butler Library, 535 W 114 St, New York, 10027. Kenneth A Lohf, Librn
Notes: Restricted use. Much on Columbia sports and athletics. Good strengths in material on Columbia's sports figures, incl Lou Gehrig, etc.

GEIGEL FAMILY

CT —UNIVERSITY OF CONNECTICUT, Library, Storrs, 06268. R H Schimmelpfeng, Dir of Special Collections
Notes: Over 3600 pieces, incl books, pamphlets, periodicals and government documents dealing with all aspects of the Island's history and culture. A collection formed through three generations of the Geigel Family of San Juan.

GEIRINGER, KARL

MA —BOSTON PUBLIC LIBRARY, Print Collection, Dartmouth St at Copley Sq, Boston, 02117. Sinclair H Hitchings, Keeper of Prints
Notes: Approx 1000 glass slides which were the basis of Prof Geiringer's book, *Musical* Instruments, and were used in his teaching. The slides represent musical instruments, portraits and caricatures of musicians, and facsimiles of musical compositions and correspondence.

GEISEL, SEUSS (DR. SEUSS)

CA —UNIVERSITY OF CALIFORNIA, LOS ANGELES, Research Library, Dept of Special Collections, 405 Hilgard Ave, Los Angeles, 90024. Edward Shreeves, Chairman, Bibliographers Group; David S Zeidberg, Head
Notes: Various collections, ranging from 18th century chapbooks to materials of Theodor Geisel (Dr Seuss) and the Hollings. Original material by Edward Ardizzone, Randolph Caldecott, Palmer Cox, Walter Crane, Alfred Henry Forrester, etc.

GEISMAR, MAXWELL

MA —BOSTON UNIVERSITY, Mugar Memorial Library, Special Collections Dept, 771 Commonwealth Ave, Boston, 02215. Howard B Gotlieb, Dir
Holdings: Cat Mss Pix Correspondence

GELLHORN, MARTHA

MA —BOSTON UNIVERSITY, Mugar Memorial Library, Special Collections Dept, 771 Commonwealth Ave, Boston, 02215. Howard B Gotlieb, Dir
Holdings: Cat Mss Pix
Notes: Mss, correspondence, etc collected in depth; incl publications by or about. Restricted.

GEMS AND GEMOLOGY

MA —HARVARD UNIVERSITY LIBRARY, Geological Sciences Library, 24 Oxford St, Cambridge, 02138. Constance Wick, Librn
Holdings: Vols (51,000) Cat Mss Maps Pix 16mm Films Microforms
Notes: The Geological Sciences Library supports the research efforts of faculty, graduate students, and upper-level undergraduate and graduate instruction in the geological sciences. Subjects collected deal with the earth sciences in general, mineralogy, petrology, geochemistry, geophysics, crystallography, structural geology, regional geology, economic geology, some geomorphology, and some gemology. The collection incl 850 serial publications and 15,000 maps.

NY —AMERICAN MUSEUM OF NATURAL HISTORY, Library Services Dept, Central Park W & 79th St, New York, 10024. Nina J Root, Chairwoman; Mary Genett, Asst Librn for Reference Services

OH —CLEVELAND PUBLIC LIBRARY, Science & Technology Dept, 325 Superior Ave, Cleveland, 44114. Jean Z Piety, Head
Holdings: cat
Notes: Part of the Handicrafts Collection, which incl crafts of many ethnic groups in Cleveland.

RI —PROVIDENCE PUBLIC LIBRARY, 150 Empire St, Providence, 02903. Lance J Bauer, Special Collections Librn
Holdings: Vols 122 // Cat
Notes: Works dating from 1670 on the history, lore and legends of precious stones, and the history and practice of jewelry and silversmithing. Restricted use.

ON —NATIONAL MUSEUMS OF CANADA, Library Services Directorate, Ottawa, K1A 0M8, Can. Valerie Monkhouse, Director
Holdings: Vols (90,000) Cat Mss Microforms
Budget: ($81,000)
Notes: Emphasis on Canadian and circumpolar natural history. Collection incl botany, herpetology, ichthyology, invertebrate zoology, malacology, mammology, mineralogy, ornithology, paleobiology, zooarchaeology. Exceptional collections in lichenology, bryology, malacology, ornithology. Research collection, interlibrary loans available, public may use on the premises.

GEMSTONES see Precious Stones

GENDARMES see Police

GENEALOGY—COLLECTIONS

AL —BIRMINGHAM PUBLIC LIBRARY, Southern History Dept, 2020 Seventh Ave N, Birmingham, 35203. Virginia K Scott, Head
Holdings: Vols (50,000) Cat Microforms
Notes: History and social conditions of the

GENEALOGY—COLLECTIONS (cont.)

southeastern US. Significant holdings on border areas such as Texas, Pennsylvania, Maryland. Strong genealogical collection with emphasis on the southeastern area of the US. Very strong Civil War Collection and early southern travel accounts. See George Ray Stewart, *The Special Collections in the Birmingham Public Library*. MA Thesis, Emory University, 1971.

AL —SAMFORD UNIVERSITY, Special Collections Library, 800 Lakeshore Dr, Birmingham, 35229. Annie Ford Wheeler, Acting Head Librn
Holdings: Vols 2500 Cat Mss Microforms
Notes: Chiefly southeast US and Ireland. Incl abstracts, printed genealogies, and census indexes (microfilm). Substantial amounts of material in the Bledsoe-Kelly mss. Incl 100,000 mss and 2000 microforms.

AL —WHEELER BASIN REGIONAL LIBRARY, 504 Cherry St NE, PO Box 1766, Decatur, 35602. Margarete Lange, Reference Librn
Holdings: Vols 300 Cat Mss Microforms
Notes: Primary emphasis on Alabama and Southern genealogy, although other areas are incl.

AL —MOBILE PUBLIC LIBRARY, Special Collections Div, 701 Government St, Mobile, 36602.
Holdings: Mss Maps Pix Microfilm
Notes: Alabama and local history; about 4500 vols, 100,000 clippings; 1750 microfilm rolls of newspapers, etc. Approx 8000 vols of genealogy, 1000 periodicals, 2000 clippings, etc. Census on 1800 microfilm rolls.

†AL —UNIVERSITY OF ALABAMA, Amelia Gayle Gorgas Library, PO Box S, University, 35486.
Notes: The Alabama Genealogy Collection incl 236 vols of Pauline Gandrud's *Alabama* Records for the following counties: Autauga, Benton, Bibb, Blount, Calhoun, Chambers, Cherokee, Clarke, Colbert, Coosa, Dallas, De Kalb, Fayette, Franklin, Greene, Jackson, Jefferson, Lauderdale, Lawrence, Limestone, Lowndes, Madison, Marengo, Marion, Marshall, Mobile, Montgomery, Morgan, Perry, Pickens, Shelby, Sumter, Talladega, Tallapossa, Tuscaloosa, Wilcox.

AZ —CHURCH OF JESUS CHRIST OF LATTER DAY SAINTS, Arizona Branch Genealogical Library, 464 E First Ave, Mesa, 85204. Joseph Lindbloom, Dir
Holdings: Vols (14,000) Cat Mss Maps Pix Microforms
Notes: Incl 25,000 microfilms with access to 1,300,000 rolls of microfilm available on loan.

AR —CENTRAL ARKANSAS LIBRARY SYSTEM, Little Rock Public Library, 700 Louisiana, Little Rock, 72201. Roberta A Muelling, Librn
Holdings: Vols 2615 Cat
Budget: $2000
Notes: General genealogy collection with specialized materials pertaining to individual states. Arkansas material makes up the largest state collection. A separate catalog.

AR —PUBLIC LIBRARY OF PINE BLUFF AND JEFFERSON COUNTY, Library System, 200 E Eighth Ave, Pine Bluff, 71601. Cora M Dorsett, Dir
Holdings: Vols 1596 Cat Maps Microforms
Notes: Census records, cemetery records, marriage records, county histories, mortality schedules, tax lists, Civil War records, records of wills, pension applications. Incls maps (30), microforms (725 rolls), periodicals (26 titles), manuscripts (21).

CA —SONS OF THE REVOLUTION IN THE STATE OF CALIFORNIA, Library, 600 S Central Ave, Glendale, 91204. Richard E Coe, Library Dir
Holdings: Vols 22,000 Mss
Notes: Incl 5000 mss and 2000 family histories. Partially cataloged.

CA —LOS ANGELES PUBLIC LIBRARY, Genealogy & Local History Dept, 630 W 5th St, Los Angeles, 90071. Lucile Lipman, Sr Librn
Holdings: Vols (55,000) Cat Mss Maps Pix Microforms
Budget: ($16,000)
Notes: Extensive collections of genealogical research materials with main strengths in North America, British and Western Europe. Includes the Orra C Monnette Collection of published books and mss. Large collection of genealogical periodicals. Family history index is maintained.

CA —MODESTO-STANISLAUS COUNTY FREE LIBRARY, 1500 I St, Modesto, 95354. Andrew L La Mance, Special Collections Librn
Holdings: Microforms
Notes: Incl 1,500 cataloged Census records (microfilm) and periodicals.

CA —POMONA PUBLIC LIBRARY, Special Collections, 625 S Garey Ave, PO Box 2271, Pomona, 91766. David Streeter, Librn
Holdings: Cat Maps Microforms
Notes: Complete California census through 1900 on microfilm; 1850 California Census index; reconstructed passenger lists; overland arrivals. Scattered censuses on microfilm from other states. All printed indexes to US Census; general US research collection. Basic heraldry and coats-of-arms.

CA —CROATIAN-SERBIAN-SLOVENE GENEALOGICAL SOCIETY, 2527 San Carlos Ave, San Carlos, 94070. Adam S Eterovich, Dir
Holdings: Vols (1000) Mss
Notes: Incl index of names of 130,000 Croatians and Serbs in the United States before 1905. Dir operates Ragusan Press.

CA —SAN DIEGO PUBLIC LIBRARY, 820 E St, San Diego, 92101. Rhoda E Kruse, Sr Librn
Notes: Also 450 bound periodicals. Incl extensive local history; papers of Foss and Kelly families; some material on John D Spreckels; papers of Southern California Exposition, San Diego 200th Anniversary Committee; Census microfilms; registers of voters 1866-1909; *San Diego Union* Index, which also incl material on Baja Califorina; records of Little Landers Colony, a 1910 Utopian group founded in the Tia Juana River Valley.

CO —DENVER PUBLIC LIBRARY, 1357 Broadway, Denver, 80203. Joanne E Classen, Genealogy Specialist, Humanities Area
Holdings: Vols (18,865) Cat Mss Maps Microforms
Budget: ($11,500)
Notes: Incl 3100 microfilm reels. Special files incl family file (a surname index to many of the collective genealogies and county histories in the collection); *Coats of Arms File* (an index to illustrations of coats of arms contained in the collection); *Obituary File* (an index to obituaries appearing in The *Denver Post*) and the *Rocky Mountain News Items File* (an index to news items, primarily anniversary announcements, appearing in the *Denver* Post) and the *Rocky Mountain News*, from 1940 to present.

CO —GREELEY PUBLIC LIBRARY, City Complex Bldg, Greeley, 80631. Esther Fromm, Librn
Notes: History of people of German-Russian ancestry.

CO —PUEBLO REGIONAL LIBRARY DISTRICT, 100 E Abriendo Ave, Pueblo, 81004. Charles E Bates, Library Dir
Holdings: Vols 4192 Cat Microforms
Notes: Materials are noncirculating.

CT —GREENWICH LIBRARY, 101 W Putnam Ave, Greenwich, 06830. Louise M Gudelis, Ref Librn
Holdings: Vols 1112 Cat Maps Pix Microforms
Notes: History and genealogy of Greenwich, Conn area.

CT —CONNECTICUT HISTORICAL SOCIETY, One Elizabeth St, Hartford, 06105. Christopher Bickford, Dir
Notes: Over 70,000 books and periodicals, 3500 bound vols of newspapers, and thousands of broadsides, maps, prints, and photographs pertaining to Connecticut. Also, more than 1 1/2 million historical mss; incl personal correspondence, diaries, account books, business records, and town materials dating from the earliest settlement. Extensive genealogical holdings, incl nearly 4000 printed genealogies and New England town and county histories.

CT —CONNECTICUT STATE LIBRARY, 231 Capitol Ave, Hartford, 06106. Mark H Jones, Archivist; T O Wohlsen, Jr, Head Archives, Hist & Genealogy Unit; Ann Barry, Ref Librn
Holdings: Cat Mss Maps
Notes: Books, maps, mss, archives pertaining to Connecticut state and local history and to the history of New England, etc. Archival collections incl state and local government records and papers of institutions and organizations in Connecticut. There are separate catalogs for archives maps, and genealogical works.

CT —NEW HAVEN COLONY HISTORICAL SOCIETY, Whitney Library, 114 Whitney Ave, New Haven, 06510. M Ottilia Koel, Librn & Cur of Mss
Notes: 25,000 printed books and pamphlets; ca 1500 linear ft of manuscript material including historic manuscripts, records of education, maritime and harbour industry, private papers, business and family records; 40,000 photographic images; maps and microforms relating to the early settlement and subsequent history of New Haven and vicinity.

CT —YALE UNIVERSITY, Beinecke Rare Book & Manuscript Library, Osborn Collection, New Haven, 06520. Stephen R Parks, Cur
Holdings: Mss

CT —STAMFORD'S PUBLIC LIBRARY, Ferguson Library, Adult Services Dept, 96 Broad St, Stamford, 06901. Ernest A DiMattia Jr, Dir; Doris Goodlett, Head Adult Servs
Holdings: Vols 4200 Cat Pix Microforms
Notes: Collection specializes in the genealogy of New England states and incl a comprehensive collection of local history. Also subscribes to many periodicals through the Stamford Genealogical Society. The Barbour Collection (Vital Record of Connecticut) is on microfilm and indexed by towns and by families. Library owns vols 1-165 of the DAR lineage books.

CT —SILAS BRONSON LIBRARY, 267 Grand St, Waterbury, 06702. Patricia L Joy, Reference Dept Head
Holdings: Vols 1500 Cat
Budget: $200
Notes: Incl are genealogies of families particularly from Connecticut and the other New England states.

DE —HISTORICAL SOCIETY OF DELAWARE, Library, 505 Market St Mall, Wilmington, 19801. Barbara E Benson, Library Dir
Holdings: Vols 1000 Cat Mss Microforms
Notes: Printed works fully cataloged. Emphasis on Delaware families, but supporting material from adjacent states. Delaware census material on microfilm; 8 linear feet of manuscript genealogical notes and charts; extensive surname file (10,000 entries); good run of *New England Historical and Genealogical Register*.

DC —HOWARD UNIVERSITY, Moorland-Spingarn Research Center, 500 Howard Place NW, Washington, 20059. Clifford L Muse, Jr, Acting Dir
Holdings: Vols (106,086) Mss Maps Pix Slides Phonorecords Audiotapes 16mm Films Filmstrips Microforms
Budget: ($854,753)
See also entry under Blacks

DC —LIBRARY OF CONGRESS, Washington, 20540.
Holdings: Vols (25,000) Cat
Notes: Local History and Genealogy Room has reference collection of 5000 volumes (1800 on genealogy). General collections contain 25,000 volumes on US and European genealogy. Additional large collection of American telephone and city directories. Card files in LH&G Room included: Family Name Index; Analytical Surname Index; US Biographical Index; Key to Rider's American Genealogical-Biographical Index; Author Catalog of Genealogy, Heraldry, and Local History. Family Name Index was published in two volumes in 1972 by Magna Carta Book Company as *Genealogies in the Library of Congress, A Bibliography*; 1977 supplement covers 3000 additional titles through July 1976.

GENEALOGY—COLLECTIONS (cont.)

DC —NATIONAL GENEALOGICAL SOCIETY, Library, 1921 Sunderland Place NW, Washington, 20036. Margaret M Redmond, Exec Dir
Holdings: Vols 13,000 Cat Mss 16mm Films
Budget: $7500
Notes: We are a nonprofit Society with librarian and some 35 volunteers. Most of the 40 mss collections are uncataloged.

FL —MIAMI-DADE PUBLIC LIBRARY SYSTEM, 1 Biscayne Blvd, Miami, 33132. Mrs Pat Warren, Cur
Holdings: Vols 6000 Cat Microforms
Notes: Incl 6691 microforms. Separate catalog. 1910 census reels for the US Census index, up to 1850.

FL —ORLANDO PUBLIC LIBRARY, Local History & Genealogy Dept, 100 Block of Central Ave, Orlando, 32806. Eileen B Willis, Librn
Holdings: Vols 11,000 Cat Maps Microforms
Budget: $8000
Notes: The

FL —FLORIDA STATE ARCHIVES, R A Gray Bldg, Tallahassee, 32301. Richard Roberts, Supervisor, Central Reference Section
Holdings: Vols 12,000 Cat Microforms
Budget: $6000
Notes: National scope, with primary emphasis on the South and Southeast, and basic source materials of New England. Incl county and family histories, vital statistics, passenger lists, abstracts of military records, and heraldry. Catalog: *Genealogy and Local History: A Bibliography.* Incl 12,000 microforms.

FL —TAMPA-HILLSBOROUGH COUNTY PUBLIC LIBRARY, 900 N Ashley St, Tampa, 33602. Joseph Hipp, Dir
Holdings: Vols (4200)
Notes: Books on genealogy (from Pennsylvania to Texas) and southern history. Florida map collection. Incl 80,000 packets on vertical file on the state of Florida.

GA —CARNEGIE LIBRARY, Henderson Room, 607 Broad St, Rome, 30161. Beatrice Millican, Librn
Holdings: Cat 16mm Films
Budget: ($2700)
Notes: Among our Genealogy Collection of 6500 items, we have the 1790 census records for the states of Maine, New Hampshire, Vermont, Massachusetts, Rhode Island, Connecticut, New York, Pennsylvania, Virginia, North Carolina, South Carolina. We have a substitute for the Georgia 1790 census. Also, we have the 1790, 1800, 1810 and 1820 census indexes for North Carolina. For Georgia we have the decennial indexes for 1820-1850. We have microfilm for Georgia, 1820-1900. Besides our general genealogy books, we have sections for the various states, particularly Virginia, South Carolina, North Carolina, and Georgia. Microfillm census for South Carolina and Alabama-1850.

IL —NEWBERRY LIBRARY, Local and Family History Dept, 60 W Walton St, Chicago, 60610. David T Thackery, Librn
Holdings: Vols 150,000 Cat Mss Maps Microforms
Notes: Family, county, and town histories, from settlement of the American Colonies through westward migration. Outstanding for military rosters, cemetery records, vital records, alumni and university directories, publications of patriotic and fraternal organizations, and federal census records. Also strong in local history of the British Isles and in European heraldry. See *Genealogical Index of the Newberry Library* (Boston: G K Hall, 1960).

IL —NORTHWESTERN UNIVERSITY, Library, Special Collections Dept, 1937 Sheridan Rd, Evanston, 60201. R Russell Maylone, Cur
Holdings: Vols 2500 Cat //
Notes: County histories, record surveys, visitations, family histories, biographies, atlases, census records, church histories and records, civil surveys and microfilms.

IL —LAKE FOREST COLLEGE, Donnelley Library, Lake Forest, 60045. Arthur H Miller Jr, College Librn
Holdings: Vols 1500 Cat
Notes: The R Douglas Stuart Collection of Scotiana. The collection consists of books dealing with the history, genealogy, and culture of Scotland. Incl basic 18th, 19th, and 20th century historical and heraldic works; numerous genealogies and histories of clans; literary works by Scottish writers; travel and settlement by Scotsmen in other areas of the world; paleography; books on Scottish art and artists; and some ephemeral works on non-Scottish subjects but which are by writers of Scottish descent or which have Scottish imprints.

IN —WILLARD LIBRARY, 21 First Ave, Evansville, 47710. Joan Elliott, Special Collections Librn
Holdings: Vols (1000) Cat Mss Microforms
Budget: ($4000)
Notes: General genealogy collection emphasizing data concerning 35 counties of southwest Indiana, southeast Illinois, and western Kentucky. Written description available.

IN —ALLEN COUNTY PUBLIC LIBRARY, Fred J Reynolds Historical Genealogy Collection, 900 Webster St, Fort Wayne, 46802. Rick J Ashton, Dir; Michael B Clegg, Manager
Holdings: Vols 200,000 Cat Mss Maps Pix Microforms
Notes: Incl state, county, regional, town and church histories. All census schedules and port of entry records released by the federal government are in the microfilm collection of 40,000 reels. The collection contains parish registers and publications of British parish register societies. Canadian, English, Scotch, Irish and Welsh records are well represented. The heraldry collection is housed with the genealogy collection. Allen County Public Library is and has been the depository for the North American Association of Directory Publishers since 1964.

IN —INDIANA STATE LIBRARY, Genealogy Div, 140 N Senate Ave, Indianapolis, 46204. William O Harris, Head
Holdings: Vols (70,000) Cat Mss Maps Microforms
Notes: Extensive collection of historical and archival material for all the Eastern, Mid-Western and Southeastern states.

IN —SOUTH BEND PUBLIC LIBRARY, Local History Dept, 122 W Wayne, South Bend, 46624.
Holdings: Vols (1317) Cat Pix Microforms Clippings
Budget: $500
Notes: Basic genealogy, with emphasis on Indiana, espec St Joseph County. Some materials are on loan from the local DAR chapter necrology file from 1838 to 1868 and 1936 to date; back-dating this service are notes concerning local individuals in service listing of local Civil War veterans, city directories, surname index, family name index.

IA —STATE HISTORICAL SOCIETY OF IOWA LIBRARY, 402 Iowa Ave, Iowa City, 52240. Darold J Brown, Librn
Holdings: Vols 5000 Cat Mss Microforms
Notes: Have many early serial publications for eastern states, federal census on microfilm, expanding collection of family histories and charts, current genealogical periodicals.

KS —NEOSHO COUNTY COMMUNITY COLLEGE, Chapman Library, 1000 S Allen, Chanute, 66720. Dan W Viergever, Library Dir
Holdings: Vols 600 Cat
Budget: $1000

KS —CENTER FOR MENNONITE BRETHREN STUDIES, Tabor College Library, 401 S Jefferson, Hillsboro, 67063. Wesley J Prieb, Dir
Holdings: Uncat Mss Maps Pix Slides Phonorecords Audiotapes 16mm Films Filmstrips Microforms
Budget: ($25,000)
Notes: Historical materials relating to Mennonite Brethern Conference of churches and its activities. Focus on US Conference of Mennonites, incl minutes and correspondence. Keeps all data for districts, except the Pacific. Collects all data on birth of Mennonites incl local church histories, family records, and genealogy. Anabaptists classics and picture collection. Periodicals and papers incl; collection partly cataloged.

KS —KANSAS STATE HISTORICAL SOCIETY LIBRARY, Memorial Bldg, 120 W Tenth, Topeka, 66612. Portia Allbert, Library Dir
Holdings: Vols 16,000 Cat Mss Microforms
Budget: ($15,000)

KS —WICHITA PUBLIC LIBRARY, 223 S Main, Wichita, 67202. Richard Rademacher, Librn
Holdings: Vols 6570 Cat Microforms
Notes: Incl approximately 2500 rolls of microfilm, 400 microcards. Not loaned.

KY —BOWLING GREEN PUBLIC LIBRARY, 1225 State St, Bowling Green, 42101. Karen A Turner, Dir
Holdings: Vols 20 Cat

KY —FILSON CLUB, 118 W Breckinridge St, Louisville, 40203. Dorothy C Rush, Librn
Holdings: Vols (40,000) Cat Mss Maps Pix Microforms
Notes: Maintain a card catalog for books, pamphlets, maps and broadsides; separate catalog for newspapers incl a chronological file; and mss incl a chronological file. Collect anything about Kentucky, including Kentucky authors. Has file on Kentucky families.

LA —R W NORTON ART GALLERY, Library, 4747 Creswell Ave, Shreveport, 71106. Jerry M Bloomer, Librn
Holdings: Cat

ME —MAINE STATE LIBRARY, Special Collections Dept, Cultural Bldg, Station 64, Augusta, 04333. Shirley Thayer, Librn
Holdings: Vols 5000 Cat Microforms
Budget: ($2,500,000)
Notes: An extensive collection of Maine genealogy with a good representation of all New England. Non-circulating.

ME —MAINE HISTORICAL SOCIETY, Library, 485 Congress St, Portland, 04101.
Holdings: Vols (60,000) Cat Mss Maps Pix
Notes: The Society's holdings cover all of Maine in its scope, with special emphasis on the Portland region.

MD —MARYLAND STATE LAW LIBRARY, Courts of Appeal Bldg, 361 Rowe Blvd, Annapolis, 21401. Michael S Miller, Dir; Shirley A Rittenhouse, Librn
Holdings: Vols (180,000) Cat Microforms
Budget: ($114,750)
Notes: Substantial out-of-state genealogy collection for original 13 colonies.

MD —JOHNS HOPKINS UNIVERSITY, Milton S Eisenhower Library, George Peabody Collection, 17 E Mt Vernon Place, Baltimore, 21201. Lyn Hart, Peabody Librn
Holdings: Vols (35,000) Cat Maps Microforms

MD —MARYLAND HISTORICAL SOCIETY, Library, 201 W Monument St, Baltimore, 21201. William B Keller, Head Librn
Holdings: Vols (65,000) Cat Maps Pix Slides
Budget: ($8000)
Notes: Also 2 million ms pieces, 300 maps, 700 slides; 10,000 musical scores. Large collection of Maryland State Colonization Papers; Maryland and Baltimore business records; Baltimore & Ohio Railroad Papers; Baltimore Theater records and programs (late 18th, early 19th century); Maryland lottery tickets; Benjamin H Latrobe (architectural) Papers; Maryland maps, plats, prints, newspapers; Baltimore history, large collection (30,000 items Maryland local history and genealogy, 100,000 mss); iron industry papers; Maryland currency; sheet music (8000 pieces, largely Baltimore publishers); Lester S Levy "Star-Spangled Banner" collection (probably the largest in the world--over 250 pieces).

MD —POLISH NOBILITY ASSOCIATION, Villa Anneslie, 529 Dunkirk Road, Baltimore, 21212.
Notes: Publish *Voice of the White Eagle,* 1965- , Annual.

MD —CHARLES COUNTY COMMUNITY COLLEGE, Learning Resource Center, PO Box 910, La Plata, 20646. J Elaine Ryan,

GENEALOGY—COLLECTIONS (cont.)

Dean
Holdings: Vols 200 Cat Microforms
Notes: Papers of Harry Wright Newman (100 cubic feet). Also incl complete census microfilm for Charles, Calvert and St Mary's Counties through 1910, and many 18th century mss. Additional points of coverage incl an index of marriages and an ongoing newspaper index of births, deaths, marriages and baptisms.
See also entry under Maryland - History

MA —JONES LIBRARY, 43 Amity St, Amherst, 01002. Daniel J Lombardo, Cur of Special Collections
Holdings: Vols (2710) Cat Maps Pix
Notes: The Boltwood Collection. Several thousand documents, cataloged, 18th and 19th centuries. The scope is primarily local, then regional, Massachusetts, New England. Several thousand local pictures, chiefly post-1926; pre-1926 not yet cataloged.

MA —FREE PUBLIC LIBRARY, Genealogy Room, 613 Pleasant St, Bedford, 02740. Paul A Cyr, Librn
Holdings: Vols (10,000) Cat Mss Maps Pix Microforms
Budget: ($1000)
Notes: Extensive collection on the history and genealogy of New England, with a strong emphasis on southeastern Massachusetts. Materials incl books, periodicals, mss, microfilms, and pictures of New England life. Unique features of the collection incl the *Leonard Papers* ms of vital records of early Bristol County, *Repertoires des Mariages* of Province Quebec, Canada, and a collection on the Society of Friends, or Quakers.

MA —NEW ENGLAND HISTORIC GENEALOGICAL SOCIETY, Library, 101 Newbury St, Boston, 02116. Ralph J Crandell, Dir
Holdings: Vols (250,000) Mss Maps Microforms Pix
Notes: New England genealogy. Especially strong Massachusetts, Maine, and New Hampshire, although all states are well represented, as are the relevancies of each subject listed in this volume with regard to British antecedent and contemporary history. Special strengths in local history and biography, obituaries, etc, incl parish registers, censuses, British and American. 3125 linear ft of mss.

MA —RADCLIFFE COLLEGE, Arthur & Elizabeth Schlesinger Library on the History of Women in America, 3 James St, Cambridge, 02138. Patricia Miller King, Dir; Eva Moseley, Cur of Mss
Notes: Incl diaries, journals, correspondence, photographs of 19th and 20th century US families.

MA —CONCORD FREE PUBLIC LIBRARY, 129 Main St, Concord, 01742. Rose Marie Mitten, Dir
Holdings: Vols 2000 Cat Mss Maps Pix
Notes: Also, town, church and cemetery records.

†MA —IRISH FAMILY HISTORY SOCIETY LIBRARY, 173 Tremont St, Newton, 02158.
Notes: Ireland--genealogy, history, literature, heraldry.

MA —SPRINGFIELD CITY LIBRARY, Genealogy and Local History Dept, 220 State St, Springfield, 01103. Joseph Carvalho III, Supervisor
Holdings: Vols (17,000) Cat Mss Maps Pix Microforms VF
Budget: ($8000)
Notes: New England, Massachusetts, local history, and genealogy collections. 18,000 pictures, 3200 microforms, ca 15,000 clippings, pamphlets, etc (280 ft of vertical files).

MA —AMERICAN ANTIQUARIAN SOCIETY LIBRARY, 185 Salisbury St, Worcester, 01609. Marcus A McCorison, Dir & Librn
Holdings: Vols 14,000 Cat
Notes: Incl heraldry, biography, genealogy, etc. Numerous special indexes and clipping files supplement the book collection.

MI —VAN BUREN COUNTY LIBRARY, Webster Memorial Library Bldg, 200 Phelps St, Decatur, 49045. David Fate, Dir
Holdings: Vols 3000 Cat Maps Microforms
Notes: Concentrating on local history, especially family histories of area families. Vital records of the county, cemetery records, births, deaths, marriages. Other area information as funds permit. Census records for Van Buren County from 1790 to 1910.

MI —DETROIT PUBLIC LIBRARY, Burton Historical Collection, 5201 Woodward Ave, Detroit, 48202. Alice Dalligan, Chief
Notes: Materials include books, charts of individual families, federal census population schedules, records of births, deaths, marriages, baptisms, cemetery inscriptions, wills and probate records, church membership lists, military records, registers of deeds, and newspaper obituaries. Biographical encyclopedias county and town histories, and various special indexes also assist patrons to research their family histories. The Reading Room is arranged to permit a self-help approach to locating this material.

MI —MONROE COUNTY LIBRARY SYSTEM, Ellis Reference and Information Center, 3700 S Custer Rd, Monroe, 48161. Marie D Chulski, Head of Reference Services
Notes: Historic Monroe County, tracing its beginnings to 1780, is a definite part of Michigan's history. Many events of the area and citizens are part of Michigan's heritage. The Michigan collection besides general works contains individual county histories, atlases, biographies, etc. The Monroe County history collection contains veteran records, plat books, oral history tapes, family histories, church records, cemetery index, atlases and census records. Genealogy emphasis is not only Monroe County but includes surrounding counties and the states with large migration to the area, such as Ohio, Kentucky, Tennessee and the New England states.

MN —MINNEAPOLIS PUBLIC LIBRARY & INFORMATION CENTER, History & Travel Dept, 300 Nicollet Mall, Minneapolis, 55401. Robert K Bruce, Head
Holdings: Vols (186,500) Cat Maps Phonorecords Audiotapes Microforms

MO —MISSOURI HISTORICAL SOCIETY, Library, Jefferson Memorial Bldg, Saint Louis, 63112. Stephanie Klein, Librn-Archivist; Peter Michel, Cur of Manuscripts
Holdings: Cat Mss Maps Pix
Notes: Extensive ms holdings relating to Missouri, US history, etc. Also ms collections of many noted persons (all but subsequent additions listed in Hamer, 1961). Library holdings described in Whitehall, Walter Muir, *Independent Historical* Societies (Boston, 1962).

MO —SAINT LOUIS PUBLIC LIBRARY, History & Genealogy Dept, 1301 Olive Blvd, Saint Louis, 63103. Noel C Holobeck, Librn
Holdings: Vols 8000 Cat Microforms
Budget: ($5000)
Notes: See Georgia Gambrill, *Genealogical Materials and Local Histories in the St Louis Public Library*, 1966; first supplement, 1971. Genealogy index (card file). Very extensive collection. Now in book form.

NE —AMERICAN HISTORICAL SOCIETY OF GERMANS FROM RUSSIA (AHSGR), 615 Twelfth St, Lincoln, 68502. Mary Lynn Tuck, Librn
Holdings: Vols (1900) Mss Maps Pix Phonorecords Videotapes Audiotapes Microforms VF
Notes: History of German people from Russia and history of people of German-Russian ancestory. Including times in Russia, Germany, US, Canada, Mexico, Argentina, Brazil, Paraguay, Korea, and Japan. This Society has fifty-six chapters in the United States. 1900 volumes, 100 maps; 500 mss; 1200 vertical files; 2000 pictures; 40,000 obituary files, 40,000 family group charts, 50 phonorecords, 20 videotapes, 50 audiotapes, 15 reel-to-reel tapes, 150 periodicals, 250 microforms, 250 family histories-published and unpublished.

NE —NEBRASKA STATE HISTORICAL SOCIETY, Archives, 1500 R St, Box 82554, Lincoln, 68501. James E Potter, State Archivist
Holdings: Cat Mss Microforms
Budget: ($290,000)
Notes: Collection

NE —OMAHA PUBLIC LIBRARY, Omaha, 68102. Michael Phipps, Dir
Holdings: Vols 3133 Cat
Budget: $2200
Notes: The collection chiefly covers the US east of the Missouri River, plus Nebraska. Census indexes.

NH —NEW HAMPSHIRE HISTORICAL SOCIETY, Library, 30 Park St, Concord, 03301. William Copeley, Assoc Librn
Holdings: Vols 10,000 Cat Mss
Budget: ($9000)
Notes: New Hampshire and New England genealogy. All genealogical material is cataloged. Separate genealogy card index lists the material in the collection alphabetically by family name.

NH —ASSOCIATION CANADO-AMERICAIN (FRATERNAL LIFE INSURANCE SOCIETY), Institute Canado-Americain, 52 Concord St, Manchester, 03101. Robert A Beaudoin, Librn
Holdings: Vols (40,000) Cat Mss Maps Pix Slides Phonorecords Audiotapes Microforms
Budget: ($2000)
Notes: Contains books, pamphlets, mss, university dissertations, newspapers, manuscripts, periodicals, and archives of various other societies (active of defunct). Subjects covered incl art, music, literature, folklore, religion, politics, sociology, history, etc of the French in France, Canada, and US (especially New England's Franco-Americans, Louisiana's Cajuns, and Quebec's French-Canadians). There is also an extensive collection of genealogical works dealing with Quebec Acadia, and New England Francophones. Articles dealing with the library are: "The Library of the Association Canado-Americaine" by Edward B Ham in *Modern Language Notes*, vol LII, no 7, November 1937 and a bilingual article "Appel d'un jeune aux jeunes en faveur de al Bibliotheque ACA" by Robert B Perreault in *Le Canado-Americain*, nouvelle serie, vol 1, no 5, julliet-aout-septembre 1975, pp 18-19.

NJ —ATLANTIC CITY FREE PUBLIC LIBRARY, Illinois & Pacific Aves, Atlantic City, 08401. Paul Nee, Adult Serv Librn
Holdings: Vols 2000 Cat
Notes: See *Colonial Genealogist*, April 1971, pp 256-57.

NJ —GLASSBORO STATE COLLEGE, Savitz Library, Stewart Room, Glassboro, 08028. Clara Kirner, Special Collection Librn
Holdings: Cat Mss
Notes: Emphasis on southern and central New Jersey. 5000 misc ms items, 500 deeds, 45 linear ft of bks and folders. Papers of Browning, Falkenburg, Haines, Hayes, Hosell, Inskeep, Ladd, Leaming, Lippincott, and Somers families. Journal of Elizabeth Haddon. Journals and ledgers of Samuel Mickle. Complete file of genealogical notes made on over 1000 families by Mrs Lois Satterthwaite.

NM —ALBUQUERQUE PUBLIC LIBRARY, 423 Central Ave NE, Albuquerque, 87102. Laurel Drew, Librn
Holdings: Vols (5000) Cat Maps Microforms Audiotapes
Notes: Collection of materials for genealogical research in the United States. Incl materials for New Mexico family research. Emphasis on New Mexico and on eastern US.

NM —ROSWELL PUBLIC LIBRARY, 301 N Pennsylvania Ave, Roswell, 88201. Sarah Beth Galloway, Library Dir
Holdings: Vols 400 Cat
Notes: Covers areas of genealogical research aids and reference tools, with source materials for various states.

NY —NEW YORK STATE LIBRARY, State Education Bldg Annex, Washington Ave, Albany, 12224.
Holdings: Cat Mss Maps Pix Microforms
Notes: Extensive collection on American local history incl books and pamphlets on American genealogy. Major strength

GENEALOGY—COLLECTIONS (cont.)

northeastern United States. Maintain unique card index to regional historical and genealogical materials in periodicals not indexed elsewhere, pamphlets, and comprehensive works; about 1912-date.

NY —ST LAWRENCE COUNTY HISTORICAL LIBRARY & ARCHIVES ASSOCIATION, Library, 3 E Main St, PO Box 506, Canton, 13617. John Baule, County Librn
Holdings: Vols (600) Uncat Mss Pix Audiotapes Microforms
Notes: Genealogical Research Collection: Saint Lawrence County printed and manuscript records, military records, diaries, account books, burial, church, school records. Complete "Alms House" of county records (1825-1975). Many scrapbooks, census microfilm, court records, etc. Housed in the Silas Wright House and Museum.

NY —NEW YORK STATE HISTORICAL ASSOCIATION, Library, Lake Rd, Cooperstown, 13326. Amy Barnum, Librn
Holdings: Vols (55,000) Cat Mss Microforms
Notes: Emphasis on New York State, more espec Otsego and contiguous counties. Noncirculating.

NY —HUNTINGTON HISTORICAL SOCIETY LIBRARY, New York Ave & High St, Huntington, 11743. Agnes K Packard, Librn
Holdings: Vols (3000) Mss Maps Pix Slides Audiotapes Microforms
Budget: ($60,000)
Notes: Huntington, NY, and Long Island history and genealogy.

NY —CORNELL UNIVERSITY LIBRARIES, Collection of Regional History, Dept of Manuscripts and Univ Archives, Ithaca, 14853.
Notes: Family histories or compilations of gealogical data for families; Allen, Angell, Baker, Barker, Barnum, Barton, Bloom, Bodine, Bradford, Bragaw, Brokaw, Brown, Browning, Bull, Chapel, Cooley, Cornell, Coshun, Crane, Creque, Cushman, Dodge, Donnelly, Doty, Easterwood, Eddy, Eustis, Fanning, Finch, Fischer, Ford, Furber, Green, Grover, Halladay, Haught, Holbrook, Holden, Horton, Howe, Ide, Ingram, Jenks, Jones, Kelsey, Ketchum, Kilmer, Lawrence, Lewis, Livingston, McMillan, Mowry, Mulks, Norton, O'Daniels, Personius, Pew, Rhodes, Sabin, Sanford, Shepherd, Smiley, Southwick, Straight, Stephens, Wheeler, Willard, and Wood.

NY —QUEENS BOROUGH PUBLIC LIBRARY, Long Island Div, 89-11 Merrick Blvd, Jamaica, 11432. Nicholas Falco, Head
Holdings: Cat Mss Maps Microforms
Budget: ($13,000)
Notes: Name index (60 drawers) of births, deaths and marriages, mainly from 19th century Long Island newspapers and books. Many cemetery records, abstracts of wills, deeds and church records. Federal Census for Long Island, 1790-1910. Soundex System 1880 and 1900.

NY —AMERICAN IRISH HISTORICAL SOCIETY, Library, 991 Fifth Ave, New York, 10028. Lisa M Hottin, Cur; William D Griffin, Librn
Holdings: Vols (20,000) Cat Maps Pix Slides
Notes: Archives and Manuscripts: The documents and papers of Friends of Irish Freedom, The Land League, the Society of the Friendly Sons of St Patrick, the Catholic Club, and the Guild of Catholic Lawyers. The papers of New York State Supreme Court Justice Daniel F Cohalan. This is the largest and most complete collection of over 20,000 American Irish and Irish history, biography and literature in the United States. Incl American-Irish Newspaper collections dating from 1811, the most comprehensive in the US; 1000 rare books and special editions. Special collections incl regular exhibits of Irish or American Irish interest incl mss, letters, books, photographs and memorabilia. Permanent collection of representative works of Irish painters.

NY —HOLLAND SOCIETY OF NEW YORK, Library, 122 E 58 St, New York, 10022. Linda Rolufs, Librn
Notes: Specializes in New Netherland (New York, New Jersey, Delaware) history during the Dutch period, materials on the Dutch Reformed Church, and Dutch-American family genealogy.

NY —NEW YORK GENEALOGICAL & BIOGRAPHICAL SOCIETY, Library, 122 E 58 St, New York, 10022. James P Gregory, Librn
Holdings: Vols 63,500 Cat Mss Maps Microforms
Notes: The Society has copied and has in its ms collections a great many church records from all parts of New York State and several from adjacent states; and many very valuable ms genealogies and family Bible records which have never been published. The Society library is noncirculating and one of the principal genealogical reference libraries in the country. It has accumulated in its collections approximately 63 thousand vols on genealogy, local history and biography. In addition it has a rapidly expanding microfilm division which presently numbers over 2000 reels and keeps four microfilm readers in continuous use.

NY —NEW YORK HISTORICAL SOCIETY, Library, 170 Central Park W, New York, 10024. James Gregory, Librn
Holdings: Mss
Notes: Incl original mss, illustrative materials, etc.

NY —NEW YORK PUBLIC LIBRARY, Local History and Genealogy Div, Fifth Ave & 42 St, New York, 10018. Gunther E Pohl, Chief
Holdings: Vols (160,000) Cat Mss Microforms
Budget: ($38,548)
Notes: Extensive collection of histories of American and European families. One of the largest collections in the country. Incl all types of resources for genealogical research.

NY —PLATTSBURGH PUBLIC LIBRARY, Local History Collection, 15 Oak St, Box 570, Plattsburgh, 12901. Katherine S Cayea, Librn
Holdings: Vols (2200) Cat Mss Maps Pix Microforms
Budget: $500
Notes: Local Plattsburgh and Clinton County, NY, history collection and some 300 genealogical items. Have city directories, postcards, newspapers, cemetery records, scrapbooks, etc. Listed in *Historical Materials Relating to Northern New York: A Union Catalog* (North Country Reference and Research Resources Council, 1976).

NY —ONONDAGA COUNTY PUBLIC LIBRARY, Local History and Genealogy Dept, 335 Montgomery St, Syracuse, 13202. Gerald James Parsons, Head
Holdings: Vols (30,000) Cat Mss Maps Pix Microforms
Budget: ($12,000)
Notes: Collection of local history and genealogy covers primarily Syracuse, Onondaga County, New York State and the northeast, ie, New England, New Jersey and Pennsylvania.

NC —PUBLIC LIBRARY OF CHARLOTTE & MECKLENBURG COUNTY, Local History and Genealogy Dept, 310 N Tryon St, Charlotte, 28202. Mary L Phillips, Librn
Holdings: Vols (2153) Cat Mss Microforms
Notes: Special interest in North Carolina, South Carolina, and Southern genealogy. Incl 5552 microforms.

NC —DUKE UNIVERSITY, William R Perkins Library, Durham, 27706. Elvin E Strowd, University Librn
Holdings: Vols 250
Notes: The Society of Mayflower Descendants in the State of North Carolina collection numbers 250 volumes. It is a collection of family history and genealogy.

NC —ROWAN PUBLIC LIBRARY, History and Genealogy Dept, Salisbury, 28144. Philip Barton, Dir
Holdings: Vols (2800) Cat Mss Maps Microforms
Budget: ($1500)
Notes: Generally, the History and Genealogy Collection is composed of materials relating to local and North Carolina State history and materials for genealogical research. Primary emphasis in on genealogical research materials. The nucleus of the genealogical collection is the McCubbins Collection. The Collection consists primarily of deed abstracts of Rowan County. Another collection is the Smith Collection, consisting of notes and correspondence collected over a wide span of years about Smiths of the US. A recent addition is the Archibald Henderson Collection of literary works of North Carolinians, Transylvania materials and materials dealing with North Carolina State history and political science. Also incl the Brawley Collection containing information on local history and families.

NC —FORSYTH COUNTY PUBLIC LIBRARY, North Carolina Collection, 660 W Fifth St, Winston-Salem, 27101. Anne R Correll, Head, North Carolina Collection
Holdings: Vols 10,000 Cat Maps Microforms
Budget: $3200
Notes: Collection newly organized 1975. Incl genealogy materials with limited materials on the Southeast. Separate card catalog for this collection.

NC —WAKE FOREST UNIVERSITY, Z Smith Reynolds Library, North Carolina Baptist Collection, PO Box 7777 Reynolda Station, Winston-Salem, 27109. John R Woodard, Jr, Dir
Holdings: Vols (7000) Cat Mss Maps Pix Slides Microforms
Budget: ($20,000)
Notes: The Ethel Taylor Crittenden Collection in Baptist History includes special index files for biographical references. Collection emphasizes the Baptists of North Carolina in particular. Much, however, from other states, the Southern Baptist Convention and the American Baptist Convention. Also Negro, Primitive and Free-Will Baptist items. There is a general card file to all holdings, an alphabetical and chronological file (incl extinct churches), the NC church file, vital statistics.

OH —BLUFFTON COLLEGE, Mennonite Historical Library, Bluffton, 45817. Delbert Gratz, Librn
Holdings: Vols (15,000) Cat Mss Maps Pix Slides Phonorecords 16mm Films Microforms
Budget: $1500
Notes: Collection incl all materials available relating to Mennonites, Anabaptist, Amish, Hutterian Brethren and related religious bodies, as well as the topic of peace. The library has a special collection and index of Mennonite and Amish family histories and genealogies; also a special index to periodical articles in non-Mennonite periodicals that relate to Mennonites, Amish, and Anabaptists. Library is a depository for the Central District of the General Conference Mennonite Church and the Africa Inter-Mennonite Mission.

OH —PUBLIC LIBRARY OF CINCINNATI & HAMILTON COUNTY, History Dept, 800 Vine St, Cincinnati, 45202. J Richard Abell, Head
Holdings: Vols 9996 Cat Microforms
Notes: Collection emphasizes Ohio, neighboring states, and Eastern seaboard states. Some material on Great Britain and Ireland. There is a genealogical index of family histories by surname only.

OH —CLEVELAND PUBLIC LIBRARY, History and Geography Department, 325 Superior Ave, Cleveland, 44114. JoAnn Petrello, Head
Notes: Incl British parish register societies' publications. *Boston Transcript, Harford* Courier genealogical column on microfilm in Microform Center. Microform Center has microfilm and computer printout of 800,000 obituaries form Cleveland newspapers: 1833-1975. 1976-date index by computer; also cemetery records to 1939 for Cuyahoga County cemeteries. Photocopying.

OH —TOLEDO-LUCAS COUNTY PUBLIC LIBRARY, Local History & Genealogy Dept, 325 Michigan St, Toledo, 43624. James Marshall, Head
Holdings: Vols 7500 Cat Mss Maps Pix Slides Microforms

OH —WILMINGTON COLLEGE, Watson Library, Quaker Collection, Pyle Center,

GENEALOGY—COLLECTIONS (cont.)

Box #1227, Wilmington, 45177. Audrey Haines, Cur
Holdings: Vols (6000) Cat Mss Maps Pix Microforms
Notes: Collection houses Wilmington College archives, 1870-present, and serves as repository for the records of the Wilmington and Ohio Valley Yearly Meetings of the Religious Society of Friends (Quakers), ca 1800-present. Also incl 120 Quaker periodical and newsletter titles, ca 1828-present; several hundred pamphlets, tracts, and epistles; 220 genealogical works, primarily Quaker families; and 3900 vols on Quaker history, philosophy, thought, and practice, particularly peace, war, slavery, education, and biography, ca 1750-present. Incl some fiction, poetry and children's books. Rare or fragile materials, reference works, pamphlets, and genealogies do not circulate. Please notify prior to visiting.

OK —OKLAHOMA HISTORICAL SOCIETY, Library, Historical Bldg, Oklahoma City, 73105. Andrea Clark, Dir, Library Resources Division
Holdings: Vols (43,000) Cat Mss Maps Pix Microforms
Notes: The Society also has the Indian Archives Collection of 2,500,000 pieces (Mary Lee Boyle, Archivist). This is an extensive collection of records, particularly of the Five Civilized Tribes. Incl tribal rolls, agency reports, manuscripts, etc.

OR —BAKER COUNTY PUBLIC LIBRARY, 2400 Resort St, Baker, 97814. Paul C Crouthamal, Librn
Holdings: Vols (1700) Cat Mss Maps Pix Microforms
Budget: ($2000)
Notes: Baker County, Oregon materials, historical and current, emphasizing genealogy, mining, agriculture and the people. Incl any fiction with Oregon as the locale. Local newspapers on microfilm, 1870-date, but incomplete for early years. 50 files on local plants, 1953-date, with separate catalog. Incl 300 maps.

PA —BUCKS COUNTY HISTORICAL SOCIETY, Spruance Library, Pine & Ashland Sts, Doylestown, 18901. Terry A McNealy, Librn
Holdings: Vols (18,000) Cat Mss Maps Pix Slides Microforms
Notes: Pennsylvania history and genealogy, especially the Bucks County area.

PA —CAMBRIA COUNTY HISTORICAL SOCIETY MUSEUM & LIBRARY, 521 W High St, Edensburg, 15931. Sara C Leishman, Cur
Holdings: Vols (2000) Cat Maps

PA —LANCASTER MENNONITE CONFERENCE HISTORICAL SOCIETY LIBRARY, 2215 Millstream Rd, Lancaster, 17602. Lloyd Zeager, Librn; David J Smucker, Genealogist
Holdings: Vols (55,000) Cat Mss Maps Pix Microforms
Budget: ($3186)
Notes: Specializes in southeastern Pennsylvania genealogy and history. Genealogical card file of over 200,000 cards. Cemetery records for all Lancaster County, Pa, cemeteries. Periodical index compiled from historical, genealogical, and theological periodicals. Census records on microfilm for 1790, 1800, 1810, 1820, 1830, 1840, 1850, 1860, 1870, 1880, 1900, and 1910 for Lancaster County and incomplete census records for other southeastern Pennsylvania counties. Complete 1850 for Pennsylvania.

PA —SNYDER COUNTY HISTORICAL SOCIETY, Library, 30 E Market St, PO Box 276, Middleburg, 17842. Kathryn G Gift, Librn
Holdings: Vols 200 Cat Microforms
Notes: Unpublished notes on genealogy by Dr C H Fisher, given to the Society some years ago. They incl genealogies of many families in the Snyder (Union-Northumberland) County area.

PA —HISTORICAL SOCIETY OF PENNSYLVANIA, Library, 1300 Locust St, Philadelphia, 19107. David Fraser, Librn
Holdings: Vols (230,000) Mss Maps Pix Microforms
Notes: Incl over 14,000,000 ms pieces. The Library Company of Philadelphia mss are on deposit with the Historical Society of Pennsylvania. Many of the Society's rare books are on deposit with the Library Company. The Society maintains the collections of the Genealogical Society of Pennsylvania, incl some 20,000 printed genealogies, original mss, family, church, and civil records.

PA —CARNEGIE LIBRARY OF PITTSBURGH, Pennsylvania Div, 4400 Forbes Ave, Pittsburgh, 15213. Maria Zini, Head
Holdings: Vols (24,000) Cat Mss Maps Pix Microforms
Budget: ($6000)
Notes: Collection contains at least one history of each county; historical atlases; biography; church histories; sociological and economic studies; journals of the General Assembly; state documents. The Pittsburgh section of the collection includes Pittsburgh directories 1815-date; newspapers on microfilm 1786-date, 30,000 photographs relating to Pittsburgh. A 65-drawer clipping collection supplements the published works. The genealogical materials (approx 5000 vols) incl individual family histories; regional and general genealogical works; periodicals; US. Census enumerations for Pennsylvania 1790-1910 (microfilm); indexes to biography, deaths and marriages. Separate catalog to entire Division. Collection is reference only.

PA —FRIENDS HISTORICAL LIBRARY OF SWARTHMORE COLLEGE, Swarthmore, 19081. J William Frost, Dir
Holdings: Vols (35,000) Cat Mss Microforms
Notes: As an official depository for the records of Philadelphia and Baltimore Yearly Meetings, the library holds either in the original manuscript or on microfilm the largest collection in the world of Quaker meeting archives, incl some records of Ohio and Illinois Yearly Meetings (Hicksite), and microfilm copies of minutes and registers of many meetings in New England, New York, North Carolina, Indiana, and Great Britain. Many, but by no means all, Friends meetings are incl in the *William Wade Hinshaw Index to Quaker Meeting Records,* a card index to genealogical data from the records of 307 Quaker meetings in the US, which supplements Hinshaw's well-known *Encyclopedia of American Quaker* Genealogy. Among the library's more than 250 mss collections are the papers of many Quaker families.

PA —CHESTER COUNTY HISTORICAL SOCIETY, 225 N High St, West Chester, 19380. Rosemary B Philips, Librn; Jack McCarthy, Archivist; Laurie Rofini, Asst Archivist
Holdings: Cat Mss Maps Pix Microforms Clippings
Notes: Almost exclusively Chester Countians. Very inclusive for Chester County. 100,000 clippings go back to 1808; 80,000 mss back to William Penn charters.

RI —RHODE ISLAND HISTORICAL SOCIETY, Library, 121 Hope St, Providence, 02906. Paul R Campbell, Library Dir
Holdings: Vols (150,000) Cat Mss Maps Pix Films Microforms
Budget: ($200,000)
Notes: Books do not circulate. No interlibrary loan.

†SC —HUGUENOT SOCIETY OF SOUTH CAROLINA LIBRARY, 25 Chalmers St, Charleston, 29401.
Notes: Genealogical data on Huguenots and allied families, especially French Huguenots.

SC —GREENVILLE COUNTY LIBRARY, 300 College St, Greenville, 29601. Joan Sorensen, Asst Dir of Public Servs
Holdings: Vols 4000 Cat Maps Microform
Notes: A Family Index and Visitors Register are maintained. The major emphasis is on the southeastern US but not restricted to this area.

SC —GREENWOOD COUNTY LIBRARY, Star Fort Chapter, DAR Collection, N Main St, Greenwood, 29646. Mary McCord, Dir
Holdings: Vols 170 Cat Mss
Notes: Genealogical and regional history of upper South Carolina.

TN —CHATTANOOGA-HAMILTON COUNTY, Bicentennial Library, Local History and Genealogy Dept, 1001 Broad St, Chattanooga, 37402. Clara W Swann, Librn
Holdings: Vols (24,561) Cat Mss Maps Pix Microforms
Budget: ($7000)
Notes: Emphasis on southern states, and eastern Tennessee counties, with considerable material on New England, Pennsylvania, and Maryland genealogy and history. Census records on microfilm. Special indexes and clipping files. Noncirculating.

TN —MEMPHIS/SHELBY COUNTY PUBLIC LIBRARY & INFORMATION CENTER, History & Travel Dept, 1850 Peabody Ave, Memphis, 38104. James R Johnson, Head
Holdings: (5100) Cat Microforms
Budget:
Notes: Covers Memphis and Shelby County, all subject areas. Features special materials and mss, groups of Memphis persons. Incl newspaper clipping file, 1930-date, of local subjects. Various indexes incl photo, biography, occupation, first facts (incl genealogy). Partial index to early Memphis newspapers in progress.

TX —AMARILLO PUBLIC LIBRARY, 413 E Fourth, Amarillo, 79101. Mary Kay Snell, Librn
Holdings: Vols 2849 Cat Microforms
Notes: The items focus on the southern and south central states east of the Mississippi River with particular emphasis on the states which had the most influence on the population of Texas: Alabama, Arkansas, Georgia, Kentucky, Mississippi, Missouri, North Carolina, Oklahoma, South Carolina, Tennessee, and Virginia. Strong retrospective coverage incl county records, immigration and passenger lists, military records, and pertinent state and federal records. This open research collection does not circulate. No ILL. We will photocopy.

TX —TEXAS STATE LIBRARY, Genealogy Collection, PO Box 12927, Capitol Station, Austin, 78711. Robin Rader, Supervisor, Genealogy Services
Holdings: Vols 9,000 Cat Microforms
Budget: $108,129
Notes: Emphasis on Texas and southern states. Census schedules (1790-1910), family histories, county data. Texas tax rolls. Index to Texas births and deaths, 1903-1973. Microfilms of municipal archives of Nuevo Leon, Mexico. Noncirculating.

TX —BEAUMONT PUBLIC LIBRARY SYSTEM, Tyrrell Historical Library, 695 Pearl St, Beaumont, 77701. Mabel Leyda, Librn; Maurine Gray, Dir of Libraries
Holdings: Vols 3451 Cat Microforms
Budget: $8000
Notes: Incl census records (1305 rolls microfilm).

TX —EAST TEXAS GENEALOGICAL ASSOCIATION, Library, 412A West College St, Carthage, 75633. L R Bagwell, Librn
Holdings: Vols (1200) Cat Mss Maps Pix Slides Microforms
Notes: Local history and genealogy; not confined to Texas.

TX —DALLAS PUBLIC LIBRARY, Texas/Dallas History and Archives Division, 1515 Young St, Dallas, 75201. Richard L Waters, Acting Dir; Wayne Gray, Manager
Notes: Dallas and Texas history.

TX —FORT WORTH PUBLIC LIBRARY, 300 Taylor St, Fort Worth, 76102. Patricia Chadwell, Social Sciences Librn; Paul Campbell, Librn, History Section
Holdings: Vols (25,000) Cat Mss Maps Microforms
Budget: $7600
Notes: Collection emphasizes southern states, but is national in scope. Substantial group of British material, and material on Huguenots.

TX —LUBBOCK CITY-COUNTY LIBRARY, 1306 Ninth St, Lubbock, 79401. Marlene M Harp, Dir, Adult Services
Holdings: Vols (10,000) Mss Microforms
Notes: Emphasis on the South and the various immigration routes used by settlers or their descendents from the Virginia-

GENEALOGY—COLLECTIONS (cont.)

Georgia coast to west Texas. Very few periodical holdings prior to 1955. Material is not available for circulation or interlibrary loan.

TX —ECTOR COUNTY LIBRARY, Texas-Southwest History & Genealogy Dept, 321 W 5th St, Odessa, 79761. Jan Carter, Head
Holdings: Vols (6968) Cat Phonorecords Microforms
Budget: ($4000)
Notes: A card catalog for the genealogy collection is located in the Genealogy Dept, along with a card file indexing Texas genealogical periodicals. Published description of collection: *Bibliography of the Genealogical Collection, Ector County Library, Odessa, Texas 1974*, compiled by Permian Basin Genealogical Society. A supplement will later update this bibliography. The monthly newsletter of PBGS lists new books, etc. The genealogy collection is non-circulating. The materials are arranged by state and all periodicals for that state are shelved with the books. National Archives Census microfilm is held, mainly, for southern states and migratory routes into Texas.

TX —SAN ANTONIO COLLEGE, Library, 1001 Howard St, San Antonio, 78284. James O Wallace, Dir
Holdings: Vols 439 Cat Mss
Notes: Southwest Genealogical Society Collection. See: San Antonio College Library. *The Southwest Genealogical Society, A Catalogue of Holdings on Deposit in the Library*. San Antonio, Texas; San Antonio College, 1967.

UT —CHURCH OF JESUS CHRIST OF LATTER-DAY SAINTS, Genealogical Dept Library, 50 E N Temple, Salt Lake City, 84150. David M Mayfield, Dir
Holdings: Vols (155,000) Cat Mss Maps Microforms
Notes: Genealogical research materials incl local history, family history, geography and original records or copies of original records. Equivalent to about 5 million vols, mostly in microform. About 100 cameras are in constant use microfilming genealogical materials. Although the collection is created and used primarily by genealogists, it is useful for many other purposes because of the kind of material collected and the size of the collection. Copies of the catalog are available at branches of the main library. Incl 1.3 million microfilm rolls.

VT —BENNINGTON MUSEUM, Genealogical Library, W Main St, Bennington, 05201. Charles G Bennett, Librn
Holdings: Vols 1400 Uncat Maps Pix
Notes: Vermont regional history and genealogy emphasis.

VT —SAINT MICHAEL'S COLLEGE, Durick Library, Winooski, 05404. Joseph Popecki, Dir; Henry Nadeau, Head of Archives & Special Collections
Holdings: Vols (5000) Cat
Notes: French Canadian genealogy, Irish genalogy, art, a complete set of Jesuit Relations and allied documents with a deluxe binding.

VA —ALEXANDRIA LIBRARY, Lloyd House, 220 N Washington St, Alexandria, 22314. Allan Robbins, Librn
Holdings: Vols 5200 Cat Mss Maps Pix Slides Audiotapes Microforms Phonorecords
Budget: $5000
Notes: Virginia history, especially local history of northern Virginia area, incl a number of rare pamphlets, etc, covering Alexandria City history. Newspaper clippings, slides, oral tapes and some primary source material.

VA —EASTERN MENNONITE COLLEGE, Menno Simons Historical Library & Archives, Harrisonburg, 22801. Grace Showalter, Librn
Holdings: Vols (15,318) Cat Mss Maps VF
Budget: ($30,500)
Notes: Anabaptist, Mennonite, and local history and genealogy.

VA —VIRGINIA STATE LIBRARY, 12 & Capitol Sts, Richmond, 23219.
Holdings: Vols 6250 Cat Mss Pix

WA —SEATTLE PUBLIC LIBRARY, 1000 Fourth Ave, Seattle, 98104. Ronald A Dubberly, City Librn
Holdings: Cat Mss Maps Microforms
Notes: Largest library of this type in Pacific Northwest. Supported by Seattle Genealogical Society, Northwest Lineage Researchers, Boone Family Association of Washington, and various patriotic societies.

WI —STATE HISTORICAL SOCIETY OF WISCONSIN, Archives, 816 State St, Madison, 53706. Harold L Miller, Reference Archivist
Holdings: Mss Maps Public Records Microforms
Notes: Incl are unpublished genealogies, records of Wisconsin cemetaries and churches, and mss, incl the Lyman C Draper Manuscripts. Also incl are Wisconsin state, county and local governmental records, incl 19th century state census records, civil war service records and some naturalization records. Collections described in *Genealogical Research: An Introduction to the Resources of the State Historical Society of Wisconsin,* (1980).

WI —STATE HISTORICAL SOCIETY OF WISCONSIN, Library, 816 State St, Madison, 53706. James L Hansen, Reference Librn
Holdings: Vols (1,600,000) Cat Mss Maps Pix Microforms
Notes: Includes individual family histories and town and county histories for all states. Special indices to Wisconsin holdings including censuses of 1820-1870. Federal census on microfilm, 1790-1910. Restricted use: noncirculating, except Wisconsin portions.

WI —MILWAUKEE PUBLIC LIBRARY, 814 W Wisconsin Ave, Milwaukee, 53233. Donald J Sager, City Librn
Holdings: Vols 5000 Cat
Notes: The largest genealogy collection in Wisconsin, excepting the State Historical Society at Madison.

MB —UNIVERSITY OF MANITOBA, Elizabeth Dafoe Library, Icelandic Collection, Winnipeg, R3T 2N2, Can. Sigrid Johnson, Librn
Holdings: Vols (22,500) Cat Mss Maps Pix Audiotapes Microforms
Notes: Material mostly in Icelandic, some in other Scandinavian languages. All subject areas incl with primary emphasis placed on language, literature and history of Icelanders in Canada, especially Manitoba (incl mss); early publications of sagas and religious literature; numerous periodicals and newspapers, incl Islandske Maanedstidender, 1773, the first Icelandic periodical, and Framfari, 1877, the first Icelandic newspaper in North America; collections of Icelandic music, such as S K Hall Collection (published and mss); Guttormur J Guttormsson and Stephan G Stephansson Memorial Collections; Vilhjalmur Stefansson publications. Cited in, Saunderson, H H, *The Chair of Icelandic Language and Literature at the University of Manitoba.* Winnipeg: University of Manitoba, 1961.

ON —PUBLIC ARCHIVES OF CANADA, Library, 395 Wellington St, Ottawa, K1A 0N3, Can. Dawn E Monroe, Collections Development Officer
Holdings: Vols (80,000) Cat
Notes: Genealogists who wish to obtain as much information as possible on the place where their ancestors lived may find some very interesting information in the Library's collection of local histories. Most of these result from the patient labors of active local historians. In order to facilitate research, the Library has a number of specialized bibliographies, usually by province, listing all the local histories published to date. For *Ontario,* there is Barbara B Aitken's *Local Histories of Ontario Municipalities 1941-1977: A Bibliography: With Representative Trans-Canada Location of Copies* (Toronto: Ontario Library Association, 1978); for *Quebec,* the bibliography of Andre Beaulieu and William F Morley *La province de* Quebec (Toronto: University of Toronto Press, 1971) in the series "Canadian Local and Regional Histories to 1950: A Bibliography"; for*Manitoba, Local History in Manitoba: A Key to Places, Districts, Schools and Transport Routes* (Winnipeg: 1976); and for Alberta, Joanna E Krotki's *Local Histories of Alberta: An Annotated Bibliography (Emonton Division of East European Studies, University of Alberta and Central and East European Studies Society of Alberta, 1980). The Library has many biographical dictionaries for those whose ancestors may have incl a eprson of some note, as well as a card index providing direct access to the information they contain.*

ON —METROPOLITAN TORONTO LIBRARY, Canadian History Dept, Baldwin Room Section, 789 Yonge St, Toronto, M4W 2G8, Can. David B Kotin, Head
Holdings: Vols (52,000) Mss Pix
Notes: This collection consists of material on Canadian history, geography, travel, archaeology, genealogy, retrospective city and telephone directories, collective biographies, native peoples (excluding customs, rights and social conditions), Arctic regions, military history and theory. It is an extremely strong collection of both current and retrospective material. Particular strengths are national and local history (especially Ontario), Arctic regions, native peoples, travel (especially Ontario), and military history. Incl 78,000 historical pictures, 235 linear meters mss, 14,000 broadsides and 3800 bound newspapers.

PQ —BIBLIOTHEQUE DE LA VILLE DE MONTREAL, Montreal City Library, Salle Gagnon Collection, 1210 Sherbrooke St E, Montreal, H2L 1L9, Can. Daniel Olivier, Dept Head
Holdings: Vols (44,055) Cat Mss Maps Slides Microforms
Budget: ($30,000)
Notes: Marriage records of Roman Catholic parishes of Province of Quebec; censuses; deeds; family histories; etc.

PQ —BIBLIOTHEQUE DES ARCHIVES NATIONALES DU QUEBEC, CP 10450, Sainte-Foy, G1V 4N1, Can. Collete Barry, Dir
Holdings: Vols (50,000) Cat Mss Maps Pix Microforms
Budget: ($25,000)
Notes: Dictionary catalog on cards (unpublished). Official Quebec documents published before 1867.

GENERAL AGREEMENT ON TARIFFS AND TRADE (GATT)

MA —BOSTON PUBLIC LIBRARY, Government Documents Department, Boston, 02117. V Lloyd Jameson, Cur
Notes: General Agreement on Tariffs and Trade depository.

GENERAL EDUCATION BOARD (GEB)

NY —ROCKEFELLER UNIVERSITY, Rockefeller Archive Center, Hillcrest, Pocantico Hills, North Tarrytown, 10591. Joseph W Ernst, Dir; J William Hess, Assoc Dir
Notes: Papers relative to the Rockefeller Family, Foundations, University, and other specific enterprises and contributions to particular areas of social, physical, educational, and historic reform, preservation, conservation, or development. Extensive records of administrative, financial, physical, or intellectual relationships.

GENERAL ELECTRIC COMPANY

NY —UNION COLLEGE, Schaffer Library, Archives of Science and Technology, Schenectady, 12308. Ellen Fladger, Archivist
Notes: Research and development. Papers of Ernst Fredrik Werner Alexanderson, Philip L Alger, Howard I Becker, Ernst Julius Berg, Gabriel Kron, Samuel P Nixdorff, Birger W Nordlander, William E Ruder, George Westinghouse, and William Comings White.

GENERAL FOODS

DC —LIBRARY OF CONGRESS, Motion Pictures, Broadcasting and Recorded Sound

GENERAL FOODS (cont.)

Div, Washington, 20540.
Notes: Broadcast recordings and scripts of General Foods' radio shows, 1930s and 1940s.

GENERAL MOTORS CORPORATION

CA —UNIVERSITY OF CALIFORNIA, LOS ANGELES, Research Library, Dept of Special Collections, 405 Hilgard Ave, Los Angeles, 90024. Edward Shreeves, Chairman, Bibliographers Group; David S Zeidberg, Head
Notes: Various collections, incl the Stuart A Work collection of automotive manuals, racing magazines, auto show brochures, etc; and the Ed Cray papers, incl correspondence, mss, etc, related to his history of General Motors Corporation.

IN —ANDERSON COLLEGE, Charles E Wilson Library, 1033 E Third St, Anderson, 46012. Richard Snyder, Dir
Holdings: Vols (120,000) Cat
Notes: The Charles E Wilson Archives (president of General Motors Corp, 1941-1953 and Secretary of Defense, 1953-1957). Incl 180 mss boxes of personal correspondence, 35 bound vols of speeches, press clippings, photographs.

GENERAL RELATIVITY (PHYSICS)

CA —UNIVERSITY OF CALIFORNIA, SANTA CRUZ, University Library, Special Collections, Santa Cruz, 95064. Rita Bottoms, Special Collections Librn; Margaret Felts, South Pacific Collection Bibliographer
Holdings: Cat
Notes: Astronomy library. Incl all major astronomical and astrophysical journals and an extensive collection of domestic and foreign observatory publications. The book collection is particularly strong in stellar structure and evolution, stellar spectroscopy, the interstellar medium, galactic structure, external galaxies, general relativity and gravitational radiation, and high-energy astrophysics.

GENERAL SEMANTICS

NY —COLUMBIA UNIVERSITY LIBRARIES, Rare Book & Manuscript Library, 801 Butler Library, 535 W 114 St, New York, 10027. Kenneth A Lohf, Librn
Holdings: Mss
Notes: Papers and correspondence of Alfred H Korzybski, 1917-1938; founder of the theory of General Semantics. 8000 items. Restricted use.

GENERAL THEOLOGICAL SEMINARY

†NY —GENERAL THEOLOGICAL SEMINARY, Saint Mark's Library, 175 Ninth Ave, New York, 10011.
Notes: The Bayne Collection of pamphllets, articles, correspondence, sermons and personal memorabilia of Episcopal Bishop Stephen F Bayne, eighth Dean of the General Theological Seminary in New York.

GENERATION see Reproduction

GENERATORS, MAGNETOHYDRODYNAMIC see Magnetohydrodynamic (Mhd) Generators

GENES see Heredity

GENESEE VALLEY, NEW YORK

NY —STATE UNIVERSITY OF NEW YORK, COLLEGE OF ARTS & SCIENCE AT GENESEO, Milne Library, Geneseo, 14454. William T Lane, Head of Information Services & Archivist
Holdings: Vols (3700) Cat Mss Maps Pix Slides Microforms
Budget: ($1000)
Notes: Genesee Valley Historical Collection. County, town, village, family and church histories for the counties of Allegany, Genesee, Livingston, Monroe, Orleans and Wyoming. Materials on the Seneca Indians, Genesee Valley Canal, and the geology of western New York state. Also, the Wadsworth Family Papers (145 linear ft, uncataloged). Business and family correspondence, account books, maps, deeds, leases, and business records of the Wadsworth Family, early landowners in the Genesee region of western New York. Major family members represented in the collection incl Jeremiah Wadsworth (1743-1804), William Wadsworth (1761-1833), Daniel Wadsworth (1771-1848), James Wadsworth (1768-1844), James Samuel Wadsworth (1807-1864), William Wolcott Wadsworth (1810-1852), Emmeline Austin Wadsworth (1808-1885), JamesWolcott Wadsworth (1846-1926), William Austin Wadsworth (1847-1918), Herbert Wadsworth (1851-1930), Martha Blow Wadsworth (1864-1934), Craig W Wadsworth (1872-1960), Charles F Wadsworth (1835-1899), James Wolcott Wadsworth, Jr (1877-1952), James Jeremiah Wadsworth (1905-), and William P Wadsworth (1906-1982). Inventory in repository. Open to qualified investigators with permission of archivist. Gift of William P Wadsworth and the Hon James J Wadsworth, Geneseo, NY, 1976- , and Michael Moukhanoff, Ashantee, NY 1976. The Wadsworth Family papers cover the years from 1790 to the early 20th century. *See also* entries under Photographs - Collections; Architecture - History.

GENETICS

CA —UNIVERSITY OF CALIFORNIA, DAVIS, General Library, Davis, 95616. Bernard Kreissman, University Librn; C Danial Elliott, Asst Head, Dept Special Collections
Holdings: Vols (5000) Cat
Notes: The collection emphasizes general works on genetics, evolution and variation. The collection is particularly strong in works dealing with plant and animal breeding.

CO —COLORADO STATE UNIVERSITY, Libraries, Fort Collins, 80523. Curtis L Gifford, Forestry & Agricultural Sciences Librn
Holdings: Vols 18,944 Cat Maps
Budget: $9000
Notes: Colorado State University Libraries are particularly strong in genetics.

CT —YALE MEDICAL LIBRARY, 333 Cedar St, New Haven, 06510.
Holdings: Vols (334,215) Cat Mss Pix Slides Microforms
Budget: ($361,650)
Notes: Incl films, audiotapes, artifacts, etc. A special subject emphasis.

CT —YALE UNIVERSITY, Dept of Human Genetics, 310 Cedar St, PO Box 3333, New Haven, 06510. Barbara J Bachmann, Cur
Holdings: Cat
Notes: Collection of *Escherichia coli K-12*, containing ampules of 6000 mutant strains of lyophilized (freeze-dried) bacteria, with explanatory cards for each.

DC —CENTER FOR BIOETHICS, Library, Kennedy Institute, Georgetown University, 3520 Prospect St NW, Washington, 20057. Doris Goldstein, Dir; Judith Mistichelli, Senior Librn
Holdings: Vols 8200
Notes: Largest library of its kind. Incl 31, 000 journal articles. Collects in the following subject areas: applied ethics; medical ethics; philosophy of medicine; science, technology and society; sociology of medicine; patient-physician care; sexuality; contraception; abortion; population policy; reproductive technologies; in vitro fertilization; genetic counseling and screening; genetic engineering; mental organ transplantation; death and dying; "baby doe" issues; euthanasia; suicide; use of chemical and biological weapons. Produces computer database *Bioethicsline,* available through MEDLARS; and the printed annual *Bibliography of Bioethics.* Other library publications are: *New Titles in Bioethics* (monthly); *Scope Notes* series on current topics.

IL —UNIVERSITY OF ILLINOIS, URBANA/CHAMPAIGN, Library, Biology Library, 101 Burrill Hall, 407 S Goodwin, Urbana, 61801. Elisabeth B Davis, Librn
Holdings: Vols (115,000) Cat Microforms
Budget: ($200,000)
Notes: The Biology Library incl books, periodicals, and reference works that cover the fields of anatomy, biophysics, botany, ecology, entomology, genetics, immunology, microbiology, physiology and zoology. About three-quarters of the total collection is made up of journals and other serials representing 2000 distinctive titles. The serial list is comprehensive for the biological sciences, contains most of the major international titles and consists of complete runs for almost all titles. Additional materials (approx 90,000 vols) in the biological sciences are available in the Natural History Survey Library and the bookstacks at the Main Library on the Urbana campus. Professional assistance is available for reference service, online searching, and library instruction. Interlibrary loan service is provided. Photocopying.

IN —INDIANA UNIVERSITY, Lilly Library, Seventh St, Bloomington, 47405. William R Cagle, Librn
Holdings: / / Mss Pix
Notes: Collections incl papers of geneticists and biologists, most notably those of Nobel Prize winner Hermann Joseph Muller, 1890-1967 and Tracy Martha Sonneborn, 1905-1981 also papers of plant geneticists Ralph Erskine Cleland, 1892-1971, and Paul Weatherwax, 1888-1976.

IN —INDIANA UNIVERSITY, Biology Library, Jordan Hall, Bloomington, 47405. Steven Sowell, Head
Holdings: Vols (105,461) Cat
Notes: 109,900 reprints on genetics.

IA —IOWA STATE UNIVERSITY, Library, Ames, 50011. Warren B Kuhn, Dean of Library Services
Holdings: Cat
Notes: Incl plant and animal genetics. Extensive serial holdings.

KY —UNIVERSITY OF KENTUCKY, Agricultural Library, Agricultural Science Center North, Lexington, 40506. Antoinette Paris Powell, Librn
Holdings: Vols (90,000) Cat Maps Microforms
Budget: ($110,385)

ME —JACKSON LABORATORY, Research Laboratory, Bar Harbor, 04609.
Notes: "Subject: *Strain Bibliography* of inbred strains of mice, transplantable tumors, and named genes in mice ..." *Mouse News* Letter. Database discontinued 1984, and has become an archival record.

MD —MEDICAL & CHIRURGICAL FACULTY OF THE STATE OF MARYLAND, Library, 1211 Cathedral St, Baltimore, 21201. Joseph E Jensen, Librn
Holdings: Vols (10,000) / / Cat Mss Maps Pix
See also entry under Medicine - History and Historic

MA —UNIVERSITY OF MASSACHUSETTS AT AMHERST, Library, Amherst, 01003. Siegfried Feller, Assoc Dir for Collection Development
Holdings: Cat
Notes: Veterinary medicine and animal sciences. Special emphases: reproductive physiology, poultry genetics, animal nutrition.

MA —MASSACHUSETTS INSTITUTE OF TECHNOLOGY, Institute Archives, Special Collections, Cambridge, 02139.
Notes: Collection incl over 100 oral history interviews with scientists, legislators, lobbyists, environmentalists, journalists, university administration, and citizen review board members concerned with recombinant DNA technology. Also incl are audiotapes, videotapes, and printed material collected in preparations for oral history interviews.

NY —ALBERT EINSTEIN COLLEGE OF MEDICINE, D Samuel Gottesman Library, 1300 Morris Park Ave, Bronx, 10461. Charlotte K Lindner, Dir

NY —COLD SPRING HARBOR LABORATORY, Library, PO Box 100,

GENETICS (cont.)

Cold Spring Harbor, 11724. Susan Gensel, Library Dir; Genemary Falvey, Librn
Holdings: Vols (30,000)
Budget: ($103,500)
Notes: The highly technical collection is comprised of 20,000 serial vols and 10,000 monographs. The library receives 500 current serial titles. Subjects covered incl molecular and cellular biology, virology, biochemistry, microbiology, oncology, neurobiology, biological risk assessment and genetic engineering/biotechnology. Special collections in eugenics and genetics are primarily historical dealing with the development of genetics in the US which had its beginnings here.

NY —NEW YORK PUBLIC LIBRARY, Research Libraries, General Research Division, Fifth Ave & 42 St, New York, 10018. Rodney Phillips, Chief
Notes: See *Bibliographic Guide to Psychology, 1976* (Boston: G K Hall, 1977). Incl publications cataloged during the year, with additional entries from MARC tapes.

NY —ROCKEFELLER UNIVERSITY, Rockefeller Archive Center, Hillcrest, Pocantico Hills, North Tarrytown, 10591. Joseph W Ernst, Dir; J William Hess, Assoc Dir
Notes: Papers of Edward L Tatum, Rockefeller University professor. Conducted research in the genetics and metabolism of bacteria, yeasts, and molds. In 1958, he was joint recipient, with Joshua Lederberg and George Beadle, of the Nobel Prize in medicine and physiology.

NY —UNIVERSITY OF ROCHESTER, Carlson Library, Hutchison Hall, River Campus, Rochester, 14627. Michael W Poulin, Librn
Holdings: Vols (48,720) Cat Microforms
Notes: Strong collection in the field and related areas.

NC —UNIVERSITY OF NORTH CAROLINA, CHAPEL HILL, Zoology Dept Library, Wilson Hall 046A, Chapel Hill, 27514. John B Darling, Librn
Holdings: Vols (31,000) Cat
Notes: Collection incl theses and dissertations.

NC —NORTH CAROLINA STATE UNIVERSITY, D H Hill Library, Box 7111, Raleigh, 27695. I T Littleton, Dir
Holdings: Vols 1260 Cat
Budget: $2000
Notes: Incl monographs.

NC —NATIONAL INSTITUTE OF ENVIRONMENTAL HEALTH SCIENCES, Library, PO Box 12233, Research Triangle Park, 27709. W Davenport Robertson, Head Librn
Holdings: Vols (9000) Cat Mss Audiotapes Microforms
Notes: The subject, "environmental health," incl toxicology, carcinogenesis, pharmacology, genetics, biophysics, and biochemistry. Special emphasis is placed on cell biology. The collection does not incl works on pollution control or law. In addition to the collection there are some 2500 vols in the laboratories. The library has an automated catalog.

OH —OHIO STATE UNIVERSITY, Biological Sciences Library, 1735 Neil Ave, Columbus, 43210. Victoria Welborn, Librn
Holdings: Vols (85,000) Cat Mss Maps Microforms

PA —AMERICAN PHILOSOPHICAL SOCIETY, Library, 105 S Fifth St, Philadelphia, 19106. Edward C Carter II, Librn
Holdings: Cat Mss
Notes: Historical emphasis.

PA —CARNEGIE LIBRARY OF PITTSBURGH, Science & Technology Dept, 4400 Forbes Ave, Pittsburgh, 15213. Catherine M Brosky, Dept Head
Notes: Of secondary interest in acquisitions because of the department's role in cooperating with Pittsburgh institutions and others across the Commonwealth in sharing resources, the cooperative acquisition of materials, and the provision of services and information. However, some aspects of the subject are emphasized. There are separate entries for each of these specialties in this vol.

TX —UNIVERSITY OF TEXAS, M D Anderson Hospital and Tumor Institute, Research Medical Library, Texas Medical Center, Houston, 77030. Marie Harvin, Research Medical Librn
Holdings: Vols (48,000) Cat
Notes: Library attempts to collect every publication in all languages related to clinical cancer (or oncology). Aim is an exhaustive collection in this field. Collect heavily (research level) in pathology, radiology, nuclear medicine, genetics and cell biology.

TX —SOUTHWEST FOUNDATION FOR RESEARCH AND EDUCATION LIBRARY, Preston C Northrup Memorial Library, Baboon Information Center, W Loop 410 at Military Dr, PO Box 28147, San Antonio, 78284. Dorothy M Brooks, Baboon
Notes: Principle field of research: Birth defects, atherosclerosis, reproductive physiology, cancer, genetics, organic chemistry, parasitology, primatology and behavioral sciences and their application to problems of drug abuse, alcoholism and ecology. Maintains the largest baboon colony in the world.

WI —UNIVERSITY OF WISCONSIN, MADISON, College of Agricultural & Life Sciences, Steenbock Memorial Library, 550 Babcock Dr, Madison, 53706. Jan Kennedy, Dir
Holdings: Vols (186,312) Cat Docs

PQ —MCGILL UNIVERSITY, Botany-Genetics Library, 1205 McGregor Ave, Montreal, H3A 1B1, Can. Eleanor MacLean, Librn
Holdings: Vols (21,000) Cat

GENETICS, BEHAVIOR see Behavior Genetics

GENEVA AWARD see Alabama Claims

GENOESE NOTARIAL ARCHIVES

DC —LIBRARY OF CONGRESS, General Reading Rooms Division, Microform Reading Room, Washington, 20540.
Holdings: Cat Mss Maps Pix Microforms
Notes: Microform materials only in this LC Division. Works of individual authors; holdings of collections; archival records, etc, press releases and translations, etc.

WI —UNIVERSITY OF WISCONSIN, MADISON, Memorial Library, Rare Books Collection, 728 State St, Madison, 53706. Gretchen Lagana, Cur
Holdings: Microforms
Notes: Photostats of the equivalent of 61 reels of microfilm (as well as the microfilms themselves). Originals in the Archivio di Stato in Genoa. These are registers or cartularies of the Genoese notaries beginning in 1154 AD. Supplements LC's collection of Pandects of Genoese Notaries to 1300.

GENSMAN, LORRAINE MICHAEL

OK —MUSEUM OF THE GREAT PLAINS, Research Center, 601 Ferris, PO Box 68, Lawton, 73502. Steve Wilson, Dir; Paula Williams, Special Collections
Notes: Papers of L M Gensman about law practice in early Lawton.
See also entry under Oklahoma - History

OK —UNIVERSITY OF OKLAHOMA, Bizzell Memorial Library, Western History Collections, 401 W Brooks, Norman, 73069. John Ezell, Cur
Holdings: Mss Documents Maps
Notes: US Representative. His papers. Guide available.

GENTHE, ARNOLD, 1869-1942

DC —LIBRARY OF CONGRESS, Prints & Photographs Div, Washington, 20540.
Notes: Photographs by Arnold Genthe and other great photographers.

GENTLEMEN'S LIBRARIES

OH —OHIO UNIVERSITY, Vernon R Alden Library, Department of Archives and Special Collections, Athens, 45701. Gary A Hunt, Head
Holdings: Vols (10,191) Uncat Mss
Notes: The Edmund Blunden Collection of Romantic and Modern Literature, being the private library assembled by Blunden during 6 decades of active collecting. The bulk of the collection (6,264 titles) consists of English imprints from the period 1750-1850, concentrating on literature but also incl contemporary works on art, natural history, philosophy and other subjects important for understanding the background of English Romanticism. Among the authors most heavily represented by first and other early editions are: Allington, Barnes, Bloomfield, Byron, Clare, Coleridge, Cowper, Dyer, Edgeworth, Goldsmith, Hazlitt, Hunt, Lamb, Landor, Scott, Thompson and Wordsworth. Books written by Blunden himself, together with his Georgian contemporaries (particularly W H Davies, Walter De la Mare, and Sigfried Sassoon) form a second major area of strength. Many ofthe modern books are inscribed to Blunden, and nearly all the volumes in the collection bear his annotations.

OH —RUTHERFORD B HAYES LIBRARY, 1337 Hayes Ave, Fremont, 43420. Watt P Marchman, Dir
Holdings: Vols 10,000 Cat Mss Maps Pix
Notes: The Rutherford B Hayes personal library collection (10,000 vols) incl the Robert Clarke Collection of Americana which Hayes purchased in 1874, and also part of the library of James Hall. Also have about 1800 vols from the personal libraries of the Hayes children. Further, correspondence, letterbooks, diaries, speeches, account books, financial and real estate records, law cases, memorabilia and ephemera of or relating to President Hayes. Much on US political activities of friends and opponents of the period (search individual names).

PA —LIBRARY COMPANY OF PHILADELPHIA, 1314 Locust St, Philadelphia, 19107. Edwin Wolf II, Librn; Kenneth Finkel, Cur of Prints
Holdings: Vols (450,000) Cat
Notes: "Cliveden," estate of the Chew Family, Germantown, Pa, books. The volumes, which constitute the only private library in America in its original state and setting since the 18th century, includes the law library of Benjamin Chew (1722-1810), Chief Justice of Pennsylvania. Some books removed from Cliveden to the Library Company's collections. Library Company also has books from Libraries of James Logan, William Byrd of Westover, Isaac Norris, John Dickinson, Benjamin Rush and Benjamin Franklin.

PA —PENNSYLVANIA STATE UNIVERSITY, Fred Lewis Pattee Library, University Park, 16802.
Holdings: Vols 2500 Cat
Notes: "The Williamscote Library" from Banbury, Oxfordshire. "Essentially complete by the end of the 18th Century". Incl books and pamphlets.

WI —UNIVERSITY OF WISCONSIN, MADISON, Memorial Library, Slavic Studies Collection, 728 State St, Madison, 53706. Aleksander Rolich, Bibliographer for Slavic Studies; Robert P Gakovich, Slavic Cataloger; Valdis J Zeps, Baltic Studies Center
Holdings: Vols 1000 // Cat
Notes: The Prince Romanovskii private library reflects his various professional and public interests as a member of the Suite of Tsar Alexander II, as President of the Mineralogical Society and as General of the Cavalry and General-Adjutant. Books on protocol, religion, science, technology, military science, transportation and mining are among the 1000 volumes in his library, as well as an unusual array of maps.

†ON —UNIVERSITY OF TORONTO, Thomas Fisher Rare Book Library, Toronto, M5S 1A5, Can.
Notes: Collection created by James Forbes (1629?-1712), English nonconformist minister. Kept as a separate library with few additions until present day. Described in

GENTLEMEN'S LIBRARIES (cont.)

Heyworth, P L *Forbes Collection* (Toronto, 1968). Also in Heyworth, P L "Unfamiliar Libraries XVI: The Forbes Library," *The Book Collector*, autumn 1970.

GENTOO LANGUAGE see Telugu Language and Literature

GENTRY, HELEN

CA —CLAREMONT COLLEGES, Ella Strong Denison Library, Scripps College, Claremont, 91711. Judy Harvey Sahak, Librn
Holdings: Vols 78 Cat
Notes: Works designed by Miss Gentry, primarily for Holiday House. Also incl Holiday House. Also incl correspondence, ephemera and items printed by Miss Gentry.

GEOCHEMISTRY

CA —UNIVERSITY OF CALIFORNIA, LOS ANGELES, Geology-Geophysics Library, 4697 Geology Bldg, Los Angeles, 90024. Sarah E How, Geology-Geophysics Librn
Holdings: Vols (85,000) Cat Maps Microforms
Notes: Incl theses and dissertations of UCLA Dept of Earth and Space Sciences; and (2000) serial titles.

CA —CALIFORNIA INSTITUTE OF TECHNOLOGY, Geology Library, Pasadena, 91125. Daphne Plane, Geology Librn
Holdings: Vols 25,000 Cat Maps Microforms
Notes: Incl 1000 microforms, 11,750 books, and 879 serials.

CO —COLORADO SCHOOL OF MINES, Arthur Lakes Library, 14 & Illinois Sts, Golden, 80401. Hartley K Phinney, Jr, Head Librn
Holdings: Vols (270,557) Cat Mss Maps Microforms

IL —UNIVERSITY OF ILLINOIS, URBANA/CHAMPAIGN, Library, Geology Library, 223 Natural History Bldg, Urbana, 61801. Dederick Ward, Librn
Holdings: Vols (105,186) Cat Maps Microforms

IN —PURDUE UNIVERSITY LIBRARIES, Geosciences Library, West Lafayette, 47907. Carolyn Lassoon, Librn
Holdings: Vols (15,000) Cat
Notes: Geosciences.

MA —HARVARD UNIVERSITY LIBRARY, Geological Sciences Library, 24 Oxford St, Cambridge, 02138. Constance Wick, Librn
Holdings: Vols (51,000) Cat Mss Maps Pix 16mm Films Microforms
Notes: The Geological Sciences Library supports the research efforts of faculty, graduate students, and upper-level undergraduate and graduate instruction in the geological sciences. Subjects collected deal with the earth sciences in general, mineralogy, petrology, geochemistry, geophysics, crystallography, structural geology, regional geology, economic geology, some geomorphology, and some gemology. The collection incl 850 serial publications and 15,000 maps.

PA —UNIVERSITY OF PITTSBURGH, Langley Library, A-217 Langley Hall, Pittsburgh, 15260. D L Johnston, Librn

PA —PENNSYLVANIA STATE UNIVERSITY, Earth & Mineral Sciences Library, 105 Deike Bldg, University Park, 16802. Emilie McWilliams, Head Librn
Holdings: Vols (58,000) Cat Maps Microforms
Budget: ($49,750)
Notes: Incl holdings on material science and engineering, mineral economy and engineering, geomechanics, mineral genergy management, processing, conservation and constitution.

GEOCHRONOLOGY see Geological Time

GEODESY

MD —NATIONAL OCEANIC & ATMOSPHERIC ADMINISTRATION, Library & Information Sciences Division, Central Library & Information Sciences Bldg, 6009 Executive Blvd, Rockville, 20852. Elizabeth J Yeates, Chief
Holdings: Vols (175,000) Cat Microforms

PQ —SERVICE DE LA DOCUMENTATION ET DES RENSEIGNEMENTS MINISTERE DE L'ENERGIE ET DES RESSOURCES, 2000B, chemin Sainte-Foy, 7th floor, Quebec, G1R 4X7, Can. Normand Guerette, Dir
Holdings: Vols (114,800) Slides Videotapes
Notes: In 1979, the Bibliotheque du ministere des Richesses naturelles du Quebec merged with the Bibliotheque du ministere des Terres et Forets. The result of this merger was the creation of the service de la Documentation et des Renseignements du ministere de l'Energie et des Ressources.
Publications: Info-Biblio Terres et Forets; Mines; Energy.

GEODETICS see Geodesy

GEOGRAPHERS, ASSOCIATION OF AMERICAN see Association of American Geographers

GEOGRAPHICAL DICTIONARIES see Geography—Dictionaries

GEOGRAPHICAL DISTRIBUTION OF ANIMALS see Zoogeography

GEOGRAPHICAL DISTRIBUTION OF HUMANOIDS see Anthropology; Ethnology

GEOGRAPHICAL MYTHS

VA —ASSOCIATION FOR RESEARCH & ENLIGHTENMENT, Library, 67 & Atlantic Avenue, PO Box 595, Virginia Beach, 23451. Stephen Jordan, Library Mgr
Holdings: Vols (1800) Cat
Notes: A R E Library Booklist incl 6000 items in 24 subject categories. This special collection is especially strong in the following subjects: astrology, spiritualism, reincarnation, healing arts, Theosophy, Atlantis, parapsychology and transpersonal psychology.

GEOGRAPHICAL NAMES see Names, Geographical

GEOGRAPHY

CA —UNIVERSITY OF CALIFORNIA, RIVERSIDE, Physical Sciences Library, Riverside, 92517. Richard W Vierich, Librn
Holdings: Vols (89,000) Cat Microforms

CT —YALE UNIVERSITY, Box 1603A, Yale Station, New Haven, 06520.
Holdings: Maps

CT —YALE UNIVERSITY, Social Science Library, 140 Prospect St, New Haven, 06520. Billie I Salter, Librn
Notes: Political, economic and social data.
See also entry under Social Sciences.

DC —NATIONAL GEOGRAPHIC SOCIETY, Library, 1146 16th St NW, Washington, 20036. Susan Fifer Canby, Dir
Holdings: Vols (63,000) Cat Mss Maps Pix
Notes: Material concerning land, sea, and space exploration--past and present. All fields of anthropology, natural history, geography, etc.

HI —BERNICE P BISHOP MUSEUM, Library, PO Box 19000-A, Honolulu, 96819. Cynthia Timberlake, Librn
Holdings: Vols (90,000) Cat Mss Maps Pix Slides Microforms
Budget: ($30,000)
Notes: Only American library devoted exclusively to the Pacific region. Collection reflects historical and contemporary research emphases of Bishop Museum; ie the natural and cultural history of the Pacific. Areas of concentration incl archaeology, ethnology, linguistics, voyages and explorations, history, vertebrate and invertebrate zoology, botany and museology. Strong special collections incl photographs, mss and archives, maps and art. Publications: Quarterly "Additions to the Catalog," *Dictionary Catalog of the* Library (9 vols and 2 suppl; Boston: G K Hall, 1964-69).

HI —PACIFIC SCIENTIFIC INFORMATION CENTER, Bernice P Bishop Library, Geography and Map Division, PO Box 19000A, Honolulu, 96819. Lee S Motteler, Geographer; Valerie T Higa, Asst Geographer
Holdings: Vols (2000) Cat Mss Maps Pix
Notes: Incl 20,000 maps and 70,000 aerial photos of Hawaii and the Pacific.

IL —NEWBERRY LIBRARY, 60 W Walton St, Chicago, 60610. Diana Haskell, Cur of Modern Mss
Holdings: Cat Maps
Notes: Historical map collection, with cut-off date of about 1900, incl 1230 atlases and 11, 050 separate maps (in 1973). Rich in classical geography, represented by almost all printed editions of Ptolemy.
See also entry under Maps and Atlases - Collections

IN —INDIANA STATE UNIVERSITY, Science Library, Terre Haute, 47809. Susan J Thompson, Science Librn
Holdings: Vols (40,000) Cat Microforms
Budget: ($160,846)

KS —UNIVERSITY OF KANSAS, Kenneth Spencer Research Library, Map Library, Lawrence, 66045. Richard L Embers, Map Cur
Holdings: Cat
Budget: ($3000)
Notes: (234,000 maps; 2500 books, atlases and gazetteers). A very strong collection for post-1900 maps in over 40 basic subjects. Depository for USGS and DMA. Maps are available for every country in the world with particular strength in North American, European, and East Asian maps. Excellent holdings for Kansas and the Mid-west. Library also has a large collection of books and serials dealing with cartography. Guide for readers available upon request.

LA —LOUISIANA STATE UNIVERSITY, Troy H Middleton Library, Louisiana Room, Baton Rouge, 70803. Evangeline Mills Lynch, Head Librn; Ruth Murray, Associate Librn
Holdings: Vols (33,500) Cat Maps VF
Notes: Louisiana Collection of history, description and travel, biography, agriculture, literature, politics and government, folklore, anthropology, geography, geology, education, language, music and natural history. Especially large subject collections may be found on Louisiana, the history of the lower Mississippi valley, Abraham Lincoln, romance languages and literatures, sugar culture and technology, Southern history, petroleum engineering, plant pathology, micropaleontology, ornithology, and various aspects of crawfish life, biology and culture. Complete depository of Louisiana State Documents; extensive newspapers clipping files; separate card catalog; items listed in Louisiana Union Catalog; restricted use (research and reference). Incl both materials about Louisiana and by Louisianians without regard to subject. LSU Press Collection(preservation copy of each title kept for exhibit purposes only). LSU theses and dissertations from 1900-date. LSU Faculty Collection. Also, 1300 maps, 104 VF drawers, 250 boxes of uncataloged pamphlets.

MD —JOHNS HOPKINS UNIVERSITY, Milton S Eisenhower Library, Charles & 34 Sts, Baltimore, 21218. Ann S Gwyn, Assistant Dir for Special Collections
Holdings: Cat Mss
Notes: Collected papers, 1904-1948.

GEOGRAPHY (cont.)

Correspondence incl council on Foreign Relations, 1931-1949, and American Geographical Society, 1915-1950. Together, about 10,000 ms pieces. Restricted access; apply in advance.

†MA —CLARK UNIVERSITY, Robert Hutchings Goddard Library, Worcester, 01610. Dorothy Mosa Kowski, Rare Books Librn
Holdings: Vols Cat Maps
Notes: Incl 55,000 maps.

MI —UNIVERSITY OF MICHIGAN, William L Clements Library, Ann Arbor, 48109. John C Dann, Dir
Notes: The William L. Clements Library of Americana is a non-circulating rare book library of original source material, printed and manuscript, dealing with America, from the discovery period into the late nineteenth century. The collection includes approximately 55,000 books and pamphlets, 550 linear feet of manuscripts, 4,100 volumes of newspapers, 36,000 maps, 40,000 pieces of sheet music, and 1,000 prints. The collection is strongest for the period of the American Revolution, and includes the papers of Thomas Gage, Sir Henry Clinton, and the Earl of Shelburne. Other areas of strength include antislavery, cartography and geography, discovery and exploration, American Indians, The Civil War, tune-books, sermons and orations, and the War of 1812. There are selective research collections dealing with Christopher Columbus, Thomas Paine, Benjamin Franklin, George Washington, Thomas Jefferson, and the Federalist Papers. Publications describing the collections of the library are: Author/Title catalog of Americana 1493-1860 in the William L. Clements Library... 7 volumes, Boston, G. K. Hall, 1970; Guide to the manuscript collections of the William L. Clements Library, by Arlene P. Shy 3d edition, Boston, G. K. Hall, 1978; Guide to the manuscript maps in the William L. Clements Library, compiled by Christian Burn, Ann Arbor, U. of Michigan, 1959; and Research catalog of maps of America, to 1860 in the William L. Clements Library...,edited by Douglas W. Marshall, 4 volumes, Boston, G. K. Hall, 1972.

MN —MINNEAPOLIS PUBLIC LIBRARY & INFORMATION CENTER, History & Travel Dept, 300 Nicollet Mall, Minneapolis, 55401. Robert K Bruce, Head
Holdings: Vols (186,500) Cat Maps Phonorecords Audiotapes Microforms

NJ —HAMMOND, Editorial Department Library, 515 Valley St, Maplewood, 07040. Ernest J Dupuy, Librn
Holdings: Vols (10,000) Cat Maps Pix
Notes: Also about 15,000 maps; 50 vertical file drawers of administrative, census, national parks, highway, and related materials. No photocopying.

NY —AMERICAN MUSEUM OF NATURAL HISTORY, Library Services Dept, Central Park W & 79th St, New York, 10024. Nina J Root, Chairwoman; Mary Genett, Asst Librn for Reference Services
Holdings: Vols (385,000) Cat Mss Maps Pix Slides Microforms
Notes: Nearly all collections are outstanding for depth of coverage and international range. Early and historic works, rare books, colored illustrations, and relevant serial publications supplement the modern scientific publications necessary to the researches of the scientific staff and the work of the educational division. Open to the public.

NY —EXPLORERS CLUB, James B Ford Memorial Library, 46 E 70 St, New York, 10021. Janet Baldwin, Librn
Holdings: Vols (24,000) Cat Maps
Notes: Additions to the collection depend upon gifts. Access by appointment only.

NY —NEW YORK PUBLIC LIBRARY, Research Libraries, General Research Division, Fifth Ave & 42 St, New York, 10018. Rodney Phillips, Chief
Holdings: Vols (2,225,000) Cat Maps Pix Microforms
Budget: ($775,718)

NY —SYRACUSE UNIVERSITY LIBRARIES, Ernest S Bird Library, George Arents Research Library for Special Collections, Syracuse, 13210. Carolyn A Davis, Manuscripts Librn; Amy S Doherty, University Archivist; Mark F Weimer, Rare Book Librn
Notes: The George Arents Research Library for Special Collections at Syracuse University contains the papers of George Babcock Cressey and Preston E James.

OH —UNIVERSITY OF CINCINNATI, Geology-Geography Library, 103 Old Tech Bldg ML 13, Cincinnati, 45221. Richard Spohn, Sr Library Assoc
Holdings: Vols (2000) Cat Maps
Budget: ($6000)
Notes: Collection covers only physical geography and cartography.

PA —UNIVERSITY OF PITTSBURGH, Hillman Library, Pittsburgh, 15260.
Holdings: Vols (6000) Cat Maps Pix Slides Microforms
Notes: The Geography collection is strengthened by US Geological Survey depository collection; US Army Map Service depository collection; US government publications depository collection; Canadian government publications; and UN depository (partial) collection.

PA —PENNSYLVANIA STATE UNIVERSITY, Earth & Mineral Sciences Library, 105 Deike Bldg, University Park, 16802. Emilie McWilliams, Head Librn
Holdings: Vols (58,000) Cat Maps Microforms
Budget: ($49,750)
Notes: This collection includes substantial numbers of geological maps, and strong periodical holdings including microform.

RI —BROWN UNIVERSITY, John Carter Brown Library, Providence, 02912. Norman Fiering, Librn; Everett C Wilkie Jr, Bibliographer; Susan Danforth, Cur Maps & Prints
Holdings: Vols (40,000)
Notes: Extensive collection of geographical materials, incl atlases, but especially of such writings pertaining to the New World in the colonial period.

TX —TEXAS STATE LIBRARY, Archives Div, 1201 Brazos, PO Box 12927, Capitol Sta, Austin, 78711. David B Gracy II, State Archivist

WA —UNIVERSITY OF WASHINGTON LIBRARIES, Geography Library, Humanities and Social Science Dept, 415 Smith Hall, DP-10, Seattle, 98195. Joan Christ, Asst Librn
Holdings: Vols (15,701) Cat Maps
Budget: ($18,627)

WI —UNIVERSITY OF WISCONSIN, MADISON, Geography Library, 280 Science Hall, Madison, 53706. Miriam E Kerndt, Librn
Holdings: Vols (40,000) Cat Microforms
Budget: ($35,000)
Notes: Geography Library collects books, journals, and atlases in all fields of regional and systematic geography to support research and university teaching. Popular works, travel accounts, and tourist literature are not collected. Maps are collected in a separate Map and Air Photo Library in the same building.

WI —UNIVERSITY OF WISCONSIN, MILWAUKEE, American Geographical Society Collection, 2311 E Hartford Ave, PO Box 399, Milwaukee, 53201. Roman Drazniowsky, Cur
Holdings: Vols (196,800)
Budget: ($270,000)
Notes: The largest special collection in the field of geography, cartography, and related fields in the Western Hemisphere. Incl 6469 atlases; 385,610 maps; 72 globes; 33,700 pamphlets; 79,000 photographs; 99,000 Landsat Images. Catalog published by G K Hall, Boston.

ON —METROPOLITAN TORONTO LIBRARY, Municipal Reference Library, City Hall, Toronto, M5H 2N1, Can. Margot Hewings, Head
Holdings: Vols (60,000) Cat Maps Pix Microforms Slides VF
Budget: ($112,600)
Notes: Community development; municipal finance; local municipal government; housing; urban pollution; urban transportation; urban affairs; urban geography.

GEOGRAPHY—DICTIONARIES

CA —LOS ANGELES PUBLIC LIBRARY, History Dept, 630 W Fifth St, Los Angeles, 90071. Dorothy Mewshaw, Librn, Map Rm
Holdings: Vols 100
Notes: A collection of gazeteers, place name books and geographical dictionaries. World-wide coverage.

CA —UNIVERSITY OF CALIFORNIA, LOS ANGELES, Map Library, Los Angeles, 90024. Carlos B Hagen, Head
Holdings: Vols (5566) Cat Maps Pix
Notes: The Library is a depository for the publications of many world-wide mapping agencies. The collection incl 507,097 maps of all areas of the world (subject and topographic maps, nautical and aeronautical charts, historical maps, and city plans), gazetteers, atlases, aerial photographs, periodicals and other basic cartographic reference tools. Incl 2550 atlases; 10,424 aerial maps; 1035 technical reports; and 311 (titles) serials subscriptions.

IL —UNIVERSITY OF ILLINOIS, URBANA/CHAMPAIGN, Library, Map & Geography Library, 418 Main Library, Urbana, 61801. David Cobb, Librn
Holdings: Vols (14,500) Cat Maps Pix Microforms Globes Relief Maps
Notes: Maps (over 325,000) of almost all types, incl topographic, soil, transportation, economic, hydrographic, weather, city, pictorial, and historical maps, are collected. Coverage is excellent for Illinois and for most parts of the United States and Canada. Good maps are available for Europe, Central America and the ocean areas. The early map collection is rich in maps of Illnois, Italy, and the western hemisphere. A large number of publishers' catalogs, particularly of foreign map publishings are kept on file. The collection of aerial photographs provides complete and sequential coverage of the State of Illinois from the late 1930s to the present. Much of the coverage is stereoscopic. Other map resources on the campus include about 50,000 geologic and topographic maps and aerial photographs in the Geology Library, a wall map collection in the Geography Department, severalhundred early maps and atlases of the Illinois area in the Illinois Historical Survey, and geologic and topographic maps and aerial photographs in the Civil Engineering Department. Publication: *Biblio* (bi-monthly acquisitions list).

KS —UNIVERSITY OF KANSAS, Kenneth Spencer Research Library, Map Library, Lawrence, 66045. Richard L Embers, Map Cur
Holdings: Cat
Budget: ($3000)
Notes: (234,000 maps; 2500 books, atlases and gazetteers). A very strong collection for post-1900 maps in over 40 basic subjects. Depository for USGS and DMA. Maps are available for every country in the world with particular strength in North American,

GEOGRAPHY—DICTIONARIES (cont.)

European, and East Asian maps. Excellent holdings for Kansas and the Mid-west. Library also has a large collection of books and serials dealing with cartography. Guide for readers available upon request.

MA —HARVARD UNIVERSITY, Harvard College Library, Map Collection, Cambridge, 02138. Frank E Trout, Cur
Holdings: Cat Mss Maps
Notes: Harvard Map Collection is comprehensive in global coverage and historical depth. Incl books on history and science of cartography, gazetteers, topographic maps, urban plans, and thematic atlases.

MI —UNIVERSITY OF MICHIGAN, Harlan Hatcher Graduate Library, Map Room, Ann Arbor, 48109. James O Minton, Map Librn
Notes: The collection consists of approx 300, 000 sheet maps incl maps and charts received on deposit from the US Geological Survey, Defense Mapping Agency, and the National Ocean Service. The collection also incl approx 5000 reference volumes related to cartography, surveying, and mapping, with emphasis on place-name literature (gazetteers, dictionaries), books on how to use and interpret maps, carto-bibliographies, and state (provincial, etc), regional, national, and international atlases. The collection is strongest geographically in materials of Michigan, Midwest, Anglo-America, and Europe; chronologically, 1850-date; and thematically, in topographic and geologic maps, although all subjects are collected. The collection maintains a separate catalog of holdings. Reference volumes are fully cataloged and classified.

OH —PUBLIC LIBRARY OF CINCINNATI & HAMILTON COUNTY, Map Collection, History Dept, 800 Vine St, Cincinnati, 45202. Carl G Marquette Jr, Librn
Holdings: Vols (1775) Cat Maps
Budget: ($4000)
Notes: The collection consists of 137,951 maps (uncataloged); 1250 atlases, with emphasis on Ohio county atlases, national atlases and facsimiles of important cartographic works; 125 bibliographies of maps or collections of maps and atlases; 400 gazetteers and other works, monographs series and journals (partially cataloged) relating to cartography and maps. The library is a depository for USGS and Defense Mapping Agency. Concentration of maps is Ohio, Hamilton County and Cincinnati. No catalog for flat maps.

OH —KENT STATE UNIVERSITY, Map Library, Kent, 44242. Julia Canan, Library Supvr
Notes: Incl gazetteers, 200,000 maps, 75 relief models, 368 folios, 974 books and 20 VF. Library temporarily closed; will be open in autumn of 1985.

WI —UNIVERSITY OF WISCONSIN, MILWAUKEE, American Geographical Society Collection, 2311 E Hartford Ave, PO Box 399, Milwaukee, 53201. Roman Drazniowsky, Cur
Holdings: Vols (196,800)
Budget. ($270,000)
Notes: The largest special collection in the field of geography, cartography, and related fields in the Western Hemisphere. Incl 6469 atlases; 385,610 maps; 72 globes; 33,700 pamphlets; 79,000 photographs; 99,000 Landsat Images. Catalog published by G K Hall, Boston.

ON —METROPOLITAN TORONTO LIBRARY, History Dept, 789 Yonge St, Toronto, M4W 2G8, Can. Michael Pearson, Head
Holdings: Maps
Notes: The collection comprises 40,000 maps: current topographic and thematic maps; depository for the Canadian National Topographic series; extensive historical collection specializing in Toronto and Ontario, incl insurance plans. 700 atlases: major world atlases, national and regional atlases; facsimiles of important early atlases, some originals. 400 current and retrospective gazetteers.

ON —VICTORIA UNIVERSITY, Library, 71 Queen's Park Crescent, Toronto, M5S 1K7, Can. Robert C Brandeis, Chief Librn
Holdings: Vols (5000) Cat
See also entry under Canada - History

PQ —MCGILL UNIVERSITY, McLennan Library, Rare Books and Special Collections Dept, 3459 McTavish St, Montreal, H3A 1Y1, Can.
Notes: 5524 sheet maps, 370 atlases, 571 folded maps, 629 guide books, 248 reference books. The coverage is worldwide, specializing in North America, Canada, Quebec, Montreal. Includes a collection of guide books from the 1800s to the present day, as well as a reference collection; there is also a large collection of modern topographical literature with worldwide coverage, and an important collection of postcards particularly of Montreal and the Province of Quebec. A finding list is available for 19th century guide books on Canada: A Preliminary Guide to Nineteenth Century Canadian Guide Books: a Survey of the Holdings of the McLennan Library with an Historical Introduction. Montreal, 1982.

GEOGRAPHY—GAZETTEERS see Geography—Dictionaries

GEOGRAPHY—HISTORY

MI —UNIVERSITY OF MICHIGAN, William L Clements Library, Ann Arbor, 48109. John C Dann, Dir
Notes: The William L. Clements Library of Americana is a non-circulating rare book library of original source material, printed and manuscript, dealing with America, from the discovery period into the late nineteenth century. The collection includes approximately 55,000 books and pamphlets, 550 linear feet of manuscripts, 4,100 volumes of newspapers, 36,000 maps, 40,000 pieces of sheet music, and 1,000 prints. The collection is strongest for the period of the American Revolution, and includes the papers of Thomas Gage, Sir Henry Clinton, and the Earl of Shelburne. Other areas of strength include antislavery, cartography and geography, discovery and exploration, American Indians, The Civil War, tune-books, sermons and orations, and the War of 1812. There are selective research collections dealing with Christopher Columbus, Thomas Paine, Benjamin Franklin, George Washington, Thomas Jefferson, and the Federalist Papers. Publications describing the collections of the library are: Author/Title catalog of Americana 1493-1860 in the William L. Clements Library... 7 volumes, Boston, G. K. Hall, 1970; Guide to the manuscript collections of the William L. Clements Library, by Arlene P. Shy 3d edition, Boston, G. K. Hall, 1978; Guide to the manuscript maps in the William L. Clements Library, compiled by Christian Burn, Ann Arbor, U. of Michigan, 1959; and Research catalog of maps of America, to 1860 in the William L. Clements Library...,edited by Douglas W. Marshall, 4 volumes, Boston, G. K. Hall, 1972.

GEOGRAPHY—STUDY AND TEACHING (SECONDARY)

CO —UNIVERSITY OF COLORADO, Libraries, Western Historical Collections, Boulder, 80309.
Holdings: / / Cat Mss
Notes: High School Geography Project Papers, 1961-1970. This collection consists of correspondence, memoranda, and unit production materials for administration, teacher education, unit production, and evaluation and school trials. 70 boxes.

GEOGRAPHY—VIEWS see Pictures—Collections; Postal Cards —Collections; Views

GEOGRAPHY, ASTRONOMICAL see Astronomical Geography

GEOGRAPHY, CULTURAL

OK —SOCIETY FOR THE NORTH AMERICAN CULTURAL SURVEY, Dept of Geography, Oklahoma State University, Stillwater, 74078. John Rooney, Dir; Todd Zdorkowski, Asst
Notes: Has produced a cultural atlas of North America. Contents incl sports and games, general cultural and popular regions, settlement patterns, land division patterns, folk and modern architecture, regional variations in social organization and behavior, language and place names, ethnicity, religion, politics, food ways, music and dance, and place perception.

GEOGRAPHY, HISTORICAL

IL —NEWBERRY LIBRARY, 60 W Walton St, Chicago, 60610. Diana Haskell, Cur of Modern Mss
Holdings: Cat Mss Maps
Notes: The E E Ayer Collection.

PA —JANKOLA LIBRARY AND SLOVAK ARCHIVES, Danville, 17821.
Holdings: Vols 1000

WI —UNIVERSITY OF WISCONSIN, MILWAUKEE, American Geographical Society Collection, 2311 E Hartford Ave, PO Box 399, Milwaukee, 53201. Roman Drazniowsky, Cur
Holdings: Vols (196,800)
Budget: ($270,000)
Notes: The largest special collection in the field of geography, cartography, and related fields in the Western Hemisphere. Incl 6469 atlases; 385,610 maps; 72 globes; 33,700 pamphlets; 79,000 photographs; 99,000 Landsat Images. Catalog published by G K Hall, Boston.

GEOGRAPHY, PHYSICAL see Physical Geography

GEOLOGICAL ENGINEERING

IN —PURDUE UNIVERSITY LIBRARIES, Geosciences Library, West Lafayette, 47907. Carolyn Lassoon, Librn
Holdings: Vols (15,000) Cat
Notes: Geosciences.

†SD —SOUTH DAKOTA SCHOOL OF MINES & TECHNOLOGY, Devereaux Library, Rapid City, 57701.
Holdings: Vols (166,200) Cat Maps Audiotapes Filmstrips Microforms
Budget: ($70,000)
Notes: Supportive collection incl an almost complete set of US Geological Survey materials (incl early Territorial Surveys); a microfilm copy (complete set) of the US Bureau of Mines "Mine Map Depository (Denver)" material; periodicals and technical reports (NASA, ACRL, JPL, etc) in engineering and geology; extensive government document materials (NBS, Bureau of Mines, etc).

MB —UNIVERSITY OF MANITOBA, Engineering Library, Winnipeg, R3T 2N2, Can. Y Cho, Head
Holdings: Vols (37,750) Cat Microforms
Notes: The Engineering Library serves four academic departments: Agricultural, Civil, Electrical and Mechanical Engineering. 27, 750 government publications, 11,500 microforms.

GEOLOGICAL PERIODICALS see Periodicals, Geological

GEOLOGICAL PHYSICS see Geophysics

GEOLOGICAL TIME

IL —UNIVERSITY OF ILLINOIS, URBANA/CHAMPAIGN, Library,

GEOLOGICAL TIME (cont.)

Geology Library, 223 Natural History Bldg, Urbana, 61801. Dederick Ward, Librn
Holdings: Vols (105,186) Cat Maps Microforms

GEOLOGISTS

AZ —NORTHERN ARIZONA UNIVERSITY, Special Collection Library, CU Box 6022, Flagstaff, 86011. Peter M Whiteley, Coordr/Archivist; William Mullane, Librn
Notes: Collection of Louis Reber, 1890-1966, first paid geologist of the United Verde Copper Company. He developed the concept of aerial photography for ore identification. Incl correspondence and records of mining activities in Arizona and the US, 1912-1950's and mining activities in South Africa and Rhodesia, 1920's.

CA —LOS ANGELES PUBLIC LIBRARY, Science & Technology Dept, 630 W Fifth St, Los Angeles, 90071. Billie M Connor, Dept Head
Notes: Extensive holdings of state geology department publications and maps of the Western states including Alaska and Hawaii, US Geological Survey, US Bureau of Mines, and the geology departments of major universities. Complete sets of publications and indexes of major geological societies including the Geological Society of America and the American Association of Petroleum Geologists. Partially cataloged.

MA —MASSACHUSETTS INSTITUTE OF TECHNOLOGY, Institute Archives, Special Collections, Cambridge, 02139.
Notes: Papers of William Barton Rogers, geologist, founder and first President of the Massachusetts Institute of Technology (1862-1870, 1878-1881). Major correspondents incl Louis Agassiz, Joseph Henry, Thomas Sterry Hunt, and Ellen Swallow Richards. Unpublished finding aid, incl correspondent index, available in Archives.

OK —ARDMORE PUBLIC LIBRARIES, Grand at E St NW, Ardmore, 73401. Carolyn Franks, Dir
Notes: 80 percent of holdings comprise private collection of Dr Charles W Tomlinson, internationally recognized geologist and civic leader. Remainder of collection is from library of the late Harold Fell and the Oklahoma University Geological Library.

TX —TEXAS A&M UNIVERSITY, Sterling C Evans Library, University Archives, College Station, 77843. Charles R Schultz, University Archivist
Notes: Papers of Michael T Halbouty, internationally renowned geologist and energy advisor.

WI —UNIVERSITY OF WISCONSIN, MADISON, Memorial Library, 728 State St, Madison, 53706. Sandra Pfahler, Librn
Notes: Leith Geological Collection. A sizeable collection of geological surveys of the United States and Canada amassed by Emeritus Professor C K Leith.

WI —UNIVERSITY OF WISCONSIN, MILWAUKEE, Greene Memorial Museum, 3367 N Downer Ave, PO Box 413, Milwaukee, 53201. Robert E Gernand, Acting Cur
Notes: Noncirculating collection of books used by Thomas A Greene in his study of minerals and fossils, 1860-1894. Incl 150,000 specimens.

GEOLOGY

AZ —NORTHERN ARIZONA UNIVERSITY, Special Collection Library, CU Box 6022, Flagstaff, 86011. Peter M Whiteley, Coordr/Archivist; William Mullane, Librn
Notes: Guy W Crane Collection; report by Crane, a mining geologist, entitled "Allison Mine, Pima County, Arizona," containing information on the mine's history, geology, production, and prospective development, 1940.

CA —KERN COUNTY LIBRARY SYSTEM, 1315 Truxtun Ave, Bakersfield, 93301. Mary Haas, Geology, Mining, Petroleum Librn
Holdings: Vols (28,256) Cat Maps Microforms
Notes: Deals with California and western states primarily. Incl 5000 maps.

CA —UNIVERSITY OF CALIFORNIA, BERKELEY, Physical Sciences Libraries, Earth Sciences Library, 230 Earth Sciences Bldg, Berkeley, 94720. Julie F Rinaldi, Librn
Holdings: Vols (83,202) Maps Microforms
Budget: ($74,880)
Notes: Library maintains a strong research collection in all aspects of geology. The collection is particularly rich in serial holdings; long runs of periodicals; approx (2850) current serial titles, and extensive foreign (espec Slavic) language coverage. Whereas coverage is world-wide in scope, emphasis is given to materials dealing with the geology of the western United States.

CA —UNION OIL CO OF CALIFORNIA, Library, 376 S Valencia Ave, Brea, 92621. Barbara Orosz, Head Librn
Holdings: Vols (40,000) Cat Maps Microforms

CA —UNIVERSITY OF CALIFORNIA, DAVIS, Physical Sciences Library, Davis, 95616. Scott Kennedy, Head
Holdings: Vols 25,000 Cat Maps
Notes: Complete files of US Geological Survey and California State geology series. Strong collection of western US geologic guide books. Excellent paleontology collection represented by catalogs of foraminifera, ostracoda and radialaria. About 4000 geologic maps including western US and basic collection of worldwide maps. Access to online reference service.

CA —UNIVERSITY OF CALIFORNIA, LIVERMORE, Lawrence Livermore National Laboratory, Library, PO Box 5500, Livermore, 94550. John B Verity, Library Mgr
Holdings: Vols (160,000) Cat 16mm Films Microforms
Budget: ($2,323,000)
Notes: The LLL library system includes a central collection in physics, chemistry, engineering, geology, mathematics, and computer science; and branch holdings in bio-medicine, environmental science, nuclear chemistry, energy research, theoretical physics, materials science, and nuclear weapons. Collections include 160,000 books, 145,000 technical reports, 530,000 reports on microfiche, and 3000 periodical subscriptions. LLL libraries are not open to the public. Unclassified materials may be borrowed on interlibrary loan.

CA —LOS ANGELES PUBLIC LIBRARY, Science & Technology Dept, 630 W Fifth St, Los Angeles, 90071. Billie M Connor, Dept Head
Holdings: Vols 18,000 Maps Microforms
Notes: Extensive holdings of state geology department publications and maps of the Western states including Alaska and Hawaii, US Geological Survey, US Bureau of Mines, and the geology departments of major universities. Complete sets of publications and indexes of major geological societies including the Geological Society of America and the American Association of Petroleum Geologists. Partially cataloged.

CA —UNIVERSITY OF CALIFORNIA, LOS ANGELES, Geology-Geophysics Library, 4697 Geology Bldg, Los Angeles, 90024. Sarah E How, Geology-Geophysics Librn
Holdings: Vols (85,000) Cat Maps Microforms
Notes: Incl theses and dissertations of UCLA Dept of Earth and Space Sciences; and (2000) serial titles.

CA —UNIVERSITY OF SOUTHERN CALIFORNIA, Seaver Science Library, University Park, Los Angeles, 90089. A Albert Baker, Head
Holdings: Vols (200,000) Microforms
Budget: ($700,000)
Notes: Includes technical reports (12,000), serial and periodical titles (3600).

CA —CALIFORNIA INSTITUTE OF TECHNOLOGY, Geology Library, Pasadena, 91125. Daphne Plane, Geology Librn
Holdings: Vols 25,000 Cat Maps Microforms
Notes: Incl 1000 microforms, 11,750 books, and 879 serials.

CA —UNIVERSITY OF CALIFORNIA, RIVERSIDE, Physical Sciences Library, Riverside, 92517. Richard W Vierich, Librn
Holdings: Vols (89,000) Cat Microforms
Budget: ($347,700)
Notes: Incl the Weaver and Putnam Collections in Geology.

CA —UNIVERSITY OF CALIFORNIA, RIVERSIDE, University Library, 4045 Canyon Crest Dr, Box 5900, Riverside, 92517.
Holdings: Vols (88,500) Cat Mss Maps Pix Microforms
Notes: Files of the US Geological Survey and California State Geology series. Strong collections of western US geological guidebooks, paleontological studies and geological maps.

CA —CALIFORNIA ACADEMY OF SCIENCES, J W Mailliard Jr Library, Golden Gate Park, San Francisco, 94118. Ray Brian, Librn
Notes: Downs no 2160.

CA —CALIFORNIA DIVISION OF MINES AND GEOLOGY LIBRARY, Ferry Bldg, Rm 2022, San Francisco, 94111. Angela Brunton, Librn
Holdings: Vols (28,500) Cat Mss Maps Pix Microforms
Budget: ($5650)
Notes: Incl theses on California geology; publications of USGS and USBM, state governments (other than California) concerning mining and geology; publications of foreign governments concerning geology and mining; history of mining in California.

CA —STANFORD UNIVERSITY, School of Earth Sciences, Branner Earth Sciences Library, Stanford, 94305. Charlotte Derksen, Head Librn
Holdings: Vols (70,000) Cat Maps
Notes: Incl 80,000 maps. Formerly the Branner Geological Library.

CO —WORLD DATA CENTER A: GLACIOLOGY (SNOW AND ICE), CIRES, University of Colorado, Boulder, 80309. Ann M Brennan, Librn
Holdings: Vols 10,000 Maps Pix Microforms
Budget: $2000
Notes: Glaciology, all forms of snow and ice. Bibliographic information will be contained in a data file which will be fully searchable. Partially cataloged (UDC).

CO —COLORADO SCHOOL OF MINES, Arthur Lakes Library, 14 & Illinois Sts, Golden, 80401. Hartley K Phinney, Jr, Head Librn
Holdings: Vols (270,557) Cat Mss Maps Microforms
Notes: Incl 118,000 maps.

CT —YALE UNIVERSITY, Geology Library, 210 Whitney Ave, PO Box 6666, New Haven, 06511. Harry Scammell, Librn
Holdings: Vols (100,000) Cat Maps Pix Microforms
Budget: ($115,000)
Notes: The O C Marsh Collection (vertebrate paleontology) is also here.

DC —NATIONAL GEOGRAPHIC SOCIETY, Library, 1146 16th St NW, Washington, 20036. Susan Fifer Canby, Dir
Holdings: Vols (63,000) Cat Mss Maps Pix
Notes: Material concerning land, sea, and space exploration--past and present. All fields of anthropology, natural history, geography, etc.

DC —NATIONAL RESEARCH COUNCIL, Transportation Research Board Library, 2101 Constitution Ave NW, Washington, 20418. Lisbeth L Luke, Librn
Holdings: Vols (17,000) Cat Microforms VF
Notes: Photocopying available.

DC —SMITHSONIAN INSTITUTION, Archives Div, Washington, 20560. William W Moss, Archivist
Holdings: Cat Mss Pix
Notes: The Archives holds the official records of the National Museum of Natural History's Department of Mineral Sciences, Department of Geology, Division of Meteorites, and Division of Mineralogy and Petrology, 1894-1977, as well as the personal papers of curators incl William F Foshag.

GEOLOGY (cont.)

GA —UNIVERSITY OF GEORGIA, Libraries, Map Collection, Athens, 30602. John Sutherland, Cur of Maps
Notes: Collection contains 291,165 cataloged maps and 192,068 aerial photographs, specializing in Georgia, Southeast US, Central and South America, and Europe. Major subject specializations are topography, geology, soils and vegetation. Special cartographic collection of Sanborn Fire Insurance Maps (7000 sheets).

IL —ILLINOIS STATE GEOLOGICAL SURVEY, Library, 615 E Peabody, Champaign, 61820. Mary Krick, Geological Librn
Holdings: Vols 13,000 Cat Documents Mss Maps Microforms
Notes: Geophysics, environmental geology, coal. Incl over 3500 maps.

IL —FIELD MUSEUM OF NATURAL HISTORY, Library, Roosevelt Rd & Lake Shore Dr, Chicago, 60605. W Peyton Fawcett, Librn; Benjamin W Williams, Assoc Librn
Holdings: Vols (210,000) Cat
Budget: ($100,000)
Notes: Extensive collections--publications of learned societies and institutions and monographic works--in all fields of natural history, with emphasis on taxonomy and evolutionary biology; and on museum publications, American and foreign: anthropology, especially archaeology and ethnology of the Americas, Africa, East Asia, and Oceania; botany, particularly strong for the Americas; geology, chiefly paleontology and meteoritic studies; and zoology, worldwide (birds, fishes, insects, mammals, mollusks, reptiles and amphibians).

IL —UNIVERSITY OF CHICAGO LIBRARIES, John Crerar Library Collections, 1100 E 57th St, Chicago, 60637. Robert Rosenthal, Special Collections Librn
Notes: The John Crerar Library's extensive science, medicine, and engineering collections have been transferred in trust to the University of Chicago Libraries. Incl rare books and special collections as listed here.

IL —NORTHWESTERN UNIVERSITY, Geology Library, 1847 Sheridan Rd, Evanston, 60201. Janet Ayers, Librn
Holdings: Vols 25,000 Cat Maps
Notes: Collection emphasizes graduate and research level material. Incl 5000 maps.

IL —UNIVERSITY OF ILLINOIS, URBANA/CHAMPAIGN, Library, Map & Geography Library, 418 Main Library, Urbana, 61801. David Cobb, Librn
Holdings: Vols (14,500) Cat Maps Pix Microforms Globes Relief Maps
Notes: Maps (over 325,000) of almost all types, incl topographic, soil, transportation, economic, hydrographic, weather, city, pictorial, and historical maps, are collected. Coverage is excellent for Illinois and for most parts of the United States and Canada. Good maps are available for Europe, Central America and the ocean areas. The early map collection is rich in maps of Illnois, Italy, and the western hemisphere. A large number of publishers' catalogs, particularly of foreign map publishings are kept on file. The collection of aerial photographs provides complete and sequential coverage of the State of Illinois from the late 1930s to the present. Much of the coverage is stereoscopic. Other map resources on the campus include about 50,000 geologic and topographic maps and aerial photographs in the Geology Library, a wall map collection in the Geography Department, severalhundred early maps and atlases of the Illinois area in the Illinois Historical Survey, and geologic and topographic maps and aerial photographs in the Civil Engineering Department. Publication: *Biblio* (bi-monthly acquisitions list).

IL —UNIVERSITY OF ILLINOIS, URBANA/CHAMPAIGN, Library, Geology Library, 223 Natural History Bldg, Urbana, 61801. Dederick Ward, Librn
Holdings: Vols (105,186) Cat Maps Microforms
Notes: Incl complete sets of outstanding geological surveys of the US, states, Canada and most foreign countries; espec strong for India and Latin America; the same is true for geological journals, incl Russia--a special strength since 1960. Extensive collection of early geological literature and rare books, perhaps the most extensive. Library houses the university's collection of 21,000 cataloged geological maps, incl many rarities. Special collection of aerial photographs.

IN —INDIANA UNIVERSITY, Dept of Geology & Indiana Geological Survey, Geology Library, 100 S E 10th St, Bloomington, 47405. Lois Heiser, Librn
Holdings: Vols (70,000) Cat Maps Microforms
Notes: All aspects of geology; incl over 250, 000 maps and 8000 microforms. Dictionary catalog for book and map materials. Technical report number index to microforms.

IN —INDIANA STATE UNIVERSITY, EVANSVILLE, Library, 8600 University Blvd, Evansville, 47712. Gina R Walker, Acting Archivist
Holdings: Uncat Mss Maps Pix Phonorecords Microforms
Notes: 120 file cabinet drawers of material pertaining to Tri-State (Indiana, Illinois, Kentucky) area donated by Sun Oil Company; 10 drawers, a gift of a local geologist. Objective: to collect and preserve materials pertaining to development of the petroleum industry in this area. Restricted use: noncirculating.

IN —INDIANA STATE UNIVERSITY, Science Library, Terre Haute, 47809. Susan J Thompson, Science Librn
Holdings: Vols (40,000) Cat Microforms
Budget: ($160,846)

IN —PURDUE UNIVERSITY LIBRARIES, Geosciences Library, West Lafayette, 47907. Carolyn Lassoon, Librn
Holdings: Vols (15,000) Cat
Notes: Geosciences.

KS —UNIVERSITY OF KANSAS, Science Library, 6040 Malott Hall, Lawrence, 66045. Sharon R Cook, Asst Science Librn
Holdings: Vols Cat Maps Microforms
Notes: Incl US Geological Survey topographical maps.

KY —UNIVERSITY OF KENTUCKY, Geology Library, 100 Bowman Hall, Lexington, 40506. Vivian S Hall, Librn
Holdings: Vols (40,000) Cat Maps Microforms
Budget: ($30,000)
Notes: Incl comprehensive collection of maps on Kentucky; 98,900 maps in all. Also, 170 journal titles, 5000 microfiche titles.

LA —LOUISIANA STATE UNIVERSITY, Troy H Middleton Library, Louisiana Room, Baton Rouge, 70803. Evangeline Mills Lynch, Head Librn; Ruth Murray, Associate Librn
Holdings: Vols (33,500) Cat Maps VF
Notes: Louisiana Collection of history, description and travel, biography, agriculture, literature, politics and government, folklore, anthropology, geography, geology, education, language, music and natural history. Especially large subject collections may be found on Louisiana, the history of the lower Mississippi Valley, Abraham Lincoln, Romance languages and literatures, sugar culture and technology, Southern history, petroleum engineering, plant pathology, micropaleontology, ornithology, and various aspects of crawfish life, biology and culture. Complete depository of Louisiana State Documents; extensive newspapers clipping files; separate card catalog; items listed in Louisiana Union Catalog; restricted use (research and reference). Incl both materials about Louisiana and by Louisianians without regard to subject. LSU Press Collection(preservation copy of each title kept for exhibit purposes only). LSU theses and dissertations from 1900-date. LSU Faculty Collection. Also, 1300 maps, 104 VF drawers, 250 boxes of uncataloged pamphlets.

ME —UNIVERSITY OF MAINE AT PRESQUE ISLE LIBRARY, 181 Main St, Presque Isle, 04769. Anna McGrath, Technical Services Librn
Holdings: Uncat
Notes: Geology of Maine. Collection not yet catalogued, but expected in 2 to 3 years.

MD —JOHNS HOPKINS UNIVERSITY, Milton S Eisenhower Library, Charles & 34 Sts, Baltimore, 21218. Ann S Gwyn, Assistant Dir for Special Collections
Holdings: Vols 38,000 Cat Microforms
Notes: Strong collection. Most fields covered. Extensive holdings in foreign as well as US journals; long runs in all languages. Practically complete in current serials. As Federal Depository, all US Geological Survey maps and serials received. Also Maryland Geological Survey. Emphasis on state geological survey publications from the Eastern coastal states.

MD —NATIONAL OCEANIC & ATMOSPHERIC ADMINISTRATION, Library & Information Sciences Division, Central Library & Information Sciences Bldg, 6009 Executive Blvd, Rockville, 20852. Elizabeth J Yeates, Chief
Holdings: Vols (175,000) Cat Microforms

MD —CALVERT MARINE MUSEUM, Library, PO Box 97, Solomons, 20688.
Holdings: Vols (2000) Uncat Maps Pix Slides 16mm Films
Notes: Geology, paleontology of southern Maryland. Primarily professional research papers, reports and Maryland State Geological Surveys.

MA —UNIVERSITY OF MASSACHUSETTS AT AMHERST, Library, Amherst, 01003. Siegfried Feller, Assoc Dir for Collection Development
Holdings: Cat Maps
Notes: Holdings of state geological survey publications.
See also entry under Maps and Atlases - Collections.

MA —STONE & WEBSTER ENGINEERING CORP, Technical Information Center, Library, 245 Summer St, PO Box 2325, Boston, 02107. Nancy M Pellini, Mgr
Holdings: Vols (10,000) Cat Pix Microforms
Notes: Also over 1200 periodicals. Extensive vertical file collection, and 5 on-line system for search.

MA —HARVARD UNIVERSITY LIBRARY, Geological Sciences Library, 24 Oxford St, Cambridge, 02138. Constance Wick, Librn
Holdings: Vols (51,000) Cat Mss Maps Pix 16mm Films Microforms
Notes: The Geological Sciences Library supports the research efforts of faculty, graduate students, and upper-level undergraduate and graduate instruction in the geological sciences. Subjects collected deal with the earth sciences in general, mineralogy, petrology, geochemistry, geophysics, crystallography, structural geology, regional geology, economic geology, some geomorphology, and some gemology. The collection incl 850 serial publications and 15,000 maps.

MA —BOSTON COLLEGE LIBRARIES, Science Library, Devlin Hall, Chestnut Hill, 02167. F Clifford McElroy, Science Librn
Holdings: Vols (54,508) Cat Maps Microforms
Budget: ($94,270)
Notes: Library is being absorbed into the general collection.

MA —WELLESLEY COLLEGE, Margaret Clapp Library, College Archives, Wellesley, 02181.
Notes: Records of the Departments of Astronomy, Biological Sciences, Botany, Chemistry, Geology, Physics, Zoology, and individuals connected with these departments at Wellesley College (27 linear feet).

MI —ANDREWS UNIVERSITY, James White Library, Berrien Springs, 49104. Marley H Soper, Dir
Holdings: Cat Mss
Notes: The George McCready Price Collection on the theory of Creation, geology, etc. Much of this material was gathered by this author and educator in preparation for numerous books and pamphlets. He is described as an ardent creationist and a vigorous opponent of the

GEOLOGY (cont.)

theory of evolution. Over 900 items. Not available by interlibrary loan, but may be used at this library.

MS —GULF COAST RESEARCH LABORATORY, Gordon Gunter Library, E Beach Rd, Ocean Springs, 39564. Malcolm Ware, Sr, Librn
Holdings: Vols (9000) Uncat Mss Pix Microforms
Notes: Also have reprint collection of 30,000 cataloged reprints, indexed by card catalog, on all aspects of marine biology.

MO —WASHINGTON UNIVERSITY, Earth and Planetary Sciences Library, Forsythe & Skinker Blvds, Saint Louis, 63130. Deborah Hartwig, Librn
Holdings: Vols (25,335) Cat Maps Pix Microforms

MT —ROCKY MOUNTAIN COLLEGE, Paul M Adams Memorial Library, 1511 Poly Dr, Billings, 59102. Sue Walker, Dir
Holdings: Cat Maps
Notes: Large collection on geology. Also, deposit of the Billings Archaeological Society, the Montana Methodist Historical Library (incl papers of Brother Van Oursdale, pioneer circuit rider) and the Montana Congregational Archives.

NV —UNIVERSITY OF NEVADA, RENO, Mines Library, Reno, 89557. Mary B Ansari, Mines Librn; Linda P Newman, Asst Mines and Map Librn
Holdings: Vols (32,000) Cat Maps Microforms
Budget: ($52,000)
Notes: Mines Library attempts to collect all PhD and Masters theses on Nevada geology. Only those originating at the University of Nevada, Reno, are available for ILL. Maintains an index of references to the literature on Nevada geology and mining.

NJ —PRINCETON UNIVERSITY, Library, Rare Books Dept, Princeton, 08544. Stephen Ferguson, Cur
Holdings: Vols 30,000 Cat Maps Pix Slides

NM —UNIVERSITY OF CALIFORNIA, Los Alamos National Laboratory, Libraries, PO Box 1663, MSP 362, Los Alamos, 87545. J Arthur Freed, Head Librn
Holdings: Vols (800,000) Cat Films Microforms
Budget: ($700,000)
Notes: Incl 500,000 classified and unclassified reports. There are 25 branch libraries and a central collection. The Medical Library contains about 40,000 vols in the areas of biomedical research.

NM —ROSWELL PUBLIC LIBRARY, 301 N Pennsylvania Ave, Roswell, 88201. Sarah Beth Galloway, Library Dir
Holdings: Vols 600 Cat Maps
Notes: Half of collection consists of bound copies of professional journals. Many items on petroleum and minerals, with empahsis on Southwestern US.

NY —PALEONTOLOGICAL INSTITUTION, Library, 1259 Trumansburg Rd, Ithaca, 14850. Peter Hoover, Dir
Holdings: Vols (60,000) Maps Pix

NY —AMERICAN MUSEUM OF NATURAL HISTORY, Library Services Dept, Central Park W & 79th St, New York, 10024. Nina J Root, Chairwoman; Mary Genett, Asst Librn for Reference Services
Holdings: Vols (385,000) Cat Mss Maps Pix Slides Microforms
Notes: Nearly all collections are outstanding for depth of coverage and international range. Early and historic works, rare books, colored illustrations, and relevant serial publications supplement the modern scientific publications necessary to the researches of the scientific staff and the work of the educational division. Open to the public.

NY —COLUMBIA UNIVERSITY LIBRARIES, Geology Library, 601 Schermerhorn, New York, 10027. Susan Klimley, Librn
Holdings: Vols 76,000 Cat
Notes: All areas of the geological sciences.

†NY —COLUMBIA UNIVERSITY LIBRARIES, Butler Library, Rare Book and Manuscript Library, 535 W 114 St, New York, 10027.
Notes: Sir Edward Crisp Bullard's research notes on Maurice Ewing which were the basis for Bullard's memoir. Incl correspondence, drafts, photographs and reprints of Ewing's scientific papers.

NY —ENGINEERING SOCIETIES LIBRARY, 345 E 47 St, New York, 10017. S Kirk Cabeen, Dir
Holdings: Vols 250,000 Cat Maps 16mm Films Microforms
Notes: One of the largest, most comprehensive engineering libraries in the world. Covers all engineering disciplines; particularly strong in electrical and electronic, mechanical mining and metallurgical, petroleum, chemical, industrial, air conditioning and refrigeration engineering. Incl Wheeler Collection of early materials on magnetism and electricity. 125, 000 bound periodical volumes; 10,000 maps; 5000 serial subscriptions (many foreign-language). Virtually all materials abstracted in *Engineering Index* (1884-date) are incl in Library. Noncirculating, except to members of professional engineering societies which support the Library. See *Engineering Societies Library, New York, Classed Subject Catalog and Index* (Boston: G K Hall, 1963); and *Supplements*, 1-10, 1964-1973.

NY —NEW YORK PUBLIC LIBRARY, Research Libraries, Science and Technology Research Center, Fifth Ave & 42 St, New York, 10018.
Holdings: Vols (1,100,000) Cat Microforms
Budget: ($647,259)

NY —SYRACUSE UNIVERSITY LIBRARIES, Ernest S Bird Library, George Arents Research Library for Special Collections, Syracuse, 13210. Carolyn A Davis, Manuscripts Librn; Amy S Doherty, University Archivist; Mark F Weimer, Rare Book Librn
Notes: The George Arents Research Library for Special Collections at Syracuse University contains the papers of Thomas Cramer Hopkins.

NC —CAMPBELL COLLEGE, Carrie Rich Memorial Library, Box 98, Buies Creek, 27506. Helen Sistrunk, Asst to Dir
Holdings: Vols 15,000 Cat Maps Pix
Budget: $717
Notes: Emphasis on Paleontology. Large collection of Geological Survey Bulletins and professional papers. Collection in process of cataloging (255,000 pieces).

NC —UNIVERSITY OF NORTH CAROLINA, CHAPEL HILL, Geology Library, Mitchell Hall 029A, Chapel Hill, 27514. Miriam L Sheaves, Librn
Holdings: Vols (41,000) Cat Maps
Notes: Earth sciences, paleontology, oceanography, geology, geophysics. Incl theses and dissertations; 103,000 map sheets.

OH —PUBLIC LIBRARY OF CINCINNATI & HAMILTON COUNTY, Science & Technology Dept, 800 Vine St, Cincinnati, 45202. Rosemary Gaiser, Head
Holdings: Vols (250,000) Cat
Notes: Pure and applied science. Incl over 1600 periodicals and serial titles and more than 100 abstracting and indexing services in major fields of science and technology.

OH —UNIVERSITY OF CINCINNATI, Geology-Geography Library, 103 Old Tech Bldg ML 13, Cincinnati, 45221. Richard Spohn, Sr Library Assoc
Holdings: Vols (35,000) Cat Maps
Budget: ($30,000)
Notes: Collection covers the broad range of geoscience topics, incl a geologic field trip guidebook collection of almost 1400 volumes.

OH —CLEVELAND PUBLIC LIBRARY, Science & Technology Dept, 325 Superior Ave, Cleveland, 44114. Jean Z Piety, Head
Holdings: Cat
Notes: Extensive collection of state and society publications; African, Australian, Canadian and other selected foreign areas; bibliography.

OK —ARDMORE PUBLIC LIBRARIES, Grand at E St NW, Ardmore, 73401. Carolyn Franks, Dir
Holdings: Vols 4000 Cat Mss Maps Pix
Notes: 80 percent of holdings comprise private collection of Dr Charles W Tomlinson, internationally recognized geologist and civic leader. Remainder of collection is from library of the late Harold Fell and the Oklahoma University Geological Library.

OK —UNIVERSITY OF OKLAHOMA, Geology Library, 830 Van Vleet Oval Rm 102, Norman, 73019. Claren Kidd, Geology Librn
Holdings: Vols 70,000 Cat Maps Microforms
Budget: $22,000
Notes: Geology Library is also the Oklahoma Geological Survey Library.

OK —OKLAHOMA STATE UNIVERSITY, Library, Stillwater, 74708. Roscoe Rouse, Dir
Holdings: Vols 8813 Cat

OK —TULSA CITY-COUNTY LIBRARY, Business & Technology Dept, 400 Civic Center, Tulsa, 74103. Craig Buthod, Head
Holdings: Vols (1600) Cat
Notes: The A I Levorsen Geology Collection. The department has a major emphasis on geology and petroleum geology. There is a catalog of the collection, which was given to the library in 1968.

OR —OREGON DEPT OF GEOLOGY & MINERAL INDUSTRIES, 1069 State Office Bldg, Portland, 97201. Beverly Vogt, Editor/Librn
Holdings: Cat Mss Maps
Notes: Chiefly publications of the USGS and the US Bureau of Mines. Emphasis on Oregon geology, and mineral industry. Partially cataloged.

PA —CARNEGIE LIBRARY OF PITTSBURGH, Science & Technology Dept, 4400 Forbes Ave, Pittsburgh, 15213. Catherine M Brosky, Dept Head
Holdings: Vols (380,000) Cat Maps Microforms
Budget: ($240,000)
Notes: Subject area well developed with emphasis on North American geology; other continents of secondary interest. Long runs of journals, reports of geological surveys and society publications. Incl abstracts, indexes, bibliographies, literature guides, dictionaries, handbooks, manuals, compilations of data, maps, history and biography. Complete sets of US topographic maps and geologic folios, climatological data, water supply papers and soil surveys.

PA —UNIVERSITY OF PITTSBURGH, Physics Library, 208 Engineering Hall, Pittsburgh, 15260. Paul J Kobulnicky, Physical Sciences Librn
Holdings: Vols (25,000) Cat Microforms
Budget: ($100,000)
Notes: The Physics Library collection is both a graduate student research-level collection in basic experimental and theoretical physics with emphasis on solid-state, nuclear, upper-atmosphere, space, and crystallography, and also a collection in the earth and planetary sciences, serving both graduate and undergraduate students. The collection is cataloged in both the University of Pittsburgh, Hillman Library union catalog and in a separate catalog in the Physics Library.

PA —UNIVERSITY OF PITTSBURGH, Langley Library, A-217 Langley Hall, Pittsburgh, 15260. D L Johnston, Librn

SC —COLLEGE OF CHARLESTON LIBRARY, Special Collections Dept, Charleston, 29401.
Notes: Carolina Geologic Society Papers, 1940.

SC —UNIVERSITY OF SOUTH CAROLINA, Thomas Cooper Library, Columbia, 29208. Kenneth E Toombs, Dir of Libraries; Roger Mortimer, Rare Book Librn
Holdings: Vols 250 Cat
Notes: Strong in early 19th century geology.

†SD —SOUTH DAKOTA SCHOOL OF MINES & TECHNOLOGY, Devereaux Library, Rapid City, 57701.
Holdings: Vols (166,200) Cat Maps Audiotapes Filmstrips Microforms
Budget: ($70,000)
Notes: Supportive collection incl an almost complete set of US Geological Survey materials (incl early Territorial Surveys); a microfilm copy (complete set) of the US

GEOLOGY (cont.)

Bureau of Mines "Mine Map Depository (Denver)" material; periodicals and technical reports (NASA, ACRL, JPL, etc) in engineering and geology; extensive government document materials (NBS, Bureau of Mines, etc).

TN —CHUCALISSA MUSEUM, 1987 Indian Village Dr, Memphis, 38109. Gerald P Smith, Cur
Holdings: Vols (1100) Cat Mss
Budget: ($200)
Notes: Collection emphasizes midsouth archaeology, but incl some regional ethnographic and geological titles. Noncirculating.

TX —UNIVERSITY OF TEXAS LIBRARIES, General Libraries, Geology Dept, PO Box P, Austin, 78712. Chestalene Pintozzi, Librn
Holdings: Vols (59,349) Cat Maps Microforms
Notes: Departmental library with a separate catalog covering broadly the earth sciences. USGS depository. Incl 126,264 maps.

TX —TEXAS A&M UNIVERSITY, Sterling C Evans Library, College Station, 77843. Judith Rieke, Map Librn; Irene B Hoadley, Dir of Libraries
Holdings: Cat
Budget: ($10,000)
Notes: Maps of all areas of the world with geographic emphasis on the US and Texas. Subject emphasis on geology, petroleum, soils, highways and streets. Depository for NOS coastal and bathymetric charts, DMA maps, and USGS topographic and geologic maps. An extensive file of publisher's catalogs is available to the public. Collection incls aerial photographs (1100), atlases and gazetteers (1500), maps (82,600).

TX —FORT WORTH PUBLIC LIBRARY, 300 Taylor St, Fort Worth, 76102. John R McCracken, Manager
Holdings: Vols (4500) Cat
Budget: ($21,000)

TX —RICE UNIVERSITY, Fondren Library, 6100 S Main St, PO Box 1892, Houston, 77251. Dr Samuel M Carrington, Jr, University Librn
Holdings: Vols 4500 Cat
Budget: $34,600
Notes: Each serial title counted once.

TX —MIDLAND COUNTY PUBLIC LIBRARY, Petroleum Dept, 301 W Missouri, PO Box 1191, Midland, 79701. Sandra Wagner, Librn
Holdings: Vols (27,000) Cat Maps
Budget: ($2000)
Notes: Scout tickets covering W Texas and New Mexico, driller's logs for the same area, Lockwood reports 1947-1970, over one hundred industry-related periodicals, publications of many State Surveys, USGS, USBM, and Geological Societies. Incl 7600 maps.

TX —ECTOR COUNTY LIBRARY, Department of Business and Technology, 321 W 5th St, Odessa, 79760. Pat Jones, Dept Head
Holdings: Vols 1000 Cat
Notes: Incl 50 vertical files, 20 periodicals, 250 Trade Specifications and Standards, 300 maps and charts, 2 manuscripts.

TX —UNIVERSITY OF TEXAS, Marine Science Institute Library, Port Aransas, 78373. Ruth Grundy, Librn
Holdings: Vols (45,000) Cat Maps Pix
Budget: ($70,000)
Notes: Current researches in marine science, especially concerning the Gulf of Mexico, the Texas Coastal Zone, and the Continental Shelf. Incl journals.

WA —UNIVERSITY OF WASHINGTON LIBRARIES, Suzzallo Library, Natural Sciences Library, FM-25, Seattle, 98195. Nancy G Blase, Head
Holdings: Vols (192,353) Cat
Budget: ($219,809)

WI —UNIVERSITY OF WISCONSIN, MADISON, Memorial Library, 728 State St, Madison, 53706. Sandra Pfahler, Librn
Notes: George White Collection of geological literature. In addition, a sizeable collection of geological surveys of the US and Canada amassed by Emeritus Professor C K Leith.

WI —MILWAUKEE PUBLIC LIBRARY, 814 W Wisconsin Ave, Milwaukee, 53233. Donald J Sager, City Librn
Holdings: Cat Maps
Notes: Or primary interest, subject area well developed with emphasis on Wisconsin geology, other states of secondary interest. Long runs of journals, reports of geological surveys and society publications. Incl abstracts, indexes, bibliographies, literature guides, dictionaries, handbooks, manuals, and climatological data. Strong general reference service.

WI —MILWAUKEE PUBLIC MUSEUM, Reference Library, 800 W Wells St, Milwaukee, 53233. Judith Campbell Turner, Museum Librn

WI —UNIVERSITY OF WISCONSIN, MILWAUKEE, Greene Memorial Museum, 3367 N Downer Ave, PO Box 413, Milwaukee, 53201. Robert E Gernand, Acting Cur
Holdings: Vols (250) Uncat
Notes: Noncirculating collection of books used by Thomas A Greene in his study of minerals and fossils, 1860-1894. Incl 150,000 specimens.

WY —NATRONA COUNTY PUBLIC LIBRARY, 307 E Second St, Casper, 82601. Kathleen Nowak, Earth Sciences/Reference Librn
Holdings: Vols (3000) Cat Maps
Notes: The earth sciences collection consists of technical literature published in energy-related fields. A map collection of topographic and geologic maps of Wyoming is maintained. State geological survey documents for the states surrounding Wyoming are collected. Also some thiry periodicals in the earth sciences.

MB —MANITOBA MUSEUM OF MAN & NATURE, Library, 190 Rupert Ave, Winnipeg, R3B 0N2, Can. V Hatten, Librn
Holdings: Vols (20,000) Cat

MB —UNIVERSITY OF MANITOBA, Science Library, Machray Hall, Winnipeg, R3T 2N2, Can. V Simosko, Head
Holdings: Vols (90,000) Cat Microforms

ON —GEOLOGICAL SURVEY OF CANADA, Library, Dept of Energy, Mines, & Resouces, 601 Booth St, Ottawa, K1A 0E8, Can. Annette E Bourgeois, Librn
Holdings: Vols (300,000) Cat Mss Maps Microforms
Notes: All aspects of Geology are collected and an attempt is made to collect all Canadian geology information. The library is a national resource collection in the geosciences. Incl 40,000 book titles (monographs), 4000 personals, 35,000 microfiche, 300,000 maps, 2000 translations of reports, 20 verrtical files, 300,000 vols of bound periodicals.

ON —METROPOLITAN TORONTO LIBRARY, Science & Technology Dept, 789 Yonge St, Toronto, M4W 2G8, Can. Margaret Walshe, Head
Holdings: Vols (120,000) Cat Maps
Notes: Most aspects of science for the specialist, the student, and the general public. The department gives high priority to Canadian materials, such as the Canadian Geological Survey.

ON —RIO ALGOM LIMITED, Library, 120 Adelaide St W, Toronto, M5H 1W5, Can. Penny Lipman, Librn
Holdings: Vols (1500) Cat
Budget: ($7000)
Notes: Espec mining of uranium and copper; geology; mining methods; nuclear energy.

ON —ROYAL ONTARIO MUSEUM, Main Library and Archives, 100 Queen's Park, Toronto, M5S 2C6, Can. Julia Matthews, Head Librn
Holdings: Vols (85,000) Cat
Notes: Since January 1977, acquisitions have been entered in UTLAS.

PQ —MCGILL UNIVERSITY, McLennan Library, Rare Books and Special Collections Dept, 3459 McTavish St, Montreal, H3A 1Y1, Can.
Holdings: Vols 1581
Notes: Early works on geology and science, housed in the Frank Dawson Adams Collection.

PQ —SERVICE DE LA DOCUMENTATION ET DES RENSEIGNEMENTS MINISTERE DE L'ENERGIE ET DES RESSOURCES, 2000B, chemin Sainte-Foy, 7th floor, Quebec, G1R 4X7, Can. Normand Guerette, Dir
Holdings: Vols (114,800) Slides Videotapes
Notes: In 1979, the Bibliotheque du ministere des Richesses naturelles du Quebec merged with the Bibliotheque du ministere des Terres et Forets. The result of this merger was the creation of the service de la Documentation et des Renseignements du ministere de l'Energie et des Ressources.
Publications: Info-Biblio Terres et Forets; Mines; Energy.

GEOLOGY—ARIZONA

AZ —NORTHERN ARIZONA UNIVERSITY, Special Collection Library, CU Box 6022, Flagstaff, 86011. Peter M Whiteley, Coordr/Archivist; William Mullane, Librn
Notes: John P Schreiber Collection; copy of "A Preliminary Survey of Obsidian Localities in The San Francisco Mountain Volcanic Field, Coconino County, Arizona," by Schreiber, 1967.

AZ —PHOENIX PUBLIC LIBRARY, Arizona Room, 12 E McDowell, Phoenix, 85004. Jeannette Brush, Librn
Holdings: Vols (30,000) Cat Maps Pix
Budget: ($12,000)
See also entry under Arizona - History.

GEOLOGY—CALIFORNIA

CA —UNIVERSITY OF CALIFORNIA, RIVERSIDE, University Library, 4045 Canyon Crest Dr, Box 5900, Riverside, 92517.
Holdings: Vols (88,500) Cat Mss Maps Pix Microforms
Notes: Files of the US Geological Survey and California State Geology series. Strong collections of western US geological guidebooks, paleontological studies and geological maps.

CA —CALIFORNIA DIVISION OF MINES AND GEOLOGY LIBRARY, Ferry Bldg, Rm 2022, San Francisco, 94111. Angela Brunton, Librn
Holdings: Vols (28,500) Cat Mss Maps Pix Microforms
Budget: ($5650)
Notes: Incl theses on California geology; publications of USGS and USBM, state governments (other than California) concerning mining and geology; publications of foreign governments concerning geology and mining; history of mining in California.

GEOLOGY—CANADA

IL —UNIVERSITY OF ILLINOIS, URBANA/CHAMPAIGN, Library, Geology Library, 223 Natural History Bldg, Urbana, 61801. Dederick Ward, Librn
Holdings: Vols (105,186) Cat Maps Micoforms

ON —GEOLOGICAL SURVEY OF CANADA, Library, Dept of Energy, Mines, & Resouces, 601 Booth St, Ottawa, K1A 0E8, Can. Annette E Bourgeois, Librn
Holdings: Vols (120,000) Cat Mss Maps Microforms
Notes: Collection incl 40,000 maps, is worldwide and in all languages. Many translations are available. *Canadian Geology* is indexed in the monthly accession list which is free and lists translations as well as being a selected current-awareness list.

ON —ONTARIO MINISTRY OF NATURAL RESOURCES, Mines Library, 77 Grenville St, Rm 812, Toronto, M5S 1B3, Can. Nancy Thurston, Librn
Holdings: Vols (40,000) Cat Maps Microforms
Budget: ($30,000)
Notes: Geology of Ontario. Incl 20,000 maps. Depository for US and Canadian federal publications in geology and mining.

ON —VICTORIA UNIVERSITY, Library, 71 Queen's Park Crescent, Toronto, M5S 1K7, Can. Robert C Brandeis, Chief Librn
Holdings: Vols 10 Cat Mss Photographs

GEOLOGY—CANADA (cont.)

Watercolors
Notes: Field notebooks, diaries, mss, photographs, and watercolors of noted Canadian geologist Dr A P Coleman.

GEOLOGY—COLORADO

CO —COLORADO GEOLOGICAL SURVEY, Library, 1313 Sherman St Rm 715, Denver, 80203. Louise Slade, Librn
Holdings: Vols (3000) Uncat Mss Maps Pix Microforms
Notes: Mineral resources of Colorado.

GEOLOGY—GUIDEBOOKS

OH —UNIVERSITY OF CINCINNATI, Geology-Geography Library, 103 Old Tech Bldg ML 13, Cincinnati, 45221. Richard Spohn, Sr Library Assoc
Holdings: Vols (35,000) Cat Maps
Budget: ($30,000)
Notes: Collection covers the broad range of geoscience topics, incl a geologic field trip guidebook collection of almost 1400 volumes.

GEOLOGY—HISTORY

FL —FLORIDA BUREAU OF GEOLOGY, Library, 903 W Tennessee St, Tallahassee, 32304. Alison Lewis, Librn
Holdings: Vols 150 // Cat Maps Pix Microforms
Notes: Special collection is mainly 19th century books dealing with a broad range of topics in the earth sciences. Some authors included are Charles Darwin, Joseph Le Conte, Thomas H Huxley, Ernst Haekel, Louis Agassiz, Archibald and James Geike, James D Dana, Sir Charles Lyell. Collection incl journals; state, federal and foreign documents; 13,000 maps and 1500 aerial photographs.

IL —UNIVERSITY OF ILLINOIS, URBANA/CHAMPAIGN, Library, Rare Book Room, 346 Library, Urbana, 61801. Norman B Brown, Asst Dir for Special Collections; N Frederick Nash, Librn
Holdings: Cat Mss Microforms
Notes: Extensive collection, described in: *Catalog of the Rare Book Room,* (Boston: G K Hall, 1972). Supplement (1978).

IL —UNIVERSITY OF ILLINOIS, URBANA/CHAMPAIGN, Library, Geology Library, 223 Natural History Bldg, Urbana, 61801. Dederick Ward, Librn
Holdings: Vols (105,186) Cat Maps Microforms
Notes: Incl complete sets of outstanding geological surveys of the US, states, Canada and most foreign countries; espec strong for India and Latin America; the same is true for geological journals, incl Russia--a special strength since 1960. Extensive collection of early geological literature and rare books, perhaps the most extensive. Library houses the university's collection of 21,000 cataloged geological maps, incl many rarities. Special collection of aerial photographs.

ME —BOWDOIN COLLEGE, Library, Brunswick, 04011. Dianne M Gutscher, Cur of Special Collections
Holdings: Cat Mss
Notes: The Parker Cleaveland Papers cover the period 1795-1858 and number about 1600 items. They are principally concerned with his tenure as professor of chemistry, mineralogy, and natural philosophy at Bowdoin. They incl personal correspondence, lecture notes, and writings on scientific subjects, incl his mss of the first American work on mineralogy and geology.

NY —CORNELL UNIVERSITY LIBRARIES, John M Olin Library, History of Science Collections, Ithaca, 14853. Lillian A Clark, Administrative Supervisor; David W Corson, History of Science Librn
Notes: Very extensive collection of history, biography and bibliography.
See also entry under Science - History

PA —CARNEGIE LIBRARY OF PITTSBURGH, Science & Technology Dept, 4400 Forbes Ave, Pittsburgh, 15213. Catherine M Brosky, Dept Head
Notes: Long runs of journals, reports of geological surveys and society publications. Incl abstracts, indexes, bibliographies, literature guides, dictionaries, handbooks, manuals, compilations of data, maps, history and biography. Complete sets of US topographic maps and geologic folios, climatological data, water supply papers and soil surveys available.

RI —BROWN UNIVERSITY, John Hay Library, 20 Prospect St, Providence, 02912. Mark N Brown, Cur Mss
Notes: See the Clarence King, 1842-1901, Manuscript Collection.

SC —UNIVERSITY OF SOUTH CAROLINA, Thomas Cooper Library, Columbia, 29208. Kenneth E Toombs, Dir of Libraries; Roger Mortimer, Rare Book Librn
Notes: Strong in early 19th century geology.

TX —SOUTHERN METHODIST UNIVERSITY, DeGolyer Library, Box 396, SMU, Dallas, 75275. Clifton H Jones, Dir
Holdings: Vols 40,000 Cat Mss Maps Pix
Notes: Includes The John Nash Collection of early works on the history of geology.

PQ —MCGILL UNIVERSITY, McLennan Library, Rare Books and Special Collections Dept, 3459 McTavish St, Montreal, H3A 1Y1, Can.
Notes: Early works on geology and science, housed in the Frank Dawson Adams Collection.

GEOLOGY—INDIA

IL —UNIVERSITY OF ILLINOIS, URBANA/CHAMPAIGN, Library, Geology Library, 223 Natural History Bldg, Urbana, 61801. Dederick Ward, Librn
Holdings: Vols (105,186) Cat Maps Microforms

GEOLOGY—LATIN AMERICA

IL —UNIVERSITY OF ILLINOIS, URBANA/CHAMPAIGN, Library, Geology Library, 223 Natural History Bldg, Urbana, 61801. Dederick Ward, Librn
Holdings: Vols (105,186) Cat Maps Microforms

GEOLOGY—LONG ISLAND, N.Y.

NY —NASSAU COUNTY MUSEUM, Sands Pt Preserve, Middleneck Rd, Sand Points, 11050.
Holdings: Vols (2500)
Notes: Collection contains almost every published reference on Long Island archaeology, ethnology, and geology, and incl most of those pertaining to the coastal New York area. Open by appointment. No photocopying.

GEOLOGY—LOUISIANA

LA —UNIVERSITY OF SOUTHERN LOUISIANA, Dupre Library, Jefferson Caffery Louisiana Room, 302 East St Mary Blvd, Lafayette, 70504. Cynthia J Rice, Louisiana Room Ref Librn
Holdings: Vols (20,000) Cat Doc Maps Microforms VF
Budget: ($3800)
Notes: Emphasis is on state, regional, and local history, genealogy, and culture; also politics and government, industry, agriculture, geology, language and literature. Collection is closed-stack and non-circulating, and is open to the public for on-site use only. Copying services are available.

GEOLOGY—MAPS

CA —KERN COUNTY LIBRARY SYSTEM, 1315 Truxtun Ave, Bakersfield, 93301. Mary Haas, Geology, Mining, Petroleum Librn
Notes: Deals with California and western states primarily. Incl 5000 maps.

†CA —UNIVERSITY OF CALIFORNIA, DAVIS, Peter J Shields Memorial Library, Map Collection, Davis, 95616.

CA —LOS ANGELES PUBLIC LIBRARY, Science & Technology Dept, 630 W Fifth St, Los Angeles, 90071. Billie M Connor, Dept Head
Holdings: Vols 18,000 Maps Microforms
Notes: Extensive holdings of state geology department publications and maps of the Western states including Alaska and Hawaii, US Geological Survey, US Bureau of Mines, and the geology departments of major universities. Complete sets of publications and indexes of major geological societies including the Geological Society of America and the American Association of Petroleum Geologists. Partially cataloged.

CA —LOS ANGELES PUBLIC LIBRARY, History Dept, 630 W Fifth St, Los Angeles, 90071. Dorothy Mewshaw, Librn, Map Rm
Holdings: Vols (3000) Cat Maps
Budget: ($75,000)
Notes: The Mary Helen Peterson Collection of Maps and Atlases. World-wide coverage, including topographic, political and special purpose maps. Depository for US Geologic Survey topographical maps, Defense Mapping Agency, and National Ocean Survey. Maps of Los Angeles City and County.

CA —US GEOLOGICAL SURVEY LIBRARY, 345 Middlefield Rd, Menlo Park, 94025.
Holdings: Vols (200,000)

CA —POMONA PUBLIC LIBRARY, Special Collections, 625 S Garey Ave, PO Box 2271, Pomona, 91766. David Streeter, Librn
Holdings: Cat Mss Maps
Notes: Some 4000 maps. Strong for Pomona Valley area: tract maps, water company maps; depository for USGS California topographic maps; California earthquake fault maps.

†CA —STANDARD OIL COMPANY OF CALIFORNIA, 225 Bush St, San Francisco, 92104.
Holdings: Maps
Notes: 8000 maps and charts.

CT —YALE UNIVERSITY, Geology Library, 210 Whitney Ave, PO Box 6666, New Haven, 06511. Harry Scammell, Librn

CT —UNIVERSITY OF CONNECTICUT, University Library, Map Room, Storrs, 06268. Thornton P McGalmery, Librn
Holdings: Vols (903) Cat Mss Pix
Budget: ($5000)
Notes: The Map Room is the largest publicly supported map library in any Connecticut institution of higher education. It is a depository library for the US Geological Survey, the Defense Mapping Agency, and the Metropolitan District (Hartford, Conn). Incl over 100,000 maps and 8523 aerial photographs. Of particular interest is the *Petersen Collection*, a group of photostats of old town maps of New England.

DC —LIBRARY OF CONGRESS, Geography and Map Division, Washington, 20540. John A Wolter, Chief
Holdings: Cat Mss Maps Pix Slides Microforms
See also entry under Maps and Atlases - Collections

ID —IDAHO STATE UNIVERSITY, Library, Pocatello, 83209. Gary Domitz, Social Science Librn
Holdings: Uncat Maps
Notes: Depository for USGS, 11 western states; depository for Defense Mapping Agency Topographic Center; Idaho county maps.

IL —UNIVERSITY OF ILLINOIS, URBANA/CHAMPAIGN, Library, Map & Geography Library, 418 Main Library, Urbana, 61801. David Cobb, Librn
Notes: Maps (over 325,000) of almost all types, incl topographic, soil, transportation, economic, hydrographic, weather, city, pictorial, and historical maps, are collected. Coverage is excellent for Illinois and for most parts of the United States and Canada. Good maps are available for Europe, Central America and the ocean areas. The early map collection is rich in maps of Illnois, Italy, and the western hemisphere. A large number of publishers' catalogs, particularly of foreign map publishings are kept on file. The collection of aerial photographs provides complete and sequential coverage of the State of Illinois from the late 1930s to the

GEOLOGY—MAPS (cont.)

present. Much of the coverage is stereoscopic. Other map resources on the campus include about 50,000 geologic and topographic maps and aerial photographs in the Geology Library, a wall map collection in the Geography Department, severalhundred early maps and atlases of the Illinois area in the Illinois Historical Survey, and geologic and topographic maps and aerial photographs in the Civil Engineering Department. Publication: *Biblio* (bi-monthly acquisitions list).

IL —UNIVERSITY OF ILLINOIS, URBANA/CHAMPAIGN, Library, Geology Library, 223 Natural History Bldg, Urbana, 61801. Dederick Ward, Librn
Notes: Incl complete sets of outstanding geological surveys of the US, states, Canada and most foreign countries; espec strong for India and Latin America; the same is true for geological journals, incl Russia--a special strength since 1960. Extensive collection of early geological literature and rare books, perhaps the most extensive. Library houses the university's collection of 21,000 cataloged geological maps, incl many rarities. Special collection of aerial photographs.

MD —JOHNS HOPKINS UNIVERSITY, Milton S Eisenhower Library, Charles & 34 Sts, Baltimore, 21218. Ann S Gwyn, Assistant Dir for Special Collections
Holdings: Cat
Notes: Depository for USGS maps and serials, Maryland Geological Survey maps, and many state geological survey maps.

MA —HARVARD UNIVERSITY LIBRARY, Geological Sciences Library, 24 Oxford St, Cambridge, 02138. Constance Wick, Librn
Holdings: Vols (51,000) Cat Mss Maps Pix 16mm Films Microforms
Notes: 15,000 geologic maps; special emphasis on New England states.

NY —BROOKLYN PUBLIC LIBRARY, History Div Map Collection, Grand Army Plaza, Brooklyn, 11238. Tsugio Yoshinaga, Map Librn
Holdings: Cat Maps
Notes: 80,000 maps and 900 atlases for general reference. Depository for US Geological Survey and Defense Mapping Agency.

NY —BUFFALO & ERIE COUNTY PUBLIC LIBRARY, History, Travel & Government Dept, Lafayette Sq, Buffalo, 14203. Ruth Willet, Head
Holdings: Cat
Notes: Depository for US Geological Survey Topographic and Geological Quadrangle Maps; US Army Service Maps; other uncataloged maps and charts.

NC —UNIVERSITY OF NORTH CAROLINA, CHAPEL HILL, Geology Library, Mitchell Hall 029A, Chapel Hill, 27514. Miriam L Sheaves, Librn
Notes: Earth sciences, paleontology, oceanography, geology, geophysics. Incl theses and dissertations; 103,000 map sheets.

PA —PENNSYLVANIA STATE UNIVERSITY, Fred Lewis Pattee Library, Maps Section, University Park, 16802. Karl Proehl, Head
Holdings: Vols (274,000) Maps
Budget: ($3000)
Notes: Depositories for US Geological Survey topographic maps; Defense mapping agency topographic maps and nautical charts; National Ocean Survey nautical and aeronautical charts; Canadian topographic maps. Sanborn Fire Insurance maps for Pennsylvania villages and towns. General coverage for foreign countries--topographic and thematic maps. Map catalog by area and subdivided by subject; atlas catalog by author-title and area-subject; shelf list catalogs for maps and atlases. See *Pennsylvania Maps and Atlases in the Pennsylvania State University Libraries*, by Ruby M Miller (Pennsylvania State University Libraries, 1972, 682 pp).

TX —UNIVERSITY OF TEXAS LIBRARIES, General Libraries, Geology Dept, PO Box P, Austin, 78712. Chestalene Pintozzi, Librn
Notes: Departmental library with a separate catalog covering broadly the earth sciences. USGS depository. Incl 126,264 maps.

TX —MIDLAND COUNTY PUBLIC LIBRARY, Petroleum Dept, 301 W Missouri, PO Box 1191, Midland, 79701. Sandra Wagner, Librn
Notes: Scout tickets covering W Texas and New Mexico, driller's Logs for the same area, Lockwood reports 1947-1970, over one hundred industry-related periodicals, publications of many State Surveys, USGS, USBM, and Geological Societies. Incl 7600 maps.

GEOLOGY—MARYLAND

MD —CALVERT MARINE MUSEUM, Library, PO Box 97, Solomons, 20688.
Notes: Geology, paleontology of southern Maryland. Primarily professional research papers, reports and Maryland State Geological Surveys.

GEOLOGY—MEXICO

TX —UNIVERSITY OF TEXAS LIBRARIES, General Libraries, Geology Dept, PO Box P, Austin, 78712. Chestalene Pintozzi, Librn
Holdings: Vols (59,349) Cat Maps Microforms

GEOLOGY—NEVADA

NV —UNIVERSITY OF NEVADA, RENO, Mines Library, Reno, 89557. Mary B Ansari, Mines Librn; Linda P Newman, Asst Mines and Map Librn
Notes: Mines Library attempts to collect all PhD and Masters theses on Nevada geology. Only those originating at the University of Nevada, Reno, are available for ILL. Maintains an index of references to the literature on Nevada geology and mining.

GEOLOGY—NEW YORK (STATE)

NY —UNIVERSITY OF ROCHESTER, Rush Rhees Library, Geology/Map Library, Rochester, 14627. Arleen N Somerville, Librn
Holdings: Vols (12,424) Cat Maps
Notes: Strong collection in the field and related areas.

NY —NASSAU COUNTY MUSEUM, Sands Pt Preserve, Middleneck Rd, Sand Points, 11050.
Holdings: Vols (2500)
Notes: Collection contains almost every published reference on Long Island archaeology, ethnology, and geology, and incl most of those pertaining to the coastal New York area. Open by appointment. No photocopying.

GEOLOGY—OHIO

OH —CLEVELAND PUBLIC LIBRARY, Science & Technology Dept, 325 Superior Ave, Cleveland, 44114. Jean Z Piety, Head
Holdings: Cat
Notes: Extensive collection of state and society publications; African, Australian, Canadian and other selected foreign areas; bibliography.

GEOLOGY—OKLAHOMA

OK —ARDMORE PUBLIC LIBRARIES, Grand at E St NW, Ardmore, 73401. Carolyn Franks, Dir
Holdings: Vols 4000 Cat Mss Maps Pix
Notes: 80 percent of holdings comprise private collection of Dr Charles W Tomlinson, internationally recognized geologist and civic leader. Remainder of collection is from library of the late Harold Fell and the Oklahoma University Geological Library.

GEOLOGY—PENNSYLVANIA

PA —PENNSYLVANIA GEOLOGICAL SOCIETY, Library, 916 Executive House, Second & Chestnut Sts, Harrisburg, 17120. Sandra Blust, Librn
Holdings: Vols (7600) Cat Mss Maps Micoroforms
Notes: Incl 200,000 aerial photographs and 250,000 maps.

GEOLOGY—RUSSIA

IL —UNIVERSITY OF ILLINOIS, URBANA/CHAMPAIGN, Library, Geology Library, 223 Natural History Bldg, Urbana, 61801. Dederick Ward, Librn
Holdings: Vols (105,186) Cat Maps Microforms

GEOLOGY—TEXAS

TX —UNIVERSITY OF TEXAS LIBRARIES, General Libraries, Geology Dept, PO Box P, Austin, 78712. Chestalene Pintozzi, Librn
Holdings: Vols (59,349) Cat Maps Microforms

GEOLOGY—WISCONSIN

WI —MILWAUKEE PUBLIC LIBRARY, 814 W Wisconsin Ave, Milwaukee, 53233. Donald J Sager, City Librn
Notes: Or primary interest, subject area well developed with emphasis on Wisconsin geology, other states of secondary interest. Long runs of journals, reports of geological surveys and society publications. Incl abstracts, indexes, bibliographies, literature guides, dictionaries, handbooks, manuals, and climatological data. Strong general reference service.

GEOLOGY—WYOMING

WY —NATRONA COUNTY PUBLIC LIBRARY, 307 E Second St, Casper, 82601. Kathleen Nowak, Earth Sciences/Reference Librn
Notes: The earth sciences collection consists of technical literature published in energy-related fields. A map collection of topographic and geologic maps of Wyoming is maintained. State geological survey documents for the states surrounding Wyoming are collected. Also some thiry periodicals in the earth sciences.

GEOLOGY, DYNAMIC see Geophysics

GEOLOGY, ECONOMIC

IL —UNIVERSITY OF ILLINOIS, URBANA/CHAMPAIGN, Library, Geology Library, 223 Natural History Bldg, Urbana, 61801. Dederick Ward, Librn
Holdings: Vols (105,186) Cat Maps Microforms

MA —HARVARD UNIVERSITY LIBRARY, Geological Sciences Library, 24 Oxford St, Cambridge, 02138. Constance Wick, Librn
Holdings: Vols (51,000) Cat Mss Maps Pix 16mm Films Microforms
Notes: The Geological Sciences Library supports the research efforts of faculty, graduate students, and upper-level undergraduate and graduate instruction in the geological sciences. Subjects collected deal with the earth sciences in general, mineralogy, petrology, geochemistry, geophysics, crystallography, structural geology, regional geology, economic geology, some geomorphology, and some gemology. The collection incl 850 serial publications and 15,000 maps.

GEOLOGY, MARINE see Submarine Geology

GEOLOGY, PALEONTOLOGIC see Paleontology

GEOLOGY, PHYSICAL see Geomorphology; Geophysics

GEOLOGY, PLANETARY

CA —UNIVERSITY OF CALIFORNIA, LOS ANGELES, Geology-Geophysics Library, 4697 Geology Bldg, Los Angeles, 90024. Sarah E How, Geology-Geophysics Librn
Holdings: Vols (85,000) Cat Maps

GEOLOGY, PLANETARY (cont.)

Microforms
Notes: Incl theses and dissertations of UCLA Dept of Earth and Space Sciences; and (2000) serial titles.

DC —SMITHSONIAN INSTITUTION LIBRARIES, National Air & Space Museum Branch, NASM Bldg, Sixth & Independence Ave SW, Washington, 20560. Frank A Pietropaoli, Branch Chief
Holdings: Vols (39,000) Cat Mss Maps Pix Slides Microforms
Notes: History of flight and aerospace development, incl biographical material on aviation pioneers, balloons and ballooning. Extensive photographic collection (600,000 pictures). Incl the Sherman Fairchild Collection of aeronautical photographs (transferred from the American Institute of Aeronautics and Astronautics). Also incl the Bella Landauer Aeronautical Sheet Music Collection (1500 pieces). 2000 films; 800,000 microforms; 9000 volumes bound.

IL —UNIVERSITY OF ILLINOIS, URBANA/CHAMPAIGN, Library, Geology Library, 223 Natural History Bldg, Urbana, 61801. Dederick Ward, Librn
Holdings: Vols (105,186) Cat Maps Microforms

GEOLOGY, STRATIGRAPHIC see Geology

GEOLOGY, STRUCTURAL see Geomorphology

GEOLOGY, SUBMARINE see Submarine Geology

GEOMAGNETISM see Magnetism, Terrestrial

GEOMORPHOLOGY

IL —UNIVERSITY OF ILLINOIS, URBANA/CHAMPAIGN, Library, Geology Library, 223 Natural History Bldg, Urbana, 61801. Dederick Ward, Librn
Holdings: Vols (105,186) Cat Maps Microforms

IN —PURDUE UNIVERSITY LIBRARIES, Geosciences Library, West Lafayette, 47907. Carolyn Lassoon, Librn
Holdings: Vols (15,000) Cat
Notes: Geosciences.

MA —HARVARD UNIVERSITY LIBRARY, Geological Sciences Library, 24 Oxford St, Cambridge, 02138. Constance Wick, Librn
Holdings: Vols (51,000) Cat mss Maps Pix 16mm Films Microforms
Notes: The Geological Sciences Library supports the research efforts of faculty, graduate students, and upper-level undergraduate and graduate instruction in the geological sciences. Subjects collected deal with the earth sciences in general, mineralogy, petrology, geochemistry, geophysics, crystallography, structural geology, regional geology, economic geology, some geomorphology, and some gemology. The collection incl 850 serial publications and 15,000 maps.

PA —UNIVERSITY OF PITTSBURGH, Hillman Library, Pittsburgh, 15260.
Holdings: Vols (6000) Cat Maps Pix Slides Microforms
Notes: The Geography collection is strengthened by US Geological Survey depository collection; US Army Map Service depository collection; US government publications depository collection; Canadian government publications; and UN depository (partial) collection.

WI —UNIVERSITY OF WISCONSIN, MADISON, Geography Library, 280 Science Hall, Madison, 53706. Miriam E Kerndt, Librn
Holdings: Vols (40,000) Cat Microforms
Budget: ($35,000)
Notes: Geography Library collects books, journals, and atlases in all fields of regional and systematic geography to support research and university teaching. Popular works, travel accounts, and tourist literature are not collected. Maps are collected in a separate Map and Air Photo Library in the same building.

ON —GEOLOGICAL SURVEY OF CANADA, Library, Dept of Energy, Mines, & Resouces, 601 Booth St, Ottawa, K1A 0E8, Can. Annette E Bourgeois, Librn
Holdings: Vols (300,000) Cat Mss Maps Microforms
Notes: All aspects of Geology are collected and an attempt is made to collect all Canadian geology information. The library is a national resource collection in the geosciences. Incl 40,000 book titles (monographs), 4000 personals, 35,000 microfiche, 300,000 maps, 2000 translations of reports, 20 verrtical files, 300,000 vols of bound periodicals.

GEOMORPHOLOGY—MAPS

CA —US GEOLOGICAL SURVEY LIBRARY, 345 Middlefield Rd, Menlo Park, 94025.
Holdings: Vols (200,000)

GEOPHYSICISTS

CA —CALIFORNIA INSTITUTE OF TECHNOLOGY, Robert A Millikan Memorial Library, Archives, 1201 E California Blvd, Pasadena, 91125. Judith R Goodstein, Archivist
Notes: Scientific correspondence, unpublished notes and data. 25,000 items, of Beno Gutenberg. Incl tape recorded interview with his widow, Herta Gutenberg.

GEOPHYSICS

CA —UNIVERSITY OF CALIFORNIA, LOS ANGELES, Geology-Geophysics Library, 4697 Geology Bldg, Los Angeles, 90024. Sarah E How, Geology-Geophysics Librn
Holdings: Vols (85,000) Cat Maps Microforms
Notes: Incl theses and dissertations of UCLA Dept of Earth and Space Sciences; and (2000) serial titles.

CA —CALIFORNIA INSTITUTE OF TECHNOLOGY, Robert A Millikan Memorial Library, Archives, 1201 E California Blvd, Pasadena, 91125. Judith R Goodstein, Archivist
Holdings: Vols (3000) Cat Mss Maps Pix Slides Phonorecords Audiotapes Videotapes 16mm Films Microforms
Notes: Ms sources for the history of astrophysics, cosmology, mathematical physics, experimental physics, radio astronomy, geophysics and biophysics. Collections incl the papers of: George Ellery Hale, Jesse Greenstein, H P Robertson, Richard Feynman, Paul Epstein, Max Delbruck, and Beno Gutenberg. Candid photos of physicists at meetings; etchings and photographs of Einstein; scientific medals; selected pieces of scientific apparatus (including the oil-drop machine constructed by Millikan at Caltech in the early 1920s); the reprint collection of Paul Epstein; over 3000 landmark books in the history of 20th century physics and mathematics. Printed publications include: Daniel Kevles, *Guide to the Microfilm Edition of the George Ellery Hale Papers* (Pasadena, Carnegie Institute of Washington and Caltech), 1968; Judith R Goodstein,*The Robert Andrews Millikan Collection at the California Institute of Technology: Guide to a Microfilm Edition* (Pasadena, Caltech), 1977; Judith R Goodstein and Carolyn Kopp, *The Theodore von Karman Collections at the California Institute of* Technology (Pasadena, Archives), 1981.

CA —CALIFORNIA INSTITUTE OF TECHNOLOGY, Geology Library, Pasadena, 91125. Daphne Plane, Geology Librn
Holdings: Vols 25,000 Cat Maps Microforms
Notes: Incl 1000 microforms, 11,750 books, and 879 serials.

CA —UNIVERSITY OF CALIFORNIA, RIVERSIDE, Physical Sciences Library, Riverside, 92517. Richard W Vierich, Librn
Holdings: Vols (89,000)
Budget: ($347,700)

CA —STANFORD UNIVERSITY, School of Earth Sciences, Branner Earth Sciences Library, Stanford, 94305. Charlotte Derksen, Head Librn
Holdings: Vols (70,000) Cat Maps
Notes: Incl 80,000 maps. Formerly the Branner Geological Library. Also incl Stanford Rock Physics Project Reports and Stanford Exploration Project Reports.

CO —COLORADO SCHOOL OF MINES, Arthur Lakes Library, 14 & Illinois Sts, Golden, 80401. Hartley K Phinney, Jr, Head Librn
Holdings: Vols (270,557) Cat Mss Maps Microforms

DC —SMITHSONIAN INSTITUTION LIBRARIES, National Air & Space Museum Branch, NASM Bldg, Sixth & Independence Ave SW, Washington, 20560. Frank A Pietropaoli, Branch Chief
Holdings: Vols (39,000) Cat Mss Maps Pix Slides Microforms
Notes: History of flight and aerospace development, incl biographical material on aviation pioneers, balloons and ballooning. Extensive photographic collection (600,000 pictures). Incl the Sherman Fairchild Collection of aeronautical photographs (transferred from the American Institute of Aeronautics and Astronautics). Also incl the Bella Landauer Aeronautical Sheet Music Collection (1500 pieces). 2000 films; 800,000 microforms; 9000 volumes bound.

GA —GEORGIA INSTITUTE OF TECHNOLOGY, Price Gilbert Memorial Library, 225 North Ave, Atlanta, 30332. Edward Graham Roberts, Dir
Holdings: Vols (1,661,559) Cat Maps Slides Microforms
Budget: ($1,383,302)
Notes: Incl (4,307,996) patents and (568, 490) government documents.

IL —ILLINOIS STATE GEOLOGICAL SURVEY, Library, 615 E Peabody, Champaign, 61820. Mary Krick, Geological Librn

IL —UNIVERSITY OF ILLINOIS, URBANA/CHAMPAIGN, Library, Geology Library, 223 Natural History Bldg, Urbana, 61801. Dederick Ward, Librn
Holdings: Vols (105,186) Cat Maps Microforms

IN —PURDUE UNIVERSITY LIBRARIES, Geosciences Library, West Lafayette, 47907. Carolyn Lassoon, Librn
Holdings: Vols (15,000) Cat
Notes: Geosciences.

MA —SMITHSONIAN INSTITUTION LIBRARIES, Astrophysical Observatory Branch, 60 Garden St, Cambridge, 02138. Joyce Rey, Librn
Holdings: Vols (10,000) Cat Maps Pix Microforms
Budget: ($94,270)

MA —BOSTON COLLEGE LIBRARIES, Science Library, Devlin Hall, Chestnut Hill, 02167. F Clifford McElroy, Science Librn
Holdings: Vols (54,508) Cat Maps Microforms
Budget: ($94,270)
Notes: Library is being absorbed into the general collection.

MA —BOSTON COLLEGE LIBRARIES, Catherine B O'Connor Geophysics Library, Weston Observatory, Weston, 02193. F Clifford McElroy, Science Librn
Holdings: Vols (10,231) Cat Maps Microforms
Budget: ($10,000)
Notes: This collection is being absorbed into the general collection.

NY —ENGINEERING SOCIETIES LIBRARY, 345 E 47 St, New York, 10017. S Kirk Cabeen, Dir
Holdings: Vols 250,000 Cat Maps 16mm Films Microforms
Notes: One of the largest, most comprehensive engineering libraries in the world. Covers all engineering disciplines; particularly strong in electrical and electronic, mechanical, mining and metallurgical, petroleum, chemical, industrial, air conditioning and refrigeration engineering. Incl Wheeler Collection of early materials on magnetism and electricity. 125, 000 bound periodical volumes; 10,000 maps;

GEOPHYSICS (cont.)

5000 serial subscriptions (many foreign-language). Virtually all materials abstracted in *Engineering Societies Library, New York, Classed Subject Catalog and Index* (Boston: G K Hall, 1963); and *Supplements*, 1-10, 1964-1973.

NY —COLUMBIA UNIVERSITY LIBRARIES, Geoscience Library, Lamont-Doherty Geological Observatory, Palisades, 10964. Susan Klimley, Librn
Holdings: Vols (20,000) Cat
Notes: Geosciences, incl geochemistry, marine geology, seismology and paleoclimatology.

NC —UNIVERSITY OF NORTH CAROLINA, CHAPEL HILL, Geology Library, Mitchell Hall 029A, Chapel Hill, 27514. Miriam L Sheaves, Librn
Holdings: Vols (41,000) Cat Maps
Notes: Earth sciences, paleontology, oceanography, geology, geophysics. Incl theses and dissertations; 103,000 map sheets.

OH —UNIVERSITY OF CINCINNATI, Geology-Geography Library, 103 Old Tech Bldg ML 13, Cincinnati, 45221. Richard Spohn, Sr Library Assoc
Holdings: Vols (35,000) Cat Maps
Budget: ($30,000)
Notes: Collection covers the broad range of geoscience topics, incl a geologic field trip guidebook collection of almost 1400 volumes.

PA —PENNSYLVANIA STATE UNIVERSITY, Earth & Mineral Sciences Library, 105 Deike Bldg, University Park, 16802. Emilie McWilliams, Head Librn
Holdings: Vols (58,000) Cat Maps Microforms
Budget: ($49,750)
Notes: This collection includes substantial numbers of geological maps, and strong periodical holdings including microform.

TX —GEOSOURCE, INC, Library, Technical Training Dept, 6909 SW Freeway, Houston, 77036. D G Lang, Training Mgr
Holdings: Cat
Notes: About 15,000 papers, etc, from libraries of Ray Geophysical/Mandrel (Houston), Petty Geophysical Engineering (San Antonio) and Geoscience (Cambridge, Mass).

WA —UNIVERSITY OF WASHINGTON LIBRARIES, Suzzallo Library, Natural Sciences Library, FM-25, Seattle, 98195. Nancy G Blase, Head
Holdings: Vols (192,353) Cat
Budget: ($219,809)

ON —ENERGY, MINES & RESOURCES CANADA, Earth Physics Branch Library, Ottawa, K1A 0Y3, Can. W M Tsang, Chief Librn
Holdings: Vols (4500) Cat Maps Pix Slides Microforms

ON —GEOLOGICAL SURVEY OF CANADA, Library, Dept of Energy, Mines, & Resouces, 601 Booth St, Ottawa, K1A 0E8, Can. Annette E Bourgeois, Librn
Holdings: Vols (300,000) Cat Mss Maps Microforms
Notes: All aspects of Geology are collected and an attempt is made to collect all Canadian geology information. The library is a national resource collection in the geosciences. Incl 40,000 book titles (monographs), 4000 personals, 35,000 microfiche, 300,000 maps, 2000 translations of reports, 20 verrtical files, 300,000 vols of bound periodicals.

GEOPHYSICS—MAPS

CA —US GEOLOGICAL SURVEY LIBRARY, 345 Middlefield Rd, Menlo Park, 94025.
Holdings: Vols (200,000)

GEOPOLITICS

KY —UNIVERSITY OF KENTUCKY, Margaret I King Library, Dept of Special Collections, Lexington, 40506. William Marshall, Head
Holdings: // Cat Mss
Notes: Geopolitics. Ellen Churchill Semple's correspondence, notes for books and articles. 4 vols, 84 pieces and 74 packages.

GEORGE, HENRY

NY —NEW YORK PUBLIC LIBRARY, Research Libraries, Economic & Public Affairs Div, Fifth Ave & 42 St, New York, 10018. Edward DiRoma, Chief

NY —NEW YORK PUBLIC LIBRARY, Rare Books and Manuscripts Div, Fifth Ave & 42 St, New York, 10018. William L Joyce, Asst Dir; Susan E Davis, Cur of Mss
Holdings: Mss
Budget: ($7161)
Notes: Incl personal and literary mss, papers, etc.

GEORGE, EARL

NY —SYRACUSE UNIVERSITY LIBRARIES, Ernest S Bird Library, George Arents Research Library for Special Collections, Syracuse, 13210. Carolyn A Davis, Manuscripts Librn; Amy S Doherty, University Archivist; Mark F Weimer, Rare Book Librn
Notes: American Music Collection. Papers of Ernst Bacon, Louis Krasner, Franklin Morris, William Henry Berwald, Earl George, and Arthur Polster.

GEORGE JUNIOR REPUBLIC

NY —CORNELL UNIVERSITY LIBRARIES, Collection of Regional History, Dept of Manuscripts and Univ Archives, Ithaca, 14853.
Holdings: Mss
Notes: Incl 82 pieces; papers, ca 1909-61; postcard views of the Republic, examples of Republic coinage, newspaper clippings, announcements and programs.

GEORGES BANKS

ME —BIGELOW LABORATORY FOR OCEAN SCIENCES & MAINE DEPT OF MARINE RESOURCES, Library, McKown Point, West Boothbay Harbor, 04575. Pamela Shephard-Lupo, Librn
Holdings: Vols Cat Periodicals Maps
Budget: ($55,000)
Notes: This library presently serves two institutions. The Maine Dept of Marine Resources has maintained the library since 1957 and thus the majority of our holdings are geared to their needs, ie fish biology and stock assessment on a local, national and international level. In 1973 Bigelow Laboratory for Ocean Sciences came to West Boothbay Harbor and began to contribute to the library with a very specialized collection on the Gulf of Maine marine chemistry, phytoplankton and nutrient cycles.

GEORGIA

GA —ATLANTA PUBLIC LIBRARY, Ivan Allen Jr Dept of Science, Industry & Government, One Margaret Mitchell Square, Atlanta, 30303. William D Munro, Head
Holdings: Vols (2000) Cat
Budget: ($180,000)
Notes: Collection concentrates on Georgia state documents in the areas of law, business, industry, and science. Major series incl Georgia Laws (1825 to date); Georgia House and Senate Journals (1810-1952); Georgia Reports and Georgia Appeals Reports. Annual reports, bulletins and circulars for selected state agencies and departments are also included.

NC —DUKE UNIVERSITY, William R Perkins Library, Durham, 27706. Elvin E Strowd, University Librn
Notes: The Flowers Collection of Southern Americana currently consists of 4,300,500 items. Additions are ongoing. Included in this collection are several types of materials, which are housed in appropriate sections of the library. The various types of materials are: manuscripts, books, pamphlets, maps, music, broadsides, newspapers, photographs, engravings, prints and memorabilia.

GEORGIA (TRANSCAUCASIA)

IN —INDIANA UNIVERSITY, Lilly Library, Seventh St, Bloomington, 47405. William R Cagle, Librn
Holdings: // Cat Mss
Notes: Emphasis on travel. Incl Russo-Turkish relations; Georgia and the Caucasus.

MA —HARVARD UNIVERSITY LIBRARY, Widener Library, Slavic Collections, Cambridge, 02138. Hugh M Olmsted, Slavic Dept Head
Holdings: Cat Mss
Notes: Collection strong in Georgian language and Russian materials, and continues to be developed actively. Houghton Library has the archive of the independent Georgian republic, 1880-1921 (on loan, 1974-2004).

GEORGIA—GENEALOGY

FL —ORLANDO PUBLIC LIBRARY, Local History & Genealogy Dept, 100 Block of Central Ave, Orlando, 32806. Eileen B Willis, Librn
Holdings: Vols 11,000 Cat Maps Microforms
Budget: $8000
Notes: Strong collection in local genealogy materials on Mass, NY, Va, Ga, and Florida. Contains exceptional holdings on all New England States, Penn, and NJ.
See also entry under Genealogy - Collections.

GA —COLQUITT-THOMAS REGIONAL LIBRARY, Moultrie-Colquitt County Library, 204 Fifth St SE, PO Box 1110, Moultrie, 31768. Melody Jenkins, Dir
Holdings: Maps Pix Slides Microforms
Notes: Emphasis on South Georgia.

GA —CARNEGIE LIBRARY, Henderson Room, 607 Broad St, Rome, 30161. Beatrice Millican, Librn
Holdings: Cat 16mm Films
Budget: ($2700)
Notes: Among our Genealogy Collection of 6500 items, we have the 1790 census records for the states of Maine, New Hampshire, Vermont, Massachusetts, Rhode Island, Connecticut, New York, Pennsylvania, Virginia, North Carolina, South Carolina. We have a substitute for the Georgia 1790 census. Also, we have the 1790, 1800, 1810 and 1820, 1830-1850 census indexes for North Carolina. For Georgia we have the decennial indexes for 1820-1850. We have microfilm for Georgia, 1820-1900. Besides our general genealogy books, we have sections for the various states, particularly Virginia, South Carolina, North Carolina, and Georgia. Also 1800-1850 South Carolina, 1800-1850 Virginia, 1830-1850 Alabama, 1830-1850 Tennessee, 1830-1850 Mississippi indexes to census.

GEORGIA—HISTORY

AL —TROY STATE UNIVERSITY, Library, Troy, 36081. Kenneth Croslin, Dir of University Libraries
Holdings: // Mss
Notes: Incl the John Horry Dent Papers, 1851-1892, 25 vols, mss, farm journals, account books, letters, legal documents, clippings and miscellaneous memorabilia of a planter, plantation owner, investor, who lived in Barbour County, Alabama from 1837 to 1867 and in Floyd County, Georgia from 1867 to 1892. Typescript from tape "Sharecropping farming in Pike County, Alabama in early 1900's" (56p). Typescript of tapes of "Source material extracted from Troy, Alabama newspapers, 1871-1935" indexed under 9 subjects by color code.

GA —UNIVERSITY OF GEORGIA, Libraries, Special Collections Division, Athens, 30602. Vesta Lee Gordon, Asst Dir for Special Collections
Holdings: Vols (75,000) Cat Mss Maps Pix
Notes: Materials on Georgia history, incl approx 3,000,000 items in 2000 collections of mss; 1200 maps; 6000 pictures and over 200 pieces of sheet music.

GA —ATLANTA PUBLIC LIBRARY, Ivan Allen Jr Dept of Science, Industry & Government, One Margaret Mitchell Square, Atlanta, 30303. William D Munro, Head
Holdings: Vols (15,000) Cat Microforms
Budget: ($180,000)
Notes: This collection incl on microform

GEORGIA—HISTORY (cont.)

annual reports and Securities Exchange Commission 10-K reports for some 11,000 companies from 1976 to date; current and retrospective stock quotations, stock reports, corporate and industry records and directories and supporting looseleaf services; information file on Atlanta's largest 15,000 with annual updates; and current plat maps for the five county Metro-Atlanta area. Atlanta and Georgia business history sections are being developed. Most material on this collection is noncirculating.

GA —EMORY UNIVERSITY, Robert W Woodruff Library, Atlanta, 30322. Herbert Johnson, Dir
Notes: Personal papers of six Atlantans who played major parts in building the city's progressive image. Incl Joel Chandler Harris (1848-1908); William B Hartsfield, mayor, 1937-61; 1961; Richard H Rich (1901-1975), business leader; Eleonore Raoul Greene (b 1888), suffragist and organizer of the Atlanta League of Women Voters; Helen Bullard (1908-1979), public relations consultant; and Josephine Wilkins (d 1970) social reformer and founder of the Georgia Citizen's Fact Finding Movement in the 1930s.

GA —EMORY UNIVERSITY, Candler School of Theology, Pitts Theology Library, Atlanta, 30322. Channing Jeschke, Librn; Anita K Delaries, Curator
Holdings: Cat Mss
Notes: Incl records (85 vols) of the Methodist Church in Georgia; 1614 mss and ms volumes dating from 1830.

GA —AUGUSTA COLLEGE & RICHMOND COUNTY HISTORICAL SOCIETY, Reese Library, Special Collections Room, 2500 Walton Way, Augusta, 30904. A Ray Rowland, Cur
Holdings: Vols 3000 Cat Mss Maps Pix Microforms
Notes: History of Augusta, Richmond County and Augusta College. Non-circulating collection, open to public. Special permission may be granted for mss upon request. Holdings of collection are listed in the main Reese Library card catalog.

GA —LAKE LANIER REGIONAL LIBRARY, Gwinnett County Library, 275 Perry St, Lawrenceville, 30245. Carolyn Fetner, Librn
Holdings: Vols 1000 Cat

GA —WESLEYAN COLLEGE, Willet Memorial Library, 4760 Forsyth Rd, Macon, 31201. Hasseltine Roberts, Librn
Holdings: Vols 4000 Cat Mss Maps Pix
Notes: The Orville A Park and Tracy McGregor Collections.

GA —GEORGIA COLLEGE, Ina Dillard Russell Library, Special Collections Dept, Milledgeville, 31061. Janice C Fennell, Dir of Libraries; Nancy Davis, Special Collections Assoc
Holdings: Vols 5000 Cat Mss Maps Pix
Notes: History of Milledgeville, Baldwin County, and middle Georgia; incl the Beeson Collection. Also incl Progressive Farmers Club of Baldwin County; minutes of meetings, photographs, letters covering 1927-1977 (44 folders).

GA —COLQUITT-THOMAS REGIONAL LIBRARY, Moultrie-Colquitt County Library, 204 Fifth St SE, PO Box 1110, Moultrie, 31768. Melody Jenkins, Dir
Holdings: Maps Pix Slides Microforms
Notes: Emphasis on Colquitt County area.

GA —CARNEGIE LIBRARY, Henderson Room, 607 Broad St, Rome, 30161. Beatrice Millican, Librn
Holdings: Vols (2500) Cat 16mm Films
Budget: ($2700)
Notes: Our Georgia Collection is a collection of books about Georgia and by Georgians. We have a fiction and biography section with the histories of Georgia and the individual county histories. We also subscribe to the Atlanta *Constitution* and Rome, Georgia newspapers. We have the Rome *News-Tribune* on microfilm, 1951 to date, from 1921-1949 bound, and some few earlier Rome newspapers on microfilm.

GA —CHATHAM-EFFINGHAM-LIBERTY REGIONAL, 2002 Bull St, Savannah, 31499. Irma Harlan, Dir; Alice Driscoll, Head Ref Dept
Holdings: Vols 4800 Cat Maps Pix Microforms Scrapbooks
Notes: Scrapbooks incl newspaper clippings, letters, photographs, pamphlets, programs of special events, postcards, typewritten mss. Emphasis on Georgia and Savannah history. Extensive microfilm collections of newspapers, censuses of Georgia counties; local and state history dissertations, etc. Incl 2100 microforms.

GA —GEORGIA HISTORICAL SOCIETY, W B Hodgson Hall, 501 Whitaker St, Savannah, 31401. Karen E Osvald, Archivist Asst
Holdings: Vols 25,000 / / Cat Mss Maps Phonorecords Audiotapes Microforms
Notes: Especially coastal Georgia and Savannah. Incl 1200 mss, 750 maps, 5000 pictures, 200 records, and 770 microforms. Collection of 560 vols transferred to Society from the Fort Frederica National Monument, St Simons Island, Georgia, on indefinite loan (1977). Restricted use.

TX —UNIVERSITY OF TEXAS LIBRARIES, General Libraries, PO Box P, Austin, 78713. Carolyn Bucknell, Asst Dir for Collection Development
Holdings: Cat Microforms

GEORGIA—MAPS

DC —LIBRARY OF CONGRESS, Geography and Map Division, Washington, 20540. John A Wolter, Chief
Notes: The American Map Collection incl 167 works produced between 1750 and 1790 incl copies of *A Map of the Most Inhabited Part of Virginia* by Joshua Fry and Peter Jefferson (1755 and 1775 editions), John Montresor's *A Map of the Province of New* York (1777), William Gerard De Brahm's *A Map of South Carolina and a Part of* Georgia (1757), and *A Plan of the City of* Philadelphia (1776) by Benjamin Easburn.

GA —UNIVERSITY OF GEORGIA, Libraries, Map Collection, Athens, 30602. John Sutherland, Cur of Maps
Notes: Collection contains 291,165 cataloged maps and 192,068 aerial photographs, specializing in Georgia, Southeast US, Central and South America, and Europe. Major subject specializations are topography, geology, soils and vegetation. Special cartographic collection of Sanborn Fire Insurance Maps (7000 sheets).

GEORGIA—POLITICS AND GOVERNMENT

GA —UNIVERSITY OF GEORGIA, Libraries, Special Collections Division, Athens, 30602. Vesta Lee Gordon, Asst Dir for Special Collections
Notes: Collection contains 1394.8 linear feet of mss: papers of US Senator Richard B Russell; US Congressmen John W Davis, Maston O'Neal, Robert G Stephens Jr, John L Pilcher, Dudley M Hughes; Governors Hoke Smith, Lester Maddox, Carl Sanders.

GEORGIA—SOCIAL LIFE AND CUSTOMS

DC —LIBRARY OF CONGRESS, American Folklife Center, Archive of Folk Culture, Washington, 20540.
Notes: Georgia vernacular architecture, food customs, storytelling, and gospel singing traditions, in local black and white communities. Thousands of color transparencies, etc.

GEORGIA AUTHORS see Authors, Georgia

GEORGIAN LANGUAGE AND LITERATURE

MA —HARVARD UNIVERSITY LIBRARY, Widener Library, Slavic Collections, Cambridge, 02138. Hugh M Olmsted, Slavic Dept Head
Holdings: Cat
Notes: Collection strong in materials written in both Georgian and Russian languages, and continues to be developed actively.

GEORGIAN POETS see Poets, Georgian

GEOSCIENCE see Earth Sciences

GEOTECTONICS see Geomorphology

GEOTHERMAL ENGINEERING

CA —STANFORD UNIVERSITY, School of Earth Sciences, Branner Earth Sciences Library, Stanford, 94305. Charlotte Derksen, Head Librn
Holdings: Vols (70,000) Cat
Notes: Incl geothermal resources; 700 technical reports.

NM —UNIVERSITY OF CALIFORNIA, Los Alamos National Laboratory, Libraries, PO Box 1663, MSP 362, Los Alamos, 87545. J Arthur Freed, Head Librn
Holdings: Vols (800,000) Cat Films Microforms
Budget: ($700,000)
Notes: Incl 500,000 classified and unclassified reports. There are 25 branch libraries and a central collection. The Medical Library contains about 40,000 vols in the areas of biomedical research.

GEOTHERMAL RESOURCES

CA —LAKE COUNTY LIBRARY, 200 Park St, Lakeport, 95453. Kathleen Jansen, Librn
Holdings: Vols (100) Cat Maps Pix
Notes: Large collection of books, articles, and reports on geothermal resources, especially in California. Partially cataloged.

NM —UNIVERSITY OF CALIFORNIA, Los Alamos National Laboratory, Libraries, PO Box 1663, MSP 362, Los Alamos, 87545. J Arthur Freed, Head Librn
Holdings: Vols (800,000) Cat Films Microforms
Budget: ($70,000)
Notes: Incl 500,000 classified and unclassified reports. There are 25 branch libraries and a central collection. The Medical Library contains about 40,000 vols in the areas of biomedical research.

TX —MCDERMOTT HUDSON ENGINEERING, Library, 5900 Hillcroft, Houston, 77036. Chris Ramirez, Librn
Holdings: Vols (750) Uncat Microforms
Notes: Emphasis is on all forms of alternative energy sources and energy conversion.

GERARD, JAMES W.

MT —UNIVERSITY OF MONTANA, Library, Missoula, 59801. Katherine Schaefer, Special Collections Librn
Holdings: Vols 6300 Cat Mss Maps Pix Slides Microforms Newspapers
Notes: About 200 ms collections, measuring 5000 feet, with emphasis on Montana business and political history (papers of Senators Joseph M Dixon, James E Murray, and US Ambassador James W Gerard). Also first editions and mss of Montana authors.

GERIATRICS AND GERONTOLOGY

CA —STANFORD UNIVERSITY LIBRARIES, Lane Medical Library, Stanford University, Medical Center, Stanford, 94305. Peter Stangl, Librn
Notes: Russel V Lee papers on group medical practice, gerontology, Agency for International Development.

DC —AMERICAN ASSOCIATION OF RETIRED PERSONS (AARP), National Gerontology Resource Center, 1909 K St NW, Washington, 20049. Paula M Lovas, Librn; Mary F Power, Coordr, Reference Service
Holdings: Vols (15,000) Cat Microforms
Budget: ($60,000)
Notes: Retirement, retirement planning and social gerontology. Incl government documents and reports, journals, and bibliographies.

DC —NATIONAL COUNCIL ON THE AGING, Library, 600 Maryland Ave SW,

GERIATRICS AND GERONTOLOGY (cont.)

Washington, 20024.
Holdings: Vols 14,000 Cat
Notes: Emphasis on psychosocial, legislative, economic and health aspects. Incl 20 vertical file drawers of Archival materials.

DC —US COMMISSION ON CIVIL RIGHTS, National Clearinghouse Library, 1121 Vermont Ave NW, Washington, 20005. Lenora McMillan, Chief Librn
Holdings: Vols (10,200) Cat Slides Microforms
Notes: The National Clearinghouse Library has a special collection of the US Commission on Civil Rights publications from its inception (1957) to present date.

IL —JACKSONVILLE STATE HOSPITAL, Training & Research Library, 1201 S Main St, Jacksonville, 62650. Lois E Wells, Librn
Notes: Concerned particularly with developmental disabilities.

MI —INSTITUTE OF GERONTOLOGY, Gerontology Library, University of Michigan, 300 N Ingalls St, Ann Arbor, 48109. Willie M Edwards, Librn
Holdings: Vols 10,000 Cat Pix Audiotapes 16mm Films
Notes: All subjects concerning the aged and aging in the US, Western Europe and strong emphasis on Great Britain. On VF (24) unpublished research papers, newsletters from elderly association, centers on aging.

MI —LAFAYETTE CLINIC LIBRARY, 951 E Lafayette, Detroit, 48207. Nancy E Ward, Librn
Holdings: Vols (7000) Cat
Notes: Special emphasis on memory disorder, dementia and Alzheimer's disease. Library's emphasis is on the biological aspects, causes and treatment of mental illness.

MO —SAINT JOSEPH STATE HOSPITAL, Professional Library, 3400 Frederick Ave, Box 263, Saint Joseph, 64502. Martha Goodding, Librn
Holdings: Vols (3000) Cat Slides Phonorecords Audiotapes 16mm Films Filmstrips Videotapes

NH —DARTMOUTH COLLEGE, Dartmouth-Hitchcock Medical Center, Dana Biomedical Library, Hanover, 03756. Shirley J Grainger, Librn
Holdings: Vols (500) // Mss
Notes: Raymond Pearl Collection on Longevity incl historical materials from the 18th and 19th centuries, as well as some popular centemporary works on aging. Partially cataloged.

NY —COLUMBIA UNIVERSITY LIBRARIES, Whitney M Young Jr Memorial Library of Social Work, 420 W 118 St, New York, 10027. Tyrone Cannon, Librn
Holdings: Vols (118,646) Cat
Notes: The collection covers the history and philosophy of social work, social work methodology, and all aspects of social welfare services, especially child welfare, mental hygiene, correction, the aging, social security and medical care, rehabilitation, aspects and problems of civil rights and automation. There is also a substantial representation of literature in psychiatry and the behavioral and social sciences. The reference section includes more than 419 periodicals, publications issued by voluntary agencies, government publications, doctoral dissertations and masters' essays in the field and standard reference works. Reference service is available.

NY —NEW YORK STATE DIVISION OF HUMAN RIGHTS, Reference Library, Two World Trade Center, Rm 5356, New York, 10047. Rosalind Spriggs, Librn
Holdings: Vols 1500 Cat
Notes: Emphasis on materials related to discrimination in employment, aged people, and antipoverty efforts. See: Simon Fediuk, *Bibliography on Employment and Related* Subjects. Special Collection No 3 of a Series. 190 pp. This special collection contains about 1500 items: books, studies, journals, pamphlets, reprints and research data.

NY —YESHIVA UNIVERSITY, Library, 500 West 185th Street, New York, 10033. Pearl Berger
Holdings: Cat

NY —CREEDMOOR PSYCHIATRIC CENTER, Health Sciences Library, Bldg 51, 80-45 Winchester Blvd, Queens Village, 11427. Susan Taubman, Dir of Library; Pushpa Bhati, Sr Librn
Holdings: Vols (12,000) Cat Slides Phonorecords Audiotapes Videotapes Filmstrips Microfiche
Budget: ($50,000)
Notes: Particularly strong in the areas of neurology, Pharmacology, psychoanalysis, and psychopharmacology.

NY —MASONIC MEDICAL RESEARCH LIBRARY, 2150 Bleecker St, Utica, 13501. Irma A Tuttle, Librn
Holdings: Vols (2000) Cat
Notes: Biochemical and basic research into the aging process. Incl 16,000 periodicals.

OR —UNIVERSITY OF OREGON LIBRARY, 1607 Agate St, Eugene, 97403. Ruth M Brewer, Resource Librn
Notes: Social and psychological aspects of aging.

PA —GRAY PANTHERS, Library, 3700 Chestnut St, Philadelphia, 19104. Jean G Hopper, Librn
Notes: Incl government publications, periodicals, internal reports, bibliographies, pamphlets, and clippings on aging and related subjects: advocacy, legislation, national health service, housing and transportation. No catalog; organized by subject.

PA —UNIVERSITY OF PITTSBURGH, Hillman Library, Pittsburgh, 15260. Glenora E Rossell, Head
Holdings: Vols (18,500) Cat
Notes: Especially strong in social theory, social history, social groups, criminology and urban sociology. Emphasis is currently being given to administration of justice, sociology of the child, sociology of the aged, sociology of education and sociology of religion. This collection is strengthened by the US government publications depository collection, the partial UN depository collection, the Canadian government publications collection and the collection of the Social Work Library.

VA —CENTRAL STATE HOSPITAL, Medical Library, PO Box 4030, Petersburg, 23803. P D Upadyaya, Medical Librn
Holdings: Vols (10,000) Cat

WI —UNIVERSITY OF WISCONSIN, MADISON, School of Social Work, Virginia L Franks Library, 425 Henry Mall, Rm 230, Madison, 53706. Thurston Davini, Librn
Holdings: Vols 12,000 Cat Journals
Budget: $16,000
Notes: Special emphasis on social gerontology and human sexuality. Incl 1200 bound journals.

†MB —UNIVERSITY OF MANITOBA, Library, Winnipeg, R3T 2N2, Can.
Notes: Especially social gerontology.

ON —UNIVERSITY OF GUELPH, Library, Guelph, N1G 2W1, Can. Margaret Beckman, Chief Librn; Ellen Pearson, Ref Librn
Holdings: Vols 4500 Cat Audiotapes Videotapes 16mm Films
Notes: 32 periodical titles currently received. Collection supports work of the Gerontology Research Centre, as well as the undergraduate and graduate teaching program of the College of Family and Consumer Studies and the College of Social Sciences. Also 200 periodical titles. Collection as a whole concentrates on behavior, clothing and textiles, foods, housing, marketing, law.

†ON —METROPOLITAN TORONTO LIBRARY, Social Sciences Dept, 789 Yonge St, Toronto, M4W 2G8, Can. Abdus Salam, Head
Holdings: Vols Cat Maps Phonorecords Audiotapes 16mm Films Microforms
Notes: Historical and contemporary Canadian material covering federal and provincial policies and programs in the fields of health care, geriatrics, child welfare, corrections, and care and rehabilitation of the physically and mentally handicapped.

ON —ONTARIO MINISTRY OF COMMUNITY & SOCIAL SERVICES, Library, 880 Bay St, Rm 663, Toronto, M7A 1E9, Can. Sandra Walsh, Chief Librn
Holdings: Vols 4000 Cat Slides Videotapes Microforms

GERGELY, TIBOR

†NY —COLUMBIA UNIVERSITY LIBRARIES, Butler Library, Rare Book and Manuscript Library, 535 W 114 St, New York, 10027.
Notes: A collection of the art work of Tibor Gergely, containing 2,824 watercolors, pen-and-ink drawings, and sketches. Gergely is best known for his illustrations of the popular Golden Book Series for children.

GERM THEORY see Life—Origin

GERMAN ALMANACS see Almanacs, German

GERMAN-AMERICAN LITERATURE

PA —HISTORICAL SOCIETY OF PENNSYLVANIA, Library, 1300 Locust St, Philadelphia, 19107. David Fraser, Librn

PA —LIBRARY COMPANY OF PHILADELPHIA, 1314 Locust St, Philadelphia, 19107. Edwin Wolf II, Librn; Kenneth Finkel, Cur of Prints

GERMAN AMERICAN NEWSPAPERS see Newspapers, German American

GERMAN AMERICANS—IMPRINTS

PA —HISTORICAL SOCIETY OF PENNSYLVANIA, Library, 1300 Locust St, Philadelphia, 19107. David Fraser, Librn

PA —LIBRARY COMPANY OF PHILADELPHIA, 1314 Locust St, Philadelphia, 19107. Edwin Wolf II, Librn; Kenneth Finkel, Cur of Prints

GERMAN AUTHORS see Authors, German

GERMAN COMPOSERS see Composers, German

GERMAN DEMOCRATIC REPUBLIC—HISTORY

CA —HOOVER INSTITUTION ON WAR, REVOLUTION & PEACE, Stanford University, Stanford, 94305. Milorad M Drachkovitch, Archivist
Holdings: Vols (16,000) Cat Mss Pix Microforms
Notes: The German history collections extend from a set of Reichstag Debates, 1870-1918, the Revolution of 1918-1919, the Weimar Government, the National Socialist State, World War II, the period of Allied Occupation to the present, incl materials for both the Federal Republic of Germany and the Democratic Republic. Particularly noteworthy are holdings of newspapers, incl *Vorwaerts, Voelkischer Beobachter,* and periodicals, incl *Sueddeutsche Monatshefte,* Einheit. Of archival interest are the microfilms of the NSDAP Hauptarchiv (155 reels). Guides: *The Hoover Library Collections on Germany*, Hildegard R Boeninger (Stanford, 1955) and *Western* Europe, Agnes F Peterson (Stanford, 1970).

CA —STANFORD UNIVERSITY LIBRARIES, Cecil H Green Library, Stanford, 94305. Peter R Frank, Cur, CDP-Germanic Collection
Notes: Stanford's holdings in all branches of the field of history are strong, from Medieval times to the present. Extensive collection of regional and city histories, regional historical journals, of historical material both for the Federal Republic of Germany and the German Democratic Republic. Broadsheet collection for the Revolution 1848/1849. Extensive collection of works on military affairs, the workers' and women's movements. Many rare items in the Stanford

GERMAN DEMOCRATIC REPUBLIC—HISTORY (cont.)

Collection of German, Austrian and Swiss Culture. Description: "The German Area Collection: A German Tradition" by Peter R Frank.

WI —UNIVERSITY OF WISCONSIN, MADISON, Memorial Library, 728 State St, Madison, 53706. Erwin K Welsch, Social Studies Bibliographer
Holdings: Vols (25,000) Cat Maps Phonorecords Microforms
Notes: A collection of printed materials covering all aspects of life and society in the GDR published in that country or elsewhere. It incl important materials in politics, eg proceedings of SED party days and congresses, and history, incl all the major and many of the minor and local historical serials and journals. The literature collection is very extensive and notable for holdings of literary periodcials. The serials collection is generally strong across the spectrum of scholarship, with many holdings dating from the immediate post-war period, and incl publications of scholarly institutes and universities as well as journals of opinion. The government documents collection is very substantial, but not comprehensive. The collection is described in "East Germany," by Erwin K Welsch, in *East Central and Southeast Europe,* ed by Paul L Horecky (Santa Barbara, 1976), pp 429-436.

GERMAN DRAMA

CT —UNIVERSITY OF CONNECTICUT, Library, Storrs, 06268. R H Schimmelpfeng, Dir of Special Collections
Holdings: Cat Microforms
Notes: 19th century drama. Expressionism, East German literature and literature since 1945 constitute major strengths in the collection. Coverage is maintained for 600 contemporary authors. Also noteworthy are holdings on popular culture of Austria and Germany, 18th and 19th century.

KY —UNIVERSITY OF KENTUCKY, Margaret I King Library, Dept of Special Collections, Lexington, 40506. William Marshall, Head
Holdings: Cat
Notes: 2000 French and approximately 2000 Spanish and German plays. 18th-19th centuries.

MD —JOHNS HOPKINS UNIVERSITY, Milton S Eisenhower Library, Charles & 34 Sts, Baltimore, 21218. Ann S Gwyn, Assistant Dir for Special Collections
Holdings: Vols 3000 / / Cat
Notes: Loewenberg Collection. Practically the complete output of German playwrights and translators, 1880-1934. Downs (1951-1960) 3580. Most are first editions.

NH —DARTMOUTH COLLEGE, Baker Memorial Library, Hanover, 03755.
Holdings: Cat
Notes: The Barrett Clark Collection.

NY —NEW YORK PUBLIC LIBRARY, Performing Arts Research Center, Billy Rose Theatre Collection, 111 Amsterdam Ave, New York, 10023. Dorothy L Swerdlove, Cur
Holdings: Cat
Notes: Described in *Catalog of the Theatre and Drama Collections,* The Research Libraries of The New York Public Library. 1967. To be Supplemented. Part 1, *Drama Collection: Listing by Cultural Origin,* 6 vols (120,000 cards), $585; Part II, *Drama Collection: Author Listing,* 6 vols (115,000 cards), $790. This catalog represents the major portion of the Research Libraries' Drama Collection. Incl are more than 120, 000 plays written in Western languages. Translations of plays published in the Cyrillic, Hebrew and Oriental alphabets are also listed. Excluded are children's plays, Christmas plays, and moralities. The catalog is in two parts: a listing by author (or title, in the case of anonymous plays); and a listing by cultural origin. An analysis of this latter section reveals the Research Libraries' interest in collecting widely from the literatures of theworld: American, 20,000 entries; English, 21,000; French, 22,000; Spanish, 16,000; German, 14,000; and a strong representation of plays written in minor languages.

TX —UNIVERSITY OF TEXAS LIBRARIES, General Libraries, PO Box P, Austin, 78713. Carolyn Bucknell, Asst Dir for Collection Development
Holdings: Cat Microforms

WI —UNIVERSITY OF WISCONSIN, MADISON, Memorial Library, Western European Humanities Collection, 728 State St, Madison, 53706. Charles Szabo, Bibliographer
Notes: An extensive special collection of approximately 1500 German plays from the 18th and 19th centuries, written by 476 dramatists. Includes not only the great personalities of the German theater, but many plays by less-known playwrights of the period. Supplements the Library's great German language literature holdings.

GERMAN EXILE COLLECTION

NY —STATE UNIVERSITY OF NEW YORK AT ALBANY, Library, Special Collections Dept, 1400 Washington Ave, Albany, 12222. Marion P Munzer, Coordr
Notes: 370 linear feet of mss; papers and personal libraries of 67 German-speaking emigres who came to the United States from 1933-1945. Collections of faculty members of the "University in Exile" of the New School for Social Research form the core. Major collections are: American Council for Emigres in the Professions, Ludwig Bachhofer, Vicki Baum, Erwin Bodky, Arnold Brecht, Emergency Rescue Committee, Helmut Hirsch, Erich Hula, Jugendbewegung, Ernst Jünger, Erich von Kahler, Emil Lederer, Hans Natonek, Hans Neisser, Fritz Neugass, Karl Otto Paetel, Yella Pessl, Richard Plant, Hans Simons, Hans Staudinger, Storm Publishers Archive, Hans Tischler, Widerstand. There are separate entries for each of these in this volume.
See also entry under Emigration and Immigration

GERMAN EXPRESSIONISM

CA —STANFORD UNIVERSITY LIBRARIES, Cecil H Green Library, Stanford, 94305. Peter R Frank, Cur, CDP-Germanic Collection
Notes: Strong collection, with many first editions, rare journals, etc. The Cassirer Collection (correspondence, autographs and typescripts by Hasenclever, Meidner, printed material) in the Stanford Collection of German, Austrian and Swiss Culture, Special Collections Register of Manuscripts.

CT —UNIVERSITY OF CONNECTICUT, Library, Storrs, 06268. R H Schimmelpfeng, Dir of Special Collections
Holdings: Cat Microforms
Notes: 19th century drama, Expressionism, East German literature and literature since 1945 constitute major strengths in the collection. Coverage is maintained for 600 contemporary authors. Also noteworthy are holdings on popular culture of Austria and Germany, 18th and 19th century.

AB —UNIVERSITY OF ALBERTA, Cameron Library, The Bruce Peel Special Collections Room, Edmonton, T6G 2J8, Can. John Charles, Special Collections Librn
Holdings: Vols 1400 Cat
Notes: German expressionism in drama.

GERMAN FRIENDLY SOCIETY

SC —COLLEGE OF CHARLESTON LIBRARY, Special Collections Dept, Charleston, 29401.
Notes: Papers, 1766-1858.

GERMAN HEBREW see Yiddish Language and Literature

GERMAN JEWS see Jews, German

GERMAN LANGUAGE AND LITERATURE

†CA —UNIVERSITY OF CALIFORNIA, DAVIS, Davis, 95616.

CA —LOS ANGELES PUBLIC LIBRARY, Foreign Languages Dept, 630 W Fifth St, Los Angeles, 90071. Sylva Manoogian, Principal Librn
Holdings: Vols (822,694)
Budget: ($41,500)

†CA —UNIVERSITY OF CALIFORNIA, LOS ANGELES, Research Library, Germanic Dept, 405 Hilgard Ave, Los Angeles, 90024. Edward Shreeves, Chairman, Bibliographers Group; Antonina Babb, Germanic Bibliographer

†CA —GOETHE INSTITUTE SAN FRANCISCO LIBRARY, 530 Bush St, San Francisco, 94108.
Notes: Germany--contemporary literature, classics, history, political science, art, economics, education.

CA —STANFORD UNIVERSITY LIBRARIES, Cecil H Green Library, Stanford, 94305. Peter R Frank, Cur, CDP-Germanic Collection
Holdings: Vols 4605 Cat
Notes: Library of Prof Rudolf Hildebran, Leipzig, the first large collection acquired by Stanford in 1895-1896, laid the foundation for an extensive German collection. Hildebrand's library is especially strong in German and Austrian philology (rare dictionaries, etc), but also in literary works. The collection is now especially strong for the period of the Reformation and Baroque, up to the present, with many rare editions, journals, almanacs, and the like. Sizable collections of women's working class and popular literature, dissertations and Schulschriften. Rare and valuable items in the Stanford Collection of German, Austrian and Swiss Culture, Special Collections. Catalog: *Katalog der Bibliothek des Herrn Prof Dr Rudolf Hildebrand.* Description: *The German Area Collection: A Stanford* Tradition by Peter R Frank.

CT —YALE UNIVERSITY, Box 1603A, Yale Station, New Haven, 06520.
Holdings: Cat Mss
Notes: See individual authors.

CT —YALE UNIVERSITY, Beinecke Rare Book & Manuscript Library, German Literature Collection, Box 1603A, Yale Sta, New Haven, 06520. Christa Sammons, Cur
Holdings: Vols 2600 Cat
Notes: The Faber du Faur Collection of 17th Century German Literature. Printed catalogues: Faber du Faur, Curt von, *German Baroque Literature,* vols 1-2 (New Haven: Yale University Press, 1958-1969); Research Publications, *Bibliography-Index to the Microfilm Edition of the Yale University Library Collection of German Baroque* Literature (New Haven: Research Publications, PO Box 3903, Amity Sta, New Haven, Conn 06525). The library allows photocopying only in rare cases and for volumes acquired after the filming project was completed.

CT —UNIVERSITY OF CONNECTICUT, Library, Storrs, 06268. R H Schimmelpfeng, Dir of Special Collections
Holdings: Cat Microforms
Notes: 19th century drama, Expressionism, East German literature and literature since 1945 constitute major strengths in the collection. Coverage is maintained for 600 contemporary authors. Also noteworthy are holdings on popular culture of Austria and Germany, 18th and 19th century.

†GA —GOETHE INSTITUTE ATLANTA LIBRARY, German Cultural Center, 400 Colony Sq, Atlanta, 30361.
Notes: Germany--contemporary literature, social science, geography, history.

IL —SOUTHERN ILLINOIS UNIVERSITY, CARBONDALE, Delyte W Morris Library, Carbondale, 62901.
Holdings: Vols (14,000) Cat
Notes: The Wilhelm Kosch Collection of German Literature, History, Biography, etc. A scholar's working library, especially strong in German monographs and standard editions from the late 19th century through the 1940s. There are some runs of German periodicals and serials. No separate catalog or index. Not maintained as a separate collection.

IL —UNIVERSITY OF CHICAGO LIBRARY, Dept of Special Collections,

GERMAN LANGUAGE AND LITERATURE (cont.)

1100 E 57 St, Chicago, 60637.
Notes: Lincke Collection of German Fiction, 1790-1850.

IL —NORTHWESTERN UNIVERSITY, Library, Special Collections Dept, 1937 Sheridan Rd, Evanston, 60201. R Russell Maylone, Cur
Holdings: Vols 6000 Cat Mss
Notes: First editions, letters, and works about major 20th-century authors. Incl books and periodicals from France and Germany and to a lesser extent from Italy, Spain, Poland, Rumania, Czechoslovakia, Sweden, Denmark, and the Netherlands. Strong in German Expressionism, Italian Futurism, Surrealism, and Dada.

IN —INDIANA UNIVERSITY, Lilly Library, Seventh St, Bloomington, 47405. William R Cagle, Librn
Holdings: Cat Mss Pix
Notes: Correspondence files of S Fischer Verlag, 1888-1975. Incl important correspondence files with such authors as Gerhardt Hauptmann, Hermann Hesse, Thomas Mann, etc. Also mss by many of the authors. 15,000 items. Incl first editions of many 19th century works and some 20th century holdings.

MD —JOHNS HOPKINS UNIVERSITY, Milton S Eisenhower Library, Charles & 34 Sts, Baltimore, 21218. Ann S Gwyn, Assistant Dir for Special Collections
Holdings: Vols (24,000) Cat Mss
Notes: Several individuals' libraries combine to make a strong collection of German literature: Leonard L Mackall's German literature, Hermann Coblitz' German linguistics, and the largest, William Kurrelmeyer's collection including incunabula and mss, and 16-18th century works on the art of warfare. Literary journals, reference works, and most important editions of all major 18th and 19th century writers.

MA —UNIVERSITY OF MASSACHUSETTS AT AMHERST, Library, Amherst, 01003. Siegfried Feller, Assoc Dir for Collection Development
Holdings: Cat Microforms
Notes: Good representation of literary periodicals; in addition to bound vols, incl microfilm of Yale's Baroque Literature Collection (Faber du Faur).

†MA —GOETHE INSTITUTE BOSTON LIBRARY, 170 Beacon St, Boston, 02116.
Notes: Germany--literature, language, geography, customs, fine arts, history and politics, sociology, philosophy, theology, and psychology.

MA —HARVARD UNIVERSITY LIBRARY, Widener Library, Cambridge, 02138. David E Silas, Specialist in Book Selection
Holdings: Cat Mss
Notes: The Hofmannsthal and Rilke collections are most noteworthy but collections for Goethe, Heine, Beer-Hofmann, Brecht, and Zweig are strong and include significant manuscripts.

MA —BRANDEIS UNIVERSITY, Goldfarb Library, 415 South St, Waltham, 02154. Bessie Hahn, Dir
Notes: George Froeschel Collection. Consists of 27 linear ft of books and 30 linear ft of mss material, correspondence, photographs and memorabilia of this novelist and former Holywood screen writer. The collection is unprocessed.

MI —UNIVERSITY OF MICHIGAN, Graduate Library, Ann Arbor, 48109. Janet White, Reference Librn
Holdings: Cat Microforms
Notes: Comprehensive collection of German language and literature; currently receives about 600 periodical titles published in Germany.

MO —UNIVERSITY OF MISSOURI-COLUMBIA, Ellis Library, Language and Literature Dept, Columbia, 65201. Jeaneice Brewer, Librn
Holdings: Vols Cat
Notes: Strong in studies of German dialects.

MO —WASHINGTON UNIVERSITY, John M Olin Library, Campus Box 1061, St Louis, 63130.
Holdings: Vols 35,000 Cat Microforms
Notes: Strongest in 19th century and early 20th century imprints. Incl the Pretorius Memorial Collection. Also the private library of the late Gert von Gontard. Incl works on art, literature (especially German), music, and theater. Contains 1200 vols Goetheana, with first editions, autographed letters and original drawings by Goethe. Also material on the Austrian writer Karl Kraus and the Belgian artist Frans Masereel.

NJ —PRINCETON UNIVERSITY, Library, Rare Books Dept, Princeton, 08544. Stephen Ferguson, Cur
Holdings: Cat

NY —HEMPSTEAD PUBLIC LIBRARY, Foreign Language Collection, 115 Nichols Court, Hempstead, 11550. Irene A Duszkiewicz, Dir
Notes: Mainly French, German, Italian, Spanish, Polish, Yiddish, Hebrew. Holdings in other languages, including Asian.

NY —NEW YORK PUBLIC LIBRARY, Research Libraries, General Research Division, Fifth Ave & 42 St, New York, 10018. Rodney Phillips, Chief
Holdings: Vols (2,225,000) Cat Maps Pix Microforms
Budget: ($775,718)

NY —NEW YORK PUBLIC LIBRARY, Donnell Foreign Language Library, 20 W 53 St, New York, 10019. Bosiljka Stevanovic, Supvr Librn
Holdings: Vols 672 Cat
Notes: German collection incl German authors of German expression. No separate catalog.

NC —DUKE UNIVERSITY, William R Perkins Library, Rare Book Room, Durham, 27706. John L Sharpe, III, Cur
Notes: Harold Jantz collection of German Baroque literature, consisting of 3600 volumes. Described in *German Baroque Literature: A Descriptive Catalogue of the Collection of Harold Jantz*. New Haven: Research Publications, Inc 1974. 2 vols.

NC —CUMBERLAND COUNTY PUBLIC LIBRARY, North Carolina Foreign Language Center, 328 Gillespie St, Fayetteville, 28301. Patrick M Valentine, Coordinator
Holdings: Vols 3800 Cat
Budget: $2000
Notes: The largest book collections are, in descending order of size, German Spanish, French, Japanese, Korean and Vietnamese, with fair sized collections in Italian, Russian, Chinese, Arabic, Greek, Hungarian, Polish, Hebrew, Thai, and Hindi. The Center has several shelves each of books in Bengali, Dutch, Marathi, Portuguese, Urdu, and Yiddish. Smaller collections of one to three shelves each incl Catalan, Croatian, Czech, Danish, Finnish, Gujarati, Icelandic, Kannada, Latin, Lithuanian, Malayalam, Norwegian, Panjabi, Persian (Farsi), Romanian, Slovak, Swedish, Tagalog, Tamil, Telegu, and Ukrianian. The Center has grammars, dictionaries and occasionally other readings in languages from Afrikaans and Albanian to Welsh, Yoruba and Zulu.

OH —UNIVERSITY OF CINCINNATI, Main Library, Cincinnati, 45221. Charles Osborn, Dir; Cecily A Johns, Dir of Info Servs
Holdings: Vols 17,300 Cat Microforms

OH —CLEVELAND PUBLIC LIBRARY, Foreign Literature Dept, 325 Superior Ave, Cleveland, 44114. Natalia Bezugloff, Head
Holdings: Vols (30,600) Cat
Notes: A popular circulating collection containing classics and the standard works with emphasis on belles lettres, history and biography. A variety of other subjects such as learning languages, how to do books, art, children's books, spoken phonodiscs and cassettes, periodicals, etc. Incl 400 ephemera.
See also entry under Foreign Language Collections

†PA —GERMAN SOCIETY OF PENNSYLVANIA, Joseph Horner Memorial Library, 611 Spring Garden St, Philadelphia, 19123.
Notes: All subjects with special emphasis on history, biography, literature (85 per cent in German), juvenile literature.

PA —UNIVERSITY OF PENNSYLVANIA, Van Pelt Library, Rare Books Collection, 34 & Walnut Sts, Philadelphia, 19104. Daniel Traister, Special Collections Librn
Notes: Especially Middle High German.

PA —BIBLIOGRAPHICAL CENTER OF GERMAN LITERATURE, University of Pittsburgh, Dept of Germanic Languages & Literatures, 102 Loeffler Bldg, Pittsburgh, 15260. Klaus W Jonas, Dir
Holdings: Cat Mss Pix Microforms
Notes: Center for the development of collections and bibliographical control of the record of publications, mss, correspondence, etc, by or relating to modern German authors. Special sections have been developed for Mann, Rilke, Hauptmann, Hesse, Broch, Sachs and others. Described by Professor Klaus W Jonas's "The German Literature Center in Pittsburgh," *Stechert-Hafner Book News*, vol 24, no 8, April 1970; "Documentation in Modern German Literature: A Progress Report," *Jahrbuch fuer Internationale Germanistik*, vol 4, no 2, 1972, and in *German and Austrian Contributions to World Literature* (1890-1970). Department of Germanic Languages and Literatures, University of Pittsburgh, 1983. 96 pp.

PA —UNIVERSITY OF PITTSBURGH, Hillman Library, Pittsburgh, 15260.
Notes: Incl the William Steinberg Collection of 800 musical scores, many signed by composers, and 1400 vols of English, French, German, Japanese, and Chinese literature.

TX —UNIVERSITY OF TEXAS LIBRARIES, General Libraries, PO Box P, Austin, 78713. Carolyn Bucknell, Asst Dir for Collection Development
Holdings: Cat Microforms

WI —UNIVERSITY OF WISCONSIN, MADISON, Memorial Library, 728 State St, Madison, 53706. Erwin K Welsch, Social Studies Bibliographer
Holdings: 140,000 Items
Notes: The

WI —UNIVERSITY OF WISCONSIN, MADISON, Memorial Library, Western European Humanities Collection, 728 State St, Madison, 53706. Charles Szabo, Bibliographer
Notes: The George B Wild Collection of Classical and Nineteenth Century German Literature. An extensive collection emphasizing history, biography, criticism, philosophy, literature, and comparative religion. Supplements the Library's great German language and literature holdings.

BC —GREATER VANCOUVER LIBRARY FEDERATION, 110-6545 Bonsor, Burnaby, Z5H 1H3, Can. Colleen Smith, Coordr
Holdings: Vols (20,350) Cat
Notes: Deposit provided by the National Library's Multilingual Biblioservice on long-term loan to libraries in the Greater Vancouver Library Federation (Burnby, New Westminster, N Vancouver City Public, N Vancouver District Public, Port Moody, Vancouver, W Vancouver).

†ON —METROPOLITAN TORONTO LIBRARY BOARD, Language Dept, 789 Yonge St, Toronto, M4W 2G8, Can.
Notes: First editions of the works of Ernst Junger (1895-), many inscribed by him. Also original editions of authors active in Germany during the Twenties, Thirties, and Forties.

GERMAN LANGUAGE AND LITERATURE—BIBLIOGRAPHY

PA —BIBLIOGRAPHICAL CENTER OF GERMAN LITERATURE, University of Pittsburgh, Dept of Germanic Languages & Literatures, 102 Loeffler Bldg, Pittsburgh, 15260. Klaus W Jonas, Dir
Holdings: Cat Mss Pix Microforms
Notes: Center for the development of collections and bibliographical control of the record of publications, mss, correspondence, etc, by or relating to modern German authors. Special sections have been developed for Mann, Rilke, Hauptmann, Hesse, Broch, Sachs and others. Described

GERMAN LANGUAGE AND LITERATURE—BIBLIOGRAPHY (cont.)

by Professor Klaus W Jonas's "The German Literature Center in Pittsburgh," *Stechert-Hafner Book News*, vol 24, no 8, April 1970; "Documentation in Modern German Literature: A Progress Report," *Jahrbuch fuer Internationale Germanistik*, vol 4, no 2, 1972, and in *German and Austrian Contributions to World Literature* (1890-1970). Department of Germanic Languages and Literatures, University of Pittsburgh, 1983. 96 pp.

GERMAN LANGUAGE AND LITERATURE—MIDDLE HIGH GERMAN

OH —CLEVELAND PUBLIC LIBRARY, Fine Arts and Special Collections Department, 325 Superior Ave, Cleveland, 44114. Alice N Loranth, Head
Holdings: Cat Mss
Notes: Part of the Medieval Literature Collection. Medieval texts, translations, facsimile reproductions, bibliographies and catalogs of mss, romances, epics, early chronicles and histories. Icelandic sagas, fabliaux (tales), legends, lives of the Saints are well represented. Monographs, scholarly journals and serials on philogy, linguistics and literature with special emphasis on Middle English, Old French, Middle High German, Middle Dutch and early Irish texts. *See also* entries under Folklore; Literature, Medieval.

PA —UNIVERSITY OF PENNSYLVANIA, Van Pelt Library, Rare Books Collection, 34 & Walnut Sts, Philadelphia, 19104. Daniel Traister, Special Collections Librn
Notes: Especially Middle High German.

GERMAN LANGUAGE AND LITERATURE—TASCHENBUCHER

IN —INDIANA UNIVERSITY, Lilly Library, Seventh St, Bloomington, 47405. William R Cagle, Librn
Holdings: Vols 1100 // Cat
Notes: From late 18th through the 19th century.

GERMAN LANGUAGE AND LITERATURE—TRANSLATIONS INTO ENGLISH

PA —PENNSYLVANIA STATE UNIVERSITY, Rare Book Room, University Park, 16802. Charles Mann, Chief, Rare Books and Special Collections
Holdings: Vols (13,000) Cat Mss Pix
Budget: ($24,000)
Notes: The Allison-Shelley Collection of translations of German literature, history, science, medicine, biography, children's literature, and other cultural manifestations into English. Incl 3000 letters and mss of British and American translations of German writings. Also phonograph records of German art songs. Further, the collection contains a large collection of Bayard Taylor's works, letters, and mss. An annotated exhibition catalog of selected items is available from the Office of the Dean of Libraries.

GERMAN METHODIST EPISCOPAL CHURCH IN THE U.S.

OH —CINCINNATI HISTORICAL SOCIETY, Library, (formerly Historical & Philosophical Society of Ohio), Eden Park, Cincinnati, 45202. Laura L Chace, Librn
Holdings: Cat Mss Pix
Notes: Entire collection of papers, printed materials, photographs, etc, of the German Methodist Episcopal Church in the US, 1835-1942 (when it merged with the United Methodist Church). Incl diaries of ministers, organizational records, church and institutional archives, etc.

GERMAN MOVING PICTURES see Moving Pictures, German

GERMAN NEWSPAPERS see Newspapers, German

GERMAN PERIODICALS see Periodicals, German

GERMAN POETRY

†NY —GOETHE HOUSE LIBRARY, 1014 Fifth Ave, New York, 10028.
Notes: German publications with special emphasis on German literature, art, history, and politics. Incl collected works of Goethe and other famous German poets.

GERMAN PROPAGANDA see Propaganda, German

GERMAN RUSSIANS see Russian Germans

GERMAN YOUTH MOVEMENT

NY —STATE UNIVERSITY OF NEW YORK AT ALBANY, Library, Special Collections Dept, 1400 Washington Ave, Albany, 12222. Marion P Munzer, Coordr
Notes: Correspondence regarding Karl Otto Paetel and his German language newspaper, *Aufbau;* mss and letters concerning the German youth movement, Ernst Jünger, German resistance, and the refugee question (3.8 linear feet). Part of the Library's German Exile Collection.
See also entries under Paetel, Karl Otto; J1nger, Ernst; Exiles, Political; German Youth Movement.

GERMANIC LANGUAGES AND LITERATURES

NJ —PRINCETON UNIVERSITY, Library, Rare Books Dept, Princeton, 08544. Stephen Ferguson, Cur
Holdings: Cat

GERMANIC LAW see Law, Germanic

GERMANIC MYTHOLOGY see Mythology, Germanic

GERMANS FROM RUSSIA

ND —NORTH DAKOTA INSTITUTE FOR REGIONAL STUDIES, North Dakota State University, Fargo, 58105. Michael M Miller, Archivist
Notes: Incl family, community and county histories, maps, cassette tapes, sound recordings, video tapes, photographs, and slides. Emphasis on the Black Sea Germans from Russia; official repository of the Germans from Russia Heritage Society. For the "Germans from Russia Heritage Collection" there has been published, *Researching the Germans from Russia* (1984), compiled by Michael M Miller.

ND —NORTH DAKOTA STATE UNIVERSITY, Library, Fargo, 58105. John E Bye, Archivist
Notes: Books, newspapers, other printed materials and audio-visual records, both in English and German. The collection documents the migration of Germans to Russia, especially the Black Sea region, in the early 19th century and their later immigration to the United States.

ND —UNIVERSITY OF NORTH DAKOTA, Chester Fritz Library, Dept of Special Collections, Grand Forks, 58202. Daniel F Rylance, Special Collections Coordr
Holdings: Vols (5500) Uncat Mss Maps Pix Microforms
Budget: ($2500)
Notes: Also the Orin G Libby Manuscript Collection (900 collections), and the Aandahl Collection of Western History on North Dakota and the Northern Great Plains. Emphasis on agriculture, politics, pioneering, etc. Guides to the collections available from the coordinator of special collections.

GERMANS IN PENNSYLVANIA see Pennsylvania Germans

GERMANS IN THE U.S.

†CO —COLORADO STATE UNIVERSITY, Germans from Russia Project, History Dept, Fort Collins, 80523.

CO —GREELEY PUBLIC LIBRARY, City Complex Bldg, Greeley, 80631. Esther Fromm, Librn
Holdings: Vols 679 Cat Maps Pix Phonorecords Microforms
Notes: American Historical Society of Germans from Russia, the history of people of German-Russian ancestry. Also, incl 105 maps, 4 phonorecords.

IL —FREEPORT PUBLIC LIBRARY, 314 W Stephenson St, Freeport, 61032. John Locascio, Head Librn
Holdings: Vols (400) Cat Microforms Clippings
Notes: Freeport, Illinois, and Stephenson County history. Incl 3 file cabinets of clippings. German language newspapers, 1854-1917; English language newspapers, 1847-date. 507 newspapers file microfilm reels.

IN —INDIANA STATE UNIVERSITY, EVANSVILLE, Library, 8600 University Blvd, Evansville, 47712. Gina R Walker, Acting Archivist
Holdings: Cat Audiotapes
Notes: 40 cassettes on the oral history of persons of German descent in the Evansville, Indiana region. This research became the basis for Dr Daniel E Bigham's book, *Reflections on a Heritage: The German Americans in Southwestern Indiana,* 1980.

IN —WILLARD LIBRARY, 21 First Ave, Evansville, 47710. Joan Elliott, Special Collections Librn
Holdings: Vols (800) Cat Mss Maps Pix Microforms
Budget: ($4000)
Notes: General local history collection, incl books, pamphlets, mss, and documents relating to the histories of Evansville and Vanderburgh and surrounding counties, with considerable material on Indiana as a whole. Incl extensive collection of German-language newspapers published in Evansville, 1850s-1918.

KS —FORT HAYS STATE UNIVERSITY, Forsyth Library, Ethnic Heritage Studies Collection, 600 Park St, Hays, 67601. Esta Lou Riley, Archivist/Special Collections Librn
Holdings: Vols 335 Microforms Pix Phonorecords Videotapes Maps
Notes: Emphasis on ethnic groups in Kansas, especially Germans from Russia. Does not circulate. Incl 1 linear foot vertical file material.

†MN —CARVER COUNTY HISTORICAL SOCIETY LIBRARY, 119 South Cherry St, Waconia, 55387.
Notes: Early 1860 library of Swedes and Germans in the locality.

MO —CONCORDIA HISTORICAL INSTITUTE, 801 DeMun Ave, Saint Louis, 63105. Aug R Suelflow, Dir
Holdings: Vols (58,000) Mss Maps Pix Slides Films Microforms
Budget: ($100,000)
Notes: A centralized collection of all information media pertaining to the history and theology of Lutheranism in North America; also German-Americana; indexes and finding aids are available; extensive microfilm collection of mss, books, periodicals, church records; the ms collection exceeds 2,500,000 pages.

NE —AMERICAN HISTORICAL SOCIETY OF GERMANS FROM RUSSIA (AHSGR), 615 Twelfth St, Lincoln, 68502. Mary Lynn Tuck, Librn
Holdings: Vols (1900) Mss Maps Pix Phonorecords Videotapes Audiotapes Microforms VF
Notes: History of German people from Russia and history of people of German-Russian ancestory. Including times in Russia, Germany, US, Canada, Mexico, Argentina, Brazil, Paraguay, Korea, and Japan. This Society has fifty-six chapters in the United States. 1900 volumes, 100 maps; 500 mss; 1200 vertical files; 2000 pictures; 40,000 obituary files, 40,000 family group charts, 50 phonorecords, 20 videotapes, 50 audiotapes, 15 reel-to-reel tapes, 150 periodicals, 250 microforms, 250 family histories-published and unpublished.

NE —NEBRASKA STATE HISTORICAL SOCIETY, Archives, 1500 R St, Box 82554, Lincoln, 68501. James E Potter, State Archivist
Holdings: // Uncat Mss
Notes: German from Russia, with emphasis

GERMANS IN THE U.S. (cont.)

on the group who settled in Lincoln, Nebraska. Collection and mss of Dr Hattie Plum Williams; also, the collection of Germans in Nebraska, collected by Dr William H Werkmeister, from the first half of the 20th century, much of it centered in the University of Nebraska.

ND —NORTH DAKOTA STATE UNIVERSITY, Library, Fargo, 58105. John E Bye, Archivist
Notes: Books, newspapers, other printed materials and audio-visual records, both in English and German. The collection documents the migration of Germans to Russia, especially the Black Sea region, in the early 19th century and their later immigration to the United States.

ND —UNIVERSITY OF NORTH DAKOTA, Chester Fritz Library, Dept of Special Collections, Grand Forks, 58202. Daniel F Rylance, Special Collections Coordr
Holdings: Vols (5500) Uncat Mss Maps Pix Microforms
Budget: ($2500)
Notes: Also the Orin G Libby Manuscript Collection (900 collections), and the Aandahl Collection of Western History on North Dakota and the Northern Great Plains. Emphasis on agriculture, politics, pioneering, Germans from Russia, etc. Guides to the collections available from the Coordinator of Special Collections.

OH —CINCINNATI HISTORICAL SOCIETY, Library, (formerly Historical & Philosophical Society of Ohio), Eden Park, Cincinnati, 45202. Laura L Chace, Librn
Holdings: Cat Mss Pix
Notes: Entire collection of papers, printed materials, photographs, etc, of the German Methodist Episcopal Church in the US, 1835-1942 (when it merged with the United Methodist Church). Incl diaries of ministers, organizational records, church and institutional archives, etc.

PA —PENNSYLVANIA DIV OF ARCHIVES & MANUSCRIPTS, State Archives, PO Box 1026, Harris, 17108. Roland M Baumann, Chief, History & Museums
Holdings: Vols (3000) // Uncat Mss Maps Pix
Budget: ($40,000)
Notes: The Harmony Society (1785-1905), a German communistic and spiritual community, which immigrated to the US in 1805 and established their community in Harmony, Pennsylvania, moved to New Harmony, Indiana, and returned to Pennsylvania to set up the town of Economy, 20 miles north of Pittsburgh on the Ohio River. The Harmonists had a vast impact on the economy of the areas in which they lived. They were involved in agriculture, manufacturing and investing. 300,000 cu ft.

PA —BALCH INSTITUTE FOR ETHNIC STUDIES, Library, 18 S Seventh St, Philadelphia, 19106. R Joseph Anderson, Library Dir
Holdings: Vols 2100 Cat Mss Pix Microforms

†PA —GERMAN SOCIETY OF PENNSYLVANIA, Joseph Horner Memorial Library, 611 Spring Garden St, Philadelphia, 19123.
Notes: All subjects with special emphasis on history, biography, literature (85 per cent in German), juvenile literature.

PA —UNIVERSITY OF PITTSBURGH, Hillman Library, Archives of Industrial Society, 363 Hillman Library, Pittsburgh, 15260. Frank A Zabrosky, Cur
Holdings: Mss Maps Pix Newpapers Audiotapes Microforms
Notes: Records of churches, fraternal/ beneficial societies, organizations.

GERMANY

†CA —GOETHE INSTITUTE SAN FRANCISCO LIBRARY, 530 Bush St, San Francisco, 94108.
Notes: Germany--contemporary literature, classics, history, political science, art, economics, education.

DC —GEORGETOWN UNIVERSITY, Library, Special Collections Div, 37 & O Sts NW, Washington, 20057. George M Barringer, Special Collections Librn; Nicholas B Sheetz, Mss Librn
Holdings: Mss Cat Maps Pix
Notes: The papers of George Crews McGhee (1912), geologist, oil producer, and diplomat. The papers incl files from McGhee's United States ambassadorships to Turkey (1951-1953) and Germany (1963-1968) as well as his extensive involvement in numerous organizations and committees incl the Combined Raw Materials Board, the Bilderberg Group, the Draper Committee, the Committee for Economic Development, and the Business Council for International Understanding, among many others. Also incl are 264 volumes from the 17th to early 20th century relating to Turkey.

†GA —GOETHE INSTITUTE ATLANTA LIBRARY, German Cultural Center, 400 Colony Sq, Atlanta, 30361.
Notes: Germany--contemporary literature, social science, geography, history.

†MA —GOETHE INSTITUTE BOSTON LIBRARY, 170 Beacon St, Boston, 02116.
Notes: Germany--literature, language, geography, customs, fine arts, history and politics, sociology, philosophy, theology, and psychology.

†PA —GERMAN SOCIETY OF PENNSYLVANIA, Joseph Horner Memorial Library, 611 Spring Garden St, Philadelphia, 19123.
Notes: All subjects with special emphasis on history, biography, literature (85 per cent in German), juvenile literature.

GERMANY—CIVILIZATION AND CULTURE

CA —STANFORD UNIVERSITY LIBRARIES, Cecil H Green Library, Stanford, 94305. Peter R Frank, Cur, CDP-Germanic Collection
Notes: An extensive collection, covering all important aspects of German civilization and culture, from art, education and economics to theatre and technology, with special emphasis on language and literature, and history. Rare and valuable items in the Stanford Collection of German, Austrian and Swiss Culture, Special Collections.
Description: "The German Area Collection: A Stanford Tradition" by Peter R Frank.

CT —UNIVERSITY OF CONNECTICUT, Library, Storrs, 06268. R H Schimmelpfeng, Dir of Special Collections
Holdings: Cat Microforms
Notes: 19th century drama, Expressionism, East German literature and literature since 1945 constitute major strengths in the collection. Coverage is maintained for 600 contemporary authors. Also noteworthy are holdings on popular culture of Austria and Germany, 18th and 19th century.

†NY —COLUMBIA UNIVERSITY LIBRARIES, Butler Library, Rare Book and Manuscript Library, 535 W 114 St, New York, 10027.
Notes: Papers relating to Prof Walter Lewis Dorn's work as special advisor to Gen Lucius D Clay on denazification of Germany.

PA —PENNSYLVANIA STATE UNIVERSITY, Rare Book Room, University Park, 16802. Charles Mann, Chief, Rare Books and Special Collections
Holdings: Vols (13,000) Cat Mss Pix
Budget: ($24,000)
Notes: The Allison-Shelley Collection of translations of German literature, history, science, medicine, biography, children's literature, and other cultural manifestations into English. Incl 3000 letters and mss of British and American translations of German writings. Also phonograph records of German art songs. Further, the collection contains a large collection of Bayard Taylor's works, letters, and mss. An annotated exhibition catalog of selected items is available from the Office of the Dean of Libraries.

WI —UNIVERSITY OF WISCONSIN, MADISON, Memorial Library, Western European Humanities Collection, 728 State St, Madison, 53706. Charles Szabo, Bibliographer
Notes: Germanic Seminary Library. The basis for Wisconsin's great Germanic collections, acquired from 1899 on and containing materials on the whole range of German culture. Strongest in German philology.

GERMANY—HISTORY

CA —CALIFORNIA STATE UNIVERSITY, FRESNO, Henry Madden Library, Dept of Special Collections, Fresno, 93740. Ronald J Mahoney, Head
Holdings: Vols 4 Cat Mss
Notes: The Joseph A Lowande Collection of Worldwide Rationing contains 20th century ration material from Germany and the United States. Especially strong on local rationing from Stadtamhof, Bavaria, 1915-1923.

CA —UNIVERSITY OF CALIFORNIA, RIVERSIDE, University Library, 4045 Canyon Crest Dr, Box 5900, Riverside, 92517.
Holdings: Vols 5,000 Cat
Notes: Printed works on Nazism, German history and politics 1918-1945, supported by two closely related collections of contemporary publications on 19th-century European socialism and labor movements; incl many NSDAP publications.

†CA —UNIVERSITY OF SAN FRANCISCO, Richard A Gleeson Library, The Countess Bernardine Murphy Donohue Rare Book Room, San Francisco, 94117. D Steven Corey, Special Collections Librn
Notes: Some highly specialized materials.

CA —HOOVER INSTITUTION ON WAR, REVOLUTION & PEACE, Stanford University, Stanford, 94305. Milorad M Drachkovitch, Archivist
Holdings: Mss Pix
Notes: Ms diaries, 1941-1924, microfolms, photographs and photostats of documents from the *Personlicher Stab Reichsfuhrer SS.* Schriftgutverwaltung dealing with the life and career of Himmler as Reichsfuhrer SS and Chef der Deutschen Polizei, 1934-1945. 6 notebooks (plus 25 loose pages), 5 microfilm reels, 2 photo albums, 14 ms boxes. Incl 24 tapes of Himmler speeches, 1940-44.

CA —HOOVER INSTITUTION ON WAR, REVOLUTION & PEACE, Stanford University, Stanford, 94305. Milorad M Drachkovitch, Archivist
Holdings: Vols (16,000) Cat Mss Pix Microforms
Notes: The German history collections extend from a set of Reichstag Debates, 1870-1918, the Revolution of 1918-1919, the Weimar Government, the National Socialist State, World War II, the period of Allied Occupation to the present, incl materials for both the Federal Republic of Germany and the Democratic Republic. Particularly noteworthy are holdings of newspapers, incl *Vorwaerts, Voelkischer Beobachter*, and periodicals, incl. *Sueddeutsche Monatshefte,* Einheit. Of archival interest are the microfilms of the NSDAP Hauptarchiv (155 reels). Guides: *The Hoover Library Collections on Germany*, Hildegard R Boeinger (Stanford, 1955) and *Western* Europe, Agnes F Peterson (Stanford, 1970).

CA —STANFORD UNIVERSITY LIBRARIES, Cecil H Green Library, Stanford, 94305. Peter R Frank, Cur, CDP-Germanic Collection
Notes: Stanford's holdings in all branches of the field of history are strong, from Medieval times to the present. Extensive collection of regional and city histories, regional historical journals, of historical material both for the Federal Republic of Germany and the German Democratic Republic. Broadsheet collection for the Revolution 1848/1849. Extensive collection of works on military affairs, the workers' and women's movements. Many rare items in the Stanford Collection of German, Austrian and Swiss Culture. Description: "The German Area Collection: A German Tradition" by Peter R Frank.

GERMANY—HISTORY (cont.)

CT —YALE UNIVERSITY, Box 1603A, Yale Station, New Haven, 06520.
Holdings: Cat Mss
Notes: Hajo Holborn's personal papers, incl correspondence, 1924-1933; mss of articles, speeches, etc, 1904-1943; printed materials on the Weimar Republic, 1919-1938.

DC —GEORGETOWN UNIVERSITY, Library, Special Collections Div, 37 & O Sts NW, Washington, 20057. George M Barringer, Special Collections Librn; Nicholas B Sheetz, Mss Librn
Holdings: Cat Mss
Notes: The papers of Heinrich A Rommen (1897-1967), educator and authority on political philosophy and international law, consisting of correspondence, mss, clippings, photographs, and printed material. Incl material on religious opposition, in particular Catholic opposition, within Germany to the Hitler regime. Papers of Goetz A Briefs (1889-1974), economist and educator, who lived in Germany (1915-1934) and in the Unted States (1934-1974). In addition to teaching, Briefs held official positions in both governments. The papers incl correspondence and manuscripts, principally in the field of economics and the "ethos problem." The bulk of the material dates from Briefs' immigration to the United States in 1934.

DC —LIBRARY OF CONGRESS, Rare Book & Special Collections Div, Washington, 20540. William Matheson, Chief
Notes: The Third Reich Collection comprises books and miscellaneous materials that originally belonged to the Reichskanzlei in Berlin or were in the Berghof, Hitler's mountain retreat. It contains some books specially printed or designed for Adolf Hitler, but principally regular trade books; periodicals; and books owned by or bearing autographs of Hitler's associates. Incl materials from the libraries of Hermann Goering, Heinrich Himmler, and Franz Xaver Schwarz.
See also entry under Hitler's Library

IL —SOUTHERN ILLINOIS UNIVERSITY, CARBONDALE, Delyte W Morris Library, Carbondale, 62901.
Holdings: Vols (14,000) Cat
Notes: The Wilhelm Kosch Collection of German Literature, History, Biography, etc. A scholar's working library, especially strong in German monographs and standard editions from the late 19th century through the 1940s. There are some runs of German periodicals and serials. No separate catalog or index. Not maintained as a separate collection.

IL —CENTER FOR RESEARCH LIBRARIES, 6050 S Kenwood Ave, Chicago, 60637. Donald B Simpson, Dir; Esther Smith, Collection Development Librn
Holdings: Microforms
Notes: Over 10,000 reels of positive microfilm of captured German archives, principally of the German Foreign Ministry for the period 1867-1945, but also of other governmental agencies and army commands, etc, for period 1920-1945, mostly 1939-1945. Microfiche of German and Prussian parliamentary proceedings and extensive hard-copy backfiles of other government documents.

IL —LAKE FOREST COLLEGE, Donnelley Library, Lake Forest, 60045. Arthur H Miller Jr, College Librn
Holdings: Vols (700) Microform
Notes: Pese Collection of books, pamphlets, and journals on Hitler, Hitler's foreign policy, and Nazi era Germany.

†MA —BOSTON PUBLIC LIBRARY, Copley Sq, Boston, 02117.
Holdings: Cat Microforms
Notes: Microform Publication by National Archives. German Foreign Ministry archives, 1920-1945; Guide: A catalog of files and microfilms of the German Foreign Ministry Archives. 1920-1945.

†MA —JOHN F KENNEDY LIBRARY, Columbia Point, Boston, 02125. Dan H Fenn Jr, Dir
Holdings: // Cat Mss
Notes: Papers of James P Warburg relating to Germany and files of Walter W Heller from his service with the American military government of Germany; 1920-1969. 37 linear ft of mss. Holdings are described in "Historical Materials in the John F Kennedy Library." Copies may be obtained by writing the Research Archivist.

MA —HARVARD UNIVERSITY LIBRARY, Widener Library, Cambridge, 02138. David E Silas, Specialist in Book Selection
Holdings: Cat
Notes: Holdings are strong for all periods; there are special collections of Bavarian local history and the Thirty Years War, as well as 2700 volumes from the working library of a reigning prince of the Holy Roman Empire. The early middle ages, Reformation, formation of the Empire, Revolution of 1848, and Nazi Regime are represented by particularly outstanding resources.

MA —BRANDEIS UNIVERSITY, Goldfarb Library, 415 South St, Waltham, 02154. Bessie Hahn, Dir
Notes: Edward Lasker Collection. Consists of 21 linear ft of mss material, correspondence and contemporary pamphlets. Eduard Lasker was a political leader during the Bismarck regime in Germany. A finding list to the collection is located in Special Collections. Also, Nazi Documents Collection: 3 linear feet of documents and letters of major Nazi officials prior to and during World War II. A finding list to the documents is in Special Collections.

MI —UNIVERSITY OF MICHIGAN, Library, Dept of Rare Books & Special Collections, Ann Arbor, 48109. Robert J Starring, Head
Holdings: Cat Mss Microforms
Notes: Espec strong in literature of the Nazi period. These have been partially described in *Checklist of Selected German Pamphlets and Booklets of the Wiemar and Nazi Period in the University of Michigan Library*, by Herbert P Rothfeder, and *German Archival Material in the Rare Book Room, University of Michigan Library* by Professor Gerhard Weinberg. Also on microfilm selected German naval records issued between 1870 and 1944, German Foreign Ministry Archives covering the period 1867-1920, and selected records from military, ministerial, and party archives covering the years 1933-1945.

MO —WASHINGTON UNIVERSITY, John M Olin Library, Campus Box 1061, St Louis, 63130.
Holdings: Vols 5200 Cat Microforms
Notes: Strongest in 19th century to date. Whitney Robson Harris Collection on the Third Reich. Primarily in English.

NE —AMERICAN HISTORICAL SOCIETY OF GERMANS FROM RUSSIA (AHSGR), 615 Twelfth St, Lincoln, 68502. Mary Lynn Tuck, Librn
Holdings: Vols (1900) Mss Maps Pix Phonorecords Videotapes Audiotapes Microforms VF
Notes: History of German people from Russia and history of people of German-Russian ancestory. Including times in Russia, Germany, US, Canada, Mexico, Argentina, Brazil, Paraguay, Korea, and Japan. This Society has fifty-six chapters in the United States. 1900 volumes, 100 maps; 500 mss; 1200 vertical files; 2000 pictures; 40,000 obituary files, 40,000 family group charts, 50 phonorecords, 20 videotapes, 50 audiotapes, 15 reel-to-reel tapes, 150 periodicals, 250 microforms, 250 family histories-published and unpublished.

NY —NEW YORK PUBLIC LIBRARY, Research Libraries, General Research Division, Fifth Ave & 42 St, New York, 10018. Rodney Phillips, Chief
Holdings: Vols (2,225,000) Cat Maps Pix Microforms
Budget: ($775,718)

NY —STATE UNIVERSITY OF NEW YORK, STONY BROOK, Melville Library, Stony Brook, 11794. John B Smith, Dir
Holdings: Cat
Notes: Modern Germany history. Part of the library's general research collections.

WI —UNIVERSITY OF WISCONSIN, MADISON, Memorial Library, 728 State St, Madison, 53706. Erwin K Welsch, Social Studies Bibliographer
Holdings: Vols (60,000) Cat Microforms
Notes: In-depth holdings of German historical source materials and related secondary works from the earliest times until the present. Strong in Medieval sources with an almost complete collection of the Monumenta and large number of printed Chartularies. Local materials from the L†nder are well represented, particularly noticeable are holdings of Bavarian parliamentary documents in the original or in microform; an almost complete collection of laws, parliamentary documents and related works from Hesse for the 19th century; the *Regierungsbl'átter* for W1rttemberg from 1806 to 1920 and for some other German states in the twentieth century. The holdings of records of the national government are equally complete, incl all of theParliamentary debates (in the original or microform) from the founding of the empire in 1871 through the present for both East and West Germany. The periodicals collection incl virtually complete holdings of all of the publications of the academies of sciences and similar scholarly bodies as well as periodicals of opinion from various groups and individuals. Materials from the Nazi period are substantial. For the post-1945 period there is a largely uncataloged collection of materials from miscellaneous groups, incl so-called "Underground" publications, and political parties. Medieval holdings are partly described in Willard T Wulff, "Preliminary List of German Chartularies in the Memorial Library, University of Wisconsin-Madison" (Madison, 1982) and in the other guides listed under related sections.

ON —VICTORIA UNIVERSITY, Library, Centre for Reformation and Renaissance Studies, 71 Queen's Park Crescent, Toronto, M5S 1K7, Can. Robert C Brandeis, Chief Librn; James Estes, Dir
Holdings: Vols (15,000) Cat Slides
Notes: The CRRS concentrates on the northern European countries and France; its chief strengths are Erasmus, 650 vols; early printed books, especially 16th century editions of Latin classics; bibliography and the history of printing. The Erasmus holdings are cataloged in W T McCready et al, "The Erasmus Collection in the Centre for Reformation and Renaissance Studies...A Catalogue"...*Reformation and Renaissance* 7 (1971), 32-76 and "A Supplementary *List"...Reformation and Renaissance,* 10 (1974), 116-119. Published catalogs. Humanist Editions of the Classics at CRRS, Toronto, 1979; Humanist Editions of Statutes and History at CRRS, Toronto, 1980; Bibles, Theological Treatises and Other Religious Literature 1491-1700 at CRRS, Toronto, 1981.

GERMANY—IMPRINTS

CA —STANFORD UNIVERSITY LIBRARIES, Cecil H Green Library, Stanford, 94305. Peter R Frank, Cur, CDP-Germanic Collection
Notes: Incl a sizable collection for book research (catalogs and histories of the booktrade), histories and Festschriften of German newspaper and periodical publishing. The Cassirer Collection also has pertinent materials.
See also entry under Germany - Civilization and Culture

GERMANY—INDUSTRY AND TRADE

WI —UNIVERSITY OF WISCONSIN, MADISON, Memorial Library, 728 State St, Madison, 53706. Erwin K Welsch, Social Studies Bibliographer
Holdings: Vols 4000 Microforms
Notes: German trade unionism; espec strong holdings of German trade union periodicals, congress proceedings and protocols, and annual reports for the Weimar Republic Period (1919-1923). Also strong for German labor in the pre-1914 period. Incl memoirs of trade union leaders and secondary

GERMANY—INDUSTRY AND TRADE (cont.)

supporting sources. Also, 50 microfilm reels. A typed list of serial holdings is available.

GERMANY—LIBRARIES

MN —SAINT JOHN'S ABBEY & UNIVERSITY, Hill Monastic Manuscript Library, Collegeville, 56321. Julian G Plante, Dir
Notes: Films of 61,000 mss. The total number of codices (bound handwritten mss) represents the holdings of several hundred libraries in Europe and elsewhere: Austria, Spain, Malta, Ethiopia, West Germany, Portugal, England, but also with concentrations of holdings from Italy, Hungary, Poland, Great Britain, Belgium, Yugoslavia, France, Switzerland and the Netherlands, and Vatican City. Also incl 70, 000 exposures.

GERMANY—POLITICS AND GOVERNMENT

CA —HOOVER INSTITUTION ON WAR, REVOLUTION & PEACE, Stanford University, Stanford, 94305. Milorad M Drachkovitch, Archivist
Holdings: Vols (16,000) Cat Mss Pix Microforms
Notes: The German history collections extend from a set of Reichstag Debates, 1870-1918, the Revolution of 1918-1919. the Weimar Government, the National Socialist State, World War II, the period of Allied Occupation to the present, incl materials for both the Federal Republic of Germany and the Democratic Republic. Particularly noteworthy are holdings of newspapers, incl *Vorwaerts, Voelkischer Beobachter*, and periodicals, incl *Sueddeutsche Monatshefte*, Einheit. Of archival interest are the microfilms of the NSDAP Hauptarchiv (155 reels). Guides: *The Hoover Library Collections on Germany*, Hildegard R Boeninger (Stanford, 1955) and *Western* Europe, Agnes F Peterson (Stanford, 1970).

MA —BRANDEIS UNIVERSITY, Goldfarb Library, 415 South St, Waltham, 02154. Bessie Hahn, Dir
Notes: Nazi Documents Collection. Consists of 3 linear ft of documents and letters of major Nazi officials prior to and during World War II. A finding list to the documents is in Special Collections.

†NY —COLUMBIA UNIVERSITY LIBRARIES, Butler Library, Rare Book and Manuscript Library, 535 W 114 St, New York, 10027.
Notes: Papers relating to Prof Walter Lewis Dorn's work as special advisor to Gen Lucius D Clay on denazification of Germany.

GERMANY, EAST see German Democratic Republic—History

GERMANY, WEST see Germany

GERMER, ADOLPH

IL —UNIVERSITY OF ILLINOIS, URBANA/CHAMPAIGN, Library, Illinois Historical Survey Library, 1408 W Gregory Dr, 1A Library, Urbana, 61801.
Holdings: Vols 50 Cat Mss Pix Microforms
Notes: Important ms collections on the labor movement and radicalism incl: Adolph Germer, papers, 1918, 1928, 1930-31, 44 folders; Thomas J Morgan, 1880-1910, 64 folders, 19 volumes; John H Walker, papers, 1910-1955, 66 boxes. Guide to the collections published in 1976.

GERMS see Bacteriology

GERONIMI, CLYDE

CA —UNIVERSITY OF CALIFORNIA, LOS ANGELES, Theater Arts Library, Los Angeles, 90024. Edward Shreeves, Chairman, Bibliographers Group; Audree Malkin, Head, Theater Arts Library
Notes: A collection of original comic books, color comic books, storyboards, and posters illustrated by Clyde Geronimi.

GERONIMO

OK —US ARMY FIELD ARTILLERY SCHOOL LIBRARY, Morris Swett Library, Snow Hall, Fort Sill, 73503. Lester L Miller Jr, Chief Librn
Notes: Incl data on Fort Sill, Indian Territory, settlement of Kiowa, Apache and Commanche tribes, imprisonment of Geronimo, Oklahoma territory, settlement of Lawton. Unit histories, incl 10th Cavalry (Buffalo Soldiers, a black unit that built Fort Sill); working papers of Sheridan, Grierson and other commanders; Field Artillery School. Photographs on army subjects, Fort Sill, Indians, Indian Territory, settlement of Southwest Oklahoma.

GERONTOLOGY see Geriatrics and Gerontology

GERSHWIN, GEORGE, 1898-1937

DC —LIBRARY OF CONGRESS, Music Division, Washington, 20540.
Notes: Music mss, papers, pictorial material, and book and record collections of George Gershwin and the papers of Ira Gershwin. The recordings are in the Motion Picture, Broadcasting, and Recorded Sound Division.

GERSON, NOEL B.

MA —BOSTON UNIVERSITY, Mugar Memorial Library, Special Collections Dept, 771 Commonwealth Ave, Boston, 02215. Howard B Gotlieb, Dir
Holdings: Cat Mss Pix
Notes: Mss, Correspondence, etc collected in depth; incl publications by or about.

GERSTACKER, F. W. C.

MD —JOHNS HOPKINS UNIVERSITY, Milton S Eisenhower Library, Charles & 34 Sts, Baltimore, 21218. Ann S Gwyn, Assistant Dir for Special Collections
Holdings: / / Cat Mss
Notes: 145 letters, cataloged in manuscript room.

GESELL, ARNOLD

DC —LIBRARY OF CONGRESS, Manuscript Division, Washington, 20540. John C Broderick, Chief
Holdings: Cat Mss Pix
Notes: Mss, papers, records, etc.

GESNER, CONRAD

†IL —UNIVERSITY OF ILLINOIS, URBANA/CHAMPAIGN, Library, Rare Book Rm, Urbana, 61801.
Notes: Collection described in: *Catalog of the Rare Book Room,* (Boston: G K Hall, 1971).

GERSHWIN, IRA

DC —LIBRARY OF CONGRESS, Music Division, Washington, 20540.
Notes: Music mss, papers, pictorial material, and book and record collections of George Gershwin and the papers of Ira Gershwin. The recordings are in the Motion Picture, Broadcasting, and Recorded Sound Division.

GESTA ROMANORUM

OH —CLEVELAND PUBLIC LIBRARY, Fine Arts and Special Collections Department, 325 Superior Ave, Cleveland, 44114. Alice N Loranth, Head
Holdings: Vols 58 Cat Mss
Notes: Early and rare 15th-19th Century editions, translations and versions. Separate "edition" catalog maintained.
See also entry under Rare Books.

GETTYSBURG, BATTLE OF, 1863

PA —ADAMS COUNTY HISTORICAL SOCIETY, Drawer A, Gettysburg, 17325. Charles H Glatfelter, Dir
Holdings: Vols 50 Cat Mss Maps Pix
Notes: Emphasis on Adams County and the Gettysburg area. Strength of collection in mss, maps, and pictorial items.

PA —GETTYSBURG NATIONAL MILITARY PARK, Gettysburg, 17325. Thomas J Harrison, Cultural Resources Specialist
Holdings: Vols (3000) Cat Mss Maps Pix Slides Microforms
Budget: $400
Notes: Civil War, especially Campaign and Battle of Gettysburg, 1863. Incl pictures (18, 000) and slides (3500).

GEVA, TAMARA

MA —BOSTON UNIVERSITY, Mugar Memorial Library, Special Collections Dept, 771 Commonwealth Ave, Boston, 02215. Howard B Gotlieb, Dir
Holdings: Cat Mss
Notes: Mss, correspondence, incl publications by or about.

GEYER, GEORGIE ANNE

MA —BOSTON UNIVERSITY, Mugar Memorial Library, Special Collections Dept, 771 Commonwealth Ave, Boston, 02215. Howard B Gotlieb, Dir
Holdings: Cat Mss
Notes: Mss, correspondence, etc collected in depth; incl publications by or about.

GHANA

DC —HOWARD UNIVERSITY, Moorland-Spingarn Research Center, 500 Howard Place NW, Washington, 20059. Clifford L Muse, Jr, Acting Dir

MI —MICHIGAN STATE UNIVERSITY, International Library, Africana Collection, East Lansing, 48824. Eugene de Benko, Librn; Onuma Ezera, Bibliographer for Africana
Holdings: Vols (82,700) Cat Mss Maps Pix Slides Phonorecords Audiotapes Videotapes Filmstrips Microforms
Budget: ($78,000)
See also entry under Africa for full description.

WI —UNIVERSITY OF WISCONSIN, MADISON, Memorial Library, 728 State St, Madison, 53706. David Henige, Librn
Holdings: Cat Microforms
Notes: Collection consists of 90 microfilm reels of extant records of the Royal African Company (T7O series in the Public Record Office, London) together with several smaller collections of materials relating to the English presence on the Gold Coast in the 17th and 18th centuries. It is the most complete collection of its kind in the US. Various parts are described in David Henige, "Some Materials on the Early Guinea Coast in the United Kingdom," *African Research and Documentation,* no 11 (1976), pp 25-28. Also incl economics and social documents relating to the Belgian Congo particularly Katanga Province.

GHENT, TREATY OF, 1814

RI —BROWN UNIVERSITY, John Hay Library, 20 Prospect St, Providence, 02912. Mark N Brown, Cur Mss
Holdings: / / Mss
Notes: Papers of Jonathan Russell, merchant, diplomat, and Massachusetts Congressman. Brown Class of 1791. A collection of 7000 items containing a diary and a letterbook (1809-1813); records of US Commissioners at Ghent (1813-1814) and of the American Legation at Stockhom (1814-1816); correspondence and documents for the period 1795-1830; and notes, largely offical, when Russell was Charge d'Affaires at Paris (1810) and for 1814-1818 when he was Minister to Sweden and Norway and a member of the US Congress.

GHOST STORIES AND GHOSTS IN LITERATURE

DC —GEORGETOWN UNIVERSITY, Library, Special Collections Div, 37 & O Sts

GHOST STORIES AND GHOSTS IN LITERATURE (cont.)

NW, Washington, 20057. George M Barringer, Special Collections Librn; Nicholas B Sheetz, Mss Librn
Holdings: Mss Cat Pix
Notes: The papers of the Irish man-of-letters Sir Shane Leslie (1885-1971) containing letters, mss, diaries, notebooks, clippings, and photographs. Extensive correspondence by Margot Asquith, countess of Oxford and Asquith; Lady Violet Bonham-Carter; Burke Cochran; Lord Alfred Douglas; Moreton Frewen; Cardinal Gasquet; Vyvyan Holland; Lady Leonie Leslie; Sir Wilfrid Meynell; Sir Horace Plunkett; John Quinn; Frederick Rolfe (Baron Corvo); and Elizabeth Russell, among others. Also incl are research files on Sir Winston Churchill (Leslie's first cousin); Leonard Jerome; Maria Anne Fitzherbet (wife of King George IV); Ghosts and Ghost stories; and Eton College.

IN —INDIANA UNIVERSITY, Lilly Library, Seventh St, Bloomington, 47405. William R Cagle, Librn
Holdings: Cat Mss
Notes: First editions of early and modern books plus some 18th and 19th century penny dreadfuls. Mss incl some original illustrations for 19th and 20th century books.

PA —TEMPLE UNIVERSITY LIBRARIES, Special Collections Dept, Rare Books & Mss Section, Philadelphia, 19122. Thomas M Whitehead, Cur
Holdings: Vols (200) Cat
Notes: Holdings include contemporary printed books, first and later editions, of 18th and early 19th century gothic fiction. Significant strength in Matthew Gregory "Monk" Lewis books.

ON —QUEEN'S UNIVERSITY, Douglas Library, Kingston, K7L 5C4, Can. William F E Morley, Cur, Special Collections
Holdings: Vols 2050 Cat
Notes: The library has purchased the H P Lovecraft collection (225 vols) and has built up a most interesting collection in Gothic Fantasy and tales of the occult. Also, 6500 pulp magazines, uncat. (List available).

GHOST TOWNS

AZ —NORTHERN ARIZONA UNIVERSITY, Special Collection Library, CU Box 6022, Flagstaff, 86011. Peter M Whiteley, Coordr/Archivist; William Mullane, Librn
Notes: David Rees Collection. "Ghost Town of the Sky, History of Standard, Arizona," (a lumbering town near Show Low) unpublished typescript, 1965. Edited excerpts from letters by Robert Grand "Bert" Binnion concerning his adventures in Texas in the late 1800's.

UT —UTAH STATE UNIVERSITY, Merrill Library, Department of Special Collections & Archives, Logan, 84322. A J Simmonds, Curator; Jeanie F Simmonds, Archivist; Bradford R Cole, Mss Librn
Holdings: Vols 3000 Uncat
Notes: Books, pamphlets, maps and periodical volumes on Western mining camps and ghost towns.

GHOSTS

DC —GEORGETOWN UNIVERSITY, Library, Special Collections Div, 37 & O Sts NW, Washington, 20057. George M Barringer, Special Collections Librn; Nicholas B Sheetz, Mss Librn
Holdings: Mss Cat Pix
Notes: The papers of the Irish man-of-letters Sir Shane Leslie (1885-1971) containing letters, mss, diaries, notebooks, clippings, and photographs. Extensive correspondence by Margot Asquith, countess of Oxford and Asquith; Lady Violet Bonham-Carter; Burke Cochran; Lord Alfred Douglas; Moreton Frewen; Cardinal Gasquet; Vyvyan Holland; Lady Leonie Leslie; Sir Wilfrid Meynell; Sir Horace Plunkett; John Quinn; Frederick Rolfe (Baron Corvo); and Elizabeth Russell, among others. Also incl are research files on Sir Winston Churchill (Leslie's first cousin); Leonard Jerome; Maria Anne Fitzherbet (wife of King George IV); Ghosts and Ghost stories; and Eton College.

IL —UNIVERSITY OF ILLINOIS, URBANA/CHAMPAIGN, Library, University Archives, 19 Library, 1408 W Gregory Drive, Urbana, 61801. Maynard Brichford, University Archivist
Holdings: Vols (5000) Cat
Budget: ($7000)
Notes: The Mandeville Collection in Parapsychology and Occult Sciences. Titles in the Merten J Mandeville Collection are purchased by funds from an endowment provided specifically for the collection on its establishment in 1966 by Merten J Mandeville, Professor Emeritus of Management, who donated 400 vols from his personal library as the nucleus of the collection. There are currently about 5000 titles in the collection, supplemented by related materials in the general collection. Topics include astrology, extrasensory perception, yoga, magic, satanism, faith healing, hypnosis, Eastern religions, witchcraft, fortune telling, reincarnation, flying saucers, ghosts, dreams, numerology, graphology, and mysticism. Biographies and reference books are a part of the collection as are journals devoted to the scientific study of parapsychology.

NY —AMERICAN SOCIETY FOR PSYCHICAL RESEARCH LIBRARY, 5 W 73 St, New York, 10023. Rhea A White, Consultant to the Library
Holdings: Vols (7000) Cat Mss Pix
Budget: ($1500)
Notes: Incl books on spiritualism, as well as works in psychology, religion, philosophy, physics, anthropology, etc which have a possible bearing on parapsychology. An attempt is made to obtain all serious books on parapsychology in English.

OH —CLEVELAND PUBLIC LIBRARY, Fine Arts and Special Collections Department, 325 Superior Ave, Cleveland, 44114. Alice N Loranth, Head
Holdings: Vols (2500) Cat
Notes: Part of the Occult Sciences Collection. Emphasis is on historical treatises, folklore aspects and the classic texts pertaining to apparitions, ghosts, divinations, oracles, omens, witchcraft, magic and sorcery in various civilizations. Astrology, palmistry, psychical research and contemporary manifestations are almost entirely omitted.
See also entries under Folklore; Occult Sciences.

GHOSTS—FICTION see Ghost Stories and Ghosts in Literature

GIAIMO, REP. ROBERT N.

CT —UNIVERSITY OF CONNECTICUT, Library, Storrs, 06268. R H Schimmelpfeng, Dir of Special Collections
Notes: Congressman Robert N Giaimo's papers. Closed for research until 1986.

GIAUQUE, WILLIAM F.

CA —UNIVERSITY OF CALIFORNIA, BERKELEY, Bancroft Library, Manuscripts Division, Berkeley, 94720. James D Hart, Dir
Notes: Correspondence and papers relative to the history of modern chemistry.

GIBBES, LEWIS REEVE, 1810-1894

SC —COLLEGE OF CHARLESTON LIBRARY, Special Collections Dept, Charleston, 29401.
Notes: Papers, 1834-1898, contain biographical material about Lewis Reeve Gibbes; material relating to his study of medicine in Paris (1836-1837), correspondence, astronomical calculations, zoological observations, scrapbooks and newsclippings regarding his scientific work and his teaching career at the College of Charleston, and his collection of prints and maps, mostly collected during his stay in Europe. Also incl materials from the Elliott Society of Natural History.

GIBBINGS, ROBERT

CA —UNIVERSITY OF CALIFORNIA, LOS ANGELES, William Andrews Clark Memorial Library, 2520 Cimarron St, Los Angeles, 90018.
Notes: The papers and library of Eric Gill, incl business correspondence, accounts, Gill's diary in 27 volumes, many of his writings in typescript or holograph, and more than 500 original drawings. Also, the Joseph Kelly Vodrey Collection of Robert Gibbings material. Consists of Gibbings' books, illustrations, wood engravings, drawings, and mss. Director of the Golden Cockerel Press (1924-1933), Gibbings worked closely with Eric Gill. The collection is described in *The Clark Newsletter,* number 5 (1983).

GIBBONS

OR —OREGON REGIONAL PRIMATE RESEARCH CENTER, Library, 505 NW 185 Ave, Beaverton, 97006. Isabel McDonald, Librn
Holdings: Vols (765) Cat Audiotapes 16mm Films Microforms
Notes: Incl small collection of dissertations and theses.

GIBBONS, EUELL

MA —BOSTON UNIVERSITY, Mugar Memorial Library, Special Collections Dept, 771 Commonwealth Ave, Boston, 02215. Howard B Gotlieb, Dir
Holdings: Cat Mss Pix
Notes: Mss, correspondence, etc collected in depth; incl publications by or about.

GIBBONS, HERBERT ADAMS, 1880-1934

NJ —PRINCETON UNIVERSITY, Library, Manuscript Collection, Nassau St, Princeton, 08540. Jean F Preston, Cur
Holdings: // Cat Mss
Notes: Incl 14 boxes of papers.

GIBBONS, STELLA

MA —BOSTON UNIVERSITY, Mugar Memorial Library, Special Collections Dept, 771 Commonwealth Ave, Boston, 02215. Howard B Gotlieb, Dir
Holdings: Cat Mss

GIBBONS FAMILY, 1767-1897

NJ —RUTGERS, THE STATE UNIVERSITY OF NEW JERSEY, Alexander Library, Special Collections and Archives, College Ave & Huntington St, New Brunswick, 08903. Ronald L Becker, Cur of Manuscripts and Rare Books
Holdings: // Mss
Notes: Papers, etc (6 linear feet).

GIBBS, ALONZO, 1915-

NY —STATE UNIVERSITY OF NEW YORK, STONY BROOK, Melville Library, Dept of Special Collections, Stony Brook, 11794. Evert Volkersz, Head
Holdings: Vols 15 Cat

GIBSON, HUGH

CA —HOOVER INSTITUTION ON WAR, REVOLUTION & PEACE, Stanford University, Stanford, 94305. Milorad M Drachkovitch, Archivist
Holdings: // Mss
Notes: Papers, 1908-1954, of Hugh Gibson, diplomat. Correspondence, diaries, journals and official papers, relating in part to the surrender of King Leopold of Belgium in 1940 and to relief activities in Europe following World War II. Correspondents incl Perrin C Galpin, Herbert, Ignace Jan

GIBSON, HUGH (cont.)

Paderewski and Maurice Pate. Ca 80 ft. Finding aid in the repository.

GIBSON, JAMES F.

DC —LIBRARY OF CONGRESS, Prints & Photographs Div, Washington, 20540.
Notes: Civil War Photograph Collection incl photographs commissioned by Mathew Brady and others. Brady employed 20 photographers at the height of his operations. His staff incl Alexander and James Gardner, James F Gibson, and Thomas C Roche.

GIBSON, WILFRID WILSON

MA —AMHERST COLLEGE, Library, Amherst, 01002. John Lancaster, Special Collections Librn

NY —HOFSTRA UNIVERSITY, Library, 1000 Fulton Ave, Hempstead, 11550. Charles R Andrews, Dean of Library Services

OH —OHIO UNIVERSITY, Vernon R Alden Library, Department of Archives and Special Collections, Athens, 45701. Gary A Hunt, Head
Holdings: Vols 44 Cat
Notes: A comprehensive collection of Gibson's published books.

GIDE, ANDRE

NY —COLUMBIA UNIVERSITY LIBRARIES, Rare Book & Manuscript Library, 801 Butler Library, 535 W 114 St, New York, 10027. Kenneth A Lohf, Librn
Notes: The Justin O'Brien papers. Restricted use.

GIERS, MIKHAIL N.

CA —HOOVER INSTITUTION ON WAR, REVOLUTION & PEACE, Stanford University, Stanford, 94305. Milorad M Drachkovitch, Archivist
Holdings: // Mss
Notes: Papers of Mikhail N Giers, diplomat, member of the Russian Political Conference, Paris, 1919, and chief diplomatic representative of the Wrangel Government, 1920. Reports of Russian diplomatic representatives in various countries including the US and Great Britain and telegraphic correspondence between these representatives and the Paris Political Conference. 10 ft.

GIFFORD, JOE

LA —LOUISIANA STATE UNIVERSITY, SHREVEPORT, Library-Archives, 8515 Youree Dr, Shreveport, 71129. Patricia L Meador, Archivist & Asst Librn
Notes: Theatre and music is documented in the John Wray and Margaret Mary Young Theatre Collection, (5 linear ft), (1929-1981), the Joe Gifford Papers (1946-1960) (3 linear ft), the Shreveport Little Theatre Records (6 linear ft), the Nathaniel S Allen Papers (1860-1930), the records of the Shreveport Symphony (1948-1978) and oral history interviews on the topics. The archives collection also incl 60 linear ft of records (1949-1981) of Holiday-In-Dixie, Shreveport-Bossier's spring-time festival.

GIFT OF TONGUES see Glossolalia

GIFTBOOKS (ANNUALS, ETC.)

FL —FLORIDA STATE UNIVERSITY, Robert Manning Strozier Library, Special Collections Dept, Tallahassee, 32306. Opal M Free, Head, Special Collections
Holdings: Vols 259 Uncat
Notes: Christmas books as gifts. Noncirculating. No photocopying.

WI —UNIVERSITY OF WISCONSIN, MADISON, Memorial Library, British & American Language & Literature Collection, 728 State St, Madison, 53706. Yvonne Schofer, Bibliographer
Notes: Nineteenth Century American and English giftbooks and annuals. A collection of some 400 volumes, initiated by the late Professor Cairns and still being increased.

GIFTED CHILDREN

CO —UNIVERSITY OF COLORADO, Libraries, Western Historical Collections, Boulder, 80309.
Holdings: Cat Mss
Notes: Papers of the Inter-University Committee on the Superior Student, which was organized before the launching of Sputnik, when a conference of 48 American educators meeting at the University of Colorado in June of 1957 called for greater utilization of talented scholars and a central clearing house for honors programs. Funded by a grant from Carnegie Corporation, ICSS was headed by Joseph Cohen. It collected and disseminated information and conducted conferences and consultations from 1958 to 1965. The collection contains administrative files, and surveys, research findings and publications dealing with honors programs. It covers the period 1957-1965 and consists of 62 boxes. A typescript inventory is available.

PQ —HOPITAL SAINTE-JUSTINE POUR LES ENFANTS, Centre d'Information sur la Sante de l'Enfant, 3175 Cote Sainte-Catherine, Montreal, H3T 1C5, Can. Louis LucLecompte, Librn
Holdings: Vols (7000) Cat Audiotapes Videotapes 16mm Films Microforms
Budget: ($11,000)
Notes: 40 percent of collection in French.

GIGANTE, CHARLES

NM —UNIVERSITY OF NEW MEXICO, Fine Arts Library, Fine Art Bldg, Albuquerque, 87131. James B Wright, Librn
Notes: The Charles Gigante Collection of orchestral scores with string bowing.

GILBERT, EDWIN

MA —BOSTON UNIVERSITY, Mugar Memorial Library, Special Collections Dept, 771 Commonwealth Ave, Boston, 02215. Howard B Gotlieb, Dir
Holdings: Cat Mss //
Notes: Mss, correspondence, etc collected in depth; incl publications by or about.

GILBERT, HENRY

CT —YALE UNIVERSITY, Music Library, 98 Wall St, New Haven, 06520. Harold E Samuel, Librn
Notes: Personal papers and musical mss. *See also* entry under music, american.

GILBERT, MICHAEL

MA —BOSTON UNIVERSITY, Mugar Memorial Library, Special Collections Dept, 771 Commonwealth Ave, Boston, 02215. Howard B Gotlieb, Dir
Holdings: Cat Mss
Notes: Mss, correspondence, etc collected in depth; incl publications by or about.

GILBERT AND SULLIVAN

IN —INDIANA UNIVERSITY, Lilly Library, Seventh St, Bloomington, 47405. William R Cagle, Librn
Holdings: // Uncat
Notes: The Carroll A Wilson Collection, etc. First and early editions of librettos and scores, as well as playbills, posters, advertising cards, etc.

NY —GENERAL SOCIETY OF MECHANICS & TRADESMEN, Library, 20 W 44 St, New York, 10036. Margery Peters, Librn
Holdings: Vols 100 Cat
Notes: Alma Watson's Collection, donated in the name of the G&S Society.

NY —NEW YORK PUBLIC LIBRARY, Performing Arts Research Center, Billy Rose Theatre Collection, 111 Amsterdam Ave, New York, 10023. Dorothy L Swerdlove, Cur
Holdings: Cat

PA —UNIVERSITY OF PITTSBURGH, Special Collections Dept, Curtis Theatre Collection, 363 Hillman Library, Pittsburgh, 15260. Jeanette Blanco, Cur
Holdings: Vols (4000) Cat Mss Pix Slides Microforms VF
Notes: The legitimate theatre of plays, musicals and vaudeville, chiefly of New York City and Pittsburgh, from 1865, and other US, community, summer, college and foreign theatre. Incl 500,000 programs, 12, 000 pictures, 300 posters, the Oliver P Merriman Scrapbooks and 300 other scrapbooks, clippings and other ephemera. Vols incl over 3000 acting editions and playscripts. Separate collections: Ralph G Allen Burlesque Skits Collection; Michael Ellis Papers; William P Halstead Theatre Collection; Kenyon Family Papers; Philip Dunning Playscripts Collection; Pittsburgh Playhouse Records; Pittsburgh Savoyards Records. Noncirculating.

GILBERT FAMILY

CT —YALE UNIVERSITY, Box 1603A, Yale Station, New Haven, 06520.
Holdings: Mss
Notes: Papers, incl correspondence and journals of Mary Goodridge Gilbert, William H, and Charles M Gilbert, 1836-1900.

GILDER, RICHARD WATSON

NY —NEW YORK PUBLIC LIBRARY, Rare Books and Manuscripts Div, Fifth Ave & 42 St, New York, 10018. William L Joyce, Asst Dir; Susan E Davis, Cur of Mss
Holdings: Mss
Budget: ($7161)
Notes: Incl personal and literary mss, papers, etc.

NY —UNIVERSITY OF ROCHESTER, Rush Rhees Library, Department of Rare Books and Special Collections, Rochester, 14627. Peter Dzwonkoski, Librn
Holdings: Cat Mss
Notes: Correspondents include Robert Underwood Johnson, Will Carlton, Henry Mills Alden, Richard Watson Gilder; Howell's proof of article on Henrik Ibsen (1906).

GILDERSLEEVE, VIRGINIA C.

NY —COLUMBIA UNIVERSITY LIBRARIES, Rare Book & Manuscript Library, 801 Butler Library, 535 W 114 St, New York, 10027. Kenneth A Lohf, Librn
Holdings: Mss
Notes: Her papers and personal library. Incl 7500 items. Restricted use.

GILIAK LANGUAGE see Gilyak Language

GILKS, AL

CA —UNIVERSITY OF CALIFORNIA, LOS ANGELES, Theater Arts Library, Los Angeles, 90024. Edward Shreeves, Chairman, Bibliographers Group; Audree Malkin, Head, Theater Arts Library
Notes: Al Gilks (cinematographer) Collection: snapshots, motion picture production stills, clippings, awards, correspondence, scripts, and periodical articles relating to his career, 1930-1960.

GILL, ERIC

CA —UNIVERSITY OF CALIFORNIA, LOS ANGELES, William Andrews Clark Memorial Library, 2520 Cimarron St, Los Angeles, 90018.
Holdings: Cat Mss Pix
Notes: The papers and library of Eric Gill, incl business correspondence, accounts, Gill's diary in 27 volumes, many of his writings in typescript or holograph, and more than 500 original drawings. Also, the Joseph Kelly Vodrey Collection of Robert Gibbings material. Consists of Gibbings' books, illustrations, wood engravings, drawings, and mss. Director of the Golden

GILL, ERIC (cont.)

Cockerel Press (1924-1933), Gibbings worked closely with Eric Gill. The collection is described in *The Clark Newsletter,* number 5 (1983).

CA —UNIVERSITY OF SAN FRANCISCO, Richard A Gleeson Library, The Countess Bernardine Murphy Donohue Rare Book Room, San Francisco, 94117. D Steven Corey, Special Collections Librn
Holdings: Vols 400 Mss Pix
Notes: Very large collection containing much correspondence of Eric Gill, a number of original wood engravings, and over half of his total output of wood engravings represented by about 400 prints. Nearly all of the published works are present, incl many unique items.

DC —GEORGETOWN UNIVERSITY, Library, Special Collections Div, 37 & O Sts NW, Washington, 20057. George M Barringer, Special Collections Librn; Nicholas B Sheetz, Mss Librn
Holdings: Mss
Notes: The Archives of the Gallery of Living Catholic Authors was founded in 1932 by Sister Mary Joseph of the Sisters of Loretto to focus attention on modern Catholic literature, and to provide a depository for manuscripts, letters, photographs, and books by contemporary Catholic writers. Contains material by hundreds of writers, incl Hilaire Belloc, Roy Campbell, Padraic Colum, Eric Gill, Paul Horgan, Mary Lavin, Marie Belloc Lowndes, Kathleen Norris, Alred Noyes, Sheila Kaye-Smith, Sigrid Undset, and Evelyn Waugh, to name only a few.

IL —ILLINOIS STATE UNIVERSITY, Milner Library, Dept of Special Collections, Normal, 61761. Robert Sokan, Librn
Notes: First editions, limited editions, ephemera, etc.

BC —UNIVERSITY OF VICTORIA, McPherson Library, Victoria, V8W 3H5, Can.
Notes: Writer, artist.

ON —UNIVERSITY OF WATERLOO, Library, Waterloo, N2L 3G1, Can. Susan Bellingham, Special Collections Librn
Holdings: Vols 250 Cat
Notes: First editions, limited editions, ephemera.

GILLESPIE, ARCHIBALD HAMILTON, 1831-1873

CA —UNIVERSITY OF CALIFORNIA, LOS ANGELES, Research Library, Dept of Special Collections, 405 Hilgard Ave, Los Angeles, 90024. Edward Shreeves, Chairman, Bibliographers Group; David S Zeidberg, Head
Holdings: Mss Microforms
Notes: One linear foot of mss and correspondence relating to his career as President Polk's special messenger to John C Fremont and his participation in the American conquest of California. Available on microfilm only.

GILLETT, CLARENCE S.

CA —UNIVERSITY OF CALIFORNIA, LOS ANGELES, Research Library, Dept of Special Collections, 405 Hilgard Ave, Los Angeles, 90024. Edward Shreeves, Chairman, Bibliographers Group; David S Zeidberg, Head
Notes: 4 linear feet of mss, correspondence, and printed material related to his efforts to relocate Japanese Americans during and after World War II.

GILLETTE, WILLIAM HOOKER, 1853-1937

†CT —CONNECTICUT STATE LIBRARY, Hartford, 06106.

CT —STOWE-DAY LIBRARY, 77 Forest St, Hartford, 06105. Diana J Royce, Librn
Holdings: Vols (15,000) Cat Mss Pix
Notes: 150,000 cataloged mss and publications concerning architecture, decorative arts, history and literature of the period 1840-1900, with emphasis on Nook Farm, Mark Twain, Harriet Beecher Stowe, Calvin E Stowe, Charles Dudley Warner, William Hooker Gillette, Isabella Beecher Hooker. Incl 5000 pictures.

GILLIS, COMMODORE JOHN P.

DE —HISTORICAL SOCIETY OF DELAWARE, Library, 505 Market St Mall, Wilmington, 19801. Barbara E Benson, Library Dir
Holdings: Cat Mss
Notes: Collection incl papers and other mss materials.

GILLIS, DON

TX —NORTH TEXAS STATE UNIVERSITY, Audio Center, Box 5188, NT Station, Denton, 76203. Morris Martin, Music Librn
Notes: Tape recordings of all of Don Gillis's compositions, some out of print or never commercially issued (50 reels) performances by Toscanini, Edward Vito, David Guilet, Doc Severinson; papers (correspondence, artifacts, scrapbooks, program notes); mss (incl scores and unpublished autobiography); tape recordings of performances and interviews with/about conductor Arturo Toscanini: NBC Radio series "Toscanini, the Man Behind the Legend" (171 reels).

GILLRAY, JAMES, 1757-1815

DC —LIBRARY OF CONGRESS, Prints & Photographs Div, Washington, 20540.
Notes: The British Cartoon collection contains 10,000 British political caricatures and satires dating from the 17th through mid 19th centuries. Incl the work of Henry Bunbury, George Cruikshank, Issac Cruikshank, Matthew Darly, James Gillray, and Thomas Rowlandson.

MD —UNIVERSITY OF MARYLAND, BALTIMORE COUNTY, Albin O Kuhn Library and Gallery, 5401 Wilkens Ave, Baltimore, 21228. Ann Copeland, Special Collections Librn
Holdings: Vols (800) // Cat Pix
Notes: The Edgar and Kathleen Merkle Collection of 19th-century English graphic satire centers around the work of George E Cruikshank. Other artists represented incl Rowlandson, Gillray, Hogarth, and "Phiz". Rare items incl. Cruikshank's lavish hand-colored films *Scraps and Sketches* (1818).

MA —BOSTON PUBLIC LIBRARY, Print Collection, Dartmouth St at Copley Sq, Boston, 02117. Sinclair H Hitchings, Keeper of Prints
Holdings: Cat
Notes: The caricature collection incl 300 American prints (colonial period to 1900), 65 of these are by Thomas Nast; 400 English prints (mostly 18th century) many by Thomas Rowlandson and James Gillray; and several thousand 19th century French items, large numbers of them by Daumier. Items are cataloged by artisit when known; or else by publisher or country. In addition, the American caricatures are arranged chronologically.

RI —BROWN UNIVERSITY, John Hay Library, 20 Prospect St, Providence, 02912. Mark N Brown, Cur Mss
Holdings: Uncat Mss Pix
Budget: ($250)
Notes: Paul Revere Bullard Collection of 185 19th century caricatures by English, French, German, Russian, and Spanish cartoonists who lampooned Napoleon throughout his career, plus 220 similar caricatures from other sources. The major English artists represented are: James Gillray, George and Isaac Cruikshank, Thomas Rowlandson, and George Woodward. Some items also part of Anne S K Brown Military Collection at Brown University.

GILMAN, CHARLOTTE PERKINS, 1860-1935

MA —RADCLIFFE COLLEGE, Arthur & Elizabeth Schlesinger Library on the History of Women in America, 3 James St, Cambridge, 02138. Patricia Miller King, Dir; Eva Moseley, Cur of Mss
Holdings: // Cat Mss Pix Microforms
Notes: This is the definitive collection, including correspondence, diaries, writings, drawings, photographs, newsclippings, etc of this feminist lecturer, author and theoretician. Collection on microfiche. Inventory published by G K Hall; see Hamilton family for citation.

WI —UNIVERSITY OF WISCONSIN, MADISON, Memorial Library, British & American Language & Literature Collection, 728 State St, Madison, 53706. Yvonne Schofer, Bibliographer
Holdings: Vols 2200 Mss Microforms Documents Periodicals
Notes: A collection of primary and secondary materials for nine major American women writers: Anne Bradstreet; Louisa May Alcott, Emily Dickinson, Kate Chopin, Mary Williams Freeman, Margaret Fuller, Sarah Orne Jewett, Charlotte Perkins Gilman, Harriet Beecher Stowe. Primary materials also collected for a list of less well known authors together with manuscripts and archives of letters of special research interest. Variety of holdings: fiction, poetry, drama, biography and autobiography, letters, memoirs, diaries, travel, domestic economy and other kinds of writings by women mostly of the 19th century. Held in Dept of Rare Books and Special Collections.

GILMAN, DANIEL COIT

MD —JOHNS HOPKINS UNIVERSITY, Milton S Eisenhower Library, Charles & 34 Sts, Baltimore, 21218. Ann S Gwyn, Assistant Dir for Special Collections
Holdings: Vols 60 Cat Mss
Notes: Incl numerous mss, letters, correspondence (5000), and journals. Cataloged in manuscript room.

GILMAN, DOROTHY

MA —BOSTON UNIVERSITY, Mugar Memorial Library, Special Collections Dept, 771 Commonwealth Ave, Boston, 02215. Howard B Gotlieb, Dir
Holdings: Cat Mss
Notes: Mss, correspondence, etc collected in depth; incl publications by or about.

GILPIN, LAURA, 1891-1979

TX —AMON CARTER MUSEUM, 3501 Camp Bowie Blvd, PO Box 2365, Fort Worth, 76113. Jan K Muhlert, Dir; Marni Sandweiss, Cur of Photographs
Holdings: Cat Pix Mss
Notes: Laura Gilpin (1891-1979) was equally adept as a portraitist, an architectural photographer, a chronicler of Southwestern Indian life, and a landscape photographer. Her bequest of her photographic estate to the Amon Carter Museum includes 26,000 negatives, 20,000 prints, a substantial photographic library, and extensive personal correspondence.

GILROY, HARRY D.

MA —BOSTON UNIVERSITY, Mugar Memorial Library, Special Collections Dept, 771 Commonwealth Ave, Boston, 02215. Howard B Gotlieb, Dir
Holdings: Mss

GILYAK LANGUAGE

WA —UNIVERSITY OF WASHINGTON LIBRARIES, Rare Books, Special Collections Dept, Seattle, 98195. Sandra Kroupa, Librn
Notes: Part of a set of Siberian primers prepared in the early 1930s by Soviet ethnographers. Some are first attempts to transcribe Siberian languages. All are in Latin phonetic script, not in Cyrillic.

GINSBERG, ALLEN, 1926-

CA —UNIVERSITY OF CALIFORNIA, BERKELEY, Bancroft Library, Manuscripts

GINSBERG, ALLEN, 1926- (cont.)

Division, Berkeley, 94720. James D Hart, Dir
Notes: Letters from Ginsberg in various collections.

MO —WASHINGTON UNIVERSITY, Libraries, Special Collections Dept, Campus Box 1061, St Louis, 63130.
Notes: A small but significant collection.

NV —UNIVERSITY OF NEVADA, RENO, University Library, Special Collections Dept, Reno, 89557. Robert E Blesse, Head
Holdings: // Vols (128) Cat
Notes: Includes individual works by author in all editions including translations; also prefaces, introductions, published correspondence, appearances in anthologies, periodicals, etc. Bibliographical research collection, part of Modern Authors Collection. Other appearances 1000 cataloged.

NY —COLUMBIA UNIVERSITY LIBRARIES, Rare Book & Manuscript Library, 801 Butler Library, 535 W 114 St, New York, 10027. Kenneth A Lohf, Librn
Holdings: Mss
Notes: Papers, incl mss, letters, reviews, etc. Incl 3000 items. Restricted use.

†NY —COLUMBIA UNIVERSITY LIBRARIES, Butler Library, Rare Book and Manuscript Library, 535 W 114 St, New York, 10027.
Notes: Papers of Louis Ginsberg, incl material relating to his son Allen Ginsberg, with tapes of poetry readings and conversations between father and son.

NY —STATE UNIVERSITY OF NEW YORK, STONY BROOK, Melville Library, Dept of Special Collections, Stony Brook, 11794. Evert Volkersz, Head
Holdings: Cat Mss

RI —BROWN UNIVERSITY, John Hay Library, Harris Collection, Prospect St, Providence, 02912. Rosemary L Cullen, Cur
Holdings: Vols (200,000) Cat Mss Pix Phonorecords Microforms
Budget: ($15,000)
Notes: The Harris Collection of American Poetry and Plays is principally composed of American and Canadian poetry and plays, 17th century-date. Extensive holdings in songsters, gift books and annuals, hymnals, pageants, broadside verse, carriers' addresses, women poets, juvenile poetry, (incl Mother Goose and *The Night Before* Christmas), sheet music with lyrics, small press publications, fine printing, black poets, "little magazines," Yiddish-American literature. All movements or schools of American poetry are represented. Incl first editions of most American poets and playwrights, notably Whitman, Poe, Wallace Stevens, Eugene O'Neill, Edward Albee, Ezra Pound, T S Eliot, William Carlos Williams, Amy Lowell, Phyllis Wheatley, Robert Frost, Allen Ginsberg, Bliss Carman, and Stephen Foster sheet music. Also incl the Saunders Walt Whitman Collection (1300 vols); the LangdonCollection of Pageants (250 vols); the Asa Cushman Collection of plays in ms and prompt copies; the MacDougall Collection of Psalters and Hymnals; 4000 plays issued by Walter H Baker Co, Boston (1890-1957); the Vaxer Collection of Yiddish Poetry, Plays and Music (1700 vols). Collections incl 200,000 vols, 30,000 broadsides, 55,000 mss, 170,000 pieces of sheet music, 450 phonorecords, and 375 microfilm reels. See *Dictionary Catalog of the Harris Collection of American Poetry and Plays* (Boston: G K Hall, 1972), 13 vols; *Supplement* (1977), 3 vols. See also, *American Poetry,* 1609-1900, *A Collection on Microfilm, Segment I* (1609-1820); *Segment II* (1821-1850); *Segment III* (1851-1870) (Woodbridge, Conn: Research Publications). Separate catalog.

BC —SIMON FRASER UNIVERSITY, Library, Burnaby, V5A 1S6, Can. Percilla Groves, Special Collections Librn
Holdings: Cat Mss
Notes: Letters written to Eshleman by Allen Ginsberg (8 pp), William Carlos Williams and Florence Williams (5 pp), Robert Duncan (4 pp), and Edward Dorn (5 pp), while Eshleman was editor of *Folio* (1959-1961). Tss from Gregory Corso (2 pp), Louis Zukofsky (8 pp), Michael Rumaker (3 pp).

BC —UNIVERSITY OF VICTORIA, McPherson Library, Victoria, V8W 3H5, Can.

GINSBERG, LOUIS

†NY —COLUMBIA UNIVERSITY LIBRARIES, Butler Library, Rare Book and Manuscript Library, 535 W 114 St, New York, 10027.
Notes: Papers, incl material relating to his son Allen Ginsberg, with tapes of poetry readings and conversations between father and son.

GIOLITO DE FERRARI, GABRIEL

WI —UNIVERSITY OF WISCONSIN, MADISON, Memorial Library, Rare Books Collection, 728 State St, Madison, 53706. Gretchen Lagana, Cur
Holdings: Vols 120// Cat
Notes: Giolito Collection. Approximately 120 titles of 16th century Italian imprints of Greek and Latin classics. Restricted use: Rare Department.

GIONO, JEAN

IN —INDIANA UNIVERSITY, Lilly Library, Seventh St, Bloomington, 47405. William R Cagle, Librn
Holdings: Cat Mss
Notes: Letters of Jean Giono, 1895-1970; and manuscript of his *Angelique* (1028 items).

GIOVANNI, NIKKI

MA —BOSTON UNIVERSITY, Mugar Memorial Library, Special Collections Dept, 771 Commonwealth Ave, Boston, 02215. Howard B Gotlieb, Dir
Holdings: Cat Mss Pix
Notes: Mss, correspondence, etc collected in depth; incl publications by or about.

GIPSIES see Gypsies and Gypsy Lore

GIRARD, STEPHEN

PA —AMERICAN PHILOSOPHICAL SOCIETY, Library, 105 S Fifth St, Philadelphia, 19106. Edward C Carter II, Librn
Holdings: Cat Microforms
Notes: The Stephen Girard Papers, 650 reels of microfilm.

GIRAUDOUX, JEAN

PA —PENNSYLVANIA STATE UNIVERSITY, Fred Lewis Pattee Library, Special Collections Dept, University Park, 16802. Charles Mann, Chief, Special Collections
Holdings: Vols 230 // Uncat Mss
Notes: The collection of 230 volumes includes many first and fine editions; there are also letters, manuscripts and proofs.

GIRL SCOUTS OF THE U.S.A.

NY —GIRL SCOUTS OF THE USA, Library Archives, 830 Third Ave, New York, 10022.
Holdings: Vols (3000)
Budget: ($2000)
Notes: Emphasis on adult education. No photocopying.

NY —ROCKEFELLER UNIVERSITY, Rockefeller Archive Center, Hillcrest, Pocantico Hills, North Tarrytown, 10591. Joseph W Ernst, Dir; J William Hess, Assoc Dir
Notes: Papers relative to the Rockefeller Family, Foundations, University, and other specific enterprises and contributions to particular areas of social, physical, educational, and historic reform, preservation, conservation, or development. Extensive records of administrative, financial, physical, or intellectual relationships.

GIRLS—EDUCATION see Education of Women

GIRLS—EMPLOYMENT see Children—Employment; Youth__Employment

GIROUX, ANDRE

ON —NATIONAL LIBRARY OF CANADA, 395 Wellington St, Ottawa, K1A 0N4, Can. Andre Preibish, Dir
Notes: Literary Manuscripts collection contains papers of several important Canadian authors writing in English and/or French eg Clare Bice (1909-1976), noted author and illustrator of children's books; Andre Giroux, novelist, writer for television and broadcaster; Roger Lemelin, well-known author of Au pied de la pente douce, Les Plouffe, and Pierre le magnifique; Gabrielle Roy (1909-1983), author of many novels, including Bonheur d'occasion, La Petite Poule d'Eau and Rue Deschambault; Laura Goodman Salverson (1890-1970), writer, public speaker and teacher; Phyllis Webb, poet.

GISBORNE, JOHN

NC —DUKE UNIVERSITY, William R Perkins Library, Durham, 27706. Elvin E Strowd, University Librn
Notes: The Shelley-Goodwin Collection of Lord Abinger is a microfilm copy of the Shelley and Godwin collection. Lord Abinger's entire manuscript collection, representing the last portion of the papers of Sir Percy Florence Shelley which is still in private hands, has been reproduced on 16 reels of film. The Bodleian Library is the only other location for this film.

GISH, LILLIAN

DC —LIBRARY OF CONGRESS, Washington, 20540.
Notes: Her personal papers, film and theatrical scripts and memorabilia.

GISSING, GEORGE

CT —YALE UNIVERSITY, Box 1603A, Yale Station, New Haven, 06520.
Holdings: Cat Mss

NY —CARL H PFORZHEIMER LIBRARY, 41 E 42 St, New York, 10017. Mihai H Handrea, Librn
Holdings: Cat Mss Pix
Notes: English Literature from Caxton to 1700; first editions of 18th and 19th centuries, incl mss material on Shelley and his circle; fine presses (Bruce Rogers); George Gissing; women writers 1790-1840, (Mary Wollstonecraft, Mary Hays, Lady Blessington).

GITLOW, BENJAMIN, 1891-1965

CA —HOOVER INSTITUTION ON WAR, REVOLUTION & PEACE, Stanford University, Stanford, 94305. Milorad M Drachkovitch, Archivist
Holdings: Mss
Notes: Papers of Benjamin Gitlow, a leader of the Communist Party in the US and later an anti-communist, incl writings, correspondence, minutes of meetings, clippings, and printed matter, 1918-1960, relating to communism and socialism in the US and Europe. 17 ms boxes.

NC —UNIVERSITY OF NORTH CAROLINA, CHARLOTTE, J Murrey Atkins Library, UNCC Station, Charlotte, 28223. Robert F Brabham Jr, Special Collections Librn
Holdings: Uncat Mss
Notes: Papers of Benjamin Gitlow, a leader in the establishment of the CPUSA and later an anti-communist. Incl correspondence, speeches, writings, clippings, and printed material, 1920-1960. Bulk of the collection (1945-60) documents Gitlow's anti-communist activities.

GLACIERS AND GLACIOLOGY

CO —WORLD DATA CENTER A: GLACIOLOGY (SNOW AND ICE), CIRES, University of Colorado, Boulder, 80309. Ann M Brennan, Librn
Holdings: Vols 10,000 Maps Pix Microforms
Budget: $2000
Notes: Glaciology, all forms of snow and ice. Bibliographic information will be contained in a data file which will be fully searchable. Partially cataloged (UDC).

IL —UNIVERSITY OF ILLINOIS, URBANA/CHAMPAIGN, Library, Geology Library, 223 Natural History Bldg, Urbana, 61801. Dederick Ward, Librn
Holdings: Vols (105,186) Cat Maps Microforms

MA —BOSTON COLLEGE LIBRARIES, Catherine B O'Connor Geophysics Library, Weston Observatory, Weston, 02193. F Clifford McElroy, Science Librn
Holdings: Vols (10,231) Cat Maps Microforms
Budget: ($10,000)
Notes: This collection is being absorbed into the general collection.

NY —AMERICAN MUSEUM OF NATURAL HISTORY, Library Services Dept, Central Park W & 79th St, New York, 10024. Nina J Root, Chairwoman; Mary Genett, Asst Librn for Reference Services
Notes: Especially strong in periodical literature.

GLADDEN, WASHINGTON

OH —RUTHERFORD B HAYES LIBRARY, 1337 Hayes Ave, Fremont, 43420. Watt P Marchman, Dir
Notes: Correspondence in the Lyman-Lincoln Collection.

GLASGOW, ELLEN

NV —UNIVERSITY OF NEVADA, RENO, University Library, Special Collections Dept, Reno, 89557. Robert E Blesse, Head
Holdings: // Vols (36) Cat Other appearances 25 Cat
Notes: Includes individual works by author in all editions including translations; also prefaces, introductions, published correspondence, appearances in anthologies, periodicals, etc. Bibliographical research collection, part of Modern Authors Collection.

VA —UNIVERSITY OF VIRGINIA, Alderman Library, Manuscripts Dept, Charlottesville, 22901. Edmund Berkeley Jr, Cur
Holdings: Cat Mss Pix
Notes: Extensive collection of mss and printed materials.

GLASS

IN —ALLEN COUNTY PUBLIC LIBRARY, 900 Webster St, Fort Wayne, 46802. Paul Deane, Reader Services Dept Head; Kay Lynn Isca, Art Music & AV Dept Head
Holdings: Vols 1257 Cat Pix

IN —PURDUE UNIVERSITY LIBRARIES, Special Collections Dept, West Lafayette, 47907. Keith Dowden, Asst Dir, Special Collections
Holdings: Vols (254) Cat
Notes: The Bitting Glass Collection, incl materials on the technology of glass-making.

MA —MASSACHUSETTS INSTITUTE OF TECHNOLOGY, Institute Archives, Special Collections, Cambridge, 02139.
Notes: Gaffield collection on glass and glassmaking.

NY —NEW YORK STATE COLLEGE OF CERAMICS AT ALFRED UNIVERSITY, Scholes Library, Harder Hall, Alfred, 14802. Bruce E Connolly, Library Dir
Holdings: Vols (70,000) Cat Mss Slides Microforms
Budget: ($134,000)
Notes: Very specialized collection incl all phases of the arts and sciences related to ceramics. Incl 1112 subscriptions.

NY —CORNING MUSEUM OF GLASS LIBRARY, Corning, 14831. Norma P H Jenkins, Librn
Holdings: Vols (30,000) Cat Slides Videotapes Microforms
Notes: Extensive and comprehensive coverage of the art, archaeology, history and early manufacture of glass, with supporting materials in art, archaeology, and the decorative arts. Collection incl some 1800 manufacturers' trade catalogs on microfiche, 10,000 periodical vols and documents. 130 videotapes, 1000 microforms. Some incumabula. Research library primarily for use on the premises.

OH —OWENS-ILLINOIS, Information Research Department, One Seagate, Toledo, 43666. Patricia Ajemian, Librn
Holdings: Vols (24,000) Cat Pix Microforms
Notes: Requests for use are handled on an individual basis. Incl information on packaging.

OH —JOHN MCINTIRE PUBLIC LIBRARY, 220 N Fifth St, Zanesville, 43701. Peg Harmon, Librn
Holdings: Vols 150 Cat

PA —FRANKLIN INSTITUTE LIBRARY, 20 & The Parkway, Philadelphia, 19103. Miriam Padusis, Dir; Charles Wilt, Readers Servs Librn
Holdings: Vols (300,000) Cat Maps Pix Microforms

PA —WILLET STAINED GLASS STUDIO, Library, 10 E Moreland Ave, Philadelphia, 19118. Helene H Weis, Librn
Holdings: Vols 1000 Cat Pix Microforms
Budget: ($180,000)
Notes: Stained glass and related subjects; leaded stained glass; historic and contemporary stained glass; new techniques (faceted, laminated, etc); original art work. The studio is the largest atelier making stained glass windows. Collection contains picture file of clippings, files of original designs, etc.

GLASS—HISTORY

LA —R W NORTON ART GALLERY, Library, 4747 Creswell Ave, Shreveport, 71106. Jerry M Bloomer, Librn
Holdings: Vols 100 Cat
Notes: Primarily histories of glass making in America and Europe and books of interest to collectors.

MA —OLD STURBRIDGE VILLAGE, Research Library, Sturbridge, 01566. Theresa Rini Percy, Librn
Holdings: Cat Mss Pix
Notes: New England glassware and manufacture to 1850.

NY —CORNING MUSEUM OF GLASS LIBRARY, Corning, 14831. Norma P H Jenkins, Librn
Holdings: Vols (30,000) Cat Slides Videotapes Microforms
Notes: Extensive and comprehensive coverage of the art, archaeology, history and early manufacture of glass, with supporting materials in art, archaeology, and the decorative arts. Collection incl some 1800 manufacturers' trade catalogs on microfiche, 10,000 periodical vols and documents. 130 videotapes, 1000 microforms. Some incumabula. Research library primarily for use on the premises.

OH —TOLEDO-LUCAS COUNTY PUBLIC LIBRARY, 325 Michigan St, Toledo, 43624. Mary B Hubbard, Head, Science-Technology Dept; Paula Baker, Head, Fine Arts Dept
Holdings: Vols (2200) Cat Pix
Notes: Antique and art glass collections are in Fine Arts Dept. Glass technology and manufacture are in Science-Technology Dept.

WV —HUNTINGTON ART GALLERIES, Library, Art Reference Library, Park Hills, Huntington, 25701. Mary McKernon, Librn
Holdings: Vols (3500) Cat Pix Slides
Notes: Large collection of pamphlets on glass and glass memorabilia. Includes literature on venetian, pressed, patterned, carnival, victorian, and depression glasses.

GLASS, CARTER

VA —UNIVERSITY OF VIRGINIA, Alderman Library, Manuscripts Dept, Charlottesville, 22901. Edmund Berkeley Jr, Cur
Holdings: Cat Mss Pix
Notes: Personal, political, and business papers.

GLASS, CUT see Cut Glass

GLASS, JOANNA

AB —UNIVERSITY OF CALGARY, Libraries, Special Collections Div, 2500 University Dr, Calgary, T2N 1N4, Can.
Notes: Papers, mss, etc. The ms collections are complemented by a book collection of some 5000 vols.

GLASS, MAUDE EMILY, 1897-

CA —UNIVERSITY OF CALIFORNIA, LOS ANGELES, Research Library, Dept of Special Collections, 405 Hilgard Ave, Los Angeles, 90024. Edward Shreeves, Chairman, Bibliographers Group; David S Zeidberg, Head
Holdings: Mss
Notes: 2.5 linear feet of mss and correspondence relating to her friendship with Ruth St Denis and with the Wilshire family.

GLASS, ORNAMENTAL

NY —CORNING MUSEUM OF GLASS LIBRARY, Corning, 14831. Norma P H Jenkins, Librn
Holdings: Vols (30,000) Cat Slides Videotapes Microforms
Notes: Extensive and comprehensive coverage of the art, archaeology, history and early manufacture of glass, with supporting materials in art, archaeology, and the decorative arts. Collection incl some 1800 manufacturers' trade catalogs on microfiche, 10,000 periodical vols and documents. 130 videotapes, 1000 microforms. Some incumabula. Research library primarily for use on the premises.

OH —TOLEDO-LUCAS COUNTY PUBLIC LIBRARY, 325 Michigan St, Toledo, 43624. Mary B Hubbard, Head, Science-Technology Dept; Paula Baker, Head, Fine Arts Dept
Holdings: Vols (2200) Cat Pix
Notes: Subject located primarily in Fine Arts Dept.

WV —HUNTINGTON ART GALLERIES, Library, Art Reference Library, Park Hills, Huntington, 25701. Mary McKernon, Librn
Holdings: Vols (3500) Cat Pix Slides
Notes: Large collection of pamphlets on glass and glass memorabilia. Includes literature on venetian, pressed, patterned, carnival, victorian, and depression glasses.

GLASS, PHILIP

TX —NORTH TEXAS STATE UNIVERSITY, Audio Center, Box 5188, NT Station, Denton, 76203. Morris Martin, Music Librn
Notes: Emphasis on Contemporary and Avant Garde music. More than 450 musical compositions (mostly manuscript, many multi-media). This is an archive of materials published in, or submitted for publication to, the contemporary music magazine *Source, the Music of the Avant Garde* which appeared from 1967-1977 (although bearing dates only through 1973). Composers represented are the editors (Larry Austin and Stanley Lunetta), John Cage, Steve Reich, Pauline Oliveros, Harry Partch, Morton Feldman, Lukas Foss, Barney Childs, David Cope, Peter Garland, Philip Glass, Ben Johnston, Alcides Lanza, Alvin Lucier, David Rosenboom, Dane Rudhyar, and Nicolas Slonimsky.

GLASS, STAINED see Glass Painting and Staining

GLASS MANUFACTURE AND TECHNOLOGY

CT —EMHART INDUSTRIES, Hartford Div, Library, 123 Day Hill Rd, Windsor, 06095.

GLASS MANUFACTURE AND TECHNOLOGY (cont.)

John P Mungovan, Dir of Engineering
Holdings: Vols 4000 Cat Mss Maps Pix Slides Phonorecords 16mm Films
Budget: $3500
Notes: Incl 2000 pictures, 500 maps, 100 slides, 100 phonorecords, and 50 films.

IN —PURDUE UNIVERSITY LIBRARIES, Special Collections Dept, West Lafayette, 47907. Keith Dowden, Asst Dir, Special Collections
Holdings: Vols (254) Cat
Notes: The Bitting Glass Collection, incl materials on the technology of glass-making.

MA —MASSACHUSETTS INSTITUTE OF TECHNOLOGY, Institute Archives, Special Collections, Cambridge, 02139.
Notes: Gaffield collection on glass and glassmaking.

NY —NEW YORK STATE COLLEGE OF CERAMICS AT ALFRED UNIVERSITY, Scholes Library, Harder Hall, Alfred, 14802. Bruce E Connolly, Library Dir
Holdings: Vols (70,000) Cat Mss Slides Microforms
Budget: ($134,000)
Notes: Very specialized collection incl all phases of the arts and sciences related to ceramics. Incl 1112 subscriptions.

NY —CORNING MUSEUM OF GLASS LIBRARY, Corning, 14831. Norma P H Jenkins, Librn
Holdings: Vols (30,000) Cat Slides Videotapes Microforms
Notes: Extensive and comprehensive coverage of the art, archaeology, history and early manufacture of glass, with supporting materials in art, archaeology, and the decorative arts. Collection incl some 1800 manufacturers' trade catalogs on microfiche, 10,000 periodical vols and documents. 130 videotapes, 1000 microforms. Some incumabula. Research library primarily for use on the premises.

NY —SYBRON CORP, Pfaudler Co, Technical Library, PO Box 1600, Rochester, 14603. Candice Johnson, Librn
Holdings: Vols (1700) Cat Slides Phonorecords Microforms
Notes: Glass and ceramic science.

OH —OWENS-ILLINOIS, Information Research Department, One Seagate, Toledo, 43666. Patricia Ajemian, Librn
Holdings: Vols 23,000 Cat Audiotapes Microforms
Notes: Collection incl laboratory notebooks and reports covering project work.

OH —TOLEDO-LUCAS COUNTY PUBLIC LIBRARY, 325 Michigan St, Toledo, 43624. Mary B Hubbard, Head, Science-Technology Dept; Paula Baker, Head, Fine Arts Dept
Holdings: Vols (2200) Cat Pix
Notes: Subject located primarily in Science-Technology Dept.

PA —FRANKLIN INSTITUTE LIBRARY, 20 & The Parkway, Philadelphia, 19103. Miriam Padusis, Dir; Charles Wilt, Readers Servs Librn
Holdings: Vols (300,000) Cat Maps Pix Microforms

PA —CARNEGIE LIBRARY OF PITTSBURGH, Science & Technology Dept, 4400 Forbes Ave, Pittsburgh, 15213. Catherine M Brosky, Dept Head
Holdings: Vols (380,000) Cat Maps Microforms
Budget: ($240,000)
Notes: Manufacturers directories, monographs, standards and specifications, periodicals, indexes, bibliographies, and symposia.

GLASS MANUFACTURE AND TECHNOLOGY—HISTORY

NJ —GLASSBORO STATE COLLEGE, Savitz Library, Stewart Room, Glassboro, 08028. Clara Kirner, Special Collection Librn
Holdings: Vols 41 Cat Mss
Notes: Has collection of 200 glass pieces also.

GLASS PAINTERS AND STAINERS see Glass Painting and Staining

GLASS PAINTING AND STAINING

IN —PURDUE UNIVERSITY LIBRARIES, Special Collections Dept, West Lafayette, 47907. Keith Dowden, Asst Dir, Special Collections
Holdings: Vols (254) Cat
Notes: The Bitting Glass Collection, incl materials on the technology of glass-making.

NY —HISTORICAL SOCIETY OF EARLY AMERICAN DECORATION, 19 Dove St, Albany, 12210. Doris Fry, Dir; Laura Olf, Librn
Holdings: Cat Pix Slides
Notes: The Library is housed with the Museum Collection of the Society. Incl examples of 19th century American country painting on tin, stenciling on wood and tin, bronzing decoration on wood, English stencilled tin and wood, bronzed items, painted objects, reverse painting on glass and examples of other decorating techniques of the period. Also included is a large collection of painted recordings of designs from early articles. Many of these were done by Esther Stevens Brazer in the 1930s. Another large collection has been added since that time. The library material is related to this interest. See *The Decorator*, official publication of the Historical Society of Early American Decoration.

NY —CORNING MUSEUM OF GLASS LIBRARY, Corning, 14831. Norma P H Jenkins, Librn
Holdings: Vols (30,000) Cat Slides Videotapes Microforms
Notes: Extensive and comprehensive coverage of the art, archaeology, history and early manufacture of glass, with supporting materials in art, archaeology, and the decorative arts. Collection incl some 1800 manufacturers' trade catalogs on microfiche, 10,000 periodical vols and documents. 130 videotapes, 1000 microforms. Some incumabula. Research library primarily for use on the premises.

NY —THE CLOISTERS, Metropolitan Museum of Art (Branch), Fort Tryon Park, New York, 10040. Suse C Childs, Librn
Holdings: Vols (5000) Cat Mss Pix Slides
Notes: A branch of the Metropolitan Museum of Art devoted solely to the literature of medieval art. Incl 16,000 slides and 5000 photographs with unique strengths in certain aspects of medieval art.

PA —WILLET STAINED GLASS STUDIO, Library, 10 E Moreland Ave, Philadelphia, 19118. Helene H Weis, Librn
Holdings: Vols 1000 Cat Pix Slides Films
Notes: Stained glass and related subjects; leaded stained glass; historic and contemporary stained glass; new techniques (faceted, laminated, etc); original work. The studio is the largest atelier making stained glass windows. Collection contains picture file of clippings, files or original designs, etc.

GLASSFORD, JOHN, AND COMPANY

DC —LIBRARY OF CONGRESS, Manuscript Division, Washington, 20540. John C Broderick, Chief
Notes: Papers.

GLASSFORD, PELHAM DAVIS, 1883-1959

CA —UNIVERSITY OF CALIFORNIA, LOS ANGELES, Research Library, Dept of Special Collections, 405 Hilgard Ave, Los Angeles, 90024. Edward Shreeves, Chairman, Bibliographers Group; David S Zeidberg, Head
Holdings: Mss
Notes: 13 linear feet of mss, correspondence, and printed materials, incl 5 linear feet of material about the Bonus Army.

GLASSWARE

IL —ART INSTITUTE OF CHICAGO, Ryerson & Burnham Libraries, Michigan Ave & Adams St, Chicago, 60603. Daphne C Roloff, Dir
Holdings: Vols (136,000) Cat Mss Slides Microforms
Budget: ($167,000)
Notes: Total collection incl 300,000 slides.

NY —CORNING MUSEUM OF GLASS LIBRARY, Corning, 14831. Norma P H Jenkins, Librn
Holdings: Vols (30,000) Cat Slides Videotapes Microforms
Notes: Extensive and comprehensive coverage of the art, archaeology, history and early manufacture of glass, with supporting materials in art, archaeology, and the decorative arts. Collection incl some 1800 manufacturers' trade catalogs on microfiche, 10,000 periodical vols and documents. 130 videotapes, 1000 microforms. Some incumabula. Research library primarily for use on the premises.

NY —GENEVA HISTORICAL SOCIETY, James Luckett Memorial Archives, 543 S Main St, Geneva, 14456. Eleanore Clise, Librn

OH —TOLEDO-LUCAS COUNTY PUBLIC LIBRARY, 325 Michigan St, Toledo, 43624. Mary B Hubbard, Head, Science-Technology Dept; Paula Baker, Head, Fine Arts Dept
Holdings: Vols (2200) Cat Pix
Notes: Antique and art glass collections are in Fine Arts Dept. Glass technology and manufacture are in Science-Technology Dept.

WI —MILWAUKEE PUBLIC LIBRARY, 814 W Wisconsin Ave, Milwaukee, 53233. Donald J Sager, City Librn
Holdings: Vols Cat
Notes: Strength in American and European decorative arts incl ceramics, glassware, jewelry, porcelain, silverware, furniture, interior decoration, textile arts and handicraft.
See also entry under Art, Decorative.

GLAZER, TOM

MA —BOSTON UNIVERSITY, Mugar Memorial Library, Special Collections Dept, 771 Commonwealth Ave, Boston, 02215. Howard B Gotlieb, Dir
Holdings: Scores Correspondence Audiotapes Pix

GLEASON, FREDERICK GRANT

IL —NEWBERRY LIBRARY, 60 W Walton St, Chicago, 60610. Diana Haskell, Cur of Modern Mss
Holdings: Cat Mss
Notes: Incl 3900 private mss; 50 ms scores; 38 scrapbooks. Chicago composer, music teacher, director of the Chicago Auditorium Conservatory, and music critic for the *Chicago Tribune* from 1887 to 1891. Restricted use: noncirculating.

GLEASON, MADELINE

CA —UNIVERSITY OF SAN FRANCISCO, Richard A Gleeson Library, The Countess Bernardine Murphy Donohue Rare Book Room, San Francisco, 94117. D Steven Corey, Special Collections Librn
Holdings: Vols 150
Notes: Madeline Gleason Archive contains collection of her own poetry and her collection of other San Francisco Bay Area poets plus much manuscript material.

GLEES, CATCHES, ROUNDS, ETC.

MA —BOSTON PUBLIC LIBRARY, Music Division, 666 Boylston St, Box 286, Boston, 02117. Ruth Bleecker, Cur of Music
Holdings: Vols 32 Cat Mss
Notes: Thomas Warren's working collection of 32 ms vols of catches, canons, and glees, 1763-1794, incl 2277 compositions, probably half unpublished.

GLENN, JOHN

DC —LIBRARY OF CONGRESS, Manuscript Division, Washington, 20540. John C Broderick, Chief
Holdings: Mss
Notes: Papers of John Glenn (90,000) pieces.

GLESSNER, FRANCES

IL —CHICAGO HISTORICAL SOCIETY, Library, Clark St at North Ave, Chicago,

GLESSNER, FRANCES (cont.)

60614. Archie Motley, Manuscript Librn
Notes: Personal papers of various members of the Crane, Laflin, Holabird, Willing, and other socially prominent Chicago families; diaries of Frances Glessner, longtime resident of the architecturally-renowned Glessner House; records of the legal firm of King, Robin, Gale, and Pillinger, dating from 1872.

GLIDERS (AERONAUTICS)

NY —NATIONAL SOARING MUSEUM, Library, Harris Hill, RD #3, Elmira, 14903.
Holdings: Cat Pix
Notes: Collection of gliding books, periodicals, pictures; also, gliders.

WY —UNIVERSITY OF WYOMING, William Robertson Coe Library, 13 & Ivinson, Laramie, 82071.
Notes: The papers of Octave Chanute (1832-1910), pioneer railroad engineer and prominent aeronautic pioneer. Incl several hundred aviation photographs, letters, articles, pamphlets, speeches, and clippings, particularly on early-day gliders, with which Chanute was greatly involved.

GLIDING AND SOARING

CA —SAN DIEGO AERO-SPACE MUSEUM, N Paul Whittier Historical Aviation Library, 2001 Pan American Plaza, Balboa Park, San Diego, 92101. B C Reynolds, Archivist
Holdings: // Uncat Microforms

MI —FRANKFORT LIBRARY, 630 Main St, Frankfort, 49635. Elsie Gilbert, Librn
Holdings: Vols (50)
Notes: Some emphasis on hang-gliding.

NY —NATIONAL SOARING MUSEUM, Library, Harris Hill, RD #3, Elmira, 14903.
Holdings: Cat Pix
Notes: Collection of gliding books, periodicals, pictures, biographies of soaring personalities; also, gliders.

GLINKA, MIKHAIL IVANOVICH

MO —UNIVERSITY OF MISSOURI-COLUMBIA, Ellis Library, Art, Archaeology and Music Dept, Columbia, 65201. Bonnie MacEwan, Librn
Holdings: Vols Cat
Notes: Russian editions of complete works of Glinka, Tchaikowsky and Rimsky-Korsakov.

GLOAG, JULIAN

MA —BOSTON UNIVERSITY, Mugar Memorial Library, Special Collections Dept, 771 Commonwealth Ave, Boston, 02215. Howard B Gotlieb, Dir
Holdings: Mss

GLOBES—COLLECTIONS

DC —LIBRARY OF CONGRESS, Geography and Map Division, Washington, 20540. John A Wolter, Chief
Holdings: Cat Maps Pix Slides Microforms
See also entry under Maps and Atlases - Collections

WI —UNIVERSITY OF WISCONSIN, MILWAUKEE, American Geographical Society Collection, 2311 E Hartford Ave, PO Box 399, Milwaukee, 53201. Roman Drazniowsky, Cur
Holdings: Vols (196,800)
Budget: ($270,000)
Notes: The largest special collection in the field of geography, cartography, and related fields in the Western Hemisphere. Incl 6469 atlases; 385,610 maps; 72 globes; 33,700 pamphlets; 79,000 photographs; 99,000 Landsat Images. Catalog published by G K Hall, Boston.

WI —UNIVERSITY OF WISCONSIN, MILWAUKEE, American Geographical Society Collection, 2311 E Hartford Ave, PO Box 399, Milwaukee, 53201. Roman Drazniowsky, Cur
Notes: Current geographical publications. Annually 10 issues. The largest special collection in geography, cartography, and related fields in the Western Hemisphere. Incl 6469 atlases; 385,610 maps; 72 globes; 33,700 pamphlets; 79,000 photographs; 99, 000 Landsat Images. Catalog published by G K Hall, Boston.

GLOBES, TERRESTRIAL see Globes—Collections

GLOETZNER, ANTON

DC —GEORGETOWN UNIVERSITY, Library, Special Collections Div, 37 & O Sts NW, Washington, 20057. George M Barringer, Special Collections Librn; Nicholas B Sheetz, Mss Librn
Holdings: Mss
Notes: Musical mss, incl a copyist's mss of the opening two movements of Beethoven's Ninth Symphony (1825); autograph mss of Rheinberger's Fantasie-Sonate fur die Orgel (before 1872); Gloetzner's Ave Regina and organ exercises; and a printed copy of his Mass, Op 12 (1910). Anton Gloetzner, Bavarian composer and musician, taught music at Georgetown College from 1873 to 1880.

GLOSSOLALIA

TN —LEE COLLEGE, Library, Ocoee St, Cleveland, 37311. Frances Arrington, Head Librn; JoAnne Sparks, Religion Librn
Holdings: Vols 28,204 Cat Slides Phonorecords Audiotapes Filmstrips
Budget: $27,000
Notes: General religion collection which supports undergraduate and graduate level curriculum. The Pentecostal Research Center houses two special collections: the Church of God (Cleveland, Tennessee) collection and the Pentecostal collection. The latter includes works about the movement and its history, works by Pentecostal authors, and specific subject areas (Holy Spirit, glossolalia, divine healing).

GLUCINIUM see Beryllium

GLUECK, SHELDON, 1896-1980 AND ELEANOR TOUROFF

MA —HARVARD UNIVERSITY LIBRARY, Law School Library, Langdell Hall, Cambridge, 02138. Erika S Chadbourn, Cur of Mss
Holdings: Cat Mss
Notes: Professional papers of Sheldon Glueck (1896-1980). Inclusive dates: 1916-1972. Also joint personal-professional papers of Sheldon Glueck and Eleanor Touroff Glueck (1898-1972). Inclusive dates: 1911-1972. Typed inventory in repository.

GLYCINE MAX see Soybean

GLYN, ANTHONY

MA —BOSTON UNIVERSITY, Mugar Memorial Library, Special Collections Dept, 771 Commonwealth Ave, Boston, 02215. Howard B Gotlieb, Dir
Holdings: Cat Mss Pix
Notes: Mss, correspondence, etc collected in depth; incl publications by or about.

GLYN, CAROLINE

MA —BOSTON UNIVERSITY, Mugar Memorial Library, Special Collections Dept, 771 Commonwealth Ave, Boston, 02215. Howard B Gotlieb, Dir
Holdings: Cat Mss Correspondence

GLYN, ELINOR

CT —LEE ASH, (personal collection), 66 Humiston Dr, Bethany, 06525.
Notes: Incl books, letters, ephemera, etc.

GNOMES (MAXIMS) see Aphorisms, Apothegms, Epigrams, Maxims, and Proverbs

GNATS

NY —AMERICAN MUSEUM OF NATURAL HISTORY, Library Services Dept, Central Park W & 79th St, New York, 10024. Nina J Root, Chairwoman; Mary Genett, Asst Librn for Reference Services
Notes: A major literature collection supplements the museum's entomology collections; perhaps the largest in the world.

GO (GAME)

NJ —PRINCETON UNIVERSITY, Library, Gest Oriental Library & East Asian Collections, 317 Palmer Hall, Princeton, 08544. D E Perushek, Cur
Holdings: Vols 500 // Cat
Notes: Gift from the American Go Association. About 500 volumes on Go; all in Japanese. Separate catalog to the collection.

NY —US MILITARY ACADEMY LIBRARY, West Point, 10996. Elaine B Eatroff, Rare Book Cur
Holdings: Vols 550 Cat Mss Pix
Notes: European imprints, beginning from the early 16th century, British, and American, incl: Hagedorn No 1, early chess periodicals. Incl: bibliography, collection of games, end games, history, openings, problems, and tournaments. Also, Chinese chess, Go, backgammon, and Checkers. Chess sets, ephemera, etc.

GOA

CA —UNIVERSITY OF CALIFORNIA, LOS ANGELES, Research Library, Indo/Pacific Collection, 405 Hilgard Ave, Los Angeles, 90024. Edward Shreeves, Chairman, Bibliographers Group; Charlotte Spence, Indo/Pacific Bibliographer
Holdings: Vols Cat Mss Maps Pix Microforms
Notes: The South Asian collection has been developed on two levels. On the research level it focuses on (1) the cultural, economic, political and social history of India from about 1859 to 1947; (2) linguistic and literary studies, with particular emphasis given to Sanskrit and Pali; and (3) the history of the Portuguese experience in South Asia. On the teaching level, materials are collected which relate to India before 1859, and from 1947 to date, as well as materials relating to the other political entities of South Asia. A description of the South Asian collection is included in the May, 1977 issue of *The Librarian,* and in *South Asian Library Resources in North* America (1975).

GOACHER, DENIS

BC —SIMON FRASER UNIVERSITY, Library, Burnaby, V5A 1S6, Can. Percilla Groves, Special Collections Librn
Holdings: Cat Mss
Notes: Incl a collection of letters from Ezra Pound to Denis Goacher, an English poet and actor who supported Pound during his years in St Elizabeths.

GOBANG (GAME) see Go (Game)

GODARD, YVES J. A. N., 1911-1975

CA —HOOVER INSTITUTION ON WAR, REVOLUTION & PEACE, Stanford University, Stanford, 94305. Milorad M Drachkovitch, Archivist
Notes: Papers of Yves Godard, officer, French Army, 19321-1961; director of police in Algeria, 1958-60; and organizer of the Organisation de l'Armee Secrete (OAS) 1961-62; incl correspondence, messages, reports, dossiers, maps photos, news clippings, speeches and writings, and other material, 1929-74. related to military and resistance operations during World War II; to military operations during Indochinese War; and to military, police, and terrorist activities during the Algerian independence struggle. Incl records of the Armee Secrete de Haute-Savoie (Secret Army of Resistance Fighters of Haute-Savoie). 13 ms boxes; 1 oversize volume; 1 envelope.

GODDARD, ROBERT HUTCHINGS

MD —US NAVAL ACADEMY, Nimitz Library, Annapolis, 21402. Alice S

GODDARD, ROBERT HUTCHINGS (cont.)

Creighton, Assistant Librn for Special Collections
Holdings: Vols 23 Cat Pix
Notes: Typescript of Goddard's research notes, 1921-1943. Incl numerous photographs of experimental equipment and tests.

†MA —CLARK UNIVERSITY, Robert Hutchings Goddard Library, Worcester, 01610. Dorothy Mosa Kowski, Rare Books Librn
Holdings: Cat Mss Maps Pix Slides
Notes: The collection of the papers, correspondence, diaries, experiment notes, etc, of Dr Robert Hutchings Goddard, "Father of American Rocketry".

NJ —PRINCETON UNIVERSITY, Library, Manuscript Collection, Nassau St, Princeton, 08540. Jean F Preston, Cur
Holdings: Cat Mss Maps Pix
Notes: Incl the collection of G Edward Pendry detailing the entry of the United States into the space age: much on early rocketry and the work of Richard H Goddard. Tape recordings and motion pictures incl Described in *Wilson Library* Bulletin, March 1968.

GODFREY, ARTHUR

DC —LIBRARY OF CONGRESS, Motion Pictures, Broadcasting and Recorded Sound Div, Washington, 20540.
Notes: The *Arthur Godfrey Time* collection is comprised of broadcast recordings of the television and radio programs from the years 1949 to 1957 and recordings of several rehearsals and warm-ups.

GODINE, DAVID R.

NC —UNIVERSITY OF NORTH CAROLINA, GREENSBORO, Walter Clinton Jackson Library, Special Collections Dept, 1000 Spring Garden St, Greensboro, 27412. Emilie W Mills, Librn
Notes: Emphasis is on American small publishers since late 19th century attention to fine printing, sound production and textual content are exemplary. Significant holdings of books published by The Typophiles, Stinehour Press, David R Godine, Jargon Society and Way and Williams are included with selective holdings of other small commercial publishers and printers, incl R H Russell, Copeland and Day, Stone and Kimball.

GODOI, JUAN-SILVANO

CA —UNIVERSITY OF CALIFORNIA, RIVERSIDE, University Library, 4045 Canyon Crest Dr, Box 5900, Riverside, 92517.
Holdings: Vols (1,000) Cat Mss Maps Pix
Notes: General research collection in the humanities and social sciences, with special strengths in history (mainly 19th and 20th centuries), literature, folklore and economic conditions, many books from the library of Julio Cesar Chaves. The Special Collections contains the papers of Juan Silvano Godoi, statesman and historian, his diaries (1897-1903, 1905-1921), the papers and correspondence of the historians Nicolas Diaz Perez, Viriato Diaz Perez, and of Hugo Rodriguez Alcala. See Thomas L Whigham and Jerry W Cooney, *Paraguayan History: Manuscript Sources in the United States*, in *Latin American Review*, vol 18 (1983) no 1: p 104-108.

GODOWSKY, LEOPOLD, 1870-1938

DC —LIBRARY OF CONGRESS, Music Division, Washington, 20540.
Notes: Music mss and papers.

GODWIN, MARY WOLLSTONECRAFT

NC —DUKE UNIVERSITY, William R Perkins Library, Durham, 27706. Elvin E Strowd, University Librn
Notes: The Shelley-Goodwin Collection of Lord Abinger is a microfilm copy of the Shelley and Godwin collection. Lord Abinger's entire manuscript collection, representing the last portion of the papers of Sir Percy Florence Shelley which is still in private hands, has been reproduced on 16 reels of film. The Bodleian Library is the only other location for this film.

GODWIN, PARKE

IL —UNIVERSITY OF ILLINOIS, URBANA/CHAMPAIGN, Library, Illinois Historical Survey Library, 1408 W Gregory Dr, 1A Library, Urbana, 61801.
Holdings: Vols 50 Cat Mss Maps Pix Microforms
Notes: Communitarianism in America. The ms material, contained in 30 separate collections (10 cubic feet), concentrates on the period 1840-70. It incl correspondence, records, minutes, ledgers and diaries. Communal societies such a Bishop Hill, Brook Farm, New Harmony, the North American Phalanx and the Sodus Bay Phalanx are represented. Among the correspondents are Albert Brisbane, Parke Godwin, Sarah Grimke, Richard Owen, Robert Owen, Robert Dale Owen, and Geeorge Ripley. Numerous pictures. Guide to the collections published in 1976.

GODWIN, WILLIAM

NC —DUKE UNIVERSITY, William R Perkins Library, Durham, 27706. Elvin E Strowd, University Librn
Notes: The Shelley-Goodwin Collection of Lord Abinger is a microfilm copy of the Shelley and Godwin collection. Lord Abinger's entire manuscript collection, representing the last portion of the papers of Sir Percy Florence Shelley which is still in private hands, has been reproduced on 16 reels of film. The Bodleian Library is the only other location for this film.

GOEBBELS, JOSEPH

CA —HOOVER INSTITUTION ON WAR, REVOLUTION & PEACE, Stanford University, Stanford, 94305. Milorad M Drachkovitch, Archivist
Holdings: Mss
Notes: Diaries, 1925-1926, 1942-1944, of Joseph Goebbels, Nazi Party member and chief of the German Ministry of Propaganda, 1933-1945 The dairy for 1925-1926 is a personal record of events, speaking engagements, appointments, trips, acquaintances, and self interpretation. The 1942-1944 diary gives a resume of the military situation and a picture of the events of the day.

GOETHE, JOHANN WOLFGANG VON

CT —YALE UNIVERSITY, Box 1603A, Yale Station, New Haven, 06520.
Holdings: Cat Mss
Notes: One of the world's most extensive collections.

CT —YALE UNIVERSITY, Beinecke Rare Book & Manuscript Library, German Literature Collection, Box 1603A, Yale Sta, New Haven, 06520. Christa Sammons, Cur
Holdings: Cat
Notes: The William A Speck Collection of Goetheana. A vast collection of books by and about Geothe. Other types of material: pamphlets, music (ms and printed) partial catalogue: Goethe's *Works with the Exception of Faust*...ed. Carl F Schreiber (New Haven: Yale University Press, 1940). "The largest Goethe collection outside of Germany, and the fourth largest in the world."

IL —UNIVERSITY OF CHICAGO LIBRARY, Dept of Special Collections, 1100 E 57 St, Chicago, 60637.
Notes: Heinemann Goethe Collection.

MA —HARVARD UNIVERSITY LIBRARY, Houghton Library, Cambridge, 02138. Rodney G Dennis, Cur of Manuscripts
Holdings: Cat Mss
Notes: Incl books given to the library by Goethe and some personal papers.

MO —WASHINGTON UNIVERSITY, Libraries, Campus Box 1061, Saint Louis, 63130.
Holdings: 4500 Vols
Notes: The private library of the late Gert von Gontard. Incl works on art, literature (especially German), music, and theater. Contains 1200 vols Goetheana, with first editions, autographed letters and original drawings by Goethe. Also material on the Austrian writer Karl Kraus and the Belgian artist Frans Masereel.

NY —COLUMBIA UNIVERSITY LIBRARIES, Rare Book & Manuscript Library, 801 Butler Library, 535 W 114 St, New York, 10027. Kenneth A Lohf, Librn
Holdings: Vols 4500 Cat

NY —NEW YORK PUBLIC LIBRARY, Research Libraries, General Research Division, Fifth Ave & 42 St, New York, 10018. Rodney Phillips, Chief
Holdings: Vols (2,225,000) Cat Maps Pix Microforms
Budget: ($775,718)

NY —STATE UNIVERSITY OF NEW YORK, COLLEGE AT OSWEGO, Penfield Library, Oswego, 13126. Anne Commerton, Dir
Holdings: Vols 448 Cat

PA —PENNSYLVANIA STATE UNIVERSITY, Rare Book Room, University Park, 16802. Charles Mann, Chief, Rare Books and Special Collections
Holdings: Vols (13,000) Cat Mss Pix
Budget: ($24,000)
Notes: The Allison-Shelley Collection of translations of German literature, history, science, medicine, biography, children's literature, and other cultural manifestations into English. Incl 3000 letters and mss of British and American translations of German writings. Also phonograph records of German art songs. Further, the collection contains a large collection of Bayard Taylor's works, letters, and mss. An annotated exhibition catalog of selected items is available from the Office of the Dean of Libraries.

GOETZ, ALEXANDER

†CA —CALIFORNIA INSTITUTE OF TECHNOLOGY, Robert A Millikan Memorial Library, Archives, 1201 E California Blvd, Pasadena, 91125.
Notes: Papers.

GOETZE, ALBRECHT

CT —YALE UNIVERSITY, Box 1603A, Yale Station, New Haven, 06520.
Holdings: Cat Mss Pix
Notes: Correspondence of Professor Albrecht Goetze, 1932-1971, incl materials relating to his work as editor of the *Journal of Cuneiform Studies*, 1947-1971.

GOGARTEN, FRIEDRICH

GA —EMORY UNIVERSITY, Candler School of Theology, Pitts Theology Library, Atlanta, 30322. Channing Jeschke, Librn; Anita K Delaries, Curator
Holdings: Vols 199 // Cat
Notes: All the published works, incl articles, by Gogarten.

GOGARTY, OLIVER ST. JOHN

PA —BUCKNELL UNIVERSITY, Ellen Clarke Bertrand Library, Lewisburg, 17837. Ann de Klerk, Librn
Holdings: Vols 300 Cat Mss
Notes: Incl books, documents and letters.

BC —UNIVERSITY OF VICTORIA, McPherson Library, Victoria, V8W 3H5, Can.
Notes: Poet, surgeon. Incl 26 pages, 1904-54; letters to G K A Bell, Ulick O'Connor and others.

GOHDES, CLARENCE

NC —DUKE UNIVERSITY, William R Perkins Library, Jay B Hubbell Center for American Literary Historiography, Durham,

GOHDES, CLARENCE (cont.)

27706. Erma Whittington, Librn
Notes: 77,312 items, including manuscripts, pictures, clippings, and correspondence. "The objective of the Center is to gather the papers and materials of significant scholars and critics in American literary history." The Center is a part of the Perkins Library Manuscripts Department.

GOIGS

MA —HARVARD UNIVERSITY LIBRARY, Widener Library, Cambridge, 02138. Ellen H Brow, Specialist in Book Selection
Holdings: Cat
Notes: Incl in *Widener Library Shelflist* No 41 (1972); also a collection of 10,000 *goigs* and *gozos.*

GOLD, HERBERT

CA —UNIVERSITY OF SAN FRANCISCO, Richard A Gleeson Library, The Countess Bernardine Murphy Donohue Rare Book Room, San Francisco, 94117. D Steven Corey, Special Collections Librn
Holdings: Vols 45 Mss
Notes: Comprehensive collection of this San Francisco author.

NY —COLUMBIA UNIVERSITY LIBRARIES, Rare Book & Manuscript Library, 801 Butler Library, 535 W 114 St, New York, 10027. Kenneth A Lohf, Librn
Holdings: Mss
Notes: Letters and mss in the James Oliver Brown Papers. Restricted use.

GOLD, FRANK

AZ —NORTHERN ARIZONA UNIVERSITY, Special Collection Library, CU Box 6022, Flagstaff, 86011. Peter M Whiteley, Coordr/Archivist; William Mullane, Librn
Notes: Collection of Frank Gold, lawyer. File on Martin F Schwab/Harry H Nash sensational murder trial, Flagstaff, 1920-1921. Also incl photographs of biographical material on Gold.

GOLD COAST see Ghana

GOLD MINES AND MINING

AZ —NORTHERN ARIZONA UNIVERSITY, Special Collection Library, CU Box 6022, Flagstaff, 86011. Peter M Whiteley, Coordr/Archivist; William Mullane, Librn
Notes: Ed McGonigle Family Collection. Incl files on the McGonigle Lumber Company, Flagstaff; Flagstaff Lumber Company and Oatman Amalgamated Gold Mining Company. Also, Mining Reports Collection, incl reports on various mines mostly located in Southern Arizona, ie, Banner Mining District, Gold Bullion Mine, and Baboquivari Mining District, 1929-1936, 1939, and 1951.

CA —UNIVERSITY OF CALIFORNIA, DAVIS, Shields Library, Dept of Special Collections, Davis, 95616. Donald Kunitz, Head; C Danial Elliott, Asst Head
Holdings: Uncat Mss Maps Pix
Notes: Business records and ms materials related to the growth of mining in the California gold fields incl account books, stock records, bullion books of mining companies such as the Empire Mine, Pioneer Reduction Company, Granite Hill Mining Company; personal correspondence, accounts, and memorabilia of pioneers; photographs of mining towns and mines in operation; related printed material. Collection covers 1849-1920. 2800 items.

CA —CALIFORNIA STATE UNIVERSITY, FRESNO, Henry Madden Library, Dept of Special Collections, Fresno, 93740. Ronald J Mahoney, Head
Holdings: // Uncat Mss Maps
Notes: Promotional material and correspondence of an unsuccessful attempt by Americans to raise capital to exploit the Torontoy, or Cercada-de-San Antonio Estate in southern Peru. The estate was said to have been the source of ancient Peruvian gold, 50 ms items.

CA —UNIVERSITY OF THE PACIFIC, Library, Stockton, 95211. Hiram L Davis, Dir of Libraries
Holdings: Vols (25,000) Cat Mss Maps Pix Slides Microforms
Budget: ($1000)
Notes: The Stuart Library of Western Americana accounts for the bulk of the special collections in the university library. Established to support the research activities of the California History Foundation under the leadership of Rockwell D Hunt in 1947 and named after Reginald R Stuart and his late wife Grace who directed the Foundation from 1956 to 1965 and contributed the nucleus of the collection. While the collection covers all of the Trans-Mississippi West, special emphasis is upon original documents and accounts of the California gold rush and subsequent development of the Central Valley of California. The most notable holdings are the John Muir papers. Research papers are published in the *Pacific* Historian, a quarterly journal.

TX —UNIVERSITY OF TEXAS LIBRARIES, Nettie Lee Benson Latin American Collection, Sid Richardson Hall 1.109, Austin, 78712. Laura Gutierrez-Witt, Head Librn
Holdings: Vols (450,000) Cat Mss
Notes: Over 1,000,000 ms pages containing the business records, 1830-1960, of the St John d'el Rey Mining Company, which operates gold and iron ore mines in Brazil.

GOLD RUSH, AFRICAN

TX —SOUTHERN METHODIST UNIVERSITY, DeGolyer Library, Box 396, SMU, Dallas, 75275. Clifton H Jones, Dir
Holdings: Vols (80,000) Cat Mss Maps Pix Slides Microforms
Notes: First editions of prominent authors; also of books in subject emphasis collections. All subjects listed in the vol are strong. Numerous collections of personal papers relating to subjects also.

GOLD RUSH, ALASKAN

†WA —WASHINGTON STATE UNIVERSITY, Library, Manuscripts, Archives & Special Collections, Pullman, 99164. John F Guido, Head
Holdings: Cat Mss Maps Pix
Notes: The manuscript collection incl business and financial records of banks, breweries, fisheries, insurance, land, lumber and livestock companies, trade and commodity associations; as well as the personal and professional papers of authors, aviators, educators, engineers, farmers, historians, pioneers, politicians and scientists; especially rich in documents relating to the exploration, settlement and development of the Palouse Country, the Inland Empire, the Columbia Basin and the Pacific Northwest. Described in *Selected Manuscript Resources in the Washington State University Library* (Pullman, 1974); and other published and unpublished inventories and registers.

GOLD RUSH, AUSTRALIAN

ON —UNIVERSITY OF TORONTO, Thomas Fisher Rare Book Library, 120 Saint George St, Toronto, M5S 1A5, Can. Richard G Landon, Head
Notes: Harcourt Brown Voltaire Collection, named for donor. Chiefly 18th century editions of Voltaire's works, including rare piracies; also includes contemporary and later works relating to Voltaire.

GOLD RUSH, CALIFORNIA

AZ —NORTHERN ARIZONA UNIVERSITY, Special Collection Library, CU Box 6022, Flagstaff, 86011. Peter M Whiteley, Coordr/Archivist; William Mullane, Librn
Notes: Henry William Bigler Collection. He was a Mormon pioneer with the Mormon Battalion, and was present at the Sutter gold discovery in Calif; incl journal, 1846-1853 (original in the Henry E Huntington Library).

CA —AZUSA PACIFIC COLLEGE, Marshburn Memorial Library, Citrus & Alosta, Azusa, 91702. Edward Peterman, Librn
Holdings: Vols (6000) Uncat
Budget: (#30,000)
Notes: Significant holdings in the George E Fullerton Library of California and Western Americana.

CA —UNIVERSITY OF CALIFORNIA, DAVIS, Shields Library, Dept of Special Collections, Davis, 95616. Donald Kunitz, Head; C Danial Elliott, Asst Head
Holdings: Uncat Mss Maps Pix
Notes: Business records and ms materials related to the growth of mining in the California gold fields incl account books, stock records, bullion books of mining companies such as the Empire Mine, Pioneer Reduction Company, Granite Hill Mining Company; personal correspondence, accounts, and memorabilia of pioneers; photographs of mining towns and mines in operation; related printed material. Collection covers 1849-1920. 2800 items.

CA —CONTRA COSTA COUNTY LIBRARY, 1750 Oak Park Blvd, Pleasant Hill, 94523. Thomas F Gates, History Specialist
Holdings: Vols (2000) Cat Maps Pix
Notes: Covers Contra Costa County and northern California history, Gold Rush memoirs, California Indian studies, county history reprints. Newspaper clippings, ephemera.

CA —CALIFORNIA STATE LIBRARY, Library & Courts Bldg, 914 Capitol Mall, Sacramento, 95809. Gary Kurutz, Head of Special Collections
Holdings: Vols (60,000) Cat Mss Maps Pix Microforms
Budget: ($41,550)
Notes: 150,000 photographs; 600 cu ft of mss; 4000 maps; 70,000 reels on microfilm; 8000 bound vols California newspapers; 500 prints of lithographs on California newpapers; 1000 posters; and vertical file materials.

CA —CALIFORNIA HISTORICAL SOCIETY, Schubert Hall Library, 2099 Pacific Ave, San Francisco, 94109. Bruce L Johnson, Library Dir
Holdings: Vols (50,000) Cat Mss Maps Pix
See also entry under California - History

CA —SOCIETY OF CALIFORNIA PIONEERS, Library, 456 McAllister St, San Francisco, 94102. Grace E Baker, Librn
Holdings: Vols (12,000) Cat Mss Maps Pix Microforms
Notes: California history, especially the gold rush and the San Francisco earthquake, Sherman collection of early California music, business letterheads of early California firms, San Francisco City Directories 1850-1944, records of California Battalion 1846-47, ms material on overland diaries, ships' logs and passenger lists. Also, large photograph collection.

CA —UNIVERSITY OF THE PACIFIC, Library, Stockton, 95211. Hiram L Davis, Dir of Libraries
Holdings: Vols (25,000) Cat Mss Maps Pix Slides Microforms
Budget: ($1000)
Notes: The Stuart Library of Western Americana accounts for the bulk of the special collections in the university library. Established to support the research activities of the California History Foundation under the leadership of Rockwell D Hunt in 1947 and named after Reginald R Stuart and his late wife Grace who directed the Foundation from 1956 to 1965 and contributed the nucleus of the collection. While the collection covers all of the Trans-Mississippi West, special emphasis is upon original documents and accounts of the California gold rush and subsequent development of the Central Valley of California. The most notable holdings are the John Muir papers. Research papers are published in the *Pacific* Historian, a quarterly journal.

GOLD RUSH, CALIFORNIA (cont.)

IN —INDIANA UNIVERSITY, Lilly Library, Seventh St, Bloomington, 47405. William R Cagle, Librn
Holdings: // Cat Mss
Notes: 1000 issues of California gold rush newspapers. Mss include some overland diaries and correspondence of miners.

NY —SAINT LAWRENCE UNIVERSITY, Owen D Young Library, Canton, 13617. Mahlon Peterson, Librn
Holdings: Mss
Notes: Collection consists of letters written home to New York State from the California gold fields and from New Orleans and Memphis during the Civil War. Approx 90 items.

NY —NEW YORK HISTORICAL SOCIETY, Library, 170 Central Park W, New York, 10024. James Gregory, Librn
Notes: One of the largest collections in the East of California newspapers printed in the 1850s.

RI —BROWN UNIVERSITY, John Hay Library, 20 Prospect St, Providence, 02912. Mark N Brown, Cur Mss
Holdings: Vols 350 // Uncat
Notes: Eberstadt Collection of Narratives of California Pioneers--personal narratives written by pioneers who crossed the Plains to California after the discovery of gold in 1849. A large portion of the books were printed in late 19th and early 20th centuries and deal with: Indian contacts, captivities, frontier lore, travel routes, topography, fauna and flora, outlaws, traders and trappers, and frontier army life.

†UT —UNIVERSITY OF UTAH, Marriott Library, Salt Lake City, 84112.
Notes: Original drawings and personal papers of John Hudson, a gold rush Forty-Niner who helped chart the Great Salt Lake with Captain Howard Stansbury.

GOLD RUSH, COLORADO

CO —COLORADO HISTORICAL SOCIETY, Research Collections, 1300 Broadway, Denver, 80203. Catherine Kane, Head Public Service and Access
Holdings: Cat Pix Slides
Budget:
Notes: 250,000 photographs of western and Colorado subjects incl gold rush, mining, Indians, natural features, transportation, cities and towns, portraits. William Henry Jackson photographs of area west of Mississippi.

GOLD RUSH, KLONDIKE

†WA —WASHINGTON STATE UNIVERSITY, Library, Manuscripts, Archives & Special Collections, Pullman, 99164. John F Guido, Head
Holdings: Cat Mss Maps Pix
Notes: The manuscript collection incl business and financial records of banks, breweries, fisheries, insurance, land, lumber and livestock companies, trade and commodity associations; as well as the personal and professional papers of authors, aviators, educators, engineers, farmers, historians, pioneers, politicians and scientists; especially rich in documents relating to the exploration, settlement and development of the Palouse Country, the Inland Empire, the Columbia Basin and the Pacific Northwest. Described in *Selected Manuscript Resources in the Washington State University Library* (Pullman, 1974); and other published and unpublished inventories and registers.

GOLD RUSH NEWSPAPERS see Newspapers, Gold Rush

GOLDBERG, LEO

NY —AMERICAN INSTITUTE OF PHYSICS, Center for the History of Physics, Niels Bohr Library, 335 E 45 St, New York, 10017. John Aubry, Librn
Notes: The Sources for History of Modern Astrophysics documents the history of 20th-century astrophysics. Incl some 400 hours of oral history interviews with astronomers, such as Bart Bok, S Chandrasekhar, Martin Schwarzschild, and A E Whitford. The project also organized and cataloged the papers of Henry Norris Russell, Frank Schlesinger, Otto Struve, Ejnar Hertzsprung, Harlow Shapley, Charles Young, Robert Atkinson, Seth Chandler, Theodore Dunham, Jr, and G C McVittie.

GOLDBERG, MOSES

AZ —ARIZONA STATE UNIVERSITY, Library, Tempe, 85287. Marilyn Wurzburger, Special Collections Librn
Holdings: Vols (108) Pix
Notes: Collection covers various aspects of Children's Theatre from 1944 through the present. Areas of emphasis incl International and National Child Drama Associations, award-winning theatres, educational programs, regional groups and prominent figures in Children's Theatre incl: Irene Vickers Baker, Isabel Burger, Virginia Lee Comer, Rita Criste, Moses Goldberg, Kenneth Graham, Aurand Harris, Paul Kozelka, George Latshaw, Rosemary Musil, Sara Spencer, Winifred Ward, Susan Zeder and Lin Wright. Publications incl newsletters, research papers, bibliographies and records of the proceedings of the Children's Theatre Association of America. 80 linear feet of scripts, documents, publications, films, tapes (oral history) programs, correspondence, photographs, working papers and clippings. Partially indexed; finding guides available.

GOLDBERG, RUBE

DC —LIBRARY OF CONGRESS, Prints & Photographs Div, Washington, 20540.
Notes: Swann Collection is strong in the work of contemporary cartoonists. Among the 400 artists represented are Peter Arno, Bil Canfield, Al Capp, Miguel Covarrubias, Louis Dalrymple, Whitney Darrow, Rube Goldberg, Thomas Nast, Jose Guadalupe Posada, Edward Sorel, and John Tenniel.

GOLDBERGER, JOSEPH

TN —VANDERBILT UNIVERSITY, Medical Center Library, Nashville, 37232. Mary H Teloh, Special Collections Librn
Holdings: Uncat Mss Pix Videotapes
Notes: The nucleus of the developing nutrition collection at Vanderbilt is the papers of medical researcher Joseph Goldberger, MD, and his associate W Henry Sebrell Jr, MD. The collection consists of first editions and translations of classic books on pellagra, and the letters, mss, and notebooks compiled by Dr Goldberger and Dr Sebrell during their years of research on pellagra. See *Nutrition Reviews,* 33(10):310-312, Oct 1975 10 linear ft of mss.

GOLDEN, HARRY

NC —PUBLIC LIBRARY OF CHARLOTTE & MECKLENBURG COUNTY, Local History and Genealogy Dept, 310 N Tryon St, Charlotte, 28202. Mary L Phillips, Librn
Holdings: Vols 75 Uncat Mss Audiotapes
Notes: Books which were consulted or read by Mr Golden during the writing of the book *Mr Kennedy and the Negroes* (World, 1964). From time to time Mr Golden gives the library other books and working papers. Cataloged copies of his books are in the North Carolina Room Collection and also in the library's circulating collection.

NC —UNIVERSITY OF NORTH CAROLINA, CHARLOTTE, J Murrey Atkins Library, UNCC Station, Charlotte, 28223. Robert F Brabham Jr, Special Collections Librn
Holdings: Cat
Notes: Papers of Harry Golden, 1945-1970. Incl 40,000 items.

GOLDEN, JOHN

NY —NEW YORK PUBLIC LIBRARY, Performing Arts Research Center, Billy Rose Theatre Collection, 111 Amsterdam Ave, New York, 10023. Dorothy L Swerdlove, Cur
Holdings: Cat Mss Pix
Notes: Papers, scrapbooks, mss, photographs, memorabilia, etc.

GOLDEN BOOKS SERIES

†NY —COLUMBIA UNIVERSITY LIBRARIES, Butler Library, Rare Book and Manuscript Library, 535 W 114 St, New York, 10027.
Notes: A collection of the art work of Tibor Gergely, containing 2,824 watercolors, pen-and-ink drawings, and sketches. Gergely is best known for his illustrations of the popular Golden Book Series for children.

GOLDER, FRANK A.

CA —HOOVER INSTITUTION ON WAR, REVOLUTION & PEACE, Stanford University, Stanford, 94305. Milorad M Drachkovitch, Archivist
Holdings: // Mss
Notes: Papers, 1743-1929, of Frank A Golder, author and professor of history. Correspondence relating the American Relief Administration in Russia and Finland, diplomatic papers from Russian archives relating to American history, articles, and other papers relating to the Civil war Alaska, the Hawaiian Islands, eastern Asia, Russian-American relations, and the Treaty of 1832. Unpublished register is available in repository.

GOLDFADEN, ABRAHAM

NY —YIVO INSTITUTE FOR JEWISH RESEARCH, Library & Archives, 1048 Fifth Ave, New York, 10028. Dina Abramowicz, Librn; Marek Web, Archivist
Holdings: Cat Mss Pix Slides
Notes: Yiddish drama in the original and in English translation from its 19th-century beginnings to the present; the Yiddish theatre in the Soviet Union and the treatrical activities in the ghettos during the Nazi regime; special collections of Sholem Perelmuter, Mendl Elkin, Maurice Schwartz, Abraham Goldfaden, Jacob Gordin, and Mark Schweid; records of the Union of Jewish Actors in Poland between the two world wars; the Vilna YIVO Collection of posters, playbills, and photographs; recordings.

GOLDIAN DIALECT

WA —UNIVERSITY OF WASHINGTON LIBRARIES, Rare Books, Special Collections Dept, Seattle, 98195. Sandra Kroupa, Librn
Notes: Part of a set of Siberian primers prepared in the early 1930s by Societ ethnographers. Some are first attempts to transcribe Siberian languages. All are in Latin phonetic script, not in Cyrillic.

GOLDING, WILLIAM

NV —UNIVERSITY OF NEVADA, RENO, University Library, Special Collections Dept, Reno, 89557. Robert E Blesse, Head
Holdings: Vols (45) Cat Other appearances 30 Cat
Notes: Includes individual works by author in all editions including translations; also prefaces, introductions, published correspondence, appearances in anthologies, periodicals, etc. Bibliographical research collection, part of Modern Authors Collection.

NY —ALFRED UNIVERSITY, Herrick Memorial Library, Alfred, 14802. June E Brown, Head Librn
Notes: The Evelyn Tennyson Openhym Collection of modern British literature and social history. Papers, incl correspondence of authors concerned with the business aspects of authorship. Gift of Evelyn Tennyson Openhym of Wellsville, NY. Also, 5300 volumes of British literature.

GOLDMAN, EDWIN FRANKO

†MD —UNIVERSITY OF MARYLAND, Library, American Bandmasters Association

GOLDMAN, EDWIN FRANKO (cont.)

Research Center, College Park, 20742. Pearl Z Tubiash, Supvr
Holdings: Cat Pix Phonorecords Audiotapes
Notes: Materials on bands and band music; organizational and personal papers, with sizable collections relating to the careers of distinguished bandmasters, notably Edwin Franko Goldman.

GOLDMAN, EMMA, 1869-1940

IN —INDIANA STATE UNIVERSITY, Cunningham Memorial Library, Dept of Rare Books & Special Collections, Terre Haute, 47809. Lawrence J McCrank, Head
Notes: The Debs Collection consists of aprox 7000 pieces of correspondence between Theodore Debs (brother of E V) and other persons, such as Sinclair Lewis, Upton Sinclair, Ethel Barrymore, Emma Goldman, Robert G Ingersoll, Carl Sandburg, Norman Thomas, Sacco and Vanzetti and many others. Many of the letters are from E V Debs to his brother; a good portion of these are from the federal penitentiary at Atlanta. Entire correspondence file has been microfilmed. 750 pamphlets cover all aspects of the labor movement, socialism and radical thought from the 19th century to appprox 1950. A collection ca 200 related books is also housed in the collection. See: J Robert Constantine and Gail Malmgreen, eds, *The Papers of Eugene V Debs, 1834-1945. A Guide to the Microfilm Edition.* NY: Microfilming Corp of America, 1983 (University Microfilms is the new distributer).

MA —BOSTON UNIVERSITY, Mugar Memorial Library, Special Collections Dept, 771 Commonwealth Ave, Boston, 02215. Howard B Gotlieb, Dir
Holdings: // Cat
Notes: Correspondence.

MA —RADCLIFFE COLLEGE, Arthur & Elizabeth Schlesinger Library on the History of Women in America, 3 James St, Cambridge, 02138. Patricia Miller King, Dir; Eva Moseley, Cur of Mss
Notes: More than 500 letters written by Emma Goldman, most to Leon Malmed (1881-1956), a comrade in the anarchist movement and for a time her lover; also photographs, writings, pamphlets, etc.

GOLDMARK FAMILY

†NY —COLUMBIA UNIVERSITY LIBRARIES, Butler Library, Rare Book and Manuscript Library, 535 W 114 St, New York, 10027.
Notes: Papers, correspondence, etc.

GOLDSCHMIDT, RICHARD BENEDIKT

CA —UNIVERSITY OF CALIFORNIA, BERKELEY, Bancroft Library, Manuscripts Division, Berkeley, 94720. James D Hart, Dir
Holdings: Cat Mss Maps Pix Microforms
Notes: Papers, correspondence, etc.

GOLDSMITH, OLIVER

CA —UNIVERSITY OF CALIFORNIA, LOS ANGELES, William Andrews Clark Memorial Library, 2520 Cimarron St, Los Angeles, 90018.
Holdings: Cat
Notes: Small collection; first editions, etc.

†CA —STANFORD UNIVERSITY LIBRARIES, Stanford, 94305.
Notes: In collection of English and American Literature.

CT —TRINITY COLLEGE LIBRARY, Watkinson Library, 300 Summit St, Hartford, 06106. Jeffrey Kaimowitz, Cur
Holdings: Cat
Notes: Over 100 editions of *The Vicar of* Wakefield.

CT —YALE UNIVERSITY, Box 1603A, Yale Station, New Haven, 06520.
Holdings: Cat Mss

MA —HARVARD UNIVERSITY LIBRARY, Houghton Library, Cambridge, 02138. Rodney G Dennis, Cur of Manuscripts
Holdings: Cat Mss

NY —NEW YORK ACADEMY OF MEDICINE, Library, 2 E 103 St, New York, 10029. Brett A Kirkpatrick, Librn
Holdings: Vols // Cat
Notes: Incl 112 copies of varying editions of The Vicar of Wakefield.

OH —OHIO UNIVERSITY, Vernon R Alden Library, Department of Archives and Special Collections, Athens, 45701. Gary A Hunt, Head
Holdings: Vols (10,191) Uncat Mss
Notes: The Edmund Blunden Collection of Romantic and Modern Literature, being the private library assembled by Blunden during 6 decades of active collecting. The bulk of the collection (6,264 titles) consists of English imprints from the period 1750-1850, concentrating on literature but also incl contemporary works on art, natural history, philosophy and other subjects important for understanding the background of English Romanticism. Among the authors most heavily represented by first and other early editions are: Allington, Barnes, Bloomfield, Byron, Clare, Coleridge, Cowper, Dyer, Edgeworth, Goldsmith, Hazlitt, Hunt, Lamb, Landor, Scott, Thompson and Wordsworth. Books written by Blunden himself, together with his Georgian contemporaries (particularly W H Davies, Walter De la Mare, and Sigfried Sassoon) form a second major area of strength. Many ofthe modern books are inscribed to Blunden, and nearly all the volumes in the collection bear his annotations.

PA —FREE LIBRARY OF PHILADELPHIA, Rare Book Dept, Logan Sq, Philadelphia, 19103. Marie E Korey, Rare Book Librn
Holdings: Vols (500) Cat
Notes: The William M Elkins Collection of important English, American and other editions of the works of Oliver Goldsmith.

VA —VIRGINIA COMMONWEALTH UNIVERSITY, James Branch Cabell Library, Richmond, 23284. Daniel Yanchisin, Special Collections Librn

GOLDSMITHS-KRESS LIBRARY OF ECONOMIC LITERATURE

CA —UNIVERSITY OF CALIFORNIA, LOS ANGELES, Graduate School of Management Library, UCLA Campus, Los Angeles, 90024. Robert Bellanti, Head Librn
Holdings: Microforms
Notes: The

GOLDWATER, BARRY MORRIS

AZ —NORTHERN ARIZONA UNIVERSITY, Special Collection Library, CU Box 6022, Flagstaff, 86011. Peter M Whiteley, Coordr/Archivist; William Mullane, Librn
Notes: Political ephemera of the presidential campaign (stickers, posters, etc).

AZ —ARIZONA STATE UNIVERSITY, Library, Arizona Collection, Tempe, 85281. Edward C Oetting, Head
Holdings: Cat Mss
Notes: Papers, etc.

IA —DRAKE UNIVERSITY, Cowles Library, 28 St & University Ave, Des Moines, 50311.
Holdings: Cat Mss Pix
Notes: Working papers and notes of Walter R Mears, Asst Bureau Chief for the Associated Press, concerning the 1964 Presidential Campaign of Senator Barry Goldwater.

NY —CORNELL UNIVERSITY LIBRARIES, Collection of Regional History, Dept of Manuscripts and Univ Archives, Ithaca, 14853.
Notes: US Senator, 1964 Presidential Candidate. Incl papers, 1964-65; 8 reels of microfilm, largely incoming letters, newspaper clippings, pamphlets and other material relating to the campaign.

GOLF

CT —YALE UNIVERSITY, Box 1603A, Yale Station, New Haven, 06520.
Notes: Papers of Walter Camp, father of American football and foremost authority on sports and physical fitness. 48 microfilm reels; incl also over 20,000 clippings, etc on sports, providing virtual history, 1866-1925. Published guide to the collection for sale.

DC —LIBRARY OF CONGRESS, Washington, 20540.

NJ —US GOLF ASSOCIATION, Library and Museum, Golf House, Route 512, PO Box Golf, Far Hills, 07936. Janet Seagle, Librn
Holdings: Vols 7000 Cat Mss Maps Pix Slides Phonorecords Audiotapes 16mm Films Microforms
Budget: $5000
Notes: Largest library on only golf in the world. Available for research and study; no loan arrangements.

NY —RACQUET & TENNIS CLUB, Library, 370 Park Ave, New York, 10022. Gerald Belliveau, Jr, Librn
Holdings: Vols (17,500) Cat
Budget: ($6000)
Notes: Specializes in court tennis, lawn tennis, early American sport. See *Dictionary Catalogue of the Library of Sports in the Racquet and Tennis Club* (Boston: G K Hall, 1971). Also, Robert W Henderson, *Early American Sport,* 3rd ed. (Cranbury, NJ: Fairleigh Dickinson University Press, 1977).

VA —JAMES RIVER GOLF MUSEUM AND LIBRARY, James River Country Club, 1500 Country Club Rd, Newport News, 23606. Weymouth Crumbler, Librn
Holdings: Vols (800)
Notes: About 900 volumes on old and modern golf; 450 gold clubs 1780-present, 150 golf balls 1820-1830.

ON —CANADIAN GOLF MUSEUM, Library, Apt No 1111, 1081 Ambleside Dr, Ottawa, K2B 8C8, Can. W Lyn Stewart, Cur
Holdings: Vols 300 Cat Mss Videotapes Filmstrips
Notes: Contains several old vols from 1875 to present day books on golf.

†ON —METROPOLITAN TORONTO LIBRARY, 789 Yonge St, Toronto, M4W 2G8, Can.
Notes: Good subject strengths.

GOLOVIN, NIKOLAI N.

CA —HOOVER INSTITUTION ON WAR, REVOLUTION & PEACE, Stanford University, Stanford, 94305. Milorad M Drachkovitch, Archivist
Holdings: // Mss
Notes: Papers, 1914-1928, of Nikolai N Golovin, Czarist Russian army officer. Reports, articles, memoranda, and other documents relating to Russian military operations in World War I, prepared by General Golovin, assistant to the chief of staff of the Russian military army on the Rumanian front, and by other military leaders; together with correspondence and other papers relating to Golovin's activities in collecting data concerning the White Russian forces in the civil war in Russia. 2 ft.

GOMEZ, FRANCISCO VAZQUEZ

IL —SOUTHERN ILLINOIS UNIVERSITY, CARBONDALE, Delyte W Morris Library, Special Collections Dept, Carbondale, 62901. David V Koch, Cur of Special Collections; Louisa Bowen, Cur of Manuscripts
Holdings: Cat Mss
Notes: Personal papers of Francisco Vazquez Gomez, 1906-1939, 27 linear feet. Collection relates almost entirely to the Mexican revolution of 1910. Inventory available at library.

GOMEZ DE LA SERNA, RAMON, 1888-1963

PA —UNIVERSITY OF PITTSBURGH, Hillman Library, Special Collections Dept, Ramon Gomez de la Serna Collection, Pittsburgh, 15260. Charles Aston Jr, Coordinator
Holdings: Vols 129 Uncat Mss Pix
Notes: Collection incl over 65 packets of published and unpublished mss and

GOMEZ DE LA SERNA, RAMON, 1888-1963 (cont.)

correspondence, 60,000 pieces, as well as material relating to *greguerias* and other works. Incl only existing copies of several works; first editions, among them Gomez de la Serna's own copies; original mss of 7 unpublished works; mss of 8 projected or incomplete works; correspondence; offprints of newspaper articles; reviews; 500 articles; and his subject clipping file. Partial inventory. 17 ft mss.

GO-MOKY see Go (Game)

GOMPERS, SAMUEL

DC —AMERICAN FEDERATION OF LABOR-CONGRESS OF INDUSTRIAL ORGANIZATIONS, Library, 815 16th St NW, Washington, 20006.
Holdings: Vols (20,000) Cat Pix Microforms
Notes: Labor, labor unions, and related subjects. Incl letters of Samuel Gompers (microfilm); constitutions and conference proceedings of international unions.

IL —SOUTHERN ILLINOIS UNIVERSITY, CARBONDALE, Delyte W Morris Library, Special Collections Dept, Carbondale, 62901. David V Koch, Cur of Special Collections; Louisa Bowen, Cur of Manuscripts
Holdings: Cat Mss
Notes: Papers and correspondence of Theodore A Schroeder, constitutional lawyer and founder, with Lincoln Steffens, of the Free Speech League, a forerunner of the American Civil Liberties Union. Contains extensive correspondence with Comstock, Gompers, Debs, H Ellis, Sanger, Sinclair, John Dewey, Darrow, Mencken, A G Hays, Emma Goldman, W E B DuBois, etc. Incl several thousand letters; notes and mss, records of legal cases and extensive files relating to the early history of psychiatry.

NY —NEW YORK PUBLIC LIBRARY, Research Libraries, Economic & Public Affairs Div, Fifth Ave & 42 St, New York, 10018. Edward DiRoma, Chief
Holdings: Vols (1,500,000) Cat Microforms

GOMPERZ, THEODOR, 1832-1912, AND HEINRICH, 1873-1942

CA —CLAREMONT COLLEGES, Honnold Library, Ninth & Dartmouth, Claremont, 91711. Tania Rizzo, Special Collections Dept Head
Holdings: Cat Mss
Notes: 362 ALsS to the Viennese philosophers Theodor and Heinrich Gomperz from Heinrich and Lily Braun, Hermann Diels, Robert Lytton, Ernst Mach, and other correspondents. Some letters have been published in the 2-vol biography of Theodor Gomperz (Vienna, 1936 and 1974). Philip and Franciszka Merlan, donors. Restricted use.

GONCOURT, EDMOND AND JULES DE

MA —HARVARD UNIVERSITY LIBRARY, Houghton Library, Cambridge, 02138. Rodney G Dennis, Cur of Manuscripts
Holdings: Cat Mss

GONDOS, VICTOR

†WY —UNIVERSITY OF WYOMING, William Robertson Coe Library, Archives of Contemporary History, 13th & Ivinson, Laramie, 82071.
Notes: The papers of Victor Gondos. Incl journals and books, several hundred folders on military and archival history, his diaries from 1920-1974, and more than 1500 letters on historical research and architecture.

GONORRHEA—HISTORY

OH —CLEVELAND MEDICAL LIBRARY ASSOCIATION/CASE WESTERN RESERVE UNIVERSITY, Cleveland Health Sciences Library, Historical Division, Allen Memorial Medical Library, 11000 Euclid Ave, Cleveland, 44106. Glen Jenkins, Rare Book Librarian & Archivist
Holdings: Vols 235 Cat
Notes: Described in "The Cole Collection of Venereals," *Bulletin of the Cleveland Medical Library*, 1954, vol 1, 4-6.

GONZAGA COLLEGE

DC —GEORGETOWN UNIVERSITY, Library, Special Collections Div, 37 & O Sts NW, Washington, 20057. George M Barringer, Special Collections Librn; Nicholas B Sheetz, Mss Librn
Holdings: Vols (100) Uncat Mss
Notes: Includes the archives of Dag Hammarskjold College, Columbia, Md; a portion of the archives of Gonzaga College, Washington, DC; records of the Fells Point Hebrew Grammar School, Baltimore, Md, and other materials (Besides these collections, students can use the Georgetown University Archives, 1787- , and the Woodstock College Archives, 1866- , qv under Jesuits in the US.)

GOOCH, JOHN SHERLOCK, 1866-1929

BC —UNIVERSITY OF VICTORIA, McPherson Library, Victoria, V8W 3H5, Can.

GOODEN, STEPHEN, 1892-1955

CA —UNIVERSITY OF CALIFORNIA, LOS ANGELES, Research Library, Dept of Special Collections, 405 Hilgard Ave, Los Angeles, 90024. Edward Shreeves, Chairman, Bibliographers Group; David S Zeidberg, Head
Notes: 88 original woodcuts, engravings, and drawings.

GOODMAN, GEORGE J. W.

MA —BOSTON UNIVERSITY, Mugar Memorial Library, Special Collections Dept, 771 Commonwealth Ave, Boston, 02215. Howard B Gotlieb, Dir
Holdings: Cat Mss Pix
Notes: Mss, correspondence, etc collected in depth; incl publications by or about. Some written under pseudonym Adam Smith.

GOODMAN, KENNETH SAWYER

IL —CHICAGO PUBLIC LIBRARY, Special Collections Div, Cultural Center, 78 E Washington St, Chicago, 60602. Laura Linard, Cur
Holdings: Mss Pix
Notes: Special Collections maintains a scarce collection of theatre broadsides, playbills, programs and other ephemera for Chicago productions, 1880-1930 as well as a recently acquired collection of contemporary material (1971-1981). These are described in *Treasures of The Chicago Public Library*, compiled by Thomas A Orlando and Marie Gecik, 1977, pp 121-33. The Archives of the Publicity Department of the Goodman Theatre (formerly of the Art Institute of Chicago) are maintained by Special Collections at The Chicago Public Library. We also have a nearly complete collection of the plays of Kenneth Sawyer Goodman, after whom the Goodman Theatre is named. Some unique pre-fire material is also to be found in these collections.A finding aid to these collections has been prepared.

IL —NEWBERRY LIBRARY, 60 W Walton St, Chicago, 60610. Diana Haskell, Cur of Modern Mss
Holdings: Uncat
Notes: Six boxes of ms and printed plays; short stories; diaries; drawings; screenplays. Noncirculating.

GOODMAN, PAUL, 1911-1972

BC —UNIVERSITY OF VICTORIA, McPherson Library, Victoria, V8W 3H5, Can.
Notes: Incl holograph and typescript of *Finite Experience.*

GOODMAN THEATRE

IL —CHICAGO PUBLIC LIBRARY, Special Collections Div, Cultural Center, 78 E Washington St, Chicago, 60602. Laura Linard, Cur
Holdings: Mss Pix
Notes: Special Collections maintains a scarce collection of theatre broadsides, playbills, programs and other ephemera for Chicago productions, 1880-1930 as well as a recently acquired collection of contemporary material (1971-1981). These are described in *Treasures of The Chicago Public Library*, compiled by Thomas A Orlando and Marie Gecik, 1977, pp 121-33. The Archives of the Publicity Department of the Goodman Theatre (formerly of the Art Institute of Chicago) are maintained by Special Collections at The Chicago Public Library. We also have a nearly complete collection of the plays of Kenneth Sawyer Goodman, after whom the Goodman Theatre is named. Some unique pre-fire material is also to be found in these collections.A finding aid to these collections has been prepared.

GOODNIGHT, CHARLES

TX —UNIVERSITY OF TEXAS LIBRARIES, General Libraries, Barker Texas History Center, PO Box P, Austin, 78712. Don Carleton, Dir

GOODNOW, FRANK J.

MD —JOHNS HOPKINS UNIVERSITY, Milton S Eisenhower Library, Charles & 34 Sts, Baltimore, 21218. Ann S Gwyn, Assistant Dir for Special Collections
Holdings: Vols 21 Cat Mss
Notes: Addresses, articles, lectures, and letters, professional and personal. Some 14, 000 pieces.

GOODRICH, CARTER

NY —COLUMBIA UNIVERSITY LIBRARIES, Rare Book & Manuscript Library, 801 Butler Library, 535 W 114 St, New York, 10027. Kenneth A Lohf, Librn
Holdings: Mss Maps
Notes: The papers of Professor Carter Goodrich, economic historian, incl his papers as chairman of the governing body of the International Labor Office, 1939-1945; chief of the United Nations economic mission in Vietnam, 1955-1956; and special representative to Bolivia for the Secretary-General of the United Nations, 1952-1953. About 28,000 items. Restricted use.

GOODRICH, SAMUEL GRISWOLD, 1793-1860

DC —LIBRARY OF CONGRESS, Rare Book & Special Collections Div, Washington, 20540. William Matheson, Chief
Notes: The Juvenile Collection covers the early 18th century to the present and is particularly strong in fiction. Authors extensively represented are: Alcott, Alger, Abbott, Goodrich, Fosdick, Lothrop and McGuffey.

MA —AMHERST COLLEGE, Library, Amherst, 01002. John Lancaster, Special Collections Librn
Notes: Collections relating to the life of Samuel Griswold Goodrich, author who wrote as "Peter Parley." Incl The Morris Cohen Collection of printed works, incl piracies, imitations under the *Peter Parley* pseudonym; also the Mrs Harmon S Boyd Collection of letters and documents, espec of his term as US Consul in Paris, 1851 to 1855.

GOODWIN, HAROLD

MA —BOSTON UNIVERSITY, Mugar Memorial Library, Special Collections Dept, 771 Commonwealth Ave, Boston, 02215. Howard B Gotlieb, Dir
Holdings: Mss Pix
Notes: Mss, correspondence, etc collected indepth; incl publications by or about.

GORDIN, JACOB

NY —YIVO INSTITUTE FOR JEWISH RESEARCH, Library & Archives, 1048 Fifth Ave, New York, 10028. Dina Abramowicz, Librn; Marek Web, Archivist
Holdings: Cat Mss Pix Slides
Notes: Yiddish drama in the original and in English translation from its 19th-century beginnings to the present; the Yiddish theatre in the Soviet Union and the theatrical activities in the ghettos during the Nazi regime; special collections of Sholem Perelmuter, Mendl Elkin, Maurice Schwartz, Abraham Goldfaden, Jacob Gordin, and Mark Schweid; records of the Union of Jewish Actors in Poland between the two world wars; the Vilna YIVO Collection of posters, playbills, and photographs; recordings.

GORDON, C. W.

MB —UNIVERSITY OF MANITOBA, Elizabeth Dafoe Library, Archives and Special Collections Dept, Winnipeg, R3T 2N2, Can. Richard E Bennett, Dept Head; Corrado A Santoro, Reference Archivist
Holdings: / / Cat Mss
Notes: The "Ralph Connor" (C W Gordon) Collection, incl the mss and working papers of 19 published and 2 unpublished works. Typed catalog only.

GORDON, CAROLINE

NV —UNIVERSITY OF NEVADA, RENO, University Library, Special Collections Dept, Reno, 89557. Robert E Blesse, Head
Holdings: Vols (18) Cat
Notes: Includes individual works by author in all editions including translations; also prefaces, introductions, published correspondence, appearances in anthologies, periodicals, etc. Bibliographical research collection, part of Modern Authors Collection. Other appearances 55 cataloged.

GORDON, GORDON AND MILDRED

MA —BOSTON UNIVERSITY, Mugar Memorial Library, Special Collections Dept, 771 Commonwealth Ave, Boston, 02215. Howard B Gotlieb, Dir
Holdings: Cat Mss
Notes: Mss, Correspondence, etc. Collected in depth; incl publications by or about.

GORDON, MAX

NY —HAMPDEN-BOOTH THEATRE LIBRARY AT THE PLAYERS, 16 Gramercy Park, New York, 10003. Louis A Rachow, Librn/Cur
Holdings: Mss Pix
Notes: The Max Gordon Collection, incl 130 typescripts of shows produced by him, routebooks, scrapbooks, playbills, and photographs. Ten linear feet; indexed.

GORE, THOMAS PRYOR

OK —UNIVERSITY OF OKLAHOMA, Bizzell Memorial Library, Western History Collections, 401 W Brooks, Norman, 73069. John Ezell, Cur
Holdings: Mss Documents Pix Maps
Notes: US Senator. His papers. Guide available.

GORELICK, MORDECAI

IL —SOUTHERN ILLINOIS UNIVERSITY, CARBONDALE, Delyte W Morris Library, Special Collections Dept, Carbondale, 62901. David V Koch, Cur of Special Collections; Louisa Bowen, Cur of Manuscripts
Holdings: Vols 110 Uncat Mss Pix Models Designs Drawings
Notes: The personal papers (75 linear feet) and art work of Mordecai Gorlik, stage designer, director, and playwright, incl a large volume of correspondence with persons of the theater, in the US and abroad, scripts of plays, and thousands of sketches, drawings, and photographs of stage settings.

GOREY, EDWARD (ST. JOHN)

CA —UNIVERSITY OF CALIFORNIA, LOS ANGELES, Research Library, Dept of Special Collections, 405 Hilgard Ave, Los Angeles, 90024. Edward Shreeves, Chairman, Bibliographers Group; David S Zeidberg, Head
Holdings: Vols 100
Notes: 100 first and other editions of his books and books he illustrated.

NM —NEW MEXICO STATE UNIVERSITY, Library, Box 3475, Las Cruces, 88003. James Dyke, Dir
Holdings: Vols 501 Cat
Notes: Collection of book covers, book illustrated works, and books by Edward St. John Gorey plus innumerable drawings.

GORGAS FAMILY

†AL —UNIVERSITY OF ALABAMA, Amelia Gayle Gorgas Library, PO Box S, University, 35486.
Notes: The Alabama Collection contains books about Alabama; by Alabama authors; scrapbooks, pamphlets, newspapers. Such ms collections as the Manly Family. Papers, 1819-1930; Samuel Townsend, Estate papers, 1829-90; Harry Mell Ayers, 1885-1964; and the Gorgas Family, papers 1821-1920.

NY —CORNELL UNIVERSITY LIBRARIES, Collection of Regional History, Dept of Manuscripts and Univ Archives, Ithaca, 14853.
Notes: Family of Dr. C R Gorgas, physician. Incl one medical ms, one cut-out silhouette of Gorgas made at the age of 15.

GORHAM, CHARLES O., 1911-1975

MA —BOSTON UNIVERSITY, Mugar Memorial Library, Special Collections Dept, 771 Commonwealth Ave, Boston, 02215. Howard B Gotlieb, Dir
Holdings: Mss Pix Audiotapes
Notes: Mss, correspondence, etc collected in depth; incl publications by or about.

GORHAM FAMILY

MA —NEW ENGLAND HISTORIC GENEALOGICAL SOCIETY, Library, 101 Newbury St, Boston, 02116. Ralph J Crandell, Dir
Notes: Family papers, likely to incl personal correspondence, diaries, business records, etc.

GORILLAS

OR —OREGON REGIONAL PRIMATE RESEARCH CENTER, Library, 505 NW 185 Ave, Beaverton, 97006. Isabel McDonald, Librn
Holdings: Vols (765) Cat Audiotapes 16mm Films Microforms
Notes: Incl small collection of dissertations and theses.

GORING, HERMANN, 1893-1946

DC —LIBRARY OF CONGRESS, Rare Book & Special Collections Div, Washington, 20540. William Matheson, Chief
Notes: The Third Reich Collection incl materials from the libraries of Hermann Goring, Heinrich Himmler, Franz Xaver Schwarz, and other Nazi leaders.

DC —LIBRARY OF CONGRESS, Prints & Photographs Div, Washington, 20540.
Notes: Personal photo albums of Hermann Goring provide detailed coverage of his activities during World War I and the years 1933-42. Biographical photographs of Hermann Goring incl pictures by Helmuth Kurth and Eitel Lange.

GORKHALI LANGUAGE see Nepali Language and Literature

GORMAN, HERBERT

IL —SOUTHERN ILLINOIS UNIVERSITY, CARBONDALE, Delyte W Morris Library, Special Collections Dept, Carbondale, 62901. David V Koch, Cur of Special Collections; Louisa Bowen, Cur of Manuscripts
Holdings: Vols 360 Cat Mss Pix Tapes
Notes: The Dr H K Croessmann Collection of James Joyce (17 linear ft) incl the papers of Joyce's biographer, Herbert Gorman, his literary agent, James Pinker, and his German translator, Georg Goyert, and more than 200 of Joyce's letters. Inventory available in library.

GOSDEN AND CORRELL

CA —UNIVERSITY OF SOUTHERN CALIFORNIA, Edward L Doheny Memorial Library, Archives of Performing Arts, University Park, Los Angeles, 90089. Robert Knutson, Librn
Holdings: Mss Pix
Notes: Personal collection of papers, pictures, etc.

GOSPEL MUSIC see Music, Gospel

GOSSE, EDMUND, 1849-1928

MA —BRANDEIS UNIVERSITY, Goldfarb Library, 415 South St, Waltham, 02154. Bessie Hahn, Dir
Notes: John Galsworthy Collection. Approx 175 letters written to Joseph Conrad, Sir Edmund Gosse and others and 15 linear ft of books consisting of first editions and books about John Galsworthy. Access to the collection of books is through the Main Card Catalog and Special Collections Catalog. A finding list to the correspondence is in Special Collections.

GOSSE, PHILIP HENRY

ON —UNIVERSITY OF TORONTO, Thomas Fisher Rare Book Library, 120 Saint George St, Toronto, M5S 1A5, Can. Richard G Landon, Head
Holdings: Vols (1700) Uncat
Notes: Popular scientific books on English natural history written in the 19th century for the amateur observer and collector. Particularly notable for holdings of Philip Henry Gosse.

GOSSETT, ED

TX —NORTH TEXAS STATE UNIVERSITY, Archives, NT Station Box 5188, Denton, 76203. Robert LaForte, University Archivist
Notes: Part of Oral History Collection. Interviews with Gossett, US Congressman (1938-51).

GOTHAM BOOK MART, NEW YORK CITY

NY —SKIDMORE COLLEGE, Lucy Scribner Library, Saratoga Springs, 12866. David Eyman, Librn
Holdings: Cat
Notes: Incl Frances Steloff's personal collection of modern first editions acquired as proprietor of the Gotham Book Mart, New York City.

GOTHIC NOVELS see Fiction, Gothic

GOTTLIEB, HARRY

IL —CHICAGO HISTORICAL SOCIETY, Library, Clark St at North Ave, Chicago, 60614. Archie Motley, Manuscript Librn
Notes: Papers of Gottlieb and Schwartz, Chicago law firm.

GOTTSCHALK, LOUIS MOREAU

NY —NEW YORK PUBLIC LIBRARY, Music Div, 111 Amsterdam Ave, New York, 10023. Frank C Campbell, Chief
Holdings: Cat Mss Pix
Notes: Composer's autographs.

GOUDAR, ANGE AND SARA

VA —RANDOLPH-MACON COLLEGE, Walter Hines Page Library, Ashland, 23005.

GOUDAR, ANGE AND SARA (cont.)

Flavia Reed Owen, Librn
Holdings: Vols 3000
Notes: Collection incl books of Casanova and other minor 18th-century European authors-Ange Goudar, Sara Goudar, Justienne Wynne. Descriptions of collection in *Cassanoviana: An Annotated Bibliography of Jacques Casanova de Seingalt and of Works Concerning Him,* by J Rives Childs (Vienna: C M Nebehay, 1956, for the Casanova Society of Virginia) and in *Casanova Gleanings,* ed by J Rives Childs (Horn, Austria: Ferdinand Berger, 1958-).

GOUDSMIT, SAMUEL A.

NY —AMERICAN INSTITUTE OF PHYSICS, Center for the History of Physics, Niels Bohr Library, 335 E 45 St, New York, 10017. John Aubry, Librn
Notes: Papers, incl correspondence, notebooks, awards, photographs, and other materials originated by Samuel A Goudsmit. Oral history interviews dealing with the discovery of and subsequent work on pulsars, collected by Steve Woolgar. Permission needed for use of the latter.

GOUDY, FREDERIC W.

CA —CLAREMONT COLLEGES, Ella Strong Denison Library, Scripps College, Claremont, 91711. Judy Harvey Sahak, Librn
Holdings: Cat Mss Pix
Notes: In addition to books and ephemera, collection includes original drawings, paper and metal patterns, matrices, and fonts for types that Frederic S Goudy designed for the Scripps College Press.

DC —LIBRARY OF CONGRESS, Rare Book & Special Collections Div, Washington, 20540. William Matheson, Chief
Holdings: Vols 1791 Cat Mss
Notes: The Frederic and Bertha Goudy Collection was purchased directly from the Goudys in 1944. Apart from the books, pamphlets, magazine articles, clippings, etc that constitute a working library, the collection includes correspondence, type specimens and typefounding equipment. This purchase was supplemented in 1975 by the acquisition of a substantial collection of Goudyana, consisting largely of correspondence and other original source material.

IL —NORTHWESTERN UNIVERSITY, Library, Special Collections Dept, 1937 Sheridan Rd, Evanston, 60201. R Russell Maylone, Cur
Holdings: Vols 2000 Cat Mss
Notes: The John J Louis Memorial Collection: works dealing with the typographic arts and extensive collections of the major typographers, especially Rogers, Dwiggins, Goudy, Clelland and Kittredge. 5000 representative examples of the work of the modern private press from Strawberry Hill to the current small printers. Additional material in the general collection.

ME —BOWDOIN COLLEGE, Library, Brunswick, 04011. Dianne M Gutscher, Cur of Special Collections
Holdings: Vols
Notes: The Frederic Wilson Main Collection contains several hundred books, pamphlets, and clippings relating to the art of printing and bookmaking. Most major contemporary presses are represented, and it incl examples of the typographic work of Bruce Rogers, Frederic W Goudy, Daniel Berkeley Updike, and Rudolph Ruzicka, to mention only a few.

MI —DETROIT PUBLIC LIBRARY, Rare Books Department, 5201 Woodward Ave, Detroit, 48202.
Holdings: Vols 40 Cat Mss
Notes: Incl some correspondence and presentation to Alfred H Zenner. Restricted use. Reference collection.

NY —COLUMBIA UNIVERSITY LIBRARIES, Rare Book & Manuscript Library, 801 Butler Library, 535 W 114 St, New York, 10027. Kenneth A Lohf, Librn
Holdings: Mss Pix
Notes: Incl many drawings and templates for his type designs.

NY —GROLIER CLUB OF NEW YORK LIBRARY, 47 E 60 St, New York, 10022. Robert Nikirk, Librn

NY —ROCHESTER INSTITUTE OF TECHNOLOGY, Melbert B Cary Jr Graphic Arts Collection, School of Printing, One Lomb Memorial Drive, Rochester, 14623. David Pankow, Cur
Holdings: Vols (11,000)
Notes: Inc books, types, mss, etc.

NY —SYRACUSE UNIVERSITY LIBRARIES, Ernest S Bird Library, George Arents Research Library for Special Collections, Syracuse, 13210. Carolyn A Davis, Manuscripts Librn; Amy S Doherty, University Archivist; Mark F Weimer, Rare Book Librn
Holdings: Vols 75 Cat Mss Pix

GOULD, GLEN

ON —NATIONAL LIBRARY OF CANADA, 395 Wellington St, Ottawa, K1A 0N4, Can. Andre Preibish, Dir
Holdings: Vols 35,000
Notes: Includes 2000 pieces of Canadian sheet music (mostly 19th century imprints), 40,000 cylinders, discs, tapes; over 600 serials titles devoted to music; 200 archival collections of composers, musicians and conductors, eg papers of Healy Willan, eminent composer; Glen Gould, well-known pianist; Sir Ernest MacMillan, conductor, director and composer. Since 1950 the Canadian imprints have been received on legal deposit. Intensive purchases aim at a comprehensive collection of Canadian music.

GOULD, JOHN

KS —UNIVERSITY OF KANSAS, Kenneth Spencer Research Library, Special Collections Dept, Lawrence, 66045. Alexandra Mason, Librn
Holdings: Vols 85 Cat Mss Pix
Notes: Part of Ellis Collection of Ornithology and Natural History. Incl over 2000 original drawings and paintings by John Gould and his artist associates. Noncirculating.

MA —BOSTON UNIVERSITY, Mugar Memorial Library, Special Collections Dept, 771 Commonwealth Ave, Boston, 02215. Howard B Gotlieb, Dir
Holdings: Cat Mss Pix
Notes: Mss, correspondence, etc collected in depth; incl publications by or about.

GOULD, NORMAN JUDD, 1877-

NY —CORNELL UNIVERSITY LIBRARIES, Collection of Regional History, Dept of Manuscripts and Univ Archives, Ithaca, 14853.
Holdings: Pix
Notes: NY Congressman, 1915-23. Incl papers, ca 1861-(1917-1923)-1938; speeches, press releases, circulars, clippings and photos.

GOUT

TX —HOUSTON ACADEMY OF MEDICINE-TEXAS MEDICAL CENTER, Library, Jesse H Jones Library Bldg, Houston, 77030. Elizabeth Borst White, Special Collections Librn
Holdings: Vols (1300) Mss Pix
Notes: Burbank Collection on Arthritis, Rheumatism and Gout. An exhaustive collection on arthritis and gout before 1957. Largely from the 16th-19th centuries (also a medical manuscript dated about 1450). Bound volumes of German, French and American offprints complement the monograph collection. In 1983 the Kevin Fraser Addition to this Collection included 130 titles published before 1900.

GOUZENKO, IGOR

BC —UNIVERSITY OF VICTORIA, McPherson Library, Victoria, V8W 3H5, Can.

GOVER, ROBERT

MA —BOSTON UNIVERSITY, Mugar Memorial Library, Special Collections Dept, 771 Commonwealth Ave, Boston, 02215. Howard B Gotlieb, Dir
Holdings: Cat Mss
Notes: Mss, correspondence, etc collected in depth; incl publications by or about.

GOVERNMENT see Political Science

GOVERNMENT, COMPARATIVE see Comparative Government

GOVERNMENT, STATE see State Government

GOVERNMENT EMPLOYEES see Civil Service

GOVERNMENT GAZETTES see Gazettes

GOVERNMENT INVESTIGATIONS see Governmental Investigations

GOVERNMENT OFFICIALS see Public Officers

GOVERNMENT PUBLICATIONS

CA —UNIVERSITY OF CALIFORNIA, BERKELEY, University Library, Government Documents Department, 350 Library Annex, Berkeley, 94720. Suzanne Gold, Collection Dept Librn
Holdings: Vols (314,000) Cat Microforms
Budget: ($85,115)
Notes: General collection of government documents, historical and current, on the federal and state levels; as well as international and foreign documents. The Library's holdings are particularly strong in foreign statistics and censuses, and US Congress. The Government Documents Department serves as a full depository for GPO, NASA, State of California, EEC, GATT, IAEA, United Nations, UNESCO, Rand Corporation (non-classified), IBRD, OECD, ILO, UNITAR, ITC, and CE. Selective depository, PL-480 Programs, or gift or exchange arrangements obtain for the states of Michigan and Washington and for Canada, India, Pakistan and Indonesia. Incl microfilm and 300,000 fiche, cards, and prints.

CA —CALIFORNIA STATE UNIVERSITY, CHICO, Library, Government Publications and Maps, Chico, 95929. William Stuve, Librn
Holdings: Vols 7200
Notes: Rand Corporation-US government publications.

CA —UNIVERSITY OF CALIFORNIA, LOS ANGELES, Research Library, Public Affairs Service, 405 Hilgard Ave, Los Angeles, 90024. Edward Shreeves, Chairman, Bibliographers Group; Eugenia Eaton, Head, Public Affairs Service
Holdings: Microforms
Notes: Depository for the official publications of California cities and counties, the state of California, the United States government, the United Nations and some of its specialized agencies (including the Food and Agricultural Organization and UNESCO), and such regional organizations as the European Communities and Organization of American States. Selected publications of other American cities and counties, of the other states and possessions of the United States, of interstate organizations, and of foreign governments (with emphasis on major world powers, Africa, Latin America and the Near and Middle East) and intergovernmental organizations.

CA —UNIVERSITY OF CALIFORNIA, LOS ANGELES, Research Library, African Studies Collection, 405 Hilgard Ave, Los Angeles, 90024. Edward Shreeves, Chairman, Bibliographers Group; Joseph J

GOVERNMENT PUBLICATIONS (cont.)

Lauer, African Studies Bibliographer
Holdings: Maps Pix Slides Phonorecords Audiotapes Microforms
Notes: General collection mainly in the humanities and social sciences, covering prehistoric times to the present. Particular strengths include: early travel and exploration, mission field, literature, vernacular languages and literatures, Portuguese Africa, slavery (have the British Foreign Office's *General Correspondence. Slave Trade* on microfilm). Extensive holdings of journals, newspapers and government publications. The collection was described in the *Handbook of American Resources for African Studies* (1967).

CO —COLORADO STATE LIBRARY, State Publications Depository & Distribution Center, 1362 Lincoln St, Denver, 80203. Tom Reynolds, Consultant
Holdings: Vols 15,000 Microforms
Notes: Incl 17,000 ERIC documents from 1977 (ED 127 417 and above) and 2000 earlier numbers, mostly below ED 002 500.

DC —DISTRICT OF COLUMBIA PUBLIC LIBRARY, Martin Luther King Memorial Library, Washingtoniana Div and Washington Star Collection, 901 G St NW, Washington, 20001. Roxanna Deane, Chief
Notes: Incl the DC Code, Regulations, the *Register,* annual reports, etc.

DC —LIBRARY OF CONGRESS, African and Middle Eastern Division, Washington, 20540.
Holdings: Cat Mss Microforms
Notes: Orientalia: the Orientalia Division contains 1,400,000 vols in Oriental languages. Chinese: more than 422,000 vols, espec strong in local histories and Ch'ing (1644-1911) period material. Japanese: over 574,000 vols, espec strong in economics, statistics, history, literature; 12,000 government, learned society, and university periodical titles, particularly science, technology, and social sciences. Korean: 56, 000 vols, espec strong in social sciences and modern history.

DC —LIBRARY OF CONGRESS, Serial and Government Publications Division, Washington, 20540.
Notes: Serials. One of the largest and most extensive collections in the world, incl periodicals; scietific and learned journals in all languages and in all fields except agriculture and medicine; US Government serials (Federal, State, County, and Municipal); national foreign government serials from all countries; provincial serials from provinces possessing autonomy; municipal serials from principal cities; newspapers (850,000 unbound issues, 75,000 bound vols, 170,000 microfilm reels), 12,000 microprint cards of early American newspapers, 1704-1820, incl 1500 titles currently received, 500 of these being representative titles from all States of the Union and 1000 from all foreign countries.

DC —US BUREAU OF THE CENSUS, Library, Federal Office Bldg 3, Rm 2451, Washington, 20233. Betty Baxtresser, Chief, ASD Library Branch
Holdings: Vols (64,000) Cat
Notes: Periodic reports from the governments of the states, counties, cities with populations of over 10,000 and selected special districts of the US. Emphasis is on the financial aspects of governments. Reports are listed in a computer print-out comprising a volume of the printed *Catalogs of the Bureau of the Census Library.*

FL —FLORIDA STATE UNIVERSITY, Robert Manning Strozier Library, Tallahassee, 32306. Judith Depew, Head, Documents-Maps Dept
Holdings: Vols (680,000) Uncat Microforms
Notes: A depository for Florida, GPO, NASA, UN, and UNESCO documents, with standing orders for British, ILO, OAS, IMF; selected documents are purchased from various government levels. The collection incl historical as well as current material, especially Florida, US, Great Britain. The Library's holdings are strong in congressional bills and hearings, decennial censuses, and British Sessional papers. Number of volumes incl microprint and microfiche, but not cataloged documents and microfilm.

ID —IDAHO STATE UNIVERSITY, Library, Pocatello, 83209. Joseph K W Lu, Librn
Holdings: Uncat Maps Microforms
Budget: ($10,000)
Notes: Over a million items. Partial depository for US Government publications (893,229 items); incl ERIC microfiche and unclassified AEC and Dept of Energy publications in microform; depository for Idaho State Government publications (1600 items); other state government publications (31,005 items); and foreign and international government bodies (24,504 items).

IL —CENTER FOR RESEARCH LIBRARIES, 6050 S Kenwood Ave, Chicago, 60637. Donald B Simpson, Dir; Esther Smith, Collection Development Librn
Holdings: Vols 700,000 Uncat Microforms
Budget: $6000
Notes: An attempt is being made to collect all official publications of all 50 states, from 1952. Also have very extensive backfiles of older material and *Microfilm Collection of Early State Records.*

IL —NORTHWESTERN UNIVERSITY, Library, Government Publications Dept, Evanston, 60201. Robert W Baumgartner, Head
Notes: Collection consits of US federal documents (depository library since 1876); state documents (emphasis on Illinois); municipal documents (emphasis on Evanston and Chicago); documents of international organizations (emphasis on United Nations, United Nations specialized agencies, Organization of American States, European Communities). Collection consists of publications of 44 international organizations. Shelflist maintained in the Government Publications Department. Most publications not incl in the library's general catalog.

KY —UNIVERSITY OF KENTUCKY, Margaret I King Library, Government Publications Dept, Lexington, 40506. Sandra McAninch, Head
Holdings: Cat Maps Microforms
Notes: The University has been a US depository since 1907 and the Kentucky Regional Depository since 1967. The library has complete holdings of the major series and the Readex microprint non-depository collection. Incl papers.

LA —NEW ORLEANS PUBLIC LIBRARY, Louisiana Div, 219 Loyola Ave, New Orleans, 70140. Collin B Hamer Jr, Head; Jean M Jones, Doc Librn
Holdings: Vols 30,000 Cat
Notes: Louisiana Documents Collection covers the period 1815 to date. Library is a legally appointed depository. The material is indexed in catalogs published and regularly cumulated by the Recorder of Documents, Louisiana State Library. Material is restricted to on-site use.

MD —MARYLAND STATE LAW LIBRARY, Courts of Appeal Bldg, 361 Rowe Blvd, Annapolis, 21401. Michael S Miller, Dir; Shirley A Rittenhouse, Librn
Holdings: Vols (180,000) Cat Microforms
Budget: ($114,750)
Notes: Strong social science, humanities and law enforcement collection. Currently select 36 percent of total available items from GPO.

MA —BOSTON PUBLIC LIBRARY, Government Documents Department, Boston, 02117. V Lloyd Jameson, Cur
Holdings: Maps Microforms
Notes: Regional depository for federal documents. Also have foreign government publications in an attempt to collect major statistical series of all countries, plus other major documents such as social and economic development plans. Collect state documents other than Mass, bluebooks, statistical abstracts and legislative research reports. Have municipal documents which are listed in *Index to Current Urban Documents.*

MI —UNIVERSITY OF MICHIGAN, Bureau of Government Library, 100A Rackman Bldg, Ann Arbor, 48109. Barbara Landay, Technical Libr Assistant
Holdings: Vols (66,000) Cat
Budget: ($10,000)
Notes: Established in 1914 to serve faculty and students of Institute of Public Policy Studies. Particularly concerned with state and local documents, but incl some federal documents. Also has a pamphlet and newspaper clipping collection on Michigan. Some information on foreign governments.

MI —MONROE COUNTY LIBRARY SYSTEM, Ellis Reference and Information Center, 3700 S Custer Rd, Monroe, 48161. Marie D Chulski, Head of Reference Services
Holdings: Vols Periodicals Microforms Pamphlets
Notes: Depository for documents of the US, Michigan, Southeast Michigan region and Monroe County, Michigan. Incl 1300 feet paper, 50 feet fiche, books, periodicals, microforms, pamphlets, etc.

MN —MINNEAPOLIS PUBLIC LIBRARY & INFORMATION CENTER, Documents Dept, 300 Nicollet Mall, Minneapolis, 55401. Julia W Copeland, Dept Head
Holdings: Documents Microforms
Budget: $24,000
Notes: Over 500,000 items; Congressional hearings on microfiche, 1869-1941; Congressional committee prints on microfiche, 1869-1981. Maintain a shelflist by Superintendent of Documents number plus a subject index. Minnesota state documents on microfiche, 1980-date.

MO —SAINT LOUIS PUBLIC LIBRARY, Documents Dept, 1301 Olive St, Saint Louis, 63103. Anne Watts, Librn
Holdings: Cat Maps Microforms
Notes: Depository for documents of the US, Missouri and St Louis, Missouri. Incl 1,600, 000 items.

NE —NEBRASKA LIBRARY COMMISSION, Publications Clearinghouse, 1420 P St, Lincoln, 68508. Patricia Sloan, Federal Documents Librn; Vern Buis, State Documents Librn
Holdings: Vols (316,000) Cat Microforms
Notes: Depository for US government publications since July 1972; regional depository for Nebraska since July 1974; Joint Regional with the University of Nebraska Libraries since September 1977. Non-depository documents acquired on microfiche from Congressional Information Service's ASI collection. Depository for all Nebraska State government publications since July 1972.
See also entries under Nebraska; State Documents.

NE —NEBRASKA STATE HISTORICAL SOCIETY, Archives, 1500 R St, Box 82554, Lincoln, 68501. James E Potter, State Archivist
Holdings: Cat Mss Microforms
Budget: ($290,000)
Notes: Collection

NY —NEW YORK STATE LIBRARY, State Education Bldg Annex, Washington Ave, Albany, 12224.
Holdings: Cat Microforms
Notes: Official depository of New York State publications; regional depository of US documents, also in microfilm; depository for Canadian government documents; strong collections of state documents, New York City documents; British sessional papers; also League of Nations, OAS documents. Extensive holdings of other domestic and foreign publications. Congressional serial set, incl hearings (1946-date).

NY —NEW YORK PUBLIC LIBRARY, Research Libraries, Economic & Public Affairs Div, Fifth Ave & 42 St, New York, 10018. Edward DiRoma, Chief
Holdings: Vols (1,500,000) Cat Microforms
Notes: Described in *Catalog of Government* Publications, The Research Libraries of The New York Public Library. Approx 700,000 cards, 40 vols, $3025. This collection comprises the fundamental documents of all national and colonial governments so far as they have been published or obtained. It incl official gazettes, parliamentary debates and papers, session laws, correspondence on

GOVERNMENT PUBLICATIONS (cont.)

foreign relations, treaties, departmental reports, statistical annuals and statistical reports, and journals and monographs relating to any major activities of government departments and agencies. The publications of state and provincial governments, principal cities, and many smaller cities, are incl. Holdings are strongest for the US, Great Britain, its related states, the Scandinavian countries, andWestern Europe. Catalog references are entered under political units, broken down by agencies under each unit's jurisdiction. The listings for each agency are in two groups: an alphabetical one for serial publications; and a dated file of monographic publications. About 1,025,000 publications cataloged through December 31, 1971. All government publications cataloged later appear in *Dictionary Catalog of the Research Libraries,* 1972.

NY —UNITED NATIONS, Dag Hammarskjold Library, Rm L382, New York, 10017. Vladimir Orlov, Librn
Holdings: Cat

OH —PUBLIC LIBRARY OF CINCINNATI & HAMILTON COUNTY, Science & Technology Dept, 800 Vine St, Cincinnati, 45202. Rosemary Gaiser, Head
Notes: Depository for US government publications since 1884 in the subject areas of science and technology. Noncirculating.

OK —OKLAHOMA DEPT OF LIBRARIES, Law Library, 109 State Capital, Oklahoma City, 73105. Robert Clark, Dir; Betty Brown, Okla Collection Librn; Virginia Collier, US Documents; Jan Blakely, State Documents; Blane Dessy, Library Science
Holdings: Vols 808,458 Cat Microforms
Notes: US document depository. Incl 911, 246 sheets microfiche; 2800 microfilm.

OR —UNIVERSITY OF OREGON LIBRARY, Documents Section, Eugene, 97403. Tom Stave, Section Head; John Shuler, Documents Librn
Holdings: Vols (250,000) Microforms
Notes: Depository for US government, Canadian government and its agencies, European Communities, and Oregon publications. Comprehensive holdings of the United Nations and its agencies plus League of Nations publications.

PA —UNIVERSITY OF PITTSBURGH, Hillman Library, Pittsburgh, 15260. Mary E Miller, Documents Librn
Holdings: Vols 212,785
Budget: $66,000
Notes: Contains Depository publications of US government, Canadian Government (1968-), Commonwealth of Pennsylvania (1970-). Comprehensive League of Nations and United Nations collection. Microforms: US Non-Depository Government Publications (1953-).

PA —SCRANTON PUBLIC LIBRARY, Vine & N Washington Sts, Scranton, 18503. Thomas McHale, Dir
Holdings: Vols (192) Cat
Budget: ($7000)
Notes: Foreign trade information service.

PA —PENNSYLVANIA STATE UNIVERSITY, Fred Lewis Pattee Library, Documents Section, University Park, 16802. Diane H Smith, Head
Notes: Depository for US Government publications; depository for Pennsylvania documents; collect United Nations and related international and intergovernmental organization publications; selected publications from Australia, Great Britain, including Parliamentary Papers; census materials; a large microform collection, including Department of Energy (formerly ERDA, AEC), Congressional publications, Patents, OAS, UN. Incl 900,000 documents. Government publications are microforms, some cataloged.

TX —TEXAS STATE LIBRARY, US Documents Collection, 1200 Brazos, PO Box 12927 Capitol Sta, Austin, 78711. Bonnie Grobar, Librn
Holdings: Vols 900,000 Microforms
Notes: The Texas State Library became a depository for US documents by law when Texas became a state in 1845. It has been a regional depository since 1963. The collection now contains many valuable and rare documents as well as one of the most complete serial sets in the state.

TX —WEST TEXAS STATE UNIVERSITY, Cornette Library, PO Box 748 WT Sta, Canyon, 79016. Annette F Nall, Documents Librn
Notes: Depository library since the 1920s. 400,000 US documents.

TX —SOUTHERN METHODIST UNIVERSITY, Fondren Library, Dallas, 75275. Curt Holleman, Librn for Collection Development

TX —NORTH TEXAS STATE UNIVERSITY, Government Documents Dept, NT Station Box 5188, Denton, 76203. Melody Kelley, Librn
Notes: Depository: 350,156 paper; 95,692 fiche. Congressional hearings 1823-1956. NTSU Libraries are also a depository for Texas State documents. Separate card catalogs for US documents.

TX —TEXAS CHRISTIAN UNIVERSITY, Mary Couts Burnett Library, Fort Worth, 76129.

WI —UNIVERSITY OF WISCONSIN, MADISON, Memorial Library, 728 State St, Madison, 53706. Erwin K Welsch, Social Studies Bibliographer
Holdings: Vols Cat Microforms
Notes: For Great Britain, incl Journals of the House of Lords and the House of Commons; Parliamentary Reports and Papers of the House of Commons; statutes, laws, and acts; Parliamentary Debates (Hansard) for Lords and Commons from 1803 to date; previous vols on microfiche. For France, Parliamentary and statistical publications. For Germany, Parliamentary (1870-1933), and of both Germanies (1949-) as well as statistical publications; also publications of German states for the 19th century.

BC —VANCOUVER PUBLIC LIBRARY, Science & Technology Div, 750 Burrard St, Vancouver, V6Z 1X5, Can. P Haffenden, Head, Science & Technology Div
Notes: We have a comprehensive collection of Canadian and British Columbian government documents in the Science and Technology subject areas as well as a selection of documents from other governments.

MB —UNIVERSITY OF MANITOBA, Elizabeth Dafoe Library, Government Publications Section, Winnipeg, R3T 2N2, Can. June Dutka, Head
Holdings: Vols 360,000 Uncat Mss Maps Microforms
Notes: Concerned mainly with supporting research programs in the arts (especially sociology, political studies, native studies, history, geography and economics), agriculture, home economics and nursing. Collection consists of Canadian federal publications; depository since 1969 (emphasis on Statistics Canada); holdings of pre-confederation documents, early parliamentary publications, and royal commissions for the post-war years are reasonably complete; provincial documents (emphasis on Manitoba); municipal documents (emphasis on Winnipeg); documents from Great Britain, India and the US (emphasis on US State Agricultural Experimental Stations); publications from international organizations (emphasis on the Food and Agricultural Organization depository since 1945), UNESCO, International Labour Organization and Commission of the EuropeanCommunities. Card catalog is maintained in the Government Publications Section. Most publications are not included in the library's general catalog.

ON —LIBRARY OF PARLIAMENT, Parliament Bldgs, Ottawa, K1A 0A9, Can. Erik J Spicer, Parliamentary Librn
Holdings: Vols 162,000 Uncat
Notes: Noncirculating; interlibrary loan restricted.

ON —NATIONAL LIBRARY OF CANADA, 395 Wellington St, Ottawa, K1A 0N4, Can. Andre Preibish, Dir
Notes: Over 1,100,000 Canadian federal and provincial government publications; about 800,000 documents from other countries, plus extensive microform collections. Strong in pre-Confederation as well as post-Confederation documents.

†ON —METROPOLITAN TORONTO LIBRARY, Social Sciences Dept, 789 Yonge St, Toronto, M4W 2G8, Can. Abdus Salam, Head
Holdings: Vols Cat Maps Phonorecords Audiotapes 16mm Films Microforms
Notes: Thecollection is a full depository for Canadian federal and Ontario provincial publications and contains an exhaustive collection of publications from the various Canadian provinces. It includes statutes, gazettes, legislative debates, journals, reports, etc. Also extensive holdings for the US and Great Britain; comprehensive holdings of treaties for Canada, Great Britain and the US; selected publications for other foreign countries. Types of publications emphasized are statutory laws, treaties, legislative proceedings, government directories and manuals, statistical materials and national yearbooks. Large collection of UN materials; full depository for UNESCO publications; selected publications of various international organizations. The collection is cited in Canada, National Library, Resources Survey *Section,Research Collections in Canadian* Libraries, Volume 5, *Collections of Official Publications in Canada* (Ottawa: Supply and Services Canada, 1976).

ON —INTERNATIONAL JOINT COMMISSION LIBRARY, 100 Ouellette Ave, Seventh Floor, Windsor, N9A 6T3, Can. Pat Murrary, Librn
Notes: Emphasis on water resources, water quality, land use, coastal zones, Great Lakes. Library includes 40,000 government reports from federal, provincial and state governments; 5000 monographs to support Great Lakes Water Quality Agreement Community. Collection also includes 243 periodicals, 1700 microfiche, 800 slides & vertical files.

†PQ —ACADIA UNIVERSITY, Library, Wolfville, B0P 1X0, Can.
Notes: Canadian document depository.

GOVERNMENTAL INVESTIGATIONS

DC —GEORGETOWN UNIVERSITY, Library, Special Collections Div, 37 & O Sts NW, Washington, 20057. George M Barringer, Special Collections Librn; Nicholas B Sheetz, Mss Librn
Holdings: Cat Mss Pix
Notes: Political assassinations, espec materials pertaining to the assissinations of John F Kennedy and Robert F Kennedy and the investigations thereof, as well as the Abraham Lincoln Assassination.

GOYEN, WILLIAM

TX —RICE UNIVERSITY, Fondren Library, Woodson Research Center, 6100 S Main St, PO Box 1892, Houston, 77251. Nancy Parker, Dir Woodson Research Center
Holdings: Mss Pix
Notes: Incl manuscripts and proofs of five novels, plus correspondence, clippings, photos and other memorabilia.

GOYERT, GEORG

IL —SOUTHERN ILLINOIS UNIVERSITY, CARBONDALE, Delyte W Morris Library, Special Collections Dept, Carbondale, 62901. David V Koch, Cur of Special Collections; Louisa Bowen, Cur of Manuscripts
Holdings: Vols 360 Cat Mss Pix Tapes
Notes: The Dr H K Croessmann Collection of James Joyce (17 linear ft) incl the papers of Joyce's biographer, Herbert Gorman, his literary agent, James Pinker, and his German translator, Georg Goyert, and more than 200 of Joyce's letters. Inventory available in library.

GOYTISOLO, JUAN

MA —BOSTON UNIVERSITY, Mugar Memorial Library, Special Collections Dept,

GOYTISOLO, JUAN (cont.)

771 Commonwealth Ave, Boston, 02215. Howard B Gotlieb, Dir
Holdings: Cat Mss Pix
Notes: Mss, correspondence, etc collected in depth; incl publications by or about.

GOZOS

MA —HARVARD UNIVERSITY LIBRARY, Widener Library, Cambridge, 02138. Ellen H Brow, Specialist in Book Selection
Holdings: Cat
Notes: Incl in *Widener Library Shelflist* No 41 (1972); also a collection of 10,000 *goigs* and *gozos.*

GRABILL, JOHN C. H.

DC —LIBRARY OF CONGRESS, Prints & Photographs Div, Washington, 20540.
Notes: The John C H Grabill collection of photographs of frontier life in Colorado, South Dakota, and Wyoming, late 19th century, incl views of hunters, prospectors, cowboys, Chinese immigrants, and US Army personnel.

GRACE, WILLIAM RUSSELL, 1832-1904

NY —COLUMBIA UNIVERSITY LIBRARIES, Rare Book & Manuscript Library, 801 Butler Library, 535 W 114 St, New York, 10027. Kenneth A Lohf, Librn
Notes: More than 32,000 items documenting the rise of William Russell Grace's shipping business and other materials relating to his career as mayor of New York. Incl records and correspondence relating to all aspects of the shipping business in New York and South America, mining interest in Peru and Chile, and transportation in Costa Rica and Nicaragua. Family memorabilia and photographs, materials concerning New York Politics, banking and insurance, real estate interests and Catholic charities, and letters from Chester A Arthur, John Jacob Astor, Andrew Carnegie, Grover Cleveland, Hamilton Fish, John Hay and J Pierpont Morgan. Restricted use.

GRACE AND CO., W. R.

NY —COLUMBIA UNIVERSITY LIBRARIES, Rare Book & Manuscript Library, 801 Butler Library, 535 W 114 St, New York, 10027. Kenneth A Lohf, Librn
Notes: More than 32,000 items documenting the rise of William Russell Grace's shipping business and other materials relating to his career as mayor of New York. Incl records and correspondence relating to all aspects of the shipping business in New York and South America, mining interest in Peru and Chile, and transportation in Costa Rica and Nicaragua. Family memorabilia and photographs, materials concerning New York Politics, banking and insurance, real estate interests and Catholic charities, and letters from Chester A Arthur, John Jacob Astor, Andrew Carnegie, Grover Cleveland, Hamilton Fish, John Hay and J Pierpont Morgan. Restricted use.

GRADY, HENRY W.

GA —EMORY UNIVERSITY, Robert W Woodruff Library, Special Collections Dept, Atlanta, 30322. Linda M Matthews, Head Special Collections; Virginia J H Cain, Processing Archivist; Richard H F Lindemann, Reference Archivist
Holdings: Cat Mss Pix Audiotapes
Notes: Extensive collections of papers of Henry W Grady, Corra Harris, Joel Chandler Harris, Julian LaRose Harris, Julia Collier Harris, Clark Howell, Ralph E McGill, and Harold H Martin, among others, most associated with the Atlanta *Constitution.* Descriptions and index available in repository.

GRAETTINGER, BOB

TX —NORTH TEXAS STATE UNIVERSITY, Audio Center, Box 5188, NT Station, Denton, 76203. Morris Martin, Music Librn
Notes: More than 1600 manuscript jazz compositions, (incl scores and parts, alternate versions, expanded arrangements) by Stan Kenton, Johnny Richards, Joe Coccia, Lennie Niehaus, Pete Rugolo, Willie Maiden, Bob Curnow, Ken Hanna, Gene Rowland, Bob Graettinger and others, used by the Stan Kenton Band and given to North Texas State University in 1962 and at Kenton's death in 1979. Unpublished catalog: Breeden, Leon, *Stan Kenton Music in the NTSU Jazz Studies Library and the NTSU Music Library,* Denton, 1983 (99 pages).

GRAHAM, BETTIE C.

TX —NORTH TEXAS STATE UNIVERSITY, Archives, NT Station Box 5188, Denton, 76203. Robert LaForte, University Archivist
Notes: Part of Business Archive Project. Interviews with founder of Liquid Paper Corporation.

GRAHAM, BILLY

IL —WHEATON COLLEGE, Billy Graham Center Library and Archives, Wheaton, 60187. Ferne Lauraine Weimer, Dir of Library; Robert Shuster, Dir of Archives
Notes: Archives of the Center.

NY —NEW YORK PUBLIC LIBRARY, Performing Arts Research Center, Rodgers & Hammerstein Archives of Recorded Sound, 111 Amsterdam Ave, New York, 10023.
Holdings: Cat Tapes
Notes: A collection of taped interviews, representing over 400 prominent figures. Incl are voices of Richard Nixon, Billy Graham, Maurice Chevalier, Sammy Davis, Jr, Dr Albert Sabin, etc.

GRAHAM, EVARTS

MO —WASHINGTON UNIVERSITY, School of Medicine, Archives, 660 S Euclid Ave, Saint Louis, 63110. Paul G Anderson, Archivist
Holdings: Mss Pix Audiotapes
Budget: ($38,000)
Notes: Institutional records and papers of faculty of Washington University School of Medicine and its predecessors and associated hospitals. Contains records of St Louis Medical College, Missouri Medical Barnard Free Skin and Cancer Hospital, Barnes Hospital, St Louis Children's Hospital and Jewish Hospital of St Louis. Incl papers of William Beaumont, Joseph Erlanger, Leo Loeb, Evarts Graham, Edmund V Cowdry, Helen Graham, Carl V Moore, Margaret Smith and others. Oral history program. See also: Anderson, Paul G and Hoolihan, Christopher, eds. *Special Collections* (St Louis: Washington University School of Medicine, 1981). 960 linear feet.

GRAHAM, HELEN

MO —WASHINGTON UNIVERSITY, School of Medicine, Archives, 660 S Euclid Ave, Saint Louis, 63110. Paul G Anderson, Archivist
Holdings: Mss Pix Audiotapes
Budget: ($38,000)
Notes: Institutional records and papers of faculty of Washington University School of Medicine and its predecessors and associated hospitals. Contains records of St Louis Medical College, Missouri Medical Barnard Free Skin and Cancer Hospital, Barnes Hospital, St Louis Children's Hospital and Jewish Hospital of St Louis. Incl papers of William Beaumont, Joseph Erlanger, Leo Loeb, Evarts Graham, Edmund V Cowdry, Helen Graham, Carl V Moore, Margaret Smith and others. Oral history program. See also: Anderson, Paul G and Hoolihan, Christopher, eds. *Special Collections* (St Louis: Washington University School of Medicine, 1981). 960 linear feet.

GRAHAM, HUGH DAVIS

MD —UNIVERSITY OF MARYLAND, BALTIMORE COUNTY, Albin O Kuhn Library and Gallery, 5401 Wilkens Ave, Baltimore, 21228. Ann Copeland, Special Collections Librn
Holdings: Vols 600// Uncat Mss
Notes: Major items in the Hugh Davis Graham papers on southern history include *Southern School News*, Southern Regional Council publications, and reports on civil rights and integration in the 1950s and 1960s.

GRAHAM, JAMES D.

PA —US ARMY MILITARY HISTORY INSTITUTE, Carlisle Barracks, 17013. Richard J Sommers, Chief Archivist-Historian
Holdings: Cat //
Notes: The James D Graham papers (Mexican War Miscellaneous Collection), his diary, 13-26 April 1848, recounting personal observations on his mission to Mexico City for President Polk.

GRAHAM, KENNETH

AZ —ARIZONA STATE UNIVERSITY, Library, Tempe, 85287. Marilyn Wurzburger, Special Collections Librn
Holdings: Vols (108) Pix
Notes: Collection covers various aspects of Children's Theatre from 1944 through the present. Areas of emphasis incl International and National Child Drama Associations, award-winning theatres, educational programs, regional groups and prominent figures in Children's Theatre incl: Irene Vickers Baker, Isabel Burger, Virginia Lee Comer, Rita Criste, Moses Goldberg, Kenneth Graham, Aurand Harris, Paul Kozelka, George Latshaw, Rosemary Musil, Sara Spencer, Winifred Ward, Susan Zeder and Lin Wright. Publications incl newsletters, research papers, bibliographies and records of the proceedings of the Children's Theatre Association of America. 80 linear feet of scripts, documents, publications, films, tapes (oral history) programs, correspondence, photographs, working papers and clippings. Partially indexed; finding guides available.

GRAHAM, MARTHA

NY —NEW YORK PUBLIC LIBRARY, Performing Arts Research Center, Dance Collection, 111 Amsterdam Ave, New York, 10023. Genevieve Oswald, Cur
Holdings: Vols (40,000) Cat Mss Pix Audiotapes Videotapes 16mm Films
Budget: ($9,280)
Notes: Extensive biographical and visual material. Includes photographs, programs, clippings, scrapbooks, original drawings, tape-recorded interviews, and films.

GRAHAM, ROBERT BONTINE CUNNINGHAME

CA —CALIFORNIA STATE UNIVERSITY, LONG BEACH, Library, Dept of Special Collections & Archives, 1250 Bellflower Blvd, Long Beach, 90840. John Ahouse, Special Collections Librn
Holdings: Vols 40 Cat
Notes: First and limited editions.

IL —ILLINOIS STATE UNIVERSITY, Milner Library, Dept of Special Collections, Normal, 61761. Robert Sokan, Librn
Notes: First editions, limited editions, ephemera, etc.

MI —UNIVERSITY OF MICHIGAN, Library, Dept of Rare Books & Special Collections, Ann Arbor, 48109. Robert J Starring, Head
Holdings: Vols 77 Cat Mss Pix
Notes: Contains 55 titles by or partly by Graham; 15 ALSS by him; ms essay on Graham by David Garnett; various presentation copies or association items; and photos.

NH —DARTMOUTH COLLEGE, Baker Memorial Library, Hanover, 03755.
Holdings: Cat Mss Pix
Notes: First editions, mss, ephemera, etc. Noncirculating.

GRAHAM, W. S.

BC —UNIVERSITY OF VICTORIA, McPherson Library, Victoria, V8W 3H5, Can.
Notes: Poet.

GRAHAM, WILLIAM A.

CT —YALE UNIVERSITY, Box 1603A, Yale Station, New Haven, 06520.
Holdings: Mss
Notes: 74 television scripts by William A Graham.

GRAIN

MB —CANADIAN GRAIN COMMISSION, Library, 303 Main St, Winnipeg, R3C 3G7, Can. Jim Blanchard, Librn
Holdings: Vols (7500) Cat Mss Maps Slides Microforms
Budget: ($20,000)

PE —AGRICULTURE CANADA, Research Station Library, PO Box 1210, Charlottetown, C1A 7M8, Can. Barrie Stanfield, Librn
Holdings: Vols (2300) Cat
Budget: ($5000)

GRAIN—ANALYSIS AND CHEMISTRY

MB —CANADIAN GRAIN COMMISSION, Library, 303 Main St, Winnipeg, R3C 3G7, Can. Jim Blanchard, Librn
Holdings: Vols (7500) Cat Mss Maps Slides Microforms
Budget: ($20,000)

GRAIN—DISEASES AND PESTS

OH —OHIO AGRICULTURAL RESEARCH & DEVELOPMENT CENTER, Dept of Plant Pathology, Madison Ave, Wooster, 44691. Richard M Ritter
Holdings: Vols 2000 Papers Journal Reprints
Notes: Virus diseases of corn. "Maize Virus Information Service."

GRAIN PESTS see Grain—Diseases and Pests

GRAMERCY BOOKSHOP

†NY —COLUMBIA UNIVERSITY LIBRARIES, Butler Library, Rare Book and Manuscript Library, 535 W 114 St, New York, 10027.
Notes: The files of Gramercy Bookshop in New York, 1940-79.

GRAMMARS—COLLECTIONS

CA —LOS ANGELES PUBLIC LIBRARY, Literature and Philology Dept, 630 W Fifth St, Los Angeles, 90071. Helene G Mochedlover, Dept Librn
Notes: Foreign Language Collection. Approximately 450 languages and dialects are represented, most of which are not included in Foreign Languages Department collection. Emphasis is on breadth of reference collection, which includes dictionaries, grammars, phrase books, and many important encyclopedias.

NY —AMERICAN MUSEUM OF NATURAL HISTORY, Library Services Dept, Central Park W & 79th St, New York, 10024. Nina J Root, Chairwoman; Mary Genett, Asst Librn for Reference Services
Holdings: / / Cat
Notes: Mostly 19th and early 20th century items; collections not kept current since there are better resources in the area. Several esoteric languages are represented, however.

OH —CLEVELAND PUBLIC LIBRARY, Fine Arts and Special Collections Department, 325 Superior Ave, Cleveland, 44114. Alice N Loranth, Head
Holdings: Vols (15,000) Cat
Notes: Part of the Language and Languages Collection. Contains many grammars, dictionaries, and works in linguistics in African, Asian and Western languages and dialects. Material in the Dewey/Brett Collection is classified by an extensively expanded language classification. Its special feature is the "Language File," indexing samples of over 7000 languages and dialects housed in Special Collections.
See also entry under Language and Languages.

WI —UNIVERSITY OF WISCONSIN, MADISON, Memorial Library, British & American Language & Literature Collection, 728 State St, Madison, 53706. Yvonne Schofer, Bibliographer
Holdings: Vols 730 Cat
Notes: Benjamin David Berry Collection of English Grammars. Consists of English grammars and grammatical treatises from the 17th to the 20th centuries, with emphasis on 19th century materials. Includes many rareties. The collection has been enlarged in succeeding years. Several volumes in Dept of Rare Books and Special Collections; the rest in stacks.

GRAN COLOMBIA

NY —STATE UNIVERSITY OF NEW YORK, COLLEGE AT BUFFALO, Poetry/Rare Books Collection, 420 Capen Hall, Buffalo, 14260. Robert J Bertholf, Cur
Holdings: Vols 4200 Cat Mss Maps Pix
Notes: Materials incl books, mss, official gazettes, and periodicals for research on the short-lived political entity known as Gran Colombia (the present-day countries of Colombia, Venezuela, and Ecuador); special emphasis is on the first half of the 19th century but earlier and later periods are incl.

GRAND CANYON

AZ —NORTHERN ARIZONA UNIVERSITY, Special Collection Library, CU Box 6022, Flagstaff, 86011. Peter M Whiteley, Coordr/Archivist; William Mullane, Librn
Notes: Various collections, incl (1) Harvey Butchart Collection. He was a Grand Canyon hiker and explorer, formerly NAU professor; photography of "Grand Canyon Trail Notes, 1957-1969." (2) Fred Harvey and US National Park Service Collection; newsletters covering the period from 1969-1978. (3) Rose Lombard Collection; "The Grand Canyon and Bucky O'Neill." Chapter from an unpublished ms written in 1949 concerning O'Neill, the Tusayan Company, Good and Company, and the Santa Fe and Grand Canyon Railroad (14 pages). (4) William McCawley Collection; typescript of article entitled "The Old Men of the Grand Canyon." Article is about Pete Berry, early settler of the Grand Canyon. Some illustrations showing Berry's ranch at the Grand Canyon today are also incl (1978). (5) C B Wilson Collection; Martin Buggelyn correspondence, files, ca 1900-1920, 1930's. Buggelyn wasa resident of the Grand Canyon and the collection incl information on the Grand Canyon railroad and Grand Canyon National Park. (6) Kolb Collection; very extensive collection of Emery Kolb's photographs (over 250,000) which concentrate on the Grand Canyon, 1902-1975. Incl photographs, motion pictures, correspondence, mss cameras, and other museum objects of Emery and Ellsworth Kolb's photographic studio at the Grand Canyon from the early 1900's to 1976. Incl the first motion picture film of the running of the Colorado River rapids. This collection is subject to restrictions pending the cataloging of the collection.

GRAND COULEE

†WA —WASHINGTON STATE UNIVERSITY, Library, Manuscripts, Archives & Special Collections, Pullman, 99164. John F Guido, Head
Holdings: Cat Mss Maps Pix
Notes: The manuscript collection incl business and financial records of banks, breweries, fisheries, insurance, land, lumber and livestock companies, trade and commodity associations; as well as the personal and professional papers of authors, aviators, educators, engineers, farmers, historians, pioneers, politicians and scientists; especially rich in documents relating to the exploration, settlement and development of the Palouse Country, the Inland Empire, the Columbia Basin and the Pacific Northwest. Described in *Selected Manuscript Resources in the Washington State University Library* (Pullman, 1974); and other published and unpublished inventories and registers.

GRAND TETON NATIONAL PARK

NY —ROCKEFELLER UNIVERSITY, Rockefeller Archive Center, Hillcrest, Pocantico Hills, North Tarrytown, 10591. Joseph W Ernst, Dir; J William Hess, Assoc Dir
Notes: Papers relative to the Rockefeller Family, Foundations, University, and other specific enterprises and contributions to particular areas of social, physical, educational, and historic reform, preservation, conservation or development. Extensive records of administrative, financial, physical, or intellectual relationships.

GRANDI, DINO, 1895-

DC —GEORGETOWN UNIVERSITY, Library, Special Collections Div, 37 & O Sts NW, Washington, 20057. George M Barringer, Special Collections Librn; Nicholas B Sheetz, Mss Librn
Holdings: Cat
Notes: A microfilm of the papers of Dino Grandi (1895-), Conte di Mordano and former Italian minister of foreign affairs and of justice; and ambassador to Great Britain. Grandi played an important role in the Mussolini government and, as president of the Grand Council, presented the resolution removing Mussolini from power in July, 1943.

GRANITE INDUSTRY AND TRADE

RI —WESTERLY PUBLIC LIBRARY, Broad St, Westerly, 02891. David J Panciera, Library Dir
Holdings: Vols (3000) Cat Mss Maps Pix Films Audiotapes Videotapes Microforms
Notes: Extensive coverage of history of Westerly and surrounding area; also general material on Rhode Island and Connecticut. Books, clippings, mss, etc. Many unique family genealogies; local photographs; postcards. Special materials on Seventh-Day Baptist Church; Westerly granite industry (holdings incl tools and mineral samples); Wilcox Park; Watch Hill. Separate catalog.

GRANT, FRANCES

NJ —RUTGERS, THE STATE UNIVERSITY OF NEW JERSEY, Alexander Library, Special Collections and Archives, College Ave & Huntington St, New Brunswick, 08903. Ronald L Becker, Cur of Manuscripts and Rare Books
Notes: Papers of the Inter-American Association for Democracy and Freedom, the Pan American Women's Association, and their director, Frances Grant (1930-). Also papers of Robert Alexander, incl transcripts of several thousand interviews with Latin American political leaders, students, etc (1950-).

GRANT, ULYSSES S.

DC —LIBRARY OF CONGRESS, Manuscript Division, Washington, 20540. John C Broderick, Chief
Notes: The Presidential Papers collection incl the papers, etc, of numerous Presidents.

IL —SOUTHERN ILLINOIS UNIVERSITY, CARBONDALE, Delyte W Morris Library, Special Collections Dept, Carbondale, 62901. David V Koch, Cur of Special Collections; Louisa Bowen, Cur of Manuscripts
Holdings: Vols 35 Cat Mss Pix
Notes: Books from the collection of General Grant; supplementing the Ulysses S Grant

GRANT, ULYSSES S. (cont.)

Association collection of photocopies, the library has collected approximately 75 original Grant letters, as well as the personal papers of Ulysses S Grant III, of his father, General Frederick Grant, and of President Grant's father-in-law Frederick Dent. 23 linear ft.

GRANTS, LAND see Land Grants

GRANTS-IN-AID

CT —HARTFORD PUBLIC LIBRARY, Reference & General Reading Dept, 500 Main St, Hartford, 06103. Beverly A Loughlin, Admin Asst
Notes: Collection is a Foundation Center cooperative collection of Grant-in-Aid for the state of Connecticut, with such holdings as soft and hard copy, IRS apperture cards, comsearch microfiche and other periodicals in support of their subject area.

MI —MONROE COUNTY LIBRARY SYSTEM, Ellis Reference and Information Center, 3700 S Custer Rd, Monroe, 48161. Bernard Margolis, Dir
Holdings: Vols 500 Cat Microforms
Budget: $5000
Notes: Incl all types of current and historical materials on foundations, foundation reports, grants-in-aid, fund raising, grant writing, sample file, periodicals, booklist, etc.

GRANTS-IN-AID, INTERNATIONAL see Economic Assistance; International Relief

GRAPE CULTURE see Viticulture

GRAPES

CA —UNIVERSITY OF CALIFORNIA, DAVIS, General Library, Davis, 95616. Bernard Kreissman, University Librn; C Danial Elliott, Asst Head, Dept Special Collections
Holdings: Vols 3200 Cat
Notes: Collection incl classic treatises and recent texts on grapes and grape growing of worldwide scope, eg, US, Europe, South Africa, South America, Australia, etc. Holdings of ampelographic works (grape variety classification) are especially significant.

CA —CALIFORNIA STATE UNIVERSITY, FRESNO, Henry Madden Library, Dept of Special Collections, Fresno, 93740. Ronald J Mahoney, Head
Holdings: Vols (3400) Cat Maps Pix
Notes: Books and pamphlets relating to the history and development of viticulture and enology. Emphasizes pre-1920 worldwide imprints. Incl 900 merchants' catalogs, 1400 pamphlets, 200 wine lists, 750 periodical issues, and ephemera. Partially cataloged.

GRAPHIC ARTS

CA —CRAFT AND FOLK ART MUSEUM, Library, 5814 Wilshire Blvd, Los Angeles, 90036. Joan M Benedetti, Museum Librn
Holdings: Vols (2000) Slides VF
Notes: Incl 2000 books; 70 journal subscriptions; artists' biographical files: 6 file drawers; clipping files: 8 file drawers; 20,000 slides. Representation of the material culture of all people, traditional and contemporary expressions. Incl visual and printed information on ethnic, traditional, popular, decorative, idiosyncratic, and contemporary crafts as well as vernacular architecture, handmade houses, and design. Information about and for professional artists on health hazards, conservation, and career management. Anthropological and art historical works; exhibition catalogues; slides, photographs, audiocassettes; clipping and pamphlet files. Contemporary Slide Registry of Craftspeople and extensive biographical files of contemporary craft artists. Information and referral files of craft related galleries, shops, festivals, organizations, etc.

CA —J PAUL GETTY MUSEUM, Photo Archives, 17985 Pacific Coast Hwy, Malibu, 90265. William Reeder, Cur
Holdings: Pix
Notes: Incl photographs of works of art at the Museum (180,000 cataloged, 500,000 uncataloged), incl ancient art, western European art (painting, sculpture, graphics) and European decorative arts, medieval and Renaissance to 19th century, and antiquities.

CA —CALIFORNIA COLLEGE OF ARTS & CRAFTS, Meyer Library, Broadway at College, Oakland, 94618. Robert L Harper, Head Librn
Holdings: Vols 1000 Cat Pix
Notes: All fields of arts and crafts. Special collection: the Sinel collection, given to Meyer Library after the death of Mr Sinel. It includes mock-ups and sketches for most of his industrial and graphic designs (penny weight scale; Safeway logo; various brochures; typewriters). It includes his correspondence dating from the early 1930s, when he entered the profession, until his death in 1975.

CA —FINE ARTS MUSEUMS OF SAN FRANCISCO, Achenbach Foundation for Graphic Arts, California Palace of the Legion of Honor, Lincoln Park, San Francisco, 94118. Jane Nelson, Librn
Holdings: Vols (3500) Cat

†CA —UNIVERSITY OF SAN FRANCISCO, Richard A Gleeson Library, The Countess Bernardine Murphy Donohue Rare Book Room, San Francisco, 94117. D Steven Corey, Special Collections Librn
Notes: Some highly specialized materials.

CA —STANFORD UNIVERSITY LIBRARIES, Cecil H Green Library, Stanford, 94305. Michael T Ryan, Cur
Holdings: Vols (12,000) Cat
Notes: The Morgan A & Aline D Gunst Memorial Library. The book arts in every century with some of the best examples. Strong collection of examples of California printers and graphic artists. Complete or nearly complete collections of works by the Kelmscott, Doves, Ashendene, Colt, Grabhorn, and Grabhorn-Hoyem presses.

CT —TRINITY COLLEGE LIBRARY, Watkinson Library, 300 Summit St, Hartford, 06106. Jeffrey Kaimowitz, Cur
Holdings: Cat Pix
Notes: Incl Trumbull-Prime Collection of early illustrated books; also material on all aspects of book design.

CT —YALE UNIVERSITY, Box 1603A, Yale Station, New Haven, 06520.
Holdings: Cat Mss Pix

DC —LIBRARY OF CONGRESS, Prints & Photographs Div, Washington, 20540.
Notes: Graphic Design Collection contains specimens of commercial and ornamental printing produced in Europe and America between 1875-1925.

DC —SMITHSONIAN INSTITUTION LIBRARIES, National Museum of American History Branch, Washington, 20560. Rhoda S Ratner, Branch Librn
Holdings: Vols 7500 Cat Mss Maps Pix

IL —NORTHWESTERN UNIVERSITY, Library, Special Collections Dept, 1937 Sheridan Rd, Evanston, 60201. R Russell Maylone, Cur
Holdings: Vols (2000) Cat Mss
Notes: The John J Louis Memorial Collection. Incl drawings and layouts. Works dealing with the typographic arts and extensive collections of major typographers, especially Rogers, Dwiggins, Goudy, Clelland and Kittredge. Additional materials in general collections.

IN —INDIANA STATE UNIVERSITY, EVANSVILLE, Library, 8600 University Blvd, Evansville, 47712. Gina R Walker, Acting Archivist
Holdings: Uncat Mss
Notes: Papers, etc of the nationally known graphic arts specialist Herbert William Simpson (1904-1970), advertising man, type designer and calligrapher. Original examples of calligraphy and graphic design executed for commercial ads and occasional pieces for personal interest. Materials of about 1940-1970.

LA —R W NORTON ART GALLERY, Library, 4747 Creswell Ave, Shreveport, 71106. Jerry M Bloomer, Librn
Holdings: Vols 101 Cat

MD —UNIVERSITY OF MARYLAND, BALTIMORE COUNTY, Albin O Kuhn Library and Gallery, 5401 Wilkens Ave, Baltimore, 21228. Ann Copeland, Special Collections Librn
Holdings: Vols (800) // Cat Pix
Notes: The Edgar and Kathleen Merkle Collection of 19th-century English graphic satire centers around the work of George E Cruikshank. Other artists represented incl Rowlandson, Gillray, Hogarth, and "Phiz." Rare items incl Cruikshank's lavish hand-colored film *Scraps and Sketches* (1828).

MA —HARVARD UNIVERSITY LIBRARY, Houghton Library, Printing and Graphic Arts Dept, Cambridge, 02138. Eleanor M Garvey, Cur
Notes: See *Harvard Library Bulletin,* I (1947), 252-253. Collection incl illustrated books, fine printing, type specimens, illuminated and calligraphic manuscripts, and drawings for book illustration.

MA —BOSTON COLLEGE LIBRARIES, Chestnut Hill, 02167.

MI —GOGEBIC COMMUNITY COLLEGE, Alex D Chisholm Learning Resources Center, Greenbush & Jackson Rd, Ironwood, 49938. Charles Tetzlaff, Dir of Learning Resources
Holdings: Vols Cat Slides
Notes: Emphasis on 20th century printmaking and on American prints. Collection is supplemented by current periodicals in the visual arts. Collection supports permanent collection of 20th century American prints.

MI —MONROE COUNTY LIBRARY SYSTEM, Bedford Branch, 8575 Jackman Road, Temperance, 48182. Paula Kaczmarek, Head, Bedford Branch
Holdings: Vols 6500 Cat Periodicals AV
Budget: $8000
Notes: Circulating general collection of popular art books, especially Western European and American painting; also includes technique, graphic arts, photography, sculpture, architecture. Periodicals held five years.

MN —MINNEAPOLIS COLLEGE OF ART & DESIGN, Library, 200 E 25 St, Minneapolis, 55404. Richard Kronstedt, Head Librn
Holdings: Vols 750 Cat Slides
Notes: Incl exhibition catalogs; collection emphasis on 20th century aspects of prints and printmaking.

MN —WALKER ART CENTER, Staff Reference Library, Vineland Place, Minneapolis, 55403. Rosemary Furtak, Librn
Holdings: Vols 5000 Cat Pix
Notes: Incl 10,000 catalogs of individual artists; museum gallery catalogs-10,000 catalogs of major exhibitions from all over the world dating back to 1940. VF material and tapes.

MO —HALLMARK CARDS, Creative Research Library, 25 & McGee, Kansas City, 64141. Sara E Wallace, Mgr of Library Services
Holdings: Vols (12,000) Cat Mss Pix Slides
Notes: Picture research collection for greeting card artists.

NH —NEW HAMPSHIRE VOCATIONAL-TECHNICAL COLLEGE, Library, Prescott Hill, Laconia, 03246. Patty Miller, Librn
Holdings: Vols 525 Cat Slides Audiotapes 16mm Films Filmstrips Microforms
Budget: $515
Notes: Incl overhead transparencies.

NJ —NEWARK PUBLIC LIBRARY, Art & Music Dept, 5 Washington St, Newark, 07101. William J Dane, Supv
Holdings: Vols (15,000) Cat
Notes: Original prints and fine facsimiles in all major media from 16th century to contemporary times. Study and special exhibition collection of the traditional and current techniques of graphic art with emphasis on late 19th and 20th century artists; ancillary collections of Japanese prints and printed books, trade cards, music covers, greeting cards, bank notes and historic maps.

NY —NEW YORK CITY TECHNICAL COLLEGE, Library, 300 Jay St, Brooklyn, 11201. Catherine T Brody, Chief Librn
Holdings: Vols 2000 Cat Pix Microforms
Notes: Incl most publications of Graphic

GRAPHIC ARTS (cont.)

Arts Technical Foundation. One bibliography available: Guide to Multi-Media Resources in Graphic Arts at the Namm Library.

NY —COLUMBIA UNIVERSITY LIBRARIES, Rare Book & Manuscript Library, 801 Butler Library, 535 W 114 St, New York, 10027. Kenneth A Lohf, Librn
Holdings: Vols (25,000) Cat
Notes: Incl allied crafts. Book arts, graphic arts and typographic libraries. Restricted use: noncirculating.

NY —COLUMBIA UNIVERSITY LIBRARIES, School of Library Service Library, 607 Butler, 535 W 114 St, New York, 10027. Olha della Cava, Librn
Holdings: Vols 12,409 Cat Microforms

NY —NEW YORK PUBLIC LIBRARY, Art, Prints, and Photographs Div, Fifth Ave & 42 St, New York, 10018. Donald Anderle, Chief
Holdings: Vols (150,000) Cat Mss Pix Microforms
Notes: History and design in the fine and applied arts. Architecture, painting, drawing, sculpture, costume, furniture, advertising art, prints, photography, crafts, and jewelry are among the subjects covered from ancient times to the present. See: New York Public Library *Dictionary Catalog of the Art and Architecture Division* (Boston, G K Hall, 1975), 30 vols. Holdings after that time are incl in the *Dictionary Catalog of the Research Libraries*. African Art and Afro-American Art are collected by the Schomburg Center for Research in Black Culture.

NY —ROCHESTER INSTITUTE OF TECHNOLOGY, Technical & Education Center of the Graphic Arts, Graphic Arts Information Service, One Lomb Memorial Dr, Rochester, 14623. Susan Clark, Technical Librn
Holdings: Vols (1500) Cat Microforms
Notes: Graphic arts (photographic and applied art aspects) with emphasis on science and technology of printing. Periodicals (265) and technical reports, pertinent to the graphic arts, are routinely scanned for articles of significant information content; articles are classified and keyworded, if needed, and the complete reference is published in *Graphic Arts Literature* Abstracts, a monthly publication of the Graphic Arts Research Center. All abstracted articles are microfilmed and in individual fiche jackets for easy storage and retrieval.

NY —VISUAL STUDIES WORKSHOP, Research Center, 31 Prince St, Rochester, 14607. Linn Underhill, Coordr; Robert Bretz, Librn
Holdings: Vols (8000) Cat Pix Slides Audiotapes Videotapes
Notes: Strong emphasis on photography (over 1,000,000 pictures) and the photographic arts in many subject areas incl in this volume. Heavy emphasis on early photographic processes and collections of examples of them. Also collections of individual photographers' works.

OH —CINCINNATI ART MUSEUM, Library, Eden Park, Cincinnati, 45202. Patrician P Rutledge, Librn
Holdings: Vols (45,850) Cat Microforms
Notes: Art library containing all subjects on art-history, graphic arts, advertising art, etc; special strength in prints, ie engravings, etc. Near Eastern art and decorative arts are also strong. At least 90,000 art exhibition catalogs. Emphasis on artists of Cincinnati and vicinity in vertical file material.

OH —PUBLIC LIBRARY OF CINCINNATI & HAMILTON COUNTY, Art & Music Dept, 800 Vine St, Cincinnati, 45202. R Jayne Craven, Head
Holdings: Vols (122,185) Cat Pix
Budget: ($56,100)
Notes: Special collections: Eda Kuhn Loeb, "Artist and the Book, 1875-Date" (now shelved in Rare Book Room); music librettos (2345); exhibition catalogs (5474); large prints and posters (5051); Cincinnati artists vertical files; picture collection (673,906 clippings).

PA —TEMPLE UNIVERSITY LIBRARIES, Special Collections Dept, Rare Books & Mss Section, Philadelphia, 19122. Thomas M Whitehead, Cur
Holdings: Vols (5000) Mss Pix
Notes: The printing and graphic arts collections stress the technological developments within the printing industry and the achievements in fine printing in the 19th and 20th centuries. Selected additions are continually made of examples and secondary works. Holdings include the Library and archives of Richard W Ellis, typographer, archives of Philadelphia printers and photoengravers. Partially cataloged.

PA —GRAPHIC ARTS TECHNICAL FOUNDATION, Edward H Wadewitz Memorial Library, 4615 Forbes Ave, Pittsburgh, 15213. Janice L Lloyd, Librn
Holdings: Vols (3500) Cat Slides Microforms
Notes: All printing processes. Also, books and periodicals on paper, ink, photography, optics, color theory, environmental control. Approximately 250 periodical titles and 35, 000 classified abstracts of selected periodical articles. Approximately 15,000 slides within the organization. Research reports from foreign graphic arts research institutes.

PA —EASTERN COLLEGE, Frank Warner Memorial Library, Saint Davids, 19087. James L Sauer, Librn
Holdings: Uncat Mss Pix
Notes: The Harry C Goebel Collection. Incl Bruce Rogers printings (over 460); press books (about 350); oriental art (over 250); bookplates (with a separate collection of an almost complete set of bookplates designed by Edwin Davis French); Christmas Books; art and graphic arts (incl the French Graphic Arts Collection of Adolph DeMilly); first editions of Christopher Morley; Print Collection (1315 prints); Oriental art realia and artifacts.

SC —WOFFORD COLLEGE, Sandor Teszler Library, N Church St, Spartanburg, 29301. Frank J Anderson, Librn
Holdings: Vols (500) Cat
Budget: ($500)
Notes: Books about the history and practice of printing, hand papermaking, bookbinding, book collecting, fine press and private press books used in conjunction with instruction at the Wofford Library Press, an experimental and bibliographic press which has been in operation since 1969. Collection contains materials on printmaking methods and related graphic arts.

TX —UNIVERSITY OF TEXAS LIBRARIES, Fine Arts Library, PO Box P, Austin, 78712. Carole L Cable, Fine Arts Librn
Holdings: Vols (55,000) Cat Pix

TX —AMON CARTER MUSEUM, Library, 3510 Camp Bowie Blvd, PO Box 2365, Fort Worth, 76113. Nancy G Wynne, Librn
Holdings: Vols (25,000) Cat Mss Pix
Notes: The book collection, microfilm and photo archives have been built toward the goal of the interpretation of American history through art. At present, the greatest strengths are in Americana, Western Canadiana, bibliography, American exhibition catalogs and history of photography. Substantial books and files on American artists of the 19th and early 20th century, and particularly of Charles M Russell and Frederic Remington. Incl 25,000 pictures; 13,000 slides.
See also entries under Newspapers, American; Pictures - Collections.

VA —UNIVERSITY OF VIRGINIA, Alderman Library, Rare Book Dept, Charlottesville, 22901. Julius P Barclay, Cur
Holdings: Vols (6500) // Mss
Notes: The Oscar Ogg Collection of Book Arts covers calligraphy, letterforms, typography, printing, and graphic arts. Contains early writing books and printed works, as well as modern manuals and other works on printing, publishing, and promotion through graphic arts. The Dept also has the Edward L Stone Collection of Printing Specimens, 3000 items. Contains materials tracing the history of printing, inks, binding styles and materials, types. Also the Tompkins Collection (2000 vols), and the Stevens Watts collection (900 vols).

WI —UNIVERSITY OF WISCONSIN, MADISON, Kohler Art Library, 800 University Ave, Madison, 53706. William C Bunce, Chief; Louise Hunning, Ref Librn
Holdings: Vols (83,000) Cat Microforms
Notes: Incl over 10,000 exhibition and auction catalogs.

AB —SOUTHERN ALBERTA INSTITUTE OF TECHNOLOGY, Learning Resources Centre, 1301 16 Ave NW, Calgary, T2M 0L4, Can. Tom Skinner, Historian
Holdings: Vols (5000) Cat Pix Slides Films Audiotapes Filmstrips Videotapes
Notes: Serves Alberta Collegeof Art (4-year professional course).

ON —NATIONAL GALLERY OF CANADA, Library, National Museums of Canada, Ottawa, K1A 0M8, Can. J Hunter, Chief Librn

ON —METROPOLITAN TORONTO LIBRARY, Fine Arts Dept, 789 Yonge St, Toronto, M4W 2G8, Can. Alan Suddon, Head
Holdings: Vols (42,000) Cat Pix Microforms
Notes: Extensive collection.

GRAPHIC ARTS, FRENCH

CT —YALE UNIVERSITY, Beinecke Rare Book & Manuscripts Library, Wall & High St, New Haven, 06520. Louis A Martz, Dir
Notes: Incl the Altschul Collection: The Arts of the French Book, 1838-1967. See *Yale Library Gazette*, October 1969 for description and catalog.

PA —EASTERN COLLEGE, Frank Warner Memorial Library, Saint Davids, 19087. James L Sauer, Librn
Holdings: Uncat Mss Pix
Notes: The Harry C Goebel Collection. Incl Bruce Rogers printings (over 460); press books (about 350); oriental art (over 250); bookplates (with a separate collection of an almost complete set of bookplates designed by Edwin Davis French); Christmas Books; art and graphic arts (incl the French Graphic Arts Collection of Adolph DeMilly); first editions of Christopher Morley; Print Collection (1315 prints); Oriental art realia and artifacts.

GRAPHIC DATA PROCESSING see Computer Graphics

GRAPHIC PUBLISHERS, OTTAWA

ON —UNIVERSITY OF TORONTO, Thomas Fisher Rare Book Library, 120 Saint George St, Toronto, M5S 1A5, Can. Richard G Landon, Head
Holdings: Vols 65 Cat
Notes: Books and pamphlets published by Graphic Publishers of Ottawa, 1924-1932.

GRAPHICS, COMPUTER see Computer Graphics

GRAPHITE

MI —ACHESON COLLOIDS, Library, 511 Port St, Port Huron, 48060. Myles T Musgrave, Librn
Holdings: Vols (5000) Cat Mss Maps Slides Microforms
Notes: Incl some original items and records of Dr E G Acheson, inventor of process of manufacturing (electric-furnace) artificial graphite and Carborundum. Incl materials on industrial manufacture and uses of graphite (natural and artificially produced) and related carbon materials, especially as solid lubricants in films, liquids, greases, etc. Incl extensive patent collection (US and foreign).

GRAPHOLOGY

IL —UNIVERSITY OF ILLINOIS, URBANA/CHAMPAIGN, Library, University Archives, 19 Library, 1408 W Gregory Drive, Urbana, 61801. Maynard Brichford, University Archivist
Holdings: Vols (5000) Cat
Budget: ($7000)
Notes: The Mandeville Collection in

GRAPHOLOGY (cont.)

Parapsychology and Occult Sciences. Titles in the Merten J Mandeville Collection are purchased by funds from an endowment provided specifically for the collection on its establishment in 1966 by Merten J Mandeville, Professor Emeritus of Management, who donated 400 vols from his personal library as the nucleus of the collection. There are currently about 5000 titles in the collection, supplemented by related materials in the general collection. Topics include astrology, extrasensory perception, yoga, magic, satanism, faith healing, hypnosis, Eastern religions, witchcraft, fortune telling, reincarnation, flying saucers, ghosts, dreams, numerology, graphology, and mysticism. Biographies and reference books are a part of the collection as are journals devoted to the scientific study of parapsychology.

GASCON, JEAN

†ON —MCMASTER UNIVERSITY, Library, Hamilton, L8S 4L6, Can.
Notes: Extensive correspondence with theatrical figures, such as Tyrone Guthrie and Jean Gascon. Collection described in *Library Research News,* vol 6, no 2, Fall 1982 and vol 7, no 1, Spring 1983.

GRASS, TURF see Turf Grasses

GRASSES

DC —SMITHSONIAN INSTITUTION LIBRARIES, Botany Branch, Washington, 20560. Ruth Schallert, Branch Librn
Holdings: Vols (21,000) Cat Mss Maps Pix Microforms
Notes: Taxonomic botany; with the J D Smith Collection of general botany, the Dawson Collection on algae, and the Hitchcock-Chase Collection on grasses.

MI —MICHIGAN STATE UNIVERSITY, Science Library, East Lansing, 48824. Carole S Armstrong, Head
Holdings: Vols 900 Cat
Notes: The collection has 100 journal titles with 650 vols, 160 monographs and 900 additional monographs on establishment, management and genetic improvement of grass.

GRASSLAND FARMING see Pastures

GRATZ FAMILY

PA —LIBRARY COMPANY OF PHILADELPHIA, 1314 Locust St, Philadelphia, 19107. Edwin Wolf II, Librn; Kenneth Finkel, Cur of Prints
Notes: The Edwin Wolf Collection of Judaica, consisting of 165 manuscripts and more than 500 books and broadsides printed in the US between 1718 and 1875. Incl literature, prayer books, Hebrew schoolbooks, reports of Jewish organizations, missionary tracts, narratives of travel to Palestine, and books on medicine. Most of the manuscripts consists of correspondence of the Gratz family, American pioneers.

GRAUPNER, J. C. G.

†IL —NEWBERRY LIBRARY, Chicago, 60610.
Notes: Charles Bradlee was a music publisher in Boston and used Graupner and Ashton plates. His music, from the J Francis Driscoll Collection.

RI —BROWN UNIVERSITY, John Hay Library, 20 Prospect St, Providence, 02912. Mark N Brown, Cur Mss
Holdings: Mss
Notes: Papers of William O Fuller (1828-1910), music teacher of Providence, comprising letters 1848 from Europe, incl a letter from Franz Liszt; papers of Johann Christian Gottlieb Graupner (1767-1836) and John Rowe Parker (fl 1820s) collected by Horace Mason Reynolds, relating to the music-publishing business in Boston, 1802-1838; papers of the American folklorist Mellinger Edward Henry (1873-1946) relating to his research and publications on American folk-songs 1910-1942; papers, 1912-1948, of Providence composer Hugh Frederick MacColl (1885-1953); papers of Frances Herriot Sargent, stage manager for "Porgy" and "Porgy and Bess", relating to productions of these, 1928-1942.

GRAVES, RICHARD L.

MA —BOSTON UNIVERSITY, Mugar Memorial Library, Special Collections Dept, 771 Commonwealth Ave, Boston, 02215. Howard B Gotlieb, Dir
Holdings: Cat Mss

GRAVES, ROBERT, 1895-

CA —UNIVERSITY OF CALIFORNIA, LOS ANGELES, Research Library, Dept of Special Collections, 405 Hilgard Ave, Los Angeles, 90024. Edward Shreeves, Chairman, Bibliographers Group; David S Zeidberg, Head
Holdings: Vols 300
Notes: 300 first and other editions of his books; 9 letters.

CA —UNIVERSITY OF SAN FRANCISCO, Richard A Gleeson Library, The Countess Bernardine Murphy Donohue Rare Book Room, San Francisco, 94117. D Steven Corey, Special Collections Librn
Holdings: Vols 400 Mss
Notes: Comprehensive collection of first editions, mss, ALS's, corrected proofs, photos and ephemera.

IL —SOUTHERN ILLINOIS UNIVERSITY, CARBONDALE, Delyte W Morris Library, Special Collections Dept, Carbondale, 62901. David V Koch, Cur of Special Collections; Louisa Bowen, Cur of Manuscripts
Holdings: Vols 88 Cat Mss
Notes: Personal papers, 1917-1965, incl mss of 62 works of fiction and approx 500 pages of poetry. Correspondents incl George Russell, Dame Edith Sitwell, E M Forster, T S Eliot, Arnold Bennett, Alec Waugh, and Siegfried Sassoon. Inventory and name index available at library.

IL —NORTHWESTERN UNIVERSITY, Library, Special Collections Dept, 1937 Sheridan Rd, Evanston, 60201. R Russell Maylone, Cur
Holdings: Vols 130 Cat Mss
Notes: Robert Graves' letters, first editions, Seizin Press books.

IN —INDIANA UNIVERSITY, Lilly Library, Seventh St, Bloomington, 47405. William R Cagle, Librn
Holdings: Cat Mss Pix
Notes: Correspondence of Robert Graves with Kenneth Charles (Karl) Gay, 1934-1968. 1332 letters and 14 Graves ms. Incl first editions of Graves' publications and several association or inscribed copies.

KS —KANSAS STATE UNIVERSITY, Library, Special Collections & University Archives, Manhattan, 66506. Antonia Q Pigno, Coordr; John J Vander Velde, Librn; Anthony R Crawford, Univ Archivist
Holdings: Vols 200 Cat Mss
Budget: ($10,000)
Notes: Works by Robert Graves, incl several rare ones. The newest segment of this collection reflects the acquisition of the Fred H and Heannette Higginson library.

NV —UNIVERSITY OF NEVADA, RENO, University Library, Special Collections Dept, Reno, 89557. Robert E Blesse, Head
Holdings: Vols (272) // Cat
Notes: Includes individual works by author in all editions including translations; also prefaces, introductions, published correspondence, appearances in anthologies, periodicals, etc. Bibliographical research collection, part of Modern Authors Collection.

NY —STATE UNIVERSITY OF NEW YORK, COLLEGE AT BUFFALO, Poetry/Rare Books Collection, 420 Capen Hall, Buffalo, 14260. Robert J Bertholf, Cur
Notes: The extensive holdings incl a complete first edition collection of Robert Graves' publications. The holdings also incl mss, letters, notes, photographs and ephemera covering Graves' career from 1911 to 1970.

†NC —WAKE FOREST UNIVERSITY, Z Smith Reynolds Library, Box 7777, Reynold Sta, Winston-Salem, 27109. Richard J Murdoch, Rare Book Librn
Holdings: Vols 133 Cat

OK —UNIVERSITY OF TULSA, McFarlin Library, Dept of Rare Books and Special Collections, 600 S College, Tulsa, 74104. David Farmer, Dir; Toby Murray, Archivist; Caroline Swinson, Cur of Manuscripts & Art
Holdings: Mss Pix Phonorecords
Notes: The Ellsworth Mason Graves/Riding Collection, incl first editions, typescripts, photographs, recordings and ephemera. The Library also has the library (8000 vols) of Cyril Connolly. Mostly modern literature; many presentation copies.

BC —UNIVERSITY OF VICTORIA, McPherson Library, Victoria, V8W 3H5, Can.
Notes: Diary (1935-39); correspondence to members of his family (1950-71), Isla Cameron, Aemilia Laracuen, Selwyn Jepson, Andrew Mylett, James Reeves, Keidrych Rhys; mss, holograph poems, worksheets, drafts, lectures and longer studies: *Hebrew Myths: The Book of Genesis; Greek Myths: The Anger of Archilles,* the collaboration with Norman Cameron: *The Pickwick* Papers and the translation of Ramon Sender: *La Luna de los Perros.* Finding aids: Gerwing, Howard. "The Robert Graves Manuscript Collection at The University of Victoria," *The Malahat Review,* No 35, July 1975, pp 180-185. *Focus on Robert Graves,* No 3, December 1973, pp 45-46. Some restrictions.

GRAVES, WILLIAM SIDNEY

CA —HOOVER INSTITUTION ON WAR, REVOLUTION & PEACE, Stanford University, Stanford, 94305. Milorad M Drachkovitch, Archivist
Holdings: // Mss
Notes: Papers, 1914-1932, of William Sidney Graves, Army officer. Correspondence, reports, monographs, photos and other material, relating to the Allied intervention in Russia and to American Expeditionary Forces in Siberia (1918-1919) of which Maj Gen Graves was commander. 3 boxes. Unpublished preliminry inventory in repository.

GRAVESTONES

MA —OLD STURBRIDGE VILLAGE, Research Library, Sturbridge, 01566. Theresa Rini Percy, Librn
Holdings: Cat
Notes: New England, 1790-1850. Incl gravestone rubbings.

GRAVITATION—CHEMISTRY

PA —ENSANIAN PHYSICOCHEMICAL INSTITUTE, Library, PO Box 98, Eldred, 16731. Elisabeth Anahid Ensanian, Chief Librn
Holdings: Vols 200 Cat Mss Slides Films Microforms
Budget: $3800
Notes: The institute has pioneered the field of Gravitation Chemistry (term coined at the institute) and has original data and reports on this phenomenon, generated from its own research, that cannot be found elsewhere in the world. Also publishes own technical journal. This special collection, which also incl the biological effects of weightlessmess, is continually being increased.

GRAVITATIONAL RADIATION

CA —UNIVERSITY OF CALIFORNIA, SANTA CRUZ, University Library, Special Collections, Santa Cruz, 95064. Rita Bottoms, Special Collections Librn; Margaret Felts, South Pacific Collection Bibliographer
Holdings: Cat
Notes: Astronomy library. Incl all major astronomical and astrophysical journals and

GRAVITATIONAL RADIATION (cont.)

an extensive collection of domestic and foreign observatory publications. The book collection is particularly strong in stellar structure and evolution, stellar spectroscopy, the interstellar medium, galactic structure, external galaxies, general relativity and gravitational radiation, and high-energy astrophysics.

GRAVITY

PA —ENSANIAN PHYSICOCHEMICAL INSTITUTE, Library, PO Box 98, Eldred, 16731. Elisabeth Anahid Ensanian, Chief Librn
Holdings: Vols 200 Cat Mss Slides Films Microforms
Budget: $3800
Notes: The institute has pioneered the field of Gravitation Chemistry (term coined at the institute) and has original data and reports on this phenomenon, generated from its own research, that cannot be found elsewhere in the world. Also publishes own technical journal. This special collection, which also incl the biological effects of weightlessness,is continually being increased.

ON —ENERGY, MINES & RESOURCES CANADA, Earth Physics Branch Library, Ottawa, K1A 0Y3, Can. W M Tsang, Chief Librn
Holdings: Vols (4500) Cat Maps Pix Slides Microforms

GRAVITY-FREE STATE—PHYSIOLOGICAL EFFECT see Weightlessness

GRAY, HAROLD

MA —BOSTON UNIVERSITY, Mugar Memorial Library, Special Collections Dept, 771 Commonwealth Ave, Boston, 02215. Howard B Gotlieb, Dir
Holdings: // Cat Mss
Notes: Mss, correspondence, etc collected in depth; incl publications by or about. Original "Orphan Annie" cartoons.

GRAY, HENRY

SC —COLLEGE OF CHARLESTON LIBRARY, Special Collections Dept, Charleston, 29401.
Notes: Program booklet and guest list of the "Dinner given to the General Society of the Cincinnati by the ... Charleston, South Carolina," April 8, 1908. Includes colored engravings of the Revolutionary War attack upon Fort Moultrie, drawn by one of its defenders, Lieutenant Henry Gray.

GRAY, JAMES, 1906-

AB —UNIVERSITY OF CALGARY, Libraries, Special Collections Div, 2500 University Dr, Calgary, T2N 1N4, Can.
Holdings: Cat Mss Audiotapes
Notes: Papers of journalist, historian James Gray, correspondence 1966-1973, draft manuscripts, duplicates of syndicated articles, research notes, and photo reproductions of historical documents, pamphlets, and taped interviews.

GRAY, JOSEPH A., 1884-1966

ON —QUEEN'S UNIVERSITY, Douglas Library, University Archives, Kingston, K7L 5C4, Can.
Notes: Physicist Joseph A Gray's papers (1908-1962).

GRAY, SIMON

MA —BOSTON UNIVERSITY, Mugar Memorial Library, Special Collections Dept, 771 Commonwealth Ave, Boston, 02215. Howard B Gotlieb, Dir
Holdings: Cat Mss
Notes: Mss, correspondence, etc collected in depth; incl publications by or about.

GRAY FRIARS see Franciscans

GRAYHOUND RACING see Greyhound Racing

GRAYSON, DAVID

MA —JONES LIBRARY, 43 Amity St, Amherst, 01002. Daniel J Lombardo, Cur of Special Collections
Holdings: Vols 250 Cat Mss Pix
Notes: The Ray Stannard Baker Collection, incl books written under the name "David Grayson." Also periodicals, clippings, letters. Does not circulate. Unpublished guide available.

GRAYSON, PETER WILLIAM

TX —ROSENBERG LIBRARY, Galveston and Texas History Center, 2310 Sealy Ave, Galveston, 77550. Jane Kenamore, Archivist
Holdings: Cat Mss
Notes: Peter W Grayson, 1788-1838, was the first Attorney General of the Republic of Texas.

GRAYSON, RICHARD

MA —BOSTON UNIVERSITY, Mugar Memorial Library, Special Collections Dept, 771 Commonwealth Ave, Boston, 02215. Howard B Gotlieb, Dir
Holdings: Mss

GRAZIANI, ANTONIO MARIA

KS —UNIVERSITY OF KANSAS, Kenneth Spencer Research Library, Special Collections Dept, Lawrence, 66045. Alexandra Mason, Librn
Holdings: Vols 200 Cat Mss Maps
Notes: Especially strong for 16th and 17th centuries, incl Polish and other imprints. Papers of Antonio Maria Graziani, Vatican emissary to court of Poland in later 16th century. Noncirculating. Unpublished list in repository. Also see Hoskins, Janina W, *Early and Rare Polonica of the 15th-17th Centuries in American Libraries,* Boston, G K Hall, 1973.

GREASE see Lubrication and Lubricants; Oils and Fats

GREAT BASIN REGION

NV —UNIVERSITY OF NEVADA, RENO, University Library, Special Collections Dept, Reno, 89557. Robert E Blesse, Head
Holdings: Vols 3500 Cat Mss Maps Pix
Notes: Incl 2100 cubic feet of mss, 25,000 photographs, maps, VF, microforms, and oral histories. Both primary and secondary materials are collected which document the history and development of Nevada and the Great Basin region from its beginnings to the present day. Areas of strength incl mining, politics, water resources, railroads, biography, land use, anthropology, architecture, Lake Tahoe, lumbering, and early Nevada imprints. Major emphasis is on the prehistory and history of Nevada with lesser emphasis on bordering states and the Great Basin region. Specialized catalogs and indexes are available in the department.

GREAT BRITAIN

NY —BOOKS-ACROSS-THE-SEA, The English-Speaking Union, 16 E 69 St, New York, 10021. Catherine Nolan, Librn
Holdings: Vols (6500) Cat
Budget: ($25,000)
Notes: Deals mainly with humanities and social sciences of Great Britain, Australia, New Zealand, and Canada; adult books. Collection started in 1942; current titles added through exchange.

NC —DUKE UNIVERSITY, William R Perkins Library, Durham, 27706. Elvin E Strowd, University Librn

GREAT BRITAIN—ANTIQUITIES

BC —VANCOUVER PUBLIC LIBRARY, History & Government Div, 750 Burrard St, Vancouver, V6Z 1X5, Can.
Holdings: Vols 200 Cat Maps Pix
Notes: Antiquities, archaeology, biography, history, description, travel, etc concerning Norfolk and East Anglia in England. (Gift of the Bulwer Family.)

GREAT BRITAIN—ARMY—MILITARY LIFE

ON —FORT MALDEN NATIONAL HISTORIC PARK, Library, 100 Laird Ave, Box 38, Amherstburg, N9V 2Z2, Can. Sally E Snyder, Librn
Holdings: Vols (400) Cat Mss Pix Slides
Notes: British and Canadian military life, weaponry, uniforms, from about 1760 to 1860.

GREAT BRITAIN—ARMY—REGIMENTAL HISTORIES

DC —GEORGETOWN UNIVERSITY, Library, Special Collections Div, 37 & O Sts NW, Washington, 20057. George M Barringer, Special Collections Librn; Nicholas B Sheetz, Mss Librn
Holdings: Vols 2000 Cat Maps Pix
Notes: Strong in British regimental histories and personal narratives.

NY —NEW YORK PUBLIC LIBRARY, Research Libraries, General Research Division, Fifth Ave & 42 St, New York, 10018. Rodney Phillips, Chief
Holdings: Vols (2,225,000) Cat Maps Pix Microforms
Budget: ($775,718)
Notes: Especially strong collection.

ON —METROPOLITAN TORONTO LIBRARY, History Dept, 789 Yonge St, Toronto, M4W 2G8, Can. Michael Pearson, Head
Holdings: Vols (11,000) Cat Phonorecords Audiotapes Microforms
Notes: Includes British army and navy lists and Prussian and French army lists from 18th century on; British regimental histories; works on military uniforms and insignia, especially European; Napoleonic and First and Second World Wars well represented.

GREAT BRITAIN—CIVILIZATION AND CULTURE

CA —UNIVERSITY OF CALIFORNIA, LOS ANGELES, William Andrews Clark Memorial Library, 2520 Cimarron St, Los Angeles, 90018.
Holdings: Cat Mss Pix
Notes: Extensive collection, first editions, etc.

WI —UNIVERSITY OF WISCONSIN, MADISON, Memorial Library, 728 State St, Madison, 53706. Erwin K Welsch, Social Studies Bibliographer
Holdings: Vols 12,500 Cat Microforms
Notes: Social history of the 19th century. Strong in pamphlet materials issued by individuals and groups between 1790 and 1914. Very large collection of periodicals.

GREAT BRITAIN—COUNTY HISTORIES

CT —TRINITY COLLEGE LIBRARY, Watkinson Library, 300 Summit St, Hartford, 06106. Jeffrey Kaimowitz, Cur
Holdings: Cat
Notes: Incl genealogical records.

MA —NEW ENGLAND HISTORIC GENEALOGICAL SOCIETY, Library, 101 Newbury St, Boston, 02116. Ralph J Crandell, Dir
Holdings: Vols (250,000) Mss Maps Microforms Pix
Notes: New England genealogy. Especially strong Massachusetts, Maine, and New Hampshire, although all states are well represented, as are the relevancies of each subject listed in this volume with regard to British antecedent and contemporary history. Special strengths in local history and biography, obituaries, etc, incl parish registers, censuses, British and American. 3125 linear ft of mss.

†NY —UNIVERSITY OF ROCHESTER, Rush Rhees Library, Rochester, 14627.

ON —METROPOLITAN TORONTO LIBRARY, History Dept, 789 Yonge St, Toronto, M4W 2G8, Can. Michael Pearson, Head
Holdings: Vols (8000) Cat Phonorecords Audiotapes Microforms
Notes: Emphasis on modern period from Tudors to present. Extensive collection of publications of local and regional historical

GREAT BRITAIN—COUNTY HISTORIES (cont.)

and record societies: Chetham Society, Lancashire and Cheshire Record Society, Harleian Society, etc. Fairly good county history collection including *Victoria History of the Counties of England.*

GREAT BRITAIN—DESCRIPTION AND TRAVEL

IN —INDIANA UNIVERSITY, Lilly Library, Seventh St, Bloomington, 47405. William R Cagle, Librn
Holdings: Cat
Notes: 18th and 19th century guidebooks and travelers' accounts; 60 vols on the Lake Country and William Wordsworth. Incl the Walkins Collection.

GREAT BRITAIN—FOREIGN RELATIONS

CA —STANFORD UNIVERSITY LIBRARIES, Jonsson Library of Government Documents, Stanford, 94305. W David Rozkuszka, Librn
Holdings: Vols 55,000 Cat Mss Microforms
Notes: Approximately 55,000 vols, incl every item published by the Public Record Office; the Historical Manuscripts Commission; the General Register Office; and very strong sets of the House of Lords and House of Commons parliamentary papers and debates (in hard copy for the nineteenth century; also 44,000 fiche of Common papers); approx 7000 microfilm reels, incl minutes and memoranda of the Cabinet Office, 1916 to date; Foreign Office records on China (3000 reels); confidential prints on China, Japan, Africa, the slave trade Tibet and Mongolia, Russia and the Soviet Union; correspondence of the British Embassy Archives in Washington, 1903-1940 (1248 microfilm reels); World War II papers of the Cabinet Office and Prime Minister's Office; Foreign Office general correspondence: Japan, 1856-1905 and 1930-1945; Russia, 1883-1948; United States, 1930-1945;China, 1906-1922; Domestic State Papers, Edward, Mary, Elizabeth, James I; Pipe Rolls, 1217-1306; English Civil War, Interregnum/Commonwealth records; Import-Export Ledgers, 1697-1780; Papers of Robert Peel; British official publications not published by HMSO, fiche collection, 1980 to date; London Corporation Journals, 1416-1694, and Repertories, 1495-1692. For more holdings, request "British Public Record Office Archival Material" at Stanford University.

NY —SYRACUSE UNIVERSITY LIBRARIES, Ernest S Bird Library, George Arents Research Library for Special Collections, Syracuse, 13210. Carolyn A Davis, Manuscripts Librn; Amy S Doherty, University Archivist; Mark F Weimer, Rare Book Librn
Notes: Microfilm copies of Benjamin Disraeli's complete papers (200,000 frames) incl family, domestic and personal papers, copies of speeches, royal and general correspondence, papers on domestic and foreign affairs, correspondence on honors and titles, Mrs Disraeli's papers, mss of his novels and proofs and notices and correspondence about the novels. Also the papers of his father Isaac D'Israeli, of his grandfather Benjamin D'Israeli and Disraeli's biographers, Monypenny and Buckle.

NC —DUKE UNIVERSITY, William R Perkins Library, Rare Book Room, Durham, 27706. John L Sharpe, III, Cur
Notes: English pamphlet collection of about 10,000 items. In the main, 17th and 18th century "political history and international relations of Great Britain." French pamphlet collection. Relating to the political, economic and social life of France from the early 18th century down to 1830.

GREAT BRITAIN—FOREIGN RELATIONS—TREATIES

CA —LOS ANGELES PUBLIC LIBRARY, Social Sciences Dept, 630 W Fifth St, Los Angeles, 90071. Marilyn C Wherley, Principal Librn
Holdings: Vols 1500 Cat
Budget: ($150,000)
Notes: Sets of treaties of League of Nations, United Nations, Great Britain, United States, currently in force, as well as historical. Cumultive indexes of world treaties. No separate catalog.

GREAT BRITAIN—GOVERNMENT PUBLICATIONS

CA —STANFORD UNIVERSITY LIBRARIES, Jonsson Library of Government Documents, Stanford, 94305. W David Rozkuszka, Librn
Holdings: Vols 55,000 Cat Mss Microforms
Notes: Approximately 55,000 vols, incl every item published by the Public Record Office; the Historical Manuscripts Commission; the General Register Office; and very strong sets of the House of Lords and House of Commons parliamentary papers and debates (in hard copy for the nineteenth century; also 44,000 fiche of Common papers); approx 7000 microfilm reels, incl minutes and memoranda of the Cabinet Office, 1916 to date; Foreign Office records on China (3000 reels); confidential prints on China, Japan, Africa, the slave trade Tibet and Mongolia, Russia and the Soviet Union; correspondence of the British Embassy Archives in Washington, 1903-1940 (1248 microfilm reels); World War II papers of the Cabinet Office and Prime Minister's Office; Foreign Office general correspondence: Japan, 1856-1905 and 1930-1945; Russia, 1883-1948; United States, 1930-1945;China, 1906-1922; Domestic State Papers, Edward, Mary, Elizabeth, James I; Pipe Rolls, 1217-1306; English Civil War, Interregnum/Commonwealth records; Import-Export Ledgers, 1697-1780; Papers of Robert Peel; British official publications not published by HMSO, fiche collection, 1980 to date; London Corporation Journals, 1416-1694, and Repertories, 1495-1692. For more holdings, request "British Public Record Office Archival Material" at Stanford University.

CT —YALE UNIVERSITY, Yale Center for Parliamentary History, 333 Sterling Memorial Library, New Haven, 06520. Maija Cole, In Charge
Holdings: Microforms

DC —LIBRARY OF CONGRESS, General Reading Rooms Division, Microform Reading Room, Washington, 20540.
Holdings: Cat Mss Maps Pix Microforms
Notes: Microform materials only in this LC Division. Works of individual authors; holdings of collections; archival records, etc, press releases and translations, etc.

FL —FLORIDA STATE UNIVERSITY, Robert Manning Strozier Library, Tallahassee, 32306. Judith Depew, Head, Documents-Maps Dept
Holdings: Vols (680,000) Uncat Microforms
Notes: A depository for Florida, GPO, NASA, UN, and UNESCO documents, with standing orders for British, ILO, OAS, IMF; selected documents are purchased from various government levels. The collection incl historical as well as current material, especially Florida, US, Great Britain. The Library's holdings are strong in congressional bills and hearings, decennial censuses, and British Sessional papers. Number of volumes incl microprint and microfiche, but not cataloged documents and microfilm.

KY —UNIVERSITY OF KENTUCKY, Margaret I King Library, Government Publications Dept, Lexington, 40506. Sandra McAninch, Head
Holdings: Uncat Microforms
Notes: Parliamentary papers and debates only. The library has IUP reprint and Readex microprint collections for 18th and 19th century sessional papers.

†MA —BOSTON PUBLIC LIBRARY, Copley Sq, Boston, 02117.
Holdings: Microforms
Notes: Microform Publication by Reader Microprint Corp British House of Commons Sessional Papers, 1731-1938; Hansard's British Parliamentary Debates, 1066-1918; Journal of the House of Commons, 1547-1900.

NY —NEW YORK STATE LIBRARY, State Education Bldg Annex, Washington Ave, Albany, 12224.
Holdings: Cat Microforms
Notes: Official depository of New York State publications; regional depository of US documents, also in microfilm; depository for Canadian government documents; strong collections of state documents, New York City documents; British sessional papers; also League of Nations, United Nations, OAS documents. Extensive holdings of other domestic and foreign publications. Congressional serial set, incl hearings (1946-date).

NY —STATE UNIVERSITY OF NEW YORK, COLLEGE AT NEW PALTZ, Sojourner Truth Library, New Paltz, 12561. W E Connors, Dir
Notes: Microform publications by Readex Microprint Corp. Sessional papers, 1801-1900; Parliamentary debates, 1803-1918.

NY —NEW YORK PUBLIC LIBRARY, Research Libraries, Economic & Public Affairs Div, Fifth Ave & 42 St, New York, 10018. Edward DiRoma, Chief
Holdings: Vols (1,500,000) Cat Microforms

OH —CLEVELAND PUBLIC LIBRARY, Social Sciences Department, 325 Superior Ave, Cleveland, 44114. Thelma Morris, Head
Holdings: Cat
Notes: Statutes of the Realm, 1810-28 (King George III); Statutes from 20th year of reign of Henry III to second session of 64th year of Queen Victoria, 1888-1909; Statutes, second rev ed, Great Britain, 1235-1900; Acts of the Parliament of Scotland, 1124-1707; Statutes passed in the Parliaments held in Ireland, 1749-1799; Sessional Papers, 1800-1900 (microprint), 1930-date (published), incl Command Papers (CD, CMD, CMND). Other vols as separates before series began in 1930.

TX —WEST TEXAS STATE UNIVERSITY, Cornette Library, PO Box 748 WT Sta, Canyon, 79016. Faye Hendrickson, Special Collections Asst
Holdings: Vols (451,253) Uncat Microforms
Notes: Includes microform collection. No photocopying.

WI —UNIVERSITY OF WISCONSIN, MADISON, Memorial Library, 728 State St, Madison, 53706. Erwin K Welsch, Social Studies Bibliographer
Holdings: Vols 16,000 Cat Microforms
Notes: Incl Journals of the House of Lords and the House of Commons; Parliamentary Reports and Papers of the House of Commons; statutes, laws, and acts; Parliamentary Debates (Hansard) for Lords and Commons from 1803 to date. Parliamentary papers set in original from 1860 to date; previous vols on microfiche.

†ON —METROPOLITAN TORONTO LIBRARY, Social Sciences Dept, 789 Yonge St, Toronto, M4W 2G8, Can. Abdus Salam, Head
Holdings: Vols Cat Maps Phonorecords Audiotapes 16mm Films Microforms
Notes: The collection is a full depository for Canadian federal and Ontario provincial publications and contains an exhaustive collection of publications from the various Canadian provinces. It includes statutes, gazettes, legislative debates, journals, reports, etc. Also extensive holdings for the US and Great Britain; comprehensive holdings of treaties for Canada, Great Britain and the US; selected publications for other foreign countries. Types of publications emphasized are statutory laws, treaties, legislative proceedings, government directories and manuals, statistical materials and national yearbooks. Large collection of UN materials; full depository for UNESCO publications; selected publications of various international organizations. The collection is cited in Canada, National Library, Resources Survey Section, *Research Collections in Canadian* LibrariesVolume 5, *Collections of Official*

GREAT BRITAIN—GOVERNMENT PUBLICATIONS (cont.)

Publications in Canada (Ottawa: Supply and Services Canada, 1976).

GREAT BRITAIN—HISTORY

CA —CALIFORNIA STATE UNIVERSITY, NORTHRIDGE, Delmar T Oviatt & South Libraries, 1811 Nordhoff St, Northridge, 91330. Donald L Read, Special Collections Dept
Holdings: Vols 2000 Uncat
Notes: Partial contents: Liberal Publication Dept, London. Pamphlets and leaflets (1893-1903; 1905-1914), Fabian tracts (1884-1904), Irish Loyal and Patriotic Union. Pamphlets and leaflets (1887). Particularly strong in letters from John Burns' personal correspondence (approx 100). Entire collection, 20 linear feet. Indexed in *Century of change, 1815-1914; a collection of original pamphlets, tracts, posters, holograph letters,* manuscripts, etc. Guernsey, Channel Islands: Guernsey Books, 1972.

†CA —UNIVERSITY OF SAN FRANCISCO, Richard A Gleeson Library, The Countess Bernardine Murphy Donohue Rare Book Room, San Francisco, 94117. D Steven Corey, Special Collections Librn
Holdings: Vols (300) Cat
Notes: Largely from the Virtue--Cahill library in England, and the collection of Charles A Fracchia. Incl important works of Bayly, Cressy, Sergeant, and Worsley. Incl a contemporary manuscript of the trial of Father Garnet, accused of complicity in the Gunpowder Plot.

CA —HUNTINGTON LIBRARY, Art Gallery & Botanical Gardens, 1151 Oxford Rd, San Marino, 91108. Robert L Middlekauff, Dir; Daniel H Woodward, Librn
Holdings: Mss Maps Pix Slides Microforms
Notes: Approx 350,000 rare books, 250,000 reference books, manuscript collection of nearly 2,500,000 pieces and between 200, 000 and 300,000 prints, rare photographs and other related materials. The fullest available survey is now *Guide to Literary Manuscripts in the Huntington Library,* a 539-page handlist published by the Library in 1979. Also *Guide to British Historical Manuscripts in the Huntington Library* (1982). Our important collections of early English printed books are partially recorded in *Short Title Catalogue of Books Printed in* England...1475-1640 (1926) and *Short Title Catalogue of Books Printed in* England...1641-1700 (1945).

CA —STANFORD UNIVERSITY LIBRARIES, Jonsson Library of Government Documents, Stanford, 94305. W David Rozkuszka, Librn
Holdings: Vols 55,000 Cat Mss Microforms
Notes: Approximately 55,000 vols, incl every item published by the Public Record Office; the Historical Manuscripts Commission; the General Register Office; and very strong sets of the House of Lords and House of Commons parliamentary papers and debates (in hard copy for the nineteenth century; also 44,000 fiche of Common papers); approx 7000 microfilm reels, incl minutes and memoranda of the Cabinet Office, 1916 to date; Foreign Office records on China (3000 reels); confidential prints on China, Japan, Africa, the slave trade Tibet and Mongolia, Russia and the Soviet Union; correspondence of the British Embassy Archives in Washington, 1903-1940 (1248 microfilm reels); World War II papers of the Cabinet Office and Prime Minister's Office; Foreign Office general correspondence: Japan, 1856-1905 and 1930-1945; Russia, 1883-1948; United States, 1930-1945;China, 1906-1922; Domestic State Papers, Edward, Mary, Elizabeth, James I; Pipe Rolls, 1217-1306; English Civil War, Interregnum/Commonwealth records; Import-Export Ledgers, 1697-1780; Papers of Robert Peel; British official publications not published by HMSO, fiche collection, 1980 to date; London Corporation Journals, 1416-1694, and Repertories, 1495-1692. For more holdings, request "British Public Record Office Archival Material" at Stanford University.

CO —UNIVERSITY OF COLORADO, Libraries, Special Collections, Boulder, 80309. Nora J Quinlan, Head
Holdings: Vols 2200
Notes: The James F Willard Collection of Pamphlets. Historical, political and religious tracts. Separate catalog.

CT —LEWIS WALPOLE LIBRARY, 154 Main St, Farmington, 06032. Catherine Jestin, Librn
Holdings: Cat Mss Maps Pix Slides Microforms Memorabilia
Notes: Research center for English eighteenth-century studies. A department of Yale University Library. Scholars may visit by appointment only.

CT —TRINITY COLLEGE LIBRARY, Watkinson Library, 300 Summit St, Hartford, 06106. Jeffrey Kaimowitz, Cur
Holdings: Cat

CT —YALE UNIVERSITY, Yale Center for Parliamentary History, 333 Sterling Memorial Library, New Haven, 06520. Maija Cole, In Charge
Holdings: Microforms
Notes: 200 reels of microfilm from Edward VI to Charles I. Microfilm of the mss in British Archives.

CT —YALE UNIVERSITY, Yale Center for British Art, Rare Book Dept, New Haven, 06520. Joan Friedman, Cur
Notes: One of the greatest assemblages of British Art of the 17th-19th centuries.

DC —FOLGER SHAKESPEARE LIBRARY, 201 E Capitol St, Washington, 20003. Philip A Knachel, Acting Dir
Holdings: Vols (223,571) Cat Mss Pix Periodicals Microfilms
Notes: Collections described in *Catalog of Printed Books of the Folger Shakespeare* Library, 28 vols; *First Supplement,* 3 vols (Boston: G K Hall, 1970, 1976); *Second* Supplement in 2 vols (Boston: G K Hall, 1981); *Catalog of Manuscripts of the Folger Shakespeare Library,* 3 vols (Boston: G K Hall, 1971); and *The Widening Circle: The Story of the Folger Library and Its* Collections (Washington, DC: Folger Shakespeare Library, 1976). Collections incl 39 vols of plays with ms annotations and stage directions by John Philip Kemble. Library use restricted to advanced research scholars.

DC —GEORGETOWN UNIVERSITY, Library, Special Collections Div, 37 & O Sts NW, Washington, 20057. George M Barringer, Special Collections Librn; Nicholas B Sheetz, Mss Librn
Holdings: Mss Cat Pix
Notes: Mss of a number of Mr Appleby's works on English medieval history (principally his *England Without Richard*) and other subjects, some correspondence pertaining thereto, and a collection of photographs of Suffolk locales (some copies of 19th century prints); together with photographic copies of medieval mss.

DC —LIBRARY OF CONGRESS, Washington, 20540.
Notes: Project of a consortium to microfilm about 200,000 pp of material on Great Britain, France, Russia and Prussia, for the period 1848-1918 in the ms and documentary collections of the Austrian State Archives. The collection will incl, among others, documents on the Austro-Prussian War of 1866, the treaty negotiations between France and Italy in 1868-1870, the Orient Question of 1877-1878, the persecution of Jews in Russia in 1882, the Congo Conference in Berlin, 1884-1887 and the British-Portuguese conflict in East Africa, 1889-1891. Copies will be available at LC, the Center for Research Libraries, the Hampshire Inter-Library Center, and the libraries of Boston College, Yale, Harvard, Duke, Stanford and the University of Virginia.

IL —CENTER FOR RESEARCH LIBRARIES, 6050 S Kenwood Ave, Chicago, 60637. Donald B Simpson, Dir; Esther Smith, Collection Development Librn
Holdings: Vols Microfilm
Notes: Extensive holdings of archival materials, especially Foreign Office, Cabinet Office, and other government agencies. Extensive holdings of parliamentary publications and other government documents.

IL —NEWBERRY LIBRARY, 60 W Walton St, Chicago, 60610. Diana Haskell, Cur of Modern Mss
Holdings: Cat
Notes: Espec English history to 1914.

IN —INDIANA UNIVERSITY, Lilly Library, Seventh St, Bloomington, 47405. William R Cagle, Librn
Holdings: Vols 480 Cat Mss
Notes: Incl contemporary printings of government publications. Strong in the period of William and Mary, 1689-1702. Mss incl a small group of Scottish materials, 1627-1707.

IN —ALLEN COUNTY PUBLIC LIBRARY, Fred J Reynolds Historical Genealogy Collection, 900 Webster St, Fort Wayne, 46802. Rick J Ashton, Dir; Michael B Clegg, Manager
Holdings: Vols 200,000 Cat Mss Maps Pix Microforms
Notes: Incl state, county, regional, town and church histories. All census schedules and port of entry records released by the federal government are in the microfilm collection of 40,000 reels. The collection contains parish registers and publications of British parish register societies. Canadian, English, Scotch, Irish and Welsh records are well represented. The heraldry collection is housed with the genealogy collection. Allen County Public Library is and has been the depository for the North American Association of Directory Publishers since 1964.

IN —PURDUE UNIVERSITY LIBRARIES, Graduate School of Management, Krannert Library, West Lafayette, 47907. Gordon Law, Librn
Notes: The collection consists of books, journals and pamphlets dating from the early 16th to late 19th century, covering to a large degree the early literature in economic thought and business practices both here and abroad. No photocopying.

KS —UNIVERSITY OF KANSAS, Kenneth Spencer Research Library, Special Collections Dept, Lawrence, 66045. Alexandra Mason, Librn
Holdings: Vols 12,000 Cat Mss Maps Pix
Notes: Particularly 18th century English imprints, incl ca 5000 pamphlets, 1000 plus vols of newspapers and periodicals, and official and private mss. Noncirculating.

MA —NEW ENGLAND HISTORIC GENEALOGICAL SOCIETY, Library, 101 Newbury St, Boston, 02116. Ralph J Crandell, Dir
Holdings: Vols (250,000) Mss Maps Microforms Pix
Notes: New England genealogy. Especially strong Massachusetts, Maine, and New Hampshire, although all states are well represented, as are the relevancies of each subject listed in this volume with regard to British antecedent and contemporary history. Special strengths in local history and biography, obituaries, etc, incl parish registers, censuses, British and American. 3125 linear ft of mss.

MA —HARVARD UNIVERSITY LIBRARY, Widener Library, Cambridge, 02138. Carolyn Fawcett, Specialist in Book Selection
Holdings: Cat Mss Microforms
Notes: An oustanding collection.

MA —BOSTON COLLEGE LIBRARIES, Chestnut Hill, 02167.
Holdings: Vols 10,345 Mss Maps Pix
Notes: The library and personal papers of Hilaire Belloc (1870-1953), whose writings on a wide range of subjects: history, travel, politics, economics, religion, social conditions and in a variety of literary forms: biography, fiction, essays, poetry, children's literature reflect both an uncommon versatility and a prophetic vision. For reference use only, by arrangement with librarian. Also 151 literary mss, over 8000 letters, notebooks, sketches, music.

MI —UNIVERSITY OF MICHIGAN, Graduate Library, Ann Arbor, 48109. Janet

GREAT BRITAIN—HISTORY (cont.)

White, Reference Librn
Holdings: Vols 17,000 Cat Maps Microforms
MN —UNIVERSITY OF MINNESOTA, O Meredith Wilson Library, 309 19 Ave S, Minneapolis, 55455. Austin J McLean, Chief, Special Collections
Holdings: Vols (9000) Cat
Notes: Special concentration on volumes from the Stuart Period. Holdings are cited in the new revisions of the STC and Wing.
MO —UNIVERSITY OF MISSOURI-COLUMBIA, Ellis Library, Special Collections Dept, Ninth & Lowry, Columbia, 65201. Margaret A Howell, Head, Special Collections
Holdings: Vols 20,000// Cat
Notes: 17th, 18th and 19th century English tracts-religious, political and historical.
MO —NORTHEAST MISSOURI STATE UNIVERSITY, Pickler Memorial Library, Kirksville, 63501. George N Hartje, Librn
Holdings: Vols 25,950 Cat Microforms
Notes: English Renaissance and Reformation history.
MO —WASHINGTON UNIVERSITY, John M Olin Library, Campus Box 1061, St Louis, 63130.
Holdings: Vols 6300 Cat Microforms
Notes: Incl important documents such as Hansard, incomplete set of *House of Commons Sessional Papers* (Irish University Press edition plus partial holdings in microprint), *Public Record Office Calendars and Indexes, Historical Manuscripts* Commission reports, etc. Strongest in early period.
NY —GENERAL THEOLOGICAL SEMINARY, Saint Marks Library, 175 Ninth Ave, New York, 10011. David Green, Dir
Holdings: Vols (200,000) Cat Mss Maps Pix Slides Microforms
Notes: Extensive collection.
NY —NEW YORK PUBLIC LIBRARY, Research Libraries, General Research Division, Fifth Ave & 42 St, New York, 10018. Rodney Phillips, Chief
Holdings: Vols (2,225,000) Cat Maps Pix Microforms
Budget: ($775,718)
NY —NEW YORK PUBLIC LIBRARY, Local History and Genealogy Div, Fifth Ave & 42 St, New York, 10018. Gunther E Pohl, Chief
Holdings: Cat Pix
Notes: Extensive collection of county, city, town and village histories of the United States and of the British Isles and the Republic of Ireland. For state and national histories of the United States refer to the American History Division. All other local histories are part of the General Research and Humanities Division. Collection includes over 60,000 mounted photographs of New York City views arranged by address and/or subject. 20,000 film and glass plate negatives depicting NYC tenement housing conditions (1902-1938). Also the Lloyd L Acker collection of 15,000 film negatives depicting NYC scenes, 1935-1975. Collection of Lewis W Hine photographic prints made by the photographer on immigration, child labor, women at work and men at work. Eugene Armbruster collection of Long Island views; D B Austin's photographs of Long Island and western Americana; scrapbooks, andpostcards of NYC and other US regions (200,000). See *United States Local History* Catalog (Boston: G K Hall, 1974), 2 vols.
NY —UNION THEOLOGICAL SEMINARY, Library, 3041 Broadway at Reinhold Niebuhr Place, New York, 10027. Richard D Spoor, Dir
Notes: McAlpin Collection of British History and Theology, 1500-1700 (18,000 items).
NY —UNIVERSITY OF ROCHESTER, Rush Rhees Library, Department of Rare Books and Special Collections, Rochester, 14627. Peter Dzwonkoski, Librn
Notes: The Robert Metzdorf Collection of material about Queen Victoria and her reign.
NC —DUKE UNIVERSITY, William R Perkins Library, Manuscript Dept, Durham, 27706. Ellen Gartrell, Cur of Mss
Holdings: Cat Mss
Notes: Incl 50,000 items, 18th-20th centuries, representing the political, diplomatic, military, ecclesiastical, and economic affairs of Great Britain and the British Empire. Incl papers of William Wilberforce, William Smith, John Wilson Croker, John Backhouse, Malet Family, etc.
OH —CLEVELAND PUBLIC LIBRARY, History and Geography Department, 325 Superior Ave, Cleveland, 44114. JoAnn Petrello, Head
Holdings: Cat
Notes: Extensive British History Collection (incl Ireland, Scotland), especially 1660-1800. Rare books. Collection of British Learned Society serials (282); English Political Pamphlet Collection (about 2000). No photocopying.
PA —TEMPLE UNIVERSITY LIBRARIES, Special Collections Dept, Rare Books & Mss Section, Philadelphia, 19122. Thomas M Whitehead, Cur
Holdings: Vols (600) Cat Mss
Notes: Seventeenth and 18th century books and pamphlets on political, religious, social and intellectual life and history of England. Strong holdings of John Cotton, Gilbert Burnet, Richard Overton, John Liburne; Civil War pamphlets, ranters and levellers. The Nordell and Simpson Collections.
PA —FRIENDS HISTORICAL LIBRARY OF SWARTHMORE COLLEGE, Swarthmore, 19081. J William Frost, Dir
Holdings: Vols (35,000) Cat Mss Pix Microforms
Notes: Library's collection contain information on the history and doctrine of the Society of Friends, Quaker contributions to literature, science, business, education, and government, plus their reform efforts in peace, Indian rights, women's rights, and abolition of slavery. The library holds, either in the original manuscript or on microfilm, the largest collection in the world of Quaker meeting archives, incl microfilm copies of minutes and registers of many meetings in Great Britain. Among the more than 250 mss collections are papers of several British Quakers and Quaker families.
SC —COLLEGE OF CHARLESTON LIBRARY, Special Collections Dept, Charleston, 29401.
Notes: This collection consists of published material, heavily illustrated, dealing with the British royal family from Queen Victoria to Queen Elizabeth II.
UT —BRIGHAM YOUNG UNIVERSITY, Harold B Lee Library, Unversity Hill, Provo, 84602. Sterling Albrecht, Dir
Notes: The David Magee Collection. About 2000 vols covering nearly every phase of life in Victorian England.
VA —VIRGINIA STATE LIBRARY, 12 & Capitol Sts, Richmond, 23219.
Holdings: Vols 16,500 Cat Maps Pix
Notes: Mostly 17th and 18th centuries. Incl early county histories and parish registers (about 9000 vols).
WI —UNIVERSITY OF WISCONSIN, MADISON, Memorial Library, 728 State St, Madison, 53706. Erwin K Welsch, Social Studies Bibliographer
Notes: Incl the Thordarson Collection, over 10,000 vols on the history and development of English science; the Guy Hayler Collection on British Temperance, an extensive collection of vols, periodicals, mss, clippings and photographs on the temperance movement in England in the 19th century; and a collection of ca 5000 18th and 20th century pamphlets reflecting contemporary opinion on some of the more controversial issues of the time. This incl 1000-pamphlet Strangford Collection and the substantial collection entitled "Economic and social pamphlets."
WI —UNIVERSITY OF WISCONSIN, MADISON, Memorial Library, Rare Books Collection, 728 State St, Madison, 53706. Gretchen Lagana, Cur
Holdings: // Mss
Notes: The English Manor Rolls number 186 in all and cover a period of more than two hundred years (1302-1506). With the exception of four rolls, each of which is dated 1302, all the rolls are from Wilberton Manor in Cambridgeshire in the bishopric of Ely. The rolls, grouped according to the regnal years of the various kings, are especially complete for the reigns of Richard II, Henry IV, Henry VI, Edward IV, and Henry VII. Housed in the Dept of Rare Books and Special Collections. No photocopying.
BC —VANCOUVER PUBLIC LIBRARY, History & Government Div, 750 Burrard St, Vancouver, V6Z 1X5, Can.
Holdings: Vols 200 Cat Maps Pix
Notes: Antiquities, archaeology, biography, history, description, travel, etc concerning Norfolk and East Anglia in England. (Gift of the Bulwer Family; additional parts of the gift are at the University of British Columbia Library.)
ON —NATIONAL LIBRARY OF CANADA, 395 Wellington St, Ottawa, K1A 0N4, Can. Andre Preibish, Dir
Holdings: Vols 44,000 Documents
Budget: $50,000
Notes: Includes 400 serials titles. Collection aims to be comprehensive and covers all aspects of Canadian history. The library has received all Canadian titles on legal deposit since 1950; intensive acquisition of earlier works and those published abroad. In addition, the collection is supported by representative resources for American, British and French history.
ON —METROPOLITAN TORONTO LIBRARY, History Dept, 789 Yonge St, Toronto, M4W 2G8, Can. Michael Pearson, Head
Holdings: Vols (8000) Cat Phonorecords Audiotapes Microforms
Notes: Emphasis on modern period from Tudors to present. Extensive collection of publications of local and regional historical and record societies: Chetham Society, Lancashire and Cheshire Record Society, Harleian Society, etc. Fairly good county history collection including *Victoria History of the Counties of England.*
ON —UNIVERSITY OF TORONTO, Thomas Fisher Rare Book Library, 120 Saint George St, Toronto, M5S 1A5, Can. Richard G Landon, Head
Notes: Strong collection.
PQ —MCGILL UNIVERSITY, McLennan Library, Rare Books and Special Collections Dept, 3459 McTavish St, Montreal, H3A 1Y1, Can.
Notes: 20,090 pamphlets on British historical, religious, and political material dating mainly from the 17th and 18th centuries, are housed in the Redpath Tracts Collection. Also the manuscripts of Carlyon Wilfroy Bellairs on early 20th century British politics and those of Henry Hardinge, first Viscount Hardinge of Lahore, are housed in the Manuscript Collection.

GREAT BRITAIN—HISTORY—STUARTS, 1603-1714

NY —UNIVERSITY OF ROCHESTER, Rush Rhees Library, Department of Rare Books and Special Collections, Rochester, 14627. Peter Dzwonkoski, Librn
Holdings: Vols 3000 Cat
Notes: Collection relating to the political, religious, and literary controversies of the period with particular emphasis on the Restoration. No photocopying.

GREAT BRITAIN—HISTORY—CIVIL WAR, 1642-1649

CA —UNIVERSITY OF CALIFORNIA, DAVIS, Shields Library, Dept of Special Collections, Davis, 95616. Donald Kunitz, Head; C Danial Elliott, Asst Head
Holdings: Vols (1100) Cat
IN —INDIANA UNIVERSITY, Lilly Library, Seventh St, Bloomington, 47405. William R Cagle, Librn
Holdings: Vols 970 // Cat
Notes: Incl contemporary printings of government publications.

GREAT BRITAIN—HISTORY—CIVIL WAR, 1642-1649 (cont.)

MA —HARVARD UNIVERSITY LIBRARY, Houghton Library, Cambridge, 02138. F Thomas Noonan, Cur, Reading Room; Lawrence Dowler, Associate Librn
Holdings: Cat
Notes: Account of Gay Collection of English Civil War Tracts, 1640-1661, published by Library in 1916.

PA —TEMPLE UNIVERSITY LIBRARIES, Special Collections Dept, Rare Books & Mss Section, Philadelphia, 19122. Thomas M Whitehead, Cur
Holdings: Vols (600) Cat Mss
Notes: Seventeenth and 18th century books and pamphlets on political, religious, social and intellectual life and history of England. Strong holdings of John Cotton, Gilbert Burnet, Richard Overton, John Liburne; Civil War pamphlets, ranters and levellers. The Nordell and Simpson Collections.

GREAT BRITAIN—HISTORY—COMMONWEALTH AND PROTECTORATE, 1649-1660

IN —INDIANA UNIVERSITY, Lilly Library, Seventh St, Bloomington, 47405. William R Cagle, Librn
Holdings: Vols (300) // Cat
Notes: Incl contemporary printings of laws and other government publications.
See also entry under Cromwell, Oliver

GREAT BRITAIN—HISTORY—RESTORATION, 1660-1688

IN —INDIANA UNIVERSITY, Lilly Library, Seventh St, Bloomington, 47405. William R Cagle, Librn
Holdings: Vols (570) // Cat Mss
Notes: Incl contemporary printings of government publications. Mss incl papers of Ignatius White, Marquis d'Albeville, 1653-1690, 335 items.

GREAT BRITAIN—HISTORY—CRIMEAN WAR, 1853-1856 see Crimean War, 1853-1856

GREAT BRITAIN—HISTORY—19TH CENTURY

CA —CLAREMONT COLLEGES, Honnold Library, Ninth & Dartmouth, Claremont, 91711. Tania Rizzo, Special Collections Dept Head
Holdings: Vols (1880) // Uncat Pamphlets
Notes: 19th century pamphlet collection, chiefly British, concerning contemporary religion, commerce, finance, politics, labor, literature, social problems. Some deal with continental problems, often in French, Italian, Portuguese, etc (indexed).

DC —LIBRARY OF CONGRESS, Prints & Photographs Div, Washington, 20540.
Notes: The Roger Fenton Collection of 265 original Crimean War photoprints.

IN —INDIANA UNIVERSITY, Lilly Library, Seventh St, Bloomington, 47405. William R Cagle, Librn
Holdings: Vols 3000 Cat Mss
Notes: Contemporary printings relating to the history of Great Britain. Strong in the periods of Anne and George I, George II and George III. Also have 1200 British pamphlets depicting the war of ideas leading to the outbreak of the American Revolution.

MA —BRANDEIS UNIVERSITY, Goldfarb Library, 415 South St, Waltham, 02154. Bessie Hahn, Dir
Notes: Benjamin Disraeli Correspondence. Contains approx 80 letters and other ephemeral items of Benjamin Disraeli, Lord Beaconsfield. A finding list is available in Special Collections.

NY —SYRACUSE UNIVERSITY LIBRARIES, Ernest S Bird Library, George Arents Research Library for Special Collections, Syracuse, 13210. Carolyn A Davis, Manuscripts Librn; Amy S Doherty, University Archivist; Mark F Weimer, Rare Book Librn
Notes: Microfilm copies of Benjamin Disraeli's complete papers (200,000 frames) incl family, domestic and personal papers, copies of speeches, royal and general correspondence, papers on domestic and foreign affairs, correspondence on honors and titles, Mrs Disraeli's papers, mss of his novels and proofs and notices and correspondence about the novels. Also the papers of his father Isaac D'Israeli, of his grandfather Benjamin D'Israeli and Disraeli's biographers, Monypenny and Buckle.

UT —BRIGHAM YOUNG UNIVERSITY, Harold B Lee Library, Unversity Hill, Provo, 84602. Sterling Albrecht, Dir
Holdings: Vols 2000 Cat
Notes: A large collection covering all phases of literature and life in the Age of Queen Victoria. Incl an unusual collection of "Yellow Backs"--1750 printer's proofs for yellow-back covers of original paperbacks of the 19th century.

WI —UNIVERSITY OF WISCONSIN, MADISON, Memorial Library, 728 State St, Madison, 53706. Erwin K Welsch, Social Studies Bibliographer
Notes: (1) Parliamentary Debates (Hansard) for Lords and Commons from 1803 to date; parliamentary papers set in original from 1860 to date, previous volumes on microfiche. (2) A collection of property of Guy Hayler, an active member of many British temperance groups in the latter part of the 19th and 20th centuries. Many items contain ms annotations by Hayler concerning individuals or organizations as well as clippings from contemporary sources which have been added. A number of the periodicals are recorded neither in the ULS or BUCOP; particularly notable are periodicals of local British temperance organizations. Incl 1500 vols cataloged; no longer expanding the collection.

GREAT BRITAIN—LIBRARIES

MN —SAINT JOHN'S ABBEY & UNIVERSITY, Hill Monastic Manuscript Library, Collegeville, 56321. Julian G Plante, Dir
Notes: Films of 61,000 mss. The total number of codices (bound handwritten mss) represents the holdings of several hundred libraries in Europe and elsewhere: Austria, Spain, Malta, Ethiopia, West Germany, Portugal, England, but also with concentrations of holdings from Italy, Hungary, Poland, Great Britain, Belgium, Yugoslavia, France, Switzerland and the Netherlands, and Vatican City. Also incl 70, 000 exposures.

GREAT BRITAIN—LOCAL HISTORY

GA —UNIVERSITY OF GEORGIA, Libraries, Special Collections Division, Athens, 30602. Vesta Lee Gordon, Asst Dir for Special Collections
Holdings: Vols (2000)
Notes: Relates to British county and parish history from the 16th through the 20th centuries with particular emphasis on architecture, natural history and travel.

IL —NEWBERRY LIBRARY, 60 W Walton St, Chicago, 60610. Diana Haskell, Cur of Modern Mss
Holdings: Cat

MI —UNIVERSITY OF MICHIGAN, Graduate Library, Ann Arbor, 48109. Janet White, Reference Librn
Holdings: Cat
Notes: Extensive collection of county histories.

†NY —UNIVERSITY OF ROCHESTER, Rush Rhees Library, Rochester, 14627.

ON —METROPOLITAN TORONTO LIBRARY, History Dept, 789 Yonge St, Toronto, M4W 2G8, Can. Michael Pearson, Head
Holdings: Vols (8000) Cat Phonorecords Audiotapes Microforms
Notes: Emphasis on modern period from Tudors to present. Extensive collection of publications of local and regional historical and record societies: Chetham Society, Lancashire and Cheshire Record Society, Harleian Society, etc. Fairly good county history collection including *Victoria History of the Counties of England.*

GREAT BRITAIN—LORD CHAMBERLAIN

†NY —STATE UNIVERSITY OF NEW YORK, COLLEGE AT BROCKPORT, Brockport, 14420.
Notes: Microfilm copy of the Lord Chamberlain's *Daybooks,* registers of plays licensed for presentation in London from 1824-1903. Originals in British Museum. Some other miscellaneous material is incl from the Lord Chamberlain's office.

GREAT BRITAIN—MAPS

CT —YALE UNIVERSITY, Box 1603A, Yale Station, New Haven, 06520.
Notes: Maps and atlas collection.

GREAT BRITAIN—NOBILITY

NY —UNIVERSITY OF ROCHESTER, Rush Rhees Library, Department of Rare Books and Special Collections, Rochester, 14627. Peter Dzwonkoski, Librn
Notes: The Robert Metzdorf Collection about Queen Victoria, her family, and the court. With first editions by Benjamin Disraeli.

GREAT BRITAIN—PARLIAMENTARY PAPERS

CA —STANFORD UNIVERSITY LIBRARIES, Jonsson Library of Government Documents, Stanford, 94305. W David Rozkuszka, Librn
Holdings: Vols 55,000 Cat Mss Microforms
Notes: Approximately 55,000 vols, incl every item published by the Public Record Office; the Historical Manuscripts Commission; the General Register Office; and very strong sets of the House of Lords and House of Commons parliamentary papers and debates (in hard copy for the nineteenth century; also 44,000 fiche of Common papers); approx 7000 microfilm reels, incl minutes and memoranda of the Cabinet Office, 1916 to date; Foreign Office records on China (3000 reels); confidential prints on China, Japan, Africa, the slave trade Tibet and Mongolia, Russia and the Soviet Union; correspondence of the British Embassy Archives in Washington, 1903-1940 (1248 microfilm reels); World War II papers of the Cabinet Office and Prime Minister's Office; Foreign Office general correspondence: Japan, 1856-1905 and 1930-1945; Russia, 1883-1948; United States, 1930-1945;China, 1906-1922; Domestic State Papers, Edward, Mary, Elizabeth, James I; Pipe Rolls, 1217-1306; English Civil War, Interregnum/Commonwealth records; Import-Export Ledgers, 1697-1780; Papers of Robert Peel; British official publications not published by HMSO, fiche collection, 1980 to date; London Corporation Journals, 1416-1694, and Repertories, 1495-1692. For more holdings, request "British Public Record Office Archival Material" at Stanford University.

CT —YALE UNIVERSITY, Box 1603A, Yale Station, New Haven, 06520.

CT —YALE UNIVERSITY, Yale Center for Parliamentary History, 333 Sterling Memorial Library, New Haven, 06520. Maija Cole, In Charge
Notes: Available to students and others for scholarly research. Now editing Parliamentary Procedings for 1638.

NY —NEW YORK STATE LIBRARY, State Education Bldg Annex, Washington Ave, Albany, 12224.
Holdings: Cat Microforms
Notes: Official depository of New York State publications; regional depository of US documents, also in microfilm; depository for

GREAT BRITAIN—PARLIAMENTARY PAPERS (cont.)

Canadian government documents; strong collections of state documents, New York City documents; British sessional papers; also League of Nations, United Nations, OAS documents. Extensive holdings of other domestic and foreign publications. Congressional serial set, incl hearings (1946-date).

PA —PENNSYLVANIA STATE UNIVERSITY, Fred Lewis Pattee Library, Documents Section, University Park, 16802. Diane H Smith, Head
Notes: Depository for US Government publications; depository for Pennsylvania documents; collect United Nations and related international and intergovernmental organization publications; selected publications from Australia, Great Britain, including Parliamentary Papers; census materials; a large microform collection, including Department of Energy (formerly ERDA, AEC), Congressional publications, Patents, OAS, UN. Incl 900,000 documents. Great Britain publications contain cataloged books and uncataloged microforms.

TX —WEST TEXAS STATE UNIVERSITY, Cornette Library, PO Box 748 WT Sta, Canyon, 79016. Faye Hendrickson, Special Collections Asst
Holdings: Vols (451,253) Uncat Microforms
Notes: Includes microform collection. No photocopying.

MB —UNIVERSITY OF MANITOBA, Elizabeth Dafoe Library, Government Publications Section, Winnipeg, R3T 2N2, Can. June Dutka, Head
Holdings: Vols 1000 //
Notes: The Irish University Press 1000 vol edition of British Parliamentary Papers 1801-1900, presents the reports with evidence of British Parliamentary enquiries, arranged in 82 "subject sets."

GREAT BRITAIN—POLITICS AND GOVERNMENT

DC —LIBRARY OF CONGRESS, Manuscript Division, Washington, 20540. John C Broderick, Chief

DC —LIBRARY OF CONGRESS, Prints & Photographs Div, Washington, 20540.
Notes: The British Cartoon collection contains 10,000 British political caricatures and satires dating from the 17th through mid 19th centuries. Incl the work of Henry Bunbury, George Cruikshank, Issac Cruikshank, Matthew Darly, James Gillray, and Thomas Rowlandson.

IN —PURDUE UNIVERSITY LIBRARIES, Graduate School of Management, Krannert Library, West Lafayette, 47907. Gordon Law, Librn
Notes: An important resource at the Krannert Library is its Special Collection of Business and Economics, consisting of some 8000 rare pre-20th century strengths in books, journals, tracts and pamphlets covering primarily the early literature of economic thought and business practices in America and abroad, 1500-1870. A catalog was issued in 1979.

MA —BRANDEIS UNIVERSITY, Goldfarb Library, 415 South St, Waltham, 02154. Bessie Hahn, Dir
Notes: Approx 80 letters and other ephemeral items of Benjamin Disraeli, Lord Beaconsfield. A finding list is available in Special Collections.

NY —UNIVERSITY OF ROCHESTER, Rush Rhees Library, Department of Rare Books and Special Collections, Rochester, 14627. Peter Dzwonkoski, Librn
Notes: The Robert Metzdorf Collection about Queen Victoria, her family, and the court. With first editions by Benjamin Disraeli.

NY —SYRACUSE UNIVERSITY LIBRARIES, Ernest S Bird Library, George Arents Research Library for Special Collections, Syracuse, 13210. Carolyn A Davis, Manuscripts Librn; Amy S Doherty, University Archivist; Mark F Weimer, Rare Book Librn
Notes: Microfilm copies of Benjamin Disraeli's complete papers (200,000 frames) incl family, domestic and personal papers, copies of speeches, royal and general correspondence, papers on domestic and foreign affairs, correspondence on honors and titles, Mrs Disraeli's papers, mss of his novels and proofs and notices and correspondence about the novels. Also the papers of his father Isaac D'Israeli, of his grandfather Benjamin D'Israeli and Disraeli's biographers, Monypenny and Buckle.

NC —DUKE UNIVERSITY, William R Perkins Library, Rare Book Room, Durham, 27706. John L Sharpe, III, Cur
Notes: English pamphlet collection of about 10,000 items. In the main, 17th and 18th century "political history and international relations of Great Britain." French pamphlet collection. Relating to the political, economic and social life of France from the early 18th century down to 1830.

RI —BROWN UNIVERSITY, John Carter Brown Library, Providence, 02912. Norman Fiering, Librn; Everett C Wilkie Jr, Bibliographer; Susan Danforth, Cur Maps & Prints
Holdings: Vols (40,000)
Notes: Extensive collections of pamphlets relating to American Revolution; other large collections of British laws; extensive collection of British writings on her colonial possissions in the New World until 1835.

TX —UNIVERSITY OF TEXAS LIBRARIES, General Libraries, PO Box P, Austin, 78713. Carolyn Bucknell, Asst Dir for Collection Development
Holdings: Cat Microforms

UT —BRIGHAM YOUNG UNIVERSITY, Harold B Lee Library, Unversity Hill, Provo, 84602. Sterling Albrecht, Dir
Notes: The David Magee Collection. About 2000 vols covering nearly every phase of life in Victorian England and 1500 vols covering literature in the Edwardian period.

†WA —WASHINGTON STATE UNIVERSITY, Library, Manuscripts, Archives & Special Collections, Pullman, 99164. John F Guido, Head
Holdings: Vols (5000) Mss Pix
Notes: The library of Virginia and Leonard Woolf (from Monk's House and Victoria Sq) forms the nucleus of the collection, which incorporates the library of Sir Leslie Stephen, Virginia's father. Leonard's interests are reflected by works concerning the Labour Party, the Fabian Society, as well as Ceylon. Partially cataloged.

ON —QUEEN'S UNIVERSITY, Douglas Library, Kingston, K7L 5C4, Can. William F E Morley, Cur, Special Collections
Holdings: Vols 200 Cat
Notes: The "Disraeli Project".

PQ —MCGILL UNIVERSITY, McLennan Library, Rare Books and Special Collections Dept, 3459 McTavish St, Montreal, H3A 1Y1, Can.
Notes: 20,090 pamphlets on British historical, religious, and political material dating mainly from the 17th and 18th centuries, are housed in the Redpath Tracts Collection. Also the manuscripts of Carlyon Wilfroy Bellairs on early 20th century British politics and those of Henry Hardinge, first Viscount Hardinge of Lahore, are housed in the Manuscript Collection.

GREAT BRITAIN—RELIGION

CA —UNIVERSITY OF CALIFORNIA, DAVIS, Shields Library, Dept of Special Collections, Davis, 95616. Donald Kunitz, Head; C Danial Elliott, Asst Head
Holdings: Vols 1700 Cat
Notes: Emphasis on Puritan and Quaker materials.

CO —UNIVERSITY OF COLORADO, Libraries, Special Collections, Boulder, 80309. Nora J Quinlan, Head
Holdings: Vols 2200
Notes: The James F Willard Collection of Pamphlets. Historical, political and religious tracts. Separate catalog.

NY —UNIVERSITY OF ROCHESTER, Rush Rhees Library, Department of Rare Books and Special Collections, Rochester, 14627. Peter Dzwonkoski, Librn
Holdings: Vols 300 Cat
Notes: A most unusual collection in size and scope of material by and about William Sherlock, Dean of St Paul's, 1691-1707, and other nonjuring writers.

NC —DUKE UNIVERSITY, Divinity School Library, Durham, 27706. Donn Michael Farris, Librn
Holdings: Vols (225,000)
Notes: Special collections and subject emphases in this library include: Archaeology, Egyptian; Archaeology, Middle Eastern; Art, Jewish; Bible; Bible-New Testament; Bible-Symbolism; Church Architecture; Egyptology; Fathers of the Church; Society of Friends; Great Britain-Religion-Methodism and Methodist Church; Hymns and Hymnals; Jansenists and Jansenism; Judaica; Mediaeval Christian Mysticism; Methodism and Methodist Church; Methodist Episcopal Church; Methodist Episcopal Church, South; Reformation; Religion-US-History; Rural Church; Theology-Great Britain-17th Century; Theology-Great Britain-18th Century; United Methodist Church; US-Church History; John Wesley.

GREAT BRITAIN—SOCIAL CONDITIONS

CA —UNIVERSITY OF CALIFORNIA, LOS ANGELES, William Andrews Clark Memorial Library, 2520 Cimarron St, Los Angeles, 90018.
Holdings: Cat Mss Pix
Notes: Extensive collection, first editions, etc.

GREAT BRITAIN—SOCIAL LIFE AND CUSTOMS

CA —CLAREMONT COLLEGES, Honnold Library, Ninth & Dartmouth, Claremont, 91711. Tania Rizzo, Special Collections Dept Head
Holdings: Vols (1880) // Uncat Pamphlets
Notes: 19th century pamphlet collection, chiefly British, concerning contemporary religion, commerce, finance, politics, labor, literature, social problems. Some deal with continental problems, often in French, Italian, Portuguese, etc (indexed).

†CA —UNIVERSITY OF SAN FRANCISCO, Richard A Gleeson Library, The Countess Bernardine Murphy Donohue Rare Book Room, San Francisco, 94117. D Steven Corey, Special Collections Librn
Holdings: Vols 1000 Cat Mss
Notes: The Eighteen-Nineties: authors and literature of the period are collected. There are specific collections of Oscar Wilde, Max Beerbohm, Arthur Symons, George Moore, Richard Le Gallienne, and Laurence Housman. The emphasis is on English rather than American literature.

CT —LEWIS WALPOLE LIBRARY, 154 Main St, Farmington, 06032. Catherine Jestin, Librn
Holdings: Cat Mss Maps Pix Slides Microforms Memorabilia
Notes: Research center for English eighteenth-century studies. A department of Yale University Library. Scholars may visit by appointment only.

CT —YALE UNIVERSITY, Yale Center for British Art, Rare Book Dept, New Haven, 06520. Joan Friedman, Cur
Notes: One of the greatest assemblages of British Art of the 17th-19th centuries.

NC —DUKE UNIVERSITY, William R Perkins Library, Durham, 27706. Elvin E Strowd, University Librn

UT —BRIGHAM YOUNG UNIVERSITY, Harold B Lee Library, Unversity Hill, Provo, 84602. Sterling Albrecht, Dir
Notes: The David Magee Collection. About 2000 vols covering nearly every phase of life in Victorian England and 1500 vols covering literature in the Edwardian period.

GREAT BRITAIN NEWSPAPERS see Newspapers, Great Britain

GREAT LAKES AREA

IL —CHICAGO HISTORICAL SOCIETY, Library, Clark St at North Ave, Chicago,

GREAT LAKES AREA (cont.)

60614. Robert L Brubaker, Librn
Holdings: Vols (150,000) Cat Mss Maps Pix
Notes: Incl the J Norman Jensen Collection, a file of approximately 8500 cards concerning ships that sank in the Great Lakes area from 1679 to 1947.

MI —GREAT LAKES COMMISSION, Institute of Science and Technology Bldg, 2200 Bonisteel Blvd, Ann Arbor, 48109. Michael J Donahue, Natural Resources Specialist
Holdings: Vols (4000)
Notes: Incl directories, reports and related documents covering Great Lakes-related natural resources management, transportation and economic development issues. The library is available for limited public use upon appointment.

MI —UNIVERSITY OF MICHIGAN, North Engineering Library, 1002 I St, Ann Arbor, 48109. Maurita Holland, Librn
Holdings: Vols 2500 Cat Maps Pix
Budget: $3500
Notes: Subject emphasis is on the natural science aspects of the Great Lakes; limnology. Also 5000 reports.

MI —MUSEUM OF THE GREAT LAKES, Bay County Historical Society, Library, 1700 Center Ave, Bay City, 48706. Eurdine Ringwelski, Librn
Holdings: Vols (800) Cat Mss Maps Pix Slides 16mm Films
Notes: Focuses on man's relationship to his environment in the Bay County region in an historical perspective. Incl books, mss, photos, maps, vertical files, and scrapbooks on the history of Bay County and the Saginaw Valley, Michigan.

MI —DETROIT PUBLIC LIBRARY, Burton Historical Collection, 5201 Woodward Ave, Detroit, 48202. Alice Dalligan, Chief
Notes: History of Great Lakes Area.

MI —MICHIGAN TECHNOLOGICAL UNIVERSITY, Archives, Copper County Historical Collections, Houghton, 49931. Theresa Sanderson Spence, University Archivist
Holdings: Uncat Mss Maps Pix
Notes: Wide variety of material on mining, fishing, lumbering and marine activities. Special interest in Great Lakes shipping, and Lake Superior. Collection is accessioned but not indexed. 637 folders (25 file boxes) of material.

MI —LANSING PUBLIC LIBRARY, Local History Room, 401 S Capitol Ave, Lansing, 48914. Jane McClary, Local History Librn
Holdings: Vols (6000) Cat Mss Maps Pix Microforms VF
Notes: Separate catalog.

MI —MACKINAC ISLAND STATE PARK COMMISSION, Library, Bos 30028, Lansing, 48909. Keith R Widder, Cur
Holdings: Vols (1000) Cat Mss Maps Pix Slides Audiotapes
Budget: ($2500)
Notes: Mackinac area history-research collection: archaeology, historic preservation, etc. Great Lakes ships and shipping.

MI —SAINT CLAIR COUNTY LIBRARY, 210 McMorran Blvd, Port Huron, 48060. Frances A Marshall, Local History Librn
Holdings: Vols 5116 Cat Mss Maps Pix Microforms
Notes: The

MI —LAKE SUPERIOR STATE COLLEGE, Library, College Dr, Sault Sainte Marie, 49783. Frederick A Michels, Dir
Holdings: Vols (500) Cat

MI —LE SAULTE DE SAINTE MARIE HISTORIC SITES, PO Box 1668, Sault Sainte Marie, 49783. Thomas Nance, Curator
Notes: 300 Great Lakes logbooks cover more than 100 years of freighter history of the local Wilson Marine Transit Company. Incl *Marine News*, 59 vols, 1900-1968, plus related reports, directoies, and yearbooks of steel industry.

NY —BUFFALO & ERIE COUNTY HISTORICAL SOCIETY, 25 Nottingham Court, Buffalo, 14216. Herman Sass, Librn
Notes: Great Lakes marine history; especially strong in Lake Erie material. In various resources departments. No separate catalog.

NY —FORT ONTARIO HISTORIC SITE, Oswego, 13126. Shelley B Weinreb, Historic Site Mgr
Holdings: Vols (400) Cat Mss Maps Pix Slides
Notes: Primary focus is upon military activities at the mouth of the Oswego River and the utilization of fortifications (Fort Ontario, Fort Oswego, and Fort George) at that point which served to control the outlet of the traditional Mohawk-Oneida-Oswego route to the Great Lakes. A limited number of sources on fortification design, weapons, uniforms, and military equipment are included. Also incl 4000 slides and 400 pictures.

NY —STATE UNIVERSITY OF NEW YORK, COLLEGE AT OSWEGO, Penfield Library, Oswego, 13126. Anne Commerton, Dir
Holdings: Cat Mss
Notes: Collection of data and newspapers, notes and correspondence for writing a book on shipwrecks on Lake Ontario and in particular, Oswego Harbor, by Richard F Palmer, Syracuse Newspapers reporter. Photographs accompanied this material but were removed to be added to our local history photograph collection. Eight inches of material.

†OH —OHIO NORTHERN UNIVERSITY, Heterick Memorial Library, 525 S Main St, Ada, 45810.

OH —BOWLING GREEN STATE UNIVERSITY, Jerome Library, Institute for Great Lakes Research, Bowling Green, 43403. Richard J Wright, Dir
Holdings: Vols (2500) Cat Mss Maps Pix Slides Phonorecords Audiotapes Videotapes 16mm Films Microforms
Budget: ($8300)
Notes: About 50 major ms collections, most of them processed; several thousand minor ms items, unprocessed. 100,000 pictures, incl several thousand film and glass plate negatives. Microforms of government vessel registries, vessel passages, 1500 maps, some mss. 6000 naval architectural drawings, 600 vols of scrapbooks. 140 periodical titles, current and op. Author/title/subject catalog.

OH —CASE WESTERN RESERVE UNIVERSITY LIBRARIES, Cleveland, 44106. Susie Hanson, Special Collections Librn
Holdings: Vols 1000 Cat
Notes: The collection was previously titled the Lake Erie Study Collection. As its scope has increased, it has been renamed the Environmental Sciences Collection and has been fully incorporated into the collection of the Sears Library, which serves the University in the areas of science and technology, economics and management. The Environmental Sciences Collection incl government and nongovernment reports, monographs and serials.

OH —CLEVELAND PUBLIC LIBRARY, Science & Technology Dept, 325 Superior Ave, Cleveland, 44114. Jean Z Piety, Head
Holdings: Cat Mss Maps Pix
Notes: Special collection covers the environmental sciences concerned with the Great Lakes-St Lawrence drainage basins. Emphasis is on limnology, ecology, meteorology, hydraulics, biology, pollution of air and water, natural history and general research. Most of the material indexed has been donated by numerous agencies around the Great Lakes. Complete set of Great Lakes Navigational charts.

OH —RUTHERFORD B HAYES LIBRARY, 1337 Hayes Ave, Fremont, 43420. Watt P Marchman, Dir
Holdings: Vols 500 Cat Mss Maps Pix Slides
Notes: The Great Lakes Marine Collection, incl the Capt Frank E Hamilton Collection; Great Lakes boats and shipping. Incl 300 charts; over 20,000 pictures (with 2500 negatives, 30 glass plates). Index and findings aids with the collection.

WI —MILWAUKEE PUBLIC LIBRARY, 814 W Wisconsin Ave, Milwaukee, 53233. Donald J Sager, City Librn
Holdings: Vols 1500 Cat Mss Maps Pix Slides
Notes: The Great Lakes Marine Collection consists of Runge Marine Collection, Wilson Marine Collection, and other collections on Great Lakes Marine History. Has data on about 85,000 ships and more than 20,000 pictures of Great Lakes vessels. Complete runs of reference material such as US List of merchant vessels, Greens, etc. Extensive collection of lake charts. Histories of cities and counties bordering Great Lakes.

ON —CANADA CENTRE FOR INLAND WATERS, Library, 867 Lakeshore Rd, Burlington, L7R 4A6, Can. Eve Dowie, Head Library Services
Holdings: Vols (20,000)
Budget: ($150,000)
Notes: A research collection oriented towards Canadian limnological research. Incl 312 subscriptions.

ON —LONDON PUBLIC LIBRARIES & MUSEUMS, London Room, 305 Queen's Ave, London, N6B 1X2, Can. W Glen Curnoe, Librn
Holdings: Cat Mss Maps Pix Slides Phonorecords Audiotapes 16mm Films Microforms
Budget: ($3700)
Notes: History of Ontario, with emphasis on London and region, from early 19th century onward. Separate catalog for books, films and microforms. Various subject indexes to materials. Special interest in London, Ontario authors and publishers.

ON —INTERNATIONAL JOINT COMMISSION LIBRARY, 100 Ouellette Ave, Seventh Floor, Windsor, N9A 6T3, Can. Pat Murrary, Librn
Notes: Emphasis on water resources, water quality, land use, coastal zones, Great Lakes. Library includes 40,000 government reports from federal, provincial and state governments; 5000 monographs to support Great Lakes Water Quality Agreement Community. Collection also includes 243 periodicals, 1700 microfiche, 800 slides & vertical files. The Great Lakes Basin Commission in Ann Arbor, Mich, which ceased operation in 1981, formerly housed some of this material.

GREAT LONDON EXHIBITION, 1851

†IN —PURDUE UNIVERSITY LIBRARIES, Krannert Library, West Lafayette, 47907.
Notes: Books, journals and pamphlets covering early literature of economic thought and business practives in America and abroad, 1500-1870.

GREAT NORTHERN RAILWAY

MN —JAMES JEROME HILL REFERENCE LIBRARY, Fourth St at Market St, Saint Paul, 55106. Virgil F Massman, Dir
Holdings: Vols (12,000) Mss
Budget: ($170,000)
Notes: Railroad history, and espec about the Great Northern Railway. James Jerome Hill papers (460 linear ft).

MN —MINNESOTA HISTORICAL SOCIETY LIBRARY, 690 Cedar St, Saint Paul, 55101. Patricia C Harpole, Chief of Reference Library; Bonnie G Wilson, Head of Special Libraries
Notes: Records.

GREAT PLAINS

IN —INDIANA UNIVERSITY, Lilly Library, Seventh St, Bloomington, 47405. William R Cagle, Librn
Holdings: // Cat Mss Maps
Notes: Description and travel of the US Plains and Rockies; overland accounts; issues of California newspapers of the gold rush era, etc.

KS —FORT HAYS KANSAS STATE UNIVERSITY, Forsyth Library, Western Collection, 600 Park St, Hays, 67601. Esta Lou Riley, Archivist/Special Collections Librn
Holdings: Vols (5500) Cat VF
Budget: ($1000)
Notes: Kansas material, emphasizing Western Kansas; the cattle industry of the Great Plains area to pre-World War I.

GREAT PLAINS (cont.)

KS —UNIVERSITY OF KANSAS, Kenneth Spencer Research Library, Kansas Collection, Lawrence, 66045. Sheryl K Williams, Cur
Holdings: Vols (92,000) Cat Mss Maps Pix
Notes: All aspects of Plains history with concentration on northern Great Plains region. Incl personal papers of conservationists, newsletter and other publications of conservation organizations.

NE —ADAMS COUNTY HISTORICAL SOCIETY, Library, 1330 N Burlington Ave, Hastings, 68901. Corinne Cody, Secretary
Holdings: Vols (200) Cat Mss Maps Pix Slides Phonorecords Audiotapes Videotapes 16mm Films Microforms
Budget: ($5000)
Notes: The most noteworthy portions of the Adams County Collection are the church and school records from the county, useful for case studies on many aspects of life on the Great Plains. The photographic collection is intensively indexed. A catalog and a guide to Adams County material available locally are in progress.

NE —KEARNEY STATE COLLEGE, Calvin T Ryan Library, Kearney, 68847. John Mayeski, Dir; Anita Norman, Reference Librn
Holdings: Vols 1700 Cat Mss Maps Pix Slides Microforms
Notes: Collection attempts to cover total historical collection incl overland journeys, Pony Express, sod houses, and the Union Pacific. Special consideration has been given to Indians of Nebraska and the cattle industry. The collection is well supported by the library's general strength of Western Americana.

NE —NEBRASKA STATE HISTORICAL SOCIETY, Archives, 1500 R St, Box 82554, Lincoln, 68501. James E Potter, State Archivist
Holdings: Cat Mss Microforms
Budget: ($290,000)
Notes: Collection estimated 4,000 cu. ft. of personal papers, business records, church records, and organizational records relating to the history of Nebraska and the Great Plains, ca. 1854-present with a particularly strong emphasis in the subject areas of Indians of North America, agriculture, railroad history, 19th century agrarian political movements, irrigation, and settlement of the Great Plains. Public records holdings of an estimated 10,000 cu. ft. of Nebraska state, county and some municipal government agencies include the official files of Nebraska governors, the Nebraska Legislature, and many territorial and state agencies 1854-present; and numerous tax records, court records, marriage records, naturalization records, and school census records for Nebraska counties. Newspaper collection of 20,000 rolls of microfilm, non-circulating but available for purchase, cataloged according to place published so specific titles must be requested. See A GUIDE TO THE NEWSPAPER COLLECTION OF THE STATE ARCHIVES (Lincoln: Nebraska State Historical Society, 1977), A GUIDE TO THE MANUSCRIPT DIVISION OF THE STATE ARCHIVES (Lincoln: Nebraska State Historical Society, 1974), and A GUIDE TO THE MANUSCRIPT DIVISION OF THE STATE ARCHIVES, a supplement (Lincoln: Nebraska State Historical Society, 1983). Microform holdings of manuscript and public records can also be purchased.

NE —NEBRASKA STATE HISTORICAL SOCIETY, Library, 1500 R St, Box 82554, Lincoln, 68501. M Ann Reinert, Library Dept Head
Holdings: Vols (100,000) Cat Maps Pix Microforms
Budget: ($200,000)
Notes: Extensive collection of Nebraska and Western Americana publications, especially Nebraska local historical and biographical materials, but also a strong emphasis in the subject areas of Indians of North America, archeology of the Great Plains, and Trans-Missouri history. A special collection of Nebraska authors, particularly Willa Cather and John G. Neihardt. Repository since 1905 of publications of state government. Approximately 30,000 vols. of genealogical materials, especially for the colonial and migration west to Nebraska period including most major genealogical and historical society periodicals. Collection of 400 atlases and 3000 separate maps primarily relating to Nebraska 1854-present including county maps; landowners maps and atlases; plans of cities and 563 sets of Sanborn Fire Insurance Maps dating back to 1883 for 135 towns in Nebraska. Repository for State Department of Roads printed maps. See Hermon Dunlap Smith Center for the history of Cartography–Newberry Library, CHECKLIST OF PRINTED MAPS OF THE MIDDLE WEST TO 1900, vol. 12 (Boston: G. K. Hall, 1981) for description of pre-1900 Nebraska separate maps. Approximately 120,000 photographs of Nebraska and Nebraskans including the 2500 photographs of sod houses in the Solomon D. Butcher Collection, the 465 photographs in the John A. Anderson collection of Brule Sioux.

NE —UNIVERSITY OF NEBRASKA-LINCOLN, Don L Love Library, University Archives and Special Collections, Lincoln, 68588. Joseph G Svoboda, University Archivist
Holdings: Pix Slides
Notes: R D Warden Collection of Charles Marion Russell. "Largest private collection of literature on Russell, 'The Cowboy Artist.'" 7000 items, incl first editions of every book and pamphlet by Russell and over 1000 periodical appearances of his art; 900 color prints; 142 drawings; color slides; scrapbooks about Russell and his family, from 1889.

ND —UNIVERSITY OF NORTH DAKOTA, Chester Fritz Library, Dept of Special Collections, Grand Forks, 58202. Daniel F Rylance, Special Collections Coordr
Holdings: Vols (5500) Uncat Mss Maps Pix Microforms
Budget: ($2500)
Notes: Also the Orin G Libby Manuscript Collection (900 collections), and the Aandahl Collection of Western History on North Dakota and the Northern Great Plains. Emphasis on agriculture, politics, pioneering, Germans from Russia, etc. Guides to the collections available from the Coordinator of Special Collections.

ND —THEODORE ROOSEVELT NATIONAL PARK, Library, PO Box 7, Medora, 58645. Susan Snow, Librn; Miki Hellickson, Chief Naturalist
Holdings: Vols (1500) Cat Mss Maps Pix Slides Audiotapes 16mm Films
Budget: ($5000)
Notes: Theodore Roosevelt, cattle country history, natural history. Also 2400 pictures and 2200 slides.

OK —MUSEUM OF THE GREAT PLAINS, Research Center, 601 Ferris, PO Box 68, Lawton, 73502. Steve Wilson, Dir; Paula Williams, Special Collections
Notes: Anthropology; archaeology; ecology and history of Trans-Mississippi West, especially Great Plains.

SD —SOUTH DAKOTA HISTORICAL RESOURCE CENTER, Library, Soldiers Memorial Bldg, Pierre, 57501. Rosemary Evetts, Librn
Holdings: Vols 1020 Cat Mss Maps Pix
Budget: $2000
Notes: South Dakota state and territorial materials. Picture collection has been cataloged and numbers approximately 20,000 items, of which we have negatives for about half. South Dakato materials include items on general state and territorial history, biographical, autobiographical, political, geological, economic and county and town materials.

SD —AUGUSTANA COLLEGE, Mikkelsen Library & Learning Resource Center, Center for Western Studies, Sioux Falls, 57197. Ronelle Thompson, Dir Library
Notes: The Center for Western Studies, located in the Mikkelsen Library, is an archival and research agency of Augustana College. Dedicated to the history and culture of the Great Plains and the Trans-Mississippi West, the Center collects and preserves materials relating to Plains Indians, immigrant settlers, Norwegiana, Western Americana, Herbert Krause, Frederick Manfred, Donald Parker, Richard F Pettigrew, Augustana College, the Episcopal Diocese of South Dakota, the South Dakota District of the American Lutheran Church, the South Dakota Penitentiary and Minnehaha County.

TX —PANHANDLE-PLAINS HISTORICAL MUSEUM, Research Center, Box 967, WT Sta, Canyon, 79016. Claire R Kuehn, Archivist-Librn
Notes: History of the Texas Panhandle. Incl interviews with early settlers taken over a 50-year period, ranch records, and business records relating to the Texas Panhandle and surrounding states.

TX —TEXAS A&M UNIVERSITY, Sterling C Evans Library, Special Collections Div, College Station, 77843. Donald H Dyal, Librn
Holdings: Vols (16,000) Mss Pix
Notes: Jeff Dykes Range Livestock Collection (incl a 600-item collection of J Frank Dobie works). Part of the Dobie Collection is described in Dykes, Jeff C *My Dobie Collection* (College Station, Tex; Friends of the Texas A&M University Library).

TX —SOUTHERN METHODIST UNIVERSITY, DeGolyer Library, Box 396, SMU, Dallas, 75275. Clifton H Jones, Dir
Holdings: Vols 50,000 Cat Mss Maps Pix
Notes: History of the trans-Mississippi West and Mexico, from discovery to present. Original editions of most of the important early collections of travels.

TX —TEXAS TECH UNIVERSITY, Library, Lubbock, 79409. David J Murrah, Assoc Dir for Special Collections

GREAT SALT LAKE

†UT —UNIVERSITY OF UTAH, Marriott Library, Salt Lake City, 84112.
Notes: Original drawings and personal papers of John Hudson, a gold rush Forty-Niner who helped chart the Great Salt Lake with Captain Howard Stansbury.

GREAT SMOKEY MOUNTAIN NATIONAL PARK

NC —WESTERN CAROLINA UNIVERSITY, Hunter Memorial Library, Cullowhee,

GREAT SMOKEY MOUNTAIN NATIONAL PARK (cont.)

28723. James B Lloyd, Cur
Notes: Incl a regional ms collection documenting the social and natural history of Appalachia in general and western North Carolina in particular. Subject emphasis incl the Cherokee Indian, the establishment of the Great Smokey Mountains National Park, and the continuing use of Appalachian wilderness.

GREBANIER, BERNARD

MA —BOSTON UNIVERSITY, Mugar Memorial Library, Special Collections Dept, 771 Commonwealth Ave, Boston, 02215. Howard B Gotlieb, Dir
Holdings: Cat Mss
Notes: Mss, correspondence, etc collected in depth; incl publications by or about.

GREECE

CA —HOOVER INSTITUTION ON WAR, REVOLUTION & PEACE, Stanford University, Stanford, 94305. Peter Duignan, Cur; Karen Fung, Deputy Cur
Holdings: Vols (100,000)
Notes: For full description of collection, see Hoover Institution entry under Near East.

GREECE—ANTIQUITIES

DC —HARVARD UNIVERSITY, Center for Hellenic Studies Library, 3100 Whitehaven St NW, Washington, 20008. Jeno Platthy, Librn
Holdings: Vols (36,000) Cat Maps
Budget: ($18,000)
Notes: In addition to a large collection of editions of ancient Greek authors, the library is well equipped to cover every aspect of ancient Greek civilization from prehistoric times to about AD 200. The subject fields covered include epigraphy, paleography, papyrology, history, literature, philosophy, religion, mythology, archaeology and art. A small collection of works on Patristics as well as all important Latin authors complete the Center's holdings.

NY —BROOKLYN MUSEUM, Wilbour Library of Egyptology, Eastern Parkway, Brooklyn, 11238. Diane Guzman, Librn
Holdings: Vols (30,000) Cat Maps
Notes: The Wilbour Library of Egyptology ranks as one of the world's finest, most complete collections of works on all aspects of the culture of Ancient Egypt (down to the Islamic conquest). A card catalog records authors, subjects, series and titles of all books, periodicals and and 12,000 pamphlets. A description of the collection, as of 1924, may be found in: William Burt Cook, Jr, *Catalogue of the Egyptological Library and other Books from the Collection of the Late Charles Edwin Wilbour* (Brooklyn, NY: Brooklyn Museum, 1924). Middle Eastern art formerly included, now transferred to the Brooklyn Museum.

GREECE—CIVILIZATION see Civilization, Greek

GREECE—HISTORY

DC —HARVARD UNIVERSITY, Center for Hellenic Studies Library, 3100 Whitehaven St NW, Washington, 20008. Jeno Platthy, Librn
Holdings: Vols (42,000)
Budget: ($76,824)
Notes: In addition to a large collection of editions of ancient Greek authors, the library is well equipped to cover every aspect of ancient Greek civilization from prehistoric times to about AD 200. The subject fields covered include epigraphy, paleography, papyrology, history, literature, philosophy, religion, mythology, archaeology and art. A small collection of works on Patristics as well as all important Latin authors complete the Center's holdings.

MN —UNIVERSITY OF MINNESOTA, O Meredith Wilson Library, 309 19 Ave S, Minneapolis, 55455. Austin J McLean, Chief, Special Collections

PA —UNIVERSITY OF PITTSBURGH, Hillman Library, Pittsburgh, 15260. Glenora E Rossell, Head
Holdings: Vols (11,550) Cat
Notes: The classics collection is particularly strong in Greek and Latin literature, Greek and Roman history, Greek philosophy, Greek and Latin language, and Greek epigraphy. In combination with the Frick Fine Arts collection it has a good collection in Greek and Roman art and archaeology. The collection of journals is also quite strong in these areas. There has been an emphasis in collecting books by and about Homer, Aristotles, Euripides, Vergil, Cicero and Petronius. It has a unique collection of unpublished PhD dissertations and Master's theses on Petronius. It has a basic collection on Greek and Latin paleography and papyrology.

GREECE, MODERN—HISTORY

MA —HARVARD UNIVERSITY LIBRARY, Widener Library, Modern Greek Collection, Cambridge, 02138. Evangelie Flessas, Librn
Holdings: Vols 80,000 Cat Mss Microforms
Notes: Oustanding collection; covers 1540-present.

OH —UNIVERSITY OF CINCINNATI, Classics Library, 320 Blegen, Cincinnati, 45221. Jean Susorney Wellington, Classics Librn; Eugenia Foster, Modern Greek Cur
Holdings: Vols (110,000) Cat Mss Maps Microforms
Notes: Niove Kyparissiotis. *The Modern Greek Collection in the Library of the University of Cincinnati; a Catalog.* Athens: Hestia Press, for the University of Cincinnati, 1960; also *Catalog of the Modern Greek Collection at the University of* Cincinnati, 5 vols. (Boston; G K Hall, 1978).

GREECE, MODERN—POLITICS AND GOVERNMENT

CA —HOOVER INSTITUTION ON WAR, REVOLUTION & PEACE, Stanford University, Stanford, 94305. Milorad M Drachkovitch, Archivist
Notes: Research files of Professor L S Stavrianos, incl reports, press releases, newspaper clippings, pamphlets, and other ephemeral publications relating to political developments in Greece and Cyprus, 1946-1960. 3 ms boxes.

GREEK ART see Art, Greek

GREEK CIVILIZATION see Civilization, Greek; Hellenism

GREEK DRAMA

NC —DUKE UNIVERSITY, William R Perkins Library, Durham, 27706. Elvin E Strowd, University Librn
Notes: The Spranger Collection of classical studies contains 2500 items. The principal dramatists, Euripides, Aeschylus, Aristophanes and Sophocles are fairly comprehensively covered by way of critical texts and studies up to 1968. Practically all the texts are represented by Loeb and Bude translations, and also Didot's 19th century series. Reference books includes a complete Pauly-Wissowa, Briquet, long runs of the Classical Review and Quarterly, the O E D and some 30 to 40 volumes of codex facsimiles of Euripides and others.

GREEK INSCRIPTIONS see Inscriptions, Greek

GREEK LANGUAGE AND LITERATURE

CA —UNIVERSITY OF CALIFORNIA, BERKELEY, University Library, Berkeley, 94720. Donald G Williams, Classics Librn
Notes: Research collections, incl a wide array of periodicals, critical editions, works of textual criticism, history, and epigraphy. Extensive coverage of 18th and 19th century classical scholarship. German and Italian research publications are particularly well represented. Main Library holdings are supplemented by significant works in the Bancroft Library: mss, incunabula, and other rare editions; especially noteworthy are the Horace Collection and the Tebtunis papyri.

CA —UNIVERSITY OF CALIFORNIA, IRVINE, Library, Irvine, 92664. Roger Berry, Dept Head
Notes: Incl the library of Professor Paul Friedlander (3000 vols). Located in general circulation collection.

CA —LOS ANGELES PUBLIC LIBRARY, Foreign Languages Dept, 630 W Fifth St, Los Angeles, 90071. Sylva Manoogian, Principal Librn
Holdings: Vols 848 Cat
Budget: ($41,500)

CT —YALE UNIVERSITY, Box 1603A, Yale Station, New Haven, 06520.
Holdings: Cat Mss

DC —CATHOLIC UNIVERSITY OF AMERICA, Mullen Library, 620 Michigan Ave NE, Washington, 20064. B Gutekunst, Humanities Librn
Holdings: Vols 6500 Cat

DC —HARVARD UNIVERSITY, Center for Hellenic Studies Library, 3100 Whitehaven St NW, Washington, 20008. Jeno Platthy, Librn
Holdings: Vols (42,000) Cat Maps
Budget: ($76,824)
Notes: In addition to a large collection of editions of ancient Greek authors, the library is well equipped to cover every aspect of ancient Greek civilization from prehistoric times to about AD 200. The subject fields covered include epigraphy, paleography, papyrology, history, literature, philosophy, religion, mythology, archaeology and art. A small collection of works on Patristics as well as all important Latin authors complete the Center's holdings.

MA —BOSTON PUBLIC LIBRARY, South End Branch, Multilingual Library, 685 Tremont St, Boston, 02118. Laura H Reyes, Librn
Holdings: Cat

MA —HARVARD UNIVERSITY LIBRARY, Widener Library, Cambridge, 02138.
Holdings: Cat
Notes: Incl particularly noteworthy collection of Aristophanes.

†MA —CLARK UNIVERSITY, Robert Hutchings Goddard Library, Worcester, 01610. Dorothy Mosa Kowski, Rare Books Librn
Holdings: Cat
Notes: Hundreds of vols of Greek and Latin classics in English translation (the Haven Darling Brackett Collection).

MI —UNIVERSITY OF MICHIGAN, Library, Dept of Rare Books & Special Collections, Ann Arbor, 48109. Robert J Starring, Head
Holdings: Cat Mss Microforms
Notes: Greek and Latin classics; classical studies periodicals.

MI —COLOMBIERE COLLEGE, Dinan Library, 9075 Big Lake Rd, Clarkston, 48016. Stephen A Meder, SJ, Librn
Holdings: Vols 2500// Cat

MN —UNIVERSITY OF MINNESOTA, O Meredith Wilson Library, 309 19 Ave S, Minneapolis, 55455. Austin J McLean, Chief, Special Collections

NC —DUKE UNIVERSITY, William R Perkins Library, Durham, 27706. Elvin E Strowd, University Librn
Notes: The Spranger Collection of classical studies contains 2500 items. The principal dramatists, Euripides, Aeschylus, Aristophanes and Sophocles are fairly comprehensively covered by way of critical texts and studies up to 1968. Practically all the texts are represented by Loeb and Bude translations, and also Didot's 19th century series. Reference books includes a complete Pauly-Wissowa, Briquet, long runs of the Classical Review and Quarterly, the O E D and some 30 to 40 volumes of codex facsimiles of Euripides and others.

OH —UNIVERSITY OF CINCINNATI, Classics Library, 320 Blegen, Cincinnati, 45221. Jean Susorney Wellington, Classics

GREEK LANGUAGE AND LITERATURE (cont.)

Librn; Eugenia Foster, Modern Greek Cur
Holdings: Vols (110,000) Cat Mss Maps Microforms

PA —UNIVERSITY OF PITTSBURGH, Hillman Library, Pittsburgh, 15260. Glenora E Rossell, Head
Holdings: Vols (11,550) Cat
Notes: The classics collection is particularly strong in Greek and Latin literature, Greek and Roman history, Greek philosophy, Greek and Latin language, and Greek epigraphy. In combination with the Frick Fine Arts collection it has a good collection in Greek and Roman art and archaeology. The collection of journals is also quite strong in these areas. There has been an emphasis in collecting books by and about Homer, Aristotle, Euripides, Vergil, Cicero and Petronius. It has a unique collection of unpublished PhD dissertations and Master's theses on Petronius. It has a basic collection on Greek and Latin paleography and papyrology.

TX —ABILENE CHRISTIAN UNIVERSITY, Margaret & Herman Brown Library, ACU Sta, Abilene, 79601. Callie Faye Milliken, Assoc Dir
Holdings: Vols (30,000) Cat Mss Slides Audiotapes Filmstrips Microforms

TX —UNIVERSITY OF TEXAS LIBRARIES, General Libraries, PO Box P, Austin, 78713. Carolyn Bucknell, Asst Dir for Collection Development
Holdings: Cat Microforms

WI —UNIVERSITY OF WISCONSIN, MADISON, Memorial Library, Rare Books Collection, 728 State St, Madison, 53706. Gretchen Lagana, Cur
Holdings: Vols 120// Cat
Notes: Giolito Collection. Approximately 120 titles of 16th century Italian imprints of Greek and Latin classics. Restricted use: Rare Book Department.

PQ —MCGILL UNIVERSITY, McLennan Library, Rare Books and Special Collections Dept, 3459 McTavish St, Montreal, H3A 1Y1, Can.
Notes: 5600 pamphlets, located in the Ribbeck Collection. Pamphlets, mostly in German, on Greek and Latin literature and philology.

GREEK LANGUAGE AND LITERATURE, MODERN

MA —HARVARD UNIVERSITY LIBRARY, Widener Library, Modern Greek Collection, Cambridge, 02138. Evangelie Flessas, Librn
Holdings: Cat
Notes: Remarkably strong collection; covers 1540-present.

MN —UNIVERSITY OF MINNESOTA, O Meredith Wilson Library, 309 19 Ave S, Minneapolis, 55455. Austin J McLean, Chief, Special Collections
Holdings: Vols 7805 Uncat
Notes: The Basil Laourdas Modern Greek Literature Collection. Most are Greek language. Most are presentation copies. Complete listing available in Division.

NY —NEW YORK PUBLIC LIBRARY, Donnell Foreign Language Library, 20 W 53 St, New York, 10019. Bosiljka Stevanovic, Supvr Librn
Holdings: Vols 1100 Cat
Notes: Greek collection incl Greek authors of Greek expression. No separate catalog.

NC —CUMBERLAND COUNTY PUBLIC LIBRARY, North Carolina Foreign Language Center, 328 Gillespie St, Fayetteville, 28301. Patrick M Valentine, Coordinator
Holdings: Vols (25,000) Cat Phonorecords Audiotapes
Notes: The largest book collections are, in descending order of size, German Spanish, French, Japanese, Korean and Vietnamese, with fair sized collections in Italian, Russian, Chinese, Arabic, Greek, Hungarian, Polish, Hebrew, Thai, and Hindi. The Center has several shelves each of books in Bengali, Dutch, Marathi, Portuguese, Urdu, and Yiddish. Smaller collections of one to three shelves each incl Catalan, Croatian, Czech, Danish, Finnish, Gujarati, Icelandic, Kannada, Latin, Lithuanian, Malayalam, Norwegian, Panjabi, Persian (Farsi), Romanian, Slovak, Swedish, Tagalog, Tamil, Telegu, and Ukrianian. The Center has grammars, dictionaries and occasionally other readings in languages from Afrikaans and Albanian to Welsh, Yoruba and Zulu.

OH —UNIVERSITY OF CINCINNATI, Classics Library, 320 Blegen, Cincinnati, 45221. Jean Susorney Wellington, Classics Librn; Eugenia Foster, Modern Greek Cur
Holdings: Vols (110,000) Cat Mss Maps Microforms
Notes: Niove Kyparissiotis. *The Modern Greek Collection in the Library of the University of Cincinnati; a Catalog.* Athens: Hestia Press, for the University of Cincinnati, 1960; also *Catalog of the Modern Greek Collection at the University of* Cincinnati, 5 vols. (Boston; G K Hall, 1978).

OH —CLEVELAND PUBLIC LIBRARY, Foreign Literature Dept, 325 Superior Ave, Cleveland, 44114. Natalia Bezugloff, Head
Holdings: Vols 3780 Cat
Notes: A popular circulating collection containing classics and the standard works with emphasis on belles lettres, history and biography. A variety of other subjects such as learning languages, how to do books, art, children's books, spoken phonodiscs and cassettes, periodicals, etc. Incl 1720 ephemera.
See also entry under Foreign Language Collections

GREEK MANUSCRIPTS see Manuscripts, Greek

GREEK MYTHOLOGY see Mythology, Greek

GREEK PAPYRI see Manuscripts (Papyri); Manuscripts, Greek

GREEK PHILOLOGY

DC —HARVARD UNIVERSITY, Center for Hellenic Studies Library, 3100 Whitehaven St NW, Washington, 20008. Jeno Platthy, Librn
Holdings: Vols (42,000) Cat Maps
Budget: ($76,824)
Notes: In addition to a large collection of editions of ancient Greek authors, the library is well equipped to cover every aspect of ancient Greek civilization from prehistoric times to about AD 200. The subject fields covered include epigraphy, paleography, papyrology, history, literature, philosophy, religion, mythology, archaeology and art. A small collection of works on Patristics as well as all important Latin authors complete the Center's holdings.

PQ —MCGILL UNIVERSITY, McLennan Library, Rare Books and Special Collections Dept, 3459 McTavish St, Montreal, H3A 1Y1, Can.
Notes: 5600 pamphlets, located in the Ribbeck Collection. Pamphlets, mostly in German, on Greek and Latin literature and philology.

GREEKS IN THE U.S.

MN —UNIVERSITY OF MINNESOTA, Immigration History Research Center, 826 Berry St, Saint Paul, 55114. Susan Griegs, Cur
Holdings: Vols (35,000) Mss Maps Pix Phonorecords Audiotapes 16mm Films Microforms
See also entry under US - Emigration and Immigration.

PA —BALCH INSTITUTE FOR ETHNIC STUDIES, Library, 18 S Seventh St, Philadelphia, 19106. R Joseph Anderson, Library Dir
Holdings: Vols 300 Cat Mss Pix Microforms

†PA —BALCH INSTITUTE FOR ETHNIC STUDIES, Library, 18 S Seventh St, Philadelphia, 19106.
Notes: Papers of Nicholas Vagionis, president of the American Greek Democratic Association.

GREELEY, REV. ANDREW M.

IL —CHICAGO HISTORICAL SOCIETY, Library, Clark St at North Ave, Chicago, 60614. Archie Motley, Manuscript Librn
Notes: Papers of: Emmet Dedmon, newspaper editor; Richard J Finnegan, newspaper editor; Rev Andres M Greeley, sociologist and author; attorney and civil liberties activist Pearl Hart; Robert J Havighurst, educator; social activist John Kearney; Kenesaw Mountain Landis, Federal Judge and first Commissioner of Baseball; Judge David F Matchett; Ivan Molek, Slovenian language publisher in Chicago; Max R Naiman, Communist Party activist; Ralph G Newman, book and autograph dealer and manuscript appraiser; Otto L Schmidt, physician and President of the Chicago and Illinois State Historical Societites; and Dempsey Travis, black mortgage banker.

GREELEY, HORACE

CO —DENVER PUBLIC LIBRARY, 1357 Broadway, Denver, 80203.
Notes: Correspondence, papers, pictures, diaries, etc.

NY —NEW YORK PUBLIC LIBRARY, Rare Books and Manuscripts Div, Fifth Ave & 42 St, New York, 10018. William L Joyce, Asst Dir; Susan E Davis, Cur of Mss
Holdings: Mss
Budget: ($7161)
Notes: Incl personal and literary mss, papers, etc.

GREEN, ALAN, 1906-1975

MA —BOSTON UNIVERSITY, Mugar Memorial Library, Special Collections Dept, 771 Commonwealth Ave, Boston, 02215. Howard B Gotlieb, Dir
Holdings: Mss Pix
Notes: Mss, correspondence, etc collected in depth; incl publications by or about.

GREEN, ALBERT L.

PA —FRIENDS HISTORICAL LIBRARY OF SWARTHMORE COLLEGE, Swarthmore, 19081. J William Frost, Dir
Holdings: Vols (31,340) Cat Mss Maps
Notes: Mss deal with Quaker Indian work under Grant's administration. Archives of Society of Friends Baltimore Yearly Meeting (Hicksite) Standing Committee on Indian Concerns; Joint Committee on Indian Affairs of Baltimore, Genesee, New York, and Philadelphia, 1836-1948; Friends Indian Aid Association of Philadelphia, 1869-1876; Philadelphia Yearly Meeting, Committee on Indian Affairs, 1887-1892. Papers of Quaker Indian agents Albert L Green and Thomas Lightfoot.

GREEN, CECIL H.

TX —NORTH TEXAS STATE UNIVERSITY, Archives, NT Station Box 5188, Denton, 76203. Robert LaForte, University Archivist
Notes: Part of Business Archive Project. Interviews with one of founders of Texas Instruments.

GREEN, COOPER

AL —BIRMINGHAM PUBLIC LIBRARY, Dept of Archives & Mss, 2020 Seventh Ave N, Birmingham, 35203. Marvin Y Whiting, Archivist & Cur
Holdings: Cat Docs Mss Photos //
Notes: Collection of correspondence, reports, memoranda, scrapbooks, other documents, and photographs of Cooper Green, Mayor, Birmingham, Alabama from 1940 to 1953. The papers reflect changes in the city during World War II, post war business expansion, and concern over growing civil rights efforts by blacks.

GREEN, GERALD

MA —BOSTON UNIVERSITY, Mugar Memorial Library, Special Collections Dept,

GREEN, GERALD (cont.)

771 Commonwealth Ave, Boston, 02215. Howard B Gotlieb, Dir
Holdings: Cat Mss Pix
Notes: Mss, correspondence, etc collected in depth; incl publications by or about.

GREEN, HENRY

NV —UNIVERSITY OF NEVADA, RENO, University Library, Special Collections Dept, Reno, 89557. Robert E Blesse, Head
Holdings: // Vols (23) Cat
Notes: Includes individual works by author in all editions including translations; also prefaces, introductions, published correspondence, appearances in anthologies, periodicals, etc. Bibliographical research collection, part of Modern Authors Collection. Other appearances 25 cataloged.

GREEN, JOSEPH COY, 1887-1978

NJ —PRINCETON UNIVERSITY, Library, Manuscript Collection, Nassau St, Princeton, 08540. Jean F Preston, Cur
Holdings: Mss
Notes: Incl 36 cartons, 1 box of papers. Terms of access: most of the records may by read by qualified scholars. A few files, incl the journals pertaining to Jordan, will not be accessible until 1988.

GREEN, MARTYN

MA —BOSTON UNIVERSITY, Mugar Memorial Library, Special Collections Dept, 771 Commonwealth Ave, Boston, 02215. Howard B Gotlieb, Dir
Holdings: Cat Mss Pix
Notes: Mss, correspondence, etc collected in depth; incl publications by or about.

GREEN, TIMOTHY

CT —CONNECTICUT COLLEGE, Library, Mohegan Ave, New London, 06320. Brian Rogers, College Librn
Holdings: Vols (382,000) Cat Mss Maps Pix
Notes: Collection includes material relating to New London and surrounding communities, including Groton, Norwich and Stonington. Includes pamphlets and broadsides printed in New London by the Greens during the Revolutionary period.

GREEN, WARREN K.

†MA —SUFFOLK UNIVERSITY, Library, Boston, 02114.
Notes: Papers.

GREEN, WILLIAM M.

MA —BOSTON UNIVERSITY, Mugar Memorial Library, Special Collections Dept, 771 Commonwealth Ave, Boston, 02215. Howard B Gotlieb, Dir
Holdings: Mss Correspondence

GREENAN, RUSSELL H.

MA —BOSTON UNIVERSITY, Mugar Memorial Library, Special Collections Dept, 771 Commonwealth Ave, Boston, 02215. Howard B Gotlieb, Dir
Holdings: Cat Mss
Notes: Mss, correspondence, etc collected in depth; incl publications by or about.

GREENAWAY,KATE,1846-1901

MI —DETROIT PUBLIC LIBRARY, Rare Books Department, 5201 Woodward Ave, Detroit, 48202.
Holdings: Vols 300 Cat Mss Pix
Notes: In addition to the 300 vols, collection incl original water colors, drawings, greeting cards and other ephemera, and memorabilia. Catalog published in 1977. Restricted use. Reference collection.

MS —UNIVERSITY OF SOUTHERN MISSISSIPPI, William David McCain Graduate Library, Box 5148, Southern Sta, Hattiesburg, 39406.
Holdings: Vols Mss Pix
Notes: Almost 300 drawings, paintings, unpublished verse, and autograph letters, together with a collection of over 100 books and memorabilia encompassing everything from first editions to wallpaper designs and costume jewelry, illustrating Greenaway's enormous influence on modern illustration and design for children. Extensive selection of her greetng cards. Catalog in progress.

NY —NEW YORK PUBLIC LIBRARY, Rare Books and Manuscripts Div, Fifth Ave & 42 St, New York, 10018. William L Joyce, Asst Dir; Bernard McTigue, Cur, Arents Collection
Holdings: Cat Mss Pix

NY —MARGARET WOODBURY STRONG MUSEUM, 1 Manhattan Square, Rochester, 14607.
Holdings: Vols (20,000) Periodicals
Notes: The Margaret Woodbury Strong Museum Library contains a collection of approx 20,000 books, periodicals and ephemera of and concerning the 19th and early 20th centuries. A large part of the library's holdings reflect the interests of Margaret Strong and her family: domestic life and literature of the 19th century and world travel, with particular emphasis on the Orient. The library's resources are available to all visitors for research. Book stacks and rare book storage are not open for browsing and do not circulate, but facilities are provided in reading room for study. Collection incl 40 books published with Kate Greenaway illustrations, 31 of which are first editions.

OH —CASE WESTERN RESERVE UNIVERSITY, M A Baxter School of Information and Library Science, 10900 Euclid Ave, Cleveland, 44106. Bettina MacAyeal, Librn; Gretchen Larson, Librn
Holdings: Vols (1100)
Notes: Incl collection of 1100 historical children's books and periodicals, housed in the Special Collections Dept of Freiberger Library, and can be used by the public. Incl *The Holy Bible Abridged* published by Isaiah Thomas in 1786, *The Life and Strange Surprising Adventures of Robinson Crusoe* of 1790, and a *Cinderella* dated 1809. There are examples of the work of illustrators Walter Crane, Randolph Caldecott, Kate Greenaway and Maurice Boutet de Monvel. The periodical collection incl a complete run of St. Nicholas Magazine.

PA —FREE LIBRARY OF PHILADELPHIA, Rare Book Dept, Logan Sq, Philadelphia, 19103. Marie E Korey, Rare Book Librn
Holdings: Vols (200) Cat Mss Pix
Notes: Contains books, annuals, autograph letters and original art.

PA —HUNT INSTITUTE FOR BOTANICAL DOCUMENTATION, Hunt Botanical Library, Frances Hooper Kate Greenaway Collection, Carnegie-Mellon University, Pittsburgh, 15213. Bernadette G Callery, Librn
Holdings: //
Notes: A collection of original watercolors, drawings, published works, and correspondence by artist and illustrator Kate Greenaway (1846-1901). For information on the collection see: *Kate Greenaway, Catalogue of an exhibition, from the Frances Hooper Collection.* Pittsburgh, Hunt Institute, 1980, which includes a summary register of the collection.

GREENBACKS

NE —NEBRASKA STATE HISTORICAL SOCIETY, Archives, 1500 R St, Box 82554, Lincoln, 68501. James E Potter, State Archivist
Holdings: Uncat Mss
Notes: Silver and the money question; also material on the Greenback Party. Printed speeches and tracts relating to the money question, 1890-1895. Many written by prominent political figures of the day. Also, pamphlets which relate to income tax, tariffs, free trade, soldiers' pensions, railroads, election laws and public lands. Collection of John Davis, Congressman from Kansas, 1891-1895.

GREENBERG, JACOB W.

†NY —COLUMBIA UNIVERSITY LIBRARIES, Butler Library, Rare Book and Manuscript Library, 535 W 114 St, New York, 10027.
Notes: Papers of Jacob W Greenberg of Greenberg Publishers.

GREENBERG, JOANNE

MA —BOSTON UNIVERSITY, Mugar Memorial Library, Special Collections Dept, 771 Commonwealth Ave, Boston, 02215. Howard B Gotlieb, Dir
Holdings: Cat Mss Pix
Notes: Mss, correspondence, etc collected in depth; incl publications by or about.

GREENBERG, NOAH

NY —NEW YORK PUBLIC LIBRARY, Performing Arts Research Center, Music Div, Lincoln Center, New York, 10018.
Notes: New York Pro Musica Archives, and personal papers of Noah Greenberg, founder.

GREENE, GAEL

MA —BOSTON UNIVERSITY, Mugar Memorial Library, Special Collections Dept, 771 Commonwealth Ave, Boston, 02215. Howard B Gotlieb, Dir
Holdings: Mss Correspondence

GREENE, GRAHAM

DC —GEORGETOWN UNIVERSITY, Library, Special Collections Div, 37 & O Sts NW, Washington, 20057. George M Barringer, Special Collections Librn; Nicholas B Sheetz, Mss Librn
Holdings: Mss
Notes: Extensive collection of mss, letters, journals and diaries by novelist Graham Greene incl correspondence to him from Evelyn Waugh and Dame Edith Sitwell. Restricted. Also, correspondence in the Christopher Sykes Collection.

KY —UNIVERSITY OF LOUISVILLE, Ekstrom Library, Rare Books & Special Collections, 2301 S Third St, Louisville, 40208. George T McWhorter, Cur; Delinda Stephens Buie, Asst Cur
Holdings: Vols 240 Cat Mss
Budget: ($1500)
Notes: Literary first editions mss, periodicals, criticism. A descriptive bibliography by Robert H Miller is available.

NV —UNIVERSITY OF NEVADA, RENO, University Library, Special Collections Dept, Reno, 89557. Robert E Blesse, Head
Holdings: // Vols (263) Cat Other appearances 340 Cat
Notes: Includes individual works by author in all editions including translations; also prefaces, introductions, published correspondence, appearances in anthologies, periodicals, etc. Bibliographical research collection, part of Modern Authors Collection.

NY —HOFSTRA UNIVERSITY, Library, 1000 Fulton Ave, Hempstead, 11550. Charles R Andrews, Dean of Library Services

OK —UNIVERSITY OF TULSA, McFarlin Library, Dept of Rare Books and Special Collections, 600 S College, Tulsa, 74104. David Farmer, Dir; Toby Murray, Archivist; Caroline Swinson, Cur of Manuscripts & Art
Holdings: Vols 888
Notes: All foreign translations of Greene's works. His personal collection.

GREENE, HARRIS

MA —BOSTON UNIVERSITY, Mugar Memorial Library, Special Collections Dept, 771 Commonwealth Ave, Boston, 02215. Howard B Gotlieb, Dir
Holdings: Cat Mss

GREENFELD, JOSH

MA —BOSTON UNIVERSITY, Mugar Memorial Library, Special Collections Dept,

GREENFELD, JOSH (cont.)

771 Commonwealth Ave, Boston, 02215.
Howard B Gotlieb, Dir
Holdings: Cat Mss Correspondence Pix

GREENHOUSES

DE —WILMINGTON GARDEN CENTER LIBRARY, 503 Market Street Mall, Wilmington, 19801. Bonnie J Swan Day, Admin Asst; Karen Bidus, Librn
Holdings: Vols (1500)
Notes: Library open to the public, only circulates to members.

MN —UNIVERSITY OF MINNESOTA, Landscape Arboretum, Andersen Horticultural Library, 3675 Arboretum Drive, Box 39, Chanhassen, 55317. June Rogier, Head
Holdings: Vols (8000)

GREENHOW, ROSE O'NEAL

DC —GEORGETOWN UNIVERSITY, Library, Special Collections Div, 37 & O Sts NW, Washington, 20057. George M Barringer, Special Collections Librn; Nicholas B Sheetz, Mss Librn
Holdings: Mss Cat
Notes: The papers of David Rankin Barbee, journalist with *The Washington Post* and authority on: Abraham Lincoln; the Lincoln assassination; Rose O'Neal Greenhow; and the Civil War. The collection incl, besides extensive correspondence with such historians as Albert J Beveridge, Henry Steele Commager, and Paul M Angle, all of Barbee's own research files and the mss of his works.

GREENLAND

NY —CORNELL UNIVERSITY LIBRARIES, John M Olin Library, Fiske Icelandic Collection, Ithaca, 14853. Louis A Pitschmann, Librn
Holdings: Vols (34,000) Cat Mss Maps Pix Microforms
Budget: ($3000)
Notes: Collection aims at comprehensive coverage of Iceland in all aspects with major emphasis on the literature and language (both old and modern). Such subjects as runology, Scandinavian and Germanic mythology, early Norwegian history and history of the Viking period and of the Norse explorations of Greenland and North America are also well represented. For printed catalogs of the Collection's holdings see Downs 3608, 3609. Records for approximately 40 percent of the collection have been entered into OCLC and RLIN.

NY —AMERICAN MUSEUM OF NATURAL HISTORY, Library Services Dept, Central Park W & 79th St, New York, 10024. Nina J Root, Chairwoman; Mary Genett, Asst Librn for Reference Services

GREENSTEIN, JESSE

CA —CALIFORNIA INSTITUTE OF TECHNOLOGY, Robert A Millikan Memorial Library, Archives, 1201 E California Blvd, Pasadena, 91125. Judith R Goodstein, Archivist
Holdings: Vols (3000) Cat Mss Maps Pix Slides Phonorecords Audiotapes Videotapes 16mm Films Microforms
Notes: Ms sources for the history of astrophysics, cosmology, mathematical physics, experimental physics, radio astronomy, geophysics and biophysics. Collections incl the papers of: George Ellery Hale, Jesse Greenstein, H P Robertson, Richard Feynman, Paul Epstein, Max Delbruck, and Beno Gutenberg. Candid photos of physicists at meetings; etchings and photographs of Einstein; scientific medals; selected pieces of scientific apparatus (including the oil-drop machine constructed by Millikan at Caltech in the early 1920s); the reprint collection of Paul Epstein; over 3000 landmark books in the history of 20th century physics and mathematics. Printed publications include: Daniel Kevles, *Guide to the Microfilm Edition of the George Ellery Hale Papers* (Pasadena, Carnegie Institute of Washington and Caltech), 1968; Judith R Goodstein, *The Robert Andrews Millikan Collection at the California Institute of Technology: Guide to a Microfilm Edition* (Pasadena, Caltech), 1977; Judith R Goodstein and Carolyn Kopp, *The Theodore von Karman Collections at the California Institute of* Technology (Pasadena, Archives), 1981.

NY —AMERICAN INSTITUTE OF PHYSICS, Center for the History of Physics, Niels Bohr Library, 335 E 45 St, New York, 10017. John Aubry, Librn
Notes: The Sources for History of Modern Astrophysics documents the history of 20th-century astrophysics. Incl some 400 hours of oral history interviews with astronomers, such as Bart Bok, S Chandrasekhar, Martin Schwarzschild, and A E Whitford. The project also organized and cataloged the papers of Henry Norris Russell, Frank Schlesinger, Otto Struve, Ejnar Hertzsprung, Harlow Shapley, Charles Young, Robert Atkinson, Seth Chandler, Theodore Dunham, Jr, and G C McVittie.

GREENWICH BOOK PUBLISHERS

NY —STATE UNIVERSITY OF NEW YORK, STONY BROOK, Melville Library, Dept of Special Collections, Stony Brook, 11794. Evert Volkersz, Head
Holdings: Vols (130) Uncat
Notes: An incomplete collection of this vanity/subsidy publisher, 1955-1959.

GREETING CARDS

IN —INDIANA UNIVERSITY, Lilly Library, Seventh St, Bloomington, 47405. William R Cagle, Librn
Holdings: Vols 500 // Cat Mss
Notes: Largely 19th century cards with emphasis on Marcus Ward and Co.

MA —AMERICAN ANTIQUARIAN SOCIETY LIBRARY, 185 Salisbury St, Worcester, 01609. Marcus A McCorison, Dir & Librn
Notes: "Sentiment Cards", from about 1830 to the Civil War. Classified as verses, sentiments, and pictorial divisions.

MO —HALLMARK CARDS, Creative Research Library, 25 & McGee, Kansas City, 64141. Sara E Wallace, Mgr of Library Services
Holdings: Vols (12,000) Cat Mss Pix Slides
Notes: Picture research collection for greeting card artists.

NJ —NEWARK PUBLIC LIBRARY, Art & Music Dept, 5 Washington St, Newark, 07101. William J Dane, Supv
Holdings: Vols (15,000) Cat
Notes: Original prints and fine facsimiles in all major media from 16th century to contemporary times. Study and special exhibition collection of the traditional and current techniques of graphic art with emphasis on late 19th and 20th century artists; ancillary collections of Japanese prints and printed books, trade cards, music covers, greeting cards, bank notes and historic maps.

NY —MARGARET WOODBURY STRONG MUSEUM, 1 Manhattan Square, Rochester, 14607.
Holdings: Vols (20,000) Cat
Notes: The Margaret Woodbury Strong Museum Library contains a collection of approx 20,000 books, periodicals and ephemera of and concerning the 19th and early 20th centuries. A large part of the library's holdings reflect the interests of Margaret Strong and her family: domestic life and literature of the 19th century and world travel, with particular emphasis on the Orient. The library's resources are available to all visitors for research. Book stacks and rare book storage are not open for browsing and do not circulate, but facilities are provided in reading room for study.

RI —BROWN UNIVERSITY, John Hay Library, 20 Prospect St, Providence, 02912. Mary T Russo, Cur of Broadsides
Notes: This is a small collection of representative types of greeting cards, mainly American.

SC —COLLEGE OF CHARLESTON LIBRARY, Special Collections Dept, Charleston, 29401.
Notes: Collection of Christmas and New Year's greeting cards cleverly designed by Robert C Aldredge, who was a high official in the US Weather Bureau in Washington, DC.

GREGG, ANDREW

CT —TRINITY COLLEGE LIBRARY, 300 Summit St, Hartford, 06106. Peter J Knapp, Archivist
Holdings: Uncat // Mss Pix
Notes: Late 18th and 19th century mss, letter, diaries, etc of the Curtis Family of Connecticut and New York, with emphasis on: William Edmond (1755-1838), US Congressman from Conn; Holbrook Curtis (1787-1858); William Edmond Curtis (1823-1880), Chief Justice of Superior Court of New York; Mary Ann Scovill Curtis (1831-1908); and William Edmond Curtis Jr, (1855-1923), US Asst Secy of the Treasury. Incl on basis of relation through marriage are late 18th and 19th century mss, letters and diaries of the Hiester, McLanahan and Muhlenberg Families of Pennsylvania, with emphasis on Joseph Hiester (1752-1832), US Congressman and Governor of Pennsylvania; and Andrew Gregg (1755-1835), US Congressman and Senator from Pennsylvania. 12 linear feet.

GREGG, DAVID L.

MI —UNIVERSITY OF MICHIGAN, Library, Dept of Rare Books & Special Collections, Ann Arbor, 48109. Robert J Starring, Head
Holdings: Cat Mss Pix
Notes: Incl in addition to miscellaneous published items, material pertaining to David L Gregg, US Commissioner of Hawaii and Minister of Finance. Gregg's diaries from 1853 to 1857, official correspondence, and private papers, all transcribed or photographed, and transcripts of Federal archival material relating to Hawaii. A few early Hawaiian periodicals.

GREGOR, ARTHUR

MA —BOSTON UNIVERSITY, Mugar Memorial Library, Special Collections Dept, 771 Commonwealth Ave, Boston, 02215. Howard B Gotlieb, Dir
Holdings: Mss
Notes: Mss, correspondence, etc collected in depth; incl publications by or about.

GREGORY, LADY AUGUSTA

DC —GEORGETOWN UNIVERSITY, Library, Special Collections Div, 37 & O Sts NW, Washington, 20057. George M Barringer, Special Collections Librn; Nicholas B Sheetz, Mss Librn
Holdings: Mss Cat Pix
Notes: A portion of the archives of the English publisher Grant Ricards (1872-1948), containing manuscripts, correspondence, photographs, clippings, and printed ephemera. Incl is extensive correspondence from such artists and authors as Neville Cardus; Frank Harris; Sir Hugh Lane; Lady Augusta Gregory; David Low; T Sturge Moore; and C R W Nevinson.

GA —EMORY UNIVERSITY, Robert W Woodruff Library, Special Collections Dept, Atlanta, 30322. Linda M Matthews, Head Special Collections; Virginia J H Cain, Processing Archivist; Richard H F Lindemann, Reference Archivist
Holdings: Mss Cat
Notes: 10 linear feet mss. Papers of Sir William Henry Gregory, of his wife, Lady Augusta Gregory, and of their son, Robert Gregory. Incl are correspondence with John Masefield, George Russell (A E), and William Butler Yeats, as well as material about the Abbey Theatre and political conditions in Ireland and Ceylon.

GREGORY, LADY AUGUSTA (cont.)

IL —SOUTHERN ILLINOIS UNIVERSITY, CARBONDALE, Delyte W Morris Library, Special Collections Dept, Carbondale, 62901. David V Koch, Cur of Special Collections; Louisa Bowen, Cur of Manuscripts
Holdings: Vols 215 Cat Mss Pix
Notes: Personal papers of Lennox Robinson, with books from his collections 1910-1954, incl play and other fiction mss; correspondence incl. 174 letters from Lady Augusta Gregory and 99 from William Butler Yeats. 12 linear feet. Inventory and name index available in library.

KY —UNIVERSITY OF LOUISVILLE, Ekstrom Library, Rare Books & Special Collections, 2301 S Third St, Louisville, 40208. George T McWhorter, Cur; Delinda Stephens Buie, Asst Cur
Holdings: Vols 3000 Cat
Budget: $1000
Notes: The Richard M Kain Collection. Literary first editions of Joyce, Yeats, A E, Lady Gregory and others; cultural and politcal documents; mss; periodical runs; clippins and related materials. Catalog in progress.

ON —UNIVERSITY OF TORONTO, Thomas Fisher Rare Book Library, 120 Saint George St, Toronto, M5S 1A5, Can. Richard G Landon, Head
Holdings: Vols 5200 Cat
Notes: DeLury Collection named for original donor, Alfred DeLury, Dean of Arts, University of Toronto. Centered on works of W B Yeats and his circle. Especially good holdings of the Yeats family. A E, Lady Gregory, and J M Synge. Incl extensive holdings of many of the minor writers.

GREGORY, ELIZABETH HIATT, 1872-1955

CA —UNIVERSITY OF CALIFORNIA, LOS ANGELES, Research Library, Dept of Special Collections, 405 Hilgard Ave, Los Angeles, 90024. Edward Shreeves, Chairman, Bibliographers Group; David S Zeidberg, Head
Holdings: Cat Mss Maps Pix
Notes: 3 linear feet of correspondence, photographs, and ephemera relating to pioneer men and women aviators, balloons, clippers, and the role of aviation in World Wars I and II, collected by Gregory.

GREGORY, SIR WILLIAM HENRY

GA —EMORY UNIVERSITY, Robert W Woodruff Library, Special Collections Dept, Atlanta, 30322. Linda M Matthews, Head Special Collections; Virginia J H Cain, Processing Archivist; Richard H F Lindemann, Reference Archivist
Holdings: Mss Cat
Notes: 10 linear feet mss. Papers of Sir William Henry Gregory, of his wife, Lady Augusta Gregory, and of their son, Robert Gregory. Incl are correspondence with John Masefield, George Russell (A E), and William Butler Yeats, as well as material about the Abbey Theatre and political conditions in Ireland and Ceylon.

GREGORY FAMILY

GA —EMORY UNIVERSITY, Robert W Woodruff Library, Special Collections Dept, Atlanta, 30322. Linda M Matthews, Head Special Collections; Virginia J H Cain, Processing Archivist; Richard H F Lindemann, Reference Archivist
Holdings: Mss Cat
Notes: 10 linear feet mss. Papers of Sir William Henry Gregory, of his wife, Lady Augusta Gregory, and of their son, Robert Gregory. Incl are correspondence with John Masefield, George Russell (A E), and William Butler Yeats, as well as material about the Abbey Theatre and political conditions in Ireland and Ceylon.

GREGUERIAS

PA —UNIVERSITY OF PITTSBURGH, Hillman Library, Special Collections Dept, Ramon Gomez de la Serna Collection, Pittsburgh, 15260. Charles Aston Jr, Coordinator
Holdings: Vols 129 Uncat Mss Pix
Notes: Ramon Gomez de la Serna's published and unpublished ms and correspondence material, 60,000 pieces, relating to *greguerias* and other works. Incl the auth's subject clipping file. Books are first editions of the author's works, his copies. Partial inventory to the collection exists in the department. 17 ft mss.

GRENADA

DC —HOWARD UNIVERSITY, Moorland-Spingarn Research Center, 500 Howard Place NW, Washington, 20059. Clifford L Muse, Jr, Acting Dir

RI —BROWN UNIVERSITY, John Carter Brown Library, Providence, 02912. Norman Fiering, Librn; Everett C Wilkie Jr, Bibliographer; Susan Danforth, Cur Maps & Prints
Notes: Works documenting slavery and slave trade in European possessions in the New World until 1833. Particular strengths are British and French abolition movements in the early nineteenth century. (Little material on slavery in what became the United States).

GRENADA—HISTORY

DC —HOWARD UNIVERSITY, Moorland-Spingarn Research Center, 500 Howard Place NW, Washington, 20059. Clifford L Muse, Jr, Acting Dir

GRENADA—POLITICS AND GOVERNMENT

DC —HOWARD UNIVERSITY, Moorland-Spingarn Research Center, 500 Howard Place NW, Washington, 20059. Clifford L Muse, Jr, Acting Dir

GRENFELL, ELTON WATTERS, 1903-

CA —HOOVER INSTITUTION ON WAR, REVOLUTION & PEACE, Stanford University, Stanford, 94305. Milorad M Drachkovitch, Archivist
Holdings: Mss Pix
Notes: Papers of Elton W Grenfell, Vice Admiral, US Navy; commander, Submarine Force, Pacific Fleet, 1956-59; and commander, Submarine Force, Atlantic Fleet, 1960-64; incl correspondence, orders, drafts of speeches and photographs, 1926-69, relating to US submarine operations during World War II and in the postwar period. 11 1/2 ms boxes, 5 binders.

GRENFELL, SIR WILFRED THOMASON, 1865-1940

CT —YALE UNIVERSITY, Box 1603A, Yale Station, New Haven, 06520.
Notes: Incl manuscripts and 44 boxes of material by or about Sir Wilfred Thomason Grenfell.

GRENVILLE FAMILY PAPERS

CA —HUNTINGTON LIBRARY, Art Gallery & Botanical Gardens, 1151 Oxford Rd, San Marino, 91108. Robert L Middlekauff, Dir; Daniel H Woodward, Librn
Holdings: Mss Maps Pix Slides Microforms
Notes: Approx 350,000 rare books, 250,000 reference books, manuscript collection of nearly 2,500,000 pieces and between 200, 000 and 300,000 prints, rare photographs and other related materials. The fullest available survey is now *Guide to Literary Manuscripts in the Huntington Library,* a 539-page handlist published by the Library in 1979. Also *Guide to British Historical Manuscripts in the Huntington Library* (1982).

GREPE, JOHN H.

CA —UNIVERSITY OF CALIFORNIA, LOS ANGELES, Research Library, Dept of Special Collections, 405 Hilgard Ave, Los Angeles, 90024. Edward Shreeves, Chairman, Bibliographers Group; David S Zeidberg, Head
Notes: 3 linear feet of legal documents and papers relating to law suits and land ownership in Tulancingo, Puebla, Mexico, 1540-1875, collected by Grepe.

GREULACH, VICTOR A.

†NC —UNIVERSITY OF NORTH CAROLINA, CHAPEL HILL, Department of Botany Library, 301 Coker Hall 010-A, Chapel Hill, 27514. William R Burk, Botany Librn
Notes: The mycology collection incl some 6000 pamphlets. It contains papers of the following scientists: William C Coker, John N Couch, Lindsay F Olive, mycologists; also, Victor A Greulach, plant pathologist. The mycology catalog is in preparation (1983), and will provide author, title, and subject access.

GREY, ZANE

OH —OHIO HISTORICAL SOCIETY, Archives Library Division, 1982 Velma Ave, Columbus, 43211. Dennis East, Division Chief
Holdings: Vols 2000// Cat Mss Pix
Notes: Collection is comprised of books by Grey, magazines in which his writings appeared, mss & typescripts, and 700 items from his personal library, incl scarce items on hunting, big-game fishing, and travel. Museum objects are at the Zane Grey Musuem, Zanesville, Ohio, operated by the Ohio Historical Society.

OH —JOHN MCINTIRE PUBLIC LIBRARY, 220 N Fifth St, Zanesville, 43701. Peg Harmon, Librn
Holdings: Vols 302 Cat

GREYHOUND RACING

KS —GREYHOUND HALL OF FAME, 407 South Buckeye, Abilene, 67410. Edward Scheele, Dir
Holdings: Vols Cat Pix
Notes: Dog racing as a sport. Incl programs, magazines, memorabilia.

GREY FRIARS see Franciscans

GRIEF

MA —NATIONAL CENTER FOR DEATH EDUCATION, New England Resource Center for Thanatology & Funeral Service, 656 Beacon St, Boston, 02215. Gail Gruner, Librn

GRIER, GEORGE M.

†NY —UNIVERSITY OF ROCHESTER, Rush Rhees Library, Rochester, 14627.

GRIEVE, CHRISTOPHER MURRAY see Macdiarmid, Hugh (Christopher Murray Grieve), 1892-1978

GRIFFES, CHARLES TOMLINSON

NY —ELMIRA COLLEGE, Gannett-Tripp Learning Center, Elmira, 14901. James D Gray, Dir
Holdings: Cat Mss Pix Phonorecords
Notes: Papers, recordings, music scores, of Charles Tomlinson Griffes, 1884-1920.

NY —NEW YORK PUBLIC LIBRARY, Music Div, 111 Amsterdam Ave, New York, 10023. Frank C Campbell, Chief
Holdings: Cat Mss Pix
Notes: Composer's autographs.

GRIFFIN, MARTIN I. J.

PA —SAINT JOSEPH'S UNIVERSITY, Drexel Library, 5600 City Ave, Philadelphia, 19131. Josephine Savaro, Dir of Library
Notes: The collection of Martin I J Griffin (1842-1911), leading figure in Catholic historiography, and founder of the American

GRIFFIN, MARTIN I. J. (cont.)

Catholic Historical Society of Philadelphia. Correspondence, scrapbooks, and pamphlets.

GRIFFIN, R. ALLEN, 1893-

CA —HOOVER INSTITUTION ON WAR, REVOLUTION & PEACE, Stanford University, Stanford, 94305. Milorad M Drachkovitch, Archivist
Holdings: Mss Pix
Notes: Papers of R Allen Griffin, Deputy Chief of ECA China Aid Mission, 1948-49, and Chief of the 1950 Economic Mission to Southeast Asia, incl correspondence, reports, memoranda, speeches and writings, photographs, and printed matter, 1945-71, relating to American technical and economic assistance missions to China and Southeast Asia. 14 ms boxes.

GRIFFITH, D. W.

NY —MUSEUM OF MODERN ART, Dept of Film, 11 W 53 St, New York, 10019. Eileen Bowser, Cur
Holdings: Mss Pix
Notes: Papers, correspondence, scrapbooks, pictures, etc. Partially cataloged.

GRIFFITH FAMILY

NY —CORNELL UNIVERSITY LIBRARIES, Collection of Regional History, Dept of Manuscripts and Univ Archives, Ithaca, 14853.
Notes: Incl 16 pieces; records, 1777-1934; family Bible and other genealogical data, incl names of inter-related families.

GRIGORIEV, SERGEI

NY —NEW YORK PUBLIC LIBRARY, Performing Arts Research Center, Dance Collection, 111 Amsterdam Ave, New York, 10023. Genevieve Oswald, Cur
Notes: Holograph ms notebooks of Sergei Grigoriev, regisseur of the Diaghilev Ballets Russes and of the De Basil Ballet Russe de Monte Carlo.

GRIMBALL, JOHN BERKELEY

SC —COLLEGE OF CHARLESTON LIBRARY, Special Collections Dept, Charleston, 29401.
Notes: Papers, incl diary covering the years 1832-1841, 1843-1884.

GRIMKE, SARAH M.

IL —UNIVERSITY OF ILLINOIS, URBANA/CHAMPAIGN, Library, Illinois Historical Survey Library, 1408 W Gregory Dr, 1A Library, Urbana, 61801.
Holdings: Vols 50 Cat Mss Maps Pix Microforms
Notes: Communitarianism in America. The ms material, contained in 30 separate collections (10 cubic feet), concentrates on the period 1840-70. It incl correspondence, records, minutes, ledgers and diaries. Communal societies such as Bishop Hill, Brook Farm, New Harmony, the North American Phalanx and the Sodus Bay Phalanx are represented. Among the correspondents are Albert Brisbane, Parke Godwin, Sarah Grimke, Richard Owen, Robert Owen, Robert Dale Owen, and George Ripley. Numerous pictures. Guide to the collections published in 1976.

PA —FRIENDS HISTORICAL LIBRARY OF SWARTHMORE COLLEGE, Swarthmore, 19081. J William Frost, Dir
Holdings: Vols (31,340) Cat Mss Pix
Notes: Works from 1654 to the present, with emphasis on the Quaker leaders in women's rights, Susan B Anthony, Sarah M Grimke, Lucretia Mott, and some non-Quakers.

GRIMM, DAVID D.

CA —HOOVER INSTITUTION ON WAR, REVOLUTION & PEACE, Stanford University, Stanford, 94305. Milorad M Drachkovitch, Archivist
Notes: Papers of David D Grimm, Professor of Law and Rector of Petersburg University, 1899-1910, Assistant Minister of Education in the Russian Provisional Government, 1917, and an amigre political activist and journalist, incl correspondence, memoranda, press reports, printed and other material, 1919-1934, relating to his service to the Russian emigre community in Finland and other parts of Europe and to the Russian Civil War. 4 ms boxes.

GRIMM FAMILY

CA —CLAREMONT COLLEGES, Honnold Library, Ninth & Dartmouth, Claremont, 91711. Tania Rizzo, Special Collections Dept Head
Holdings: Cat Mss
Notes: 30 ALsS and mss by Wilhelm, Jacob, and Wilibald Grimm to their publisher, Salomon Hirzel, written between 1814 and 1859. Restricted use.

GRINNELL, JOSEPH

CA —UNIVERSITY OF CALIFORNIA, BERKELEY, Bancroft Library, Manuscripts Division, Berkeley, 94720. James D Hart, Dir
Holdings: Cat Mss Maps Pix Microforms
Notes: Papers, correspondence, etc.

GRISWOLD, A. WHITNEY

CT —YALE UNIVERSITY, Box 1603A, Yale Station, New Haven, 06520.
Notes: Private papers, correspondence, mss, lecture notes and memorabilia.

GRISWOLD, ERWIN NATHANIEL, 1904-

MA —HARVARD UNIVERSITY LIBRARY, Law School Library, Langdell Hall, Cambridge, 02138. Erika S Chadbourn, Cur of Mss
Holdings: Cat Mss
Notes: Professional papers. Typed inventory in repository. Inclusive dates: 1934-present. Additions expected.

GROCERS AND GROCERY TRADE—HISTORY

AZ —NORTHERN ARIZONA UNIVERSITY, Special Collection Library, CU Box 6022, Flagstaff, 86011. Peter M Whiteley, Coordr/Archivist; William Mullane, Librn
Notes: Account book with most of the entries for meat or ice, 1892.

TX —UNIVERSITY OF TEXAS LIBRARIES, General Libraries, PO Box P, Austin, 78713. Carolyn Bucknell, Asst Dir for Collection Development
Notes: Papers of retail grocers, Heidenheimer Brothers, of Galveston, being travelling salesmen's correspondence and other papers, bound by month and year, measuring 35 linear feet.

GROLIER, JEAN

NY —GROLIER CLUB OF NEW YORK LIBRARY, 47 E 60 St, New York, 10022. Robert Nikirk, Librn
Notes: Subject strength.

GROLIG, MORIZ, 1873-

CA —UNIVERSITY OF CALIFORNIA, LOS ANGELES, Research Library, Dept of Special Collections, 405 Hilgard Ave, Los Angeles, 90024. Edward Shreeves, Chairman, Bibliographers Group; David S Zeidberg, Head
Notes: Collection of *Dialogues of the Dead* and 3-volume holograph bibliography of material, 1495-1792.

GROPIUS, WALTER

MA —HARVARD UNIVERSITY LIBRARY, Widener Library, Cambridge, 02138.
Holdings: Cat Mss Pix Microforms

GROS VENTRES INDIANS see Atsina Indians

GROSS, MARTIN L.

MA —BOSTON UNIVERSITY, Mugar Memorial Library, Special Collections Dept, 771 Commonwealth Ave, Boston, 02215. Howard B Gotlieb, Dir
Holdings: Cat Mss
Notes: Mss, correspondence, etc collected in depth; incl publications by or about.

GROSSETESTE, ROBERT

†IL —UNIVERSITY OF CHICAGO LIBRARIES, Joseph Regenstein Library, Dept of Special Collections, 1100 E 57th St, Chicago, 60637.
Notes: A collection of photostats and microfilms of 383 medieval mss gathered by Prof S Harrison Thomson in the course of his research on Robert Grosseteste and John Wyclyf. Inventory index of the collection available.

GROSSMAN, ALFRED

MA —BOSTON UNIVERSITY, Mugar Memorial Library, Special Collections Dept, 771 Commonwealth Ave, Boston, 02215. Howard B Gotlieb, Dir
Holdings: Mss

GROSSMAN, KURT RICHARD, 1897-1972

CA —HOOVER INSTITUTION ON WAR, REVOLUTION & PEACE, Stanford University, Stanford, 94305. Milorad M Drachkovitch, Archivist
Notes: Papers of Kurt R Grossman, 1926-73, incl mss of writings, correspondence, clippings, and serial issues, relating to Jewish refugees from Nazi Germnay, postwar German and Austrian restitution payments to Jewish war victims, German-Israeli relations, the condition of Jews throughout the world, and civil liberties in the US and Germany. 53 ms boxes, 8 scrapbooks.

GROSVENOR, GILBERT H.

DC —LIBRARY OF CONGRESS, Manuscript Division, Washington, 20540. John C Broderick, Chief
Holdings: 140,000 Items
Notes: The papers of Alexander Graham Bell and his family. Incl Bell's diaries, correspondence, printed matter, financial and legal records, and several hundred vols of laboratory notebooks which record his daily work from 1865 to 1922. Also, materials of Alexander Melville Bell, Mabel Hubbard Bell, and Gilbert H Grosvenor.

GROT, ANTON

CA —UNIVERSITY OF CALIFORNIA, LOS ANGELES, Research Library, Dept of Special Collections, 405 Hilgard Ave, Los Angeles, 90024. Edward Shreeves, Chairman, Bibliographers Group; David S Zeidberg, Head
Notes: 7 linear feet of original drawings for motion picture set designs.

GROTIUS, HUGO

RI —BROWN UNIVERSITY, John Hay Library, 20 Prospect St, Providence, 02912. Mark N Brown, Cur Mss
Holdings: Vols 68 Cat
Notes: Grotius Collection contains 68 of the 79 recorded complete editions of *De Jure Belli ac Pacis* printed between 1625 and 1939. It lacks 6 of the 49 Latin editions and one each of the English, Dutch, German and Spanish editions.

WI —UNIVERSITY OF WISCONSIN, MADISON, Memorial Library, Rare Books Collection, 728 State St, Madison, 53706. Gretchen Lagana, Cur
Holdings: Vols (58) Cat
Notes: Grotius Collection. Some 58 volumes

GROTIUS, HUGO (cont.)

by, about, or associated with the Dutch jurist and humanist Hugo Grotius. A number of the volumes comprise classical writings edited by Grotius. Certain of the volumes issued by Jansson, Elzevier, and Estienne are, in addition, valuable as specimens illustrating the history of printing. Restricted use: Rare Book Department.

GROUEFF, STEPHANE

MA —BOSTON UNIVERSITY, Mugar Memorial Library, Special Collections Dept, 771 Commonwealth Ave, Boston, 02215. Howard B Gotlieb, Dir
Holdings: Cat Mss Pix
Notes: Mss, correspondence, etc collected in depth; incl publications by or about.

GROUND WATER see Water, Underground

GROUP FOR THE ADVANCEMENT OF PSYCHIATRY

KS —MENNINGER FOUNDATION, Archives, 5600 W Sixth St, Box 829, Topeka, 66601. Alice Brand, Librn; Mark West, Archivist
Notes: 25 boxes, 1946-66. The collection incl correspondence, committee reports, proceedings from national meetings, and miscellaneous materials. Most of the papers date from the presidencies of William Menninger and Henry Brosin.

GROUP HEALTH see Medical Care, Prepaid

GROUP MEDICAL PRACTICE

CO —MEDICAL GROUP MANAGEMENT ASSOCIATION, Information Service, 1355 S Colorado Blvd, Suite 900, Denver, 80222. Barbara V Hamilton, Dir; Linda S Elinoff, Asst Dir
Holdings: Vols (3000) Cat
Budget: ($7825)
Notes: Administration of medical group practice and health maintenance organization. Also, the professional papers of the Fellows of the American College of Medical Group Administrators.

GROUP MEDICAL SERVICE see Medical Care, Prepaid

GROVE, FREDERICK PHILIP, 1879-1948

MB —UNIVERSITY OF MANITOBA, Elizabeth Dafoe Library, Archives and Special Collections Dept, Winnipeg, R3T 2N2, Can. Richard E Bennett, Dept Head; Corrado A Santoro, Reference Archivist
Holdings: // Cat Mss
Notes: Incl mss of 8 published and 12 unpublished works and approx 1000 letters between Grove and his publishers, his friends, also personal letters to his wife. In addition photographs of Grove at various times in his life.
See also entry under Stobie, Margaret R

GROVES, GEN. LESLIE RICHARD, 1856-1939

IL —UNIVERSITY OF CHICAGO LIBRARY, Dept of Special Collections, 1100 E 57 St, Chicago, 60637.
Holdings: Mss
Notes: Argonne National Laboratory deposit of 46 linear ft of materials dealing with the construction of Argonne and the Manhattan Project at the University of Chicago.

MA —MASSACHUSETTS INSTITUTE OF TECHNOLOGY, Institute Archives, Special Collections, Cambridge, 02139.
Notes: Correspondence, newsletters, fact-sheets, newspaper and magazine articles, books and reports of the Citizens' League Against the Sonic Boom, established in 1967 by William Shurcliff to oppose the sonic boom, stop commercial supersonic transport production, and influence public opinion and policy decisions on the SST. Major correspondents incl Bo Lundberg, Richard Wiggs, several US congressmen, and CLASB members.

NY —CORNELL UNIVERSITY LIBRARIES, Collection of Regional History, Dept of Manuscripts and Univ Archives, Ithaca, 14853.
Notes: Chaplain. Letters (microfilm, 35mm, 1 neg, 1 pos), ca 1895-1901; 2 reels.

GROWERS see Nurseries (Horticulture)

GROWTH

IL —UNIVERSITY OF ILLINOIS, URBANA/CHAMPAIGN, Library, Applied Life Studies Library, 1408 W Gregory Dr, Urbana, 61801.
Holdings: Vols (38,000) Cat Microforms
See also entry under Physical Education and Training.

GRUNDTVIG, N. F. S.

IL —NORTHWESTERN UNIVERSITY, Library, Special Collections Dept, 1937 Sheridan Rd, Evanston, 60201. R Russell Maylone, Cur
Holdings: Vols 500 Cat //
Notes: First editions of Grundtvig and works about him.

GRUNEBAUM, GUSTAVE EDMUND VON, 1909-1972

CA —UNIVERSITY OF CALIFORNIA, LOS ANGELES, Research Library, Dept of Special Collections, 405 Hilgard Ave, Los Angeles, 90024. Edward Shreeves, Chairman, Bibliographers Group; David S Zeidberg, Head
Notes: 8.5 linear feet of mss, correspondence, and papers of the founder of UCLA's Near Eastern Center.

GRYPHONS see Heraldry

GUADALUPE HIDALGO, TREATY OF, 1848

CA —CALIFORNIA STATE UNIVERSITY, FULLERTON, Library, Box 4150, Fullerton, 92634. Alfredo H Zuniga, Coord
Notes: Some materials on the subject; not maintained as a separate collection.

GUADELOUPE

CT —YALE UNIVERSITY, Sterling Memorial Library, Latin American Collections, New Haven, 06520. Lee H Williams Jr, Cur
Holdings: Vols (300,000) Cat Maps Pix Slides Phonorecords 16mm Films Filmstrips
See also entry under Latin America

GUAM

DC —GEORGETOWN UNIVERSITY, Library, Special Collections Div, 37 & O Sts NW, Washington, 20057. George M Barringer, Special Collections Librn; Nicholas B Sheetz, Mss Librn
Holdings: Cat
Notes: Papers of Chauncey Brewster Chapman, Jr (1919-1980), attorney, from his early legal career in private practice and his years in the Department of Interior where he served as solicitor for territories from 1967-1979. The bulk of the papers concerns judicial and legal matters in regard to territories outside the United States, as well as internal departmental affairs. Of particular interest is material concerning Samoa from 1969-1980.

DC —LIBRARY OF CONGRESS, Manuscript Division, Washington, 20540. John C Broderick, Chief
Holdings: Cat Mss
Notes: Microfilm of records of the Spanish Colonial Government in the Mariana Islands, 1678-1899. Originals (5.5 linear ft) of these varied materials are in the Manuscript Divison. See *LC Information* Bulletin, 18 July 1968.

PI —NIEVES M FLORES MEMORIAL LIBRARY, PO Box 652, Agana, Guam, 96910. Magdalena S Taitano, Territorial Librn
Holdings: Vols 3975 Cat Slides Microforms
Budget: $1000
Notes: Guam Micronesian collection. Incl 500 slides, 15,000 images and 249 microforms. Photocopying available.

GUARDIAN BOSTON (NEWSPAPER)

MA —BOSTON UNIVERSITY, Mugar Memorial Library, Special Collections Dept, 771 Commonwealth Ave, Boston, 02215. Howard B Gotlieb, Dir
Holdings: // Cat Mss Pix

GUATEMALA

KS —UNIVERSITY OF KANSAS, Kenneth Spencer Research Library, Special Collections Dept, Lawrence, 66045. Alexandra Mason, Librn
Holdings: Vols 4400 Uncat Mss
Notes: William Griffith Collection on Central America, especially Guatemalan imprints, late 18th to mid-20th century, incl many newpapers and broadsides. Noncirculating.

KS —UNIVERSITY OF KANSAS, Watson Library, Lawrence, 66045. George Jerkovich, Cur Slavic Collections
Notes: Over 6000 valuable Central American titles, of which fewer than half in a random sample are presently located in OCLC, and over half not incl in published holdings of the University of Texas or Tulane University. A special grant is supporting cataloging of the collection.

MA —PAN AMERICAN SOCIETY OF NEW ENGLAND, Shattuck Library, 152 North Street, Boston, 02109. Vivian Ingrao, Dir
Holdings: Vols (10,000) Cat Slides Phonorecords
Notes: Books on art, literature, history, and economy of Pan American countries.

GUATEMALA—CIVILIZATION AND CULTURE

MA —HARVARD UNIVERSITY LIBRARY, Botanical Museum Library, Cambridge, 02138.
Holdings: Vols (2400) Mss Pix
Notes: The Tina and Gordon Wisson Ethnomycological Collection, one of the most important modern collections, acquired as an adjunct to the Museum's Economic Botany Library of Oakes Ames. From 15th to 20th century, it deals with hallucinogenic mushrooms in art, religion, and folklore; chemistry, pharmacology, linguistics, archaeological artifacts of Mexico, Guatemala, India, Japan, China, etc. Personal papers, etc.

GUATEMALA—HISTORY

CT —YALE UNIVERSITY, Sterling Memorial Library, Latin American Collections, New Haven, 06520. Lee H Williams Jr, Cur
Holdings: Vols (300,000) Cat Maps Pix Slides Phonorecords 16mm Films Filmstrips
See also entry under Latin America

LA —TULANE UNIVERSITY, Howard-Tilton Memorial Library, Latin American Library, New Orleans, 70118. Thomas Niehaus, Dir
Holdings: Vols (150,000) Cat Mss Maps Pix Microforms VF
Budget: ($67,000)
Notes: *Catalog of the Latin American* Library (Boston: G K Hall, 1970, suppl. 1973,1975,1978); Downs 5338-41; suppl (1961), 2727, 2737. The Latin American Library is a general collection, but specializes in Central American, Mexican, and Brazilian materials. The disciplines which are most strongly represented are history, anthropology, and archaeology. The Viceregal Ecclesiastical Mexican Collection contains manuscripts from the colonial

GUATEMALA—HISTORY (cont.)

period. The France V Scholes Collection contains a large number of photoprints and microfilm of colonial documents from the archives of Spain and Mexico. The Merle Greene Robertson Rubbings Collection contains nearly five hundred rubbings of relief sculpture from Mayan archaeological sites in Mexico and Guatemala. The Photographic Collection contains photos of archaeological sites inMeso-America, of pre-Columbian Peruvian architecture, and a general group of historic photos from Latin America.

PA —UNIVERSITY OF PITTSBURGH, Hillman Library, Pittsburgh, 15260. Glenora E Rossell, Head
Holdings: Vols (172,000) Cat Microforms
Notes: The Latin American collection, although it contains good coverage of all countries and subjects related to those countries, has been developed giving special emphasis to materials related to Cuba, Ecuador, Guatemala, Mexico, Bolivia, and Peru. The collection is outstanding for research on Bolivia and contemporary Cuba. It incl 1700 periodical titles, 600 of which are currently being received. Especially strong on revolutionary and radical movements, and social change. The collection is very strong in pre-Columbian archaeology and Indian cultures from the historical and anthropological point of view. Emphasis on contemporary history, politics and socio-economical problems.

TX —UNIVERSITY OF TEXAS LIBRARIES, Nettie Lee Benson Latin American Collection, Sid Richardson Hall 1.109, Austin, 78712. Laura Gutierrez-Witt, Head Librn
Holdings: Vols (450,000) Cat Mss Maps Pix Videotapes Microforms
Notes: Private library of Arturo Taracena Flores, providing extensive coverage of all Central American countries. Incl nearly all Guatemala imprints, 1800-1964; also incl broadsides.
See also entry under Latin America.

GUAYULE

CA —UNIVERSITY OF CALIFORNIA, RIVERSIDE, University Library, Bio-Agricultural Library, Batchelor Hall, Riverside, 92521. Barbara Montanary, Head
Holdings: Vols (130,000) Cat Mss Maps Pix Microforms
Notes: The Bio-Agricultural Library (formerly the Library of Citrus Experiment Station of the University of California) is well known for its complete collections in the fields of the agriculture sciences. It is especially known for its emphasis on entomology, incl bio-control; botany, citriculture, plant sciences, nematology and plant pathology; arid and semi-arid lands research and subtropical agriculture. Specific areas of interest are avocados, dates, desert flora, jojoba, guayule and carob.

MD —US DEPT OF AGRICULTURE, National Agricultural Library, 10301 Baltimore Blvd, Beltsville, 20705. Joseph H Howard, Director
Holdings: Vols (2,000,000) Mss Maps Pix Slides Microforms
Notes: Crop Fiber Collection. A special collection of approximately 50,000 reference cards, thousands of reprints, manuscript materials, photographs, and specimens relating to more than 300 genera of plants. Contains the most complete record of information in the country, if not the world, on fiber crops of the world. The collection is particularly vital to research interests and projects involving the use of natural fibers (i. e. rubber, guayule).

GUDE, GILBERT

DC —GEORGE WASHINGTON UNIVERSITY, Gelman Library, 2130 H St NW, Washington, 20052.
Holdings: / / Cat Mss
Notes: The Gilbert Gude Congressional papers cover his terms in the House of Representatives from the 90th to the 94th Congresses (1967-76). During his tenure in office as representative from the 8th District, Maryland, Mr Gude served on the Government Operations Committee and its Conservation, Energy, and Natural Resources Subcommittee; the House Environmental Study; the FDR Memorial Commission; the Select Committee on Aging; and the House District of Columbia Committee. Papers reflect the working files of a congressional office and include bills, voting records, correspondence, press materials, special projects, record statements, speeches, testimony, subject files, and case studies (restricted). Cataloged as a collection with unpublished inventory for access.

GUENTHER, CHARLES

MO —WASHINGTON UNIVERSITY, Libraries, Special Collections Dept, Campus Box 1061, St Louis, 63130.
Notes: A small but significant collection.

GUERILLA WARFARE

NC —US ARMY SPECIAL WARFARE CENTER, Marquat Library, Fort Bragg, 28307. Frank Lundgren, Librn
Holdings: Vols (45,000) Cat Microforms
Notes: Guerilla warfare, unconventional warfare, strategy, etc. International aspect in political science. 425 periodicals, serial subject collections; newspapers, HRAF microfiche subscription.

VA —MACARTHUR MEMORIAL, Library & Archives, MacArthur Sq, Norfolk, 23510. Ellen E Folkama, Asst Archivist
Holdings: Vols (4000) Cat Maps Pix Slides Phonorecords Audiotapes 16mm Films Microforms
Notes: Everything relating to the life and related activities of MacArthur. The Archives of the collection consist of 600 shelf-feet of documents from Gen MacArthur's official headquarters files over the period 1941-1951. These papers pertain to all matters with which his various commands were involved: military, naval and air matters; international relations; political science; Japanese occupation, peace treaty and Constitution, etc. Each Record Group is indexed. The indexes are retained here since they are being expanded. They are available for researchers.

GUERRERO, MANUEL

TX —NORTH TEXAS STATE UNIVERSITY, Archives, NT Station Box 5188, Denton, 76203. Robert LaForte, University Archivist
Notes: Part of Oral History Collection. Intervew with governor of Guam (1963-72).

GUERRERO, VICENTE

IN —INDIANA UNIVERSITY, Lilly Library, Seventh St, Bloomington, 47405. William R Cagle, Librn
Holdings: Vols (10,000) / / Cat Mss
Notes: Historical pronouncements and documents by the leaders of the movement of Mexican independence. Partially cataloged.
See also entry under Mexico - History.

GUESTS see Etiquette

GUEVARA, ERNESTO (CHE), 1928-1967

CA —HOOVER INSTITUTION ON WAR, REVOLUTION & PEACE, Stanford University, Stanford, 94305. Milorad M Drachkovitch, Archivist
Holdings: Vols (1600) Mss Pix Microfilm
Notes: About 1600 titles on contemporary Cuba. Intensive collecting of political, social and economic works covering the Castro period, especially writings and speeches of Castro and Guevara. Some 30 periodical and newspaper titles currently received from the island. General description of the Latin American Collection and complete listing of the serial and newspaper holdings available in: Joseph W Bingaman, *Latin America: a Survey of Holdings at the Hoover Institution on War, Revolution and Peace*. Stanford, California: Hoover Institution, Stanford University, 1972. 96 pp.

GUGGENHEIM, HARRY F.

DC —LIBRARY OF CONGRESS, Manuscript Division, Washington, 20540. John C Broderick, Chief
Notes: Papers; additions, 1977- .

GUGGENHEIMER, RICHARD

NC —UNIVERSITY OF NORTH CAROLINA, GREENSBORO, Walter Clinton Jackson Library, Special Collections Dept, 1000 Spring Garden St, Greensboro, 27412. Emilie W Mills, Librn
Holdings: Cat Mss
Notes: Letters by Etta Cone to her cousin Richard Guggenheimer, written from Baltimore and Europe, 1927-1935, and two letters by Richard to Etta, one of which is dated 24 August 1949 and relays the news of Nina Stein's death. Etta never received the letter, dying herself just one week later. There are four letters to Richard from other members of the Cone family written from Baltimore, North Carolina, and Europe. Etta's letters to Richard are concerned chiefly with his progress as a painter.

GUGGIASBERG, HENS R.

MO —CENTER FOR REFORMATION RESEARCH, 6477 San Bonita Ave, Saint Louis, 63105. William S Meltby, Dir
Notes: Papers.

GUIANA, FRENCH see French Guiana

GUIDANCE, STUDENT see Vocational Guidance

GUIDANCE, VOCATIONAL see Vocational Guidance

GUIDANCE SYSTEMS (FLIGHT)

CA —LOGICON INC, Strategic & Information Systems Division, Information Center, 255 W Fifth St, Box 471, San Pedro, 90731. Constance B Davenport, Supervisor
Holdings: Vols (3000) Cat Mss Microforms
Notes: Incl about 3000 books, 250 periocial titles, 5000 technical reports, 10,000 microfiche, 750 standards and specifications. Catalog is computerized. Interactive search capability with Dialog, Orbit, DMS on-line, NASA Recon. Material on computer programming, systems analysis, military systems and operations research.

GUIDEBOOKS, GEOLOGICAL see Geology—Guidebooks

GUIDED MISSILES

HI —PACIFIC SUBMARINE MUSEUM, Library, Naval Submarine Base, Pearl Harbor, 96860. Ray W de Yarmin, Cur
Holdings: Vols (1500) Cat Mss Maps Pix Slides Phonorecords 16mm Films
Budget: ($600)
Notes: Incl 3000 pictures. Extensive missile and torpedo collection; submarine models; salvage/deep-sea diver exhibit; Arctic exploration by submarines Worl War II submarine components. Research program for students, authors, lecturers, etc.

WA —BOEING COMPANY, Boeing Technical Libraries, PO Box 3707, Seattle, 98124. Corrine Campbell, Mgr Technical Library
Holdings: Vols (75,000) Cat Microforms
Notes: Books are distributed between 3 libraries, Kent, Renton, and Bellevue. Also contains many periodicals and Boeing Documents Library restricted to Boeing Personnel.

GUIDE-POSTS see Signs and Signboards

GUILD OF CATHOLIC LAWYERS

NY —AMERICAN IRISH HISTORICAL SOCIETY, Library, 991 Fifth Ave, New

GUILD OF CATHOLIC LAWYERS (cont.)

York, 10028. Lisa M Hottin, Cur; William D Griffin, Librn
Holdings: Vols (20,000) Cat Maps Pix Slides
Notes: Archives and Manuscripts: The documents and papers of Friends of Irish Freedom, The Land League, the Society of the Friendly Sons of St Patrick, the Catholic Club, and the Guild of Catholic Lawyers. The papers of New York State Supreme Court Justice Daniel F Cohalan. This is the largest and most complete collection of over 20,000 American Irish and Irish history, biography and literature in the United States. Incl American-Irish Newspaper collections dating from 1811, the most comprehensive in the US; 1000 rare books and special editions. Special collections incl regular exhibits of Irish or American Irish interest incl mss, letters, books, photographs and memorabilia. Permanent collection of representative works of Irish painters.

GUILFORD, J. P.

NY —STATE UNIVERSITY OF NEW YORK, COLLEGE AT BUFFALO, E H Butler Library, 1300 Elmwood Ave, Buffalo, 14222. Jerome Earley, Librn
Holdings: Microforms
Notes: The work of J P Guilford, on microfilm, relating to his research on the Structure of the Intellect (SOI) model. 200 reels of microfilm contain the tests, answer sheets, and supporting data for his SOI theory. Corresponds to the Psychological Laboratory Reports at UCLA.

GUILIAK LANGUAGE see Gilyak Language

GUINEA

DC —HOWARD UNIVERSITY, Moorland-Spingarn Research Center, 500 Howard Place NW, Washington, 20059. Clifford L Muse, Jr, Acting Dir

WI —UNIVERSITY OF WISCONSIN, MADISON, Memorial Library, 728 State St, Madison, 53706. David Henige, Librn
Holdings: Cat Microforms
Notes: Collection consists of 90 microfilm reels of extant records of the Royal African Company (T7O series in the Public Record Office, London) together with several smaller collections of materials relating to the English presence on the Gold Coast in the 17th and 18th centuries. It is the most complete collection of its kind in the US. Various parts are described in David Henige, "Some Materials on the Early Guinea Coast in the United Kingdom," *African Research and Documentation,* no 11 (1976), pp 25-28. Also incl economics and social documents relating to the Belgian Congo particularly Katanga Province.

GUINEA-BISSAU

DC —HOWARD UNIVERSITY, Moorland-Spingarn Research Center, 500 Howard Place NW, Washington, 20059. Clifford L Muse, Jr, Acting Dir

GUINEY, LOUISE IMOGEN, 1861-1920

MA —COLLEGE OF THE HOLY CROSS, Dinand Library, College St, Worcester, 01610. James M Mahoney, Cur of Special Collection
Holdings: Cat Mss Pix
Notes: Collection contains mss; letters to and from L I Guiney; notebooks; scrapbooks; photos; association items (books and letters); about 3000 items. Restricted use; noncirculating.

GUION FAMILY

LA —NICHOLLS STATE UNIVERSITY, Ellender Memorial Library, Thibodaux, 70310. Randall A Detro, Dir; Philip D Uzee, Archivist
Holdings: Uncat Mss Maps Pix Microforms
Notes: Louisiana and local history; family papers of the period, etc.

GUITAR MUSIC

CA —UNIVERSITY OF CALIFORNIA, LOS ANGELES, Music Library, Schonberg Hall, Los Angeles, 90024. Stephen M Fry, Music Librn
Notes: Broad collection of guitar music anthologies and methods, studies, and exercises. Ca 4000 scores.

GUITEAU, CHARLES

IL —CHICAGO HISTORICAL SOCIETY, Library, Clark St at North Ave, Chicago, 60614. Archie Motley, Manuscript Librn
Notes: Papers of Charles J Guiteau (Presidents Garfield's assassin).

GUIZOT, FRANCOIS PIERRE GUILLAUME

MI —UNIVERSITY OF MICHIGAN, Library, Dept of Rare Books & Special Collections, Ann Arbor, 48109. Robert J Starring, Head
Holdings: // Cat
Notes: Incl more that 600 pamphlets bound in 68 vols gathered by the French historian in preparation for the writing of his *History of France.* Dated from 1769 to 1862, many of the pamphlets relate to the period when Guizot was Prime Minister under Louis Phillippe.

GUJARATI LANGUAGE AND LITERATURE

NY —NEW YORK PUBLIC LIBRARY, Oriental Div, Fifth Ave & 42 St, New York, 10018. E Christian Filstrup, Chief
Holdings: Cat Mss Microforms
Budget: ($56,455)
Notes: Published catalog of holdings.

NY —NEW YORK PUBLIC LIBRARY, Donnell Foreign Language Library, 20 W 53 St, New York, 10019. Bosiljka Stevanovic, Supvr Librn
Holdings: Vols 672 Cat
Notes: Gujarati collection incl Gujarati authors of Gujarati expression. No separate catalog.

GULF, MOBILE AND OHIO RAILROAD

MS —UNIVERSITY OF SOUTHERN MISSISSIPPI, William David McCain Graduate Library, Box 5148, Southern Sta, Hattiesburg, 39406.
Holdings: Cat Mss
Notes: Records (1869-1965; bulk: 1925-1955; 72 cubic feet) of the G M & O, Railroad and its predecessors, notable the Mobile and Ohio Railroad and the Gulf, Mobile and Northern Railroad. A guide to the records is available for loan.

GULF OF MAINE

ME —BIGELOW LABORATORY FOR OCEAN SCIENCES & MAINE DEPT OF MARINE RESOURCES, Library, McKown Point, West Boothbay Harbor, 04575. Pamela Shephard-Lupo, Librn
Holdings: Cat
Budget: ($55,000)
Notes: This library presently serves two institutions. The Maine Dept of Marine Resources has maintained the library since 1957 and thus the majority of our holdings are geared to their needs, ie fish biology and stock assessment on a local, national and international level. In 1973 Bigelow Laboratory for Ocean Sciences came to West Boothbay Harbor and began to contribute to the library with a very specialized collection on the Gulf of Maine marine chemistry, phytoplankton and nutrient cycles.

GULF OF MEXICO

TX —UNIVERSITY OF TEXAS, Marine Science Institute Library, Port Aransas, 78373. Ruth Grundy, Librn
Holdings: Vols (45,000) Cat Maps Pix
Budget: ($70,000)
Notes: Current researches in marine science, especially concerning the Gulf of Mexico, the Texas Coastal Zone, and the Continental Shelf. Incl journals.

GULF STATES

TX —UNIVERSITY OF HOUSTON, M D Anderson Memorial Library, University Park, Houston, 77004. David Farmer, Cur, Special Collections; Jean Jackson, Assistant Cur
Holdings: Vols 650 Cat Maps Pix
Notes: Emphasis is on 20th century Houston and Harris County, with other local, county, and church histories. Some company histories and family histories are also purchased for this collection. Gulf Coast Area is another subject emphasis.

GULFS see Bays

GULIK, ROBERT H. VAN, 1910-1967

MA —BOSTON UNIVERSITY, Mugar Memorial Library, Special Collections Dept, 771 Commonwealth Ave, Boston, 02215. Howard B Gotlieb, Dir
Holdings: // Cat Mss
Notes: Mss, correspondence, etc collected in depth; incl publications by or about.

GULLETTE, REV. J. C.

NM —MUSEUM OF NEW MEXICO, Photo Archives, Box 2087, Santa Fe, 87503. Arthur L Olivas, Cur; Richard Rudisill, Photo Historian
Holdings: Cat Pix Slides
Notes: Extensive collection of his work.

GUMS AND RESINS

CA —KELCO DIV OF MERCK, Library, 8355 Aero Dr, San Diego, 92123. Ann A Jenkins, Librn
Holdings: Cat Mss Maps Pix Slides Microforms
Notes: Kelco, as the largest producer of algin and xanthan gum in the world, supports a library specialized in the subject of natural gums and polysaccharides, incl all aspects of the subject: chemistry, biology, microbiology, applications (food, industrial, petroleum), etc.

GUN DOGS see Hunting Dogs

GUN POWDER

DE —HAGLEY MUSEUM AND LIBRARY, Eleutherian Mills-Hagley Foundation Inc, PO Box 3630, Greenville, 19807. Richmond D Williams, Dir; Heddy A Richter, Imprints Librn
Notes: Records of E I du Pont de Nemours & Company (1801-1958; 2500 cubic feet). The collection traces the founding of the company in Paris, its evolution into an American partnership during the early nineteenth century and its first incorporation in 1899. Details concerning the financial and business negotiations which led to the founding of the company, the selection of a site for operations, the erection of the mills, and methods of manufacturing, production, marketing and labor relations are well described. Records of Atlas Powder Company (1912-1955; 500 cubic feet) document the history of one of the United States' largest manufacturers of gun powder which was split off from the Du Pont Company as a result of a 1912 antitrust case.

GUNN, JAMES E.

KS —UNIVERSITY OF KANSAS, Kenneth Spencer Research Library, Special Collections Dept, Lawrence, 66045. Alexandra Mason, Librn
Holdings: Vols 2500 Cat Mss
Notes: Particularly strong in periodicals (1920s to present), and mss of James E Gunn. Incl fan literature (uncataloged). Noncirculating.

GUNN, THOMAS

NV —UNIVERSITY OF NEVADA, RENO, University Library, Special Collections Dept,

GUNN, THOMAS (cont.)

Reno, 89557. Robert E Blesse, Head
Holdings: Vols (48) Cat
Notes: Includes individual works by author in all editions including translations; also prefaces, introductions, published correspondence, appearances in anthologies, periodicals, etc. Bibliographical research collection, part of Modern Authors Collection Other appearances 500 cataloged.

GUNNING see Hunting

GUNPOWDER see Gun Powder

GUNS see Firearms; Ordnance; Rifles; Shotguns

GUNSMITHING

CO —TRINIDAD STATE JUNIOR COLLEGE, Samuel Freudenthal Memorial Library, Trinidad, 81082. Ena M Sroat, Librn
Holdings: Vols 900 Cat 16mm Films
Notes: Incl almost all gunsmithing books in print as well as many rare, out of print items. No separate catalog or index.

GUNTER, JOT

TX —UNIVERSITY OF TEXAS LIBRARIES, General Libraries, Barker Texas History Center, PO Box P, Austin, 78712. Don Carleton, Dir

GUNTRIP, HARRY, 1901-1975

KS —MENNINGER FOUNDATION, Archives, 5600 W Sixth St, Box 829, Topeka, 66601. Alice Brand, Librn; Mark West, Archivist
Notes: 1 box, 1945-74. The collection consists of unpublished autobiography, mss and research notes.

GUSTATION see Taste

GUTENBERG, BENO

CA —CALIFORNIA INSTITUTE OF TECHNOLOGY, Robert A Millikan Memorial Library, Archives, 1201 E California Blvd, Pasadena, 91125. Judith R Goodstein, Archivist
Holdings: Vols (3000) Cat Mss Maps Pix Slides Phonorecords Audiotapes Videotapes 16mm Films Microforms
Notes: Ms sources for the history of astrophysics, cosmology, mathematical physics, experimental physics, radio astronomy, geophysics and biophysics. Collections incl the papers of: George Ellery Hale, Jesse Greenstein, H P Robertson, Richard Feynman, Paul Epstein, Max Delbruck, and Beno Gutenberg. Candid photos of physicists at meetings; etchings and photographs of Einstein; scientific medals; selected pieces of scientific apparatus (including the oil-drop machine constructed by Millikan at Caltech in the early 1920s); the reprint collection of Paul Epstein; over 3000 landmark books in the history of 20th century physics and mathematics. Printed publications include: Daniel Kevles, *Guide to the Microfilm Edition of the George Ellery Hale Papers* (Pasadena, Carnegie Institute of Washington and Caltech), 1968; Judith R Goodstein, *The Robert Andrews Millikan Collection at the California Institute of Technology: Guide to a Microfilm Edition* (Pasadena, Caltech), 1977; Judith R Goodstein and Carolyn Kopp, *The Theodore von Karman Collections at the California Institute of* Technology (Pasadena, Archives), 1981.

GUTENBERG, JOHANNES

IL —NEWBERRY LIBRARY, John M Wing Foundation on the History of Printing, 60 W Walton St, Chicago, 60610. Diana Haskell, Cur of Modern Mss
Holdings: Vols (30,000) Cat Mss
Budget: ($50,000)
Notes: The collection covers printing and printing history of Western Europe and the Americas from its invention to the present. It is particularly rich in incunabula (about 2000); including imprints and books by Gutenberg. The works of the great printers, among others Aldus, Bodini, Baskerville, and Rogers. Printed catalog: *A Dictionary* Catalogue. (Boston G K Hall, 1961); *Supplements* (1981). Brief descriptions: James M Wells, "The John M Wing Foundation of The Newberry Library," *The Book Collector,* VIII, 2 (Summer 1959), pp 157-162; Lawrence W Towner, *An Uncommon Collection of Uncommon* Collections (Chicago: The Newberry Library, 1977), pp 25-26.

GUTHRIE, ISOBEL see Macdiarmid, Hugh (Christopher Murray Grieve), 1892-1978

GUTHRIE, TYRONE

†ON —MCMASTER UNIVERSITY, Library, Hamilton, L8S 4L6, Can.
Notes: Extensive correspondence with theatrical figures, such as Tyrone Guthrie and Jean Gascon. Collection described in *Library Research News,* vol 6, no 2, Fall 1982 and vol 7, no 1, Spring 1983.

GUTHRIE, WOODY

DC —LIBRARY OF CONGRESS, American Folklife Center, Archive of Folk Culture, Washington, 20540.
Notes: Recordings and papers of Woody Guthrie.

GUYANA

CT —YALE UNIVERSITY, Sterling Memorial Library, Latin American Collections, New Haven, 06520. Lee H Williams Jr, Cur
Holdings: Vols (300,000) Cat Maps Pix Slides Phonorecords 16mm Films Filmstrips
See also entry under Latin America

DC —HOWARD UNIVERSITY, Moorland-Spingarn Research Center, 500 Howard Place NW, Washington, 20059. Clifford L Muse, Jr, Acting Dir

NY —AMERICAN MUSEUM OF NATURAL HISTORY, Library Services Dept, Central Park W & 79th St, New York, 10024. Nina J Root, Chairwoman; Mary Genett, Asst Librn for Reference Services

TX —UNIVERSITY OF TEXAS LIBRARIES, Nettie Lee Benson Latin American Collection, Sid Richardson Hall 1.109, Austin, 78712. Laura Gutierrez-Witt, Head Librn
Holdings: Vols (450,000) Cat Mss Maps Pix Phonorecords Filmstrips Microforms
See also entry under Latin America.

GUYANA—HISTORY

DC —HOWARD UNIVERSITY, Moorland-Spingarn Research Center, 500 Howard Place NW, Washington, 20059. Clifford L Muse, Jr, Acting Dir

GUYANA—POLITICS AND GOVERNMENT

DC —HOWARD UNIVERSITY, Moorland-Spingarn Research Center, 500 Howard Place NW, Washington, 20059. Clifford L Muse, Jr, Acting Dir

GUYANE see French Guiana

GUYON, RENE

CA —RENE GUYON SOCIETY, Library, 256 S Robertson Blvd, Beverly Hills, 09211. Tim O'Hara, Cur
Notes: The Rene Guyon Society. Reference materials incl circulating treatises and books, incl law brief, re sex, children, pornography, and law relaxation reform.

GYMNASTICS

IL —AMERICAN SOKOL EDUCATIONAL AND PHYSICAL CULTURE, 6424 W Cermak Road, Berwyn, 60402. Annette Schabowski, Librn
Holdings: Vols 2000 Pix
Notes: Incl theses and dissertations on Czech life, folk dancing, gymnastics, etc.

MA —UNIVERSITY OF MASSACHUSETTS AT AMHERST, Library, Amherst, 01002.
Notes: Strong collections in physical education, sports studies, exercise, gymnastics, etc.

NC —UNIVERSITY OF NORTH CAROLINA, GREENSBORO, Walter Clinton Jackson Library, Special Collections Dept, 1000 Spring Garden St, Greensboro, 27412. Emilie W Mills, Librn
Holdings: Vols 2000// Cat
Notes: Incl 1000 pamphlets. The Homans Collection of historical materials acquired from Wellesley College, dating from 16th century to early 1900s. Emphasis on history of physical education for women. Incl early dance books and landmark works on all types of physical activity, training, theory; gymnastics books date from the 16th century.

PA —PENNSYLVANIA STATE UNIVERSITY, Fred Lewis Pattee Library, University Park, 16802.
Notes: Numerous and large collections on many sports. Also, materials supporting every aspect of the program of the Center for Women and Sport, incl research into kinetics, endocrinology, physiology, psychology, etc.

GYNECOLOGY

CT —YALE MEDICAL LIBRARY, 333 Cedar St, New Haven, 06510.
Holdings: Vols (334,215) Cat Mss Pix Slides Microforms
Budget: ($361,650)
Notes: Incl films, audiotapes, artifacts, etc.

CT —YALE UNIVERSITY, School of Medicine, Dept of Obstetrics & Gynecology Library, Farnam Memorial Bldg, New Haven, 06510.
Holdings: Cat Mss Pix Slides
Notes: X-ray plates, 10,00 slides of monkey and human tissue and about 1000 slides of gynecologocial and obstetrical pathology, used as teaching and research materials. Other large collections of X-rays and radiotherapy photographs are in the Hunter Radiation Therapy Center.

IL —UNIVERSITY OF CHICAGO LIBRARIES, John Crerar Library Collections, 1100 E 57th St, Chicago, 60637. Robert Rosenthal, Special Collections Librn
Notes: The John Crerar Library's extensive science, medicine, and engineering collections have been transferred in trust to the University of Chicago Libraries. Incl rare books and special collections as listed here.

MA —FRANCIS A COUNTWAY LIBRARY OF MEDICINE, Boston Medical Library/Harvard Medical Library, 10 Shattuck St, Boston, 02115. C Robin LeSueur, Librn; Richard J Wolfe, Cur, Rare Books & Manuscripts
Holdings: Vols (500,000) Cat Mss Maps Pix Microforms
Notes: Combines resources of the Harvard Medical School and the Boston Medical Library. Strong in serials and medical history in all fields of medicine, incl incunabula, non-medical books by doctors, travel books by doctors. 500,000 medical dissertations and theses. Special strength in all medical subjects listed in this volume.

NJ —ORTHO PHARMACEUTICAL CORP, Hartman Library, U S Highway 202, Raritan, 08869. June Bente, Mgr
Holdings: Vols (15,000) Cat Microforms
See also entry under Medicine.

†NY —MEDICAL RESEARCH LIBRARY OF BROOKLYN, Academy of Medicine of Brooklyn & The State University of New York Downstate Medical Center, 450 Clarkson St, Brooklyn, 11203. Kenneth E Moody, Dir
See also entry under Medicine.

NY —FLUSHING HOSPITAL & MEDICAL CENTER, Medical Library, Parsons Blvd & 45 Ave, Flushing, 11355. Maria Czechowicz, Dir
Holdings: Vols (5741) Cat Audiotapes
Budget: ($11,000)

GYNECOLOGY—HISTORY

CA —UNIVERSITY OF CALIFORNIA, SAN FRANCISCO, Library, Special Collections, San Francisco, 94143. Nancy Witten Zinn, Librn
Holdings: Vols (23,000) Cat Mss Pix
Budget: ($8500)

GA —MEDICAL COLLEGE OF GEORGIA, Library, Laney Walker Blvd, Augusta, 30902. Dorothy H Mims, Librn for Special Collections
Holdings: Vols (2500) Cat
Notes: Special collection of late 18th and early 19th century medical works, incl both the typical and the classic books on midwifery and diseases of women.

MD —MEDICAL & CHIRURGICAL FACULTY OF THE STATE OF MARYLAND, Library, 1211 Cathedral St, Baltimore, 21201. Joseph E Jensen, Librn
Holdings: Vols (10,000) // Cat Mss Maps Pix
See also entry under Medicine - History and Historic

NE —UNIVERSITY OF NEBRASKA MEDICAL CENTER, Library, 42 & Dewey Ave, Omaha, 68105. Robert M Braude, Dir
Holdings: Vols (196,313)
Budget: ($320,000)
Notes: History of Medicine Collection particularly strong in obstetrics and gynecology.

OH —CLEVELAND MEDICAL LIBRARY ASSOCIATION/CASE WESTERN RESERVE UNIVERSITY, Cleveland Health Sciences Library, Historical Division, Allen Memorial Medical Library, 11000 Euclid Ave, Cleveland, 44106. Glen Jenkins, Rare Book Librarian & Archivist
Notes: Incl 15,000 historical vols, 6000 in the supporting collection. Incl about 1000 16th-18th century titles. Strength of collection: diseases, epidemiology, anatomy, surgery, medicine, obstetrics, gynecology, pediatrics and yellow fever. Incl also medical Americana, listed in Robert B Austin *Early American Medical Imprints*, 1668-1820 (Washington, DC, HEW, Public Health Service, 1961) and ca 7000 19th century works. Our total medical Americana collection also incl journals (not counted), mss and archives (900 linear ft) and 5000 pictures, especially of the Western Reserve. Anatomical works discussed in I Ebner and G Jenkins *Skeletons in Our Closet* (Cleveland, Cleveland Health Sciences Library, 1983)

ON —UNIVERSITY OF TORONTO, Thomas Fisher Rare Book Library, 120 Saint George St, Toronto, M5S 1A5, Can. Richard G Landon, Head
Holdings: Vols (6000) Cat
Notes: Hannah Collection named in honour of Jason A Hannah, the founder of the Hannah Institute for the History of Medical and Related Sciences at the University of Toronto. Collection comprises a wide range of works in medicine, surgery, anatomy, physiology and other related sciences published in the major European countries and Great Britain from 1500 to 1900. Areas of special strength are psychology, gynecology and obstetrics. Highlights of collection described in two exhibition catalogues published by the Thomas Fisher Rare Book Library: *The Early History of Medicine; An Exhibition of Books Selected from the Jason A Hannah Collection in the History of Medical and Related Sciences* (March, 1974) and *The Byrth of Mankynd* (1981).

GYPSIES AND GYPSY LORE

CT —TRINITY COLLEGE LIBRARY, 300 Summit St, Hartford, 06106. Ralph S Emerick, Librn
Holdings: // Cat

IL —NEWBERRY LIBRARY, John M Wing Foundation on the History of Printing, 60 W Walton St, Chicago, 60610. Diana Haskell, Cur of Modern Mss
Holdings: Cat
Notes: Incl the Alfred E Hamill collection, bequeathed to the library.

NY —NEW YORK PUBLIC LIBRARY, Research Libraries, General Research Division, Fifth Ave & 42 St, New York, 10018. Rodney Phillips, Chief
Holdings: Vols (2,225,000) Cat Maps Pix Microforms
Budget: ($775,718)

OH —CLEVELAND PUBLIC LIBRARY, Fine Arts and Special Collections Department, 325 Superior Ave, Cleveland, 44114. Alice N Loranth, Head
Holdings: Vols 650 Cat Mss
Notes: A comprehensive collection incl most of the titles listed in Black's bibliography as well as titles recorded since in the *Journal of the Gypsy Lore Society*. Good collection of newspaper clippings relating to British gypsies at the turn of the century.
See also entry under Folklore

PA —UNIVERSITY OF PITTSBURGH, Hillman Library, Pittsburgh, 15260.
Holdings: Vols 500
Notes: A Rumanian collection, which deals with the country's history; racial, ethnic and religious minorities; folklore; art; literature; customs; agriculture; politics.

GYPSY LANGUAGE AND LITERATURE

NY —NEW YORK PUBLIC LIBRARY, Oriental Div, Fifth Ave & 42 St, New York, 10018. E Christian Filstrup, Chief
Holdings: Cat Mss Microforms
Budget: ($56,455)
Notes: Published catalog of holdings.

H

HABE, HANS

MA —BOSTON UNIVERSITY, Mugar Memorial Library, Special Collections Dept, 771 Commonwealth Ave, Boston, 02215. Howard B Gotlieb, Dir
Holdings: Cat Mss Pix
Notes: Mss, correpsondence, etc collected in depth; incl publications by or about.

HABITS OF ANIMALS see Animals, Habits and Behavior of

HABSBURG EMPIRE

CA —STANFORD UNIVERSITY LIBRARIES, Cecil H Green Library, Stanford, 94305. Peter R Frank, Cur, CDP-Germanic Collection
Notes: Extensive holdings, covering Austrian history of the Habsburg Empire to the present. Especially strong for the period of Maria Theresia and Joseph II, 19th & 20th century. Extremely rich in the Josephinic pamphlets (Broschuren-Literatur), broadsheets of the Napoleonic Wars and of the Revolution 1848/1849, rare periodicals. This and other rare material in the Stanford Collection of German, Austrian and Swiss Culture, Special Collections. Over 4,000 vols entered in RLIN. Description: "Narrative on a Good Meal: A Collection of Austriaca at Stanford University Libraries" by Peter R Frank.

HACKETT, JAMES W.

MA —BOSTON UNIVERSITY, Mugar Memorial Library, Special Collections Dept, 771 Commonwealth Ave, Boston, 02215. Howard B Gotlieb, Dir
Holdings: Mss
Notes: Mss, correspondence, incl publications by or about.

HACKS (CARRIAGES) see Carriages and Carts

HACKWORTH, JONNIE MAE

TX —TEXAS A&M UNIVERSITY, Sterling C Evans Library, University Archives, College Station, 77843. Charles R Schultz, University Archivist
Notes: The Archives of Modern Politics: Political candidate and religious zealot Jonnie Mae Hackworth, ca 1945-1980.

HADES see Future Life

HADLEY, HENRY K.

DC —LIBRARY OF CONGRESS, Music Division, Washington, 20540.
Notes: The business papers and music mss of the Arthur P Schmidt Company. Numerous works by important composers.

HAFFENDEN, HENRY

BC —UNIVERSITY OF VICTORIA, McPherson Library, Victoria, V8W 3H5, Can.

HAGEMEYER, JOHAN

AZ —UNIVERSITY OF ARIZONA, Center for Creative Photography, 843 E University Blvd, Tucson, 85721. James Enyeart, Dir; Terence Pitts, Cur and Librn
Notes: Center has significant collections consisting of more than 25 photographs plus other archival material such as negatives, contact sheets, work prints, correspondence, financial records, diaries, project files, etc. Inventories of the collections are available to researchers. Published guides available for some collections.

HAGEN, REV. JOHN, S.J., 1847-1930

DC —GEORGETOWN UNIVERSITY, Library, Special Collections Div, 37 & O Sts NW, Washington, 20057. George M Barringer, Special Collections Librn; Nicholas B Sheetz, Mss Librn
Holdings: Mss Cat
Notes: The papers of Rev. John Hagen, SJ (1847-1930), noted Jesuit astronomer and a native of Austria. While in this country he was stationed at Prarie du Chien, Wisconsin and at Georgetown University, Washington, DC. In 1905 he has called to Rome by Pope Pius X and named Director of the Vatican Observatory. During his lifetime, Fr Hagen received numerous honors from the scientific community. The papers incl notebooks of calculations and observations kept by Fr Hagen.

HAGGADAH

FL —UNIVERSITY OF FLORIDA LIBRARY, Isser and Rae Price Library of Judaica, 18 Libr East, Gainesville, 32611. Robert Singerman, Head Librn
Budget: ($30,000)
Notes: Total holdings estimated at 55,000 vols dealing with the political, social, economic and intellectual history of the Jews in the ancient, medieval and modern periods and in all geographic areas. The following areas are especially well represented by printed matter in all relevant languages: Bibliography, Festschriften, History, Bible, Judaism and Jewish theology, liturgy, responsa, rabbinical literature, Jewish law, Hebrew language and literature, Yiddish language and literature, anti-semitism, Zionism, Palestine and the *Yishuv,* and the State of Israel. German and American Judaica form a collecting emphasis with holdings for all the standard histories as well as histories of individual synagogues, institutions and local communities. Works in Hebrew and Yiddish comprise about 60 percent of the collection (estimated 30,000 vols). With few exceptions, holdingsare limited to nineteenth and twentieth century imprints, with complete sets of journals and thousands of ephemeral pamphlets, many of them commemorating anniversaries, enhancing the research value of the collection, the largest Judaica research library in the southeastern United States. Only about half of the collection is cataloged; the collection is a circulating one and vols may be borrowed on interlibrary loan. Incl the Leonard C Mishkin Collection (40,000 vols), the largest personal Judaica collection in the United States, the Shlomo Marenof Collection (3500 vols), and the inventory of Bernard Morgenstern's Lower East Side Book Store (8000 vols). Scholars should inquire in advance of their visit. *The Isser and Rae Price Library of Judaica* Report (circulation 2900 copies) is mailed gratis twice a year to all interested parties. Special catalogs:Pre-1881 Hebrew imprints recorded in a chronological card file.

OH —HEBREW UNION COLLEGE-JEWISH INSTITUTE OF RELIGION, Klau Library, 3101 Clifton Ave, Cincinnati, 45220. David J Gilner, Reference Librn
Holdings: Cat Mss
Notes: Hebrew illuminated mss, especially illuminated Passover Haggadot (incl the Cincinnati Haggadah), Esther Scrolls, etc.

HAGGARD, H. RIDER, 1856-1925

†CA —UNIVERSITY OF CALIFORNIA, BERKELEY, Bancroft Library, Berkeley, 94720. James D Hart, Director
Notes: Underground comics, 500. Max Brand and H Rider Haggard Collections.

CA —UNIVERSITY OF CALIFORNIA, LOS ANGELES, Research Library, Dept of Special Collections, 405 Hilgard Ave, Los Angeles, 90024. Edward Shreeves, Chairman, Bibliographers Group; David S Zeidberg, Head
Holdings: Vols 650
Notes: 650 first and other editions of his books; 400 pieces of correspondence.

CA —UNIVERSITY OF CALIFORNIA, RIVERSIDE, University Library, 4045 Canyon Crest Dr, Box 5900, Riverside, 92517.
Holdings: Vols (30,000)
Notes: The Eaton Collection of science fiction and fantasy materials, incl 5,600 pulp magazines; also horror, supernatural, and Gothic mystery fiction; boys' books; utopian and dystopian fiction, imaginary voyages, future war and lost race fiction; large holdings in French language science fiction and fantasy; critical and scholarly works pertaining to these genres; videotapes of science fiction/fantasy films and shooting scripts. Collection covers science fiction/ fantasy literature from the 16th-17th centuries to the present. Strong individual author collections of Jules Verne, H Rider Haggard, H G Wells, Edgar Rice Burroughs, and Philip K Dick. For a complete description of the collection see: George Slusser, "The J Lloyd Eaton Collection," *Special Collections,* II, 1/2, 25-38 (1983), and*Dictionary Catalog of the J Lloyd Eaton Collection of Science Fiction and Fantasy* Literature (Boston: G K Hall) 1982.

CT —TRINITY COLLEGE LIBRARY, Watkinson Library, 300 Summit St, Hartford, 06106. Jeffrey Kaimowitz, Cur
Holdings: Cat
Notes: First editions, etc.

NY —COLUMBIA UNIVERSITY LIBRARIES, Rare Book & Manuscript Library, 801 Butler Library, 535 W 114 St, New York, 10027. Kenneth A Lohf, Librn
Holdings: Cat Mss
Notes: A large collection of his letters, mss, and publications. Also incl an important series of his letters to his brother John and his wife Agnes Barber Haggard, etc. Restricted use.

HAGIOGRAPHY

DC —DOMINICAN HOUSE OF STUDIES, Dominican College Library, 487 Michigan Ave NE, Washington, 20017. J Raymond Vandegrift, OP, Librn
Holdings: Vols (5000) Cat
Budget: ($1350)
Notes: The Dominican Order (its history, spirituality, government, liturgy), its members (directories, biographies, bibliographies, lives of saints) and works written by Dominicans: incunabula, rare books, dissertations, periodicals (2300 vols), monographs. Incl periodicals either about the Order or edited by Dominicans. Does not incl titles about the congregations of Dominican Sisters. The Library's catalog contains analytics for Dominican contributors to monographs.

MD —JOHNS HOPKINS UNIVERSITY, Milton S Eisenhower Library, George Peabody Collection, 17 E Mt Vernon Place, Baltimore, 21201. Lyn Hart, Peabody Librn
Notes: Noncirculating.

HAGIOLOGY see Hagiography

HAGUE PEACE CONFERENCE

PA —SWARTHMORE COLLEGE, Peace Collection, Swarthmore, 19081. Jean R Soderlund, Cur of Peace Collection
Notes: International arbitration has been one of the central subject emphases of the Peace Collection since its inception in 1930. Incl books and other materials on the Hague Peace Conferences of 1899 and 1907, and other peace congresses and conventions. For descriptions of major document groups, see the *Guide to the Swarthmore College Peace* Collection, second ed (1981).

HAHN, EMILY

IN —INDIANA UNIVERSITY, Lilly Library, Seventh St, Bloomington, 47405. William R Cagle, Librn
Holdings: Mss Pix
Notes: Correspondence, writings, and research materials for writings of author Emily Hahn, 1905- . Incl correspondence with family, friends, editors, writers; photographs of family and friends as well as for use in publications; mss, galleys, and page proofs for several of her books, etc. 6133 items.

HAHNEMANN, SAMUEL

MA —WORCESTER HAHNEMANN HOSPITAL, Medical Library, 281 Lincoln

HAHNEMANN, SAMUEL (cont.)

St, Worcester, 01605. Roger Manahan, Librn
Holdings: Vols 30 Uncat Pix
Notes: Collection of medical history, incl books written by and about Dr Samuel Hahnemann from 1829.

HAIG, ALEXANDER M.

DC —LIBRARY OF CONGRESS, Manuscript Division, Washington, 20540. John C Broderick, Chief
Notes: The papers of former Secretary of State Alexander M Haig. Access to the collection is restricted.

HAILMANN, WILLIAM NICHOLAS, 1836-1920

CA —UNIVERSITY OF CALIFORNIA, LOS ANGELES, Research Library, Dept of Special Collections, 405 Hilgard Ave, Los Angeles, 90024. Edward Shreeves, Chairman, Bibliographers Group; David S Zeidberg, Head
Notes: 20 linear feet of books and educational play material related to his work with kindergarten training, ca 1880-1920.

HAINES FAMILY

NJ —GLASSBORO STATE COLLEGE, Savitz Library, Stewart Room, Glassboro, 08028. Clara Kirner, Special Collection Librn
Notes: Papers.

HAIRDRESSING

FL —BREVARD COMMUNITY COLLEGE, Learning Resources Center, Cocoa Campus, Clearlake Rd, Cocoa, 32922. John S French, Ref Librn
Holdings: Vols 29 Cat
Notes: All materials both print and nonprint supportive of instruction in cosmetology.

HAITI

CT —LEE ASH, (personal collection), 66 Humiston Dr, Bethany, 06525.
Holdings: Mss Maps Pix

CT —YALE UNIVERSITY, Sterling Memorial Library, Latin American Collections, New Haven, 06520. Lee H Williams Jr, Cur
Holdings: Vols (300,000) Cat Maps Pix Slides Phonorecords 16mm Films Filmstrips
See also entry under Latin America

DC —HOWARD UNIVERSITY, Moorland-Spingarn Research Center, 500 Howard Place NW, Washington, 20059. Clifford L Muse, Jr, Acting Dir

MA —BOSTON PUBLIC LIBRARY, Rare Books and Manuscripts, Copley Square, Boston, 02117. Laura V Monti, Keeper of Rare Books
Holdings: Vols (700) Cat Mss Maps Pix
Notes: The Benjamin P Hunt Collection, formed prior to the Civil War, with particular reference to Haiti, to which substantial additions have been made. Also about 3000 mss. Use restricted to qualified scholars.

PA —BUCKNELL UNIVERSITY, Ellen Clarke Bertrand Library, Lewisburg, 17837. Ann de Klerk, Librn
Holdings: Vols 150 Cat
Notes: Special emphasis on titles published in Haiti

RI —BROWN UNIVERSITY, John Carter Brown Library, Providence, 02912. Norman Fiering, Librn; Everett C Wilkie Jr, Bibliographer; Susan Danforth, Cur Maps & Prints
Holdings: Vols (40,000)
Notes: Documentation of life on the island through 1833, incl slave revolt and refugees that arrived in the United States.

TX —UNIVERSITY OF TEXAS LIBRARIES, Nettie Lee Benson Latin American Collection, Sid Richardson Hall 1.109, Austin, 78712. Laura Gutierrez-Witt, Head Librn
Holdings: Vols (450,000) Cat Mss Maps Pix Phonorecords Filmstrips Microforms
See also entry under Latin America.

HAITI—HISTORY

DC —HOWARD UNIVERSITY, Moorland-Spingarn Research Center, 500 Howard Place NW, Washington, 20059. Clifford L Muse, Jr, Acting Dir

FL —UNIVERSITY OF FLORIDA, Libraries, Special Collections, W University Ave, Gainesville, 32611. Sidney Ives, Librn & Rare Books
Holdings: Cat Mss Maps
Notes: This collection, of manuscripts only, deals especially with Haiti, revolutionary period and after. Also a very large group of notaries' papers useful for research in trade and slavery, etc.

HAITI—POLITICS AND GOVERNMENT

DC —HOWARD UNIVERSITY, Moorland-Spingarn Research Center, 500 Howard Place NW, Washington, 20059. Clifford L Muse, Jr, Acting Dir

HAITIAN AUTHORS see Authors, Haitian

HAITIAN LANGUAGE AND LITERATURE (FRENCH)

DC —HOWARD UNIVERSITY, Moorland-Spingarn Research Center, 500 Howard Place NW, Washington, 20059. Clifford L Muse, Jr, Acting Dir

NY —NEW YORK PUBLIC LIBRARY, Donnell Foreign Language Library, 20 W 53 St, New York, 10019. Bosiljka Stevanovic, Supvr Librn
Notes: Haitian materials incl in the French collection. No separate catalog.

HAL ROACH STUDIO

CA —UNIVERSITY OF SOUTHERN CALIFORNIA, Edward L Doheny Memorial Library, Archives of Performing Arts, University Park, Los Angeles, 90089. Robert Knutson, Librn
Holdings: Mss
Notes: Hal Roach Studio Collection incl studio records, 1916-mid fifties.

HALACHA see Jewish Law

HALACHIC LITERATURE

IL —HEBREW THEOLOGICAL COLLEGE, Saul Silber Memorial Library, 7135 N Carpenter Rd, Skokie, 60077. Leah Mishkin, Head Librn/Cur
Holdings: Vols (58,000) Cat Mss Microforms
Notes: Main subject is rabbinics (Halachic literature). We also have a very large and important Holocaust Collection.

OH —HEBREW UNION COLLEGE-JEWISH INSTITUTE OF RELIGION, Klau Library, 3101 Clifton Ave, Cincinnati, 45220. David J Gilner, Reference Librn
Holdings: Cat Mss
Notes: About 6000 mss in Hebrew characters representing various languages, such as Hebrew, Ladino, Yiddish, Spanish, Italian, German; also mss in Arabic, Ethiopian, Chinese and Persian alphabets. Incl literary, archival, sermonic and halakhic mss.

HALAKHA see Jewish Law

HALBERSTAM, DAVID

MA —BOSTON UNIVERSITY, Mugar Memorial Library, Special Collections Dept, 771 Commonwealth Ave, Boston, 02215. Howard B Gotlieb, Dir
Holdings: Cat Mss
Notes: Mss, correspondence, etc collected in depth; incl publications by or about. Restricted.

HALBERSTAM, MICHAEL

MA —BOSTON UNIVERSITY, Mugar Memorial Library, Special Collections Dept, 771 Commonwealth Ave, Boston, 02215. Howard B Gotlieb, Dir
Holdings: Mss Correspondence

HALBOUTY, MICHEL T.

TX —TEXAS A&M UNIVERSITY, Sterling C Evans Library, University Archives, College Station, 77843. Charles R Schultz, University Archivist
Notes: The Archives of Southwestern Technology: Papers of geologist and independent oil producer Michel T Halbouty, ca 1930-1983. Records of the Texas Section of the American Society of Civil Engineers, ca 1914-1980; and records of the Texas Engineering Experiment Station, ca 1914-1970.

HALDEMAN-JULIUS COLLECTION

CA —UNIVERSITY OF CALIFORNIA, LOS ANGELES, Research Library, Dept of Special Collections, 405 Hilgard Ave, Los Angeles, 90024. Edward Shreeves, Chairman, Bibliographers Group; David S Zeidberg, Head
Holdings: Vols 1200
Notes: 1200 Little Blue Books and other publications, ca 1920-1940.

CA —UNIVERSITY OF CALIFORNIA, SAN DIEGO, Central University Library, Mandeville Dept of Special Collections, La Jolla, 92093. Lynda Corey Claassen, Head
Notes: Rare Book Collection incl 5000 Little Blue Books and related materials published by Haldeman-Julius of Girard, Kansas.

IL —NORTHWESTERN UNIVERSITY, Library, Special Collections Dept, 1937 Sheridan Rd, Evanston, 60201. R Russell Maylone, Cur
Holdings: Vols 1500 //
Notes: "Little Blue Books" and "Big Blue Books."

IN —INDIANA UNIVERSITY, Lilly Library, Seventh St, Bloomington, 47405. William R Cagle, Librn
Holdings: // Cat Mss
Notes: First printings incl 1847 Little Blue Books; 437 Big Blue Books. Mss incl papers of Emanual and his wife Anna Marcet (Haldeman) Haldeman--Julius and of her mother Sarah Alice (Addams) Haldeman. 5892 items. Partially cataloged.

IA —IOWA STATE UNIVERSITY, Library, Dept of Special Collections, Ames, 50011. Stanley M Yates, Head
Holdings: Vols 2210 Cat
Notes: The Gilkey-Kehlenbeck Collection of the "Little Blue Books," incl variants.

KS —UNIVERSITY OF KANSAS, Kenneth Spencer Research Library, Kansas Collection, Lawrence, 66045. Sheryl K Williams, Cur
Holdings: Vols 6048 Cat
Notes: Publications of the Haldeman-Julius Press, Girard, Kansas. A separate book catalog is maintained--volumes in the collection are identified by author, title, series, and number within each series. All 12 series of the Haldeman-Julius press are included in the collection. The most notable of the series are the Little Blue Books, the Big Blue Books, and the Appeal to Reason Library.

MI —MICHIGAN STATE UNIVERSITY, Libraries, Special Collections Div, East Lansing, 48824. Jannette Fiore, Librn
Holdings: Vols 2800 Cat
Notes: The Russel B Nye Popular Culture Collection in the Michigan State Univ Libraries incl over (45,000) items. Most of the collection is organized into 4 categories: comic art, popular fiction, popular information materials and materials relating to the popular performing arts. About 3900 items. Almanacs, Blue Books, and works popularizing knowledge or offering self-help and how-to advice. There are ca 350 issues of 100 19th and 20th century almanacs. The Blue Books incl ca 2000 Little Blue Books, over 600 Big Blue Books and a good number of issues of the various Haldeman-Julius magazines. In addition to almanacs and Blue Books, Popular Information incl books of advice on etiquette, life and love, how-to-succeed books, popular history, science and

HALDEMAN-JULIUS PUBLICATIONS (cont.)

biography, and several hundred public schooltextbooks from the 19th and early 20th centuries.

HALE, EDWARD EVERETT

NY —UNIVERSITY OF ROCHESTER, Rush Rhees Library, Department of Rare Books and Special Collections, Rochester, 14627. Peter Dzwonkoski, Librn
Holdings: Vols 150

HALE, GEORGE ELLERY

CA —CALIFORNIA INSTITUTE OF TECHNOLOGY, Robert A Millikan Memorial Library, Archives, 1201 E California Blvd, Pasadena, 91125. Judith R Goodstein, Archivist
Holdings: Vols (3000) Cat Mss Maps Pix Slides Phonorecords Audiotapes Videotapes 16mm Films Microforms
Notes: Ms sources for the history of astrophysics, cosmology, mathematical physics, experimental physics, radio astronomy, geophysics and biophysics. Collections incl the papers of: George Ellery Hale, Jesse Greenstein, H P Robertson, Richard Feynman, Paul Epstein, Max Delbruck, and Beno Gutenberg. Candid photos of physicists at meetings; etchings and photographs of Einstein; scientific medals; selected pieces of scientific apparatus (including the oil-drop machine constructed by Millikan at Caltech in the early 1920s); the reprint collection of Paul Epstein; over 3000 landmark books in the history of 20th century physics and mathematics. Printed publications include: Daniel Kevles, *Guide to the Microfilm Edition of the George Ellery Hale Papers* (Pasadena, Carnegie Institute of Washington and Caltech), 1968; Judith R Goodstein,*The Robert Andrews Millikan Collection at the California Institute of Technology: Guide to a Microfilm Edition* (Pasadena, Caltech), 1977; Judith R Goodstein and Carolyn Kopp, *The Theodore von Karman Collections at the California Institute of* Technology (Pasadena, Archives), 1981.

IA —HERBERT HOOVER PRESIDENTIAL LIBRARY, West Branch, 52358. Dale C Mayer, Archivist
Notes: Papers.

HALE, GEN. IRVING

CO —DENVER PUBLIC LIBRARY, 1357 Broadway, Denver, 80203.
Notes: Correspondence, papers, pictures, diaries, etc.

HALE, JOHN PARKER

NH —NEW HAMPSHIRE HISTORICAL SOCIETY, Manuscripts Library, 30 Park St, Concord, 03301. Thomas E Camden, Cur
Holdings: Cat Mss
Notes: John Parker Hale (1806-1873) was a US Representative and Senator from New Hampshire. Papers are chiefly correspondence but incl a scrapbook, copies of speeches, certificates and misc memorabilia. Quite comprehensive; material relates to all periods of Hale's life and political activity. About 5000 items.

HALE, L. DE WITT

TX —NORTH TEXAS STATE UNIVERSITY, Archives, NT Station Box 5188, Denton, 76203. Robert LaForte, University Archivist
Notes: Part of Oral History Collection. Interviews 1967-77 with Hale, member of Texas legislature. Open access after June, 1987.

HALE, NATHAN

CT —YALE UNIVERSITY, Box 1603A, Yale Station, New Haven, 06520.

HALE, ROBERT, 1889-1976

ME —BOWDOIN COLLEGE, Library, Brunswick, 04011. Dianne M Gutscher, Cur of Special Collections
Notes: The Robert Hale Papers contain more than 1000 items relating to this US Congressman, incl correspondence, speeches, addresses, articles, and newsclippings covering the period 1938-1975.

HALE-KING PAPERS

ME —BOWDOIN COLLEGE, Library, Brunswick, 04011. Dianne M Gutscher, Cur of Special Collections
Notes: Besides a general collection of 13,000 volumes relating to the State of Maine, there are also many ms collections touching on the political, economic and social history of Maine. These incl Hale-King Papers; 700 letters, 1787-1880, concerning these two Maine families and incl letters of William King, first governor of the State of Maine.

HALEY, REP. JAMES A.

FL —FLORIDA SOUTHERN COLLEGE, Roux Library, Johnson at McDonald, Lakeland, 33802. Larry Stallings, Special Collections Librn
Holdings: // Uncat Mss Maps Pix Audiotapes 16mm Films
Notes: Incl papers, speeches, correspondence, etc, of Congressman James A Haley of Florida's 8th District. 1989 file folders. Separate subject index.

HALFWAY HOUSES

MA —MASSACHUSETTS REHABILITATION COMMISSION, Library, 20 Park Plaza, Boston, 02116. June C Holt, Librn
Holdings: Vols (15,000) Cat Audiotapes 16mm Films Microforms
Budget: ($18,000)
Notes: For staff and community interested in rehabilitation literature, defined as publications which deal with impairments resulting in disabling conditions; mental and behavioral disorders; employment of the handicapped; counseling techniques with handicapped populations; sheltered workshops, rehabilitation facilities; halfway houses and independent living arrangements; psychological aspects of disability; attitudes toward the handicapped; and other material on services for the handicapped. Library subscribes to 70 journals relating to disability and rehabilitation.

HALIBURTON, THOMAS CHANDLER

NS —DALHOUSIE UNIVERSITY LIBRARY, Halifax, B3H 4H8, Can.
Holdings: 150 Cat Pix
Notes: A representative collection of the British, American and Canadian first editions and later editions of the important and popular 19th humorist and Nova Scotian historian, Thomas Chandler Haliburton. Critical works, biogrpahies of Haliburton, and prints of his major literary creation "Sam Slick" are incl in the collection.

HALL, BARRY

BC —SIMON FRASER UNIVERSITY, Library, Burnaby, V5A 1S6, Can. Percilla Groves, Special Collections Librn
Holdings: Cat Mss
Notes: Letters of Charles Olson to Robin Blaser, Andrew Crozier, Barry Hall, Le Roi Jones (Amiri Baraka), Ed Sanders. Typescript and galleys for *Maximus IV, V,* VI, mss published in *Pacific Nation* and *Wivenhoe Park Review*. See *Line*, vol 1, no 1, spring 1983, for a complete list of Olson mss at SFU.

HALL, BERNARD H., 1919-

KS —MENNINGER FOUNDATION, Archives, 5600 W Sixth St, Box 829, Topeka, 66601. Alice Brand, Librn; Mark West, Archivist
Notes: 14 boxes, 1948-70. Consists mostly of professional correspondence.

HALL, GRANVILLE STANLEY

†MA —CLARK UNIVERSITY, Robert Hutchings Goddard Library, Worcester, 01610. Dorothy Mosa Kowski, Rare Books Librn
Holdings: Mss
Notes: His papers. Described in *G Stanley Hall Papers, Clark University*, comp by William A Koelsch and Suzanne M Hamel (Worcester: Goddard Library, Clark University, 1972?), (Register Series, No 1; 13 pp). Incl correspondence with Sigmund Freud, 1908-1923.

HALL, HARVEY MONROE

CA —UNIVERSITY OF CALIFORNIA, BERKELEY, Bancroft Library, Manuscripts Division, Berkeley, 94720. James D Hart, Dir
Holdings: Cat Mss Maps Pix Microforms
Notes: Papers, correspondence, etc.

HALL, JOHN S.

†MA —SUFFOLK UNIVERSITY, Library, Boston, 02114.
Notes: Papers.

HALL, MANLY P.

AZ —WORLD UNIVERSITY, Library, 711 E Blacklidge Dr, Tucson, 85719. Howard John Zitko, Cur
Holdings: Vols (15,000) Cat Mss Maps Audiotapes
Notes: Collection concerns what are generally called the "frontier sciences." No interlibrary loan.

HALLECK, CHARLES ABRAHAM

IN —INDIANA UNIVERSITY, Lilly Library, Seventh St, Bloomington, 47405. William R Cagle, Librn
Holdings: // Mss Pix
Notes: Correspondence and congressional papers of Indiana congressman Charles Halleck, 1900-. Incl several original pen and ink political cartoons of Halleck and/or of issues involving him. 191,978 items.

HALLINAN, NANCY

MA —BOSTON UNIVERSITY, Mugar Memorial Library, Special Collections Dept, 771 Commonwealth Ave, Boston, 02215. Howard B Gotlieb, Dir
Holdings: Mss Pix
Notes: Mss, correspondence, etc collected in depth; incl publications by or about.

HALLIWELL-PHILLIPPS, JAMES ORCHARD, 1820-1889

BC —UNIVERSITY OF VICTORIA, McPherson Library, Victoria, V8W 3H5, Can.

HALLMARK HALL OF FAME SCRIPTS (TELEVISION PROGRAM)

CA —UNIVERSITY OF CALIFORNIA, LOS ANGELES, Theater Arts Library, Los Angeles, 90024. Edward Shreeves, Chairman, Bibliographers Group; Audree Malkin, Head, Theater Arts Library
Notes: Hallmark Hall of Fame Collection, consists of *Hallmark Hall of Fame* radio and television scripts, incl property procurements, releases and properties dropped.

NY —NEW YORK PUBLIC LIBRARY, Performing Arts Research Center, Billy Rose Theatre Collection, 111 Amsterdam Ave, New York, 10023. Dorothy L Swerdlove, Cur
Holdings: Cat
See also entry under Television.

HALLOCK, LILLIAN

†CO —DENVER BOTANIC GARDENS, Helen Fowler Library, 909 York St, Denver, 80206. Solange G Gignac, Librn
Notes: Emphasis on Bromeliada Literature; horticulture; Colorado, Oregon, and Rocky Mountains Region botany; landscape architecture; juvenile horticultural and botanical literature. Incl over 5000 pamphlets on botany and horticulture; also, 197 watercolors of Colorado wildflowers by Emma Irvine, and 250 of Oregon by Lillian Hallock.

HALLS OF FAME (SPORTS)

CA —FIRST INTERSTATE BANK, Athletic Foundation, 2141 W Adams, Los Angeles, 90018. W R Schroeder, Managing Dir
Notes: One of the most extensive library and museum collections relating to sports, the Olympic Games, etc. Bound vols of sports sections from several newspapers. Large collection of college and university annuals and yearbooks; souvenir publications from amateur, college, and professional sporting events. Also, large museum collection of sports memorabilia, ledger of halls of fame with thousands of names of outstanding athletes in all sports. Repository for the Association of Sports Museums and Halls of Fame. Noncirculating.

HALLUCINOGENIC DRUGS

CA —FITZ HUGH LUDLOW MEMORIAL LIBRARY, PO Box 99346, San Francisco, 94109. Michael R Aldrich, Exec Cur
Holdings: Vols (1000) Cat Mss Maps Pix Slides Phonorecords Audiotapes Videotapes
Notes: Collection stored. Important mail inquiries only. No interlibrary lending or telephone inquiries. Hallucinogens as used in historical and contemporary cultures. Nearly complete collection of books and articles by or about Timothy Leary, incl manuscripts; also nearly complete collection of the writings of Aldous Huxley concerning drugs. Much autographed or inscribed material, mostly popular music from the 1960s but also incl ethnographic music. Emphasis on psychoactive drugs relative to religion, literature, art. Also an excellent collection of research papers (chemistry, pharmacology, epidemiology, sociology, ethnobotany) in this field, as well as artifacts and artwork relating to the field.

MA —HARVARD UNIVERSITY LIBRARY, Botanical Museum Library, Cambridge, 02138.
Holdings: Vols (2400) Mss Pix
Notes: The Tina and Gordon Wisson Ethnomycological Collection, one of the most important modern collections, acquired as an adjunct to the Museum's Economic Botany Library of Oakes Ames. From 15th to 20th century, it deals with hallucinogenic mushrooms in art, religion, and folklore; chemistry, pharmacology, linguistics, archaeological artifacts of Mexico, Guatemala, India, Japan, China, etc. Personal papers, etc.

HALPER, ALBERT

DE —UNIVERSITY OF DELAWARE, Hugh M Morris Library, S College Ave, Newark, 19711. T Stuart Dick, Special Collections
Holdings: Cat Mss Pix
Notes: Manuscripts, etc, incl literary correspondence.

HALSELL, GRACE

MA —BOSTON UNIVERSITY, Mugar Memorial Library, Special Collections Dept, 771 Commonwealth Ave, Boston, 02215. Howard B Gotlieb, Dir
Holdings: Cat Mss Pix
Notes: Mss, correspondence, etc collected in depth; incl publications by or about.

HALSTEAD, MURAT

IL —LOYOLA UNIVERSITY OF CHICAGO, E M Cudahy Memorial Library, 6525 N Sheridan Rd, Chicago, 60626.
Notes: Incl letters from Matthew Hale Carpenter, lawyer and US Senator from Wisconsin, to Murat Halstead, prominent 19th century journalist, war correspondent, author and editor. Also, other letters and collection of clipped signatures of prominent individuals.

HAMBLETON, T. EDWARD

NY —NEW YORK PUBLIC LIBRARY, Performing Arts Research Center, Billy Rose Theatre Collection, 111 Amsterdam Ave, New York, 10023. Dorothy L Swerdlove, Cur
Holdings: Cat Mss Pix
Notes: Papers, scrapbooks, mss, photographs, memorabilia, etc.

HAMILTON, ALEXANDER

DC —LIBRARY OF CONGRESS, Manuscript Division, Washington, 20540. John C Broderick, Chief
Holdings: Cat Mss Pix
Notes: Mss, papers, records, etc.

MI —NATIONAL HAMILTONIAN PARTY, Library, 3314 Dillon Rd, Flushing, 48433.
Holdings: Vols Cat
Notes: The life and writings of Alexander Hamilton. The National Hamiltonian Library is a part of the offices of the Hamiltonian National Committee, the governing body of the National Hamiltonian Party, a Neo-Federalist political movement. Incl 4835 vols. Also the Kelly Collection, a group of over 10,000 pieces of American political memorabilia covering presidents and presidential hopefuls of major and minor parties as well as special sectons on women, minorities and families in politics.

NJ —PASSAIC COUNTY HISTORICAL SOCIETY, Lamhurt Castle, Valley Rd, Paterson, 07503. Helen D Hamilton, Dir
Holdings: Vols (5000) Cat Mss Maps Pix
Notes: Material on the Society for the Establishment of Useful Manufacturing (founded) by Alexander Hamilton, papers relating to John Holland, who developed the submarine, the industrial magnates of the area who were active in the manufacture of locomotives, Colt revolvers, and textiles, especially silk.

NY —COLUMBIA UNIVERSITY LIBRARIES, Rare Book & Manuscript Library, 801 Butler Library, 535 W 114 St, New York, 10027. Kenneth A Lohf, Librn
Holdings: Vols 900 Mss Pix
Notes: Editions of Alexander Hamilton's writings, works about him, the *Federalist* Papers, books from his library, autograph letters and mss. Also a collection of papers of his son, historian John Church Hamilton (AB, Columbia, 1809), incl transcripts of papers of Alexander Hamilton which have been lost since the transcripts were made. Incl 5500 items. Restricted use.

HAMILTON, ALICE

MA —RADCLIFFE COLLEGE, Arthur & Elizabeth Schlesinger Library on the History of Women in America, 3 James St, Cambridge, 02138. Patricia Miller King, Dir; Eva Moseley, Cur of Mss
Holdings: Vols (23,000) Cat Mss Pix Microforms
Budget: ($300,000)
Notes: Ms collection incl Blackwell family, Beecher-Stowe family, Betty Friedan, Charlotte Perkins Gilman, Emma Goldman, Dr Alice Hamilton and the Hamilton family, the National Abortion Rights Action League, the National Organization for Women, Leonora O'Reilly, and the Women's Equity Action League.

HAMILTON, DONALD, 1916-

CA —UNIVERSITY OF CALIFORNIA, LOS ANGELES, Research Library, Dept of Special Collections, 405 Hilgard Ave, Los Angeles, 90024. Edward Shreeves, Chairman, Bibliographers Group; David S Zeidberg, Head
Holdings: Mss
Notes: 21 linear feet of mss, papers, and correspondence.

HAMILTON, EDMOND

NM —EASTERN NEW MEXICO UNIVERSITY, Golden Library, Special Collections, Portales, 88130. Mary Jo Walker, Special Collections Librn
Holdings: Vols 11,940 Cat Mss Pix Audiotapes
Notes: Incl 700 magazine titles (10,318 issues), 11,940 vols, mss and correspondences of the following science fiction writers: Jack Williamson, Edmond Hamilton, Leigh Brackett, Forrest J Ackerman and Piers Anthony (Jacob), plus *Astounding/Analog* ms files (1954-1975). Also serves as a depository for Science Fiction Writers of America. Incl separate catalog for published books and unpublished registers to personal papers. The Williamson Register is being prepared for publication. Collection is described in *Anatomy of* Wonder, by Neil Barron (NY: Bowker, 1981); and *Special Collections, II* (winter, 1982), pp 49-57.

HAMILTON, EW. B.

BC —UNIVERSITY OF VICTORIA, McPherson Library, Victoria, V8W 3H5, Can.
Notes: Governor of Antigua. Incl letters to Henry Labouchere, MP.

HAMILTON, CAPT. FRANK E.

OH —RUTHERFORD B HAYES LIBRARY, 1337 Hayes Ave, Fremont, 43420. Watt P Marchman, Dir
Holdings: Vols 500 Cat Mss Maps Pix Slides
Notes: The Great Lakes Marine Collection, incl the Capt Frank E Hamilton Collection; Great Lakes boats and shipping. Incl 300 charts; over 20,000 pictures (with 2500 negatives, 30 glass plates). Index and findings aids with the collection.

HAMILTON, JOHN CHURCH

NY —COLUMBIA UNIVERSITY LIBRARIES, Rare Book & Manuscript Library, 801 Butler Library, 535 W 114 St, New York, 10027. Kenneth A Lohf, Librn
Holdings: Mss
Notes: A collection of papers of John Church Hamilton (AB, Columbia, 1809), the son of Alexander Hamilton, incl transcripts of papers of Alexander Hamilton which have been lost since the transcripts were made. Restricted use.

HAMILTON, JOSEPH GILBERT

CA —UNIVERSITY OF CALIFORNIA, BERKELEY, Bancroft Library, Manuscripts Division, Berkeley, 94720. James D Hart, Dir
Holdings: Mss
Notes: His papers.

HAMILTON, THOMAS GLENDENNING, 1873-1935

MB —UNIVERSITY OF MANITOBA, Elizabeth Dafoe Library, Archives and Special Collections Dept, Winnipeg, R3T 2N2, Can. Richard E Bennett, Dept Head; Corrado A Santoro, Reference Archivist
Notes: Emphasis is on psychic research with a limited amount of materials regarding his medical and political careers. Seance attendance registers, records and affidavits, lecture notes, correspondence, newspaper clippings, books and journal articles. Also some photos. 19 boxes, 9 linear ft.

HAMLIN, SONYA

MA —BOSTON UNIVERSITY, Mugar Memorial Library, Special Collections Dept, 771 Commonwealth Ave, Boston, 02215. Howard B Gotlieb, Dir
Holdings: Mss Correspondence videotapes

HAMILTON FAMILY

MA —RADCLIFFE COLLEGE, Arthur & Elizabeth Schlesinger Library on the History

HAMILTON FAMILY (cont.)

of Women in America, 3 James St, Cambridge, 02138. Patricia Miller King, Dir; Eva Moseley, Cur of Mss
Holdings: Mss Pix Microforms
Notes: Papers of Alice Hamilton (1869-1970) incl correspondence, etc about work at Hull House, as first woman professor at Harvard Medical School, work in industrial toxicology for US Dept of Labor, member of League of Nations Health Organization and Pres Hoover's Committee on Social Trends, Inventory published by G K Hall, *The Manuscript Inventories and the Catalogs of the Books and Manuscripts of the Arthur and Elizabeth Schlesinger Library*, 1984. Family papers incl correspondence, etc of Alice, sister Edith (1867-1963), the classicist and author, and other family members; photographs, etc. Letters concern Alice's work, life in Fort Wayne, at Miss Porter's School, social work in Philadelphia, etc. 10 linear ft. Family papers available only on microfilm.

HAMLIN, CHARLES, 1861-1938

†DC —LIBRARY OF CONGRESS, Manuscript Division, Washington, 20540.
Notes: The papers, etc, of Charles Hamlin.

HAMLIN, CYRUS, 1811-1900

ME —BOWDOIN COLLEGE, Library, Brunswick, 04011. Dianne M Gutscher, Cur of Special Collections
Holdings: Mss
Notes: A small collection of Cyrus Hamlin material is supplemented by about 500 letters in the Abbott Memorial Collection from and to this missionary, founder of Robert College in Bebek, Turkey, and president of Middlebury College (Vermont).

HAMMARSKJOLD COLLEGE

DC —GEORGETOWN UNIVERSITY, Library, Special Collections Div, 37 & O Sts NW, Washington, 20057. George M Barringer, Special Collections Librn; Nicholas B Sheetz, Mss Librn
Holdings: Vols (100) Uncat Mss
Notes: Includes the archives of Dag Hammarskjold College, Columbia, Md; a portion of the archives of Gonzaga College, Washington, DC; records of the Fells Point Hebrew Grammar School, Baltimore, Md, and other materials (Besides these collections, students can use the Georgetown University Archives, 1787- , and the Woodstock College Archives, 1866- , qv under Jesuits in the US.)

HAMMERED STRING INSTRUMENTS see Stringed Instruments

HAMMERSTEIN, OSCAR, II, 1895-1960

DC —LIBRARY OF CONGRESS, Music Division, Washington, 20540.
Notes: Collection contains scripts, notes, librettos, correspondence, printed music, pictorial material, playbills and press notices. The productions *South Pacific, Flower Drum Song,* and *The Sound of Music* are particularly well documented. A few dictaphone belts on which Hammerstein recorded drafts for *The Sound of Music* and *Flower Drum Song* are kept in the Motion Picture, Broadcasting, and Recorded Sound Division.

HAMMETT, DASHIELL

CA —UNIVERSITY OF CALIFORNIA, SAN DIEGO, Central University Library, Mandeville Dept of Special Collections, La Jolla, 92093. Lynda Corey Claassen, Head
Notes: The Ira Wolff Collection numbers some 6000 volumes and emphasizes English-language detective fiction from the mid-19th century to the present, containing important or first editions of the works of Agatha Christie, Dorothy Sayers, Raymond Chandler, Dashiell Hammett, and Wilkie Collins.

HAMOND, SIR ANDREW SNAPE

VA —UNIVERSITY OF VIRGINIA, Alderman Library, Manuscripts Dept, Charlottesville, 22901. Edmund Berkeley Jr, Cur
Holdings: Cat Mss Maps Pix
Notes: Personal and official papers of Sir Andrew Snape Hamond and Graham Eden Hamond concern British naval operations during the American Revolution and in the Mediterranean during the Napoleonic Wars. Paul P Hoffman (ed) *Guide to the Naval Papers of Sir Andrew Snape Hamond . . . and Sir Graham Eden Hamond . . .* (Charlottesville, Va: Microfilm Publications, University of Virginia, 1966). Papers of US and Confederate naval officer Samuel Barron; US fleet surgeon and Brooklyn Navy Yard surgeon Gustavus R B Horner; US naval surgeon John S Whittle on a scientific expedition to the Pacific, 1838-1841; and US naval officer William Conway Whittle on West Indies and Mediterranean cruises, 1823-1831.

HAMOND, SIR GRAHAM EDEN

VA —UNIVERSITY OF VIRGINIA, Alderman Library, Manuscripts Dept, Charlottesville, 22901. Edmund Berkeley Jr, Cur
Holdings: Cat Mss Maps Pix
Notes: Personal and official papers of Sir Andrew Snape Hamond and Graham Eden Hamond concern British naval operations during the American Revolution and in the Mediterranean during the Napoleonic Wars. Paul P Hoffman (ed) *Guide to the Naval Papers of Sir Andrew Snape Hamond . . . and Sir Graham Eden Hamond . . .* (Charlottesville, Va: Microfilm Publications, University of Virginia, 1966). Papers of US and Confederate naval officer Samuel Barron; US fleet surgeon and Brooklyn Navy Yard surgeon Gustavus R B Horner; US naval surgeon John S Whittle on a scientific expedition to the Pacific, 1838-1841; and US naval officer William Conway Whittle on West Indies and Mediterranean cruises, 1823-1831.

HAMMOND, JOHN HAYS, JR.

CT —YALE UNIVERSITY, Box 1603A, Yale Station, New Haven, 06520.
Notes: Some 80 bound volumes of clippings and articles about him, his home, and his inventions.

HAMMOND FAMILY

NY —CORNELL UNIVERSITY LIBRARIES, Collection of Regional History, Dept of Manuscripts and Univ Archives, Ithaca, 14853.
Notes: Incl business papers, 1835-1916; considerable correspondence, journals, and legal documents relating to the family's businesses.

HAMPDEN, WALTER

NY —HAMPDEN-BOOTH THEATRE LIBRARY AT THE PLAYERS, 16 Gramercy Park, New York, 10003. Louis A Rachow, Librn/Cur
Holdings: Mss Pix
Notes: Numerous promptbooks and annotated scripts, official company records of Walter Hampden, Inc, letters and correspondence dating from 1896, photographs and clippings, and blueprints and sketches of productions by Claude Bragdon. 55 boxes of indexed material. Described in *The Players Bulletin* (autumn 1968), pp 15-16. Described in *Theatre & Performing Arts Collections* (New York: Haworth Press, 1981).

HANCOCK, GEN. WINFIELD SCOTT, 1824-1886

DC —GEORGETOWN UNIVERSITY, Library, Special Collections Div, 37 & O Sts NW, Washington, 20057. George M Barringer, Special Collections Librn; Nicholas B Sheetz, Mss Librn
Holdings: Mss
Notes: Correspondence and printed ephemera from the papers of John D Crimmins (1844-1917), New York financier and philanthropist. The correspondence incl letters from Henry Gabriels (1844-1917), James Cardinal Gibbons (1834-1921), General Winfield Scott Hancock (1824-1886), and Patrick J Ryan (1831-1911), Archbishop of Philadelphia. The printed material primarily concerns Irish-American organizations and activities.

HANCOCK FAMILY

MA —NEW ENGLAND HISTORIC GENEALOGICAL SOCIETY, Library, 101 Newbury St, Boston, 02116. Ralph J Crandell, Dir
Notes: Business papers of John and Thomas Hancock, incl those of Daniel Henchman (brother-in-law and Boston bookseller).

HANCOCK HOUSE PUBLISHING LIMITED

AB —UNIVERSITY OF CALGARY, Libraries, Special Collections Div, 2500 University Dr, Calgary, T2N 1N4, Can.
Holdings: Mss
Notes: Mss (6 meters), proofs, layouts, boards, galleys and correspondence for Hancock House publications, 1970-77.

HAND—SURGERY

MD —UNION MEMORIAL HOSPITAL, Library Services, 201 E University Pkwy, Baltimore, 21218. Rena M Snyder, Dir
Holdings: Vols 100 Cat Slides Audiotapes Videotapes

HAND, LEARNED, 1872-1961

MA —HARVARD UNIVERSITY LIBRARY, Law School Library, Langdell Hall, Cambridge, 02138. Erika S Chadbourn, Cur of Mss
Holdings: Cat Mss
Notes: Personal, professional and judicial papers. Typed inventory in repository. Inclusive dates, 1892-1961.

HAND, WAYLAND D.

†CA —UNIVERSITY OF CALIFORNIA LOS ANGELES, Center for the Study of Comparative Folklore and Mythology, Los Angeles, 90024.
Notes: Archive, consisting of nearly 500,000 entries and cross-references, developed by Prof Wayland D Hand over the past 40 years as part of his monumental *Dictionary of American Popular Beliefs and* Superstitions. Entries have been drawn from both field collections and from printed and published sources. Analytical data stress both the historical component and the comparative approach. Of special interest is the emphasis on magical medicine, although natural and botanical medicine are also well represented.

HANDBELL RINGING

MI —GUILD OF CARILLONNEURS IN NORTH AMERICA, Archives, 900 Burton Tower, University of Michigan, Ann Arbor, 48109. William De Turk, Archivist
Holdings: Mss Pix Phonorecords
Notes: Emphasis is on carillons.

NY —SOCIETAS CAMPANARIORUM (SOCIETY OF BELL-RINGERS), Campanological Library, Riverside Church, 490 Riverside Dr, New York, 10027. James R Lawson, Librn
Holdings: Vols 1000 Cat
Notes: One of the largest collections of books, pamphlets, periodicals, etc on bells and bell music (chimes, carillons, change-ringing, handbells, electronic carillons, etc) in North America. Examined by appointment only.

HANDEL, GEORGE FREDERICK

IN —INDIANA UNIVERSITY, Lilly Library, Seventh St, Bloomington, 47405. William R Cagle, Librn
Holdings: Vols 185 Cat
Notes: The William C Smith collection.

†MD —UNIVERSITY OF MARYLAND, Library, Coopersmith Collection, College Park, 20742. Frederic A Heutte, Head, Music Room
Holdings: Vols 2000 Cat
Notes: The working library of the late Jacob Coopersmith, a specialist in the music of Handel.

MA —BOSTON PUBLIC LIBRARY, Music Division, 666 Boylston St, Box 286, Boston, 02117. Ruth Bleecker, Cur of Music
Notes: The Handel and Haydn Society officially transferred its collection to the library in 1978. The Society gave its books, scores, and archives to the Trustees of the Library to be maintained and preserved as part of the permanent research collection. Presently the collection ranges from early imprints of Handel's music and copies of the *Handel and Haydn Society Collection of Church Music* to the holographs of commissioned works. The archives incl copies off bills and disbursements dating back to 1815, printers' plates for tickets, programs from 1815-1912, membership lists, and by-laws.

MI —UNIVERSITY OF MICHIGAN, School of Music, Music Library, Moore Bldg, Ann Arbor, 48109. Peggy Daub, Head
Holdings: / / Uncat Mss Pix Slides Microforms
Notes: The Coopersmith Handel Collection. A unique collection of the late J M Coopersmith containing music, facsimiles, photostats, letters, microfilms, slides, and extensive bibliographic records relating to Dr Coopersmith's Handelian scholarship. Included in the collection are records of his investigation of Leclair.

NJ —PRINCETON UNIVERSITY, Library, Rare Books Dept, Princeton, 08544. Stephen Ferguson, Cur
Notes: For particulars refer to: J Merrill Knapp, "The Hall Handel Collection" in the *Princeton University Library Chronicle* XXXVI, 1 (autumn, 1974) pp 3-18. The collection is in the process of being cataloged. There is a checklist of the collection in the special files of the Music Librarian.

NY —NEW YORK PUBLIC LIBRARY, Music Div, 111 Amsterdam Ave, New York, 10023. Frank C Campbell, Chief
Notes: Composers' autographs on microfilm. Works of 17-20th century composers. Major holdings: Bach, Handel, Beethoven. Original music mss, association items, etc.

HANDEL AND HAYDN SOCIETY

MA —BOSTON PUBLIC LIBRARY, Music Division, 666 Boylston St, Box 286, Boston, 02117. Ruth Bleecker, Cur of Music
Notes: The Handel and Haydn Society officially transferred its collection to the library in 1978. The Society gave its books, scores, and archives to the Trustees of the Library to be maintained and preserved as part of the permanent research collection. Presently the collection ranges from early imprints of Handel's music and copies of the *Handel and Haydn Society Collection of Church Music* to the holographs of commissioned works. The archives incl copies of bills and disbursements dating back to 1815, printers' plates for tickets, programs from 1815-1912, membership lists, and by-laws.

HANDICAPPED

CA —UNIVERSITY OF CALIFORNIA, LOS ANGELES, Research Library, Dept of Special Collections, 405 Hilgard Ave, Los Angeles, 90024. Edward Shreeves, Chairman, Bibliographers Group; David S Zeidberg, Head
Notes: 270 linear feet of papers and printed material of the attorney active in cases involving civil liberties, obscenity, and rights of the disabled.

DC —LIBRARY OF CONGRESS, National Library Service for Blind Physically Handicapped, 1291 Taylor St NW, Washington, 20542. Frank Kunt Cylke, Director; Hylda Kamisar, Head Reference Section
Holdings: Cat
Budget: $35,099,000
Notes: The Library of Congress National Library Service for the Blind and Physically Handicapped administers a free national library service to provide reading materials for persons who cannot read or use conventional print because of visual or physical handicapping conditions. The materials are distributed through a cooperating network of 56 regional and more than 100 subregional (local) libraries. Titles issued in multiple copies under this program total 5100 in braille, 11,200 on disc recordings, and 9700 on cassettes. Additional titles in braille and on tape are made available through a national volunteer program. Other special materials incl books in foreign languages in both braille and recorded form. Other special collections incl a musiccollection for the blind and physically handicapped and a print reference collection on blindness and physical handicapping conditions. The following publications describe the program: *Reading is for Everyone, Fact Sheet; Books for Blind and Physically Handicapped Individuals,* and *A Music Library for Blind and Physically Handicapped Individuals.*

DC —US COMMISSION ON CIVIL RIGHTS, National Clearinghouse Library, 1121 Vermont Ave NW, Washington, 20005. Lenora McMillan, Chief Librn
Holdings: Vols (10,200) Cat Slides Microforms
Notes: The National Clearinghouse Library has a special collection of the US Commission on Civil Rights publications from its inception (1957) to present date.

IA —WOODWARD STATE HOSPITAL-SCHOOL, Staff Library, Box 600, Woodward, 50276. Joy Averill, Librn
Holdings: Vols 3568 Cat Audiotapes Videotapes 16mm Films Microfiche
Budget: $3000
Notes: Developmental Disabilities.

KS —KANSAS NEUROLOGICAL INSTITUTE, Menninger Professional Library, 3107 W 21 St, Topeka, 66604. Richard Gray, Librn
Holdings: Vols 1224 Cat
Notes: Incl development disabilities; special education; nursing care for the handicapped; programs for the mentally retarded; behavioral psychology; supervision in mental health/mental retardation; staff training in mental health/mental retardation.

ME —LEARNING INC, Library, Learning Place, Manset, 04656. A L Welles, Librn; E R Welles, Cur
Holdings: Vols (2000) Uncat Mss
Notes: Materials that will help people understand the various learning handicaps and some of the remedial methods for overcoming them. Anyone wishing to visit the collection telephone (207) 244-5015 to make arrangements.

MA —CHILDREN'S MUSEUM, Resource Center, Museum Wharf, 300 Congress St, Boston, 02210. Marie Ariel, Librn; Maria Russell, Resource Services Mgr
Holdings: Vols 400 Cat Mss Filmstrips
Notes: Curriculum materials and materials for children and adults. Available for reference use by the public; borrowing privileges for Museum members; activity and curriculum kits available to public, schools and community groups for rental fee. Subject-related programs and services offered by Museum staff.

MA —MASSACHUSETTS REHABILITATION COMMISSION, Library, 20 Park Plaza, Boston, 02116. June C Holt, Librn
Holdings: Vols (15,000) Cat Audiotapes 16mm Films Microforms
Budget: ($18,000)
Notes: For staff and community interested in rehabilitation literature, defined as publications which deal with impairments resulting in disabling conditions; mental and behavioral disorders; employment of the handicapped; counseling techniques with handicapped populations; sheltered workshops, rehabilitation facilities; halfway houses and independent living arrangements; psychological aspects of disability; attitudes toward the handicapped; and other material on services for the handicapped. Library subscribes to 70 journals relating to disability and rehabilitation.

NV —NEVADA MENTAL HEALTH INSTITUTE, Library, 480 Galletti Way, Reno, 89512. Robert D Armstrong, Librn
Holdings: Vols 500 Cat
Notes: Developmental disabilities.

NY —SAINT MARY'S SCHOOL FOR THE DEAF, Professional Library, 2253 Main St, Buffalo, 14214. Collette Sangster, Librn
Holdings: Vols (8939) Cat Audiotapes Microforms
Budget: ($11,802)
Notes: Medical and educational aspects of deafness.

NY —NEW YORK PUBLIC LIBRARY, Mid-Manhattan Library, Project ACCESS, 455 Fifth Ave, New York, 10016. Rebecca Adler, Sr Librn
Holdings: Vols 150 Uncat
Notes: Reference collection of directories and pamphlets on organizations and services for the disabled; information on various disabilities, legislation, independent living, aids and devices, new technology, sources for special formats, etc. Provides special equipment (Kurzweil Reading Machines, TDD, enlargers, etc.) to aid in the use of the library's collections. Services by appointment.

†ON —METROPOLITAN TORONTO LIBRARY, Social Sciences Dept, 789 Yonge St, Toronto, M4W 2G8, Can. Abdus Salam, Head
Holdings: Vols Cat Maps Phonorecords Audiotapes 16mm Films Microforms
Notes: Historical and contemporary Canadian material covering federal and provincial policies and programs in the fields of health care, geriatrics, child welfare, corrections, and care and rehabilitation of the physically and mentally handicapped.

HANDICAPPED—BIOGRAPHY

MN —MAYO MEDICAL LIBRARY, History of Medicine Collection, Rochester, 55905. Nancy R Hensel, Librn
Holdings: Vols 800 Cat
Notes: The Walter C Alvarez Collection of autobiographies of the physically and mentally handicapped. Collection described: Mann, Ruth J: The Shelf of Walter C Alvarez, MD, *Mayo Clin Proc* 47:125-127, Fed 1972.

HANDICAPPED—EMPLOYMENT

ON —ONTARIO MINISTRY OF LABOUR, Library, 400 University Ave, Toronto, M7A 1T7, Can. Jean Collins-Williams, Librn
Holdings: Vols (80,000) Microforms Films

HANDICAPPED—REHABILITATION

see Rehabilitation; Vocational Rehabilitation

HANDICAPPED CHILDREN

MA —MEDFORD PUBLIC LIBRARY, 111 High St, Medford, 02155. Phyllis Breslow, Children's Librn
Holdings: Cat
Notes: Instructional materials center for children with special needs. Major portion of collection is made up of learning games and toys designed to be used by a parent or tutor with a child who has a physical, mental or learning disability. Books are selected to help the parent understand the child's disability. Incl films and cassettes.

OR —OREGON STATE SCHOOL FOR THE BLIND, Library, 700 Church St SE, Salem, 97310. Delphie Schuberg, Librn
Holdings: Vols 200 Cat
Notes: Professional materials related to visually and multiply handicapped children.

HANDICAPPED CHILDREN (cont.)

TX —SOUTHWEST FOUNDATION FOR RESEARCH AND EDUCATION LIBRARY, Preston C Northrup Memorial Library, Baboon Information Center, W Loop 410 at Military Dr, PO Box 28147, San Antonio, 78284. Dorothy M Brooks, Baboon
Notes: Principle field of research: Birth defects, atherosclerosis, reproductive physiology, cancer, genetics, organic chemistry, parasitology, primatology and behavioral sciences and their application to problems of drug abuse, alcoholism and ecology. Maintains the largest baboon colony in the world.

PQ —HOPITAL SAINTE-JUSTINE POUR LES ENFANTS, Centre d'Information sur la Sante de l'Enfant, 3175 Cote Sainte-Catherine, Montreal, H3T 1C5, Can. Louis LucLecompte, Librn
Holdings: Vols (7000) Cat Audiotapes Videotapes 16mm Films Microforms
Budget: ($11,000)
Notes: 40 percent of collection in French.

HANDICRAFTS

CA —CRAFT AND FOLK ART MUSEUM, Library, 5814 Wilshire Blvd, Los Angeles, 90036. Joan M Benedetti, Museum Librn
Holdings: Vols (2000) Slides VF
Notes: Incl 2000 books; 70 journal subscriptions; artists' biographical files: 6 file drawers; clipping files: 8 file drawers; 20,000 slides. Representation of the material culture of all people, traditional and contemporary expressions. Incl visual and printed information on ethnic, traditional, popular, decorative, idiosyncratic, and contemporary crafts as well as vernacular architecture, handmade houses, and design. Information about and for professional artists on health hazards, conservation, and career management. Anthropological and art historical works; exhibition catalogues; slides, photographs, audiocassettes; clipping and pamphlet files. Contemporary Slide Registry of Craftspeople and extensive biographical files of contemporary craft artists. Information and referral files of craft related galleries, shops, festivals, organizations, etc.

CA —CALIFORNIA COLLEGE OF ARTS & CRAFTS, Meyer Library, Broadway at College, Oakland, 94618. Robert L Harper, Head Librn
Holdings: Vols (29,000) Cat Pix
Budget: ($10,000)
Notes: All fields of arts and crafts.

DC —NATIONAL ENDOWMENT FOR THE ARTS, Library, 1100 Pen Ave NW, Rm 213, Washington, 20506. Christine Morrison, Arts Librn
Holdings: Vols (6000) Cat
Notes: Incl arts and education and public policy in the arts.

IL —CHICAGO PUBLIC LIBRARY, Art Section, Fine Arts Division, 78 E Washington St, Chicago, 60602. Rosalinda I Hack, Fine Arts Division Chief; Yvonne S Brown, Head, Art Section
Holdings: Vols 42,000
Notes: Reference and circulating collection of books, periodicals, exhibition catalogs, dissertations, picture collections, and microforms on all aspects of the visual arts. Major concentration of art history, especially European, with concentration on 19th and 20th century art movements and artists. We attempt to represent the works of recognized artists past and present. The Decorative Arts are well represented especially in the areas of antiques, interior decoration, and handicrafts. The collection is supplemented by a strong periodical collection, consisting of 330 current English and Foreign subscriptions, the majority of these titles we bind, as well as strong bound retrospective collections. The visual arts is supported by a clipping File on Chicago Artists, a current exhibition catalogs collection, as well as by the microfilm collections of the*Chicago Art Institute Scrapbooks,* the *Scrapbook on Art,* Artists, and the *Index of American Design.*

IN —THE ART CENTER, Library, 120 St Joseph St, South Bend, 46601. Judy Oberhausen, Cur
Holdings: Vols (1010) Cat Slides
Notes: 500 slides. This Art Center has a specific, separate collection--"The Arts of the United States"--which has its own index and is geared toward American painting, graphics, architecture, design and decorative arts, from the 19th to the 20th century, and sculpture works on paper. Incl 32 periodical titles.

MA —MELROSE PUBLIC LIBRARY, 69 W Emerson St, Melrose, 02176. Diane E Shaw, Art Librn
Holdings: Vols (8500) Cat Pix Slides Phonorecords
Budget: ($6900)
Notes: Framed and unframed art reproductions (110), slides (2773), periodicals, clippings, sound recordings (3000). Incl the Mary Livermore Collection of Sacred Art, the Odlin Collection, and the Pierre Gendrot Collection of Fine Art.

MA —OLD STURBRIDGE VILLAGE, Research Library, Sturbridge, 01566. Theresa Rini Percy, Librn
Holdings: Cat Mss
Notes: New England hand industries, to 1840; textile crafts, ceramics, wood, metal work, etc.

MI —EDISON INSTITUTE, Greenfield Village and Henry Ford Museum, Archives & Research Library, PO Box 1970, Dearborn, 48121. Steve Hamp, Dir; Joan W Gartland, Librn
Holdings: Vols 400,000 Cat Mss Maps Microforms
Notes: 400,000 vols incl pamphlets. The Archives and research library supports the program of Greenfield Village and the Henry Ford Museum. Special collections incl: automotive literature, ephemera, McGuffey Readers, trade catalogs, photographs and graphics.

MI —PORTAGE LAKE DISTRICT LIBRARY, 105 Huron, Houghton, 49931. Bethany Patterson, Dir
Holdings: Vols 100 Cat Pix
Notes: Weaving and related crafts, spinning, etc. Some foreign language materials.

NJ —ENGLEWOOD LIBRARY, 31 Engle St, Englewood, 07631. N E Rhoades, Reference Librn
Holdings: Vols (8200) Cat

NY —NEW YORK STATE HISTORICAL ASSOCIATION, Library, Lake Rd, Cooperstown, 13326. Amy Barnum, Librn
Holdings: Vols (55,000) Cat Mss Slides Audiotapes
Notes: American hand industries to 1860. Noncirculating.

NY —AMERICAN CRAFT COUNCIL, Library and Artists Registry, 44 W 53 St, New York, 10019. Joanne Polster, Librn
Holdings: Vols 3300 Cat Pix Slides Films
Notes: Crafts and craft-related subjects, incl portfolios for approx 2000 contemporary American craftspeople consisting of biographical material and photographs, indexed by media, geographic location, and a visual index. Over 1500 exhibition catalogs. The collection incl 35mm slide kits available for purchase. Catagories covered are: exhibitions of ACC's American Craft Museum from 1958 to date; kits in all media: fiber, metal, wood, clay, glass and multimedia; kits covering crafts processes. The Library also holds catalogs of craft school and art centers offering craft courses; newsletters, by-laws, and other materials of craft organizations and groups; the Archives and Photo-Archives of the American Craft Museum. No photocopying.

NY —INTERNATIONAL PAPER CO, Corporate Information Center, 77 W 45 St, New York, 10036. Elizabeth Skerritt, Corporate Librn
Holdings: Vols 25

NY —NEW YORK PUBLIC LIBRARY, Mid-Manhattan Library, Science & Business Dept, 455 Fifth Ave, New York, 10016. Frederick E Dusold, Sr Principal Librn
Holdings: Vols (110,000) Cat Microforms
Budget: ($134,000)
Notes: All works are in English. Material is current; policy precludes archival collecting. Collection is geared toward the undergraduate college student, with consideration given to the professional, the lay reader and the beginning graduate student. Collection incl monographs, texts, treatises, standard reference works and periodicals in agriculture, horticulture, home economics, crafts, engineering, industrial chemistry, construction and other technologies. Books are available for circulation in addition to an extensive reference collection.

OH —PUBLIC LIBRARY OF CINCINNATI & HAMILTON COUNTY, Art & Music Dept, 800 Vine St, Cincinnati, 45202. R Jayne Craven, Head
Holdings: Vols (122,185) Cat Pix
Budget: ($56,100)
Notes: Special collections: Eda Kuhn Loeb, "Artist and the Book, 1875-Date" (now shelved in Rare Book Room); music librettos (2345); exhibition catalogs (5474); large prints and posters (5051); Cincinnati artists vertical files; picture collection (673,906 clippings).

OH —CLEVELAND PUBLIC LIBRARY, Science & Technology Dept, 325 Superior Ave, Cleveland, 44114. Jean Z Piety, Head
Holdings: Cat
Notes: Incl crafts of many ethnic groups in Cleveland.

OH —GRANDVIEW HEIGHTS PUBLIC LIBRARY, 1685 W First Ave, Columbus, 43212. Kathryn M Hannon, Librn
Holdings: Vols (418) Cat

PA —BUCKS COUNTY HISTORICAL SOCIETY, Spruance Library, Pine & Ashland Sts, Doylestown, 18901. Terry A McNealy, Librn
Holdings: Vols (18,000) Cat

PA —INDEPENDENCE NATIONAL HISTORICAL PARK, Library, 313 Walnut St, Philadelphia, 19106. David C G Dutcher, Chief Historian; Shirley A Mays, Librn
Holdings: Vols 5000 Cat Mss Videotapes Films
Budget: ($25,000)
Notes: Emphasis on Pennsylvania and Philadelphia, incl arts and crafts to early 19th century. Incl some 2000 ms pieces; 25, 000 pictures; 3000 slides; 600 microfilm reels. No photocopying.

PA —CARNEGIE LIBRARY OF PITTSBURGH, Science & Technology Dept, 4400 Forbes Ave, Pittsburgh, 15213. Catherine M Brosky, Dept Head
Holdings: Vols (380,000) Cat Maps Microforms
Budget: ($240,000)
Notes: Incl much of the material in *Index to* Handicrafts. Books for the home owner, repairman and craftsman and the general builder and mechanics are emphasized. Information on the use of tools and materials especially for woodworking and metal crafts; also optical instruments, clocks, guns, and other mechanic trades. Maintains supplement to *Index to Handicrafts.*

TX —UNIVERSITY OF TEXAS LIBRARIES, Fine Arts Library, PO Box P, Austin, 78712. Carole L Cable, Fine Arts Librn
Holdings: Vols (55,000) Cat Pix
Notes: Emphasis is on historical as well as practical aspects.

VA —COLONIAL WILLIAMSBURG FOUNDATION, Abby Aldrich Rockefeller Folk Art Center, PO Box C, Williamsburg, 23187. Anne E Watkins, Registrar
Holdings: Vols (5000) Cat
Notes: American folk arts and crafts. Periodicals of current art, antiques, and history. Researchers wishing to use the library are requested to call the museum for an appointment.

ON —METROPOLITAN TORONTO LIBRARY, Fine Arts Dept, 789 Yonge St, Toronto, M4W 2G8, Can. Alan Suddon, Head
Holdings: Vols (42,000) Cat Pix Microforms
Notes: Extensive collection.

HANDICRAFTS—BIOGRAPHY see Craftspeople—Biography

HANDICRAFTS—HISTORY

RI —BROWN UNIVERSITY, John Carter Brown Library, Providence, 02912. Norman

HANDICRAFTS—HISTORY (cont.)

Fiering, Librn; Everett C Wilkie Jr, Bibliographer; Susan Danforth, Cur Maps & Prints
Notes: Children's and pedagogical materials available in America through the colonial period (ca 1800).

HANDLER, MILTON

†NY —COLUMBIA UNIVERSITY LIBRARIES, Butler Library, Rare Book and Manuscript Library, 535 W 114 St, New York, 10027.
Notes: Prof Milton Handler's papers, correspondence, etc, largely on antitrust and trademark law.

HANDMADE HOUSES

CA —CRAFT AND FOLK ART MUSEUM, Library, 5814 Wilshire Blvd, Los Angeles, 90036. Joan M Benedetti, Museum Librn
Holdings: Vols (2000) Slides VF
Notes: Incl 2000 books; 70 journal subscriptions; artists' biographical files: 6 file drawers; clipping files: 8 file drawers; 20,000 slides. Representation of the material culture of all people, traditional and contemporary expressions. Incl visual and printed information on ethnic, traditional, popular, decorative, idiosyncratic, and contemporary crafts as well as vernacular architecture, handmade houses, and design. Information about and for professional artists on health hazards, conservation, and career management. Anthropological and art historical works; exhibition catalogues; slides, photographs, audiocassettes; clipping and pamphlet files. Contemporary Slide Registry of Craftspeople and extensive biographical files of contemporary craft artists. Information and referral files of craft related galleries, shops, festivals, organizations, etc.

HANDY, LEVIN C., 1855?-1932

DC —LIBRARY OF CONGRESS, Prints & Photographs Div, Washington, 20540.
Notes: The Brady-Handy Collection consists of some 10,000 negatives from the files of photographers Levin C Handy (1855?-1932) and Mathew B Brady (1823?-1896), most of which are portrait photographs and views of Washington, DC from the 19th and early 20th centuries. Incl portraits of congressmen and government leaders (1855-90).

HANES, THOMAS ANDREW

VA —UNIVERSITY OF VIRGINIA, Alderman Library, Manuscripts Dept, Charlottesville, 22901. Edmund Berkeley Jr, Cur
Holdings: Cat Mss Pix
Notes: Papers, etc.

HANLEY, JAMES

IL —NORTHERN ILLINOIS UNIVERSITY, Founders Memorial Library, Rare Books and Special Collections Dept, De Kalb, 60115. William R DuBois, Dept Head
Holdings: Vols (297) Uncat Mss
Notes: Manuscripts and/or typescripts of several Hanley novels, stories and plays as well as almost all his published works in sequential editions. Some of the manuscripts are unpublished; Mr Hanley retains all copyrights. Collection includes Hanely's correspondece with Norman Unger.

PA —BRYN MAWR COLLEGE, Canaday Library, Bryn Mawr, 19010. James Tanis, Dir
Notes: Rare books in the Adelman Collection.

HANNA, KEN

TX —NORTH TEXAS STATE UNIVERSITY, Audio Center, Box 5188, NT Station, Denton, 76203. Morris Martin, Music Librn
Notes: More than 1600 manuscript jazz compositions, (incl scores and parts, alternate versions, expanded arrangements) by Stan Kenton, Johnny Richards, Joe Coccia, Lennie Niehaus, Pete Rugolo, Willie Maiden, Bob Curnow, Ken Hanna, Gene Rowland, Bob Graettinger and others, used by the Stan Kenton Band and given to North Texas State University in 1962 and at Kenton's death in 1979. Unpublished catalog: Breeden, Leon, *Stan Kenton Music in the NTSU Jazz Studies Library and the NTSU Music Library,* Denton, 1983 (99 pages).

HANNIBAL, EDWARD

MA —BOSTON UNIVERSITY, Mugar Memorial Library, Special Collections Dept, 771 Commonwealth Ave, Boston, 02215. Howard B Gotlieb, Dir
Holdings: Cat Mss Correspondence

HANOVER, NEW HAMPSHIRE

NH —DARTMOUTH COLLEGE, Baker Memorial Library, Hanover, 03755.
Holdings: Cat Mss Maps Pix Microforms
Notes: Microfilm copy of Dr Gilman Frost's extensive records of Hanover family genealogies.

HANSEATIC LEAGUE

CA —CLAREMONT COLLEGES, Honnold Library, Ninth & Dartmouth, Claremont, 91711. Franklin D Scott, Cur, Nordic Collection; Penelope Garris, Librn
Holdings: Vols (25,000) Cat Maps Pix Slides Audiotapes Videotapes
Notes: Nordic Collections are broadly inclusive, but emphasize history of Scandinavia, Baltic countries, and Hanseatic cities. Nucleus of collections from gifts and endowment of Waldemar Westergaard, supplemented with relevant collections of David Bjork, John H Wuorinen, Ingolf Olsen, Henry Steele Commager, Franklin Scott and other gifts and purchases. Eight vertical file drawers of news bulletins in English or vernaculars, 1941-. See: Franklin D Scott, "The Westergaard-Bjork Collection at the Honnold Library, the Claremont Colleges," *Scandinavian Studies,* 41 (1969), 346-354.

HANSEN, ROBERT P.

MA —BOSTON UNIVERSITY, Mugar Memorial Library, Special Collections Dept, 771 Commonwealth Ave, Boston, 02215. Howard B Gotlieb, Dir
Holdings: //Cat Mss Correspondence

HANSEN'S DISEASE

LA —US PUBLIC HEALTH SERVICE, National Hansen's Disease Center, Medical Library and Archives of Leprosy, Carville, 70721. Anna Belle Steinbach, Librn (Medical and Biological Sciences)
Holdings: Vols (8000) Cat
Notes: Only institution in the continental US devoted entirely to the treatment of leprosy and to worldwide educations about this disease. Unique collection of over 5000 reprints collected from earliest times to the present. There are books, historical documents, newspaper clippings, scrapbooks and bibliographies in all languages; as well as current books, journals and research materials.

MD —MEDICAL & CHIRURGICAL FACULTY OF THE STATE OF MARYLAND, Library, 1211 Cathedral St, Baltimore, 21201. Joseph E Jensen, Librn
Holdings: Vols (10,000) // Cat Mss Maps Pix
See also entry under Medicine - History and Historic

MD —NATIONAL LIBRARY OF MEDICINE, 8600 Rockville Pike, Bethesda, 20209. Harold M Schoolinam, Actg Dir
Budget: ($46,400)

HANSEN, JULIA BUTLER

WA —UNIVERSITY OF WASHINGTON LIBRARIES, Suzzallo Library, Manuscripts Section, FM-25, Seattle, 98195. Karyl Winn, Librn
Notes: Incl 217 linear feet, circa 1961-1974.

HANSON, KENNETH

SC —COLLEGE OF CHARLESTON LIBRARY, Special Collections Dept, Charleston, 29401.
Notes: The Kenneth Hanson Archives of Sound Recordings chronicling the growth of the recording industry through the 1940s. Over 400 cylinder records of marches, popular songs, vaudeville acts, and speeches.

HAN SUYIN

MA —BOSTON UNIVERSITY, Mugar Memorial Library, Special Collections Dept, 771 Commonwealth Ave, Boston, 02215. Howard B Gotlieb, Dir
Holdings: Cat Mss Pix
Notes: Mss, correspondence, etc collected in depth; incl publications by or about.

HAPGOOD, ELIZABETH REYNOLDS

NY —NEW YORK PUBLIC LIBRARY, Performing Arts Research Center, Billy Rose Theatre Collection, 111 Amsterdam Ave, New York, 10023. Dorothy L Swerdlove, Cur
Holdings: Cat
Notes: Includes several portfolios of correspondence.

HAPPENINGS

CA —CALIFORNIA INSTITUTE OF THE ARTS, Library, 24700 McBean Pkwy, Valencia, 91355. James Elrod, Dir
Holdings: Vols (61,000) Slides
Budget: ($11,000)
Notes: Modern art, incl abstract, conceptual, concrete, environment, minimal, and pop art; art; dadaism; surrealism; happenings; and caricatures and cartoons. Slides (61,683).

MI —APPLE TREE PRESS, Library, Box 1012, Flint, 48501. W D Chase, Editor/Librn
Holdings: Vols (1200) Uncat Mss Maps Pix Microforms

HARBISON, JOHN S.

CA —UNIVERSITY OF CALIFORNIA, DAVIS, Shields Library, Dept of Special Collections, Davis, 95616. Donald Kunitz, Head; C Danial Elliott, Asst Head
Holdings: Vols 100 Cat Mss Pix
Notes: Mss, patent papers and daybooks of John S Harbison, pioneer. Described in: USDA Agricultural Research Service, *Beekeeping in the United States* (Agricultural Handbook, no 335, rev ed 1977); and Johansson, Tag Sigvard Kjell, *Apicultural Literature Published in Canada and the United States* (New York, 1972).

HARBOR DEFENSES see Coast Defenses

HARBORS AND PORTS

MA —AMERICAN ANTIQUARIAN SOCIETY LIBRARY, 185 Salisbury St, Worcester, 01609. Marcus A McCorison, Dir & Librn
Holdings: Vols 5200 Cat
Notes: Incl the Thomas Winthrop Streeter Collection on Transportation. The finest and most complete documentation of early American railroads, canals, bridges, turnpikes, and harbors in existence.

NY —STATE UNIVERSITY OF NEW YORK, Maritime College, Stephen B Luce Library, Fort Schuyler, Bronx, 10465. Richard H Corson, Librn
Holdings: Vols (68,000) Cat Maps Slides Phonorecords Audiotapes Videotapes 16mm Films Filmstrips Microforms
Budget: ($90,000)
Notes: Incl extensive holdings in periodical literature with long and complete runs of many titles. Approximately 3500 recent research reports in paper and microfiche format. Mainly English language.

HARBORS AND PORTS (cont.)

VA —MARINERS MUSEUM, Library, Newport News, 23606. Ardie L Kelly, Librn
Holdings: Vols (60,000) Cat Mss Maps Pix Slides
Notes: Incl collections of over 150,000 photographs of merchant ships, naval vessels, sailing ships, lighthouses, portraits of naval men, harbors, canals, etc, and maps, ships' papers, and log books. Catalogs of various parts of the collection published by G K Hall, Boston.

ON —MCMASTER UNIVERSITY, Mills Memorial Library, Div of Archives & Research Collections, Hamilton, L8S 4L6, Can. G R Hill, Univ Librn
Holdings: // Mss Maps Pix
Notes: Colonel Steer-Webster played a leading part in the invention, design, and development of the Mulberry artificial harbor installations used for the invasion of Europe in WW II. The collection comprises memoranda, drawings, photographs, and maps.

HARBURG, E. Y.

CT —YALE UNIVERSITY, Sterling Memorial Library, Yale Collection of Historical Sound Recordings, 120 High St, New Haven, 06520. Richard Warren Jr, Cur
Holdings: Mss Phonorecords Audiotapes
Notes: Documenting his career as a lyricist in the fields of American musical theatre and film.

HARD, WILLIAM, 1878-1962

NJ —PRINCETON UNIVERSITY, Library, Manuscript Collection, Nassau St, Princeton, 08540. Jean F Preston, Cur
Holdings: // Cat Mss
Notes: Incl 2 cartons. The papers cover the period 1914-1928.

HARD COAL see Coal

HARDIN, JOHN WESLEY

TX —SOUTHWEST TEXAS STATE UNIVERSITY, Library, San Marcos, 78666. Bob Harris, Special Collections Librn
Holdings: Vols 12 // Cat Mss Pix
Notes: Incl pictures.

HARDING, EARL

DC —GEORGETOWN UNIVERSITY, Library, Special Collections Div, 37 & O Sts NW, Washington, 20057. George M Barringer, Special Collections Librn; Nicholas B Sheetz, Mss Librn
Holdings: Cat Mss pix
Notes: Panama Canal, and papers of Harry W Frantz, Thomas Herran, Earl Harding, Thomas E Martin, William McCan, Clark Thompson, Leonor K Sullivan, and Capt Miles Duval.

HARDING, WARREN GAMALIEL

DC —LIBRARY OF CONGRESS, Manuscript Division, Washington, 20540. John C Broderick, Chief
Notes: Over 100 letters in the controversial series of love letters and love poems to and from President Harding and Mrs Hames (Carrie) Phillips; unpublished (except for some unauthorized phrases in newspapers), and under seal until the year 2014.

OH —OHIO HISTORICAL SOCIETY, Archives Library Division, 1982 Velma Ave, Columbus, 43211. Dennis East, Division Chief
Holdings: Vols 2000 Cat Mss Pix Microforms
Notes: This is essentially the Presidential library for Harding. The papers have been microfilmed (1971) and are available by loan or purchase from the Ohio Historical Society. The microfilm edition totals 263 rolls; a printed inventory to the microfilm edition is avaialable.

HARDINGE, HENRY

PQ —MCGILL UNIVERSITY, McLennan Library, Rare Books and Special Collections Dept, 3459 McTavish St, Montreal, H3A 1Y1, Can.
Notes: 20,090 pamphlets on British historical, religious, and political material dating mainly from the 17th and 18th centuries, are housed in the Redpath Tracts Collection. Also the manuscripts of Carlyon Wilfroy Bellairs on early 20th century British politics and those of Henry Hardinge, first Viscount Hardinge of Lahore, are housed in the Manuscript Collection.

HARDS, IRA A. AND INA HAMMER

†NY —COLUMBIA UNIVERSITY LIBRARIES, Butler Library, Rare Book and Manuscript Library, 535 W 114 St, New York, 10027.
Notes: The papers, etc, of Ira A Hards, American theatre producer and his actress wife Ina Hammer Hards.

HARDY, THOMAS, 1840-1928

CA —UNIVERSITY OF CALIFORNIA, LOS ANGELES, Research Library, Dept of Special Collections, 405 Hilgard Ave, Los Angeles, 90024. Edward Shreeves, Chairman, Bibliographers Group; David S Zeidberg, Head
Holdings: Vols 150
Notes: 150 first and other editions of his books; 2 letters.

CA —UNIVERSITY OF CALIFORNIA, RIVERSIDE, University Library, 4045 Canyon Crest Dr, Box 5900, Riverside, 92517.
Holdings: Cat Mss Pix
Notes: Collection of playscripts and materials related to the production of stage adaptations of Hardy's novels and stories, made by A H Evans and T H Tilley, with some ms changes by Hardy, and 5 dramatizations by Hardy. Incl correspondence, photo albums of the productions, drawings and press clippings.

CT —YALE UNIVERSITY, Box 1603A, Yale Station, New Haven, 06520.
Holdings: Cat Mss

FL —FLORIDA STATE UNIVERSITY, Robert Manning Strozier Library, Special Collections Dept, Tallahassee, 32306. Opal M Free, Head, Special Collections
Holdings: Vols 128 // Uncat
Notes: 71 titles in 98 volumes of first edition and presentation copies of all major works. Also 30 volumes of bibliography, criticism, some modern editions.

NJ —PRINCETON UNIVERSITY, Library, Morris L Parrish Collection, Princeton, 08540. Alexander D Wainwright, Cur
Notes: Princeton has a virtually complete set of English and American first editions of the Wessex novels, most of the Hardy serials, and the collected works. More than 300 vols. The collection is rounded out by bibliographies of Hardy's works and the significant biographical and critical studies. Refer to: Glenn J Christensen, "The Thomas Hardy Collection" in the *Chronicle* VIII, 1 (November, 1946) pp 24-27.

NY —ALFRED UNIVERSITY, Herrick Memorial Library, Alfred, 14802. June E Brown, Head Librn
Notes: The Evelyn Tennyson Openhym Collection of modern British literature and social history. Papers, incl correspondence of authors concerned with the business aspects of authorship. Gift of Evelyn Tennyson Openhym of Wellsville, NY. Also, 5300 volumes of British literature.

NC —DUKE UNIVERSITY, William R Perkins Library, Rare Book Room, Durham, 27706. John L Sharpe, III, Cur
Notes: Thomas J Wise collection. Many rare pieces, including works of Byron, Coleridge, Dryden, Pope and Hardy. 135 political and religious broadsides, mostly of the 17th century.

HARE, MICHAEL M.

CT —YALE UNIVERSITY, Box 1603A, Yale Station, New Haven, 06520.
Holdings: Mss
Notes: Mss, notes, correspondence, etc.

HARE'S HILL, VIRGINIA, BATTLE OF, 1865 see Stedman, Fort, Battle of, 1865

HARING, FIRTH

MA —BOSTON UNIVERSITY, Mugar Memorial Library, Special Collections Dept, 771 Commonwealth Ave, Boston, 02215. Howard B Gotlieb, Dir
Holdings: Mss
Notes: Mss, correspondence, etc collected in depth; incl publications by or about.

HARKINS, CLIFFORD

AZ —NORTHERN ARIZONA UNIVERSITY, Special Collection Library, CU Box 6022, Flagstaff, 86011. Peter M Whiteley, Coordr/Archivist; William Mullane, Librn
Notes: Correspondence, subject files, printed matter (1914), 1931-1975. Arizona educator, former Arizona State Superintendent of Public Instruction, NAU graduate, 1932.

HARLAN, JOHN MARSHALL, 1899-1971

NJ —PRINCETON UNIVERSITY, Seeley G Mudd Manuscript Library, Public Affairs Papers Collection, Princeton, 08544. Nancy Bressler, Cur
Notes: Incl 681 boxes. The papers cover the period 1884-1972. An unpublished 634p guide is available in the Library.

HARLEM RENAISSANCE

RI —BROWN UNIVERSITY, John Hay Library, 20 Prospect St, Providence, 02912. Mary T Russo, Cur of Broadsides
Notes: A major collection of 30,000 pieces of American verse in broadside form dating from the 18th through 20th century. Ephemeral in nature and all inclusive, it covers a broad spectrum of American life. Numerous examples of early American poetry, admonishing, proclaiming, celebrating, advertising and mourning are represented. Poets range from the anonymous to major figures, incl Cummings, Eliot, Emerson, Frost, Pound and Whitman as well as contemporary authors. The Beat Movement, Black Mountain School, Concrete Poetry and Poetry of the Harlem Renaissance are represented as well as that of the young black poets published by the Detroit Broadside Press and a good selection of poetry by women. Retrospective and current pieces are added annually. Partial catalog.

HARLESTON FAMILY

SC —COLLEGE OF CHARLESTON LIBRARY, Special Collections Dept, Charleston, 29401.
Notes: Papers, 1780, incl correspondence of members of the Harleston family with each other and with Francis Marion.

HARLEQUIN AND HARLEQUINADES

CA —UNIVERSITY OF CALIFORNIA, LOS ANGELES, Research Library, Dept of Special Collections, 405 Hilgard Ave, Los Angeles, 90024. Edward Shreeves, Chairman, Bibliographers Group; David S Zeidberg, Head
Holdings: Cat
Notes: 50 British and American turn-ups or Harlequinades.

IN —INDIANA UNIVERSITY, Lilly Library, Seventh St, Bloomington, 47405. William R Cagle, Librn
Holdings: Vols 55 Uncat
Notes: The Elisabeth Ball Collection consists of more than 7,000 books and many manuscripts from the late seventeenth to the early twentieth centuries. Strengths include Newbery and other early imprints, chapbooks, horn books, harlequinades, street cries, and miniature books.

HARMONISTS AND HARMONY SOCIETY see Harmony Society and Harmonists

HARMONY, KEYBOARD

CA —CALIFORNIA INSTITUTE OF THE ARTS, Library, 24700 McBean Pkwy,

HARMONY, KEYBOARD (cont.)

Valencia, 91355. James Elrod, Dir
Holdings: Vols (61,000) Cat Phonorecords Audiotapes
Budget: ($8500)
Notes: Incl 11,656 audiotapes. Cataloged.

HARMONY SOCIETY AND HARMONISTS

IN —INDIANA UNIVERSITY, Lilly Library, Seventh St, Bloomington, 47405. William R Cagle, Librn
Holdings: // Cat Mss
Notes: First and early printings of the Icarian communities (1840-1880) and of works by Rappites and the Owenites; also New Harmony, Indiana. Mss relating to the Shaker community in Kentucky (1826-1828) in the Charles Willing Byrd collection.

PA —OLD ECONOMY VILLAGE, 14th & Church St, Great House Square, Ambridge, 15003. Raymond V Shepherd Jr, Archivist
Notes: Incl 5000 vols in German and English on original society of Harmonists. Library open to researchers by prior arrangement.

PA —PENNSYLVANIA DIV OF ARCHIVES & MANUSCRIPTS, State Archives, PO Box 1026, Harris, 17108. Roland M Baumann, Chief, History & Museums
Holdings: Vols (3000) // Uncat Mss Maps Pix
Budget: ($40,000)
Notes: The Harmony Society (1785-1905), a German communistic and spiritual community, which immigrated to the US in 1805 and established their community in Harmony, Pennsylvania, moved to New Harmony, Indiana, and returned to Pennsylvania to set up the town of Economy, 20 miles north of Pittsburgh on the Ohio River. The Harmonists had a vast impact on the economy of the areas in which they lived. They were involved in agriculture, manufacturing and investing. 300,000 cu ft.

PA —BALCH INSTITUTE FOR ETHNIC STUDIES, Library, 18 S Seventh St, Philadelphia, 19106. R Joseph Anderson, Library Dir

HARMOUNT, WILLIAM

LA —NICHOLLS STATE UNIVERSITY, Ellender Memorial Library, Thibodaux, 70310. Randall A Detro, Dir; Philip D Uzee, Archivist
Holdings: Uncat Mss Maps Pix Microforms
Notes: Louisiana and local history; family papers of the period, etc.

HARNESS RACING

NY —HALL OF FAME OF THE TROTTER, Library, 240 Main St, Goshen, 10924. Philip Pines, Dir
Holdings: Vols 2000 Cat Mss Pix Slides
Notes: Harness horses (trotters and pacers). Incl history of harness racing. Assembling videotape collection of famous races, interviews with prominent horsemen, film-to-tape. Not yet cataloged.

ON —CANADIAN TROTTING ASSOCIATION, Standardbred Canada Library, 233 Evans Ave, Toronto, M8Z 1J6, Can. David Hornell, Librn; Margaret Neal, Coordinator
Notes: Books, magazines, photographs, microfilm, audiotapes, videotapes, slides, 16mm films, etc relating to harness racing in Canada.

HARPER, ALVAN S.

FL —FLORIDA DEPT OF STATE, Florida State Archives, Florida Photographic Collection, R A Gray Bldg, Tallahassee, 32301. Mrs Allen Morris, Archives Supervisor
Holdings: Maps Pix Slides Films Audiotapes
Notes: Alvan S Harper, Tallahassee portrait artist; 1700 glass negatives of Tallahassee people, 1885-1910.

HARPER, GEORGE MCLEAN, 1863-1947

NJ —PRINCETON UNIVERSITY, Library, Manuscript Collection, Nassau St, Princeton, 08540. Jean F Preston, Cur
Holdings: // Mss
Notes: The collection totals 1300 pieces. See *Princeton University Libary Chronicle,* v 11, p 89-94.

HARPER AND BROTHERS (PUBLISHERS)

NJ —PRINCETON UNIVERSITY, Library, Manuscript Collection, Nassau St, Princeton, 08540. Jean F Preston, Cur
Holdings: Mss Pix Cat
Notes: The archive of Harper & Brothers, publishers, fills 34 ms boxes. An unpublished typescript guide is available in the Library. Also the archives of Henry Holt, publishers, and Scribner (qv).

NY —COLUMBIA UNIVERSITY LIBRARIES, Rare Book & Manuscript Library, 801 Butler Library, 535 W 114 St, New York, 10027. Kenneth A Lohf, Librn
Holdings: Mss
Notes: Publishing records of Harper & Bros, chiefly 19th century contract files. Restricted use.

HARPER AND ROW (PUBLISHERS)

NY —COLUMBIA UNIVERSITY LIBRARIES, Rare Book & Manuscript Library, 801 Butler Library, 535 W 114 St, New York, 10027. Kenneth A Lohf, Librn
Holdings: Mss
Notes: 23,000 item publishing archive of Harper & Row Publishing Co, 1935-65. Restricted use.

HARPER'S (MAGAZINE)

DC —LIBRARY OF CONGRESS, Manuscript Division, Washington, 20540. John C Broderick, Chief
Notes: Records; additions, 1977- .

HARPOOL, TOM, SEED COMPANY

TX —NORTH TEXAS STATE UNIVERSITY, Archives, NT Station Box 5188, Denton, 76203. Robert LaForte, University Archivist
Notes: Morrison Milling Company Collection (14 linear feet), Tom Harpool Seed Company Collection (17 linear feet). The development of agriculture and businesses dependent on agriculture in the North Texas area is a collecting strength at the NTSU Archives. The Morrison Milling Company Collection and the Tom Harpool Seed Company Collection focus on agricultural businesses in the city of Denton from the 1930s to the early 1980s.

HARPSICHORD MUSIC

IN —INDIANA UNIVERSITY, Music Library, Bloomington, 47401. David E Fenske, Head
Holdings: Vols 400 // Cat Microforms
Notes: Keyboard music to 1800. See Dominique-Rene de Lerma, *An Annotated Catalog of Early Keyboard Literature Contained within the Apel Collection.* Bloomington (Indiana): The Music Library, Indiana University, 1973.

HARRELD, JOHN WILLIAM

OK —UNIVERSITY OF OKLAHOMA, Bizzell Memorial Library, Western History Collections, 401 W Brooks, Norman, 73069. John Ezell, Cur
Holdings: Mss
Notes: US Senator. His papers. Guide available.

HARRINGTON, ALAN

MA —BOSTON UNIVERSITY, Mugar Memorial Library, Special Collections Dept, 771 Commonwealth Ave, Boston, 02215. Howard B Gotlieb, Dir
Holdings: Cat Mss
Notes: Mss, correspondence, etc collected in depth; incl publications by or about.

HARRINGTON, JOSEPH

MA —BOSTON UNIVERSITY, Mugar Memorial Library, Special Collections Dept, 771 Commonwealth Ave, Boston, 02215. Howard B Gotlieb, Dir
Holdings: Cat Mss
Notes: Mss, correspondence, etc collected in depth; incl publications by or about.

HARRIS, AURAND

AZ —ARIZONA STATE UNIVERSITY, Library, Tempe, 85287. Marilyn Wurzburger, Special Collections Librn
Holdings: Vols (108) Pix
Notes: Collection covers various aspects of Children's Theatre from 1944 through the present. Areas of emphasis incl International and National Child Drama Associations, award-winning theatres, educational programs, regional groups and prominent figures in Children's Theatre incl: Irene Vickers Baker, Isabel Burger, Virginia Lee Comer, Rita Criste, Moses Goldberg, Kenneth Graham, Aurand Harris, Paul Kozelka, George Latshaw, Rosemary Musil, Sara Spencer, Winifred Ward, Susan Zeder and Lin Wright. Publications incl newsletters, research papers, bibliographies and records of the proceedings of the Children's Theatre Association of America. 80 linear feet of scripts, documents, publications, films, tapes (oral history) programs, correspondence, photographs, working papers and clippings. Partially indexed; finding guides available.

HARRIS, CHRISTIE, 1908-

AB —UNIVERSITY OF CALGARY, Libraries, Special Collections Div, 2500 University Dr, Calgary, T2N 1N4, Can.
Holdings: Cat Mss
Notes: Manuscripts, proofs, research notes, and correspondence for Christie Harris's books. Also included are personal diaries, personal correspondence, and copies of Canadian Broadcasting Corporation scripts, short stories, articles, and speeches, 1940-1974.

HARRIS, COL. COLLAS

†VA —GEORGE C MARSHALL RESEARCH FOUNDATION AND LIBRARY, Drawer 920, Lexington, 24450. Royster Lyle Jr, Cur Collections
Holdings: Cat Mss Maps Pix
Notes: The Collas Harris papers incl 1000 pages of SCAP Civil Information and Educations Series; miscellaneous papers concerning SCAP and the occupation of Japan, 1945-1947. The Francis P Miller papers incl intelligence papers from OSS and Operation Sussex, SHAEF (incl Battle of the Bulge), Germany's occupations; and the US Senate's investigation of military government in occupied Europe.

HARRIS, FRANK, 1855-1931

DC —GEORGETOWN UNIVERSITY, Library, Special Collections Div, 37 & O Sts NW, Washington, 20057. George M Barringer, Special Collections Librn; Nicholas B Sheetz, Mss Librn
Holdings: Mss Cat Pix
Notes: A portion of the archives of the English publisher Grant Ricards (1872-1948), containing manuscripts, correspondence, photographs, clippings, and printed ephemera. Incl is extensive correspondence from such artists and authors as Neville Cardus; Frank Harris; Sir Hugh Lane; Lady Augusta Gregory; David Low; T Sturge Moore; and C R W Nevinson.

NC —UNIVERSITY OF NORTH CAROLINA, CHARLOTTE, J Murrey

HARRIS, FRANK, 1855-1931 (cont.)

Atkins Library, UNCC Station, Charlotte, 28223. Robert F Brabham Jr, Special Collections Librn
Holdings: Vols 100 Cat
Notes: Incl scholarly works on sex, classics by such writers as D H Lawrence, Frank Harris, and Norman Douglas, and about 40 novels published between 1890 and 1930.

OH —OHIO UNIVERSITY, Vernon R Alden Library, Department of Archives and Special Collections, Athens, 45701. Gary A Hunt, Head
Holdings: Vols 47 Cat
Notes: A comprehensive collection of first and other significant editions.

NS —DALHOUSIE UNIVERSITY LIBRARY, Halifax, B3H 4H8, Can.
Notes: The collection of numerous editions from Dr Henry Hicks, past president of Dalhousie.

HARRIS, FRED

OK —MUSEUM OF THE GREAT PLAINS, Research Center, 601 Ferris, PO Box 68, Lawton, 73502. Steve Wilson, Dir; Paula Williams, Special Collections
Notes: Papers about Oklahoma and national politics in 1960's.

OK —UNIVERSITY OF OKLAHOMA, Bizzell Memorial Library, Western History Collections, 401 W Brooks, Norman, 73069. John Ezell, Cur
Holdings: Vols Mss Documents Maps Pix Newspapers
Notes: US Senator; Chairman, Democratic National Committee. His papers.

HARRIS, JED

TN —MEMPHIS STATE UNIVERSITY, John Willard Brister Library, Memphis, 38152. John Terreo, Special Collections Librn
Notes: Theatre Collection, 1789-1972. Correspondence, scripts, programs, handbills, musical scores, clippings, drawings, sketches, and photographs, documenting careers of artists, production of plays, ballett and theatre companies, and theaters and opera houses centering in New York and London, England. Incl drawings, prints, publications, and other personal papers of British producer and designer Edward Gordon Craig (1872-1966), relating to his career, radio talks (1951-1961) for the BBC, acting school in Florence, Italy, and his mother, actress Ellen Terry; and correspondence, scripts, programs, reviews, scrapbooks, photos, and other materials, of American producer Jed Harris (?)-1979, relating to his stage productions (1926-1945).

HARRIS, JOEL CHANDLER

GA —EMORY UNIVERSITY, Robert W Woodruff Library, Atlanta, 30322. Herbert Johnson, Dir
Holdings: Mss Pix Cat
Notes: Personal papers of six Atlantans who played major parts in building the city's progressive image. Incl Joel Chandler Harris (1848-1908); William B Hartsfield, mayor, 1937-61; 1961; Richard H Rich (1901-1975), business leader; Eleonore Raoul Greene (b 1888), suffragist and organizer of the Atlanta League of Women Voters; Helen Bullard (1908-1979), public relations consultant; and Josephine Wilkins (d 1970) social reformer and founder of the Georgia Citizen's Fact Finding Movement in the 1930s. 15 linear ft mss.

VA —UNIVERSITY OF VIRGINIA, Alderman Library, Clifton Waller Barrett Collection, Charlottesville, 22901. Joan St C Crane, Cur of American Literature Collections
Notes: Papers.

HARRIS, JOHN

MA —BOSTON UNIVERSITY, Mugar Memorial Library, Special Collections Dept, 771 Commonwealth Ave, Boston, 02215. Howard B Gotlieb, Dir
Holdings: Cat Mss Correspondence

HARRIS, LANCELOT MINOR

SC —COLLEGE OF CHARLESTON LIBRARY, Special Collections Dept, Charleston, 29401.
Notes: Papers, 1872-1940, incl genealogical materials of the Harris family of Virginia and biographical material regarding Lancelot Minor Harris; incl correspondence with numerous individuals; among them Felix Adler, Thomas Della Torre, James Easterby, E M Fitzsimmons, DuBose Heyward, Ludwig Lewisohn (incl typescripts of unpublished poetry), Harrison Randolph, Herbert Ravenel Sass, Albert Simmons, Nathaniel Stephenson and Thomas Tobias; contains also material from travels in America and Europe, the Bel-Aire School in Virginia, and numerous photographs of family and friends. Within the collection are found the correspondence of Harris' wife, Carlotta, and of their family and friends not addressed to either of them.

HARRIS, LEE V.

CA —HOOVER INSTITUTION ON WAR, REVOLUTION & PEACE, Stanford University, Stanford, 94305. Milorad M Drachkovitch, Archivist
Holdings: // Mss Maps Pix
Notes: Papers, 1944-1952, of Lee V Harris, Army officer. Correspondence, memoirs, maps, photos, flags, clippings and scrapbooks, dealing with events in Vietnam, Laos and Cambodia. Incl material relating to Col Harris' military service in the China-Burma-India Theater (1944-1945); with the Marshall Mission and the Truce Team 37, Manchruia (1946-1947); and as senior military and Army attache to Vietnam and the Kingdoms of Laos and Cambodia (1950-1952). 2 boxes. Unpublished preliminary inventory in library.

HARRIS, O. H.

TX —NORTH TEXAS STATE UNIVERSITY, Archives, NT Station Box 5188, Denton, 76203. Robert LaForte, University Archivist
Notes: Part of Oral History Collection. Interviews 1969-78 with Harris, member of Texas legislature.

HARRIS, ROY

DC —LIBRARY OF CONGRESS, Music Division, Washington, 20540.
Notes: Music mss.

HARRIS, SEYMOUR

†MA —JOHN F KENNEDY LIBRARY, Columbia Point, Boston, 02125. Dan H Fenn Jr, Dir
Holdings: // Cat
Notes: Seymour Harris's collection of books and other printed materials relating to economics and public affairs. 60 linear ft of mss. Holdings are described in Historical Materials in the John F Kennedy Library. Copies may be obtained by writing the Research Archivist.

HARRIS, TOWNSEND

NY —CITY UNIVERSITY OF NEW YORK, City College, Morris R Cohen Library, North Academic Center, Convent Ave & 137th St, New York, 10031. Barbara J Dunlap, Archivist
Holdings: // Mss Microforms
Notes: Townsend Harris, the founder of the Free Academy of New York (later City College) was the first US minister to Japan. A primary record of Harris' years in Japan consists of his personal papers: five volumes of his private letterbooks, his four-volume journal, 443 letters to him, presentation letters in Japanese, his account books, and Japanese prints depicting him in his official role. These materials (except those in Japanese) have been microfilmed, and the papers may be consulted in microfilm to spare the fragile originals. The collection also contains some books about Harris, but this, of course, is not unique.

HARRIS, WILLIAM JORREY

MA —CONCORD FREE PUBLIC LIBRARY, 129 Main St, Concord, 01742. Rose Marie Mitten, Dir
Notes: Letters to W T Harris are incl in the Elizabeth Peabody and William Ellery Channing (the younger) Collections.

HARRIS FAMILY

GA —EMORY UNIVERSITY, Robert W Woodruff Library, Special Collections Dept, Atlanta, 30322. Linda M Matthews, Head Special Collections; Virginia J H Cain, Processing Archivist; Richard H F Lindemann, Reference Archivist
Holdings: Cat Mss Pix Audiotapes
Notes: Extensive collections of papers of Henry W Grady, Corra Harris, Joel Chandler Harris, Julian LaRose Harris, Julia Collier Harris, Clark Howell, Ralph E McGill, and Harold H Martin, among others, most associated with the Atlanta *Constitution.* Descriptions and index available in repository.

HARRISON, BENJAMIN

DC —LIBRARY OF CONGRESS, Manuscript Division, Washington, 20540. John C Broderick, Chief
Notes: The Presidential Papers collection incl the papers, etc, of numerous Presidents.

OH —MIAMI UNIVERSITY, King Library, Walter Havighurst Special Collections Library, Oxford, 45056. Helen Ball, Cur of Special Collections
Holdings: Uncat
Notes: Microfilms and some memorabilia. Papers of William Henry Harrison and Benjamin Harrison.

HARRISON, CARTER H.

IL —NEWBERRY LIBRARY, 60 W Walton St, Chicago, 60610. Diana Haskell, Cur of Modern Mss
Holdings: // Cat Mss
Notes: His papers. 4000 mss. Noncirculating.

HARRISON, HARRY

MD —UNIVERSITY OF MARYLAND, BALTIMORE COUNTY, Albin O Kuhn Library and Gallery, 5401 Wilkens Ave, Baltimore, 21228. Ann Copeland, Special Collections Librn
Holdings: Cat Mss
Notes: Science fiction mss.
See also entry under Science Fiction.

HARRISON, WILLIAM HENRY

DC —LIBRARY OF CONGRESS, Manuscript Division, Washington, 20540. John C Broderick, Chief
Notes: The Presidential Papers collection incl the papers, etc, of numerous Presidents.

IN —INDIANA HISTORICAL SOCIETY, Library, 315 W Ohio St, Indianapolis, 46202. Robert K O'Neill, Dir
Holdings: Vols Cat Mss Maps Pix Slides Microforms

OH —MIAMI UNIVERSITY, King Library, Walter Havighurst Special Collections Library, Oxford, 45056. Helen Ball, Cur of Special Collections
Holdings: Uncat
Notes: Microfilms and some memorabilia. Papers of William Henry Harrison and Benjamin Harrison.

HARRISSE, HENRY

MD —JOHNS HOPKINS UNIVERSITY, Milton S Eisenhower Library, Charles & 34 Sts, Baltimore, 21218. Ann S Gwyn, Assistant Dir for Special Collections
Holdings: Vols Cat
Notes: Specially strong in the works of

HARRISSE, HENRY (cont.)

Henry Harrisse. 83 titles, some rare, belonged to the author.

HARROD, SIR ROY

DC —GEORGETOWN UNIVERSITY, Library, Special Collections Div, 37 & O Sts NW, Washington, 20057. George M Barringer, Special Collections Librn; Nicholas B Sheetz, Mss Librn
Holdings: Cat Mss
Notes: The papers of the English author, journalist, and historian Douglas Woodruff (1897-1978), containing correspondence, mss, and photographs. Incl is considerable material concerning his years at Oxford University; his editorship for many years of The "Tablet"; English Catholic society in general and English Catholic literature in particular. Also present are research files on the Tichborne Claimant, one of the most famous cases of impersonation in English legal history. There is extensive correspondence from such figures as: Hilaire Belloc; Tom Burns; Rev Martin D'Arcy, SJ; Christopher Dawson; Sir Roy Harrod; Christopher Hollis; Msgr Ronald Knox; Sir Shane Leslie; Sir Arnold Lunn; Rebecca West; and Evelyn Waugh.

HARROUN, P. E.

NM —MUSEUM OF NEW MEXICO, Photo Archives, Box 2087, Santa Fe, 87503. Arthur L Olivas, Cur; Richard Rudisill, Photo Historian
Holdings: Cat Pix Slides
Notes: Extensive collection of his work.

HART, B. H. LIDDELL

CA —CLAREMONT COLLEGES, Honnold Library, Ninth & Dartmouth, Claremont, 91711. Tania Rizzo, Special Collections Dept Head
Holdings: Vols 50 Cat Mss
Notes: Correspondence to Merle Armitage now in the George E Fullerton collection.

HART, HENRY MELVIN, 1904-1969

MA —HARVARD UNIVERSITY LIBRARY, Law School Library, Langdell Hall, Cambridge, 02138. Erika S Chadbourn, Cur of Mss
Holdings: Cat Mss
Notes: Professional papers. Typed inventory in repository. Inclusive dates: 1927-1969.

HART, MOSS, AND GEORGE S. KAUFMAN

NY —HAMPDEN-BOOTH THEATRE LIBRARY AT THE PLAYERS, 16 Gramercy Park, New York, 10003. Louis A Rachow, Librn/Cur
Holdings: Mss Pix
Notes: The Franklin Heller Collection, incl correspondence, photographs; playscripts by Moss Hart and George S Kaufman, John Steinbeck, Thomas Wolfe, and others. (110 items). Described in *Theatre & Performing Arts Collections* (New York: Haworth Press, 1981).

HART, PEARL

IL —CHICAGO HISTORICAL SOCIETY, Library, Clark St at North Ave, Chicago, 60614. Archie Motley, Manuscript Librn
Notes: Papers of: Emmet Dedmon, newspaper editor; Richard J Finnegan, newspaper editor; Rev Andres M Greeley, sociologist and author; attorney and civil liberties activist Pearl Hart; Robert J Havighurst, educator; social activist John Kearney; Kenesaw Mountain Landis, Federal Judge and first Commissioner of Baseball; Judge David F Matchett; Ivan Molek, Slovenian language publisher in Chicago; Max R Naiman, Communist Party activist; Ralph G Newman, book and autograph dealer and manuscript appraiser; Otto L Schmidt, physician and President of the Chicago and Illinois State Historical Societites; and Dempsey Travis, black mortgage banker.

HART, ROSA

LA —MCNEESE STATE UNIVERSITY, Lether E Frazar Library, Ryan St, Lake Charles, 70609. Kathie Bordelon, Special Collections Librn
Notes: Personal collection of Rosa Hart including Little Theatre scrapbooks, correspondence, playbills, photographs. Rosa Hart was director of the Little Theatre in Lake Charles for over 30 years achieving national recognition for her talents.

HARTE, BRET, 1836-1902

CA —UNIVERSITY OF CALIFORNIA, LOS ANGELES, Research Library, Dept of Special Collections, 405 Hilgard Ave, Los Angeles, 90024. Edward Shreeves, Chairman, Bibliographers Group; David S Zeidberg, Head
Holdings: Vols 650
Notes: 650 first and other editions of his books; 300 letters; 7 linear feet of articles and ephemera.

IN —DEPAUW UNIVERSITY, Roy O West Library, PO Box 137, Greencastle, 46135. James A Martindale, Dir
Holdings: Vols // Uncat Mss
Notes: Described in: Dozer, Russell S *The Bret Harte Library of First Editions.* Greencastle, Ind: DePauw University, 1958 (21 pp unbound pamphlet) available upon request. Downs 1698; Suppl 1950-1961.

NY —HOFSTRA UNIVERSITY, Library, 1000 Fulton Ave, Hempstead, 11550. Charles R Andrews, Dean of Library Services

†NY —COLUMBIA UNIVERSITY LIBRARIES, Butler Library, Rare Book and Manuscript Library, 535 W 114 St, New York, 10027.
Notes: Works by Bret Harte, first editions, etc.

PA —FREE LIBRARY OF PHILADELPHIA, Rare Book Dept, Logan Sq, Philadelphia, 19103. Marie E Korey, Rare Book Librn
Holdings: Vols (70) Uncat
Notes: The Edward F R Wood Collection of first editions.

PA —UNIVERSITY OF PENNSYLVANIA, Van Pelt Library, Rare Books Collection, 34 & Walnut Sts, Philadelphia, 19104. Daniel Traister, Special Collections Librn
Holdings: Vols 100 Cat
Notes: Downs (Supplement) 1699.

TX —SOUTHERN METHODIST UNIVERSITY, DeGolyer Library, Box 396, SMU, Dallas, 75275. Clifton H Jones, Dir
Holdings: Vols (80,000) Cat Mss Maps Pix Slides Microforms
Notes: First editions of prominent authors; also of books in subject emphasis collections. All subjects listed in this vol are strong. Numerous collections of personal papers relating to subjects also.

VA —UNIVERSITY OF VIRGINIA, Alderman Library, Clifton Waller Barrett Collection, Charlottesville, 22901. Joan St C Crane, Cur of American Literature Collections
Holdings: Vols 300 Cat Mss
Notes: Bibliography: Lucy Trimble Clark, comp, *The Barrett Library Bret Hartes: A Checklist of Printed and Manuscript Works of Francis Bret Harte in the Library of the University of Virginia* (Charlottesville: University of Virginia Press, 1957).

HARTFORD, CONNECTICUT

CT —CONNECTICUT HISTORICAL SOCIETY, One Elizabeth St, Hartford, 06105. Christopher Bickford, Dir
Notes: Over 70,000 books and periodicals, 3500 bound vols of newspapers, and thousands of broadsides, maps, prints, and photographs pertaining to Connecticut. Also, more than 1 1/2 million historical mss; incl personal correspondence, diaries, account books, business records, and town materials dating from the earliest settlement. Extensive New England town and county histories.

CT —HARTFORD PUBLIC LIBRARY, Reference & General Reading Dept, 500 Main St, Hartford, 06103. Beverly A Loughlin, Admin Asst
Holdings: Vols (3000) Cat Mss Maps Pix Slides Phonorecords Audiotapes Videotapes 16mm Films
Notes: The Hartford Collection is a noncirculating multimedia collection encompassing Hartford: histories of businesses, churches, schools, and organizations; Hartford authors; and Hartford imprints. Separate catalog.

CT —TRINITY COLLEGE LIBRARY, Watkinson Library, 300 Summit St, Hartford, 06106. Jeffrey Kaimowitz, Cur
Holdings: Cat Mss Maps Pix Slides Microforms
Notes: Incl Hartford Imprints.

HARTLEY, LESLIE POLES

NV —UNIVERSITY OF NEVADA, RENO, University Library, Special Collections Dept, Reno, 89557. Robert E Blesse, Head
Holdings: // Vols (44) Cat
Notes: Includes individual works by author in all editions including translations; also prefaces, introductions, published correspondence, appearances in anthologies, periodicals, etc. Bibliographical research collection, part of Modern Authors Collection. Other appearances 65 cataloged.

HARTLEY, MARSDEN

CT —YALE UNIVERSITY, Box 1603A, Yale Station, New Haven, 06520.
Holdings: Cat Mss

HARTMANN, SADAKICHI

CA —UNIVERSITY OF CALIFORNIA, RIVERSIDE, University Library, 4045 Canyon Crest Dr, Box 5900, Riverside, 92517.
Holdings: Cat Mss Pix Offprints
Notes: In-depth collection of manuscripts, printed works and correspondence by and about Sadakichi Hartmann. Much of the material concerns photography, incl an extensive collection of offprints and photographs; 7 letters from Ezra Pound. There is a 140p published guide to the collection.
See also entry under Pound, Ezra Loomis

HARTNELL, WILLIAM EDWARD PETTY

CA —UNIVERSITY OF SAN FRANCISCO, Richard A Gleeson Library, The Countess Bernardine Murphy Donohue Rare Book Room, San Francisco, 94117. D Steven Corey, Special Collections Librn
Holdings: Mss
Notes: Papers of William Edward Petty Hartnell was an early settler of Monterey, Calif. His business ledger for June 1822 to January 1826 and his litterbook for July 1823 to September 1831.

HARVARD UNIVERSITY—LIBRARIES

IL —UNIVERSITY OF ILLINOIS, URBANA/CHAMPAIGN, Library, 1408 W Gregory Drive, Urbana, 61801. Norman B Brown, Asst Dir for Special Collections
Notes: The Alfred Kaimang Chiu Collection of books on Chinese library administration (240 in Chinese; 170 in English), with pamphlets, manuscripts, etc, incl essays on Chinese economics. Chiu was the first librarian of the Harvard-Yenching Library at Harvard University, 1931-1965.

HARVARD-YENCHING LIBRARY see Harvard University—Libraries

HARVESTING MACHINES

CA —UNIVERSITY OF CALIFORNIA, DAVIS, Shields Library, Dept of Special

HARVESTING MACHINES (cont.)

Collections, Davis, 95616. Donald Kunitz, Head; C Danial Elliott, Asst Head
Notes: Farming equipment: Manufacturer's catalogs, manuals, parts lists, ephemera, and literature pertaining to historical as well as current data on such items as tractors, engines, combines, hay equipment, etc. Described in "The Higgins Library: A Source for the Study of Agricultural History," Don Kunitz, *Agricultural History,* vol 49, 1975, pp 89-91.

HARVEY, FRED, INCORPORATED

AZ —NORTHERN ARIZONA UNIVERSITY, Special Collection Library, CU Box 6022, Flagstaff, 86011. Peter M Whiteley, Coordr/Archivist; William Mullane, Librn
Notes: Newsletters covering the period from 1969-1978.

HARVEY, WILLIAM, 1578-1657

CT —YALE UNIVERSITY, Medical Historical Library, 333 Cedar St, New Haven, 06510. Ferenc A Gyorgyey, Librn
Holdings: Vols 220 Cat
Notes: Plus 161 Harveian orations.

NY —NEW YORK ACADEMY OF MEDICINE, Library, 2 E 103 St, New York, 10029. Brett A Kirkpatrick, Librn
Holdings: Vols 45 Cat
Notes: Copies of varying editions of Harvey's writings, including two first editions of De Motu Cordis; part ofthe Robert L Levy Collection on cardiology.

PA —COLLEGE OF PHYSICIANS OF PHILADELPHIA, Library, 19 S 22 St, Philadelphia, 19103. Christine Ruggere, Cur, Historical Collections
Holdings: Vols (316,223) Cat Mss
Budget: ($1,096,557)
Notes: Very strong collection.
See also entry under Medicine.

HARWOOD FORESTRY RESEARCH FELLOWSHIP PROGRAM

GA —UNIVERSITY OF GEORGIA, Libraries, Athens, 30602. Arlene E Luchsinger, Asst Dir Branch Libraries
Notes: Collection of over 1000 photographs on Southern forestry and the Southern logging industry, 1939-46. This gift, from the Southern Forest Institute, includes the records and files of four groups formed to solve specific problems of Southern forests.

HASHISH

CA —FITZ HUGH LUDLOW MEMORIAL LIBRARY, PO Box 99346, San Francisco, 94109. Michael R Aldrich, Exec Cur
Holdings: Vols (500) Cat Mss Maps Pix Slides Phonorecords Audiotapes Videotapes
Notes: Collection stored. Important mail inquiries only. No interlibrary loan or telephone queries. We collect many old pharmacopoeias, dispensatories, formularies, medical history books and records, old pharmaceutical bottles and labels, etc valuable for researching the history of psychoactive drug use. Incl a small but valuable collection of works on anesthesia and toxicology.

HASIDISM

FL —UNIVERSITY OF FLORIDA LIBRARY, Isser and Rae Price Library of Judaica, 18 Libr East, Gainesville, 32611. Robert Singerman, Head Librn
Budget: ($30,000)
Notes: Total holdings estimated at 55,000 vols dealing with the political, social, economic and intellectual history of the Jews in the ancient, medieval and modern periods and in all geographic areas. The following areas are especially well represented by printed matter in all relevant languages: Bibliography, Festschriften, History, Bible, Judaism and Jewish theology, liturgy, responsa, rabbinical literature, Jewish law, Hebrew language and literature, Yiddish language and literature, anti-semitism, Zionism, Palestine and the *Yishuv,* and the State of Israel. German and American Judaica form a collecting emphasis with holdings for all the standard histories as well as histories of individual synagogues, institutions and local communities. Works in Hebrew and Yiddish comprise about 60 percent of the collection (estimated 30,000 vols). With few exceptions, holdingsare limited to nineteenth and twentieth century imprints, with complete sets of journals and thousands of ephemeral pamphlets, many of them commemorating anniversaries, enhancing the research value of the collection, the largest Judaica research library in the southeastern United States. Only about half of the collection is cataloged; the collection is a circulating one and vols may be borrowed on interlibrary loan. Incl the Leonard C Mishkin Collection (40,000 vols), the largest personal Judaica collection in the United States, the Shlomo Marenof Collection (3500 vols), and the inventory of Bernard Morgenstern's Lower East Side Book Store (8000 vols). Scholars should inquire in advance of their visit. *The Isser and Rae Price Library of Judaica* Report (circulation 2900 copies) is mailed gratis twice a year to all interested parties. Special catalogs:Pre-1881 Hebrew imprints recorded in a chronological card file.

IA —UNIVERSITY OF IOWA, University Libraries, Iowa City, 52242.
Holdings: Vols 1850 Mss
Notes: The Leo W Schwarz Collection, a valuable and rare group of books dealing with Hasidic literature, a portion on Old Testament studies and works on Jewish history, philosophy and culture, the Jews in Nazi Germany, Jewish folklore and the history of the Jews in the US. Incl about 850 books in Hebrew and 1000 in other languages, mss of several of Schwarz's books and articles, correspondence, notes, and background research relating to his publications.

MA —HEBREW COLLEGE, Jacob & Rose Grossman Library and Lawrence Jay & Anne Cable Rubenstein Library, 43 Hawes St, Brookline, 02146. Maurice Tuchman, Librn
Holdings: Vols 600 Cat Mss
Notes: Hassidic and Cabalistic literature.

NY —NEW YORK PUBLIC LIBRARY, Jewish Division, Fifth Ave & 42 St, New York, 10018. Leonard S Gold, Chief
Holdings: Vols (200,000) Cat Mss Microforms
Budget: ($33,383)
Notes: A collection of material in all languages on Judaism, Jewish history, literature and traditions from the earliest times to date and works in the Hebrew alphabet (mainly Hebrew and Yiddish) on a variety of subjects. The division has extensive files of Jewish periodicals and newspapers. The collection of rare Hebraica incl medieval texts, cabalistic works, ethical and philosophical tracts in book form. See *Dictionary Catalog of the Jewish Collection* (Boston: G K Hall, 1960), 14 vols. First Supplement (Boston: G K Hall, 1975), 8 vols.

HASKELL, ARTHUR

MA —SOCIETY FOR THE PRESERVATION OF NEW ENGLAND ANTIQUITIES, Library, 141 Cambridge St, Boston, 02114. Ellie Reichlin, Librn & Cur of Photographic Collections
Notes: Over 125 sets of survey sheets (full-scale, some originals) for historic buildings throughout New England, strongest for Massachusetts and New Hampshire; original photographs of Massachusetts structures by HABS photographer Arthur Haskell; office files of Massachusetts HABS Director, Frank Chouteau Brown, with measured details, sketchbooks, correspondence, notes for surveys, not all of them reported to HABS in Washington. Original measured drawings of historic structures by the Emergency Planning and Research Bureau, Architectural Division, predecessor to HABS. Ca 2000 pieces; 1200 photographs.

HASKINS, CHARLES HOMER, 1870-1937

NJ —PRINCETON UNIVERSITY, Library, Manuscript Collection, Nassau St, Princeton, 08540. Jean F Preston, Cur
Holdings: / / Cat Mss
Notes: Incl 35 boxes; 30 cartons of papers. An unpublished typescript guide (21p) is available in the Library.

HASSID, WILLIAM ZEV

CA —UNIVERSITY OF CALIFORNIA, BERKELEY, Bancroft Library, Manuscripts Division, Berkeley, 94720. James D Hart, Dir
Notes: Correspondence and papers relative to the history of modern chemistry.

HASSLER, FERDINAND RUDOLF

NY —NEW YORK PUBLIC LIBRARY, Rare Books and Manuscripts Div, Fifth Ave & 42 St, New York, 10018. William L Joyce, Asst Dir; Susan E Davis, Cur of Mss
Holdings: Mss
Budget: ($7161)
Notes: Incl personal and literary mss, papers, etc.

HASTIC, WILLIAM HENRY

MA —HARVARD UNIVERSITY LIBRARY, Law School Library, Langdell Hall, Cambridge, 02138. Harry S Martin III, Librn
Notes: Personal and legal papers of William Henry Hastic, Governor of the Virgin Islands, Judge of the US Court of Appeals, Third Circuit, who died in April 1976. Much on his involvement in civic and antidiscrimination cases.

HASTIE, WILLIAM HENRY, 1904-1976

MA —HARVARD UNIVERSITY LIBRARY, Law School Library, Langdell Hall, Cambridge, 02138. Erika S Chadbourn, Cur of Mss
Holdings: Cat Mss
Notes: Personal-professional and judicial papers. Printed inventory: *William Henry Hastie: An Inventory of His Papers in the Harvard Law School Library,* Manuscript Division, Harvard Law School Library, 1984. Inclusive dates: 1916-1976.

HASTINGS, MACDONALD

MA —BOSTON UNIVERSITY, Mugar Memorial Library, Special Collections Dept, 771 Commonwealth Ave, Boston, 02215. Howard B Gotlieb, Dir
Holdings: Mss
Notes: Mss, correspondence, etc collected in depth; incl publications by or about.

HASTINGS, MICHAEL, 1937-

NY —STATE UNIVERSITY OF NEW YORK, STONY BROOK, Melville Library, Dept of Special Collections, Stony Brook, 11794. Evert Volkersz, Head
Holdings: Cat Mss

HATCH, CARL ATWOOD

OK —UNIVERSITY OF OKLAHOMA, Bizzell Memorial Library, Western History Collections, 401 W Brooks, Norman, 73069. John Ezell, Cur
Holdings: Documents
Notes: US Senator. His papers. Guide available.

HATCH, ERIC

MA —BOSTON UNIVERSITY, Mugar Memorial Library, Special Collections Dept, 771 Commonwealth Ave, Boston, 02215. Howard B Gotlieb, Dir
Holdings: Cat Mss Pix
Notes: Mss, correspondence, etc collected in depth; incl publications by or about.

HATHAWAY, HENRY

CA —AMERICAN FILM INSTITUTE, Louis B Mayer Library, 2021 N Western Ave, PO Box 27999, Los Angeles, 90027. Anne G Schlosser, Dir
Holdings: Vols (3500) Cat
Notes: The Henry Hathaway Collection contains scripts (annotated) and scrapbooks with clippings, memos, photographs, etc.

HATHEWAY FAMILY

NY —CORNELL UNIVERSITY LIBRARIES, Collection of Regional History, Dept of Manuscripts and Univ Archives, Ithaca, 14853.
Notes: Incl papers, 1788-ca 1900. Samuel Gilbert Hatheway (1780-1867) was a US Congressman, Senator, and holder of other governmental positions. His papers consist mainly of correspondence, commission certificates, petitions, and other records. Papers of his eldest son, Samuel Gilbert, Jr., (1810-64), attorney, assemblyman, and Civil War officer, incl personal and professional correspondence, certificates, political speeches, and military records. Also incl are papers of several other family members.

HAUGEN, GILBERT

IA —STATE HISTORICAL SOCIETY OF IOWA LIBRARY, 402 Iowa Ave, Iowa City, 52240. Darold J Brown, Librn
Holdings: Cat
Notes: Thousands of individual items and smaller collections. Two hundred larger collections incl the papers of Cyrus C Carpenter, Jonathan P Dolliver, Gilbert Haugen, W W Waymack, Ephraim Adams, A C Dodge, Dorothy Houghton, Jesse Macy, Agnes Samuelson, Donald Johnson, Jack Miller, Ruth Sayre, Samuel Kirkwood, Thomas McKnight, Robert Lucas, Dwight McCarty, William Larrabee. Includes church, school, company and organization records, Civil War materials.

HAUNTED HOUSES see Ghosts

HAUPTMANN, GERHART

CT —YALE UNIVERSITY, Box 1603A, Yale Station, New Haven, 06520.
Notes: See Gerhart Hauptmann Collection in American and England, by Klau W Jonas, *Stechert-Hafner Book News,* xxvi, no 6, (February 1971), pp 77-82.

DC —LIBRARY OF CONGRESS, Washington, 20540.

IN —INDIANA UNIVERSITY, Lilly Library, Seventh St, Bloomington, 47405. William R Cagle, Librn
Holdings: Cat Mss Pix
Notes: Correspondence of Gerhart Hauptmann and his wife with his publisher Samuel Fischer, 1890-1949 (686 items). Collection includes 9 Hauptmann manuscripts.

MA —HARVARD UNIVERSITY LIBRARY, Cambridge, 02138.

NY —STATE UNIVERSITY OF NEW YORK, BINGHAMTON, Glenn G Bartle Library, Binghamton, 13901. Marion Hanscom, Special Collections Librn
Holdings: Cat

NY —ADELPHI UNIVERSITY, Library, Garden City, 11530. Jerome Yavarkovsky, Dean of Libraries
Holdings: Vols 347// Cat Mss Pix Phonorecords

NY —COLUMBIA UNIVERSITY LIBRARIES, Rare Book & Manuscript Library, 801 Butler Library, 535 W 114 St, New York, 10027. Kenneth A Lohf, Librn
Holdings: Mss
Notes: Mss of Frederick William Justus Heuser, chiefly relating to his studies of Gerhart Hauptmann. 2500 items. Restricted use.

PA —BIBLIOGRAPHICAL CENTER OF GERMAN LITERATURE, University of Pittsburgh, Dept of Germanic Languages & Literatures, 102 Loeffler Bldg, Pittsburgh, 15260. Klaus W Jonas, Dir
Holdings: Cat Mss Pix Microforms
Notes: Center for the development of collections and bibliographical control of the record of publications, mss, correspondence, etc, by or relating to modern German authors. Special sections have been developed for Mann, Rilke, Hauptmann, Hesse, Broch, Sachs and others. Described by Professor Klaus W Jonas's "The German Literature Center in Pittsburgh," *Stechert-Hafner Book News,* vol 24, no 8, April 1970; "Documentation in Modern German Literature: A Progress Report," *Jahrbuch fuer Internationale Germanistik,* vol 4, no 2, 1972, and in *German and Austrian Contributions to World Literature* (1890-1970). Department of Germanic Languages and Literatures, University of Pittsburgh, 1983. 96 pp.

HAUSA LANGUAGE AND LITERATURE

IL —NORTHWESTERN UNIVERSITY, Melville J Herskovits Library of African Studies, Evanston, 60201. Hans E Panofsky, Cur
Notes: Collected in depth. Incl a complete set of the recordings by and on African authors assembled by the Transcription Centre, London. Also, about 3000 books and pamphlets on African languages.

NY —NEW YORK PUBLIC LIBRARY, Oriental Div, Fifth Ave & 42 St, New York, 10018. E Christian Filstrup, Chief
Holdings: Cat Mss Microforms
Budget: ($56,455)
Notes: Published catalog of holdings.

PA —DUQUESNE UNIVERSITY, Library, 600 Forbes Ave, Pittsburgh, 15219.
Holdings: Vols (7407) Cat Maps Slides Microforms
Notes: Mostly concerned with Africa south of the Sahara. CIDESA file (Centre International de Documentation Economique et Social Africaine) contains material dealing with economic and social problems of the African continent. Collection strong in materials of economics and Hausa and Swahili languages.

HAUSDORFER, WALTER, 1898-1970

PA —TEMPLE UNIVERSITY LIBRARIES, Special Collections Dept, Conwellana-Templana Collection, 13 & Berks St, Philadelphia, 19122. Miriam I Crawford, Cur
Holdings: Vols 22 // Cat Mss Pix
Budget: ($30,000)
Notes: Papers of Walter Hausdorfer, librarian of the Columbia University School of Business, 1930-46 and Temple University from 1946-61, professor of bibliography from 1961-63, and a noted linguist and authority on rare books and mss.

HAVASUPAI INDIANS

AZ —NORTHERN ARIZONA UNIVERSITY, Special Collection Library, CU Box 6022, Flagstaff, 86011. Peter M Whiteley, Coordr/Archivist; William Mullane, Librn
Holdings: Mss Pix
Notes: H C Whitener Collection: Zuni language research notes and religious and Biblical translations in the Zuni language. Incl one folder on the Havasupai language. Florence Barker Collection: She was a missionary nurse for the Navajo, Havasupai, Acoma and Laguna Indian Reservations. Incl diaries, 1922-1927.

HAVIGHURST, ROBERT J.

IL —CHICAGO HISTORICAL SOCIETY, Library, Clark St at North Ave, Chicago, 60614. Archie Motley, Manuscript Librn
Notes: Papers of: Emmet Dedmon, newspaper editor; Richard J Finnegan, newspaper editor; Rev Andres M Greeley, sociologist and author; attorney and civil liberties activist Pearl Hart; Robert J Havighurst, educator; social activist John Kearney; Kenesaw Mountain Landis, Federal Judge and first Commissioner of Baseball; Judge David F Matchett; Ivan Molek, Slovenian language publisher in Chicago; Max R Naiman, Communist Party activist; Ralph G Newman, book and autograph dealer and manuscript appraiser; Otto L Schmidt, physician and President of the Chicago and Illinois State Historical Societites; and Dempsey Travis, black mortgage banker.

HAWAII

CA —LOS ANGELES PUBLIC LIBRARY, Science & Technology Dept, 630 W Fifth St, Los Angeles, 90071. Billie M Connor, Dept Head
Holdings: Vols 18,000 Maps Microforms
Notes: Extensive holdings of state geology department publications and maps of the Western state including Alaska and Hawaii, US Geology Survey, US Bureau of Mines, and the geology departments of major universities. Complete sets of publications and indexes of major geological societies including the Geological Society of American and the American Association of Petroleum Geologists. Partially cataloged.

CT —YALE UNIVERSITY, Box 1603A, Yale Station, New Haven, 06520.

HI —BERNICE P BISHOP MUSEUM, Library, PO Box 19000-A, Honolulu, 96819. Cynthia Timberlake, Librn
Holdings: Vols (90,000) Cat Mss Maps Pix Slides Microforms
Budget: ($30,000)
Notes: Only American library devoted exclusively to the Pacific region. Collection reflects historical and contemporary research emphases of Bishop Museum; ie the natural and cultural history of the Pacific. Areas of concentration incl archaeology, ethnology, linguistics, voyages and explorations, history, vertebrate and invertebrate zoology, botany and museology. Strong special collections incl photographs, mss and archives, maps and art. Publications: Quarterly "Additions to the Catalog," *Dictionary Catalog of the* Library (9 vols and 2 suppl; Boston: G K Hall, 1964-69).

†HI —EAST-WEST POPULATION INSTITUTE RESOURCE MATERIALS COLLECTION, 1777 East-West Rd, Honolulu, 96848.
Notes: Demography, population problems and policy in Hawaii, Asian countries and Pacific area, family planning programs, environment.

HI —HAWAII STATE LIBRARY, Hawaii & Pacific Collection, 478 S King St, Honolulu, 96813. Proserfina Strona, Acting Head
Holdings: Vols (93,834) Cat Microforms
Budget: ($30,000)
Notes: Publish cumulative index of Hawaii State Documents biennially and an index to the *Honolulu Advertiser* and *Honolulu* Star-Bulletin annually. Also print bibliographies of special interest, such as ethnic bibliographies, Aloha Week celebrations, etc. Depository for county and state documents.

HI —LEGISLATIVE REFERENCE BUREAU, Library, State Capitol, Rm 005, Honolulu, 96813. Ms Hanako Kobayashi, Research Librn
Holdings: Vols (70,000) Cat
Budget: $12,450

†HI —PACIFIC BIO-MEDICAL RESEARCH CENTER, 41 Ahui St, Honolulu, 96813.

HI —PACIFIC SCIENTIFIC INFORMATION CENTER, Bernice P Bishop Library, Geography and Map Division, PO Box 19000A, Honolulu, 96819. Lee S Motteler, Geographer; Valerie T Higa, Asst Geographer
Holdings: Vols (2000) Cat Mss Maps Pix
Notes: Incl 20,000 maps and 70,000 aerial photos of Hawaii and the Pacific.

HI —UNIVERSITY OF HAWAII, Library, 2550 The Mall, Honolulu, 96822. David Kittelson, Hawaiian Cur
Holdings: Vols (65,000) Cat Microforms
Budget: ($2000)
Notes: This is a comprehensive collection of material published in and about Hawaii,

HAWAII (cont.)

including especially 20th century publications, and University of Hawaii publications and theses. The Collection publishes *Current Hawaiiana*, a quarterly bibliography of recently available publications. There is a separate Hawaiian Collection card catalog; it was published in 1963 by G K Hall as a 4-volume set.

MA —HARVARD UNIVERSITY LIBRARY, Widener Library, Cambridge, 02138.
Holdings: Cat Mss Microforms
Notes: Incl files or early newspapers.

MA —AMERICAN ANTIQUARIAN SOCIETY LIBRARY, 185 Salisbury St, Worcester, 01609. Marcus A McCorison, Dir & Librn
Holdings: Vols 18,000 Cat
Notes: Strongest for New York, Pennsylvania, Massachusetts and Connecticut. Incl Canada, Hawaii, Mexico, the West Indies; also Pennsylvania German. About 18,000 or 90 percent of the almanacs and yearbooks known to have been printed in the United States before 1850; the Latin American and Canadian collections are the most complete in this country.

MI —UNIVERSITY OF MICHIGAN, Library, Dept of Rare Books & Special Collections, Ann Arbor, 48109. Robert J Starring, Head
Holdings: Cat Mss
Notes: Incl in addition to miscellaneous published items, material pertaining to David L Gregg, US Commissioner of Hawaii and Minister of Finance. Gregg's diaries from 1853 to 1857, official correspondence, and private papers, all transcribed or photographed, and transcripts of Federal archival material relating to Hawaii. A few early Hawaiian periodicals.

NY —AMERICAN MUSEUM OF NATURAL HISTORY, Library Services Dept, Central Park W & 79th St, New York, 10024. Nina J Root, Chairwoman; Mary Genett, Asst Librn for Reference Services

HAWAII—ECONOMIC DEVELOPMENT

HI —BANK OF HAWAII, Information Ctr, PO Box 2900, Honolulu, 96846. Sally Campbell, Information Mgr
Holdings: Vols 4000 Cat Maps VF
Notes: Economics research in developing areas of Hawaii, US Pacific Islands, Asian and other foreign countries. Emphasis on economics, business statistics, demography, finance, banking, tourist industry, construction, domestic and foreign trade. Incl 1000 serial titles.

HAWAII—HISTORY

CA —HOOVER INSTITUTION ON WAR, REVOLUTION & PEACE, Stanford University, Stanford, 94305. Milorad M Drachkovitch, Archivist
Notes: Typewritten documentation of events and conditions leading up to the Japanese attack on Pearl Harbor, December 7, 1941, assembled by Lt Gen W C Short, Commanding General, US Army Hawaiian Department, for his defense before the Roberts Commission, which investigated the attack.

DC —LIBRARY OF CONGRESS, Rare Book & Special Collections Div, Washington, 20540. William Matheson, Chief
Notes: 19th century government documents, schoolbooks, religious books, missionary tracts that are the first results of the effort to form an Hawaiian printed language.

HI —LYMAN HOUSE MEMORIAL MUSEUM, 276 Haili St, Hilo, 96720. Christina Lothian, Librn & Archivist
Holdings: Vols 5000 Cat Maps Pix Slides
Notes: Incl some 10,000 pictures, 2000 bound books, letters, maps, documents. Old New England newspapers (500) 1806-1900. Reference Library only.

HI —BERNICE P BISHOP MUSEUM, Library, PO Box 19000-A, Honolulu, 96819. Cynthia Timberlake, Librn
Notes: Early voyages, natural and general history, archaeology, and ethnology of the Pacific area. Hawaiian materials incl mss, maps, 360,000 photographs dating from 1845, and Hawaiian language newspapers.

HI —HAWAIIAN HISTORICAL SOCIETY LIBRARY, 560 Kawaiahao St, Honolulu, 96813. Barbara E Dunn, Librn
Holdings: Vols (11,000) Cat Mss Maps Pix Microforms Newspapers Scrapbooks
Notes: Particular strength in Hawaiian materials--voyages and travels; guidebooks; city directories; histories of Hawaii; both primary and secondary sources. Collection also incl Oceania; Polynesia, Micronesia, Melanesia. No photocopying.

HI —HAWAIIAN MISSION CHILDREN'S SOCIETY LIBRARY, 553 S King St, Honolulu, 96813. Mary Jane Knight, Librn
Holdings: Vols 15,000 Cat Mss Pix
Notes: Missionary period of Hawaiian history, 1819-1864, plus family and Congregational Church in Hawaii to 1947, incl a general collection of Hawaiian history and travel, an outstanding collection of early voyages to the Pacific, and an almost complete collection of early Hawaiian imprints, ie, publications in the Hawaiian language during the 19th century. Ms material incl letters, journals and reports of the Protestant missionaries who came to Hawaii (the Sandwich Islands) under the auspices of the American Board of Commissioners for Foreign Missions. The material is for research only; the stacks are closed. Unpublished papers may be examined by qualified researchers on application to the librarian. Published material is cataloged. Hawaiian imprints are cataloged,except for the Dewey classification 300's which are mainly government documents. Ms collections are cataloged or in the process of being completely arranged and cataloged.

†HI —HAWAII CHINESE HISTORY CENTER, 111 North King St, No 410, Honolulu, 96817.
Notes: Chinese in Hawaii and mainland US.

HI —HAWAII STATE LIBRARY, Hawaii & Pacific Collection, 478 S King St, Honolulu, 96813. Proserfina Strona, Acting Head
Holdings: Vols (93,834) Cat Microforms
Budget: ($30,000)
Notes: Publish cumulative index of Hawaii State Documents biennially and an Index to the *Honolulu Advertiser* and *Honolulu* Star-Bulletin annually. Also print bibliographies of special interest, such as ethnic bibliogrhies, Aloha Week celebrations, etc. Depository for county and state documents.

HI —UNIVERSITY OF HAWAII, Library, 2550 The Mall, Honolulu, 96822. David Kittelson, Hawaiian Cur
Holdings: Vols (65,000) Cat Microforms
Budget: ($2000)
Notes: This is a comprehensive collection of material published in and about Hawaii, including especially 20th century publications, and University of Hawaii publications and theses. The Collection publishes *Current Hawaiiana*, a quarterly bibliography of recently available publications. There is a separate Hawaiian Collection card catalog; it was published in 1963 by G K Hall as a 4-volume set.

HI —MAUI HISTORICAL SOCIETY, Research Library, 2375A Main St, PO Box 1018, Wailuku, 96793. Virginia Wirtz, Museum Dir
Holdings: Vols (300) Cat Mss Maps Pix
Budget: ($500)
Notes: History of Hawaii, especially Maui County. Incl newspaper clipping file, 1957-date. Incl state government publications.

IL —NEWBERRY LIBRARY, 60 W Walton St, Chicago, 60610. Diana Haskell, Cur of Modern Mss
Holdings: Cat Mss Pix
Notes: History and linguistics to 1915. Consult published lists. Very strong in early imprints.

HAWAII—IMPRINTS

DC —LIBRARY OF CONGRESS, Rare Book & Special Collections Div, Washington, 20540. William Matheson, Chief
Notes: 19th century government documents, schoolbooks, religious books, missionary tracts that are the first results of the effort to form an Hawaiian printed language.

HI —HAWAIIAN MISSION CHILDREN'S SOCIETY LIBRARY, 553 S King St, Honolulu, 96813. Mary Jane Knight, Librn
Holdings: Vols (15,000) Cat
Notes: Almost complete collection of early Hawaiian imprints.

HI —UNIVERSITY OF HAWAII, Library, 2550 The Mall, Honolulu, 96822. David Kittelson, Hawaiian Cur
Holdings: Vols (65,000) Cat Microforms
Budget: ($2000)
Notes: This is a comprehensive collection of material published in and about Hawaii, including especially 20th century publications, and University of Hawaii publications and theses. The Collection publishes *Current Hawaiiana*, a quarterly bibliography of recently available publications. There is a separate Hawaiian Collection card catalog; it was published in 1963 by G K Hall as a 4-volume set.

IL —NEWBERRY LIBRARY, 60 W Walton St, Chicago, 60610. Diana Haskell, Cur of Modern Mss
Holdings: Cat
Notes: Very strong in early imprints.

HAWAII—MAPS

CA —LOS ANGELES PUBLIC LIBRARY, Science & Technology Dept, 630 W Fifth St, Los Angeles, 90071. Billie M Connor, Dept Head
Notes: Extensive holdings of state geology department publications and maps of the Western states including Alaska and Hawaii, US Geological Survey, US Bureau of Mines, and the geology departments of major universities. Complete sets of publications and indexes of major geological societies including the Geological Society of American and the American Association of Petroleum Geologists. Partially cataloged.

HI —PACIFIC SCIENTIFIC INFORMATION CENTER, Bernice P Bishop Library, Geography and Map Division, PO Box 19000A, Honolulu, 96819. Lee S Motteler, Geographer; Valerie T Higa, Asst Geographer
Notes: Incl 20,000 maps and 70,000 aerial photos of Hawaii and the Pacific.

HAWAII—PICTURES, ILLUSTRATIONS, ETC.

HI —BERNICE P BISHOP MUSEUM, Library, PO Box 19000-A, Honolulu, 96819. Cynthia Timberlake, Librn
Notes: Early voyages, natural and general history, archaeology, and ethnology of the Pacific area. Hawaiian materials incl mss, maps, 360,000 photographs dating from 1845, and Hawaiian language newspapers.

HAWAII ART see Art, Hawaiian

HAWAIIAN LANGUAGE AND LITERATURE

HI —HAWAIIAN MISSION CHILDREN'S SOCIETY LIBRARY, 553 S King St, Honolulu, 96813. Mary Jane Knight, Librn
Holdings: Vols 15,000 Cat Mss Pix
Notes: Missionary period of Hawaiian history, 1819-1880, incl a general collection of Hawaiian history and travel, an outstanding collection of early voyages to the Pacific, and an almost complete collection of early Hawaiian imprints, ie, publications in the Hawaiian language during the 19th century. Ms material incl letters, journals and reports of the Protestant missionaries who came to Hawaii (the Sandwich Islands) under the auspices of the American Board of Commissioners for Foreign Missions. The material is for research only; the stacks are closed. Unpublished papers may be examined by qualified researchers on application to the librarian. Published material is cataloged.

HAWAIIAN LANGUAGE AND LITERATURE (cont.)

Hawaiian imprints are cataloged, except for the Dewey classification 300's which are mainly governmentdocuments. Ms collections are cataloged or in the process of being completely arranged and cataloged.

HI —HAWAII STATE LIBRARY, Hawaii & Pacific Collection, 478 S King St, Honolulu, 96813. Proserfina Strona, Acting Head
Holdings: Vols (93,834) Cat Microforms
Budget: ($30,000)
Notes: Publish cumulative index of Hawaii State Documents biennially and an index to the *Honolulu Advertiser* and *Honolulu* Star-Bulletin annually. Also print bibliographies of special interest, such as ethnic bibliographies, Aloha Week celebrations, etc. Depository for county and state documents.

IL —NEWBERRY LIBRARY, 60 W Walton St, Chicago, 60610. Diana Haskell, Cur of Modern Mss
Holdings: Cat Mss
Notes: The Ayer Collection.

HAWKES, JOHN

NV —UNIVERSITY OF NEVADA, RENO, University Library, Special Collections Dept, Reno, 89557. Robert E Blesse, Head
Holdings: Vols (21) Cat
Notes: Includes individual works by author in all editions including translations; also prefaces, introductions, published correspondence, appearances in anthologies, periodicals, etc. Bibliographical research collection, part of Modern Authors Collection. Other appearances 45 cataloged.

HAWKING see Falconry and Falcons

HAWKINS, GERALD

MA —BOSTON UNIVERSITY, Mugar Memorial Library, Special Collections Dept, 771 Commonwealth Ave, Boston, 02215. Howard B Gotlieb, Dir
Holdings: Cat Mss Pix
Notes: Mss, correspondence, etc collected in depth; incl publications by or about.

HAWKINS, MAUDE M.

DC —LIBRARY OF CONGRESS, Washington, 20540.
Notes: Three collections are pertinent to Housman: (1) The AE Housman Collection, with most of the surviving fragments of the poetry notebooks, along with some of the letters AEH received on publication of *Last* Poems; (2) The Laurence Housman Collection, Chiefly of correspondence LH had with Maude M Hawkins, one of AEH's biographers. (3) The Grant Richards Collection preserves over a hundred autograph letters from AEH and several hundred typescript copies of his letters; copies of to AEH from Grant Richards; letters to GR about AEH; and drafts and proofs of Richard's memoir. Scattered in other LC collections (Cyril Clemens, Van Doren, etc) are other letters from AEH. LC has only a few books from Housman's library.

HAWKINS, RUSH CHRISTOPHER, 1831-1920

RI —BROWN UNIVERSITY, John Hay Library, 20 Prospect St, Providence, 02912. Mark N Brown, Cur Mss
Holdings: Mss
Notes: Materials relative to the history of the US Army.

HAWLEY, CAMERON

MA —BOSTON UNIVERSITY, Mugar Memorial Library, Special Collections Dept, 771 Commonwealth Ave, Boston, 02215. Howard B Gotlieb, Dir
Holdings: // Cat Mss
Notes: Mss, correspondence, etc collected in depth; incl publications by or about.

HAWLEY, WILLIS

BC —SIMON FRASER UNIVERSITY, Library, Burnaby, V5A 1S6, Can. Percilla Groves, Special Collections Librn
Holdings: Cat Mss
Notes: Incl a collection of 75 letters from Ezra Pound to Agnes Bedford and five letters to Wyndham Lewis, 1950-1959, plus 46 letters to Denis Goacher, his literary agent, and 140 pages to Sinologist Willis Hawley with carbons of Hawley's letters to Pound, also graphics for *Confucius: The Great Digest and Unwobbling Pivet,* and for *The Cantos.*

HAWORTH, LELAND

NY —AMERICAN INSTITUTE OF PHYSICS, Center for the History of Physics, Niels Bohr Library, 335 E 45 St, New York, 10017. John Aubry, Librn
Notes: Papers and records.

HAWTHORNE, JULIAN

DC —GEORGETOWN UNIVERSITY, Library, Special Collections Div, 37 & O Sts NW, Washington, 20057. George M Barringer, Special Collections Librn; Nicholas B Sheetz, Mss Librn
Holdings: Cat Mss

NY —UNIVERSITY OF ROCHESTER, Rush Rhees Library, Department of Rare Books and Special Collections, Rochester, 14627. Peter Dzwonkoski, Librn
Holdings: Vols 60 // Cat Mss Pix
Notes: No photocopying.

NC —DUKE UNIVERSITY, William R Perkins Library, Rare Book Room, Durham, 27706. John L Sharpe, III, Cur
Holdings: Vols 100
Notes: Turner Hawthorne Collection. Collection of first and important editions of all the major works of Nathaniel Hawthorne, as well as a number of titles by Julian Hawthorne.

HAWTHORNE, NATHANIEL, 1804-1864

CT —TRINITY COLLEGE LIBRARY, Watkinson Library, 300 Summit St, Hartford, 06106. Jeffrey Kaimowitz, Cur
Holdings: Cat
Notes: First editions, etc.

CT —YALE UNIVERSITY, Box 1603A, Yale Station, New Haven, 06520.

DE —UNIVERSITY OF DELAWARE, Hugh M Morris Library, S College Ave, Newark, 19711. T Stuart Dick, Special Collections
Holdings: Cat
Notes: Incl original issues of *Salem Gazette* as well as first and variant editions and bindings.

ME —BOWDOIN COLLEGE, Library, Brunswick, 04011. Dianne M Gutscher, Cur of Special Collections
Holdings: Vols 700 Cat Mss Pix
Notes: The Hawthorne Collection contains approximately 700 volumes by and about Hawthorne, 180 manuscripts, incl his letters to Horatio Bridge and William B Pike, and numerous scrapbooks and ephemeral items. Most writings are represented in first and subsequent editions, including books, magazines, and newspapers. Included is an important group of 59 volumes from the Hawthorne family library, a number with Hawthorne's signature, presentation copies and books inscribed by his wife, his sister and his three children.

MA —HARVARD UNIVERSITY LIBRARY, Houghton Library, Cambridge, 02138. Rodney G Dennis, Cur of Manuscripts
Holdings: Cat Mss

MA —CONCORD FREE PUBLIC LIBRARY, 129 Main St, Concord, 01742. Rose Marie Mitten, Dir
Holdings: Cat Mss Maps Pix Slides
Notes: Extensive collection.

MA —ESSEX INSTITUTE, James Duncan Phillips Library, 132-34 Essex St, Salem, 01970. Prudence K Backman, Manuscript Librn
Holdings: Vols Mss
Notes: Holdings incl works by and about Nathaniel Hawthorne, the personal library of preeminent Hawthorne collector and bibliographer C E Frazer Clark, first editions of all writings (incl *Fanshawe*) and Hawthorne's correspondence and handwritten newspaper, *Spectator.* Finding aid available for manuscripts.

NY —SAINT LAWRENCE UNIVERSITY, Owen D Young Library, Canton, 13617. Mahlon Peterson, Librn
Holdings: Vols Cat Mss Pix Slides
Notes: The Ulysses Sumner Milburn Collection. The collection incl first editions of all Hawthorne's works as well as letters written by Hawthorne and family members between 1837 and 1863. Also incl are manuscripts by Hawthorne and members of his family, documents relating to Hawthorne's business and financial affairs, and pamphlets and photos relating to his literary career. Over 1200 items.

NC —DUKE UNIVERSITY, William R Perkins Library, Rare Book Room, Durham, 27706. John L Sharpe, III, Cur
Holdings: Vols 100
Notes: Turner Hawthorne Collection. Collection of first and important editions of all the major works of Nathaniel Hawthorne, as well as a number of titles by Julian Hawthorne.

OH —OHIO STATE UNIVERSITY, William Oxley Thompson Memorial Library, 1858 Neil Ave Mall, Columbus, 43210. Robert A Tibbetts, Cur of Special Collections
Holdings: Vols 1000 Cat Mss
Notes: Editions of Hawthorne's work, photocopies of mss, drafts, and letters, and relevant secondary materials which support a textual edition published by the Ohio State University Press.

VA —UNIVERSITY OF VIRGINIA, Alderman Library, Clifton Waller Barrett Collection, Charlottesville, 22901. Joan St C Crane, Cur of American Literature Collections
Holdings: Vols 350 Cat Mss
Notes: Includes important correspondence between Hawthorne and Longfellow.

WA —UNIVERSITY OF WASHINGTON LIBRARIES, Suzzallo Library, Special Collections Division, Rare Book Collection, FM-25, Seattle, 98195. Gary Menges, Coordinator for Special Collections
Notes: Printing history, including early printed books and modern fine printing; book arts, including papermaking, decorated papers, bookbinding, book design, and artist's books; American literature, 19th century includes: Stephen Crane, Ralph Waldo Emerson, Nathaniel Hawthorne, Henry James, Henry Wadsworth Longfellow, Herman Melville, Frank Norris, Harriet Beecher Stowe and Walt Whitman and 20th century includes: Theodore Roethke; illustrated books, including emblem books, historical children's illustration, books illustrated with prints, and artist's books; costume history; voyages and travels; preservation of library materials.

HAWTHORNE FAMILY

MA —ESSEX INSTITUTE, James Duncan Phillips Library, 132-34 Essex St, Salem, 01970. Prudence K Backman, Manuscript Librn
Holdings: Mss
Notes: Papers, incl documents relating to Nathaniel Hawthorne

OH —ANTIOCH COLLEGE, Olive Kettering Library, Livermore St, Yellow Springs, 45387. Nina Myatt, Cur
Holdings: Vols 14// Mss
Notes: Letters of the Peabody, Mann, Hawthorne and related families. Collected by Robert Straker from many sources, arranged in chronological order and well indexed.

HAY, JOHN

DC —LIBRARY OF CONGRESS, Manuscript Division, Washington, 20540. John C Broderick, Chief
Holdings: Cat Mss Pix
Notes: Mss, papers, records, etc.

HAY, JOHN (cont.)

NY —COLUMBIA UNIVERSITY LIBRARIES, Rare Book & Manuscript Library, 801 Butler Library, 535 W 114 St, New York, 10027. Kenneth A Lohf, Librn
Notes: More than 32,000 items documenting the rise of William Russell Grace's shipping business and other materials relating to his career as mayor of New York. Incl records and correspondence relating to all aspects of the shipping business in New York and South America, mining interest in Peru and Chile, and transportation in Costa Rica and Nicaragua. Family memorabilia and photographs, materials concerning New York Politics, banking and insurance, real estate interests and Catholic charities, and letters from Chester A Arthur, John Jacob Astor, Andrew Carnegie, Grover Cleveland, Hamilton Fish, John Hay and J Pierpont Morgan. Restricted use.

RI —BROWN UNIVERSITY, John Hay Library, 20 Prospect St, Providence, 02912. Mark N Brown, Cur Mss
Holdings: Vols 1000 Cat Mss Pix
Notes: A virtually complete collection of the writings of John Hay incl periodical contributions, separately published books, broadsides, and pamphlets plus critical and biographical works on Hay and his period. The collection is especially rich in association items and personal papers incl: diaries kept while Assistant Secretary to President Lincoln and Secreatry of Legations in Paris, Vienna, and Madrid plus letterpress books reflecting diplomatic service in Paris and Vienna (1866-1867), Madrid (1869-1879), and London (1897-1898); mss of prose and poetry incl corrected galley proofs for *Abraham Lincoln, A History* (1890); and correspondence to and from major literary and political figures such as: Henry Adams, Arthur Balfour, Salmon Chase, John C Fremont, Richard Gilder, Bret Harte, William Herndon, William Dean Howells, Henry James, Clarence King,Henry Cabot Lodge, Seth Low, Thomas Stanton, and James Wadsworth.

HAY AND HAYING—EQUIPMENT AND SUPPLIES

CA —UNIVERSITY OF CALIFORNIA, DAVIS, Shields Library, Dept of Special Collections, Davis, 95616. Donald Kunitz, Head; C Danial Elliott, Asst Head
Notes: Farming equipment: Manufacturer's catalogs, manuals, parts lists, ephemera, and literature pertaining to historical as well as current data on such items as tractors, engines, combines, hay equipment, etc. Described in "The Higgins Library: A Source for the Study of Agricultural History," Don Kunitz, *Agricultural History,* vol 49, 1975, pp 89-91.

HAY FEVER

†CO —NATIONAL JEWISH HOSPITAL AND RESEARCH CENTER-NATIONAL ATHSMA CENTER, Gerald Tucker Memorial Medical Library, 3800 Colfax Ave, Denver, 80206. Helen-Ann Brown, Librn
Holdings: Vols (8500)
Notes: Allergy, asthma, immunology, research in molecular and cellular biology, medicine, tuberculosis and diseases of the chest.

HAYCOX, ERNEST, 1899-1950

OR —UNIVERSITY OF OREGON LIBRARY, Special Collections Div, Eugene, 97403. Kenneth W Duckett, Curator
Holdings: Vols 2,000 // Cat
Notes: Professional library belonging to Ernest Haycox, primarily Western Americana.

HAYCRAFT, MOLLY COSTAIN

MA —BOSTON UNIVERSITY, Mugar Memorial Library, Special Collections Dept, 771 Commonwealth Ave, Boston, 02215. Howard B Gotlieb, Dir
Holdings: Cat Mss
Notes: Mss, correspondence, incl publications by or about.

HAYDEN, CARL T.

AZ —NORTHERN ARIZONA UNIVERSITY, Special Collection Library, CU Box 6022, Flagstaff, 86011. Peter M Whiteley, Coordr/Archivist; William Mullane, Librn
Notes: Arizona Cattle Feeders Association Collection; correspondence (some from Carl Hayden, US Senator from Arizona) concerning grain sorghum reserves in Arizona, 1965.

AZ —ARIZONA STATE UNIVERSITY, Library, Arizona Collection, Tempe, 85281. Edward C Oetting, Head
Holdings: Cat Mss
Notes: Papers, etc.

HAYDN, JOSEF

MA —BOSTON PUBLIC LIBRARY, Music Division, 666 Boylston St, Box 286, Boston, 02117. Ruth Bleecker, Cur of Music
Notes: The Handel and Haydn Society officially transferred its collection to the library in 1978. The Society gave its books, scores, and archives to the Trustees of the Library to be maintained and preserved as part of the permanent research collection. Presently the collection ranges from early imprints of Handel's music and copies of the *Handel and Haydn Society Collection of Church Music* to the holographs of commissioned works. The archives incl copies off bills and disbursements dating back to 1815, printers' plates for tickets, programs from 1815-1912, membership lists, and by-laws.

HAYES, HELEN

NY —NEW YORK PUBLIC LIBRARY, Performing Arts Research Center, Billy Rose Theatre Collection, 111 Amsterdam Ave, New York, 10023. Dorothy L Swerdlove, Cur
Holdings: Cat Mss Pix
Notes: Papers, scrapbooks, mss, photographs, memorabilia, etc.

HAYES, JOEL ADDISON, JR.

TN —MEMPHIS STATE UNIVERSITY, John Willard Brister Library, Memphis, 38152. John Terreo, Special Collections Librn
Notes: Jefferson Davis-Joel Addison Family papers, 1864-1889. President of the Confederacy. Personal and business correspondence, receipts, notes, cancelled checks, and other papers, of Davis, following the Civil War (primarily 1877-1889) and his son-in-law, Joel Addison Hayes (1848-1919), banker of Memphis, TN, relating chiefly to management of Davis' plantation, Brierfield, near Vicksburg, MS, stocks and mining investments, and land sales. Incl correspondence between Davis' wife Varina (Howell) Davis and her daughter Margaret Howell (Davis) (1848-1908), and between Addison Hayes and members of his family.

HAYES, MAX S.

OH —OHIO HISTORICAL SOCIETY, Archives Library Division, 1982 Velma Ave, Columbus, 43211. Dennis East, Division Chief

HAYES, PATRICK

PA —PHILADELPHIA MARITIME MUSEUM, Library, 321 Chestnut St, Philadelphia, 19106. Dorothy H Mueller, Librn
Holdings: // Mss
Notes: Hepburn Collection, Consists of the family papers of John Barry, Patrick Hayes, and the Sommers and Keene families of Philadelphia. Includes personal correspondence, financial and business papers, and diaries and journals. Dates range from 1723-1876. 300 ms pieces.

HAYES, RUTHERFORD B., AND FAMILY

OH —RUTHERFORD B HAYES LIBRARY, 1337 Hayes Ave, Fremont, 43420. Watt P Marchman, Dir
Holdings: Vols (10,000) Cat Mss Maps Pix Slides Audiotapes Microforms
Notes: The Rutherford B Hayes Family Collections. The collections comprise papers, books, correspondence, diaries, speeches, account books, financial and real estate records, law cases, ephemera, and memorabilia of members of the Rutherford B Hayes family; his wife, Lucy Webb Hayes; their children: Birchard Austin Hayes; Webb C Hayes I; Rutherford Platt Hayes; Scott Russell Hayes; Fanny Hayes; grandchildren: Dalton Hayes; Webb C Hayes, II; daughter-in-law, Mary Miller Hayes. Mss of the collection are described in *Guide to Manuscripts of the Ohio Historical Society,* 208, 209, 210, 211, 212, 214, 216, 217, 218, 219. Indexed, listed. The collections are housed in the mss division and newspapers division. Ms materials of 256 linear feet; 50, 000 pictures; slides; tapes; moving pictures, maps. The papers ofRutherford Birchard Hayes available on 304 rolls of microfilm. The collection described in *Guide to the Microfilm Edition of the Papers of Rutherford Birchard Hayes, the Nineteenth President of the United States.* Fremont, Ohio: The Rutherford B Hayes Presidential Center, 1983.

HAYES FAMILY

NJ —GLASSBORO STATE COLLEGE, Savitz Library, Stewart Room, Glassboro, 08028. Clara Kirner, Special Collection Librn
Notes: Papers.

HAYMAN, RONALD

MA —BOSTON UNIVERSITY, Mugar Memorial Library, Special Collections Dept, 771 Commonwealth Ave, Boston, 02215. Howard B Gotlieb, Dir
Holdings: Mss Pix
Notes: Mss, correspondence, etc collected in depth; incl publications by or about.

HAYMARKET SQUARE RIOT, CHICAGO, 1886 see Chicago—Haymarket Square Riot, 1886

HAYNE, PAUL HAMILTON

NC —DUKE UNIVERSITY, William R Perkins Library, Manuscript Dept, Durham, 27706. Ellen Gartrell, Cur of Mss
Holdings: Cat Mss
Notes: Papers, correspondence, etc.

SC —COLLEGE OF CHARLESTON LIBRARY, Special Collections Dept, Charleston, 29401.
Notes: Papers, 1859-1896.

HAYNES, JOHN RANDOLPH

CA —UNIVERSITY OF CALIFORNIA, LOS ANGELES, Research Library, Dept of Special Collections, 405 Hilgard Ave, Los Angeles, 90024. Edward Shreeves, Chairman, Bibliographers Group; David S Zeidberg, Head
Holdings: // Uncat Mss
Notes: 90 linear feet of personal papers, 1890-1937, containing materials on direct legislation, the progressive period in California politics, public ownership of water and power, politics and government in Los Angeles, and women's suffrage.

HAYNES, WILLIAM E.

OH —RUTHERFORD B HAYES LIBRARY, 1337 Hayes Ave, Fremont, 43420. Watt P Marchman, Dir
Holdings: Vols 300 Cat Mss
Notes: Ten boxes of ms materials. The

HAYNES, WILLIAM E. (cont.)

Congressman's correspondence, business agreements, papers, pamphlets, circulars, etc. Index. The mss are incl in *Guide to Manuscripts of the Ohio Historical Society,* 220.

HAYS, ARTHUR GARFIELD, 1881-1954

NJ —PRINCETON UNIVERSITY, Library, Manuscript Collection, Nassau St, Princeton, 08540. Jean F Preston, Cur
Holdings: // Mss
Notes: Incl 85 boxes.

HAYS, BROOKS

†MA —JOHN F KENNEDY LIBRARY, Columbia Point, Boston, 02125. Dan H Fenn Jr, Dir
Holdings: // Cat Mss
Notes: Congressional papers, official and personal correspondence, and scrapbooks of Brooks Hays, 1934-1966. 75 linear ft of mss. Holdings are described in "Historical Materials in the John F Kennedy Library." Copies may be obtained by writing the Research Archivist.

NC —WAKE FOREST UNIVERSITY, Z Smith Reynolds Library, North Carolina Baptist Collection, PO Box 7777 Reynolda Station, Winston-Salem, 27109. John R Woodard, Jr, Dir
Notes: Baptists Historical Collection of papers, mss, speeches, etc, in 24 document boxes, covering the Southern Baptists, mainly the period 1963-1966. Other segments of the Brooks Hays papers are deposited at the John F Kennedy Library, Boston, and with the Historical Commission of the Southern Baptist Convention, Nashville, Tennessee.

HAYS, MARY

NY —CARL H PFORZHEIMER LIBRARY, 41 E 42 St, New York, 10017. Mihai H Handrea, Librn
Holdings: Cat Mss Pix
Notes: English Literature from Caxton to 1700; first editions of 18th and 19th centuries, incl mss material on Shelley and his circle; fine presses (Bruce Rogers); George Gissing; women writers 1790-1840, (Mary Wollstonecraft, Mary Hays, Lady Blessington).

HAYWARD, BROOKE

MA —BOSTON UNIVERSITY, Mugar Memorial Library, Special Collections Dept, 771 Commonwealth Ave, Boston, 02215. Howard B Gotlieb, Dir
Holdings: Cat Mss

HAYWARD, JOHN

DC —GEORGETOWN UNIVERSITY, Library, Special Collections Div, 37 & O Sts NW, Washington, 20057. George M Barringer, Special Collections Librn; Nicholas B Sheetz, Mss Librn
Holdings: Mss Pix
Notes: The papers of Christopher Sykes, biographer, journalist, and novelist; containing mss, letters, photographs, and drawings. With extensive correspondence from Harold Acton; Angela, Countess of Antrim; Sir John Betjeman; Ivy Compton-Burnett; Alick Dru; T S Eliot; Max Beerbohm; Graham Greene; John Hayward; Lord Patrick Kinross; Compton Mackenzie; Nancy Mitford; Anthony Powell; Dame Flora Robson; Cecil Roth; Sir John Russell; Osbert Sitwell; John Sparrow; Freya Stark; James Stern; and Evelyn Waugh, among others. Also, considerable research material about Evelyn Waugh, Adam von Trott, Robert Byron, Lady Nancy Astor; and the foundation of the state of Israel.

HAYWARD, LELAND

NY —NEW YORK PUBLIC LIBRARY, Performing Arts Research Center, Billy Rose Theatre Collection, 111 Amsterdam Ave, New York, 10023. Dorothy L Swerdlove, Cur
Holdings: Cat Mss Pix
Notes: Papers, scrapbooks, mss, photographs, memorabilia, etc.

HAYWARD, WILLIAM MATTHEW

BC —UNIVERSITY OF VICTORIA, McPherson Library, Victoria, V8W 3H5, Can.
Notes: Incl 32 pages, 1912; diary of a trip from Quebec to Vancouver.

HAZARD, JOHN N.

†NY —COLUMBIA UNIVERSITY LIBRARIES, Butler Library, Rare Book and Manuscript Library, 535 W 114 St, New York, 10027.
Notes: Prof John N Hazard's papers, incl 20 notebooks of class notes while a student at the Moscow Juridical Institute, 1934-37.

HAZARDOUS GEOGRAPHIC ENVIRONMENTS

CA —ASSOCIATION OF BAY AREA GOVERNMENTS, MTC/ABAG Library, 101 Eighth St, Oakland, 94607. Diane Gillman, Information Coord
Notes: Concentrates heavily on the nine-county Bay Area region. About 10,000 monographs and serials. Title catalog, OCLC/ATS. Central collection of documents for six transit properties in Bay Area. Incl material on hazardous geographic environments.

HAZARDOUS MATERIALS see Hazardous Substances

HAZARDOUS SUBSTANCES

AR —NATIONAL CENTER FOR TOXICOLOGICAL RESEARCH, Library, Jefferson, 72079. Susan Laney-Sheehan, Supvr Librn
Holdings: Vols (15,000) Cat Mss Slides Audiotapes 16mm Films Microforms
Notes: Incl (860) journal titles, (230) current subscriptions.

CA —UNIVERSITY OF CALIFORNIA, BERKELEY, Life Sciences Libraries, Public Health Library, 42 Earl Warren Hall, Berkeley, 94720. Thomas J Alexander, Librn
Holdings: Vols (75,000) Cat Microforms
Notes: Research collection covering all aspects of public health. Health Department annual reports from all 50 states are acquired, as well as such reports from all California health units and from major US cities. Serial publications issued by Health Departments in the 13 western states are being received.

CA —UNIVERSITY OF CALIFORNIA, DAVIS, Environmental Toxicology Library, Davis, 95616. Ming-yu Li, Documentation Specialist
Holdings: Vols (5000) Cat
Notes: Library is open to public for reference only. In addition to the cataloged holdings, the library also maintains a pamphlet collection of 50 file drawers on agricultural chemicals, environmental pollution, heavy metals, food toxicants, toxicology, pesticides and trace elements.

CA —ASSOCIATION OF BAY AREA GOVERNMENTS, MTC/ABAG Library, 101 Eighth St, Oakland, 94607. Diane Gillman, Information Coord
Notes: Concentrates heavily on the nine-county Bay Area region. About 10,000 monographs and serials. Title catalog, OCLC/ATS. Central collection of documents for six transit properties in Bay Area. Incl material on hazardous geographic environments.

MD —RACHEL CARSON COUNCIL INC, Library, 8940 Jones Mill Rd, Chevy Chase, 20815. Shirley A Briggs, Exec Dir
Notes: Bioassays of pesticides and other toxic substances for carcinogenicity by National Cancer Institute; government regulatory documents. Holdings approx 1500 books; 1000 documents and unbound reports; 40 drawers of specialized files. Also have Environmental Protection Agency Pesticide Product Information. Subscribe to 54 journals and others serials. Also publish on pesticides, toxic substances and alternatives to use of pesticides. Have index to pesticides by chemical formula, trade names and CAS number.

MA —CAMP, DRESSER & MCKEE, Herman G Dresser Library, One Center Plaza, Boston, 02108. Virginia L Carroll, Librn
Holdings: Vols (15,000) Cat Maps Slides Microforms
Notes: Air, land, and water pollution; environmental engineering; hazardous wastes; water resources; solid wastes; resource recycling.

PA —PENNSYLVANIA DEPT OF ENVIRONMENTAL RESOURCES, Office of Environmental Protection, Technical Reference Library, Fulton Bldg, 17th Floor, Box 2063, Harrisburg, 17120. Wanda R Bell, Librn
Holdings: Vols (2000) Cat Slides Microfilm Microfiche
Notes: 10,000 technical reports; water and wastewater feasibility plans; PA Bulletin, 1970-Present; water pollution; solid waste; mining and reclamation; air quality; acid mine drainage.

ON —ONTARIO MINISTRY OF HEALTH, Laboratory Services Branch, Library, Box 9000, Terminal A, Toronto, M5W 1R5, Can. Doris A Standing, Librn
Notes: Medical laboratory technology and related subjects: microbiology, bacteriology, mycology, parasitology, virology, immunology, serology, biochemistry, automated laboratory techniques, environmental bacteriology, quality control and laboratory safety, incl biohazard control.

HAZEN, HERVEY CROSBY, 1841-1914

NY —CORNELL UNIVERSITY LIBRARIES, Collection of Regional History, Dept of Manuscripts and Univ Archives, Ithaca, 14853.
Notes: Presbyterian clergyman, missionary. Incl papers, 1853-1914; several diaries describe his voyages to and missionary work in India; notes, sermons, scrapbooks, and personal and professional correspondence.

HAZLITT, WILLIAM

DE —UNIVERSITY OF DELAWARE, Hugh M Morris Library, S College Ave, Newark, 19711. T Stuart Dick, Special Collections
Holdings: Vols 155// Cat Mss

OH —OHIO UNIVERSITY, Vernon R Alden Library, Department of Archives and Special Collections, Athens, 45701. Gary A Hunt, Head
Holdings: Vols (10,191) Uncat Mss
Notes: The Edmund Blunden Collection of Romantic and Modern Literature, being the private library assembled by Blunden during 6 decades of active collecting. The bulk of the collection (6,264 titles) consists of English imprints from the period 1750-1850, concentrating on literature but also incl contemporary works on art, natural history, philosophy and other subjects important for understanding the background of English Romanticism. Among the authors most heavily represented by first and other early editions are: Allington, Barnes, Bloomfield, Byron, Clare, Coleridge, Cowper, Dyer, Edgeworth, Goldsmith, Hazlitt, Hunt, Lamb, Landor, Scott, Thompson and Wordsworth. Books written by Blunden himself, together with his Georgian contemporaries (particularly W H Davies, Walter De la Mare, and Sigfried Sassoon) form a second major area of strength. Many ofthe modern books are inscribed to Blunden, and nearly all the volumes in the collection bear his annotations.

HAZZARD, FLORENCE WOOLSEY, 1903-

NY —CORNELL UNIVERSITY LIBRARIES, Collection of Regional History, Dept of

HAZZARD, FLORENCE WOOLSEY, 1903- (cont.)

Manuscripts and Univ Archives, Ithaca, 14853.
Notes: Writer, psychologist. Incl papers, 1819-(1925-65); 2 reels microfilm; 3 unpublished works, several short biographical sketches, transcripts, notes, bibliographies, pamphlets, offprints and clippings.

HEAD, BESSIE

MA —BOSTON UNIVERSITY, Mugar Memorial Library, Special Collections Dept, 771 Commonwealth Ave, Boston, 02215. Howard B Gotlieb, Dir
Holdings: Cat Mss

HEAD, EDITH

CA —ACADEMY OF MOTION PICTURE ARTS & SCIENCES, Margaret Herrick Library, 8949 Wilshire Blvd, Beverly Hills, 90211. Linda Harris Mehr, Library Administrator
Notes: Papers.
See also entry under Moving Pictures.

HEADINGS, SUBJECT see Subject Headings

HEALD, TIM

MA —BOSTON UNIVERSITY, Mugar Memorial Library, Special Collections Dept, 771 Commonwealth Ave, Boston, 02215. Howard B Gotlieb, Dir
Holdings: Mss

HEALEY, BEN

MA —BOSTON UNIVERSITY, Mugar Memorial Library, Special Collections Dept, 771 Commonwealth Ave, Boston, 02215. Howard B Gotlieb, Dir
Holdings: Cat Mss
Notes: Mss, correspondence, etc collected in depth; incl publications by or about.

HEALEY, DOROTHY, 1914-

CA —UNIVERSITY OF CALIFORNIA, LOS ANGELES, Research Library, Dept of Special Collections, 405 Hilgard Ave, Los Angeles, 90024. Edward Shreeves, Chairman, Bibliographers Group; David S Zeidberg, Head
Notes: 2 linear feet of copies of federal documents obtained under the Freedom of Information Act; oral history transcript (3 volumes).

HEALING, FAITH see Faith Cure

HEALING, MENTAL see Mental Healing

HEALTH, COMMUNITY see Public Health

HEALTH, ENVIRONMENTAL see Environmental Health

HEALTH, INDUSTRIAL see Industrial Hygiene; Occupational Diseases

HEALTH, PUBLIC see Public Health

HEALTH AND BEAUTY AIDS

IL —J WALTER THOMPSON CO, Information Center, 875 N Michigan Ave, Chicago, 60611. Edward G Strable, Dir
Holdings: Vols 75 Cat Microforms
Notes: Basis of collection is fugitive materials (reports, studies, clippings, articles, releases) on consumer markets and use patterns of health and beauty aids-about 20 file drawers. Indexing and organization make for immediate access.

HEALTH CARE see Medical Care

HEALTH EDUCATION

CA —LOS ANGELES PUBLIC LIBRARY, Science & Technology Dept, 630 W Fifth St, Los Angeles, 90071. Billie M Connor, Dept Head
Holdings: Vols (7500)
Notes: A well-rounded collection of materials related to consumer health, medicine and drugs as well as materials for the allied health and medical professions. Includes a sound representative selection of basic texts covering various aspects of medical treatment, drugs, diseases and syndromes. Indexes are collected as well as a basic collection of journals. The directories collection is strong. The broadest possible collection of books oriented toward consumer health, medicine, diets and nutrition is maintained, both traditional and alternative. Texts and examination study books are collected for nurses, laboratory technicians, physcial therapists, speech therapists, paramedics and other allied health professions.

CA —KAISER-PERMANENTE MEDICAL CENTER, Health Library, 280 W McArthur Blvd, Oakland, 94611. Eileen McAdam, Librn
Holdings: Vols Audiotapes Videotapes 16mm Films
Notes: Lists of books, pamphlets, films, journals, and micro computer software available upon request.

CO —WESTERN INTERSTATE COMMISSION FOR HIGHER EDUCATION, Wiche Library, PO Drawer P, Boulder, 80302. Karon M Kelly, Dir Library Services
Holdings: Vols (10,000) Cat Microforms
Notes: Incl medical and nursing education, student exchange programs, minority involvement in education, management systems in higher education.

IL —UNIVERSITY OF ILLINOIS, URBANA/CHAMPAIGN, Library, Applied Life Studies Library, 1408 W Gregory Dr, Urbana, 61801.
Holdings: Vols (38,000) Cat Microforms
Notes: Library has own card catalog and shelf list for this collection; it is also represented in the main card catalog and shelf list of the University of Illinois Library. Card indexes to games and sports are incl in books in the collection, also to folk and national dances. Try to have fairly complete coverage of books published in all aspects of the field of physical education which would be of interest to students, as well as a lot of more general books on sports. Coverage of health education and recreation is also quite complete. This is one of the few (if not only) departmental libraries in the US devoted to this field. Published catalog: *Dictionary Catalog of the Applied Life Studies Library* (formerly Physical Education Library) *University of Illinois at Urbana-Champaign* v 1-4 (Boston: G K Hall, 1977) and *First* Supplement v 1-2 (Boston: G K Hall, 1982).

MN —MINNESOTA DEPT OF HEALTH, R N Barr Public Health Library, 717 Delaware St SE, PO Box 9441, Minneapolis, 55440. Barbara Brian, Librn
Holdings: Vols (26,000) Cat Microforms
Notes: Public health.

NC —CAROLINA POPULATION CENTER, Library, University Sq E, Chapel Hill, 27514. Patricia Shipman, Head Librn
Holdings: Vols (20,000) Cat
Budget: ($10,500)
Notes: Try to acquire everything published in English on population, with particular emphasis on the US and developing countries. Also acquire conference proceedings, seminar papers. These and journal articles are indexed and the analytics are incl in the catalog. Incl 13,000 reprints and other pieces of ephemera. Most extensive area files are on India, Africa, Thailand, Iran, Korea, and Latin America. Holdings are recorded on an automated data base. A microfiche catalog is available for use in the Library and for purchase. Access by subject & geographic area are available through the Library's own thesaurus-based indexing systems.

VA —UNITED WAY OF AMERICA INFORMATION CENTER, 701 North Fairfax St, United Way Plaza, Alexandria, 22314. Henry M Smith, Dir; Barbara L Owen, Librn
Holdings: Vols (1200) Cat Microforms
Notes: Incl 5000 research reports and studies on microfiche; 100 vertical file drawers. Services primarily for United Way organizations--United Funds, Community Chests, Health and Welfare Planning Councils.

HEALTH INSURANCE see Insurance, Health

HEALTH MANPOWER

IL —LIBRARY OF THE AMERICAN HOSPITAL ASSOCIATION, Asa S Bacon Memorial, 840 N Lake Shore Dr, Chicago, 60611. Eloise C Foster, Dir
Holdings: Vols (39,000) Cat
Budget: ($95,000)
Notes: Literature on non-clinical aspects of health care administration, planning and financing of hospitals and related health care institutions; administrative aspects of the medical, paramedical, and prepayment fields. Special Collection: Ray E Brown Management Collection. *Hospital Literature* Index prepared by the Library of the American Hospital Association in cooperation with the National Library of Medicine; *Catalog of the Library of the American Hospital Association*, published by G K Hall, Boston.

HEALTH OF CHILDREN see Children—Care and Hygiene

HEALTH OF WORKERS see Industrial Hygiene

HEALTH PHYSICS SOCIETY

NY —AMERICAN INSTITUTE OF PHYSICS, Center for the History of Physics, Niels Bohr Library, 335 E 45 St, New York, 10017. John Aubry, Librn
Notes: Papers and records.

HEALTH POLICY see Medical Policy

HEALTH RESORTS, WATERING PLACES, ETC.

NH —NEW HAMPSHIRE COLLEGE, Harry A B and Gertrude C Shapiro Library, 2500 N River Rd, Manchester, 03104. Richard Pantano, Dir
Notes: Hotel and restaurant management. Library is a selective US Government Documents depository, and New Hampshire State Documents depository. Subscribe to microfiche SEC 10K reports to AMEX and NYSE (1975-), as well as AMEX and NYSE company annual reports (1977-); AICPA publications and cassettes. Strong collections in accounting; business; business education; computers; hotel and restaurant management; and social service.

†NY —MEDICAL RESEARCH LIBRARY OF BROOKLYN, Academy of Medicine of Brooklyn & The State University of New York Downstate Medical Center, 450 Clarkson St, Brooklyn, 11203. Kenneth E Moody, Dir
See also entry under Medicine.

HEALTH SCIENCES

AK —ALASKA HEALTH SCIENCES LIBRARY, 3211 Providence Dr, Anchorage, 99508. Stanley Truelson, Dir
Budget: ($56,000)
Notes: A unit of the Division of State Libraries and Museums, State of Alaska, but located in the University of Alaska, Anchorage Library, whose collection it shares.

CA —ALTA BATES HOSPITAL, Stuart Memorial Library, One Colby Plaza, Berkeley, 94705. Kathryn Kammerer, Librn
Holdings: Vols 1000 Cat
Budget: $5000

CA —BURBANK COMMUNITY HOSPITAL, Medical Library, 466 E Olive Ave, Burbank, 91501. Narciso Merioles Garganta, Medical

HEALTH SCIENCES (cont.)

Librn
Holdings: Vols 1000 Cat Audiotapes Videotapes

CA —LOMA LINDA UNIVERSITY, Dell E Webb Memorial Library, Loma Linda, 92350. H Maynard Lowrey, Librn
Holdings: Vols Cat
Notes: History of Health Sciences; 19th century health reform.

CA —LOS ANGELES PUBLIC LIBRARY, Science & Technology Dept, 630 W Fifth St, Los Angeles, 90071. Billie M Connor, Dept Head
Holdings: Vols (7500)
Notes: A well-rounded collection of materials related to consumer health, medicine and drugs as well as materials for the allied health and medical professions. Includes a sound representative selection of basic texts covering various aspects of medical treatment, drugs, diseases and syndromes. Indexes are collected as well as a basic collection of journals. The directories collection is strong. The broadest possible collection of books oriented toward consumer health, medicine, diets and nutrition is maintained, both traditional and alternative. Texts and examination study books are collected for nurses, laboratory technicians, physcial therapists, speech therapists, paramedics and other allied health professions.

CA —RIVERSIDE GENERAL HOSPITAL-UNIVERSITY MEDICAL CENTER, Medical Library, 9851 Magnolia Ave, Riverside, 92503. Rosalie Reed, Library Asst
Holdings: Vols (898) Cat Audiotapes
Budget: $40,000
Notes: Incl 209 journal subscriptions, (4737) bound vols and 5 audiodigest titles.

CA —ROSEVILLE COMMUNITY HOSPITAL, Medical Library, 333 Sunrise Ave, Roseville, 95678. Helen R Asher, Librn
Holdings: Vols 1654 Cat Slides Audiotapes Videotapes Microforms
Budget: $3500
Notes: Incl 407 slides and 302 audiotapes.

CO —UNIVERSITY OF COLORADO, Health Sciences Center, Charles Denison Memorial Library, 4200 E Ninth Ave, Denver, 80262. Margaret Butkovich, Interim Dir
Holdings: Vols 179,128 Cat
Budget: $351,749

CT —MIDDLESEX MEMORIAL HOSPITAL, Health Sciences Library, 28 Crescent St, Middletown, 06457. Evelyn M Breck, Dir
Holdings: Vols (2000) Cat
Budget: ($20,000)
Notes: 125 journals are kept for 10 year runs.

FL —SAINT MARY'S HOSPITAL INC, Health Services Library, 901 45th St W, Palm Beach, 33407. Jennie Glock, Librn
Holdings: Vols (7000) Cat Slides Audiotapes

FL —UNIVERSITY OF SOUTH FLORIDA, Medical Center Library, 12901 N 30 St, Tampa, 33612. Maxyne Grimes, Dir
Holdings: Vols (75,383) Cat
Budget: ($325,000)

IL —ARLINGTON HEIGHTS MEMORIAL LIBRARY, 500 N Dunton Ave, Arlington Heights, 60004. Caryl Mobley, Reference Librn
Holdings: Vols (5000) Cat
Budget: ($8000)
Notes: Medical sciences, nursing, and patient education.

IL —ROSELAND COMMUNITY HOSPITAL, Health Science Library, 45 W 111 St, Chicago, 60628. Mary T Hanlon, Librn
Holdings: Vols (800) Cat
Budget: $3200

IL —LUTHERAN GENERAL HOSPITAL LIBRARY, 1775 Dempster St, Park Ridge, 60068. Joanne Crispen, Dir of Library Services
Holdings: Vols (21,298) Cat Slides Audiotapes Videotapes 16mm Films Filmstrips
Budget: ($52,600)

IN —SAINT VINCENT HOSPITAL & HEALTH CARE CENTER, Garceau Library, 20001 W 86 St, Indianapolis, 46260. Virginia Durkin, Librn
Holdings: Vols (7500) Cat Pix Slides Phonorecords Audiotapes Videotapes 16mm Films Filmstrips Microforms
Notes: Building a collection on the history of the hospital.

IN —PURDUE UNIVERSITY LIBRARIES, Pharmacy, Nursing and Health Sciences Library, Pharmacy Bldg, West Lafayette, 47907. Theodora Andrews, Librn
Notes: Industrial hygiene and environmental science.

IA —MARIAN HEALTH CENTER, Health Science Library, 801 Fifth St, Sioux City, 51101. Donna Phillips, Dir
Holdings: Vols 6500 Cat Slides Phonorecords Audiotapes Videotapes 16mm Films Filmstrips Journals
Budget: $40,000

KS —UNIVERSITY OF KANSAS MEDICAL CENTER, College of Health Sciences & Hospital, Dykes Library of Health Sciences, Rainbow Blvd at 39th, Kansas City, 66103. Earl Farley, Dir
Holdings: Vols 119,117 Cat

LA —TOURO INFIRMARY, Hospital Library, 1401 Foucher, New Orleans, 70115. Patricia J Greenfield, Head
Holdings: Vols (3000) Cat Audiotapes
Budget: $80,752
Notes: Clinical medicine and nursing. Photocopying.

MD —JOHNS HOPKINS UNIVERSITY, William H Welch Medical Library, 1900 E Monument St, Baltimore, 21205. Richard A Polacsek, Dir & Librn
Holdings: Vols (270,000) Cat Pix Slides Phonorecords Audiotapes Videotapes 16mm Films Filmstrips Microforms
Budget: ($497,000)

MD —PROVIDENT HOSPITAL, Health Sciences Library, 2600 Liberty Heights Ave, Baltimore, 21215. Bertha G Wilson, Librn
Holdings: Vols (5077) Cat Slides Audiotapes Microforms
Notes: Incl 1000 slides, 300 audiotapes and 104 microforms.

MA —FRANCIS A COUNTWAY LIBRARY OF MEDICINE, Boston Medical Library/Harvard Medical Library, 10 Shattuck St, Boston, 02115. C Robin LeSueur, Librn; Richard J Wolfe, Cur, Rare Books & Manuscripts
Holdings: Vols (500,000) Mss Maps Pix
Budget: ($1,160,000)
Notes: Second largest medical library in the nation. Combines the resources of the Harvard Medical School and the Boston Medical Library, as well as the medical collections of many regional libraries. Outstanding in all areas of medical science. Author-title catalog of imprints through 1959 published by G K Hall, 1973. Strong in serials and medical history in all fields of medicine. Especially strong in subject areas incl incunabula, medical Judaica, Osleriana, O W Holmes, William Rimmer, non-medical books by doctors, travel books by physicians, X-ray (Dr Lloyd E Hawes, Hon Curator), prints and medical satire (Dr Mark D Altschule, Hon Curator), phrenology, witchcraft, gynecology and obstetrics, medical illustrations, birth control and sex research, medical numismatics, European imprints before 1850 and American imprints before 1870, Chinese and Japanese medicine, medicaldissertations (500,000), anatomy, anesthesia, botany, biochemistry and chemistry, alchemy, dental medicine, legal medicine, physiology, dental medicine, legal medicine, physiology, psychiatry, plastic surgery, surgery, zoology, ms collections, which incl the Harvard Medical Archives, probably the strongest in America.

MA —LAWRENCE GENERAL HOSPITAL, Health Sciences Library, One General St, Lawrence, 01842. Carmel Gran, Librn
Holdings: Vols 1500 Cat Slides Audiotapes Videotapes 16mm Films Filmstrips
Budget: $18,000

MA —BERKSHIRE MEDICAL CENTER, Medical Library, 725 North St, Pittsfield, 01201. Jutta Luhde, Medical Librn
Holdings: Vols (15,000) Cat
Notes: Medicine and allied health sciences.

MI —WAYNE STATE UNIVERSITY, Vera Parshall Shiffman Medical Library, 4325 Brush St, Detroit, 48201. Faith Van Toll, Acting Head Librn
Holdings: Vols (158,612)
Budget: ($381,153)
Notes: Resource Library in Greater Midwest Regional Medical Library Network Program.

MI —EDWARD W SPARROW HOSPITAL, Medical Library, 1215 E Michigan Ave, PO Box 30480, Lansing, 48909. Doris H Asher, Medical Librn
Holdings: Vols (1800) Cat Audiotapes Videotapes
Budget: ($10,000)
Notes: Hospital employees and health sciences professionals only.

MO —SAINT JOHN'S SCHOOL OF NURSING LIBRARY, 1930 S National Ave, Springfield, 65804. Marty Osredker, Librn
Holdings: Vols 5200 Cat Audiotapes Microforms
Budget: $5000
Notes: Nursing library with emphasis on nursing, medicine and allied health.

NJ —UNIVERSITY OF MEDICINE AND DENTISTRY OF NEW JERSEY, George F Smith Library of the Health Sciences, 100 Bergen St, Newark, 07103. Philip Rosenstein, Dir of Libraries
Holdings: Vols (110,000) Cat Slides Audiotapes Videotapes 8mm Films Filmstrips Microforms
Budget: ($380,880)
Notes: There is a separate a/v catalog available, arranged by main entry and incl a tracings index. Incl 70,648 slides, 19,298 microforms, 395 8mm films, 2150 audiotapes.

NM —UNIVERSITY OF NEW MEXICO, Medical Center Library, North Campus, Albuquerque, 87131. Erika Love, Dir
Notes: Health sciences collection, principally medicine, but incl nursing, pharmacy, and allied health sciences, in book, journal, and multimedia formats. Library holdings include 33,427 book titles; 37,266 vols; 2,260 periodical subscriptions; 71,303 bound vols.

NY —ERIE COUNTY MEDICAL CENTER, Medical Library, 462 Grider St, Buffalo, 14215. Anthony Ciko, Sr Medical Librn
Holdings: Vols (13,000) Cat Slides Audiotapes Videotapes
Budget: ($42,000)

NY —SUFFOLK ACADEMY OF MEDICINE, Health Sciences Library, 850 Veterans Memorial Highway, Hauppauge, 11788. Isabel V Hathorn, Dir
Holdings: Vols (13,000) Cat Videotapes Microforms

NC —UNIVERSITY OF NORTH CAROLINA, CHAPEL HILL, Health Sciences Library, 223 H, Chapel Hill, 27514. Samuel Hitt, Dir
Holdings: Vols (200,000) Cat Slides Journals Documents Audiotapes Videotapes Microforms
Budget: ($560,000)

ND —SAINT LUKE'S HOSPITAL, Medical Library, Fifth St at Mills Ave, Fargo, 58122. Marcia Stephens, Dir
Holdings: Vols (3300) Cat Slides Audiotapes Videotapes 16mm Films Filmstrips

OH —MOUNT SINAI MEDICAL CENTER, George H Hays Library, University Circle, Cleveland, 44106. Pamela Alderman, Librn
Holdings: Vols (6000) Cat Mss Slides Phonorecords Filmstrips Audiotapes
Notes: Bound journals 4000; incl on-line reference service with Dialog database.

OK —UNIVERSITY OF OKLAHOMA, Health Sciences Center, Library, 1000 Stanton L Young Blvd, PO Box 26901, Oklahoma City, 73190. C M Thompson, Jr, Dir
Holdings: Vols (155,434) Cat Slides Audiotapes Videotapes 16mm Films
Budget: ($374,960)
Notes: Incl physical therapy, occupational therapy, radiologic technology, clinical dietetic.

OR —OREGON HEALTH SCIENCES, University Libraries, PO Box 573, Portland, 97207. James E Morgan, Dir
Holdings: Vols (178,373) Cat Mss Pix Slides

HEALTH SCIENCES (cont.)

Audiotapes Videotapes Microforms
Notes: Libraries incl a medical/nursing library and a separate dental library. Medical history collection of books and artifacts emphasizes the Pacific Northwest.

PA —LANCASTER GENERAL HOSPITAL, Mueller Health Sciences Library, 555 N Duke St, Lancaster, 17604. Claudette Strohm, Librn
Holdings: Vols (4431) Cat Audiotapes Microforms

PA —OHIO VALLEY GENERAL HOSPITAL, Health Library, McKees Rocks, 15136. Mary G Evans, Librn
Holdings: Vols (1900) Cat Slides
Budget: ($3300)

PA —PENNSYLVANIA HOSPITAL HISTORICAL LIBRARY, Eighth & Spruce Sts, Philadelphia, 19107. Caroline Morris, Librn
Holdings: Vols (13,009)
Budget: ($15,000)
Notes: 20th century journals and current medical books. Strong collection of nursing journals. Some historical nursing textbooks and a good collection on the history of nursing.

SC —BAPTIST MEDICAL CENTER, Amelia White Pitts Memorial Library, Taylor at Marion Sts, Columbia, 29220. Lois W Smith, Medical Librn
Holdings: Vols (3000) Cat

TX —TEXAS TECH UNIVERSITY HEALTH SCIENCES CENTER, Amarillo Branch, Harrington Library of Health Sciences, 1400 Wallace Blvd, Amarillo, 79106. Carolyn Patrick, Assoc Dir
Holdings: Vols (12,000) Cat
Budget: ($6600)
Notes: Supports Diploma School of Nursing (Northwest Texas Hospital School of Nursing). Also incl 13,000 bound journals, 5100 audiovisual items.

TX —SAINT PAUL HOSPITAL, C B Sacher Library, 5909 Harry Hines Blvd, Dallas, 75235. Barbara J Miller, Medical Librn; Michael Zimmerman, Library Asst
Holdings: Cat Audiotapes
Budget: $3000

TX —TEXAS CHIROPRACTIC COLLEGE, Mae Hilty Memorial Library, 5912 Spencer Highway, Pasadena, 77505. Michelle Larson, Librn
Holdings: Vols 5000 Cat Pix Slides
Notes: Chiropractic science and practice. 200 currently received periodical titles; 250 paperbacks; 6000 vols directly related subjects; slides; no separate catalog. Archives Dept incl a collection on chiropractic history with 450 items of audiovisual material, and 3000 bound periodicals.

†UT —LDS HOSPITAL MEDICAL LIBRARY, 325 Eighth Ave, Salt Lake City, 84143. Terry L Heyer, Librn
Holdings: Vols (2200) Cat Slides Phonorecords Audiotapes Videotapes

VT —UNIVERSITY OF VERMONT, Charles A Dana Medical Library, Given Bldg, Burlington, 05405. Ellen Nagle, Medical Librn
Notes: Resource Library in the Greater Northeastern Regional Medical Library Program.

VA —RICHMOND MEMORIAL HOSPITAL, Medical Library, 1300 Westwood Ave, Richmond, 23227. Lynn Turman, Librn
Holdings: Vols (7000) Cat Slides Phonorecords Audiotapes Videotapes 16mm Films Filmstrips

WA —UNIVERSITY OF WASHINGTON LIBRARIES, Health Sciences Library, SB-55, Seattle, 98195. Gerald J Oppenheimer, Dir
Holdings: Vols (232,000) Cat Slides Audiotapes Microforms
Budget: ($550,000)

WA —CENTRAL WASHINGTON HOSPITAL, Rose A Heminger Health Sciences Library, PO Box 1887, Wenatchee, 98801. Jane Belt, Librn & Coordr of Continuing Education
Holdings: Cat Slides Phonorecords Audiotapes Videotapes 16mm Films Filmstrips
Budget: ($5000)
Notes: Incl 100 slide sets, 500 audiotapes, 100 videotapes, and 50 filmstrip programs.

WI —SACRED HEART HOSPITAL, Medical Library, 900 W Clairemont Ave, Eau Claire, 54701. Bruno Warner, Librn
Holdings: Vols (2006) Cat Slides Phonorecords Audiotapes Videotapes
Notes: Incl 212 audiotapes and 93 videotapes.

WI —BLACKHAWK TECHNICAL INSTITUTE, PO Box 5009, 6004 Prairie Rd, Janesville, 53547. Grace M Sweeney, Libn
Holdings: Vols 6000 Cat
Budget: $2000
See also entry under Nurses and Nursing.

WI —MERCY HOSPITAL, Medical Library, 1000 Mineral Point, Janesville, 53545. Lois Zuehlke, Librn
Holdings: Vols (565) Cat Slides Phonorecords Audiotapes Videotapes 16mm Films Filmstrips
Budget: $1000

WI —KENOSHA MEMORIAL HOSPITAL, Health Sciences Library, 6308 Eighth Ave, Kenosha, 53140. Esther L Puhek, Librn
Holdings: Vols (1825) Cat Slides Audiotapes Videotapes
Notes: Incl 300 videotapes.

WI —SAINT JOSEPH'S HOSPITAL, School of Nursing, Learning Resource Center, 611 St Joseph's Ave, Marshfield, 54449. Margaret A Allen, Librn
Holdings: Vols (3600) Cat Slides Phonorecords Audiotapes Videotapes 16mm Films Filmstrips
Budget: ($9,000)
Notes: Collection supports nursing education. Historical material incl nursing journals, 1914-date.

AB —SOUTHERN ALBERTA INSTITUTE OF TECHNOLOGY, Learning Resources Centre, 1301 16 Ave NW, Calgary, T2M 0L4, Can. Tom Skinner, Historian
Holdings: Vols (40,000) Cat Maps Pix Films Videotapes Microforms
Budget: ($50,000)
Notes: Wide range of current technical information about electronics and engineering (mechanical, electrical, chemical); emphasis on vocational-technical material. Incl (50,000) slides, (300) videotapes, and (500) films.

ON —UNIVERSITY OF OTTAWA, Health Sciences Library, 451 Smyth Road, Ottawa, K1H 8L5, Can. Myra Owen, Librn
Holdings: Vols (70,000) Slides Audiotapes Films Filmstrips
Budget: ($325,000)
Notes: This collection is made up of works in support of clinical and research studies in all branches of medicine, nursing and kinanthropology. Incl 1500 periodicals.

HEALTH SERVICES see Public Health

HEALTH SERVICES, INFANT AND MATERNAL see Maternal Health Services

HEALTH SERVICES ADMINISTRATION

CT —YALE UNIVERSITY, Beinecke Rare Book & Manuscript Library, Osborn Collection, New Haven, 06520. Stephen R Parks, Cur
Holdings: Mss

FL —SAINT MARY'S HOSPITAL INC, Health Services Library, 901 45th St W, Palm Beach, 33407. Jennie Glock, Librn
Holdings: Vols (7000) Cat Slides Audiotapes

IL —BLUE CROSS AND BLUE SHIELD ASSOCIATION, Library, 804 N Lake Shore Dr, Chicago, 60611. Mary T Drazba, Librn
Holdings: Vols (15,000) Cat Microforms
Notes: Health care financing.

PA —UNIVERSITY OF PENNSYLVANIA, Bio-Medical Library, Johnson Pavilion/G2, Philadelphia, 19104. Eleanor Goodchild, Librn
Holdings: Vols (139,000) Cat Slides Audiotapes Videotapes

HEALTH SURVEYS

CT —YALE UNIVERSITY, Medical Historical Library, 333 Cedar St, New Haven, 06510. Ferenc A Gyorgyey, Librn
Notes: Records of the Milbank Memorial Fund for the years 1922-1977. A part of the Contemporary Medical Care and Health Policy Collection.

MA —HARVARD MEDICAL SCHOOL, Schering Foundation Library of Health Care, 643 Huntington Ave, Boston, 02115. Anne Alach, Librn
Holdings: Cat
Budget: ($3000)
Notes: Socioeconomic aspects of health care.

HEALTH THOUGHTS see Mental Healing

HEALY, G. P. A.

IL —NEWBERRY LIBRARY, 60 W Walton St, Chicago, 60610. Diana Haskell, Cur of Modern Mss
Holdings: Vols 35
Notes: Original oil paintings on permanent display.

HEALY, JAMES A.

CA —STANFORD UNIVERSITY LIBRARIES, Cecil H Green Library, Stanford, 94305. Michael T Ryan, Cur
Holdings: Vols (2300) Uncat Mss Pix
Notes: The James A Healy Collection of Irish Literature. Incl books, magazines, prints, photgraphs, ephemera, and about 3000 unpublished letters. Among the books are complete sets of Dun Emer and Cuala Press publications. Individuals represented in the Healy ms collection incl: A E, Oliver St John Gogarty, James Joyce, Elizabeth C Yeats, George Yeats, and William Butler Yeats.

HEALY, REV. PATRICK F., S.J., 1836-1910

DC —GEORGETOWN UNIVERSITY, Library, Special Collections Div, 37 & O Sts NW, Washington, 20057. George M Barringer, Special Collections Librn; Nicholas B Sheetz, Mss Librn
Holdings: Mss Cat Pix
Notes: The papers of Rev Patrick F Healy, SJ (1836-1910), Georgetown University's twenty-eighth president from 1873-1882 - a period of great quantitative and qualitative expansion for the college. Healy was born in Georgia, the son of an Irish plantation owner and a mulatto slave, and is reportedly the first black in the United States to hold a PhD. The papers consist of correspondence (1853-1906), diaries (18 7, 1879-80, 1891-1906), academic notebooks and misc documents. Also incl is material regarding Bishop James A Healy, photographs of the Healy brothers, and newspaper clippings about the Healy family.

HEARD, GERALD, 1889-1971

CA —UNIVERSITY OF CALIFORNIA, LOS ANGELES, Research Library, Dept of Special Collections, 405 Hilgard Ave, Los Angeles, 90024. Edward Shreeves, Chairman, Bibliographers Group; David S Zeidberg, Head
Holdings: Vols 75
Notes: 75 first and other editions of his books; 16 linear feet of mss, correspondence, and ephemera.

NY —PARAPSYCHOLOGY SOURCES OF INFORMATION CENTER, 2 Plane Tree Lane, Dix Hills, 11746. Rhea A White, Dir
Holdings: Vols (4000)
Notes: The PSI Center includes 4000 books, 100 periodical titles, cassette tapes, and unpublished mss dealing with parapsychology and the transformation of consciousness, also 12,000 articles, reprints, etc. There is a charge for reference service and bibliographies.

HEARING

CT —YALE MEDICAL LIBRARY, 333 Cedar St, New Haven, 06510.
Notes: A special subject emphasis.

HEARING (cont.)

MA —MASSACHUSETTS INSTITUTE OF TECHNOLOGY, Research Laboratory of Electronics, Document Room 36-412, Cambridge, 02139. J E Woore, Head
Holdings: Vols (15,000)
Notes: Incl World War II technical reports on radar. Current electromagnetism and electric engineering, radar, etc.

MO —WASHINGTON UNIVERSITY, School of Medicine, Library, 660 South Euclid Ave, Saint Louis, 63110. Christopher Hoolihan, Rare Book Librn
Holdings: Vols 850 Cat
Budget: ($40,000)
Notes: The CID-Max A Goldstein Collection in Speech and Hearing. Incl printed books from the 16th through 19th centuries on deafness, deaf education, ear diseases, hearing, speech and speech disorders.

OK —PHILLIPS UNIVERSITY, Zollars Memorial Library, University Sta, Enid, 73701. John L Sayre, Dir of University Libraries
Holdings: Vols 2050 Cat Pix Slides Microforms Games
Notes: Works on speech and hearing disorders, research, and therapy.

PA —EYE & EAR HOSPITAL OF PITTSBURGH, Blair-Lippincott Library, 230 Lothrop St, Pittsburgh, 15213. Bruce A Johnston, Medical Librn
Holdings: Vols (6000) Cat
Notes: Special emphasis on ophthalmology, otorhinolaryngology, audiology, and speech pathology.

HEARN, LAFCADIO

AL —SAMFORD UNIVERSITY, Special Collections Library, 800 Lakeshore Dr, Birmingham, 35229. Annie Ford Wheeler, Acting Head Librn
Holdings: Vols 200 Cat
Notes: Mostly noncirculating.

†AL —UNIVERSITY OF ALABAMA, Amelia Gayle Gorgas Library, PO Box S, University, 35486.
Notes: Incl a collection of Sir Walter Scott first editions, 41 vols; Robinson Jeffers collection of 37 vols and mss; Lafcadio Hearn Collection of 110 vols and pamphlets.

CA —CLAREMONT COLLEGES, Ella Strong Denison Library, Scripps College, Claremont, 91711. Judy Harvey Sahak, Librn
Holdings: Vols 150// Uncat
Notes: First editions in mint condition.

CT —LEE ASH, (personal collection), 66 Humiston Dr, Bethany, 06525.
Notes: First editions, mss, ephemera, memorabilia.

IL —ILLINOIS STATE UNIVERSITY, Milner Library, Dept of Special Collections, Normal, 61761. Robert Sokan, Librn
Notes: First editions, limited editions, ephemera, etc.

LA —TULANE UNIVERSITY, Howard-Tilton Memorial Library, Special Collections Div, 7001 Freret St, New Orleans, 70118. Wilbur E Meneray, Librn
Holdings: Vols 257 Cat Mss Pix
Notes: Published works by and about Lafcadio Hearn. See *Lafcadio Hearn A Catalogue of the Collection at the Howard-Tilton Memorial Library Tulane University* (New Orleans, 1977)

MA —HARVARD UNIVERSITY LIBRARY, Houghton Library, Cambridge, 02138. F Thomas Noonan, Cur, Reading Room; Lawrence Dowler, Associate Librn
Holdings: Cat Mss
Notes: See *Harvard Library Notes,* IV (1941), 38-45.

NY —PIERPONT MORGAN LIBRARY, 29 E 36 St, New York, 10016. Herbert Cahoon, Librn
Holdings: Cat Mss
Notes: Mss only.

OH —OHIO UNIVERSITY, Vernon R Alden Library, Department of Archives and Special Collections, Athens, 45701. Gary A Hunt, Head
Holdings: Vols 124 Cat
Notes: First editions, some of them early, and incl many of the posthumously published works by Hearn.

VA —UNIVERSITY OF VIRGINIA, Alderman Library, Clifton Waller Barrett Collection, Charlottesville, 22901. Joan St C Crane, Cur of American Literature Collections
Holdings: Vols 800 Cat Mss Pix
Notes: Works by and about him. First editions, nearly 700 mss, etc. This collection includes some exquisite books which Hearn himself collected in the Orient. Many books from Hearn's own library.

HEARST, WILLIAM RANDOLPH

CA —CALIFORNIA POLYTECHNIC STATE UNIVERSITY LIBRARY, Special Collections and University Archives, San Luis Obispo, 93407. Nancy E Loe, Head Librn
Holdings: Vols (100) Cat
Notes: Herpersonal papers covering her architectural career of forty years, which incl several Hearst estates as well as private residences in the California Arts and Crafts style. Incl Hearst/Morgan correspondence and telegrams; business correspondence, travel accounts, sketchbooks, awards, photographs and several hundred architectural drawings. Hearst Castle Collection incl 8500 architectural drawings for Hearst's residences at San Simeon, Jolon, Wyntoon, and Santa Monica and approx 100 vols of secondary source material. The Asilomar Collection contains 145 architectural drawings for the Morgan-designed YWCA facility near Monterey, California. Incl blueprints, diplomas, personal papers. Finding aid in progress. Incl 10,000 pieces of ms material, 10,000 architectural drawings and blueprints.

NY —C W POST CENTER OF LONG ISLAND UNIVERSITY, B Davis Schwartz Memorial Library, Greenvale, 11548. Jean Goldberg, Special Collections Librn
Holdings: Pix
Notes: Photographs of his collection. Incl extensive collection of auction catalogs.

HEART—DISEASES

MA —FRANCIS A COUNTWAY LIBRARY OF MEDICINE, Boston Medical Library/ Harvard Medical Library, 10 Shattuck St, Boston, 02115. C Robin LeSueur, Librn; Richard J Wolfe, Cur, Rare Books & Manuscripts
Holdings: Cat

TX —AMERICAN HEART ASSOCIATION, Library, 7320 Greenville Ave, Dallas, 75231. Katie Trickey, Librn; Barbara Lightfoot, Info Spec
Holdings: Vols (4000) Cat
Budget: ($20,000)
Notes: Cardiovascular diseases.

HEART—SURGERY

†TN —SAINT THOMAS HOSPITAL, Health Sciences Library, Box 380, Nashville, 37202. Dee Platt, Dir
Holdings: Vols (2600) Cat Slides

HEARTMAN, CHARLES F.

MS —UNIVERSITY OF SOUTHERN MISSISSIPPI, William David McCain Graduate Library, Box 5148, Southern Sta, Hattiesburg, 39406.
Holdings: Uncat Mss
Notes: The personal and business records (1913-1953) of the noted bookseller, Charles F Heartman. Incl 15 cubic feet of correspondence, auction and books catalogs, the Heartman Historical Series, and copies of articles, pamphlets and books written or published by Heartman.

HEAT—TRANSMISSION

IL —ARGONNE NATIONAL LABORATORY, Reactor Science/ Engineering Branch Library, 9700 S Cass Ave, Argonne, 60439. Marion Benson, Librn
Notes: Incl 10,000 vols monographs, 200 current journals, a comprehensive collection of AEC, ERDA, DOE, and NRC scientific and technical reports. Materials may be used by the public in the library by prior arrangement. Photocopies may be supplied for interlibrary loan, for which a processing and handling charge is made.

KY —UNIVERSITY OF KENTUCKY, Robert E Shaver Library of Engineering, 355 Anderson Hall, Lexington, 40506. Russell H Powell, Engineering Librn
Holdings: Vols (48,000) Cat Microforms

HEAT EXCHANGERS

KY —UNIVERSITY OF KENTUCKY, Robert E Shaver Library of Engineering, 355 Anderson Hall, Lexington, 40506. Russell H Powell, Engineering Librn
Holdings: Vols (48,000) Cat Microforms

HEAT TRANSFER

OH —GOODYEAR ATOMIC CORP, Technical Library, PO Box 628, Piketon, 45661. Robert Holland, Supvr
Holdings: Vols (50,000) Cat Mss Microforms
Notes: Uranium enrichment; gas flow, heat transfer, isotope analyses, uranium-floride chemistry.

PA —UNIVERSITY OF PENNSYLVANIA, Towne Scientific Library, 220 S 33 St, Philadelphia, 19104. Charles Meyers, Librn
Holdings: Vols (65,000) Cat

HEATH, CATHERINE

MA —BOSTON UNIVERSITY, Mugar Memorial Library, Special Collections Dept, 771 Commonwealth Ave, Boston, 02215. Howard B Gotlieb, Dir
Holdings: Mss Pix

HEATH, D. C., AND COMPANY

MA —AMERICAN ANTIQUARIAN SOCIETY LIBRARY, 185 Salisbury St, Worcester, 01609. Marcus A McCorison, Dir & Librn
Holdings: Cat
Notes: Papers of D C Heath & Company.

HEATH, ROYAL VALE

RI —BROWN UNIVERSITY, John Hay Library, 20 Prospect St, Providence, 02912. Mark N Brown, Cur Mss
Notes: The Royal Vale Heath Collection of about 200 of his designs, drawings, models, ocular, and verbal descriptions of simultaneous solutions to linear Diophantine equations in such examples as magic squares, Platonic solids, etc. These curious designs often were devised as talismans in ancient India and were first developed as mathematical problems by the Chinese.

HEATH, WILLIAM

MA —MASSACHUSETTS HISTORICAL SOCIETY LIBRARY, 1154 Boylston St, Boston, 02215. John D Cushing, Librn
Notes: One of more than 5000 individual collections in the Library, this collection incl the Adams Family papers and materials relating to Massachusetts and New England. The Library's collection of mss has been cataloged and issued in nine folio vols by G K Hall & Co of Boston. It is widely distributed throughout the United States and Europe.

HEATH-STUBBS, JOHN FRANCIS ALEXANDER

IN —INDIANA UNIVERSITY, Lilly Library, Seventh St, Bloomington, 47405. William R Cagle, Librn
Holdings: // Cat Mss
Notes: Correspondence of Heath-Stubbs with other poets concerning his books and writings. Also mss of many of his poems and essays. 75 items. Incl first editions.

HEATING

KY —UNIVERSITY OF KENTUCKY, Robert E Shaver Library of Engineering, 355

HEATING (cont.)

Anderson Hall, Lexington, 40506. Russell H Powell, Engineering Librn
Holdings: Vols (48,000) Cat Microforms

NY —ENGINEERING SOCIETIES LIBRARY, 345 E 47 St, New York, 10017. S Kirk Cabeen, Dir
Holdings: Vols 250,000 Cat Maps 16mm Films Microforms
Notes: One of the largest, most comprehensive engineering libraries in the world. Covers all engineering disciplines; particularly strong in electrical and electronic, mechanical, mining and metallurgical, petroleum, chemical, industrial, air conditioning and refrigeration engineering. Incl Wheeler Collection of early materials on magnetism and electricity. 125, 000 bound periodical volumes; 10,000 maps; 5000 serial subscriptions (many foreign-lanugage). Virtually all materials abstracted in *Engineering Index* (1884-date) are incl in Library. Noncirculating, except to members of professional engineering societies which support the Library. See *Engineering Societies Library, New York, Classed Subject Catalog and Index* (Boston: G K Hall, 1963); and *Supplements,* 1-10, 1964-1973.

NY —CARRIER CORPORATION, Logan Lewis Library, Research Division, Carrier Parkway, Syracuse, 13221. Christine Greene, Librn
Holdings: Vols (5000)
Notes: Emphasis on technical and research and development aspects of the air conditioning, heating and refrigeration industry.

NY —YONKERS PUBLIC LIBRARY, Information Services, 7 Main St, Yonkers, 10701. Martita Schwarz, Dept Head
Holdings: Vols (21,500) Cat Maps Microforms
Budget: ($30,000)

NC —TECHNICAL INSTITUTE OF ALAMANCE, Learning Resources Center, Jimmy Kerr Rd, PO Box 623, Haw River, 27258. Ron Plummer, Coordr
Holdings: Vols (265) Cat Pix Phonorecords Audiotapes 16mm Films Filmstrips Microforms
Budget: ($180,000)

PA —FRANKLIN INSTITUTE LIBRARY, 20 & The Parkway, Philadelphia, 19103. Miriam Padusis, Dir; Charles Wilt, Readers Servs Librn
Holdings: Vols (300,000) Cat Maps Pix Microforms

PA —CARNEGIE LIBRARY OF PITTSBURGH, Science & Technology Dept, 4400 Forbes Ave, Pittsburgh, 15213. Catherine M Brosky, Dept Head
Notes: Collection incl material on general construction, carpentry, masonry, plumbing, heating, air conditioning, corrosion and painting and numerous other building trades. Sweets Architectural File complete except for a few years. *Car Builders Encyclopedia of American Practice,* most editions since 1879.

SC —HORRY GEORGETOWN TECHNICAL COLLEGE, Library, Hwy 501, Box 1966, Conway, 29526. Barbara Brittain, Librn
Holdings: Vols (20,000) Cat Maps Slides Microforms

HEATING—HISTORY

IN —PURDUE UNIVERSITY LIBRARIES, Graduate School of Management, Krannert Library, West Lafayette, 47907. Gordon Law, Librn
Notes: Business history. The collection consist of books, journals and pamphlets dating from the early 16th to late 19th century, covering to a large degree early literature in economic thought and business practices both here and abroad. No photocopying.

HEATING, SOLAR see Solar Heating and Cooling

HEAVY METALS

AR —NATIONAL CENTER FOR TOXICOLOGICAL RESEARCH, Library, Jefferson, 72079. Susan Laney-Sheehan, Supvr Librn
Holdings: Microforms
Notes: Incl (860) journal titles, (230) current subscriptions.

CA —UNIVERSITY OF CALIFORNIA, DAVIS, Environmental Toxicology Library, Davis, 95616. Ming-yu Li, Documentation Specialist
Holdings: Vols (5000) Cat
Notes: Library is open to the public for reference only. In addition to the cataloged holdings, the library also maintains a pamphlet collection of 50 file drawers on agricultural chemcials, environmental pollution, heavy metals, food toxicants, toxicology, pesticides and trace elements.

HEAVY WATER REACTORS

ON —ATOMIC ENERGY OF CANADA LIMITED, Main Library, Technical Information Branch, Chalk River Nuclear Laboratories, Chalk River, K0J 1J0, Can. Harry Greenshields, Chief Librn
Holdings: Vols (128,700) Microforms
Budget: ($662,400)
Notes: The Main Library, Atomic Energy of Canada Limited, is the Canadian repository for the literature of nuclear science and technology. Its collections reflect both fundamental and nuclear aspects of biology, chemistry, electronics, engineering, mathematics, computers, metallurgy, physics and other specific areas of science involving nuclear technology with special emphasis on heavy water reactor systems. 512,000 research reports are available in paper copy and microfiche form. Incl US DOE, INIS and other offshore nuclear research reports. 386,000 microforms.

HEBERT, FELIX EDWARD

LA —TULANE UNIVERSITY, Howard-Tilton Memorial Library, Special Collections Div, 7001 Freret St, New Orleans, 70118. Wilbur E Meneray, Librn
Holdings: Cat Mss Pix Audiotapes Videotapes
Notes: Papers of Louisiana politicians, including Thomas Hale Boggs, Felix Edward Hebert, Sam Houston Jones and deLesseps Story Morrison.

HEBRAICA

CA —UNIVERSITY OF CALIFORNIA, LOS ANGELES, Research Library, Jewish Studies Collection, 405 Hilgard Ave, Los Angeles, 90024. Edward Shreeves, Chairman, Bibliographers Group; Shimeon Brisman, Jewish Studies Bibliographer
Holdings: Vols (100,000) Cat Mss Microforms

CO —UNIVERSITY OF DENVER LIBRARIES, Denver, 80210. Steve Fisher, Librn
Holdings: Vols 10,000 Cat Mss Pix
Notes: The Rabbi I Edward Kiev Collection, incl many areas and all periods of Judaica: history, religion, philosophy, mysticism, law, sociology, linguistics and Hebrew literature, also rare books.

DC —LIBRARY OF CONGRESS, African and Middle Eastern Division, Washington, 20540.
Holdings: Cat Mss Microforms
Notes: Hebraica: about 109,000 vols in Hebrew, Yiddish, Judeo-Arabic, Judeo-Persian, Ladino, Syriac, Ethiopic; espec strong in Biblical subjects, responsa literature, and socio-political aspects.

FL —UNIVERSITY OF FLORIDA LIBRARY, Isser and Rae Price Library of Judaica, 18 Libr East, Gainesville, 32611. Robert Singerman, Head Librn
Budget: ($30,000)
Notes: Total holdings estimated at 55,000 vols dealing with the political, social, economic and intellectual history of the Jews in the ancient, medieval and modern periods and in all geographic areas. The following areas are especially well represented by printed matter in all relevant languages: Bibliography, Festschriften, History, Bible, Judaism and Jewish theology, liturgy, responsa, rabbinical literature, Jewish law, Hebrew language and literature, Yiddish language and literature, anti-semitism, Zionism, Palestine and the *Yishuv,* and the State of Israel. German and American Judaica form a collecting emphasis with holdings for all the standard histories as well as histories of individual synagogues, institutions and local communities. Works in Hebrew and Yiddish comprise about 60 percent of the collection (estimated 30,000 vols). With few exceptions, holdingsare limited to nineteenth and twentieth century imprints, with complete sets of journals and thousands of ephemeral pamphlets, many of them commemorating anniversaries, enhancing the research value of the collection, the largest Judaica research library in the southeastern United States. Only about half of the collection is cataloged; the collection is a circulating one and vols may be borrowed on interlibrary loan. Incl the Leonard C Mishkin Collection (40,000 vols), the largest personal Judaica collection in the United States, the Shlomo Marenof Collection (3500 vols), and the inventory of Bernard Morgenstern's Lower East Side Book Store (8000 vols). Scholars should inquire in advance of their visit. *The Isser and Rae Price Library of Judaica* Report (circulation 2900 copies) is mailed gratis twice a year to all interested parties. Special catalogs:Pre-1881 Hebrew imprints recorded in a chronological card file.

IL —SPERTUS COLLEGE OF JUDAICA, Asher Library, 618 S Michigan Ave, Chicago, 60605. Richard W Marcus, Librn
Holdings: Vols 60,000 Cat Maps Microforms
Budget: $130,000

IL —HEBREW THEOLOGICAL COLLEGE, Saul Silber Memorial Library, 7135 N Carpenter Rd, Skokie, 60077. Leah Mishkin, Head Librn/Cur
Holdings: Vols (58,000) Cat Mss Microforms
Notes: Main subject is rabbinics (Halachic literature). We also have a very large and important Holocaust Collection.

IA —UNIVERSITY OF IOWA, University Libraries, Iowa City, 52242.
Holdings: Vols 1850 Mss
Notes: The Leo W Schwarz Collection, a valuable and rare group of books dealing with Hasidic literature, a portion on Old Testament studies and works on Jewish history, philosophy and culture, the Jews in Nazi Germany, Jewish folklore and the history of the Jews in the US. Incl about 850 books in Hebrew and 1000 in other languages, mss of several of Schwarz's books and articles, correspondence, notes, and background research relating to his publications.

MD —JOHNS HOPKINS UNIVERSITY, Milton S Eisenhower Library, Charles & 34 Sts, Baltimore, 21218. Ann S Gwyn, Assistant Dir for Special Collections
Holdings: Cat Mss Maps
Notes: Strong collection, espec in Biblical studies, Hebraica, and Assyriology, but with some omissions. Includes Leopold Strouse Rabbinical Library with Hebrew and Oriental mss.

MD —JOHNS HOPKINS UNIVERSITY, Milton S Eisenhower Library, George Peabody Collection, 17 E Mt Vernon Place, Baltimore, 21201. Lyn Hart, Peabody Librn
Notes: Emphasis on materials published before 1950. Strength is a good collection through the 19th century.

†MA —HARVARD UNIVERSITY LIBRARY, Widener Library, Judaica Collection, Room M, Cambridge, 02138. Charles Berlin, Bibliographer
Holdings: Cat Mss
Notes: 50,000 vols in Hebrew, plus related items. *Catalogue of Hebrew Books* (6 vols) published by Library in 1968, with 3-volume *Supplement* in 1972. *Catalogue of Hebrew Manuscripts* published by library in 1975. See also *Jewish Book Annual,* XXVI (1968/9) 58-63.

MA —BRANDEIS UNIVERSITY, Goldfarb Library, 415 South St, Waltham, 02154. Bessie Hahn, Dir

MI —UNIVERSITY OF MICHIGAN, Library, Dept of Rare Books & Special Collections,

HEBRAICA (cont.)

Ann Arbor, 48109. Robert J Starring, Head
Holdings: Mss
Notes: Over 1200 mss chiefly in Arabic, but also in Persian, Turkish, Coptic, Syriac, Ethiopic, Hebrew, and Armenian. Incl the McGregor collection on mathematics and astronomy, the Tiflis collection, and portions of the Abdul Hamid and Yahuda collections.

NY —HEBREW UNION COLLEGE, Jewish Institute of Religion, Klau Library, 1 W 4th St, New York, 10012. Philip Miller, Librn
Holdings: Vols (115,000) Cat Mss Microforms
Notes: Hebrew literature--ancient, medieval and modern.

NY —NEW YORK PUBLIC LIBRARY, Jewish Division, Fifth Ave & 42 St, New York, 10018. Leonard S Gold, Chief
Holdings: Vols (200,000) Cat Mss Microforms
Budget: ($33,383)
Notes: A collection of material in all languages on Judaism, Jewish history, literature and traditions from the earliest times to date and works in the Hebrew alphabet (mainly Hebrew and Yiddish) on a variety of subjects. The division has extensive files of Jewish periodicals and newspapers. The collection of rare Hebraica incl medieval texts, cabalistic works, ethical and philosophical tracts in book form. See *Dictionary Catalog of the Jewish Collection* (Boston: G K Hall, 1960), 14 vols. First Supplement (Boston: G K Hall, 1975), 8 vols.

NY —YESHIVA UNIVERSITY, Library, 500 West 185th Street, New York, 10033. Pearl Berger
Holdings: Cat

NY —YESHIVA UNIVERSITY-STERN COLLEGE FOR WOMEN, Hedi Steinberg Library, 245 Lexington Ave, New York, 10016. Edith Lubetski, Librn
Holdings: Vols (9000) Cat Maps Phonorecords
Notes: Incl a graded Hebrew Reading Collection.

NY —YIVO INSTITUTE FOR JEWISH RESEARCH, Library & Archives, 1048 Fifth Ave, New York, 10028. Dina Abramowicz, Librn; Marek Web, Archivist
Holdings: Cat Mss Pix

NC —UNIVERSITY OF NORTH CAROLINA, CHAPEL HILL, Wilson Library, Rare Book Collection, Chapel Hill, 27514. Paul S Koda, Cur of Rare Books
Holdings: Cat
Notes: Books, periodicals, and articles from 1523 on, chiefly in Hebrew and English, with many volumes from the 17th and 18th centuries. In addition, a portion of the Jacob Sarna library.

OH —HEBREW UNION COLLEGE-JEWISH INSTITUTE OF RELIGION, Klau Library, 3101 Clifton Ave, Cincinnati, 45220. David J Gilner, Reference Librn
Holdings: Cat Mss
Notes: Major collection of Hebrew literature; incl some Agnon manuscripts and Agnon works in many languages.

OH —OHIO STATE UNIVERSITY, William Oxley Thompson Memorial Library, 1858 Neil Ave, Columbus, 43210. Amnon Zipin, Jewish Studies Bibliographer
Holdings: Vols (43,000) Cat Maps Microfilms
Budget: ($35,000)
Notes: Collection emphasis is materials on Jewish history (especially US, Israel and Europe) and Hebrew language and literature. Small collection of Yiddish materials.

PA —FREE LIBRARY OF PHILADELPHIA, Education, Philosophy and Religion Department, Logan Sq, Philadelphia, 19103. Esther J Maurer, Head
Holdings: Vols 2200 // Cat
Notes: Judaica and Hebraica library formerly owned by Moses Marx. Contains source material on local German-Jewish communities pre-World War II. Bibliographies, festschriften and works on liturgy are notable. Most of the collection is in German and Hebrew. Also incl books in French, Latin and Spanish.

†PA —GRATZ COLLEGE LIBRARY, Tenth St & Tabor Rd, Philadelphia, 19141.
Notes: Hebraica, Judaica, education.

PA —LIBRARY COMPANY OF PHILADELPHIA, 1314 Locust St, Philadelphia, 19107. Edwin Wolf II, Librn; Kenneth Finkel, Cur of Prints
Notes: The Edwin Wolf Collection of Judaica, consisting of 165 manuscripts and more than 500 books and broadsides printed in the US between 1718 and 1875. Incl literature, prayer books, Hebrew schoolbooks, reports of Jewish organizations, missionary tracts, narratives of travel to Palestine, and books on medicine. Most of the manuscripts consists of correspondence of the Gratz family, American pioneers.

PA —DUQUESNE UNIVERSITY, Library, Pittsburgh, 15282. Dena F Jacobson, Music and Reference Librn
Holdings: Vols 3000 Cat
Notes: Main emphasis of collection is on history of Jewish philosophy in the Middle Ages and relationship between Jewish and Christian scholars; collection incl works by 14th century writer Nicolas de Lyra and general Judaica, history of the Jews, theology, Bible texts and commentaries, literature, grammatical works and dictionaries, etc.

TX —UNIVERSITY OF TEXAS LIBRARIES, General Libraries, PO Box P, Austin, 78713. Carolyn Bucknell, Asst Dir for Collection Development
Holdings: Cat Microforms

TX —TEXAS TECH UNIVERSITY, Library, Lubbock, 79409. David J Murrah, Assoc Dir for Special Collections

UT —UNIVERSITY OF UTAH, Middle East Library, Salt Lake City, 84112. Ragai N Makar, Librn
Holdings: Vols 4000 Cat
Budget: ($40,000)
Notes: From the library of Samuel Mendelson.

ON —NATIONAL LIBRARY OF CANADA, 395 Wellington St, Ottawa, K1A 0N4, Can. Andre Preibish, Dir
Notes: *The Jacob M Lowy Collection* over 2000 works of very rare Hebraica and Judaica. Among outstanding items are 30 incunabula - the first printed edition of the Babylonian Talmud, many editions of Flavius Josephus, including first edition of 1470 Early Bibles in many languages. *The Saul Hayes Collection* of Hebraic Manuscripts and microforms. Manuscripts from North Africa and the Orient; 300 reels of manuscripts held by libraries in Poland, USSR and Hungary. This collection is held in the Jacob M Lowy Room.

HEBREW ART see Art, Jewish

HEBREW ARTISTS see Artists, Jewish

HEBREW CHRISTIAN ALLIANCE OF AMERICA

IL —WHEATON COLLEGE, Buswell Memorial Library, Wheaton, 60187. Paul Snezek, Library Dir
Holdings: Mss
Notes: Collection includes publications of pamphlets and articles. *Related Topics:* Hebrew Christian Alliance of America.

HEBREW IMPRINTS

FL —UNIVERSITY OF FLORIDA LIBRARY, Isser and Rae Price Library of Judaica, 18 Libr East, Gainesville, 32611. Robert Singerman, Head Librn
Budget: ($30,000)
Notes: Total holdings estimated at 55,000 vols dealing with the political, social, economic and intellectual history of the Jews in the ancient, medieval and modern periods and in all geographic areas. The following areas are especially well represented by printed matter in all relevant languages: Bibliography, Festschriften, History, Bible, Judaism and Jewish theology, liturgy, responsa, rabbinical literature, Jewish law, Hebrew language and literature, Yiddish language and literature, anti-semitism, Zionism, Palestine and the *Yishuv*, and the State of Israel. German and American Judaica form a collecting emphasis with holdings for all the standard histories as well as histories of individual synagogues, institutions and local communities. Works in Hebrew and Yiddish comprise about 60 percent of the collection (estimated 30,000 vols). With few exceptions, holdingsare limited to nineteenth and twentieth century imprints, with complete sets of journals and thousands of ephemeral pamphlets, many of them commemorating anniversaries, enhancing the research value of the collection, the largest Judaica research library in the southeastern United States. Only about half of the collection is cataloged; the collection is a circulating one and vols may be borrowed on interlibrary loan. Incl the Leonard C Mishkin Collection (40,000 vols), the largest personal Judaica collection in the United States, the Shlomo Marenof Collection (3500 vols), and the inventory of Bernard Morgenstern's Lower East Side Book Store (8000 vols). Scholars should inquire in advance of their visit. *The Isser and Rae Price Library of Judaica* Report (circulation 2900 copies) is mailed gratis twice a year to all interested parties. Special catalogs:Pre-1881 Hebrew imprints recorded in a chronological card file.

HEBREW LANGUAGE AND LITERATURE

CA —JUDAH L MAGNES MEMORIAL MUSEUM, Morris Goldstein Library, 2911 Russell St, Berkeley, 94705. Jane Levy, Archivist
Holdings: Vols 7000 Cat Mss Maps 16mm Films
Notes: Judaica, incl Hebrew manuscripts, Yiddish literature, and Jewish music and art.

†CA —HEBREW UNION COLLEGE, Jewish Institute of Religion, 3077 University Ave, Los Angeles, 90007.
Notes: Bible, Talmud, Rabbinics, Jewish history, philosophy, art and communal science, Hebrew literature, religion, Zionism.

CA —LOS ANGELES PUBLIC LIBRARY, Foreign Languages Dept, 630 W Fifth St, Los Angeles, 90071. Sylva Manoogian, Principal Librn
Holdings: Vols 2386 Cat
Budget: ($41,500)

CA —UNIVERSITY OF CALIFORNIA, LOS ANGELES, Research Library, Jewish Studies Collection, 405 Hilgard Ave, Los Angeles, 90024. Edward Shreeves, Chairman, Bibliographers Group; Shimeon Brisman, Jewish Studies Bibliographer
Holdings: Vols (100,000) Cat Mss Microforms

DC —LIBRARY OF CONGRESS, African and Middle Eastern Division, Washington, 20540.
Holdings: Cat Mss Microforms
Notes: Hebraica: about 109,000 vols in Hebrew, Yiddish, Judeo-Arabic, Judeo-Persian, Ladino, Syriac, Ethiopic; espec strong in Biblical subjects, responsa literature, and socio-political aspect.

FL —UNIVERSITY OF FLORIDA LIBRARY, Isser and Rae Price Library of Judaica, 18 Libr East, Gainesville, 32611. Robert Singerman, Head Librn
Budget: ($30,000)
Notes: Total holdings estimated at 55,000 vols dealing with the political, social, economic and intellectual history of the Jews in the ancient, medieval and modern periods and in all geographic areas. The following areas are especially well represented by printed matter in all relevant languages: Bibliography, Festschriften, History, Bible, Judaism and Jewish theology, liturgy, responsa, rabbinical literature, Jewish law, Hebrew language and literature, Yiddish language and literature, anti-semitism, Zionism, Palestine and the *Yishuv*, and the State of Israel. German and American Judaica form a collecting emphasis with holdings for all the standard histories as well as histories of individual synagogues,

HEBREW LANGUAGE AND LITERATURE (cont.)

institutions and local communities. Works in Hebrew and Yiddish comprise about 60 percent of the collection (estimated 30,000 vols). With few exceptions, holdingsare limited to nineteenth and twentieth century imprints, with complete sets of journals and thousands of ephemeral pamphlets, many of them commemorating anniversaries, enhancing the research value of the collection, the largest Judaica research library in the southeastern United States. Only about half of the collection is cataloged; the collection is a circulating one and vols may be borrowed on interlibrary loan. Incl the Leonard C Mishkin Collection (40,000 vols), the largest personal Judaica collection in the United States, the Shlomo Marenof Collection (3500 vols), and the inventory of Bernard Morgenstern's Lower East Side Book Store (8000 vols). Scholars should inquire in advance of their visit. *The Isser and Rae Price Library of Judaica* Report (circulation 2900 copies) is mailed gratis twice a year to all interested parties. Special catalogs:Pre-1881 Hebrew imprints recorded in a chronological card file.

IL —HEBREW THEOLOGICAL COLLEGE, Saul Silber Memorial Library, 7135 N Carpenter Rd, Skokie, 60077. Leah Mishkin, Head Librn/Cur
Holdings: Vols (58,000) Cat Mss Microforms
Notes: Main subject is rabbinics (Halachic literature). We also have a very large and important Holocaust Collection.

IA —UNIVERSITY OF IOWA, University Libraries, Iowa City, 52242.
Holdings: Vols 1850 Mss
Notes: The Leo W Schwarz Collection, a valuable and rare group of books dealing with Hasidic literature, a portion on Old Testament studies and works on Jewish history, philosophy and culture, the Jews in Nazi Germany, Jewish folklore and the history of the Jews in the US. Incl about 850 books in Hebrew and 1000 in other languages, mss of several of Schwarz's books and articles, correspondence, notes, and background research relating to his publications.

MA —HEBREW COLLEGE, Jacob & Rose Grossman Library and Lawrence Jay & Anne Cable Rubenstein Library, 43 Hawes St, Brookline, 02146. Maurice Tuchman, Librn
Notes: Jewish history, Hebrew literature, Israel Rabbinic literature.

NY —ALFRED UNIVERSITY, Herrick Memorial Library, Alfred, 14802. June E Brown, Head Librn
Holdings: Vols (1200) // Cat Mss
Notes: The Bergren Collection. A comprehensive collection on Biblical Studies in the Old and New Testaments. Includes material on the Dead Sea Scrolls, Eastern religions, and Hebrew and Aramaic languages.

NY —HEMPSTEAD PUBLIC LIBRARY, Foreign Language Collection, 115 Nichols Court, Hempstead, 11550. Irene A Duszkiewicz, Dir
Notes: Mainly French, German, Italian, Spanish, Polish, Yiddish, Hebrew. Holdings in other languages, including Asian.

NY —HEBREW UNION COLLEGE, Jewish Institute of Religion, Klau Library, 1 W 4th St, New York, 10012. Philip Miller, Librn
Holdings: Vols (115,000) Cat Mss Microforms
Notes: Hebrew literature--ancient, medieval and modern.

NY —JEWISH BRAILLE INSTITUTE OF AMERICA, 110 E 30St, New York, 10016. Richard Borgersen, Library Dir
Holdings: Vols (50,000) Cat Audiotapes
Budget: ($75,000)
Notes: A worldwide circulating library of English and Hebrew Braille, English, Hebrew and Yiddish tape talking books and English and Hebrew large type books. All books sent free of charge. Loan period 90 days.

†NY —JEWISH THEOLOGICAL SEMINARY OF AMERICA LIBRARY, 3080 Broadway, New York, 10027.

NY —NEW YORK PUBLIC LIBRARY, Donnell Foreign Language Library, 20 W 53 St, New York, 10019. Bosiljka Stevanovic, Supvr Librn
Holdings: Vols 915 Cat
Notes: Hebrew collection incl Hebrew authors of Hebrew expression. No separate catalog.

NY —NEW YORK PUBLIC LIBRARY, Jewish Division, Fifth Ave & 42 St, New York, 10018. Leonard S Gold, Chief
Holdings: Vols (200,000) Cat Mss Microforms
Budget: ($33,383)
Notes: A collection of material in all languages on Judaism, Jewish history, literature and traditions from the earliest times to date and works in the Hebrew alphabet (mainly Hebrew and Yiddish) on a variety of subjects. The division has extensive files of Jewish periodicals and newspapers. The collection of rare Hebraica incl medieval texts, cabalistic works, ethical and philosophical tracts in book form. See *Dictionary Catalog of the Jewish Collection* (Boston: G K Hall, 1960), 14 vols. First Supplement (Boston: G K Hall, 1975), 8 vols.

NY —YIVO INSTITUTE FOR JEWISH RESEARCH, Library & Archives, 1048 Fifth Ave, New York, 10028. Dina Abramowicz, Librn; Marek Web, Archivist
Holdings: Cat Mss Pix

NC —CUMBERLAND COUNTY PUBLIC LIBRARY, North Carolina Foreign Language Center, 328 Gillespie St, Fayetteville, 28301. Patrick M Valentine, Coordinator
Holdings: Vols (25,000) Cat Phonorecords Audiotapes
Notes: The largest book collections are, in descending order of size, German Spanish, French, Japanese, Korean and Vietnamese, with fair sized collections in Italian, Russian, Chinese, Arabic, Greek, Hungarian, Polish, Hebrew, Thai, and Hindi. The Center has several shelves each of books in Bengali, Dutch, Marathi, Portuguese, Urdu, and Yiddish. Smaller collections of one to three shelves each incl Catalan, Croatian, Czech, Danish, Finnish, Gujarati, Icelandic, Kannada, Latin, Lithuanian, Malayalam, Norwegian, Panjabi, Persian (Farsi), Romanian, Slovak, Swedish, Tagalog, Tamil, Telegu, and Ukrianian. The Center has grammars, dictionaries and occasionally other readings in languages from Afrikaans and Albanian to Welsh, Yoruba and Zulu.

OH —HEBREW UNION COLLEGE-JEWISH INSTITUTE OF RELIGION, Klau Library, 3101 Clifton Ave, Cincinnati, 45220. David J Gilner, Reference Librn
Holdings: Cat Mss
Notes: Major collection of Hebrew literature; incl some Agnon manuscripts and Agnon works in many languages.

OH —CLEVELAND PUBLIC LIBRARY, Foreign Literature Dept, 325 Superior Ave, Cleveland, 44114. Natalia Bezugloff, Head
Holdings: Vols 3830 Cat
Notes: A popular circulating collection containing classics and the standard works with emphasis on belles lettres, history and biography. A variety of other subjects such as learning languages, how to do books, art, children's books, spoken phonodiscs and cassettes, periodicals, etc. Incl 1720 ephemera.
See also entry under Foreign Language Collections

OH —OHIO STATE UNIVERSITY, William Oxley Thompson Memorial Library, 1858 Neil Ave, Columbus, 43210. Amnon Zipin, Jewish Studies Bibliographer
Holdings: Vols (43,000) Cat Maps Microfilms
Budget: ($35,000)
Notes: Collection emphasis is materials on Jewish history (especially US, Israel and Europe) and Hebrew language and literature. Small collection of Yiddish materials.

TX —UNIVERSITY OF TEXAS LIBRARIES, General Libraries, PO Box P, Austin, 78713. Carolyn Bucknell, Asst Dir for Collection Development
Holdings: Cat Microforms

UT —UNIVERSITY OF UTAH, Middle East Library, Salt Lake City, 84112. Ragai N Makar, Librn
Holdings: Vols 4000 Cat
Budget: ($40,000)
Notes: From the library of Samuel Mendelson.

WA —UNIVERSITY OF WASHINGTON LIBRARIES, Suzzallo Library, Near East Section, FM-25, Seattle, 98195. Fawzi W Khoury, Head
Holdings: Vols 13,000 Cat
Budget: ($52,752)
Notes: Includes a collection of 13,000 Hebrew language materials.

HEBREW LAW see Jewish Law

HEBREW MANUSCRIPTS see Manuscripts, Hebrew

HEBREW THEATRE see Theatre—Jews

HEBREWS see Jews

HECHT, BEN, 1893-1964

IL —NEWBERRY LIBRARY, 60 W Walton St, Chicago, 60610. Diana Haskell, Cur of Modern Mss
Holdings: Mss Pix
Notes: Primary repository. 100 boxes containing correspondence, screenplays, book mss, photographs. Restricted use: noncirculating.

†IL —UNIVERSITY OF ILLINOIS, URBANA/CHAMPAIGN, Library, Wright St, 230 Library UIUC, Urbana, 61801.
Notes: The Ben Hecht Collection incl all first editions, most first British and paperback editions, reprints, screenplays, letters, typescripts, playbills, and pressbooks.

HECKENWELDER, JONATHAN

OH —RUTHERFORD B HAYES LIBRARY, 1337 Hayes Ave, Fremont, 43420. Watt P Marchman, Dir
Notes: Correspondence in the Lyman-Lincoln Collection.

HEDGEROW THEATRE (MOYLAN, PENNSYLVANIA)

MA —BOSTON UNIVERSITY, Mugar Memorial Library, Special Collections Dept, 771 Commonwealth Ave, Boston, 02215. Howard B Gotlieb, Dir
Notes: Archives of America's longest running repertory theatre.

HEDGEROWS see Windbreaks, Shelterbelts, Etc.

HEELEY, DESMOND

ON —METROPOLITAN TORONTO LIBRARY, Theatre Dept, 789 Yonge St, Toronto, M4W 2G8, Can. Heather McCallum, Head
Notes: Theatre Department is one of eleven subject departments of the Metropolitan Toronto Library, which is generally acknowledged to be the most comprehensive of Canadian public library collections. The collection balances book and nonbook material in all areas of the performing arts. Production history is the special emphasis of the dance collection, as it is for all the material in the Theatre Department. This is supported by the department's extensive holdings of programs, posters, photographs and press clippings for Canadian productions and dancers, as well as a representative selection of material for non-Canadian dance. Important original stage designs in the collection incl work by Mstislav Dobujinsky for the Canadian ballet *Red Ear of Corn,* which was produced by Boris Volkoff in 1949; Maurice Strike's work for the National Ballet of Canada's productionof *Coppelia,* and Desmond Heeley's designs for that company's *Swan Lake.* Ms collections incl: The Boris Volkoff Collection (qv); papers of the Toronto dance teacher Bettina

HEELEY, DESMOND (cont.)

Byers; the papers of two Canadian dance critics, Ralph Hicklin and John Fraser; and the Mary Wigman Collection, consisting of xerox copies of letters exchanged between Miss Wigman and her Canadian pupil Judy Jarvis, and a taped conversation with Miss Wigman.

HEFLIN, WOODFORD

†ON —UNIVERSITY OF WESTERN ONTARIO, School of Library and Information Science, Special Collections Room, London, N6A 5B9, Can.
Notes: Archive of lexicographical materials of the Committee on Lexicography of the Modern Language Association. Incl lexicographical slips for *The United States Air Force Dictionary* and The *Second Aerospace Glossary*, by Woodford Heflin. 13 cartons of slips.

HEGEL, GEORGE W. F.

MA —HARVARD UNIVERSITY LIBRARY, Houghton Library, Cambridge, 02138. Rodney G Dennis, Cur of Manuscripts
Holdings: Cat Mss

HEIDENHEIMER BROTHERS, GROCERS, GALVESTON

TX —UNIVERSITY OF TEXAS LIBRARIES, General Libraries, PO Box P, Austin, 78713. Carolyn Bucknell, Asst Dir for Collection Development
Notes: Papers of retail grocers, Heidenheimer Brothers, of Galveston, being travelling salesmen's correspondence and other papers, bound by month and year, measuring 35 linear feet.

HEIFETZ, JASCHA

DC —LIBRARY OF CONGRESS, Music Division, Washington, 20540.
Holdings: Cat Mss Maps Pix Slides Microforms

HEINE, HEINRICH

CT —YALE UNIVERSITY, Beinecke Rare Book & Manuscript Library, Osborn Collection, New Haven, 06520. Stephen R Parks, Cur
Holdings: Mss

MA —HARVARD UNIVERSITY LIBRARY, Houghton Library, Cambridge, 02138. F Thomas Noonan, Cur, Reading Room; Lawrence Dowler, Associate Librn
Holdings: Cat Mss
Notes: See *Harvard Library Notes*, III (1935), 71-80.

HEINECKEN, ROBERT

AZ —UNIVERSITY OF ARIZONA, Center for Creative Photography, 843 E University Blvd, Tucson, 85721. James Enyeart, Dir; Terence Pitts, Cur and Librn
Notes: Center has significant collections consisting of more than 25 photographs plus other archival material such as negatives, contact sheets, work prints, correspondence, financial records, diaries, project files, etc. Inventories of the collections are available to researchers. Published guides available for some collections.

HEINLEIN, ROBERT

CA —UNIVERSITY OF CALIFORNIA, SANTA CRUZ, University Library, Special Collections, Santa Cruz, 95064. Rita Bottoms, Special Collections Librn; Margaret Felts, South Pacific Collection Bibliographer
Notes: Archives of Robert Heinlein. Mss and published works noncirculating. Scholarly research only.

†LA —TULANE UNIVERSITY, Libraries, Rare Books Dept, New Orleans, 70118. Sylvia V Metzinger, Librn
Notes: Science fiction, 1000 vols and growing. Rosel George Brown and Robert A Heinlein special collections.

HEINRICH, WILLI

MA —BOSTON UNIVERSITY, Mugar Memorial Library, Special Collections Dept, 771 Commonwealth Ave, Boston, 02215. Howard B Gotlieb, Dir
Holdings: Cat Mss
Notes: Mss, correspondence, etc collected in depth; incl publications by or about.

HEINSEN FAMILY

CA —CALIFORNIA STATE UNIVERSITY, HAYWARD, Library, Hayward, 94542. Melissa Rose, Dir
Holdings: Vols (14,000) // Cat Mss Pix
Budget: ($7408)
Notes: Jensen Family Papers (about 3000 leaves) consisting of letters, journals, original watercolors, are the papers of a pioneer German family (Jensen-Hensen) who settled in the 1860s in the Hayward-Castro Valley, Calif, area. Covering the approx period 1830-1920, the collection incl both sides of the correspondence, a large part of which is written in German script.

HELLEGERS, ANDRE E.

DC —GEORGETOWN UNIVERSITY, Library, Special Collections Div, 37 & O Sts NW, Washington, 20057. George M Barringer, Special Collections Librn; Nicholas B Sheetz, Mss Librn
Holdings: Mss Cat Pix
Notes: Papers of Andre E Hellegers, obstetrician, gynecologist and leading authority in bioethics. The major bulk of the papers concerns Dr Helleger's directorship of the Joseph and Rose Kennedy Institute for Ethics, 1971-1979. Incl are numerous publications and mss written by Hellegers and others on abortion, birth control, population research, and bioethics.

HELLENISM

DC —HARVARD UNIVERSITY, Dumbarton Oaks, Research Library, 1703 32nd St NW, Washington, 20007. Irene Vaslef, Librn
Holdings: Vols (91,000) Cat Maps Pix Slides Microforms
Budget: ($219,000)
Notes: Byzantine civilization (including art, archaeology, literature, history, religion, law, music, etc). Extensive supplemental material on Classical, Hellenistic, Medieval, Islamic, Medieval Slavic cultures. 62,000 b/w photographs, 25,000 slides and transparencies, 1000 microfilms of books and manuscripts. Printed description of collection in *Harvard Library Bulletin*, vol 19, no 1 (Jan 1971), pp 25-35 and vol 19, no 2 (April 1971), pp 204-214, pp 25-35 and vol 19, no 2 (April 1971), pp 204-214.

DC —HARVARD UNIVERSITY, Center for Hellenic Studies Library, 3100 Whitehaven St NW, Washington, 20008. Jeno Platthy, Librn
Holdings: Vols (42,000) Cat Maps
Budget: ($76,824)
Notes: In addition to a large collection of editions of ancient Greek authors, the library is well equipped to cover every aspect of ancient Greek civilization from prehistoric times to about AD 200. The subject fields covered include epigraphy, paleography, papyrology, history, literature, philosophy, religion, mythology, archaeology and art. A small collection of works on Patristics as well as all important Latin authors complete the Center's holdings.

HELLER, FRANKLIN

NY —HAMPDEN-BOOTH THEATRE LIBRARY AT THE PLAYERS, 16 Gramercy Park, New York, 10003. Louis A Rachow, Librn/Cur
Holdings: Mss Pix
Notes: The Franklin Heller Collection, incl correspondence, photographs; playscripts by Moss Hart and George S Kaufman, John Steinbeck, Thomas Wolfe, and others. (110 items). Described in *Theatre & Performing Arts Collections* (New York: Haworth Press, 1981).

HELLER, JOSEPH, 1923-

MA —BRANDEIS UNIVERSITY, Goldfarb Library, 415 South St, Waltham, 02154. Bessie Hahn, Dir
Notes: 3 linear ft of first and signed editions of Joseph Heller, 19 linear ft of mss material incl the original mss of "Catch-22". The collection has not been processed as yet, spring 1984.

NV —UNIVERSITY OF NEVADA, RENO, University Library, Special Collections Dept, Reno, 89557. Robert E Blesse, Head
Holdings: Vols (23) Cat
Notes: Includes individual works by author in all editions including translations; also prefaces, introductions, published correspondence, appearances in anthologies, periodicals, etc. Bibliographical research collection, part of Modern Authors Collection. Other appearances 50 cataloged.

HELLER, SELIG

TX —TEXAS TECH UNIVERSITY, Library, Lubbock, 79409. David J Murrah, Assoc Dir for Special Collections

HELLER, WALTER W.

†MA —JOHN F KENNEDY LIBRARY, Columbia Point, Boston, 02125. Dan H Fenn Jr, Dir
Holdings: // Cat Mss
Notes: Walter W Heller's correspondence and other papers relating to national economic policy, 1940-1971. 50 linear ft of mss. Holdings are described in "Historical Materials in the John F Kennedy Library." Copies may be obtained by writing the Research Archivist.

HELLMAN, GEOFFREY T.

NY —NEW YORK UNIVERSITY, Elmer Holmes Bobst Library, Div of Special Collections, Washington Sq S, New York, 10012. Frank Walker, Librn; Patrick McGuire, Asst Librn
Notes: Extensive Geoffrey T Hellman collection of articles, letters and memorabilia; much material concerning Harold Ross; a great deal on New York City.

HELLMAN, LILLIAN

NY —COLUMBIA UNIVERSITY LIBRARIES, Rare Book & Manuscript Library, 801 Butler Library, 535 W 114 St, New York, 10027. Kenneth A Lohf, Librn
Holdings: Mss
Notes: Forty years of literary correspondence between the Harold Matson Literary Agency and numerous notable authors. Restricted use.

HELLZAPOPPIN

CA —LOS ANGELES PUBLIC LIBRARY, Frances Howard Goldwyn Hollywood Regional Library, 1623 Ivar Ave, Los Angeles, 90028. Sally Dumaux, Librn
Holdings: Vols (100,000) Cat Mss Pix VF
Budget: ($60,000)
Notes: A general and a research collection on theatre history, US and foreign, with special emphasis on Los Angeles, Chicago, and New York theatre from the late 1800s to the present. Other aspects of the collection include theatre design, make-up, costume, and acting and directing techniques. Also includes biographies of actors and actresses (many signed). The play collection of over 15,000 titles covers mainly English and American plays of the 19th and 20th century. There are over 5000 playbills, scrapbooks, posters, and programs. Special Collections: "Hellzapoppin," NY, 1938-40. Includes photographs, clippings, and programs.

HELMINTHOLOGY

IA —IOWA STATE UNIVERSITY, Library, Ames, 50011. Warren B Kuhn, Dean of Library Services
Holdings: Cat
Notes: Extensive serial holdings supplement this strong collection.

HELWIG, CARL

FL —FLORIDA STATE UNIVERSITY, Warren D Allen Music Library, Tallahassee, 32306. Dale L Hudson, Music Librn
Holdings: // Uncat
Notes: The Carl Helwig Hungarian-Slavic-Americana Recorded Sound Collection is in accessible storage, with 6000 discs and 1400 tapes arranged as nearly as possible according to Helwig's plan. Tapes dated, but not yet shelved in any visible order. Special equipment would be required to do any transcription; hence study of the contents needs to be made before attempt to rerecord. Some materials are deteriorating. Mr Helwig made radio transcriptions, recorded speeches and celebrations, choral concerts and many other perhaps unique performances. Some commercial recordings, but the great bulk of collection produced by Mr Helwig himself. Also some correspondence, espec concerning recording contracts.

HEMATOLOGY

CT —YALE MEDICAL LIBRARY, 333 Cedar St, New Haven, 06510.
Notes: A special subject emphasis.

MD —US ARMED FORCES RADIOBIOLOGY RESEARCH INSTITUTE, Naval Medical Command, Bethesda, 20014. Nannette M Pope, Head, Library Division
Holdings: Vols (50,000)
Budget: ($150,000)
Notes: Collection consists of monographs, technical reports, serials, and microfiche related to radiation effects on human and animal biology.

MA —INSTRUMENTATION LABORATORY, Library, 113 Hartwell Ave, Lexington, 02173. Jacqueline R Kates, Librn
Holdings: Vols (6000) Cat Microforms Reprints

PA —CARDEZA FOUNDATION, Tocantins Memorial Library, 1015 Walnut St, Philadelphia, 19107. Doris Riso, Librn
Holdings: Vols 1800 Cat Mss Pix
Notes: Extensive collection of hematology. Mss of the late hematologist, Leandro M Tocantins, renowned for his work in coagulation. Part of the Jefferson University. Currently 39 periodicals in the field of hematology and related biochemistry and immunology are received.

RI —MIRIAM HOSPITAL MEDICAL LIBRARY, 164 Summit Ave, Providence, 02906. Ann LeClaire, Dir of Library Services
Holdings: Cat Audiotapes
Notes: Special collection on the renal system with emphasis on kidney transplantation and dialysis.

TX —HOUSTON ACADEMY OF MEDICINE-TEXAS MEDICAL CENTER, Library, Jesse H Jones Library Bldg, Houston, 77030. Elizabeth Borst White, Special Collections Librn
Holdings: Vols (250) Cat
Notes: Historic texts and classic works are collected with emphasis on surgical intervention in cardiovascular disorders and on replacement with artificial materials or transplantation. About 55 of the titles are 19th century works on hematology.

HEMATOLOGY, FORENSIC see Forensic Hematology

HEMINGWAY, ERNEST, 1899-1961

CA —AZUSA PACIFIC COLLEGE, Marshburn Memorial Library, Citrus & Alosta, Azusa, 91702. Edward Peterman, Librn
Holdings: Vols (150) Uncat
Notes: The Odo B Stade Collection of Literary First Editions. No photocopying.

CA —CLAREMONT COLLEGES, Honnold Library, Ninth & Dartmouth, Claremont, 91711. Tania Rizzo, Special Collections Dept Head
Holdings: Vols 120 // Cat Periodicals
Notes: First and limited editions of works by and about Hemingway. Obscure publications and 66 periodicals, incl *The Little Review* (1920s), containing introductions, comments, articles of Hemingway.

CA —UNIVERSITY OF CALIFORNIA, SAN DIEGO, Central University Library, Mandeville Dept of Special Collections, La Jolla, 92093. Lynda Corey Claassen, Head
Notes: First and/or important editions of his writings are included in the Rare Book Collection.

CA —BIBLIOGRAPHIC RESEARCH LIBRARY, 964 Chapel Hill Way, San Jose, 95122. Robert B Harmon, Bibliographer
Holdings: Vols (759) Uncat Microforms
Budget: ($500)
Notes: Private research library emphasizing bibliography, political science, John Steinbeck and Ernest Hemingway.

IL —NORTHWESTERN UNIVERSITY, Library, Special Collections Dept, 1937 Sheridan Rd, Evanston, 60201. R Russell Maylone, Cur
Holdings: Vols 160 Cat Mss
Notes: First editions, letters, ephemera.

IL —KNOX COLLEGE, Henry M Seymour Library, Galesburg, 61401. Douglas L Wilson, Dir
Holdings: Cat Mss Pix
Notes: The Mr and Mrs James H Hughes Collection. Over 1500 items by or about Hemingway, incl a complete set of his books, scarce vols, mss, fugitive pieces, 14 holograph letters, programs, photographs, etc.

IL —OAK PARK PUBLIC LIBRARY, 834 Lake St, Oak Park, 60301. Barbara Ballinger, Librn
Notes: Part of Local Authors Collection. Incl books, photographs, correspondence, prints and drawings cataloged.

IN —INDIANA UNIVERSITY, Lilly Library, Seventh St, Bloomington, 47405. William R Cagle, Librn
Holdings: Vols 188 Cat Mss
Notes: First and limited editions of works by Hemingway. 47 letters Hemingway wrote to members of his family from his childhood years to 1934; also letters to Ezra Pound, 1922-1924.

MA —JOHN F KENNEDY LIBRARY, Columbia Point on Dorchester Bay, Boston, 02125. Joan L O'Connor, Cur
Holdings: Vols (1575) Cat Mss Maps Pix Slides Audiotapes Microforms
Notes: The papers of Ernest Hemingway. Incl mss for almost all his works, published and unpublished, and a large volume of correspondence, photographs (10,000), clippings, and scrapbooks. It covers his entire life. A complete catalog is available. No photocopying.

MO —WASHINGTON UNIVERSITY, Libraries, Special Collections Dept, Campus Box 1061, St Louis, 63130.
Notes: A small but significant collection of secondary material.

NV —UNIVERSITY OF NEVADA, RENO, University Library, Special Collections Dept, Reno, 89557. Robert E Blesse, Head
Holdings: // Vols (197) Cat
Notes: Includes individual works by author in all editions including translations; also prefaces, introductions, published correspondence, appearances in anthologies, periodicals, etc. Bibliographical research collection, part of Modern Authors Collection. Other appearances 525 cataloged.

NJ —PRINCETON UNIVERSITY, Library, Rare Books Dept, Princeton, 08544. Stephen Ferguson, Cur
Notes: Princeton received a gift of a virtually complete set of Hemingway first editions in 1974, from Archibald S Alexander, '28. There is a total of some 150 vols by and about Hemingway in the A-floor vault and in the Gallery. Besides monographs the Library has periodicals, magazines, and journals to which Hemingway contributed. In the General Rare Books Collections, there is a small collection of periodicals in which works by this author appear. Consult special card file "Index of Periodical Appearances" for details. The file of periodicals are shelved in B-10-B-2, Range 11. They are usually boxed in flat, red boxes. The Alexander collection is uncataloged as of January 24, 1984 and shelved in the Gallery.

VA —UNIVERSITY OF VIRGINIA, Alderman Library, Clifton Waller Barrett Collection, Charlottesville, 22901. Joan St C Crane, Cur of American Literature Collections
Holdings: Vols 400
Notes: Mss. Holograph "Green Hills of Africa", copy mss "Sun Also Rises".

HEMIPTERA

DC —SMITHSONIAN INSTITUTION LIBRARIES, Entomology Branch, Washington, 20560. Jean C Smith, Asst Dir for Bureau Services
Holdings: Vols (17,000) Cat Maps Pix

NC —NORTH CAROLINA STATE UNIVERSITY, D H Hill Library, Box 7111, Raleigh, 27695. I T Littleton, Dir
Holdings: Vols 7370 Cat
Notes: The Friedrich F Tippman Collection of 6200 volumes on entymology incl many unique and rare volumes which make the collection one of the best in the U S. Incl the Z P Metcalf collection on Homoptera and Hemiptera: 1100 vols and 24 VF cabinets.

HEMON, LOUIS

ON —METROPOLITAN TORONTO LIBRARY, Literature Dept, 789 Yonge St, Toronto, M4W 2G8, Can. Katherine McCook, Head
Holdings: Vols 70 Cat
Notes: Marie Chapdelaine Collection. Over 70 editions of the Quebec classic by Louis Hemon.

HEMORRHAGIC FEVERS

OH —MIAMI UNIVERSITY, Science Library, Oxford, 45056.
Notes: Zoonoses and related diseases. Collection partially transferred from Parker-Davis Memorial Library, Hamilton, Mont.

HENCH, ATCHESON LAUGHLIN

VA —UNIVERSITY OF VIRGINIA, Alderman Library, Manuscripts Dept, Charlottesville, 22901. Edmund Berkeley Jr, Cur
Holdings: Cat Mss Pix
Notes: The Atcheson Laughlin Hench Memorial Collection of Richard Doddridge Blackmore manuscripts consists of ca 1035 items, 1812-1973, by, about, and relating to the English poet, novelist, and agricultural experimenter. The collection chiefly contains correspondence but also includes bills; exercises; examination questions and answers from Exeter College, Oxford; proofs for the novels *Cradock Nowell* and *Perlycross*; a patent; and some printed materials. An additional part of the collection consists of miscellanea from the files of Atcheson L Hench, longtime University of Virginia professor of English, who acquired the major portion of this collection and presented it to the Library. The most significant part of the collection is the correspondence which illuminates the most important facets of Blackmore's life: his strong family ties; hisfruit growing and gardening; his novels and poetry, and his negotiations with editors, illustrators, and publishers. An unpublished register is available in the repository.

HENCHMAN, DANIEL

MA —NEW ENGLAND HISTORIC GENEALOGICAL SOCIETY, Library, 101

HENCHMAN, DANIEL (cont.)

Newbury St, Boston, 02116. Ralph J Crandell, Dir
Notes: Business papers of John and Thomas Hancock, incl those of Daniel Henchman (brother-in-law and Boston bookseller).

HENDERSON, LAURENCE

MA —BOSTON UNIVERSITY, Mugar Memorial Library, Special Collections Dept, 771 Commonwealth Ave, Boston, 02215. Howard B Gotlieb, Dir
Holdings: Cat Mss

HENDERSON, MALCOLM COLBY

CA —UNIVERSITY OF CALIFORNIA, BERKELEY, Bancroft Library, Manuscripts Division, Berkeley, 94720. James D Hart, Dir
Holdings: Mss
Notes: His papers.

HENDERSON, THOMAS S., 1789-1854

SC —COLLEGE OF CHARLESTON LIBRARY, Special Collections Dept, Charleston, 29401.
Notes: Papers, incl correspondence between Thomas Henderson and Samuel Prioleau regarding political and financial matters, June 23 and August 31, 1832.

TX —UNIVERSITY OF TEXAS LIBRARIES, General Libraries, Barker Texas History Center, PO Box P, Austin, 78712. Don Carleton, Dir

HENDERSON (THEATRE) STOCK COMPANY

MI —MICHIGAN STATE UNIVERSITY, Libraries, Special Collections Div, East Lansing, 48824. Jannette Fiore, Librn
Holdings: Uncat Mss Pix
Notes: The Russel B Nye Popular Culture Collection in the Michigan State Univ Libraries incl over (45,000) items. Most of the collection is organized into 4 categories: comic art, popular fiction, popular information materials and materials relating to the popular performing arts. Materials relating to popular theatre, music, television, radio, and film. Theatre is best represented. A significant collection of primary materials relating to the tent show incl photographs, financial and other records of the Henderson Stock Company, correspondence, leaflets, handbills and other ephemera from many of the companies playing in the upper midwest in the 1920s and 1930s, and photocopies of 250 tent show scripts.

HENDRICKS PAPERS

NY —NEW YORK HISTORICAL SOCIETY, Library, 170 Central Park W, New York, 10024. James Gregory, Librn
Holdings: Cat Mss
Notes: The Hendricks Collections traces the development of the copper industry in the U S, and reflects the life of an old and prominent Sephardic family.

HENKEL FAMILY

PA —LUTHERAN THEOLOGICAL SEMINARY, Krauth Memorial Library, 7301 Germantown Ave, Philadelphia, 19119. Rev David J Wartluft, Dir Libr
Holdings: Vols (3500) Cat Mss Microforms
Notes: Incl published minutes of United Lutheran Church in American, Lutheran Church in America, General Council and General Synod affiliated churches. Archives of General Council housed in library, also New Jersey Synod, and Slovak Zion Synod. Also incl papers of early Lutheran leaders: Muhlenbergs, Henkels, etc.

HENLE, JAKOB, 1809-1885

KS —UNIVERSITY OF KANSAS MEDICAL CENTER, College of Health Sciences & Hospital, Clendening History of Medicine Library, Rainbow Blvd at 39th, Kansas City, 66103. Robert P Hudson, Chmn/Cur
Holdings: Vols (15,725) Cat Mss
Notes: Papers, ca 1707-ca 1935. 228 ft (ca 4050 items). German histologist and anatomist. Correspondence, portraits, signatures, scientific material, and other papers, chiefly in German, but incl Dutch, English, French, Latin and Swedish. Incl letters to Adolf Henle. Unpublished finding aid in the repository. Access restricted.

HENNACY, AMMON

AZ —NORTHERN ARIZONA UNIVERSITY, Special Collection Library, CU Box 6022, Flagstaff, 86011. Peter M Whiteley, Coordr/Archivist; William Mullane, Librn
Notes: Collection of Cline Platt, president of the *Arizona Daily Sun*, Flagstaff, local historian. Historical files concerning Flagstaff and Coconino County, Incl pioneer reminiscences of Black Family, Babbitt Brothers Trading Company records, correspondence and business papers of J Gutherie Savage, 1880's-1890's, Flagstaff attorney; and Ammon Hennacy, correspondence and subject files, 1950's-1960's. Hennacy (Phoenix, Arizona, and Salt Lake City, Utah) was a noted Christian anarchist.

HENNING, ERVIN, 1910-1982

MA —BOSTON UNIVERSITY, Mugar Memorial Library, Special Collections Dept, 771 Commonwealth Ave, Boston, 02215. Howard B Gotlieb, Dir
Holdings: Cat Mss Audiotapes
Notes: Mss, correspondence, musical scores, etc collected in depth; incl publications by or about.

HENREY, MADELEINE

MA —BOSTON UNIVERSITY, Mugar Memorial Library, Special Collections Dept, 771 Commonwealth Ave, Boston, 02215. Howard B Gotlieb, Dir
Holdings: Cat Mss Correspondence

TX —TEXAS WOMAN'S UNIVERSITY, Bralley Memorial Library, Box 23715, TWU Sta, Denton, 76204. Metta Nicewarner, Spec Collections Libn
Holdings: Cat Mss Pix
Notes: Autographed copies, special limited editions, edited manuscripts, galleys, and some personal items, incl letters. No photocopying.

HENRY, AARON

MI —WAYNE STATE UNIVERSITY, Walter P Reuther Library, Archives of Labor & Urban Affairs, Detroit, 482C . Philip Mason, Dir
Notes: Papers, etc of Aaron Henry, President of the Mississippi Freedom Democratic Party.

MS —TOUGALOO COLLEGE, L Zenobia Coleman Library, Tougaloo, 39174. Virgia Brocks-Shedd, Acting Dir
Budget: ($142,650)
Notes: Civil rights cases and legal papers; lawsuits; Mississippi, 1960-1968. Local attorneys have donated papers of cases they have handled, espec attorneys of two government-funded legal services offices. Individual collections: Papers of Aaron Henry, Rev Robert L T Smith, Sr, Annie B Rankin and the Howard Kester Papers. Incl VF holdings of articles from 1930 and on.

HENRY, JOSEPH

DC —SMITHSONIAN INSTITUTION, Archives Div, Washington, 20560. William W Moss, Archivist
Holdings: Cat Mss Pix
Notes: The Archives holds the personal papers of Joseph Henry, first Secretary of the Smithsonian, as well as the existing official records of his tenure as Secretary, 1846-1878.

MA —MASSACHUSETTS INSTITUTE OF TECHNOLOGY, Institute Archives, Special Collections, Cambridge, 02139.
Notes: Papers of William Barton Rogers, geologist, founder and first President of the Massachusetts Institute of Technology (1862-1870, 1878-1881). Major correspondents incl Louis Agassiz, Joseph Henry, Thomas Sterry Hunt, and Ellen Swallow Richards. Unpublished finding aid, incl correspondent index, available in Archives.

HENRY, MELLINGER EDWARD

RI —BROWN UNIVERSITY, John Hay Library, 20 Prospect St, Providence, 02912. Mark N Brown, Cur Mss
Holdings: Mss
Notes: Papers of William O Fuller (1828-1910), music teacher of Providence, comprising letters 1848 from Europe, incl a letter from Franz Liszt; papers of Johann Christian Gottlieb Graupner (1767-1836) and John Rowe Parker (fl 1820s) collected by Horace Mason Reynolds, relating to the music-publishing business in Boston, 1802-1838; papers of the American folklorist Mellinger Edward Henry (1873-1946) relating to his research and publications on American folk-songs 1910-1942; papers, 1912-1948, of Providence composer Hugh Frederick MacColl (1885-1953); papers of Frances Herriot Sargent, stage manager for "Porgy" and "Porgy and Bess", relating to productions of these, 1928-1942.

HENRY, O. see O. Henry

HENRY, PATRICK

†AL —MUSEUMS OF THE CITY OF MOBILE, Reference Library, 355 Government St, Mobile, 36602. Caldwell Delaney, Adminr

VA —PATRICK HENRY MEMORIAL FOUNDATION, Library, Red Hill Shrine, Box 27, Brookneal, 24528. Patrick T Daily, Administrator
Holdings: Vols Cat Mss Pix Videotapes Maps
Notes: Collection includes the Robert Douthat Meade Papers which consist of over 4000 index cards, manuscripts, and copies of records used in research for 2-volume biography of Patrick Henry. Compiled 1945-1970. The Fontaine-Winston Papers contain nearly 3000 letters, writings, publications, and clippings pertaining to Patrick Henry Fontaine (1775-1855) and descendants. Compiled 1925-1975.

HENRY, WILL

CA —UNIVERSITY OF CALIFORNIA, LOS ANGELES, Research Library, Dept of Special Collections, 405 Hilgard Ave, Los Angeles, 90024. Edward Shreeves, Chairman, Bibliographers Group; David S Zeidberg, Head
Notes: 25 linear feet of mss and books written by Henry Allen under the pseudonym, Will Henry.

HENRY STREET SETTLEMENT

NY —COLUMBIA UNIVERSITY LIBRARIES, Rare Book & Manuscript Library, 801 Butler Library, 535 W 114 St, New York, 10027. Kenneth A Lohf, Librn
Holdings: Mss
Notes: Papers of Lillian D Wald, relating to the founding and adminstration of the Henry Street Settlement, and other philanthropic and liberal causes in which she was active. 30,000 items. Restricted use.

HENS see Poultry

HENSLEY, STEWART

DC —LIBRARY OF CONGRESS, Manuscript Division, Washington, 20540. John C Broderick, Chief
Notes: Correspondence, memoranda, transcriptions of interviews, research files,

HENSLEY, STEWART (cont.)

clippings, speeches, and notebooks of Stewart Hensley.

HENTOFF, NAT

MA —BOSTON UNIVERSITY, Mugar Memorial Library, Special Collections Dept, 771 Commonwealth Ave, Boston, 02215. Howard B Gotlieb, Dir
Holdings: Cat Mss Pix
Notes: Mss, correspondence, etc collected in depth; incl publications by or about.

HENTY, GEORGE ALFRED

CA —SAN DIEGO STATE UNIVERSITY, Malcolm A Love Library, 5300 Campanile Dr, San Diego, 92182. D Dickinson, Univ Librn; Don L Bosseau, Dir
Notes: Collected works in first edition of certain prominent authors, as H G Wells, Somerset Maugham, William Dean Howells, Gertrude Atherton, Tom Stoppard, James Clavell, G A Henty, Henry Raup Wagner.

FL —UNIVERSITY OF SOUTH FLORIDA, Library, Tampa, 33620. J B Dobkin, Special Collections Librn
Holdings: Vols 412 Cat
Budget: ($7500)
Notes: James Baird Herndon, Jr and Willilam B Poage Collection of American and British editions of the juvenile literature of George Alfred Henty. Collection incl juvenile periodicals edited by Henty. Present in the collection are bibliographical and biographical works relating to Henty and diverse items of Hentyana. Also incl are Henty's adult novels.

IN —INDIANA UNIVERSITY, Lilly Library, Seventh St, Bloomington, 47405. William R Cagle, Librn
Holdings: Vols 400 // Cat
Notes: Ms include materials collected by Peter Martin for a projected biography of Henty.

MA —HARVARD UNIVERSITY LIBRARY, Houghton Library, Cambridge, 02138. F Thomas Noonan, Cur, Reading Room; Lawrence Dowler, Associate Librn
Holdings: Cat

MS —UNIVERSITY OF SOUTHERN MISSISSIPPI, William David McCain Graduate Library, Box 5148, Southern Sta, Hattiesburg, 39406.
Holdings: Vols 550
Notes: The Lena Y de Grummond Collection of Children's Literature. Incl the Robert L Dartt Collection of over 1800 books for boys from the late 19th and early 20th centuries. Extensive Henty (over 550 vols), Alger, Brereton, Castlemon, Fenn, Kingston, Optic, and Stratemeyer holdings. Catalog in progress.

OH —OHIO UNIVERSITY, Vernon R Alden Library, Department of Archives and Special Collections, Athens, 45701. Gary A Hunt, Head
Holdings: Vols (1400) Uncat
Notes: A miscellaneous collection of children's books by American and English authors, with most imprint dates in the period 1870-1930; numerous series books. Authors incl Jacob Abbott (196 v), "Oliver Optic" (84 v), Horatio Alger (89 v), J H Ewing (53 v), Martha Finley (47 v), G A Henty (46 v), Frank V Webster (38 v), and many others.

SC —FRANCIS MARION COLLEGE, James A Rogers Library, Florence, 29501. H Paul Dove, Dir; Roger K Hux, Special Collections Librn

HEPATICAE see Liverworts

HEPPLE, ALEX

IL —NORTHWESTERN UNIVERSITY, Melville J Herskovits Library of African Studies, Evanston, 60201. Hans E Panofsky, Cur
Holdings: Vols (85,000) Mss
Budget: ($70,000)
Notes: Papers, etc. Mostly southern Africa.
See also entry under Africa.
See also entry under Africa

HERALD, LEON SRABIAN

WI —UNIVERSITY OF WISCONSIN, MADISON, Memorial Library, Rare Books Collection, 728 State St, Madison, 53706. Gretchen Lagana, Cur
Holdings: // Uncat
Notes: The Leon Srabian Herald Collection of manuscripts, letters, and memorabilia of the Armenian-American poet, philosopher, and writer, active in Madison, Wisconsin, in the first quarter of the 20th Century and thereafter in New York City. Active in the creation of the Federal Writer's Project of the NRA, contributor to *Pagany, The Dial,* O'Brien's short stories collections, and friend of Harriet Monroe, Marianne Moore, Kenneth Fearing, Horace Gregory, Zona Gale, and many other literary and cultural figures of the period. Housed in Dept of Rare Books and Special Collections.

HERALD OF TRUTH ARCHIVES

TX —ABILENE CHRISTIAN UNIVERSITY, Margaret & Herman Brown Library, ACU Sta, Abilene, 79601. Callie Faye Milliken, Assoc Dir
Holdings: Mss Audiotapes Videotapes 16mm Films
Notes: Extensive collection of films, audiotapes, and scripts used in developing the religious radio-television program "Herald of Truth," which has been aired by Members of Churches of Christ since 1952.

HERALDIC BOOKPLATES see Bookplates

HERALDRY

CA —LOS ANGELES PUBLIC LIBRARY, Genealogy & Local History Dept, 630 W 5th St, Los Angeles, 90071. Lucile Lipman, Sr Librn
Holdings: Vols (55,000) Cat Mss Maps Pix
Budget: ($16,000)
Notes: Extensive collection of American, British and European materials on personal, civic and corporate arms. Coats-of-arms index is maintained.

CA —POMONA PUBLIC LIBRARY, Special Collections, 625 S Garey Ave, PO Box 2271, Pomona, 91766. David Streeter, Librn
Holdings: Cat Maps Microforms
Notes: Complete California census through 1900 on microfilm; 1850 California Census index; reconstructed passenger lists; overland arrivals. Scattered censuses on microfilm from other states. All printed indexes to US Census; general US research collection. Basic heraldry and coats-of-arms.

CO —DENVER PUBLIC LIBRARY, 1357 Broadway, Denver, 80203. Joanne E Classen, Genealogy Specialist, Humanities Area
Holdings: Vols 18,865 Cat Mss Maps Microforms
Budget: ($11,500)
Notes: Incl 3100 microfilm reels. Special files incl family file (a surname index to many of the collective genealogies and county histories in the collection); *Coats of Arms File* (an index to illustrations of coats of arms contained in the collection); *Obituary File* (an index to obituaries appearing in The *Denver Post*) and the *Rocky Mountain News Items File* (an index to news items, primarily anniversary announcements, appearing in the *Denver* Post) and the *Rocky Mountain News,* from 1940 to present.

CT —YALE UNIVERSITY, Box 1603A, Yale Station, New Haven, 06520.
Notes: Historical works on heraldry; mss, books, pamphlets.

DC —LIBRARY OF CONGRESS, Washington, 20540.
Holdings: Vols 3800 Cat
Notes: Local History and Genealogy Room has reference collection of 5000 volumes (200 on heraldry). Card files in LH&G Room include: Coats of Arms Index; Author Catalog of Genealogy, Heraldry, and Local History.

FL —ORLANDO PUBLIC LIBRARY, Local History & Genealogy Dept, 100 Block of Central Ave, Orlando, 32806. Eileen B Willis, Librn
Holdings: Vols 11,000 Cat Maps Microforms
Budget: $8000
Notes: The

FL —FLORIDA STATE ARCHIVES, R A Gray Bldg, Tallahassee, 32301. Richard Roberts, Supervisor, Central Reference Section
Holdings: Vols 12,000 Cat Microforms
Budget: $6000
Notes: National scope, with primary emphasis on the South and Southeast, and basic source materials of New England. Incl county and family histories, vital statistics, passenger lists, abstracts of military records, and heraldry. Catalog: *Genealogy and Local History: A Bibliography.* Incl 12,000 microforms.

IL —NEWBERRY LIBRARY, 60 W Walton St, Chicago, 60610. Diana Haskell, Cur of Modern Mss
Holdings: Cat Pix
Notes: Heraldic card index of 33,000 cards referring to illustrations of family and public arms.

IN —ALLEN COUNTY PUBLIC LIBRARY, Fred J Reynolds Historical Genealogy Collection, 900 Webster St, Fort Wayne, 46802. Rick J Ashton, Dir; Michael B Clegg, Manager
Holdings: Vols 200,000 Cat Mss Maps Pix Microforms
Notes: Incl state, county, regional, town and church histories. All census schedules and port of entry records released by the federal government are in the microfilm collection of 40,000 reels. The collection contains parish registers and publications of British parish register societies. Canadian, English, Scotch, Irish and Welsh records are well represented. The heraldry collection is housed with the genealogy collection. Allen County Public Library is and has been the depository for the North American Association of Directory Publishers since 1964.

LA —R W NORTON ART GALLERY, Library, 4747 Creswell Ave, Shreveport, 71106. Jerry M Bloomer, Librn
Holdings: Cat

MD —POLISH NOBILITY ASSOCIATION, Villa Anneslie, 529 Dunkirk Road, Baltimore, 21212.
Notes: Publish *Voice of the White Eagle,* 1965- , Annual.

MA —NEW ENGLAND HISTORIC GENEALOGICAL SOCIETY, Library, 101 Newbury St, Boston, 02116. Ralph J Crandell, Dir
Holdings: Vols (250,000) Mss Maps Microforms Pix
Notes: New England genealogy. Especially strong Massachusetts, Maine, and New Hampshire, although all states are well represented, as are the relevancies of each subject listed in this volume with regard to British antecedent and contemporary history. Special strengths in local history and biography, obituaries, etc, incl parish registers, censuses, British and American. 3125 linear ft of mss.

†MA —IRISH FAMILY HISTORY SOCIETY LIBRARY, 173 Tremont St, Newton, 02158.
Notes: Ireland--genealogy, history, literature, heraldry.

MA —SPRINGFIELD CITY LIBRARY, Genealogy and Local History Dept, 220 State St, Springfield, 01103. Joseph Carvalho III, Supervisor
Holdings: Vols (17,000) Cat Mss Maps Pix Microforms
Budget: ($8000)
Notes: New England, Massachusetts, local history (Springfield), and genealogy collections. collections. 18,000 pictures, 3200 microforms, ca 15,000 clippings, pamphlets, etc (280 ft of vertical files).

MA —AMERICAN ANTIQUARIAN SOCIETY LIBRARY, 185 Salisbury St, Worcester, 01609. Marcus A McCorison,

HERALDRY (cont.)

Dir & Librn
Holdings: Vols 14,000 Cat
Notes: Incl heraldry, biography, genealogy, etc. Numerous special indexes and clipping files supplement the book collection.

MO —SAINT LOUIS PUBLIC LIBRARY, History & Genealogy Dept, 1301 Olive Blvd, Saint Louis, 63103. Noel C Holobeck, Librn
Holdings: Cat
Notes: Heraldry index (card file); See also *Genealogical Materials and Local Histories in the St Louis Library,* by Georgia Gambrill, 1966; first supplement, 1971; Heraldry Index of the St Louis Public Library, 1980, G K Hall, 6 vols.

NY —NEW YORK STATE LIBRARY, Manuscripts and Special Collections, Albany, 12230. Peter R Christoph, Associate Librn
Holdings: 200 Cat Mss Maps Pix

NY —NEW YORK PUBLIC LIBRARY, Local History and Genealogy Div, Fifth Ave & 42 St, New York, 10018. Gunther E Pohl, Chief
Holdings: Vols (160,000) Cat Pix
Budget: ($38,548)
Notes: Extensive collection of personal, civic and corporate arms (international). The Division has prepared a personal arms index to coats of arms, illustrated in its book material.

OH —PUBLIC LIBRARY OF CINCINNATI & HAMILTON COUNTY, History Dept, 800 Vine St, Cincinnati, 45202. J Richard Abell, Head
Holdings: Vols 9996 Cat Microforms
Notes: Collection emphasizes Ohio, neighboring states, and Eastern seaboard states. Some material on Great Britain and Ireland. There is a genealogical index of family histories by surname only.

OH —CLEVELAND PUBLIC LIBRARY, History and Geography Department, 325 Superior Ave, Cleveland, 44114. JoAnn Petrello, Head
Holdings: Cat
Notes: Strong in Normandy, Britanny, Gascony. Nearly complete collection of historical memoirs (analyzed). Mazarinade collection. Contemporary political pamphlets of the period of the Fronde, 1648-1653 (about 2000 pamphlets). No photocopying.

SC —COLLEGE OF CHARLESTON LIBRARY, Special Collections Dept, Charleston, 29401.
Notes: Coat of arms granted by the English College of Heralds, in 1745, to Francis Salvador, the grandfather of the Francis Salvador who brought it from England to South Carolina.

ON —QUEEN'S UNIVERSITY, Douglas Library, Kingston, K7L 5C4, Can. William F E Morley, Cur, Special Collections
Holdings: Vols 100 Uncat
Notes: The MacGillivray Collection. Scottish books, especially those dealing with clans, tartans and heraldry. Also, the Buchan Collection, 5000 vols.

ON —PUBLIC ARCHIVES OF CANADA, Library, 395 Wellington St, Ottawa, K1A 0N3, Can. Dawn E Monroe, Collections Development Officer
Holdings: Vols (80,000) Cat
Notes: The Library's heraldic sources can be divdied into two main categories: heraldic treatises and manuals, which deal primarily with the representation of coats of arms; and lists of armorial bearings for Canada, Great Britain and France. The latter category incl *Armorial du Canada francais* by Edouard-Zotiquue Massicotte and Regis Roy, *Armorial des eveques du Canada* by Gerard Brassard, *Armorial du Canada francais* by Aegedius Fauteux, and *A Collection of the Armorial Bearings of the Baronets of Nova* Scotia... by James Haig.

HERBAGE see Grasses

HERBALS see Herbs and Herbals

HERBARIA

†AK —UNIVERSITY OF ALASKA, Museum Herbarium, 907 Yucan Dr, Fairbanks, 99701.

MI —UNIVERSITY OF MICHIGAN, Museums Library, Ann Arbor, 48109. Patricia B Yocum, Librn
Holdings: Vols 11,000 Cat Pix Microforms
Notes: Taxonomy.

OR —BAKER COUNTY PUBLIC LIBRARY, 2400 Resort St, Baker, 97814. Paul C Crouthamal, Librn
Holdings: Vols (1700) Cat Mss Maps Pix Microforms
Budget: ($2000)
Notes: Baker County, Oregon materials, historical and current, emphasizing genealogy, mining, agriculture and the people. Incl any fiction with Oregon as the locale. Local newspapers on microfilm, 1870-date, but incomplete for early years. 50 files on local plants, 1953-date, with separate catalog. Incl 300 maps.

TX —SOUTHERN METHODIST UNIVERSITY, Science/Engineering Library, Dallas, 75275. Devertt D Bickston, Librn
Holdings: Vols (140,000) Cat Maps Pix Microforms
Budget: ($150,000)
Notes: Also maintain an herbarium.

WI —US FOREST SERVICE, Forest Products Laboratory Library, Box 5130, Madison, 53705. Roger Schurmer, Librn; Dr Regis Miller, Librn; Dr Harold H Burdsall, Jr, Librn
Notes: Mostly Tropical New World. Incl (30,000) sheets (MAD).

HERBERT, GEORGE

MA —HARVARD UNIVERSITY LIBRARY, Widener Library, Cambridge, 02138.
Holdings: Cat Mss
Notes: Catalog in Harvard University Library, *Bibliographical Contributions,* 59 (1911).

NC —UNIVERSITY OF NORTH CAROLINA, GREENSBORO, Walter Clinton Jackson Library, Special Collections Dept, 1000 Spring Garden St, Greensboro, 27412. Emilie W Mills, Librn
Holdings: Vols (100) Cat Pix Microforms
Notes: First, early and later editions of George Herbert, 17th to 20th centuries. Early manuscripts and documents relating to Nicolas Ferrar and the Herbert family (microfilm). Also incl are early works of Edward, Lord Herbert of Cherbury, Izaak Walton and Nicolas Ferrar; items issued by the Friends of Bemerton are added as published.

HERBERT, HENRY WILLIAM (FRANK FORESTER)

CT —YALE UNIVERSITY, Box 1603A, Yale Station, New Haven, 06520.
Holdings: Cat Mss

HERBERT, VICTOR

DC —LIBRARY OF CONGRESS, Music Division, Washington, 20540.
Notes: Music and music mss of Victor Herbert.

IN —INDIANA UNIVERSITY, Lilly Library, Seventh St, Bloomington, 47405. William R Cagle, Librn
Holdings: // Uncat
Notes: In the Starr Collection of American Sheet Music.

WI —UNIVERSITY OF WISCONSIN, MADISON, Mills Music Library, 728 State St, Madison, 53706. Arne Arneson, Music Librn
Holdings: // Uncat Mss
Notes: Tams-Witmark Collection formed part of the rental collection of the firm bearing that name. Incl piano-conductor scores (some in mss); ca 65 sets of orchestral parts for operas; 70 vocal scores of works by American composers incl Herbert, Sousa, Edwards and De Koven; ca 100 sets of orchestral parts of comic operas; ca 4000 vocal scores of European operas. Restricted use.

HERBERT OF CHERBURY, EDWARD, LORD

NC —UNIVERSITY OF NORTH CAROLINA, GREENSBORO, Walter Clinton Jackson Library, Special Collections Dept, 1000 Spring Garden St, Greensboro, 27412. Emilie W Mills, Librn
Holdings: Vols (100) Cat Pix Microforms
Notes: First, early and later editions of George Herbert, 17th to 20th centuries. Early manuscripts and documents relating to Nicolas Ferrar and the Herbert family (microfilm). Also incl are early works of Edward, Lord Herbert of Cherbury, Izaak Walton and Nicolas Ferrar; items issued by the Friends of Bemerton are added as published.

HERBS AND HERBALS

†AK —UNIVERSITY OF ALASKA, Museum Herbarium, 907 Yucan Dr, Fairbanks, 99701.

CA —UNIVERSITY OF SOUTHERN CALIFORNIA, School of Medicine, Norris Medical Library, 2025 Zonal Ave, Los Angeles, 90033. Nelson J Gilman, Librn
Holdings: Vols 275 Cat
Budget: $200
Notes: The Collection of American Indian Ethnopharmcology.

†CA —HUNTINGTON BOTANICAL GARDENS LIBRARY, 1151 Oxford Rd, San Marino, 91108. Ann Ravenscroft, Secretary
Notes: Emphases on history of botanical science; papers and notes of American botanists and naturalists of The West; botanical illustration, etc. Subtropical horticulture, incl cacti and succulents of Australia, South Africa, and Mexico.

CT —YALE UNIVERSITY, Box 1603A, Yale Station, New Haven, 06520.

CT —YALE UNIVERSITY, Medical Historical Library, Klebs Collection, 333 Cedar St, New Haven, 06520. Ferenc A Gyorgyey, Librn
Notes: The Arnold Carl Klebs Medical Collection books, pamphlets, etc, incl the library of his father, Edwin T A Klebs, pathologist. Strong in bibliography of early printed medical books, herbals, plague tracts, inoculation, vaccination and tubercular diseases.

†CT —UNIVERSITY OF CONNECTICUT LIBRARY, Special Collections Dept, Storrs, 06268. Richard H Schimmelpfeng, Dir of Special Collections

DE —UNIVERSITY OF DELAWARE, Hugh M Morris Library, S College Ave, Newark, 19711. T Stuart Dick, Special Collections
Holdings: Cat
Notes: Unidel History of Horticulture and Landscape Architecture Collection. Focus is on the origins of horticulture and landscape architecture in America. Particularly strong in early American, English and continental works. Landscape architecture is represented by of the great English and American works as well as the French and Italian ones. There is a small but important group of American works on botanic medicine. Some of the great herbals are also present as well as a number of early American periodicals.

FL —FLORIDA STATE UNIVERSITY, Robert Manning Strozier Library, Special Collections Dept, Tallahassee, 32306. Opal M Free, Head, Special Collections
Holdings: Vols 176 Cat Mss Maps
Notes: Noncirculating. No photocopying.

IL —UNIVERSITY OF ILLINOIS AT CHICAGO, Library of the Health Sciences, 1750 W Polk St, PO Box 7509, Chicago, 60612. Robert J Adelsperger, Cur, Special Collections
Holdings: Vols (6000) Cat Mss
Notes: Emphasis on pharmacopoeias, formularies and dispensatories, and American and foreign herbals. Description of collection in *Pharmacopeias, Formularies,* Dispensatories, (Chicago: Library of the Health Sciences, 1975).

IL —MORTON ARBORETUM, Sterling Morton Library, Lisle, 60532. Ian MacPhail, Librn
Holdings: Vols (20,000) Cat Maps Pix
Budget: ($10,000)
Notes: The library is especially concerned with the literature of woody plants (trees and shrubs) of north temperate zones but has

HERBS AND HERBALS (cont.)

substantial holdings in the taxonomy and systematics of plants in general, both wild and cultivated, flora of different parts of the world, and a growing collection on plant monographs. Also about 2000 pictures. Described in *The Morton Arboretum* Quarterly, vol 9, no 4 (Winter 1973), pp 56-61.

IN —PURDUE UNIVERSITY LIBRARIES, Pharmacy, Nursing and Health Sciences Library, Pharmacy Bldg, West Lafayette, 47907. Theodora Andrews, Librn
Holdings: Vols 400 Cat
Notes: There is a separate catalog to the colelction. Contains research level materials as well as undergraduate.

KS —UNIVERSITY OF KANSAS, Kenneth Spencer Research Library, Special Collections Dept, Lawrence, 66045. Alexandra Mason, Librn
Holdings: Vols (5600) Cat Mss
Notes: About (2600) items before 1800. Espec strong in herbals, medical botany, Linnaeus, early American botanists (William Darlington, C S Refinesque). Incl material from T J Fitzpatrick collection. Noncirculating.

MA —HARVARD UNIVERSITY LIBRARY, Gray Herbarium Library, 22 Divinity Ave, Cambridge, 02138. Barbara A Callahan, Librn
Holdings: Vols (61,445) Microforms
Notes: Flowering plants and ferns are emphasized. *Gray Herbarium Index,* 10 volumes (published 1968) reproduces 265, 000 cards giving names and literature citations of newly described or established vascular plants of the Western Hemisphere.

MA —HERB SOCIETY OF AMERICA, Library, 2 Independence Court, Concord, 01742. Julie Macksoud, Exec Dir
Holdings: Vols (600)

MA —SMITH COLLEGE, Library, Northampton, 01063. Ruth Mortimer, Cur of Rare Books
Holdings: Vols 145 // Cat
Notes: Thornton Collection of 15th-19th century herbals, early microscopy, Linneaus, biography.

MI —UNIVERSITY OF MICHIGAN, Herbarium Library, University Herbarium, 2003 N University Bldg, Ann Arbor, 48109. Robert L Shaffer, Dir, Herbarium
Holdings: Vols 2311 Cat
Notes: Gift from Parke Davis and Co in 1933. Many are very rare and noncirculating, housed in the Dept of Rare Books and Special Collections or in the Medical Center Library. Others added through gifts and purchase.

MN —UNIVERSITY OF MINNESOTA, Owen H Wangensteen Historical Library of Biology & Medicine, Diehl Hall, Minneapolis, 55455. Judith Overmier, Cur
Holdings: Vols (35,000) Cat
Budget: ($80,000)
Notes: Incl historic materials.

MO —UNIVERSITY OF MISSOURI-COLUMBIA, Ellis Library, Special Collections Dept, Ninth & Lowry, Columbia, 65201. Margaret A Howell, Head, Special Collections
Holdings: Vols Cat
Notes: Rare early works in Latin, German, Italian, French and English.

MO —MISSOURI BOTANICAL GARDEN LIBRARY, PO Box 299, Saint Louis, 63166. M R Crosby, Dir of Research

NY —NEW YORK PUBLIC LIBRARY, Rare Books and Manuscripts Div, Fifth Ave & 42 St, New York, 10018. William L Joyce, Asst Dir; Bernard McTigue, Cur, Arents Collection
Holdings: Cat Mss Maps Pix
Notes: Arents Tobacco Collection; incl 16th century herbals.

OH —LLOYD LIBRARY & MUSEUM, 917 Plum St, Cincinnati, 45202. John B Griggs, Librn
Notes: Extensive collection of original editions.

OH —CLEVELAND MEDICAL LIBRARY ASSOCIATION/CASE WESTERN RESERVE UNIVERSITY, Cleveland Health Sciences Library, Historical Division, Allen Memorial Medical Library, 11000 Euclid Ave, Cleveland, 44106. Glen Jenkins, Rare Book Librarian & Archivist
Holdings: Vols 500 Cat
Notes: Partially described in Fisch, Ruth E and Max H, "The Marshall Collection of Herbals in the Cleveland Medical Library" (checklist), *Bulletin of the History of* Medicine, 1947, vol 21, pp 224-261.

OH —CLEVELAND PUBLIC LIBRARY, Fine Arts and Special Collections Department, 325 Superior Ave, Cleveland, 44114. Alice N Loranth, Head
Holdings: Vols (1356) Cat
Notes: Part of the Tobacco Collection. Incl numerous rare items: 16th century herbals; official proclamations issued by the English, French, Portuguese, Dutch governments. The manners and customs aspect of smoking is emphasized. Some museum objects. Separate shelf list and separate dictionary catalog maintained.
See also entry under Tobacco.

OH —KINGWOOD CENTER, Library, 900 Park Ave W, Mansfield, 44906. Timothy Gardner, Horticulturist
Holdings: Vols 8500
Notes: Espec ornamental horticulture, home gardening, landscaping, and floral arrangements. Incl 12,000 35mm slides of plants.

OH —MASSILLON PUBLIC LIBRARY, 208 Lincoln Way E, Massillon, 44646. Camille Leslie, Dir
Holdings: Vols (580,000) Cat Maps Microforms
Budget: ($735,000)
Notes: Of secondary interest in acquistions because of the department's role in cooperating with Pittsburgh institutions and others across the Commonwealth in sharing resources, the cooperative acqusition of materials, and the provision of services and information. However, some aspects of the subjects are emphasized. There are separate entries for each of these specialties in this vol.

OH —HOLDEN ARBORETUM, Warren H Corning Library, 9500 Sperry Rd, Mentor, 44060. Paul C Spector, Dir of Education
Holdings: Vols (5500) // Cat
Notes: Extensive collection of horticultural classics, floras, herbals and monographs prior to 1850. Primarily European works.

OR —UNIVERSITY OF OREGON LIBRARY, Special Collections Div, Eugene, 97403. Kenneth W Duckett, Curator
Holdings: Vols 100 Cat
Notes: European and American printed herbals, 15th-20th centuries.

PA —PENNSYLVANIA HORTICULTURAL SOCIETY, Library, 325 Walnut St, Philadelphia, 19106. Mary Lou Wolfe, Librn
Notes: Publications: *Selected Books From the Library of the Pennsylvania Horticultural Society*, 1976; *From Seed to Flower, Philadelphia 1681-1876*, 1976.

PA —PENNSYLVANIA HOSPITAL HISTORICAL LIBRARY, Eighth & Spruce Sts, Philadelphia, 19107. Caroline Morris, Librn
Holdings: Vols (12,963) // Cat Mss
Notes: First medical library in US. Rich in runs of 19th century medical journals. Some early botany books. Some incunabula. Printed catalog was made in 1876. This collection is important because it reflects the history of medicine by the nature of the materials that were acquired. However, *no attempt is made to keep a current history of medicine library.*

PA —TEMPLE UNIVERSITY LIBRARIES, Special Collections Dept, Rare Books & Mss Section, Philadelphia, 19122. Thomas M Whitehead, Cur
Holdings: Vols (500) Cat Mss
Notes: Incl the Louise Bush-Brown Horticulture Collection; 15th-20th century rare herbals, animal husbandry and landscape gardening. List of majority of collection available.

PA —HUNT INSTITUTE FOR BOTANICAL DOCUMENTATION, Hunt Botanical Library, Carnegie-Mellon University, Pittsburgh, 15213. Bernadette G Callery, Librn
Holdings: Vols (23,000) Cat Pix
Notes: Collection of primarily historical botany and plant taxonomy, especially 1730-1840. Includes approximately 500 15th through 17th century herbals, extensive collection of 18th and 19th century color-plate works, floras and monographic works, and other works on natural history, early gardening and horticulture, and travel, particularly that dealing with plant exploration and introduction. Extensive biographical materials, on people in the plant sciences. Reference collection and extensive documentation in botanical bibliography, especially concerning books published before 1850. Includes as separate collections, the Strandell Collection of Linnaeana and the Michel Adanson Library. Over 800 items described in *Catalogue of Botanical Books in the Collection of Rachel McMasters Miller Hunt, 1477-1800* (Pittsburgh, 1958-1960).

RI —UNIVERSITY OF RHODE ISLAND, Library, Special Collections, Kingston, 02881. David Maslyn, Head
Notes: Extensive collections.

HERBS AND HERBALS—THERAPEUTIC USE see Botany, Medical

HERD REGISTERS see Cattle—Herd Registers

HEREDITY

CT —YALE MEDICAL LIBRARY, 333 Cedar St, New Haven, 06510.
Notes: A special subject emphasis.

HEREDITY, HUMAN

PA —CARNEGIE LIBRARY OF PITTSBURGH, Science & Technology Dept, 4400 Forbes Ave, Pittsburgh, 15213. Catherine M Brosky, Dept Head
Notes: Of secondary interest in acquisitions because of the department's role in cooperating with Pittsburgh institutions and others across the Commonwealth in sharing resources, the cooperative acquisition of materials, and the provision of services and information. However, some aspects of the subject are emphasized. There are separate entries for each of these specialties in this vol.

HERFORD, OLIVER

CA —CLAREMONT COLLEGES, Ella Strong Denison Library, Scripps College, Claremont, 91711. Judy Harvey Sahak, Librn
Holdings: 67 Uncat

†MA —WILLIAMS COLLEGE, Chapin Library of Rare Books, PO Box 426, Williamstown, 01267. Robert L Volz, Custodian
Holdings: Vols 91 Cat
Notes: By and about him; incl variant editions, inscribed copies, etc. The Carry F Denny Collection. No ILL.

HERGESHEIMER, JOSEPH

CT —YALE UNIVERSITY, Box 1603A, Yale Station, New Haven, 06520.
Holdings: Cat Mss

NC —UNIVERSITY OF NORTH CAROLINA, CHAPEL HILL, Wilson Library, Rare Book Collection, Chapel Hill, 27514. Paul S Koda, Cur of Rare Books
Holdings: Cat
Notes: Fully representative collection.

VA —UNIVERSITY OF VIRGINIA, Alderman Library, Manuscripts Dept, Charlottesville, 22901. Edmund Berkeley Jr, Cur
Holdings: Cat Mss Pix
Notes: First editions, correspondence.

HERLIHY, JAMES LEO

MA —BOSTON UNIVERSITY, Mugar Memorial Library, Special Collections Dept,

HERLIHY, JAMES LEO (cont.)

771 Commonwealth Ave, Boston, 02215. Howard B Gotlieb, Dir
Holdings: Cat Mss Pix
Notes: Mss, correspondence, etc collected in depth; incl publications by or about.

HERMANT, ABEL

MN —CARLETON COLLEGE LIBRARY, Northfield, 55057.
Holdings: Vols 7000 Cat
Notes: Books and periodicals relating to French literature of the second half of the 19th century, incl the French symbolist and decadent writers and critical works about them. Major writers are well represented as are some of the relatively minor figures, such as Paul Adam, Rene Boylesve, Abel Hermant, Pierre Louys, and others. The collection incl 69 plays written and produced in the period.

HERMETIC ART AND PHILOSOPHY see Occult Sciences

HEROINES see Women in Literature

HEROYS, B. V.

CA —HOOVER INSTITUTION ON WAR, REVOLUTION & PEACE, Stanford University, Stanford, 94305. Milorad M Drachkovitch, Archivist
Holdings: / / Mss
Notes: Papers, 1919-1920, of B V Heroys, White Russian army officer. Correspondence, reports, and other documents relating to anti-Bolshevik antivities in northwest Russia. Incl correspondence with the British War Office and reports by Heroys as chief of the Special Military Mission to London for General Nikolai Yudenich, commander of the White Russian forces in northwest Russia. 3 ft.

HERPETOLOGY

DC —NATIONAL GEOGRAPHIC SOCIETY, Library, 1146 16th St NW, Washington, 20036. Susan Fifer Canby, Dir
Holdings: Vols (63,000) Cat Mss Maps Pix
Notes: Material concerning land, sea, and space exploration--past and present. All fields of anthropology, natural history, geography, etc.

IL —FIELD MUSEUM OF NATURAL HISTORY, Library, Roosevelt Rd & Lake Shore Dr, Chicago, 60605. W Peyton Fawcett, Librn; Benjamin W Williams, Assoc Librn
Holdings: Vols (210,000) Cat
Budget: ($100,000)
Notes: Extensive collections--publications of learned societies and institutions and monographic works--in all fields of natural history, with emphasis on taxonomy and evolutionary biology; and on museum publications, American and foreign: anthropology, especially archaeology and ethnology of the Americas, Africa, East Asia, and Oceania; botany, particularly strong for the Americas; geology, chiefly paleontology and meteoritic studies; and zoology, worldwide (birds, fishes, insects, mammals, mollusks, reptiles and amphibians).

MI —UNIVERSITY OF MICHIGAN, Museums Library, Ann Arbor, 48109. Patricia B Yocum, Librn
Holdings: Vols 2500 Cat

NY —NEW YORK ZOOLOGICAL SOCIETY LIBRARY, Bronx Zoo, Bronx, 10460. Steven P Johnson, Archivist and Librn
Holdings: Vols (6000) Cat Mss
Budget: ($50,000)
Notes: Collection consists primarily of journals in captive management of animals, vertebrate zoology, and veterinary medicine. Primarily intended for the scientific staff, the collection is open to the public on a noncirculating basis, by appointment, (212) 220-6874.

NY —AMERICAN MUSEUM OF NATURAL HISTORY, Library Services Dept, Central Park W & 79th St, New York, 10024. Nina J Root, Chairwoman; Mary Genett, Asst Librn for Reference Services
Holdings: Vols (385,000) Cat Mss Maps Pix Slides Microforms
Notes: Nearly all collections are outstanding for depth of coverage and international range. Early and historic works, rare books, colored illustrations, and relevant serial publications supplement the modern scientific publications necessary to the researches of the scientific staff and the work of the educational division. Open to the public.

PA —ACADEMY OF NATURAL SCIENCES LIBRARY, 19 Benjamin Franklin Parkway, Philadelphia, 19103.
Holdings: Vols (180,000) Cat Mss Maps Pix Slides Microforms
Notes: Incl (250,000) mss. Described in *Academy of Natural Sciences of Philadelphia: Catalog* (Boston: G K Hall, 1972); *Guide to the Manuscript Collections in the Academy of Natural Sciences of* Philadelphia by Venia T Phillips (Philadelphia: Academy of Natural Sciences, 1963).

ON —NATIONAL MUSEUMS OF CANADA, Library Services Directorate, Ottawa, K1A 0M8, Can. Valerie Monkhouse, Director
Holdings: Vols (90,000) Cat Mss Microforms
Budget: ($81,000)
Notes: Emphasis on Canadian and circumpolar natural history. Collection incl botany, herpetology, ichthyology, invertebrate zoology, malacology, mammology, mineralogy, ornithology, paleobiology, zooarchaeology. Exceptional collections in lichenology, bryology, malacology, ornithology. Research collection, interlibrary loans available, public may use on the premises.

HERRAN, TOMAS

DC —GEORGETOWN UNIVERSITY, Library, Special Collections Div, 37 & O Sts NW, Washington, 20057. George M Barringer, Special Collections Librn; Nicholas B Sheetz, Mss Librn
Holdings: Cat Mss Pix
Notes: Panama Canal, and papers of Tomas Herran, Earl Harding, Thomas E Martin, William McCan, Clark Thompson, Leonor K Sullivan, and Capt Miles Duval.

HERRESHOFF MANUFACTURING CO., 1870-1945

MA —MASSACHUSETTS INSTITUTE OF TECHNOLOGY MUSEUM, Hart Nautical Collections, 77 Massachusetts Ave, Rm 5-329, Cambridge, 02139. John W Waterhouse, Cur
Holdings: Vols (800) Cat Maps Pix
Notes: Ship and marine engineering development. Museum is under jurisdiction of MIT'S Dept of Ocean Engineering. Collection incl various collections of prints and photographs of ships and yachts; working drawings from the Herreshoff Manufacturing Co, 1870-1945, and of George Lawley and Son Corp; working drawings and models from the Munro, Owen, and Paine Collections.

HERREY, HERMAN, 1904-1968

NY —CORNELL UNIVERSITY LIBRARIES, Collection of Regional History, Dept of Manuscripts and Univ Archives, Ithaca, 14853.
Notes: Theatrical director, architect and city planner. Papers, ca 1939-71; 16.5 ft. Unpublished guide available. Restricted.

HERRICK, MARY

MI —WAYNE STATE UNIVERSITY, Walter P Reuther Library, Archives of Labor & Urban Affairs, Detroit, 48202. Philip Mason, Dir
Notes: The records of the American Federation of Teachers, as well as the files of the Detroit, Toledo, East Detroit, and other Federations of Teachers, are now preserved in the Archives. The personal papers of several teacher union leaders, incl Arthur Elder, Selma M Borchardt, Henry R Linville, Mary Herrick, and others are important supplements to the national union's file.

HERRICK, MYRON T.

DC —GEORGETOWN UNIVERSITY, Library, Special Collections Div, 37 & O Sts NW, Washington, 20057. George M Barringer, Special Collections Librn; Nicholas B Sheetz, Mss Librn
Holdings: Mss Cat
Notes: Correspondence written to Edythe Patten Corbin, prominent Washington socialite and wife of General Henry Clark Corbin. Extensive correspondence, spanning numerous years, is incl from William Howard Taft, Philip Bunau-Varilla, Myron T Herrick, General John Pershing, and Elihu Root, among others. The correspondence contains extensive discussions of national and international affairs.

HERRICK, WILLIAM

MA —BOSTON UNIVERSITY, Mugar Memorial Library, Special Collections Dept, 771 Commonwealth Ave, Boston, 02215. Howard B Gotlieb, Dir
Holdings: Cat Mss Correspondence

HERRING-CURTIS COMPANY

NY —CORNELL UNIVERSITY LIBRARIES, Collection of Regional History, Dept of Manuscripts and Univ Archives, Ithaca, 14853.
Notes: Incl papers, 1891-(1909-31); legal documents relating to the company, and a scrapbook, a notebook, blueprints, photos, pamphlets and clippings relating to aviation development.

HERRMANN, BERNARD, 1911-1975

CA —UNIVERSITY OF CALIFORNIA, SANTA BARBARA, Arts Library, Music Section, Santa Barbara, 93106. Susan Sonnet Bower, Asst Music Librn
Holdings: Mss
Notes: Collection of holograph music manuscripts of the late American composer, Bernard Herrmann, 1911-1975. Collection contains 53 manuscript scores of both music written for the films and non-film music. Incl the film scores for "Vertigo," "Pschyo," "North by Northwest," "Marnie," "Magnificent Ambersons," "Devil and Daniel Webster (All That Money Can Buy)" Academy Award, 1941. Non-film Music: Symphony (1941) Moby Dick (Dramatic Cantata), Wuthering Heights (Opera in 4 Acts, 1950) with text by Lucille Fletcher, first performed by Portland Opera Association, Nov 6, 1982.

HERRNHUTER see Moravian Church and Moravians

HERRON, GEORGE DAVIS

CA —HOOVER INSTITUTION ON WAR, REVOLUTION & PEACE, Stanford University, Stanford, 94305. Milorad M Drachkovitch, Archivist
Holdings: / / Mss
Notes: Papers, 1917-1919, of George Davis Herron, Congregational minister, educator, journalist, and socialist who served as an unofficial adviser to Woodrow Wilson. Correspondence and interviews with leaders in the US, Austria, Germany, Czechoslovakia, Hungary, Bulgaria, Rumania, Russia, Serbia, and Switzerland, relating to World War I, peace proposals and settlements, territorial questions, and the Paris Peace Conference, 1919. 3 ft. Transcripts (typewritten) of originals preserved in the Hoover Institute.

HERSCHEL, SIR WILLIAM

MA —HARVARD UNIVERSITY LIBRARY, Houghton Library, Cambridge, 02138.

HERSCHEL, SIR WILLIAM (cont.)

Rodney G Dennis, Cur of Manuscripts
Holdings: Cat Mss

HERSCHEL, WILLIAM JAMES

†TX —UNIVERSITY OF TEXAS LIBRARIES, General Libraries, Humanities Research Center, PO Box 7219, Austin, 78712. John Chalmers, Librn
Notes: Part of the History of Science Collection. Incl papers of various members of the Herschel Family.

HERSCHEL FAMILY

†TX —UNIVERSITY OF TEXAS LIBRARIES, General Libraries, Humanities Research Center, PO Box 7219, Austin, 78712. John Chalmers, Librn
Notes: Part of the History of Science Collection. Incl papers of various members of the Herschel Family.

HERSEY, JOHN RICHARD

NV —UNIVERSITY OF NEVADA, RENO, University Library, Special Collections Dept, Reno, 89557. Robert E Blesse, Head
Holdings: Vols (78) Cat
Notes: Includes individual works by author in all editions including translations; also prefaces, introductions, published correspondence, appearances in anthologies, periodicals, etc. Bibliographical research collection, part of Modern Authors Collection. Other appearances 100 cataloged.

HERSH, BURTON

MA —BOSTON UNIVERSITY, Mugar Memorial Library, Special Collections Dept, 771 Commonwealth Ave, Boston, 02215. Howard B Gotlieb, Dir
Holdings: Cat Mss

HERSHEY, LEWIS

PA —US ARMY MILITARY HISTORY INSTITUTE, Carlisle Barracks, 17013. Richard J Sommers, Chief Archivist-Historian
Holdings: Mss Cat
Notes: The World War II collection, personal letters, daily logs, reminiscences, speeches, and official papers of American officers and soldiers serving in the European, Mediterranean, Middle Eastern, China-Burma-India, Southwest Pacific, and Central Pacific Theaters and in the Zone of the Interior during the Second World War. Most of these collections are manuscripts of General officers, incl Omar Bradley, Stephen Chamberlin, Lewis Hershey, John Lucas, William Simpson, and Brehon Somervell.

HERSHOLT, JEAN

DC —LIBRARY OF CONGRESS, Rare Book & Special Collections Div, Washington, 20540. William Matheson, Chief
Notes: See description of collection under Andersen, Hans Christian; Lewis, Sinclair; Walpole, Hugh.

HERSKOVITS, MELVILLE J.

IL —NORTHWESTERN UNIVERSITY, Melville J Herskovits Library of African Studies, Evanston, 60201. Hans E Panofsky, Cur
Holdings: Vols (85,000) Mss
Budget: ($70,000)
Notes: Although the collection incl the papers of Melville J Herskovits, the last ten years of this archive is closed until 1988. Also have papers of the African Studies Association, Carter/Karis, Abdullah Abdurahman, Alex Hepple, Leo Kuper, Dennis Brutus; further, on West Africa--John Paden, Umar Falke, Liberian economic survey. Supplements for 1972-1977 for our book catalog (8 vols) was published by G K Hall in 1978; unlike 1972, the supplement to the *Joint Acqusitions List of Africana* will be published in seperate vols from the Northwestern Catalog supplement. There are, in 1978, 16,000 additional vols.

HERTER, CHRISTIAN

†MA —JOHN F KENNEDY LIBRARY, Columbia Point, Boston, 02125. Dan H Fenn Jr, Dir
Holdings: // Cat Mss
Notes: The White House staff files of Christian Herter during his term as Special Representative for Trade Negotiations, 1962-1967. 16 linear ft of mss. Holdings are described in "Historical Materials in the John F Kennedy Library." Copies may be obtained by writing the Research Archivist.

HERTY, CHARLES HOLMES

GA —EMORY UNIVERSITY, Robert W Woodruff Library, Special Collections Dept, Atlanta, 30322. Linda M Matthews, Head Special Collections; Virginia J H Cain, Processing Archivist; Richard H F Lindemann, Reference Archivist
Holdings: Cat Mss Maps Pix Microforms
Notes: Correspondence and other materials of Charles Holmes Herty (1867-1937), who was known for his work in applying chemistry to the improvement of industry and who served as president of the American Chemical Association; items reflect Herty's naval stores and other forestry products. 300,000 items.

HERTZBERG, GERHARD, 1904-

†ON —PUBLIC ARCHIVES OF CANADA, Library, 395 Wellington St, Ottawa, K1A 0N3, Can. Dawn E Monroe, Collections Dept Officer
Holdings: 13 Feet
Notes: His papers (1928-1940, 1950-1962).

HERTZIAN WAVES see Microwaves

HERTZOG, CARL

TX —HARDIN-SIMMONS UNIVERSITY, Richardson Library, Abilene, 79601. Joe F Dahlstrom, Dir
Holdings: Vols (10,000) Cat Mss Maps Pix Microforms
Notes: Special collection name is Richardson Research Center, named in honor of Dr Rupert N Richardson. Collect in the areas of his own research interests, especially that portion of the US that was once a part of Mexico. Emphases on the history of ranching, railroads, discovery and exploration, Texas county histories, etc. Incl 350 items printed and/or designed by El Paso printer Cart Hertzog; the Judge R C Crane collection of Texana and a similar collection of Louise Kelley's; and the Research Publication's Western Americana collection (microfilm).

TX —EL PASO PUBLIC LIBRARY, Southwest Collection, 501 N Oregon, El Paso, 79901. Mary A Sarber, Head
Holdings: Vols (12,000) Cat Mss Maps Pix
Budget: ($11,000)
Notes: Research collection includes rare books and mss journals, vertical files, index to El Paso newspapers, microfilmed newspapers, photographs, and architectural plans. Separate catalog. Limited to materials on Texas, New Mexico, Arizona and Mexico. Special collections of material by and about Tom Lea Jr, and Carl Hertzog. Aultman Collection of photographs includes 3500 on El Paso Southwest and 2500 on Mexican Revolution. Cited in Lovelace, Lisa, "The Southwest Collection of the El Paso Public Library". *Great Plains Journal,* vol 2, no 2, pp 161-166; Aultman, Otis A *Photographs from the Border: The Otis A Aultman Collection,* El Paso Public Library Association, 1977.

TX —UNIVERSITY OF TEXAS, EL PASO, Library, Special Collections Dept, El Paso, 79968. Cesar Caballero, Dept Head
Holdings: Vols 1370 Cat
Budget: ($5000)
Notes: Carl Hertzog Collection. More than three hundred books produced by the prominent printer/book designer Carl Hertzog and over a thousand books on books about books, typography, and the history of printing make up this collection. It also contains many Southwestern classics by Frank Dobie and Tom Lea.

TX —UNIVERSITY OF HOUSTON, M D Anderson Memorial Library, University Park, Houston, 77004. David Farmer, Cur, Special Collections; Jean Jackson, Assistant Cur
Holdings: Vols (600) Cat
Notes: This collection is confined to books in some way distinguished by their typographic qualities and produced within the borders of Texas at any time, past or present. Larger portions of the collection incl the work of the Encino Press, William Holman, Carl Hertzog, Edwin Hill, and other private and fine printers.

HERTZSPRUNG, EJNAR

NY —AMERICAN INSTITUTE OF PHYSICS, Center for the History of Physics, Niels Bohr Library, 335 E 45 St, New York, 10017. John Aubry, Librn
Notes: The Sources for History of Modern Astrophysics documents the history of 20th-century astrophysics. Incl some 400 hours of oral history interviews with astronomers, such as Bart Bok, S Chandrasekhar, Martin Schwarzschild, and A E Whitford. The project also organized and cataloged the papers of Henry Norris Russell, Frank Schlesinger, Otto Struve, Ejnar Hertzsprung, Harlow Shapley, Charles Young, Robert Atkinson, Seth Chandler, Theodore Dunham, Jr, and G C McVittie.

HERZ, JOHN HERMAN, 1908-

NY —STATE UNIVERSITY OF NEW YORK AT ALBANY, Library, Special Collections Dept, 1400 Washington Ave, Albany, 12222. Marion P Munzer, Coordr
Notes: Correspondence, mss, lecture notes, and materials of John Herman Herz on the United Nations Commission to study the Organization of Peace, 1972-1974 (8 linear feet). Part of the Library's German Exile Collection.
See also entry under United Nations

HERZ, MARTIN F., 1917-1983

DC —GEORGETOWN UNIVERSITY, Library, Special Collections Div, 37 & O Sts NW, Washington, 20057. George M Barringer, Special Collections Librn; Nicholas B Sheetz, Mss Librn
Holdings: Mss Cat
Notes: The papers of Ambassador Martin F Herz (1917-1983), containing correspondence, reports, memoranda, posters, propaganda leaflets, and other ephemeral material relating to psychological warfare in World War II and Vietnam; also much material on the Cold War and American foreign policy in the years following World War II.

HERZOG, ARTHUR

MA —BOSTON UNIVERSITY, Mugar Memorial Library, Special Collections Dept, 771 Commonwealth Ave, Boston, 02215. Howard B Gotlieb, Dir
Holdings: Cat Mss Pix Audiotapes Correspondence

HESSE, HERMANN

CA —UNIVERSITY OF CALIFORNIA, BERKELEY, Bancroft Library, Manuscripts Division, Berkeley, 94720. James D Hart, Dir
Holdings: Vols (2000) Uncat Mss
Notes: A comprehensive collection of the published works of Hermann Hesse. Particuarly strong in first editions, as well as magazines and books edited by Hesse. Also represented are book reviews and other contributions to periodicals. Ms materials incl Tschudy correspondence and original water colors.

HESSE, HERMANN (cont.)

IN —INDIANA UNIVERSITY, Lilly Library, Seventh St, Bloomington, 47405. William R Cagle, Librn
Holdings: Cat Mss Pix
Notes: Correspondence, 1926-1950, of Hermann Hesse with his publisher Gottfried Bermann Fischer (62 items). Collection includes 20 manuscripts by Hesse. Incl first editions of many 19th century works, and some 20th century holdings.

MI —WAYNE STATE UNIVERSITY, G Flint Purdy Library, Detroit, 48202. K L Kaul, Asst Dir & Head
Holdings: Cat Mss
Notes: The Hans Popp collection of books, mss, letters, etc.

PA —BIBLIOGRAPHICAL CENTER OF GERMAN LITERATURE, University of Pittsburgh, Dept of Germanic Languages & Literatures, 102 Loeffler Bldg, Pittsburgh, 15260. Klaus W Jonas, Dir
Holdings: Cat Mss Pix Microforms
Notes: Center for the development of collections and bibliographical control of the record of publications, mss, correspondence, etc, by or relating to modern German authors. Special sections have been developed for Mann, Rilke, Hauptmann, Hesse, Broch, Sachs and others. Described by Professor Klaus W Jonas's "The German Literature Center in Pittsburgh," *Stechert-Hafner Book News*, vol 24, no 8, April 1970; "Documentation in Modern German Literature: A Progress Report," *Jahrbuch fuer Internationale Germanistik*, vol 4, no 2, 1972, and in *German and Austrian Contributions to World Literature* (1890-1970). Department of Germanic Languages and Literatures, University of Pittsburgh, 1983. 96 pp.

HESSER, EDWIN BOWER

CA —UNIVERSITY OF CALIFORNIA, LOS ANGELES, Research Library, Dept of Special Collections, 405 Hilgard Ave, Los Angeles, 90024. Edward Shreeves, Chairman, Bibliographers Group; David S Zeidberg, Head
Notes: 10 linear feet of business records and photographs relating to the invention of "Hessercolor."

HESTON, CHARLTON

CA —UNIVERSITY OF CALIFORNIA, LOS ANGELES, Theater Arts Library, Los Angeles, 90024. Edward Shreeves, Chairman, Bibliographers Group; Audree Malkin, Head, Theater Arts Library
Notes: The Charlton Heston Archives, incl correspondence, scripts, movie posters, still photographs, scrapbooks, interviews, awards, etc, covering his forty-year acting career in fifty-four films. He served six terms as President of the Screen Actors Guild, longer than anyone else.

HETEROCERA see Butterflies and Moths

HETEROGENESIS see Life-Origin

HEWITT, HELEN

TX —NORTH TEXAS STATE UNIVERSITY, Audio Center, Box 5188, NT Station, Denton, 76203. Morris Martin, Music Librn
Notes: Supports wide range of music curricula and research with over 100,000 volumes incl music books, periodicals, scores, sheet music of all kinds, chamber music, recordings; special collections incl the libraries of musicologists Lloyd Hibberd and Helen Hewitt, bandleader Stan Kenton, composer Don Gillis, radio stations WFAA and WBAP; archives of *Source* magaine, mss of Arnold Schoenberg, recording collections (Arturo Toscanini, Don Gillis, Duke Ellington and other jazz musicians).

HEWLETT, CLARENCE WILSON, 1886-1976

NY —UNION COLLEGE, Schaffer Library, Archives of Science and Technology, Schenectady, 12308. Ellen Fladger, Archivist

HEWLETT, MAURICE HENRY, 1861-1923

CT —YALE UNIVERSITY, Box 1603A, Yale Station, New Haven, 06520.

NY —HOFSTRA UNIVERSITY, Library, 1000 Fulton Ave, Hempstead, 11550. Charles R Andrews, Dean of Library Services
Notes: Strong collection. Incl some mss.

OH —OHIO UNIVERSITY, Vernon R Alden Library, Department of Archives and Special Collections, Athens, 45701. Gary A Hunt, Head
Holdings: Vols 70 Cat
Notes: A comprehensive collection of first and other significant early editions.

HEWLETT FAMILY

NY —WHALING MUSEUM SOCIETY, Cold Spring Harbor Whaling Museum, Main St, Cold Spring Harbor, 11724. Robert D Farwell, Dir
Holdings: Cat Mss Maps Pix
Notes: Library of bound and printed books covers Cold Spring Harbor whaling industry, in general, and maritime affairs. Archives contain thousands of original documents concerning whaling activities, the Cold Spring Harbor Whaling Company, and the extensive maritime coastal trade conducted out of Cold Spring Harbor after the whaling era (latter 1800s). Considerable material deals with the Jones and Hewlett families, important in both local commerce and Long Island and New York affairs.

HEXAPODA see Insects

HEYEN, WILLIAM, 1940-

MA —BOSTON UNIVERSITY, Mugar Memorial Library, Special Collections Dept, 771 Commonwealth Ave, Boston, 02215. Howard B Gotlieb, Dir
Holdings: Cat Mss Correspondence

NY —UNIVERSITY OF ROCHESTER, Rush Rhees Library, Department of Rare Books and Special Collections, Rochester, 14627. Peter Dzwonkoski, Librn
Holdings: Vols Cat Ephemera

OH —OHIO UNIVERSITY, Vernon R Alden Library, Department of Archives and Special Collections, Athens, 45701. Gary A Hunt, Head
Holdings: Vols 103 Cat Mss
Notes: An exhaustive collection of Heyen's published works, incl some letters and mss.

HEYWARD, DUBOSE, 1885-1940

SC —COLLEGE OF CHARLESTON LIBRARY, Special Collections Dept, Charleston, 29401.
Notes: Correspondence within the Lancelot Minor Harris Papers.

HIBBERD, LLOYD

TX —NORTH TEXAS STATE UNIVERSITY, Audio Center, Box 5188, NT Station, Denton, 76203. Morris Martin, Music Librn
Notes: Supports wide range of music curricula and research with over 100,000 volumes incl music books, periodicals, scores, sheet music of all kinds, chamber music, recordings; special collections incl the libraries of musicologists Lloyd Hibberd and Helen Hewitt, bandleader Stan Kenton, composer Don Gillis, radio stations WFAA and WBAP; archives of *Source* magaine, mss of Arnold Schoenberg, recording collections (Arturo Toscanini, Don Gillis, Duke Ellington and other jazz musicians).

HIBBERT, CHRISTOPHER

MA —BOSTON UNIVERSITY, Mugar Memorial Library, Special Collections Dept, 771 Commonwealth Ave, Boston, 02215. Howard B Gotlieb, Dir
Holdings: Cat Mss Pix
Notes: Mss, correspondence, etc collected in depth; incl publications by or about.

HICHBORN, FRANKLIN, 1869-1963

CA —UNIVERSITY OF CALIFORNIA, LOS ANGELES, Research Library, Dept of Special Collections, 405 Hilgard Ave, Los Angeles, 90024. Edward Shreeves, Chairman, Bibliographers Group; David S Zeidberg, Head
Holdings: // Uncat Mss
Notes: 63 linear feet of personal papers, 1890-1940, covering his career as a legislative reporter and observer of California political history.

HICKEY, MARGARET

MO —UNIVERSITY OF MISSOURI-SAINT LOUIS, Thomas Jefferson Library, Manuscript and Historical Society Collection, 8001 Natural Bridge Rd, Saint Louis, 63121.
Holdings: Mss
Notes: Margaret Hickey's papers.

HICKLIN, RALPH

ON —METROPOLITAN TORONTO LIBRARY, Theatre Dept, 789 Yonge St, Toronto, M4W 2G8, Can. Heather McCallum, Head
Notes: Theatre Department is one of eleven subject departments of the Metropolitan Toronto Library, which is generally acknowledged to be the most comprehensive of Canadian public library collections. The collection balances book and nonbook material in all areas of the performing arts. Production history is the special emphasis of the dance collection, as it is for all the material in the Theatre Department. This is supported by the department's extensive holdings of programs, posters, photographs and press clippings for Canadian productions and dancers, as well as a representative selection of material for non-Canadian dance. Important original stage designs in the collection incl work by Mstislav Dobujinsky for the Canadian ballet *Red Ear of Corn,* which was produced by Boris Volkoff in 1949; Maurice Strike's work for the National Ballet of Canada's productionof *Coppelia,* and Desmond Heeley's designs for that company's *Swan Lake.* Ms collections incl: The Boris Volkoff Collection (qv); papers of the Toronto dance teacher Bettina Byers; the papers of two Canadian dance critics, Ralph Hicklin and John Fraser; and the Mary Wigman Collection, consisting of xerox copies of letters exchanged between Miss Wigman and her Canadian pupil Judy Jarvis, and a taped conversation with Miss Wigman.

HICKS, ELIAS, 1748-1830

PA —FRIENDS HISTORICAL LIBRARY OF SWARTHMORE COLLEGE, Swarthmore, 19081. J William Frost, Dir
Holdings: Mss
Notes: Ms collection of approx 400 letters, a journal, and other items of this farmer, surveyor, antislavery worker, and Quaker minister from Jericho, NY, active in the Separation of 1827-8 among Quakers.

HIDALGO, MIGUEL

IN —INDIANA UNIVERSITY, Lilly Library, Seventh St, Bloomington, 47405. William R Cagle, Librn
Holdings: Vols (10,000) // Cat Mss
Notes: Historical pronouncements and documents by the leaders of the movement of Mexican independence. Partially cataloged.
See also entry under Mexico - History

HIERATIC INSCRIPTIONS see Egyptian Language and Literature

HIEROGLYPHICS

NY —NEW YORK PUBLIC LIBRARY, Oriental Div, Fifth Ave & 42 St, New York,

HIEROGLYPHICS (cont.)

10018. E Christian Filstrup, Chief
Holdings: Cat Mss Microforms
Budget: ($56,455)
Notes: Published catalog of holdings.

OH —CLEVELAND PUBLIC LIBRARY, Fine Arts and Special Collections Department, 325 Superior Ave, Cleveland, 44114. Alice N Loranth, Head
Holdings: Vols (5200) Cat Mss
Notes: Part of the Egyptology Collection. Extensive collection of scholarly research material on Egyptian antiquities and philogical studies. Strong holdings in French, British and German series, excavation reports, etc.

HIEROGLYPHICS, EGYPTIAN see Egyptian Language and Literature

HIESTER, JOSEPH

CT —TRINITY COLLEGE LIBRARY, 300 Summit St, Hartford, 06106. Peter J Knapp, Archivist
Holdings: Uncat Mss Pix
Notes: Late 18th and 19th century mss, letter, diaries, etc of the Curtis Family of Connecticut and New York, with emphasis on: William Edmond (1755-1838), US Congressman from Conn; Holbrook Curtis (1787-1858); William Edmond Curtis (1823-1880), Chief Justice of Superior Court of New York; Mary Ann Scovill Curtis (1831-1908); and William Edmond Curtis Jr, (1855-1923), US Asst Secy of the Treasury. Incl on basis of relation through marriage are late 18th and 19th century mss, letters and diaries of the Hiester, McLanahan and Muhlenberg Families of Pennsylvania, with emphasis on Joseph Hiester (1752-1832), US Congressman and Governor of Pennsylvania; and Andrew Gregg (1755-1835), US Congressman and Senator from Pennsylvania. 12 linear feet.

HIGGINBOTTOM, SAMUEL

VA —UNIVERSITY OF VIRGINIA, Alderman Library, Manuscripts Dept, Charlottesville, 22901. Edmund Berkeley Jr, Cur
Holdings: Cat Mss Pix
Notes: Papers of Samuel Higginbottom and his family; missionary to India. (30 linear feet).

HIGGINS, AIDAN

BC —UNIVERSITY OF VICTORIA, McPherson Library, Victoria, V8W 3H5, Can.
Notes: Mss of novels, notebooks, typescripts, galley proofs, *Felo de Se; Langrishe, Go Down Balcony of Europe; Images of Africa; Scenes from a Receding Past;* tapes and transcripts of radio plays, "The Assassination of Franz Ferdinand," "Uncontrollable Laughter," "B S Johnson interviews Aidan Higgins."

HIGGINS, RAYMOND

OH —GREENE COUNTY DISTRICT LIBRARY, 76 E Market St, PO Box 520, Xenia, 45385. Julie M Overton, Local History Coordr
Notes: Collection of papers of Raymond Higgins, editor emeritus of the Xenia Daily Gazette, and historian for the Xenia area until the mid-1970's. Correspondence includes letters written in response to his historical column and are unusually good depictions of Xenia's Catholic population in the 1920's and 1930's.

HIGGINSON, ELLA RHOADS, 1862-1940

WA —BELLINGHAM PUBLIC LIBRARY, 210 Central Ave, Bellingham, 98225. Claudia McCain, Dir
Holdings: Cat Mss Pix
Notes: Ella Higginson was a poet of the Pacific Coast who is claimed by Oregon and Washington. Her published writing was done in Bellingham. Collection of her works incl all her published poetry except for her first book, a miniature paper-bound brochure written in 1894. Published description of her collected works in *History of Oregon* Literature, by Alfred Powers (Metropolitan Press, 1935), pp 427-431.

HIGGINSON, THOMAS WENTWORTH

MA —HARVARD UNIVERSITY LIBRARY, Houghton Library, Cambridge, 02138. Rodney G Dennis, Cur of Manuscripts
Holdings: Cat Mss

HIGH ALTITUDE PHENOMENOLOGY

CA —UNIVERSITY OF CALIFORNIA, SANTA CRUZ, University Library, Special Collections, Santa Cruz, 95064. Rita Bottoms, Special Collections Librn; Margaret Felts, South Pacific Collection Bibliographer
Holdings: Cat
Notes: Astronomy library. Incl all major astronomical and astrophysical journals and an extensive collection of domestic and foreign observatory publications. The book collection is particularly strong in stellar structure and evolution, stellar spectroscopy, the interstellar medium, galactic structure, external galaxies, general relativity and gravitational radiation, and high-energy astrophysics.

NM —UNIVERSITY OF CALIFORNIA, Los Alamos National Laboratory, Libraries, PO Box 1663, MSP 362, Los Alamos, 87545. J Arthur Freed, Head Librn
Holdings: Vols (800,000) Cat Films Microforms
Budget: ($700,000)
Notes: Incl 481,000 classified and unclassified reports. There are 33 branch libraries and a central collection. The Medical Library contains about 40,000 vols in the areas of biomedical research.

HIGH BLOOD PRESSURE see Hypertension

HIGH ENERGY PHYSICS

CA —UNIVERSITY OF CALIFORNIA, LOS ANGELES, Physics Library, 213 Kinsey Hall, Los Angeles, 90024. J Wally Pegram, Librn
Holdings: Vols (37,000) Cat
Notes: UCLA physics theses; current SLAC preprints in high-energy physics. (592) current serials subscriptions.

CA —UNIVERSITY OF CALIFORNIA, SANTA CRUZ, University Library, Special Collections, Santa Cruz, 95064. Rita Bottoms, Special Collections Librn; Margaret Felts, South Pacific Collection Bibliographer
Holdings: Vols (30,000) Cat
Notes: Incl all major astronomical and astrophysical journals and an extensive collection of domestic and foreign observatory publications. The book collection is particularly strong in stellar structure and evolution, stellar spectroscopy, the interstellar medium, galactic structure, external galaxies, general relativity and gravitational radiation, and high-energy astrophysics.

CA —STANFORD LINEAR ACCELERATOR CENTER, Library, PO Box 4349, Stanford, 94305. Robert C Gex, Librn
Holdings: Cat Microforms
Notes: High energy physics and particle accelerators.

CO —UNIVERSITY OF COLORADO, Duane Physical Laboratories G140, Mathematics-Physics Library, Boulder, 80309. Allen Wynne, Head Librn
Holdings: Vols Cat Microforms
Notes: All areas of mathematics and physics with special emphasis on astrophysics, astrogeophysics, theoretical high energy physics and theoretical computer science. Also basic astronomy. The most comprehensive general mathematics and physics collection in the Rocky Mountain area, although not having sufficient depth to allow doctoral research in some specific areas. Excellent bibliographic control for current and retrospective searching as complete runs of most major subject indexing and abstracting services are present. ILL for businesses through the Colorado Technical Reference Center in main library building.

IL —ARGONNE NATIONAL LABORATORY, High-Energy Physics/Environmental Sciences Branch Library, 9700 S Cass Ave, Argonne, 60439. Jean Castle, Library Assistant
Notes: Incl 9000 vols monographs, 207 current journals, a comprehensive collection of high-energy physics pre-prints. Materials may be used by the public in the library by prior arrangement. Photocopies may be supplied for interlibrary loan, for which a processing and handling charge is made.

IL —FERMI NATIONAL ACCELERATOR LABORATORY (FERMILAB), Library, PO Box 500, Batavia, 60510. Roger S Thompson, Manager, Technical Information
Holdings: Vols 12,000 Cat
Budget: ($140,000)

IL —UNIVERSITY OF ILLINOIS, URBANA/CHAMPAIGN, Library, Physics/Astronomy Library, 204 Loomis Laboratory, 1110 West Green St, Urbana, 61801. Bernice Lord Hulsizer, Librn
Holdings: Vols (34,000) Cat Microforms
Budget: ($130,000)
Notes: We collect heavily in high-energy physics, incl books, journals, and 400,000 microforms. (No longer collected except in demand).

HIGH SCHOOL EDUCATION see Education, Secondary

HIGH SOCIETY see Upper Classes

HIGH SPEED CINEMATOGRAPHY see Cinematography, High Speed

HIGH SPEED PHOTOGRAPHY see Photography, High Speed

HIGH TEMPERATURE MATERIALS see Materials at High Temperatures

HIGH VACUUM TECHNIQUE see Vacuum Science and Technology

HIGH VOLTAGE, HIGH FREQUENCY PHOTOGRAPHY see Kirlian Photography

HIGHAM, CHARLES

MA —BOSTON UNIVERSITY, Mugar Memorial Library, Special Collections Dept, 771 Commonwealth Ave, Boston, 02215. Howard B Gotlieb, Dir
Holdings: Cat Mss

HIGHER EDUCATION see Education, Higher

HIGHET, GILBERT

†NY —COLUMBIA UNIVERSITY LIBRARIES, Butler Library, Rare Book and Manuscript Library, 535 W 114 St, New York, 10027.
Notes: Papers, mss, correspondence, etc of Prof Gilbert Highet.

HIGH-JACKING see Terrorism and Terrorists

HIGHLAND CLANS see Clans and Clan Systems

HIGHLAND COSTUME see Tartans

HIGHTOWER, JIM

IA —IOWA STATE UNIVERSITY, Library, Dept of Special Collections, Ames, 50011. Stanley M Yates, Head
Holdings: // Mss
Notes: Founded in 1970, the Agribusiness

HIGHTOWER, JIM (cont.)

Accountability Project was a non-profit, non-partisan, public-interest research organization which investigated various aspects of agribusiness. 15 linear ft, finding aid available.

HIGHWAY ACCIDENTS see Traffic Accidents

HIGHWAY CONSTRUCTION see Road Construction

HIGHWAY DESIGN see Roads—Design

HIGHWAY ENGINEERING see Roads; Road Construction

HIGHWAY SIGNS see Signs and Signboards

HIGHWAY TRANSPORTATION see Transportation, Automotive

HIGHWAYMEN see Brigands and Robbers

HIGHWAYS see Roads

HIJACKING see Terrorism and Terrorists

HIKING

MA —APPALACHIAN MOUNTAIN CLUB, 5 Joy St, Boston, 02108. Fran Belcher, Librn
Holdings: Vols (6500) Cat Maps Pix Slides
Budget: ($3000)
Notes: Mountaineering, espec the White Mountains. Bound editions of other countries, mountaineering journals.

WA —MOUNTAINEERS INC, Library, 300 3rd Ave West, Seattle, 98119. Verna M Ness, Library Cur
Holdings: Vols (3000) Cat
Notes: Collection incl some 19th century vols of Alpine information, incl the first issue of *The Alpine Journal* (1863). Bound serials of many important American climbing publications. Small sub-collections for American Alpine Club members and for The Mountaineer Foundation, the latter on conservation and ecology. In the main collection backpacking, skiing and natural history are also represented.

HILGARD, EUGENE W.

CA —UNIVERSITY OF CALIFORNIA, BERKELEY, Bancroft Library, Manuscripts Division, Berkeley, 94720. James D Hart, Dir
Holdings: Cat Mss Maps Pix Microforms
Notes: Papers, correspondence, etc.

HILL, DRAPER

OH —OHIO STATE UNIVERSITY, Library for Communication and Graphic Arts, 242 W 18th St, Columbus, 43210. Lucy S Caswell, Curator
Notes: The original works of editorial cartoonists Art Poinier, Scott Willis, Brian Basset, Billy Ireland, Frank Williams, Charles Werner, Ned Beard, L D Warren, Edward D Kuekes, Ray Osrin, Mike Peters, Draper Hill, Eugene Craig and Bert Whitman.

HILL, JAMES JEROME

MN —JAMES JEROME HILL REFERENCE LIBRARY, Fourth St at Market St, Saint Paul, 55106. Virgil F Massman, Dir
Holdings: Vols 800 Cat Mss Pix
Notes: Books collected by James J Hill as well as works about him. Incl memorabilia, clippings, ephemera.

HILL, JOHN WESLEY

NY —COLUMBIA UNIVERSITY LIBRARIES, Rare Book & Manuscript Library, 801 Butler Library, 535 W 114 St, New York, 10027. Kenneth A Lohf, Librn
Holdings: Mss
Notes: Mss, prints, portraits and memorabilia relating to Lincoln.

HILL, KNUTE

†WA —WASHINGTON STATE UNIVERSITY, Library, Manuscripts, Archives & Special Collections, Pullman, 99164. John F Guido, Head
Holdings: Vols Cat Mss Maps Pix
Notes: The personal and political papers of Fred C Ashley, William Edward Carty, Knute Hill, Walter Franklin Horan, William Lon Johnson, Catherine May, and Austin Mires are among the holdings of the library. Most collections described in printed registers.

HILL, MARTHA

KS —WICHITA PUBLIC LIBRARY, Art & Music Division, 223 S Main, Wichita, 67202. Leonard Messineo, Jr, Head, Art & Music Division; Deborah Hamilton, Special Collections Librn
Holdings: Uncat Audiotapes Vidoetape Pix
Notes: Alice Bauman Dance Symposia Collection. Contains 300 hours of audio tapes, 1 hour-long video tape, several hundred photographs, and fugitive material of the American Dance Symposia held in Wichita from 1968-1972. The symposia covered all dance idioms-ballet, modern, jazz, folk, ethnic, dance education and therapy-and featured such notable figures such as Leonide Massine, Martha Hill, William Christensen, Alfonso Cimber, Toni Intravaia, James Clouser, Eleo Pomare, Juana de Laban, and many others. Characterized by the *Kansas City Star* as the "most distinguished faculties of fine artists ever assembled in the contemporary world of dance."

HILL, REGINALD

MA —BOSTON UNIVERSITY, Mugar Memorial Library, Special Collections Dept, 771 Commonwealth Ave, Boston, 02215. Howard B Gotlieb, Dir
Holdings: Mss

HILL, WALTER NICKERSON, 1846-1884

RI —BROWN UNIVERSITY, John Hay Library, 20 Prospect St, Providence, 02912. Mark N Brown, Cur Mss
Holdings: / / Mss
Notes: Papers of Walter Nickerson Hill, American chemist, incl correspondence, letters, autograph drafts of articles for scientific journals, lectures, letter press copy books, scrapbook with inserted A Ls S, pamphlets, photographs, and memorabilia. The correspondence deals with personal, familial, and business matters (the latter during Hill's tenure as instructor in explosives at the U S Torpedo Station in Newport, R I, and while he was chief chemist for the Rapauno Nitroglycerine Works, near Philadelphia, owned by the duPont Family). There is scientific correspondence between Hill and leading scientists, ordnance specialists, and influential figures. See also Papers of Augustus W Smith, Hill's father-in-law, also at Brown.

HILL, WILLIAM HENRY, 1876-1972

NY —CORNELL UNIVERSITY LIBRARIES, Collection of Regional History, Dept of Manuscripts and Univ Archives, Ithaca, 14853.
Notes: NY State Senator, US Congressman, and holder of governmental positions. Incl papers, 1878-(1918-1964); citations, awards, photos, phonograph records, and related pamphlets and other printed matter.

HILLERS, JOHN K.

NM —MUSEUM OF NEW MEXICO, Photo Archives, Box 2087, Santa Fe, 87503. Arthur L Olivas, Cur; Richard Rudisill, Photo Historian
Holdings: Cat Pix Slides
Notes: Extensive collection of his work.

HILLHOUSE, JAMES A.

CT —YALE UNIVERSITY, Box 1603A, Yale Station, New Haven, 06520.
Holdings: Cat Mss

HILLQUIT, MORRIS

WI —STATE HISTORICAL SOCIETY OF WISCONSIN, Archives, 816 State St, Madison, 53706. Harold L Miller, Reference Archivist
Holdings: Mss Pix Microforms
Notes: Records and papers documenting the history of the labor and Socialist movements in the United States from 1850s to the present. Incl are records of labor and socialist organizations incl American Federation of Labor and the Socialist Labor Party, and papers of individual labor and socialist leaders such as Morris Hillquit and John L Lewis. Collections are described in *A Guide to Labor Papers in the State Historical Society of Wisconsin* (1978) and in current accession notes in the *Wisconsin Magazine of History.* Major collections are also listed in Hamer, *Guide to Manuscripts and Archives in the United States,* (1961) and in the *National Union Catalog of Manuscript Collections,* (1959-date).

HILSMAN, ROGER

†MA —JOHN F KENNEDY LIBRARY, Columbia Point, Boston, 02125. Dan H Fenn Jr, Dir
Holdings: / / Cat Mss
Notes: His papers as Assistant Secretary of State for Far Eastern Affairs and Director of Intelligence and Research, State Department, 1961-1965. 6 linear ft of mss. Holdings are described in "Historical Materials in the John F Kennedy Library." Copies may be obtained by writing the Research Archivist.

HILTON, JOHN BUXTON

MA —BOSTON UNIVERSITY, Mugar Memorial Library, Special Collections Dept, 771 Commonwealth Ave, Boston, 02215. Howard B Gotlieb, Dir
Holdings: Cat Mss Correspondence

HILTON, RONALD

†TX —TRINITY UNIVERSITY, Library, 715 Stadium Dr, San Antonio, 78284.
Holdings: Vols (10,000)
Notes: The library of Professor Ronald Hilton on Latin America and the Carribbean. Incl 270 audiotapes of interviews with prominent Latin Americans, 34 autograph letters, and photographs of Cuba during the Spanish-American War.

HIMALAYAN LANGUAGES see Tibeto-Burman Languages and Literatures

HIMALAYAN MOUNTAINS

NC —UNIVERSITY OF NORTH CAROLINA, CHARLOTTE, J Murrey Atkins Library, UNCC Station, Charlotte, 28223. Robert F Brabham Jr, Special Collections Librn
Notes: Part of the Suzuki Collection of books on Mahayana Buddhism. It incl 10 vols and 25 paintings and sketches of Himalayan scenes. Cataloged.

HIMMLER, HEINRICH, 1900-1945

CA —HOOVER INSTITUTION ON WAR, REVOLUTION & PEACE, Stanford University, Stanford, 94305. Milorad M Drachkovitch, Archivist
Holdings: Mss Pix
Notes: Ms diaries, 1914-1924, microfilms, photographs and photostats of documents

HIMMLER, HEINRICH, 1900-1945 (cont.)

from the *Personlicher Stab Reichsfuhrer, SS, Schriftgutverwaltung* dealing with the life and career of Himmler as Reichsfuhrer SS and Chef der Deutschen Polizei, 1934-1945. 6 notebooks (plus 25 loose pages), 5 microfilm reels, 2 photo albums, 14 ms boxes. Incl 24 tapes of Himmler speeches, 1940-44.

DC —LIBRARY OF CONGRESS, Rare Book & Special Collections Div, Washington, 20540. William Matheson, Chief
Notes: The Third Reich Collection incl materials from the libraries of Hermann Goring, Heinrich Himmler, Franz Xaver Schwarz, and other Nazi leaders.

HINCKLEY, ROBERT O'DONNEL

DC —GEORGETOWN UNIVERSITY, Library, Special Collections Div, 37 & O Sts NW, Washington, 20057. George M Barringer, Special Collections Librn; Nicholas B Sheetz, Mss Librn
Holdings: Mss Pix
Notes: Correspondence, documents, journals, diaries, financial accounts, mss, photographs, and art work comprising the personal and professional papers of McCeney Werlich, diplomat, as well as those of his wife, Gladys Hinckley Werlich; Thomas Hinckley, and Robert 0'Donnel Hinckley, both diplomats; papers of Eleanor O'Donnell Hinckley, mother of Gladys Werlich, and her husband Robert Hinckley, noted portrait painter. The papers incl: State Department correspondence and other material relating to McCeney Werlich's posts in Latvia (1926-1927), Poland (1927-1931), Costa Rica (1931-1932), Liberia (1932-1933), and France (1934-1936); correspondence from Robert O'Donnell Hinckley from his travels in the Orient, 1919; correspondence from Thomas Hinckley, incl accounts of the Austro-Hungarian empire, 1914-1915; as well as numerous journalsand diaries kept by Gladys Werlich regarding her extensive travels and variety of experiences.

HIND, E. CORA, 1861-1942

MB —UNIVERSITY OF MANITOBA, Elizabeth Dafoe Library, Archives and Special Collections Dept, Winnipeg, R3T 2N2, Can. Richard E Bennett, Dept Head; Corrado A Santoro, Reference Archivist
Notes: Papers relating to Miss Hind's career in journalism as Commercial and Agricultural Editor of the Winnipeg Free Press. Includes materials on her two world tours (1935-37) sponsored by the Free Press.

HINDEMITH, PAUL

CT —YALE UNIVERSITY, Music Library, 98 Wall St, New Haven, 06520. Harold E Samuel, Librn
Holdings: Vols (118,000) Cat Mss Pix Phonorecords Audiotapes
Notes: Personal papers and musical mss.
See also entry under Music, American

HINDI LANGUAGE AND LITERATURE

AZ —UNIVERSITY OF ARIZONA, Library, Oriental Studies Collection, Tucson, 85721. Mary J McWhorter, Actg Head Librn
Holdings: Vols (95,000) Cat Microforms
Budget: ($30,000)
See also entry under Oriental Languages and Literatures

DC —LIBRARY OF CONGRESS, African and Middle Eastern Division, Washington, 20540.
Holdings: Cat Mss Microforms
Notes: Southern Asian: over 137,000 vols of literature of the area from Pakistan to Philippines.

HI —UNIVERSITY OF HAWAII, Library, 2550 The Mall, Honolulu, 96822. Joyce Wright, Head, Asia Collection; Masato Matsu, Head, East Asia Vernacular Collection
Holdings: Vols 75,215
Notes: The Asia Collection holds material from and relating to Bangladesh, India, Nepal, Pakistan, and Sri Lanka in western and Asian languages. South Asian languages currently acquired: Bengali, Hindi, Marathi, Nepali, Pali, Prakrit, Sanskrit, Tamil. Period emphasis is post-World War II. Subject emphases: social sciences and the humanities (literature, economics, history, religion/ philosophy). Holdings are supplemented by a large uncataloged backlog, much of it accessible through the Library of Congress Accessions Lists for the area and by over 7000 cataloged titles in the main library collection. *South Asian Library Resources in North America: A Survey Prepared for the Boston Conference, 1974* ed by M L P Patterson (Zug, Switzerland: Tutes Documentation Company, 1975). (Bibliotheca Asiatica 12-), "University of Hawaii," pp 103-114.

MI —UNIVERSITY OF MICHIGAN, Graduate Library, South Asian Dept, Ann Arbor, 48109. Om P Sharma, Librn
Holdings: Vols (365,000) Cat Maps Slides Microforms
Notes: The major emphasis is on social sciences and humanitites. Besides materials in classsical languages, South Asian vernaculars being retained are Hindi, Bengali, Urdu, Marathi and Tamil; strong in classical languages, especially Sanskrit, Pali, and Prakrit.

MI —MICHIGAN STATE UNIVERSITY, International Library, South and Southeast Asia Collection, East Lansing, 48824. Clinton Lockert, Bibliographer
Holdings: Vols 55,700 / / Cat Mss Maps Audiotapes Microforms
Notes: Serials and monographs of South Asia received on PL 480 for India, Pakistan, Sri Lanka, and Nepal since 1968. Emphasis is upon social sciences, humanities, and science. Areas of strength are anthropology and rural development. This subject has been de-emphasized, additions are not being made.

MO —UNIVERSITY OF MISSOURI-COLUMBIA, Ellis Library, Ninth and Lowry, Columbia, 65201. Murari Lal Nagar, Librn
Holdings: Vols 100,000 Maps Microforms
Notes: The South Asia Studies Program at the University of Missouri-Columbia, is an interdepartmental, multi-disciplinary area studies program on India, Pakistan, Bangladesh, Sri Lanka and Nepal. Depository for the PL480 Program of the Library of Congress in many languages from South Asia. There are library resources in Sankskrit, Hindi, Bengali, Panjabi, and Malayalam. The library is particularly strong in Baroda, Bengal and the Punjab.

NY —NEW YORK PUBLIC LIBRARY, Oriental Div, Fifth Ave & 42 St, New York, 10018. E Christian Filstrup, Chief
Holdings: Cat Mss Microforms
Budget: ($56,455)
Notes: Published catalog of holdings.

NY —NEW YORK PUBLIC LIBRARY, Donnell Foreign Language Library, 20 W 53 St, New York, 10019. Bosiljka Stevanovic, Supvr Librn
Holdings: Vols 997 Cat
Notes: Hindi collection incl Hindi authors of Hindi expression. No separate catalog.

NY —UNIVERSITY OF ROCHESTER, Rush Rhees Library, Rochester, 14627. Datta S Kharbas, Head
Holdings: Vols 100,000 Cat Maps Microforms
Notes: Area studies collection on East Asia and South Asia. Major emphasis is on social sciences and humanities. Extensive holdings in Sanskrit, Hindi, and Marathi.

NC —CUMBERLAND COUNTY PUBLIC LIBRARY, North Carolina Foreign Language Center, 328 Gillespie St, Fayetteville, 28301. Patrick M Valentine, Coordinator
Holdings: Vols (25,000) Cat Phonorecords Audiotapes
Notes: The largest book collections are, in descending order of size, German Spanish, French, Japanese, Korean and Vietnamese, with fair sized collections in Italian, Russian, Chinese, Arabic, Greek, Hungarian, Polish, Hebrew, Thai, and Hindi. The Center has several shelves each of books in Bengali, Dutch, Marathi, Portuguese, Urdu, and Yiddish. Smaller collections of one to three shelves each incl Catalan, Croatian, Czech, Danish, Finnish, Gujarati, Icelandic, Kannada, Latin, Lithuanian, Malayalam, Norwegian, Panjabi, Persian (Farsi), Romanian, Slovak, Swedish, Tagalog, Tamil, Telegu, and Ukrianian. The Center has grammars, dictionaries and occasionally other readings in languages from Afrikaans and Albanian to Welsh, Yoruba and Zulu.

PA —UNIVERSITY OF PENNSYLVANIA, Van Pelt Library, South Asia Collection, 34 and Walnut Sts, Philadelphia, 19104. Kanta Bhatia, Bibliographer
Holdings: Vols 160,000 Cat
Notes: Incl South Asia social sciences, history, politics, economics and anthroplogy. Extensive holdings in vernacular languages, especially Hindi, Tamil and Sanskrit. Incl 3400 mss.

TX —UNIVERSITY OF TEXAS LIBRARIES, Asian Collection, PO Box P, Austin, 78712. Kevin Lin, Asian Librn; Merry Burlingham, South Asian Librn
Holdings: Vols (56,000) Microforms
Notes: Materials in Hindi, Sanskrit, Urdu, Prakrit, and Pali (acquired chiefly through the Special Foreign Acquisitions Program) and selected English-language materials, including Indian censuses and district gazetteers and Pakistani censuses.

HINDU LANGUAGE AND LITERATURE

†CA —CALIFORNIA INSTITUTE OF ASIAN STUDIES LIBRARY, 3494 21 St, San Francisco, 94110.
Notes: Philosophy, psychology, religion, Hindu and Buddhist literature, Yoga and Zen discipline, art, Asian languages.

HINDUISM

CA —GRADUATE THEOLOGICAL UNION LIBRARY, New Religious Movements Research Collection, Public Services and Special Collections Dept, 2400 Ridge Road, Berkeley, 94709. Diane Choquette, Dept Head
Holdings: Vols (3000) Mss Pix
Notes: Begun in 1977, the collection focuses on religious movements new to America since 1960, and unorthodox religious movements resurgent since 1960. American forms of Hinduism, Buddhism, Sikhism, and Sufism are included along with occultism, Neo-Paganism, esoteric and alternative forms of Christianity, feminist spirituality, and human potential movements having a spiritual aspect. Legal issues, such as deprogramming, and the question of church/ state relations are an important part of the collection. The Library is a depository for publications of the Unification Church in America, the Church of Scientology, and the International Society for Krishna Consciousness (America). The responses of mainstream religions and concerned citizens groups are also included. Besides 3000 monographs, the library has 400 periodical titles, 200 posters from the San FranciscoBay Area, 1965-77, 300 research papers, and 31 linear feet of ephemera.

CA —LOS ANGELES PUBLIC LIBRARY, Philosophy & Religion Dept, 630 W Fifth St, Los Angeles, 90071. Marilyn C Wherley, Librn
Holdings: Vols 250 Cat
Budget: ($60,000)
Notes: Historical, theological, and biographical works relating to the religion. Many English translations of sacred works with revelent criticism. Includes scholarly and popular materials on comparative religion. Emphasis on groups active in Southern California including much ephemera.

MD —JOHNS HOPKINS UNIVERSITY, Milton S Eisenhower Library, George

HINDUISM (cont.)

Peabody Collection, 17 E Mt Vernon Place, Baltimore, 21201. Lyn Hart, Peabody Librn
Notes: Emphasis on materials published before 1950. Strength is a good collection through the 19th century.

NY —NEW YORK PUBLIC LIBRARY, Oriental Div, Fifth Ave & 42 St, New York, 10018. E Christian Filstrup, Chief
Holdings: Cat Mss Microforms
Budget: ($56,455)
Notes: Described in *Dictionary Catalog of the Oriental Collection,* The Research Libraries of the New York Public Library, 1960, 16 vols, and *First Supplement,* 1976, 8 vols (144,000 cards). This catalog incl 318, 000 entries for works in about 100 languages of the East, and all works in Western languages on Oriental subjects. The Oriental Collection numbers about 120,000 vols; its Arabic and Indic holdings and those on ancient Egypt and the ancient Near East are among the largest in the US. There is also a collection of 30,000 vols of PL 480 material from Egypt, Pakistan, and India to which there is main entry access, but which is not incorporated into the dictionary catalog. Other outstanding features of the Oriental Collection incl extensive holdings of Japanese technical and scientific periodicals; a unique collection of linguistic works, grammars, anddictionaries; and unusually good coverage of the field of Oriental religions and philosophies. The catalog contains numerous subject references to periodical articles in all languages. All entries are arranged alphabetically according to the Roman alphabet.

NY —INSTITUTE FOR ADVANCED STUDIES OF WORLD RELIGIONS (IASWR), Melville Memorial Library, State University of New York, Stony Brook, 11794. C T Shen, Dir
Holdings: Vols 8000 Periodicals Maps Microforms
Notes: Incl reference facilities. Modern imprints and reprints in English, Sanskrit, Hindi, Marathi and Bengali from the 1960s to date. Microforms: *University of Pennsylvania Indic Manuscripts,* descriptive catalogs available.
See also entry under Indic Languages and Literature

OH —CLEVELAND PUBLIC LIBRARY, Fine Arts and Special Collections Department, 325 Superior Ave, Cleveland, 44114. Alice N Loranth, Head
Holdings: Vols (7000) Cat Mss
Notes: Part of the Oriental Religion Collection. Emphasis is on religious texts in their original languages and Western translations. Treatises on religious beliefs and practices are also incl. Strong holdings in Buddhism, Egyptian religion, Hinduism, Judaica, Lamaistic texts, Islam, Sikhism and Zoroastrianism. Works on primitive religion cover aspects of animism, totemism, fetishism, etc. Special emphasis on Islam in China.
See also entries under India; Religion, Oriental.

PA —UNIVERSITY OF PENNSYLVANIA, Van Pelt Library, Rare Books Collection, 34 & Walnut Sts, Philadelphia, 19104. Daniel Traister, Special Collections Librn
Holdings: Cat Mss
Notes: Almost 3000 mss, from the 15th to the 19th centuries, mostly on philosophy, religion and grammar.

VA —ASSOCIATION FOR RESEARCH & ENLIGHTENMENT, Library, 67 & Atlantic Avenue, PO Box 595, Virginia Beach, 23451. Stephen Jordan, Library Mgr
Holdings: Vols (3000) Cat
Notes: Emphasis on Christian, Buddist, Hindu religions, mysticism, comparative religion, psychological approach to biofeedback, autogenics, etc.

HINE, DARYL

IN —INDIANA UNIVERSITY, Lilly Library, Seventh St, Bloomington, 47405. William R Cagle, Librn
Notes: Ms collection incl editorial and correspondence files of *Poetry*, 1945-80.

HINE, LEWIS W.

DC —LIBRARY OF CONGRESS, Prints & Photographs Div, Washington, 20540.
Notes: One of photographers represented in the American National Red Cross Collection.

MD —UNIVERSITY OF MARYLAND, BALTIMORE COUNTY, Albin O Kuhn Library and Gallery, Edward L Bafford Photography Collection, 5401 Wilkens Ave, Baltimore, 21228. Tom Beck, Cur
Holdings: Uncat Pix
Notes: The Edward L Bafford Photography Collection contains more than 200,000 images, negatives, cameras and books representing the entire history and aesthetics of photography. A main theme of the collection is photography as a social force, as represented by the 4000 photographs and negatives by Lewis Hine and by William Henry Jackson's *Photographs of the Yellowstone National Park and Views of Montana and Wyoming Territories.* Another important historical document is the rare *Photographic Sketchbook of the Civil War* by Alexander Gardner.
See also entry under Photographs - Collections.

NY —COLUMBIA UNIVERSITY LIBRARIES, Rare Book & Manuscript Library, 801 Butler Library, 535 W 114 St, New York, 10027. Kenneth A Lohf, Librn
Holdings: Mss
Notes: Papers of the Community Service Society of New York. Incl files, books, photographs (1000) and bound volumes of periodicals and conference proceedings. Among the papers are central and district administrative records, committee correspondence and minutes, and files of programs sponsored by the organization. Also more than 1000 photographs by Jessie Tarbox Beals and Lewis W Hine depicting conditions of the poor. 276,000 items. Restricted use.

NY —NEW YORK PUBLIC LIBRARY, Local History and Genealogy Div, Fifth Ave & 42 St, New York, 10018. Gunther E Pohl, Chief
Holdings: Vols (160,000) Cat Pix
Budget: ($38,548)
Notes: Collection includes over 60,000 mounted photographs of New York City views arranged by address and/or subject. 20,000 film and glass plate negatives depicting NYC tenement housing conditions (1902-1938). Also the Lloyd L Acker collection of 48,000 film negatives depicting NYC buildings, 1935-1975. Collection of 443 Lewis W Hine photographic prints made by the photographer on immigration, child labor, women at work and men at work. Eugene Armbruster collection of Long Island views; D B Austin's photographs of Long Island and western Americana; scrapbooks, and postcards of NYC and other US regions (200,000). See *United States Local History Catalog* (Boston: G K Hall, 1974), 2 vols.

RI —SLATER MILL HISTORIC SITE, SMHS Library, Roosevelt Ave, Pawtucket, 02962. TE Leary, Cur
Holdings: Vols 500 Mss Maps Pix Oral History
Budget: $500
Notes: Lewis Hine photos of child labor in RI (1909-1912).

HINES, JOHN L., 1868-1968

DC —LIBRARY OF CONGRESS, Manuscript Division, Washington, 20540. John C Broderick, Chief
Notes: Papers and World War I maps of General John L Hines.

HIPPIES see Youth Movement

HIPPOCRATES

CT —YALE UNIVERSITY, Medical Historical Library, 333 Cedar St, New Haven, 06510. Ferenc A Gyorgyey, Librn
Holdings: Vols 300 Cat
Notes: Incl numerous editions of his writings.

HIPPOLOGY see Horses

HIROSHIMA, JAPAN

OH —WILMINGTON COLLEGE, Peace Resource Center, Hiroshima/Nagasaki Memorial Collection, Pyle Center Box 1183, Wilmington, 45177. Helen Redding, Librn
Holdings: Vols Pix Audiotapes Videotapes Film Slides Art Reproductions VF
Notes: The Hiroshima/Nagasaki Memorial Collection is nationally known and respected as a major source of information, films, slides and audiotapes about the atomic bombings of Hiroshima and Nagasaki. An especially signifciant part of the Collection is a continually growing library in Japanese currently numbering more than 500 vols. Here are recorded eyewitness account of the atomic bombings, as well as details of what life has been like in the intervening years for the thousands of survivors (*hibakusha*). Also incl are books of poetry, photo books, juvenile literature, and books dealing with medical information, peace research, peace education, nuclear power, etc. All books in the Hiroshima/Nagasaki Memorial Collection are available for interlibrary loan. An *Annotated Bibliography of Japanese A-Bomb Literature* may be purchased or borrowed from the PRC. In it are briefsummaries in English of each book in the Collection.

HIRSCH, HELMUT, 1907-

NY —STATE UNIVERSITY OF NEW YORK AT ALBANY, Library, Special Collections Dept, 1400 Washington Ave, Albany, 12222. Marion P Munzer, Coordr
Notes: Mss, correspondence of Helmut Hirsch; reprints of articles (2.5 linear feet). Part of the Library's German Exile Collection.

HIRSHBERG, AL

MA —BOSTON UNIVERSITY, Mugar Memorial Library, Special Collections Dept, 771 Commonwealth Ave, Boston, 02215. Howard B Gotlieb, Dir
Holdings: // Cat Mss Pix
Notes: Mss, correspondence, etc collected in depth; incl publications by or about.

HISCOCK, IRA V.

CT —YALE UNIVERSITY, Box 1603A, Yale Station, New Haven, 06520.
Holdings: Mss Pix
Notes: The Contemporary Medical Care and Health Policy Collection. Letters, memos, records, photographs, etc of the principal strategists of the social medical movement in the U S.

HISPANIC AMERICAN NEWSPAPERS see Newspapers, Hispanic American

HISPANIC AMERICANS

LA —AMISTAD RESEARCH CENTER, 400 Esplanade Ave, New Orleans, 70116. Clifton H Johnson, Exec Dir; Florence E Borders, Senior Archivist
Budget: ($315,000)
Notes: Originally established at Fisk University, in Nashville, by the American Missionary Association (AMA), this research center on Black American History consists of mss, photographs, clippings, books, pamphlets, taped speeches and interviews; also, the papers of such leaders as WEB DuBois, Countee Cullen, and Mary McLeod Bethune. Also materials on other American minorities, such as Native Americans, Asian Americans, Hispanics, etc.

WI —STATE HISTORICAL SOCIETY OF WISCONSIN, Library, Newspaper and Periodicals Section, 816 State St, Madison, 53706. James P Danky, Librn
Notes: One of the largest collections of Hispanic American periodicals and newspapers in the US. Holdings described in

HISPANIC AMERICANS (cont.)

Hispanic Americans in the United States: A Union List.... Madison, The Society, 1979. (ERIC Report 220 110).

HISPANIC CIVILIZATION see Civilization, Hispanic

HISPANIC LANGUAGES AND LITERATURES

DC —LIBRARY OF CONGRESS, Hispanic Division, Washington, 20540.
Notes: The Archive of Hispanic Literature on Tape is a repository of recorded poetry and prose from the Spanish- and Portuguese-speaking world. Most of the outstanding Hispanic literary figures of the last 30 years are included.

HISPANO-AMERICAN WAR, 1898 see U.S.—History—War of 1898

HISS, ALGER, 1904-

MA —HARVARD UNIVERSITY LIBRARY, Law School Library, Langdell Hall, Cambridge, 02138. Erika S Chadbourn, Cur of Mss
Holdings: Cat Mss
Notes: Personal papers; government and legal documents. Typed folder list in repository. Inclusive dates: 1930s-present.

HISTOLOGY

PA —CARNEGIE LIBRARY OF PITTSBURGH, Science & Technology Dept, 4400 Forbes Ave, Pittsburgh, 15213. Catherine M Brosky, Dept Head
Notes: Of secondary interest in acquisitions because of the department's role in cooperating with Pittsburgh institutions and others across the Commonwealth in sharing resources, the cooperative acquisition of materials, and the provision of services and information. However, some aspects of the subject are emphasized. There are separate entries for each of these specialties in this vol.

HISTOPLASMOSIS

OH —MIAMI UNIVERSITY, Science Library, Oxford, 45056.
Notes: Zoonoses and related diseases. Collection partially transferred from Parker-Davis Memorial Library, Hamilton, Mont.

HISTORIC AMERICAN BUILDINGS SURVEY

DC —LIBRARY OF CONGRESS, Prints and Photographs Div, Historic American Buildings Survey, Washington, 20540.
Holdings: Cat Mss Pix Drawings
Notes: Details of some 17,000 American buildings in 81,000 photographs, 42,000 measured drawings and 44,000 pp of written documentation.

IL —CHICAGO PUBLIC LIBRARY, Art Section, Fine Arts Division, 78 E Washington St, Chicago, 60602. Rosalinda I Hack, Fine Arts Division Chief; Yvonne S Brown, Head, Art Section
Holdings: Vols 6000
Notes: Reference and circulating collection, with special emphasis on general architectural history, modern architecture, architecture of the United States, and Chicago architectural history. Collections is supported by the Chicago Architecture File, a card file that lists citations to information on buildings that been recognized for their architectural significance. The Section's picture Collection has extensive documentation on Chicago area architecture, and incorporates a collection of architectural photographs by Stephen Beal. Archival copies of these photographs are to be found in Special Collections. The collections is also supplemented by the microform collections of *The Historic American Buildings Survey,* and *American Architectural Books.*

MA —SOCIETY FOR THE PRESERVATION OF NEW ENGLAND ANTIQUITIES, Library, 141 Cambridge St, Boston, 02114. Ellie Reichlin, Librn & Cur of Photographic Collections
Notes: Over 125 sets of survey sheets (full-scale, some originals) for historic buildings throughout New England, strongest for Massachusetts and New Hampshire; original photographs of Massachusetts structures by HABS photographer Arthur Haskell; office files of Massachusetts HABS Director, Frank Chouteau Brown, with measured details, sketchbooks, correspondence, notes for surveys, not all of them reported to HABS in Washington. Original measured drawings of historic structures by the Emergency Planning and Research Bureau, Architectural Division, predecessor to HABS. Ca 2000 pieces; 1200 photographs.

NY —LANDMARK SOCIETY OF WESTERN NEW YORK, Wenrich Memorial Library, 130 Spring Rd, Rochester, 14608.
Holdings: Vols (2000) Cat Maps Pix Slides
Budget: ($500)
Notes: Paintings, slides, drawings, as well as the Society's archives of local architecture and information on preservation and restoration techniques. Much on preservation ordinances; legal, physical and financial aspects of building preservation; local and regional history, especially of Rochester and Monroe County.

OR —SOUTHERN OREGON HISTORICAL SOCIETY, Jacksonville Museum Library, 206 N Fifth St, PO Box 480, Jacksonville, 97530. Richard H Engeman, Librn
Holdings: Vols (200) Cat Mss Pix Slides 16mm Films
Budget: ($5200)

HISTORIC HOUSES, ETC.

MA —SOCIETY FOR THE PRESERVATION OF NEW ENGLAND ANTIQUITIES, Library, 141 Cambridge St, Boston, 02114. Ellie Reichlin, Librn & Cur of Photographic Collections
Holdings: Vols (3000) Cat Pix Microforms
Budget: ($75,000)
Notes: Photograph collections, all media (incl daguerreotypes, ambrotypes, etc, stereographic views, carte de visite) depicting New England buildings; interiors; street and town views; occupations; pastimes; transport and personalities. Covers 1840s-1930s, with some more recent additons. Amateur and professional photographers represented. Cataloged in part, otherwise arranged by localities, subject, personal name. Special collections incl: marine photographs by N L Stebbins and Henry Peabody (1880s-1920s); Boston and Albany railroad photographic archive, early 1900s; Quabbin Valley views; historic American Buildings Survey photographs (17th to early 19th century architecture) by Arthur Haskell; Baldwin College collection, and many others. Size: 500,000 prints, ca 75,000 negatives (glass plates and copy negs). These are cataloged. Some special indexes incllandscape design (arbors, conservatories, flower beds, bandstands etc); photographers represented; architects represented (partial), and pending, interiors (specific features of); occupations.

MA —HISTORIC DEERFIELD-POCUMTUCK VALLEY MEMORIAL ASSOCIATION, Libraries, Memorial St, Box 53, Deerfield, 01342. David R Proper, Librn
Holdings: Vols (17,000) Cat Mss Maps Pix Microforms
Notes: Local and regional history, especially western Massachusetts. Also, remnants of several collection of books available to early Deerfield and Greenfield residents. Strong ms collection dealing with the region's families, businesses, etc. These consist of sermons, diaries, town and church records, voluntary societies' archives, etc. Extensive collection of photographs of the people and buildings of Deerfield and its environs, and travels in Maine, California, and England (1880s to 1920s). Also, large collection of glassplate negatives. Houses the Connecticut Valley Bibliography, a comprehensive card file on the history and culture of the Connecticut Valley of Massachusetts.

MA —OLD STURBRIDGE VILLAGE, Research Library, Sturbridge, 01566. Theresa Rini Percy, Librn
Holdings: Vols (23,000) Cat
Notes: Preservation of books, papers, fabrics, artifacts of every description, and of buildings.

MI —EDISON INSTITUTE, Greenfield Village and Henry Ford Museum, Archives & Research Library, PO Box 1970, Dearborn, 48121. Steve Hamp, Dir; Joan W Gartland, Librn
Holdings: Vols 400,000 Cat Mss Maps Microforms
Notes: 400,000 vols incl pamphlets. The Archives and research library supports the program of Greenfield Village and the Henry Ford Museum. Special collections incl: automotive literature, ephemera, McGuffey Readers, trade catalogs, photographs and graphics.

NY —LANDMARK SOCIETY OF WESTERN NEW YORK, Wenrich Memorial Library, 130 Spring Rd, Rochester, 14608.
Holdings: Vols (2000) Cat Maps Pix Slides
Budget: ($500)
Notes: Paintings, slides, drawings, as well as the Society's archives of local architecture and information on preservation and restoration techniques. Much on preservation ordinances; legal, physical and financial aspects of building preservation; local and regional history, especially of Rochester and Monroe County.

OR —SOUTHERN OREGON HISTORICAL SOCIETY, Jacksonville Museum Library, 206 N Fifth St, PO Box 480, Jacksonville, 97530. Richard H Engeman, Librn
Holdings: Vols (200) Cat Mss Maps Pix Slides 16mm Films
Budget: ($5200)

VA —BELLE GROVE, INC, Library, PO Box 137, Middletown, 22645. Wynn Lee, Exec Dir
Holdings: Vols (500) Mss
Notes: Belle Grove is a historic property of the National Trust. It maintains no library but has a small collection of manuscript and secondary source materials related to the construction of the house and the family who built it.

VA —MOUNT VERNON LADIES' ASSOCIATION OF THE UNION, Research & Reference Library, Mount Vernon, 22121. Ellen McCallister Clark, Librn; John Rhodehamel, Dir of Education
Holdings: Vols (12,000) Cat Mss Maps Pix Slides
Notes: The Washington family and Mount Vernon. The history of the Mount Vernon Ladies' Association and historic preservation.

BC —UNIVERSITY OF VICTORIA, Maltwood Art Museum & Gallery, Finnerty Rd, Victoria, V8W 2Y2, Can. Martin Segger, Dir/Cur
Holdings: Vols 700
Notes: The Museum maintains a special archival collection of architectural plans and drawings, mainly of regional historic interest. Its library and archives are now housed and administered by the McPherson Library, University of Victoria.

HISTORIC HOUSES, SITES, ETC., PRESERVATION OF see Preservation of Historic Houses, Sites, Etc.

HISTORIC SITES

NC —GREENSBORO PUBLIC LIBRARY, Oral History Program Library, Drawer X-4, Greensboro, 27402. Eugene Edwin Pfaff, Jr, Librn
Holdings: Videotapes Audiotapes
Notes: Oral history on the cultural, social, and economic development of Greensboro and Guilford County; the program is expanding to incl prominent North Carolinians throughout the State. Collection

HISTORIC SITES (cont.)

consists of 42 videotapes and 93 audiotapes which are uncataloged.

VA —US NATIONAL PARK SERVICE, Harpers Ferry Center, Library, Harpers Ferry, 25425. David Nathanson, Chief Librn
Holdings: Vols (8000) Cat Mss Maps Pix Slides Phonorecords Audiotapes 16mm Films Microforms
Budget: ($105,000)

HISTORICAL CRITICISM see Historiography

HISTORICAL FICTION

PA —UNIVERSITY OF PITTSBURGH, Hillman Library, Special Collections Dept, Hervey Allen Collection, Pittsburgh, 15260. Charles E Aston, Jr, Coordr
Holdings: Vols (2747) Cat Mss Memorabilia Pix
Notes: Substantially all of the author's mss, from first draft to published first edition, of his major works. Incl author's entire personal library. Mss incl correspondence form contemporary writers and poets. Occasional additions to this collection, of lacunae.

HISTORICAL GEOGRAPHY see Geography, Historical

HISTORICAL MARKERS

†WA —WASHINGTON STATE UNIVERSITY, Library, Manuscripts, Archives & Special Collections, Pullman, 99164. John F Guido, Head
Holdings: Cat Mss Maps Pix
Notes: The Carl Parcher Russell papers, a vast resource (24,916 items; 45 linear feet) on American Indian and Western pioneer activities and artifacts. Much on the fur trade; pioneer life; mountain men and trapping; wildlife; primitive life in detail. Also the National Park Service, parks, monuments, etc. Described in *Carl Parcher Russell: An Indexed Register of His Scholarly and Professional Papers, 1920-1967, in the Washington State University* Library (Pullman, 1970), 149 pp.

HISTORICAL MONUMENTS see Monuments and Statues

HISTORICAL RECORDS—PRESERVATION see Archives

HISTORICAL SITES see Historic Sites

HISTORICAL SOCIETIES

†AL —MUSEUMS OF THE CITY OF MOBILE, Reference Library, 355 Government St, Mobile, 36602. Caldwell Delaney, Adminr
Notes: Iberville Historical Society Papers.

IA —STATE HISTORICAL SOCIETY OF IOWA LIBRARY, 402 Iowa Ave, Iowa City, 52240. Darold J Brown, Librn
Holdings: Vols 8200 Cat
Notes: Good collection of early publications of eastern states historical societies and other organizations. Continuing collection of all major historical publications.

HISTORIOGRAPHY

CT —LEE ASH, (personal collection), 66 Humiston Dr, Bethany, 06525.
Holdings: Mss Maps Pix
Notes: First editions, mss, ephemera, memorabilia.

NY —NEW YORK PUBLIC LIBRARY, Research Libraries, General Research Division, Fifth Ave & 42 St, New York, 10018. Rodney Phillips, Chief
Holdings: Vols (2,225,000) Cat Maps Pix Microforms
Budget: ($775,718)

NY —SYRACUSE UNIVERSITY LIBRARIES, Ernest S Bird Library, George Arents Research Library for Special Collections, Syracuse, 13210. Carolyn A Davis, Manuscripts Librn; Amy S Doherty, University Archivist; Mark F Weimer, Rare Book Librn
Notes: Private library of Leopold von Ranke, father of modern historical scholarship, acquired in 1886. More than 17,000 volumes, 4000 pamphlets, and 430 mss, and private papers and letters. A complete catalogue of the ms collection published in 1983. Incl more than 100 dispatches (Relazioni) from Venetian ambassadors, 1500-1800, etc. Much unpublished primary source material.

NC —DUKE UNIVERSITY, William R Perkins Library, Durham, 27706. Elvin E Strowd, University Librn
Notes: The J Walter Lambeth collection consists of writings of statesmen and historians of countries in Asia, Africa, Europe and South America; its purpose is to increase our knowledge of world problems and to promote international understanding. Additions are ongoing.

NC —DUKE UNIVERSITY, William R Perkins Library, Jay B Hubbell Center for American Literary Historiography, Durham, 27706. Erma Whittington, Librn
Holdings: Mss Pix
Notes: 77,312 items, incl mss, pictures, clippings, and correspondence. "The objective of the Center is to gather the papers and materials of significant scholars and critics in American literary history." The Center is a part of the Perkins Library Manuscript Department.

OH —CLEVELAND PUBLIC LIBRARY, History and Geography Department, 325 Superior Ave, Cleveland, 44114. JoAnn Petrello, Head
Holdings: Cat Microforms
Notes: Research collections plus circulating books, incl all basic sources as, *Monumenta Germaniae; British State Papers and Rolls Series; Archivio Storico Italiano; Coleccion de Documentos Ineditos para la Historia de Espana; Muratori (Rerum Italicarum* Scriptores), etc. Valuable contemporary political pamphlets on World War I and World War II.

†PA —CARNEGIE-MELLON UNIVERSITY, Pittsburgh, 15213.
Notes: Studies of the use of psychology.

†WY —UNIVERSITY OF WYOMING, William Robertson Coe Library, Archives of Contemporary History, 13th & Ivinson, Laramie, 82071.
Notes: The papers of Victor Gondos. Incl journals and books, several hundred folders on military and archival history, his diaries from 1920-1974, and more than 1500 letters on historical research and architecture.

HISTORY

CA —ABC-CLIO, Inge Boehm Library, 2040 Alameda Padre Serra, PO Box 4397, Santa Barbara, 93103. Hope Smith, Librn
Holdings: Vols (2000) Uncat
Budget: $10,000
Notes: Current serials (2000) and reference works on histroy: world history, history, 1450-present; US and Canadian history, prehistory-present; and history-related social science and humanities. Library serves as support unit in the publication of *Historical* Abstracts and *America: History and Life.*

HI —BERNICE P BISHOP MUSEUM, Library, PO Box 19000-A, Honolulu, 96819. Cynthia Timberlake, Librn
Holdings: Vols (90,000) Cat Mss Maps Pix Slides Microforms
Budget: ($30,000)
Notes: Only American library devoted exclusively to the Pacific region. Collection reflects historical and contemporary research emphases of Bishop Museum; ie the natural and cultural history of the Pacific. Areas of concentration incl archaeology, ethnology, linguistics, voyages and explorations, history, vertebrate and invertebrate zoology, botany and museology. Strong special collections incl photographs, mss and archives, maps and art. Publications: Quarterly "Additions to the Catalog," *Dictionary Catalog of the* Library (9 vols and 2 suppl; Boston: G K Hall, 1964-69).

†MI —WESTERN MICHIGAN UNIVERSITY, Dwight B Waldo Library, Kalamazoo, 49008. Carl H Sachtleben, Dir
Notes: Regional history.

MN —MINNEAPOLIS PUBLIC LIBRARY & INFORMATION CENTER, History & Travel Dept, 300 Nicollet Mall, Minneapolis, 55401. Robert K Bruce, Head
Holdings: Vols (186,500) Cat Maps Phonorecords Audiotapes Microforms

MO —SAINT LOUIS UNIVERSITY, Pius XII Memorial Library, 3655 W Pine Blvd, Saint Louis, 63108. William Cole, Dir
Holdings: Slides Microforms
Notes: Collection covers all areas of learning and European history from Classical Antiquity to early modern period. Researchers using collection receive assistance in paleography, bibliography and reference search. Approx 10,000 1000-foot reels of microfilm (not counting master negatives) reproducing Vatican Library's Latin, Greek, Hebrew, Arabic and Ethiopic mss. Some 8000 100-foot reels of microfilm (again not counting master negative) reproducing rare and out of print books relating to subject areas in the mss. Over 50, 000 color slides of medieval and Renaissance mss illuminations. A reference collection of modern materials relating to ms research.

NY —MUSEUM OF THE AMERICAN INDIAN, Library, 9 Westchester Square, Bronx, 10401. Mary B Davis, Librn
Holdings: Vols Cat
Notes: Incl information in Indians of North, Central, and South America; archaeology of North, Central, and South America; American Indian ethnology; anthropology, history.

NY —CORNELL UNIVERSITY LIBRARIES, Collection of Regional History, Dept of Manuscripts and Univ Archives, Ithaca, 14853.
Notes: Files of the Department of History of Cornell University.

NY —NEW YORK PUBLIC LIBRARY, Research Libraries, General Research Division, Fifth Ave & 42 St, New York, 10018. Rodney Phillips, Chief
Holdings: Vols (2,225,000) Cat Maps Pix Microforms
Budget: ($775,718)

NY —SYRACUSE UNIVERSITY LIBRARIES, Ernest S Bird Library, George Arents Research Library for Special Collections, Syracuse, 13210. Carolyn A Davis, Manuscripts Librn; Amy S Doherty, University Archivist; Mark F Weimer, Rare Book Librn
Notes: Private library of Leopold von Ranke, father of modern historical scholarship, acquired in 1886. More than 17,000 volumes, 4000 pamphlets, and 430 mss, and private papers and letters. A complete catalogue of the ms collection published in 1983. Incl more than 100 dispatches (Relazioni) from Venetian ambassadors, 1500-1800, etc. Much unpublished primary source material.

NC —NEW BERN-CRAVEN COUNTY PUBLIC LIBRARY, 400 Johnson St, New Bern, 28560. Elinor D Hawkins, Dir
Holdings: Vols (3926) Cat Pix

NC —WAKE FOREST UNIVERSITY, Z Smith Reynolds Library, Artom Collection,

HISTORY (cont.)

Box 7777, Reynolds Station, Winston-Salem, 27109. Elen Knott, Archivist
Holdings: Cat Pix
Notes: World history, from 1949. Incl newspaper clippings, periodical tearsheets, press releases, research studies, documents, and pamphlets, covering domestic and foreign politics, government, economics, health, housing, civil rights, education, conservation, business, finance, the arts and humanities. Biographical file of over 1000 names. The collection was the news morgue of *The Reporter,* 1949-1968. Separate book catalog.

OH —CLEVELAND PUBLIC LIBRARY, History and Geography Department, 325 Superior Ave, Cleveland, 44114. JoAnn Petrello, Head
Holdings: Cat Microforms
Notes: Research collections plus circulating books, incl all basic sources as, *Monumenta* Germaniae; *British State Papers and Rolls* Series; *Archivio Storico Italiano; Coleccion de Documentos Ineditos para la Historia de* Espana; *Muratori* (*Rerum Italicarum* Scriptores), etc. Valuable contemporary political pamphlets on World War I and World War II.

TX —TRINITY UNIVERSITY, Elizabeth Coates Maddux Library, 715 Stadium Dr, San Antonio, 78284. Richard Hume Werking, Library Dir; Craig Likness, Head Bibliographer
Notes: General reference.

WA —SEATTLE PUBLIC LIBRARY, 1000 Fourth Ave, Seattle, 98104. Ronald A Dubberly, City Librn
Holdings: Cat

WI —MILWAUKEE PUBLIC MUSEUM, Reference Library, 800 W Wells St, Milwaukee, 53233. Judith Campbell Turner, Museum Librn
Holdings: Vols (90,000) Cat Maps Microforms

PQ —CONCORDIA UNIVERSITY LIBRARIES, 1455 de Maisonneuve Blvd W, Montreal, H3G 1M8, Can. Martin Cohen, Special Collections Librn
Holdings: Vols 60 // Cat Mss
Notes: The Maximilien Bibaud Collection contains the author's memoirs and correspondence as well as his writing on diverse subjects such as religion, theology, Canadian, European and ancient history, and the French language. 51 vols of ms materials.

PQ —TROIS-RIVIERES COLLEGE LIBRARY, CEGEP de Trois-Rivieres-Bibliotheque, 3500 de Courval, Trois-Rivieres, G9A 5E6, Can. Denis Simard, Librn
Holdings: Vols (95,000) Cat Maps Pix Slides Phonorecords Audiotapes Videotapes 16mm Films Filmstrips Microforms

HISTORY—CRITICISM see Historiography

HISTORY—EARLY WORKS TO 1800

PA —ALLEGHENY COLLEGE, Lawrence Lee Pelletier Library, Meadville, 16335. Margaret L Moser, Librn
Holdings: Vols (3000) Cat
Notes: James Winthrop's original collection. History, science, language among principal subject fields. Part of original gift to this library, 1819-23. Listed in Timothy Alden, *Catalogus Bibliothecae Collegii* Alleghaniensis 1823. Downs 180.

HISTORY—HISTORIOGRAPHY see Historiography

HISTORY—16TH CENTURY

MO —CENTER FOR REFORMATION RESEARCH, 6477 San Bonita Ave, Saint Louis, 63105. William S Meltby, Dir
Holdings: Cat Mss Maps Pix Microforms
Notes: Bibliography series, 23 vol.

HISTORY—19TH CENTURY

CT —YALE UNIVERSITY, Beinecke Rare Book & Manuscript Library, Osborn Collection, New Haven, 06520. Stephen R Parks, Cur
Holdings: Mss

HISTORY, ANCIENT

IL —UNIVERSITY OF ILLINOIS, URBANA/CHAMPAIGN, Library, Classics Library, 419A Main Library, Urbana, 61801. Suzanne N Griffiths, Librn
Holdings: Vols (10,000) Cat
Notes: Ancient history section of Classics Library is strong in numismatics and in inscription materials; also incl ancient archaeology.

HISTORY, CHURCH see Church History

HISTORY, ECCLESIASTICAL see Church History

HISTORY, ECONOMIC see Economic History

HISTORY, MEDIEVAL see Middle Ages—History

HISTORY, MILITARY see Military History

HISTORY, NATURAL see Natural History

HISTORY, NAVAL see Naval History

HISTORY, PSYCHOLOGY IN see Psychology in History

HISTORY, WORLD see World History

HISTRIONICS see Theatre; Theatre—History

HITCHCOCK, ROMYN, 1851-1923

NY —CORNELL UNIVERSITY LIBRARIES, Collection of Regional History, Dept of Manuscripts and Univ Archives, Ithaca, 14853.
Holdings: Maps
Notes: Chemist, lecturer on the Orient. Incl papers, 1882-1900; lecture notes, correspondence, monographs, newspaper clippings and maps; concerned mainly with Chinese-American problems, arts and customs.

HITCHENS, DOLORES, 1907-1973

MA —BOSTON UNIVERSITY, Mugar Memorial Library, Special Collections Dept, 771 Commonwealth Ave, Boston, 02215. Howard B Gotlieb, Dir
Holdings: Cat Mss

HITCHMAN, JANET

MA —BOSTON UNIVERSITY, Mugar Memorial Library, Special Collections Dept, 771 Commonwealth Ave, Boston, 02215. Howard B Gotlieb, Dir
Holdings: Cat Mss Correspondence

HITLER, ADOLF, 1889-1945

CA —HOOVER INSTITUTION ON WAR, REVOLUTION & PEACE, Stanford University, Stanford, 94305. Milorad M Drachkovitch, Archivist
Holdings: Mss Pix
Notes: Two collections: (1) Ms diaries, 1914-1924, microfilms, photographs and photostats of documents from the *Personlicher Stab Reichsfuhrer SS,* Schriftgutverwaltung dealing with the file and career of Himmler as Reichsfuhrer SS and Chef der Deutschen Polizei, 1934-1945. 6 notebooks (plus 25 loose pages), 5 microfilm reels, 2 photo albums, 14 ms boxes. Incl 24 tapes of Himmler speeches, 1940-44. (2) Papers of Princess Stephanie zu Hohenlohe, confidant and intermediary of Lord Rothermere, owner of the *Daily Mail,* London, and Adolf Hitler, incl correspondence, memoranda, telegrams, clippings, and printed matter, 1914-1972, relating in the 1930s, political developments in Hungary, and Princess Hohenlohe's personal life in Europe and the US, as well as her associations with various publishing houses. 4 ms boxes.

IL —LAKE FOREST COLLEGE, Donnelley Library, Lake Forest, 60045. Arthur H Miller Jr, College Librn
Holdings: Vols (700) Microforms
Notes: Pese Collection of books, pamphlets, and journals on Hitler, Hitler's foreign policy, and Nazi era Germany.

MA —BRANDEIS UNIVERSITY, Goldfarb Library, 415 South St, Waltham, 02154. Bessie Hahn, Dir
Notes: Nazi Documents Collection. Consists of 3 linear ft of documents and letters of major Nazi officials prior to and during World War II. A finding list to the documents is in Special Collections.

HITLER LIBRARY

DC —LIBRARY OF CONGRESS, Rare Book & Special Collections Div, Washington, 20540. William Matheson, Chief
Notes: Part of the Third Reich Collection. The so-called Hitler Library was shipped to the Library of Congress in 1946. Incl 1019 vols, many of which bear dedications, notes of transmittal, or Hitler's Eagle bookplate.

HITOPADESA

OH —CLEVELAND PUBLIC LIBRARY, Fine Arts and Special Collections Department, 325 Superior Ave, Cleveland, 44114. Alice N Loranth, Head
Holdings: Vols (700) Cat Mss
Notes: Part of the Fables Collection, which is strong in Medieval European and Oriental works. Numerous rare and early editions of Reynard the Fox (200 vols), Panchatantra, Bidpai, Hitopadesa, etc, are incl. Aesop and the modern fabulists are incl only by representative editions.
See also entries under Fables; Oriental Languages and Literatures.

HITTITE LANGUAGE AND LITERATURE

NY —NEW YORK PUBLIC LIBRARY, Oriental Div, Fifth Ave & 42 St, New York, 10018. E Christian Filstrup, Chief
Holdings: Cat Mss Microforms
Budget: ($56,455)
Notes: Published catalog of holdings.

HLAVATY, VACLAV, 1894-1969

IN —INDIANA UNIVERSITY, Lilly Library, Seventh St, Bloomington, 47405. William R Cagle, Librn
Notes: Correspondence and manuscripts, 1942-1969, of mathematician Vaclav Hlavaty. 8000 items.

HOAR, GEORGE FRISBEE

MA —CONCORD FREE PUBLIC LIBRARY, 129 Main St, Concord, 01742. Rose Marie Mitten, Dir
Holdings: Cat Mss Pix
Notes: Well-known lawyer in Concord and Washington (Senator 1877-1904).

HOAXES

NY —MORRIS N & CHESLEY V YOUNG LIBRARY OF MNEMONICS, 270 Riverside Dr, New York, 10025. Morris N Young, Cur
Holdings: Cat Mss Maps Pix Phonorecords Audiotapes 16mm Films Microform
Notes: Collection of 5000 books, pamphlets, pictures, memorabilia, etc incl medieval art of memory; psychology of memory, forgetting and reading; medical aspects of memory, amnesia, dyslexia; biomedical aspects of learning and memory; information storage, retrieval and cybernetics; memory prodigies, lightning calculators, calendars;

HOAXES (cont.)

remembrance cups and memory mementos. All languages. Memorabilia incl engravings, posters, programs, advertisements, birthday cards, teaching cards, ASLs, and Mark Twain's Memory Builder game and other games. Items range from 1410 to 1980s.

HOBBES, THOMAS

ON —UNIVERSITY OF TORONTO, Thomas Fisher Rare Book Library, 120 Saint George St, Toronto, M5S 1A5, Can. Richard G Landon, Head
Holdings: Vols 500 Cat Mss
Notes: First and early editions of works by Thomas Hobbes and of contemporary commentaries on his work. An unpublished holograph poem, *De Motu Solis*.

HOBBIES

OH —PUBLIC LIBRARY OF CINCINNATI & HAMILTON COUNTY, Art & Music Dept, 800 Vine St, Cincinnati, 45202. R Jayne Craven, Head
Holdings: Vols (122,185) Cat Pix
Budget: ($56,100)
Notes: Special collections: Eda Kuhn Loeb, "Artist and the Book, 1875-Date" (now shelved in Rare Book Room); music librettos (2345); exhibition catalogs (5474); large prints and posters (5051); Cincinnati artists vertical files; picture collection (673,906 clippings).

OH —GRANDVIEW HEIGHTS PUBLIC LIBRARY, 1685 W First Ave, Columbus, 43212. Kathryn M Hannon, Librn
Holdings: Vols (364) Cat

HOBBS, WILLIAM H.

MI —UNIVERSITY OF MICHIGAN, Library, Dept of Rare Books & Special Collections, Ann Arbor, 48109. Robert J Starring, Head
Holdings: Cat Mss Maps Pix
Notes: Includes over 100 books, mostly autographed presentation copies from polar explorers to donor William H Hobbs, and 62 scrapbooks, notebooks, albums, and made-up volumes of pamphlets, documents and correspondence, 11 relating to Admiral Peary. Also there are such primary records from Professor Hobbs' own expeditions as his journals, radio logs, purchase requisitions, pilot balloon ascension reports and graphs, and anemoscope records. In addition there are an estimated 3500 items of correspondence with explorers and other notables, 800 photographs, and maps.

HOBBY, OVETA CULP

DC —LIBRARY OF CONGRESS, Manuscript Division, Washington, 20540. John C Broderick, Chief
Notes: Papers of Oveta Culp Hobby, incl correspondence, contracts, memos, programs, play typescripts, notes and photographs; much on the WACS.

HOBSBAUM, PHILIP

BC —UNIVERSITY OF VICTORIA, McPherson Library, Victoria, V8W 3H5, Can.
Notes: Poet, editor. Incl mss and typescript of The Group: Taner Baybars, Martin bell, Alan Brownjohn, Julian Cooper, Anne Dyke, Christopher Hampton, Philip Hobsbaum, Arthur Jacobs, Rosemary Joseph, Owen Leeming, Christopher Levenson, Edward Lucie-Smith, George MacBeth, Robin McLaren, Adrian Mitchell, M Pickering, Peter Porter, George Raphael, Peter Redgrove; mss of *A Theory of* Communication with holograph corrections by William Empson; mss of poems.

HOBSON-JOBSON

MA —HARVARD UNIVERSITY LIBRARY, Cambridge, 02138.
Holdings: Cat

HOCKEY

MN —US HOCKEY HALL OF FAME, Library, Hat Trick Ave, Eveleth, 55734. Roger A Godin, Librn
Holdings: Vols 20 Uncat Pix Phonorecords Audiotapes Videotapes 16mm Films

ON —INTERNATIONAL HOCKEY HALL OF FAME AND MUSEUM, PO Box 82, York and Alfred Sts, Kingston, K7L 4V6, Can. Doug Nichols, Pres
Notes: Hockey books from 1886; scrapbooks, programs, guides, and magazines.

ON —HOCKEY HALL OF FAME AND MUSEUM LIBRARY, Exhibition Place, Toronto, M6K 3C3, Can. M H Reid, Dir and Cur
Holdings: Uncat Pix Slides Audiotapes Videotapes 16mm Films
Notes: Incl extensive library of scrapbooks, programs and publications. Research by personal visit only.

†ON —METROPOLITAN TORONTO LIBRARY, 789 Yonge St, Toronto, M4W 2G8, Can.
Notes: Good subject strengths.

HODES, AUBREY

MA —BOSTON UNIVERSITY, Mugar Memorial Library, Special Collections Dept, 771 Commonwealth Ave, Boston, 02215. Howard B Gotlieb, Dir
Holdings: Cat Mss
Notes: Mss, correspondence, etc collected in depth; incl publications by or about.

HODGINS, ERIC

MA —BOSTON UNIVERSITY, Mugar Memorial Library, Special Collections Dept, 771 Commonwealth Ave, Boston, 02215. Howard B Gotlieb, Dir
Holdings: Cat Mss

HODGSON, RALPH

PA —BRYN MAWR COLLEGE, Canaday Library, Bryn Mawr, 19010. James Tanis, Dir
Notes: Manuscript and printed material in the Adelman Collection.

HOE, RICHARD, AND COMPANY

DC —LIBRARY OF CONGRESS, Manuscript Division, Washington, 20540. John C Broderick, Chief
Notes: Papers of Richard Hoe and Company, printers.

NY —COLUMBIA UNIVERSITY LIBRARIES, Rare Book & Manuscript Library, 801 Butler Library, 535 W 114 St, New York, 10027. Kenneth A Lohf, Librn
Holdings: Mss
Notes: 10,500 pieces of archival material of the printing firm of R Hoe & Co. Restricted use.

HOEY, CLYDE R.

NC —DUKE UNIVERSITY, William R Perkins Library, Manuscript Dept, Durham, 27706. Ellen Gartrell, Cur of Mss
Holdings: Cat Mss
Notes: Papers, etc.

HOFFMAN, JUDGE JULIUS H.

IL —CHICAGO HISTORICAL SOCIETY, Library, Clark St at North Ave, Chicago, 60614. Archie Motley, Manuscript Librn
Notes: Correspondence and papers of Julius H Hoffman, judge at Chicago Seven Conspiracy Trial.

HOFMANNSTHAL, HUGO VON

MA —HARVARD UNIVERSITY LIBRARY, Houghton Library, Cambridge, 02138. F Thomas Noonan, Cur, Reading Room; Lawrence Dowler, Associate Librn
Holdings: Cat
Notes: *Catalogue of Collection,* James E Walsh (Heidelberg: Luther Stiehm Verlag, 1974). See also *Harvard Library Bulletin,* VIII (1954), pp 54-64.

HOG CHOLERA see Swine Fever

HOGAN, FRANK S.

†NY —COLUMBIA UNIVERSITY LIBRARIES, Butler Library, Rare Book and Manuscript Library, 535 W 114 St, New York, 10027.
Notes: Papers of New York City's District Attorney, 1942-74, Frank S Hogan.

HOGARTH, WILLIAM

MD —UNIVERSITY OF MARYLAND, BALTIMORE COUNTY, Albin O Kuhn Library and Gallery, 5401 Wilkens Ave, Baltimore, 21228. Ann Copeland, Special Collections Librn
Holdings: Vols (800) / / Cat Pix
Notes: The Edgar and Kathleen Merkle Collection of 19th-century English graphic satire centers around the work of George E Cruikshank. Other artists represented incl Rowlandson, Gillray, Hogarth, and "Phiz." Rare items incl Cruikshank's lavish hand-colored film *Scraps and Sketches* (1828).

MD —HOOD COLLEGE, Joseph Henry Apple Library, Rosemont Ave, Frederick, 21701.
Notes: The Samuel J Cole Hogarth Print Collection (116 prints).

MA —HARVARD UNIVERSITY LIBRARY, Houghton Library, Cambridge, 02138. F Thomas Noonan, Cur, Reading Room; Lawrence Dowler, Associate Librn
Holdings: Cat
Notes: Catalog in Harvard University Library, *Bibliographical Contributions,* 37 (1890).

HOGG, JAMES STEPHEN

CT —YALE UNIVERSITY, Beinecke Rare Book & Manuscript Library, Osborn Collection, New Haven, 06520. Stephen R Parks, Cur
Holdings: Mss

TX —UNIVERSITY OF TEXAS LIBRARIES, General Libraries, Barker Texas History Center, PO Box P, Austin, 78712. Don Carleton, Dir

HOGS see Swine

HOHENBERGER, FRANK M.

IN —INDIANA UNIVERSITY, Lilly Library, Seventh St, Bloomington, 47405. William R Cagle, Librn
Notes: Photographs, etc, of actors and actresses are located in ms collections: (1) Johnson, William Spencer, 1813-1897, printer. Correspondence and photographs from actors and actresses, 1846-1894. 129 items; (2) Stock, Keith Lievesley, 1911-, professor. Autographs, etc of people associated with 19th-early 20th century theatre in England. 279 items; and (3) Woodward, Sidney C, journalist. Correspondence, autographs, and pictures, 1769-1961, of actors, actresses, and other theatre people, mostly American and British. 1235 items. Also, in Printed Books Division: small pictures (largely engravings excerpted from books) of Shakespearean actors and actresses, 18th into 20th century. The Hohenberger collection includes the negatives and original prints of Brown County, Indiana photographer Frank M Hohenberger, 1876-1963.

HOHENHEIM, THEOPHRASTUS BOMBASTUS VON see Paracelsus

HOHENLOHE, PRINCESS STEPHANIE ZU

CA —HOOVER INSTITUTION ON WAR, REVOLUTION & PEACE, Stanford University, Stanford, 94305. Milorad M Drachkovitch, Archivist
Notes: Papers of Princess Stephanie zu

HOHENLOHE, PRINCESS STEPHANIE ZU (cont.)

Hohenlohe, confidant and intermediary of Lord Rothermere, owner of the *Daily Mail*, London, and Adolf Hitler, incl correspondence, memoranda, telegrams, clippings, and printed matter, 1914-1972, relating to improvement of German-English relations in the 1930s, political developments in Hungary, and Princess Hohenlohe's personal life in Europe and the US, as well as her associations with various publishing houses. 4 ms boxes.

HOHOKAM CULTURE

AZ —COLORADO RIVER INDIAN TRIBES MUSEUM/LIBRARY, Rte One, Box 23-B, Parker, 85344. Priscilla Johnson, Librn
Holdings: Cat Mss Maps Pix Slides Audiotapes Microforms
Notes: Library deals with the four tribes of the Colorado River Indian Reservation: Mohave, Chemehuevi, Navajo, and Hopi. Emphasis is also given to the prehistoric culture of this area; Patayan and Hohokam. Library collections include original manuscripts and other documents, photographs, oral history tape recordings, cultural items and artifacts. Copies of many documents relating to the reservation from various other collections are copied in our collection. Of particular interest is the museum basket collection which incl about 1000 Chemehuevi baskets. Other artifacts give special emphasis to the Mojave culture.

HOIT, PRICE AND BARNES

MO —UNIVERSITY OF MISSOURI-KANSAS CITY, General Library, State Historical Society of Missouri Manuscripts, 5100 Rockhill Road, Kansas City, 64110. Kenneth J LaBudde, Dir; Gordon Hendrickson, Assoc Dir
Holdings: Mss
Notes: Joint Collection Western Historical Manuscript Collection and the State Historical of Missouri Manuscripts, University of Missouri-Kansas City General Library, 5100 Rockhill Road, Kansas City, MO 64110. Ca 2,500 linear feet of manuscripts, blueprints and oral history tapes.
Notes: The manuscript collection includes material which documents the history, growth and development of Missouri, especially the Greater Kansas City area. The personal papers of business, civic, cultural, political and community leaders; local historians and other individuals of families from the area are within the collection as are the records of associations, organizations and institutions which reflect the history of the area. Prominent among the collections are the papers of Charles B. Wheeler, Jr., Charles N. Kimball, Arthur Mag, Oscar D. Nelson, Lou B. Holland, J. C. Nichols, Perry Cookingham, Blevins Davis and Daniel Macmorris and the records of the Kansas City Board of Trade. Architectural designs and plans for approximately 3,500 Kansas City buildings and the records of the Hoit, Price and Barnes architectural firm and the papers of Asa Beebe Cross, early Kansas City architect as well as a number of oral histories with Kansas City Jazz figures are in the collection.

HOKAIDO

HI —UNIVERSITY OF HAWAII, Library, 2550 The Mall, Honolulu, 96822. Joyce Wright, Head, Asia Collection; Masato Matsu, Head, East Asia Vernacular Collection
Holdings: Vols 64,481 Cat Microforms
Notes: The Asia Collection includes materials from and relating to Japan in all languages. In addition to the cataloged Japanese language volumes (above), there are estimated 15,000 not yet processed. No figures are available for western language volumes about Japan, which are supplemented by retrospective materials in the main library collection. Scope: social sciences and humanities. Subject strengths: Japanese history, especially Tokugawa period, Buddhism, Ryukyus and Satsuma (Sakamaki Collection), Hokkaido. *Catalog of the Glenn Shaw Collection at the East West Center Library*, by H Arai & M Gibu, Honolulu, 1967 (East West Center Library Occasional Paper No 8); *Research Resources on Hokkaido, Sakhalen and the Kuriles at the East West Center Library*, by M Matsui and K Shimanaka, Honolulu, 1967 (East West Center Library Occasional Paper No 9);*Research Resources at the University of* Hawaii, by Shunzo Sakamaki, Honolulu, 1965 (Ryukyuan Research Center. Research Series No 1).

HOLABIRD AND ROOT

IL —CHICAGO HISTORICAL SOCIETY, Library, Clark St at North Ave, Chicago, 60614. Archie Motley, Manuscript Librn
Notes: Chicago Architectural Archive contains the papers of Chicago architects Barry Byrne and Earl H Reed, the records of the Illinois Society of Architects, and the voluminous files of two leading Chicago architectural firms, Holabird & Root and Harry M Weese and Associates. Access to these collections is by arrangement with Frank Jewell, The Society's Curator of Architectural Collections.

HOLBEIN, HANS

DC —FOLGER SHAKESPEARE LIBRARY, 201 E Capitol St, Washington, 20003. Philip A Knachel, Acting Dir
Notes: A major collection.
See also entry under Reformation.

NY —METROPOLITAN MUSEUM OF ART, Dept of Prints & Photographs, 82 St & Fifth Ave, New York, 10028. Colta Ives, Cur

HOLBORN, HAJO

CT —YALE UNIVERSITY, Box 1603A, Yale Station, New Haven, 06520.
Holdings: Cat Mss
Notes: A collection of Hajo Holborn's personal papers, consisting of correspondence, 1924-1933; mss of articles speechs, etc, 1904-1943 and printed materials on the Weimar Republic, 1919-1938.

HOLDEN, PERRY G.

MI —MICHIGAN STATE UNIVERSITY, Libraries, Special Collections Div, East Lansing, 48824. Jannette Fiore, Librn
Holdings: / / Mss Pix
Notes: Publications, mss, personal correspondence and scrapbooks of Perry G Holden, relating to the development of hybrid corn.

HOLIDAY IN DIXIE

LA —LOUISIANA STATE UNIVERSITY, SHREVEPORT, Library-Archives, 8515 Youree Dr, Shreveport, 71129. Patricia L Meador, Archivist & Asst Librn
Notes: Theatre and music is documented in the John Wray and Margaret Mary Young Theatre Collection, (5 linear ft), (1929-1981), the Joe Gifford Papers (1946-1960) (3 linear ft), the Shreveport Little Theatre Records (6 linear ft), the Nathaniel S Allen Papers (1860-1930), the records of the Shreveport Symphony (1948-1978) and oral history interviews on the topics. The archives collection also incl 60 linear ft of records (1949-1981) of Holiday-In-Dixie, Shreveport-Bossier's spring-time festival.

HOLIDAYS

LA —NEW ORLEANS PUBLIC LIBRARY, Louisiana Div & City Archives Dept, Louisiana History Collection, 219 Loyola Ave, New Orleans, 70140. Collin B Hamer Jr, Head
Holdings: Cat Mss Pix
Notes: The Carnival Collection incl 11,000 programs, costume designs and memorabilia relative to annual Mardi Gras festivities, 1852-date. Use is restricted to on-site research by adults.

MI —APPLE TREE PRESS, Library, Box 1012, Flint, 48501. W D Chase, Editor/ Librn
Holdings: Vols (1200) Uncat Mss Maps Pix Microforms

NY —US COMMITTEE FOR UNICEF, Information Center on Children's Cultures, 331 E 38 St, New York, 10016. Melinda Greenblatt, Chief Librn
Holdings: Vols (17,500) Cat Pix Slides Films Filmstrips
Notes: Social and cultural aspects of lives of children from developing countries. Especially strong in the area of school textbooks from Near Eastern Asian, African, Latin American, Caribbean, and Pacific Area countries; holidays and celebrations related to children all over the world; children's books in English which describe child life in other countries. Especially strong collection of folklore, and folklore of children, from all regions mentioned above.

HOLIDAYS (VACATIONS) see Vacations

HOLINESS

CA —POINT LOMA NAZARENE COLLEGE, Ryan Library, 3900 Lomaland Dr, San Diego, 92106. Esther Schandorff, Librn
Holdings: Vols 1600 Cat Mss Pix
Notes: Historical material from the period of the Wesleyan revival to the present day.

IN —FREE METHODIST CHURCH OF NORTH AMERICA, Marston Memorial Historical Center Library, 901 College Ave, Winona Lake, 46590. Evelyn L Mottweiler, Librn
Holdings: Vols (6000) Cat Mss
Budget: ($16,000)
Notes: Denominational headquarters of the Free Methodist Church in North America. Works on the Wesleyan doctrine of holiness and the Holy Spirit. Includes historical holiness classics as well as contemporary authors. Methodist and Free Methodist holdings of the Library are included in the Methodist Union Catalog: *Pre-1976* Imprints, by Kenneth E Rowe.
See also entry under Wesley, John.

KY —ASBURY THEOLOGICAL SEMINARY, B L Fisher Library, Wilmore, 40390. D William Faupel, Dir of Library Services
Holdings: Vols 1000 Cat
Budget: ($72,000)
Notes: Special emphasis is on holiness from the Arminian-Wesleyan point of view, but other view points are also well represented.

HOLINESS AND PENTECOSTAL CHURCHES

CA —AZUSA PACIFIC COLLEGE, Marshburn Memorial Library, Citrus & Alosta, Azusa, 91702. Edward Peterman, Librn
Holdings: Vols 583 Cat
Notes: Historical collection of Holiness and Pentecostal movement with writings of early leaders. Incl considerable history of churches in the movement, etc.

CA —POINT LOMA NAZARENE COLLEGE, Ryan Library, 3900 Lomaland

HOLINESS AND PENTECOSTAL CHURCHES (cont.)

Dr, San Diego, 92106. Esther Schandorff, Librn
Holdings: Vols 1600 Cat Mss Pix
Notes: Historical material from the period of the Wesleyan revival to the present day.

NC —DUKE UNIVERSITY, William R Perkins Library, Manuscript Dept, Durham, 27706. Ellen Gartrell, Cur of Mss
Holdings: Cat Mss
Notes: Especially US South, eg Methodist Church Papers (records of local and regional units) also many personal and professional papers of clergy, missionaries and laymen, 19th-20th centuries, eg Methodist John Lakin Brasher (holiness movement leader), Carlyle Marney (Southern Baptist minister), Methodist Bishop James Cannon, missionary Martha Foster Crawford.

TN —LEE COLLEGE, Library, Ocoee St, Cleveland, 37311. Frances Arrington, Head Librn; JoAnne Sparks, Religion Librn
Holdings: Vols 5086 Cat Slides Phonorecords Audiotapes Filmstrips
Notes: The Pentecostal Research Center houses two special collections: the Church of God (Cleveland, Tennessee) collection and the Pentecostal collection. The latter includes works about the movement and its history, works by Pentecostal authors, and specific subject areas (Holy Spirit, glossolalia, divine healing).

TX —MESSENGER CHRISTIAN COLLEGE, McDonald Library, 10950 Beaumont Highway, Houston, 77078. Judy Mitchell, Dir
Holdings: Vols 300 Cat Mss
Notes: Collection is in two divisions; regular trade books on Pentecostal Church history and pamphlets and paperback books written by ministers and evangelists in the movement. There has been no attempt to catalog or index the second collection. Messenger Christian College incl the former Southern Bible College at this location.

TX —P C NELSON MEMORIAL LIBRARY, Southwestern Assemblies of God College, 1200 Sycamore, Waxahachie, 75165. Murl M Winters, Dir
Holdings: Vols (21,877) Cat
Budget: ($11,358)
Notes: Incl William Burton McCafferty Pentecostal Periodical Collection (mostly before 1950; while several titles have moderate runs, many titles are represented by only one or two issues). Holdings: one 4-drawer filing cabinet. Index to the following Pentecostal periodicals: "Pentecostal Evangel," "Church of God Evangel," "Pentecost" (published by Donald Gree), "Christ's Ambassadors Herald," and "Missionary Challenge." Format: card catalog. Entries to date: 60,872.

HOLLAND see Netherlands—History

HOLLAND, ERNEST OTTO

†WA —WASHINGTON STATE UNIVERSITY, Library, Manuscripts, Archives & Special Collections, Pullman, 99164. John F Guido, Head
Holdings: Vols Cat Mss Maps Pix Microforms
Notes: Ms resources in the Washington State Library for the study of Pacific Northwest history incl the personal papers of Ernest Otto Holland. All ms collections are described in a catalog, a published register or an unpublished finding aid.

HOLLAND, JOHN

NJ —PASSAIC COUNTY HISTORICAL SOCIETY, Lamhurt Castle, Valley Rd, Paterson, 07503. Helen D Hamilton, Dir
Holdings: Vols (5000) Cat Mss Maps Pix
Notes: Material on the Society for the Establishment of Useful Manufacturing (founded) by Alexander Hamilton, papers relating to John Holland, who developed the submarine, the industrial magnates of the area who were active in the manufacture of locomotives, Colt revolvers, and textiles, especially silk.

HOLLAND, LOU B.

MO —UNIVERSITY OF MISSOURI-KANSAS CITY, General Library, State Historical Society of Missouri Manuscripts, 5100 Rockhill Road, Kansas City, 64110. Kenneth J LaBudde, Dir; Gordon Hendrickson, Assoc Dir
Holdings: Mss
Notes: Western Historical Manuscript Collection incl papers of Charles B Wheeler, Jr, Charles N Kimball, Arthur Mag, Oscar D Nelson, Lou B Holland, J C Nichols, Perry Cookingham, Blevins Davis, Daniel MacMorris, and the records of the Kansas City Board of Trade.

HOLLAND, VYVYAN

DC —GEORGETOWN UNIVERSITY, Library, Special Collections Div, 37 & O Sts NW, Washington, 20057. George M Barringer, Special Collections Librn; Nicholas B Sheetz, Mss Librn
Holdings: Mss Cat Pix
Notes: The papers of the Irish man-of-letters Sir Shane Leslie (1885-1971) containing letters, mss, diaries, notebooks, clippings, and photographs. Extensive correspondence by Margot Asquith, countess of Oxford and Asquith; Lady Violet Bonham-Carter; Burke Cochran; Lord Alfred Douglas; Moreton Frewen; Cardinal Gasquet; Vyvyan Holland; Lady Leonie Leslie; Sir Wilfrid Meynell; Sir Horace Plunkett; John Quinn; Frederick Rolfe (Baron Corvo); and Elizabeth Russell, among others. Also incl are research files on Sir Winston Churchill (Leslie's first cousin); Leonard Jerome; Maria Anne Fitzherbet (wife of King George IV); Ghosts and Ghost stories; and Eton College.

HOLLAR, WENCESLAUS, 1607-1677

ON —UNIVERSITY OF TORONTO, Thomas Fisher Rare Book Library, 120 Saint George St, Toronto, M5S 1A5, Can. Richard G Landon, Head
Holdings: Vols 100 // Cat Maps Pix
Notes: Fisher Collection of etchings by Wenceslaus Hollar. Collection named for donor Sidney T Fisher. Collection includes copies of most books in which Hollar's plates were published. About 3500 loose prints include various states of many etchings; some proofs; group of 19th century forgeries by Peter Thompson; original chalk and wash sketch for Hollar's etching of John the Baptist. See: Pennington, Richard, *A Descriptive Catalogue of the Etched Work of Wenceslaus Hollar, 1607-1677.* Cambridge: 1982. Based in part on Fisher holdings.

HOLLING, HOLLING CLANCY

CA —UNIVERSITY OF CALIFORNIA, LOS ANGELES, Research Library, Dept of Special Collections, 405 Hilgard Ave, Los Angeles, 90024. Edward Shreeves, Chairman, Bibliographers Group; David S Zeidberg, Head
Notes: 25 linear feet of mss, correspondence, illustrations, and memorabilia of Holling Clancey Holling and Lucille Webster Holling, authors and illustrators of modern children's books.

HOLLING, LUCILLE WEBSTER

CA —UNIVERSITY OF CALIFORNIA, LOS ANGELES, Research Library, Dept of Special Collections, 405 Hilgard Ave, Los Angeles, 90024. Edward Shreeves, Chairman, Bibliographers Group; David S Zeidberg, Head
Notes: 25 linear feet of mss, correspondence, illustrations, and memorabilia of Holling Clancey Holling and Lucille Webster Holling, authors and illustrators of modern children's books.

HOLLIS, CHRISTOPHER

DC —GEORGETOWN UNIVERSITY, Library, Special Collections Div, 37 & O Sts NW, Washington, 20057. George M Barringer, Special Collections Librn; Nicholas B Sheetz, Mss Librn
Holdings: Cat Mss
Notes: The papers of the English author, journalist, and historian Douglas Woodruff (1897-1978), containing correspondence, mss, and photographs. Incl is considerable material concerning his years at Oxford University; his editorship for many years of The "Tablet"; English Catholic society in general and English Catholic literature in particular. Also present are research files on the Tichborne Claimant, one of the most famous cases of impersonation in English legal history. There is extensive correspondence from such figures as: Hilaire Belloc; Tom Burns; Rev Martin D'Arcy, SJ; Christopher Dawson; Sir Roy Harrod; Christopher Hollis; Msgr Ronald Knox; Sir Shane Leslie; Sir Arnold Lunn; Rebecca West; and Evelyn Waugh.

HOLLOW WARE, SILVER see Silverware

HOLLYWOOD BOWL, LOS ANGELES

CA —LOS ANGELES PUBLIC LIBRARY, Frances Howard Goldwyn Hollywood Regional Library, 1623 Ivar Ave, Los Angeles, 90028. Sally Dumaux, Librn
Holdings: Vols (100,000) Cat Pix VF
Budget: ($60,000)
Notes: Over 2000 playbills, photographs, posters, and programs of Los Angeles area theatre from the 1920s to the present. Collection includes *Turnabout Theatre Monthly Bulletin,* 1942-48, souvenir programs and flyers. Also Pilgrimage Theatre and Hollywood Bowl programs, 1922 to present. Gladys Littell Collection. Hollywood Bowl Sunrise Services, 1920s-1940s. Hollywood Conservatory of Music, 1920s. Hollywood Chamber of Commerce. Including correspondence, programs, working papers, and photographs.

HOLM, HANYA

NY —NEW YORK PUBLIC LIBRARY, Performing Arts Research Center, Dance Collection, 111 Amsterdam Ave, New York, 10023. Genevieve Oswald, Cur
Notes: Extensive biographical and visual documentation. Includes photographs, clippings, programs, scrapbooks, dance notation scores, motion pictures, tape-recorded discussions, manuscripts, and letters.

HOLMAN, LIBBY

MA —BOSTON UNIVERSITY, Mugar Memorial Library, Special Collections Dept, 771 Commonwealth Ave, Boston, 02215. Howard B Gotlieb, Dir
Holdings: // Cat Mss Pix
Notes: Mss, correspondence, etc collected in depth; incl publications by or about.

HOLME, FRANK, 1868-1904

AZ —UNIVERSITY OF ARIZONA, Library, Tucson, 85721. W David Laird, Librn
Notes: Frank Holme and 2 complete collections of books from the Bandarlog Press, numerous original drawings for newspapers and other media, books from Holme's library.

CA —UNIVERSITY OF CALIFORNIA, LOS ANGELES, Research Library, Dept of Special Collections, 405 Hilgard Ave, Los Angeles, 90024. Edward Shreeves, Chairman, Bibliographers Group; David S Zeidberg, Head
Notes: 1.5 linear feet of ephemera, correspondence, and publications of the Bandar Log Press.

HOLMES, FRANCIS S.

SC —COLLEGE OF CHARLESTON LIBRARY, Special Collections Dept, Charleston, 29401.
Notes: Papers, 1842-1853, incl correspondence of Mitchell King with Henry

HOLMES, FRANCIS S. (cont.)

C King (son), F S Holmes, J L Petigru, and John Pennington.

HOLMES, JOHN CLELLON

MA —BOSTON UNIVERSITY, Mugar Memorial Library, Special Collections Dept, 771 Commonwealth Ave, Boston, 02215. Howard B Gotlieb, Dir
Holdings: Cat Mss
Notes: Mss, correspondence, etc collected in depth; incl publications by or about.

HOLMES, OLIVER WENDELL, 1809-1894

DC —LIBRARY OF CONGRESS, Rare Book & Special Collections Div, Washington, 20540. William Matheson, Chief
Notes: The division houses the cataloged portions of the libraries of several generations of a distinguished American family. Incl American literary works inscribed to Oliver Wendell Holmes and studies in law, history, and politics inscribed to Mr Justice Holmes.

DC —LIBRARY OF CONGRESS, Manuscript Division, Washington, 20540. John C Broderick, Chief
Holdings: Cat Mss Pix
Notes: Mss, papers, records, etc.

MD —JOHNS HOPKINS UNIVERSITY, Milton S Eisenhower Library, Charles & 34 Sts, Baltimore, 21218. Ann S Gwyn, Assistant Dir for Special Collections
Holdings: Vols 330 // Mss
Notes: 2 ms, 23 letters, many first editions and some unpublished pamphlets.

MA —HARVARD UNIVERSITY LIBRARY, Houghton Library, Cambridge, 02138. Rodney G Dennis, Cur of Manuscripts
Holdings: Cat Mss

VA —UNIVERSITY OF VIRGINIA, Alderman Library, Clifton Waller Barrett Collection, Charlottesville, 22901. Joan St C Crane, Cur of American Literature Collections
Notes: Papers.

HOLMES, OLIVER WENDELL, JR., 1841-1935

MA —HARVARD UNIVERSITY LIBRARY, Law School Library, Langdell Hall, Cambridge, 02138. Erika S Chadbourn, Cur of Mss
Holdings: Cat Mss
Notes: Personal and judicial papers. Typed inventory in repository. Inclusive dates, 1861-1967.

HOLMES, SHERLOCK

CA —SAN FRANCISCO ACADEMY OF COMIC ART, Library, 2850 Ulloa, San Francisco, 94116.
Notes: Incl largest collection of pulp magazines in US. Paper copies of all major American newspapers, emphasis on Hearst papers. Extensive collection of Sherlockiana and a member of the National Sherlockiana Society. Also extensive collection of early motion picture tapes, books, magazines and posters. 19th and early 20th century children's books also in the holdings. Collection incl 1,000,000 comic strips, 22, 000 comic books, 12,500 hard cover mystery books, 8000 hard cover science fiction books and copies of all science fiction pulp magazines.

†NC —UNIVERSITY OF NORTH CAROLINA, CHAPEL HILL, Wilson Library, Chapel Hill, 27514.
Notes: Crime and detective fiction, 10,000 vols. Mary Shore Cameron Collection of Sherlock Holmes, 800 vols.

HOLMES, THOMAS J.

OH —OHIO STATE UNIVERSITY, William Oxley Thompson Memorial Library, 1858 Neil Ave Mall, Columbus, 43210. Robert A Tibbetts, Cur of Special Collections
Holdings: Cat Mss
Notes: The papers of Thomas J Holmes.

HOLMES BOOK COMPANY

CA —UNIVERSITY OF CALIFORNIA, LOS ANGELES, Research Library, Dept of Special Collections, 405 Hilgard Ave, Los Angeles, 90024. Edward Shreeves, Chairman, Bibliographers Group; David S Zeidberg, Head
Notes: 71 linear feet of correspondence and business records of this Los Angeles bookseller.

HOLOCAUST, JEWISH, 1939-1945

†CT —YALE UNIVERSITY, Library, Box 1603A, Yale Station, New Haven, 06520.
Notes: A collection of more than 200 videotaped interviews with survivors of the Holocaust.

FL —UNIVERSITY OF FLORIDA LIBRARY, Isser and Rae Price Library of Judaica, 18 Libr East, Gainesville, 32611. Robert Singerman, Head Librn
Budget: ($30,000)
Notes: Total holdings estimated at 55,000 vols dealing with the political, social, economic and intellectual history of the Jews in the ancient, medieval and modern periods and in all geographic areas. The following areas are especially well represented by printed matter in all relevant languages: Bibliography, Festschriften, History, Bible, Judaism and Jewish theology, liturgy, responsa, rabbinical literature, Jewish law, Hebrew language and literature, Yiddish language and literature, anti-semitism, Zionism, Palestine and the *Yishuv*, and the State of Israel. German and American Judaica form a collecting emphasis with holdings for all the standard histories as well as histories of individual synagogues, institutions and local communities. Works in Hebrew and Yiddish comprise about 60 percent of the collection (estimated 30,000 vols). With few exceptions, holdingsare limited to nineteenth and twentieth century imprints, with complete sets of journals and thousands of ephemeral pamphlets, many of them commemorating anniversaries, enhancing the research value of the collection, the largest Judaica research library in the southeastern United States. Only about half of the collection is cataloged; the collection is a circulating one and vols may be borrowed on interlibrary loan. Incl the Leonard C Mishkin Collection (40,000 vols), the largest personal Judaica collection in the United States, the Shlomo Marenof Collection (3500 vols), and the inventory of Bernard Morgenstern's Lower East Side Book Store (8000 vols). Scholars should inquire in advance of their visit. *The Isser and Rae Price Library of Judaica* Report (circulation 2900 copies) is mailed gratis twice a year to all interested parties. Special catalogs:Pre-1881 Hebrew imprints recorded in a chronological card file.

IL —HEBREW THEOLOGICAL COLLEGE, Saul Silber Memorial Library, 7135 N Carpenter Rd, Skokie, 60077. Leah Mishkin, Head Librn/Cur
Holdings: Vols (58,000) Cat Mss Microforms
Notes: Main subject is rabbinics (Halachic literature). We also have a very large and important Holocaust Collection.

MA —BRANDEIS UNIVERSITY, Goldfarb Library, 415 South St, Waltham, 02154. Bessie Hahn, Dir
Notes: JewishResistance Collection: Contains 21 linear ft of books, periodical articles and contemporary ephemera emphasizing the role Jews played in armed resistance to the Nazi regime. A catalog of the books is in the Special Colections Catalog and Main Card Catalog. Theresienstadt Concentration Camp Documents: Consists of over 200 "daily order" bulletins issued by the German command. Many of them contain lists of arrival and departure of internees. A finding list to the documents is located in Special Collections. No photocopying of the documents is permitted. Holocaust Survivors Collection: Consists of 20 linear ft of recorded interviews with survivors of the Holocaust, now living in the US. The tapes are not transcribed and the collection is unprocessed, but the tapes are arranged alphabetically by interviewee.

NY —CORNELL UNIVERSITY LIBRARIES, Collection of Regional History, Dept of Manuscripts and Univ Archives, Ithaca, 14853.
Notes: Interviews by A Gerd Korman, 1967-68; 4 trs. with transcripts.

NY —YIVO INSTITUTE FOR JEWISH RESEARCH, Library & Archives, 1048 Fifth Ave, New York, 10028. Dina Abramowicz, Librn; Marek Web, Archivist
Holdings: Cat Mss Pix Slides
Notes: Special collection of books and periodicals, incl government publications, which appeared in Germany between the years 1933-1945. Extensive library and archives collection on history of Jews under Nazi rule in Europe, 1933-1945, in all languages. Hundreds of memorial volumes for towns destroyed by Nazis.

OH —HEBREW UNION COLLEGE-JEWISH INSTITUTE OF RELIGION, Klau Library, 3101 Clifton Ave, Cincinnati, 45220. David J Gilner, Reference Librn
Holdings: Cat
Notes: The Jewish Holocaust (1939-1945) collection. Incl large collections of memorial books, curricula and juvenile fiction.

HOLT, HAMILTON

FL —ROLLINS COLLEGE, Mills Memorial Library, Winter Park, 32789. Patricia J Delks, Dir of Libraries
Holdings: // Cat Mss Pix
Notes: The Hamilton Holt Papers, composed of 93 ms boxes and 35 scrapbooks of correspondence, diaries and appointment books, pamphlets, topical folders, *The* Independent, memorabilia and newspaper clippings, speechs and writings. Indexed. Noncirculating.

HOLT, HENRY, PUBLISHERS

NJ —PRINCETON UNIVERSITY, Library, Manuscript Collection, Nassau St, Princeton, 08540. Jean F Preston, Cur
Holdings: // Mss Pix Cat
Notes: The collection incl 300 ms boxes, ledgers, and letterbooks. See *Princeton University Library Chronicle,* v 27, p 86-106. An unpublished typescript guide is available in the Library.

HOLTZMAN, REP. ELIZABETH

MA —RADCLIFFE COLLEGE, Arthur & Elizabeth Schlesinger Library on the History of Women in America, 3 James St, Cambridge, 02138. Patricia Miller King, Dir; Eva Moseley, Cur of Mss
Notes: Papers of New York's Democratic Representative Elizabeth Holtzman, graduate of Radcliffe. Most are restricted.

HOLY GHOST see Holy Spirit

HOLY LAND

PA —LIBRARY COMPANY OF PHILADELPHIA, 1314 Locust St, Philadelphia, 19107. Edwin Wolf II, Librn; Kenneth Finkel, Cur of Prints
Notes: The Edwin Wolf Collection of Judaica, consisting of 165 manuscripts and more than 500 books and broadsides printed in the US between 1718 and 1875. Incl literature, prayer books, Hebrew schoolbooks, reports of Jewish organizations, missionary tracts, narratives of travel to Palestine, and books on medicine. Most of the manuscripts consists of correspondence of the Gratz family, American pioneers.

HOLY OFFICE see Inquisition

HOLY PLACES see Shrines

HOLY ROMAN EMPIRE

MA —HARVARD UNIVERSITY LIBRARY, Widener Library, Cambridge, 02138.
Holdings: Cat
Notes: Stolberg collection incl 2700 vols

HOLY ROMAN EMPIRE (cont.)

from the working library of a reigning prince of the Holy Roman Empire.

HOLY SCRIPTURES see Bible

HOLY SPIRIT

CA —POINT LOMA NAZARENE COLLEGE, Ryan Library, 3900 Lomaland Dr, San Diego, 92106. Esther Schandorff, Librn
Holdings: Vols 1600 Cat Mss Pix
Notes: Person and work of the Holy Spirit and the doctrine of Christian Perfection.

MO —CENTRAL BIBLE COLLEGE LIBRARY, 3000 N Grant, Springfield, 65802. G J Flokstra Jr, Librn
Holdings: Vols 1975 Cat Mss Audiotapes Microforms
Notes: Holy Spirit theology.

TN —LEE COLLEGE, Library, Ocoee St, Cleveland, 37311. Frances Arrington, Head Librn; JoAnne Sparks, Religion Librn
Holdings: Vols 28,204 Cat Slides Phonorecords Audiotapes Filmstrips
Budget: $27,000
Notes: General religion collection which supports undergraduate and graduate level curriculum. The Pentecostal Research Center houses two special collections: the Church of God (Cleveland, Tennessee) collection and the Pentecostal collection. The latter includes works about the movement and its history, works by Pentecostal authors, and specific subject areas (Holy Spirit, glossolalia, divine healing).

HOMAGE VOLUMES see Festschriften

HOME DECORATION see Interior Decoration

HOME ECONOMICS

IL —UNIVERSITY OF ILLINOIS, URBANA/CHAMPAIGN, Library, Home Economics Library, 314 Bevier Hall, Champaign, 61820. Barbara C Swain, Librn
Holdings: Vols Cat

IL —GLENVIEW PUBLIC LIBRARY, 1930 Glenview Rd, Glenview, 60025. Peter Bury, Librn
Holdings: Vols (4100) Cat Filmstrips Audiotapes
Notes: Maintained as health and domestic science subject center. Incl 1840 cookbooks.

IN —INDIANAPOLIS-MARION COUNTY PUBLIC LIBRARY, Arts Div, 40 E Saint Clair St, PO Box 211, Indianapolis, 46204. Daniel H Gann, Head
Holdings: Vols 2500 Cat
Budget: $5000
Notes: The Julia Connor Thompson Collection on the Fine Arts of Homemaking. Restricted use. Reference only.

IN —PURDUE UNIVERSITY LIBRARIES, Consumer & Family Sciences Library, Stone Hall W, West Lafayette, 47907. Emily Alward, Librn
Holdings: Vols (14,000) Cat

IA —IOWA STATE UNIVERSITY, Library, Ames, 50011. Warren B Kuhn, Dean of Library Services
Holdings: Cat
Notes: Specific strength: costume history.

KS —KANSAS STATE UNIVERSITY, Library, Special Collections & University Archives, Manhattan, 66506. Antonia Q Pigno, Coordr; John J Vander Velde, Librn; Anthony R Crawford, Univ Archivist
Holdings: Vols 4500 Cat Mss
Budget: ($10,000)
Notes: Cookbooks and related items on home economics, nutrition and domestic economy. Nucleus of the collection is from the Abby Lillian Marlatt collection augmented by a sizable bequest from the estate of Clementine Paddleford. Includes about 600 volumes of rare cookbooks from the 16th, 17th, and 18th centuries as well as unprocessed papers (scrapbooks, recipe files and correspondence of Clementine Paddleford). A chronological bibliography is available for the pre-1900 portion of the collection: *The Kansas State University Receipt Book and Household Manual* (1968) by G A Rudolph.

NE —UNIVERSITY OF NEBRASKA-LINCOLN, C Y Thompson Library, East Campus, Lincoln, 68583. Lyle Schreiner, Librn
Holdings: Vols (220,000) Cat
Notes: Agriculture, with major strength in entomology, agronomy, and animal science; medicine; veterinary medicine; and home economics.

NY —CORNELL UNIVERSITY LIBRARIES, Collection of Regional History, Dept of Manuscripts and Univ Archives, Ithaca, 14853.
Notes: Correspondence and printed matter, 1935-41, 1948, of Cornell University, NY.

NY —NEW YORK PUBLIC LIBRARY, Mid-Manhattan Library, Science & Business Dept, 455 Fifth Ave, New York, 10016. Frederick E Dusold, Sr Principal Librn
Holdings: Vols (110,000) Cat Microforms
Budget: ($134,000)
Notes: All works are in English. Material is current; policy precludes archival collecting. Collection is geared toward the undergraduate college student, with consideration given to the professional, the lay reader and the beginning graduate student. Collection incl monographs, texts, treatises, standard reference works and periodicals in agriculture, horticulture, home economics, crafts, engineering, industrial chemistry, construction and other technologies. Books are available for circulation in addition to an extensive reference collection.

OH —OHIO STATE UNIVERSITY, Home Economics Library, Campbell Hall Rm 325, 1787 Neil Ave, Columbus, 43210. Neosha Mackey, Librn
Holdings: Vols (14,000) Cat Microforms
Notes: Separate catalog. Also, book catalog: *Catalog of the Home Economics Library* (Boston; G K Hall, 1976), 3 vols.

PA —DREXEL UNIVERSITY LIBRARIES, General Division, 32 & Chestnut Sts, Philadelphia, 19104. Tung Chu Chen, General Division Librn
Holdings: Vols (1226) Cat
Notes: Emphasis on home economics study and teaching, consumer education, and early childhood education.

WI —UNIVERSITY OF WISCONSIN, MADISON, College of Agricultural & Life Sciences, Steenbock Memorial Library, 550 Babcock Dr, Madison, 53706. Jan Kennedy, Dir
Holdings: Vols (186,312) Cat Docs
Notes: Collection supports the School of Family Resources and Consumer Sciences in areas of textiles and fashion design, interior decorating, consumer science, and nutrition; USDA documents and experiment station publications.

WI —UNIVERSITY OF WISCONSIN-STOUT, Library Learning Center, Menomonie, 54751. Philip Sawin Jr, Coll Develop Librn
Notes: This collection is the major collection in the library. It was begun in 1883. The Home Economics Education Graduate Program was begun in 1935.

NS —MOUNT SAINT VINCENT UNIVERSITY, Library, 166 Bedford Hwy, Halifax, B3M 2J6, Can. Lucian Bianchini, University Librn
Holdings: Vols 3000 Cat
Budget: ($125,000)
Notes: Collection to support the program for a Master's Degree.

HOME ECONOMICS—STUDY AND TEACHING

IL —UNIVERSITY OF ILLINOIS, URBANA/CHAMPAIGN, Library, Home Economics Library, 314 Bevier Hall, Champaign, 61820. Barbara C Swain, Librn
Holdings: Vols Cat
Budget: $20,283

OH —OHIO STATE UNIVERSITY, Home Economics Library, Campbell Hall Rm 325, 1787 Neil Ave, Columbus, 43210. Neosha Mackey, Librn
Holdings: Vols (14,000) Cat Microforms
Notes: Separate catalog. Also, book catalog: *Catalog ofthe Home Economics Library* (Boston: G K Hall, 1976), 3 vols.

HOME REPAIRING see Repair Manuals

HOMEOPATHY

CA —UNIVERSITY OF CALIFORNIA, SAN FRANCISCO, Library, Special Collections, San Francisco, 94143. Nancy Witten Zinn, Librn
Holdings: Vols (23,000) Cat

CT —YALE MEDICAL LIBRARY, 333 Cedar St, New Haven, 06510.

MD —MEDICAL & CHIRURGICAL FACULTY OF THE STATE OF MARYLAND, Library, 1211 Cathedral St, Baltimore, 21201. Joseph E Jensen, Librn
Holdings: Vols (10,000) / / Cat Mss Maps Pix
See also entry under Medicine - History and Historic

MA —WORCESTER HAHNEMANN HOSPITAL, Medical Library, 281 Lincoln St, Worcester, 01605. Roger Manahan, Librn
Holdings: Vols 30 Uncat Pix
Notes: Collection of medical history, incl books written by and about Dr Samuel Hahnemann from 1829.

PA —COLLEGE OF PHYSICIANS OF PHILADELPHIA, Library, 19 S 22 St, Philadelphia, 19103. Christine Ruggere, Cur, Historical Collections
Holdings: Vols (316,223) Cat Mss
Budget: ($1,096,557)
Notes: Very strong collection.
See also entry under Medicine.

HOMER

PA —UNIVERSITY OF PITTSBURGH, Hillman Library, Pittsburgh, 15260. Glenora E Rossell, Head
Holdings: Vols (11,550) Cat
Notes: The classics collection is particularly strong in Greek and Latin literature, Greek and Roman history, Greek philosophy, Greek and Latin language, and Greek epigraphy. In combination with the Frick Fine Arts collection it has a good collection in Greek and Roman art and archaelolgy. The collection of journals is also quite strong in these areas. There has been an emphasis in collecting books by and about Homer, Aristotles, Euripides, Vergil, Cicero and Petronius. It has a unique collection of unpublished PhD dissertations and Master's theses on Petronius. It has a basic collection on Greek and Latin paleography and papyrology.

HOMES (INSTITUTIONS) see Charitable Uses, Trusts, and Foundations

HOMICIDE

NY —NEW YORK HISTORICAL SOCIETY, Library, 170 Central Park W, New York, 10024. James Gregory, Librn
Notes: Books and pamphlets devoted to homicide and murder.

HOMICULTURE see Eugenics

HOMILETICS see Preaching

HOMILIES see Sermons—Collections

HOMOPHILE MOVEMENT see Gay Liberation Movement

HOMOPHILES see Homosexuals and Homosexuality

HOMOPTERA

NC —NORTH CAROLINA STATE UNIVERSITY, D H Hill Library, Box 7111, Raleigh, 27695. I T Littleton, Dir
Holdings: Vols 7370 Cat
Budget: $5000
Notes: The Friedrich F Tippman Collection

HOMOPTERA (cont.)

of 6200 volumes on entomology incl many unique and rare volumes which make the collection one of the best in the US. Incl the Z P Metcalf collection on Homoptera and Hemiptera: 1100 vols and 24 VF cabinets.

HOMOSEXUAL ART see Art, Homosexual

HOMOSEXUALS AND HOMOSEXUALITY

CA —NATIONAL GAY ARCHIVES, 1654 North Hudson, Hollywood, 90028. Jim Kipner, Archivist
Notes: One of the most important collections.

CA —HOMOSEXUAL INFORMATION CENTER, Library, 6758 Hollywood Blvd Rm 208, Los Angeles, 90028. Don Slater, Librn
Holdings: Vols Periodicals Unpublished Mss Pix Phonorecords Clippings
Notes: Contains over 5000 mss, periodicals, and pamphlets on the homosexual movement, from 1948 and records the movement's organizational, social, and political history. Incl are periodicals in Japanese, French, German, Dutch, and other European languages, and newsletters records, and reports of homosexual organizations probably not to be found in any other archive. The Library publishes bibliographies, selected reading lists, a directory of homosexual movement organizations and publications, and a newsletter. It participates in an ILL network.

CA —LOS ANGELES PUBLIC LIBRARY, Social Sciences Dept, 630 W Fifth St, Los Angeles, 90071. Marilyn C Wherley, Principal Librn
Holdings: Vols 3000 Cat
Budget: ($150,000)
Notes: Books, clippings, pamphlets, periodicals, government publications, bibliogrpahies, popular and scholarly works on homosexuality, husband-wife relations, abortion, rape, and sex education.

CA —ONE, INCORPORATED, Blanche M Baker Memorial Library, 3340 Country Club Dr, Los Angeles, 90019. David G Moore, Dir
Holdings: Vols (7600) Cat Mss Pix Slides Phonorecords Audiotapes
Notes: Nonfiction in numerous disciplines relating to homosexuality, homophile movement, sexual minorities, and human sexuality; biography, gay and lesbian fiction, poetry, erotica; standard reference works; 200 periodicals in many languages; 65 file drawers and containers of VF materials (clippings, fliers, brochures, newsletters, correspondence, archival collections). Partially cataloged.

CA —UNIVERSITY OF CALIFORNIA, LOS ANGELES, Research Library, Dept of Special Collections, 405 Hilgard Ave, Los Angeles, 90024. Edward Shreeves, Chairman, Bibliographers Group; David S Zeidberg, Head
Notes: 11 linear feet of books, clippings, audio tapes, and ephemera concerning sexual minorities, collected by Frank E Schreck.

CA —CALIFORNIA STATE UNIVERSITY, NORTHRIDGE, Delmar T Oviatt & South Libraries, 1811 Nordhoff St, Northridge, 91330. Donald L Read, Special Collections Dept
Holdings: Vols 1800 Cat
Notes: Books and other materials devoted to all aspects of human sexuality, particularly strong in prostitution and homosexuals and homosexuality.

†CA —INSTITUTE FOR THE ADVANCED STUDY OF HUMAN SEXUALITY, 1523 Franklin St, San Francisco, 94109.

CA —SAN FRANCISCO STATE UNIVERSITY, Center for Homosexual Education, Evaluation, and Research (CHEER), San Francisco, 94132. Salvatore J Licata, Dir
Notes: Homosexuality in its historical and contemporary contexts; its social sex-role, and the increase of public awareness in American society.

FL —LESBIAN AND GAY ARCHIVES OF NAIAD PRESS, INC, PO Box 10543, Tallahassee, 32302. Barbara Grier, Librn; Donna J McBride, Librn
Holdings: Vols 22,000
Budget: $2500
Notes: The Lesbian and Gay Archives of Naiad Press. A private collection of lesbian and gay literature. Open to researchers on appointment basis.

IL —NORTHWESTERN UNIVERSITY, Library, Special Collections Dept, 1937 Sheridan Rd, Evanston, 60201. R Russell Maylone, Cur
Holdings: Cat / /
Notes: Newspapers, newsletters, pamphlets, posters, ephemera written and distributed by women active in lesbian organizations or the Gay Liberation Movement from the early 1960's to the present. Additional material available in the Women's Liberation Collection.

IN —INDIANA UNIVERSITY, Institute for Sex Research Library, 416 Morrison Hall, Bloomington, 47401. Douglas Freeman, Collections and Services Librn; Joan Brewer, Information Services Librn
Holdings: Vols (62,000) Cat Mss Pix Phonorecords Audiotapes Slides Films Microforms
Budget: ($20,000)
Notes: One of the greatest and most extensive collections on sexual behavior, the library collects materials on all aspects of sex activity, with special emphasis on behavioral and social aspects. Also collects erotic literature and sexual ephemera. Incl 105 audiotapes, 23 vertical file drawers, 108 phonorecords, 55,000 pictures, 5000 slides and 1700 films. Rich in French, German and American sources; also much Oriental. Semitraditional erotic poetry and song of 17th-18th century England. Bawdy limericks, double-entendre, puns, slang, erotic literature, graffiti, slang and special dictionaries, proverbs and sayings, epigrams and research materials of the Kinsey Studies, etc. Contact Information Service for: literature searching, preparation of bibliographies, permission to use collection. Limited photocopying.

MI —UNIVERSITY OF MICHIGAN, Dept of Rare Books & Special Collections, Ann Arbor, 48109. Edward C Weber, Head, Labadie Collection
Holdings: Vols (40,000) Cat Mss Phonorecords Audiotapes
Notes: Particularly material concerned with radical Gay Liberation. Mostly serials and pamphlets, many of which represent homosexual protest before the official designation of Gay Liberation.

NY —GAY PEOPLE AT COLUMBIA, Library, Broadway & 116 St, New York, 10027.

NY —LESBIAN HERSTORY EDUCATIONAL FOUNDATION INC, Lesbian Herstory Archives, PO Box 1258, New York, 10116. Deborah Edel, Treasurer
Notes: Lesbian, feminist, and Gay books and periodicals on all aspects of Lesbian culture, photographs and slides of Lesbians and Lesbian art, records, tapes, graphics and crafts. Also, unpublished materials such as first drafts, term papers from Lesbian and Gay studies courses, diaries, letters, poetry, and conference notes.

NY —YWCA NATIONAL BOARD, Library, 726-730 Broadway, New York, 10012. Elizabeth Norris, Librn
Holdings: Vols (3000) Cat Mss
Budget: ($2400)
Notes: Women and their contemporary interests.

PA —TEMPLE UNIVERSITY LIBRARIES, Special Collections Dept, Contemporary Culture Collection, Philadelphia, 19122. Patricia J Case, Cur
Notes: The Contemporary Culture Collection. See full entry under US-Social Life and Customs.

ON —CANADIAN GAY ARCHIVES, 54 Wolsley St, Box 639, Station A, Toronto, M5T 1A5, Can.
Notes: One of the best collections, incl memorabilia, such as buttons and other historically important material.

ON —WOMEN'S MOVEMENT ARCHIVES, PO Box 928, Station Q, Toronto, M5W 1G2, Can.
Holdings: Vols (250) Pix
Notes: Graphics, individual files, 250 periodicals and newsletters, 450 group files.

HONDURAS

CT —YALE UNIVERSITY, Sterling Memorial Library, Latin American Collections, New Haven, 06520. Lee H Williams Jr, Cur
Holdings: Vols (300,000) Cat Maps Pix Slides Phonorecords 16mm Films Filmstrips
See also entry under Latin America

KS —UNIVERSITY OF KANSAS, Watson Library, Lawrence, 66045. George Jerkovich, Cur Slavic Collections
Notes: Over 6000 valuable Central American titles, of which fewer than half in a random sample are presently located in OCLC, and over half not incl in published holdings of the University of Texas or Tulane University. A special grant is supporting cataloging of the collection.

MA —PAN AMERICAN SOCIETY OF NEW ENGLAND, Shattuck Library, 152 North Street, Boston, 02109. Vivian Ingrao, Dir
Holdings: Vols (10,000) Cat Slides Phonorecords
Notes: Books on art, literature, history, and economy of Pan American countries.

HONDURAS, BRITISH see Belize

HONEYBEES see Bees and Beekeeping

HONEYWELL, MARK C.

IN —WABASH CARNEGIE PUBLIC LIBRARY, Oral History Program, 188 W Hill St, Wabash, 46992. Linda Robertson, Librn
Holdings: Cat
Budget: $100
Notes: The collection will be of major concern to those interested in local history; however, effort is made to get information on Ku Klux Klan activities in Indiana, Spanish-American War remembraces, and depression days, as well as local history. The Honeywell Company has expanded the collection by interviewing former employees about the company and its founder, Mark C Honeywell. Collection is cited in the *Indiana Magazine of History,* vol LXVIII, no 4 (December 1972): 315- 337.

HONG KONG

HI —UNIVERSITY OF HAWAII, Library, 2550 The Mall, Honolulu, 96822. Joyce Wright, Head, Asia Collection; Masato Matsu, Head, East Asia Vernacular Collection
Holdings: Vols 60,394 Cat Microforms
Notes: The Asia Collection includes materials from and about China (People's Republic, Taiwan, Hong Kong) in all languages. No figures are available for western language materials relating to China, which are supplemented by retrospective materials in the main library collection. Scope: social sciences and the humanities, traditional and contemporary.

IL —CENTER FOR RESEARCH LIBRARIES, 6050 S Kenwood Ave, Chicago, 60637. Donald B Simpson, Dir; Esther Smith, Collection Development Librn
Holdings: Vols Cat Microforms
Notes: Mainland China newspapers, periodicals and clippings, early western language newspapers in China, Hong Kong newspapers in English, British Foreign Office and US State Dept records relating to China, Dunhuang manuscripts, missionary periodicals. Microfilm and reprints of newspapers, serials and monographs from Center for Chinese Research Materials. Hunter collection of Chinese communist propaganda (ca 1000 vols). Microfilm and originals of Maritime Customs publications. Microfilm of press summaries prepared by US Consulate, Hong Kong, archives of

HONG KONG (cont.)

missionary organizations, Chinese folk literature, etc. Descriptive pamphlet available.

HONNEGER, ARTHUR

DC —LIBRARY OF CONGRESS, Music Division, Washington, 20540.
Notes: Mss in Koussevitzky Archives.

HONOR, DECORATIONS OF see Decorations of Honor

HOO, VICTOR

CA —HOOVER INSTITUTION ON WAR, REVOLUTION & PEACE, Stanford University, Stanford, 94305. Milorad M Drachkovitch, Archivist
Holdings: Mss Pix
Notes: Papers of Victor Chi-tsai Hoo, Nationalist Chinese diplomat and statesman, 1919-1945, and United Nations official, 1945-1972, incl diaries, correspondence, clippings, reports, memoranda, photographs, and other material, 1930-1972, relating to his government service for China, Chinese political events and foreign relations, Sino-Soviet relations, and his career with the United Nations. 7 1/2 ms boxes.

HOOD, THOMAS, 1799-1845

CA —UNIVERSITY OF CALIFORNIA, LOS ANGELES, Research Library, Dept of Special Collections, 405 Hilgard Ave, Los Angeles, 90024. Edward Shreeves, Chairman, Bibliographers Group; David S Zeidberg, Head
Holdings: Vols 100
Notes: 100 first and other editions of his books; 75 letters and drawings.

OH —OHIO UNIVERSITY, Vernon R Alden Library, Department of Archives and Special Collections, Athens, 45701. Gary A Hunt, Head
Holdings: Vols 54 Cat
Notes: The collection incl various editions of Hood's works, periodicals and some drawings and page proofs.

HOOK, SIDNEY

IL —SOUTHERN ILLINOIS UNIVERSITY, CARBONDALE, Delyte W Morris Library, Special Collections Dept, Carbondale, 62901. David V Koch, Cur of Special Collections; Louisa Bowen, Cur of Manuscripts
Holdings: Cat Mss
Notes: Twenty Collections related to 20th century philosophy, incl the papers of John Dewey, Henry Nelson Wieman, Stephen C Pepper and Toyohiko Kagawa; the archives of the *Library of Living Philosophers* and the Open Court Publishing Company; and small collections of James H Tufts, Edward Scribner Ames and Sidney Hook.

HOOK, THEODOR EDWARD, 1788-1841

CA —UNIVERSITY OF CALIFORNIA, LOS ANGELES, Research Library, Dept of Special Collections, 405 Hilgard Ave, Los Angeles, 90024. Edward Shreeves, Chairman, Bibliographers Group; David S Zeidberg, Head
Holdings: Vols 50 Mss
Notes: 50 first and other editions of his books; 38 letters; 1 manuscript.

HOOKE, ROBERT

ON —UNIVERSITY OF TORONTO, Thomas Fisher Rare Book Library, 120 Saint George St, Toronto, M5S 1A5, Can. Richard G Landon, Head
Holdings: Vols 4000
Notes: The Science Collection is especially rich in works on Renaissance astronomy, physics and mechanics and has noteworthy holdings of works of English experimental scientists in the 17th and 18th centuries with excellent collections of the works of Robert Boyle, Robert Hooke, and Sir Isaac Newton. Includes virtually all important early editions of Euclid; alchemical works of the 16th and 17th centuries together with the works of 18th century chemists like Lavoisier and Priestly; works on agriculture with special emphasis on British agriculture in the 18th century; and a variety of other works important in the history of science in all its branches. In addition the Fisher Library has many other specialized scientific collections which are listed separately.

HOOKER, ISABELLA BEECHER, 1822-1907

CT —STOWE-DAY LIBRARY, 77 Forest St, Hartford, 06105. Diana J Royce, Librn
Holdings: Vols (15,000) Cat Mss Pix
Notes: 150,000 cataloged mss and publications concerning architecture, decorative arts, history and literature of the period 1840-1900, with emphasis on Nook Farm, Mark Twain, Harriet Beecher Stowe, Calvin E Stowe, Charles Dudley Warner, William Hooker Gillette, Isabella Beecher Hooker. Incl 5000 pictures.

HOOKER, THOMAS

MI —NORTHERN MICHIGAN UNIVERSITY, Lydia M Olson Library, Elizabeth L Harden Drive, Marquette, 49855. Stephen H Peters, Cataloger
Notes: A section of the personal library of Moses Coit Tyler, incl works by Thomas Hooker, John Cotton, Cotton Mather, and Jonathan Edwards.

HOOKER FAMILY PAPERS

CT —YALE UNIVERSITY, Box 1603A, Yale Station, New Haven, 06520.
Holdings: Cat Mss
Notes: The family papers.

HOOPES, TOWNSEND

MA —BOSTON UNIVERSITY, Mugar Memorial Library, Special Collections Dept, 771 Commonwealth Ave, Boston, 02215. Howard B Gotlieb, Dir
Holdings: Cat Mss Pix
Notes: Mss, correspondence, etc collected in depth; incl publications by or about.

HOOSAC TUNNEL

MA —NORTH ADAMS PUBLIC LIBRARY, Houghton Memorial Bldg, Church & Main Sts, North Adams, 01247. Constance Griffin, Librn
Holdings: Vols 57 // Cat Mss Pix Microforms
Notes: Books on the building on the Hoosac Tunnel; reports made during the construction; ledgers kept by men working on the tunnel; pictures of the construction (both photographs and lithographs); and a partial collection of the original plans of the tunnel. No seperate catalog.

HOOVER, HERBERT CLARK

CA —CLAREMONT COLLEGES, Norman F Sprague Memorial Library, 12 & Dartmouth, Claremont, 91711. David Kuhner, Librn
Notes: President Herbert Hoover's personal collection of rare mining books-about 1000 vols of the 15th-17th centuries.

CA —HOOVER INSTITUTION ON WAR, REVOLUTION & PEACE, Stanford University, Stanford, 94305. Milorad M Drachkovitch, Archivist
Holdings: Mss Pix
Notes: Four collections: (1) Correspondence between Herbert Hoover and Woodrow Wilson, 1915-1920. 152 items. Also the Paul Ahill Collection of some 300 letters from famous people concerning their opinions of Wilson. (2) Records of the Commission for Relief in Belgium organized in 1914 under the chairmanship of Herbert Hoover, incl correspondence, reports, memoranda, accounts, pamphlets, bulletins and photographs, 1914-1924, relating to procurement of food and other supplies in the US and their distribution in German-occupied Belgium and northern France during and immediately aft.er World War I. 265 ft (3) Records of the US Executive Branch Organization Commissions (Hoover Commissions), 1947-1949 and 1953-1955, incl correspondence, reports, minutes, pressreleases, and printed matter, relating to the Commissions' efforts to rationalize the organization of the executive branch of the federal government and especially to the work of the Chairman Herbert Hoover. 27 ms boxes. Also, records of the National Citizens Committee for the Reorganization of the Executive Branch of the Government and the Citizens Committee for the Hoover Report, 1949-1958. 103 ms boxes (4) Records of the Famine Emergency Committee, an organization for the coordination of international famine relief after World War II, incl correspondence, reports, notes and clippings, 1946-47, relating to US food conservation and to famine conditions throughout the world. Incl memoranda and diaries of Herbert Hoover, Honorary Chairman of the Committee. 30 ms boxes, 2 envelopes.

OR —GEORGE FOX COLLEGE, Shambaugh Library, Newberg, 97132. F E Walls, Libr Dir
Holdings: Vols 3300 Cat Pix Microforms
Budget: $300
Notes: Incl periodicals, scrapbooks, pamphlets, etc and books relating to Herbert Hoover.

HOOVER COMMISSIONS

CA —HOOVER INSTITUTION ON WAR, REVOLUTION & PEACE, Stanford University, Stanford, 94305. Milorad M Drachkovitch, Archivist
Holdings: Mss
Notes: Records of the US Executive Branch Organization Commissions (Hoover Commissions), 1947-1949 and 1953-1955, incl correspondence, reports, minutes, press releases, and printed matter, relating to the Commissions' efforts to rationalize the organization of the executive branch of the federal goverment and especially to the work of the chairman, Herbert Hoover. 27 ms boxes. Also, records of the National Citizens Committee for the Reorganization of the Executive Branch of the Goverment and the Citizens Committee for the Hoover Report, 1949-1958. 103 ms boxes.

HOOVER DAM

CA —POMONA PUBLIC LIBRARY, Special Collections, 625 S Garey Ave, PO Box 2271, Pomona, 91766. David Streeter, Librn
Holdings: // Uncat Pix
Notes: Some 600 photographs taken during the construction of Hoover Dam, also known as Boulder Dam.

HOPE, BOB

CA —UNIVERSITY OF CALIFORNIA, LOS ANGELES, Theater Arts Library, Los Angeles, 90024. Edward Shreeves, Chairman, Bibliographers Group; Audree Malkin, Head, Theater Arts Library
Holdings: Cat Mss Pix
Notes: Radio Scripts Collection incl *The Bob Hope Show,* 29 scripts, 1949-1950.

HOPEDALE COMMUNITY

NY —SYRACUSE UNIVERSITY LIBRARIES, Ernest S Bird Library, George Arents Research Library for Special Collections, Syracuse, 13210. Carolyn A Davis, Manuscripts Librn; Amy S Doherty, University Archivist; Mark F Weimer, Rare Book Librn
Holdings: Vols 225 Cat Pix
Notes: A collection of publications by and about the Hopeland and Oneida communities and their forerunners; supplemented by reference works dealing

HOPEDALE COMMUNITY (cont.)

with Communistic societies in general. Contains ephemeral handbooks, annual reports and periodicals; particularly relating to John Humphrey Noyes.

HOPI INDIANS

AZ —NORTHERN ARIZONA UNIVERSITY, Special Collection Library, CU Box 6022, Flagstaff, 86011. Peter M Whiteley, Coordr/Archivist; William Mullane, Librn
Holdings: Mss Pix
Notes: Affidavits of Hopis and Navajos regarding the "moral character of the Hopi ceremonial dances." Incl related files on other Pueblo Indians and files concerning William E "Pussyfoot" Johnson, and correspondence of Herbert Welsh of the Indian Rights Association (1915-1925). Also Hopi Extension Work Reports Collection: Annual reports, 1938-1939, 1941-1950 (photocopies) on livestock, grazing and agricultural conditions of the Hopi Indian Reservation. NAU also has the following collection regarding the Hopi tribe: (1) White Bear Fredericks Collection of tapes and mss; (2) David P Seaman Collection of mss on the Hopi language. Incl books on anthropology collected by H C Diehl, an amateur anthropologist who was especially interested in the Hopi Indians. (3) Fred Eggan Collection of microfilms(BIA letterbooks from Hopi Agency, 1899-1916); (4) Winnifred Frey Stryker Collection of photographs; (5) Leo Crane Collection of photographs and mss; (6) Michael W Lomatuway'ma Collection of tapes and photographs. (7) James Biglin Collection containing computer printout data for his publication, *Cultural Values in Indian Education: A Study of Parental Attitudes and Values Towards Education on the Navajo and Hopi Reservations,* Flagstaff: Southwest Behavioral Institute, 1971-1972. (8) Mennonite Library and Archives Collection contains a photocopy of H R Voth mss, *Hopi-English Vocabulary,* 1902, and *Hopi Field Notes,* 1990's. (9) Frier Collection; incl materials on the development of the Flagstaff Cemetery and an account of the 1911 Hopi Snake Dance attended by Teddy Roosevelt.

AZ —COLORADO RIVER INDIAN TRIBES MUSEUM/LIBRARY, Rte One, Box 23-B, Parker, 85344. Priscilla Johnson, Librn
Holdings: Cat Mss Maps Pix Slides Audiotapes Microforms
Notes: Library deals with the four tribes of the Colorado River Indian Reservation: Mojave, Chemehuevi, Navajo, and Hopi. Emphasis is also given to the prehistoric culture of this area; Patayan and Hohokam. Library collections include original manuscripts and other documents, photographs, oral history tape recordings, cultural items and artifacts. Copies of many documents relating to the reservation are in bound volumes, microfilm, and photocopies. Photos relative to the reservation from various other collections are copied in our collection. Of particular interest is the museum basket collection which incl about 1000 Chemehuevi baskets-the largest Chemehuevi basket collection. Other artifacts give special emphasis to the Mojave culture.

AZ —UNIVERSITY OF ARIZONA, Center for Creative Photography, 843 E University Blvd, Tucson, 85721. James Enyeart, Dir; Terence Pitts, Cur and Librn
Holdings: Pix
Notes: The Marion Palfi Photo Archive. Famous portrayals of, espec, poverty-stricken and victimized persons in the US, 1940 through 1970s, incl Hopi, Navajo, and Papago Indians on reservations, in urban relocation, and acculturation centers. Over 1500 master prints, 10,000 work prints, hundreds of glass plate and film negatives, manuscripts, etc.

CO —FORT LEWIS COLLEGE, Library, Southwest Collection, College Heights, Durango, 81301. Daniel W Lester, Dir
Holdings: Vols (7000) Cat Mss Maps Pix Slides Microforms
Budget: ($3800)
Notes: Also have seperate catalog of the special collections concerning the Southwest, Indians, mine records, railroad records, etc.

NM —ALBUQUERQUE PUBLIC LIBRARY, 501 Copper Ave NW, Albuquerque, 87102. Alan B Clark, Dir
Holdings: Vols (4000) Cat Microforms Records Maps VF
Notes: Large collection of materials on all aspects of New Mexico history and cultures. In-house index accesses VF materials and local and regional periodicals. Special emphasis on Indians of New Mexico and northeastern Arizona, particularly the Navajo, Hopi, Pueblos and Apache. Reference copies of many works are housed at the Special Collections Library, 423 Central Ave NE, Albuquerque, NM 87102.

NM —GALLUP PUBLIC LIBRARY, 115 W Hill Ave, Gallup, 87301. Octavia Fellin, Dir
Holdings: Vols (8000) Cat Maps Pix

HOPI INDIANS—PICTURES, ILLUSTRATIONS, ETC.

NM —MUSEUM OF NEW MEXICO, Photo Archives, Box 2087, Santa Fe, 87503. Arthur L Olivas, Cur; Richard Rudisill, Photo Historian
Holdings: Cat Pix Slides
Budget: ($9000)
Notes: 90,000 photographs, cataloged, and 1000 slides. Photographs may be ordered as research copies for set fees. Reproduction or publication requires written permission plus additional required fees. Incl. special groups of photographs, e.g. T. Harmon Parkhurst Collection-ca. 15,000 photos, 1915-1950, Southwest Indians, scenic views, town views; H. F. Robinson Collection-ca. 1000 items, ca. 1910-1920, Southwest Indians, esp. Hopi and Blackfoot; Ben Wittick Collection-ca. 1500 items, 1879-1903, Southwest Indians, military, town views. Many other of the important early photographers are represented, especially large collections of the work of G. C. Bennett, William H. Brown, Dana B. Chase, Edward S. Curtis, H. H. Dorman, Rev. J. C. Gullette, P. E. Harroun, William H. Jackson, Charles F. Lummis, Jesse L. Nussbaum, Henry A. Schmidt, and about a hundred others.

HOPKINS, GERARD MANLEY, 1844-1899

MD —LOYOLA/NOTRE DAME LIBRARY, 200 Winston Ave, Baltimore, 21212. Jack Ray, Dir
Holdings: Vols 115 Cat Mss Pix
Notes: Incl 250 periodical issues; family letters, etc.

HOPKINS, KENNETH

OK —UNIVERSITY OF TULSA, McFarlin Library, Dept of Rare Books and Special Collections, 600 S College, Tulsa, 74104. David Farmer, Dir; Toby Murray, Archivist; Caroline Swinson, Cur of Manuscripts & Art
Holdings: Vols 5000
Notes: His library collection of 18th and 19th century English poetry.

HOPKINS, THOMAS CRAMER

NY —SYRACUSE UNIVERSITY LIBRARIES, Ernest S Bird Library, George Arents Research Library for Special Collections, Syracuse, 13210. Carolyn A Davis, Manuscripts Librn; Amy S Doherty, University Archivist; Mark F Weimer, Rare Book Librn
Notes: The George Arents Research Library for Special Collections at Syracuse University contains the papers of Thomas Cramer Hopkins.

HOPWOOD, AVERY

MI —UNIVERSITY OF MICHIGAN, Library, Dept of Rare Books & Special Collections, Ann Arbor, 48109. Robert J Starring, Head
Holdings: Cat Mss Pix
Notes: 7200 manuscript items. The collection comprises chiefly correspondence with noted writers and critics concerning participation as judges in the annual University of Michigan Hopwood Awards contests in dramatic writing, fiction, poetry, and the essay, or as lectures at the annual award ceremony. It also includes 32 book manuscripts of former award winners, manuscripts of 16 of the lectures, and correspondence with several award winners about publication of their later work, as well as the papers of Broadway playwright Avery Hopwood whose bequest has funded the Avery Hopwood and Jule Hopwood Awards since their inception in 1931.

HORACE

CA —UNIVERSITY OF CALIFORNIA, BERKELEY, University Library, Berkeley, 94720. Donald G Williams, Classics Librn
Notes: Research collections, incl a wide array of periodicals, critical editions, works of textual criticism, history, and epigraphy. Extensive coverage of 18th and 19th century classical scholarship. German and Italian research publications are particularly well represented. Main Library holdings are supplemented by significant works in the Bancroft Library: mss, incunabula, and other rare editions; especially noteworthy are the Horace Collection and the Tebtunis papyri.

IL —DE PAUL UNIVERSITY, Library, 2323 N Seminary, Chicago, 60614. Kathryn De Graff, Special Collections Librn
Holdings: Vols 212// Uncat
Notes: The Hamil and Barker Collection consists of 212 volumes of various printings of the works of Horace, 1554-1934.

IL —NORTHWESTERN UNIVERSITY, Library, Special Collections Dept, 1937 Sheridan Rd, Evanston, 60201. R Russell Maylone, Cur
Holdings: Vols 2200 Cat Mss
Notes: Historical collection of editions of Horace, published from 1482 to date. Additional materials in general collection.

IA —LORAS COLLEGE, Wahlert Memorial Library, 14 & Alta Vista, Dubuque, 52001. Robert F Klein, Librn
Holdings: Vols 800 Cat
Notes: Collection gathered by Horace Howard Furness, editor of the Shakespeare "Variorum." Vols in the collection date from 1482 to the present, the majority being pre-19th century. Incl editions of works (574 vols) and critical studies (237 vols).

MA —HARVARD UNIVERSITY LIBRARY, Widener Library, Cambridge, 02138.
Holdings: Cat

NH —DARTMOUTH COLLEGE, Baker Memorial Library, Hanover, 03755.
Notes: Extensive collection of Marjorie Dana Barlow of works by and about Horace. The collection had originally been formed by Mrs Barlow's father, Charles Loomis Dana.

NJ —PRINCETON UNIVERSITY, Library, Rare Books Dept, Princeton, 08544. Stephen Ferguson, Cur
Notes: Robert Patterson Collection of Editions of Horace. About 1200 vols. For particulars refer to: *A Preliminary Catalogue of the Horace Collection Presented to the Library of Princeton University by Robert Wilson Patterson, Class of 1876.* (Princeton, 1917). The collection is noteworthy for its extent and variety no less than for the rarity of individual items, and illustrates the history of bookmaking as well as the scholarly study of Horace. It ranges from 15th century mss to the most recent editions, imitations and translations.

HORACE (cont.)

PA —FREE LIBRARY OF PHILADELPHIA, Rare Book Dept, Logan Sq, Philadelphia, 19103. Marie E Korey, Rare Book Librn
Holdings: Vols (1100) Cat
Notes: The Moncure Biddle Collection of significant editions of Horace containing many examples of fine printing and binding.

RI —BROWN UNIVERSITY, John Hay Library, 20 Prospect St, Providence, 02912. Mark N Brown, Cur Mss
Holdings: Vols 600 // Cat
Notes: Foster Horace Collection of editions and translations of Horace from the 15th to the 20th century.

HORAN, JAMES D.

MA —BOSTON UNIVERSITY, Mugar Memorial Library, Special Collections Dept, 771 Commonwealth Ave, Boston, 02215. Howard B Gotlieb, Dir
Holdings: Cat Mss Pix
Notes: Mss, correspondence, etc collected in depth; incl publications by or about.

HORAN, WALTER FRANKLIN

†WA —WASHINGTON STATE UNIVERSITY, Library, Manuscripts, Archives & Special Collections, Pullman, 99164. John F Guido, Head
Holdings: Vols Cat Mss Maps Pix
Notes: The personal and political papers of Fred C Ashley, William Edward Carty, Knute Hill, Walter Franklin Horan, William Lon Johnson, Catherine May, and Austin Mires are among the holdings of the library. Most collections described in printed registers.

HORGAN, PAUL

AZ —UNIVERSITY OF ARIZONA, University Library, Special Collections, Tucson, 85721. Louis A Hieb, Head
Holdings: Vols (7000) Cat Mss Microforms
Budget: ($30,000)
Notes: Incl the belle lettres of the American Southwest. The collection covers the complete scope of works by Southwest authors and those works which are set in the Southwest. The major authors are Edward Abbey, Coolidge, Eastlake, Fergusson, Garfield, Horgan, King, McMurtry, Nichols and Rhodes.

CT —YALE UNIVERSITY, Box 1603A, Yale Station, New Haven, 06520.
Holdings: Cat Mss
Notes: First editions, some containing inscriptions.

DC —GEORGETOWN UNIVERSITY, Library, Special Collections Div, 37 & O Sts NW, Washington, 20057. George M Barringer, Special Collections Librn; Nicholas B Sheetz, Mss Librn
Holdings: Mss
Notes: The Archives of the Gallery of Living Catholic Authors was founded in 1932 by Sister Mary Joseph of the Sisters of Loretto to focus attention on modern Catholic literature, and to provide a depository for manuscripts, letters, photographs, and books by contemporary Catholic writers. Contains material by hundreds of writers, incl Hilaire Belloc, Roy Campbell, Padraic Colum, Eric Gill, Paul Horgan, Mary Lavin, Marie Belloc Lowndes, Kathleen Norris, Alred Noyes, Sheila Kaye-Smith, Sigrid Undset, and Evelyn Waugh, to name only a few.

NV —UNIVERSITY OF NEVADA, RENO, University Library, Special Collections Dept, Reno, 89557. Robert E Blesse, Head
Holdings: Vols (53) Cat
Notes: Includes individual works by author in all editions including translations; also prefaces, introductions, published correspondence, appearances in anthologies, periodicals, etc. Bibliographical research collection, part of Modern Authors Collection.

HORMONES

AR —NATIONAL CENTER FOR TOXICOLOGICAL RESEARCH, Library, Jefferson, 72079. Susan Laney-Sheehan, Supvr Librn
Holdings: Vols (15,000) Cat Mss Slides Audiotapes 16mm Films Microforms
Notes: Incl (860) journal titles, (230) current subscriptions.

CT —YALE MEDICAL LIBRARY, 333 Cedar St, New Haven, 06510.
Notes: A special subject emphasis.

HORN BOOKS see Hornbooks

HORN MUSIC

IN —BALL STATE UNIVERSITY, Alexander M Bracken Library, Muncie, 47306. Nyal Williams, Music Librn
Holdings: Vols (30,000) Cat Mss
Budget: ($20,000)
Notes: Incl archives of International Horn Society, Tubists Universal Brotherhood Association Library, Cecil Leeson Archival Saxophone Collection, and Archives of Buescher Music Instrument Manufacturing Company.

HORNADAY, WILLIAM T.

DC —LIBRARY OF CONGRESS, Manuscript Division, Washington, 20540. John C Broderick, Chief
Notes: Papers of William T Hornaday, Naturalist.

HORNBECK, STANLEY KUHL

CA —HOOVER INSTITUTION ON WAR, REVOLUTION & PEACE, Stanford University, Stanford, 94305. Milorad M Drachkovitch, Archivist
Holdings: // Mss Pix
Notes: Papers, 1919-1966, of Stanley Kuhl Hornbeck, diplomat and educator. Correspondence, diaries, reports, memoranda and other papers chiefly relating to Hornbeck's career with the US State Dept. Incl reports of a conference with Winston Churchill, reports and recommendations prior to and following Pearl Harbor, Hornbeck's interests as a Rhodes Scholar and teacher, and impressions of numerous conferences, committees and people. Correspondents incl Cordell Hull, Henry L Stimson, ambassadors to China and Japan, and leading figures in the political, educational, and business life of the US. 550 ms boxes.

HORNBERGER, THEODORE

NC —DUKE UNIVERSITY, William R Perkins Library, Jay B Hubbell Center for American Literary Historiography, Durham, 27706. Erma Whittington, Librn
Notes: 77,312 items, including manuscripts, pictures, clippings, and correspondence. "The objective of the Center is to gather the papers and materials of significant scholars and critics in American literary history." The Center is a part of the Perkins Library Manuscripts Department.

HORNBOOKS

CA —CLAREMONT COLLEGES, Ella Strong Denison Library, Scripps College, Claremont, 91711. Judy Harvey Sahak, Librn
Holdings: Vols 452 Cat
Notes: Early books for children published 1790 to early 20th century. Emphasis on moralistic and didactic literature of 1790s-1840s, tracts, alphabet books, school books, readers, chap books, horn books, verse and riddles. 150 vols uncataloged.

IN —INDIANA UNIVERSITY, Lilly Library, Seventh St, Bloomington, 47405. William R Cagle, Librn
Holdings: Uncat Mss
Notes: The Elisabeth Ball Collection consists of more than 7,000 books and many manuscripts from the late seventeenth to the early twentieth centuries. Strengths include Newbery and other early imprints, chapbooks, horn books, harlequinades, street cries, and miniature books.

PA —FREE LIBRARY OF PHILADELPHIA, Rare Book Dept, Logan Sq, Philadelphia, 19103. Marie E Korey, Rare Book Librn
Holdings: Vols 168 // Uncat
Notes: The Elizabeth Ball Collection of hornbooks, consisting mainly of 19th century facsimiles.

TX —ROSENBERG LIBRARY, Fox Rare Book Room, 2310 Sealy Ave, Galveston, 77550. Fernando Basilza, Rare Book Librn
Holdings: Vols (200) Cat Mss Pix
Notes: The Col Milo Pitcher Fox and Agnes Peel Fox Rare Book Room contains 2000 vols incunabula, first printings, and modern fine printing. Incl tablets, horn books, parchment material, illuminated books and mss fine printing (principally 15th-18th centuries), fine binding, fore-edge paintings, etc.

ON —TORONTO PUBLIC LIBRARY, Osborne Collection of Early Children's Books, 40 St George St, Toronto, M5S 2E4, Can. Margaret Crawford Maloney, Special Collections Librn
Holdings: Vols 21,500 Cat Mss Pix Slides
Notes: *Osborne Collection of Early Children's Books: A Catalogue,* 2 vols, published by the Toronto Public Library, 1958; 1975. The Osborne Collection is chiefly books published in England from the fourteenth century through 1910, with first or early editions in the original languages of books adopted by English-speaking children. The Lillian H Smith Collection comprises distinguished children's books in English published since 1910, selected for both literary and artistic qualities. The Canadiana Collection consists of 3500 children's books in English by Canadians, about Canada or published in Canada. Friends of the Osborne and Lillian H Smith Collections organized in 1966. Worldwide membership (over 600 in 1983). Publishes an annual gift-book for members (16 titles to date).

HORNE, MARILYN

CA —LONG BEACH PUBLIC LIBRARY, Performing Arts Dept, 101 Pacific Ave, Long Beach, 90802. Barbara Davis, Dept Librn
Holdings: Cat Pix Phonorecords Audiotapes
Notes: Recordings (65 discs; 7 audiotapes), programs and pictures (75) of Miss Horne, who attended Long Beach schools and graduated from Long Beach Polytechnic in 1955. Long Beach Public Library will be a depository for all the material written about Miss Horne, designated as the Marilyn Horne Archive Collection.

HORNER, GUSTAVUS R. B.

VA —UNIVERSITY OF VIRGINIA, Alderman Library, Manuscripts Dept, Charlottesville, 22901. Edmund Berkeley Jr, Cur
Holdings: Cat Mss Maps Pix
Notes: Personal and official papers of Sir Andrew Snape Hamond and Graham Eden Hamond concern British naval operations during the American Revolution and in the Mediterranean during the Napoleonic Wars. Paul P Hoffman (ed) *Guide to the Naval Papers of Sir Andrew Snape Hamond . . . and Sir Graham Eden Hamond . . .* (Charlottesville, Va: Microfilm Publications, University of Virginia, 1966). Papers of US and Confederate naval officer Samuel Barron; US fleet surgeon and Brooklyn Navy Yard surgeon Gustavus R B Horner; US naval surgeon John S Whittle on a scientific expedition to the Pacific, 1838-1841; and US naval officer William Conway Whittle on West Indies and Mediterranean cruises, 1823-1831.

HORNER, HARRY

CA —AMERICAN FILM INSTITUTE, Louis B Mayer Library, 2021 N Western Ave, PO Box 27999, Los Angeles, 90027. Anne G Schlosser, Dir
Notes: Harry Horner's a• direction materials, incl his personal location notebooks, original sketches and designs, set

HORNER, HARRY (cont.)

lists, continuity sketches, blue prints and other architectural plans.

HOROLOGY

CT —TRINITY COLLEGE LIBRARY, Watkinson Library, 300 Summit St, Hartford, 06106. Jeffrey Kaimowitz, Cur
Holdings: Cat
Notes: The Karl Vogel Collection of Horology.

IL —ADLER PLANETARIUM, History of Astronomy Collection, 1300 S Lake Shore Dr, Chicago, 60605. Roderick Webster, Cur; Marjorie Webster, Cur; Sara Schechner Genuth, Asst Cur
Holdings: Vols (430) Uncat Mss Maps Pix
Notes: Historical time-telling instruments. Price Photographic Archives (2800) containing prints of instruments. Incl (1000) scientific instruments. Noncirculating.
See also entries under Astronomy - History; Navigation - History; Surveying - History.

PA —FRANKLIN INSTITUTE LIBRARY, 20 & The Parkway, Philadelphia, 19103. Miriam Padusis, Dir; Charles Wilt, Readers Servs Librn
Holdings: Vols 2400 Cat Mss
Notes: One of the finest collections of horology in the world.

HOROSCOPE see Astrology

HOROVITZ, ISRAEL

NY —NEW YORK PUBLIC LIBRARY, Performing Arts Research Center, Billy Rose Theatre Collection, 111 Amsterdam Ave, New York, 10023. Dorothy L Swerdlove, Cur
Holdings: Uncat
Notes: Material incl one or more versions, usually annotated, of almost all play and film scripts to date. Most of the items are available for use, though uncataloged.

HORROR TALES

CA —OCCIDENTAL COLLEGE, Library, 1600 Campus Rd, Los Angeles, 90041. Michael C Sutherland, Special Collections Librn
Notes: Mystery and detective fiction. Samples of fantasy, gothic romance, horror and pulps.

CA —UNIVERSITY OF CALIFORNIA, RIVERSIDE, University Library, 4045 Canyon Crest Dr, Box 5900, Riverside, 92517.
Holdings: Vols (30,000)
Notes: The Eaton Collection of science fiction and fantasy materials, incl 5,600 pulp magazines; also horror, supernatural, and Gothic mystery fiction; boys' books; utopian and dystopian fiction, imaginary voyages, future war and lost race fiction; large holdings in French language science fiction and fantasy; critical and scholarly works pertaining to these genres; videotapes of science fiction/fantasy films and shooting scripts. Collection covers science fiction/fantasy literature from the 16th-17th centuries to the present. Strong individual author collections of Jules Verne, H Rider Haggard, H G Wells, Edgar Rice Burroughs, and Philip K Dick. For a complete description of the collection see: George Slusser, "The J Lloyd Eaton Collection," *Special Collections*, II, 1/2, 25-38 (1983), and*Dictionary Catalog of the J Lloyd Eaton Collection of Science Fiction and Fantasy* Literature (Boston: G K Hall) 1982.

IN —INDIANA UNIVERSITY, Lilly Library, Seventh St, Bloomington, 47405. William R Cagle, Librn
Holdings: Cat Mss
Notes: First editions of early and modern books plus some 18th and 19th century penney dreadfuls. Mss incl some original illustrations for 19th and 20th century books.

MI —MICHIGAN STATE UNIVERSITY, Libraries, Special Collections Div, East Lansing, 48824. Jannette Fiore, Librn
Notes: The Russel B Nye Popular Culture Collection in the Michigan State Univ Libraries incl over (45,000) items. Most of the collection is organized into 4 categories: comic art, popular fiction, popular information materials and materials relating to the popular performing arts. Popular fiction in the collection is organized into juvenile, detective-mystery, and science fiction, westerns and women's fiction. In addition, there is a sample collection of dime novels and story papers (ca 400 issues representing nearly 100 titles). Pulp magazines which fall into none of the separate categories are housed with the dime novels and story papers. Juvenile Fiction: ca 4000 vols. Emphasis is on juvenile series fiction of the 19th and 20th centuries, with nearly 200 girls and 300 boys series represented. 19th-century "Sunday School" books andboth fiction and non-fiction scouting books are also included. Western Fiction: An exceptionally fine institutional collection, with over 3000 novels (most published between 1900 and 1950), almost all hardbound and in dust jackets, and nearly 500 pulp magazine issues representing more than fifty titles. The most important pulp runs are Street and Smith's *Western Story* Magazine and Warner Publications's *Ranch* Romances. Women's Fiction: Over 3000 novels and ca 1000 issues of romance, confession and movie magazines and pulps from the 1920s through the 1970s. Most of the novels are in the romance category, with over 2000 Harlequin novels, a good representation of other modern best-selling romances, and several dozen titles from late 19th-century romance series. Science Fiction: ca 3000 books and periodicals. MSU is a depository for the Science Fiction Writersof America, which contributes review copies of new books. The bulk of the collection is periodicals, with 71 titles represented. Most issues come from the period from the late 1940s to the present. The collection subscribes to most major science fiction magazines and holds a fanzine collection which now numbers over 2500. Detective-Mystery Fiction: ca 3500 novels, in paper and hardback, and pulps representing 28 titles from 1920-1950. Complete runs of *The London Mystery* Magazine and *Ellery Queen's Mystery* Magazine are included, along with a large sample collection of the more sensational detective and crime fiction magazines from the 1930s through the present.

†NY —SYRACUSE UNIVERSITY LIBRARIES, E S Bird Library, George Arents Research Library, Rm 600, Syracuse, 13210. Mr Sidney Huttner, Librn
Notes: Samples or selections of cartoon art, comic strips, Disney, fantasy, fanzines, horror (Ackerman mss), mystery pulps, series books and westerns.

PA —TEMPLE UNIVERSITY LIBRARIES, Special Collections Dept, Rare Books & Mss Section, Philadelphia, 19122. Thomas M Whitehead, Cur
Holdings: Vols (200) Cat
Notes: Holdings include contemporary printed books, first and later editions, of 18th and early 19th century gothic fiction. Significant strength in Matthew Gregory "Monk" Lewis books.

RI —BROWN UNIVERSITY, John Hay Library, 20 Prospect St, Providence, 02912. Mark N Brown, Cur Mss
Holdings: Vols (600) Cat Mss Pix Phonorecords Audiotpes
Notes: Howard Phillips Lovecraft Collection of books amateur and professional magazines, plus mss/typescripts by and about Howard Phillips Lovecraft, incl first and subsequent editions of Lovecraft's work in 12 languages; complete runs of *Weird Tales, Marvel Tales, The Californian, Driftwind, Rainbow, Leaves* and *Amateur Fantasy Correspondent* plus scattered issues of 50 amateur and professional magazines; 1500 letters written by Lovecraft to more than 200 correspondents, 270 mss/typescripts of his essays, fiction and poetry plus over 3000 mss/typescripts of essays, fiction, letters, and poetry written by his correspondents. Photocopying of mss is restricted.

WI —UNIVERSITY OF WISCONSIN, LA CROSSE, Murphy Library, 1631 Pine St, La Crosse, 54601. Edwin L Hill, Special Collections Librn
Holdings: Vols 1000 Cat
Notes: The Paul W Skeeters Collection of science fiction, fantasy, and horror literature. Complements the library's complete collection of Arkham House books, which contains many titles autographed by August Derleth, and H P Lovecraft's complete fiction and poetic works.

†MB —UNIVERSITY OF WINNIPEG, Library, 515 Portage Avenue, Winnipeg, R3B 2E9, Can. Raymond C Wright, Librn
Notes: Edgar Rice Burroughs special collection. Extensive collection of books on film. Sample Gothic, Romance and Horror collections.

HORSE see Horses

HORSE BREEDING

IA —IOWA STATE UNIVERSITY, Library, Ames, 50011. Warren B Kuhn, Dean of Library Services
Holdings: Cat
Notes: Incl horse husbandry and horsemanship. Substantial serial holdings.

KY —KEENELAND LIBRARY, Keeneland Race Course, PO Box 1690, Lexington, 40592. Doris J Waren, Librn
Holdings: Vols 8000 Cat Mss Maps Pix Slides Microforms
Notes: Thoroughbred horse breeding and racing, horse sports. Incl large photographic negative collection covering American racing 1900-1960. Prints available at nominal cost for publication purposes only. No lending. Amelia K Buckley. *The Keeneland Association Library: a Guide to the* Collection. Lexington: University Press of Kentucky, 1958.

MD —PRINCE GEORGE'S COUNTY MEMORIAL LIBRARY SYSTEM, Bowie Branch Library, Selima Room, 15210 Annapolis Rd, Bowie, 20715. Suzan H Stephenson, Librn
Holdings: Vols (3000) Cat Maps Pix
Notes: General subject is horses with emphasis on horse-racing and breeding particularly as it pertains to Maryland.

NY —NEW YORK PUBLIC LIBRARY, Research Libraries, General Research Division, Fifth Ave & 42 St, New York, 10018. Rodney Phillips, Chief
Holdings: Vols (2,225,000) Cat Maps Pix Microforms
Budget: ($775,718)

NY —NATIONAL MUSEUM OF RACING, The Thoroughbred Racing Hall of Fame, Union Ave, Saratoga Springs, 12866. Elaine E Mann, Dir
Notes: Founded in 1950 to collect materials on the origin, history, and development of breeding and racing thoroughbred horses.

WV —SALEM COLLEGE, Library, Salem, 26426. Myron J Smith, Jr, Librn
Notes: Collection supports "the most complete equestrian studies program available anywhere". *Myron J Smith, Equestrian Studies:* the Salem College [Bibliographical] Guide to Sources in English, 1950-1980. Metuchen, NJ: Scarecrow Press, 1981; 4645 entries.

HORSE RACING

CT —YALE UNIVERSITY, Box 1603A, Yale Station, New Haven, 06520.

IL —DE PAUL UNIVERSITY, Library, 2323 N Seminary, Chicago, 60614. Kathryn De Graff, Special Collections Librn
Holdings: Vols (900) // Uncat
Notes: The Anita Peabody Sports Collection of approx 900 volumes, incl about 250 periodical volumes, covering such topics as foxhunting, gambling, horse racing, and breeding, along with rule books and song books. Materials cover the middle to late 19th century. A complete run of *The Sporting Magazine,* begun in 1792, is also part of the collection. In addition, collection of ca 1000 vols on British field sports. Also, 20 hand-colored sets of prints by Edward Troye (1808-1874) on American thoroughbred horses.

HORSE RACING (cont.)

KY —KEENELAND LIBRARY, Keeneland Race Course, PO Box 1690, Lexington, 40592. Doris J Waren, Librn
Holdings: Vols 8000 Cat Mss Maps Pix Slides Microforms
Notes: Thoroughbred horse breeding and racing, horse sports. Incl large photographic negative collection covering American racing 1900-1960. Prints available at nominal cost for publication purposes only. No lending. Amelia K Buckley. *The Keeneland Association Library: a Guide to the* Collection. Lexington: University Press of Kentucky, 1958.

KY —KENTUCKY DERBY MUSEUM, 700 Central Ave, Louisville, 40208. William W Ray, Exec Dir
Notes: Books, programs, photographs, Archival materials relating to the Kentucky Derby and International Thoroughbred Racing.

MD —PRINCE GEORGE'S COUNTY MEMORIAL LIBRARY SYSTEM, Bowie Branch Library, Selima Room, 15210 Annapolis Rd, Bowie, 20715. Suzan H Stephenson, Librn
Holdings: Vols (3000) Cat Maps Pix
Notes: General subject is horses with emphasis on horse-racing and breeding particularly as it pertains to Maryland.

NY —MERCY COLLEGE LIBRARY, Dobbs Ferry, 10522. Larry Earle Bone, Dir
Holdings: Vols (406) Cat Pix
Notes: General collection of American and British books and periodicals on horses, hounds and hunting, with special emphasis on the Millbrook Hunt. 15 percent of the collection is rare books and periodicals. Rare photographs and paintings also incl. Many of the books are from the private libraries of members of the Millbrook Hunt. Collection formerly at Bennett College, Millbrook, New York.

NY —NATIONAL MUSEUM OF RACING, The Thoroughbred Racing Hall of Fame, Union Ave, Saratoga Springs, 12866. Elaine E Mann, Dir

PA —UNIVERSITY OF PENNSYLVANIA, Jean Austin duPont Libary, New Bolton Center, 382 W Street Rd, Kennett Square, 19348. Alice K Holton, Librn
Holdings: Vols (1200) // Cat Mss Pix
Notes: The Fairman Rogers Library of Horsemanship. Collection covers 16th-20th centuries. There is a seperate catalog; also, Claire G Fox, *The Fairman Rogers Collection on the Horse and Equitation* (Medical Documentation Service, College of Physicians and Surgeons of Philadelphia, 1975) Noncirculating.

VA —NATIONAL SPORTING LIBRARY, Chronicle of the Horse Bldg Publishing Offices, PO Box 1335, Middleburg, 22117. Judith Ozment, Librn
Holdings: Vols (11,000) Cat Mss Pix
Notes: A research center for turf and field sports, their history and social significance.

WV —SALEM COLLEGE, Library, Salem, 26426. Myron J Smith, Jr, Librn
Notes: Collection supports "the most complete equestrian studies program available anywhere". *Myron J Smith, Equestrian Studies:* the Salem College [Bibliographical] Guide to Sources in English, 1950-1980. Metuchen, NJ: Scarecrow Press, 1981; 4645 entries.

ON —CANADIAN TROTTING ASSOCIATION, Standardbred Canada Library, 233 Evans Ave, Toronto, M8Z 1J6, Can. David Hornell, Librn; Margaret Neal, Coordinator
Notes: Books, magazines, photographs, microfilm, audiotapes, videotapes, slides, 16mm films, etc relating to harness racing in Canada.

HORSE RAILROADS see Street Railroads

HORSEMANSHIP

†CT —UNIVERSITY OF CONNECTICUT LIBRARY, Special Collections Dept, Storrs, 06268. Richard H Schimmelpfeng, Dir of Special Collections

IA —IOWA STATE UNIVERSITY, Library, Ames, 50011. Warren B Kuhn, Dean of Library Services
Holdings: Cat
Notes: Incl horse husbandry and horsemanship. Substantial serial holdings.

KY —KEENELAND LIBRARY, Keeneland Race Course, PO Box 1690, Lexington, 40592. Doris J Waren, Librn
Holdings: Vols 8000 Cat Mss Maps Pix Slides Microforms
Notes: Thoroughbred horse breeding and racing, horse sports. Incl large photographic negative collection covering American racing 1900-1960. Prints available at nominal cost for publication purposes only. No lending. Amelia K Buckley. *The Keeneland Association Library: a Guide to the* Collection. Lexington: University Press of Kentucky, 1958.

NY —RACQUET & TENNIS CLUB, Library, 370 Park Ave, New York, 10022. Gerald Belliveau, Jr, Librn
Holdings: Vols (17,500) Cat
Budget: ($6000)
Notes: Specializes in court tennis, lawn tennis, early American sport. See *Dictionary Catalogue of the Library of Sports in the Racquet and Tennis Club* (Boston: G K Hall, 1971). Also, Robert W Henderson, *Early American Sport,* 3rd ed. (Cranbury, NJ: Fairleigh Dickinson University Press, 1977).

PA —UNIVERSITY OF PENNSYLVANIA, Jean Austin duPont Libary, New Bolton Center, 382 W Street Rd, Kennett Square, 19348. Alice K Holton, Librn
Holdings: Vols (1200) // Cat Mss Pix
Notes: The Fairman Rogers Library of Horsemanship. Collection covers 16th-20th centuries. There is a separate catalog; also, Claire G Fox, *The Fairman Rogers Collection on the Horse and Equitation* (Medical Documentatin Service, College of Physicians and Surgeons of Philadelphia, 1975). Noncirculating.

WV —SALEM COLLEGE, Library, Salem, 26426. Myron J Smith, Jr, Librn
Notes: Collection supports "the most complete equestrian studies program available anywhere". *Myron J Smith, Equestrian Studies:* the Salem College [Bibliographical] Guide to Sources in English, 1950-1980. Metuchen, NJ: Scarecrow Press, 1981; 4645 entries.

HORSES

CA —CALIFORNIA STATE POLYTECHNIC UNIVERSITY, POMONA, University Library, 3801 W Temple Ave, Pomona, 91768. Harold Schleiser, Actg Dir
Holdings: Vols (2000) Cat Mss Pix Filmstrips
Notes: Among the finest Arabian horse collections in the world. Collector's items and rare books are featured, in addition to the working materials used in tracing pedigrees or in research specific problems, such as immunodeficiency disease which is endemic to the Arab breed. The collection is made available, upon request, to persons outside the academic community. Located on the site of the W. K. Kellogg Arabian Horse Ranch founded in 1926. Collection also incl. the Ranch papers and copies of the papers of Kellogg dating from his purchase of the stock herd from Lady Judith Wentworth of Crabbet stud. Arabia of the 18th and 19th centuries is also featured in the collection. Mainly in books of European and American travelers who incl. descriptions of the "horse of the desert" in their writings. Official studbooks from 22 countries, numerous private studbooks, histories of the Arabian Horse, and backfiles of serial publications are also important segments of the collection. Maintain a current desiderata list available on request. Interested in exchange programs with other libraries. Information or list of holdings is available.

CT —TRINITY COLLEGE LIBRARY, 300 Summit St, Hartford, 06106. Ralph S Emerick, Librn

CT —YALE UNIVERSITY, Box 1603A, Yale Station, New Haven, 06520.

†CT —UNIVERSITY OF CONNECTICUT LIBRARY, Special Collections Dept, Storrs, 06268. Richard H Schimmelpfeng, Dir of Special Collections

IL —DE PAUL UNIVERSITY, Library, 2323 N Seminary, Chicago, 60614. Kathryn De Graff, Special Collections Librn
Notes: About 1000 vols on British field sports. Also, 20 hand-colored sets of prints by Edward Troye (1808-1874) of American thoroughbred horses.

IA —IOWA STATE UNIVERSITY, Library, Ames, 50011. Warren B Kuhn, Dean of Library Services
Holdings: Cat
Notes: Incl horse husbandry and horsemanship. Substantial serial holdings.

MD —PRINCE GEORGE'S COUNTY MEMORIAL LIBRARY SYSTEM, Bowie Branch Library, Selima Room, 15210 Annapolis Rd, Bowie, 20715. Suzan H Stephenson, Librn
Holdings: Vols (3000) Cat Maps Pix
Notes: General subject is horses with emphasis on horse-racing and breeding particularly as it pertains to Maryland.

MI —MICHIGAN STATE UNIVERSITY, Science Library, East Lansing, 48824. Carole S Armstrong, Head
Holdings: Vols 600 Cat

NE —UNIVERSITY OF NEBRASKA-LINCOLN, Don L Love Library, University Archives and Special Collections, Lincoln, 68588. Joseph G Svoboda, University Archivist
Holdings: Pix Slides
Notes: R D Warden Collection of Charles Marion Russell. "Largest private collection of literature on Russell, 'The Cowboy Artist'." 7000 items, incl first editions of every book and pamphlet by Russell and over 1000 periodicals appearances of his art; 900 color prints; 142 drawings; color slides; scrapbooks about Russell and his family, from 1889.

NY —MERCY COLLEGE LIBRARY, Dobbs Ferry, 10522. Larry Earle Bone, Dir
Holdings: Vols (406) Cat Pix
Notes: General collection of American and British books and periodicals on horses, hounds and hunting, with special emphasis on the Millbrook Hunt. 15 percent of the collection is rare books and periodicals. Rare photographs and paintings also incl. Many of the books are from the private libraries of members of the Millbrook Hunt. Collection formerly at Bennett College, Millbrook, New York.

NY —HALL OF FAME OF THE TROTTER, Library, 240 Main St, Goshen, 10924. Philip Pines, Dir
Holdings: Vols 2000 Cat Mss Pix Slides
Notes: Harness horses (trotters and pacers). Incl history of harness racing. Assembling videotape collection of famous races, interviews with prominent horsemen, film-to-tape. Not cataloged as yet.

NY —NEW YORK PUBLIC LIBRARY, Research Libraries, General Research Division, Fifth Ave & 42 St, New York, 10018. Rodney Phillips, Chief
Holdings: Vols (2,225,000) Cat Maps Pix Microforms
Budget: ($775,718)

NY —RACQUET & TENNIS CLUB, Library, 370 Park Ave, New York, 10022. Gerald Belliveau, Jr, Librn
Holdings: Vols (17,500) Cat
Budget: ($6000)
Notes: Specializes in court tennis, lawn tennis, early American sport. See *Dictionary*

HORSES (cont.)

Catalogue of the Library of Sports in the Racquet and Tennis Club (Boston: G K Hall, 1971). Also, Robert W Henderson, *Early American Sport,* 3rd ed. (Cranbury, NJ: Fairleigh Dickinson University Press, 1977).

NY —NATIONAL MUSEUM OF RACING, The Thoroughbred Racing Hall of Fame, Union Ave, Saratoga Springs, 12866. Elaine E Mann, Dir
Notes: Founded in 1950 to collect materials on the origin, history, and development of breeding and racing thoroughbred horses.

PA —UNIVERSITY OF PENNSYLVANIA, Jean Austin duPont Libary, New Bolton Center, 382 W Street Rd, Kennett Square, 19348. Alice K Holton, Librn
Holdings: Vols (1200) // Cat Mss Pix
Notes: The Fairman Rogers Library of Horsemanship. Collection covers 16th-20th centuries. There is a separate catalog; also, Claire G Fox, *The Fairman Rogers Collection on the Horse and Equitation* (Medical Documentation Service, College of Physicians and Surgeons of Philadelphia, 1975). Noncirculating.

VA —NATIONAL SPORTING LIBRARY, Chronicle of the Horse Bldg Publishing Offices, PO Box 1335, Middleburg, 22117. Judith Ozment, Librn
Holdings: Vols (11,000) Cat Mss Pix
Notes: A research center for turf and fields sports, their history and social significance.

†WA —WASHINGTON STATE UNIVERSITY, Library, Manuscripts, Archives & Special Collections, Pullman, 99164. John F Guido, Head
Holdings: Cat Mss Maps Pix
Notes: The Carl Parcher Russell papers, a vast resource (24,916 items; 45 linear feet) on American Indian and Western pioneer activities and artifacts. Much on the fur trade; pioneer life; mountain men and trapping; wildlife; primitive life in detail. Also thc National Park Service, parks, monuments, etc. Described in *Carl Parcher Russell: An Indexed Register of His Scholarly and Professional papers, 1920-1967, in the Washington State University* Library (Pullman, 1970), 149 pp.

WV —SALEM COLLEGE, Library, Salem, 26426. Myron J Smith, Jr, Librn
Notes: Collection supports "the most complete equestrian studies program available anywhere". *Myron J Smith, Equestrian Studies:* the Salem College [Bibliographical] Guide to Sources in English, 1950-1980. Metuchen, NJ: Scarecrow Press, 1981; 4645 entries.

ON —CANADIAN TROTTING ASSOCIATION, Standardbred Canada Library, 233 Evans Ave, Toronto, M8Z 1J6, Can. David Hornell, Librn; Margaret Neal, Coordinator
Notes: Books, magazines, photographs, microfilm, audiotapes, videotapes, slides, 16mm films, etc relating to harness racing in Canada.

HORSES—DAM-BOOKS see Horses—Stud-Books

HORSES—STUD-BOOKS

ON —CANADIAN TROTTING ASSOCIATION, Standardbred Canada Library, 233 Evans Ave, Toronto, M8Z 1J6, Can. David Hornell, Librn; Margaret Neal, Coordinator
Notes: Books, magazines, photographs, microfilm, audiotapes, videotapes, slides, 16mm films, etc relating to harness racing in Canada.

HORSES, ARABIAN see Arabian Horses

HORSKY, CHARLES

†MA —JOHN F KENNEDY LIBRARY, Columbia Point, Boston, 02125. Dan H Fenn Jr, Dir
Notes: The White House staff files of Charles Horsky, advisor to President Kennedy for National Capitol Affairs, 1961-1965; the personal papers of Louis Brownlow, journalist and public administrator, relating to the District of Columbia, 1915-1920; and records of the District of Columbia, 1961-1963. 14 linear ft of mss Holdings are described in "Historical Materials in the John F Kennedy Library". Copies may be obtained by writing the Research Archivist.

HORST, LOUIS, 1884-1964

NY —NEW YORK PUBLIC LIBRARY, Performing Arts Research Center, Dance Collection, 111 Amsterdam Ave, New York, 10023. Genevieve Oswald, Cur
Notes: Extensive biographical and visual material, relating to his association as pianist-accompanist with Denishawn, Martha Graham, Agnes De Mille, Ruth Page, and many other modern dance artists. Includes correspondence, notebooks, scrapbooks, programs and clippings, photographs, musical scores, and motion pictures.

HORTICULTURE

AL —BIRMINGHAM BOTANICAL GARDENS, Horace Hammond Memorial Library, 2612 Lane Park Road, Birmingham, 35223. Ida Burns, Librn
Holdings: Vols 2800 Cat Pix Films Slides VF
See also entries under Botany; Flower Arrangement; Landscape-Architecture.

AZ —DESERT BOTANICAL GARDEN, Richter Memorial Library, 1201 North Galvin Pkwy, Phoenix, 85008. J B Cole, Librn
Holdings: Vols (4000)
Notes: Emphasis on desert and arid regions ecology and horticulture.

CA —LOS ANGELES STATE & COUNTY ARBORETUM, Plant Science Library, 301 N Baldwin Ave, Arcadia, 91006. Joan DeFato, Librn
Holdings: Vols (24,000) Cat 16mm Films
Budget: ($6000)
Notes: Emphasis on woody plants, particularly of Australia and South Africa. Botany is weighted toward taxonomy rather than plant physiology.

CA —UNIVERSITY OF CALIFORNIA, BERKELEY, Environmental Design Library, (The General Library), 210 Wurster Hall, Berkeley, 94720. Arthur B Waugh, Head
Holdings: Vols (9000) Cat
Budget: ($4900)
Notes: Research collection emphasizing the following areas: Park and garden design; site planning; spatial planning; professional practice. Lesser emphasis on horticulture. The Library also includes the Beatrix Farrand Collection of rare books in the field of landscape architecture.

CA —RANCHO SANTA ANA BOTANIC GARDEN LIBRARY, 1500 N College Ave, Claremont, 91711. Beatrice M Beck, Librn
Holdings: Vols 30,000 Cat Maps Microforms
Notes: Incl emphasis on California flora, floras of the world, evolutionary biology and ethnobotany.

CA —UNIVERSITY OF CALIFORNIA, DAVIS, Shields Library, Dept of Special Collections, Davis, 95616. Donald Kunitz, Head; C Danial Elliott, Asst Head
Holdings: Cat Mss Pix
Notes: The E J Wickson Collection contains correspondence between Burbanks and E J Wickson, regarding Burbanks's developments and Wickson's writing about him; copies of Burbank's scrapbook's related ephemera. The Nursery Catalog Collection, with catalogs from both foreign and domestic seed and plant dealers, spans the late 19th and 20th centuries. Records, photographs, seed posters, and scrapbooks of the Ferry-Morse Company document the success of this well-known nursery. 12,000 items.

CA —UNIVERSITY OF CALIFORNIA, IRVINE, Library, Irvine, 92664. Roger Berry, Dept Head
Notes: The Emma D Menninger extensive collection of 19th and 20th century information on horticulture, with special emphasis on orchids.

CA —UNIVERSITY OF CALIFORNIA, LOS ANGELES, Biomedical Library, Center for Health Sciences, Los Angeles, 90024. Louise Darling, Biomedical Librn

CA —CONTRA COSTA COUNTY LIBRARY, 1750 Oak Park Blvd, Pleasant Hill, 94523. Barbara Potter, Librn
Holdings: Vols (18,000)

CA —CALIFORNIA STATE POLYTECHNIC UNIVERSITY, POMONA, University Library, 3801 W Temple Ave, Pomona, 91768. Harold Schleiser, Actg Dir
Notes: General reference materials on agricultural business management, agricultural engineering, animal science, horticulture and plant and soil science.

†CA —ZOOLOGICAL SOCIETY OF SAN DIEGO, Ernst Schwarz Library, San Diego Zoo, Box 551, San Diego, 92112.

CA —STRYBING ARBORETUM SOCIETY, Golden Gate Park Library, Jane Gates, Librn, 9th Ave at Lincoln Way, San Francisco, 94122.
Holdings: Vols (10,000)

CA —CALIFORNIA POLYTECHNIC STATE UNIVERSITY LIBRARY, Special Collections and University Archives, San Luis Obispo, 93407. Nancy E Loe, Head Librn
Holdings: Mss
Notes: The Barton Collection incl the personal and professional papers of Arthur G Barton, a noted Southern California landscape architect, incl his office files, bids, and drawings and designs (collection in rough sorting stage). 55,000 pieces of ms material.

†CA —HUNTINGTON BOTANICAL GARDENS LIBRARY, 1151 Oxford Rd, San Marino, 91108. Ann Ravenscroft, Secretary
Notes: Emphases on history of botanical science; papers and notes of American botanists and naturalists of The West; botanical illustration, etc. Subtropical horticulture, incl cacti and succulents of Australia, South Africa, and Mexico.

CA —SANTA BARBARA BOTANIC GARDEN, Library, 1212 Mission Canyon Rd, Santa Barbara, 93105. Margaret Connors, Librn
Holdings: Vols 5500 Cat Mss Maps Slides
Notes: Botany and horticulture with emphasis on California native flora. Restricted to use by the staff and members of the Garden; limited use by public is permitted. Incl seed catalogs.

CO —HORTICULTURAL ART SOCIETY OF COLORADO SPRINGS, Library, Orchard House, 3202 Chambers Way, Colorado Springs, 80904. Ernestine H Fagan, Librn
Holdings: Vols (950)
Notes: Horticulture of the Pikes Peak Region.

CO —DENVER BOTANIC GARDENS, Helen Fowler Library, 909 York St, Denver, 80206. Solange G Gignac, Librn
Holdings: Vols (13,500)
Budget: ($15,000)

DE —UNIVERSITY OF DELAWARE, Agriculture Library, 2 Townsend Hall, Newark, 19717. Frederick Getze, Assoc Librn
Holdings: Vols (32,500) Cat Pix Microforms
Notes: Strong in entomology and ornamental horticulture. Extensive collection of state agriculture documents for each US state and Puerto Rico. Library subscribes to 600 serials (English and foreign).

DE —UNIVERSITY OF DELAWARE, Hugh M Morris Library, S College Ave, Newark, 19711. T Stuart Dick, Special Collections
Holdings: Cat Mss Pix
Notes: Unidel History of Horticulture and Landscape Architecture Collection. Focus is on the origins of horticulture and landscape architecture in America. Particularly strong in early American, English and continental works. Landscape architecture is represented by of the great English and American works as well as the French and Italian ones. There is a small but important group of American works on botanic medicine. Some of the great herbals are also present as well as a number of early American periodicals.

DE —WILMINGTON GARDEN CENTER LIBRARY, 503 Market Street Mall,

HORTICULTURE (cont.)

Wilmington, 19801. Bonnie J Swan Day, Admin Asst; Karen Bidus, Librn
Holdings: Vols (1500)
Notes: Library open to the public, only circulates to members.

DC —SMITHSONIAN INSTITUTION LIBRARIES, Botany Branch, Washington, 20560. Ruth Schallert, Branch Librn
Notes: Taxonomic botany; with the J D Smith Collection of general botany, the Dawson Collection on algae, and the Hitchcock-Chase Collection on grasses.

DC —US NATIONAL ARBORETUM, Library, 3501 New York Ave NE, Washington, 20002. Judi Ho, Librn
Holdings: Vols (6000) Cat Microforms
Notes: Separate catalog. Botany and horticulture, especially of woody plants. Library is a branch of the National Agricultural Library. No photocopying.

FL —UNIVERSITY OF FLORIDA, Institute of Food & Agricultural Sciences, Hume Library, Gainesville, 32611. Albert C Strickland, Librn
Holdings: Vols (135,000) Cat Mss Microforms
Notes: Including journals and monographs, this collection is a general agricultural one. The emphasis is on tropical agriculture, especially Latin America. Entomology is very strong. The library offers on-line information retrieval using Lockheed and SDC data bases.

GA —CHEROKEE GARDEN LIBRARY, 3101 Andrews Dr NW, Atlanta, 30305. Sally Bruce McClatchey, Librn
Holdings: Vols 2700
Notes: Southern history and horticulture. Emphasis on the historical development of American horticulture, 1634 to 1900.

GA —FERNBANK SCIENCE CENTER LIBRARY, 156 Heaton Park Dr NE, Atlanta, 30307. Mary Larsen, Librn; Janice MacLeod, Bibliographic Instructor
Holdings: Vols (12,000) Cat Maps Pix Slides Microforms
Budget: ($35,000)
Notes: Science with emphasis on astronomy, biology, outdoor education. Incl 5500 color slides; periodicals on microfilm.

IL —CHICAGO BOTANIC GARDEN LIBRARY, PO Box 400, Glencoe, 60022. Virginia Henrichs, Librn
Holdings: Vols 6000

IL —MORTON ARBORETUM, Sterling Morton Library, Lisle, 60532. Ian MacPhail, Librn
Holdings: Vols (20,000) Cat Maps Pix
Budget: ($10,000)
Notes: The library is especially concerned with the literature of woody plants (trees and shrubs) of north temperate zones but has substantial holdings in the taxonomy and systematics of plants in general, both wild and cultivated, flora of different parts of the world, and a growing collection on plant monographs. Also about 2000 pictures. Described in *The Morton Arboretum* Quarterly, vol 9, no 4 (Winter 1973), pp 56-61.

†IL —UNIVERSITY OF ILLINOIS, URBANA/CHAMPAIGN, Agricultural Library, 226 Mumford Hall, 1301 W Gregory Dr, Urbana, 61801.

IN —PURDUE UNIVERSITY LIBRARIES, Life Sciences Library, Lilly Hall of Life Sciences, West Lafayette, 47907. Martha J Bailey, Librn
Holdings: Vols (73,404) Cat Microforms
Budget: ($223,445)
Notes: Incl materials in agronomy, animal sciences, botany, entomology, forestry, horticulture, biological sciences and agricultural engineering.

IA —IOWA STATE UNIVERSITY, Library, Ames, 50011. Warren B Kuhn, Dean of Library Services
Holdings: Cat
Notes: Extensive serial holdings.

IA —BICKELHAUPT ARBORETUM FREE LENDING LIBRARY, 340 S Fourteenth St, Clinton, 52732. Francie B Hill, Librn
Notes: Strong on indoor plants, horticulture, ecology, energy conservation, plant entomology and pathology, urban tree planting; also curriculum materials. Over 3000 slides available for lending.

KY —UNIVERSITY OF KENTUCKY, Agricultural Library, Agricultural Science Center North, Lexington, 40506. Antoinette Paris Powell, Librn
Holdings: Vols (90,000) Cat Microforms
Budget: ($110,385)

MA —MASSACHUSETTS HORTICULTURAL SOCIETY, 300 Massachusetts Ave, Boston, 02115. Becky Ellis, Librn
Holdings: Vols (37,000)
Notes: Garden history, pomology, flora, landscape design. Print collection of many centuries; nursery catalogues from the mid-18th century. In storage, remodeling, will be available in about a year. Open to the public.

MA —HARVARD UNIVERSITY LIBRARY, Gray Herbarium Library, 22 Divinity Ave, Cambridge, 02138. Barbara A Callahan, Librn
Holdings: Vols (61,445) Cat Mss Maps Pix Microforms
Notes: Downs 2325. Research in evolutionary and systematic botany. Arnold Arboretum and Gray Herbarium Libraries hold one of the nation's largest collections (149,000 items).

MA —NEW ENGLAND WILD FLOWER SOCIETY, INC, Lawrence Newcomb Library, Hemenway Rd, Framingham, 01701. Mary M Walker, Librn
Holdings: Vols (2500)
Budget: ($1000)
Notes: Incl 15,000 slides (35mm) and 4 vertical files.

MA —HARVARD UNIVERSITY, Arnold Arboretum, Horticultural Library, The Arborway, Jamaica Plain, 02130.
Holdings: Vols Pix Slides
Notes: Arnold Arboretum and Gray Herbarium Libraries hold one of the nation's largest collections (149,000 items).

MI —UNIVERSITY OF MICHIGAN, Matthaei Botanical Gardens, 1800 N Dixboro Rd, Ann Arbor, 48105. Annie Hannan, Collections Botanist
Holdings: Vols (1750)
Notes: Computer inventory of indoor collections. 30 scientific (botanical) journals.

MN —UNIVERSITY OF MINNESOTA, Landscape Arboretum, Andersen Horticultural Library, 3675 Arboretum Drive, Box 39, Chanhassen, 55317. June Rogier, Head
Holdings: Vols (8000)

MO —MISSOURI BOTANICAL GARDEN LIBRARY, PO Box 299, Saint Louis, 63166. M R Crosby, Dir of Research
Holdings: Vols 82,000 Cat Pix Microforms
Notes: Incl 80,000 pamphlets and reprints and George Engelmann's botanical notebooks and correspondence, incl 6000 letters.

NH —STRAWBERY BANKE, Thayer Cumings Historical Reference Library, Portsmouth, 03801. Nicole R Osborn, Librn
Notes: The Library is a small, highly specialized library with holdings in American art, architecture and decorative arts. The collection is especially strong in the American decorative arts, with additional concentration in European decorative arts. In addition, the collection contains books on American painting, American architecture, archaeology, technology, maritime history and boatbuilding, landscape gardening and design, as well as books on local and regional history and social and material culture of the 17th-19th centuries. Collection of mss microfilm and documents is related to important properties and personages of Portsmouth and the surrounding area.

NY —NEW YORK BOTANICAL GARDEN LIBRARY, Bronx, 10458. Charles R Long, Asst Vice Pres & Dir
Holdings: Vols 45,000 Cat Mss Pix Slides Microforms VF
Budget: ($356,000)
Notes: One of the largest botanical collections in the world. Over 900,000 items. Covers botany (150,000 vols), botanists (3000), horticulture (45,000) plant diseases (25,000), plant physiology (15,000), history of botany (1500), conservation of natural resources (15,000), gardening (13,000), paleobotany (7000), ecology (20,000), forestry (5000) medical botany (3000), agriculture (9000) and biology (20,000). Reference library; materials do not circulate, except for member circulating collection (1200) and standard inter-library loan. About 5000 vols uncataloged. Incl art, books, serials, pamphlets, archives and manuscripts, vertical files, microfiche and microfilm, nursery and seed catalogs, photographs, paintings, prints, drawings and engravings. Covers all areas of botanical sciences. This is an OCLC library with fullresource services incl photocopying and photography.

NY —BROOKLYN BOTANIC GARDEN, 1000 Washington Ave, Brooklyn, 11225. Marie Giasi, Librn
Notes: A reference library of approx 55,000 vols of horticultural and botanical interest. Also, all publications of the Garden, incl annual reports, quarterly magazine "Plants & Gardens," pamphlets, newsletters, contributions and handbook series.

NY —PLANTING FIELDS ARBORETUM HORTICULTURAL LIBRARY, Oyster Bay, 11771. Elizabeth K Reilley, Dir; Helen S Moskowitz, Librn
Holdings: Vols 4500
Notes: Incl periodicals and vertical file material.

NY —MONROE COUNTY PARKS ARBORETUM, Library, 375 Westfall Road, Rochester, 14620. Mr Kelly, Special Collections Librn
Holdings: Vols (1000)

NY —UNIVERSITY OF ROCHESTER, Rush Rhees Library, Department of Rare Books and Special Collections, Rochester, 14627. Peter Dzwonkoski, Librn
Holdings: Vols 1000 // Cat Mss
Notes: Ellwanger and Barry Horticultural Library: American and European books and pomological journals of the 19th century. Also have records of the Ellwanger and Barry Nursery of Rochester, NY.

†NC —UNIVERSITY OF NORTH CAROLINA, CHAPEL HILL, Department of Botany Library, 301 Coker Hall 010-A, Chapel Hill, 27514. William R Burk, Botany Librn
Notes: The mycology collection incl some 6000 pamphlets. It contains papers of the following scientists: William C Coker, John N Couch, Lindsay F Olive, mycologists; also, Victor A Greulach, plant pathologist. The mycology catalog is in preparation (1983), and will provide author, title, and subject access.

OH —PUBLIC LIBRARY OF CINCINNATI & HAMILTON COUNTY, Science & Technology Dept, 800 Vine St, Cincinnati, 45202. Rosemary Gaiser, Head
Holdings: Vols (250,000) Cat
Notes: Pure and applied science. Incl over 1600 periodicals and serial titles and more than 100 abstracting and indexing services in major fields of science and technology.

OH —GARDEN CENTER OF GREATER CLEVELAND, Eleanor Squire Library, 11030 East Blvd, Cleveland, 44106. Richard T Isaacson, Librn
Holdings: Vols 11,000 Cat Pix Slides
Budget: $5000
Notes: The Warren C Corning Collection of Horticultural Classics. The Flowering Plant Index of Illustration and Information.

OH —KINGWOOD CENTER, Library, 900 Park Ave W, Mansfield, 44906. Timothy Gardner, Horticulturist
Holdings: Vols 8500 Cat Slides
Budget: $1500

OH —MASSILLON PUBLIC LIBRARY, 208 Lincoln Way E, Massillon, 44646. Camille Leslie, Dir
Holdings: Vols 379 Cat

OH —HOLDEN ARBORETUM, Warren H Corning Library, 9500 Sperry Rd, Mentor, 44060. Paul C Spector, Dir of Education
Holdings: Vols (5500) // Cat
Notes: Extensive collection of horticultural classics, floras, herbals and monographs prior to 1850. Primarily European works.

OH —WARREN H CORNING LIBRARY, 9500 Sperry Rd, Mentor, 44060. Paul C

HORTICULTURE (cont.)

Spector, Dir of Education
Holdings: Vols (5400) Cat VF
Notes: 1500 vols of Warren H Corning Horticulture Classics. Also 80 periodicals and 10 vertical files.

OH —THE DAWES ARBORETUM LIBRARY, 7770 Jacksontown Rd SE, Newark, 43055. Alan D Cook, Senior Horticulturist
Holdings: Vols 5000

PA —TEMPLE UNIVERSITY, Ambler Campus Library, Meetinghouse Road, Ambler, 19002. Esther G Bloomsburgh, Librn
Notes: Rare herbals are housed in Special Collections, Paley Library, Temple University (Thomas Whitehead, Curator). Incl 2500 items.

PA —DELAWARE VALLEY COLLEGE, Joseph Krauskopf Library, Doylestown, 18901. Constance Shook, Dir

PA —LONGWOOD GARDENS, INC, Library, Kennett Square, 19348. Enola Jane N Teeter, Librn

PA —PENNSYLVANIA HORTICULTURAL SOCIETY, Library, 325 Walnut St, Philadelphia, 19106. Mary Lou Wolfe, Librn
Holdings: Vols (200) Cat Pix Slides
Notes: Books about horticulture published by Pennsylvanians, about Pennsylvania, or which bear a Philadelphia imprint. Descriptive catalog which highlights the collection: *From Seed to Flower: Philadelphia 1681-1876; A Horticultural Point of View* (Philadelphia: Pennsylvania Horticultural Society, 1976).

PA —TEMPLE UNIVERSITY LIBRARIES, Special Collections Dept, Rare Books & Mss Section, Philadelphia, 19122. Thomas M Whitehead, Cur
Holdings: Vols (500) Cat Mss
Notes: Incl the Louise Bush-Brown Horticulture Collection; 15th-20th century rare herbals, animal husbandry and landscape gardening. List of majority of collection available.

PA —UNIVERSITY OF PENNSYLVANIA, Morris Arboretum Library, 9414 Meadowbrook Ave, Philadelphia, 19118.
Holdings: Vols 6000

PA —HUNT INSTITUTE FOR BOTANICAL DOCUMENTATION, Hunt Botanical Library, Carnegie-Mellon University, Pittsburgh, 15213. Bernadette G Callery, Librn
Holdings: Vols (23,000) Cat Pix
Notes: Collection of primarily historical botany and plant taxonomy, especially 1730-1840. Includes approximately 500 15th through 17th century herbals, extensive collection of 18th and 19th century color-plate works, floras and monographic works, and other works on natural history, early gardening and horticulture, and travel, particularly that dealing with plant exploration and introduction. Extensive biographical materials, on people in plant sciences. Reference collection and extensive documentation in botanical bibliography, especially concerning books published before 1850. Includes as separate collections, the Strandell Collection of Linnaeana and the Michel Adanson Library. Over 800 items described in *Catalogue of Botanical Books in the Collection of Rachel McMasters Miller Hunt, 1477-1800* (Pittsburgh, 1958-1960).

TN —THE BOTANICAL GARDENS, Minnie Ritchie and Joel Owsley Cheek Memorial Library, Forrest Park Drive, Nashville, 37205. Richard C Page, Dir Botanical Gardens
Holdings: Vols (3500) Cat Pix Slides
Budget: $2500

TX —SLOVANSKA PODPORUJICI JEDNOTA STATU TEXAS, Slavonic Benevolent Order of the State of Texas, SPJST Library, Archives, Museum, 520 N Main St, Temple, 76501. Otto Hanus, Cur-Librn; Thelma Bartosh, Asst Cur-Librn
Holdings: Vols (400) Cat
Notes: Our agricultural section contains US Dept of Agriculture books plus many bound magazines dealing with agriculture, gardening and flower growing.

VA —CHRISTOPHER NEWPORT COLLEGE, Captain John Smith Library, 50 Shoe Lane, PO Box 6070, Newport News, 23606.
Holdings: Vols 177 Cat
Notes: Woodroof Hiden Hussey Memorial Collection.

VA —NORFOLK BOTANICAL GARDENS LIBRARY, Airport Rd, Norfolk, 23518. Marian Cole, Librn
Holdings: Vols 1903 Cat Pix

VA —COLLEGE OF WILLIAM AND MARY, Earl Gregg Swem Library, Williamsburg, 23185. Margaret C Cook, Cur of Manuscripts & Rare Books
Holdings: Vols 50 // Cat
Notes: The Hetty Cary Harrison Memorial Collection. The majority of volumes in this collection are 17th-19th centuries. Also, uncataloged American seedmen's catalogs, 19th-20 centuries; 7 running ft.

WA —JOHN A FINCH ARBORETUM, W3404 Wodland Blvd, Spokane, 99204. John Dodson, Arboriculturist
Holdings: Vols 600 Cat
Notes: No photocopying. Incl books on plants and horticulture.

WI —UNIVERSITY OF WISCONSIN, MADISON, College of Agricultural & Life Sciences, Steenbock Memorial Library, 550 Babcock Dr, Madison, 53706. Jan Kennedy, Dir
Holdings: Vols (186,312) Cat Docs Microforms
Notes: Collection supports horticulture and landscape architecture, and includes plant genetics, physiology and pathology.

ON —CIVIC GARDEN CENTRE LIBRARY, 777 Lawrence Ave E, Don Mills, M3C 1P2, Can. Pamela MacKenzie, Librn
Holdings: Vols (5000) Cat
Budget: ($3200)

ON —ROYAL BOTANICAL GARDENS, Library, Box 399, Hamilton, L8N 3H8, Can. Ina Vrugtman, Librn
Holdings: Vols (5000) Cat
Budget: ($13,000)
Notes: Botany and ornamental horticulture. Incl 10,000 slides. Periodicals are not yet union listed. Collection of nursery and seed trade catalogs; *Gray Herbarium Index;* Centre for Canadian Historical Horitcultural Studies. The library is located in the headquarters building of the Royal Botanical Gradens, 680 Plains Road West (Highway No 2) Burlington, Ontario. Phone: (416) 527-1158. Road West (Highway No 2) Burlington, Ontario. Phone: (416) 527-1158.

HORTICULTURE—BIOGRAPHY see Horticulturists

HORTICULTURE—HISTORY

†DC —HARVARD UNIVERSITY, Dumbarton Oaks, Garden Library, 1703 32nd Street NW, Washington, 20007. Laura Byers, Librn

GA —CHEROKEE GARDEN LIBRARY, 3101 Andrews Dr NW, Atlanta, 30305. Sally Bruce McClatchey, Librn
Holdings: Vols 2700
Notes: Southern history and horticulture. Emphasis on the historical development of American horticulture, 1634 to 1900.

IL —MORTON ARBORETUM, Sterling Morton Library, Lisle, 60532. Ian MacPhail, Librn
Holdings: Vols (22,000)
Notes: Emphasis is on Woody plants. Print collection of 3000 pieces; 2000 botanical and horticultural rare books; Linnaeana. The Jens Jensen Archive of letters, photographs, blueprints, landscape plans.

MA —HERB SOCIETY OF AMERICA, Library, 2 Independence Court, Concord, 01742. Julie Macksoud, Exec Dir
Holdings: Vols (600)

MA —OLD STURBRIDGE VILLAGE, Research Library, Sturbridge, 01566. Theresa Rini Percy, Librn
Holdings: Cat
Notes: Northeastern US 1790-1850.

MO —MISSOURI BOTANICAL GARDEN LIBRARY, PO Box 299, Saint Louis, 63166. M R Crosby, Dir of Research

NY —NEW YORK BOTANICAL GARDEN LIBRARY, Bronx, 10458. Charles R Long, Asst Vice Pres & Dir
Notes: One of the largest botanical collections in the world. Over 900,000 items. Covers botany (150,000 vols), botanists (3000), horticulture (45,000) plant diseases (25,000), plant physiology (15,000), history of botany (1500), conservation of natural resources (15,000), gardening (13,000), paleobotany (7000), ecology (20,000), forestry (5000) medical botany (3000), agriculture (9000) and biology (20,000). Reference library; materials do not circulate, except for member circulating collection (1200) and standard inter-library loan. About 5000 vols uncataloged. Incl art, books, serials, pamphlets, archives and manuscripts, vertical files, microfiche and microfilm, nursery and seed catalogs, photographs, paintings, prints, drawings and engravings. Covers all areas of botanical sciences. This is an OCLC library with fullresource services incl photocopying and photography.

HORTICULTURE—U.S.

†PA —LIBRARY COMPANY OF PHILADELPHIA, 1314 Locust St, Philadelphia, 19107. Edwin Wolf II, Librn
Holdings: Vols (450,000)

HORTICULTURISTS

DC —LIBRARY OF CONGRESS, Manuscript Division, Washington, 20540. John C Broderick, Chief
Notes: The papers of Luther Burbank (1849-1926), incl approximately 10,000 items range in date over much of his life span. Contains correspondence, writings, scientific notes and records, ledgers, account books, scrapbooks, photographs, and journal reprints and other printed matter.

PA —HUNT INSTITUTE FOR BOTANICAL DOCUMENTATION, Hunt Botanical Library, Carnegie-Mellon University, Pittsburgh, 15213. Bernadette G Callery, Librn
Holdings: Vols (23,000) Cat Pix
Notes: Collection of primarily historical botany and plant taxonomy, especially 1730-1840. Includes approximately 500 15th through 17th century herbals, extensive collection of 18th and 19th century color-plate works, floras and monographic works, and other works on natural history, early gardening and horticulture and travel, particularly that dealing with plant exploration and introduction. Extensive biographical materials, on people in the plant sciences. Reference collection and extensive documentation in bibliography, especially concerning books published before 1850. Includes as separate collections, the Strandell Collection of Linnaeana and the Michel Adanson Library. Over 800 items described in *Catalogue of Botanical Books in the Collection of Rachel McMasters Miller Hunt, 1477-1800* (Pittsburgh, 1958-1960).

HORWITZ, JULIUS

MA —BOSTON UNIVERSITY, Mugar Memorial Library, Special Collections Dept, 771 Commonwealth Ave, Boston, 02215. Howard B Gotlieb, Dir
Holdings: Cat Mss Pix
Notes: Mss, correspondence, etc collected in depth; incl publications by or about.

HORWOOD, HAROLD, 1923-

AB —UNIVERSITY OF CALGARY, Libraries, Special Collections Div, 2500 University Dr, Calgary, T2N 1N4, Can.
Holdings: Mss
Notes: Mss (3 meters) of articles, radio talks, television documentaries, short stories, novels and non-fiction works as well as journals, periodicals and financial records, 1942-78.

HOSACK, DAVID, M.D.

NY —NEW YORK BOTANICAL GARDEN LIBRARY, Bronx, 10458. Charles R Long,

HOSACK, DAVID, M.D. (cont.)

Asst Vice Pres & Dir
Holdings: Vols 100 Cat VF
Budget: ($356,000)
Notes: Over 900,000 items, incl books, serials, pamphlets, archives and manuscripts, vertical files, microfiche and microfilm, nursery and seed catalogs, photographs, paintings, prints, drawings and engravings. Covering all areas of botanical sciences.

HOSIERY

NC —PUBLIC LIBRARY OF CHARLOTTE & MECKLENBURG COUNTY, 310 N Tyron St, Charlotte, 28202. Mae S Tucker, Asst Dir
Holdings: Vols (3950) Cat Slides 16mm Films Filmstrips
Notes: Weaving, chemistry, dyes and dyeing, and color are emphasized. Also hosiery, knitting, machinery, manufacturing, directories and statistics. Have specialized dictionaries in the subject field in both English and other languages. 110 periodical titles.

HOSKINS, ARTHUR C.

MO —WASHINGTON UNIVERSITY, Libraries, Special Collections Dept, Campus Box 1061, St Louis, 63130.
Notes: Family and business correspondence.

HOSKINS, GAYLE PORTER

DE —DELAWARE ART MUSEUM, Library, 2301 Kentmere Pkwy, Wilmington, 19806. Anne Hoslam, Librn
Holdings: Vols (25,000) Cat Mss
Notes: The collection is rich in the following subjects: Howard Pyle and his pupils; John Sloan and the eight; history of the book and printing; and English and American illustrated books. There is also a section on contemporary photography. Archival material on Albert Mumford Lindsay, Jerome Myers, Everett Shinn, Gayle Porter Hoskins, Frank Schoonover.

HOSMER, HARRIET GOODHUE, 1830-1908

MA —RADCLIFFE COLLEGE, Arthur & Elizabeth Schlesinger Library on the History of Women in America, 3 James St, Cambridge, 02138. Patricia Miller King, Dir; Eva Moseley, Cur of Mss
Holdings: / / Cat Mss Pix
Notes: Correspondence, writings, photographs, etc of the sculptor Harriet Goodhue Hosmer. Probably the largest collection of her papers. Available only on microfilm. Inventory published by G K Hall; see Hamilton Family for citation.

HOSPICES (TERMINAL CARE) see Terminal Care Facilities

HOSPITAL ADMINISTRATION see Hospitals—Administration

HOSPITAL ENDOWMENTS see Endowments

HOSPITAL PERSONNEL ADMINISTRATION see Hospitals—Personnel Management

HOSPITAL PHARMACIES

NY —LONG ISLAND UNIVERSITY, Brooklyn Center, Pharmacy Library Collection, University Plaza, Brooklyn, 11201. Barbara Chanton, Dir & Health Sciences Librn
Holdings: Vols (17,500) Cat Mss
Notes: Pharmacy, drug abuse, hospital pharmacy, medicinal chemistry.

HOSPITAL RECORDS

NY —UNITED HOSPITAL FUND OF NEW YORK, Library, 3 E 54th St, New York, 10022. Christine Bahr, Librn
Holdings: Vols (4000) Cat Mss Maps Pix Slides Microforms
Notes: Incl 100 journal titles.

HOSPITAL SERVICE (WAR) see Red Cross

HOSPITAL SOCIAL WORK see Medical Social Work

HOSPITALS

†CT —YALE UNIVERSITY, Medical Library, 333 Cedar St, New Haven, 06520.
Notes: Hospital, clinic, and dispensary collection of extensive, uncatalogued materials, descriptive pamphlets, annual reports, etc. This is a large collection with much on institutional histories of European and American hospitals.

HOSPITALS—ADMINISTRATION

CA —UNIVERSITY OF CALIFORNIA, BERKELEY, Life Sciences Libraries, Public Health Library, 42 Earl Warren Hall, Berkeley, 94720. Thomas J Alexander, Librn
Holdings: Vols (75,000) Cat Microforms
Notes: Research collection covering all aspects of public health. Health Department annual reports from all 50 states are acquired, as well as such reports from all California health units and from major US cities. Serial publications issued by Health Departments in the 13 western states are being received.

CA —HOLLYWOOD PRESBYTERIAN MEDICAL CENTER, Health Sciences Library, 1300 N Vermont Ave, Los Angeles, 90027. Erika M Hansen, Chief Medical Librn
Holdings: Vols (9200) Cat
Budget: ($130,000)
Notes: Medicine, nursing and allied health personnel, hospital administration. Incl audiovisual material.

CA —STANFORD UNIVERSITY LIBRARIES, Lane Medical Library, Stanford University, Medical Center, Stanford, 94305. Peter Stangl, Librn
Holdings: Mss Cat
Notes: Mss Lane and Stanford hospitals; R L Wilbur's work on Commission on Hospital Care, and course on medical economics, California hospitals regulation under.

CO —SWEDISH MEDICAL CENTER LIBRARY, 501 E Hampden Ave, Englewood, 80110. Sandra Parker, Dir
Holdings: Vols (6000) Cat
Budget: ($40,000)

†CT —YALE UNIVERSITY, Medical Library, 333 Cedar St, New Haven, 06520.
Notes: Extensive collection of books, illustrations, pamphlets, etc, incl three vols of Charles F Neergaard's "Occasional Papers on Hospital Adminstration."

IL —BLUE CROSS AND BLUE SHIELD ASSOCIATION, Library, 804 N Lake Shore Dr, Chicago, 60611. Mary T Drazba, Librn
Holdings: Vols (15,000) Cat Microforms
Notes: Health care financing.

IL —LIBRARY OF THE AMERICAN HOSPITAL ASSOCIATION, Asa S Bacon Memorial, 840 N Lake Shore Dr, Chicago, 60611. Eloise C Foster, Dir
Holdings: Vols (39,000) Cat
Budget: ($95,000)
Notes: Literature on non-clinical aspects of health care administration, planning and financing of hospitals and related health care institutions; administrative aspects of the medical, paramedical, and prepayment fields. Special Collection: Ray E Brown Management Collection. *Hospital Literature* Index prepared by the Library of the American Hospital Association in cooperation with the National Library of Medicine; *Catalog of the Library of the American Hospital Association*, published by G K Hall, Boston.

IN —SAINT VINCENT HOSPITAL & HEALTH CARE CENTER, Garceau Library, 20001 W 86 St, Indianapolis, 46260. Virginia Durkin, Librn
Holdings: Vols (7500) Cat Pix Slides Phonorecords Audiotapes Videotapes 16mm Films Filmstrips Microforms
Notes: Building a collection on the history of the hospital

IN —WISHARD MEMORIAL HOSPITAL, Professional Library, 1001 W Tenth St, Indianapolis, 46202. Fran Bischoff, Library Dir; Kirsten Quam, Librn
Holdings: Vols 92 Cat

IA —IOWA LUTHERAN HOSPITAL, Department of Educational Media, University at Penn, Des Moines, 50316. Wayne Pedersen, Dir of Educational Media
Holdings: Vols 2695 Cat Audiocassettes Videotapes Slides 16mm Films
Budget: ($15,000)
Notes: The department consists of 3 libraries: Levitt Health Sciences, Nursing Administrative. The Audio-Visual Division is also part of the department. Holdings incl 524 audiocassettes (cat); 177 videotapes (cat); 13 slide-tape kits (cat); 2 16mm films (cat).

KY —NKC HOSPITALS, Medical Library, PO Box 35070, Louisville, 40232. Holly Shipp Buchanan, Dir
Holdings: Vols (4500) Cat Audiotapes Videotapes 16mm Films
Budget: $200,000
Notes: The Library has a special historical collection, corporate archives in honor of Dr Morris Flexner.

MD —PROVIDENT HOSPITAL, Health Sciences Library, 2600 Liberty Heights Ave, Baltimore, 21215. Bertha G Wilson, Librn
Holdings: Vols (5077) Cat Slides Audiotapes Microforms

MI —UNIVERSITY OF MICHIGAN, Public Health Library, Ann Arbor, 48109. Mary Townsend, Head
Holdings: Vols (55,000) Cat Maps Pix
Budget: ($24,000)

MN —MINNESOTA DEPT OF HEALTH, R N Barr Public Health Library, 717 Delaware St SE, PO Box 9441, Minneapolis, 55440. Barbara Brian, Librn
Holdings: Vols (26,000) Cat Microforms
Notes: Public health.

MN —UNIVERSITY OF MINNESOTA, Bio-Medical Library, Diehl Hall, Minneapolis, 55455. Gertrude Foreman, Acting Dir
Holdings: Vols (263,361)
Budget: ($500,000)

NY —US VETERANS ADMINISTRATION HOSPITAL, Medical Library, 130 W Kingsbridge Rd, Bronx, 10468. Margaret M Kinney, Chief Librn
Holdings: Vols (23,000) Cat
Notes: No photocopying.

NY —BOOTH MEMORIAL MEDICAL CENTER, Health Education Library, Main St at Booth Memorial Ave, Flushing, 11355. Rita Maier, Library Dir
Holdings: Vols (3000) Cat Audiotapes
Notes: Incl 7000 bound journals; software slide tape programs.

NY —CORNELL UNIVERSITY LIBRARIES, Graduate School of Management, Malott Hall, Ithaca, 14853. Betsy Ann Olive, Librn
Holdings: Vols (135,000) Cat Microforms
Budget: ($130,000)

NY —AMERICAN JOURNAL OF NURSING CO, Sophia F Palmer Library, 555 W 57th St, New York, 10019. Frederick W Pattison, Librn
Holdings: Cat Mss Pix
Notes: Collection described in *Catalog of the Sophia F Palmer Memorial Library, American Journal of Nursing Co, New York City* (Boston G K Hall, 1973) 2 vols.

NY —UNITED HOSPITAL FUND OF NEW YORK, Library, 3 E 54th St, New York, 10022. Christine Bahr, Librn
Holdings: Vols (4000) Cat Mss Maps Pix
Notes: Incl 100 journal titles.

OH —MOUNT SINAI MEDICAL CENTER, George H Hays Library, University Circle, Cleveland, 44106. Pamela Alderman, Librn
Holdings: Vols (6000) Cat Mss Slides Phonorecords Filmstrips Audiotapes
Notes: Bound journals 4000; incl on line reference service with Dialog database.

OH —KETTERING COLLEGE OF MEDICAL ARTS, Learning Resources Center, 3737 Southern Blvd, Kettering, 45429. Edward Collins, Librn
Holdings: Vols 200 Cat Audiotapes Videotapes

HOSPITALS—ADMINISTRATION (cont.)

PA —WESTERN PSYCHIATRIC INSTITUTE & CLINIC, Library, 3811 O'Hara St, Pittsburgh, 15261. Lucile Stark, Dir
Holdings: Vols 50,000 Cat Mss Pix Films Microforms Audiotapes
Budget: ($180,000)
Notes: Also incl the archives of the Institute and other ms material relating to the development of psychiatry in Western Pennsylvania, specifically in Pittsburgh. Incl 12,000 pamphlets on all aspects of psychiatry, etc. Rich in bibliographies and reference materials. Incl 750 journal titles.

†TN —SAINT THOMAS HOSPITAL, Health Sciences Library, Box 380, Nashville, 37202. Dee Platt, Dir
Holdings: Vols (2600) Cat Slides

WA —SWEDISH HOSPITAL MEDICAL CENTER, Medical Library, 747 Summit Ave, Seattle, 98104.
Holdings: Vols (2072) Cat

WA —CENTRAL WASHINGTON HOSPITAL, Rose A Heminger Health Sciences Library, PO Box 1887, Wenatchee, 98801. Jane Belt, Librn & Coordr of Continuing Education
Holdings: Cat Slides Audiotapes Videotapes 16mm Films Filmstrips
Budget: ($5000)
Notes: Incl 100 slide sets, 500 audiotapes, 100 videotapes, and 50 filmstrip programs.

WI —WAUKESHA MEMORIAL HOSPITAL, Medical Staff Library, 725 American Ave, Waukesha, 53186. Linda A Oddon, Medical Librn
Holdings: Vols (3336) Cat Pix Audiotapes Videotapes
Budget: ($4919)

ON —CANADIAN HOSPITAL ASSOCIATION, Blackader Library, 410 Laurier W, Suite 800, Ottawa, K1R 7T6, Can. Linda Solomon, Dir
Holdings: Vols 2800 Cat Pix Audiotapes 16mm Films
Budget: $8300
Notes: The most comprehensive specialized collection in Canada on hospital management. Incl over 1000 vertical file boxes. In storage at this time.

ON —SUNNYBROOK HOSPITAL, Health Sciences Library, 2075 Bayview Ave, Toronto, M4N 3M5, Can. Linda McFarlane, Librn
Holdings: Vols (20,000) Cat Audiotapes Videotapes
Notes: Emphasis on clinical medicine; also have nursing and hospital administration.

PQ —UNIVERSITY OF MONTREAL, Bibliotheque Para-medicale, 2375 Chemin de la Cote Ste Catherine, Montreal, H3C 3J7, Can. Johanne Hopper, Head Librn
Holdings: Vols 1050 Cat
Budget: $6000
Notes: 15 percent of collection in French.

HOSPITALS—FINANCE

NY —CORNELL UNIVERSITY LIBRARIES, Graduate School of Management, Malott Hall, Ithaca, 14853. Betsy Ann Olive, Librn
Holdings: Vols (135,000) Cat Microforms
Budget: ($130,000)

HOSPITALS—HISTORY

CA —UNIVERSITY OF CALIFORNIA, SAN FRANCISCO, Library, Special Collections, San Francisco, 94143. Nancy Witten Zinn, Librn
Holdings: Vols (2300) Cat Mss Pix
Budget: ($8500)

†CT —YALE UNIVERSITY, Medical Library, 333 Cedar St, New Haven, 06520.
Notes: Hospital, clinic, and dispensary collection of extensive, uncatalogued materials, descriptive pamphlets, annual reports, etc. This is a large collection with much on institutional histories of European and American hospitals.

MO —WASHINGTON UNIVERSITY, School of Medicine, Archives, 660 S Euclid Ave, Saint Louis, 63110. Paul G Anderson, Archivist
Holdings: Mss Pix Audiotapes
Budget: ($38,000)
Notes: Institutional records and papers of faculty of Washington University School of Medicine and its predecessors and associated hospitals. Contains records of St Louis Medical College, Missouri Medical Barnard Free Skin and Cancer Hospital, Barnes Hospital, St Louis Children's Hospital and Jewish Hospital of St Louis. Incl papers of William Beaumont, Joseph Erlanger, Leo Loeb, Evarts Graham, Edmund V Cowdry, Helen Graham, Carl V Moore, Margaret Smith and others. Oral history program. See also: Anderson, Paul G and Hoolihan, Christopher, eds. *Special Collections* (St Louis: Washington University School of Medicine, 1981). 960 linear feet.

NY —COLUMBIA UNIVERSITY LIBRARIES, Teachers College, Milbank Memorial Library, 525 W 120 St, New York, 10027. Jane P Franck, Dir
Holdings: Cat Pix
Notes: A small collection of rare books on French hospitals.

†NY —COLUMBIA UNIVERSITY LIBRARIES, Butler Library, Rare Book and Manuscript Library, 535 W 114 St, New York, 10027.
Notes: Papers of the American Bureau for Medical Aid to China, incl correspondence, memoranda, reports, minutes, membership and financial records, photographs, posters and printed material. Approx 45,000 pieces. Also, some 6000 photographs of Chinese medical colleges, hospitals, laboratories, and personnel.

HOSPITALS—MANAGEMENT AND REGULATION see Hospitals—Administration

HOSPITALS—NURSES see Nurses and Nursing

HOSPITALS—OUTPATIENT SERVICES

IN —WISHARD MEMORIAL HOSPITAL, Professional Library, 1001 W Tenth St, Indianapolis, 46202. Fran Bischoff, Library Dir; Kirsten Quam, Librn
Holdings: Vols 56 Cat

HOSPITALS—PERSONNEL MANAGEMENT

CA —HOLLYWOOD PRESBYTERIAN MEDICAL CENTER, Health Sciences Library, 1300 N Vermont Ave, Los Angeles, 90027. Erika M Hansen, Chief Medical Librn
Notes: Medicine, nursing and allied health personnel, hospital administration. Incl audiovisual material.

MA —MOUNT AUBURN HOSPITAL, Health Sciences Library, 330 Mount Auburn St, Cambridge, 02138. Cherie Haitz, Librn
Holdings: Vols (3000) Cat Audiotapes
Notes: Incl 300 periodical subscriptions.

HOSPITALS—RECORDS see Hospital Records

HOSPITALS, FIELD see Medicine, Military

HOSPITALS, FRENCH see France—Hospitals; Hospitals—History

HOSTILITIES see War

HOTHOUSES see Greenhouses

HOT SPRINGS see Springs (Thermal)

HOTCHKISS, JEDEDIAH, 1828-1899

DC —LIBRARY OF CONGRESS, Manuscript Division, Washington, 20540. John C Broderick, Chief
Notes: The Jedediah Hotchkiss Collection of his papers and Civil War maps.

HOTCHNER, A. E.

MO —WASHINGTON UNIVERSITY, Libraries, Special Collections Dept, Campus Box 1061, St Louis, 63130.
Notes: A major collection, incl mss, correspondence, literary papers, photographs, etc. Described in *Special Collections: an Annotated Guide to the Holdings of the Manuscript Division and the University Archives and Research Collection.*

HOTEL ADMINISTRATION see Hotel and Restaurant Management

HOTEL MANAGEMENT see Hotel and Restaurant Management

HOTEL AND RESTAURANT MANAGEMENT

CA —CITY COLLEGE OF SAN FRANCISCO, Alice Statler Library, Hotel & Restaurant Dept, 50 Phelan Ave, San Francisco, 94112. Mary B Smyth, Librn
Holdings: Vols (7300) Cat Slides 16mm Films Filmstrips Microforms
Budget: ($5000)
Notes: The collection covers all aspects of the public hospitality industry. In addition to the book collection, it has 6000 cataloged pamphlets, 1500 menus. It also has bound hotel and restaurant magazines dating back to the 19th century. Receives 85 current periodicals in hospitality industry.

DE —WIDENER UNIVERSITY, Delaware Campus Library, Box 7139, Concord Pike, Wilmington, 19803. Jane E Hukill, Library Dir
Holdings: Vols (48,000) Microforms
Notes: Incl food service, restaurants, motels, volume feeding, cookery.

IL —UNIVERSITY OF ILLINOIS, URBANA/CHAMPAIGN, Library, Home Economics Library, 314 Bevier Hall, Champaign, 61820. Barbara C Swain, Librn
Holdings: Vols Cat
Notes: Foods and Nutrition.

IN —HURTY-PECK LIBRARY OF BEVERAGE LITERATURE, 5650 W Raymond Street, PO Box 41167, Indianapolis, 46208. Ben Wilson, Librn
Holdings: Vols (6000) Cat //
Notes: The most comprehensive collection, in English, in the world on beverages of all types. History, manufacture, formulae, customs. Books on beer and brewing; cocoa and chocolate; coffee; liquors and spirits; soft drinks; tea; and wine.

IN —PURDUE UNIVERSITY LIBRARIES, Consumer & Family Sciences Library, Stone Hall W, West Lafayette, 47907. Emily Alward, Librn
Holdings: Vols (14,000) Cat

NH —NEW HAMPSHIRE COLLEGE, Harry A B and Gertrude C Shapiro Library, 2500 N River Rd, Manchester, 03104. Richard Pantano, Dir
Holdings: Vols (66,000) Cat Maps Slides Audiotapes Videotapes 16mm films Filmstrips Microforms
Budget: ($133,173)
Notes: Library is a selective US Government Documents depository, and New Hampshire State Documents depository. Subscribe to microfiche SEC 10K reports to AMEX and NYSE (1975-), as well as AMEX and NYSE company annual reports (1977-); AICPA publications and cassettes. Strong collections in accounting; business; business education; computers; hotel and restaurant management; and social service.

NY —NEW YORK CITY TECHNICAL COLLEGE, Library, 300 Jay St, Brooklyn, 11201. Catherine T Brody, Chief Librn
Holdings: Vols 1500 Cat Pix Microforms Menus
Notes: Incl menus representing restaurants of the US and many other countries. One bibliography available: Guide to Hotel and Restaurant Management Resources in the Namm Hall Library.

NY —CULINARY INSTITUTE OF AMERICA, Katharine Angell Library, North Rd, Hyde Park, 12538. Gertrude Trani, Asst Librn
Holdings: Vols (23,000) Cat Slides Videotapes 16mm Films Filmstrips
Notes: Culinary arts, incl cookery,

HOTEL AND RESTAURANT MANAGEMENT (cont.)

beverages, and food service management. AV materials housed in separate Learning Resources Center. Henry Woods, Dir.

NY —CORNELL UNIVERSITY LIBRARIES, Hotel Administration Library, Statler Hall, Ithaca, 14853. Margaret J Oaksford, Librn
Holdings: Vols (25,000) Cat Mss Maps
Budget: ($60,000)
Notes: Extensive collections on management, travel, hotels, food and beverage, wine, real estate and tourism. Incl menu collection.

NY —PAUL SMITHS COLLEGE, Frank L Cubley Library, Paul Smiths, 12970. Theodore Mack, Librn
Holdings: Vols (1000) Cat

OH —OHIO STATE UNIVERSITY, Home Economics Library, Campbell Hall Rm 325, 1787 Neil Ave, Columbus, 43210. Neosha Mackey, Librn
Holdings: Vols (14,000) Cat Microforms
Notes: Separate catalog. Also, book catalog: *Catalog of the Home Economics Library* (Boston: G K Hall, 1976), 3 vols.

PA —LUZERNE COUNTY COMMUNITY COLLEGE, Library, Prospect St & Middle Rd, Nanticoke, 18634. Robert N Cohee, Library Dir
Holdings: Vols 1500 Cat Slides Audiotapes Films Filmstrips Microforms
Budget: ($26,000)
Notes: Selected bibliographic listing in: James P Malkames, et al, *Hotel and Restaurant Management; A Bibliography of Books and Audio-visual Materials.* (Nanticoke, Pa: Luzerne County Community College, 1975).

RI —JOHNSON AND WALES COLLEGE, Hospitality Center, 1150 Narragansett Blvd, Cranston, 02905. Margaret A Thomas, Librn
Budget: ($15,000)
Notes: The Paul Fritzsche Cookbook Collection, incl more than 8000 cookbooks, with some rare and valuable items. Many 19th and early 20th century items; particularly strong in fund raising cookbooks. Collection is partially cataloged.

RI —BRYANT COLLEGE, Edith M Hodgson Memorial Library, Rte 7, Douglas Pike, Smithfield, 02917. John P Hannon, Dir
Holdings: Vols (103,000) Cat Phonorecords Audiotapes Videotapes 16mm Films Filmstrips Microforms
Budget: ($175,000)
Notes: Incl 6000 bound periodical vols, 250 phonorecords, 220 audiotapes, 120 videotapes, 30 16mm films, 150 filmstrips and 7500 microforms.

SC —HORRY GEORGETOWN TECHNICAL COLLEGE, Library, Hwy 501, Box 1966, Conway, 29526. Barbara Brittain, Librn
Holdings: Vols (20,000) Cat Maps Slides Microforms

TX —NORTHWOOD INSTITUTE, Library, Box 58, Cedar Hill, 75104. Jennifer Cope, Librn
Holdings: Vols (300) Cat Audiotapes Filmstrips
Budget: ($1000)

WI —UNIVERSITY OF WISCONSIN-STOUT, Library Learning Center, Menomonie, 54751. Philip Sawin Jr, Coll Develop Librn
Notes: Comprehensive collection for Hotel and Restaurant Management. Because there is a large undergraduate enrollment, this collection is quite substantial. Much of the emphasis for this collection is on the management of the various hotel and restaurant systems. This program was begun in 1967.

ON —UNIVERSITY OF GUELPH, Library, Guelph, N1G 2W1, Can. Margaret Beckman, Chief Librn; Ellen Pearson, Ref Librn
Holdings: Vols 10,000 Cat Audiotapes Videotapes Microforms
Budget: $14,000
Notes: 100 periodical titles. Special aspects are food services, hospitality, industry, management studies, law, travel and tourism, recreation, marketing.

HOTELS, TAVERNS, ETC.

RI —JOHNSON AND WALES COLLEGE, Hospitality Center, 1150 Narragansett Blvd, Cranston, 02905. Margaret A Thomas, Librn
Budget: ($15,000)
Notes: The Paul Fritzsche Cookbook Collection, incl more than 8000 cookbooks, with some rare and valuable items. Many 19th and early 20th century items; particularly strong in fund raising cookbooks. Collection is partially cataloged.

HOTELS, TAVERNS, ETC. —MANAGEMENT see Hotel and Restaurant Management

HOTMAN, FRANCOIS

NY —UNIVERSITY OF ROCHESTER, Rush Rhees Library, Department of Rare Books and Special Collections, Rochester, 14627. Peter Dzwonkoski, Librn
Holdings: Vols (450) Cat
Notes: Collection of materials on 16th and 17th century European law and political theory with special emphasis on works emanating from the French Civil Wars of the works of Francois Hotman and the editions of the Corpus Juris Civilis printed in Lyon. No photocopying.

HOUDINI, HARRY, 1874-1926

NY —CORNELL UNIVERSITY LIBRARIES, Collection of Regional History, Dept of Manuscripts and Univ Archives, Ithaca, 14853.
Holdings: Pix
Notes: Magician. Incl 2 letters (1924), and 2 photos, in one of which "two ghosts appear."

HOUGHTON, CLAUDE, PSEUD., 1889-

CA —CLAREMONT COLLEGES, Honnold Library, Ninth & Dartmouth, Claremont, 91711. Tania Rizzo, Special Collections Dept Head
Holdings: Vols 30 // Cat Mss
Notes: First and special British and American editions; 17 with original dust jackets; 9 inscribed; one ALS.
See also entry under Oldfield, Claude Houghton

HOUGHTON, DOROTHY

IA —STATE HISTORICAL SOCIETY OF IOWA LIBRARY, 402 Iowa Ave, Iowa City, 52240. Darold J Brown, Librn
Holdings: Cat
Notes: Thousands of individual items and smaller collections. Two hundred larger collections incl the papers of Cyrus C Carpenter, Jonathan P Dolliver, Gilbert Haugen, W W Waymack, Ephraim Adams, A C Dodge, Dorothy Houghton, Jesse Macy, Agnes Samuelson, Donald Johnson, Jack Miller, Ruth Sayre, Samuel Kirkwood, Thomas McKnight, Robert Lucas, Dwight McCarty, William Larrabee. Includes church, school, company and organization records, Civil War materials.

HOUNDS

NY —MERCY COLLEGE LIBRARY, Dobbs Ferry, 10522. Larry Earle Bone, Dir
Holdings: Vols (406) Cat Pix
Notes: General collection of American and British books and periodicals on horses, hounds and hunting, with special emphasis on the Millbrook Hunt. 15 percent of the collection is rare books and periodicals. Rare photographs and paintings also incl. Many of the books are from the private libraries of members of the Millbrook Hunt. Collection formerly at Bennett College, Millbrook, New York.

HOURS (TIME) see Horology

HOUSE, EDWARD M.

CT —YALE UNIVERSITY, Box 1603A, Yale Station, New Haven, 06520.
Holdings: Cat Mss

CT —YALE UNIVERSITY, Sterling Memorial Library, Latin American Collections, New Haven, 06520. Lee H Williams Jr, Cur
Holdings: Vols (300,000) Cat Maps Pix Slides Phonorecords 16mm Films Filmstrips
See also entry under Latin America

HOUSE DECORATION see Interior Decoration

HOUSE DRAINAGE see Sanitation; Sewage Disposal and Treatment

HOUSE FLIES see Flies

HOUSE ORGANS

PA —CARNEGIE LIBRARY OF PITTSBURGH, Science & Technology Dept, 4400 Forbes Ave, Pittsburgh, 15213. Catherine M Brosky, Dept Head
Holdings: Vols (380,000) Cat Maps Microforms
Budget: ($240,000)
Notes: Approx 100 house organs received currently. A few titles bound and cataloged for permanent reference.

HOUSE PAINTING

PA —CARNEGIE LIBRARY OF PITTSBURGH, Science & Technology Dept, 4400 Forbes Ave, Pittsburgh, 15213. Catherine M Brosky, Dept Head
Notes: Collection incl material on general construction, carpentry, masonry, plumbing, heating, air conditioning, corrosion and painting and numerous other building trades. Sweets Architectural File complete except for a few years. *Car Builders Encyclopedia of America Practice,* most editions since 1879.

HOUSE PLANTS

IA —BICKELHAUPT ARBORETUM FREE LENDING LIBRARY, 340 S Fourteenth St, Clinton, 52732. Francie B Hill, Librn
Notes: Strong on indoor plants, horticulture, ecology, energy conservation, plant entomology and pathology, urban tree planting; also curriculum materials. Over 3000 slides available for lending.

HOUSEHOLD, GEOFFREY EDWARD WEST

IN —INDIANA UNIVERSITY, Lilly Library, Seventh St, Bloomington, 47405. William R Cagle, Librn
Holdings: // Cat Mss
Notes: Correspondence and writings of British author Geoffrey Household, 1944-1952. 250 items. Incl first editions of author's works.

HOUSEHOLD MANAGEMENT see Home Economics

HOUSEHOLD REPAIRS see Repair Manuals

HOUSEHOLD SCIENCE see Home Economics

HOUSEHOLD WORKERS see Servants

HOUSEKEEPING see Home Economics

HOUSEMAIDS see Servants

HOUSEMAN, JOHN, 1902-

CA —UNIVERSITY OF CALIFORNIA, LOS ANGELES, Research Library, Dept of Special Collections, 405 Hilgard Ave, Los Angeles, 90024. Edward Shreeves, Chairman, Bibliographers Group; David S Zeidberg, Head
Holdings: Mss Pix
Notes: 12 linear feet of correspondence, scripts and ephemera. No photocopying; Mr Houseman's permission is required to consult the correspondence.

HOUSES see Architecture, Domestic

HOUSES, EARTH see Earth Houses

HOUSES, HISTORIC see Historic Houses, Etc.

HOUSES, SOD see Sod Houses

HOUSING

CA —ASSOCIATION OF BAY AREA GOVERNMENTS, MTC/ABAG Library, 101 Eighth St, Oakland, 94607. Diane Gillman, Information Coord
Notes: Concentrates heavily on the nine-county Bay Area region. About 10,000 monographs and serials. Title catalog, OCLC/ATS. Central collection of documents for six transit properties in Bay Area.

CA —HOOVER INSTITUTION ON WAR, REVOLUTION & PEACE, Stanford University, Stanford, 94305. Milorad M Drachkovitch, Archivist
Holdings: Mss
Notes: Records of the President's Conference on Home Building and Home Ownership, established by President Hoover as a fact-finding conference on housing incl memoranda, reports, correspondence, pamphlets, clippings, press releases and expense statements, 1929-33, relating to housing conditions in the US and to proposals for improving them. 40 ms boxes, 3 ledgers, oversize report.

DC —GEORGETOWN UNIVERSITY, Library, Special Collections Div, 37 & O Sts NW, Washington, 20057. George M Barringer, Special Collections Librn; Nicholas B Sheetz, Mss Librn
Holdings: Mss
Notes: Papers of John Ihlder, consisting of correspondence, reports, mss, and printed material, principally pertaining to his work with the Committee on Evaluation of Public Housing of the National Capitol Housing Authority. Incl are reports from the New Jersey Board of Tenement House Supervision (1916), a guide for the evaluation of public housing (1943), correspondence concerning the Hillside low-rent housing project in Washington (1944), and material on postwar housing. A small quantity of family papers completes the collection. Collection of personal and professional papers, mss, and related items concerning housing and urban affairs. Carl Coan (1911-1976) served as staff director of the Senate Subcommittee on Housing and Urban Affairs from 1961-1976. Supplemented by related documents received since 1979.

DC —NATIONAL ASSOCIATION OF HOUSING AND REDEVELOPMENT OFFICIALS, Resource Center, 2600 Virginia Ave NW, Washington, 20037. Mary L Pike, Librn
Holdings: Vols 1000
Notes: Public housing and community development, incl urban renewal and housing code enforcement.

DC —URBAN LAND INSTITUTE, Library, 1090 Vermont Ave, Washington, 20005. Ann Benson, Librn
Holdings: Vols (9000) Cat
Budget: ($6000)
Notes: Incl 200 serials.

DC —US DEPT OF HOUSING & URBAN DEVELOPMENT, HUD Library, 451 Seventh St SW Room 8141, Washington, 20410. Carol A Johnson, Project Manager
Holdings: Vols Cat Documents Microforms
Notes: 600,000 pieces. Strong in all phases of community planning. Extensive coverage of the production and financing of housing. Emphasis on federal legislation.

IL —ILLINOIS STATE UNIVERSITY, Milner Library, Dept of Special Collections, Normal, 61761. Robert Sokan, Librn
Holdings: Vols 2100 // Uncat
Notes: Sigmund Livingston Collection on Intergroup Relations, 1944 to the present. The material is divided into subject headings which contain pamphlets, newsletters and commission reports.

MD —MARYLAND-NATIONAL CAPITAL PARK & PLANNING COMMISSION, Montgomery County Planning Department Library, 8787 Georgia Ave, Silver Spring, 20907. Janice C Holt, Librn
Holdings: Vols (5000) Cat
Notes: Specific subject areas include: community facilities, conservation, economics, flood control, highways, housing, human and natural resources. landscape architecture, open space, parks, pollution, population, recreation, transportation, urban renewal, and zoning. Commission's publications are maintained by Records Management (not Library).

MI —INSTITUTE OF GERONTOLOGY, Gerontology Library, University of Michigan, 300 N Ingalls St, Ann Arbor, 48109. Willie M Edwards, Librn
Holdings: Vols (10,000) Cat Pix Audiotapes 16mm Films
Notes: All subjects concerning the aged and aging in the US, Western Europe and strong emphasis on Great Britain. On VF (24) unpublished research papers, newsletters from elderly association, centers on aging.

MI —UNIVERSITY OF DETROIT, Main Library, 4001 W McNichols Rd, Detroit, 48221.
Notes: Architecture Library was closed in 1981. Collection consolidated in main library.

MI —OAKLAND COUNTY REFERENCE LIBRARY, 1200 N Telegraph Rd, Pontiac, 48053. Phyllis Jose, Library Dir
Holdings: Vols (11,000) Cat
Budget: ($34,000)

MN —UNIVERSITY OF MINNESOTA, Architecture Library, 89 Church St, Minneapolis, 55455. A Kristine Johnson, Librn
Holdings: Vols (27,000) Cat Mss
Budget: ($20,000)
Notes: Incl architecture, architectural history, landscape architecture, design methodology, housing, urban sociolgy, interior design, etc.

NJ —MIDDLESEX COUNTY PLANNING BOARD, Library, 40 Livingston Ave, New Brunswick, 08901. Lou Mattei, Planning Supervisor, Data Mgt
Holdings: Vols (3500) Cat
Budget: ($500)

NJ —RUTGERS, THE STATE UNIVERSITY OF NEW JERSEY, Center for Urban Policy Research Library, Bldg 4051-Kilmer, New Brunswick, 08903. Edward E Duensing, Jr
Holdings: Vols 3500 Cat Periodicals VF
Budget: ($4000)
Notes: Collection focuses on the subjects of housing, municipal finance, and planning in American cities. The emphasis is on current material. Incl 5000 cataloged vertical files, 157 periodical subscriptions.

NJ —PRINCETON UNIVERSITY, Firestone Library, Afro-American Studies Collection, Princeton, 08540. William Wellburn, Cur
Holdings: Vols (2000) Cat Pix Phonorecords Audiotapes Microforms
Notes: Our emphasis is primarily Afro-American: catalogs of other collections, biographical and vertical files, reference materials, indexes, bibliographies and serials.

NY —CORNELL UNIVERSITY LIBRARIES, Fine Arts Library, Sibley Hall, Ithaca, 14853. Judith Holliday, Librn
Holdings: Vols (115,000) Cat Maps Pix

NY —COLUMBIA UNIVERSITY LIBRARIES, Avery Architectural and Fine Arts Library, 201 Avery Hall, New York, 10027. Angela Giral, Librn
Holdings: Vols 4000
Notes: Restricted use: noncirculating.

NY —NEW YORK STATE DIVISION OF HOUSING & COMMUNITY RENEWAL, Library, 2 World Trade Center, New York, 10047. Carole Williams, Asst Librn, Special Reference Room
Holdings: Vols 2100 Cat Pix
Budget: $1500
Notes: No photocopying.

NY —NEW YORK STATE DIVISION OF HUMAN RIGHTS, Reference Library, Two World Trade Center, Rm 5356, New York, 10047. Rosalind Spriggs, Librn
Holdings: Vols 1200 // Cat
Notes: Emphasis on materials which deal with the problems of discrimination in housing, the development of cities, and urban unrest. See *Bibliography on Housing and Urban Renewal* by Simon Fediuk. Special Collection, No 1 of a Series. 2nd printing, New York, 1972. 92 pp. This special collection contains about 1200 items: books, studies, journals, pamphlets, reports, reprints, and research data.

NY —ROCKEFELLER UNIVERSITY, Rockefeller Archive Center, Hillcrest, Pocantico Hills, North Tarrytown, 10591. Joseph W Ernst, Dir; J William Hess, Assoc Dir
Notes: Papers relative to the Rockefeller Family, Foundations, University, and other specific enterprises and contributions to particular areas of social, physical, educational, and historic reform, preservation, conservation, or development. Extensive records of administrative, financial, physical, or intellectual relationships.

OH —OHIO STATE UNIVERSITY, Home Economics Library, Campbell Hall Rm 325, 1787 Neil Ave, Columbus, 43210. Neosha Mackey, Librn
Holdings: Vols (14,000) Cat Microforms
Notes: Separate catalog. Also, book catalog: *Catalog of the Home Economics Library* (Boston: G K Hall, 1976), 3 vols.

OR —UNIVERSITY OF OREGON LIBRARY, 1607 Agate St, Eugene, 97403. Ruth M Brewer, Resource Librn
Notes: Social and psychological aspects of aging.

PA —DELAWARE COUNTY PLANNING DEPT, Library, Third & Orange St, Media, 19063. Jane Taggart Quin, Librn
Holdings: Vols 4800 Cat
Budget: $1500

†PA —TEMPLE UNIVERSITY LIBRARIES, Special Collections Dept, Urban Archives Center, Philadelphia, 19122. Thomas Whitehead, Cur of Mss
Holdings: Cat
Notes: Incl the records of several separate collections which are deposited in the Urban Archives Center. Many collections contain photographs, maps and pamphlets in addition to manuscripts. All collections in the Urban Archives are separately cataloged.

PA —UNIVERSITY OF PITTSBURGH, Economics/Center for Regional Economics Studies Library, 4956 Forbes Quad, Pittsburgh, 15260. Patricia Suozzi-Crehan, Librn
Holdings: Vols 20,000
Budget: ($25,724)
Notes: Card catalog for collection. Cards for Economics Collection are in Hillman Library catalog. Collections are working collections reflecting the research and teaching interests of the Dept of Economics faculty and graduate students. The collection covers all aspects of the field of economics and demography.

WI —LEGISLATIVE REFERENCE BUREAU LIBRARY, City of Milwaukee, City Hall Rm 404, 200 E Wells St, Milwaukee, 53202. Ronald Leonhardt, Dir
Holdings: Vols (50,000) Cat Mss Maps Pix Microforms
Budget: ($8000)

ON —CANADIAN HOUSING INFORMATION CENTER, Canada Mortgage and Housing Corp, CMHC Annex Bldg Ground Floor, Montreal Rd, Ottawa, K1A 0P7, Can. Leslie Jones, Mgr
Holdings: Vols 7210 Cat
Budget: $27,000
Notes: Housing--all aspects: general, US Canada, Great Britain, France. 5000 pamphlets; 400 periodicals.

ON —METROPOLITAN TORONTO LIBRARY, Municipal Reference Library, City Hall, Toronto, M5H 2N1, Can. Margot Hewings, Head
Holdings: Vols (60,000) Cat Maps Pix Microforms Slides VF
Budget: ($112,600)
Notes: Community development; municipal finance; local municipal government;

HOUSING (cont.)

housing; urban pollution; urban transportation; urban affairs; urban geography.

HOUSING—STATISTICS

DC —US BUREAU OF THE CENSUS, Library, Federal Office Bldg 3, Rm 2451, Washington, 20233. Betty Baxtresser, Chief, ASD Library Branch
Holdings: Cat Microforms
Notes: Emphases on statistics of agriculture, business, construction, economics, foreign trade, governments, housing, industry, population, transportation, statistical methodology, and data processing. Library holdings are largely current materials covering the Bureau's programs. Outdated materials are withdrawn regularly.

HOUSMAN, A. E.

CA —UNIVERSITY OF SAN FRANCISCO, Richard A Gleeson Library, The Countess Bernardine Murphy Donohue Rare Book Room, San Francisco, 94117. D Steven Corey, Special Collections Librn
Holdings: Vols 50
Notes: All of his first editions, incl the first American edition of *A Shropshire Lad,* many later editions, plus 3 ALS's.

CT —YALE UNIVERSITY, Box 1603A, Yale Station, New Haven, 06520.

DC —LIBRARY OF CONGRESS, Washington, 20540.
Notes: Three collections are pertinent to Housman: (1) The AE Housman Collection, with most of the surviving fragments of the poetry notebooks, along with some of the letters AEH received on publication of *Last* Poems; (2) The Laurence Housman Collection, Chiefly of correspondence LH had with Maude M Hawkins, one of AEH's biographies; (3) The Grant Richards Collection preserves over a hundred autograph letters from AEH, and several hundred typescript copies of his letters; copies of to AEH from Grant Richards; letters to GR about AEH; and drafts and proofs of Richard's memoir. Scattered in other LC collections (Cyril Clemens; Van Doren, etc) are other letters from AEH. LC has only a few books from Housman's library.

IL —SOUTHERN ILLINOIS UNIVERSITY, CARBONDALE, Delyte W Morris Library, Carbondale, 62901.

IL —UNIVERSITY OF ILLINOIS, URBANA/CHAMPAIGN, Library, 1408 W Gregory Drive, Urbana, 61801. Norman B Brown, Asst Dir for Special Collections
Holdings: Mss
Notes: Some 110 letters of A E Housman to Grant Richards, and the Grant Richards Letter Books.

ME —COLBY COLLEGE, Library, Waterville, 04901.
Notes: A number of letters from A E Housman, and a large collection of editions of *A Shropshire Lad.*

MA —HARVARD UNIVERSITY LIBRARY, Houghton Library, Cambridge, 02138. Rodney G Dennis, Cur of Manuscripts
Holdings: Cat Mss
Notes: Incl some 90 letters from A E Housman, as well as a few books from his library.

†NJ —PRINCETON UNIVERSITY, Library, Princeton, 08540.

NY —COLUMBIA UNIVERSITY LIBRARIES, Rare Book & Manuscript Library, 801 Butler Library, 535 W 114 St, New York, 10027. Kenneth A Lohf, Librn
Holdings: Mss
Notes: A E Housman letters to Cyril Clemens, who planned a biography of A E Housman; also a few other Housman letters. Restricted use.

PA —BRYN MAWR COLLEGE, Canaday Library, Bryn Mawr, 19010. James Tanis, Dir
Notes: Manuscript and printed material in the Adelman Collection.

†TX —UNIVERSITY OF TEXAS LIBRARIES, General Libraries, Humanities Research Center, PO Box 7219, Austin, 78712. John Chalmers, Librn

WI —MARQUETTE UNIVERSITY, Memorial Library, 1415 W Wisconsin Ave, Milwaukee, 53233. Jay Kirk, Health Sciences Librn

HOUSMAN, LAURENCE

CA —UNIVERSITY OF SAN FRANCISCO, Richard A Gleeson Library, The Countess Bernardine Murphy Donohue Rare Book Room, San Francisco, 94117. D Steven Corey, Special Collections Librn
Holdings: Vols 120
Notes: First editions, ALS's, original drawings.

DC —LIBRARY OF CONGRESS, Washington, 20540.
Notes: Three collections are pertinent to Housman: (1) The AE Housman Collection, with most of the surviving fragments of the poetry notebooks, along with some of the letters AEH received on publication of *Last* Poems; (2) The Laurence Housman Collection, Chiefly of correspondence LH had with Maude M Hawkins, one of AEH's biographies; (3) The Grant Richards Collection preserves over a hundred autograph letters from AEH, and several hundred typescript copies of his letters; copies of to AEH from Grant Richards; letters to GR about AEH; and drafts and proofs of Richard's memoir. Scattered in other LC collections (Cyril Clemens; Van Doren, etc) are other letters from AEH. LC has only a few books from Housman's library.

PA —BRYN MAWR COLLEGE, Canaday Library, Bryn Mawr, 19010. James Tanis, Dir
Notes: Manuscript and printed material in the Adelman Collection.

HOUSTON, WILLIAM V.

IA —HERBERT HOOVER PRESIDENTIAL LIBRARY, West Branch, 52358. Dale C Mayer, Archivist
Notes: Papers.

TX —RICE UNIVERSITY, Fondren Library, 6100 S Main St, PO Box 1892, Houston, 77251. Dr Samuel M Carrington, Jr, University Librn
Holdings: // Cat Mss Pix
Notes: Papers of William V Houston, incl his research papers in spectroscopy, theory of solid state, quantum mechanics and superconductivity (15 linear ft).

HOVHANESS, ALAN

DC —LIBRARY OF CONGRESS, Music Division, Washington, 20540.
Notes: Music mss.

HOW, SAMUEL B., 1790-1868

NJ —RUTGERS, THE STATE UNIVERSITY OF NEW JERSEY, Alexander Library, Special Collections and Archives, College Ave & Huntington St, New Brunswick, 08903. Ronald L Becker, Cur of Manuscripts and Rare Books
Holdings: // Mss
Notes: Papers, etc (10 linear feet).

HOWARD, CHARLES HENRY, 1838-1908

ME —BOWDOIN COLLEGE, Library, Brunswick, 04011. Dianne M Gutscher, Cur of Special Collections
Holdings: Mss
Notes: The Charles Henry Howard Papers contain more than 400 pieces of correspondence, articles, and addresses, 1852-1907, of this Civil War officer and Secretary of the American Missionary Association. The papers complement those of his brother, Oliver Otis Howard.

HOWARD, GEORGE AND ELEANOR

CA —UNIVERSITY OF CALIFORNIA, LOS ANGELES, Research Library, Dept of Special Collections, 405 Hilgard Ave, Los Angeles, 90024. Edward Shreeves, Chairman, Bibliographers Group; David S Zeidberg, Head
Holdings: Mss
Notes: 70 letters to George and Eleanor Howard from Henry Miller and Anais Nin; 9 mss by Miller and Nin.

HOWARD, JOHN

†PA —FRIENDS HISTORICAL LIBRARY OF SWARTHMORE COLLEGE, Swarthmore, 19081.
Notes: Works on prison conditions, capital punishment, and works by and about Quaker prison reformers, Elizabeth Fry, John Howard, Richard Vaux, Robert Vaux, American Friends Service Committee, and others.

HOWARD, JOHN TASKER

NJ —NEWARK PUBLIC LIBRARY, Art & Music Dept, 5 Washington St, Newark, 07101. William J Dane, Supv
Holdings: Vols (25,000) Cat Mss Audiotapes Microforms VF
Notes: Music literature, scores, librettos, extensive vertical file, song sheets, special indexes, music periodicals. John Tasker Howard collection of notes and letters. Some special material on New Jersey and Newark music.

NY —CORNELL UNIVERSITY LIBRARIES, Collection of Regional History, Dept of Manuscripts and Univ Archives, Ithaca, 14853.
Notes: City planner. Papers, 1968-70; .2 ft.

HOWARD, MINNIE

ID —IDAHO STATE UNIVERSITY, Library, Pocatello, 83209. Gary Domitz, Social Science Librn
Holdings: Uncat Mss Pix //
Notes: Papers, etc.

HOWARD, OLIVER OTIS, 1830-1909

ME —BOWDOIN COLLEGE, Library, Brunswick, 04011. Dianne M Gutscher, Cur of Special Collections
Holdings: Mss Pix
Notes: The Oliver Otis Howard Papers consist of more than 150,000 pieces of correspondence, articles, lectures, and ephemera for the period 1843-1908, covering his services as a Civil War officer, as founder of the Freedmen's Bureau, as president of Howard University, and as superintendent of the US Military Academy at West Point.

HOWARD, ROWLAND BAILEY, 1834-1892

ME —BOWDOIN COLLEGE, Library, Brunswick, 04011. Dianne M Gutscher, Cur of Special Collections
Holdings: Mss
Notes: The Rowland Bailey Howard Papers contain about 250 letters, as well as diaries, newsclippings, and ephemera, primarily for the period 1848-1891, of this clergyman and Secretary of the American Peace Society. The collection contains almost exclusively family letters and complements those of Rowland's brothers, Oliver Otis Howard and Charles Henry Howard.

HOWARD, ROY W.

DC —LIBRARY OF CONGRESS, Manuscript Division, Washington, 20540. John C Broderick, Chief
Notes: Papers of Roy W Howard (1883-1964), past president and chairman of the board of Scripps--Howard Newspapers. Some 85,000 items for the years 1923-64, incl business and personal correspondence, maintained under state and city of origin, with separate files in each year for the various Scripps--Howard newspapers, especially for the *World Telegram* (New York City).

HOWARD FAMILY

IN —INDIANA UNIVERSITY, Lilly Library, Seventh St, Bloomington, 47405. William R Cagle, Librn
Holdings: // Mss Pix
Notes: Business papers and correspondence of Howard Ship Yards & Dock Co, Jeffersonville, Ind, 1834-1942. Incl correspondence with captains, ship owners, Howard family members, etc; some photos of Howard-built ships during construction; ca 10,000 blueprints, drawings and scale specifications for riverboat construction; business ledgers and cash books; general office files. 265,600 items.

HOWARD UNIVERSITY

ME —BOWDOIN COLLEGE, Library, Brunswick, 04011. Dianne M Gutscher, Cur of Special Collections
Holdings: Mss Pix
Notes: The Oliver Otis Howard Papers consist of more than 150,000 pieces of correspondence, articles, lectures, and ephemera for the period 1843-1908, covering his services as a Civil War officer, as founder of the Freedmen's Bureau, as president of Howard University, and as superintendent of the US Military Academy at West Point.

HOWARTH, R. G.

†TX —UNIVERSITY OF TEXAS LIBRARIES, General Libraries, Humanities Research Center, PO Box 7219, Austin, 78712. John Chalmers, Librn

HOWE, REP. ALLAN

UT —UNIVERSITY OF UTAH, Marriott Library, Special Collections, Salt Lake City, 84112. Gregory C Thompson, Cur
Holdings: Cat Mss Microfilm Film Oral History
Notes: Papers.

HOWE,CHAUNCEY J., O.D.

MI —FERRIS STATE COLLEGE ARCHIVES, 901 S State St, Big Rapids, 49307. R Lawrence Martin, Coordr
Holdings: Vols 26 Cat Mss Pix
Notes: 4 boxes of papers and books of Dr Chauncey J Howe, OD, practicing optometrist in Hillsdale, Mich, 1920-1968, secretary, Michigan Board of Examiners in Optometry, 1941-1972, founder of Omega Delta, professional optometric fraternity. Includes professional papers of Dr Howe, papers of the State Board and 7 vols of minutes of the State Board, 1909-1970.

HOWE, DONALD

MA —SOCIETY FOR THE PRESERVATION OF NEW ENGLAND ANTIQUITIES, Library, 141 Cambridge St, Boston, 02114. Ellie Reichlin, Librn & Cur of Photographic Collections
Notes: Photographs of communities inundated by the development of the Quabbin Reservoir in Western Massachusetts. 300 pieces.

HOWE, ELLIC

MO —WASHINGTON UNIVERSITY, Libraries, Special Collections Dept, Campus Box 1061, St Louis, 63130.
Notes: Family and business correspondence.

HOWE, JULIA WARD, 1819-1910

MA —CONCORD FREE PUBLIC LIBRARY, 129 Main St, Concord, 01742. Rose Marie Mitten, Dir
Notes: Letters.

HOWE, LOIS LILLEY, 1864-1964

MA —MASSACHUSETTS INSTITUTE OF TECHNOLOGY, Institute Archives, Special Collections, Cambridge, 02139.
Notes: Papers of Howe, Manning and Almy, an architectural firm that started in 1913 as Lois Lilley Howe and Manning, was an unusual and successful partnership of women architects. The collection incl correspondence, financial data, reports, specifications, photographs, blueprints, drawings, and research material from the firm. Housing projects incl Mariemont, Ohio, as well as designs and renovations for New England especially in the Colonial Revival style.

HOWE, MANNING AND ALMY, 1913-1937

MA —MASSACHUSETTS INSTITUTE OF TECHNOLOGY, Institute Archives, Special Collections, Cambridge, 02139.
Notes: Papers of Howe, Manning and Almy, an architectural firm that started in 1913 as Lois Lilley Howe and Manning, was an unusual and successful partnership of women architects. The collection incl correspondence, financial data, reports, specifications, photographs, blueprints, drawings, and research material from the firm. Housing projects incl Mariemont, Ohio, as well as designs and renovations for New England especially in the Colonial Revival style.

HOWE, MARK DEWOLFE, 1906-1967

MA —HARVARD UNIVERSITY LIBRARY, Law School Library, Langdell Hall, Cambridge, 02138. Erika S Chadbourn, Cur of Mss
Holdings: Cat Mss
Notes: Personal-professional papers. Typed inventory in repository. Inclusive dates: 1930-1967.

HOWELL, CLARK

GA —EMORY UNIVERSITY, Robert W Woodruff Library, Special Collections Dept, Atlanta, 30322. Linda M Matthews, Head Special Collections; Virginia J H Cain, Processing Archivist; Richard H F Lindemann, Reference Archivist
Holdings: Cat Mss Pix Audiotapes
Notes: Extensive collections of papers of Henry W Grady, Corra Harris, Joel Chandler Harris, Julian LaRose Harris, Julia Collier Harris, Clark Howell, Ralph E McGilll, Harold H Martin, Mildred Seydell, and Claude Sitton, among others, most associated with the Atlanta *Constitution.* Descriptions and index are availalbe in repository.

HOWELL, WILSON S.

LA —NEW ORLEANS PUBLIC LIBRARY, Louisiana Div, 219 Loyola Ave, New Orleans, 70140. Collin B Hamer Jr, Head; Brenda M Osbey, Library Associate
Holdings: Cat Maps Pix
Notes: Louisiana and New Orleans Picture File Collection ranges from the late 19th century-date and incl the following separate collections: Alexander Allison (ca 1898-1951, 337 pieces); Charles Franck (ca 1920-50, 170 pieces); Leda Plauche (ca 1935-53, 220 pieces); C Milo Williams (ca 1910, 85 pieces); Wilson S Howell (ca 1890, 49 pieces); Grauman Marks (ca 1960, 268 pieces); Robert Tallant (ca 1940-50, 70 pieces); Robert E Tracy (1959, 87 pieces); Anthony J Flaherty (ca 1970-84, 83 pieces); George F Mugnier (1880-1920, 186 pieces); Color Slides (ca 1945-date, 500 pieces); 30, 000 photographs incl 500 color slides and 104 negatives. Use of the material is restricted to on-site research. Publication must be accompanied by credit cut line.

HOWELL FAMILY

NJ —GLASSBORO STATE COLLEGE, Savitz Library, Stewart Room, Glassboro, 08028. Clara Kirner, Special Collection Librn
Holdings: Cat Mss
Notes: Correspondence, personal and business (fisheries), account books, diaries, commissions and appointments, other misc papers of Anna Blackwell Howell, Benjamin Betterton Howell, Benjamin Paschall Howell, John Ladd Howell, Joshua Ladd Howell, Governor Richard Howell, Samuel Ladd Howell and others.

NJ —GLOUCESTER COUNTY HISTORICAL SOCIETY LIBRARY, 17 Hunter St, PO Box 409, Woodbury, 08096. Edith E Hoelle, Librn
Notes: Cataloged mss pertaining to the Howell Family of Fancy Hill, Gloucester County, NJ from 1739-1890. Incl letters, bills, account books and memorabilia of the Shad Fisheries along the Delaware River and Etna Furnace at Tuckahoe, NJ, a 19th century bog iron furnace; lists of (State of) Delaware suppliers to the Continental Army, Revolutionary War, etc, as well as household memorabilia of Anna Blackwood Howell (1769-1855), ca 3800 items.

HOWELLS, J. HARVEY

MA —BOSTON UNIVERSITY, Mugar Memorial Library, Special Collections Dept, 771 Commonwealth Ave, Boston, 02215. Howard B Gotlieb, Dir
Holdings: Cat Mss Pix
Notes: Mss, correspondence, etc collected in depth; incl publications by or about.

HOWELLS, WILLIAM DEAN, 1837-1920

CA —UNIVERSITY OF CALIFORNIA, LOS ANGELES, Research Library, Dept of Special Collections, 405 Hilgard Ave, Los Angeles, 90024. Edward Shreeves, Chairman, Bibliographers Group; David S Zeidberg, Head
Holdings: Vols 150
Notes: 150 first and other editions of his books; 5 letters.

CA —SAN DIEGO STATE UNIVERSITY, Malcolm A Love Library, 5300 Campanile Dr, San Diego, 92182. D Dickinson, Univ Librn; Don L Bosseau, Dir
Notes: Collected works in first edition of certain prominent authors, as H G Wells, Somerset Maugham, William Dean Howells, Gertrude Atherton, Tom Stoppard, James Clavell, G A Henty, Henry Raup Wagner.

CT —YALE UNIVERSITY, Box 1603A, Yale Station, New Haven, 06520.
Holdings: Cat Mss

MA —BOSTON UNIVERSITY, Mugar Memorial Library, Special Collections Dept, 771 Commonwealth Ave, Boston, 02215. Howard B Gotlieb, Dir
Holdings: Cat Vols
Notes: About 85 titles and publications by.

MA —HARVARD UNIVERSITY LIBRARY, Widener Library, Cambridge, 02138.
Holdings: Cat Mss
Notes: Incl in *Harvard Library Notes,* III (1938), 147-153.

NY —ALFRED UNIVERSITY, Herrick Memorial Library, Alfred, 14802. June E Brown, Head Librn
Notes: The Howells/Frechette Collection. Family documents, 7000 letters of William Cooper Howells (American consul to Quebec, later to Toronto), William Dean Howells, his sister Annie Frechette, Achille Frechette (official translator, Canadian House of Commons), and Louis Frechette (poet laureate of Canada).

NY —CORNELL UNIVERSITY LIBRARIES, Collection of Regional History, Dept of Manuscripts and Univ Archives, Ithaca, 14853.
Notes: Letters to Mrs Lewis, 1887, and to Prof William Strunk, 1911; novelist.

NY —SAINT JOHN'S UNIVERSITY, Special Collections Dept, Grand Central & Utopia Pkwys, Jamaica, 11439. Szilvia E Szmuk, Librn
Holdings: // Cat
Notes: No photocopying.

NY —UNIVERSITY OF ROCHESTER, Rush Rhees Library, Department of Rare Books and Special Collections, Rochester, 14627. Peter Dzwonkoski, Librn
Holdings: Cat Mss
Notes: Correspondents include Robert

HOWELLS, WILLIAM DEAN, 1837-1920 (cont.)

Underwood Johnson, Will Carlton, Henry Mills Alden, Richard Watson Gilder; Howell's proof of article on Henrik Ibsen (1906).

OH —BOWLING GREEN STATE UNIVERSITY, Jerome Library, Center for Archival Collections, Bowling Green, 43403. Paul D Yon, Dir; Elaine R Ezell, Reference Archivist; Nancy Steen, Rare Books Librn
Holdings: Vols 125 Cat
Budget: ($3000)
Notes: Most of these vols autographed by Howells; most in fine bindings.

OH —RUTHERFORD B HAYES LIBRARY, 1337 Hayes Ave, Fremont, 43420. Watt P Marchman, Dir
Holdings: Vols 505 Cat Mss Maps Pix Microforms
Notes: Mss of W D Howells, consisting of correspondence, literary mss, genealogical and biographical materials; clippings, etc. Part is listed in *Guide to Manuscripts of the Ohio Historical Society,* 239. Indexed. Also, correspondence in the Lyman-Lincoln Collection.

OH —MIAMI UNIVERSITY, King Library, Walter Havighurst Special Collections Library, Oxford, 45056. Helen Ball, Cur of Special Collections
Holdings: Vols 663 Uncat
Notes: Incl over 120 autographs and letters.

PA —BUCKNELL UNIVERSITY, Ellen Clarke Bertrand Library, Lewisburg, 17837. Ann de Klerk, Librn
Holdings: Vols 175 Cat

PA —UNIVERSITY OF PENNSYLVANIA, Van Pelt Library, Rare Books Collection, 34 & Walnut Sts, Philadelphia, 19104. Daniel Traister, Special Collections Librn
Holdings: Vols 250 Cat
Notes: The Kirk-Howells Collection incl 10 boxes of related material and 6 scrapbooks. Descriptive case file available in library.

VA —UNIVERSITY OF VIRGINIA, Alderman Library, Clifton Waller Barrett Collection, Charlottesville, 22901. Joan St C Crane, Cur of American Literature Collections
Holdings: Vols 300 Cat Mss
Notes: Works by and about him. Over 300 manuscript pieces, etc. Bibliography: Fannie Mae Elliott and Lucy Clark, comps, *The Barrett Library W D Howells: A Checklist of Printed and Manuscript Works of William Dean Howells in the Library of the University of Virginia* (Charlottesville: University of Virginia Press, 1959).

HOWELLS, WILLIAM COOPER

NY —ALFRED UNIVERSITY, Herrick Memorial Library, Alfred, 14802. June E Brown, Head Librn
Notes: The Howells/Frechette Collection. Family documents, 7000 letters of William Cooper Howells (American consul to Quebec, later to Toronto), William Dean Howells, his sister Annie Frechette, Achille Frechette (official translator, Canadian House of Commons), and Louis Frechette (poet laureate of Canada).

HOWES, ESTELLA E.

CA —POMONA PUBLIC LIBRARY, Special Collections, 625 S Garey Ave, PO Box 2271, Pomona, 91766. David Streeter, Librn
Holdings: // Uncat Pix Slides
Notes: Brooking Tatum collection of California Flora: 125 8x10 color prints and 50 35mm color transparencies; Estella E Howes water color paintings of local flora (98 paintings); Cyril Albritt oil painting.

HOWLAND, HENRY R.

NY —BUFFALO MUSEUM OF SCIENCE, Buffalo Society of Natural Sciences, Research Library, Humboldt Park, Buffalo, 14211. Marcia T Morrison, Chief Librn
Notes: Henry R Howland Manuscript Collection. 1824-1926. Autographs and letters to Howland and others in French and English, from scientists and others, incl Charles Darwin; Thomas Huxley; and Louis Agassiz. Many items from or about John James Audubon, incl his original ms description of the Canada Jay Young and his notes for the Blue Jay. Howland served on the Board of Directors of the Museum, 1878-1930. He He was corresponding secretary 1921-29 and author of a history of the Museum.

HOWSON, ROGER

†NY —COLUMBIA UNIVERSITY LIBRARIES, Butler Library, Rare Book and Manuscript Library, 535 W 114 St, New York, 10027.
Notes: The papers of Dwight Carroll Miner, comprising the extensive files of correspondence, mss, notes, and printed materials relating to the history of Columbia University. Incl the papers of University Librarian and historian Roger Howson.

HOYEM, ANDREW

CA —CLAREMONT COLLEGES, Honnold Library, Ninth & Dartmouth, Claremont, 91711. Tania Rizzo, Special Collections Dept Head
Holdings: Vols (75) Cat VF
Notes: The combined holdings of Honnold and Denison Libraries at the Claremont Colleges contain a complete set but one of the books published by the Arion Press as well as commissioned books and pamphlets, and a comprehensive collection of books printed by Andrew Hoyem for Grabhorn-Hoyem and others. Complete ephemera since 1979. Extensive files of advertising, prospectuses, correspondence, and broadsides.

HOYT, EDWIN P.

MA —BOSTON UNIVERSITY, Mugar Memorial Library, Special Collections Dept, 771 Commonwealth Ave, Boston, 02215. Howard B Gotlieb, Dir
Holdings: Cat Mss Correspondence

HOYT, RICHARD D.

MA —BOSTON UNIVERSITY, Mugar Memorial Library, Special Collections Dept, 771 Commonwealth Ave, Boston, 02215. Howard B Gotlieb, Dir
Holdings: Mss

HSIANG CHI (GAME) see Chinese Chess

HUARTE DE SAN JUAN, JUAN

OH —CLEVELAND PUBLIC LIBRARY, Fine Arts and Special Collections Department, 325 Superior Ave, Cleveland, 44114. Alice N Loranth, Head
Holdings: Vols 42 Cat
Notes: Early and rare 16th-19th Century editions, translations and versions. Separate "edition" catalog is maintained.
See also entry under Rare Books.

HUAVE INDIANS

NY —HOFSTRA UNIVERSITY, Library, 1000 Fulton Ave, Hempstead, 11550. Charles R Andrews, Dean of Library Services
Notes: The personal library of Paul Radin. See description of the American Philosophical Society Library's collection of his anthropological papers under this entry (Pa).

PA —AMERICAN PHILOSOPHICAL SOCIETY, Library, 105 S Fifth St, Philadelphia, 19106. Edward C Carter II, Librn
Notes: The anthropological papers of Paul Radin in fields of ethnology, social organization, primitive religion, linguistics, and mythology. He worked mostly among the Winnebao, Ojibwa, Fox Zapotec, Wappo, Wintun, and Huave Indian tribes; also Italian and other ethnic minorities of San Francisco.

HUBARD FAMILY

VA —UNIVERSITY OF VIRGINIA, Alderman Library, Manuscripts Dept, Charlottesville, 22901. Edmund Berkeley Jr, Cur
Holdings: Cat Mss Maps Pix
Notes: 19th century Virginia Family Papers Collections enable a researcher to obtain an excellent picture of the economic and social interactions on large plantations in Virginia during the 19th century. They are invaluable as research sources in the study of slavery, women's history, economic history, agrarian and political history.

HUBBARD, ELBERT

AZ —NORTHERN ARIZONA UNIVERSITY, Special Collection Library, CU Box 6022, Flagstaff, 86011. Peter M Whiteley, Coordr/Archivist; William Mullane, Librn
Holdings: Vols 659 // Cat
Notes: Lloyd C Henning Collection: extensive collection of Roycroft Press Books, incl several unique and several very rare items.

IL —ILLINOIS STATE UNIVERSITY, Milner Library, Dept of Special Collections, Normal, 61761. Robert Sokan, Librn
Notes: First editions, limited editions, ephemera, etc.

NY —BUFFALO & ERIE COUNTY PUBLIC LIBRARY, Rare Book Room, Lafayette Sq, Buffalo, 14203. William H Loos, Cur
Holdings: Vols 450 Cat Mss Pix
Notes: First and limited editions, some mss, incl that of *A Message to Garcia.*

NY —AURORA HISTORICAL SOCIETY, Library-Museum, 571 Main St, Village Hall, East Aurora, 14052. Genevieve Steffen, Cur
Holdings: Vols 1500 Cat Mss Pix Audiotapes
Budget: ($400)
Notes: A one-room Library-Museum dedicated to the preservation of Hubbard/Roycroft memorabila. In addition to beautifully printed and bound books, we have collections of metalcraft and leathercraft items and furniture made in the Roycroft shops 1895-1938. The collection belongs to the Village of East Aurora. Check for opening hours.

†ON —UNIVERSITY OF WESTERN ONTARIO, School of Library and Information Science, Special Collections Room, London, N6A 5B9, Can.
Notes: Representative colection incl some early items from the Roycrofters private press.

HUBBARD, GURDON S.

IL —CHICAGO HISTORICAL SOCIETY, Library, Clark St at North Ave, Chicago, 60614. Archie Motley, Manuscript Librn
Notes: Gurdon S Hubbard, fur trader and Chicago commission merchant.

HUBBARD, JOHN, 1794-1869

ME —BOWDOIN COLLEGE, Library, Brunswick, 04011. Dianne M Gutscher, Cur of Special Collections
Holdings: Mss
Notes: The Hubbard Family Papers contain more than 12,000 pieces of correspondence and other mss materials relating to the Hubbard Family, for the period 1794-1915. Of principal interest are extensive files of letters to and from John Hubbard (1794-1869), governor of Maine, who signed the "Maine Law" (prohibition law) in 1851, and was a commissioner under the Reciprocity Treaty with Great Britain.

HUBBARD, KIN

IN —INDIANA UNIVERSITY, Lilly Library, Seventh St, Bloomington, 47405. William R Cagle, Librn
Holdings: Vols 130 // Cat Mss Pix
Notes: First and early editions, many signed. Mss incl pen and ink drawings and scrapbooks of Abe Martin cartoons, photographs, and correspondence. 112 items.

HUBBARD, KIN (cont.)

IN —BUTLER UNIVERSITY, Irwin Library, Hugh Thomas Miller Rare Book Room, 4600 Sunset Ave, Indianapolis, 46208. Gisela Terrell, Rare Books Librn
Holdings: Cat Mss Pix
Notes: *Gaar Williams/Kin Hubbard* Collection. This collection was presented to the library by Blanche Stillson in 1964. It contains original cartoons and other drawings, books (many of them inscribed), magazines, letters and other manuscripts, photographs, and memorabilia by both Hoosier cartoonists and humorists. A catalogue of the Gaar Williams ("Abe Martin") items was printed in 1981. It is available upon request.

HUBBARD FAMILY

ME —BOWDOIN COLLEGE, Library, Brunswick, 04011. Dianne M Gutscher, Cur of Special Collections
Holdings: Mss
Notes: The Hubbard Family Papers contain more than 12,000 pieces of correspondence and other mss materials relating to the Hubbard Family, for the period 1794-1915. Of principal interest are extensive files of letters to and from John Hubbard (1794-1869), governor of Maine, who signed the "Maine Law" (prohibition law) in 1851, and was a commissioner under the Reciprocity Treaty with Great Britain.

HUBBELL, JAY BROADUS, 1885-1979

NC —DUKE UNIVERSITY, William R Perkins Library, Manuscript Dept, Durham, 27706. Ellen Gartrell, Cur of Mss
Holdings: Cat Mss
Notes: Papers, correspondence, etc.

NC —DUKE UNIVERSITY, William R Perkins Library, Jay B Hubbell Center for American Literary Historiography, Durham, 27706. Erma Whittington, Librn
Notes: 77,312 items, including manuscripts, pictures, clippings, and correspondence. "The objective of the Center is to gather the papers and materials of significant scholars and critics in American literary history." The Center is a part of the Perkins Library Manuscripts Department.

HUBLER, RICHARD G.

MA —BOSTON UNIVERSITY, Mugar Memorial Library, Special Collections Dept, 771 Commonwealth Ave, Boston, 02215. Howard B Gotlieb, Dir
Holdings: Cat Mss

HUBLEY, FRANK

CA —UNIVERSITY OF CALIFORNIA, LOS ANGELES, Theater Arts Library, Los Angeles, 90024. Edward Shreeves, Chairman, Bibliographers Group; Audree Malkin, Head, Theater Arts Library
Notes: Collection of Frank Hubley, animator: storyboards, cels and watercolor sketches for the production of animated films, 1950-1970.

HUDSON, JOHN

†UT —UNIVERSITY OF UTAH, Marriott Library, Salt Lake City, 84112.
Notes: Original drawings and personal papers of John Hudson, a gold rush Forty-Niner who helped chart the Great Salt Lake with Captain Howard Stansbury.

HUDSON, MANLEY OTTMER, 1886-1960

MA —HARVARD UNIVERSITY LIBRARY, Law School Library, Langdell Hall, Cambridge, 02138. Erika S Chadbourn, Cur of Mss
Holdings: Cat Mss
Notes: Professional papers; international documents. Typed inventory in repository. Inclusive dates: 1905-1960.

RI —US NAVAL WAR COLLEGE, Historical Collection & Museum, Newport, 02841. Anthony S Nicolosi, Dir; Evelyn Cherpak, Cur
Holdings: Mss
Notes: A collection of official letters, research notes and legal case files dealing with the Supreme Court case, US vs California (1947) and supplemental proceedings; the Anglo-Egyptian dispute before the UN (1947); various international law issues and studies and international law at the Naval War College. Manley O Hudson was a noted jurist and and professor of international law at the Naval War College, 1946-1952.

HUDSON, STEPHEN

CA —UNIVERSITY OF CALIFORNIA, LOS ANGELES, Research Library, Dept of Special Collections, 405 Hilgard Ave, Los Angeles, 90024. Edward Shreeves, Chairman, Bibliographers Group; David S Zeidberg, Head
Holdings: Vols 15
Notes: 15 first and other editions of his books; 35 letters.

HUDSON, WILLIAM HENRY

IL —ILLINOIS STATE UNIVERSITY, Milner Library, Dept of Special Collections, Normal, 61761. Robert Sokan, Librn
Notes: First editions, limited editions, ephemera, etc.

MI —UNIVERSITY OF MICHIGAN, Library, Dept of Rare Books & Special Collections, Ann Arbor, 48109. Robert J Starring, Head
Holdings: Vols 120 Cat Mss Pix
Notes: Includes scarce first editions, presentation copies, and association items; copies of *Ralph Herne* and *Fan*, with revisions in the author's hand for republication. There are also 75 manuscript items including 32 letters in Hudson's holograph and photocopies of 17 early letters (1866-70), and photographs.

NH —DARTMOUTH COLLEGE, Baker Memorial Library, Hanover, 03755.
Holdings: Cat
Notes: Noncirculating.

†NC —WAKE FOREST UNIVERSITY, Z Smith Reynolds Library, Box 7777, Reynold Sta, Winston-Salem, 27109. Richard J Murdoch, Rare Book Librn
Holdings: Vols 120 Cat Mss Pix
Notes: A significant collection.

PA —BRYN MAWR COLLEGE, Canaday Library, Bryn Mawr, 19010. James Tanis, Dir
Notes: Rare books in the Adelman Collection.

HUDSON, J. L., COMPANY

MI —DETROIT PUBLIC LIBRARY, Burton Historical Collection, 5201 Woodward Ave, Detroit, 48202. Alice Dalligan, Chief

HUDSON REVIEW

VT —UNIVERSITY OF VERMONT, Guy W Bailey/David W Howe Library, Burlington, 05405. John Buehler, Asst Dir for Special Collections
Notes: The papers of Hayden Carruth (1921-), poet and poetry editor for the *Hudson* Review.

HUDSON RIVER SCHOOL

VT —SAINT JOHNSBURY ATHENAEUM, Library, 30 Main St, Saint Johnsbury, 05819. Jean F Marcy, Librn
Holdings: Vols (41,000) Cat
Notes: American artists of the late 19th century, with emphasis on artists whose works are in the Institution's art gallery.

HUDSON RIVER VALLEY—HISTORY

NY —GREENE COUNTY HISTORICAL SOCIETY, Vedder Memorial Library, RD, Coxsackie, 12051. Raymond Beecher, Librn
Holdings: Vols (3500) Cat Mss Maps Pix Slides
Budget: ($500)
Notes: Collection strong in Greene County, the mid-Hudson region and the Catskill Mountains. County newspapers, pictorial county file, very large mss, 1800-1900.

NY —NEW YORK STATE OFFICE OF PARKS & RECREATION, TACONIC REGION, Clermont State Historic Park, Library, RR 1, Box 215, Germantown, 12526. Bruce E Naramore, Historic Site Manager
Holdings: Vols (5000) Cat Mss Maps Slides Audiotapes
Notes: Many period editions of pre - and post-American Revolutionary War history of the Hudson River Valley. Incl political, social, agricultural, editions. No photocopying.

NY —MOUNT SAINT MARY COLLEGE, Curtin Memorial Library, Liberty St, Newburgh, 12550. Estelle McKeever, Librn
Holdings: Vols (110) Cat
Notes: Monihan Collection of Hudson Valley History. Emphasis on Orange County and Newburgh.

NY —VASSAR COLLEGE, Library, Rare Books & Manuscripts Collection, Box 20, Poughkeepsie, 12601. Lisa Browar, Cur
Holdings: Mss Pix
Notes: Predominantly 19th and early 20th centuries. Incl books, mss, photographs.

NY —HISTORICAL SOCIETY OF THE TARRYTOWNS, Library, One Grove St, Tarrytown, 10591. Ruth Neuendorffer, Librn
Holdings: Vols (3000) Cat Mss Maps Pix Microforms
Notes: History of the Tarrytowns and vicinity. Incl newspapers, 1875-1946, on microfilm. Bound volumes of Tarrytown *Daily News,* 1916-1937.

NY —YONKERS PUBLIC LIBRARY, Information Services, 7 Main St, Yonkers, 10701. Martita Schwarz, Dept Head
Notes: Hudson River Museum branch has closed. Materials on history of Yonkers, with some materials on Hudson River history have been distributed to several other branches in the library system.

HUDSON'S BAY COMPANY

MN —GRAND PORTAGE NATIONAL MONUMENT, Library, Box 666, Grand Marais, 55604.
Holdings: Vols (1000) Cat Mss Pix
Notes: Deals primarily with the Canadian fur trade, especially the activities of the North West Co and the Hudson's Bay Co.

†WA —WASHINGTON STATE UNIVERSITY, Library, Manuscripts, Archives & Special Collections, Pullman, 99164. John F Guido, Head
Holdings: Cat Mss Maps Pix
Notes: The Carl Parcher Russell papers, a vast resource (24,916 items; 45 linear feet) on American Indian and Western pioneer activities and artifacts. Much on the fur trade; pioneer life; mountain men and trapping; wildlife; primitive life in detail. Also the National Park Service, parks monuments, etc. Described in *Carl Parcher Russell: An Indexed Register of His Scholarly and Professional Papers, 1920-1967, in the Washington State University* Library (Pullman 1970), 149 pp.

MB —HUDSON'S BAY CO, Library, 77 Main St, Winnipeg, R3C 2R1, Can. Carol Preston, Librn Hudson's Bay House
Holdings: Vols (6000) Cat Mss Maps Pix Slides
Notes: Main purpose is to provide research materials for production of the historical quarterly *The Beaver,* and to answer inquiries about the Company's history. Incl 250,000 pictures and 7000 VF pieces. No published catalog, but Library maintains author/subject/title card catalog. Limited photocopying. Mss of HBC Archives held by the Manitoba Provincial Archives. Published descriptions: Dowdall, Judi, "Hudson's Bay Company Library," *Canadian Library* Journal, June 1974, p 179; Preston, Carol, "Hudson's Bay Company Library," *Manitoba Library Association Bulletin,* June 1976, pp 24-25.

HUDSON'S BAY COMPANY (cont.)

MB —UNIVERSITY OF MANITOBA, Elizabeth Dafoe Library, Archives and Special Collections Dept, Winnipeg, R3T 2N2, Can. Richard E Bennett, Dept Head; Corrado A Santoro, Reference Archivist
Notes: History of Hudson's Bay Company.

ON —PUBLIC ARCHIVES OF CANADA, Library, 395 Wellington St, Ottawa, K1A 0N3, Can. Dawn E Monroe, Collections Development Officer
Holdings: Vols (80,000) Cat
Notes: The Public Archives Library's extensive collection covers almost all historical disciplines. Accounts of explorations and discoveries certainly represent the core of the Public Archives Library's Rare Book Collection. Indeed, the works of early explorers such as Champlain, Bacqueville de la Potherie, Lahontan, La Perouse, Le Clerq, Hakluyt, Cook, Mackenzie, Heriot, Hearne and many others can be consulted. The Library also holds both the original Swedish edition and the rare English translation of Pehr Kalm's voyages in North America: Kalm, Pehr. An important, well-documented area concerns the settlement of the French in Canada, their dealings with native people, and descriptions of New France's natural environment. This early material on indigenous people is further supplemented by prayer and books such as Henry Aaron Hill's translation of*A Collection of Hymns for the Use of Native Christians of the Mohawk Language; To Which Are Added a Number of Hymns for Sabbath Schools* (New York: Printed by M'Elrath & Bangs, 1832, various pagings); Micmac, Algonquin and Iroquois dictionaries; and an illustrated reading book entitled *Indian Child's Book: A Primer in English and Cree Languages* (np, nd, 37 pp). Military strategy and naval construction are areas which are well documented in the Rare Book Collection.

HUEBERT, DIANA

IL —NEWBERRY LIBRARY, 60 W Walton St, Chicago, 60610. Carolyn A Sheehy, Administrator
Holdings: Cat Mss Pix Posters
Notes: Extensive holdings in the areas of dance history (including important first editions) and dance music. Newly formed Midwest Dance Archive contains the papers of Ann Barzel, Walter Camryn, Diana Huebert and Edna McRae.

HUEBSCH, BENJAMIN W.

DC —LIBRARY OF CONGRESS, Manuscript Division, Washington, 20540. John C Broderick, Chief
Holdings: Cat Mss Pix
Notes: Mss, papers, records, etc.

NY —COLUMBIA UNIVERSITY LIBRARIES, Rare Book & Manuscript Library, 801 Butler Library, 535 W 114 St, New York, 10027. Kenneth A Lohf, Librn
Holdings: Vols 400 Uncat
Notes: Over 1000 vols published by him.

HUEGEL, BARON FRIEDRICH VON, 1852-1925

†CA —UNIVERSITY OF SAN FRANCISCO, Richard A Gleeson Library, The Countess Bernardine Murphy Donohue Rare Book Room, San Francisco, 94117. D Steven Corey, Special Collections Librn
Holdings: Vols 1200 Uncat Pix
Notes: Modernism in the Catholic Church. Incl extensive holdings concerning George Tyrrell, Alfred Loisy, and Baron Friedrich von Huegel.

HUFFMAN, EUGENE

CA —UNIVERSITY OF CALIFORNIA, BERKELEY, Bancroft Library, Manuscripts Division, Berkeley, 94720. James D Hart, Dir
Notes: Correspondence and papers relative to the history of modern chemistry.

HUGGINS, SIR WILLIAM, 1824-1910

MA —WELLESLEY COLLEGE, Whitin Observatory, Astronomy Dept, Wellesley, 02181.
Notes: Sir William Huggins' (1824-1910) diaries, ca 5 inches (1856-1900) plus scientic instruments and apparatus.

HUGHES, CHARLES EVANS, 1862-1948

DC —LIBRARY OF CONGRESS, Manuscript Division, Washington, 20540. John C Broderick, Chief
Holdings: Cat Mss Pix
Notes: Mss, papers, records, etc.

RI —BROWN UNIVERSITY, John Hay Library, 20 Prospect St, Providence, 02912. Mark N Brown, Cur Mss
Holdings: / / Mss
Notes: Some papers of Charles Evans Hughes, Governor of New York, Secretary of State, and Chief Justice of the US Supreme Court. Brown Class of 1881. More than 100 papers incl college notebooks, memorabilia, and letters, of which 44 are to his parents while a student at Brown University (1878-1881) and 9 are to Hughes about conferring on him the Degree of Grand Cross Knight of the Crown of Italy.

HUGHES, DUDLEY M.

GA —UNIVERSITY OF GEORGIA, Libraries, Special Collections Division, Athens, 30602. Vesta Lee Gordon, Asst Dir for Special Collections
Notes: Collection contains 1394.8 linear feet of mss: papers of US Senator Richard B Russell; US Congressmen John W Davis, Maston O'Neal, Robert G Stephens Jr, John L Pilcher, Dudley M Hughes; Governors Hoke Smith, Lester Maddox, Carl Sanders.

HUGHES, JOHN

MA —BOSTON UNIVERSITY, Mugar Memorial Library, Special Collections Dept, 771 Commonwealth Ave, Boston, 02215. Howard B Gotlieb, Dir
Holdings: Cat Mss Pix

HUGHES, LANGSTON

CT —YALE UNIVERSITY, Box 1603A, Yale Station, New Haven, 06520.
Holdings: Cat Mss

IL —CHICAGO PUBLIC LIBRARY, G Woodson Regional Library, George C Hall Branch, 9525 S Halsted, Chicago, 60628. Steven C Newsome, Cur; Hattie L Power, Regional Library Dir
Holdings: Vols 8000 Cat Mss Audiotapes Microforms
Notes: The Vivian G Harsh Collectioon on Afro-American History and Literature, in the George Cleveland Hall Branch of the Chicago Public Library, contains books, in print and on microfilm, periodicals, recordings, tapes, pamphlets and mss. Specializes in Afro-Americana, but contains a sizeable number of books on Africa. Also contains these noteworthy items: *The Negro in Illinois: the Illinois Writers Project Files; The Chicago Afro-American Union Analytic Catalog; Big Boy Leaves Home*, by Richard Wright (an original typewritten ms); *The Big Sea*, by Langston Hughes (3 original typewritten mss of this work). 7800 vols on microfilm.

KS —UNIVERSITY OF KANSAS, Kenneth Spencer Research Library, Kansas Collection, Lawrence, 66045. Sheryl K Williams, Cur
Holdings: Vols 120 Cat Mss Microforms
Notes: His published works, regardless of the language, 80 items of sheet music, single copies of periodicals, offprints of articles, etc, some 25 playbills, advertisements, phonograph records, as well as 12 unpublished plays and librettos, correspondence.

MA —BOSTON UNIVERSITY, Mugar Memorial Library, Special Collections Dept, 771 Commonwealth Ave, Boston, 02215. Howard B Gotlieb, Dir
Holdings: Cat Mss
Notes: Mss, correspondence, incl publications by or about.

NV —UNIVERSITY OF NEVADA, RENO, University Library, Special Collections Dept, Reno, 89557. Robert E Blesse, Head
Holdings: Vols (69) Cat Other appearances 640 Cat
Notes: Includes individual works by author in all editions including translations; also prefaces, introductions, published correspondence, appearances in anthologies, periodicals, etc. Bibliographical research collection, part of Modern Authors Collection.

BC —UNIVERSITY OF VICTORIA, McPherson Library, Victoria, V8W 3H5, Can.

HUGHES, RUPERT, 1872-1956

CA —CLAREMONT COLLEGES, Honnold Library, Ninth & Dartmouth, Claremont, 91711. Tania Rizzo, Special Collections Dept Head
Holdings: / / Cat Mss Pix
Notes: Photostats, typescripts, clippings, journal articles used by Rupert Hughes in preparation for publication of his 3-vol *George Washington, 1926-1930.* Scrapbook incl clippings Apr 30, May 1, 1889--celebration of centenary of Washington's first inaugural. Seven boxes and scrapbook. List available. Restricted use.

†CA —UNIVERSITY OF SOUTHERN CALIFORNIA LIBRARY, American Literature Collection, Los Angeles, 90089.
Notes: His manuscripts and literary correspondence.

HUGHES, SARAH

TX —NORTH TEXAS STATE UNIVERSITY, Archives, NT Station Box 5188, Denton, 76203. Robert LaForte, University Archivist
Notes: Part of Oral History Collection. Interviews with Hughes, former member of Texas legislature and state and federal district judge.

HUGHES, TED

†MD —UNIVERSITY OF MARYLAND, Library, College Park, 20742. Donald Farren, Assoc Dir for Special Collections
Holdings: Cat
Notes: First appearances in book form, in anthologies, and in periodicals; subsequent editions, with differences in text, etc; works edited or translated; association items, especially with marginalia. Secondary works are generally excluded.

NV —UNIVERSITY OF NEVADA, RENO, University Library, Special Collections Dept, Reno, 89557. Robert E Blesse, Head
Holdings: Vols (52) Cat Other appearances 600 Cat
Notes: Includes individual works by author in all editions including translations; also prefaces, introductions, published correspondence, appearances in anthologies, periodicals, etc. Bibliographical research collection, part of Modern Authors Collection.

BC —UNIVERSITY OF VICTORIA, McPherson Library, Victoria, V8W 3H5, Can.
Notes: Incl holograph drafts of four poems, "Dully Gumtion's Addendum," "Fishing at Dawn," "New Moon," and "Remembrance Day," several on verso of letters and ts of other titles, incl some by Sylvia Plath; 4 letters to Graham T Ackroyd.

HUGHES, THOMAS

IL —CHICAGO PUBLIC LIBRARY, Special Collections Div, Cultural Center, 78 E Washington St, Chicago, 60602. Laura Linard, Cur
Holdings: Vols 45 Cat
Notes: Since Thomas Hughes, MP and author of *Tom Brown's Schooldays,* was instrumental in the founding of The Chicago Public Library in 1871, the Library has

HUGHES, THOMAS (cont.)

begun to collect him in depth. The collection is small at present but several bookdealers in the US and Great Britain are searching for Hughes material and we purchase nearly 90 per cent of what is quoted. The Hughes Collection supplements the English Book Donation of 1871, originally about 7000 volumes (now only 500 are preserved), sponsored by Hughes. The Donation comprises primarily books donated by Oxford University and bears Oxford's gift-stamp and bookplate; the other extant books are late editions of Victorian literary and historical writers.

NJ —PRINCETON UNIVERSITY, Library, Morris L Parrish Collection, Princeton, 08540. Alexander D Wainwright, Cur
Holdings: Vols 92
Notes: The collection contains over 6500 vols, as well as many theatre programs, playbills, photographs, clippings and other miscellanea. Parrish's goal was to assemble in both the English and the American first editions, in the original condition as issued, everything that a given author published. He was also interested in a high standard of condition for his books. Many additions have been acquired since the Parrish collection came to the Library as a bequest in 1944. The collection is an assemblage of author collections, consisting of books by: William Harrison Ainsworth, James Matthew Barrie, William Black, The Brontes, William Wilkie Collins, Dinah Mulock Craik, Marie de la Ramee ("Ouida"), Benjamin Disraeli, Charles Dickens, Charles Dodgson, George du Maurier, George Eliot (ie Mary Ann Evans), Elizabeth Gaskell, Thomas Hardy, Thomas Hughes,Charles Kingsley, Charles Lever, Edward George Earle Bulwer-Lytton, Mary Maxwell, George Meredith, Charles Reade, Walter Scott, Robert Louis Stevenson, William Makepeace Thackeray, Trollope Family, Ellen Wood, and Charlotte Yonge.

HUGO, VICTOR

MA —HARVARD UNIVERSITY LIBRARY, Houghton Library, Cambridge, 02138. Rodney G Dennis, Cur of Manuscripts
Holdings: Mss

ON —QUEEN'S UNIVERSITY, Douglas Library, Kingston, K7L 5C4, Can. William F E Morley, Cur, Special Collections
Holdings: Vols 145 Cat Mss Pix
Notes: Books and manuscripts by and about Victor Hugo; photographs.

HUGUENOTS

IL —NEWBERRY LIBRARY, 60 W Walton St, Chicago, 60610. Diana Haskell, Cur of Modern Mss
Holdings: Cat

ME —BOWDOIN COLLEGE, Library, Brunswick, 04011. Dianne M Gutscher, Cur of Special Collections
Holdings: Vols 800
Notes: 110 volumes printed before 1800 supplement about 700 in the general library collection.

MA —HARVARD UNIVERSITY, Baker Library of the Graduate School of Business Administration, Kress Library of Business and Economics, Soldiers Field, Boston, 02163. Ruth E Rogers, Cur
Notes: For Huguenot merchant materials, see *Harvard Library Bulletin,* X (1956), 94-118.

NH —ASSOCIATION CANADO-AMERICAIN (FRATERNAL LIFE INSURANCE SOCIETY), Institute Canado-Americain, 52 Concord St, Manchester, 03101. Robert A Beaudoin, Librn
Holdings: Vols (40,000) Cat Mss Maps Pix Slides Phonorecords Audiotapes Microforms
Budget: ($2000)
Notes: Contains books, pamphlets, mss, university dissertations, newspapers, manuscripts, periodicals, and archives of various other societies (active of defunct). Subjects covered incl art, music, literature, folklore, religion, politics, sociology, history, etc of the French in France, Canada, and US (especially New England's Franco-Americans, Louisiana's Cajuns, and Quebec's French-Canadians). There is also an extensive collection of genealogical works dealing with Quebec Acadia, and New England Francophones. Articles dealing with the library are: "The Library of the Association Canado-Americaine" by Edward B Ham in *Modern Language Notes*, vol LII, no 7, November 1937 and a bilingual article "Appel d'un jeune aux jeunes en faveur de al Bibliotheque ACA" by Robert B Perreault in *Le Canado-Americain*, nouvelle serie, vol 1, no 5, julliet-aout-septembre 1975, pp 18-19.

†NY —HUGUENOT HISTORICAL SOCIETY, New Paltz Library, 6 Broadhead Ave, Box 339, New Paltz, 12561.

†NY —HUGUENOT SOCIETY OF AMERICA LIBRARY, 122 E 58 St, New York, 10022.
Notes: French Huguenot migration to America, Huguenot history in France and elsewhere, biography, genealogy.

NY —UNIVERSITY OF ROCHESTER, Rush Rhees Library, Department of Rare Books and Special Collections, Rochester, 14627. Peter Dzwonkoski, Librn
Holdings: Vols 450 Cat
Notes: Collection of materials on 16th and 17th century European law and political theory with special emphasis on works emanating from the French Civil Wars of the late 16th century. Particularly notable are the editions of the works of Francois Hotman and the editions of the Corpus Juris Civilis printed in Lyon. No photocopying.

PA —BALCH INSTITUTE FOR ETHNIC STUDIES, Library, 18 S Seventh St, Philadelphia, 19106. R Joseph Anderson, Library Dir

†SC —HUGUENOT SOCIETY OF SOUTH CAROLINA LIBRARY, 25 Chalmers St, Charleston, 29401.
Notes: Genealogical data on Huguenots and allied families, especially French Huguenots.

TX —FORT WORTH PUBLIC LIBRARY, 300 Taylor St, Fort Worth, 76102. Patricia Chadwell, Social Sciences Librn; Paul Campbell, Librn, History Section
Holdings: Vols (25,000) Cat Mss Maps Microforms
Budget: $7600
Notes: Collection emphasizes southern states, but is national in scope. Substantial group of British material, and material on Huguenots.

WI —UNIVERSITY OF WISCONSIN, MADISON, Memorial Library, Western European Humanities Collection, 728 State St, Madison, 53706. Charles Szabo, Bibliographer
Notes: Montauban Collection. Formerly the private library of a prominent Huguenot family long connected with the University of Montauban and organized to document the origin and development of Calvinism in France, and other fugitive materials. Supplements the Tank Collection (Calvinism) and the Chwalibog Collection (theology).

HULA, ERICH, 1900-

NY —STATE UNIVERSITY OF NEW YORK AT ALBANY, Library, Special Collections Dept, 1400 Washington Ave, Albany, 12222. Marion P Munzer, Coordr
Notes: Articles, typescripts, and pamphlets by Erich Hula on international relations; lecture notes and mss; clipping file (21 linear feet). Part of the Library's German Exile Collection.

HULL, CORDELL

DC —LIBRARY OF CONGRESS, Manuscript Division, Washington, 20540. John C Broderick, Chief
Holdings: Cat Mss Pix
Notes: Mss, papers, records, etc.

HULL, JOHN

MA —NEW ENGLAND HISTORIC GENEALOGICAL SOCIETY, Library, 101 Newbury St, Boston, 02116. Ralph J Crandell, Dir
Notes: Large collection of printed British and American parish registers; some American ms parish records. Strong collection of early censuses, incl the Massachusetts Direct Tax Record of 1798, actually a census of Maine and Massachusetts and more informative than the Federal decennial record of early national censuses. Earlier similarly useful records incl the Accounts of Pay for King Philip's War (1675-1676) kept by John Hull, War Treasurer.

HULSIUS, LEVINUS

NY —NEW YORK PUBLIC LIBRARY, Rare Books and Manuscripts Div, Fifth Ave & 42 St, New York, 10018. William L Joyce, Asst Dir; Francis O Mattson, Curator
Holdings: Cat
Budget: ($7161)
Notes: Incl one of the most extensive collections of De Bry and Hulsius and one of the finest sets of Canadian Jesuit Relations. Most editions of Columbus' "Letter."

HUMAN BEHAVIOR

DC —US DEPT OF JUSTICE, Drug Enforcement Administration, Library, 1405 I St NW, Washington, 20537. Morton S Goren, Librn
Holdings: Vols (10,000) Cat Microforms
Notes: Narcotics and dangerous drugs control.

MI —UNIVERSITY OF MICHIGAN, Transportation Research Institute, Library, 2901 Baxter Rd, Ann Arbor, 48109. Ann C Grimm, Librn
Holdings: Vols (57,000) Cat Mss Maps Pix Slides Microforms
Budget: ($25,000)

MO —SAINT LOUIS POLICE LIBRARY, 315 S Tucker Blvd, Saint Louis, 63102. Cathy Reilly, Librn
Holdings: Vols (21,000) Cat Mss Pix Microforms
Budget: ($18,400)
Notes: Library on all subjects of police work is open to the public for general reference use.

HUMAN BODY see Body, Human

HUMAN DEVELOPMENT see Personality

HUMAN ECOLOGY

IL —UNIVERSITY OF ILLINOIS, URBANA/CHAMPAIGN, Library, Applied Life Studies Library, 1408 W Gregory Dr, Urbana, 61801.
Holdings: Vols (38,000) Cat Microforms
See also entry under Physical Education and Training

IL —UNIVERSITY OF ILLINOIS, URBANA/CHAMPAIGN, Library, Biology Library, 101 Burrill Hall, 407 S Goodwin, Urbana, 61801. Elisabeth B Davis, Librn
Holdings: Vols (115,000) Cat Microforms
Budget: ($200,000)
Notes: The Biology Library incl books, periodicals, and reference works that cover the fields of anatomy, biophysics, botany, ecology, entomology, genetics, immunology, microbiology, physiology and zoology. About three-quarters of the total collection is made up of journals and other serials representing 2000 distinctive titles. The serial list is comprehensive for the biological sciences, contains most of the major international titles and consists of complete runs for almost all titles. Additional materials (approx 90,000 vols) in the biological sciences are available in the Natural History Survey Library and the bookstacks at the Main Library on the Urbana campus. Professional assistance is available for reference service, online searching, and library instruction. Interlibrary loan service is provided. Photocopying.

HUMAN ECOLOGY (cont.)

NV —FORESTA INSTITUTE FOR OCEAN AND MOUNTAIN STUDIES, Library, 6205 Franktown Rd, Carson City, 89701. Shannon Porter, Librn
Holdings: Vols (3000) Cat Mss Maps Pix Slides
Notes: Material on plant, animal, and human ecology with special emphasis on far western US and Nevada ecology and environmental problems. Also hold about 2000 reprints, pamphlets, reports, etc.

HUMAN ENGINEERING

CT —YALE MEDICAL LIBRARY, 333 Cedar St, New Haven, 06510.

IL —UNIVERSITY OF ILLINOIS, URBANA/CHAMPAIGN, Library, Applied Life Studies Library, 1408 W Gregory Dr, Urbana, 61801.
Holdings: Vols (38,000) Cat Microforms
See also entry under Physical Education and Training

IN —MILES LABORATORIES, Library Resources and Services, 1127 Myrtle St, PO Box 40, Elkhart, 46515. Allam Hagopian, Mgr
Holdings: Vols (16,500) Cat Audiotapes Microforms
Notes: Incl files of pharmaceutical product advertising pieces, extensive literature files on company related drugs; domestic and international marketing files. 32,000 bound periodicals.

MA —INSTRUMENTATION LABORATORY, Library, 113 Hartwell Ave, Lexington, 02173. Jacqueline R Kates, Librn
Holdings: Vols (6000) Cat Microforms

MI —UNIVERSITY OF MICHIGAN, Transportation Research Institute, Library, 2901 Baxter Rd, Ann Arbor, 48109. Ann C Grimm, Librn
Holdings: Vols (57,000) Cat Mss Maps
Budget: ($25,000)
Notes: Special emphasis on accident investigation and data analysis, vehicle dynamics, biomechanical aspects of trauma, vision and visibility, alcohol and driving.

NY —COLD SPRING HARBOR LABORATORY, Library, PO Box 100, Cold Spring Harbor, 11724. Susan Gensel, Library Dir; Genemary Falvey, Librn
Holdings: Vols (30,000)
Budget: ($103,500)
Notes: The highly technical collection is comprised of 20,000 serial vols and 10,000 monographs. The library receives 500 current serial titles. Subjects covered incl molecular and cellular biology, virology, biochemistry, microbiology, oncology, neurobiology, biological risk assessment and genetic engineering/biotechnology. Special collections in eugenics and genetics are primarily historical dealing with the development of genetics in the US which had its beginnings here.

NY —ENGINEERING SOCIETIES LIBRARY, 345 E 47 St, New York, 10017. S Kirk Cabeen, Dir
Holdings: Vols 250,000 Cat Maps 16mm Films Microforms
Notes: One of the largest, most comprehensive engineering libraries in the world. Covers all engineering disciplines; particularly strong in electrical and electronic, mechanical, mining and metallurgical, petroleum, chemical, industrial, air conditioning and refrigeration engineering. Incl Wheeler Collection of early materials on magnetism and electricity. 125, 000 bound periodical volumes; 10,000 maps; 5000 serial subscriptions (many foreign-language). Virtually all materials abstracted in *Engineering Index* (1884-date) are incl in Library. Noncirculating, except to members of professional engineering societies which support the Library. See *Engineering Societies Library, New York, Classed Subject Catalog and Index* (Boston: G K Hall, 1963); and *Supplements*, 1-10, 1964-1973.

NC —DUKE UNIVERSITY, School of Engineering, Library, Durham, 27706. Eric J Smith, Librn
Holdings: Vols (72,000) Cat Microforms
Budget: ($110,000)

PA —FRANKLIN INSTITUTE LIBRARY, 20 & The Parkway, Philadelphia, 19103. Miriam Padusis, Dir; Charles Wilt, Readers Servs Librn
Holdings: Vols (300,000) Cat Maps Pix Microforms

TX —US AIR FORCE, School of Aerospace Medicine, Strughold Aeromedical Library, Brooks AFB, 78235. Fred W Todd, Chief Librn
Holdings: Vols (119,188) Cat Mss Maps Pix Microforms
Budget: ($499,000)
Notes: Aviation and space medicine and physiology, including the physiological effects of altitude and decompression. Biomedical and and human engineering. Military medicine, including chemical and biological warfare. Emergency medicine in both professional and technical areas. Radiobiology, including atomic medicine, nuclear medicine, and space radiation. Material not oriented to the School of Aerospace Medicine are excluded. Incl also 45,787 microforms and 142,371 technical documents.

ON —AGRICULTURE CANADA, Research Branch, Neatby Library, Rm 3032, K W Neatby Bldg, CEF, Ottawa, K1A 0C6, Can. Marcel Charette, Library Technician
Holdings: Vols 1500 Cat
Notes: Nitrogen Fixation. All phases of cell biology.

PQ —UNIVERSITY OF MONTREAL, Physical Education Library, Montreal, H3C 3J7, Can. Lisa Mayrand, Dir

HUMAN FACTORS IN ENGINEERING DESIGN see Human Engineering

HUMAN FERTILITY see Fertility, Human

HUMAN GENETICS

CT —YALE MEDICAL LIBRARY, 333 Cedar St, New Haven, 06510.
Holdings: Vols (334,215) Cat Mss Pix Slides Microforms
Budget: ($361,650)
Notes: Incl films, audiotapes, artifacts, etc.

HUMAN MECHANICS

CA —UNIVERSITY OF CALIFORNIA, LOS ANGELES, Biomedical Library, Center for Health Sciences, Los Angeles, 90024. Louise Darling, Biomedical Librn

CA —UNIVERSITY OF CALIFORNIA, LOS ANGELES, Education & Psychology Library, 390 Powell Library Bldg, Los Angeles, 90024. Barbara Duke, Librn
Holdings: Vols (133,000) Cat Audiotapes Microforms
Notes: Research collection serving graduate students and faculty in Education, Psychology, Kinesiology and Teaching English as a Second Language. Areas of emphasis incl higher education, education and work, comparative education, early childhood development, reading, second language acquisition, cognition, perception, personality, social psychology, motor control and learning. Library has Univ of Oregon microfiche collection of unpublished research in sports, physical education, and recreation and is a depository for ERIC microfiche.

CA —STANFORD UNIVERSITY LIBRARIES, Lane Medical Library, Stanford University, Medical Center, Stanford, 94305. Peter Stangl, Librn
Notes: Papers of William Stroebel Hunter on human locomotion.

CT —YALE UNIVERSITY, Box 1603A, Yale Station, New Haven, 06520.

ON —UNIVERSITY OF OTTAWA, Health Sciences Library, 451 Smyth Road, Ottawa, K1H 8L5, Can. Myra Owen, Librn
Holdings: Vols (70,000) Audiotapes Films Filmstrips
Budget: $325,000
Notes: This collection is made up of works in support of clinical and research studies in all branches of medicine, nursing and kinanthropology. Incl 1500 periodicals.

ON —UNIVERSITY OF WINDSOR, Leddy Library, Windsor, N9B 3P4, Can. P Jerome Malone, Librn
Notes: Human kinetics, with emphasis on the history, psychology, sociology, philosophy, and administration of sports and their organization. Also hold archival records, etc of numerous Canadian sports organizations: Canadian Intercollegiate Athletic Union (CIAU), Ontario-Quebec AA, Ontario Universities AA, etc. Local and Regional history. 40 feet of materials.

HUMAN MOVEMENTS see Human Mechanics

HUMAN PALEONTOLOGY see Fossil Man

HUMAN RIGHTS see Civil Rights

HUMANE SOCIETIES see Child Welfare

HUMANISM AND HUMANISTS

CA —GRADUATE THEOLOGICAL UNION LIBRARY, New Religious Movements Research Collection, Public Services and Special Collections Dept, 2400 Ridge Road, Berkeley, 94709. Diane Choquette, Dept Head
Holdings: Vols (3000) Mss Pix
Notes: Begun in 1977, the collection focuses on religious movements new to America since 1960, and unorthodox religious movements resurgent since 1960. American forms of Hinduism, Buddhism, Sikhism, and Sufism are included along with occultism, Neo-Paganism, esoteric and alternative forms of Christianity, feminist spirituality, and human potential movements having a spiritual aspect.

CA —SAN FRANCISCO STATE UNIVERSITY, Frank V de Bellis Collection, 1630 Holloway Ave, San Francisco, 94132. Serena de Bellis, Cur
Holdings: Vols (5000) Cat Mss Maps Pix
Notes: Emphasis on history, and history of the fine arts.

CA —STANFORD UNIVERSITY LIBRARIES, Cecil H Green Library, Stanford, 94305. Michael T Ryan, Cur
Holdings: Vols Cat
Notes: An emphasis in the Rare Book Collection.

IL —NEWBERRY LIBRARY, 60 W Walton St, Chicago, 60610. Diana Haskell, Cur of Modern Mss
Holdings: Cat Mss
Notes: Special strength in monographs and in 16th and 17th century books. Restricted use; noncirculating.

MN —SAINT JOHN'S ABBEY & UNIVERSITY, Hill Monastic Manuscript Library, Collegeville, 56321. Julian G Plante, Dir
Holdings: Vols (61,000) Microforms
Notes: Films of 61,000 mss. The total number of codices or bound handwritten mss represents the holdings of several hundred libraries in Europe, mostly Austria, Spain, Ethiopia, West Germany, Portugal, and also Italy, Hungary, Poland, Great Britain, Belgium, Yugoslavia, France, Switzerland, and the Netherlands.

PA —HAVERFORD COLLEGE, Magill Library, Quaker Collection, Haverford, 19041. Edwin B Bonner, Librn & Cur
Holdings: Vols 3250 //
Notes: Works from the 15th through the 19th centuries by and about the humanistic Latin writers of the 14th and 15th centuries.

TX —SOCIETY OF SEPARATIONISTS, Library, 2210 Hancock Dr, PO Box 2117, Austin, 78756. R Murray-O'Hair, Dir
Holdings: Vols (50,000)
Notes: Atheism, separation of church and state, biographical archives on Atheists, agnostics, humanists, and iconoclasts.

HUMANITARIANISM (RELIGION) see Unitarianism

HUMANITIES

CA —UNIVERSITY OF CALIFORNIA, SAN DIEGO, Central University Library,

HUMANITIES (cont.)

Mandeville Dept of Special Collections, La Jolla, 92093. Lynda Corey Claassen, Head
Notes: Rare Book Collection preserves special materials for research in the humanities. Approx 25,000 vols of diverse materials.

CA —UNIVERSITY OF CALIFORNIA, LOS ANGELES, Library, Slavic Collection, 405 Hilgard Ave, Los Angeles, 90024. Edward Shreeves, Chairman, Bibliographers Group; Leon Ferder, Slavic Bibliographer
Holdings: Vols (250,000) Cat Maps Microforms
Notes: The entire range of humanities, social sciences, and the arts. One of the most comprehensive US collections for material not only on Russia and the Soviet Union, but also on Bulgaria, Czechoslovakia, Poland, Yugoslavia, the non-Slavic countries of Eastern Europe (Romania, Hungary, Albania) and Soviet Central Asia. Holdings in Russian and Slavic linguistics, Russian literature, and Russian history are particularly strong, covering all periods. The collections are described in some detail in Paul Horecky's book on US Slavic collections.

CA —CALIFORNIA INSTITUTE OF TECHNOLOGY, Humanities and Social Sciences Library, Millikan Library 1-32, Pasadena, 91125. Janet Casebier, Librn
Holdings: Vols (140,000) Cat Microforms
Notes: Incl 57,000 microforms.

†CA —UNIVERSITY OF SAN FRANCISCO, Richard A Gleeson Library, The Countess Bernardine Murphy Donohue Rare Book Room, San Francisco, 94117. D Steven Corey, Special Collections Librn
Notes: Some highly specialized materials.

DC —CATHOLIC UNIVERSITY OF AMERICA, Mullen Library, 620 Michigan Ave NE, Washington, 20064. B Gutekunst, Humanities Librn
Holdings: Vols (20,000) Cat

IL —NEWBERRY LIBRARY, 60 W Walton St, Chicago, 60610. Lawrence W Towner, Pres & Librn
Holdings: Vols 1,300,000 Cat Mss Maps Pix Microforms
Notes: An independent research library in the humanities and the history of Western Europe and the Americas from the late Middle Ages to the 20th century. Particularly rich in a number of fields: the Renaissance; Americana; history of printing and calligraphy; music and musicology; English and American literature and history; colonial Latin American history; the American Indian; the American West; history of the Portuguese empire; travel, exploration, and the history of cartography; family and local history; and the mss of Midwestern writers, historical figures, and institutions.

MD —JOHNS HOPKINS UNIVERSITY, Milton S Eisenhower Library, George Peabody Collection, 17 E Mt Vernon Place, Baltimore, 21201. Lyn Hart, Peabody Librn
Holdings: Vols (40,000) Cat Mss

MA —SWAIN SCHOOL OF DESIGN LIBRARY, 140 Orchard St, Sch add: 19 Hawthorn St, New Bedford, 02740. Martha Maier, Librn
Notes: Rare book collection.

NY —STATE UNIVERSITY OF NEW YORK, COLLEGE AT BUFFALO, E H Butler Library, 1300 Elmwood Ave, Buffalo, 14222. George C Newman, Dir
Holdings: Vols (465,130) Cat Maps Microforms
Budget: ($466,000)
Notes: Fully cataloged collections in education, incl education of exceptional children, art education, social sciences education, etc, are strong since the College was formerly a college of education and approx 60 percent of current graduates still obtain some degree enabling them to teach. Incl Curriculum Laboratory containing courses of study, elementary and secondary textbooks, and collections for children's literature courses (MA in Children's Literature offered). Collection consists of 465,130 volumes incl 64,255 bound periodical volumes, plus 19,120 microfilm reels and 457,988 microtext pieces other than reels. Subscribe to 2263 periodicals.

NY —NEW YORK PUBLIC LIBRARY, Research Libraries, General Research Div, Fifth Ave & 42 St, New York, 10018. Keith McKinney, Assistant Div Chief
Holdings: Cat
Notes: Current periodicals. Subjects incl advertising, business and professional periodicals, international affairs, labor and trade unions, political and social sciences, humanities in general. Division holds 10,000 titles. Incl little magazines.

†RI —UNIVERSITY OF RHODE ISLAND, Library, Kingston, 02881.
Notes: Extensive collections.

†TX —UNIVERSITY OF TEXAS LIBRARIES, General Libraries, Humanities Research Center, PO Box 7219, Austin, 78712. John Chalmers, Librn

TX —TRINITY UNIVERSITY, Elizabeth Coates Maddux Library, 715 Stadium Dr, San Antonio, 78284. Richard Hume Werking, Library Dir; Craig Likness, Head Bibliographer
Notes: General reference.

ON —QUEEN'S UNIVERSITY, Douglas Library, Kingston, K7L 5C4, Can. William F E Morley, Cur, Special Collections
Holdings: Vols 746// Uncat Pix
Notes: The MacDonnel and Cartwright Collections of history, literature, art, classics, checklist available.

ON —TORONTO SCHOOL OF THEOLOGY, Consortium of Libraries, University of Toronto, Toronto, M5S 1A5, Can. R Grane Bracewell, Library Coordr
Holdings: Cat
Notes: A consortium of 7 theological college and faculty libraries at the University of Toronto.

PQ —TROIS-RIVIERES COLLEGE LIBRARY, CEGEP de Trois-Rivieres-Bibliotheque, 3500 de Courval, Trois-Rivieres, G9A 5E6, Can. Denis Simard, Librn
Holdings: Vols (95,000) Cat Maps Pix Slides Phonorecords Audiotapes Viedotpes 16mm Films Filmdstrips Microfilms

HUMANOIDS—ORIGIN

MI —ANDREWS UNIVERSITY, James White Library, Berrien Springs, 49104. Marley H Soper, Dir
Holdings: Cat Mss
Notes: The George McCready Price Collection on the theory of Creation, geology, etc. Much of this material was gathered by this author and educator in preparation for numerous books and pamphlets. He is described as an ardent creationist and a vigorous opponent of the theory of evolution. Over 900 items. Not available by interlibrary loan, but may be used at this library.

PA —CARNEGIE LIBRARY OF PITTSBURGH, Science & Technology Dept, 4400 Forbes Ave, Pittsburgh, 15213. Catherine M Brosky, Dept Head
Notes: Of secondary interest in acquisitions because of the department's role in cooperating with Pittsburgh institutions and others across the Commonwealth in sharing resources, the cooperative acquistion of materials, and the provision of services and information. However, some aspects of the subject are emphasized. There are separate entries for each of these specialties in this vol.

HUMBLE OIL AND REFINING COMPANY

TX —LEE COLLEGE, Library, PO Box 818, Baytown, 77522. William K Peace, Librn
Notes: Oral history tapes covering the area of east Harris County, Texas. Early history of Baytown, Goose Creek, and Pelly, with some relating to the early development of Humble Oil and Refining Company as remembered by early residents of the area. Also in the western area of Chambers County, Texas, known as Barbers Hill. The original tapes are housed in the Lee College Library, with copies located in the Sterling Municipal Library of Baytown. Incl 75 tapes; 50 transcripts.

HUMBOLDT, ALEXANDER VON, 1769-1859

SC —COLLEGE OF CHARLESTON LIBRARY, Special Collections Dept, Charleston, 29401.
Notes: Newsclippings of von Humboldt's correspondence, 1858-1860.

HUME, DAVID, 1711-1776

PQ —MCGILL UNIVERSITY, McLennan Library, Rare Books and Special Collections Dept, 3459 McTavish St, Montreal, H3A 1Y1, Can.
Notes: Books by and about the philosopher.

HUMOR see Wit and Humor

HUMOR, AMERICAN see American Wit and Humor

HUMOROUS ILLUSTRATIONS see Caricatures and Cartoons

HUMPHREY, DORIS, 1895-1958

NY —NEW YORK PUBLIC LIBRARY, Performing Arts Research Center, Dance Collection, 111 Amsterdam Ave, New York, 10023. Genevieve Oswald, Cur
Notes: Extensive biographical and visual material. Includes photographs, original drawings, clippings and programs, scrapbooks, tape-recorded lectures and interviews, dance notation scores, and 40 films. The Doris Humphrey Collection, 1911-1958, comprises 7000 ms items, including correspondence, business records, scenarios, choreographic notes, and memorabilia. Register published in *Bulletin of The New York Public Library,* vol 77, no 1 (Autumn, 1973). The Humphrey-Weidman Collection of more than 800 photographs, 30 volumes of press clippings, 200 programs, set designs, and playbills mirrors dance of the 1930s. Early career before 1930 documented by the Denishawn Collection of programs, clippings, photographs, and manuscripts. Materials in the Pauline Lawrence Limon Collection also document the Humphrey-Weidman Company and Miss Humphrey's career.

HUMPHREY, HUBERT H.

MN —MINNESOTA HISTORICAL SOCIETY LIBRARY, 690 Cedar St, Saint Paul, 55101. Patricia C Harpole, Chief of Reference Library; Bonnie G Wilson, Head of Special Libraries
Notes: Materials by such well-known figures as Hubert H. Humphrey, Eugene J. McCarthy, Orville L Freeman, Maurice H. Stans, Donald M Fraser, Albert H Quie, Clark MacGregor and John A Blatnik. A list of these holdings is on file in the Audio-Visual Library, the tapes are housed in the MHS Research Center, 1500 Mississippi Street, St Paul, Minn.

HUMPHRIES, ROLFE

MA —AMHERST COLLEGE, Library, Amherst, 01002. John Lancaster, Special Collections Librn
Holdings: Vols 175 Uncat Mss
Notes: Amherst College holds literary rights to all unpublished works of Rolfe Humphries, including letters. 7 ft of mss.

HUNEKER, JAMES GIBBONS

NH —DARTMOUTH COLLEGE, Baker Memorial Library, Hanover, 03755.
Holdings: Cat Mss Pix
Notes: First editions, mss, etc. Noncirculating.

HUNGARIAN AMERICAN NEWSPAPERS see Newspapers, Hungarian American

HUNGARIAN LANGUAGE AND LITERATURE

CA —UNIVERSITY OF CALIFORNIA, BERKELEY, University Library, Hispanic

HUNGARIAN LANGUAGE AND LITERATURE (cont.)

Collections, Berkeley, 94720. Gaston Somoshegyi-Szokol, Librn
Holdings: Vols (6000)
Notes: Strong research collection with strength in belles-lettres covering authors of all literary periods. Of particular importance is the wealth of literary periodicals: journals, yearbooks, annals, etc with complete holdings.

CA —LOS ANGELES PUBLIC LIBRARY, Foreign Languages Dept, 630 W Fifth St, Los Angeles, 90071. Sylva Manoogian, Principal Librn
Holdings: Vols 5972 Cat
Budget: ($41,500)

IL —UNIVERSITY OF ILLINOIS, URBANA/CHAMPAIGN, Slavic and East European Library, Urbana, 61801. Marianna Tax Choldin, Head
Holdings: Vols (18,000) Cat Maps Microforms

MA —HARVARD UNIVERSITY LIBRARY, Widener Library, Cambridge, 02138.
Holdings: Cat
Notes: Some 5500 vols on Hungarian history, language, and literature are listed by *Widener Library Shelflist,* No 44 (1973).

NY —NEW YORK PUBLIC LIBRARY, Donnell Foreign Language Library, 20 W 53 St, New York, 10019. Bosiljka Stevanovic, Supvr Librn
Holdings: Vols 1516 Cat
Notes: Hungarian collection incl Hungarian authors of Hungarian expression. No separate catalog.

NC —CUMBERLAND COUNTY PUBLIC LIBRARY, North Carolina Foreign Language Center, 328 Gillespie St, Fayetteville, 28301. Patrick M Valentine, Coordinator
Holdings: Vols (25,000) Cat Phonorecords Audiotapes
Notes: The largest book collections are, in descending order of size, German Spanish, French, Japanese, Korean and Vietnamese, with fair sized collections in Italian, Russian, Chinese, Arabic, Greek, Hungarian, Polish, Hebrew, Thai, and Hindi. The Center has several shelves each of books in Bengali, Dutch, Marathi, Portuguese, Urdu, and Yiddish. Smaller collections of one to three shelves each incl Catalan, Croatian, Czech, Danish, Finnish, Gujarati, Icelandic, Kannada, Latin, Lithuanian, Malayalam, Norwegian, Panjabi, Persian (Farsi), Romanian, Slovak, Swedish, Tagalog, Tamil, Telegu, and Ukrianian. The Center has grammars, dictionaries and occasionally other readings in languages from Afrikaans and Albanian to Welsh, Yoruba and Zulu.

OH —CLEVELAND PUBLIC LIBRARY, Foreign Literature Dept, 325 Superior Ave, Cleveland, 44114. Natalia Bezugloff, Head
Holdings: Vols 9100 Cat
Notes: A popular circulating collection containing classics and the standard works with emphasis on belles lettres, history and biography. A variety of other subjects such as learning languages, how to do books, art, children's books, spoken phonodiscs and cassettes, periodicals, etc. Incl 1720 ephemera.
See also entry under Foreign Language Collections

OH —KENT STATE UNIVERSITY, Libraries, Ethnic Collections, Kent, 44242.
Holdings: Vols 250 Cat
See also entry under Foreign Langauge Collections

HUNGARIAN LAW see Law, Hungarian

HUNGARIAN MUSIC see Music, Hungarian

HUNGARIANS IN THE U.S.

†IL —SZATHMARY ARCHIVES, 2218 North Lincoln Ave, Chicago, 60614.
Notes: Hungary and Hungarian Americans.

MN —UNIVERSITY OF MINNESOTA, Immigration History Research Center, 826 Berry St, Saint Paul, 55114. Susan Griegs, Cur
Holdings: Vols (35,000) Mss Maps Pix Phonorecords Audiotapes 16mm Films Microforms
See also entry under U.S.--Emigration and Immigration

PA —BALCH INSTITUTE FOR ETHNIC STUDIES, Library, 18 S Seventh St, Philadelphia, 19106. R Joseph Anderson, Library Dir
Holdings: Vols 150 Pix Microforms

HUNGARY

†GA —HUNGARIAN CULTURAL FOUNDATION, 755 Columbia Dr, Suite 612, Decatur, 30030.

†IL —SZATHMARY ARCHIVES, 2218 North Lincoln Ave, Chicago, 60614.
Notes: Hungary and Hungarian Americans.

IL —UNIVERSITY OF ILLINOIS, URBANA/CHAMPAIGN, Slavic and East European Library, Urbana, 61801. Marianna Tax Choldin, Head
Holdings: Vols (18,000) Cat Maps Microforms

MA —HARVARD UNIVERSITY LIBRARY, Widener Library, Cambridge, 02138.
Holdings: Cat
Notes: Some 5500 vols on Hungarian history, language, and literature are listed by *Widener Library Shelflist,* No 44 (1973).

†NJ —AMERICAN HUNGARIAN STUDIES FOUNDATION LIBRARY, 177 Somerset St, New Brunswick, 08903.
Notes: Hungarian history and culture.

HUNGARY—HISTORY

CA —UNIVERSITY OF CALIFORNIA, BERKELEY, University Library, Hispanic Collections, Berkeley, 94720. Gaston Somoshegyi-Szokol, Librn
Holdings: Vols (6000)
Notes: Strong research collection with strength in belles-lettres covering authors of all literary periods. Of particular importance is the wealth of literary periodicals: journals, yearbooks, annals, etc with complete holdings.

CA —CALIFORNIA INSTITUTE OF TECHNOLOGY, Robert A Millikan Memorial Library, Archives, 1201 E California Blvd, Pasadena, 91125. Judith R Goodstein, Archivist
Holdings: Vols (3000) Uncat Mss Maps Pix Slides Phonorecords Audiotapes Videotapes 16mm Films Microforms
Notes: Over 60 collections (1830s-present) relating to history of 19th-20th centuries science and technology and the history of the Institute. There are also family letters relating to 19th century social conditions in Russia and Hungary (the Paul Epstein papers and Theodore von Karman papers).

CA —HOOVER INSTITUTION ON WAR, REVOLUTION & PEACE, Stanford University, Stanford, 94305. Milorad M Drachkovitch, Archivist
Notes: Two collections: (1) Papers of Princess Stephanie zu Hohenlohe, confidant and intermediary of Lord Rothermere, owner of the *Daily Mail*, London, and Adolf Hitler, incl correspondence, memoranda, telegrams, clippings, and printed matter, 1914-1972, relating to improvement of German-English relations in the 1930s, political developments in Hungary, and Princess Hohenlohe's personal life in Europe and the US, as well as her associations with various publishing houses. 4 ms boxes. (2) Papers of Rusztem Vambery, Hungarian author, lawyer, and Minister to the US, 1947-48, incl correspondence, speeches and writings, reports, printed matter, and other material, 1905-48, relating to his legal and political careers, to criminology, and to Hungarian domestic and foreign affairs. 9 ms boxes.

IL —UNIVERSITY OF ILLINOIS, URBANA/CHAMPAIGN, Slavic and East European Library, Urbana, 61801. Marianna Tax Choldin, Head
Holdings: Vols (18,000) Cat

IN —INDIANA UNIVERSITY, University Libraries, Bloomington, 47401. Murlin Croucher, Librn for Slavic Studies
Holdings: Vols (300,000) Cat Maps Microforms
Budget: ($63,000)
Notes: The collection, established after World War II, covers material of, and on, the Soviet Union (55 percent) and Eastern Europe (45 percent) in the languages of the area and in western European languages as well. Material is chiefly in the fields of humanities and social sciences. Many other Slavic and East European books are located in the Lilly Library (rare book library).

†NJ —HUNGARIAN FREEDOM FIGHTERS FEDERATION, USA, Library, 201 Raymond Ave, South Orange, 07079.
Notes: Hungarian history and the Hungarian Revolution of 1956.

†PA —VARDY COLLECTION, 5740 Aylesboro Ave, Pittsburgh, 15217.

HUNGARY—HISTORY—AUSTRO-HUNGARIAN EMPIRE, 1867-1918

TX —RICE UNIVERSITY, Fondren Library, 6100 S Main St, PO Box 1892, Houston, 77251. Dr Samuel M Carrington, Jr, University Librn
Holdings: Vols 21,500 // Cat Maps Pix
Notes: The Austro-Hungarian Empire of Franz Josef. Historical and literary materials. Incl newspapers. Downs 2706.

HUNGATE, WILLIAM

MO —UNIVERSITY OF MISSOURI-SAINT LOUIS, Thomas Jefferson Library, Manuscript and Historical Society Collection, 8001 Natural Bridge Rd, Saint Louis, 63121.

HUNLEY, CSS see CSS Hunley

HUNT, EDWARD E.

CA —HOOVER INSTITUTION ON WAR, REVOLUTION & PEACE, Stanford University, Stanford, 94305. Milorad M Drachkovitch, Archivist
Holdings: // Mss
Notes: Papers, 1914-1946, of Edward E Hunt, public official. Papers concerning Hunt's work with the Dept of Commerce, the restoration of Italy following World War I, and the mission to Poland of the European Children's Fund of the American Relief Administration. Incl typescript of *The Food Problem in Germany*, by J E Johansson and the archival copy of *Rapport du Comite Executif pour le mois de november 1914* of the Commission for Relief in Belgium. 11 ft. Unpublished register is available in repository.

HUNT, GEORGE W. P.

AZ —ARIZONA STATE UNIVERSITY, Library, Arizona Collection, Tempe, 85281. Edward C Oetting, Head
Holdings: Cat Mss Diaries
Notes: Papers, etc.

HUNT, LEIGH

IA —UNIVERSITY OF IOWA, University Libraries, Iowa City, 52242. Frank Paluka, Head, Special Collections Dept
Holdings: Vols 2385 Cat Mss Pix
Notes: The Luther A Brewer Collection, incl 1924 mss of or letters by or to Leigh Hung; 100 association books; nearly 600 editions and variant issues of Hunt's published writings. Probably the most extensive Leigh Hunt collection anywhere. Described in "The Brewer-Leigh Hunt Collection at the State University of Iowa," by Frank S Hanlin in the *Keats-Shelley Journ.!* (Autumn 1959); *My Leigh Hunt Library,* by Luther A Brewer, 2 vols (1932, 1938); *A Bibliographical Description of the Leigh Hunt Collection at the University of Iowa,* by Gail C Colburn (MA thesis, Univ of Iowa, 1965); and *A Catalogue of the Leigh Hunt Manuscripts in the University of Iowa* Libraries, O M Brack, Jr and D H Stefanson (Iowa City, 1973), 32 pp.

HUNT, LEIGH (cont.)

MA —AMHERST COLLEGE, Library, Amherst, 01002. John Lancaster, Special Collections Librn
Holdings: Vols 150 Cat

OH —OHIO UNIVERSITY, Vernon R Alden Library, Department of Archives and Special Collections, Athens, 45701. Gary A Hunt, Head
Holdings: Vols 90 Cat
Notes: A comprehensive collection of first editions, most in uniform bindings by Riviere.

HUNT, GEN. MEMUCAN

TX —ROSENBERG LIBRARY, Galveston and Texas History Center, 2310 Sealy Ave, Galveston, 77550. Jane Kenamore, Archivist
Holdings: Cat Mss
Notes: General Memucan Hunt, 1807-1856, received high appointments to military and political posts during the period of the Texas Republic.

HUNT, RICHARD MORRIS

DC —AMERICAN INSTITUTE OF ARCHITECTS, Library, 1735 New York Ave, Washington, 20006. Stephanie C Byrnes, Librn
Holdings: Vols (22,000) Cat Mss Pix Slides Microforms
Notes: Emphasis of current acquisitions is on American architecture and its practice. Incl the library of R M Hunt and considerable other material. Photocopying.

HUNT, ROCKWELL D.

CA —UNIVERSITY OF THE PACIFIC, Library, Stockton, 95211. Hiram L Davis, Dir of Libraries
Holdings: Vols (15,000) Cat Mss Maps Pix Slides
Budget: ($1000)
Notes: The Stuart Library of Western Americana contains a strong basic collection of published material on California history plus numerous special collections of unpublished material. The papers of Rockwell D Hunt, historian, teacher, author, 20 shelf feet of correspondence, mss, etc. Several other smaller collections of a similar nature.

HUNT, THOMAS STERRY

MA —MASSACHUSETTS INSTITUTE OF TECHNOLOGY, Institute Archives, Special Collections, Cambridge, 02139.
Notes: Papers of William Barton Rogers, geologist, founder and first President of the Massachusetts Institute of Technology (1862-1870, 1878-1881). Major correspondents incl Louis Agassiz, Joseph Henry, Thomas Sterry Hunt, and Ellen Swallow Richards. Unpublished finding aid, incl correspondent index, available in Archives.

HUNTER, BEATRICE TRUM

MA —BOSTON UNIVERSITY, Mugar Memorial Library, Special Collections Dept, 771 Commonwealth Ave, Boston, 02215. Howard B Gotlieb, Dir
Holdings: Cat Mss Correspondence

HUNTER, CHARLES N.

NC —DUKE UNIVERSITY, William R Perkins Library, Manuscript Dept, Durham, 27706. Ellen Gartrell, Cur of Mss
Holdings: Cat Mss
Notes: Especially strong for Southern states, 19th-20th centuries. Education of women and blacks, regional and national organizations, public and private schools. Papers of black educator Charles N Hunter; Alliance for the Guidance of Rural Youth; NEA official Belmont Farley, and much more.

HUNTER, DARD

CA —CLAREMONT COLLEGES, Ella Strong Denison Library, Scripps College, Claremont, 91711. Judy Harvey Sahak, Librn
Holdings: Vols (200) Uncat
Notes: In addition to books, the Kimberly Stuart Collection on the history of paper and papermaking includes trade journals, examples of handmade papers and watermarks and a distinguished collection of Dard Hunter books and ephemera.

CA —UNIVERSITY OF CALIFORNIA, SANTA BARBARA, Library, Dept of Special Collections, Santa Barbara, 93106. Christian F Brun, Head
Holdings: Cat Pix
Notes: A small but distinctive Dard Hunter collection. All major works.

IL —NEWBERRY LIBRARY, John M Wing Foundation on the History of Printing, 60 W Walton St, Chicago, 60610. Diana Haskell, Cur of Modern Mss
Holdings: Vols (30,000) Cat Mss
Budget: ($50,000)
Notes: The collection covers printing and printing history of Western Europe and the Americas from its invention to the present, as well as papermaking, binding, and other ancillary fields. It is particularly rich in incunabula (about 2000); the works of the great printers, among others Aldus, Bodoni, Baskerville, and Rogers. Printed catalog: *A Dictionary Catalogue.* (Boston: G K Hall, 1961); *Supplements* (1981). Brief descriptions: James M Wells, "The John M Wing Foundation of The Newberry Library," *The Book Collector,* VIII, 2 (Summer 1959), pp 157-162; Lawrence W Towner, *An Uncommon Collection of Uncommon* Collections (Chicago: The Newberry Library, 1977), pp 25-26.

NY —BUFFALO & ERIE COUNTY PUBLIC LIBRARY, Rare Book Room, Lafayette Sq, Buffalo, 14203. William H Loos, Cur
Holdings: Vols 16 Cat Mss
Notes: Nearly all Dard Hunter's major works, incl some letters.

NY —ROCHESTER INSTITUTE OF TECHNOLOGY, Melbert B Cary Jr Graphic Arts Collection, School of Printing, One Lomb Memorial Drive, Rochester, 14623. David Pankow, Cur
Holdings: Vols (11,000) Cat Pix
Notes: Incl most of the volumes produced by Dard Hunter; also specimens.

OH —OHIO UNIVERSITY, Vernon R Alden Library, Department of Archives and Special Collections, Athens, 45701. Gary A Hunt, Head
Holdings: Vols 20 Cat
Notes: A comprehensive collection of Dard Hunter's books on paper, incl all the Mountain House Press imprints. Also a number of the Roycrofters books designed by Hunter.

RI —BROWN UNIVERSITY, John Hay Library, 20 Prospect St, Providence, 02912. Mark N Brown, Cur Mss
Holdings: Vols 75 Cat
Notes: All works by or about artists, papermaker, and paper historian Dard Hunter are incl in the Dard Hunter Collection.

HUNTER, EVAN

MA —BOSTON UNIVERSITY, Mugar Memorial Library, Special Collections Dept, 771 Commonwealth Ave, Boston, 02215. Howard B Gotlieb, Dir
Holdings: Cat Mss Pix
Notes: Mss, correspondence, etc collected in depth; incl publications by or about.

HUNTER, JOHN

NY —NEW YORK ACADEMY OF MEDICINE, Library, 2 E 103 St, New York, 10029. Brett A Kirkpatrick, Librn
Holdings: Cat //
Notes: Many editions of Hunter's works on blood, venereal diseases dentistry, animal economy.

HUNTER, ROBERT M. T.

VA —UNIVERSITY OF VIRGINIA, Alderman Library, Manuscripts Dept, Charlottesville, 22901. Edmund Berkeley Jr, Cur
Holdings: Mss Pix Phonorecords Audiotapes Videotapes 16mm Films
Notes: Papers, personal and political, etc.

HUNTER, WILLIAM STROEBEL

CA —STANFORD UNIVERSITY LIBRARIES, Lane Medical Library, Stanford University, Medical Center, Stanford, 94305. Peter Stangl, Librn
Notes: William Stroebel Hunter papers on human locomotion.

HUNTING

CT —TRINITY COLLEGE LIBRARY, 300 Summit St, Hartford, 06106. Ralph S Emerick, Librn

CT —YALE UNIVERSITY, Box 1603A, Yale Station, New Haven, 06520.

DC —LIBRARY OF CONGRESS, Rare Book & Special Collections Div, Washington, 20540. William Matheson, Chief
Notes: President Theodore Roosevelt's library of late 19th and early 20th century works on hunting, exploration, and natural history, with a few earlier classics in these fields.

IL —DE PAUL UNIVERSITY, Library, 2323 N Seminary, Chicago, 60614. Kathryn De Graff, Special Collections Librn
Notes: About 1000 vols on British field sports. Also, 20 hand-colored sets of prints by Edward Troye (1808-1874) of American thoroughbred horses.

IN —UNIVERSITY OF NOTRE DAME, University Libraries, Notre Dame, 46556.
Notes: Very likely the largest collection of sporting materials in the world. Over 500 sports and games are represented in a half-million documents. All physical forms of records are included, and there is no geographical restriction. Major center for research into all aspects of games and sports.

KY —UNIVERSITY OF KENTUCKY, Margaret I King Library, Dept of Special Collections, Lexington, 40506. William Marshall, Head

NJ —PRINCETON UNIVERSITY, Library, Rare Books Dept, Princeton, 08544. Stephen Ferguson, Cur
Notes: Laurence Roberts Carton Hunting Collection. Consists of over 1000 vols, comprising a portion of the Library's sizable Sporting Books Collection. See: William Dix, "The Hunting Library of Laurence Roberts Carton '07" in the *Princeton University Library Chronicle* XV, 1 (Autumn, 1953) pp 43-45. The books are a discriminating and representative collection of the literature of fox hunting and related subjects, particularly in England and America. Works from the 15th century are represented by facsimiles and other modern printed version. There are a number of first editions of notable 16th, 17th and 18th century books, especially in English. The verse and fiction of sport are extensively represented, and biographies of dozens of notable figures and histories of scores of individual packs and hunting territories can be found. Incidental to the collection is thefine collection of illustrated hunting books. It is rich in examples of the work of the major illustrators of the period who helped make, and in turn were made by, the popularity of the sporting book. Especially notable are the works of Henry Alken.

NY —C W POST CENTER OF LONG ISLAND UNIVERSITY, B Davis Schwartz Memorial Library, Greenvale, 11548. Manju Prasad-Rao, Media Librn
Notes: The Franklin B Lord Collection of some 600 vols on hunting and fishing. Many 19th century.

NY —AMERICAN MUSEUM OF NATURAL HISTORY, Library Services Dept, Central Park W & 79th St, New York, 10024. Nina J Root, Chairwoman; Mary Genett, Asst Librn for Reference Services
Notes: Especially the Ernest Thompson Seton diaries.

NY —RACQUET & TENNIS CLUB, Library, 370 Park Ave, New York, 10022. Gerald

HUNTING (cont.)

Belliveau, Jr, Librn
Holdings: Vols (17,500) Cat
Budget: ($6000)
Notes: Specializes in court tennis, lawn tennis, early American sport. See *Dictionary Catalogue of the Library of Sports in the Racquet and Tennis Club* (Boston: G K Hall, 1971). Also, Robert W Henderson, *Early American Sport*, 3rd ed. (Cranbury, NJ: Fairleigh Dickinson University Press, 1977).

NY —UNIVERSITY CLUB, Library, One W 54 St, New York, 10019. Guy St Clair, Library Dir
Holdings: Vols (100,000) Cat Mss Maps Pix
Notes: A private library for the members of the University Club, their guests, and serious scholars upon written application to the Library Director. Holds the Carroll O Bickelhaupt Collection of Books on Hunting and Firearms.

NY —SAGAMORE HILL NATIONAL HISTORIC SITE, Library, 304 Cove Neck Rd, Oyster Bay, 11771.
Holdings: Cat

OH —PUBLIC LIBRARY OF CINCINNATI & HAMILTON COUNTY, Dept of Rare Books & Special Collections, 800 Vine St, Library Square, Cincinnati, 45202. Yeatman Anderson III, Cur
Notes: Large hunting and fishing collection, and a nearly complete set of Derrydale Press publications.

OH —OHIO HISTORICAL SOCIETY, Archives Library Division, 1982 Velma Ave, Columbus, 43211. Dennis East, Division Chief
Holdings: Vols 2000// Cat Mss Pix
Notes: Collection is comprised of books by Grey, magazines in which his writings appeared, mss & typescripts, and 700 items from his personal library, incl scarce items on hunting, big-game fishing, and travel. Museum objects are at the Zane Grey Museum, Zanesville, Ohio, operated by the Ohio Historical Society.

SC —FRANCIS MARION COLLEGE, James A Rogers Library, Florence, 29501. H Paul Dove, Dir; Roger K Hux, Special Collections Librn
Holdings: Vols (400) Cat
Notes: Includes publications of the Small Arms Technical Pub Co, emphasis on hunting and fishing.

VA —NATIONAL SPORTING LIBRARY, Chronicle of the Horse Bldg Publishing Offices, PO Box 1335, Middleburg, 22117. Judith Ozment, Librn
Holdings: Vols (11,000) Cat Mss Pix
Notes: A research center for turf and field sports, their history and social significance.

HUNTING, CONSTANCE

MA —BOSTON UNIVERSITY, Mugar Memorial Library, Special Collections Dept, 771 Commonwealth Ave, Boston, 02215. Howard B Gotlieb, Dir
Holdings: Cat Mss Correspondence

HUNTING DOGS

NY —MERCY COLLEGE LIBRARY, Dobbs Ferry, 10522. Larry Earle Bone, Dir
Holdings: Vols (406) Cat Pix
Notes: General collection of American and British books and periodicals on horses, hounds and hunting, with special emphasis on the Millbrook Hunt. 15 percent of the collection is rare books and periodicals. Rare photographs and paintings also incl. Many of the books are from the private libraries of members of the Millbrook Hunt. Collection formerly at Bennett College, Millbrook, New York.

OH —CLEVELAND PUBLIC LIBRARY, Science & Technology Dept, 325 Superior Ave, Cleveland, 44114. Jean Z Piety, Head
Holdings: Cat
Notes: Emphases: history of the dog; dog show catalogs; stud books of the American Kennel Club, the Canadian Kennel Club, the Kennel Club, the field dog, the foxhound, and the Irish terrier.

HUNTINGTON, COLLIS POTTER

†NY —SYRACUSE UNIVERSITY LIBRARIES, Ernest S Bird Library, 222 Waverly Ave, Syracuse, 13210.
Notes: Papers, etc.

HUNTINGTON, ELLSWORTH

CT —YALE UNIVERSITY, Box 1603A, Yale Station, New Haven, 06520.
Holdings: Mss

HUNTON, EPPA

VA —UNIVERSITY OF VIRGINIA, Alderman Library, Manuscripts Dept, Charlottesville, 22901. Edmund Berkeley Jr, Cur
Holdings: Cat Mss Maps Pix
Notes: About 1500 collections have material pertaining to the Civil War and particularly to the Army of Northern Virginia and campaigns and battles in Virginia. There are letters, diaries, reminiscences, maps, and pictorial material of Confederate soldiers and civilians, as well as papers of Robert E Lee, J E B Stuart, Thomas L Rosser, Jubal A Early, John Daniel Imboden, William "Extra Billy" Smith, Henry Alexander Wise, Eppa Hunton, and John S Mosby.

HUNTOON, MARY

KS —UNIVERSITY OF KANSAS, Kenneth Spencer Research Library, Kansas Collection, Lawrence, 66045. Sheryl K Williams, Cur
Holdings: Vols (92,000) Mss Pix Audiotapes
Notes: All aspects of women's history in Kansas and the region. The collection incl personal papers, such as those of Peggy Hull Deuell (first accredited woman war correspondent), and Mary Huntoon (art therapist); diaries; and organizational records of many women's organizations, such as the Kansas League of Women Voters, the Missouri State Association of Parliamentarians and women's literary and service clubs.

HURBAN, VLADIMIR

†PA —BALCH INSTITUTE FOR ETHNIC STUDIES, Library, 18 S Seventh St, Philadelphia, 19106.
Notes: Papers of Vladimir Hurban, Czechoslovak ambassador to the United States.

HURON INDIANS

KS —WYANDOTTE COUNTY HISTORICAL SOCIETY, Museum, Trowbridge Research Library, 631 N 126 St, Bonner Springs, 66012. Stephen J Allie, Archivist
Holdings: Vols 3000 Mss Maps Pix Slides Audiotapes Microforms
Budget: $12,500
Notes: Emphasis on Wyandotte County. Cataloged. Incl 100 maps, 4000 photographs. Also County Records 1855-1820. Cataloged.

KS —KANSAS CITY PUBLIC LIBRARY, 625 Minnesota Ave, Kansas City, 66101. Eleanor Fox, Librn
Holdings: Mss
Notes: Wyandot (Huron) Indians.

ON —ONTARIO MINISTRY OF TOURISM & RECREATION, Huronia Historical Resource Centre, PO Box 160, Midland, L4R 4K8, Can. M Quealey, Supervisor, Library Services
Holdings: Vols 11,000 Cat Mss Maps Pix Slides Phonorecords Audiotapes Filmstrips Microforms Videotapes
Notes: Reference collection; interlibrary loan; non-circulating. Research facility for reconstruction of historic sites: Historic Naval and Military Establishments, 19th century British base on the Great Lakes; and Sainte-Marie among the Hurons, an early 17th century French Jesuit mission to the Huron Indians. Also, local history collection and archaeological reports for Simcoe County, Ont, Canada.

HURRIAN LANGUAGE

NY —NEW YORK PUBLIC LIBRARY, Oriental Div, Fifth Ave & 42 St, New York, 10018. E Christian Filstrup, Chief
Holdings: Cat Mss Microforms
Budget: ($56,455)
Notes: Published catalog of holdings.

HURST, FANNIE, 1889-1968

MA —BRANDEIS UNIVERSITY, Goldfarb Library, 415 South St, Waltham, 02154. Bessie Hahn, Dir
Notes: 48 linear ft of books, mss, photographs and memorabilia of Fannie Hurst. The collection is unprocessed, spring 1984.

MO —MISSOURI HISTORICAL SOCIETY, Library, Jefferson Memorial Bldg, Saint Louis, 63112. Stephanie Klein, Librn-Archivist; Peter Michel, Cur of Manuscripts
Notes: A collection of material on 119 women who lived or worked in St Louis and Missouri as educators, artists, and homemakers, or played significant roles in US politics and social reform. Incl Sacajawea, Susan B Anthony, Fannie Hurst, Carry Nation, Patience Worth, etc.

MO —SAINT LOUIS PUBLIC LIBRARY, Gardner Rare Book Room, 1301 Olive St, Saint Louis, 63103. Julanne M Good, Supervisor; Martha Riley, Rare Books Librn
Holdings: Vols (2300) Cat
Budget: ($5573)
Notes: First editions of authors having some association with William Marion Reedy and *Reedy's Mirror*, such as Sara Teasdale, Zoe Akins, Fannie Hurst, Edgar Lee Masters, Babette Deutsch, Richard LeGallienne, etc. Also first editions of selected St Louis and/or Missouri authors such as T S Eliot, Samuel L Clemens, Theodore Dreiser and Tennessee Williams. Noncirculating.

MO —WASHINGTON UNIVERSITY, Libraries, Special Collections Dept, Campus Box 1061, St Louis, 63130.
Notes: A major collection, incl books, mss, correspondence, literary papers, photographs, etc. Described in *Special Collections: an Annotated Guide to the Holdings of the Manuscript Division and the University Archives and Research Collection.*

HUS, JAN

MA —HARVARD UNIVERSITY LIBRARY, Widener Library, Cambridge, 02138.
Holdings: Cat

HUSBAND AND WIFE

CA —LOS ANGELES PUBLIC LIBRARY, Social Sciences Dept, 630 W Fifth St, Los Angeles, 90071. Marilyn C Wherley, Principal Librn
Holdings: Vols 3000 Cat
Budget: ($150,000)
Notes: Books, clippings, pamphlets, periodicals, government publications, bibliogrpahies, popular and scholarly works on homosexuality, husband-wife relations, abortion, rape, and sex education.

WI —UNIVERSITY OF WISCONSIN-STOUT, Library Learning Center, Menomonie, 54751. Philip Sawin Jr, Coll Develop Librn
Notes: One of eleven graduate programs in Marriage and Family Therapy in the United States. The program was begun in 1975. This special collection also includes video tapes of outstanding therapists and a specialized 16mm film collection.

HUSBANDRY see Agriculture

HUSSERL, EDMUND

NY —NEW SCHOOL FOR SOCIAL RESEARCH, Raymond Fogelman Library, 65 Fifth Ave, New York, 10003. Michael Lordi, Director
Holdings: Mss
Notes: The papers, etc, of Edmund Husserl. Copies of unpublished notebooks.

HUSSEY, MARY FIELD

IL —NEWBERRY LIBRARY, 60 W Walton St, Chicago, 60610. Diana Haskell, Cur of Modern Mss
Notes: Holdings include the Mary Field Parton correspondence and work files of biographers Arthur and Lila Weinberg.

HUSSITES

IL —UNIVERSITY OF ILLINOIS, URBANA/CHAMPAIGN, Slavic and East European Library, Urbana, 61801. Marianna Tax Choldin, Head
Holdings: Vols (35,000) Cat
Notes: Extensive coverage.

HUSTON, JAY CALVIN

CA —HOOVER INSTITUTION ON WAR, REVOLUTION & PEACE, Stanford University, Stanford, 94305. Milorad M Drachkovitch, Archivist
Holdings: // Mss
Notes: The J Calvin Huston Collection. Handwritten papers, pamphlets, placards, leaflets, and newspaper clippings, chiefly in English and Russian, dealing with cultural, political, and economic conditions in China, with special reference to communism and the influence of Soviet Russia, 1917-1931. 14 boxes. Unpublished register is available in repository.

HUSTON, JOHN

CA —ACADEMY OF MOTION PICTURE ARTS & SCIENCES, Margaret Herrick Library, 8949 Wilshire Blvd, Beverly Hills, 90211. Linda Harris Mehr, Library Administrator
Notes: Papers.
See also entry under Moving Pictures.

HUTCHINS, MAUDE

MA —BOSTON UNIVERSITY, Mugar Memorial Library, Special Collections Dept, 771 Commonwealth Ave, Boston, 02215. Howard B Gotlieb, Dir
Holdings: Cat Mss
Notes: Mss, correspondence, etc collected in depth; incl publications by or about.

HUTCHISON, ALEXANDER

BC —UNIVERSITY OF VICTORIA, McPherson Library, Victoria, V8W 3H5, Can.
Notes: Correspondence. Alexander Hutchinson with George Woodcock re reviews of Robin Skelton's poetry and with Will and Sebastian Carter (The Rampant Lions Press) re printing a collection of broadsides.

HUTCHISON, BRUCE, 1901-

AB —UNIVERSITY OF CALGARY, Libraries, Special Collections Div, 2500 University Dr, Calgary, T2N 1N4, Can.
Holdings: Cat Mss
Notes: The papers of Bruce Hutchison, Canadian journalist and editor, consisting of draft manuscripts, speeches, newspaper clippings, and correspondence (1934-1976) with eminent persons in the scholarly, political, theatrical and publishing worlds.

BC —UNIVERSITY OF VICTORIA, McPherson Library, Victoria, V8W 3H5, Can.

HUTCHISSON, ELMER

NY —AMERICAN INSTITUTE OF PHYSICS, Center for the History of Physics, Niels Bohr Library, 335 E 45 St, New York, 10017. John Aubry, Librn
Notes: Papers and records.

HUTTEN, ULRICH VON

CA —STANFORD UNIVERSITY LIBRARIES, Cecil H Green Library, Stanford, 94305. Peter R Frank, Cur, CDP-Germanic Collection
Notes: Extensive holdings in the field of Reformation and Counter-Reformation. First and early editions by Luther, Melanchthon, Bugenhagen, Cochleus, Eck, Hutten, Reuchlin, and minor figures in Special Collections.

HUTTERIAN BRETHREN

OH —BLUFFTON COLLEGE, Mennonite Historical Library, Bluffton, 45817. Delbert Gratz, Librn
Holdings: Vols (15,000) Cat Mss Maps Pix Slides Phonorecords 16mm Films Microforms
Budget: $1500
Notes: Collection incl all materials available relating to Mennonites, Anabaptists, Amish, Hutterian Brethren and related religious bodies, as well as the topic of peace. The library has a special collection and index of Mennonite and Amish family histories and genealogies; also a special index to periodical articles in non-Mennonite periodicals that relate to Mennonites, Amish, and Anabaptists. Library is a depository for the Central District of the General Conference Mennonite Church and the Africa Inter-Mennonite Mission. Incl archives of the Africa Inter-Mennonite Mission.

HUXLEY, ALDOUS, 1894-1963

CA —UNIVERSITY OF CALIFORNIA, BERKELEY, Bancroft Library, Manuscripts Division, Berkeley, 94720. James D Hart, Dir
Notes: Letters from Huxley in various collections.

CA —UNIVERSITY OF CALIFORNIA, SAN DIEGO, Central University Library, Mandeville Dept of Special Collections, La Jolla, 92093. Lynda Corey Claassen, Head
Notes: First and/or important editions of his writings are included in the Rare Book Collection.

CA —UNIVERSITY OF CALIFORNIA, LOS ANGELES, Research Library, Dept of Special Collections, 405 Hilgard Ave, Los Angeles, 90024. Edward Shreeves, Chairman, Bibliographers Group; David S Zeidberg, Head
Holdings: Vols 450 Cat Mss
Notes: 450 first and other editions of his books; 4 linear feet of mss, correspondence, etc. No photocopying.

CA —FITZ HUGH LUDLOW MEMORIAL LIBRARY, PO Box 99346, San Francisco, 94109. Michael R Aldrich, Exec Cur
Holdings: Cat Mss Maps Pix Slides Phonorecords Audiotapes Videotapes
Notes: Collection stored. Important mail inquiries only. No interlibrary lending or telephone inquiries. Hallucinogens as used in historical and contemporary cultures. Nearly complete collection of books and articles by or about Timothy Leary, incl manuscripts; also nearly complete collection of the writings of Aldous Huxley concerning drugs. Much autographed or inscribed material, mostly popular music from the 1960s but also incl ethnographic music. Emphasis on psychoactive drugs relative to religion, literature, art. Also an excellent collection of research papers (chemistry, pharmacology, epidemiology, sociology, ethnobotany) in this field, as well as artifacts and artwork relating to the field.

CA —UNIVERSITY OF CALIFORNIA, SANTA BARBARA, Library, Dept of Special Collections, Santa Barbara, 93106. Christian F Brun, Head
Holdings: Cat Mss Pix

IN —BALL STATE UNIVERSITY, University Libraries, Special Collections Dept, University Ave, Muncie, 47306. David C Tambo, Head of Special Collections
Holdings: Vols 94 Cat
Notes: First editions.

MI —DETROIT PUBLIC LIBRARY, Rare Books Department, 5201 Woodward Ave, Detroit, 48202.
Holdings: Vols 120 Cat
Notes: Incl many first editions inscribed to Crosby Gaige. Restricted use. Reference collection.

NV —UNIVERSITY OF NEVADA, RENO, University Library, Special Collections Dept, Reno, 89557. Robert E Blesse, Head
Holdings: // Vols (230) Cat
Notes: Includes individual works by author in all editions including translations; also prefaces, introductions, published correspondence, appearances in anthologies, periodicals, etc. Bibliographical research collection, part of Modern Authors Collection. Other appearances 370 cataloged.

NY —ALFRED UNIVERSITY, Herrick Memorial Library, Alfred, 14802. June E Brown, Head Librn
Notes: The Evelyn Tennyson Openhym Collection of modern British literature and social history. Correspondence addressed to Ursula Roberts ("Susan Miles"), many pieces concerning the British peace movement of the 1930s.

NY —STATE UNIVERSITY OF NEW YORK, COLLEGE OF ARTS & SCIENCE AT GENESEO, Milne Library, Geneseo, 14454. William T Lane, Head of Information Services & Archivist
Holdings: Vols 575 Cat Pix Microforms
Budget: $200
Notes: First English and American editions, variant editions, some inscribed and autographed by the author. Huxley's contributions to periodicals, anthologies, etc. *By and About Aldous Huxley: a checklist of the Aldous Huxley Collection of Milne* Library, by Barry Lash (Geneseo, 1973), 38 pp.

†NC —DUKE UNIVERSITY, Archives, 341 Perkins Library, Durham, 27706.
Notes: Incl psychic phenomena, the plight of emigres and the growth of the police state in Nazi Germany, euthanasia and eugenics, behaviorism and John Watson, and such figures as Aldous Huxley and C G Jung. 1800 items and 24 vols. Correspondence with individuals significant in the fields of psychology, psychic research, and social sciences.

†NC —WAKE FOREST UNIVERSITY, Z Smith Reynolds Library, Box 7777, Reynold Sta, Winston-Salem, 27109.
Notes: A significant collection.

TX —UNIVERSITY OF HOUSTON, M D Anderson Memorial Library, University Park, Houston, 77004. David Farmer, Cur, Special Collections; Jean Jackson, Assistant Cur
Holdings: Vols 300 Cat Mss Pix
Notes: This collection represents the most comprehensive bibliographical author collection at the University. Actively sought are ephemeral pieces, reprints, variants, and letters.

ON —UNIVERSITY OF TORONTO, Thomas Fisher Rare Book Library, 120 Saint George St, Toronto, M5S 1A5, Can. Richard G Landon, Head
Holdings: Vols 5400 Cat Mss
Notes: Three collections. Duncan Collection is named for donor, Douglas Duncan, art dealer and collector, Toronto. Contains first and subsequent important editions of Richard Aldington, Max Beerbohm, Norman Douglas, Aldoux Huxley, and D H Lawrence. Manuscripts by Beerbohm, Aldington, Lawrence, William Sharp. Endicott Collection named in honor of Norman J Endicott, Professor of English, University of Toronto, contains first and significant later editions of over fifty British writers whose major work falls into the period from 1880 to 1930. Fisher Collection named for donor, Charles B Fisher, contains first and significant editions of Kipling, Norman Douglas, and Lord Dunsany.

HUXLEY, SIR JULIAN SORELL, 1887-1975

TX —RICE UNIVERSITY, Fondren Library, Woodson Research Center, 6100 S Main St, PO Box 1892, Houston, 77251. Nancy Parker, Dir Woodson Research Center
Notes: The papers of Julian Huxley, eminent biologist, Director of the London Zoo, first Director-General of UNESCO, and prolific writer.

HUZVARESH see Pahlavi Language and Literature

HYBRIDITY OF RACES see Miscegenation

HYDER, BULLOCK

TX —NORTH TEXAS STATE UNIVERSITY, Archives, NT Station Box 5188, Denton, 76203. Robert LaForte, University Archivist
Notes: Texas political manuscript collections housed in the NTSU Archives include the Fred H Minor Collection (former Texas Speaker of the House), the Alvin M Owsley Collection (former US diplomat from Texas), the Hermine Tobolowsky Equal Legal Rights Collection (leader of women's equal legal rights in Texas), and the Bullock Hyder Collection (former representative to Texas House from Lewisville). The collections cover Texas politics from the 1920's to the 1970's. Published Description: Fred H Minor Collection, *The National Union Catalog of Manuscript Collections: Catalog* 1979 Washington: Library of Congress, 1980. Page 214. Alvin M Owsley Collection, Ibid, p 215. Hermine Tobolowsky Equal Legal Rights Collection, Ibid.

HYDRAULIC ENGINEERING

CA —RAYMOND KAISER ENGINEERS INC, Engineering Library, 300 Lakeside Dr, PO Box 23210, Oakland, 94623. Elaine Zacher, Librn
Holdings: Vols 500 Cat

IA —UNIVERSITY OF IOWA, University Libraries, Iowa City, 52242. Frank Paluka, Head, Special Collections Dept
Holdings: Vols 395 Cat
Notes: Hydraulic engineering and the history of hydraulics. Hunter Rouse, "Highlights in the History Hydraulics", *Books at Iowa*, April 1983.

MA —MASSACHUSETTS INSTITUTE OF TECHNOLOGY, Institute Archives, Special Collections, Cambridge, 02139.
Notes: Papers of John Ripley Freeman, a hydraulic engineer, President of Associated Factory Mutual Fire Insurance Companies, and a consulting engineer. Collection primarily documents his activities as a consultant on hydraulics projects in the United States, Canada, China, Columbia, Mexico and Panama. Also, his work on the hydraulics of fire prevention, safety precautions for theaters, and seismology; his promotion of the National Hydraulics Laboratory and of European engineering practices; his involvement with the Engineering Foundation, the National Bureau of Standards, and the National Research Council; and his investments in mining, manufacturing, and land speculation. Unpublished finding aid available in Archives.

MS —US ARMY ENGINEER WATERWAYS EXPERIMENT STATION, Library Branch, PO Box 631, Vicksburg, 39180. Bernice Black, Chief Librn
Holdings: Vols (350,000) Cat Mss Maps Microforms

NY —ENGINEERING SOCIETIES LIBRARY, 345 E 47 St, New York, 10017. S Kirk Cabeen, Dir
Holdings: Vols 250,000 Cat Maps 16mm Films Microforms
Notes: One of the largest, most comprehensive engineering libraries in the world. Covers all engineering disciplines; particularly strong in electrical and electronic, mechanical, mining and metallurgical, petroleum, chemical, industrial, air conditioning and refrigeration engineering. Incl Wheeler Collection of early materials on magnetism and electricity. 125, 000 bound periodical volumes; 10,000 maps; 5000 serial subscriptions (many foreign-language). Virtually all materials abstracted in *Engineering Index* (1884-date) are incl in Library. Noncirculating, except to members of professional engineering societies which support the Library. See *Engineering Societies Library, New York, Classed Subject Catalog and Index* (Boston: G K Hall, 1963); and *Supplements*, 1-10, 1964-1973.

PA —FRANKLIN INSTITUTE LIBRARY, 20 & The Parkway, Philadelphia, 19103. Miriam Padusis, Dir; Charles Wilt, Readers Servs Librn
Holdings: Vols (300,000) Cat Maps Pix Microforms

PA —ROCKWELL INTERNATIONAL, General Industries Operations, Technical Information Center, 400 N Lexington Ave, Pittsburgh, 15208. Kathleen H Witkowski, Library Coordr
Holdings: Vols Cat Microforms Mss Documents Periodicals VF
Budget: ($5100)

TX —TEXAS DEPT OF WATER RESOURCES, Library, 1700 N Congress, PO Box 13087, Capitol Sta, Austin, 78711. Sylvia von Fange, Head Librn
Holdings: Vols (58,000) Cat Pix Microforms
Notes: A comprehensive technical collection which incl information on all aspects of water resources. Publications Catalog; Library Bulletin (monthly).

ON —NATIONAL RESEARCH COUNCIL OF CANADA, Aeronautical/Mechanical Engineering Branch Library, Montreal Rd, Ottawa, K1A 0R6, Can. Louise Fletcher, Head
Notes: This branch library of the Canada Institute for Scientific and Technical Information (CISTI) of the National Research Council of Canada, Ottawa, has a collection strong in aeronautical engineering, automatic control, CAD/CAM, robotics, ocean, wind, and solar energy power, hydraulic and coastal engineering, icing, low temperature research, naval engineering, metals and metallurgy, incl composites, tribology, and air, railroad, marine transportation. Library supported the Council contribution to the development of the remote manipular Canadarm for NASA's Space Shuttle Orbiters and more recently, the Canadian Astronaut Program which will contribute payload specialists to NASA's Space Shuttle Program in 1984. 35, 000 monographs, 1200 serials. Report collection: over 500,000 items.

HYDRAULICS

MS —US ARMY ENGINEER WATERWAYS EXPERIMENT STATION, Library Branch, PO Box 631, Vicksburg, 39180. Bernice Black, Chief Librn
Holdings: Vols (350,000) Cat Mss Maps Microforms

OH —CLEVELAND PUBLIC LIBRARY, Science & Technology Dept, 325 Superior Ave, Cleveland, 44114. Jean Z Piety, Head
Holdings: Cat Pix
Notes: Special collection covers the environmental sciences concerned with the Great Lakes-St Lawrence drainage basins. Emphasis is on limnology, ecology, meteorology, hydraulics, biology, pollution of air and water, natural history and general research. Most of the material indexed has been donated by numerous agencies around the Great Lakes.

PQ —SERVICE DE LA DOCUMENTATION ET DES RENSEIGNEMENTS MINISTERE DE L'ENERGIE ET DES RESSOURCES, 2000B, chemin Sainte-Foy, 7th floor, Quebec, G1R 4X7, Can. Normand Guerette, Dir
Holdings: Vols (114,800) Slides Videotapes
Notes: In 1979, the Bibliotheque du ministere des Richesses naturelles du Quebec merged with the Bibliotheque du ministere des Terres et Forets. The result of this merger was the creation of the service de la Documentation et des Renseignements du ministere de l'Energie et des Ressources. Publications: Info-Biblio Terres et Forets; Mines; Energy.

HYDRAULICS—HISTORY

IA —UNIVERSITY OF IOWA, University Libraries, Iowa City, 52242. Frank Paluka, Head, Special Collections Dept
Holdings: Vols 395 Cat
Notes: Hydraulic engineering and the history of hydraulics.

HYDROBIOLOGY see Freshwater Biology; Marine Biology

HYDRODYNAMICS

NM —UNIVERSITY OF CALIFORNIA, Los Alamos National Laboratory, Libraries, PO Box 1663, MSP 362, Los Alamos, 87545. J Arthur Freed, Head Librn
Holdings: Vols (800,000) Cat Films Micorforms
Budget: ($700,000)
Notes: Incl 500,000 classified and unclassified reports. There are 25 branch libraries and a central collection. The Medical Library contains about 40,000 vols in the areas of biomedical research.

PA —FRANKLIN INSTITUTE LIBRARY, 20 & The Parkway, Philadelphia, 19103. Miriam Padusis, Dir; Charles Wilt, Readers Servs Librn
Holdings: Vols (300,000) Cat Maps Pix Microforms

HYDROGEN BOMB

MI —UNIVERSITY OF MICHIGAN, Libraries, Michigan Historical Collections, Ann Arbor, 48109. Mary Jo Pugh, Reference Archivist
Notes: Ralph A Sawyer's papers (1918-78). Incl material relating to his work as consultant at the test of the hydrogen bomb at the Naval Proving Grounds, Bikini Atoll.

NM —UNIVERSITY OF CALIFORNIA, Los Alamos National Laboratory, Libraries, PO Box 1663, MSP 362, Los Alamos, 87545. J Arthur Freed, Head Librn
Holdings: Vols (800,000) Cat Films Microforms
Budget: ($700,000)
Notes: Incl 500,000 classified and unclassified reports. There are 25 branch libraries and a central collection. The Medical Library contains about 40,000 vols in the areas of biomedical research.

HYDROGRAPHIC CHARTS see Nautical Charts

HYDROLOGY

AZ —PHOENIX PUBLIC LIBRARY, Arizona Room, 12 E McDowell, Phoenix, 85004. Jeannette Brush, Librn
Holdings: Vols (30,000) Cat Maps Pix
Budget: ($12,000)
See also entry under Arizona - History.

CA —UNIVERSITY OF CALIFORNIA, DAVIS, Physical Sciences Library, Davis, 95616. Scott Kennedy, Head
Holdings: Vols (170,000) Cat VF
Notes: Collection covers aeronautical, agricultural, chemical, civil, electrical, mechanical, water science, hydrology, nuclear reactor, extensive cold regions collection in vertical file drawers, and computer science engineering academic programs. Good strength in journal runs.

FL —SOUTH FLORIDA WATER MANAGEMENT DISTRICT, Library, PO Box V, West Palm Beach, 33402. Cynthia H Plockelman, Research Librn
Holdings: Cat Slides Microforms Periodicals
Budget: ($13,000)
Notes: A state agency dealing in all aspects of water management, flood control, hydrology, changing environmental conditions, etc. Emphasis is changing from flood control to general water management.

IN —PURDUE UNIVERSITY LIBRARIES, Geosciences Library, West Lafayette, 47907. Carolyn Lassoon, Librn
Holdings: Vols (15,000) Cat
Notes: Geosciences.

MD —NATIONAL OCEANIC & ATMOSPHERIC ADMINISTRATION, Library & Information Sciences Division, Central Library & Information Sciences Bldg, 6009 Executive Blvd, Rockville, 20852. Elizabeth J Yeates, Chief
Holdings: Vols (175,000) Cat Maps Microforms

NM —US GEOLOGICAL SURVEY, Water Resources Division Library, Western Bank,

HYDROLOGY (cont.)

505 Marquette, Rm 714, Albuquerque, 87102. Janie S Jones, Librn
Holdings: Vols (38,000) Mss Maps
Budget: ($15,000)
Notes: Primarily hydrology and geology of New Mexico. Incl 20,000 maps.

NC —UNIVERSITY OF NORTH CAROLINA, CHAPEL HILL, Geology Library, Mitchell Hall 029A, Chapel Hill, 27514. Miriam L Sheaves, Librn
Holdings: Vols (41,000) Cat Maps
Notes: Earth sciences, paleontology, oceanography, geology, geophysics. Incl theses and dissertations; 103,000 map sheets.

PA —CARNEGIE LIBRARY OF PITTSBURGH, Science & Technology Dept, 4400 Forbes Ave, Pittsburgh, 15213. Catherine M Brosky, Dept Head
Notes: Long runs of journals, reports of geological surveys and society publications. Incl abstracts, indexes, bibliographies, literature guides, dictionaries, handbooks, manuals, compilations of data, maps, history and biography. Complete sets of US topographic maps and geologic folios, climatological data, water supply papers and soil surveys available.

TN —TENNESSEE VALLEY AUTHORITY (TVA), Technical Library, 400 W Summit Hill Dr, E2 B7, Knoxville, 37902. Jesse C Mills, Chief Librn
Holdings: Vols (106,900) Cat Mss Maps Pix Audiotapes Microforms
Budget: ($2,025,000)
Notes: The Technical Library Headquarters Staff (order, cataloging, information, and administration) is located in Knoxville, Tenn. In addition there are branch libraries in Knoxville, Norris, and Chattanooga, Tennessee, and Muscle Shoals, Alabama.

AB —CANADIAN FORESTRY SERVICE, Northern Forest Research Centre Library, 5320 122nd, Edmonton, T6H 3S5, Can. David J S Robinson, Librn
Holdings: Vols (7000) Cat Microforms
Budget: ($25,000)
Notes: Also 23,000 government documents, 2600 research reports, 3000 pamphlets and reprints.

BC —CANADIAN FORESTRY SERVICE, Pacific Forest Research Centre, Library, 506 West Burnside Rd, Victoria, V8Z 1M5, Can. Alice Solyma, Librn
Holdings: Vols (60,500) Cat Microforms
Notes: Forest hydrology; incl selective collection in general hydrology. meteorology, mensuration, fire research, hydrology, environmental science and ecology, biometrics, land use and classification, soil science, and forest economics. 400 microforms; 40,000 documents and reports.

PQ —SERVICE DE LA DOCUMENTATION ET DES RENSEIGNEMENTS MINISTERE DE L'ENERGIE ET DES RESSOURCES, 2000B, chemin Sainte-Foy, 7th floor, Quebec, G1R 4X7, Can. Normand Guerette, Dir
Holdings: Vols (114,800) Slides Videotapes
Notes: In 1979, the Bibliotheque du ministere des Richesses naturelles du Quebec merged with the Bibliotheque du ministere des Terres et Forets. The result of this merger was the creation of the service de la Documentation et des Renseignements du ministere de l'Energie et des Ressources.
Publications: Info-Biblio Terres et Forets; Mines; Energy.

SK —CANADA PRAIRIE FARM REHABILITATION ADMINISTRATION LIBRARY, Motherwell Bldg, Regina, S4P 0R5, Can. C Kosack, Head
Holdings: Vols (10,000) Cat
Budget: ($8000)
Notes: PFRA is a Canadian federal government agency initiated to alleviate the effects of drought and water shortages on the prairies. The collection covers engineering (dams), agricultural economics, hydrology, irrigation, community pastures, and soil and water conservation.

HYDROLOGY—MAPS

CA —US GEOLOGICAL SURVEY LIBRARY, 345 Middlefield Rd, Menlo Park, 94025.
Holdings: Vols (200,000)

HYDROMAGNETIC WAVES see Magnetohydrodynamics (MHD)

HYDROMECHANICS see Fluid Mechanics

HYDROPATHY see Hydrotherapy

HYDROPHYTES see Algae; Marine Flora

HYDROTHERAPY

CA —LOMA LINDA UNIVERSITY, Dell E Webb Memorial Library, Loma Linda, 92350. H Maynard Lowrey, Librn
Holdings: Vols Cat
Notes: Incl works on hydrotherapy and works by William Beaumont and Daniel Drake.

MD —MEDICAL & CHIRURGICAL FACULTY OF THE STATE OF MARYLAND, Library, 1211 Cathedral St, Baltimore, 21201. Joseph E Jensen, Librn
Holdings: Vols (10,000) // Cat Mss Maps Pix
See also entry under Medicine - History and Historic

†NY —MEDICAL RESEARCH LIBRARY OF BROOKLYN, Academy of Medicine of Brooklyn & The State University of New York Downstate Medical Center, 450 Clarkson St, Brooklyn, 11203. Kenneth E Moody, Dir
Notes: Extensive collection of 18th-19th century material.
See also entry under Medicine

HYGIENE

OH —PUBLIC LIBRARY OF CINCINNATI & HAMILTON COUNTY, Science & Technology Dept, 800 Vine St, Cincinnati, 45202. Rosemary Gaiser, Head
Holdings: Vols 16,000 Cat
Notes: Books in this subject area are mainly for the general reader rather than physicians or medical students.

TX —HOUSTON ACADEMY OF MEDICINE-TEXAS MEDICAL CENTER, Library, Jesse H Jones Library Bldg, Houston, 77030. Elizabeth Borst White, Special Collections Librn
Holdings: Vols (900) Cat
Notes: Mading Collection on Public Health. English-language materials dealing with American public health conditions before 1925. Emphasis is on epidemiology and infectious diseases (excluding venereal disease), incl material on sanitation and climatology. Federal, state or municipal reports on health, mortality and sanitation are included. Also 500 pamphlets.

VA —UNITED WAY OF AMERICA INFORMATION CENTER, 701 North Fairfax St, United Way Plaza, Alexandria, 22314. Henry M Smith, Dir; Barbara L Owen, Librn
Holdings: Vols (1200) Cat Microforms
Notes: Incl 5000 research reports and studies on microfiche; 100 vertical file drawers. Services primarily for United Way organizations--United Funds, Community Chests, Health and Welfare Planning Councils.

HYGIENE—STUDY AND TEACHING see Health Education

HYGIENE, DENTAL see Dental Hygiene

HYGIENE, INDUSTRIAL see Industrial Hygiene

HYGIENE, MENTAL see Mental Hygiene

HYGIENE, ORAL see Dental Hygiene

HYGIENE, PUBLIC see Public Health

HYGIENE, PUBLIC—ADMINISTRATION see Public Health

HYGIENE, SOCIAL see Prostitution; Public Health

HYMENOPTERA

DC —SMITHSONIAN INSTITUTION LIBRARIES, Entomology Branch, Washington, 20560. Jean C Smith, Asst Dir for Bureau Services
Holdings: Vols (17,000) Cat Maps Pix

HYMNOLOGY see Hymns and Hymnals

HYMNS, AMERICAN see Hymns, English

HYMNS, ENGLISH

ON —VICTORIA UNIVERSITY, Library, 71 Queen's Park Crescent, Toronto, M5S 1K7, Can. Robert C Brandeis, Chief Librn
Holdings: Vols 1150 Uncat
Notes: Collection consists of British and North American hymnbooks from the 19th and 20th centuries. The emphasis is on Protestant denominations. Some liturgical works are incl.

HYMNS AND HYMNALS

CA —CLAREMONT COLLEGES, Honnold Library, Ninth & Dartmouth, Claremont, 91711. Tania Rizzo, Special Collections Dept Head
Holdings: Vols 3500 Cat Mss Periodicals Phonorecords
Notes: Card index by Mr and Mrs Robert Guy McCutchan, donors. Mainly American, 17th century to present. Most complete for Methodist hymnbooks. Donor was editor of 1935 edition of Methodist Hymnal. Scrapbooks of McCutchan's life, accomplishments, and tributes, compiled by his widow. Restricted use.

CA —CALIFORNIA STATE UNIVERSITY, HAYWARD, Library, Hayward, 94542. Melissa Rose, Dir
Holdings: Vols (15,986) Cat Phonorecords
Budget: ($21,000)
Notes: The score collection covers the entire range of instrumental and vocal concert music, incl collected works of various composers, and representative collections of hymnals, folk music, musical comedy, and some popular music. Sound recordings range from ethnomusicological collections to electronic music. Emphasis is on concert music, but there is a large collection of jazz and a selective collection of popular music. Separate catalog.

CA —BIOLA UNIVERSITY, Rose Memorial Library, 13800 Biola Ave, La Mirada, 90639. A Lawrence Marshburn
Holdings: Vols (178,000) Cat Maps Pix Microforms
Budget: ($430,000)
Notes: Biblical and evangelical materials.

CA —UNIVERSITY OF CALIFORNIA, LOS ANGELES, Research Library, Dept of Special Collections, 405 Hilgard Ave, Los Angeles, 90024. Edward Shreeves, Chairman, Bibliographers Group; David S Zeidberg, Head
Holdings: Vols 500
Notes: Contains 19th century American hymns and hymnals.

CT —YALE UNIVERSITY, Music Library, 98 Wall St, New Haven, 06520. Harold E Samuel, Librn
Holdings: Vols (118,000) Cat Mss Pix Phonorecords Audiotapes
Notes: Manuscript and archive collection comprising over 500 individual musical mss as well as the personal papers and musical mss of such American musicians and composers as Charles Ives, Carl Ruggles, Haratio Parker, Quincy Porter, Richard Donovan and David Stanley Smith, Leo Ornstein, Armin Loos, Duane Davidson, Alonzo Elliott, John Rosamund Johnson, Hope Leroy Baumgartner, Gustave Stoeckel, Hershy Kay, Virgil Thomson, Kurt Weill, Lotte Lenya, Lowell Mason, Parker Bailey, Henry Gilbert, Seymour Shifrin, Lehman Engel, Ernest Trow Carter, and Alec Templeton. Extensive Paul Hindemith Collection. Also ca 35,000 pieces of American sheet music, both instrumental and vocal as well as extensive holdings of 17th & 18th century American hymn books.

DC —LIBRARY OF CONGRESS, American Folklife Center, Archive of Folk Culture,

HYMNS AND HYMNALS (cont.)

Washington, 20540.
Notes: Georgia vernacular architecture, food customs, storytelling, and gospel singing traditions, in local black and white communities. Thousands of color transparencies, etc.

FL —FLORIDA SOUTHERN COLLEGE, Roux Library, Johnson at McDonald, Lakeland, 33802. Larry Stallings, Special Collections Librn
Holdings: Vols (5100) Cat Mss
Notes: Incl Florida church histories and minutes of District Conventions. Methodist-related books and hymnals, and many old Bibles, are included. Separate indexes.

FL —FLORIDA STATE UNIVERSITY, Robert Manning Strozier Library, Childhood in Poetry Collection, Tallahassee, 32306. Frederick Korn, Cur
Holdings: Vols (25,000) Cat
Notes: The Childhood in Poetry Collection consists of the books of all the great poets and hundreds of minor poets of all periods, in first or other early and illustrated editions, in children's periodicals and "juveniles." There are more than 300 hymnals, incl the personal collection of Dr Robert Lowry, author of "Shall We Gather at the River" and other popular hymns.

GA —EMORY UNIVERSITY, Candler School of Theology, Pitts Theology Library, Atlanta, 30322. Channing Jeschke, Librn; Anita K Delaries, Curator
Holdings: Vols 8786 Cat
Notes: Primarily English and American imprints, incl denominational as well as nondenominational works. Described in *The* Hymn, 28:1, Jan, 1977, p. 24.

IL —NEWBERRY LIBRARY, 60 W Walton St, Chicago, 60610. Diana Haskell, Cur of Modern Mss
Holdings: Vols 2400 Cat
Notes: Incl library of Hubert P Main. Mostly 18th century and early 19th century American song books and hymnals. Restricted use: noncirculating.

IL —WHEATON COLLEGE, Buswell Memorial Library, Wheaton, 60187. Paul Snezek, Library Dir
Holdings: Vols 1500
Notes: Nearly half are 19th century publications.

LA —NEW ORLEANS BAPTIST THEOLOGICAL SEMINARY, Martin Music Library, 4110 Seminary Place, New Orleans, 70126. Douglas G Broomoe, Music Librn
Holdings: Vols 38,000 Cat Mss Microforms
Budget: ($10,000)
Notes: Martin Music Library serves the Division of Church Music Ministries of the New Orleans Baptist Theological Seminary. As such, its holdings lean toward church music: books (7500); scores (11,000); anthems (15,000); records (4500). Martin Music Library is maintained as a separate division of the Seminary's library and is housed in the main library. Separate catalog.

MA —EPISCOPAL DIOCESE OF MASSACHUSETTS, Diocesan Library, 1 Joy St, Boston, 02108. Mark J Duffy, Archivist; Margaret A Dempsey, Asst Archivist
Holdings: Mss Pix
Budget: $37,000
Notes: Official material of the Diocese of Massachusetts, incl parish histories, biographies and writings of bishops and clergymen; prayer books and hymnals of the American Church; Americana; colonial Church histories; materials relating to the Society for the Propagation of the Gospel (SPG); 18th and 19th century pamphlets.

MA —BERKSHIRE ATHENAEUM, 1 Wendell Ave, Pittsfield, 01201. Ruth T Degenhardt, Head Local History & Literature
Holdings: Vols 200 Cat Mss
Budget: ($2000)
Notes: Large and representative collection. Specific area of focus in Hancock, Massachusetts, and New Lebanon, New York, Shaker communities. Also contains 500 unbound pamphlets; 20 handwritten hymnals. Published guide to collection: Richmond, Mary L comp, *Shaker Literature: A Bibliography* (Hanover, NH: University Press of New England, 1977).

MA —AMERICAN ANTIQUARIAN SOCIETY LIBRARY, 185 Salisbury St, Worcester, 01609. Marcus A McCorison, Dir & Librn
Holdings: Vols (10,000) Cat
Notes: Presumably the most extensive collection of American psalmody in the country. Over 5000 volumes before 1880. Incl the Bay Psalm Book.

MI —ANDREWS UNIVERSITY, James White Library, Berrien Springs, 49104. Marley H Soper, Dir
Holdings: Vols 110// Cat
Notes: Hymns of the Seventh-Day Adventist faith. The collection begins with the 1849 edition of the hymnal and continues to the present. Not available by interlibrary loan, but may be used at this library.

MO —UNIVERSITY OF MISSOURI-KANSAS CITY, General Library, Conservatory of Music Library, 5100 Rockhill Road, Kansas City, 64110. Kenneth J LaBudde, Dir; Richard Belanger, Librn
Holdings: Vols 46,337 Cat
Notes: 276 current serial subscriptions, 7462 microforms, 16,702 sound recordings, some 70,000 other items with specialists in American Music, Virgil Thomson and hymnology.

NJ —DREW UNIVERSITY, Library, Madison, 07940. Caroline Coughlin, Assoc Dir
Notes: Collection of hymnals for all of the major Methodist churches in the US, with additional foreign materials.

NY —UNION THEOLOGICAL SEMINARY, Library, 3041 Broadway at Reinhold Niebuhr Place, New York, 10027. Richard D Spoor, Dir
Holdings: Vols (550,000) Cat Mss Microforms
Budget: ($350,000)

†NY —COLGATE ROCHESTER DIVINITY SCHOOL, Ambrose Swasey Library, 1100 S Goodman St, Rochester, 14620.
Notes: Incl general works about worship, its history and practice and contains manuals of worship, liturgies of primarily Protestant denomination, a sizable collection of hymn books, with particular emphasis upon the Anglican tradition.

NC —UNIVERSITY OF NORTH CAROLINA, CHAPEL HILL, Music Library, Hill Hall, Chapel Hill, 27514.
Holdings: Vols (90,000) Cat Mss Pix Slides Phonorecords Audiotapes Microforms
Budget: ($60,000)
Notes: Extensive holdings of early theoretical treatises; complete editions; performing scores; music periodicals; reference works. Special interests reflected in holdings of sonatas; oratorios; requiems; operas; microfilms of Vatican Library holdings of mss containing hymns; microfilms from the Deutsches Musikgeschichtliches Archiv; microfilms of important European primary sources; contemporary chamber music. Approx 5000 pieces of early American sheet music, primarily antebellum. Substantial collection of shape-note hymnals, 19th and 20th century. Dictionary catalog of books, scores, microforms and recordings. Separate card catalog of early American music and song anthologies held by Music Library. Partial book catalog of libretto collection.

NC —DUKE UNIVERSITY, Divinity School Library, Durham, 27706. Donn Michael Farris, Librn
Holdings: Vols (225,000)
Notes: Special collections and subject emphases in this library include: Archaeology, Egyptian; Archaeology, Middle Eastern; Art, Jewish; Bible; Bible-New Testament; Bible-Symbolism; Church Architecture; Egyptology; Fathers of the Church; Society of Friends; Great Britain-Religion-Methodism and Methodist Church; Hymns and Hymnals; Jansenists and Jansenism; Judaica; Mediaeval Christian Mysticism; Methodism and Methodist Church; Methodist Episcopal Church; Methodist Episcopal Church, South; Reformation; Religion-US-History; Rural Church; Theology-Great Britain-17th Century; Theology-Great Britain-18th Century; United Methodist Church; US-Church History; John Wesley.

NC —MORAVIAN MUSIC FOUNDATION, Peter Memorial Library, 20 Cascade Ave, Winston-Salem, 27107. James Boeringer, Dir
Holdings: Vols (6000) Cat Phonorecords
Budget: ($2500)
Notes: Emphasis on 18th and 19th century music, incl hymns, Moravian music, etc.

OH —CLEVELAND PUBLIC LIBRARY, Fine Arts and Special Collections Department, 325 Superior Ave, Cleveland, 44114. Alice N Loranth, Head
Holdings: Vols 2000 Cat
Notes: Mostly in English, representing various denominations. Department maintains its own index by first line and/or tune name.

OH —OBERLIN COLLEGE LIBRARY, Oberlin, 44074. William A Moffett, Dir of Libraries
Holdings: Cat
Notes: Of special interest are sermons, hymn books, and hymnals of the late 18th and early 19th centuries.

PA —FREE LIBRARY OF PHILADELPHIA, Music Dept, Logan Sq, Philadelphia, 19103. Frederick James Kent, Head
Holdings: Vols 2000
Notes: The American Hymnody Collection incl early psalters, hymn books and anthologies of sacred music published in the 18th and 19th centuries. Examples of holdings are Lyon's *Urania* (1761), Billings' *Singing Master's Assistant* (1778), and Wyeth's *Repository of Sacred Music*. Arrangements to use the collection should be made in advance.

PA —LUTHERAN THEOLOGICAL SEMINARY, Krauth Memorial Library, 7301 Germantown Ave, Philadelphia, 19119. Rev David J Wartluft, Dir Libr
Holdings: Vols (2800) Cat
Notes: Lutheran, of all countries. American publications of many denominations also represented. Incl the Luther D Reed collection of Lutheran hymnals.

RI —BROWN UNIVERSITY, John Hay Library, Harris Collection, Prospect St, Providence, 02912. Rosemary L Cullen, Cur
Holdings: Vols (175,000) Cat Mss Pix Phonorecords Microforms
Budget: ($15,000)
Notes: The Harris Collection of American Poetry and Plays is principally composed of American and Canadian poetry and plays from the 17th century to the present. Extensive holdings in hymnals of the 17th to the 20th centuries, incl a number of Pennsylvania German hymnals. Collection incl the MacDougall Collection of Psalters and Hymnals. See *Dictionary Catalog of The Harris Collection of American Poetry and* Plays (Boston: G K Hall, 1972), 13 vols; Supplement (1976), 3 vols. Separate catalog.

SC —WOFFORD COLLEGE, Sandor Teszler Library, N Church St, Spartanburg, 29301. Frank J Anderson, Librn
Holdings: Vols 1247 Uncat
Notes: Haynes-Brown Hymnal Collection consists of all denominations of rare items and colonial imprints, incl Christopher Saur and Isaiah Thomas imprints. Collection is being augmented by Pierce Gault of Washington, DC.

TX —ABILENE CHRISTIAN UNIVERSITY, Margaret & Herman Brown Library, ACU Sta, Abilene, 79601. Callie Faye Milliken, Assoc Dir
Holdings: Vols 500
Notes: Early American songbooks and hymnals.

TX —SOUTHWESTERN BAPTIST THEOLOGICAL SEMINARY, Music Library, Fort Worth, 76122. Phillip W Sims, Librn
Holdings: Vols (19,000) Cat
Budget: ($30,000)
Notes: Incl in the Treasure Section are approx 250 tune books, plus many very old hymnals and other antiquarian items. Incl 97,000 pieces of sheet music, 24,000 scores,

HYMNS AND HYMNALS (cont.)

7500 phonograph records and 3500 audiocassettes. The entire collection is cataloged except the periodicals and about one fourth of the sheet music.

TX —BAYLOR UNIVERSITY, Moody Memorial Library, Crouch Music Library, 1312 S Third St, PO Box 6307, Waco, 76706. Avery T Sharp, Librn
Holdings: Vols (75,000) Cat Phonorecords Audiotapes Microforms
Budget: ($48,000)
Notes: Areas of strength: The Frances G Spencer Collection of American Printed Music, 30,000 items of popular sheet music of the 19th and 20th centuries, completely cataloged; complete collection of Denkmaler, Gesamtausgeben and other historical sets, periodicals, dictionaries, library catalogs, thematic indexes, etc; 55,000 volumes of music scores and music literature; 20,000 phonorecords, tapes and microfilm; 400 early American hymn books. Collection has separate catalog.

VA —CBN UNIVERSITY, Virginia Beach, 23463. Jack L Ralston, Fine Arts Librn
Holdings: Vols 9000
Notes: The Keith C Clark Collection of hymnology; hymnals, psazlters, oblong tune-books, hymnody, church music, composers, early sermons on church music, and journals. See Clark's *Selective Bibliography for the Study of Hymns* (1980).

ON —UNIVERSITY OF TORONTO, Thomas Fisher Rare Book Library, 120 Saint George St, Toronto, M5S 1A5, Can. Richard G Landon, Head
Holdings: Vols 300 Cat
Notes: Noels Collection of French carols and hymns in a variety of dialects, 18th and 19th centuries.

ON —VICTORIA UNIVERSITY, Library, 71 Queen's Park Crescent, Toronto, M5S 1K7, Can. Robert C Brandeis, Chief Librn
Holdings: Vols (1000)// Cat Mss Maps Pix
Notes: Collection consists of books, pamphlets, and government reports mainly dealing with North American Indians and western explorations and missionary enterprises among the Indian in Canada. Incl, Indian Bibles and hymnbooks, and mss and vols by Peter Jones (an Indian missionary) and James Evans (inventor of the Cree syllabic alphabet).

HYMNS AND HYMNALS—INDEXES

OH —CLEVELAND PUBLIC LIBRARY, Fine Arts and Special Collections Department, 325 Superior Ave, Cleveland, 44114. Alice N Loranth, Head
Notes: 71 drawers of index cards, incl 37 drawers of songs, 31 drawers of hymns and 3 drawers of Christmas carols. A "Spanish Ballad Index" on cards is in the Special Collections were extensive indexes for French, Provencal and Italian songs are also maintained.

HYPERBOREAN LANGUAGES AND LITERATURES

MA —HARVARD UNIVERSITY LIBRARY, Cambridge, 02138.
Holdings: Cat
Notes: Languages and literatures of the Arctic Regions.

NY —NEW YORK PUBLIC LIBRARY, Slavonic Div, Fifth Ave & 42 St, New York, 10018. Edward Kasinec, Chief
Holdings: Cat Microforms
Notes: See New York Public Library, *Dictionary Catalog of the Slavonic* Collection (Boston: G K Hall, 1974), 44 vols.

WA —UNIVERSITY OF WASHINGTON LIBRARIES, Rare Books, Special Collections Dept, Seattle, 98195. Sandra Kroupa, Librn
Notes: Part of a set of Siberian primers prepared in the early 1930s by Soviet ethnographers. Some are first attempts to transcribe Siberian languages. All are in Latin phonetic script, not in Cyrillic.

HYPERBOREANS see Arctic Races

HYPERTENSION

TX —AMERICAN HEART ASSOCIATION, Library, 7320 Greenville Ave, Dallas, 75231. Katie Trickey, Librn; Barbara Lightfoot, Info Spec
Holdings: Vols (4000) Cat
Budget: ($20,000)

TX —SOUTHWEST FOUNDATION FOR RESEARCH AND EDUCATION LIBRARY, Preston C Northrup Memorial Library, Baboon Information Center, W Loop 410 at Military Dr, PO Box 28147, San Antonio, 78284. Dorothy M Brooks, Baboon
Notes: Principle field of research: Birth defects, atherosclerosis, reproductive physiology, cancer, genetics, organic chemistry, parasitology, primatology and behavioral sciences and their application to problems of drug abuse, alcoholism and ecology. Maintains the largest baboon colony in the world.

HYPNOTIC TRANCE see Hypnotism; Trance

HYPNOTISM

AZ —WORLD UNIVERSITY, Library, 711 E Blacklidge Dr, Tucson, 85719. Howard John Zitko, Cur
Holdings: Vols (15,000) Cat Mss Maps Audiotapes
Notes: Collection concerns what are generally called the "frontier sciences." No interlibrary loan.

CA —AMERICAN HYPNOTISTS' ASSOCIATION, 1159 Green St, San Francisco, 94109. Raphael M Bertuccelli, Pres
Holdings: Vols 4000 Cat
Notes: Methods and history of hypnosis.

IL —UNIVERSITY OF ILLINOIS, URBANA/CHAMPAIGN, Library, University Archives, 19 Library, 1408 W Gregory Drive, Urbana, 61801. Maynard Brichford, University Archivist
Holdings: Vols (5000) Cat
Budget: ($7000)
Notes: The Mandeville Collection in Parapsychology and Occult Sciences. Titles in the Merten J Mandeville Collection are purchased by funds from an endowment provided specifically for the collection on its establishment in 1966 by Merten J Mandeville, Professor Emeritus of Management, who donated 400 vols from his personal library as the nucleus of the collection. There are currently about 5000 titles in the collection, supplemented by related materials in the general collection. Topics include astrology, extrasensory perception, yoga, magic, satanism, faith healing, hypnosis, Eastern religions, witchcraft, fortune telling, reincarnation, flying saucers, ghosts, dreams, numerology, graphology, and mysticism. Biographies and reference books are a part of the collection as are journals devoted to the scientific study of parapsychology.

KS —WICHITA STATE UNIVERSITY, Ablah Library, Box 68, Wichita, 67208. Michael T Kelly, Cur of Special Collections
Holdings: Vols Cat Pamphlets
Notes: Includes the Maurice M Tinterow Collection.

MD —JOHNS HOPKINS UNIVERSITY, Milton S Eisenhower Library, George Peabody Collection, 17 E Mt Vernon Place, Baltimore, 21201. Lyn Hart, Peabody Librn
Notes: Noncirculating.

MA —MASSACHUSETTS INSTITUTE OF TECHNOLOGY, Institute Archives, Special Collections, Cambridge, 02139.
Notes: Vail collection incl many early works on telecommunications, electricity, ballooning, aeronautics, and animal magnetism.

NY —PARAPSYCHOLOGY FOUNDATION, Eileen J Garrett Library, 228 E 71st St, New York, 10021. Wayne Norman, Librn
Holdings: Vols (9300) Cat
Notes: Books, periodicals, pamphlets on parapsychology, its history, and books in other subjects that relate to parapsychology, eg, altered states of consciousness, hypnosis, dreams, time theories, etc.

TN —VANDERBILT UNIVERSITY, Medical Center Library, Nashville, 37232. Mary H Teloh, Special Collections Librn
Holdings: Vols (900)// Cat
Notes: The Moll Collection contains about 900 items on hypnosis and sleep: books, reprints, inaugural theses, lectures, and newspaper clippings. The collection was accumulated by Dr Albert Moll (1862-1939), a prominent Berlin neurologist. The newspaper clippings date from 1880 through 1906 and are mostly German. The books, lectures, reprints, and theses date from the 16th to the early 20th century. See *Bulletin of the Medical Library Association,* 65(1) :65-66, Jan 1977.

VA —ASSOCIATION FOR RESEARCH & ENLIGHTENMENT, Library, 67 & Atlantic Avenue, PO Box 595, Virginia Beach, 23451. Stephen Jordan, Library Mgr
Holdings: Vols (3000) Cat
Notes: Emphasis on Christian, Buddhist, Hindu religions, mysticism, comparative religion, psychological approach to biofeedback, autogenics, etc.

HYRNE, EDWARD

SC —COLLEGE OF CHARLESTON LIBRARY, Special Collections Dept, Charleston, 29401.
Notes: Papers, incl correspondence, (October 19, 1700) of Hyrne to his wife in England, detailing his experiences in the colony of Charles Town. Photocopy of typescript, original to be found in Taurus Gallery, London.

I

IBERIA

MA —COLLEGE OF THE HOLY CROSS, Dinand Library, College St, Worcester, 01610. James M Mahoney, Cur of Special Collection
Holdings: Vols 1000 Cat Maps
Notes: Early Christian Iberia (Roman-Visigothic Hispania). History and culture of southwestern Europe and northern Africa AD 50-711; 1100 topographic maps of Instituto Geografico y Catastral; offprints.

IBERO-AMERICAN LANGUAGE AND LITERATURE

DC —LIBRARY OF CONGRESS, Hispanic Division, Washington, 20540.
Notes: The Archive of Hispanic Literature on Tape is a repository of recorded poetry and prose from the Spanish- and Portuguese-speaking world. Most of the outstanding Hispanic literary figures of the last 30 years are included.

ICARIA (UTOPIAN COMMUNITY)

IN —INDIANA UNIVERSITY, Lilly Library, Seventh St, Bloomington, 47405. William R Cagle, Librn
Holdings: // Cat Mss
Notes: First and early printings of the Icarian communities (1840-1880) and of works by Rappites and the Owenites; also New Harmony, Indiana. Mss relating to the Shaker community in Kentucky (1826-1828) in the Charles Willing Byrd collection.

NE —UNIVERSITY OF NEBRASKA, OMAHA, Library, 60 & Dodge Sts, Omaha, 68132. Mel Bohn, Librn
Holdings: Vols 800 // Uncat Mss
Notes: 100 mss.

ICE AND ICING

CO —WORLD DATA CENTER A: GLACIOLOGY (SNOW AND ICE), CIRES, University of Colorado, Boulder, 80309. Ann M Brennan, Librn
Holdings: Vols 10,000 Maps Pix Microforms
Budget: $2000
Notes: Glaciology, all forms of snow and ice. Bibliographic information will be contained in a data file which will be fully searchable. Partially cataloged (UDC).

ON —NATIONAL RESEARCH COUNCIL OF CANADA, Aeronautical/Mechanical Engineering Branch Library, Montreal Rd, Ottawa, K1A 0R6, Can. Louise Fletcher, Head
Notes: This branch library of the Canada Institute for Scientific and Technical Information (CISTI) of the National Research Council of Canada, Ottawa, has a collection strong in aeronautical engineering, automatic control, CAD/CAM, robotics, ocean, wind, and solar energy power, hydraulic and coastal engineering, icing, low temperature research, naval engineering, metals and metallurgy, incl composites, tribology, and air, railroad, marine transportation. Library supported the Council contribution to the development of the remote manipular Canadarm for NASA's Space Shuttle Orbiters and more recently, the Canadian Astronaut Program which will contribute payload specialists to NASA's Space Shuttle Program in 1984. 35, 000 monographs, 1200 serials. Report collection: over 500,000 items.

ICE HOCKEY see Hockey

ICE MACHINERY see Refrigeration and Refrigerating Machinery

ICE SKATING see Skating

ICELAND

CT —LEE ASH, (personal collection), 66 Humiston Dr, Bethany, 06525.
Holdings: Mss Maps Pix
Notes: Does not include saga literature. Mostly travel, history, reference.

NY —CORNELL UNIVERSITY LIBRARIES, John M Olin Library, Fiske Icelandic Collection, Ithaca, 14853. Louis A Pitschmann, Librn
Holdings: Vols (34,000) Cat Mss Maps Pix Microforms
Budget: ($3000)
Notes: Collection aims at comprehensive coverage of Iceland in all aspects with major emphasis on the literature and language (both old and modern). Such subjects as runology, Scandinavian and Germanic mythology, early Norwegian history and history of the Viking period and of the Norse explorations of Greenland and North America are also well represented. For printed catalogs of the Collection's holdings see Downs 3608, 3609. Records for approximately 40 percent of the collection have been entered into OCLC and RLIN.

MB —UNIVERSITY OF MANITOBA, Elizabeth Dafoe Library, Icelandic Collection, Winnipeg, R3T 2N2, Can. Sigrid Johnson, Librn
Holdings: Vols (23,000) Cat
Notes: Material mostly in Icelandic, some in other Scandinavian languages. All subject areas incl with primary emphasis placed on language, literature and history of Icelanders in Canada, especially Manitoba (incl mss); early publications of sagas and religious literature; numerous periodicals and newspapers, incl Islandske Maanedstidender, 1773, the first Icelandic periodical, and Framfari, 1877, the first Icelandic newspaper in North America; collections of Icelandic music, such as S K Hall Collection (published and mss); Guttormur J Guttormsson and Stephan G Stephansson Memorial Collections; Vilhjalmur Stefansson publications. Cited in, Saunderson, H H, *The Chair of Icelandic Language and Literature at the University of Manitoba.* Winnipeg: University of Manitoba, 1961.

ICELAND—HISTORY

CA —CLAREMONT COLLEGES, Honnold Library, Ninth & Dartmouth, Claremont, 91711. Franklin D Scott, Cur, Nordic Collection; Penelope Garris, Librn
Holdings: Vols (25,000) Cat Maps Pix Slides Audiotapes Videotapes
Notes: Nordic Collections are broadly inclusive, but emphasize history of Scandinavia, Baltic countries, and Hanseatic cities. Nucleus of collections from gifts and endowment of Waldemar Westergaard, supplemented with relevant collections of David Bjork, John H Wuorinen, Ingolf Olsen, Henry Steele Commager, Franklin Scott and other gifts and purchases. Eight vertical file drawers of news bulletins in English or vernaculars, 1941-. See: Franklin D Scott, "The Westergaard-Bjork Collection at the Honnold Library, the Claremont Colleges," *Scandinavian Studies,* 41 (1969), 346-354." Collection incl complete publications of Nordic Council.

WA —UNIVERSITY OF WASHINGTON LIBRARIES, Suzzallo Library, Scandinavian Collections, FM-25, Seattle, 98195. A Gerald Anderson, Librn
Holdings: Vols (50,000) Cat Mss Pix
Budget: ($15,546)
Notes: Research collections with emphasis on languages and literatures, and auxiliary strengths in history, political science, social science. Archival and other special materials relating to Scandinavian-Americans in the Pacific Northwest are located in other appropriate collections.

WI —UNIVERSITY OF WISCONSIN, MADISON, Memorial Library, Rare Books Collection, 728 State St, Madison, 53706. Gretchen Lagana, Cur
Holdings: // Cat Mss
Notes: The core of this extensive collection consists of books from the libraries of Chester H Thordarson and Rasmus B Anderson. Very strong in Old Norse language and literature, incl important editions of saga literature and manuscript series in facsimile. Also incl works on modern Icelandic, important works in Icelandic history, and a good collection of Icelandic literature through the mid-twentieth century. Some of the early and rare material is kept in the Dept of Rare Books and Special Collections.

MB —UNIVERSITY OF MANITOBA, Elizabeth Dafoe Library, Icelandic Collection, Winnipeg, R3T 2N2, Can. Sigrid Johnson, Librn
Holdings: Vols (23,000) Cat
Notes: Material mostly in Icelandic, some in other Scandinavian languages. All subject areas incl with primary emphasis placed on language, literature and history of Icelanders in Canada, especially Manitoba (incl mss); early publications of sagas and religious literature; numerous periodicals and newspapers, incl Islandske Maanedstidender, 1773, the first Icelandic periodical, and Framfari, 1877, the first Icelandic newspaper in North America; collections of Icelandic music, such as S K Hall Collection (published and mss); Guttormur J Guttormsson and Stephan G Stephansson Memorial Collections; Vilhjalmur Stefansson publications. Cited in, Saunderson, H H, *The Chair of Icelandic Language and Literature at the University of Manitoba.* Winnipeg: University of Manitoba, 1961.

ICELAND—RELIGION

MB —UNIVERSITY OF MANITOBA, Elizabeth Dafoe Library, Icelandic Collection, Winnipeg, R3T 2N2, Can. Sigrid Johnson, Librn
Holdings: Vols (22,500) Cat Mss Maps Pix Audiotapes Microforms
Budget: ($4200)
Notes: Material mostly in Icelandic, some in other Scandinavian languages. All subject areas incl with primary emphasis placed on language, literature and history of Icelanders in Canada, especially Manitoba (incl mss); early publications of sagas and religious literature; numerous periodicals and newspapers, incl Islandske Maanedstidender, 1773, the first Icelandic periodical, and Framfari, 1877, the first Icelandic newspaper in North America; collections of Icelandic music, such as S K Hall Collection (published and mss); Guttormur J Guttormsson and Stephan G Stephansson Memorial Collections; Vilhjalmur Stefansson publications. Cited in, Saunderson, H H, *The Chair of Icelandic Language and Literature at the University of Manitoba.* Winnipeg: University of Manitoba, 1961.

ICELANDERS IN CANADA

WA —UNIVERSITY OF WASHINGTON LIBRARIES, Suzzallo Library, Scandinavian Collections, FM-25, Seattle, 98195. A Gerald Anderson, Librn
Holdings: Vols (50,000) Cat Mss Pix
Budget: ($15,546)
Notes: Research collections with emphasis on languages and literatures, and auxiliary strengths in history, political science, social science. Archival and other special materials relating to Scandinavian-Americans in the Pacific Northwest are located in other appropriate collections.

MB —UNIVERSITY OF MANITOBA, Elizabeth Dafoe Library, Icelandic Collection, Winnipeg, R3T 2N2, Can. Sigrid Johnson, Librn
Holdings: Vols (22,500) Cat Mss Maps Pix Audiotapes Microforms
Notes: Material mostly in Icelandic, some in other Scandinavian languages. All subject areas incl with primary emphasis placed on language, literature and history of Icelanders in Canada, especially Manitoba (incl mss); early publications of sagas and religious literature; numerous periodicals and newspapers, incl Islandske Maanedstidender, 1773, the first Icelandic periodical, and Framfari, 1877, the first Icelandic newspaper in North America; collections of Icelandic music, such as S K Hall Collection (published and mss); Guttormur J Guttormsson and Stephan G Stephansson Memorial Collections; Vilhjalmur Stefansson publications. Cited in, Saunderson, H H, *The Chair of Icelandic Language and Literature*

ICELANDERS IN CANADA (cont.)

at the University of Manitoba. Winnipeg: University of Manitoba, 1961.

ON —PUBLIC ARCHIVES OF CANADA, Library, 395 Wellington St, Ottawa, K1A 0N3, Can. Dawn E Monroe, Collections Development Officer
Holdings: Vols (80,000) Cat
Notes: The Public Archives Library has collected certain published documents, general works and specialized studies pertinent to the study of the historical and sociological development of native peoples. These documents incl accounts of the trips made by missionaries, explorers and others into Inuit or Amerindian territory, territory, specialized bibliographies, and ethnographic reference works incl dictionaries of native languages, studies on customs and and habits, and specialized periodicals.

ICELANDERS IN THE U.S.

ND —UNIVERSITY OF NORTH DAKOTA, Chester Fritz Library, Dept of Special Collections, Grand Forks, 58202. Daniel F Rylance, Special Collections Coordr
Holdings: Vols (5500) Uncat Mss Maps Pix Microforms
Budget: ($2500)
Notes: Also the Orin G Libby Manuscript Collection (900 collections), and the Aandahl Collection of Western History on North Dakota and the Northern Great Plains. Emphasis on agriculture, politics, pioneering, Germans from Russia, etc. Guides to the collections available from the Coordinator of Special Collections.

WA —UNIVERSITY OF WASHINGTON LIBRARIES, Suzzallo Library, Scandinavian Collections, FM-25, Seattle, 98195. A Gerald Anderson, Librn
Holdings: Vols (50,000) Cat Mss Pix
Budget: ($15,546)
Notes: Research collections with emphasis on languages and literatures, and auxiliary strengths in history, political science, social science. Archival and other special materials relating to Scandinavian-Americans in the Pacific Northwest are located in other appropriate collections.

ICELANDIC AND OLD NORSE LANGUAGES AND LITERATURE

CA —UNIVERSITY OF CALIFORNIA, BERKELEY, University Library, Scandinavian Collections, Berkeley, 94720. Helvi M Bessenyei, Librn
Holdings: Vols 20,000
Budget: $15,530
Notes: Research collections covering the full range of Scandinavian languages and literatures, with extensive periodical holdings. Particular strengths are Old Norse and Swedish. Moreover, special emphasis is on the late 19th century Scandinavian authors from Kierkegaard to Strinberg. The language and literature collections are supplemented by substantial resources in related disciplines. Some rare book materials are housed in the Bancroft Library.

IL —NORTH PARK COLLEGE LIBRARY, 5125 N Spaulding Ave, Chicago, 60625. Dorothy-Ellen Gross, Dir
Holdings: Vols (4500) Cat
Notes: Scandinavian Collection, with materials mostly Swedish, but some titles in Norwegian, Danish, Finnish and Icelandic. Separate shelf list, but also incl in union catalog. General collection with emphasis on literature and history. Other Swedish books in the field of religion available through Mellander Library on same campus.

MD —JOHNS HOPKINS UNIVERSITY, Milton S Eisenhower Library, Charles & 34 Sts, Baltimore, 21218. Ann S Gwyn, Assistant Dir for Special Collections
Holdings: Vols Cat // Mss Maps
Notes: The Nikulas Ottenson Collection. Chiefly modern works, printed in Iceland, Denmark and Canada. Bibles and devotional works 16-19th century, some very rare. All early Icelandic presses represented; 18th and 19th century periodicals strongly represented. Mss of post-medieval popular poetry. Cards in main catalog.

MA —HARVARD UNIVERSITY LIBRARY, Widener Library, Cambridge, 02138.
Holdings: Cat
Notes: Catalog (of Konrad von Maurer collection) published (Munich, Junge & Sohn) 1903; see also *Harvard Library Notes,* II (1931): pp, 247-267. See also *Distributable Union Catalog* (Harvard).

NY —CORNELL UNIVERSITY LIBRARIES, John M Olin Library, Fiske Icelandic Collection, Ithaca, 14853. Louis A Pitschmann, Librn
Holdings: Vols (34,000) Cat Mss Maps Pix Microforms
Budget: ($3000)
Notes: Collection aims at comprehensive coverage of Iceland in all aspects with major emphasis on the literature and language (both old and modern). Such subjects as runology, Scandinavian and Germanic mythology, early Norwegian history and history of the Viking period and of the Norse explorations of Greenland and North America are also well represented. For printed catalogs of the Collection's holdings see Downs 3608, 3609. Records for approximately 40 percent of the collection have been entered into OCLC and RLIN.

NC —DUKE UNIVERSITY, William R Perkins Library, Durham, 27706. Elvin E Strowd, University Librn
Notes: The Scandinavian collection of 3000 items is a collection of Scandinavian literature, primarily representing the latter half of the 18th century and early 19th century.

OH —CLEVELAND PUBLIC LIBRARY, Fine Arts and Special Collections Department, 325 Superior Ave, Cleveland, 44114. Alice N Loranth, Head
Holdings: Vols 1100 Cat
Notes: Sagas and philological studies are emphasized. One of the notable collections is Tegner's Frithjof's saga which alone is represented by about 225 editions.
See also entry under Folklore; Literature, Medieval

WA —UNIVERSITY OF WASHINGTON LIBRARIES, Suzzallo Library, Scandinavian Collections, FM-25, Seattle, 98195. A Gerald Anderson, Librn
Holdings: Vols (50,000) Cat Mss Pix
Budget: ($15,546)
Notes: Research collections with emphasis on languages and literatures, and auxiliary strengths in history, political science, social science. Archival and other special materials relating to Scandinavian-Americans in the Pacific Northwest are located in other appropriate collections.

WI —UNIVERSITY OF WISCONSIN, MADISON, Memorial Library, 728 State St, Madison, 53706. Erwin K Welsch, Social Studies Bibliographer
Holdings: Vols (3500) Cat Mss Phonorecords
Notes: The holdings in Icelandic and Old Norse are substantial (although the modern Icelandic collections is not) with some unique ms materials from the 17th and 18th centuries collected by Chester Thordarson. Special collections incl the "Mimer's Collection," consisting of 1000 vols collected by Rasmus B Anderson, founder of the UW Scandinavian Studies Department, with the aid of the Norwegian violinist Ole Bull and which consists largely of Old Norse materials.

MB —UNIVERSITY OF MANITOBA, Elizabeth Dafoe Library, Icelandic Collection, Winnipeg, R3T 2N2, Can. Sigrid Johnson, Librn
Holdings: Vols (22,500) Cat Mss Maps Pix Audiotapes Microforms
Notes: Material mostly in Icelandic, some in other Scandinavian languages. All subject areas incl with primary emphasis placed on language, literature and history of Icelanders in Canada, especially Manitoba (incl mss); early publications of sagas and religious literature; numerous periodicals and newspapers, incl Islandske Maanedstidender, 1773, the first Icelandic periodical, and Framfari, 1877, the first Icelandic newspaper in North America; collections of Icelandic music, such as S K Hall Collection (published and mss); Guttormur J Guttormsson and Stephan G Stephansson Memorial Collections; Vilhjalmur Stefansson publications. Cited in, Saunderson, H H, *The Chair of Icelandic Language and Literature at the University of Manitoba.* Winnipeg: University of Manitoba, 1961.

ICELANDIC LANGUAGE AND LITERATURE see Icelandic and Old Norse Languages and Literature

ICELANDIC NEWSPAPERS—CANADA see Newspapers, Icelandic—Canada

ICHTHYOLOGY

CA —CALIFORNIA STATE UNIVERSITY, FULLERTON, Library, Box 4150, Fullerton, 92634. Linda Herman, Special Collections Librn
Holdings: Cat
Notes: Dr Leonard B Schultz Ichthyology Collection of 13,000 pieces incl books, pamphlets, articles and ephemera. It is supplemented by the Ecology of Bay and Estuarine Fishes Collections.

CA —CALIFORNIA ACADEMY OF SCIENCES, J W Mailliard Jr Library, Golden Gate Park, San Francisco, 94118. Ray Brian, Librn
Notes: Downs No 2160.

CT —YALE UNIVERSITY, Medical Historical Library, 333 Cedar St, New Haven, 06510. Ferenc A Gyorgyey, Librn
Holdings: Vols 600 Cat
Notes: The George Milton Smith Collection of early ichthyology.

DC —SMITHSONIAN INSTITUTION, Archives Div, Washington, 20560. William W Moss, Archivist
Holdings: Cat Mss Pix
Notes: The Archives holds the records the National Museum of Natural History's Division of Fishes, 1865-1964, as well as the personal papers of curators incl Leonard Peter Schultz, ca 1915-1970, and George Sprague Myers.

DC —SMITHSONIAN INSTITUTION LIBRARIES, Natural History Branch, Washington, 20560. Sylvia Churgin, Chief Librn
Holdings: Vols 2400 Cat Maps Pix Slides

FL —UNIVERSITY OF MIAMI, Otto G Richter Library, PO Box 248214, Coral Gables, 33124. Frank Rodgers, Dir of Libraries
Holdings: Vols Microforms
Notes: The Rosenstiel School of Marine and Atmospheric Sciences Library is one of the major marine science collections in the United States and is especially strong in the literature of tropical oceanography. Special collections in the library incl 200 oceanographic atlases and more than 50 sets of the world's major expedition reports. The library also maintains a nautical chart collection. 3000 microforms; 1000 current subscriptions.

FL —ARCHBOLD BIOLOGICAL STATION, Library, Rt 2, Box 180, Lake Placid, 33852. Fred E Lohrer, Librn
Holdings: Vols (2000) Cat Periodicals

HI —BERNICE P BISHOP MUSEUM, Library, PO Box 19000-A, Honolulu, 96819. Cynthia Timberlake, Librn
Holdings: Vols (90,000) Cat Mss Maps Pix Slides Microforms
Budget: ($30,000)
Notes: Only American library devoted exclusively to the Pacific region. Collection reflects historical and contemporary research emphases of Bishop Museum; ie the natural and cultural history of the Pacific. Areas of concentration incl archaeology, ethnology, linguistics, voyages and explorations, history, vertebrate and invertebrate zoology, botany and museology. Strong special collections incl photographs, mss and archives, maps and art. Publications: Quarterly "Additions to the Catalog," *Dictionary Catalog of the* Library (9 vols and 2 suppl; Boston: G K Hall, 1964-69).

ICHTHYOLOGY (cont.)

IL —FIELD MUSEUM OF NATURAL HISTORY, Library, Roosevelt Rd & Lake Shore Dr, Chicago, 60605. W Peyton Fawcett, Librn; Benjamin W Williams, Assoc Librn
Holdings: Vols (210,000) Cat
Budget: ($100,000)
Notes: Extensive collections--publications of learned societies and institutions and monographic works--in all fields of natural history, with emphasis on taxonomy and evolutionary biology; and on museum publications, American and foreign: anthropology, especially archaeology and ethnology of the Americas, Africa, East Asia, and Oceania; botany, particularly strong for the Americas; geology, chiefly paleontology and meteoritic studies; and zoology, worldwide (birds, fishes, insects, mammals, mollusks, reptiles and amphibians).

MD —NATIONAL AQUARIUM IN BALTIMORE, Pier 3, 501 East Pratt St, Baltimore, 21202. Lee Campbell, Librn
Notes: Staff members only.

MI —UNIVERSITY OF MICHIGAN, Museums Library, Ann Arbor, 48109. Patricia B Yocum, Librn
Holdings: Vols 8000 Cat

MS —GULF COAST RESEARCH LABORATORY, Gordon Gunter Library, E Beach Rd, Ocean Springs, 39564. Malcolm Ware, Sr, Librn
Holdings: Vols (9000) Uncat Mss Pix Microforms
Notes: Also have reprint collection of 30,000 cataloged reprints, indexed by card catalog, on all aspects of marine biology.

NV —FORESTA INSTITUTE FOR OCEAN AND MOUNTAIN STUDIES, Library, 6205 Franktown Rd, Carson City, 89701. Shannon Porter, Librn
Holdings: Vols 500 Cat Maps Slides
Notes: Collection is international in scope; incl material on fish of the far western US, espec Nevada from prehistoric times to the present. Also, about 1000 pamphlets, etc.

NJ —PRINCETON UNIVERSITY, Library, Rare Books Dept Princeton, 08544. Stephen Ferguson, Cur
Notes: (1) Kenneth H Rockey Angling Collection; about 4300 volumes, of which 350 are considered rare. Main strength is in the American and English 19th and 20th century literature of angling in fresh and salt water. (2) Otto von Kienbusch Angling Collection; incl the earliest angling book in English, Dame Juliana Berners, *A Treatysse on Fysshynge Wyth an Angle,* printed by Wynkyn de Worde, assistant to England's first printer, William Caxton, 1496. Also the unique copy of the second angling book printed in English (anonymous), *The Art of* Angling, London: Henry Middleton, 1577. For particulars refer to: *Fresh Water Angling; 50 Books and Other Materials Tracing its Development: An Exhibition.* Princeton, 1946. A more recent exhibition of sporting books also featured angling. For particulars refer to: Stephen Ferguson, "The Gentelman's Recreation:Sporting Books in the Princeton University Library" in the *Chronicle* XL, 3 (spring, 1979). A catalog of the exhibition is available.
See also entry under Fishing and Angling

NY —AMERICAN MUSEUM OF NATURAL HISTORY, Library Services Dept, Central Park W & 79th St, New York, 10024. Nina J Root, Chairwoman; Mary Genett, Asst Librn for Reference Services
Holdings: Vols (385,000) Cat Mss Maps Pix Slides Microforms
Notes: Nearly all collections are outstanding for depth of coverage and international range. Early and historic works, rare books, colored illustrations, and relevant serial publications supplement the modern scientific publications necessary to the researchers of the scientific staff and the work of the educational division. Open to the public.

PA —ACADEMY OF NATURAL SCIENCES LIBRARY, 19 Benjamin Franklin Parkway, Philadelphia, 19103.
Holdings: Vols (180,000) Cat Mss Maps Pix Slides Microforms
Notes: Incl (250,000) mss. Described in *Academy of Natural Sciences of Philadelphia: Catalog* (Boston: G K Hall, 1972); *Guide to the Manuscript Collections in the Academy of Natural Sciences of* Philadelphia, by Venia T Phillips (Philadelphia: Academy of Natural Sciences, 1963).

TX —UNIVERSITY OF TEXAS, Marine Science Institute Library, Port Aransas, 78373. Ruth Grundy, Librn
Holdings: Vols (45,000) Cat Maps Pix
Budget: ($70,000)
Notes: Current researches in marine science, especially concerning the Gulf of Mexico, the Texas Coastal Zone, and the Continental Shelf. Incl journals.

WV —US FISH & WILDLIFE SERVICE, National Fisheries Center, Technical Information Services, Route 3 Box 700, Kearneysville, 25430. Joyce A Mann-Grim, Librn
Holdings: Vols (22,900) Slides
Notes: Collection topics incl fish virology, histology bacteriology, immunology, nutrition and parasitology. Publish *Fish Heath News.* Incl 20,000 reprints, 5000 slides.

ON —NATIONAL MUSEUMS OF CANADA, Library Services Directorate, Ottawa, K1A 0M8, Can. Valerie Monkhouse, Director
Holdings: Vols (90,000) Cat Mss Microforms
Budget: ($81,000)
Notes: Emphasis on Canadian and circumpolar natural history. Collection incl botany, herpetology, ichthyology, invertebrate zoology, malacology, mammology, mineralogy, ornithology, paleobiology, zooarchaeology. Exceptional collections in lichenology, bryology, malacology, ornithology. Research collection, interlibrary loans available, public may use on the premises.

ICKES, HAROLD

DC —LIBRARY OF CONGRESS, Manuscript Division, Washington, 20540. John C Broderick, Chief
Holdings: Cat Mss Pix
Notes: Mss, papers, records, etc.

ICONOCLASTS

TX —SOCIETY OF SEPARATIONISTS, Library, 2210 Hancock Dr, PO Box 2117, Austin, 78756. R Murray-O'Hair, Dir
Holdings: Vols (50,000)
Notes: Atheism, separation of church and state, biographical archives on Atheists, agnostics, humanists, and iconoclasts.

ICONOGRAPHY see Christian Art and Symbolism

IDAHO

ID —IDAHO STATE HISTORICAL SOCIETY, Library, 610 N Julia Davis Dr, Boise, 83706. Elizabeth Jacox, Librn
Holdings: Vols 2500 Cat Mss Maps Pix Slides Microforms
Notes: Oral history collection, 700 hours of taped interviews. Catalog on microfiche, also newspapers and documents.

ID —IDAHO STATE LIBRARY, 325 W State, Boise, 83702. Charles A Bolles, Dir
Holdings: Vols 3500 Cat Maps
Notes: Also documents collection.

ID —IDAHO FALLS PUBLIC LIBRARY, 457 Broadway, Idaho Falls, 83402. Craig Anderson, Head Reference Librn
Holdings: Vols 482 Cat Mss Maps Pix Pamphlets
Notes: Incl 54 fiction and 428 nonfiction titles.

ID —UNIVERSITY OF IDAHO, Library, Dept of Special Collections & Archives, Moscow, 83843.
Holdings: Vols (11,000) Cat Mss Maps Pix Slides Microforms
Budget: ($4000)
Notes: Emphasis on Idaho and the Pacific Northwest. Incl 20,000 pictures and 700 slides. Charles A Webbert, *Check List of Western Americana in the Day-NW Collection, University of Idaho Library, July 1, 1969* (University of Idaho Publication No 8, June 1970).

UT —UNIVERSITY OF UTAH, Marriott Library, Special Collections, Salt Lake City, 84112. Gregory C Thompson, Cur

WA —WASHINGTON STATE LIBRARY, Washington/Northwest Rm, State Library Bldg, Olympia, 98504. Nancy B Pryor, Research Consultant
Holdings: Vols 8000 Cat Mss Maps Pix Microforms
Notes: Mss, photographs and microfilm largely limited to Washington territorial and state materials as is the file of pamphlets and newspaper clippings, which includes both historical and current material. The book collection incl works on the four Pacific Northwest States, Alaska, and British Columbia, and books by Washington authors.

WA —UNIVERSITY OF WASHINGTON LIBRARIES, Pacific Northwest Collection, Seattle, 98195. Andrew F Johnson, Librn
Holdings: Vols (50,000) Cat Mss Maps Pix
Budget: ($12,000)
Notes: The Pacific Northwest Collection contains printed materials documenting the historic and contemporary life and culture of the region in a broad range of subject areas. The Pacific Northwest is defined as the geographic region including Washington, Oregon, Idaho, Montana, British Columbia, Yukon Territory, and Alaska. Printed materials including books, periodicals, government documents, maps, weekly and local regional newspapers, theses and dissertations, as well as photographs and architectural drawings are included in the Pacific Northwest Collection. Photographic works of over 200 photographers active in the Pacific Northwest, Alaska, and the Yukon Territory (Canada) during the period 1860-1930, including Asahel and Edward S Curtis, Eric Hegg, and Clark Kinsey, are represented in a print collection of more than 300,000 images. The architecturaldrawings collection includes over 19,000 original plans, drawings, sketches, renderings and blue prints pertaining to the history of architecture and urban planning and landscape gardening in the Pacific Northwest ca 1880-1940. Areas of particular strength are the holdings of over 1100 published journals of Pacific Northwest exploration expeditions, photographs of Northwest Coast Native Americans and of historic Seattle, newspapers issued within the Japanese-American relocation camps, 1942-1945, materials relating to the 1980 eruption of Mt St Helens, and Sanborne fire insurance maps for Washington. A unique feature of the Collection is the subject index to regional periodicals and local newspapers maintained by the PNW Collection staff; over 100 titles are currently indexed. G K Hall Company published a books catalog of the Pacific Northwest Collectionin 1973.

IDAHO—GENEALOGY

ID —IDAHO STATE HISTORICAL SOCIETY, Library, 610 N Julia Davis Dr, Boise, 83702.
Holdings: Vols 9000 Cat Mss Maps Microforms
Budget: ($400,000)
Notes: Incl 28,000 ft of mss, 48,000 maps, 100,000 pictures, and newspapers.

IDAHO—GOVERNMENT PUBLICATIONS

ID —UNIVERSITY OF IDAHO, Library, Dept of Special Collections & Archives, Moscow, 83843.
Holdings: Vols 8000 Cat
Notes: A collection of the official publications of the State of Idaho.

ID —IDAHO STATE UNIVERSITY, Library, Pocatello, 83209. Joseph K W Lu, Librn
Holdings: Uncat Microforms Documents

IDAHO—GOVERNMENT PUBLICATIONS (cont.)

Maps
Budget: ($10,000)
Notes: Over a million items. Partial depository for US Government publications (1,053,430 items); incl ERIC microfiche and unclassified AEC and Dept of Energy publications in microform; depository for Idaho State Government publications (16, 000 items); international government bodies (11,000 items).

IDAHO—HISTORY

ID —IDAHO STATE HISTORICAL SOCIETY, Library, 610 N Julia Davis Dr, Boise, 83702.
Holdings: Vols 9000 Cat Mss Maps Microforms
Budget: ($400,000)
Notes: Incl 28,000 ft of mss, 48,000 maps, 100,000 pictures, and newspapers.

ID —IDAHO STATE UNIVERSITY, Library, Pocatello, 83209. Gary Domitz, Social Science Librn
Holdings: Cat
Budget: ($2500)
Notes: Idaho and Intermountain West History Collection; incl the Lemhi Indian Reservation's miscellaneous papers. Extensive collections.

UT —UTAH STATE UNIVERSITY, Merrill Library, Department of Special Collections & Archives, Logan, 84322. A J Simmonds, Curator; Jeanie F Simmonds, Archivist; Bradford R Cole, Mss Librn
Holdings: Vols 750 Cat Mss Maps Pix Microforms
Notes: Emphasis is on southern Idaho, especially Oneida, Bear Lake, Franklin, Bannock, Bingham, Bonneville, and Teton counties. Incl 30 feet of ms items; 200 rolls of microfilm; 50 maps.

IDAHO—MAPS

ID —IDAHO STATE UNIVERSITY, Library, Pocatello, 83209. Gary Domitz, Social Science Librn
Holdings: Uncat Maps
Notes: Depository for USGS, 11 western states; depository for Defense Mapping Agency Topographic Center; Idaho county maps.

OK —TULSA CITY-COUNTY LIBRARY, Business & Technology Dept, 400 Civic Center, Tulsa, 74103. Craig Buthod, Head
Notes: Original General Land Office survey maps for the states of Arizona, Arkansas, Colorado, Illinois, Indiana, Idaho, Kansas, Michigan, Missouri, Montana, Nebraska, Nevada, New Mexico, North Dakota, Ohio, Oklahoma, South Dakota, Utah and Wyoming. Incomplete coverage of each state.

IDEAL STATES see Utopias

IDEOGRAPHY see Hieroglyphics; Picture Writing

IGO (GAME) see Go (Game)

IHLDER, JOHN

DC —GEORGETOWN UNIVERSITY, Library, Special Collections Div, 37 & O Sts NW, Washington, 20057. George M Barringer, Special Collections Librn; Nicholas B Sheetz, Mss Librn
Holdings: Mss
Notes: Papers of John Ihlder, consisting of correspondence, reports, mss, and printed material, principally pertaining to his work with the Committee on Evaluation of Public Housing of the National Capitol Housing Authority. Incl are reports from the New Jersey Board of Tenement House Supervision (1916), a guide for the evaluation of public housing (1943), correspondence concerning the Hillside low-rent housing project in Washington (1944), and material on postwar housing. A small quantity of family papers completes the collection.

ILLEGAL LITERATURE see Underground Literature

ILLINOIS

IL —SOUTHERN ILLINOIS UNIVERSITY, CARBONDALE, Morris Library, Carbondale, 62901. Jean M Ray, Map Librn
Holdings: Cat Maps Pix
Budget: ($1070)
Notes: Emphasis of map collection is Southern Illinois and Mississippi Valley. Incl 158,000 maps; 47,000 aerial photographs of Southern Illinois; 2000 atlases, reference books, etc; 4000 issues of weather map series (historical, daily, monthly); and 360 Illinois county platbooks. Includes Sang Collection--60 early maps of North America, especially Mississippi Valley, 1584-1840.

IL —CHICAGO HISTORICAL SOCIETY, Library, Clark St at North Ave, Chicago, 60614. Robert L Brubaker, Librn
Holdings: Vols (150,000) Cat Mss Maps Pix

IL —GALESBURG PUBLIC LIBRARY, 40 E Simmons St, Galesburg, 61401. Jane M Willenborg, Special Collections Librn
Holdings: Vols (6113) Cat Mss Maps Pix Slides Phonorecords Audiotapes Microforms
Budget: ($10,500)
Notes: Incl extensive collection of Illinois histories--state, county, city, town, and village; Illinois laws and statutes, 1829-1977; state and county atlases and plat books (listed in *United States Atlases,* vol II, Library of Congress, 1953); Lincoln books; works of Illinois authors; Civil War Illinois regimental histories; photographs of local interest (incl numerous photos of Carl Sandburg); and local newspapers and city directories on microfilm. Incl mss (26 ft), 79 maps, 4371 pictures, 3515 slides. 3053 negatives (some are duplicates of the photographs). Separate catalog. Restricted use: noncirculating; limited photocopying.

IL —SCHAUMBURG TOWNSHIP PUBLIC LIBRARY, 32 W Library Lane, Schaumburg, 60194. Michael Madden, Librn
Notes: Illinois Setting Collection. Maintains reference and circulating collection of current and out-of-print materials in history, economics, business, biography, art, architecture representing entire state with special emphasis on Chicago. Materials for both adults and children, includes slides, dioramas, and realia as well as books, manuscripts, and maps.

ILLINOIS—AERIAL PHOTOGRAPHS

IL —UNIVERSITY OF ILLINOIS, URBANA/CHAMPAIGN, Library, Map & Geography Library, 418 Main Library, Urbana, 61801. David Cobb, Librn
Holdings: Vols (14,500) Cat Maps Pix Microforms
Notes: Maps (over 325,000) of almost all types, incl topographic, soil, transportation, economic, hydrographic, weather, city, pictorial, and historical maps, are collected. Coverage is excellent for Illinois and for most parts of the United States and Canada. Good maps are available for Europe, Central America and the ocean areas. The early map collection is rich in maps of Illnois, Italy, and the western hemisphere. A large number of publishers' catalogs, particularly of foreign map publishings are kept on file. The collection of aerial photographs provides complete and sequential coverage of the State of Illinois from the late 1930s to the present. Much of the coverage is stereoscopic. Other map resources on the campus include about 50,000 geologic and topographic maps and aerial photographs in the Geology Library, a wall map collection in the Geography Department, severalhundred early maps and atlases of the Illinois area in the Illinois Historical Survey, and geologic and topographic maps and aerial photographs in the Civil Engineering Department. Publication: *Biblio* (bi-monthly acquisitions list).

ILLINOIS—DESCRIPTION AND TRAVEL

IL —UNIVERSITY OF ILLINOIS, URBANA/CHAMPAIGN, Library, Illinois Historical Survey Library, 1408 W Gregory Dr, 1A Library, Urbana, 61801.
Holdings: Vols 150 Cat Mss Maps
Notes: Travel and description in the Midwest, particularly Illinois. The majority of these items were published in the 19th century. Guide to the collections published in 1976.

ILLINOIS—DESCRIPTION AND TRAVEL—VIEWS

IL —ILLINOIS STATE HISTORICAL SOCIETY, Library, Old State Capitol, Springfield, 62706. Roger D Bridges, Head Librn
Holdings: Cat Pix
Notes: Incl an unusual collection of Illinois pictorial history--some 12,000 scenes and portraits preserved on glass photographic negatives dating from the 1890s to the 1920s acquired from the estate of Herbert W Georg, Springfield photographer. Also, a collection of 100,000 pictures.
See also entry under Illinois - History

ILLINOIS—GENEALOGY

FL —ORLANDO PUBLIC LIBRARY, Local History & Genealogy Dept, 100 Block of Central Ave, Orlando, 32806. Eileen B Willis, Librn
Holdings: Vols 11,000 Cat Maps Microforms
Budget: $8000
Notes: Genealogy collection on Md, Del, W Va, NC, SC, Ala, Miss, La, Texas, Ark, Ky, Ohio, Ill, Ind, and Mich are well represented. Most other states are covered by smaller collections.
See also entry under Genealogy - Collections.

IL —MCLEAN COUNTY HISTORICAL SOCIETY LIBRARY & MUSEUM, 201 E Grove, Bloomington, 61701. Barbara Dunbar, Dir; Greg Koos, Archivist
Holdings: Vols (3000) Cat Mss Maps Pix
Notes: Illinois history, emphasis on McLean County. Strong in military heritage of Illinois, particularly the 33rd and 94th regiments (Ill Vol Inf) in the Civil War. Incl 150 LF archives and 1000 pictures. Photocopying.

IL —FREEPORT PUBLIC LIBRARY, 314 W Stephenson St, Freeport, 61032. John Locascio, Head Librn
Holdings: Vols 353 Cat

IL —QUINCY PUBLIC LIBRARY, 526 Jersey, Quincy, 62301. Michael G Garrison, Admin Librn
Holdings: Cat Mss Maps Pix Microforms
Notes: Local history and genealogy collection for city of Quincy and Adams County, Illinois. Incl Illinois and Adams County histories, area census records for 1820-1910 (microfilm), local cemetery records, probate papers and wills with index (microfilm), mss, church records (microfilm/microfiche), Quincy newspapers (1835-date), city directories, local atlases and plat books. Also incl over 250 books written by Quincy/Adams County authors. Collection does not circulate; reference only.

IL —ILLINOIS STATE HISTORICAL SOCIETY, Library, Old State Capitol, Springfield, 62706. Roger D Bridges, Head Librn
Holdings: Cat Pix
Notes: Incl an unusual collection of Illinois pictorial history--some 12,000 scenes and portraits preserved on glass photographic negatives dating from the 1890s to the 1920s acquired from the estate of Herbert W Georg, Springfield photographer. Also, a collection of 180,000 pictures.
See also entry under Illinois - History

IL —WINNETKA PUBLIC LIBRARY, 768 Oak St, Winnetka, 60093. Donna Sundstrom, Dir
Holdings: Vols 4500 Cat Mss
Notes: Incl 1500 mss. Separate catalog.

ILLINOIS—GENEALOGY (cont.)

IN —WILLARD LIBRARY, 21 First Ave, Evansville, 47710. Joan Elliott, Special Collections Librn
Holdings: Vols (1000) Cat Mss Microforms
Budget: ($4000)
Notes: General genealogy collection emphasizing data concerning 35 counties of southwest Indiana, southeast Illinois, and western Kentucky. Written description available.

ILLINOIS—GOVERNMENT PUBLICATIONS

IL —UNIVERSITY OF ILLINOIS, URBANA/CHAMPAIGN, College of Law, Library, Champaign, 61820. Richard Surles, Law Librn
Holdings: Vols (425,000) Cat Mss Microforms
Notes: Plus 800 reels of microfilm; 150,000 microfiches. Research collection covering both Anglo-American and foreign law. Depository for documents of the US Government, Illinois, and European Economic Communities.

IL —NORTHWESTERN UNIVERSITY, Library, Government Publications Dept, Evanston, 60201. Robert W Baumgartner, Head
Notes: Collection consists of US federal documents (depository library since 1876); state documents (emphasis on Illinois); municipal documents (emphasis on Evanston and Chicago); documents of international organizations (emphasis on United Nations, United Nations specialized agencies, Organization of American States, European Communities). Collection consists of publications of 44 international organizations. Shelflist maintained in the Government Publications Department. Most publications not incl in the library's general catalog.

NC —DUKE UNIVERSITY, William R Perkins Library, Public Documents and Maps Department, Durham, 27706. Jaia Barrett, Head
Notes: A selective depository for US Government publications since 1890, the Department currently holds well over 500, 000 items, plus publications of the European Community (a depository collection), the League of Nations, the UN and UN-affiliated agencies. Other international organizations, publications are acquired also, as are state government publications, especially from the Southeast, California, New York and Illinois. The Documents Department holds services the major map collections of Perkins Library. These collections include topographic, geologic, and special subject maps which are worldwide in coverage. The department is a depository for the US Defense Mapping Agency and the US Geological Survey. In addition, there are many other maps of general and specific interest, including US and foreign road maps. As appropriate, maps are also held in the Perkins Library's Rare BookRoom and Manuscript Department. Atlases are shelved in the Reference Department and in the bookstacks of Perkins Library.

ILLINOIS—HISTORY

IL —MCLEAN COUNTY HISTORICAL SOCIETY LIBRARY & MUSEUM, 201 E Grove, Bloomington, 61701. Barbara Dunbar, Dir; Greg Koos, Archivist
Holdings: Vols (3000) Cat Mss Maps Pix
Notes: Illinois history, emphasis on McLean County. Strong in military heritage of Illinois, particularly the 33rd and 94th regiments (Ill Vol Inf) in the Civil War. Incl 150 LF archives and 1000 pictures. Photocopying.

IL —CHICAGO HISTORICAL SOCIETY, Library, Clark St at North Ave, Chicago, 60614. Robert L Brubaker, Librn
Holdings: Vols (150,000) Cat Mss Maps Pix Microfilm
Notes: Incl most of the histories and atlases of the state, counties, and larger towns.

IL —CHICAGO HISTORICAL SOCIETY, Library, Clark St at North Ave, Chicago, 60614. Archie Motley, Manuscript Librn
Notes: Nineteenth and eighteenth century collection of papers incl; American Colonization Society (anti-slavery group); American Field Service (World War I European ambulance service); American Fur Company; Chicago Cubs (National League baseball team); Chicago Fire of 1871; Will J Davis (theatre manager); Declaration of Independence (complete set of autographs of signers of the Declaration); Finley Peter Dunne (journalist, satirist); Robert Fergus (printer and publisher); firearms agents; French settlers in North America; Melville Weston Fuller (Chief Justice of the US); Grand Army of the Republic; Charles J Guiteau (President Garfield's assassin); Haymarket Riot, May 4, 1886; Illinois Central Railroad (1836-1969); Indians of North America; Leander Hamilton McCormick (author, inventor); Harold Fowler McCormick(manufacturer, philanthropist, son of inventor Cyrus Hall McCormick); Mormons (chiefly Illinois materials); Richard Parker (judge at the trial of abolitionist John Brown); Zebulon Pike and Zebulon Montgomery Pike (US Army officers, explorers); George Mortimer Pullman (inventor, designer of Pullman cars and the Pullman and Fluhrer families).

IL —CHICAGO HISTORICAL SOCIETY, Library, Clark St at North Ave, Chicago, 60614. Archie Motley, Manuscript Librn
Notes: Twentieth century collections incl these papers: Aero Club of Illinois (aviation promoters); American Legion, Illinois Branch; Paul M Angle; Business and Professional People for the Public Interest, a public interest law firm; Chicago Municipal Court; Chicago Peace Council; Chicago Peace Society; Herma Clark (*Chicago* Tribune columnist); Frances Crane Lillie (social activist); Frank Rattray Lillie (zoologist), the Crane Company; Charles R Crane and other members of the Crane family; France Forever, Chicago Chapter; Frances MacBeth Glessner; William Walter Husband (Commissioner of Immigration); Irish Fellowship Club of Chicago; Albert E Jenner, Jr (member of the Warren Commission, minority counsel during the Nixon impeachment hearing); materials on opera in Chicago and elsewhere; Kenesaw Mountain Landis(US District Judge, first Commissioner of Baseball); Nathan F Leopold (convicted murderer); Philip Lord (actor); Harry A Musham (naval architect); Military Training Camps Association of the United States; Ivan Molek; Ruth Moore; Ralph G Newman; Northeastern Illinois Planning Commission; Len O'Connor (television news commentator); Open Lands Project; Oral History Archives of Chicago Polonia; Donald R Richberg; letterbooks of Chicago law firms involving Julius and Lessing Rosenthal, Charles Hammill, and George F Wormser; Otto L Schmidt; Studs Terkel (author, oral historian); Henry A Voegeli; Jacob J Weinstein; White City Construction Co; Elmer Lynn Williams; World Federalists USA Inc.

IL —DE PAUL UNIVERSITY, College of Law Library, 25 E Jackson Blvd, Chicago, 60604. Judith G Gecas, Dir
Holdings: (300) Cat
Notes: Territorial laws: Northwest Territory; Indiana territory; Illinois Territory. "Farthing Collection of Illinois Statutory Laws." *33 Chicago Bar Record*, pp 451-454 (1952).

IL —LOYOLA UNIVERSITY OF CHICAGO, E M Cudahy Memorial Library, 6525 N Sheridan Rd, Chicago, 60626.
Notes: Dorr E Felt Pamphlet and Clipping Collection. Emphasizes political and economic issues, 1902-35, and documents Illinois Manufacturers Association Conference, September 8-9, 1919; Air Board of Chicago, April 16, 1921-August 1, 1930; Allied Debts to the US, May 15, 1923-September 30, 1926; Bolshevism, Communism, "Red" Russia, 1924-27; Child Labor Bill, March 30, 1915, 1914-20; Labor, March, 1902-March, 1932; Railroad Strike, August 25, 1916-August 7, 1920; The War, August, 1914-October 23, 1930; War Industries Commission, June, 1918-November 23, 1928. A pamphlet list is available for each topic.

IL —NORTHERN ILLINOIS REGIONAL HISTORY CENTER, Sven Parson Hall, Northern Illinois University, De Kalb, 60115. Glen Gildemeister, Dir
Holdings: Cat Mss Maps Pix Slides Phonorecords Audiotapes 16mm Films Microforms
Notes: "A research center for advanced research in the humanities. This northern area of Illinois (excluding Cook County) has been virtually untouched by collecting agencies and we hope to fill that void. We will be strong in agribusiness, agricultural implement business, and hybrid farming mechanics....Will be primarily a ms repository, but [have] already taken responsibility for many artifacts and books, some rare."

IL —DES PLAINES HISTORICAL SOCIETY, John Byrne Memorial Library, 777 Lee St, Des Plaines, 60016. Donald S Johnson, Librn
Holdings: Vols 1000 Cat Maps Pix Slides Filmstrips Microforms
Budget: $1,000
Notes: Census-1840-50-60-70-80-1900.

IL —EVANSTON HISTORICAL SOCIETY, Library, 225 Greenwood, Evanston, 60201.
Holdings: Vols 5000 Cat Mss Maps Pix Slides
Notes: Evanston history, with clipping files, 1872-date, 150 maps and 5000 pictures. Also incl collection of Evanston authors.

IL —FREEPORT PUBLIC LIBRARY, 314 W Stephenson St, Freeport, 61032. John Locascio, Head Librn
Holdings: Vols (400) Cat Microforms
Notes: Freeport, Illinois, and Stephenson County history. Incl 3 file cabinets of clippings. German language newspapers, 1854-1917; English language newspapers, 1847-date. 507 newspaper file microfilm reels.

IL —GALESBURG PUBLIC LIBRARY, 40 E Simmons St, Galesburg, 61401. Jane M Willenborg, Special Collections Librn
Holdings: Vols (6113) Cat Mss Maps Pix Slides Phonorecords Audiotapes Microforms
Budget: ($10,500)
Notes: Incl extensive collection of Illinois histories--state, county, city, town, and village; Illinois laws and statutes, 1829-1977; state and county atlases and plat books (listed in *United States Atlases,* vol II, Library of Congress, 1953); Lincoln books; works of Illinois authors; Civil War Illinois regimental histories; photographs of local interest (incl numerous photos of Carl Sandburg); and local newspapers and city directories on microfilm. Incl mss (26 ft), 79 maps, 4371 pictures, 3515 slides. 3053 negatives (some are duplicates of the photographs). Separate catalog. Restricted use: noncirculating; limited photocopying.

IL —JOLIET PUBLIC LIBRARY, 150 N Ottawa, Joliet, 60431. James R Johnston, Dir
Notes: The emphasis of the collection is on Joliet and Will County in Illinois. We have an incomplete run of the *Joliet City* Directory back to 1875. We own the Federal population censuses for Will County 1840-1910 on microfilm.

IL —QUINCY COLLEGE LIBRARY, Quincy, 62301. Victor Kingery, OFM, Librn
Holdings: Vols 30 Cat Mss
Notes: Emphasis on Quincy and Adams County.

IL —QUINCY PUBLIC LIBRARY, 526 Jersey, Quincy, 62301. Michael G Garrison, Admin Librn
Holdings: Cat Mss Maps Pix Microforms
Notes: Local history and genealogy collection for city of Quincy and Adams County, Illinois. Incl Illinois and Adams County histories, area census records for 1820-1910 (microfilm), local cemetery records, probate papers and wills with index (microfilm), mss, church records (microfilm/microfiche), Quincy newspapers (1835-date), city directories, local atlases and plat books. Also incl over 250 books written by Quincy/

ILLINOIS—HISTORY (cont.)

Adams County authors. Collection does not circulate; reference only.

IL —SCHAUMBURG TOWNSHIP PUBLIC LIBRARY, 32 W Library Lane, Schaumburg, 60194. Michael Madden, Librn
Notes: Illinois Setting Collection. Maintains reference and circulating collection of current and out-of-print materials in history, economics, business, biography, art, architecture representing entire state with special emphasis on Chicago. Materials for both adults and children, includes slides, dioramas, and realia as well as books, manuscripts, and maps.

IL —ILLINOIS STATE HISTORICAL SOCIETY, Library, Old State Capitol, Springfield, 62706. Roger D Bridges, Head Librn
Holdings: Vols (160,000) Cat Mss Maps Pix Microforms
Budget: ($40,000)
Notes: Incl 8 million mss, nearly 2000 maps, 180,000 pictures and 60,000 microfilm reels. Downs 2546, 2606, 2612, 187, 188. See also *Guide to the Microfilm Edition of the Pierre Menard Collection in the Illinois State Historical Library*. Separate catalogs (card) for printed material, mss, broadsides.

IL —UNIVERSITY OF ILLINOIS, URBANA/CHAMPAIGN, Library, Rare Book Room, 346 Library, Urbana, 61801. Norman B Brown, Asst Dir for Special Collections; N Frederick Nash, Librn
Holdings: Cat Mss Maps
Notes: Extensive collection, described in: *Catalog of the Rare Book Room,* (Boston: G K Hall, 1972). Supplement (1978).

IL —UNIVERSITY OF ILLINOIS, URBANA/CHAMPAIGN, Library, Illinois Historical Survey Library, 1408 W Gregory Dr, 1A Library, Urbana, 61801.
Holdings: Vols (6500) Cat Mss Maps Pix Microforms
Notes: Important ms collections incl: Randolph County Records, 1720-1853, 91 items, 59 reels of microfilm; St Clair County Records, 1722-1809, 6 items, 5 reels of microfilm; George Morgan, papers, 1766-1826, 280 items, 5 reels of microfilm; William Morrison, papers, 1805-1855, 7 reels of microfilm. Pierre Menard, papers, 1780, 1802-1859, 155 items, 27 volumes, 29 reels microfilm; Illinois Surveyors' field notes and plat maps, 1805-1850, 56 reels microfilm. Numerous county and local histories and plat books. 1733 maps, and thousands of Illinois pictures. Guide to the collections published in 1976.

ILLINOIS—HISTORY—BLACK HAWK WAR, 1832 see Black Hawk War, 1832

ILLINOIS—HISTORY—COLONIAL PERIOD

IL —UNIVERSITY OF ILLINOIS, URBANA/CHAMPAIGN, Library, Illinois Historical Survey Library, 1408 W Gregory Dr, 1A Library, Urbana, 61801.
Holdings: Vols 500 Cat Mss Maps Microforms
Notes: Colonial and Revolutionary Period--Midwest, particularly Illinois. Important ms collections (75 cubic feet) under this subject incl: Baynton, Wharton and Morgan, papers, 1757-1799, 6 reels of microfilm; British Archives, 1547-1858, 7000 items, 40 reels of microfilm; Cunningham Collection, 1600-1836, 40 cubic feet (typed copies from Archives in Spain and South America); French Archives, 1671-1796, 3500 items; Gage, Thomas, papers, 1759-1773, 1300 items; Morgan, George, papers, 1766-1826, 280 items, 5 reels of microfilm; Randolph County Records, 1720-1853, 91 items, 59 reels of microfilm; St Clair County Records, 1722-1809, 6 items, 5 reels of microfilm. Guide to the collections published: Maynard J Brichford, Robert M Sutton, Dennis F Walle, *Manuscripts Guide to Collections at the University of Illnois at* Urbana-Champaign(Urbana, Chicago, London: University of Illnois Press, 1976).

ILLINOIS—HISTORY—REVOLUTION

IL —UNIVERSITY OF ILLINOIS, URBANA/CHAMPAIGN, Library, Illinois Historical Survey Library, 1408 W Gregory Dr, 1A Library, Urbana, 61801.
Holdings: Vols 500 Cat Mss Maps Microforms
Notes: Colonial and Revolutionary Period--Midwest, particularly Illinois. Important ms collections (75 cubic feet) under this subject incl: Baynton, Wharton and Morgan, papers, 1757-1799, 6 reels of microfilm; British Archives, 1547-1858, 7000 items, 40 reels of microfilm; Cunningham Collection, 1600-1836, 40 cubic feet (typed copies from Archives in Spain and South America); French Archives, 1671-1796, 3500 items; Gage, Thomas, papers, 1759-1773, 1300 items; Morgan, George, papers, 1766-1826, 280 items, 5 reels of microfilm; Randolph County Records, 1720-1853, 91 items, 59 reels of microfilm; St Clair County Records, 1722-1809, 6 items, 5 reels of microfilm. Guide to the collections published: Maynard J Brichford, Robert M Sutton, Dennis F Walle, *Manuscripts Guide to Collections at the University of Illinois at* Urbana-Champaign(Urbana, Chicago, London: University of Illinois Press, 1976).

ILLINOIS—LAWS AND LEGISLATION

IL —DE PAUL UNIVERSITY, College of Law Library, 25 E Jackson Blvd, Chicago, 60604. Judith G Gecas, Dir
Holdings: (300) Cat
Notes: Territorial laws: Northwest Territory; Indiana Territory; Illinois Territory. "Farthing Collection of Illinois Statutory Laws." *33 Chicago Bar Record*, pp 451-454 (1952).

ILLINOIS—MAPS

IL —SOUTHERN ILLINOIS UNIVERSITY, CARBONDALE, Morris Library, Carbondale, 62901. Jean M Ray, Map Librn
Notes: Emphasis of map collection is Southern Illinois and Mississippi Valley. Incl 158,000 maps; 47,000 aerial photographs of Southern Illinois; 2000 atlases, reference books, etc; 4000 issues of weather map series (historical, daily, monthly); and 360 Illinois county platbooks. Includes Sang Collection--60 early maps of North America, especially Mississippi Valley, 1584-1840.

IL —CHICAGO HISTORICAL SOCIETY, Library, Clark St at North Ave, Chicago, 60614. Robert L Brubaker, Librn
Notes: About 10,000 maps and 640 atlases. Especially strong for Chicago, Illinois, and the Midwest. Also substantial holdings of general maps of the Americas from the 16th century to 1850, general maps of the US for the period to 1900, US transportation, and the Civil War. Incl most county altases for Illinois.

IL —GALESBURG PUBLIC LIBRARY, 40 E Simmons St, Galesburg, 61401. Jane M Willenborg, Special Collections Librn
Holdings: Vols (6113) Cat Mss Maps Pix Slides Phonorecords Audiotapes Microforms
Budget: ($10,500)
Notes: Incl extensive collection of Illinois histories--state, county, city, town, and village; Illinois laws and statutes, 1829-1977; state and county atlases and plat books (listed in *United States Atlases,* vol II, Library of Congress, 1953); Lincoln books; works of Illinois authors; Civil War Illinois regimental histories; photographs of local interest (incl numerous photos of Carl Sandburg); and local newspapers and city directories on microfilm. Incl mss (26 ft), 79 maps, 4371 pictures, 3515 slides. 3053 negatives (some are duplicates of the photographs). Separate catalog. Restricted use: noncirculating; limited photocopying.

IL —ILLINOIS STATE HISTORICAL SOCIETY, Library, Old State Capitol, Springfield, 62706. Roger D Bridges, Head Librn
Notes: Incl 4.6 million mss, nearly 2000 maps, 100,000 pictures and 52,000 microfilm reels. Downs 2546, 2606, 2612, 187, 188. See also *Guide to the Microfilm Edition of the Pierre Menard Collection in the Illinois State Historical Library*. Separate catalogs (card) for printed material, mss, broadsides.

IL —UNIVERSITY OF ILLINOIS, URBANA/CHAMPAIGN, Library, Illinois Historical Survey Library, 1408 W Gregory Dr, 1A Library, Urbana, 61801.
Notes: Important ms collections incl: Randolph County Records, 1720-1853, 91 items, 59 reels of microfilm; St Clair County Records, 1722-1809, 6 items, 5 reels of microfilm; George Morgan, papers, 1766-1826, 280 items, 5 reels of microfilm. Pierre Menard, papers, 1780, 1802-1859, 155 items, 27 volumes, 29 reels of microfilm; Illinois Surveyors' field notes and plat maps, 1805-1850, 56 reels microfilm. Numerous county and local histories and plat books. 1733 maps, and thousands of Illinois pictures. Guide to the collections published in 1976.

OK —TULSA CITY-COUNTY LIBRARY, Business & Technology Dept, 400 Civic Center, Tulsa, 74103. Craig Buthod, Head
Notes: Original General Land Office survey maps for the states of Arizona, Arkansas, Colorado, Illinois, Indiana, Idaho, Kansas, Michigan, Missouri, Montana, Nebraska, Nevada, New Mexico, North Dakota, Ohio, Oklahoma, South Dakota, Utah and Wyoming. Incomplete coverage of each state.

ILLINOIS—POLITICS AND GOVERNMENT

IL —CHICAGO HISTORICAL SOCIETY, Library, Clark St at North Ave, Chicago, 60614. Archie Motley, Manuscript Librn
Notes: Twentieth century political materials incl these papers: Better Government Association, Chicago; Fred W Blaisdell (Dir, Better Government Association, Chicago, member The Crusaders, a national Prohibition-repeal organization); Citizens' Association of Chicago (civic improvement organization); City Club of Chicago (civic improvement organization); William G Clark (Attorney General); Leon M Despres (attorney, Chicago alderman); William E Dever, (lawyer, judge, Chicago alderman, mayor of Chicago); Richard E Friedman (Executive Director, Better Government Association, Chicago; Chicago mayoral candidate); Harold F Gosnell (political scientist, author); John Gutknecht (attorney, judge, Cook County State's Attorney); Illinois League of Women Voters; Independent Voters of Illinois (affiliate of Americans for Democratic Action); Joint Civic Committeeon Elections, Chicago (honest election organization); Clarence Manion (attorney, conservative leader and broadcaster, founder of the Manion Forum radio and television series); Joseph T Meek (President Illinois Retail Merchants Association, Republican senatorial candidate 1954, Delegate, Illinois Constitutional Convention); Robert E Merriam (businessman, Chicago alderman, Chicago mayoral candidate); Municipal Voters' League, Chicago (better government group); James C Murray (attorney, Chicago alderman, Assistant Cook County State's Attorney); Polish American Democratic Organization, Chicago; Seymour Simon (attorney, Chicago alderman, Cook County Commissioner); Peter A Tomei (attorney, delegate, Illinois Constitutional Convention).

IL —NORTHERN ILLINOIS REGIONAL HISTORY CENTER, Sven Parson Hall, Northern Illinois University, De Kalb, 60115. Glen Gildemeister, Dir
Notes: "A research center for advanced research in the humanities. This northern area of Illinois (excluding Cook County) has been virtually untouched by collecting agencies and we hope to fill that void. We will be strong in agribusiness, agricultural implement business, and hybrid farming mechanics....Will be primarily a ms repository, but [have] already taken

responsibility for many artifacts and books, some rare."

†IL —ILLINOIS STATE HISTORICAL SOCIETY, Library, Old State Capitol, Springfield, 62706.
Notes: Papers, incl letters and mss of US Senator Lyman Trumball (1813-1896).

ILLINOIS—RELIGIOUS LIFE AND CUSTOMS

IL —CHICAGO HISTORICAL SOCIETY, Library, Clark St at North Ave, Chicago, 60614. Archie Motley, Manuscript Librn
Notes: Collections relative to religion and society incl papers of Chicago Sunday Evening Club (American preaching ministry); Church Federation of Chicago; Clifford W Barnes, Congregational minister and social reformer; Msgr Daniel M Cantwell, Roman Catholic priest, social and civil rights activist, a founder and chaplain of the following four Catholic groups: Catholic Adult Education Center, Catholic Council on Working Life, Catholic Interracial Council of Chicago, Friendship House; Bishop Bernard J Sheil, Roman Catholic priest, social and civil rights activist, founder of the Catholic Youth Organization.

ILLINOIS—SOCIAL LIFE AND CUSTOMS

IL —CHICAGO HISTORICAL SOCIETY, Library, Clark St at North Ave, Chicago, 60614. Archie Motley, Manuscript Librn
Notes: Collections relative to religion and society: Msgr Daniel M Cantwell (Roman Catholic priest, social and civil rights activist. A founder and chaplain of the following four Catholic groups: Catholic Adult Education Center, Chicago; Catholic Council on Working Life, Chicago; Catholic Interracial Council of Chicago; Friendship House). Also Chicago Sunday Evening Club (American preaching ministry); Church Federation of Greater Chicago. Bishop Bernard J Sheil (Roman Catholic priest, social and civil rights activist, founder of the Catholic Youth Organization).

IL —CHICAGO HISTORICAL SOCIETY, Library, Clark St at North Ave, Chicago, 60614. Archie Motley, Manuscript Librn
Notes: Lyric Opera of Chicago and the Apollo Musical Club of Chicago, and in audio tapes of Herman Kogan's "Critic's Choice" radio programs.

IL —NORTHERN ILLINOIS REGIONAL HISTORY CENTER, Sven Parson Hall, Northern Illinois University, De Kalb, 60115. Glen Gildemeister, Dir
Notes: "A research center for advanced research in the humanities. This northern area of Illinois (excluding Cook County) has been virtually untouched by collecting agencies and we hope to fill that void. We will be strong in agribusiness, agricultural implement business, and hybrid farming mechanics....Will be primarily a ms repository, but [have] already taken responsibility for many artifacts and books, some rare."

ILLINOIS AND MICHIGAN CANAL

IL —CHICAGO HISTORICAL SOCIETY, Library, Clark St at North Ave, Chicago, 60614. Archie Motley, Manuscript Librn
Notes: Papers of William K Swift on the Illinois and Michigan Canal.

ILLINOIS AUTHORS see Authors, Illinois

ILLINOIS CENTRAL RAILROAD

IL —NEWBERRY LIBRARY, 60 W Walton St, Chicago, 60610. Diana Haskell, Cur of Modern Mss
Holdings: / / Mss Maps
Notes: Collection of 350 sq feet of archival material is particularly valuable for the long series of letters from the President, Stuyvesant Fish, 1887-1906 (80 vols). The richest part of the collection runs from 1880 to 1905. There are no "working papers" dealing with railway operations or personnel for this period, but rather administrative detail at the higher levels. Carolyn Curtis Mohr, comp, *Guide to the Illinois Central Archives in the Newberry Library,* 1851-1906. Chicago: The Newberry Library, 1951.

MS —UNIVERSITY OF SOUTHERN MISSISSIPPI, William David McCain Graduate Library, Box 5148, Southern Sta, Hattiesburg, 39406.
Holdings: Cat Mss
Notes: Primarily records (1913-1961; 23 cubic feet) of the Vicksburg, Mississippi Division. Incl are maintenance reports, freight train performance reports, station reports, and other documents relating to division operations. A guide to the records is available for loan.

ILLINOIS HOME ECONOMICS ASSOCIATION

IL —CHICAGO HISTORICAL SOCIETY, Library, Clark St at North Ave, Chicago, 60614. Archie Motley, Manuscript Librn
Notes: Papers of the Illinois Home Economics Association

ILLINOIS LEAGUE OF WOMEN VOTERS

IL —CHICAGO HISTORICAL SOCIETY, Library, Clark St at North Ave, Chicago, 60614. Robert L Brubaker, Librn
Holdings: Vols (150,000) Cat Mss Maps Pix Microforms
Notes: Early Municipal documents, incl some not in the Municipal Reference Library, and selected later documents; archives of the City Club of Chicago, the Illinois League of Women Voters, Independent Voters of Illinois, and other organizations; papers of Chicago aldermen and other political leaders from Chicago; broadsides concerning political campaigns; ward maps; and other publications.

ILLINOIS MANUFACTURERS' ASSOCIATION

IL —CHICAGO HISTORICAL SOCIETY, Library, Clark St at North Ave, Chicago, 60614. Archie Motley, Manuscript Librn
Notes: Business history acquisitions incl the records of the Illinois Manufacturers' Association; customer complaint files of the Better Business Bureau of Metropolitan Chicago; Chicago Board of Underwriters; papers of George S Bowen, Illinois capitalist; and Ernest J Stevens.

ILLINOIS NEWSPAPERS see Newspapers, Illinois

ILLINOIS SOCIETY OF ARCHITECTS

IL —CHICAGO HISTORICAL SOCIETY, Library, Clark St at North Ave, Chicago, 60614. Archie Motley, Manuscript Librn
Notes: Chicago Architectural Archive contains the papers of Chicago architects Barry Byrne and Earl H Reed, the records of the Illinois Society of Architects, and the voluminous files of two leading Chicago architectural firms, Holabird & Root and Harry M Weese and Associates. Access to these collections is by arrangement with Frank Jewell, The Society's Curator of Architectural Collections.

ILLITERACY AND LITERACY

CA —HUMAN RESOURCES RESEARCH ORGANIZATION (HUMRRO), Western Div Library, 27857 Berwick Dr, Carmel, 93923. Dianalee Stickler, Librn
Notes: Citations for HumRRO reports appear in *HumRRO Bibliography of* Publications, 1971 and *HumRRO Bibliography of Publications and Presentations During FY,* 1972-77. Library is inactive.

ILLUMINATED BOOKS AND MANUSCRIPTS

CA —SAINT JOHN'S SEMINARY, Edward Laurence Doheny Memorial Library, The Estelle Doheny Collection, 5012 E Seminary Rd, Camarillo, 93010. Rita S Faulders, Cur

CA —CLAREMONT COLLEGES, Ella Strong Denison Library, Scripps College, Claremont, 91711. Judy Harvey Sahak, Librn
Holdings: Vols (10,000) Cat Mss Pix
Notes: Emphasizes the history of the book and fine printing; includes illuminated manuscripts, incunabula, fine bindings, representative examples of modern fine presses, first editions, and literary ALS.

CA —SAN DIEGO PUBLIC LIBRARY, Wangenheim Rm, 820 E St, San Diego, 92101. Eileen Boyle, Librn
Holdings: Vols (7500) Cat
Notes: A collection on the history of the book and the development of printing with specimens ranging from Babylonian tablets to cassettes.

†CT —UNIVERSITY OF CONNECTICUT LIBRARY, Special Collections Dept, Storrs, 06268. Richard H Schimmelpfeng, Dir of Special Collections
Notes: Good and unusual collection.

DC —LIBRARY OF CONGRESS, Rare Book & Special Collections Div, Washington, 20540. William Matheson, Chief
Notes: The collection incl mss from the 13th to the 16th century in a variety of hands and texts. Some classical and medieval texts are represented, but a proportionately larger number of Bibles, lectionaries, psalters, and books of hours (often with illumination, or illuminated initials or borders) are found. *See also* entry under Manuscripts, Medieval

FL —FLORIDA STATE UNIVERSITY, Robert Manning Strozier Library, Special Collections Dept, Tallahassee, 32306. Opal M Free, Head, Special Collections
Holdings: Vols (12,254) Cat
Notes: Noncirculating. No photocopying.

IN —INDIANA UNIVERSITY, Lilly Library, Seventh St, Bloomington, 47405. William R Cagle, Librn
Holdings: / / Mss Pix Slides
Notes: Ms holdings incl collections of C L Ricketts and George A Poole of Chicago. Both are described in De Ricci, *Census of Medieval and Renaissance* Manuscripts...(Polle collection is in supplement vol). Individual illuminated leaves are also in the ms holdings as the Ege Collection, and a few other mss are scattered in other collections. No photocopying.

KS —SAINT MARY COLLEGE, Library, Leavenworth, 66048. Therese Deplazes, Special Collections Librn
Holdings: / / Cat Pix

MD —WALTERS ART GALLERY, Library & Manuscripts & Rare Book Collection, 600 N Charles St, Baltimore, 21201. Muriel L Toppan, Reference Librn; Lilian M C Randall, Cur of Mss & Rare Books
Holdings: Vols (80,000) Cat Mss
Budget: ($35,000)
Notes: The collection supports the gallery's collections of art objects which date from 4000 BC to the end of the 19th century. The collection of medieval and renaissance illuminated mss (782 in number), incunabula (about 1400) and rare books are considered art objects. There are card catalogs providing indexing to the collection. The mss are listed in De Ricci and the incunabula in Goff. Photocopying permitted for Reference Library materials only.

MA —HARVARD UNIVERSITY LIBRARY, Houghton Library, Printing and Graphic Arts Dept, Cambridge, 02138. Eleanor M Garvey, Cur
Notes: Collection incl illustrated books, fine printing, type specimens, illuminated and calligraphic manuscripts, and drawings for book illustration.

MI —MICHIGAN STATE UNIVERSITY, Art Library, East Lansing, 48824. Shirlee A Studt, Librn
Holdings: Vols (45,000) Cat
Notes: The Illuminated Manuscript

ILLUMINATED BOOKS AND MANUSCRIPTS (cont.)

Facsimile Collection includes examples of religious and secular works from the earliest codex to the age of printing. It has particular strengths in Carolingian, Ottonian, French Gothic and works from the British Isles. The facsimile collection is strengthened by related research materials (biographical material, critical studies, etc) The facsimile collection and related materials are part of a 45,000 volume separately housed and staffed collection on the visual and decorative arts (including photography) serving the curricular and research needs of the University community. A guide to full facsimiles in the collection is available in the Art Library and in the Special Collections division. A strong collection of architectural history.

MN —SAINT JOHN'S ABBEY & UNIVERSITY, Hill Monastic Manuscript Library, Collegeville, 56321. Julian G Plante, Dir
Holdings: Cat Mss Slides Microforms
Notes: Films of 61,000 mss. The total number of codices (bound handwritten mss) represents the holdings of several hundred libraries in Europe and elsewhere: Austria, Spain, Malta, Ethiopia, West Germany, Portugal, England, but also with concentrations of holdings from Italy, Hungary, Poland, Great Britain, Belgium, Yugoslavia, France, Switzerland and the Netherlands, and Vatican City. Also incl 70, 000 exposures.

MO —SAINT LOUIS PUBLIC LIBRARY, Gardner Rare Book Room, 1301 Olive St, Saint Louis, 63103. Julanne M Good, Supervisor; Martha Riley, Rare Books Librn
Holdings: Vols 1300 Cat Mss
Budget: ($5573)
Notes: Collection of rare materials, 350 specimen leaves and supporting reference materials on history of the book, history of printing, bibliography, book collecting, book and document conservation, papermaking, and bookbinding. The 350 specimen leaves are from illuminated manuscript books and incunabula. Noncirculating.

NJ —PRINCETON UNIVERSITY, Library, Manuscript Collection, Nassau St, Princeton, 08540. Jean F Preston, Cur
Holdings: Mss Pix
Notes: The collection of Medieval and Renaissance manuscripts, totaling 350 books manuscripts, incl items collected by Robert Garrett and Grenville Kane. The collection is supplemented by several single leaves. See *Princeton University Library Chronicle*, v. 3, p 123-35; v 11, p 37-44. Ricci, Seymour de. *Census of Medieval and Renaissance Manuscripts in the United States and* Canada (New York: H W Wilson Co 1935-40); and *Supplement* ed by H W Bond, 1962.

NJ —PRINCETON UNIVERSITY, Library, Graphic Arts Collection, Princeton, 08540. Dale Roylance, Cur
Notes: Sinclair Hamilton Collection. One of the largest collections of American Illustrated Books in the US. 2 vols published; catalog available. Also, large collection of illustrated books of all countries, for all periods.

NY —FRICK ART REFERENCE LIBRARY, 10 E 71 St, New York, 10021. Helen Sanger, Librn
Holdings: Vols (154,384) Cat Pix Per
Notes: History of painting, drawing, sculpture and illuminated mss of US and western Europe from 4th century AD to about 1860. 54,862 art auction catalogs; 420, 507 study photographs.

NY —GENERAL THEOLOGICAL SEMINARY, Saint Marks Library, 175 Ninth Ave, New York, 10011. David Green, Dir
Holdings: Vols (200,000) Cat Mss Maps Pix Slides Microforms
Notes: Extensive collection.

NY —NEW YORK PUBLIC LIBRARY, Spencer Collection, Fifth Ave & 42 St, New York, 10018. Joseph T Rankin, Cur
Holdings: Vols (8000) Cat Mss
Notes: Rare illustrated and illuminated mss and books, in fine bindings, in all languages, of all countries, and of all periods, constituting the development of book illustration and the book arts the world around. See *Dictionary Catalog and Shelf List of the Spencer Collection,* New York Public Library, 1970. 2 vols, $155.

NY —PIERPONT MORGAN LIBRARY, 29 E 36 St, New York, 10016. John H Plummer, Cur
Notes: One of the largest collections, with many rarities, unique works and mss.

OH —HEBREW UNION COLLEGE-JEWISH INSTITUTE OF RELIGION, Klau Library, 3101 Clifton Ave, Cincinnati, 45220. David J Gilner, Reference Librn
Holdings: Cat Mss
Notes: Hebrew illuminated mss, especially illuminated Passover Haggadot (incl the Cincinnati Haggadah), Esther Scrolls, etc.

PA —FREE LIBRARY OF PHILADELPHIA, Rare Book Dept, Logan Sq, Philadelphia, 19103. Marie E Korey, Rare Book Librn
Holdings: Cat Mss
Notes: The John Frederick Lewis and Joseph E Widener Collections of European Manuscripts incl 2200 bound volumes and seperate illuminated leaves and text leaves.

PA —UNIVERSITY OF PITTSBURGH, Henry Clay Frick Fine Arts Library, Pittsburgh, 15260. Anne W Gordon, Fine Arts Librn
Holdings: Vols (55,000) Cat Pix Slides Microforms
Notes: Emphasis is on the art of the Western World--Architecture, sculpture, painting, minor arts, archaeology, with special strength in the Byzantine, early Christian, medieval, renaissance and modern periods. The Oriental field is represented, incl replicas of scrolls. Studio arts are also covered. Illuminated ms facsimiles. Extensive collections of slides and photographs for study of art history are available in the building but not administered by the art library.

VA —LYNCHBURG COLLEGE, Knight-Capron Library, Lynchburg, 24501. Mary C Scudder, Dir
Holdings: Vols (847) Cat Maps
Notes: Religious works and history, 15th-19th century. Part of the Capron Collection.

MB —UNIVERSITY OF MANITOBA, Elizabeth Dafoe Library, Archives and Special Collections Dept, Winnipeg, R3T 2N2, Can. Richard E Bennett, Dept Head; Corrado A Santoro, Reference Archivist
Holdings: / / Uncat Mss
Notes: The Dysart Memorial Library collection or rare books representative of the development and the art of book-making and fine printing, with several illuminated mss and examples of the works of famous printers from the 15th century to the present day.

ILLUMINATED MANUSCRIPTS see Illuminated Books and Manuscripts

ILLUMINATION see Lighting

ILLUMINATION OF BOOKS AND MANUSCRIPTS

CT —YALE UNIVERSITY, Box 1603A, Yale Station, New Haven, 06520.

DC —LIBRARY OF CONGRESS, General Reading Rooms Division, Microform Reading Room, Washington, 20540.
Holdings: Cat Mss Maps Pix Microforms
Notes: Microform materials only in this LC Division. Works of individual authors; holdings of collections; archival records, etc, press releases and translations, etc.

KY —UNIVERSITY OF KENTUCKY, Margaret I King Library, Dept of Special Collections, Lexington, 40506. William Marshall, Head
Holdings: Cat Mss Pix Slides Microforms
Notes: Comprehensive collection of books on typography and history of printing; fine press books (incl Lexington imprints); ms books and illumination, paleography; mss of W A Dwiggins (gift of C H Griffith); James Anderson papers; bookbinding; 2 hand-presses and working collection for summer seminars in hand-press printing; bookplates, bookmarks, book jackets, etc.

MO —SAINT LOUIS UNIVERSITY, Pius XII Memorial Library, 3655 W Pine Blvd, Saint Louis, 63108. William Cole, Dir
Holdings: Slides Microforms
Notes: Collection covers all areas of learning and European history from Classical Antiquity to early modern period. Researchers using collection receive assistance in paleography, bibliography and reference search. Approx 10,000 1000-foot reels of microfilm (not counting master negatives) reproducing Vatican Library's Latin, Greek, Hebrew, Arabic and Ethiopic mss. Some 8000 100-foot reels of microfilm (again not counting master negative) reproducing rare and out of print books relating to subject areas in the mss. Over 50, 000 color slides of medieval and Renaissance mss illuminations. A reference collection of modern materials relating to ms research.

ILLUSTRATED BOOKS

CA —UNIVERSITY OF CALIFORNIA, LOS ANGELES, Research Library, Dept of Special Collections, 405 Hilgard Ave, Los Angeles, 90024. Edward Shreeves, Chairman, Bibliographers Group; David S Zeidberg, Head
Holdings: Vols 225 Cat Pix
Notes: 100 books with color illustrations, and 100 color prints, printed by George Baxter. Also 125 books by and illustrated by Thomas Bewick; 16 original woodblocks.

CA —MILLS COLLEGE LIBRARY, Oakland, 94613. Steven P Pandolfo, Librn
Holdings: Vols 500 Cat Pix
Notes: Early printed books with emphasis on works important for their illustrations, representative of the history of the book, and landmark volumes in the history of art.

CA —HUNTINGTON LIBRARY, Art Gallery & Botanical Gardens, 1151 Oxford Rd, San Marino, 91108. Robert L Middlekauff, Dir; Daniel H Woodward, Librn
Holdings: Mss Maps Pix Slides Microforms
Notes: Approx 350,000 rare books, 250,000 reference books, manuscript collection of nearly 2,500,000 pieces and between 200, 000 and 300,000 prints, rare photographs and other related materials. The fullest available survey is now *Guide to Literary Manuscripts in the Huntington Library,* a 539-page handlist published by the Library in 1979.

CA —UNIVERSITY OF CALIFORNIA, SANTA BARBARA, Library, Dept of Special Collections, Santa Barbara, 93106. Christian F Brun, Head
Notes: Emphasis of Skofield Printers Collection.

CO —UNIVERSITY OF COLORADO, Libraries, Special Collections, Boulder, 80309. Nora J Quinlan, Head
Holdings: Vols Uncat
Notes: George Creamer Collection. Over two thousand books on 19th century English literature (Dickens), and 19th and 20th centuries British and American book illustration. In addition, approx 250 children's illustrated books.

CT —TRINITY COLLEGE LIBRARY, Watkinson Library, 300 Summit St, Hartford, 06106. Jeffrey Kaimowitz, Cur
Holdings: Cat Pix
Notes: Incl Trumbull-Prime Collection of early illustrated books; also material on all aspects of book design.

DE —DELAWARE ART MUSEUM, Library, 2301 Kentmere Pkwy, Wilmington, 19806. Anne Hoslam, Librn
Holdings: Cat Mss Pix
Notes: The Frank E Schoonover and other collections. Archives, letters, sketches, photographs, memorabilia, clippings.

DC —LIBRARY OF CONGRESS, Rare Book & Special Collections Div, Washington, 20540. William Matheson, Chief
Holdings: Vols 2600
Notes: The Lessing J Rosenwald Collection. Outstanding copies of the major Western illustrated books printed from the 15th to the 20th centuries with a special emphasis

ILLUSTRATED BOOKS (cont.)

on early printed books, 18th century French luxury books, the illuminated books of William Blake, and the modern *livre* d'artiste. A group of ten block books, a selection of 15th and 16th century Dutch and Flemish books from the Library of the Dukes of Arenberg, and modern publications by Ambroise Vollard illustrated with original prints by Pierre Bonnard, Pablo Picasso, and Joan Miro are noteworthy among these holdings. See *The Lessing J Rosenwald Collection: A Catalog of the Gifts of Lessing J Rosenwald to the Library of Congress, 1943 to 1975* (Washington, Library of Congress, 1977). The collection is complemented by a large reference library focused on the history of the graphic arts.

FL —FLORIDA STATE UNIVERSITY, Robert Manning Strozier Library, Special Collections Dept, Tallahassee, 32306. Opal M Free, Head, Special Collections
Holdings: Vols (5176) Cat
Notes: Noncirculating. No photocopying.

IL —CHICAGO PUBLIC LIBRARY, Special Collections Div, Cultural Center, 78 E Washington St, Chicago, 60602. Laura Linard, Cur
Holdings: Vols (1000) Cat
Notes: A general collection on the history of typography, including a specimen collection of works printed before 1700, books about books, private press productions (primarily Chicago), limited editions, illustrated and extra-illustrated books and fine bindings. Outstanding items described in *Treasures of The Chicago Public Library*, compiled by Thomas A Orlando and Marie Gecik, 1977, pp. 6-29.

IL —NEWBERRY LIBRARY, John M Wing Foundation on the History of Printing, 60 W Walton St, Chicago, 60610. Diana Haskell, Cur of Modern Mss
Holdings: Vols (30,000) Cat Mss Pix
Budget: ($30,000)
Notes: Part of the John M Wing Foundation on the History of Printing, which collects western European and American printing from the invention to the present day. Includes some 2,000 incunabula, excellent collections of the major printers, modern illustrated books, etc. Especially strong in periodicals and illustrated books of the Victorian period, G K Hall has published *A Dictionary Catalogue of the John M. Wing Foundation and two Supplements.* Parts have been described in various articles, etc., notable J.M. Wells, *The Scholar Printers* and an article by Wells in *The Book Collector.*

KS —TOPEKA PUBLIC LIBRARY, Special Collections & Local History Dept, 1515 W Tenth, Topeka, 66604. Warren Taylor, Librn
Holdings: Vols 500
Notes: Emphasis on illustrated books adult and children's.

KY —UNIVERSITY OF LOUISVILLE, Allen R Hite Art Institute, Library, Belknap Campus, Louisville, 40292. Gail Gilbert, Librn
Holdings: Vols (40,000) Cat Pix
Budget: ($29,000)
Notes: Incl books on art, architecture, landscape architecture and gardening, prints, printing, illustrated books and brass rubbings. Library subscribes to 200 periodical titles in these and other areas. Collection circulates to faculty and staff only, with same restrictions placed on interlibrary loan. Library also has collections of bookplates, posters, original prints, hand-made Christmas cards and clippings file filling 56 VF drawers.

ME —WILLIAM A FARNSWORTH LIBRARY & ART MUSEUM, 19 Elm St, Rockland, 04841. Marius B Peladeau, Dir
Holdings: Vols (4000) Cat Pix Microforms
Notes: Emphasis on American and European fine and decorative arts of all periods (largely modern). Other areas include marine history and Maine history (local); illustrated books and rare books also a part of our collection, which has its own catalog. Also, Louise Nevelsen, N C Wyeth Archives.

MD —US NAVAL ACADEMY, Nimitz Library, Annapolis, 21402. Alice S Creighton, Assistant Librn for Special Collections
Holdings: Vols (900)// Uncat
Notes: Wiedorn Collection of illustrated books, chiefly of the 19th century.

MD —JOHNS HOPKINS UNIVERSITY, Milton S Eisenhower Library, Special Collections, John Work Garrett Library, 4545 N Charles St, Baltimore, 21210. Jane Katz, Garrett Librn
Holdings: Vols Cat Mss Maps
Notes: The John Work Garrett Library incl 100 maps; 1500 autograph letters; early voyages and travels; Americana; early Maryland imprints and Marylandia; Bible collection; 17th century English Literature (4 Shakespeare folios, 2 quartos); ornithology and natural history (complete set of Gould's Birds); early illustrated books; 19th and 20th century adult and children's illustrated books; typography (Kent Currie), limited editions, incl Bruce Rogers proof sheets; Fowler Architectural Collection (has own book catalog); Sidney Lanier Personal Library, books he wrote and his ms music collection. Downs (1961-70) 444.

MA —BOSTON PUBLIC LIBRARY, Print Collection, Dartmouth St at Copley Sq, Boston, 02117. Sinclair H Hitchings, Keeper of Prints
Holdings: Vols (500) Cat
Notes: Fine illustrated books, mainly English, of the 18th, 19th and 20th centuries, containing original prints of photographs. Also, 250 books with fore-edge paintings and books with fine bindings. No photocopying.

MA —HARVARD UNIVERSITY LIBRARY, Houghton Library, Printing and Graphic Arts Dept, Cambridge, 02138. Eleanor M Garvey, Cur
Holdings: Cat
Notes: Collection incl illustrated books, fine printing, type specimens, illuminated and calligraphic manuscripts, and drawings for book illustration.

†MA —WILLIAMS COLLEGE, Chapin Library of Rare Books, PO Box 426, Williamstown, 01267. Robert L Volz, Custodian
Holdings: Vols 2000 Cat
Notes: 15th-20th centuries. No material available on interlibrary loan.

MN —MINNEAPOLIS PUBLIC LIBRARY & INFORMATION CENTER, 300 Nicollet Mall, Minneapolis, 55401. Richard J Hofstad, Athenaeum Librn
Holdings: Vols (300) Cat
Notes: 19th century color plate books.

MO —WASHINGTON UNIVERSITY, John M Olin Library, Campus Box 1061, St Louis, 63130.
Notes: Representative collection of European, British and American books from the sixteenth to twentieth century; especially strong in 20th century American, British and German illustrated editions of poetry and fiction.

NH —DARTMOUTH COLLEGE, Baker Memorial Library, Hanover, 03755.
Holdings: Cat
Notes: Esp New England imprints, 1769-1869. Noncirculating. Publication: *Sampler of Illustrated Books Published in New England, 1769-1869.*

NJ —NEWARK PUBLIC LIBRARY, Art & Music Dept, 5 Washington St, Newark, 07101. William J Dane, Supv
Holdings: Mss Maps Pix Slides
Notes: 1,000,000 pictures with supporting collections of postcards, 2000 portfolios of plates of design, fine and circulating print collections (incl Japanese), 1400 illustrated books, 4000 posters. The classification scheme and headings used are listed in *The Picture Collection Subject Headings* (Shoe String Press, 1968).

NJ —PRINCETON UNIVERSITY, Library, Graphic Arts Collection, Princeton, 08540. Dale Roylance, Cur
Notes: Sinclair Hamilton Collection. One of the largest collections of American Illustrated Books in the US. 2 vols published; catalog available. Also, large collection of illustrated books of all countries, for all periods.

NY —PRATT INSTITUTE LIBRARY, Art & Architecture Dept, 200 Willoughby Ave, Brooklyn, 11205. Sydney Star Keaveney, Prof
Holdings: Vols (30,000) Cat Pix Slides
Budget: ($50,000)
Notes: Art and architecture, incl sculpture, photography, painting, design, costume, and commercial art. Incl 60,000 art slides. Use restricted to Pratt faculty and students.

NY —ALBRIGHT-KNOX ART GALLERY, Art Reference Library, 1285 Elmwood Ave, Buffalo, 14222. Annette Masling, Librn
Holdings: Vols (20,000) Cat
Notes: Special strength in American 19th and 20th century art. Excellent collection of exhibition catalogs for contemporary art.

NY —BUFFALO & ERIE COUNTY PUBLIC LIBRARY, Rare Book Room, Lafayette Sq, Buffalo, 14203. William H Loos, Cur
Holdings: Vols 900 Cat Pix

NY —METROPOLITAN MUSEUM OF ART, Dept of Prints & Photographs, 82 St & Fifth Ave, New York, 10028. Colta Ives, Cur
Holdings: Vols (10,000)
Notes: Contained in a collection of 500,000 prints from 15th to 20th century. Approx 10, 000 illustrated books; European and American. No photocopying.

NY —NEW YORK PUBLIC LIBRARY, Rare Books and Manuscripts Div, Fifth Ave & 42 St, New York, 10018. William L Joyce, Asst Dir; Bernard McTigue, Cur, Arents Collection
Holdings: Cat Maps Pix
Notes: The Arents Collections of Books in Parts incl original drawings by illustrators (John Leech, Thomas Rowlandson, George Cruikshank, and others); autograph letters relating to the books and their illustrators, incl Dickens, Thackeray, Ainsworth, Trollope, Collins, Kate Greenaway, etc.

NY —NEW YORK PUBLIC LIBRARY, Spencer Collection, Fifth Ave & 42 St, New York, 10018. Joseph T Rankin, Cur
Holdings: Vols (8000) Cat Mss
Notes: Rare illustrated and illuminated mss and books, in fine bindings, in all languages, of all countries, and of all periods, constituting the development of book illustration and the book arts the world around. See *Dictionary Catalog and Shelf List of the Spencer Collection,* New York Public Library, 1970. 2 vols, $155.

NY —NEW YORK PUBLIC LIBRARY, Print Collection, Fifth Ave & 42 St, New York, 10018. Robert Rainwater, Keeper
Holdings: Vols 12,000 Cat
Notes: Incl 175,000 prints and drawings. A representative collection of fine prints from the 15th century to the present, cataloged by artist, with strong holdings in 19th century French prints and Americana. See Stokes-Haskell, *American Historical Prints, Etc New York* (New York Public Library, 1933) and Weitenkampf, Frank, *The Eno Collection of New York City Views* (New York Public Library, 1925). See *Dictionary Catalog of the Prints Division* (Boston: G K Hall, 1975), 5 vols.

NY —UNIVERSITY CLUB, Library, One W 54 St, New York, 10019. Guy St Clair, Library Dir
Holdings: Vols (100,000) Cat Mss Maps Pix
Notes: A private library for the members of the University Club, their guests, and serious scholars upon written application to the Library Director. Holds the Edward Larocque Tinker Collection of Illustrated Books Between the Two World Wars, A Milton Runyon Collection on the History of Printing and Publishing, the Frederic R Coudert "Les Bibliophiles des Paris" Collection, The University Club Rare Book Collection, and the Frederick G Rudge Collection of Books Designed by William E Rudge and Bruce Rogers.

NY —UNIVERSITY OF ROCHESTER, Rush Rhees Library, Department of Rare Books and Special Collections, Rochester, 14627. Peter Dzwonkoski, Librn
Holdings: Vols 600 Cat
Notes: Hubbell Collection of 19th century illustrated books with mounted photographs. No photocopying.

OH —CASE WESTERN RESERVE UNIVERSITY, M A Baxter School of

ILLUSTRATED BOOKS (cont.)

Information and Library Science, 10900 Euclid Ave, Cleveland, 44106. Bettina MacAyeal, Librn; Gretchen Larson, Librn
Holdings: Vols (1100)
Notes: Incl collection of 1100 historical children's books and periodicals, housed in the Special Collections Dept of Freiberger Library, and can be used by the public. Incl *The Holy Bible Abridged* published by Isaiah Thomas in 1786, *The Life and Strange Surprising Adventures of Robinson Crusoe* of 1790, and a *Cinderella* dated 1809. There are examples of the work of illustrators Walter Crane, Randolph Caldecott, Kate Greenaway and Maurice Boutet de Monvel. The periodical collection incl a complete run of St. Nicholas Magazine.

OH —GARDEN CENTER OF GREATER CLEVELAND, Eleanor Squire Library, 11030 East Blvd, Cleveland, 44106. Richard T Isaacson, Librn
Notes: The Warren C Corning Collection of Horticultural Classics. The Flowering Plant Index of Illustration and Information.

OR —UNIVERSITY OF OREGON, Library, Eugene, 97403. Kenneth W Duckett, Curator
Holdings: Mss
Notes: The paper, etc, of Edwin Tunis.

PA —FREE LIBRARY OF PHILADELPHIA, Rare Book Dept, Logan Sq, Philadelphia, 19103. Marie E Korey, Rare Book Librn
Holdings: Vols (1000) Cat Mss Pix
Notes: The Thornton Oakley Collection containing 1000 pieces of original art, autograph letters, and books and periodicals, illustrated by Howard Pyle and his students, incl Maxfield Parish, Frank Schoonover, Jessie Wilcox Smith, and N C Wyeth.

PA —PENNSYLVANIA STATE UNIVERSITY, Fred Lewis Pattee Library, Special Collections Dept, University Park, 16802. Charles Mann, Chief, Special Collections
Holdings: Vols (122,533) Cat Mss Maps Pix Slides
Budget: ($37,000)
Notes: Special Collections and Rare Books includes several collections described separately. The holdings are particularly strong in literature, the 18th century, aeronautics, facsimiles, atlases, 19th century illustrated works on birds, botany and traveller's view. Special strengths are Emblem Books, Utopias, Fantastic Fiction, Australiana, Fine Presses, Labor Archives, Landscape Architecture, Pennsylvaniana. These collections are strengthened by parallel holdings in the open stacks. It also includes the collections of the Penn State Room. Several mineographed lists are available. Audiotapes are listed in *Voices and Events, A Catalog of Audio Tapes* (Pennsylvania State University Libraries, 1975), 45 pp.

RI —PROVIDENCE PUBLIC LIBRARY, 150 Empire St, Providence, 02903. Lance J Bauer, Special Collections Librn
Holdings: Vols 400 // Cat
Notes: The Wetmore Illustrated Books Collection. This historical collection of more than 400 volumes was given to Providence Public Library in 1955 by Newport, Rhode Island, Collector Edith Wetmore. An extremely fine collection of *livres d'artiste,* examples of fine illustration, printing and bindings. This collection incl the works of such notable artists as William Blake, Pablo Picasso, Giorgio DiChirico, Aubrey Beardsley, Jean Cocteau, William Hogarth, Raoul Dufy, Pierre Bonnard and numerous others. Although especially strong in the French illustrated books, English and German illustrated books are amply represented also. Partially cataloged. Material must be used in-house.

VT —UNIVERSITY OF VERMONT, Guy W Bailey/David W Howe Library, Burlington, 05405. John Buehler, Asst Dir for Special Collections
Notes: Illustrated editions of Ovid.

ON —VICTORIA UNIVERSITY, Library, 71 Queen's Park Crescent, Toronto, M5S 1K7, Can. Robert C Brandeis, Chief Librn
Holdings: Vols (400) //
Notes: A major collection of George Baxter's woodblock and metal plate prints and book illustration in watercolor and oil color. Listed in *Starr Collection of Baxter* Prints. Toronto: Ryerson Press,1946.

ILLUSTRATED BOOKS, BRITISH

CA —UNIVERSITY OF CALIFORNIA, LOS ANGELES, Research Library, Dept of Special Collections, 405 Hilgard Ave, Los Angeles, 90024. Edward Shreeves, Chairman, Bibliographers Group; David S Zeidberg, Head
Holdings: Vols 2500 Cat
Notes: 2500 books; a list of illustrators of books in Michael Sadleir's collection is available.

CT —YALE UNIVERSITY, Beinecke Rare Book & Manuscript Library, Osborn Collection, New Haven, 06520. Stephen R Parks, Cur
Holdings: Mss

DE —DELAWARE ART MUSEUM, Library, 2301 Kentmere Pkwy, Wilmington, 19806. Anne Hoslam, Librn
Holdings: Cat Mss Pix
Notes: The Frank E Schoonover and other collections. Archives, letters, sketches, photographs, memorabilia, clippings.

ILLUSTRATED BOOKS, CHILDREN'S

CA —UNIVERSITY OF CALIFORNIA, LOS ANGELES, Research Library, Dept of Special Collections, 405 Hilgard Ave, Los Angeles, 90024. Edward Shreeves, Chairman, Bibliographers Group; David S Zeidberg, Head
Notes: Various collections, ranging from 18th century chapbooks to materials of Theodor Geisel (Dr Seuss) and the Hollings. Original material by Edward Ardizzone, Randolph Caldecott, Palmer Cox, Walter Crane, Alfred Henry Forrester, etc.

CO —UNIVERSITY OF COLORADO, Libraries, Special Collections, Boulder, 80309. Nora J Quinlan, Head
Holdings: Vols Uncat
Notes: George Creamer Collection. Over two thousand books on 19th century English literature (Dickens), and 19th and 20th centuries British and American book illustration. In addition, approx 250 children's illustrated books.

DC —DISTRICT OF COLUMBIA PUBLIC LIBRARY, Martin Luther King Memorial Library, Children's Div, 901 G St NW, Washington, 20001. Maria B Salvadore, Coordr, Children's Service
Holdings: Vols (13,000)
Notes: Collection incl examples of illustrated children's books from the 18th century to the present, mainly English and American, as well as general titles about illustrations and biographical information on illustrators. Collection is cited in *Subject Collections in Children's Literature,* ed by Carolyn Field (Bowker, 1969). "Source Collection" of folk literature is currently being developed to aid research. Partially cataloged. No photocopying.

FL —FLORIDA STATE UNIVERSITY, Robert Manning Strozier Library, Special Collections Dept, Tallahassee, 32306. Opal M Free, Head, Special Collections
Holdings: Uncat Mss Pix Tapes
Notes: The Lois Lenski collection contains 867 items, many first editions of books written and illustrated by Miss Lenski and other editions of her books, incl foreign-language editions: books illustrated by Lois Lenski; books containing selections from her works; articles by and about her; original drawings, block prints, lithographs, rough sketches. Many items autographed. Two editions of a catalog of the collection, *The Lois Lenski Collection in the Florida State University Library,* were published in 1966, both limited editions and now out-of-print. Noncirculating. No photocopying.

IL —WHEATON COLLEGE, Buswell Memorial Library, Wheaton, 60187. Paul Snezek, Library Dir
Holdings: Vols 150 Cat Mss Pix
Budget: $1500
Notes: Mss number over 60 linear feet and dates from Madeleine L'Engle's childhood through 1984. Included are correspondence, examples of her artwork, and non-print media resources. *Related Topics:* Illustrated Children's Books.

IN —INDIANA UNIVERSITY, Lilly Library, Seventh St, Bloomington, 47405. William R Cagle, Librn
Holdings: Uncat Mss
Notes: The Elisabeth Ball Collection consists of more than 7,000 books and many manuscripts from the late seventeenth to the early twentieth centuries. Strengths include Newbery and other early imprints, chapbooks, horn books, harlequinades, street cries, and miniature books.

IN —INDIANAPOLIS-MARION COUNTY PUBLIC LIBRARY, Riley Room for Young People, PO Box 211, Indianapolis, 46206. Margaret Barks, Head
Holdings: Vols 831 Cat

MI —WAYNE STATE UNIVERSITY, Kresge Library (Education), Detroit, 48202. Theodore Manheim, Librn
Holdings: Vols (65,000) Cat Mss Microforms
Budget: ($2000)
Notes: The Eloise Ramsey Collection (10, 000 vols). See, *The Eloise Ramsey Collection of Literature for Young People: A Catalogue;* compiled by Joan Cusenza (Detroit: Wayne State University Libraries, 1967). Besides the Ramsey Collection, which is housed separately and does not circulate, the Education Library has approx 55,000 volumes of children's and young adults' literature, with a very large picture-book collection, a large poetry collection; all with special emphasis on urban and ethnic materials.

MS —UNIVERSITY OF SOUTHERN MISSISSIPPI, William David McCain Graduate Library, Box 5148, Southern Sta, Hattiesburg, 39406.
Holdings: Vols 20,000 Mss Pix
Notes: The Lena Y de Grummond Collection. Literary mss, correspondence and original illustrations for children's books, original editions of children's books and magazines, 1530-date. Approx 2100 feet. Incl works by over 900 authors and illustrators, among them Kate Greenaway, Randolph Caldecott, Maud and Miska Petersham, Merritt Mauzey, Berta and Elmer Hader, Scott O'Dell, Lois Lenski, Roger Duvoisin, Lynd Ward, Taro Yashima, Marcia Brown, Adrienne Adams, Madeleine L'Engle, Barbara Cooney and Nonny Hogrogian. Robert L Dartt Collection of over 1800 books for boys from the late 19th and early 20th centuries. Extensive Henty (over 550 vols), Alger, Brereton, Castlemon, Fenn, Kingston, Optic, and Stratemeyer holdings. Catalog in progress.

NE —KEENE MEMORIAL LIBRARY, Children's Library, 1030 N Broad St, Fremont, 68025. Mary Scheele, Children's Librn
Holdings: Vols (35,000) Cat Phonorecords Filmstrips
Budget: ($10,000)
Notes: Keene Memorial Library (Fremont Public Library) combined with former Nebraska Library Commission Juvenile collection. It is a working collection, nearly all 20th century, English-language materials. Strengths incl multiple editions of standard children's titles, such as Robin Hood, tales of King Arthur, and examples of the work of most children's book illustrators from 1900 to present.

NM —NEW MEXICO STATE UNIVERSITY, Library, Box 3475, Las Cruces, 88003. James Dyke, Dir
Holdings: Vols 675// Cat
Notes: The Herman llfeld Bacharach Collection includes both American and foreign imprints published during the late 19th and early 20th centuries.

NY —COLUMBIA UNIVERSITY LIBRARIES, Teachers College, Milbank Memorial Library, 525 W 120 St, New York, 10027. Jane P Franck, Dir
Holdings: Vols 300 // Cat
Notes: Incl the Annie E Moore Collection of illustrated children's books. Noncirculating. Shows development of children's book illustration; catalog arranged by illustrator.

ILLUSTRATED BOOKS, CHILDREN'S (cont.)

†NY —COLUMBIA UNIVERSITY LIBRARIES, Butler Library, Rare Book and Manuscript Library, 535 W 114 St, New York, 10027.
Notes: A collection of the art work of Tibor Gergely, containing 2,824 watercolors, pen-and-ink drawings, and sketches. Gergely is best known for his illustrations of the popular Golden Book Series for children.

OH —CASE WESTERN RESERVE UNIVERSITY, M A Baxter School of Information and Library Science, 10900 Euclid Ave, Cleveland, 44106. Bettina MacAyeal, Librn; Gretchen Larson, Librn
Holdings: Vols (1100)
Notes: Incl collection of 1100 historical children's books and periodicals, housed in the Special Collections Dept of Freiberger Library, and can be used by the public. Incl *The Holy Bible Abridged* published by Isaiah Thomas in 1786, *The Life and Strange Surprising Adventures of Robinson Crusoe* of 1790, and a *Cinderella* dated 1809. There are examples of the work of illustrators Walter Crane, Randolph Caldecott, Kate Greenaway and Maurice Boutet de Monvel. The periodical collection incl a complete run of St. Nicholas Magazine.

OR —UNIVERSITY OF OREGON LIBRARY, Special Collections Div, Eugene, 97403. Kenneth W Duckett, Curator
Holdings: Vols (11,500) Cat Mss Pix
Notes: Collection contains 250,000 pieces, incl original mss, correspondence, dummy books, and original illustrations from Harriet Stratemayer Adams, Clyde Bulla, Ruth Robinson Carroll, Edgar and Ingri d'Aulaire, James Daugherty, Roger Duvoisin, Leonard Everett Fisher, Jean Fritz, Hardie Gramatky, Berta and Elmer Hader, Holling C Holling, Evelyn Sibley Lampman, Maud Hart Lovelace, James Marshall, Walt Morey, Clare Newberry, Scott O'Dell, Lucille Ogle, Willy Pogany, Kate Seredy, Yoshiko Uchida, Lynd Ward, Kurt Wiese and many others. Incl 5,000 vols uncat of c19-c20 children's books in the Ogle collection. Publication: Martin Schmitt, Comp. *Catalogue of Manuscripts in the University of Oregon* Library (Eugene: University of Oregon Books, 1971).

PA —FREE LIBRARY OF PHILADELPHIA, Central Children's Dept, Logan Sq, Philadelphia, 19103. Ellen Whitney, Head
Holdings: Vols (30,382) Cat Mss Pix
Notes: Special collections of children's literature dating from 1837 to the present are maintained by the Central Children's Department. These collections include Historical Bibliography, the Kathrine M McAlarney Collection of Illustrated Children's Books, the Folklore Collection, the Historical Collection which includes children's periodicals and the Series Collection. Featured in these non-circulating research collections are works of outstanding illustrators in the field of children's books, books by Philadelphia and Pennsylvania authors, books about Philadelphia and Pennsylvania people and places, and books published in Philadelphia and Pennsylvania. Included also are framed originals as well as manuscripts and typescripts by Evaline Ness, material for Lloyd Alexander books, Virginia Lee Burton, Marguerite (Lofft) deAngeli, Beatrice Schenk (Freedman) DeRegniers, EulalieOsgood Grover, Carolyn Haywood, Elizabeth Hoffman Honness, Kristin (Eggleston) Hunter [on loan to Free Library], Margaret Oldroyd Hyde, Katherine Milhous, Scott O'Dell, Lucy Fitch Perkins, Elizabeth Blake Ripley, Tomi Ungerer, Hendrik Willem Van Loon and Lucille Wallower. *The Checklist of Children's* Books, 1837-1876, published in 1975 and available in limited supply in book form, but also available in microform from the Office of Work with Children, Free Library of Philadelphia, lists all books in Special Collections during this period at date of publication. These special collections supplement the Rosenbach Collection of Early American Children's Books, the American Sunday School Union Collection, the Elisabeth Ball Collection of Hornbooks, and other children's books published prior to 1837, all of which are housed in the Rare Book Department of the Free Library ofPhiladelphia.

PA —HUNT INSTITUTE FOR BOTANICAL DOCUMENTATION, Hunt Botanical Library, Frances Hooper Kate Greenaway Collection, Carnegie-Mellon University, Pittsburgh, 15213. Bernadette G Callery, Librn
Notes: A substantial collection of original watercolors, drawings, published works, and correspondence by artist and illustrator Kate Greenaway (1846-1901).

VA —ARLINGTON COUNTY LIBRARIES, Children's Room, Central Room, 1015 N Quincy St, Arlington, 22201. Caroline Parr, Head
Holdings: Vols (305) Cat
Notes: The Francis and Elizabeth Booth Silver illustrator's collection; outstanding examples of illustration in children's books. Collection was begun in 1962. Incl. framed original illustrations by contemporary illustrators. Anniversary brochure listing holdings was published in 1972. Collection incl early 19th century and contemporary illustrators. Books not available for interlibrary loan. No photocopying.

WA —UNIVERSITY OF WASHINGTON LIBRARIES, Suzzallo Library, Special Collections Division, Rare Book Collection, FM-25, Seattle, 98195. Gary Menges, Coordinator for Special Collections
Notes: Printing history, including early printed books and modern fine printing; book arts, including papermaking, decorated papers, bookbinding, book design, and artist's books; American literature, 19th century includes: Stephen Crane, Ralph Waldo Emerson, Nathaniel Hawthorne, Henry James, Henry Wadsworth Longfellow, Herman Melville, Frank Norris, Harriet Beecher Stowe and Walt Whitman and 20th century includes: Theodore Roethke; illustrated books, including emblem books, historical children's illustration, books illustrated with prints, and artist's books; costume history; voyages and travels; preservation of library materials.

BC —VANCOUVER PUBLIC LIBRARY, Boys & Girls Div, 750 Burrard St, Vancouver, V6Z 1X5, Can.
Holdings: Vols 1000
Notes: The Illustrated Collection. Children's books illustrated by internationally renowned illustrators. It incl examples of some of the best children's books published since 1900. Some books in this collection are catalogued. A shelf list and illustrator index provides additional access.

ILLUSTRATED BOOKS, FRENCH

CT —YALE UNIVERSITY, Beinecke Rare Book & Manuscripts Library, Wall & High St, New Haven, 06520. Louis A Martz, Dir
Notes: Incl the Altschul Collection: The Arts of the French Book, 1838-1967. See *Yale Library Gazette*, October 1969 for description and catalog.

IN —INDIANA UNIVERSITY, Lilly Library, Seventh St, Bloomington, 47405. William R Cagle, Librn
Holdings: Cat
Notes: French illustrated books of the nineteenth and twentieth centuries. including a strong collection of *livres d'artiste*. See *Beyond Illustration: The Livre D'artiste in the Twentieth Century* (Bloomington: The Lilly Library, 1976).

RI —PROVIDENCE PUBLIC LIBRARY, 150 Empire St, Providence, 02903. Lance J Bauer, Special Collections Librn
Holdings: Vols 400 // Cat
Notes: The Wetmore Illustrated Books Collection. This historical collection of more than 400 volumes was given to Providence Public Library in 1955 by Newport, Rhode Island, Collector Edith Wetmore. An extremely fine collection of *livres d'artiste,* examples of fine illustration, printing and bindings. This collection incl the works of such notable artists as William Blake, Pablo Picasso, Giorgio DiChirico, Aubrey Beardsley, Jean Cocteau, William Hogarth, Raoul Dufy, Pierre Bonnard and numerous others. Although especially strong in the French illustrated books, English and German illustrated books are amply represented also. Partially cataloged. Material must be used in-house.

ILLUSTRATED BOOKS, JAPANESE

DC —LIBRARY OF CONGRESS, Asian Division, Washington, 20540.
Notes: Japanese Section. Crosby Stuart Noyes Collection.

ILLUSTRATED CHILDREN'S BOOKS see Illustrated Books, Children'S

ILLUSTRATED FLOWER BOOKS see Flower Books, Illustrated

ILLUSTRATION, MEDICAL see Medical Illustration

ILLUSTRATION, TECHNICAL

NY —VISUAL STUDIES WORKSHOP, Research Center, 31 Prince St, Rochester, 14607. Linn Underhill, Coordr; Robert Bretz, Librn
Holdings: Vols (8000) Cat Pix Slides Audiotapes Videotapes
Notes: Strong emphasis on photography (over 1,000,000 pictures) and the photographic arts in many subject areas incl in this volume. Heavy emphasis on early photographic processes and collections of examples of them. Also collections of individual photographers' works.

NC —TECHNICAL INSTITUTE OF ALAMANCE, Learning Resources Center, Jimmy Kerr Rd, PO Box 623, Haw River, 27258. Ron Plummer, Coordr
Holdings: Vols (465) Cat Slides Filmstrips Microforms
Notes: Commercial art and advertising design--technical illustration.

ILLUSTRATION OF BOOKS

CA —STANFORD UNIVERSITY LIBRARIES, Cecil H Green Library, Stanford, 94305. Michael T Ryan, Cur
Holdings: Vols (12,000) Cat
Notes: The Morgan A & Aline D Gunst Memorial Library. The book arts in every century with some of the best examples. Strong collection of examples of California printers and graphic artists. Complete or nearly complete collections of works by the Kelmscott, Doves, Ashendene, Colt, Grabhorn, and Grabhorn--Hoyem presses.

CO —UNIVERSITY OF COLORADO, Libraries, Special Collections, Boulder, 80309. Nora J Quinlan, Head
Holdings: Vols Uncat
Notes: George Creamer Collection. Over two thousand books on 19th century English literature (Dickens), and 19th and 20th centuries British and American book illustration. In addition, approx 250 children's illustrated books.

DC —LIBRARY OF CONGRESS, Prints & Photographs Div, Washington, 20540.
Notes: The Cabinet of American Illustration contains over 4000 cartoons, cover designs, sketches for posters, and illustrations for magazines, novels, and children's books that were executed chiefly between 1880 and 1910.

†MD —UNIVERSITY OF MARYLAND, Library, R D Remley Collection, College Park, 20742. Donald Farren, Cur Rare Books
Holdings: Vols (2000) Cat
Notes: *Exempla* and secondary works in the areas of typography, calligraphy, book design, book illustration, the history of books, and of publishing, etc. Catalog entries for designers, printing types, private presses, etc.

MA —HARVARD UNIVERSITY LIBRARY, Houghton Library, Printing and Graphic

ILLUSTRATION OF BOOKS (cont.)

Arts Dept, Cambridge, 02138. Eleanor M Garvey, Cur
Notes: Collection incl illustrated books, fine printing, type specimens, illuminated and calligraphic manuscripts, and drawings for book illustration.

NJ —PRINCETON UNIVERSITY, Library, Graphic Arts Collection, Princeton, 08540. Dale Roylance, Cur
Notes: Sinclair Hamilton Collection. One of the largest collections of American Illustrated Books in the US. 2 vols published; catalog available. Also, large collection of illustrated books of all countries, for all periods.

NY —GRADUATE CENTER OF THE CITY UNIVERSITY OF NEW YORK, William H and Gwynne K Crouse Library for Publishing Arts, 33 W 42 St, New York, 10036. Alfred H Lane, Dir
Notes: Recently established and still growing, but intended to become the authoritative source of materials in the field, of particular value in research about the publishing industry. Open to staff members of publishing houses, students, scholars, authors, printers, and booksellers. Primarily 20th century materials, and particularly useful for research on technical, financial, and historical matters. Much on the history of individual houses, economics of authorship; marketing and distribution of books; etc.

ON —NATIONAL LIBRARY OF CANADA, 395 Wellington St, Ottawa, K1A 0N4, Can. Andre Preibish, Dir
Notes: The collection on History and Art of the Book consists of over 10,000 volumes. Areas of concentration are: early imprints, special editions, examples of private presses works, book industry and trade books illustrating the aesthetic and technical aspects of the field, collection of books illustrated by Bartlett.

ILLUSTRATIONS, HUMOROUS see Caricatures and Cartoons

ILLUSTRATORS

DC —GEORGETOWN UNIVERSITY, Library, Special Collections Div, 37 & O Sts NW, Washington, 20057. George M Barringer, Special Collections Librn; Nicholas B Sheetz, Mss Librn
Holdings: Mss
Notes: A collection of letters, documents, original artwork, and books by and about John W Thomason, Jr (1893-1944), a Colonel in the Marines as well as an author and illustrator.

OH —CASE WESTERN RESERVE UNIVERSITY, M A Baxter School of Information and Library Science, 10900 Euclid Ave, Cleveland, 44106. Bettina MacAyeal, Librn; Gretchen Larson, Librn
Holdings: Vols (1100)
Notes: Incl collection of 1100 historical children's books and periodicals, housed in the Special Collections Dept of Freiberger Library, and can be used by the public. Incl *The Holy Bible Abridged* published by Isaiah Thomas in 1786, *The Life and Strange Surprising Adventures of Robinson Crusoe* of 1790, and a *Cinderella* dated 1809. There are examples of the work of illustrators Walter Crane, Randolph Caldecott, Kate Greenaway and Maurice Boutet de Monvel. The periodical collection incl a complete run of St. Nicholas Magazine.

PA —FREE LIBRARY OF PHILADELPHIA, Rare Book Dept, Logan Sq, Philadelphia, 19103. Marie E Korey, Rare Book Librn
Holdings: Cat Mss Pix
Notes: The Grace Clark Haskell Collection, with additions, containing 500 pieces of original art, autograph letters, books and periodicals illustrated by Arthur Rackham.

ILLUSTRATORS, AMERICAN

DC —LIBRARY OF CONGRESS, Prints & Photographs Div, Washington, 20540.
Notes: The Cabinet of American Illustration contains over 4000 cartoons, cover designs, sketches for posters, and illustrations for magazines, novels, and children's books that were executed chiefly between 1880 and 1910.

OR —UNIVERSITY OF OREGON LIBRARY, Special Collections Div, Eugene, 97403. Kenneth W Duckett, Curator
Holdings: Cat Mss
Notes: Over 50 mss collections of artists and illustrators, about half being illustrators primarily for children's books, and two being cartoonists. Collections usually contain some artwork, such as sketchbooks and original illustrations in various mediums, and might also contain personal and professional correspondence, diaries, or mss. Notable illustrators incl Frederic Gruger, Willy Pogany, James Daugherty, Edwin Tunis, John O'Hara Cosgrave, and Robert Riggs.
Publication: Martin Schmitt, comp. *Catalogue of Manuscripts in the University of Oregon Library* (Eugene: University of Oregon Books, 1971).
See also entry under Artists, American; Illustrated Books; Children's Books

PA —FREE LIBRARY OF PHILADELPHIA, Rare Book Dept, Logan Sq, Philadelphia, 19103. Marie E Korey, Rare Book Librn
Holdings: Vols (1000) Cat Mss Pix
Notes: The Thornton Oakley Collection containing 1000 pieces of original art, autograph letters, and books and periodicals, illustrated by Howard Pyle and his students, incl Maxfield Parish, Frank Schoonover, Jessie Wilcox Smith, and N C Wyeth.

TX —TEXAS A&M UNIVERSITY, Sterling C Evans Library, Special Collections Div, College Station, 77843. Donald H Dyal, Librn
Notes: The Western Illustrators Collection is comprised of approximately 3500 illustrated books, pamphlets, and other items. The collection incl illustrated works by Charles Marion Russell, Frederic Sackrider Remington, and other artists of the American West. Numerous other artists of the West and Southwest are represented, many of them contemporary moderns. Quite a lot of the books have additional unique original drawings by the artists.

ILLUSTRATORS, BLACK

NY —NEW YORK PUBLIC LIBRARY, Schomburg Center for Research in Black Culture, 515 Lenox Ave, New York, 10037. Catherine J Lenix Hooker, Interim Administrator
Notes: Research collection of children's books relating to Blacks, by or about Blacks and Black illustrators. Transferred from the James Weldon Johnson Memorial Collection, formerly the Countee Cullen Regional Branch Library.

ILLYRIAN LANGUAGE AND LITERATURE (SLAVIC) see Serbo-Croatian Language and Literature

IMAGINARY ANIMALS see Animal Lore

IMAGINARY BATTLES see Imaginary Wars and Battles

IMAGINARY CITIES see Geographical Myths

IMAGINARY CONVERSATIONS

CA —UNIVERSITY OF CALIFORNIA, LOS ANGELES, Research Library, Dept of Special Collections, 405 Hilgard Ave, Los Angeles, 90024. Edward Shreeves, Chairman, Bibliographers Group; David S Zeidberg, Head
Holdings: Vols 200 Cat
Notes: 150 volumes, based on the Moriz Grolig Collection, mostly in German or French, incl Grolig's ms bibliography of material, 1495-1792.

IMAGINARY IMPRINTS see Imprints (In Books), Fictitious

IMAGINARY ISLANDS see Geographical Myths

IMAGINARY VOYAGES

CA —CLAREMONT COLLEGES, Norman F Sprague Memorial Library, 12 & Dartmouth, Claremont, 91711. David Kuhner, Librn
Holdings: Vols (3500) Cat Mss Pix
Notes: Gift of Mr and Mrs John F B Carruthers. Major concentrations are European and American World War I aeronautical history; strong emphasis on ballooning, and early experiments with real or imaginary flight. Restricted use.

CA —UNIVERSITY OF CALIFORNIA, RIVERSIDE, University Library, 4045 Canyon Crest Dr, Box 5900, Riverside, 92517.
Holdings: Vols (30,000)
Notes: The Eaton Collection of science fiction and fantasy materials, incl 5,600 pulp magazines; also horror, supernatural, and Gothic mystery fiction; boys' books; utopian and dystopian fiction, imaginary voyages, future war and lost race fiction; large holdings in French language science fiction and fantasy; critical and scholarly works pertaining to these genres; videotapes of science fiction/fantasy films and shooting scripts. Collection covers science fiction/fantasy literature from the 16th-17th centuries to the present. Strong individual author collections of Jules Verne, H Rider Haggard, H G Wells, Edgar Rice Burroughs, and Philip K Dick. For a complete description of the collection see: George Slusser, "The J Lloyd Eaton Collection," *Special Collections*, II, 1/2, 25-38 (1983), and*Dictionary Catalog of the J Lloyd Eaton Collection of Science Fiction and Fantasy* Literature (Boston: G K Hall) 1982.

CO —US AIR FORCE ACADEMY, Library, USAF Academy, Colorado Springs, 80840. Reiner H Schaeffer, Dir
Holdings: Vols 6000 Cat Mss Maps Pix
Notes: The Colonel Richard Gimbel Aeronautical History Collection. Incl material from ancient myth to 1903 on manned flight: early scientific works on physical properties of the atmosphere, and imaginative literature on moon voyages. Collection is most complete in manned pioneer balloon ascents (1783ff). Also the Richard Upjohn Light Collection formerly at Culver Military Academy. Separate catalog, index to be published. 250 mss, 100 maps, 2000 pictures, 5000 prints, 7000 clippings.

DC —LIBRARY OF CONGRESS, Rare Book & Special Collections Div, Washington, 20540. William Matheson, Chief
Notes: Late 19th and early 20th century English and American editions of Jules Verne, many with distinctive illustrations and bindings.

IL —NEWBERRY LIBRARY, 60 W Walton St, Chicago, 60610. Diana Haskell, Cur of Modern Mss
Holdings: Cat Maps Pix
Notes: Voyages and travels to 1914, incl imaginary voyages.

IN —INDIANA UNIVERSITY, Lilly Library, Seventh St, Bloomington, 47405. William R Cagle, Librn
Holdings: Vols 230 // Cat
Notes: First and early English editions, Hetzil publications, etc.

MD —UNIVERSITY OF MARYLAND, BALTIMORE COUNTY, Albin O Kuhn Library and Gallery, 5401 Wilkens Ave, Baltimore, 21228. Ann Copeland, Special Collections Librn
Holdings: Vols (4500) Cat Mss Pix Phonorecords
Notes: The Azriel Rosenfeld Science Fiction Research Collection of about 20,000 items incl a developed section of indexes, reference books and criticisms of science fiction makes this a valuable research collection.
See also entry under Science Fiction.

MI —UNIVERSITY OF MICHIGAN, Library, Dept of Rare Books & Special Collections, Ann Arbor, 48109. Robert J Starring, Head
Holdings: Vols 3024 Cat
Notes: Almost half of the Hubbard Collection of Imaginary Voyages consists of various editions, translations, adaptations, and imitations of *Robinson Crusoe.* The works of Jonathan Swift, principally *Gulliver's Travels,* form another large part. The Defoe collection of George Hough was added in 1959.

IMAGINARY VOYAGES (cont.)

PA —PENNSYLVANIA STATE UNIVERSITY, Fred Lewis Pattee Library, Special Collections Dept, University Park, 16802. Charles Mann, Chief, Special Collections
Holdings: Vols 3856 Cat
Budget: ($37,000)
Notes: Fantastic Fiction of all genres. Collection also has 607 paperback volumes. There is also a substantial number of science fiction titles in the general stacks.

RI —BROWN UNIVERSITY, John Carter Brown Library, Providence, 02912. Norman Fiering, Librn; Everett C Wilkie Jr, Bibliographer; Susan Danforth, Cur Maps & Prints
Notes: Spurious, imaginary, visionary, or utopian works dealing with the New World or set in the New World, published before 1835.

IMAGINARY WARS AND BATTLES

CO —COLORADO STATE UNIVERSITY, Libraries, Fort Collins, 80523. John Newman, Special Collections Librn
Holdings: Vols (900) Cat
Notes: The Imaginary Wars Collection incl fictional accounts of future wars, imaginary wars in the past and the greatly altered outcomes of real wars. Stories must depict known societies on Earth or close parallels to known societies. At present, the collection consists primarily of monographs. Future plans call for the identification of appropriate short stories. For an annotated bibliography of American imprints in the collection see John Newman, "America at War: Horror Stories for a Society," *Extrapolation*, XVI, No 1 and 2 (December 1974 and May 1975).

IMAGIST POETRY

IL —UNIVERSITY OF ILLINOIS, URBANA/CHAMPAIGN, Slavic and East European Library, Urbana, 61801. Marianna Tax Choldin, Head
Holdings: Cat Microforms
Notes: IDC microfiche collection. (959) titles of symbolism, futurism, contructivism, acmeism, imagism, and zemstvo publications.

IMAGO (PERIODICAL)

AB —UNIVERSITY OF CALGARY, Libraries, Special Collections Div, 2500 University Dr, Calgary, T2N 1N4, Can.
Notes: Archives of the literary periodicals: *Tish, Imago, Ariel, Descant, Canadian Review Magazine* and *Canadian Short Story* Magazine.

IMBECILITY see Mentally Handicapped

IMBODEN, JOHN DANIEL

VA —UNIVERSITY OF VIRGINIA, Alderman Library, Manuscripts Dept, Charlottesville, 22901. Edmund Berkeley Jr, Cur
Holdings: Cat Mss Maps Pix
Notes: About 1500 collections have material pertaining to the Civil War and particularly to the Army of Northern Virginia and campaigns and battles in Virginia. There are letters, diaries, reminiscences, maps, and pictorial material of Confederate soldiers and civilians, as well as papers of Robert E Lee, J E B Stuart, Thomas L Rosser, Jubal A Early, John Daniel Imboden, William "Extra Billy" Smith, Henry Alexander Wise, Eppa Hunton, and John S Mosby.

IMMACULATE CONCEPTION

OH —UNIVERSITY OF DAYTON, Marian Library, 300 College Park Ave, Dayton, 45469. Rev Theodore Koehler, SM, Dir/Cur
Holdings: Vols (65,000) Cat Mss Pix Slides Phonorecords Audiotapes Filmstrips Microforms
Budget: ($12,000)
Notes: Largest and most comprehensive collections of literature on Virgin Mary in the world. Covers all five centuries of printing. Some 50 languages represented. Incl doctrinal, polemical, popular works, children's books. Catholic and non-Catholic. Especially strong in publications on French shrines (Clugnet collection), on the Immaculate Conception, and materials after 1950. Has Vloberg collection of pictures, ms notes and offprints on Marian iconography. Complete files of major journals in Mariology and partial runs of more than 100 others. Files of 48,000 clippings from domestic and foreign periodicals. 10,000 holy cards from 19th and 20th centuries. 2600 postcard views of shrines. 3000 postcards of Marian art. Philatelic collection of 1000 stamps and 200 first-day covers. 1000 photographs. 300 medals. General reference collection strong inpatristic sources, biblical literature, religious inconography (especially of Eastern Churches), general bibliography, and bibliography of religious orders. Union catalog of Marian holdings in American and other libraries. Library publishes *Marian Library Studies* and *Marian Library* Newsletter. Has had scholars in residence since 1972. Since 1975 recognized as a Pontifical Institute in affiliation with the Marianum in Rome empowered to prepare candidates for pontifical degree with specialization in Marian studies. In 1976 began summer schools in Mariology. History of the Library and description of its holdings in Fackovec, William, S M, "The Marian Library of the University of Dayton," in *Marian Library Studies* (New Series) vol 1 (1969), pp 9-76.

IMMERSION, BAPTISMAL see Baptism

IMMIGRANTS see Emigration and Immigration

IMMIGRATION see Emigration and Immigration

IMMORTALITY

MI —ANDREWS UNIVERSITY, James White Library, Berrien Springs, 49104. Marley H Soper, Dir
Holdings: Cat Microforms
Notes: Belief in immortality of the soul in historical context. This collection of about 1247 items on condition immortality was gathered originally by Dr L E Froom in the preparation of his work *Conditionalist Faith of Our Fathers*, ca 1965-1966. Not available by interlibrary loan, but may be used at this library

IMMUNODEFICIENCY DISEASE

CA —CALIFORNIA STATE POLYTECHNIC UNIVERSITY, POMONA, University Library, 3801 W Temple Ave, Pomona, 91768. Harold Schleiser, Actg Dir
Notes: Among the finest Arabian horse collections in the world. Collector's items and rare books are featured, in addition to the working materials used in tracing pedigrees or in researching specific problems, such as immunodeficiency disease, which is endemic to the Arab breed.
See also entry under Arabian Horses.

IMMUNOLOGY

†CO —NATIONAL JEWISH HOSPITAL AND RESEARCH CENTER-NATIONAL ATHSMA CENTER, Gerald Tucker Memorial Medical Library, 3800 Colfax Ave, Denver, 80206. Helen-Ann Brown, Librn
Holdings: Vols (8500)
Notes: Allergy, asthma, immunology, research in molecular and cellular biology, medicine, tuberculosis and diseases of the chest.

IL —UNIVERSITY OF ILLINOIS, URBANA/CHAMPAIGN, Library, Biology Library, 101 Burrill Hall, 407 S Goodwin, Urbana, 61801. Elisabeth B Davis, Librn
Holdings: Vols (115,000) Cat Microforms
Budget: ($200,000)
Notes: The Biology Library incl books, periodicals, and reference works that cover the fields of anatomy, biophysics, botany, ecology, entomology, genetics, immunology, microbiology, physiology and zoology. About three-quarters of the total collection is made up of journals and other serials representing 2000 distinctive titles. The serial list is comprehensive for the biological sciences, contains most of the major international titles and consists of complete runs for almost all titles. Additional materials (approx 90,000 vols) in the biological sciences are available in the Natural History Survey Library and the bookstacks at the Main Library on the Urbana campus. Professional assistance is available for reference service, online searching, and library instruction. Interlibrary loan service is provided. Photocopying.

MD —US ARMED FORCES RADIOBIOLOGY RESEARCH INSTITUTE, Naval Medical Command, Bethesda, 20014. Nannette M Pope, Head, Library Division
Holdings: Vols (50,000)
Budget: ($150,000)
Notes: Collection consists of monographs, technical reports, serials, and microfiche related to radiation effects on human and animal biology.

MA —UNIVERSITY OF MASSACHUSETTS AT AMHERST, Library, Amherst, 01003. Siegfried Feller, Assoc Dir for Collection Development
Holdings: Cat
Notes: Microbiology, incl bacteriology, immunology, virology, and pathology.

MA —HARVARD MEDICAL SCHOOL, New England Primate Research Center Library, 1 Pine Hill Dr, Southborough, 01772. Sydney Fingold, Librn
Holdings: Vols (4000)

NY —US DEPT OF AGRICULTURE, Agriculture Research Service, Plum Island Animal Disease Laboratory, PO Box 848, Greenport, 11944. Stephen Perlman, Librn
Holdings: Vols (15,000) Cat Pix Slides Microforms
Budget: ($37,000)

NY —NASSAU COUNTY DEPARTMENT OF HEALTH, Division of Laboratories & Research, 209 Main St, Hempstead, 11550. Madeline Burston, Librn; Beatrice R Sewald, Asst Librn
Holdings: Vols (4076) Cat Mss Slides Microforms

OH —CHRIST HOSPITAL INSTITUTE OF MEDICAL RESEARCH, Research Library, 2141 Auburn Ave, Cincinnati, 45219. Lisa L McCormick, Research Librn
Holdings: Vols 16,000
Budget: $36,000

ON —ONTARIO MINISTRY OF HEALTH, Laboratory Services Branch, Library, Box 9000, Terminal A, Toronto, M5W 1R5, Can. Doris A Standing, Librn
Holdings: Vols (4000)
Budget: ($50,000)
Notes: Medical laboratory technology and related subjects: microbiology; environmental bacteriology (limited to testing of milk, food and water for bacterial quality, etc); biological chemistry (clinical); mycology; parasitology; virology; immunology; serology; automated laboratory techniques; biohazard control.

IMMUNOLOGY—HISTORY

MD —UNIVERSITY OF MARYLAND, BALTIMORE COUNTY, Albin O Kuhn Library and Gallery, 5401 Wilkens Ave, Baltimore, 21228. Ann Copeland, Special Collections Librn
Holdings: Vols (3000) Cat
Notes: The Archives of the American Society for Microbiology (ASM) are strong in 20th century English-language immunological and bacteriological works, incl nearly every edition of every major microbiological title published in England and the US. The reprint collection is also excellent, incl significant material published in non-bacteriological journals. The theses are largely European, pre-1900 inaugural

IMMUNOLOGY—HISTORY (cont.)

dissertations. The collection also incl mss, proceedings, memorabilia and correspondence of the Society.

MN —MAYO MEDICAL LIBRARY, History of Medicine Collection, Rochester, 55905. Nancy R Hensel, Librn
Holdings: Vols (18,000) Cat Mss Maps Pix Slides
Notes: The collection consists of over 18,000 vols, 6500 of which are considered source material (rare or reprint editions of classics). 4308 items from Garrison-Morton are available in the collection. Appropriate bibliographies, biographies and histories of medicine are a part of the collection. Fields of collecting interest are anesthesiology, dermatology, cardiology, neurology, immunology and radiology. Eight medical incunabula.

IMPERIAL RUSSIAN SECRET POLICE (OKHRANA)

CA —HOOVER INSTITUTION ON WAR, REVOLUTION & PEACE, Stanford University, Stanford, 94305. Milorad M Drachkovitch, Archivist
Holdings: / / Mss
Notes: Records of the Imperial Russian Secret Police (Okhrana) headquarters in Paris, 1883-1917. Materials incl reports of agents in the field, Paris office reports, dispatches, circulars, studies, correspondence, and other material. 203 ms. box, 10 clipping volumes, 163,802 biographical and reference cards, and 16 boxes of photographs. Unpublished register is available in repository.

IMPERIALISM

MI —UNIVERSITY OF MICHIGAN, Dept of Rare Books & Special Collections, Ann Arbor, 48109. Edward C Weber, Head, Labadie Collection
Holdings: Vols (40,000) Cat Microforms Records Tapes
Notes: Incl 20th-century protest against policies of the Western nations; mostly recent materials.

MN —UNIVERSITY OF MINNESOTA, James Ford Bell Library, 309 19th Ave S, Minneapolis, 55455. John Parker, Cur
Holdings: Vols (11,000) Cat Mss Maps
Notes: Collection of original materials relating to European expansion, 1400-1800.

IMPORTS see Commerce

IMPRINTS (IN BOOKS)

IL —NEWBERRY LIBRARY, John M Wing Foundation on the History of Printing, 60 W Walton St, Chicago, 60610. Diana Haskell, Cur of Modern Mss
Holdings: Vol (30,000) Cat Mss
Budget: ($50,000)
Notes: The collection covers printing and printing history of Western Europe and the Americas from its invention to the present. It is particularly rich in incunabula (about 2000); the works of the great printers, among others Aldus, Bodoni, Baskerville, and Rogers. Printed catalog: *A Dictionary* Catalogue. (Boston: G K Hall, 1961); *Supplements* (1981). Brief descriptions: James M Wells, "The John M Wing Foundation of the Newberry Library," *The Book Collector, VIII,* 2 (Summer 1959), pp 157-162; Lawrece W Towner, *An Uncommon Collection of Uncommon* Collections (Chicago: The Newberry Library, 1977), pp 25-26.

IMPRINTS (IN BOOKS), FICTITIOUS

CA —UNIVERSITY OF CALIFORNIA, LOS ANGELES, Research Library, Dept of Special Collections, 405 Hilgard Ave, Los Angeles, 90024. Edward Shreeves, Chairman, Bibliographers Group; David S Zeidberg, Head
Holdings: Vols 2000

IMPRINTS, CIVIL WAR see U.S. —History—Civil War—Imprints

IMPRINTS, IMAGINARY see Imprints (In Books), Fictitious

IMPROVISATION (MUSIC)

CA —CALIFORNIA INSTITUTE OF THE ARTS, Library, 24700 McBean Pkwy, Valencia, 91355. James Elrod, Dir
Holdings: Vols (61,000) Cat Phonorecords Audiotapes
Budget: ($8500)
Notes: Incl 11,656 audiotapes. Cataloged.

INCANTATIONS

OH —CLEVELAND PUBLIC LIBRARY, Fine Arts and Special Collections Department, 325 Superior Ave, Cleveland, 44114. Alice N Loranth, Head
Holdings: Vols (1600) Cat
Notes: Part of the Witchcraft Collection, which incl witchcraft, magic, sorcery, magical manuals, devil worship, incantations, charms, talismans, amulets and spells. Contemporary urban practices are almost entirely omitted.
See also entry under Witchcraft.

INCAS

PA —UNIVERSITY OF PITTSBURGH, Hillman Library, Pittsburgh, 15260. Glenora E Rossell, Head
Holdings: Vols (172,000) Cat Microforms
Notes: A general collection on Peruvian studies, but particularly strong in the history of the conquest, the discovery, the colonial period, and indian civilizations and cultures. Emphasis also is on contemporary history, politics, sociology, and anthropology.

TX —UNIVERSITY OF TEXAS LIBRARIES, Nettie Lee Benson Latin American Collection, Sid Richardson Hall 1.109, Austin, 78712. Laura Gutierrez-Witt, Head Librn
Holdings: Vols (450,000) Cat Mss Maps Pix Phonorecords Filmstrips Microforms
See also entry under Latin America

†VA —GEORGE C MARSHALL RESEARCH FOUNDATION AND LIBRARY, Drawer 920, Lexington, 24450. Royster Lyle Jr, Cur Collections
Holdings: Vols Uncat Mss
Notes: Examples of ancient writings of Europe, Crete, and Easter Island, and material on the Aztecs, Incas, and particularly the Mayans.

INCE, THOMAS H.

CA —ACADEMY OF MOTION PICTURE ARTS & SCIENCES, Margaret Herrick Library, 8949 Wilshire Blvd, Beverly Hills, 90211. Linda Harris Mehr, Library Administrator
Notes: Stills collection.
See also entry under Moving Pictures.

CA —UNIVERSITY OF CALIFORNIA, LOS ANGELES, Theater Arts Library, Los Angeles, 90024. Edward Shreeves, Chairman, Bibliographers Group; Audree Malkin, Head, Theater Arts Library
Notes: Thomas Ince (producer, director, screenwriter, actor) Collection: portraits, studio photographs, and production stills for 20 Ince productions. Total of 949 stills covering the period 1916-1925.

NY —MUSEUM OF MODERN ART, Dept of Film, 11 W 53 St, New York, 10019. Eileen Bowser, Cur
Holdings: Mss Pix
Notes: Papers, correspondence, scrapbooks, pictures, etc. Partially cataloged.

INCEST

IN —INDIANA UNIVERSITY, Institute for Sex Research Library, 416 Morrison Hall, Bloomington, 47401. Douglas Freeman, Collections and Services Librn; Joan Brewer, Information Services Librn
Holdings: Vols (62,000) Cat Mss Pix Microforms
See also entry under Sex.

INCIDENTAL MUSIC see Music, Incidental

INCIPITS

NY —HISPANIC SOCIETY OF AMERICA, Library, 613 W 155 St, New York, 10032. Martha M de Narvaez, Cur of Mss; Irene S Frye, Asst Librn
Holdings: Vols (150,000) Cat Mss Maps Pix Slides Phonorecords Microforms

INCOME DISTRIBUTION

WI —UNIVERSITY OF WISCONSIN, MADISON, Land Tenure Center Library, 434 Steenbock Memorial Library, 550 Babcock Dr, Madison, 53706. Teresa J Anderson, Librn
Holdings: Vols (60,000) Cat Mss Maps Microforms
Budget: ($65,000)
Notes: Socio-economic aspects of agricultural development in the Third World. All materials in the collection are cataloged and classified. The library has its own catalog.

INCOME TAX

NE —NEBRASKA STATE HISTORICAL SOCIETY, Archives, 1500 R St, Box 82554, Lincoln, 68501. James E Potter, State Archivist
Holdings: Uncat Mss
Notes: Silver and the money question; also material on the Greenback party. Printed speeches and tracts relating to the money question, 1890-1895. Many written by prominent political figures of the day. Also, pamphlets which relate to income tax, tariffs, free trade, soldiers' pensions, railroads, election laws and public lands. Collection of John Davis, Congressman from Kansas, 1891-1895.

INCUNABULA

CA —SAINT JOHN'S SEMINARY, Edward Laurence Doheny Memorial Library, The Estelle Doheny Collection, 5012 E Seminary Rd, Camarillo, 93010. Rita S Faulders, Cur

CA —CLAREMONT COLLEGES, Norman F Sprague Memorial Library, 12 & Dartmouth, Claremont, 91711. David Kuhner, Librn
Notes: President Herbert Hoover's personal collection of rare mining books-about 1000 vols of the 15th-17th centuries.

CA —CLAREMONT COLLEGES, Ella Strong Denison Library, Scripps College, Claremont, 91711. Judy Harvey Sahak, Librn
Holdings: Vols (10,000) Cat Mss Pix
Notes: Emphasizes the history of the book and fine printing; includes illuminated manuscripts, incunabula, fine bindings, representative examples of modern fine presses, first editions, and literary ALS.

CA —CLAREMONT COLLEGES, Honnold Library, Ninth & Dartmouth, Claremont, 91711. Tania Rizzo, Special Collections Dept Head
Holdings: Vols 400 Cat
Notes: Greatest strength of incunabula collection is Italian Renaissance publications. Some uncataloged. Some are listed by Goff.

CA —UNIVERSITY OF CALIFORNIA, SAN DIEGO, Central University Library, Mandeville Dept of Special Collections, La Jolla, 92093. Lynda Corey Claassen, Head
Notes: Incl in the Rare Book Collection.

CA —UNIVERSITY OF CALIFORNIA, LOS ANGELES, Biomedical Library, Center for the Health Sciences, Los Angeles, 90024. Alison Bunting, Acting Biomedical Librn; Victoria Steele, Head, History & Special Collections Div
Holdings: Vols (36,000) Cat Mss Pix Slides Microforms
Notes: Early imprints (approx 13,000 volumes) comprising landmarks in biomedical history, 15th through 19th centuries. Approx 23,000 supporting monographs and serial volumes related to

INCUNABULA (cont.)

the history of medicine, dentistry, nursing, public health and other life sciences. Special historical collections in urology, ophthalmology, neurology, ornithology, mammalogy, Oriental medicine, Nicholas Culpeper, Silas Weir Mitchell, Florence Nightingale, Juan de Valverde (qv). Also, a collection of 19th century German and Austrian medical works (Franklin E Murphy Fund). Rare books for reference use only.

CA —UNIVERSITY OF CALIFORNIA, LOS ANGELES, William Andrews Clark Memorial Library, 2520 Cimarron St, Los Angeles, 90018.
Holdings: Vols 37 / /

CA —SAN DIEGO PUBLIC LIBRARY, Wangenheim Rm, 820 E St, San Diego, 92101. Eileen Boyle, Librn
Holdings: Vols (7500) Cat
Notes: A collection on the history of the book and the development of printing with specimens ranging from Babylonian tablets to cassettes.

CA —UNIVERSITY OF SAN FRANCISCO, Richard A Gleeson Library, The Countess Bernardine Murphy Donohue Rare Book Room, San Francisco, 94117. D Steven Corey, Special Collections Librn
Holdings: Vols 40
Notes: Our holdings of titles in Goff have hot yet been listed. We also have the 5-vol set of incunabula leaves assembled by Konrad Haebler, 1927-28, one of 100 sets with the text in English.

CA —HUNTINGTON LIBRARY, Art Gallery & Botanical Gardens, 1151 Oxford Rd, San Marino, 91108. Robert L Middlekauff, Dir; Daniel H Woodward, Librn
Holdings: Mss Maps Pix Slides Microforms
Notes: See *Incunabula in the Huntington* Library, compiled by Herman Ralph Mead (1937).

CT —TRINITY COLLEGE LIBRARY, Watkinson Library, 300 Summit St, Hartford, 06106. Jeffrey Kaimowitz, Cur
Holdings: Vols 200 Cat

CT —YALE UNIVERSITY, Box 1603A, Yale Station, New Haven, 06520.

DC —DOMINICAN HOUSE OF STUDIES, Dominican College Library, 487 Michigan Ave NE, Washington, 20017. J Raymond Vandegrift, OP, Librn
Holdings: Vols (5000) Cat
Budget: ($1350)
Notes: The Dominican Order (its history, spirituality, government, liturgy), its members (directories, biographies, bibliographies, lives of saints) and works written by Dominicans: incunabula, rare books, dissertations, periodicals (2300 vols), monographs. Incl periodicals either about the Order or edited by Dominicans. Does not incl titles about the congregations of Dominican Sisters. The Library's catalog contains analytics for Dominican contributors to monographs.

DC —GEORGETOWN UNIVERSITY, Library, Special Collections Div, 37 & O Sts NW, Washington, 20057. George M Barringer, Special Collections Librn; Nicholas B Sheetz, Mss Librn
Holdings: Cat

DC —LIBRARY OF CONGRESS, Rare Book & Special Collections Div, Washington, 20540. William Matheson, Chief
Holdings: Vols 5628 Cat
Notes: The Library has more than 5600 incunabula, representing the largest single holding in the Western hemisphere. The bulk of the items are found in the following collections: (1) The Otto H Vollbehr Collection. Purchased by Congress in 1930. The collection numbers 3000 incunabula from all European countries, but chiefly Germany and northern Europe. Contains a perfect vellum copy of the Gutenberg Bible; (2) The John Boyd Thacher Collection of Books, Pamphlets, Broadsides, and Manuscripts is divided into four groups: early Americana and works regarding Christopher Columbus, books and manuscripts relating to the French Revolution, autographs of European notables, and early examples of printing in the Western World, the latter represented by some 904 incunabula (incl 64 duplicates); (3) The original LC collection represents the early holdings of the Library from thenineteenth century to present day, largely increased by purchases in the first quarter of this century. Numbering 602 vols, the collection tends to complement subjects and authors considered important for research already in the Library. (4) The Lessing J Rosenwald Collection, one of the chief treasures of the Library, is largely dedicated to the illustrated book and contains over 570 incunabula representing some of the most notable examples of the early book art, more than one hundred of which are unique in this country; (5) The John Davis Batchelder Collection contains books, magazines, newspapers, manuscripts, bindings, illustrations, and some non-print material, etc, selected to exemplify human activities and institutions from early times to present day. The collection includes 42 incunabula, copies of the 1599 quarto edition of Shakespeare's *Romeo and Juliet* and theFirst Folio edition (1623) of his plays.
Publications: Incunabula holdings are reported in *Incunabula in American Libraries-A Third Census of Fifteenth Century Books Recorded in North American Collections,* comp and ed by Frederick R Goff (NY, 1964) and *Supplement* (NY, 1972). For the incunabula in the Thacher Collection see the Library of Congress published catalog: *The Collection of John Boyd Thacher in the Library of Congress,* vol 1 (Washington, 1915). See also *The Lessing J Rosenwald Collection: A Catalog of the Gifts of Lessing J Rosenwald to the Library of Congress, 1943 to 1975,* 2nd ed, pp 13-111 (Washington, 1978), devoted to incunabula.

FL —FLORIDA STATE UNIVERSITY, Robert Manning Strozier Library, Special Collections Dept, Tallahassee, 32306. Opal M Free, Head, Special Collections
Holdings: Vols (12,254) Cat Mss Maps
Notes: Noncirculating. No photocopying.

GA —EMORY UNIVERSITY, Candler School of Theology, Pitts Theology Library, Atlanta, 30322. Channing Jeschke, Librn; Anita K Delaries, Curator
Holdings: Vols 101 Cat

IL —NEWBERRY LIBRARY, John M Wing Foundation on the History of Printing, 60 W Walton St, Chicago, 60610. Diana Haskell, Cur of Modern Mss
Holdings: Vols (30,000) Cat Mss
Budget: ($50,000)
Notes: The collection covers printing and printing history of Western Europe and the Americas from its invention to the present. It is particularly rich in incunabula (about 2000); the works of the great printers, among others Aldus, Bodoni, Baskerville, and Rogers. Printed catalog: *A Dictionary* Catalogue. (Boston: G K Hall, 1961); *Supplements* (1981). Brief descriptions: James M Wells, "The John M Wing Foundation of the Newberry Library," *The Book Collector, VIII,* 2 (Summer 1959), pp 157-162; Lawrece W Towner, *An Uncommon Collection of Uncommon* Collections (Chicago: The Newberry Library, 1977), pp 25-26.

IL —NORTHWESTERN UNIVERSITY, Library, Special Collections Dept, 1937 Sheridan Rd, Evanston, 60201. R Russell Maylone, Cur
Holdings: Vols 27,000 Cat Mss
Notes: Representative collection with emphasis on the humanities and 19th century English and American literature in first editions. Incl Elzeviers, Aldines, Deism, German classics, Fichte, Gruntig, Ibsen, Kant, Kiekegaard, Mark Twain, Walt Whitman, economic history, Siege and Commune of Paris, 1870-1871, etc. Also rare law books (4000)-- British, European, Roman, Canon, American law; incunabula; Blackstone collection.

IL —QUINCY COLLEGE LIBRARY, Quincy, 62301. Victor Kingery, OFM, Librn
Holdings: Vols (4000)
Notes: Collection of rare books, incl 40 incunabula.

IL —UNIVERSITY OF ILLINOIS, URBANA/CHAMPAIGN, Library, Rare Book Room, 346 Library, Urbana, 61801. Norman B Brown, Asst Dir for Special Collections; N Frederick Nash, Librn
Holdings: Cat Mss Maps Pix Slides Microforms
Notes: Extensive collection, described in: *Catalog of the Rare Book Room,* (Boston: G K Hall, 1972). Supplement (1978).

IN —INDIANA UNIVERSITY, Lilly Library, Seventh St, Bloomington, 47405. William R Cagle, Librn
Holdings: Vols 700 Cat

†IN —UNIVERSITY OF NOTRE DAME, Library, 221 Memorial Library, Notre Dame, 46556.
Notes: The Astrik L Gabriel Collection of incunabula.

IA —LORAS COLLEGE, Wahlert Memorial Library, 14 & Alta Vista, Dubuque, 52001. Robert F Klein, Librn
Holdings: Vols 55 Cat
Notes: Printed catalog available: *Printed Books, 1471-1500.*

KS —BAKER UNIVERSITY, Library, Quayle Rare Bible Collection, Eighth St, Baldwin City, 66006. John Forbes, Dir
Holdings: Vols (600) Cat Mss
Notes: This collection of rare Bibles was given by Bishop William A Quayle (1860-1925), representative collection of books and other writings before advent (in the western world) of printing by moveable type, incunabula, Biblical works since 1501, and a few non-Biblical works since 1500. See *The William Alfred Qualyle Bible Collection: A Descriptive Catalog,* by Margaret Stutzman; also *The William A Quayle Rare Bible Collection: A Self-Guided Tour Manual* (preliminary ed) by Ray Firestone. Persons desiring to visit the collection are advised to make an appointment or phone ahead to Baker University (913-6451 ext 414) to assure that collection is open.

KS —UNIVERSITY OF KANSAS MEDICAL CENTER, College of Health Sciences & Hospital, Clendening History of Medicine Library, Rainbow Blvd at 39th, Kansas City, 66103. Robert P Hudson, Chmn/Cur
Holdings: Vols (15,725) Cat Mss
Notes: Strong in all fields of medical history. Incl incunabula and series. Mss incl Jakob Henie, 1809-1885, papers (ca 4050 items); Howard Atwood Kelly, 1858-1943, correspondence (ca 90 items); Joseph Lister, 1827-1912, letters (7); Florence Nightingale, 1820-1910, letters (20); and Samuel Jay Crumbine, 1862-1954, papers (ca 2365 items).

KS —SAINT MARY COLLEGE, Library, Leavenworth, 66048. Therese Deplazes, Special Collections Librn
See also entry under Bible.

MD —JOHNS HOPKINS UNIVERSITY, Milton S Eisenhower Library, Special Collections, John Work Garrett Library, 4545 N Charles St, Baltimore, 21210. Jane Katz, Garrett Librn
Holdings: Vols 150 Cat

MD —MEDICAL & CHIRURGICAL FACULTY OF THE STATE OF MARYLAND, Library, 1211 Cathedral St, Baltimore, 21201. Joseph E Jensen, Librn
Holdings: Vols (10,000) / / Cat Mss Maps Pix
Notes: The history of medicine and rare medical book collection incl early literature (some medical incunabula), texts, and periodicals (strong in Garrison & Morton items), histories, bibliographies, reprints, lecture notes, health department reports, hospital and physician records, medical society transactions, etc. Materials generally span the 16th through the 19th centuries. Very strong in Early American imprints relating to medicine (Austin items), European medical classics, and 18th and 19th century medical periodicals. Also incl the archives of the Medical and Chirugical Faculty of the State of Maryland, biographical information about Maryland physicians, and much material on the history of Maryland as it relates to medicine. Many items were donations from the collections of Osler, Steiner, Ruhrah, Chatard, Thayer, Welch, etc.

INCUNABULA (cont.)

MD —WALTERS ART GALLERY, Library & Manuscripts & Rare Book Collection, 600 N Charles St, Baltimore, 21201. Muriel L Toppan, Reference Librn; Lilian M C Randall, Cur of Mss & Rare Books
Holdings: Vols (80,000) Cat Mss
Budget: ($35,000)
Notes: The collections supports the gallery's collections of art objects which date from 4000 BC to the end of the 19th century. The collection of medieval and renaissance illuminated mss (782 in number), incunabula (about 1400) and rare books are considered art objects. There are card catalogs providing indexing to the collection. The mss are listed in De Ricci and the incunabula in Goff. Photocopying permitted for Reference Library materials only.

MD —NATIONAL LIBRARY OF MEDICINE, 8600 Rockville Pike, Bethesda, 20209. Harold M Schoolinam, Actg Dir
Holdings: Vols (3,150,000) Cat Mss Audiotapes Videotapes 16mm Films Filmstrips Microforms
Budget: ($46,400)
Notes: The world's largest medical library. Materials are collected exhaustively in some 40 biomedical areas and, to a lesser degree, in related subject areas such as general chemistry, physics, zoology, botany, and instrumentation. Holdings include 82,000 monographic volumes, pre-1871; 438,000 monographic volumes, 1871-present; 714,000 bound serial volumes; 281,000 theses; 172, 000 pamphlets; 1,207,000 manuscripts; 156, 000 microforms; 12,000 audiovisuals; and 75, 000 prints and photographs. Pre-1871 material is in a separate historical collection. Approximately 24,000 serial titles are currenlty received.

MD —UNIVERSITY OF MARYLAND, Library, Rare Book Collection, College Park, 20742. Donald Farren, Assoc Dir for Special Collections
Holdings: Vols (10,000) Cat
Notes: Ranging from incunabula to modern first editions, the Rare Book Collection is particularly strong in materials relating to the history of France and in *exempla* of interest to students of bibliography. Related collections include sizable groups of books and other items relating to the Savoy, to *Expressionismus*, and to Pompeii. Pamphlet collections include many Mazarinades, many pamphlets relating to slavery and abolition, numerous French plays, and press books.

MA —HARVARD UNIVERSITY LIBRARY, Houghton Library, Cambridge, 02138. F Thomas Noonan, Cur, Reading Room; Lawrence Dowler, Associate Librn
Holdings: Cat
Notes: The University Library has more than 3700 volumes printed before 1501, of which most are in the Houghton Library.

MA —SAINT HYACINTH COLLEGE & SEMINARY, Kolbe Memorial Library, 66 School St, Granby, 01033. Brother Christian Katusz, OFM Conv, Librn
Holdings: Uncat

†MA —WILLIAMS COLLEGE, Chapin Library of Rare Books, PO Box 426, Williamstown, 01267. Robert L Volz, Custodian
Holdings: Vols 527 Cat
Notes: No material available on interlibrary loan.

†MA —CLARK UNIVERSITY, Robert Hutchings Goddard Library, Worcester, 01610. Dorothy Mosa Kowski, Rare Books Librn
Holdings: Vols Cat Mss
Notes: Rare books, first editions, mss, incunabula (50), bindings, fore-edge paintings.

MI —UNIVERSITY OF MICHIGAN, Library, Dept of Rare Books & Special Collections, Ann Arbor, 48109. Robert J Starring, Head
Holdings: Vols 439 Cat
Notes: 443 titles in 439 vols. Divided between the Dept of Rare Books and Special Collections and the Medical Center Library. Together with incunables in the Clements and Law libraries, 513 titles in 513 vols available in U of M libraries.

MI —WESTERN MICHIGAN UNIVERSITY, Dwight B Waldo Library, Institute of Cistercian Studies Library, Kalamazoo, 49008. Beatrice H Beck, Librn
Notes: The Abbot Obrecht Collection of mss, incunabula, and other books from the Cistercian Abbey of Gethsemane at Trappist, Kentucky. On indefinite loan (1976).

MN —UNIVERSITY OF MINNESOTA, O Meredith Wilson Library, 309 19 Ave S, Minneapolis, 55455. Austin J McLean, Chief, Special Collections
Holdings: Vols 191 //
Notes: Listed in Goff's census of Incunabula.

MN —MAYO MEDICAL LIBRARY, History of Medicine Collection, Rochester, 55905. Nancy R Hensel, Librn
Holdings: Vols (18,000) Cat Mss Maps Pix Slides
Notes: The collection consists of over 18,000 vols, 6500 of which are considered source material (rare or reprint editions of classics). 4308 items from Garrison-Morton are available in the collection. Appropriate bibliographies, biographies and histories of medicine are a part of the collection. Fields of collecting interest are anesthesiology, dermatology, cardiology, neurology, immunology and radiology. Eight medical incunabula.

MO —CONCEPTION ABBEY, Library, Conception, 64433.
Holdings: Vols (2425)// Uncat Mss Microforms
Budget: ($20,000)
Notes: Rare Roman Catholic theological books and mss, mostly 16th-19th centuries. A partial catalog of the collection exists. Basically this is a donation received in the last quarter of the 19th century from a 900-year-old Swiss abbey, Engleberg Abbey. Most of our mss are listed in De Ricci census. The incunabula are for the most part listed in Goff's census. No photocopying.

MO —SAINT LOUIS PUBLIC LIBRARY, Gardner Rare Book Room, 1301 Olive St, Saint Louis, 63103. Julanne M Good, Supervisor; Martha Riley, Rare Books Librn
Holdings: Vols 1300 Cat Mss
Budget: ($5573)
Notes: Collection of rare materials, 350 specimen leaves and supporting reference materials on history of the book, history of printing, bibliography, book collecting, book and document conservation, papermaking, and bookbinding. The 350 specimen leaves are from illuminated manuscript books and incunabula. Noncirculating.

MO —WASHINGTON UNIVERSITY, School of Medicine, Library, 660 South Euclid Ave, Saint Louis, 63110. Christopher Hoolihan, Rare Book Librn
Holdings: Vols 600 Cat Pix
Budget: $2500
Notes: The Bernard Becker, MD Library of Ophthalmology. Incl first German, French, British, and American works in ophthalmology. Collection ranges from about 300 incunabula to later publications. Printed catalog in preparation; will contain microfiche reproductions of all the title-pages of works in collection. All items cataloged and in OCLC data base.

MO —WASHINGTON UNIVERSITY, John M Olin Library, Campus Box 1061, St Louis, 63130.
Holdings: Vols 54
Notes: Principally in the Philip M Arnold Semeiology Collection and the general rare book collection.

NH —DARTMOUTH COLLEGE, Baker Memorial Library, Hanover, 03755.
Holdings: Vols 170
Notes: Published catalog: *Incunabula in the Dartmouth College Library*, 1980.

NJ —JAMES H JOHNSON MEMORIAL LIBRARY, 670 Popular Ave, Deptford Township, 08096. Lois B Greene, Library Dir
Holdings: Vols 265 Cat Mss
Notes: Antique book collection.

NJ —NEWARK PUBLIC LIBRARY, Art & Music Dept, 5 Washington St, Newark, 07101. William J Dane, Supv
Holdings: Vols (3500) Cat
Notes: R C Jenkinson Collection of Finely Printed Books. Shows the physical form of the book and its development through the centuries. There is always a related exhibit in this section of the library covering such subjects as letter forms, printing, individual presses and publishers, papermaking, etc. Extensive Bruce Rogers collection.

NY —BUFFALO & ERIE COUNTY PUBLIC LIBRARY, Rare Book Room, Lafayette Sq, Buffalo, 14203. William H Loos, Cur
Holdings: Vols 44 Cat
Notes: Collection incl 116 specimen leaves.

NY —CORNING MUSEUM OF GLASS LIBRARY, Corning, 14831. Norma P H Jenkins, Librn
Holdings: Vols (30,000) Cat Slides Videotapes Microforms
Notes: Extensive and comprehensive coverage of the art, archaeology, history and early manufacture of glass, with supporting materials in art, archaeology, and the decorative arts. Collection incl some 1800 manufacturers' trade catalogs on microfiche, 10,000 periodical vols and documents. 130 videotapes, 1000 microforms. Some incunabula. Research library primarily for use on the premises.

NY —GENERAL THEOLOGICAL SEMINARY, Saint Marks Library, 175 Ninth Ave, New York, 10011. David Green, Dir
Holdings: Vols (200,000) Cat Mss Maps Pix Slides Microforms
Notes: Extensive collection.

NY —HISPANIC SOCIETY OF AMERICA, Library, 613 W 155 St, New York, 10032. Martha M de Narvaez, Cur of Mss; Irene S Frye, Asst Librn
Holdings: Vols (150,000) Cat Mss Maps Pix Slides Phonorecords Microforms
Notes: History, art, literature and general culture of the Hispanic countries (where Spanish or Portuguese is spoken). Incl (18, 000) vols printed before 1701, incl (250) incunabula; over (100,000) later vols, plus thousands of periodicals. About (200,000) mss incl ms maps. Printed atlases are in the Book Collection. Some microfilms, chiefly of our early books. Engraved and printed separate maps; reference collection of over 100,000 photographs; slides: all in Department of Iconography, not in library. Catalogs: *Catalogue of the Hispanic Society of America* (Boston: G K Hall, 1962), 10 vols; *First Supplement* (Boston, 1970), 4 vols. Early books: *Printed Books 1468-1700;* Mss: *Catalogo de los Manuscritos Poeticos* Castellanos (15th-17th centuries; 3 vols); *Medieval Manuscripts in the Library; Golden Age Drama Manuscripts*(the latter in press).

NY —NEW YORK ACADEMY OF MEDICINE, Library, 2 E 103 St, New York, 10029. Brett A Kirkpatrick, Librn
Holdings: Vols 139 Cat
Notes: One of the strongest collections of medical literature, the history of medicine, medical classics, public health, and all paramedical subjects.

NY —NEW YORK PUBLIC LIBRARY, Music Div, 111 Amsterdam Ave, New York, 10023. Frank C Campbell, Chief
Notes: Incunabula related to music and music theory.

NY —PIERPONT MORGAN LIBRARY, 29 E 36 St, New York, 10016. Paul Needham, Cur
Notes: One of the largest collections, with many rarities, unique works and mss.

NY —YESHIVA UNIVERSITY, Library, 500 West 185th Street, New York, 10033. Pearl Berger
Notes: Hebrew.

NY —UNIVERSITY OF ROCHESTER, Rush Rhees Library, Department of Rare Books and Special Collections, Rochester, 14627. Peter Dzwonkoski, Librn
Holdings: Cat
Notes: Approx 90.

NY —SYRACUSE UNIVERSITY LIBRARIES, Ernest S Bird Library, George Arents Research Library for Special Collections, Syracuse, 13210. Carolyn A Davis, Manuscripts Librn; Amy S Doherty, University Archivist; Mark F Weimer, Rare Book Librn
Notes: Incl a 2 vol set of 100 original leaves

INCUNABULA (cont.)

from various German incunabula dating from 1468 to 1500.

NC —BELMONT ABBEY COLLEGE, Abbot Vincent Taylor Library, Belmont, 28012. Marjorie McDermott, Dir
Holdings: Vols (10,000) Cat Mss Pix
Notes: Patristics (incl Migne's *Patrologie*), Roman Catholic Church history, philosophy, literature (American and British), and both US and North Carolina history. A substantial number of the books date from the 15th, 16th, and 17th centuries. Most of the source material in Catholic studies particularly could not be obtained elsewhere in the Southeast.

NC —DUKE UNIVERSITY, William R Perkins Library, Rare Book Room, Durham, 27706. John L Sharpe, III, Cur
Holdings: Vols 250
Notes: Ranges from Anton Koberger's 1427 Bible and the 1493 Nuernberg Chronicle to a leaf from the Gutenberg Bible.

OH —HEBREW UNION COLLEGE-JEWISH INSTITUTE OF RELIGION, Klau Library, 3101 Clifton Ave, Cincinnati, 45220. David J Gilner, Reference Librn
Holdings: Cat
Notes: Collection consists of 142 Hebrew and non-Hebrew works. Listed in Marx, Moses. "A Catalogue of Hebrew Books Printed in the 15th Century Now in the Library of the Hebrew Union College," *Studies in Bibliography and Booklore*, 1 (1953-54), pp 21-52; and Marx, Moses, "A Catalogue of Non-Hebrew Books Printed in the 15th Century Now in the Library of Hebrew Union College," *Studies in Bibliography and Booklore*, 5 (1961), pp 62-91.

OH —CLEVELAND MEDICAL LIBRARY ASSOCIATION/CASE WESTERN RESERVE UNIVERSITY, Cleveland Health Sciences Library, Historical Division, Allen Memorial Medical Library, 11000 Euclid Ave, Cleveland, 44106. Glen Jenkins, Rare Book Librarian & Archivist
Holdings: Vols 43 Cat
Notes: Incl Nicolaus Pol Collection of Incunabula; see Max H Fisch, *Nicolaus Pol Doctor 1494* (Bibliography) (New York; Reichner, 1947).

OH —CLEVELAND PUBLIC LIBRARY, Fine Arts and Special Collections Department, 325 Superior Ave, Cleveland, 44114. Alice N Loranth, Head
Holdings: Vols 63 Cat
Notes: Most incunabula in the John G White Collection deal with chess, and history. No photocopying.
See also entry under Rare Books.

OR —OREGON STATE UNIVERSITY, Library, Corvallis, 97331. Melvin George, Dir

OR —UNIVERSITY OF OREGON LIBRARY, Special Collections Div, Eugene, 97403. Kenneth W Duckett, Curator
Holdings: Vols 1000// Cat
Notes: The Edward S Burgess Collection of Rare Books and Manuscripts. Incunabula and early printed books of the 15th and 16th centuries. Incl 13th and 14th century mss. Use restricted to the library.

PA —BRYN MAWR COLLEGE, Canaday Library, Bryn Mawr, 19010. James Tanis, Dir
Notes: Over 1000 incunabula.

PA —COLLEGE OF PHYSICIANS OF PHILADELPHIA, Library, 19 S 22 St, Philadelphia, 19103. Christine Ruggere, Cur, Historical Collections

PA —FREE LIBRARY OF PHILADELPHIA, Rare Book Dept, Logan Sq, Philadelphia, 19103. Marie E Korey, Rare Book Librn
Holdings: Vols 795 Cat
Notes: The Copinger-Widener Collection of incunabula, and additions: a collection representative to the evolution of printing.

PA —PENNSYLVANIA HOSPITAL HISTORICAL LIBRARY, Eighth & Spruce Sts, Philadelphia, 19107. Caroline Morris, Librn
Holdings: Vols (12,963)// Cat Mss
Notes: First medical library in US. Rich in runs of 19th century medical journals. Some early botany books. Some incunabula. Printed catalog was made in 1876. This collection is important because it reflects the history of medicine by the nature of the materials that were acquired. However, *no attempt is made to keep a current history of medicine library.*

PA —UNIVERSITY OF PENNSYLVANIA, Van Pelt Library, Rare Books Collection, 34 & Walnut Sts, Philadelphia, 19104. Daniel Traister, Special Collections Librn
Holdings: Vols 450 Cat
Notes: See (University of Pennsylvania) *Library Chronicle*, Vol 32, no 2, Spring 1966, pp 148-152. Riley, Lyman W "Incunabula at the University of Pennsylvania."

PA —DUQUESNE UNIVERSITY, Library, Pittsburgh, 15282. Dena F Jacobson, Music and Reference Librn
Holdings: Vols 3000 Cat
Notes: Main emphasis of collection is on history of Jewish philosophy in the Middle Ages and relationship between Jewish and Christian scholars; collection incl works by 14th century writer Nicolas de Lyra and general Judaica, history of the Jews, theology, Bible texts and commentaries, literature, grammatical works and dictionaries, etc.

PA —UNIVERSITY OF PITTSBURGH, Hillman Library, Special Collections Dept, Hervey Allen Collection, Pittsburgh, 15260. Charles E Aston, Jr, Coordr
Holdings: Vols 11 Cat
Notes: Incunabula listed in M R Desiderio, *A Census of Incunabula in Pittsburgh* Libraries, University of Pittsburgh, Graduate School of Library and Information Sciences, 1971.

PA —PENNSYLVANIA STATE UNIVERSITY, Fred Lewis Pattee Library, University Park, 16802.
Notes: Placed on deposit at the library by Walter Goldwater, is his extensive collection of incunabula.

RI —BROWN UNIVERSITY, John Hay Library, 20 Prospect St, Providence, 02912. Mark N Brown, Cur Mss
Notes: The Harris Collection of American Poetry & Plays provides a major source for the study of fine printing from the 18th Century through the present. It contains deluxe as well as trade editions, broadsides and ephemera from presses ranging from the well know to the fugitive. The 800 incunables held by Brown University offer a history of the spread of printing in Europe and a foundation in typographical, bibliographical and textual studies of the book.

RI —PROVIDENCE ATHENAEUM, 251 Benefit St, Providence, 02903. Sally Duplaix, Dir
Holdings: (152,000) Vols
Notes: Material available on interlibrary loan under certain conditions.

TX —ROSENBERG LIBRARY, Fox Rare Book Room, 2310 Sealy Ave, Galveston, 77550. Fernando Basilza, Rare Book Librn
Holdings: Vols (2000) Cat Mss Pix
Notes: The Col Milo Pitcher Fox and Agnes Peel Fox Rare Book Room contains 2000 vols incunabula, first printings, and modern fine printing. Incl clay tablets, horn books, parchment material, illuminated books and mss, fine printing (principally 15th-18th centuries), fine binding, fore-edge paintings, etc.

UT —BRIGHAM YOUNG UNIVERSITY, Harold B Lee Library, Unversity Hill, Provo, 84602. Sterling Albrecht, Dir
Holdings: Vols 320 Cat
Notes: The Marco Heidner Collection of representative works of the great printers of the 15th-16th centuries. With additions.

VA —SWEET BRIAR COLLEGE, Library, Sweet Briar, 24595. John Jaffe, Librn
Holdings: Vols (400) Cat
Budget: ($2000)

†WA —WASHINGTON STATE UNIVERSITY, Library, Manuscripts, Archives & Special Collections, Pullman, 99164. John F Guido, Head
Holdings: Cat
Notes: Described in "Incunabula in the Library" by John MacEachern, *The Record* (1959): pp 22-28. Fifty-five incunabula.

WA —UNIVERSITY OF WASHINGTON LIBRARIES, Suzzallo Library, Special Collections Division, Rare Book Collection, FM-25, Seattle, 98195. Gary Menges, Coordinator for Special Collections
Holdings: Vols (12,000) Cat Maps
Notes: American, British, French, German and Italian books printed before 1800, chiefly in the fields of history and literature. Fine bindings and illustrated works are represented. Incl incunabula, emblemata, history of travel, and first editions of the works of major poets: Spencer, Blake, Whitman, Yeats, Roethke, etc.

MB —UNIVERSITY OF MANITOBA, Elizabeth Dafoe Library, Archives and Special Collections Dept, Winnipeg, R3T 2N2, Can. Richard E Bennett, Dept Head; Corrado A Santoro, Reference Archivist
Holdings: // Uncat Mss
Notes: The Dysart Memorial Library collection of rare books representative of the development and the art of book-making and fine printing, with several illuminated mss and examples of the works of famous printers from the 15th century to the present day.

ON —UNIVERSITY OF WESTERN ONTARIO, School of Library and Information Science, Special Collections Room, London, N6A 5B9, Can.
Holdings: Vols 27
Notes: Small collection of mainly post 1476 Italian imprints, incl some leaves.

ON —NATIONAL LIBRARY OF CANADA, 395 Wellington St, Ottawa, K1A 0N4, Can. Andre Preibish, Dir
Holdings: Vols 18,000
Notes: The collection contains 42 incunabula. The core collection consists of early Canadiana (1752-1867) and 16th and 17th century books on Canada. The books printed in native languages are a very valuable part of the collection. Canadian Livres d'Artistes collection of limited editions and Canadian *livres d'artistes* received on legal deposit as well as examples of private press publications from other countries also form part of the Rare Book collection.

ON —UNIVERSITY OF TORONTO, Thomas Fisher Rare Book Library, 120 Saint George St, Toronto, M5S 1A5, Can. Richard G Landon, Head
Notes: Strong collection.

INDECENT EXPOSURE

IN —INDIANA UNIVERSITY, Institute for Sex Research Library, 416 Morrison Hall, Bloomington, 47401. Douglas Freeman, Collections and Services Librn; Joan Brewer, Information Services Librn
Holdings: Vols (62,000) Cat Mss Pix Microforms
See also entry under Sex.

INDEPENDENCE, DECLARATION OF see U.S.—Declaration of Independence

INDEPENDENCE DAY (U.S.) see Fourth of July

INDEPENDENCY (CHURCH POLITY) see Congregationalism

INDEPENDENT VOTERS OF ILLINOIS

IL —CHICAGO HISTORICAL SOCIETY, Library, Clark St at North Ave, Chicago, 60614. Robert L Brubaker, Librn
Holdings: Vols (15,000) Cat Mss Maps Pix Microforms
Notes: Early municipal documents, incl some not in the Municipal Reference Library, and selected later documents; archives of the City Club of Chicago, the Illinois League of Women Voters, Independent Voters of Illinois, and other organizations; papers ofChicago aldermen and other political leaders from Chicago; broadsides concerning political campaigns; ward maps and other publications.

INDETERMINATE ANALYSIS see Diophantine Analysis

INDEX OF CHRISTIAN ART see Princeton Index of Christian Art

INDEXING, AUTOMATIC

CA —INTERNATIONAL BUSINESS MACHINES RESEARCH LIBRARY, 5600 Cottle Rd, San Jose, 95193. Phil Grincewich, Mgr Technical Information
Holdings: Vols (13,5000) Cat
Notes: Incl 21,000 vols of 770 journals. On-line search facility. Vols are divided into three libraries, Technical Research, Technical Information, and Programing. Not open to public.

INDIA

CA —UNIVERSITY OF CALIFORNIA, BERKELEY, University Library, 438 Main Library, Berkeley, 94720. Kenneth R Logan, South Asia Librn
Notes: South Asia collection (India, Pakistan, Bangladesh, Nepal, Sri Lanka) contain 150,000-200,000 titles. Covers at research level the social sciences and humanities in western languages and 20 South Asian languages. Subject areas: history, political science, lanugage and literature (especially strong in Hindi, Urdu, Tamil, Sanskrit and Nepali), art and art history, sociology, education, music, environmental design, philosophy and religion, anthropology, geography, national and local government publications. Formats: monographs, periodicals, newspapers, microforms, maps, sound recordings, video-tapes, pamphlets. Special strengths: modern Hindi literature; history of South Asian countries; government publications of India, late 19th and 20th centuries. Member of South Asia Microform Project; Participant in Library of Congress AcquistionsPrograms for India, Pakistan, Nepal, and Bangladesh.

CT —YALE UNIVERSITY, Box 1603A, Yale Station, New Haven, 06520.

HI —UNIVERSITY OF HAWAII, Library, 2550 The Mall, Honolulu, 96822. Joyce Wright, Head, Asia Collection; Masato Matsu, Head, East Asia Vernacular Collection
Holdings: Vols 75,215 Cat Microforms
Notes: The Asia Collection holds material from and relating to Bangladesh, India, Nepal, Pakistan, and Sri Lanka in western and Asian languages. South Asian languages currently acquired: Bengali, Hindi, Marathi, Nepali, Pali, Prakrit, Sanskrit, Tamil. Period emphasis is post-World War II. Subject emphases: social sciences and humanities (literature, economics, history, religion/philosophy). Holdings are supplemented by a large uncataloged backlog, much of it accessible through the Library of Congress Accessions List for the area and by over 7000 cataloged titles in the main library collection. *South Asian Library Resources in North America: A Survey Prepared for the Boston Conference, 1974*, ed by M L P Patterson (Zug, Switzerland: Tutes Documentation Company, 1975). (Bibliotheca Asiatica 12-), "University of Hawaii," pp 103-114.

IL —CENTER FOR RESEARCH LIBRARIES, 6050 S Kenwood Ave, Chicago, 60637. Donald B Simpson, Dir; Esther Smith, Collection Development Librn
Holdings: Microforms
Notes: Monographs, serials beginning 1969, government documents beginning 1958, received on PL 480. Newspapers and periodicals on microfilm, mostly 1962.

KS —SOUTHWESTERN COLLEGE, Memorial Library, 100 College St, Winfield, 67156. Daniel L Nutter, Librn
Holdings: Vols 1000 Cat
Notes: The Watumull India Collection; also the Fisher India Collection with artifacts from India and a few pieces from China.

MI —UNIVERSITY OF MICHIGAN, Graduate Library, South Asian Dept, Ann Arbor, 48109. Om P Sharma, Librn
Holdings: Vols (365,000) Cat Maps Slides Microforms
Notes: The major emphasis is on social sciences and humanities. Besides materials in classical languages, South Asian vernaculars being retained are Hindi, Bengali, Urdu, Marathi and Tamil; strong in classical languages, especially Sanskrit, Pali, and Prakrit.

MI —MICHIGAN STATE UNIVERSITY, International Library, South and Southeast Asia Collection, East Lansing, 48824. Clinton Lockert, Bibliographer
Holdings: Vols 55,700 Cat Mss Maps Audiotapes Microforms
Notes: Serials and monographs of South Asia received on PL 480 for India, Pakistan, Sri Lanka, and Nepal since 1968. Emphasis in upon Social Sciences, Humanities, and Science. Areas of strength are Anthropology and rural development.

MO —UNIVERSITY OF MISSOURI-COLUMBIA, Ellis Library, Ninth and Lowry, Columbia, 65201. Murari Lal Nagar, Librn
Holdings: Vols 100,000 Maps Microforms
Notes: The South Asia Studies Program at the University of Missouri-Columbia, is an interdepartmental, multi-disciplinary area studies program on India, Pakistan, Bangladesh, Sri Lanka and Nepal. Depository for the PL480 Program of the Library of Congress in many languages from South Asia. There are library resources in Sankskrit, Hindi, Bengali, Panjabi, and Malayalam. The library is particularly strong in Baroda, Bengal and the Punjab.

NY —NEW YORK PUBLIC LIBRARY, Oriental Div, Fifth Ave & 42 St, New York, 10018. E Christian Filstrup, Chief
Holdings: Cat Mss Microforms
Budget: ($56,455)
Notes: Described in *Dictionary Catalog of the Oriental Collection,* The Research Libraries of the New York Public Library, 1960, 16 vols, and *First Supplement,* 1976, 8 vols (144,000 cards). This catalog incl 318, 000 entries for works in about 100 languages of the East, and all works in Western languages on Oriental subjects. The Oriental Collection numbers about 120,000 vols; its Arabic and Indic holdings and those on ancient Egypt and the ancient Near East are among the largest in the US. There is also a collection of 30,000 vols of PL 480 material from Egypt, Pakistan, and India to which there is main entry access, but which is not incorporated into the dictionary catalog. Other outstanding features of the Oriental Collection incl extensive holdings of Japanese technical and scientific periodicals; a unique collection of linguistic works, grammars, anddictionaries; and unusually good coverage of the field of Oriental religions and philosophies. The catalog contains numerous subject references to periodical articles in all languages. All entries are arranged alphabetically according to the Roman alphabet.

NC —DUKE UNIVERSITY, William R Perkins Library, Durham, 27706. Elvin E Strowd, University Librn

OH —CLEVELAND PUBLIC LIBRARY, Fine Arts and Special Collections Department, 325 Superior Ave, Cleveland, 44114. Alice N Loranth, Head
Holdings: Vols 10,000 Cat Mss Maps Microforms
Notes: All aspects of Indian civilization up to the mid-19th century. The more than 5400 vols of Indic language texts and their translations, the rich representation of the various literary languages of India, and the more than 19,000 pages of ms records of the East India Company referring to British Indian affairs (1741-1859) are the strengths of the collection. Important serials, periodicals, ms catalogs, bibliographies. English titles pertaining to modern history, politics, and economics are currently added to the respective departmental collections of the library. See M B Emeneau, *Union List of Printed Indic Texts and Translation in American Libraries* (New Haven, 1935). Separate catalogs of main entries for materials in Indic languages are maintained. *See also* entries under Indic Language and Literature; Oriental Languages and Literatures; Sanskrit Language and Literature.

TX —UNIVERSITY OF TEXAS LIBRARIES, Asian Collection, PO Box P, Austin, 78712. Kevin Lin, Asian Librn; Merry Burlingham, South Asian Librn
Holdings: Vols (58,000) Cat Microforms
Notes: Materials in Hindi, Sanskrit, Urdi, Prakrit, and Pali (aquired chiefly through the Special Foreign Acquisitions Program) and selected English-language materials, incl Indian censuses and district gazetteers and Pakistani censuses.

INDIA—CENSUSES

NC —CAROLINA POPULATION CENTER, Library, University Sq E, Chapel Hill, 27514. Patricia Shipman, Head Librn
Holdings: // Cat
Notes: On microfiche, 1890-1960.

TX —UNIVERSITY OF TEXAS LIBRARIES, Asian Collection, PO Box P, Austin, 78712. Kevin Lin, Asian Librn; Merry Burlingham, South Asian Librn
Holdings: Vols (56,000) Microforms
Notes: Materials in Hindi, Sanskrit, Urdu, Prakrit, and Pali (acquired chiefly through the Special Foreign Acquisitions Program) and selected English-language materials, including Indian censuses and district gazetteers and Pakistani censuses.

INDIA—CIVILIZATION AND CULTURE

IL —FIELD MUSEUM OF NATURAL HISTORY, The Berthold Laufer Library, Roosevelt Rd & Lake Shore Dr, Chicago, 60605. W Peyton Fawcett, Librn
Holdings: Vols (12,000)// Cat Mss Maps
Notes: The part of the museum's collection of Berthold Laufer (1874-1934), Curator of Anthropology, dealing with the peoples of the pre-19th century Chinese Empire (incl Manchuria, Mongolia, Sinkiang and Tibet); their anthropology, art and religion; influences upon their cultures by those of India, Siberia, Japan, Indonesia, and Oceania--and vice versa. Incl about 500 books in Tibetan. About 2/3 of the collection is cataloged.

INDIA—COLONIZATION

IN —INDIANA UNIVERSITY, Lilly Library, Seventh St, Bloomington, 47405. William R Cagle, Librn
Holdings: Cat
Notes: First and early printings of 15th through 17th century. European voyages to the western hemisphere, incl such collections as the *Decades* of Peter Martyr, the *Grands and Petits Voyages* gathered by Debry, and Hakluyt's *Prinicpall Navigations;* travels to the Orient, incl first printed accounts of Marco Polo; the Portuguese in India from the time of the arrival of Vasco da Gama; 18th century voyages by Captain James Cook, Le Comte de Laperouse and others; and the great scientific expeditions of the 18th and 19th centuries.

INDIA—GOVERNMENT PUBLICATIONS

NC —DUKE UNIVERSITY, William R Perkins Library, Durham, 27706. Elvin E Strowd, University Librn

MB —UNIVERSITY OF MANITOBA, Elizabeth Dafoe Library, Government Publications Section, Winnipeg, R3T 2N2, Can. June Dutka, Head
Holdings: Uncat
Notes: Dates from the mid-1960s. Over 4000 items.

INDIA—HISTORY

CA —UNIVERSITY OF CALIFORNIA, LOS ANGELES, Research Library, Indo/Pacific Collection, 405 Hilgard Ave, Los Angeles,

INDIA—HISTORY (cont.)

90024. Edward Shreeves, Chairman, Bibliographers Group; Charlotte Spence, Indo/Pacific Bibliographer
Holdings: Vols Cat Mss Maps Pix Microforms
Notes: The South Asian collection has been developed on two levels. On the research level it focuses on (1) the cultural, economic, political and social history of India from about 1859 to 1947; (2) linguistic and literary studies, with particular emphasis given to Sanskrit and Pali; and (3) the history of the Portuguese experience in South Asia. On the teaching level, materials are collected which relate to India before 1859, and from 1947 to date, as well as materials relating to the other political entities of South Asia. A description of the South Asian collection is included in the May, 1977 issue of *The Librarian,* and in *South Asian Library Resources in North America* (1975).

CA —HOOVER INSTITUTION ON WAR, REVOLUTION & PEACE, Stanford University, Stanford, 94305. Milorad M Drachkovitch, Archivist
Holdings: Mss Pix
Notes: Papers of Robert Norton, US attorney and journalist (editor of China Today), incl correspondence, speeches and writings, clippings, printed matter, photographs, and other materials, 1935-1948, relating to US relations with China and Japan, India's independence from Great Britain, Japanese military incursions into China, and United Nations assistance to China. 3 1/2 ms boxes.

OH —CLEVELAND PUBLIC LIBRARY, Fine Arts and Special Collections Department, 325 Superior Ave, Cleveland, 44114. Alice N Loranth, Head
Holdings: Vols 10,000 Cat Mss Maps Microforms
Notes: All aspects of Indian civilization up to the mid-19th century. The more than 5400 vols of Indic language texts and their translations, the rich representation of the various literary languages of India, and the more than 19,000 pages of ms records of the East India Company referring to British Indian affairs (1741-1859) are the strengths of the collection. Important serials, periodicals, ms catalogs, bibliographies. English titles pertaining to modern history, politics, and economics are currently added to the respective departmental collections of the library. See M B Emeneau, *Union List of Printed Indic Texts and Translation in American Libraries* (New Haven, 1935). Separate catalogs of main entries for materials in Indic languages are maintained. *See also* entries under Indic Language and Literature; Oriental Languages and Literatures; Sanskrit Language and Literature.

WI —UNIVERSITY OF WISCONSIN, MADISON, Memorial Library, South Asian Collection, 728 State St, Madison, 53706. Jack C Wells, Bibliographer
Holdings: Cat Microforms
Notes: Madras history sources. Filmed collections of 112,000 documents (400 reels of positive microfilm) from the Revenue, Public, Judicial, Ecclesiastical, Political, Military, and Financial Departments of the Madras Presidency. Public and private papers of Governors of Madras: George Hay Tweedale (1842-1848); John Elphenstone (1837-1842); William Bentinck (1803-1807), Thomas Munro (1761-1827). District gazetteers and manuals. Survey and settlement reports of selected districts. Administrative reports of the Revenue Department (1892-1926). Madras Native Newspaper Reports (1877-1921). South of India observer, 1864-1887; Madras Times, 1858-61, 1863-69, 1871-77.

INDIA—LANGUAGES AND LITERATURES see Indic Languages and Literatures

INDIA—NATURAL RESOURCES

OH —ANTIOCH COLLEGE, Olive Kettering Library, Livermore St, Yellow Springs, 45387. Nina Myatt, Cur
Notes: Personal papers and correspondence (1920-1975) of Arthur E Morgan former President of Antioch (1920-1936), first director of Ohio's Miami Valley Conservancy District, and first Chairman of the Tennessee Valley Authority (TVA). Mss, film, out-takes, much on the engineering of over 50 water-control projects in this country, Africa, and India. Materials on Edward Bellamy (Morgan wrote biography of Bellamy). Incl family papers. About 175 file boxes.

INDIA—POLITICS AND GOVERNMENT

CA —UNIVERSITY OF CALIFORNIA, BERKELEY, University Library, 438 Main Library, Berkeley, 94720. Kenneth R Logan, South Asia Librn
Notes: South Asia collection (India, Pakistan, Bangladesh, Nepal, Sri Lanka) contain 150,000-200,000 titles. Covers at research level the social sciences and humanities in western languages and 20 South Asian languages. Subject areas: history, political science, lanugage and literature (especially strong in Hindi, Urdu, Tamil, Sanskrit and Nepali), art and art history, sociology, education, music, environmental design, philosophy and religion, anthropology, geography, national and local government publications. Formats: monographs, periodicals, newspapers, microforms, maps, sound recordings, video-tapes, pamphlets. Special strengths: modern Hindi literature; history of South Asian countries; government publications of India, late 19th and 20th centuries. Member of South Asia Microform Project; Participant in Library of Congress AcquisitionsPrograms for India, Pakistan, Nepal, and Bangladesh.

NY —UNIVERSITY OF ROCHESTER, Rush Rhees Library, Rochester, 14627. Datta S Kharbas, Head
Holdings: Vols 100,000 Cat Maps Microforms
Notes: Area studies collection on East Asia and South Asia. Major emphasis is on social sciences and humanities. Over 57,000 volumes on East Asia, out of which 29,000 volumes are in Chinese and 15,000 in Japanese. Extensive holdings on Chinese and Japanese histories. Catalog of East Asian collection consisting of Chinese and Japanese language holdings published in 1968, with two subsequent supplements. Over 33,000 volumes on South Asia. Considerable depth in social sciences, history, politics and anthropology. Extensive holdings in Sanskrit, Hindi, and Marathi.

NC —DUKE UNIVERSITY, William R Perkins Library, Durham, 27706. Elvin E Strowd, University Librn

INDIA—POPULATION

NC —CAROLINA POPULATION CENTER, Library, University Sq E, Chapel Hill, 27514. Patricia Shipman, Head Librn
Holdings: Vols (20,000) Cat
Budget: ($10,500)
Notes: Try to acquire everything published in English on population, with particular emphasis on the US and developing countries. Also acquire conference proceedings, seminar papers. These and journal articles are indexed and the analytics are incl in the catalog. Incl 13,000 reprints and other pieces of ephemera. Most extensive area files are on India, Africa, Thailand, Iran, Korea, and Latin America. Holdings are recorded on an automated data base. A microfiche catalog is available for use in the Library and for purchase. Access by subject & geographic area are available through the Library's own thesaurus-based indexing systems.

INDIA—SOCIAL LIFE AND CUSTOMS

CA —UNIVERSITY OF CALIFORNIA, BERKELEY, University Library, 438 Main Library, Berkeley, 94720. Kenneth R Logan, South Asia Librn
Notes: South Asia collection (India, Pakistan, Bangladesh, Nepal, Sri Lanka) contain 150,000-200,000 titles. Covers at research level the social sciences and humanities in western languages and 20 South Asian languages. Subject areas: history, political science, lanugage and literature (especially strong in Hindi, Urdu, Tamil, Sanskrit and Nepali), art and art history, sociology, education, music, environmental design, philosophy and religion, anthropology, geography, national and local government publications. Formats: monographs, periodicals, newspapers, microforms, maps, sound recordings, video-tapes, pamphlets. Special strengths: modern Hindi literature; history of South Asian countries; government publications of India, late 19th and 20th centuries. Member of South Asia Microform Project; Participant in Library of Congress AcquisitionsPrograms for India, Pakistan, Nepal, and Bangladesh.

NC —DUKE UNIVERSITY, William R Perkins Library, Durham, 27706. Elvin E Strowd, University Librn

INDIA, PORTUGUESE see Goa

INDIA LANGUAGES AND LITERATURES see Indic Languages and Literatures

INDIA RUBBER INDUSTRY see Rubber Industry and Trade

INDIAN CAPTIVITIES

IL —NEWBERRY LIBRARY, 60 W Walton St, Chicago, 60610. Diana Haskell, Cur of Modern Mss
Holdings: Cat Mss
Notes: The Ayer Collection. One of the most extensive collections extant.

MA —NEW ENGLAND HISTORIC GENEALOGICAL SOCIETY, Library, 101 Newbury St, Boston, 02116. Ralph J Crandell, Dir
Holdings: Vols (250,000) Mss Maps Microforms Pix
Notes: New England genealogy. Especially strong Massachusetts, Maine, and New Hampshire, although all states are well represented, as are the relevancies of each subject listed in this volume with regard to British antecedent and contemporary history. Special strengths in local history and biography, obituaries, etc, incl parish registers, censuses, British and American. 3125 linear ft of mss.

NY —NEW YORK STATE LIBRARY, State Education Bldg Annex, Washington Ave, Albany, 12224.
Holdings: Vols (110,500) Cat
Notes: Strong collection emphasis on North American Indians, especially Indians of New York. Incl books and pamphlets on Indian captivities, treaties, conferences, lives of noted Indians, laws. Bible and catechisms, prayerbooks, grammars, etc in native languages. Outstanding collection on Iroquois Indians. Incl original treaties between the State of New York and the Iroquois, papers of Cornplanter, drawings by Jesse Cornplanter.

NY —NEW YORK HISTORICAL SOCIETY, Library, 170 Central Park W, New York, 10024. James Gregory, Librn
Holdings: Mss
Notes: Incl original mss, illustrative materials, etc.

NY —UNIVERSITY OF ROCHESTER, Rush Rhees Library, Department of Rare Books and Special Collections, Rochester, 14627. Peter Dzwonkoski, Librn

RI —BROWN UNIVERSITY, John Hay Library, 20 Prospect St, Providence, 02912. Mark N Brown, Cur Mss
Notes: Eberstadt Collection of Narratives of California Pioneers--personal narratives written by pioneers who crossed the Plains to California after the discovery of gold in 1849. A large portion of the books were printed in late 19th and early 20th centuries and deal with: Indian contacts, captivities,

INDIAN CAPTIVITIES (cont.)

frontier lore, travel routes, topography, fauna and flora, outlaws, traders and trappers, and frontier army life.

TX —AMARILLO PUBLIC LIBRARY, 413 E Fourth, Amarillo, 79101. Mary Kay Snell, Librn
Holdings: Vols Cat Mss Maps Pix
Notes: The southwest collections incl materials on the history of Texas, Louisiana, New Mexico, Arkansas, Missouri and Kansas. General subjects covered incl overland journeys, early narratives, early biographies, Indian captivities, outlaws, US government reports, Mississippi and Ohio Rivers, the Mexican War, reports of Catholic missionaries, Niles Register, early publications, fur trade, western trails, Texas Rangers, sheriffs and Texas as a sovereign state, buffalo hunting, Indian wars, cowboys, the arrival of farmers, fences, and towns. Over 1600 items which incl books, documents, maps, mss, pamphlets, unpublished theses, interviews and photographs. The three major collections are the William Henry Bush Collection, the Laurence J Fitzsimon Collection and the Calendar of John L McCarty.

INDIAN LANGUAGES see Indic Languages and Literatures

INDIAN TERRITORY

OK —FIVE CIVILIZED TRIBES MUSEUM, Library, Agency Hill, Honor Hts Dr, Muskogee, 74401. Mrs Spencer Denton, Dir
Holdings: Maps Pix
Notes: The collection pertains to the history, culture, and traditions of the Five Civilized Tribes plus history of Indian Territory prior to statehood.

INDIAN TERRITORY—IMPRINTS

OK —UNIVERSITY OF TULSA, McFarlin Library, Dept of Rare Books and Special Collections, 600 S College, Tulsa, 74104. David Farmer, Dir; Toby Murray, Archivist; Caroline Swinson, Cur of Manuscripts & Art
Holdings: Cat
Notes: The Indian collection of John W Shleppey. Indian materials of some 6000 bibliographic items, excl of mss and photographs. Emphasis on Indian Territory imprints, laws, Cherokee and Choctaw tribes, etc.

INDIANA

IN —INDIANA STATE UNIVERSITY, EVANSVILLE, Library, 8600 University Blvd, Evansville, 47712. Gina R Walker, Acting Archivist
Holdings: Vols 50 Cat Mss Pix Slides Audiotapes
Notes: Daily radio programs broadcast (1949-1954) over several Evansville, Indiana, stations concerning activities of the local United Electrical and Radio and Machine Workers of America union; other local union news; state, national, and international events; editorial commentary. Prepared and presented by Sadelle Berger, community leader. 4 document cases. Also materials collected during year-long Indiana Labor History Project. Oral history interviews, photographs, slides, brochures, newspaper clippings.

IN —FRANKLIN COLLEGE OF INDIANA, Library, Special Collections Dept, Franklin, 46131. Mary Alice Medlicott, Cur
Holdings: Vols (12,000) Cat Mss Maps Pix
Budget: ($151,189)
Notes: David Demaree Banta Indiana Collection. Contains material relating to the area which became the Northwest Territory, the State of Indiana, its official publications; description, incl county and city histories, atlases and biographies; literary and scientific works of Hoosier authors. Printed catalog of collection available on request. Third edition of catalog is completed in manuscript.

IN —HAMMOND PUBLIC LIBRARY, 564 State St, Hammond, 46320. Kathryn Fhegze, Librn
Holdings: Vols 400 Cat Mss Maps Pix Slides Audiotapes Microforms
Budget: $1000
Notes: Hammond, Indiana, and the Calumet region.

IN —INDIANA HISTORICAL SOCIETY, Library, 315 W Ohio St, Indianapolis, 46202. Robert K O'Neill, Dir
Holdings: Vols (12,000) Cat Mss Maps Pix Slides Microforms
Notes: Incl rare books, mss, pictures, maps, and ephemera relating to the history of Indiana and the Old Northwest. Manuscripts dealing with the Old Northwest, incl a large collection of William Henry Harrison materials; papers of leading nineteenth-century Indiana figures; letters of Civil War soldiers; records of 20th century social welfare organizations. Rare book collection incl Jesuit *Relations*, early travel accounts, and early Indiana imprints. Pictures include Indiana small-town life; Monon Railroad Collection; Callis Steamboat Collection; Bretzman Collection, dealing with Indianapolis; and the Ken Martin Collection, dealing with Terre Haute. Maps incl 18th century maps of North America; 19th century maps of Indiana; Sanborn real estate atlases for Indianapolis. Special collections in Indiana black, ethnic, and architectural history.

IN —INDIANA STATE LIBRARY, Indiana Div, 140 N Senate Ave, Indianapolis, 46204. Robert Logsdon, Acting Head
Holdings: Vols (60,541)
Budget: ($242,431)
Notes: Incl books, pamphlets (50,564), mss (3,000,000), microfilm (1641 reels), photographs (5000), records (37), audiotapes (22), films (107), slides (55 sets), maps (10, 160), VF (37), broadsides (920), newspapers (10,000 bound and wrapped files and 43,000 reels of microfilm). Collects information and materials both current and historical, about Indiana. Separate catalog for printed materials, separate indexes for mss, Indianapolis newspapers and pictures. Other indexes for smaller collections and special subjects.

IN —MUNCIE PUBLIC LIBRARY, 301 E Jackson St, Muncie, 47305. Arthur S Meyers, Librn
Holdings: Vols 1100 Cat
Notes: Mary Hough Goddard Memorial Reference Collection of Indiana Authors established in 1904. Collection contains material both by and about Indiana authors. It attempts to be representative rather than inclusive. Some vols are autographed, some are first editions. The collection is kept in a separate room and is noncirculating. Seperate shelf list and accession book.

IN —TIPTON COUNTY PUBLIC LIBRARY, 127 E Madison St, Tipton, 46072. Jean Parks, Ref Librn
Holdings: Vols (1200) Cat Maps Pix Microforms

INDIANA—DESCRIPTION AND TRAVEL

IN —INDIANA HISTORICAL SOCIETY, Library, 315 W Ohio St, Indianapolis, 46202. Robert K O'Neill, Dir
Holdings: Vols Cat Maps
Notes: A collection of 17th - 19th century maps and travel accounts covering the region which is now the Midwest.

INDIANA—DESCRIPTION AND TRAVEL—VIEWS

IN —INDIANA STATE UNIVERSITY, EVANSVILLE, Library, 8600 University Blvd, Evansville, 47712. Gina R Walker, Acting Archivist
Holdings: // Cat Pix Slides
Notes: Collection of photographs, negatives and slides by John Waring Doane (1915-1972), Mt Vernon, Indiana, photographer. Also a group of glass negatives taken by earlier photographers; people, places, and events of Posey County and Evansville, Indiana. 1900-1972. Unpublished index.

INDIANA—GENEALOGY

FL —ORLANDO PUBLIC LIBRARY, Local History & Genealogy Dept, 100 Block of Central Ave, Orlando, 32806. Eileen B Willis, Librn
Holdings: Vols 11,000 Cat Maps Microforms
Budget: $8000
Notes: Genealogy collection on Md, Del, W Va, NC, SC, Ala, Miss, La, Texas, Ark, Ky, Ohio, Ill, Ind, and Mich are well represented. Most other states are covered by smaller collections.
See also entry under Genealogy - Collections.

IN —MONROE COUNTY PUBLIC LIBRARY, 303 E Kirkwood, Bloomington, 47401. Roberta Taylor, Indiana Room Librn
Holdings: Vols 1900 Cat Mss Maps Pix Microforms
Budget: $2500
Notes: The Indiana Collection also contains the following types of materials: books by and about Indiana authors, books and clippings about famous Indiana people, large vertical file containing clippings about state and local activities, Indiana magazines, and Monroe County on microfilm back to 1824. Indiana Federal Census Records on microfilm 1820-1910 (complete through 1850 for all counties, not complete thereafter except for Monroe County). Many Monroe County records of genealogical interest on microfilm and indexed. Special collections of oral histories, city directories, government documents, old atlases, photographs and slides (color transparencies), and historic preservation materials.

IN —WILLARD LIBRARY, 21 First Ave, Evansville, 47710. Joan Elliott, Special Collections Librn
Holdings: Vols (1000) Cat Mss Microforms
Budget: ($4000)
Notes: General genealogy collection emphasizing data concerning 35 counties of southwest Indiana, southeast Illinois, and western Kentucky. Written description available.

IN —ALLEN COUNTY PUBLIC LIBRARY, Fred J Reynolds Historical Genealogy Collection, 900 Webster St, Fort Wayne, 46802. Rick J Ashton, Dir; Michael B Clegg, Manager
Holdings: Vols 200,000 Cat Mss Maps Pix Microforms
Notes: Incl state, county, regional, town and church histories. All census schedules and port of entry records released by the federal government are in the microfilm collection of 40,000 reels. The collection contains parish registers and publications of British parish register societies. Canadian, English, Scotch, Irish and Welsh records are well represented. The heraldry collection is housed with the genealogy collection. Allen County Public Library is and has been the depository for the North American Association of Directory Publishers since 1964.

IN —INDIANA STATE LIBRARY, Genealogy Div, 140 N Senate Ave, Indianapolis, 46204. William O Harris, Head
Holdings: Vols (70,000) Cat Mss Maps Microforms
Notes: The largest collection of Indiana county archival material in existence. Microfilm of courthouse records through 1920 available now for many Indiana counties. Records for all.

IN —HENRY HISTORICAL SOCIETY MUSEUM, 608 S 14 St, New Castle, 47362. Evelyn S Clift, Cur
Holdings: Vols 600 Maps Pix Audiotapes
Notes: Genealogy, primarily of Henry County, Indiana. Incl family records and 19th century newspaper clippings. Cataloging in process.

IN —JENNINGS COUNTY PUBLIC LIBRARY, 143 E Walnut St, North Vernon, 47265. Helen Horstman, Genealogy & Local History Librn
Holdings: Vols (700) Cat Mss Pix Audiotapes
Budget: ($300)
Notes: Incl family histories, scrapbooks,

INDIANA—GENEALOGY (cont.)

diaries, bible records, newspapers, atlases, platbooks, and cemetery records.

IN —WAYNE COUNTY HISTORICAL MUSEUM, Library, 1150 N A St, Richmond, 47374. Don Goodwell, Dir
Holdings: Vols (1000) Cat Mss Maps Pix Slides Phonorecords Audiotapes 16mm Films Microforms
Notes: Local history and genealogy of Wayne County, Indiana.

IN —SOUTH BEND PUBLIC LIBRARY, Local History Dept, 122 W Wayne, South Bend, 46624.
Holdings: Vols (1317) Cat Pix Microforms
Notes: Basic genealogy, with emphasis on Indiana, espec St Joseph County. Some materials are on loan from the local DAR chapter necrology file from 1838 to 1868 and 1936 to date; back-dating this service are notes concerning local individuals in service listing of local Civil War veterans, city directories, surname index, family name index.

INDIANA—HISTORY

IL —DE PAUL UNIVERSITY, College of Law Library, 25 E Jackson Blvd, Chicago, 60604. Judith G Gecas, Dir
Holdings: (300) Cat
Notes: Territorial laws: Northwest Territory; Indiana territory; Illinois Territory. "Farthing Collection of Illinois Statutory Laws." *33 Chicago Bar Record*, pp 451-454 (1952).

IL —UNIVERSITY OF CHICAGO LIBRARY, Dept of Special Collections, 1100 E 57 St, Chicago, 60637.
Notes: Personal papers of William H English relating to Indiana history.

IN —INDIANA UNIVERSITY, Lilly Library, Seventh St, Bloomington, 47405. William R Cagle, Librn
Holdings: Cat Mss Maps Pix
Notes: Business papers and correspondence of Howard Ship Yards & Dock Co, Jeffersonville, Ind, 1834-1942. Incl correspondence with captains, ship owners. Howard family members, etc; some photos of Howard-built ships during construction; ca 10,000 blueprints, drawings and scale specifications for riverboat constructions; business ledgers and cash books; general office files. 265,600 items. Also, early description and travel; county histories. Mss incl some early church records, business files, papers of Indiana cultural, political, and social leaders. Emphasis is late 19th through 20th century.

IN —MONROE COUNTY PUBLIC LIBRARY, 303 E Kirkwood, Bloomington, 47401. Roberta Taylor, Indiana Room Librn
Holdings: Vols 1900 Cat Mss Maps Pix Microforms
Budget: $2500
Notes: The Indiana Collection also contains the following types of materials: books by and about Indiana authors, books and clippings about famous Indiana people, large vertical file containing clippings about state and local activities, Indiana magazines, and Monroe County on microfilm back to 1824. Indiana Federal Census Records on microfilm 1820-1910 (complete through 1850 for all counties, not complete thereafter except for Monroe County). Many Monroe County records of genealogical interest on microfilm and indexed. Special collections of oral histories, city directories, government documents, old atlases, photographs and slides (color transparencies), and historic preservation materials.

IN —INDIANA STATE UNIVERSITY, EVANSVILLE, Library, 8600 University Blvd, Evansville, 47712. Gina R Walker, Acting Archivist
Holdings: Vols (3000) Cat Mss Maps Pix Audiotapes
Notes: Restricted use: some items available on interilibrary loan. Incl oral history interviews (32 cat cassettes) of Evansville, Indiana natives. These interviews were used in a slide-tape presentation entitled, "Growing Up in Evansville."

IN —WILLARD LIBRARY, 21 First Ave, Evansville, 47710. Joan Elliott, Special Collections Librn
Holdings: Vols (800) Cat Mss Maps Pix Microforms
Budget: ($4000)
Notes: General local history; collection, incl books, pamphlets, mss and documents relating to the histories of Evansville and Vanderburgh and surrounding counties, with considerable material on Indiana as a whole Incl extensive collection of German-language newspapers published in Evansville, 1850-1918.

IN —FRANKLIN COLLEGE OF INDIANA, Library, Special Collections Dept, Franklin, 46131. Mary Alice Medlicott, Cur
Holdings: Vols (12,000) Cat Mss Maps Pix
Budget: ($151,189)
Notes: David Demaree Banta Indiana Collection. Contains material relating to the area which became the Northwest Territory, the State of Indiana, its official publications; description, incl county and city histories, atlases and biographies; literary and scientific works of Hoosier authors. Printed catalog of collection available on request. Third edition of catalog is completed in manuscript.

IN —GARY PUBLIC LIBRARY, 220 W Fifth Ave, Gary, 46402. Lyle Warrick, Local History Librn
Holdings: Vols 6000 Cat Maps Pix Slides Audiotapes Microforms
Budget: $850
Notes: Emphasis on Gary local history, plus some Lake County, Calumet region, and Indiana. In main card catalog plus duplicate in Indiana Room. *Old WPA newspaper index, 1907-1939.* Continuation of subject index to local daily newspaper. The *Post-Tribune* begun by WPA workers and maintained by library staff to date, with hiatus during World War II years.

IN —DEPAUW UNIVERSITY, Roy O West Library, University Archives, PO Box 137, Greencastle, 46135. Virginia C Brann, Sr Archives Asst
Holdings: Vols (2000) Cat Mss Maps Pix Slides Microforms
Notes: Archives of DePauw University and Indiana United Methodism. *Select Bibliographic Guide* available upon request.

IN —HAMMOND PUBLIC LIBRARY, 564 State St, Hammond, 46320. Kathryn Fhegze, Librn
Holdings: Vols 400 Cat Mss Maps Pix Slides Audiotapes Microforms
Budget: $1000
Notes: Hammond, Indiana, and the Calumet region.

IN —HUNTINGTON PUBLIC LIBRARY, 50 E Park Dr, Huntington, 46750. C Kathryn Holst, Head Librn
Holdings: Vols 800 Cat Pix Microforms

IN —INDIANA HISTORICAL SOCIETY, Library, 315 W Ohio St, Indianapolis, 46202. Robert K O'Neill, Dir
Holdings: Vols (12,000) Cat Mss Maps Pix Slides Microforms
Notes: Incl rare books, mss, pictures, maps, and ephemera relating to the history of Indiana and the Old Northwest. Manuscripts dealing with the Old Northwest, incl a large collection of William Henry Harrison materials; papers of leading nineteenth-century Indiana figures; letters of Civil War soldiers; records of 20th century social welfare organizations. Rare book collection incl Jesuit *Relations*, early travel accounts, and early Indiana imprints. Pictures include Indiana small-town life; Monon Railroad Collection; Callis Steamboat Collection; Bretzman Collection, dealing with Indianapolis; and the Ken Martin Collection, dealing with Terre Haute. Maps incl 18th century maps of North America; 19th century maps of Indiana; Sanborn real estate atlases for Indianapolis. Special collections in Indiana black, ethnic, and architectural history.

IN —INDIANA MEDICAL HISTORY MUSEUM, Old Pathology Bldg, 3000 W Washington St, Indianapolis, 46222. Katherine Mandusic McDonell, Cur
Budget: ($24,000)
Notes: Over 1000 volumes of mid-to-late 19th century medical works; bound volumes of the proceedings of Indiana State Medical Society (1857-1907); 100 volumes pertaining to the history of medicine; 50 volumes pertaining to museum studies; approximately 200 prints, paintings, and photographs relating to history of medicine in Indiana; early medical school diplomas; vertical files on history of medicine; materials (printed and manuscripts) pertaining to state's first mental hosptial-Central State Hospital.

IN —INDIANAPOLIS NEWSPAPERS, Library, 307 N Penn St, Indianapolis, 46206. Sandra Fitzgerald, Librn
Holdings: Vols (1200) Cat
Notes: No space or personnel to serve the public, but will give the name of the newspaper, page, and column number for specific information. Patron can then use the microfilm copy of the *Indianapolis News* (evening paper) at the public library. Index (not published) to *News*, 1912-1947; *Star*, 1929-1947; both, 1948-date.

IN —INDIANA STATE LIBRARY, Indiana Div, 140 N Senate Ave, Indianapolis, 46204. Robert Logsdon, Acting Head
Holdings: Vols (60,541)
Budget: ($242,431)
Notes: Incl books, pamphlets (50,564), mss (3,000,000), microfilm (1641 reels), photographs (5000), records (37), audiotapes (22), films (107), slides (55 sets), maps (10, 160), VF (37), broadsides (920), newspapers (10,000 bound and wrapped files and 43,000 reels of microfilm). Collects information and materials both current and historical, about Indiana. Separate catalog for printed materials, separate indexes for mss, Indianapolis newspapers and pictures. Other indexes for smaller collections and special subjects.

IN —BALL STATE UNIVERSITY, University Libraries, Special Collections Dept, University Ave, Muncie, 47306. David C Tambo, Head of Special Collections
Holdings: Mss Maps Pix Audiotapes Videotapes Slides Microforms Film
Notes: Incl one half million feet of film. Center for Middletown Studies holdings include materials by Robert and Helen Lynd, Middletown III Project and Peter Davis' Middletown Film Project. Also Stoeckel Archives holdings incl primarily Delaware County, Indiana family, organization and local government records.

IN —NEW CASTLE-HENRY COUNTY PUBLIC LIBRARY, 376 S 15 St, PO Box J, New Castle, 47362. Marjorie J Johnson, Library Dir
Holdings: Vols 165,000 Cat Maps Pix Slides
Notes: Emphasis on Henry County and New Castle.

IN —JENNINGS COUNTY PUBLIC LIBRARY, 143 E Walnut St, North Vernon, 47265. Helen Horstman, Genealogy & Local History Librn
Holdings: Vols (700) Cat Mss Maps Pix Audiotapes
Budget: ($300)
Notes: Incl family histories, scrapbooks, diaries, bible records, newspapers, atlases, platbooks, and cemetery records.

IN —WAYNE COUNTY HISTORICAL MUSEUM, Library, 1150 N A St, Richmond, 47374. Don Goodwell, Dir
Holdings: Vols (1000) Cat Mss Maps Pix Slides Phonorecords Audiotapes 16mm Films Microforms
Notes: Local history and genealogy of Wayne County, Indiana.

IN —SOUTH BEND PUBLIC LIBRARY, Local History Dept, 122 W Wayne, South Bend, 46624.
Holdings: Vols (5900) Cat Maps Pix Microforms
Notes: Indiana, with emphasis on St Joseph County and South Bend. Collection incl material on the Studebaker family and plant.

IN —INDIANA STATE UNIVERSITY, Cunningham Memorial Library, Dept of Rare Books & Special Collections, Terre Haute, 47809. Lawrence J McCrank, Head
Holdings: Vols (2800) Cat Maps
Budget: ($1500)
Notes: The Indiana collection covers entire state with special emphasis on Terre Haute

INDIANA—HISTORY (cont.)

and the Wabash Valley in the following categories: first or special limited editions of major writers associated with Indiana for a significant portion of their productive lives; publications of private presses in Indiana; early Indiana imprints; other materials pertinent to Indiana, eg diaries, broadsides, early travel literature, etc; county, local and regional histories-chiefly 18th and 19th century; early atlases of Indiana locations; other materials (not rare) which depict the life of the state in a significant way in such areas as education, religion, industry, sports, social life, etc.

IN —WABASH CARNEGIE PUBLIC LIBRARY, Oral History Program, 188 W Hill St, Wabash, 46992. Linda Robertson, Librn
Holdings: Cat
Budget: $100
Notes: The collection will be of major concern to those interested in local history; however, effort is made to get information on Ku Klux Klan activities in Indiana, Spanish-American War remembrances, and depression days, as well as local history. The Honeywell Company has expanded the collection by interviewing former employees about the company and its founder, Mark C Honeywell. Collection is cited in the *Indiana Magazine of History*, vol LXVIII, no 4 (December 1972): 315-337.

PA —PENNSYLVANIA DIV OF ARCHIVES & MANUSCRIPTS, State Archives, PO Box 1026, Harris, 17108. Roland M Baumann, Chief, History & Museums
Holdings: Vols (3000) // Uncat Mss Maps Pix
Budget: ($40,000)
Notes: The Harmony Society (1785-1905), a German communistic and spiritual community, which immigrated to the US in 1805 and established their community in Harmony, Pennsylvania, moved to New Harmony, Indiana, and returned to Pennsylvania to set up the town of Economy, 20 miles north of Pittsburgh on the Ohio River. The Harmonists had a vast impact on the economy of the areas in which they lived. They were involved in agriculture, manufacturing and investing. 300,000 cu ft.

INDIANA—IMPRINTS

IN —INDIANA UNIVERSITY, Lilly Library, Seventh St, Bloomington, 47405. William R Cagle, Librn
Holdings: Vols 170 // Cat
Notes: Vols printed before 1860.

IN —INDIANA STATE UNIVERSITY, EVANSVILLE, Library, 8600 University Blvd, Evansville, 47712. Gina R Walker, Acting Archivist
Holdings: Vols (3000) Cat Mss Maps Pix
Notes: Restricted use: some items available on interlibrary loan.

IN —INDIANA HISTORICAL SOCIETY, Library, 315 W Ohio St, Indianapolis, 46202. Robert K O'Neill, Dir
Holdings: Vols Cat
Notes: Collection of early Indiana imprints, covering 1815 - 1850.

IN —INDIANA STATE UNIVERSITY, Cunningham Memorial Library, Dept of Rare Books & Special Collections, Terre Haute, 47809. Lawrence J McCrank, Head
Holdings: Vols (2800) Cat Maps
Budget: ($1500)
Notes: The Indiana collection covers entire state with special emphasis on Terre Haute and the Wabash Valley in the following categories: first or special limited editions of major writers associated with Indiana for a significant portion of their productive lives; publications of private presses in Indiana; early Indiana imprints; other materials pertinent to Indiana, eg diaries, broadsides, early travel literature, etc; county, local and regional histories-chiefly 18th and 19th century; early atlases of Indiana locations; other materials (not rare) which depict the life of the state in a significant way in such areas as education, religion, industry, sports, social life, etc.

INDIANA—LABOR

IN —INDIANA STATE UNIVERSITY, EVANSVILLE, Library, 8600 University Blvd, Evansville, 47712. Gina R Walker, Acting Archivist
Holdings: Vols 50 Cat Mss Pix Slides Audiotapes
Notes: Daily radio programs broadcast (1949-1954) over several Evansville, Indiana, stations concerning activities of the local United Electrical and Radio and Machine Workers of America union; other local union news; state, national, and international events; editorial commentary. Prepared and presented by Sadelle Berger, community leader. 4 document cases. Also materials collected during year-long Indiana Labor History Project. Oral history interviews, photographs, slides, brochures, newspaper clippings.

INDIANA—LAWS, STATUTES, ETC.

IN —FRANKLIN COLLEGE OF INDIANA, Library, Special Collections Dept, Franklin, 46131. Mary Alice Medlicott, Cur
Holdings: Vols (12,000) Cat Mss Maps Pix
Budget: ($151,189)
Notes: David Demaree Banta Indiana Collection. Contains material relating to the area which became the Northwest Territory, the State of Indiana, its official publications; description, incl county and city histories, atlases and biographies; literary and scientific works of Hoosier authors. Printed catalog of collection available on request. Third edition of catalog is completed in manuscript.

INDIANA—MAPS

OK —TULSA CITY-COUNTY LIBRARY, Business & Technology Dept, 400 Civic Center, Tulsa, 74103. Craig Buthod, Head
Notes: Original General Land Office survey maps for the states of Arizona, Arkansas, Colorado, Illinois, Indiana, Idaho, Kansas, Michigan, Missouri, Montana, Nebraska, Nevada, New Mexico, North Dakota, Ohio, Oklahoma, South Dakota, Utah and Wyoming. Incomplete coverage of each state.

INDIANA—POLITICS AND GOVERNMENT

DC —LIBRARY OF CONGRESS, Manuscript Division, Washington, 20540. John C Broderick, Chief
Notes: The John Brademas Papers, etc. About 361,000 items.

IN —INDIANA UNIVERSITY, Lilly Library, Seventh St, Bloomington, 47405. William R Cagle, Librn
Holdings: // Mss
Notes: Papers, correspondence, etc of several Indiana legislators, congressmen and senators. See entries under Cravens, James Addison; Dunn, George Grundy; Fairbanks, Charles Warren; and Halleck, Charles Abraham. Also the papers of former US Senator Birch Evans Bayh (D-Ind), 1962-1980. Bayh collection closed until 1990.

IN —INDIANA STATE UNIVERSITY, EVANSVILLE, Library, 8600 University Blvd, Evansville, 47712. Gina R Walker, Acting Archivist
Holdings: Cat Mss Pix
Notes: Evansville municipal documents, incl city ordinances, minutes of council sessions, court records, city treasurer's books, Board of Public Works, tax receipts, cemetery records, assessor's records, reports of special commissions. Also Vanderburgh County. Dates incl 1842 to 1978. Restricted use: noncirculating. Also, collection of Winfield K Denton (1896-1972), Evansville attorney, legislator, congressman; correspondence and papers mainly concerning 1941 session of Indiana Legislature; also law school lecture notes and typed briefs. Covers ca 1922-1967.

IN —UNIVERSITY OF EVANSVILLE, Clifford Memorial Library & Learning Resources, 1800 Lincoln Ave, Evansville, 47714. P Grady Morein, University Librn
Holdings: Vols 45 // Uncat Mss
Notes: Incl approx 10,000 cartoons by Karl K Knecht.

IN —FRANKLIN COLLEGE OF INDIANA, Library, Special Collections Dept, Franklin, 46131. Mary Alice Medlicott, Cur
Holdings: Cat Mss Pix
Budget: ($151,189)
Notes: Governor Roger D Branigan papers. Incl correspondence reports, mementos, and pictures of Roger Douglas Branigan, mostly from the years 1964-1968, while he was governor of the State of Indiana. Considerable additional material from the years prior to 1964 and subsequent to 1968 have recently been added. A finding aid for use with the collection is available; 414 ft, 193 boxes.

INDIANA—SOCIAL CONDITIONS

IN —INDIANA STATE UNIVERSITY, EVANSVILLE, Library, 8600 University Blvd, Evansville, 47712. Gina R Walker, Acting Archivist
Holdings: Uncat Mss Pix
Notes: Visiting Nurse Association of Southwestern Indiana's scrapbooks (sometimes called "Business Diaries" and "Publicity Books") covering the activities of the Association and its staff; also clippings concerning other local social problems. 1927-1971. Unpublished guide.

INDIANA AUTHORS see Authors, Indiana

INDIANA NORMAL SCHOOL

IN —INDIANA STATE UNIVERSITY, Cunningham Memorial Library, Dept of Rare Books & Special Collections, Terre Haute, 47809. Lawrence J McCrank, Head
Notes: The University Archives holds copies of all publications of the Indiana Normal School which became the Indiana State Teachers College and Indiana State University, plus collections of faculty publications and papers. The K Martin sub-collection contains 10,000 photographs relating to ISU from the 1890s to the 1950s. Incl 300 feet of mss.

INDIANA STATE TEACHERS COLLEGE

IN —INDIANA STATE UNIVERSITY, Cunningham Memorial Library, Dept of Rare Books & Special Collections, Terre Haute, 47809. Lawrence J McCrank, Head
Notes: The University Archives holds copies of all publications of the Indiana Normal School which became the Indiana State Teachers College and Indiana State University, plus collections of faculty publications and papers. The K Martin sub-collection contains 10,000 photographs relating to ISU from the 1890s to the 1950s. Incl 300 feet of mss.

INDIANA STATE UNIVERSITY

IN —INDIANA STATE UNIVERSITY, Cunningham Memorial Library, Dept of Rare Books & Special Collections, Terre Haute, 47809. Lawrence J McCrank, Head
Holdings: Vols 750 Mss
Budget: $500
Notes: The University Archives holds copies of all publications of the Indiana Normal School which became the Indiana State Teachers College and Indiana State University, plus collections of faculty publications and papers. The K Martin sub-collection contains 10,000 photographs relating to ISU from the 1890s to the 1950s. Incl 300 feet of mss.

INDIANAPOLIS, INDIANA

IN —INDIANA UNIVERSITY, Lilly Library, Seventh St, Bloomington, 47405. William R Cagle, Librn
Notes: Incl papers of an Indianapolis

INDIANAPOLIS, INDIANA (cont.)

cannery, the Columbia Conserve Company, 1903-1953 (qv).

IN —INDIANA HISTORICAL SOCIETY, Library, 315 W Ohio St, Indianapolis, 46202. Robert K O'Neill, Dir
Holdings: Vols Mss Maps Pix
Notes: Incl Indianapolis city directories; Sanborn real estate atlases; city histories; photographs, most notable the Bretzman Collection; personal papers of local individuals, mostly 19th century; records of various Indianapolis social welfare organizations; the Shortridge High School Collection.

IN —INDIANAPOLIS NEWSPAPERS, Library, 307 N Penn St, Indianapolis, 46206. Sandra Fitzgerald, Librn
Holdings: Vols (1200) Cat
Notes: No space or personnel to serve the public, but will give the name of the newspaper, page, and column number for specific information. Patron can then use the microfilm copy of the *Indianapolis News* (evening paper) at the public library. Index (not published) to *News*, 1912-1947; *Star*, 1929-1947; both, 1948-date.

INDIANS

AZ —NORTHERN ARIZONA UNIVERSITY, Special Collection Library, CU Box 6022, Flagstaff, 86011. Peter M Whiteley, Coordr/Archivist; William Mullane, Librn
Notes: Roger Kelly Collection; notes and files for book *American Indians in Small Cities: A Survey of Urban Acculturation in Two Northern Arizona Communities* (Flagstaff: Northern Arizona University, 1966).

CA —UNIVERSITY OF CALIFORNIA, SANTA BARBARA, Library, Dept of Special Collections, Santa Barbara, 93106. Christian F Brun, Head
Holdings: Vols (95,980) Cat Mss
Notes: The Pearl Chase Collections of Community Development and Conservation. Papers of outstanding California leaders in conservation, community planning, Indian affairs, national parks.

CT —TRINITY COLLEGE LIBRARY, Watkinson Library, 300 Summit St, Hartford, 06106. Jeffrey Kaimowitz, Cur
Holdings: Cat

CT —YALE UNIVERSITY, Beincke Rare Book & Manuscript Library, Western Americana Collection, Wall & High St, New Haven, 06520. George Miles, Cur
Holdings: Cat Mss Maps Pix
Notes: Incl much historical ephemeral material.

DC —SMITHSONIAN INSTITUTION LIBRARIES, Anthropology Branch, Washington, 20560. Jean C Smith, Asst Dir for Bureau Services
Holdings: Vols (54,000) Cat Mss Maps Pix Slides Microforms
Budget: ($7041)
Notes: Physical anthropology, archaeology, ethnology, language and languages; Indians of both continents.

IL —FIELD MUSEUM OF NATURAL HISTORY, Library, Roosevelt Rd & Lake Shore Dr, Chicago, 60605. W Peyton Fawcett, Librn; Benjamin W Williams, Assoc Librn
Holdings: Vols (210,000) Cat
Budget: ($100,000)
Notes: Extensive collections--publications of learned societies and institutions and monographic works--in all fields of natural history, with emphasis on taxonomy and evolutionary biology; and on museum publications, American and foreign: anthropology, especially archaeology and ethnology of the Americas, Africa, East Asia, and Oceania; botany, particularly strong for the Americas; geology, chiefly paleontology and meteoritic studies; and zoology, worldwide (birds, fishes, insects, mammals, mollusks, reptiles and amphibians).

LA —AMISTAD RESEARCH CENTER, 400 Esplanade Ave, New Orleans, 70116. Clifton H Johnson, Exec Dir; Florence E Borders, Senior Archivist
Notes: Originally established at Fisk University, in Nashville, by the American Missionary Association (AMA), this research center on Black American History consists of mss, photographs, clippings, books, pamphlets, taped speeches and interviews; also, the papers of such leaders as WEB DuBois, Countee Cullen, and Mary McLeod Bethune. Also materials on other American minorities, such as Native Americans, Asian Americans, Hispanics, etc.

MI —UNIVERSITY OF MICHIGAN, Museums Library, Ann Arbor, 48109. Patricia B Yocum, Librn
Holdings: Vols 15,000 Cat
Notes: Especially Indians and archaeology of the Americas.

MI —MONROE COUNTY LIBRARY SYSTEM, Ellis Reference and Information Center, 3700 S Custer Rd, Monroe, 48161. Marie D Chulski, Head of Reference Services
Holdings: Vols (35,000) Cat
Budget: ($15,000)
Notes: The George Armstrong Custer Collection is a burgeoning archive of materials on General Custer and the events surrounding and shaping his life. This incl the Lawrence A Frost Collection of Custerania acquired by the library system in 1977. The Custer Monograph Series is produced by the Monroe County Library System. Publications are printed in limited numbered editions, aimed at providing insight into the life and times of General George Armstrong Custer. The continuing series consists of reprints of significant publications and original items.

NY —EXPLORERS CLUB, James B Ford Memorial Library, 46 E 70 St, New York, 10021. Janet Baldwin, Librn
Holdings: Vols (24,000) Cat Maps
Notes: Additions to the collection depend upon gifts. Access by appointment only.

NY —HISPANIC SOCIETY OF AMERICA, Library, 613 W 155 St, New York, 10032. Martha M de Narvaez, Cur of Mss; Irene S Frye, Asst Librn
Holdings: Vols (150,000) Cat Mss Maps Pix Slides Phonorecords Microforms

NY —NEW YORK PUBLIC LIBRARY, Mid-Manhattan Library, History and Social Sciences Dept, 455 Fifth Ave, New York, 10016. Robert Sheehan, Sr Principal Librn
Holdings: Vols 5,000 Cat Phonorecords Audiotapes Microforms
Budget: $5,000
Notes: Strong in material on American Indians and US history in general. Incl the *Library of American Civilization* on microfiche.

NY —NEW YORK PUBLIC LIBRARY, Research Libraries, American History Div, Fifth Ave & 42 St, New York, 10018.
Holdings: Vols (10,000) Cat Maps Microforms
Notes: Archaeology, anthropology, linguistics, ethnology, and sociology of the American Indian. Comprehensive coverage. Much material on Indian languages, incl numerous syllabaries. Coverage ranges from the Eskimos to the Indians of Tierra del Fuego.

PA —FRIENDS HISTORICAL LIBRARY OF SWARTHMORE COLLEGE, Swarthmore, 19081. J William Frost, Dir
Holdings: Vols (35,000) Cat Mss Pix Microforms
Notes: Library's collections contain information on the history and doctrine of the Society of Friends, Quaker contributions to literature, science, business, education, and government, plus their reform efforts in peace, Indian rights, women's rights, and abolition of slavery. Among the more than 250 mss collections are records of several Quaker agencies, established by Philadelphia, Baltimore, and other Hicksite Yearly Meetings to aid Indians, particularly during the administration of Ulysses S Grant. Also incl are papers of Quaker Indian agents Albert L Green and Thomas Lightfoot, and journals of Quaker ministers who visited Indians.

RI —BROWN UNIVERSITY, John Carter Brown Library, Providence, 02912. Norman Fiering, Librn; Everett C Wilkie Jr, Bibliographer; Susan Danforth, Cur Maps & Prints
Holdings: Vols (40,000) Cat Mss Maps Pix
Notes: European contacts with and writings about native Americans until 1833; incl much mss material on Indian linguistics.

WI —STATE HISTORICAL SOCIETY OF WISCONSIN, Library, Newspaper and Periodicals Section, 816 State St, Madison, 53706. James P Danky, Librn
Notes: The largest collection of Native American periodicals and newspapers in the US. Holdings described i: *Native American Periodicals and Newspapers, 1828-1982. Bibliography, Publishing Record and* Holdings. Westport, Conn, Greenwood Press, 1983. Describes over 1160 currently published and ceased titles, over 800 of which are in the Society's collection.

INDIANS—ANTIQUITIES

DC —NATIONAL GEOGRAPHIC SOCIETY, Library, 1146 16th St NW, Washington, 20036. Susan Fifer Canby, Dir
Holdings: Vols (63,000) Cat Mss Maps Pix
Notes: Material concerning land, sea, and space exploration--past and present. All fields of anthropology, natural history, geography, etc.

MI —UNIVERSITY OF MICHIGAN, Museums Library, Ann Arbor, 48109. Patricia B Yocum, Librn
Holdings: Vols 15,000 Cat
Notes: Especially Indians and archaeology of the Americas.

NY —MUSEUM OF THE AMERICAN INDIAN, Library, 9 Westchester Square, Bronx, 10401. Mary B Davis, Librn
Holdings: Vols (40,000) Cat Mss Maps Pix Microforms VF
Notes: Collections cover all aspects of the Indians of the Western Hemisphere; some materials on Eskimos. For scholarly research only.

PA —UNIVERSITY OF PENNSYLVANIA, University Museum Library, 33 & Spruce Sts, Philadelphia, 19104. Jean S Adelman, Librn
Holdings: Vols (80,000) Cat Microforms
Notes: Incl the Daniel Garrison Brinton collection of about 2000 vols, on aboriginal American linguistics and ethnology. Espec strong in Maya language materials.

INDIANS—ART

CA —FINE ARTS MUSEUMS OF SAN FRANCISCO, M H de Young Memorial Museum, Golden Gate Park, San Francisco, 94118. Jane Nelson, Librn
Holdings: Vols Cat

CO —UNIVERSITY OF COLORADO, Libraries, Art & Architecture Library, Campus Box 184, Boulder, 80309. Liesel Nolan, Librn/Dept Head
Holdings: Vols (57,647) Cat Pix
Budget: ($39,000)
Notes: Special feature: art exhibition catalog collection 1963-1971, 1972-date. Good general collection with some special emphasis on environmental design, Islamic architecture, Indian art and South American Indian art. Fair collection of periodical backfiles in art and in architecture. Separate catalog for materials in collection. Rare books in main library, listed only in central union catalog.

OH —GREENE COUNTY DISTRICT LIBRARY, 76 E Market St, PO Box 520, Xenia, 45385. Julie M Overton, Local History Coordr
Holdings: // Uncat
Notes: Galloway Collection of Ohio history is housed in a five-drawer filing cabinet, incl letters, some at the time of the Gold Rush; family letters of the Galloways, Lyons, Worthingtons and others; material about William Maxwell, editor and publisher of the first newspaper in the Northwest Territory, also legal papers concerning him; papers, some legal, concerning Galloways, incl "The Galloway Lands in 1812," and papers about

INDIANS—ART (cont.)

the Worthingtons and Lyons; indentures; Civil War diary of Clark Galloway, MD, a surgeon in the war; pictures of families, covered bridges, mills etc; material about Tecumseh and some other Indians and their traditions; galley sheets and correspondence concerning the publishing of the New Testament in the Shawnee language; material about the railroad, OVCH (formerly OS&OS Home) Antioch College, Wilberforce University and other items about Ohiohistory; many notes, papers and correspondence acquired when William Galloway was preparing to write the book "Old Chillicothe," published posthumously in 1934.

TX —EL PASO PUBLIC LIBRARY, Southwest Collection, 501 N Oregon, El Paso, 79901. Mary A Sarber, Head
Holdings: Vols (7000) Cat Pix
Budget: ($6000)
Notes: Emphasis on art and artists of the Southwest, particularly Tom Lea Jr, and Southwestern Indian arts and crafts.

INDIANS—BIOGRAPHY

NY —NEW YORK STATE LIBRARY, State Education Bldg Annex, Washington Ave, Albany, 12224.
Holdings: Vols (110,500) Cat
Notes: Strong collection emphasis on North American Indians, especially Indians of New York. Incl books and pamphlets on Indian captivities, treaties, conferences, lives of noted Indians, laws. Bibles and catechisms, prayerbooks, grammars, etc in native languages. Outstanding collection on Iroquois Indians. Incl original treaties between the State of New York and the Iroquois, papers of Cornplanter, drawings by Jesse Cornplanter.

INDIANS—LANGUAGES

CT —TRINITY COLLEGE LIBRARY, Watkinson Library, 300 Summit St, Hartford, 06106. Jeffrey Kaimowitz, Cur
Holdings: Cat
Notes: Incl the J Hammond Trumbull Collection of works on the American Indians and their languages.

DC —GEORGETOWN UNIVERSITY, Library, Special Collections Div, 37 & O Sts NW, Washington, 20057. George M Barringer, Special Collections Librn; Nicholas B Sheetz, Mss Librn
Holdings: Cat Mss
Notes: Papers of John Gilmary Shea (1824-1892), noted Catholic historian and linguist of Indian languages who published over two hundred titles during his lifetime. The papers incl correspondence to Shea, manuscripts and notes reflecting his research, collected documents and manuscripts, and various photographs. Correspondence written to Shea incl letters from George Bancroft, Francis Parkman, Jared Sparks, Harriet Beecher Stowe, E B O'Callahan, Hanry Schoolcraft, Charles White, D D, Charles Currier, P T Barnum, Frederick Douglass, Thomas A Edison, Oliver Wendell Holmes, as well as noted members of the Church hierarchy. A long span of correspondence from Shea to the historian, Edmund Mallet contains many insights into Shea's life and work. Photographs incl likenesses of Elizabeth Seton, Isaac Hecker and George Bancroft. Also incl in the papers are numerous documents andmss concerning Shea's work in the field of Native American history, language, and culture.

IL —NEWBERRY LIBRARY, 60 W Walton St, Chicago, 60610. Diana Haskell, Cur of Modern Mss
Holdings: Cat Mss
Notes: The Ayer Collection. One of the most extensive collections extant.

IN —INDIANA UNIVERSITY, Lilly Library, Seventh St, Bloomington, 47405. William R Cagle, Librn
Holdings: Vols 6000 // Cat Mss
Notes: This exceptional collection, incl 10,000 broadsides, contains material from the establishment of the press in the New World, in Mexico City, through the revolutionary process of 1910. Incl works in Indian languages, incl the invaluable first linguistic works of the 16th century in America.

KS —SAINT MARY COLLEGE, Library, Leavenworth, 66048. Therese Deplazes, Special Collections Librn
Notes: In the Sir John and Mary Craig Collection of Holy Scripture are minor items in some thirty languages of Indians of North and South America.

MO —UNIVERSITY OF MISSOURI-COLUMBIA, Museum of Anthropology Archives, 104 Swallow Hall, Columbia, 65201. Lawrence H Feldman, Museum Dir
Holdings: Vols (30) Cat Mss Maps Slides Microforms
Notes: Copies of Latin American and colonial mss. Many of the ms copies are census, or census-like, documents of late colonial Verapaz; a few are from Sonsonate, El Salvador or Chiapas, Mexico. Additional material in the archives incl an original Eskimo manuscript (ca 1930) and an original Dieguено Yuman card vocabulary (ca 1964) and the Museum archives (papers on old accession systems, etc). Uncataloged microfilm copies of colonial Otomi and other vocabularies are also part of the collection will appear in the Annual Report of the Museum of Anthropology, beginning with the 1976-77 volume.

NY —NEW YORK STATE LIBRARY, State Education Bldg Annex, Washington Ave, Albany, 12224.
Holdings: Vols (110,500) Cat
Notes: Strong collection emphasis on North American Indians, especially Indians of New York. Incl books and pamphlets on Indian captivities, treaties, conferences, lives of noted Indians, laws. Bibles and catechisms, prayerbooks, grammars, etc in native languages. Outstanding collection on Iroquois Indians. Incl original treaties between the State of New York and the Iroquois, papers of Cornplanter, drawings by Jesse Cornplanter.

NY —AMERICAN MUSEUM OF NATURAL HISTORY, Library Services Dept, Central Park W & 79th St, New York, 10024. Nina J Root, Chairwoman; Mary Genett, Asst Librn for Reference Services
Holdings: Cat Mss Pix Microforms
Notes: The Ernest Thompson Seton diaries. Thousands of pages of an unpublished 67-year (1879-1946) diary record of one of the world's most famous naturalists, the gift of Joseph F Cullman III, a Trustee of the Museum. Preserved in 35 protective cases, the gift incl unpublished diaries, notebooks, and some other writings. Research will reveal information on the Indian sign language.

NY —HISPANIC SOCIETY OF AMERICA, Library, 613 W 155 St, New York, 10032. Martha M de Narvaez, Cur of Mss; Irene S Frye, Asst Librn
Holdings: Vols (150,000) Cat Mss Maps Pix Slides Phonorecords Microforms

NY —NEW YORK PUBLIC LIBRARY, Research Libraries, American History Div, Fifth Ave & 42 St, New York, 10018.
Holdings: Vols (10,000) Cat Maps Microforms
Notes: Archaeology, anthropology, linguistics, ethnology, and sociology of the American Indian. Comprehensive coverage. Much material on Indian languages, incl numerous syllabaries. Coverage ranges from the Eskimos to the Indians of Tierra del Fuego.

PA —AMERICAN PHILOSOPHICAL SOCIETY, Library, 105 S Fifth St, Philadelphia, 19106. Edward C Carter II, Librn
Holdings: Cat Mss Maps
Notes: The Boas Family Papers, incl 60,000 pieces of correspondence of Franz Boas' Also 600 groups of items in honor of Dr Boas chiefly field notes, lexical files, dictionaries, texts, etc concerning the American Indian and, especially, Indian linguistics. Numerous papers of other anthropologists are also in the APS Library: Sylvanus G Morley, Frans M Olbrechts, Ely S Parker, Elsie Clews Parsons, Paul Radin, Frank G Speck, etc. See *A Guide to Manuscripts Relating to the American Indian in the Library of the American Philosophical Society*, by John F Freeman and Murphy D Smith (1966).

PA —UNIVERSITY OF PENNSYLVANIA, University Museum Library, 33 & Spruce Sts, Philadelphia, 19104. Jean S Adelman, Librn
Holdings: Vols (80,000) Cat Mss
Notes: Incl the Daniel Garrison Brinton collection of about 2000 vols, on aboriginal American linguistics and ethnology. Espec strong in Maya language materials.

ON —NATIONAL LIBRARY OF CANADA, 395 Wellington St, Ottawa, K1A 0N4, Can. Andre Preibish, Dir
Holdings: Vols 18,000
Notes: The collection contains 42 incunabula. The core collection consists of early Canadiana (1752-1867) and 16th and 17th century books on Canada. The books printed in native languages are a very valuable part of the collection. Canadian Livres d'Artistes collection of limited editions and Canadian *livres d'artistes* received on legal deposit as well as examples of private press publications from other countries also form part of the Rare Book collection.

ON —NATIONAL MUSEUMS OF CANADA, Library Services Directorate, Ottawa, K1A 0M8, Can. Valerie Monkhouse, Director
Holdings: Vols (70,000) Cat Mss Maps Pix Slides Microforms
Budget: ($60,000)
Notes: Collection includes anthropology, archaeology, ethnology, folklore, history, Indians of North America, Inuit, linguistics of North American Indians, material history, military and naval history, museology. Research collection, interlibrary loans available, public may use on the premises.

INDIANS—MISSIONS

AZ —COOK CHRISTIAN TRAINING SCHOOL, Mary M McCarthy Library, 708 S Lindon Lane, Tempe, 85281. Mark E Thomas, Librn
Holdings: Vols 800 Cat Audiotapes Videotapes 16mm Films Filmstrips VF
Notes: Cook is an interdenominational school for the preparation of Native American adults for positions of church leadership. The school at times has been under contract with the Institute for the Development of Indian Law, Washington, DC for the production of filmstrips and workshops dealing with Indian issues. Visitors are welcomed but all materials must be used within the library.

CA —AZUSA PACIFIC COLLEGE, Marshburn Memorial Library, Citrus & Alosta, Azusa, 91702. Edward Peterman, Librn
Holdings: Vols 175 Cat Mss
Notes: The Clifford M Drury Collection on the Protestant Missionary in the Far West. No photocopying.

KS —WYANDOTTE COUNTY HISTORICAL SOCIETY, Museum, Trowbridge Research Library, 631 N 126 St, Bonner Springs, 66012. Stephen J Allie, Archivist
Holdings: Vols 3000 Mss Maps Pix Slides Audiotapes Microforms
Budget: $12,500
Notes: Emphasis on Wyandotte County. Cataloged. Incl 100 maps, 4000 photographs. Also County Records 1855-1820. Cataloged.

PA —HAVERFORD COLLEGE, Magill Library, Quaker Collection, Haverford, 19041. Edwin B Bonner, Librn & Cur
Holdings: Vols (32,000) Cat Mss Maps Pix Phonorecords Audiotapes Microforms
Notes: Incl material about Society of Friends from inception in England, 1650, to the present. Formats incl periodicals, diaries, documents of individual Friends, families, Quaker Meetings and institutions, incl archives of Haverford College. Emphases on

INDIANS—MISSIONS (cont.)

American Indians, antislavery, women, minorities, the Rufus M Jones Mysticism collection, Quaker fiction, and Delaware Valley, Pennsylvania.

TX —AMARILLO PUBLIC LIBRARY, 413 E Fourth, Amarillo, 79101. Mary Kay Snell, Librn
Holdings: Vols Cat Mss Maps Pix
Notes: The southwest collections incl materials on the history of Texas, Louisiana, New Mexico, Arkansas, Missouri and Kansas. General subjects covered incl overland journeys, early narratives, early biographies, Indian captivities, outlaws, US government reports, Mississippi and Ohio Rivers, the Mexican War, reports of Catholic missionaries, Niles Register, early publications, fur trade, western trails, Texas Rangers, sheriffs and Texas as a sovereign state, buffalo hunting, Indian wars, cowboys, the arrival of farmers, fences, and towns. Over 1600 items which incl books, documents, maps, mss, pamphlets, unpublished theses, interviews and photographs. The three major collections are the William Henry Bush Collection, the Laurence J Fitzsimon Collection and the Calendar of John L McCarty.

INDIANS—SIGN LANGUAGE

NY —AMERICAN MUSEUM OF NATURAL HISTORY, Library Services Dept, Central Park W & 79th St, New York, 10024. Nina J Root, Chairwoman; Mary Genett, Asst Librn for Reference Services
Holdings: Cat Mss Pix Microforms
Notes: The Ernest Thompson Seton diaries. Thousands of pages of an unpublished 67-year (1879-1946) diary record of one of the world's most famous naturalists, the gift of Joseph F Cullman III, a Trustee of the Museum. Preserved in 35 protective cases, the gift incl unpublished diaries, notebooks, and some other writings. Research will reveal information on the Indian sign language.

INDIANS—TREATIES

NY —NEW YORK STATE LIBRARY, State Education Bldg Annex, Washington Ave, Albany, 12224.
Holdings: Vols (110,500) Cat
Notes: Strong collection emphasis on north American Indians, especially Indians of New York. Incl books and pamphlets on Indians captivities, treaties, conferences, lives of noted Indians, laws. Bibles and catechisms, prayerbooks, grammars, etc in native languages. Outstanding collection on Iroquois Indians. Incl original treaties between the State of New York and the Iroquois, papers of Cornplanter, drawings by Jesse Cornplanter.

INDIANS, TREATMENT OF

IN —EARLHAM COLLEGE, Lilly Library, Richmond, 47374.
Holdings: Vols 10,000 Cat Mss Maps Pix Microforms Audiotapes
Notes: The Quaker Collection in the archives is cataloged separately. In addition the archives incl the Earlham College Historical Collection. The Earlham Archives is the designated depository for materials relating to Young Friends organizations and activities. Its collection of materials relating to the work of Friends with the American Indians is probably the largest anywhere. Sources for Quaker genealogical research are good. See "Earlham's Quaker Collection" by Opal Thornburg, *Quaker History*, Autumn 1965, Vol 54, No 2.

INDIANS OF CANADA see Indians of North America and Mexico—Canada

INDIANS OF CENTRAL AMERICA

CA —UNIVERSITY OF CALIFORNIA, SAN DIEGO, Central University Library, Mandeville Dept of Special Collections, La Jolla, 92093. Lynda Corey Claassen, Head
Holdings: Vols (2400) Cat Mss Maps
Notes: The Hill Collection of Pacific Voyages, including reports and commentaries of important voyages in the Pacific, from those of Magellan and Sir Francis Drake to exploration through the first half of the 19th century. Includes many rare overland accounts to the Pacific across North America, Mexico, and Panama.
Bibliography: Silveira de Braganza, Ronald, *The Hill Collection of Pacific Voyages* (La Jolla: Calif, 1974-1983).

CA —UNIVERSITY OF CALIFORNIA, LOS ANGELES, Research Library, Dept of Special Collections, 405 Hilgard Ave, Los Angeles, 90024. Edward Shreeves, Chairman, Bibliographers Group; David S Zeidberg, Head
Notes: Various collections on languages of the Indians of Central America, incl the John H Grepe and Byron McAfee Collections.

CT —TRINITY COLLEGE LIBRARY, Watkinson Library, 300 Summit St, Hartford, 06106. Jeffrey Kaimowitz, Cur
Holdings: Cat

CT —YALE UNIVERSITY, Anthropology Library, Peabody Museum of Natural History, C-8 KBT, New Haven, 06511.
Holdings: Vols (16,000) Cat
Budget: ($11,000)

CT —YALE UNIVERSITY, Sterling Memorial Library, Latin American Collections, New Haven, 06520. Lee H Williams Jr, Cur
Holdings: Vols (300,000) Cat Maps Pix Slides Phonorecords 16mm Films Filmstrips
See also entry under Latin America

DC —SMITHSONIAN INSTITUTION LIBRARIES, Anthropology Branch, Washington, 20560. Jean C Smith, Asst Dir for Bureau Services
Holdings: Vols (54,000) Cat Mss Maps Pix Slides Microforms
Budget: ($7041)
Notes: Physical anthropology, archaeology, ethnology, language and languages; Indians of both continents.

IL —NEWBERRY LIBRARY, 60 W Walton St, Chicago, 60610. Diana Haskell, Cur of Modern Mss
Holdings: Vols 2100 Cat Mss Maps Pix
Notes: Restricted use; noncirculating.

IN —INDIANA UNIVERSITY, Lilly Library, Seventh St, Bloomington, 47405. William R Cagle, Librn
Holdings: Vols (40,000) Cat Mss Maps
Notes: Research and rare book collection (Bernardo Mendel) of first or only editions, mostly printed in Latin America, from the discovery of the New World through 1830. Special strength in discoveries and exploration, history (mainly period of independence), Inquisition, missionary works by the Augustinians, Dominicans, Franciscans, and the Jesuits, and the history of the Catholic Church in these countries. Major geographic concentration is on the three great viceroyalties of Mexico (ca 10, 000 titles, plus over 10,000 official Mexican broadsides), Peru (2000 titles), and Argentina (4000 titles), incl in Argentina a substantial amount of printings from the Imprenta de Ninos Expositos, and the Coleccion Santamaria. A special Bolivian Collection (2500 titles), mostly history, from the establishment of the press there, ca 1826, through the beginning of the 20th century. Part of theMendel Collection is the select Bibliotheca Boxeriana from Charles R Boxer (1000 titles) on European expansion into Asia, and into the New World, mainly Brazil, during the 16th-18th centuries. The collection is supplemented by substantial material from the private collection of Josiah K Lilly.
See also entries under Spain - History; Portugal - History; Mexico - History.

LA —TULANE UNIVERSITY, Howard-Tilton Memorial Library, Latin American Library, New Orleans, 70118. Thomas Niehaus, Dir
Holdings: Vols (150,000) Cat Mss Maps Pix Microforms VF
Budget: ($67,000)
Notes: *Catalog of the Latin American Library* (Boston: G K Hall, 1970, suppl. 1973,1975,1978); Downs 5338-41; suppl (1961), 2727, 2737. The Latin American Library is a general collection, but specializes in Central American, Mexican, and Brazilian materials. The disciplines which are most strongly represented are history, anthropology, and archaeology. The Viceregal Ecclesiastical Mexican Collection contains manuscripts from the colonial period. The France V Scholes Collection contains a large number of photoprints and microfilm of colonial documents from the archives of Spain and Mexico. The Merle Greene Robertson Rubbings Collection contains nearly five hundred rubbings of relief sculpture from Mayan archaeological sites in Mexico and Guatemala. The Photographic Collection contains photos of archaeological sites inMeso-America, of pre-Columbian Peruvian architecture, and a general group of historic photos from Latin America.

MA —HARVARD UNIVERSITY LIBRARY, Botanical Museum Library, Cambridge, 02138.
Holdings: Vols (2400) Mss Pix
Notes: The Tina and Gordon Wisson Ethnomycological Collection, one of the most important modern collections, acquired as an adjunct to the Museum's Economic Botany Library of Oakes Ames. From 15th to 20th century, it deals with hallucinogenic mushrooms in art, religion, and folklore; chemistry, pharmacology, linguistics, archaeological artifacts of Mexico, Guatemala, India, Japan, China, etc. Personal papers, etc.

MA —PEABODY MUSEUM OF SALEM, Phillips Library, E India Sq, Salem, 01970. Gregor Trinkaus-Randall, Librn
Holdings: Vols (100,000) Cat Mss Pix
Notes: Ethnology of Non-European Peoples Collection. Composed of separate divisions relating to the Pacific Islands, China, Japan and the American Indian. No published indexes.

MO —UNIVERSITY OF MISSOURI-COLUMBIA, Museum of Anthropology Archives, 104 Swallow Hall, Columbia, 65201. Lawrence H Feldman, Museum Dir
Holdings: Vols (30) Cat Mss Maps Slides Microforms
Notes: Copies of Latin American and colonial mss. Many of the ms copies are of census, or census-like, documents of late colonial Verapaz; a few are from Sonsonate, El Salvador or Chiapas, Mexico. Additional material in the archives incl an original Eskimo manuscript (ca 1930) and an original Diegueno Yuman card vocabulary (ca 1964) and the Museum archives (papers on old accession systems, etc). Uncataloged microfilm copies of colonial Otomi and other vocabularies are also part of the collection. A catalog of material in this collection will appear in the Annual Report of the Museum of Anthropology, beginning with the 1976-77 volume.

NJ —PRINCETON UNIVERSITY, Library, Princeton, 08540. Alfred Bush, Cur
Holdings: Cat Mss

NY —MUSEUM OF THE AMERICAN INDIAN, Library, 9 Westchester Square, Bronx, 10401. Mary B Davis, Librn
Holdings: Vols (40,000) Cat Mss Maps Pix Microforms VF
Notes: Incl information in Indians of North, Central, and South America; archaeology of North, Central, and South America; American Indian ethnology; anthropology, history.

NY —AMERICAN MUSEUM OF NATURAL HISTORY, Library Services Dept, Central Park W & 79th St, New York, 10024. Nina J Root, Chairwoman; Mary Genett, Asst Librn for Reference Services
Holdings: Vols (385,000) Cat Mss Maps Pix Slides Microforms
Notes: Nearly all collections are outstanding for depth of coverage and international range. Early and historic works, rare books, colored illustrations, and relevant serial publications supplement the modern scientific publications necessary to the researchers of the scientific staff and the

INDIANS OF CENTRAL AMERICA (cont.)

work of the educational division. Open to the public.

NY —HISPANIC SOCIETY OF AMERICA, Library, 613 W 155 St, New York, 10032. Martha M de Narvaez, Cur of Mss; Irene S Frye, Asst Librn
Holdings: Vols (150,000) Cat Mss Maps Pix Slides Phonorecords Microforms

NY —NEW YORK PUBLIC LIBRARY, Research Libraries, American History Div, Fifth Ave & 42 St, New York, 10018.
Holdings: Vols (10,000) Cat Mss Maps Pix Slides Microforms
Notes: Archaeology, anthropology, linguistics, ethnology, and sociology of the American Indian. Comprehensive coverage. Much material on Indian languages, incl numerous syllabaries. Coverage ranges from the Eskimos to the Indians of Tierra del Fuego.

OK —THOMAS GILCREASE INSTITUTE OF AMERICAN HISTORY & ART LIBRARY, 1400 North 25th West Ave, Tulsa, 74127. Sarah Hirsch, Librn
Holdings: Vols Cat Mss Maps Pix
Notes: Trans-Mississippi West, US, Indian and Hispanic history. The Gilcrease Library contains a total of about 40,000 mss; 10,000 imprints; 5000 photographs; 600 maps and 50,000 vols.

PA —UNIVERSITY OF PITTSBURGH, Hillman Library, Pittsburgh, 15260. Glenora E Rossell, Head
Holdings: Vols (172,000) Cat Microforms
Notes: The collection is very strong in pre-Columbian archaeology and Indian cultures from the historical and anthropological point of view. Emphasis on contemporary history, politics and socio-economical problems.

RI —BROWN UNIVERSITY, John Hay Library, 20 Prospect St, Providence, 02912. Mark N Brown, Cur Mss
Holdings: Vols (3500) // Cat Mss Maps
Notes: George Earl Church Collection, formed by a civil engineer, explorer and Fellow of the Royal Geographic Society, who specialized in railroad construction. Although part of the collection is devoted to American Revolutionary and Civil War history, the majority, over 2000 volumes, pertains to Central and South America. The imprints, which are predominantly 18th century, include Lima, Madrid, Rome, Mexico City, Seville, Barcelona, Lisbon, and Cadiz as well as *Nova orbis regionum ac insularum veteribus incognitarum* (Basle: 1537). Major subject areas are: anthropology. commerce, economics, engineering, ethnology, geography, history, law, mineral resources, railroad surveys, voyages of exploration and dictionaries of the South American Indian languages. The most significant ms is an historical account of the Bolivian mining town of Potosi from 1545-1737.

RI —BROWN UNIVERSITY, John Carter Brown Library, Providence, 02912. Norman Fiering, Librn; Everett C Wilkie Jr, Bibliographer; Susan Danforth, Cur Maps & Prints
Notes: Incl pre-Columbia materials; large mss holdings pertaining to Indian linguistics. *See also* entry under Indians of South America.

TX —UNIVERSITY OF TEXAS LIBRARIES, Nettie Lee Benson Latin American Collection, Sid Richardson Hall 1.109, Austin, 78712. Laura Gutierrez-Witt, Head Librn
Holdings: Vols (450,000) Cat Mss Maps Pix Phonorecords Filmstrips Microforms
See also entry under Latin America.

INDIANS OF CENTRAL AMERICA—ANTIQUITIES

†AL —UNIVERSITY OF ALABAMA, Amelia Gayle Gorgas Library, PO Box S, University, 35486.
Notes: This collection consists of 119 reels of microfilm. Separately published bibliography: *A Catalog of the Yucatan* Collection on Microfilm in the University of Alabama Libraries (University: University of Alabama Press), 1972.

DC —LIBRARY OF CONGRESS, Geography and Map Division, Washington, 20540. John A Wolter, Chief
Notes: Ephraim George Squier's papers and maps of Central America. Maps are located in the Geography and Maps Division; mss in the Manuscripts Division.

IL —NEWBERRY LIBRARY, 60 W Walton St, Chicago, 60610. Diana Haskell, Cur of Modern Mss
Holdings: Vols (1000) Cat Mss Pix
Notes: Western continent antiquities.

NJ —PRINCETON UNIVERSITY, Library, Princeton, 08540. Alfred Bush, Cur
Holdings: Cat Mss

PA —UNIVERSITY OF PENNSYLVANIA, University Museum Library, 33 & Spruce Sts, Philadelphia, 19104. Jean S Adelman, Librn
Holdings: Vols (80,000) Cat Mss Microforms
Notes: World archaeology, with special emphasis on North and Central America, Egyptology, Sumerology, and the classical world. All holdings are listed in the University of Pennsylvania main library (union) catalog.

PA —UNIVERSITY OF PITTSBURGH, Hillman Library, Pittsburgh, 15260. Glenora E Rossell, Head
Holdings: Vols (172,000) Cat Microforms
Notes: The collection is very strong in pre-Columbian archaeology and Indian cultures from the historical and anthropological point of view. Emphasis on contemporary history, politics and socio-economical problems.

INDIANS OF CENTRAL AMERICA—ART

NY —METROPOLITAN MUSEUM OF ART, Robert Goldwater Library, Fifth Ave at 82nd St, New York, 10028. Allan D Chapman, Librn
Holdings: Vols (27,000) Cat
Notes: Primitive art: African, Indians of the Americans (incl Pre-Columbian), Oceanic, Polynesian, etc. 150,000 photographs.

INDIANS OF CENTRAL AMERICA—LANGUAGES

CA —UNIVERSITY OF CALIFORNIA, BERKELEY, University Library, Hispanic Collections, Berkeley, 94720. Gaston Somoshegyi-Szokol, Librn
Holdings: Vols (1000)
Notes: Strong research collection covering both literature (chronicles, histories, poetry, mythologies, etc) and linguistics (grammars, lexicons, dictionaries, etc) with special strength in Nahuatl and Maya.

MA —HARVARD UNIVERSITY LIBRARY, Tozzer Library, 21 Divinity Ave, Cambridge, 02138. Nancy J Schmidt, Librn
Holdings: Cat Mss Microforms
Notes: Tozzer Library was formerly the Peabody Museum Library.

RI —BROWN UNIVERSITY, John Hay Library, 20 Prospect St, Providence, 02912. Mark N Brown, Cur Mss
Holdings: Vols 3500 // Cat Mss Maps
Notes: George Earl Church Collection, formed by a civil engineer, explorer and Fellow of the Royal Geographic Society. Incl dictionaries of the South American Indian languages.

INDIANS OF MEXICO see Indians of North America and Mexico

INDIANS OF NORTH AMERICA—ETHNOLOGY see Ethnology; Indians of North America and Mexico

INDIANS OF NORTH AMERICA AND MEXICO

AL —SAMFORD UNIVERSITY, Special Collections Library, 800 Lakeshore Dr, Birmingham, 35229. Annie Ford Wheeler, Acting Head Librn
Holdings: Uncat Mss Maps Pix Microforms
Notes: The William H Brantley Collection is in superb condition, consisting of early works on travels, Indians, and law in the southeast, plus scarce imprints of Alabama.

AL —MOBILE PUBLIC LIBRARY, Special Collections Div, 701 Government St, Mobile, 36602.
Notes: The Mobile area; incl papers of the Forbes Trading Co, 1795-1840; Bank of Mobile papers, 1820-.

AZ —NORTHERN ARIZONA UNIVERSITY, Special Collection Library, CU Box 6022, Flagstaff, 86011. Peter M Whiteley, Coordr/Archivist; William Mullane, Librn
Notes: Flagstaff All-Indian Pow Wow Collection; correspondence, files, 1947; programs, blurbs, 1930's-1970's.

AZ —COOK CHRISTIAN TRAINING SCHOOL, Mary M McCarthy Library, 708 S Lindon Lane, Tempe, 85281. Mark E Thomas, Librn
Holdings: Vols 800 Cat Audiotapes Videotapes 16mm Films Filmstrips VF
Notes: Cook is an interdenominational school for the preparation of Native American adults for positions of church leadership. The school at times has been under contract with the Institute for the Development of Indian Law, Washington, DC for the production of filmstrips and workshops dealing with Indian issues. Visitors are welcomed but all materials must be used within the library.

AZ —NAVAJO COMMUNITY COLLEGE, Naaltsoos Ba' Hoogan, Library, Tsaile, 86556. Marvin E Pollard Jr, Dir, Library Services
Holdings: Vols (10,000) Cat Mss Maps Pix Slides Phonorecords Audiotapes Videotapes 16mm Films Filmstrips Microforms
Budget: ($15,000)
Notes: The Moses/Donner Collection emphasizes Navajos and other tribes of the Southwest; also, all Indians of North America and Mexico. All aspects of the geology, geography, sociology, archaeology, anthropology, etc, of the Four Corners region. The Collection includes a comprehensive collection of Doctoral dissertations dealing with Indians of North America and Mexico.

AZ —ARIZONA STATE MUSEUM, Library, University of Arizona, Tucson, 85721. Hans R Bart, Museum Librn
Holdings: Vols (35,000) Cat Mss Maps Pix Slides Phonorecords Microforms

CA —AZUSA PACIFIC COLLEGE, Marshburn Memorial Library, Citrus & Alosta, Azusa, 91702. Edward Peterman, Librn
Holdings: Vols (6000) Uncat
Budget: ($30,000)
Notes: Significant holdings in the George E Fullerton Library of Californiana and Western Americana.

CA —UNIVERSITY OF CALIFORNIA, BERKELEY, Bancroft Library, Manuscripts Division, Berkeley, 94720. James D Hart, Dir
Holdings: Vols Cat Mss Maps Pix Slides Microforms
Notes: Approxi. twelve million pieces, with primary emphasis on California, with a lesser emphasis on the other Pacific States, incl. Alaska and the Province of British Columbia. In general, the Bancroft Library seeks to acquire historical and biographical works and primary source materials, documenting: the development of a geographic area or political unit; man and his activities, and his impact on the land and on his institutions. Methodological and theoretical work and texts in the physical and biological sciences are not collected, as a rule; exceptions here are publications essential to the study of an area's historical development and those providing general background information. Hubert Howe Bancroft's own distinguished holdings, assembled 1860-1880, constitute the core of the collection. The Bancroft Library's collections are noncirculating. A. G. K. Hall catalog has been published. The Bolton Collection (146,000 pages of archival material) contains ms. materials for the history of the Pacific

INDIANS OF NORTH AMERICA AND MEXICO (cont.)

Coast and the Southwest, gathered by Herbert Eugene Bolton. There is a comprehensive key to the arrangement of the collection.

CA —HARRISON MEMORIAL LIBRARY, Ocean & Lincoln Sts, Carmel, 93921. Keith Brehmer, Ref Librn
Holdings: Vols 450 Cat
Notes: All aspects of Indian life.

CA —UNIVERSITY OF CALIFORNIA, SAN DIEGO, Central University Library, Mandeville Dept of Special Collections, La Jolla, 92093. Lynda Corey Claassen, Head
Holdings: Vols (2400) Cat Mss Maps
Notes: The Hill Collection of Pacific Voyages, including reports and commentaries of important voyages in the Pacific, from those of Magellan and Sir Francis Drake to exploration through the first half of the 19th century. Includes many rare overland accounts to the Pacific across North America, Mexico, and Panama.
Bibliography: Silveira de Braganza, Ronald, *The Hill Collection of Pacific Voyages* (La Jolla: Calif, 1974-1983).

CA —LAKE COUNTY LIBRARY, 200 Park St, Lakeport, 95453. Kathleen Jansen, Librn
Holdings: Vols (300) Cat
Notes: Collection of books and articles dealing with the Pomo Indians of California.

CA —LOS ANGELES PUBLIC LIBRARY, History Dept, 630 W Fifth St, Los Angeles, 90071. Leah Simon Kornbluth, Librn
Holdings: Vols (6000) Cat Maps Phonorecords Microforms
Budget: ($85,000)
Notes: The core of the American Indian collection is in the History Dept.; it includes descriptions of contemporary life, social commentary, legends, religious thought, political studies, as well as history and biography. There are sizeable sections of material outside the dept. as well; notable are anthropology in the Science Dept., art in the Art Dept., phonograph records in Audio-Visual. The History Dept.'s older holdings are particularly strong in folklore and descriptive accounts of Indian life. There are many full sets of monographs and society publications; the Bureau of American Ethnology Reports and Bulletins, the U.S. Office of Indian Affairs Reports, California Publications in American Archaeology and Ethnology among them, and the Indian Claims Commission Decisions and Expert Testimony on microfiche. Present acquisitions are strong in books written by Indian authors and material published by smaller and regional publishers. There are old and new journal runs and the History Dept. currently subscribes to 28 Indian periodicals. An index has been started within the last 2 years dealing with such topics as land tenure and claims, fishing rights, television programs, biographical information, etc. The material indexed is from periodicals, newspapers and books.

CA —UNIVERSITY OF CALIFORNIA, LOS ANGELES, William Andrews Clark Memorial Library, 2520 Cimarron St, Los Angeles, 90018.
Holdings: // Cat Mss
Notes: 18th and early 19th century mss, incl reports and correspondence on missions, Indians, New Mexico, Alta and Baja California.

CA —UNIVERSITY OF SOUTHERN CALIFORNIA, School of Medicine, Norris Medical Library, 2025 Zonal Ave, Los Angeles, 90033. Nelson J Gilman, Librn
Holdings: Vols (275) Cat
Budget: $200
Notes: The Collection of American Indian Ethnopharmacology.

CA —SAN DIEGO PUBLIC LIBRARY, 820 E St, San Diego, 92101. Marion L Buckner, Supervising Librn
Holdings: Vols 2500 Cat Maps Pix

CA —CALIFORNIA HISTORICAL SOCIETY, Schubert Hall Library, 2099 Pacific Ave, San Francisco, 94109. Bruce L Johnson, Library Dir
Holdings: Vols (50,000) Cat Mss Maps Pix
See also entry under California - History

CO —COLORADO HISTORICAL SOCIETY, Research Collections, 1300 Broadway, Denver, 80203. Catherine Kane, Head Public Service and Access
Holdings: Cat Pix Slides
Notes: 250,000 photographs of western and Colorado subjects incl gold rush, mining, Indians, natural features, transportation, cities and towns, portraits. William Henry Jackson photographs of area west of Mississippi.

CO —DENVER PUBLIC LIBRARY, Western History Department, 1357 Broadway, Denver, 80203. Eleanor M Gehres, Head
Holdings: Vols (50,000) Cat Mss Maps Pix Audiotapes Microforms
Notes: Western US History. The department has a separate catalog, published in 1970 in 7 vols by G K Hall Co. First supplement published in 1975 in 1 vol. There is a subject index of some 3 million entries to newspapers and magazines of the Rocky Mountain region, added to daily. The Western Newspaper Microfilm Center contains approx 7000 reels of Western US newspapers. Collection has ca 275,000 negatives and prints of Western life; and ca 2500 maps, cataloged and classified.

CT —LEE ASH, (personal collection), 66 Humiston Dr, Bethany, 06525.
Holdings: Mss Maps Pix

CT —TRINITY COLLEGE LIBRARY, Watkinson Library, 300 Summit St, Hartford, 06106. Jeffrey Kaimowitz, Cur
Holdings: Cat

CT —YALE UNIVERSITY, Anthropology Library, Peabody Museum of Natural History, C-8 KBT, New Haven, 06511.
Holdings: Vols (16,000) Cat
Budget: ($11,000)

CT —YALE UNIVERSITY, Beincke Rare Book & Manuscript Library, Western Americana Collection, Wall & High St, New Haven, 06520. George Miles, Cur
Holdings: Cat Mss Maps Pix
Notes: Incl much historical ephemeral material.

DC —GEORGETOWN UNIVERSITY, Library, Special Collections Div, 37 & O Sts NW, Washington, 20057. George M Barringer, Special Collections Librn; Nicholas B Sheetz, Mss Librn
Holdings: Cat Mss
Notes: Papers of John Gilmary Shea (1824-1892), noted Catholic historian and linguist of Indian languages who published over two hundred titles during his lifetime. The papers incl correspondence to Shea, manuscripts and notes reflecting his research, collected documents and manuscripts, and various photographs. Correspondence written to Shea incl letters from George Bancroft, Francis Parkman, Jared Sparks, Harriet Beecher Stowe, E B O'Callahan, Hanry Schoolcraft, Charles White, D D, Charles Currier, P T Barnum, Frederick Douglass, Thomas A Edison, Oliver Wendell Holmes, as well as noted members of the Church hierarchy. A long span of correspondence from Shea to the historian, Edmund Mallet contains many insights into Shea's life and work. Photographs incl likenesses of Elizabeth Seton, Isaac Hecker and George Bancroft. Also incl in the papers are numerous documents andmss concerning Shea's work in the field of Native American history, language, and culture.

DC —SMITHSONIAN INSTITUTION LIBRARIES, Anthropology Branch, Washington, 20560. Jean C Smith, Asst Dir for Bureau Services
Holdings: Vols (54,000) Cat Mss Maps Pix Slides Microforms
Budget: ($7041)
Notes: Physical anthropology, archaeology, ethnology, language and languages; Indians of both continents.

FL —HISTORICAL ASSOCIATION OF SOUTHERN FLORIDA, Charlton W Tebeau Library of Florida History, 101 W Flager St, Miami, 33130. Rebecca A Smith, Cur of Research Materials
Holdings: Vols (3000) Cat Mss Maps Pix Slides Audiotapes 16mm Films Microfilms
Notes: History of Florida, with emphasis on southern area. Less extensively, history of the Caribbean area, especially as related to Florida. Florida materials incl anthropology, archaeology, Indians of south Florida, incl Seminole Indians, Dade County history, and a complete run of the newspaper *The American Eagle* (1906-date), printed by Koreshan Unity, Estero, Florida. Incl 300 feet of mss, 1500 maps, 75,000 pictures, 2000 slides, 125 audiotapes, 25 16mm films, 200 microforms, 50 feet of vertical files, and 7000 postcards. Work in progress on guide to ms collection and on indexing of photographs. Also incl books and journals on museum science: conservation and preservation of museum materials.

GA —CARNEGIE LIBRARY, Henderson Room, 607 Broad St, Rome, 30161. Beatrice Millican, Librn
Holdings: Cat Maps 16mm Films
Budget: ($2700)
Notes: There is a special catalog to the Indian collection. The collection (5000 items) includes, books, maps, excerpts of other books, copies of documents, etc.

IL —NEWBERRY LIBRARY, 60 W Walton St, Chicago, 60610. Diana Haskell, Cur of Modern Mss
Holdings: Cat Mss
Notes: The Ayer Collection. One of ths most extensive collections.

IL —UNIVERSITY OF CHICAGO LIBRARY, Dept of Special Collections, 1100 E 57 St, Chicago, 60637.
Notes: Source material regarding first contact of White men and Indians in Mississippi Valley. Part of Ethno-History Collection.

IL —KNOX COLLEGE, Henry M Seymour Library, Galesburg, 61401. Douglas L Wilson, Dir
Holdings: Vols 4780 Cat Mss Maps Pix
Notes: Special emphasis on the earliest European contacts in the upper Mississippi, early settlement in Illinois.

IL —AUGUSTANA COLLEGE, Library, Rock Island, 61201. Marjorie M Miller, Special Collections Librn
Holdings: Vols 2000 Cat Mss
Notes: The John Hauberg Upper Mississippi Valley Collection. Incl strong collection of immigrant guide books for the Midwestern states. Fine collection relative to the Sauk and Fox tribes and Black Hawk in particular.

IL —UNIVERSITY OF ILLINOIS, URBANA/CHAMPAIGN, Library, Urbana, 61801.

IN —INDIANA UNIVERSITY, Lilly Library, Seventh St, Bloomington, 47405. William R Cagle, Librn
Holdings: Vols (40,000) Cat Mss Maps
Notes: Research and rare book collection

INDIANS OF NORTH AMERICA AND MEXICO (cont.)

(Bernardo Mendel) of first or only editions, mostly printed in Latin America, from the dicsovery of the New World through 1830. Special strength in discoveries and exploration, history (mainly period of independence), Inquisition, missionary works by the Augustinians, Dominicans, Franciscans, and the Jesuits, and the history of the Catholic Church in these countries. Major geographic concentration is on the three great viceroyalties of Mexico (ca 10, 000 titles, plus over 10,000 official Mexican broadsides), Peru (2000 titles), and Argentina (4000 titles), incl in Argentina a substantial amount of printings from the Imprenta de Ninos Expositos, and the Colleccion Santamarina. A special Bolivian Collection (2500 titles), mostly history, from the establishment of the press there, ca 1826, through the beginning of the 20th century. Part of the Mendel Collection is the select Bibliotheca Boxeriana from Charles R Boxer (1000 titles) on European expansion into Asia, and into the New World, mainly Brazil, during the 16th-18th centuries. The collection is supplemented by substantial material from the private collection of Josiah K Lilly.
See also entries under Spain - History; Portugal - History; Mexico - History.

IA —STATE HISTORICAL SOCIETY OF IOWA LIBRARY, 402 Iowa Ave, Iowa City, 52240. Darold J Brown, Librn
Holdings: Vols 1500 Cat Mss Pix
Notes: Manuscript materials and pictures are very limited in number. Primarily, a book collection which incl many older publications.

IA —UNIVERSITY OF IOWA, University Libraries, Iowa City, 52242. Frank Paluka, Head, Special Collections Dept
Holdings: Vols 500 // Cat Pix
Notes: Especially the Midwestern regions. The Harvey Ingham Collection, described by Charles Gibson, in *Books at Iowa*, No 4, April 1966, pp 3-8.

KS —KANSAS CITY PUBLIC LIBRARY, 625 Minnesota Ave, Kansas City, 66101. Eleanor Fox, Librn
Holdings: Mss
Notes: Wyandot (Huron) Indians.

KS —UNIVERSITY OF KANSAS, Kenneth Spencer Research Library, Kansas Collection, Lawrence, 66045. Sheryl K Williams, Cur
Holdings: Vols (92,000) Cat Mss Maps Pix
Notes: Several photographic collections devoted exclusively to American Indian subjects, collections of personal papers, contemporary American Indian periodicals, 19th century tracts and treatises. Wars, missionary contracts, reservation life, etc in Kansas, Oklahoma and Nebraska. Good holdings treating Potawatomie Indians (Prairie Band), Sauk, Fox, Osage.

KS —KANSAS STATE HISTORICAL SOCIETY LIBRARY, Memorial Bldg, 120 W Tenth, Topeka, 66612. Portia Allbert, Library Dir
Holdings: Vols (3900) Cat Maps Microforms
Budget: ($15,000)

KS —WICHITA PUBLIC LIBRARY, 223 S Main, Wichita, 67202. Richard Rademacher, Librn
Holdings: Vols (400) Cat
Notes: Selection based on the American Indian viewpoint and impartial analysis. Scope: art, legends, historical works. Many 19th century publications. Not loaned.

LA —AMISTAD RESEARCH CENTER, 400 Esplanade Ave, New Orleans, 70116. Clifton H Johnson, Exec Dir; Florence E Borders, Senior Archivist
Holdings: Vols (10,000) Cat Mss Pix Audiotapes Microforms
Budget: ($315,000)
Notes: 8,000,000 ms pieces, 10,000 pictures, 3500 microforms, and 500 audiotapes. Amistad Research Center is an historical research library devoted to the collection and use of primary source materials on the history of America's ethnic minorities, with particular emphasis on Afro-Americans, American Indians, and immigrant groups. Originally established at Fisk University, in Nashville, by the American Missionary Association (AMA), this research center on Black American History incl papers of such leaders as W E B DuBois, Countee Cullen, and Mary McLeod Bethune. Among the larger institutional collections held are the archives and records of the American Missionary Assoc, the American Home Missionary Society, the Race Relations Dept of the Anti-Defamation League, the Catholic Committee of the South, and the National Assoc of Human Rights Workers, (formerly NAIRO).

LA —TULANE UNIVERSITY, Howard-Tilton Memorial Library, Latin American Library, New Orleans, 70118. Thomas Niehaus, Dir
Holdings: Vols (150,000) Cat Mss Maps Pix Microforms VF
Budget: ($67,000)
Notes: *Catalog of the Latin American* Library (Boston: G K Hall, 1970, suppl. 1973,1975,1978); Downs 5338-41; suppl (1961), 2727, 2737. The Latin American Library is a general collection, but specializes in Central American, Mexican, and Brazilian materials. The disciplines which are most strongly represented are history, anthropology, and archaeology. The Viceregal Ecclesiastical Mexican Collection contains manuscripts from the colonial period. The France V Scholes Collection contains a large number of photoprints and microfilm of colonial documents from the archives of Spain and Mexico. The Merle Greene Robertson Rubbings Collection contains nearly five hundred rubbings of relief sculpture from Mayan archaeological sites in Mexico and Guatemala. The Photographic Collection contains photos of archaeological sites inMeso-America, of pre-Columbian Peruvian architecture, and a general group of historic photos from Latin America.

LA —R W NORTON ART GALLERY, Library, 4747 Creswell Ave, Shreveport, 71106. Jerry M Bloomer, Librn
Holdings: Vols 114 Cat

MA —CHILDREN'S MUSEUM, Resource Center, Museum Wharf, 300 Congress St, Boston, 02210. Marie Ariel, Librn; Maria Russell, Resource Services Mgr
Holdings: Vols 350 Cat Mss Slides Phonorecords Audiotapes Filmstrips
Notes: Curriculum materials and materials for children and adults. Available for reference use by the public; borrowing privileges for Museum members; activity and curriculum kits available to public, schools and community groups for rental fee. Collection of Northeast Indian objects housed in Study Storage facility for use by appointment with Curator; incl is a Folk Arts collection of oral history interviews with 40 Native American craftspeople, with supporting audio-visual materials. Subject-related programs and services offered by Museum staff.

MA —HARVARD UNIVERSITY LIBRARY, Botanical Museum Library, Cambridge, 02138.
Holdings: Vols (2400) Mss Pix
Notes: The Tina and Gordon Wisson Ethnomycological Collection, one of the most important modern collections, acquired as an adjunct to the Museum's Economic Botany Library of Oakes Ames. From 15th to 20th century, it deals with hallucinogenic mushrooms in art, religion, and folklore; chemistry, pharmacology, linguistics, archaeological artifacts of Mexico, Guatemala, India, Japan, China, etc. Personal papers, etc.

MA —PEABODY MUSEUM OF SALEM, Phillips Library, E India Sq, Salem, 01970. Gregor Trinkaus-Randall, Librn
Holdings: Vols (100,000) Cat Mss Pix
Notes: Ethnology of Non-European Peoples Collection. Composed of separate divisions relating to the Pacific Islands, China, Japan and the American Indian. No published indexes.

MA —AMERICAN ANTIQUARIAN SOCIETY LIBRARY, 185 Salisbury St, Worcester, 01609. Marcus A McCorison, Dir & Librn
Holdings: Cat

MI —UNIVERSITY OF MICHIGAN, William L Clements Library, Ann Arbor, 48109. John C Dann, Dir
Notes: The William L. Clements Library of Americana is a non-circulating rare book library of original source material, printed and manuscript, dealing with America, from the discovery period into the late nineteenth century. The collection includes approximately 55,000 books and pamphlets, 550 linear feet of manuscripts, 4,100 volumes of newspapers, 36,000 maps, 40,000 pieces of sheet music, and 1,000 prints. The collection is strongest for the period of the American Revolution, and includes the papers of Thomas Gage, Sir Henry Clinton, and the Earl of Shelburne. Other areas of strength include antislavery, cartography and geography, discovery and exploration, American Indians, The Civil War, tune-books, sermons and orations, and the War of 1812. There are selective research collections dealing with Christopher Columbus, Thomas Paine, Benjamin Franklin, George Washington, Thomas Jefferson, and the Federalist Papers. Publications describing the collections of the library are: Author/Title catalog of Americana 1493-1860 in the William L. Clements Library... 7 volumes, Boston, G. K. Hall, 1970; Guide to the manuscript collections of the William L. Clements Library, by Arlene P. Shy 3d edition, Boston, G. K. Hall, 1978; Guide to the manuscript maps in the William L. Clements Library, compiled by Christian Burn, Ann Arbor, U. of Michigan, 1959; and Research catalog of maps of America, to 1860 in the William L. Clements Library...,edited by Douglas W. Marshall, 4 volumes, Boston, G. K. Hall, 1972.

MI —HACKLEY PUBLIC LIBRARY, 316 W Webster Ave, Muskegon, 49440. Dale H Pretzer, Dir
Holdings: // Cat
Notes: Incl *The North American Indians* by Edward Curtis, in 20 vols plus 20 portfolios of numbered plates.

MI —LAKE SUPERIOR STATE COLLEGE, Library, College Dr, Sault Sainte Marie, 49783. Frederick A Michels, Dir
Holdings: Vols (400) Cat Maps Pix Slides
Notes: Michigan History with emphasis on Sault Ste Marie, Eastern end of Upper Peninsula, and area Indians (Chippewa or Ojibway).

MN —MINNEAPOLIS PUBLIC LIBRARY & INFORMATION CENTER, 300 Nicollet Mall, Minneapolis, 55401. Richard J Hofstad, Athenaeum Librn
Holdings: Vols (300) Cat Maps Pix
Notes: Incl rare books in the field.

MN —COLLEGE OF SAINT CATHERINE, Library, 2004 Randolph Ave, Saint Paul, 55105. Sister Elizabeth Delmore, Library Dir
Holdings: Vols (800) Cat Mss Slides Phonorecords Audiotapes Filmstrips Microforms
Budget: ($800)
Notes: Both historical and cultural aspects. Special emphasis on Chippewa and Sioux Indian tribes.

MN —JAMES JEROME HILL REFERENCE LIBRARY, Fourth St at Market St, Saint

INDIANS OF NORTH AMERICA AND MEXICO (cont.)

Paul, 55106. Virgil F Massman, Dir
Holdings: Vols 1000 Cat Maps Pix

MN —MINNESOTA HISTORICAL SOCIETY LIBRARY, 690 Cedar St, Saint Paul, 55101. Patricia C Harpole, Chief of Reference Library; Bonnie G Wilson, Head of Special Libraries

MO —UNIVERSITY OF MISSOURI-COLUMBIA, Museum of Anthropology Archives, 104 Swallow Hall, Columbia, 65201. Lawrence H Feldman, Museum Dir
Holdings: Vols (30) Cat Mss Maps Slides Microforms
Notes: Copies of Latin American and colonial mss. Many of the ms copies are of census and census-like, documents of late colonial Verapaz; a few are from Sonsonate, El Salvador or Chiapas, Mexico. Additional material in the archives incl an original Eskimo manuscript (ca 1930) an original Diegueno Yuman card vocabulary (ca 1964) and the Museum archives (papers on old accession systems, etc). Uncataloged microfilm copies of colonial Otomi and other vocabularies are also part of the collection. A catalog of material in this collection will appear in the Annual Report of the Museum of Anthropology, beginning with the 1976-77 volume.

MO —UNIVERSITY OF MISSOURI-KANSAS CITY, General Library, Snyder Collection of Americana, 5100 Rockhill Road, Kansas City, 64110. Kenneth J LaBudde, Dir; Robert Paustian, Asst Dir
Holdings: Vols 25,000 Cat
Notes: Nucleus was Robert M Snyder, Jr Americana Collection of some 14,000 items. Contains printed materials on 19th-century American history, especially the Trans-Mississippi West. Strengths include the history of Kansas City and Jackson County, Missouri, Kansas and Missouri county and state histories, American frontier religion (esp the Mormons and Alexander Campbell's Disciples of Christ), the history of railroads and transportation, the cattle trade, 19th-Century biography and autobiography, North American Indians and early Kansas and Missouri imprints.

MO —WASHINGTON UNIVERSITY, John M Olin Library, Campus Box 1061, St Louis, 63130.
Holdings: Vols (1800) Cat Mss
Notes: Incl material from the Arthur C Hoskins, Richard S Hawes, Ernst C Krohn, George N Meissner, Stratford Lee Morton, and Edgar M Queeny collections; strong in early travel literature of the US and Latin America; accounts of exploration in the Mississippi Valley and Trans-Mississippi West; misc accounts of exploration in the Trans-Mississippi West; misc accounts of history, pioneer life, and travel in the Ohio Valley, Old Southwest, and California; material on the American Indian; 18th century American music; early American imprints.

MT —MONTANA STATE UNIVERSITY, Library, Bozeman, 59717. Minnie Ellen Paugh, Special Collections Librn
Holdings: Vols (7000) // Mss Maps Pix
Notes: Leggat-Donahoe Collection. Collection of Alexander Leggat of Butte, whose father was active in opening the mines. Mr Leggat's interests were mining, exploration, and the fur trade. There are excellent Indian materials in the collection. Also the manuscript and picture collections of James Willard Schultz, Harry James (about James Willard Schultz), and Olga Ross Hannon on Blackfeet Indian tepees. Land claim clase files and manuscripts about Blackfeet, Gros Ventre, Assiniboine and Crow Indians collected by Dr Thomas R Wessell, Edward E Barry and Dr Merrill G Burlingame.

NE —UNIVERSITY OF NEBRASKA-LINCOLN, Don L Love Library, University Archives and Special Collections, Lincoln, 68588. Joseph G Svoboda, University Archivist
Holdings: Pix Slides
Notes: R D Warden Collection of Charles Marion Russell. "Largest private collection of literature on Russell, 'The Cowboy Artist.'" 700 items, incl first editions of every book and pamphlet by Russell and over 1000 periodical appearances of his art; 900 color prints; 142 drawings; color slides; scrapbooks about Russell and his family, from 1889.

NE —JOSLYN ART REFERENCE LIBRARY, Joslyn Art Museum, 2200 Dodge St, Omaha, 68102. Ann Birney, Librn; Marie Sedlacek, Cataloger-Slide Librn
Holdings: Vols (17,000) Cat Slides
Notes: Incl catalogs of exhibitions and western US materials, especially early Omaha and Nebraska. Large collections of vertical files on subjects and artists; also mounted prints, reproductions, slides. filmstrips.

NV —UNIVERSITY OF NEVADA SYSTEM, Elko Community College, Learning Resources Center, Elko, 89801. Juanita R Karr, Dir
Holdings: Vols 1200 Cat Maps Pix Microforms
Budget: $500

NJ —GLASSBORO STATE COLLEGE, Savitz Library, Stewart Room, Glassboro, 08028. Clara Kirner, Special Collection Librn
Holdings: Vols 400 Cat Mss Pix
Notes: Some New Jersey Indian deeds and artifacts of southern New Jersey.

NJ —PRINCETON UNIVERSITY, Library, Princeton, 08540. Alfred Bush, Cur
Holdings: Cat Mss

NM —ALBUQUERQUE PUBLIC LIBRARY, 501 Copper Ave NW, Albuquerque, 87102. Alan B Clark, Dir
Holdings: Vols (4000) Cat Microforms Records Maps VF
Notes: Large collection of materials on all aspects of New Mexico history and cultures. In-house index accesses VF materials and local and regional periodicals. Special emphasis on Indians of New Mexico and northeastern Arizona, particularly the Navajo, Hopi, Pueblos and Apache. Reference copies of many works are housed at the Special Collections Library, 423 Central Ave NE, Albuquerque, NM 87102.

NM —AZTEC RUINS NATIONAL MONUMENT, Library, PO Box U, Aztec, 87410. William L Schart, Park Ranger
Holdings: Vols (500) // Cat Mss Maps Pix Slides
Notes: Archaeology of the Anasazi ruins.

NM —NEW MEXICO HIGHLANDS UNIVERSITY, Donnelly Library, National Ave, Las Vegas, 87701. Karen Jaggers, Assoc Librn
Holdings: Vols (5000) Cat Mss Maps Pix Microforms
Notes: The outstanding collection is the Arrott Collection on Fort Union, New Mexico, 1851-1891.

NY —NEW YORK STATE LIBRARY, State Education Bldg Annex, Washington Ave, Albany, 12224.
Holdings: Vols (110,500) Cat
Notes: Strong collection emphasis on North American Indians, especially Indians of New York. Incl books and pamphlets on Indian captivities, treaties, conferences, lives of noted Indians, laws. Bibles and catechisms, prayerbooks, grammars, etc in native languages. Outstanding collection on Iroquois Indians. Incl original treaties between the State of New York and the Iroquois, papers of Cornplanter, drawings by Jesse Cornplanter. Also incl papers of William Beauchamp (ca 1860-1930), consisting mainly of his notebooks and scrapbooks concerning the history of the Iroquois Indians. Incl 13 boxes of material on Indian language, folklore, and place names, the Moravians, and New York State archeology.

NY —MUSEUM OF THE AMERICAN INDIAN, Library, 9 Westchester Square, Bronx, 10401. Mary B Davis, Librn
Holdings: Vols (40,000) Cat Mss Maps Pix Microforms VF
Notes: Collections cover all aspects of the Indians of the Western Hemisphere; some materials on Eskimos. For scholarly research only.

NY —HOFSTRA UNIVERSITY, Library, 1000 Fulton Ave, Hempstead, 11550. Charles R Andrews, Dean of Library Services
Notes: The personal library of Paul Radin. See description of the American Philosophical Society Library's collection of his anthropological papers under this entry (Pa).

NY —AMERICAN MUSEUM OF NATURAL HISTORY, Library Services Dept, Central Park W & 79th St, New York, 10024. Nina J Root, Chairwoman; Mary Genett, Asst Librn for Reference Services
Holdings: Vols (385,000) Cat Mss Maps Pix Slides Microforms
Notes: Nearly all collections are outstanding for depth of coverage and international range. Early and historic works, rare books, colored illustrations, and relevant serial publications supplement the modern scientific publications necessary to the researches of the scientific staff and the work of the educational division. Open to the public. Incl a card index of about 800 entries of portraits of named American Indians, indexed from various publications. Indexing ended, apparently, about 1955.

NY —NEW YORK HISTORICAL SOCIETY, Library, 170 Central Park W, New York, 10024. James Gregory, Librn
Holdings: Mss
Notes: Incl original mss, illustrative materials, etc.

NY —NEW YORK PUBLIC LIBRARY, Mid-Manhattan Library, History and Social Sciences Dept, 455 Fifth Ave, New York, 10016. Robert Sheehan, Sr Principal Librn
Holdings: Vols 5,000 Cat Phonorecords Audiotapes Microforms
Budget: $5,000
Notes: Strong in material on American Indians and US history in general. Incl the *Library of American Civilization* on microfiche.

NY —NEW YORK PUBLIC LIBRARY, Research Libraries, American History Div, Fifth Ave & 42 St, New York, 10018.
Holdings: Vols (10,000) Cat Maps Microforms
Notes: Archaeology, anthropology, linguistics, ethnology, and sociology of the American Indian. Comprehensive coverage. Much material on Indian lanugages, incl numerous syllabaries. Coverage ranges from the Eskimos to the Indians of Tierra del Fuego.

NY —HARTWICK COLLEGE, Library, Oneonta, 13820. Eric von Brockdorff, Dir
Holdings: Vols (5000) Cat Maps Pix Microforms
Budget: ($6000)
Notes: Emphasis is on eastern Woodland Indians. Cited in *Indians of North and South America: A Bibliography Based on the Collection in the Willard E Yager Library-Museum, Hartwick College, Oneonta, NY*, by Carolyn E Wolf and Karen Folk (Metuchen, NJ: Scarecrow Pr, 1977).

NC —MUSEUM OF THE CHEROKEE INDIAN, Library, PO Box 770-A, Cherokee, 28719. Juanita H Hughes, Archivist
Holdings: Vols 1400 Cat Mss Microforms
Budget: $500

ND —MINOT STATE COLLEGE, Memorial Library, Minot, 58701. Ronald J Rudser, Dir
Holdings: Vols 1000 Cat Microforms
Notes: Primarily North Central States area.

OH —CLEVELAND PUBLIC LIBRARY, Fine Arts and Special Collections Department, 325 Superior Ave, Cleveland, 44114. Alice N Loranth, Head
Holdings: Vols 8000 Cat
Notes: Part of the research collection on the Indians of North, Central and South America and Mexico; holds materials on tribal histories, archaeology and antiquities, arts, costumes, folklore, manners and customs, etc. Special strength is in the extensive holdings on Indian languages, dictionaries and linguistics. Some rare books and first editions on travel among the Indians. Current acquisitions in subject departments and rare book collection only. *See also* entries under Folklore; Language and Languages; Rare Books.

INDIANS OF NORTH AMERICA AND MEXICO (cont.)

OH —OHIO HISTORICAL SOCIETY, Archives Library Division, 1982 Velma Ave, Columbus, 43211. Dennis East, Division Chief
Holdings: Vols (96,000) Cat Mss Maps Pix Slides Microforms
Budget: ($18,000)
Notes: This library is the primary collection for Ohio. Most purchases are on the rare and op market. Collecting area is early American history, esp relating to exploration into the Northwest Territory. Major media collections are books (96,000), newspapers (25,000 vols and 22,000 microfilm), pictures (50,000), maps (2500), manuscripts (1,500, 000). Library is noncirculating except through interlibrary loan of microfilm.

OH —FLESH PUBLIC LIBRARY, 124 W Greene St, Piqua, 45356. Wallace White, Librn
Holdings: Vols (1400) // Cat Maps
Notes: The Jerome C Smiley Collection.

OK —UNIVERSITY OF SCIENCE & ARTS OF OKLAHOMA, Nash Library, Chickasha, 73018. William A Martin, Jr, Librn
Holdings: // Uncat Mss Pix Audiotapes
Notes: Papers of Hugh D Corwin, writer on Indian life and history, incl conversations with elderly Kiowa Indians, with audiotapes, some pictures and mss; also reprints of Corwin's historical articles from local newspapers.

OK —FIVE CIVILIZED TRIBES MUSEUM, Library, Agency Hill, Honor Hts Dr, Muskogee, 74401. Mrs Spencer Denton, Dir
Holdings: Maps Pix
Notes: The collection pertains to the history, culture, and traditions of the Five Civilized Tribes plus history of Indian Territory prior to statehood.

OK —UNIVERSITY OF OKLAHOMA, Bizzell Memorial Library, Western History Collections, 401 W Brooks, Norman, 73069. John Ezell, Cur
Holdings: Cat Mss Maps Pix Microforms

OK —OKLAHOMA HISTORICAL SOCIETY, Library, Historical Bldg, Oklahoma City, 73105. Andrea Clark, Dir, Library Resources Division
Holdings: Vols (43,000) Cat Mss Maps Pix Microforms
Notes: The Society also has the Indian Archives Collection of 2,500,000 pieces (Mary Lee Boyle, Archivist). This is an extensive collection of records, particularly of the Five Civilized Tribes. Incl tribal rolls, agency reports, manuscripts, etc.

OK —CHEROKEE NATIONAL HISTORICAL SOCIETY, Archives & Library, PO Box 515 TSA-LA-GI, Tahlequah, 74464. Duane King, Dir
Holdings: Vols (1000) Uncat Mss Maps Pix Slides Audiotapes Microforms
Notes: An embryonic collection, directly or indirectly related to Cherokee history, culture and genealogy. Slide collection depicts copies of material from the collection, from the Cherokee National Museum Village (Cherokee, 1650 AD) and the Cultural Theatre ("Trail of Tears Drama"). Newspaper collection incl several hundred newspapers dating back to 1762, each of which contains some reference to the Cherokees. The Cherokee National Archives also contains the non-current 1975 files of the Cherokee Nation of Oklahoma and the Keeler Collection (papers and personal files of W W Keeler, former Principal Chief of the Cherokee Nation for 26 years).

OK —PHILBROOK ART CENTER, Library, 2727 S Rockford Rd, Tulsa, 74114. Thomas E Young, Librn
Holdings: Vols (1000) Uncat Pix
Notes: The Roberta C Lawson Collection is mainly books, with some serials, and an uncounted group of photographs. The books are organized and partially cataloged; photographs are not. They deal with Indians and western Americana.

OK —THOMAS GILCREASE INSTITUTE OF AMERICAN HISTORY & ART LIBRARY, 1400 North 25th West Ave, Tulsa, 74127. Sarah Hirsch, Librn
Holdings: Vols Cat Mss Maps Pix
Notes: Trans-Mississippi West, US, Indian and Hispanic history. The Gilcrease Library contains a total of about 40,000 mss; 10,000 imprints; 5000 photographs; 600 maps and 50,000 vols.

OK —UNIVERSITY OF TULSA, McFarlin Library, Dept of Rare Books and Special Collections, 600 S College, Tulsa, 74104. David Farmer, Dir; Toby Murray, Archivist; Caroline Swinson, Cur of Manuscripts & Art
Holdings: Cat
Notes: The Indian collection of John W Shleppey. Indian materials of some 6000 bibliographic items, excl of mss and photographs. Emphasis on Indian Territory imprints, laws, Cherokee and Choctaw tribes, etc.

OR —UNIVERSITY OF OREGON LIBRARY, Social Science Dept, Eugene, 97403. Holway R Jones, Head Dept Librn
Holdings: Cat
Notes: Western tribes.

PA —GETTYSBURG COLLEGE, Musselman Library, Gettysburg, 17325. Willis M Hubbard, College Librn
Holdings: Vols 1200 Cat Phonorecords

PA —HAVERFORD COLLEGE, Magill Library, Quaker Collection, Haverford, 19041. Edwin B Bonner, Librn & Cur
Holdings: Vols (32,000) Cat Mss Maps Pix Phonorecords Audiotapes Microforms
Notes: Incl material about Society of Friends from inception in England, 1650, to the present. Formats incl periodicals, diaries, documents of individual Friends, families, Quaker Meetings and institutions, incl archives of Haverford College. Emphases on American Indians, antislavery, women, minorities, the Rufus M Jones Mysticism collection, Quaker fiction, and Delaware Valley, Pennsylvania.

PA —AMERICAN PHILOSOPHICAL SOCIETY, Library, 105 S Fifth St, Philadelphia, 19106. Edward C Carter II, Librn
Notes: The anthropological papers of Paul Radin in fields of ethnology, social organization, primitive religion, linguistics, and mythology. He worked mostly among the Winnebago, Ojibwa, Fox, Zapotec, Wappo, Wintun, and Huave Indian tribes; also Italian and other ethnic minorities of San Francisco.

PA —FREE LIBRARY OF PHILADELPHIA, Social Science and History Dept, Logan Sq, Philadelphia, 19103. William Handley, Head
Holdings: Vols 6000 Cat
Notes: With the Wilberforce Eames Collection as nucleus.

PA —UNIVERSITY OF PITTSBURGH, Hillman Library, Pittsburgh, 15260. Glenora E Rossell, Head
Holdings: Vols 3500 Cat Microforms
Notes: The collection is very strong in pre-Columbian archaeology and Indian cultures from the historical and anthropological point of view. Emphasis on contemporary history, politics and socio-economical problems.

PA —UNIVERSITY OF PITTSBURGH, Darlington Memorial Library, Special Collections, 601 Cathedral of Learning, Pittsburgh, 15260. Dennis Lambert, Darlington Librn
Holdings: Vols (17,000) Cat Mss Maps Pix
Notes: The Darlington Collection is especially rich in American history of the colonial period, the French and Indian War, the Revolution, and the War of 1812 with geographical emphasis on Western Pennsylvania and Ohio Valley history to 1870 and on Pittsburgh history to 1900. Indian treaties, captivity accounts, US and Pennsylvania travel and description, and early American fiction and prose are represented. A partial guide to the Darlington Manuscript Collections is available by writing for *Darlington Memorial Library: A Descriptive Checklist of its Manuscript Collections,* University of Pittsburgh Bibliographic Series 5, 1969. Noncirculating.

PA —FRIENDS HISTORICAL LIBRARY OF SWARTHMORE COLLEGE, Swarthmore, 19081. J William Frost, Dir
Holdings: Vols (35,000) Cat Mss Pix Microforms
Notes: Library's collections contain information on the history and doctrine of the Society of Friends, Quaker contributions to literature, science, business, education, and government, plus their reform efforts in peace, Indian rights, women's rights, and abolition of slavery. Among the more than 250 mss collections are records of several Quaker agencies, established by Philadelphia, Baltimore, and other Hicksite Yearly Meetings to aid Indians, particularly during the administration of Ulysses S Grant. Also incl are papers of Quaker Indian agents Albert L Green and Thomas Lightfoot, and journals of Quaker ministers who visited Indians.

PA —WASHINGTON AND JEFFERSON COLLEGE, Library, Washington, 15301. Robert E Connell, Librn
Holdings: Vols 2100 Cat Mss Maps Pix
Notes: A general subject and author card catalog has been prepared for the ms collection. Published description of the collection appears in: Pennsylvania, Historical and Museum Commission, *Historical Manuscript Depositories in* Pennsylvania (Harrisburg, 1965), compiled by Irwin Richman. Incl are materials concerning the "Westward movement"--letters, land grants, etc. Much on the Revolutionary War, the "Whiskey Rebellion" of 1794. Many other small collections of mss, some containing American Indian and Western Pennsylvania history.

RI —BROWN UNIVERSITY, John Carter Brown Library, Providence, 02912. Norman Fiering, Librn; Everett C Wilkie Jr, Bibliographer; Susan Danforth, Cur Maps & Prints
Notes: Materials documenting contact between native Americans and Europeans; incl works on Indian liguistics.

RI —PROVIDENCE ATHENAEUM, 251 Benefit St, Providence, 02903. Sally Duplaix, Dir
Holdings: (152,000) Vols
Notes: Material available on interlibrary loan under certain conditions.

SC —COLLEGE OF CHARLESTON LIBRARY, Special Collections Dept, Charleston, 29401.
Notes: Papers incl report of the committee regarding sending Catawba Indian officials to New York "to make a peace with the Six Nations" of Indians, May 17, 1758.

SD —NORTHERN STATE COLLEGE, Beulah Williams Library, Documents & Reference Dept, Aberdeen, 57401. Keith W Warne, Librn
Holdings: Cat Mss Audiotapes
Notes: American Indian History Research Project.

†SD —SOUTH DAKOTA SCHOOL OF MINES & TECHNOLOGY, Devereaux Library, Rapid City, 57701.
Holdings: Vols 153 Cat
Notes: Indians of North America with emphasis on the Sioux Indians. Some of the books concern wars and battles with Indians, especially the Custer Massacre.

SD —AUGUSTANA COLLEGE, Mikkelsen Library & Learning Resource Center, Center for Western Studies, Sioux Falls, 57197. Ronelle Thompson, Dir Library
Notes: The Center for Western Studies, located in the Mikkelsen Library, is an archival and research agency of Augustana College. Dedicated to the history and culture of the Great Plains and the Trans-Mississippi West, the Center collects and preserves materials relating to Plains Indians, immigrant settlers, Norwegiana, Western Americana, Herbert Krause, Frederick Manfred, Donald Parker, Richard F Pettigrew, Augustana College, the Episcopal Diocese of South Dakota, the South Dakota District of the American Lutheran Church, the South Dakota Penitentiary and Minnehaha County.

SD —W H OVER MUSEUM, 414 E Clark, University of South Dakota, Vermillion, 57069. Julia Vodicka, Dir
Holdings: Cat Pix
Notes: The Stanley J Morrow Collection of

INDIANS OF NORTH AMERICA AND MEXICO (cont.)

Stereographs; frontier military posts, Indians, riverboats, pioneer life in Dakota Territory. The 440 stereographs of this collection were made in Dakota Territory and the Upper Missouri region between 1868 and 1883 by Stanley J Morrow, Yankton, DT. Copy photographs may be ordered. The collection is described in Wesley Hurt's *Stanley J Morrow: Pioneer Photographer*.

TX —AMARILLO PUBLIC LIBRARY, 413 E Fourth, Amarillo, 79101. Mary Kay Snell, Librn
Holdings: Vols Cat Mss Maps Pix
Notes: The southwest collections incl materials on the history of Texas, Louisiana, New Mexico, Arkansas, Missouri and Kansas. General subjects covered incl overland journeys, early narratives, early biographies, Indian captivities, outlaws, US government reports, Mississippi and Ohio Rivers, the Mexican War, reports of Catholic missionaries, Niles Register, early publications, fur trade, western trails, Texas Rangers, sheriffs and Texas as a sovereign state, buffalo hunting, Indian wars, cowboys, the arrival of farmers, fences, and towns. Over 1600 items which incl books, documents, maps, mss, pamphlets, unpublished theses, interviews and photographs. The three major collections are the William Henry Bush Collection, the Laurence J Fitzsimon Collection and the Calendar of John L McCarty.

TX —UNIVERSITY OF TEXAS LIBRARIES, General Libraries, Barker Texas History Center, PO Box P, Austin, 78712. Don Carleton, Dir
Notes: Major center for the study of Texas history, incl the Eberstadt Collection.

TX —WEST TEXAS STATE UNIVERSITY, Cornette Library, PO Box 748 WT Sta, Canyon, 79016. Faye Hendrickson, Special Collections Asst
Holdings: Vols (1850) Uncat Microforms
Notes: Includes microforms collection.

TX —TEXAS A&M UNIVERSITY, Sterling C Evans Library, Special Collections Div, College Station, 77843. Donald H Dyal, Librn
Holdings: Vols (16,000) Mss Pix
Notes: Jeff Dykes Range Livestock Collection (incl a 600-item collection of J Frank Dobie works). Part of the Dobie Collection is described in Dykes, Jeff C *My Dobie Collection* (College Station, Tex: Friends of the Texas A & M University Library).

TX —DALLAS PUBLIC LIBRARY, Texas/Dallas History and Archives Division, 1515 Young St, Dallas, 75201. Richard L Waters, Acting Dir; Wayne Gray, Manager
Holdings: Vols (152,442) Cat Maps Pix Slides Microforms
Budget: ($38,540)
Notes: Dallas and Texas history.

TX —SOUTHERN METHODIST UNIVERSITY, DeGolyer Library, Box 396, SMU, Dallas, 75275. Clifton H Jones, Dir
Holdings: Vols (80,000) Cat Mss Maps Pix Slides Microforms
Notes: First editions of prominent authors; also of books in subject emphasis collections. All subjects listed in this vol are strong. Numerous collections of personal papers relating to subjects also.

TX —AMON CARTER MUSEUM, Library, 3510 Camp Bowie Blvd, PO Box 2365, Fort Worth, 76113. Nancy G Wynne, Librn
Holdings: Vols (25,000) Cat Mss Pix
Notes: The book collection, microfilm and photo archives have been built toward the goal of the interpretation of American history through art. At present, the greatest strengths are in Americana, Western Canadiana, bibliography, American exhibition catalogs and history of photography. Substantial books and files on American artists of the 19th and early 20th century, and particularly of Charles M Russell and Frederic Remington. Incl 25,000 pictures; 13,000 slides.
See also entries under Newspapers, American; Pictures - Collections.

UT —UNIVERSITY OF UTAH, Marriott Library, Special Collections, Salt Lake City, 84112. Gregory C Thompson, Cur

†WA —WASHINGTON STATE UNIVERSITY, Library, Manuscripts, Archives & Special Collections, Pullman, 99164. John F Guido, Head
Holdings: Cat Mss Maps Pix
Notes: The Carl Parcher Russell papers, a vast resource (24,916 items; 45 linear feet) on American Indian and Western pioneer activities and artifacts. Much on the fur trade; pioneer life; mountain men and trapping; wildlife; primitive life in detail. Also the National Park Service, parks, monuments, etc. Described in *Carl Parcher Russell: An Indexed Register of His Scholarly and Professional Papers, 1920-1967, in the Washington State University* Library (Pullman, 1970), 149 pp.

WI —MILWAUKEE PUBLIC LIBRARY, 814 W Wisconsin Ave, Milwaukee, 53233. Donald J Sager, City Librn
Holdings: Vols 2000 Cat
Notes: Includes sets of McKenny-Hall, Catlin, Lewis, Eastman.

WI —MILWAUKEE PUBLIC MUSEUM, Reference Library, 800 W Wells St, Milwaukee, 53233. Judith Campbell Turner, Museum Librn
Holdings: Vols (90,000) Cat Maps Microforms

WI —SHAWANO CITY-COUNTY LIBRARY, 128 S Sawyer St, Shawano, 54166. Michael Hille, Dir
Holdings: Vols 400 Cat Mss Slides
Notes: This collection is known by the general name of Indians of North America. However, the library specializes in materials of all sorts on the Menominee Indians. Some general books on the topic are paperback and uncataloged--perhaps 75 titles.

ON —NATIONAL MUSEUMS OF CANADA, Library Services Directorate, Ottawa, K1A 0M8, Can. Valerie Monkhouse, Director
Holdings: Vols (70,000) Cat Mss Maps Pix Slides Microforms
Budget: ($60,000)
Notes: Collection includes anthropology, archaeology, ethnology, folklore, history, Indians of North America, Inuit, linguistics of North American Indians, material history, military and naval history, museology. Research collection, interlibrary loans available, public may use on the premises.

ON —CANADIAN ASSOCIATION IN SUPPORT OF THE NATIVE PEOPLES, Library, 277 Victoric St, Toronto, M5V 1W2, Can. Frances Davidson-Arnott, Librn
Holdings: Vols 4000 Cat Mss Maps Pix Slides Microforms
Notes: Native peoples of North America, especially of Canada.

ON —ROYAL ONTARIO MUSEUM, Main Library and Archives, 100 Queen's Park, Toronto, M5S 2C6, Can. Julia Matthews, Head Librn
Holdings: Vols (85,000) Cat
Notes: Since January 1977, acquisitions have been entered in UTLAS.

ON —NORTH YORK PUBLIC LIBRARY, Canadiana Collection, 35 Fairview Mall Dr, Willowdale, M2J 4S4, Can. Ian C Ross, Head
Holdings: Vols (70,000) Cat Microforms
See also entry under Canada.

†SK —UNIVERSITY OF REGINA, Library, Regina, S4S 0A2, Can. Margarett Hammond, Librn
Notes: Native peoples of North America, especially of Canada. Collection formerly held by Canadian Association in Support of the Native Peoples.

INDIANS OF NORTH AMERICA AND MEXICO—ALASKA

AK —ALASKA STATE LIBRARY, Alaska Historical Library Collection, Pouch G, Juneau, 99811. Phyllis Demuth, Readers Services Librn
Holdings: Vols (24,000) Cat Mss Maps Pix Slides Phonorecords Audiotapes Videotapes 16mm Films Microforms

TX —AMON CARTER MUSEUM, Library, 3510 Camp Bowie Blvd, PO Box 2365, Fort Worth, 76113. Nancy G Wynne, Librn
Holdings: Vols (25,000) Cat Mss Pix
Notes: The book collection, microfilm and photo archives have been built toward the goal of the interpretation of American history through art. At present, the greatest strengths are in Americana, Western Canadiana, bibliography, American exhibition catalogs and history of photography. Substantial books and files on American artists of the 19th and early 20th century, and particularly of Charles M Russell and Frederic Remington. Incl 25,000 pictures; 13,000 slides.
See also entries under Newspapers, American; Pictures - Collections.

INDIANS OF NORTH AMERICA AND MEXICO—ANTIQUITIES

†AL —UNIVERSITY OF ALABAMA, Amelia Gayle Gorgas Library, PO Box S, University, 35486.
Notes: This collection consists of 119 reels of microfilm. Separately published bibliography: *A Catalog of the Yucatan Collection on Microfilm in the University of Alabama Libraries* (University: University of Alabama Press), 1972.

AZ —FULTON-HAYDEN MEMORIAL LIBRARY, Dragoon, 85609. Mario Nick Klimiades, Librn
Holdings: Vols 17,000 Cat Mss Maps Pix Microforms
Budget: $2500
Notes: The Fulton-Hayden Memorial Library is a special collection of books about archaeology and ethnology specifically as they pertain to the western hemisphere and particularly to Mexico and the greater American Southwest.

AZ —HEARD MUSEUM, Library, 22 E Monte Vista Rd, Phoenix, 85004. Mary Graham, Librn
Holdings: Vols (40,000) Cat
Notes: Anthropology and primitive art. Incl 124 periodical titles and contemporary Native American Art.

AZ —NAVAJO COMMUNITY COLLEGE, Naaltsoos Ba' Hoogan, Library, Tsaile, 86556. Marvin E Pollard Jr, Dir, Library Services
Holdings: Vols (10,000) Cat Mss Maps Pix Slides Phonorecords Audiotapes Videotapes 16mm Films Filmstrips Microforms
Budget: ($15,000)
Notes: The Moses/Donner Collection emphasizes Navajos and other tribes of the Southwest; also, all Indians of North America and Mexico. All aspects of the geology, geography, sociology, archaeology, anthropology, etc, of the Four Corners region. The Collection includes a comprehensive collection of Doctoral dissertations dealing with Indians of North Aemrica and Mexico.

AZ —ARIZONA STATE MUSEUM, Library, University of Arizona, Tucson, 85721. Hans R Bart, Museum Librn
Holdings: Vols (35,000) Cat Mss Maps Pix Slides Phonorecords Microforms

CO —COLORADO SPRINGS FINE ARTS CENTER LIBRARY, 30 W Dale St, Colorado Springs, 80903. Roderick Dew, Librn
Holdings: Vols (20,000) Cat
Budget: ($4000)
Notes: Specialize in fine arts and anthropology of the Southwest. Incl auction and exhibition catalogs.

IL —NEWBERRY LIBRARY, 60 W Walton St, Chicago, 60610. Diana Haskell, Cur of Modern Mss
Holdings: Vols (1000) Cat Mss Pix
Notes: Western continent antiquities.

MI —MACKINAC ISLAND STATE PARK COMMISSION, Library, Bos 30028, Lansing, 48909. Keith R Widder, Cur
Holdings: Vols (1000) Cat Mss Maps Pix Slides Audiotapes
Budget: ($2500)
Notes: Mackinac area history-research collection: archeology, historic preservation, etc. Great Lakes ships and shipping.

INDIANS OF NORTH AMERICA AND MEXICO—ANTIQUITIES (cont.)

MO —SCHOOL OF THE OZARKS, Lois Brownell Research Library, Ralph Foster Museum, Point Lookout, 65726. Robert Esworthy, Librn
Holdings: Vols (1300) Cat Mss Maps Pix
Notes: Archaeology of North America.

NJ —BRIDGETON FREE PUBLIC LIBRARY, George J Woodruff Museum of Indian Artifacts, 150 E Commerce St, Bridgeton, 08302. Anthony M Butler, Library Dir
Holdings: Vols (150) Cat Mss Maps Videotapes
Notes: Among the 20,000 artifacts, the oldest items are Folsom points, other items of the Adena and Hopewell periods, with the most recent items those of the Lenni Lenape (after 900 AD) and other local Delaware Indians being represented. Supportive book collection.

NJ —SETON HALL UNIVERSITY MUSEUM, Archaeological Research Center, S Orange Ave, South Orange, 07079. Herbert C Craft, Dir
Holdings: Vols (750) Cat
Notes: Primarily books and periodicals related to New Jersey and northeastern states prehistory and archaeology.

NM —AZTEC RUINS NATIONAL MONUMENT, Library, PO Box U, Aztec, 87410. William L Schart, Park Ranger
Holdings: Vols (500) // Cat Mss Maps Pix Slides
Notes: Archaeology of the Anasazi ruins.

NM —MUSEUM OF NEW MEXICO, Laboratory of Anthropology Library, PO Box 2087, Santa Fe, 87503. Laura Holt, Librn
Holdings: Vols (16,000) Cat Mss Maps
Notes: Southwestern archaeology, anthropology, ethnology. Noncirculating. Also incl the personal Library (2000 vols) of Sylvanus Morley, Meso-American archaeologist and historian. Some materials on Indians of Middle America.

NY —NASSAU COUNTY MUSEUM, Sands Pt Preserve, Middleneck Rd, Sand Points, 11050.
Holdings: Vols (2500)
Notes: Collection contains almost every published reference on Long Island archaeology, ethnology, and geology, and incl most of those pertaining to the coastal New York area. Open by appointment. No photocopying.

NY —HISTORICAL SOCIETY OF THE TARRYTOWNS, Library, One Grove St, Tarrytown, 10591. Adelaide R Smith, Cur
Notes: The Leslie V Case collection of material on the American Indian is displayed in two adjoining rooms. Stone weapons and tools, articles of clothing, pipes, jewelry, pottery and rugs; findings from local archeological studies, incl the remains of an Indian who once lived at Croton.

OH —OHIO HISTORICAL SOCIETY, Archives Library Division, 1982 Velma Ave, Columbus, 43211. Dennis East, Division Chief
Holdings: Mss Maps Pix
Notes: Collection begun in 1885 to support work of the Division of Archaeology, Ohio Historical Society.
See also entry under Ohio - History

PA —UNIVERSITY OF PENNSYLVANIA, University Museum Library, 33 & Spruce Sts, Philadelphia, 19104. Jean S Adelman, Librn
Holdings: Vols (80,000) Cat Mss
Notes: World archaeology, with special emphasis on North and Central America, Egyptology, Sumerology, and the classical world. All holdings are listed in museum library catalog and are also listed in University of Pennsylvania main library (union) catalog.

PA —UNIVERSITY OF PITTSBURGH, Hillman Library, Pittsburgh, 15260. Glenora E Rossell, Head
Holdings: Vols 3500 Cat Microforms
Notes: The collection is very strong in pre-Columbian archaeology and Indian cultures from the historical and anthropological point of view. Emphasis on contemporary history, politics and socio-economical problems.

SC —UNIVERSITY OF SOUTH CAROLINA, Institute of Archaeology and Anthropology, Research Report Library, Maxcy College, Columbia, 29208. Kenn Pinson, Ms Archivist
Holdings: Mss Maps Pix Slides
Notes: Reports of research performed by the Institute of Archeology and Anthropology. Incl four series: the *Institute of Archeology and Anthropology Notebook; Research Manuscript Series;* and *Anthropological Studies, Popular Series.* Partially cataloged.

TX —UNIVERSITY OF TEXAS LIBRARIES, Nettie Lee Benson Latin American Collection, Sid Richardson Hall 1.109, Austin, 78712. Laura Gutierrez-Witt, Head Librn
Holdings: Vols (450,000) Cat Mss Maps Pix Phonorecords Filmstrips Microforms
Notes: Incl 950 linear feet of mss, 15,800 maps, 18,250 reels of microfilm, and 11,400 microfiche.
See also entry under Latin America

TX —FORT WORTH PUBLIC LIBRARY, 300 Taylor St, Fort Worth, 76102. Patricia Chadwell, Social Sciences Librn; Paul Campbell, Librn, History Section
Holdings: Cat
Notes: Strong collection with emphasis on classical archaeology and archaeology of the Americas.

INDIANS OF NORTH AMERICA AND MEXICO—ARCHITECTURE

†AL —UNIVERSITY OF ALABAMA, Amelia Gayle Gorgas Library, PO Box S, University, 35486.
Notes: This collection consists of 119 reels of microfilm. Separately published bibliography: *A Catalog of the Yucatan Collection on Microfilm in the University of Alabama Libraries* (University: University of Alabama Press, 1972).

INDIANS OF NORTH AMERICA AND MEXICO—ART

AK —TONGASS HISTORICAL SOCIETY, Library, 629 Dock St, Ketchikan, 99901. Marjorie Anne Voss, Librn
Holdings: Vols 400 Cat Pix
Notes: Alaskan and regional hsitory and art, as well as Northwest Coast Indian history and art. Extensive photograph collection.

AZ —NORTHERN ARIZONA UNIVERSITY, Special Collection Library, CU Box 6022, Flagstaff, 86011. Peter M Whiteley, Coordr/Archivist; William Mullane, Librn
Notes: Guy and Doris Monthan Collection; mss, notes, correspondence, and other data for the book, *Art and Indian Individualists,* 1972-1975.

NJ —MONTCLAIR ART MUSEUM LIBRARY, 3 South Mountain Ave, PO Box 1582, Montclair, 07042. Edith A Rights, Librn
Holdings: Vols (10,000) Cat Pix Slides Audiotapes
Budget: ($3500)
Notes: American painting and sculpture. Incl 5000 pictures; 10,000 slides; posters. Audiotapes on American art and artists.

NY —METROPOLITAN MUSEUM OF ART, Robert Goldwater Library, Fifth Ave at 82nd St, New York, 10028. Allan D Chapman, Librn
Holdings: Vols (27,000) Cat
Notes: Primitive art: African, Indians of the Americans (incl Pre-Columbian), Oceanic, Polynesian, etc. 150,000 photographs.

OH —CLEVELAND PUBLIC LIBRARY, Fine Arts and Special Collections Department, 325 Superior Ave, Cleveland, 44114. Alice N Loranth, Head
Holdings: Vols 8000 Cat
Notes: Part of the research collection on the Indians of North, Central and South America and Mexico; holds materials on tribal histories, archaeology and antiquities, arts, costumes, folklore, manners and customs, etc. Special strength is in the extensive holdings on Indian languages, dictionaries and linguistics. Some rare books and first editions on travel among the Indians. Current acquisitions in subject departments and rare book collection only.

TX —SOUTHERN METHODIST UNIVERSITY, DeGolyer Library, Box 396, SMU, Dallas, 75275. Clifton H Jones, Dir
Holdings: Vols (80,000) Cat Mss Maps Pix Slides Microforms
Notes: First editions of prominent authors; also of books in subject emphasis collections. All subjects listed in this vol are strong. Numerous collections of personal papers relating to subjects also.

TX —EL PASO PUBLIC LIBRARY, Southwest Collection, 501 N Oregon, El Paso, 79901. Mary A Sarber, Head
Holdings: Vols (7000) Cat Pix
Budget: ($6000)
Notes: Emphasis in art and artists of the Southwest, particularly Tom Lea Jr, and Southwestern Indian arts and crafts.

INDIANS OF NORTH AMERICA AND MEXICO—BRITISH COLUMBIA

BC —UNIVERSITY OF VICTORIA, McPherson Library, Victoria, V8W 3H5, Can.
Notes: Victoria, BC. Phootocopies. Incl 9 cm, 1975-76; mss of linguistic and ethnographic studies relating to British Columbia Indians. Restriction: use with the permission of British Columbia Indian Language Project only.

INDIANS OF NORTH AMERICA AND MEXICO—CALIFORNIA

CA —EUREKA-HUMBOLDT COUNTY LIBRARY, 636 F St, Eureka, 95503. Dierdre Sockbeson, Reference Librn
Holdings: Vols (5000) Cat Mss Maps Pix Microforms
Budget: ($5000)
Notes: Humboldt County history, with particular emphasis on Indians of northwest California. Do not offer telephone reference service.

CA —LOS ANGELES PUBLIC LIBRARY, History Dept, 630 W Fifth St, Los Angeles, 90071. Leah Simon Kornbluth, Librn
Holdings: Vols (6000) Cat Maps Phonorecords Microforms
Budget: ($85,000)
Notes: See entry under Indians of North America and Mexico for full description of collection.

CA —CONTRA COSTA COUNTY LIBRARY, 1750 Oak Park Blvd, Pleasant Hill, 94523. Thomas F Gates, History Specialist
Holdings: Vols (2000) Cat Maps Pix
Notes: Covers Contra Costra County and northern California history, Gold Rush memoirs, California Indian studies, county history reprints. Newspaper clippings, ephemera.

CA —A K SMILEY PUBLIC LIBRARY, 125 W Vine St, Redlands, 92373. Larry E Burgess, Archivist
Holdings: Vols (3500) Mss Maps Pix Phonorecords Microforms
Budget: ($45,000)
Notes: Emphasis on San Bernadino County and the Redlands area. Especially prized is *The Citrographic*, 1887-1908 (bound vols and microfilm) edited by Scipio Craig, prominent in state, national, and newspaper circles. The ms collection (250,000 pieces) incl the Smily Family papers, much on water development, and onthe citrus industry. The photograph collection (over 5000) covers the history of the area; there are many stereographs and glass slides. The collection on Indians of California and the Southwest was begun from a special gift by Andrew Carnegie honoring his friend, Albert K Smiley.

CA —CALIFORNIA HISTORICAL SOCIETY, Schubert Hall Library, 2099 Pacific Ave, San Francisco, 94109. Bruce L Johnson, Library Dir
Holdings: Uncat Pix
Notes: California Historica Society's Title

INDIANS OF NORTH AMERICA AND MEXICO—CALIFORNIA (cont.)

Insurance and Trust Corporation Collection of Historical Photographs in Los Angeles contains 20,000 photographs centered around pictures of Southern California by noted photographer C C Pierce. Copies of photographs by other pioneer Los Angeles photographers, such as Godfrey, Wolfenstein and Parker are incl, as well as 2000 glass plate negatives of local Indians by George Wharton James.

INDIANS OF NORTH AMERICA AND MEXICO—CANADA

TX —AMON CARTER MUSEUM, Library, 3510 Camp Bowie Blvd, PO Box 2365, Fort Worth, 76113. Nancy G Wynne, Librn
Holdings: Vols (25,000) Cat Mss Pix
Notes: The book collection, microfilm and photo archives have been built toward the goal of the interpretation of American history through art. At present, the greatest strengths are in Americana, Western Canadiana, bibliography, American exhibition catalogs and history of photography. Substantial books and files on American artists of the 19th and early 20th century, and particularly of Charles M Russell and Frederic Remington. Incl 25,000 pictures; 13,000 slides.
See also entries under Newspapers, American; Pictures - Collections.

†WA —WASHINGTON STATE UNIVERSITY, Library, Manuscripts, Archives & Special Collections, Pullman, 99164. John F Guido, Head
Holdings: // Mss Maps Pix
Notes: Papers, 1821-1873, covering Father De Smet's early sojourns at Whitemarsh and St Louis, his founding of the Rocky Mountain Missions, his long service as Procurator and Socius of the Missouri Province, and his many travels. Correspondence with his family in Belgium, mss of his published journals, 2 small maps, sketches and engravings used to illustrate his books. Incl about 100 small pencil sketches by Father Nicholas Point depicting the 1841 journey from Westport to St Mary's Mission in the Bitterroot Valley. Described in *The* Record, 30 (1969) 6-40; and 32 (1971) 47-63.

AB —PETER WHYTE FOUNDATION, Archives of the Canadian Rockies, Box 160, Banff, T0L 0C0, Can. Mary Andrews, ACR Librn
Holdings: Vols (4247) Cat Mss Maps Pix Slides Phonorecords Audiotapes Videotapes 16mm Films Filmstrips Microforms
Budget: ($1500)
Notes: Collect all available material which touches on the Rocky Mountains of Canada (from the US border to the Peace River in the north; from the west of Calgary on the east to the town of Revelstoke, BC on the west). This material incl history (the early explorers, Indians, construction of the railroads, mountaineering, and development of the national parks), natural history (geology, botany, wildlife) and poetry and fiction with the Rockies as a setting. Collect maps of the area, photographs, tape recordings of the pioneers. We also house on our premises the Alpine Club of Canada's library, which is one of the most comprehensive collections on the subject of mountaineering worldwide. Noncirculating.

AB —GLENBOW-ALBERTA INSTITUTE, Historical Library & Archives, 130 9th Avenue SE, Calgary, T2G 0P3, Can. Leonard J Gottseleg, Chief Librn
Holdings: Vols (60,000) Cat Mss Maps Pix Microforms
Notes: Main emphasis is on Western Canadian history. Equally important emphasis is placed on the Canadian Arctic and Alaska, Northwest Coast explorations, Aboriginal peoples of the North and Canadian West, and the fur trade in the US Northwest.

BC —TERRACE PUBLIC LIBRARY, 4610 Park Ave, Terrace, V8G 1V6, Can. Ed Curell, Librn; Gillian Campbell, Librn, Terrace Collection
Holdings: Vols (270) Cat
Budget: ($250)
Notes: The collection is limited to books and pamphlets relating to Terrace, Skeena, and Nass River District history and geography. Emphasis on art and sociology of the Niska and Tsimshian and lives of early missionaries.

BC —VANCOUVER PUBLIC LIBRARY, History & Government Div, 750 Burrard St, Vancouver, V6Z 1X5, Can.

MB —MANITOBA MUSEUM OF MAN & NATURE, Library, 190 Rupert Ave, Winnipeg, R3B 0N2, Can. V Hatten, Librn
Holdings: Vols (20,000) Cat Maps Slides Audiotapes Videotapes Microforms
Notes: Human and natural history of Manitoba.

NT —NORTHWEST TERRITORIES PUBLIC LIBRARY SERVICES, Bos 1100, Hay River, X0E 0R0, Can.
Holdings: Vols (1235) Cat Maps Audiotapes
Notes: Originally intended to provide items of historical significance on the Northwest Territories. It contains a number of first editions, some of which have since become available in reprint form. Copies of material in relevant native languages and on learning languages.

ON —CHATHAM PUBLIC LIBRARY, 120 Queen St, Chatham, N7M 2G6, Can. Arlene Mason, Head of Reference
Holdings: Mss
Notes: Materials on the Indians of Kent County, Ont, incl articles and books on the Pottawatamis and Chippewas of Walpole Island Reserve and on the Delaware Indians brought to Canada by the Moravian Missionaries in 1792 (the Fairfield Mission).

ON —ONTARIO MINISTRY OF TOURISM & RECREATION, Huronia Historical Resource Centre, PO Box 160, Midland, L4R 4K8, Can. M Quealey, Supervisor, Library Services
Holdings: Vols 11,000 Cat Mss Maps Pix Slides Phonorecords Audiotapes Filmstrips Microforms Videotapes
Notes: Reference collection; interlibrary loan; non-circulating. Research facility for reconstruction of historic sites: Historic Naval and Military Establishments, 19th century British base on the Great Lakes; and Sainte-Marie among the Hurons, an early 17th century French Jesuit mission to the Huron Indians. Also, local history collection and archaeological reports for Simcoe County, Ont, Canada.

ON —NATIONAL MUSEUMS OF CANADA, Library Services Directorate, Ottawa, K1A 0M8, Can. Valerie Monkhouse, Director
Holdings: Vols (70,000) // Cat Mss Maps Pix Slides Microforms
Budget: ($60,000)
Notes: Collection includes anthropology, archaeology, ethnology, folklore, history, Indians of North America, Inuit, linguistics of North American Indians, material history, military and naval history, museology. Also 13,500 periodical titles; vertical files of Canadian Association in Support of Native Peoples (microfilm); over 22,000 items covering every facet of contemporary native life. Mss, pictures and theses are held in Archives (National Museum of Man). Research collection, interlibrary loans available, public may use on the premises.

ON —PUBLIC ARCHIVES OF CANADA, Library, 395 Wellington St, Ottawa, K1A 0N3, Can. Dawn E Monroe, Collections Development Officer
Holdings: Vols (80,000) Cat
Notes: The Public Archives Library has collected certain published documents, general works and specialized studies pertinent to the study of the historical and sociological development of native peoples. These documents incl accounts of the trips made by missionaries, explorers and others into Inuit or Amerindian territory, territory, specialized bibliographies, and ethnographic reference works incl dictionaries of native languages, studies on customs and and habits, and specialized periodicals.

ON —SAULT SAINTE MARIE PUBLIC LIBRARY, 50 East St, Sault Sainte Marie, P6A 3C3, Can. Brian R Ingram, Dir
Holdings: Vols 720 Cat Slides Videotapes 16mm Films Filmstrips

ON —CANADIAN ASSOCIATION IN SUPPORT OF THE NATIVE PEOPLES, Library, 277 Victoric St, Toronto, M5V 1W2, Can. Frances Davidson-Arnott, Librn
Holdings: Vols (20,000) Cat Mss Pix Slides Microforms
Notes: Native peoples of North America, especially of Canada.

†ON —METROPOLITAN TORONTO LIBRARY, Social Sciences Dept, 789 Yonge St, Toronto, M4W 2G8, Can. Abdus Salam, Head
Holdings: Vols Cat Maps Phonorecords Audiotapes 16mm Films Microforms
Notes: Strong collection on folklore, education, religion, anthropology. Also includes bibles in Canadian Indian languages.

ON —METROPOLITAN TORONTO LIBRARY, Canadian History Dept, Baldwin Room Section, 789 Yonge St, Toronto, M4W 2G8, Can. David B Kotin, Head
Holdings: Vols (52,000) Mss Pix
Notes: This collection consists of material on Canadian history, geography, travel, archaeology, genealogy, retrospective city and telephone directories, collective biographies, native peoples (excluding customs, rights and social conditions), Arctic regions, military history and theory. It is an extremely strong collection of both current and retrospective material. Particular strengths are national and local history (especially Ontario), Arctic regions, native peoples, travel (especially Ontario), and military history. Incl 78,000 historical pictures, 235 linear meters mss, 14,000 broadsides and 3800 bound newspapers.

ON —VICTORIA UNIVERSITY, Library, 71 Queen's Park Crescent, Toronto, M5S 1K7, Can. Robert C Brandeis, Chief Librn
Holdings: Vols (1000) // Cat Mss Maps Pix
Notes: Collection consists of books, pamphlets, and government reports mainly dealing with North American Indians and western explorations and missionary enterprises among the Indian tribes in Canada. Incl Indian Bibles and hymnbooks, and mss and vols by Peter Jones (an Indian missionary) and James Evans (inventor of the Cree syllabic alphabet).

†SK —UNIVERSITY OF REGINA, Library, Regina, S4S 0A2, Can. Margarett Hammond, Librn
Notes: Native peoples of North America, especially of Canada. Collection formerly held by Canadian Association in Support of the Native Peoples.

INDIANS OF NORTH AMERICA AND MEXICO—COSTUME AND ADORNMENT

OH —CLEVELAND PUBLIC LIBRARY, Fine Arts and Special Collections Department, 325 Superior Ave, Cleveland, 44114. Alice N Loranth, Head
Holdings: Vols 8000 Cat
Notes: Part of the research collection on the Indians of North, Central and South America and Mexico; holds materials on tribal histories, archaeology and antiquities, arts, costumes, folklore, manners and customs, etc. Special strength is in the extensive holdings on Indian languages, dictionaries and linguistics. Some rare books and first editions on travel among the Indians. Current acquisitions in subject departments and rare book collection only.

INDIANS OF NORTH AMERICA AND MEXICO—CULTURE

†IL —NEWBERRY LIBRARY, 60 W Walton St, Chicago, 60610.
Notes: Collection of color slides of the early 1950s. Photographs by the eight-year Superintendent of the Fort Belknap Indian Reservation in Montana, J W "Duke" Wellington, who was allowed to take pictures of some of the most important

INDIANS OF NORTH AMERICA AND MEXICO—CULTURE (cont.)

rituals of the Assiniboine and Gros Ventres Indians, dances, renewals, etc. An annotated collection.

NM —MUSEUM OF NEW MEXICO, Laboratory of Anthropology Library, PO Box 2087, Santa Fe, 87503. Laura Holt, Librn
Holdings: Vols (16,000) Cat Mss Maps
Notes: Southwestern archaeology, anthropology, ethnology. Noncirculating. Also incl the personal Library (2000 vols) of Sylvanus Morley, Meso-American archaeologist and historian. Some materials on Indians of Middle America.

†WA —WASHINGTON STATE UNIVERSITY, Library, Manuscripts, Archives & Special Collections, Pullman, 99164. John F Guido, Head
Holdings: Cat Mss Maps Pix
Notes: The Carl Parcher Russell papers, a vast resource (24,916 items; 45 linear feet) on American Indian and Western pioneer activities and artifacts. Much of the fur trade; pioneer life; mountain men and trapping; wildlife; primitive life in detail. Also the National Park Service, parks, monuments, etc. Described in *Carl Parcher Russell: An Indexed Register of His Scholarly and Professional Papers, 1920-1967, in the Washington State University* Library (Pullman, 1970), 149 pp.

INDIANS OF NORTH AMERICA AND MEXICO—GOVERNMENT RELATIONS

CO —NATIVE AMERICAN RIGHTS FUND, National Indian Law Library, 1506 Broadway, Boulder, 80302. Diana Lim Garry, Librn
Holdings: Vols Case Files Law Review Articles Studies Monographs
Budget: ($125,000)
Notes: A National Library of Indian Law, originally made possible by a grant from the Carnegie Corporation, now funded by the Administration for Native Americans (DHHS). Emphasizes information about treaties and rulings in cases involving Indian Country jurisdiction, economic development, hunting, land and water rights. Incl over 2000 case files and 4400 other monographs. Library publishes the *National Indian Law Library Catalogue: An Index to Indian Legal Materials and Resources.* Cumulative edition published in 1982, supplemented biannually. Catalog lists library holdings indexed by subject, author-title and case name.

NM —UNIVERSITY OF NEW MEXICO, School of Law Library, 1117 Stanford Dr NE, Albuquerque, 87131. Myron Fink, Law Librn
Holdings: Vols (3000) Cat Mss
Notes: Collection supports the work of the American Indian Law Center, established by the law school. Has separate catalog with extensive subject analysis. Incl papers of William Zimmerman, Asst Commissioner of Indian Affairs, 1934-1950. Emphasis is on government relations, tribal government (especially tribal codes for all Indian tribes in US). Incl materials on indigenous peoples world-wide. Periodical literature is subject indexed. Bibliography: Sabatini, Joseph D, *American Indian Law: A Bibliography of Books, Law Review Articles and Indian* Periodicals. (Albuquerque, 1973), Supplement, 1975.

INDIANS OF NORTH AMERICA AND MEXICO—GREAT BASIN

NV —UNIVERSITY OF NEVADA, RENO, University Library, Special Collections Dept, Reno, 89557. Robert E Blesse, Head
Holdings: Vols (1100) Mss Pix
Notes: Includes over 5000 photographs, government documents, periodicals, 80 cu ft manuscripts, and audiotapes. The Great Basin Indian Collection contains materials on the anthropology, archeology, and ethnohistory of the Great Basin region. Materials are collected for a defined group of 65 tribes including Washo, Shoshone, Northern and Southern Paiute, the major tribes of the region. Collections of importance include the Sven Liljeblad Collection, linguistics and ethnography; papers of US Indian agent Lorenzo D Creel, 1902-1922; Robert Leland Collection, Indian water rights.

INDIANS OF NORTH AMERICA AND MEXICO—GREAT PLAINS

†IL —NEWBERRY LIBRARY, 60 W Walton St, Chicago, 60610.
Notes: Collection of color slides of the early 1950s. Photographs by the eight-year Superintendent of the Fort Belknap Indian Reservation in Montana, J W "Duke" Wellington, who was allowed to take pictures of some of the most important rituals of the Assiniboine and Gros Ventres Indians, dances, renewals, etc. An annotated collection.

IA —IOWA FALLS PUBLIC LIBRARY, 520 Rocksylvania, Iowa Falls, 50126. Deanne Keller, Librn
Holdings: Vols (500) Cat

MO —UNIVERSITY OF MISSOURI-COLUMBIA, Ellis Library, Language and Literature Dept, Columbia, 65201. Jeaneice Brewer, Librn
Holdings: Vols (3500) Cat
Notes: Consists of the personal library of John G Neihardt, 1881-1973, poet, literary critic, and lecturer. Lived among Omaha Indians and Ogalala Sioux Indians to study their character and history. Poet laureate of Nebraska. Literary editor of *St Louis* Post-Dispatch, 1926-38. Poet in residence and lecturer in English, U of Missouri, 1949-66. Manuscripts are housed separately in Western Historical Manuscripts Collection of Ellis Library.

NE —NEIHARDT STUDY CENTER, Library, Bancroft, 68004. John Lindahl, Cur; Ann Reinert, Librn
Notes: The Center will preserve the published works and papers of John G Neihardt, State Poet Laureate and authority on Plains Indians.

NE —NEBRASKA STATE HISTORICAL SOCIETY, Fort Robinson Museum, Box 304, Crawford, 69339. Vance Nelson, Cur
Holdings: Vols (1500) Cat Mss Maps Pix Slides Phonorecords Audiotapes 16mm Films Microforms
Notes: Materials related to the history of Fort Robinson, and incl the Post Medical Library, reference books on state government, etc, Western Americana: books on ranching, homesteaders, Indian wars, etc; microfilm records for Fort Robinson records, Red Cloud and Spotted Tail Indian Agency records, Crawford and Chadron, Nebraska newspapers, diaries and interviews. Library incl the E Kopac collection of books dealing with Western Americana; particularly Indian wars, transportation, guns and railroads.

NE —NEBRASKA STATE HISTORICAL SOCIETY, Archives, 1500 R St, Box 82554, Lincoln, 68501. James E Potter, State Archivist
Holdings: Cat Mss Microforms
Budget: ($290,000)
Notes: Collection estimated 4,000 cu. ft. of personal papers, business records, church records, and organizational records relating to the history of Nebraska and the Great Plains, ca. 1854-present with a particularly strong emphasis in the subject areas of Indians of North America, agriculture, railroad history, 19th century agrarian political movements, irrigation, and settlement of the Great Plains. Public records holdings of an estimated 10,000 cu. ft. of Nebraska state, county and some municipal government agencies include the official files of Nebraska governors, the Nebraska Legislature, and many territorial and state agencies 1854-present; and numerous tax records, court records, marriage records, naturalization records, and school census records for Nebraska counties. Newspaper collection of 20,000 rolls of microfilm, non-circulating but available for purchase, cataloged according to place published so specific titles must be requested. See A GUIDE TO THE NEWSPAPER COLLECTION OF THE STATE ARCHIVES (Lincoln: Nebraska State Historical Society, 1977), A GUIDE TO THE MANUSCRIPT DIVISION OF THE STATE ARCHIVES (Lincoln: Nebraska State Historical Society, 1974), and A GUIDE TO THE MANUSCRIPT DIVISION OF THE STATE ARCHIVES, a supplement (Lincoln: Nebraska State Historical Society, 1983). Microform holdings of manuscript and public records can also be purchased.

NE —UNIVERSITY OF NEBRASKA-LINCOLN, Don L Love Library, University Archives and Special Collections, Lincoln, 68588. Joseph G Svoboda, University Archivist
Holdings: Vols (1000) / / Cat Mss Maps Pix Audiotapes 16mm Films
Notes: The Mari Sandoz Collection consists of four basic parts. The first contains correspondence files, 25,000 letters in all, including letters received from 1925 on and carbon copies of letters sent. The correspondence files are a rich source of information about the author's life and career, creative writing, and Plains Indian and western American history. The second portion of the collection is the author's personal library of books and periodicals, many annotated. Part three contains the author's published works, including most of the editions, foreign and domestic and some unpublished manuscripts as well. Many of the early drafts of books, copy-edited manuscripts, and galley and proofs are also contained in this portion of the collection. The final part of the collections consists of the author's resource files, research and reading notes, clippings, and related materials. These materials fill over fifty standard letter boxes. In addition, the prepared 45,000 index cards refering to information contained both in and out of the collection.

ND —UNIVERSITY OF NORTH DAKOTA, Chester Fritz Library, Dept of Special Collections, Grand Forks, 58202. Daniel F Rylance, Special Collections Coordr
Holdings: Vols (5500) Uncat Mss Maps Pix Microforms
Budget: ($2500)
Notes: Also the Orin G Libby Manuscript Collection (900 collections), and the Aandahl Collection of Western History on North Dakota and the Northern Great Plains. Emphasis on agriculture, politics,

INDIANS OF NORTH AMERICA AND MEXICO—GREAT PLAINS (cont.)

pioneering, Germans from Russia, etc. Guides to the collections available from the Coordinator of Special Collections.

OK —US ARMY FIELD ARTILLERY SCHOOL LIBRARY, Morris Swett Library, Snow Hall, Fort Sill, 73503. Lester L Miller Jr, Chief Librn
Notes: Incl data on Fort Sill, Indian Territory, settlement of Kiowa, Apache and Commanche tribes, imprisonment of Geronimo, Oklahoma territory, settlement of Lawton. Unit histories, incl 10th Cavalry (Buffalo Soldiers, a black unit that built Fort Sill); working papers of Sheridan, Grierson and other commanders; Field Artillery School. Photographs on army subjects, Fort Sill, Indians, Indian Territory, settlement of Southwest Oklahoma.

SD —SOUTH DAKOTA HISTORICAL RESOURCE CENTER, Library, Soldiers Memorial Bldg, Pierre, 57501. Rosemary Evetts, Librn
Holdings: Vols 1000 Cat Pix
Budget: $2000
Notes: Collection is aobut evenly divided between Sioux and other tribes and Indian subjects in general, such as art, wars, etc, 1650 audiotapes duplicating one-third of the Indian history project at the University of South Dakota, Vermillion.

SD —SIOUXLAND HERITAGE MUSEUMS, Pettigrew Museum Library, 131 N Duluth Ave, Sioux Falls, 57104. Ms Lee N McLaird, Cur of Collections
Holdings: Vols (7500) Cat Mss Maps Pix
Budget: ($900)
Notes: Pettigrew Museum Library is a support service of the Siouxland Heritage Museums. US Senator R F Pettigrew established the core collection in 1926, covering natural history (incl North American Indian anthropology) and state-local history (concentrating on exploration and settlement to about 1900). The collection also incl the Senator's private papers (ca 1870-1926). Additions to the collection since 1926 have emphasized Plains Indian anthropology, state-local history, baseball and museology, supporting the work of the Museum staff. The collection is mostly cataloged and is inter-indexed with Augustana College, Sioux Falls College, and Sioux Falls Public Libraries (as well as having its own catalog). The photograph collection includes prints by D F Barry as well as other photographers' work with native peoples.

†WA —WASHINGTON STATE UNIVERSITY, Library, Manuscripts, Archives & Special Collections, Pullman, 99164. John F Guido, Head
Holdings: // Mss Maps Pix
Notes: Papers, 1821-1873, covering Father De Smet's early sojourns at Whitemarsh and St Louis, his founding of the Rocky Mountain Missions, his long service as Procurator and Socius of the Missouri Province, and his many travels. Correspondence with his family in Belgium, mss of his published journals, 2 small maps, sketches and engravings used to illustrate his books. Incl about 100 small pencil sketches by Father Nicholas Point depicting the 1841 journey from Westport to St Mary's Mission in the Bitterroot Valley. Described in *The* Record, 30 (1969) 6-40; and 32 (1971) 47-63.

INDIANS OF NORTH AMERICA AND MEXICO—HEALTH AND HYGIENE

NE —NEBRASKA STATE HISTORICAL SOCIETY, Fort Robinson Museum, Box 304, Crawford, 69339. Vance Nelson, Cur
Holdings: Vols (1500) Cat Mss Maps Pix Slides Phonorecords Audiotapes 16mm Films Microforms
Notes: Materials related to the history of Fort Robinson, and incl the Post Medical Library, reference books on state government, etc, Western Americana: books on ranching, homesteaders, Indian wars, etc; microfilm records for Fort Robinson records, Red Cloud and Spotted Tail Indian Agency records, Crawford and Chadron, Nebraska newspapers, diaries and interviews. Library incl the E Kopac Collection of books dealing with Western Americana; particularly Indian wars, transportation, guns and railroads.

†NM —UNIVERSITY OF NEW MEXICO, Medical Center Library, Albuquerque, 87131. Beatrice Kovacs, Chief, Collections and Resource Development
Notes: Concern is health care and health services in New Mexico; medicine and medicine men of Indian tribes of the Southwest; and history of medicine and health in the Southwest.

OK —UNIVERSITY OF OKLAHOMA, Health Sciences Center, Library, 1000 Stanton L Young Blvd, PO Box 26901, Oklahoma City, 73190. C M Thompson, Jr, Dir
Holdings: Vols (750) Cat
Notes: Health and well-being of the American Indian-historically and currently.

INDIANS OF NORTH AMERICA AND MEXICO—LAND TRANSFERS

CO —NATIVE AMERICAN RIGHTS FUND, National Indian Law Library, 1506 Broadway, Boulder, 80302. Diana Lim Garry, Librn
Holdings: Vols Case Files Law Review Articles Studies Monographs
Budget: ($125,000)
Notes: A National Library of Indian Law, originally made possible by a grant from the Carnegie Corporation, now funded by the Administration for Native Americans (DHHS). Emphasizes information about treaties and rulings in cases involving Indian Country jurisdiction, economic development, hunting, land and water rights. Incl over 2000 case files and 4400 other monographs. Library publishes the *National Indian Law Library Catalogue: An Index to Indian Legal Materials and Resources.* Cumulative edition published in 1982, supplemented biannually. Catalog lists library holdings indexed by subject, author-title and case name.

NM —UNIVERSITY OF NEW MEXICO, School of Law Library, 1117 Stanford Dr NE, Albuquerque, 87131. Myron Fink, Law Librn
Holdings: Vols (3000) Cat Mss
Notes: Collection supports the work of the American Indian Law Center, established by the law school. Has separate catalog with extensive subject analysis. Incl papers of William Zimmerman, Asst Commissioner of Indian Affairs, 1934-1950. Emphasis is on government relations, tribal government (especially tribal codes for all Indian tribes in US). Incl materials on indigenous peoples world-wide. Periodical literature is subject indexed. Bibliography: Sabatini, Joseph D, *American Indian Law: A Bibliography of Books, Law Review Articles and Indian* Periodicals. (Albuquerque, 1973), Supplement, 1975.

INDIANS OF NORTH AMERICA AND MEXICO—LANGUAGES

AZ —NORTHERN ARIZONA UNIVERSITY, Special Collection Library, CU Box 6022, Flagstaff, 86011. Peter M Whiteley, Coordr/Archivist; William Mullane, Librn
Notes: (1) Apachean Languages and Music Collection. A music collection compiled by Werner Winter, Universitaet Kiel, Germany. Incl uses of language, stories, recipes, jokes, etc. (2) Faye and Faith Hill Collection of mss and notes of the translation of the New Testament into the Apache and Navajo Languages, 1940's-1960's. (3) Dean Saxton Collection; corrected Papago Hymnal, first edition, 1959. Concise Papago-English dictionary with corrections, dated ca 1950's or 1960's. (4) David L Shaul Collection; mss titled "An English-Shoshone Dictionary of Nineteenth Century Sources," compiled by Shaul, 1976. (5) H C Whitener Collection; Zuni language research notes and religious and Biblical translations in the Zuni Language. Incl onefolder on the Havasupai language. Inventory available.

CA —UNIVERSITY OF CALIFORNIA, LOS ANGELES, Research Library, Dept of Special Collections, 405 Hilgard Ave, Los Angeles, 90024. Edward Shreeves, Chairman, Bibliographers Group; David S Zeidberg, Head
Notes: Various collections, incl the John H Grepe, Byron McAfee, and Lorraine Miller Sherer collections.

DC —GEORGETOWN UNIVERSITY, Library, Special Collections Div, 37 & O Sts NW, Washington, 20057. George M Barringer, Special Collections Librn; Nicholas B Sheetz, Mss Librn
Holdings: Cat
Notes: Papers of John Gilmary Shea (1824-1892), noted Catholic historian and linguist of Indian languages who published over two hundred titles during his lifetime. The papers incl correspondence to Shea, manuscripts and notes reflecting his research, collected documents and manuscripts, and various photographs. Correspondence written to Shea incl letters from George Bancroft, Francis Parkman, Jared Sparks, Harriet Beecher Stowe, E B O'Callahan, Hanry Schoolcraft, Charles White, D D, Charles Currier, P T Barnum, Frederick Douglass, Thomas A Edison, Oliver Wendell Holmes, as well as noted members of the Church hierarchy. A long span of correspondence from Shea to the historian, Edmund Mallet contains many insights into Shea's life and work. Photographs incl likenesses of Elizabeth Seton, Isaac Hecker and George Bancroft. Also incl in the papers are numerous documents andmss concerning Shea's work in the field of Native American history, language, and culture.

IL —NEWBERRY LIBRARY, 60 W Walton St, Chicago, 60610. Diana Haskell, Cur of Modern Mss
Holdings: Cat Mss
Notes: The Ayer Collection.

IN —INDIANA UNIVERSITY, Lilly Library, Seventh St, Bloomington, 47405. William R Cagle, Librn
Holdings: Vols 6000 // Cat Mss
Notes: Research and rare book collection (Bernardo Mendel) of first or only editions, mostly printed in Latin America, from the discovery of the New World through 1830. Special strength in discoveries and exploration, history (mainly period of independence), Inquisition, missionary works by the Augustinians, Dominicans, Franciscans, and the Jesuits, and the history of the Catholic Church in these countries. Major geographic concentration is on the three great viceroyalties of Mexico (ca. 10,000 titles, plus over 10,000 official Mexican broadsides), Peru (2000 titles), and Argentina (4000 titles), incl. in Argentina a substantial amount of printings from the Imprenta de Ninos Expositos, and the Coleccion Santamarina. A special Bolivian Collection (2500 titles), mostly history, from the establishment of the press there, ca. 1826, through the beginning of the 20th century. Part of the Mendel Collection is the select Bibliotheca Boxeriana from Charles R. Boxer (1000 titles) on European expansion into Asia, and into the New World, mainly Brazil, during the 16th-18th centuries. The collection is supplemented by substantial material from the private collection of Josiah K. Lilly. See also entries under Spain-History, Portugal-History, and Mexico-History.

INDIANS OF NORTH AMERICA AND MEXICO—LANGUAGES (cont.)

MA —HARVARD UNIVERSITY LIBRARY, Tozzer Library, 21 Divinity Ave, Cambridge, 02138. Nancy J Schmidt, Librn
Holdings: Cat Mss Microforms
Notes: Tozzer Library was formerly the Peabody Museum Library.

MA —GORDON COLLEGE, Winn Library, Vining Collection, 255 Grapevine Rd, Wenham, 01984. John Beauregard, Dir
Holdings: Vols 3000 Cat
Notes: The Vining Collection (or rare books).

NV —UNIVERSITY OF NEVADA, RENO, University Library, Special Collections Dept, Reno, 89557. Robert E Blesse, Head
Holdings: Vols 1100 Mss Pix
Notes: Incl over 5000 photographs, government documents, periodicals, 80 cubic feet, mss, and audiotapes. The Great Basin Indian Collection contains materials on the anthropology, archaeology, and ethnohistory of the Great Basin region. Materials are collected for a defined group of 65 tribes incl Washo, Shoshone, Northern and Southern Paiute, the major tribes of the region. Collection of importance incl the Sven Liljeblad Collection, linguistics and ethnography; papers of US agent Lorenzo D Greel, 1902-22; Robert Leland Collection, Indian water rights.

OH —CLEVELAND PUBLIC LIBRARY, Fine Arts and Special Collections Department, 325 Superior Ave, Cleveland, 44114. Alice N Loranth, Head
Holdings: Vols (8000) Cat
Notes: Part of the research collection on the Indians of North, Central and South America and Mexico; holds materials on tribal histories, archaeology and antiquities, arts, costumes, folklore, manners and customs, etc. Special strength is in the extensive holdings on Indian languages, dictionaries and linguistics. Some rare books and first editions on travel among the Indians. Current acquisitions in subject departments and rare book collection only. *See also* entry under Language and Languages.

PA —AMERICAN PHILOSOPHICAL SOCIETY, Library, 105 S Fifth St, Philadelphia, 19106. Edward C Carter II, Librn
Holdings: Cat Mss
Notes: American Indian: linguistics and general ethnohistory.

PA —UNIVERSITY OF PENNSYLVANIA, University Museum Library, 33 & Spruce Sts, Philadelphia, 19104. Jean S Adelman, Librn
Holdings: Vols (80,000) Cat Mss Microforms
Notes: Incl (5000) pamphlets, fully cataloged. Mss (primarily American Indian word lists) in Brinton collection.

BC —UNIVERSITY OF VICTORIA, McPherson Library, Victoria, V8W 3H5, Can.
Notes: Victoria, BC. Phootocopies. Incl 9 cm, 1975-76; mss of linguistic and ethnographic studies relating to British Columbia Indians. Restriction: use with the permission of British Columbia Indian Language Project only.

†ON —METROPOLITAN TORONTO LIBRARY, Social Sciences Dept, 789 Yonge St, Toronto, M4W 2G8, Can. Abdus Salam, Head
Holdings: Vols Cat Maps Phonorecords Audiotapes 16mm Films Microforms
Notes: Strong collection on folklore, education, religion, anthropology. Also includes bibles in Canadian Indian languages.

ON —METROPOLITAN TORONTO LIBRARY, Languages Centre, 789 Yonge St, Toronto, M4W 2G8, Can. Barbara Gunther, Head
Holdings: Vols (90,000) Cat Phonorecords Audiotapes
Notes: Original literature in over 80 languages; books, records, cassettes, microfilm on language studies; newspapers and periodicals from 50 counties. Language study materials. Issue quarterly additions lists by language. Collect North American Indian and Eskimo language materials. Occasional bibliographies.

ON —VICTORIA UNIVERSITY, Library, 71 Queen's Park Crescent, Toronto, M5S 1K7, Can. Robert C Brandeis, Chief Librn
Holdings: Vols (1000)// Cat Mss Maps Pix
Notes: Collection consists of books, pamphlets, and government reports mainly dealing with North American Indians and western explorations and missionary enterprises among the Indian tribes in Canada. Incl Indian Bibles and hymnbooks, and mss and vols by Peter Jones (an Indian missionary) and James Evans (inventor of the Cree syllabic alphabet).

INDIANS OF NORTH AMERICA AND MEXICO—LEGAL STATUS AND LAWS

AZ —COOK CHRISTIAN TRAINING SCHOOL, Mary M McCarthy Library, 708 S Lindon Lane, Tempe, 85281. Mark E Thomas, Librn
Holdings: Vols 800 Cat Audiotapes Videotapes 16mm Films Filmstrips VF
Notes: Cook is an interdenominational school for the preparation of Native American adults for positions of church leadership. The school at times has been under contract with the Institute for the Development of Indian Law, Washington, DC for the production of filmstrips and workshops dealing with Indian issues. Visitors are welcomed but all materials must be used within the library.

CA —LOS ANGELES PUBLIC LIBRARY, History Dept, 630 W Fifth St, Los Angeles, 90071. Leah Simon Kornbluth, Librn
Holdings: Vols (6000) Cat Maps Phonorecords Microforms
Budget: ($85,000)

CO —NATIVE AMERICAN RIGHTS FUND, National Indian Law Library, 1506 Broadway, Boulder, 80302. Diana Lim Garry, Librn
Holdings: Vols Cat
Budget: ($125,000)
Notes: A National Library of Indian Law, originally made possible by a grant from the Carnegie Corporation, now funded by the Administration for Native Americans (DHHS). Emphasizes information about treaties and rulings in cases involving Indian Country jurisdiction, economic development, hunting, land and water rights. Incl over 2000 case files and 4400 other monographs. Library publishes the *National Indian Law Library Catalog: An Index to Indian Legals Materials and Resources.* Cumulative edition published in 1982, supplemented biannually. Catalog lists library holdings indexed by subject, author-title and case name.

MI —UNIVERSITY OF MICHIGAN, Law Library, Legal Research Bldg, 801 Monroe St, Ann Arbor, 48109. Beverley J Pooley, Dir
Holdings: Vols (570,000) Cat Microforms
Budget: $575,000
Notes: Unusually strong in legal history, canon law, US state constitutional proceedings, Indian nations, and foreign and international law. Also 300,000 microforms.

NM —UNIVERSITY OF NEW MEXICO, School of Law Library, 1117 Stanford Dr NE, Albuquerque, 87131. Myron Fink, Law Librn
Holdings: Vols (3000) Cat Mss
Notes: Collection supports the work of the American Indian Law Center, established by the law school. Has separate catalog with extensive subject analysis. Incl papers of William Zimmerman, Asst Commissioner of Indian Affairs, 1934-1950. Emphasis is on government relations, tribal government (especially tribal codes for all Indian tribes in US). Incl materials on indigenous peoples world-wide. Periodical literature is subject indexed. Bibliography: Sabatini, Joseph D, *American Indian Law: A Bibliography of Books, Law Review Articles and Indian* Periodicals. (Albuquerque, 1973), Supplement, 1975.

OK —UNIVERSITY OF OKLAHOMA, Law Library, 300 Timberdell Rd, Norman, 73019. Laura N Gasaway, Dir
Holdings: Vols 4500 Cat Microforms
Notes: Basic historical legal materials, incl rare materials. Some non-legal materials.

OK —UNIVERSITY OF TULSA, McFarlin Library, Dept of Rare Books and Special Collections, 600 S College, Tulsa, 74104. David Farmer, Dir; Toby Murray, Archivist; Caroline Swinson, Cur of Manuscripts & Art
Holdings: Cat
Notes: The Indian collection of John W Shleppey. Indian materials of some 6000 bibliographic items, excl of mss and photographs. Emphasis on Indian Territory imprints, laws, Cherokee and Choctaw tribes, etc.

INDIANS OF NORTH AMERICA AND MEXICO—MAINE

MA —COLLEGE OF THE HOLY CROSS, Dinand Library, College St, Worcester, 01610. James M Mahoney, Cur of Special Collection
Holdings: Uncat Mss Pix
Notes: The John J William SJ Collection contains correspondence, notes on history of Passamaquoddy tribe; (86) letters and copies of documents concerning Maine Indians from 1778-1913; pictures and 3 notebooks. Restricted use, noncirculating.

INDIANS OF NORTH AMERICA AND MEXICO—MASSACHUSETTS

MA —DUKES COUNTY HISTORICAL SOCIETY, School & Cooke Sts, Edgartown, 02539. Thomas E Norton, Dir
Holdings: Cat Mss Maps Pix Audiotapes Microforms
Notes: History and genealogy of Massachusetts, especially Martha's Vineyard. Also, materials on whaling and Indians of the region.

INDIANS OF NORTH AMERICA AND MEXICO—MISSIONS

AZ —NORTHERN ARIZONA UNIVERSITY, Special Collection Library, CU Box 6022, Flagstaff, 86011. Peter M Whiteley, Coordr/Archivist; William Mullane, Librn
Notes: Florence Barker Collection. She was a missionary nurse on the Navajo, Havasupai, Acoma and Laguna Indian Reservations. Incl diaries, 1922-1927 (Immanuel Mission, Navajo Reservation), also some copied textual material of interest concerning the Immanuel Mission during the 1920's. Inventory available.

IL —NEWBERRY LIBRARY, 60 W Walton St, Chicago, 60610. Diana Haskell, Cur of Modern Mss
Holdings: Vols 1500 Cat
Notes: Work among Indians. Missions of all sects in the US and Canada. The Edward E Ayer Collection.

INDIANS OF NORTH AMERICA AND MEXICO—MONTANA

†IL —NEWBERRY LIBRARY, 60 W Walton St, Chicago, 60610.
Notes: Collection of color slides of the early 1950s. Photographs by the eight-year Superintendent of the Fort Belknap Indian Reservation in Montana, J W "Duke" Wellington, who was allowed to take pictures of some of the most important rituals of the Assiniboine and Gros Ventres Indians, dances, renewals, etc. An annotated collection.

INDIANS OF NORTH AMERICA AND MEXICO—MUSIC

AZ —NORTHERN ARIZONA UNIVERSITY, Special Collection Library, CU Box 6022, Flagstaff, 86011. Peter M Whiteley, Coordr/Archivist; William Mullane, Librn
Notes: Apachean Languages and Music Collection. A music collection compiled by

INDIANS OF NORTH AMERICA AND MEXICO—MUSIC (cont.)

Werner Winter, Universitaet Kiel, Germany. Incl uses of language, stories, recipes, jokes, etc.

AZ —PHOENIX PUBLIC LIBRARY, Arizona Room, 12 E McDowell, Phoenix, 85004. Jeannette Brush, Librn
Holdings: Vols (30,000) Cat Maps Pix
Budget: ($12,000)
See also entry under Arizona - History.

AZ —NAVAJO COMMUNITY COLLEGE, Naaltsoos Ba' Hoogan, Library, Tsaile, 86556. Marvin E Pollard Jr, Dir, Library Services
Holdings: Vols (10,000) Cat Mss Maps Pix Slides Phonorecords Audiotapes Videotapes 16mm Films Filmstrips Microforms
Budget: ($15,000)
Notes: The Moses/Donner Collection emphasizes Navajos and other tribes of the Southwest; also, all Indians of North America and Mexico. All aspects of the geology, geography, sociology, archaeology, anthropology, etc, of the Four Corners region. The Collection includes a comprehensive collection of Doctoral dissertations dealing with Indians of North America and Mexico.

CA —LOS ANGELES PUBLIC LIBRARY, History Dept, 630 W Fifth St, Los Angeles, 90071. Leah Simon Kornbluth, Librn
Holdings: Vols (6000) Cat Maps Phonorecords Microforms
Budget: ($85,000)

Notes: The core of the American Indian collection is in the History Dept.; it includes descriptions of contemporary life, social commentary, legends, religious thought, political studies, as well as history and biography. There are sizeable sections of material outside the dept. as well; notable are anthropology in the Science Dept., art in the Art Dept., phonograph records in Audio-Visual. The History Dept.'s older holdings are particularly strong in folklore and descriptive accounts of Indian life. There are many full sets of monographs and society publications; the Bureau of American Ethnology Reports and Bulletins, the U.S. Office of Indian Affairs Reports, California Publications in American Archaeology and Ethnology among them, and the Indian Claims Commission Decisions and Expert Testimony on microfiche. Present acquisitions are strong in books written by Indian authors and material published by smaller and regional publishers. There are old and new journal runs and the History Dept. currently subscribes to 28 Indian periodicals. An index has been started within the last 2 years dealing with such topics as land tenure and claims, fishing rights, television programs, biographical information, etc. The material indexed is from periodicals, newspapers and books.

DC —LIBRARY OF CONGRESS, American Folklife Center, Archive of Folk Culture, Washington, 20540.
Notes: Frances Densmore's archive of 2500 recordings of 35 tribal groups. Also, her personal papers, annotated notebooks, etc. Also, William Rhodes Collection of field recordings of North American Indian music, 1940-52.

INDIANS OF NORTH AMERICA AND MEXICO—NEBRASKA

NE —KEARNEY STATE COLLEGE, Calvin T Ryan Library, Kearney, 68847. John Mayeski, Dir; Anita Norman, Reference Librn
Holdings: Vols (1700) Cat Mss Maps Pix Slides Microforms
Notes: Collection attempts to cover total historical development of Nebraska. Special strengths incl overland journeys, pony express, sod houses, and the Union Pacific. Special consideration has been given to Indians of Nebraska and the cattle industry. The collection is well supported by the library's general strength of Western Americana.

INDIANS OF NORTH AMERICA AND MEXICO—NEW ENGLAND

MA —NEW ENGLAND HISTORIC GENEALOGICAL SOCIETY, Library, 101 Newbury St, Boston, 02116. Ralph J Crandell, Dir
Holdings: Vols (250,000) Mss Maps Microforms Pix
Notes: New England genealogy. Especially strong Massachusetts, Maine, and New Hampshire, although all states are well represented, as are the relevancies of each subject listed in this volume with regard to British antecedent and contemporary history. Special strengths in local history and biography, obituaries, etc, incl parish registers, censuses, British and American. 3125 linear ft of mss.

INDIANS OF NORTH AMERICA AND MEXICO—NEW MEXICO

NM —ALBUQUERQUE PUBLIC LIBRARY, 423 Central Ave NE, Albuquerque, 87102. Laurel Drew, Librn
Holdings: Vols (5000) Cat Maps Microforms Audiotapes

NM —AZTEC RUINS NATIONAL MONUMENT, Library, PO Box U, Aztec, 87410. William L Schart, Park Ranger
Holdings: Vols (500) // Cat Mss Maps Pix Slides
Notes: Archaeology of the Anasazi ruins.

INDIANS OF NORTH AMERICA AND MEXICO—NEW YORK (STATE)

NY —NEW YORK STATE LIBRARY, State Education Bldg Annex, Washington Ave, Albany, 12224.
Holdings: Vols (110,500) Cat
Notes: Strong collection emphasis on North American Indians, especially Indians of New York. Incl books and pamphlets on Indian captivities, treaties, conferences, lives of noted Indians, laws. Bibles and catechisms, prayerbooks, grammars, etc in native languages. Outstanding collection on Iroquois Indians. Incl original treaties between the State of New York and the Iroguois, papers of Cornplanter, drawings by Jesse Cornplanter.

NY —NEW YORK STATE LIBRARY, Manuscripts and Special Collections, Albany, 12230. Peter R Christoph, Associate Librn
Holdings: Cat Mss Maps Pix Microforms
Notes: Strong collection, all aspects: social, political, legislative, economic history of the State and its people, incl Indians. Particularly valuable and extensive collection of historical mss, Colonial and State.

NY —STATE UNIVERSITY OF NEW YORK, COLLEGE OF ARTS & SCIENCE AT GENESEO, Milne Library, Geneseo, 14454. William T Lane, Head of Information Services & Archivist
Holdings: Vols (3700) Cat Mss Maps Slides
Budget: ($1000)
Notes: Genesee Valley Historical Collection. County, town, village, family and church histories for the counties of Allegany, Genesee, Livingston, Monroe, Orleans and Wyoming. Materials on the Seneca Indians, Genesee Valley Canal, and the geology of western New York state.
See also entry under Wadsworth Family

NY —SAINT JOHN FISHER COLLEGE, Library, Rochester, 14618.
Notes: George Deck Papers. 1000 correspondence papers pertaining to the Indians of New York and Canada.

INDIANS OF NORTH AMERICA AND MEXICO—NORTHEAST

NJ —SETON HALL UNIVERSITY MUSEUM, Archaeological Research Center, S Orange Ave, South Orange, 07079. Herbert C Craft, Dir
Holdings: Vols (750) Cat
Notes: Primarily books and periodicals related to New Jersey and northeastern states prehistory and archaeology.

INDIANS OF NORTH AMERICA AND MEXICO—NORTHWEST, PACIFIC

AK —TONGASS HISTORICAL SOCIETY, Library, 629 Dock St, Ketchikan, 99901. Marjorie Anne Voss, Librn
Holdings: Vols 400 Cat Pix
Notes: Alaskan and regional history and art, as well as Northwest Coast Indian history and art. Extensive photograph collection.

OR —COLLIER STATE PARK LOGGING MUSEUM LIBRARY, PO Box 428, Klamath Falls, 97601. Alfred D Collier, Cur; Lowell N Jones, Asst Cur
Holdings: Uncat Mss Maps Pix Slides
Notes: 600 pieces of equipment showing evolution of logging. 800 pictures of logging. 15 pioneer log cabins. 500 Indian Stone artifacts. Collection of cruisers marks and sleighs.

†OR —LEWIS AND CLARK COLLEGE, Library, 615 SW Palatine Hill Rd, Portland, 97219.

WA —WASHINGTON STATE LIBRARY, Washington/Northwest Rm, State Library Bldg, Olympia, 98504. Nancy B Pryor, Research Consultant
Holdings: Cat Mss Maps Pix Microforms
Notes: The Library has a large collection of books and government publications on Indians of North America and Mexico in the general loan collection and in the documents section. The Pacific Northwest Indian books are located in the Washington/Northwest Room. We try to collect everything possible on the Indians of Washington State.

†WA —WASHINGTON STATE UNIVERSITY, Library, Manuscripts, Archives & Special Collections, Pullman, 99164. John F Guido, Head
Holdings: Cat Mss Maps Pix
Notes: The collection is especially rich in documents relating to the exploration, settlement and development of the Palouse Country, the Inland Empire, the Columbia Basin and the Pacific Northwest. Described in *Selected Manuscript Resources in the Washington State University Library* (Pullman, 1974); and other published and unpublished inventories and registers. Also incl papers, 1821-1873, covering Father De Smet's early sojourns at Whitemarsh and St Louis, his founding of the Rocky Mountain Missions, his long service as Procurator and Socius of the Missouri Province, and his many travels. Correspondence with his family in Belgium, mss of his published journals, 2 small maps, sketches and engravings used to illustrate his books. Incl about 100 small pencil sketches by Father Nicholas Point depicting the 1841 journey from Westport to St Mary's Mission in theBitterroot Valley. Described in *The* Record, 30 (1969) 6-40; and 32 (1971) 47-63.

WA —UNIVERSITY OF WASHINGTON LIBRARIES, Pacific Northwest Collection, Seattle, 98195. Andrew F Johnson, Librn
Holdings: Vols (50,000) Cat Maps Pix
Budget: ($12,000)
Notes: The Pacific Northwest Collection contains printed materials documenting the historic and contemporary life and culture of the region in a broad range of subject areas. The Pacific Northwest is defined as the geographic region including Washington, Oregon, Idaho, Montana, British Columbia, Yukon Territory, and Alaska. Printed materials including books, periodicals, government documents, maps, weekly and

INDIANS OF NORTH AMERICA AND MEXICO—NORTHWEST, PACIFIC (cont.)

local regional newspapers, theses and dissertations, as well as photographs and architectural drawings are included in the Pacific Northwest Collection. Photographic works of over 200 photographers active in the Pacific Northwest, Alaska, and the Yukon Territory (Canada) during the period 1860-1930, including Asahel and Edward S Curtis, Eric Hegg, and Clark Kinsey, are represented in a print collection of more than 300,000 images. The architecturaldrawings collection includes over 19,000 original plans, drawings, sketches, renderings and blue prints pertaining to the history of architecture and urban planning and landscape gardening in the Pacific Northwest ca 1880-1940. Areas of particular strength are the holdings of over 1100 published journals of Pacific Northwest exploration expeditions, photographs of Northwest Coast Native Americans and of historic Seattle, newspapers issued within the Japanese-American relocation camps, 1942-1945, materials relating to the 1980 eruption of Mt St Helens, and Sanborne fire insurance maps for Washington. A unique feature of the Collection is the subject index to regional periodicals and local newspapers maintained by the PNW Collection staff; over 100 titles are currently indexed. G K Hall Company published a books catalog of the Pacific Northwest Collectionin 1973.

INDIANS OF NORTH AMERICA AND MEXICO—PICTURES, ILLUSTRATIONS, ETC.

DC —LIBRARY OF CONGRESS, Prints & Photographs Div, Washington, 20540.
Notes: The Edward S Curtis collection of photographs of North American Indians, early 20th century. About 1600 photoprints.

KS —UNIVERSITY OF KANSAS, Kenneth Spencer Research Library, Kansas Collection, Lawrence, 66045. Sheryl K Williams, Cur
Holdings: Cat Pix
Notes: The Floyd Schultz Photographic Collection mainly treating Potawatomie Indians (Prairie Band). About 450 photographs.

NV —UNIVERSITY OF NEVADA, RENO, University Library, Special Collections Dept, Reno, 89557. Robert E Blesse, Head
Holdings: Vols 1100 Mss Pix
Notes: Incl over 5000 photographs, government documents, periodicals, 80 cubic feet, mss, and audiotapes. The Great Basin Indian Collection contains materials on the anthropology, archaeology, and ethnohistory of the Great Basin region. Materials are collected for a defined group of 65 tribes incl Washo, Shoshone, Northern and Southern Paiute, the major tribes of the region. Collection of importance incl the Sven Liljeblad Collection, linguistics and ethnography; papers of US agent Lorenzo D Greel, 1902-22; Robert Leland Collection, Indian water rights.

NM —MUSEUM OF NEW MEXICO, Photo Archives, Box 2087, Santa Fe, 87503. Arthur L Olivas, Cur; Richard Rudisill, Photo Historian
Holdings: Cat Pix Slides
Budget: ($9000)
Notes: 90,000 photographs, cataloged, and 1000 slides. Photographs may be ordered as research copies for set fees. Reproduction or publication requires written permission plus additional required fees. Incl. special groups of photographs, e.g. T. Harmon Parkhurst Collection-ca. 15,000 photos, 1915-1950, Southwest Indians, scenic views, town views; H. F. Robinson Collection-ca. 1000 items, ca. 1910-1920, Southwest Indians, esp. Hopi and Blackfoot; Ben Wittick Collection-ca. 1500 items, 1879-1903, Southwest Indians, military, town views. Many other of the important early photographers are represented, especially large collections of the work of G. C. Bennett, William H. Brown, Dana B. Chase, Edward S. Curtis, H. H. Dorman, Rev. J. C. Gullette, P. E. Harroun, William H. Jackson, Charles F. Lummis, Jesse L. Nussbaum, Henry A. Schmidt, and about a hundred others.

NY —AMERICAN MUSEUM OF NATURAL HISTORY, Library Services Dept, Central Park W & 79th St, New York, 10024. Nina J Root, Chairwoman; Mary Genett, Asst Librn for Reference Services
Holdings: Cat Pix
Notes: Incl a card index of about 800 entries of portraits of named American Indians, indexed from various publications. Indexing ended, apparently, about 1955.

INDIANS OF NORTH AMERICA AND MEXICO—RESERVATIONS

AZ —NORTHERN ARIZONA UNIVERSITY, Special Collection Library, CU Box 6022, Flagstaff, 86011. Peter M Whiteley, Coordr/Archivist; William Mullane, Librn
Notes: Various collections, incl: (1) Florence Barker Collection. She was a missionary nurse on the Navajo, Havasupai, Acoma and Laguna Indian Reservations. Incl diaries, 1922-1927. (2) Day Family Collection. They were Anglo traders on the eastern Navajo Reservation. Incl correspondence, files of trading and other activities. Also unpublished mss on Navajo ceremonies and correspondence relating to the looting of Canyon del Muerto. (3) Phillip Johnston Collection; correspondence, files on Arizona, Navajo Reservation, Mexico and Southern California, 1920's-1970's (incl thousands of photo negatives of the Navajo Reservation, 1920's-1930's and slide shows of the Navajo Reservation and Mexico).

AZ —COLORADO RIVER INDIAN TRIBES MUSEUM/LIBRARY, Rte One, Box 23-B, Parker, 85344. Priscilla Johnson, Librn
Holdings: Cat Mss Maps Pix Slides Audiotapes Microforms
Notes: Library deals with the four tribes of the Colorado River Indian Reservation: Mojave, Chemehuevi, Navajo, and Hopi. Emphasis is also given to the prehistoric cultures of this area; Patayan and Hohokam. Library collections include original manuscripts and other documents, photographs, oral history tape recordings, cultural items and artifacts. Copies of many documents relating to the reservation are in bound volumes, microfilm, and photocopies. Photos relative to the reservation form various other collections are copied in our collection. Of particular interest is the museum basket collection which incl about 1000 Chemehuevi baskets--the largest Chemehuevi basket collection. Other artifacts give special emphasis to the Mojave culture.

ID —IDAHO STATE UNIVERSITY, Library, Pocatello, 83209. Gary Domitz, Social Science Librn
Holdings: Cat
Budget: ($2500)
Notes: Idaho and intermountain west history collection; incl the Lemhi Indian reservation's miscellaneous papers. Extensive collections.

†IL —NEWBERRY LIBRARY, 60 W Walton St, Chicago, 60610.
Notes: Collection of color slides of the early 1950s. Photographs by the eight-year Superintendent of the Fort Belknap Indian Reservation in Montana, J W "Duke" Wellington, who was allowed to take pictures of some of the most important rituals of the Assiniboine and Gros Ventres Indians, dances, renewals, etc. An annotated collection.

INDIANS OF NORTH AMERICA AND MEXICO—SOUTH CAROLINA

SC —UNIVERSITY OF SOUTH CAROLINA, Institute of Archaeology and Anthropology, Research Report Library, Maxcy College, Columbia, 29208. Kenn Pinson, Ms Archivist
Holdings: Mss Maps Pix Slides
Notes: Reports of research performed by the Institute of Archeology and Anthropology. Incl four series: the *Institute of Archeology and Anthropology Notebook; Research Manuscript Series;* and *Anthropological Studies, Popular Series*. Partially cataloged.

INDIANS OF NORTH AMERICA AND MEXICO—SOUTHERN STATES

TN —UNIVERSITY OF TENNESSEE, KNOXVILLE, Library, Knoxville, 37996. John Dobson, Special Collections Librn
Holdings: Vols (20,000) Cat Mss Maps Pix
Notes: Tennesseana; 19th century American fiction; southern Indians; early imprints. Separate catalog; holdings also listed in comprehensive public catalog in main library. Rare books card catalog with special headings calling attention to unusual features of the books; unpublished registers and calendars to ms collection. Also, 18 vols of extremely rare southwest territory and *Tennessee Official Acts and Journals*, printed in Knoxville, 1794-1796. The rare *Acts and Journals* are described in *The Lost Roulstone Imprints*, by John Dobson (Knoxville: Univ of Tennessee Libraries, 1975), 70 pp.

TX —UNIVERSITY OF TEXAS LIBRARIES, General Libraries, Barker Texas History Center, PO Box P, Austin, 78712. Don Carleton, Dir
Holdings: Vols (132,000) Cat Mss Maps Pix Slides Phonorecords Audiotapes Microforms
Notes: See description of collection under Texas-History.

TX —PANHANDLE-PLAINS HISTORICAL MUSEUM, Research Center, Box 967, WT Sta, Canyon, 79016. Claire R Kuehn, Archivist-Librn
Holdings: Vols 516 Cat Slides Phonorecords Microforms
Budget: $500
Notes: Supplements Indian customs and artifacts in the museum collection.

INDIANS OF NORTH AMERICA AND MEXICO—SOUTHWEST

AZ —NORTHERN ARIZONA UNIVERSITY, Special Collection Library, CU Box 6022, Flagstaff, 86011. Peter M Whiteley, Coordr/Archivist; William Mullane, Librn
Holdings: Cat Mss Pix
Notes: Various collections, incl: (1) Florence Barker Collection. She was a missionary nurse on the Navajo, Havasupai, Acoma and Laguna Indian Reservations. Incl diaries, 1922-1927. (2) Day Family Collection. They were Anglo traders on the eastern Navajo Reservation. Incl correspondence, files of trading and other activities. Also unpublished mss on Navajo ceremonies and correspondence relating to the looting of Canyon del Muerto. (3) Faye and Faith Hill Edgerton Collection; mss and notes of the translation of the New Testament into the Apache and Navajo languages. (4) Flagstaff All-Indian Pow-Wow Collection; correspondence, files (1947), programs, births, 1930's-1970's. (5) Phillip Johnston Collection; correspondence, files files on Arizona, Navajo Reservation, Mexico and Southern California, 1920's-1970's(incl thousands of photo negatives of the Navajo Reservation, 1920's-1930's and slide shows of the Navajo Reservation and Mexico). (6) Mennonite Library and Archives Collection incl photocopy of H R Voth mss *Hopi-English Vocabulary,* 1902, and *Hopi*

INDIANS OF NORTH AMERICA AND MEXICO—SOUTHWEST (cont.)

Field Notes, 1890's. (7) Saxton Collection; corrected Papago Hymnal, first edition, 1959 and concise Papago-English dictionary with corrections, undated, ca 1950-1960. (8) David L Shaul Collection; ms titled *An English-Shoshone Dictionary of Nineteenth Century Sources,* 1976. (9) H C Whitener Collection; Zuni language research notes and religious and Biblical translations in the Zuni language. Incl one folder on the Havasupai language.

AZ —FORT HUACHUCA HISTORICAL ASSOCIATION, Fort Huachuca, 85705. James P Finley, Dir
Holdings: Cat Mss Maps Pix Slides Microforms Artifacts
Notes: Voluminous collection of documents concerning Fort Huachuca, southeastern Arizona, Indians, pioneer settlements, and military history. About 50,000 manuscript pieces and documents.

AZ —HUBBELL TRADING POST NATIONAL HISTORIC SITE, Library, PO Box 150, Ganado, 86505. L Edward Gastellum, Supt
Holdings: Vols (500) Cat Mss Maps Pix Slides Audiotapes
Notes: Incl archives and mss of Hubbell Trading Post and much on Navajo Indian life.

AZ —HEARD MUSEUM, Library, 22 E Monte Vista Rd, Phoenix, 85004. Mary Graham, Librn
Holdings: Vols (40,000) Cat
Notes: Anthropology and primitive art. Incl 124 periodical titles and contemporary Native American Art.

AZ —PHOENIX PUBLIC LIBRARY, Arizona Room, 12 E McDowell, Phoenix, 85004. Jeannette Brush, Librn
Holdings: Vols (30,000) Cat Maps Pix
Budget: ($12,000)
See also entry under Arizona - History.

AZ —SCOTTSDALE COMMUNITY COLLEGE, Library, 9000 E Chaparral Rd, Scottsdale, 85253.
Holdings: Vols (1100) Cat Audiotapes Microforms
Notes: Incl 75 audiotapes.

AZ —NAVAJO COMMUNITY COLLEGE, Naaltsoos Ba' Hoogan, Library, Tsaile, 86556. Marvin E Pollard Jr, Dir, Library Services
Holdings: Vols (10,000) Cat Mss Maps Pix Slides Phonorecords Audiotapes Videotapes 16mm Films Filmstrips Microforms
Budget: ($15,000)
Notes: The Moses/Donner Collection emphasizes Navajos and other tribes of the southwest; also, all Indians of North America and Mexico. All aspects of the geology, geography, sociology, archaeology, anthropology, etc, of the Four Corners region. The collection includes a comprehensive collection of doctoral dissertations dealing with Indians of North America and Mexico.

AZ —ARIZONA HERITAGE CENTER, Library, 949 E Second St, Tucson, 85719. Michael Weber, Dir
Notes: Espec with reference to Arizona, the West, and the Southwest.

AZ —UNIVERSITY OF ARIZONA, Center for Creative Photography, 843 E University Blvd, Tucson, 85721. James Enyeart, Dir; Terence Pitts, Cur and Librn
Holdings: Pix
Notes: The Marion Palfi Photo Archive. Famous portrayals of, espec, poverty-stricken and victimized persons in the US, 1940 through 1970s, incl Hopi, Navajo, and Papago Indians on reservations, in urban relocation, and acculturation centers. Over 1500 master prints, 10,000 work prints, hundreds of glass plate and film negatives, manuscripts, etc.

AZ —NAVAJO TRIBAL MUSEUM, Navajo Historical Library, Window Rock, 86515. Russell P Hartman, Cur
Notes: Navajo history, art, social life and customs.

CA —HEMET PUBLIC LIBRARY, 510 E Florida Ave, Hemet, 92343. James P Boulton, Chief Librn
Holdings: Vols (3000) Cat Mss Maps Pix
Notes: Special emphasis on southern California and Indians of the Southwest. Local newspaper collection from 1907 to date.

CA —LOS ANGELES PUBLIC LIBRARY, History Dept, 630 W Fifth St, Los Angeles, 90071. Leah Simon Kornbluth, Librn
Holdings: Vols (6000) Cat Maps Phonorecords Microforms
Budget: ($85,000)
Notes: See entry under Indians of North America and Mexico for full description of collection.

CA —UNIVERSITY OF CALIFORNIA, LOS ANGELES, Research Library, Dept of Special Collections, 405 Hilgard Ave, Los Angeles, 90024. Edward Shreeves, Chairman, Bibliographers Group; David S Zeidberg, Head
Holdings: Mss Pix Phonorecords
Notes: Various collections, incl the Jaime de Angulo (Pit River) and Lorraine Miller Sherer (Mojave) collections.

CA —UNIVERSITY OF SOUTHERN CALIFORNIA, School of Medicine, Norris Medical Library, 2025 Zonal Ave, Los Angeles, 90033. Nelson J Gilman, Librn
Holdings: Vols (275) Cat
Budget: $200
Notes: The Collection of American Indian Ethnopharmacology.

CA —A K SMILEY PUBLIC LIBRARY, 125 W Vine St, Redlands, 92373. Larry E Burgess, Archivist
Holdings: Vols (3500) Mss Maps Pix Phonorecords Microforms
Budget: ($45,000)
Notes: Emphasis on San Bernadino County and the Redlands area. Especially prized is *The Citrograph*, 1887-1908 (bound vols and microfilm) edited by Scipio Craig, prominent in state, national, and newspaper circles. The ms collection (250,000 pieces) incl the Smiley Family Papers, much on water development, and on the citrus industry. The photograph collection (over 5000) covers the history of the area; there are many stereographs and glass slides. The collection on Indians of California and the southwest was begun from a special gift by Andrew Carnegie honoring his friend, Albert K Smiley.

CO —COLORADO SPRINGS FINE ARTS CENTER LIBRARY, 30 W Dale St, Colorado Springs, 80903. Roderick Dew, Librn
Holdings: Vols (20,000) Cat
Budget: ($4000)
Notes: Specialize in fine arts and anthropology of the Southwest. Incl auction and exhibition catalogs.

CO —FORT LEWIS COLLEGE, Library, Southwest Collection, College Heights, Durango, 81301. Daniel W Lester, Dir
Holdings: Vols (7000) Cat Mss Maps Pix Slides Microforms
Budget: ($3800)
Notes: Also have separate catalog of the special collections concerning the Southwest, Indians, mine records, railroads, etc.

†NM —UNIVERSITY OF NEW MEXICO, Medical Center Library, Albuquerque, 87131. Beatrice Kovacs, Chief, Collections and Resource Development
Notes: Concern is health care and health services in New Mexico; medicine and medicine men of Indian tribes of the Southwest; and history of medicine and health in the Southwest.

NM —AZTEC RUINS NATIONAL MONUMENT, Library, PO Box U, Aztec, 87410. William L Schart, Park Ranger
Holdings: Vols (500) // Cat Mss Maps Pix Slides
Notes: Archaeology of the Anasazi ruins.

NM —GALLUP PUBLIC LIBRARY, 115 W Hill Ave, Gallup, 87301. Octavia Fellin, Dir
Holdings: Vols (8000) Cat Maps Pix

NM —MUSEUM OF NEW MEXICO, Laboratory of Anthropology Library, PO Box 2087, Santa Fe, 87503. Laura Holt, Librn
Holdings: Vols (16,000) Cat Mss Maps
Notes: Southwestern archaeology, anthropology, ethnology. Noncirculating. Also incl the personal Library (2000 vols) of Sylvanus Morley, Meso-American archaeologist and historian. Some materials on Indians of Middle America.

NM —MUSEUM OF NEW MEXICO, Photo Archives, Box 2087, Santa Fe, 87503. Arthur L Olivas, Cur; Richard Rudisill, Photo Historian
Holdings: Cat Pix Slides
Budget: ($9000)
Notes: 90,000 photographs, cataloged, and 1000 slides. Photographs may be ordered as research copies for set fees. Reproduction or publication requires written permission plus additional required fees. Incl. special groups of photographs, e.g. T. Harmon Parkhurst Collection-ca. 15,000 photos, 1915-1950, Southwest Indians, scenic views, town views; H. F. Robinson Collection-ca. 1000 items, ca. 1910-1920, Southwest Indians, esp. Hopi and Blackfoot; Ben Wittick Collection-ca. 1500 items, 1879-1903, Southwest Indians, military, town views. Many other of the important early photographers are represented, especially large collections of the work of G. C. Bennett, William H. Brown, Dana B. Chase, Edward S. Curtis, H. H. Dorman, Rev. J. C. Gullette, P. E. Harroun, William H. Jackson, Charles F. Lummis, Jesse L. Nussbaum, Henry A. Schmidt, and about a hundred others.

NY —STATE UNIVERSITY OF NEW YORK, COLLEGE OF ARTS & SCIENCE AT GENESEO, Milne Library, Geneseo, 14454. William T Lane, Head of Information Services & Archivist
Holdings: // Pix
Notes: The Martha Blow Wadsworth Collection. Photographs taken or collected by Mrs Wadsworth from the 1890s to around 1910. There are 33 albums containing 4561 mounted photographs, and 3 boxes containing 345 hand-tinted lantern slides. Subjects include horseback rides from Washington, DC to Avon, NY (1905-1909); US Army packtrain trips in the southwestern US (1907-1910); Hopi, Navajo, and Zuni Indians (1910); motor trip through France and England (1909); Panama Canal construction; Alaskan boundary survey trip; and the Wadsworth family of Livingston County, NY. There are no negatives. Inventory in repository. Open to qualified investigators with permission of archivist. Gift of Michael Moukhanoff, Ashantee, NY, 1976.

OK —WOOLAROC MUSEUM, Library, Rte 3, Bartlesville, 74003. Robert R Lansdown, Museum Dir
Holdings: Vols (300) Cat

OK —US ARMY FIELD ARTILLERY SCHOOL LIBRARY, Morris Swett Library, Snow Hall, Fort Sill, 73503. Lester L Miller Jr, Chief Librn
Notes: Incl data on Fort Sill, Indian Territory, settlement of Kiowa, Apache and Commanche tribes, imprisonment of Geronimo, Oklahoma territory, settlement of Lawton. Unit histories, incl 10th Cavalry (Buffalo Soldiers, a black unit that built Fort Sill); working papers of Sheridan, Grierson and other commanders; Field Artillery School. Photographs on army subjects, Fort Sill, Indians, Indian Territory, settlement of Southwest Oklahoma.

OK —UNIVERSITY OF OKLAHOMA, Bizzell Memorial Library, Western History Collections, 401 W Brooks, Norman, 73069. John Ezell, Cur
Holdings: Cat Mss Maps Pix Microforms

TX —EL PASO PUBLIC LIBRARY, Southwest Collection, 501 N Oregon, El Paso, 79901. Mary A Sarber, Head
Holdings: Vols (12,000) Cat Mss Maps Pix
Budget: ($11,000)
Notes: Research collection includes rare

INDIANS OF NORTH AMERICA AND MEXICO—SOUTHWEST (cont.)

books and mss journals, vertical files, index to El Paso newspapers, microfilmed newspapers, photographs, and architectural plans. Separate catalog. Limited to materials on Texas, New Mexico, Arizona and Mexico. Special collections of material by and about Tom Lea Jr, and Carl Hertzog. Aultman Collection of photographs includes 3500 on El Paso Southwest and 2500 on Mexican Revolution. Cited in Lovelace, Lisa, "The Southwest Collection of the El Paso Public Library". *Great Plains Journal,* vol 2, no 2, pp 161-166; Aultman, Otis A *Photographs from the Border: The Otis A Aultman Collection,* El Paso Public Library Association, 1977.

INDIANS OF NORTH AMERICA AND MEXICO—TRADING POSTS

AZ —HUBBELL TRADING POST NATIONAL HISTORIC SITE, Library, PO Box 150, Ganado, 86505. L Edward Gastellum, Supt
Holdings: Vols (500) Cat Mss Maps Pix Slides Audiotapes
Notes: Incl copies of the Hubbell Trading Post manuscripts and archives. Much on Navajo Indian life.

†WA —WASHINGTON STATE UNIVERSITY, Library, Manuscripts, Archives & Special Collections, Pullman, 99164. John F Guido, Head
Holdings: Cat Mss Maps Pix
Notes: The Carl Parcher Russell papers, a vast resource (24,916 items; 45 linear feet) on American Indian and Western pioneer activities and artifacts. Much on the fur trade; pioneer life; mountain men and trapping; wildlife; primitive life in detail. Also the National Park Service, parks, monuments, etc. Described in *Carl Parcher Russell: An Indexed Register of His Scholarly and Professional Papers, 1920-1967, in the Washington State University* Library (Pullman, 1970), 149 pp.

INDIANS OF NORTH AMERICA AND MEXICO—TRAPPING

†WA —WASHINGTON STATE UNIVERSITY, Library, Manuscripts, Archives & Special Collections, Pullman, 99164. John F Guido, Head
Holdings: Cat Mss Maps Pix
Notes: The Carl Parcher Russell papers, a vast resource (24,916 items; 45 linear feet) on American Indian and Western pioneer activities and artifacts. Much on the fur trade; pioneer life; mountain men and trapping; wildlife; primitive life in detail. Also the National Park Service, parks, monuments, etc. Described in *Carl Parcher Russell: An Indexed Register of His Scholarly and Professional Papers, 1920-1967, in the Washington State University* Library (Pullman, 1970), 149 pp.

INDIANS OF NORTH AMERICA AND MEXICO—TREATIES

CO —NATIVE AMERICAN RIGHTS FUND, National Indian Law Library, 1506 Broadway, Boulder, 80302. Diana Lim Garry, Librn
Holdings: Vols Case Files Law Review Articles Studies Monographs
Budget: ($125,000)
Notes: A National Library of Indian Law, originally made possible by a grant from the Carnegie Corportation, now funded by the Administration for Native Amercians (DHHS). Emphasizes information about treaties and rulings in cases involving Indian Country jurisdiciton, economic development, hunting, land and water rights. Incl over 2000 case files and 4400 other monographs. Library publishes the *National Indian Law Library Catalogue: An Index to Indian Legal Materials and Resources.* Cumulative edition published in 1982, supplemented biannually. Catalog lists library holdings indexed by subject, author-title and case name.

NM —UNIVERSITY OF NEW MEXICO, School of Law Library, 1117 Stanford Dr NE, Albuquerque, 87131. Myron Fink, Law Librn
Holdings: Vols (3000) Cat Mss
Notes: Collection supports the work of the American Indian Law Center, established by the law school. Has separate catalog with extensive subject analysis. Incl papers of William Zimmerman, Asst Commissioner of Indian Affairs, 1934-1950. Emphasis is on government relations, tribal government (especially tribal codes for all Indian tribes in US). Incl materials on indigenous peoples world-wide. Periodical literature is subject indexed. Bibliography: Sabatini, Joseph D, *American Indian Law: A Bibliography of Books, Law Review Articles and Indian* Periodicals. (Albuquerque, 1973), Supplement, 1975.

PA —UNIVERSITY OF PITTSBURGH, Darlington Memorial Library, Special Collections, 601 Cathedral of Learning, Pittsburgh, 15260. Dennis Lambert, Darlington Librn
Holdings: Vols (17,000) Cat Mss Maps Pix
Notes: The Darlington Collection is especially rich in American history of the colonial period, the French and Indian War, the Revolution, and the War of 1812 with geographical emphasis on Western Pennsylvania and Ohio Valley history to 1870 and on Pittsburgh history to 1900. Indian treaties, captivity accounts, US and Pennsylvania travel and description, and early American fiction and prose are represented. A partial guide to the Darlington Manuscript Collections is available by writing for *Darlington Memorial Library: A Descriptive Checklist of its Manuscript Collections,* University of Pittsburgh Bibliographic Series 5, 1969. Noncirculating.

RI —BROWN UNIVERSITY, John Hay Library, 20 Prospect St, Providence, 02912. Mark N Brown, Cur Mss
Holdings: Vols 111// Cat
Notes: US State Dept treaties with the Indian nations (1833-1868) by which the US acquired claims to tracts of land, incl 13 treaties proclaimed by President Lincoln.

INDIANS OF NORTH AMERICA AND MEXICO—TRIBAL GOVERNMENT

NM —UNIVERSITY OF NEW MEXICO, School of Law Library, 1117 Stanford Dr NE, Albuquerque, 87131. Myron Fink, Law Librn
Holdings: Vols (3000) Cat Mss
Notes: Collection supports the work of the American Indian Law Center, established by the law school. Has separate catalog with extensive subject analysis. Incl papers of William Zimmerman, Asst Commissioner of Indian Affairs, 1934-1950. Emphasis is on government relations, tribal government (especially tribal codes for all Indian tribes in US). Incl materials on indigenous peoples world-wide. Periodical literature is subject indexed. Bibliography: Sabatini, Joseph D, *American Indian Law: A Bibliography of Books, Law Review Articles and Indian* Periodicals. (Albuquerque, 1973), Supplement, 1975.

INDIANS OF NORTH AMERICA AND MEXICO—WARS

AZ —NORTHERN ARIZONA UNIVERSITY, Special Collection Library, CU Box 6022, Flagstaff, 86011. Peter M Whiteley, Coordr/Archivist; William Mullane, Librn
Notes: Letters concerning placement of monument at the Battle of Big Dry Wash, last major Indian battle in Arizona, 1882, located near the Mogollon Rim. Incl letters written by W C Barnes, author of *Arizona Place Names,* and E G Miller, former Coconino National Forest supervisor, 1929-1934.

CO —UNIVERSITY OF COLORADO, Libraries, Western Historical Collections, Boulder, 80309.
Holdings: // Cat Mss Maps Pix
Notes: The collection contains correspondence, diaries, military papers, maps, publications, scrapbooks, addresses, photographs, and newspaper clippings relating to Gen William Carey Brown's military career, which incl campaigns against the Indians, service in the Spanish-American War and the Philippine Insurrection, and participation in the Mexican Punitive Expedition. The material, in 49 boxes, covers virtually all of Brown's life. A published guide is available.

IL —NEWBERRY LIBRARY, 60 W Walton St, Chicago, 60610. Diana Haskell, Cur of Modern Mss
Holdings: Vols (500) Cat
Notes: Incl source and secondary works. Restricted use: noncirulating.

ME —BOWDOIN COLLEGE, Library, Brunswick, 04011. Dianne M Gutscher, Cur of Special Collections
Holdings: Mss
Notes: The Oliver Otis Howard Papers consist of more than 150,000 pieces of correspondence, articles, lectures, and ephemera for the period 1843-1908, covering his services as a Civil War officer, as founder of the Freedmen's Bureau, as president of Howard University, as commander of the Department of the Columbia during the Northwest Indian Wars, and as superintendent of the US Military Academy at West Point.

MA —NEW ENGLAND HISTORIC GENEALOGICAL SOCIETY, Library, 101 Newbury St, Boston, 02116. Ralph J Crandell, Dir
Holdings: Vols (250,000) Mss Maps Microforms Pix
Notes: New England genealogy. Especially strong Massachusetts, Maine, and New Hampshire, although all states are well represented, as are the relevancies of each subject listed in this volume with regard to British antecedent and contemporary history. Special strengths in local history and biography, obituaries, etc, incl parish registers, censuses, British American. 3125 linear ft of mss.

MI —MONROE COUNTY LIBRARY SYSTEM, Ellis Reference and Information Center, 3700 S Custer Rd, Monroe, 48161. Marie D Chulski, Head of Reference Services
Holdings: Vols 35,000 Cat Mss Maps Pix Slides 16mm Films Microforms Periodicals Sound Recordings Paintings Memorabilia
Budget: ($15,000)
Notes: Historic Monroe County, tracing its beginnings to 1780, is a definite part of Michigan's history. Many events of the area and citizens are part of Michigan's heritage. The Michigan collection besides general works contains individual county histories, atlases, biographies, etc. The Monroe County history collection contains veteran records, plat books, oral history tapes, family histories, church records, cemetery index, atlases and census records. Genealogy emphasis is not only Monroe County but includes surrounding counties and the states with large migration to the area, such as Ohio, Kentucky, Tennessee and the New England states.

MI —CENTRAL MICHIGAN UNIVERSITY, Clarke Historical Library, Mount Pleasant, 48859. William H Mulligan, Jr, Dir; William Miles, Biography Collections Librn
Holdings: Vols 1200 Mss Pix
Notes: Incl material on life and times of Gen George Custer and general subject of Indian-Army relations.

MN —BROWN COUNTY HISTORICAL SOCIETY, Museum and Archives, Center St and Broadway, Box 116, New Ulm, 56073. Paul Klammer, Dir
Holdings: Vols (250) Mss Maps Pix Slides Phonorecords Audiotapes Videotapes 16mm Films Filmstips Microforms
Notes: History of Brown County, Minn. Also have *Historical Files,* about 500 pieces in vertical files incl newspaper clippings, advertising, letterheads, etc, pertaining to Brown County businesses, industry, schools,

INDIANS OF NORTH AMERICA AND MEXICO—WARS (cont.)

governmental units, etc. *Family Files,* about 2500 pioneer families. Files incl obituaries, pictures, documents, letters, etc. Also collection on Siouan Uprising of 1862-clippings, copies of treaties, letters, etc (65 vols, 10 mss, 25 maps, 40 pix, 50 slides).

NE —NEBRASKA STATE HISTORICAL SOCIETY, Fort Robinson Museum, Box 304, Crawford, 69339. Vance Nelson, Cur
Holdings: Vols (1500) Cat Mss Maps Pix Slides Phonorecords Audiotapes 16mm Films Microforms
Notes: Materials related to the history of Fort Robinson, and incl the Post Medical Library, reference books on state government, etc, Western Americana: books on ranching, homesteaders, Indian wars, etc; microfilm records for Fort Robinson records, Red Cloud and Spotted Tail Indian Agency records, Crawford and Chadron, Nebraska newspapers, diaries and interviews. Library incl the E Kopac Collection of books dealing with Western Americana; particularly Indian wars, transportation, guns and railroads.

PA —US ARMY MILITARY HISTORY INSTITUTE, Carlisle Barracks, 17013. Richard J Sommers, Chief Archivist-Historian
Holdings: Mss Cat
Notes: 450 folders and 50 boxes of mss. The Indian Wars collection, personal correspondence, diaries, and reminscences of officers of US cavalry, infantry, and artillery regiments serving in the American West, 1865-1898.

INDIANS OF NORTH AMERICA AND MEXICO—WASHINGTON (STATE)

WA —WASHINGTON STATE LIBRARY, Washington/Northwest Rm, State Library Bldg, Olympia, 98504. Nancy B Pryor, Research Consultant
Holdings: Cat Mss Maps Pix Microforms
Notes: The Library has a large collection of books and government publications on Indians of North America and Mexico in the general loan collection and in the documents section. The Pacific Northwest Indian books and other material indicated above are located in the Washington/Northwest Room. We try to collect everything possible on the Indians of Washington State.

INDIANS OF NORTH AMERICA AND MEXICO—WATER RIGHTS

NV —UNIVERSITY OF NEVADA, RENO, University Library, Special Collections Dept, Reno, 89557. Robert E Blesse, Head
Holdings: Vols 1100 Mss Pix
Notes: Incl over 5000 photographs, government documents, periodicals, 80 cubic feet, mss, and audiotapes. The Great Basin Indian Collection contains materials on the anthropology, archaeology, and ethnohistory of the Great Basin region. Materials are collected for a defined group of 65 tribes incl Washo, Shoshone, Northern and Southern Paiute, the major tribes of the region. Collection of importance incl the Sven Liljeblad Collection, linguistics and ethnography; papers of US agent Lorenzo D Greel, 1902-22; Robert Leland Collection, Indian water rights.

INDIANS OF SOUTH AMERICA

CT —TRINITY COLLEGE LIBRARY, Watkinson Library, 300 Summit St, Hartford, 06106. Jeffrey Kaimowitz, Cur
Holdings: Cat

CT —YALE UNIVERSITY, Anthropology Library, Peabody Museum of Natural History, C-8 KBT, New Haven, 06511.
Holdings: Vols (16,000)
Budget: ($11,000)

CT —YALE UNIVERSITY, Sterling Memorial Library, Latin American Collections, New Haven, 06520. Lee H Williams Jr, Cur
Holdings: Vols (300,000) Cat Maps Pix Slides Phonorecords 16mm Films Filmstrips
See also entry under Latin America

DC —SMITHSONIAN INSTITUTION LIBRARIES, Anthropology Branch, Washington, 20560. Jean C Smith, Asst Dir for Bureau Services
Holdings: Vols (54,000) Cat Mss Maps Pix Slides Microforms
Budget: ($7041)
Notes: Physical anthropology, archaeology, ethnology, language and languages; Indians of both continents.

IL —NEWBERRY LIBRARY, 60 W Walton St, Chicago, 60610. Diana Haskell, Cur of Modern Mss
Holdings: Vols 1000 Cat Mss Maps Pix
Notes: Incl South American linguistic books. Restricted use: noncirculating.

IN —INDIANA UNIVERSITY, Lilly Library, Seventh St, Bloomington, 47405. William R Cagle, Librn
Holdings: Vols (40,000) Cat Mss Maps
Notes: Research and rare book collection (Bernardo Mendel) of first or only editions, mostly printed in Latin America, from the discovery of the New World through 1830. Special strength in discoveries and exploration, history (mainly period of independence), Inquisition, missionary works by the Augustinians, Dominicans, Franciscanss, and the Jesuits, and the history of the Catholic Church in these countries. Major geographic concentration is on the three great viceroyalties of Mexico (ca 10, 000 titles, plus over 10,000 official Mexican broadsides), Peru (2000 titles), and Argentina (4000 titles), incl in Argentina a substantial amount of printings from the Imprenta de Ninos Espositos, and the Coleccion Santamarina. A special Bolivian Collection (2500 titles), mostly history, from the establishment of the press there, ca 1829, through the beginning ofthe 20th century. Part of the Mendel Collection is the select Bibliotheca Boxeriana from Charles R Boxer (1000 titles) on European expansion into Asia, and into the New World, mainly Brazil, during the 16th-18th centuries. The collection is supplemented by substantial material from the private collection of Josiah K Lilly.
See also entries under Spain - History, Portugal - History, and Mexico - History.

LA —TULANE UNIVERSITY, Howard-Tilton Memorial Library, Latin American Library, New Orleans, 70118. Thomas Niehaus, Dir
Holdings: Vols (150,000) Cat Mss Maps Pix Microforms VF
Budget: ($67,000)
Notes: *Catalog of the Latin American* Library (Boston: G K Hall, 1970, suppl. 1973,1975,1978); Downs 5338-41; suppl (1961), 2727, 2737. The Latin American Library is a general collection, but specializes in Central American, Mexican, and Brazilian materials. The disciplines which are most strongly represented are history, anthropology, and archaeology. The Viceregal Ecclesiastical Mexican Collection contains manuscripts from the colonial period. The France V Scholes Collection contains a large number of photoprints and microfilm of colonial documents from the archives of Spain and Mexico. The Merle Greene Robertson Rubbings Collection contains nearly five hundred rubbings of relief sculpture from Mayan archaeological sites in Mexico and Guatemala. The Photographic Collection contains photos of archaeological sites inMeso-America, of pre-Columbian Peruvian architecture, and a general group of historic photos from Latin America.

MA —PEABODY MUSEUM OF SALEM, Phillips Library, E India Sq, Salem, 01970. Gregor Trinkaus-Randall, Librn
Holdings: Vols (100,000) Cat Mss Pix
Notes: Ethnology of Non-European Peoples Collection. Composed of separate divisions relating to the Pacific Islands, China, Japan and the American Indian. No published indexes.

NV —UNIVERSITY OF NEVADA SYSTEM, Elko Community College, Learning Resources Center, Elko, 89801. Juanita R Karr, Dir
Holdings: Vols 1200 Cat Maps Pix Microforms
Budget: $500

NJ —PRINCETON UNIVERSITY, Library, Princeton, 08540. Alfred Bush, Cur
Holdings: Cat Mss

NY —MUSEUM OF THE AMERICAN INDIAN, Library, 9 Westchester Square, Bronx, 10401. Mary B Davis, Librn
Holdings: Vols (40,000) Cat Mss Maps Pix Microforms VF
Notes: Incl information in Indians of North, Central, and South America; archaeology of North, Central, and South America; American Indian ethnology; anthropology, history.

NY —AMERICAN MUSEUM OF NATURAL HISTORY, Library Services Dept, Central Park W & 79th St, New York, 10024. Nina J Root, Chairwoman; Mary Genett, Asst Librn for Reference Services
Holdings: Vols (385,000) Cat Mss Maps Pix Slides Microforms
Notes: Nearly all collections are outstanding for depth of coverage and international range. Early and historic works, rare books, colored illustrations, and relevant serial publications supplement the modern scientific publications necessary to the researches of the scientific staff and the work of the educational division. Open to the public.

NY —HISPANIC SOCIETY OF AMERICA, Library, 613 W 155 St, New York, 10032. Martha M de Narvaez, Cur of Mss; Irene S Frye, Asst Librn
Holdings: Vols (150,000) Cat Mss Maps Pix Slides Phonorecords Microforms

NY —NEW YORK PUBLIC LIBRARY, Research Libraries, American History Div, Fifth Ave & 42 St, New York, 10018.
Holdings: Vols (10,000) Cat Mss Maps Pix Slides Microforms
Notes: Archaeology, anthropology, linguistics, ethnology, and sociology of the American Indian. Comprehensive coverage. Much material on Indian languages, incl numerous syllabaries. Coverage ranges from the Eskimos to the Indians of Tierra del Fuego.

PA —UNIVERSITY OF PITTSBURGH, Hillman Library, Pittsburgh, 15260. Glenora E Rossell, Head
Holdings: Vols (172,000) Cat Microforms
Notes: A general collection on Peruvian studies, but particularly strong in the history of the conquest, the discovery, the colonial period, and Indian civilizations and cultures. Emphasis also is on contemporary history, politics, sociology, and anthropology.

RI —BROWN UNIVERSITY, John Hay Library, 20 Prospect St, Providence, 02912. Mark N Brown, Cur Mss
Holdings: Vols (3500) // Cat Mss Maps
Notes: George Earl Church Collection, formed by a civil engineer, explorer and Fellow of the Royal Geographic Society, who specialized in railroad construction. Although part of the collection is devoted to American Revolutionary and Civil War history, the majority, over 2000 volumes, pertains to Central and South America. The imprints, which are predominantly 18th century, include Lima, Madrid, Rome, Mexico City, Seville, Barcelona, Lisbon, and Cadiz as well as *Nova orbis regionum ac insularum veteribus incognitarum* (Basle: 1537). Major subject areas are: anthropology, commerce, economics, engineering, ethnology, geography, history, law, mineral resources, railroad surveys, voyages of exploration and dictionaries of the South American Indian languages. The most significant ms is an historical account of the Bolivian mining town of Potosi from 1545-1737.

RI —BROWN UNIVERSITY, John Carter Brown Library, Providence, 02912. Norman Fiering, Librn; Everett C Wilkie Jr, Bibliographer; Susan Danforth, Cur Maps & Prints
Notes: Incl pre-Columbian materials; large mss holdings pertaining to Indian linguistics.
See also entry under Indians of Central America.

TX —UNIVERSITY OF TEXAS LIBRARIES, Nettie Lee Benson Latin American Collection, Sid Richardson Hall 1.109, Austin, 78712. Laura Gutierrez-Witt, Head

INDIANS OF SOUTH AMERICA (cont.)

Librn
Holdings: Vols (450,000) Cat Mss Maps Pix Phonorecords Filmstrips Microforms
See also entry under Latin America.

ON —ROYAL ONTARIO MUSEUM, Main Library and Archives, 100 Queen's Park, Toronto, M5S 2C6, Can. Julia Matthews, Head Librn
Holdings: Vols (85,000) Cat
Notes: Since January 1977, acquisitions have been entered in UTLAS.

INDIANS OF SOUTH AMERICA—ANTIQUITIES

IL —NEWBERRY LIBRARY, 60 W Walton St, Chicago, 60610. Diana Haskell, Cur of Modern Mss
Holdings: Vols (1000) Cat Mss Pix
Notes: Western continent antiquities.

INDIANS OF SOUTH AMERICA—ART

CO —UNIVERSITY OF COLORADO, Libraries, Art & Architecture Library, Campus Box 184, Boulder, 80309. Liesel Nolan, Librn/Dept Head
Holdings: Vols (57,647) Cat Pix
Budget: ($39,000)
Notes: Special feature: art exhibition catalog collection 1963-1971, 1972-date. Good general collection with some special emphasis on environmental design, Islamic architecture, Indian art and South American Indian art. Fair collection of periodical backfiles in art and in architecture. Separate catalog for materials in collection. Rare books in main library, listed only in central union catalog.

NY —METROPOLITAN MUSEUM OF ART, Robert Goldwater Library, Fifth Ave at 82nd St, New York, 10028. Allan D Chapman, Librn
Holdings: Vols (27,000) Cat
Notes: Primitive art: African, Indians of the Americans (incl Pre-Columbian), Oceanic, Polynesian, etc. 150,000 photographs.

INDIANS OF SOUTH AMERICA—LANGUAGES

CA —UNIVERSITY OF CALIFORNIA, BERKELEY, University Library, Hispanic Collections, Berkeley, 94720. Gaston Somoshegyi-Szokol, Librn
Holdings: Vols (1000)
Notes: Strong research collection covering both literature (chronicles, histories, poetry, mythologies, etc) and linguistics (grammars, lexicons, dictionaries, etc) with special strength in Nahuatl and Maya.

IL —NEWBERRY LIBRARY, 60 W Walton St, Chicago, 60610. Diana Haskell, Cur of Modern Mss
Holdings: Vols 1000 Cat Mss Maps Pix
Notes: Incl South American linguistic books. Restricted use: noncirculating.

MA —HARVARD UNIVERSITY LIBRARY, Tozzer Library, 21 Divinity Ave, Cambridge, 02138. Nancy J Schmidt, Librn
Holdings: Cat Mss Microforms
Notes: Tozzer Library was formerly the Peabody Museum Library.

RI —BROWN UNIVERSITY, John Hay Library, 20 Prospect St, Providence, 02912. Mark N Brown, Cur Mss
Holdings: Vols 3500// Cat Mss Maps
Notes: George Earl Church Collection, formed by a civil engineer, explorer and Fellow of the Royal Geographic Society. Incl dictionaries of the South American Indian languages.

INDIANS OF THE SOUTHWEST see Indians of North America and Mexico—Southwest

INDIANS OF THE U.S. see Indians of North America and Mexico

INDIC LANGUAGES AND LITERATURES

CA —UNIVERSITY OF CALIFORNIA, BERKELEY, University Library, 438 Main Library, Berkeley, 94720. Kenneth R Logan, South Asia Librn
Notes: South Asia collection (India, Pakistan, Bangladesh, Nepal, Sri Lanka) contain 150,000-200,000 titles. Covers at research level the social sciences and humanities in western languages and 20 South Asian languages. Subject areas: history, political science, lanugage and literature (especially strong in Hindi, Urdu, Tamil, Sanskrit and Nepali), art and art history, sociology, education, music, environmental design, philosophy and religion, anthropology, geography, national and local government publications. Formats: monographs, periodicals, newspapers, microforms, maps, sound recordings, video-tapes, pamphlets. Special strengths: modern Hindi literature; history of South Asian countries; government publications of India, late 19th and 20th centuries. Member of South Asia Microform Project; Participant in Library of Congress AcquisitionsPrograms for India, Pakistan, Nepal, and Bangladesh.

NY —INSTITUTE FOR ADVANCED STUDIES OF WORLD RELIGIONS (IASWR), Melville Memorial Library, State University of New York, Stony Brook, 11794. C T Shen, Dir
Holdings: Vols 30,000 Periodicals Mss Maps Microforms
Notes: Reference and research facilities on religious and related subjects in Arabic, Bengali, Gujarati, Hindi, Marathi, Pali, Persian, Prakit, Punjabi, Sanskrit, and Urdu and English. Microforms: 3400 Indic mss in microfiche; 80 percent Hinduism, 20 percent Buddhism. Catalogs available. Refer inquiries to H Robinson.

OH —CLEVELAND PUBLIC LIBRARY, Fine Arts and Special Collections Department, 325 Superior Ave, Cleveland, 44114. Alice N Loranth, Head
Holdings: Vols (10,000) Cat Mss Maps
Notes: Part of the collection on India. All aspects of Indian civilization up to the mid-19th century. The more than 5400 vols of Indic language texts and their translations, the rich representation of the various literary languages of India, and the more than 19, 000 pages of ms records of the East India Company referring to British Indian affairs (1741-1859) are the strengths of the collection. Important serials, periodicals, ms catalogs, bibliographies. English titles pertaining to modern history, politics and economics are currently added to the respective departmental collections of the library. See M B Emeneau, *Union List of Printed Indic Texts and Translations in American Libraries* (New Haven, 1935). Separate catalogs of main entries for materials in Indic languages are maintained. *See also* entries under India; Oriental Languages and Literatures; Sanskrit Language and Literature.

PA —PENNSYLVANIA STATE UNIVERSITY, Fred Lewis Pattee Library, University Park, 16802. Stuart Forth, Dean of Libraries
Holdings: Vols Cat Phonorecords Microforms
Notes: Strong in Australian Literature, lesser holdings in Canadian, Caribbean, New Zealand, Indian and West African. Special collections of African Plays, Australian Literature.

RI —BROWN UNIVERSITY, John Hay Library, 20 Prospect St, Providence, 02912. Mark N Brown, Cur Mss
Holdings: Vols (53) //
Notes: Indic Manuscripts Collection. Codices written in Burmese, Cambodian, Telugu, Skandhas, Bengali, and Sinhalese script on palm leaves, encased within wood covers, some lacquered. Subjects include: Buddhist canon, Pali grammar and lexicons, epics, dance drama, and a treatise on midwifery. Recorded in *A Census of Indic Manuscripts in the United States and* Canada compiled by Horace I Poleman (New Haven: American Oriental Society, 1938).

INDIC MANUSCRIPTS see Manuscripts, Indic

INDIGO

SC —FRANCIS MARION COLLEGE, James A Rogers Library, Florence, 29501. H Paul Dove, Dir; Roger K Hux, Special Collections Librn
Holdings: Vols (600) Cat Maps Audiotapes Microforms
Notes: The Pee Dee Region of South Carolina. Emphasis on Colonial and Revolutionary periods, rice and indigo culture, plantations. Includes old rural church library with children's books.

INDIRECT TAXATION see Taxation

INDO-ARYAN LANGUAGES

NY —NEW YORK PUBLIC LIBRARY, Oriental Div, Fifth Ave & 42 St, New York, 10018. E Christian Filstrup, Chief
Holdings: Cat Mss Microforms
Budget: ($56,455)
Notes: Published catalog of holdings.

INDOCHINA

NY —CORNELL UNIVERSITY LIBRARIES, Collection of Regional History, Dept of Manuscripts and Univ Archives, Ithaca, 14853.
Notes: Tapes, ca 1973; Indochina peace campaign; 2 items.

NY —STATE UNIVERSITY OF NEW YORK, COLLEGE AT NEW PALTZ, Sojourner Truth Library, World Study Center, William J Haggerty Collection of French Colonial History, New Paltz, 12561. Corinne Nyquist, Librn
Holdings: Vols (19,153)// Uncat Mss Maps Pix
Notes: French colonial history. In 1966 this college acquired the research Library of the Comite Francais pour l'outre-mer. This library served the needs of a society in Paris whose membership incl French colonial administrators, scholars, and students. The more than 19,000 books and pamphlets and 135 sets of periodicals date from 1830, and cover the administration and development of the former colonies of France. Much of the material is economic, statistical, or agricultural, reflecting the interests of the collectors. British colonial history is well represented. Described in *Africana Library* Journal, Winter 1971.

INDOCHINA, FRENCH

DC —HOWARD UNIVERSITY, Founders Library, Bernard B Fall Collection (Southeast Asia Collection), Washington, 20059. Steven Ilsang Yoon, Cur
Holdings: Vols (6000) Cat Microforms
Budget: $15,000
Notes: The Bernard B Fall Collection has more than 6000 books, incl 1200 books purchased from the Kendric N Marshall Estate, 3000 items in vertical files, 300 pamphlets, and 800 microfilms, about Southeastern Asia and China. In addition, there are nearly 100 current periodicals and another 100 older periodicals about Indochina in the Collection.

INDOCHINESE LANGUAGES

CA —CLAREMONT COLLEGES, Honnold Library, Ninth & Dartmouth, Claremont, 91711. Tania Rizzo, Special Collections Dept Head
Holdings: Vols 150 // Uncat
Notes: Grammars and dictionaries (some dual-language with French or Dutch) of mainly Malayo-Polynesian, some Sino-Tibetan, and other languages, dating from the late 19th to mid-20th centuries. Checklisted.

NY —NEW YORK PUBLIC LIBRARY, Oriental Div, Fifth Ave & 42 St, New York, 10018. E Christian Filstrup, Chief
Holdings: // Cat Mss Microforms
Budget: ($56,455)
Notes: Published catalog of holdings. Currently collected in Western language materials only.

INDOCHINESE IN THE U.S.

†WA —TACOMA COMMUNITY HOUSE MINI LIBRARY, 1311 South M St,

INDOCHINESE IN THE U.S. (cont.)

Tacoma, 98405.
Notes: A special collection of books, periodicals, and audio-visual materials documents the history of the Vietnamese in America and provides resources for Indochinese educational and social activities.

INDO-IRANIAN LANGUAGES AND LITERATURES

MA —HARVARD UNIVERSITY LIBRARY, Cambridge, 02138.
Holdings: Cat

INDONESIA

CA —UNIVERSITY OF CALIFORNIA, LOS ANGELES, Research Library, Indo/Pacific Collection, 405 Hilgard Ave, Los Angeles, 90024. Edward Shreeves, Chairman, Bibliographers Group; Charlotte Spence, Indo/Pacific Bibliographer
Holdings: Vols Cat Mss Maps Pix Microforms
Notes: The Southeast Asian collection has been developed on a combination of the research and teaching levels; it focuses on the cultural, economic, political and social history of the area from ancient times to the present day. Although all the individual countries of the region are represented, some priority is given to Malaysia, Singapore, Indonesia and the Philippines. The majority of the materials is in Western languages except for a collection of several thousand books in Thai, and a smaller collection of materials in Vietnamese, Indonesian, Malaysian, and the Philippine languages.

CA —HOOVER INSTITUTION ON WAR, REVOLUTION & PEACE, Stanford University, Stanford, 94305. Milorad M Drachkovitch, Archivist
Holdings: Mss
Notes: Papers of Howard Palfrey Jones, 1930-1973, incl mss, correspondence, reports, research files, studies, and printed matter, relating primarily to public finance and post-war reconstruction in Germany, 1945-1951, to US foreign relations in East Asia, 1951-73, and to his service as Ambassador to Indonesia, 1958-1965. Ca 60 ms boxes.

CT —YALE UNIVERSITY, Box 1603A, Yale Station, New Haven, 06520.
Notes: Special strength in vernacular collections.

HI —UNIVERSITY OF HAWAII, Library, 2550 The Mall, Honolulu, 96822. Joyce Wright, Head, Asia Collection; Masato Matsu, Head, East Asia Vernacular Collection
Holdings: Vols 331,620 Cat Microforms
Notes: The Asia Collection holds materials from and about Southeast Asia: Brunei, Burma, Cambodia (Kampuchea), Indonesia, Laos, Malaysia, Philippines, Singapore, Thailand. Large contemporary Indonesian language collection. Several thousand vols in Thai and in Vietnamese. Minimal holdings in Burmese, Khmer, Lao languages. Social sciences and humanities emphasis for the post-World War II period. Western language coverage supplemented by retrospective holdings in the main library collection.

IL —CENTER FOR RESEARCH LIBRARIES, 6050 S Kenwood Ave, Chicago, 60637. Donald B Simpson, Dir; Esther Smith, Collection Development Librn
Holdings: Microforms
Notes: Monographs, serials and government documents from 1969, received on NPAC. Newspapers on microfilm, mostly from 1966.

IL —FIELD MUSEUM OF NATURAL HISTORY, The Berthold Laufer Library, Roosevelt Rd & Lake Shore Dr, Chicago, 60605. W Peyton Fawcett, Librn
Holdings: Vols (12,000)/ / Cat Mss Maps
Notes: The part of the museum's collection of Berthold Laufer (1874-1934), Curator of Anthropology, dealing with the peoples of the pre-19th century Chinese Empire (incl Manchuria, Mongolia, Sinkiang and Tibet); their anthropology, art and religion; influences upon their cultures by those of India, Siberia, Japan, Indonesia, and Oceania--and vice versa. Incl about 500 books in Tibetan. About 2/3 of the collection is cataloged.

IL —NORTHERN ILLINOIS UNIVERSITY, Founders Memorial Library, Southeast Asia Collection, Normal Rd, De Kalb, 60115. Lee S Dutton Dr, Cur
Holdings: Vols (34,000) Cat Maps Microforms
Notes: An extensive collection of books, periodicals, newspapers, maps, and microforms from or about Southeast Asia. Areas of concentration incl Thailand, Malaysia, Indonesia, Singapore, Brunei, Philippines, Laos, and Burma. Holdings (except rare books, maps, and microforms) are housed in a separate area collection within the Founders Library. A departmental card catalog and specialized reference collection support reference services. A Thai collection of several thousand vols is the largest vernacular component. Extensive Malaysia, Indonesia, Singapore, and Brunei holdings have been acquired through the NPAC program. A collection of Filipino-American newspapers, and a growing collection of children's literature in common and uncommon Southeast Asian languages are available. Resources are accessible to borrowers through OCLC.

MI —UNIVERSITY OF MICHIGAN, Harlan Hatcher Graduate Library, Ann Arbor, 48109. Susan Go, Librn
Holdings: Vols (250,000) Cat Mss Maps Pix Slides Microforms
Notes: Incl in the Michigan Historical Collections (primarily archival material) are papers of Michiganders in southeast Asia, mostly the Philipines, eg papers of Joseph R Hayden, Frank Murphy and G Mennen Williams, also, on film, the selected papers of Philippines president Manuel Quezon. All aspects of the countries, cultures and peoples of Brunei, Burma, Khymer, Indonesia, Laos, Malaysia, Philippines, Singapore, Thailand, Portuguese Timor and Vietnam. Also the Malayo-Polynesian (Austronesian), Mon-Khmer (Austroasiatic), and Sino-Tibetan language groupings.

NY —CORNELL UNIVERSITY LIBRARIES, John M Olin Library, John M Echols Collection on Southeast Asia, Ithaca, 14853. Giok Po Oey, Curator
Holdings: Vols (167,000) Cat Mss Maps Pix Microforms
Budget: ($90,000)
Notes: Additions published in monthly *John M Echols Collection on Southeast Asia Accessions List* (Ithaca: Cornell University, Southeast Asia Program, 1959-). Described partially in the following publications: Anderson, Benedict R *Bibliography of Indonesia Publications; Newspapers, Non-government Periodicals and Bulletins 1945-1958 at Cornell University.* Ithica, NY: Cornell University, Southeast Asia Program, 1959 (data paper no 33); Echols, John M *Preliminary Checklist of Indonesian Imprints (1945-1949), with Cornell University* Holdings. Ithica, NY: Cornell University, Modern Indonesia Project, 1965; Leigh, Michael B *Checklist of Holdings on Borneo in the Cornell University Libraries,* 1966 (data paper no 62); Lev, Daniel SA *Bibliography of Indonesian Government Documents and Selected Indonesian Writings on Government in the Cornell University Library,* 1958 (data paper no 31); Thung, Yvonne and John M Echols, *A Checklist of Indonesian Serials in the Cornell University Library, 1945-1970* (Ithica: Cornell University, Southeast Asia Program, 1973) (Data Paper no 89); and Nakamura, Mitsuo, *Checklist of Microfilm Holdings on the Japanese Occupation of Indonesia in the Cornell University Library, Wason Collection* (Ithica, 1970). Holdings through June 1975 listed in *Cornell University Libraries Southeast Asia Catalog* (Boston: G K Hall, 1976), vols 2, 4 and 7.

NY —NEW YORK PUBLIC LIBRARY, Oriental Div, Fifth Ave & 42 St, New York, 10018. E Christian Filstrup, Chief
Holdings: Cat Mss Microforms
Budget: ($56,455)
Notes: Described in *Dictionary Catalog of the Oriental Collection,* The Research Libraries of the New York Public Library, 1960, 16 vols, and *First Supplement,* 1976, 8 vols (144,000 cards). This catalog incl 318, 000 entries for works in about 100 languages of the East, and all works in Western languages on Oriental subjects. The Oriental Collection numbers about 120,000 vols; its Arabic and Indic holdings and those on ancient Egypt and the ancient Near East are among the largest in the US. There is also a collection of 30,000 vols of PL 480 material from Egypt, Pakistan, and India to which there is main entry access, but which is not incorporated into the dictionary catalog. Other outstanding features of the Oriental Collection incl extensive holdings of Japanese technical and scientific periodicals; a unique collection of linguistic works, grammars, anddictionaries; and unusually good coverage of the field of Oriental religions and philosophies. The catalog contains numerous subject references to periodical articles in all languages. All entries are arranged alphabetically according to the Roman alphabet. The Library currently collects materials about Indonesia in Western languages only.

OH —OHIO UNIVERSITY, Vernon R Alden Library, Southeast Asia Collection, Athens, 45701. Lian The-Mulliner, Head
Holdings: Vols (68,000) Cat Maps Slides Phonorecords Videotapes 16mm Films Filmstrips Microforms
Budget: ($35,000)
Notes: Emphasis on Indonesia, Malaysia, Singapore, Brunei and the Philippines. Incl language and literature, history, civilization and culture, art, medicine, philosophy and economic conditions. Separate catalog.

OH —CLEVELAND PUBLIC LIBRARY, Fine Arts and Special Collections Department, 325 Superior Ave, Cleveland, 44114. Alice N Loranth, Head
Holdings: Vols 2000 Cat Mss Maps
Notes: Emphasis is on materials concerning Dutch East India. Complete runs of the Dutch serials and periodicals, such as the publications of the *Indisch Genootschnap, Instituut voor Taal-, Land- en Volkenkunde,* etc are the strengths of this collection.
See also entry under Oriental Languages and Literatures.

INDONESIA—CURRENT EVENTS

DC —LIBRARY OF CONGRESS, General Reading Rooms Division, Microform Reading Room, Washington, 20540.
Holdings: Cat Mss Maps Pix Microforms
Notes: Microform materials only in this LC Division. Works of individual authors; holdings of collections; archival records, etc, press releases and translations, etc.

INDONESIA—HISTORY

CA —HOOVER INSTITUTION ON WAR, REVOLUTION & PEACE, Stanford University, Stanford, 94305. Milorad M Drachkovitch, Archivist
Holdings: Mss
Notes: Proceedings of the Indonesian Special Military Tribunal, 1965-67, relating to the trials of Indonesian communists and others implicated in the attempted coup of 1965, incl Politbureau member Sudisman, Foreign Minister Subandrio, Air Force Chief of Staff Omar Bhani. 22 ms boxes.

INDONESIAN LANGUAGE AND LITERATURE

CA —UNIVERSITY OF CALIFORNIA, LOS ANGELES, Research Library, Indo/Pacific Collection, 405 Hilgard Ave, Los Angeles, 90024. Edward Shreeves, Chairman, Bibliographers Group; Charlotte Spence, Indo/Pacific Bibliographer
Holdings: Vols Cat Mss Maps Pix Microforms
Notes: The Southeast Asian collection has been developed on a combination of the research and teaching levels; it focuses on the cultural, economic, political and social

INDONESIAN LANGUAGE AND LITERATURE (cont.)

history of the area from ancient times to the present day. Although all the individual countries of the region are represented, some priority is given to Malaysia, Singapore, Indonesia and the Philippines. The majority of the materials is in Western languages except for a collection of several thousand books in Thai, and a smaller collection of materials in Vietnamese, Indonesian, Malaysian, and the Philippine languages.

DC —LIBRARY OF CONGRESS, African and Middle Eastern Division, Washington, 20540.
Holdings: Cat Mss Microforms
Notes: Southern Asian: over 137,000 vols of literature of the area from Pakistan to the Philippines.

HI —UNIVERSITY OF HAWAII, Library, 2550 The Mall, Honolulu, 96822. Joyce Wright, Head, Asia Collection; Masato Matsu, Head, East Asia Vernacular Collection
Holdings: Vols 331,620 Cat Microforms
Notes: The Asia Collection holds materials from and about Southeast Asia: Brunei, Burma, Cambodia (Kampuchea), Indonesia, Laos, Malaysia, Philippines, Singapore, Thailand. Large contemporary Indonesian language collection. Several thousand vols in Thai and in Vietnamese. Minimal holdings in Burmese, Khmer, Lao languages. Social sciences and humanities emphasis for the post-World War II period. Western language coverage supplemented by retrospective holdings in the main library collection.

INDONESIAN SPECIAL MILITARY TRIBUNAL

CA —HOOVER INSTITUTION ON WAR, REVOLUTION & PEACE, Stanford University, Stanford, 94305. Milorad M Drachkovitch, Archivist
Holdings: Mss
Notes: Papers, correspondence, etc.

INDOOR PLANTS see House Plants

INDUCTION (LOGIC) see Logic

INDUSTRIAL ACCIDENTS—PREVENTION see Industrial Safety

INDUSTRIAL ADMINISTRATION see Industrial Management

INDUSTRIAL ARBITRATION see Arbitration, Industrial

INDUSTRIAL ARTS

CA —CRAFT AND FOLK ART MUSEUM, Library, 5814 Wilshire Blvd, Los Angeles, 90036. Joan M Benedetti, Museum Librn
Holdings: Vols (2000) Slides VF
Notes: Incl 2000 books; 70 journal subscriptions; artists' biographical files: 6 file drawers; clipping files: 8 file drawers; 20,000 slides. Representation of the material culture of all people, traditional and contemporary expressions. Incl visual and printed information on ethnic, traditional, popular, decorative, idiosyncratic, and contemporary crafts as well as vernacular architecture, handmade houses, and design. Information about and for professional artists on health hazards, conservation, and career management. Anthropological and art historical works; exhibition catalogues; slides, photographs, audiocassettes; clipping and pamphlet files. Contemporary Slide Registry of Craftspeople and extensive biographical files of contemporary craft artists. Information and referral files of craft related galleries, shops, festivals, organizations, etc.

DE —HAGLEY MUSEUM AND LIBRARY, Eleutherian Mills-Hagley Foundation Inc, PO Box 3630, Greenville, 19807. Richmond D Williams, Dir; Heddy A Richter, Imprints Librn
Notes: Strong collection.

MA —OLD STURBRIDGE VILLAGE, Research Library, Sturbridge, 01566. Theresa Rini Percy, Librn
Holdings: Vols (23,000) Cat Mss Pix
Notes: Hand and mechanized methods and products in New England, 1790-1850; agriculture, ceramics, leatherwork, metal-work, mill-work, needlework, printing, textile crafts and manufacture, woodworking.

MI —EDISON INSTITUTE, Greenfield Village and Henry Ford Museum, Archives & Research Library, PO Box 1970, Dearborn, 48121. Steve Hamp, Dir; Joan W Gartland, Librn
Holdings: Vols 400,000 Cat Mss Maps Microforms
Notes: 400,000 vols incl pamphlets. The Library, a memorial to Robert Hudson Tannahill, supports the programs of Greenfield Village and the Henry Ford Museum. The Library is open to Friends of Greenfield Village and the Henry Ford Museum (a membership organization) and to qualified students and faculty by appointment.

PA —CARNEGIE LIBRARY OF PITTSBURGH, Science & Technology Dept, 4400 Forbes Ave, Pittsburgh, 15213. Catherine M Brosky, Dept Head
Holdings: Vols (380,000) Cat Maps Microforms
Budget: ($240,000)
Notes: Incl much of the material in *Index to Handicrafts*. Books for the home owner, repairman and craftsman and the general builder and mechanics are emphasized. Information on the use of tools and materials especially for woodworking and metal crafts; also optical instruments, clocks, guns, and other mechanic trades. Maintains supplement to *Index to Handicrafts*.
See also entry under Technology.

WI —UNIVERSITY OF WISCONSIN-STOUT, Library Learning Center, Menomonie, 54751. Philip Sawin Jr, Coll Develop Librn
Notes: This collection is a major one, including the Verne C Fryklund Papers. The program was begun in 1883 as an original purpose of the University. The collection contains original editions on sloyd, a 19th century Swedish system of manual training based on wood carving and carpentry.

ON —METROPOLITAN TORONTO LIBRARY, Science & Technology Dept, 789 Yonge St, Toronto, M4W 2G8, Can. Margaret Walshe, Head
Holdings: Vols (120,000) Cat
Notes: Industrial science. All aspects of science and technology for the specialist, the student and the general public. The department gives high priority to Canadian material.

INDUSTRIAL ARTS—EXHIBITIONS see Exhibitions and Expositions

INDUSTRIAL ARTS—HISTORY

DE —HAGLEY MUSEUM AND LIBRARY, Eleutherian Mills-Hagley Foundation Inc, PO Box 3630, Greenville, 19807. Richmond D Williams, Dir; Heddy A Richter, Imprints Librn
Notes: Strong collection.

INDUSTRIAL BANKING see Loans, Personal

INDUSTRIAL CHEMISTRY see Chemical Engineering; Chemistry, Technical

INDUSTRIAL DESIGN see Design, Industrial

INDUSTRIAL DEVELOPMENT CENTERS see Industrial Productivity Centers

INDUSTRIAL DISEASES see Occupational Diseases

INDUSTRIAL DRAWING see Mechanical Drawing

INDUSTRIAL EDUCATION see Technical Education

INDUSTRIAL EFFICIENCY see Efficiency, Industrial

INDUSTRIAL ENGINEERING

CA —KAISER FOUNDATION HOSPITAL, Management Effectiveness Library, 4747 Sunset Blvd, Los Angeles, 90027. Marilyn Crawford, Librn
Holdings: Vols (1000) Cat Maps Slides Audiotapes
Notes: Small, selective management, business, and health care collection, with many US and state health-related reports and a few health newsletters. Internal index to printed materials and audiotapes.

CA —CALIFORNIA STATE POLYTECHNIC UNIVERSITY, POMONA, University Library, 3801 W Temple Ave, Pomona, 91768. Harold Schleiser, Actg Dir
Notes: General reference materials on aerospace, chemical, civil, electrical, electronics, industrial, mechanical and manufacturing engineering.

GA —GEORGIA INSTITUTE OF TECHNOLOGY, Price Gilbert Memorial Library, 225 North Ave, Atlanta, 30332. Edward Graham Roberts, Dir
Holdings: Vols (1,661,559) Cat Maps Slides Microforms
Budget: ($1,383,302)
Notes: Incl (4,307,996) patents and (568, 490) government documents.

IL —UNIVERSITY OF ILLINOIS, URBANA/CHAMPAIGN, Library, 221 Engineering Hall, Urbana, 61801. William Mischo, Librn
Holdings: Vols (175,000) Cat Slides Microforms
Notes: Incl 3500 periodicals. Collection designed to serve teaching and research programs. Supports instructional faculty research. Also, 470 microfilm reels and 6000 microfiche sheets.

IN —PURDUE UNIVERSITY LIBRARIES, Engineering Library, A A Potter Engineering Center, West Lafayette, 47907. Edwin D Posey, Engineering Librn
Holdings: Vols (225,178) Cat Maps Audiotapes Microforms
Budget: ($300,000)

MI —UNIVERSITY OF MICHIGAN, Engineering-Transportation Library, 312 Undergraduate Library, Ann Arbor, 48109. Maurita Holland, Librn
Holdings: Vols (400,000) Cat Microforms
Budget: ($225,000)

NY —ENGINEERING SOCIETIES LIBRARY, 345 E 47 St, New York, 10017. S Kirk Cabeen, Dir
Holdings: Vols 250,000 Cat Maps 16mm Films Microforms
Notes: One of the largest, most comprehensive engineering libraries in the world. Covers all engineering disciplines; particularly strong in electrical and electronic, mechanical, mining and metallurgical, petroleum, chemical, industrial, air conditioning and refrigeration engineering. Incl Wheeler Collection of early materials on magnetism and electricity. 125, 000 bound periodical volumes; 10,000 maps; 5000 serial subscriptions (many foreign-language). Virtually all materials abstracted in *Engineering Index* (1884-date) are in in Library. Noncirculating, except to members of professional engineering societies which support the Library. See *Engineering Societies Library, New York, Classed Subject Catalog and Index* (Boston: G K Hall, 1963); and *Supplements*, 1-10, 1964-1973.

NC —NORTH CAROLINA STATE UNIVERSITY, D H Hill Library, Box 7111, Raleigh, 27695. I T Littleton, Dir
Holdings: Vols 10,800 Cat
Budget: $2000

OH —UNIVERSITY OF CINCINNATI, Engineering Library, 880 Baldwin Hall, Cincinnati, 45221. Dorothy Furber Byers, Head
Holdings: Vols (50,000) Cat Videotapes Microforms
Budget: ($100,000)
Notes: Have NASA and DOE microfiche collections.

OH —OHIO STATE UNIVERSITY, Engineering Library, 2024 Neil Ave, Columbus, 43210. Mary Jo V Arnold, Librn
Holdings: Vols (132,000) Cat Microforms
Budget: ($110,000)

PA —PENNSYLVANIA STATE UNIVERSITY, Engineering Library, 325

INDUSTRIAL ENGINEERING (cont.)

Hammond St, University Park, 16802. Tom Conkling, Librn
Holdings: Vols (60,000) Microforms
Notes: This collection includes substantial microform holdings and extensive runs of periodicals.

RI —BROWN UNIVERSITY, John Hay Library, 20 Prospect St, Providence, 02912. Mark N Brown, Cur Mss
Holdings: Mss
See also entry under George Henry Corliss, 1817-1883; Elmer Lawrence Corthell, 1840-1916,

TN —TENNESSEE VALLEY AUTHORITY (TVA), Technical Library, 400 W Summit Hill Dr, E2 B7, Knoxville, 37902. Jesse C Mills, Chief Librn
Holdings: Vols (106,900) Cat Mss Maps Pix Audiotapes Microforms
Budget: ($2,025,000)
Notes: The Technical Library Headquarters Staff (order, cataloging, information, and administration) is located in Knoxville, Tenn. In addition there are branch libraries in Knoxville, Norris, and Chattanooga, Tennessee, and Muscle Shoals, Alabama.

INDUSTRIAL EQUIPMENT—MAINTENANCE AND REPAIR

NC —TECHNICAL INSTITUTE OF ALAMANCE, Learning Resources Center, Jimmy Kerr Rd, PO Box 623, Haw River, 27258. Ron Plummer, Coordr
Holdings: Vols 282 Cat Microforms

INDUSTRIAL EXHIBITIONS see Exhibitions and Expositions

INDUSTRIAL HEALTH see Industrial Hygiene; Occupational Diseases

INDUSTRIAL HEALTH ENGINEERING see Industrial Hygiene

INDUSTRIAL HYGIENE

CA —UNIVERSITY OF CALIFORNIA, BERKELEY, Life Sciences Libraries, Public Health Library, 42 Earl Warren Hall, Berkeley, 94720. Thomas J Alexander, Librn
Holdings: Vols (75,000) Cat Microforms
Notes: Research collection covering all aspects of public health. Health Department annual reports from all 50 states are acquired, as well as such reports from all California health units and from major US cities. Serial publications issued by Health Departments in the 13 western states are being received.

CO —COLORADO STATE UNIVERSITY, Libraries, Fort Collins, 80523. K Suzanne Johnson, Biomedical Sciences, Librn
Holdings: Vols (2000) Cat Microforms
Budget: ($2000)

CT —YALE UNIVERSITY, Medical Historical Library, 333 Cedar St, New Haven, 06510. Ferenc A Gyorgyey, Librn
Notes: Records of the Milbank Memorial Fund for the years 1922-1977. A part of the Contemporary Medical Care and Health Policy Collection.

IL —NATIONAL SAFETY COUNCIL, Library, 444 N Michigan Ave, Chicago, 60611. Ruth K Hammersmith, Mgr, Library
Holdings: Cat Microforms
Budget: ($22,000)
Notes: NSC Library has a comprehensive collection of accident prevention, occupational and industrial safety and health material. The Safety Research Information Section (SRIS) begun in 1968 has a collection of over 12,000 indexed and cataloged research documents. The Library also has a collection of over 5000 safety-related books, 12,000 Research Reports, 60, 000 general information items, a collection of historically valuable safety-related information. The Library data is part of an inhouse computer system.

IN —PURDUE UNIVERSITY LIBRARIES, Pharmacy, Nursing and Health Sciences Library, Pharmacy Bldg, West Lafayette, 47907. Theodora Andrews, Librn
Holdings: Vols (1000) Cat
Notes: There is a separate catalog to the collection. Contains research level materials as well as undergraduate.

MI —UNIVERSITY OF MICHIGAN, Public Health Library, Ann Arbor, 48109. Mary Townsend, Head
Holdings: Vols (55,000) Cat Maps Pix
Budget: ($24,000)

NM —UNIVERSITY OF CALIFORNIA, Los Alamos National Laboratory, Libraries, PO Box 1663, MSP 362, Los Alamos, 87545. J Arthur Freed, Head Librn
Holdings: Vols (800,000) Cat Films Microforms
Budget: ($700,000)
Notes: Incl 500,000 classified and unclassified reports. There are 25 branch libraries and a central collection. The Medical Library contains about 40,000 vols in the areas of biomedical research.

PQ —UNIVERSITY OF MONTREAL, Bibliotheque Para-medicale, 2375 Chemin de la Cote Ste Catherine, Montreal, H3C 3J7, Can. Johanne Hopper, Head Librn
Holdings: Vols 1700 Cat
Budget: $12,000
Notes: Social medicine, preventive medicine, epidemiology, industrial health and hygiene, and environmental factors (pollution) as related to health. Depository for World Health Organization publications.

PQ —NORANDA RESEARCH CENTRE, Library, 240 Hymus Blvd, Pointe-Claire, H9R 1G5, Can. Shirley Courtis, Librn
Holdings: Vols (7000)

INDUSTRIAL MANAGEMENT

CA —UNIVERSITY OF CALIFORNIA, LOS ANGELES, Graduate School of Management Library, UCLA Campus, Los Angeles, 90024. Robert Bellanti, Head Librn
Holdings: Vols (128,000) Cat Mss Microforms
Notes: The

CA —UNIVERSITY OF SOUTHERN CALIFORNIA, Crocker Business Library, Hoffman Hall, University Park, Los Angeles, 90007. Judith A Truelson, Head Librn
Holdings: Vols (100,000) Cat Microforms
Notes: The Roy P Crocker Library of Business Administration, located in Hoffman Hall, houses more than 100,000 volumes and regularly receives approximately 1500 trade, financial, economics, labor, and general business periodicals and newspapers. The areas of subject concentration include business economics, finance and investments, general management/management theory, international business, finance and management, marketing/food marketing, and quantitative business analysis.

CT —YALE UNIVERSITY, Social Science Library, 140 Prospect St, New Haven, 06520. Billie I Salter, Librn
Holdings: Cat

GA —GEORGIA INSTITUTE OF TECHNOLOGY, Price Gilbert Memorial Library, 225 North Ave, Atlanta, 30332. Edward Graham Roberts, Dir
Holdings: Vols (1,661,559) Cat Maps Slides Microforms
Budget: ($1,383,302)
Notes: Incl (4,307,996) patents and (568, 490) government documents.

IN —PURDUE UNIVERSITY LIBRARIES, Special Collections Dept, West Lafayette, 47907. Keith Dowden, Asst Dir, Special Collections
Holdings: Vols (500) // Cat Mss Pix Slides
Notes: The Gilbreth Collection. Incl motion study equipment and personal working papers and photographs of Frank B and Lillian Gilbreth's work in the development of the field of industrial management. Also, correspondence, certificates, diplomas, memorabilia, published and nonprint material.

MA —HARVARD UNIVERSITY, Graduate School of Business Administration, Baker Library, Soldiers Field, Boston, 02163. Mary V Chatfield, Librn; Florence Bartoshesky, Cur of Manuscripts and Archives

NJ —STEVENS INSTITUTE OF TECHNOLOGY, Samuel C Williams Library, Castle Point Sta, Hoboken, 07030. Jane G Hartye, Special Collections Librn
Holdings: Vols (180) Cat Pix Slides
Budget: ($1500)
Notes: Frederick Winslow Taylor is known as the "father of scientific mangagement," and we have in our collection volumes of correspondence relating to the introduction of this system into industry, government, the army and navy, etc. This collection also includes many personal items belonging to and used by Mr Taylor. Our collection is the most complete one of the subject of scientific management.

PA —UNIVERSITY OF PENNSYLVANIA, Lippincott Library of the Wharton School, Philadelphia, 19104. Michael Halperin, Librn
Holdings: Cat
Notes: Incl labor management.

WI —UNIVERSITY OF WISCONSIN-STOUT, Library Learning Center, Menomonie, 54751. Philip Sawin Jr, Coll Develop Librn
Notes: Supports the Packaging concentration of the Master's Degree in Industrial Management. Concentration was authorized at the graduate level in 1974, but specialized collection since 1965.

INDUSTRIAL MATERIALS see Materials

INDUSTRIAL MEDICINE see Medicine, Industrial

INDUSTRIAL POISONS see Industrial Toxicology

INDUSTRIAL PROCESS CONTROL see Process Control

INDUSTRIAL PRODUCTIVITY CENTERS

TN —TENNESSEE VALLEY AUTHORITY (TVA), Technical Library, 400 W Summit Hill Dr, E2 B7, Knoxville, 37902. Jesse C Mills, Chief Librn
Holdings: Vols (106,900) Cat Mss Maps Pix Audiotapes Microforms
Budget: ($2,025,000)
Notes: The Technical Library Headquarters Staff (order, cataloging, information, and administration) is located in Knoxville, Tenn. In addition there are branch libraries in Knoxville, Norris, and Chattanooga, Tennessee, and Muscle Shoals, Alabama.

ON —DEPT OF REGIONAL INDUSTRIAL EXPANSION, Ottawa Library, 235 Queen St, Ottawa, K1A 0H5, Can. Steven Rush, Librn
Holdings: Vols (100,000) Cat Maps Microforms
Notes: Contains 1500 reports of ARDA projects (Agricultural Rehabilitation and Development Agency); also NEWSTART project reports. There is a published book catalog and two supplements. 15,000 documents; 3000 periodical subscriptions.

INDUSTRIAL PSYCHOLOGY see Psychology, Industrial

INDUSTRIAL REFORM

NY —ROCKEFELLER UNIVERSITY, Rockefeller Archive Center, Hillcrest, Pocantico Hills, North Tarrytown, 10591. Joseph W Ernst, Dir; J William Hess, Assoc Dir
Notes: Papers relative to the Rockefeller Family, Foundations, University, and other specific enterprises and contributions to particular areas of social, physical, educational, and historic reform, preservation, conservation, or development. Extensive records of administrative, financial, physical, or intellectual relationships.

INDUSTRIAL RELATIONS

CA —UNIVERSITY OF CALIFORNIA, BERKELEY, Institute of Industrial

INDUSTRIAL RELATIONS (cont.)

Relations Library, 2521 Channing Way Room 110, Berkeley, 94720. Nanette Sand, Librn
Holdings: Vols 50,000 Cat
Notes: Industrial relations, labor, organizational behavior and related subjects. Institute of Industrial Relations Library has separate card catalog (author, title, subject interfiled) but there is no published catalog. Library has a selective collection of books, periodicals, government documents, union and employer publications, publications of university industrial relations institutes and similar research organizations, pamphlets (50,000), etc. It does not incl archival and manuscript materials, or much material published prior to 1950.

CA —KAISER FOUNDATION HOSPITAL, Management Effectiveness Library, 4747 Sunset Blvd, Los Angeles, 90027. Marilyn Crawford, Librn
Holdings: Vols (1000) Cat Maps Slides Audiotapes
Notes: Small, selective management, business, and health care collection, with many US and state health-related reports and a few health newsletters. Internal index to printed materials and audiotapes.

CA —UNIVERSITY OF CALIFORNIA, LOS ANGELES, Graduate School of Management Library, UCLA Campus, Los Angeles, 90024. Robert Bellanti, Head Librn
Holdings: Vols (128,000) Cat Mss Microforms
Notes: The

CA —UNIVERSITY OF CALIFORNIA, LOS ANGELES, Research Library, Public Affairs Service, 405 Hilgard Ave, Los Angeles, 90024. Edward Shreeves, Chairman, Bibliographers Group; Eugenia Eaton, Head, Public Affairs Service
Holdings: Uncat
Notes: Current non-governmental English-language pamphlets (192,819), broadsides, leaflets and other ephemera on public affairs, from 1960, representing a wide spectrum of political and social opinions. Social welfare and industrial relations are strong fields. Legal loose-leaf labor services, such as the *Daily Labor Report,* the *Government Employee Relations Report* and the *Labor Relations Reporter,* as well as labor pamphlets from the mid-1940s, reflect a long-standing responsibility to the University's Institute of Industrial Relations.

CT —YALE UNIVERSITY, Social Science Library, 140 Prospect St, New Haven, 06520. Billie I Salter, Librn

DC —INTERNATIONAL LABOR ORGANIZATION, International Labor Office, Washington Branch Library, 1750 New York Ave NW, Rm 330, Washington, 20006. Karen J Mark, Librn
Holdings: Vols (13,500) Cat Pix 16mm Films Monographs
Notes: Wide range of titles dealing with worldwide labor and social matters. The library contains ILO publications and documentation only, dating back to 1919. Also, a collection of ILO films and photos. See *Subject Guide to Publications of the ILO, 1919-1964* and *ILO Catalogue of Publications in Print, 1982* (ILO).

DC —US DEPT OF LABOR, Library, 200 Constitution Ave NW, Washington, 20210. Sabina Jacobson, Dir
Holdings: Vols (550,000) Cat

IL —UNIVERSITY OF ILLINOIS, URBANA/CHAMPAIGN, Institute of Labor and Industrial Relations, Library, 504 E Armory, Champaign, 61820. Margaret A Chaplan, Librn
Holdings: Vols (11,597) Cat Audiotapes Microforms
Budget: ($7500)
Notes: Collection incl four subject areas within industrial relations: collective bargaining and labor-management relations; manpower and labor economics; international and comparative labor movements; and organizational behavior. There is an extensive vertical file containing information on individual labor unions. The resources of the library which are relevant to the study of labor history are described in "Labor History Resources of the University of Illinois," by Patricia Wilson Onsi, *Labor* History, vol 7, Spring 1966, pp 209-215.

IN —PURDUE UNIVERSITY LIBRARIES, Graduate School of Management, Krannert Library, West Lafayette, 47907. Gordon Law, Librn
Holdings: Vols (142,727) Cat Microforms
Budget: ($69,700)
Notes: There is an extensive collection of corporate reports and labor information material (some 115,000 items). Over 2500 periodicals are currently received.

MD —INTERNATIONAL ASSOCIATION OF CHIEFS OF POLICE, 13 Firstfield Rd, PO Box 6010, Gaithersburg, 20760.
Holdings: Vols (6000) Cat Mss
Notes: Collection heavy in criminal investigation, crime prevention, police administration and management. Collecting in public sector labor relations, family violence, terrorism.

MA —HARVARD UNIVERSITY LIBRARY, John F Kennedy School of Government Library, Manpower and Industrial Relations Collection, Littauer Library, Cambridge, 02138. James C Damaskos, Librn
Holdings: Vols (120,000) Cat
Notes: Major strength is in publications of labor unions and government documents relating to labor.

MI —UNIVERSITY OF MICHIGAN, Graduate School of Business Administration, Business Administration Library, Institute for International Commerce Reading Rm, Ann Arbor, 48109. Carol Holbrook, Dir
Notes: The collection contains historical and current materials published by business, government, US labor unions and associations on employer-employee relationship, absenteeism, employee benefits, executive compensation, fair employment practices, job satisfaction, management development and performance appraisal. Labor union publications incl convention proceedings, constitutions, histories, manuals for officers and stewards, newspapers, and research reports. Incl approx (61,000) cataloged vertical file items.

MI —MICHIGAN STATE UNIVERSITY, Labor and Industrial Relations Library, East Lansing, 48824. Martha Jane Soltow, Librn
Holdings: Vols (55,000) Cat Microforms
Notes: All aspects of employer/employee relations.

NJ —RUTGERS, THE STATE UNIVERSITY OF NEW JERSEY, Institute of Management & Labor Relations, Ryders Lane & Clifton Ave, New Brunswick, 08903. Bernard F Downey, Librn
Holdings: Vols (18,530) Cat Slides Phonorecords 16mm Films Filmstrips
Budget: ($7300)
Notes: Separate card catalog for collection. Particular emphasis on dispute settlement. Strong collection on public sector labor relations, emphasizing New Jersey publications.

NJ —PRINCETON UNIVERSITY, Library, Rare Books Dept, Princeton, 08544. Stephen Ferguson, Cur
Holdings: Cat

NY —NEW YORK STATE DEPT OF STATE, Community Affairs Library, 162 Washington Ave, Albany, 12231. M L Johnson, Librn
Holdings: Vols (14,640) Cat
Notes: Local government. Serves as research arm for official activities. 16,000 items in vertical files; 150 periodicals. Unique Community File collection of about 1600 local governments arranged by counties in the state.

NY —CORNELL UNIVERSITY, New York State School of Industrial & Labor Relations, Martin P Catherwood Library, Ives Hall, Ithaca, 14853. Shirley F Harper, Dir
Holdings: Vols 101,000 Cat Mss Pix Slides Phonorecords Audiotapes Microforms
Notes: The library has a Labor Management Documentation Center, which collects, processes, and services original mss, constitutions, collective bargaining agreements, audiovisual materials, rare pamphlets and books. Also acquires and services microfilm copies of primary source materials. Its holdings of rare books, pamphlets, constitutions and agreements are incl in the library catalog. The materials in the ms holdings are accessible through finding aids available only in the Center. The card catalog has been printed by G K Hall & Co of Boston and is entitled *Library Catalog of the Martin P Catherwood Library of the NYSSILR, Cornell University.* There are presently 12 vols in the basic set and 5 annual cumulations. It represents all of the books and a selected number of the more important pamphlets. Periodical titles and holdings are not incl, buta feature of the catalog is the inclusion of author and subject entries for selected articles from 100 periodicals dating back to 1952. Additionally, the library has a heavy concentration of author and subject analytics for serial publications.

NY —AMALGAMATED CLOTHING & TEXTILE WORKERS UNION, Research Dept Library, 15 Union Sq, New York, 10003. Mohammad Homayon Pour, Librn
Holdings: Vols (3200) Cat Pix
Notes: Collective bargaining and economic conditions in the men's and boys' apparel industries and the textile industry.

NY —NEW YORK PUBLIC LIBRARY, Research Libraries, Economic & Public Affairs Div, Fifth Ave & 42 St, New York, 10018. Edward DiRoma, Chief
Holdings: Vols (1,500,000) Cat Microforms

NY —NEW YORK UNIVERSITY, Elmer Holmes Bobst Library, Div of Special Collections, Tamiment Library of Labor History, Washington Sq, New York, 10012. Dorothy Swanson, Librn
Holdings: Cat Mss Maps Pix Microforms
Notes: Books, pamphlets, newspapers, periodicals and mss. Large microfilm collection. Described in Daniel Bell's *The Tamiment Library* (1969), available free from the Tamiment librarian, and *Elmer Holmes Bobst Library Information Bulletin 8* (updated periodically).

ON —CANADA DEPT OF LABOUR, Library, Ottawa, K1A 0J2, Can. Monique Marchand, Chief Librn
Holdings: Vols (100,000) Cat Microforms

ON —ONTARIO MINISTRY OF LABOUR, Library, 400 University Ave, Toronto, M7A 1T7, Can. Jean Collins-Williams, Librn
Holdings: Vols (80,000) Microforms Films

INDUSTRIAL REVOLUTION see Industry—History

INDUSTRIAL SAFETY

DC —INTERNATIONAL LABOR ORGANIZATION, International Labor Office, Washington Branch Library, 1750 New York Ave NW, Rm 330, Washington, 20006. Karen J Mark, Librn
Holdings: Vols (13,500) Cat Pix 16mm Films Monographs
Notes: Wide range of titles dealing with worldwide labor and social matters. The library contains ILO publications and documentation only, dating back to 1919. Also, a collection of ILO films and photos. See *Subject Guide to Publications of the ILO, 1919-1964* and *ILO Catalogue of Publications in Print, 1982* (ILO).

IL —NATIONAL SAFETY COUNCIL, Library, 444 N Michigan Ave, Chicago, 60611. Ruth K Hammersmith, Mgr, Library
Holdings: Cat Microforms
Budget: ($22,000)
Notes: NSC Library has a comprehensive collection of accident prevention, occupational and industrial safety and health material. The Safety Research Information Section (SRIS) begun in 1968 has a collection of over 12,000 indexed and cataloged research documents. The Library also has a collection of over 5000 safety-related books, 12,000 Research Reports, 60, 000 general information items, a collection of historically valuable safety-related information. The Library data is part of an inhouse computer system.

INDUSTRIAL SAFETY (cont.)

IN —PURDUE UNIVERSITY LIBRARIES, Pharmacy, Nursing and Health Sciences Library, Pharmacy Bldg, West Lafayette, 47907. Theodora Andrews, Librn
Holdings: Vols (1000) Cat
Notes: There is a separate catalog to the collection. Contains research level materials as well as undergraduate.

NY —CENTER FOR LABOR STUDIES, SUNY, Empire State College, Labor College Library, 330 W 42nd St, New York, 10036. Jayne Adler, Librn
Holdings: Vols (3000) Cat Videotapes VF
Budget: ($4000)
Notes: Areas being emphasized in development of the library are: Women and labor, occupational health and safety, and trade union leadership.

WV —NATIONAL INSTITUTE FOR OCCUPATIONAL SAFETY & HEALTH, NIOSH/ALOSH Library, 944 Chestnut Ridge Rd, Morgantown, 26505. Colleen M Herrington, Librn
Holdings: Vols (6000) Cat Microforms
Notes: Occupational safety and health. Main Library located at 4676 Columbia Pkwy, Cincinnati, Ohio. Incl 120,000 microforms.

WI —WAUSAU INSURANCE COMPANIES, Library, 2000 Westwood Dr, Wausau, 54401. Douglas Ley, Dir of Library Services; Donna Nuernberg, Ref Librn
Holdings: Vols (15,000) Cat
Budget: $130,000
Notes: Library also maintains corporate history collection of materials dating from 1911.

ON —ONTARIO MINISTRY OF LABOUR, Library, 400 University Ave, Toronto, M7A 1T7, Can. Jean Collins-Williams, Librn
Holdings: Vols (80,000) Microforms Films

INDUSTRIAL SALVAGE see Salvage (Waste, Etc.)

INDUSTRIAL STATISTICS

DC —US BUREAU OF THE CENSUS, Library, Federal Office Bldg 3, Rm 2451, Washington, 20233. Betty Baxtresser, Chief, ASD Library Branch
Holdings: Cat Microforms
Notes: Emphases on statistics of agriculture, business, construction, economics, foreign trade, governments, housing, industry, population, transporation, statistical methodology, and data processing. Library holdings are largely current materials covering the Bureau's programs. Outdated materials are withdrawn regularly.

INDUSTRIAL TOXICOLOGY

NY —US ENVIRONMENTAL PROTECTION AGENCY, Region II, Technical Library, 26 Federal Plaza, New York, 10278. Audrey Thomas, Regional Librn
Holdings: Vols 4200 Cat
Notes: Incl 16,000 reports, 225,000 microfiche, 100 current subscriptions.

INDUSTRIAL UNIONS see Trade Unions

INDUSTRIAL VACUUM see Vacuum Science and Technology

INDUSTRIAL WASTES see Factory and Trade Waste; Waste Products

INDUSTRIAL WATER SUPPLY see Water Supply, Industrial

INDUSTRIAL WORKERS OF THE WORLD (IWW)

MI —UNIVERSITY OF MICHIGAN, Dept of Rare Books & Special Collections, Ann Arbor, 48109. Edward C Weber, Head, Labadie Collection
Holdings: Vols (40,000) Cat Mss Pix Audiotapes Microforms

MI —WAYNE STATE UNIVERSITY, Walter P Reuther Library, Archives of Labor & Urban Affairs, Detroit, 48202. Philip Mason, Dir
Notes: The Archives of Labor History and Urban Affairs of Wayne State University has long been known for its large and extensive ms collections related to the labor movement and to the city in 20th century America. As the official deposity for the United Automobile, Aerospace and Agriculture Implement Workers, Congress of Industrial Organizations, United Farm Workers Organizing Committee, American Newspaper Guild, Air Line Pilots Association, and Industrial Workers of the World, the Archives has established itself as a distinguished research institution.

INDUSTRIES see Industrial Arts

INDUSTRIES, CHEMICAL see Chemical Industries

INDUSTRY

AL —MOBILE PUBLIC LIBRARY, Special Collections Div, 701 Government St, Mobile, 36602.
Notes: The Mobile area; incl papers of the Forbes Trading Co, 1795-1840; Bank of Mobile papers, 1820-.

FL —FLORIDA DEPT OF COMMERCE, Research Library, 408 Fletcher Bldg, Tallahassee, 32301. Dennis Hitchens, Librn
Notes: Collect materials related to the 2 divisions of the Florida Dept of Commerce: Economic Development and Tourism, incl titles on Florida (historical and current), international trade, transportation, education, employment, management, industrial development and business. The Florida and US documents collection covers population, manufacturing, employment, agriculture, retail trade, wholesale trade and labor. VF incl files on every city and county, especially local economic data, SIC coded material, out-of-state information, county files, Florida specific material and general subject material. 100 VF drawers.

GA —ATLANTA PUBLIC LIBRARY, Ivan Allen Jr Dept of Science, Industry & Government, One Margaret Mitchell Square, Atlanta, 30303. William D Munro, Head
Holdings: Vols (15,000) Cat Microforms
Budget: ($180,000)
Notes: This collection incl on microform annual reports and Securities Exchange Commission 10-K reports for some 11,000 companies from 1976 to date; current and retrospective stock quotations, stock reports, corporate and industry records and directories and supporting looseleaf services; information file on Atlanta's largest 15,000 with annual updates; and current plat maps for the five county Metro-Atlanta area. Atlanta and Georgia business history sections are being developed. Most material on this collection is noncirculating.

IL —CENTER FOR RESEARCH LIBRARIES, 6050 S Kenwood Ave, Chicago, 60637. Donald B Simpson, Dir; Esther Smith, Collection Development Librn
Holdings: Vols Cat
Notes: Very extensive holdings of older scientific journals, especially in medicine, applied science, technology, industry and trade. Currently 5,000 titles.

IN —PURDUE UNIVERSITY LIBRARIES, Graduate School of Management, Krannert Library, West Lafayette, 47907. Gordon Law, Librn
Holdings: Vols (142,727) Cat Microforms
Budget: ($69,700)
Notes: There is an extensive collection of corporate reports and labor information material (some 115,000 items). Over 2500 periodicals are currently received.

LA —UNIVERSITY OF SOUTHERN LOUISIANA, Dupre Library, Jefferson Caffery Louisiana Room, 302 East St Mary Blvd, Lafayette, 70504. Cynthia J Rice, Louisiana Room Ref Librn
Holdings: Vols (20,000) Cat Doc Maps Microforms VF
Budget: ($3800)
Notes: Emphasis is on state, regional, and local history, genealogy, and culture; also politics and government, industry, agriculture, geology, language and literature. Collection is closed-stack and non-circulating, and is open to the public for on-site use only. Copying services are available.

MA —HARVARD UNIVERSITY, Graduate School of Business Administration, Baker Library, Soldiers Field, Boston, 02163. Mary V Chatfield, Librn; Florence Bartoshesky, Cur of Manuscripts and Archives
Holdings: Vols (470,805) Cat Mss Microforms
Notes: Catalog (32 volumes) published in 1971 by G K Hall; 3-volume supplement published in 1974 (out of print).

NJ —H M BAKER ASSOCIATES, Research Collection, 266 E Dudley Ave, Westfield, 07090. Helen Baker Cushman, Managing Associate
Holdings: Vols 5000 Cat Mss Maps Pix Slides Periodicals
Notes: Baker Associates publishes *The Business History Letter* The Anniversary Manual, "Remember the Year," business histories and anniversary studies which are based on the contents of the collection. Emphasis of the collection is on industrial and business history.

NY —MERRILL LYNCH, CAPITAL MARKETS, Securities Research Library, One Liberty Plaza (165 Broadway), New York, 10006. Rita A Hughes, Chief Librn
Holdings: Vols 10,000 Cat Microforms
Notes: Subject files by industry; corporate files; all NYSE and AMEX companies on DISCLOSURE microfiches plus approx 1000 OTC companies. *Wall Street Journal* quotation pages on microfiche or microfilm from 1928 to present. as well as *Toronto Globe & Mail* and *Financial Post* Quotations. *Moody's* and *Standard & Poor's Manual* from 1916 to present. Incl 800,000 microfiche.

NY —NEW YORK PUBLIC LIBRARY, Research Libraries, Economic & Public Affairs Div, Fifth Ave & 42 St, New York, 10018. Edward DiRoma, Chief
Holdings: Vols (1,500,000) Cat Microforms

NC —GREENSBORO PUBLIC LIBRARY, Oral History Program Library, Drawer X-4, Greensboro, 27402. Eugene Edwin Pfaff, Jr, Librn
Notes: Oral history on the cultural, social, and economic development of Greensboro and Guilford County; the program is expanding to incl prominent North Carolinians throughout the State. Collection consists of 42 videotapes and 93 audiotapes which are uncataloged.

RI —UNIVERSITY OF RHODE ISLAND, Library, Special Collections, Kingston, 02881. David Maslyn, Head
Notes: Extensive collections.

WI —STATE HISTORICAL SOCIETY OF WISCONSIN, Archives, 816 State St, Madison, 53706. Harold L Miller, Reference Archivist
Holdings: Cat Mss Microforms
Notes: About 22 million pieces. Major ms emphasis is American, with special collections in the history of anti-Vietnam War, agriculture, civil rights, industry, labor, mass communications, motion pictures and theatre, and Wisconsin. There is a separate card catalog to mss. Collections are described in the *Guide to Manuscripts of the State Historical Society of Wisconsin* (3 vols, 1944, 1957, 1966), *Guide to the Wisconsin State Archives* (1966), in current accession notes in the *Wisconsin Magazine of History,* and in other special Society publications. Major collections are also listed in Hamer, *Guide to Manuscripts and Archives in the United States* (1961) and in the *National Union Catalog of Manuscript Collections* (1959-date).

ON —TORONTO DOMINION BANK, Department of Economic Research, 55 King St W, Toronto, M5K 1A2, Can. Ruth P Smith, Librn
Holdings: Vols (6000) Cat

INDUSTRY—DIRECTORIES

NY —NEW YORK PUBLIC LIBRARY, Research Libraries, Economic & Public

INDUSTRY—DIRECTORIES (cont.)

Affairs Div, Fifth Ave & 42 St, New York, 10018. Edward DiRoma, Chief
Holdings: Vols (1,500,000) Cat Microforms

INDUSTRY—HISTORY

CA —THE HAGGIN MUSEUM, Petzinger Library of Californiana, 1201 N Pershing Ave, Stockton, 95203. Diane Freggiaro, Librn/Archivist
Holdings: Vols (7000) Cat Mss Maps Pix Slides Audiotapes 16mm Films
Notes: The Petzinger Library is open by appointment only. Special emphasis on Stockton and San Joaquin County and Valley area, local biography, agriculture, agricultural history, industrial history, farm machinery (especially Holt Manufacturing Co, Stockton). There is a photograph collection of 8500 pictures, and extensive manuscript holdings (about 17,000 pieces).

DC —SMITHSONIAN INSTITUTION LIBRARIES, Business & Industry Collections, Washington, 20560.
Notes: The Warshaw Collection of illustrative materials.

IN —PURDUE UNIVERSITY LIBRARIES, Graduate School of Management, Krannert Library, West Lafayette, 47907. Gordon Law, Librn
Notes: An important resource at the Krannert Library is its Special Collection of Business and Economics, consisting of some 8000 rare pre-20th century strengths in books, journals, tracts and pamphlets covering primarily the early literature of economic thought and business practices in America and abroad, 1500-1870. A catalog was issued in 1979. No photocopying.

MA —HARVARD UNIVERSITY, Baker Library of the Graduate School of Business Administration, Kress Library of Business and Economics, Soldiers Field, Boston, 02163. Ruth E Rogers, Cur
Holdings: Cat Mss Microforms

MA —UNIVERSITY OF LOWELL, Library, One University Ave, Lowell, 01854. Martha Mayo, Special Collections Librn
Holdings: Vols (24,000) Cat Mss Maps Pix
Notes: The Olney Collections contain books and journals on all aspects of textile technology particularly textile chemistry and textile engineering. The Flather Collection of the Boott Mill company papers 1835-1954. Photographic collections with emphasis on Lowell's textile industry.

MA —OLD STURBRIDGE VILLAGE, Research Library, Sturbridge, 01566. Theresa Rini Percy, Librn
Holdings: Cat Mss
Notes: Mainly American technology before 1850, incl building, engineering, lighting, mills, manufacturers, printing, invention.

NC —DUKE UNIVERSITY, William R Perkins Library, Manuscript Dept, Durham, 27706. Ellen Gartrell, Cur of Mss
Holdings: Cat Mss
Notes: Strongest for textile and tobacco industries in Southeastern US, 19th- 20th centuries. Incl papers of B N Duke, Richard H Wright, British- American Tobacco Co; business records of textile mills and several lumber companies, Romeo Guest papers on development of Research Triangle Park, North Carolina.

PA —LIBRARY COMPANY OF PHILADELPHIA, 1314 Locust St, Philadelphia, 19107. Edwin Wolf II, Librn; Kenneth Finkel, Cur of Prints
Holdings: Vols (400,000) Cat Maps Pix
Budget: ($25,000)
Notes: American science and industry before 1860. Books, pamphlets, etc on science incl math, pysics, astronomy, and industry, incl business and engineering. Incl many 18th century books printed in England and France but used by American colonials in their study and research. Impossible to estimate the exact size of collection since it is not separated from general collection.

INDUSTRY—SOCIAL ASPECTS

IL —INSTITUTE ON THE CHURCH IN URBAN-INDUSTRIAL SOCIETY, Library, 5700 S Woodlawn, Chicago, 60637.
Holdings: Vols 1000 Cat Microforms
Notes: Urban-industrial involvement of the churches world-wide, international urban literature, corporate responsibility, human factors of urbanization and industrialization. Library holdings are dorment at present.

INDUSTRY—STATISTICS see Industrial Statistics

INDUSTRY—VOCATIONAL GUIDANCE see Vocational Guidance

INDUSTRY, CANADIAN see Canada—Industry

INDUSTRY AND THE CHURCH see Church and Industry

INEBRIETY see Alcoholism

INERTIAL NAVIGATION SYSTEMS

CA —LOGICON INC, Strategic & Information Systems Division, Information Center, 255 W Fifth St, Box 471, San Pedro, 90731. Constance B Davenport, Supervisor
Holdings: Vols (3000) Cat Mss Microforms
Notes: Incl about 3000 books, 250 periocial titles, 5000 technical reports, 10,000 microfiche, 750 standards and specifications. Catalog is computerized. Interactive search capability with Dialog, Orbit, DMS on-line, NASA Recon. Material on computer programming, systems analysis, military systems and operations research.

INFANT AND MATERNAL HEALTH SERVICES see Maternal Health Services

INFANT WELFARE see Maternal and Infant Welfare

INFANTILE PARALYSIS see Poliomyelitis

INFANTRY

GA —US ARMY INFANTRY CENTER, National Infantry Museum, Fort Benning, 31905. Dick D Grube, Dir; Z Frank Hanner, Cur; Carol Sims, Librn
Holdings: Vols (6000) Cat Mss Maps Pix Slides
Notes: Published and unpublished works dealing with infantry history, equipment, and units, for research on the Museum's collections of artifacts. Items cannot be checked out except under unusual and compelling circumstances. The collection traces the two centuries of history of the US Infantry. Of special interest are: unpublished reports of tests conducted on US Army Infantry equipment; photographs showing the history of Fort Benning; books and periodical articles dealing with Infantry small arms, both American and foreign, especially Japanese, Soviet, Chinese, and British; US Army manuals, incl many from the early 20th and late 19th centuries; WWII battlefield maps; WWI and WWII posters; histories of WWI; US Army insignia and medals; WWII era German uniforms and insignia. Also, over 2500 weapons.

GA —US ARMY INFANTRY SCHOOL LIBRARY, Fort Benning, 31905. Vivian S Dodson, Chief Librn
Holdings: Vols 165,000 Microforms
Budget: $47,000
Notes: Each Army service school and branch school has an academic library. Incl books, classified and unclassified documents, periodicals (cat).

INFANTS (NEWBORN)

AR —NATIONAL CENTER FOR TOXICOLOGICAL RESEARCH, Library, Jefferson, 72079. Susan Laney-Sheehan, Supvr Librn
Holdings: Vols (15,000) Cat Mss Slides Audiotapes 16mm Films Microforms
Notes: Incl (860) journal titles, (230) current subscriptions.

CA —STANFORD UNIVERSITY LIBRARIES, Lane Medical Library, Stanford University, Medical Center, Stanford, 94305. Peter Stangl, Librn
Notes: Papers of Adelaide Brown, sanitation and prenatal care.

WA —CHILDREN'S ORTHOPEDIC HOSPITAL & MEDICAL CENTER, Medical Library, 4800 Sand Point Way NE, Seattle, 98105. Tamara A Turner, Librn
Holdings: Vols (10,000)
Notes: Specialize in pediatric texts and journals, with an emphasis on neontology, perinatology and childhood cancer.

INFANTS—CHARITIES, PROTECTION, ETC. see Maternal and Infant Welfare

INFECTIOUS DISEASES see Communicable Diseases

INFLATION (FINANCE)

DC —US DEPT OF LABOR, Library, 200 Constitution Ave NW, Washington, 20210. Sabina Jacobson, Dir
Holdings: Vols (550,000) Cat

ON —CANADA DEPT OF LABOUR, Library, Ottawa, K1A 0J2, Can. Monique Marchand, Chief Librn
Holdings: Vols (100,000) Cat Microforms

INFORMATION CENTERS see Information Storage and Retrieval Systems

INFORMATION PROCESSING SYSTEMS see Information Storage and Retrieval Systems

INFORMATION RETRIEVAL SYSTEMS see Computers; Information Storage and Retrieval Systems

INFORMATION SCIENCE

CA —UNIVERSITY OF CALIFORNIA, BERKELEY, Humanities-Social Sciences Libraries, Library School Library, 2 South Hall, Berkeley, 94720. Virginia Pratt, Head
Holdings: Vols (41,500) Cat Microforms
Notes: Research collection with special strengths in general library science; history of libraries; history of printing and book arts, and publishing; information systems and services; history, criticism, and bibliography of children's literature. The collections in printing and the book arts are complemented by significant holdings both in the Main Library and in the Bancroft Library. Incl collection of 5000 pamphlets.

CA —INTERNATIONAL BUSINESS MACHINES RESEARCH LIBRARY, 5600 Cottle Rd, San Jose, 95193. Phil Grincewich, Mgr Technical Information
Holdings: Vols (13,500) Cat
Notes: Incl 21,000 vols of 770 journals. On-line search facility. Vols are divided into three libraries, Technical Research, Technical Information, and Programing. Not open to public.

DC —CATHOLIC UNIVERSITY OF AMERICA, Library and Information Science Library, Marist Hall 132, 620 Michigan Ave NE, Washington, 20064. Patsy Haley Stann, Head; Lisa Navidi, Asst Head
Holdings: Vols 9000 Cat Periodicals Microfilm
Notes: Materials on Library and Information Science, history of books, information retrieval, automation, book selection, cataloging. Historical children's collection; depository for the International Federation for Documentation (FID).

GA —GEORGIA INSTITUTE OF TECHNOLOGY, Price Gilbert Memorial Library, 225 North Ave, Atlanta, 30332. Edward Graham Roberts, Dir
Holdings: Vols (1,661,559) Cat Maps Slides Microforms
Budget: ($1,383,302)
Notes: Incl (4,307,996) patents and (568, 490) government documents.

IN —INDIANA UNIVERSITY, Graduate School Library, Bloomington, 47401. Patricia

INFORMATION SCIENCE (cont.)

Steele, Librn
Holdings: Vols 13,000 Cat Pix Slides Phonorecords Audiotapes 16mm Films Filmstrips Microforms
Budget:

MA —MASSACHUSETTS BOARD OF LIBRARY COMMISSIONERS, Professional Library, 648 Beacon St, Boston, 02215. Brian Donoghue, Ref Asst
Holdings: Vols (16,500) Cat Audiotapes Videotapes Microforms
Budget: (15,000)
Notes: The library science emphasis does not stress the history of libraries. The collection embraces all other aspects of library and information science with an emphasis on public libraries, library administration and library technology. Subscriptions to 300 library science periodicals. Microforms: approx 1000 microfiche titles; the ERIC/IR Collection 1968-Date. Vertical files: approx 100 drawers. Dialog and BRS search service provided.

MA —MASSACHUSETTS INSTITUTE OF TECHNOLOGY, Institute Archives, Special Collections, Cambridge, 02139.
Notes: Papers of Norbert Wiener, renowned mathematician, was instrumental in the development of communication and control theories. He coined the word "cybernetics" to describe this new science. Professional papers document the development of this theory, his development as a mathematician, and his effective collaboration with students and colleagues including Vannevar Bush and John von Neumann. Unpublished finding aid with correspondent index is available in the Institute Archives.

MN —OFFICE OF LIBRARY DEVELOPMENT AND SERVICES, 440 Capitol Square, 550 Cedar St, Saint Paul, 55101. Darlene M Arnold, Sr Librn
Holdings: Vols 12,000 Cat Slides Phonorecords Audiotapes Videotapes 16mm Films Filmstrips Microforms
Budget: $13,000

NY —PRATT INSTITUTE, Library Science Library, 200 Willoughby Ave, Brooklyn, 11205. Margot Karp, Library Science Librn
Holdings: Vols (10,000) Cat Microforms
Budget: ($15,000)
Notes: Separate catalog.

NY —SCIENCE ASSOCIATES/ INTERNATIONAL, Library, 1841 Broadway, New York, 10023. Roxy Bauer, Librn
Holdings: Vols 2000 Uncat Microforms
Notes: No photocopying.

OH —CASE WESTERN RESERVE UNIVERSITY, M A Baxter School of Information and Library Science, 10900 Euclid Ave, Cleveland, 44106. Bettina MacAyeal, Librn; Gretchen Larson, Librn
Holdings: Vols (15,000) Cat
Budget: ($40,000)
Notes: Western Reserve University merged with Case Institute of Technology to form Case Western Reserve University. The University Libraries do have a library science collection, but the Library Science Library is a separate department on campus, and does not have the same address. Noncirculating historical children's literature collection is established and cataloged.

PA —DREXEL UNIVERSITY LIBRARIES, W W Hagerty Library, 32 & Chestnut Sts, Philadelphia, 19104. R L Snyder, Dir
Holdings: Vols (1350) Cat Microforms
Budget: ($9400)

PA —UNIVERSITY OF PENNSYLVANIA, Moore School of Electrical Engineering Library, 203 Moore School, 33 & Walnut Sts, Philadelphia, 19104. Charles Myers, Head Librn
Holdings: Vols (30,000) Cat Microforms

†PA —UNIVERSITY OF PITTSBURGH, Graduate School of Library & Information Sciences Library, L I S Bldg, Third Fl, Pittsburgh, 15260. Jean Kindlin, Librn
Notes: Extensive collection on the historical development of school libraries, media services, and evaluation of materials for use in all types of schools. Incl 54,800 vols, 7524 bound periodicals, 630 periodical subscriptions.

RI —RHODE ISLAND DEPARTMENT OF STATE LIBRARY SERVICES, 95 Davis St, Providence, 02908. Frank P Iacono, Reference Librn
Holdings: Vols 4000 Cat VF
Budget: $15,000
Notes: Collection incl over 200 vertical files.

WI —UNIVERSITY OF WISCONSIN, MADISON, Library School Library, 600 N Park St, Madison, 53706. Sally Davis, Librn
Holdings: Vols 59,000

ON —UNIVERSITY OF WESTERN ONTARIO, Schoool of Library and Information Science, Library, London, N6G 1H1, Can. Victoria Ripley, Librn
Holdings: Vols (50,000)
Notes: Auction and antiquarian booksellers' catalogs from Canadian, American and European firms, some dating back to the 18th century. A special strength is 19th and early 20th century American booksellers' catalogs, recently augmented by a collection of pre-1920 catalogs formed by the late H O Teisberg. Current emphasis is on Canadian catalogs.

INFORMATION SERVICES see Information Storage and Retrieval Systems

INFORMATION STORAGE AND RETRIEVAL SYSTEMS

CA —HEWLETT-PACKARD CORP, Data Systems Div, Cupertino Library, 11000 Wolfe Rd, Cupertino, 95014. Katherine Biggs, Librn
Holdings: Vols 2000 Cat

CA —UNIVERSITY OF CALIFORNIA, LOS ANGELES, Graduate School of Management Library, UCLA Campus, Los Angeles, 90024. Robert Bellanti, Head Librn
Holdings: Vols (128,000) Cat Mss Microforms
Notes: The

CA —UPDATA PUBLICATIONS INC, Library, 1756 Westwood Blvd, Los Angeles, 90024. Sara Ferguson, Dir; Judith Harrington, Librn
Holdings: Vols (300) Uncat Maps Microforms
Notes: Incl 800,000 microforms, 35 periodicals.

CA —INTERNATIONAL BUSINESS MACHINES RESEARCH LIBRARY, 5600 Cottle Rd, San Jose, 95193. Phil Grincewich, Mgr Technical Information
Holdings: Vols (13,500) Cat
Notes: Incl 21,000 vols of 770 journals. On-line search facility. Vols are divided into three libraries, Technical Research, Technical Information, and Programing. Not open to public.

CO —IBM, Boulder Library, PO Box 1900, Boulder, 80302. Beverly Jorman, Library Mgr
Holdings: Vols (10,000) Cat Microforms
Notes: Emphasis in chemistry, physics, computer sciences and technology.

CT —AETNA LIFE & CASUALTY, Corporate Data Processing Library, 151 Farmington Ave, Hartford, 06156. Kathryn Porter, Chief Librn
Holdings: Vols 10

DC —US BUREAU OF THE CENSUS, Library, Federal Office Bldg 3, Rm 2451, Washington, 20233. Betty Baxtresser, Chief, ASD Library Branch
Holdings: Cat Microforms
Notes: Emphases on statistics of agriculture, business, construction, economics, foreign trade, governments, housing, industry, population, transportation, statistical methodology, and data processing. Library holdings are largely current materials covering the Bureau's programs. Outdated materials are withdrawn regularly.

NJ —AT&T BELL LABORATORIES, Libraries and Information Systems Center, 600 Mountain Ave, Murray Hill, 07974. W D Penniman, Dir
Holdings: Vols (346,000) Cat Microforms
Notes: Restricted use to AT&T employees. Catalogs/*Indexes*: Bell Laboratories Library Network and Book Serial Catalogs; Bell Laboratories Translations. Bell Laboratories Library Network with New Jersey libraries located in Holmdel, Murray Hill, Piscataway, Whippany, Princeton, Short Hills, Summit, West Long Branch, Crawford Hill; libraries also in Allentown, Pennsylvania; Reading, Pennsylvania; New York, New York; Atlanta, Georgia; Columbus, Ohio; Naperville, Illinois; Indianapolis, Indiana; North Andover, Massachusetts.

NJ —DATA SYSTEMS ANALYSTS, Library, 6981 North Park Dr, Pennsauken, 08109. Elise Colabrese, Librn
Holdings: Vols (2300) Cat
Budget: ($15,000)
Notes: Incl technical reports and programming manuals relating to data communications, computer programming and computer networks.

NY —MORRIS N & CHESLEY V YOUNG LIBRARY OF MNEMONICS, 270 Riverside Dr, New York, 10025. Morris N Young, Cur
Holdings: Cat Mss Maps Pix Phonorecords Audiotapes 16mm Films Microforms
Notes: Collection of 5000 books, pamphlets, pictures, memorabilia, etc incl medieval art of memory; psychology of memory, forgetting and reading; medical aspects of memory, amnesia, dyslexia; biomedical aspects of learning and memory; information storage, retrieval and cybernetics; memory prodigies, lightning calculators, calendars; remembrance cups and memory mementos. All languages. Memorabilia incl engravings, posters, programs, advertisements, birthday cards, teaching cards, ASLs, and Mark Twain's Memory Builder game and other games. Items range from 1410 to 1980s.

NC —TECHNICAL INSTITUTE OF ALAMANCE, Learning Resources Center, Jimmy Kerr Rd, PO Box 623, Haw River, 27258. Ron Plummer, Coordr
Holdings: Vols 233 Cat Microforms
Notes: Business data processing.

OH —OHIO STATE UNIVERSITY, Engineering Library, 2024 Neil Ave, Columbus, 43210. Mary Jo V Arnold, Librn
Holdings: Vols (132,000) Cat Microforms
Budget: ($110,000)

PA —DREXEL UNIVERSITY LIBRARIES, W W Hagerty Library, 32 & Chestnut Sts, Philadelphia, 19104. R L Snyder, Dir
Holdings: Vols (13,500) Cat Microforms
Budget: ($9400)

RI —BRYANT COLLEGE, Edith M Hodgson Memorial Library, Rte 7, Douglas Pike, Smithfield, 02917. John P Hannon, Dir
Holdings: Vols (103,000) Cat Phonorecords Audiotapes Videotapes 16mm Films Filmstrips Microforms
Budget: ($175,000)
Notes: Incl 6000 bound periodical vols, 250 phonorecords, 220 audiotapes, 120 videotapes, 30 16mm films, 150 filmstrips and 7500 microforms.

ON —INSTITUTE OF CHARTERED ACCOUNTANTS OF ONTARIO, The Merrilees Library, 69 Bloor St E, Toronto, M4W 1B3, Can. Theresa Wolak, Librn
Holdings: Vols 36 Cat

INFORMATION THEORY

IL —UNIVERSITY OF ILLINOIS, URBANA/CHAMPAIGN, Library, Communications Library, 122 Gregory Hall, Urbana, 61801. Nancy Allen, Librn
Holdings: Vols (18,000) Cat
Budget: ($27,000)

INFORMED CONSENT (MEDICAL LAW)

MD —NATIONAL LIBRARY OF MEDICINE, 8600 Rockville Pike, Bethesda, 20209. Harold M Schoolinam, Actg Dir
Budget: ($46,400)

INGE, WILLIAM

KS —INDEPENDENCE COMMUNITY JUNIOR COLLEGE, Library, Independence, 67301. Del Singleton, Librn
Holdings: Vols 2000 Mss
Notes: Official archival repository for his

INGE, WILLIAM (cont.)

books, plays, letters, photographs, etc. Incl 385 mss, some correspondence, and a large poster collection.

INGERSOLL, RALPH

MA —BOSTON UNIVERSITY, Mugar Memorial Library, Special Collections Dept, 771 Commonwealth Ave, Boston, 02215. Howard B Gotlieb, Dir
Holdings: Cat Mss Correspondence Pix Family Papers

INGERSOLL, ROBERT GREEN, 1833-1899

DC —GEORGETOWN UNIVERSITY, Library, Special Collections Div, 37 & O Sts NW, Washington, 20057. George M Barringer, Special Collections Librn; Nicholas B Sheetz, Mss Librn
Holdings: Vols 50 Uncat Mss

IL —SOUTHERN ILLINOIS UNIVERSITY, CARBONDALE, Delyte W Morris Library, Special Collections Dept, Carbondale, 62901. David V Koch, Cur of Special Collections; Louisa Bowen, Cur of Manuscripts
Holdings: Vols 275 Cat Mss
Notes: Gordon Stein Collection of Robert G Ingersoll incl 5 linear feet of mss, 1968-1921. Inventory available at library.

IN —INDIANA STATE UNIVERSITY, Cunningham Memorial Library, Dept of Rare Books & Special Collections, Terre Haute, 47809. Lawrence J McCrank, Head
Notes: The Debs Collection consists of aprox 7000 pieces of correspondence between Theodore Debs (brother of E V) and other persons, such as Sinclair Lewis, Upton Sinclair, Ethel Barrymore, Emma Goldman, Robert G Ingersoll, Carl Sandburg, Norman Thomas, Sacco and Vanzetti and many others. Many of the letters are from E V Debs to his brother; a good portion of these are from the federal penitentiary at Atlanta. Entire correspondence file has been microfilmed. 750 pamphlets cover all aspects of the labor movement, socialism and radical thought from the 19th century to appprox 1950. A collection ca 200 related books is also housed in the collection. See: J Robert Constantine and Gail Malmgreen, eds, *The Papers of Eugene V Debs, 1834-1945. A Guide to the Microfilm Edition.* NY: Microfilming Corp of America, 1983 (University Microfilms is the new distributor).

NY —CORNELL UNIVERSITY LIBRARIES, Collection of Regional History, Dept of Manuscripts and Univ Archives, Ithaca, 14853.
Notes: Attorney, lecturer. Letters, 1877-98; 1 reel microfilm, 9 items.

INHALATION INJURIES

MD —NATIONAL LIBRARY OF MEDICINE, 8600 Rockville Pike, Bethesda, 20209. Harold M Schoolinam, Actg Dir
Budget: ($46,400)

INHALATION THERAPY

OH —KETTERING COLLEGE OF MEDICAL ARTS, Learning Resources Center, 3737 Southern Blvd, Kettering, 45429. Edward Collins, Librn
Holdings: Vols 276 Cat Audiotapes Videotapes

INHERITANCE (BIOLOGY) see Heredity

INJURIES see Traffic Accidents; First Aid

INJURIES (LAW) see Medical Jurisprudence

INK

IL —NEWBERRY LIBRARY, John M Wing Foundation on the History of Printing, 60 W Walton St, Chicago, 60610. Diana Haskell, Cur of Modern Mss
Holdings: Vols (30,000) Cat Mss
Budget: ($50,000)
Notes: The collection covers printing and printing history of Western Europe and the Americas from its invention to the present. It is particularly rich in incunabula (about 2000); the works of the great printers, among others Aldus, Bodoni, Baskerville, and Rogers. Printed catalog: *A Dictionary* Catalogue. (Boston: G K Hall, 1961); *Supplements* (1981). Brief descriptions: James M Wells, "The John M Wing Foundation of the Newberry Library," *The Book Collector, VIII,* 2 (Summer 1959), pp 157-162; Lawrece W Towner, *An Uncommon Collection of Uncommon* Collections (Chicago: The Newberry Library, 1977), pp 25-26.

PA —GRAPHIC ARTS TECHNICAL FOUNDATION, Edward H Wadewitz Memorial Library, 4615 Forbes Ave, Pittsburgh, 15213. Janice L Lloyd, Librn
Holdings: Vols (3500) Cat Slides Microforms
Notes: All printing processes. Also, books and periodicals on paper, ink, photography, optics, color theory, environmental control. Approximately 250 periodical titles and 35, 000 classified abstracts of selected periodical articles. Approximately 15,000 slides within the organization. Research reports from foreign graphic arts research institutes.

VA —UNIVERSITY OF VIRGINIA, Alderman Library, Rare Book Dept, Charlottesville, 22901. Julius P Barclay, Cur
Holdings: Vols (6500) // Mss
Notes: The Oscar Ogg Collection of Book Arts covers calligraphy, letterforms, typography, printing, and graphic arts. Contains early writing books and printed works, as well as modern manuals and other works on printing, publishing, and promotion through graphic arts. The Dept also has the Edward L Stone Collection of Printing Specimens, 3000 items. Contains materials tracing the history of printing, inks, binding styles and materials, types. Also the Tompkins Collection (2000 vols), and the Stevens Watts collection (900 vols).

INKLINGS (OXFORD UNIVERSITY)

IL —WHEATON COLLEGE, Library, Marion E Wade Collection, Irving & Franklin Sts, Wheaton, 60187. Lyle Dorsett, Cur; Marjorie Mead, Associate Cur
Holdings: Vols (6500)
Notes: Extensive Marion E Wade Collection contains a wide variety of materials on the lives and writings of the Oxford literary circle, the Inklings. Concerns C S Lewis, Owen Barfield J R R Tolkien and Charles Williams.

INLAND NAVIGATION

IL —NORTHWESTERN UNIVERSITY, Transportation Center Library, Evanston, 60201. Mary Roy, Librn
Holdings: Vols (116,000)
Notes: The emphasis in this collection is on current developments in transportation operations and socioeconomics--management, planning, impact and regulation. All modes of transportation and containerization are incl; the geographic scope covers domestic and foreign activity at the urban, intercity and international levels. Publications on new systems developments and the application of analytic techniques to operations are well represented. Incl 19,000 pamphlets; 9000 company reports. *Services are offered on research conducted outside Northwestern. A fee schedule is available on request.* Publications: *Current Literature in Traffic and Transportation* (bi-monthly accessions bulletin citing 625 books, reports and periodical articles per issue).

MD —STEAMSHIP HISTORICAL SOCIETY OF AMERICA (SSHSA), University of Baltimore Library, 1420 Maryland Ave, Baltimore, 21201.
Holdings: Vols (3500) Cat Maps Pix Slides 16mm Films
Budget: ($15,000)
Notes: Powered Maritime Transportation Collection. Photo bank of over 15,000 negatives and 25,000 prints, arranged alphabetically by vessel name. Extensive blueprint and tracing collection. Collection documents history of steam navigation from the early 19th century to the present. Emphasis upon East Coast American vessels of late 19th and early 20th centuries and upon transatlantic vessels. Some coverage of Great Lakes and inland river steamboats. Very little about sailing vessels. No published catalog. Books listed in OCLC. Collection located at University of Baltimore. Address for Society is 414 Pelton Ave, Staten Island, NY 10310, attention: Alice S Wilson, Secretary and SSHSA Librn.

MA —HARVARD UNIVERSITY, Baker Library of the Graduate School of Business Administration, Kress Library of Business and Economics, Soldiers Field, Boston, 02163. Ruth E Rogers, Cur
Notes: An extensive collection. Historical emphasis on railroads and canals.

OH —PUBLIC LIBRARY OF CINCINNATI & HAMILTON COUNTY, Dept of Rare Books & Special Collections, 800 Vine St, Library Square, Cincinnati, 45202. Yeatman Anderson III, Cur
Holdings: Cat Mss Maps Pix Slides Microforms
Notes: Inland River Collection. Incl logbooks, account books, personal correspondence, diaries, etc. Also, a picture collection of 14,000 items (steamboats, towboats, river views, crews, construction, barges, etc.)

OH —RUTHERFORD B HAYES LIBRARY, 1337 Hayes Ave, Fremont, 43420. Watt P Marchman, Dir
Holdings: Vols 500 Cat Mss Maps Pix Slides
Notes: The Great Lakes Marine Collection, incl the Capt Frank E Hamilton Collection; Great Lakes boats and shipping. Incl 300 charts; over 20,000 pictures (with 2500 negatives, 30 glass plates). Index and findings aids with the collection.

INLAND SHIPPING see Inland Water Transportation

INLAND WATER TRANSPORTATION

CO —COLORADO STATE UNIVERSITY, Libraries, Fort Collins, 80523. Marjorie Rhoades, Engineering Sciences Librn
Notes: Not significant amount of material. Water and Soil in Arid Regions (WASAR) is an index with citations of selected items dealing with soils, water, arid lands, crops, foods and nutrition, with certain economic, political, ecological, and historical considerations also included.

IL —NORTHWESTERN UNIVERSITY, Transportation Center Library, Evanston, 60201. Mary Roy, Librn
Holdings: Vols (116,000)
Notes: The emphasis in this collection is on current developments in transportation operations and socioeconomics--management, planning, impact and regulation. All modes of transportation and containerization are incl; the geographic scope covers domestic and foreign activity at the urban, intercity and international levels. Publications on new systems developments and the application of analytic techniques to operations are well represented. Incl 19,000 pamphlets; 9000 company reports. *Services are offered on research conducted outside Northwestern. A fee schedule is available on request.* Publications: *Current Literature in Traffic and Transportation* (bi-monthly accessions bulletin citing 625 books, reports and periodical articles per issue).

LA —TULANE UNIVERSITY, Howard-Tilton Memorial Library, Special Collections Div, 7001 Freret St, New Orleans, 70118. Wilbur E Meneray, Librn
Holdings: Vols 950 Mss Pix 30,000
Notes: Photographs of river vessels, published works about river transportation, correspondence and mementos of riverboat captains, and papers of the Mississippi Valley Association and the Gulf Intracoastal Canal Association.

INLAND WATER TRANSPORTATION (cont.)

MI —LE SAULTE DE SAINTE MARIE HISTORIC SITES, PO Box 1668, Sault Sainte Marie, 49783. Thomas Nance, Curator
Notes: 300 Great Lakes logbooks cover more than 100 years of freighter history of the local Wilson Marine Transit Company. Incl *Marine News*, 59 vols, 1900-1968, plus related reports, directoies, and yearbooks of steel industry.

OH —RUTHERFORD B HAYES LIBRARY, 1337 Hayes Ave, Fremont, 43420. Watt P Marchman, Dir
Holdings: Vols 500 Cat Mss Maps Pix Slides
Notes: The Great Lakes Marine Collection, incl the Capt Frank E Hamilton Collection; Great Lakes boats and shipping. Incl 300 charts; over 20,000 pictures (with 2500 negatives, 30 glass plates). Index and findings aids with the collection.

INNOVATIONS, TECHNOLOGICAL see Technological Innovations

INNOVATIVE POETRY

CA —UNIVERSITY OF CALIFORNIA, DAVIS, Shields Library, Dept of Special Collections, Davis, 95616. Donald Kunitz, Head; C Danial Elliott, Asst Head
Holdings: Vols 4700 Cat
Notes: Ephemeral and rare post-1946 titles which are experimental or innovative in nature. Incl Bukowski, Dorn, Everson, Ferlinghetti, Ashbery, DiPrima, Snyder, etc.

CA —UNIVERSITY OF CALIFORNIA, SAN DIEGO, Central University Library, Mandeville Dept of Special Collections, La Jolla, 92093. Lynda Corey Claassen, Head; Michael Davidson, Cur, Archive for New Poetry
Notes: An extensive collection of modern English-language poetry published since World War II, the Archive contains over 28, 000 books, over 1000 magazine titles, and some 900 tapes and records. The Archive maintains substantial collections of papers from Paul Blackburn, Charles Reznikoff, Lew Welch, Jerome Rothenberg, Louis Zukofsky, and other major contemporary American poets. The collection of papers belonging to editor and publisher Donald Allen represents the work of one of the first publishers to make innovative poetry available through his anthology, *The New American Poetry, 1945-1960,* and through his two presses, The Four Seasons Foundation and Grey Fox Press.

INNS see Hotels, Taverns, Etc.

INNUIT see Eskimos and Inuits

INOCULATION—HISTORY

CT —YALE UNIVERSITY, Medical Historical Library, Klebs Collection, 333 Cedar St, New Haven, 06520. Ferenc A Gyorgyey, Librn
Notes: The Arnold Carl Klebs Medical Collection books, pamphlets, etc, incl the library of his father, Edwin T A Klebs, pathologist. Strong in bibliography of early printed medical books, herbals, plague tracts, inoculation, vaccination and tubercular diseases.

MD —JOHNS HOPKINS UNIVERSITY, Institute of the History of Medicine, 1900 E Monument St, Baltimore, 21205. Doris Thibodeau, Librn
Holdings: Vols 1053 Cat

INORGANIC CHEMISTRY see Chemistry, Inorganic

THE INQUIRY

CT —YALE UNIVERSITY, Box 1603A, Yale Station, New Haven, 06520.
Holdings: Cat Mss Maps
Notes: Gift of the records of "The Inquiry," from the National Geographic Society, in honor of Charles Seymour who was a member of the group.

INQUISITION

†DC —DOMINICAN HOUSE OF STUDIES, Dominican College Library, 487 Michigan Ave NE, Washington, 20017.
Holdings: Vols (5000) Cat
Budget: ($1350)
Notes: The Dominican Order (its history, spirituality, government, liturgy), its members (directories, biographies, bibliographies, lives of saints) and works written by Dominicans: incunabula, rare books, dissertations, periodicals (2300 vols), monographs. Incl periodicals either about the Order or edited by Dominicans. Does not incl titles about the congregations of Dominican Sisters. The Library's catalog contains analytics fro Dominican contributors to monographs.

DC —LIBRARY OF CONGRESS, Manuscript Division, Washington, 20540. John C Broderick, Chief
Notes: The Hans P Kraus Collection of documents relating to colonial Spanish America, 1492-1819. Focusing on colonial Mexico, incl material on exploration, government, activities of the Inquisition, taxation and economic conditions, relations with the Indians and the French, and the impending loss of land to Anglo-American settlers. Also contains items concerning the history of Spanish Florida, Tezozomoc's chronicle on the history of the Aztecs, and mss describing the explorations of Amerigo Vespucci, Giovanni da Verrazzano, Alvar Nunez Cabeza de Vaca, Pedro de Ursua, and Lope de Aguirre.

IL —NEWBERRY LIBRARY, 60 W Walton St, Chicago, 60610. Diana Haskell, Cur of Modern Mss
Holdings: Cat Mss
Notes: A collection of mss photoduplicated from libraries all over the world dealing with the Roman Inquisition, 16th and 17th centuries.

IN —INDIANA UNIVERSITY, Lilly Library, Seventh St, Bloomington, 47405. William R Cagle, Librn
Holdings: Vols (40,000) Cat Mss Maps
Notes: Research and rare book collection (Bernardo Mendel) of first or only editions, mostly printed in Latin America, from the discovery of the New World through 1830. Special strength in discoveries and exploration, history (mainly period of independence), Inquisition, missionary works by the Augustinians, Dominicans, Franciscans, and the Jesuits, and the history of the Catholic Church in these countries. Major geographic concentration is on the three great viceroyalities of Mexico (ca 10, 000 titles, plus over 10,000 official Mexican broadsides), Peru (2000 titles), and Argentina (4000 titles), incl in Argentina a substantial amount of printings from the Imprenta de Ninos Expositos, and the Coleccion Santamarina. A special Bolivian Collection (2500 titles), mostly history, from the establishment of the press there, ca 1826, through the beginning of the 20th century. Part of the Mendel Collection is the selected Bibliotheca Boxeriana from Charles R Boxer (1000 titles) on European expansion into Asia, and into the New World, mainly Brazil, during the 16th-18th centuries. *See also* entries under Spain - History, Portugal - History, and Mexico - History.

MD —JOHNS HOPKINS UNIVERSITY, Milton S Eisenhower Library, George Peabody Collection, 17 E Mt Vernon Place, Baltimore, 21201. Lyn Hart, Peabody Librn
Notes: Emphasis on materials published before 1950. Strength is a good collection through the 19th century.

NY —NEW YORK PUBLIC LIBRARY, Research Libraries, General Research Division, Fifth Ave & 42 St, New York, 10018. Rodney Phillips, Chief
Holdings: Vols (2,225,000) Cat Maps Pix Microforms
Budget: ($775,718)

OH —HEBREW UNION COLLEGE-JEWISH INSTITUTE OF RELIGION, Klau Library, 3101 Clifton Ave, Cincinnati, 45220. David J Gilner, Reference Librn
Holdings: Cat Mss
Notes: Incl papal bulls, edicts of inquisitions, royal letters, inquistorial instructions, sermons preached at the autos-da-fe held by the Portuguese Inquisition at Lisbon, Colombia, etc. Early and late histories.

PA —UNIVERSITY OF PENNSYLVANIA, Lea Library, 3420 Walnut St, Philadelphia, 19104. Daniel Traister, Special Collections Librn
Holdings: Vols 20,000 Cat Mss
Notes: One of the great collections. See Downs 4241, 4234.

INQUISITION—MEXICO

IN —INDIANA UNIVERSITY, Lilly Library, Seventh St, Bloomington, 47405. William R Cagle, Librn
Holdings: Vols 6000 / / Cat Mss

Notes: Begins with the conquest of Mexico by Cortes and his letters to Charles V, in first and subsequent editions and translations, through the Revolution of 1910. Incl. the most important reforms of the Enlightenment concerning the economy, commerce, mining, science, and the expulsion of the Jesuits. The period of independence, the best represented aspects of which are the effect of the Napoleonic invasion of Spain in 1808, the constitutional crisis in Spain and the colonies provoked by the capture of the Spanish royal family by Napoleon, the policy of Ferdinand VII and the most important decisions by all the viceroys, bishops and archbishops. From the revolutionary side, the historical pronouncements and documents by the leaders of the movement of independence, such as Hidalgo, Morelos, Guerrero, and Iturbide, and the legal and political documents that gave structure to the Revolution. The empire with Iturbide and the period of political instability and strife that followed the independence, the reforms of Juarez, Maximillian's Empire, and its corollary, the dictatorial regime of Porfirio Diaz through the Revolution of 1910, are also well documented.

INQUISITION—SPAIN

CA —UNIVERSITY OF CALIFORNIA, SANTA BARBARA, Library, Dept of Special Collections, Santa Barbara, 93106. Christian F Brun, Head
Holdings: Vols 322 Uncat Mss
Notes: Judaica and the Spanish Inquisition.

DC —HARVARD UNIVERSITY, Center for Hellenic Studies Library, 3100 Whitehaven

INSCRIPTIONS (cont.)

St NW, Washington, 20008. Jeno Platthy, Librn
Holdings: Vols (42,000) Cat Maps
Budget: ($76,824)
Notes: In addition to a large collection of editions of ancient Greek authors, the library is well equipped to cover every aspect of ancient Greek civilization from prehistoric times to about AD 200. The subject fields covered include epigraphy, paleography, papyrology, history, literature, philosophy, religion, mythology, archaeology and art. A small collection of works on Patristics as well as all important Latin authors complete the Center's holdings.

IL —UNIVERSITY OF ILLINOIS, URBANA/CHAMPAIGN, Library, Classics Library, 419A Main Library, Urbana, 61801. Suzanne N Griffiths, Librn
Holdings: Vols (10,000) Cat
Notes: Ancient history section of Classics Library is strong in numismatics and in inscription materials; also incl ancient archaeology.

NY —AMERICAN NUMISMATIC SOCIETY LIBRARY, Broadway between 155 & 156 Sts, New York, 10032. Francis D Campbell Jr, Chief Librn
Holdings: Vols (50,000) Cat Mss Maps Pix Slides 16mm Films Microforms
Budget: ($6000)
Notes: Incl materials devoted to coins, medals, decorations, orders, tokens, paper money, seals, heraldry. Aids materials incl history, economic history, art history, archaeology, inscriptions and a number of encyclopedias and biographical dictionaries. Dictionary card catalog provides access to the materials: *Dictionary Catalogue of the Library of the American Numismatic* Society. (Boston: G K Hall, 1962). 6 vols and vol listing the auction catalogs in our collection; *First Supplement: 1962-1967; Second Supplement: 1968-1972; Third Supplement: 1973-1977* (Boston: G K Hall, 1967, 1973, 1978). Noncirculating.

NY —COLUMBIA UNIVERSITY LIBRARIES, Rare Book & Manuscript Library, 801 Butler Library, 535 W 114 St, New York, 10027. Kenneth A Lohf, Librn
Notes: Books and specimens in the history of papyrology and epigraphy. Incl 250 papyri fragments of Egyptian origin.

INSCRIPTIONS, ASSYRIAN see Cuneiform Inscriptions

INSCRIPTIONS, BABYLONIAN see Cuneiform Inscriptions

INSCRIPTIONS, BEHISTUN see Cuneiform Inscriptions

INSCRIPTIONS, CUNEIFORM see Cuneiform Inscriptions

INSCRIPTIONS, EGYPTIAN see Egyptian Language and Literature

INSCRIPTIONS, GREEK

CA —UNIVERSITY OF CALIFORNIA, BERKELEY, University Library, Berkeley, 94720. Donald G Williams, Classics Librn
Notes: Research collections, incl a wide array of periodicals, critical editions, works of textual criticism, history, and epigraphy. Extensive coverage of 18th and 19th century classical scholarship. German and Italian research publications are particularly well represented. Main Library holdings are supplemented by significant works in the Bancroft Library: mss, incunabula, and other rare editions; especially noteworthy are the Horace Collection and the Tebtunis papyri.

DC —HARVARD UNIVERSITY, Center for Hellenic Studies Library, 3100 Whitehaven St NW, Washington, 20008. Jeno Platthy, Librn
Holdings: Vols 5000 Cat
Notes: Emphasis on Greek text editions, epigraphy, literature and linguistics; more than 200 periodicals devoted to classical scholarship.

PA —UNIVERSITY OF PITTSBURGH, Hillman Library, Pittsburgh, 15260. Glenora E Rossell, Head
Holdings: Vols (11,550) Cat
Notes: The classics collection is particularly strong in Greek and Latin literature, Greek and Roman history, Greek philosophy, Greek and Latin language, and Greek epigraphy. In combination with the Frick Fine Arts collection it has a good collection in Greek and Roman art and archaeology. The collection of journals is also quite strong in these areas. There has been an emphasis in collecting books by and about Homer, Aristotles, Euripides, Vergil, Cicero and Petronius. It has a unique collection of unpublished PhD dissertations and Master's theses on Petronius. It has a basic collection on Greek an Latin paleography and papyrology.

INSCRIPTIONS, LATIN

CA —UNIVERSITY OF CALIFORNIA, BERKELEY, University Library, Berkeley, 94720. Donald G Williams, Classics Librn
Notes: Research collections, incl a wide array of periodicals, critical editions, works of textual criticism, history, and epigraphy. Extensive coverage of 18th and 19th century classical scholarship. German and Italian research publications are particularly well represented. Main Library holdings are supplemented by significant works in the Bancroft Library: mss, incunabula, and other rare editions; especially noteworthy are the Horace Collection and the Tebtunis papyri.

DC —HARVARD UNIVERSITY, Center for Hellenic Studies Library, 3100 Whitehaven St NW, Washington, 20008. Jeno Platthy, Librn
Holdings: Vols (42,000) Cat Maps
Budget: ($76,824)
Notes: In addition to a large collection of editions of ancient Greek authors, the library is well equipped to cover every aspect of ancient Greek civilization from prehistoric times to about AD 200. The subject fields covered include epigraphy, paleography, papyrology, history, literature, philosophy, religion, mythology, archaeology and art. A small collection of works on Patristics as well as all important Latin authors complete the Center's holdings.

INSCRIPTIONS, PALM-LEAF see Palm Leaf Inscriptions

INSECTICIDES

MI —MICHIGAN STATE UNIVERSITY, Science Library, East Lansing, 48824. Carole S Armstrong, Head
Holdings: Vols 700 Cat
Notes: Both books and journals include titles in English, French, German and Russian, with a few in other languages. The scope includes general toxicology, industrial toxicology, veterinary toxicology, the toxicology of metals and insecticides, and poisons as studied in experimental pharmacology.

INSECTS

CA —UNIVERSITY OF CALIFORNIA, BERKELEY, Life Sciences Library, Entomology Library, 201 Wellman Hall, Berkeley, 94720. Nancy Axelrod, Librn
Holdings: Vols (12,000) Cat Microforms
Notes: A highly specialized collection limited to materials on insects, arachnida and animal parasites. Special emphasis is given to works on pest control, particularly on biological methods of control. The library's holdings in the field of parasitology emphasize medical parasitology. Incl over (17,000) pamphlets.

CA —UNIVERSITY OF CALIFORNIA, DAVIS, General Library, Davis, 95616. Bernard Kreissman, University Librn; C Danial Elliott, Asst Head, Dept Special Collections
Holdings: Vols (14,000) Cat Mss Maps Slides
Notes: Relatively strong in materials published from 1920 to date. Areas of entomology that are emphasized incl bees (apiculture), nematology, parasitology and the control of insect publications. The slides and specimens in the collection are housed in the research collection of the Department of Entomology.

CA —CALIFORNIA ACADEMY OF SCIENCES, J W Mailliard Jr Library, Golden Gate Park, San Francisco, 94118. Ray Brian, Librn
Notes: Downs no 2160.

DC —SMITHSONIAN INSTITUTION, Archives Div, Washington, 20560. William W Moss, Archivist
Holdings: Cat Mss Pix
Notes: The Archives holds the records of the National Museum of Natural History's Division of Insects and the Department of Entomology, 1850-1974, as well as some papers of entomologists, incl Charles P Alexander.

DC —SMITHSONIAN INSTITUTION LIBRARIES, Entomology Branch, Washington, 20560. Jean C Smith, Asst Dir for Bureau Services
Holdings: Vols (17,000) Cat Maps Pix

FL —FLORIDA DEPARTMENT OF AGRICULTURE & CONSUMER SERVICES, Div of Plant Industry, Library, PO Box 1269, Gainesville, 32602. June B Jacobson, Librn; Alice Richards, Asst Librn
Holdings: Vols (11,455) Cat Mss Microforms
Budget: ($23,798)
Notes: Collection is primarily taxonomic. 464 periodical, current and antiquariat titles.

IL —ILLINOIS NATURAL HISTORY SURVEY LIBRARY, 196 Natural Resources Bldg, Champaign, 61820. Carla G Heister, Librn
Holdings: Vols (36,000) Cat Microforms
Budget: ($25,500)
Notes: A Research and Science Branch of the State of Illinois, the Natural History Survey maintains a library of books, journals and reports on various aspects of natural history. Material is collected in all major languages. The library maintains its own exchange arrangements with some 600 worldwide institutions and organizations. Interlibrary loans and photocopy services are available through the University of Illinois Library. Publications issued regularly by the Survey incl *Biological Notes, The Bulletin, and Circulars.*

IL —FIELD MUSEUM OF NATURAL HISTORY, Library, Roosevelt Rd & Lake Shore Dr, Chicago, 60605. W Peyton Fawcett, Librn; Benjamin W Williams, Assoc Librn
Holdings: Vols (210,000) Cat
Budget: ($100,000)
Notes: Extensive collections--publications of learned societies and institutions and monographic works--in all fields of natural history, with emphasis on taxonomy and evolutionary biology; and on museum publications, American and foreign: anthropology, especially archaeology and ethnology of the Americas, Africa, East Asia, and Oceania; botany, particularly strong for the Americas; geology, chiefly paleontology and meteoritic studies; and zoology, worldwide (birds, fishes, insects, mammals, mollusks, reptiles and amphibians).

IA —IOWA STATE UNIVERSITY, Library, Ames, 50011. Warren B Kuhn, Dean of Library Services
Holdings: Cat
Notes: Specific strengths: flies, mosquitoes and ticks.

MA —UNIVERSITY OF MASSACHUSETTS AT AMHERST, Library, Amherst, 01003. Siegfried Feller, Assoc Dir for Collection Development
Holdings: Cat
Notes: Incl the Guy C Crampton Collection; also, extensive holdings on bees and beekeeping.

MA —HARVARD UNIVERSITY, Museum of Comparative Zoology, Library, 26 Oxford St, Cambridge, 02138. Eva S Jonas, Librn
Holdings: Cat Mss Pix Microforms

INSECTS (cont.)

MI —UNIVERSITY OF MICHIGAN, Museums Library, Ann Arbor, 48109. Patricia B Yocum, Librn
Holdings: Vols 10,000 Cat

NY —CORNELL UNIVERSITY LIBRARIES, Comstock Memorial Library of Entomology, Ithaca, 14853. Edwin Spragg, Librn
Holdings: Vols (30,000) Cat Maps Pix Audiotapes Microforms
Budget: ($13,500)
Notes: Major topics: general and applied entomology. Minor topics: parasitology, medical entomology, ecology, zoological nomenclature and allied orders of arthropods. Separate catalog to the collection, also extensive collection of reprints. Apiculture material kept at nearby A R Mann Library.

NY —AMERICAN MUSEUM OF NATURAL HISTORY, Library Services Dept, Central Park W & 79th St, New York, 10024. Nina J Root, Chairwoman; Mary Genett, Asst Librn for Reference Services
Holdings: Vols (385,000) Cat Mss Maps Pix Slides Microforms
Notes: Nearly all collections are outstanding for depth of coverage and international range. Early and historic works, rare books, colored illustrations, and relevant serial publications supplement the modern scientific publications necessary to the researches of the scientific staff and the work of the educational division. Open to the public.

NC —NORTH CAROLINA STATE UNIVERSITY, D H Hill Library, Box 7111, Raleigh, 27695. I T Littleton, Dir
Holdings: Vols 7950 Cat
Budget: $5000
Notes: The Friedrich F Tippman Collection of 6200 volumes of entomology incl many unique and rare volumes which make the collection one of the best in the US. Incl the Z P Metcalf collection of Homoptera and Hemiptera: 1100 vols and 24 VF cabinets.

OK —OKLAHOMA STATE UNIVERSITY, Library, Stillwater, 74708. Roscoe Rouse, Dir
Holdings: Vols 3650 Cat

OR —OREGON STATE UNIVERSITY, Library, Corvallis, 97331. Melvin George, Dir
Holdings: Vols (980,000) Cat Pix

BC —CANADIAN FORESTRY SERVICE, Pacific Forest Research Centre, Library, 506 West Burnside Rd, Victoria, V8Z 1M5, Can. Alice Solyma, Librn
Holdings: Vols (60,500) Cat Microforms
Notes: Incl rearing, biological control, identification, dispersal, insect pest management, comprehensive collection re Mountain Pine Beetle, Western Spruce Budworm, Douglas Fir Tussack Moth.

ON —AGRICULTURE CANADA, Entomology Research Library, K W Neatby Bldg, Ottawa, K1A 0C6, Can. J P Miska, Area Coordinator, NCR/Ontario
Holdings: Vols 26,000 Cat Mss Maps Pix Slides Microforms
Budget: $30,000
Notes: Also 41,000 pamphlets, reprints, etc.

INSECTS, AQUATIC

HI —BERNICE P BISHOP MUSEUM, Library, PO Box 19000-A, Honolulu, 96819. Cynthia Timberlake, Librn
Holdings: Vols (90,000) Cat Mss Maps Pix Slides Microforms
Budget: ($30,000)
Notes: Only American library devoted exclusively to the Pacific region. Collection reflects historical and contemporary research emphases of Bishop Museum; ie the natural and cultural history of the Pacific. Areas of concentration incl archaeology, ethnology, linguistics, voyages and explorations, history, vertebrate and invertebrate zoology, botany and museology. Strong special collections incl photographs, mss and archives, maps and art. Publications: Quarterly "Additions to the Catalog," *Dictionary Catalog of the Library* (9 vols and 2 suppl; Boston: G K Hall, 1964-69).

IL —ILLINOIS NATURAL HISTORY SURVEY LIBRARY, 196 Natural Resources Bldg, Champaign, 61820. Carla G Heister, Librn
Holdings: Vols (36,000) Cat Microforms
Budget: ($25,500)
Notes: A Research and Science Branch of the State of Illinois, the Natural History Survey maintains a library of books, journals and reports on various aspects of natural history. Material is collected in all major languages. The library maintains its own exchange arrangements with some 600 worldwide institutions and organizations. Interlibrary loans and photocopy services are available through the University of Illinois Library. Publications issued regularly by the Survey incl *Biological Notes, The Bulletin, and Circulars.*

IN-SERVICE TRAINING see Employees, Training of

INSHORE UNDERSEA WARFARE see Undersea Warfare Inshore

INSIGNIA

CA —WESTERN COSTUME COMPANY, Research Library, 5335 Melrose Ave, Hollywood, 90038. Nancy S Kinney, Dir of Research
Holdings: Vols 3000
Notes: Incl 25 vertical file drawers of photographs, 30 bound periodical volumes, bound uniform regulations, insignia and decorations charts, 27 periodical subscriptions. Card file index on selected military uniform pictures from periodicals holdings. Collection can be used only by the customers of Western Costume Company. All other use is on a fee basis. Collection is non-circulating. Photocopying available.

MA —HARVARD UNIVERSITY LIBRARY, Cambridge, 02138.
Holdings: Cat

ON —METROPOLITAN TORONTO LIBRARY, History Dept, 789 Yonge St, Toronto, M4W 2G8, Can. Michael Pearson, Head
Holdings: Vols (11,000) Cat Phonorecords Audiotapes Microforms
Notes: Includes British army and navy lists and Prussian and French army lists from 18th century on; British regimental histories; works on military uniforms and insignia, especially European; Napoleonic and First and Second World Wars well represented.

INSKEEP FAMILY

NJ —GLASSBORO STATE COLLEGE, Savitz Library, Stewart Room, Glassboro, 08028. Clara Kirner, Special Collection Librn
Notes: Papers.

INSOLATION see Solar Radiation

INSPECTION OF SCHOOLS see School Management and Organization

INSTITUTE OF PACIFIC RELATIONS (IPR)

CA —HOOVER INSTITUTION ON WAR, REVOLUTION & PEACE, Stanford University, Stanford, 94305. Milorad M Drachkovitch, Archivist
Holdings: Mss Pix
Notes: Collection of correspondence, reports, memoranda, study papers, press releases, printed matter and photographs, 1925-1960, relating to the study of political, social and economic conditions in the Far East and of US foreign policy in the Far East by the American Council of the Institute of Pacific Relations, collected by Ray Lyman Wilbur. 21 ms boxes, 1 album, 1 envelope.

MI —MICHIGAN STATE UNIVERSITY, International Library, South and Southeast Asia Collection, East Lansing, 48824. Clinton Lockert, Bibliographer
Holdings: Vols (13,500) Cat Mss Maps Pix Audiotapes Microforms
Notes: Emphasis is upon South Vietnam (1955-1962), Thailand (1964-1968) and the Philippines (1898-). Complete holdings of MSU Vietnam Advisory Group, *Reports and Documents.* Extensive materials related to Thailand Project in Educational Planning, 1964-1968. Extensive holdings of the institute of Pacific Relations.

INSTITUTION MANAGEMENT

CA —LOS ANGELES PUBLIC LIBRARY, Science & Technology Dept, 630 W Fifth St, Los Angeles, 90071. Billie M Connor, Dept Head
Holdings: Vols 3500 Cat
Notes: Books on the cookery of all nationalities and ethnic groups. Strong collection of California cookery. Some early works in Spanish. Additional materials on wines and other beverages, quantity and institutional cookery, food technology, and special diets. Menu collection of approximately 1000 concentrates on Southern California.

CA —UNIVERSITY OF SOUTHERN CALIFORNIA, Crocker Business Library, Hoffman Hall, University Park, Los Angeles, 90007. Judith A Truelson, Head Librn
Holdings: Vols (100,000) Cat Microforms
Notes: The Roy P Crocker Library of Business Administration, located in Hoffman Hall, houses more than 100,000 volumes and regularly receives approximately 1500 trade, financial, economics, labor, and general business periodicals and newspapers. The areas of subject concentration include business economics, finance and investments, general management/management theory, international business, finance and management, marketing/food marketing, and quantitative business analysis.

IL —UNIVERSITY OF ILLINOIS, URBANA/CHAMPAIGN, Library, Home Economics Library, 314 Bevier Hall, Champaign, 61820. Barbara C Swain, Librn
Holdings: Vols Cat
Budget: $20,283
Notes: Foods and Nutrition.
See also entry under Restaurant and Hotel Management

IN —PURDUE UNIVERSITY LIBRARIES, Consumer & Family Sciences Library, Stone Hall W, West Lafayette, 47907. Emily Alward, Librn
Holdings: Vols (14,000) Cat

NY —CORNELL UNIVERSITY LIBRARIES, Collection of Regional History, Dept of Manuscripts and Univ Archives, Ithaca, 14853.
Notes: Incl records, 1929-66; correspondence, reports, minutes, plans, memoranda, blueprints, photos, and mimeographed matter concerning the Cornell University Department of Institution Management.

OH —OHIO STATE UNIVERSITY, Home Economics Library, Campbell Hall Rm 325, 1787 Neil Ave, Columbus, 43210. Neosha Mackey, Librn
Holdings: Vols (14,000) Cat Microforms
Notes: Separate catalog. Also, books catalog: *Catalog of the Home Economics Library* (Boston: G K Hall, 1976), 3 vols.

RI —BRYANT COLLEGE, Edith M Hodgson Memorial Library, Rte 7, Douglas Pike, Smithfield, 02917. John P Hannon, Dir
Holdings: Vols (103,000) Cat Phonorecords Audiotapes Videotapes 16mm Films Filmstrips Microforms
Budget: ($175,000)
Notes: Incl 6000 bound periodical vols, 250 phonorecords, 220 audiotapes, 120 videotapes, 30 16mm films, 150 filmstrips and 7500 microforms.

INSTITUTIONAL CHURCH see Church Work

INSTITUTIONS, ASSOCIATIONS, ETC. see Associations, Institutions, Etc.

INSTITUTIONS, CHARITABLE AND PHILANTHROPIC see Charitable Uses, Trusts, and Foundations

INSTITUTIONS, INTERNATIONAL see International Agencies; International Cooperation

INSTRUMENTAL MUSIC

CA —UNIVERSITY OF CALIFORNIA, BERKELEY, Humanities-Social Sciences

INSTRUMENTAL MUSIC (cont.)

Libraries, Music Library, 24 Morrison Hall, Berkeley, 94720. Michael A Keller, Head Librn
Holdings: Vols 115,000 Cat Mss Slides Microforms
Notes: The Library maintains an outstanding music reference collection. It is rich in primary source materials for research, particularly in the areas of opera, 18th-century instrumental music, music theory. Incl 20,000 sound recordings. See the following: Vincent Duckles and Minnie Elmer, *Thematic Catalogue of a Collection of 18th-Century Italian Instrumental Music in the Music Library of the University of Califonia, Berkeley* (Univ of California Press, 1963); Alan Curtis, "Musique classique francaise a Berkeley," in *Revue de* Musicologie, 56 (1970) pp 123-164. Minnie Elmer, *Autograph Manuscripts of Ernest Bloch at the University of California*; *Cum Notis Variorum, the Newsletter of the Music Library of the University of California* (Published 10 times annually since April 1976).

CA —CALIFORNIA STATE UNIVERSITY, HAYWARD, Library, Hayward, 94542. Melissa Rose, Dir
Holdings: Vols (15,986) Cat Phonorecords
Budget: ($21,000)
Notes: The score collection covers the entire range of instrumental and vocal concert music, incl collected works of various composers, and representative collections of hymnals, folk music, musical comedy, and some popular music. Sound recordings range from ethnomusicological collections to electronic music. Emphasis is on concert music, but there is a large collection of jazz and a selective collection of popular music. Separate catalog.

CA —OAKLAND PUBLIC LIBRARY, Art, Music and Recreation Section, 125 14 St, Oakland, 94612. Richard Colvig, Senior Librn
Holdings: Vols (5000) Cat Phonorecords Audiotapes
Budget: ($6700)
Notes: 10,000 scores, incl chamber music, instrumental music (piano and organ collections especially strong), miniature scores, opera scores, songs and song collections; 30,000 octavos (anthems and choral music of all kinds); 5000 books about music; 8000 phonorecords; and audiocassettes.

CA —PASADENA PUBLIC LIBRARY, Alice Coleman Batchelder Music Library, Reference Services, 285 E Walnut, Pasadena, 91101. Anne Cain, Principal Librn
Holdings: Vols (8012) Cat Pix
Notes: Separate record catalog of over 10, 000 phonorecords; over 4400 music scores. Special index of songs in collection. Over 150,000 pictures.

CT —YALE UNIVERSITY, Music Library, 98 Wall St, New Haven, 06520. Harold E Samuel, Librn
Holdings: Vols (118,000) Cat Mss Pix Phonorecords Audiotapes
Notes: Manuscript and archive collection comprising over 500 individual musical mss as well as the personal papers and musical mss of such American musicians and composers as Charles Ives, Carl Ruggles, Haratio Parker, Quincy Porter, Richard Donovan and David Stanley Smith, Leo Ornstein, Armin Loos, Duane Davidson, Alonzo Elliott, John Rosamund Johnson, Hope Leroy Baumgartner, Gustave Stoeckel, Hershy Kay, Virgil Thomson, Kurt Weill, Lotte Lenya, Lowell Mason, Parker Bailey, Henry Gilbert, Seymour Shifrin, Lehman Engel, Ernest Trow Carter, and Alec Templeton. Extensive Paul Hindemith Collection. Also ca 35,000 pieces of American sheet music, both instrumental and vocal as well as extensive holdings of 17th & 18th century American hymn books.

IL —UNIVERSITY OF ILLINOIS, URBANA/CHAMPAIGN, Library, Bands & Busch Instrument Collection, 1103 S Sixth St, Champaign, 61820. John Cranford, Librn
Holdings: Vols (8600) Cat Mss
Notes: Printed music, about 8400; plus the Sousa Library, 1900 vols, printed music about 1500; also the Clarke Library, 400 vols, printed music, approximately 375. No photocopying.

IL —CHICAGO PUBLIC LIBRARY, Music Section, Fine Arts Division, 78 E Washington St, Chicago, 60602. Rosalinda I Hack, Fine Arts Division Chief; Richard C Schwegel, Head, Music Section
Holdings: Vols 15,000 Cat
Notes: Circulating and reference collection of solo instrumental and chamber music with parts. Small collection of orchestral sets.

IN —INDIANA UNIVERSITY, Lilly Library, Seventh St, Bloomington, 47405. William R Cagle, Librn
Holdings: Cat
Notes: First editions. Also in the Starr American Sheet Music Collection; the Fritz Busch collection; etc. Partially cataloged.

MD —PEABODY CONSERVATORY LIBRARY, 21 E Mt Vernon Place, Baltimore, 21202. Edwin A Quist, Librn
Holdings: Vols 70,000 Cat Mss Pix Phonorecords Audiotapes Videotapes Microforms
Budget: $30,000
Notes: The Peabody Conservatory Library, formerly a part of the Peabody Institute Library (now the George Peabody Library of the Johns Hopkins University) supplies the library needs of the faculty and student body of the Peabody Conservatory of Music. While the collection has numerous research capabilities, it is basically a collection of musical scores. The entire history of Western music is represented through collected editions, monumental anthologies, study scores, performing editions and a large collection of books and music periodicals. This collection is supplemented by a listening facility containing 14,000 discs and an ensembles library containing scores and parts of orchestral, band and chorus works.

MA —HARVARD UNIVERSITY LIBRARY, Eda Kuhn Loeb Music Library, Isham Memorial Library of Early Instrumental Music, Harvard University Music Library Bldg, Cambridge, 02138. Michael Ochs, Librn
Holdings: Cat Microforms
Notes: Collection of Early Instrumental Music in microform. See *Harvard Library* Bulletin, VI (1952), 376-380.

MI —DETROIT PUBLIC LIBRARY, Music & Performing Arts Dept, 5201 Woodward, Detroit, 48202. Agatha Pfeiffer Kalkanis, Chief
Holdings: Vols 19,000 Cat Mss Pix Microforms
Notes: Also incl (77,000) scores. General collection intended for practical use in performance and for scholarly research. Good working collection of bibliographies, thematic catalogs, dictionaries and encyclopedias, periodical indexes. Many sets of collected works, monumental editions, historical anthologies. Good representation of opera and operetta, art song and folk song, solo instrumental literature and chamber music in practical editions. 2575 titles of choral music, chiefly sacred, for use by choirs. 17,000 titles of popular sheet music, uncataloged but thoroughly indexed. Considerable recent holdings of books and periodicals in foreign languages. Special collections of black and local materials. 25, 000 recordings and extensive discographical literature. Collection of publishers' trade catalogs.

NY —NEW YORK PUBLIC LIBRARY, Music Div, 111 Amsterdam Ave, New York, 10023. Frank C Campbell, Chief

OH —CLEVELAND PUBLIC LIBRARY, Fine Arts and Special Collections Department, 325 Superior Ave, Cleveland, 44114. Alice N Loranth, Head
Holdings: Vols (21,350) Cat
Notes: Incl part sets for chamber music and orchestral music, indexed by instrumentation or form. Collected works editions of major composers or periods in music. Study scores, piano, violin, organ, and other instrumental music. Also incl 3080 dance band orchestrations.

PA —FREE LIBRARY OF PHILADELPHIA, Music Dept, Drinker Library of Choral Music, Logan Sq, Philadelphia, 19103. Frederick James Kent, Head
Holdings: Cat Mss
Budget: ($27,754)
Notes: The collection has approx 18,000 sets of chamber music parts for ensembles.

RI —BROWN UNIVERSITY, John Hay Library, 20 Prospect St, Providence, 02912. Mark N Brown, Cur Mss
Holdings: Uncat
Notes: The Sheet Music Collection concentrates on music of American imprint, incl 170,000 vocal pieces filed by title, plus 80,000 instrumental pieces filed by composer. Major strengths are in 19th century music, especially prior to 1830; Civil War music, both Union and Confederate; lithographic covers; World War I songs; political campaign music; and band music. An additional 100,000 pieces of American and European imprint remain unprocessed.

WA —UNIVERSITY OF WASHINGTON LIBRARIES, Music Library, DN-10, Seattle, 98195. David A Wood, Music Librn
Budget: ($7373)
Notes: The Melvin Harris Collection of pre-LP recordings of brass and woodwind music, 1,700 items.

INSTRUMENTAL MUSIC—INSTRUCTION AND STUDY

CA —SAN DIEGO PUBLIC LIBRARY, Art, Music & Recreation Sect, 820 E St, San Diego, 92101. Barbara A Tuhill, Supvr
Holdings: Cat
Notes: Score collection of 17,000 pieces covers all types of music incl religious works, opera scores, musical plays, miniature scores. Complete works of Bach, Berlioz, Beethoven, Mozart, and others are added as published in German reprint. Also, thematic indexes, and study and instructions for playing various musical instruments. General circulation.

INSTRUMENTATION (MECHANICAL)

AR —UNIVERSITY OF ARKANSAS, Technology Campus Library, 1201 McAlmont St, PO Box 3017, Little Rock, 72203. Brent Nelson, Librn
Holdings: Vols (20,849) Cat Slides Microforms
Budget: ($35,000)

CA —BECKMAN INSTRUMENTS, Research Library, 2500 Harbor Blvd, Fullerton, 92634. Jean R Miller, Librn
Holdings: Vols (7000) Cat Slides Audiotapes Videotapes Microforms
Budget: ($9000)
Notes: Strong collection in scientific and analytic instrumentation, electrochemistry, analytical chemistry, optics and spectroscopy, chromatography, clinical chemistry and biochemistry.

PA —ROCKWELL INTERNATIONAL, General Industries Operations, Technical Information Center, 400 N Lexington Ave, Pittsburgh, 15208. Kathleen H Witkowski, Library Coordr
Holdings: Vols Cat Microforms Mss Documents Periodicals VF
Budget: ($5100)

INSTRUMENTS, ASTRONAUTICAL see Astronautical Instruments

INSTRUMENTS, ELECTRIC see Electric Apparatus and Appliances

INSTRUMENTS, ASTRONOMICAL see Astronomical Instruments

INSTRUMENTS, ELECTRONIC see Electronic Instruments

INSTRUMENTS, MEDICAL see Medical Instruments and Apparatus

INSTRUMENTS, MUSICAL see Musical Instruments

INSTRUMENTS, OPTICAL see Optical Instruments

INSTRUMENTS, PERCUSSION see Percussion Instruments and Music

INSTRUMENTS, SCIENTIFIC see Scientific Instruments and Apparatus

INSTRUMENTS, WIND see Wind Instruments

INSTRUMENTS AND INSTRUMENT MAKERS, MUSIC see Musical Instruments; Musical Instruments—Makers

INSULL, SAMUEL

IL —LOYOLA UNIVERSITY OF CHICAGO, E M Cudahy Memorial Library, 6525 N

INSULL, SAMUEL (cont.)

Sheridan Rd, Chicago, 60626.
Holdings: Mss
Notes: General correspondence and personal papers. Collection also incl papers of the Middle West Utilities Company 1913-1933, and misc materials from other Samuel Insull controlled enterprises. Transcript of United States vs Insull and his memoirs are also available. To be used under the direct supervision of the archivist at all times.

INSURANCE

CA —ALAMEDA COUNTY LIBRARY SYSTEM, Business & Government Library, 2201 Broadway, Oakland, 94612. David Lewallen, Manager
Holdings: Vols (10,000) Cat Maps Microforms
Budget: ($50,000)

CT —AETNA LIFE & CASUALTY, Corporate Data Processing Library, 151 Farmington Ave, Hartford, 06156. Kathryn Porter, Chief Librn
Holdings: Vols 1500

CT —HARTFORD INSURANCE GROUP, Loss Control Dept Library, Hartford Plaza, Hartford, 06115. Laurice Klemarczyk, Librn
Holdings: Vols (2000) Cat

CT —PHOENIX MUTUAL LIFE INSURANCE COMPANY, Library, One American Row, Hartford, 06115. Margaret Colton, Librn
Holdings: Vols (15,000) Cat

CT —TRAVELERS INSURANCE CO, Corporate Library, One Tower Sq, Hartford, 06115. Margaret Orloske, Librn
Holdings: Vols 40,000 Cat
Budget: $20,000
Notes: Information on all lines of insurance. Open to the outside users by appointment.

CT —UNIVERSITY OF CONNECTICUT, HARTFORD, School of Business Administration, Library, 39 Woodland St, Hartford, 06105.
Holdings: Vols (17,000) Cat Audiotapes Microforms
Notes: Incl 8 vertical file drawers of pamphlets, etc; 60 of annual reports.

IL —ILLINOIS FARM BUREAU LIBRARY, 1701 Towanda Ave, PO Box 1901, Bloomington, 61701. Rue E Olson, Librn
Holdings: Vols (24,000) Cat Microforms
Budget: ($25,000)
Notes: Emphasis on Illinois.

IL —KEMPER INSURANCE LIBRARY, Long Grove, 60049. Evelyn Giannini, Librn
Holdings: Vols 4000 Cat

MA —MASSACHUSETTS INSTITUTE OF TECHNOLOGY, Institute Archives, Special Collections, Cambridge, 02139.
Notes: Papers of John Ripley Freeman, a hydraulic engineer, President of Associated Factory Mutual Fire Insurance Companies, and a consulting engineer. Collection primarily documents his activities as a consultant on hydraulics projects in the United States, Canada, China, Columbia, Mexico and Panama. Also, his work on the hydraulics of fire prevention, safety precautions for theaters, and seismology; his promotion of the National Hydraulics Laboratory and of European engineering practices; his involvement with the Engineering Foundation, the National Bureau of Standards, and the National Research Council; and his investments in mining, manufacturing, and land speculation. Unpublished finding aid available in Archives.

NY —COLLEGE OF INSURANCE, Library, 123 William St, New York, 10038. Donald Carson, Chief Librn
Holdings: Vols (52,543) Cat Pix
Budget: ($50,000)
Notes: Collection contains 53,322 pieces of VF material. Included in the collection are 6374 bound vols of US and foreign periodicals dating back to 19th century; laws and regulations of the insurance departments of all 50 states, as well as those of Canada and other foreign countries; 16th century treatise on marine insurance.

NY —NEW YORK PUBLIC LIBRARY, Research Libraries, Economic & Public Affairs Div, Fifth Ave & 42 St, New York, 10018. Edward DiRoma, Chief
Holdings: Vols (1,500,000) Cat Microforms

NC —GREENSBORO PUBLIC LIBRARY, Business Library, 201 Greene St, Drawer X-4, Greensboro, 27402. Lebby B Lamb, Business Librn
Holdings: Vols (6000) Cat Microforms
Budget: ($12,000)

OH —AKRON-SUMMIT COUNTY PUBLIC LIBRARY, Business, Labor & Government Div, 55 S Main St, Akron, 44326. William G Johnson, Head
Holdings: Vols (10,000) Cat Microforms
Budget: ($20,000)

OH —CLEVELAND PUBLIC LIBRARY, Business, Economics and Labor Department, 325 Superior Ave, Cleveland, 44114. Joan Sorger, Head
Holdings: Cat
Notes: Particulary comprehensive for life insurance: manuals, directories, underwriters' and buyers' guides, tax and legal aspects, association proceedings, annual reports of state departments of insurance.

PA —UNIVERSITY OF PENNSYLVANIA, Lippincott Library of the Wharton School, Philadelphia, 19104. Michael Halperin, Librn
Holdings: Cat
Notes: Long files of annual reports of insurance commissions for several states. Annual reports from all major US insurance companies. Extensive collection of insurance company manuals and insurance annuals and handbooks.

TX —ECTOR COUNTY LIBRARY, Department of Business and Technology, 321 W 5th St, Odessa, 79760. Pat Jones, Dept Head
Holdings: Vols 100 Cat VF

TX —UNITED SERVICES AUTOMOBILE ASSOCIATION, Library, USAA Bldg, San Antonio, 78288. Fran Day, Librn
Holdings: Vols (3600) Cat
Notes: Principally property and casualty insurance. 300 subscriptions.

WI —UNIVERSITY OF WISCONSIN, MILWAUKEE, Library, Box 604, Milwaukee, 53201. William C Roselle, Dir
Holdings: Cat Microforms
Notes: Wisonsin Legislative Reference Bureau Clippings File. Special strength in a collection mostly of Wisconsin emphasis. 440 reels of 16mm microfilm. A subject-chronological arrangement (approximately 1200 subjects covering the years from the 1890s through 1970) of pamphlets and a variety of fugitive materials and of clippings from national and Wisconsin newspapers, popular magazines and scholarly journals, and federal, state, and local government documents.

WI —WAUSAU INSURANCE COMPANIES, Library, 2000 Westwood Dr, Wausau, 54401. Douglas Ley, Dir of Library Services; Donna Nuernberg, Ref Librn
Holdings: Vols (15,000) Cat
Budget: $130,000
Notes: Library also maintains corporate history collection of materials dating from 1911.

ON —REED STENHOUSE, Research Dept, PO Box 250, T-D Centre, Toronto, M5K 1J6, Can. G R E Bromwich, VP & Mgr Research Dept
Holdings: Vols 400 Cat
Notes: All types of insurance covered incl unusual ones. Considerable quantity of material on law related to insurance. Extensive clipping and pamphlet files.

INSURANCE—HISTORY

MA —INSURANCE LIBRARY ASSOCIATION OF BOSTON, 156 State St, Boston, 02109. Jean Lucey, Head Librn
Holdings: Vols (15,000) Cat Maps Pix
Budget: ($63,000)
Notes: Also rare historical source material relating to early insurance.

MA —NORTHEASTERN UNIVERSITY LIBRARIES, Special Collections, 360 Huntington Ave, Boston, 02115. Nieves F Farin, Head Collection Development Librn
Holdings: Vols 400
Notes: Hardy Insurance Collection. 200 items covering history of insurance, 1790-1945.

NH —PORTSMOUTH ATHENAEUM, 9 Market Sq, Box 848, Portsmouth, 03801. Joseph P Copley, Cur
Holdings: Vols Cat Mss
Notes: Incl Larkin Papers, 1758-1798 (235 items); papers of Daniel and John Peirce, ca 1730-1800 (115 items); and papers of NH Fire and Marine Insurance Co, 1803-1823 (1800 items). Collection relates to ships, insurances; War of 1812 claims; all contain business transactions, commerce, shipping, claims.

NY —COLLEGE OF INSURANCE, Library, 123 William St, New York, 10038. Donald Carson, Chief Librn
Holdings: Vols (52,543) Cat Pix
Budget: ($50,000)
Notes: Collection contains 53,322 pieces of VF material. Included in the collection are 6374 bound vols of US and foreign periodicals dating back to 19th century; laws and regulations of the insurance departments of all 50 states, as well as those of Canada and other foreign countries; 16th century treatise on marine insurance.

UT —UNIVERSITY OF UTAH, Marriott Library, Special Collections, Salt Lake City, 84112. Gregory C Thompson, Cur
Notes: Approx 1000 maps, historical of Utah, incl Sanborn Maps.

INSURANCE—ILLINOIS

IL —CENTER FOR RESEARCH LIBRARIES, 6050 S Kenwood Ave, Chicago, 60637. Donald B Simpson, Dir; Esther Smith, Collection Development Librn
Holdings: Vols 27,000 Uncat
Notes: Comprises annual reports submitted to the State Department of Insurance by companies licensed to do business in Illinois.

INSURANCE—NEW YORK (CITY)

NY —COLUMBIA UNIVERSITY LIBRARIES, Rare Book & Manuscript Library, 801 Butler Library, 535 W 114 St, New York, 10027. Kenneth A Lohf, Librn
Notes: More than 32,000 items documenting the rise of William Russell Grace's shipping business and other materials relating to his career as mayor of New York. Incl records and correspondence relating to all aspects of the shipping business in New York and South America, mining interest in Peru and Chile, and transportation in Costa Rica and Nicaragua. Family memorabilia and photographs, materials concerning New York Politics, banking and insurance, real estate interests and Catholic charities, and letters from Chester A Arthur, John Jacob Astor, Andrew Carnegie, Grover Cleveland, Hamilton Fish, John Hay and J Pierpont Morgan. Restricted use.

INSURANCE—MATHEMATICS

MI —UNIVERSITY OF MICHIGAN, Mathematics Library, 3027 Angell Hall, Ann Arbor, 48109. John W Weigel II, Physical Sciences Librn
Holdings: Vols 2000 Cat
Budget: $1300

INSURANCE—RISK see Risk (Insurance)

INSURANCE, ACCIDENT

CT —TRAVELERS INSURANCE CO, Corporate Library, One Tower Sq, Hartford, 06115. Margaret Orloske, Librn
Notes: Information on all lines of insurance. Open to the outside users by appointment.

INSURANCE, AUTOMOBILE

MI —UNIVERSITY OF MICHIGAN, Transportation Research Institute, Library, 2901 Baxter Rd, Ann Arbor, 48109. Ann C Grimm, Librn
Holdings: Vols (57,000) Cat Mss Maps Pix Slides Microforms
Budget: ($25,000)
Notes: Books, periodicals, documents, reports, patents, etc. Incl the C Donald Kennedy Collection (separate card catalog).

INSURANCE, CASUALTY

CA —FIREMAN'S FUND INSURANCE LIBRARY, PO Box 777, Novato, 94998.
Holdings: Cat

MA —INSURANCE LIBRARY ASSOCIATION OF BOSTON, 156 State St, Boston, 02109. Jean Lucey, Head Librn
Holdings: Vols (15,000) Cat Maps Pix
Budget: ($63,000)
Notes: Also rare historical source material relating to early insurance.

TX —UNITED SERVICES AUTOMOBILE ASSOCIATION, Library, USAA Bldg, San Antonio, 78288. Fran Day, Librn
Holdings: Vols (3600) Cat
Notes: Principally property and casualty insurance. 300 subscriptions.

INSURANCE, FIRE

OH —OHIO STATE UNIVERSITY, Commerce Library, Columbus, 43210.
Notes: 18 British, 10 American and 8 German insurance firemarks, with 23 from fifteen other countries.

INSURANCE, FIRE—MAPS AND SURVEYS

†CA —CALIFORNIA STATE UNIVERSITY, NORTHRIDGE, Map Library, Northridge, 91324.

DC —LIBRARY OF CONGRESS, Geography and Map Division, Washington, 20540. John A Wolter, Chief
Holdings: Cat Mss Maps Pix Slides Microforms
See also entry under Maps and Atlases - Collections.

GA —UNIVERSITY OF GEORGIA, Libraries, Map Collection, Athens, 30602. John Sutherland, Cur of Maps
Holdings: Cat
Notes: Collection contains 291,165 cataloged maps and 192,068 aerial photographs, specializing in Georgia, Southeast US, Central and South America, and Europe. Major subject specializations are topography, geology, soils and vegetation. Special cartographic collection of Sanborn Fire Insurance Maps (7000 sheets).

KY —UNIVERSITY OF KENTUCKY, Margaret I King Library, Map Collection, Lexington, 40506. Gwen Curtis, Head
Holdings: Maps Microforms Uncat
Notes: Collection of Sanborn Insurance Maps of Kentucky cities, 99 percent complete.

PA —PENNSYLVANIA STATE UNIVERSITY, Fred Lewis Pattee Library, Maps Section, University Park, 16802. Karl Proehl, Head
Holdings: Vols (274,000) Maps
Budget: ($3000)
Notes: Depositories for US Geological Survey topographic maps; Defense mapping agency topographic maps and nautical charts; National Ocean Survey nautical and aeronautical charts; Canadian topographic maps. Sanborn Fire Insurance maps for Pennsylvania villages and towns. General coverage for foreign countries--topographic and thematic maps. Map catalog by area and subdivided by subject; atlas catalog by author-title and area-subject; shelf list catalogs for maps and atlases. See *Pennsylvania Maps and Atlases in The Pennsylvania State University Libraries*, by Ruth M Miller (Pennsylvania State University Libraries, 1972. 682 pp).

ON —UNIVERSITY OF TORONTO, Thomas Fisher Rare Book Library, 120 Saint George St, Toronto, M5S 1A5, Can. Richard G Landon, Head
Notes: A large group of fire insurance plans for cities, town, and villages across Canada, 1876-1973. About 1200 items.

INSURANCE, FIRE—OFFICE MARKS see Fire Marks

INSURANCE, HEALTH

CA —FIREMAN'S FUND INSURANCE LIBRARY, PO Box 777, Novato, 94998.
Holdings: Cat

CA —STANFORD UNIVERSITY LIBRARIES, Lane Medical Library, Stanford University, Medical Center, Stanford, 94305. Peter Stangl, Librn
Notes: Phillip King Brown's papers on health insurance and socialized medicine.

CA —BLUE CROSS OF SOUTHERN CALIFORNIA, Library, PO Box 70,000, Van Nuys, 91470. Frances Linke, Head Librn
Holdings: Vols (9500) Cat Mss Slides Audio Tapes Videotapes 16mm Films Filmstrips Microforms
Budget: ($19,000)
Notes: Strong law collection.

CO —MEDICAL GROUP MANAGEMENT ASSOCIATION, Information Service, 1355 S Colorado Blvd, Suite 900, Denver, 80222. Barbara V Hamilton, Dir; Linda S Elinoff, Asst Dir
Holdings: Vols (3000) Cat
Budget: ($7825)
Notes: Administration of medical group practices and health maintainance organization. Also, the professional papers of the Fellows of the American College of Medical Group Administrators.

DC —AMERICAN COUNCIL OF LIFE INSURANCE & HEALTH INSURANCE ASSOCIATION OF AMERICA, General Library, 1850 K St, NW, Washington, 20006. Kim Lowry, Head Librn
Holdings: Vols (5000) Cat
Notes: Library shared by the two organizations. Reference service to the public. Incl 400 periodicals.

MD —US SOCIAL SECURITY ADMINISTRATION, Library, Library Information & Graphics Services Branch, Altmeyer Bldg Rm 571, 6401 Security Blvd, Baltimore, 21235. Rowena S Sadler, Chief
Holdings: Vols Cat
Notes: All phases of social insurance incl OASI pensions, welfare health insurance and medical economics.

MA —INSURANCE LIBRARY ASSOCIATION OF BOSTON, 156 State St, Boston, 02109. Jean Lucey, Head Librn
Holdings: Vols (15,000) Cat Maps Pix
Budget: ($63,000)
Notes: Also collect information on life insurance and employee benefit planning.

MN —NORTHWESTERN NATIONAL LIFE INSURANCE CO, Library, Box 20, Minneapolis, 55440. Beth Soener, Librn
Holdings: Vols (8000) Cat
Notes: Incl a small collection of annuities and life insurance published 1731-1864. Also materials about employee benefits.

NE —WOODMEN ACCIDENT & LIFE CO, Library, 1526 K St, PO Box 82288, Lincoln, 68501. Virgene Sloan, Librn
Holdings: Vols (3000) Cat 16mm Films Filmstrips
Budget: ($43,000)
Notes: No photocopying.

NY —UNITED HOSPITAL FUND OF NEW YORK, Library, 3 E 54th St, New York, 10022. Christine Bahr, Librn
Holdings: Vols (4000) Cat Mss Maps Pix
Notes: Incl 100 journal titles.

INSURANCE, LIFE

CA —FIREMAN'S FUND INSURANCE LIBRARY, PO Box 777, Novato, 94998.
Holdings: Cat

CT —LIFE INSURANCE MARKETING & RESEARCH ASSOCIATION, Library, 170 Sigourney St, PO Box 208, Hartford, 06141. William J Mortimer, Mgr, Library and Reference Services
Holdings: Vols 5000 Cat Audiotapes
Budget: ($10,000)
Notes: Incl 150-drawer vertical file on life insurance marketing and 250 audiotapes.

CT —PHOENIX MUTUAL LIFE INSURANCE COMPANY, Library, One American Row, Hartford, 06115. Margaret Colton, Librn
Holdings: Vols (15,000) Cat

DC —AMERICAN COUNCIL OF LIFE INSURANCE & HEALTH INSURANCE ASSOCIATION OF AMERICA, General Library, 1850 K St, NW, Washington, 20006. Kim Lowry, Head Librn
Holdings: Vols (5000) Cat
Notes: Library shared by the two organizations. Reference service to the public. Incl 400 periodicals.

MA —INSURANCE LIBRARY ASSOCIATION OF BOSTON, 156 State St, Boston, 02109. Jean Lucey, Head Librn
Holdings: Vols (15,000) Cat Maps Pix
Budget: ($63,000)
Notes: Also collect information on health insurance and employee benefit planning.

MA —MASSACHUSETTS MUTUAL LIFE INSURANCE CO, Library, 1295 State St, Springfield, 01111. Yvette Jensen, Librn
Holdings: Vols 225 Cat

MN —NORTHWESTERN NATIONAL LIFE INSURANCE CO, Library, Box 20, Minneapolis, 55440. Beth Soener, Librn
Holdings: Vols (8000) Cat
Notes: Incl a small collection of annuities and life insurance published 1731-1864. Also materials about employee benefits.

NY —MUTUAL LIFE INSURANCE CO OF NEW YORK, Corporate Library, 1740 Broadway, New York, 10028. Marion Koshar, Librn
Holdings: Vols (6000) Cat Periodicals Microforms
Notes: Incl Mutual's company history and archives; over 200 periodical titles.

OH —CLEVELAND PUBLIC LIBRARY, Business, Economics and Labor Department, 325 Superior Ave, Cleveland, 44114. Joan Sorger, Head
Holdings: Cat
Notes: Particulary comprehensive for life insurance: manuals, directories, underwriters' and buyers' guides, tax and legal aspects, association proceedings, annual reports of state departments of insurance.

VT —NATIONAL LIFE INSURANCE CO LIBRARY, Montpelier, 05602. Saba L Foster, Chief Librn
Holdings: Vols 6250 Cat Periodicals Mss Maps Pix
Budget: $58,100
Notes: Incl general reference, business, and government documents; 176 periodicals.

INSURANCE, MARINE

NH —PORTSMOUTH ATHENAEUM, 9 Market Sq, Box 848, Portsmouth, 03801. Joseph P Copley, Cur
Holdings: Vols Cat Mss
Notes: Incl Larkin Papers, 1758-1798 (235 items); papers of Daniel and John Peirce, ca 1730-1800 (115 items); and papers of NH Fire and Marine Insurance Co, 1803-1823 (1800 items). Collection relates to ships, insurances; War of 1812 claims; all contain business transactions, commerce, shipping, claims.

NY —COLLEGE OF INSURANCE, Library, 123 William St, New York, 10038. Donald Carson, Chief Librn
Holdings: Vols (52,543) Cat Pix
Budget: ($50,000)
Notes: Collection contains 53,522 pieces of VF material. Included in the collection are 6374 bound vols of US and foreign periodicals dating back to 19th century; laws and regulations of the insurance departments of all 50 states, as well as those of Canada and other foreign countries; 16th century treatise on marine insurance.

INSURANCE, MUTUAL see Insurance

INSURANCE, POSTAL LIFE see Insurance, Life

INSURANCE, PROPERTY

CA —FIREMAN'S FUND INSURANCE LIBRARY, PO Box 777, Novato, 94998.
Holdings: Cat

CT —HARTFORD INSURANCE GROUP, Loss Control Dept Library, Hartford Plaza, Hartford, 06115. Laurice Klemarczyk, Librn
Holdings: Vols (2000) Cat

MA —INSURANCE LIBRARY ASSOCIATION OF BOSTON, 156 State St, Boston, 02109. Jean Lucey, Head Librn
Holdings: Vols (15,000) Cat Maps Pix
Budget: ($63,000)
Notes: Also rare historical source material relating to early insurance.

INSURANCE, PROPERTY (cont.)

TX —UNITED SERVICES AUTOMOBILE ASSOCIATION, Library, USAA Bldg, San Antonio, 78288. Fran Day, Librn
Holdings: Vols (3000) Cat Microforms
Budget: ($10,000)
Notes: Principally property and casualty insurance.

INSURANCE, SICKNESS see Insurance, Health

INSURANCE, SOCIAL

DC —INTERNATIONAL LABOR ORGANIZATION, International Labor Office, Washington Branch Library, 1750 New York Ave NW, Rm 330, Washington, 20006. Karen J Mark, Librn
Holdings: Vols (13,500) Cat Pix 16mm Films Monographs
Notes: Wide range of titles dealing with worldwide labor and social matters. The library contains ILO publications and documentation only, dating back to 1919. Also, a collection of ILO films and photos. See *Subject Guide to Publications of the ILO, 1919-1964* and *ILO Catalogue of Publications in Print, 1982* (ILO).

FL —FLORIDA STATE UNIVERSITY, Robert Manning Strozier Library, Special Collections Dept, Tallahassee, 32306. Opal M Free, Head, Special Collections
Notes: The official papers, documents, photographs, recordings, and memorabilia of US Representative Claude Pepper. Incl the papers, photographs, and memorabilia of his wife, Mildred Irene Webster Pepper (706, 536 items).

MD —US SOCIAL SECURITY ADMINISTRATION, Library, Library Information & Graphics Services Branch, Altmeyer Bldg Rm 571, 6401 Security Blvd, Baltimore, 21235. Rowena S Sadler, Chief
Holdings: Vols Cat
Notes: All phases of social insurance incl OASI pensions, welfare health insurance and medical economics.

MI —INSTITUTE OF GERONTOLOGY, Gerontology Library, University of Michigan, 300 N Ingalls St, Ann Arbor, 48109. Willie M Edwards, Librn
Holdings: Vols (10,000) Cat Pix Audiotapes 16mm Films
Notes: All subjects concerning the aged and aging in the US, Western Europe and strong emphasis on Great Britain. On VF (24) unpublished research papers, newsletters from elderly association, centers on aging.

NY —COLUMBIA UNIVERSITY LIBRARIES, Whitney M Young Jr Memorial Library of Social Work, 420 W 118 St, New York, 10027. Tyrone Cannon, Librn
Holdings: Vols (118,646) Cat
Notes: The collection covers the history and philosophy of social work, social work methodology, and all aspects of social welfare services, especially child welfare, mental hygiene, correction, the aging, social security and medical care, rehabilitation, aspects and problems of civil rights and automation. There is also a substantial representation of literature in psychiatry and the behavioral and social sciences. The reference section includes more than 419 periodicals, publications issued by voluntary agencies, government publications, doctoral dissertations and masters' essays in the field and standard reference works. Reference service is available.

NY —UNIVERSITY OF ROCHESTER, Rush Rhees Library, Department of Rare Books and Special Collections, Rochester, 14627. Peter Dzwonkoski, Librn
Holdings: Cat Mss
Notes: Material related to the creation, passage, and subsequent amendments to the Social Security Act of 1935; also correspondence, printed material, and reports related to Folsom's career as an Eastman Kodak executive, Under Secretary of the Treasury (1953-55), and Secretary of Health, Education, and Welfare (1955-58).

ON —CANADA, DEPT OF EMPLOYMENT & IMMIGRATION LIBRARY, Ottawa, K1A 0J9, Can. P E Sunder-Raj, Dir Library Services
Holdings: Vols (35,000)// Cat

PQ —CENTRE DE DOCUMENTATION, REGIE DES RENTES DU QUEBEC, CP 5200, Quebec, G1K 7S9, Can. Michel Dupuis, Bibliothecaine en Chef; Nicole Paquin, Bibliotechnicienne
Holdings: Vols 5000 Cat
Budget: $60,500
Notes: Social security, incl private pension plans literature. 80 vertical file drawers.

INSURANCE, STATE AND COMPULSORY see Insurance, Social

INSURANCE, UNEMPLOYMENT

ON —CANADA, DEPT OF EMPLOYMENT & IMMIGRATION LIBRARY, Ottawa, K1A 0J9, Can. P E Sunder-Raj, Dir Library Services
Holdings: Vols (35,000)// Cat

INSURANCE, WORKERS see Insurance, Social

INSURANCE LAW

ON —REED STENHOUSE, Research Dept, PO Box 250, T-D Centre, Toronto, M5K 1J6, Can. G R E Bromwich, VP & Mgr Research Dept
Holdings: Vols 400 Cat
Notes: All types of insurance covered incl unusual ones. Considerable quantity of material on law related to insurance. Extensive clipping and pamphlet files.

INSURANCE PERIODICALS see Periodicals, Insurance

INSURRECTIONS see Revolutions

INTAGLIOS

NY —NEW YORK PUBLIC LIBRARY, Rare Books and Manuscripts Div, Fifth Ave & 42 St, New York, 10018. William L Joyce, Asst Dir; Susan E Davis, Cur of Mss
Holdings: Cat Mss

INTEGRATED CIRCUITS

AZ —MOTOROLA INC, Technical Library, 2200 W Broadway, Mesa, 85202. Denise Ashford, Managing Sr Librn
Holdings: Vols (5500) Cat Maps

INTEGRATED DATA PROCESSING see Electronic Data Processing

INTEGRATION, EUROPEAN see European Integration

INTEGRATION, INTERNATIONAL ECONOMIC see International Economic Integration

INTEGRATION, RACIAL see Segregation and Desegregation

INTEGRATION, SOCIAL see Social Integration

INTELLECT

NY —STATE UNIVERSITY OF NEW YORK, COLLEGE AT BUFFALO, E H Butler Library, 1300 Elmwood Ave, Buffalo, 14222. Jerome Earley, Librn
Notes: The work of J P Guilford, on microfilm, relating to his research on the Structure of the Intellect (SOI) model. 200 reels of microfilm contain the tests, answer sheets, and supporting data for his SOI theory. Corresponds to the Psychological Laboratory Reports at UCLA.

NY —NEW YORK PUBLIC LIBRARY, Research Libraries, General Research Division, Fifth Ave & 42 St, New York, 10018. Rodney Phillips, Chief
Notes: See *Bibliographic Guide to Psychology, 1976* (Boston: G K Hall, 1977). Incl publications cataloged during the year, with additional entries from MARC tapes.

INTELLECTUAL FREEDOM see Censorship

INTELLECTUAL LIFE

CA —HOOVER INSTITUTION ON WAR, REVOLUTION & PEACE, Stanford University, Stanford, 94305. Milorad M Drachkovitch, Archivist
Holdings: Mss
Notes: Records of Aid Refugee Chinese Intellectuals (ARCI), a private US relief organization, incl correspondence, reports, minutes of meetings, financial records and photographs, 1952-1970, relating to ARCI relief work for Chinese refugees. 44 ms boxes, 3 albums.

INTELLECTUAL PROPERTY see Copyright; Inventions and Inventors

INTELLIGENCE see Intellect

INTELLIGENCE, ARTIFICIAL see Artificial Intelligence

INTELLIGENCE LEVELS—TESTING see Mental Tests

INTELLIGENCE OF ANIMALS see Animal Intelligence

INTELLIGENCE SERVICE

CA —HARVEY G WOLFE LIBRARY, PO Box 3514, Grand Central Sta, Glendale, 91201. Douglas L Evans, Librn
Holdings: Vols (6580) Mss Maps Pix
Budget: ($4500)
Notes: Main emphasis on espionage, military intelligence, and sabotage.

DC —GEORGETOWN UNIVERSITY, Library, Special Collections Div, 37 & O Sts NW, Washington, 20057. George M Barringer, Special Collections Librn; Nicholas B Sheetz, Mss Librn
Holdings: Cat
Notes: The Russell J Bowen Collection on Intelligence, Security, and Covert Activities. The collection extends over several hundred years, and incl early wars and conflicts in Europe, the American Revolutionary era, the Civil War in the United States, the World Wars, and other events. Intelligence and espionage activities during World War II, the Cold War, and recent events are extensively documented. See *Scholar's Guide to Intelligence Literature: Bibliography of the Russell J Bowen Collection* (1983).

INTEMPERANCE see Alcoholism; Temperance

INTENSIVE CARE, MEDICAL

MD —NATIONAL LIBRARY OF MEDICINE, 8600 Rockville Pike, Bethesda, 20209. Harold M Schoolinam, Actg Dir
Budget: ($46,400)

INTER-ALLIED FOOD COUNCIL, 1918

CA —HOOVER INSTITUTION ON WAR, REVOLUTION & PEACE, Stanford University, Stanford, 94305. Milorad M Drachkovitch, Archivist
Holdings: // Mss
Notes: Records of the Inter-Allied Food Council, 1918, relating to the work of the Council in Great Britain, France, Italy, and the US. 21 boxes. Unpublished register is available in repository.

INTER-ALLIED GAMES

ON —UNIVERSITY OF WESTERN ONTARIO, Dept of Special Collections, London, N6A 5B9, Can. Beth Miller, Librn
Notes: Large and important collection on

INTER-ALLIED GAMES (cont.)

Canadian participation in pre-Olympic and other Game series. Incl minutes of annual meetings of the Athletic Union of Canada, 1884-1898, 1908-1954.

INTER-AMERICAN ASSOCIATION FOR DEMOCRACY AND FREEDOM

NJ —RUTGERS, THE STATE UNIVERSITY OF NEW JERSEY, Alexander Library, Special Collections and Archives, College Ave & Huntington St, New Brunswick, 08903. Ronald L Becker, Cur of Manuscripts and Rare Books
Notes: Papers of the Inter-American Association for Democracy and Freedom, the Pan American Women's Association, and their director, Frances Grant (1930-). Also papers of Robert Alexander, incl transcripts of several thousand interviews with Latin American political leaders, students, etc (1950-).

INTER-AMERICAN RELATIONS see Pan-Americanism

INTERGOVERNMENTAL RELATIONS

KY —COUNCIL OF STATE GOVERNMENTS, States Information Center, Iron Works Pike, PO Box 11910, Lexington, 40578. Sue Stoltz, Dir
Holdings: Vols 18,000 Cat
Notes: State government administration and procedures. Major portion of collection is research reports of state legislatures, other state government agencies, and current affairs topics of interest to state governments. Incl 200 current journals.

ON —ONTARIO MINISTRY OF TREASURY & ECONOMICS, Library Services, Frost Bldg N, Queen's Park, Toronto, M7A 1Y8, Can. Barbara Weatherhead, Head Librn
Holdings: Vols (100,000) Cat Microforms
Budget: ($76,500)
Notes: Index to Ontario regulations.

INTERGROUP RELATIONS

IL —ILLINOIS STATE UNIVERSITY, Milner Library, Dept of Special Collections, Normal, 61761. Robert Sokan, Librn
Holdings: Vols 2100 // Uncat
Notes: Sigmund Livingston Collection on Intergroup Relations, 1944 to the present. The material is divided into subject headings which contain pamphlets, newsletters and commission reports.

INTERIOR DECORATION

CA —BURBANK PUBLIC LIBRARY, 110 N Glenoaks Blvd, Burbank, 91502. Mary Ann Grasso, Coordr; Barbara Stones, Coordr, Media Project
Holdings: Vols (32,000) Cat Clippings Pix VF
Notes: The Warner Research Collection is a full service research division designed to serve the production needs of the motion picture, television, theatrical, and creative arts communities. This is a see-based service available by appointment only. Subject specialties include costumes, U.S. military, crime and criminals, transportation, license plates, and Sears catalogues.

†CA —WED ENTERPRISES, Research Library, 1401 Flower St, Glendale, 91201.
Notes: A subject emphasis.

CA —CRAFT AND FOLK ART MUSEUM, Library, 5814 Wilshire Blvd, Los Angeles, 90036. Joan M Benedetti, Museum Librn
Holdings: Vols (2000) Slides VF
Notes: Incl 2000 books; 70 journal subscriptions; artists' biographical files: 6 file drawers; clipping files: 8 file drawers; 20,000 slides. Representation of the material culture of all people, traditional and contemporary expressions. Incl visual and printed information on ethnic, traditional, popular, decorative, idiosyncratic, and contemporary crafts as well as vernacular architecture, handmade houses, and design. Information about and for professional artists on health hazards, conservation, and career management. Anthropological and art historical works; exhibition catalogues; slides, photographs, audiocassettes; clipping and pamphlet files. Contemporary Slide Registry of Craftspeople and extensive biographical files of contemporary craft artists. Information and referral files of craft related galleries, shops, festivals, organizations, etc.

CT —STOWE-DAY LIBRARY, 77 Forest St, Hartford, 06105. Diana J Royce, Librn
Holdings: Vols (15,000) Cat Mss
Notes: Incl (6000) additional pamphlets. The entire collection covers architecture, decorative arts, history, literature, woman suffrage, and Harriet Beecher Stowe, through the 19th century.

DE —HENRY F DUPONT WINTERTHUR MUSEUM LIBRARY, Winterthur, 19735. Frank H Sommer, III, Head
Holdings: Cat
Notes: Strong collections.

DC —LIBRARY OF CONGRESS, Washington, 20540.
Notes: Papers and working materials of Charles Eames (1907-1978), American architect and designer. Incl are original negatives and prints of the 106 educational films he created, business correspondence 1944 to 1978, some 400,000 color slides, 31, 000 black and white photographs, production materials for exhibits and drawings for all his major furniture designs.

IL —UNIVERSITY OF ILLINOIS, URBANA/CHAMPAIGN, Library, Home Economics Library, 314 Bevier Hall, Champaign, 61820. Barbara C Swain, Librn
Holdings: Vols Cat Microforms
Budget: $20,283
Notes: Textiles, apparel and interior design. *See also* entry under Furniture

IL —CHICAGO PUBLIC LIBRARY, Art Section, Fine Arts Division, 78 E Washington St, Chicago, 60602. Rosalinda I Hack, Fine Arts Division Chief; Yvonne S Brown, Head, Art Section
Holdings: Vols 42,000
Notes: Reference and circulating collection of books, periodicals, exhibition catalogs, dissertations, picture collections, and microforms on all aspects of the visual arts. Major concentration of art history, especially European, with concentration on 19th and 20th century art movements and artists. We attempt to represent the works of recognized artists past and present. The Decorative Arts are well represented especially in the areas of antiques, interior decoration, and handicrafts. The collection is supplemented by a strong periodical collection, consisting of 330 current English and Foreign subscriptions, the majority of these titles we bind, as well as strong bound retrospective collections. The visual arts is supported by a clipping File on Chicago Artists, a current exhibition catalogs collection, as well as by the microfilm collections of the*Chicago Art Institute Scrapbooks,* the *Scrapbook on Art,* Artists, and the *Index of American Design.*

LA —LOUISIANA STATE UNIVERSITY, College of Design, Design Resource Center, 102 College of Design Bldg, Baton Rouge, 70803. Doris A Wheeler, Librn
Holdings: Vols 8500 Cat Maps Slides VF
Budget: $6000
Notes: Architecture, interior design, city planning, landscape architecture.

MA —SOCIETY FOR THE PRESERVATION OF NEW ENGLAND ANTIQUITIES, Library, 141 Cambridge St, Boston, 02114. Ellie Reichlin, Librn & Cur of Photographic Collections
Holdings: Vols (3000) Cat Pix Microforms
Budget: ($75,000)
Notes: Incl two types of mss: (1) Family papers relating to historic properties administered by SPNEA. Ca 125 linear feet, incl the Codman family archive, 1700s-1960s, with associated family photograph collection. (2) Misc mss with emphasis on topics relating to building, interior designs, material culture (ca 3500 items, cataloged). For further information, an *Annotated Checklist to Special Collections of SPNEA* Library is available. See also entry in *Architectural Records in Boston: A Guide to Architectural Research* (1983, Garland Publishing Co, New York). Additional collections incl prints, original artwork (largely by NE artists, engravers) relating to architectural subjects; maps; architectural periodicals (19th century).

MN —UNIVERSITY OF MINNESOTA, Architecture Library, 89 Church St, Minneapolis, 55455. A Kristine Johnson, Librn
Holdings: Vols (27,000) Cat Mss
Budget: ($20,000)
Notes: Incl architecture, architectural history, landscape architecture, design methodology, housing, urban sociology, interior design, etc.

NY —MUSEUM OF THE CITY OF NEW YORK, Photo Archives, Fifth Ave & 103 St, New York, 10029. Esther Brumberg, Librn
Holdings: Mss Maps Pix
Notes: All aspects of New York City--history, costume, social life and customs, etc. Also, Byron Collection--about 10,000 prints, 1880-1930, of views of New York, commercial interiors, interiors and exteriors of private residences, social events, shipping, immigration; Wurts Collection--15,000 glass negatives, 1890-1940, mostly architectural; 100,000 Wurts Architectural Photographs, to be cataloged. Underhill Collection--about 900 glass negatives, mostly architectural, 1896-1936; McKim, Mead & White Collection--1000 glass negatives of the work of the firm, 1880-1915; and Berenice Abbott Collection, Changing New York--about 350 negatives taken by Miss Abbott for the Federal Arts Project, 1930s. Other FAP photographs incl a series on Coney Island, one on Harlem, Sewing Project, and Sabbath Studies.

NY —TRAPHAGEN SCHOOL OF FASHION LIBRARY, 257 Park Ave S, New York, 10010. Allyn Bloeme, Librn
Holdings: Vols (17,000) Cat Pix Slides
Notes: Costume history, design, construction and illustration. Collection incl old and rare bound fashion periodicals: French, English and American, also continuing run of *Vogue* and *Harper's Bazaar.* No photocopying.

OR —UNIVERSITY OF OREGON LIBRARY, Architecture & Allied Arts Branch, Eugene, 97403. Reyburn R McCready, Head Librn
Holdings: Cat
Notes: House decoration. Farmington Plan assignment.

OR —BASSIST COLLEGE LIBRARY, 2000 SW Fifth Ave, Portland, 97201. Norma Bassist, Librn
Holdings: Vols (4200) Cat Mss Pix Slides
Notes: Some material on the history of the subject also.

PA —ATHENAEUM OF PHILADELPHIA, 219 S Sixth St, Philadelphia, 19106. Roger W Moss Jr, Librn
Notes: Interior design 2500 vols.

WI —UNIVERSITY OF WISCONSIN, MADISON, College of Agricultural & Life Sciences, Steenbock Memorial Library, 550 Babcock Dr, Madison, 53706. Jan Kennedy, Dir
Holdings: Vols (186,312) Cat Docs
Notes: Collection supports the School of Family Resources and Consumer Sciences in areas of textiles and fashion design, interior decorating, consumer science, and nutrition; USDA documents and experiment station publications.

WI —MILWAUKEE PUBLIC LIBRARY, 814 W Wisconsin Ave, Milwaukee, 53233. Donald J Sager, City Librn
Holdings: Vols Cat Pix Slides
Notes: The collection incl all fields of art, with emphasis on architecture, incl: Frank Lloyd Wright and local city planning documents; interior decoration; art history; American art; Oriental art; art instruction; decorative arts; numismatics and philately; photography, incl local photo archives and

INTERIOR DECORATION (cont.)

instruction manuals; costume; art exhibition and auction ctalogs; and local newspaper clippings on art subjects. Also, circulating mounted and framed art prints and sculpture reproductions.

BC —VANCOUVER PUBLIC LIBRARY, Art Div, 750 Burrard St, Vancouver, V6Z 1X5, Can.
Holdings: Cat Pix
Notes: Besides the book and pamphlet collection, special files incl *Newspaper Clippings File*--31 drawers of relevant clippings from major newspapers, incl the *Sun, Province, Toronto Globe and Mail, Christian Science Monitor, New York* Times, etc on arts, music, architecture; incl biographical material (16 drawers); *Picture* File--about 500,000 pictures in 150 cabinet drawers; strong in architecture, costume, interior decoration.

MB —UNIVERSITY OF MANITOBA, Architecture & Fine Arts Library, Winnipeg, R3T 2N2, Can. Peter Anthony, Head
Holdings: Vols (50,000) Pix
Notes: Incl product catalogs.

ON —METROPOLITAN TORONTO LIBRARY, Fine Arts Dept, 789 Yonge St, Toronto, M4W 2G8, Can. Alan Suddon, Head
Holdings: Vols (42,000) Cat Pix Microforms
Notes: Extensive collection.

INTERIOR DESIGN see Interior Decoration

INTERIOR NAVIGATION see Inland Navigation

INTERLAKEN SCHOOL, INDIANA

IN —INDIANA UNIVERSITY, Lilly Library, Seventh St, Bloomington, 47405. William R Cagle, Librn
Holdings: // Mss Pix
Notes: Ms holdings incl papers of Edward A Rumely, founder of Interlaken School in Indiana and apostle of the New School Movement in the US. 10,000 items in this nearly 100,000 item collection relate to Interlaken and to such college preparatory training as represented by Interlaken.

INTERMARRIAGE, RACIAL see Miscegenation

INTERMITTENT FEVER see Malarial Fever

INTERMOUNTAIN WEST—HISTORY

ID —IDAHO STATE UNIVERSITY, Library, Pocatello, 83209. Gary Domitz, Social Science Librn
Holdings: Cat
Budget: ($2500)
Notes: Idaho and Intermountain West History Collection; incl the Lemhi Indian Reservation's miscellaneous papers. Extensive collections.

INTERNAL COMBUSTION ENGINES see Gas and Oil Engines

INTERNAL IMPROVEMENT MOVEMENT see Public Works

INTERNAL MEDICINE see Medicine, Internal

INTERNAL SECURITY

CA —HARVEY G WOLFE LIBRARY, PO Box 3514, Grand Central Sta, Glendale, 91201. Douglas L Evans, Librn
Holdings: Vols (6580) Mss Maps Pix
Budget: ($4500)
Notes: Main emphasis on espionage, military intelligence, and sabatoge.

INTERNATIONAL, FOURTH

MI —UNIVERSITY OF MICHIGAN, Dept of Rare Books & Special Collections, Ann Arbor, 48109. Edward C Weber, Head, Labadie Collection
Holdings: Vols (40,000) Cat Mss Pix Phonorecords Audiotapes Microforms
Notes: Strong on publications on the Fourth International.

INTERNATIONAL, SECOND

MA —HARVARD UNIVERSITY LIBRARY, Cambridge, 02138.
Holdings: Cat Mss

INTERNATIONAL ADMINISTRATION see International Agencies; International Organization

INTERNATIONAL AGENCIES

CA —UNIVERSITY OF CALIFORNIA, BERKELEY, University Library, Government Documents Department, 350 Library Annex, Berkeley, 94720. Suzanne Gold, Collection Dept Librn
Holdings: Vols (314,000) Cat Microforms
Budget: ($85,115)
Notes: General collection of government documents, historical and current, on the federal and state levels; as well as international and foreign documents. The Library's holdings are particularly strong in foreign statistics and censuses, and US Congress. The Government Documents Department serves as a full depository for GPO, NASA, State of California, EEC, GATT, IAEA, United Nations, UNESCO, Rand Corporation (non-classified), IBRD, OECD, ILO, UNITAR, ITC, and CE. Selective depository, PL-480 Programs, or gift or exchange arrangements obtain for the states of Michigan and Washington and for Canada, India, Pakistan and Indonesia. Incl microfilm and 300,000 fiche, cards, and prints.

CA —LOS ANGELES PUBLIC LIBRARY, Social Sciences Dept, 630 W Fifth St, Los Angeles, 90071. Marilyn C Wherley, Principal Librn
Holdings: Vols 2000 Cat
Budget: ($150,000)
Notes: International relations, incl documents of international agencies and governments, long runs of periodicals, indexes, pamphlets, bibliographies. No separate catalog. Many items uncataloged.

CA —UNIVERSITY OF CALIFORNIA, LOS ANGELES, Research Library, Public Affairs Service, 405 Hilgard Ave, Los Angeles, 90024. Edward Shreeves, Chairman, Bibliographers Group; Eugenia Eaton, Head, Public Affairs Service
Holdings: Microforms
Notes: Depository for the official publications of California cities and counties, the state of California, the United States government, the United Nations and some of its specialized agencies (including the Food and Agricultural Organization and UNESCO), and such regional organizations as the European Communities and Organization of American States. Selected publications of other American cities and counties, of the other states and possessions of the United States, of interstate organizations, and of foreign governments (with emphasis on major world powers, Africa, Latin America and the Near and Middle East) and intergovernmental organizations.

DC —US BUREAU OF THE CENSUS, Library, Federal Office Bldg 3, Rm 2451, Washington, 20233. Betty Baxtresser, Chief, ASD Library Branch
Holdings: Vols (23,000) Cat Microforms
Notes: Incl censuses, statistical yearbooks, and statistical bulletins from about 100 foreign countries printed in nearly 40 languages. The span of coverage varies, depending upon the publication program of each country and on publications exchange arrangements. Materials in this collection are arranged first by geographic unit, then by subject. Publications of the international organizations are arranged by organizational unit, then by subject.

FL —FLORIDA STATE UNIVERSITY, Robert Manning Strozier Library, Tallahassee, 32306. Judith Depew, Head, Documents-Maps Dept
Holdings: Vols (680,000) Uncat Microforms
Notes: A depository for Florida, GPO, NASA, UN, and UNESCO documents, with standing orders for British, ILO, OAS, IMF; selected documents are purchased from various government levels. The collection incl historical as well as current material, especially Florida, US, Great Britain. The Library's holdings are strong in congressional bills and hearings, decennial censuses, and British Sessional papers. Number of volumes incl microprint and microfiche, but not cataloged documents and microfilm.

IL —NORTHWESTERN UNIVERSITY, Library, Government Publications Dept, Evanston, 60201. Robert W Baumgartner, Head
Notes: Collection consists of US federal documents (depository library since 1876); state documents (emphasis on Illinois); municipal documents (emphasis on Evanston and Chicago); documents of international organizations (emphasis on United Nations, United Nations specialized agencies, Organization of American States, European Communities). Collection consists of publications of 44 international organizations. Shelflist maintained in the Government Publications Department. Most publications not incl in the library's general catalog.

IL —WHEATON COLLEGE, Buswell Memorial Library, Wheaton, 60187. Paul Snezek, Library Dir
Notes: The collection includes mss, correspondence, lecture tapes, (40), (25 linear feet). 1945 UN conference on International Organization, Canadian Rebellion, 1837-1838, Wheaton Scholastic Society.

MA —HARVARD UNIVERSITY LIBRARY, Law School Library, Langdell Hall, Cambridge, 02138. Harry S Martin III, Librn

NY —UNITED NATIONS, Dag Hammarskjold Library, Rm L382, New York, 10017. Vladimir Orlov, Librn
Holdings: Cat Microforms
Notes: Also incl documents.

NC —DUKE UNIVERSITY, William R Perkins Library, Public Documents and Maps Department, Durham, 27706. Jaia Barrett, Head
Holdings: Vols Maps Pamphlets Microforms
Notes: A selective depository for US Government publications since 1890, the Department currently holds well over 500, 000 items, plus publications of the European Community (a depository collection), the League of Nations, the UN and UN-affiliated agencies. Other international organizations, publications are acquired also, as are state government publications, especially from the Southeast, California, New York and Illinois. The Documents Department holds services the major map collections of Perkins Library. These collections include topographic, geologic, and special subject maps which are worldwide in coverage. The department is a depository for the US Defense Mapping Agency and the US Geological Survey. In addition, there are many other maps of general and specific interest, including US and foreign road maps. As appropriate, maps are also held in the Perkins Library's Rare BookRoom and Manuscript Department. Atlases are shelved in the Reference Department and in the bookstacks of Perkins Library.

TX —UNIVERSITY OF TEXAS LIBRARIES, General Libraries, Barker Texas History Center, PO Box P, Austin, 78712. Don Carleton, Dir
Notes: Papers, etc, documenting the career of Luther H Evans.

MB —UNIVERSITY OF MANITOBA, Elizabeth Dafoe Library, Government Publications Section, Winnipeg, R3T 2N2, Can. June Dutka, Head
Holdings: Vols 300,000 Uncat Mss Maps Microforms
Notes: Concerned mainly with supporting

INTERNATIONAL AGENCIES (cont.)

research programs in the arts (especially sociology, political studies, native studies, history, geography and economics), agriculture, home economics and nursing. Collection consists of Canadian federal publications; depository since 1969 (emphasis on Statistics Canada); holdings of pre-confederation documents, early parliamentary publications, and royal commissions for the post-war years are reasonably complete; provincial documents (emphasis on Manitoba); municipal documents (emphasis on Winnipeg); documents from Great Britain, India and the US (emphasis on US State Agricultural Experimental Stations); publications from international organizations (emphasis on the Food and Agricultural Organization depository since 1945), UNESCO, International Labour Organization and Commission of the EuropeanCommunities. Card catalog is maintained in the Government Publications Section. Most publications are not included in the library's general catalog.

†ON —METROPOLITAN TORONTO LIBRARY, Social Sciences Dept, 789 Yonge St, Toronto, M4W 2G8, Can. Abdus Salam, Head
Holdings: Vols Cat Maps Phonorecords Audiotapes 16mm Films Microforms
Notes: General collection of documents of international organizations with emphasis on the United Nations and UNESCO. Collection ranges from international relations to social conditions in underdeveloped countries. Selected League of Nations publications. Both current and historical in scope.

INTERNATIONAL AGRICULTURAL COOPERATION

OH —OHIO STATE UNIVERSITY, Agriculture Library, 2120 Fyffe Rd, Agricultural Administration Bldg, Columbus, 43210. Mary P Key, Head
Holdings: Vols (12,000) Cat Mss Maps Pix
Notes: The Arnold Agriculture Credit Collection. There is a special catalog which is not being kept up-to-date. Much of the material is in a pamphlet file arranged by country or other geographical unit. All interlibrary loan requests are handled through the interlibrary loan department of our main library. Address: Interlibrary Loan; Main Library, Ohio State University, 1858 Neil Ave, Columbus, Ohio 43210.

INTERNATIONAL ANIMATED FILM SOCIETY (ASIFA)

CA —UNIVERSITY OF CALIFORNIA, LOS ANGELES, Theater Arts Library, Los Angeles, 90024. Edward Shreeves, Chairman, Bibliographers Group; Audree Malkin, Head, Theater Arts Library
Notes: Incl many rare cels and sketches which have never been produced anywhere. Represented are Hanna-Barbera, Walt Disney, Chuck Jones, DePatie-Freleng, J R Bray, Ralph Bakshi, Frederic Back, Furlong, John Hubley, Fritz Fleleng, John Weldon, Tex Aveny, and Bosustow.

INTERNATIONAL ARBITRATION see Arbitration, International

INTERNATIONAL BROADCASTING

DC —GEORGE WASHINGTON UNIVERSITY, Gelman Library, Telecommunications Information Center, Washington, 20052. Cathy Haworth, Librn
Holdings: Vols (1500) Periodicals
Notes: Incl

NY —COLUMBIA UNIVERSITY LIBRARIES, Lehman Library, Bureau of Applied Social Research Archive, 420 W 118th St, New York, 10027. David Lewis, Librn
Holdings: Uncat Pix
Notes: Current information file of Radio Free Europe publications. There is significant coverage of the period 1956-1973. The current file incl Radio Free Europe Situation Reports, which are published for selected countries on a weekly basis, Background Reports dealing with themes of broader significance, and Media Surveys which are translations of important East European press articles. The retrospective files incl these research products arranged on a country-by-country basis.

INTERNATIONAL BUSINESS ENTERPRISES

CA —UNIVERSITY OF CALIFORNIA, LOS ANGELES, Graduate School of Management Library, UCLA Campus, Los Angeles, 90024. Robert Bellanti, Head Librn
Holdings: Vols (128,000) Cat Mss Microforms
Notes: The

CA —UNIVERSITY OF SOUTHERN CALIFORNIA, Crocker Business Library, Hoffman Hall, University Park, Los Angeles, 90007. Judith A Truelson, Head Librn
Holdings: Vols (100,000) Cat Microforms
Notes: The Roy P Crocker Library of Business Administration, located in Hoffman Hall, houses more than 100,000 volumes and regularly receives approximately 1500 trade, financial, economics, labor, and general business periodicals and newspapers. The areas of subject concentration include business economics, finance and investments, general management/management theory, international business, finance and management, marketing/food marketing, and quantitative business analysis.

IN —PURDUE UNIVERSITY LIBRARIES, Graduate School of Management, Krannert Library, West Lafayette, 47907. Gordon Law, Librn
Holdings: Vols (7000) Cat Mss Maps Pix Microforms
Notes: The collection consists of books, journals and pamphlets dating from the early 16th to late 19th century, covering to a large degree the early literature in economic thought and business practices both here and abroad. No photocopying.

MA —HARVARD UNIVERSITY, Graduate School of Business Administration, Baker Library, Soldiers Field, Boston, 02163. Mary V Chatfield, Librn; Florence Bartoshesky, Cur of Manuscripts and Archives

MN —UNIVERSITY OF MINNESOTA, James Ford Bell Library, 309 19th Ave S, Minneapolis, 55455. John Parker, Cur
Holdings: Vols (11,000) Cat Mss Maps
Notes: Collection of original materials relating to European expansion, 1400-1800.

TX —TEXAS TECH UNIVERSITY, Library, Lubbock, 79409. David J Murrah, Assoc Dir for Special Collections

WY —US AIR FORCE INSTITUTE OF TECHNOLOGY, Library, Dept 9 Bldg 831, FE, Warren AFB, 82001. Patricia A Johnson, Librn
Holdings: Vols (7000) Cat Microforms
Budget: ($9000)
Notes: The Library supports graduate programs for students (Air Force Missile-Combat Crewmen) seeking a Master of Business Administration Degree. Civilian students and other military personnel are also admitted.

INTERNATIONAL CENTER FOR ARID AND SEMI-ARID LAND STUDIES

†NY —UNITED NATIONS, Library, Grand Central Station, PO Box 20, New York, 10017.

INTERNATIONAL COOPERATION

CA —WORLD AFFAIRS COUNCIL OF NORTH CALIFORNIA, Library, 312 Sutter St, San Francisco, 94108. Lone C Beeson, Head Librn; Edith Malamud, Circulation Librn
Holdings: Vols 6500 Cat Maps

MA —HARVARD UNIVERSITY LIBRARY, Law School Library, Langdell Hall, Cambridge, 02138. Harry S Martin III, Librn
Holdings: Cat

NY —COLUMBIA UNIVERSITY LIBRARIES, Rare Book & Manuscript Library, 801 Butler Library, 535 W 114 St, New York, 10027. Kenneth A Lohf, Librn
Holdings: Mss
Notes: Archival material of the Carnegie Endowment for International Peace through 1954. 712,500 items. Restricted use.

NY —UNITED NATIONS, Dag Hammarskjold Library, Rm L382, New York, 10017. Vladimir Orlov, Librn

ON —CANADIAN INSTITUTE OF INTERNATIONAL AFFAIRS, 15 King's College Circle, Toronto, M5S 2V9, Can. Jane Barrett, Librn
Holdings: Vols (23,000) Cat Mss Microforms Books VF
Budget: ($8800)
Notes: Incl both historical and current material on all subjects relevant to a study of Canadian foreign relations.

PQ —CANADIAN INTERNATIONAL DEVELOPMENT AGENCY, Development Information Centre, 200 Promenade du Portage, Hull, K1A 0G4, Can. Nicole Smith, Librn
Holdings: Vols 3000 Cat
Notes: International economic development.

INTERNATIONAL COOPERATION IN AGRICULTURE see International Agricultural Cooperation

INTERNATIONAL COURTS

NY —NEW YORK PUBLIC LIBRARY, Research Libraries, Economic & Public Affairs Div, Fifth Ave & 42 St, New York, 10018. Edward DiRoma, Chief
Holdings: Vols (1,500,000) Cat Microforms

NY —UNITED NATIONS, Dag Hammarskjold Library, Rm L382, New York, 10017. Vladimir Orlov, Librn

INTERNATIONAL ECONOMIC INTEGRATION

DC —COMMISSION OF THE EUROPEAN COMMUNITIES, European Community Information Service Library, 2100 M St NW Suite 707, Washington, 20037. Barbara Sloan, Head of Public Inquiries
Holdings: Vols (35,000) Cat Maps Pix Microforms
Notes: Library contains all of the official documents and occasional publications of the Institutions of the European Communities: ie, European Economic Community (Common Market), European Atomic Energy Community (Euratom), European Coal and Steel Community (ECSC). It collects non-Community publications about European integration, international trade and monetary affairs. Also has the publications of the General Agreements for Tariffs and Trade (GATT), Western European Union, and Council of Europe. Also, 1000 vertical files.

NY —UNITED NATIONS, Dag Hammarskjold Library, Rm L382, New York, 10017. Vladimir Orlov, Librn

INTERNATIONAL ECONOMIC RELATIONS

MA —HARVARD UNIVERSITY, Center for International Affairs, Library, Coolidge Hall, 1737 Cambridge St, Cambridge, 02138. Barbara Mitchell, Librn
Holdings: Vols (13,000) Periodicals
Notes: Collection emphasizes international politics and also contains considerable statistical material on individual countries. Library currently receives 115 periodical titles.

MA —HARVARD UNIVERSITY, Institute for International Development, Library, Coolidge Hall, 1737 Cambridge St, Cambridge, 02138. Barbara Mitchell, Librn
Holdings: Vols (17,000)
Notes: Economic development, rural development, statistical material on selected

INTERNATIONAL ECONOMIC RELATIONS (cont.)

underdeveloped countries. Incl 75 periodical titles.

MI —UNIVERSITY OF MICHIGAN, Center for Research on Economic Development, Library, 240 Lorch Hall, Ann Arbor, 48109. Carol Wilson, Information/Resources Coordinator
Holdings: Vols (21,000) Cat 16mm Films Microforms
Notes: Publications that list library and its collection: *Directory of Third World Studies in the US* (African Studies Assn, 1981), *National Reference Center Directory* 1983 (NRC), *World Guide to Libraries* 1983 (Saur Verlag), *Research Centers Directory 1983* (Gale Research), and *A Directory of Information Resources in US* (Library of Congress, 1978). Collection's focus is Third World economic development. Other areas of interest are economic planning, developing countries, Africa (specifically francophone Africa), the Sahel, African agricultural economics, commodities production, financial statistics, development plans from less developed countries (LDC), and international development. Each part of the library's collection (working papers/reports, periodicals and government documents) has its own catalog and cataloging system.

NY —UNITED NATIONS, Dag Hammarskjold Library, Rm L382, New York, 10017. Vladimir Orlov, Librn

PQ —CANADIAN INTERNATIONAL DEVELOPMENT AGENCY, Development Information Centre, 200 Promenade du Portage, Hull, K1A 0G4, Can. Nicole Smith, Librn
Notes: International economic development.

INTERNATIONAL ECONOMICS see International Economic Relations

INTERNATIONAL EDUCATION

CO —WESTERN INTERSTATE COMMISSION FOR HIGHER EDUCATION, Wiche Library, PO Drawer P, Boulder, 80302. Karon M Kelly, Dir Library Services
Holdings: Vols (10,000) Cat Microforms
Notes: Incl medical and nursing education, student exchange programs, minority involvement in education, management systems in higher education.

MA —NORTHEASTERN UNIVERSITY LIBRARIES, Center for International Higher Education Documentation, 360 Huntington Ave, Boston, 02115. Solveig M Turner, Dir; Nieves F Farin, Head Collection Development Librn
Notes: Collection based on files of the International Encyclopedia of Higerh Education. Emphasis on international higher education. Subjects incl: national systems of higher education (administrative concerns, planning, enrollments, equivalences of credentials). Also incl international university catalogs. Extensive subject index maintained.

INTERNATIONAL EXHIBITIONS see Exhibitions and Expositions

INTERNATIONAL FEDERATION see International Organization

INTERNATIONAL FINANCE

DC —EXPORT-IMPORT BANK OF THE UNITED STATES, EXIMBANK Library, 811 Vermont Ave NW, Washington, 20571. Theodora McGill, Librn; John Posniak, Asst Librn
Holdings: Vols (15,000) Maps Audiotapes
Notes: The library has almost a complete set of the Economist Intelligence unit of London's *Quarterly Economic Reviews;* various types of materials with general, economic and statistical data on virtually every country of the world; incl foreign government publications, publications of various international organizations, and US Government documents.

DC —INTERNATIONAL MONETARY FUND AND WORLD BANK, Joint Bank-Fund Library, Washington, 20431. Maureen M Moore, Librn
Holdings: Vols Cat Films Microforms
Notes: Incl foreign trade and statistical bulletins and yearbooks, central bank reports and bulletins, budget papers, security yearbooks, economic development plans and reports on economic conditions from the 132 member countries. An index of periodical material compiled by the Library staff has been published as: *Economics and Finance; Index to Periodical Articles, 1947-1971;* First Supplement, 1972, 1973, 1974 (Second Supplement, 1975, 1976, 1977, in preparation), 5 vols. (Boston: G K Hall, 1972, 1975). Also, The Developing Areas: *A Classed Bibliography of the Joint Bank-Fund Library,* Vol 1: *Latin America and the* Caribbean; Vol 2: *Africa and the Middle* East; Vol 3: *Asia and Oceania* (Boston: G K Hall, 1976).

MA —HARVARD UNIVERSITY, Center for International Affairs, Library, Coolidge Hall, 1737 Cambridge St, Cambridge, 02138. Barbara Mitchell, Librn
Holdings: Vols (13,000) Periodicals
Notes: Collection emphasizes international politics and also contains considerable statistical material on individual countries. Library currently receives 115 periodical titles.

NY —SALOMON BROTHERS, Library, One New York Plaza, 46th Floor, New York, 10004. Lydia P Davies, Library Mgr
Holdings: Vols (4750) Cat
Notes: Library contains a collection of reference sources relating to corporate finance, investment banking and international finance. Extensive domestic and international corporate documents on microfiche. 11,000 corporate document files; 406,700 microforms.

NY —UNITED NATIONS, Dag Hammarskjold Library, Rm L382, New York, 10017. Vladimir Orlov, Librn

OH —MARATHON OIL CO, Law Library, 539 S Main St, Room 854-M, Findlay, 45840. Durand S Dudley, Sr Law Librn
Holdings: Vols (18,000) Cat
Budget: ($100,000)
Notes: Library serves the informational needs of the staff attorneys of a major oil company operating in both domestic and foreign areas. Includes all of the domestic law reports and digests. Includes statutes of 25 states. Particular emphasis is given to the acquisition of mineral (petroleum) law and energy legislation and regulation. Library open to the public by permission.

ON —CANADIAN IMPERIAL BANK OF COMMERCE, Information Centre, Commerce Court, Toronto, M5L 1A2, Can. Jane Cooney, Librn Head Office
Holdings: Vols (22,000) Cat Microforms
Notes: Canadian and international banking. Annual reports of Canadian chartered banks from 19th century. Government reports and proceedings on Canadian banking laws and legislation from mid-19th century. Central bank reports from around the world. All major Canadian and international banking periodicals.

INTERNATIONAL GRANTS IN AID see Economic Assistance; International Relief

INTERNATIONAL HORN SOCIETY

IN —BALL STATE UNIVERSITY, Alexander M Bracken Library, Muncie, 47306. Nyal Williams, Music Librn
Holdings: Vols (30,000) Cat Mss
Budget: ($20,000)
Notes: Incl archives of International Horn Society Tubists Universal Brotherhood Association Library, Cecil Leeson Archival Saxophone Collection, and Archival Saxophone Collection, and Archives of Buescher Music Instrument Manufacturing Company.

INTERNATIONAL INSTITUTE OF AGRICULTURE

NY —NEW YORK PUBLIC LIBRARY, Research Libraries, Economic & Public Affairs Div, Fifth Ave & 42 St, New York, 10018. Edward DiRoma, Chief
Holdings: Vols (1,500,000) Cat Microforms

INTERNATIONAL INSTITUTIONS see International Agencies; International Cooperation

INTERNATIONAL LABOR ORGANIZATION

DC —INTERNATIONAL LABOR ORGANIZATION, International Labor Office, Washington Branch Library, 1750 New York Ave NW, Rm 330, Washington, 20006. Karen J Mark, Librn
Holdings: Vols (13,500) Cat Pix 16mm Films Monographs
Notes: Wide range of titles dealing with worldwide labor and social matters. The library contains ILO publications and documentation only, dating back to 1919. Also, a collection of ILO films and photos. See *Subject Guide to Publications of the ILO, 1919-1964 and ILO Catalogue of Publications in print, 1982* (ILO).

MA —BOSTON PUBLIC LIBRARY, Government Documents Department, Boston, 02117. V Lloyd Jameson, Cur
Holdings: Maps Microforms
Notes: International Labor Organization documents.

†MA —JOHN F KENNEDY LIBRARY, Columbia Point, Boston, 02125. Dan H Fenn Jr, Dir
Holdings: / / Cat Microforms
Notes: Copies of AFL-CIO press releases and records relating to legislation, relations with the Federal government, and international affairs, 1955-1968. 9 rolls of microfilm. Holdings are described in "Historical Materials in the John F Kennedy Library." Copies may be obtained by writing the Research Archivist.

NY —COLUMBIA UNIVERSITY LIBRARIES, Rare Book & Manuscript Library, George Dunlop Collection of Letters & Manuscripts, 801 Butler Library, 535 W 114 St, New York, 10027. Kenneth A Lohf, Librn
Holdings: Cat Mss Maps Pix
Notes: The papers of Professor Carter Goodrich economic historian, incl his papers as chairman of the governing body of the International Labor Office, 1939-1945; chief of the United Nations economic mission in Vietnam, 1955-1956, and special representative to Bolivia for the Secretary-General of the United Nations, 1952-1953. About 28,000 items.

NY —NEW YORK PUBLIC LIBRARY, Research Libraries, Economic & Public Affairs Div, Fifth Ave & 42 St, New York, 10018. Edward DiRoma, Chief
Holdings: Vols (1,500,000) Cat Microforms

NY —UNITED NATIONS, Dag Hammarskjold Library, Rm L382, New York, 10017. Vladimir Orlov, Librn

ON —METROPOLITAN TORONTO LIBRARY, Business Dept, 789 Yonge St, Toronto, M4W 2G8, Can. Patricia Dye, Head
Holdings: Vols (63,682) Cat Microforms
Notes: Extensive current and historical information with emphasis on Canadian companies incl annual reports, clippings and pamphlets files, and a collection of business and trade directories. Also international directories. Approximately 1000 current periodicals, and up-dating services giving corporation information. Statistics collection.

INTERNATIONAL LANGUAGES see Languages, International

INTERNATIONAL LAW

CT —YALE UNIVERSITY, Law Library, 127 Wall St, New Haven, 06520. Morris L Cohen, Librn

INTERNATIONAL LAW (cont.)

DC —AMERICAN SOCIETY OF INTERNATIONAL LAW LIBRARY, 2223 Massachusetts Ave NW, Washington, 20008. Helen S Philos, Librn
Holdings: Vols (22,000) Cat
Budget: $7500
Notes: Public international law. (22,000 books, pamphlets, etc. Over 300 current foreign and domestic periodicals). Briefs and/or opinions in many international law cases. Documents of international organizations.

DC —GEORGETOWN UNIVERSITY, Library, Special Collections Div, 37 & O Sts NW, Washington, 20057. George M Barringer, Special Collections Librn; Nicholas B Sheetz, Mss Librn
Holdings: Mss Cat
Notes: Incl the Heinrich Kronstein Memorial Collection of International and Foreign Trade Law; papers of James Brown Scott, international jurist; papers of Heinrich A Rommen (1897-1967), educator and authority on political philosphy and international law, consisting of correspondence, mss, clippings, photographs, and printed material; material on religious opposition, in particular Catholic opposition, within Germany to the Hitler regime.

DC —GEORGE WASHINGTON UNIVERSITY, Gelman Library, 2130 H St NW, Washington, 20052.
Holdings: Vols (50,000)// Cat Mss Microforms
Notes: The Carnegie Endownment for International Peace library was purchased in 1950. The collection has been cataloged and assimilated in the University Library and the Law Library's holdings. It includes monographs, a few bound manuscripts, conference proceedings, and periodicals. Certain periodicals are available on microfilm through Clearwater Publishing Co. Holdings are catalogued individually.

DC —LIBRARY OF CONGRESS, Law Library, 101 Independence Ave, SE, Washington, 20540. Carleton W Kenyon, Dir
Holdings: Vols 1,800,000 Cat Mss Microforms
Notes: The collection, comprising the legal sources and literature of all foreign nations, covers all legal systems incl common, civil, international, religious, and historic law.

DC —US DEPT OF STATE, Library, Rm 3239 NS, Washington, 20520. Conrad P Eaton, Librn
Holdings: Vols (750,000) Cat Microforms
Notes: Incl 7200 microfilm reels.

IL —NORTHWESTERN UNIVERSTIY, School of Law, Library, 357 E Chicago Ave, Chicago, 60611. George S Grossman, Dir
Holdings: Cat
Notes: Comprehensive collections of Anglo-American and foreign (especially European) law; Roman and Canon law (selective); international law; European Common Market; Williams Collection of Legal Instruments (AD 1300-1700); George W Shaw Collection of Early European Law. Incl 500 ms legal documents.

MA —HARVARD UNIVERSITY LIBRARY, Law School Library, Langdell Hall, Cambridge, 02138. Harry S Martin III, Librn
Holdings: Cat Mss Maps Pix Slides
Notes: Downs 1687, 1763, 1774, 1776-1779, 1782-1784, 1790-1793, 1809, 1764, 1768, 1796; Downs Supplement 789. Comprehensive collection of English common law, American Law (historical and current), foreign law, comparative law, international law, Roman law and Canon law. Over a million vols.

MA —BOSTON COLLEGE, Law School Library, 885 Centre St, Newton Centre, 02159. Sharon Hamby, Librn
Holdings: Vols (160,000) Cat Maps Pix
Notes: Emphasizes Anglo-American law and international law and relations.

MI —UNIVERSITY OF MICHIGAN, Law Library, Legal Research Bldg, 801 Monroe St, Ann Arbor, 48109. Beverley J Pooley, Dir
Holdings: Vols (570,000) Cat Microforms
Budget: $575,000
Notes: Unusually strong in legal history, canon law, US state constitutional proceedings, Indian nations, and foreign and international law. Also 300,000 microforms.

MI —WAYNE STATE UNIVERSITY, Arthur Neef Law Library, Detroit, 48202. Georgia Clark, Law Librn
Holdings: Vols (165,587) Cat Microforms

NJ —PRINCETON UNIVERSITY, Library, Rare Books Dept, Princeton, 08544. Stephen Ferguson, Cur
Holdings: Cat

NY —COLUMBIA UNIVERSITY LIBRARIES, Law School Library, Law Building, 435 W 116 St, New York, 10027. James L Hoover, Librn
Holdings: Vols 70,000 Cat

NY —UNITED NATIONS, Dag Hammarskjold Library, Rm L382, New York, 10017. Vladimir Orlov, Librn
Holdings: Cat Microforms

NC —DUKE UNIVERSITY, William R Perkins Library, Durham, 27706. Elvin E Strowd, University Librn
Notes: The Louis Strisower collection on international law contains 5000 volumes dealing with international law dating from the 17th to the 20th centuries; there are monographs and periodicals in the collection.

OH —CASE WESTERN RESERVE UNIVERSITY, Franklin Thomas Backus School of Law Library, 11075 East Blvd, Cleveland, 44106. Kathleen Carrick, Law Librn; Marsha Tittlebaum, Reader Serv Librn
Holdings: Vols (191,000)

OH —CLEVELAND PUBLIC LIBRARY, Social Sciences Department, 325 Superior Ave, Cleveland, 44114. Thelma Morris, Head
Holdings: Vols (200,000) Cat
Notes: Extensive collection. Full runs of periodicals.

PA —UNIVERSITY OF PENNSYLVANIA, Biddle Law Library, 3400 Chestnut St, Philadelphia, 19104. Elizabeth S. Kelly, Libn
Holdings: Vols (350,000) Cat
Notes: Comprehensive collection of Anglo-American law. Legal materials from selected foreign countries, particularly in Common Market area. International law incl UN documents and other regional organizations Substantial holdings in historical sources particularly early English law and Canon law.

RI —US NAVAL WAR COLLEGE, Historical Collection & Museum, Newport, 02841. Anthony S Nicolosi, Dir; Evelyn Cherpak, Cur
Holdings: Mss
Notes: Collections incl over 200,000 separate pieces; chiefly papers of naval officers and records of organizations associated with the US Navy, the Naval War College, the college's major study areas, and the Navy in the Narragansett Bay region; oral history collection; Naval War College Archives, 1884-present; records of conferences held at the College; newspaper collections treating with naval themes and military conflicts.

RI —BROWN UNIVERSITY, John Hay Library, 20 Prospect St, Providence, 02912. Mark N Brown, Cur Mss
Holdings: Vols 68 Cat
Notes: Grolius Collection contains 68 of the 79 recorded complete editions of *De Jure Belli ac Pacis* printed between 1625 and 1939. It lacks 6 of the 49 Latin editions and one each of the English, Dutch, German and Spanish editions. See description for the Henry Wheaton, 1785-1848, Manuscript Collection.

ON —CANADA DEPT OF EXTERNAL AFFAIRS, Library Services Div, 125 Sussex Dr, Ottawa, K1A 0G2, Can. Ruth Margaret Thompson, Dir
Holdings: Vols (40,000) Cat Maps Phonorecords Audiotapes Microforms
Notes: Incl 1000 maps, 250,000 microforms, and 550,000 documents.

INTERNATIONAL MANAGEMENT CONFERENCE, 1948-1954

†MA —MASSACHUSETTS INSTITUTE OF TECHNOLOGY, Cambridge, 02139.
Notes: Archival collections and papers at MIT.

INTERNATIONAL MILITARY TRIBUNAL FOR THE FAR EAST

IL —CENTER FOR RESEARCH LIBRARIES, 6050 S Kenwood Ave, Chicago, 60637. Donald B Simpson, Dir; Esther Smith, Collection Development Librn
Holdings: Vols Cat Microforms
Notes: Microfilm holdings of newspapers, official gazette. Microfilm and reprint of Imperial and National Diet proceedings. Archival material, Tokugwa period forward. Microfilm of annual reports of over 2,000 companies, 1872-1945. Meiji and Taisho prefectural statistics. Prange collection of censored periodicals, occupation period. Fairly complete collection of records of the International Military Tribunal for the Far East. 520 current periodical subscriptions. Descriptive pamphlet available.

INTERNATIONAL MONETARY AFFAIRS

DC —COMMISSION OF THE EUROPEAN COMMUNITIES, European Community Information Service Library, 2100 M St NW Suite 707, Washington, 20037. Barbara Sloan, Head of Public Inquiries
Holdings: Vols (35,000) Cat Maps Pix Microforms
Notes: Library contains all of the official documents and occasional publications of the institutions of the European Communities: ie European Economic Community (Common Market), European Atomic Energy Community (Euratom), European Coal and Steel Community (ECSC). It collects non-Community publications about European integration, international trade and monetary affairs. Also, has the publications of the General Agreements for Tariffs and Trade (GATT). Western European union, and Council of Europe. Also 1000 vertical files.

INTERNATIONAL ORGANIZATION

CA —WORLD AFFAIRS COUNCIL OF NORTH CALIFORNIA, Library, 312 Sutter St, San Francisco, 94108. Lone C Beeson, Head Librn; Edith Malamud, Circulation Librn
Holdings: Vols 6500 Cat Maps

DC —AMERICAN SOCIETY OF INTERNATIONAL LAW LIBRARY, 2223 Massachusetts Ave NW, Washington, 20008. Helen S Philos, Librn
Holdings: Vols (22,000) Cat
Budget: $7500
Notes: Public international law. (22,000 books, pamphlets, etc. Over 300 current foreign and domestic periodicals). Briefs and/or opinions in many international law cases. Documents of international organizations.

DC —COMMISSION OF THE EUROPEAN COMMUNITIES, European Community Information Service Library, 2100 M St NW Suite 707, Washington, 20037. Barbara Sloan, Head of Public Inquiries
Holdings: Vols (35,000) Cat Maps Pix Microforms
Notes: Library contains all of the official documents and occasional publications of the institutions of the European Communities: ie, European Economic Community (Common Market). European Atomic Energy Community (Euratom), European Coal and Steel Community (ECSC). It collects non-Community publications about European integration, international trade and monetary affairs. Also, has the publications the General Agreements for Tariffs and Trade (GATT), Western European Union, and Council of Europe. Also 1000 vertical files.

DC —US DEPT OF STATE, Library, Rm 3239 NS, Washington, 20520. Conrad P Eaton, Librn
Holdings: Vols (750,000) Cat Microforms
Notes: Incl 7200 microfilm reels.

ID —IDAHO STATE UNIVERSITY, Library, Pocatello, 83209. Joseph K W Lu, Librn
Holdings: Uncat Microforms Documents
Budget: ($10,000)
Notes: Over a million items. Partial

INTERNATIONAL ORGANIZATION (cont.)

depository for US Government publications (1,053,430 items); incl ERIC microfiche and unclassified AEC and Dept of Energy publications in microform; depository for Idaho State Government publications (16, 000 items); international government bodies (11,000 items).

IL —NORTHWESTERN UNIVERSITY, Library, Government Publications Dept, Evanston, 60201. Robert W Baumgartner, Head
Notes: Collection consists of US federal documents (depository library since 1876); state documents (emphasis on Illinois); municipal documents (emphasis on Evanston and Chicago); documents of international organizations (emphasis on United Nations, United Nations specialized agencies, Organization of American States, European Communities). Collection consists of publications of 44 international organizations. Shelflist maintained in the Government Publications Department. Most publications not incl in the library's general catalog.

MA —BOSTON PUBLIC LIBRARY, Government Documents Department, Boston, 02117. V Lloyd Jameson, Cur
Holdings: Microforms
Notes: We have major publications for many international organizations and most publications of UN, UNESCO, ILO, OAS, GATT, WHO IAEA, EC, OECD, WMO, FAO, IBRD and IMF. Also depository for the DANUBE Commission.

MA —HARVARD UNIVERSITY, Center for International Affairs, Library, Coolidge Hall, 1737 Cambridge St, Cambridge, 02138. Barbara Mitchell, Librn
Holdings: Vols (13,000) Periodicals
Notes: Collection emphasizes international politics and also contains considerable statistical material on individual countries. Library currently receives 115 periodical titles.

MA —HARVARD UNIVERSITY LIBRARY, Law School Library, Langdell Hall, Cambridge, 02138. Harry S Martin III, Librn

NJ —PRINCETON UNIVERSITY, Woodrow Wilson School Library, Princeton, 08544. Linda Oppenheim, Special Librn
Holdings: Vols (17,345)
Notes: This is a convenience collection primarily for Woodrow Wilson School of Public and International Affairs students. It is a functional special library, intended to support courses by providing reserve readings, journals and reference works. Faculty and students alike are expected to use the central campus library for research.

NY —CARNEGIE ENDOWMENT FOR INTERNATIONAL PEACE, James Thomson Shotwell Library, Formerly, New York, 10017.
Holdings: Vols (8500) Cat
Notes: This important collection has been dispersed (Summer 1983). The United Nations documents collections has gone to the University of the West Indies, St Augustine, Trinidad. The rest of the library has been given to special collections in the New York area or to the USBE.

NY —COUNCIL ON FOREIGN RELATIONS, Library, 58 E 68 St, New York, 10021. Janet M Rigney, Librn
Holdings: Vols (45,000) Cat Maps Microforms
Notes: Incl extensive newspaper clipping files and microform records. Strong in aspects of international relations and organization. Catalog of the foreign relations library (Boston: G K Hall, 1969), 9 vols. Supplement 3V UN and EEC limited depository.

NY —NEW YORK PUBLIC LIBRARY, Research Libraries, Economic & Public Affairs Div, Fifth Ave & 42 St, New York, 10018. Edward DiRoma, Chief
Holdings: Vols (1,500,000) Cat Microforms
Notes: Publications of most international organizations are fully or partially represented in holdings.

NY —UNITED NATIONS, Dag Hammarskjold Library, Rm L382, New York, 10017. Vladimir Orlov, Librn
Holdings: Cat Microforms

OR —UNIVERSITY OF OREGON LIBRARY, Documents Section, Eugene, 97403. Tom Stave, Section Head; John Shuler, Documents Librn
Holdings: Vols (250,000) Microforms
Notes: Depository for Canadian government and its agencies, and European Communities publications. Comprehensive holdings of the United Nations and its agencies plus League of Nations publications.

ON —CANADA DEPT OF EXTERNAL AFFAIRS, Library Services Div, 125 Sussex Dr, Ottawa, K1A 0G2, Can. Ruth Margaret Thompson, Dir
Holdings: Vols (40,000) Cat Maps Phonorecords Audiotapes Microforms
Notes: Incl 1000 maps, 250,000 microforms, and 550,000 documents.

†ON —METROPOLITAN TORONTO LIBRARY, Social Sciences Dept, 789 Yonge St, Toronto, M4W 2G8, Can. Abdus Salam, Head
Holdings: Vols Cat Maps Phonorecords Audiotapes 16mm Films Microforms
Notes: Thecollection is a full depository for Canadian federal and Ontario provincial publications and contains an exhaustive collection of publications from the various Canadian provinces. It includes statutes, gazettes, legislative debates, journals, reports, etc. Also extensive holdings for the US and Great Britain; comprehensive holdings of treaties for Canada, Great Britain and the US; selected publications for other foreign countries. Types of publications emphasized are statutory laws, treaties, legislative proceedings, government directories and manuals, statistical materials and national yearbooks. Large collection of UN materials; full depository for UNESCO publications; selected publications of various international organizations. The collection is cited in Canada, National Library, Resources Survey *Section,Research Collections in Canadian* Libraries, Volume 5, *Collections of Official Publications in Canada* (Ottawa: Supply and Services Canada, 1976).

INTERNATIONAL ORGANIZATIONS see International Agencies

INTERNATIONAL PAYMENTS, BALANCE OF see Balance of Payments

INTERNATIONAL POLITICS see World Politics

INTERNATIONAL RELATIONS

CA —LOS ANGELES PUBLIC LIBRARY, Social Sciences Dept, 630 W Fifth St, Los Angeles, 90071. Marilyn C Wherley, Principal Librn
Holdings: Vols 2000 Cat
Budget: ($150,000)
Notes: International relations, incl documents of international agencies and governments, long runs of periodicals, indexes, pamphlets, bibliographies. No separate catalog. Popular and scholarly works.

CA —COMMONWEALTH CLUB OF CALIFORNIA, Library, 681 Market St, San Francisco, 94105. Virginia Rees, Librn
Holdings: Vols (6500) Cat Maps Pix
Budget: ($2000)

CA —WORLD AFFAIRS COUNCIL OF NORTH CALIFORNIA, Library, 312 Sutter St, San Francisco, 94108. Lone C Beeson, Head Librn; Edith Malamud, Circulation Librn
Holdings: Vols 6500 Cat Maps

CA —ABC-CLIO, Inge Boehm Library, 2040 Alameda Padre Serra, PO Box 4397, Santa Barbara, 93103. Hope Smith, Librn
Holdings: Vols (2000) Uncat
Budget: $10,000
Notes: Current serials (2000) and reference works on history; 1450-present; US and Canadian history, prehistory-present; and history-related social science and humanities. Library serves as support unit in the publication of *Historical Abstracts* and *America: History and Life.*

CA —HOOVER INSTITUTION ON WAR, REVOLUTION & PEACE, Stanford University, Stanford, 94305. Milorad M Drachkovitch, Archivist
Holdings: Cat Mss Maps Pix Slides Microforms
Notes: One of the nation's most extensive collections in many specialized areas. Described in *Archival and Manuscript Materials at the Hoover Institution...A Checklist of Major Collections (July 1977)* $2.00.

DC —COMMISSION OF THE EUROPEAN COMMUNITIES, European Community Information Service Library, 2100 M St NW Suite 707, Washington, 20037. Barbara Sloan, Head of Public Inquiries
Holdings: Vols (35,000) Cat Maps Pix Microforms
Notes: Library contains all of the official documents and occasional publications of the institutions of the European Communities: ie, European Economic Community (Common Market), European Atomic Energy Community (Euratom), European Coal and Steel Community (ECSC). It collects non-Community publications about European integration, international trade and monetary affairs. Also, has the publications of the General Agreements for Tariffs and Trade (GATT), Western European Union, and Council of Europe. Also 1000 vertical files.

DC —EXPORT-IMPORT BANK OF THE UNITED STATES, EXIMBANK Library, 811 Vermont Ave NW, Washington, 20571. Theodora McGill, Librn; John Posniak, Asst Librn
Holdings: Vols (15,000) Maps Audiotapes
Notes: The library has almost a complete set of the *Economist Intelligence* unit of London's *Quarterly Economic Reviews*; various types of materials with general, economic and statistical data on virtually every country of the world; incl foreign government publications, publications of various international organizations, and US Government documents.

DC —GEORGETOWN UNIVERSITY, Library, Special Collections Div, 37 & O Sts NW, Washington, 20057. George M Barringer, Special Collections Librn; Nicholas B Sheetz, Mss Librn
Notes: The Heinrich Kronstein Memorial Collection of International and Foreign Trade Law, as well as the papers of various American diplomats, incl those of George C McGhee, John J Jova, Richard T Crane, Hamilton King, and Martin F Herz.

DC —GEORGETOWN UNIVERSITY, Library, Special Collections Div, 37 & O Sts NW, Washington, 20057. George M Barringer, Special Collections Librn; Nicholas B Sheetz, Mss Librn
Holdings: Cat Mss Pix
Notes: The papers of James Brown Scott (1866-1945), internationalist and authority in international law, consisting of correspondence, memoranda, documents, minutes, printed material, manuscripts of articles and addresses, photographs, and newspaper clippings. Incl is material from Scott's activities as Solicitor (1906-1910) and Special Advisor (1914-1917) for the State Department, as delegate to the Second Hague Conference (1907) and the Paris Peace Conference (1919), his membership and offices in the Carnegie Endowment for International Peace, the American Society of International Law, and the Institut de Droit International, as well as Scott's involvement in numerous courts of international arbitration. Also incl is material relating to Pan-American law. Correspondence incl letters from Charles Evans Hughes, Robert Bacon, William Jennings Bryan,James Bryce, Nicholas Murray Butler, Andrew Carnegie, Charles Francis Adams, Frank B Kellogg, Robert Lansing, Franklin Roosevelt, Elihu Root, and Woodrow Wilson, among many others. The papers of George Crews McGhee (1912), geologist, oil producer, and diplomat. The papers incl files from

INTERNATIONAL RELATIONS (cont.)

McGhee's United States ambassadorships to Turkey (1951-1953) and Germany (1963-1968) as well as his extensive involvement in numerous organizations and committees incl the Combined Raw Materials Board, the Bilderberg Group, the Draper Committee, the Committee for Economic Development, and the Business Council for International Understanding, among many others. Also incl are 264 volumes from the 17th to early 20th century relating to Turkey. The Archives of the Society for Historians of Foreign Relations, contain correspondence, minutes, agenda, constitutionsand by-laws, rosters, publications, and reports. The records concern the founding and organization of SHER, its membership, meetings, and activities. Founded in 1967, and incorporated in 1972, the Society's primary concern is the advancement of historical analysis of foreign relations.

DC —GEORGE WASHINGTON UNIVERSITY, Gelman Library, 2130 H St NW, Washington, 20052.
Holdings: Vols (50,000)// Cat Mss Microforms
Notes: The Carnegie Endowment for International Peace library was purchased in 1950. The collection has been cataloged and assimilated in the University Library and the Law Library's holdings. It includes monographs, a few bound manuscripts, conference proceedings, and periodicals. Certain periodicals are available on microfilm through Clearwater Publishing Co. Holdings are cataloged individually.

DC —LIBRARY OF CONGRESS, Washington, 20540.
Notes: Project of a consortium to microfilm about 200,000 pp of material on Great Britain, France, Russia and Prussia, for the period 1848-1918 in the ms and documentary collections of the Austrian State Archives. The collection will incl, among others, documents on the Austro-Prussian War of 1866, the treaty negotiations between France and Italy in 1868-1870, the Orient Question of 1877-1878, the persecution of Jews in Russia in 1882, the Congo Conference in Berlin, 1884-1887 and the British-Portuguese conflict in East Africa, 1889-1891. Copies are available at LC the Center for Research Libraries, the Hampshire Inter-Library Center, and the libraries of Boston College, Yale, Harvard, Duke, Stanford and the University of Virginia.

DC —US DEPT OF STATE, Library, Rm 3239 NS, Washington, 20520. Conrad P Eaton, Librn
Holdings: Vols (750,000) Cat Microforms
Notes: Incl 7200 microfilm reels.

†HI —PACIFIC AND ASIAN AFFAIRS COUNCIL, Pacific House Library, 2004 University Ave, Honolulu, 96816.
Notes: Asia and the Pacific. Pacific and Asian foreign policy.

†MA —JOHN F KENNEDY LIBRARY, Columbia Point, Boston, 02125. Dan H Fenn Jr, Dir
Holdings: Cat Mss Pix Audiotapes Videotapes 16mm Films Microforms
Notes: 20,000,000 pages of papers of President John F Kennedy, his staff, his associates, congressmen and ambassadors. Holdings are described in "Historical Materials in the John F Kennedy Library." Copies may be obtained by writing the Research Archivist. Also copies of AFL-CIO press releases and records relating to legislation, relations with the Federal government and international affairs, 1955-1968. 9 rolls of microfilm.

MA —HARVARD UNIVERSITY, Center for International Affairs, Library, Coolidge Hall, 1737 Cambridge St, Cambridge, 02138. Barbara Mitchell, Librn
Holdings: Vols (13,000)
Notes: Collection emphasizes international politics and also contains considerable statistical material on individual countries. Library currently receives 115 periodical titles.

MA —HARVARD UNIVERSITY LIBRARY, Law School Library, Langdell Hall, Cambridge, 02138. Harry S Martin III, Librn
Holdings: Mss Microforms
Notes: Library's 20-vol *Catalog of International Law and Relations* published 1965-1967.

MA —TUFTS UNIVERSITY, Fletcher School of Law & Diplomacy, Murrow Center of Public Diplomacy, Medford, 02155. Natalie Schatz, Cur of Special Collections
Holdings: Vols (1500)// Cat Mss Pix Phonorecords Audiotapes 16mm Films
Notes: Professional papers and diaries of John Moors Cabot.

MA —BOSTON COLLEGE, Law School Library, 885 Centre St, Newton Centre, 02159. Sharon Hamby, Librn
Holdings: Vols (160,000) Cat Maps Pix
Notes: Emphasizes Anglo-American law and international law and relations.

NJ —PRINCETON UNIVERSITY, Library, Manuscript Collection, Nassau St, Princeton, 08540. Jean F Preston, Cur
Holdings: Cat Mss Pix
Notes: The John Foster Dulles Collection of personal papers, 1907-1959, fills 621 boxes. Unpublished typescript guide (938 p) is available in library. Also oral history collection made 1964-67 by Dulles' friends and colleagues. 275 typescripts. Published catalog: *Dulles Oral History Collection, A Descriptive Catalogue* (Princeton, 1967). Terms of access: each author controls his transcript, most are open, some are closed. Limited photocopying. See published catalog.

NJ —PRINCETON UNIVERSITY, Woodrow Wilson School Library, Princeton, 08544. Linda Oppenheim, Special Librn
Holdings: Vols 17,345
Budget: $30,000
Notes: This is a convenience collection primarily for Woodrow Wilson School of Public and International Affairs students. It is a functional special library, intended to support courses by providing reserve readings, journals and reference works. Faculty and students alike are expected to use the central campus library for research.

NY —STATE UNIVERSITY OF NEW YORK AT ALBANY, Library, Special Collections Dept, 1400 Washington Ave, Albany, 12222. Marion P Munzer, Coordr
Notes: Articles, typescripts, and pamphlets by Erich Hula on international relations; lecture notes and mss; clipping file (21 linear feet). Part of the Library's German Exile Collection.
See also entry under Hula, Erich

NY —CARNEGIE ENDOWMENT FOR INTERNATIONAL PEACE, James Thomson Shotwell Library, Formerly, New York, 10017.
Holdings: Vols (8500) Cat
Notes: This important collection has been dispersed (Summer 1983). The United Nations documents collection has gone to the University of the West Indies, St Augustine, Trinidad. The rest of the library has been given to special collections in the New York area or to the USBE.

NY —COLUMBIA UNIVERSITY LIBRARIES, Rare Book & Manuscript Library, 801 Butler Library, 535 W 114 St, New York, 10027. Kenneth A Lohf, Librn
Holdings: Mss
Notes: A strong collection in this area incl, for example, the Archives of the Carnegie Endowment for International Peace (712,500 items), Council on Religion and International Affairs (318,000 items), Declaration of Atlantic Unity (20,000 items), the papers of James T Shotwell (60,000 items), Andrew W Cordier (200,000 items) and V K Wellington Koo (50,000 items). Restricted use.

NY —COUNCIL ON FOREIGN RELATIONS, Library, 58 E 68 St, New York, 10021. Janet M Rigney, Librn
Holdings: Vols (45,000) Cat Maps Microforms
Notes: Incl extensive newspaper clipping files and microform records. Strong in aspects of international relations and organization. Catalog of the foreign relations library (Boston: G K Hall, 1969), 9 vols. Supplement 3V UN and EEC limited depository.

NY —NEW YORK PUBLIC LIBRARY, Research Libraries, Economic & Public Affairs Div, Fifth Ave & 42 St, New York, 10018. Edward DiRoma, Chief
Holdings: Vols (1,500,000) Cat Microforms

NY —NEW YORK PUBLIC LIBRARY, Research Libraries, General Research Div, Fifth Ave & 42 St, New York, 10018. Keith McKinney, Assistant Div Chief
Holdings: Cat
Notes: Current periodicals. Subjects incl advertising, business and professional periodicals, international affairs, labor and trade unions, political and social sciences, humanities in general. Division holds 10,000 titles.

NY —UNITED NATIONS, Dag Hammarskjold Library, Rm L382, New York, 10017. Vladimir Orlov, Librn
Holdings: Cat Microforms

NC —DUKE UNIVERSITY, William R Perkins Library, Durham, 27706. Elvin E Strowd, University Librn
Notes: The J Walter Lambeth collection consists of writings of statesman and historians of countries in Asia, Africa, Europe and South America; its purpose is to increase our knowledge of world problems and to promote international understanding. Additions are ongoing.

OH —PUBLIC LIBRARY OF CINCINNATI & HAMILTON COUNTY, Government and Business Dept, 800 Vine St, Cincinnati, 45202. Paul T Hudson, Head
Holdings: Vols 120,000 Cat
Notes: Department receives over 1200 periodical and loose-leaf service titles, 1500 serial titles and over 1500 telephone directories. Subjects include political science, especially foreign relations, economics, law, public administration and business management. Dept houses Murray Seasongood collection of local government. Dept has extensive census material from 1790. Library is a full depository for US Government Publications, 1884 to date.

PA —US ARMY WAR COLLEGE LIBRARY, Carlisle Barracks, 17013. Barbara E Stevens, Dir

PA —UNIVERSITY OF PITTSBURGH, Library, Graduate School of Public and International Affairs, Forbes Quadrangle, 1st floor West, Pittsburgh, 15260. Nicholas C Caruso, Librn
Holdings: Vols (80,000) Cat
Budget: ($150,000)
Notes: The library attempts to collect as many national economic and social development plans as possible from the developing countries of the world. It also holds city, regional and state plans for Pennsylvania particularly, the 9 southwestern counties of Pennsylvania.

SD —NATIONAL COLLEGE OF BUSINESS, Thomas Jefferson Learning Resource Center, 321 Kansas City St, Rapid City, 57701. Linda Watson, Library Dir
Holdings: Vols (26,000) Cat
Notes: Analyses (Index) of national and international issues. Published at irregular, frequent intervals, produced by the American Enterprise institute for Public Policy Research.

TX —UNIVERSITY OF TEXAS LIBRARIES, General Libraries, Barker Texas History Center, PO Box P, Austin, 78712. Don Carleton, Dir
Notes: Papers, etc, documenting the career of Luther H Evans.

UT —BRIGHAM YOUNG UNIVERSITY, Harold B Lee Library, Unversity Hill, Provo, 84602. Sterling Albrecht, Dir
Notes: Diplomacy.

ON —CANADA DEPT OF EXTERNAL AFFAIRS, Library Services Div, 125 Sussex Dr, Ottawa, K1A 0G2, Can. Ruth Margaret Thompson, Dir
Holdings: Vols (40,000) Cat Maps Phonorecords Audiotapes Microforms
Notes: Incl 1000 maps, 250,000 microforms, and 550,000 documents.

ON —LIBRARY OF PARLIAMENT, Parliament Bldgs, Ottawa, K1A 0A9, Can.

INTERNATIONAL RELATIONS (cont.)

Erik J Spicer, Parliamentary Librn
Holdings: Vols 35,000 Cat

ON —CANADIAN INSTITUTE OF INTERNATIONAL AFFAIRS, 15 King's College Circle, Toronto, M5S 2V9, Can. Jane Barrett, Librn
Holdings: Vols (23,000) Cat Mss Microforms Books VF
Budget: ($8800)
Notes: Incl both historical and current material on all subjects relevant to a study of Canadian foreign relations.

INTERNATIONAL RELIEF

†NY —COLUMBIA UNIVERSITY LIBRARIES, Butler Library, Rare Book and Manuscript Library, 535 W 114 St, New York, 10027.
Notes: Papers of the US Solicitor General, 1930-33, relating to the American Red Cross Mission to Russia, 1917-18.

NY —UNITED NATIONS, Dag Hammarskjold Library, Rm L382, New York, 10017. Vladimir Orlov, Librn

INTERNATIONAL RESCUE COMMITTEE

MI —MICHIGAN STATE UNIVERSITY, International Library, South and Southeast Asia Collection, East Lansing, 48824. Clinton Lockert, Bibliographer
Holdings: Vols (3500) Cat Mss Maps Pix Audiotapes Microforms
Notes: Emphasis is on South Vietnam (1955-1962). The University had a Vietnam Advisory Group headquartered in Saigon during this period. Have complete holdings of *Reports and Documents Serie* of the MSU Vietnam Advisory Group. Extensive correspondence, documents and publications of the American Friends of Vietnam, and of the International Rescue Committee. Very extensive clippings, correspondence, documents, and photographs from the Gilbert Jonas Collection, and the Wesley Fishel Collection. Significant unique items. Representative selection of Vietnamese literature.

INTERNATIONAL SECURITY see Security, International

INTERNATIONAL SOCIETY FOR KRISHNA CONSCIOUSNESS (AMERICA)

CA —GRADUATE THEOLOGICAL UNION LIBRARY, New Religious Movements Research Collection, Public Services and Special Collections Dept, 2400 Ridge Road, Berkeley, 94709. Diane Choquette, Dept Head
Holdings: Vols (3000) Mss Pix
Notes: Begun in 1977, the collection focuses on religious movements new to America since 1960, and unorthodox religious movements resurgent since 1960. American forms of Hinduism, Buddhism, Sikhism, and Sufism are included along with occultism, Neo-Paganism, esoteric and alternative forms of Christianity, feminist spirituality, and human potential movements having a spiritual aspect. Legal issues, such as deprogramming, and the question of church/state relations are an important part of the collection. The Library is a depository for publications of the Unification Church in America, the Church of Scientology, and the International Society for Krishna Consciousness (America). The responses of mainstream religions and concerned citizens groups are also included. Besides 3000 monographs, the library has 400 periodical titles, 200 posters from the San FranciscoBay Area, 1965-77, 300 research papers, and 31 linear feet of ephemera.

INTERNATIONAL STATISTICS see Statistics, Foreign and International

INTERNATIONAL THEATRE

IL —NORTHWESTERN UNIVERSITY, Library, Special Collections Dept, 1937 Sheridan Rd, Evanston, 60201. R Russell Maylone, Cur
Holdings: Cat
Notes: 12,000 plays.

NY —NEW YORK PUBLIC LIBRARY, Performing Arts Research Center, Billy Rose Theatre Collection, 111 Amsterdam Ave, New York, 10023. Dorothy L Swerdlove, Cur
Holdings: Cat
See also entry under Theatre - History.

NY —THEATRE COLLECTION OF THE INTERNATIONAL THEATRE INSTITUTE OF THE UNITED STATES, INC, Library, Suite 1510, 1860 Broadway, New York, 10023. Elizabeth B Burdick, Dir
Holdings: Vols (4525) Cat Mss Pix
Budget: ($35,000)
Notes: The International Theatre Institute was founded by UNESCO to "promote the exchange of knowledge and practice in the theatre arts." In 1948, eleven nations, incl the United States, became charter members of the international organization, which today has national centers or affiliates in 64 countries. The American center is the International Theatre Institute of the United States (ITI/US). In 1970, as one of its programs to strengthen communication among theatre people, ITI/US opened a library devoted to international theatre since World War II. The Collection's main holdings have been amassed over the 35-year operation of ITI/US through its world-wide exchange of information, publications, and people. Holdings document theatre activity in 140 countries. The 4525 vols on American and foreign theatre(covering history, management, design, stagecraft, theory, criticism, biography, playscripts) represent only a small part of the total collection. Focus is on foreign theatre companies, directors, playwrights, designers, managers, actors. The emphasis is on the acquisition of material which is generally unavailable in this country: foreign yearbooks, house organs, newsletters, programs, press releases, production schedules, brochures, periodicals, monographs, articles, newspaper clippings. While these fugitive items have never been counted, they have been cataloged by country, then indexed by title, subject, or name of theatre. The library receives regularly 250 periodicals on the performing arts (cataloged by country, then indexed by title). It now owns 6417 foreign plays from 80 countries in ms or publishedmss or published editions, in collections and anthologies, and in periodicals. Each play is cataloged by author, title, and country of origin. The section on American theatre incl books, programs, reviews, over 60 periodicals, 2061 American plays. The activities of approx 700 theatres across the country are documented by annual files containing production schedules, press releases, programs, brochures for each theatrical season.

PA —UNIVERSITY OF PITTSBURGH, Special Collections Dept, Curtis Theatre Collection, 363 Hillman Library, Pittsburgh, 15260. Jeanette Blanco, Cur
Holdings: Vols (4000) Cat Mss Documents Microforms Pix Slides VF
Notes: The legitimate theatre of plays, musicals and vaudeville, chiefly of New York City and Pittsburgh, from 1865, and other US, community, summer, college and foreign theatre. Incl 500,000 programs, 12, 000 pictures, 300 posters, the Oliver P Merriman Scrapbooks and 300 other scrapbooks, clippings and other ephemera. Vols incl over 3000 acting editions and playscripts. Separate collections: Ralph G Allen Burlesque Skits Collection; Michael Ellis Papers; William P Halstead Theatre Collection; Kenyon Family Papers; Philip Dunning Playscripts Collection; Pittsburgh Playhouse Records; Pittsburgh Savoyards Records. Noncirculating.

TX —SOUTHERN METHODIST UNIVERSITY, Fondren Library, McCord Theater Collection, Room 301, Dallas, 75275. Edyth Renshaw, Cur; Linda Sellers, Pub Serv
Holdings: Vols (2000) Uncat Mss Pix Slides Phonorecords
Notes: See *Theatre Collections in Libraries and Museums*, Gilder and Freedley (Theatre Arts, 1936). The McCord Theatre Collection encompasses the entire spectrum of the performing arts. The central purpose is to gather records of our regional theater before such ephemeral material is lost. Records of over two hundred early Texas theaters, some fragmentary and some relatively complete, are in the files. These records incl photographs of buildings, stagehands, orchestras, and performers. Local theatre history incl the once famous Dallas Little Theatre and the Margo Jones Theatre. The national theatre, opera, ballet, and circus archives incl pictures (some autographed), programs, posters, throw-aways, tear sheets, clippings, and letters. Our international archives are small, but we have some excellent material, eg, artifacts from Max Reinhardt's production of"The Miracle" which happened to go bankrupt in Dallas. After a few years the items were given to us. There are posters, tear sheets, souvenir programs, and other colorful items from Morris Gest and the Artef Collection. We have about 200 19th century English playbills and a few from the 18th century. There is a collection of modern English, French, and other European programs, many of them illustrated souvenir programs. Also, magazines on theater, cinema, and television (1800). Scrapbooks covering both southwest and Dallas theater, 1890s-1950s. Special Collections: artifacts and documents on puppets; masks; costume design; circus; and ballet and dance. The Harriet Bacon MacDonald Collection of over 200 photographs of musicians appearing in Dallas during the first three decades of the 20th century. Many autographed. Affiliated with Meadow Theatre of the Arts.

WI —UNIVERSITY OF WISCONSIN, MADISON, Memorial Library, British & American Language & Literature Collection, 728 State St, Madison, 53706. Yvonne Schofer, Bibliographer
Holdings: // Cat Mss Pix
Notes: Thomas H Dickinson Collection. An extensive collection of special interest to scholars and students of the American and European theatre. Includes books, photographs, diaries, memorabilia, individual author collections, prints, sketches, playbills, ephemera concerning the drama and theatre of the US, England, France, Spain, Germany, Italy, Czechoslovakia, Poland, Russia, Rumania, Yugoslavia, Austria, and Japan. Books held by Library: other materials housed in Communication Arts Dept, 6117 Vilas Communication Hall, UW-Madison.

ON —MCMASTER UNIVERSITY, Mills Memorial Library, Div of Archives & Research Collections, Hamilton, L8S 4L6, Can. G R Hill, Univ Librn
Holdings: //Cat Mss Pix
Notes: Thomas H Dickinson Collection. An extensive collection of special interest to scholars and students of the American, diaries, memorabilia, individual author collections prints, sketches, playballs, ephemera concerning the drama and theatre of the US England, France, Spain, Germany, Italy, Czechoslovakia, Poland, Russia, Rumania, Yugoslavia, Austria, and Japan.

INTERNATIONAL TRADE

CA —GOLDEN GATE UNIVERSITY, One Embarcadero Center, No 216, San Francisco, 94111. Jeanne Nichols, Librn
Notes: World Trade Libraries and archives.

CT —YALE UNIVERSITY, Social Science Library, Economic Growth Center Collection, 140 Prospect St, New Haven, 06520. Billie I Salter, Librn
Holdings: Vols (47,600) Cat
Notes: Economic data on national economies and their development: budgets, plans, statistical yearbooks and bulletins, censuses, national accounts, trade, monetary data, statistics, etc. The focus is primarily on less-developed countries. Mostly government documents 3800 serials currently received.

INTERNATIONAL TRADE (cont.)

Shelf list organized by country and LC number, in addition to dictionary catalog.

DC —COMMISSION OF THE EUROPEAN COMMUNITIES, European Community Information Service Library, 2100 M St NW Suite 707, Washington, 20037. Barbara Sloan, Head of Public Inquiries
Holdings: Vols (35,000) Cat Maps Pix Microforms
Notes: Library contains all of the official documents and occasional publications of the institutions of the European Communities: ie, European Economic Community (Common Market), European Atomic Energy Community (Euratom), European Coal and Steel Community (ECSC). It collects non-Community publications about European integration, international trade and monetary affairs. Also, has the publications of the General Agreements for Tariffs and Trade (GATT). Western European Union, and Council of Europe. Also 1000 vertical files.

HI —BANK OF HAWAII, Information Ctr, PO Box 2900, Honolulu, 96846. Sally Campbell, Information Mgr
Holdings: Vols 4000 Cat Maps
Notes: Economics research in developing areas of Hawaii, US Pacific islands. Asian and other foreign countries. Emphasis on economics, business statistics, demography, finance, banking, tourist industry, construction, domestic and foreign trade.

MA —BOSTON PUBLIC LIBRARY, Government Documents Department, Boston, 02117. V Lloyd Jameson, Cur
Holdings: Microforms
Notes: International trade statistics.

MA —HARVARD UNIVERSITY, Graduate School of Business Administration, Baker Library, Soldiers Field, Boston, 02163. Mary V Chatfield, Librn; Florence Bartoshesky, Cur of Manuscripts and Archives
Holdings: Cat Mss
Notes: Incl strong collection on the China trade. See *American Neptune,* XIII (1953), 118-124.

†MA —JOHN F KENNEDY LIBRARY, Columbia Point, Boston, 02125. Dan H Fenn Jr, Dir
Holdings: / / Cat Mss
Notes: Files and papers of JFK and his key foreign trade advisors Christian Herter and Howard Petersen, 1961-1967. 40 linear ft of mss. Holdings are described in "Historical Materials in the John F Kennedy Library." Copies may be obtained by writing the Research Archivist.

NY —UNITED NATIONS, Dag Hammarskjold Library, Rm L382, New York, 10017. Vladimir Orlov, Librn

INTERNATIONAL TRIBUNALS see International Courts

INTERNATIONAL UNION OF MINE, MILL, AND SMELTER WORKERS

CO —UNIVERSITY OF COLORADO, Libraries, Western Historical Collections, Boulder, 80309.
Holdings: workers
Notes: The Western Federation of Miners was a radical hard-rock miners' union that began in Montana and spread to Idaho, Washington, Utah, Colorado, Arizona, New Mexico, Nevada, and California. Its successor Mine-Mill, resurged during the New Deal years. It merged with the United Steelworkers in 1967. This collection consists of 700 boxes of files, correspondence, and publications; 500 bound vols of minutes, ledgers, magazines, and court proceedings; the library of the Research Department, consisting of approx. 360 linear feet of books, pamphlets, and periodicals; a number of artifacts and curios incl union banners and seals, convention delegates' ribbons, photographs and membership cards. Most of the materials are for the period 1936-1967. A typescript guide, name indexes and other finding aides are available.

INTERNATIONAL UNION OF RADIO SCIENCE

CA —UNIVERSITY OF CALIFORNIA, BERKELEY, Bancroft Library, Manuscripts Division, Berkeley, 94720. James D Hart, Dir
Holdings: Mss
Notes: Papers of Samuel Silver, specialist on applied electromagnetic, microwave, and radio astronomical problems. Incl much on the International Union of Radio Science. 48 linear ft.

INTERNATIONAL UNIONS see International Agencies

INTEROCEANIC CANALS see Canals, Interoceanic

INTERPLANETARY PHENOMENA

AZ —WORLD UNIVERSITY, Library, 711 E Blacklidge Dr, Tucson, 85719. Howard John Zitko, Cur
Holdings: Vols (15,000) Cat Mss Maps Audiotapes
Notes: Collection concerns what are generally called the "frontier sciences." No interibrary loan.

INTERPLANETARY VOYAGES

AL —UNIVERSITY OF ALABAMA, HUNTSVILLE, Library, Box 2600, Huntsville, 35807. John Warren, Dir
Holdings: Vol (4500)
Notes: The Willy Ley Collection of Rocketry and Space Travel.

CO —US AIR FORCE ACADEMY, Library, USAF Academy, Colorado Springs, 80840. Reiner H Schaeffer, Dir
Holdings: Vols 6000 Cat Mss Maps Pix
Notes: The Colonel Richard Gimbel Aeronautical History Collection. Incl material from ancient myth to 1903 on manned flight; early scientific works on physical properties of the atmosphere, and imaginative literature on moon voyages. Collection is most complete in manned pioneer balloon ascents (1783ff). Also the Richard Upjohn Light Collection formerly at Culver Military Academy. Separate catalog, index to be published. 250 mss, 100 maps, 2000 pictures, 5000 prints, 7000 clippings.

INTERPRETATION, BIBLICAL see Bible—Criticism, Interpretation, Etc.

INTERSTELLAR VOYAGES see Interplanetary Voyages

INTERUNIVERSITY COMMITTEE ON THE SUPERIOR STUDENT

CO —UNIVERSITY OF COLORADO, Libraries, Western Historical Collections, Boulder, 80309.
Holdings: Cat Mss
Notes: Papers of the Inter-University Committee on the Superior Student, which was organized before the launching of Sputnik, when a conference of 48 American educators meeting at the University of Colorado in June of 1957 called for greater utilization of talented scholars and a central clearing house for honors programs. Funded by a grant from Carnegie Corporation, ICSS was headed by Joseph Cohen. It collected and disseminated information and conducted conferences and consultations from 1958 to 1965. The collection contains administrative files, and surveys, research findings and publications dealing with honors programs. It covers the period 1957-1965 and consists of 62 boxes. A typescript inventory is available.

INTERURBAN RAILROADS see Street Railroads

INTOLERANCE see Religious Liberty

INTOXICANTS see Alcohol; Drugs; Liquors

INTOXICATION see Alcoholism; Drug Habit; Temperance

INTRAVAIA, TONI

KS —WICHITA PUBLIC LIBRARY, Art & Music Division, 223 S Main, Wichita, 67202. Leonard Messineo, Jr, Head, Art & Music Division; Deborah Hamilton, Special Collections Librn
Holdings: Uncat Audiotapes Videotape Pix
Notes: Alice Bauman Dance Symposia Collection. Contains 300 hours of audio tapes, 1 hour-long video tape, several hundred photographs, and fugitive material of the American Dance Symposia held in Wichita from 1968-1972. The symposia covered all dance idioms-ballet, modern, jazz, folk, ethnic, dance education and therapy-and featured such notable figures such as Leonide Massine, Martha Hill, William Christensen, Alfonso Cimber, Toni Intravaia, James Clouser, Eleo Pomare, Juana de Laban, and many others. Characterized by the *Kansas City Star* as the "most distinguished faculties of fine artists ever assembled in the contemporary world of dance."

INTUITION OF DURATION see Time Perception

INUITS see Eskimos and Inuits

INUNDATIONS see Floods

INVENTIONS AND INVENTORS

DC —GEORGETOWN UNIVERSITY, Library, Special Collections Div, 37 & O Sts NW, Washington, 20057. George M Barringer, Special Collections Librn; Nicholas B Sheetz, Mss Librn
Holdings: Cat
Notes: Papers of James Harris Rogers (1850-1929) consisting of newspaper clippings, photographs, and correspondence about his work and reputation as an inventor. Incl are several photographs of General John J Pershing's visit to Roger's lab when the latter was honored for his invention of the underground and subsea wireless and its contribution to the war effort.

IN —INDIANA UNIVERSITY, Lilly Library, Seventh St, Bloomington, 47405. William R Cagle, Librn
Holdings: Cat Mss
Notes: First appearances in print of great scientific discoveries. Mss incl papers of many scientists, particularly the biological sciences; also of some inventors.

MA —OLD STURBRIDGE VILLAGE, Research Library, Sturbridge, 01566. Theresa Rini Percy, Librn
Holdings: Cat
Notes: US to 1900.

NY —NEW YORK HISTORICAL SOCIETY, Library, 170 Central Park W, New York, 10024. James Gregory, Librn
Notes: Randall J LeBoeuf Jr's collection of Robert Fulton and related material, 1764-1857, consisting of correspondence, drawings, legal papers, etc, relating to steam engines and boats, canals, and torpedoes. The correspondents incl John Quincy Adams, Henry Clay, De Witt Clinton, Albert Gallatin, Benjamin H Latrobe, James Madison, James Monroe, John Livingston, Robert R Livingston, and William Thornton. Also incl are Fulton's expense and note book, 1803-1808, and Robert R Livingston's receipt book, 1808-1812. Approx 215 items, cataloged.

ON —METROPOLITAN TORONTO LIBRARY, Science & Technology Dept, 789 Yonge St, Toronto, M4W 2G8, Can. Margaret Walshe, Head
Holdings: Vols (120,000) Cat
Notes: Some aspects of technology for the specialist, the student, and the general public. The department gives high priority to Canadian material.

INVENTORY MANAGEMENT

†MA —BABSON COLLEGE LIBRARY, Horn Library, Wellesley, 02181.
Notes: Special collection on production and inventory management.

INVERTEBRATES

CA —CALIFORNIA ACADEMY OF SCIENCES, J W Mailliard Jr Library,

INVERTEBRATES (cont.)

Golden Gate Park, San Francisco, 94118. Ray Brian, Librn
Notes: Downs No 2160.

DC —SMITHSONIAN INSTITUTION, Archives Div, Washington, 20560. William W Moss, Archivist
Holdings: Cat Mss Maps Pix Slides
Notes: The Archives holds the records of the National Museum of Natural History's Dept of Invertebrate Zoology, Division of Echinoderms, Division of Marine Invertebrates, and Division of Mollusks, ca 1853-1975, as well as the personal papers of William H Dall, Paul Bartsch, Austin H Clark, and Waldo LaSalle Schmitt.

DC —SMITHSONIAN INSTITUTION LIBRARIES, Natural History Branch, Washington, 20560. Sylvia Churgin, Chief Librn
Holdings: Cat Mss Maps Pix Slides Microforms
Notes: Invertebrate zoology, Systematics. Incl crustacea, echinoderms, mollusks, worms, Cushman collection of foraminifera; Springer collection on crinoids; Wilson collection on copepoda.

HI —BERNICE P BISHOP MUSEUM, Library, PO Box 19000-A, Honolulu, 96819. Cynthia Timberlake, Librn
Holdings: Vols (90,000) Cat Mss Maps Pix Slides Microforms
Notes: Only American library devoted exclusively to the Pacific region. Collection reflects historical and contemporary research emphases of Bishop Museum; ie the natural and cultural history of the Pacific. Areas of concentration incl archaeology, ethnology, linguistics, voyages and explorations, history, vertebrate and invertebrate zoology, botany and museology. Strong special collections incl photographs, mss and archives, maps and art. Publications: Quarterly "Additions to the Catalog," *Dictionary Catalog of the* Library (9 vols and 2 suppl; Boston: G K Hall, 1964-69).

IA —IOWA STATE UNIVERSITY, Library, Ames, 50011. Warren B Kuhn, Dean of Library Services
Holdings: Cat
Notes: Extensive serial holdings supplement this strong collection.

NY —AMERICAN MUSEUM OF NATURAL HISTORY, Library Services Dept, Central Park W & 79th St, New York, 10024. Nina J Root, Chairwoman; Mary Genett, Asst Librn for Reference Services
Holdings: Vols (385,000) Cat Mss Maps Pix Slides Microforms
Notes: Nearly all collections are outstanding for depth of coverage and international range. Early and historic works, rare books, colored illustrations, and relevant serial publications supplement the modern scientific publications necessary to the researches of the scientific staff and the work of the educational division.

OR —OREGON STATE UNIVERSITY, Marine Science Center, Library, Newport, 97365. Marilyn Guin, Librn
Holdings: Vols (8000) Cat Maps Microforms
Budget: ($15,000)
Notes: Collection emphasizes marine ecology, invertebrate zoology and marine ecology, invertebrate zoology and marine algae. The portion of the collection concerned with fisheries emphasizes aquaculture. Collection is divided between the Marine Science Library and the Main OSU Library.

TX —UNIVERSITY OF TEXAS, Marine Science Institute Library, Port Aransas, 78373. Ruth Grundy, Librn
Holdings: Vols (45,000) Cat Maps Pix
Budget: ($70,000)
Notes: Current researches in marine science, especially concerning the Gulf of Mexico, the Texas Coastal Zone, and the Continental Shelf. Incl journals.

INVERTEBRATES, AQUATIC

MO —US FISH & WILDLIFE SERVICE, Columbia National Fisheries Research Laboratory, Rte One, Columbia, 65201. Axie Hindman, Librn
Holdings: Vols (2000) Cat Microforms
Budget: ($7000)
Notes: Pesticides in aquatic biota; fisheries research; fresh-water ecology. Also incl collection in water pollution, acid rain, aquatic invertebrets, environment and 10,000 reprints.

INVERTEBRATES, FOSSIL

CA —UNIVERSITY OF CALIFORNIA, BERKELEY, Physical Sciences Libraries, Earth Sciences Library, 230 Earth Sciences Bldg, Berkeley, 94720. Julie F Rinaldi, Librn
Holdings: Vols (83,202) Cat Microforms
Budget: ($74,880)
Notes: A strong collection, giving particular emphasis to vertebrates and invertebrates. Especially rich in serials; approx (2850) current titles received on subscription, and in foreign-language publications.

NY —AMERICAN MUSEUM OF NATURAL HISTORY, Library Services Dept, Central Park W & 79th St, New York, 10024. Nina J Root, Chairwoman; Mary Genett, Asst Librn for Reference Services
Holdings: Vols (385,000) Cat Mss Maps Pix Slides Microforms
Notes: Nearly all collections are outstanding for depth of coverage and international range. Early and historic works, rare books, colored illustrations, and relevant serial publications supplement the modern scientific publications necessary to the researches of the scientific staff and the work of the educational division. Open to the public.

PA —CARNEGIE LIBRARY OF PITTSBURGH, Science & Technology Dept, 4400 Forbes Ave, Pittsburgh, 15213. Catherine M Brosky, Dept Head
Notes: Subject of secondary interest with emphasis on North America. Covers paleobotany, vertebrates and invertebrates, foraminifera, mollusks, fish, reptiles, mammals. Abstracts, indexes, catalogs, bibliographies, journals, continuations, federal, state and society publications available.

INVESTIGATIONS, GOVERNMENT see Governmental Investigations

INVESTMENT IN REAL ESTATE see Real Estate Investment

INVESTMENTS

CA —UNIVERSITY OF SOUTHERN CALIFORNIA, Crocker Business Library, Hoffman Hall, University Park, Los Angeles, 90007. Judith A Truelson, Head Librn
Holdings: Vols (100,000) Cat Microforms
Notes: The Roy P Crocker Library of Business Administration, located in Hoffman Hall, houses more than 100,000 volumes and regularly receives approximately 1500 trade, financial, economics, labor, and general business periodicals and newspapers. The areas of subject concentration include business economics, finance and investments, general management/management theory, international business, finance and management, marketing/food marketing, and quantitative business analysis.

CA —ALAMEDA COUNTY LIBRARY SYSTEM, Business & Government Library, 2201 Broadway, Oakland, 94612. David Lewallen, Manager
Holdings: Vols (10,000) Cat Maps Microforms
Budget: ($50,000)

CA —PASADENA PUBLIC LIBRARY, Business-Technology Division, 285 E Walnut St, Pasadena, 91101. Anne Cain, Librn for Reference Services
Holdings: Vols (19,000) Cat Microforms
Budget: ($35,000)
Notes: Investment and financial services (current and historical); trade and industrial directories; corporate annual reports; current economic statistics in business services and in state and federal government publications. Special index to directory collection.

CA —CONTRA COSTA COUNTY LIBRARY, 1750 Oak Park Blvd, Pleasant Hill, 94523. Lyn Talme, Business Specialist
Holdings: Vols (7000)
Notes: Incl 76 periodicals, 1000 corporate annual reports, and 316 telephone directories.

DC —EDISON ELECTRIC INSTITUTE, Library-8th Floor, 1111 19th St NW, Washington, 20036. Ethel Tiberg, Mgr, Library Services
Holdings: Vols (13,321) Cat Maps Pix Microforms

GA —ATLANTA PUBLIC LIBRARY, Ivan Allen Jr Dept of Science, Industry & Government, One Margaret Mitchell Square, Atlanta, 30303. William D Munro, Head
Holdings: Vols (15,000) Cat Microforms
Budget: ($180,000)
Notes: This collection incl on microform annual reports and Securities Exchange Commission 10-K reports for some 11,000 companies from 1976 to date; current and retrospective stock quotations, stock reports, corporate and industry records and directories and supporting looseleaf services; information file on Atlanta's largest 15,000 with annual updates; and current plat maps for the five county Metro-Atlanta area. Atlanta and Georgia business history sections are being developed. Most material on this collection is noncirculating.

IL —CHICAGO PUBLIC LIBRARY, Business/Science/Technology Div, Science/Technology Information Center, 425 North Michigan Ave, Chicago, 60611. Lynda Sanford, Head; John R Moore, Environment Collection Coordinator & Engineering Librn
Holdings: Vols
Budget: $205,000
Notes: Collection incl all subject areas of business within HB-HJ Library of Congress classifications scheme. Emphases are on current materials in management, careers, investments, and reference. Collection is also strong in labor history. 2200 periodical titles; 60,000 vols monographs.

IL —NORTHERN TRUST COMPANY LIBRARY, 50 S LaSalle St, Chicago, 60675. Marianne Lee, Head Librn
Holdings: Vols (2500) Cat Audiotapes Microforms

MA —BOSTON PUBLIC LIBRARY, Kirstein Business Branch, 20 City Hall Ave, Boston, 02108. Joseph E Walsh, Business Branch Librn
Holdings: Vols 42,900 Cat
Notes: City and telephone directories, trade directories, investment manuals and services, law reporting services, trade periodicals and newspapers, government periodicals, periodical indexes, books on all aspects of business incl accounting, advertising, banking, retail and wholesale trade, marketing, real estate, etc. No separate catalog or index to the collection.

MA —HARVARD UNIVERSITY, Graduate School of Business Administration, Baker Library, Soldiers Field, Boston, 02163. Mary V Chatfield, Librn; Florence Bartoshesky, Cur of Manuscripts and Archives

MN —JAMES JEROME HILL REFERENCE LIBRARY, Fourth St at Market St, Saint Paul, 55106. Virgil F Massman, Dir
Holdings: Vols (197,000)
Budget: ($170,000)
Notes: Sources of current and historical information.

NY —BROOKLYN PUBLIC LIBRARY, Business Library, 280 Cadman Plaza W, Brooklyn, 11201. Sylvia Mechanic, Business Librn
Holdings: Vols (107,000) Cat
Notes: Library received about 1800 periodicals, 3000 serials, 2700 directories, 1600 telephone books from all over the world with a complete back file on microfilm for greater New York. Library is a selective US Government Documents depository. Subscribes to microfiche SEC 10K reports for AMEX, NYSE and OTC from 1976 to date; annual reports for earlier years. Transnational annual reports, on fiche from 1982-to date. 78 vertical file trays; Sanborn maps for Brooklyn, special collection of corporation histories. Publish monthly

INVESTMENTS (cont.)

newsletter, *Service to Business and Industry* with our Science Division.

NY —CORNELL UNIVERSITY LIBRARIES, Graduate School of Management, Malott Hall, Ithaca, 14853. Betsy Ann Olive, Librn
Holdings: Vols (135,000) Cat Microforms
Budget: ($130,000)

NY —SALOMON BROTHERS, Library, One New York Plaza, 46th Floor, New York, 10004. Lydia P Davies, Library Mgr
Holdings: Vols (4750) Cat
Notes: Library contains a collection of reference sources relating to corporate finance, investment banking and international finance. Extensive domestic and international corporate documents on microfiche. 11,000 corporate document files; 406,700 microforms.

NC —GREENSBORO PUBLIC LIBRARY, Business Library, 201 Greene St, Drawer X-4, Greensboro, 27402. Lebby B Lamb, Business Librn
Holdings: Vols (6000) Cat Microforms
Budget: ($12,000)

OH —CLEVELAND PUBLIC LIBRARY, Business, Economics and Labor Department, 325 Superior Ave, Cleveland, 44114. Joan Sorger, Head
Holdings: Cat
Notes: Collection extends from 1800s. Strong in periodicals, services, corporate and investment manuals, both domestic and foreign information; long runs of annual reports and data for SEC listed companies. Disclosure microfiche of Annual Reports, 10-K's and Proxy statements for SEC filing companies; years vary.

PA —UNIVERSITY OF PENNSYLVANIA, Lippincott Library of the Wharton School, Philadelphia, 19104. Michael Halperin, Librn
Holdings: Cat
Notes: Complete files of financial manuals from mid-19th century; long bound files of many financial and investment advisory services. Complete bound file of NYSE listing applications from no A-1 to date.

BC —VANCOUVER PUBLIC LIBRARY, Business and Economics Div, 750 Burrard St, Vancouver, V6Z 1X5, Can. Barbara Bell, Librn
Notes: Incl numerous special files for *Quick Reference, Subject Clippings, Companies* (information of major Canadian, US and international corporations; index to new British Columbia and Canadian company corporations, 1951 to 1978; 160,000 cards); company file, *Province Index* and *Association File* (particulars of Canadian trade and professional associations). *International Collection of Trade* directories and telephone books.

INVESTMENTS, FOREIGN

MI —UNIVERSITY OF MICHIGAN, Graduate School of Business Administration, Business Administration Library, Institute for International Commerce Reading Rm, Ann Arbor, 48109. Carol Holbrook, Dir
Holdings: Cat
Notes: International business.

OH —CLEVELAND PUBLIC LIBRARY, Business, Economics and Labor Department, 325 Superior Ave, Cleveland, 44114. Joan Sorger, Head
Holdings: Cat
Notes: Collection extends from 1800s. Strong in periodicals, services, corporate and investment manuals, both domestic and foreign information; long runs of annual reports and data for SEC listed companies. Disclosure microfiche of Annual Reports, 10-K's and Proxy statements for SEC filing companies; years vary.

IO ARCHIVE

BC —SIMON FRASER UNIVERSITY, Library, Burnaby, V5A 1S6, Can. Percilla Groves, Special Collections Librn
Holdings: Uncat Mss
Notes: *IO* Archive incl mss, correspondence, proofs, and business records of this little magazine, 1966-1976.

IONIZED GASES see Plasma (Ionized Gases)

IOWA

IA —IOWA STATE UNIVERSITY, Library, Dept of Special Collections, Ames, 50011. Stanley M Yates, Head

IOWA—CHURCH HISTORY

IA —STATE HISTORICAL SOCIETY OF IOWA LIBRARY, 402 Iowa Ave, Iowa City, 52240. Darold J Brown, Librn
Holdings: Vols 2000 Cat Mss
Notes: Incl records, proceedings of conferences, histories, centennial booklets. Representative, but very incomplete.

IOWA—GENEALOGY

IA —IOWA STATE HISTORICAL DEPT, Iowa Historical Library, Iowa Historical Bldg, E 12 & Grand Ave, Des Moines, 50319. Lowell R Wilbur, Librn
Holdings: Vols (62,000) Cat Mss Maps

IA —STATE HISTORICAL SOCIETY OF IOWA LIBRARY, 402 Iowa Ave, Iowa City, 52240. Darold J Brown, Librn
Holdings: Vols 5000 Cat Mss Microforms
Notes: Have many early serial publications for eastern states, federal census on microfilm, expanding collection of family histories and charts, current genealogical periodicals.

IOWA—HISTORY

IA —IOWA STATE UNIVERSITY, Library, Dept of Special Collections, Ames, 50011. Stanley M Yates, Head
Holdings: / / Mss
Notes: (1) Austin Adams Family Papers. Collection contains correspondence, diaries (1872-1874, 1900) notes, and lectures and essays of Mary Newbury Adams (1837-1901) and her husband, Austin Adams (1827-1890), lawyer and Iowa Supreme Court Justice, of Dubuque, Iowa. Contains references to Ralph Waldo Emerson and A Bronson Alcott (including letters from him). 2 linear feet. Finding aid available. (2) Papers of Roswell Garst, Iowa's most famous farmer. Initiator of experimental feeding of corncobs to produce beef, use of hybrid seedcorn and commercial fertilizers. Credited with opening of agricultural sales and exchanges with Russia in the 1950s.

IA —GRAND LODGE OF IOWA, AF & AM Iowa Masonic Library, 813 First Ave SE, Cedar Rapids, 52406. Tom Eggleston, Librn
Holdings: Vols 4000 Cat Maps

IA —CLINTON PUBLIC LIBRARY, 306 Eighth Ave S, Clinton, 52732. Robert M Seger, Dir
Holdings: Vols (100) Cat Microforms
Notes: Local history, emphasizing Clinton County. Incl Clinton newspapers. 1854-date (microfilm).

IA —IOWA STATE HISTORICAL DEPT, Iowa Historical Library, Iowa Historical Bldg, E 12 & Grand Ave, Des Moines, 50319. Lowell R Wilbur, Librn
Holdings: Vols (62,000) Cat Mss Maps

IA —LORAS COLLEGE, Wahlert Memorial Library, 14 & Alta Vista, Dubuque, 52001. Robert F Klein, Librn
Holdings: Vols (5000) Uncat Mss Maps Pix Phonorecords Audiotapes Videotapes 16mm Films Microforms
Notes: Incl 250 vols of Dubuque County records, 1853-1900. Also incl Dubuque municipal resolutions, petitions, reports, and other communications, 1837-1941 (not indexed).

IA —STATE HISTORICAL SOCIETY OF IOWA LIBRARY, 402 Iowa Ave, Iowa City, 52240. Darold J Brown, Librn
Holdings: Vols 17,000 Cat Mss Maps Pix Microforms
Notes: All aspects of Iowa history incl industry, organizations, city and county history, state documents, Iowa periodical publications. Large collections of Iowa pamphlets and maps; thousands of mss, incl 200 large collections of personal papers. Large newspaper collection.

IA —UNIVERSITY OF IOWA, University Libraries, Iowa City, 52242. Frank Paluka, Head, Special Collections Dept
Holdings: Cat Mss
Notes: The Iowa Historical Manuscripts Collection comprises 4260 linear feet of ms materials concerning the history of institutions, people and business. Holdings are reported to the *National Union Catalog of Manuscript Collections.* Boyd K Swigger, *A Guide to Resources for the Study of the Recent History of the United States.* (Iowa City, 1977).

IA —IOWA FALLS PUBLIC LIBRARY, 520 Rocksylvania, Iowa Falls, 50126. Deanne Keller, Librn
Holdings: Vols (400) Cat Maps Microforms
Notes: Iowa history and local history. Microforms are microfilm of the local papers dating back to 1862-date. Maps include plat maps of surrounding counties; pictorial atlases of surrounding counties.

IA —SIOUX CITY PUBLIC LIBRARY, 705 Sixth St, Sioux City, 51105. Betsy Thompson, Head Librn
Holdings: Vols 3700 Cat Mss Maps Pix Microforms
Notes: Emphasis on Sioux City and Iowa history, the Missouri River region. Microfilm copies of early newspapers, etc.

SD —AUGUSTANA COLLEGE, Mikkelsen Library & Learning Resource Center, Center for Western Studies, Sioux Falls, 57197. Ronelle Thompson, Dir Library
Notes: The Center for Western Studies, located in the Mikkelsen Library, is an archival and research agency of Augustana College. Dedicated to the history and culture of the Great Plains and the Trans-Mississippi West, the Center collects and preserves materials relating to Plains Indians, immigrant settlers, Norwegiana, Western Americana, Herbert Krause, Frederick Manfred, Donald Parker, Richard F Pettigrew, Augustana College, the Episcopal Diocese of South Dakota, the South Dakota District of the American Lutheran Church, the South Dakota Penitentiary and Minnehaha County.

IOWA—MAPS

IA —STATE HISTORICAL SOCIETY OF IOWA LIBRARY, 402 Iowa Ave, Iowa City, 52240. Darold J Brown, Librn
Notes: Iowa plat atlases cataloged. Approx 100 atlases of Iowa counties pre-1900 and approx 300 Iowa county atlases for the 20th century. Incl approx 1200 maps.

IOWA—PARKS

IA —IOWA STATE UNIVERSITY, Library, Dept of Special Collections, Ames, 50011. Stanley M Yates, Head
Notes: Louis H Pammel (1862-1931) was professor of botany (1889-1931) and head of department of botany. Collection incl correspondence, collected works, speeches, interviews and articles. Collection is 39 linear feet. Important in conservation movement; founder of Iowa State Park System; teacher and friend of George Washington Carver.

IOWA—SCHOOLS

IA —STATE HISTORICAL SOCIETY OF IOWA LIBRARY, 402 Iowa Ave, Iowa City, 52240. Darold J Brown, Librn
Holdings: Vols 1000 Cat Mss
Notes: 19th and 20th century materials on Iowa schools, incl catalogs, directories, histories, and records of public schools, academies, and colleges.

IOWA—SOCIAL LIFE AND CUSTOMS

IA —DRAKE UNIVERSITY, Cowles Library, 28 St & University Ave, Des Moines, 50311.
Notes: Nearly 3000 musical works used by orchestras and musicians to accompany silent films, donated by Dorman Hundling

IOWA—SOCIAL LIFE AND CUSTOMS (cont.)

who had played in orchestras in theatres owned by his family in South Dakota and Iowa.

IOWA ACADEMY OF SCIENCE

IA —IOWA STATE UNIVERSITY, Library, Dept of Special Collections, Ames, 50011. Stanley M Yates, Head
Holdings: Mss
Notes: The Academy was organized in 1875 and has endeavored to develop interest in science, strengthen the bonds between scientists and stimulate scientific research and work in Iowa. 18 linear ft, finding aid available.

IOWA AUTHORS see Authors, Iowa

IOWA BANKERS ASSOCIATION

IA —IOWA STATE UNIVERSITY, Library, Dept of Special Collections, Ames, 50011. Stanley M Yates, Head
Holdings: Mss Pix
Notes: Iowa Bankers Association Records (1910-1973). Collection contains correspondence, printed matter, minutes, reports, financial records, photographs and newspaper clippings relating to financial and economic conditions. Also contains files and photographs relating to crimes against Iowa banks. About 700 linear feet. Finding aid available.

IOWA COMPOSERS see Composers, Iowa

IOWA FARM BUREAU FEDERATION

IA —IOWA STATE UNIVERSITY, Library, Dept of Special Collections, Ames, 50011. Stanley M Yates, Head
Holdings: // Mss
Notes: The Federation was organized in 1918 and used the services of the Extension County Agents of the USDA and the State agricultural department until 1955 when the USDA separated Extension from private farm organizations. 16 linear ft, finding aid available.

IOWA FARMERS UNION

IA —IOWA STATE UNIVERSITY, Library, Dept of Special Collections, Ames, 50011. Stanley M Yates, Head
Holdings: Mss
Notes: A division of the National Farmers Union, the Iowa chapter was reorganized and recharted in 1957. 19 linear ft, finding aid available.

IOWA MANUSCRIPTS see Manuscripts, Iowa

IOWA NEWSPAPERS see Newspapers, Iowa

IRAN

CA —HOOVER INSTITUTION ON WAR, REVOLUTION & PEACE, Stanford University, Stanford, 94305. Peter Duignan, Cur; Karen Fung, Deputy Cur
Holdings: Vols (100,000)
Notes: For full description of collection, see Hoover Institution entry under Near East.

DC —LIBRARY OF CONGRESS, African and Middle Eastern Division, Washington, 20540.
Holdings: Cat Mss Microforms
Notes: Near East: Over 75,000 vols, Arabic, Armenian, Turkish, Persian, and related languages. Special subject strengths incl islamic philosophy, history, and literature.

MA —HARVARD UNIVERSITY LIBRARY, Widener Library, Cambridge, 02138.
Holdings: Cat
Notes: The Library's published *Catalogue of Arabic, Persian, and Ottoman Turkish Books* (1968) lists some 5500 vols in Persian; see also *Harvard Library Bulletin,* XVI (313-325).

IRAN—CENSUSES

NC —CAROLINA POPULATION CENTER, Library, University Sq E, Chapel Hill, 27514. Patricia Shipman, Head Librn
Holdings: Vols 172 // Cat
Notes: 1966 census.

IRAN—POPULATION

NC —CAROLINA POPULATION CENTER, Library, University Sq E, Chapel Hill, 27514. Patricia Shipman, Head Librn
Holdings: Vols (20,000) Cat
Budget: ($10,500)
Notes: Try to acquire everything published in English on population, with particular emphasis on the US and developing countries. Also acquire conference proceedings, seminar papers. These and journal articles are indexed and the analytics are incl in the catalog. Incl 13,000 reprints and other pieces of ephemera. Most extensive area files are on India, Africa, Thailand, Iran, Korea, and Latin America. Holdings are recorded on an automated data base. A microfiche catalog is available for use in the Library and for purchase. Access by subject & geographic area are available through the Library's own thesaurus-based indexing systems.

IRANIAN LANGUAGES

NY —NEW YORK PUBLIC LIBRARY, Oriental Div, Fifth Ave & 42 St, New York, 10018. E Christian Filstrup, Chief
Holdings: Cat Mss Microforms
Budget: ($56,455)
Notes: Published catalog of holdings.

IRANIANS

CA —CALIFORNIA STATE COLLEGE, STANISLAUS, Library, 801 W Monte Vista Ave, Turlock, 95380. J Carlyle Parker, Actg Library Dir
Holdings: Vols 100 // Uncat
Notes: The Sayad Collection of Assyriana consists of books in the Syriac dialect of the modern Assyrians, often called Nestorians, who are natives of northwestern Iran. Other books in English relating to the modern Assyrians are also in the collection. Also books on Mesopotamian civilizations.

IRAQ

CA —HOOVER INSTITUTION ON WAR, REVOLUTION & PEACE, Stanford University, Stanford, 94305. Peter Duignan, Cur; Karen Fung, Deputy Cur
Holdings: Vols (100,000)
Notes: For full description of collection, see Hoover Institution entry under Near East.

IRELAND

MA —HARVARD UNIVERSITY LIBRARY, Widener Library, Cambridge, 02138.
Holdings: Cat Mss Microforms
Notes: Microfilms of archives and manuscripts described in *Harvard Library Bulletin, VIII* (1954), 111-114.

MA —BOSTON COLLEGE LIBRARIES, Thomas P O'Neill Library, Irish Collection, Chestnut Hill, 02167. Ralph Coffman, Cur
Holdings: Vols (10,000) Cat Mss Maps Pix
Notes: Nearly every aspect of Irish history and literature are covered in this collection. Items of special interest are the many papers of Patrick Andrew Collins, president of the Irish Land League, and letters of Jeremiah O'Donovan Rossa, poet, editor and leader in the Fenian and related organizations. Holdings also incl a facsimile of the famous illuminated ms of the Gospels, the *Book of* Kells; a complete vol of *Malton's Views of Dublin, 1799; The Ordinance Surveys;* a complete set of the *Irish Bulletin;* and Colgan's *Acta Sanctorum Hiberniae* describing the lives of the Irish saints.

RI —PROVIDENCE PUBLIC LIBRARY, 150 Empire St, Providence, 02903. Lance J Bauer, Special Collections Librn
Holdings: Vols 2000 Cat Mss Maps Pix
Notes: The George W Potter and Alfred M Williams Memorial on Irish Culture. Covers various aspects of Irish culture in the English language with emphasis on 19th and 20th centuries. Incl an original Easter Proclamation, over 1000 19th century street ballads, and the Charles James Fox Collection of approx 400 pamphlets covering Irish history, education, emancipation, agriculture and tithes for the period 1740-1890. This collection is particularly strong in Irish literature (especially the Irish Renaissance), history, politics (incl the Irish Question), and genealogy. Photocopying when condition of material allows. Material must be used in-house. Genealogical searches are not performed, although assistance is provided.

BC —UNIVERSITY OF VICTORIA, McPherson Library, Victoria, V8W 3H5, Can.
Notes: Dublin Co, Lusk. Incl 48 pages, 1876; notebook: copied by Mark Perrin from the *Journal of Antiquarian Rambles in the County of Dublin,* written by the late Austin Cooper (1759-1930).

IRELAND—CIVILIZATION AND CULTURE

NY —CANISIUS COLLEGE, Andrew L Bouwhuis Library, 2001 Main St, Buffalo, 14208. Peter J Laux, Dir
Holdings: Vols 1675 Cat
Budget: $2000
Notes: Joseph P Desmond Collection in Irish literature, history and culture.

IRELAND—GENEALOGY

AL —SAMFORD UNIVERSITY, Special Collections Library, 800 Lakeshore Dr, Birmingham, 35229. Annie Ford Wheeler, Acting Head Librn
Holdings: Vols 1000 Cat Miss Maps Microforms
Notes: Nucleus is Albert E Casey Collection, incl important and rare volumes. Extensive ms materials pertaining primarily to counties Cork and Kerry (mostly transcriptions from church registers and county records), and 250 reels of ms materials. Most of this has been indexed and printed in the O'Kief series of Dr A E Casey. Also incl Griffith's valuations for 155 unions in 24 vols. Published catalog of the collection.

IL —NORTHWESTERN UNIVERSITY, Library, Special Collections Dept, 1937 Sheridan Rd, Evanston, 60201. R Russell Maylone, Cur
Holdings: Vols 2500 Cat //
Notes: County histories, record surveys, visitations, family histories, biographies, atlases, census records, church histories and records, civil surveys and microfilms.

†MA —IRISH FAMILY HISTORY SOCIETY LIBRARY, 173 Tremont St, Newton, 02158.
Notes: Ireland--genealogy, history, literature, heraldry.

VT —SAINT MICHAEL'S COLLEGE, Durick Library, Winooski, 05404. Joseph Popecki, Dir; Henry Nadeau, Head of Archives & Special Collections
Holdings: Vols (5000) Cat
Notes: French Canadian genealogy, Irish genealogy, art, a complete set of Jesuit Relations and allied documents with a deluxe binding.

IRELAND—HISTORY

AL —SAMFORD UNIVERSITY, Special Collections Library, 800 Lakeshore Dr, Birmingham, 35229. Annie Ford Wheeler, Acting Head Librn
Holdings: Vols 1000 Cat Mss Maps Microforms
Notes: Nucleus is Albert E Casey Collection, incl important and rare volumes. Extensive ms materials pertaining primarily to counties Cork and Kerry (mostly transcriptions from church registers and county records), and 250 reels of ms materials. Most of this has been indexed and printed in the O'Kief series of Dr A E Casey. Also incl Griffith's valuations for 155 unions in 24 vols. Published catalog of the collection.

IRELAND—HISTORY (cont.)

CA —UNIVERSITY OF CALIFORNIA, BERKELEY, Bancroft Library, Manuscripts Division, Berkeley, 94720. James D Hart, Dir
Holdings: Vols 2000 Uncat
Notes: A major collection of pamphlets and printed ephemera published primarily in the 18th and 19th centuries. Writings on political and religious controversy are well represented.

CA —CALIFORNIA STATE UNIVERSITY, NORTHRIDGE, Delmar T Oviatt & South Libraries, 1811 Nordhoff St, Northridge, 91330. Donald L Read, Special Collections Dept
Holdings: Vols 2000 Uncat
Notes: Partial contents: Liberal Publication Dept, London. Pamphlets and leaflets (1893-1903; 1905-1914). Fabian tracts (1884-1904), Irish Loyal and Patriotic Union. Pamphlets and leaflets (1887). Particularly strong in letters from John Burns' personal correspondence (approx 100). Entire collection, 20 linear feet. Indexed in *Century of change, 1815-1914; a Collection of Original Pamphlets. Tracts, Posters, Holograph Letters, Manuscripts, etc* (Guernsey, Channel Islands: Guernsey Books, 1972).

†CA —UNITED IRISH CULTURAL CENTER, 2700 45th Ave, San Francisco, 94116.
Notes: Irish history, poetry, literature, drama and Irish heritage in the US.

CA —UNIVERSITY OF SANTA CLARA, Michel Orradre Library, Santa Clara, 95053. Alice Whistler, Ref Librn
Holdings: Cat Mss Microforms
Notes: The Hiberniana collection is cataloged and the cards are interfiled in the main card catalog; also a separate catalog.

FL —UNIVERSITY OF FLORIDA, Libraries, Special Collections, W University Ave, Gainesville, 32611. Sidney Ives, Librn & Rare Books
Holdings: Vols (8000) Cat Mss
Notes: Incl Irish authors from the revival, as well as history, travel, and religious books.

†IL —IRISH-AMERICAN CULTURAL ASSOCIATION LIBRARY, 10415 South Western, Chicago, 60643.
Notes: Irish literature, history, biography, art, music.

IL —NEWBERRY LIBRARY, 60 W Walton St, Chicago, 60610. Diana Haskell, Cur of Modern Mss
Holdings: Cat
Notes: Incl Irish history and literature to 1900. Also a collection on Gaelic linguistics, particularly Irish, Cornish, Welsh and Manx.

IL —NORTHWESTERN UNIVERSITY, Library, Special Collections Dept, 1937 Sheridan Rd, Evanston, 60201. R Russell Maylone, Cur
Holdings: Vols 2000 Cat Mss Per
Notes: Pamphlets, broadsides, photographs focusing on the period from the Easter Uprising of 1916 to 1924. Margaret Falley Collection of Irish Genealogy and local history.

†IL —SAINT MARY OF THE LAKE SEMINARY, Feehan Memorial Library, Mundelein, 60060.
Notes: History of Ireland, the Irish language and literature.

IN —ALLEN COUNTY PUBLIC LIBRARY, Fred J Reynolds Historical Genealogy Collection, 900 Webster St, Fort Wayne, 46802. Rick J Ashton, Dir; Michael B Clegg, Manager
Holdings: Vols 200,000 Cat Mss Maps Pix Microforms
Notes: Incl state, county, regional, town and church histories. All census schedules and port of entry records released by the federal government are in the microfilm collection of 40,000 reels. The collection contains parish registers and publications of British parish register societies. Canadian, English, Scotch, Irish and Welsh records are well represented. The heraldry collection is housed with the genealogy collection. Allen County Public Library is and has been the depository for the North American Association of Directory Publishers since 1964.

KS —UNIVERSITY OF KANSAS, Kenneth Spencer Research Library, Special Collections Dept, Lawrence, 66045. Alexandra Mason, Librn
Holdings: Cat Mss Maps
Notes: Part of 25,000 vol P S O'Hegarty collection. Especially strong in late 18th century through 1926. Noncirculating.

MA —BOSTON COLLEGE LIBRARIES, Thomas P O'Neill Library, Irish Collection, Chestnut Hill, 02167. Ralph Coffman, Cur
Holdings: Vols (10,000) Cat Mss Maps Pix
Notes: Nearly every aspect of Irish history and literature are covered in this collection. Items of special interest are the many papers of Patrick Andrew Collins, president of the Irish Land League, and letters of Jeremiah O'Donovan Rossa, poet, editor and leader in the Fenian and related organizations. Holdings also incl a facsimile of the famous illuminated ms of the Gospels, the *Book of* Kells; a complete vol of *Malton's Views of Dublin, 1799; The Ordinance Surveys;* a complete set of the *Irish Bulletin;* and Colgan's *Acta Sanctorum Hiberniae* describing the lives of the Irish saints.

†MA —IRISH FAMILY HISTORY SOCIETY LIBRARY, 173 Tremont St, Newton, 02158.
Notes: Ireland--genealogy, history, literature, heraldry.

MA —COLLEGE OF THE HOLY CROSS, Dinand Library, College St, Worcester, 01610. James M Mahoney, Cur of Special Collection
Holdings: Vols 2000 Cat Maps Pix

MI —UNIVERSITY OF MICHIGAN, Library, Dept of Rare Books & Special Collections, Ann Arbor, 48109. Robert J Starring, Head
Holdings: Uncat Mss
Notes: The Irish Papers of John F Finerty, long-time friend of President Eamon de Valera and his legal counsel in the Irish Republican bond litigation, comprise over 3 ft of records, 1921-60, documenting the struggle for the establishment of the Republic of Ireland and related Irish-American activities. Included are correspondence, legal documents, speeches, clippings, and pamphlets on a range of subjects including the Irish bond drive and litigation, the Irish Free State, civil strife, recognition of the Irish Republic, Irish neutrality in World War II, and Finerty's trips to Ireland in the 1950s.

†MN —COLLEGE OF SAINT THOMAS CELTIC LIBRARY, O'Shaughnessy Library, Saint Paul, 55105.
Notes: Irish language, history, and literature.

MO —SAINT LOUIS UNIVERSITY, Pius XII Memorial Library, 3655 W Pine Blvd, Saint Louis, 63108. William Cole, Dir
Holdings: Vols 250 Cat Mss Slides //
Notes: Fundamental source material for the study of every aspect of Catholic religious, political, and social thought during nearly five hundred years of English, Scottish, and Irish history (early sixteenth century to modern times). Approximately 2220 volumes do not appear in card catalog, and researchers must write ahead to make arrangements, since these volumes are not readily available for public use.

NJ —SETON HALL UNIVERSITY, McLaughlin Library, South Orange, 07079. James Sharp, University Librn
Holdings: Vols (9000) Cat Mss Maps
Notes: McManus Collection of Irish History and Literature.

NY —CANISIUS COLLEGE, Andrew L Bouwhuis Library, 2001 Main St, Buffalo, 14208. Peter J Laux, Dir
Holdings: Vols 1675 Cat
Budget: $2000
Notes: Joseph P Desmond Collection in Irish literature, history and culture.

NY —SAINT JOHN'S UNIVERSITY, Special Collections Dept, Grand Central & Utopia Pkwys, Jamaica, 11439. Szilvia E Szmuk, Librn
Holdings: // Uncat Mss
Notes: O'Dwyer Collections: papers dealing with Northern Ireland. 1973-1977; American Friends of Irish Neutrality, World War II. a) The Paul O'Dwyer Papers deal with conditions in Northern Ireland, incl correspondence, speeches, press releases, and periodical articles contain in 18 labeled manila envelopes and roughly indexed. b) American Friends of Irish Neutrality collection consist of 109 letters, membership and donation cards, minutes, press clippings, post cards, speechs, pamphlets, in 6 manila envelopes. No photocopying.

NY —AMERICAN IRISH HISTORICAL SOCIETY, Library, 991 Fifth Ave, New York, 10028. Lisa M Hottin, Cur; William D Griffin, Librn
Holdings: Vols (20,000) Cat Maps Pix Slides
Notes: Archives and Manuscripts: The documents and papers of Friends of Irish Freedom, The Land League, the Society of the Friendly Sons of St Patrick, the Catholic Club, and the Guild of Catholic Lawyers. The papers of New York State Supreme Court Justice Daniel F Cohalan. This is the largest and most complete collection of over 20,000 American Irish and Irish history, biography and literature in the United States. Incl American-Irish Newspaper collections dating from 1811, the most comprehensive in the US; 1000 rare books and special editions. Special collections incl regular exhibits of Irish or American Irish interest incl mss, letters, books, photographs and memorabilia. Permanent collection of representative works of Irish painters.

NY —NEW YORK PUBLIC LIBRARY, Rare Books and Manuscripts Div, Fifth Ave & 42 St, New York, 10018. William L Joyce, Asst Dir; Susan E Davis, Cur of Mss
Holdings: Cat Mss
Budget: ($7161)
Notes: The Maloney Irish Historical Collections.

NY —NEW YORK PUBLIC LIBRARY, Local History and Genealogy Div, Fifth Ave & 42 St, New York, 10018. Gunther E Pohl, Chief
Holdings: Cat Pix
Notes: Extensive collection of county, city, town and village histories of the United States and of the British isles and the Republic of Ireland. For state and national histories of the United States refer to the American History Division. All other local histories are part of the General Research and Humanities Division. See *United States Local History Catalog* (Boston: G K Hall, 1974), 2 vols.

NY —STATE UNIVERSITY OF NEW YORK, STONY BROOK, Melville Library, Dept of Special Collections, Stony Brook, 11794. Evert Volkersz, Head
Holdings: Uncat
Notes: Irish Political Pamphlets Collection. 503 pamphlets in 78 vols, mainly of the period 1789-1829, with a few from 1776. A few are French, some English, mainly from Ireland. Excellent source material for research on the period which was one of great English-Irish and Protestant-Catholic tension.

OH —CLEVELAND PUBLIC LIBRARY, History and Geography Department, 325 Superior Ave, Cleveland, 44114. JoAnn Petrello, Head
Holdings: Cat
Notes: Extensive British History Collection (incl Ireland, Scotland), especially 1660-1800. Rare books. Collection of British Learned Society serials (282); English Political Pamphlet Collection (about 2000). No photocopying.

†PA —BALCH INSTITUTE FOR ETHNIC STUDIES, Library, 18 S Seventh St, Philadelphia, 19106.
Notes: Papers of Patrick Stanton (1907-1976), an activist in Irish-American cultural and social programs. Incl in the collection is a unique manuscript volume of poetry by Donal O'Herlihy, Fenian activist of the 1860s.

PA —CHESTNUT HILL COLLEGE, Logue Library, Germantown & Northwestern Aves, Philadelphia, 19118. Helen M Hayes, Librn
Holdings: Vols (3500) Cat Mss
Budget: ($2500)
Notes: Irish history and literature collection, incl 8 letters from G B Shaw to James G Huneker.

IRELAND—HISTORY (cont.)

PA —FREE LIBRARY OF PHILADELPHIA, Rare Book Dept, Logan Sq, Philadelphia, 19103. Marie E Korey, Rare Book Librn
Holdings: Vols 3500 Uncat
Notes: A collection of pamphlets printed in Ireland between 1701 and 1879 dealing with contemporary events and topics of local interest. The collection also incl pamphlets printed in England from 1701 through 1866 which bear on Irish topics (1500).

PA —CARLOW COLLEGE, Grace Library, Fifth Ave, Pittsburgh, 15213. Joan M Mitchell, Dir of Library Services
Holdings: Vols 543 // Cat Phonorecords Audiotapes
Notes: The Gladys Wholey Curran Collection, which consists primarily of titles in the area of Irish Literature, specifically those titles concerned with the study of the Irish playwrights and poets. The collection is particularly strong in volumes related to the study of Jonathan Swift, John M Synge, and William B Yeats. In addition, there is notable focus upon Irish history of the 17th and 18th centuries. No photocopying.

RI —PROVIDENCE PUBLIC LIBRARY, 150 Empire St, Providence, 02903. Lance J Bauer, Special Collections Librn
Holdings: Vols 2000 Cat Mss Maps Pix
Notes: The George W Potter and Alfred M Williams Memorial on Irish Culture. Covers various aspects of Irish culture in the English language with emphasis on 19th and 20th centuries. Incl an original Easter Proclamation, over 1000 19th century street ballads, and the Charles James Fox Collection of approx 400 pamphlets covering Irish history, education, emancipation, agriculture and tithes for the period 1740-1890. This collection is particularly strong in Irish literature (especially the Irish Renaissance), history, politics (incl the Irish Question), and genealogy. Photocopying when condition of material allows. Material must be used in-house. Genealogical searches are not performed, although assistance is provided.

WI —UNIVERSITY OF WISCONSIN, MADISON, Memorial Library, 728 State St, Madison, 53706. Erwin K Welsch, Social Studies Bibliographer
Notes: Probably one of the five best collections of Celtic materials in the country, acquired from 1914 onward, and incl both printed vols and photostats.

IRELAND, BILLY

OH —OHIO STATE UNIVERSITY, Library for Communication and Graphic Arts, 242 W 18th St, Columbus, 43210. Lucy S Caswell, Curator
Notes: The original works of editorial cartoonists Art Poinier, Scott Willis, Brian Basset, Billy Ireland, Frank Williams, Charles Werner, Ned Beard, L D Warren, Edward D Kuekes, Ray Osrin, Mike Peters, Draper Hill, Eugene Craig and Bert Whitman.

IRELAND, JOHN

MN —CATHOLIC HISTORICAL SOCIETY OF SAINT PAUL, John Ireland Memorial Library, 2260 Summit Ave, Saint Paul, 55105. Leo J Tibesar, Dir
Holdings: Mss //
Notes: The John Ireland papers, extant correspondence, sermons, clippings. Microfilm edition for research. Index by Minnesota Historical Society (1983) where copy of microfilm edition may be acquired: 1500 Mississippi St, St Paul, Minnesota 55101.

MS —UNIVERSITY OF SOUTHERN MISSISSIPPI, William David McCain Graduate Library, Box 5148, Southern Sta, Hattiesburg, 39406.
Holdings: Cat Mss Pix
Notes: Correspondence and records (1847-1892) relating to Alexander Melvorne Jackson's participation in the Mexican War, his service as Secretary of the State of the New Mexico Territory (1857-1861), and his participation in the Civil War on the side of the Confederacy. Among his correspondents were Albert Gallatin Brown, Reuben Davis, Miguel A Otero, Jacob Thompson, and John Ireland. Incl are photographs of Austin, Texas, ca 1890. 1.1 cubic feet holdings.

IRELAND, WILLIAM HENRY

IN —INDIANA UNIVERSITY, Lilly Library, Seventh St, Bloomington, 47405. William R Cagle, Librn
Holdings: // Mss
Notes: Mss incl a collection of William Henry Ireland fabrications of Shakespeare. 69 items, 1805.

IRENITY see Christian Union

IRIMESCU, RADU

CA —HOOVER INSTITUTION ON WAR, REVOLUTION & PEACE, Stanford University, Stanford, 94305. Milorad M Drachkovitch, Archivist
Holdings: Mss Pix
Notes: Papers of Radu Irimescu, Rumanian Minister of Air and Navy, 1932-38, and Rumanian Ambassador to the United States, 1938-40, incl correspondence, reports, dispatches, memoranda, clippings, photos, and other material, 1918-40, relating to his service in the Rumanian government and to the development of aviation in Rumania. Primarily in Rumanian. 5 ms boxes.

IRISH AMERICAN NEWSPAPERS see Newspapers, Irish American

IRISH ART see Art, Irish

IRISH AMERICAN CLUB

†PA —BALCH INSTITUTE FOR ETHNIC STUDIES, Library, 18 S Seventh St, Philadelphia, 19106.
Notes: Papers of Dennis Clark, incl copies of minute books of two organizations, Clan na Gaol and the Irish American Club (c 1886-1923).

IRISH AUTHORS see Authors, Irish

IRISH FOLK MUSIC see Folk Music, Irish

IRISH FOLK SONGS see Folk Songs, Irish

IRISH FOLKLORE see Folklore, Irish

IRISH BALLADS AND SONGS

FL —UNIVERSITY OF FLORIDA, Libraries, Special Collections, W University Ave, Gainesville, 32611. Sidney Ives, Librn & Rare Books
Holdings: Vols (8000) Cat Mss
Notes: Incl Irish authors from the revival, as well as history, travel, and religious books.

RI —PROVIDENCE PUBLIC LIBRARY, 150 Empire St, Providence, 02903. Lance J Bauer, Special Collections Librn
Holdings: Vols 2000 Cat Mss Maps Pix
Notes: The George W Potter and Alfred M Williams Memorial on Irish Culture. Covers various aspects of Irish culture in the English language with emphasis on 19th and 20th centuries. Incl an original Easter Proclamation, over 1000 19th century street ballads, and the Charles James Fox Collection of approx 400 pamphlets covering Irish history, education, emancipation, agriculture and tithes for the period 1740-1890. This collection is particularly strong in Irish literature (especially the Irish Renaissance), history, politics (incl the Irish Question), and genealogy. Photocopying when condition of material allows. Material must be used in-house. Genealogical searches are not performed, although assistance is provided.

IRISH IN CANADA

PA —BALCII INSTITUTE FOR ETHNIC STUDIES, Library, 18 S Seventh St, Philadelphia, 19106. R Joseph Anderson, Library Dir
Notes: Ethnic heritage collection.

IRISH IN THE U.S.

†CA —UNITED IRISH CULTURAL CENTER, 2700 45th Ave, San Francisco, 94116.
Notes: Irish history, poetry, literature, drama and Irish heritage in the US.

DC —GEORGETOWN UNIVERSITY, Library, Special Collections Div, 37 & O Sts NW, Washington, 20057. George M Barringer, Special Collections Librn; Nicholas B Sheetz, Mss Librn
Notes: Historical archives of the Maryland Province. Incl the letters of Abp John Carroll and Fr John McElroy. Correspondence addressed to Thomas F Meehan (1854-1943), historian, journalist and editor who served on the editorial staff of numerous publications, incl *Irish-American*, *America*, and the *Catholic* Encyclopedia. Correspondence contains letters from prominent Irish-American Catholic politicians, journalists, and Church prelates, Patrick Andrew Collins, Martin Griffin, and John Boyle O'Reilly are among the correspondents. Correspondence and printed ephemera from the papers of John D Crimmins (1844-1917), New York financier and philanthropist. The correspondence incl letters from Henry Gabriels (1844-1917), James Cardinal Gibbons (1834-1921), General Winfield Scott Hancock (1824-1886), and PatrickJ Ryan (1831-1911), Archbishop of Philadelphia. The printed material primarily concerns Irish-American organizations and activities.

IL —NORTHWESTERN UNIVERSITY, Library, Special Collections Dept, 1937 Sheridan Rd, Evanston, 60201. R Russell Maylone, Cur
Holdings: Vols 2500 Cat //
Notes: County histories, record surveys, visitations, family histories, biographies, atlases, census records, church histories and records, civil surveys and microfilms.

NY —STATE UNIVERSITY OF NEW YORK AT ALBANY, Library, Special Collections Dept, 1400 Washington Ave, Albany, 12222. Marion P Munzer, Coordr
Notes: Correspondence and financial records of Abraham Bell and Son, New York shipping line which exported cotton and brought back British and English immigrants in the 1830s and 1840s. Additional correspondence and papers of James W Bell from 1862-1917; James C Bell from 1864-1899; and Bell Brothers, a money-lending business in Yonkers (22 linear feet). Part of the Library's German Exile Collection.

NY —SAINT JOHN'S UNIVERSITY, Special Collections Dept, Grand Central & Utopia Pkwys, Jamaica, 11439. Szilvia E Szmuk, Librn
Holdings: // Uncat Mss
Notes: O'Dwyer Collections: papers dealing with Northern Ireland. 1973-1977; American Friends of Irish Neutrality, World War II. a) The Paul O'Dwyer Papers deal with conditions in Northern Ireland, incl correspondence, speeches, press releases, and periodical articles contain in 18 labeled manila envelopes and roughly indexed. b) American Friends of Irish Neutrality collection consist of 109 letters, membership and donation cards, minutes, press clippings, post cards, speechs, pamphlets, in 6 manila envelopes. No photocopying.

NY —AMERICAN IRISH HISTORICAL SOCIETY, Library, 991 Fifth Ave, New York, 10028. Lisa M Hottin, Cur; William D Griffin, Librn
Holdings: Vols (20,000) Cat Maps Pix Slides
Notes: Archives and Manuscripts: The documents and papers of Friends of Irish Freedom, The Land League, the Society of the Friendly Sons of St Patrick, the Catholic Club, and the Guild of Catholic Lawyers. The papers of New York State Supreme Court Justice Daniel F Cohalan. This is the largest and most complete collection of over 20,000 American Irish and Irish history, biography and literature in the United States.

IRISH IN THE U.S. (cont.)

Incl American-Irish Newspaper collections dating from 1811, the most comprehensive in the US; 1000 rare books and special editions. Special collections incl regular exhibits of Irish or American Irish interest incl mss, letters, books, photographs and memorabilia. Permanent collection of representative works of Irish painters.

PA —BALCH INSTITUTE FOR ETHNIC STUDIES, Library, 18 S Seventh St, Philadelphia, 19106. R Joseph Anderson, Library Dir
Holdings: Vols 550 Cat Mss Pix Microforms

†PA —BALCH INSTITUTE FOR ETHNIC STUDIES, Library, 18 S Seventh St, Philadelphia, 19106.
Notes: Papers of Patrick Stanton (1907-1976), an activist in Irish-American cultural and social programs. Incl in the collection is a unique manuscript volume of poetry by Donal O'Herlihy, Fenian activist of the 1860s. Papers of Dennis Clark, incl copies of minute books of two organizations, Clan na Gaol and the Irish American Club (c 1886-1923).

PA —TEMPLE UNIVERSITY LIBRARIES, Special Collections Dept, Conwellana-Templana Collection, 13 & Berks St, Philadelphia, 19122. Miriam I Crawford, Cur
Holdings: Vols 5 Cat Mss
Budget: ($30,000)
Notes: Published novels, magazine writings, typescripts, galley and page proofs, and correspondence of Mary Wallace, popular contemporary novelist, including extended correspondence with her literary agent, Muriel Fuller, and examples of her detailed work and painstaking rewriting in her stories of the close-knit family lives of Irish-Americans.

PA —UNIVERSITY OF PITTSBURGH, Hillman Library, Archives of Industrial Society, 363 Hillman Library, Pittsburgh, 15260. Frank A Zabrosky, Cur
Holdings: Mss Pix Microforms
Notes: Incl documents; newspapers; records of Irish Catholic churches and organizations.

IRISH LANGUAGE AND LITERATURE

CA —SONOMA STATE UNIVERSITY, Salazar Library, 1801 E Cotati Ave, Rohnert Park, 94928. Sandra Walton, Librn
Holdings: Vols (650)
Notes: The W W Lyman Collection of Celtic literature, consisting of Irish, Scottish and Welsh fiction, poetry and play.

†CA —UNITED IRISH CULTURAL CENTER, 2700 45th Ave, San Francisco, 94116.
Notes: Irish history, poetry, literature, drama and Irish heritage in the US.

CA —UNIVERSITY OF SANTA CLARA, Michel Orradre Library, Santa Clara, 95053. Alice Whistler, Ref Librn
Holdings: Cat Mss Microforms
Notes: The Hiberniana collection is cataloged and the cards are interfiled in the main card catalog; also a separate catalog.

CA —STANFORD UNIVERSITY LIBRARIES, Cecil H Green Library, Stanford, 94305. Michael T Ryan, Cur
Holdings: Vols (2300) Uncat Mss Pix
Notes: The James A Healy Collection of Irish Literature. Incl books, magazines, prints, photgraphs, ephemera, and about 3000 unpublished letters. Among the books are complete sets of Dun Emer and Cuala Press publications. Individuals represented in the Healy ms collection incl: A E, Oliver St John Gogarty, James Joyce, Elizabeth C Yeats, George Yeats, and William Butler Yeats.

DE —UNIVERSITY OF DELAWARE, Hugh M Morris Library, S College Ave, Newark, 19711. T Stuart Dick, Special Collections
Holdings: Cat Maps Pix
Notes: Extensive Yeats holdings, incl a collection of personal correspondence which features 67 unpublished letters and telegrams written in 1931-39 to Swami Shri Purohit, an Indian mystic, who with Yeats cotranslated the *Upanishads* into English.

FL —UNIVERSITY OF FLORIDA, Libraries, Special Collections, W University Ave, Gainesville, 32611. Sidney Ives, Librn & Rare Books
Holdings: Vols (8000) Cat Mss
Notes: Incl Irish authors from the revival, as well as history, travel, and religious books.

IL —SOUTHERN ILLINOIS UNIVERSITY, CARBONDALE, Delyte W Morris Library, Special Collections Dept, Carbondale, 62901. David V Koch, Cur of Special Collections; Louisa Bowen, Cur of Manuscripts
Holdings: Vols 2200 Cat Mss Pix
Notes: The papers of Lennox Robinson, Irish playwright and producer, incl in addition to his own mss, letters from William Butler Yeats, Lady Augusta Gregory, George Bernard Shaw, Sean O'Casey, Sara Allgood, and others associated with the Abbey Theatre. The Irish collection also has extensive correspondence between philosopher-author, Arland Ussher, and Yeats' biographer Joseph Hone, covering some 30 years, and correspondence relating to the affairs of the Abbey from the files of Abbey Director, Gabriel Fallon. Tape recordings of Eoin O'Mahony give background and identify figures in the Irish Renaissance. (*The Irish Collection, Rare Book Room, Morris Library, Southern Illinois University at Carbondale,* 1970; Donald Peake, *The Big House Themes in Plays of Lennox Robinson,* 1972.)

†IL —IRISH-AMERICAN CULTURAL ASSOCIATION LIBRARY, 10415 South Western, Chicago, 60643.
Notes: Irish literature, history, biography, art, music.

IL —NEWBERRY LIBRARY, 60 W Walton St, Chicago, 60610. Diana Haskell, Cur of Modern Mss
Holdings: Cat
Notes: Incl Irish history and literature to 1900. Also, a collection on Gaelic linguistics, particularly Irish, Cornish, Welsh and Manx.

IL —NORTHWESTERN UNIVERSITY, Library, Special Collections Dept, 1937 Sheridan Rd, Evanston, 60201. R Russell Maylone, Cur
Holdings: Cat Mss
Notes: First, limited, special editions, letters, ephemera of major 20th century Irish writers such as James Joyce and W B Yeats, as well as representative minor writers. Incl the Dublin Gate Theatre Archive, several paintings by Jack B Yeats, as well as representative minor writers Incl the Dublin Gate Theatre Archive, several paintings by Jack B Yeats and a large collection of Kate O'Brien mss. Literature: Tina Howe, *A Guide to the Books and Collection of Manuscripts of Novels, Plays, Short Stories, Articles, Talks, and Letters of Kate O'Brien in the Special Collections Department, Northwestern University Library* (January, 1975).

†IL —SAINT MARY OF THE LAKE SEMINARY, Feehan Memorial Library, Mundelein, 60060.
Notes: History of Ireland, the Irish language and literature.

KS —UNIVERSITY OF KANSAS, Kenneth Spencer Research Library, Special Collections Dept, Lawrence, 66045. Alexandra Mason, Librn
Holdings: Vols 2000 Cat Mss
Notes: Joyce Collection (800 vols), Yeats Collection (500 vols), and parts of the P S O'Hegarty Collection of some 25,000 vols. Noncirculating.

KY —UNIVERSITY OF LOUISVILLE, Ekstrom Library, Rare Books & Special Collections, 2301 S Third St, Louisville, 40208. George T McWhorter, Cur; Delinda Stephens Buie, Asst Cur
Holdings: Vols 3000 Cat
Budget: $1000
Notes: The Richard M Kain Collection. Literary first editions of Joyce, Yeats, A E, Lady Gregory and others; cultural and political documents; mss; periodical runs; clippings and related materials. Catalog in progress.

†ME —COLBY COLLEGE, Miller Library, Special Collections, Waterville, 04901.
Notes: James A Healy Collection of Irish Literature.

MA —HARVARD UNIVERSITY LIBRARY, Widener Library, Cambridge, 02138.
Holdings: Cat
Notes: *Widener Library Shelflist* No 25 (1970) lists 8147 titles in Celtic languages and literatures, of which some 4800 are Welsh and 2000 are Irish. See *Harvard Library Bulletin,* I (1947), 52-65. There is also a Celtic seminar room in Widener Library containing 1200 vols. For microfilms of Irish manuscripts, see *Harvard Library* Bulletin, VIII (1954), 111-114.

MA —BOSTON COLLEGE LIBRARIES, Thomas P O'Neill Library, Irish Collection, Chestnut Hill, 02167. Ralph Coffman, Cur
Holdings: Vols (10,000) Cat Mss Maps Pix
Notes: Nearly every aspect of Irish history and literature are covered in this collection. Items of special interest are the many papers of Patrick Andrew Collins, president of the Irish Land League, and letters of Jeremiah O'Donovan Rossa, poet, editor and leader in the Fenian and related organizations. Holdings also incl a facsimile of the famous illuminated ms of the Gospels, the *Book of* Kells; a complete vol of *Malton's Views of Dublin, 1799; The Ordinance Surveys;* a complete set of the *Irish Bulletin;* and Colgan's *Acta Sanctorum Hiberniae* describing the lives of the Irish saints.

†MA —IRISH FAMILY HISTORY SOCIETY LIBRARY, 173 Tremont St, Newton, 02158.
Notes: Ireland--genealogy, history, literature, heraldry.

MA —STONEHILL COLLEGE, Donahue Hall, Washington St, North Easton, 02356. Louise M Kenneally, Archivist & Special Collections Librn
Holdings: Vols Cat Periodicals
Notes: Mary Joan Glynn Institute of Irish Studies. Collection of Irish literature containing about 1000 items.

MI —MICHIGAN STATE UNIVERSITY, Libraries, Special Collections Div, East Lansing, 48824. Jannette Fiore, Librn
Holdings: Cat
Notes: Irish Literary Renaissance through Joyce. First and subsequent editions of works of Irish authors, most nearly complete.

†MN —COLLEGE OF SAINT THOMAS CELTIC LIBRARY, O'Shaughnessy Library, Saint Paul, 55105.
Notes: Irish language, history, and literature.

NJ —SETON HALL UNIVERSITY, McLaughlin Library, South Orange, 07079. James Sharp, University Librn
Holdings: Vols (9000) Cat Mss Maps
Notes: McManus Collection of Irish History and Literature.

NY —FORDHAM UNIVERSITY LIBRARY, Bronx, 10458. Joseph A LoSchiavo, Reference Librn
Holdings: Vols 700 // Uncat
Notes: The McLees Gaelic Collection.

NY —CANISIUS COLLEGE, Andrew L Bouwhuis Library, 2001 Main St, Buffalo, 14208. Peter J Laux, Dir
Holdings: Vols 1675 Cat
Budget: $2000
Notes: Joseph P Desmond Collection in Irish literature, history and culture.

NY —AMERICAN IRISH HISTORICAL SOCIETY, Library, 991 Fifth Ave, New York, 10028. Lisa M Hottin, Cur; William D Griffin, Librn
Holdings: Vols (20,000) Cat Maps Pix Slides
Notes: Archives and Manuscripts: The documents and papers of Friends of Irish Freedom, The Land League, the Society of the Friendly Sons of St Patrick, the Catholic Club, and the Guild of Catholic Lawyers. The papers of New York State Supreme Court Justice Daniel F Cohalan. This is the largest and most complete collection of over 20,000 American Irish and Irish history, biography and literature in the United States. Incl American-Irish Newspaper collections dating from 1811, the most comprehensive in the US; 1000 rare books and special editions. Special collections incl regular exhibits of Irish or American Irish interest incl mss, letters, books, photographs and memorabilia. Permanent collection of representative works of Irish painters.

NY —NEW YORK PUBLIC LIBRARY, Berg Collection of English & American Literature,

IRISH LANGUAGE AND LITERATURE (cont.)

Fifth Ave & 42 St, New York, 10018. Lola L Szladits, Cur
Holdings: Cat Mss
Notes: Largest known assemblage of Sean O'Casey's literary papers. Complements the Lady Gregory archive and makes the library a center for study of the Irish Literary Revival.

NY —LE MOYNE COLLEGE, Library, Le Moyne Heights, Syracuse, 13214. James J Simonis, Dir; Annette M Monaco, Special Colelctions Librn
Holdings: Vols (1614) // Cat Mss Slides
Notes: Incl 614 monographs and 1000 pamphlets, reprint articles, and periodical issues. Represents the Irish Literature Collection, covering the modern Irish Literature period from 1880 to 1950, and the Rev William T Noon SJ Collection. Father Noon had James Joyce as his main interest. Manuscripts of Noon's books *Joyce and* Aquinas (Yale University, 1957) and *Poetry and Prayer* (Rutgers University, 1957) are incl. There are several hundred pieces of correspondence which incl authors who had similar interests. The collection also incl his class notes and cutouts from newspapers, pamphlets, periodical articles, many of which have notes written by him. Monographs are represented by an author file. Pamphlets and reprint articles are organized in boxes and numbered numerically.

†NC —WAKE FOREST UNIVERSITY, Z Smith Reynolds Library, Box 7777, Reynold Sta, Winston-Salem, 27109. Richard J Murdoch, Rare Book Librn
Holdings: Cat
Notes: Literature collections with emphasis on a select list of English, Irish and American authors total 13,000 vols incl are first and significant editions, works about the authors and some ephemera. Noncirculating.

OH —CLEVELAND PUBLIC LIBRARY, Fine Arts and Special Collections Department, 325 Superior Ave, Cleveland, 44114. Alice N Loranth, Head
Holdings: Vols (1000) Cat
Notes: Part of the Celtic Language and Literature Collection. Medieval texts, translations, folk songs, linguistics are emphasized. The important scholarly journals, and the serials and publications of the Cymmrodorian Society, Irish Texts Society, Ossianic Society, etc, are well represented.
See also entries under Folklore; Literature, Medieval.

PA —BUCKNELL UNIVERSITY, Ellen Clarke Bertrand Library, Lewisburg, 17837. Ann de Klerk, Librn
Notes: Irish authors.

PA —CHESTNUT HILL COLLEGE, Logue Library, Germantown & Northwestern Aves, Philadelphia, 19118. Helen M Hayes, Librn
Holdings: Vols (3500) Cat Mss
Budget: ($2500)
Notes: Irish history and literature collection, incl 8 letters from G B Shaw to James G Huneker.

PA —CARLOW COLLEGE, Grace Library, Fifth Ave, Pittsburgh, 15213. Joan M Mitchell, Dir of Library Services
Holdings: Vols 543 // Cat Phonorecords Audiotapes
Notes: The Gladys Wholey Curran Collection, which consists primarily of titles in the area of Irish Literature, specifically those titles concerned with the study of the Irish playwrights and poets. The collection is particularly strong in volumes related to the study of Jonathan Swift, John M Synge, and William B Yeats. In addition, there is notable focus upon Irish history of the 17th and 18th centuries. No photocopying.

WI —UNIVERSITY OF WISCONSIN, MADISON, Memorial Library, British & American Language & Literature Collection, 728 State St, Madison, 53706. Yvonne Schofer, Bibliographer
Holdings: Cat Mss Maps
Notes: An extensive collection of Celtic materials acquired from 1914 onward Includes important philological and historical journals, the principal editions of texts and photostats of the Royal Irish Academy's collection of manuscripts, approximately 60 17th and 18th century maps.

NS —SAINT FRANCIS XAVIER UNIVERSITY, Angus L MacDonald Library, Antigonish, B0H 1C0, Can. Maureen Lonergan, Librn
Holdings: Vols 5298 Cat Mss Maps Pix Phonorecords Audiotapes
Notes: Books on or about Scotland and Scottish people; books and pamphlets dealing with Scottish immigrants to Canada; books newspaper published in Cape Breton; reports and records of Scottish societies. Separate catalog. See "The St Francis Xavier University Celtic Collection," by Calum I N MacLeod in Special Collections in Canadian Libraries (Ottawa: Canadian Library Assn, 1963) (Occasional Paper, 53).

ON —QUEEN'S UNIVERSITY, Douglas Library, Kingston, K7L 5C4, Can. William F E Morley, Cur, Special Collections
Holdings: Vols (3250) Cat
Notes: Collection incl all the original vols in the Cuala Press series and a facsimile reprint of each plus about 170 other works by and about W B Yeats, 200 by and about James Joyce, 240 by and about G B Shaw, 100 by and about "A E," George W Russell.

IRISH LITERARY RENAISSANCE

CA —STANFORD UNIVERSITY LIBRARIES, Cecil H Green Library, Stanford, 94305. Michael T Ryan, Cur
Holdings: Vols (2300) Uncat Mss Pix
Notes: The James A Healy Collection of Irish Literature. Incl books, magazines, prints, photgraphs, ephemera, and about 3000 unpublished letters. Among the books are complete sets of Dun Emer and Cuala Press publications. Individuals represented in the Healy ms collection incl: A E, Oliver St John Gogarty, James Joyce, Elizabeth C Yeats, George Yeats, and William Butler Yeats.

DE —UNIVERSITY OF DELAWARE, Hugh M Morris Library, S College Ave, Newark, 19711. T Stuart Dick, Special Collections
Holdings: Vols (35,000) Cat Maps Pix

FL —UNIVERSITY OF FLORIDA, Libraries, Special Collections, W University Ave, Gainesville, 32611. Sidney Ives, Librn & Rare Books
Holdings: Vols (8000) Cat Mss
Notes: Incl Irish authors from the revival, as well as history, travel, and religious books.

IL —SOUTHERN ILLINOIS UNIVERSITY, CARBONDALE, Delyte W Morris Library, Special Collections Dept, Carbondale, 62901. David V Koch, Cur of Special Collections; Louisa Bowen, Cur of Manuscripts
Holdings: Vols 2200 Cat Mss Pix
Notes: The papers of Lennox Robinson, Irish playwright and producer, incl, in addition to his own mss, letters from William Butler Yeats, Lady Augusta Gregory, George Bernard Shaw, Sean O'Casey, Sara Allgood, and others associated with the Abbey Theatre. The Irish collection also has extensive correspondence between philosopher-author, Arland Ussher, and Yeats' biographer Joseph Hone, covering some 30 years, and correspondence relating to the affairs of the Abbey from the files of Abbey Director, Gabriel Fallon. Tape recordings of Eoin O'Mahony give background and identity figures in the Irish Renaissance. (*The Irish Collection, Rare Book Room, Morris Library, Southern Illinois University at Carbondale*, 1970; Donald Peake, *The Big House Themes in Plays of Lennox Robinson*, 1972.)

IL —NEWBERRY LIBRARY, 60 W Walton St, Chicago, 60610. Diana Haskell, Cur of Modern Mss
Holdings: Cat
Notes: Good collection of first editions with supportive material.

IL —NORTHERN ILLINOIS UNIVERSITY, Founders Memorial Library, Rare Books and Special Collections Dept, De Kalb, 60115. William R DuBois, Dept Head
Holdings: Vols 30 // Cat Mss
Notes: The Alan Denson Collection. Emphasis on George Russell, "A.E." Includes Denson's correspondence with many mid-20th century literary figures. Mss indexed but not cataloged.

IN —INDIANA UNIVERSITY, Lilly Library, Seventh St, Bloomington, 47405. William R Cagle, Librn
Holdings: Cat Mss
Notes: First editions.

KY —UNIVERSITY OF LOUISVILLE, Ekstrom Library, Rare Books & Special Collections, 2301 S Third St, Louisville, 40208. George T McWhorter, Cur; Delinda Stephens Buie, Asst Cur
Holdings: Vols 3000 Cat
Budget: $1000
Notes: The Richard M Kain Collection. Literary first editions of Joyce, Yeats, A E, Lady Gregory and others; cultural and political documents; mss; periodical runs; clippings and related materials. Catalog in progress.

†ME —COLBY COLLEGE, Miller Library, Special Collections, Waterville, 04901.
Notes: James A Healy Collection of Irish Literature.

MA —SMITH COLLEGE, Library, Northampton, 01063. Ruth Mortimer, Cur of Rare Books
Holdings: Vols 250 // Cat

MI —MICHIGAN STATE UNIVERSITY, Libraries, Special Collections Div, East Lansing, 48824. Jannette Fiore, Librn
Holdings: Cat
Notes: Irish Literary Renaissance through Joyce. First and subsequent editions of works of Irish authors, most nearly complete.

NY —STATE UNIVERSITY OF NEW YORK, BINGHAMTON, Glenn G Bartle Library, Binghamton, 13901. Marion Hanscom, Special Collections Librn
Notes: The Colum Collection, consisting of the notebooks, mss, galley proofs of Padraic Colum, and letters to both Padraic and Mary Colum. Books by the Colums (in variant editions), and about them.

NY —NEW YORK PUBLIC LIBRARY, Rare Books and Manuscripts Div, Fifth Ave & 42 St, New York, 10018. William L Joyce, Asst Dir; Susan E Davis, Cur of Mss
Holdings: Cat Mss
Budget: ($7161)
Notes: The John Quinn Memorial Collection, incl 72 letterfile boxes, 16 letterfile boxes, 16 folders and 30 letterpress copy books of letters, notes, telegrams and cables, 1900-1924. Also, Foster-Murphy Collection.

NY —NEW YORK PUBLIC LIBRARY, Berg Collection of English & American Literature, Fifth Ave & 42 St, New York, 10018. Lola L Szladits, Cur
Holdings: Vols 20,000 Cat Mss
Notes: The preface to the Collection's G K Hall catalog, 1969 (5 vols) prints an outline of history and guide to the catalog: "The Berg Collection of English and American Literature is one of America's most celebrated collections of first editions, rare books, autograph letters, and mss. Among the 20,000 printed items and 50,000 mss, covering the entire range of English and American literature, there can be found rarities considered museum pieces by the book world. . . .The Irish Literary Remaissance survives in the papers of Lady Gregory."

NY —LE MOYNE COLLEGE, Library, Le Moyne Heights, Syracuse, 13214. James J Simonis, Dir; Annette M Monaco, Special Colelctions Librn
Holdings: Vols (1614) // Cat Mss Slides
Notes: Incl 614 monographs and 1000 pamphlets, reprint articles, and periodical issues. Represents the Irish Literature Collection, covering the modern Irish Literature period from 1880 to 1950, and the Rev William T Noon SJ Collection. Father Noon had James Joyce as his main interest. Manuscripts of Noon's books *Joyce and* Aquinas (Yale University, 1957) and *Poetry and Prayer* (Rutgers University, 1957) are incl. There are several hundred pieces of correspondence which incl authors who had similar interests. The collection also incl his

IRISH LITERARY RENAISSANCE (cont.)

class notes and cutouts from newspapers, pamphlets, periodical articles, many of which have notes written by him. Monographs are represented by an author file. Pamphlets and reprint articles are organized in boxes and numbered numerically.

PA —CHESTNUT HILL COLLEGE, Logue Library, Germantown & Northwestern Aves, Philadelphia, 19118. Helen M Hayes, Librn
Holdings: Vols (3500) Cat Mss
Budget: ($2500) Cat Mss
Notes: Irish history and literature collection, incl 8 letters from G B Shaw to James G Huneker.

PA —CARLOW COLLEGE, Grace Library, Fifth Ave, Pittsburgh, 15213. Joan M Mitchell, Dir of Library Services
Holdings: Vols 543 // Cat Phonorecords Audiotapes
Notes: The Gladys Wholey Curran Collection, which consists primarily of titles in the area of Irish Literature, specifically those titles concerned with the study of the Irish playwrights and poets. The collection is particularly strong in volumes related to the study of Jonathan Swift, John M Synge, and William B Yeats. In addition, there is notable focus upon Irish history of the 17th and 18th centuries. No photocopying.

ON —MCMASTER UNIVERSITY, Mills Memorial Library, Div of Archives & Research Collections, Hamilton, L8S 4L6, Can. G R Hill, Univ Librn
Holdings: Cat Mss
Notes: The main part of this collection consists of works from the Anglo-Irish renaissance, 1890 to 1939. There is also a small archival collection, as well as extensive runs of some Irish periodicals.

ON —UNIVERSITY OF TORONTO, Thomas Fisher Rare Book Library, 120 Saint George St, Toronto, M5S 1A5, Can. Richard G Landon, Head
Holdings: Vols 5200 Cat
Notes: DeLury Collection named for original donor, Alfred DeLury, Dean of Arts, University of Toronto. Centered on works of W B Yeats and his circle. Especially good holdings of the Yeats family. A E, Lady Gregory, and J M Synge. Incl extensive holdings of many of the minor writers.

IRISH LOYAL AND PATRIOTIC UNION

CA —CALIFORNIA STATE UNIVERSITY, NORTHRIDGE, Delmar T Oviatt & South Libraries, 1811 Nordhoff St, Northridge, 91330. Donald L Read, Special Collections Dept
Holdings: Vols 2000 Uncat
Notes: Partial contents; Liberal Publication Dept, London. Pamphlets and leaflets (1893-1903; 1905-1914), Fabian tracts (1884-1904), Irish Loyal and Patriotic Union. Pamphlets and leaflets (1887). Particularly strong in letters from John Burns' personal correspondence (approx 100). Entire collection, 20 linear feet. Indexed in *Century of Change,* 1815-1914; *a Collection of original Pamphlets, Tracts, Posters, Holograph Letters, Manuscripts, etc* (Guernsey, Channel Islands: Guernsey Books, 1972).

IRISH PERIODICALS see Periodicals, Irish

IRISH PLAYWRIGHTS see Playwrights, Irish

IRISH TERRIERS

OH —CLEVELAND PUBLIC LIBRARY, Science & Technology Dept, 325 Superior Ave, Cleveland, 44114. Jean Z Piety, Head
Holdings: Cat
Notes: Emphases: history of the dog; dog show catalogs; stud books of the American Kennel Club, the Canadian Kennel Club, the Kennel Club, the field dog, the foxhound, and the Irish terrier.

IRISH VOLUNTEERS

SC —COLLEGE OF CHARLESTON LIBRARY, Special Collections Dept, Charleston, 29401.
Notes: Papers, 1884-1917, incl a history for the period 1789-1836.

IRON

DE —HAGLEY MUSEUM AND LIBRARY, Eleutherian Mills-Hagley Foundation Inc, PO Box 3630, Greenville, 19807. Richmond D Williams, Dir; Heddy A Richter, Imprints Librn
Notes: Records of the Lukens Steel Co of Coatsville, Pa (1798-1944; 750 cubic feet) incl administrative, accounting, payroll, production and sales records documenting the history of one of America's oldest iron and steel companies. Records of the Phoenix Steel Corporation (1827-1962; 335 cubic feet) incl minute books, financial records, payroll and production records documenting the history of this important Delaware Valley steel producer. Also, Alan Wood Steel Company of Conshohocken, Pa (1728-1937; 250 cubic feet).

†OH —GENERAL MOTORS CORP, Inland Manufacturing Div, Engineering Library, PO Box 1224, Dayton, 45401.

PA —FRANKLIN INSTITUTE LIBRARY, 20 & The Parkway, Philadelphia, 19103. Miriam Padusis, Dir; Charles Wilt, Readers Servs Librn
Holdings: Vols (300,000) Cat Maps Pix Microforms

PA —CARNEGIE LIBRARY OF PITTSBURGH, Science & Technology Dept, 4400 Forbes Ave, Pittsburgh, 15213. Catherine M Brosky, Dept Head
Holdings: Vols (380,000)
Budget: ($240,000)
Notes: Chemistry, metallurgy, manufacture and history. Long runs of periodicals, monographs, serials.

TX —AUSTIN PUBLIC LIBRARY, Austin History Center, 810 Guadalupe Street, PO Box 2287, Austin, 78768. Audray Bateman, Cur

VA —UNIVERSITY OF VIRGINIA, Alderman Library, Manuscripts Dept, Charlottesville, 22901. Edmund Berkeley Jr, Cur
Holdings: Cat Mss
Notes: Papers, 1873-1927, of the Low Moor Iron Company, an Allegheny County, Virginia pig iron company.

IRON INDUSTRY AND TRADE

AL —UNITED STATES PIPE & FOUNDRY CO, Technical Services Library, PO Box 10406, Birmingham, 35202. Phil McGrath, Mgr
Holdings: Vols (3100) Cat
Notes: Books and periodicals on ferrous metallurgy and allied subjects. Restricted use: company personnel and interlibrary loan only.

IN —PURDUE UNIVERSITY LIBRARIES, Graduate School of Management, Krannert Library, West Lafayette, 47907. Gordon Law, Librn
Notes: An important resource at the Krannert Library is its Special Collection of Business and Economics, consisting of some 8000 rare pre-20th century strengths in books, journals, tracts and pamphlets covering primarily the early literature of economic thought and business practices in America and abroad, 1500-1870. A catalog was issued in 1979.

OH —TIMKEN CO, Timken Research Library, 1835 Dueber Ave SW, Canton, 44706. Joellen A Hadbavny, Librn
Holdings: Vols (20,000) Cat Mss Slides
Notes: Incl (7500) translations, reports, etc.

PA —UNITED STATES STEEL CORP, Research Laboratory, Technical Information Center, MS 88, Monroeville, 15146. Angela R Pollis, Staff Supvr of Technical Information Services
Holdings: Vols 30,000 Cat Mss Microforms
Notes: Ferrous metallurgy.

PA —CARNEGIE LIBRARY OF PITTSBURGH, Science & Technology Dept, 4400 Forbes Ave, Pittsburgh, 15213. Catherine M Brosky, Dept Head
Holdings: Vols (380,000) Cat Maps Microforms
Budget: ($240,000)
Notes: General information acquired relating to iron and steel and other metals. Manufacturers directories, including old editions, standards and specifications, trade catalogs, basic periodicals, indexes, and bibliographies.
See also entry under Technology.

PA —COLT INDUSTRIES, Crucible Research Center Library, Box 88, Pittsburgh, 15230. Patricia J Aducci, Technical Librn

VA —UNIVERSITY OF VIRGINIA, Alderman Library, Manuscripts Dept, Charlottesville, 22901. Edmund Berkeley Jr, Cur
Holdings: Cat Mss
Notes: Papers, 1873-1927, of the Low Moor Iron Company, an Allegheny County, Virginia pig iron company.

IRON INDUSTRY AND TRADE—HISTORY

†AL —UNIVERSITY OF ALABAMA, Amelia Gayle Gorgas Library, PO Box S, University, 35486.
Notes: Incl the T P Thompson Collection on the Southern States; Shelby Iron Works Collection, Papers 1862-1923. Unpublished guide in the library for ms collections.

DE —HAGLEY MUSEUM AND LIBRARY, Eleutherian Mills-Hagley Foundation Inc, PO Box 3630, Greenville, 19807. Richmond D Williams, Dir; Heddy A Richter, Imprints Librn
Notes: Records of the Lukens Steel Co of Coatsville, Pa (1798-1944; 750 cubic feet) incl administrative, accounting, payroll, production and sales records documenting the history of one of America's oldest iron and steel companies. Records of the Phoenix Steel Corporation (1827-1962; 335 cubic feet) incl minute books, financial records, payroll and production records documenting the history of this important Delaware Valley steel producer. Also, Alan Wood Steel Company of Conshohocken, Pa (1728-1937; 250 cubic feet).

MD —MARYLAND HISTORICAL SOCIETY, Library, 201 W Monument St, Baltimore, 21201. William B Keller, Head Librn
Holdings: Cat Mss Maps Pix Slides Microforms
Notes: Espec relating to Maryland and Baltimore. Extensive collection.

VA —LYNCHBURG COLLEGE, Knight-Capron Library, Lynchburg, 24501. Mary C Scudder, Dir
Holdings: Vols (847) Cat Maps
Notes: History of the early iron industry in Europe and America. The Capron Collection.

IRON MINES AND MINING

AL —BIRMINGHAM PUBLIC LIBRARY, Dept of Archives & Mss, 2020 Seventh Ave N, Birmingham, 35203. Marvin Y Whiting, Archivist & Cur
Holdings: Cat Docs Mss //
Notes: Business and personal papers of Harry Welles Coffin covering the period from 1878 to 1938 in Birmingham, Alabama. Coffin was a vice president of The Alabama Company, a coal mining and iron products manufacturing firm. The business records incl correspondence, reports, financial records, and other documents relating to iron, steel, and coal industries in North Central Alabama. The personal papers mainly consist of love letters from Coffin to Minnie Everist Smith. These and other letters describe life on Birmingham's Southside area from 1885-1938.

MN —MINNESOTA HISTORICAL SOCIETY LIBRARY, 690 Cedar St, Saint Paul, 55101. Patricia C Harpole, Chief of Reference Library; Bonnie G Wilson, Head of Special Libraries

IRON MINES AND MINING (cont.)

TX —UNIVERSITY OF TEXAS LIBRARIES, Nettie Lee Benson Latin American Collection, Sid Richardson Hall 1.109, Austin, 78712. Laura Gutierrez-Witt, Head Librn
Holdings: Vols (450,000) Cat Mss
Notes: Over 1,000,000 ms pages containing the business records, 1830-1960, of the St John d'el Rey Mining Company, which operates gold and iron ore mines in Brazil.

IRONCLAD, U.S. see Monitor (U.s. Ironclad)

IRONWORK

MA —OLD STURBRIDGE VILLAGE, Research Library, Sturbridge, 01566. Theresa Rini Percy, Librn
Holdings: Cat Pix
Notes: New England, 1790-1850.

IROQUOIS INDIANS

NY —NEW YORK STATE LIBRARY, State Education Bldg Annex, Washington Ave, Albany, 12224.
Holdings: Vols (110,500) Cat
Notes: Strong collection emphasis on North American Indians, especially Indians of New York. Incl books and pamphlets on Indian captivities, treaties, conferences, lives of noted Indians, laws. Bibles and catechisms, prayerbooks, grammars, etc in native languages. Outstanding collection on Iroquois Indians. Incl original treaties between the State of New York and the Iroquois, papers of Cornplanter, drawings by Jesse Cornplanter. Also the papers of William Beauchamp (ca 1860-1930), consisting mainly of his notebooks and scrapbooks concerning the history of the Iroquois Indians. Incl 13 boxes material on Indian language, folklore, and place names, the Moravians, and the New York State archeology.

NY —SAINT LAWRENCE UNIVERSITY, Owen D Young Library, Canton, 13617. Mahlon Peterson, Librn
Holdings: Mss
Notes: Correspondence between Edmund Wilson and William Fenton during the years 1857-1872. The letters are concerned primarily with New York State Indians and Wilson's book *Apologies to the Iroquois.* Approx 60 items.

NY —UNIVERSITY OF ROCHESTER, Rush Rhees Library, Department of Rare Books and Special Collections, Rochester, 14627. Peter Dzwonkoski, Librn
Holdings: Vols 200 Cat Mss
Notes: The printed material includes editions of Lewis Henry Morgan's works, and material about him. Also have his papers (approximately 12 feet of manuscript material) and a collection of several hundred pamphlets which were owned by him. Each letter in the collection has been indexed by the name of the letter writer. Includes most editions of Seavers *Life of Mary Jemison.* Unpublished register is available in the repository.

IRREVERSIBLE COMA see Brain Death

IRRIGATION

CA —UNIVERSITY OF CALIFORNIA, BERKELEY, Giannini Foundation of Agricultural Economics, Library, 248 Giannini Hall, Berkeley, 94720. Grace Dote, Librn
Holdings: Vols (18,000) Cat Mss Maps Microforms
Notes: Noncirculating collection. No interlibrary loans. Also about 124,000 unbound vols. Open to graduate students and faculties of universities and colleges, research workers and interested public. Mostly English language materials, primarily 1900 to date. Card catalog published by G K Hall Co *Dictionary Catalog of the Giannini Foundation of Agricultural Economics Library. Univ of California*, 12 vols (Holdings thru 7/71).

CA —UNIVERSITY OF CALIFORNIA, BERKELEY, Water Resources Center Archives, 410 O'Brien Hall, Berkeley, 94720. Gerald J Giefer, Librn
Holdings: Vols (83,000) Cat Mss Maps
Notes: The engineering, economic, social and legal aspects of water: water as a natural resource and its utilization; irrigation and reclamation; flood control; municipal and industrial water uses and problems; water rights; and water development projects. Particular concentration is on California and the West. Much ephemeral material. See *Dictionary Catalog of the Water Resources Center Archives, University of California* (Boston: G K Hall, 5 vols; First Supp, 1971; Second Supp, 1972; Third Supp, 1973; Fourth Supp, 1974; Fifth Supp, 1976; and Sixth Supp, 1978).

CA —UNIVERSITY OF CALIFORNIA, DAVIS, Shields Library, Dept of Special Collections, Davis, 95616. Donald Kunitz, Head; C Danial Elliott, Asst Head
Notes: Farming equipment: Manufacturer's catalogs, manuals, parts lists, ephemera, and literature pertaining to historical as well as current data on such items as tractors, engines, combines, hay equipment, etc. Described in "The Higgins Library: A Source for the Study of Agricultural History," Don Kunitz, *Agricultural History,* vol 49, 1975, pp 89-91.

CO —COLORADO STATE UNIVERSITY, Libraries, Fort Collins, 80523. Marjorie Rhoades, Engineering Sciences Librn
Holdings: Vols (6000) Cat
Budget: ($5000)
Notes: Water and Soil in Arid Regions (WASAR) is an index and guide to books, conference papers, journal articles, government documents and technical reports, mostly in English, within the appropriate subject areas and held by Colorado State University Libraries. The bibliographical citations are of selected items dealing with soils, water, arid lands, crops, foods and nutrition with certain economic, political, ecological and historical parameters also included. The information needs of developing countries and of those who serve them are the prime criteria for inclusion.

NE —NEBRASKA STATE HISTORICAL SOCIETY, Archives, 1500 R St, Box 82554, Lincoln, 68501. James E Potter, State Archivist
Holdings: / / Uncat Mss Maps Pix
Notes: Agriculture, reclamation, and irrigation on the Great Plains from 1910 to 1957. Collection of Val Kuska, agricultural development for CB&O Railroad.

SK —CANADA PRAIRIE FARM REHABILITATION ADMINISTRATION LIBRARY, Motherwell Bldg, Regina, S4P 0R5, Can. C Kosack, Head
Holdings: Vols (10,000) Cat
Budget: ($8000)
Notes: PFRA is a Canadian federal government agency initiated to alleviate the effects of drought and water shortages on the prairies. The collection covers engineering (dams), agricultural economics, hydrology, irrigation, community pastures, and soil and water conservation.

IRRIGATION, TRICKLE see Trickle Irrigation

IRVIN, EMMA

†CO —DENVER BOTANIC GARDENS, Helen Fowler Library, 909 York St, Denver, 80206. Solange G Gignac, Librn
Notes: Emphasis on Bromeliada Literature; horticulture; Colorado, Oregon, and Rocky Mountains Region botany; landscape architecture; juvenile horticultural and botanical literature. Incl over 5000 pamphlets on botany and horticulture; also, 197 watercolors of Colorado wildflowers by Emma Irvine, and 250 of Oregon by Lillian Hallock.

IRVING, SIR HENRY, 1838-1905

CA —UNIVERSITY OF CALIFORNIA, DAVIS, Shields Library, Dept of Special Collections, Davis, 95616. Donald Kunitz, Head; C Danial Elliott, Asst Head
Holdings: Cat Mss Pix
Notes: Memorabilia from Irving's career as actor-manager; incl programs, scrapbooks, photographs, original scripts and lighting plots. 175 items.

CA —UNIVERSITY OF CALIFORNIA, SANTA CRUZ, University Library, Special Collections, Santa Cruz, 95064. Rita Bottoms, Special Collections Librn; Margaret Felts, South Pacific Collection Bibliographer
Holdings: Cat Mss Pix
Notes: The Robert McNulty Collection of books by Sir Henry Irving, also photographs, hand-written letters, biographies, prompt books and programs.

IL —NORTHWESTERN UNIVERSITY, Library, Special Collections Dept, 1937 Sheridan Rd, Evanston, 60201. R Russell Maylone, Cur
Holdings: Vols 210 Cat Mss Pix Phonorecords
Notes: Collection is being cataloged according to the Craig bibliography of Fletcher & Rood. Collection incl material about Ellen Terry and Henry Irving, as well as original art work by Craig, stage designs and other ephemera. Collection created by J Wesley Swanson and given to Northwestern University Library by his sister.

NY —UNIVERSITY OF ROCHESTER, Rush Rhees Library, Department of Rare Books and Special Collections, Rochester, 14627. Peter Dzwonkoski, Librn
Holdings: Vols (300) Cat Mss Pix
Notes: 19th century English and American plays and works on theatre. Also includes manuscript collections on theatre, and papers of Clement William Scott, John Lawrence Toole, Arthur Wing Pinero, George Alexander, Henry Irving, Charles Kean, Lillian Russell and Leon Marks Lion, collection of 130 lithographic theatre posters, and collection of programs and playbills, chiefly Rochester, NY, and New York City, 1870-1950. Unpublished guides to ms collections available in repository.

IRVING, JULES

NY —NEW YORK PUBLIC LIBRARY, Performing Arts Research Center, Billy Rose Theatre Collection, 111 Amsterdam Ave, New York, 10023. Dorothy L Swerdlove, Cur
Holdings: Cat

IRVING, WASHINGTON

AZ —UNIVERSITY OF ARIZONA, University Library, Special Collections, Tucson, 85721. Louis A Hieb, Head
Holdings: Vols (7000) Cat Mss Microforms
Budget: ($30,000)
Notes: Major authors collected are Twain, Garland, Hart, Irving, Melville and James.

CT —YALE UNIVERSITY, Box 1603A, Yale Station, New Haven, 06520.
Holdings: Cat Mss

NY —NEW YORK PUBLIC LIBRARY, Rare Books and Manuscripts Div, Fifth Ave & 42 St, New York, 10018. William L Joyce, Asst Dir; Susan E Davis, Cur of Mss
Holdings: Mss
Budget: ($7161)
Notes: Incl personal and literary mss, papers, etc. Also, Hellman-Seligman Collection.

NY —UNIVERSITY OF ROCHESTER, Rush Rhees Library, Department of Rare Books and Special Collections, Rochester, 14627. Peter Dzwonkoski, Librn
Holdings: Vols 190 Cat

NY —HISTORICAL SOCIETY OF THE TARRYTOWNS, Library, One Grove St, Tarrytown, 10591. Ruth Neuendorffer, Librn
Holdings: Vols (3000) Cat Mss Maps Pix Microforms VF
Notes: History of the Tarrytowns and vicinity. Incl newspapers, 1875-1946, on microfilm. Bound volumes of Tarrytown *Daily News,* 1916-1937.

VA —UNIVERSITY OF VIRGINIA, Alderman Library, Clifton Waller Barrett Collection, Charlottesville, 22901. Joan St C Crane, Cur of American Literature

IRVING, WASHINGTON (cont.)

Collections
Holdings: Vols 250 Cat Mss
Notes: First editions, important manuscript collection, including *The Sketch Book*. Critical works.

ISHERWOOD, CHRISTOPHER

NV —UNIVERSITY OF NEVADA, RENO, University Library, Special Collections Dept, Reno, 89557. Robert E Blesse, Head
Holdings: Vols (116) Cat Other appearances 210 Cat
Notes: Includes individual works by author in all editions including translations; also prefaces, introductions, published correspondence, appearances in anthologies, periodicals, etc. Bibliographical research collection, part of Modern Authors Collection.

ISHILL, JOSEPH

NJ —BERKELEY HEIGHTS PUBLIC LIBRARY, 290 Plainfield Ave, Berkeley Heights, 07922. Caren Brown, Dir
Holdings: Vols 250 //
Notes: Joseph Ishill had his press in Berkeley Heights for many years. The collection incl examples of most of his work from 1931 to 1966. Also a tape of an interview with him.

ISLA, JOSE FRANCISCO DE, S. J. see De Isla, Jose Francisco, S.j., 1703-1781

ISLAM

CA —LOS ANGELES PUBLIC LIBRARY, Philosophy & Religion Dept, 630 W Fifth St, Los Angeles, 90071. Marilyn C Wherley, Librn
Holdings: Vols 300 Cat
Budget: ($60,000)
Notes: General works on the history, theology, biography and current reference of the religion. Includes many translations of the Koran with related materials.

CA —UNIVERSITY OF CALIFORNIA, LOS ANGELES, Research Library, Near Eastern Collection, Los Angeles, 90024. Edward Shreeves, Chairman, Bibliographers Group; Dunning Wilson, Near Eastern Bibliographer
Holdings: Vols (200,000) Cat Mss Maps Microforms
Budget: ($12,000)
Notes: Incl ancient cultures and history.

†CO —AMERICAN INSTITUTE OF ISLAMIC STUDIES, Muslim Bibliographic Center, Box 10398, Denver, 80210.

†DC —AHMADIYYA MOVEMENT IN ISLAM, Muslim Library, 2141 Leroy Place, NW, Washington, 20008.

DC —LIBRARY OF CONGRESS, African and Middle Eastern Division, Washington, 20540.
Holdings: Cat Mss Microforms
Notes: Over 75,000 vols, Arabic Armenian, Turkish, Persian, and related languages. Special subject strengths incl islamic philosophy, history, and literature.

†IN —NORTH AMERICAN ISLAMIC TRUST INC, Library, 10900 West Washington St, Indianapolis, 46227.

LA —UNIVERSITY OF NEW ORLEANS, Earl K Long Library, New Orleans, 70148. Susan LaHaye, Cataloger
Notes: Approximately 450 pieces (including monographs, pamphlets, serials, newspaper reprints). The Judge Pierre Crabites collection of Egyptology consisting mainly of late 19th and early 20th century imprints. Some signed editions.

MA —HARVARD UNIVERSITY LIBRARY, Widener Library, Middle Eastern Dept, Cambridge, 02138. David H Partington, Librn
Holdings: Cat
Budget: ($55,000)
Notes: The Library's published *Catalogue of Arabic, Persian, and Ottoman Turkish Books* (1968) lists some 40,000 vols in the languages named; many of these are on Islam, as are thousands of Western-language works. See *Harvard Library Bulletin,* XVI (1968), 313-325. The 1983 six-volume catalog of the Arabic Collection lists thousands of additional titles.

MI —UNIVERSITY OF MICHIGAN, Graduate Library, Near East Dept, Ann Arbor, 48109. John A Eilts, Bibliographer
Holdings: Vols (150,000) Cat Mss Maps Microforms
Notes: Excludes Islam in the Far East, Judaism in general, though it does incl specifically Near Eastern Judaism, Incl Bahaism and Arab philosophy, fields of study connected with Islamic or Arabic studies. Turkish language and literature.

NJ —PRINCETON UNIVERSITY, Library, Near East Collections, Princeton, 08540. James Weinberger, Cur
Holdings: Vols (100,000) Cat Mss Maps Phonorecords
Budget: ($72,000)
Notes: Princeton has the largest collection of Arabic mss in the US Collections are particularly rich in classical Arabic and Persian texts, encompassing all the traditional genres. Of special note are collections in Arabic and Persian literature, language, history, philosophy and theology and the religious sciences of Islam, both in ms and printed formats. A separate, additional collection of Arabic mss (about 2000 items) is being cataloged. It is especially rich in theology and philosophy of the classical Islamic period. Two printed catalogs are available: *Descriptive Catalog of the Garrett Collection of Arabic* Manuscripts, Philip K Hitti et al. (Princeton: Princeton Univ Press, 1938); and *Catalogue of Arabic Manuscripts* (Yahuda Section) *in the Garrett Collection, Princeton University,* Rudolf Mach (Princeton: Princeton Univ Press, 1977).

NY —ISLAMIC CENTER OF NEW YORK LIBRARY, 1 Riverside Dr, New York, 10023. Elsayed M I Elkasaby,Dir
Holdings: Vols (8000) Cat
Notes: Islamic life and culture.

NY —NEW YORK PUBLIC LIBRARY, Oriental Div, Fifth Ave & 42 St, New York, 10018. E Christian Filstrup, Chief
Holdings: Cat Mss Microforms
Budget: ($56,455)
Notes: Described in *Dictionary Catalog of the Oriental Collection,* The Research Libraries of the New York Public Library, 1960, 16 vols, and *First Supplement,* 1976, 8 vols (144,000 cards). This catalog incl 318, 000 entries for works in about 100 languages of the East, and all works in Western languages on Oriental subjects. The Oriental Collection numbers about 120,000 vols; its Arabic and Indic holdings and those on ancient Egypt and the ancient Near East are among the largest in the US. There is also a collection of 30,000 vols of PL 480 material from Egypt, Pakistan, and India to which there is main entry access, but which is not incorporated into the dictionary catalog. Other outstanding features of the Oriental Collection incl extensive holdings of Japanese technical and scientific periodicals; a unique collection of linguistic works, grammars, anddictionaries; and unusually good coverage of the field of Oriental religions and philosophies. The catalog contains numerous subject references to periodical articles in all languages. All entries are arranged alphabetically according to the Roman alphabet.

OH —CLEVELAND PUBLIC LIBRARY, Fine Arts and Special Collections Department, 325 Superior Ave, Cleveland, 44114. Alice N Loranth, Head
Holdings: Vols 8600 Cat Mss
Notes: Strong collection of material on religion, literature, folklore, early history, travel and geography prior to the impact of European influence. Classic texts in their original languages and Western translations are emphasized. Important Western language serial publications are well represented. Special emphasis is on Islamic law and Islam in China.
See also entry under Religion, Oriental.

OH —OHIO STATE UNIVERSITY, Library, 1858 Neil Mall, Columbus, 43210. Dona Straley, Islamica Librn
Holdings: Vols (25,000) Cat Maps Microforms
Budget: ($30,000)
Notes: The bulk of the Arabic language collection is in the field of language and literature, with large and medium collections in the fields of Islamica and Middle East history. There are also approx 2000 Persian language vols and approx 3000 vols in Turkish. Scholarly translations of Arabic, Persian and Turkish materials are acquired as available. Also a substantial supporting collection of materials on Arabic language and literature, Islamica, and Middle East history in all of the major European languages. PL 480 recipient since 1975. No ms holdings.

ISLAM IN CHINA

OH —CLEVELAND PUBLIC LIBRARY, Fine Arts and Special Collections Department, 325 Superior Ave, Cleveland, 44114. Alice N Loranth, Head
Holdings: Vols 8500 Cat Mss Pix
Notes: Strong collection of material on Mohammedan religion, literature, folklore, early history, travel and geography prior to European influence. Classic texts in their original languages and Western translations are emphasized. Important Western language serial publications are well represented. Special emphasis is on aspects of Mohammedan law, and Mohammedanism in China.
See also entry under Religion, Oriental.

ISLAMIC ARCHITECTURE see Architecture, Islamic

ISLAMIC ART see Art, Islamic

ISLAMIC CIVILIZATION see Civilization, Islamic

ISLAMIC COUNTRIES

†CO —AMERICAN INSTITUTE OF ISLAMIC STUDIES, Muslim Bibliographic Center, Box 10398, Denver, 80210.

†DC —AHMADIYYA MOVEMENT IN ISLAM, Muslim Library, 2141 Leroy Place, NW, Washington, 20008.

NY —ISLAMIC CENTER OF NEW YORK LIBRARY, 1 Riverside Dr, New York, 10023. Elsayed M I Elkasaby,Dir
Holdings: Vols (8000) Cat
Notes: Islamic life and culture.

†PA —DROPSIE UNIVERSITY, Library, Broad & York Sts, Philadelphia, 19132.

ISLAMIC MANUSCRIPTS see Manuscripts, Islamic

ISLAMIC PHILOSOPHY see Philosophy, Islamic

ISLANDS OF THE PACIFIC

CA —AZUSA PACIFIC COLLEGE, Marshburn Memorial Library, Citrus & Alosta, Azusa, 91702. Edward Peterman, Librn
Holdings: Vols (6000) Uncat
Budget: ($30,000)
Notes: Significant holdings in the George E Fullerton Library of Californiana and Western Americana.

CA —CLAREMONT COLLEGES, Honnold Library, Ninth & Dartmouth, Claremont, 91711. Tania Rizzo, Special Collections Dept Head
Holdings: Vols 150 // Uncat
Notes: Grammars and dictionaries (some dual-language with French or Dutch) of mainly Malayo-Polynesian, some Sino-Tibetan, and other languages, dating from the late 19th to mid-20th centuries. Checklisted.

CA —UNIVERSITY OF CALIFORNIA, SAN DIEGO, Central University Library, Mandeville Dept of Special Collections, La Jolla, 92093. Lynda Corey Claassen, Head
Holdings: Vols (2400) Cat Mss Maps
Notes: The Hill Collection of Pacific

ISLANDS OF THE PACIFIC (cont.)

Voyages, including reports and commentaries of important voyages in the Pacific, from those of Magellan and Sir Francis Drake to exploration through the first half of the 19th century. Includes many rare overland accounts to the Pacific across North America, Mexico, and Panama. Bibliography: Silveira de Braganza, Ronald, *The Hill Collection of Pacific Voyages* (La Jolla: Calif, 1974-1983). In addition, the Pacific Collection incl descriptive works on various cultures of Pacifc rim and Pacific islands. The Melanesian Archive preserves published and unpublished research materials documenting the culture of this archipelago.

CA —UNIVERSITY OF CALIFORNIA, LOS ANGELES, Research Library, Indo/Pacific Collection, 405 Hilgard Ave, Los Angeles, 90024. Edward Shreeves, Chairman, Bibliographers Group; Charlotte Spence, Indo/Pacific Bibliographer
Holdings: Vols Cat Mss Maps Pix Microforms
Notes: The Pacific area collection has been developed on a combination of the research and teaching levels. It focuses on the cultural, economic, political and social history of Australia, New Zealand and the various island groups. The accounts of the early European voyagers are well represented, with the highlight being the Captain Cook collection. An effort has also been made to collect the novels, poetry, drama, etc, of Australian and New Zealand authors.

CA —PACIFIC GROVE PUBLIC LIBRARY, 550 Central Ave, Pacific Grove, 93950. Margaret McBride, Library Dir
Holdings: Vols (1200) // Cat
Notes: Alvin Seale South Seas Collection, incl rare and unusual items, accounts of early voyages, ships' logs and artifacts. Separate catalog. Gift of Alvin Seale, curator of Steinhart Aquarium, San Francisco, 1937.

CA —UNIVERSITY OF CALIFORNIA, SANTA CRUZ, University Library, Special Collections, Santa Cruz, 95064. Rita Bottoms, Special Collections Librn; Margaret Felts, South Pacific Collection Bibliographer
Holdings: Vols (10,000) Cat
Notes: South Pacific Collection. Monographs, rare books, serials, documents and atlases which treat of the Pacific areas of Polynesia, Melanesia, Micronesia, Australia and New Zealand, but excluding western New Guinea (Irian Jaya), the Philippines and Southeast Asia. Approximately 10 percent of the titles are multi-volume documents such as parliamentary papers, legislative journals, official yearbooks, statistical sourcebooks, laws and statutes. The collection includes an exhaustive selection of current journals and monographic series from and about the Pacific: early serials, South Pacific Commission publications, US Government and US Trust Territory publications, serials from museums, universities and scholarly societies. Chief emphasis has been placed on acquisition of the literature of history, description and travel, ethnology andanthropology, literature and literary criticism, political and constitutional histories. Other extensive holdings are in the fields of geography and maps, voyages, mission histories, mythology and folklore, art, linguistics, and science fields of natural history, environmental studies, biology, zoology, botany, geology and astronomy. Printed catalog is available. This is an on-going, growing collection.

DE —UNIVERSITY OF DELAWARE, Hugh M Morris Library, S College Ave, Newark, 19711. T Stuart Dick, Special Collections
Holdings: Cat Mss Pix
Notes: The George Handy Bates Samoan Papers (about 400 items). Calendared mss Berlin Samoan Conference Papers Downs 5382.

DC —LIBRARY OF CONGRESS, Manuscript Division, Washington, 20540. John C Broderick, Chief
Holdings: Cat Mss
Notes: Microfilm of records of the Spanish Colonial Government in the Mariana Islands, 1678-1899. Originals (5.5 linear ft) of these varied materials are in the Manuscript Division. See *LC Information* Bulletin, 18 July 1968.

HI —BERNICE P BISHOP MUSEUM, Library, PO Box 19000-A, Honolulu, 96819. Cynthia Timberlake, Librn
Holdings: Vols (90,000) Cat Mss Maps Pix Slides Microforms
Budget: ($30,000)
Notes: Only American library devoted exclusively to the Pacific region. Collection reflects historical and contemporary research emphases of Bishop Museum; ie the natural and cultural history of the Pacific. Areas of concentration incl archaeology, ethnology, linguistics, voyages and explorations, history, vertebrate and invertebrate zoology, botany and museology. Strong special collections incl photographs, mss and archives, maps and art. Publications: Quarterly "Additions to the Catalog," *Dictionary Catalog of the* Library (9 vols and 2 suppl; Boston: G K Hall, 1964-69).

HI —HAWAIIAN HISTORICAL SOCIETY LIBRARY, 560 Kawaiahao St, Honolulu, 96813. Barbara E Dunn, Librn
Holdings: Vols (11,000) Cat Mss Maps Pix Microforms
Notes: Particular strength in Hawaiian materials-voyages and travels; guidebooks; city directories; histories of Hawaii; both primary and secondary sources. Collection also incl Oceania; Polynesia, Micronesia, Melanesia. No photocopying.

HI —HAWAIIAN MISSION CHILDREN'S SOCIETY LIBRARY, 553 S King St, Honolulu, 96813. Mary Jane Knight, Librn
Holdings: Voils 15,000 Cat Mss Pix
Notes: Missionary period of Hawaiian history, 1819-1880, incl a general collection of Hawaiian history and travel, an outstanding collection of early voyages to the Pacific, and an almost complete collection of early Hawaiian imprints, ie, publications in the Hawaiian language during the 19th century. Ms material incl letters, journals and reports of the Protestant missionaries who came to Hawaii (the Sandwich Islands) under the auspices of the American Board of Commissioners for Foreign Missions. The material is for research only; the stacks are closed. Unpublished papers may be examined by qualified researchers on application to the librarian. Published material is cataloged. Hawaiian imprints are cataloged, except for the Dewey classification 300's which are mainly governmentdocuments. Ms collections are cataloged or in the process of being completely arranged and cataloged.

HI —HAWAII STATE LIBRARY, Hawaii & Pacific Collection, 478 S King St, Honolulu, 96813. Proserfina Strona, Acting Head
Holdings: Vols (93,834) Cat Microforms
Budget: ($30,000)
Notes: Publish cumulative index of Hawaii State Documents biennially and an Index to the *Honolulu Advertiser and Honolulu* Star-Bulletin annually. Also print bibliographies of special interest, such as ethnic bibliographies, Aloha Week celebrations, etc. Depository for county and state documents.

†HI —PACIFIC AND ASIAN AFFAIRS COUNCIL, Pacific House Library, 2004 University Ave, Honolulu, 96816.
Notes: Asia and the Pacific. Pacific and Asian foreign policy.

HI —PACIFIC SCIENTIFIC INFORMATION CENTER, Bernice P Bishop Library, Geography and Map Division, PO Box 19000A, Honolulu, 96819. Lee S Motteler, Geographer; Valerie T Higa, Asst Geographer
Holdings: Vols (2000) Cat Mss Maps Pix
Notes: Incl 20,000 maps and 70,000 aerial photos of Hawaii and the Pacific.

HI —UNIVERSITY OF HAWAII, Library, 2550 The Mall, Honolulu, 96822. R Renee Heyum, Pacific Cur
Holdings: Vols (45,000) Cat Audiotapes Microforms
Budget: ($30,000)
Notes: There is a separate Pacific Collection card catalog, for items cataloged up to 1980, after which all additions are on the Library's microfiche catalog. This is a comprehensive collection of Pacific Islands material with special emphasis on government documents, linguistics, anthropology, economics and cultural change. An acquisitions list is issued quarterly.

HI —BRIGHAM YOUNG UNIVERSITY, HAWAII CAMPUS, Joseph F Smith Library, 55-220 Kulanui St, Laie, 96762. E Curtis Fawson, Dir
Holdings: Vols 9000 Cat Mss Maps Pix Slides Phonorecords Audiotapes Videotapes 16mm Films Filmstrips Microforms
Notes: Incl Melanesia and Micronesia.

IL —FIELD MUSEUM OF NATURAL HISTORY, The Berthold Laufer Library, Roosevelt Rd & Lake Shore Dr, Chicago, 60605. W Peyton Fawcett, Librn
Holdings: Vols (12,000) // Cat Mss Maps
Notes: The part of the museum's collection of Berthold Laufer (1874-1934), Curator of Anthropology, dealing with the peoples of the pre-19th century Chinese Empire (incl Manchuria, Mongolia, Sinkiang and Tibet); their anthropology, art and religion; influences upon their cultures by those of India, Siberia, Japan, Indonesia, and Oceania--and vice versa. Incl about 500 books in Tibetan. About 2/3 of the collection is cataloged.

IL —NEWBERRY LIBRARY, 60 W Walton St, Chicago, 60610. Diana Haskell, Cur of Modern Mss
Holdings: Vols 400 Cat Mss Maps Pix
Notes: Incl circumnavigations of the world, the many travelers to the Philippines and the Northwest Coast.

IN —BUTLER UNIVERSITY, Irwin Library, Hugh Thomas Miller Rare Book Room, 4600 Sunset Ave, Indianapolis, 46208. Gisela Terrell, Rare Books Librn
Holdings: Vols 2500 Cat Maps Pix
Notes: *The William F Charters South Seas* Collection. With the additions made by Butler University since the acceptance of this collection in 1931, we are housing circa 2500 volumes pertaining to the Pacific islands and their peoples; materials range from the earliest explorers' and circumnavigators' reports to detailed studies in anthropology, history, religion, art, socio-political structures, botany and zoology.

MA —PEABODY MUSEUM OF SALEM, Phillips Library, E India Sq, Salem, 01970. Gregor Trinkaus-Randall, Librn
Holdings: Vols (100,000) Cat Mss Pix
Notes: Ethnology of Non-European Peoples Collection. Composed of separate divisions relating to the Pacific Islands, China, Japan and the American Indian. No published indexes.

MN —UNIVERSITY OF MINNESOTA, James Ford Bell Library, 309 19th Ave S, Minneapolis, 55455. John Parker, Cur
Holdings: Vols (11,000) Cat Mss Maps
Notes: Collection of original materials relating to European expansion, 1400-1800.

NE —UNIVERSITY OF NEBRASKA-LINCOLN, Don L Love Library, University Archives and Special Collections, Lincoln, 68588. Joseph G Svoboda, University Archivist
Notes: Collection consists mainly of pamphlets, clippings, posters, and other World War II ephemera; 2000 items.

NY —AMERICAN MUSEUM OF NATURAL HISTORY, Library Services Dept, Central Park W & 79th St, New York, 10024. Nina J Root, Chairwoman; Mary Genett, Asst Librn for Reference Services

NY —NEW YORK PUBLIC LIBRARY, Research Libraries, General Research Division, Fifth Ave & 42 St, New York, 10018. Rodney Phillips, Chief
Holdings: Vols (2,225,000) Cat Maps Pix Microforms
Budget: ($775,718)
Notes: Also strong for ethnology of the islands.

NY —SYRACUSE UNIVERSITY LIBRARIES, Ernest S Bird Library, George Arents Research Library for Special Collections, Syracuse, 13210. Carolyn A Davis, Manuscripts Librn; Amy S Doherty,

ISLANDS OF THE PACIFIC (cont.)

University Archivist; Mark F Weimer, Rare Book Librn
Holdings: Vols 2000 Cat Pix Microforms
Notes: Collection of material relating to Okinawa and the Southern Ryukyus, largely in Japanese, Library has published *Catalog of the Ryukyu Research Collection*, compiled by Douglas G Haring, 1969.

PA —PENNSYLVANIA STATE UNIVERSITY, Fred Lewis Pattee Library, University Park, 16802. Stuart Forth, Dean of Libraries
Holdings: Vols Cat Mss Maps Pix
Notes: The Pennsylvania State University has for several years had a strong interest in the South Pacific, based on Australia but extending to New Zealand and other island groups, together with an interest in voyages of exploration and scientific discovery. The collection is particularly strong in literature but extends to history, political science, the arts and humanities generally. Holdings housed in Special Collections includes the Moody gift of 90 prints and paintings, press collections including the Wattle Grove Press, and Fanfrolico Press publications associated with Norman Lindsay. The special collection of Australiana is dedicated to Bruce Sutherland and was described in his publication *Australiana in the PSU Libraries* (Pennsylvania State University Libraries, 1969), 390 pp.

PI —NIEVES M FLORES MEMORIAL LIBRARY, PO Box 652, Agana, Guam, 96910. Magdalena S Taitano, Territorial Librn
Holdings: Vols 3975 Cat Slides Microforms
Budget: $1000
Notes: Guam Micronesian collection. Incl 500 slides, 15,000 images and 249 microforms. Photocopying available.

ON —UNIVERSITY OF TORONTO, Thomas Fisher Rare Book Library, 120 Saint George St, Toronto, M5S 1A5, Can. Richard G Landon, Head
Holdings: Vols 1500 Uncat
Notes: Sheldon Collection of Australiana, named for collector William Sheldon. Especially rich in 19th century accounts of the exploration of the South Pacific and the interior of the Australian continent. Includes narratives of exiled Canadians who took part in the Rebellion of 1837 in Canada. Includes works on colonization and settlement, the gold-rush of the mid 19th century, and on the life of the indigenous peoples. Includes literature written by Australians or about Australia.

ISLANDS OF THE PACIFIC—ECONOMIC DEVELOPMENT

HI —BANK OF HAWAII, Information Ctr, PO Box 2900, Honolulu, 96846. Sally Campbell, Information Mgr
Holdings: Vols 4000 Cat Maps
Notes: Economics research in developing areas of Hawaii, US Pacific Islands, Asian and other foreign countries. Emphasis on economics, business statistics, demography, finance, banking, tourist industry, construction, domestic and foreign trade. Incl 1000 serial titles.

ISLE OF MAN

NC —DUKE UNIVERSITY, William R Perkins Library, Rare Book Room, Durham, 27706. John L Sharpe, III, Cur
Holdings: Vols 200
Notes: Manx Collection. Collection of items published in the Isle of Man and outside relating to its history and culture.

ISLE ROYALE, MICHIGAN

MI —MICHIGAN TECHNOLOGICAL UNIVERSITY, Archives, Copper County Historical Collections, Houghton, 49931. Theresa Sanderson Spence, University Archivist
Holdings: Uncat Mss Maps Pix
Notes: Wide variety of material on mining, fishing, lumbering and marine activities. Special interest in Great Lakes shipping. Collection is accessioned but not indexed. 637 folders (25 file boxes) of material.

ISLEY, DWIGHT

IA —IOWA STATE UNIVERSITY, Library, Dept of Special Collections, Ames, 50011. Stanley M Yates, Head
Holdings: / / Mss
Notes: Papers of Dwight Isley (1887-1974) who worked at the Bureau of Entomology at the USDA (1915-1921), then at the University of Arkansas (1921-1951), and finally as the Associate Director of the Agriculture Experiment Station at the University of Arkansas (1951-1953). Seven linear feet; finding aid available.

ISOGONIC LINES see Magnetism, Terrestrial

ISOLATIONISM, NATIONAL

CA —HOOVER INSTITUTION ON WAR, REVOLUTION & PEACE, Stanford University, Stanford, 94305. Milorad M Drachkovitch, Archivist
Holdings: Mss
Notes: Records of the America First Committee, 1940-1941. Correspondence of General Robert F Wood, chairman, and R Douglas Stuart, Jr, national director, contributors' correspondence, letters of criticism, research files. State chapter records, speakers bureau files, financial ledgers, and newspaper clippings, relating to the work of the America First Committee to influence US foreign policy, 205 ft. Unpublished register is available in repository.

ISOPTERA see Termites

ISOTOPES

OH —GOODYEAR ATOMIC CORP, Technical Library, PO Box 628, Piketon, 45661. Robert Holland, Supvr
Holdings: Vols (50,000) Cat Mss Microforms
Notes: Uranium enrichment; gas flow, heat transfer, isotope analyses, uranium-floride chemistry.

ON —ATOMIC ENERGY OF CANADA LIMITED, Main Library, Technical Information Branch, Chalk River Nuclear Laboratories, Chalk River, K0J 1J0, Can. Harry Greenshields, Chief Librn
Holdings: Vols (128,700) Microforms
Budget: ($662,400)
Notes: The Main Library, Atomic Energy of Canada Limited, is the Canadian repository for the literature of nuclear science and technology. Its collections reflect both fundamental and nuclear aspects of biology, chemistry, electronics, engineering, mathematics, computers, metallurgy, physics and other specific areas of science involving nuclear technology with special emphasis on heavy water reactor systems. 512,000 research reports are available in paper copy and microfiche form. Incl US DOE, INIS and other offshore nuclear research reports. 386,000 microforms.

ISRAEL

CA —HOOVER INSTITUTION ON WAR, REVOLUTION & PEACE, Stanford University, Stanford, 94305. Peter Duignan, Cur; Karen Fung, Deputy Cur
Holdings: Vols (100,000)
Notes: For full description of collection, see Hoover Institution entry under Near East.

DC —LIBRARY OF CONGRESS, African and Middle Eastern Division, Washington, 20540.
Holdings: Cat Mss Microforms
Notes: Hebraica: about 109,000 vols in Hebrew, Yiddish, Judeo-Arabic, Judeo-Persian, Ladino, Syriac, Ethiopic; espec strong in Biblical subjects, responsa literature, and socio-political aspcets.

FL —UNIVERSITY OF FLORIDA LIBRARY, Isser and Rae Price Library of Judaica, 18 Libr East, Gainesville, 32611. Robert Singerman, Head Librn
Budget: ($30,000)
Notes: Total holdings estimated at 55,000 vols dealing with the political, social, economic and intellectual history of the Jews in the ancient, medieval and modern periods and in all geographic areas. The following areas are especially well represented by printed matter in all relevant languages: Bibliography, Festschriften, History, Bible, Judaism and Jewish theology, liturgy, responsa, rabbinical literature, Jewish law, Hebrew language and literature, Yiddish language and literature, anti-semitism, Zionism, Palestine and the *Yishuv*, and the State of Israel. German and American Judaica form a collecting emphasis with holdings for all the standard histories as well as histories of individual synagogues, institutions and local communities. Works in Hebrew and Yiddish comprise about 60 percent of the collection (estimated 30,000 vols). With few exceptions, holdingsare limited to nineteenth and twentieth century imprints, with complete sets of journals and thousands of ephemeral pamphlets, many of them commemorating anniversaries, enhancing the research value of the collection, the largest Judaica research library in the southeastern United States. Only about half of the collection is cataloged; the collection is a circulating one and vols may be borrowed on interlibrary loan. Incl the Leonard C Mishkin Collection (40,000 vols), the largest personal Judaica collection in the United States, the Shlomo Marenof Collection (3500 vols), and the inventory of Bernard Morgenstern's Lower East Side Book Store (8000 vols). Scholars should inquire in advance of their visit. *The Isser and Rae Price Library of Judaica* Report (circulation 2900 copies) is mailed gratis twice a year to all interested parties. Special catalogs:Pre-1881 Hebrew imprints recorded in a chronological card file.

MA —HEBREW COLLEGE, Jacob & Rose Grossman Library and Lawrence Jay & Anne Cable Rubenstein Library, 43 Hawes St, Brookline, 02146. Maurice Tuchman, Librn
Notes: Jewish history, Hebrew literature, Israel Rabbinic literature.

†MA —HARVARD UNIVERSITY LIBRARY, Widener Library, Judaica Collection, Room M, Cambridge, 02138. Charles Berlin, Bibliographer
Holdings: Cat Mss Microforms
Notes: Library has published *Catalogue of Hebrew Books*, 6 vols (1968), and *Supplement*, 3 vols (1972); shelflist for Judaica *Widener Library Shelflist*, No 39 (1971) lists 11,800 vols in western languages. See also *Jewish Book Annual*, XXVI (1968/9), 58-63.

NY —NEW YORK PUBLIC LIBRARY, Jewish Division, Fifth Ave & 42 St, New York, 10018. Leonard S Gold, Chief
Holdings: Vols (200,000) Cat Mss Microforms
Budget: ($33,383)
Notes: A collection of material in all languages on Judaism, Jewish history, literature and traditions from the earliest times to date and works in the Hebrew alphabet (mainly Hebrew and Yiddish) on a variety of subjects. The division has extensive files of Jewish periodicals and newspapers. The collection of rare Hebraica incl medieval texts, cabalistic works, ethical and philosophical tracts in book form. See *Dictionary Catalog of the Jewish Collection* (Boston: G K Hall, 1960), 14 vols. First Supplement (Boston: G K Hall, 1975), 8 vols.

NY —YESHIVA UNIVERSITY, Library, 500 West 185th Street, New York, 10033. Pearl Berger
Holdings: Cat

NY —YIVO INSTITUTE FOR JEWISH RESEARCH, Library & Archives, 1048 Fifth Ave, New York, 10028. Dina Abramowicz, Librn; Marek Web, Archivist
Holdings: Vols 315,000 Mss Maps Pix Slides
Notes: The most extensive collection in existence of Yiddish books and periodicals.

ISRAEL (cont.)

Covers American, European, Soviet, Israel and other publications from 16th century to the present. Scholarship in the Yiddish field, as well as translations from Yiddish into other languages are incl The Archives Division contains unpublished mss, correspondence and pictures, incl the library and archives of Max Weinreich.
Publications: *Guide to the YIVO Library,* 1975; *Guide to Major Collections in the YIVO Archives,* 1973.

OH —HEBREW UNION COLLEGE-JEWISH INSTITUTE OF RELIGION, Klau Library, 3101 Clifton Ave, Cincinnati, 45220. David J Gilner, Reference Librn
Holdings: Cat

ISRAEL—HISTORY

CA —HOOVER INSTITUTION ON WAR, REVOLUTION & PEACE, Stanford University, Stanford, 94305. Milorad M Drachkovitch, Archivist
Notes: Papers of Kurt R Grossman, 1926-73, incl mss of writings, correspondence, clippings, and serial issues, relating to Jewish refugees from Nazi Germany, postwar German and Austrian restitution payments to Jewish war victims, German-Israeli relations, the condition of Jews throughout the world, and civil liberties in the US and Germany. 53 ms boxes. 8 scrapbooks.

DC —GEORGETOWN UNIVERSITY, Library, Special Collections Div, 37 & O Sts NW, Washington, 20057. George M Barringer, Special Collections Librn; Nicholas B Sheetz, Mss Librn
Holdings: Mss Pix
Notes: The papers of Christopher Sykes, biographer, journalist, and novelist; containing mss, letters, photographs, and drawings. With extensive correspondence from Harold Acton; Angela, Countess of Antrim; Sir John Betjeman; Ivy Compton-Burnett; Alick Dru; T S Eliot; Max Beerbohm; Graham Greene; John Hayward; Lord Patrick Kinross; Compton Mackenzie; Nancy Mitford; Anthony Powell; Dame Flora Robson; Cecil Roth; Sir John Russell; Osbert Sitwell; John Sparrow; Freya Stark; James Stern; and Evelyn Waugh, among others. Also, considerable research material about Evelyn Waugh, Adam von Trott, Robert Byron, Lady Nancy Astor; and the foundation of the state of Israel.

OH —HEBREW UNION COLLEGE-JEWISH INSTITUTE OF RELIGION, Klau Library, 3101 Clifton Ave, Cincinnati, 45220. David J Gilner, Reference Librn
Holdings: Cat

OH —OHIO STATE UNIVERSITY, William Oxley Thompson Memorial Library, 1858 Neil Ave, Columbus, 43210. Amnon Zipin, Jewish Studies Bibliographer
Holdings: Vols (43,000) Cat Maps Microfilms
Budget: ($35,000)
Notes: Collection emphasis is materials on Jewish history (especially US, Israel and Europe) and Hebrew language and literature. Small collection of Yiddish materials.

ISRAEL—MAPS

OH —HEBREW UNION COLLEGE-JEWISH INSTITUTE OF RELIGION, Klau Library, 3101 Clifton Ave, Cincinnati, 45220. David J Gilner, Reference Librn
Notes: About 200 pre-1900 maps, some as old as early 16th century. About 400 post-1900, most in color. Primarily of Israel/Palestine.

ISRAELI LITERATURE

NY —HEBREW UNION COLLEGE, Jewish Institute of Religion, Klau Library, 1 W 4th St, New York, 10012. Philip Miller, Librn
Holdings: Volsl (115,000) Cat Mss Microforms
Notes: Hebrew literature--ancient, medieval and modern.

ISSEI

CA —UNIVERSITY OF CALIFORNIA, LOS ANGELES, Research Library, Dept of Special Collections, 405 Hilgard Ave, Los Angeles, 90024. Edward Shreeves, Chairman, Bibliographers Group; David S Zeidberg, Head
Notes: 63 linear feet of administrative records, reports, and camp newspapers of the US War Relocation Authority, Relocation Center, Manzanar, Calif. Incl records of Ralph Palmer Merritt, director of the Center. Also 170 photographs taken by Ansel Adams at that Relocation Center for the book, *Born Free and Equal.*

ITALIAN AMERICAN NEWSPAPERS see Newspapers, Italian American

ITALIAN ARCHITECTURE see Architecture, Italian

ITALIAN ARCHIVES see Archives, Italian

ITALIAN DRAMA

CT —YALE UNIVERSITY, Box 1603A, Yale Station, New Haven, 06520.

IA —UNIVERSITY OF IOWA, University Libraries, Iowa City, 52242. Frank Paluka, Head, Special Collections Dept
Holdings: Vols (13,170) Cat
Notes: Florindo Cerreta, "Italian Plays of the Renaissance", *Books at Iowa,* April 1965.

NC —DUKE UNIVERSITY, William R Perkins Library, Durham, 27706. Elvin E Strowd, University Librn
Notes: The Mazzoni collection of approximately 23,000 books and 67,000 reprints and pamphlets is strong in, but not limited by any means to, Italian literature. A special aspect of this collection is a group of essays, studies, or small works published on the occasion of a marriage. These "per la nozze di" range from a poem published in post card form to a scientific or literary work. The manuscript catalog of the pamphlet collection has been published by the library in book form; the 23,000 volumes have been cataloged and are shelved in the library's bookstacks.

ON —UNIVERSITY OF TORONTO, Thomas Fisher Rare Book Library, 120 Saint George St, Toronto, M5S 1A5, Can. Richard G Landon, Head
Holdings: Vols 6500 Cat Mss
Notes: Italian Play Collection comprises editions of Italian plays performed before 1815, with particular emphasis on the Renaissance period. Holdings partially described in Corrigan, Beatrice. *Catalogue of Italian Plays, 1500-1700, in the Library of the University of Toronto* (Toronto, 1961). Some unpublished ms material. Libretti collection comprises libretti for operas performed in Italian after 1815.

ITALIAN LANGUAGE AND LITERATURE

CA —UNIVERSITY OF CALIFORNIA, BERKELEY, University Library, French and Italian Collections, Berkeley, 94720. Donald G Williams, Dir
Notes: Research collection with special strengths in early Italian literature (to 1400), and Italian literature of the Renaissance. Strong holdings for such authors as Dante, Petrarch, Boccaccio, Ariosto, Machiavelli, Tasso, and many others. The collections in the Main Library are complemented by significant incunabula, rare books and ms holdings in the Bancroft Library.

CA —LOS ANGELES PUBLIC LIBRARY, Foreign Languages Dept, 630 W Fifth St, Los Angeles, 90071. Sylva Manoogian, Principal Librn
Holdings: Vols 9332 Cat
Budget: ($41,500)

CA —SAN FRANCISCO STATE UNIVERSITY, Frank V de Bellis Collection, 1630 Holloway Ave, San Francisco, 94132. Serena de Bellis, Cur
Holdings: Vols 3000 Cat Mss
Notes: Frank V de Bellis Collection. There is a separate catalog of the collection which incl rare and current materials, with literature by Italian authors and medieval through contemporary literary criticism.

CA —SAN JOSE PUBLIC LIBRARY, 180 W San Carlos St, San Jose, 95113. Homer Fletcher, Dir
Holdings: Vols 650 // Cat
Notes: The Guglielmo Marconi Memorial Collection (incl in the general collection).

CA —STANFORD UNIVERSITY LIBRARIES, Cecil H Green Library, Stanford, 94305. Michael T Ryan, Cur
Holdings: Vols Cat
Notes: An emphasis in the Rare Book Collection.

CT —YALE UNIVERSITY, Beinecke Rare Book & Manuscript Library, Osborn Collection, New Haven, 06520. Stephen R Parks, Cur
Holdings: Mss

DC —GEORGETOWN UNIVERSITY, Library, Special Collections Div, 37 & O Sts NW, Washington, 20057. George M Barringer, Special Collections Librn; Nicholas B Sheetz, Mss Librn
Holdings: Cat
Notes: Strength in Italian dialectoloty.

IL —NEWBERRY LIBRARY, 60 W Walton St, Chicago, 60610. Diana Haskell, Cur of Modern Mss
Holdings: Cat Mss
Notes: Several thousand vols. Espec strong for 1400-1600.

IL —NORTHWESTERN UNIVERSITY, Library, Special Collections Dept, 1937 Sheridan Rd, Evanston, 60201. R Russell Maylone, Cur
Holdings: Vols 6000 Cat Mss
Notes: First editions, letters and works about major 20th-century authors. Incl books and periodicals from France and Germany and to a lesser extent from Italy, Spain, Poland, Rumania, Czechoslovakia, Sweden, Denmark, and the Netherlands. Strong in German Expressionism, Italian Futurism, Surrealism, and Dada.

KS —UNIVERSITY OF KANSAS, Kenneth Spencer Research Library, Special Collections Dept, Lawrence, 66045. Alexandra Mason, Librn
Holdings: Cat Mss
Notes: 15th-17th century Italian language imprints in Summerfield collection; 15th-18th Italian mss. Noncirculating.

MA —BOSTON PUBLIC LIBRARY, North End Branch, 25 Pamenter St, Boston, 02113. Rhoda Blacker, Librn
Holdings: Vols Cat
Notes: Old collection of vols, wide assortment of reading material, incl fiction and classics. Approx 1500 vols.

MA —HARVARD UNIVERSITY LIBRARY, Widener Library, Cambridge, 02138. Assunta S Pisani, Specialist in Book Selection
Holdings: Cat
Notes: See *Harvard Library Notes,* III (1935), 81-86. Collections on Dante, Petrarch, and Tasso are noteworthy, as is 19th-century drama.

NY —HEMPSTEAD PUBLIC LIBRARY, Foreign Language Collection, 115 Nichols Court, Hempstead, 11550. Irene A Duszkiewicz, Dir
Notes: Mainly French, German, Italian, Spanish, Polish, Yiddish, Hebrew. Holdings in other languages, including Asian.

†NY —COLUMBIA UNIVERSITY LIBRARIES, Paterno Library, 1161 Amsterdam Ave, New York, 10027.
Notes: Italian literature and culture. One of the most extensive collections in the United States.

†NY —ISTITUTO ITALIANO DI CULTURA LIBRARY, 686 Park Ave, New York, 10021.
Notes: Italian philosophy, social sciences concerning Italy, Italian language and literature, science and technology, Italian arts, history, geography and biography.

NY —NEW YORK PUBLIC LIBRARY, Research Libraries, General Research Division, Fifth Ave & 42 St, New York, 10018. Rodney Phillips, Chief
Holdings: Vols (2,225,000) Cat Maps Pix Microforms
Budget: ($775,718)

ITALIAN LANGUAGE AND LITERATURE (cont.)

NY —NEW YORK PUBLIC LIBRARY, Donnell Foreign Language Library, 20 W 53 St, New York, 10019. Bosiljka Stevanovic, Supvr Librn
Holdings: Vols 1974 Cat
Notes: Italian collection incl Italian authors of Italian expression. No separate catalog.

NC —DUKE UNIVERSITY, William R Perkins Library, Durham, 27706. Elvin E Strowd, University Librn
Notes: The Mazzoni collection of approximately 23,000 books and 67,000 reprints and pamphlets is strong in, but not limited by any means to, Italian literature. A special aspect of this collection is a group of essays, studies, or small works published on the occasion of a marriage. These "per la nozze di" range from a poem published in post card form to a scientific or literary work. The manuscript catalog of the pamphlet collection has been published by the library in book form; the 23,000 volumes have been cataloged and are shelved in the library's bookstacks.

NC —CUMBERLAND COUNTY PUBLIC LIBRARY, North Carolina Foreign Language Center, 328 Gillespie St, Fayetteville, 28301. Patrick M Valentine, Coordinator
Holdings: Vols 800 Cat
Budget: $300
Notes: The largest book collections are, in descending order of size, German Spanish, French, Japanese, Korean and Vietnamese, with fair sized collections in Italian, Russian, Chinese, Arabic, Greek, Hungarian, Polish, Hebrew, Thai, and Hindi. The Center has several shelves each of books in Bengali, Dutch, Marathi, Portuguese, Urdu, and Yiddish. Smaller collections of one to three shelves each incl Catalan, Croatian, Czech, Danish, Finnish, Gujarati, Icelandic, Kannada, Latin, Lithuanian, Malayalam, Norwegian, Panjabi, Persian (Farsi), Romanian, Slovak, Swedish, Tagalog, Tamil, Telegu, and Ukrianian. The Center has grammars, dictionaries and occasionally other readings in languages from Afrikaans and Albanian to Welsh, Yoruba and Zulu.

OH —CLEVELAND PUBLIC LIBRARY, Foreign Literature Dept, 325 Superior Ave, Cleveland, 44114. Natalia Bezugloff, Head
Holdings: Vols 6920 Cat
Notes: A popular circulating collection containing classics and the standard works with emphasis on belles lettres, history and biography. A variety of other subjects such as learning languages, how to do books, art, children's books, spoken phonodiscs and cassettes, periodicals, etc. Incl 80 ephemera.
See also entry under Foreign Language Collections

PA —UNIVERSITY OF PENNSYLVANIA, Van Pelt Library, Rare Books Collection, 34 & Walnut Sts, Philadelphia, 19104. Daniel Traister, Special Collections Librn
Holdings: Cat
Notes: Strong collections of 15th and 16th century imprints, especially Boccaccio and Tasso.

†PA —CABRINI COLLEGE, Holy Spirit Library, Eagle & King of Prussia Rds, Radnor, 19087.

PA —PENNSYLVANIA STATE UNIVERSITY, Fred Lewis Pattee Library, Library Hispanic Program, University Park, 16802. Donald C Henderson, Head
Holdings: Vols (50,000) Cat Mss
Budget: ($21,000)
Notes: A good general collection covers all periods with emphasis on Dante and on contemporary writers; supports doctoral programs.

RI —WESTERLY PUBLIC LIBRARY, Broad St, Westerly, 02891. David J Panciera, Library Dir
Holdings: Vols 500 Cat Phonorecords
Notes: Recreational reading in the Italian language, incl juveniles, periodicals, records.

BC —GREATER VANCOUVER LIBRARY FEDERATION, 110-6545 Bonsor, Burnaby, Z5H 1H3, Can. Colleen Smith, Coordr
Holdings: Vols (20,350) Cat
Notes: Deposit provided by the National Library's Multilingual Biblioservice on long-term loan to libraries in the Greater Vancouver Library Federation (Burnaby, New Westminister, N Vancouver City Public, N Vancouver District Public, Port Moody, Vancouver, W Vancouver).

ON —UNIVERSITY OF TORONTO, Thomas Fisher Rare Book Library, 120 Saint George St, Toronto, M5S 1A5, Can. Richard G Landon, Head
Holdings: Vols 6500 Cat Mss
Notes: Italian Play Collection comprises editions of Italian plays performed before 1815, with particular emphasis on the Renaissance period. Holdings partially described in Corrigan, Beatrice. *Catalogue of Italian Plays, 1500-1700, in the Library of the University of Toronto* (Toronto, 1961). Some unpublished ms material. Libretti collection comprises libretti for operas performed in Italian after 1815.

ITALIAN MANUSCRIPTS see Manuscripts, Italian

ITALIAN MUSIC see Music, Italian

ITALIAN NEWSPAPERS see Newspapers, Italian

ITALIAN PERIODICALS see Periodicals, Italian

ITALIAN RENAISSANCE ART see Art, Italian Renaissance

ITALIAN SONS AND DAUGHTERS OF AMERICA

PA —UNIVERSITY OF PITTSBURGH, Hillman Library, Archives of Industrial Society, 363 Hillman Library, Pittsburgh, 15260. Frank A Zabrosky, Cur
Holdings: Documents Mss Pix Newspapers Audiotapes Microforms
Notes: Records of Italian churches, fraternal/beneficial, social organizations.
Unique: Italian Sons and Daughters of America, Records, 1929-1970.

ITALIANS IN THE U.S.

LA —LOUISIANA STATE UNIVERSITY, SHREVEPORT, Library-Archives, 8515 Youree Dr, Shreveport, 71129. Patricia L Meador, Archivist & Asst Librn
Notes: Archives incl catalogued manuscripts and records, 500 maps, more than 5000 photographs, 1000 architectural drawings, slides. The archives has on microfilm more than 200 letters (1827-1842) of Henry Miller Shreve, relating to the improvement of the Ohio, Mississippi and Red Rivers. Microfilm records also include those of the Shreveport City Council, Caddo and Bossier Parish Police Juries, Caddo Levee Board, the Shreveport Chamber of Commerce, and the Louisiana State Fair. Original and microfilm copies of the *Italia Moderna,* an Italian newspaper published by Frank Fulco in Shreveport, 1929-1946, are available for use in the archives. Other area newspapers are on microfilm and available for use.

MN —UNIVERSITY OF MINNESOTA, Immigration History Research Center, 826 Berry St, Saint Paul, 55114. Susan Griegs, Cur
Holdings: Vols (35,000) Mss Maps Pix Phonorecords Audiotapes 16mm Films Microforms
See also entry under US - Emigration and Immigration

NY —HOFSTRA UNIVERSITY, Library, 1000 Fulton Ave, Hempstead, 11550. Charles R Andrews, Dean of Library Services
Notes: The personal library of Paul Radin. See description of the American Philosophical Society Library's collection of his anthropological papers under this entry (Pa).

†NY —CENTER FOR MIGRATION STUDIES LIBRARY, 209 Flagg Place, Staten Island, 10304.
Notes: Human migration and ethnic group relations, especially strong in Italian-American affairs.

PA —AMERICAN PHILOSOPHICAL SOCIETY, Library, 105 S Fifth St, Philadelphia, 19106. Edward C Carter II, Librn
Notes: The anthropological papers of Paul Radin in fields of ethnology, social orgainization, primitive religion, linguistics, and mythology. He worked mostly among the Winnebago, Ojibwa, Fox, Zapotec, Wappo, Wintun, and Huave Indian tribes; also Italian and other ethnic minorities of San Francisco.

PA —BALCH INSTITUTE FOR ETHNIC STUDIES, Library, 18 S Seventh St, Philadelphia, 19106. R Joseph Anderson, Library Dir
Holdings: Vols 650 Cat Mss Pix Microforms
Notes: The Ethnic Heritage Studies Clearinghouse Collection of over 2000 reports, print and a/v materials, instructional kits, and scholarly monographs developed since 1974 under the federal government's Ethnic Heritage Studies Act, to encourage support of ethnic studies in public school and college curricula. Supplemented by the Leonard Covello (Italian-American educator) papers.
See also entry under Covello, Leonard

PA —UNIVERSITY OF PITTSBURGH, Hillman Library, Archives of Industrial Society, 363 Hillman Library, Pittsburgh, 15260. Frank A Zabrosky, Cur
Holdings: Documents Mss Pix Newspapers Audiotapes Microforms
Notes: Records of Italian churches, fraternal/beneficial, social organizations.
Unique: Italian Sons and Daughters of America, Records, 1929-1970.

ITALLIE, JEAN-CLAUDE VAN

OH —KENT STATE UNIVERSITY, Libraries, Dept of Special Collections, Kent, 44242. Dean H Keller, Cur
Holdings: Vols 60 Cat Mss

ITALY—ANTIQUITIES

CA —SAN FRANCISCO STATE UNIVERSITY, Frank V de Bellis Collection, 1630 Holloway Ave, San Francisco, 94132. Serena de Bellis, Cur
Holdings: // Cat
Notes: Catalog: Becker-Colonna, Andreina, *Etruscan, Greek and Roman Artifacts in the Frank V de Bellis Collection of the California State University,* rev and ed by Rosefannie Grabstein (San Francisco State University, 1976).

ITALY—CIVILIZATION AND CULTURE

CA —SAN FRANCISCO STATE UNIVERSITY, Frank V de Bellis Collection, 1630 Holloway Ave, San Francisco, 94132. Serena de Bellis, Cur
Holdings: Vols (5000) Cat Mss Maps Pix
Notes: Rare and current materials. Emphasis on history, and history of the fine arts. General descriptive pamphlet: *The Frank V de Bellis Collection* (San Francisco, 1967).

CT —UNIVERSITY OF CONNECTICUT, Library, Storrs, 06268. R H Schimmelpfeng, Dir of Special Collections
Holdings: // Cat
Notes: The collection incl 1900 books, about 4400 contemporary pamphlets, periodicals, and more than 7000 broadsides, the latter not yet cataloged. A checklist of the author file is available. The collection does not incl the secondary source which are cataloged for the general library.

†NY —COLUMBIA UNIVERSITY LIBRARIES, Paterno Library, 1161 Amsterdam Ave, New York, 10027.
Notes: Italian literature and culture. One of the most extensive collections in the United States.

†NY —ISTITUTO ITALIANO DI CULTURA LIBRARY, 686 Park Ave, New York, 10021.
Notes: Italian philosophy, social sciences

ITALY—CIVILIZATION AND CULTURE (cont.)

concerning Italy, Italian language and literature, science and technology, Italian arts, history, geography and biography.

NC —DUKE UNIVERSITY, William R Perkins Library, Durham, 27706. Elvin E Strowd, University Librn

†PA —CABRINI COLLEGE, Holy Spirit Library, Eagle & King of Prussia Rds, Radnor, 19087.

ITALY—DESCRIPTION AND TRAVEL

CT —YALE UNIVERSITY, Box 1603A, Yale Station, New Haven, 06520.

ITALY—HISTORY

CA —UNIVERSITY OF CALIFORNIA, BERKELEY, University Library, French and Italian Collections, Berkeley, 94720. Donald G Williams, Librn
Notes: General research collection, emphasizing cultural, local and recent political history; incl 1500 pamphlets. Special strength in the *Risorgimento.*

†CA —CLAREMONT COLLEGES, Honnold Library, Claremont, 91711.
Notes: Florentine Renaissance, particularly 1450-1500. Angelo Poliziano (1454-1494), the humanist scholars and writers of the Medici circle, and the Platonic Academy.

CA —UNIVERSITY OF CALIFORNIA, LOS ANGELES, Research Library, Medieval and Renaissance Collection, 405 Hilgard Ave, Los Angeles, 90024. Edward Shreeves, Chairman, Bibliographers Group; Frances K Zeitlin, Medievan and Renaissance Bibliographer
Holdings: Mss
Notes: Histories and statutes of Italian cities and towns from the Middle Ages to the 17th century.

CA —UNIVERSITY OF CALIFORNIA, LOS ANGELES, Research Library, Western European Collection, Los Angeles, 90024. Edward Shreeves, Chairman, Bibliographers Group; Mary E Greco, Western European Bibliographer
Holdings: Mss Maps Pix Microforms
Notes: Special strengths in Italian local history, medieval to modern, as well as religion, politics, popular culture, and urbanism of the 19th and 20th centuries.

CA —SAN FRANCISCO STATE UNIVERSITY, Frank V de Bellis Collection, 1630 Holloway Ave, San Francisco, 94132. Serena de Bellis, Cur
Holdings: Vols (5000) Cat Mss Maps Pix
Notes: Rare and current materials. Emphasis on history, and history of the fine arts. General descriptive pamphlet: *The Frank V de Bellis Collection* (San Francisco, 1967).

CT —YALE UNIVERSITY, Box 1603A, Yale Station, New Haven, 06520.
Holdings: Cat Mss Pix

DC —GEORGETOWN UNIVERSITY, Library, Special Collections Div, 37 & O Sts NW, Washington, 20057. George M Barringer, Special Collections Librn; Nicholas B Sheetz, Mss Librn
Holdings: Cat
Notes: A microfilm of the papers of Dino Grandi (1895-), Conte di Mordano and former Italian minister of foreign affairs and of justice; and ambassador to Great Britain. Grandi played an important role in the Mussolini government and, as president of the Grand Council, presented the resolution removing Mussolini from power in July, 1943.

DC —LIBRARY OF CONGRESS, General Reading Rooms Division, Microform Reading Room, Washington, 20540.
Holdings: Cat Mss Maps Pix Microforms
Notes: Microform materials only in this LC Division Works of individual authors; holdings of collection; archival records, etc, press releases and translations, etc.

IL —NEWBERRY LIBRARY, 60 W Walton St, Chicago, 60610. Diana Haskell, Cur of Modern Mss
Holdings: Cat Mss
Notes: Several hundred vols on the Italian Reformers. The entire field of Italian history is especially strong for 1400-1600, represented by several thousand vols.

KS —UNIVERSITY OF KANSAS, Kenneth Spencer Research Library, Special Collections Dept, Lawrence, 66045. Alexandra Mason, Librn
Holdings: Cat Mss Maps
Notes: Great Britain, Italy, France, Spain, Eastern Europe (especially Poland), mediaeval to late 18th century. Noncirculating. Incl the Rubinstein Collection of the papers of the Orsetti Family of Lucca, Tuscany, 1180-1950 (mostly before 1650). 117 linear ft.

MA —HARVARD UNIVERSITY LIBRARY, Widener Library, Cambridge, 02138. Assunta S Pisani, Specialist in Book Selection
Holdings: Cat
Notes: Particular strength for Florence, Sicily, and Venice; the Gay Risorgimento collection is outstanding.

NY —HOFSTRA UNIVERSITY, Library, 1000 Fulton Ave, Hempstead, 11550. Charles R Andrews, Dean of Library Services
Holdings: Vols (5000) Cat
Notes: The personal collection of Professor Shepard Clough of Columbia University. Especially strong in French and Italian modern history, Italian Fascism and European economic statistics.

NY —AMERICAN INSTITUTE FOR VERDI STUDIES, New York University, Bobst Library, Music Div, New York, 10023. Ruth B Hilton, Librn
Holdings: Mss Maps Pix Slides Microforms
Notes: Contains the archives of the Institute for Verdi Studies.

†NY —COLUMBIA UNIVERSITY LIBRARIES, Paterno Library, 1161 Amsterdam Ave, New York, 10027.
Notes: Italian literature and culture. One of the most extensive collections in the United States.

NY —NEW YORK PUBLIC LIBRARY, Research Libraries, General Research Division, Fifth Ave & 42 St, New York, 10018. Rodney Phillips, Chief
Holdings: Vols (2,225,000) Cat Maps Pix Microforms
Budget: ($775,718)

NY —SYRACUSE UNIVERSITY LIBRARIES, Ernest S Bird Library, George Arents Research Library for Special Collections, Syracuse, 13210. Carolyn A Davis, Manuscripts Librn; Amy S Doherty, University Archivist; Mark F Weimer, Rare Book Librn
Notes: The Van Ranke Collection.

PA —TEMPLE UNIVERSITY LIBRARIES, Special Collections Dept, Rare Books & Mss Section, Philadelphia, 19122. Thomas M Whitehead, Cur
Holdings: Vols 200 Cat Mss
Notes: Extensive collection of printed books and mss, 900 AD-1900 AD; Cochran History of Business Collection. Original documents, ledgers, contracts, business letters, indentures, statutes, etc. Emphasis on Italy, 13th-17th centuries. Partial listings and descriptions published in the *Temple University Library Bulletin,* 1950-1963. Catalog in preparation.

PA —UNIVERSITY OF PENNSYLVANIA, Lea Library, 3420 Walnut St, Philadelphia, 19104. Daniel Traister, Special Collections Librn
Notes: Lea Collection of Medieval and Renaissance periond incl statutes of the city-states and the Medici-Gondi account books. See *(University of Pennsylvania) Library* Chronicle, vol 36, no 2, spring 1970. Hirsch, Rudolf. Catalogue of Manuscripts in the Libraries of the University ofPennsylvania to 1800: Supplement A (3) Medici-Gondi Archive II and *Library Chronicle,* vol 37, no 1 winter 1971. Catalogue...Supplement A (4). Zacour, Norman P and Rudolf Hirsch. *Catalogue of Manuscripts in the Libraries of the University of Pennsylvania to 1800.* Philadelphia: University of Pennsylvania Press, 1965.

ITALY—HISTORY—RISORGIMENTO, 1830-1870

CT —UNIVERSITY OF CONNECTICUT, Library, Storrs, 06268. R H Schimmelpfeng, Dir of Special Collections
Holdings: / / Cat
Notes: The collection incl 1900 books, about 4400 contemporary pamphlets, periodicals, and more than 7000 broadsides, the latter not yet cataloged. A checklist of the author file is available. The collection does not incl the secondary sources which are cataloged for the general library.

MA —HARVARD UNIVERSITY LIBRARY, Widener Library, Cambridge, 02138. Assunta S Pisani, Specialist in Book Selection
Holdings: Cat
Notes: Henry Nelson Gay Risorgimento collection (40,000 items) described in *Catholic Historical Review,* XXIX (1943): pp 347-356.

MI —MICHIGAN STATE UNIVERSITY, Libraries, Special Collections Div, East Lansing, 48824. Jannette Fiore, Librn
Notes: The primary emphasis of this collection is on the central period of the Italian Risorgimento, 1845-1870. It includes account by eyewitnesses, works by significant polical figures, many scarce political pamphlets and complete runs of several key serial publications. The library is actively acquiring additional materials to support and expand this subject collection. 1500 pamphlets; 7000 issues of newspapers and periodicals.

ITALY—POLITICS AND GOVERNMENT

CA —UNIVERSITY OF CALIFORNIA, LOS ANGELES, Research Library, Dept of Special Collections, 405 Hilgard Ave, Los Angeles, 90024. Edward Shreeves, Chairman, Bibliographers Group; David S Zeidberg, Head
Notes: 8.5 linear feet of Italian broadsides, ca 1676-1821, primarily from the period of Napoleonic domination of Italy. Texts incl edicts, decrees, proclamations, etc, of church, military, and local governments.

KS —UNIVERSITY OF KANSAS, Kenneth Spencer Research Library, Special Collections Dept, Lawrence, 66045. Alexandra Mason, Librn
Holdings: Cat Mss Maps
Notes: Great Britain, Italy, France, Spain, Eastern Europe (especially Poland), mediaeval to late 18th century. Noncirculating. Incl the Rubinstein Collection of the papers of the Orsetti Family of Lucca, Tuscany, 1180-1950 (mostly before 1650). 117 linear ft.

†NY —COLUMBIA UNIVERSITY LIBRARIES, Paterno Library, 1161 Amsterdam Ave, New York, 10027.
Notes: Italian literature and culture. One of the most extensive collections in the United States.

†PA —CABRINI COLLEGE, Holy Spirit Library, Eagle & King of Prussia Rds, Radnor, 19087.

ITELMES LANGUAGE see Kamchadal Language

ITHACA FESTIVAL

NY —CORNELL UNIVERSITY LIBRARIES, Collection of Regional History, Dept of Manuscripts and Univ Archives, Ithaca, 14853.
Notes: Incl records, 1962-66; 2 tape recordings, correspondence, financial statements, memoranda, resolutions, newspaper clippings, 9 interviews and an incomplete run (1965-66) of the newsletter "From the Wings."

ITHACA STREET RAILWAY COMPANY

NY —CORNELL UNIVERSITY LIBRARIES, Collection of Regional History, Dept of Manuscripts and Univ Archives, Ithaca, 14853.
Notes: Incl business records, ca 1887- 1914, of the company and its subsidiaries.

ITURBIDE, AGUSTIN DE

DC —GEORGETOWN UNIVERSITY, Library, Special Collections Div, 37 & O Sts

ITURBIDE, AGUSTIN DE (cont.)

NW, Washington, 20057. George M Barringer, Special Collections Librn; Nicholas B Sheetz, Mss Librn
Holdings: Vols (100) Cat Mss Pix
Notes: Includes papers of Mexican Emperor Iturbide; President and General Santa Anna; and of Revs Richard Tierney, SJ; Edmund A Walsh, SJ, and Wilfrid Parsons, SJ.

IN —INDIANA UNIVERSITY, Lilly Library, Seventh St, Bloomington, 47405. William R Cagle, Librn
Holdings: Vols (10,000) / / Cat Mss
Notes: Historical pronouncements and documents by the leaders of the movement of Mexican independence. Partially cataloged.
See also entry under Mexico - History

IVES, BURL

NY —NEW YORK PUBLIC LIBRARY, Performing Arts Research Center, Billy Rose Theatre Collection, 111 Amsterdam Ave, New York, 10023. Dorothy L Swerdlove, Cur
Holdings: Cat Mss Pix
Notes: Papers, scrapbooks, mss, photographs, memorabilia, etc.

IVES, CHARLES EDWARD, 1874-1954

CT —YALE UNIVERSITY, Music Library, 98 Wall St, New Haven, 06520. Harold E Samuel, Librn
Holdings: Vols (118,000) Cat Mss Pix Phonorecords Audiotapes
Notes: Comprises the complete musical and literary mss of Charles Ives, as well as his personal papers. See John Kirkpatrick, *Temporary Mimeographed Catalog of Music Manuscripts and Related Materials of C E Ives, 1874-1954* (New Haven: Yale University Library, 1960).

IVES, IRVING MC NEIL, 1896-1962

NY —CORNELL UNIVERSITY LIBRARIES, Collection of Regional History, Dept of Manuscripts and Univ Archives, Ithaca, 14853.
Notes: US Senator, 1947-59, NY assemblyman, author. Incl papers, 1946-58; correspondence, memoranda, clippings, speeches, press releases, honorary materials, etc.

IVORY COAST

DC —HOWARD UNIVERSITY, Moorland-Spingarn Research Center, 500 Howard Place NW, Washington, 20059. Clifford L Muse, Jr, Acting Dir

IXODIDAE see Ticks

IZARD, RALPH, 1688-1743

SC —COLLEGE OF CHARLESTON LIBRARY, Special Collections Dept, Charleston, 29401.
Notes: This ms vol appears to have been compiled by Sen Ralph Izard's (1741-1804) grandfather, Ralph Izard (1688-1743), while studying, as a youth, in England. As a merchant's lesson book, it begins with simple arithmetical computations and quickly moves on to more complex matters, such as profit and loss, discounting, currency exchange, compounding interest, etc. Among the products mentioned are wine, indigo, linen, silk, and hops.

J

JACKMAN, SYDNEY W.

BC —UNIVERSITY OF VICTORIA, McPherson Library, Victoria, V8W 3H5, Can.
Notes: Mss for several monographs. Restrictions on the unpublished portions of the transcripts.

JACKSON, ALAN R.

MA —BOSTON UNIVERSITY, Mugar Memorial Library, Special Collections Dept, 771 Commonwealth Ave, Boston, 02215. Howard B Gotlieb, Dir
Holdings: Cat Mss

JACKSON, ALEXANDER MELVORNE

MS —UNIVERSITY OF SOUTHERN MISSISSIPPI, William David McCain Graduate Library, Box 5148, Southern Sta, Hattiesburg, 39406.
Holdings: Cat Mss Pix
Notes: Correspondence and records (1847-1892) relating to Alexander Melvorne Jackson's participation in the Mexican War, his service as Secretary of the State of the New Mexico Territory (1857-1861), and his participation in the Civil War on the side of the Confederacy. Among his correspondents were Albert Gallatin Brown, Reuben Davis, Miguel A Otero, Jacob Thompson, and John Ireland. Incl are photographs of Austin, Texas, ca 1890. 1.1 cubic feet holdings.

JACKSON, ANDREW

DC —LIBRARY OF CONGRESS, Manuscript Division, Washington, 20540. John C Broderick, Chief
Notes: The Presidential Papers collection incl the papers, etc, of numerous Presidents.

TN —UNIVERSITY OF TENNESSEE, KNOXVILLE, Library, Knoxville, 37996. John Dobson, Special Collections Librn
Holdings: Mss
Notes: Joint member in a project planning a comprehensive new edition of the papers of Andrew Jackson.

TN —MEMPHIS STATE UNIVERSITY, John Willard Brister Library, Memphis, 38152. John Terreo, Special Collections Librn
Notes: Andrew Jackson Letters, 1804-1844.

JACKSON, CHARLES BACON

IN —INDIANA UNIVERSITY, Lilly Library, Seventh St, Bloomington, 47405. William R Cagle, Librn
Notes: Contemporary with and depicting Lincoln; the War of 1812 and other periods. Incl significant mss of the modern cartoonists and caricaturists Ardizzone, Beerbohm, Fontane Fox, Kin Hubbard, Charles Bacon Jackson, McCutcheon, Messick, Nast, Rothenstein, Sendak, and many miscellaneous items.

JACKSON, DUGALD CALEB, 1865-1951

MA —MASSACHUSETTS INSTITUTE OF TECHNOLOGY, Institute Archives, Special Collections, Cambridge, 02139.
Notes: Papers of Dugald Caleb Jackson, electrical engineer, important in development of American engineering education. Significant is material recording the ties between industry and engineering education and the growth of the Department of Electrical Engineering. Bulk of collection dates 1899 to 1948. Unpublished finding aid and correspondence index available in Archives.

JACKSON, GLENDA

MA —BOSTON UNIVERSITY, Mugar Memorial Library, Special Collections Dept, 771 Commonwealth Ave, Boston, 02215. Howard B Gotlieb, Dir
Holdings: Cat Correspondence

JACKSON, HELEN HUNT

MA —JONES LIBRARY, 43 Amity St, Amherst, 01002. Daniel J Lombardo, Cur of Special Collections
Holdings: Vols 108 Cat Mss Pix
Notes: Editions, mss, newspaper clippings, letters, ephemera, etc. Does not circulate. Unpublished guide available.

JACKSON, HENRY M.

WA —UNIVERSITY OF WASHINGTON LIBRARIES, Suzzallo Library, Manuscripts Section, FM-25, Seattle, 98195. Karyl Winn, Librn
Notes: Incl papers from 1940-1983, not processed and not open for use as of 1984.

JACKSON, JOSEPH HENRY

CA —UNIVERSITY OF CALIFORNIA, SANTA CRUZ, University Library, Special Collections, Santa Cruz, 95064. Rita Bottoms, Special Collections Librn; Margaret Felts, South Pacific Collection Bibliographer
Notes: Joseph Henry Jackson's personal library. Strong in California. Noncirculating, for scholarly research only.

JACKSON, LAURA RIDING

NY —ADELPHI UNIVERSITY, Library, Garden City, 11530. Jerome Yavarkovsky, Dean of Libraries
Holdings: Vols 160 Cat Mss
Notes: Expatriate American writers of the 1920s and 1930s, with primary emphasis on the works of Gertrude Stein and Laura Riding Jackson.

JACKSON, STANLEY

MA —BOSTON UNIVERSITY, Mugar Memorial Library, Special Collections Dept, 771 Commonwealth Ave, Boston, 02215. Howard B Gotlieb, Dir
Holdings: Cat Mss

JACKSON, WILLIAM HENRY

CO —COLORADO HISTORICAL SOCIETY, Research Collections, 1300 Broadway, Denver, 80203. Catherine Kane, Head Public Service and Access
Holdings: Cat Pix Sides
Notes: 250,000 photographs of western and Colorado subjects incl gold rush, mining, Indians, natural features, transportation, cities and towns, portraits. William Henry Jackson photographs of area west of Mississippi.

MD —UNIVERSITY OF MARYLAND, BALTIMORE COUNTY, Albin O Kuhn Library and Gallery, Edward L Bafford Photography Collection, 5401 Wilkens Ave, Baltimore, 21228. Tom Beck, Cur
Holdings: Vols Pix
Notes: The Edward L Bafford Photography Collection contains more than 200,000 images, negatives, cameras and books representing the entire history and aesthetics of photography. A main theme of the collection is photography as a social force, as represented by the 4000 photographs and negatives by Lewis Hine and by William Henry Jackson's *Photographs of the Yellowstone National Park and Views of Montana and Wyoming Territories.*
See also entry under Photographs - Collections.

NM —MUSEUM OF NEW MEXICO, Photo Archives, Box 2087, Santa Fe, 87503. Arthur L Olivas, Cur; Richard Rudisill, Photo Historian
Holdings: Cat Pix Slides
Notes: Extensive collection of his work.

JACKSON HOLE, WYOMING

NY —ROCKEFELLER UNIVERSITY, Rockefeller Archive Center, Hillcrest, Pocantico Hills, North Tarrytown, 10591. Joseph W Ernst, Dir; J William Hess, Assoc Dir
Notes: Papers relative to the Rockefeller Family, Foundations, University, and other specific enterprises and contributions to particular areas of social, physical, educational, and historic reform, preservation, conservation, or development. Extensive records of administrative, financial, physical, or intellectual relationships.

JACOBI, LOTTE

MD —UNIVERSITY OF MARYLAND, BALTIMORE COUNTY, Albin O Kuhn Library and Gallery, Edward L Bafford Photography Collection, 5401 Wilkens Ave, Baltimore, 21228. Tom Beck, Cur
Holdings: Vols Pix
Notes: The Edward L Bafford Photography Collection contains more than 200,000 images, negatives, cameras and books representing the entire history and aesthetics of photography. Incl are a large number of photographs by both 19th and 20th century photographers, such as Lucien Clergue, Barbara Crane, Eadward Muybridge, Alfred Stieglitz, Diane Arbus, Lotte Jacobi and many others.
See also entry under Photographs - Collections.

JACOBI, MARY PUTNAM

MA —RADCLIFFE COLLEGE, Arthur & Elizabeth Schlesinger Library on the History of Women in America, 3 James St, Cambridge, 02138. Patricia Miller King, Dir; Eva Moseley, Cur of Mss
Holdings: Cat Mss
Notes: Correspondence, writings, photographs of the New York City physician.

JACOBINS (DOMINICANS) see Dominicans

JACOBS, FLORENCE B.

ME —WESTBROOK COLLEGE, Library, 716 Stevens Ave, Portland, 04103. Dorothy M Healy, Special Collections Librn
Holdings: Vols (3000) Cat Mss Pix
Notes: Collection incl work of Maine women writers. Many mss and scrapbooks are incl. Memorabilia of Mrs Robert E Peary, Mary Ellen Chase, Florence B Jacobs, Celia Thaxter, and Edna St Vincent Millay are notable items. Some rare books, ie Madame Wood novels, are part of the collection.

JACOBS, PAUL

MA —BOSTON UNIVERSITY, Mugar Memorial Library, Special Collections Dept, 771 Commonwealth Ave, Boston, 02215. Howard B Gotlieb, Dir
Holdings: Cat Mss
Notes: Mss, correspondence, etc collected in depth; incl publications by or about.

JACOBS, W. W., 1863-1943

OH —OHIO UNIVERSITY, Vernon R Alden Library, Department of Archives and Special Collections, Athens, 45701. Gary A Hunt, Head
Holdings: Vols 28 Cat
Notes: A collection of first and other important early editions.

JACOBSEN, JOSEPHINE

MA —BOSTON UNIVERSITY, Mugar Memorial Library, Special Collections Dept, 771 Commonwealth Ave, Boston, 02215. Howard B Gotlieb, Dir
Holdings: Mss Pix
Notes: Mss, correspondence, etc collected in depth; incl publications by or about.

MO —WASHINGTON UNIVERSITY, Libraries, Special Collections Dept, Campus Box 1061, St Louis, 63130.
Notes: Extensive collection.

JACOBY, NEIL

MA —BOSTON UNIVERSITY, Mugar Memorial Library, Special Collections Dept,

JACOBY, NEIL (cont.)

771 Commonwealth Ave, Boston, 02215. Howard B Gotlieb, Dir
Holdings: Mss
Notes: Mss, correspondence, etc collected in depth; incl publications by or about.

JACQUARD POINT PAPER

NY —FASHION INSTITUTE OF TECHNOLOGY, Edward C Blum Design Laboratory, 227 W 27 St, New York, 10001. Laura Sinderbrand, Dir
Holdings: Cat Pix Slides
Notes: The largest resource of it kind consisting of 4 million indexed swatches and 300 swatch books, jacquard point paper, croquis, quilts, rug samples, laces, embroideries, and color swatch cards. A collection of international scope incl antique and contemporary textiles; woven and printed patterns created for apparel and home furnishings which may be adapted to china, giftware, floor covering, wallpaper, and package design. A comprehensive research facility comprised of over one million articles of dress dating from the 17th Century to the present, incl men's, women's, children's clothes, furs, foundation garments and lingerie, as well as an outstanding grouping of 19th and 20th century designer clothing. Accessories as diverse as hats, handbags, gloves, hosiery, shoes, shawls, and costume jewelry offer an additonal resource to this international collection.

JAFFE, LOUIS I.

VA —UNIVERSITY OF VIRGINIA, Alderman Library, Manuscripts Dept, Charlottesville, 22901. Edmund Berkeley Jr, Cur
Holdings: Cat Mss Pix
Notes: Papers, etc.

JAGATAIC LANGUAGE AND LITERATURE

NY —NEW YORK PUBLIC LIBRARY, Oriental Div, Fifth Ave & 42 St, New York, 10018. E Christian Filstrup, Chief
Holdings: Cat Mss Microforms
Budget: ($56,455)
Notes: Published catalog of holdings.

JAILS see Prisons and Prisoners

JAJOBA see Jojoba

JAKUT LANGUAGE see Yakut Language and Literature

JAMAICA

CT —TRINITY COLLEGE LIBRARY, 300 Summit St, Hartford, 06106. Ralph S Emerick, Librn
Holdings: // Cat
CT —YALE UNIVERSITY, Sterling Memorial Library, Latin American Collections, New Haven, 06520. Lee H Williams Jr, Cur
Holdings: Vols (300,000) Cat Maps Pix Slides Phonorecords 16mm Films Filmstrips
See also entry under Latin America
DC —HOWARD UNIVERSITY, Moorland-Spingarn Research Center, 500 Howard Place NW, Washington, 20059. Clifford L Muse, Jr, Acting Dir
FL —UNIVERSITY OF MIAMI, Otto G Richter Library, PO Box 248214, Coral Gables, 33124. Frank Rodgers, Dir of Libraries
Notes: Unique special collections on Cuba, the Cuban exiles, and Jamaica are supported by a growing general Caribbean collection. See *Catalog of the Cuban and Caribbean Library, University of Miami* (Boston: G K Hall, 1977).
MA —BOSTON COLLEGE LIBRARIES, Thomas P O'Neill Library, Nicholas M Williams Ethnological Collection, Chestnut Hill, 02167. Frank J Seegraber, Special Collections Librn
Holdings: Vols 10,000 // Cat Mss Maps
Notes: Collection emphasizes Caribbeana, especially Jamaica, to 1940. Incl discovery, exploration and natural history of the British, French and Spanish settlements; the slave question; piracy. There are over 6000 mss, 5000 of which are Anansi folk tales recorded by native school children. Also small ancillary sections of Africana and Judaica. For reference use only, by arrangement with librarian.

JAMAICA—HISTORY

DC —HOWARD UNIVERSITY, Moorland-Spingarn Research Center, 500 Howard Place NW, Washington, 20059. Clifford L Muse, Jr, Acting Dir

JAMAICA—POLITICS AND GOVERNMENT

DC —HOWARD UNIVERSITY, Moorland-Spingarn Research Center, 500 Howard Place NW, Washington, 20059. Clifford L Muse, Jr, Acting Dir

JAMES, DANIEL

CA —UNIVERSITY OF THE PACIFIC, Holt-Atherton Pacific Center for Western Studies, Stockton, 95211. Hiram L Davis, Dir of Libraries
Holdings: // Cat Mss
Notes: The Daniel James papers contain ms correspondence, notes and printed matter collected by a US freelance journalist who traveled and lived in Latin America in the 1960s. Emphasis is on politics and government. Ca 50 linear ft.

JAMES, GEORGE WHARTON

CA —CALIFORNIA HISTORICAL SOCIETY, Schubert Hall Library, 2099 Pacific Ave, San Francisco, 94109. Bruce L Johnson, Library Dir
Holdings: Pix
Notes: California Historica Society's Title Insurance and Trust Corporation Collection of Historical Photographs in Los Angeles contains 20,000 photographs centered around pictures of Southern California by noted photographer C C Pierce. Copies of photographs by other pioneer Los Angeles photographers, such as Godfrey, Wolfenstein and Parker are incl, as well as 2000 glass plate negatives of local Indians by George Wharton James.
TX —SOUTHERN METHODIST UNIVERSITY, DeGolyer Library, Box 396, SMU, Dallas, 75275. Clifton H Jones, Dir
Holdings: Vols (80,000) Cat Mss Maps Pix Slides Microforms
Notes: First editions of prominent authors; also of books in subject emphasis collections. All subjects listed in this vol are strong. Numerous collections of personal papers relating to subjects also.

JAMES, HENRY, 1843-1916

CA —UNIVERSITY OF CALIFORNIA, LOS ANGELES, Research Library, Dept of Special Collections, 405 Hilgard Ave, Los Angeles, 90024. Edward Shreeves, Chairman, Bibliographers Group; David S Zeidberg, Head
Holdings: Vols 100
Notes: 100 first and other editions of his books; 8 letters.
CT —LEE ASH, (personal collection), 66 Humiston Dr, Bethany, 06525.
Notes: First editions, mss, ephemera, memorabilia.
CT —YALE UNIVERSITY, Box 1603A, Yale Station, New Haven, 06520.
Holdings: Cat Mss
Notes: Incl correspondence.
DC —LIBRARY OF CONGRESS, Rare Book & Special Collections Div, Washington, 20540. William Matheson, Chief
Holdings: Vols 132 Cat
Notes: Contains a large number of first editions, American and British, of James' writings, together with copies of significant later revisions. Incl a selection, as well, of volumes to which he contributed prefaces, essays and stories; plus proof pages of several novels.
IL —NEWBERRY LIBRARY, 60 W Walton St, Chicago, 60610. Diana Haskell, Cur of Modern Mss
Holdings: Cat
Notes: The Morton Zabel Collection.
MD —JOHNS HOPKINS UNIVERSITY, Milton S Eisenhower Library, Charles & 34 Sts, Baltimore, 21218. Ann S Gwyn, Assistant Dir for Special Collections
Holdings: Vols 500 Cat Mss
Notes: Strong collection. Many first editions. Cards in main catalog.
MA —HARVARD UNIVERSITY LIBRARY, Houghton Library, Cambridge, 02138. F Thomas Noonan, Cur, Reading Room; Lawrence Dowler, Associate Librn
Holdings: Cat Mss
Notes: For account of ms letters, see *Harvard Library Notes,* IV (1942), 7-60.
MA —BRANDEIS UNIVERSITY, Goldfarb Library, 415 South St, Waltham, 02154. Bessie Hahn, Dir
Notes: 24 linear ft of first editions of Henry James as well as books about Henry James. Access to the collection is through the Special Collections Catalog.
MI —UNIVERSITY OF MICHIGAN, Library, Dept of Rare Books & Special Collections, Ann Arbor, 48109. Robert J Starring, Head
Holdings: Vols 125 Cat
Notes: Incl over 50 first editions.
NY —BUFFALO & ERIE COUNTY PUBLIC LIBRARY, Rare Book Room, Lafayette Sq, Buffalo, 14203. William H Loos, Cur
Holdings: // Cat Mss
Notes: Nearly all of his first editions and the manuscript of his essay on Ivan Turgenev.
NY —UNIVERSITY OF ROCHESTER, Rush Rhees Library, Department of Rare Books and Special Collections, Rochester, 14627. Peter Dzwonkoski, Librn
Holdings: Vols 250 Cat
PA —BRYN MAWR COLLEGE, Canaday Library, Bryn Mawr, 19010. James Tanis, Dir
Notes: Rare books and manuscripts.
RI —BROWN UNIVERSITY, John Hay Library, 20 Prospect St, Providence, 02912. Mark N Brown, Cur Mss
Notes: Within the John Hay Manuscript Collection (qv) are found 30 personal letters written by James to Hay.
VA —UNIVERSITY OF VIRGINIA, Alderman Library, Clifton Waller Barrett Collection, Charlottesville, 22901. Joan St C Crane, Cur of American Literature Collections
Holdings: Vols 700 Cat Mss Pix
Notes: First editions; books by and about him. Includes 1500 manuscript pieces. Published description: *Henry James, 1843-1916: An Exhibition of Books, Manuscripts and Portraits Arranged in the Fiftieth Year of His Death* (Charlottesville, VA: The Clifton Waller Barrett Library of the University of Virginia, 1966).
WA —UNIVERSITY OF WASHINGTON LIBRARIES, Suzzallo Library, Special Collections Division, Rare Book Collection, FM-25, Seattle, 98195. Gary Menges, Coordinator for Special Collections
Notes: Printing history, including early printed books and modern fine printing; book arts, including papermaking, decorated papers, bookbinding, book design, and artist's books; American literature, 19th century includes: Stephen Crane, Ralph Waldo Emerson, Nathaniel Hawthorne, Henry James, Henry Wadsworth Longfellow, Herman Melville, Frank Norris, Harriet Beecher Stowe and Walt Whitman and 20th century includes: Theodore Roethke; illustrated books, including emblem books, historical children's illustration, books illustrated with prints, and artist's books; costume history; voyages and travels; preservation of library materials.
ON —MCMASTER UNIVERSITY, Mills Memorial Library, Div of Archives & Research Collections, Hamilton, L8S 4L6, Can. G R Hill, Univ Librn
Holdings: Vols 200 Cat
Notes: The Simon Nowell-Smith Collection.

JAMES, HOWARD

MA —BOSTON UNIVERSITY, Mugar Memorial Library, Special Collections Dept, 771 Commonwealth Ave, Boston, 02215. Howard B Gotlieb, Dir
Holdings: Cat Mss
Notes: Mss, correspondence, etc collected in depth; incl publications by or about.

JAMES, JOHN

WI —SEVENTH DAY BAPTIST HISTORICAL SOCIETY, Library, 3120 Kennedy Rd, PO Box 1678, Janesville, 53547. D Scott Smith, Historian
Holdings: Vols 200 Uncat Mss Pix
Notes: English Seventh Day Baptist Collection. These materials have to do with early and middle years of Baptist movement (1662-1920) in England, incl work of John James, Joseph Stennett, Peter Chamberlen, et al, Sabbatarians or Seventh Day Baptists. About 300 items incl record books, tracts, correspondence.

JAMES, PRESTON E.

NY —SYRACUSE UNIVERSITY LIBRARIES, Ernest S Bird Library, George Arents Research Library for Special Collections, Syracuse, 13210. Carolyn A Davis, Manuscripts Librn; Amy S Doherty, University Archivist; Mark F Weimer, Rare Book Librn
Notes: The George Arents Research Library for Special Collections at Syracuse University contains the papers of George Babcock Cressey and Preston E James.

JAMES, ROBERT LEIGH

MA —BOSTON UNIVERSITY, Mugar Memorial Library, Special Collections Dept, 771 Commonwealth Ave, Boston, 02215. Howard B Gotlieb, Dir
Holdings: Cat Mss
Notes: Mss, correspondence, etc collected in depth; incl publications by or about.

JAMES, WILL (COWBOY)

CA —AZUSA PACIFIC COLLEGE, Marshburn Memorial Library, Citrus & Alosta, Azusa, 91702. Edward Peterman, Librn
Holdings: Vols (150) Uncat
Notes: The Odo B Stade Collection of Literary First Editions. No photocopying.

JAMES, WILLIAM, 1842-1910

KS —MENNINGER FOUNDATION, Archives, 5600 W Sixth St, Box 829, Topeka, 66601. Alice Brand, Librn; Mark West, Archivist
Notes: 1 box, 1894-1910. Incl correspondence and a ms entitled, *Some Mental Effects of the San Francisco* Earthquake.

MA —HARVARD UNIVERSITY LIBRARY, Houghton Library, Cambridge, 02138. F Thomas Noonan, Cur, Reading Room; Lawrence Dowler, Associate Librn
Holdings: Cat Mss
Notes: For account of ms letters, see *Harvard Library Notes,* IV (1942), pp 57-60.

JANIN, JULES

IL —NORTHWESTERN UNIVERSITY, Library, Special Collections Dept, 1937 Sheridan Rd, Evanston, 60201. R Russell Maylone, Cur
Holdings: Mss
Notes: 734 letters; 250 notes and memoranda.

JANSENISTS AND JANSENISM

CA —UNIVERSITY OF CALIFORNIA, LOS ANGELES, Research Library, Western European Collection, Los Angeles, 90024. Edward Shreeves, Chairman, Bibliographers Group; Mary E Greco, Western European Bibliographer
Holdings: Mss Maps Pix Microforms
Notes: Special strengths in intellectual and religious history of the 17th and 18th centuries, Jansenism in particular.

CT —YALE UNIVERSITY, Beinecke Rare Book & Manuscript Library, Osborn Collection, New Haven, 06520. Stephen R Parks, Cur
Holdings: Mss

IL —NEWBERRY LIBRARY, 60 W Walton St, Chicago, 60610. Diana Haskell, Cur of Modern Mss
Holdings: Cat
Notes: Several thousand volumes. Espec on France and the Netherlands, 17th and 18th centuries.

MA —HARVARD UNIVERSITY LIBRARY, Cambridge, 02138.
Holdings: Cat

NC —DUKE UNIVERSITY, Divinity School Library, Durham, 27706. Donn Michael Farris, Librn
Holdings: Vols (225,000)
Notes: Special collections and subject emphases in this library include: Archaeology, Egyptian; Archaeology, Middle Eastern; Art, Jewish; Bible; Bible-New Testament; Bible-Symbolism; Church Architecture; Egyptology; Fathers of the Church; Society of Friends; Great Britain-Religion-Methodism and Methodist Church; Hymns and Hymnals; Jansenists and Jansenism; Judaica; Mediaeval Christian Mysticism; Methodism and Methodist Church; Methodist Episcopal Church; Methodist Episcopal Church, South; Reformation; Religion-US-History; Rural Church; Theology-Great Britain-17th Century; Theology-Great Britain-18th Century; United Methodist Church; US-Church History; John Wesley.

JAPAN

CA —UNIVERSITY OF CALIFORNIA, BERKELEY, University Library, East Asiatic Library, Room 208, Durant Hall, Berkeley, 94720. Donald Shively, Head
Holdings: Vols 215,000 Cat Mss Maps Pix Microforms
Notes: The largest collection of Japanese-language materials at any American university. Subject coverage is universal in scope, but works in the humanities and the social sciences predominate. All historical periods are represented. The East Asiatic Library (like the Library of Congress) serves as a full depository for Japanese Government publications. The Library maintains a distinguisehd rare book collection, comprising, for instance, ancient woodblock color maps, manuscripts, early Buddhist Sutras, and rare and early editions. Outstanding resources include: the Murakami Collection of Meiji Literature; the Mitsui Library; and the Japanese Military Map Collection. Western-language materials in related fields are located in the Main Library. A G K Hall catalog of East Asiatic Library holdings has been published.

CA —CLAREMONT COLLEGES, Honnold Library, Asian Studies Collection, Ninth & Dartmouth, Claremont, 91711. Frances D Wang, Cur
Holdings: Vols (69,658) Cat Mss Maps Pix Microforms
Budget: ($50,000)
Notes: Incl 62,476 vols in Chinese and Japanese; 6276 in Western languages. About 13,000 uncataloged. Collection incl artifacts, original mss, rare, original editions of Chinese, Japanese, Korean and Western language and literature, history, and archaeology, which are today totally unavailable to acquire. The most distinguished work is the collection of some 200 Chinese gazetteers (fang-chih) which is one of the best in the US. Another valuable collection is the Frederick McCormick Collection of 214 titles in 896 vols of movable-type editions of Korean printed books, 15th-19th centuries. The Western-language collection on the Far East is probably one of the strongest in the US. Recently added was a collection of Japanese books on Shinto (125 titles), periodicals, and artifacts. Separate catalog.

†CA —AMERICAN ACADEMY OF ASIAN STUDIES LIBRARY, 134-140 Church St, San Francisco, 94114.

†CA —ASIA FOUNDATION LIBRARY, 550 Kearny St, San Francisco, 94114.

CA —HOOVER INSTITUTION ON WAR, REVOLUTION & PEACE, East Asian Collection, Stanford University, Stanford, 94305. Ramon H Myers, Cur
Holdings: Vols 102,436 Cat Microforms
Notes: The emphasis of this Japanese collection is on social science subjects related to 20th century Japan. *Catalog of the Japanese Collection, The Library Catalogs of the Hoover Institution on War, Revolution, and Peace, Stanford University* was published by G K Hall Co, in 1969 (7 vols). Its first supplement was published in 1972 (1 vol) and the second supplement in 1977 (1 vol).

CT —TRINITY COLLEGE LIBRARY, 300 Summit St, Hartford, 06106. Ralph S Emerick, Librn
Holdings: Cat
Notes: Moore Collection of the Far East.

CT —YALE UNIVERSITY LIBRARY, East Asian Collection, 120 High St, New Haven, 06520. Hideo Kaneko, Cur
Holdings: Vols 140,000 Cat Maps Pix

DC —HOWARD UNIVERSITY, Founders Library, Bernard B Fall Collection (Southeast Asia Collection), Washington, 20059. Steven Ilsang Yoon, Cur
Holdings: Vols (6000) Cat Microforms
Budget: $15,000
Notes: The Bernard B Fall Collection has more than 6000 books, incl 1200 books purchased from the Kendric N Marshall Estate, 3000 items in vertical files, 300 pamphlets, and 800 microfilms, about Southeastern Asia and China. In addition, there are nearly 100 current periodicals and another 100 older periodicals about Indochina in the Collection.

DC —LIBRARY OF CONGRESS, African and Middle Eastern Division, Washington, 20540.
Holdings: Cat Mss Microforms
Notes: Orientalia: the Orientalia Division contains 1,400,000 vols in Oriental languages. Chinese: more than 422,000 vols, espec strong in local histories and Ch'ing (1644-1911) period material. Japanese: over 574,000 vols, espec strong in economics, statistics, history, literature; 12,000 government, learned society, and university periodical titles, particularly science, technology, and social sciences. Korean: 56, 000 vols, espec strong in social sciences and modern history.

GA —OGLETHORPE UNIVERSITY, Library, 4484 Peachtree RD, NE, Atlanta, 30319. Thomas W Chandler, Librn
Holdings: Vols (1200) Cat Pix Microforms
Notes: English language collection; emphasis on history, humanities, and social sciences; also a collection of Japanese prints (25), principally by contemporary artists.

HI —UNIVERSITY OF HAWAII, Library, 2550 The Mall, Honolulu, 96822. Joyce Wright, Head, Asia Collection; Masato Matsu, Head, East Asia Vernacular Collection
Holdings: Vols 64,481 Cat Microforms
Notes: The Asia Collection includes materials from and relating to Japan in all languages. In addition to the cataloged Japanese language volumes (above), there are estimated 15,000 not yet processed. No figures are available for western language volumes about Japan, which are supplemented by retrospective materials in the main library collection. Scope: social sciences and humanities. Subject strengths: Japanese history, especially Tokugawa period, Buddhism, Ryukyus and Satsuma (Sakamaki Collection), Hokkaido. *Catalog of the Glenn Shaw Collection at the East West Center Library,* by H Arai & M Gibu, Honolulu, 1967 (East West Center Library Occasional Paper No 8); *Research Resources on Hokkaido, Sakhalen and the Kuriles at the East West Center Library,* by M Matsui and K Shimanaka, Honolulu, 1967 (East

JAPAN (cont.)

West Center Library Occasional Paper No 9);*Research Resources at the University of* Hawaii, by Shunzo Sakamaki, Honolulu, 1965 (Ryukyuan Research Center. Research Series No 1).

IL —CENTER FOR RESEARCH LIBRARIES, 6050 S Kenwood Ave, Chicago, 60637. Donald B Simpson, Dir; Esther Smith, Collection Development Librn
Holdings: Vols Cat Microforms
Notes: Microfilm holdings of newspapers, official gazette. Microfilm and reprint of Imperial and National Diet proceedings. Archival material, Tokugwa period forward. Microfilm of annual reports of over 2,000 companies, 1872-1945. Meiji and Taisho prefectural statistics. Prange collection of censored periodicals, occupation period. Fairly complete collection of records of the International Military Tribunal for the Far East. 520 current periodical subscriptions. Descriptive pamphlet available.

IL —QUINCY COLLEGE LIBRARY, Quincy, 62301. Victor Kingery, OFM, Librn
Notes: In general collection.

MA —CHILDREN'S MUSEUM, Resource Center, Museum Wharf, 300 Congress St, Boston, 02210. Marie Ariel, Librn; Maria Russell, Resource Services Mgr
Holdings: Vols 200 Cat Mss Slides Phonorecords Audiotapes Videotapes Filmstrips
Notes: Curriculum materials and materials for children and adults. Available for reference use by the public; borrowing privileges for Museum members; activity and curriculum kits available to public, schools and community groups for rental fee. Subject-related programs and services offered by Museum staff.

MI —UNIVERSITY OF MICHIGAN, Asia Library, Ann Arbor, 48109. Wei-Ying Wan, Head
Holdings: Vols 170,000 Cat Microforms
Notes: Strong collection (incl 5700 microfilm reels and 5100 microfiche) on all aspects of Japan and Japanese culture; holdings on bibliography, local history, legislation, education, and statistical compilations outstanding; collection of materials on the occupation of Japan, both in English and in Japanese, is very strong. Special collections incl the proceedings of the Japanese Diet, 8000 scripts of Japanese folk drama, early Meiji newspapers on microfilm, Bartlett Collection of old Japanese botanical books and mss, and the Foreign Office Archives for the Meiji period up to 1945.

NJ —PRINCETON UNIVERSITY, Library, Gest Oriental Library & East Asian Collections, 317 Palmer Hall, Princeton, 08544. D E Perushek, Cur
Holdings: Vols 83,000 Cat Maps Pix Microforms
Notes: Mostly in Japanese. Subject areas incl Japanese civilization, language, philosophy, religion, history, geography, economics, sociology, and other social sciences. With regard to Japanese art and archaeology, only works of a general or cultural nature and primary textual sources are acquired. Subject areas in science and technology, except those materials dealing with indigenous developments and historical aspects, are excluded. No historical period is excluded. Some Western-language reference works as well as Western-language works on Japanese literature, language, and linguistics. Emphasis is on current publications. Separate card catalog. Publications on collection: *List of Periodicals in Japanese in the Gest Oriental Library and East Asian* Collections (Princeton: Princeton University Library, 1980).

NM —UNIVERSITY OF NEW MEXICO, Zimmerman Library, Albuquerque, 87131.
Notes: English-language materials about Japan, purchased on a Japanese government grant.

NY —CORNELL UNIVERSITY LIBRARIES, John M Olin Library, Wason Collection of China & the Chinese, Ithaca, 14853. James Cole, Cur; Paul P W Cheng, East Asia Librn
Holdings: Vols (330,000) Cat Mss Maps Pix Microforms
Notes: The collection has three major components: Western language collection; Chinese language collection; and the Japanese language collection. Volumes: Western, 40,000; Chinese 207,000; and Japanese, 35,000. The scope of the collection incl materials on all disciplines in the humanities and social sciences. Materials on the natural sciences are generally not included. A complete main entry catalog for the Wason Collection is in the Wason Reading Room. Author, title, and subject cards for all books are interfiled in the Cornell University Library Catalog. For description see: Cornell University Libraries. *The Wason Collection* (Ithaca, N Y, 1969), 8 pp, illus. (Its *Special Collection,* No 1); and *Cornell University Libraries Bulletin,* No 193 (Jan/Feb 1975), pp 36-43.

†NY —ASIA SOCIETY LIBRARY, 725 Park Ave, New York, 10021.

NY —COLUMBIA UNIVERSITY LIBRARIES, C V Strarr East Asian Library, 300 Kent Hall, New York, 10027. James Reardon-Anderson, Librn
Holdings: Vols 171,168 Cat
Notes: Publications in major East Asian and Western languages in all subjects comprising the social sciences and humanities.

NY —COLUMBIA UNIVERSITY LIBRARIES, Lehman Library, Japan Documentation Center, 420 W 118 St, New York, 10027. Lawrence C Reardon, Librn
Holdings: Vols 5200 Cat Mss Microforms
Notes: The total holdings of the Japan Documentation Center is roughly 5200 titles comprised of Japanese and English titles. The emphasis is on collecting current materials; holdings do not go back much further than 1970. Materials are selected from fugitive social science materials from modern Japan. Incl are seminar and conference reports, in-house publications and not-for-sale items made available by governmental and non-governmental organizations, papers and documents of political parties and labor unions, and reports from some 30 different banks dealing with aspects of the Japanese economy. Access to the collection is by appointment only.

NY —CONSULATE GENERAL OF JAPAN, Japan Information Center, Library, 299 Park Ave, New York, 10017. Masakatsu Wajima, Librn
Holdings: Vols 4000 Cat Pix Slides
Notes: No photocopying. Reference library for staff use only.

NY —EXPLORERS CLUB, James B Ford Memorial Library, 46 E 70 St, New York, 10021. Janet Baldwin, Librn
Notes: Ted Banks Collection was begun by Prof Harley H Bartlett, bequeathed to American Institute for Exploration, with additions by Prof Ted Bank II, and subsequently acquired by the Explorers Club. Incl field notes, diaries, and photographs of Bank, who led more than 30 scientific expeditions to the Arctic, Aleutians, Sea of Okhotsk, Japan, Taiwan, Southeast Asia and Africa.

NY —JAPAN SOCIETY LIBRARY, 333 E 47 St, New York, 10017. Tomie Mochizuki, Librn
Holdings: Vols 9000 Cat
Notes: Limited photocopying.

NY —NEW YORK PUBLIC LIBRARY, Oriental Div, Fifth Ave & 42 St, New York, 10018. E Christian Filstrup, Chief
Holdings: Cat Mss Microforms
Budget: ($56,455)
Notes: Described in *Dictionary Catalog of the Oriental Collection,* The Research Libraries of the New York Public Library, 1960, 16 vols, and *First Supplement,* 1976, 8 vols (144,000 cards). This catalog incl 318, 000 entries for works in about 100 languages of the East, and all works in Western languages on Oriental subjects. The Oriental Collection numbers about 120,000 vols; its Arabic and Indic holdings and those on ancient Egypt and the ancient Near East are among the largest in the US. There is also a collection of 30,000 vols of PL 480 material from Egypt, Pakistan, and India to which there is main entry access, but which is not incorporated into the dictionary catalog. Other outstanding features of the Oriental Collection incl extensive holdings of Japanese technical and scientific periodicals; a unique collection of linguistic works, grammars, anddictionaries; and unusually good coverage of the field of Oriental religions and philosophies. The catalog contains numerous subject references to periodical articles in all languages. All entries are arranged alphabetically according to the Roman alphabet.

PA —BUCKNELL UNIVERSITY, Ellen Clarke Bertrand Library, Lewisburg, 17837. Ann de Klerk, Librn
Holdings: Vols (3000) Cat
Notes: Incl about 400 titles in the Japanese language.

PA —UNIVERSITY OF PITTSBURGH, Hillman Library, Pittsburgh, 15260. Glenora E Rossell, Head
Holdings: Vols (9250) Cat
Notes: Emphasis is on cultural anthropology and archaeology.

TX —UNIVERSITY OF TEXAS LIBRARIES, Asian Collection, PO Box P, Austin, 78712. Kevin Lin, Asian Librn; Merry Burlingham, South Asian Librn
Holdings: Vols 34,000 Cat Microforms
Notes: Anthropology, economics, government, history, and language and literature of Japan. Incl 250 periodical titles.

JAPAN—CIVILIZATION AND CULTURE

CA —UNIVERSITY OF CALIFORNIA, BERKELEY, University Library, East Asiatic Library, Room 208, Durant Hall, Berkeley, 94720. Donald Shively, Head
Holdings: Vols 215,000 Cat Mss Maps Pix Microforms
Notes: The largest collection of Japanese-language materials at any American university. Subject coverage is universal in scope, but works in the humanities and the social sciences predominate. All historical periods are represented. The East Asiatic Library (like the Library of Congress) serves as a full depository for Japanese Government publications. The Library maintains a distinguished rare book collection, comprising, for instance, ancient woodblock color maps, manuscripts, early Buddhist Sutras, and rare and early editions. Outstanding resources include: the Murakami Collection of Meiji Literature; the Mitsui Library; and the Japanese Military Map Collection. Western-language materials in related fields are located in the Main Library. A G K Hall catalog of East Asiatic Library holdings has been published.

DC —AMERICAN UNIVERSITY LIBRARY, Bender Library, 4400 Massachusetts Ave NW, Washington, 20016.
Holdings: Vols 1200 Cat Mss Maps Pix
Notes: The Charles Nelson Spinks Library was donated to the University Library. The collection, many items beautifully hand-bound, is devoted chiefly to the field of Japanese local history, ukiyoe (Japanese color prints), and the civilization of the Tokugawa Period. A selected annotated bibliography for this collection is in progress. A complete shelflist is available at the American University Library.

IL —FIELD MUSEUM OF NATURAL HISTORY, The Berthold Laufer Library, Roosevelt Rd & Lake Shore Dr, Chicago, 60605. W Peyton Fawcett, Librn
Holdings: Vols (12,000)// Cat Mss Maps
Notes: The part of the museum's collection of Berthold Laufer (1874-1934), Curator of Anthropology, dealing with the peoples of the pre-19th century Chinese Empire (incl Manchuria, Mongolia, Sinkiang and Tibet); their anthropology, art and religion; influences upon their cultures by those of India, Siberia, Japan, Indonesia, and Oceania--and vice versa. Incl about 500 books in Tibetan. About 2/3 of the collection is cataloged.

KS —UNIVERSITY OF KANSAS, Watson Library, East Asian Library, Lawrence,

JAPAN—CIVILIZATION AND CULTURE (cont.)

66045. Eugene Carvalho, Librn
Holdings: Vols 40,000 Cat
Notes: Japanese language materials with special emphasis on literature, political science, history, anthropology, sociology and economics.

MA —PEABODY MUSEUM OF SALEM, Phillips Library, E India Sq, Salem, 01970. Gregor Trinkaus-Randall, Librn
Holdings: Vols (100,000) Cat Mss Pix
Notes: Ethnology of Non-European Peoples Collection. Composed of separate divisions relating to the Pacific Islands, China, Japan and the American Indian. No published indexes.

†NY —COLUMBIA UNIVERSITY LIBRARIES, Butler Library, Rare Book and Manuscript Library, 535 W 114 St, New York, 10027.
Notes: Papers of Dr Ivan Morris, American Section chairman of Amnesty International, his researches into Japanese literature and culture, and his books on puzzles.

NC —NORTH CAROLINA STATE UNIVERSITY, School of Education, Curriculum Materials Center, 400 Poe, Box 7801, Raleigh, 27695. James Jarrell, Coordr
Holdings: Vols (80) Cat Slides Phonorecords Audiotapes Videotapes 16mm Films Filmstrips
Budget: ($8500)
Notes: *SASASAAS Review,* v 2, no 2, Spring 1977. Incl curriculum guides and teachers' kits. Distributor for 1 14-part TV course; *Japan, Pt 1: The Living Tradition.*

OH —CLEVELAND PUBLIC LIBRARY, Fine Arts and Special Collections Department, 325 Superior Ave, Cleveland, 44114. Alice N Loranth, Head
Holdings: Vols 3000 Cat Pix
Notes: Emphasis is on Western editions and translations of literary and religious texts prior to the impact of European influence. Additional materials on archaeology and antiquities, early description and travel, and early history. Incl 1750 vols in Japanese. Separate catalog of author entries for titles in Japanese is maintained.
See also entry under East (Far East)

JAPAN—COMMERCE—U.S.

†CA —FAR EAST MERCHANTS ASSOCIATION, Femas Trade Library, 1597 Curtis St, Berkeley, 94702.
Notes: Trade with Far Eastern countries, esp China, Japan, Philippine Islands and Singapore.

†DC —JAPAN ECONOMIC INSTITUTE OF AMERICA LIBRARY, 1000 Connecticut Ave, NW, Washington, 20036.
Notes: Japan - United States trade.

JAPAN—HISTORY

CA —PACIFIC UNION COLLEGE, Nelson Memorial Library, Angwin, 94508. Taylor D Ruhl, Dir
Holdings: Uncat Mss
Notes: Mimeographed copies of all Japanese war crime trials.

CA —UNIVERSITY OF CALIFORNIA, BERKELEY, University Library, East Asiatic Library, Room 208, Durant Hall, Berkeley, 94720. Donald Shively, Head
Holdings: Vols 215,000 Cat Mss Maps Pix Microforms
Notes: The largest collection of Japanese-language materials at any American university. Subject coverage in universal in scope, but works in the humanities and the social sciences predominate. All historical periods are represented, The East Asiatic Library (like the Library of Congress) serves as a full depository for Japanese Government publications. The library maintains a distinguished rare book collection, comprising, for instance, ancient woodblock color maps, manuscripts, early Buddhist Sutras, and rare and early editions. Outstanding resources include: the Murakami Collection of Meiji Leterature; the Mitsui Library; and the Japanese Military Map Collection. Western-language materials in related fields are located in the Main Library. A G K Hall catalog of East Asiatic Library holdings has been published.

CA —UNIVERSITY OF CALIFORNIA, LOS ANGELES, Oriental Library, 405 Hilgard Ave, Los Angeles, 90024. Ik-Sam Kim, Head
Holdings: Vols 30,000 Cat

CA —HOOVER INSTITUTION ON WAR, REVOLUTION & PEACE, Stanford University, Stanford, 94305. Milorad M Drachkovitch, Archivist
Holdings: Mss Pix
Notes: Four collections: (1) Papers of Eugene H Dooman, US diplomat, Counsellor or Embassy at Tokyo, 1937-41, and Special Assistant to the Assistant Secretary of State for Far Eastern Affairs, 1944-45, incl mss of writings, transcripts of speeches, correspondence, diaries and printed matter, 1913-1966, relating to US foreign policy in the Far East, US-Japanese relations, the decision to drop the atomic bomb on Japan. 1 1/2 ms boxes. (2) Records of the Japanese Legation in Korea, 1894-1905, the Japanese Residency General in Korea, 1906-1910, and the Japanese Government-General in Korea, 1910, incl diplomatic correspondence, dispatches and instructions, reports, treaties, and agreements, lists, charts, and personal correspondence relating to Japanese policy and actions in Korea during the 15 years preceding annexations, international relations in the Far East, the Koreandomestic politics. 1 file cabinet. (3) Papers of Robert Norton, US attorney and journalist (editor of *China Today*), incl correspondence speeches and writings, clippings, printed matter, photographs, and other materials, 1935-1948, relating to US relations with China and Japan, India's independence from Great Britian, Japanese military incursions into China, and United Nations assistance to China. 3 1/2 ms boxes. (4) Papers of Milo E Rowell, Lt Col, US Army, and lawyer in the Government Section of General Headquarters, Supreme Commander for the Allied Powers, incl reports, drafts, and memoranda, December 1945-March 1946, relating to the writings of the revised Japanese constitution, as required in the Potsdam Declaration of 1945. 1/2 ms box.

†CT —PHILIPPINE-AMERICAN RESEARCH CENTER, Library, PO Box507, Sharoni, 06069. John Silva, Dir
Holdings: Vols 200 Maps Pix
Notes: Philippine history and culture from pre-colonial times to the present, as well as under Spanish, Japanese, and American regimes, and post-independence. Mostly rare works of the late 19th and early 20th century; history and anthropology. Over 2, 500 photographs. Incl maps, posters, memorabilia. Limited copying. Visits by appointment.

DC —AMERICAN HISTORICAL COLLECTION, US Embassy, Manilla, Philippines, c/o US Dept of State, Washington, 20525. Aurora P Galvez, Librn; Lewis E Gleeck Jr, Cur
Notes: The American Historical Collection is located at 1201 Roxas Blvd, Metro Manilla, Philippines. Incl the William Cameron Forbes, Eugene A Perkins Memorial Library, Leonard Dawson, and Sternberg Collections. Considerable on Japanese in WW II and the Japanese-supported Philippine Republic (approx 1946-53).

DC —AMERICAN UNIVERSITY LIBRARY, Bender Library, 4400 Massachusetts Ave NW, Washington, 20016.
Holdings: Vols 1200 Cat Mss Maps Pix
Notes: The Charles Nelson Spinks Library was donated to the University Library. The collection, many items beautifully hand-bound, is devoted chiefly to the field of Japanese local history, ukiyoe (Japanese color prints), and the civilization of the Tokugawa Period. A selected annotated bibliography for this collection is in progress. A complete shelflist is available at the American University Library.

DC —NATIONAL ARCHIVES AND RECORDS SERVICE, National Archives Library, Pennsylvania Ave & Eighth St NW, Washington, 20408.
Notes: Journals kept by Commodore Matthew C Perry (1794-1858) on his expedition to Japan in 1852-1854. The three journals were kept by Perry as his personal account of the trip, undertaken as a diplomatic mission to establish trade relations with Japan. Incl numerous illustrations of rare birds, flowers, fish, animals, and the life and ceremonies of trade ports along Perry's route.

GA —OGLETHORPE UNIVERSITY, Library, 4484 Peachtree RD, NE, Atlanta, 30319. Thomas W Chandler, Librn
Holdings: Vols (1200) Cat Pix Microforms
Notes: English language collection; emphasis on history, humanities, and social sciences; also a collection of Japanese prints (25), principally by contemporary artists.

HI —UNIVERSITY OF HAWAII, Library, 2550 The Mall, Honolulu, 96822. Joyce Wright, Head, Asia Collection; Masato Matsu, Head, East Asia Vernacular Collection
Holdings: Vols 64,487 Cat Microforms
Notes: The Asia Collection includes materials from and relating to Japan in all languages. In addition to the cataloged Japanese language volumes (above), there are an estimated 15,000 not yet processed. No figures are avaialable for western language volumes about Japan, which are supplemented by retrospective materials in the main library collection. Scope: social sciences and humanitites. Subject strengths: Japanese history, especially Tokugawa period, Buddhism, Ryukyus and Satsuma (Sakamaki Collection), Hokkaido. *Catalog of the Glenn Shaw Collection at the East West Center Library,* by H Arai & M Gibu, Honolulu, 1967 (East West Center Library Occasional Paper No 8); *Research Resources on Hokkaido, Sakhalen and the Kuriles at the East-West Center Library,* by Matsui and K Shimanaka, Honolulu, 1967 (East West Center Library Occasional Paper No 9);*Ryukyuan Research Resources at the University of Hawaii,* by Shunzo Sakamaki, Honolulu, 1965 (Ryukyuan Research Center. Research Series No 1).

IN —INDIANA UNIVERSITY, Lilly Library, Seventh St, Bloomington, 47405. William R Cagle, Librn
Holdings: Vols (2000) // Cat
Notes: The core of the collection is the specialized library of Charles R Boxer (1000 titles) dealing with the history of the Iberians in the East, 16th-18th century. Mainly incl works on China, Japan and the Phillippines during the period of their early intercourse with the West through 1800, as well as materials on the English and Dutch naval wars. Special mention should be made of the valuable letters from missions by the Jesuits, and the works in this area by the Augustinians, Franciscans, and Dominicans, from the time of the arrival of the Iberians in Asia. The collection is a valuable source of information for the study of the European expansion into the area, including Southeast Asia.

MD —UNIVERSITY OF MARYLAND, Library, East Asia Collection, College Park, 20742. Frank Joseph Shulman, Curator and Head
Holdings: Vols (90,000) // Mss
Notes: Japanese books, newspapers, periodicals, etc, of the Allied Occupation period (1945-1952), including files of censored publications. Books number 40,000; periodical titles, 13,000; newspaper titles, ca 16,500. The special collection relating to the Occupation period is supplemented by a growing collection (now ca 50,000 vols) of Chinese, Japanese, and Korean publications which form the basis of the University's general collection in East Asian language materials.

MI —UNIVERSITY OF MICHIGAN, Asia Library, Ann Arbor, 48109. Wei-Ying Wan, Head
Holdings: Vols 170,000 Cat Microforms
Notes: Strong collection (incl 5700 microfilm reels and 5100 microfiche) on all aspects of Japan and Japanese culture;

JAPAN—HISTORY (cont.)

holdings on bibliography, local history, legislation, education, and statistical compilations outstanding; collection of materials on the occupation of Japan, both in English and in Japanese, is very strong. Special collections incl the proceedings of the Japanese Diet, 8000 scripts of Japanese folk drama, early Meiji newspapers on microfilm, Bartlett Collection of old Japanese botanical books and mss, and the Foreign Office Archives for the Meiji period up to 1945.

MI —MICHIGAN STATE UNIVERSITY, International Library, East Asia Collection, East Lansing, 48824. Eugene deBenko, Librn
Holdings: Vols (34,000) Cat Mss Maps Phonorecords Audiotapes Microforms
Budget: ($11,000)
Notes: Priority given to East Asian publications on contemporary China, Japan and Korea. Principal subject emphasis on language, literature and history. Important resources also on politics and government, economics, anthropology, sociology, geography and agriculture.

NE —AMERICAN HISTORICAL SOCIETY OF GERMANS FROM RUSSIA (AHSGR), 615 Twelfth St, Lincoln, 68502. Mary Lynn Tuck, Librn
Holdings: Vols (1900) Mss Maps Pix Phonorecords Videotapes Audiotapes Microforms VF
Notes: History of German people from Russia and history of people of German-Russian ancestory. Including times in Russia, Germany, US, Canada, Mexico, Argentina, Brazil, Paraguay, Korea, and Japan. This Society has fifty-six chapters in the United States. 1900 volumes, 100 maps; 500 mss; 1200 vertical files; 2000 pictures; 40,000 obituary files, 40,000 family group charts, 50 phonorecords, 20 videotapes, 50 audiotapes, 15 reel-to-reel tapes, 150 periodicals, 250 microforms, 250 family histories-published and unpublished.

NJ —RUTGERS, THE STATE UNIVERSITY OF NEW JERSEY, Alexander Library, Special Collections and Archives, College Ave & Huntington St, New Brunswick, 08903. Ronald L Becker, Cur of Manuscripts and Rare Books
Notes: An extensive collection of mss and over 450 books and pamphlets from the library of William Elliot Griffis (1843-1928). They deal primarily with oriental history and culture, especially that of Japan. Official records of the US Naval Expedition to Japan, 1852-1854, are in 6 volumes.

NY —CONSULATE GENERAL OF JAPAN, Japan Information Center, Library, 299 Park Ave, New York, 10017. Masakatsu Wajima, Librn
Holdings: Vols 4000 Cat Pix Slides
Notes: No photocopying. Reference library for staff use only.

NY —UNIVERSITY OF ROCHESTER, Rush Rhees Library, Rochester, 14627. Datta S Kharbas, Head
Holdings: Vols 100,000 Cat Maps Microforms
Notes: Area studies collection on East Asia and South Asia. Major emphasis is on social sciences and humanities. Over 57,000 volumes on East Asia, out of which 29,000 volumes are in Chinese and 15,000 in Japanese. Extensive holdings on Chinese and Japanese histories. Catalog of East Asian collection consisting of Chinese and Japanese language holdings published in 1968, with two subsequent supplements. Over 33,000 volumes on South Asia. Considerable depth in social sciences, history, politics and anthropology. Extensive holdings in Sanskrit, Hindi, and Marathi.

OH —WILMINGTON COLLEGE, Peace Resource Center, Hiroshima/Nagasaki Memorial Collection, Pyle Center Box 1183, Wilmington, 45177. Helen Redding, Librn
Holdings: Vols Pix Slides Audiotapes Videotapes Film Art Reproductions VF
Notes: The Hiroshima/Nagasaki Memorial Collection is nationally known and respected as a major source of information, films, slides and audiotapes about the atomic bombings of Hiroshima and Nagasaki. An especially signifciant part of the Collection is a continually growing library in Japanese currently numbering more than 500 vols. Here are recorded eyewitness account of the atomic bombings, as well as details of what life has been like in the intervening years for the thousands of survivors (*hibakusha*). Also incl are books of poetry, photo books, juvenile literature, and books dealing with medical information, peace research, peace education, nuclear power, etc. All books in the Hiroshima/Nagasaki Memorial Collection are available for interlibrary loan. An *Annotated Bibliography of Japanese A-Bomb Literature* may be purchased or borrowed from the PRC. In it are briefsummaries in English of each book in the Collection.

PA —UNIVERSITY OF PITTSBURGH, East Asian Library, 234 Hillman Library, Pittsburgh, 15260. Thomas C Kuo, Cur
Holdings: Vols (118,000) Periodicals Microfilms
Budget: ($210,000)
Notes: Contains Chinese and Japanese language publications on all social sciences and humanities, with special emphasis on history and source materials on both traditional and modern China, as well as research materials on language, literature, history, anthropology, economics and sociology of modern Japan. Catalogs of Chinese local history, East Asian periodicals and serials, and microforms in the collection have been published by the library. Also, *A Brief Guide to the Use of the East Asian* Library (1983). Incl 1600 periodicals and 2900 reels of microfilms.

RI —BROWN UNIVERSITY, John Hay Library, 20 Prospect St, Providence, 02912. Mark N Brown, Cur Mss
Holdings: Vols (74,000) Cat Microforms
Budget: ($10,000)
Notes: East Asia Collection. The primary focus is on Chinese studies with a small segment of approx 700 vols devoted to Japanese studies. Major subject areas, in descending order of strength, are: literature (incl classics), history, geography, social sciences, philosophy and religion, fine arts, science and technology. This incl the personal collection (20,000 vols) formed by Harvard University Sinologist Dr Charles Sideny Gardner, which is especially rich in materials relating to the Ch'ing Dynasty (1644-1912). In addition to books, there are 500 reels of microfilm, plus runs of 8 Chinese newspapers and 25 current Chinese periodicals.

TX —UNIVERSITY OF TEXAS LIBRARIES, Asian Collection, PO Box P, Austin, 78712. Kevin Lin, Asian Librn; Merry Burlingham, South Asian Librn
Holdings: Vols 34,000 Cat Microforms
Notes: Anthropology, economics, government, history, and language and literature of Japan. Incl 250 periodical titles.

VA —MACARTHUR MEMORIAL, Library & Archives, MacArthur Sq, Norfolk, 23510. Ellen E Folkama, Asst Archivist
Holdings: Vols (4000) Cat Maps Pix Slides Phonorecords Audiotapes 16mm Films Microfilms
Notes: Everything relating to the life and related activities of MacArthur. The Archives of the collection consist of 600 shelf-feet of documents from Gen MacArthur's official headquarters files over the period 1941-1951. These papers pertain to all matters with which his various commands were involved: military, naval and air matters; international relations; political science; Japanese occupation, peace treaty and Constitution, etc. Each Record Group is indexed. The indexes are retained here since they are being expanded. They are available for researchers.

WA —UNIVERSITY OF WASHINGTON LIBRARIES, East Asia Library, DO-27, Seattle, 98195. Karl Lo, Head
Holdings: Vols (300,000) Cat Microforms
Budget: ($200,000)
Notes: Southwest China: Joseph Rock Collection, ca 2000 vols; modern Chinese poetry, 1919 to date: ca 700 titles; Asian art, esp Japanese painting: 4097 vols; Tiao-yu-t'ai movement in the US: ca 400 items of periodicals and pamphlets; modern Korean poetry, ancient and modern: ca 1000 titles; Mu-yu-shu folk literature: ca 1000 items.

JAPAN—HISTORY—ALLIED OCCUPATION, 1945-1952

VA —MACARTHUR MEMORIAL, Library & Archives, MacArthur Sq, Norfolk, 23510. Ellen E Folkama, Asst Archivist
Holdings: Vols (4000) Cat Mss Maps Pix Slides Phonorecords Audiotapes 16mm Films Microforms
Notes: Everything relating to the life and related activities of MacArthur. The Archives of the collection consist of 600 shelf-feet of documents from Gen MacArthur's official headquarters files over the period 1941-1951. These papers pertain to all matters with which his various commands were involved: military, naval and air matters; international relations; political science; Japanese occupation, peace treaty and Constitution, etc. Each Record Group is indexed. The indexes are retained here since they are being expanded. They are available for researchers.

JAPAN—IMPRINTS

MD —UNIVERSITY OF MARYLAND, Library, East Asia Collection, College Park, 20742. Frank Joseph Shulman, Curator and Head
Holdings: Vols (90,000) // Mss
Notes: Japanese books, newspapers, periodicals, etc, of the Allied Occupation period (1945-1952), including files of censored publications. Books number 40,000; periodical titles, 13,000; newspaper titles, ca 16,500. The special collection relating to the Occupation period is supplemented by a growing collection (now ca 50,000 vols) of Chinese, Japanese, and Korean publications which form the basis of the University's general collection in East Asian language materials.

JAPAN—INDUSTRIES

MI —GENERAL MOTORS, Research Laboratories Library, General Motors Technical Center, Warren, 48090. Robert W Gibson, Librn

JAPAN—POLITICS AND GOVERNMENT

NY —UNIVERSITY OF ROCHESTER, Rush Rhees Library, Rochester, 14627. Datta S Kharbas, Head
Holdings: Vols 100,000 Cat Maps Microforms
Notes: Area studies collection on East Asia and South Asia. Major emphasis is on social sciences and humanities. Over 57,000 volumes on East Asia, out of which 29,000 volumes are in Chinese and 15,000 in Japanese. Extensive holdings on Chinese and Japanese histories. Catalog of East Asian collection consisting of Chinese and Japanese language holdings published in 1968, with two subsequent supplements. Over 33,000 volumes on South Asia. Considerable depth in social sciences, history, politics and anthropology. Extensive holdings in Sanskrit, Hindi, and Marathi.

JAPAN—POSTAGE STAMPS

CA —JAPANESE-AMERICAN PHILATELIC SOCIETY, Library, PO Box 24561, San Jose, 95154.
Notes: Philatelic history of the Japanese empire and associated areas. Research materials in English, Japanese, French and German available to society members only.

JAPAN—RELIGION

†CA —INSTITUTE OF BUDDHISTS STUDIES LIBRARY, 2717 Haste St, Berkeley, 94704.

JAPAN—RELIGION (cont.)

NY —INSTITUTE FOR ADVANCED STUDIES OF WORLD RELIGIONS (IASWR), Melville Memorial Library, State University of New York, Stony Brook, 11794. C T Shen, Dir
Holdings: Vols 15,000 Cat Periodicals Maps
Notes: Incl works on Buddhism and related subjects in history, art, etc, in Chinese, Japanese, English and other European languages. Buddhist canon: Chinese version in Japanese edition; Pali version in Japanese translation. Chinese Buddhist works in Japanese editions and in Japanese translations. Reference works, collected works and traditional commentaries and modern critical studies of Buddhist texts. Works on Shinto, new religions (Shin shukyo), Tenrikyo. Refer inquiries to L L Yang.

JAPAN—SOCIAL LIFE AND CUSTOMS

MS —UNIVERSITY OF SOUTHERN MISSISSIPPI, William David McCain Graduate Library, Box 5148, Southern Sta, Hattiesburg, 39406.
Holdings: Cat Mss
Notes: The Paul Yoder Collection (1940-1980; 30 cubic feet) contains original musical scores and published copies of band music which Yoder composed or arranged. Some of the band music was written for foreign bands, especially Japanese. Catalog in progress.

JAPAN—SOCIAL PROBLEMS

IL —SOUTHERN ILLINOIS UNIVERSITY, CARBONDALE, Delyte W Morris Library, Carbondale, 62901.
Notes: Extensive file of papers relating to the life and work of Japanese social reformer Toyohiko Kagawa, collected by his secretary, Helen F Topping. Also incl files documenting her work in Japan.

JAPAN, OCCUPATION OF, 1945-1951 see Japan—History—Allied Occupation, 1945-1952

JAPANESE AMERICAN NEWSPAPERS see Newspapers, Japanese American

JAPANESE AMERICANS

CA —UNIVERSITY OF CALIFORNIA, LOS ANGELES, Research Library, Dept of Special Collections, 405 Hilgard Ave, Los Angeles, 90024. Edward Shreeves, Chairman, Bibliographers Group; David S Zeidberg, Head
Notes: Various collections, incl the Japanese American Research Project, the records of the US Relocation Center (Manzanar, Calif), and personal papers of many individuals, incl T Scott Miyakawa, first director of the Japanese-American Research Center at UCLA (1962-1965).

CA —UNIVERSITY OF CALIFORNIA, LOS ANGELES, University Research Library, 405 Hilgard Ave, Los Angeles, 90024. Edward Shreeves, Chairman, Bibliographers Group
Notes: Papers of the liberal and politically active Japanese American, Prof T Scott Miyakawa of the University of California and of Boston University. He worked extensively on studies of Japanese Americans, and for their causes before, during, and after WWII. Considerable on Japanese and Chinese history, and studies of important historical personages in his field.

JAPANESE AMERICANS RESEARCH PROJECT (JARP)

CA —UNIVERSITY OF CALIFORNIA, LOS ANGELES, Research Library, Dept of Special Collections, 405 Hilgard Ave, Los Angeles, 90024. Edward Shreeves, Chairman, Bibliographers Group; David S Zeidberg, Head
Notes: Various collections, incl the Japanese American Research Project, the records of the US Relocation Center (Manzanar, Calif), and personal papers of many individuals, incl T Scott Miyakawa, first director of the Japanese-American Research Center at UCLA (1962-1965).

JAPANESE ART see Art, Japanese

JAPANESE AUTHORS see Authors, Japanese

JAPANESE BANKING see Banks and Banking—Japan

JAPANESE CHILDREN'S LITERATURE see Children's Literature, Japanese

JAPANESE COLOR PRINTS see Color Prints, Japanese

JAPANESE DRAMA

MA —HARVARD UNIVERSITY LIBRARY, Theatre Collection, Cambridge, 02138. Jeanne T Newlin, Cur
Holdings: Cat
Notes: For account of Noh dance prints, see *Harvard Library Notes,* III (1938): pp 158-159.

MI —UNIVERSITY OF MICHIGAN, Asia Library, Ann Arbor, 48109. Wei-Ying Wan, Head
Holdings: Cat
Notes: The principal Japanese authors and their works are represented; special collection of 8000 scripts of Japanese folk drama, modern Japanese literature and literary criticism.

NY —NEW YORK PUBLIC LIBRARY, Performing Arts Research Center, Dance Collection, 111 Amsterdam Ave, New York, 10023. Genevieve Oswald, Cur
Notes: Incl scenarios and texts for Bunraku, Kabuki, and Noh dramas of Japan.
See also entry under Asian Dance.

JAPANESE IN CANADA

MB —UNIVERSITY OF MANITOBA, Elizabeth Dafoe Library, Archives and Special Collections Dept, Winnipeg, R3T 2N2, Can. Richard E Bennett, Dept Head; Corrado A Santoro, Reference Archivist
Notes: Correspondence, reports and various papers of Dr Bruce H Chown. Haemolitic diseases of the newborn, especially erthroblastosis fetalis and the maternal Rh-factor. Incl correspondence with Dr Louis Diamond of Boston. Also incl are human anthropological blood group studies of Eskimo, Indian and Canadian-Japanese communities.

JAPANESE IN THE U.S.

†CA —INSTITUTE OF BUDDHISTS STUDIES LIBRARY, 2717 Haste St, Berkeley, 94704.

CA —UNIVERSITY OF CALIFORNIA, BERKELEY, Bancroft Library, Manuscripts Division, Berkeley, 94720. James D Hart, Dir
Holdings: Vols Cat Mss Microforms
Notes: In addition to numerous mss relating to the history of western North America (western plains to the Pacific Coast, Alaska to Panama), The Bancroft Library has many ms collections of significance in other areas. The following collections are large enough to justify the attention of serious researchers; most are analyzed in unpublished keys to arrangement. History collections incl Archives of California (1757-1822), Archives of Mexico and Spain (microcopies); Herbert Eugene Bolton; British West Indies Documents, Danish West Indies Documents, Dutch West Indies Documents; John Charles Fremont; Japanese American Evacuation and Resettlement. Scientific and technological collections incl the papers of many important modern scientists.

CA —CLAREMONT COLLEGES, Honnold Library, Ninth & Dartmouth, Claremont, 91711. Tania Rizzo, Special Collections Dept Head
Holdings: Vols 60 // Cat Mss Pix
Notes: Incl 40 serial titles, often incomplete, some in Japanese, from War Relocation centers, 1941-1945. One document case of miscellaneous newspaper clippings and pamphlets; 8 document cases, part of a Carey McWilliams collection, incl press releases, private agency and governmental reports, newspaper clippings, pamphlets, and over 150 pieces of correspondence, 1942-1945, to and from McWilliams, some with evacuees. Restricted use.

CA —LOS ANGELES PUBLIC LIBRARY, Social Sciences Dept, 630 W Fifth St, Los Angeles, 90071. Marilyn C Wherley, Principal Librn
Holdings: Vols 4000 Microforms
Budget: ($150,000)
Notes: Emphasis on minorities; immigration policies, background and social problems of ethnic minorities in the US and the Southwest in particular. Incl periodicals, government publications and documents, popular and scholarly works on Blacks, Hispanics and Asians predominantly.

CA —UNIVERSITY OF CALIFORNIA, LOS ANGELES, Research Library, Dept of Special Collections, 405 Hilgard Ave, Los Angeles, 90024. Edward Shreeves, Chairman, Bibliographers Group; David S Zeidberg, Head
Holdings: Cat Mss Maps Pix Audiotapes
Notes: Various collections, incl the Japanese American Research Project, the records of the US Relocation Center (Manzanar, Calif), and personal papers of many individuals, incl T Scott Miyakawa, first director of the Japanese-American Research Center at UCLA (1962-1965).

†CA —JAPANESE-AMERICAN LIBRARY, 1759 Sutter St, San Francisco, 94115.

CA —HOOVER INSTITUTION ON WAR, REVOLUTION & PEACE, Stanford University, Stanford, 94305. Milorad M Drachkovitch, Archivist
Holdings: // Mss
Notes: The Conard-Duveneck Collection. Letters, documents, pamphlets, notebooks, and mimeographed data, concerning conditions in the war relocation centers for Japanese during World War II. Also, correspondence, questionnaires, student education records, and miscellaneous items pertaining to the National Japanese American Student Relocation Council, 1942-1946. 101 cartons and 17 drawers of index cards.

CA —UNIVERSITY OF THE PACIFIC, Library, Stockton, 95211. Hiram L Davis, Dir of Libraries
Holdings: // Mss Pix
Notes: Nisei collection, collected by Harold S Jacoby, two ft of typescripts, clippings, newsletters, articles, reports, and other materials relating to Japanese-American relocation during World War II. Also a collection of 60 items from Guy W Cook, teacher at the Tule Lake relocation camp, incl correspondence, field reports, articles, yearbooks, etc.

IL —NORTHWESTERN UNIVERSITY, Library, Special Collections Dept, 1937 Sheridan Rd, Evanston, 60201. R Russell Maylone, Cur
Holdings: Vols 733 Pix
Notes: Papers and records of the World War II Japanese-American relocation camp at Manzanar, California. Incl newspapers, manuals, directories, forms, posters, photographs, personal accounts, background material predating World War II.

MA —CHILDREN'S MUSEUM, Resource Center, Museum Wharf, 300 Congress St, Boston, 02210. Marie Ariel, Librn; Maria Russell, Resource Services Mgr
Holdings: Vols 200 Cat Mss Slides Phonorecords Audiotapes Videotapes Filmstrips
Notes: Curriculum materials and materials for children and adults. Available for reference use by the public; borrowing privileges for Museum members; activity and curriculum kits available to public, schools and community groups for rental fee.

JAPANESE IN THE U.S. (cont.)

Subject-related programs and services offered by Museum staff.

NY —CORNELL UNIVERSITY LIBRARIES, Collection of Regional History, Dept of Manuscripts and Univ Archives, Ithaca, 14853.
Notes: Records of Japanese-American Relocation Centers, 1935-53; 54 ft.

PA —BALCH INSTITUTE FOR ETHNIC STUDIES, Library, 18 S Seventh St, Philadelphia, 19106. R Joseph Anderson, Library Dir
Holdings: Vols 280 Cat Mss Pix Microforms

WA —UNIVERSITY OF WASHINGTON LIBRARIES, Pacific Northwest Collection, Seattle, 98195. Andrew F Johnson, Librn
Holdings: Vols (50,000) Cat Maps Pix
Budget: ($12,000)
Notes: The Pacific Northwest Collection contains printed materials documenting the historic and contemporary life and culture of the region in a broad range of subject areas. The Pacific Northwest is defined as the geographic region including Washington, Oregon, Idaho, Montana, British Columbia, Yukon Territory, and Alaska. Printed materials including books, periodicals, government documents, maps, weekly and local regional newspapers, theses and dissertations, as well as photographs and architectural drawings are included in the Pacific Northwest Collection. Photographic works of over 200 photographers active in the Pacific Northwest, Alaska, and the Yukon Territory (Canada) during the period 1860-1930, including Asahel and Edward S Curtis, Eric Hegg, and Clark Kinsey, are represented in a print collection of more than 300,000 images. The architecturaldrawings collection includes over 19,000 original plans, drawings, sketches, renderings and blue prints pertaining to the history of architecture and urban planning and landscape gardening in the Pacific Northwest ca 1880-1940. Areas of particular strength are the holdings of over 1100 published journals of Pacific Northwest exploration expeditions, photographs of Northwest Coast Native Americans and of historic Seattle, newspapers issued within the Japanese-American relocation camps, 1942-1945, materials relating to the 1980 eruption of Mt St Helens, and Sanborne fire insurance maps for Washington. A unique feature of the Collection is the subject index to regional periodicals and local newspapers maintained by the PNW Collection staff; over 100 titles are currently indexed. G K Hall Company published a books catalog of the Pacific Northwest Collectionin 1973.

JAPANESE LANGUAGE AND LITERATURE

AZ —UNIVERSITY OF ARIZONA, Library, Oriental Studies Collection, Tucson, 85721. Mary J McWhorter, Actg Head Librn
Holdings: Vols (95,000) Cat Microforms
Budget: ($30,000)
See also entry under Oriental Languages and Literatures.

CA —UNIVERSITY OF CALIFORNIA, BERKELEY, University Library, East Asiatic Library, Room 208, Durant Hall, Berkeley, 94720. Donald Shively, Head
Holdings: Vols 215,000 Cat Mss Maps Pix Microforms
Notes: The largest collection of Japanese-language materials in any American university. Subject coverage is universal in scope, but works in the humanitites and the social sciences predominate. All historical periods are represented. The East Asiatic Library (like the Library of Congress) serves as a full depository for Japanese Government publications. The Library maintains a distinguished rare book collection, comprising, for instance, ancient woodblock color maps, manuscripts, early Buddhist Sutras, and rare and early editions. Outstanding resources include: the Murakami Collection of Meiji Literature; the Mitsui Library; and the Japanese Military Map Collection. Western-language materials in related fields are located in the Main Library. A G K Hall catalog of East Asiatic Library holdings has been published.

CA —CLAREMONT COLLEGES, Honnold Library, Asian Studies Collection, Ninth & Dartmouth, Claremont, 91711. Frances D Wang, Cur
Holdings: Vols (69,658) Cat Mss Maps Pix Microforms
Budget: ($50,000)
Notes: Incl 62,476 vols in Chinese and Japanese; 6276 in Western languages. About 13,000 uncataloged. Collection incl artifacts, original mss, rare, original editions of Chinese, Japanese, Korean and Western language and literature, history, and archaeology, which are today totally unavailable to acquire. The most distinguished work is the collection of some 200 Chinese gazetteers (fang-chih) which is one of the best in the US. Another valuable collection is the Frederick McCormick Collection of 214 titles in 896 vols of movable-type editions of Korean printed books, 15th-19th centuries. The Western-language collection on the Far East is probably one of the strongest in the US. Recently added was a collection of Japanese books on Shinto (125 titles), periodicals, and artifacts. Separate catalog.

†CA —LOS ANGELES COUNTY PUBLIC LIBRARY, Gardena Library, 1731 W Gardena Blvd, Gardena, 90247.
Notes: Japanese language materials, incl World War II period Japanese-American newspapers; Japanese-American monographs on microfilm; Japanese-American newspapers.

CA —LOS ANGELES PUBLIC LIBRARY, Foreign Languages Dept, 630 W Fifth St, Los Angeles, 90071. Sylva Manoogian, Principal Librn
Holdings: Vols 2994 Cat
Budget: ($41,500)

CA —UNIVERSITY OF CALIFORNIA, LOS ANGELES, Oriental Library, 405 Hilgard Ave, Los Angeles, 90024. Ik-Sam Kim, Head
Holdings: Vols 35,000 Cat

CA —SAN JOSE PUBLIC LIBRARY, 180 W San Carlos St, San Jose, 95113. Homer Fletcher, Dir
Holdings: Vols 7000 Cat

DC —LIBRARY OF CONGRESS, African and Middle Eastern Division, Washington, 20540.
Holdings: Cat Mss Microforms
Notes: Orientalia: the Orientalia Division contains 1,400,000 vols in Oriental languages. Chinese: more than 422,000 vols, espec strong in local histories and Ch'ing (1644-1911) period material. Japanese: over 574,000 vols, espec strong in economics, statistics, history, literature; 12,000 government, learned society, and university periodical titles, particularly science, technology, and social sciences. Korean: 56, 000 vols, espec strong in social sciences and modern history.

FL —UNIVERSITY OF FLORIDA, Libraries, Gainesville, 32611. Ray Jones, Research Librn; Max Willocks, Librn
Holdings: Vols (2000)
Notes: An extensive collection of modern and premodern Japanese prose fiction in English translation and Japanese. Incl complete works of a number of important modern Japanese authors such as Yasunari Kawabata, Naoya Shiga, Junichiro Tanizaki, and Yukio Mishima.

HI —UNIVERSITY OF HAWAII, Library, 2550 The Mall, Honolulu, 96822. Joyce Wright, Head, Asia Collection; Masato Matsu, Head, East Asia Vernacular Collection
Holdings: Vols 64,487 Cat Microforms
Notes: The Asia Collection includes materials from and relating to Japan in all languages. In addition to the cataloged Japanese language volumes (above), there are estimated 15,000 not yet processed. No figures are available for western language volumes about Japan, which are supplemented by retrospective materials in the main library collection. Scope: social sciences and humanities. Subject strengths: Japanese history, especially Tokugawa period, Buddhism, Ryukyus and Satsuma (Sakamaki Collection), Hokkaido. *Catalog of the Glenn Shaw Collection at the East West Center Library,* by H Arai & M Gibu, Honolulu, 1967 (East West Center Library Occasional Paper No 8); *Research Resources on Hokkaido, Sakhalen and the Kuriles at the East West Center Library,* by M Matsui and K Shimanaka, Honolulu, 1967 (East West Center Library Occasional Paper No 9);*Research Resources at the University of* Hawaii, by Shunzo Sakamaki, Honolulu, 1965 (Ryukyuan Research Center. Research Series No 1).

IL —UNIVERSITY OF ILLINOIS, URBANA/CHAMPAIGN, Asian Library, Urbana, 61801. William S Wong, Asian Librn
Holdings: Vols 130,000
Notes: East Asian Collection. Primarily a collection of Chinese, Japanese, and Korean language materials.

IN —EARLHAM COLLEGE, Lilly Library, Richmond, 47374. Evan Ira Farber, Librn
Holdings: Vols (7000) Cat Slides Phonorecords Videotapes 16mm Films Microforms
Notes: The collection is predominately in English, but incl some material in Japanese.

KS —UNIVERSITY OF KANSAS, Watson Library, East Asian Library, Lawrence, 66045. Eugene Carvalho, Librn
Holdings: Vols 26,500 Cat
Notes: Japanese language materials with special emphasis on literature, political science, history, anthropology, sociology and economics.

MD —UNIVERSITY OF MARYLAND, Library, East Asia Collection, College Park, 20742. Frank Joseph Shulman, Curator and Head
Holdings: Vols (90,000) / / Mss
Notes: Japanese books, newspapers, periodicals, etc, of the Allied Occupation period (1945-1952), including files of censored publications. Books number 40,000; periodical titles, 13,000; newspaper titles, ca 16,500. The special collection relating to the Occupation period is supplemented by a growing collection (now ca 50,000 vols) of Chinese, Japanese, and Korean publications which form the basis of the University's general collection in East Asian language materials.

MA —BOSTON PUBLIC LIBRARY, South End Branch, Multilingual Library, 685 Tremont St, Boston, 02118. Laura H Reyes, Librn
Holdings: Cat

MA —HARVARD UNIVERSITY LIBRARY, Harvard-Yenching Library, 2 Divinity Ave, Cambridge, 02138. Eugene W Wu, Librn
Notes: *Japanese Collected Works and Series* in the Libary published by Harvard-Yenching Institute (1954). Strong in philology and all literary genres.

MI —UNIVERSITY OF MICHIGAN, Asia Library, Ann Arbor, 48109. Wei-Ying Wan, Head
Holdings: Cat
Notes: The principal Japanese authors and their works are represented; special collection of 8000 scripts of Japanese folk drama, modern Japanese literature and literary criticism.

MI —MICHIGAN STATE UNIVERSITY, International Library, East Asia Collection, East Lansing, 48824. Eugene deBenko, Librn
Holdings: Vols (34,000) Cat Mss Maps Phonorecords Audiotapes Microforms
Budget: ($11,000)
Notes: Priority given to East Asian publications on contemporary China, Japan and Korea. Principal subject emphasis on language, literature and history. Important resources also on politics and government, economics, anthropology, sociology, geography and agriculture.

NJ —FORT LEE PUBLIC LIBRARY, 320 Main St, Fort Lee, 07024. Nancy V Gallo, Dir
Holdings: Vols (1109) Cat
Notes: The greater part of this collection is juvenile literature. The adult collection is mostly fiction.

JAPANESE LANGUAGE AND LITERATURE (cont.)

NJ —PRINCETON UNIVERSITY, Library, Gest Oriental Library & East Asian Collections, 317 Palmer Hall, Princeton, 08544. D E Perushek, Cur
Holdings: Vols 83,000 Cat Maps Pix Microforms
Notes: Mostly in Japanese. Subject areas incl Japanese civilization, language, philosophy, religion, history, geography, economics, sociology, and other social sciences. With regard to Japanese art and archaeology, only works of a general or cultural nature and primary textual sources are acquired. Subject areas in science and technology, except those materials dealing with indigenous developments and historical aspects, are excluded. No historical period is excluded. Some Western-language reference works as well as Western-language works on Japanese literature, language, and linguistics. Emphasis is on current publications. Separate card catalog. Publications on collection: *List of Periodicals in Japanese in the Gest Oriental Library and East Asian* Collections (Princeton: Princeton University Library, 1980).

NY —CORNELL UNIVERSITY LIBRARIES, John M Olin Library, Wason Collection of China & the Chinese, Ithaca, 14853. James Cole, Cur; Paul P W Cheng, East Asia Librn
Holdings: Vols (330,000) Cat Mss Maps Pix Microforms
See also entry under Japan.

NY —COLUMBIA UNIVERSITY LIBRARIES, C V Strarr East Asian Library, 300 Kent Hall, New York, 10027. James Reardon-Anderson, Librn
Holdings: Vols 171,168 Cat
Notes: Publications in major East Asian and Western languages in all subjects comprising the social sciences and humanities.

†NY —COLUMBIA UNIVERSITY LIBRARIES, Butler Library, Rare Book and Manuscript Library, 535 W 114 St, New York, 10027.
Notes: Papers of Dr Ivan Morris, American Section chairman of Amnesty International, his researches into Japanese literature and culture, and his books on puzzles.

NY —CONSULATE GENERAL OF JAPAN, Japan Information Center, Library, 299 Park Ave, New York, 10017. Masakatsu Wajima, Librn
Holdings: Vols 4000 Cat Pix Slides
Notes: No photocopying. Reference library for staff use only.

NY —NEW YORK PUBLIC LIBRARY, Oriental Div, Fifth Ave & 42 St, New York, 10018. E Christian Filstrup, Chief
Holdings: Cat Mss Microforms
Budget: ($56,455)
Notes: Published catalog of holdings.

NY —NEW YORK PUBLIC LIBRARY, Donnell Foreign Language Library, 20 W 53 St, New York, 10019. Bosiljka Stevanovic, Supvr Librn
Holdings: Vols 2653 Cat
Notes: Japanese collection incl Japanese authors of Japanese expression. No separate catalog.

NY —UNIVERSITY OF ROCHESTER, Rush Rhees Library, Rochester, 14627. Datta S Kharbas, Head
Holdings: Vols 100,000 Cat Maps Microforms
Notes: Area studies collection on East Asia and South Asia. Major emphasis is on social sciences and humanities. Over 57,000 volumes on East Asia, out of which 29,000 volumes are in Chinese and 15,000 in Japanese. Extensive holdings on Chinese and Japanese histories. Catalog of East Asian collection consisting of Chinese and Japanese language holdings published in 1968, with two subsequent supplements. Over 33,000 volumes on South Asia. Considerable depth in social sciences, history, politics and anthropology. Extensive holdings in Sanskrit, Hindi, and Marathi.

NY —US MILITARY ACADEMY LIBRARY, Special Collections Division, West Point, 10996. Angela H Kao, Orientalia Librn
Notes: Primarily military and general history of China, incl biographies of Chinese military leaders of different political backgrounds from the early years of the Chinese Republic to recent times. Books as well as periodicals are mostly in Chinese with a few additional works in English and Japanese. Described in *Catalog of the Orientalia Collection of the USMA Library, West Point, 1978.*

NC —CUMBERLAND COUNTY PUBLIC LIBRARY, North Carolina Foreign Language Center, 328 Gillespie St, Fayetteville, 28301. Patrick M Valentine, Coordinator
Holdings: Vols 1750 Cat
Budget: $1000
Notes: The largest book collections are, in descending order of size, German Spanish, French, Japanese, Korean and Vietnamese, with fair sized collections in Italian, Russian, Chinese, Arabic, Greek, Hungarian, Polish, Hebrew, Thai, and Hindi. The Center has several shelves each of books in Bengali, Dutch, Marathi, Portuguese, Urdu, and Yiddish. Smaller collections of one to three shelves each incl Catalan, Croatian, Czech, Danish, Finnish, Gujarati, Icelandic, Kannada, Latin, Lithuanian, Malayalam, Norwegian, Panjabi, Persian (Farsi), Romanian, Slovak, Swedish, Tagalog, Tamil, Telegu, and Ukrianian. The Center has grammars, dictionaries and occasionally other readings in languages from Afrikaans and Albanian to Welsh, Yoruba and Zulu.

OH —CLEVELAND PUBLIC LIBRARY, Fine Arts and Special Collections Department, 325 Superior Ave, Cleveland, 44114. Alice N Loranth, Head
Holdings: Vols 3000 Cat Pix
Notes: Part of the Japan Collection. Emphasis is on Western editions and translations of literary and religious texts prior to European influence. Additional material on archaeology and antiquities, early description and travel, and early history. Incl 1750 vols in Japanese. Separate catalog of main entries for titles in Japanese is maintained.
See also entries under East (Far East); Oriental Languages and Literatures.

OH —CLEVELAND PUBLIC LIBRARY, Foreign Literature Dept, 325 Superior Ave, Cleveland, 44114. Natalia Bezugloff, Head
Holdings: Vols 960 Cat
Notes: A popular circulating collection containing classics and the standard works with emphasis on belles lettres, history and biography. A variety of other subjects such as learning languages, how to do books, art, children's books, spoken phonodiscs and cassettes, periodicals, etc. Incl 110 ephemera.
See also entry under Foreign Language Collections

PA —BUCKNELL UNIVERSITY, Ellen Clarke Bertrand Library, Lewisburg, 17837. Ann de Klerk, Librn
Holdings: Vols (3000) Cat
Notes: Incl about 400 titles in the Japanese language.

PA —UNIVERSITY OF PITTSBURGH, East Asian Library, 234 Hillman Library, Pittsburgh, 15260. Thomas C Kuo, Cur
Holdings: Vols (118,000) Periodicals Microfilms
Budget: ($210,000)
Notes: Contains Chinese and Japanese language publications on all social sciences and humanities, with special emphasis on history and source materials on both traditional and modern China, as well as research materials on language, literature, history, anthropology, economics and sociology of modern Japan. Catalogs of Chinese local history, East Asian periodicals and serials, and microforms in the collection have been published by the library. Also, *A Brief Guide to the Use of the East Asian* Library (1983). Incl 1600 periodicals and 2900 reels of microfilms.

RI —BROWN UNIVERSITY, John Hay Library, 20 Prospect St, Providence, 02912. Mark N Brown, Cur Mss
Holdings: Vols (74,000) Cat Microforms
Budget: ($10,000)
Notes: East Asia Collection. The primary focus is on Chinese studies with a small segment of approx 700 vols devoted to Japanese studies. Major subject areas, in descending order of strength, are: literature (incl classics), history, geography, social sciences, philosophy and religion, fine arts, science and technology. This incl the personal collection (20,000 vols) formed by Harvard University Sinologist Dr Charles Sideny Gardner, which is especially rich in materials relating to the Ch'ing Dynasty (1644-1912). In addition to books, there are 500 reels of microfilm, plus runs of 8 Chinese newspapers and 25 current Chinese periodicals.

TX —UNIVERSITY OF TEXAS LIBRARIES, Asian Collection, PO Box P, Austin, 78712. Kevin Lin, Asian Librn; Merry Burlingham, South Asian Librn
Holdings: Vols 34,000 Cat Microforms
Notes: Anthropology, economics, government, history, language and literature of Japan. Incl 250 periodical titles.

WA —UNIVERSITY OF WASHINGTON LIBRARIES, East Asia Library, DO-27, Seattle, 98195. Karl Lo, Head
Holdings: Vols (300,000) Cat Microforms
Budget: ($200,000)
Notes: Southwest China: Joseph Rock Collection, ca 2000 vols; modern Chinese poetry, 1919 to date: ca 700 titles; Asian art, esp Japanese painting: 4097 vols; Tiao-yu-t'ai movement in the US: ca 400 items of periodicals and pamphlets; modern Korean poetry, ancient and modern: ca 1000 titles; Mu-yu-shu folk literature: ca 1000 items.

JAPANESE MEDICINE see Medicine, Japanese

JAPANESE MOVING PICTURES see Moving Pictures, Japanese

JAPANESE MUSIC see Music, Japanese

JAPANESE NEWSPAPERS see Newspapers, Japanese

JAPANESE PAINTING see Painting, Japanese

JAPANESE PERIODICALS see Periodicals, Japanese

JAPANESE PRINTS see Color Prints, Japanese

JAPANESE STUDENT RELOCATION see Student Relocation (Japanese)

JARCHO, SAUL, M.D.

MD —NATIONAL LIBRARY OF MEDICINE, 8600 Rockville Pike, Bethesda, 20209. Harold M Schoolinam, Actg Dir
Budget: ($46,400)
Notes: Papers of the eminent internist and medical historian.

JARGONS see Languages, Mixed

JARRE, MAURICE

CA —UNIVERSITY OF SOUTHERN CALIFORNIA, Edward L Doheny Memorial Library, Archives of Performing Arts, University Park, Los Angeles, 90089. Robert Knutson, Librn
Holdings: Mss Pix
Notes: Personal collection of papers, pictures, etc.

JARRELL, RANDALL

NV —UNIVERSITY OF NEVADA, RENO, University Library, Special Collections Dept, Reno, 89557. Robert E Blesse, Head
Holdings: // Vols (57) Cat Other appearances 550 Cat
Notes: Includes individual works by author in all editions including translations; also prefaces, introductions, published correspondence, appearances in anthologies, periodicals, etc. Bibliographical research collection, part of Modern Authors Collection.

JARRELL, RANDALL (cont.)

NY —NEW YORK PUBLIC LIBRARY, Berg Collection of English & American Literature, Fifth Ave & 42 St, New York, 10018. Lola L Szladits, Cur
Notes: A significant body of his papers, incl mss, etc.

NC —UNIVERSITY OF NORTH CAROLINA, GREENSBORO, Walter Clinton Jackson Library, Special Collections Dept, 1000 Spring Garden St, Greensboro, 27412. Emilie W Mills, Librn
Holdings: Vols (200) Cat Mss Pix Phonorecords Audiotapes
Notes: Randall Jarrell taught here from 1947 until his death in 1965. Over 3000 ms items were the gift of the author and incl various drafts of poems, translations, critical works and essays. Books incl first, foreign, and variant editions, association books and many other heavily annotated by Jarrell readings, conversations (tapes) with other poets, incl John Crowe Ransom and Robert Frost. A one-hour color film made after the poet's death incl readings of his poems made from the earlier tapes, and an interview with the poet's widow, Mary Jarrell. Jarrell memorabilia is also included.

JARVIS, JUDY

ON —METROPOLITAN TORONTO LIBRARY, Theatre Dept, 789 Yonge St, Toronto, M4W 2G8, Can. Heather McCallum, Head
Notes: Theatre Department is one of eleven subject departments of the Metropolitan Toronto Library, which is generally acknowledged to be the most comprehensive of Canadian public library collections. The collection balances book and nonbook material in all areas of the performing arts. Production history is the special emphasis of the dance collection, as it is for all the material in the Theatre Department. This is supported by the department's extensive holdings of programs, posters, photographs and press clippings for Canadian productions and dancers, as well as a representative selection of material for non-Canadian dance. Important original stage designs in the collection incl work by Mstislav Dobujinsky for the Canadian ballet *Red Ear of Corn,* which was produced by Boris Volkoff in 1949; Maurice Strike's work for the National Ballet of Canada's productionof *Coppelia,* and Desmond Heeley's designs for that company's *Swan Lake.* Ms collections incl: The Boris Volkoff Collection (qv); papers of the Toronto dance teacher Bettina Byers; the papers of two Canadian dance critics, Ralph Hicklin and John Fraser; and the Mary Wigman Collection, consisting of xerox copies of letters exchanged between Miss Wigman and her Canadian pupil Judy Jarvis, and a taped conversation with Miss Wigman.

JAUVOISH, SIMON, M.D.

MB —UNIVERSITY OF MANITOBA, Elizabeth Dafoe Library, Archives and Special Collections Dept, Winnipeg, R3T 2N2, Can. Richard E Bennett, Dept Head; Corrado A Santoro, Reference Archivist
Notes: Literary manuscripts (unpublished?) of several of his works of both prose and poetry. Most of the drafts are in typewritten form with several bearing his handwritten notes and corrections. Three folders.

JAVA see Indonesia

JAVANESE LANGUAGE AND LITERATURE

NY —NEW YORK PUBLIC LIBRARY, Oriental Div, Fifth Ave & 42 St, New York, 10018. E Christian Filstrup, Chief
Holdings: // Cat Mss Microforms
Budget: ($56,455)
Notes: Published catalog of holdings. Currently collected in Western language materials only.

JAVITS, JACOB K., 1904-

NY —NEW YORK STATE LIBRARY, State Education Bldg Annex, Washington Ave, Albany, 12224.
Notes: The papers of former Senator Jacob Javits, covering his press releases, speeches, and campaign materials for the years 1957-1978. Incl 6 boxes materials.

NY —STATE UNIVERSITY OF NEW YORK, STONY BROOK, Melville Library, Dept of Special Collections, Stony Brook, 11794. Evert Volkersz, Head
Holdings: Mss Pix Audiotapes Videotapes Memorabilia
Notes: The political papers of New York State Republican Jacob K Javits, who served in the US House of Representatives from 1948-54 and in the US Senate from 1956-81. The collection is expected to be open for research in 1985, when finding aids will be available.

JAY, JOHN

MI —NORTHERN MICHIGAN UNIVERSITY, Lydia M Olson Library, Elizabeth L Harden Drive, Marquette, 49855. Stephen H Peters, Cataloger
Notes: A major section of the personal library of Moses Coit Tyler. Strong in the Colonial and Early National periods. Includes biographies and published letters and writings of such figures as Benjamin Franklin, John Adams, John Jay, Thomas Jefferson, Charles Sumner.

NY —COLUMBIA UNIVERSITY LIBRARIES, Rare Book & Manuscript Library, 801 Butler Library, 535 W 114 St, New York, 10027. Kenneth A Lohf, Librn
Holdings: Mss
Notes: His papers (10,500 ms letters and documents); the pre-eminent collection. Restricted use. Also, the Jay Family Papers (14,678 mss, letters and documents).

PA —FREE LIBRARY OF PHILADELPHIA, Rare Book Dept, Logan Sq, Philadelphia, 19103. Marie E Korey, Rare Book Librn
Holdings: // Uncat Mss
Notes: The William M Elkins Collection of 2000 letters relating to the treaty which ended the US quasi-war with France.

JAY, LEONARD

IL —ILLINOIS STATE UNIVERSITY, Milner Library, Dept of Special Collections, Normal, 61761. Robert Sokan, Librn
Holdings: Vols 191 // Cat
Notes: The city of Birmingham, School of Printing collection incl all the items that were produced by the School of Printing under the direction of Leonard Jay from 1925-1953.

PA —TEMPLE UNIVERSITY, Samuel Paley Library, Berks & 13 Sts, Philadelphia, 19122.
Notes: Collection of works of the City of Birmingham School of Printing (England). Books and ephemera of the students and Leonard Jay, Master Printer. Also the William Danner Collection of periodical issues from amateur printers and presses.

JAZZ

CA —CALIFORNIA STATE UNIVERSITY, HAYWARD, Library, Hayward, 94542. Melissa Rose, Dir
Holdings: Vols (15,986) Cat Phonorecords
Budget: ($21,000)
Notes: The score collection covers the entire range of instrumental and vocal concert music, incl collected works of various composers, and representative collection of hymnals, folk music, musical comedy, and some popular music. Sound recordings range from ethnomusicological collections to electronic music. Emphasis is on concert music, but there is a large collection of jazz and a selecltive collection of popular music. Separate catalog.

CA —SANTA CRUZ PUBLIC LIBRARY, Art, Music, Film Dept, 224 Church St, Santa Cruz, 95060. Alma Westberg, Librn
Holdings: Phonorecords Videotapes
Notes: The Edward Podesta Jazz Collection incl about 250 jazz periodicals of the 1960s and 1970s and about 200 jazz records, all cataloged. For reference use only.

CT —TRINITY COLLEGE LIBRARY, Watkinson Library, 300 Summit St, Hartford, 06106. Jeffrey Kaimowitz, Cur
Holdings: Cat Mss Phonorecords
Notes: Edward Abbe Niles Collection of books and sheet music, Also 200 78 rpm records.

FL —UNIVERSITY OF MIAMI, Music Library, PO Box 248165, Coral Gables, 33124. Nancy Kobialke, Librn
Holdings: Vols Cat Phonorecords
Budget: ($25,000)
Notes: Emphasis on research editions and performing editions with parts for 2-8 players. Nearly 24,000 musical scores. Recordings are mostly classical, but incl 1200 jazz LPs and 1200 ethnic LPs from all parts of world. *Inter-American Music* Archive is special catalog of Latin American holdings. Collection incl 15,500 cataloged phonorecords.

FL —ORLANDO PUBLIC LIBRARY, 100 Block of Central Ave, Orlando, 32806. Helen M Struthers, AV Librn
Holdings: Cat Phonorecords Audiotapes
Budget: ($5500)
Notes: 7155 LP recordings with emphasis on classical music; also jazz, country-western, easy-listening, spoken arts, foreign language study, dictation. Young Adult Dept has additional 850 contemporary and rock records. Library serves as subregional talking book library for the blind and physically handicapped, maintaining 7858 titles. Also, 681 audiotapes on all subjects. All materials circulate for 3 weeks.

IL —CHICAGO PUBLIC LIBRARY, Music Section, Fine Arts Division, 78 E Washington St, Chicago, 60602. Rosalinda I Hack, Fine Arts Division Chief; Richard C Schwegel, Head, Music Section
Notes: Comprehensive collection of books and disserations. Strong periodical and discography holdings. Phonorecord collection (primarily LP) extensive and covers most types of jazz. Small but growing score collection including arrangements. Balaban & Katz Orchestral Collection has 6000 arrangements of dance band music 1920-1950 (limited access).

IL —NORTH CENTRAL COLLEGE, Oesterle Library, 320 E School Ave, Naperville, 60540. Harriet Arklie, Dir
Holdings: Vols 250 Cat //
Notes: The Sang Jazz Collection, mostly first editions. Incl misc articles and clippings.

IL —UNIVERSITY OF ILLINOIS, URBANA/CHAMPAIGN, Library, Music Library, Urbana, 61801. William M McClellan, Librn
Holdings: Vols (200,000) Cat Mss Slides Sound Recordings Microforms Books Scores
Budget: ($65,000)
Notes: Introductory, instructive, research and reference materials to support work at graduate level in ethnomusicology,, musicology, music education, performance areas. Special areas incl about 2500 pre-1800 music mss and editions of music on microfilm, 2400 graduate music theses on microfilm, a special collection of 30,000 titles of American vocal sheet music covering the period 1790-1970, the Rafael Joseffy Collection of about 2000 pieces of 19th century piano music (incl performer markings), the Joseph Szigeti Collection (700 items: published music, mss, recordings), mainly violin and piano music by various commposers. Also incl a special collection of 45,000 78 rpm sound recordings (uncat) of classical music and jazz; a collection of 2900 titles from Chicago radio station WGN. Incl orchestrations, a collection of 500,000 items (uncat) from stock of Hunleth Music Store, St Louis, Missouri, mainly early 20th century imprints of songs, wind music, string music, piano, sets of theatre orchestra parts, dance band orchestrations. A separate collection of choral octavos and instrumental parts is maintained, incl 135,000 pieces of choral music, 30,500 orchestral parts, and 5500 wind ensemble parts. Also, music publishers' catalogues (mainly European and American), ca 126 cubic feet, 1860s-1950s.

JAZZ (cont.)

IN —INDIANA UNIVERSITY, Lilly Library, Seventh St, Bloomington, 47405. William R Cagle, Librn
Holdings: // Uncat
Notes: In the Starr American Sheet Music Collection.

IN —MORRISSON-REEVES LIBRARY, 80 N Sixth St, Richmond, 47374. Harriet E Bard, Librn
Holdings: Cat
Notes: All recordings circulate and are long playing, monaural and stereo--4527 adult and 392 juvenile discs. Mainly classical music but incl spoken records, musical, folk music and historical jazz.

KY —UNIVERSITY OF KENTUCKY, Music Library, 116 Fine Arts Bldg, Lexington, 40506. Cathy S Hunt, Music Librn
Holdings: Vols 18,000 Cat Microforms Scores Recordings
Notes: Collection incl books (14,000), includes music history, theory, music eduction, jazz, etc cat. Music Scores (18, 000) cat. Serials (3200 vols) cat. Microforms (6300) cat. Recordings (9100) cat. Collected Editions (complete Works of composers, large sets, etc) (7100) cat. The Alfred Cortot Collection (about 300 vols of rare, early music theory books) is housed in the Rare Books Room of the Main Library.

LA —TULANE UNIVERSITY, Howard-Tilton Memorial Library, Special Collections Div, William Ransom Hogan Jazz Archive, 7001 Freret, New Orleans, 70118. Richard B Allen, Acting Cur; Alma D Williams, Assistant to the Cur
Holdings: Vols (100,000) Cat Mss Pix Slides Phonorecords Audiotapes Videotapes 16mm Films Microforms
Budget: ($90,000)
Notes: A major collection of New Orleans Jazz, other jazz music, and history of jazz. Incl recorded interviews on audiotape reels (1509), recorded music on audiotape reels (815), phonograph records (24,000), sheet music (16,205 pieces), books (1601), serials (12,000), photographs (6,273), catalogs (285), manuscripts (18), microforms (6) and other archival material (37,500 items). These materials emphasize the origin and development of New Orleans jazz, but also cover related fields, incl biographical details, as well as description of this music and the way it functions in society. Transcriptions or digests of these interviews are made with added explanatory comments and cross-references. Researchers may refer to original taped interviews. For photocopies of transcriptions and digests write to the Archive.Only materials which are in the public domain or are copyrighted by Tulane University may be copied at this time. There are at least two dozen published descriptions of the collection.

MD —JOHNS HOPKINS UNIVERSITY, Milton S Eisenhower Library, Charles & 34 Sts, Baltimore, 21218. Ann S Gwyn, Assistant Dir for Special Collections
Holdings: Vols 4700 Cat Phonorecords
Notes: The best American and foreign music recordings are added each year. Rose and Morris Light Record Collection, and the Salmieri Jazz Record Collection.

MD —UNIVERSITY OF MARYLAND, BALTIMORE COUNTY, Albin O Kuhn Library and Gallery, 5401 Wilkens Ave, Baltimore, 21228. Ann Copeland, Special Collections Librn
Holdings: 900 Cat Phonorecords and Audiotapes
Notes: Collection is catalogued by subject and incl blues, historical (pre 1950), big band, ragtime, modern and fusion jazz.

MA —BOSTON UNIVERSITY, Mugar Memorial Library, Special Collections Dept, 771 Commonwealth Ave, Boston, 02215. Howard B Gotlieb, Dir
Holdings: Cat Mss Pix
Notes: Incl personal papers and literary productions of numerous modern actors, actresses, musicians (composers and performers) of all kinds and of music critics. A complete list is available.

MI —DETROIT PUBLIC LIBRARY, Music & Performing Arts Dept, 5201 Woodward, Detroit, 48202. Agatha Pfeiffer Kalkanis, Chief
Holdings: Vols 19,000 Cat Mss Pix Microforms
Notes: Also incl (77,000) scores. General collection intended for practical use in performance and for scholarly research. Good working collection of bibliographies, thematic catalogs, dictionaries and encyclopedias, periodical indexes. Many sets of collected works, monumental editions, historical anthologies. Good representation of opera and operetta, art song and folk song, solo instrumental literature and chamber music in practical editions. 2575 titles of choral music, chiefly sacred, for use by choirs. 17,000 titles of popular sheet music, uncataloged but thoroughly indexed. Considerable recent holdings of books and periodicals in foreign languages. Special collections of black and local materials. 25, 000 recordings and extensive discographical literature. Collection of publishers' trade catalogs.

MO —UNIVERSITY OF MISSOURI-KANSAS CITY, General Library, State Historical Society of Missouri Manuscripts, 5100 Rockhill Road, Kansas City, 64110. Kenneth J LaBudde, Dir; Gordon Hendrickson, Assoc Dir
Holdings: Mss
Notes: Joint Collection Western Historical Manuscript Collection and the State Historical of Missouri Manuscripts, University of Missouri-Kansas City General Library, 5100 Rockhill Road, Kansas City, MO 64110. Ca 2,500 linear feet of manuscripts, blueprints and oral history tapes. Notes: The manuscript collection includes material which documents the history, growth and development of Missouri, especially the Greater Kansas City area. The personal papers of business, civic, cultural, political and community leaders; local historians and other individuals of families from the area are within the collection as are the records of associations, organizations and institutions which reflect the history of the area. Prominent among the collections are the papers of Charles B. Wheeler, Jr., Charles N. Kimball, Arthur Mag, Oscar D. Nelson, Lou B. Holland, J. C. Nichols, Perry Cookingham, Blevins Davis and Daniel Macmorris and the records of the Kansas City Board of Trade. Architectural designs and plans for approximately 3,500 Kansas City buildings and the records of the Hoit, Price and Barnes architectural firm and the papers of Asa Beebe Cross, early Kansas City architect as well as a number of oral histories with Kansas City Jazz figures are in the collection.

MO —MISSOURI HISTORICAL SOCIETY, Library, Jefferson Memorial Bldg, Saint Louis, 63112. Stephanie Klein, Librn-Archivist; Peter Michel, Cur of Manuscripts
Holdings: Vols (500) Cat
Notes: Five hundred volumes of sheet music. In additions, over 5000 pieces of individual sheet music. Most of this music was published in St Louis, and many have St Louis themes. Collection will remain in storage until 1986.

NJ —RUTGERS, THE STATE UNIVERSITY OF NEW JERSEY, Institute of Jazz Studies, 135 Bradley Hall, Newark, 07102. Dan Morgenstern, Dir; Edward Berger, Cur; Maxie Griffin, Librn
Holdings: Vols 3000 Cat Pix Phonorecords Audiotapes Films Microforms VF
Notes: Incl jazz records, books, periodicals etc as well as some roots and peripheral material--African music, gospel music, rhythm and blues, rock etc (both written and recorded). Incl 60,000 records.

NM —NEW MEXICO STATE UNIVERSITY, Library, Box 3475, Las Cruces, 88003. James Dyke, Dir
Holdings: Vols 4000// Cat
Notes: Jazz, Blues, and music history. Collection of music periodicals and monographs of the 1930s, 1940s and 1950s.

NY —STATE UNIVERSITY OF NEW YORK, BUFFALO, Baird Music Library, Baird Hall, Amherst, 14260. James B Coover, Dir
Holdings: Vols (104,000) Cat Mss Pix Slides Phonorecords Microforms
Notes: Nearly complete collections of *Denkmaeler and Gesamtausgaben* and other historical sets. Strong collection of dictionaries, bibliographies, biographies, facsimiles, works on the "new" music, organology and ethnomusicology. Special emphasis on operas, scores of the avant-garde, jazz and urban popular music, discography and music librarianship. Good collection of medieval and Renaissance anthologies, contemporary and avant-garde recordings. Houses Archives of the Center of the Creative and Performing Arts. Collections incl 2100 slides, 22,000 phonorecords, 46,000 scores and parts, 29, 000 books, 4900 microforms. Computerized record catalog in process.

NY —STATE UNIVERSITY OF NEW YORK, COLLEGE AT BUFFALO, E H Butler Library, 1300 Elmwood Ave, Buffalo, 14222. Sister Martin Joseph Jones, Assoc Librn
Holdings: Uncat Phonorecords
Notes: The William H Tallmadge Collection of jazz, pop, and country music (691 phonorecords) incl 46 Hill and Dale records with standing record player.

NY —NEW YORK PUBLIC LIBRARY, Schomburg Center for Research in Black Culture, 515 Lenox Ave, New York, 10037. Catherine J Lenix Hooker, Interim Administrator
Notes: A repository for 10,000 phonodiscs and 2000 tapes covering African and West Indian folk music, early blues, and jazz.

NY —NEW YORK PUBLIC LIBRARY, Performing Arts Research Center, Rodgers & Hammerstein Archives of Recorded Sound, 111 Amsterdam Ave, New York, 10023.
Holdings: Cat Phonorecords Audiotapes
Notes: 400,000 sound recordings on disc, tape, wire, and cylinder; classical and popular music, jazz, speech, etc. Printed materials related to the subject.

NY —NEW YORK PUBLIC LIBRARY, Music Div, 111 Amsterdam Ave, New York, 10023. Frank C Campbell, Chief
Holdings: Cat Mss Pix Microforms
Notes: Extensive holdings of jazz and popular music books, sheet music, books, archival collections, periodicals, recordings, pictures. Holdings are concentrated in the Americana Collection.

OH —AKRON-SUMMIT COUNTY PUBLIC LIBRARY, 55 S Main St, Akron, 44326. Steven Hawk, Dir
Holdings: Cat Pix Phonorecords
Budget: ($9600)
Notes: General music and fine arts collection, incl 16,515 phonorecords, 2951 music scores, 3000 pieces of sheet music and 55,472 pictures.

OH —CLEVELAND PUBLIC LIBRARY, Fine Arts and Special Collections Department, 325 Superior Ave, Cleveland, 44114. Alice N Loranth, Head
Holdings: Vols (72,050) Cat Phonorecords
Notes: Part of the Music Collection which incl books, scores and 15,300 recordings on classical, modern, jazz and popular music.

TN —COUNTRY MUSIC FOUNDATION, Library & Media Center, 4 Music Sq E, Nashville, 37203. Charlie Seemann, Dir
Holdings: Vols (6000) Mss Pix Slides

JAZZ (cont.)

Phonorecords Audiotapes Videotapes 16mm Films Microforms
Notes: The largest collection in the world dealing with American country music. Related subject areas are also included--Anglo-American folk song, popular music in general (soul, jazz, rock and roll, rhythm and blues, etc), recorded sound technology, music law.

TX —NORTH TEXAS STATE UNIVERSITY, Audio Center, Box 5188, NT Station, Denton, 76203. Morris Martin, Music Librn
Notes: More than 1600 manuscript jazz compositions, (incl scores and parts, alternate versions, expanded arrangements) by Stan Kenton, Johnny Richards, Joe Coccia, Lennie Niehaus, Pete Rugolo, Willie Maiden, Bob Curnow, Ken Hanna, Gene Rowland, Bob Graettinger and others, used by the Stan Kenton Band and given to North Texas State University in 1962 and at Kenton's death in 1979. Unpublished catalog: Breeden, Leon, *Stan Kenton Music in the NTSU Jazz Studies Library and the NTSU Music Library,* Denton, 1983 (99 pages). In addition, books, recordings, tapes, and discographies concerning or by Duke Ellington. Incl some 600 78 rpm records and 400 LP, 45 rpm records, transcriptions and tapes. In Music Library.

WI —MILWAUKEE PUBLIC LIBRARY, 814 W Wisconsin Ave, Milwaukee, 53233. Donald J Sager, City Librn
Holdings: Vols Cat
Notes: An extensive general music literature collection incl classical, contemporary, jazz, and musical biographies, as well as the most significant reference works in music. Also incl 46,708 sound recordings, 73,150 historical recorded sound collection, 20,000 historic popular song collection, and WPA copied music. Local area music materials incl concert programs and newspaper clippings.

JAZZ—HISTORY

CA —SANTA CRUZ PUBLIC LIBRARY, Art, Music, Film Dept, 224 Church St, Santa Cruz, 95060. Alma Westberg, Librn
Holdings: Phonorecords Videotapes
Notes: The Edward Podesta Jazz Collection incl about 250 jazz periodicals of the 1960s and 1970s and about 200 jazz records, all cataloged. For reference use only.

DC —LIBRARY OF CONGRESS, American Folklife Center, Archive of Folk Culture, Washington, 20540.
Notes: Recordings of jazz musician Jelly Roll Morton, 1938.

LA —LOUISIANA STATE MUSEUM, Louisiana Historical Center, 400 Esplanade Ave, (Mailing add: 751 Chartres St, New Orleans, 70116). Edward F Haas, Chief Cur
Holdings: Vols 2000 Cat Pix Slides Phonorecords Audiotapes
Notes: New Orleans Jazz Museum and Archives Collection. Donated to the Louisiana State Museum by the New Orleans Jazz Club in 1977. It was formerly a private museum sponsored by the Jazz Club and housed at 833 Conti St, New Orleans, LA 70130. Emphasis is New Orleans jazz, incl 8000 pieces of sheet music; 12,000 phonorecords; 15,000 pictures; 1000 slides; and 1000 audiotapes. A guide to the collection is in preparation.

LA —TULANE UNIVERSITY, Howard-Tilton Memorial Library, Special Collections Div, William Ransom Hogan Jazz Archive, 7001 Freret, New Orleans, 70118. Richard B Allen, Acting Cur; Alma D Williams, Assistant to the Cur
Holdings: Vols (100,000) Cat Mss Pix Slides Phonorecords Audiotapes Videotapes 16mm Films Microforms
Budget: ($90,000)
Notes: Jazz music and musicians. Outstanding collection, incl books, music scores, serials, catalogs and other archival material. Music, history, etc.
See also entry under Jazz

NJ —RUTGERS, THE STATE UNIVERSITY OF NEW JERSEY, Institute of Jazz Studies, 135 Bradley Hall, Newark, 07102. Dan Morgenstern, Dir; Edward Berger, Cur; Maxie Griffin, Librn
Holdings: Vols 2500 Cat Mss Pix Phonorecords
Notes: Original collection from Marshall Stearns who founded the Institute. Incl archives of George Hoefer, Charles Edward Smith, Walter C Allen, and other jazz scholars. 60,000 phonorecords. Oral history project.

JAZZ DANCE

CA —CALIFORNIA INSTITUTE OF THE ARTS, Library, 24700 McBean Pkwy, Valencia, 91355. James Elrod, Dir
Holdings: Vools (61,000) Cat
Budget: ($2868)
Notes: Incl classical and modern dance forms.

IL —CHICAGO PUBLIC LIBRARY, Art Section, Fine Arts Division, 78 E Washington St, Chicago, 60602. Rosalinda I Hack, Fine Arts Division Chief; Yvonne S Brown, Head, Art Section
Holdings: Vols 2500
Notes: Reference and circulating collection of books, periodicals, pamphlets, and videotapes on all aspects of the dance eg ballet, social dance, square dance, jazz and folkdance. Focus of the collection is on ballet, history, biographies of dancers, and dance instruction. Subject is supplemented by a dance videotape collection, the *Folk Dance Index* a comprehensive index to descriptions of folkdances of all nations. Special Collections: Eliza Stigler Dance Collection of 200 dance books on ballet and dance history with particular emphasis on Spanish Dance. Ruth Page Archives: small collection of memorabilia documents the career of Ms Page. Reference collection of 85 dance videotapes that document notable dance performances, from the past and present by well known dancers and dance groups. Subject concentration is that of ballet, with some examples of ethnic dance. There is alsoa collection of tapes that document Chicago area dance groups, dancers, and choreographers. A file to the contents of the tapes is available.

KS —WICHITA PUBLIC LIBRARY, Art & Music Division, 223 S Main, Wichita, 67202. Leonard Messineo, Jr, Head, Art & Music Division; Deborah Hamilton, Special Collections Librn
Holdings: Uncat Audiotapes Videotape Pix
Notes: Alice Bauman Dance Symposia Collection. Contains 300 hours of audio tapes, 1 hour-long video tape, several hundred photographs, and fugitive material of the American Dance Symposia held in Wichita from 1968-1972. The symposia covered all dance idioms-ballet, modern, jazz, folk, ethnic, dance education and therapy-and featured such notable figures such as Leonide Massine, Martha Hill, William Christensen, Alfonso Cimber, Toni Intravaia, James Clouser, Eleo Pomare, Juana de Laban, and many others. Characterized by the *Kansas City Star* as the "most distinguished faculties of fine artists ever assembled in the contemporary world of dance."

JEANNERET-GRIS, CHARLES EDOUARD see le Corbusier (Charles Edouard Jeanneret-Gris)

JEDNODNIOWKA

MA —HARVARD UNIVERSITY LIBRARY, Cambridge, 02138.
Notes: Incl nearly 1000 Yiddish books, pamphlets and periodicals, acquired in 1972, many of which were the period just before World War II. Incl in these materials are popular novels, plays, historical and political works, incl some 50 jednodniowka (occasional publications similar to periodicals in appearance but issued in response to specific events).

JEDNOTA FRATERNAL ORGANIZATION

PA —THE SLOVAK MUSEUM AND ARCHIVES AT JEDNOTA ESTATES, Rosedale & Jednota Sts, PO Box 150, Middletown, 17057. Edward A Tuleya, Cur & Archivist
Notes: Incl periodicals and artifacts; rich collection of the history of the Jednota Fraternal Organization, its branches and districts; pamphlets on convention activities, banners, uniforms, badges. Phonograph recordings; mining equipment; paintings of mining scenes; letters. Photographs of Jednota officers and groups, of Jednota Orphanage and equipment used by children; pictures of classes. Desk used by Father Mathew Jankola, priest, patriot and educator. Confessional, cymbal, and maps.

JEEPS see Automobiles

JEFFCOTT, PERCIVAL R.

WA —WESTERN WASHINGTON UNIVERSITY, Center for Pacific Northwest Studies, High St, Bellingham, 98225. James W Scott, Dir
Holdings: Cat Mss Maps Pix
Notes: The Percival R Jeffcott Collection of Local History is particularly rich in photogrpahic materials, incl about 1800 negatives and about 1100 photographs, which deal with pioneer settlement and economic and cultural developments in Whatcom County, Washington, and a few adjacent areas, such as the Lower Mainland of British Columbia to the north and neighboring counties of Washington to the south and west. Incl also ms versions of Jeffcott's published works: *Nooksack Tales and Trails, Chechaco and Sourdough* and *Blanket Bill Jarman* and numerous unpublished papers and workbooks. A small collection of Jeffcott materials is housed in the Washington State Historical Society, Tacoma, and for this there is an unpublished inventory. An inventory of the present collection is being prepared for publication by the Center for Pacific Northwest Studies.

JEFFERIES, RICHARD, 1848-1887

GA —EMORY UNIVERSITY, Robert W Woodruff Library, Special Collections Dept, Atlanta, 30322. Linda M Matthews, Head Special Collections; Virginia J H Cain, Processing Archivist; Richard H F Lindemann, Reference Archivist
Holdings: Vols 100 Cat
Notes: First and variant editions.

JEFFERS, LANCE

MS —TOUGALOO COLLEGE, L Zenobia Coleman Library, Tougaloo, 39174. Virgia Brocks-Shedd, Acting Dir
Budget: ($142,650)
Notes: Civil rights cases and legal papers; lawsuits; Mississippi, 1960-1968. Local attorneys have donated papers of cases they have handled, espec attorneys of two government-funded legal services offices. Individual collections: Jerry W Ward, Lance Jeffers, (Ret) Lt Col Jesse Johnson on Blacks in the military. Incl VF holdings of articles from 1930 and on.

JEFFERS, ROBINSON

†AL —UNIVERSITY OF ALABAMA, Amelia Gayle Gorgas Library, PO Box S, University, 35486.
Notes: Incl a collection of Sir Walter Scott first editions, 41 vols; Robinson Jeffers collection of 37 vols and mss; Lafcadio Hearn Collection of 100 vols and pamphlets.

CA —HARRISON MEMORIAL LIBRARY, Ocean & Lincoln Sts, Carmel, 93921. Keith Brehmer, Ref Librn
Holdings: Vols 70 Cat Pix

CA —CALIFORNIA STATE UNIVERSITY, LONG BEACH, Library, Dept of Special Collections & Archives, 1250 Bellflower Blvd, Long Beach, 90840. John Ahouse, Special Collections Librn
Holdings: Vols 220 Cat Mss
Notes: Incl first issues, many signed; presentation copies; prospectuses; ALS (10).

CA —OCCIDENTAL COLLEGE, Library, 1600 Campus Rd, Los Angeles, 90041.

JEFFERS, ROBINSON (cont.)

Michael C Sutherland, Special Collections Librn
Holdings: Vols (500) Cat Mss Pix Slides Phonorecords Audiotapes 16mm Films
Notes: Robinson Jeffers, California Poet, was a student at Occidental College around 1900. The College has attempted to build a collection of major importance by collecting mss, letters, various editions of Jeffers' works, and books and correspondence about him. Photocopying is allowed under strict supervision.

CA —UNIVERSITY OF SAN FRANCISCO, Richard A Gleeson Library, The Countess Bernardine Murphy Donohue Rare Book Room, San Francisco, 94117. D Steven Corey, Special Collections Librn
Holdings: Vols 200 Mss
Notes: Comprehensive collection of first editions, ALS's, particularly of Una Jeffers, photos, magazine appearances, ephemera.

CA —UNIVERSITY OF CALIFORNIA, SANTA BARBARA, Library, Dept of Special Collections, Santa Barbara, 93106. Christian F Brun, Head
Holdings: Cat Mss Pix
Notes: The Armstrong Collection of books, photographs, mss, ephemera.

NV —UNIVERSITY OF NEVADA, RENO, University Library, Special Collections Dept, Reno, 89557. Robert E Blesse, Head
Holdings: // Vols (55) Cat Other appearances 400 Cat
Notes: Includes individual works by author in all editions including translations; also prefaces, introductions, published correspondence, appearances in anthologies, periodicals, etc. Bibliographical research collection, part of Modern Authors Collection.

TX —UNIVERSITY OF HOUSTON, M D Anderson Memorial Library, University Park, Houston, 77004. David Farmer, Cur, Special Collections; Jean Jackson, Assistant Cur
Holdings: Vols 150 Cat
Notes: A published catalog exists for the initial group of Jeffers material that was acquired by the University Library. The collection, however, has grown to more than double its original size since that time. Copies of the catalog, *Robinson Jeffers at the University of Houston,* are available by the Department of Special Collections. Additions are actively sought for this collection. Current needs are primarily for periodical appearances, obscure reprints, foreign translations, variant editions, and ephemera.

VA —UNIVERSITY OF VIRGINIA, Alderman Library, Clifton Waller Barrett Collection, Charlottesville, 22901. Joan St C Crane, Cur of American Literature Collections
Holdings: Vols 600

JEFFERSON, JOSEPH

CA —UNIVERSITY OF CALIFORNIA, DAVIS, Shields Library, Dept of Special Collections, Davis, 95616. Donald Kunitz, Head; C Danial Elliott, Asst Head
Holdings: Uncat Mss Pix
Notes: Photographs, clippings, and correspondence of personalities of American and British theatre in the 19th and 20th centuries, such as Edwin Booth, Joseph Jefferson, Julia Marlowe, E H Sothern, Ellen Terry, Henry Irving, McKee Rankin, Fanny Davenport, and Zero Mostel.

JEFFERSON, MARK SYLVESTER WILLIAM

MI —EASTERN MICHIGAN UNIVERSITY, Center of Educational Resources, Ypsilanti, 48197.
Notes: Collection of Mark S W Jefferson's correspondence, papers and notes--also incl the Paris Peace Conference Diary.

JEFFERSON, THOMAS

CT —UNIVERSITY OF CONNECTICUT, Library, Storrs, 06268. R H Schimmelpfeng, Dir of Special Collections
Holdings: Vols 4600// Uncat Mss Maps
Notes: The library of Pierce Welch Gaines of Federalist material, chiefly contemporary books and mss. Emphasis on Washington, Jefferson and Adams.

DC —LIBRARY OF CONGRESS, Rare Book & Special Collections Div, Washington, 20540. William Matheson, Chief
Holdings: Vols 2465 Cat
Notes: The collection represents the survivors of ca 6500 vols that constituted Thomas Jefferson's personal library as sold to the nation in 1815. The works are chiefly 18th century British, French and American publications on a wide variety of subjects: classics, law, history, architecture, philososphy, economics, and especially politics. Several items with ms notes incl Jefferson's own copy of his *Summary View* (Williamsburg: 1774); presentation copies; association items incl several with notes of Benjamin Franklin. Catalog published: *Catalogue of the Library of Thomas* Jefferson, (Washington, DC: US Library of Congress, 1952-1959), 5 vols. Descriptions of the collection are found in: *Quarterly Journal of the Library of Congress,* vol 8 (Nov 1950):no 1. *Quarterly Journal of the Library of Congress,* vol 14, (Nov 1956): no 1.

DC —LIBRARY OF CONGRESS, Manuscript Division, Washington, 20540. John C Broderick, Chief
Notes: The Presidential Papers collection incl the papers, etc, of numerous Presidents.

IL —NEWBERRY LIBRARY, 60 W Walton St, Chicago, 60610. Diana Haskell, Cur of Modern Mss
Notes: Letters; association books. Incl The Herbert Strauss Collection. 45 ms pieces.

MI —UNIVERSITY OF MICHIGAN, William L Clements Library, Ann Arbor, 48109. John C Dann, Dir
Notes: The William L. Clements Library of Americana is a non-circulating rare book library of original source material, printed and manuscript, dealing with America, from the discovery period into the late nineteenth century. The collection includes approximately 55,000 books and pamphlets, 550 linear feet of manuscripts, 4,100 volumes of newspapers, 36,000 maps, 40,000 pieces of sheet music, and 1,000 prints. The collection is strongest for the period of the American Revolution, and includes the papers of Thomas Gage, Sir Henry Clinton, and the Earl of Shelburne. Other areas of strength include antislavery, cartography and geography, discovery and exploration, American Indians, The Civil War, tune-books, sermons and orations, and the War of 1812. There are selective research collections dealing with Christopher Columbus, Thomas Paine, Benjamin Franklin, George Washington, Thomas Jefferson, and the Federalist Papers. Publications describing the collections of the library are: Author/Title catalog of Americana 1493-1860 in the William L. Clements Library... 7 volumes, Boston, G. K. Hall, 1970; Guide to the manuscript collections of the William L. Clements Library, by Arlene P. Shy 3d edition, Boston, G. K. Hall, 1978; Guide to the manuscript maps in the William L. Clements Library, compiled by Christian Burn, Ann Arbor, U. of Michigan, 1959; and Research catalog of maps of America, to 1860 in the William L. Clements Library..., edited by Douglas W. Marshall, 4 volumes, Boston, G. K. Hall, 1972.

MI —NORTHERN MICHIGAN UNIVERSITY, Lydia M Olson Library, Elizabeth L Harden Drive, Marquette, 49855. Stephen H Peters, Cataloger
Notes: A major section of the personal library of Moses Coit Tyler. Strong in the Colonial and Early National periods. Includes biographies and published letters and writings of such figures as Benjamin Franklin, John Adams, John Jay, Thomas Jefferson, Charles Sumner.

OH —OBERLIN COLLEGE LIBRARY, Clarence Ward Art Library, Allen Art Bldg, Oberlin, 44074. Jeffrey Weidman, Librn
Holdings: Vols (62,000) Cat Microforms
Notes: Strong in medieval European architecture and American architecture. Incl the Jefferson Collection, an almost complete duplication of the architectural books in Thomas Jefferson's library. Also incl Frederick B Artz Collection of books on architecture and gardening dating from the 16th through the 19th centuries. Significant holdings in early serials (see *ARLO Union List of Serials).*

†UT —UNIVERSITY OF UTAH, Marriott Library, Salt Lake City, 84112.
Notes: Manuscripts and papers of historian-biographer Fawn M Brodie (d 1981). Incl taped interviews with Richard Nixon, and notes, clippings, reviews, articles, and about 400 books used in her researches on Nixon, Thomas Jefferson, and Sir Richard Burton, in preparation of their biographies.

VA —UNIVERSITY OF VIRGINIA, Alderman Library, Manuscripts Dept, Charlottesville, 22901. Edmund Berkeley Jr, Cur
Holdings: Cat Mss
Notes: Jefferson's papers are divided among family collections and University archives. More than half are from the post-Presidential years. The establishment of the University of Virginia, family events, and personal business are the chief topics. Thurlow, Berkeley, Freudenberg, and Casteen (comps) *The Jefferson Papers of the University of Virginia* (Charlottesville, VA: The University Press of Virginia, 1973).

VA —CENTRAL VIRGINIA COMMUNITY COLLEGE, Library, 3506 Wards Rd, Lynchburg, 24502. John B St Leger, Dir of Library Servs
Holdings: Vols (6000)

VA —VIRGINIA STATE LIBRARY, 12 & Capitol Sts, Richmond, 23219.
Holdings: Vols 2900 Cat Mss Pix

VA —COLLEGE OF WILLIAM AND MARY, Earl Gregg Swem Library, Williamsburg, 23185. Margaret C Cook, Cur of Manuscripts & Rare Books
Holdings: Vols 1500 Cat Mss
Notes: Tucker-Coleman Papers (1675-1956): Family, literary, and business papers of the Tucker Family, particularly St George Tucker (1752-1827) and Nathaniel Beverley Tucker (1784-1851). This collection, which incl 600 Jefferson items, is particularly important for the study of Virginia social, economic, and political history during the period 1770-1850. Also, 30,000 ms items.

JEFFERSON NATIONAL EXPANSION MEMORIAL

†WA —WASHINGTON STATE UNIVERSITY, Library, Manuscripts, Archives & Special Collections, Pullman, 99164. John F Guido, Head
Holdings: Cat Mss Maps Pix
Notes: The Carl Parcher Russell papers, a vast resource (24,916 items; 45 linear feet) in American Indian and Western pioneer activities and artifacts. Much on the fur trade; pioneer life; mountain men and trapping; wildlife; primitive life in detail. Also the National Park Service, parks, monuments, etc. Described in *Carl Parcher Russell: An Indexed Register of His Scholarly and Professional Papers, 1920-*

JEFFERSON NATIONAL EXPANSION MEMORIAL (cont.)

1967, in the Washington State University Library (Pullman, 1970), 149 pp.

JEFFREY, HOWARD

MA —BOSTON UNIVERSITY, Mugar Memorial Library, Special Collections Dept, 771 Commonwealth Ave, Boston, 02215. Howard B Gotlieb, Dir
Holdings: Mss Correspondence

JELLIFFE, SMITH ELY, 1866-1945

DC —LIBRARY OF CONGRESS, Manuscript Division, Washington, 20540. John C Broderick, Chief
Holdings: 9000 Items
Notes: Correspondence, photographs, notes, and reprints of Smith Ely Jelliffe (1896-1944).

JEMISON, ROBERT, JR.

AL —BIRMINGHAM PUBLIC LIBRARY, Dept of Archives & Mss, 2020 Seventh Ave N, Birmingham, 35203. Marvin Y Whiting, Archivist & Cur
Holdings: Mss Pix Slides Audiotapes Microforms
Notes: Especially Birmingham history. Largest avaialable collections are the Robert Jemison, Jr. Papers (ca 1.2 million items) and the Donald Comer Papers (ca 390,000 items). Photographs incl ca one million negatives from the collection of Birmingham photographer Charles Preston.

NY —CORNELL UNIVERSITY LIBRARIES, Collection of Regional History, Dept of Manuscripts and Univ Archives, Ithaca, 14853.
Notes: Real estate developer. Records, 1903-68; 33 items, 2 reels microfilm.

JENKINS, GEOFFREY

MA —BOSTON UNIVERSITY, Mugar Memorial Library, Special Collections Dept, 771 Commonwealth Ave, Boston, 02215. Howard B Gotlieb, Dir
Holdings: // Cat Mss
Notes: Mss, correspondnece, etc collected in depth; incl publications by or about.

JENKINS, GEORGE

CA —UNIVERSITY OF CALIFORNIA, LOS ANGELES, Theater Arts Library, Los Angeles, 90024. Edward Shreeves, Chairman, Bibliographers Group; Audree Malkin, Head, Theater Arts Library
Notes: The George Jenkins Collection is comprised of his archive of art direction materials for more than 30 films and television specials. Incl scripts, set lists, 1/4" ground plans, budget records, research photographs and notes, original set sketches, storyboards, blueprints, construction and prop stills, and other production materials.

JENKINS, JAMES ANGUS

CA —UNIVERSITY OF CALIFORNIA, BERKELEY, Bancroft Library, Manuscripts Division, Berkeley, 94720. James D Hart, Dir
Holdings: Cat Mss Maps Pix Microforms
Notes: Papers, correspondence, etc.

JENKINS, WILL F., 1896-

NY —SYRACUSE UNIVERSITY LIBRARIES, Ernest S Bird Library, George Arents Research Library for Special Collections, Syracuse, 13210. Carolyn A Davis, Manuscripts Librn; Amy S Doherty, University Archivist; Mark F Weimer, Rare Book Librn
Notes: Papers 1915-1968 (35 linear feet). *See also* entry under Science Fiction

JENNER, ALBERT E.

IL —CHICAGO HISTORICAL SOCIETY, Library, Clark St at North Ave, Chicago, 60614. Archie Motley, Manuscript Librn
Notes: Papers of Albert E Jenner, member of Warren Commission, minority counsel during Nixon impeachment hearing.

JENNINGS, ELIZABETH

DE —UNIVERSITY OF DELAWARE, Hugh M Morris Library, S College Ave, Newark, 19711. T Stuart Dick, Special Collections
Holdings: Cat Mss Pix
Notes: Manuscripts, etc, incl literary correspondence.

MO —WASHINGTON UNIVERSITY, Libraries, Campus Box 1061, Saint Louis, 63130.
Holdings: Vols 100 Cat Mss Pix
Notes: Her papers incl 5 notebooks, autobiographical sketches, drafts of essays and poems, notes on visits to Rome, and loose ms drafts of poems described in *Special Collections: an Annotated Guide to the Holdings of the Manuscript Division and the University Archives and Research* Collection.

JENNINGS, W. N.

PA —FRANKLIN INSTITUTE LIBRARY, Dept of Historical Programs, 20th St and Parkway, Philadelphia, 19103.
Notes: Papers.

JENSEN, JENS

IL —MORTON ARBORETUM, Sterling Morton Library, Lisle, 60532. Ian MacPhail, Librn
Holdings: Vols (22,000)
Notes: Emphasis is on Woody plants. Print collection of 3000 pieces; 2000 botanical and horticultural rare books; Linnaeana. The Jens Jensen Archive of letters, photographs, blueprints, landscape plans.

JENSEN FAMILY

CA —CALIFORNIA STATE UNIVERSITY, HAYWARD, Library, Hayward, 94542. Melissa Rose, Dir
Holdings: Vols (14,000) // Cat Mss Pix
Budget: ($7408)
Notes: Jensen Family Papers (about 3000 leaves) consisting of letters, journals, original watercolors, are the papers of a pioneer German family (Jensen-Hensen) who settled in the 1860s in the Hayward-Castro Valley, Calif, area. Covering the approx period 1830-1920, the collection incl both sides of the correspondence, a large part of which is written in German script. Noncirculating.

JEROME, ARIZONA

AZ —NORTHERN ARIZONA UNIVERSITY, Special Collection Library, CU Box 6022, Flagstaff, 86011. Peter M Whiteley, Coordr/Archivist; William Mullane, Librn
Notes: Various collections, incl (1) J P Connolly Collection; Home Owners Loan Corporation, Jerome, Ariz. Incl bank statements, correspondence, 1920's-1940's and photos of appraised buildings in Jerome and the Verde Valley, 1930's. (2) Hotel Sullivan, Jerome, Ariz, Collection; financial records, 1917-1931, 1943. Hotel register, 1916-1917. Also incl some records of the Yavapai Drug Store of Jerome, 1927-1932. (3) Jerome and Prescott Stage Line Collection; page from ledger in account with United Verde Copper Company, 1891. (4) Jerome Fire Collection; letter written by H J Allen to W A Clark concerning the fire in Jerome in 1898. (5) Jerome Public Library Collection; Shea Copper Company, Jerome, Ariz; records, 1916-1920's, incl payroll and stockholders records. (6) Herbert V Young Collection (historian, Jerome); typescript of published books: *They Came to* Jerome(1972) and *Ghosts of Cleopatra Hill* (1964). (7) Joe Larson Collection; correspondence and files concerning mining in Jerome, Ariz, 1897, 1950's. Incl the files on the Calumet and Jerome Copper Companies and the United Verde Extension Copper Company. Correspondents incl Lewis and James Douglas. (8) Perry Ling Collection; correspondence and files relating to Jerome and the Verde Valley, 1917-1940's. Incl records of the "Town of Jerome," Verde Valley Game Protection Association, Shea Copper Company, and United Verde Extension Mining Company.

JEROME, JUDSON

MA —BOSTON UNIVERSITY, Mugar Memorial Library, Special Collections Dept, 771 Commonwealth Ave, Boston, 02215. Howard B Gotlieb, Dir
Holdings: Cat Mss Pix
Notes: Mss, correspondence, etc collected in depth; incl publications by or about.

JEROME, LEONARD

DC —GEORGETOWN UNIVERSITY, Library, Special Collections Div, 37 & O Sts NW, Washington, 20057. George M Barringer, Special Collections Librn; Nicholas B Sheetz, Mss Librn
Holdings: Mss Cat Pix
Notes: The papers of the Irish man-of-letters Sir Shane Leslie (1885-1971) containing letters, mss, diaries, notebooks, clippings, and photographs. Extensive correspondence by Margot Asquith, countess of Oxford and Asquith; Lady Violet Bonham-Carter; Burke Cochran; Lord Alfred Douglas; Moreton Frewen; Cardinal Gasquet; Vyvyan Holland; Lady Leonie Leslie; Sir Wilfrid Meynell; Sir Horace Plunkett; John Quinn; Frederick Rolfe (Baron Corvo); and Elizabeth Russell, among others. Also incl are research files on Sir Winston Churchill (Leslie's first cousin); Leonard Jerome; Maria Anne Fitzherbet (wife of King George IV); Ghosts and Ghost stories; and Eton College.

JEROME STATE HISTORIC PARK

AZ —NORTHERN ARIZONA UNIVERSITY, Special Collection Library, CU Box 6022, Flagstaff, 86011. Peter M Whiteley, Coordr/Archivist; William Mullane, Librn
Notes: United Verde Copper Company and Phelps Dodge mining record books and files of day-to-day mining operations, 1900-1952. Also incl inquest files of Jerome Precinct Justice of the Peace, 1932-1947. Inventory available.

JERVIS, JOHN B.

NY —JERVIS PUBLIC LIBRARY, 613 N Washington St, Rome, 13440. William A Dillon, Dir
Holdings: Vols (1500) // Cat Mss Maps Slides
Notes: John Bloomfield Jervis Collection contains personal library (1500 vols) and papers (1300 items) of chief engineer of Croton aqueduct and other waterworks, canals, and railroads circa 1825-1860. Papers available from Jervis Public Library.

JESSUP, RICHARD

MA —BOSTON UNIVERSITY, Mugar Memorial Library, Special Collections Dept, 771 Commonwealth Ave, Boston, 02215. Howard B Gotlieb, Dir
Holdings: Cat Mss Pix
Notes: Mss, correspondence, etc collected in depth; incl publications by or about.

JEST-BOOKS see Chapbooks; Wit and Humor

JESTS see Wit and Humor

JESUIT 'RELATIONS'

IL —LOYOLA UNIVERSITY OF CHICAGO, E M Cudahy Memorial Library, 6525 N Sheridan Rd, Chicago, 60626.
Notes: Incl books by and about Jesuits, 16th-18th centuries, province catalogs and *Jesuit* Relations. Emphasis on theological topics.

JESUIT 'RELATIONS' (cont.)

Some items in main collection and others to be used under the direct supervision of a librarian at all times.

IN —INDIANA HISTORICAL SOCIETY, Library, 315 W Ohio St, Indianapolis, 46202. Robert K O'Neill, Dir
Notes: Incl rare books, mss, pictures, maps, and ephemera relating to the history of Indiana and the Old Northwest. Mss dealing with the Old Northwest, incl a large collection of William Henry Harrison materials; papers of leading nineteenth-century Indiana figures; letters of Civil War soldiers; records of twentieth-century social welfare organizations. Rare books collection incl Jesuit *Relations,* early travel accounts, and early Indiana imprints. Pictures incl Indiana small-town life; Monon Railroad Collection; Callis Steamboat Collection, dealing with Terre Haute. Maps of Indiana; Sanborn real estate atlases for Indianapolis. Special collections in Indiana black, ethnic, and architectural history.

MA —BOSTON COLLEGE LIBRARIES, Thomas P O'Neill Library, Chestnut Hill, 02167. Frank J Seegraber, Special Collections Librn
Holdings: Vols (1500) Cat
Notes: Jesuitana Collection of early and rare works by and about Jesuits, 1540-1773. Incl annual letters from Jesuit missionaries in the Far East, Jesuit missionary activities in the New World, anti-Jesuit materials. Complete set of *Jesuit Relations.* For reference use only, by arrangement with librarian.

MI —DETROIT PUBLIC LIBRARY, Burton Historical Collection, 5201 Woodward Ave, Detroit, 48202. Alice Dalligan, Chief

MN —UNIVERSITY OF MINNESOTA, James Ford Bell Library, 309 19th Ave S, Minneapolis, 55455. John Parker, Cur
Holdings: Vols (11,000) Cat Mss Maps
Notes: Collection of original materials relating to European expansion, 1400-1800.

NY —NEW YORK STATE LIBRARY, State Education Bldg Annex, Washington Ave, Albany, 12224.
Holdings: Cat
Notes: 33 vols of original relations.

NY —NEW YORK PUBLIC LIBRARY, Rare Books and Manuscripts Div, Fifth Ave & 42 St, New York, 10018. William L Joyce, Asst Dir; Francis O Mattson, Curator
Holdings: Cat
Budget: ($7161)
Notes: Incl one of the most extensive collections of De Bry and Hulsius and one of the finest sets of Canadian Jesuit Relations. Most editions of Columbus' "Letter."

PA —UNIVERSITY OF PENNSYLVANIA, Van Pelt Library, Rare Books Collection, 34 & Walnut Sts, Philadelphia, 19104. Daniel Traister, Special Collections Librn
Holdings: Vols 2500//
Notes: Robert Dechert Collection: early exploration, 17th and 18th centuries; western Americana, 19th century; Canadiana, incl Jesuit relations.

RI —BROWN UNIVERSITY, John Carter Brown Library, Providence, 02912. Norman Fiering, Librn; Everett C Wilkie Jr, Bibliographer; Susan Danforth, Cur Maps & Prints
Notes: Nearly complete holdings of "Jesuit relations" before 1800.
See also entry under Jesuits.

VT —SAINT MICHAEL'S COLLEGE, Durick Library, Winooski, 05404. Joseph Popecki, Dir; Henry Nadeau, Head of Archives & Special Collections
Holdings: Vols (5000) Cat
Notes: French Canadian generalogy, Irish genealogy, art, a complete set of Jesuit Relations and allied documents with a deluxe binding.

ON —METROPOLITAN TORONTO LIBRARY, Canadian History Dept, Baldwin Room Section, 789 Yonge St, Toronto, M4W 2G8, Can. David B Kotin, Head
Holdings: Vols (52,000) Mss Pix
Notes: This collection consists of material on Canadian history, geography, travel, archaeology, genealogy, retrospective city and telephone directories, collective biographies, native peoples (excluding customs, rights and social conditions), Arctic regions, military history and theory. It is an extremely strong collection of both current and retrospective material. Particular strengths are national and local history (especially Ontario), Arctic regions, native peoples, travel (especially Ontario), and military history. Incl 78,000 historical pictures, 235 linear meters mss, 14,000 broadsides and 3800 bound newspapers.

JESUITS

DC —GEORGETOWN UNIVERSITY, Library, Special Collections Div, 37 & O Sts NW, Washington, 20057. George M Barringer, Special Collections Librn; Nicholas B Sheetz, Mss Librn
Holdings: Cat Mss Pix
Notes: Incl runs of Province catalogs; works by Jesuit authors; works about or against the order. A collection of typescripts containing Fr Repetti's unpublished history of the Society of Jesus in the Philippines, 1589-1615; with other ms material and correspondence dealing with Fr Repetti's researches in Philippine Jesuit and seismological history and on the life of Pye Neale.

IL —LOYOLA UNIVERSITY OF CHICAGO, E M Cudahy Memorial Library, 6525 N Sheridan Rd, Chicago, 60626.
Notes: Source materials of Jesuit history of the Middle US. Collected, organized, cataloged and published by the Institute of Jesuit History.

IL —NEWBERRY LIBRARY, 60 W Walton St, Chicago, 60610. Diana Haskell, Cur of Modern Mss
Holdings: Cat
Notes: Missions, particularly in North America, but also in the Orient, 16th-19th centuries.

IN —INDIANA UNIVERSITY, Lilly Library, Seventh St, Bloomington, 47405. William R Cagle, Librn
Holdings: Vols (2000) // Cat Mss
Notes: The core of the collection is the specialized library of Charles R Boxer (1000 titles) dealing with the history of the Iberians in the East, 16th-18th century. Mainly incl works on China, Japan and the Philippines during the period of their early intercourse with the West through 1800, as well as materials on the English and Dutch East India Companies, and the 17th century Anglo-Dutch naval wars. Special mention should be made of the valuable letters from missions by the Jesuits, and the works in this area by the Augustinians, Franciscans, and Dominicans, from the time of the arrival of the Iberians in Asia. The collection is a valuable source of information for the study of the European expansion into the area, including Southeast Asia. Ms collections include materials by and about Jesuitsin Latin America and the Philippines.

MD —JOHNS HOPKINS UNIVERSITY, Milton S Eisenhower Library, George Peabody Collection, 17 E Mt Vernon Place, Baltimore, 21201. Lyn Hart, Peabody Librn
Notes: Emphasis on materials published before 1950. Strength is a good collection through the 19th century.

MA —BOSTON COLLEGE LIBRARIES, Thomas P O'Neill Library, Chestnut Hill, 02167. Frank J Seegraber, Special Collections Librn
Holdings: Vols (1500) Cat
Notes: Jesuitana Collection of early and rare works by and about Jesuits, 1540-1773. Incl annual letters from Jesuit missionaries in the Far East, Jesuit missionary activities in the New World, anti-Jesuit materials. Complete set of *Jesuit Relations.* For reference use only, by arrangement with librarian.

MA —COLLEGE OF THE HOLY CROSS, Dinand Library, College St, Worcester, 01610. James M Mahoney, Cur of Special Collection
Holdings: Vols 2500 Cat Pix
Notes: Collection contains books by Jesuit authors of the 16th-17th century in the field of belle-letters. Restricted use; noncirculating.

MN —UNIVERSITY OF MINNESOTA, O Meredith Wilson Library, 309 19 Ave S, Minneapolis, 55455. Austin J McLean, Chief, Special Collections
Holdings: Vols 556// Cat
Notes: This collection contains a great number of publications critical of the Jesuits, including histories of the order, edicts and proclamations against them, hundreds of defamatory pamphlets, and other material published in the years just prior to the suppression of the Society in 1773.

MO —SAINT LOUIS UNIVERSITY, Pius XII Memorial Library, Vatican Film Library Collection, 3655 W Pine Blvd, Saint Louis, 63108. Charles J Ermatinger, Librn
Holdings: Mss Slides Microforms
Notes: Vatican Film Library has 75 percent of the Greek, Latin and western European vernacular holdings in the Vatican Library, plus all the Hebrew, Arabic and Ethiopic holdings on film. Covers 5th-19th centuries. Sizable collection of western European books. In addition, has largest collection on the work of the Jesuits in Latin America, the US and the Philippines, filmed from European Jesuit archives. Excellent catalogs and guides to all collections. Also, 50,608 slides of illuminated mss; 26,470 reels of microfilm.

MO —SAINT LOUIS UNIVERSITY, Pius XII Memorial Library, Saint Louis Room Collection, 3655 W Pine Blvd, Saint Louis, 63108. Catherine E Weidle, Rare Books Librn
Holdings: Vols Cat Mss
Notes: Books on early education, Jesuitica and Western Americana. Related collections of works by Peter Ramus (University is center for Ramist studies) and Omer Talon; also collections on the Spiritual Exercises of St Ignatius Loyola and on the Sodality of Our Lady. Mss uncataloged.

RI —BROWN UNIVERSITY, John Carter Brown Library, Providence, 02912. Norman Fiering, Librn; Everett C Wilkie Jr, Bibliographer; Susan Danforth, Cur Maps & Prints
Notes: Extensive holdings of Jesuit letters from missions and ecclesiatical histories of Jesuit activities in the New World.
See also entry under Jesuit Relations.

†WA —WASHINGTON STATE UNIVERSITY, Library, Manuscripts, Archives & Special Collections, Pullman, 99164. John F Guido, Head
Holdings: // Cat Mss Maps
Notes: Regla, Counts of: The papers of the Romero de Terreros family, to whom were granted the titles of Regla, San Cristoval, and San Francisco, include wills, deeds, titles, property maps, litigation over such things as sheep walks, water rights, and the titles themselves. Incl also is much detailed correspondence between hacienda administrators and the family concerning weather, crops, and commodity prices. Several large vols, bound in 1783, document the history of land acquisitions by the Jesuit Colegio Maximo de San Pedro y San Pablo of Mexico City, especially the hacienda of Santa Lucia, from 1576 to the time of the Expulsion. Other early papers deal with the holdings and genealogy of the Marquisates of Salinas, Salvatierra, and Santiago. Described by J Horace Nunemaker in the *Hispanic American Historical Review* (August 1945) 25:409; and by Jacquelyn M Gaines in*Three Centuries of the Ragla* Papers (Pullman, Washington, 1963).

ON —ONTARIO MINISTRY OF TOURISM & RECREATION, Huronia Historical Resource Centre, PO Box 160, Midland, L4R 4K8, Can. M Quealey, Supervisor, Library Services
Holdings: Vols 11,000 Cat Mss Maps Pix Slides Phonorecords Audiotapes Filmstrips Microforms Videotapes
Notes: Reference collection; interlibrary loan; non-circulating. Research facility for reconstruction of historic sites: Historic Naval and Military Establishments, 19th century British base on the Great Lakes; and Sainte-Marie among the Hurons, an early 17th century French Jesuit mission to the Huron Indians. Also, local history collection

JESUITS (cont.)

and archaeological reports for Simcor County, Ont, Canada.

JESUITS IN THE U.S.

DC —GEORGETOWN UNIVERSITY, Library, Special Collections Div, 37 & O Sts NW, Washington, 20057. George M Barringer, Special Collections Librn; Nicholas B Sheetz, Mss Librn
Holdings: Vols (500) Cat Mss Maps Pix Slides
Notes: Includes the archives of Woodstock College (1866-); seminary of the Maryland Province, on deposit; the archives (1640-) of the Maryland Province of the Society of Jesus, on deposit; personal papers of Revs John LaFarge, SJ, Wilfrid Parsons, SJ, Edmund A Walsh, SJ, among others. In the Woodstock archives are included papers of Revs John Courtney Murray, SJ, and Gustave Weigel, SJ. Also present are editorial files (1900-1920, incomplete later) of *America* magazine.

JESUS, SOCIETY OF see Jesuits

JESUS CHRIST

CA —WESTMONT COLLEGE, Roger John Voskuyl Library, Santa Barbara, 93108. John D Murray, Librn
Holdings: Cat Microforms
Notes: The Christ and Culture Collection contains materials which express and illustrate the interaction between Christian faith (as both faith and life, doctrine and practice) and the liberal arts and sciences.

MD —JOHNS HOPKINS UNIVERSITY, Milton S Eisenhower Library, George Peabody Collection, 17 E Mt Vernon Place, Baltimore, 21201. Lyn Hart, Peabody Librn
Notes: Christology. Noncirculating.

JESUS CHRIST—BIRTH see Virgin Birth

JESUS CHRIST—SECOND ADVENT see Second Advent

JEWELRY

CA —CALIFORNIA COLLEGE OF ARTS & CRAFTS, Meyer Library, Broadway at College, Oakland, 94618. Robert L Harper, Head Librn
Notes: All fields of arts and crafts, incl art metal work.

IN —ALLEN COUNTY PUBLIC LIBRARY, 900 Webster St, Fort Wayne, 46802. Paul Deane, Reader Services Dept Head; Kay Lynn Isca, Art Music & AV Dept Head
Holdings: Vols 1257 Cat Pix

†MA —MELROSE PUBLIC LIBRARY, 63 W Emerson St, Melrose, 02176. Diane E Shaw, Art Librn
Holdings: Vols (8500) Cat Pix Slides Phonorecords
Budget: ($6900)
Notes: Framed and unframed art reproductions (110), slides (2773), periodicals, clippings, sound recordings (3000). Incl the Mary Livermore Collection of Sacred Art, the Odlin Collection and the Pierre Gendrot Collection of Fine Art.

NY —NEW YORK PUBLIC LIBRARY, Art, Prints, and Photographs Div, Fifth Ave & 42 St, New York, 10018. Donald Anderle, Chief
Holdings: Vols (150,000) Cat Mss Pix Microforms
Notes: History and design in the fine and applied arts. Architecture, painting, drawing, sculpture, costume, furniture, advertising art, prints, photography, crafts, and jewelry are among the subjects covered from ancient times to the present. See: New York Public Library *Dictionary Catalog of the Art and Architecture Division* (Boston, G K Hall, 1975), 30 vols. Holdings after that time are incl in the *Dictionary Catalog of the Research Libraries.* African Art and Afro-American Art are collected by the Schomburg Center for Research in Black Culture.

RI —PROVIDENCE PUBLIC LIBRARY, 150 Empire St, Providence, 02903. Lance J Bauer, Special Collections Librn
Holdings: Vols 122 // Cat
Notes: Works dating from 1670 on the history, lore and legends of precious stones, and the history and practice of jewelry and silversmithing. Restricted use.

RI —RHODE ISLAND SCHOOL OF DESIGN, Library, Two College St, Providence, 02903. James A Findlay, Dir
Holdings: Vols (70,000) Cat Pix Slides
Budget: ($50,000)

WI —MILWAUKEE PUBLIC LIBRARY, 814 W Wisconsin Ave, Milwaukee, 53233. Donald J Sager, City Librn
Holdings: Vols Cat
Notes: Strength in American and European decorative arts incl ceramics, glassware, jewelry, porcelain, silverware, furniture, interior decoration, textile arts and handicraft.
See also entry under Art, Decorative.

AB —SOUTHERN ALBERTA INSTITUTE OF TECHNOLOGY, Learning Resources Centre, 1301 16 Ave NW, Calgary, T2M 0L4, Can. Tom Skinner, Historian
Holdings: Vols (5000) Cat Pix Slides Films Audiotapes Filmstrips Videotapes
Notes: Serves Alberta College of Art (4-year professional course).

JEWELS see Insignia; Jewelry

JEWETT, SARAH ORNE, 1849-1909

ME —PORTLAND PUBLIC LIBRARY, 5 Monument Sq, Portland, 04101. Edward V Chenevert, Library Dir
Holdings: Vols 53 // Cat
Notes: Incl fiction, letters and poetry by Sarah Orne Jewett.

MA —HARVARD UNIVERSITY LIBRARY, Houghton Library, Cambridge, 02138. F Thomas Noonan, Cur, Reading Room; Lawrence Dowler, Associate Librn
Holdings: Cat Mss
Notes: Described in *Harvard Alumni* Bulletin, XXXV (1933), 474-476.

VA —UNIVERSITY OF VIRGINIA, Alderman Library, Clifton Waller Barrett Collection, Charlottesville, 22901. Joan St C Crane, Cur of American Literature Collections
Notes: Papers.

WI —UNIVERSITY OF WISCONSIN, MADISON, Memorial Library, British & American Language & Literature Collection, 728 State St, Madison, 53706. Yvonne Schofer, Bibliographer
Holdings: Vols 2200 Mss Microforms Documents Periodicals
Notes: A collection of primary and secondary materials for nine major American women writers: Anne Bradstreet; Louisa May Alcott, Emily Dickinson, Kate Chopin, Mary Williams Freeman, Margaret Fuller, Sarah Orne Jewett, Charlotte Perkins Gilman, Harriet Beecher Stowe. Primary materials also collected for a list of less well known authors together with manuscripts and archives of letters of special research interest. Variety of holdings: fiction, poetry, drama, biography and autobiography, letters, memoirs, diaries, travel, domestic economy and other kinds of writings by women mostly of the 19th century. Held in Dept of Rare Books and Special Collections.

JEWETT CITY COTTON MANUFACTURING COMPANY

CT —UNIVERSITY OF CONNECTICUT, Historical Manuscripts and Archives Division, Box U-205, Storrs, 06268. Randall Jimerson, Librn
Holdings: Mss
Notes: The business records of Jewett City Cotton Mfg Co founded in 1810 and later purchased by John and Samuel Slater in 1825.

JEWISH-ARAB RELATIONS

MA —HARVARD UNIVERSITY, Center for Middle Eastern Studies, Library, Coolidge Hall, 1737 Cambridge St, Cambridge, 02138. Barbara Mitchell, Librn
Holdings: Vols (5000) Periodicals
Notes: Some history of countries of the Middle East; increasingly emphasizes culture and politics of the current Middle Eastern area. Special collection of Energy Economics Research. Library currently receives 15 periodical titles.

JEWISH ART see Art, Jewish

JEWISH ARTISTS see Artists, Jewish

JEWISH AUTHORS see Authors, Jewish

JEWISH BOOKS AND RECORDINGS FOR THE BLIND

NY —JEWISH BRAILLE INSTITUTE OF AMERICA, 110 E 30St, New York, 10016. Richard Borgersen, Library Dir
Holdings: Vols (50,000) Cat Audiotapes
Budget: ($75,000)
Notes: A worldwide circulating library of English and Hebrew Braille, English, Hebrew and Yiddish tape talking books and English and Hebrew large type books. All books sent free of charge. Loan period 90 days.

JEWISH-CHRISTIAN RELATIONS

NY —NEW YORK PUBLIC LIBRARY, Jewish Division, Fifth Ave & 42 St, New York, 10018. Leonard S Gold, Chief
Holdings: Vols (200,000) Cat Mss Microforms
Budget: ($33,383)
Notes: A collection of material in all languages on Judaism, Jewish history, literature and traditions from the earliest times to date and works in the Hebrew alphabet (mainly Hebrew and Yiddish) on a variety of subjects. The division has extensive files of Jewish periodicals and newspapers. The collection of rare Hebraica incl medieval texts, cabalistic works, ethical and philosophical tracts in book form. See *Dictionary Catalog of the Jewish Collection* (Boston: G K Hall, 1960), 14 vols. First Supplement (Boston: G K Hall, 1975), 8 vols.

PA —DUQUESNE UNIVERSITY, Library, Pittsburgh, 15282. Dena F Jacobson, Music and Reference Librn
Holdings: Vols 3000 Cat
Notes: Main emphasis of collection is on history of Jewish philosophy in the Middle Ages and relationship between Jewish and Christian scholars; collection incl works by 14th century writer Nicolas de Lyra and general Judaica, history of the Jews, theology, Bible texts and commentaries, literature, grammatical works and dictionaries, etc.

JEWISH CONVERTS TO CHRISTIANITY see Converts From Judaism

JEWISH FOLKLORE see Folklore, Jewish

JEWISH HOLOCAUST, 1939-1945 see Holocaust, Jewish, 1939-1945

JEWISH LABOR BOARD

†NY —BUND ARCHIVES OF THE JEWISH LABOR MOVEMENT, 25 East 78 St, New York, 10021.
Notes: History of the Jewish labor movement, labor movement in Eastern Europe, socialism, Yiddish culture, history of the Jewish Labor Bund.

JEWISH LAW

FL —UNIVERSITY OF FLORIDA LIBRARY, Isser and Rae Price Library of Judaica, 18 Libr East, Gainesville, 32611. Robert Singerman, Head Librn
Budget: ($30,000)
Notes: Total holdings estimated at 55,000 vols dealing with the political, social,

JEWISH LAW (cont.)

economic and intellectual history of the Jews in the ancient, medieval and modern periods and in all geographic areas. The following areas are especially well represented by printed matter in all relevant languages: Bibliography, Festschriften, History, Bible, Judaism and Jewish theology, liturgy, responsa, rabbinical literature, Jewish law, Hebrew language and literature, Yiddish language and literature, anti-semitism, Zionism, Palestine and the *Yishuv*, and the State of Israel. German and American Judaica form a collecting emphasis with holdings for all the standard histories as well as histories of individual synagogues, institutions and local communities. Works in Hebrew and Yiddish comprise about 60 percent of the collection (estimated 30,000 vols). With few exceptions, holdingsare limited to nineteenth and twentieth century imprints, with complete sets of journals and thousands of ephemeral pamphlets, many of them commemorating anniversaries, enhancing the research value of the collection, the largest Judaica research library in the southeastern United States. Only about half of the collection is cataloged; the collection is a circulating one and vols may be borrowed on interlibrary loan. Incl the Leonard C Mishkin Collection (40,000 vols), the largest personal Judaica collection in the United States, the Shlomo Marenof Collection (3500 vols), and the inventory of Bernard Morgenstern's Lower East Side Book Store (8000 vols). Scholars should inquire in advance of their visit. *The Isser and Rae Price Library of Judaica* Report (circulation 2900 copies) is mailed gratis twice a year to all interested parties. Special catalogs:Pre-1881 Hebrew imprints recorded in a chronological card file.

IL —HEBREW THEOLOGICAL COLLEGE, Saul Silber Memorial Library, 7135 N Carpenter Rd, Skokie, 60077. Leah Mishkin, Head Librn/Cur
Holdings: Vols (58,000) Cat Mss Microforms
Notes: Main subject is rabbinics (Halachic literature). We also have a very large and important Holocaust Collection.

MA —HEBREW COLLEGE, Jacob & Rose Grossman Library and Lawrence Jay & Anne Cable Rubenstein Library, 43 Hawes St, Brookline, 02146. Maurice Tuchman, Librn
Holdings: Vols 700 Cat Mss
Notes: Responsa literature.

OH —HEBREW UNION COLLEGE-JEWISH INSTITUTE OF RELIGION, Klau Library, 3101 Clifton Ave, Cincinnati, 45220. David J Gilner, Reference Librn
Holdings: Cat

JEWISH LITERATURE

NY —NEW YORK PUBLIC LIBRARY, Jewish Division, Fifth Ave & 42 St, New York, 10018. Leonard S Gold, Chief
Holdings: Vols (200,000) Cat Mss Microforms
Budget: ($33,383)
Notes: A collection of material in all languages on Judaism, Jewish history, literature and traditions from the earliest times to date and works in the Hebrew alphabet (mainly Hebrew and Yiddish) on a variety of subjects. The division has extensive files of Jewish periodicals and newspapers. The collection of rare Hebraica incl medieval texts, cabalistic works, ethical and philosophical tracts in book form. See *Dictionary Catalog of the Jewish Collection* (Boston: G K Hall, 1960), 14 vols. First Supplement (Boston: G K Hall, 1975), 8 vols.

NY —YIVO INSTITUTE FOR JEWISH RESEARCH, Library & Archives, 1048 Fifth Ave, New York, 10028. Dina Abramowicz, Librn; Marek Web, Archivist
Holdings: Cat Mss Pix

OH —HEBREW UNION COLLEGE-JEWISH INSTITUTE OF RELIGION, Klau Library, 3101 Clifton Ave, Cincinnati, 45220. David J Gilner, Reference Librn
Holdings: Cat

PA —BALCH INSTITUTE FOR ETHNIC STUDIES, Library, 18 S Seventh St, Philadelphia, 19106. R Joseph Anderson, Library Dir
Holdings: Vols 1000
Notes: Much of the collection is in Yiddish.

RI —BROWN UNIVERSITY, John Hay Library, Harris Collection, Prospect St, Providence, 02912. Rosemary L Cullen, Cur
Holdings: Vols (200,000) Cat Mss Pix Phonorecords Microforms
Budget: ($15,000)
Notes: The Harris Collection of American Poetry and Plays is principally composed of American and Canadian poetry and plays from the 17th century to the present. Extensive holdings in Yiddish-American literature, particularly of the late 19th and early 20th centuries. Incl the Vaxer Collection of Yiddish Poetry, Plays and Music (1700 vols), See *Dictionary Catalog of the Harris Collection of American Poetry and Plays* (Boston:G K Hall 1972), 13 vols; Supplement (1977), 3 vols. Separate catalog. Also, a virtually separate complete collection (1500 vols) of the literature dealing with the Legend of the Wandering Jew printed from the 17th century to date. In addition to historical discussion of the legend, there are sections devoted to the appearance of Ahasuerus in drama, fiction, illustrations, poetry, song, and music.

JEWISH MEDICINE see Medicine, Jewish—History and Historic

JEWISH MISSIONS see Missions—Jews

JEWISH MUSIC see Music, Jewish

JEWISH PERIODICALS see Periodicals, Jewish

JEWISH PHILOSOPHY see Philosophy, Jewish

JEWISH QUESTION

AZ —NORTHERN ARIZONA UNIVERSITY, Special Collection Library, CU Box 6022, Flagstaff, 86011. Peter M Whiteley, Coordr/Archivist; William Mullane, Librn
Holdings: Vols 9000 Cat Mss Phonorecords Microforms
Notes: The large Allderdice Collection of thousands of books, pamphlets, periodicals, and organizational files reflects the conservative, communist, socialist, facist, anarchist, and other viewpoints, etc, during the 20th century.

NY —YIVO INSTITUTE FOR JEWISH RESEARCH, Library & Archives, 1048 Fifth Ave, New York, 10028. Dina Abramowicz, Librn; Marek Web, Archivist
Notes: Jews in contemporary world. Anti-semitism. Many periodicals and pamphlets.

OH —HEBREW UNION COLLEGE-JEWISH INSTITUTE OF RELIGION, Klau Library, 3101 Clifton Ave, Cincinnati, 45220. David J Gilner, Reference Librn
Holdings: Cat
Notes: Incl extensive collections of Russian and Zionist controversial literature.

JEWISH REFUGEES see Refugees, Jewish

JEWISH SECTS

NY —NEW YORK PUBLIC LIBRARY, Jewish Division, Fifth Ave & 42 St, New York, 10018. Leonard S Gold, Chief
Holdings: Vols (200,000) Cat Mss Microforms
Budget: ($33,383)
Notes: A collection of material in all languages on Judaism, Jewish history, literature and traditions from the earliest times to date and works in the Hebrew alphabet (mainly Hebrew and Yiddish) on a variety of subjects. The division has extensive files of Jewish periodicals and newspapers. The collection of rare Hebraica incl medieval texts, cabalistic works, ethical and philosophical tracts in book form. See *Dictionary Catalog of the Jewish Collection* (Boston: G K Hall, 1960), 14 vols. First Supplement (Boston: G K Hall, 1975), 8 vols.

OH —HEBREW UNION COLLEGE-JEWISH INSTITUTE OF RELIGION, Klau Library, 3101 Clifton Ave, Cincinnati, 45220. David J Gilner, Reference Librn
Holdings: Cat

†PA —DROPSIE UNIVERSITY, Library, Broad & York Sts, Philadelphia, 19132.

JEWISH SYMBOLISM AND ART see Art, Jewish

JEWS

CA —JUDAH L MAGNES MEMORIAL MUSEUM, Morris Goldstein Library, 2911 Russell St, Berkeley, 94705. Jane Levy, Archivist
Holdings: Vols 7000 Cat Mss Maps Pix Slides Audiotapes Microforms
See also entry under Jews - History

CA —LOS ANGELES PUBLIC LIBRARY, Philosophy & Religion Dept, 630 W Fifth St, Los Angeles, 90071. Marilyn C Wherley, Librn
Holdings: Vols 2000 Cat
Budget: ($60,000)
Notes: Popular and scholarly archeological material and biographical material on this ethnic group in Biblical and early modern times. Does not include the holocaust or the modern state of Israel. Emphasis on Jews and Judaism in the United States.

CA —UNIVERSITY OF CALIFORNIA, LOS ANGELES, Research Library, Jewish Studies Collection, 405 Hilgard Ave, Los Angeles, 90024. Edward Shreeves, Chairman, Bibliographers Group; Shimeon Brisman, Jewish Studies Bibliographer
Holdings: Vols (100,000) Cat Mss Microforms

FL —UNIVERSITY OF FLORIDA LIBRARY, Isser and Rae Price Library of Judaica, 18 Libr East, Gainesville, 32611. Robert Singerman, Head Librn
Budget: ($30,000)
Notes: Total holdings estimated at 55,000 vols dealing with the political, social, economic and intellectual history of the Jews in the ancient, medieval and modern periods and in all geographic areas. The following areas are especially well represented by printed matter in all relevant languages: Bibliography, Festschriften, History, Bible, Judaism and Jewish theology, liturgy, responsa, rabbinical literature, Jewish law, Hebrew language and literature, Yiddish language and literature, anti-semitism, Zionism, Palestine and the *Yishuv*, and the State of Israel. German and American Judaica form a collecting emphasis with holdings for all the standard histories as well as histories of individual synagogues, institutions and local communities. Works in Hebrew and Yiddish comprise about 60 percent of the collection (estimated 30,000 vols). With few exceptions, holdingsare limited to nineteenth and twentieth century imprints, with complete sets of journals and thousands of ephemeral pamphlets, many of them commemorating anniversaries, enhancing the research value of the collection, the largest Judaica research library in the southeastern United States. Only about half of the collection is cataloged; the collection is a circulating one and vols may be borrowed on interlibrary loan. Incl the Leonard C Mishkin Collection (40,000 vols), the largest personal Judaica collection in the United States, the Shlomo Marenof Collection (3500 vols), and the inventory of Bernard Morgenstern's Lower East Side Book Store (8000 vols). Scholars should inquire in advance of their visit. *The Isser and Rae Price Library of Judaica* Report (circulation 2900 copies) is mailed gratis twice a year to all interested parties. Special catalogs:Pre-1881 Hebrew imprints recorded in a chronological card file.

IL —ILLINOIS STATE UNIVERSITY, Milner Library, Dept of Special Collections, Normal, 61761. Robert Sokan, Librn
Holdings: Vols 2100 // Uncat
Notes: Sigmund Livingston Collection on

JEWS (cont.)

Intergroup Relations, 1944 to the present. The material is divided into subject headings which contain pamphlets, newsletters and commission reports.

MA —BRANDEIS UNIVERSITY, Goldfarb Library, 415 South St, Waltham, 02154. Bessie Hahn, Dir
Budget:
Notes: Jewish Resistance Collection. Contains 21 linear feet of books, periodical articles and contemporary ephemera emphasizing the role Jews played in armed resistance to the Nazi regime. A catalog of the books is in the Special Collections Catalog and Main Card Catalog.

NY —NEW YORK PUBLIC LIBRARY, Jewish Division, Fifth Ave & 42 St, New York, 10018. Leonard S Gold, Chief
Holdings: Vols (200,000) Cat Mss Microforms
Budget: ($33,383)
Notes: A collection of material in all languages on Judaism, Jewish history, literature and traditions from the earliest times to date and works in the Hebrew alphabet (mainly Hebrew and Yiddish) on a variety of subjects. The division has extensive files of Jewish periodicals and newspapers. The collection of rare Hebraica incl medieval texts, cabalistic works, ethical and philosophical tracts in book form. See *Dictionary Catalog of the Jewish Collection* (Boston: G K Hall, 1960), 14 vols. First Supplement (Boston: G K Hall, 1975), 8 vols.

OH —HEBREW UNION COLLEGE-JEWISH INSTITUTE OF RELIGION, Klau Library, 3101 Clifton Ave, Cincinnati, 45220. David J Gilner, Reference Librn
Holdings: Cat Mss
Notes: Over 250,000 items on every phase of Jewish life, worldwide.

†PA —DROPSIE UNIVERSITY, Library, Broad & York Sts, Philadelphia, 19132.

PA —FREE LIBRARY OF PHILADELPHIA, Education, Philosophy and Religion Department, Logan Sq, Philadelphia, 19103. Esther J Maurer, Head
Holdings: Vols 2200// Cat
Notes: Judaica and Hebraica library formerly owned by Moses Marx. Contains source material on local German-Jewish communities pre-World War II. Bibliographies, festschiften and works on liturgy are notable. Most of the collection is in German and Hebrew. Also incl books in French, Latin and Spanish.

PA —UNIVERSITY OF PITTSBURGH, Hillman Library, Pittsburgh, 15260. Glenora E Rossell, Head
Holdings: Vols (3500) cat
Notes: Most of the collection on Judaism is in the English, French, and German languages. There are a few Hebrew titles. It contains Jewish reference works and materials on all subjects relating to Jews and Judaism--history, religion, sociology, and philosophy. The collection is integrated into the general library catalog.

TX —ABILENE CHRISTIAN UNIVERSITY, Margaret & Herman Brown Library, ACU Sta, Abilene, 79601. Callie Faye Milliken, Assoc Dir
Holdings: Vols 5000 // Cat
Notes: Donner Library of Americanism. Books, pamphlets, documents, and periodical materials dealing with American politics of the far right collected by Robert Donner during and after World War II. Also incl materials on Jews and Freemasonry.

JEWS—CABALA see Cabala

JEWS—CONVERTS TO CHRISTIANITY see Converts From Judaism

JEWS—CUSTOMS see Jews—Social Life and Customs

JEWS—EDUCATION

MA —HEBREW COLLEGE, Jacob & Rose Grossman Library and Lawrence Jay & Anne Cable Rubenstein Library, 43 Hawes St, Brookline, 02146. Maurice Tuchman, Librn
Holdings: Vols 2000 Cat Maps Slides
Notes: The Herman and Peggy Vershbow Pedagogic Center.

NY —YIVO INSTITUTE FOR JEWISH RESEARCH, Library & Archives, 1048 Fifth Ave, New York, 10028. Dina Abramowicz, Librn; Marek Web, Archivist
Holdings: Cat Mss Pix Slides
Notes: Emphasis is on immigration history. Incl archives of Jewish organizations which served immigrant masses, such as Educational Alliance, Hias, Hicem, Jewish Desertion Bureau and others. Yiddish language general and labor periodicals in originals and on microfilm. The Yiddish school movement in the US is covered, as well as other cultural activities in the field of the Yiddish theatre, Literature and the arts. Correspondence of outstanding authors with parties in the US and abroad is an important source of information on Yiddish cultural life and communal affairs.

JEWS—FOLKLORE see Folklore, Jewish

JEWS—HISTORY

CA —JUDAH L MAGNES MEMORIAL MUSEUM, Morris Goldstein Library, 2911 Russell St, Berkeley, 94705. Jane Levy, Archivist
Holdings: Vols 7000 Cat Mss Maps Pix Slides Audiotapes Microforms
Notes: Most of our special collections have been deposited in our archives by Western Jewish families or institutions. The collection focuses on the contribution of Western Jews and Jewish institutions (California, Nevada, Oregon, Utah, Washington, Colorado, Texas, New Mexico, Arizona, etc, incl some material from Canada, Mexico, and Latin America) to the cultural, intellectual, commercial, civic, etc growth of the American West. 135 ms collections. The collection is cataloged, many of the documents being indexed and inventoried. The collection has been noted in the Western Jewish History Center's published bibliographies by Sara Cogan, *Pioneer Jews of the California Mother Lode* and *The Jews of San Francisco and the Greater Bay Area, 1849-1919*; also, *A Selective History of San Francisco Eastern European Jewish Life, 1880-1940*, by RuthKelson Rafael (Berkeley: Magnes Museum, 1976; rev 1977); *Catalog of Manuscripts Collections in the Western Jewish History Center, Judah L Magnes Memorial Museum, Berkeley*, by Suzanne Nemiroff (Berkeley: Magnes Museum, 1977); and *Catalog of Western Jewish Periodicals, 1849-1945, at the Western Jewish History Center* by Suzanne Nemiroff (Berkeley: Magnes Museum, 1976).

CA —STANFORD UNIVERSITY LIBRARIES, Cecil H Green Library, Stanford, 94305. Peter R Frank, Cur, CDP-Germanic Collection
Notes: Strong collection on important aspects of Jewish history and culture in the German area (Germany, the Austrian Empire and Austria, German part of Switzerland). Emphasis on the period from Enlightenment up to the present. Also sizeable collection of Anti-Semitica. Rare items in the Stanford Collection of German, Austrian and Swiss Culture, Special Collections.

†CT —YALE UNIVERSITY, Library, Box 1603A, Yale Station, New Haven, 06520.
Notes: A collection of more than 200 videotaped interviews with survivors of the Holocaust.

FL —UNIVERSITY OF FLORIDA LIBRARY, Isser and Rae Price Library of Judaica, 18 Libr East, Gainesville, 32611. Robert Singerman, Head Librn
Budget: ($30,000)
Notes: Total holdings estimated at 55,000 vols dealing with the political, social, economic and intellectual history of the Jews in the ancient, medieval and modern periods and in all geographic areas. The following areas are especially well represented by printed matter in all relevant languages: Bibliography, Festschriften, History, Bible, Judaism and Jewish theology, liturgy, responsa, rabbinical literature, Jewish law, Hebrew language and literature, Yiddish language and literature, anti-semitism, Zionism, Palestine and the *Yishuv*, and the State of Israel. German and American Judaica form a collecting emphasis with holdings for all the standard histories as well as histories of individual synagogues, institutions and local communities. Works in Hebrew and Yiddish comprise about 60 percent of the collection (estimated 30,000 vols). With few exceptions, holdingsare limited to nineteenth and twentieth century imprints, with complete sets of journals and thousands of ephemeral pamphlets, many of them commemorating anniversaries, enhancing the research value of the collection, the largest Judaica research library in the southeastern United States. Only about half of the collection is cataloged; the collection is a circulating one and vols may be borrowed on interlibrary loan. Incl the Leonard C Mishkin Collection (40,000 vols), the largest personal Judaica collection in the United States, the Shlomo Marenof Collection (3500 vols), and the inventory of Bernard Morgenstern's Lower East Side Book Store (8000 vols). Scholars should inquire in advance of their visit. *The Isser and Rae Price Library of Judaica* Report (circulation 2900 copies) is mailed gratis twice a year to all interested parties. Special catalogs:Pre-1881 Hebrew imprints recorded in a chronological card file.

IL —UNIVERSITY OF CHICAGO LIBRARY, Dept of Special Collections, 1100 E 57 St, Chicago, 60637.
Notes: Ludwig Rosenberger Library of Judaica. Covers history of Jewish social and political thought from 1200 to the present.

IA —UNIVERSITY OF IOWA, University Libraries, Iowa City, 52242.
Holdings: Vols 1850 Mss
Notes: The Leo W Schwarz Collection, a valuable and rare group of books dealing with Hasidic literature, a portion on Old Testament studies and works on Jewish history, philosophy and culture, the Jews in Nazi Germany, Jewish folklore and the history of the Jews in the US. Incl about 850 books in Hebrew and 1000 in other languages, mss of several of Schwarz's books and articles, correspondence, notes, and background research relating to his publications.

MA —HEBREW COLLEGE, Jacob & Rose Grossman Library and Lawrence Jay & Anne Cable Rubenstein Library, 43 Hawes St, Brookline, 02146. Maurice Tuchman, Librn
Notes: Jewish history, Hebrew literature, Israel Rabbinic literature.

MA —BRANDEIS UNIVERSITY, Goldfarb Library, 415 South St, Waltham, 02154. Bessie Hahn, Dir
Notes: Consistoire Israelite Archives contains 12 linear ft of original documents relating to the French-Jewish community from the 18th to 20th century. A finding list of the documents is in Special Collections. Also, the Jewish Resistance Collection. Contains 21 linear feet of books, periodical articles and contemporary ephemera emphasizing the role Jews played in armed resistance to the Nazi regime. A catalog of the books is in the Special Collections Catalog and Main Card Catalog.

†NY —ANTI-DEFAMATION LEAGUE OF B'NAI B'RITH, 823 United Nations Plaza, New York, 10017.

NY —HEBREW UNION COLLEGE, Jewish Institute of Religion, Klau Library, 1 W 4th St, New York, 10012. Philip Miller, Librn
Holdings: Vols (115,000) Cat Mss Microforms
Notes: Hebrew literature--ancient, medieval and modern.

NY —LEO BAECK INSTITUTE, Library, 129 E 73 St, New York, 10021. Fred Grubel, Secretary & Dir
Holdings: Vols (50,000)
Notes: History and philosophy of European German-speaking Jewry, 18th to 20th

JEWS—HISTORY (cont.)

century. Publications: LBI Archives and Library News, free, 2 issues a year. Provides an update of collections. Also, LBI News incl more general info for members only. $35.00 per year dues.

NY —NEW YORK PUBLIC LIBRARY, Jewish Division, Fifth Ave & 42 St, New York, 10018. Leonard S Gold, Chief
Holdings: Vols (200,000) Cat Mss Microforms
Budget: ($33,383)
Notes: A collection of material in all languages on Judaism, Jewish history, literature and traditions from the earliest times to date and works in the Hebrew alphabet (mainly Hebrew and Yiddish) on a variety of subjects. The division has extensive files of Jewish periodicals and newspapers. The collection of rare Hebraica incl medieval texts, cabalistic works, ethical and philosophical tracts in book form. See *Dictionary Catalog of the Jewish Collection* (Boston: G K Hall, 1960), 14 vols. First Supplement (Boston: G K Hall, 1975), 8 vols.

†NY —WORLD ZIONIST ORGANIZATION - AMERICAN SECTION, Zionist Archives and Library, 515 Park Ave, New York, 10022.
Notes: Israel, Zionism, Middle East, history of the Jews and Jewish life.

NY —YESHIVA UNIVERSITY, Library, 500 West 185th Street, New York, 10033. Pearl Berger
Holdings: Cat

NY —YIVO INSTITUTE FOR JEWISH RESEARCH, Library & Archives, 1048 Fifth Ave, New York, 10028. Dina Abramowicz, Librn; Marek Web, Archivist
Holdings: Cat Mss Pix Slides
Notes: Books and periodicals on modern Jewish history with special emphasis on Eastern European history, the mass migration to the US and the Holocaust period. Archives of national Jewish organizations, memoirs, eye-witness reports.

OH —HEBREW UNION COLLEGE-JEWISH INSTITUTE OF RELIGION, Klau Library, 3101 Clifton Ave, Cincinnati, 45220. David J Gilner, Reference Librn
Holdings: Cat Mss

OH —OHIO STATE UNIVERSITY, William Oxley Thompson Memorial Library, 1858 Neil Ave, Columbus, 43210. Amnon Zipin, Jewish Studies Bibliographer
Holdings: Vols (43,000) Cat Maps Microfilms
Budget: ($35,000)
Notes: Collection emphasis is materials on Jewish history (especially US, Israel and Europe) and Hebrew language and literature. Small collection of Yiddish materials.

PA —LIBRARY COMPANY OF PHILADELPHIA, 1314 Locust St, Philadelphia, 19107. Edwin Wolf II, Librn; Kenneth Finkel, Cur of Prints
Notes: The Edwin Wolf Collection of Judaica, consisting of 165 manuscripts and more than 500 books and broadsides printed in the US between 1718 and 1875. Incl literature, prayer books, Hebrew schoolbooks, reports of Jewish organizations, missionary tracts, narratives of travel to Palestine, and books on medicine. Most of the manuscripts consists of correspondence of the Gratz family, American pioneers.

PA —CARNEGIE-MELLON UNIVERSITY, Hunt Library, Schenley Park, Pittsburgh, 15213. Richard L Schoewald, Supvr
Holdings: Vols 700 Cat
Budget: $13,000
Notes: The Hirschfield Judaica Collection. All books are in English. Also Hunt Library Judaica holdings.

PA —DUQUESNE UNIVERSITY, Library, Pittsburgh, 15282. Dena F Jacobson, Music and Reference Librn
Holdings: Vols 3000 Cat
Notes: Main emphasis of collection is on history of Jewish philosophy in the Middle Ages and relationship between Jewish and Christian scholars; collection incl works by 14th century writer Nicolas de Lyra and general Judaica, history of the Jews, theology, Bible texts and commentaries, literature, grammatical works and dictionaries, etc.

TX —UNIVERSITY OF TEXAS, EL PASO, Library, El Paso, 79968. Fred W Hanes, Dir
Holdings: Vols 1730 Cat
Budget: ($5000)
Notes: The Judaica Collection. Jewish history and culture, as well as religion, philosophy and literature are documented by the collection.

TX —FORT WORTH PUBLIC LIBRARY, 300 Taylor St, Fort Worth, 76102. Patricia Chadwell, Social Sciences Librn; Paul Campbell, Librn, History Section
Holdings: Cat
Notes: Collection incl all periods of Jewish history and culture, American and European.

WA —UNIVERSITY OF WASHINGTON LIBRARIES, Suzzallo Library, Manuscripts Section, FM-25, Seattle, 98195. Karyl Winn, Librn
Holdings: Mss Audiotapes
Notes: Personal papers and organizational records of the Jewish population of the greater Seattle, Washington area and to a lesser extent, Washington state. Holdings includes synagogue records, philanthropic and educational organization records, papers of community leaders and families, and recorded interviews. Photographs administered by the Libraries' Pacific Northwest Collection. Many interviews have been transcribed. Inventories for all larger accessions. Includes 260 linear feet of manuscript and 250 audiotapes.

JEWS—LAW see Jewish Law

JEWS—MEDICINE see Medicine, Jewish—History and Historic

JEWS—MISSIONS see Missions—Jews

JEWS—MUSIC see Music, Jewish

JEWS—ORAL HISTORIES

MA —BRANDEIS UNIVERSITY, Goldfarb Library, 415 South St, Waltham, 02154. Bessie Hahn, Dir
Notes: Holocaust Survivors Collection. 20 linear feet of recorded interviews with survivors of the Holocaust, now living in the US. The tapes are not transcribed and the collection is unprocessed, but the tapes are arranged alphabetically by interviewee.

JEWS—PERSECUTIONS

IL —HEBREW THEOLOGICAL COLLEGE, Saul Silber Memorial Library, 7135 N Carpenter Rd, Skokie, 60077. Leah Mishkin, Head Librn/Cur
Holdings: Vols (58,000) Cat Mss Microforms
Notes: Main subject is rabbinics (Halachic literature). We also have a very large and important Holocaust Collection.

MA —BRANDEIS UNIVERSITY, Goldfarb Library, 415 South St, Waltham, 02154. Bessie Hahn, Dir
Notes: Alfred Dreyfus Trial Collection. Approx 1000 books, pamphlets, newspapers and photographs as well as some correspondence of French notables dealing with the Alfred Dreyfus trial at the turn of the century. An author-title card catalog can be found in the Special Collections Card Catalog.

OH —HEBREW UNION COLLEGE-JEWISH INSTITUTE OF RELIGION, Klau Library, 3101 Clifton Ave, Cincinnati, 45220. David J Gilner, Reference Librn
Holdings: Cat
Notes: The Jewish Holocaust (1939-1945) collection. Incl large collections of memorial books, curricula and juvenile fiction.

JEWS—PERSECUTIONS—RUSSIA, 1882

DC —LIBRARY OF CONGRESS, Washington, 20540.
Notes: Project of a consortium to microfilm about 200,000 pp of material on Great Britain, France, Russia and Prussia, for the period 1848-1918 in the ms and documentary collections of the Austrian State Archives. The collection will incl, among others, documents on the Austro-Prussian War of 1866, the treaty negotiations between France and Italy in 1868-1870, the Orient Question of 1877-1878, the persecution of Jews in Russia in 1882, the Congo Conference in Berlin, 1884-1887 and the British-Portuguese conflict in East Africa, 1889-1891. Copies are available at LC, the Center for Research Libraries, the Hampshire Inter-Library Center, and the libraries of Boston College, Yale, Harvard, Duke, Stanford and the University of Virginia.

JEWS—PHILOSOPHY see Philosophy, Jewish

JEWS—RELIGION see Judaism

JEWS—RITES AND CEREMONIES

NY —NEW YORK PUBLIC LIBRARY, Jewish Division, Fifth Ave & 42 St, New York, 10018. Leonard S Gold, Chief
Holdings: Vols (200,000) Cat Mss Microforms
Budget: ($33,383)
Notes: A collection of material in all languages on Judaism, Jewish history, literature and traditions from the earliest times to date and works in the Hebrew alphabet (mainly Hebrew and Yiddish) on a variety of subjects. The division has extensive files of Jewish periodicals and newspapers. The collection of rare Hebraica incl medieval texts, cabalistic works, ethical and philosophical tracts in book form. See *Dictionary Catalog of the Jewish Collection* (Boston: G K Hall, 1960), 14 vols. First Supplement (Boston: G K Hall, 1975), 8 vols.

OH —HEBREW UNION COLLEGE-JEWISH INSTITUTE OF RELIGION, Klau Library, 3101 Clifton Ave, Cincinnati, 45220. David J Gilner, Reference Librn
Holdings: Cat Mss

JEWS—RITUALS see Jews—Social Life and Customs

JEWS—SECTS see Jewish Sects

JEWS—SOCIAL LIFE AND CUSTOMS

FL —UNIVERSITY OF FLORIDA LIBRARY, Isser and Rae Price Library of Judaica, 18 Libr East, Gainesville, 32611. Robert Singerman, Head Librn
Budget: ($30,000)
Notes: Total holdings estimated at 55,000 vols dealing with the political, social, economic and intellectual history of the Jews in the ancient, medieval and modern periods and in all geographic areas. The following areas are especially well represented by printed matter in all relevant languages: Bibliography, Festschriften, History, Bible, Judaism and Jewish theology, liturgy, responsa, rabbinical literature, Jewish law, Hebrew language and literature, Yiddish language and literature, anti-semitism, Zionism, Palestine and the *Yishuv,* and the State of Israel. German and American Judaica form a collecting emphasis with holdings for all the standard histories as well as histories of individual synagogues, institutions and local communities. Works in Hebrew and Yiddish comprise about 60 percent of the collection (estimated 30,000 vols). With few exceptions, holdingsare limited to nineteenth and twentieth century imprints, with complete sets of journals and thousands of ephemeral pamphlets, many of them commemorating anniversaries, enhancing the research value of the collection, the largest Judaica research library in the southeastern United States. Only about half of the collection is cataloged; the collection is a circulating one and vols may be borrowed on interlibrary loan. Incl the Leonard C Mishkin Collection

JEWS—SOCIAL LIFE AND CUSTOMS (cont.)

(40,000 vols), the largest personal Judaica collection in the United States, the Shlomo Marenof Collection (3500 vols), and the inventory of Bernard Morgenstern's Lower East Side Book Store (8000 vols). Scholars should inquire in advance of their visit. *The Isser and Rae Price Library of Judaica* Report (circulation 2900 copies) is mailed gratis twice a year to all interested parties. Special catalogs:Pre-1881 Hebrew imprints recorded in a chronological card file.

NY —NEW YORK PUBLIC LIBRARY, Jewish Division, Fifth Ave & 42 St, New York, 10018. Leonard S Gold, Chief
Holdings: Vols (200,000) Cat Mss Microforms
Budget: ($33,383)
Notes: A collection of material in all languages on Judaism, Jewish history, literature and traditions from the earliest times to date and works in the Hebrew alphabet (mainly Hebrew and Yiddish) on a variety of subjects. The division has extensive files of Jewish periodicals and newspapers. The collection of rare Hebraica incl medieval texts, cabalistic works, ethical and philosophical tracts in book form. See *Dictionary Catalog of the Jewish Collection* (Boston: G K Hall, 1960), 14 vols. First Supplement (Boston: G K Hall, 1975), 8 vols.

NY —YIVO INSTITUTE FOR JEWISH RESEARCH, Library & Archives, 1048 Fifth Ave, New York, 10028. Dina Abramowicz, Librn; Marek Web, Archivist
Holdings: Cat Pix
Notes: Extensive collections on Yiddish folklore, incl folk songs, folk tales, art and music. Scholarship: monographs, periodicals, bibliographies in Yiddish and other languages.

OH —HEBREW UNION COLLEGE-JEWISH INSTITUTE OF RELIGION, Klau Library, 3101 Clifton Ave, Cincinnati, 45220. David J Gilner, Reference Librn
Holdings: Cat Mss

TX —UNIVERSITY OF TEXAS, EL PASO, Library, El Paso, 79968. Fred W Hanes, Dir
Holdings: Vols 1730 Cat
Budget: ($5000)
Notes: The Judaica Collection. Jewish history and culture, as well as religion, philosophy and literature are documented by the collection.

JEWS—ZIONISM see Zionism

JEWS, AMERICAN

MN —MINNESOTA HISTORICAL SOCIETY LIBRARY, 690 Cedar St, Saint Paul, 55101. Patricia C Harpole, Chief of Reference Library; Bonnie G Wilson, Head of Special Libraries
Notes: Representatives of ethnic groups in Minnesota interviewed as a part of special projects include Blacks, Mexican-Americans, Finns in northern Minnesota, and Jews in Minneapolis.

OH —HEBREW UNION COLLEGE-JEWISH INSTITUTE OF RELIGION, Klau Library, 3101 Clifton Ave, Cincinnati, 45220. David J Gilner, Reference Librn
Holdings: Cat

†PA —BALCH INSTITUTE FOR ETHNIC STUDIES, Library, 18 S Seventh St, Philadelphia, 19106.
Notes: Papers of Edwin Lukas, head of the civil rights and social action department of the American Jewish Committee.

JEWS, CHINESE

OH —HEBREW UNION COLLEGE-JEWISH INSTITUTE OF RELIGION, Klau Library, 3101 Clifton Ave, Cincinnati, 45220. David J Gilner, Reference Librn
Holdings: Vols 59// Cat Mss
Notes: Only Chinese Hebrew ms collection extant. Incl community roster of Kai-Feng-fu in Hebrew and Chinese, and many mss in fanfold form.

JEWS, EXTERMINATION OF, 1939-1945 see Holocaust, Jewish, 1939-1945

JEWS, GERMAN

CA —STANFORD UNIVERSITY LIBRARIES, Cecil H Green Library, Stanford, 94305. Peter R Frank, Cur, CDP-Germanic Collection
Notes: Strong collection on important aspects of Jewish history and culture in the German area (Germany, the Austrian Empire and Austria, German part of Switzerland). Emphasis on the period from Enlightenment up to the present. Also sizeable collection of Anti-Semitica. Rare items in the Stanford Collection of German, Austrian and Swiss Culture, Special Collections.

NY —YIVO INSTITUTE FOR JEWISH RESEARCH, Library & Archives, 1048 Fifth Ave, New York, 10028. Dina Abramowicz, Librn; Marek Web, Archivist
Holdings: Cat Mss Pix Slides
Notes: Special collection of books and periodicals, incl government publications, which appeared in Germany between the years 1933-1945. Extensive library and archives collections on history of Jews under Nazi rule in Europe, 1933-1945, in all languages. Hundreds of memorial volumes for towns destroyed by Nazis.

PA —FREE LIBRARY OF PHILADELPHIA, Education, Philosophy and Religion Department, Logan Sq, Philadelphia, 19103. Esther J Maurer, Head
Holdings: Vols 2200// Cat
Notes: Judaica and Hebraica library formerly owned by Moses Marx. Contains source material on local German-Jewish communities pre-World War II. Bibliogrphies, festschriften and works on liturgy are notable. Most of the collection is in German and Hebrew. Also incl books in French, Latin and Spanish.

JEWS, POLISH

NY —YIVO INSTITUTE FOR JEWISH RESEARCH, Library & Archives, 1048 Fifth Ave, New York, 10028. Dina Abramowicz, Librn; Marek Web, Archivist
Holdings: Cat Mss Pix Slides
Notes: Jewish life in Eastern Europe is one of the areas of emphasis. The books and periodicals include the literature of the Jewish Enlightenment in Russia (first half of the 19th century), first periodicals of Russian Jewry in Yiddish, Hebrew and Russian Jewry in the last century: *Voskhod,* underground publications of Jewish labor and radical groups in the Czarist Empire, extensive collection of the Soviet-Yiddish press and literature, publications of the refugee groups outside Russia in the Far East and the West and in present-day Israel. Jewish life in Poland of the interbellum period is presented by the press in Yiddish, Hebrew and Polish, by publications of numerous Jewish organizations and political parties in the fields of education, economy, medicine and the arts. Source materials on Jews in the Baltic countries and Rumania are also represented. Music,folklore and art of Jews in Eastern Europe is well covered.

JEWS, RUSSIAN

NY —YIVO INSTITUTE FOR JEWISH RESEARCH, Library & Archives, 1048 Fifth Ave, New York, 10028. Dina Abramowicz, Librn; Marek Web, Archivist
Holdings: Cat Mss Pix Slides
Notes: Jewish life in Eastern Europe is one of the areas of emphasis. The books and periodicals include the literature of the Jewish Enlightenment in Russia (first half of the 19th century), first periodicals of Russian Jewry in Yiddish, Hebrew and Russian, a complete set of the main organ of Russian Jewry in the last century: *Voskhod,* underground publications of Jewish labor and radical groups in the Czarist Empire, extensive collection of the Soviet- Yiddish press and literature, publications of the refugee groups outside Russia in the Far East and the West and in present-day Israel. Jewish life in Poland of the interbellum period is presented by the press in Yiddish, Hebrew and Polish, by publications of numerous Jewish organizations and political parties in the fields of education, economy, medicine and the arts. Source materials on Jewsin the Baltic countries and Rumania are also represented. Music folklore and art of Jews in Eastern Europe is well covered.

JEWS, SEPHARDIM see Sephardim

JEWS AND CHRISTIANS see Jewish—Christian Relations

JEWS IN CANADA

CA —JUDAH L MAGNES MEMORIAL MUSEUM, Morris Goldstein Library, 2911 Russell St, Berkeley, 94705. Jane Levy, Archivist
Holdings: Vols 7000 Cat Mss Maps Pix Slides Audiotapes Microforms
Notes: Most of our special collections have been deposited in our archives by Western Jewish families or institutions. The collection focuses on the contribution of Western Jews and Jewish institutions (California, Nevada, Oregon, Utah, Washington, Colorado, Texas, New Mexico, Arizona, etc, incl some material from Canada, Mexico, and Latin America) to the cultural, intellectual, commercial, civic, etc growth of the American West. 135 ms collections. The collection is cataloged, many of the documents being indexed and inventoried. The collection has been noted in the Western Jewish History Center's published bibliographies by Sara Cogan, *Pioneer Jews of the California Mother Lode* and *The Jews of San Francisco and the Greater Bay Area,* 1849-1919; also, *A Selective History of San Francisco Eastern European Jewish Life,* 1880-1940, by RuthKelson Rafael (Berkeley: Magnes Museum, 1976; rev 1977); *Catalog of Manuscripts Collections in the Western Jewish History Center, Judah L Magnes Memorial Museum, Berkeley,* by Suzanne Nemiroff (Berkeley: Magnes Museum, 1977); and *Catalog of Western Jewish Periodicals, 1849-1945, at the Western Jewish History Center* by Suzanne Nemiroff (Berkeley: Magnes Museum, 1976).

PA —BALCH INSTITUTE FOR ETHNIC STUDIES, Library, 18 S Seventh St, Philadelphia, 19106. R Joseph Anderson, Library Dir

†ON —METROPOLITAN TORONTO LIBRARY, Social Sciences Dept, 789 Yonge St, Toronto, M4W 2G8, Can. Abdus Salam, Head
Holdings: Vols Cat Maps Phonorecords Audiotapes 16mm Films Microforms
Notes: The collection is strong in the history and philosophy of religion and comparative religions; literature of all the major religions of the world; works on the devotional and practical aspects of religion; and books on such sacred scripture as the Bible. In addition, our holdings contain many denominational studies on religion in Canada, as well as more than 300 congregational histories, particularly Ontario churches and synagogues.

JEWS IN CHINA

OH —HEBREW UNION COLLEGE-JEWISH INSTITUTE OF RELIGION, Klau Library, 3101 Clifton Ave, Cincinnati, 45220. David J Gilner, Reference Librn
Holdings: Vols 59// Cat Mss
Notes: Only Chinese Hebrew ms collection extant. Incl community roster of Kai-Feng-fu in Hebrew and Chinese, and many mss in fanfold form.

JEWS IN EASTERN EUROPE

IA —UNIVERSITY OF IOWA, University Libraries, Iowa City, 52242.
Holdings: Vols 1850 Mss
Notes: The Leo W Schwarz Collection, a

JEWS IN EASTERN EUROPE (cont.)

valuable and rare group of books dealing with Hasidic literature, a portion on Old Testament studies and works on Jewish history, philosophy and culture, the Jews in Nazi Germany, Jewish folklore and the history of the Jews in the US. Incl about 850 books in Hebrew and 1000 in other languages, mss of several of Schwarz's books and articles, correspondence, notes, and background research relating to his publications.

NY —NEW YORK PUBLIC LIBRARY, Slavonic Div, Fifth Ave & 42 St, New York, 10018. Edward Kasinec, Chief
Holdings: Cat Microforms
Notes: See: New York Public Library, Slavic Div, *Dictionary Catalog of the Slavonic* Collection, 2nd ed, rev and enl (Boston: G K Hall, 1974), 44 vols; and New York Public Library, *Dictionary Catalog of the Research* Libraries (New York, 1972-).

NY —YIVO INSTITUTE FOR JEWISH RESEARCH, Library & Archives, 1048 Fifth Ave, New York, 10028. Dina Abramowicz, Librn; Marek Web, Archivist
Holdings: Cat Mss Pix Slides
Notes: Jewish life in Eastern Europe is one of the areas of emphasis. The books and periodicals include the literature of the Jewish Enlightenment in Russia (first half of the 19th century), first periodicals of Russian Jewry in Yiddish, Hebrew and Russian, a complete set of the main organ of Russian Jewry in the last century: *Voskhod*, underground publications of Jewish labor and radical groups in the Czarist Empire, extensive collection of the refugee groups outside Russia in the Far East and the West and in present-day Israel. Jewish life in Poland of the interbellum period is presented by the press in Yiddish, Hebrew and Polish, by publications of numerous Jewish organizations and political parties in the fields of education, economy, medicine and the arts. Source materials on Jews in the Baltic countries and Rumania are alsorepresented. Music, folklore and art of Jews in Eastern Europe is well covered.

JEWS IN FRANCE

MA —BRANDEIS UNIVERSITY, Goldfarb Library, 415 South St, Waltham, 02154. Bessie Hahn, Dir
Notes: JewishResistance Collection: Contains 21 linear ft of books, periodical articles and contemporary ephemera emphasizing the role Jews played in armed resistance to the Nazi regime. A catalog of the books is in the Special Colections Catalog and Main Card Catalog. Theresienstadt Concentration Camp Documents: Consists of over 200 "daily order" bulletins issued by the German command. Many of them contain lists of arrival and departure of internees. A finding list to the documents is located in Special Collections. No photocopying of the documents is permitted. Holocaust Survivors Collection: Consists of 20 linear ft of recorded interviews with survivors of the Holocaust, now living in the US. The tapes are not transcribed and the collection is unprocessed, but the tapes are arranged alphabetically by interviewee.

JEWS IN GERMANY

CA —HOOVER INSTITUTION ON WAR, REVOLUTION & PEACE, Stanford University, Stanford, 94305. Milorad M Drachkovitch, Archivist
Notes: Papers of Kurt R Grossman, 1926-73, incl mss of writings, correspondence, clippings, and serial issues, relating to Jewish refugees from Nazi Germany, postwar German and Austrian restitution payments to Jewish war victims, German-Israeli relations, the condition of Jews throughout the world, and civil liberties in the US and Germany. 53 ms boxes, 8 scrapbooks.

CA —STANFORD UNIVERSITY LIBRARIES, Cecil H Green Library, Stanford, 94305. Peter R Frank, Cur, CDP-Germanic Collection
Notes: Strong collection on important aspects of Jewish history and culture in the German area (Germany, Austrian Empire and Austria, German part of Switzerland). Emphasis on the period from Enlightenment up to the present. Also sizeable collection of Anti-Semitica.

IA —UNIVERSITY OF IOWA, University Libraries, Iowa City, 52242.
Holdings: Vols 1850 Mss
Notes: The Leo W Schwarz Collection, a valuable and rare group of books dealing with Hasidic literature, a portion on Old Testament studies and works on Jewish history, philosophy and culture, the Jews in Nazi Germany, Jewish folklore and the history of the Jews in the US. Incl about 850 books in Hebrew and 1000 in other languages, mss of several of Schwarz's books and articles, correspondence, notes, and background research relating to his publications.

MA —BRANDEIS UNIVERSITY, Goldfarb Library, 415 South St, Waltham, 02154. Bessie Hahn, Dir
Notes: JewishResistance Collection: Contains 21 linear ft of books, periodical articles and contemporary ephemera emphasizing the role Jews played in armed resistance to the Nazi regime. A catalog of the books is in the Special Colections Catalog and Main Card Catalog. Theresienstadt Concentration Camp Documents: Consists of over 200 "daily order" bulletins issued by the German command. Many of them contain lists of arrival and departure of internees. A finding list to the documents is located in Special Collections. No photocopying of the documents is permitted. Holocaust Survivors Collection: Consists of 20 linear ft of recorded interviews with survivors of the Holocaust, now living in the US. The tapes are not transcribed and the collection is unprocessed, but the tapes are arranged alphabetically by interviewee.

NY —LEO BAECK INSTITUTE, Library, 129 E 73 St, New York, 10021. Fred Grubel, Secretary & Dir
Holdings: Vols (50,000)
Notes: History and philosophy of European German-speaking Jewry, 18th to 20th century. Publications: LBI Archives and Library News, free, 2 issues a year. Provides an update of collections. Also, LBI News incl more general info for members only. $35.00 per year dues.

NY —YIVO INSTITUTE FOR JEWISH RESEARCH, Library & Archives, 1048 Fifth Ave, New York, 10028. Dina Abramowicz, Librn; Marek Web, Archivist
Holdings: Cat Mss Pix Slides
Notes: Special collection of books and periodicals, incl government publications, which appeared in Germany between the years 1933-1945. Extensive library and archives collections on history of Jews under Nazi rule in Europe, 1933-1945, in all languages. Hundreds of memorial volumes for towns destroyed by Nazis.

OH —HEBREW UNION COLLEGE-JEWISH INSTITUTE OF RELIGION, Klau Library, 3101 Clifton Ave, Cincinnati, 45220. David J Gilner, Reference Librn
Holdings: Cat Mss
Notes: Incl the Kirschstein Collection, containing mss of a private, business, communal and government nature, as well as religious documents, primarily from Prussia and Mecklenburg.

JEWS IN GREAT BRITAIN

NY —SYRACUSE UNIVERSITY LIBRARIES, Ernest S Bird Library, George Arents Research Library for Special Collections, Syracuse, 13210. Carolyn A Davis, Manuscripts Librn; Amy S Doherty, University Archivist; Mark F Weimer, Rare Book Librn
Notes: Microfilm copies of Benjamin Desraeli's complete papers (200,000 frames) incl family, domestic and personal papers, copies of speeches, royal and general correspondence, papers on domestic and foreign affairs, correspondence on honors and titles, Mrs Disraeli's papers, mss of his novels and proofs and notices and correspondence about the novels. Also the papers of his father Isaac D'Israeli, of his grandfather Benjamin D'Israeli and Disraeli's biographers, Monypenny and Buckle.

JEWS IN LATIN AMERICA

CA —JUDAH L MAGNES MEMORIAL MUSEUM, Morris Goldstein Library, 2911 Russell St, Berkeley, 94705. Jane Levy, Archivist
Holdings: Vols 7000 Cat Mss Maps Pix Slides Audiotapes Microforms
Notes: Most of our special collections have been deposited in our archives by Western Jewish families or institutions. The collection focuses on the contribution of Western Jews and Jewish institutions (California, Nevada, Oregon, Utah, Washington, Colorado, Texas, New Mexico, Arizona, etc, incl some material from Canada, Mexico, and Latin America) to the cultural, intellectual, commercial, civic, etc growth of the American West. 135 ms collections. The collection is cataloged, many of the documents being indexed and inventoried. The collection has been noted in the Western Jewish History Center's published bibliographies by Sara Cogan, *Pioneer Jews of the California Mother Lode* and *The Jews of San Francisco and the Greater Bay Area*, 1849-1919; also, *A Selective History of San Francisco Eastern European Jewish Life*, 1880-1940, by RuthKelson Rafael (Berkeley: Magnes Museum, 1976; rev 1977); *Catalog of Manuscripts Collections in the Western Jewish History Center, Judah L Magnes Memorial Museum, Berkeley*, by Suzanne Nemiroff (Berkeley: Magnes Museum, 1977); and *Catalog of Western Jewish Periodicals, 1849-1945, at the Western Jewish History Center* by Suzanne Nemiroff (Berkeley: Magnes Museum, 1976).

JEWS IN MEXICO

CA —JUDAH L MAGNES MEMORIAL MUSEUM, Morris Goldstein Library, 2911 Russell St, Berkeley, 94705. Jane Levy, Archivist
Holdings: Vols 7000 Cat Mss Maps Pix Slides Audiotapes Microforms
Notes: Most of our special collections have been deposited in our archives by Western Jewish families or institutions. The collection focuses on the contribution of Western Jews and Jewish institutions (California, Nevada, Oregon, Utah, Washington, Colorado, Texas, New Mexico, Arizona, etc, incl some material from Canada, Mexico, and Latin America) to the cultural, intellectual, commercial, civic, etc growth of the American West. 135 ms collections. The collection is cataloged, many of the documents being indexed and inventoried. The collection has been noted in the Western Jewish History Center's published bibliographies by Sara Cogan, *Pioneer Jews of the California Mother Lode* and *The Jews of San Francisco and the Greater Bay Area*, 1849-1919; also, *A Selective History of San Francisco Eastern European Jewish Life*, 1880-1940, by RuthKelson Rafael (Berkeley: Magnes Museum, 1976; rev 1977); *Catalog of Manuscripts Collections in the Western Jewish History Center, Judah L Magnes Memorial Museum, Berkeley*, by Suzanne Nemiroff (Berkeley: Magnes Museum, 1977); and *Catalog of Western Jewish Periodicals, 1849-1945, at the Western Jewish History Center* by Suzanne Nemiroff (Berkeley: Magnes Museum, 1976).

JEWS IN POLAND

NY —NEW YORK PUBLIC LIBRARY, Slavonic Div, Fifth Ave & 42 St, New York, 10018. Edward Kasinec, Chief
Holdings: Cat Microforms
Notes: See: New York Public Library, Slavic Div, *Dictionary Catalog of the Slavonic*

JEWS IN POLAND (cont.)

Collection, 2nd ed, rev and enl (Boston: G K Hall, 1974), 44 vols; and New York Public Library, *Dictionary Catalog of the Research* Libraries (New York, 1972-).

JEWS IN RUSSIA

NY —NEW YORK PUBLIC LIBRARY, Slavonic Div, Fifth Ave & 42 St, New York, 10018. Edward Kasinec, Chief
Holdings: Cat Microforms
Notes: See: New York Public Library, Slavonic Div, *Dictionary Catalog of the Slavonic Collection*, 2nd ed, rev and enl (Boston: G K Hall, 1974), 44 vols; and New York Public Library, *Dictionary Catalog of the Research Libraries* (New York, 1972-).

OH —HEBREW UNION COLLEGE-JEWISH INSTITUTE OF RELIGION, Klau Library, 3101 Clifton Ave, Cincinnati, 45220. David J Gilner, Reference Librn
Holdings: Cat
Notes: Excellent collection of pre-revolutionary monographs and periodicals; recent "exile" literature.

JEWS IN THE U.S.

CA —JUDAH L MAGNES MEMORIAL MUSEUM, Morris Goldstein Library, 2911 Russell St, Berkeley, 94705. Jane Levy, Archivist
Holdings: Vols 7000 Cat Mss Maps Pix Slides Audiotapes Microforms
Notes: Most of our special collections have been deposited in our archives by Western Jewish families or institutions. The collection focuses on the contribution of Western Jews and Jewish institutions (California, Nevada, Oregon, Utah, Washington, Colorado, Texas, New Mexico, and Latin America) to the cultural, intellectual, commercial, civic, etc growth of the American West. 135 ms collections. The collection is cataloged, many of the documents being indexed and inventoried. The collection has been noted in the Western Jewish History Center's published bibliographies by Sara Cogan, *Pioneer Jews of the California Mother Lode* and *The Jews of San Francisco and the Greater Bay Area, 1849-1919,* also, *A Selective History of San Francisco Eastern European Jewish Life, 1880-1940,* by Ruth Kelson Rafael (Berkeley: Magnes Museum, 1976; rev 1977);*Catalog of Manuscripts Collections in the Western Jewish History Center, Judah L Magnes Memorial Museum, Berkeley,* by Suzanne Nemiroff (Berkeley: Magnes Museum, 1977); and *Catalog of Western Jewish Periodicals, 1849-1945, at the Western Jewish History Center...,* by Suzanne Nemiroff (Berkeley: Magnes Museum, 1976).

†CA —JEWISH FEDERATION COUNCIL OF GREATER LOS ANGELES, Jewish Community Library, 6505 Wilshire Blvd, Los Angeles, 90048.
Notes: Jewish culture, life in America. Incl historical documents and pictures pertaining to the history of the Jewish community in Los Angeles and vicinity.

CA —LOS ANGELES PUBLIC LIBRARY, Philosophy & Religion Dept, 630 W Fifth St, Los Angeles, 90071. Marilyn C Wherley, Librn
Holdings: Vols 2000 Cat
Budget: ($60,000)
Notes: Popular and scholarly archeological material and biographical material on this ethnic group in Biblical and early modern times. Does not include the holocaust or the modern state of Israel. Emphasis on Jews and Judaism in the United States.

IN —INDIANA STATE UNIVERSITY, EVANSVILLE, Library, 8600 University Blvd, Evansville, 47712. Gina R Walker, Acting Archivist
Holdings: Uncat Mss Audiotapes
Notes: Small collection dealing with the Evanville, Indiana, Jewish Community (including neighboring counties): people, businesses, temples, burial records. Covers 1840s to present.

IA —UNIVERSITY OF IOWA, University Libraries, Iowa City, 52242.
Holdings: Vols 1850 Mss
Notes: The Leo W Schwarz Collection, a valuable and rare group of books dealing with Hasidic literature, a portion on Old Testament studies and works on Jewish history, philosophy and culture, the Jews in Nazi Germany, Jewish folklore and the history of the Jews in the US. Incl about 850 books in Hebrew and 1000 in other languages, mss of several of Schwarz's books and articles, correspondence, notes, and background research relating to his publications.

MA —AMERICAN JEWISH HISTORICAL SOCIETY, Library, 2 Thornton Rd, Waltham, 02154. Nathan M Kaganoff, Librn-Editor
Holdings: Vols 78,000 Cat Mss Pix Microforms
Budget: ($9000)
Notes: American Jewish history; incl paintings (100), theatre posters (500), sheet music (3500), mss (4 million). Calendar to individual collection published (2 vols).

MA —AMERICAN ANTIQUARIAN SOCIETY LIBRARY, 185 Salisbury St, Worcester, 01609. Marcus A McCorison, Dir & Librn
Holdings: Cat
Notes: The Society holds over 90 percent of the 685 titles in Rosenbach's bibliography of American Jewish books to 1850, plus many early items not included in the list.

MN —UNIVERSITY OF MINNESOTA, Immigration History Research Center, 826 Berry St, Saint Paul, 55114. Susan Griegs, Cur
Holdings: Vols (35,000) Mss Maps Pix Microforms
See also entry under US - Emigration and Immigration

†NY —AMERICAN JEWISH COMMITTEE, William E Wiener Oral History Library, 165 E 56 St, New York, 10022.
Notes: All aspects of the American Jewish experience in the 20th century. Other materials located in the Blaustein Library.

NY —NEW YORK HISTORICAL SOCIETY, Library, 170 Central Park W, New York, 10024. James Gregory, Librn
Holdings: Cat Mss
Notes: The Hendricks Collection traces the development of the copper industry in the US, and relects the life of an old and prominent Sephardic family.

NY —YIVO INSTITUTE FOR JEWISH RESEARCH, Library & Archives, 1048 Fifth Ave, New York, 10028. Dina Abramowicz, Librn; Marek Web, Archivist
Holdings: Cat Mss Pix Slides
Notes: Emphasis is on immigration history. Incl archives of Jewish organizations which served immigrant masses, such as Educational Alliance, Hias, Hicem, Jewish Desertion Bureau and others. Yiddish language general and labor periodicals in originals and on microfilm. The Yiddish school movement in the US is covered, as well as other cultural activities in the field of the Yiddish theater, literature and the arts. Correspondence of outstanding authors with parties in the US and abroad is an important source of information on Yiddish cultural life and communal affairs.

NY —UNIVERSITY OF ROCHESTER, Rush Rhees Library, Department of Rare Books and Special Collections, Rochester, 14627. Peter Dzwonkoski, Librn
Holdings: Vols Mss
Notes: Correspondence, drafts of sermon, speeches and other records that relate to Philip Bernstein's career as a rabbi of Temple Brith Kodest (Rochester, NY), as head of the Committee on Army and Navy Religious Activities of the National Jewsih Welfare Board during World War II, as the advisor on Jewish Affairs to the US Army Commanders in Europe following the War, as President of the Central Conference of American Rabbis, and as Chairman of the American Israel Public Affairs Committee.

NC —UNIVERSITY OF NORTH CAROLINA, CHARLOTTE, J Murrey Atkins Library, UNCC Station, Charlotte, 28223. Robert F Brabham Jr, Special Collections Librn
Notes: Papers of Harry Golden, 1945-1970 and of Benjamin Gitlow, 1920-1960. Gitlow Papers incl material on Jewish anti-communist groups of the 1950s.

NC —NORTH CAROLINA DIV OF ARCHIVES & HISTORY, 109 E Jones St, Raleigh, 27611.
Holdings: Mss
Notes: The papers of Gertrude Weil, correspondence, material about her activities in various organizations, particularly for women's interests. 51 cubic ft of mss.

OH —HEBREW UNION COLLEGE-JEWISH INSTITUTE OF RELIGION, Klau Library, 3101 Clifton Ave, Cincinnati, 45220. David J Gilner, Reference Librn
Holdings: Cat
Notes: Incl the first Hebrew Bible printed in the US. (Philadelphia, 1814); first printed Jewish Prayerbook; first Jewish periodical in the US (*The Jew*).

PA —BALCH INSTITUTE FOR ETHNIC STUDIES, Library, 18 S Seventh St, Philadelphia, 19106. R Joseph Anderson, Library Dir
Holdings: Vols 2000 Vols Cat Mss Pix Microforms

PA —UNIVERSITY OF PITTSBURGH, Hillman Library, Archives of Industrial Society, 363 Hillman Library, Pittsburgh, 15260. Frank A Zabrosky, Cur
Holdings: Mss Maps Pix Phonorecords Audiotapes Microforms
Notes: Incl documents; newspapers; records of organizations and synagogues.

RI —BROWN UNIVERSITY, John Hay Library, Harris Collection, Prospect St, Providence, 02912. Rosemary L Cullen, Cur
Holdings: Vols (200,000) Cat Mss Pix Phonorecords Microforms
Budget: ($15,000)
Notes: The Harris Collection of American Poetry and Plays is principally composed of American and Canadian poetry and plays, 17th century-date. Extensive holdings in songsters, gift books and annuals, hymnals, pageants, broadside verse, carriers' addresses, women poets, juvenile poetry, (incl Mother Goose and *The Night Before* Christmas), sheet music with lyrics, small press publications, fine printing, black poets, "little magazines," Yiddish-American literature. All movements or schools of American poetry are represented. Incl first editions of most American poets and playwrights, notably Whitman, Poe, Wallace Stevens, Eugene O'Neill, Edward Albee, Ezra Pound, T S Eliot, William Carlos Williams, Amy Lowell, Phyllis Wheatley, Robert Frost, Allen Ginsberg, Bliss Carman, and Stephen Foster sheet music. Also incl the Saunders Walt Whitman Collection (1300 vols); the LangdonCollection of Pageants (250 vols); the Asa Cushman Collection of plays in ms and prompt copies; the MacDougall Collection of Psalters and Hymnals; 4000 plays issued by Walter H Baker Co, Boston (1890-1957); the Vaxer Collection of Yiddish Poetry, Plays and Music (1700 vols). Collections incl 200,000 vols, 30,000 broadsides, 55,000 mss, 170,000 pieces of sheet music, 450 phonorecords, and 375 microfilm reels. See *Dictionary Catalog of the Harris Collection of American Poetry and Plays* (Boston: G K Hall, 1972), 13 vols; *Supplement* (1977), 3 vols. See also, *American Poetry,* 1609-1900, *A Collection on Microfilm, Segment I* (1609-1820); *Segment II* (1821-1850); *Segment III* (1851-1870) (Woodbridge, Conn: Research Publications). Separate catalog.

†RI —RHODE ISLAND JEWISH HISTORICAL ASSOCIATION, 130 Sessions St, Providence, 02906.
Notes: History of Rhode Island Jews and Jews in the US.

TX —ABILENE CHRISTIAN UNIVERSITY, Margaret & Herman Brown Library, ACU Sta, Abilene, 79601. Callie Faye Milliken, Assoc Dir
Holdings: Vols 5000 // Cat
Notes: Donner Library of Americanism. Books, pamphlets, documents, and periodical materials dealing with American politics of

JEWS IN THE U.S. (cont.)

the far right collected by Robert Donner during and after World War II. Also incl materials on Jews and Freemasonry.
†WA —UNIVERSITY OF WASHINGTON LIBRARIES, Seattle, 98195.

JIMENEZ, JUAN RAMON

PR —UNIVERSITY OF PUERTO RICO, Jose M Lazaro Memorial Library, Sala Zenobia y Juan Ramon Jimenez, Rio Piedras, 00931. Raquel Sarraga, Librn
Holdings: Vols (8000) Cat Mss Phonorecords Audiotapes Filmstrips
Notes: Personal library and papers of Jimenez. Bibliographical data on the "Modernismo" period is very rich. The collection incl rare books, first editions autographed by their authors, magazines (some are rare collections), thousands of Juan Ramon's originals and manuscripts, letters of some of the top literary writers of the century, photographs (3061), paper clippings (32,000), paintings, furniture and personal belongings.

JINGHPAW LANGUAGE see Kachin Language

JITNEY BUSES see Motor Buses

JOAN OF ARC, ST.

MA —HARVARD UNIVERSITY LIBRARY, Widener Library, Cambridge, 02138.
Holdings: Cat
NY —COLUMBIA UNIVERSITY LIBRARIES, Rare Book & Manuscript Library, 801 Butler Library, 535 W 114 St, New York, 10027. Kenneth A Lohf, Librn
Holdings: Vols 1769 // Cat Mss
Notes: Restricted use: noncirculating. Incl 15th-16th century mss.

JOAO III, KING OF PORTUGAL

MA —HARVARD UNIVERSITY LIBRARY, Houghton Library, Cambridge, 02138. Rodney G Dennis, Cur of Manuscripts
Holdings: Mss

JOB DISCRIMINATION see Discrimination in Employment

JOB SATISFACTION AND ENRICHMENT

DC —US DEPT OF LABOR, Library, 200 Constitution Ave NW, Washington, 20210. Sabina Jacobson, Dir
Holdings: Vols (550,000) Cat
ON —CANADA DEPT OF LABOUR, Library, Ottawa, K1A 0J2, Can. Monique Marchand, Chief Librn
Holdings: Vols (100,000) Cat Microforms

JOB VACANCIES

NY —FEDERATION EMPLOYMENT & GUIDANCE SERVICE, Richard J Bernhard Memorial Library, 510 Sixth Ave, 4th Floor, New York, 10011. Otto Kanocz, Chief Librn
Holdings: Vols (4000) Cat Microforms Videotapes Audiotapes VF
Notes: Occupational information, guidance and counseling, vocational rehabilitation. Incl 30,000 pamphlets; 200 periodical titles. Also incl 50 vertical files and microfiche. Open to the public.

JOBS see Professions

JOHN, HENRY J., 1912-1968

NE —UNIVERSITY OF NEBRASKA-LINCOLN, Don L Love Library, University Archives and Special Collections, Lincoln, 68588. Joseph G Svoboda, University Archivist
Holdings: // Cat
Notes: The basic collection consists of 500 items from the collection of Dr Henry J John given to the University of Nebraska-Lincoln Libraries by Senator Roman Hruska. Includes mss and correspondence of Dr John.
NE —UNIVERSITY OF NEBRASKA-LINCOLN, Don L Love Library, Czech Heritage Collection, Lincoln, 68588. Joseph G Svoboda, University Archivist
Holdings: Vols (3000) Cat Mss Pix Audiotapes Microforms
Notes: The Czech Heritage Collection.

JOHN BIRCH SOCIETY

CA —UNIVERSITY OF CALIFORNIA, LOS ANGELES, Research Library, Dept of Special Collections, 405 Hilgard Ave, Los Angeles, 90024. Edward Shreeves, Chairman, Bibliographers Group; David S Zeidberg, Head
Holdings: Cat Mss Pix
Notes: 11 cartons of materials, recordings, etc, relating to the John Birch Society, incl runs of many relevant periodicals, government documents, etc.
MD —UNIVERSITY OF MARYLAND, BALTIMORE COUNTY, Albin O Kuhn Library and Gallery, 5401 Wilkens Ave, Baltimore, 21228. Ann Copeland, Special Collections Librn
Holdings: // Uncat
Notes: The collection includes 1000 pamphlets on communism, fascism, Trotskyism, socialism, etc.

JOHN NEWBERY MEDAL BOOKS see Newbery Award Books

JOHNNY APPLESEED

MA —LEOMINSTER PUBLIC LIBRARY, 30 West St, Leominster, 01453.
Holdings: Mss Pix
Notes: Index. All information filed under Chapman, John (legal name of Johnny Appleseed).

JOHNPOLL, BERNARD

MA —BOSTON UNIVERSITY, Mugar Memorial Library, Special Collections Dept, 771 Commonwealth Ave, Boston, 02215. Howard B Gotlieb, Dir
Holdings: Mss Cat Correspondence

JOHNS HOPKINS UNIVERSITY

NY —ROCKEFELLER UNIVERSITY, Rockefeller Archive Center, Hillcrest, Pocantico Hills, North Tarrytown, 10591. Joseph W Ernst, Dir; J William Hess, Assoc Dir
Notes: Papers relative to the Rockefeller Family, Foundations, University, and other specific enterprises and contributions to particular areas of social, physical, educational, and historic reform, preservation, conservation, or development. Extensive records of administrative, financial, physical, or intellectual relationships.

JOHNSON, A. E.

NY —SYRACUSE UNIVERSITY LIBRARIES, Ernest S Bird Library, George Arents Research Library for Special Collections, Syracuse, 13210. Carolyn A Davis, Manuscripts Librn; Amy S Doherty, University Archivist; Mark F Weimer, Rare Book Librn
Holdings: Mss
Notes: Personal papers of the poet, A E Johnson, incl correspondence with many notable "modern" literary persons.

JOHNSON, AMANDUS, 1877-1974

PA —BALCH INSTITUTE FOR ETHNIC STUDIES, Library, 18 S Seventh St, Philadelphia, 19106. R Joseph Anderson, Library Dir
Holdings: Mss Cat Pix Audiovisual Materials
Notes: The Amandus Johnson Collection of his papers, incl biographical material on 20th century Swedish-Americans, records from the American Swedish Historical Museum in South Philadelphia, and source documents on the early Swedish settlement of the Delaware Valley, and historical writings based on these documents.

JOHNSON, ANDREW

DC —LIBRARY OF CONGRESS, Manuscript Division, Washington, 20540. John C Broderick, Chief
Notes: The Presidential Papers collection incl the papers, etc, of numerous Presidents.

JOHNSON, BYRON I., 1890-1964

BC —UNIVERSITY OF VICTORIA, McPherson Library, Victoria, V8W 3H5, Can.
Notes: Byron Johnson (1890-1964); Premier of British Columbia. Incl correspondence; reports; clippings; ephemera; photographs (1914-57).

JOHNSON, DONALD

IA —STATE HISTORICAL SOCIETY OF IOWA LIBRARY, 402 Iowa Ave, Iowa City, 52240. Darold J Brown, Librn
Holdings: Cat
Notes: Thousands of individual items and smaller collections. Two hundred larger collections incl the papers of Cyrus C Carpenter, Jonathan P Dolliver, Gilbert Haugen, W W Waymack, Ephraim Adams, A C Dodge, Dorothy Houghton, Jesse Macy, Agnes Samuelson, Donald Johnson, Jack Miller, Ruth Sayre, Samuel Kirkwood, Thomas McKnight, Robert Lucas, Dwight McCarty, William Larrabee. Includes church, school, company and organization records, Civil War materials.

JOHNSON, E. RICHARD

MA —BOSTON UNIVERSITY, Mugar Memorial Library, Special Collections Dept, 771 Commonwealth Ave, Boston, 02215. Howard B Gotlieb, Dir
Holdings: Cat Mss
Notes: Mss, correspondence, etc collected in depth; incl publications by or about.

JOHNSON, EDDIE BERNICE

TX —NORTH TEXAS STATE UNIVERSITY, Archives, NT Station Box 5188, Denton, 76203. Robert LaForte, University Archivist
Notes: Part of Oral History Collection. Interviews with the Texas legislator, Black Caucus, and Women's Caucus. Restricted.

JOHNSON, EDWARD

ON —UNIVERSITY OF TORONTO, Edward Johnson Music Library, Toronto, M5S 1A1, Can. Kathleen McMorow, Librn; James Creighton, Sound Archivist
Holdings: Cat
Notes: Scores, memorabilia, etc.

JOHNSON, ELDRIDGE R., RECORDS

DC —LIBRARY OF CONGRESS, Motion Pictures, Broadcasting and Recorded Sound Div, Washington, 20540.
Holdings: Cat
Notes: 133 Berliner Gramophone Co records, 1896-1900; 31 Zonophone records, 1899-1904; 2 rare Vitaphone records, 1899; 67 Eldridge R Johnson records, 1900-1901; and 30 Victor Talking Machine Co records, 1902-1909.

JOHNSON, EMILY PAULINE, 1862-1913

ON —MCMASTER UNIVERSITY, Mills Memorial Library, Div of Archives & Research Collections, Hamilton, L8S 4L6, Can. G R Hill, Univ Librn
Holdings: // Mss
Notes: Correspondence, mss of poems and stories, clippings, programs, and cards from recitals.

JOHNSON, FERD

MA —BOSTON UNIVERSITY, Mugar Memorial Library, Special Collections Dept, 771 Commonwealth Ave, Boston, 02215. Howard B Gotlieb, Dir
Holdings: Cat
Notes: Cartoons, drawings, proofs incl "Moon Mullins".

JOHNSON, GEORGE P., 1885- ?

CA —UNIVERSITY OF CALIFORNIA, LOS ANGELES, Research Library, Dept of Special Collections, 405 Hilgard Ave, Los Angeles, 90024. Edward Shreeves, Chairman, Bibliographers Group; David S Zeidberg, Head
Holdings: Cat Mss Pix Slides
Notes: 6 linear feet of correspondence, playbills, advertising, and business records reflecting the early involvement of Blacks in the moving picture industry.

JOHNSON, GEORGE F.

NY —GEORGE F JOHNSON MEMORIAL LIBRARY, 1001 Park St, Endicott, 13760. S Judson Locke, Dir
Holdings: Pix
Notes: Most of the material is housed in the George F Johnson Memorial Room. Incl tapes, memorabilia.

JOHNSON, HAROLD K.

PA —US ARMY MILITARY HISTORY INSTITUTE, Carlisle Barracks, 17013. Richard J Sommers, Chief Archivist-Historian
Holdings: Mss Cat
Notes: 2000 boxes mss. The Viet Nam War collection, personal letters, daily logs, memoirs, speeches, and official papers of American officers and soldiers serving in Viet Nam or elsewhere in the world during the era. Almost all these papers are from Generals, incl William DePuy, Harold K Johnson, Bruce Palmer, Jonathan Seaman, and William Westmoreland.

JOHNSON, JACK

NY —COLUMBIA UNIVERSITY LIBRARIES, Rare Book & Manuscript Library, 801 Butler Library, 535 W 114 St, New York, 10027. Kenneth A Lohf, Librn
Notes: Restricted use. The Paul Magriel Boxing Collection on the history and literature of pugilism. The L S Alexander Gumby Collection, which incl much on Jack Johnson.

JOHNSON, JAMES G.

OH —OHIO HISTORICAL SOCIETY, Archives Library Division, 1982 Velma Ave, Columbus, 43211. Dennis East, Division Chief
Notes: His papers.

JOHNSON, JAMES WELDON

CT —YALE UNIVERSITY, Box 1603A, Yale Station, New Haven, 06520.
Holdings: Cat Mss Pix

JOHNSON, JED JOSEPH, SR.

OK —UNIVERSITY OF OKLAHOMA, Bizzell Memorial Library, Western History Collections, 401 W Brooks, Norman, 73069. John Ezell, Cur
Holdings: Mss
Notes: US Representative. His papers. Guide available.

JOHNSON, JESSE J.

MA —BOSTON UNIVERSITY, Mugar Memorial Library, Special Collections Dept, 771 Commonwealth Ave, Boston, 02215. Howard B Gotlieb, Dir
Holdings: Mss Pix
Notes: Mss, correspondence, etc collected in depth; incl publications by or about.

MS —TOUGALOO COLLEGE, L Zenobia Coleman Library, Tougaloo, 39174. Virgia Brocks-Shedd, Acting Dir
Budget: ($142,650)
Notes: Civil rights cases and legal papers; lawsuits; Mississippi, 1960-1968. Local attorneys have donated papers of cases they have handled, espec attorneys of two government-funded legal services offices. Individual collections: Jerry W Ward, Lance Jeffers, (Ret) Lt Col Jesse Johnson on Blacks in the military. Incl VF holdings of articles from 1930 and on.

JOHNSON, JOHN

VT —UNIVERSITY OF VERMONT, Guy W Bailey/David W Howe Library, Burlington, 05405. John Buehler, Asst Dir for Special Collections
Notes: The papers of John Johnson (1771-1842), Surveyor General of Vermont, 1813-23, 1832-38.

JOHNSON, JOHN ROSAMUND

CT —YALE UNIVERSITY, Music Library, 98 Wall St, New Haven, 06520. Harold E Samuel, Librn
Notes: Personal papers and musical mss. *See also* entry under Music, American.

CT —YALE UNIVERSITY, Beinecke Rare Book & Manuscript Library, Osborn Collection, New Haven, 06520. Stephen R Parks, Cur
Holdings: Mss

JOHNSON, JOSEPHINE

MO —WASHINGTON UNIVERSITY, Libraries, Campus Box 1061, Saint Louis, 63130.
Holdings: Mss
Notes: Professional correspondence and literary mss of the Pulitzer Prize novelist. Incl books, mss, etc described in *Special Collections: an Annotated Guide to the Holdings of the Manuscript Division and the University Archives and Research* Collection.

JOHNSON, LOUIS A.

VA —UNIVERSITY OF VIRGINIA, Alderman Library, Manuscripts Dept, Charlottesville, 22901. Edmund Berkeley Jr, Cur
Holdings: Cat Mss Pix Phonorecords 16mm Films
Notes: Personal, political, and business papers.

JOHNSON, LYNDON BAINES

NY —NEW YORK PUBLIC LIBRARY, Fifth Ave & 42 St, New York, 10018.
Notes: Supported by a special Lyndon Baines Johnson Memorial Fund, to acquire materials by and about him.

TX —UNIVERSITY OF TEXAS, Lyndon Baines Johnson Presidential Library, 2813 Red River St, Austin, 78712. Harry J Middleton, Dir
Holdings: Vols (14,164) Cat Mss Pix Phonorecords Audiotapes Videotapes Films VF
Budget: ($856,500)
Notes: A collection containing the papers and materials of President Lyndon Baines Johnson; his life, associates, family and administration. Incl 34,699,837 ms pages; 593,417 still photographs; 824,076 feet of motion picture film; 5711 videotapes; 11,146 audiotapes; 607 audio disks; oral history transcripts; 37,836 museum objects. 7731 cataloged vertical files.

TX —UNIVERSITY OF TEXAS LIBRARIES, General Libraries, Barker Texas History Center, PO Box P, Austin, 78712. Don Carleton, Dir
Holdings: Vols (132,000) Cat Mss Maps Pix Slides Phonorecords Audiotapes Microforms
See also entry under Texas-History.

JOHNSON, NUNNALLY

MA —BOSTON UNIVERSITY, Mugar Memorial Library, Special Collections Dept, 771 Commonwealth Ave, Boston, 02215. Howard B Gotlieb, Dir
Holdings: Cat Mss Pix
Notes: Mss, correspondence, etc collected in depth; incl publications by or about.

JOHNSON, PAMELA HANSFORD

NV —UNIVERSITY OF NEVADA, RENO, University Library, Special Collections Dept, Reno, 89557. Robert E Blesse, Head
Holdings: Vols (54) Cat
Notes: Includes individual works by author in all editions including translations; also prefaces, introductions, published correspondence, appearances in anthologies, periodicals, etc. Bibliographical research collection, part of Modern Authors Collection. Other appearances 100 cataloged.

JOHNSON, PAUL B.

MS —UNIVERSITY OF SOUTHERN MISSISSIPPI, William David McCain Graduate Library, Box 5148, Southern Sta, Hattiesburg, 39406.
Holdings: Vols 12,000 Cat Mss Maps Pix Microforms
Notes: Mississippiana Collection incl government publications, newspapers, works on geography, literature, history, politics and travel. Also incl papers of Theodore G Bilbo, William M Colmer, Paul B Johnson, Sr and Paul B Johnson, Jr, Con Sellers, the University of Southern Mississippi Archives, an oral history collection, and a genealogy collection. See also entries under individual names and subjects.

JOHNSON, PAUL B., JR.

MS —UNIVERSITY OF SOUTHERN MISSISSIPPI, William David McCain Graduate Library, Box 5148, Southern Sta, Hattiesburg, 39406.
Holdings: Vols 12,000 Cat Mss Maps Pix Microforms
Notes: Mississippiana Collection incl government publications, newspapers, works on geography, literature, history, politics and travel. Also incl papers of Theodore G Bilbo, William M Colmer, Paul B Johnson, Sr and Paul B Johnson, Jr, Con Sellers, the University of Southern Mississippi Archives, an oral history collection, and a genealogy collection. See also entries under individual names and subjects.

JOHNSON, ROBERT UNDERWOOD

DE —UNIVERSITY OF DELAWARE, Hugh M Morris Library, S College Ave, Newark, 19711. T Stuart Dick, Special Collections
Holdings: Cat Mss Pix
Notes: Manuscripts, etc, incl literary correspondence.

NY —NEW YORK PUBLIC LIBRARY, Rare Books and Manuscripts Div, Fifth Ave & 42 St, New York, 10018. William L Joyce, Asst Dir; Susan E Davis, Cur of Mss
Holdings: Mss
Budget: ($7161)
Notes: Incl personal and literary mss, papers, etc.

NY —UNIVERSITY OF ROCHESTER, Rush Rhees Library, Department of Rare Books and Special Collections, Rochester, 14627. Peter Dzwonkoski, Librn
Holdings: Cat Mss
Notes: Correspondents include Robert Underwood Johnson, Will Carlton, Henry Mills Alden, Richard Watson Gilder; Howell's proof of article on Henrik Ibsen (1906).

JOHNSON, SAMUEL

CA —UNIVERSITY OF CALIFORNIA, SAN DIEGO, Central University Library, Mandeville Dept of Special Collections, La Jolla, 92093. Lynda Corey Claassen, Head
Notes: Rare Book Collection incl 2000 vols of 18th century English literature, with special emphasis on the works of Daniel Defoe and Samuel Johnson.

CA —UNIVERSITY OF CALIFORNIA, LOS ANGELES, William Andrews Clark

JOHNSON, SAMUEL (cont.)

Memorial Library, 2520 Cimarron St, Los Angeles, 90018.
Holdings: Cat Pix
Notes: Extensive collection, first editions, etc.

CT —YALE UNIVERSITY, Box 1603A, Yale Station, New Haven, 06520.

IL —NORTHWESTERN UNIVERSITY, Library, Special Collections Dept, 1937 Sheridan Rd, Evanston, 60201. R Russell Maylone, Cur
Holdings: Vols 900 Cat
Notes: The Elmer A Smith Memorial Collection. Works of Samuel Johnson and those of his contemporaries touching upon him, especially Boswell. Additional material in general collection.

MA —HARVARD UNIVERSITY LIBRARY, Houghton Library, Cambridge, 02138. F Thomas Noonan, Cur, Reading Room; Lawrence Dowler, Associate Librn
Holdings: Cat Mss
Notes: See *Harvard Library Notes,* III (1935), 20-29.

NV —UNIVERSITY OF NEVADA, RENO, University Library, Special Collections Dept, Reno, 89557. Robert E Blesse, Head
Holdings: Vols (60) Cat
Notes: First and early editions. Works about Johnson. Boswell's *Life of Samuel Johnson* in four editions.

NY —CORNELL UNIVERSITY LIBRARIES, John M Olin Library, Dept of Rare Books, Ithaca, 14853. Donald D Eddy, Librn
Notes: A collection of materials by and about Samuel Johnson.

NY —UNIVERSITY OF ROCHESTER, Rush Rhees Library, Department of Rare Books and Special Collections, Rochester, 14627. Peter Dzwonkoski, Librn
Holdings: Vols 250 // Cat
Notes: Works by and about him. No photocopying.

NC —UNIVERSITY OF NORTH CAROLINA, CHAPEL HILL, Wilson Library, Rare Book Collection, Chapel Hill, 27514. Paul S Koda, Cur of Rare Books
Holdings: Vols 300 Cat
Notes: The Whitaker Collection of Samuel Johnson and James Boswell contains 600 first and rare editions of the writings of Johnson and his friends. Important works of James Boswell, as well as Chesterfield, Goldsmith, and Fanny Burney are included, as well as reference, critical, and bibliographical material.

VA —VIRGINIA COMMONWEALTH UNIVERSITY, James Branch Cabell Library, Richmond, 23284. Daniel Yanchisin, Special Collections Librn

†ON —UNIVERSITY OF WESTERN ONTARIO, School of Library and Information Science, Special Collections Room, London, N6A 5B9, Can.
Holdings: Vols 103
Notes: Contains about 67 different editions from folio to miniature of Samuel Johnson's *A Dictionary of the English Language.*

ON —METROPOLITAN TORONTO LIBRARY, Literature Dept, 789 Yonge St, Toronto, M4W 2G8, Can. Katherine McCook, Head
Holdings: Vols 206 Cat
Notes: More than 200 editions of Samuel Johnson's allegorical romance *Rasselas,* beginning with the first (1759). No photocopying.

JOHNSON, SONIA

UT —UNIVERSITY OF UTAH, Marriott Library, Special Collections, Salt Lake City, 84112. Gregory C Thompson, Cur
Notes: Papers, correspondence, and manuscripts, of Sonia Johnson, excommunicated Mormon feminist. Part of the collection has a time seal on it.

JOHNSON, WALTER, 1915-

NJ —PRINCETON UNIVERSITY, Library, Manuscript Collection, Nassau St, Princeton, 08540. Jean F Preston, Cur
Holdings: // Mss
Notes: Incl 6 boxes of papers.

JOHNSON, WILLIAM LON

†WA —WASHINGTON STATE UNIVERSITY, Library, Manuscripts, Archives & Special Collections, Pullman, 99164. John F Guido, Head
Holdings: Vols Cat Mss Maps Pix Microforms
Notes: Ms resources in the Washington State University Library for the study of Pacific Northwest history incl the personal papers of Frank A Banks, William Compton Brown, Enoch Albert Bryan, Ernest Otto Holland, William Lon Johnson, Catherine May, Lucullus Virgil McWhorter, Austin Mires, Carl Parcher Russell, Pierre Jean de Smet, Henry Harmon Spalding, Elkanah Walker, John McAdam Webster, Marcus Whitman, as well as many business records of banks, insurance firms and agencies, breweries, lumber mills, merchants, entrepreneurs and farmers. All ms collections are described in a catalog, a published register or an unpublished finding aid.

JOHNSON, WILLIAM SAMUEL, 1727-1819

†DC —LIBRARY OF CONGRESS, Manuscript Division, Washington, 20540.
Notes: The papers, etc, of William Samuel Johnson.

JOHNSON, WILLIAM SPENCER, 1813-1897

IN —INDIANA UNIVERSITY, Lilly Library, Seventh St, Bloomington, 47405. William R Cagle, Librn
Holdings: // Mss Pix
Notes: Photographs, etc, of actors and actresses are located in ms collection of William Spencer Johnson, 1813-1897, printer. Correspondence and photographs from actors and actresses, 1846-1894. 120 items.

JOHNSTON, ALBERT SIDNEY

LA —TULANE UNIVERSITY, Howard-Tilton Memorial Library, Special Collections Div, 7001 Freret St, New Orleans, 70118. Wilbur E Meneray, Librn
Holdings: Cat Mss
Notes: Official, personal and family correspondence of Johnston including letter and order books. Includes the Mexican War, the Utah Campaign and the Civil War. Indexed.

JOHNSTON, CLEMENT D.

VA —VIRGINIA POLYTECHNIC INSTITUTE AND STATE UNIVERSITY LIBRARY, Blacksburg, 24061. Glenn L McMullen, Special Collections Librn
Holdings: Vols (2000) Cat Mss Maps Pix Audiotapes
Notes: Primarily Southwest Virginia materials. Collection incl ca 200 mss, account books and other archival records of nineteenth century area businesses and other mining operations; the extant archival records of several Southwest Virginia railroads, incl the Virginia and Tennessee Railroad and the Norfolk and Western Railroad; and papers of historically prominent Southwest Virginians, incl John Apperson, Dr Harvy Black, James P Charlton, W Graham Claytor, Henley Fugate, Clement D Johnston, Germanicus Kent, William Preston, J Hoge Tyler, and William C Wampler. Several oral history collections incl material on Appalachian customs and folklore, particularly in Patrick County.

JOHNSTON, DENIS

MA —BOSTON UNIVERSITY, Mugar Memorial Library, Special Collections Dept, 771 Commonwealth Ave, Boston, 02215. Howard B Gotlieb, Dir
Holdings: Cat Mss
Notes: Mss, correspondence, incl publications by or about.

BC —UNIVERSITY OF VICTORIA, McPherson Library, Victoria, V8W 3H5, Can.

JOHNSTON, FRANCES BENJAMIN

DC —LIBRARY OF CONGRESS, Prints & Photographs Div, Washington, 20540.
Notes: The Carnegie Survey of the Architecture of the South is a photographic record of the early buildings and gardens of Maryland, Virginia, the Carolinas, Georgia, Alabama, Louisiana, Florida and Mississippi, executed by Frances Benjamin Johnston between 1933 and 1940. Incl photographs and papers of photojournalist and portrait photographer Frances Benjamin Johnston.

JOHNSTON, MARY

VA —UNIVERSITY OF VIRGINIA, Alderman Library, Clifton Waller Barrett Collection, Charlottesville, 22901. Joan St C Crane, Cur of American Literature Collections
Holdings: Cat Mss Pix
Notes: Extensive collection of mss and printed materials.

JOHNSTON, RONALD

MA —BOSTON UNIVERSITY, Mugar Memorial Library, Special Collections Dept, 771 Commonwealth Ave, Boston, 02215. Howard B Gotlieb, Dir
Holdings: Cat Mss Pix Memorabilia

JOHNSTON, THOMAS

MA —JOHN F KENNEDY LIBRARY, Columbia Point, Boston, 02125. Henry J Gwiazda II, Cur
Notes: The Burke Marshall papers, 50 archives boxes re civil rights, 1961-1964 and the Bedford-Stuyvesant Development and Restoration Corporations; the Joseph Dolan papers, 1 box; the Thomas Johnston papers, 3 boxes; the James Mc Shane papers, 2 boxes; the Frank Mankiewicz papers, 15 boxes; and the Scott Rafferty papers, 4 boxes.

JOHNSTON, WILLIAM PRESTON

LA —TULANE UNIVERSITY, Howard-Tilton Memorial Library, Special Collections Div, 7001 Freret St, New Orleans, 70118. Wilbur E Meneray, Librn
Holdings: Cat Mss
Notes: Official, personal and family correspondence relating to the Civil War and Tulane University.

JOJOBA

CA —UNIVERSITY OF CALIFORNIA, RIVERSIDE, University Library, Bio-Agricultural Library, Batchelor Hall, Riverside, 92521. Barbara Montanary, Head
Holdings: Vols (130,000) Cat Mss Maps Pix Microforms
Notes: The Bio-Agricultural Library (formerly the Library of Citrus Experiment Station of the University of California) is well known for its complete collections in the fields of the agriculture sciences. It is especially known for its emphasis on entomology, incl bio-control; botany, citriculture, plant sciences, nematology and plant pathology; arid and semi-arid lands research and subtropical agriculture. Specific areas of interest are avocados, dates, desert flora, jojoba, guayule and carob.

JOKES see Wit and Humor

JOLLEY, A. B.

TX —NORTH TEXAS STATE UNIVERSITY, Archives, NT Station Box 5188, Denton, 76203. Robert LaForte, University Archivist
Notes: A B Jolley Collection (15 linear feet). The development of agriculture and businesses dependent on agriculture in the North Texas area is a collection strength at the NTSU Archives. The A B Jolley

JOLLEY, A. B. (cont.)

Collection contains extensive information on the development of Dallas County agriculture from the perspective of the County Agricultural Agent from 1929-1953. A B Jolley Collection, *The National Union Catalog of Manuscript Collections: Catalog* 1979 Washington: Library of Congress, 1980. Page 214.

JONAS, GILBERT

MI —MICHIGAN STATE UNIVERSITY, International Library, South and Southeast Asia Collection, East Lansing, 48824. Clinton Lockert, Bibliographer
Holdings: Vols (13,500) Cat Mss Maps Pix Audiotapes Microforms
Notes: Correspondence and papers of Frederick Field, Gilbert Jonas, and Wesley Fishel.

JONAS, OSWALD

CA —UNIVERSITY OF CALIFORNIA, RIVERSIDE, University Library, 4045 Canyon Crest Dr, Box 5900, Riverside, 92517.
Notes: The Oswald Jonas Memorial Collection holds the musicological mss, letters, biographical materials, and notebooks of Heinrich Schenker and also the papers of the late Oswald Jonas, musicologist and leading authority on the life and work of Schenker. Incl Schenker's diary; correspondence with Anthony van Hoboken, Reinhard Oppel, Moriz Violin, Eugen d'Albert, and Oswald Jonas; the proofs and mss of his published works; printed editions from his library with notes, marginalia, and critical annotations; *Urlinie* tables; and miscellanea. A guide to the collection will be published by the library.

JONES, DAVID MICHAEL, 1895-1974

NV —UNIVERSITY OF NEVADA, RENO, University Library, Special Collections Dept, Reno, 89557. Robert E Blesse, Head
Holdings: // Vols (18) Cat Other appearances 32 Cat
Notes: Includes individual works by author in all editions including translations; also prefaces, introductions, published correspondence, appearances in anthologies, periodicals, etc. Bibliographical research collection, part of Modern Authors Collection.

BC —UNIVERSITY OF VICTORIA, McPherson Library, Victoria, V8W 3H5, Can.

JONES, ERNEST LARUE, 1879-1958

DC —GEORGETOWN UNIVERSITY, Library, Special Collections Div, 37 & O Sts NW, Washington, 20057. George M Barringer, Special Collections Librn; Nicholas B Sheetz, Mss Librn
Holdings: Cat
Notes: The Ernest Larue Jones Collection consists of seven large volumes of photographs which document the development of American aeronautics from 1863-1917. The majority of the pictures are of the period 1907-1915 when Jones was publisher of the pioneer technical journal "Aeronautics".

KS —UNIVERSITY OF KANSAS MEDICAL CENTER, College of Health Sciences & Hospital, Clendening History of Medicine Library, Rainbow Blvd at 39th, Kansas City, 66103. Robert P Hudson, Chmn/Cur
Notes: Papers, 1895-1958. Ca 20 items. British psychoanalyst. Notebooks and papers written while a medical student at Cardiff, Wales. Unpublished finding aid in the repository. Access restricrted. Purchased from Mrs Katherine Jones, 1958.

JONES, GAYL

MA —BOSTON UNIVERSITY, Mugar Memorial Library, Special Collections Dept, 771 Commonwealth Ave, Boston, 02215. Howard B Gotlieb, Dir
Holdings: Cat Mss

JONES, HILARY POLLARD

DC —LIBRARY OF CONGRESS, Manuscript Division, Washington, 20540. John C Broderick, Chief
Notes: His papers; Naval Historical Foundation Collection.

JONES, HOWARD MUMFORD, 1892-1980

NC —DUKE UNIVERSITY, William R Perkins Library, Jay B Hubbell Center for American Literary Historiography, Durham, 27706. Erma Whittington, Librn
Notes: 77,312 items, including manuscripts, pictures, clippings, and correspondence. "The objective of the Center is to gather the papers and materials of significant scholars and critics in American literary history." The Center is a part of the Perkins Library Manuscripts Department.

JONES, HOWARD PALFREY, 1899-1973

CA —HOOVER INSTITUTION ON WAR, REVOLUTION & PEACE, Stanford University, Stanford, 94305. Milorad M Drachkovitch, Archivist
Holdings: Mss
Notes: Papers of Howard Palfrey Jones, 1930-1973, incl mss, correspondence, reports, research files, studies, and printed matter, relating primarily to public finance and post-war reconstruction in Germany, 1945-1951, to US foreign relations in East Asia, 1951-73, and to his service as Ambassador to Indonesia, 1958-1965. Ca 60 Ms Boxes.

NY —STATE UNIVERSITY OF NEW YORK AT ALBANY, Library, Special Collections Dept, 1400 Washington Ave, Albany, 12222. Marion P Munzer, Coordr
Notes: Personal and family records of Howard Palfrey Jones (12 linear feet); correspondence, articles, and texts of speeches relating to municipal reform; proposals on tax reforms.
See also entries under Municipal Government; Taxation

JONES, JAMES

NV —UNIVERSITY OF NEVADA, RENO, University Library, Special Collections Dept, Reno, 89557. Robert E Blesse, Head
Holdings: Vols (47) Cat Other appearances 50 Cat
Notes: Includes individual works by author in all editions including translations; also prefaces, introductions, published correspondence, appearances in anthologies, periodicals, etc. Bibliographical research collection, part of Modern Authors Collection.

†TX —UNIVERSITY OF TEXAS LIBRARIES, General Libraries, Humanities Research Center, PO Box 7219, Austin, 78712. John Chalmers, Librn
Notes: All but one of his literary manuscripts; incl correspondence, contracts, etc.

JONES, JESSE HOLMAN, 1914-1957

TX —UNIVERSITY OF TEXAS LIBRARIES, General Libraries, Barker Texas History Center, PO Box P, Austin, 78712. Don Carleton, Dir
Holdings: Cat Mss Pix
Notes: Personal and business papers of Jesse Holman Jones (1874-1956), publisher of the Houston *Chronicle,* director of the Reconstruction Finance Corporation, and Secretary of Commerce (1940-1945); 42 linear feet.

JONES, JOHN PAUL

DC —LIBRARY OF CONGRESS, Manuscript Division, Washington, 20540. John C Broderick, Chief
Holdings: Cat Mss Pix
Notes: Mss, papers, records, etc.

MA —GRAND LODGE OF MASONS IN MASSACHUSETTS, Library, 186 Tremont St, Boston, 20111. Roberta Hankamer, Librn
Holdings: Vols 60,000 Cat Mss Maps Pix Slides Microforms
Notes: Collection incl philosophy, religion, local history, biography, etc, as they might further Masonic research, in addition to strictly Masonic works--transactions of research lodges worldwide, lodge histories, theory, origins, Masonic jurisprudence, Masonic music, etc. Museum collection of aprons, jewels, diplomas and other artifacts is a prime research source. No estimate has been made of the depth of these holdings. John Paul Jones materials are notable. Inc scrapbooks and clippings.

JONES, JOHN PERCIVAL

CA —UNIVERSITY OF CALIFORNIA, LOS ANGELES, Research Library, Dept of Special Collections, 405 Hilgard Ave, Los Angeles, 90024. Edward Shreeves, Chairman, Bibliographers Group; David S Zeidberg, Head
Notes: 12 linear feet of mss and correspondence of the Nevada senator, John Percival Jones, founder of Santa Monica, and of the related Morton and Conger families.

JONES, JOSEPH

LA —TULANE UNIVERSITY, Howard-Tilton Memorial Library, Special Collections Div, 7001 Freret St, New Orleans, 70118. Wilbur E Meneray, Librn
Holdings: Vols (700) Cat Mss Pix
Notes: Publications of 19th and 20th century New Orleans and Louisana medical associations and physicians. Correspondence and diaries of Louisiana physicians from the 18th century to the present including those of Charles Cassidy Bass, Stanford Emerson Chaille, Joseph Jones, Edmund Kells, Rudolph Matas, Joseph Montegut, John Leonard Riddell and Edmond Souchon.

JONES, L. ROGAN

WA —WESTERN WASHINGTON UNIVERSITY, Center for Pacific Northwest Studies, High St, Bellingham, 98225. James W Scott, Dir
Holdings: Mss Pix Phonorecords
Notes: The L Rogan Jones Collection: Broadcasting executive and community leader, Rogan Jones died in 1972. Owner, operator and sr executive of various radio, television and cable transmitting companies, Jones was involved during the 1930s in a famous lawsuit brought by various Washington newspapers and Associated Press against Station KVOS, which he then operated. In a case of changing fortunes, first for, then against KVOS, the case was argued before the US Supreme Court in 1936. A unanimous verdict was finally handed down in favor of the station. It is regarded as a landmark verdict in the history of public broadcasting. Papers on this and other radio and television issues are included in the collection. An *Informational Paper* is presently being prepared on this collection.

JONES, LEROI (IMAMU AMIRI BARAKA), 1934-

CT —YALE UNIVERSITY, Box 1603A, Yale Station, New Haven, 06520.
Notes: Extensive file; newspaper, magazine contributions by and about Jones (Imanu Amiri Baraka).

IN —INDIANA UNIVERSITY, Lilly Library, Seventh St, Bloomington, 47405. William R Cagle, Librn
Holdings: // Cat Mss
Notes: Editorial office records for *Yugen,* 1958-1961, and for *The Floating Bear,* 1961. Incl correspondence of Jones, Hettie Cohen and Diane DePrima with various authors

JONES, LEROI (IMAMU AMIRI BARAKA), 1934- (cont.)

and some mss and proofs of items published by Totem Press. Also typescipts with autograph changes and corrections of Jones' *The Baptism* and *Dutchman*, as well as galleys and manuscript for his *Preface to a Twenty Volume Suicide Note*. 572 items. Incl first editions of Jones and most issues of *Yugen* and *Floating Bear*.

NY —NEW YORK UNIVERSITY, Elmer Holmes Bobst Library, Div of Special Collections, Washington Sq S, New York, 10012. Frank Walker, Librn; Patrick McGuire, Asst Librn
Holdings: Vols (100,000) Cat Mss Pix
Notes: The Fales Collection of first (and other) editions of English and American novels from about 1750 to date (about 70, 000 titles). Mss (30,000) pieces.

NY —SYRACUSE UNIVERSITY LIBRARIES, Ernest S Bird Library, George Arents Research Library for Special Collections, Syracuse, 13210. Carolyn A Davis, Manuscripts Librn; Amy S Doherty, University Archivist; Mark F Weimer, Rare Book Librn
Notes: His correspondence, papers and works. Papers 1957-65 (25 linear feet).

BC —SIMON FRASER UNIVERSITY, Library, Burnaby, V5A 1S6, Can. Percilla Groves, Special Collections Librn
Holdings: Cat Mss
Notes: Letters of Charles Olson to Robin Blaser, Andrew Crozier, Barry Hall, Le Roi Jones (Amiri Baraka), Ed Sanders. Typescript and galleys for *Maximus IV, V,* VI, mss published in *Pacific Nation* and *Wivenhoe Park Review*. See *Line*, vol 1, no 1, spring 1983, for a complete list of Olson mss at SFU.

JONES, LOUISE SEYMOUR

CA —CLAREMONT COLLEGES, Ella Strong Denison Library, Scripps College, Claremont, 91711. Judy Harvey Sahak, Librn
Holdings: Vols 50 Cat
Notes: About 5000 examples of bookplates, the Louise Seymour Jones Collections. Incl her papers.

JONES, MARCUS

†CA —RANCHO SANTA ANA BOTANIC GARDEN LIBRARY, 1500 N College Ave, Claremont, 91711. Beatrice M Beck, Librn
Holdings: Vols (20,000)
Notes: California flora nd gardening, world floras, taxonomic literature, evolutionary biology, and the papers and collections of Marcus Jones and Philip Munz.

JONES, MARGO

TX —DALLAS PUBLIC LIBRARY, Fine Arts Div, 1515 Young St, Dallas, 75201. Richard L Waters, Acting Dir; Jane Holahan, Manager
Holdings: // Uncat Mss Pix
Notes: *The Margo Jones Theatre Collection* (75 linear ft) contains the office papers of this theatre: financial, business, legal records, scripts, programs, photos of productions, reviews and clippings, personal correspondence; organizational records. Gift of the Dallas Civic Theatre, Inc, 1962 after theatre ceased operation. Described in L C card catalog MS 66-1622.

JONES, PETER

ON —VICTORIA UNIVERSITY, Library, 71 Queen's Park Crescent, Toronto, M5S 1K7, Can. Robert C Brandeis, Chief Librn
Holdings: Vols (1000) // Cat Mss Maps Pix
Notes: Collection consists of books, pamphlets, and government reports mainly dealing with North American Indians and western explorations and missionary enterprises among the Indian tribes in Canada. Incl Indian Bibles and hymnbooks, and mss and vols by Peter Jones (an Indian missionary) and James Evans (inventor of the Cree syllabic alphabet).

JONES, ROBERT E.

AL —UNIVERSITY OF ALABAMA, HUNTSVILLE, Library, Box 2600, Huntsville, 35807. John Warren, Dir
Holdings: Mss
Notes: The congressman's papers, etc.

JONES, ROGER

DC —LIBRARY OF CONGRESS, Manuscript Division, Washington, 20540. John C Broderick, Chief
Notes: Roger Jones Family Papers, 1662-1820.

JONES, SAM HOUSTON

LA —TULANE UNIVERSITY, Howard-Tilton Memorial Library, Special Collections Div, 7001 Freret St, New Orleans, 70118. Wilbur E Meneray, Librn
Holdings: Cat Mss Pix Audiotapes Videotapes
Notes: Papers of Louisiana politicians, including Thomas Hale Boggs, Felix Edward Hebert, Sam Houston Jones and deLesseps Story Morrison.

JONES, THOMAS S.

NY —COLUMBIA UNIVERSITY LIBRARIES, Rare Book & Manuscript Library, 801 Butler Library, 535 W 114 St, New York, 10027. Kenneth A Lohf, Librn
Holdings: Pix
Notes: 163 photographs of and relating to the poet, Thomas S Jones, and his friend John L Foley. Restricted use.

JONES, WESLEY L.

WA —UNIVERSITY OF WASHINGTON LIBRARIES, Suzzallo Library, Manuscripts Section, FM-25, Seattle, 98195. Karyl Winn, Librn
Notes: Incl 147 linear feet, 1898-1932.

JONES, WILLIAM ATKINSON

VA —UNIVERSITY OF VIRGINIA, Alderman Library, Manuscripts Dept, Charlottesville, 22901. Edmund Berkeley Jr, Cur
Holdings: Cat Mss Pix
Notes: Papers, personal and political, etc.

JONES FAMILY (NEW YORK)

NY —WHALING MUSEUM SOCIETY, Cold Spring Harbor Whaling Museum, Main St, Cold Spring Harbor, 11724. Robert D Farwell, Dir
Holdings: Cat Mss Maps Pix
Notes: Library of bound printed books covers Cold Spring Harbor whaling industry, in general, and maritime affairs. Archives contain thousands of original documents concerning whaling activities, the Cold Spring Harbor Whaling Company, and the extensive maritime coastal trade conducted out of Cold Spring Harbor after the whaling era (latter 1800s). Considerable material deals with the Jones and Hewlett families, important in both local commerce and Long Island and New York affairs.

JORDAN

CA —HOOVER INSTITUTION ON WAR, REVOLUTION & PEACE, Stanford University, Stanford, 94305. Milorad M Drachkovitch, Archivist
Holdings: Vols (100,000)
See also entry under Near East

JORDAN, B. EVERETT

NC —DUKE UNIVERSITY, William R Perkins Library, Manuscript Dept, Durham, 27706. Ellen Gartrell, Cur of Mss
Holdings: Cat Mss
Notes: Papers, etc.

JORDAN, BARBARA

TX —NORTH TEXAS STATE UNIVERSITY, Archives, NT Station Box 5188, Denton, 76203. Robert LaForte, University Archivist
Notes: Part of Oral History Collection. Interviews with Jordan, member of Texas legislature. Restricted.

JORDAN, DAVID STARR, 1851-1931

CA —HOOVER INSTITUTION ON WAR, REVOLUTION & PEACE, Stanford University, Stanford, 94305. Milorad M Drachkovitch, Archivist
Holdings: // Mss
Notes: 1913-1925, of David Starr Jordan, president and chancellor of Stanford University, author, and naturalist. Correspondence with leaders of the international peace movement and with scientists and statesmen; together with reports, memoranda, and other papers relating to the Japanese in California, the California alien land law, the effects of war, education for peace, efforts to maintain the neutrality of the US, and international problems arising from the Peace Conference of 1919. 30 ft.

NY —CORNELL UNIVERSITY LIBRARIES, Collection of Regional History, Dept of Manuscripts and Univ Archives, Ithaca, 14853.
Notes: Poem (handwritten, autographed), 1921; 1 item.

JORDAN, MILDRED

MA —BOSTON UNIVERSITY, Mugar Memorial Library, Special Collections Dept, 771 Commonwealth Ave, Boston, 02215. Howard B Gotlieb, Dir
Holdings: Cat Mss
Notes: Mss, correspondence, etc collected in depth; incl publications by or about.

JOSEPH II OF AUSTRIA

CA —STANFORD UNIVERSITY LIBRARIES, Cecil H Green Library, Stanford, 94305. Peter R Frank, Cur, CDP-Germanic Collection
Notes: Extensive holdings, covering Austrian history of the Habsburg Empire to the present. Especially strong for the period of Maria Theresia and Joseph II, 19th & 20th century. Extremely rich in the Josephinic pamphlets (Broschuren-Literatur), broadsheets of the Napoleonic Wars and of the Revolution 1848/1849, rare periodicals. This and other rare material in the Stanford Collection of German, Austrian and Swiss Culture, Special Collections. Over 4,000 vols entered in RLIN. Description: "Narrative on a Good Meal: A Collection of Austriaca at Stanford University Libraries" by Peter R Frank.

JOSEPHAT see Barlaam and Josephat

JOSEPHINIC LITERATURE

CA —STANFORD UNIVERSITY LIBRARIES, Cecil H Green Library, Stanford, 94305. Peter R Frank, Cur, CDP-Germanic Collection
Notes: Extensive collection of works by Austrian writers and secondary literature, literary periodicals, anthologies, and the like. Baroque items, especially rich in Josephinic literature, 19th and 20th century, with rare first editions. Autographs and typescripts (P Hanke, eg). Rare material in the Stanford Collection of German, Austrian and Swiss Culture, Special Collections. Description: "Narrative on a Good Meal: A Collection of Austriaca at Stanford University Libraries" by Peter R Frank.

JOSEPHSON, MATTHEW

CT —YALE UNIVERSITY, Box 1603A, Yale Station, New Haven, 06520.
Notes: Papers.

JOSEPHSON, WILLIAM

†MA —JOHN F KENNEDY LIBRARY, Columbia Point, Boston, 02125. Dan H Fenn

JOSEPHSON, WILLIAM (cont.)

Jr, Dir
Holdings: // Cat Mss Microforms
Notes: Papers of JFK; microfilm copies (20 rolls) of papers of Public Information Director Edwin Bayley, General Counsel William Josephson; and records of the Peace Corp, 1961-1966. 2 linear ft of mss. Holdings are described in "Historical Materials in the John F Kennedy Library." Copies may be obtained by writing the Research Archivist.

JOSEPHUS

OH —HEBREW UNION COLLEGE-JEWISH INSTITUTE OF RELIGION, Klau Library, 3101 Clifton Ave, Cincinnati, 45220. David J Gilner, Reference Librn
Holdings: Vols 500 Cat
Notes: Six 15th century editions; over 50 16th century editions and issues. In Latin, Greek, Dutch, English, French, German, Italian and Spanish.

ON —NATIONAL LIBRARY OF CANADA, 395 Wellington St, Ottawa, K1A 0N4, Can. Andre Preibish, Dir
Notes: *The Jacob M Lowy Collection* over 2000 works of very rare Hebraica and Judaica. Among outstanding items are 30 incunabula - the first printed edition of the Babylonian Talmud, many editions of Flavius Josephus, including first edition of 1470 Early Bibles in many languages. *The Saul Hayes Collection* of Hebraic Manuscripts and microforms. Manuscripts from North Africa and the Orient; 300 reels of manuscripts held by libraries in Poland, USSR and Hungary. This collection is held in the Jacob M Lowy Room.

JOSEPHUS, WILLIAM

IL —SOUTHERN ILLINOIS UNIVERSITY, CARBONDALE, Delyte W Morris Library, Carbondale, 62901.
Holdings: Cat Mss Pix
Notes: Incl the papers of Drs William Josephus and Victor Robinson; with the papers of Theodore A Schroeder. Much on sex instruction and birth control.

JOSLYN, ALLYN

CA —UNIVERSITY OF CALIFORNIA, LOS ANGELES, Theater Arts Library, Los Angeles, 90024. Edward Shreeves, Chairman, Bibliographers Group; Audree Malkin, Head, Theater Arts Library
Notes: Allyn Joslyn (actor) Collection: scripts for stage, motion picture and television dramas and comedies; related production material; production stills and portraits; press clippings; souvenir programs and recordings.

JOSTEN, WERNER

MA —SMITH COLLEGE, Werner Josten Library for the Performing Arts, Northampton, 01063. Marlene M Wong, Librn
Notes: Holographs and published scores of music by Werner Josten. Letters to him.

JOUDRY, PATRICIA, 1921-

AB —UNIVERSITY OF CALGARY, Libraries, Special Collections Div, 2500 University Dr, Calgary, T2N 1N4, Can.
Holdings: Mss
Notes: Correspondence, diaries, writer's logs and journals, notes, mss (4 meters), setting copies, galleys, page proofs, playbills, and reviews for nonfiction, fiction and drama, 1940s-82.

JOURNALISM

AZ —ARIZONA STATE UNIVERSITY, Library, Tempe, 85287. Marilyn Wurzburger, Special Collections Librn
Notes: Reflecting his roles of reporter, photographer and novelist, Ted Schwarz's papers cover subject areas such as investigative journalism, psychology, criminal justice, law, numismatics, visual communication, photography and writing as a career. Collection incl extensive research materials from the author's study and reporting of the "Hillside Strangler" case which deals with multiple personalities. Partially cataloged and indexed, the collection consists of 140 linear feet of multi-media materials: vols, magazines, newspaper articles, galley proofs, interviews and correspondence, reel-to-reel tapes, audiotapes and videotapes.

CT —YALE UNIVERSITY, Beinecke Rare Book & Manuscript Library, Osborn Collection, New Haven, 06520. Stephen R Parks, Cur
Holdings: Mss

DC —LIBRARY OF CONGRESS, Manuscript Division, Washington, 20540. John C Broderick, Chief
Notes: Papers of Roy W Howard (1883-1964), past president and chairman of the board of Scripps-Howard Newspapers. Some 85,000 items for the years 1923-64, incl business and personal correspondence, maintained under state and city of origin, with separate files in each year for the various Scripps-Howard newspaper, especially for the *World Telegram* (New York City). Also, the papers of Joseph Wood Krutch, incl correspondence; Joseph Alsop; Stewart Hensley.

DC —LIBRARY OF CONGRESS, Prints & Photographs Div, Washington, 20540.
Holdings: Cat Pix
Notes: Complete photographic files of *Look* magazine: the history of 35 years in pictures. Incl 17.5 million black and white negatives, 1.5 million color transparencies, 450,000 contact sheets, and 25,000 movie stills.

IL —UNIVERSITY OF ILLINOIS, URBANA/CHAMPAIGN, Library, Communications Library, 122 Gregory Hall, Urbana, 61801. Nancy Allen, Librn
Holdings: Vols (18,000) Cat
Budget: ($27,000)
Notes: Journalism history, theory and skills. Studies of individual journalists, newspapers, and other news media.

IA —IOWA STATE UNIVERSITY, Library, Dept of Special Collections, Ames, 50011. Stanley M Yates, Head
Holdings: // Mss
Notes: Papers of Lauren K Soth, editor of Des Moines *Register and Tribune* from 1954-75, winning a Pulitzer Prize for Editorial Writing in 1956 for his editorials which helped establish agricultural exchanges with the Soviet Union. 20 linear ft, finding aid available. Also, papers of Frank Rinehart Eyerly, managing editor for *Register and* Tribune.

MA —BOSTON UNIVERSITY, Mugar Memorial Library, Special Collections Dept, 771 Commonwealth Ave, Boston, 02215. Howard B Gotlieb, Dir
Holdings: Cat Mss Pix
Notes: Incl literary and personal papers of some 75 prominent modern journalists: Daniel Lang, Georgie Anne Geyer, Flora Lewis, Carleton Beals, Alistair Cooke, Ralph Ingersoll, Richard Tregaskis, Far Eastern journalists John Hughes of the *Christian Science Monitor* and Dennis Bloodworth of the *Observer* of London, etc. A complete list is available.

NY —COLUMBIA UNIVERSITY LIBRARIES, Journalism Library, New York, 10027. Wade Doares, Librn
Holdings: Vols 13,000 Cat
Notes: Incl clipping files.

NY —NEW YORK PUBLIC LIBRARY, Research Libraries, General Research Division, Fifth Ave & 42 St, New York, 10018. Rodney Phillips, Chief
Holdings: Vols (2,225,000) Cat Maps Pix Microforms
Budget: ($775,718)

OR —AMERICAN PRIVATE PRESS ASSOCIATION, 112 E Burnett St, Stayton, 97383. Martin M Horvat, Librn
Notes: The collection is divided into two primary segments: the first is the traditional one of Amateur Journalism, the second is science fiction and fantasy oriented. The collection was once at New York University Libraries but moved in 1981.

SC —COLLEGE OF CHARLESTON LIBRARY, Special Collections Dept, Charleston, 29401.
Notes: Robert Walter Marks Papers, 1890-1980: a collection of correspondence, mss, published material, notes, and photographs reflecting Marks' multifarious career in Charlestown, New York, and Europe as a journalist covering a wide variety of fields.

TX —ROSENBERG LIBRARY, Galveston and Texas History Center, 2310 Sealy Ave, Galveston, 77550. Jane Kenamore, Archivist
Holdings: Vols 7368 Cat Mss Maps Pix Slides Microforms
Budget: $60,000
Notes: Emphasis on upper Texas coast material; Republic of Texas period; Civil War period; Shipping; Texas Navy; Jean Laffite; Texas politics; 19th-20th century; Railroads; Texas journalism, incl microfilms of Galveston newspapers, 1838-date.

VA —AMERICAN NEWSPAPER PUBLISHERS ASSOCIATION, ANPA, Library, 11600 Sunrise Valley Dr, Reston, (Mailing add: PO Box 17407, Dulles Intl AP, Washington, DC, 20041). Yvonne Egertson, Librn
Holdings: Vols (5000) Cat Microforms
Notes: Newspaper publishing. Newspaper history.

WI —STATE HISTORICAL SOCIETY OF WISCONSIN, Archives, 816 State St, Madison, 53706. Harold L Miller, Reference Archivist
Holdings: Mss Pix Films Microforms
Notes: Areas represented in collection incl radio, television, the press, public relations and advertising. Emphasis is on development of media in the 20th century; materials are mainly professional papers of individuals or organization or organizational records of firms or associations in the media. Collections are described in *Sources for Mass Communications, Film and Theater Research: A Guide,* (1982) and in current accession notes in the *Wisconsin Magazine of History.* Major collections are also listed in Hamer, *Guide to Manuscripts and Archives in the United States,* (1961) and in the *National Union Catalog of Manuscripts* Collections, (1959-date). Also incl, disc recordings and tape recordings.

WI —UNIVERSITY OF WISCONSIN, MADISON, Journalism Reading Room (Nieman-Grant), (formerly Bleyer Memorial Reading Room, School of Journalism), Vilas Communication Hall, Rm 2130, Madison, 53706. Arthur Cran, Librn; Mary Nagel, Asst Librn
Holdings: Vols 750 Cat
Budget: ($500)
Notes: Incl international mass communication, television, radio.

JOURNALISM—HISTORY

CT —YALE UNIVERSITY, Box 1603A, Yale Station, New Haven, 06520.

IL —UNIVERSITY OF ILLINOIS, URBANA/CHAMPAIGN, Library, Communications Library, 122 Gregory Hall, Urbana, 61801. Nancy Allen, Librn
Holdings: Vols (18,000) Cat
Notes: Journalism history, theory and skills. Studies of individual journalists, newspapers, and other news media.

MA —AMERICAN ANTIQUARIAN SOCIETY LIBRARY, 185 Salisbury St, Worcester, 01609. Marcus A McCorison, Dir & Librn
Holdings: cat
Notes: Center for research in the history of early American journalism.
See also entry under Newspapers, American

NY —ALFRED UNIVERSITY, Herrick Memorial Library, Alfred, 14802. June E Brown, Head Librn
Notes: The Howells/Frechette Collection. Family documents, 7000 letters of William Cooper Howells (American consul to Quebec, later to Toronto), William Dean Howells, his sister Annie Frechette, Achille Frechette (official translator, Canadian

JOURNALISM—HISTORY (cont.)

House of Commons), and Louis Frechette (poet laureate of Canada).

†OK —OKLAHOMA STATE UNIVERSITY, Library, Stillwater, 74074.
Notes: Papers of Paul Miller, chairman emeritus of the Gannett Company. Incl personal papers reflecting his career in journalism and as president of the Associated Press.

JOURNALISM, NONPRINT

WA —UNIVERSITY OF WASHINGTON LIBRARIES, Suzzallo Library, Manuscripts Section, FM-25, Seattle, 98195. Karyl Winn, Librn
Notes: Files of locally produced newsfilm from station KOMO-TV in Seattle, from 1954.

WY —UNIVERSITY OF WYOMING, William Robertson Coe Library, 13 & Ivinson, Laramie, 82071.
Notes: The papers of Morgan Beatty (1902-1975), an eminent newsman in print and broadcast journalism. Contains several thousand letters, many from prominent personalities, extensive background files of his "News of the World" and other broadcasts, and several thousand radio scripts and feature news stories.

JOURNALISM, PICTORIAL

IL —UNIVERSITY OF ILLINOIS, URBANA/CHAMPAIGN, Library, Communications Library, 122 Gregory Hall, Urbana, 61801. Nancy Allen, Librn
Holdings: Vols (18,000) Cat
Notes: Photojournalism theory and methods.

PA —TEMPLE UNIVERSITY LIBRARIES, Special Collections Dept, Rare Books & Mss Section, Philadelphia, 19122. Thomas M Whitehead, Cur
Holdings: Vols (10,000) Mss Pix
Notes: The private library of Charles Blockson established as a collection at Temple University. Approximately 25,000 items of Afro-American literature, history of slavery and African and Carribbean histroy and history and culture. Selective catalog (exhibition) available.

JOURNALISTS

AZ —NORTHERN ARIZONA UNIVERSITY, Special Collection Library, CU Box 6022, Flagstaff, 86011. Peter M Whiteley, Coordr/Archivist; William Mullane, Librn
Notes: Collection of Robert Eunson, journalist, vice president, and assistant general manager of United Press International. NAU graduate. Incl correspondence, scrapbooks, subject files, photos, 1930's-1975. Eunson was a World War II correspondent. Also incl information on the Pacific and European theatres, Generals MacArthur and Eisenhower, and Arizona AP news articles from the Korean War era. Inventory available. Also, Paul Sweitzer Collection; subject files and mss relating to Flagstaff area stories of the *Arizona Daily Sun,* Flagstaff, 1960's-1977. Sweitzer was a Flagstaff journalist.

AZ —ARIZONA STATE UNIVERSITY, Library, Tempe, 85287. Marilyn Wurzburger, Special Collections Librn
Notes: (1) The A T Steele Collection is a unique compilation of articles and documents dealing with events in China from 1932-1949. The collection is divided into five parts: dispatches, newspaper clippings, pamphlets and books, original documents of the Communist Party (circa 1945) and memorabilia, written and/or collected by American journalist A T Steele. Dispatches cover events in China from 1940-1949 and are mostly first-hand experiences of Steele. These dispatches, not all of which were published, often contain details absent in the final copy. Post-war topics incl trucc negotiations between the Nationalists and Chinese Communists and the "Manchurian Question." Incl 12 linear feet of materials. Index available. (2) Reflecting his roles of reporter, photographer and novelist, Ted Schwarz's papers cover subject areas such as investigative journalism, psychology, criminal justice, law,numismatics, visual communication, photography, and writing as a career. Collection incl extensive research materials from the author's study and reporting of the "Hillside Strangler" case which deals with multiple personalities. Partially cataloged and indexed, the collection consists of books, magazines, newspaper articles, galley proofs, interviews and correspondence, reel-to-reel tapes, audiotapes and videocassettes. (3) The Jimmy Starr Film History Collection contains the personal library and working materials of Jimmy Starr, Hollywood movie columnist from the 1920s-1960s. In addition to working as a press agent, Mr Starr was a columnist for the now defunct *Los Angeles* Record and the *Los Angeles Herald &* Express, and his columsn were widely syndicated; he also wrote silent comedies for Mack Sennett, scripts for the talkies, as well asseveral mystery novels.

CA —HOOVER INSTITUTION ON WAR, REVOLUTION & PEACE, Stanford University, Stanford, 94305. Milorad M Drachkovitch, Archivist
Holdings: Mss
Notes: Nine collections: (1) Papers of Gaston Bergery, French attorney, diplomat, author, journalist, politician, with service as Secretary-General for the Inter-Allied Commission for Reparations, 1918-1924, Director of the Cabinet of the Ministry of Foreign Affairs, 1924-25, and French Ambassador to Moscow, 1941, incl correspondence, telegrams, reports, memoranda, lists, speeches and writings, posters, leaflets, and other material, 1924-1973, relating to his government service in France and abroad, his literary and legal careers, French political events and foreign relations, France during World War II, and his activities in the Front Populaire. Primarily in French. 28 ms boxes. (2) Unpublished memoirs (photocopy of typewritten draft with handwritten annotations, in French), by Pierre Daye, Belgian writer, politician, and journalist, concerning his lifeand professional career, world history, and international affairs, 1892-1953. Chapters 60, 61, and conclusion are missing. 2 ms boxes. (3) Papers of Julius Epstein, journalist, research associate at the Hoover Institution, and author of *Operation Keelhaul: The Story of Forced Repatriation,* incl correspondence, speeches and writings, clippings, photographs, and printed matter. 1939-71, relating to his research on the events of World War II, communism, forced repatriation of Russian prisioners of the Soviet Union following World War II, Katyn forest massacres, and unreported deaths of Soviet Cosmonauts, as well as his efforts to obtain restricted government documents on these subjects. 180 ms boxes. (4) Collection of sound recordings of interviews with British, Portuguese and South African diplomats, politicians, economic advisors, journalists, and businessmen,1970-76, relating to political events in Portugal and Southern Africa, collected by Keith Middlemas, Professor at the University of Sussex, England. Also incl are documents and correspondence pertaining to British, Portuguese and South African relations and various political events, 1966-1973. 7 ms boxes. (5) Papers of Robert Norton, US attorney and journalist (editor of *China* Today), incl correspondence, speeches and writings, clippings, printed matter, photographs, and other materials, 1935-1948, relating to US relations with China and Japan, India's independence from Great Britain, Japanese military incursions into China, and United Nations assistance to China. 3 1/2 ms boxes. (6) Papers of Herbert Solow, American journalist, and editor of *Fortune*, 1945-1964, incl correspondence, speeches, drafts of writings, memoranda, depositions, clippings andother printed matter, 1924-76, relating to the communist movement in the US, the Non-Partisan Defense League, the Commission of Inquiry into the Charges Made Against Leon Trotsky in the Moscow Trials, Soviet espionage in the US, Zionism, and post-World War II international business enterprises. Incl some papers of Mrs Herbert Solow, 1964-76. 8 ms boxes. (7) Papers of Mark Sullivan, editor of *Collier's Weekly*, 1912-19, and newspaper columnist for the *New York Herald-Tribune*, 1923-52, incl correspondence, diaries, speeches and writings, memoranda, and printed matter, 1883-1952, relating to the career of Mark Sullivan; journalism in the US; and social, political, and economic developments in the US from 1900 to 1952. 62 ms boxes, 10 scrapbooks, 3 envelopes. (8) Papers of Karl H von Wiegand, Hearst newspaper foreign correspondent, 1917-61, inclcorrespondence, dispatches, mss of writings, photos, clippings, and printed matter, 1911-61, relating to European diplomacy and German politics between the world war, the Sino-Japanese War, the postwar Middle Eastern situation, and US foreign policy. In English and German. 88 ms boxes, 6 binders, 1 stack of oversize mounted clippings, 2 swords, 1 shield. (9) Papers of Nym Wales (Helen Foster Snow), journalist and writer, incl personal and collected correspondence, speeches and writings, news dispatches, interviews, reports, memoranda, organization records, and other material, 1931-1954, related primarily to her experiences in China with the Chinese communists, industrial cooperative movement, student movement, labor movement, Sian incident (1936), Sino-Japanese conflict, and art and literature. 37 ms boxes; 30 photo envelopes.

CA —UNIVERSITY OF THE PACIFIC, Holt-Atherton Pacific Center for Western Studies, Stockton, 95211. Hiram L Davis, Dir of Libraries
Holdings: // Cat Mss
Notes: The Daniel James papers contain ms correspondence, notes and printed matter collected by a US freelance journalist who traveled and lived in Latin America in the 1960s. Emphasis is on politics and government. Ca 50 linear ft.

CT —YALE UNIVERSITY, Box 1603A, Yale Station, New Haven, 06520.
Holdings: Cat Mss

DC —GEORGETOWN UNIVERSITY, Library, Special Collections Div, 37 & O Sts NW, Washington, 20057. George M Barringer, Special Collections Librn; Nicholas B Sheetz, Mss Librn
Holdings: Mss Cat
Notes: The papers of David Rankin Barbee, journalist with *The Washington Post* and authority on: Abraham Lincoln; the Lincoln assassination; Rose O'Neal Greenhow; and the Civil War. The collection incl, besides extensive correspondence with such historians as Albert J Beveridge, Henry Steele Commager, and Paul M Angle, all of Barbee's own research files and the mss of his works. The papers of Andre Vission, journalist and writer about American-European relations from the beginning of World War II through the Cold War years. The papers of the journalist and author, Count Michael de la Bedoyere, who edited for many years the English periodical, "The Catholic Herald". Contains for the most part correspondence from contributors and readers. Correspondence and manuscripts (incl an autobiography) ofEdwin Emerson (1869-1959), journalist and miscellaneous writer, touching on his experiences in the Spanish-American, Russo-Japanese, and First World Wars. Incl photographic materials. Also present is an extensive correspondence by Emerson about the novelist Stephen Crane. The papers of Christopher Sykes, biographer, journalist, and novelist; containing mss, letters, photographs, and drawings.

DC —GEORGE WASHINGTON UNIVERSITY, Gelman Library, 2130 H St NW, Washington, 20052.
Holdings: // Cat Mss Pix
Notes: The Frederick Kuh papers cover the period 1924-1967, although the

JOURNALISTS (cont.)

preponderance of mss range from 1938-1967. Kuh was a foreign correspondent for UPI and then the Chicago *Sun-Times*, and wrote numerous articles for periodicals, notably the *New Republic, The Nation*, and *Foreign Report*. The collection includes diaries, biographical information, correspondence, articles, speeches, subject files, misc papers, notebooks, and scrapbooks. Cataloged as a collection with unpublished inventory for access and a name index covering all people mentioned in the diaries and correspondence.

DC —LIBRARY OF CONGRESS, Manuscript Division, Washington, 20540. John C Broderick, Chief
Notes: Papers of Roy W Howard (1883-1964), past president and chairman of the board of Scripps-Howard Newspapers. Some 85,000 items for the years 1923-64, incl business and personal correspondence, maintained under state and city of origin, with separate files in each year for the various Scripps-Howard newspaper, especially for the *World Telegram* (New York City). Also, the papers of Joseph Wood Krutch, incl correspondence; Joseph Alsop; Stewart Hensley.

DC —LIBRARY OF CONGRESS, Washington, 20540.
Holdings: Cat Mss Pix
Notes: The Arthur Mann papers, incl correspondence, 1923-1962, clippings and drafts and notes for books and articles, by the noted sports writer and baseball authority.

DC —LIBRARY OF CONGRESS, Motion Pictures, Broadcasting and Recorded Sound Div, Washington, 20540.
Notes: Over 5600 papers and broadcast recordings of Raymond Swing (1887-1968).

GA —EMORY UNIVERSITY, Robert W Woodruff Library, Special Collections Dept, Atlanta, 30322. Linda M Matthews, Head Special Collections; Virginia J H Cain, Processing Archivist; Richard H F Lindemann, Reference Archivist
Holdings: Cat Mss Pix Audiotapes
Notes: Extensive collections of papers of Henry W Grady, Corra Harris, Joel Chandler Harris, Julian LaRose Harris, Julia Collier Harris, Clark Howell, Ralph E McGilll, Harold H Martin, Mildred Seydell, and Claude Sitton, among others, most associated with the Atlanta *Constitution*. Descriptions and index are availalbe in repository.

IL —CHICAGO HISTORICAL SOCIETY, Library, Clark St at North Ave, Chicago, 60614. Archie Motley, Manuscript Librn
Notes: Publishing and literary collections incl these papers: *Chicago Journalism* Review; *Chicago Seed*; *The Chicagoan*; Friends of American Writers, Chicago literary group; Emmett Dedmon (Chicago newspaper executive, journalist, author); Interviews of 97 Chicago journalists conducted by students in Northwestern University's Medill School.

IL —NEWBERRY LIBRARY, 60 W Walton St, Chicago, 60610. Diana Haskell, Cur of Modern Mss
Holdings: Cat Mss Pix
Notes: Personal and working papers of 30 Chicago journalists, mainly from the *Daily* News.

IL —UNIVERSITY OF ILLINOIS, URBANA/CHAMPAIGN, Library, Communications Library, 122 Gregory Hall, Urbana, 61801. Nancy Allen, Librn
Holdings: Vols (18,000) Cat
Notes: Journalism history, theory and skills. Studies of individual journalists, newspapers, and other news media.

IA —COE COLLEGE, Stewart Memorial Library, Cedar Rapids, 52402. R Doyle, Dir of Library Services
Holdings: // Uncat
Notes: Incl in 5 ms boxes the original ms, supplementary outlines and notes of his best seller, *The Rise and Fall of the Third Reich*, donated by William L Shirer. Also incl some correspondence and a bibliography.

KS —EMPORIA STATE UNIVERSITY, William Allen White Library, Emporia, 66801. Mary E Bogan, Special Collections Librn
Holdings: Vols (233)// Cat Mss Pix Phonorecords Audiotapes
Notes: The William Allen White Collection contains books by and about Mr White as well as inscribed volumes from his personal library, manuscripts, photographs, newspaper and periodical articles, memorabilia, as well as letters and telegrams exchanged between Mr White and such national figures as Herbert Hoover, Calvin Coolidge, Theodore Roosevelt, Franklin D Roosevelt, William Dean Howells, William Howard Taft, Robert Taft and many others.

MA —BOSTON UNIVERSITY, Mugar Memorial Library, Special Collections Dept, 771 Commonwealth Ave, Boston, 02215. Howard B Gotlieb, Dir
Holdings: Cat Mss Pix
Notes: Incl literary and personal papers of some 75 prominent modern journalists: Daniel Lang, Georgie Anne Geyer, Flora Lewis, Carleton Beals, Alistair Cooke, Ralph Ingersoll, Richard Tregaskis, Far Eastern journalists John Hughes of the *Christian Science Monitor* and Dennis Bloodworth of the *Observer* of London, etc. A complete list is available.

MA —TUFTS UNIVERSITY, Fletcher School of Law & Diplomacy, Murrow Center of Public Diplomacy, Medford, 02155. Natalie Schatz, Cur of Special Collections
Holdings: Vols (1500)// Cat Mss Pix Phonorecords Audiotapes 16mm Films
Notes: Professional correspondence, reports, speeches, scripts and interviews relating to Edward R Murrow's career in broadcasting: reports, hearings and speeches from his years as Director of USIA, as well as personal correspondence, memorabilia, books, some films and audiotapes. 43,300 pieces.

NJ —PRINCETON UNIVERSITY, Library, Rare Books Dept, Princeton, 08544. Stephen Ferguson, Cur
Notes: Correspondence of Arthur Krock. Also, papers of Louis Fischer, journalist and authority on the Soviet Union.

NY —STATE UNIVERSITY OF NEW YORK AT ALBANY, Library, Special Collections Dept, 1400 Washington Ave, Albany, 12222. Marion P Munzer, Coordr
Notes: Mss, publications, photographs relating to the work of Fritz Neugass as art correspondent for foreign newspapers and periodicals, specializing in the American art market (53 linear feet, 25 feet of auction catalogs). Also, correspondence regarding Karl Otto Paetel and his German language newspaper, *Aufbau;* mss and letters concerning the German Youth Movement, Ernst Jüunger, German resistance, and the refugee question (3.8 linear feet). Part of the Library's German Exile Collection.
See also entries under Neugass, Fritz; Photographers; German Youth Movement; Paetel, Karl Otto; Exiles, Political

NY —STATE UNIVERSITY OF NEW YORK, BINGHAMTON, Glenn G Bartle Library, Binghamton, 13901. Marion Hanscom, Special Collections Librn
Notes: Papers, correspondence, etc of the Washington, DC speech writer and journalist.

NY —NEW YORK PUBLIC LIBRARY, Rare Books and Manuscripts Div, Fifth Ave & 42 St, New York, 10018. William L Joyce, Asst Dir; Susan E Davis, Cur of Mss
Budget: ($7161)
Notes: The papers of Jacob A Riis, H L Mencken, and many others.

NY —NEW YORK PUBLIC LIBRARY, Fifth Ave & 42 St, New York, 10018.
Notes: One of the world's largest collections of H L Mencken's correspondence, some 30, 000 letters to and from the American writer and editor.

NY —UNIVERSITY OF ROCHESTER, Rush Rhees Library, Department of Rare Books and Special Collections, Rochester, 14627. Peter Dzwonkoski, Librn
Notes: Thurlow Weed, 1797-1882. Papers of this American journalist; editor of the *Albany (NY) Evening Journal*. Influential in 19th century American politics. Each letter in the collection has been indexed by name of letter writer. Unpublished register available in the repository.

NC —DUKE UNIVERSITY, William R Perkins Library, Manuscript Dept, Durham, 27706. Ellen Gartrell, Cur of Mss
Holdings: Cat Mss
Notes: Large collections of James T Williams, William Watts Ball, John Sanford Martin, Francis Warrington Dawson, Hemphill Family, Josephus Daniels II, and others.

OH —RUTHERFORD B HAYES LIBRARY, 1337 Hayes Ave, Fremont, 43420. Watt P Marchman, Dir
Holdings: Cat Mss Pix
Notes: Papers, correspondence and literary mss (approx 6 linear ft) pertaining to "Petroleum V Nasby" and his son, Robinson Locke, both of the Toledo *Blade*. Index in the collection. Also, a collection of newspaper clippings, poems and some ms materials written by women journalists in the latter half of the 19th century, eg, Mary Clemmer Ames, Austine and Fayette Snead, C H Mohun, who wrote as "Raymonde." The Ames papers are listed in *Guide to Manuscripts of the Ohio Historical Society*. 304.

OH —GREENE COUNTY DISTRICT LIBRARY, 76 E Market St, PO Box 520, Xenia, 45385. Julie M Overton, Local History Coordr
Notes: Collection of papers on Fred Kelley, noted newspaper journalist and author born in Greene Co, Ohio. Papers include many published articles and books as well as some correspondence.

OR —AMERICAN PRIVATE PRESS ASSOCIATION, 112 E Burnett St, Stayton, 97383. Martin M Horvat, Librn
Notes: The collection is divided into two primary segments: the first is the traditional one of Amateur Journalism, the second is science fiction and fantasy oriented. The collection was once at New York University Libraries but moved in 1981.

PA —TEMPLE UNIVERSITY LIBRARIES, Special Collections Dept, Conwellana-Templana Collection, 13 & Berks St, Philadelphia, 19122. Miriam I Crawford, Cur
Holdings: Vols 6 // Cat Mss Pix
Budget: ($30,000)
Notes: Frank Brookhouser, news reporter, columnist, and film and book critic, emphasized the human interest in his stories, which included daily columns in the Philadelphia newspapers from 1936 to 1975 and a large number of magazine stories. Philadelphia and its people provide the focus for much of his writing.

SC —COLLEGE OF CHARLESTON LIBRARY, Special Collections Dept, Charleston, 29401.
Notes: Robert Walter Marks Papers, 1890-1980: a collection of correspondence, mss, published material, notes, and photographs reflecting Marks' multifarious career in Charlestown, New York, and Europe as a journalist covering a wide variety of fields.

SC —CLEMSON UNIVERSITY, Libraries, Clemson, 29631. Michael F Kohl, Head of Special Collections
Holdings: Cat Mss Pix
Notes: Papers of Ben Robertson, a newsman and war correspondent for *PM*, the *New York Herald Tribune*, and the Associated Press. Collection incl news-clippings, incl reviews of his books, magazine travel articles and news stories; and notes by him; 2 log books and pictures. Partial inventory, unpublished.

TX —DALLAS PUBLIC LIBRARY, Fine Arts Div, 1515 Young St, Dallas, 75201. Richard L Waters, Acting Dir; Jane Holahan, Manager
Notes: Papers of John Rosenfield, eminent Dallas critic for 41 years.

VA —UNIVERSITY OF VIRGINIA, Alderman Library, Manuscripts Dept, Charlottesville, 22901. Edmund Berkeley Jr, Cur
Holdings: Cat Mss Pix Audiotapes
Notes: The collection includes papers of persons prominent in the field of journalism

JOURNALISTS (cont.)

chiefly in Virginia, but also nationally in some instances. The papers of the following persons are included: Walter Scott Copeland, editor and publisher of the Newport News *Daily Press and Times-Herald;* Virginia Dabney, editor of the Richmond *Times-Dispatch;* Douglas Southall Freeman, editor of the Richmond *News-Leader;* Thomas Andrew Hanes, editor of the Norfolk *Ledger-Star;* Louis I Jaffe, editor of the Norfolk *Virginia Pilot;* James J Kilpatrick, editor of the Richmond *News-Leader,* and currently a print and broadcast columnist; Philip Lightfoot Scruggs, editor of the Lynchburg, Virginia, *Daily Advance;* and Louis Spilman, publisher of the Waynesboro, Virginia, *New-Virginian.* 130 linear ft.

WY —UNIVERSITY OF WYOMING, William Robertson Coe Library, 13 & Ivinson, Laramie, 82071.
Notes: The papers of Morgan Beatty (1902-1975), an eminent newsman in print and broadcast journalism. Contains several thousand letters, many from prominent personalities, extensive background files of his "News of the World" and other broadcasts, and several thousand radio scripts and feature news stories.

AB —UNIVERSITY OF CALGARY, Libraries, Special Collections Div, 2500 University Dr, Calgary, T2N 1N4, Can.
Holdings: (5000) Cat Mss
Notes: The Division has extensive collections of the papers of modern Canadian authors (qv individuals), incl Hugh MacLennan, Mordecai Richler, Brian Moore, W O Mitchell, Cliff Faulknor, Christie Harris, Robert Kroetsch, Rudy Wiebe, Claude Peloquin, George Ryga, Andre Langevin, Malcolm Ross, Bruce Hutchison, John Mellor, Grant MacEwan, James Gray, Ernest Watkins, Len Peterson, Michael Cook, & Joanna Glass. The papers of musician Morris Surdin contain hundreds of Canadian Broadcasting Corporation scripts, and constitute a valuable addition to the purely literary ms collections. The Division's holdings also incl collections of scores by Canadian musicians R Murray Schafer and Bruce Mather. In addition, the records of the following Canadian publishing houses are on deposit: E C W Press, Hancock House Publishers Ltd and Coach House Press. The Division alsohouses small collections of letters and mss of Canadian poets such as Earle Birney and George Bowering as well as the archives of the literary periodicals *Tish, Imago, Ariel, Descant, Canadian Review Magazine,* and *Canadian Short Story Magazine.* The ms collections are complemented by a book collection of some 5000 vols.

ON —MCMASTER UNIVERSITY, Mills Memorial Library, Div of Archives & Research Collections, Hamilton, L8S 4L6, Can. G R Hill, Univ Librn
Holdings: // Mss
Notes: Pierre Berton's mss and research files. Collection partially described in *Library Research News,* vol 2, no 5, May 1974.

JOURNALISTS, WOMEN see Women Journalists

JOURNALS see Periodicals—Collections

JOURNEYS see Discovery and Exploration; Travel; Voyages and Travels

JOUSTS AND JOUSTING

WV —SALEM COLLEGE, Library, Salem, 26426. Myron J Smith, Jr, Librn
Notes: Collection supports "the most complete equestrian studies program available anywhere". *Myron J Smith, Equestrian Studies:* the Salem College [Bibliographical] Guide to Sources in English, 1950-1980. Metuchen, NJ: Scarecrow Press, 1981; 4645 entries.

JOWETT, BENJAMIN, 1817-1893

CA —CLAREMONT COLLEGES, Honnold Library, Ninth & Dartmouth, Claremont, 91711. Tania Rizzo, Special Collections Dept Head
Holdings: Cat Mss
Notes: 7 ALsS, 6 to Mrs Humphry Ward (Mary Augusta Arnold Ward, qv). Several privately printed limited editions; printed but unpublished books; others by and about him. Restricted use.

JOY, CHARLES TURNER, 1895-1956

CA —HOOVER INSTITUTION ON WAR, REVOLUTION & PEACE, Stanford University, Stanford, 94305. Milorad M Drachkovitch, Archivist
Holdings: Mss
Notes: Three handwritten diaries, July 10, 1951-May 22, 1952, by Admiral Charles Turner Joy, Chief United Nations negotiator at the Korean military armistice negotiations at Panmunjom, 1951-53, mainly concerning prisoner of war issues and repatriation questions. 3 vols in 1/2 ms box.

JOY, JAMES F.

MI —DETROIT PUBLIC LIBRARY, Burton Historical Collection, 5201 Woodward Ave, Detroit, 48202. Alice Dalligan, Chief

JOYCE, JAMES

CA —UNIVERSITY OF CALIFORNIA, SANTA BARBARA, Library, Dept of Special Collections, Santa Barbara, 93106. Christian F Brun, Head

CT —YALE UNIVERSITY, Box 1603A, Yale Station, New Haven, 06520.
Holdings: Cat Mss Pix

IL —SOUTHERN ILLINOIS UNIVERSITY, CARBONDALE, Delyte W Morris Library, Special Collections Dept, Carbondale, 62901. David V Koch, Cur of Special Collections; Louisa Bowen, Cur of Manuscripts
Holdings: Vols 360 Cat Mss Pix Tapes
Notes: The Dr H K Croessmann Collection of James Joyce (17 linear ft) incl the papers of Joyce's biographer, Herbert Gorman, his literary agent, James Pinker, and his German translator, Georg Goyert, and more than 200 of Joyce's letters. Inventory available in library.

IL —NORTHWESTERN UNIVERSITY, Library, Special Collections Dept, 1937 Sheridan Rd, Evanston, 60201. R Russell Maylone, Cur
Holdings: Vols 360 Cat Mss Pix
Notes: First editions, letters, drawings, paintings.

KS —UNIVERSITY OF KANSAS, Kenneth Spencer Research Library, Special Collections Dept, Lawrence, 66045. Alexandra Mason, Librn
Holdings: Vols 950 Cat
Notes: Based on James F Spoerri collection. All first editions except 5 minor items, many later editions, very good for periodical appearances. Noncirculating.

KY —UNIVERSITY OF LOUISVILLE, Ekstrom Library, Rare Books & Special Collections, 2301 S Third St, Louisville, 40208. George T McWhorter, Cur; Delinda Stephens Buie, Asst Cur
Holdings: Vols 3000 Cat
Budget: $1000
Notes: The Richard M Kain Collection. Literary first editions of Joyce, Yeats, A E, Lady Gregory and others; cultural and political documents; mss; periodical runs; clippings and related materials. Catalog in progress.

MA —HARVARD UNIVERSITY LIBRARY, Houghton Library, Cambridge, 02138. Rodney G Dennis, Cur of Manuscripts
Holdings: Cat Mss

NY —STATE UNIVERSITY OF NEW YORK, COLLEGE AT BUFFALO, Poetry/Rare Books Collection, 420 Capen Hall, Buffalo, 14260. Robert J Bertholf, Cur
Holdings: Cat Mss Pix Phonorecords
Notes: The Wickser and Sylvia Beach Collections. Material by and about James Joyce, incl his personal library and family portraits. See: Spielberg: *James Joyces's Mss and Letters at the University of Buffalo: a* Catalogue (1962).

NY —CORNELL UNIVERSITY LIBRARIES, John M Olin Library, Dept of Rare Books, Ithaca, 14853. Donald D Eddy, Librn
Holdings: Cat Mss
Notes: Downs 2186. Robert E Schules, *The Cornell Joyce Collection, A Catalogue* (Ithaca, Cornell Univeristy Press, 1961).

NY —NEW YORK UNIVERSITY, Elmer Holmes Bobst Library, Div of Special Collections, Washington Sq S, New York, 10012. Frank Walker, Librn; Patrick McGuire, Asst Librn
Holdings: Vols (100,000) Cat Mss Pix
Notes: The Fales Collection of first (and other) editions of English and American novels from about 1750 to date (about 70, 000 titles). Mss (30,000) pieces.

NY —LE MOYNE COLLEGE, Library, Le Moyne Heights, Syracuse, 13214. James J Simonis, Dir; Annette M Monaco, Special Colelctions Librn
Holdings: Vols (1614) // Cat Mss Slides
Notes: Incl 614 monographs and 1000 pamphlets, reprint articles, and periodical issues. Represents the Irish Literature Collection, covering the modern Irish Literature period from 1880 to 1950, and the Rev William T Noon SJ Collection. Father Noon had James Joyce as his main interest. Manuscripts of Noon's books *Joyce and* Aquinas (Yale University, 1957) and *Poetry and Prayer* (Rutgers University, 1957) are incl. There are several hundred pieces of correspondence which incl authors who had similar interests. The collection also incl his class notes and cutouts from newspapers, pamphlets, periodical articles, many of which have notes written by him. Monographs are represented by an author file. Pamphlets and reprint articles are organized in boxes and numbered numerically.

OK —UNIVERSITY OF TULSA, McFarlin Library, Dept of Rare Books and Special Collections, 600 S College, Tulsa, 74104. David Farmer, Dir; Toby Murray, Archivist; Caroline Swinson, Cur of Manuscripts & Art
Notes: The Harriet Shaw Weaver Collection of James Joyce materials (from the Nation Book League, London).

TX —MIDWESTERN STATE UNIVERSITY, Moffett Library, 3400 Taft St, Wichita Falls, 76308.
Holdings: Vols 80// Uncat
Notes: This collection appears to be a complete collection of Joyce's works. The volumes are first editions or copies of limited editions.

VA —MARY WASHINGTON COLLEGE, E Lee Trinkle Library, Fredericksburg, 22401. Ruby Y Weinbrecht, Librn
Holdings: Vols 264 Cat
Budget: $800

WI —UNIVERSITY OF WISCONSIN, MILWAUKEE, Library, Box 604, Milwaukee, 53201. William C Roselle, Dir
Holdings: Vols (68,000) Cat Mss Phonorecords Audiotapes
Notes: Special strengths of the literature collection include Shakespeare Research Collection (600 volumes), William Blake, James Joyce, Howard Fast (English-language translations), contemporary small press poetry publications, etc.

ON —QUEEN'S UNIVERSITY, Douglas Library, Kingston, K7L 5C4, Can. William F E Morley, Cur, Special Collections
Holdings: Vols (3250) Cat
Notes: Collection incl all the original vols in the Cuala Press series and a facsimile reprint of each plus about 170 other works by and about W B Yeats, 200 by and about James Joyce, 240 by and about G B Shaw, 100 by and about "A E," George W Russell.

JUAREZ, BENITO

CA —COPLEY NEWSPAPERS, James S Copley Library, 1134 Kline St, PO Box 1530, La Jolla, 92038. Richard Reilly, Cur; Suzanne Carnes, Librn
Holdings: Vols (10,000) Cat
Notes: Collection incl materials on American Revolutionary period, Benito Juarez correspondence, California and western Americana. Library open to graduate students who obtain reading privileges from curator or librarian.

JUAREZ, BENITO (cont.)

IN —INDIANA UNIVERSITY, Lilly Library, Seventh St, Bloomington, 47405. William R Cagle, Librn
Holdings: Vols (10,000) // Cat Mss
Notes: Historical pronouncements and documents by the leaders of the movement of Mexican independence. Partially cataloged.

JUBILEE VOLUMES see Festschriften

JUDAEO-ARABIC LANGUAGE AND LITERATURE

†MA —HARVARD UNIVERSITY LIBRARY, Widener Library, Judaica Collection, Room M, Cambridge, 02138. Charles Berlin, Bibliographer
Holdings: Cat

JUDAEO-GERMAN LANGUAGE see Yiddish Language and Literature

JUDAEO-PERSIAN LANGUAGE AND LITERATURE

OH —HEBREW UNION COLLEGE-JEWISH INSTITUTE OF RELIGION, Klau Library, 3101 Clifton Ave, Cincinnati, 45220. David J Gilner, Reference Librn
Holdings: Cat Mss
Notes: Described in Spicehandler, Ezra, "A Descriptive List of Judeo-Persian Manuscripts at the Klau Library of the Hebrew Union College," *Studies in Bibliography and Booklore*, 8 (1968), pp 114-136.

JUDAEO-SPANISH LANGUAGE see Ladino Language and Literature

JUDAICA

CA —JUDAH L MAGNES MEMORIAL MUSEUM, Morris Goldstein Library, 2911 Russell St, Berkeley, 94705. Jane Levy, Archivist
Holdings: Vols 7000 Cat Mss Maps 16mm Films
Notes: Judaica, incl Hebrew manuscripts, Yiddish literature, and Jewish music and art.

†CA —HEBREW UNION COLLEGE, Jewish Institute of Religion, 3077 University Ave, Los Angeles, 90007.
Notes: Bible, Talmud, Rabbinics, Jewish history, philosophy, art and communal science, Hebrew literature, religion, Zionism.

CA —LOS ANGELES PUBLIC LIBRARY, Philosophy & Religion Dept, 630 W Fifth St, Los Angeles, 90071. Marilyn C Wherley, Librn
Holdings: Vols 600 Cat
Budget: ($60,000)
Notes: Historical, theological and biographical works relating to the faith. Includes popular and scholarly materials on comparative religions. Some serials and periodicals. Emphasis on Judaism in the United States.

CA —UNIVERSITY OF CALIFORNIA, LOS ANGELES, Research Library, Jewish Studies Collection, 405 Hilgard Ave, Los Angeles, 90024. Edward Shreeves, Chairman, Bibliographers Group; Shimeon Brisman, Jewish Studies Bibliographer
Holdings: Vols (100,000) Cat Mss Microforms

CA —UNIVERSITY OF CALIFORNIA, SANTA BARBARA, Library, Dept of Special Collections, Santa Barbara, 93106. Christian F Brun, Head
Holdings: Vols 322 Uncat Mss
Notes: Judaica and the Spanish Inquisition.

CO —UNIVERSITY OF DENVER LIBRARIES, Denver, 80210. Steve Fisher, Librn
Holdings: Vols 10,000 Cat Mss Pix
Notes: The Rabbi I Edward Kiev Collection, incl many areas and all periods of Judaica: history, religion, philosophy, mysticism, law, sociology, linguistics and Hebrew literature, also rare books.

DC —LIBRARY OF CONGRESS, African and Middle Eastern Division, Washington, 20540.
Holdings: Cat Mss Microforms
Notes: Hebraica: about 109,000 vols in Hebrew, Yiddish, Judeo-Arabic, Judeo-:Arabic, Judeo-Persian, Ladino, Syriac, Ethiopic; espec strong in Biblical subjects, responsa literature, and socio-political aspects.

FL —UNIVERSITY OF FLORIDA LIBRARY, Isser and Rae Price Library of Judaica, 18 Libr East, Gainesville, 32611. Robert Singerman, Head Librn
Budget: ($30,000)
Notes: Total holdings estimated at 55,000 vols dealing with the political, social, economic and intellectual history of the Jews in the ancient, medieval and modern periods and in all geographic areas. The following areas are especially well represented by printed matter in all relevant languages: Bibliography, Festschriften, History, Bible, Judaism and Jewish theology, liturgy, responsa, rabbinical literature, Jewish law, Hebrew language and literature, Yiddish language and literature, anti-semitism, Zionism, Palestine and the *Yishuv*, and the State of Israel. German and American Judaica form a collecting emphasis with holdings for all the standard histories as well as histories of individual synagogues, institutions and local communities. Works in Hebrew and Yiddish comprise about 60 percent of the collection (estimated 30,000 vols). With few exceptions, holdingsare limited to nineteenth and twentieth century imprints, with complete sets of journals and thousands of ephemeral pamphlets, many of them commemorating anniversaries, enhancing the research value of the collection, the largest Judaica research library in the southeastern United States. Only about half of the collection is cataloged; the collection is a circulating one and vols may be borrowed on interlibrary loan. Incl the Leonard C Mishkin Collection (40,000 vols), the largest personal Judaica collection in the United States, the Shlomo Marenof Collection (3500 vols), and the inventory of Bernard Morgenstern's Lower East Side Book Store (8000 vols). Scholars should inquire in advance of their visit. *The Isser and Rae Price Library of Judaica* Report (circulation 2900 copies) is mailed gratis twice a year to all interested parties. Special catalogs:Pre-1881 Hebrew imprints recorded in a chronological card file.

IL —SPERTUS COLLEGE OF JUDAICA, Asher Library, 618 S Michigan Ave, Chicago, 60605. Richard W Marcus, Librn
Holdings: Vols 60,000 Cat Maps Microforms
Budget: $130,000
Notes: Incl Chicago Jewish history, 200 vols; mss and archives.

IL —UNIVERSITY OF CHICAGO LIBRARY, Dept of Special Collections, 1100 E 57 St, Chicago, 60637.
Notes: Ludwig Rosenberger Library of Judaica. Covers history of Jewish social and political thought from 1200 to the present.

IL —HEBREW THEOLOGICAL COLLEGE, Saul Silber Memorial Library, 7135 N Carpenter Rd, Skokie, 60077. Leah Mishkin, Head Librn/Cur
Holdings: Vols (58,000) Cat Mss Microforms
Notes: Main subject is rabbinics (Halachic literature). We also have a very large and important Holocaust Collection.

IN —EVANSVILLE & VANDERBURGH COUNTY PUBLIC LIBRARIES, Adult Information Dept, 22 S E Fifth St, Evansville, 47708. Judith Hanefeldt, Dept Head
Holdings: Cat
Notes: The Marcus and Mina Ravdin Memorial Judaica Collection was established in 1948 as a separate collection at Central Library. In 1968, this collection was integrated into the full collection of books at Central Library. Thus the 400 vol (1968) Ravdin Collection, as such, no longer exists. Additions are made to the subject emphasis.

MD —JOHNS HOPKINS UNIVERSITY, Milton S Eisenhower Library, George Peabody Collection, 17 E Mt Vernon Place, Baltimore, 21201. Lyn Hart, Peabody Librn
Notes: Emphasis on materials published before 1950. Strength is a good collection through the 19th century.

MA —HEBREW COLLEGE, Jacob & Rose Grossman Library and Lawrence Jay & Anne Cable Rubenstein Library, 43 Hawes St, Brookline, 02146. Maurice Tuchman, Librn
Holdings: Vols 2000 Cat Maps Slides Records
Notes: Emphasis on Jewish education. Also Russian Judaica; books of Jewish interest in Russian.

†MA —HARVARD UNIVERSITY LIBRARY, Widener Library, Judaica Collection, Room M, Cambridge, 02138. Charles Berlin, Bibliographer
Holdings: Cat Mss Microforms
Notes: Library has published *Catalogue of Hebrew Books*, 6 vols (1968), and *Supplement*, 3 vols (1972); shelflist for Judaica *Widener Library Shelflist*, No 39 (1971) lists 11,800 vols in western languages. See also *Jewish Book Annual*, XXVI (1968/9), 58-63.

†MA —HARVARD UNIVERSITY LIBRARY, Judaica Dept, Cambridge, 02138. Charles Berlin, Librn
Notes: Harvard's Judaica Collections have been helped by a special grant from the S H and Helen R Scheuer Family Foundation (NY) to develop its Jewish children's literature collection to encourage research in literature for and about Jewish children.

MA —BOSTON COLLEGE LIBRARIES, Thomas P O'Neill Library, Nicholas M Williams Ethnological Collection, Chestnut Hill, 02167. Frank J Seegraber, Special Collections Librn
Holdings: Vols 10,000 // Cat Mss Maps
Notes: Collection emphasizes Caribbeana, especially Jamaica, to 1940. Incl discovery, exploration and natural history of the British, French and Spanish settlements; the slave question; piracy. There are over 6000 mss, 5000 of which are Anansi folk tales recorded by native school children. Also small ancillary sections of Africana and Judaica. For reference use only, by arrangement with librarian.

MA —BRANDEIS UNIVERSITY, Goldfarb Library, 415 South St, Waltham, 02154. Bessie Hahn, Dir

MA —AMERICAN ANTIQUARIAN SOCIETY LIBRARY, 185 Salisbury St, Worcester, 01609. Marcus A McCorison, Dir & Librn
Holdings: Cat
Notes: The Society holds over 90 percent of the 685 titles in Rosenbach's bibliography of American Jewish books to 1850, plus many early items not included in the list.

MI —UNIVERSITY OF MICHIGAN, Graduate Library, Near East Dept, Ann Arbor, 48109. John A Eilts, Bibliographer
Holdings: Vols (150,000) Cat Mss Maps Microforms
Notes: Excludes Islam in the Far East, Judism in general, though it does incl specifically Near Eastern Judaism. Incl Bahaism and Arab philosophy, fields of study connected with Islamic or Arabic studies, Turkish language and lterature.

MO —UNIVERSITY OF MISSOURI-KANSAS CITY, General Library, 5100 Rockhill Road, Kansas City, 64110. Kenneth J LaBudde, Dir; Gordon Hendrickson, Assoc Dir; Marilyn Carbonell, Ref Librn
Holdings: Vols 6000 Cat

NJ —ENGLEWOOD LIBRARY, 31 Engle St, Englewood, 07631. Jean Grushkin, Reference Dept
Holdings: Vols 1000 Cat
Budget: $1000
Notes: Sociology, art, literature, history, juvenile, biography, fiction.

NY —HEBREW UNION COLLEGE, Jewish Institute of Religion, Klau Library, 1 W 4th St, New York, 10012. Philip Miller, Librn
Holdings: Vols (115,000) Cat Mss Microforms
Notes: Hebrew literature-ancient, medieval and modern.

NY —JEWISH BRAILLE INSTITUTE OF AMERICA, 110 E 30St, New York, 10016.

JUDAICA (cont.)

Richard Borgersen, Library Dir
Holdings: Vols (50,000) Cat Audiotapes
Budget: ($75,000)
Notes: A worldwide circulating library of English and Hebrew Braille, English, Hebrew and Yiddish tape talking books and English, Hebrew and Yiddish tape talking books and English and Hebrew large type books. All books sent free of charge. Loan period 90 days.

†NY —JEWISH THEOLOGICAL SEMINARY OF AMERICA LIBRARY, 3080 Broadway, New York, 10027.

NY —YESHIVA UNIVERSITY, Library, 500 West 185th Street, New York, 10033. Pearl Berger
Holdings: Cat Mss

NY —YESHIVA UNIVERSITY-STERN COLLEGE FOR WOMEN, Hedi Steinberg Library, 245 Lexington Ave, New York, 10016. Edith Lubetski, Librn
Holdings: Vols (9000) Cat Maps Phonorecords
Notes: Incl a graded Hebrew Reading Collection.

NY —YIVO INSTITUTE FOR JEWISH RESEARCH, Library & Archives, 1048 Fifth Ave, New York, 10028. Dina Abramowicz, Librn; Marek Web, Archivist
Holdings: Cat Mss Pix

NC —UNIVERSITY OF NORTH CAROLINA, CHAPEL HILL, Wilson Library, Rare Book Collection, Chapel Hill, 27514. Paul S Koda, Cur of Rare Books
Holdings: Cat
Notes: Books, periodicals, and articles from 1523 on, chiefly in Hebrew and English, with many volumes from the 17th and 18th centuries. In addition, a portion of the Jacob Sarna library.

NC —DUKE UNIVERSITY, Divinity School Library, Durham, 27706. Donn Michael Farris, Librn
Holdings: Vols (225,000)
Notes: Special collections and subject emphases in this library include: Archaeology, Egyptian; Archaeology, Middle Eastern; Art, Jewish; Bible; Bible-New Testament; Bible-Symbolism; Church Architecture; Egyptology; Fathers of the Church; Society of Friends; Great Britain-Religion-Methodism and Methodist Church; Hymns and Hymnals; Jansenists and Jansenism; Judaica; Mediaeval Christian Mysticism; Methodism and Methodist Church; Methodist Episcopal Church; Methodist Episcopal Church, South; Reformation; Religion-US-History; Rural Church; Theology-Great Britain-17th Century; Theology-Great Britain-18th Century; United Methodist Church; US-Church History; John Wesley.

OH —HEBREW UNION COLLEGE-JEWISH INSTITUTE OF RELIGION, Klau Library, 3101 Clifton Ave, Cincinnati, 45220. David J Gilner, Reference Librn
Holdings: Vols 250,000 Cat Mss Maps
Notes: Hebrew Union College-Jewish Institute of Religion, *Dictionary Catalog of the Klau Library,* Cincinnati, 1964, 32 vols. Emphasis on Jewish history, American literature, philosophy, art, etc.

OH —CLEVELAND PUBLIC LIBRARY, Fine Arts and Special Collections Department, 325 Superior Ave, Cleveland, 44114. Alice N Loranth, Head
Holdings: Vols 1600 Cat mss
Notes: Religious texts, folklore, philology and the classic aspects of the subjectr are emphasized. 620 vols in Hebrew.
See also entry under Oriental Languages and Literatures.

OH —OHIO STATE UNIVERSITY, William Oxley Thompson Memorial Library, 1858 Neil Ave, Columbus, 43210. Amnon Zipin, Jewish Studies Bibliographer
Holdings: Vols (43,000) Cat Maps Microfilms
Budget: ($35,000)
Notes: Collection enphasis is materials on Jewish history (especially US, Isreal and Europe) and Hebrew language and literature. Small collection of Yiddish materials.

†PA —DROPSIE UNIVERSITY, Library, Broad & York Sts, Philadelphia, 19132.

PA —FREE LIBRARY OF PHILADELPHIA, Education, Philosophy and Religion Department, Logan Sq, Philadelphia, 19103. Esther J Maurer, Head
Holdings: Vols 2200// Cat
Notes: Judaica and Hebraica library formerly owned by Moses Marx. Contains source material on local German-Jewish communities pre-World War II. Bibliographies, festschriften and works on liturgy are notable. Most of the collection is in German and Hebrew. Also incl books in French, Latin and Spanish.

†PA —GRATZ COLLEGE LIBRARY, Tenth St & Tabor Rd, Philadelphia, 19141.
Notes: Hebraica, Judaica, education.

PA —LIBRARY COMPANY OF PHILADELPHIA, 1314 Locust St, Philadelphia, 19107. Edwin Wolf II, Librn; Kenneth Finkel, Cur of Prints
Holdings: Vols (450,000) Cat
Notes: The Edwin Wolf Collection of Judaica, consisting of 165 manuscripts and more than 500 books and broadsides printed in the US between 1718 and 1875. Incl literature, prayer books, Hebrew schoolbooks, reports of Jewish organizations, missionary tracts, narratives of travel to Palestine, and books on medicine. Most of the manuscripts consists of correspondence of the Gratz family, American pioneers.

PA —DUQUESNE UNIVERSITY, Library, Pittsburgh, 15282. Dena F Jacobson, Music and Reference Librn
Holdings: Vols 3000 Cat
Notes: Main emphasis of collection is on history of Jewish philosophy in the Middle Ages and relationship between Jewish and Christian scholars; collection incl works by 14th century writer Nicolas de Lyra and general Judaica, history of the Jews, theology, Bible texts and commentaries, literature, grammatical works and dictionaries, etc.

PA —UNIVERSITY OF PITTSBURGH, Hillman Library, Pittsburgh, 15260. Glenora E Rossell, Head
Holdings: Vols (3500) Cat
Notes: Most of the collection on Judiaism is in the English, French, and German languages. There are a few Hebrew titles. It contains Jewish reference works and materials on all subjects relating to Jews and Judiaism--history, religion, sociology, and philosophy. The collection is integrated into the general library catalog.

TX —UNIVERSITY OF TEXAS LIBRARIES, General Libraries, PO Box P, Austin, 78713. Carolyn Bucknell, Asst Dir for Collection Development
Holdings: Cat Microforms

TX —UNIVERSITY OF TEXAS, EL PASO, Library, El Paso, 79968. Fred W Hanes, Dir
Holdings: Vols 1730 Cat
Budget: ($5000)
Notes: The Judaica Collection. Jewish history and culture, as well as religion, philosophy and literature are documented by the collection.

TX —FORT WORTH PUBLIC LIBRARY, Humanities Division, 300 Taylor St, Fort Worth, 76102. Linda Bostic, Manager
Holdings: Cat
Notes: Collection incl all periods of Jewish history and culture, American and European.

UT —UNIVERSITY OF UTAH, Middle East Library, Salt Lake City, 84112. Ragai N Makar, Librn
Holdings: Vols 4000 Cat
Budget: ($28,000)
Notes: From the library of Samuel Mendelson.

WA —UNIVERSITY OF WASHINGTON LIBRARIES, Suzzallo Library, Manuscripts Section, FM-25, Seattle, 98195. Karyl Winn, Librn
Notes: More than 600 monographs and serials on Byzantine studies from the library of the late professor Paul Alexander. His Jewish studies collection is included.

WI —UNIVERSITY OF WISCONSIN, MADISON, Memorial Library, Western European Humanities Collection, 728 State St, Madison, 53706. Charles Szabo, Bibliographer
Notes: The Joseph L Baron Collection of Judaica. Includes volumes in Hebrew, German and English in the field of Semitic studies. Supplements the Library's Judaica holdings.

ON —NATIONAL LIBRARY OF CANADA, 395 Wellington St, Ottawa, K1A 0N4, Can. Andre Preibish, Dir
Notes: *The Jacob M Lowy Collection* over 2000 works of very rare Hebraica and Judaica. Among outstanding items are 30 incunabula - the first printed edition of the Babylonian Talmud, many editions of Flavius Josephus, including first edition of 1470 Early Bibles in many languages. *The Saul Hayes Collection* of Hebraic Manuscripts and microforms. Manuscripts from North Africa and the Orient; 300 reels of manuscripts held by libraries in Poland, USSR and Hungary. This collection is held in the Jacob M Lowy Room.

PQ —CONCORDIA UNIVERSITY LIBRARIES, 1455 de Maisonneuve Blvd W, Montreal, H3G 1M8, Can. Dorothy Cameron, Reference Librn
Notes: Collection incl Judaism History, Talmudie Period (17 titles), Medieval and early modern (106 titles), modern 1750- (9 titles); Philosophy - Jewish (38 titles); Ethics (2000 titles); Christianity modern period 1453- (278 titles).

JUDAICA, AMERICAN

PA —LIBRARY COMPANY OF PHILADELPHIA, 1314 Locust St, Philadelphia, 19107. Edwin Wolf II, Librn; Kenneth Finkel, Cur of Prints
Notes: An extensive collection of American Judaica formerly owned by Edwin Wolf, II. Contains 165 mss and over 500 books and broadsides, printed in this country from 1718 to 1875, by and relating to Jews.

JUDAICA, MEDICAL

MA —FRANCIS A COUNTWAY LIBRARY OF MEDICINE, Boston Medical Library/Harvard Medical Library, 10 Shattuck St, Boston, 02115. C Robin LeSueur, Librn; Richard J Wolfe, Cur, Rare Books & Manuscripts
Holdings: Cat Mss Microforms
Notes: Outstanding collection, 14th to 19th century.

MA —HEBREW COLLEGE, Jacob & Rose Grossman Library and Lawrence Jay & Anne Cable Rubenstein Library, 43 Hawes St, Brookline, 02146. Maurice Tuchman, Librn
Holdings: Vols (700) Cat Mss
Notes: Harry A and Beatrice C Savitz Medical History Collection. Collection of material on Jewish Medical history.

JUDAISM

CA —LOS ANGELES PUBLIC LIBRARY, Philosophy & Religion Dept, 630 W Fifth St, Los Angeles, 90071. Marilyn C Wherley, Librn
Holdings: Vols 600 Cat
Budget: ($60,000)
Notes: Historical, theological and biographical works relating to the faith. Includes popular and scholarly materials on comparative religions. Some serials and periodicals. Emphasis on Judaism in the United States.

CA —UNIVERSITY OF CALIFORNIA, LOS ANGELES, Research Library, Jewish Studies Collection, 405 Hilgard Ave, Los Angeles, 90024. Edward Shreeves, Chairman, Bibliographers Group; Shimeon Brisman, Jewish Studies Bibliographer
Holdings: Vols (100,000) Cat Mss Microforms

FL —UNIVERSITY OF FLORIDA LIBRARY, Isser and Rae Price Library of Judaica, 18 Libr East, Gainesville, 32611. Robert Singerman, Head Librn
Budget: ($30,000)
Notes: Total holdings estimated at 55,000 vols dealing with the political, social, economic and intellectual history of the Jews

JUDAISM (cont.)

in the ancient, medieval and modern periods and in all geographic areas. The following areas are especially well represented by printed matter in all relevant languages: Bibliography, Festschriften, History, Bible, Judaism and Jewish theology, liturgy, responsa, rabbinical literature, Jewish law, Hebrew language and literature, Yiddish language and literature, anti-semitism, Zionism, Palestine and the *Yishuv*, and the State of Israel. German and American Judaica form a collecting emphasis with holdings for all the standard histories as well as histories of individual synagogues, institutions and local communities. Works in Hebrew and Yiddish comprise about 60 percent of the collection (estimated 30,000 vols). With few exceptions, holdingsare limited to nineteenth and twentieth century imprints, with complete sets of journals and thousands of ephemeral pamphlets, many of them commemorating anniversaries, enhancing the research value of the collection, the largest Judaica research library in the southeastern United States. Only about half of the collection is cataloged; the collection is a circulating one and vols may be borrowed on interlibrary loan. Incl the Leonard C Mishkin Collection (40,000 vols), the largest personal Judaica collection in the United States, the Shlomo Marenof Collection (3500 vols), and the inventory of Bernard Morgenstern's Lower East Side Book Store (8000 vols). Scholars should inquire in advance of their visit. *The Isser and Rae Price Library of Judaica* Report (circulation 2900 copies) is mailed gratis twice a year to all interested parties. Special catalogs:Pre-1881 Hebrew imprints recorded in a chronological card file.

MA —AMERICAN ANTIQUARIAN SOCIETY LIBRARY, 185 Salisbury St, Worcester, 01609. Marcus A McCorison, Dir & Librn
Holdings: Cat
Notes: The Society holds over 90 percent of the 685 titles in Rosenbach's bibliography of American Jewish books to 1850, plus many early items not included in the list.

†NY —JEWISH THEOLOGICAL SEMINARY OF AMERICA LIBRARY, 3080 Broadway, New York, 10027.

NY —NEW YORK PUBLIC LIBRARY, Jewish Division, Fifth Ave & 42 St, New York, 10018. Leonard S Gold, Chief
Holdings: Vols (200,000) Cat Mss Microforms
Budget: ($33,383)
Notes: A collection of material in all languages on Judaism, Jewish history, literature and traditions from the earliest times to date and works in the Hebrew alphabet (mainly Hebrew and Yiddish) on a variety of subjects. The division has extensive files of Jewish periodicals and newspapers. The collection of rare Hebraica incl medieval texts, cabalistic works, ethical and philosophical tracts in book form. See *Dictionary Catalog of the Jewish Collection* (Boston: G K Hall, 1960), 14 vols. First Supplement (Boston: G K Hall, 1975), 8 vols.

NY —YESHIVA UNIVERSITY, Library, 500 West 185th Street, New York, 10033. Pearl Berger
Holdings: Cat Mss

NY —YIVO INSTITUTE FOR JEWISH RESEARCH, Library & Archives, 1048 Fifth Ave, New York, 10028. Dina Abramowicz, Librn; Marek Web, Archivist
Notes: Rabbinics collection, embracing publications from the 16th to the 20th century, incl rare books. Cataloged by subject and title.

OH —HEBREW UNION COLLEGE-JEWISH INSTITUTE OF RELIGION, Klau Library, 3101 Clifton Ave, Cincinnati, 45220. David J Gilner, Reference Librn
Holdings: Cat
Notes: Broad coverage of Orthodox, Conservative, and especially Reform Judaism.

PA —UNIVERSITY OF PITTSBURGH, Hillman Library, Pittsburgh, 15260. Glenora E Rossell, Head
Holdings: Vols (3500) Cat
Notes: Most of the collection on Judaism is in the English, French, and German languages. There are a few Hebrew titles. It contains Jewish reference works and materials on all subjects relating to Jews and Judaism--history, religion, sociology, and philosophy. The collection is integrated into the general library catalog.

TX —UNIVERSITY OF TEXAS, EL PASO, Library, El Paso, 79968. Fred W Hanes, Dir
Holdings: Vols 1730 Cat
Budget: ($5000)
Notes: The Judaica Collection. Jewish history and culture, as well as religion, philosophy and literature are documented by the collection.

PQ —CONCORDIA UNIVERSITY LIBRARIES, 1455 de Maisonneuve Blvd W, Montreal, H3G 1M8, Can. Dorothy Cameron, Reference Librn
Notes: Collection incl Judaism History, Talmudie Period (17 titles), Medieval and early modern (106 titles), modern 1750- (9 titles); Philosophy - Jewish (38 titles); Ethics (2000 titles); Christianity modern period 1453- (278 titles).

JUDESMO see Ladino Language and Literature

JUDGES—PORTRAITS

MA —HARVARD UNIVERSITY LIBRARY, Law School Library, Langdell Hall, Cambridge, 02138. Harry S Martin III, Librn
Notes: Prints and portraits.

JUDGMENT DAY

MI —ANDREWS UNIVERSITY, James White Library, Berrien Springs, 49104. Marley H Soper, Dir
Holdings: Cat Mss Pix
Notes: Advent Source Collection. Deals with prophecy of the Bible and the Advent hope in historical context. About 3700 items. Materials gathered by Dr L R Froom in the preparation of his four-volume set entitled *Prophetic Faith of Our Fathers*, ca 1946-1954. Not available by interlibrary loan, but may be used at this library.

JUDICIAL ADMINISTRATION see Law

JUDICIARY see Courts

JUGENDBEWEGUNG

NY —STATE UNIVERSITY OF NEW YORK AT ALBANY, Library, Special Collections Dept, 1400 Washington Ave, Albany, 12222. Marion P Munzer, Coordr
Notes: Primarily newspaper clippings assembled by Karl Otto Paetel over a period of about 25 years (2.5 linear feet). Also incl newsletters of pre- and postwar German youth groups. Part of the Library's German Exile Collection.
See also entry under German Youth Movement

JUGENDSTIL see Art Nouveau

JUGOSLAVIA see Yugoslavia

JULES-BOIS, HENRI ANTOINE, 1869-1943

DC —GEORGETOWN UNIVERSITY, Library, Special Collections Div, 37 & O Sts NW, Washington, 20057. George M Barringer, Special Collections Librn; Nicholas B Sheetz, Mss Librn
Holdings: Mss
Notes: The papers of Henri Antoine Jules-Bois (1869-1943), French poet, novelist, essayist, and dramatist, who lived for many years in the United States.

JULY FOURTH see Fourth of July

JUNG, CARL GUSTAV

DC —LIBRARY OF CONGRESS, Rare Book & Special Collections Div, Washington, 20540. William Matheson, Chief
Notes: An archival set of the Foundation's publications, supporting the papers of the Foundation in the Library's Manuscript Division. Focused originally on writings of Carl Jung on myth, symbol, and the collective unconsciousness, but expanded to incl "works that increase human consciousness" in aesthetics, cultural and art history, philosophy, poetry, psychology, and religion.

NY —ANALYTICAL PSYCHOLOGY CLUB OF NEW YORK, Kristine Mann Library, 28 E 39 St, New York, 10016. Doris Albrecht, Librn

JUNGER, ERNST, 1895-

NY —STATE UNIVERSITY OF NEW YORK AT ALBANY, Library, Special Collections Dept, 1400 Washington Ave, Albany, 12222. Marion P Munzer, Coordr
Notes: Correspondence between Jünger and Karl Otto Paetel; mss and clippings of articles; reviews of Jünger's works. Part of the Library's German Exile Collection.
See also entry under Paetel, Karl Otto

†ON —METROPOLITAN TORONTO LIBRARY BOARD, Language Dept, 789 Yonge St, Toronto, M4W 2G8, Can.
Notes: First editions of the works of Ernst Junger (1895-), many inscribed by him. Also original editions of authors active in Germany during the Twenties, Thirties, and Forties.

JUNK see Waste Products

JURGEMEYER, LOUIS LEROY

†IA —UNIVERSITY OF IOWA, Libraries, Iowa City, 52242.
Notes: Papers, etc.

JURICIC, ZELIMIR B.

BC —UNIVERSITY OF VICTORIA, McPherson Library, Victoria, V8W 3H5, Can.

JURISPRUDENCE

KY —UNIVERSITY OF KENTUCKY, Law Library, L-124 College of Law Bldg, Lexington, 40506. William James, Law Librn
Holdings: Vols (246,842) Cat Microforms
Budget: ($265,532)
Notes: Special collection on jurisprudence; hold briefs of Kentucky Court of Appeals since 1950-1977; Kentucky Supreme Court, 1977-.

MI —MICHIGAN STATE UNIVERSITY, Libraries, Special Collections Div, East Lansing, 48824. Jannette Fiore, Librn
Holdings: Vols 1440// Uncat Mss
Notes: Works from 15th to 19th centuries on criminology, criminal law and jurisprudence, including witchcraft, demonology, et al, chiefly in German and Latin.

JURISPRUDENCE—HISTORY

PA —UNIVERSITY OF PENNSYLVANIA, Lea Library, 3420 Walnut St, Philadelphia, 19104. Daniel Traister, Special Collections Librn
Holdings: Vols (20,000) Cat Mss
Notes: Collection incl works on Church history, the history of jurisprudence, political theory, Byzantine history, the Crusades and medieval urban history. See Downs 4241, 4234.

JURISPRUDENCE, COMPARATIVE see Comparative Law

JURISPRUDENCE, MEDICAL see Medical Jurisprudence

JURISTIC PERSONS, FOREIGN see Corporations, Foreign

JUSTICE, DONALD

DE —UNIVERSITY OF DELAWARE, Hugh M Morris Library, S College Ave, Newark,

JUSTICE, DONALD (cont.)

19711. T Stuart Dick, Special Collections
Holdings: Cat Mss
Notes: Manuscripts, notebooks, drafts, galleys and page proofs of all published works of Pulitzer Prize poet. Incl literary correspondence from 1953-1982.

JUSTMAN, ROBERT

CA —UNIVERSITY OF CALIFORNIA, LOS ANGELES, Theater Arts Library, Los Angeles, 90024. Edward Shreeves, Chairman, Bibliographers Group; Audree Malkin, Head, Theater Arts Library
Notes: Robert Justman (producer) Collection: complementing the Gene Roddenberry *Star Trek* Collection are the 66 annotated *Star Trek* scripts and production material.

JUSTUM PRETIUM see Prices

JUVENILE ARTHRITIS DEFORMANS see Rheumatoid Arthritis in Children

JUVENILE DELINQUENTS AND DELINQUENCY

IN —INDIANA LAW ENFORCEMENT ACADEMY, David F Allen Memorial Learning Resources Center, Rd 700 E, PO Box 313, Plainfield, 46168. Donna K Zimmerman, Librn
Holdings: Vols (4500) Cat Slides 16mm Films
Budget: ($8500)
Notes: Concentrated in the areas of police science, criminology, and law.

†MA —JOHN F KENNEDY LIBRARY, Columbia Point, Boston, 02125. Dan H Fenn Jr, Dir
Holdings: // Cat Mss
Notes: Background papers of Richardson White for his study "Youth and Opportunity: The Federal Anti-Delinquency Program" and Daniel Knapp's papers relating to the President's Commission on Juvenile Delinquency, late 1950s-late 1960s. 21 linear ft of mss. Holdings are described in "Historical Materials in the John F Kennedy Library." Copies may be obtained by writing the Research Archivist.

†MA —SECRETARY OF THE COMMONWEALTH, Archives Division, State House, Boston, 02133.

MA —HARVARD UNIVERSITY LIBRARY, Law School Library, Langdell Hall, Cambridge, 02138. Harry S Martin III, Librn
Holdings: cat

MO —SAINT LOUIS POLICE LIBRARY, 315 S Tucker Blvd, Saint Louis, 63102. Cathy Reilly, Librn
Holdings: Vols (21,000) Cat Mss Pix Microforms
Budget: ($18,400)
Notes: Library on all subjects of police work is open to the public for general reference use.

MO —CENTRAL MISSOURI STATE UNIVERSITY, Ward Edwards Library, Warrensburg, 64093. Nancy E Littlejohn, Social Sciences Librn
Holdings: Vols (8000) Cat Microforms
Budget: ($7500)
Notes: Extensive criminal justice and law collection. In addition, a 7593 title microfiche collection of criminal justice and juvenile delinquency.

NJ —RUTGERS, THE STATE UNIVERSITY OF NEW JERSEY, John Cotton Dana Library, 185 University Ave, Newark, 07102. Phyllis Schultze, Librn
Holdings: Vols 40,000 Cat
Notes: National Council on Crime and Delinquency. Criminology, as applied, means all phases of crime and delinquency prevention, control and treatment, ie, the whole "criminal justice" gamut: police, courts, probation and parole, prisons, community rehabilitation centers, etc. In short, everything except police laboratory materials. Collection completely cataloged; all criminological and correctional journals indexed. Incl many reports of correctional agencies, research reports, unpublished monographs, publications in the field by all government agencies, federal, state, county and local. Information file contains over 40, 000 such items, as well as about 10,000 uncataloged clippings and other pieces of information stored by specific subjects.

OH —OHIO STATE UNIVERSITY, Social Work Library, 1947 N College Rd, Columbus, 43210. Toyo S Kawakami, Librn
Holdings: Vols (46,410) Cat
Budget: ($11,960)
Notes: VF incl approx 4500 pamphlets, arranged by LC subject headings. 278 serial titles on social work, social and public service, crime and delinquency, corrections, criminal justice, marriage and the family, probation, and related topics, are received.

TX —WEST TEXAS STATE UNIVERSITY, Cornette Library, PO Box 748 WT Sta, Canyon, 79016. Faye Hendrickson, Special Collections Asst
Holdings: Vols (451,253) Uncat Microforms
Notes: Includes microform collection.

WI —UNIVERSITY OF WISCONSIN, MADISON, Law School Library, Criminal Justice Reference & Information Center, Madison, 53706. Sue Center, Librn
Holdings: Vols (29,000) Cat Mss
Budget: ($45,000)
Notes: In-depth subject access is provided to collection by our own cataloging and classification systems. Incl are periodical articles which are selectively cataloged to supplement the collection. Special items in collection incl penal press (prisoner newspapers); annual and statistical reports from criminal justice agencies throughout the US and Canada; theses and dissertations; and 280 periodical titles in the field of criminal justice.

ON —ONTARIO MINISTRY OF COMMUNITY & SOCIAL SERVICES, Library, 880 Bay St, Rm 663, Toronto, M7A 1E9, Can. Sandra Walsh, Chief Librn
Holdings: Vols (30,000) Cat Slides Videotapes 16mm Films Microforms
Notes: Probation and aftercare.

ON —UNIVERSITY OF TORONTO, Centre of Criminology, Library, 130 St George St, Rm 8001, Toronto, M5S 1A5, Can. Catherine J Matthews, Librn
Holdings: Vols (20,000) Cat
Notes: Over 4500 research reports, article reprints, theses, etc. Extensive newspaper clippings file from 1963 to present indexed under 350 subject headings. The collection covers criminology, law enforcement and policing, delinquency, criminal justice system, penology and corrections. Acquisitions list published three times a year subscription.

JUVENILE LITERATURE see Children's Literature

JUVENILE NOVELS see Children's Literature

JUVENILE PERIODICALS see Periodicals, Children's

JUVENILE RHEUMATOID ARTHRITIS see Rheumatoid Arthritis in Children

JUVENILE SERIES (BOOKS) see Children'S Literature—Juvenile Series

K

KABBALA see Cabala

KACHIN LANGUAGE

NY —NEW YORK PUBLIC LIBRARY, Oriental Div, Fifth Ave & 42 St, New York, 10018. E Christian Filstrup, Chief
Holdings: Cat Mss Microforms
Budget: ($56,455)
Notes: Published catalog of holdings.

KAFKA, FRANZ

OH —CASE WESTERN RESERVE UNIVERSITY LIBRARIES, Freiberger Library, 11161 East Blvd, Cleveland, 44106.
Notes: First editions, criticism, and ephemera.

KAGAWA, TOYOHIKO

IL —SOUTHERN ILLINOIS UNIVERSITY, CARBONDALE, Delyte W Morris Library, Carbondale, 62901.
Notes: Extensive file of papers relating to the life and work of Japanese social reformer Toyohiko Kagawa, collected by his secretary, Helen F Topping.

KAHGAN, PHILIP

CA —UNIVERSITY OF CALIFORNIA, LOS ANGELES, Music Library, Schonberg Hall, Los Angeles, 90024. Stephen M Fry, Music Librn
Notes: The Philip Kahgan Collection of music films, letters, programs, and photographs important to the Southern California classical music scene. Incl 16mm "home movies" of more than thirty renowned conductors and performers during Hollywood Bowl rehearsals in the late 1930s. Incl Kahgan correspondence, memorabilia, 35 scrapbooks, etc.

KAHLER, ERICH VON, 1885-1970

NY —STATE UNIVERSITY OF NEW YORK AT ALBANY, Library, Special Collections Dept, 1400 Washington Ave, Albany, 12222. Marion P Munzer, Coordr
Notes: Correspondence of Erich von Kahler; mss, reviews (12 linear feet). Part of the Library's German Exile Collection.

KAHN, ELY JACQUES

†NY —COLUMBIA UNIVERSITY LIBRARIES, Butler Library, Rare Book and Manuscript Library, 535 W 114 St, New York, 10027.
Notes: Located in the Avery Architectural Library. The architectural drawings of the New York firm of Kahn and Jacobs. A record of much of New York architecture from the 1890s through 1972. Incl works by Ely Jacques Kahn.

KAHN, OTTO HERMANN, 1867-1934

NJ —PRINCETON UNIVERSITY, Library, Manuscript Collection, Nassau St, Princeton, 08540. Jean F Preston, Cur
Holdings: // Mss Pix
Notes: The collection totals over 300,000 pieces in 536 ms boxes. It is indexed on 3 x 5 cards.

KAISER, GEORG

AB —UNIVERSITY OF ALBERTA, Cameron Library, The Bruce Peel Special Collections Room, Edmonton, T6G 2J8, Can. John Charles, Special Collections Librn
Notes: 157 vols cataloged; 28 boxes of photocopies of mss, newspapers cuttings, letters, etc; 10 boxes unsorted; 14 reels microfilm of primary and secondary material from journals.

KALER, JAMES OTIS

ME —SOUTH PORTLAND PUBLIC LIBRARY, 482 Broadway, South Portland, 04106. Carol Scheffler, Cataloger
Holdings: Vols 1900 Mss Pix
Notes: Papers and books of James Otis Kaler, famous Maine children's author of the 19th century, author of *Toby Tyler*. Also, other books, pre-1920. Separate shelflist.

KALIMANTAN see Indonesia

KALKA LANGUAGE see Khalkha Language

KAMARCK, LAWRENCE

MA —BOSTON UNIVERSITY, Mugar Memorial Library, Special Collections Dept, 771 Commonwealth Ave, Boston, 02215. Howard B Gotlieb, Dir
Holdings: Cat Mss

KAMCHADAL LANGUAGE

NY —NEW YORK PUBLIC LIBRARY, Oriental Div, Fifth Ave & 42 St, New York, 10018. E Christian Filstrup, Chief
Holdings: Cat Mss Microforms
Budget: ($56,455)
Notes: Published catalog of holdings.

WA —UNIVERSITY OF WASHINGTON LIBRARIES, Rare Books, Special Collections Dept, Seattle, 98195. Sandra Kroupa, Librn
Notes: Part of a set of Siberian primers prepared in the early 1930s by Soviet ethnographers. Some are first attempts to transcribe Siberian languages. All are in Latin phonetic script, not in Cyrillic.

KAMEN, MARTIN D.

CA —UNIVERSITY OF CALIFORNIA, BERKELEY, Bancroft Library, Manuscripts Division, Berkeley, 94720. James D Hart, Dir
Notes: Papers and research notes relative to the history of modern chemistry.

KAMI LANGUAGE see Syryenian Language and Literature

KAMPEN, IRENE

MA —BOSTON UNIVERSITY, Mugar Memorial Library, Special Collections Dept, 771 Commonwealth Ave, Boston, 02215. Howard B Gotlieb, Dir
Holdings: Cat Mss

KAMPUCHEA see Cambodia

KANARESE LANGUAGE AND LITERATURE

MI —MICHIGAN STATE UNIVERSITY, International Library, South and Southeast Asia Collection, East Lansing, 48824. Clinton Lockert, Bibliographer
Holdings: Vols 55,700 // Cat Mss Maps Audiotapes Microforms
Notes: Serials and monographs of South Asia received on PL 480 for India, Pakistan, Sri Lanka, and Nepal since 1968. Emphasis is upon social sciences, humanities, and science. Areas of strength are anthropology and rural development. This subject has been de-emphasized, additions are not being made.

NY —NEW YORK PUBLIC LIBRARY, Oriental Div, Fifth Ave & 42 St, New York, 10018. E Christian Filstrup, Chief
Holdings: Cat Mss Microforms
Budget: ($56,455)
Notes: Published catalog of holdings.

KANE, ELISHA KENT

PA —AMERICAN PHILOSOPHICAL SOCIETY, Library, 105 S Fifth St, Philadelphia, 19106. Edward C Carter II, Librn
Holdings: Cat Mss

KANJUR

MA —HARVARD UNIVERSITY LIBRARY, Harvard-Yenching Library, 2 Divinity Ave, Cambridge, 02138. Eugene W Wu, Librn
Notes: See *Harvard Library Bulletin*, IV (1950); p 286. Contains the three rare editions of the *Tripitaka:* The Narthang edition (1732) of both the Kanjur and the Tanjur, the Peking edition of the Kanjur, and the Lhasa edition (1933?) of the Kanjur; also Tibetan-language publications received under the PL480 program.

NY —COLUMBIA UNIVERSITY LIBRARIES, C V Strarr East Asian Library, 300 Kent Hall, New York, 10027. James Reardon-Anderson, Librn
Notes: Incl Narthang edition of the Kanjur and Tanjur. Restricted use.

NY —INSTITUTE FOR ADVANCED STUDIES OF WORLD RELIGIONS (IASWR), Melville Memorial Library, State University of New York, Stony Brook, 11794. C T Shen, Dir
Notes: Incl, in hard cover, Japanese reduced-size reprint of Peking edition of Kanjur and Tanjur, 168 vols containing 6439 titles and detailed catalog. Kanjur also in Derge, Tog Palace editions and in Mongolian translation. Tanjur in Derge edition arriving in stages. Various catalogs available. In microform: Lhasa ed of Kanjur (Bka-gyur), Cone ed of Tanjur (Bstan-gyur). Refer inquiries to H Robinson.
See also entries under Tantrism, Buddhist; Tibetan Buddhism; Tanjur

KANNADA LANGUAGE see Kanarese Language and Literature

KANSAS

KS —FORT HAYS KANSAS STATE UNIVERSITY, Forsyth Library, Western Collection, 600 Park St, Hays, 67601. Esta Lou Riley, Archivist/Special Collections Librn
Holdings: Vols (5500) Cat VF
Budget: ($1000)
Notes: Kansas material, emphasizing Western Kansas; the cattle industry of the Great Plains area to pre-World War I.

KS —KANSAS STATE HISTORICAL SOCIETY LIBRARY, Memorial Bldg, 120 W Tenth, Topeka, 66612. Portia Allbert, Library Dir
Holdings: Vols 145,000 Cat Mss Maps Pix Microforms
Budget: ($15,000)

KS —WICHITA PUBLIC LIBRARY, 223 S Main, Wichita, 67202. Richard Rademacher, Librn
Holdings: Vols (5560) Cat Pix Maps
Notes: Books by Kansas authors and books about Kansas, old and new. Not loaned.

KS —WICHITA PUBLIC LIBRARY, Art & Music Division, 223 S Main, Wichita, 67202. Leonard Messineo, Jr, Head, Art & Music Division; Deborah Hamilton, Special Collections Librn
Holdings: Audiotapes
Notes: Joan O'Bryant Kansas Folklore Collection. Contains approximately 200 hours of folkmusic and oral histories on tape; over 27,000 note cards covering topics such as anecdotes, beliefs, customs, games, jokes, medicines and cures, proverbs, recipes, rhymes, riddles, sayings, songs, speech and dialect, etc; 102 research papers covering family histories, town and area histories, biographies, tales, recipes, etc; and well over 70 mounted quilt blocks-covering the folk history of Kansas. This material was collected by Joan O'Bryant and her students from 1947-1964, the period in which she taught Folklore and English at Wichita State University.

KANSAS PSYCHIATRIC SOCIETY

KS —MENNINGER FOUNDATION, Archives, 5600 W Sixth St, Box 829, Topeka, 66601. Alice Brand, Librn; Mark West, Archivist
Notes: 10 boxes, 1942-date. Consists of correspondence, membership lists, financial records, minutes, newsletters, and miscellaneous materials.

KANSAS—GENEALOGY

KS —WICHITA PUBLIC LIBRARY, 223 S Main, Wichita, 67202. Richard Rademacher,

KANSAS—GENEALOGY (cont.)

Librn
Holdings: Vols (6570) Cat Microfilms
Notes: Incl approximately 2500 rolls of microfilm, 400 microcards. Not loaned.

KANSAS—GOVERNMENT PUBLICATIONS

KS —WICHITA PUBLIC LIBRARY, 223 S Main, Wichita, 67202. Larry DePiesse, Head, Business & Technology Dept; Jayne F Young, Business & Technology Dept
Holdings: Documents
Notes: All state documents designated as depository since 1977. Both cat and uncat. The majority of the collection is in the Business and Technology Dept arranged by the Kansas document classification scheme. Some have been distributed to various departments for Dewey cataloging or vertical file information.

KANSAS—HISTORY

KS —BAKER UNIVERSITY, Library, Eighth St, Baldwin City, 66006. Ray Firestone, Dir of Libraries
Holdings: Vols 200 Cat Mss Maps Pix Microforms
Notes: Housed in the United Methodist Historical Collection/Library room. Visitors are advised to make an appointment or check in advance to assure that collection is open. Archives of Baker University are incl in this collection.

KS —WYANDOTTE COUNTY HISTORICAL SOCIETY, Museum, Trowbridge Research Library, 631 N 126 St, Bonner Springs, 66012. Stephen J Allie, Archivist
Holdings: Vols 3000 Mss Maps Pix Slides Audiotapes Microforms
Budget: $12,500
Notes: Emphasis on Wyandotte County. Cataloged. Incl 100 maps, 4000 photographs. Also County Records 1855-1820. Cataloged.

KS —GREAT BEND PUBLIC LIBRARY, 1409 Williams St, Great Bend, 67530. James A Swan, Assoc Dir
Holdings: Vols 1000 Cat Mss Maps

KS —SANTA FE TRAIL CENTER, Library, Rte 3, Larned, 67550. Kim Keiswetter, Archivist/Education Dir
Holdings: Uncat Mss Maps Pix Slides
Budget: ($2500)
Notes: Archives and history of Pawnee County, Kansas, and the Santa Fe Trail. Strong slide and picture collections.

KS —UNIVERSITY OF KANSAS, Kenneth Spencer Research Library, Kansas Collection, Lawrence, 66045. Sheryl K Williams, Cur
Holdings: Vols (92,000) Cat Mss Maps Pix Microforms
Notes: In addition to printed book holdings there are more than 700,000 mss, 8000 maps, nearly 1 million photos and negatives, 1500 serial titles covering all aspects of Kansas history. Also state publications. Also, the J J Pennell Collection. Joseph Judd Pennell (1866-1922) was a commercial photographer living and working in Junction City, Kansas from 1888 to 1922. This collection of more than 30,000 glass negatives and nearly 6000 prints is a pictorial record of Junction City, Kansas and nearby Ft Riley. The residents of Junction City have been photographed in their various business, professional, social, and cultural activities, while the army post, Fort Riley, has been documented as a cavalry and light artillery post, as well as an important military post during the First World War and after. The various ethnic groups which made up the population of Junction City, whites, blacks, and Mexican-Americans are represented in the collection. Pennell's day books accompany the photographic collection.

KS —KANSAS STATE UNIVERSITY, Library, Special Collections & University Archives, Manhattan, 66506. Antonia Q Pigno, Coordr; John J Vander Velde, Librn; Anthony R Crawford, Univ Archivist
Holdings: Vols 1925 Cat
Notes: Subjects of collection are Kansas and Kansas State University.

KS —RILEY COUNTY HISTORICAL SOCIETY & MUSEUM, Seaton Memorial Library, 2309 Claflin Rd, Manhattan, 66502. Jean C Dallas, Dir
Holdings: Cat Mss Maps Pix Slides Audiotapes 16mm Films Videotapes Books VF
Budget: $2000
Notes: History of Kansas, primarily Riley County and Manhattan. Incl scrapbooks, bound and indexed newspapers, official records.

KS —HARVEY COUNTY HISTORICAL SOCIETY, Historical Library & Museum, 203 Main St, Newton, 67114. Mike Smurr, Dir
Holdings: Maps Pix
Notes: Our Library-Museum is limited to literature, pictures, and artifacts of interest to this locality, Harvey County, KS. Newton has been a railroad point since the Santa Fe built here in 1871, so we have an unusually good collection of railroad items. Hundreds of pictures, many timetables, passes, and items small enough to be housed in our building. Attention is also given to early-day agriculture in mid-Kansas, especially wheat-raising by early settlers in central Kansas. We have all the Harvey County newspapers through the year 1930 on microfilm. We have many photographs of scenes in Harvey County from the late 1800s to the present.

KS —POTTAWATOMIE-WABAUNSEE REGIONAL LIBRARY, 605 W Bertrand St, Saint Marys, 66536. Judith A Muck, Dir
Holdings: Cat Mss Maps Pix
Notes: Most of the collection is of maps bound in elephant volumes. While the whole state is covered, emphasis is on Pottawatomie and Wabaunsee counties. County atlases from 1868 to 1935 comprise the largest part of the collection.

KS —KANSAS STATE HISTORICAL SOCIETY LIBRARY, Memorial Bldg, 120 W Tenth, Topeka, 66612. Portia Allbert, Library Dir
Holdings: Vols 145,000 Cat Mss Maps Pix Microforms
Budget: ($15,000)

KS —TOPEKA PUBLIC LIBRARY, Special Collections & Local History Dept, 1515 W Tenth, Topeka, 66604. Warren Taylor, Librn
Holdings: Vols 1100 Cat Mss Maps Pix Slides Phonorecords Audiotapes 16mm Films Filmstrips Post Cards Trade Cards Sheet Music Periodicals
Budget: $2000
Notes: The Topeka Room is a local history collection and the primary goal is to acquire materials written by Topeka/Shawnee County authors, as well as material about the history, presses and ethnic groups of the area.

KS —WICHITA PUBLIC LIBRARY, Local History Dept, 223 S Main, Wichita, 67202. William Clark Ellington, Jr, Dept Head & City Historian
Notes: The Local History collection consists of a photographic archive of Wichita and Sedgwick county subjects and views. Many early Wichita and Sedgwick county town builders are represented in this extensive collection. The photographic archive also includes the prints and glass plates of pioneer photographers, W S Rogers of Wichita and John R Salmon of Mount Hope, Ks. Manuscripts, diarys and a general file of historical information covering Wichita and Sedgwick county history are maintained for public use. Rare early editions of the Wichita Beacon are also part of the Local History section.

KS —WICHITA STATE UNIVERSITY, Ablah Library, Box 68, Wichita, 67208. Michael T Kelly, Cur of Special Collections
Holdings: Vols Cat Maps
Notes: Incl the Robert W Baughman Collection of Kansas Maps.

MO —UNIVERSITY OF MISSOURI-KANSAS CITY, General Library, Snyder Collection of Americana, 5100 Rockhill Road, Kansas City, 64110. Kenneth J LaBudde, Dir; Robert Paustian, Asst Dir
Holdings: Vols 25,000 Cat
Notes: Nucleus was Robert M Snyder, Jr Americana Collection of some 14,000 items. Contains printed materials on 19th-century American history, especially the Trans-Mississippi West. Strengths include the history of Kansas City and Jackson County, Missouri, Kansas and Missouri county and state histories, American frontier religion (esp the Mormons and Alexander Campbell's Disciples of Christ), the history of railroads and transportation, the cattle trade, 19th-Century biography and autobiography, North American Indians and early Kansas and Missouri imprints.

RI —BROWN UNIVERSITY, John Hay Library, 20 Prospect St, Providence, 02912. Mark N Brown, Cur Mss
Holdings: / /
Notes: See the Eli Thayer Manuscript Collection.

TX —AMARILLO PUBLIC LIBRARY, 413 E Fourth, Amarillo, 79101. Mary Kay Snell, Librn
Holdings: Vols Cat Mss Maps Pix
Notes: The southwest collections incl materials on the history of Texas, Louisiana, New Mexico, Arkansas, Missouri and Kansas. General subjects covered incl overland journeys, early narratives, early biographies, Indian captivities, outlaws, US government reports, Mississippi and Ohio Rivers, the Mexican War, reports of Catholic missionaries, Niles Register, early publications, fur trade, western trails, Texas Rangers, sheriffs and Texas as a sovereign state, buffalo hunting, Indian wars, cowboys, the arrival of farmers, fences, and towns. Over 1600 items which incl books, documents, maps, mss, pamphlets, unpublished theses, interviews and photographs. The three major collections are the William Henry Bush Collection, the Laurence J Fitzsimon Collection and the Calendar of John L McCarty.

†WA —WASHINGTON STATE UNIVERSITY, Library, Manuscripts, Archives & Special Collections, Pullman, 99164. John F Guido, Head
Holdings: / / Mss Maps Pix
Notes: Papers, 1821-1873, covering Father De Smet's early sojourns at Whitemarsh and St Louis, his founding of the Rocky Mountain Missions, his long service as Procurator and Socius of the Missouri Province, and his many travels. Correspondence with his family in Belgium, mss of his published journals, 2 small maps, sketches and engravings used to illustrate his books. Incl about 100 small pencil sketches by Father Nicholas Point depicting the 1841 journey from Westport to St Mary's Mission in the Bitterroot Valley. Described in *The* Record, 30 (1969) 6-40; and 32 (1971) 47-63.

KANSAS—IMPRINTS

KS —UNIVERSITY OF KANSAS, Kenneth Spencer Research Library, Kansas Collection, Lawrence, 66045. Sheryl K Williams, Cur
Holdings: Vols 550 Cat
Notes: Kansas imprints, 1854-1876. See *Checklist of Kansas Imprints, 1854-1876* (American Imprints Inventory No 10), Topeka, Kansas, WPA Historical Records Survey Project, 1939 and Hawley, L A and Farley, Alan W, *Kansas Imprints,, 1854-1876; a Supplement* Topeka, Kansas: Kansas State Historical Society, 1958.

KANSAS—MAPS

KS —POTTAWATOMIE-WABAUNSEE REGIONAL LIBRARY, 605 W Bertrand St, Saint Marys, 66536. Judith A Muck, Dir
Notes: Most of the collection is of maps bound in elephant volumes. While the whole state is covered, emphasis is on Pottawatomie and Wabaunsee counties. County atlases from 1868 to 1935 comprise the largest part of the collection.

KS —WICHITA STATE UNIVERSITY, Ablah Library, Box 68, Wichita, 67208. Michael T

KANSAS—MAPS (cont.)

Kelly, Cur of Special Collections
Holdings: Cat Maps
Notes: Incl the Robert W Baughman Collection of Kansas Maps.

OK —TULSA CITY-COUNTY LIBRARY, Business & Technology Dept, 400 Civic Center, Tulsa, 74103. Craig Buthod, Head
Notes: Original General Land Office survey maps for the states of Arizona, Arkansas, Colorado, Illinois, Indiana, Idaho, Kansas, Michigan, Missouri, Montana, Nebraska, Nevada, New Mexico, North Dakota, Ohio, Oklahoma, South Dakota, Utah and Wyoming. Incomplete coverage of each state.

KANSAS—PICTURES, ILLUSTRATIONS, ETC.

KS —WICHITA PUBLIC LIBRARY, Local History Dept, 223 S Main, Wichita, 67202. William Clark Ellington, Jr, Dept Head & City Historian
Notes: The Local History collection consists of a photographic archive of Wichita and Sedgwick county subjects and views. Many early Wichita and Sedgwick county town builders are represented in this extensive collection. The photographic archive also includes the prints and glass plates of pioneer photographers, W S Rogers of Wichita and John R Salmon of Mount Hope, Ks. Manuscripts, diarys and a general file of historical information covering Wichita and Sedgwick county history are maintained for public use. Rare early editions of the Wichita Beacon are also part of the Local History section.

KANSAS—SOCIAL LIFE AND CUSTOMS

KS —WICHITA PUBLIC LIBRARY, Art & Music Division, 223 S Main, Wichita, 67202. Leonard Messineo, Jr, Head, Art & Music Division; Deborah Hamilton, Special Collections Librn
Holdings: Audiotapes
Notes: Joan O'Bryant Kansas Folklore Collection. Contains approximately 200 hours of folkmusic and oral histories on tape; over 27,000 note cards covering topics such as anecdotes, beliefs, customs, games, jokes, medicines and cures, proverbs, recipes, rhymes, riddles, sayings, songs, speech and dialect, etc; 102 research papers covering family histories, town and area histories, biographies, tales, recipes, etc; and well over 70 mounted quilt blocks-covering the folk history of Kansas. This material was collected by Joan O'Bryant and her students from 1947-1964, the period in which she taught Folklore and English at Wichita State University.

KANSAS AUTHORS see Authors, Kansas

KANSAS CITY—CULTURAL HISTORY

MO —UNIVERSITY OF MISSOURI-KANSAS CITY, General Library, State Historical Society of Missouri Manuscripts, 5100 Rockhill Road, Kansas City, 64110. Kenneth J LaBudde, Dir; Gordon Hendrickson, Assoc Dir
Holdings: Mss
Notes: Joint Collection Western Historical Manuscript Collection and the State Historical of Missouri Manuscripts, University of Missouri-Kansas City General Library, 5100 Rockhill Road, Kansas City, MO 64110. Ca 2,500 linear feet of manuscripts, blueprints and oral history tapes.
Notes: The manuscript collection includes material which documents the history, growth and development of Missouri, especially the Greater Kansas City area. The personal papers of business, civic, cultural, political and community leaders; local historians and other individuals of families from the area are within the collection as are the records of associations, organizations and institutions which reflect the history of the area. Prominent among the collections are the papers of Charles B. Wheeler, Jr., Charles N. Kimball, Arthur Mag, Oscar D. Nelson, Lou B. Holland, J. C. Nichols, Perry Cookingham, Blevins Davis and Daniel Macmorris and the records of the Kansas City Board of Trade. Architectural designs and plans for approximately 3,500 Kansas City buildings and the records of the Hoit, Price and Barnes architectural firm and the papers of Asa Beebe Cross, early Kansas City architect as well as a number of oral histories with Kansas City Jazz figures are in the collection.

KANSAS CITY—HISTORY

MO —UNIVERSITY OF MISSOURI-KANSAS CITY, General Library, Snyder Collection of Americana, 5100 Rockhill Road, Kansas City, 64110. Kenneth J LaBudde, Dir; Robert Paustian, Asst Dir
Holdings: Vols 25,000 Cat
Notes: Nucleus was Robert M Snyder, Jr Americana Collection of some 14,000 items. Contains printed materials on 19th-century American history, especially the Trans-Mississippi West. Strengths include the history of Kansas City and Jackson County, Missouri, Kansas and Missouri county and state histories, American frontier religion (esp the Mormons and Alexander Campbell's Disciples of Christ), the history of railroads and transportation, the cattle trade, 19th-Century biography and autobiography, North American Indians and early Kansas and Missouri imprints.

MO —UNIVERSITY OF MISSOURI-KANSAS CITY, General Library, State Historical Society of Missouri Manuscripts, 5100 Rockhill Road, Kansas City, 64110. Kenneth J LaBudde, Dir; Gordon Hendrickson, Assoc Dir
Holdings: Mss
Notes: Joint Collection Western Historical Manuscript Collection and the State Historical of Missouri Manuscripts, University of Missouri-Kansas City General Library, 5100 Rockhill Road, Kansas City, MO 64110. Ca 2,500 linear feet of manuscripts, blueprints and oral history tapes.
Notes: The manuscript collection includes material which documents the history, growth and development of Missouri, especially the Greater Kansas City area. The personal papers of business, civic, cultural, political and community leaders; local historians and other individuals of families from the area are within the collection as are the records of associations, organizations and institutions which reflect the history of the area. Prominent among the collections are the papers of Charles B. Wheeler, Jr., Charles N. Kimball, Arthur Mag, Oscar D. Nelson, Lou B. Holland, J. C. Nichols, Perry Cookingham, Blevins Davis and Daniel Macmorris and the records of the Kansas City Board of Trade. Architectural designs and plans for approximately 3,500 Kansas City buildings and the records of the Hoit, Price and Barnes architectural firm and the papers of Asa Beebe Cross, early Kansas City architect as well as a number of oral histories with Kansas City Jazz figures are in the collection.

KANSAS CITY BOARD OF TRADE

MO —UNIVERSITY OF MISSOURI-KANSAS CITY, General Library, State Historical Society of Missouri Manuscripts, 5100 Rockhill Road, Kansas City, 64110. Kenneth J LaBudde, Dir; Gordon Hendrickson, Assoc Dir
Holdings: Mss
Notes: Western Historical Manuscript Collection incl papers of Charles B Wheeler, Jr, Charles N Kimball, Arthur Mag, Oscar D Nelson, Lou B Holland, J C Nichols, Perry Cookingham, Blevins Davis, Daniel MacMorris, and the records of the Kansas City Board of Trade.

KANT, IMMANUEL

IL —NORTHWESTERN UNIVERSITY, Library, Special Collections Dept, 1937 Sheridan Rd, Evanston, 60201. R Russell Maylone, Cur
Holdings: Vols 123 Cat
Notes: Incl first editions. Additional material in general collection.

MD —JOHNS HOPKINS UNIVERSITY, Milton S Eisenhower Library, George Peabody Collection, 17 E Mt Vernon Place, Baltimore, 21201. Lyn Hart, Peabody Librn
Notes: Emphasis on materials published before 1950. Strength is a good collection through the 19th century.

MA —HARVARD UNIVERSITY LIBRARY, Widener Library, Cambridge, 02138.
Holdings: Cat

KARA KIRGHIZ LANGUAGE see Kirghiz Language and Literature

KARAGHIOZES

MA —HARVARD UNIVERSITY LIBRARY, Widener Library, Milman Parry Collection of Oral Literature & the James A Notopoulos Collection, Cambridge, 02138. Albert B Lord, Cur
Holdings: Cat Mss Pix Slides Microforms
Notes: First known systematic collection of Karaghiozes, incl 100 tapes of live and filmed performances and of professional life histories, pictures, and 245 actual shadow puppets. See *Harvard Library Bulletin, XIX* (1971): pp 242-243.

KARAIM DIALECTS see Karaitic Language and Literature

KARAITES

OH —HEBREW UNION COLLEGE-JEWISH INSTITUTE OF RELIGION, Klau Library, 3101 Clifton Ave, Cincinnati, 45220. David J Gilner, Reference Librn
Holdings: Cat

KARAITIC LANGUAGE AND LITERATURE

NY —NEW YORK PUBLIC LIBRARY, Oriental Div, Fifth Ave & 42 St, New York, 10018. E Christian Filstrup, Chief
Holdings: Cat Mss Microforms
Budget: ($56,455)
Notes: Published catalog of holdings.

KARDEX

DE —HAGLEY MUSEUM AND LIBRARY, Eleutherian Mills-Hagley Foundation Inc, PO Box 3630, Greenville, 19807. Richmond

KARDEX (cont.)

D Williams, Dir; Heddy A Richter, Imprints Librn
Notes: Sperry Univac has deposited a large amount of historical records. Approximately 2000 cubic feet of records, files and photographs that document the invention and development of computers and the rapid growth of the industry were officially released by Sperry Corporation to the Library. The collection includes technical and legal documents relating to the ENIAC and UNIVAC computers as well as records of the founding of the E Remington Typewriter Company and other predecessor companies of the Sperry organization, such as The Library Bureau, Kardex, Rodic Rubber and the Powers Accounting Machinery Company. Thus our knowledge of the Sperry predecessors dates back in this collection to 1902.

KAREN LANGUAGE

NY —NEW YORK PUBLIC LIBRARY, Oriental Div, Fifth Ave & 42 St, New York, 10018. E Christian Filstrup, Chief
Holdings: / / Cat Mss Microforms
Budget: ($56,455)
Notes: Published catalog of holdings.

KARLAN, RICHARD

MA —BOSTON UNIVERSITY, Mugar Memorial Library, Special Collections Dept, 771 Commonwealth Ave, Boston, 02215. Howard B Gotlieb, Dir
Holdings: Cat Mss

KARMAN, THEODORE VON

CA —CALIFORNIA INSTITUTE OF TECHNOLOGY, Robert A Millikan Memorial Library, Archives, 1201 E California Blvd, Pasadena, 91125. Judith R Goodstein, Archivist
Holdings: Vols (3000) Uncat Mss Maps Pix Slides Phonorecords Audiotapes Videotapes 16mm Films Microforms
Notes: Over 60 collections (1830s-present) relating to history of 19th-20th centuries science and technology and the history of the Institute. Included are personal and professional papers of Caltech scientists and adminstrative officers; divisional records and faculty committees; over 5000 photographs of American and European scientists. Mss collections document more than a century of American political, social, and intellectual history; the development of the physical sciences, aeronautics, molecular biology, and seismology in the US and abroad; and social and political conditions in Europe between the two World Wars. There are also family letters relating to 19th century American life before and during the Civil War (the Morley papers); to 19th century social conditions in Russia and Hungary (the Paul Epstein papers and Theodore von Karman papers); and toth development of 20th century Italian mathematics. The archive of Theodore von Karman, aerodynamicist incl 145,000 pages of letters, documents, scientific manuscripts, unpublished speeches, lecture notes, medals, photographs, and pictorial material. A microfiche copy of the archive is at the Smithsonian Institution's National Air and Space Museum.

KAROLYI, CATHERINE AND MICHAEL

MA —BOSTON UNIVERSITY, Mugar Memorial Library, Special Collections Dept, 771 Commonwealth Ave, Boston, 02215. Howard B Gotlieb, Dir
Holdings: Cat Mss Pix Correspondence

KARP, DAVID

MA —BOSTON UNIVERSITY, Mugar Memorial Library, Special Collections Dept, 771 Commonwealth Ave, Boston, 02215. Howard B Gotlieb, Dir
Holdings: Cat Mss Pix
Notes: Mss, correspondence, etc collected in depth; incl publications by or about.

KARR, JACK, 1916-1979

†ON —METROPOLITAN TORONTO LIBRARY, Theatre Dept, Toronto, M4W 2G8, Can.
Notes: Papers of Jack Karr, Canadian film and theatre critic, and public relations director for Stratford Festival and O'Keefe Centre.

KARSAVINA, TAMARA, 1885-

NY —NEW YORK PUBLIC LIBRARY, Performing Arts Research Center, Dance Collection, 111 Amsterdam Ave, New York, 10023. Genevieve Oswald, Cur
Notes: Extensive biographical and visual material. Includes photographs, clippings, reviews, scrapbooks, programs, posters, and tape-recorded interviews.
See also entry under Ballets Russes de Diaghilev.

KARZITIC

NY —NEW YORK PUBLIC LIBRARY, Oriental Div, Fifth Ave & 42 St, New York, 10018. E Christian Filstrup, Chief
Holdings: Cat Mss Microforms
Budget: ($56,455)
Notes: Published catalog of holdings.

KASER, DAVID

CO —UNIVERSITY OF DENVER, Center for the Study of Library Architecture, Graduate School of Librarianship and Information Management, University Park, Denver, 80208.
Notes: Architectural consultation papers, plans and programs of David Kaser for the years 1958-1975. Kaser has advised in the development of over 60 college and university library buildings in the US, Africa, Asia, and the Middle East.

KASHMIRI LANGUAGE AND LITERATURE

NY —NEW YORK PUBLIC LIBRARY, Oriental Div, Fifth Ave & 42 St, New York, 10018. E Christian Filstrup, Chief
Holdings: Cat Mss Microforms
Budget: ($56,455)
Notes: Published catalog of holdings.

KATCHER, LEO

MA —BOSTON UNIVERSITY, Mugar Memorial Library, Special Collections Dept, 771 Commonwealth Ave, Boston, 02215. Howard B Gotlieb, Dir
Holdings: Cat Mss

KATY KEENE

OH —OHIO STATE UNIVERSITY, Library for Communication and Graphic Arts, 242 W 18th St, Columbus, 43210. Lucy S Caswell, Curator
Notes: Original comic art of Caniff, Foster, Dunn, Dudley T Fisher. Extensive original cartoon art. Shel Dorf Collection of comic strips and related material. A small but growing collection of comic books especially those featuring *Katy Keene,* is available in the Library. Movie posters and stills, 110, 000. Incl Milton Caniff Research Room.

KATYN FOREST MASSACRE, 1940

CA —HOOVER INSTITUTION ON WAR, REVOLUTION & PEACE, Stanford University, Stanford, 94305. Milorad M Drachkovitch, Archivist
Holdings: Mss Pix
Notes: Two collections: (1) Papers of Julius Epstein, journalist, research associate at the Hoover Institution, and author of *Operation Keelhaul: The Story of Forced Repatriation,* incl correspondence, speeches and writings, clippings, photographs, and printed matter, 1939-72, relating to his research on the events of World War II, communism, forced repatriation of Russian prisoners of the Soviet Union following World War II, Katyn Forest Massacres, and unreported deaths of Soviet Cosmonauts, as well as his efforts to obtain restricted government documents on these subjects. 180 ms boxes. (2) Records of the Polish Embassy at Moscow and Kuibyshev, incl reports, correspondence, accounts, lists, testimonies, questionnaires, certificates, petitions, card files, maps, circulars, graphs, protocols, and clippings1941-1944, relating to World War II, the Soviet occupation of Poland the Polish-Soviet military and diplomatic agreements of 1941, the reestablishment of the Polish Embassy in Moscow, Polish prisoners-of-war in the USSR, deportations of Polish citizens to the USSR, labor camps and settlements, relief work by Polish Social Welfare Department delegations among the deportees, the Polish Armed Forces formed in the USSR, evacuation of the Polish Embassy to Kuibyshev, evacuation of Polish citizens to the Middle East, the Katyn massacre of Polish officers, and the break-down of Polish-Soviet relations in April, 1943. Also incl material on the Communist Party of the Soviet Union and the Soviet government, 1928-1929. 54 ms boxes.

KATZ, LEON, 1909-

SK —UNIVERSITY OF SASKATCHEWAN, Murray Library, University Archives, Third Floor, Saskatoon, S7N 0W0, Can. Stan Hanson, Univ Archivist
Notes: Two meters of materials. Personal papers and office prints.

KATZENELLENBOGEN, ADOLF

MD —JOHNS HOPKINS UNIVERSITY, Milton S Eisenhower Library, Charles & 34 Sts, Baltimore, 21218. Ann S Gwyn, Assistant Dir for Special Collections
Holdings: Cat Mss
Notes: 100 mss of lectures on art and architecture, based on research done in Germany before World War II (many sites no longer extant).

KAUFFMANN, LANE

MA —BOSTON UNIVERSITY, Mugar Memorial Library, Special Collections Dept, 771 Commonwealth Ave, Boston, 02215. Howard B Gotlieb, Dir
Holdings: Cat Mss

KAUFMAN, GEORGE S. see Hart, Moss, and George S. Kaufman

KAUFMAN, HARRY, 1894-1961

CA —UNIVERSITY OF CALIFORNIA, LOS ANGELES, Research Library, Dept of Special Collections, 405 Hilgard Ave, Los Angeles, 90024. Edward Shreeves, Chairman, Bibliographers Group; David S Zeidberg, Head
Notes: 10 linear feet of correspondence, photographs, and albums relating to his career as a pianist and music teacher.

KAUFMAN, LENARD

MA —BOSTON UNIVERSITY, Mugar Memorial Library, Special Collections Dept, 771 Commonwealth Ave, Boston, 02215. Howard B Gotlieb, Dir
Holdings: Cat Mss

KAUFMANN, ALOYS P.

MO —WASHINGTON UNIVERSITY, Libraries, Special Collections Dept, Campus Box 1061, St Louis, 63130.
Notes: St Louis Mayoral Papers Collection: Papers of Aloys P Kaufmann, 1944-49; Raymond R Tucker, 1953-65; Alphonso J Cervantes, 1965-73; John H Poelker, 1973-77; James F Conway, 1977-81.

KAVANAGH, PATRICK, 1905-1967

BC —UNIVERSITY OF VICTORIA, McPherson Library, Victoria, V8W 3H5, Can.

KAWABATA, YASUNARI

FL —UNIVERSITY OF FLORIDA, Libraries, Gainesville, 32611. Ray Jones, Research Librn; Max Willocks, Librn
Holdings: Vols (2000)
Notes: An extensive collection of modern and premodern Japanese prose fiction in English translation and Japanese. Incl complete works of a number of important modern Japanese authors such as Yasunari Kawabata, Naoya Shiga, Junichiro Tanizaki, and Yukio Mishima.

KAY, HERSHY

CT —YALE UNIVERSITY, Music Library, 98 Wall St, New Haven, 06520. Harold E Samuel, Librn
Notes: Personal papers and musical mss. *See also* entry under Music, American.

KAYAKS see Canoes and Canoeing

KAYE, MARVIN

MA —BOSTON UNIVERSITY, Mugar Memorial Library, Special Collections Dept, 771 Commonwealth Ave, Boston, 02215. Howard B Gotlieb, Dir
Holdings: Cat Mss

KAYE-SMITH, SHEILA

DC —GEORGETOWN UNIVERSITY, Library, Special Collections Div, 37 & O Sts NW, Washington, 20057. George M Barringer, Special Collections Librn; Nicholas B Sheetz, Mss Librn
Holdings: Mss
Notes: The Archives of the Gallery of Living Catholic Authors was founded in 1932 by Sister Mary Joseph of the Sisters of Loretto to focus attention on modern Catholic literature, and to provide a depository for manuscripts, letters, photographs, and books by contemporary Catholic writers. Contains material by hundreds of writers, incl Hilaire Belloc, Roy Campbell, Padraic Colum, Eric Gill, Paul Horgan, Mary Lavin, Marie Belloc Lowndes, Kathleen Norris, Alred Noyes, Sheila Kaye-Smith, Sigrid Undset, and Evelyn Waugh, to name only a few.

IL —ILLINOIS STATE UNIVERSITY, Milner Library, Dept of Special Collections, Normal, 61761. Robert Sokan, Librn
Notes: First editions, limited editions, ephemera, etc.

KAZAK KIRGHIZ LANGUAGE see Kazakh Language and Literature

KAZIN, ALFRED

NY —NEW YORK PUBLIC LIBRARY, Fifth Ave & 42 St, New York, 10018.
Notes: His papers, incl typescripts of his books, 2350 pages of journal entries, articles, sketches and stories written since 1930, the unpublished rough draft of a novelette with a war background, and letters from other writers of recent years, incl Sherwood Anderson, Van Wyck Brooks, Edmund Wilson, Saul Bellow, William Faulkner, Ernest Hemingway and John Updike.

KAZAKH LANGUAGE AND LITERATURE

NY —NEW YORK PUBLIC LIBRARY, Oriental Div, Fifth Ave & 42 St, New York, 10018. E Christian Filstrup, Chief
Holdings: Cat Mss Microforms
Budget: ($56,455)
Notes: Published catalog of holdings.

KEAN, CHARLES

NY —UNIVERSITY OF ROCHESTER, Rush Rhees Library, Department of Rare Books and Special Collections, Rochester, 14627. Peter Dzwonkoski, Librn
Holdings: Cat Mss Pix
Notes: Papers, etc, incl books by and about, etc.

KEAN, EDMUND

NY —NEW YORK PUBLIC LIBRARY, Performing Arts Research Center, Billy Rose Theatre Collection, 111 Amsterdam Ave, New York, 10023. Dorothy L Swerdlove, Cur
Holdings: Cat
Notes: Includes many autograph letters, prints, programs, etc.

KEARNEY, JOHN

IL —CHICAGO HISTORICAL SOCIETY, Library, Clark St at North Ave, Chicago, 60614. Archie Motley, Manuscript Librn
Notes: Papers of: Emmet Dedmon, newspaper editor; Richard J Finnegan, newspaper editor; Rev Andres M Greeley, sociologist and author; attorney and civil liberties activist Pearl Hart; Robert J Havighurst, educator; social activist John Kearney; Kenesaw Mountain Landis, Federal Judge and first Commissioner of Baseball; Judge David F Matchett; Ivan Molek, Slovenian language publisher in Chicago; Max R Naiman, Communist Party activist; Ralph G Newman, book and autograph dealer and manuscript appraiser; Otto L Schmidt, physician and President of the Chicago and Illinois State Historical Societites; and Dempsey Travis, black mortgage banker.

KEATING, KENNETH B.

NY —UNIVERSITY OF ROCHESTER, Rush Rhees Library, Department of Rare Books and Special Collections, Rochester, 14627. Peter Dzwonkoski, Librn
Notes: Mss, documents, photographs, films (1200 linear ft) documenting his career as congressman, senator, federal judge, and ambassador. Closed until January 1, 1985.

KEATON, BUSTER

CA —AMERICAN FILM INSTITUTE, Louis B Mayer Library, 2021 N Western Ave, PO Box 27999, Los Angeles, 90027. Anne G Schlosser, Dir
Holdings: Vols (3500) Cat
Notes: The Buston Keaton Scrapbook documents the Keaton family in vaudeville.

KEATS, JOHN

CA —OCCIDENTAL COLLEGE, Library, 1600 Campus Rd, Los Angeles, 90041. Michael C Sutherland, Special Collections Librn
Holdings: Vols (2000) // Cat
Notes: The Weller Collection of Romantic Literature was given by Earl V Weller. Primary emphasis is on John Keats, but first or other important editions of many Romantic Poets of this period are also included.

CA —UNIVERSITY OF CALIFORNIA, LOS ANGELES, William Andrews Clark Memorial Library, 2520 Cimarron St, Los Angeles, 90018.
Holdings: Cat Mss
Notes: Small collection, original editions, etc.

CA —STANFORD UNIVERSITY LIBRARIES, Cecil H Green Library, Stanford, 94305. Michael T Ryan, Cur
Holdings: Vols (23,000) Cat
Notes: The Charlotte Ashley Felton Memorial Library. Incl first editions.

FL —UNIVERSITY OF SOUTH FLORIDA, Library, Tampa, 33620. J B Dobkin, Special Collections Librn
Notes: Microfilm of mss at Keats House, Hampstead, England. Many unpublished documents; incl letters, etc of the Keats circle.

MD —JOHNS HOPKINS UNIVERSITY, Milton S Eisenhower Library, Charles & 34 Sts, Baltimore, 21218. Ann S Gwyn, Assistant Dir for Special Collections
Holdings: Vols Cat Mss Microforms
Notes: The Osler Collection (Tudor and Stuart Club) contains original editions of Shelley, Milton, Keats, Donne, Defoe, Thomas Fuller, Golden Book of Marcus Aurelilus (1559). A collection of his articles made by Walt Whitman. 17th and 18th century commonplace books in English and French, in ms. Most English translations of Jakob Boehme. Cards in main catalog. Also, not included in the above figure, Pollard and Redgrave's and Wing's Early English Books on microfilm.

MA —HARVARD UNIVERSITY LIBRARY, Houghton Library, Cambridge, 02138. Rodney G Dennis, Cur of Manuscripts
Holdings: Cat Mss
Notes: An unequalled collection of mss of poems and letters, books, from the poet's own library, editions of his work, and related materials, combining collections made by Amy Lowell and Arthur A Houghton, Jr. A catalog is being prepared for publication. See *Harvard Library Notes, I* (1921), 78-81, and *Harvard Library Bulletin, VI* (1952), 161-175.

NJ —PRINCETON UNIVERSITY, Library, Rare Books Dept, Princeton, 08544. Stephen Ferguson, Cur
Notes: Uncataloged collection of about 100 vols in the Department of Rare Books and Special Collections. Gift of Archibald S Alexander in 1974.

PA —BRYN MAWR COLLEGE, Canaday Library, Bryn Mawr, 19010. James Tanis, Dir
Notes: Manuscript and printed material in the Adelman Collection.

KECSKEMETI, PAUL

MA —BRANDEIS UNIVERSITY, Goldfarb Library, 415 South St, Waltham, 02154. Bessie Hahn, Dir
Notes: 6 linear ft of research and working papers of American sociologist, Paul Kecskemeti. This collection is unprocessed, spring 1984.

KEELER, LUCY ELLIOT

OH —RUTHERFORD B HAYES LIBRARY, 1337 Hayes Ave, Fremont, 43420. Watt P Marchman, Dir
Holdings: Vols 100 Cat Mss Pix Microforms
Notes: Papers of Lucy Elliot Keeler who was a niece of President Rutherford B Hayes. Considerable on American literature and local history. Index in collection; listed in *Guide to Manuscripts of the Ohio Historical Society,* 269.

KEELER, W. W.

OK —CHEROKEE NATIONAL HISTORICAL SOCIETY, Archives & Library, PO Box 515 TSA-LA-GI, Tahlequah, 74464. Duane King, Dir
Holdings: Vols (1000) Uncat Mss Maps Pix Slides Audiotapes Microforms
Notes: An embryonic collection, directly or indirectly related to Cherokee history, culture and genealogy. Slide collection depicts copies of material from the collection, from the Cherokee National Museum Village (Cherokee, 1650 AD) and the Cultural Theatre ("Trail of Tears Drama"). Newspaper collection incl several hundred newspapers dating back to 1762, each of which contains some reference to the Cherokees. The Cherokee National Archives also contains the non-current 1975 files of the Cherokee Nation of Oklahoma and the Keeler Collection (papers and personal files of W W Keeler, former Principal Chief of the Cherokee Nation for 26 years).

KEEN, WILLIAM WILLIAMS, 1837-1932

RI —BROWN UNIVERSITY, John Hay Library, 20 Prospect St, Providence, 02912. Mark N Brown, Cur Mss
Holdings: // Mss
Notes: Papers of William Williams Keen, American surgeon, Brown Class of 1859. Of the 13,700 items in this collection. 13,200 consist of correspondence for the period

KEEN, WILLIAM WILLIAMS, 1837-1932 (cont.)

1858 to 1932 with noted scientists, physicians, and public figures. Also diaries, mss, and typescripts of articles, addresses, and lectures. A source for the history of medicine and surgery in the U S, 1860-1930. Registar available.

KEENE FAMILY

PA —PHILADELPHIA MARITIME MUSEUM, Library, 321 Chestnut St, Philadelphia, 19106. Dorothy H Mueller, Librn
Holdings: // Mss
Notes: Hepburn Collection. Consists of the family papers of John Barry, Patrick Hayes, and the Sommers and Keene families of Philadelphia. Includes personal correspondence, financial and business papers, and diaries and journals. Dates range from 1723-1876. 300 ms pieces.

KEEPSAKES (BOOKS) see Literary Annuals and Giftbooks; Giftbooks (Annuals, Etc.)

KEES, WELDON

NE —UNIVERSITY OF NEBRASKA, OMAHA, Library, 60 & Dodge Sts, Omaha, 68132. Mel Bohn, Librn
Holdings: Cat
Notes: 39 items; books and periodicals.

KEFAUVER, ESTES

TN —UNIVERSITY OF TENNESSEE, KNOXVILLE, Library, Knoxville, 37996. John Dobson, Special Collections Librn
Holdings: Vols (20,000) Cat Mss Maps Pix
Notes: Tennesseana; 19th century American fiction; southern Indians; early Imprints. Separate catalog; holdings also listed in comprehensive public catalog in Main Library. Rare books card catalog with special headings calling attention to unusual features of the books; unpublished registers and calendars to ms collection. *Kefauver* collection, 59,000 pounds of political papers and memorabilia, reconstructed Senate office; *Radiation Biology Archives* (ca 60, 000 pieces), papers of scientists from several countries dealing with the development of radiation biology. Also, 18 vols of extremely rare Southwest Territory and *Tennessee Official Journals,* printed in Knoxville, 1794-1796. The rare *Acts and Journals* are described in *The Lost Roulstone Imprints*, by John Dobson (Knoxville: Univ of Tennessee Libraries, 1975), 70 pp.

KEFAUVER, GRAYSON N.

CA —HOOVER INSTITUTION ON WAR, REVOLUTION & PEACE, Stanford University, Stanford, 94305. Milorad M Drachkovitch, Archivist
Holdings: // Mss
Notes: The Grayson N Kefauver Collection. Papers documenting the founding, background, and early history of the United Nations Educational, Scientific, and Cultural Organization. Incl memoranda and reports of individuals, press clippings, and minutes of meetings of organizations participating in its founding. 16 ft.

KEIL, CHARLES M. H.

MA —BOSTON UNIVERSITY, Mugar Memorial Library, Special Collections Dept, 771 Commonwealth Ave, Boston, 02215. Howard B Gotlieb, Dir
Holdings: Cat Mss

KEITH, BENJAMIN FRANKLIN, 1846-1914

IA —UNIVERSITY OF IOWA, University Libraries, Iowa City, 52242. Robert A McCown, Mss Librn
Holdings: Mss
Notes: Keith/Albee Vaudeville Collection. Records of a vaudeville, theatre, and moving-pictures business established by Benjamin Franklin Keith, 1846-1914, and Edward Franklin Albee, 1857-1930. The collection includes clipping books, report books, cash books, subject files, signs and posters. Theatres in the following cities are represented in the collection: Providence, RI, Pawtucket, RI, Woonsocket, RI, and Webster, Mass. The business was later part of RKO Pictures, Inc. Unpublished register in the library. 50 ft of mss.

KEITH, JOSEPH JOEL

CO —UNIVERSITY OF COLORADO, Libraries, Special Collections, Boulder, 80309. Nora J Quinlan, Head
Holdings: // Cat Mss
Notes: Incl 104 poems and 8 notebooks.

KEITH, WILLIAM

†CA —UNIVERSITY OF THE PACIFIC, Library, Stockton, 95211.

KELLER, HELEN

CA —FRANCIS BACON LIBRARY, 655 N Dartmouth Ave, Claremont, 91711. Elizabeth S Wrigley, Dir
Holdings: Mss Pix
Notes: Arensberg's miscellaneous correspondence with American literary figures (1920's-50's) including Bruce Bliven, Catherine Drinker Bowen, Kay Boyle, Witter Bynner, Edwin Corle, Helen A Keller, Lysander Kemp, Kenneth Macgowan, John Macy, Henry Miller, Lewis Mumford, Clifford Odets, Kenneth Patchen, Irving Stone, and William Carlos Williams.

NY —AMERICAN FOUNDATION FOR THE BLIND, M C Migel Memorial Library and Information Center, 15 W 16 St, New York, 10011. Diane Wolfe, Head Librn & Info Ctr Coordr; Marguerite Levine, Supvr Archives
Holdings: Mss Pix Slides Audiotapes 16mm Film
Notes: Helen Keller's papers in Helen Keller Archives. A collection relating to Helen Adams Keller. Incl are correspondence with friends and admirers, speeches, literary mss, legal and genealogical material, photographs, sound recordings, and one film: about Helen Keller, her teacher Anne Sullivan Macy, her companion Polly Thomson, and John Albert Macy, husband of Anne Sullivan Macy. Among the subjects represented are work on behalf of the blind, deaf-blind, and deaf; children and women in factories; planned parenthood; labor movements; peace; and suffrage.

KELLER, ROBERT

DC —LIBRARY OF CONGRESS, Music Division, Washington, 20540.
Notes: A large collection of letters from Brahms to Robert Keller.

KELLOGG, CHARLES E.

MD —NATIONAL AGRICULTURAL LIBRARY, Rare Books Dept, 10301 Baltimore Blvd, Beltsville, 20705. Alan Susoni, Librn
Notes: A special collection of soil science publications, manuscripts, maps, slides, and unpublished journals from the personal library of the late Charles E Kellogg. Incl some rare copies of important works in the field and journals Kellogg kept on his many foreign travels.

KELLOGG, ELIJAH

ME —BOWDOIN COLLEGE, Library, Brunswick, 04011. Dianne M Gutscher, Cur of Special Collections
Holdings: Vols Mss
Notes: The Kellogg Collection contains the diaries of Elijah Kellogg (1761-1842) for the years of 1821, 1822, and 1825-1827, during the time of his missionary work with the Passamaquoddies. Collection also contains more than 80 volumes of the adventure stories for boys written by Elijah Kellogg (1813-1901).

KELLEY, FRED

OH —GREENE COUNTY DISTRICT LIBRARY, 76 E Market St, PO Box 520, Xenia, 45385. Julie M Overton, Local History Coordr
Notes: Collection of papers on Fred Kelley, noted newspaper journalist and author born in Greene Co, Ohio. Papers include many published articles and books as well as some correspondence.

KELLEY, ROBERT

NY —STATE UNIVERSITY OF NEW YORK, COLLEGE AT BUFFALO, Poetry/Rare Books Collection, 420 Capen Hall, Buffalo, 14260. Robert J Bertholf, Cur
Notes: The extensive holdings incl a complete first edition collection for Robert Kelley's publications. The holdings also incl notebooks, typescripts, notes, letters, photographs and ephemera of Kelley's career through 1978.

KELLEY, ROBERT F., 1894-1975

DC —GEORGETOWN UNIVERSITY, Library, Special Collections Div, 37 & O Sts NW, Washington, 20057. George M Barringer, Special Collections Librn; Nicholas B Sheetz, Mss Librn
Holdings: Mss Cat Pix
Notes: Correspondence, memoranda, reports, mss of articles and addresses, pamphlets, and newspaper clippings constituting the papers of Robert F Kelley (1894-1975). Kelley served as US Military Attache to the Baltic Provinces from 1920-22, before entering the foreign service in 1922. From 1926-37 he served as Chief of the Division of Eastern European Affairs in the State Department. In 1937 he was transferred to Ankara, Turkey where he remained until his retirement from foreign service in 1945. The papers most directly concern USSR internal affairs as well as US - USSR relations from the years immediately prior to recognition in 1933 through the cold war years of the early 1960's. Apart from State Department material, additional material is incl from Kelley's involvement in the American Committee for Liberation from Bolshevism and the establishment of Radio Liberty.

KELLY, GENE

MA —BOSTON UNIVERSITY, Mugar Memorial Library, Special Collections Dept, 771 Commonwealth Ave, Boston, 02215. Howard B Gotlieb, Dir
Holdings: Cat Mss Pix
Notes: Mss, correspondence, etc collected in depth; incl publications by or about.

KELLY, HOWARD ATWOOD, 1858-1943

KS —UNIVERSITY OF KANSAS MEDICAL CENTER, College of Health Sciences & Hospital, Clendening History of Medicine Library, Rainbow Blvd at 39th, Kansas City, 66103. Robert P Hudson, Chmn/Cur
Holdings: Vols (15,725) Cat Mss
Notes: Strong in all fields of medical history. Incl incunabula and serials. Mss incl Jakob Henie, 1809-1885, papers (ca 4050 items); Howard Atwood Kelly, 1858-1943, correspondence (ca 90 items); Joseph Lister, 1827-1912, letters (7); Florence Nightingale, 1820-1910, letters (20); and Samuel Jay Crumbine, 1862-1954, papers (ca 2365 items).

KELLY, JOHN B.

PA —FREE LIBRARY OF PHILADELPHIA, Rare Book Dept, Logan Sq, Philadelphia, 19103. Marie E Korey, Rare Book Librn
Holdings: Vols (2000) // Uncat
Notes: Newspaper and periodical clippings

KELLY, JOHN B. (cont.)

(2000) and materials relating to the Philadelphia politician and his family.

KELLY, JOSEPH J.

PA —LIBRARY COMPANY OF PHILADELPHIA, 1314 Locust St, Philadelphia, 19107. Edwin Wolf II, Librn; Kenneth Finkel, Cur of Prints
Holdings: 2500 Prints
Notes: Incl 2500 prints by Joseph J Kelly's firm, The Photo-Illustrators; with a large proportion on the Sesquicentennial and other Philadelphia views.

KELLY, KEVIN

†IA —UNIVERSITY OF IOWA, Libraries, Iowa City, 52242.
Notes: Papers, etc.

KELLY, MARY

MA —BOSTON UNIVERSITY, Mugar Memorial Library, Special Collections Dept, 771 Commonwealth Ave, Boston, 02215. Howard B Gotlieb, Dir
Holdings: Cat Mss

KELLY, WILLIAM AIKEN

SC —COLLEGE OF CHARLESTON LIBRARY, Special Collections Dept, Charleston, 29401.
Notes: Papers, incl two diaries for 1864 of Kelly's experiences as a captain in the army of Northern Virginia during the Civil War.

KELLY FAMILY

CA —SAN DIEGO PUBLIC LIBRARY, 820 E St, San Diego, 92101. Rhoda E Kruse, Sr Librn
Notes: Extensive local history collection. Incl papers of the Kelly and Foss families.

KELLY PLOW COMPANY

TX —STEPHEN F AUSTIN STATE UNIVERSITY, Ralph W Steen Library, Special Collections Dept, Box 13055, SFA Sta, Nacogdoches, 75962. Linda Cheves Nicklas, Special Collections Librn
Holdings: Mss Maps Pix
Budget: ($5000)
Notes: Incl personal and business papers, letters, diaries, and other records of East Texans and East Texas institutions and businesses. Major collections incl papers of Karl Wilson Baker, George L Crocket, Bennett Blake, McFarland-Russell family, Orton family, Samuel E Asbury; and records of Nacogdoches University, East Texas Historical Association, Kelly Plow Company and many local organizations; 60 Thomas J Rusk letters. Indexes, calendars and inventories are available. Description: SFASU, *A Guide to Special Collections,* 1980.

KEMBLE, 'FANNY'

MA —LENOX LIBRARY ASSOCIATION, Main St, Lenox, 01240. Denis J Lesieur, Dir
Holdings: Mss Pix
Notes: Frances Anne "Fanny" Kemble (Mrs Pierce M Butler), the English actress who lived in Lenox. Some of her books.

KEMBLE, JOHN PHILIP

DC —FOLGER SHAKESPEARE LIBRARY, 201 E Capitol St, Washington, 20003. Philip A Knachel, Acting Dir
Holdings: Vols (223,571) Cat Mss Pix Periodicals Microfilms
Notes: Collections described in *Catalog of Printed Books of the Folger Shakespeare* Library, 28 vols; *First Supplement,* 3 vols (Boston: G K Hall, 1970, 1976); *Second* Supplement in 2 vols (Boston: G K Hall, 1981); *Catalog of Manuscripts of the Folger Shakespeare Library,* 3 vols (Boston: G K Hall, 1971); and *The Widening Circle: The Story of the Folger Library and Its* Collections (Washington, DC: Folger Shakespeare Library, 1976). Collections incl 39 vols of plays with ms annotations and stage directions by John Philip Kemble. Library use restricted to advanced research scholars.

KEMMERER, EDWIN WALTER, 1875-1945

NJ —PRINCETON UNIVERSITY, Library, Manuscript Collection, Nassau St, Princeton, 08540. Jean F Preston, Cur
Notes: The papers of the late Edwin W Kemmerer. Incl are papers spanning nearly a half-century dating from student days in 1897: letters, diaries, drafts of articles, speech texts, financial records, offprints, clippings, academic notes, photographs, and personal copies of numerous reports. Also incl are scrapbooks, diplomas, maps and charts, books from his own library, and a wealth of memoranda and mementos. Incl 147 letter boxes; 240 boxes; 4 cartons; appprox 125 vols.

KEMP, DONALD C.

DC —GEORGETOWN UNIVERSITY, Library, Special Collections Div, 37 & O Sts NW, Washington, 20057. George M Barringer, Special Collections Librn; Nicholas B Sheetz, Mss Librn
Holdings: Cat Pix
Notes: Collection of photgraphs taken by Captain Donald C Kemp, Signal Corps. The photographs document the people, land and culture of Panama, ca 1928-32.

KEMP, HARRY

IN —INDIANA UNIVERSITY, Lilly Library, Seventh St, Bloomington, 47405. William R Cagle, Librn
Notes: Writings by author Harry Kemp.

KEMP, LYSANDER

CA —FRANCIS BACON LIBRARY, 655 N Dartmouth Ave, Claremont, 91711. Elizabeth S Wrigley, Dir
Holdings: Mss Pix
Notes: Arensberg's miscellaneous correspondence with American literary figures (1920's-50's) including Bruce Bliven, Catherine Drinker Bowen, Kay Boyle, Witter Bynner, Edwin Corle, Helen A Keller, Lysander Kemp, Kenneth Macgowan, John Macy, Henry Miller, Lewis Mumford, Clifford Odets, Kenneth Patchen, Irving Stone, and William Carlos Williams.

KEMPER, JAMES LAWSON

VA —UNIVERSITY OF VIRGINIA, Alderman Library, Manuscripts Dept, Charlottesville, 22901. Edmund Berkeley Jr, Cur
Holdings: Cat Mss
See also entry under Virginia - History.

KEMPIS, THOMAS A. see Thomas a Kempis

KENNAN, GEORGE FROST, 1904-

DC —LIBRARY OF CONGRESS, Manuscript Division, Washington, 20540. John C Broderick, Chief
Notes: Correspondence in the J Robert Oppenheimer Collection.
NJ —PRINCETON UNIVERSITY, Library, Manuscript Collection, Nassau St, Princeton, 08540. Jean F Preston, Cur
Holdings: Mss
Notes: The George Frost Kennan Collection incl 38 boxes of papers. Reproduction not permitted.

KENNEDY, ADAM

MA —BOSTON UNIVERSITY, Mugar Memorial Library, Special Collections Dept, 771 Commonwealth Ave, Boston, 02215. Howard B Gotlieb, Dir
Holdings: Cat Mss Pix
Notes: Mss correspondence, etc collected in depth: incl publications by or about.

KENNEDY, C. DONALD

MI —UNIVERSITY OF MICHIGAN, Transportation Research Institute, Library, 2901 Baxter Rd, Ann Arbor, 48109. Ann C Grimm, Librn
Holdings: Vols (57,000) Cat Mss Maps Pix Slides Microforms
Budget: ($25,000)

KENNEDY, CHARLES RANN, 1871-1950

CA —UNIVERSITY OF CALIFORNIA, LOS ANGELES, Research Library, Dept of Special Collections, 405 Hilgard Ave, Los Angeles, 90024. Edward Shreeves, Chairman, Bibliographers Group; David S Zeidberg, Head
Holdings: Vols 75 Mss
Notes: 75 books; 31 linear feet of clippings, mss, and carbons of correspondence, 1887-1947.

KENNEDY, EVA

MA —BOSTON UNIVERSITY, Mugar Memorial Library, Special Collections Dept, 771 Commonwealth Ave, Boston, 02215. Howard B Gotlieb, Dir
Holdings: Mss Pix
Notes: Mss, correspondence, etc collected in depth; incl publications by or about.

KENNEDY, JAY RICHARD

MA —BOSTON UNIVERSITY, Mugar Memorial Library, Special Collections Dept, 771 Commonwealth Ave, Boston, 02215. Howard B Gotlieb, Dir
Holdings: Cat Mss Pix
Notes: Mss, correspondence, etc collected in depth; incl publications by or about.

KENNEDY, JOHN F.

CA —LONG BEACH PUBLIC LIBRARY, Literature & History Dept, 101 Pacific Ave, Long Beach, 90802. Harriet J Friis, Head
Holdings: Vols 110 // Cat Microforms
Notes: In addition to books and ephemera in the John F Kennedy Collection, there are 185 newspapers from all over the U S. There is also a collection of 45 recordings, collection of 45 phonorecords, some of which circulate. Books, pamphlets, newspapers and periodicals do not circulate. No additions to the collection are contemplated because of the opening of the Kennedy Library in Massachusetts.
CA —LOS ANGELES COUNTY PUBLIC LIBRARY SYSTEM, 320 W Temple St, Los Angeles, 90012. Barbara Parks, Librn
Holdings: Vols 250 Cat Pix
KS —WICHITA PUBLIC LIBRARY, 223 S Main, Wichita, 67202. Larry DePiesse, Head, Business & Technology Dept; Jayne F Young, Business & Technology Dept
Holdings: Vols (200) // Cat
Notes: Primarily books in print at time of his death; includes report of US President's Commission on the Assassination of President Kennedy, 26 v.
†MA —JOHN F KENNEDY LIBRARY, Columbia Point, Boston, 02125. Dan H Fenn Jr, Dir
Holdings: Vols 20,000 Cat Mss Maps Pix Slides Phonorecords Audiotapes Videotapes 16mm Films Microforms
Notes: *The* major collection about JFK, his life, family and adminstration. It contains personal papers, audiovisual materials, books, oral history interviews. Collection is described in "Historical Materials in the John F Kennedy Library." "The Kennedy Collection," a subject guide to the book collection, is available for sale.
NY —CORNELL UNIVERSITY LIBRARIES, Collection of Regional History, Dept of

KENNEDY, JOHN F. (cont.)

Manuscripts and Univ Archives, Ithaca, 14853.
Notes: Incl announcements, 1965; statement of purpose of the Kennedy Scholarship, established by the Cornell University Class of 1964.

PA —DICKINSON COLLEGE, Boyd Lee Spahr Library, W High St, Carlisle, 17013. Yates M Forbis, Dir
Holdings: Vols 700
Notes: Memorabilia.

TX —TEXAS CHRISTIAN UNIVERSITY, Mary Couts Burnett Library, Fort Worth, 76129.
Notes: The Marguerite Oswald Collection (mother of Lee Harvey Oswald), incl the full Warren Commission Report, with her own annotations and comments. Also, some 200 vols, many inscribed or dedicated to her.

KENNEDY, JOHN PENDLETON

MD —JOHNS HOPKINS UNIVERSITY, Milton S Eisenhower Library, George Peabody Collection, 17 E Mt Vernon Place, Baltimore, 21201. Lyn Hart, Peabody Librn
Holdings: Mss
Notes: Noncirculating.

VA —UNIVERSITY OF VIRGINIA, Alderman Library, Clifton Waller Barrett Collection, Charlottesville, 22901. Joan St C Crane, Cur of American Literature Collections
Holdings: Cat Mss Pix
Notes: Extensive collection of mss and printed materials.

KENNEDY, LAWTON AND ALFRED

†CA —UNIVERSITY OF SAN FRANCISCO, Richard A Gleeson Library, The Countess Bernardine Murphy Donohue Rare Book Room, San Francisco, 94117. D Steven Corey, Special Collections Librn
Notes: About 1000 items in the archival collection of this San Francisco firm. Extensive ephemera.

KENNEDY, ROBERT F.

MA —JOHN F KENNEDY LIBRARY, Columbia Point, Boston, 02125. Henry J Gwiazda II, Cur
Holdings: Cat Mss Maps Pix Slides Phonorecords Audiotapes Videotapes 16mm Films Microforms
Notes: The Robert F Kennedy Papers cover the period from 1937-1968 and are divided into four subcollections: the Pre-Administration, Attorney General's, Senate, and 1968 Presidential Campaign Papers. In the Pre-Administration Papers, over 140 archives boxes or 70 percent of the materials are open to research. The Personal and Political Papers of this subcollection are almost entirely open. Most of the unprocessed mss are in the Working Files and involve investigative work on labor racketeering. Seventy five percent or 185 archives boxes of the Attorney General's Papers are open, incl the correspondence, the John F Kennedy Library File, the Speech and Trip Files for 1961-1964. For the Senate Papers, 200 boxes are open for the 1964 Senate Campaign, the Legislative Subject File, and the Speech and Trip Files for 1964-1968. The speeches and press releases(incl in the Senate subcollection Speech File) and "The Black Books" (16 boxes) on state and delegate information are open for the 1968 campaign. Each subcollection has its own finding aid. The Library also has available for research about 100 audiotapes of Robert F Kennedy's public addresses from 1962-1966 and some 50 oral history interviews on RFK and one (1000 pages) by RFK. There are also available the major documentaries on RFK and a number of films donated by the major networks for research use in the Library.

KENNEDY FAMILY

†TX —UNIVERSITY OF TEXAS LIBRARIES, Hoblitzelle Theatre Arts Library, Austin, 78712.
Notes: A 100,000-item collection of correspondence and documents related to the career and personal life of Gloria Swanson, one of the largest archives from 1913 to 1983. Correspondence with Mary Pickford, William Faulkner, and the Kennedy Family, the latter to remain sealed until the year 2000.

KENNELS AND KENNEL CLUBS

OH —CLEVELAND PUBLIC LIBRARY, Science & Technology Dept, 325 Superior Ave, Cleveland, 44114. Jean Z Piety, Head
Holdings: Cat
Notes: Emphases: history of the dog; dog show catalogs; stud books of the American Kennel Club, the field dog, the foxhound, and the Irish terrier.

KENNER, HUGH

VA —UNIVERSITY OF VIRGINIA, Alderman Library, Clifton Waller Barrett Collection, Charlottesville, 22901. Joan St C Crane, Cur of American Literature Collections
Notes: Papers.

KENT, FRED I., 1869-1954

NJ —PRINCETON UNIVERSITY, Library, Manuscript Collection, Nassau St, Princeton, 08540. Jean F Preston, Cur
Holdings: / / Cat Mss
Notes: Incl 50 boxes of papers. An unpublished typescript guide (8p) is available in the Library.

KENT, GERMANICUS

VA —VIRGINIA POLYTECHNIC INSTITUTE AND STATE UNIVERSITY LIBRARY, Blacksburg, 24061. Glenn L McMullen, Special Collections Librn
Holdings: Vols (2000) Cat Mss Maps Pix Audiotapes
Notes: Primarily Southwest Virginia materials. Collection incl ca 200 mss, account books and other archival records of nineteenth century area businesses and other mining operations; the extant archival records of several Southwest Virginia railroads, incl the Virginia and Tennessee Railroad and the Norfolk and Western Railroad; and papers of historically prominent Southwest Virginians, incl John Apperson, Dr Harvy Black, James P Charlton, W Graham Claytor, Henley Fugate, Clement D Johnston, Germanicus Kent, William Preston, J Hoge Tyler, and William C Wampler. Several oral history collections incl material on Appalachian customs and folklore, particularly in Patrick County.

KENT, ROCKWELL, 1882-1971

MA —BRANDEIS UNIVERSITY, Goldfarb Library, 415 South St, Waltham, 02154. Bessie Hahn, Dir
Notes: 50 or more letters from Rockwell Kent to Dr Bern Dibner and others. A schedule of the letters is located in Special Collections.

NY —COLUMBIA UNIVERSITY LIBRARIES, Rare Book & Manuscript Library, 801 Butler Library, 535 W 114 St, New York, 10027. Kenneth A Lohf, Librn
Holdings: Mss Maps Pix
Notes: Mss, correspondence, publications, sketches, drawings, designs, art pieces and memorabilia. Much unusual ephemera. Restricted use.

KENT-DELORD PAPERS

NY —STATE UNIVERSITY OF NEW YORK, COLLEGE AT PLATTSBURGH, Feinberg Library, Special Collections, 153 Hawkins Hall, Plattsburgh, 12901. Joseph G Swinyer, Librn
See also entry under New York (State) - History

KENT STATE UNIVERSITY INCIDENT, 1970

OH —KENT STATE UNIVERSITY, University Archives, Kent, 44242. Stephen C Morton, University Archivist
Holdings: Cat Mss Maps Pix Microforms
Notes: The May 4, 1970 incident; 50 linear ft. Separate catalog. Partial description in *Cleveland State Law Review*, Winter, 1973.

KENTON, STAN

TX —NORTH TEXAS STATE UNIVERSITY, Audio Center, Box 5188, NT Station, Denton, 76203. Morris Martin, Music Librn
Notes: More than 1600 manuscript jazz compositions, (incl scores and parts, alternate versions, expanded arrangements) by Stan Kenton, Johnny Richards, Joe Coccia, Lennie Niehaus, Pete Rugolo, Willie Maiden, Bob Curnow, Ken Hanna, Gene Rowland, Bob Graettinger and others, used by the Stan Kenton Band and given to North Texas State University in 1962 and at Kenton's death in 1979. Unpublished catalog: Breeden, Leon, *Stan Kenton Music in the NTSU Jazz Studies Library and the NTSU Music Library,* Denton, 1983 (99 pages).

KENTUCKY

KY —HOPKINSVILLE COMMUNITY COLLEGE, Library, North Dr, Hopkinsville, 42240. Marjanna J Frising, Librn
Holdings: Vols 750 Cat Maps Pix Slides Microforms
Notes: Books about Kentucky and by Kentucky authors.

KY —UNIVERSITY OF KENTUCKY, Margaret I King Library, Dept of Special Collections, Lexington, 40506. William Marshall, Head
Holdings: Cat Mss Maps Pix Microforms
Notes: Kentucky history and travel. Incl the Samuel M Wilson Library, Kentucky imprints, Kentucky authors, biography and autobiography, regional history (Ohio Valley), Kentucky maps. Also sheet music, clippings, etc.

KY —LOUISVILLE FREE PUBLIC LIBRARY, Fourth & York Sts, Louisville, 40203. Mark Harris, Head, Kentucky Division
Holdings: Vols 10,500 Cat Maps Microforms
Notes: The Kentucky Division incl a complete microfilm of *The Louisville* Courier-Journal newspaper which has been selectively card indexed for state and local items since 1918; also a complete microfilm file of *The Louisville Times.* Holdings of local newspapers on microfilm have been submitted to the Library of Congress' *Newspapers on Microfilm.* Noncirculating.

KY —EASTERN KENTUCKY UNIVERSITY, Crabbe Library, Richmond, 40475. Sharon Brown McConnell, Cur
Holdings: Vols (10,000) Mss Maps Pix Microforms
Notes: The John Wilson Townsend Collection is a Kentuckiana collection and contains books, mss, letters, maps by Kentuckians and/or about Kentucky.

KY —CUMBERLAND COLLEGE, Norma P Hagan Memorial Library, 821 Walnut St, Williamsburg, 40769. Robert B Williams, Dir
Holdings: Vols 3500 Cat
Budget: ($3000)
Notes: Kentucky, Appalachia Collection.

†TX —UNIVERSITY OF TEXAS LIBRARIES, General Libraries, Humanities Research Center, PO Box 7219, Austin, 78712. John Chalmers, Librn
Holdings: Vols Cat Mss Maps Pix Microforms

KENTUCKY—DESCRIPTION AND TRAVEL—VIEWS

KY —WESTERN KENTUCKY UNIVERSITY, Kentucky Library, Bowling Green, 42101. Riley Handy, Head, Special Collections; Connie Mills, Maps & Music

KENTUCKY—DESCRIPTION AND TRAVEL—VIEWS (cont.)

Librn; Nancy Baird, Photographs Librn; Nancy Solley, Conservation Librn
Holdings: Vols (25,000) Cat Mss Maps Pix Microforms
Notes: Besides Kentucky history, other strengths are Mammoth Cave, South Union Shakers, Kentucky religion; and steamboat photos (3300 cataloged pictures); 8000 Kentucky postal cards, etc.

KENTUCKY—GENEALOGY

FL —ORLANDO PUBLIC LIBRARY, Local History & Genealogy Dept, 100 Block of Central Ave, Orlando, 32806. Eileen B Willis, Librn
Holdings: Vols 11,000 Cat Maps Microforms
Budget: $8000
Notes: Genealogy collection on Md, Del, W Va, NC, SC, Ala, Miss, La, Texas, Ark, Ky, Ohio, Ill, Ind, and Mich are well represented. Most other states are covered by smaller collections.
See also entry under Genealogy - Collections.

IN —WILLARD LIBRARY, 21 First Ave, Evansville, 47710. Joan Elliott, Special Collections Librn
Holdings: Vols (1000) Cat Mss Microforms
Budget: ($4000)
Notes: General genealogy collection emphasizing data concerning 35 counties of southwest Indiana, southeast Illinois, and western Kentucky. Written description available.

KY —BOWLING GREEN PUBLIC LIBRARY, 1225 State St, Bowling Green, 42101. Karen A Turner, Dir
Holdings: Vols 57 Cat

KY —WESTERN KENTUCKY UNIVERSITY, Kentucky Library, Bowling Green, 42101. Riley Handy, Head, Special Collections; Connie Mills, Maps & Music Librn; Nancy Baird, Photographs Librn; Nancy Solley, Conservation Librn
Holdings: Vols (25,000) Cat Mss Maps Pix Microforms
Notes: Besides Kentucky history, other strengths are Mammoth Cave, South Union Shakers, Kentucky religion; and steamboat photos (3300 cataloged pictures); 8000 Kentucky postal cards, etc.

KY —FILSON CLUB, 118 W Breckinridge St, Louisville, 40203. Dorothy C Rush, Librn
Holdings: Vols (40,000) Cat Mss Maps Pix Microforms
Notes: Maintain a card catalog for books, pamphlets, maps and broadsides; separate catalog for newspapers incl a chronological file; and mss incl a chronological file. Collect anything about Kentucky, including Kentucky authors. Has file on Kentucky families.

MI —MONROE COUNTY LIBRARY SYSTEM, Ellis Reference and Information Center, 3700 S Custer Rd, Monroe, 48161. Marie D Chulski, Head of Reference Services
Notes: Incl individual county histories, atlases, biographies, etc. The Monroe County history collection contains veteran records, plat books, oral history tapes, family histories, church records, cemetery index, atlases and census records. Genealogy emphasis is not only Monroe County but incl surrounding counties and the states with large migration to the area, such as Ohio, Kentucky, Tennessee and the New England states.

KENTUCKY—GOVERNMENT PUBLICATIONS

KY —UNIVERSITY OF KENTUCKY, Margaret I King Library, Government Publications Dept, Lexington, 40506. Sandra McAninch, Head
Holdings: Cat 16mm Films
Notes: All Kentucky State publications and selectively, other state publications. Incl papers.

KENTUCKY—HISTORY

IL —UNIVERSITY OF CHICAGO LIBRARY, Dept of Special Collections, 1100 E 57 St, Chicago, 60637.

IN —LOUIS A WARREN LINCOLN LIBRARY AND MUSEUM, 1300 S Clinton St, Fort Wayne, 46801. Mark E Neely Jr, Dir
Holdings: Vols (17,000) Cat Mss Maps pix
Notes: Acquire all books on Abraham Lincoln, most on his contemporaries, as many as possible on his times, and historical journals. Constantly acquiring unpublished mss of Lincoln, Lincoln's associates, correspondents, and collateral figures. Have some Kentucky Court Records, Richard Thompson Papers. Publish a monthly bulletin of historical research on Lincoln's life and times called *Lincoln Lore,* which includes an annually updated bibliography of Lincolniana.

KY —BOWLING GREEN PUBLIC LIBRARY, 1225 State St, Bowling Green, 42101. Karen A Turner, Dir
Holdings: Vols 123 Cat

KY —WESTERN KENTUCKY UNIVERSITY, Kentucky Library, Bowling Green, 42101. Riley Handy, Head, Special Collections; Connie Mills, Maps & Music Librn; Nancy Baird, Photographs Librn; Nancy Solley, Conservation Librn
Holdings: Vols (25,000) Cat Mss Maps Pix Microforms
Notes: Beside Kentucky history, other strengths are Mammoth Cave, South Union Shakers, Kentucky religion; and steamboat photos (3300 cataloged pictures); 8000 Kentucky postal cards, etc.

KY —KENTUCKY DEPARTMENT OF LIBRARY AND ARCHIVES, Div of Public Services, Kentuckiana Collection, Cotton Tree Rd, PO Box 534, Frankfurt, 40602. Jim Nelson, Librn
Holdings: Vols 2500 Cat

KY —GEORGETOWN COLLEGE, Cooke Memorial Library, Georgetown, 40324. Darlene Cummins, Librn
Holdings: Vols 1200 Mss Pix
Notes: Partially cataloged.

KY —LEXINGTON PUBLIC LIBRARY, 251 W Second St, Lexington, 40507. Rebecca Croft, Librn
Holdings: Vols 2700 Cat Mss Maps Pix
Budget: $3000
Notes: Collection of original newspapers as well as microfilm covering Lexington's history from 1787 to the present. Local History Index of newspapers.

KY —UNIVERSITY OF KENTUCKY, Margaret I King Library, Dept of Special Collections, Lexington, 40506. William Marshall, Head
Holdings: Cat Mss Maps Pix
Notes: History of Kentucky, Ohio Valley and Presbyterian Church. Consists of books, letters, maps, etc; about 10,000 pieces. Also incl a collection (310 vols) assembled by Dr Emmet Field Horine to document the work and writings of Daniel Drake in medicine and history and education; includes Drake's own publications. (Daniel Drake is important to Ohio and Kentucky history in particular.) Incl oil portrait and bust. Also, early Kentucky maps to 1900 and basic maps of America to 1800.

KY —FILSON CLUB, 118 W Breckinridge St, Louisville, 40203. Dorothy C Rush, Librn
Holdings: Vols (40,000) Cat Mss Maps Pix Microforms
Notes: Maintain a card catalog for books, pamphlets, maps and broadsides; separate catalog for newspapers incl a chronological file; and mss incl a chronological file. Collect anything about Kentucky, including Kentucky authors. Has file on Kentucky families.

KY —MIDWAY COLLEGE, Marrs Library, Stephens St, Midway, 40347. Kay Cordoves, Librn
Holdings: Vols (450) Cat
Notes: Incl books by Kentucky writers and Kentucky history.

KY —MOREHEAD STATE UNIVERSITY, Johnson Camden Library, Morehead, 40351. Jack D Ellis, Dir
Holdings: Vols 6003 Cat

KY —KENTUCKY WESLEYAN COLLEGE LIBRARY, 3000 Frederica, Owensboro, 42301. Stuart Stiffler, Dir
Notes: The Dr and Mrs M David Orrahood Collection.

KENTUCKY—IMPRINTS

KY —UNIVERSITY OF KENTUCKY, Margaret I King Library, Dept of Special Collections, Lexington, 40506. William Marshall, Head
Holdings: Cat Mss Maps Pix Microforms
Notes: Kentucky history and travel. Incl the Samuel M Wilson Library, Kentucky imprints, Kentucky authors, biography and autobiography, regional history (Ohio Valley), Kentucky maps. Also sheet music, clippings, etc.

KENTUCKY—MAPS

KY —UNIVERSITY OF KENTUCKY, Margaret I King Library, Dept of Special Collections, Lexington, 40506. William Marshall, Head
Notes: Emphasis is on early Kentucky maps to 1900 and basic maps of America to 1800.

KY —UNIVERSITY OF KENTUCKY, Margaret I King Library, Map Collection, Lexington, 40506. Gwen Curtis, Head
Holdings: Vols
Notes: Post-1870, general collection excluding geology and hydrology, depository for Kentucky Geological Survey topographic. 69,654 maps and books, cataloged and uncataloged.

KENTUCKY—PICTURES, ILLUSTRATIONS, ETC.

KY —UNIVERSITY OF KENTUCKY, Margaret I King Library, Dept of Special Collections, Lexington, 40506. William Marshall, Head
Holdings: Cat Pix
Notes: Incl original prints, negatives and direct positives. Most of the images are Kentucky-related; period covered: 1840's to present. Index to majority of collection. Ca 60,000 pieces.

KY —UNIVERSITY OF LOUISVILLE, Ekstrom Library, Photographic Archives, Louisville, 40292. J C Anderson, Cur; David G Horvath, Asst Cur
Holdings: Vols (750,000) Cat Pix Slides
Budget: ($60,000)
Notes: Photographs in three broad areas: works of outstanding photographers; examples of major developments in the art and technology of photography; photographs important as sociological, historical, or behavioral documents. Actors and actresses, Louisville's Macauley Theatre. Standard Oil of New Jersey Collection, 85,000 pictures of oil industry's effect on life in the 20th century (1943-1950, directed by Roy Stryker); Stryker's collection from Farm Security Adminstration series on rural conditions, 1935-1942; Jones and Laughlin Steel Corp. Picture Library, by Stryker. Stryker manuscripts, 1934-1972. Caufield and Shook commerical photographs, Louisville area, 1920-1949. Jean Thomas "The Traipsin' Woman" photographs of Kentucky mountain folkways. Kate Matthews' (1870-1956) photographs incl prototypes for "Little Colonel" Series. Other collectionsdescribed in unpublished brochure. Print duplication service.

KENTUCKY—RELIGION

KY —WESTERN KENTUCKY UNIVERSITY, Kentucky Library, Bowling Green, 42101. Riley Handy, Head, Special Collections; Connie Mills, Maps & Music Librn; Nancy Baird, Photographs Librn; Nancy Solley, Conservation Librn
Holdings: Vols (25,000) Cat Mss Maps Pix Microforms
Notes: Besides Kentucky history, other strengths are Mammoth Cave, South Union Shakers, Kentucky religion; and steamboat photos (3300 cataloged pictures); 8000 Kentucky postal cards, etc.

KENTUCKY—SOCIAL LIFE AND CUSTOMS

KY —WESTERN KENTUCKY UNIVERSITY, Kentucky Library, Bowling

KENTUCKY—SOCIAL LIFE AND CUSTOMS (cont.)

Green, 42101. Riley Handy, Head, Special Collections; Connie Mills, Maps & Music Librn; Nancy Baird, Photographs Librn; Nancy Solley, Conservation Librn
Holdings: Vols (25,000) Cat Mss Maps Pix Microforms
Notes: Besides Kentucky history, other strengths are Mammoth Cave, South Union Shakers, Kentucky religion; and steamboat photos (3300 cataloged pictures); 8000 Kentucky postal cards, etc.

KY —KENTUCKY DERBY MUSEUM, 700 Central Ave, Louisville, 40208. William W Ray, Exec Dir
Notes: Books, programs, photographs, Archival materials relating to the Kentucky Derby and International Thoroughbred Racing.

KY —UNIVERSITY OF LOUISVILLE, Ekstrom Library, Photographic Archives, Louisville, 40292. J C Anderson, Cur; David G Horvath, Asst Cur
Holdings: Vols (750,000) Cat Pix Slides
Budget: ($60,000)
Notes: Photographs in three broad areas: works of outstanding photographers; examples of major developments in the art and technology of photography; photographs important as sociological, historical, or behavioral documents. Actors and actresses, Louisville's Macauley Theatre. Standard Oil of New Jersey Collection, 85,000 pictures of oil industry's effect on life in the 20th century (1943-1950, directed by Roy Stryker); Stryker's collection from Farm Security Administration series on rural conditions, 1935-1942; Jones and Laughlin Steel Corp Picture Library, by Stryker. Stryker manuscripts, 1934-1972. Caufield and Shook commercial photographs, Louisville area, 1920-1949. Jean Thomas "The Traipsin' Woman" photographs of Kentucky mountain folkways. Kate Matthews' (1870-1956) photographs incl prototypes for "Little Colonel" Series. Other collections describedin unpublished brochure. Print duplication service.

KENTUCKY AUTHORS see Authors, Kentucky

KENTUCKY COMPOSERS see Composers, Kentucky

KENYA

DC —HOWARD UNIVERSITY, Moorland-Spingarn Research Center, 500 Howard Place NW, Washington, 20059. Clifford L Muse, Jr, Acting Dir

MI —MICHIGAN STATE UNIVERSITY, International Library, Africana Collection, East Lansing, 48824. Eugene de Benko, Librn; Onuma Ezera, Bibliographer for Africana
Holdings: Vols (82,700) Cat Mss Maps Pix Slides Phonorecords Audiotapes Videotapes Filmstrips Microforms
Budget: ($78,000)
See also entry under Africa for full description.

KENYON FAMILY

NY —CORNELL UNIVERSITY LIBRARIES, Collection of Regional History, Dept of Manuscripts and Univ Archives, Ithaca, 14853.
Notes: Papers, 1828-1915; 4 in.

PA —UNIVERSITY OF PITTSBURGH, Special Collections Dept, Curtis Theatre Collection, 363 Hillman Library, Pittsburgh, 15260. Jeanette Blanco, Cur
Holdings: Cat Mss Pix
Notes: The legitimate theatre of plays, musicals and vaudeville, chiefly of New York City and Pittsburgh, from 1865, and other US, community, summer, college and foreign theatre. Incl 500,000 programs, 12, 000 pictures, 300 posters, the Oliver P Merriman Scrapbooks and 300 other scrapbooks, clippings and other ephemera. Vols incl over 3000 acting editions and playscripts. Separate collections: Ralph G Allen Burlesque Skits Collection; Michael Ellis Papers; William P Halstead Theatre Collection; Kenyon Family Papers; Philip Dunning Playscripts Collection; Pittsburgh Playhouse Records; Pittsburgh Savoyards Records. Noncirculating.
See also entry under Theatre - Pittsburgh.

KEPHART, HORACE

NC —PACK MEMORIAL PUBLIC LIBRARY, North Carolina Collection, 67 Haywood St, Asheville, 28801. John Toms, Dept Head
Notes: Collection incl early ms accounts of western North Carolina; Civil War letters; letters, diary, and mss of Horace Kephart; mss of Thomas Dixon; Thomas Wolfe Collection; contemporary North Carolina authors; North Carolina censuses, 1790-1910; rare newspapers and runs of local newspapers, and clippings from Asheville newspapers, from 1920s; early maps; information on Cherokee Indians; approx 400 vols of North Carolina genealogy and file of unpublished genealogies. Collection concentrates on western North Carolina, with some general Appalachian materials. Incl 4000 local and state photographs, separate catalog.

KEPLER, JOHANN

CA —CALIFORNIA INSTITUTE OF TECHNOLOGY, Robert A Millikan Memorial Library, 1201 E California Blvd, Pasadena, 91125. Judith R Goodstein, Archivist
Holdings: Vols (2300) Cat
Notes: Emphasis on the period of Galileo and Kepler. Incl the Watson History of Science Collection and the Rocco Collection. Catalogs.

KEPPEL, FREDERICK PAUL

†NY —COLUMBIA UNIVERSITY LIBRARIES, Butler Library, Rare Book and Manuscript Library, 535 W 114 St, New York, 10027.
Notes: Papers, etc.

KERAMICS see Ceramics

KERN, JEROME

IN —INDIANA UNIVERSITY, Lilly Library, Seventh St, Bloomington, 47405. William R Cagle, Librn
Holdings: // Uncat
Notes: In the Starr Collection of American Sheet Music.

KERNAN, JULIA K.

DC —GEORGETOWN UNIVERSITY, Library, Special Collections Div, 37 & O Sts NW, Washington, 20057. George M Barringer, Special Collections Librn; Nicholas B Sheetz, Mss Librn
Holdings: Mss Pix
Notes: Papers of Julia K Kernan, editor, translator, and author of *Our Friend, Jacques Maritain - A Personal Memoir.* Miss Karnan was instrumental in establishing the French Book Club and later served on the editorial staff of Longmans, Green and Company and P J Kennedy and Sons. Among the papers are letters from Paul Claudel, Marie Belloc, and Francois Mauriac, as well as extensive correspondence from Jacques Maritain. Also incl are numerous photographs of such celebrities as Colette, Leon Bloy, Charles Peguy, Sigrid Undset and Marie Belloc Lowndes, in addition to photographs of Jacques Maritain used in *Our Friend.*

KEROUAC, JACK

MA —POLLARD MEMORIAL LIBRARY, 401 Merrimack St, Lowell, 01852. Walter V Hickey, Libr Asst
Holdings: Vols (3000) Cat Pix
Notes: A full collection of Jack Kerouac's work.

NV —UNIVERSITY OF NEVADA, RENO, University Library, Special Collections Dept, Reno, 89557. Robert E Blesse, Head
Holdings: // Vols (110) Cat Other appearances 340 Cat
Notes: Includes individual works by author in all editions including translations; also prefaces, introductions, published correspondence, appearances in anthologies, periodicals, etc. Bibliographical research collection, part of Modern Authors Collection.

NY —COLUMBIA UNIVERSITY LIBRARIES, Rare Book & Manuscript Library, 801 Butler Library, 535 W 114 St, New York, 10027. Kenneth A Lohf, Librn
Holdings: Mss
Notes: Papers, incl mss, letters, reviews, etc. Restricted use.

BC —UNIVERSITY OF VICTORIA, McPherson Library, Victoria, V8W 3H5, Can.
Notes: John Kerouac, writer. Incl 4 leaves, 1959; 4 poems from *Mexico City Blues* (113th, 146th, 182nd, 221st chorus); typescript signed.

KERR, LOIS REYNOLDS, 1908-

AB —UNIVERSITY OF CALGARY, Libraries, Special Collections Div, 2500 University Dr, Calgary, T2N 1N4, Can.
Holdings: Mss
Notes: Correspondence, diaries, scrapbooks, photographs and mss (2 meters) for nonfiction, fiction and drama, 1920s-79.

KERR, LOWELL

MI —UNIVERSITY OF MICHIGAN, Library, Dept of Rare Books & Special Collections, Ann Arbor, 48109. Robert J Starring, Head
Holdings: Vols (390) Cat Mss Pix
Notes: Includes many first editions and association copies of Swinburne. In addition there are 235 manuscript items, over 70 in Swinburne's holograph, and including as a special series 65 items of correspondence of major donor Lowell Kerr with Swinburne scholars; also photographs and Swinburneana.

KERR, ROBERT SAMUEL

OK —UNIVERSITY OF OKLAHOMA, Bizzell Memorial Library, Western History Collections, 401 W Brooks, Norman, 73069. John Ezell, Cur
Holdings: Mss Documents Newspapers Maps Pix
Notes: Governor of Oklahoma; US Senator. His papers. Guide available (1986). Restrictions on use.

KERR, SOPHIE

NY —COLUMBIA UNIVERSITY LIBRARIES, Rare Book & Manuscript Library, 801 Butler Library, 535 W 114 St, New York, 10027. Kenneth A Lohf, Librn
Holdings: Mss
Notes: Nearly 500 mss, drafts and typescripts of her novels, short stories, plays and essays. Also first editions; presentation copies, etc.

KERSCHENSTEINER, GEORG MICHAEL, 1854-1932

CA —UNIVERSITY OF CALIFORNIA, LOS ANGELES, Research Library, Dept of Special Collections, 405 Hilgard Ave, Los Angeles, 90024. Edward Shreeves, Chairman, Bibliographers Group; David S Zeidberg, Head
Notes: 53 books and 2 linear feet of pamphlets and ephemera by and about Georg Michael Kerschensteiner (1854-1932), German educator.

KERST, DONALD W.

IL —UNIVERSITY OF ILLINOIS, URBANA/CHAMPAIGN, Library, University Archives, 19 Library, 1408 W

KERST, DONALD W. (cont.)

Gregory Drive, Urbana, 61801. Maynard Brichford, University Archivist
Holdings: Mss
Notes: Papers of Donald W Kerst, incl correspondence on the betatron, 1943-1952.

KESEY, KEN

NV —UNIVERSITY OF NEVADA, RENO, University Library, Special Collections Dept, Reno, 89557. Robert E Blesse, Head
Holdings: Vols (13) Cat
Notes: Includes individual works by author in all editions including translations; also prefaces, introductions, published correspondence, appearances in anthologies, periodicals, etc. Bibliographical research collection, part of Modern Authors Collection. Other appearances 37 cataloged.

KESSLER, GRAF HARRY

IL —NEWBERRY LIBRARY, John M Wing Foundation on the History of Printing, 60 W Walton St, Chicago, 60610. Diana Haskell, Cur of Modern Mss
Holdings: Vols 50 Cat Mss Pix
Notes: Incl correspondence among Kessler and Eric Gill, Gordon Craig, Emery Walker, Edward Johnston, et al; proofs and sketches for Cranach books and types. Complements the Kessler collection at Cambridge, with which microfilms have been exchanged.

KESTER, HOWARD

MS —TOUGALOO COLLEGE, L Zenobia Coleman Library, Tougaloo, 39174. Virgia Brocks-Shedd, Acting Dir
Budget: ($142,650)
Notes: Civil rights cases and legal papers; lawsuits; Mississippi, 1960-1968. Local attorneys have donated papers of cases they have handled, espec attorneys of two government-funded legal services offices. Individual collections: Papers of Aaron Henry, Rev Robert L T Smith, Sr, Annie B Rankin and the Howard Kester Papers. Incl VF holdings of articles from 1930 and on.

KETCHAM, HANK

MA —BOSTON UNIVERSITY, Mugar Memorial Library, Special Collections Dept, 771 Commonwealth Ave, Boston, 02215. Howard B Gotlieb, Dir
Holdings: Cat Mss
Notes: Mss, cartoons of "Dennis the Menace," correspondence, etc collected in depth; incl publications by or about.

KETTERING, CHARLES F.

MI —G M I ENGINEERING AND MANAGEMENT INSTITUTE, 1700 W 3rd Ave, Flint, 48502. Richard Scharchburg, Archivist
Notes: Material by and about Charles F Kettering, founder of the Research Laboratories. Collection available to serious students of the history of science and technology.

MI —GENERAL MOTORS, Research Laboratories Library, General Motors Technical Center, Warren, 48090. Robert W Gibson, Librn
Notes: The Oral History Project incl taped interviews with people who knew and worked with Mr Kettering. Collection available to serious students of the history of science and technology.

KETTLES

†WA —WASHINGTON STATE UNIVERSITY, Library, Manuscripts, Archives & Special Collections, Pullman, 99164. John F Guido, Head
Holdings: Cat Mss Maps Pix
Notes: The Carl Parcher Russell papers, a vast resource (24,916 items; 45 linear feet) on American Indian and Western pioneer activities and artifacts. Much on the fur trade; pioneer life; mountain men and trapping; wildlife; primitive life in detail. Also the National Park Service, parks, monuments, etc. Described in *Carl Parcher Russell: An Indexed Register of His Scholarly and Professional Papers, 1920-1967, in the Washington State University* Library (Pullman, 1970), 149 pp.

KEY, FRANCIS SCOTT

MD —MARYLAND HISTORICAL SOCIETY, Library, 201 W Monument St, Baltimore, 21201. William B Keller, Head Librn
Holdings: Cat Mss Maps Pix
Notes: The Lester S Levy "Star Spangled Banner" Collection, probably the largest in the world--over 250 pieces.

KEY, V. O.

†MA —JOHN F KENNEDY LIBRARY, Columbia Point, Boston, 02125. Dan H Fenn Jr, Dir
Holdings: / / Cat Mss
Notes: Papers of JFK and other holdings of the Kennedy Library, specifically the papers of Louis Brownlow and V O Key, 1902-1963. 70 linear ft of mss. Holdings are described in "Historical Materials in the John F Kennedy Library." Copies may be obtained by writing the Research Archivist.

KEYBOARD HARMONY see Harmony, Keyboard

KEYBOARD MUSIC

IN —INDIANA UNIVERSITY, Music Library, Bloomington, 47401. David E Fenske, Head
Holdings: Vols 700 Cat Microforms
Budget:
Notes: Collection comprises an exhaustive repertoire of early keyboard music from original sources in photocopy up to that music written by ca 1700.

MA —UNIVERSITY OF MASSACHUSETTS AT AMHERST, Music Library, Fine Arts Center, Amherst, 01003.
Holdings: Uncat
Notes: The personal library of Howard M Lebow (once an outstanding concert pianist). The collection (over 5000 items) incl primarily keyboard music, as well as many unusual early editions.

PA —WEST CHESTER UNIVERSITY, Music Library, Swope Hall, University Ave, West Chester, 19383. Ruth I Weidner, Music Librn
Budget: ($26,000)
Notes: Large basic music collection (scores, sheet music, and 21,000 phonorecords) which is especially strong in collected works, historical editions, opera, keyboard music, and miniature scores. Incl 24,000 music scores. All music is fully cataloged. Scope of collection is broad and excludes only music education and curriculum materials. Collection does not include books about music or periodicals but does have about 500 reference books. For the most part collection is music published during or availalbe within the past twenty years.

RI —BROWN UNIVERSITY, John Hay Library, 20 Prospect St, Providence, 02912. Mark N Brown, Cur Mss
Holdings: Uncat
Notes: The Sheet Music Collection concentrates on music of American imprints, incl 170,000 vocal pieces filed by title, plus 80,000 instrumental pieces filed by composer. Major strengths are in 19th century music, especially prior to 1830; Civil War music, both Union and Confederate; lithographic covers; World War I songs; political campaign music; and band music. An additional 100,000 pieces of American and European imprint remain unprocessed.

KEYES, FRANCES PARKINSON

VA —UNIVERSITY OF VIRGINIA, Alderman Library, Manuscripts Dept, Charlottesville, 22901. Edmund Berkeley Jr, Cur
Holdings: Cat Mss Pix
Notes: Extensive collection of mss and printed materials.

KEYNES, JOHN MAYNARD

IL —NORTHWESTERN UNIVERSITY, Library, Special Collections Dept, 1937 Sheridan Rd, Evanston, 60201. R Russell Maylone, Cur
Holdings: Mss
Notes: 79 letters to Vanessa Bell from J M Keynes.

NY —HOFSTRA UNIVERSITY, Library, 1000 Fulton Ave, Hempstead, 11550. Charles R Andrews, Dean of Library Services

KEYS, DAVID A.

†ON —PUBLIC ARCHIVES OF CANADA, Library, 395 Wellington St, Ottawa, K1A 0N3, Can. Dawn E Monroe, Collections Dept Officer
Notes: Papers.

KHAKASS LANGUAGE

NY —NEW YORK PUBLIC LIBRARY, Oriental Div, Fifth Ave & 42 St, New York, 10018. E Christian Filstrup, Chief
Holdings: Cat Mss Microforms
Budget: ($56,455)
Notes: Published catalog of holdings.

KHALDIAN LANGUAGE see Vannic Language

KHALKHA LANGUAGE

NY —NEW YORK PUBLIC LIBRARY, Oriental Div, Fifth Ave & 42 St, New York, 10018. E Christian Filstrup, Chief
Holdings: Cat Mss Microforms
Budget: ($56,455)
Notes: Published catalog of holdings.

KHAS LANGUAGE see Nepali Language and Literature

KHMER LANGUAGE AND LITERATURE

HI —UNIVERSITY OF HAWAII, Library, 2550 The Mall, Honolulu, 96822. Joyce Wright, Head, Asia Collection; Masato Matsu, Head, East Asia Vernacular Collection
Holdings: Vols 331,620 Cat Microforms
Notes: The Asia Collection holds materials from and about Southeast Asia: Brunei, Burma, Cambodia (Kampuchea), Indonesia, Laos, Malaysia, Philippines, Singapore, Thailand. Large contemporary Indonesian language collection. Several thousand vols in Thai and in Vietnamese. Minimal holdings in Burmese, Khmer, Lao languages. Social sciences and humanities emphasis for the post-World War II period. Western language coverage supplemented by retrospective holdings in the main library collection.

NY —INSTITUTE FOR ADVANCED STUDIES OF WORLD RELIGIONS (IASWR), Melville Memorial Library, State University of New York, Stony Brook, 11794. C T Shen, Dir
Holdings: Vols 400 Periodicals Maps
Notes: Incl Pali Buddhist Canon in Khmer script and translation. Works in Cambodian, French and English on history, culture, art and Buddhism.

KHMER REPUBLIC see Cambodia

KIDNEY, ARTIFICIAL see Artificial Kidney

KIDNEYS—TRANSPLANTATION

RI —MIRIAM HOSPITAL MEDICAL LIBRARY, 164 Summit Ave, Providence, 02906. Ann LeClaire, Dir of Library Services
Holdings: Cat Cassettes
Notes: Special collection on the renal system

KIDNEYS—TRANSPLANTATION (cont.)

with emphasis on kidney transplantation and dialysis.

KIERKEGAARD, SOREN AABYE, 1813-1855

CA —UNIVERSITY OF CALIFORNIA, BERKELEY, University Library, Scandinavian Collections, Berkeley, 94720. Helvi M Bessenyei, Librn
Holdings: Vols 20,000
Budget: $15,530
Notes: Research collections covering the full range of Scandinavian languages and literatures, with extensive periodical holdings. Particular strengths are Old Norse and Swedish. Moreover, special emphasis is on the late 19th century Scandinavian authors from Kierkegaard to Strinberg. The language and literature collections are supplemented by substantial resources in related disciplines. Some rare book materials are housed in the Bancroft Library.

IL —NORTHWESTERN UNIVERSITY, Library, Special Collections Dept, 1937 Sheridan Rd, Evanston, 60201. R Russell Maylone, Cur
Holdings: Vols 170 Cat
Notes: First editions; criticism in Danish. Additional material in general collection.

IN —INDIANA UNIVERSITY, Lilly Library, Seventh St, Bloomington, 47405. William R Cagle, Librn
Holdings: Vols 42 // Cat
Notes: The Henry Helsen Collection of first editions, etc.

MA —HARVARD UNIVERSITY LIBRARY, Widener Library, Cambridge, 02138.
Holdings: Cat

MA —HARVARD UNIVERSITY LIBRARY, Robbins Library of Philosophy, Dept of Philosophy, Emerson Hall, Cambridge, 02138. M Pakaluk, Asst in Charge
Holdings: Vols (8677) Cat Mss
Budget: ($9000)
Notes: In the care of the library is the Bechtel Collection of first edition 19th and 20th century works in philosophy (430 volumes) and a special collection of Kierkegaard's works and important secondary literature, largely in Danish and German (140 volumes). Major research collection for philosophy is in general collection of Harvard Library.

PQ —MCGILL UNIVERSITY, McLennan Library, Rare Books and Special Collections Dept, 3459 McTavish St, Montreal, H3A 1Y1, Can.
Holdings: Vols 1551
Notes: Books by and about this Danish philosopher; includes books owned by him.

KIFIOTI LANGUAGE see Congo Languages and Literature

KI-KONGO LANGUAGE see Congo Languages and Literature

KILDAY, PAUL

TX —NORTH TEXAS STATE UNIVERSITY, Archives, NT Station Box 5188, Denton, 76203. Robert LaForte, University Archivist
Notes: Part of Oral History Collection. Interview with Kilday, US Congressman (1939-49).

KILLIAN, CARL DAN, SR.

NC —WESTERN CAROLINA UNIVERSITY, Hunter Memorial Library, Cullowhee, 28723. James B Lloyd, Cur
Notes: The papers of former North Carolina state senators William E Breese, Jr (1875-1939), W Frank Forsyth (1913-70), and Carl Dan Killian, Sr (1903-76).

KILLENS, JOHN OLIVER

MA —BOSTON UNIVERSITY, Mugar Memorial Library, Special Collections Dept, 771 Commonwealth Ave, Boston, 02215. Howard B Gotlieb, Dir
Holdings: Cat Mss
Notes: Mss, correspondence, etc collected in depth; incl publications by or about.

KILMER, ALINE

DC —GEORGETOWN UNIVERSITY, Library, Special Collections Div, 37 & O Sts NW, Washington, 20057. George M Barringer, Special Collections Librn; Nicholas B Sheetz, Mss Librn
Holdings: Mss Cat Pix
Notes: The papers of the Kilmer family incl letters and mss by the poet Joyce Kilmer and his wife, Aline Kilmer, also a poet and essayist. The papers incl correspondence by various authors, among them Rev James J Daly, SJ and Rev Charles L O'Donnell, CSC.

KILMER, JOYCE

DC —GEORGETOWN UNIVERSITY, Library, Special Collections Div, 37 & O Sts NW, Washington, 20057. George M Barringer, Special Collections Librn; Nicholas B Sheetz, Mss Librn
Holdings: Mss Cat
Notes: The papers of the Kilmer family incl letters and mss by the poet Joyce Kilmer and his wife, Aline Kilmer, also a poet and essayist. The papers incl correspondence by various authors, among them Rev James J Daly, SJ and Rev Charles L O'Donnell, CSC.

VA —UNIVERSITY OF VIRGINIA, Alderman Library, Clifton Waller Barrett Collection, Charlottesville, 22901. Joan St C Crane, Cur of American Literature Collections
Notes: Paper.

KILPATRICK, JAMES J.

VA —UNIVERSITY OF VIRGINIA, Alderman Library, Manuscripts Dept, Charlottesville, 22901. Edmund Berkeley Jr, Cur
Holdings: Cat Mss Pix
Notes: Papers, etc.

KIMBALL, CHARLES N.

MO —UNIVERSITY OF MISSOURI-KANSAS CITY, General Library, State Historical Society of Missouri Manuscripts, 5100 Rockhill Road, Kansas City, 64110. Kenneth J LaBudde, Dir; Gordon Hendrickson, Assoc Dir
Holdings: Mss
Notes: Western Historical Manuscript Collection incl papers of Charles B Wheeler, Jr, Charles N Kimball, Arthur Mag, Oscar D Nelson, Lou B Holland, J C Nichols, Perry Cookingham, Blevins Davis, Daniel MacMorris, and the records of the Kansas City Board of Trade.

KINANTHROPOLOGY

ON —UNIVERSITY OF OTTAWA, Health Sciences Library, 451 Smyth Road, Ottawa, K1H 8L5, Can. Myra Owen, Librn
Holdings: Vols (70,000) Slides Audiotapes Films Filmstrips
Budget: ($325,000)
Notes: This collection is made up of works in support of clinical and research studies in all branches of medicine, nursing and kinanthropology. Incl 1500 periodicals.

ON —SIRLS, Faculty of Human Kinetics & Leisure Studies, University of Waterloo, Waterloo, N2L 3G1, Can. Betty Smith, Database Mgr
Notes: Information Retrieval System for the Sociology of Leisure and Sport (SIRLS) is a computerized online database of about 13, 000 entries (1983). Incl dance as a leisure time activity.

KINDERGARTEN

CA —UNIVERSITY OF CALIFORNIA, LOS ANGELES, Research Library, Dept of Special Collections, 405 Hilgard Ave, Los Angeles, 90024. Edward Shreeves, Chairman, Bibliographers Group; David S Zeidberg, Head
Notes: 20 linear feet of books and educational play material related to his work with kindergarten training, ca 1880-1920.

ME —BOWDOIN COLLEGE, Library, Brunswick, 04011. Dianne M Gutscher, Cur of Special Collections
Holdings: Vols 425 Cat Mss
Notes: The Kate Douglas Wiggin Collection incl 115 first and later editions of her works, 310 volumes from her library, chiefly presentation copies; 2 albums of periodical and newspaper appearances; 16 scrapbooks of clippings and notices; 4 boxes of mss, and about 100 letters of this author and pioneer kindergarten worker.

NY —ADELPHI UNIVERSITY, Library, Garden City, 11530. Jerome Yavarkovsky, Dean of Libraries
Holdings: // Mss
Notes: The collection includes 183 items consisting primarily of letters and some memorabilia. Mrs Maria Kraus-Boelte was one of the earliest and most influential apostles of the kindergarten in the U S employing the Froebelian method. Collection contains letters to a pupil Carrie Coit Meleney and memorabilia relating to the Kraus Alumni Kindergarten Association.

NY —BANK STREET COLLEGE OF EDUCATION LIBRARY, 610 W 112 St, New York, 10025. Eleanor Kule Seid, Library Dir
Holdings: Vols (80,000) Cat Microforms
Budget: ($29,000)
Notes: Education, guidance, psychology, educational psychology, curricula, textbooks, Black Studies, etc. All subjects are intergrated in one professional collection; in addition there are two separately cataloged and shelved collections: Children's and Elementary Curriculum Materials.

KINDNESS TO ANIMALS see Animals, Treatment of

KINESIOLOGY see Human Mechanics

KINETICS see Dynamics

KING, CECIL

MA —BOSTON UNIVERSITY, Mugar Memorial Library, Special Collections Dept, 771 Commonwealth Ave, Boston, 02215. Howard B Gotlieb, Dir
Holdings: Mss Maps Pix
Notes: Mss, correspondence, etc collected in depth; incl publications by or about.

KING, CHARLES

WI —MILWAUKEE PUBLIC LIBRARY, 814 W Wisconsin Ave, Milwaukee, 53233. Donald J Sager, City Librn
Holdings: Cat
Notes: Just about all the editions and formats listed in Dornbusch plus a quantity not known to him.

KING, CLARENCE, 1842-1901

RI —BROWN UNIVERSITY, John Hay Library, 20 Prospect St, Providence, 02912. Mark N Brown, Cur Mss
Holdings: // Mss
Notes: Within the John Hay Manuscript Collection (qv) are found about 90 letters written by King to Hay, concerning personal and social matters, politics and travel.

KING, ERNEST J.

RI —US NAVAL WAR COLLEGE, Historical Collection & Museum, Newport, 02841. Anthony S Nicolosi, Dir; Evelyn Cherpak, Cur
Holdings: Mss
Notes: Research source materials collected by Thomas Buell for his biograph of King, *Masters of Seapower.* Incl are *A Naval* Record by Walter M Whitehill, Adm King's

KING, ERNEST J. (cont.)

autobiography, personal papers, oral histories, photographs and drafts of the book. Adm King was Fleet Admiral and Chief of Naval Operations during World War II.

KING, HAMILTON, 1852-1912

DC —GEORGETOWN UNIVERSITY, Library, Special Collections Div, 37 & O Sts NW, Washington, 20057. George M Barringer, Special Collections Librn; Nicholas B Sheetz, Mss Librn
Holdings: Mss Cat Pix
Notes: The papers of Hamilton King (1852-1912), American Minister to Siam from 1898-1912. The papers contain correspondence, letter books, diary (1903), mss of articles, reports, and addresses, and newspaper clippings dealing specifically with King's years as ambassador. Correspondence incl letters from George Dewey, Douglas MacArthur, William Alden Smith, J C Burrows, Frank Seward, and members of the Siamese royal family and ministry, incl King Chulalongkorn, Crown Prince Vajiravudh, Prince Dwanwongse, and Prince Damron, among others. Apart from material concerning official diplomatic matters, the papers provide detailed accounts of life in Siam. Of patricular interest is a series of diaries kept by Mrs Hamilton King for the years, 1885, 1898-1915.

KING, HELEN DEAN, 1896-1955

MA —MASSACHUSETTS INSTITUTE OF TECHNOLOGY, Institute Archives, Special Collections, Cambridge, 02139.
Notes: Correspondence, newsletters, fact-sheets, newspaper and magazine articles, books and reports of the Citizens' League Against the Sonic Boom, established in 1967 by William Shurcliff to oppose the sonic boom, stop commercial supersonic transport production, and influence public opinion and policy decisions on the SST. Major correspondents incl Bo Lundberg, Richard Wiggs, several US congressmen, and CLASB members.

KING, MARIAN

CT —YALE UNIVERSITY, Box 1603A, Yale Station, New Haven, 06520.
Holdings: Cat

KING, MARTIN LUTHER, JR.

DC —HOWARD UNIVERSITY, Moorland-Spingarn Research Center, 500 Howard Place NW, Washington, 20059. Clifford L Muse, Jr, Acting Dir
Holdings: Vols (106,086) Mss Maps Pix Slides Phonorecords Audiotapes 16mm Films Filmstrips Microforms
Budget: ($854,753)
See also entry under Blacks

GA —MARTIN LUTHER KING, JR, CENTER FOR NONVIOLENT SOCIAL CHANGE, INC, King Library and Archives, 449 Auburn Ave, Atlanta, 30312. D Louise Cook, Dir of Library and Archives
Holdings: Vols 4000 Cat Mss Audiotapes Microforms
Notes: The philosophy of Martin Luther King and the movement he led. Emphasis on obscure information and ephemeral pieces. Oral history project has over 500 tapes. Incl collection of mss of various civil rights organizations of the 1950s and 1960s. All materials are noncirculating.

IL —SOUTHERN ILLINOIS UNIVERSITY, CARBONDALE, Delyte W Morris Library, Special Collections Dept, Carbondale, 62901. David V Koch, Cur of Special Collections; Louisa Bowen, Cur of Manuscripts
Holdings: Vols 30 Cat Mss Pix
Notes: The archives of Henry Nelson Wieman, American theologian and philosopher consist of some 30 vols which Wieman authored or co-authored, together with mss (published and unpublished), autobiographical materials, letters, lecture notes, and other papers. See Martin Luther King, *A Comparison of the Conception of God in the Thinking of Paul Tillich and Henry Nelson Wieman,* 1955. Inventory and name index at the library.

MA —BOSTON UNIVERSITY, Mugar Memorial Library, Special Collections Dept, 771 Commonwealth Ave, Boston, 02215. Howard B Gotlieb, Dir
Holdings: Cat Mss Pix
Notes: Mss, correspondence, etc collected in depth; incl publications by or about. Personal papers of Martin Luther King, Jr.

SC —COLLEGE OF CHARLESTON LIBRARY, Special Collections Dept, Charleston, 29401.
Notes: Includes material relating to Martin Luther King, Jr, Esau Jenkins, and Rosa Parks.

TN —MEMPHIS STATE UNIVERSITY, John Willard Brister Library, Memphis, 38152. John Terreo, Special Collections Librn
Notes: 1968 Memphis Sanitation Workers Strike. A collection of audiotape interviews with Memphis governmental officals and administrators, strikers, union leaders, religious leaders, and other significant persons involved in the strike, during which civil rights leader Dr Martin Luther King, Jr was assassinated. Also incl are photographic prints and negatives and the news outakes from the news departments of the three Memphis television stations as well as clippings from newspapers and periodicals. Published finding aid can be found in the Mississippi Valley Collection.

WI —BELOIT COLLEGE LIBRARIES, Beloit, 53511. Dennis W Dickinson, Dir
Holdings: Vols 700 Cat
Notes: The Martin Luther King Jr Collection on Nonviolence. This small collection was given by H Vail Deale, Director, at the time of the assassination of Dr King in 1968. Comprises books by and about: M K Gandhi, H D Thoreau, M L King, world peace, pacifism, nonviolence, etc. Contains a 35-year bound file of *Fellowship,* the magazine of US pacifism. At present time there is only a local card index of the collection, though items are fully cataloged in the Public Card Catalog. A specially designed bookplate by local artist, O Vernon Shaffer, is used for books in this collection.

KING, MITCHELL, 1783-1862

SC —COLLEGE OF CHARLESTON LIBRARY, Special Collections Dept, Charleston, 29401.
Notes: Papers, 1842-1853, incl correspondence of Mitchell King with Henry C King (son), F S Holmes, J L Petigru, and John Pennington.

KING, ROBIN, GALE, AND PILLINGER

IL —CHICAGO HISTORICAL SOCIETY, Library, Clark St at North Ave, Chicago, 60614. Archie Motley, Manuscript Librn
Notes: Personal papers of various members of the Crane, Laflin, Holabird, Willing, and other socially prominent Chicago families; diaries of Frances Glessner, longtime resident of the architecturally-renowned Glessner House; records of the legal firm of King, Robin, Gale, and Pillinger, dating from 1872.

KING, SLATER

TN —FISK UNIVERSITY, Library, Special Collections, 17 & Jackson St, Nashville, 37203. Ann Allen Shockley, Assoc Librn
Holdings: Cat Mss Pix
Notes: Papers of the late Slater King, leader of the Albany, Georgia, Civil Rights Movement.

KING, STODDARD

OR —UNIVERSITY OF OREGON, Library, Eugene, 97403. Kenneth W Duckett, Curator
Notes: Papers of Stoddard King incl a number of Vachel Lindsay letters and broadsides.

KING, WAYNE

AZ —ARIZONA STATE UNIVERSITY, Music Library, Tempe, 85281. Arlys L McDonald, Music Librn
Holdings: Vols 5446 // Uncat Phonorecords 16mm Films
Notes: The Wayne King Collection of popular music titles arranged for and used by the Wayne King Orchestra from the 1930s-1960s. It includes full score arrangements with parts, charts, recordings and 16mm films of his television shows originating from Chicago, 1949-1952. The collection is indexed by title. No photocopying.

KING, GOV. WILLIAM

ME —BOWDOIN COLLEGE, Library, Brunswick, 04011. Dianne M Gutscher, Cur of Special Collections
Holdings: Vols (13,000)
Notes: Besides a general collection of 13,000 volumes relating to the State of Maine, there are also many mss collections touching on the political, economic, and social history of Maine. These incl Hale-King papers, 700 letters (1787-1880), concerning these two Maine families and incl letters of Gov William King, first governor of Maine.

ME —MAINE HISTORICAL SOCIETY, Library, 485 Congress St, Portland, 04101.
Holdings: Vols (60,000) Cat Mss Maps Pix
Notes: The Society's holdings cover all of Maine in its scope, with special emphasis on the Portland region.

KING, SEN. WILLIAM

UT —UNIVERSITY OF UTAH, Marriott Library, Special Collections, Salt Lake City, 84112. Gregory C Thompson, Cur
Holdings: Cat Mss Microfilm Film Oral History
Notes: Papers.

KING-HALL, SIR STEPHEN, 1893-1966

BC —UNIVERSITY OF VICTORIA, McPherson Library, Victoria, V8W 3H5, Can.

KING PHILIP'S WAR, 1675-1676

MA —NEW ENGLAND HISTORIC GENEALOGICAL SOCIETY, Library, 101 Newbury St, Boston, 02116. Ralph J Crandell, Dir
Notes: Large collection of printed British and American parish registers; some American ms parish records. Strong collection of early censuses, incl the Massachusetts Direct Tax Record of 1798, actually a census of Maine and Massachusetts and more informative than the Federal decennial record of early national censuses. Early similarly useful records incl the Accounts of Pay for King Philip's War (1675-1676) kept by John Hull, War Treasurer.

KINGS see Rulers (Kings, Queens, Etc.)

KINGSLEY, CHARLES, 1819-1875

NJ —PRINCETON UNIVERSITY, Library, Morris L Parrish Collection, Princeton, 08540. Alexander D Wainwright, Cur
Notes: The finest collection of the works of Charles Kingsley, incl many first editions and first American editions. Almost 200 vols. For particulars refer to: Morris L Parrish and B K Mann. *Charles Kingsley and Thomas Hughes: First Editions in the Library of Dormy House* (Pine Valley, NJ, 1936) as well as Margaret Farrand Thorp, "The Kingsley Collection" in the *Chronicle* VIII, 1 (November, 1946) pp 18-20.

KINGSLEY, HENRY

MA —HARVARD UNIVERSITY LIBRARY, Houghton Library, Cambridge, 02138. Rodney G Dennis, Cur of Manuscripts
Holdings: Mss

KINGSTON, WILLIAM H. G.

MS —UNIVERSITY OF SOUTHERN MISSISSIPPI, William David McCain Graduate Library, Box 5148, Southern Sta, Hattiesburg, 39406.
Holdings: Vols 56
Notes: The Lena Y de Grummond Collection of Children's Literature. Incl the Robert L Dartt Collection of over 1800 books for boys from the late 19th and early 20th centuries. Extensive Henty (over 550 vols), Alger, Brereton, Castlemon, Fenn, Kingston, Optic, and Stratemeyer holdings. Catalog in progress.

KINNELL, GALWAY

IN —INDIANA UNIVERSITY, Lilly Library, Seventh St, Bloomington, 47405. William R Cagle, Librn
Notes: Papers, incl mss, letters, etc, 1948-1980.

KINROSS, LORD PATRICK

DC —GEORGETOWN UNIVERSITY, Library, Special Collections Div, 37 & O Sts NW, Washington, 20057. George M Barringer, Special Collections Librn; Nicholas B Sheetz, Mss Librn
Holdings: Mss Pix
Notes: The papers of Christopher Sykes, biographer, journalist, and novelist; containing mss, letters, photographs, and drawings. With extensive correspondence from Harold Acton; Angela, Countess of Antrim; Sir John Betjeman; Ivy Compton-Burnett; Alick Dru; T S Eliot; Max Beerbohm; Graham Greene; John Hayward; Lord Patrick Kinross; Compton Mackenzie; Nancy Mitford; Anthony Powell; Dame Flora Robson; Cecil Roth; Sir John Russell; Osbert Sitwell; John Sparrow; Freya Stark; James Stern; and Evelyn Waugh, among others. Also, considerable research material about Evelyn Waugh, Adam von Trott, Robert Byron, Lady Nancy Astor; and the foundation of the state of Israel.

KINSEY STUDIES

IN —INDIANA UNIVERSITY, Institute for Sex Research Library, 416 Morrison Hall, Bloomington, 47401. Douglas Freeman, Collections and Services Librn; Joan Brewer, Information Services Librn
Holdings: Vols (62,000) Cat Mss Pix Phonorecords Audiotapes Slides Films Microforms
Budget: ($20,000)
Notes: One of the greatest and most extensive collections on sexual behavior, the library collects materials on all aspects of sex activity, with special emphasis on behavioral and social aspects. Also collects erotic literature and sexual ephemera. Incl 105 audiotapes, 23 vertical file drawers, 108 phonorecords, 55,000 pictures, 5000 slides, and 1700 films. Rich in French, German and American sources; also much Oriental. Semitraditional erotic poetry and song of 17th-18th century England. Bawdy limericks, double-entendre, puns, slang, erotic literature, graffiti, slang and special dictionaries, proverbs and sayings, epigrams and research materials of the Kinsey Studies, etc. Contact Information Service for: literature searching, preparation of bibliographies, permission to use collection. Limited photocopying.

KIOWA INDIANS

OK —UNIVERSITY OF SCIENCE & ARTS OF OKLAHOMA, Nash Library, Chickasha, 73018. William A Martin, Jr, Librn
Holdings: // Uncat Mss Pix Audiotapes
Notes: Papers of Hugh D Corwin, writer on Indian life and history, incl conversations with elderly Kiowa Indians, with audiotapes, some pictures and mss; also reprints of Corwin's historical articles from local newspapers.

OK —US ARMY FIELD ARTILLERY SCHOOL LIBRARY, Morris Swett Library, Snow Hall, Fort Sill, 73503. Lester L Miller Jr, Chief Librn
Notes: Incl data on Fort Sill, Indian Territory, settlement of Kiowa, Apache and Commanche tribes, imprisonment of Geronimo, Oklahoma territory, settlement of Lawton. Unit histories, incl 10th Cavalry (Buffalo Soldiers, a black unit that built Fort Sill); working papers of Sheridan, Grierson and other commanders; Field Artillery School. Photographs on army subjects, Fort Sill, Indians, Indian Territory, settlement of Southwest Oklahoma.

KIP, FRANCIS EVERINGTON

NY —SAINT LAWRENCE UNIVERSITY, Owen D Young Library, Canton, 13617. Mahlon Peterson, Librn
Holdings: Mss
Notes: Collection consists of letters written home to New York State from the California gold fields and from New Orleans and Memphis during the Civil War. Approx 90 items.

KIPLING, RUDYARD

CT —TRINITY COLLEGE LIBRARY, Watkinson Library, 300 Summit St, Hartford, 06106. Jeffrey Kaimowitz, Cur
Holdings: Cat
Notes: First editions, etc.

CT —YALE UNIVERSITY, Beinecke Rare Book & Manuscript Library, Osborn Collection, New Haven, 06520. Stephen R Parks, Cur
Holdings: Mss

DE —UNIVERSITY OF DELAWARE, Hugh M Morris Library, S College Ave, Newark, 19711. T Stuart Dick, Special Collections
Holdings: Cat Mss
Notes: First English, American, Indian and variant editions.

DC —LIBRARY OF CONGRESS, Rare Book & Special Collections Div, Washington, 20540. William Matheson, Chief
Holdings: Cat
Notes: (A) The William M Carpenter Collection of 923 vols, considered one of the outstanding Kipling collections, consists of 120 first and later editions, autograph mss of 13 stories and poems, and more than 85 original letters and sketches. Incl the earliest draft of *Mowgli's Brothers.* (B) The Lloyd Chandler Collection consists of 415 pieces, basically of a research character. Contains 294 loose-leaf vols representing the printed texts of 846 prose and 1013 verse pieces written by (or ascribed to) Kipling, together with bibliographical notes and statements. The Chandler Collection is described in his *Summary,* printed by the Grolier Club (New York: 1930).

IL —ILLINOIS STATE UNIVERSITY, Milner Library, Dept of Special Collections, Normal, 61761. Robert Sokan, Librn
Notes: First editions, limited editions, ephemera, etc.

IN —INDIANA UNIVERSITY, Lilly Library, Seventh St, Bloomington, 47405. William R Cagle, Librn
Holdings: Vols 250 // Cat

MA —HARVARD UNIVERSITY LIBRARY, Houghton Library, Cambridge, 02138. Rodney G Dennis, Cur of Manuscripts
Holdings: Mss

†MA —WILLIAMS COLLEGE, Chapin Library of Rare Books, PO Box 426, Williamstown, 01267. Robert L Volz, Custodian
Holdings: Vols 750 Cat
Notes: No material available on interlibrary loan.

OH —OHIO UNIVERSITY, Vernon R Alden Library, Department of Archives and Special Collections, Athens, 45701. Gary A Hunt, Head
Holdings: Vols 166 Cat
Notes: A representative collection, incl some of the earliest works, and American as well as English first editions of many titles.

PA —BRYN MAWR COLLEGE, Canaday Library, Bryn Mawr, 19010. James Tanis, Dir
Notes: Rare books in the Adelman Collection.

TX —TEXAS TECH UNIVERSITY, Library, Lubbock, 79409. David J Murrah, Assoc Dir for Special Collections

VA —UNIVERSITY OF VIRGINIA, Alderman Library, Rare Book Dept, Charlottesville, 22901. Julius P Barclay, Cur
Holdings: Vols 450 // Cat
Notes: First editions and other books by or about him.

MB —UNIVERSITY OF MANITOBA, Elizabeth Dafoe Library, Archives and Special Collections Dept, Winnipeg, R3T 2N2, Can. Richard E Bennett, Dept Head; Corrado A Santoro, Reference Archivist
Holdings: Vols 350 // Cat
Notes: The Edwin A Pridham Collection. Writings and works of criticism, also periodical material.

NS —DALHOUSIE UNIVERSITY LIBRARY, Halifax, B3H 4H8, Can.
Holdings: 5000 Cat Mss Pix
Notes: The collection consists of Kipling mss, letters, monographs, periodical publications of works, newspapers and illustrations. Main strength lies in number of original letters, literary mss and first editions. Highlights of the collection are original drafts of *Our Lady of the Snows, Mandalay,* and *In Ambush;* inscribed first editions of *Echoes* and *Schoolboy Lyrics;* and over 700 letters by Kipling to business associates, family members and friends. Published catalog: *Rudyard Kipling: A bibliographical catalog,* by James McG Stewart. Edited by A W Yeats, Toronto: Dalhousie University Press, University of Toronto Press, 1959.

ON —UNIVERSITY OF TORONTO, Thomas Fisher Rare Book Library, 120 Saint George St, Toronto, M5S 1A5, Can. Richard G Landon, Head
Holdings: Vols 5400 Cat Mss
Notes: Three collections. Duncan Collection is named for donor, Douglas Duncan, art dealer and collector,, Toronto. Contains first and subsequent important editions of Richard Aldington, Max Beerbohm, Norman Douglas, Aldoux Huxley, and D H Lawrence. Manuscripts by Beerbohm, Aldington, Lawrence, William Sharp. Endicott Collection named in honor of Norman J Endicott, Professor of English, University of Toronto, contains first and significant later editions of over fifty British writers whose major work falls into the period from 1880 to 1930. Fisher Collection named for donor, Charles B Fisher, contains first and significant editions of Kipling, Norman Douglas, and Lord Dunsany.

KIRBY, ROLLIN

KS —UNIVERSITY OF KANSAS, Kenneth Spencer Research Library, Kansas Collection, Lawrence, 66045. Sheryl K Williams, Cur
Holdings: Cat
Notes: The Albert T Reid Cartoon Collection. Nucleus of collection was Reid's personal collection of political and comic cartoons. Later cartoonists presented samples of their work. Bill Mauldin, Rollin Kirby, Daniel B Dowling, Thomas Nast, and other political cartoonists represented. Comic strips from the late 1920s and 1930s. The collection of cartoons is cataloged and represented in the Kansas Collection card catalog. A separate book catalog is maintained also. For description see: *Albert T Reid Cartoon Collection.* Lawrence, Kan, Published for the Journalistic Historical Center, University of Kansas by the William Allen White Foundation, University of Kansas, ca 1957. Originally maintained by the Journalistic Historical Center, William Allen White School of Journalism, the collection was transferred to the Kansas Collection, Kenneth Spencer Library in 1969.

KIRCHHEIMER, OTTO

NY —STATE UNIVERSITY OF NEW YORK AT ALBANY, Library, Special Collections Dept, 1400 Washington Ave, Albany, 12222. Marion P Munzer, Coordr
Notes: Correspondence of Otto Kirchheimer;

KIRCHHEIMER, OTTO (cont.)

notes, mss (6 linear feet), publications, and reviews. Part of the Library's German Exile Collection.

KIRCHIZ-KAISSAK LANGUAGE see Kazakh Language and Literature

KIRGHIZ LANGUAGE AND LITERATURE

NY —NEW YORK PUBLIC LIBRARY, Oriental Div, Fifth Ave & 42 St, New York, 10018. E Christian Filstrup, Chief
Holdings: Cat Mss Microforms
Budget: ($56,455)
Notes: Published catalog of holdings.

KIRKCONNELL, WATSON

BC —UNIVERSITY OF VICTORIA, McPherson Library, Victoria, V8W 3H5, Can.

KIRKLAND, MURIEL

NY —HAMPDEN-BOOTH THEATRE LIBRARY AT THE PLAYERS, 16 Gramercy Park, New York, 10003. Louis A Rachow, Librn/Cur
Holdings: Uncat Mss Pix
Notes: The Muriel Kirkland Collection, incl her correspondence, photographs, and playbills. 4 boxes; presently uncataloged. Described in *Theatre & Performing Arts* Collections (New York: Haworth Press, 1981).

KIRKWOOD, SAMUEL

IA —STATE HISTORICAL SOCIETY OF IOWA LIBRARY, 402 Iowa Ave, Iowa City, 52240. Darold J Brown, Librn
Holdings: Cat
Notes: Thousands of individual items and smaller collections. Two hundred larger collections incl the papers of Cyrus C Carpenter, Jonathan P Dolliver, Gilbert Haugen, W W Waymack, Ephraim Adams, A C Dodge, Dorothy Houghton, Jesse Macy, Agnes Samuelson, Donald Johnson, Jack Miller, Ruth Sayre, Samuel Kirkwood, Thomas McKnight, Robert Lucas, Dwight McCarty, William Larrabee. Includes church, school, company and organization records, Civil War materials.

KIRLIAN PHOTOGRAPHY

NY —PARAPSYCHOLOGY SOURCES OF INFORMATION CENTER, 2 Plane Tree Lane, Dix Hills, 11746. Rhea A White, Dir
Holdings: Vols (4000)
Notes: The PSI Center includes 4000 books, 100 periodical titles, cassette tapes, and unpublished mss dealing with parapsychology and the transformation of consciousness, also 12,000 articles, reprints, etc. There is a charge for reference service and bibliographies.

KIRSCH, ROBERT

MA —BOSTON UNIVERSITY, Mugar Memorial Library, Special Collections Dept, 771 Commonwealth Ave, Boston, 02215. Howard B Gotlieb, Dir
Holdings: Cat Mss Correspondence

KIRST, HANS HELLMUT

MA —BOSTON UNIVERSITY, Mugar Memorial Library, Special Collections Dept, 771 Commonwealth Ave, Boston, 02215. Howard B Gotlieb, Dir
Holdings: Cat Mss

KIRSTEIN, LINCOLN

NY —NEW YORK PUBLIC LIBRARY, Performing Arts Research Center, Dance Collection, 111 Amsterdam Ave, New York, 10023. Genevieve Oswald, Cur
Notes: A comprehensive historical collection on the dance in the 18th-19th centuries was given in 1961, forming the core of the Lincoln Kirstein Collection. Additions have been continuously received with extensive gifts of prints, original stage and costume designs, drawings, manuscripts, rare books, and films.

KISSINGER, HENRY A.

DC —LIBRARY OF CONGRESS, Manuscript Division, Washington, 20540. John C Broderick, Chief
Holdings: 208,000 Items
Notes: Papers of Henry A Kissinger.

KITCHELT, FLORENCE LEDYARD CROSS, 1874-1961

NY —CORNELL UNIVERSITY LIBRARIES, Collection of Regional History, Dept of Manuscripts and Univ Archives, Ithaca, 14853.
Notes: Incl papers, 1896-(1898-1910)-1954; 53 pieces; letters, notes and reminiscences concerning the beginnings of the George Junior Republic; and family letters and printed items.

KITCHEN-GARDENS see Vegetable Gardening

KITIMAUG PRESS

SC —WOFFORD COLLEGE, Sandor Teszler Library, N Church St, Spartanburg, 29301. Frank J Anderson, Librn
Notes: Books about the history and practice of printing, hand papermaking, bookbinding, book collecting, fine press and private press books used in conjunction with instruction at the Wofford Library Press, an experimental and bibliographic press which has been in operation since 1969. Collection contains materials on printmaking methods and related graphic arts. Collection incl imprints of: Briarpatch Press, Anthoensen Press, Mosher Press, Kitimaug Press, Windhover Press, Penman Press, Unicorn Press, Wofford Library Press and others.

KITTREDGE, TRACY B.

CA —HOOVER INSTITUTION ON WAR, REVOLUTION & PEACE, Stanford University, Stanford, 94305. Milorad M Drachkovitch, Archivist
Holdings: // Mss
Notes: Papers of Tracy B Kittredge, official historian of the Commission for Relief in Belgium. Correspondence, clippings, photos, and ms drafts of a history of the commission. Unpublished register is available in repository.

KLAMT, FRANCES

MA —BOSTON UNIVERSITY, Mugar Memorial Library, Special Collections Dept, 771 Commonwealth Ave, Boston, 02215. Howard B Gotlieb, Dir
Holdings: Mss Pix
Notes: Mss, correspondence, etc collected in depth; incl publications by or about.

KLEBS, ARNOLD CARL, 1870-1943

CT —YALE UNIVERSITY, Medical Historical Library, Klebs Collection, 333 Cedar St, New Haven, 06520. Ferenc A Gyorgyey, Librn
Notes: The Arnold Carl Klebs Medical Collection books, pamphlets, etc, incl the library of his father, Edwin T A Klebs, pathologist. Strong in bibliography of early printed medical books, herbals, plague tracts, inoculation, vaccination and tubercular diseases.

KLEINE, GEORGE, 1864?-1931

DC —LIBRARY OF CONGRESS, Manuscript Division, Washington, 20540. John C Broderick, Chief
Notes: Film library and business papers.

KLEMIN, ALEXANDER, 1888-1950

CA —UNIVERSITY OF CALIFORNIA, LOS ANGELES, Research Library, Dept of Special Collections, 405 Hilgard Ave, Los Angeles, 90024. Edward Shreeves, Chairman, Bibliographers Group; David S Zeidberg, Head
Holdings: Cat Mss Maps Pix
Notes: 115 linear feet of mss, photographs, and printed material concerning the technical and historical aspects of aeronautics, incl the development of the helicopter and gyroscope.

KLEMMER, HERBERT, 1911-

KS —MENNINGER FOUNDATION, Archives, 5600 W Sixth St, Box 829, Topeka, 66601. Alice Brand, Librn; Mark West, Archivist
Notes: 12 boxes, 1957-71. Papers consist of reports, correspondence, and miscellaneous materials.

KLINE, ALMA

MA —RADCLIFFE COLLEGE, Arthur & Elizabeth Schlesinger Library on the History of Women in America, 3 James St, Cambridge, 02138. Patricia Miller King, Dir; Eva Moseley, Cur of Mss
Notes: Correspondence, writings, etc of the sculptor Harriet Goodhue Hosmer. (1830-1908). Probably largest collection of her papers. Available on microfilm. Inventory published by G K Hall; see Hamilton Family for citation. Also papers of Alma Kline and Cornelia Van Auken Chapin (1893-).

KLINK, THOMAS W., 1920-1970

KS —MENNINGER FOUNDATION, Archives, 5600 W Sixth St, Box 829, Topeka, 66601. Alice Brand, Librn; Mark West, Archivist
Notes: 25 boxes, 1947-70. Contains mss, sermons, lecture notes, and correspondence.

KLONDIKE GOLD RUSH see Gold Rush, Klondike

KNAPP, DANIEL

†MA —JOHN F KENNEDY LIBRARY, Columbia Point, Boston, 02125. Dan H Fenn Jr, Dir
Holdings: // Cat Mss
Notes: Background papers of Richardson White for his study "Youth and Opportunity: The Federal Anti-Delinquency Program" and Daniel Knapp's papers relating to the President's Commission on Juvenile Delinquency, late 1950s-late 1960s. 21 linear ft of mss. Holdings are described in "Historical Materials in the John F Kennedy Library." Copies may be obtained by writing the Research Archivist.

KNAPP, ADM. HARRY S.

MD —US NAVAL ACADEMY, Nimitz Library, Annapolis, 21402. Alice S Creighton, Assistant Librn for Special Collections
Holdings: Mss
Notes: Papers, etc.

KNAPP, JOSEPH GRANT, 1900-

NY —CORNELL UNIVERSITY LIBRARIES, Collection of Regional History, Dept of Manuscripts and Univ Archives, Ithaca, 14853.
Notes: Papers, 1924-71; 4.5 ft. Administrator of the Farm Cooperative Service, USDA; author.

KNEBEL, FLETCHER

MA —BOSTON UNIVERSITY, Mugar Memorial Library, Special Collections Dept, 771 Commonwealth Ave, Boston, 02215. Howard B Gotlieb, Dir
Holdings: Cat Mss Pix
Notes: Mss, correspondence, etc collected in depth; incl publications by or about.

KNECHT, KARL K., 1906-1960

IN —UNIVERSITY OF EVANSVILLE, Clifford Memorial Library & Learning Resources, 1800 Lincoln Ave, Evansville, 47714. P Grady Morein, University Librn
Holdings: Vols 45 // Uncat Mss
Notes: Incl approximately 10,000 cartoons by Karl K Knecht.

KNEIPP CURE see Hydrotherapy

KNIGHT, CHARLES R.

NY —AMERICAN MUSEUM OF NATURAL HISTORY, Library Services Dept, Central Park W & 79th St, New York, 10024. Nina J Root, Chairwoman; Mary Genett, Asst Librn for Reference Services
Holdings: Cat Mss Maps Pix Slides 16mm Films
Notes: Manuscripts, diaries, correspondence, artifacts, some art work, and collected materials. Not all cataloged as of 1983.

KNIGHT, FRANCES G.

MA —BOSTON UNIVERSITY, Mugar Memorial Library, Special Collections Dept, 771 Commonwealth Ave, Boston, 02215. Howard B Gotlieb, Dir
Holdings: Mss Pix
Notes: Mss, correspondence, etc collected in depth; incl publications by or about.

KNIGHT, JONATHAN, 1789-1864

CT —YALE UNIVERSITY, Medical Historical Library, 333 Cedar St, New Haven, 06510. Ferenc A Gyorgyey, Librn
Holdings: Vols 124 Cat
Notes: Books from Knight's library.

KNIGHTHOOD, ORDERS OF see Military Religious Orders; Orders of Knighthood and Chivalry

KNIGHTS OF COLUMBUS

AZ —NORTHERN ARIZONA UNIVERSITY, Special Collection Library, CU Box 6022, Flagstaff, 86011. Peter M Whiteley, Coordr/Archivist; William Mullane, Librn
Notes: (1) Knights of Columbus, Da Silva Council, Flagstaff, Ariz, Collection; minutes, financial records, correspondence, bank statements and other documents, 1907-1969. (2) Knights of Columbus, Verde Council, Jerome, Ariz, Collection; correspondence and financial records, 1920's, 1940's.

KNIGHTS OF LABOR

MI —MICHIGAN STATE UNIVERSITY, Labor and Industrial Relations Library, East Lansing, 48824. Martha Jane Soltow, Librn
Holdings: Cat Microforms
Notes: This material is composed primarily of special collections of papers on microfilm or microfiche.

KNIGHTS OF MALTA

DC —CATHOLIC UNIVERSITY OF AMERICA, Mullen Library, Washington, 20064. Carolyn Lee, Cur
Holdings: Vols 300 Cat
Notes: The Foster Stearns Collection of Militensa. There is a printed catalog of the original gift collection containing 281 vols.

KNISTER, RAYMOND

ON —VICTORIA UNIVERSITY, Library, 71 Queen's Park Crescent, Toronto, M5S 1K7, Can. Robert C Brandeis, Chief Librn
Notes: The collection is very strong in 19th-20th century poetry, drama and fiction; it contains gazetteers, travel books, biographies, and works on history and geography. Nucleus of collection listed in James, C C, *A Bibliography of Canadian Poetry (English)* (Victoria University Library Publication No 1, Toronto, 1899); and Horning, L E and Burpee, L J, *A Bibliography of Canadian Fiction (English)* (Victoria University Library Publication No 2, Toronto, 1904). Collection incl mss and vols by Canadian writers Helena Coleman, Raymond Knister, and Marjorie L C Pickthall and letters of Bliss Carman, and Duncan Campbell Scott.

KNIT GOODS INDUSTRY

NY —STATE UNIVERSITY OF NEW YORK, COLLEGE AT OSWEGO, Penfield Library, Oswego, 13126. Anne Commerton, Dir
Holdings: Cat Mss Maps Pix
Notes: Hayes Textile Co papers, 1913 to 1929. The company was founded in 1911 by Thomas Hayes. The papers contain the business records of the company incl ledgers of adminstration, general accounts, sales and purchases, etc. Unpublished guide.

KNITTING

NC —PUBLIC LIBRARY OF CHARLOTTE & MECKLENBURG COUNTY, 310 N Tyron St, Charlotte, 28202. Mae S Tucker, Asst Dir
Holdings: Vols (3950) Cat Slides 16mm Films Filmstrips
Notes: Weaving, chemistry, dyes and dyeing, and color are emphasized. Also, hosiery, knitting, machinery, manufacturing, directories and statistics. Have specialized dictionaries in the subject field in both English and other languages. 110 periodical titles.

KNIVES

†WA —WASHINGTON STATE UNIVERSITY, Library, Manuscripts, Archives & Special Collections, Pullman, 99164. John F Guido, Head
Holdings: Cat Mss Maps Pix
Notes: The Carl Parcher Russell papers, a vast resource (24,916 items; 45 linear feet) on American Indian and Western pioneer activities and artifacts. Much on the fur trade; pioneer life; mountain men and trapping; wildlife; primitive life in detail. Also the National Park Service, parks, monuments, etc. Described in *Carl Parcher Russell: An Indexed Register of His Scholarly and Professional Papers, 1920-1967, in the Washington State University* Library (Pullman, 1970), 149 pp.

KNOEPFLE, JOHN

MO —WASHINGTON UNIVERSITY, Libraries, Special Collections Dept, Campus Box 1061, St Louis, 63130.
Notes: A small but significant collection.

KNOLES, TOM, JR.

AZ —NORTHERN ARIZONA UNIVERSITY, Special Collection Library, CU Box 6022, Flagstaff, 86011. Peter M Whiteley, Coordr/Archivist; William Mullane, Librn
Notes: Collection of Tom Knoles, Jr, Flagstaff, Ariz, state senator. Impeachment trial of A P Buzard and E T Williams, Jr, members of the Arizona Corporation Commission, 1964. Court transcripts, volumes 1-32. Also incl one scrapbook concerning the history and development of the Central Arizona Project.

KNOPF, ALFRED A. AND BLANCHE

NE —UNIVERSITY OF NEBRASKA-LINCOLN, Don L Love Library, University Archives and Special Collections, Lincoln, 68588. Joseph G Svoboda, University Archivist
Notes: Virginia Faulkner was recognized as one of Nebraska's most distinguished writers and scholars. The Virginia Faulkner Collection, containing over 2000 titles, is housed in the Special Collections Department of Love Library. It is especially strong in twentieth century writers and in University of Nebraska Press publications. Of especial value to scholars are her extensive holdings of Willa Cather, Wright Morris, and John Neihardt. Her correspondence with S N Behrman, E B White, Edward Wagenknecht, Donald Sutherland, Wright Morris, Louise Pound, Mari Sandoz, Hazel Barnes, Alfred A and Blanche Knopf, and others provide insight into the literary development of these figures, as well as chronicle the intellectual thought of the period. Amassed in a separate file, these letters are available to interested scholars.

†TX —UNIVERSITY OF TEXAS LIBRARIES, General Libraries, Humanities Research Center, PO Box 7219, Austin, 78712. John Chalmers, Librn
Notes: The Alfred A and Blanche Knopf Archive, incl their personal library collection with numerous inscribed and association copies of their own and other publications.

KNOWLEDGE, BOOK OF see Encyclopedias and Dictionaries

KNOWLEDGE, THEORY OF see Epistemology

KNOWLES, JOHN

CT —YALE UNIVERSITY, Box 1603A, Yale Station, New Haven, 06520.
Holdings: Mss

KNOW-NOTHING PARTY see American Party

KNOX, FRANK

DC —LIBRARY OF CONGRESS, Manuscript Division, Washington, 20540. John C Broderick, Chief
Holdings: Cat Mss Pix
Notes: Mss, papers, records, etc.

KNOX, MSGR. RONALD

CT —SACRED HEART UNIVERSITY, Library, 5229 Park Ave, PO Box 6460, Bridgeport, 06606. Roch-Josef di Lisio, Actg Dir
Holdings: Vols 61 Cat
Notes: Books and articles by Msgr Ronald Knox, noted British wit, writer of detective fiction, apologist, and translater of the Bible. Almost all of the collection was described in the *Catalog Library World* (Jan 1967, March 1967).

DC —GEORGETOWN UNIVERSITY, Library, Special Collections Div, 37 & O Sts NW, Washington, 20057. George M Barringer, Special Collections Librn; Nicholas B Sheetz, Mss Librn
Holdings: Cat Mss
Notes: The papers of the English author, journalist, and historian Douglas Woodruff (1897-1978), containing correspondence, mss, and photographs. Incl is considerable material concerning his years at Oxford University; his editorship for many years of The "Tablet"; English Catholic society in general and English Catholic literature in particular. Also present are research files on the Tichborne Claimant, one of the most famous cases of impersonation in English legal history. There is extensive correspondence from such figures as: Hilaire Belloc; Tom Burns; Rev Martin D'Arcy, SJ; Christopher Dawson; Sir Roy Harrod; Christopher Hollis; Msgr Ronald Knox; Sir Shane Leslie; Sir Arnold Lunn; Rebecca West; and Evelyn Waugh.

KNOX, WILLIAM

MA —BOSTON UNIVERSITY, Mugar Memorial Library, Special Collections Dept, 771 Commonwealth Ave, Boston, 02215. Howard B Gotlieb, Dir
Holdings: Cat Mss Pix
Notes: Mss, correspondence, etc collected in depth; incl publications by or about.

KNOX FAMILY

†MA —UNIVERSITY OF MASSACHUSETTS AT AMHERST,

KNOX FAMILY (cont.)

Library, Amherst, 01003.
Notes: Microform collections of materials in other American libraries.

KNUDSEN, VERN OLIVER, 1893-1974

CA —UNIVERSITY OF CALIFORNIA, LOS ANGELES, Research Library, Dept of Special Collections, 405 Hilgard Ave, Los Angeles, 90024. Edward Shreeves, Chairman, Bibliographers Group; David S Zeidberg, Head
Holdings: Mss
Notes: 21 linear feet of papers, correspondence, mss, and other material related to his activities as physicist, acoustical consultant, and UCLA administrator.

KOCH, CLAUDE

MA —BOSTON UNIVERSITY, Mugar Memorial Library, Special Collections Dept, 771 Commonwealth Ave, Boston, 02215. Howard B Gotlieb, Dir
Holdings: Cat Mss

KOCH, KENNETH

BC —UNIVERSITY OF VICTORIA, McPherson Library, Victoria, V8W 3H5, Can.

KODAK see Eastman Kodak Company

KOEHLER, HERMANN

MI —UNIVERSITY OF MICHIGAN, Library, Dept of Rare Books & Special Collections, Ann Arbor, 48109. Robert J Starring, Head
Holdings: Uncat Mss Pix
Notes: Especially the period 1920-1945. The Myers Collection contains over 3,000 German pamphlets, brochures, serials, and circulars of the Weimar and Nazi period. Partially listed in H P Rothfeder, *Checklist of Selected German Pamphlets...of the Weimar and Nazi Period in the University of Michigan Library* (Ann Arbor, 1961). The German Archival Papers include the offical papers, chiefly correspondence, 1931-1944, of Hermann Kohler, District leader ofthe Nationalsozialistische Deutsche Arbeiter-Partei, Eisenach District, consisting of 3300 items plus 3 feet, and 7 photograph albums. Described in G L Weinberg, *German Archival Material in the Rare Book Room, the University of Michigan Library* (Ann Arbor, n d).

KOESTLER, ARTHUR

NV —UNIVERSITY OF NEVADA, RENO, University Library, Special Collections Dept, Reno, 89557. Robert E Blesse, Head
Holdings: Vols (89) Cat Other appearances 150 Cat
Notes: Includes individual works by author in all editions including translations; also prefaces, introductions, published correspondence, appearances in anthologies, periodicals, etc. Bibliographical research collection, part of Modern Authors Collection.

NY —COLUMBIA UNIVERSITY LIBRARIES, Rare Book & Manuscript Library, 801 Butler Library, 535 W 114 St, New York, 10027. Kenneth A Lohf, Librn
Notes: Forty years of literary correspondence between the Harold Matson Literary Agency and numerous notable authors. Restricted use.

KOGAN, HERMAN

IL —CHICAGO HISTORICAL SOCIETY, Library, Clark St at North Ave, Chicago, 60614. Archie Motley, Manuscript Librn
Notes: Lyric Opera of Chicago and the Apollo Musical Club of Chicago, and in audio tapes of Herman Kogan's "Critic's Choice" radio programs.

KOHN, JOHN

OK —UNIVERSITY OF TULSA, McFarlin Library, Dept of Rare Books and Special Collections, 600 S College, Tulsa, 74104. David Farmer, Dir; Toby Murray, Archivist; Caroline Swinson, Cur of Manuscripts & Art
Notes: The Robert Frost Collection, assembled by the late John Kohn, a friend of Frost and proprietor of Seven Gables Book Shop in New York. Incl all first editions of Frost's works, his appearances in anthologies and periodicals, translations into other languages, and critical works.

KOLB, EMERY

AZ —NORTHERN ARIZONA UNIVERSITY, Special Collection Library, CU Box 6022, Flagstaff, 86011. Peter M Whiteley, Coordr/Archivist; William Mullane, Librn
Notes: Kolb Collection of Photographs; very extensive collection of Kolb's photographs (over 250,000) which concentrate on the Grand Canyon, between 1902-1975. Incl an undetermined amount of photographs, motion pictures, correspondence, mss cameras, and other museum objects of Emery and Ellsworth Kolb's photographic studio at the Grand Canyon from the early 1900's to 1976. Incl the first motion picture film of the running of the Colorado River Rapids. This collection is subject to restrictions pending the cataloging of the collection.

KOLB, KEN

MA —BOSTON UNIVERSITY, Mugar Memorial Library, Special Collections Dept, 771 Commonwealth Ave, Boston, 02215. Howard B Gotlieb, Dir
Holdings: Cat Mss

KOLB BROTHERS

AZ —NORTHERN ARIZONA UNIVERSITY, Special Collection Library, CU Box 6022, Flagstaff, 86011. Peter M Whiteley, Coordr/Archivist; William Mullane, Librn
Holdings: Cat Mss Pix
Notes: More than 15,000 photographs of the Grand Canyon taken by the Kolb Brothers, 1902-1970.
See also entry under Kolb, Emery

KOLISCH, RUDOLF

DC —LIBRARY OF CONGRESS, Music Division, Washington, 20540.
Notes: Papers and recordings of composer Arnold Schoenberg. Extensive correspondence with other composers, writers, etc.

KOLLER, JAMES

CT —UNIVERSITY OF CONNECTICUT, Library, Storrs, 06268. George F Butterick, Cur of Literary Archives
Holdings: Mss

KOMADINIC, MILAN, 1882-1944

WI —UNIVERSITY OF WISCONSIN, MADISON, Memorial Library, Slavic Studies Collection, 728 State St, Madison, 53706. Aleksander Rolich, Bibliographer for Slavic Studies; Robert P Gakovich, Slavic Cataloger; Valdis J Zeps, Baltic Studies Center
Holdings: Vols (1000) Cat
Notes: The Komadinish Collection in Serbian and Yugoslav social and political history embraces publications and pamphlets of peasant, socialist and other radical movements of the last half of the nineteenth century up to World War II. It consists of some 1000 items, mostly in Serbo-Croatian, and represents only part of the private library acquired from the survivors of Milan Komadinic (1882-1944).

KOMI LANGUAGE see Syryenian Language and Literature

KOMO-TV

WA —UNIVERSITY OF WASHINGTON LIBRARIES, Suzzallo Library, Manuscripts Section, FM-25, Seattle, 98195. Karyl Winn, Librn
Notes: Files of locally produced newsfilm from station KOMO-TV in Seattle, from 1954.

KOMROFF, MANUEL

†NY —COLUMBIA UNIVERSITY LIBRARIES, Butler Library, Rare Book and Manuscript Library, 535 W 114 St, New York, 10027.
Notes: Papers, correspondence, mss, and first editions. Also a collection of 42 photographs Komroff took of writers and close friends.

KONANTZ, MARGARET, 1899-1967

MB —UNIVERSITY OF MANITOBA, Elizabeth Dafoe Library, Archives and Special Collections Dept, Winnipeg, R3T 2N2, Can. Richard E Bennett, Dept Head; Corrado A Santoro, Reference Archivist
Notes: Papers, diaries, etc, concerning her work and travels with UNICEF. Memoranda and pictures of her with governmental leaders such as Prime Minister Pearson and President John F Kennedy.

KONING, HANS

MA —BOSTON UNIVERSITY, Mugar Memorial Library, Special Collections Dept, 771 Commonwealth Ave, Boston, 02215. Howard B Gotlieb, Dir
Holdings: Cat Mss Pix
Notes: Mss, correspondence, etc collected in depth; incl publications by or about.

KOOPMAN, HARRY LYMAN, 1860-1937

RI —BROWN UNIVERSITY, John Hay Library, 20 Prospect St, Providence, 02912. Mark N Brown, Cur Mss
Holdings: // Mss
Notes: Papers of Harry Lyman Koopman, writer, librarian, and Professor of Bibliography at Brown University. Incl mss and typescripts of prose and poetry for the period 1877 to 1937, account books, journals, essays, speeches, articles, translations, a novel, short stories, poetry, articles written for *The Providence Journal* 1926-1937, and correspondence by Koopman as Librarian. 30,000 items.

KORAN

CA —LOS ANGELES PUBLIC LIBRARY, Philosophy & Religion Dept, 630 W Fifth St, Los Angeles, 90071. Marilyn C Wherley, Librn
Holdings: Vols 300 Cat
Budget: ($60,000)
Notes: General works on the history, theology, biography and current reference of the religion. Includes many translations of the Koran with related materials.

NY —COLUMBIA UNIVERSITY LIBRARIES, Rare Book & Manuscript Library, 801 Butler Library, 535 W 114 St, New York, 10027. Kenneth A Lohf, Librn
Holdings: Vols (5000)
Notes: Incl the Arthur Jeffrey Collection of numerous extremely rare printed editions and mss. Especially strong various texts, translations and commentaries. Restricted use.

OH —CLEVELAND PUBLIC LIBRARY, Fine Arts and Special Collections Department, 325 Superior Ave, Cleveland, 44114. Alice N Loranth, Head
Holdings: Vols 201 Cat Mss
Notes: 38 language versions are represented, incl Chinese, Georgian, Javanese and Swahili.
See also entries under Islam; Religion, Oriental.

KOREA

CA —UNIVERSITY OF CALIFORNIA, BERKELEY, University Library, East

KOREA (cont.)

Asiatic Library, Room 208, Durant Hall, Berkeley, 94720. Donald Shively, Head
Holdings: Vols 30,000 Cat Mss Maps Pix Microforms
Notes: Research collection of Korean-language materials, treating a broad range of subjects in the humanities and the social sciences. All historical periods, from ancient times to the present, are covered. The Library holds many rare and fine editions, such as the records of the Yi Dynasty. A major resource is the distinguished Asami Library of Korean literature (from the 16th through the 20th century), described by Chaoying Fang in *The Asami Library, a descriptive Catalogue* (Berkeley and Los Angeles: University of California Press, 1969). A G K Hall catalog of East Asiatic Library holdings is available.

CA —CLAREMONT COLLEGES, Honnold Library, Ninth & Dartmouth, Claremont, 91711. Tania Rizzo, Special Collections Dept Head
Holdings: Vols (792) // Mss Pix
Notes: Collected by Frederick McCormick while a newspaper correspondent in Korea in the early 20th century. Incl 16th to 19th century handwritten and printed volumes, some rare, of literary works, biography, history, philosophy, government, geography, calligraphy, children's textbooks. Indexed. Restricted use.

†CA —AMERICAN ACADEMY OF ASIAN STUDIES LIBRARY, 134-140 Church St, San Francisco, 94114.

†CA —ASIA FOUNDATION LIBRARY, 550 Kearny St, San Francisco, 94114.

CA —YONGSAN LIBRARY-KOREANA COLLECTION, Area Library Office, Seoul, Korea, APO, San Francisco, 96301.
Notes: The Koreana Collection of the Yongsan Library in Seoul, is a special reference collection of mostly English-language materials about Korea and the Korean War. A 319-page catalogue is free upon request from the Area Library Office, US Army Recreational Services Operations-Central, APO San Francisco 96301.

CT —TRINITY COLLEGE LIBRARY, 300 Summit St, Hartford, 06106. Ralph S Emerick, Librn
Holdings: Cat
Notes: Moore Collection of the Far East.

DC —LIBRARY OF CONGRESS, African and Middle Eastern Division, Washington, 20540.
Holdings: Cat Mss Microforms
Notes: Orientalia: the Orientalia Division contains 1,400,000 vols in Oriental languages. Chinese: more than 422,000 vols, espec strong in local histories and Ch'ing (1644-1911) period material. Japanese: over 574,000 vols, espec strong in economics, statistics, history, literature; 12,000 government, learned society, and university periodical titles, particularly science, technology, and social sciences. Korean: 56, 000 vols, espec strong in social sciences and modern history.

HI —UNIVERSITY OF HAWAII, Library, 2550 The Mall, Honolulu, 96822. Joyce Wright, Head, Asia Collection; Masato Matsu, Head, East Asia Vernacular Collection
Holdings: Vols 18,549 Cat Microforms
Notes: The Asia Collection includes materials from and about Korea in all languages. In addition to the cataloged Korean language volumes (above), there are an estimated 2000 not yet processed. No figures are available for western language volumes relating to Korea, which are supplemented by retrospective materials in the main library collection. Scope: social sciences and the humanities, traditional and modern.

IL —QUINCY COLLEGE LIBRARY, Quincy, 62301. Victor Kingery, OFM, Librn
Notes: In general collection.

IL —WHEATON COLLEGE, Buswell Memorial Library, Wheaton, 60187. Paul Snezek, Library Dir
Holdings: Vols 200
Notes: A wide rings of topic relating to missionary work. Most of the publications are from the late 19th and early 20th centuries.

NJ —PRINCETON UNIVERSITY, Library, Gest Oriental Library & East Asian Collections, 317 Palmer Hall, Princeton, 08544. D E Perushek, Cur
Holdings: Vols 8000 Cat Mss Maps Pix Microforms
Notes: Mostly in Korean. Subject areas incl Korean civilization, language, literature, philosophy, religion, history, geography, and social sciences. Some Western-language reference works and Western-language works on Korean literature and language. The Library maintains its Korean collection in a holding position with a minimum budget allocation. Emphasis is on current publications. Only the major academic journals, essential bibliographies, reference books and major works of research value are collected. Separate card catalog. Also incl serials.

†NY —ASIA SOCIETY LIBRARY, 725 Park Ave, New York, 10021.

NY —COLUMBIA UNIVERSITY LIBRARIES, C V Strarr East Asian Library, 300 Kent Hall, New York, 10027. James Reardon-Anderson, Librn
Holdings: Vols 27,682 Cat
Notes: Publications in major East Asian and Western languages in all subjects comprising the social sciences and humanities.

NY —NEW YORK PUBLIC LIBRARY, Oriental Div, Fifth Ave & 42 St, New York, 10018. E Christian Filstrup, Chief
Holdings: Cat Mss Microforms
Budget: ($56,455)
Notes: Described in *Dictionary Catalog of the Oriental Collection,* The Research Libraries of the New York Public Library, 1960, 16 vols, and *First Supplement,* 1976, 8 vols (144,000 cards). This catalog incl 318, 000 entries for works in about 100 languages of the East, and all works in Western languages on Oriental subjects. The Oriental Collection numbers about 120,000 vols; its Arabic and Indic holdings and those on ancient Egypt and the ancient Near East are among the largest in the US. There is also a collection of 30,000 vols of PL 480 material from Egypt, Pakistan, and India to which there is main entry access, but which is not incorporated into the dictionary catalog. Other outstanding features of the Oriental Collection incl extensive holdings of Japanese technical and scientific periodicals; a unique collection of linguistic works, grammars, anddictionaries; and unusually good coverage of the field of Oriental religions and philosophies. The catalog contains numerous subject references to periodical articles in all languages. All entries are arranged alphabetically according to the Roman alphabet.

KOREA—CIVILIZATION AND CULTURE

CA —UNIVERSITY OF CALIFORNIA, BERKELEY, University Library, East Asiatic Library, Room 208, Durant Hall, Berkeley, 94720. Donald Shively, Head
Holdings: Vols 30,000 Cat Mss Maps Pix Microforms
Notes: Research collection of Korean-language materials, treating a broad range of subjects in the humanities and the social sciences. All historical periods, from ancient times to the present, are covered. The Library holds many rare and fine editions, such as the records of the Yi Dynasty. A major resource is the distinguished Asami Library of Korean literature (from the 16th through the 20th century), described by Chaoying Fang in *The Asami Library, A Descriptive Catalogue* (Berkeley and Los Angeles: University of California Press, 1969). A G K Hall catalog of East Asiatic Library holdings is available.

KS —UNIVERSITY OF KANSAS, Watson Library, East Asian Library, Lawrence, 66045. Eugene Carvalho, Librn
Holdings: Vols 1000 // Cat
Notes: Language materials with emphasis on general culture.

KOREA—HISTORY

CA —UNIVERSITY OF CALIFORNIA, BERKELEY, University Library, East Asiatic Library, Room 208, Durant Hall, Berkeley, 94720. Donald Shively, Head
Holdings: Vols 30,000 Cat Mss Maps Pix Microforms
Notes: Research collection of Korean-language materials, treating a broad range of subjects in the humanities and the social sciences. All historical periods, from ancient times to the present, are covered. The Library holds many rare and fine editions, such as the records of the Yi Dynasty. A major resource is the distinguished Asami Library of Korean literature (from the 16th through the 20th century), described by Chaoying Fang in *The Asami Library, A Descriptive Catalogue* (Berkeley and Los Angeles: University of California Press, 1969). A G K Hall catalog of East Asiatic Library holdings is available.

CA —UNIVERSITY OF CALIFORNIA, LOS ANGELES, Oriental Library, 405 Hilgard Ave, Los Angeles, 90024. Ik-Sam Kim, Head
Holdings: Vols 6000 Cat

CA —HOOVER INSTITUTION ON WAR, REVOLUTION & PEACE, Stanford University, Stanford, 94305. Milorad M Drachkovitch, Archivist
Holdings: Mss
Notes: Records of the Japanese Legation in Korea, 1894-1905, the Japanese Residency General in Korea, 1906-1910, and the Japanese Government-General in Korea, 1910, incl diplomatic correspondence, dispatches and instructions, reports, treaties and agreements, lists, charts, and personal correspondence relating to Japanese policy and actions in Korea during the 15 years preceding annexation, international relations in the Far East, the Korea domestic politics. 1 file cabinet.

MD —UNIVERSITY OF MARYLAND, Library, East Asia Collection, College Park, 20742. Frank Joseph Shulman, Curator and Head
Holdings: Vols (90,000) // Mss
Notes: Japanese books, newspapers, periodicals, etc, of the Allied Occupation period (1945-1952), including files of censored publications. Books number 40,000; periodical titles, 13,000; newspaper titles, ca 16,500. The special collection relating to the Occupation period is supplemented by a growing collection (now ca 50,000 vols) of Chinese, Japanese, and Korean publications which form the basis of the University's general collection in East Asian language materials.

MI —MICHIGAN STATE UNIVERSITY, International Library, East Asia Collection, East Lansing, 48824. Eugene deBenko, Librn
Holdings: Vols (34,000) Cat Mss Maps Phonorecords Audiotapes Microforms
Budget: ($11,000)
Notes: Priority given to East Asian publications on contemporary China, Japan and Korea. Principal subject emphasis on language, literature and history. Important resources also on politics and government, economics, anthropology, sociology, geography and agriculture.

NE —AMERICAN HISTORICAL SOCIETY OF GERMANS FROM RUSSIA (AHSGR), 615 Twelfth St, Lincoln, 68502. Mary Lynn Tuck, Librn
Holdings: Vols (1900) Mss Maps Pix Phonorecords Videotapes Audiotapes Microforms VF
Notes: History of German people from Russia and history of people of German-Russian ancestory. Including times in Russia, Germany, US, Canada, Mexico, Argentina, Brazil, Paraguay, Korea, and Japan. This Society has fifty-six chapters in the United States. 1900 volumes, 100 maps; 500 mss; 1200 vertical files; 2000 pictures; 40,000 obituary files, 40,000 family group charts, 50 phonorecords, 20 videotapes, 50 audiotapes, 15 reel-to-reel tapes, 150 periodicals, 250 microforms, 250 family histories-published and unpublished.

NY —NEW YORK PUBLIC LIBRARY, Rare Books and Manuscripts Div, Fifth Ave & 42

KOREA—HISTORY (cont.)

St, New York, 10018. William L Joyce, Asst Dir; Susan E Davis, Cur of Mss
Holdings: Cat Mss
Notes: The division holds over 9 million pieces, incl medieval, Renaissance, and Oriental examples. Major emphasis on American, incl exploration, discovery. Spanish expansion, U S history and historical persons; political, economic, and literary materials up to the 20th century, especially post-Civil War period; diaries of interest to social historians; theatrical history; science and engineering in 19th century America. Also the Maloney Irish Historical Collections; collections on Korean history, 1870-1948; Archives of the N Y World's Fairs, 1939-1940 and 1964-1965. Autograph collections, and fraudulent signatures and documents. See *Dictionary Catalog of the Manuscript Division.* The Research Libraries of the New York Public Library. 1967. 1155 pp 2 vols $110.

VA —MACARTHUR MEMORIAL, Library & Archives, MacArthur Sq, Norfolk, 23510. Ellen E Folkama, Asst Archivist
Holdings: Vols (4000) Cat Maps Pix Slides Phonorecords Audiotapes 16mm Films Microforms
Notes: Everything relating to the life and related activities of MacArthur. The Archives of the collection consist of 600 shelf-feet of documents from Gen MacArthur's official headquarters files over the period 1941-1951. These papers pertain to all matters with which his various commands were involved: military, naval and air matters; international relations; political science; Japanese occupation, peace treaty and Constitution, etc. Each Record Group is indexed. The indexes are retained here since they are being expanded. They are available for researchers.

WA —UNIVERSITY OF WASHINGTON LIBRARIES, East Asia Library, DO-27, Seattle, 98195. Karl Lo, Head
Holdings: Vols (300,000) Cat Microforms
Budget: ($200,000)
Notes: Southwest China: Joseph Rock Collection, ca 2000 vols; modern Chinese poetry, 1919 to date: ca 700 titles; Asian art, esp Japanese painting: 4097 vols; Tiao-yu-t'ai movement in the US: ca 400 items of periodicals and pamphlets; modern Korean poetry, ancient and modern: ca 1000 titles; Mu-yu-shu folk literature: ca 1000 items.

KOREA—HISTORY—WAR AND INTERVENTION, 1950-1953 see Korean War, 1950-1953

KOREA—MAPS

DC —LIBRARY OF CONGRESS, Geography and Map Division, Washington, 20540. John A Wolter, Chief
Holdings: Cat Mss Maps Pix Slides Microforms
Notes: *Cartographic Materials.* One of the largest cartographic collections in the world, all-inclusive in coverage. Early original manuscript maps, navigation charts by Italian, Portuguese, and Spanish 15th, 16th, and 17th-century cartographers; the Hummel & Warner Collections of rare manuscript and printed maps and atlases of China and Korea from the 17th, 18th, and 19th centuries; manuscript and printed maps of colonial America, the Revolutionary War, the War of 1812, the Civil War, and wars of the 20th century; individual sheets of large and medium-scale set maps and charts published in the 19th and 20th centuries, including official topographic, geologic, soil, mineral, and resource maps, and nautical and aeronautical charts for most countries of the world; special subject maps of the world and its various political entities; maps of the United States and the separateStates; county maps and plans of cities and towns, and the Sanborn Fire Insurance Maps, dating back to 1866 for some 13,000 cities in the United States. Atlases include earliest printed editions of Ptolemy's Geography (1482), and representative volumes of leading atlas publishers of the last five centuries covering individual continents, countries, states, counties, cities, and the world. Total: 3,800, 000 maps, 49,000 atlases, 400 globes and 2000 relief models. See *The Geography and Map Division: A Guide to Its Collections and Services*, rev ed, 1975 (LC 5.2:SE6/975).

KOREA—POPULATION

NC —CAROLINA POPULATION CENTER, Library, University Sq E, Chapel Hill, 27514. Patricia Shipman, Head Librn
Holdings: Vols (20,000) Cat
Budget: ($10,500)
Notes: Try to acquire everything published in English on population, with particular emphasis on the US and developing countries. Also acquire conference proceedings, seminar papers. These and journal articles are indexed and the analytics are incl in the catalog. Incl 13,000 reprints and other pieces of ephemera. Most extensive area files are on India, Africa, Thailand, Iran, Korea, and Latin America. Holdings are recorded on an automated data base. A microfiche catalog is available for use in the Library and for purchase. Access by subject & geographic area are available through the Library's own thesaurus-based indexing systems.

KOREAN AMERICAN NEWSPAPERS see Newspapers, Korean American

KOREAN ART see Art, Korean

KOREAN LANGUAGE AND LITERATURE

CA —AZUSA PACIFIC COLLEGE, Marshburn Memorial Library, Citrus & Alosta, Azusa, 91702. Edward Peterman, Librn
Holdings: Vols 300 Cat Mss Pix

CA —UNIVERSITY OF CALIFORNIA, BERKELEY, University Library, East Asiatic Library, Room 208, Durant Hall, Berkeley, 94720. Donald Shively, Head
Holdings: Vols 30,000 Cat Mss Maps Pix Microforms
Notes: Research collection of Korean-language materials, treating a broad range of subjects in the humanities and the social sciences. All historical periods, from ancient times to the present, are covered. The Library holds many rare and fine editions, such as the records of the Yi Dynasty. A major resource is the distinguished Asami Library of Korean literature (from the 16th through the 20th century), described by Chaoying Fang in *The Asami Library, A Descriptive Catalogue* (Berkeley and Los Angeles: University of California Press, 1969). A G K Hall catalog of East Asiatic Library holdings is available.

CA —CLAREMONT COLLEGES, Honnold Library, Asian Studies Collection, Ninth & Dartmouth, Claremont, 91711. Frances D Wang, Cur
Holdings: Vols (68,658) Cat Mss Maps Pix Microforms
Budget: ($50,000)
Notes: Incl 62,476 vols in Chinese and Japanese; 6276 in Western languages. About 13,000 uncataloged. Collection incl artifacts, original mss, rare, original editions of Chinese, Japanese, Korean and Western language and literature, history, and archaeology, which are today totally unavailable to acquire. The most distinguished work is the collection of some 200 Chinese gazetteers (fang-chih) which is one of the best in the US. Another valuable collection is the Frederick McCormick Collection of 214 titles in 896 vols of movable-type editions of Korean printed books, 15th-19th centuries. The Western-language collection on the Far East is probably one of the strongest in the US. Recently added was a collection of Japanese books on Shinto (125 titles), periodicals, and artifacts. Separate catalog.

CA —LOS ANGELES PUBLIC LIBRARY, Foreign Languages Dept, 630 W Fifth St, Los Angeles, 90071. Sylva Manoogian, Principal Librn
Holdings: Vols 1128 Cat
Budget: ($41,500)

CA —UNIVERSITY OF CALIFORNIA, LOS ANGELES, Oriental Library, 405 Hilgard Ave, Los Angeles, 90024. Ik-Sam Kim, Head
Holdings: Vols 7000 Cat

CA —SAN JOSE PUBLIC LIBRARY, 180 W San Carlos St, San Jose, 95113. Homer Fletcher, Dir
Holdings: Vols 7000 Cat

DC —LIBRARY OF CONGRESS, African and Middle Eastern Division, Washington, 20540.
Holdings: Cat Mss Microforms
Notes: Orientalia: the Orientalia Division contains 1,400,000 vols in Oriental languages. Chinese: more than 422,000 vols, espec strong in local histories and Ch'ing (1644-1911) period material. Japanese: over 574,000 vols, espec strong in economics, statistics, history, literature; 12,000 government, learned society, and university periodical titles, particularly science, technology, and social sciences. Korean: 56, 000 vols, espec strong in social sciences and modern history.

HI —UNIVERSITY OF HAWAII, Library, 2550 The Mall, Honolulu, 96822. Joyce Wright, Head, Asia Collection; Masato Matsu, Head, East Asia Vernacular Collection
Holdings: Vols 18,549 Cat Microforms
Notes: The Asia Collection includes material from and about Korea in all languages. In addition to the cataloged Korean language volumes (above), there are an estimated 2000 not yet processed. No figures are available for western language volumes relating to Korea, which are supplemented by retrospective materials in the main library collection. Scope: social sciences and the humanities, traditional and modern.

IL —UNIVERSITY OF ILLINOIS, URBANA/CHAMPAIGN, Asian Library, Urbana, 61801. William S Wong, Asian Librn
Holdings: Vols 130,000
Notes: East Asian Collection. Primarily a collection of Chinese, Japanese, and Korean language materials.

IL —WHEATON COLLEGE, Library, Marion E Wade Collection, Irving & Franklin Sts, Wheaton, 60187. Lyle Dorsett, Cur; Marjorie Mead, Associate Cur

KS —UNIVERSITY OF KANSAS, Watson Library, East Asian Library, Lawrence, 66045. Eugene Carvalho, Librn
Holdings: Vols 1000 // Cat
Notes: Language materials with emphasis on general culture.

MD —UNIVERSITY OF MARYLAND, Library, East Asia Collection, College Park, 20742. Frank Joseph Shulman, Curator and Head
Holdings: Vols (90,000) // Mss
Notes: Japanese books, newspapers, periodicals, etc, of the Allied Occupation period (1945-1952), including files of censored publications. Books number 40,000; periodical titles, 13,000; newspaper titles, ca 16,500. The special collection relating to the Occupation period is supplemented by a growing collection (now ca 50,000 vols) of Chinese, Japanese, and Korean publications which form the basis of the University's general collection in East Asian language materials.

MA —HARVARD UNIVERSITY LIBRARY, Harvard-Yenching Library, 2 Divinity Ave, Cambridge, 02138. Eugene W Wu, Librn
Notes: Three volumes of *A Classified Catalogue of Korean Books* have been published by the Library (1962, 1966, and 1980). Strong in philology and all literary genres.

MI —MICHIGAN STATE UNIVERSITY, International Library, East Asia Collection, East Lansing, 48824. Eugene deBenko, Librn
Holdings: Vols (34,000) Cat Maps Phonorecords Audiotapes Microforms
Budget: ($11,000)
Notes: Priority given to East Asian

KOREAN LANGUAGE AND LITERATURE (cont.)

publications on contemporary China, Japan and Korea. Principal subject emphasis on language, literature and history. Important resources also on politics and government, economics, anthropology, sociology, geography and agriculture.

NJ —PRINCETON UNIVERSITY, Library, Gest Oriental Library & East Asian Collections, 317 Palmer Hall, Princeton, 08544. D E Perushek, Cur
Holdings: Vols 8000 Cat Mss Maps Pix Microforms
Notes: Mostly in Korean. Subject areas incl Korean civilization, language, literature, philosophy, religion, history, geography, and social sciences. Some Western-language reference works and Western-language works on Korean literature and language. The Library maintains its Korean collection in a holding position with a minimum budget allocation. Emphasis is on current publications. Only the major academic journals, essential bibliographies, reference books and major works of research value are collected. Separate card catalog. Also incl serials.

NY —COLUMBIA UNIVERSITY LIBRARIES, C V Strarr East Asian Library, 300 Kent Hall, New York, 10027. James Reardon-Anderson, Librn
Holdings: Vols 27,682 Cat
Notes: Publications in major East Asian and Western languages in all subjects comprising the social sciences and humanities.

NY —NEW YORK PUBLIC LIBRARY, Oriental Div, Fifth Ave & 42 St, New York, 10018. E Christian Filstrup, Chief
Holdings: Cat Mss Microforms
Budget: ($56,455)
Notes: Published catalog of holdings.

NY —NEW YORK PUBLIC LIBRARY, Donnell Foreign Language Library, 20 W 53 St, New York, 10019. Bosiljka Stevanovic, Supvr Librn
Holdings: Vols 798 Cat
Notes: Korean collection incl Korean authors of Korean expression. No separate catalog.

NC —CUMBERLAND COUNTY PUBLIC LIBRARY, North Carolina Foreign Language Center, 328 Gillespie St, Fayetteville, 28301. Patrick M Valentine, Coordinator
Holdings: Vols 1000 Cat
Budget: $1000
Notes: The largest book collections are, in descending order of size, German Spanish, French, Japanese, Korean and Vietnamese, with fair sized collections in Italian, Russian, Chinese, Arabic, Greek, Hungarian, Polish, Hebrew, Thai, and Hindi. The Center has several shelves each of books in Bengali, Dutch, Marathi, Portuguese, Urdu, and Yiddish. Smaller collections of one to three shelves each incl Catalan, Croatian, Czech, Danish, Finnish, Gujarati, Icelandic, Kannada, Latin, Lithuanian, Malayalam, Norwegian, Panjabi, Persian (Farsi), Romanian, Slovak, Swedish, Tagalog, Tamil, Telegu, and Ukrianian. The Center has grammars, dictionaries and occasionally other readings in languages from Afrikaans and Albanian to Welsh, Yoruba and Zulu.

OH —CLEVELAND PUBLIC LIBRARY, Foreign Literature Dept, 325 Superior Ave, Cleveland, 44114. Natalia Bezugloff, Head
Holdings: Vols 310 Cat
Notes: A popular circulating collection containing classics and the standard works with emphasis on belles lettres, history and biography. A variety of other subjects such as learning languages, how to do books, art, children's books, spoken phonodiscs and cassettes, periodicals, etc. Incl 370 ephemera.
See also entry under Foreign Language Collections

WA —UNIVERSITY OF WASHINGTON LIBRARIES, East Asia Library, DO-27, Seattle, 98195. Karl Lo, Head
Holdings: Vols (300,000) Cat Microforms
Budget: ($200,000)
Notes: Southwest China: Joseph Rock Collection, ca 2000 vols; modern Chinese poetry, 1919 to date: ca 700 titles; Asian art, esp Japanese painting: 4097 vols; Tiao-yu-t'ai movement in the U S: ca 400 items of periodicals and pamphlets; Korean poetry, ancient and modern: ca 1000 titles; Mu-yu-shu folk literature: ca 1000 items.

KOREAN POETRY see Poetry, Korean

KOREAN WAR, 1950-1953

AZ —NORTHERN ARIZONA UNIVERSITY, Special Collection Library, CU Box 6022, Flagstaff, 86011. Peter M Whiteley, Coordr/Archivist; William Mullane, Librn
Notes: Collection of Robert Eunson, journalist, vice president, and assistant general manager of United Press International. NAU graduate. Incl correspondence, scrapbooks, subject files, photos, 1930's-1975. Eunson was a World War II correspondent. Also incl information on the Pacific and European theatres, Generals MacArthur and Eisenhower, and Arizona AP news articles from the Korean War era. Inventory available.

CA —YONGSAN LIBRARY-KOREANA COLLECTION, Area Library Office, Seoul, Korea, APO, San Francisco, 96301.
Notes: The Koreana Collection of the Yongsan Library in Seoul, is a special reference collection of mostly English-language materials about Korea and the Korean War. A 319-page catalogue is free upon request from the Area Library Office, US Army Recreational Services Operations-Central, APO San Francisco 96301.

CA —HOOVER INSTITUTION ON WAR, REVOLUTION & PEACE, Stanford University, Stanford, 94305. Milorad M Drachkovitch, Archivist
Holdings: Mss Pix Slides
Notes: Two collections: (1) Three handwritten diaries, July 10, 1951-May 22, 1952, by Admiral Charles Turner Joy, Chief United Nations negotiator at the Korean military armistice negotiations at Panmunjom, 1951-53, mainly concerning prisoner of war issues and repatriation questions. 3 vols in 1/2 mss box. (2) Papers of W H Vatcher, Jr, 1939-65, incl correspondence, mss, pamphlets, leaflets, slides, photographs, and other material, relating to South African political parties; Afrikaner and African nationalism; Afrikaner Broederbond; US, Japanese, and North Korean propaganda and psychological warfare methods during World War II and the Korean war. Incl "Siberian Sketchbook," a ms with photos by W H Vatcher. 18 ms boxes, 1 box, envelopes.

PA —US ARMY MILITARY HISTORY INSTITUTE, Carlisle Barracks, 17013. Richard J Sommers, Chief Archivist-Historian
Holdings: Mss Cat
Notes: TheKorean War collection, personal correspondence, daily logs, recollections, and official papers of US officers and soldiers serving in the Korean War, incl Generals Edward Almond, George Barth Bruce Clarke, Matthew Ridgway, and Arthur Trudeau.

PA —ERIE COUNTY HISTORICAL SOCIETY LIBRARY, 417 State St, Erie, 16501. Helen Andrews, Librn
Notes: World War II and Korean War Veterans. 66 vertical file drawers containing mostly newspaper clippings.

TX —UNIVERSITY OF TEXAS, EL PASO, Special Collections Dept, The S L A Marshall Military History Collection, El Paso, 79968. Thomas Burdett, Cur
Holdings: Vols 7000 Cat Periodicals Mss
Budget: $2000
Notes: The collection contains all of General Samuel Lyman Atwood Marshall's published works, his personal library and his personal papers. General Marshall was a prolific military historian and journalist. The collection's strengths are in its coverage of the wars of the twentieth century, specifically the two world wars, the Korean conflict and the war in Vietnam. The Marshall Room where the collection is housed is opened to the public.

VA —MACARTHUR MEMORIAL, Library & Archives, MacArthur Sq, Norfolk, 23510. Ellen E Folkama, Asst Archivist
Holdings: Vols (4000) Cat Maps Pix Slides Phonorecords Audiotapes 16mm Films Microfilms
Notes: Everything relating to the life and related activities of MacArthur. The Archives of the collection consist of 600 shelf-feet of documents from Gen MacArthur's official headquarters files over the period 1941-1951. These papers pertain to all matters with which his various commands were involved: military, naval and air matters; international relations; political science; Japanese occupation, peace treaty and Constitution, etc. Each Record Group is indexed. The indexes are retained here since they are being expanded. They are available for researchers.

KOREANS IN THE U.S.

PA —BALCH INSTITUTE FOR ETHNIC STUDIES, Library, 18 S Seventh St, Philadelphia, 19106. R Joseph Anderson, Library Dir
Holdings: Vols Cat

KORESHAN UNITY

FL —HISTORICAL ASSOCIATION OF SOUTHERN FLORIDA, Charlton W Tebeau Library of Florida History, 101 W Flager St, Miami, 33130. Rebecca A Smith, Cur of Research Materials
Holdings: Vols (3000) Cat Mss Maps Pix Slides Audiotapes 16mm Films Microforms
Notes: History of Florida, with emphasis on southern area. Less extensively, history of the Caribbean area, especially as related to Florida. Florida materials incl anthropology, archaeology, Indians of south Florida, incl Seminole Indians, Dade County history, and a complete run of the newspaper *The American Eagle* (1906-date), printed by Koreshan Unity, Estero, Florida. Incl 300 feet of mss, 1500 maps, 75,000 pictures, 2000 slides, 125 audiotapes, 25 16mm films, 200 microforms, 50 feet of vertical files, and 7000 postcards. Work in progress on guide to ms collection and on indexing of photographs. Also incl books and journals on museum science: conservation and preservation of museum materials.

KORNGOLD, ERIC WOLFGANG

DC —LIBRARY OF CONGRESS, Music Division, Washington, 20540.
Notes: A group of seven holograph musical scores by Eric Wolfgang Korngold.

KORNMANN AFFAIR

MA —UNIVERSITY OF MASSACHUSETTS AT AMHERST, Library, Amherst, 01003. Siegfried Feller, Assoc Dir for Collection Development
Holdings: Cat
Notes: Collection Binet. Mostly contemporary works, 1524 periodicals, and pamphlets, including a 99 vol contemporary nonce collection with quite strong Dauphine representation and pamphlets on important prerevolutionary events, viz, the Diamond Necklace affair, the Kornmann affair, etc. Some cataloged, some calendared and indexed.

KORSON, GEORGE

DC —LIBRARY OF CONGRESS, American Folklife Center, Archive of Folk Culture, Washington, 20540.
Notes: 100 songs and ballads largely from the bituminous coal regions of Appalachia; songs recorded near Pottsville, PA. George Korson's original recordings and field notes are at King's College, Wilkes-Barre, PA.

PA —KING'S COLLEGE, D Leonard Corgan Library, 14 W Jackson St, Wilkes-Barre, 18711. Judith Tierney, Special Collections Librn
Holdings: Cat Mss Tapes
Notes: The entire collection of tapes, mss,

KORSON, GEORGE (cont.)

books and letters of the folklorist, George Korson. Covers period 1918-1969.

KORYAK LANGUAGE

WA —UNIVERSITY OF WASHINGTON LIBRARIES, Rare Books, Special Collections Dept, Seattle, 98195. Sandra Kroupa, Librn
Notes: Part of a set of Siberian primers prepared in the early 1930s by Soviet ethnographers. Some are first attempts to transcribe Siberian languages. All are in Latin phonetic script, not in Cyrillic.

KORZYBSKI, ALFRED HABDANK

NY —COLUMBIA UNIVERSITY LIBRARIES, Rare Book & Manuscript Library, 801 Butler Library, 535 W 114 St, New York, 10027. Kenneth A Lohf, Librn
Holdings: Mss
Notes: Papers and correspondence of Alfred H Korzybski, 1917-1938; founder of the theory of General Semantics. 8000 items. Restricted use.

KOSCIUSZKO, TADEUSZ, 1746-1817

NY —KOSCIUSZKO FOUNDATION, Book Service, 15 E 65 St, New York, 10021.
Holdings: Vols 1500
Notes: Published guide available. Materials on Tadeusz Kosciuszko (1746-1817), Polish history, and Poles in the United States.

KOSIK, MICHAEL

PA —PENNSYLVANIA STATE UNIVERSITY, Fred Lewis Pattee Library, Labor History Collection, University Park, 16802. Peter Gottlieb, Archivist
Holdings: Cat Mss Pix
Notes: Personal papers.

KOSSUTH, LAJOS, 1802-1894

†IN —BUTLER UNIVERSITY, Kossuth Foundation, Hungarian Research Library, Indianapolis, 46208.
Notes: Hungarian culture, social sciences, American-Hungarian relations, and Hungarians in the US.

†NY —AMERICAN HUNGARIAN LIBRARY AND HISTORICAL SOCIETY, 215 East 82 St, New York, 10028.

KOUDELKA COLLECTION

MA —BOSTON PUBLIC LIBRARY, Music Division, 666 Boylston St, Box 286, Boston, 02117. Ruth Bleecker, Cur of Music
Notes: The library acquired the Koudelka Collection at a Berlin auction of the Koudelka estate in 1859 with funds provided by Joshua Bates and his friends. The collection contains some rare musical works from the fifteenth to the eighteenth centuries as well as contemporary imprints and reference materials.

KOUSSEVITZKY, SERGE

DC —LIBRARY OF CONGRESS, Music Division, Washington, 20540.
Holdings: Cat Mss Maps Pix Slides Microforms
Notes: Serge Koussevitzky (1874-1951), conductor of the Boston Symphony Orchestra from 1924-49. In 1950 he established a permanent endowment at the Library of Congress to commission new musical compositions and continue the annual programming of commissions begun by the original Koussevitzky Foundation formed in Brookline, Massachusetts, in 1942. All original scores commissioned by both foundations as well as a small number of pieces owned or written by the conductor have been brought together at the Library of Congress in the Koussevitzky Archives. This important collection contains mss of nearly 150 20th-century composers, some of whom are represented by several works.

MA —BOSTON PUBLIC LIBRARY, Rare Books and Manuscripts, Copley Square, Boston, 02117. Laura V Monti, Keeper of Rare Books
Holdings: Mss Pix
Notes: Incl memorabilia, annotated scores of works he conducted, books, archival materials, etc. Gift of Mrs Olga Koussevitzky in 1974.

KOVACS, ERNIE, 1919-1962

CA —UNIVERSITY OF CALIFORNIA, LOS ANGELES, Research Library, Dept of Special Collections, 405 Hilgard Ave, Los Angeles, 90024. Edward Shreeves, Chairman, Bibliographers Group; David S Zeidberg, Head
Notes: 45 linear feet of scripts, recordings, and "Profuselies" of his television shows.

KOZELKA, PAUL

AZ —ARIZONA STATE UNIVERSITY, Library, Tempe, 85287. Marilyn Wurzburger, Special Collections Librn
Holdings: Vols (108) Pix
Notes: Collection covers various aspects of Children's Theatre from 1944 through the present. Areas of emphasis incl International and National Child Drama Associations, award-winning theatres, educational programs, regional groups and prominent figures in Children's Theatre incl: Irene Vickers Baker, Isabel Burger, Virginia Lee Comer, Rita Criste, Moses Goldberg, Kenneth Graham, Aurand Harris, Paul Kozelka, George Latshaw, Rosemary Musil, Sara Spencer, Winifred Ward, Susan Zeder and Lin Wright. Publications incl newsletters, research papers, bibliographies and records of the proceedings of the Children's Theatre Association of America. 80 linear feet of scripts, documents, publications, films, tapes (oral history) programs, correspondence, photographs, working papers and clippings. Partially indexed; finding guides available.

KRAMER, STANLEY

CA —UNIVERSITY OF CALIFORNIA, LOS ANGELES, Research Library, Dept of Special Collections, 405 Hilgard Ave, Los Angeles, 90024. Edward Shreeves, Chairman, Bibliographers Group; David S Zeidberg, Head
Holdings: Mss Pix
Notes: 200 linear feet of production files for most of his films; correspondence.

KRAMM, JOSEPH

MA —BOSTON UNIVERSITY, Mugar Memorial Library, Special Collections Dept, 771 Commonwealth Ave, Boston, 02215. Howard B Gotlieb, Dir
Holdings: Cat Mss Pix
Notes: Mss, correspondence, etc collected in depth; incl publications by or about.

KRAPPE, ALEXANDER HAGGERTY

IL —SOUTHERN ILLINOIS UNIVERSITY, CARBONDALE, Delyte W Morris Library, Carbondale, 62901.
Holdings: Vols 1000 Cat
Notes: The Alexander Haggerty Krappe Folklore Collection is a scholar's working library; international in scope. Strong in monographs of the 19th through mid-20th centuries. A complete set of off-prints of Dr Krappe's voluminous periodical output have been bound in 3 large vols. There is a mimeographed checklist of the collection which is not maintained as a separate collection.

KRASNER, WILLIAM

MO —WASHINGTON UNIVERSITY, Libraries, Special Collections Dept, Campus Box 1061, St Louis, 63130.
Notes: A major collection, incl mss, correspondence, literary papers, photographs, etc. Described in *Special Collections: an Annotated Guide to the Holdings of the Manuscript Division and the University Archives and Research Collection.*

KRASNER, LOUIS

NY —SYRACUSE UNIVERSITY LIBRARIES, Ernest S Bird Library, George Arents Research Library for Special Collections, Syracuse, 13210. Carolyn A Davis, Manuscripts Librn; Amy S Doherty, University Archivist; Mark F Weimer, Rare Book Librn
Notes: Incl the Louis Krasner Collection, with original scores by classic composers and an original death mask of Alban Berg made by Anna Mahler. There is also a collection of Napoleana.

KRAUS, KARL, 1874-1936

CT —TRINITY COLLEGE LIBRARY, 300 Summit St, Hartford, 06106. Ralph S Emerick, Librn
Holdings: // Cat
Notes: Incl a run of *Die Fackel.*

IL —NORTHWESTERN UNIVERSITY, Library, Special Collections Dept, 1937 Sheridan Rd, Evanston, 60201. R Russell Maylone, Cur
Holdings: Vols 75 Cat
Notes: Incl a complete set and an index to *Die Fackel.* Additional material in general collection.

MA —BRANDEIS UNIVERSITY, Goldfarb Library, 415 South St, Waltham, 02154. Bessie Hahn, Dir
Notes: Oskar Samek Collecion of Karl Krausiana. Approx 10 linear ft of books by and about Karl Kraus as well as some original mss. Kraus was a leading Austrian poet and satirist. Access to the collection is through the Special Collections Card Catalog.

MO —WASHINGTON UNIVERSITY, Libraries, Campus Box 1061, Saint Louis, 63130.
Holdings: 4500 Vols
Notes: The private library of the late Gert von Gontard. Incl works on art, literature (especially German), music, and theater. Contains 1200 vols Goetheana, with first editions, autographed letters and original drawings by Goethe. Also material on the Austrian writer Karl Kraus and the Belgian artist Frans Masereel.

KRAUS-BOELTE, MARIA

NY —ADELPHI UNIVERSITY, Library, Garden City, 11530. Jerome Yavarkovsky, Dean of Libraries
Holdings: // Mss
Notes: The collection includes 183 items consisting primarily of letters and some memorabilia. Mrs Maria Kraus-Boelte was one of the earliest and most influential apostles of the kindergarten in the US employing the Froebelian method. Collection contains letters to a pupil Carrie Coit Meleney and memorabilia relating to the Krus Alumni Kindergarten Association.

KRAUSE, HERBERT

SD —AUGUSTANA COLLEGE, Mikkelsen Library & Learning Resource Center, Center for Western Studies, Sioux Falls, 57197. Ronelle Thompson, Dir Library
Holdings: Vols (40,000) Cat Mss Maps Pix Slides Microforms
Budget: ($130,000)
Notes: The Center for Western Studies, located in the Mikkelsen Library, is an archival and research agency of Augustana College. Dedicated to the history and culture of the Great Plains and the Trans-Mississippi West, the Center collects and preserves materials relating to Plains Indians, immigrant settlers, Norwegiana, Western Americana, Herbert Krause, Frederick Manfred, Donald Parker, Richard F Pettigrew, Augustana College, the Episcopal Diocese of South Dakota, the South Dakota District of the American Lutheran Church, the South Dakota Penitentiary and Minnehaha County.

KRAUSS, FRIEDRICH SALOMO, 1859-1938

CA —UNIVERSITY OF CALIFORNIA, LOS ANGELES, Research Library, Dept of Special Collections, 405 Hilgard Ave, Los Angeles, 90024. Edward Shreeves, Chairman, Bibliographers Group; David S Zeidberg, Head
Holdings: Vols 10 Mss
Notes: Incl 18 linear feet of mss and letters relating to Slavic and Balkan folklore and ethnology.

KREDEL, FRITZ

CT —YALE UNIVERSITY, Beinecke Rare Book & Manuscripts Library, Wall & High St, New Haven, 06520. Louis A Martz, Dir

CT —YALE UNIVERSITY, Sterling Memorial Library, Arts of the Book Collection, New Haven, 06520. Gay Walker, Cur
Notes: Most all illustrated books, engraved blocks, and drawings.

KREISLER, FRITZ

DC —LIBRARY OF CONGRESS, Music Division, Washington, 20540.
Holdings: Cat Mss Maps Pix Slides Microforms

KRENEK, ERNST

CA —UNIVERSITY OF CALIFORNIA, SAN DIEGO, Central University Library, Mandeville Dept of Special Collections, La Jolla, 92093. Lynda Corey Claassen, Head
Notes: Manuscript Collection incl the correspondence and writings of composer Ernst Krenek and musicologist Peter Yates.

DC —LIBRARY OF CONGRESS, Music Division, Washington, 20540.
Notes: Papers and recordings of composer Arnold Schoenberg. Extensive correspondence with other composers, writers, etc.

KRIEGSSPIEL see War Games

KRIPPNER, STANLEY

OH —KENT STATE UNIVERSITY, Libraries, Dept of Special Collections, Kent, 44242. Dean H Keller, Cur
Holdings: Vols 20 Cat Mss
Notes: Collection contains over 350 off-prints of articles by Krippner.

KROCK, ARTHUR, 1886-1974

NJ —PRINCETON UNIVERSITY, Seeley G Mudd Manuscript Library, Public Affairs Papers Collection, Princeton, 08544. Nancy Bressler, Cur
Holdings: Mss
Notes: Incl 93 boxes. A guide (946 p) is available in the Library.

KROEBER, ALFRED LOUIS

CA —UNIVERSITY OF CALIFORNIA, BERKELEY, Bancroft Library, Manuscripts Division, Berkeley, 94720. James D Hart, Dir
Holdings: Cat Mss Pix
Notes: Scientific and personal papers.

KROETSCH, ROBERT

AB —UNIVERSITY OF CALGARY, Libraries, Special Collections Div, 2500 University Dr, Calgary, T2N 1N4, Can.
Holdings: Cat Mss
Notes: Research notes, drafts, galley sheets, proofs and reviews, of Robert Kroestch's novels, poetry, short stories, and critical essays, as well as his editiorial correspondence for *Boundary 2,* (1945-1976).

KRON, GABRIEL

NY —UNION COLLEGE, Schaffer Library, Archives of Science and Technology, Schenectady, 12308. Ellen Fladger, Archivist
Notes: Papers etc.

KRONENBERGER, LOUIS, 1904-1980

MA —BRANDEIS UNIVERSITY, Goldfarb Library, 415 South St, Waltham, 02154. Bessie Hahn, Dir
Notes: 5 linear ft of literary mss.

KRUSI, HERMANN

NY —STATE UNIVERSITY OF NEW YORK, COLLEGE AT OSWEGO, Penfield Library, Oswego, 13126. Anne Commerton, Dir
Holdings: Cat Mss
Notes: Krusi was an educator.

KRULAK, VICTOR H., 1913-

CA —HOOVER INSTITUTION ON WAR, REVOLUTION & PEACE, Stanford University, Stanford, 94305. Milorad M Drachkovitch, Archivist
Notes: Papers of Victor H Krulak, Lt Gen, US Marine Corps, and vice-president of Copley News Service, incl writings, speeches, interviews, and newspapers clippings, 1958-1977, relating to Marine Corps activities in China in the 1930s and during World War II, the Korean War, and the Vietnamese Conflict. 1 ms box.

KRUTCH, JOSEPH WOOD

DC —LIBRARY OF CONGRESS, Manuscript Division, Washington, 20540. John C Broderick, Chief
Holdings: Vols 1500 Cat
Notes: Papers of Joseph Wood Krutch, incl correspondence.

KU KLUX KLAN

IN —BALL STATE UNIVERSITY, University Libraries, Special Collections Dept, University Ave, Muncie, 47306. David C Tambo, Head of Special Collections
Holdings: Vols 81 Cat Mss Pix
Notes: Ephemera, manuals, mss, pictures, etc. Incl catalog.

IN —WABASH CARNEGIE PUBLIC LIBRARY, Oral History Program, 188 W Hill St, Wabash, 46992. Linda Robertson, Librn
Holdings: Cat
Budget: $100
Notes: The collection will be of major concern to those interested in local history; however, effort is made to get information on Ku Klux Klan activities in Indiana, Spanish-American War remembrances, and depression days, as well as local history. The Honeywell Company has expanded the collection by interviewing former employees about the company and its founder, Mark C Honeywell. Collection is cited in the *Indiana Magazine of History,* vol LXVIII, no 4 (December 1974): 315-337.

MI —MICHIGAN STATE UNIVERSITY, Libraries, Special Collections Div, East Lansing, 48824. Jannette Fiore, Librn
Notes: Ku Klux Klan pamphlets, magazines, and ephemera dating from the late 1920s and early 1930s. Incl issues of the *Kourier,* the official monthly magazine of the Klan; a Klan newspaper published in Alma, Mich; position pamphlets and leaflets; advertisements for Klan merchandise; and Michigan Klan ephemera.

NC —DUKE UNIVERSITY, William R Perkins Library, Manuscript Dept, Durham, 27706. Ellen Gartrell, Cur of Mss
Holdings: Cat Mss
Notes: Papers.

PA —BALCH INSTITUTE FOR ETHNIC STUDIES, Library, 18 S Seventh St, Philadelphia, 19106. R Joseph Anderson, Library Dir
Holdings: Vols 50 Cat

SC —COLLEGE OF CHARLESTON LIBRARY, Special Collections Dept, Charleston, 29401.
Notes: Papers, ca 1920s, incl a circular regarding "The Affair at Mer Rouge," condemning Irish and Italian Catholics as agents of the Pope, seeking to "make America Catholic" by undermining education, "law and order," and the Volstead Act.

TX —TEXAS A&M UNIVERSITY, Sterling C Evans Library, Special Collections Div, College Station, 77843. Donald H Dyal, Librn
Holdings: Uncat Mss Pix Microforms
Notes: About 350 items. Now in circulating collection.

KUCHEAN LANGUAGE see Tokharian Languages

KUEKES, EDWARD D.

OH —OHIO STATE UNIVERSITY, Library for Communication and Graphic Arts, 242 W 18th St, Columbus, 43210. Lucy S Caswell, Curator
Notes: The original works of editorial cartoonists Art Poinier, Scott Willis, Brian Basset, Billy Ireland, Frank Williams, Charles Werner, Ned Beard, L D Warren, Edward D Kuekes, Ray Osrin, Mike Peters, Draper Hill, Eugene Craig and Bert Whitman.

KUH, FREDERICK R.

DC —GEORGE WASHINGTON UNIVERSITY, Gelman Library, 2130 H St NW, Washington, 20052.
Holdings: // Cat Mss Pix
Notes: The Frederick Kuh papers cover the period 1924-1967, although the preponderance of mss range from 1938-1967. Kuh was a foreign correspondent for UPI and then the Chicago *Sun-Times,* and wrote numerous articles for periodicals, notably the *New Republic, The Nation, and Foreign Report.* The collection includes diaries, biographical information, correspondence, articles, speeches, subject files, misc papers, notebooks, and scrapbooks. Cataloged as a collection with unpublished inventory for access and a name index covering all people mentioned in the diaries and correspondence.

KUHLER, OTTO

MA —BOSTON UNIVERSITY, Mugar Memorial Library, Special Collections Dept, 771 Commonwealth Ave, Boston, 02215. Howard B Gotlieb, Dir
Holdings: Mss Pix
Notes: Mss, correspondence, etc collected in depth; incl publications by or about.

MI —UNIVERSITY OF MICHIGAN, Engineering-Transportation Library, 312 Undergraduate Library, Ann Arbor, 48109. Sharon A Balius, Assoc Librn
Holdings: Pix
Notes: Kuhler was the designer of the first streamlined steam locomotives. The collection contains 100 etchings, watercolors and pen and ink drawings.

KULANAPAN INDIANS see Pomo Indians

KUMIN, MAXINE

MA —BOSTON UNIVERSITY, Mugar Memorial Library, Special Collections Dept, 771 Commonwealth Ave, Boston, 02215. Howard B Gotlieb, Dir
Holdings: Cat Mss

†TX —UNIVERSITY OF TEXAS LIBRARIES, General Libraries, Humanities Research Center, PO Box 7219, Austin, 78712. John Chalmers, Librn
Notes: Complete archives of the Pulitzer Prize poet, Anne Sexton (1928-1974). Includes some of her suicide notes; also correspondence with Maxine Kumin, another Pulitzer winner.

KUMYK LANGUAGE AND LITERATURE

NY —NEW YORK PUBLIC LIBRARY, Oriental Div, Fifth Ave & 42 St, New York,

KUMYK LANGUAGE AND LITERATURE (cont.)

10018. E Christian Filstrup, Chief
Holdings: Cat Mss Microforms
Budget: ($56,455)
Notes: Published catalog of holdings.

KUNICZAK, W. S.

MA —BOSTON UNIVERSITY, Mugar Memorial Library, Special Collections Dept, 771 Commonwealth Ave, Boston, 02215. Howard B Gotlieb, Dir
Holdings: Cat Mss

KUNITZ, STANLEY JASSPON

NV —UNIVERSITY OF NEVADA, RENO, University Library, Special Collections Dept, Reno, 89557. Robert E Blesse, Head
Holdings: Vols (32) Cat
Notes: Includes individual works by author in all editions including translations; also prefaces, introductions, published correspondence, appearances in anthologies, periodicals, etc. Bibliographical research collection, part of Modern Authors Collection. Other appearances 420 cataloged.

KUNSTLER, WILLIAM

MA —BOSTON UNIVERSITY, Mugar Memorial Library, Special Collections Dept, 771 Commonwealth Ave, Boston, 02215. Howard B Gotlieb, Dir
Holdings: Cat Mss

KUPER, LEO

IL —NORTHWESTERN UNIVERSITY, Melville J Herskovits Library of African Studies, Evanston, 60201. Hans E Panofsky, Cur
Holdings: Vols (85,000) Mss
Budget: ($70,000)
Notes: Papers, etc. Mostly southern Africa. See also entry under Africa.

KURDISH LANGUAGE AND LITERATURE

MA —HARVARD UNIVERSITY LIBRARY, Widener Library, Middle Eastern Dept, Cambridge, 02138. David H Partington, Librn
Holdings: Vols (70,000) Cat
Budget: ($55,000)
Notes: The Middle Eastern Collections consist of separately housed and cataloged books in Arabic, Turkish, Persian, Kurdish, and Urdu. Approx 4000 titles are added per year in the principal subject fields of language, literature, Islamic studies, and the modern social science disciplines. The Armenian collection is especially strong in classical and medieval texts.

KURMANJI LANGUAGE AND LITERATURE see Kurdish Language and Literature

KURTH, BETTY, 1878-1948

MA —BRANDEIS UNIVERSITY, Goldfarb Library, 415 South St, Waltham, 02154. Bessie Hahn, Dir
Notes: Betty Kurth Collection: 2 linear ft of mss and book material relating to the author's first published book written pseudonymously in Vienna at the turn of the century. Apparently the book caused a controversy at the time. This collection is unprocessed, spring 1984.

KURTH, HELMUTH

DC —LIBRARY OF CONGRESS, Prints & Photographs Div, Washington, 20540.
Notes: Personal photo albums of Hermann Goring provide detailed coverage of his activities during World War I and the years 1933-42. Biographical photographs of Hermann Goring incl pictures by Helmuth Kurth and Eitel Lange.

KURZMAN, DAN

MA —BOSTON UNIVERSITY, Mugar Memorial Library, Special Collections Dept, 771 Commonwealth Ave, Boston, 02215. Howard B Gotlieb, Dir
Holdings: Cat Mss Pix
Notes: Mss, correspondence, etc collected in depth; incl publications by or about.

KUWAIT

CA —HOOVER INSTITUTION ON WAR, REVOLUTION & PEACE, Stanford University, Stanford, 94305. Peter Duignan, Cur; Karen Fung, Deputy Cur
Holdings: Vols (100,000)
Notes: For fully description of collection, see Hoover Institution entry under Near East.

KYGER, JOANNE

BC —SIMON FRASER UNIVERSITY, Library, Burnaby, V5A 1S6, Can. Percilla Groves, Special Collections Librn
Holdings: // Cat
Notes: Letters from Gary Snyder to Joanne Kyger, 1959-1960, and carbon copies of Kyger's letters to Snyder.

L

LABAN, JUANA DE

KS —WICHITA PUBLIC LIBRARY, Art & Music Division, 223 S Main, Wichita, 67202. Leonard Messineo, Jr, Head, Art & Music Division; Deborah Hamilton, Special Collections Librn
Holdings: Uncat Audiotapes Vidoetape Pix
Notes: Alice Bauman Dance Symposia Collection. Contains 300 hours of audio tapes, 1 hour-long video tape, several hundred photographs, and fugitive material of the American Dance Symposia held in Wichita from 1968-1972. The symposia covered all dance idioms-ballet, modern, jazz, folk, ethnic, dance education and therapy-and featured such notable figures such as Leonide Massine, Martha Hill, William Christensen, Alfonso Cimber, Toni Intravaia, James Clouser, Eleo Pomare, Juana de Laban, and many others. Characterized by the *Kansas City Star* as the "most distinguished faculties of fine artists ever assembled in the contemporary world of dance."

LABANOTATION

CA —CALIFORNIA INSTITUTE OF THE ARTS, Library, 24700 McBean Pkwy, Valencia, 91355. James Elrod, Dir
Holdings: Vols (61,000) Cat
Budget: ($2868)
Notes: Incl classical and modern dance forms.

NY —NEW YORK PUBLIC LIBRARY, Performing Arts Research Center, Dance Collection, 111 Amsterdam Ave, New York, 10023. Genevieve Oswald, Cur
Notes: Multi-media collection with full documentation on various systems devised to record dance movement. Includes treatises and technical manuals, as well as over 480 dance notation scores recording the choreography of specific dances--ballets, modern dance works, musical comedies, folk and social dances.

OH —OHIO STATE UNIVERSITY, William Oxley Thompson Memorial Library, 1858 Neil Ave Mall, Columbus, 43210. Robert A Tibbetts, Cur of Special Collections
Holdings: Cat Mss
Notes: Dance Notation Bureau collection, incl choreographic scores and papers on systems of notation. Emphasis on Labanotation.

ON —NATIONAL LIBRARY OF CANADA, 395 Wellington St, Ottawa, K1A 0N4, Can. Andre Preibish, Dir
Holdings: Vols 8000
Notes: Includes 100 serial titles, also programs, play bills etc on microfilm. Performing arts collection consists of Canadian titles received on legal deposit and purchased. Areas of concentration: Canadian theatre and dance; European and American performing arts tradition; theatre architecture; stage craft; costume history, dance history and notation etc.

LABELS, INCLUDING TRADE UNION LABELS

CA —UNIVERSITY OF CALIFORNIA, DAVIS, Shields Library, Dept of Special Collections, Davis, 95616. Donald Kunitz, Head; C Danial Elliott, Asst Head
Holdings: Uncat
Notes: Graphic collection of 2500 fruit box labels used by California citrus growers in marketing their produce. Also the Cebis Wine Collections (2500 items) incl brochures, wine lists, and labels from Eastern Europe, clippings and brochures on wine by subject. The California Wineries Records (24,000 items) incl correspondence, inspection reports with emphasis on wine production, the physical nature of specific wineries, import/export involvement. These records, filed with the Federal Bureau of Alcohol, Tobacco and Firearms, cover 1922-1953. Wine bottle labels for wines and liquors imported into the United States or bottled here which were submitted to the Alcohol and Tobacco Tax Division of the Internal Revenue Service for approval, 1963-1968, are held in the Wine Bottle Label Collection (21,000).

CA —POMONA PUBLIC LIBRARY, Special Collections, 625 S Garey Ave, PO Box 2271, Pomona, 91766. David Streeter, Librn
Holdings: Cat
Notes: 4000 citrus box labels (world wide) indexed by brand name and packing house; 6000 California wine labels indexed by winery.

DC —LIBRARY OF CONGRESS, Prints & Photographs Div, Washington, 20540.
Notes: Packaging for American tobacco products, 1840s-1880s. Approx 1000 tobacco labels, arranged by subject.

LA —LOUISIANA STATE UNIVERSITY, SHREVEPORT, Library-Archives, 8515 Youree Dr, Shreveport, 71129. Patricia L Meador, Archivist & Asst Librn
Notes: The collection incl 25 linear ft of records of the United Brotherhood of Carpenterss and Joiners of America, Local No 764, (1900-1980), two reels of the Louisiana State Council of Carpenters (1941-1980) and two linear ft of records of the Woman's Union Label League (1907-1940).

MA —MERRIMACK VALLEY TEXTILE MUSEUM, Library, 800 Massachusetts Ave, North Andover, 01845. Clare Sheridan, Librn; Laurence Gross, Cur
Holdings: Vols (35,000) Cat Mss Maps Pix Slides
Notes: *Checklist of Prints, Drawings and Painting in the Merrimack Valley Textile* Museum, Helena E Wright, 1972; *Checklist of Finished Textiles,* Katherine R Koob, 1980; *New City on the Merrimack: Prints of Lawrence 1845-1876,* Helena Wright, 1974; *Homespun to Factory Made: Woolen Textiles in America 1776-1876* (exhibit catalog) 1978; *Textile Technology Prints: A Checklist of Prints, Drawings and Paintings in the Merrimack Valley Textile Museum,* Helena E Wright, 1980; *All Sorts of Good Sufficient Cloth: Linen-making in New England, 1640-1860,* (exhibit catalogue) 1980; *The Merrimack Valley Textile Museum: A Guide to the Manuscript* Collections Helena E Wright, Garland Press 1983.

LABOR

CA —UNIVERSITY OF CALIFORNIA, BERKELEY, University Library, Social Science Library, 30 Stephens Hall, Berkeley, 94720. Bette Erskine, Librn
Holdings: Vols 11,000 Cat Mss Microforms
Notes: The Labor Union Collection consists primarily of labor union journals, newspapers, proceedings and constitutions. Holdings are largely national in scope, with emphasis on Northern California. Approximately 850 current serials are being received. This collection is complemented by labor union materials in the Institute of Industrial Relations Library and in The Bancroft Library, and by holdings in Labor History in the Main Library. Incl 1683 microfilm reels.

CA —UNIVERSITY OF CALIFORNIA, BERKELEY, Institute of Industrial Relations Library, 2521 Channing Way Room 110, Berkeley, 94720. Nanette Sand, Librn
Holdings: Vols 50,000 Cat
Notes: Industrial relations, labor, organizational behavior and related subjects. Institute of Industrial Relations Library has separate card catalog (author, title, subject interfiled) but there is no published catalog. Library has a selective collection of books, periodicals, government documents, union and employer publications, publications of university industrial relations institutes and similar research organizations, pamphlets (50,000), etc. It does not incl archival and manuscript materials, or much material published prior to 1950.

CA —UNIVERSITY OF CALIFORNIA, DAVIS, Shields Library, Dept of Special Collections, Davis, 95616. Donald Kunitz, Head; C Danial Elliott, Asst Head
Notes: Overview of American political movements from the 1890s to the present: socialism, communism, labor, to ecology and women's liberation.

CA —CALIFORNIA STATE UNIVERSITY, FULLERTON, Library, Box 4150, Fullerton, 92634. Linda Herman, Special Collections Librn
Holdings: Cat
Notes: Mostly American (some British) newspapers and journals of labor organizations, late 1800s to present. Incl official labor association publications as well as early Marxist newspapers and bulletins. Approx 800 labor and labor-related publications.

CA —SOUTHERN CALIFORNIA LIBRARY FOR SOCIAL STUDIES & RESEARCH, 6120 S Vermont Ave, Los Angeles, 90044. Sarah Cooper, Dir
Holdings: Vols (15,000) Mss Maps Pix Slides Phonorecords Audiotapes 16mm Films News Clips
Budget: ($30,000)
Notes: Marxist, non-Marxist and anti-Marxist approaches to social change. Other important functions of the library: to make available source materials to those engaged in the Marxist vs no-Marxist dialog; to aid historians, economists, sociologists, writers, students and labor organizations researching the history of grassroots social movements; and to preserve primary and secondary sources on labor, minorities, women and radicalism. Collection incl 50 mss, 75 maps, 500 pictures, 1000 slides, 100 phonorecords, 2000 audiotapes, 50 16mm films and 150, 000 newspaper clippings.

CA —UNIVERSITY OF CALIFORNIA, LOS ANGELES, Research Library, Public Affairs Service, 405 Hilgard Ave, Los Angeles, 90024. Edward Shreeves, Chairman, Bibliographers Group; Eugenia Eaton, Head, Public Affairs Service
Holdings: Uncat
Notes: Current non-governmental English-language pamphlets (192,819), broadsides, leaflets and other ephemera on public affairs, from 1960, representing a wide spectrum of political and social opinions. Social welfare and industrial relations are strong fields. Legal loose-leaf labor services, such as the *Daily Labor Report,* the *Government Employee Relations Report* and the *Labor Relations Reporter,* as well as labor pamphlets from the mid-1940s, reflect a long-standing responsibility to the University's Institute of Industrial Relations.

CA —UNIVERSITY OF SOUTHERN CALIFORNIA, Crocker Business Library, Hoffman Hall, University Park, Los Angeles, 90007. Judith A Truelson, Head Librn
Holdings: Vols (100,000) Cat Microforms
Notes: The Roy P Crocker Library of Business Administration, located in Hoffman Hall, houses more than 100,000 volumes and regularly receives approximately 1500 trade, financial, economics, labor, and general business periodicals and newspapers. The areas of subject concentration include business economics, finance and investments, general management/management theory, international business, finance and management, marketing/food marketing, and quantitative business analysis.

CA —CONTRA COSTA COUNTY LIBRARY, 1750 Oak Park Blvd, Pleasant Hill, 94523. Lyn Talme, Business Specialist
Holdings: Vols (7000)
Notes: Incl 76 periodicals, 1000 corporate annual reports, and 316 telephone directories.

CA —SACRAMENTO PUBLIC LIBRARY, 828 I St, Sacramento, 95814. Dorothy Harvey, Librn, Special Collections
Holdings: Vols (8000) Cat
Notes: Incl 800 periodicals and services. Emphasis is on business subjects and economics and labor. Technology not incl. Incl about 1000 corporation reports.

CA —HOOVER INSTITUTION ON WAR, REVOLUTION & PEACE, Stanford University, Stanford, 94305. Milorad M Drachkovitch, Archivist
Holdings: Mss
Notes: Papers of Alice Park, 1883-1957, incl

LABOR (cont.)

diaries, correspondence, pamphlets, clippings, and leaflets, relating to Pacifism and the peace movement, the Ford Peace Ship Expedition of 1915-1916, feminism, socialism, the labor movement, prison reform, child labor legislation, civil liberties, and a variety of other reform movements in the US. 30 ms boxes, 3 envelopes.

CA —STANFORD UNIVERSITY LIBRARIES, Cecil H Green Library, Stanford, 94305. Michael T Ryan, Cur
Notes: Correspondence, papers, and material on farm labor and migrant workers of recent years. Incl papers of Ernesto Galarza and the National Agricultural Workers Union (NAWU), Fr Victor Salandini and Fr James L Vizzard.
See also entry under Chicano Studies

CO —UNIVERSITY OF COLORADO, Libraries, Western Historical Collections, Boulder, 80309.
Holdings: Cat Mss Pix
Notes: The Archive of the Colorado State Federation of Labor for the period 1896-1955, incl correspondence, reports, publications, photographs, and totaling approx 40 shelf feet. These papers deal with a wide range of labor subjects and extensively document the Federation's legal, social and political activities since the 1890s. A typescript inventory is available.

CT —YALE UNIVERSITY, Social Science Library, 140 Prospect St, New Haven, 06520. Billie I Salter, Librn
Holdings: Cat

DC —AMERICAN FEDERATION OF LABOR-CONGRESS OF INDUSTRIAL ORGANIZATIONS, Library, 815 16th St NW, Washington, 20006.
Holdings: Vols (20,000) Cat Pix Microforms
Notes: Labor, labor unions, and related subjects. Incl letters of Samuel Gompers (microfilm); constitutions and conference proceedings of international unions.

DC —HOWARD UNIVERSITY, Moorland-Spingarn Research Center, 500 Howard Place NW, Washington, 20059. Clifford L Muse, Jr, Acting Dir
Holdings: Vols (106,086) Mss Maps Pix Slides Phonorecords Audiotapes 16mm Films Filmstrips Microforms
Budget: ($854,753)
See also entry under Blacks

DC —INTERNATIONAL LABOR ORGANIZATION, International Labor Office, Washington Branch Library, 1750 New York Ave NW, Rm 330, Washington, 20006. Karen J Mark, Librn
Holdings: Vols (13,500) Cat Pix 16mm Films Monographs
Notes: Wide range of titles dealing with worldwide labor and social matters. The library contains worldwide labor and social matters. The library contains ILO publications and documentation only, dating back to 1919. Also, a collection of ILO films and photos. See *Subject Guide to Publications of the ILO, 1919-1964* and *ILO Catalogue of Publications in Print, 1982* (ILO).

DC —US DEPT OF LABOR, Library, 200 Constitution Ave NW, Washington, 20210. Sabina Jacobson, Dir
Holdings: Vols 535,000 Cat Audiotapes Microforms
Notes: Economics, especially labor, incl much historical material. Receive 3200 current periodical titles.

IL —UNIVERSITY OF ILLINOIS, URBANA/CHAMPAIGN, Institute of Labor and Industrial Relations, Library, 504 E Armory, Champaign, 61820. Margaret A Chaplan, Librn
Holdings: Vols (11,597) Cat Audiotapes Microforms
Budget: ($7500)
Notes: Collection incl four subject areas within industrial relations: collective bargaining and labor-management relations; manpower and labor economics; international and comparative labor movements; and organizational behavior. There is an extensive vertical file containing information on individual labor unions. The resources of the library which are relevant to the study of labor history are described in "Labor History Resources of the University of Illinois," by Patricia Wilson Onsi, *Labor History*, vol 7, Spring 1966, pp 209-215.

IL —LOYOLA UNIVERSITY OF CHICAGO, E M Cudahy Memorial Library, 6525 N Sheridan Rd, Chicago, 60626.
Notes: Dorr E Felt Pamphlet and Clipping Collection. Emphasizes political and economic issues, 1902-35, and documents Illinois Manufacturers Association Conference, September 8-9, 1919; Air Board of Chicago, April 16, 1921-August 1, 1930; Allied Debts to the US, May 15, 1923-September 30, 1926; Bolshevism, Communism, "Red" Russia, 1924-27; Child Labor Bill, March 30, 1915, 1914-20; Labor, March, 1902-March, 1932; Railroad Strike, August 25, 1916-August 7, 1920; The War, August, 1914-October 23, 1930; War Industries Commission, June, 1918-November 23, 1928. A pamphlet list is available for each topic.

IL —NORTHWESTERN UNIVERSITY, Library, Special Collections Dept, 1937 Sheridan Rd, Evanston, 60201. R Russell Maylone, Cur
Holdings: Vols (14,000) Cat
Notes: Periodicals and pamphlets concerning many social and political movements in the 20th century, with emphasis on anarachism, struggles of the working class, women's rights, and student protest of the 1960s. Foreign material incl. An additional 10,000 pieces arranged by subject.

IL —UNIVERSITY OF ILLINOIS, URBANA/CHAMPAIGN, Library, Illinois Historical Survey Library, 1408 W Gregory Dr, 1A Library, Urbana, 61801.
Holdings: Vols 50 Cat Mss Pix Microforms
Notes: Important ms collections on the labor movement and radicalism incl: Adolph Germer, papers, 1918, 1928, 1930-32, 44 folders; Thomas J Morgan, 1880-1910, 64 folders, 19 volumes; John H Walker, papers, 1910-1955, 66 boxes. Guide to the collections published in 1976.

IN —INDIANA STATE UNIVERSITY, EVANSVILLE, Library, 8600 University Blvd, Evansville, 47712. Gina R Walker, Acting Archivist
Holdings: Vols 50 Cat Mss Pix Slides Audiotapes
Notes: Daily radio programs broadcast (1949-1954) over several Evansville, Indiana, stations concerning activities of the local United Electrical and Radio and Machine Workers of America union; other local union news; state, national, and international events; editorial commentary. Prepared and presented by Sadelle Berger, community leader. 4 document cases. Also materials collected during year-long Indiana Labor History Project. Oral history interviews, photographs, slides, brochures, newspaper clippings.

IN —PURDUE UNIVERSITY LIBRARIES, Graduate School of Management, Krannert Library, West Lafayette, 47907. Gordon Law, Librn
Holdings: Vols (115,000) Cat Microforms
Budget: ($71,900)
Notes: There is an extensive collection of corporate reports and labor information material (some 110,000 items). Over 2500 periodicals are currently received.

MD —INTERNATIONAL ASSOCIATION OF CHIEFS OF POLICE, 13 Firstfield Rd, PO Box 6010, Gaithersburg, 20760.
Holdings: Vols (6000) Cat Mss
Notes: Collection heavy in criminal investigation, crime prevention, police administration and management. Collecting in public sector labor relations, family violence, terrorism.

†MA —JOHN F KENNEDY LIBRARY, Columbia Point, Boston, 02125. Dan H Fenn Jr, Dir
Holdings: / / Cat Microforms
Notes: Copies of AFL-CIO press releases and records relating to legislation, relations with the Federal government, and international affairs, 1955-1969. 9 rolls of microfilm. Holdings are described in "Historical Materials in the John F Kennedy Library." Copies may be obtained by writing the Research Archivist.

MA —HARVARD UNIVERSITY LIBRARY, John F Kennedy School of Government Library, Manpower and Industrial Relations Collection, Littauer Library, Cambridge, 02138. James C Damaskos, Librn
Holdings: Vols (120,000) Cat
Notes: Major strength is in publications of labor unions and government documents relating to labor.

MA —MERRIMACK VALLEY TEXTILE MUSEUM, Library, 800 Massachusetts Ave, North Andover, 01845. Clare Sheridan, Librn; Laurence Gross, Cur
Holdings: Vols (35,000) Cat Mss Maps Pix Slides
Notes: *Checklist of Prints, Drawings and Painting in the Merrimack Valley Textile* Museum, Helena E Wright, 1972; *Checklist of Finished Textiles,* Katherine R Koob, 1980; *New City on the Merrimack: Prints of Lawrence 1845-1876,* Helena Wright, 1974; *Homespun to Factory Made: Woolen Textiles in America 1776-1876* (exhibit catalog) 1978; *Textile Technology Prints: A Checklist of Prints, Drawings and Paintings in the Merrimack Valley Textile Museum,* Helena E Wright, 1980; *All Sorts of Good Sufficient Cloth: Linen-making in New England, 1640-1860,* (exhibit catalogue) 1980; *The Merrimack Valley Textile Museum: A Guide to the Manuscript* Collections Helena E Wright, Garland Press 1983.

MI —WAYNE STATE UNIVERSITY, Walter P Reuther Library, Archives of Labor & Urban Affairs, Detroit, 48202. Philip Mason, Dir
Holdings: Vols Cat Mss Pix Slides Phonorecords Audiotapes Videotapes
Budget: ($450,000)
Notes: 95,000 mss; 750,000 photos; cartoons and other illustrations; 20,000 tapes; films; 20,000 books, journals, and pamphlets. See Warner Pflug, *A Guide to the Archives of Labor History and Urban Affairs* (Wayne State University Press, 1974). Philip P Mason, "The Archives of Labor and Urban Affairs, Walter P Reuther Library, Wayne State University." *Labor History,* Number 4, Vol 23, Fall 1982.

MI —SUOMI COLLEGE, Finnish-American Historical Archives, Hancock, 49930. Kenneth Niemi, Archives Librn
Notes: Collection incl 8000 vols, 152,000 mss, 2000 photographs, 760 audiotapes; microforms and maps; 14,000 holdings are cataloged. Subject interests: coop movement, labor, pioneer library of rare books and church records, socialist and communist movements, temperance societies. Special Collections: Finnish language newspapers (includes 100 titles from 1876-present); Suomi Synod Archives; Finnish-American Oral History.

MI —WESTERN MICHIGAN UNIVERSITY, Business Library, N Hall, Kalamazoo, 49008. David H McKee, Head
Holdings: Vols (71,977) Cat Phonorecords Microforms
Notes: Incl 14,570 vols of bound periodicals, 33,041 monographs, 14,605 government documents, 1796 microfilm and 7u965 microfiche/microcards. Large collection of corporate annual reports is separate.

MN —MINNESOTA HISTORICAL SOCIETY LIBRARY, 690 Cedar St, Saint Paul, 55101. Patricia C Harpole, Chief of Reference Library; Bonnie G Wilson, Head of Special Libraries
Notes: Activities of such groups as the Women's International League for Peace and Freedom, labor organizations, and the Izaak Walton League are discussed in interviews.

MO —UNIVERSITY OF MISSOURI-SAINT LOUIS, Thomas Jefferson Library, Manuscript and Historical Society Collection, 8001 Natural Bridge Rd, Saint Louis, 63121.
Holdings: Mss Pix Tapes
Notes: ca

NJ —RUTGERS, THE STATE UNIVERSITY OF NEW JERSEY, Institute of

LABOR (cont.)

Management & Labor Relations, Ryders Lane & Clifton Ave, New Brunswick, 08903. Bernard F Downey, Librn
Holdings: Vols (18,530) Cat Slides Phonorecords 16mm Films Filmstrips
Budget: ($7300)
Notes: Separate card catalog for collection. Particular emphasis on dispute settlement. Strong collection on public sector labor relations, emphasizing New Jersey publications.

NY —STATE UNIVERSITY OF NEW YORK, Maritime College, Stephen B Luce Library, Fort Schuyler, Bronx, 10465. Richard H Corson, Librn
Holdings: Vols (68,000) Cat Audiotapes Videotapes 16mm Films Filmstrips Microforms
Budget: ($90,000)
Notes: Incl full runs of newspapers of the major maritime unions on microfilm.

NY —CORNELL UNIVERSITY, New York State School of Industrial & Labor Relations, Martin P Catherwood Library, Ives Hall, Ithaca, 14853. Shirley F Harper, Dir
Holdings: Vols (150,000) Cat Mss Pix Phonorecords Microforms
Notes: Collection incl approx 1000 periodicals and union journals currently received, and ms collections of labor unions, arbitrators, and scholars. 6000 linear ft. *Library Catalog of the New York State School of Industrial and Labor Relations* (Boston: G K Hall, 1967), 12 volumes; *Cumulation of the Library Catalog Supplements of the New York State School of Industrial and Labor Relations* (Boston: G K Hall, 1976), 8 volumes.

NY —AMALGAMATED CLOTHING & TEXTILE WORKERS UNION, Research Dept Library, 15 Union Sq, New York, 10003. Mohammad Homayon Pour, Librn
Holdings: Vols (3200) Cat Pix
Notes: Collective bargaining and economic conditions in the men's and boys' apparel industries and the textile industry.

NY —CENTER FOR LABOR STUDIES, SUNY, Empire State College, Labor College Library, 330 W 42nd St, New York, 10036. Jayne Adler, Librn
Holdings: Vols (3000) Cat Periodicals Videotapes VF
Budget: ($4000)
Notes: Periodical holdings incl a cross-section of trade union newspapers, scholarly labor serials, and alternative press journals.

NY —NEW YORK PUBLIC LIBRARY, Research Libraries, Economic & Public Affairs Div, Fifth Ave & 42 St, New York, 10018. Edward DiRoma, Chief
Holdings: Vols (1,500,000) Cat Microforms

NY —NEW YORK PUBLIC LIBRARY, Research Libraries, General Research Div, Fifth Ave & 42 St, New York, 10018. Keith McKinney, Assistant Div Chief
Holdings: Cat
Notes: Current periodicals. Subjects incl advertising, business and professional periodicals, international affairs, labor and trade unions, political and social sciences, humanities in general. Division holds 10,000 titles.

NY —ROCKEFELLER UNIVERSITY, Rockefeller Archive Center, Hillcrest, Pocantico Hills, North Tarrytown, 10591. Joseph W Ernst, Dir; J William Hess, Assoc Dir
Notes: Papers relative to the Rockefeller Family, Foundations, University, and other specific enterprises and contributions to particular areas of social, physical, educational, and historic reform, preservation, conservation, or development. Extensive records of administrative, financial, physical, or intellectual relationships.

NC —GREENSBORO PUBLIC LIBRARY, Business Library, 201 Greene St, Drawer X-4, Greensboro, 27402. Lebby B Lamb, Business Librn
Holdings: Vols (6000) Cat Microforms
Budget: ($12,000)

OH —AKRON-SUMMIT COUNTY PUBLIC LIBRARY, Business, Labor & Government Div, 55 S Main St, Akron, 44326. William G Johnson, Head
Holdings: Vols (10,000) Cat Microforms
Budget: ($20,000)

OH —CLEVELAND PUBLIC LIBRARY, Business, Economics and Labor Department, 325 Superior Ave, Cleveland, 44114. Joan Sorger, Head
Holdings: Vols (115,703) Cat
Notes: Currently receiving over 1700 periodicals and 1300 serial titles; 1000 individual trade, industrial and professional directories, worldwide; 324 file drawers annual reports of old companies, many local; 24 drawers historical information on Cleveland companies. Annual reports, 10-K's, Proxy Statements (disclosure SEC filings on fiche); over 200 loose-leaf services; 1700 current telephone and city directories. Emphasis on current material. Areas of special strength are banking, investments, marketing and management. Also strong insurance, accounting, real estate and transportation collections. Computerized sources available incl Dow Jones News Service and a variety of Dialog business-related databases.

PA —BALCH INSTITUTE FOR ETHNIC STUDIES, Library, 18 S Seventh St, Philadelphia, 19106. R Joseph Anderson, Library Dir

PA —SCRANTON PUBLIC LIBRARY, Vine & N Washington Sts, Scranton, 18503. Thomas McHale, Dir
Holdings: Vols (975) Cat
Budget: ($6000)

TX —ECTOR COUNTY LIBRARY, Department of Business and Technology, 321 W 5th St, Odessa, 79760. Pat Jones, Dept Head
Notes: 25,000 Corporate Annual Reports microfilmed reports are complete from 1978-1983. 200 vertical files, 30 periodicals. Collection includes the subjects of Business, Management, Real Estate Accounting, Land Economics, Labor Economics, Finance, Personal Finance and Environmental Economics. Also included are stock and dividend reports, commodities and bond reports as well as business rankings. All items are referenced and cataloged.

WI —UNIVERSITY OF WISCONSIN, GREEN BAY, Library/Learning Center, Green Bay, 54301. Marian A Gould, Acting Dir, Special Collections/University Archives
Holdings: Vols 700 // Cat
Notes: This represents the collection of Leon Kramer, "idealist, philosophical anarchist and bookseller." Much of the material concerns radical literature and small socialist and communist parties in the US, although there is a considerable amount of books, booklets, and pamphlets published in Germany, Italy, and other parts of Europe. Incl uncounted pamphlets.

WI —STATE HISTORICAL SOCIETY OF WISCONSIN, Archives, 816 State St, Madison, 53706. Harold L Miller, Reference Archivist
Holdings: Mss Pix Microforms
Notes: Records and papers documenting the history of the labor and Socialist movements in the United States from 1850s to the present. Incl are records of labor and socialist organizations incl American Federation of Labor and the Socialist Labor Party, and papers of individual labor and socialist leaders such as Morris Hillquit and John L Lewis. Collections are described in *A Guide to Labor Papers in the State Historical Society of Wisconsin* (1978) and in current accession notes in the *Wisconsin Magazine of History.* Major collections are also listed in Hamer, *Guide to Manuscripts and Archives in the United States,* (1961) and in the *National Union Catalog of Manuscript Collections,* (1959-date).

WI —STATE HISTORICAL SOCIETY OF WISCONSIN, Library, Newspaper and Periodicals Section, 816 State St, Madison, 53706. James P Danky, Librn
Notes: One of the largest collections of Labor newspapers in the US. Holdings described in *Labor papers on Microfilm: A Combined List,* (Madison, The Society, 1965) and in Naas and Sakr's *American Labor Union Periodicals: A Guide to Their Location.* Only positive microfilm circulates on ILL.

WI —UNIVERSITY OF WISCONSIN, MADISON, School for Workers Library, 610 Langdon St, Madison, 53706. Eleanor Nugent, Program Coord
Holdings: Vols 2000 Cat

WI —UNIVERSITY OF WISCONSIN, MILWAUKEE, Library, Box 604, Milwaukee, 53201. William C Roselle, Dir
Holdings: Cat Microforms
Notes: Wisconsin Legislative Reference Bureau Clippings File. Special strength in a collection mostly of Wisconsin emphasis. 440 reels of 16mm microfilm. A subject-chronological arrangement (approximately 1200 subjects covering the years from the 1890s through 1970) of pamphlets and a variety of fugitive materials and of clippings from national and Wisconsin newspapers, populr magazines and scholarly journals, and federal, state, and local government documents.

PR —CARIBBEAN REGIONAL LIBRARY, General Library, University of Puerto Rico, Rio Piedras, (Mailing add: PO Box 21917, University Station, San Juan, 00931). Carmen M Costa de Ramos, Librn
Holdings: Vols (115,605) Cat Maps Pix Microforms
Notes: Collection is specialized in the Caribbean with emphasis in the areas of interest to developing countries: social sciences, politics, economics, labor, education, commerce, tourism, literature, etc. The *Current Caribbean Bibliography* is compiled at the Caribbean Regional Library, with card contributions from all countries of the Caribbean; it also lists all the new additions to the library.

ON —MCMASTER UNIVERSITY, Mills Memorial Library, Div of Archives & Research Collections, Hamilton, L8S 4L6, Can. G R Hill, Univ Librn
Holdings: Mss
Notes: Archives and records of several constituents of Canadian business and labour: General Steel Wares (42 linear ft); Hamilton and District Labour Council, 1888-1971 (75 linear ft); US Steel Workers of America, Local 1005, 1937-1972 (55 linear ft) and District 6, 1953-1972 (273 linear ft); Service Employees International Union, Local 204, 1944-1971 (105 linear ft).

ON —CANADA DEPT OF LABOUR, Library, Ottawa, K1A 0J2, Can. Monique Marchand, Chief Librn
Holdings: Vols (100,000) Cat Microforms

LABOR—CHILD LABOR see Children—Employment

LABOR—HISTORY

AL —BIRMINGHAM PUBLIC LIBRARY, Dept of Archives & Mss, 2020 Seventh Ave N, Birmingham, 35203. Marvin Y Whiting, Archivist & Cur
Holdings: Mss
Notes: Collection consists mainly of the Philip Taft Research Papers and labor newspapers of Birmingham, 14,000 ms pieces.

CA —UNIVERSITY OF CALIFORNIA, BERKELEY, University Library, Social Science Library, 30 Stephens Hall, Berkeley, 94720. Bette Erskine, Librn
Holdings: Vols 11,000 Cat Mss Microforms
Notes: The Labor Union Collection consists primarily of labor union journals, newspapers, preceedings and constitutions. Holdings are largely national in scope, with emphasis on Northern California. Approximately 850 current serials are being received. This collection is complemented by labor union materials in the Institute of Industrial Relations Library and in The Bancroft Library, and by holdings in Labor History in the Main Library. Incl 1683 microfilm reels.

CA —HOOVER INSTITUTION ON WAR, REVOLUTION & PEACE, Stanford University, Stanford, 94305. Milorad M Drachkovitch, Archivist
Holdings: Mss
Notes: Two collections: (1) Papers of Walter

LABOR—HISTORY (cont.)

Schevenels, Belgian syndicalist and international trade union official, General Secretary of the International Federation of Trade Unions, 1929-1945, and General Secretary for the European Regional Organization of the International Condederation of Free Trade Unions, 1951-1966, incl correspondence, reports, speeches, writings, telegrams, bulletins, interviews, pamphlets, clippings, and printed materials, 1930-1966, relating to syndicalism and free European trade unions, labor and laboring classes in Europe, and international labor problems. 12 ms boxes. (2) Stenographic transcripts of the minutes of the First and Second National Industrial Conferences of 1919-1920. 15 ms boxes.

CO —UNIVERSITY OF COLORADO, Libraries, Western Historical Collections, Boulder, 80309.
Holdings: Mss
Notes: Papers of Herrick Roth (b 1916), who was one of the founders in 1946 of the American Federation of Teachers local in Denver. In 1951 he left teaching to devote himself full-time to the labor movement. From 1962 until his ouster by George Meany in 1973 he served as President of the Colorado Labor Council. Since then he has taught at Denver University, run unsuccessfully for the US Senate and served as head of the State Employment Service. The collection contains correspondence, pamphlets, clippings and other material on Roth's labor union, political and social interests. The largest portion of the material deals with the Colorado Labor Council and the American Federation of Teachers. 25 boxes, 1950s-1970s. A typescript inventory is available.

DC —AMERICAN FEDERATION OF LABOR-CONGRESS OF INDUSTRIAL ORGANIZATIONS, Library, 815 16th St NW, Washington, 20006.
Holdings: Vols (20,000) Cat Pix Microforms
Notes: Labor, labor unions, and related subjects. Incl letters of Samuel Gompers (microfilm); constitutions and conference proceedings of international unions.

DC —GEORGE WASHINGTON UNIVERSITY, Gelman Library, 2130 H St NW, Washington, 20052.
Holdings: Cat Mss Pix
Notes: The Eli L. Oliver labor papers cover the period 1930-1952 and particularly concern labor's involvement in politics. The correspondence contains letters from union officials nationwide. Organizational papers of Labor's Non-Partisan League incl financial records, memos, campaign pamphlets, press releases, etc. Oliver's papers also include reports discussing primary and general election strategies for 1938-1940; similar material is present for the American Labor Party of New York relating to the 1940 campaign and for the Labor Committee's backing of the Truman-Barkley and the Stevenson-Sparkman campaigns of 1948-1952, respectively. The collection also contains some of Oliver's speeches, addresses, etc and some personal files including photos, financial records, clippings, etc. Cataloged as a collection with unpublished inventory for access.

DC —HOWARD UNIVERSITY, Moorland-Spingarn Research Center, 500 Howard Place NW, Washington, 20059. Clifford L Muse, Jr, Acting Dir
Holdings: Vols (106,086) Mss Maps Pix Slides Phonorecords Audiotapes 16mm Films Filmstrips Microforms
Budget: ($854,753)
See also entry under Blacks

DC —INTERNATIONAL LABOR ORGANIZATION, International Labor Office, Washington Branch Library, 1750 New York Ave NW, Rm 330, Washington, 20006. Karen J Mark, Librn
Holdings: Vols (13,500) Cat Pix 16mm Films Monographs
Notes: Wide range of titles dealing with worldwide labor and social matters. The library contains ILO publications and documentation only, dating back to 1919. Also, a collection of ILO films and photos. See *Subject Guide to Publications of the ILO, 1919-1964* and *ILO Catalogue of Publications in Print, 1982* (ILO).

DC —LIBRARY OF CONGRESS, Manuscript Division, Washington, 20540. John C Broderick, Chief
Notes: Papers.

DC —LIBRARY OF CONGRESS, Music Division, Washington, 20540.
Notes: Musical aspects of the revolutionary workers' movement represented in the Workers Music League's publications and activities; also, the Composers' Collective, etc.

DC —LIBRARY OF CONGRESS, American Folklife Center, Archive of Folk Culture, Washington, 20540.
Notes: The Charles Todd and Robert Sonkin Collection of field recordings made in California migratory labor camps, 1940-41.

DC —US DEPT OF LABOR, Library, 200 Constitution Ave NW, Washington, 20210. Sabina Jacobson, Dir
Holdings: Vols 535,000 Cat Audiotapes Microforms
Notes: Economics, especially labor, incl much historical material. Receive 3200 current periodical titles.

GA —EMORY UNIVERSITY, Robert W Woodruff Library, Atlanta, 30322. Herbert Johnson, Dir
Holdings: Mss Cat
Notes: A collection of materials relating to the history of the Communist Party in the US and the Communist International, gathered by author Theodore Draper. Incl periodicals, pamphlets, party documents, and books, as well as taped interviews that Draper conducted with party leaders and correspondence relating to his research. 80 linear ft mss.

IL —CHICAGO HISTORICAL SOCIETY, Library, Clark St at North Ave, Chicago, 60614. Archie Motley, Manuscript Librn
Notes: Labor history collections incl these papers: Chicago Newspaper Guild (labor union); Ernest DeMaio (President of District Council 11 United Electrical, Radio & Machine Workers of American UE, leading activist of the political left, international trade unionist); John Fitzpatrick (labor leader, President Chicago Federation of Labor, member Chicago Journeymen Horse Shoers Union); minutes of the Chicago Federation of Labor; Ben Meyers (labor union counsel, particularly those of the politcial left); Irving Meyers (brother of Ben) and his law partner David Rothstein (labor union counsel, particularly those of the politcal left); Agnes Nestor (labor leader, President International Glove Workers Union and the Women's Trade Union League of Chicago); Victor A Olander(Secretary-Treasurer, Illinois State Federation of Labor and the International Seaman's Union of America; member of the Illinois Emergency Relief Commmission); United Scenic Artists Union Local 350; Chicago Typographical Union No 16.

IL —CHICAGO PUBLIC LIBRARY, Business/Science/Technology Div, Science/Technology Information Center, 425 North Michigan Ave, Chicago, 60611. Lynda Sanford, Head; John R Moore, Environment Collection Coordinator & Engineering Librn
Holdings: Vols
Budget: $205,000
Notes: Collection incl all subject areas of business within HB-HJ Library of Congress classifications scheme. Emphases are on current materials in management, careers, investments, and reference. Collection is also strong in labor history. 2200 periodical titles; 60,000 vols monographs.

IN —INDIANA STATE UNIVERSITY, Cunningham Memorial Library, Dept of Rare Books & Special Collections, Terre Haute, 47809. Lawrence J McCrank, Head
Holdings: Uncat Mss Pix
Budget: ($1350)
Notes: The Debs Collection consists of aprox 7000 pieces of correspondence between Theodore Debs (brother of E V) and other persons, such as Sinclair Lewis, Upton Sinclair, Ethel Barrymore, Emma Goldman, Robert G Ingersoll, Carl Sandburg, Norman Thomas, Sacco and Vanzetti and many others. Many of the letters are from E V Debs to his brother; a good portion of these are from the federal penitentiary at Atlanta. Entire correspondence file has been microfilmed. 750 pamphlets cover all aspects of the labor movement, socialism and radical thought from the 19th century to appprox 1950. A collection ca 200 related books is also housed in the collection. See: J Robert Constantine and Gail Malmgreen, eds, *The Papers of Eugene V Debs, 1834-1945. A Guide to the Microfilm Edition.* NY: Microfilming Corp of America, 1983 (University Microfilms is the new distributer).

MD —UNIVERSITY OF MARYLAND, Library, Archives & Manuscripts Dept, College Park, 20742. Mary A Boccaccio, Head
Holdings: Mss Pix
Notes: University of Maryland publications and archives; collections of organizational papers (eg, Baltimore & Ohio Railroad; various organizations concerned with the Chesapeake Bay and environs; various labor unions, particularly those involving the tobacco industry), mostly associated with Maryland; collections of papers and mss associated with literary and public figures (eg,the Senator Millard Tydings); oral histories relating to the archival and mss collections; associated memorabilia; photographs, mainly associated with Maryland. A guide to collections of personal, family, and organizational papers relating to Maryland is being prepared.

MD —SEAFARER'S HARRY LUNDEBERG SCHOOL OF SEAMANSHIP, Paul Hall Library and Maritime Museum, Piney Point, 20674. Janice McAteer Smolek, Librn
Holdings: Mss Pix Slides Audiotapes Videotapes 16mm Films Filmstrips
Notes: Special collection on maritime studies incl books, mss, periodicals, audiovisuals, and archival materials pertaining to maritime history and maritime labor union history and vocational skills required by the maritime industry. Incl some rare books.

MA —HARVARD UNIVERSITY, Graduate School of Business Administration, Baker Library, Soldiers Field, Boston, 02163. Mary V Chatfield, Librn; Florence Bartoshesky, Cur of Manuscripts and Archives
Holdings: Cat Mss Pix
Notes: Personnel and labor record series in original company records, 1810-1950. Industries represented include textile, agriculture, railroad, metal manufacture, engineering construction. See Robert W Lovett and Eleanor C Bishop, compilers, *Manuscripts in Baker Library* (Boston: The Library, 1978), 382 pp.

MA —JOHN F KENNEDY LIBRARY, Columbia Point, Boston, 02125. Henry J Gwiazda II, Cur
Notes: The Robert F Kennedy Papers cover the period from 1937-1968 and are divided into four subcollections: the Pre-Administration, Attorney General's, Senate, and 1968 Presidential Campaign Papers. In the Pre-Administration Papers, over 140 archives boxes or 70 percent of the materials are open to research. The Personal and Political Papers of this subcollection are almost entirely open. Most of the unprocessed mss are in the Working Files and involve investigative work on labor racketeering. Seventy five percent or 185 archives boxes of the Attorney General's Papers are open, incl the correspondence, the John F Kennedy Library File, the Speech and Trip Files for 1961-1964. For

LABOR—HISTORY (cont.)

the Senate Papers, 200 boxes are open for the 1964 Senate Campaign, the Legislative Subject File, and the Speech and Trip Files for 1964-1968. The speeches and press releases(incl in the Senate subcollection Speech File) and "The Black Books" (16 boxes) on state and delegate information are open for the 1968 campaign. Each subcollection has its own finding aid. The Library also has available for research about 100 audiotapes of Robert F Kennedy's public addresses from 1962-1966 and some 50 oral history interviews on RFK and one (1000 pages) by RFK. There are also available the major documentaries on RFK and a number of films donated by the major networks for research use in the Library.

MA —HARVARD UNIVERSITY LIBRARY, Widener Library, Cambridge, 02138.
Holdings: Cat
Notes: For account of holdings, see *Labor* History, IV (1963), 273-279.

MA —HARVARD UNIVERSITY LIBRARY, Law School Library, Langdell Hall, Cambridge, 02138. Erika S Chadbourn, Cur of Mss
Notes: Legal documents, pictorial material, microfilms. Incl holograph letters of Sacco and Vanzetti, 1920-1928. Typed chronological list in repository.

MA —RADCLIFFE COLLEGE, Arthur & Elizabeth Schlesinger Library on the History of Women in America, 3 James St, Cambridge, 02138. Patricia Miller King, Dir; Eva Moseley, Cur of Mss
Notes: The papers of the 1974 class action suit against *The New York Times* that charged the newspaper with "a pattern and practice of discrimination in employment on the basis of sex." The *Times* agreed to an affirmative action plan, and the suit was resolved in 1978.

MA —RADCLIFFE COLLEGE, Arthur & Elizabeth Schlesinger Library on the History of Women in America, 3 James St, Cambridge, 02138. Patricia Miller King, Dir; Eva Moseley, Cur of Mss
Holdings: Mss Pix
Notes: Several mss collections of organizations and individuals concerned with women in trade unions, protective legislation, wages and working conditions for women and children. Among them are papers of labor organizers Pauline M Newman (ca 1890-) (restricted) and Leonora O'Reilly (1870-1927) and records of the Consumers' Leagues of Connecticut and Massachusetts, of the National Women's Trade Union League, and of 9 to 5: Organization for Women Office Workers (restricted). Also papers of labor educators Hilda Worthington Smith (1888-) and Margaret (Earhart) Smith (1902-1960), and of federal and state officials concerned with labor issues, notably Clara (Mortenson) Beyer (1892-), Ethel McLean Johnson (1882-1978), Frieda Segelke Miller (1889-1973), Frances Perkins (1880-1965), and Esther (Eggertsen) Peterson (1906-).

MA —UNIVERSITY OF LOWELL, Library, One University Ave, Lowell, 01854. Martha Mayo, Special Collections Librn
Holdings: 15,000 Cat Pix
Notes: Lowell History Collection contains photographs, lithographs, post cards, stereoviews, and lanternslides pertaining to the history of the area with special focus on the textile industry and the men and women who worked in the mills from New England Yankee farm girls to the Irish, French-Canadian, and Greek immigrants. The Locks and Canals Collection contains photographs taken from 1875-1947 showing the day to day operations of the company.

MA —BRANDEIS UNIVERSITY, Goldfarb Library, 415 South St, Waltham, 02154. Bessie Hahn, Dir
Notes: Sacco and Vanzetti Case Collection. Incl 23 linear feet of material collected by both Tom O'Connor and Francis Russell relating to this celebrated American trial. This collection is unprocessed, spring 1984.

†MA —CLARK UNIVERSITY, Robert Hutchings Goddard Library, Worcester, 01610. Dorothy Mosa Kowski, Rare Books Librn
Holdings: Cat Mss Pix
Notes: The papers of Carroll Davidson Wright, first US Commissioner of Labor, establisher of the Bureau of Labor Statistics, distinguished economist and sociologist.

MI —UNIVERSITY OF MICHIGAN, Dept of Rare Books & Special Collections, Ann Arbor, 48109. Edward C Weber, Head, Labadie Collection
Holdings: Vols (40,000) Cat Mss Pix Phonorecords Audiotapes Microforms
Notes: Emphasis is on US labor history up to 1940.

MI —WAYNE STATE UNIVERSITY, Walter P Reuther Library, Archives of Labor & Urban Affairs, Detroit, 48202. Philip Mason, Dir
Holdings: Vols (4000) Cat Mss Pix Slides Phonorecords Audiotapes Videotapes 16mm Films Filmstrips Microforms
Budget: ($450,000)
Notes: See Warner Pflug, *A Guide to the Archives of Labor History and Urban Affairs* (Wayne State University Press, 1974).

MI —MICHIGAN STATE UNIVERSITY, Labor and Industrial Relations Library, East Lansing, 48824. Martha Jane Soltow, Librn
Holdings: Cat Microforms
Notes: This material is composed primarily of special collections on microfilm and microfiche. The following are some of the collections: all constitutions and proceedings of most of the major unions, 1836-present; papers of John Mitchell (United Mine Workers), 1885-1919; radical pamphlet literature from Tamiment Library (New York University), 1900-1945; Knights of Labor Papers, 1800-1921; Socialist Party of America Papers, 1896-1969; Earl Browder Papers, 1891-1975; American Association for Labor Legislation Papers, 1905-1943; and the Committee on Fair Employment Practices Papers, 1941-1946.

MS —MISSISSIPPI STATE UNIVERSITY, Mitchell Memorial Library, Box 5408, Mississippi State, 39762. Frances N Coleman, Head, Special Collections
Holdings: Cat Mss
Notes: The Holt E Ross papers, a collection dealing with labor organization in Mississippi, incl correspondence, speeches, poems, legal papers, published materials and newspaper clippings collected by Mr Ross during his career as a labor leader, the collection also pertains to the state, national and international labor scene.

NJ —RUTGERS, THE STATE UNIVERSITY OF NEW JERSEY, Alexander Library, Special Collections and Archives, College Ave & Huntington St, New Brunswick, 08903. Ronald L Becker, Cur of Manuscripts and Rare Books
Holdings: / /
Notes: American Labor Party of the State of New York. Ms records, 1947-1956 (72 linear feet).

NY —STATE UNIVERSITY OF NEW YORK, BINGHAMTON, Glenn G Bartle Library, Binghamton, 13901. Marion Hanscom, Special Collections Librn
Notes: Papers, correspondence, etc of the former aide to the Rockefeller enterprises. Incl much on the Colorado mine strikes.

NY —CORNELL UNIVERSITY, New York State School of Industrial & Labor Relations, Martin P Catherwood Library, Ives Hall, Ithaca, 14853. Shirley F Harper, Dir
Holdings: Vols (150,000) Cat Mss Pix Phonorecords Microforms
Notes: Collection incl approx 1000 periodicals and union journals currently received, and ms collections of labor unions, arbitrators, and scholars. 6000 linear ft. *Library Catalog of the New York State School of Industrial and Labor Relations* (Boston: G K Hall, 1967), 12 volumes; *Cumulation of the Library Catalog Supplements of the New York State School of Industrial and Labor Relations* (Boston: G K Hall, 1976), 8 volumes.

†NY —CORNELL UNIVERSITY LIBRARIES, Ithaca, 14853.
Notes: Papers of Sidney Hillman, Amalgamated Clothing and Textile Workers Union.

NY —CENTER FOR LABOR STUDIES, SUNY, Empire State College, Labor College Library, 330 W 42nd St, New York, 10036. Jayne Adler, Librn
Holdings: Vols (3000) Cat Videotapes VF
Budget: ($4000)
Notes: Areas being emphasized in development of the library are: Women and Labor, Occupational Health and Safety, and Trade Union Leadership.

NY —NEW YORK UNIVERSITY, Elmer Holmes Bobst Library, Div of Special Collections, Tamiment Library of Labor History, Washington Sq, New York, 10012. Dorothy Swanson, Librn
Holdings: Cat Mss Maps Pix Microforms
Notes: Books, pamphlets, newspapers, periodicals and mss. Large microfilm collection. Described in Daniel Bell's *The Tamiment Library* (1969), available free from the Tamiment librarian, and *Elmer Holmes Bobst Library Information Bulletin 8* (updated periodically).

NY —STATE UNIVERSITY OF NEW YORK, STONY BROOK, Melville Library, Dept of Special Collections, Stony Brook, 11794. Evert Volkersz, Head
Holdings: Uncat
Notes: About 150 pamphlets.

NC —UNIVERSITY OF NORTH CAROLINA, CHARLOTTE, J Murrey Atkins Library, UNCC Station, Charlotte, 28223. Robert F Brabham Jr, Special Collections Librn
Holdings: Cat Mss Pix
Notes: Papers of Boyd E Payton, documenting strike (1958-61) at Harriett-Henderson Textile Mill in Henderson, NC; Payton's imprisonment for conspiring to dynamite the mill; and the ensuing controversy over the legitimacy of Payton's conviction amidst allegations of a state-supported frame-up.

NC —DUKE UNIVERSITY, William R Perkins Library, Manuscript Dept, Durham, 27706. Ellen Gartrell, Cur of Mss
Holdings: Cat Mss
Notes: Emphasis on US South, especially CIO Organizing Committee papers, 1946-1953 (143,000 items). Large percentage have been commercially microfilmed under title "Operation Dixie." Also papers of Lucy Randolph Mason, Frank deVyver, Frank Morrison.

OH —KENT STATE UNIVERSITY, University Archives, Kent, 44242. Stephen C Morton, University Archivist
Holdings: Uncat Mss Pix
Notes: Books, periodical articles, and correspondence from various members of the Fuller Family of Austinburg, Ohio. The collection includes correspondence of Ira Fuller (1840s), his son Allen O Fuller, his wife, and their daughter Jeannette Fuller (1868-1952), a midwestern temperance lecturer and union organizer and interested correspondent in the Non-Tobacco League of America.

OH —ALLEN COUNTY HISTORICAL SOCIETY, Elizabeth M MacDonell Memorial Library, 620 W Market St, Lima, 45801. Raymond F Schuck, Cur, Allen County Museum; Anna B Selfridge, Asst Cur, Manuscripts & Archives
Holdings: Vols (6824) Cat Mss Maps Pix Slides Audiotapes Microforms
Notes: History of Allen County.

†PA —TEMPLE UNIVERSITY LIBRARIES, Special Collections Dept, Urban Archives Center, Philadelphia, 19122. Thomas Whitehead, Cur of Mss
Holdings: Cat
Notes: Incl the records of several separate collections which are deposited in the Urban Archives Center. Many collections contain photographs, maps and pamphlets, in addition to manuscripts. All collections in the Urban Archives are separately cataloged.

PA —UNIVERSITY OF PITTSBURGH, Hillman Library, Archives of Industrial Society, 363 Hillman Library, Pittsburgh, 15260. Frank A Zabrosky, Cur
Holdings: Documents Mss Pix Newspapers Audiotapes Microforms
Notes: Records of trade unions, service employee unions, teacher unions in the 20th

LABOR—HISTORY (cont.)

century; personal papers of individuals involved in the labor union movement. Unique collection: Msgr Charles Owen Rice Papers, 1935-.
See also entry under United Electrical, Radio and Machine Workers.

PA —PENNSYLVANIA STATE UNIVERSITY, Fred Lewis Pattee Library, Labor History Collection, University Park, 16802. Peter Gottlieb, Archivist
Holdings: Cat Mss Pix
Notes: Penn State is "provisional repository" for papers and records of the United Steel Workers of America, incl records from the USWA international headquarters in Pittsburgh and from 29 district offices. A comprehensive oral history program with union members is underway.

TX —UNIVERSITY OF TEXAS, ARLINGTON, Library, Arlington, 76019. Charles A Colley, Dir of Special Collections; Robert A Gamble, Head of Archives
Holdings: Mss Pix Microforms
Notes: History

TX —NORTH TEXAS STATE UNIVERSITY, Archives, NT Station Box 5188, Denton, 76203. Robert LaForte, University Archivist

WI —STATE HISTORICAL SOCIETY OF WISCONSIN, Archives, 816 State St, Madison, 53706. Harold L Miller, Reference Archivist
Holdings: Mss Pix Microforms
Notes: Records and papers documenting the history of the labor and Socialist movements in the United States from 1850s to the present. Incl are records of labor and socialist organizations incl American Federation of Labor and the Socialist Labor Party, and papers of individual labor and socialist leaders such as Morris Hillquit and John L Lewis. Collections are described in *A Guide to Labor Papers in the State Historical Society of Wisconsin* (1978) and in current accession notes in the *Wisconsin Magazine of History.* Major collections are also listed in Hamer, *Guide to Manuscripts and Archives in the United States,* (1961) and in the *National Union Catalog of Manuscript Collections,* (1959-date).

BC —UNIVERSITY OF BRITISH COLUMBIA, Library, Special Collections Div, 1956 Main Mall, Vancouver, V6T 1Y3, Can. Anne Yandle, Head
Holdings: Mss
Notes: Mss relating to British Columbia.

ON —CANADA DEPT OF LABOUR, Library, Ottawa, K1A 0J2, Can. Monique Marchand, Chief Librn
Holdings: Vols (100,000) Cat Microforms

ON —UNIVERSITY OF TORONTO, Thomas Fisher Rare Book Library, 120 Saint George St, Toronto, M5S 1A5, Can. Richard G Landon, Head
Holdings: Vols 700 Cat Mss Audiotapes
Notes: Woodsworth Collection fo books, pamphlets, and broadsides relating to the history of socialist and labour movements in Canada with particular emphasis on the CCF party in Ontario. Presented by the Ontario Woodsworth Memorial Foundation and designated as part of its official archives. Ms material from the files of the Ontario Woodsworth House in Toronto, and from former party members. Incl some private papers.

LABOR—INSURANCE see Old Age Pensions

LABOR, FORCED see Forced Labor

LABOR, KNIGHTS OF see Knights of Labor

LABOR, MARITIME see Merchant Seamen

LABOR, MIGRANT see Migrant Labor

LABOR, ORGANIZED see Trade Unions

LABOR AND CAPITAL see Industrial Relations

LABOR AND LABORING CLASSES—U.S.

DC —LIBRARY OF CONGRESS, Manuscript Division, Washington, 20540. John C Broderick, Chief
Notes: Papers.

LABOR COLONIES see Agricultural Colonies

LABOR FORCE see Labor Supply

LABOR LAWS AND LEGISLATION

CA —UNIVERSITY OF CALIFORNIA, LOS ANGELES, Research Library, Dept of Special Collections, 405 Hilgard Ave, Los Angeles, 90024. Edward Shreeves, Chairman, Bibliographers Group; David S Zeidberg, Head
Notes: 8 linear feet of correspondence, pamphlets, and clippings concerning women's suffrage, the Progressive and Republican parties, minimum wage laws, etc.

DC —INTERNATIONAL LABOR ORGANIZATION, International Labor Office, Washington Branch Library, 1750 New York Ave NW, Rm 330, Washington, 20006. Karen J Mark, Librn
Holdings: Vols (13,500) Cat Pix 16mm Films Monographs
Notes: Wide range of titles dealing with worldwide labor and social matters. The library contains ILO publications and documentation only, dating back to 1919. Also, a collection of ILO films and photos. See *Subject Guide to Publications of the ILO, 1919-1964* and *ILO Catalogue of Publications in Print, 1982* (ILO).

DC —US DEPT OF LABOR, Library, 200 Constitution Ave NW, Washington, 20210. Sabina Jacobson, Dir
Holdings: Vols (550,000) Cat

MI —MICHIGAN STATE UNIVERSITY, Labor and Industrial Relations Library, East Lansing, 48824. Martha Jane Soltow, Librn
Holdings: Vols 850 Cat
Notes: Included in this collection are all court, board, and arbitration decisions published by the Bureau of National Affairs and Commerce Clearing House; decisions of the National Labor Relations Board; decisions of the Michigan Employment Relations Commission and the Michigan Civil Service Commission; and the fact-finding decisions for Michigan police and firemen. *Shepard's Federal Labor Law* Citations and some legal labor periodicals have been included. Excluded from the total size of the collection are the state and federal court decisions which are available adjacent to the Labor and Industrial Relations library.

ON —CANADA DEPT OF LABOUR, Library, Ottawa, K1A 0J2, Can. Monique Marchand, Chief Librn
Holdings: Vols (100,000) Cat Microforms

LABOR LEGISLATION, AMERICAN ASSOCIATION FOR see American Association for Labor Legislation

LABOR NEWSPAPERS see Newspapers, Labor

LABOR ORGANIZATIONS see Trade Unions

LABOR PARTY OF N.Y., AMERICAN see American Labor Party of New York

LABOR PERIODICALS see Periodicals, Labor

LABOR PROGRESSIVE PARTY, CANADA

ON —UNIVERSITY OF TORONTO, Thomas Fisher Rare Book Library, 120 Saint George St, Toronto, M5S 1A5, Can. Richard G Landon, Head
Holdings: Vols 2500 Mss Pix Phonorecords
Notes: Kenny Collection named for original collector, Robert Kenny of Toronto. Chiefly material on and by the Labor Progressive Party and the Communist Party of Canada, including their constitutions, reports of national conventions, leaflets, posters, election material, ephemera. Manuscript material of A E Smith, Tim Buck and other Canadian communists.

LABOR RELATIONS see Industrial Relations

LABOR SUPPLY

ON —CANADA, DEPT OF EMPLOYMENT & IMMIGRATION LIBRARY, Ottawa, K1A 0J9, Can. P E Sunder-Raj, Dir Library Services
Holdings: Vols (35,000) Cat
Notes: Also have 1800 current journals and serials.

LABOR UNIONS see Trade Unions

LABORATORIES—SAFETY MEASURES

ON —ONTARIO MINISTRY OF HEALTH, Laboratory Services Branch, Library, Box 9000, Terminal A, Toronto, M5W 1R5, Can. Doris A Standing, Librn
Holdings: Vols (4000) Cat
Budget: ($50,000)
Notes: Medical laboratory technology and related subjects: microbiology; environmental bacteriology (limited to testing of milk, food and water for bacterial quality, etc); biological chemistry (clinical); mycology; parasitology; virology; immunology; serology; automated laboratory techniques; biohazard control.

LABORATORIES, MEDICAL see Medical Laboratories

LABORATORY ANIMALS

AL —UNIVERSITY OF ALABAMA, BIRMINGHAM, Lister Hill Library of the Health Sciences, University Sta, Birmingham, 35294. Richard B Fredericksen, Dir

AR —NATIONAL CENTER FOR TOXICOLOGICAL RESEARCH, Library, Jefferson, 72079. Susan Laney-Sheehan, Supvr Librn
Holdings: Vols (15,000) Cat Mss Slides Audiotapes 16mm Films Microforms
Notes: Incl (860) journal titles, (230) current subscriptions.

CA —UNIVERSITY OF CALIFORNIA, LOS ANGELES, Biomedical Library, Center for Health Sciences, Los Angeles, 90024. Louise Darling, Biomedical Librn

CT —YALE MEDICAL LIBRARY, 333 Cedar St, New Haven, 06510.

CT —YALE UNIVERSITY, School of Medicine, Dept of Obstetrics & Gynecology Library, Farnam Memorial Bldg, New Haven, 06510.
Holdings: Cat Mss Pix Slides X-Rays
Notes: X-ray plates, 10,000 slides of monkey and human tissue and about 1000 slides of gynecological and obstetrical pathology, used as teaching and research materials. Other large collections of X-rays and radiotherapy photographs are in the Hunter Radiation Therapy Center.

IN —PURDUE UNIVERSITY LIBRARIES, Veterinary Medical Library, C J Lynn Hall of Veterinary Medicine, West Lafayette, 47907. Gretchen Stephens, Librn
Holdings: Vols (31,022) Cat
Budget: ($106,281)
Notes: The collection contains the outstanding books and serials in English that are germane to comparative and veterinary medicine. Foreign language materials are added selectively. Subjects of particular strength are laboratory animal medicine, pathology, comparative anatomy, animal behavior and clinical veterinary medicine.

IA —IOWA STATE UNIVERSITY, College of Veterinary Medicine, Veterinary Medical Library, Ames, 50011. Sara R Peterson, Librn
Holdings: Vols (17,000) Cat Microforms
Notes: Incl comparative and veterinary medicine with emphasis in the fields of mammalian anatomy and physiology, laboratory animal medicine, pathology,

LABORATORY ANIMALS (cont.)

toxicology, biomedical engineering and clinical veterinary medicine. Incl 2000 uncataloged German theses.

ME —JACKSON LABORATORY, Research Laboratory, Bar Harbor, 04609.
Notes: "Subject: *Strain Bibliography* of inbred strains of mice, transplantable tumors, and named genes in mice ..." *Mouse News* Letter. Database discontinued 1984, and has become an archival record.

MD —MEDICAL & CHIRURGICAL FACULTY OF THE STATE OF MARYLAND, Library, 1211 Cathedral St, Baltimore, 21201. Joseph E Jensen, Librn
Holdings: Vols (10,000) // Cat Mss Maps Pix
See also entry under Medicine - History and Historic

MD —US ARMED FORCES RADIOBIOLOGY RESEARCH INSTITUTE, Naval Medical Command, Bethesda, 20014. Nannette M Pope, Head, Library Division
Holdings: Vols (50,000)
Budget: ($150,000)
Notes: Collection consists of monographs, technical reports, serials, and microfiche related to radiation effects on human and animal biology.

MA —HARVARD MEDICAL SCHOOL, New England Primate Research Center Library, 1 Pine Hill Dr, Southborough, 01772. Sydney Fingold, Librn
Holdings: Vols (4000)

†NY —MEDICAL RESEARCH LIBRARY OF BROOKLYN, Academy of Medicine of Brooklyn & The State University of New York Downstate Medical Center, 450 Clarkson St, Brooklyn, 11203. Kenneth E Moody, Dir
Notes: Extensive collection of 18th-19th century material.
See also entry under Medicine

LABORATORY ANIMALS—MONKEYS see Monkeys As Laboratory Animals

LABORATORY DIAGNOSIS see Diagnosis, Laboratory

LABOR'S NON-PARTISAN LEAGUE

DC —GEORGE WASHINGTON UNIVERSITY, Gelman Library, 2130 H St NW, Washington, 20052.
Holdings: Cat Mss Pix
Notes: The Eli L Oliver labor papers cover the period 1930-1952 and particularly concern labor's involvement in politics. The correspondence contains letters from union officials nationwide. Organizational papers of Labor's Non-Partisan League include financial records, memos, campaign pamphlets, press releases, etc. Oliver's papers also include reports discussing primary and general election strategies for 1938 and 1940; similar material is present for the American Labor Party of New York relating to the 1940 campaign and for the Labor Committee's backing of the Truman-Barkley and the Stevenson-Sparkman campaigns of 1948 and 1952, respectively. The collection also contains some of Oliver's speeches, addresses, etc and some personal files including photos, financial records, clippings, etc. Cataloged as a collection with unpublished inventory for access.

LABOULAYE, EDOUARD

MD —JOHNS HOPKINS UNIVERSITY, Milton S Eisenhower Library, Charles & 34 Sts, Baltimore, 21218. Ann S Gwyn, Assistant Dir for Special Collections
Holdings: // Cat Mss
Notes: Incl part of library of J C Bluntschli, his complete works, mss and notebooks. Annotated works and mss of Francis Lieber. Ms lecture notes of Edouard Laboulaye.

LABRADOR

CT —YALE UNIVERSITY, Box 1603A, Yale Station, New Haven, 06520.
Holdings: Uncat Mss Pix
Notes: Incl 44 boxes of material by and about Sir Wilfred Grenfell.

ME —BOWDOIN COLLEGE, Library, Brunswick, 04011. Dianne M Gutscher, Cur of Special Collections
Holdings: Mss Pix
Notes: A miscellaneous collection of ten logs and journals kept by members of the Bowdoin expeditions to Labrador in 1860 and 1891; as well as 29 letters, a log book, and about 100 newsclippings from the John C Parker Papers, concerning the Labrador expedition of 1891; and about 200 nitrate negatives and 200 mounted prints of those negatives done by Alfred O Gross, professor of biology at Bowdoin, when he accompanied Donald B MacMillan on an expedition to Labrador in 1934. Most of the pictures are of native birds and nesting sites.

NY —AMERICAN MUSEUM OF NATURAL HISTORY, Library Services Dept, Central Park W & 79th St, New York, 10024. Nina J Root, Chairwoman; Mary Genett, Asst Librn for Reference Services

RI —BROWN UNIVERSITY, John Hay Library, 20 Prospect St, Providence, 02912. Mark N Brown, Cur Mss
Holdings: // Mss
Notes: Papers of Augustus William Smith, Professor of Astronomy and Mathematics and President of Wesleyan University; Professor of Natural Philosophy, United States Naval Academy. Approx 335 items with inclusive dates 1816-1918. There are letters and autograph mss of scientific import written by Smith while at Hamilton and Wesleyan colleges; a notebook, part of which records Smith's journey to Labrador in 1860 as a member of the US government expedition to observe the solar eclipse; diplomas; civilian commissions, deeds, and photographs.

NF —MEMORIAL UNIVERSITY OF NEWFOUNDLAND, University Library, Centre for Newfoundland Studies, Elizabeth Ave, Saint John's, A1C 5S7, Can. Anne Hart, Head
Holdings: Vols (48,000) Cat Map Microforms
Budget: ($50,000)
Notes: Materials about Newfoundland, by Newfoundlanders, or published in Newfoundland, incl Labrador. Also, Saint Pierre and Miquelon. Bibliography of Newfoundland materials is being compiled (now over 7,000 items).

LACE AND LACE MAKING

IL —BLACK HAWK COLLEGE, Learning Resources Center, 6600 34 Ave, Moline, 61265. Donald C Rowland, Dir
Holdings: Vols 773 Cat Pix Audiotapes
Notes: Emphasis on fine arts. Entire college collection a gift of the Belgian Consul.

NY —FASHION INSTITUTE OF TECHNOLOGY, Edward C Blum Design Laboratory, 227 W 27 St, New York, 10001. Laura Sinderbrand, Dir
Holdings: Cat Pix Slides
Notes: The largest resource of it kind consisting of 4 million indexed swatches and 300 swatch books, jacquard point paper, croquis, quilts, rug samples, laces, embroideries, and color swatch cards. A collection of international scope incl antique and contemporary textiles; woven and printed patterns created for apparel and home furnishings which may be adapted to china, giftware, floor covering, wallpaper, and package design. A comprehensive research facility comprised of over one million articles of dress dating from the 17th Century to the present, incl men's, women's, children's clothes, furs, foundation garments and lingerie, as well as an outstanding grouping of 19th and 20th century designer clothing. Accessories as diverse as hats, handbags, gloves, hosiery, shoes, shawls, and costume jewelry offer an additonal resource to this international collection.

WA —UNIVERSITY OF WASHINGTON LIBRARIES, Costume and Textile Collection, FM-25, Seattle, 98195. Krista Jensen Turnbull, Cur
Holdings: Vols (1500) Cat Pix Slides
Notes: Incl the Elizabeth Bayley Willis Collection of more than 1000 textiles from India, and the Seattle Weavers' Guild Collection of Guatemalan textiles. Coptic textiles are on loan from Yale University, and the Boston Museum of Fine Arts gave the Choate Collection of lace. There are also good collections of ecclasiastical vestments and embroideries from many nations, ranging from 1500 BC to the present.

LACKEY, S. E., LUMBER COMPANY

MS —UNIVERSITY OF SOUTHERN MISSISSIPPI, William David McCain Graduate Library, Box 5148, Southern Sta, Hattiesburg, 39406.
Holdings: Uncat Mss Pix
Notes: The business records of the S E Lackey Lumber Company document the Southern yellow pine lumber industry in Mississippi from the 1920s through the 1950s. Forty-five August 1920 photographs of the Goodyear Yellow Pine Lumber Company of Picayune, Mississippi depict all phases of lumbering, from logging and skidder operations to milling and curing. Incl are photographs of lumber camps and "houses on wheels." 44 cubic feet holdings.

LACROSSE

MD —LACROSSE FOUNDATION HALL OF FAME AND LIBRARY, Newton H White Jr, Athletic Center, Homeswood, Baltimore, 21218. Ann Gwyn, Librn
Holdings: Microforms
Notes: Large collection of books and memorabilia.

OK —SOCIETY FOR THE NORTH AMERICAN CULTURAL SURVEY, Dept of Geography, Oklahoma State University, Stillwater, 74078. John Rooney, Dir; Todd Zdorkowski, Asst
Notes: Producing a cultural survey of North American sports and games. John Rooney has published several books on the geography of sports. SWAC's current project involves mapping the continent-wide distributions and the participation patterns for the major and minor professional, college and high school sports.

BC —CANADIAN LACROSSE HALL OF FAME AND LIBRARY, Box 308, New Westminster, V3L 4Y6, Can. Archie W Miller, Cur
Notes: Incl a large collection of memorabilia, archival material and a small library of lacrosse around the world, particularly in Canada.

LACY, ED

MA —BOSTON UNIVERSITY, Mugar Memorial Library, Special Collections Dept, 771 Commonwealth Ave, Boston, 02215. Howard B Gotlieb, Dir
Holdings: // Cat Mss
Notes: Mss, correspondence, etc collected in depth; incl publications by or about.

LADD, BRUCE D.

MA —BOSTON UNIVERSITY, Mugar Memorial Library, Special Collections Dept, 771 Commonwealth Ave, Boston, 02215. Howard B Gotlieb, Dir
Holdings: Cat Mss

LADD FAMILY

NJ —GLASSBORO STATE COLLEGE, Savitz Library, Stewart Room, Glassboro, 08028. Clara Kirner, Special Collection Librn
Holdings: Vols (200) Cat Mss
Notes: Correspondence, account books, manumission papers, transfers of indentured servantes, deeds, surveys, commissions and appointments, and misc papers of Hannah (Mickle) Ladd, John Ladd (d 1740), John Ladd Jr (d 1770), Samuel Ladd and others.

LADENBURG, RUDOLF

NJ —PRINCETON UNIVERSITY, Library, Rare Books Dept, Princeton, 08544. Stephen Ferguson, Cur
Holdings: Mss
Budget: Some of his papers and lectures
Notes: Some of his papers and lectures.

LADIN LANGUAGE see Raeto-Romance Language and Literature

LADINO LANGUAGE AND LITERATURE

DC —LIBRARY OF CONGRESS, African and Middle Eastern Division, Washington, 20540.
Holdings: Cat Mss Microforms
Notes: Hebraica: about 109,000 vols in Hebrew, Yiddish, Judeo-Arabic, Judeo-Persian, Ladino, Syriac, Ethiopic; espec strong in Biblical subjects, responsa literature, and socio-political aspects.

†MA —HARVARD UNIVERSITY LIBRARY, Widener Library, Judaica Collection, Room M, Cambridge, 02138. Charles Berlin, Bibliographer
Holdings: Cat

OH —HEBREW UNION COLLEGE-JEWISH INSTITUTE OF RELIGION, Klau Library, 3101 Clifton Ave, Cincinnati, 45220. David J Gilner, Reference Librn
Holdings: Cat Mss
Notes: About 6000 mss in Hebrew characters representing various languages, such as Hebrew, Ladino, Yiddish, Spanish, Italian, German; also mss in Arabic, Ethiopian, Chinese and Persian alphabets. Incl literary, archival, sermonic and halakhic mss.

LA FARGE, JOHN

NY —NEW YORK HISTORICAL SOCIETY, Library, 170 Central Park W, New York, 10024. James Gregory, Librn
Notes: 4 linear ft of correspondence and papers, 1842-1920, of Stanford White (architect). Incl a great many letters from American artists and sculptors such as Augustus Saint-Gaudens and John La Farge.

LA FARGE, REV. JOHN, S.J.

DC —GEORGETOWN UNIVERSITY, Library, Special Collections Div, 37 & O Sts NW, Washington, 20057. George M Barringer, Special Collections Librn; Nicholas B Sheetz, Mss Librn
Holdings: Cat Mss
Notes: Correspondence, documents, manuscripts, and newspaper clippings comprising the personal papers of Ref John LaFarge, SJ (1880-1963), noted Catholic social thinker. The bulk of the papers dates from LaFarge's ministry in Southern Maryland and from his years as editor *America* in New York. Incl is material from his extensive involvement with the Catholic Interracial Council, Catholic Layman's Union, and other interracial and social organizations. LaFarge, son of artist John LaFarge, was a member of an unusually gifted family. Incl among the family correspondence are letters from Oliver LaFarge, author and anthropologist, and from Christopher LaFarge, author.

LAFOLLETTE, CHARLES MARION

IN —INDIANA STATE UNIVERSITY, EVANSVILLE, Library, 8600 University Blvd, Evansville, 47712. Gina R Walker, Acting Archivist
Holdings: Cat Mss Recordings
Notes: Correspondence and papers, newspaper clippings and taped interviews. Period largely 1940s. Restricted use: noncirculating.

LA FOLLETTE, ROBERT M., AND FAMILY

DC —LIBRARY OF CONGRESS, Manuscript Division, Washington, 20540. John C Broderick, Chief
Notes: Their papers; more than 1400 ms containers; period of 1850s to 1967. Incl biographical, personal, legislative and political materials.

LA FORTE, BENOIST

NY —CORNELL UNIVERSITY LIBRARIES, John M Olin Library, History of Science Collections, Ithaca, 14853. Lillian A Clark, Administrative Supervisor; David W Corson, History of Science Librn
Holdings: // 3000 Uncat Mss
Notes: La Forte Archive: official correspondence of Benoist La Forte (b 1761), *commissionaire*, then *inspecteur des poudres et salpetres* of France, 1784-1797. Typed checklists exist.

LAFARGE FAMILY PAPERS

CT —YALE UNIVERSITY, Box 1603A, Yale Station, New Haven, 06520.
Holdings: Cat Mss
Notes: Primarily papers of John La Farge.

LAFAYETTE, MARQUIS DE

†AL —MUSEUMS OF THE CITY OF MOBILE, Reference Library, 355 Government St, Mobile, 36602. Caldwell Delaney, Adminr

CT —YALE UNIVERSITY, Beinecke Rare Book & Manuscript Library, Osborn Collection, New Haven, 06520. Stephen R Parks, Cur
Holdings: Mss

DC —SOCIETY OF THE CINCINNATI, Library, 2118 Massachusetts Ave NW, Washington, 20008. John D Kilbourne, Dir of Museum & Library
Holdings: Vols (12,000) Cat Mss Maps Pix Slides Microforms
Budget: ($65,000)
Notes: Because of the French connections of the Society of the Cincinnati, a particular effort is made to incl information about the French contribution to the American Revolution. The collection is also rich in biographical materials concerning the officer personnel of the American and French armies of the American Revolution. There are two significant sub-sections of this collection: The George Rogers Clark Collection concerning the history of the Old Northwest (to 1820); and the Member-Author Collection, writings of members of the Society of the Cincinnati in various fields. It is advisable to make an appointment for use of the collections.

IN —INDIANA UNIVERSITY, Lilly Library, Seventh St, Bloomington, 47405. William R Cagle, Librn
Holdings: // Cat Mss Pix
Notes: First editions. Incl pamphlets relative to the 1824-1825 visit to the US. Ms collections incl Lafayette collection formerly owned by Judge Walter P Gardner. Most of the items appear in Gottschalk's *Lafayette: A Guide to the Letters, Documents, and Manuscripts in the United States* (Cornell University, 1975).

NY —CORNELL UNIVERSITY LIBRARIES, John M Olin Library, Dept of Rare Books, Ithaca, 14853. Donald D Eddy, Librn
Holdings: Cat Mss
Notes: The Arthur H and Mary Marden Dean Lafayette Collection (formerly Fabius and Blancheteau collections). The principal American repository for papers by and about Lafayette. See *Quarterly Journal of the Library of Congress*, vol 29, April 1972.

PA —LAFAYETTE COLLEGE, David Bishop Skillman Library, Easton, 18042. Dorothy Cieslicki, Librn
Holdings: Vols 2200 Cat Mss Pix
Budget: $300
Notes: Incl 636 engravings; also, artifacts.

LAFFERTY, R. A.

†OK —UNIVERSITY OF TULSA, McFarlin Library, Dept of Rare Books and Special Collections, 600 South College Avenue, Tulsa, 74104. Dr David Farmer, Librn
Notes: R A Lafferty Manuscript Collection.

LAFFITE, JEAN

TX —ROSENBERG LIBRARY, Galveston and Texas History Center, 2310 Sealy Ave, Galveston, 77550. Jane Kenamore, Archivist
Holdings: Vols 7368 Cat Mss Maps Pix Slides Microforms
Budget: $60,000
Notes: Emphasis on upper Texas coast material; Republic of Texas period; Civil War period; Shipping; Texas Navy; Jean Laffite; Texas politics, 19th-20th century; Railroads; Texas journalism, incl microfilms of Galveston newspapers, 1838-date.

LAGAKOS FAMILY

PA —BALCH INSTITUTE FOR ETHNIC STUDIES, Library, 18 S Seventh St, Philadelphia, 19106. R Joseph Anderson, Library Dir

LAGERQVIST, PAR

MN —UNIVERSITY OF MINNESOTA, O Meredith Wilson Library, 309 19 Ave S, Minneapolis, 55455. Austin J McLean, Chief, Special Collections
Holdings: Vols 165// Uncat
Notes: First editions and translations. Complete listing available in the Division.

LAGOUDAKIS, HARILAOS

MA —BOSTON UNIVERSITY, Mugar Memorial Library, Special Collections Dept, 771 Commonwealth Ave, Boston, 02215. Howard B Gotlieb, Dir
Holdings: Mss Correspondence Pix

LAGRANGE'S EQUATIONS see Dynamics

LAHR, BERT

NY —NEW YORK PUBLIC LIBRARY, Performing Arts Research Center, Billy Rose Theatre Collection, 111 Amsterdam Ave, New York, 10023. Dorothy L Swerdlove, Cur
Holdings: Cat Mss Pix
Notes: Scripts, photographs, posters, scrapbooks, and other papers and memorabilia.

LAHR, JOHN

MA —BOSTON UNIVERSITY, Mugar Memorial Library, Special Collections Dept, 771 Commonwealth Ave, Boston, 02215. Howard B Gotlieb, Dir
Holdings: Cat Mss
Notes: Mss, correspondence, etc collected in depth; incl publications by or about.

LAIDLAW, A. K. see Macdiarmid, Hugh (Christopher Murray Grieve), 1892-1978

LAING SCHOOL

SC —COLLEGE OF CHARLESTON LIBRARY, Special Collections Dept, Charleston, 29401.
Notes: This collection consists of photocopied material from the papers of the Pennsylvania Abolition Society housed at the Historical Society of Pennsylvania, dealing with the establishment (1866), maintenance and eventual relinquishing of the Laing School to the local Public School Board (1940). Collection guide available.

LAIRD, CHARLETON

NV —UNIVERSITY OF NEVADA, RENO, University Library, Special Collections Dept, Reno, 89557. Robert E Blesse, Head
Holdings: Vols (25) Cat Pix Mss
Notes: Papers of Laird, writer for more than 40 years, published novels, language studies, literary criticism, reference works and textbooks. Collection includes manuscripts, correspondence, personal papers.

LAKE, AUSTEN

MA —BOSTON UNIVERSITY, Mugar Memorial Library, Special Collections Dept, 771 Commonwealth Ave, Boston, 02215. Howard B Gotlieb, Dir
Holdings: Mss Correspondence Pix

LAKE CHAMPLAIN TRANSPORTATION COMPANY

VT —UNIVERSITY OF VERMONT, Guy W Bailey/David W Howe Library, Burlington, 05405. John Buehler, Asst Dir for Special Collections

LAKE ERIE

NY —BUFFALO & ERIE COUNTY HISTORICAL SOCIETY, 25 Nottingham Court, Buffalo, 14216. Herman Sass, Librn
Notes: Great Lakes marine history; especially strong in Lake Erie material. In various resources departments. No separate catalog.

OH —CASE WESTERN RESERVE UNIVERSITY LIBRARIES, Cleveland, 44106. Susie Hanson, Special Collections Librn
Holdings: Vols 1000 Cat
Notes: The collection was previously titled the Lake Erie Study Collection. As its scope has increased, it has been renamed the Environmental Sciences Collection and has been fully incorporated into the collection of the Sears Library, which serves the University in the area of science and technology, economics and management. The Environmental Sciences Collection incl government and nongovernment reports, monographs and serials.

ON —LONDON PUBLIC LIBRARIES & MUSEUMS, London Room, 305 Queen's Ave, London, N6B 1X2, Can. W Glen Curnoe, Librn
Holdings: Cat Mss Maps Pix Slides Phonorecords Audiotapes 16mm Films Microforms
Budget: ($3700)
Notes: History of Ontario, with emphasis on London and region, from early 19th century onward. Separate catalog for books, films and microforms. Various subject indexes to materials. Special interest in London, Ontario authors and publishers.

LAKE ONTARIO—SHIPWRECKS

NY —STATE UNIVERSITY OF NEW YORK, COLLEGE AT OSWEGO, Penfield Library, Oswego, 13126. Anne Commerton, Dir
Holdings: Mss Cat
Notes: Collection of data and newspapers, notes and correspondence for writing a book on shipwrecks on Lake Ontario and in particular, Oswego Harbor, by Richard F Palmer, Syracuse Newspapers reporter. Photographs accompanied this material but were removed to be added to our local history photograph collection. Eight inches of material.

LAKE MOHONK ARBITRATION CONFERENCES

PA —SWARTHMORE COLLEGE, Peace Collection, Swarthmore, 19081. Jean R Soderlund, Cur of Peace Collection
Holdings: Vols (10,000) Cat Mss Pix Microforms
Notes: International arbitration has been one of the central subject emphases of the Peace Collection since its inception in 1930. A large proportion of the total book collection deals with international arbitration. In addition, major records and document collections in this area incl those of the Women's Peace Party (1915-1919), and its successor, the Women's International League for Peace and Freedom (1919-); the Lake Mohonk (New York) Arbitration Conferences (1895-1917); the American Peace Society and its branches (1828-1947); the World Peace Foundation (1911-); the Post War World Council (1942-1967); also, books and other materials on the Hague Peace Conferences of 1899 and 1907, and other peace congresses and conventions. The Peace Collection has been described in Downs 972, 978, 4633, and in Downs 1950-1961 Supplement 507 and 916. Fordescriptions of major document groups, see the *Guide to the Swarthmore College Peace Collection,* 2nd ed (1981).
See also entry under Pacifism - History.

LAKE TAHOE

NV —UNIVERSITY OF NEVADA, RENO, University Library, Special Collections Dept, Reno, 89557. Robert E Blesse, Head
Holdings: Vols (100) Cat Pix Mss
Notes: Books, manuscripts (115 cu ft), photographs (500), dealing with Lake Tahoe and the surrounding region. Included are papers of organizations concerned with the environmental quality of the lake, eg, the Lake Tahoe Area Council records, the Tahoe Regional Planning Association records. Records of two 19th-20th century business involved with logging and lumber production in the Tahoe region, the Carson, Tahoe Lumber and Fluming Company, and the El Dorado Wood and Flume Company. Photographs include many early 19th century views of the lake and structures surrounding it.

LAKES

MI —UNIVERSITY OF MICHIGAN, North Engineering Library, 1002 I St, Ann Arbor, 48109. Maurita Holland, Librn
Holdings: Vols 2500 Cat Maps Pix
Budget: $3500
Notes: Subject emphasis is on the natural science aspects of the Great Lakes; limnology. Also 5000 reports.

OH —CLEVELAND PUBLIC LIBRARY, Science & Technology Dept, 325 Superior Ave, Cleveland, 44114. Jean Z Piety, Head
Holdings: Cat
Notes: Special collection covers the environmental sciences concerned with the Great Lakes-St Lawrence drainage basins. Emphasis is on limnology, ecology, meteorology, hydraulics, biology, pollution of air and water, natural history and general research. Most of the material indexed has been donated by numerous agencies around the Great Lakes.

LAM-QUA PAINTINGS

CT —YALE UNIVERSITY, Medical Historical Library, 333 Cedar St, New Haven, 06510. Ferenc A Gyorgyey, Librn
Holdings: Pix
Notes: Pictures of 86 patients with pronounced pathological conditions, painted in China by Lam-Qua in the 19th century, commissioned by Dr Peter Parker, a medical missionary.

LAMAISM

†NY —INSTITUTE FOR ADVANCED STUDIES OF WORLD RELIGIONS (IASWR), Library, State University of New York at Stony Brook, Stony Brook, 11794. C T Shen, Librn
Holdings: Vols 4400 Mss Microforms

OH —CLEVELAND PUBLIC LIBRARY, Fine Arts and Special Collections Department, 325 Superior Ave, Cleveland, 44114. Alice N Loranth, Head
Holdings: Vols (7000) Cat Mss
Notes: Part of the Oriental Religion Collection. Emphasis is on religious texts in their original languages and Western translations. Treatises on religious beliefs and practices are also incl. Strong holdings in Buddhism, Egyptian religion, Hinduism, Judaica, Lamaistic texts, Islam, Sikhism and Zoroastrianism. Works on primitive religion cover aspects of animism, totemism, fetishism, etc. Special emphasis on Islam in China.
See also entry under Religion, Oriental.

LA MAMA EXPERIMENTAL THEATRE CLUB

NY —HAMPDEN-BOOTH THEATRE LIBRARY AT THE PLAYERS, 16 Gramercy Park, New York, 10003. Louis A Rachow, Librn/Cur
Holdings: Mss
Notes: La Mama Experimental Theatre Club. The holdings include printed, typescript and manuscript material and relate chiefly to the period when La Mama, under the guidance of Ellen Stewart, was located at 122 Second Avenue--a symbol of the Off-Off Broadway movement of the 1960s. The collection is divided into three sections (1) Chronological records of productions containing approximately 140 manuscript and typescript leaves as well as some additional eighty pages of source material and worksheets, (2) Clippings and press coverage including 123 clippings from Scottish, English, German and American newspapers and periodicals, and (3) Playbills and programs consisting of 143 broadsides and handbills together with miscellaneous bills of productions and lectures by La Mama artists. Each section has its own calendar and the holdings as a whole are considered to be the mostcomplete in existence for the years 1965-68, since no systematic archives were maintained until after La Mama's move from Second Avenue in 1968. The collection has been designated the Paul F Cranefield Collection of the La Mama Experimental Theatre Club. Described in *Theatre & Performing Arts* Collections (New York: Haworth Press, 1981)

LAMAR, MIRABEAU B.

TX —RICE UNIVERSITY, Fondren Library, Woodson Research Center, 6100 S Main St, PO Box 1892, Houston, 77251. Nancy Parker, Dir Woodson Research Center

LAMARTINE, ALPHONSE DE, 1790-1869

NY —SYRACUSE UNIVERSITY LIBRARIES, Ernest S Bird Library, George Arents Research Library for Special Collections, Syracuse, 13210. Carolyn A Davis, Manuscripts Librn; Amy S Doherty, University Archivist; Mark F Weimer, Rare Book Librn
Notes: His correspondence, 1829-1867 (194 items).

LAMB, CHARLES

KY —UNIVERSITY OF KENTUCKY, Margaret I King Library, Dept of Special Collections, Lexington, 40506. William Marshall, Head
Holdings: Vols (8000) Cat Mss
Notes: W Hugh Peal Collection of mss and books chiefly relating to British and American literature. Particularly strong in Lamb, Wordsworth, Coleridge and Southey. Incl 4 cubic feet of mss. Incl 16th-20th centuries.

MA —HARVARD UNIVERSITY LIBRARY, Houghton Library, Cambridge, 02138. F Thomas Noonan, Cur, Reading Room; Lawrence Dowler, Associate Librn
Holdings: Cat Mss
Notes: Described in *Harvard Library* Bulletin, X (1956), 208-239, 367-402.

MA —MOUNT HOLYOKE COLLEGE, Williston Memorial Library, South Hadley, 01075. Anne C Edmonds, Librn
Holdings: (100) Cat
Notes: Books by and about him, incl first editions and original drawings.

OH —OHIO UNIVERSITY, Vernon R Alden Library, Department of Archives and Special Collections, Athens, 45701. Gary A Hunt, Head
Holdings: Vols (10,191) Uncat Mss
Notes: The Edmund Blunden Collection of Romantic and Modern Literature, being the private library assembled by Blunden during 6 decades of active collecting. The bulk of the collection (6,264 titles) consists of English imprints from the period 1750-1850, concentrating on literature but also incl contemporary works on art, natural history, philosophy and other subjects important for understanding the background of English Romanticism. Among the authors most heavily represented by first and other early editions are: Allington, Barnes, Bloomfield, Byron, Clare, Coleridge, Cowper, Dyer, Edgeworth, Goldsmith, Hazlitt, Hunt, Lamb, Landor, Scott, Thompson and Wordsworth. Books written by Blunden himself, together with his Georgian contemporaries (particularly W H Davies, Walter De la Mare, and Sigfried Sassoon) form a second major area of strength. Many ofthe modern books are inscribed to Blunden, and nearly all the volumes in the collection bear his annotations.

ON —VICTORIA UNIVERSITY, Library, 71 Queen's Park Crescent, Toronto, M5S 1K7, Can. Robert C Brandeis, Chief Librn
Holdings: Vols 1100 Cat Mss
Notes: A significant collection (second only to the British Museum) of books, mss, notebooks, correspondence, etc of Samuel Taylor Coleridge and his circle and family, including letters and mss of Wordsworth, Lamb and Southey. Catalog of collection by H O Dendurent in *The Wordsworth Circle* (Temple University, Philadelphia, Pa) 5:4 (Autumn 1974).

LAMB, EDWARD

OH —BOWLING GREEN STATE UNIVERSITY, Jerome Library, Center for Archival Collections, Bowling Green, 43403. Paul D Yon, Dir; Elaine R Ezell, Reference Archivist; Nancy Steen, Rare Books Librn
Notes: Incl pamphlets; records of 25 major labor unions document labor history in northwest Ohio. Complemented also by the papers of Edward Lamb, a noted Toledo lawyer active in labor affairs.

LAMB, HAROLD, 1892-1962

CA —UNIVERSITY OF CALIFORNIA, LOS ANGELES, Research Library, Dept of Special Collections, 405 Hilgard Ave, Los Angeles, 90024. Edward Shreeves, Chairman, Bibliographers Group; David S Zeidberg, Head
Holdings: Vols 50
Notes: 50 books; 14 linear feet of typescripts, clippings, etc.

LAMBERT, DEREK

MA —BOSTON UNIVERSITY, Mugar Memorial Library, Special Collections Dept, 771 Commonwealth Ave, Boston, 02215. Howard B Gotlieb, Dir
Holdings: Cat Mss

LAMBERT, ERIC

BC —UNIVERSITY OF VICTORIA, McPherson Library, Victoria, V8W 3H5, Can.
Notes: Biologist, cricket coach and freelance writer. Incl corrected typescript of novel *Hiroshima Reef.*

LAMBERT, GAVIN

MA —BOSTON UNIVERSITY, Mugar Memorial Library, Special Collections Dept, 771 Commonwealth Ave, Boston, 02215. Howard B Gotlieb, Dir
Holdings: Cat Mss
Notes: Mss, correspondence, etc collected in depth; incl publications by or about.

LAMBS CLUB

NY —NEW YORK PUBLIC LIBRARY, Performing Arts Research Center, Billy Rose Theatre Collection, 111 Amsterdam Ave, New York, 10023. Dorothy L Swerdlove, Cur
Holdings: Cat
Notes: Most of the archives of this important theatrical club, 1883-1970, incl historical records, mss, and correspondence. Much of the special material has been cataloged under Lambs; other items were integrated into regular Theatre Collection's subjects.

LAMONT, CORLISS

†NY —COLUMBIA UNIVERSITY LIBRARIES, Butler Library, Rare Book and Manuscript Library, 535 W 114 St, New York, 10027.
Notes: Dr Corliss Lamont's correspondence with John Dewey, as well as related correspondence.

†NY —COLUMBIA UNIVERSITY LIBRARIES, Law Library, Law Bldg, New York, 10027.
Notes: Collection to support the civil liberties program under a new Corliss Lamont chair.

LAMONT, THOMAS W.

MA —HARVARD UNIVERSITY, Graduate School of Business Administration, Baker Library, Soldiers Field, Boston, 02163. Mary V Chatfield, Librn; Florence Bartoshesky, Cur of Manuscripts and Archives
Holdings: Mss
Notes: Business papers.

LAMPE, ALEKSEI ALEKSANDROVICH VON

CA —HOOVER INSTITUTION ON WAR, REVOLUTION & PEACE, Stanford University, Stanford, 94305. Milorad M Drachkovitch, Archivist
Holdings: / / Mss
Notes: Papers, 1917-1926, of Aleksei Aleksandrovich von Lampe, Czarist general, chief of the Russian Military Agency in Berlin and military writer. Correspondence, reports, documents and printed material, dealing with the activities of the agency which was headed by Lampe and served as a headquarters for Gens Wrangel, Yudenich, and Denikin, Adm Kolchak and others, ca 1917-1926. 9 boxes. Unpublished preliminary inventory in repository.

LAMPE, DAVID

MA —BOSTON UNIVERSITY, Mugar Memorial Library, Special Collections Dept, 771 Commonwealth Ave, Boston, 02215. Howard B Gotlieb, Dir
Holdings: Cat Mss Correspondence

LAMPLAND, CARL O.

AZ —NORTHERN ARIZONA UNIVERSITY, Special Collection Library, CU Box 6022, Flagstaff, 86011. Peter M Whiteley, Coordr/Archivist; William Mullane, Librn
Notes: Typewritten journal, written by Lampland, incl episode occurring at the Lowell Observatory in Flagstaff, Ariz.

LAMPMAN, ARCHIBALD

BC —SIMON FRASER UNIVERSITY, Library, Burnaby, V5A 1S6, Can. Percilla Groves, Special Collections Librn
Holdings: / / Cat Mss Pix
Notes: Holograph essay on Keats and book of poems, correspondence to and from Lampman's wife, correspondence from Bliss Carman, Hamlin Garland, and Charles G D Roberts, photographs of Lampman family, small group of miscellaneous correspondence.

LAMUT LANGUAGE

WA —UNIVERSITY OF WASHINGTON LIBRARIES, Rare Books, Special Collections Dept, Seattle, 98195. Sandra Kroupa, Librn
Notes: Part of a set of Siberian primers prepared in the early 1930s by Soviet ethnographers. Some are first attempts to transcribe Siberian languages. All are in Latin phonetic script, not in Cyrillic.

LANCASTER INDUSTRIAL SCHOOL

†MA —SECRETARY OF THE COMMONWEALTH, Archives Division, State House, Boston, 02133.

LAND

AZ —ARIZONA HERITAGE CENTER, Library, 949 E Second St, Tucson, 85719. Michael Weber, Dir
Notes: Espec with reference to Arizona, the West, and the Southwest.

CA —UNIVERSITY OF CALIFORNIA, BERKELEY, Giannini Foundation of Agricultural Economics, Library, 248 Giannini Hall, Berkeley, 94720. Grace Dote, Librn
Holdings: Vols (18,000) Cat Mss Maps Microforms
Notes: Noncirculating collection. No interlibrary loans. Also about 124,000 unbound vols. Open to graduate students and faculties of universities and colleges, research workers and interested public. Mostly English language materials, primarily 1900 to date. Card catalog published by G K Hall Co. *Dictionary Catalog of the Giannini Foundation of Agricultural Economics Library, Univ of California*, 12 vols (Holdings thru 7/71).

CA —UNIVERSITY OF CALIFORNIA, DAVIS, Agricultural Economics Library, Davis, 95616. Susan Casement, Head
Holdings: Vols 6200 Maps
Budget: $10,000
Notes: Agricultural business; Land

LAND (cont.)

economics and development; soil survey maps. 170,000 pamphlets.

CA —UNIVERSITY OF CALIFORNIA, LOS ANGELES, Graduate School of Management Library, UCLA Campus, Los Angeles, 90024. Robert Bellanti, Head Librn
Holdings: Vols (128,000) Cat Mss Microforms
Notes: The collection is broad in scope covering all aspects of business and management; emphasis is placed on in-depth collecting in the Graduate School of Management's core curriculum areas: accounting, behavioral and organizational science, business economics, computers and information science, finance, management science/operations research, marketing, organization and strategic studies, production and operations managements, public/non-profit management and urban land economics.

CA —ASSOCIATION OF BAY AREA GOVERNMENTS, MTC/ABAG Library, 101 Eighth St, Oakland, 94607. Diane Gillman, Information Coord
Notes: Concentrates heavily on the nine-county Bay Area region. About 10,000 monographs and serials. Title catalog, OCLC/ATS. Central collection of documents for six transit properties in Bay Area.

CA —UNIVERSITY OF CALIFORNIA, SANTA BARBARA, Map and Imagery Laboratory, Santa Barbara, 93106. Larry Carver, Dept Head
Notes: Worldwide coverage of Landsat imagery donated by US Dept of Agriculture Aerial Photography Field Office. Consists of 153,000 scenes, covering most of the earth's surface between the years 1975 and 1980. Incl 300,000 maps, 1800 atlases, 9 globes, 300 relief models, 1,500,000 satellite imagery and aerial photographs, 700 reference books and gazetteers, 25 serials (titles received), and 21,000 microforms.

CT —YALE UNIVERSITY, Forestry Library, 205 Prospect St, New Haven, 06511. Joseph A Miller, Librn
Holdings: Vols (115,000) Cat Microforms
Notes: The Forestry Library is a unit of the Yale University Library, housed in and serving primarily the School of Forestry and Environmental Studies. Founded in 1900, it has become one of the largest forestry libraries in the world. Forestry is construed broadly to incl underlying or closely related social, physical, and biological sciences. The literature of North American forestry and forest products is most completely covered, though other countries and foreign languages are well represented. Environmental studies and allied fields of natural resources management have been emphasized during the past 10 years. See *Dictionary Catalog of the Yale Forestry Library*, 12 vols (Boston: G K Hall, 1962).

DC —CONSERVATION FOUNDATION, Library, 1717 Massachusetts Ave NW, Washington, 20036. Barbara K Rodes, Librn
Holdings: Vols (8000) Cat Maps
Notes: Collection incl natural resources, ecology, city and regional planning, land use, recreation, energy conservation, environmental economics, pollution control, water resources.

DC —METROPOLITAN WASHINGTON COUNCIL OF GOVERNMENTS, Map Library, 1875 Eye St NW, Suite 200, Washington, 20006. Susan Kalish, Librn
Holdings: Cat Maps
Notes: 3000 current and retrospective maps covering metropolitan Washington region, incl the District of Columbia; Montgomery and Prince George's counties in Maryland; and Arlington, Fairfax, Prince William and Loudoun counties and the City of Alexandria in Virginia. Maps cover land use, community facilities, transportation, topography, statistical units, and socioeconomic information. Record of holdings on computer printout.

DC —URBAN LAND INSTITUTE, Library, 1090 Vermont Ave, Washington, 20005. Ann Benson, Librn
Holdings: Vols (9000) Cat
Budget: ($6000)
Notes: Incl 200 serials.

FL —ARCHBOLD BIOLOGICAL STATION, Library, Rt 2, Box 180, Lake Placid, 33852. Fred E Lohrer, Librn
Holdings: Cat Slides
Notes: Florida natural history. Emphasis on south central peninsular Florida. Habitats, plants, vertebrates, land use changes. About 8000 2x2 color transparencies and 35mm films.

IL —LAKE FOREST COLLEGE, Donnelley Library, Lake Forest, 60045. Arthur H Miller Jr, College Librn
Holdings: Vols (500) Cat Maps
Budget: ($1200)
Notes: Focus on development of suburban fringe areas, particularly Lake Co, Ill, and Chicago region: local documents (plans, transit, zoning maps, etc), US documents, and special studies of suburban issues, such as historic preservation and land use.

IA —IOWA STATE UNIVERSITY, Library, Ames, 50011. Warren B Kuhn, Dean of Library Services
Holdings: Cat Mss
Notes: Incl agriculture finance and policy, agricultural marketing, farm management, land valuation, and rural development. Extensive serial holdings.

MD —MARYLAND-NATIONAL CAPITAL PARK & PLANNING COMMISSION, Montgomery County Planning Department Library, 8787 Georgia Ave, Silver Spring, 20907. Janice C Holt, Librn
Holdings: Vols (5000) Cat Slides Microforms
Notes: Specific subject areas include: community facilities, conservation, economics, flood control, highways, housing, human and natural resources. landscape architecture, open space, parks, pollution, population, recreation, transportation, urban renewal, and zoning. Commission's publications are maintained by Records Management (not Library).

MI —MICHIGAN STATE UNIVERSITY, Urban Policy & Planning Library, East Lansing, 48824. Dale E Casper, Librn
Holdings: Vols (12,800) Cat
Budget: ($35,000)
Notes: Serves the curricular and research needs of faculty and students involved in urban and regional policy analysis and community planning.

NV —UNIVERSITY OF NEVADA, RENO, University Library, Special Collections Dept, Reno, 89557. Robert E Blesse, Head
Holdings: Vols 3500 Cat Mss Maps Pix
Notes: Incl 2100 cubic feet of mss, 25,000 photographs, maps, VF, microforms, and oral histories. Both primary and secondary materials are collected which document the history and development of Nevada and the Great Basin region from its beginnings to the present day. Areas of strength incl mining, politics, water resources, railroads, biography, land use, anthropology, architecture, Lake Tahoe, lumbering, and early Nevada imprints. Major emphasis is on the prehistory and history of Nevada with lesser emphasis on bordering states and the Great Basin region. Specialized catalogs and indexes are available in the department.

OR —UNIVERSITY OF OREGON, Library, Eugene, 97403. Kenneth W Duckett, Curator
Notes: Papers of James C Rettie, Senior Economist of the Department of the Interior.

OR —UNIVERSITY OF OREGON, Bureau of Governmental Research Library, Box 3177, Eugene, 97403. Katherine G Eaton, Head Librn
Holdings: Vols (25,000) Cat Microforms
Budget: ($5000)
Notes: Separate catalog and classification system.

TX —ECTOR COUNTY LIBRARY, Department of Business and Technology, 321 W 5th St, Odessa, 79760. Pat Jones, Dept Head
Notes: 25,000 Corporate Annual Reports microfilmed reports are complete from 1978-1983. 200 vertical files, 30 periodicals. Collection includes the subjects of Business, Management, Real Estate Accounting, Land Economics, Labor Economics, Finance, Personal Finance and Environmental Economics. Also included are stock and dividend reports, commodities and bond reports as well as business rankings. All items are referenced and cataloged.

BC —CANADIAN FORESTRY SERVICE, Pacific Forest Research Centre, Library, 506 West Burnside Rd, Victoria, V8Z 1M5, Can. Alice Solyma, Librn
Holdings: Vols (60,500) Cat Microforms
Notes: Incl forest and plant pathology, entomology, silviculture, meteorology, mensuration, fire research, hydrology, environmental science and ecology, biometrics, land use and classification, soil science, and forest economics. 400 microforms; 40,000 documents and reports.

ON —ONTARIO MINISTRY OF NATURAL RESOURCES, Natural Resources Library, Whitney Block 4540, Toronto, M5S 1B3, Can. Sandra Louet, Librn
Holdings: Cat

ON —INTERNATIONAL JOINT COMMISSION LIBRARY, 100 Ouellette Ave, Seventh Floor, Windsor, N9A 6T3, Can. Pat Murrary, Librn
Notes: Emphasis on water resources, water quality, land use, coastal zones, Great Lakes. Library includes 40,000 government reports from federal, provincial and state governments; 5000 monographs to support Great Lakes Water Quality Agreement Community. Collection also includes 243 periodicals, 1700 microfiche, 800 slides & vertical files.

LAND—POLLUTION

MA —CAMP, DRESSER & MCKEE, Herman G Dresser Library, One Center Plaza, Boston, 02108. Virginia L Carroll, Librn
Holdings: Vols (15,000) Cat Maps Slides Microforms
Notes: Air, land, and water pollution; environmental engineering; hazardous wastes; water resources; solid wastes; resource recycling.

LAND—MAPS

†CA —UNIVERSITY OF CALIFORNIA, DAVIS, Peter J Shields Memorial Library, Map Collection, Davis, 95616.

LAND, MYRICK E.

MA —BOSTON UNIVERSITY, Mugar Memorial Library, Special Collections Dept, 771 Commonwealth Ave, Boston, 02215. Howard B Gotlieb, Dir
Holdings: Cat Mss Pix
Notes: Mss, correspondence, etc collected in depth; incl publications by or about.

LAND, RECLAMATION OF see Reclamation of Land

LAND CREDIT see Agricultural Credit

LAND DRAINAGE see Drainage

LAND GRANTS

CA —CALIFORNIA STATE ARCHIVES, 1020 O St, Room 130, Sacramento, 95814. John F Burns, Chief of Archives; Joseph Samora, Head of Reference
Holdings: Vols (19)
Notes: A special collection of Spanish and Mexican land grants, ca 1784-1846.

FL —SAINT PETERSBURG PUBLIC LIBRARY, 3745 Ninth Ave N, Saint Petersburg, 33713. Luccille Bostfofff, Reference Supvr
Holdings: Vols 2240 Cat Maps Pix Microforms
Notes: Florida document depository. Spanish land grants on microfilm. Local newspapers on microfilm. Approximately 196,000 cards indexing local newspapers and Florida magazines by subject. Incl 125 pictures, 2474 microfilm reels; 30,943 pamphlets and documents.

LAND GRANTS (cont.)

NY —CORNELL UNIVERSITY LIBRARIES, Collection of Regional History, Dept of Manuscripts and Univ Archives, Ithaca, 14853.
Notes: Incl records, 1959-63, concerning the simultaneous observance (1961-62) of the 100th anniversary of the Morrill Act by Cornell University and other land-grant colleges and universities. Also, pamphlets, magazine and newspaper articles, and clippings concerning land-grant colleges and the Centennial.

SC —COLLEGE OF CHARLESTON LIBRARY, Special Collections Dept, Charleston, 29401.
Notes: Indenture for the sale of a tract of land in Prince Willliam Parish, Granville County, SC, granted to Hugh Bryan by King George II and given to Rev George Whitefield and then by Rev Whitefield to Mary Bryan, Nov 24, 1752, and a plat of the tract dated Dec 29, 1747, Property conveyances, 1776-1800 incl leases, releases, deeds, grants, and renunciations of dower for properties located in South Carolina (Charleston, Prince William Parish, Christ Church Parish), involving Thomas Barksdale, Ebenezer Coffin, Janet Cumming, Martha Godin, John Harleston, Benjamin Huger, John Huger, Ralph Izard the Younger, William Logan, Spencer Man, Charlotte Martin, Thomas Martin, Jacob Motte, Benjamin Stead, Ann Timothy, John Wells, Patience Wise, Sarah Young; Court of Common Pleas, papers, 1819.

LAND LEAGUE

NY —AMERICAN IRISH HISTORICAL SOCIETY, Library, 991 Fifth Ave, New York, 10028. Lisa M Hottin, Cur; William D Griffin, Librn
Holdings: Vols (20,000) Cat Maps Pix Slides
Notes: Archives and Manuscripts: The documents and papers of Friends of Irish Freedom, The Land League, the Society of the Friendly Sons of St Patrick, the Catholic Club, and the Guild of Catholic Lawyers. The papers of New York State Supreme Court Justice Daniel F Cohalan. This is the largest and most complete collection of over 20,000 American Irish and Irish history, biography and literature in the United States. Incl American-Irish Newspaper collections dating from 1811, the most comprehensive in the US; 1000 rare books and special editions. Special collections incl regular exhibits of Irish or American Irish interest incl mss, letters, books, photographs and memorabilia. Permanent collection of representative works of Irish painters.

LAND PATENTS see Land Grants

LAND QUESTION see Land Tenure

LAND RECLAMATION see Reclamation of Land

LAND REFORM—HISTORY

IN —PURDUE UNIVERSITY LIBRARIES, Graduate School of Management, Krannert Library, West Lafayette, 47907. Gordon Law, Librn
Notes: An important resource at the Krannert Library is its Special Collection of Business and Economics, consisting of some 8000 rare pre-20th century strengths in books, journals, tracts and pamphlets covering primarily the early literature of economic thought and business practices in America and abroad, 1500-1870. A catalog was issued in 1979.

WI —UNIVERSITY OF WISCONSIN, MADISON, Land Tenure Center Library, 434 Steenbock Memorial Library, 550 Babcock Dr, Madison, 53706. Teresa J Anderson, Librn
Notes: Socio-economic aspects of agricultural development in the Third World. All materials in the collection are cataloged and classified. The library has its own catalog.

LAND SURVEYING see Surveying

LAND TENURE

CA —UNIVERSITY OF CALIFORNIA, BERKELEY, Giannini Foundation of Agricultural Economics, Library, 248 Giannini Hall, Berkeley, 94720. Grace Dote, Librn
Holdings: Vols (18,000) Cat Mss Maps Microforms
Notes: Noncirculating collection. No interlibrary loans. Also about 124,000 unbound vols. Open to graduate students and faculties of universities and colleges, research workers and interested public. Mostly English language materials, primarily 1900 to date. Card catalog published by G K Hall Co. *Dictionary Catalog of the Giannini Foundation of Agriculatural Economics Library, Univ of California*, 12 vols (Holdings thru 7/71).

IN —PURDUE UNIVERSITY LIBRARIES, Graduate School of Management, Krannert Library, West Lafayette, 47907. Gordon Law, Librn
Holdings: Vols (7000) Cat Mss Maps Pix Microforms
Notes: The collection consists of books, journals and pamphlets dating from the early 16th to late 19th century, covering to a large degree the early literature in economic thought and business practices both here and abroad. No photocopying.

OR —US DEPT OF ENERGY, Bonneville Power Administration Library, 1002 NE Holladay St, PO Box 3621, Portland, 97232. Karen Hadman, Chief of Library Branch
Holdings: Vols (1000)
Notes: Emphasis is on Federal and Pacific Northwest law and in subject areas of interest to the Departments of Energy and Interior.

WI —UNIVERSITY OF WISCONSIN, MADISON, Land Tenure Center Library, 434 Steenbock Memorial Library, 550 Babcock Dr, Madison, 53706. Teresa J Anderson, Librn
Holdings: Vols (60,000) Cat Mss Maps Microforms
Budget: ($65,000)
Notes: Socio-economic aspects of agricultural development in the Third World. All materials in the collection are cataloged and classified. The library has its own catalog.

LAND USE see Land

LAND UTILIZATION see Land; Regional Planning

LANDIS, JAMES MCCAULEY, 1899-1964

MA —HARVARD UNIVERSITY LIBRARY, Law School Library, Langdell Hall, Cambridge, 02138. Erika S Chadbourn, Cur of Mss
Holdings: Cat Mss
Notes: Professional papers. Typed inventory in repository. Inclusive dates: 1924-1945.

LANDIS, KENESAW MOUNTAIN

IL —CHICAGO HISTORICAL SOCIETY, Library, Clark St at North Ave, Chicago, 60614. Archie Motley, Manuscript Librn
Notes: Papers of: Emmet Dedmon, newspaper editor; Richard J Finnegan, newspaper editor; Rev Andres M Greeley, sociologist and author; attorney and civil liberties activist Pearl Hart; Robert J Havighurst, educator; social activist John Kearney; Kenesaw Mountain Landis, Federal Judge and first Commissioner of Baseball; Judge David F Matchett; Ivan Molek, Slovenian language publisher in Chicago; Max R Naiman, Communist Party activist; Ralph G Newman, book and autograph dealer and manuscript appraiser; Otto L Schmidt, physician and President of the Chicago and Illinois State Historical Societies; and Dempsey Travis, black mortgage banker.

LANDON, H. C. ROBBINS

MA —BOSTON UNIVERSITY, Mugar Memorial Library, Special Collections Dept, 771 Commonwealth Ave, Boston, 02215. Howard B Gotlieb, Dir
Holdings: Cat Mss Correspondence Phonorecords Family Papers

LANDSAT IMAGERY

CA —UNIVERSITY OF CALIFORNIA, SANTA BARBARA, Map and Imagery Laboratory, Santa Barbara, 93106. Larry Carver, Dept Head
Notes: Worldwide coverage of Landsat imagery donated by US Dept of Agriculture Aerial Photography Field Office. Consists of 153,000 scenes, covering most of the earth's surface between the years 1975 and 1980. Incl 300,000 maps, 1800 atlases, 9 globes, 300 relief models, 1,500,000 satellite imagery and aerial photographs, 700 reference books and gazetteers, 25 serials (titles received), and 21,000 microforms.

DC —LIBRARY OF CONGRESS, Geography and Map Division, Washington, 20540. John A Wolter, Chief
Notes: Not a comprehensive collection. Samples of Landsat imagery.

WI —UNIVERSITY OF WISCONSIN, MADISON, Kurt F Wendt Library, 215 N Randall Ave, Madison, 53706. LeRoy G Zweifel, Librn
Notes: Incl LANDSAT Remote Imagery; also, complete US patent collection.

WI —UNIVERSITY OF WISCONSIN, MILWAUKEE, American Geographical Society Collection, 2311 E Hartford Ave, PO Box 399, Milwaukee, 53201. Roman Drazniowsky, Cur
Holdings: Vols (196,800)
Budget: ($270,000)
Notes: The largest special collection in geography, cartography and related fields in the Western Hemisphere. Incl 6469 atlases; 385,610 maps; 71 globes; 33,700 pamphlets; 79,000 photographs; 99,000 Landsat Images. Catalog published by G K Hall, Boston.

LANDSCAPE ARCHITECTURE

AL —BIRMINGHAM BOTANICAL GARDENS, Horace Hammond Memorial Library, 2612 Lane Park Road, Birmingham, 35223. Ida Burns, Librn
Holdings: Vols 2800 Cat Pix Films Slides VF

CA —UNIVERSITY OF CALIFORNIA, BERKELEY, Environmental Design Library, (The General Library), 210 Wurster Hall, Berkeley, 94720. Arthur B Waugh, Head
Holdings: Vols (9000) Cat
Budget: ($4900)
Notes: Research collection emphasizing the following areas: Park and garden design; site planning; spatial planning; professional practice. Lesser emphasis on horticulture. The Library also includes the Beatrix Farrand Collection of rare books in the field of landscape architecture.

CA —CALIFORNIA STATE POLYTECHNIC UNIVERSITY, POMONA, University Library, 3801 W Temple Ave, Pomona, 91768. Harold Schleiser, Actg Dir
Holdings: Vols 1600 Cat
Budget: $3200

CA —STRYBING ARBORETUM SOCIETY, Golden Gate Park Library, Jane Gates, Librn, 9th Ave at Lincoln Way, San Francisco, 94122.
Holdings: Vols (10,000)

CA —CALIFORNIA POLYTECHNIC STATE UNIVERSITY LIBRARY, Special Collections and University Archives, San Luis Obispo, 93407. Nancy E Loe, Head Librn
Holdings: Mss
Notes: The Barton Collection incl the personal and professional papers of Arthur G

LANDSCAPE ARCHITECTURE (cont.)

Barton, a noted Southern California landscape architect, incl his office files, bids, and drawings and designs (collection in rough sorting stage). 55,000 pieces of ms material. 6000 landscape architecture designs and drawings.

CO —UNIVERSITY OF COLORADO, Libraries, Art & Architecture Library, Campus Box 184, Boulder, 80309. Liesel Nolan, Librn/Dept Head
Holdings: Vols (57,647) Cat Pix
Budget: ($39,000)
Notes: Special feature: art exhibition catalog collection 1963-1971, 1972-date. Good general collection with some special emphasis on environmental design, Islamic architecture, Indian art and South American Indian art. Fair collection of periodical backfiles in art and in architecture. Separate catalog for materials in collection. Rare books in main library, listed only in central union catalog.

†CO —DENVER BOTANIC GARDENS, Helen Fowler Library, 909 York St, Denver, 80206. Solange G Gignac, Librn
Notes: Emphasis on Bromeliada Literature; horticulture; Colorado, Oregon, and Rocky Mountains Region botany; landscape architecture; juvenile horticultural and botanical literature. Incl over 5000 pamphlets on botany and horticulture; also, 197 watercolors of Colorado wildflowers by Emma Irvine, and 250 of Oregon by Lillian Hallock.

DE —UNIVERSITY OF DELAWARE, Hugh M Morris Library, S College Ave, Newark, 19711. T Stuart Dick, Special Collections
Holdings: Cat Mss Pix
Notes: Personal and business letters and receipts, of the Albertson family, Quaker lumber and lime merchants (1782-1862) residing in Plymouth, Montgomery Co, Pa. Included are many letters concerning the Plymouth RR and rules and regulations for its administration.

DE —WILMINGTON GARDEN CENTER LIBRARY, 503 Market Street Mall, Wilmington, 19801. Bonnie J Swan Day, Admin Asst; Karen Bidus, Librn
Holdings: Vols (1500)
Notes: Library open to the public, only circulates to members.

DC —LIBRARY OF CONGRESS, Manuscript Division, Washington, 20540. John C Broderick, Chief
Notes: More than 150,000 items added to the records of Olmsted Associates, Inc, of Brookline, Massachusetts, landscape architects.

IL —MORTON ARBORETUM, Sterling Morton Library, Lisle, 60532. Ian MacPhail, Librn
Holdings: Vols (20,000) Cat Maps Pix
Budget: ($10,000)
Notes: The library is especially concerned with the literature of woody plants (trees and shrubs) of north temperate zones but has substantial holdings in the taxonomy and systematics of plants in general, both wild and cultivated, flora of different parts of the world, and a growing collection on plant monographs. Also about 2000 pictures. Described in *The Morton Arboretum* Quarterly, vol 9, no 4 (Winter 1973), pp 56-61.

IL —NORTHBROOK PUBLIC LIBRARY, 1201 Cedar Lane, Northbrook, 60062. Donna Hicks, Librn
Holdings: Vols (3500) Cat Slides
Notes: Maintained as architecture subject center under the North Suburban Library System's Coordinated Acquisitions Program through 1977. Library will attempt to maintain collection through its own budget.

IL —UNIVERSITY OF ILLINOIS, URBANA/CHAMPAIGN, Library, City Planning & Landscape Architecture Library, 203 Mumford Hall, 1301 West Gregory Drive, Urbana, 61801. Mary D Ravenhall, Librn
Holdings: Vols (20,000) Cat
Budget: ($11,000)
Notes: Urban and regional planning; landscape architecture.

IN —BALL STATE UNIVERSITY, College of Architecture & Planning, Architecture Library, Muncie, 47306. Marjorie Hake Joyner, Librn
Holdings: Vols (25,000) Cat Maps Slides Microforms
Budget: ($17,360)
Notes: Strong emphasis on history of all aspects of architecture. Also, for other major areas, architecture and landscape architecture and planning 50,000 35 mm color slides, over half cataloged.

KY —UNIVERSITY OF LOUISVILLE, Allen R Hite Art Institute, Library, Belknap Campus, Louisville, 40292. Gail Gilbert, Librn
Holdings: Vols (40,000) Cat Pix
Budget: ($29,000)
Notes: Incl books on art, architecture, landscape architecture and gardening, prints, printing, illustrated books and brass rubbings. Library subscribes to 200 periodical titles in these and other areas. Collection circulates to faculty and staff only, with same restrictions placed on interlibrary loan. Library also has collections of bookplates, posters, original prints, hand-made Christmas cards and clippings file filling 56 VF drawers.

LA —LOUISIANA STATE UNIVERSITY, College of Design, Design Resource Center, 102 College of Design Bldg, Baton Rouge, 70803. Doris A Wheeler, Librn
Holdings: Vols 8500 Cat Maps Slides VF
Budget: $6000
Notes: Architecture, interior design, city planning, landscape architecture.

MD —MARYLAND-NATIONAL CAPITAL PARK & PLANNING COMMISSION, Montgomery County Planning Department Library, 8787 Georgia Ave, Silver Spring, 20907. Janice C Holt, Librn
Holdings: Vols (5000) Cat Microforms
Notes: Specific subject areas include: community facilities, conservation, economics, flood control, highways, housing, human and natural resources. landscape architecture, open space, parks, pollution, population, recreation, transportation, urban renewal, and zoning. Commission's publications are maintained by Records Management (not Library).

MA —MASSACHUSETTS HORTICULTURAL SOCIETY, 300 Massachusetts Ave, Boston, 02115. Becky Ellis, Librn
Holdings: Vols (37,000)
Notes: Garden history, pomology, flora, landscape design. Print collection of many centuries; nursery catalogues from the mid-18th century. In storage, remodeling, will be available in about a year. Open to the public.

MA —SOCIETY FOR THE PRESERVATION OF NEW ENGLAND ANTIQUITIES, Library, 141 Cambridge St, Boston, 02114. Ellie Reichlin, Librn & Cur of Photographic Collections
Holdings: Vols (3000) Cat Pix Microforms
Budget: ($75,000)
Notes: Photograph collections, all media (incl daguerreotypes, ambrotypes, etc, stereographic views, carte de visite) depicting New England buildings; interiors; street and town views; occupations; pastimes; transport and personalities. Covers 1840s-1930s, with some more recent additons. Amateur and professional photographers represented. Cataloged in part, otherwise arranged by localities, subject, personal name. Special collections incl: marine photographs by N L Stebbins and Henry Peabody (1880s-1920s); Boston and Albany railroad photographic archive, early 1900s; Quabbin Valley views; historic American Buildings Survey photographs (17th to early 19th century architecture) by Arthur Haskell; Baldwin Coolidge collection, and many others. Size: 500,000 prints, ca 75,000 negatives (glass plates and copy negs). These are cataloged. Some special indexes inclandscape design (arbors, conservatories, flower beds, bandstands etc); photographers represented; architects represented (partial), and pending, interiors (specific features of); occupations.

MA —HARVARD UNIVERSITY, Graduate School of Design, Frances Loeb Library, Gund Hall, Cambridge, 02138. James Hodgson, Librn
Holdings: Vols (225,000) Cat Mss Pix Slides Microforms
Budget: ($500,000)
Notes: Covers architecture, landscape architecture, city and regional planning, and urban design. Catalog, in 44 volumes, published in 1968, with 2-volume supplement in 1970, 5-volume supplement in 1974, and 3-volume supplement in 1979. It also analyzes periodical articles. Architecture collection described in *Harvard Library* Bulletin, VI (1952): pp 263-269. Noteworthy holdings incl those on Abbey of Cluny, Le Corbusier, amd Henry Hobson Richardson. Landscape Architecture described in *Harvard Library Bulletin,* VII (1953), 188-195. Incl books and papers of Charles Eliot.

MA —UNIVERSITY OF LOWELL, Library, One University Ave, Lowell, 01854. Martha Mayo, Special Collections Librn
Holdings: Cat Mss Maps Pix
Notes: Warren H Manning was a founding member of the American Society of Landscape Architects. This collection contains his personal and professional papers incl project and client lists, business records, correspondence, plans, and photographs.

MI —OAKLAND COMMUNITY COLLEGE, Auburn Hills Campus, Learning Resources Center, 2900 Featherstone Rd, Auburn Hills, 48057. Eugene F Larson, Dept Chairman
Holdings: Vols 500 Cat Slides Audiotapes Videotapes 16mm Films

MI —UNIVERSITY OF DETROIT, Main Library, 4001 W McNichols Rd, Detroit, 48221.
Notes: Architecture Library was closed in 1981. Collection consolidated in main library.

MI —MICHIGAN STATE UNIVERSITY, Libraries, Special Collections Div, East Lansing, 48824. Jannette Fiore, Librn
Notes: The published works of Humphrey Repton renowned British landscape designer.

MN —UNIVERSITY OF MINNESOTA, Landscape Arboretum, Andersen Horticultural Library, 3675 Arboretum Drive, Box 39, Chanhassen, 55317. June Rogier, Head
Holdings: Vols (8000)

MN —UNIVERSITY OF MINNESOTA, Architecture Library, 89 Church St, Minneapolis, 55455. A Kristine Johnson, Librn
Holdings: Vols (27,000) Cat Mss
Budget: ($20,000)
Notes: Incl architecture, architectural history, landscape architecture, design methodology, housing, urban sociology, interior design, etc.

NY —CITY UNIVERSITY OF NEW YORK, City College, Architecture Library, 3300 Broadway, New York, 10031. Sylvia Wright, Assoc Prof
Holdings: Vols (15,000) Cat Pix Microforms
Budget: ($15,000)
Notes: Architecture, landscape architecture, urban planning and other related areas. 11, 000 pamphlets.

NY —GARDEN CENTER OF ROCHESTER INC, Library, 5 Castle Park, Rochester, 14620. Dorothea Baschnagel, Librn
Holdings: Vols (3000)
Notes: Gardening and home landscaping; plant identification; decorative use of plants; 19th century gardening. 700 bound periodicals, 30 periodical subscriptions.

NY —LANDMARK SOCIETY OF WESTERN NEW YORK, Wenrich Memorial Library, 130 Spring Rd, Rochester, 14608.
Holdings: Vols (2000) Cat Maps Pix Slides
Budget: ($500)
Notes: Paintings, slides, drawings, as well as the Society's archives of local architecture and information on preservation and restoration techniques. Much on preservation ordinances; legal, physical and financial aspects of building preservation; local and regional history, especially of Rochester and Monroe County.

NY —STATE UNIVERSITY OF NEW YORK, COLLEGE OF ENVIRONMENTAL SCIENCE AND

LANDSCAPE ARCHITECTURE (cont.)

FORESTRY, F Franklin Moon Library, Syracuse, 13210. Donald F Webster, Librn
Holdings: Vols (86,430) Cat
Budget: ($120,000)

NC —NORTH CAROLINA STATE UNIVERSITY, Harry B Lyons Design Library, P. O. Box 7701, Raleigh, 27607. Maryellen LoPresti, Librn
Notes: Collection covers architecture, landscape architecture, design and related professions. Additional materials may be found on art, painting, sculpture, photography and solar energy design. The library presently houses a total of 28,000 books, periodical and serial volumes to support the curriculum. A product and trade literature file and a vertical file of pamplets are also locally cataloged in the library representing an additional 3000 items of materials available for use. A significant collection of over 50,000 cataloged slides primarily representing the areas of art and architectural history are also contained in the library facility. See *Directory of Special Libraries and Information Centers.*

OH —OHIO STATE UNIVERSITY, Engineering Library, 2024 Neil Ave, Columbus, 43210. Mary Jo V Arnold, Librn
Holdings: Vols (132,000) Cat Microforms
Budget: ($110,000)

OH —KINGWOOD CENTER, Library, 900 Park Ave W, Mansfield, 44906. Timothy Gardner, Horticulturist
Holdings: Vols 8500
Notes: Espec ornamental horticulture, home gardening, landscaping, and floral arrangements. Incl 12,000 35mm slides of plants.

OH —THE DAWES ARBORETUM LIBRARY, 7770 Jacksontown Rd SE, Newark, 43055. Alan D Cook, Senior Horticulturist
Holdings: Vols 5000

PA —TEMPLE UNIVERSITY, Ambler Campus Library, Meetinghouse Road, Ambler, 19002. Esther G Bloomsburgh, Librn
Notes: Rare herbals are housed in Special Collections, Paley Library, Temple University (Thomas Whitehead, Curator). Incl 2500 items.

PA —PENNSYLVANIA STATE UNIVERSITY, Fred Lewis Pattee Library, Special Collections Dept, University Park, 16802. Charles Mann, Chief, Special Collections
Holdings: Vols (122,533) Cat Mss Maps Pix Slides Phonorecords Audiotapes Videotapes 16mm Films Microforms
Budget: ($37,000)
Notes: Special Collections and Rare Books includes several collections described separately. The holdings are particularly strong in literature, the 18th century, aeronautics, facsimiles, atlases, 19th century illustrated works on birds, botany and traveller's views. Special strengths are Emblem Books, Utopias, Fantastic Fiction, Australiana, Fine Presses, Labor Archives, Landscape Architecture, Pennsylvaniana. These collections are strengthened by parallel holdings in the open stacks. It also includes the collections of the Penn State Room. Several mimeographed lists are available. Audiotapes are listed in *Voices and Events, A Catalog of Audio Tapes* (Pennsylvania State University Libraries, 1975), 45 pp.

RI —RHODE ISLAND SCHOOL OF DESIGN, Library, Two College St, Providence, 02903. James A Findlay, Dir
Holdings: Vols (70,000) Cat Pix Slides
Budget: ($50,000)
Notes: Strong architecture and architectural history collection.

TN —THE BOTANICAL GARDENS, Minnie Ritchie and Joel Owsley Cheek Memorial Library, Forrest Park Drive, Nashville, 37205. Richard C Page, Dir Botanical Gardens
Holdings: Vols (3500) Cat Pix Slides
Budget: $2500

WA —UNIVERSITY OF WASHINGTON LIBRARIES, Pacific Northwest Collection, Seattle, 98195. Andrew F Johnson, Librn
Holdings: Vols (50,000) Cat Maps Pix
Budget: ($12,000)
Notes: The Pacific Northwest Collection contains printed materials documenting the historic and contemporary life and culture of the region in a broad range of subject areas. The Pacific Northwest is defined as the geographic region including Washington, Oregon, Idaho, Montana, British Columbia, Yukon Territory, and Alaska. Printed materials including books, periodicals, government documents, maps, weekly and local regional newspapers, theses and dissertations, as well as photographs and architectural drawings are included in the Pacific Northwest Collection. Photographic works of over 200 photographers active in the Pacific Northwest, Alaska, and the Yukon Territory (Canada) during the period 1860-1930, including Asahel and Edward S Curtis, Eric Hegg, and Clark Kinsey, are represented in a print collection of more than 300,000 images. The architecturaldrawings collection includes over 19,000 original plans, drawings, sketches, renderings and blue prints pertaining to the history of architecture and urban planning and landscape gardening in the Pacific Northwest ca 1880-1940. Areas of particular strength are the holdings of over 1100 published journals of Pacific Northwest exploration expeditions, photographs of Northwest Coast Native Americans and of historic Seattle, newspapers issued within the Japanese-American relocation camps, 1942-1945, materials relating to the 1980 eruption of Mt St Helens, and Sanborne fire insurance maps for Washington. A unique feature of the Collection is the subject index to regional periodicals and local newspapers maintained by the PNW Collection staff; over 100 titles are currently indexed. G K Hall Company published a books catalog of the Pacific Northwest Collectionin 1973.

WI —UNIVERSITY OF WISCONSIN, MADISON, College of Agricultural & Life Sciences, Steenbock Memorial Library, 550 Babcock Dr, Madison, 53706. Jan Kennedy, Dir
Holdings: Vols (186,312) Cat Docs Slides
Notes: Literature on historic preservation, landscape design, and horticulture. Twentieth century domestic architecture.

MB —UNIVERSITY OF MANITOBA, Architecture & Fine Arts Library, Winnipeg, R3T 2N2, Can. Peter Anthony, Head
Holdings: Vols (50,000) Maps Microforms
Notes: Incl government publications.

ON —UNIVERSITY OF GUELPH, Library, Guelph, N1G 2W1, Can. Margaret Beckman, Chief Librn; Ellen Pearson, Ref Librn
Holdings: Vols 25,000 Cat Audiotapes Videotapes 16mm Films Slides Maps Microforms
Budget: $9500
Notes: 250 periodical titles. Additional material in archival collection, including archives of the Association of Canadian Landscape Architects and of individual Canadian landscape architects.
See also entry under Agriculture

ON —UNIVERSITY OF TORONTO, Faculty of Architecture, Landscape Architecture Library, 230 College St, Toronto, M5S 1A1, Can. Pamela Manson-Smith, Librn
Holdings: Vols (14,401) Cat Slides
Notes: Incl architecture and landscape architecture.

LANDSCAPE ARCHITECTURE—HISTORY

†DC —HARVARD UNIVERSITY, Dumbarton Oaks, Garden Library, 1703 32nd Street NW, Washington, 20007. Laura Byers, Librn
early wartime broadcasts. Since 1967 the Library has received AFRTS's complete radio program package.

LANDSCAPE DESIGN see Landscape Architecture

LANDSCAPE GARDENING

CA —UNIVERSITY OF CALIFORNIA, BERKELEY, Environmental Design Library, (The General Library), 210 Wurster Hall, Berkeley, 94720. Arthur B Waugh, Head
Holdings: Vols (9000) Cat
Budget: ($4900)
Notes: Research collection emphasizing the following areas: Park and garden design; site planning; spatial planning; professional practice. Lesser emphasis on horticulture. The Library also includes the Beatrix Farrand Collection of rare books in the field of landscape architecture.

CA —CALIFORNIA POLYTECHNIC STATE UNIVERSITY LIBRARY, Special Collections and University Archives, San Luis Obispo, 93407. Nancy E Loe, Head Librn
Holdings: Mss
Notes: The Barton Collection incl the personal and professional papers of Arthur G Barton, a noted Southern California landscape architect, incl his office files, bids, and drawings and designs (collection in rough sorting stage). 55,000 pieces of ms material. 6000 landscape architecture designs and drawings.

IN —BALL STATE UNIVERSITY, College of Architecture & Planning, Architecture Library, Muncie, 47306. Marjorie Hake Joyner, Librn
Notes: Strong emphasis on history of all aspects of architecture. Also, for other major areas, architecture and landscape architecture and planning, 50,000 35mm color slides, over half cataloged.

KY —UNIVERSITY OF LOUISVILLE, Allen R Hite Art Institute, Library, Belknap Campus, Louisville, 40292. Gail Gilbert, Librn
Holdings: Vols (40,000) Cat Pix
Budget: ($29,000)
Notes: Incl books on art, architecture, landscape architecture and gardening, prints, printing, illustrated books and brass rubbings. Library subscribes to 200 periodical titles in these and other areas. Collection circulates to faculty and staff only, with same restrictions placed on interlibrary loan. Library also has collections of bookplates, posters, original prints, hand-made Christmas cards and clippings file filling 56 VF drawers.

MA —HARVARD UNIVERSITY, Graduate School of Design, Frances Loeb Library, Gund Hall, Cambridge, 02138. James Hodgson, Librn
Holdings: Vols (225,000) Cat Mss Pix Slides Microforms
Budget: ($500,000)
Notes: Covers architecture, landscape architecture, city and regional planning, and urban design. Catalog, in 44 volumes, published in 1968, with 2-volume supplement in 1970, 5-volume supplement in 1974, and 3-volume supplement in 1979. It also analyzes periodical articles. Architecture collection described in *Harvard Library* Bulletin, VI (1952): pp 263-269. Noteworthy holdings incl those on Abbey of Cluny, Le Corbusier, amd Henry Hobson Richardson. Landscape Architecture described in *Harvard Library Bulletin,* VII (1953), 188-195. Incl books and papers of Charles Eliot.

MI —OAKLAND COMMUNITY COLLEGE, Auburn Hills Campus, Learning Resources Center, 2900 Featherstone Rd, Auburn Hills, 48057. Eugene F Larson, Dept Chairman
Holdings: Vols 500 Cat Slides Audiotapes Videotapes 16mm Films

OH —CLEVELAND PUBLIC LIBRARY, Science & Technology Dept, 325 Superior Ave, Cleveland, 44114. Jean Z Piety, Head
Holdings: Cat
Notes: Part of the Gardening Collection,

LANDSCAPE GARDENING (cont.)

which emphasizes the history of gardens around the world, domestic landscape planning and planting, incl flower gardening, annuals and perennials, and indoor plants.

OH —MASSILLON PUBLIC LIBRARY, 208 Lincoln Way E, Massillon, 44646. Camille Leslie, Dir
Holdings: Vols 250 Cat

PA —PENNSYLVANIA HORTICULTURAL SOCIETY, Library, 325 Walnut St, Philadelphia, 19106. Mary Lou Wolfe, Librn
Notes: Publications: *Selected Books From the Library of the Pennsylvania Horticultural Society*, 1976; *From Seed to Flower, Philadelphia 1681-1876*, 1976.

PA —TEMPLE UNIVERSITY LIBRARIES, Special Collections Dept, Rare Books & Mss Section, Philadelphia, 19122. Thomas M Whitehead, Cur
Holdings: Vols (500) Cat Mss
Notes: Incl the Louise Bush-Brown Horticulture Collection; 15th-20th century rare herbals, animal husbandry and landscape gardening. List of majority of collection available.

VA —NORFOLK BOTANICAL GARDENS LIBRARY, Airport Rd, Norfolk, 23518. Marian Cole, Librn
Holdings: Vols 1903 Cat Pix

WA —UNIVERSITY OF WASHINGTON LIBRARIES, Pacific Northwest Collection, Seattle, 98195. Andrew F Johnson, Librn
Holdings: Vols (50,000) Cat Maps Pix
Budget: ($12,000)
Notes: The Pacific Northwest Collection contains printed materials documenting the historic and contemporary life and culture of the region in a broad range of subject areas. The Pacific Northwest is defined as the geographic region including Washington, Oregon, Idaho, Montana, British Columbia, Yukon Territory, and Alaska. Printed materials including books, periodicals, government documents, maps, weekly and local regional newspapers, theses and dissertations, as well as photographs and architectural drawings are included in the Pacific Northwest Collection. Photographic works of over 200 photographers active in the Pacific Northwest, Alaska, and the Yukon Territory (Canada) during the period 1860-1930, including Asahel and Edward S Curtis, Eric Hegg, and Clark Kinsey, are represented in a print collection of more than 300,000 images. The architecturaldrawings collection includes over 19,000 original plans, drawings, sketches, renderings and blue prints pertaining to the history of architecture and urban planning and landscape gardening in the Pacific Northwest ca 1880-1940. Areas of particular strength are the holdings of over 1100 published journals of Pacific Northwest exploration expeditions, photographs of Northwest Coast Native Americans and of historic Seattle, newspapers issued within the Japanese-American relocation camps, 1942-1945, materials relating to the 1980 eruption of Mt St Helens, and Sanborne fire insurance maps for Washington. A unique feature of the Collection is the subject index to regional periodicals and local newspapers maintained by the PNW Collection staff; over 100 titles are currently indexed. G K Hall Company published a books catalog of the Pacific Northwest Collectionin 1973.

LANE, ARTHUR BLISS

CT —YALE UNIVERSITY, Sterling Memorial Library, Latin American Collections, New Haven, 06520. Lee H Williams Jr, Cur
Holdings: Vols (300,000) Cat Maps Pix Slides Phonorecords 16mm Films Filmstrips
See also entry under Latin America

LANE, DANIEL

MA —BOSTON UNIVERSITY, Mugar Memorial Library, Special Collections Dept, 771 Commonwealth Ave, Boston, 02215. Howard B Gotlieb, Dir
Holdings: Mss

LANE, FERDINAND COLE

MA —BOSTON UNIVERSITY, Mugar Memorial Library, Special Collections Dept, 771 Commonwealth Ave, Boston, 02215. Howard B Gotlieb, Dir
Holdings: Cat Mss Correspondence

LANE, SIR HUGH

DC —GEORGETOWN UNIVERSITY, Library, Special Collections Div, 37 & O Sts NW, Washington, 20057. George M Barringer, Special Collections Librn; Nicholas B Sheetz, Mss Librn
Holdings: Mss Cat Pix
Notes: A portion of the archives of the English publisher Grant Ricards (1872-1948), containing manuscripts, correspondence, photographs, clippings, and printed ephemera. Incl is extensive correspondence from such artists and authors as Neville Cardus; Frank Harris; Sir Hugh Lane; Lady Augusta Gregory; David Low; T Sturge Moore; and C R W Nevinson.

LANE, JOHN

CA —UNIVERSITY OF CALIFORNIA, LOS ANGELES, William Andrews Clark Memorial Library, 2520 Cimarron St, Los Angeles, 90018.
Holdings: Cat Mss Pix
Notes: Extensive collection of books published by Lane along with mss and correspondence collected by J Lewis May for his biography, *John Lane and the* Nineties (1936).

LANE, LEVI COOPER

CA —STANFORD UNIVERSITY LIBRARIES, Lane Medical Library, Stanford University, Medical Center, Stanford, 94305. Peter Stangl, Librn
Notes: Papers of Levi Cooper Lane, founder of Cooper Medical College.

LANE, MARGARET

MA —BOSTON UNIVERSITY, Mugar Memorial Library, Special Collections Dept, 771 Commonwealth Ave, Boston, 02215. Howard B Gotlieb, Dir
Holdings: Cat Mss

LANE, PATRICK, 1939-

†ON —MCMASTER UNIVERSITY, Library, Hamilton, L8S 4L6, Can.
Notes: Correspondence and poetry mss.

LANG, ANDREW, 1844-1912

CA —CLAREMONT COLLEGES, Honnold Library, Ninth & Dartmouth, Claremont, 91711. Tania Rizzo, Special Collections Dept Head
Holdings: Vols 180 Cat Mss
Notes: The William W Clary Collection. First, limited, and special editions of books, pamphlets, offprints by or about him. Several holograph essays and some correspondence.

IN —INDIANA UNIVERSITY, Lilly Library, Seventh St, Bloomington, 47405. William R Cagle, Librn
Holdings: // Cat Mss
Notes: A small collection (76 items) of Andrew Lang letters and writings, 1886-1913. Incl first and early editions of Andrew Lang.

IN —INDIANAPOLIS-MARION COUNTY PUBLIC LIBRARY, Arts Div, 40 E Saint Clair St, PO Box 211, Indianapolis, 46204. Daniel H Gann, Head
Holdings: Vols 138 // Cat
Notes: Lang illustrated books, etc. Restricted use. Reference only.

†MA —CLARK UNIVERSITY, Robert Hutchings Goddard Library, Worcester, 01610. Dorothy Mosa Kowski, Rare Books Librn
Holdings: Cat
Notes: An extensive collection of his writings in the first editions.

NC —UNIVERSITY OF NORTH CAROLINA, CHARLOTTE, J Murrey Atkins Library, UNCC Station, Charlotte, 28223. Robert F Brabham Jr, Special Collections Librn
Holdings: Vols 500 Cat Mss
Notes: Principally American and English. Strength of the collection is US, 1800-1850. Incl 200 vols from the collection of Elizabeth Botteme Lewis. Also incl first editions of Andrew Lang's fairy books, several series of books for boys (early 20th century), and 1960s comic books. Also incl small collection of papers of and ephemera collected by Wilbur Macey Stone, collector and writer about historical children's books.

LANG, FRITZ

CA —UNIVERSITY OF SOUTHERN CALIFORNIA, Edward L Doheny Memorial Library, Archives of Performing Arts, University Park, Los Angeles, 90089. Robert Knutson, Librn
Holdings: Mss Pix
Notes: Personal collection of papers, pictures, etc.

LANGDON, JOHN

NH —NEW HAMPSHIRE HISTORICAL SOCIETY, Library, 30 Park St, Concord, 03301. William Copeley, Assoc Librn
Notes: The Langdon-Elwyn Family papers, incl espec those of John Langdon, New Hampshire's 18th century premier merchant-shipbuilder and politician.

LANGDON, WILLIAM CHAUNCEY, 1871-1947

RI —BROWN UNIVERSITY, John Hay Library, 20 Prospect St, Providence, 02912. Mark N Brown, Cur Mss
Holdings: Vols 4000 Mss Pix
Notes: Papers of William Chauncey Langdon (1871-1947), incl over 300 pageants, some written and directed by him, 1911-1921.

LANGDON-ELWYN FAMILY

NH —NEW HAMPSHIRE HISTORICAL SOCIETY, Library, 30 Park St, Concord, 03301. William Copeley, Assoc Librn
Notes: The Langdon-Elwyn Family papers, incl espec those of John Langdon, New Hampshire's 18th century premier merchant-shipbuilder and politician.

LANGE, EITEL

DC —LIBRARY OF CONGRESS, Prints & Photographs Div, Washington, 20540.
Notes: Personal photo albums of Hermann Goring provide detailed coverage of his activities during World War I and the years 1933-42. Biographical photographs of Hermann Goring incl pictures by Helmuth Kurth and Eitel Lange.

LANGEVIN, ANDRE

AB —UNIVERSITY OF CALGARY, Libraries, Special Collections Div, 2500 University Dr, Calgary, T2N 1N4, Can.
Holdings: Cat Mss
Notes: Manuscripts, galleys, and proofs for Andre Langevin's novels *Evade de la Nuit, Le Temps des Hommes, l'Elan d'Amerique, Poussiere sur la Ville* and *Une Chaine dans le Parc.*

LANGLEY, ADRIA LOCKE

MA —BOSTON UNIVERSITY, Mugar Memorial Library, Special Collections Dept, 771 Commonwealth Ave, Boston, 02215. Howard B Gotlieb, Dir
Holdings: Mss
Notes: Mss, correspondence, etc collected in depth; incl publications by or about.

LANGLEY, SAMUEL PIERPONT

DC —SMITHSONIAN INSTITUTION, Archives Div, Washington, 20560. William

LANGLEY, SAMUEL PIERPONT (cont.)

W Moss, Archivist
Holdings: Cat Mss Pix
Notes: The Archives holds a small amount of the papers of the third Smithsonian Secretary, Samuel Pierpont Langley, as well as the official records of this tenure, 1887-1906.
See also entries under Astronomy; Astrophysics

LANGSTROTH, REV. L. L.

NY —CORNELL UNIVERSITY LIBRARIES, Everett Franklin Phillips Beekeeping Library, Ithaca, 14853. Jan Olsen, Librn
Holdings: Vols 4200 Cat Mss
Notes: Incl collections of Moses Quimby, first commercial beekeeper in America, and Rev L L Langstroth.

LANGTON, JANE

MA —BOSTON UNIVERSITY, Mugar Memorial Library, Special Collections Dept, 771 Commonwealth Ave, Boston, 02215. Howard B Gotlieb, Dir
Holdings: Mss Correspondence Research

LANGUAGE AND LANGUAGES

CA —UNIVERSITY OF CALIFORNIA, BERKELEY, Humanities-Social Sciences Libraries, Anthropology Library, 230 Kroeber Hall, Berkeley, 94720. Dorothy A Koenig, Librn
Holdings: Vols (55,000) Cat Microforms
Notes: The library maintains general research collections covering all aspects of social and physical anthropology, anthropological linguistics and archaeology (excluding classical archaeology). Serials constitute the collection's special strength.

CA —UNIVERSITY OF CALIFORNIA, BERKELEY, University Library, Slavic Collections, Berkeley, 94720. Edward Kasinec, Librn
Holdings: Vols (210,000) Cat Maps Microforms
Budget: ($40,000)
Notes: Strong research collections for Bulgaria, Czechoslovakia, Poland, Russia-USSR, and Yugoslavia. Holdings are excellent in economics, folklore, history, linguistics, and literature. Publications issued by academies, major universities, and principal scholarly institutions are well represented. Extensive periodical holdings have been built up, largely as a result of early exchange arrangements. More than 4000 Slavic-language serials are currently being received. Farmington Plan and PL480 commitments have augmented Yugoslav resources. Sizable Slavic-language collections are to be found in Branch Libraries as well, in such subjects as agriculture, biology, earth sciences, forestry, and mathematics.

CA —LOS ANGELES PUBLIC LIBRARY, Central Library, Audio Visual Dept, 630 W Fifth St, Los Angeles, 90071. Richard V Partlow, Principal Librn
Budget: ($71,989)
Notes: Includes 16mm film (4300), VHS video (300), audio recordings (20,000), audio cassettes (5500), picture file (220,000 estimated clippings), filmstrips (60), periodicals (65). Material on all subject areas are included.

CA —LOS ANGELES PUBLIC LIBRARY, Literature and Philology Dept, 630 W Fifth St, Los Angeles, 90071. Helene G Mochedlover, Dept Librn
Holdings: Cat
Notes: Foreign Language Collection. Approximately 450 languages and dialects are represented, most of which are not included in Foreign Languages Department collection. Emphasis is on breadth of reference collection, which includes dictionaries, grammars, phrase books, and many important encyclopedias.

CA —UNIVERSITY OF CALIFORNIA, LOS ANGELES, Research Library, Indo/Pacific Collection, 405 Hilgard Ave, Los Angeles, 90024. Edward Shreeves, Chairman, Bibliographers Group; Charlotte Spence, Indo/Pacific Bibliographer
Holdings: Vols Cat Mss Maps Pix Microforms
Notes: The South Asian collection has been developed on two levels. On the research level it focuses on (1) the cultural, economic, political and social history of India from about 1859 to 1947; (2) linguistic and literary studies, with particular emphasis given to Sanskrit and Pali; and (3) the history of the Portuguese experience in South Asia. On the teaching level, materials are collected which relate to India before 1859, and from 1947 to date, as well as materials relating to the other political entities of South Asia. A description of the South Asian collection is included in the May, 1977 issue of *The Librarian,* and in *South Asian Library Resources in North* America (1975).

CA —DEFENSE LANGUAGE INSTITUTE FOREIGN LANGUAGE CENTER, Academic Library, Presidio of Monterey, Monterey, 93944. Gary D Walter, Librn
Holdings: Vols (85,000) Cat Videotapes
Budget: ($90,000)
Notes: Linguistics and foreign languages. Formerly US Army Language School Technical Library, Monterey, Calif.

CT —TRINITY COLLEGE LIBRARY, Watkinson Library, 300 Summit St, Hartford, 06106. Jeffrey Kaimowitz, Cur
Holdings: Cat
Notes: Espec American Indian languages.

DC —CENTER FOR APPLIED LINGUISTICS, ERIC Clearinghouse on Language & Linguistics, 3520 Prospect St NW, Washington, 20007. Martha Clarke, Coordr
Budget: $4500
Notes: ERIC microfiche, ED 000/001 to date.

DC —GEORGETOWN UNIVERSITY, Library, Special Collections Div, 37 & O Sts NW, Washington, 20057. George M Barringer, Special Collections Librn; Nicholas B Sheetz, Mss Librn
Holdings: Cat Mss
Notes: Representative of American Indian languages.

DC —LIBRARY OF CONGRESS, African and Middle Eastern Division, Washington, 20540.
Holdings: Cat

HI —BERNICE P BISHOP MUSEUM, Library, PO Box 19000-A, Honolulu, 96819. Cynthia Timberlake, Librn
Holdings: Vols (90,000) Cat Mss Maps Pix Slides Microforms
Budget: ($30,000)
Notes: Only American library devoted exclusively to the Pacific region. Collection reflects historical and contemporary research emphases of Bishop Museum; ie the natural and cultural history of the Pacific. Areas of concentration incl archaeology, ethnology, linguistics, voyages and explorations, history, vertebrate and invertebrate zoology, botany and museology. Strong special collections incl photographs, mss and archives, maps and art. Publications: Quarterly "Additions to the Catalog," *Dictionary Catalog of the* Library (9 vols and 2 suppl; Boston: G K Hall, 1964-69).

IL —NEWBERRY LIBRARY, 60 W Walton St, Chicago, 60610. Diana Haskell, Cur of Modern Mss
Holdings: Cat
Notes: Bonaparte Collection of historical linguistics, to 1900.

IN —INDIANA UNIVERSITY, Lilly Library, Seventh St, Bloomington, 47405. William R Cagle, Librn
Holdings: Mss
Notes: Papers of lexicographer and philologist Eric Partridge, 1894-1979. Correspondence, research materials for publications, and mss of writings. 6757 items.

IN —INDIANA STATE UNIVERSITY, Cunningham Memorial Library, Dept of Rare Books & Special Collections, Terre Haute, 47809. Lawrence J McCrank, Head
Holdings: Mss
Notes: Papers of Mitford Mathews. Supplements the Cordell Collection of rare dictionaries.

LA —LOUISIANA STATE UNIVERSITY, Troy H Middleton Library, Louisiana Room, Baton Rouge, 70803. Evangeline Mills Lynch, Head Librn; Ruth Murray, Associate Librn
Holdings: Vols (33,500) Cat Maps VF
Notes: Louisiana Collection of history, description and travel, biography, agriculture, literature, politics and government, folklore, anthropology, geography, geology, education, language, music and natural history. Especially large subject collections may be found on Louisiana, the history of the lower Mississippi Valley, Abraham Lincoln, Romance languages and literatures, sugar culture and technology, Southern history, petroleum engineering, plant pathology, micropaleontology, ornithology, and various aspects of crawfish life, biology and culture. Complete depository of Louisiana State Documents; extensive newspapers clipping files; separate card catalog; items listed in Louisiana Union Catalog; restricted use (research and reference). Incl both materials about Louisiana and by Louisianians without regard to subject. LSU Press Collection(preservation copy of each title kept for exhibit purposes only). LSU theses and dissertations from 1900-date. LSU Faculty Collection. Also, 1300 maps, 104 VF drawers, 250 boxes of uncataloged pamphlets.

MA —HARVARD UNIVERSITY, Graduate School of Education, Monroe C Gutman Library, 6 Appian Way, Cambridge, 02138. Susan S Baughman, Associate Librn
Holdings: Vols (150,000) Cat Mss Microforms
Budget: ($95,000)
Notes: A comprehensive research collection that seeks to acquire all scholarly works published in the English language in the fields of education, educational administration, educational psychology, and human development. Selective coverage in the related areas of counseling and psychology, business administration, finance, forecasting, statistical analysis and survey design, public and social policy, linguistics, demographics, and international and economic development. Incl 4000 educational and psychological tests.

MA —HARVARD UNIVERSITY LIBRARY, Widener Library, Cambridge, 02138.
Holdings: Cat

MA —HARVARD UNIVERSITY LIBRARY, Botanical Museum Library, Cambridge, 02138.
Holdings: Vols (2400) Mss Pix
Notes: The Tina and Gordon Wisson Ethnomycological Collection, one of the most important modern collections, acquired as an adjunct to the Museum's Economic Botany Library of Oakes Ames. From 15th to 20th century, it deals with hallucinogenic mushrooms in art, religion, and folklore; chemistry, pharmacology, linguistics, archaeological artifacts of Mexico, Guatemala, India, Japan, China, etc. Personal papers, etc.

MI —UNIVERSITY OF MICHIGAN, English Language Institute/Linguistics Library, 1013 N University Bldg, Ann Arbor, 48109. Patricia M Aldridge, Librn
Holdings: Vols (4500) Cat Maps VF Videotapes
Notes: The collection of teaching English as a foreign language is fairly complete; in modern language study it is also quite good. Supporting subjects are linguistics and English grammar; psychology, American culture, education, foreign student adjustment, and bibliography are covered.

MI —MICHIGAN STATE UNIVERSITY, International Library, Africana Collection, East Lansing, 48824. Eugene de Benko, Librn; Onuma Ezera, Bibliographer for Africana
Holdings: Vols (82,700) Cat Mss Maps Pix Slides Phonorecords Audiotapes Videotapes Filmstrips Microforms
Budget: ($78,000)
See also entry under Africa for full description.

LANGUAGE AND LANGUAGES (cont.)

MN —MINNEAPOLIS PUBLIC LIBRARY & INFORMATION CENTER, Literature & Language Dept, 300 Nicollet Mall, Minneapolis, 55401. Dorothy D Thews, Head
Holdings: Vols (210,000) Cat Microforms Phonorecords Audiotapes
Budget: ($49,124)
Notes: Foreign language collection: 30,000 vols, special emphasis on Scandinavian languages, separate catalog. Theatre collection: 9 vertical file drawers. Books integrated with department collection.

NY —NEW YORK PUBLIC LIBRARY, Research Libraries, General Research Division, Fifth Ave & 42 St, New York, 10018. Rodney Phillips, Chief
Holdings: Vols (2,225,000) Cat Maps Pix Microforms
Budget: ($775,718)

NY —NEW YORK PUBLIC LIBRARY, Oriental Div, Fifth Ave & 42 St, New York, 10018. E Christian Filstrup, Chief
Holdings: Cat Mss Microforms
Budget: ($56,455)
Notes: Described in *Dictionary Catalog of the Oriental Collection,* The Research Libraries of the New York Public Library, 1960, 16 vols, and *First Supplement,* 1976, 8 vols (144,000 cards). This catalog incl 318, 000 entries for works in about 100 languages of the East, and all works in Western languages on Oriental subjects. The Oriental Collection numbers about 120,000 vols; its Arabic and Indic holdings and those on ancient Egypt and the ancient Near East are among the largest in the US. There is also a collection of 30,000 vols of PL 480 material from Egypt, Pakistan, and India to which there is main entry access, but which is not incorporated into the dictionary catalog. Other outstanding features of the Oriental Collection incl extensive holdings of Japanese technical and scientific periodicals; a unique collection of linguistic works, grammars, anddictionaries; and unusually good coverage of the field of Oriental religions and philosophies. The catalog contains numerous subject references to periodical articles in all languages. All entries are arranged alphabetically according to the Roman alphabet.

NY —NEW YORK PUBLIC LIBRARY, Mid-Manhattan Library, Literature and Language Dept, 455 Fifth Ave, New York, 10016. Eric Steele, Sr Principal Librn
Holdings: Vols (160,000) Cat Phonorecords Microforms Audiotapes
Budget: ($92,000)
Notes: Broad coverage for the study of over 100 languages and dialects, materials on most areas of theoretical and applied linguistics. Extensive runs of major journals. 3000 records and cassettes aid in the learning of 40 languages, in addition to English.

NC —DUKE UNIVERSITY, William R Perkins Library, Jay B Hubbell Center for American Literary Historiography, Durham, 27706. Erma Whittington, Librn
Notes: 77,312 items, including manuscripts, pictures, clippings, and correspondence. "The objective of the Center is to gather the papers and materials of significant scholars and critics in American literary history." The Center is a part of the Perkins Library Manuscripts Department.

OH —CLEVELAND PUBLIC LIBRARY, Fine Arts and Special Collections Department, 325 Superior Ave, Cleveland, 44114. Alice N Loranth, Head
Holdings: Vols (15,000) Cat Mss
Notes: Contains many grammars, dictionaries, and works on linguistics in African, Asian and Western languages and dialects. Material in Dewey/Brett Collection is classified by an extensively expanded language classification scheme. Its special feature is the "Language File," indexing samples of over 7000 languages and dialects housed in Special Collections.

OR —UNIVERSITY OF OREGON, Library, Eugene, 97403. Kenneth W Duckett, Curator
Holdings: Vols (3000) Cat
Notes: Incl 475 serial runs. The George Alan Connor Collection of Esperanto literature features local, regional, national, and international publications in Esperanto, mainly from the period 1910-1960. Catalog available. Also the Rev M Whipple Bishop papers which incl 31 vols and 27 serial titles as well as mss.

PA —UNIVERSITY OF PENNSYLVANIA, University Museum Library, 33 & Spruce Sts, Philadelphia, 19104. Jean S Adelman, Librn
Holdings: Vols (80,000) Cat Mss Microforms
Notes: Incl the Daniel Garrison Brinton collection of about 2000 vols, on aboriginal American linguistics and ethnology. Espec strong in Maya language materials.

WA —UNIVERSITY OF WASHINGTON LIBRARIES, Suzzallo Library, Slavic & East European Section, FM-25, Seattle, 98195. Barbara A Galik, Head
Holdings: Vols (250,000) Cat Mss Maps Pix Phonorecords Audiotapes Microforms
Budget: ($85,000)
Notes: Strong research collections for Eastern Europe, especially Poland. Holdings are notably excellent in historical source materials. There are extensive holdings of the publications of academies, major universities, and principal scholarly institutions, especially of long serial runs.

WI —UNIVERSITY OF WISCONSIN, MADISON, Memorial Library, British & American Language & Literature Collection, 728 State St, Madison, 53706. Yvonne Schofer, Bibliographer
Notes: Miles L Hanley Collection of English and American Linguistics. 600 phonorecords, close to 1,000,000 rhyme slips in 300 file boxes, 115,000 cards of assembled rhymes, 293 books, 22 cartons of rhyme pairs, materials on American surnames, usage and pronunciations, and in general data on pronunciation of the English language in the modern period, acquired in 1955.

BC —VANCOUVER PUBLIC LIBRARY, Language & Literature Div, 750 Burrard St, Vancouver, V6Z 1X5, Can. B Kinnear, Head
Holdings: Books Pamphlets Audiotapes
Notes: A good general collection of language dictionaries supplemented by clippings and a word file compiled by the staff. Collection of language learning materials.

ON —CANADA PUBLIC SERVICE COMMISSION, Library, Room 930 W Tower, Esplande Laurier, Ottawa, K1A 0M7, Can. A Campbell, Chief Librn
Holdings: Vols 7000 Cat
Budget: $20,000
Notes: Library supports the research, administrative, and instructional needs of the Commission. English and French materials.

ON —METROPOLITAN TORONTO LIBRARY, Languages Centre, 789 Yonge St, Toronto, M4W 2G8, Can. Barbara Gunther, Head
Holdings: Vols (90,000) Cat Phonorecords Audiotapes
Notes: Original literature in over 80 languages; books, records, cassettes, microfilm on language studies; newspapers and periodicals from 50 counties. Language study materials. Issue quarterly additions lists by language. Collect North American Indian and Eskimo language materials. Occasional bibliographies.

LANGUAGE AND LANGUAGES—DICTIONARIES AND GRAMMARS

CA —LOS ANGELES PUBLIC LIBRARY, Literature and Philology Dept, 630 W Fifth St, Los Angeles, 90071. Helene G Mochedlover, Dept Librn
Holdings: Cat
Notes: Foreign Language Collection. Approximately 450 languages and dialects are represented, most of which are not included in Foreign Languages Department collection. Emphasis is on breadth of reference collection, which includes dictionaries, grammars, phrase books, and many important encyclopedias.

NY —NEW YORK PUBLIC LIBRARY, Mid-Manhattan Library, Literature and Language Dept, 455 Fifth Ave, New York, 10016. Eric Steele, Sr Principal Librn
Holdings: Vols (10,000) Cat Phonorecords Microforms
Budget: ($10,000)
Notes: Broad coverage for the study of over 100 language and dialects, materials on most areas of theoretical and applied linguistics, incl philology, speech and the teaching of languages, especially of English as a second language. Extensive runs of major journals. Records and cassettes aid in the learning of 40 languages, in addition to English. Strong in materials on the history of American and English language and pronunciation. In Old, Middle and Early Modern English, Department has a representative collection of primary and secondary source materials in microfiche.

LANGUAGE AND LANGUAGES—EARLY WORKS TO 1800

PA —ALLEGHENY COLLEGE, Lawrence Lee Pelletier Library, Meadville, 16335. Margaret L Moser, Librn
Holdings: Vols (3000) Cat
Notes: James Winthrop's original collection. History, science, language among principal subject fields. Part of original gift to this library, 1819-23. Listed in Timothy Alden, *Catalogus Bibliothecae Collegii* Alleghaniensis, 1823. Downs 180.

LANGUAGE AND LANGUAGES—HISTORY

IL —NEWBERRY LIBRARY, 60 W Walton St, Chicago, 60610. Diana Haskell, Cur of Modern Mss
Holdings: Cat Maps
Notes: The bulk of the collection (about 15, 000 vols) is in the Prince Lucien Bonaparte group, which deals with western European linguistics. In this group the major rare categories are Etruscan and Basque linguistic studies, although the bulk of the group treats the major European languages and their dialects, ie French, German, English, Spanish, Italian and Russian. There is also strong representation in Gaelic linguistics, particularly Irish, Cornish, Welsh and Manx. In other collections of the library, there are major groups of books and mss dealing with American Indian languages and Philippine languages (about 4500 books and mss).

LANGUAGE AND LANGUAGES—STUDY AND TEACHING

NY —NEW YORK PUBLIC LIBRARY, Mid-Manhattan Library, Literature and Language Dept, 455 Fifth Ave, New York, 10016. Eric Steele, Sr Principal Librn
Holdings: Vols (160,000) Cat Phonorecords Microforms Audiotapes
Budget: ($92,000)
Notes: Broad coverage for the study of over 100 languages and dialects, materials on most areas of theoretical and applied linguistics. Extensive runs of major journals. 3000 records and cassettes aid in the learning of 40 languages, in addition to English.

NT —NORTHWEST TERRITORIES PUBLIC LIBRARY SERVICES, Bos 1100, Hay River, X0E 0R0, Can.
Holdings: Vols (1235) Cat Maps Audiotapes
Notes: Originally intended to provide items of historical significance on the Northwest Territories. It contains a number of first editions, some of which have since become available in reprint form. Copies of material in relevant native languages and on learning languages.

†ON —UNIVERSITY OF WESTERN ONTARIO, School of Library and Information Science, Special Collections

LANGUAGE AND LANGUAGES—STUDY AND TEACHING (cont.)

Room, London, N6A 5B9, Can.
Notes: Archive of lexicographical materials of the Committee on Lexicography of the Modern Language Association. Incl lexicographical slips for *The United States Air Force Dictionary* and The *Second Aerospace Glossary,* by Woodford Heflin. 13 cartons of slips.

LANGUAGE AND LANGUAGES—TERMINOLOGY see Language and Languages—Dictionaries and Grammars

LANGUAGE AND SOCIETY see Sociolinguistics

LANGUAGE ART (FINE ARTS) see Art, Conceptual

LANGUAGE ARTS see Communications; English Language; Reading

LANGUAGE OF FLOWERS see Flower Language

LANGUAGE PERIODICALS see Periodicals, Language

LANGUAGES—SOCIOLOGICAL ASPECTS see Sociolinguistics

LANGUAGES, ARTIFICIAL

MO —WASHINGTON UNIVERSITY, John M Olin Library, Campus Box 1061, St Louis, 63130.
Holdings: Vols (1300) Cat Mss
Notes: The Philip M Arnold Semeiology Collection is concerned with the study of signs and symbols. Topics incl cryptography; artificial memory; decipherment of unknown languages; universal languages; early developments in stenography, telegraphy; and communication systems for the blind, the deaf and the mute; and various forms of nonverbal communication. Limited photocopying. Noncirculating.

LANGUAGES, INTERNATIONAL

OR —UNIVERSITY OF OREGON, Library, Eugene, 97403. Kenneth W Duckett, Curator
Holdings: Vols (3000) Cat
Notes: Incl 475 serial runs. The George Alan Connor Collection of Esperanto literature features local, regional, national, and international publications in Esperanto, mainly from the period 1910-1960. Catalog available. Also the Rev M Whipple Bishop papers which incl 31 vols and 27 serial titles as well as mss.

LANGUAGES, MIXED

MA —HARVARD UNIVERSITY LIBRARY, Cambridge, 02138.
Holdings: Cat

NY —NEW YORK PUBLIC LIBRARY, Mid-Manhattan Library, Literature and Language Dept, 455 Fifth Ave, New York, 10016. Eric Steele, Sr Principal Librn
Holdings: Vols (160,000) Cat Phonorecords Microforms Audiotapes
Budget: ($92,000)
Notes: Broad coverage for the study of over 100 languages and dialects, materials on most areas of theoretical and applied linguistics. Extensive runs of major journals. 3000 records and cassettes aid in the learning of 40 languages, in addition to English.

OR —UNIVERSITY OF OREGON, Library, Eugene, 97403. Kenneth W Duckett, Curator
Holdings: Vols (3000) Cat
Notes: Incl 475 serial runs. The George Alan Connor Collection of Esperanto literature features local, regional, national, and international publications in Esperanto, mainly from the period 1910-1960. Catalog available. Also the Rev M Whipple Bishop papers which incl 31 vols and 27 serial titles as well as mss.

LANGUAGES, MODERN—CONVERSATION AND PHRASE BOOKS

CA —LOS ANGELES PUBLIC LIBRARY, Literature and Philology Dept, 630 W Fifth St, Los Angeles, 90071. Helene G Mochedlover, Dept Librn
Holdings: Cat
Notes: Foreign Language Collection. Approximately 450 languages and dialects are represented, most of which are not included in Foreign Languages Department collection. Emphasis is on breadth of reference collection, which includes dictionaries, grammars, phrase books, and many important encyclopedias.

NY —NEW YORK PUBLIC LIBRARY, Mid-Manhattan Library, Literature and Language Dept, 455 Fifth Ave, New York, 10016. Eric Steele, Sr Principal Librn
Holdings: Vols (160,000) Cat Phonorecords Microforms Audiotapes
Budget: ($92,000)
Notes: Broad coverage for the study of over 100 languages and dialects, materials on most areas of theoretical and applied linguistics, incl philology, speech and the teaching of langauges, especially of English as a second language. Extensive runs of major journals. Records and cassettes aid in the learning of 40 langauges, in addition to English. Strong in materials on the history of American and English language and pronunciation. In Old, Middle and Early Modern English, Department has a representative collection of primary and secondary source materials in microfiche.

LANGUAGES, ORIENTAL see Oriental Languages and Literatures

LANGUAGES, SEMITIC see Semitics

LANGUAGES, UNKNOWN

MO —WASHINGTON UNIVERSITY, John M Olin Library, Campus Box 1061, St Louis, 63130.
Holdings: Vols (1300) Cat Mss
Notes: The Philip M Arnold Semeiology Collection is concerned with the study of signs and symbols. Topics incl cryptography; artificial memory; decipherment of unknown languages; universal languages; early developments in stenography, telegraphy; and communication systems for the blind, the deaf and the mute; and various forms of nonverbal communication. Limited photocopying. Noncirculating.

LANGUE D'OC see Provencal Language and Literature

LANGUE D'OIL see French Language and Literature

LANHAM, EDWIN

MA —BOSTON UNIVERSITY, Mugar Memorial Library, Special Collections Dept, 771 Commonwealth Ave, Boston, 02215. Howard B Gotlieb, Dir
Holdings: Cat Mss
Notes: Mss, correspondence, etc collected in depth; incl publications by or about.

LANIER, SIDNEY

GA —OGLETHORPE UNIVERSITY, Library, 4484 Peachtree RD, NE, Atlanta, 30319. Thomas W Chandler, Librn
Holdings: Vols 75 Cat Pix Slides
Notes: Incl first and later editions of the works of Lanier; also biographical and critical materials.

MD —JOHNS HOPKINS UNIVERSITY, Milton S Eisenhower Library, Charles & 34 Sts, Baltimore, 21218. Ann S Gwyn, Assistant Dir for Special Collections
Holdings: Vols 125 Cat Mss
Notes: The best source on the poet and his work. Incl 229 mss, 3800 letters and correspondence, journals and documents. First editions, critical works, his own library, music mss and memorabilia. Cataloged in manuscript room. Music mss at the John Work Garrett Library, 4545 N Charles St; letters, etc, at Eisenhower Library, manuscript room.

NC —DUKE UNIVERSITY, William R Perkins Library, Durham, 27706. Elvin E Strowd, University Librn
Notes: The Ethel Carr Peacock collection of 7000 volumes is strong in holdings of 19th century American literature.

VA —UNIVERSITY OF VIRGINIA, Alderman Library, Clifton Waller Barrett Collection, Charlottesville, 22901. Joan St C Crane, Cur of American Literature Collections
Notes: Papers.

LANKES, J. J.

NY —BUFFALO & ERIE COUNTY PUBLIC LIBRARY, Rare Book Room, Lafayette Sq, Buffalo, 14203. William H Loos, Cur
Notes: 100 original woodcuts; memorabilia, photographs and letters.

LANSBURY, ANGELA

MA —BOSTON UNIVERSITY, Mugar Memorial Library, Special Collections Dept, 771 Commonwealth Ave, Boston, 02215. Howard B Gotlieb, Dir
Holdings: Cat Mss Pix Correspondence Audiotapes

LANSING, MICHIGAN

MI —R E OLDS MUSEUM LIBRARY, 240 Museum Drive, Lansing, 48933.
Notes: Emphasizes the contributions that Lansing has made to transportation history; materials on Oldsmobile, Reo, Star, Durant, and Bates cars. Incl books, manuals, magazines, advertisements, photographs, films, slides, audiotapes, videotapes, VF, and art reproductions.

LANSING, ROBERT, 1864-1928

DC —LIBRARY OF CONGRESS, Manuscript Division, Washington, 20540. John C Broderick, Chief
Holdings: Cat Mss Pix
Notes: Mss, papers, records, etc.

NJ —PRINCETON UNIVERSITY, Library, Manuscript Collection, Nassau St, Princeton, 08540. Jean F Preston, Cur
Holdings: / / Mss
Notes: Incl 16 boxes of papers. Terms of Access: May be read by qualified scholars; special permission from the Library is required to publish material based upon the papers.

†TX —UNIVERSITY OF TEXAS LIBRARIES, General Libraries, Humanities Research Center, PO Box 7219, Austin, 78712. John Chalmers, Librn
Notes: The John W F Dulles collection of correspondence, diaries, autographs, speeches, and paintings by famous historical figures from the 17th century to the present. Much of the material is related to Mr Dulles' three relatives who served as Secretaries of State: John Foster Dulles, Robert Lansing, and John W Foster.

LANTZ, WALTER

CA —UNIVERSITY OF CALIFORNIA, LOS ANGELES, Theater Arts Library, Los Angeles, 90024. Edward Shreeves, Chairman, Bibliographers Group; Audree Malkin, Head, Theater Arts Library
Notes: Scripts, posters, comic books, music, models, original sketches, research, drawings, cels, storyboards, and films of cartoon producer Walter Lantz. Extensive collection.

LANTZ, WALTER (cont.)

Also, a collection of original comic books, color comic books, storyboards, and posters illustrated by Clyde Geronimi.

LAO LANGUAGE AND LITERATURE

HI —UNIVERSITY OF HAWAII, Library, 2550 The Mall, Honolulu, 96822. Joyce Wright, Head, Asia Collection; Masato Matsu, Head, East Asia Vernacular Collection
Holdings: Vols 331,620 Cat Microforms
Notes: The Asia Collection holds materials from and about Southeast Asia: Brunei, Burma, Cambodia (Kampuchea), Indonesia, Laos, Malaysia, Philippines, Singapore, Thailand. Large contemporary Indonesian language collection. Several thousand vols in Thai and in Vietnamese. Minimal holdings in Burmese, Khmer, Lao languages. Social sciences and humanities emphasis for the post-World War II period. Western language coverage supplemented by retrospective holdings in the main library collection.

IL —NORTHERN ILLINOIS UNIVERSITY, Founders Memorial Library, Southeast Asia Collection, Normal Rd, De Kalb, 60115. Lee S Dutton Dr, Cur
Holdings: Vols (34,000) Cat Maps Microforms
Notes: An extensive collection of books, periodicals, newspapers, maps, and microforms from or about Southeast Asia. Areas of concentration incl Thailand, Malaysia, Indonesia, Singapore, Brunei, Philippines, Laos, and Burma. Holdings (except rare books, maps, and microforms) are housed in a separate area collection within the Founders Library. A departmental card catalog and specialized reference collection support reference services. A Thai collection of several thousand vols is the largest vernacular component. Extensive Malaysia, Indonesia, Singapore, and Brunei holdings have been acquired through the NPAC program. A collection of Filipino-American newspapers, and a growing collection of children's literature in common and uncommon Southeast Asian languages are available. Resources are accessible to borrowers through OCLC.

NY —NEW YORK PUBLIC LIBRARY, Oriental Div, Fifth Ave & 42 St, New York, 10018. E Christian Filstrup, Chief
Holdings: // Cat Mss Microforms
Budget: ($56,455)
Notes: Published catalog of holdings. Currently collected in Western language materials only.

LAOS

HI —UNIVERSITY OF HAWAII, Library, 2550 The Mall, Honolulu, 96822. Joyce Wright, Head, Asia Collection; Masato Matsu, Head, East Asia Vernacular Collection
Holdings: Vols 331,620 Cat Microforms
Notes: The Asia Collection holds materials from and about Southeast Asia: Brunei, Burma, Cambodia (Kampuchea), Indonesia, Laos, Malaysia, Philippines, Singapore, Thailand. Large contemporary Indonesian language collection. Several thousand vols in Thai and in Vietnamese. Minimal holdings in Burmese, Khmer, Lao languages. Social sciences and humanities emphasis for the post-World War II period. Western language coverage supplemented by retrospective holdings in the main library collection.

IL —SOUTHERN ILLINOIS UNIVERSITY, CARBONDALE, Delyte W Morris Library, Carbondale, 62901.
Holdings: Vols (4100) Cat Maps Audiotapes Microforms
Notes: The Vietnamese collection has been transferred to the general library. It incl 1200 cataloged titles in the Vietnamese language, plus 56 Vietnamese language microfilms. A profile of the area emphasis on the collection appears from the following distribution of the 2987 titles entered in the holdings and accessions lists published by the Southern Illinois University Center for Vietnamese Studies: Vietnam, 1965; Cambodia and Laos, 63; Other Southeast Asia (incl Indonesia), 916; East Asia (mostly China), 246; General (reference works, bibliographies, etc), 197. Also over 1000 maps.

IL —NORTHERN ILLINOIS UNIVERSITY, Founders Memorial Library, Southeast Asia Collection, Normal Rd, De Kalb, 60115. Lee S Dutton Dr, Cur
Holdings: Vols (34,000) Cat Maps Microforms
Notes: An extensive collection of books, periodicals, newspapers, maps, and microforms from or about Southeast Asia. Areas of concentration incl Thailand, Malaysia, Indonesia, Singapore, Brunei, Philippines, Laos, and Burma. Holdings (except rare books, maps, and microforms) are housed in a separate area collection within the Founders Library. A departmental card catalog and specialized reference collection support reference services. A Thai collection of several thousand vols is the largest vernacular component. Extensive Malaysia, Indonesia, Singapore, and Brunei holdings have been acquired through the NPAC program. A collection of Filipino-American newspapers, and a growing collection of children's literature in common and uncommon Southeast Asian languages are available. Resources are accessible to borrowers through OCLC.

MI —UNIVERSITY OF MICHIGAN, Harlan Hatcher Graduate Library, Ann Arbor, 48109. Susan Go, Librn
Holdings: Vols (250,000) Cat Mss Maps Pix Slides Microforms
Notes: Incl in the Michigan Historical Collections (primarily archival material) are papers of Michiganders in southeast Asia, mostly the Philipines, eg papers of Joseph R Hayden, Frank Murphy and G Mennen Williams, also, on film, the selected papers of Philippines president Manuel Quezon. All aspects of the countries, cultures and peoples of Brunei, Burma, Khymer, Indonesia, Laos, Malaysia, Philippines, Singapore, Thailand, Portuguese Timor and Vietnam. Also the Malayo-Polynesian (Austronesian), Mon-Khmer (Austroasiatic), and Sino-Tibetan language groupings.

NY —CORNELL UNIVERSITY LIBRARIES, John M Olin Library, John M Echols Collection on Southeast Asia, Ithaca, 14853. Giok Po Oey, Curator
Holdings: Vols (167,000) Cat Mss Maps Pix Microforms
Budget: ($90,000)
Notes: Additions published in the collection's monthly accessions list (Ithaca: Cornell University, Southeast Asia Program, 1959-). Holdings through December 1980 listed in *Cornell University Libraries Southeast Asia Catalog* (Boston: G K Hall, 1976, First supplement, 1983), 10 vols.

LAOS LANGUAGE see Lao Language and Literature

LAOTIAN LANGUAGE see Lao Language and Literature

LA RAZA UNIDA PARTY see Raza Unida Party

LARCOM, LUCY

MA —WHEATON COLLEGE, Library, Norton, 02766. Sherrie S Bergman, College Librn
Holdings: Vols (280) Cat Mss
Notes: The Larcom Collection, books by and about Lucy Larcom, and her personal library. Mss, poetry, correspondence with John Greenleaf Whittier and others, diaries, watercolors.

MA —ESSEX INSTITUTE, James Duncan Phillips Library, 132-34 Essex St, Salem, 01970. Prudence K Backman, Manuscript Librn
Holdings: Mss
Notes: Correspondence and poetry of mill girl, poet and author.

LARDNER, RINGGOLD (RING) WILMER, 1885-1933

CT —YALE UNIVERSITY, Box 1603A, Yale Station, New Haven, 06520.
Holdings: Cat Mss Pix
Notes: First editions, etc.

IL —NEWBERRY LIBRARY, 60 W Walton St, Chicago, 60610. Diana Haskell, Cur of Modern Mss
Holdings: // Cat Mss Pix
Notes: 3050 mss. Noncirculating.

LARGE PRINT BOOKS

DC —LIBRARY OF CONGRESS, National Library Service for Blind Physically Handicapped, 1291 Taylor St NW, Washington, 20542. Frank Kunt Cylke, Director; Hylda Kamisar, Head Reference Section
Holdings: Cat
Budget: ($434,000)
Notes: Collection of instructional recordings, music scores, and books about music in large print and braille. Instructional recordings incl recorded books, recorded methods for the guitar, piano, and other instruments, lectures, master classes, rehearsals, and a small collection of slow tapes for piano. Large print and braille books incl college texts, biographies, histories, and music appreciation and other general interest books. The collection consists of over 30,000 items. The publication series, *Music and* Musicians, lists holdings by medium and by instrument. All material is available on free loan to blind and partially sighted persons or physically handicapped persons notable to read conventionally printed materials.

MA —HEBREW COLLEGE, Jacob & Rose Grossman Library and Lawrence Jay & Anne Cable Rubenstein Library, 43 Hawes St, Brookline, 02146. Maurice Tuchman, Librn
Holdings: Vols 60 Cat
Notes: Bessie Berkowitz Large Print Books Collection. Large print books of Jewish interest.

NY —BUFFALO & ERIE COUNTY PUBLIC LIBRARY, Fiction Dept, Lafayette Sq, Buffalo, 14203. Irene Dwigans, Head
Holdings: Vols 8419 Cat
Notes: Books in 18 point type.

NY —WILLARD PSYCHIATRIC CENTER, Patients Library, Willard, 14588. Helen Bunting, Chief Library Services
Holdings: Vols (23,025) Cat Phonorecords

TX —PHARR MEMORIAL LIBRARY, 200 S Athol, Pharr, 78577. Karen Mier, Asst Librn
Holdings: Vols 360 Cat

LARKIN, GEORGE AND OLIVE

CA —UNIVERSITY OF CALIFORNIA, LOS ANGELES, Research Library, Dept of Special Collections, 405 Hilgard Ave, Los Angeles, 90024. Edward Shreeves, Chairman, Bibliographers Group; David S Zeidberg, Head
Notes: 2.5 linear feet of scripts for radio, stage, and moving picture productions.

LARKIN, THOMAS OLIVER, 1802-1858

NH —PORTSMOUTH ATHENAEUM, 9 Market Sq, Box 848, Portsmouth, 03801. Joseph P Copley, Cur
Holdings: Vols Cat Mss
Notes: Incl Larkin Papers, 1758-1798 (235 items); papers of Daniel and John Peirce, ca 1730-1800 (115 items); and papers of NH Fire and Marine Insurance Co, 1803-1823 (1800 items).

LARNER, JEREMY

MA —BOSTON UNIVERSITY, Mugar Memorial Library, Special Collections Dept, 771 Commonwealth Ave, Boston, 02215. Howard B Gotlieb, Dir
Holdings: Cat Mss Correspondence

LARRABEE, WILLIAM

IA —STATE HISTORICAL SOCIETY OF IOWA LIBRARY, 402 Iowa Ave, Iowa

LARRABEE, WILLIAM (cont.)

City, 52240. Darold J Brown, Librn
Holdings: Cat
Notes: Thousands of individual items and smaller collections. Two hundred larger collections incl the papers of Cyrus C Carpenter, Jonathan P Dolliver, Gilbert Haugen, W W Waymack, Ephraim Adams, A C Dodge, Dorothy Houghton, Jesse Macy, Agnes Samuelson, Donald Johnson, Jack Miller, Ruth Sayre, Samuel Kirkwood, Thomas McKnight, Robert Lucas, Dwight McCarty, William Larrabee. Includes church, school, company and organization records, Civil War materials.

LARRICK, JIM

OH —OHIO STATE UNIVERSITY, Library for Communication and Graphic Arts, 242 W 18th St, Columbus, 43210. Lucy S Caswell, Curator
Notes: Original cartoons by Winsor McCay, John T McCutcheon, Dick Moores, Ned White, Walter Berndt, Jim Larrick, Carl Rose and Bill Crawford.

LASERS

CA —UNIVERSITY OF CALIFORNIA, LIVERMORE, Lawrence Livermore National Laboratory, Library, PO Box 5500, Livermore, 94550. John B Verity, Library Mgr
Holdings: Vols (160,000) Cat 16mm Films Microforms
Budget: ($2,323,000)
Notes: The LLL library system includes a central collection in physics, chemistry, engineering, geology, mathematics, and computer science; and branch holdings in bio-medicine, environmental science, nuclear chemistry, energy research, theoretical physics, materials science, and nuclear weapons. Collections include 160,000 books, 145,000 technical reports, 530,000 reports on microfiche, and 3000 periodical subscriptions. LLL libraries are not open to the public. Unclassified materials may be borrowed on interlibrary loan.

CA —INTERNATIONAL BUSINESS MACHINES RESEARCH LIBRARY, 5600 Cottle Rd, San Jose, 95193. Phil Grincewich, Mgr Technical Information
Holdings: Vols (13,500) Cat
Notes: Collection includes emphasis on laser spectroscopy, organic photomaterial and chemical dynamics. Incl 21,000 vols of 770 journals. On-line search facility. Vols are divided into three libraries, Technical Research, Technical Information, and Programing. Not open to public.

MA —AVCO EVERETT RESEARCH LABORATORY, INC, Library, 2385 Revere Beach Parkway, Everett, 02149. Lorraine T Nazzaro, Librn
Holdings: Vols (24,000) Cat Maps Microforms
Budget: ($150,000)
Notes: Incl 50,000 reports.

MN —MINNEAPOLIS COLLEGE OF ART & DESIGN, Library, 200 E 25 St, Minneapolis, 55404. Richard Kronstedt, Head Librn

NM —UNIVERSITY OF CALIFORNIA, Los Alamos National Laboratory, Libraries, PO Box 1663, MSP 362, Los Alamos, 87545. J Arthur Freed, Head Librn
Holdings: Vols (800,000) Cat Films Microforms
Budget: ($700,000)
Notes: Incl 500,000 classified and unclassified reports. There are 25 branch libraries and a central collection. The Medical Library contains about 40,000 vols in the areas of biomedical research.

NY —UNIVERSITY OF ROCHESTER, Engineering Library, Gavett Hall, River Campus, Rochester, 14627. Isabel Kaplan, Librn
Holdings: Vols (25,000) Cat
Notes: Strong collection in the field and related areas.

NY —UNIVERSITY OF ROCHESTER, Physics-Optics-Astronomy Library, Bausch & Lomb Bldg, River Campus, Rochester, 14627. Loretta Caren, Librn
Holdings: Vols (20,000) Cat
Notes: Strong research level collection in the field and related areas. Also, at Laser Laboratory, 1000 vols on nuclear fusion and applied laser technology.

LASERS—HISTORY

MA —LASER HISTORY PROJECT, 25 Stoddard St, Woburn, 01801. Joan Lisa Bromberg, Dir
Notes: Four professional societies--the American Physical Society, The Laser Institute of America, The Optical Society of America and the IEEE Quantum Electronics and Applications Society have joined with the American Institute of Physics' Center for History of Physics and the Institute of Electrical and Electronics Engineers' Center for the History of Electrical Engineering to initiate a project on the history of lasers. The project's central activities will be the taking of oral histories, and the locating of papers, photographs, tapes, and equipment of historical significance.

LASERS IN CHEMISTRY

CA —INTERNATIONAL BUSINESS MACHINES RESEARCH LIBRARY, 5600 Cottle Rd, San Jose, 95193. Phil Grincewich, Mgr Technical Information
Notes: Collection includes emphasis on laser spectroscopy, organic photomaterial and chemical dynamics. Incl 21,000 vols of 770 journals. On-line search facility. Vols are divided into three libraries, Technical Research, Technical Information, and Programing. Not open to public.

LASKER, EDWARD, 1829-1884

MA —BRANDEIS UNIVERSITY, Goldfarb Library, 415 South St, Waltham, 02154. Bessie Hahn, Dir
Notes: Edward Lasker Collection. Consists of 21 linear ft of mss material, correspondence and contemporary pamphlets. Eduard Lasker was a political leader during the Bismarck regime in Germany. A finding list to the collection is located in Special Collections.

LASKY, JESSE L., JR.

MA —BOSTON UNIVERSITY, Mugar Memorial Library, Special Collections Dept, 771 Commonwealth Ave, Boston, 02215. Howard B Gotlieb, Dir
Holdings: Cat Mss
Notes: Mss, correspondence, etc collected in depth; incl publications by or about.

LAST JUDGMENT see Judgment Day

LATIMER, GEORGE

UT —UNIVERSITY OF UTAH, Marriott Library, Special Collections, Salt Lake City, 84112. Gregory C Thompson, Cur
Notes: Papers of George Latimer, attorney for Lt William Calley. Complete record of court-martial trial 1968-1973.

LATIMER, MARGERY BODINE

WI —UNIVERSITY OF WISCONSIN, MADISON, Memorial Library, Rare Books Collection, 728 State St, Madison, 53706. Gretchen Lagana, Cur
Holdings: / / Mss
Notes: Matthias Collection of 136 letters of Margery Bodine Latimer, author of such works as *The Guardian Angel and Other Stories, Nellie Bloom and Other Stories, This Is My Body, and We Are Incredible,* written in the late 1920s and early 1930s, and wife of the black poet Jean Toomer. Some 136 typescript and manuscript letters, mainly by Latimer but including as well nine from Jean Toomer and one each from Zona Gale, George Whitsett, and Donald Douglas, probing the feelings and philosophy of a writer and discussing such literary and artistic friends as Hergesheimer, Wolfe, Zona Gale, Orage, Starrett, Matisse, and many others. Housed in Dept of Rare Books and Special Collections.

LATIMER, WENDELL M.

CA —UNIVERSITY OF CALIFORNIA, BERKELEY, Bancroft Library, Manuscripts Division, Berkeley, 94720. James D Hart, Dir
Notes: Correspondence and papers relative to the history of modern chemistry.

LATIN AMERICA

AZ —UNIVERSITY OF ARIZONA, Library, Tucson, 85721. W David Laird, Librn
Notes: Latin American materials in the University of Arizona Library system may be found in all of the campus libraries. The largest collection is located in the Main Library and concentrates primarily on the history, literature, political science and economics of Mexico, Panama, Colombia, Argentina, Brazil and Chile. Special Collections specializes in the colonial period in the areas of law, religion, and economics. They also incl numerous manuscript collections, photographs, and 4000 broadsides from Mexico covering the late 18th century through the 20th century revolutionary period. There are also strong map, music and phonorecord collections primarily on Mexico. The greatest collecting effort is current materials on contemporary Latin America. Materials are fully accessible through the main card catalog as there is no separate catalog of the collection.

CA —UNIVERSITY OF CALIFORNIA, BERKELEY, University Library, Hispanic Collections, Berkeley, 94720. Gaston Somoshegyi-Szokol, Librn
Holdings: Vols (300,000)
Notes: General research collection in the humanities and social sciences, with special strengths in history, literature, economics, and political developments. Major emphasis on Argentina, Brazil, Chile, Mexico, and Peru. Main Library holdings are supplemented by subject coverage in branch libraries. Extensive government document holdings are maintained in the Government Documents Department (strength in statistics). The Bancroft Library contains outstanding research collections for Mexico and the Central American republics.

CA —CLAREMONT COLLEGES, Honnold Library, Ninth & Dartmouth, Claremont, 91711. Tania Rizzo, Special Collections Dept Head
Holdings: Vols 200 Cat Mss Pix
Notes: The papers of former Democratic Congressman Jerry Voorhis, from the 1930s to present, occupying nearly 100 document boxes. The papers reflect his life and career, incl biographical material, the history of the Voorhis School for Boys, his involvement in the Dies Committee, and his wide-ranging interests in American economic and social issues, such as cooperatives, monopolies and cartels, Latin American relations, consumers, and senior citizens. Books by and about him, with research files. Correspondence with political leaders. Inventory available. Restricted use.

CA —UNIVERSITY OF CALIFORNIA, SAN DIEGO, Central University Library, Mandeville Dept of Special Collections, La Jolla, 92093. Lynda Corey Claassen, Head
Notes: Hispanic Collection: Approx 6000 vols describe cultures of Spain, Portugal, Mexico, Latin America, and South America. Works of literature, history, philosophy and art date from the 15th to the mid-19th century. Highlights of the collection include rare 18th century Spanish provincial dramas and works on the history of Seville and Andalusia.

CA —UNIVERSITY OF CALIFORNIA, LOS ANGELES, Research Library, Dept of Special Collections, 405 Hilgard Ave, Los Angeles, 90024. Edward Shreeves, Chairman, Bibliographers Group; David S Zeidberg, Head
Notes: 90 linear feet in various collections

LATIN AMERICA (cont.)

pertaining to political and social activities in the US, Europe, Latin America, and the USSR.

CA —UNIVERSITY OF THE PACIFIC, Holt-Atherton Pacific Center for Western Studies, Stockton, 95211. Hiram L Davis, Dir of Libraries
Holdings: // Cat Mss
Notes: The Daniel James papers contain ms correspondence, notes and printed matter collected by a US freelance journalist who traveled and lived in Latin America in the 1960s. Emphasis is on politics and government. Ca 50 linear ft.

CT —YALE UNIVERSITY, Box 1603A, Yale Station, New Haven, 06520.
Holdings: Cat Mss Maps

CT —YALE UNIVERSITY, Sterling Memorial Library, Latin American Collections, New Haven, 06520. Lee H Williams Jr, Cur
Holdings: Vols (300,000) Cat Mss Maps Pix Slides Phonorecords 16mm Films Filmstrips Microforms
Notes: Collecting policy is to collect in depth (about 5000 vols a year) in the humanities and social sciences over the whole continental and Caribbean area without emphasizing any one country or subject area. Science and medicine are collected only as they relate to the historical development of the area. Monographs, periodicals, newspapers, pamphlets, government publications, mss, broadsides, posters, photographs, films, musical recordings, maps, and pre-Columbian artifacts form part of the collection. Areas of unusual strength are 19th century Mexico and Peru, Castro Cuba, the Allende period in Chile, and Central America, with recent gift of some 5000 items from Frederick R Mayer, Yale 1950, along with the earlier gift of Central American documents from Lindley and Charles Eberstadt. The Manuscripts and Archives Collectioncontains the following collections related to the Latin America area: (1) Latin American Manuscripts Collection, with 170 bound volumes, and 130 boxes of manuscripts relating primarily to the civil and religious history of Peru and Mexico from the 16th through the 19th centuries; (2) the Puebla Archives Collection, 50 boxes of legal manuscripts relating to church and state affairs of the Mexican state of Puebla; (3) the Columbus Collection, containing briefs, documents and mss covering the lawsuit initiated by Columbus's descendants to determine who was entitled to his estate; (4) a number of smaller collections containing handwritten journals, family papers and log books touching all periods of Latin American history. Of special interest are the personal papers of important diplomats and statesmen, such as Henry L Stimson, Edward M House, James Rockwell Sheffield, and Arthur BlissLane. For a partial listing of Chilean imprints in the collection for the years 1970-1973, see: *The Allende Years, A Union List of Chilean Imprints,* 1970-1973, "in selected North American Libraries, with a Supplemented Holdings List of Books Published Elsewhere for the Same Period by Chileans or about Chile or Chileans", comp by Lee H Williams, Jr (Boston: G K Hall, 1977).

DC —PAN AMERICAN HEALTH ORGANIZATION, Library, 525 23 St NW, Washington, 20037. Dr Carlos Gamboa, Chief of Library and Reference Services
Holdings: Vols 50,000 Cat Maps Slides Filmstrips

FL —UNIVERSITY OF MIAMI, Otto G Richter Library, PO Box 248214, Coral Gables, 33124. Frank Rodgers, Dir of Libraries
Notes: Special collections on Cuba, Jamaica, Colombia, Brazil, Panama and Mexico are supported by a general collection pertaining to the history and culture of Latin America. The collection incl the Agencia Latinoamericana papers. Emphasis is on Cuba and the Caribbean area.

FL —UNIVERSITY OF FLORIDA, Institute of Food & Agricultural Sciences, Hume Library, Gainesville, 32611. Albert C Strickland, Librn
Holdings: Vols (135,000) Cat Mss Microforms
Notes: Including journals and monographs, this collection is a general agricultural one. The emphasis is on tropical agriculture, especially Latin America. Entomology is very strong. The library offers on-line information retrieval using Lockheed and SDC data bases.

FL —MIAMI-DADE PUBLIC LIBRARY SYSTEM, 1 Biscayne Blvd, Miami, 33132. Alicia Godoy, Foreign Language Librn
Holdings: Vols 32,000 Cat Maps Microforms Phonorecords Audiotapes VF
Notes: Incl books in 17 languages, mainly Spanish; fiction, technical, biography, travel, history, mysteries, westerns, science-fiction and grammar; 200 language records, 100 language cassettes, 3 vertical files of clippings related to Latin America, Spain, Miami, etc; 35 magazines, 10 newspapers (daily local paper: Diario las Americas, El Miami Herald-El Mundo Puerto Rico); Sunday editions of Latin American newspapers from Argentina, Colombia, Chile, Mexico and Brazil; 1 Yiddish and 1 German newspaper.

FL —ROLLINS COLLEGE, Mills Memorial Library, Winter Park, 32789. Patricia J Delks, Dir of Libraries
Holdings: Vols 2450 // Cat Pix
Notes: Incl the Hispanic Institute Library. Latin American Collection. Circulating.

KS —UNIVERSITY OF KANSAS, Watson Library, Lawrence, 66045. George Jerkovich, Cur Slavic Collections
Notes: Over 6000 valuable Central American titles, of which fewer than half in a random sample are presently located in OCLC, and over half not incl in published holdings of the University of Texas or Tulane University. A special grant is supporting cataloging of the collection. Approximately 200,000 vols related to Spain, Portugal and Latin America are integrated into the libraries' collections. Emphasis for the past 25 years has been on literature and history, but there are notable strengths in social sciences and biological sciences as well. There is a full and growing collection on theatre in Central and South America.

MD —NATIONAL LIBRARY OF MEDICINE, 8600 Rockville Pike, Bethesda, 20209. Harold M Schoolinam, Actg Dir
Holdings: Vols (3,150,000) Cat Mss Audiotapes Videotapes 16mm Films Filmstrips Microforms
Budget: ($46,400)
Notes: The world's largest medical library. Materials are collected exhaustively in some 40 biomedical areas and, to a lesser degree, in related subject areas such as general chemistry, physics, zoology, botany, and instrumentation. Holdings include 82,000 monographic volumes, pre-1871; 438,000 monographic volumes, 1871-present; 714,000 bound serial volumes; 281,000 theses; 172, 000 pamphlets; 1,207,000 manuscripts; 156, 000 microforms; 12,000 audiovisuals; and 75, 000 prints and photographs. Pre-1871 material is in a separate historical collection. Approximately 24,000 serial titles are currenlty received.

MA —UNIVERSITY OF MASSACHUSETTS AT AMHERST, Library, Amherst, 01003.
Holdings: Cat Microforms
Notes: Latin American studies. Special strengths: Literature, history (especially Argentine history), anthropology. Newspapers on microfilm.

MO —UNIVERSITY OF MISSOURI-COLUMBIA, Museum of Anthropology Archives, 104 Swallow Hall, Columbia, 65201. Lawrence H Feldman, Museum Dir
Holdings: Vols (30) Cat Mss Maps Slides Microforms
Notes: Copies of Latin American and colonial mss. Many of the ms copies are of census, or census-like, documents of late colonial Verapaz; a few are from Sonsonate, El Salvador or Chiapas, Mexico. Additional material in the archives incl an original Eskimo manuscript (ca 1930) and an original Diegueno Yuman card vocabulary (ca 1964) and the Museum archives (papers on old accession systems, etc). Uncataloged microfilm copies of colonial Otomi and other vocabularies are also part of the collection. A catalog of material in this collection will appear in the Annual Report of the Museum of Anthropology, beginning with the 1976-77 volume.

MO —WASHINGTON UNIVERSITY, John M Olin Library, Campus Box 1061, St Louis, 63130.
Holdings: Vols 50,000 Cat Microforms
Notes: Geographical areas stressed are Argentina, Brazil, Cuba, Mexico, Uruguay and the Andean region. Subject strengths are Spanish-American literature, Brazilian literature, history, political science, economics, sociology and music. Areas of specialization in the field of literature are Argentine and Uruguayan (especially Gaucho materials, 19th and 20th century literary and general cultural reviews), Mexican, Cuban (Jose Marti) and Brazilian; Modernismo. Libraries hold 75 percent of the journal titles listed in Sturgis E Leavitt's *Revistas Hispanoamericanas; Indice Bibliografico, 1843-1935.* Areas of specialization in the fields of the social sciences are congressional documents (Argentina, Brazil, Mexico, Uruguay); statistical yearbooks, reviews, and bulletins(especially for Argentina, Brazil, Chile, Colombia, El Salvador, Panama, Peru, and Venezuela); Peronism (over 500 monographs, reports, and speeches published by the Peron government).

NJ —RUTGERS, THE STATE UNIVERSITY OF NEW JERSEY, Alexander Library, Special Collections and Archives, College Ave & Huntington St, New Brunswick, 08903. Ronald L Becker, Cur of Manuscripts and Rare Books
Notes: Papers of the Inter-American Association for Democracy and Freedom, the Pan American Women's Association, and their director, Frances Grant (1930-). Also papers of Robert Alexander, incl transcripts of several thousand interviews with Latin American political leaders, students, etc (1950-).

NJ —PRINCETON UNIVERSITY, Library, Rare Books Dept, Princeton, 08544. Stephen Ferguson, Cur
Holdings: Cat

NY —CORNELL UNIVERSITY LIBRARIES, John M Olin Library, Ithaca, 14853.
Holdings: Vols 190,000 Cat Mss Maps 16mm Films Microforms
Budget: $40,000
Notes: Latin American materials in the Cornell University Libraries may be found in all of the campus libraries. The largest single collection is located in the John M Olin Library, and the holdings and budget statements above refer *only* to this collection. The Olin Library collection incl both materials published in Latin America as well as those published anywhere in the world dealing with Latin America. Its central focus is on social science materials for South America, particularly the central Andes (Ecuador, Peru, Bolivia), Brazil, and the River Plate countries. Although the collection is historical in scope, with materials dating back to the "Columbus letter" of 1493, the greatest collecting effort is directed toward materials on contemporary Latin America: its culture, society, politics, etc. The materials are fully integrated into the generalcollections of the libraries, and there is no separate catalog of the collection. Deborah A Wood's *Directed Cultural Change in Peru: A Guide to the Vicos Collection* (1975) describes this archival collection, located in the Library's Dept of Manuscripts and University Archives.

NY —ROCKEFELLER UNIVERSITY, Rockefeller Archive Center, Hillcrest, Pocantico Hills, North Tarrytown, 10591. Joseph W Ernst, Dir; J William Hess, Assoc Dir
Notes: Papers relative to the Rockefeller Family, Foundations, University, and other specific enterprises and contributions to

LATIN AMERICA (cont.)

particular areas of social, physical, educational, and historic reform, preservation, conservation, or development. Extensive records of administrative, financial, physical, or intellectual relationships.

NY —STATE UNIVERSITY OF NEW YORK, STONY BROOK, Melville Library, Dept of Special Collections, Stony Brook, 11794. Evert Volkersz, Head
Holdings: // Uncat
Notes: 19th century Latin American pamphlets. 145 bound vols with about 1215 pamphlets.

NC —DUKE UNIVERSITY, William R Perkins Library, Durham, 27706. Elvin E Strowd, University Librn
Notes: The Perez de Velasco collection of 3000 titles relates to all phases of Latin American life. Emphasis is on colonial Peru.

OR —UNIVERSITY OF OREGON, Map Library, Eugene, 97403. Peter L Stark, Map Librarian
Holdings: Cat Maps Pix
Budget: ($4000)
Notes: 2500 atlases, 247,000 maps, 330,000 aerial photos. Specializations for maps are Pacific Northwest, Latin America and West Africa. Incl topographic maps. Specialization for aerial photos is Oregon. Separate catalog and index. Atlases are fully cataloged; maps are classified with shelf list cards; aerial photographs are fully indexed.

PA —BRYN MAWR COLLEGE, Canaday Library, Bryn Mawr, 19010. James Tanis, Dir
Notes: Rare books: The Dillingham Collection on Latin America, 16th - 19th centuries.

PA —UNIVERSITY OF PITTSBURGH, Hillman Library, Pittsburgh, 15260. Glenora E Rossell, Head
Holdings: Vols (172,000) Cat Microforms
Notes: The Latin American collection, although it contains good coverage of all countries and subjects related to those countries, has been developed giving special emphasis to materials related to Cuba, Ecuador, Guatemala, Mexico, Bolivia, and Peru. The collection is outstanding for research on Bolivia and contemporary Cuba. It incl 1700 periodical titles, 600 of which are currently being received. Especially strong on revolutionary and radical movements, and social change.

TX —TEXAS STATE LIBRARY, Archives Div, 1201 Brazos, PO Box 12927, Capitol Sta, Austin, 78711. David B Gracy II, State Archivist

TX —UNIVERSITY OF TEXAS LIBRARIES, Nettie Lee Benson Latin American Collection, Sid Richardson Hall 1.109, Austin, 78712. Laura Gutierrez-Witt, Head Librn
Holdings: Vols (450,000) Cat Mss Maps Pix Pix Phonorecords Filmstrips Microforms
Notes: Library acquires as exhaustively as possible materials relating to Latin America or written by Latin American authors. Related materials deal with states of the US during the period when they were part of the Spanish Empire or Mexico and with all aspects of Spanish-speaking people in the US. Downs 5289, 5336, 5337; suppl, 1950-1961, 2726. *Catalog of the Nettie Lee Benson Latin American Collection*, 31 volumes, 4 supplements in 19 vols (Boston: G K Hall, 1974). G K Hall also publishes annually the *Bibliographic Guide to Latin American Studies*, which incl the General Libraries' OCLC input of Latin American cataloging.

TX —SOUTHERN METHODIST UNIVERSITY, Fondren Library, Dallas, 75275. Curt Holleman, Librn for Collection Development

LATIN AMERICA—DESCRIPTION AND TRAVEL

MO —WASHINGTON UNIVERSITY, John M Olin Library, Campus Box 1061, St Louis, 63130.
Holdings: Vols (1800) Cat Mss
Notes: Incl material from the Arthur C Hoskins, Richard S Hawes, Ernst C Krohn, George N Meissner, Stratford Lee Morton, and Edgar M Queeny collections; strong in early travel literature of the US and Latin America; accounts of exploration in the Mississippi Valley and Trans-Mississippi West; miscellaneous accounts of history, pioneer life, and travel in the Ohio Valley, Old Southwest, and California; material on the American Indian; 18th century Americn music; early American imprints.

RI —BROWN UNIVERSITY, John Hay Library, 20 Prospect St, Providence, 02912. Mark N Brown, Cur Mss
Holdings: Vols (3500) // Cat Mss Maps
Notes: George Earl Church Collection, formed by a civil engineer, explorer and Fellow of the Royal Geographic Society, who specialized in railroad construction. Although part of the collection is devoted to American Revolutionary and Civil War history, the majority, over 2000 volumes, pertains to Central and South America. The imprints, which are predominantly 18th century, include Lima, Madrid, Rome, Mexico City, Seville, Barcelona, Lisbon, and Cadiz as well as *Nova orbis regionum ac insularum veteribus incognitarum* (Basle: 1537). Major subject areas are: anthropology, commerce, economics, engineering, ethnology, geography, history, law, mineral resources, railroad surveys, voyages of exploration and dictionaries of the South American Indian languages. The most significant ms is an historical account of the Bolivian mining town of Potosi from 1545-1737.

LATIN AMERICA—GAZETTES

NY —NEW YORK PUBLIC LIBRARY, Research Libraries, Economic & Public Affairs Div, Fifth Ave & 42 St, New York, 10018. Edward DiRoma, Chief
Holdings: Vols (1,500,000) Cat Microforms

LATIN AMERICA—GOVERNMENT PUBLICATIONS

CA —UNIVERSITY OF CALIFORNIA, BERKELEY, University Library, Hispanic Collections, Berkeley, 94720. Gaston Somoshegyi-Szokol, Librn
Notes: A significant research collection, emphasizing statistical publications and newspaper coverage.

CA —UNIVERSITY OF CALIFORNIA, LOS ANGELES, Research Library, Public Affairs Service, 405 Hilgard Ave, Los Angeles, 90024. Edward Shreeves, Chairman, Bibliographers Group; Eugenia Eaton, Head, Public Affairs Service
Holdings: Microforms
Notes: Depository for the official publications of California cities and counties, the state of California, the United States government, the United Nations and some of its specialized agencies (including the Food and Agricultural Organization and UNESCO), and such regional organizations as the European Communities and Organization of American States. Selected publications of other American cities and counties, of the other states and possessions of the United States, of interstate organizations, and of foreign governments (with emphasis on major world powers, Africa, Latin America and the Near and Middle East) and intergovernmental organizations.

NM —UNIVERSITY OF NEW MEXICO, Zimmerman Library, Albuquerque, 87131.
Holdings: Mss
Notes: The T Lynn Smith Collection (20,000 pieces).

LATIN AMERICA—HISTORY

AZ —UNIVERSITY OF ARIZONA, Library, Tucson, 85721. W David Laird, Librn
Notes: Latin American materials in the University of Arizona Library system may be found in all of the campus libraries. The largest collection is located in the Main Library and concentrates primarily on the history, literature, political science and economics of Mexico, Panama, Colombia, Argentina, Brazil and Chile. Special Collections specializes in the colonial period in the areas of law, religion, and economics. They also incl numerous manuscript collections, photographs, and 4000 broadsides from Mexico covering the late 18th century through the 20th century revolutionary period. There are also strong map, music and phonorecord collections primarily on Mexico. The greatest collecting effort is current materials on contemporary Latin America. Materials are fully accessible through the main card catalog as there is no separate catalog of the collection.

CA —UNIVERSITY OF CALIFORNIA, BERKELEY, University Library, Hispanic Collections, Berkeley, 94720. Gaston Somoshegyi-Szokol, Librn
Holdings: Vols (45,000)
Notes: Research collection of works dealing with the history of Latin America, especially Argentina, Brazil, Chile and Peru. The Main Library holdings are supplemented by strong government document and newspaper coverage. The Bancroft Library maintains excellent collections in the fields of Mexican and Central American history, incl primary source materials.

CA —UNIVERSITY OF CALIFORNIA, SAN DIEGO, Central University Library, Mandeville Dept of Special Collections, La Jolla, 92093. Lynda Corey Claassen, Head
Holdings: Vols (5000) Cat Maps Pix
Notes: The Jose and Maria Teresa Fernandez de Miranda Collection of about 5000 vols, incl history of Mexico, Spain, and Latin America. Also archaeology, anthropology, and linguistics of Mesoamerica.

CA —OCCIDENTAL COLLEGE, Library, 1600 Campus Rd, Los Angeles, 90041. Michael C Sutherland, Special Collections Librn
Holdings: Vols 2000 Cat
Notes: Cleland Library of Hispanic American History relating to Mexican and Latin American History, given in honor of Dr Robert Glass Cleland. Additions to the collection are being made from time to time by Occidental alumnus Arthur H Clark, Jr.

CT —YALE UNIVERSITY, Box 1603A, Yale Station, New Haven, 06520.

CT —UNIVERSITY OF CONNECTICUT, Library, Storrs, 06268. R H Schimmelpfeng, Dir of Special Collections
Holdings: Cat
Notes: Collection of newspapers and periodicals formerly belonging to the Duque de T'Serclaes. Ranging from the 17th century through the 20th, the bulk of titles are from 1800-1840, covering the Napoleonic period and the Latin American wars of independence.

DE —UNIVERSITY OF DELAWARE, Hugh M Morris Library, S College Ave, Newark, 19711. T Stuart Dick, Special Collections
Holdings: // Mss
Notes: Personal and business papers of the Potter Family, a Philadelphia merchant family prominent in the import trade with Central America, particularly Nicaragua (1801-1943).

DC —LIBRARY OF CONGRESS, General Reading Rooms Division, Microform Reading Room, Washington, 20540.
Holdings: Cat Mss Maps Pix Microforms
Notes: Microform materials only in this LC Division. Works of individual authors; holdings of collections; archival records, ect, press releases and translations, etc.

FL —UNIVERSITY OF MIAMI, Otto G Richter Library, PO Box 248214, Coral Gables, 33124. Frank Rodgers, Dir of Libraries
Notes: Special collections on Cuba, Jamaica, Colombia, Brazil, Panama and Mexico are supported by a general collection pertaining to the history and culture of Latin America. The collection incl the Agencia Latinoamericana papers. Emphasis is on Cuba and the Caribbean area.

FL —BETHUNE-COOKMAN COLLEGE LIBRARY, Daytona Beach, 32015. Albert M Bethune, Jr, College Archivist
Notes: Papers and private library of the historian, Joseph Henry Taylor.

LATIN AMERICA—HISTORY (cont.)

FL —UNIVERSITY OF WEST FLORIDA, John C Pace Library, Pensacola, 32514. Dean Debolt, Head, Special Collections
Holdings: Vols 180 Cat
Notes: The James B Lockey Collection of pre-1900 Latin American History.

IL —SOUTHERN ILLINOIS UNIVERSITY, CARBONDALE, Delyte W Morris Library, Carbondale, 62901.
Holdings: Vols (19,000) Cat
Notes: Described in Woodbridge, Hensley C, "Faculty and library collaboration in developing the Latin American collection for area studies programs at Southern Illinois University," Twelfth Seminar on the Acquisition of Latin American Library Materials, Final Report and Working Papers, vol 2, pp 99-108 (1967).

IL —CENTER FOR RESEARCH LIBRARIES, 6050 S Kenwood Ave, Chicago, 60637. Donald B Simpson, Dir; Esther Smith, Collection Development Librn
Holdings: Microforms
Notes: Newspaper files, Mexican parliamentary debates 1876-1914, statistical publications, US State Department and British Foreign Office records relating to Latin America, especially to Mexico and Central America. There is also a Latin American Microform Project, for which borrowing is restricted to subscribers to the project, but anyone may purchase prints where LAMP owns negative. LAMP materials cataloged, listed in *Materials aquired by LAMP.* There are 966 reels of microfilm.

IL —NEWBERRY LIBRARY, 60 W Walton St, Chicago, 60610. Diana Haskell, Cur of Modern Mss
Holdings: Cat Mss
Notes: Latin American colonial history, incl Brazil. See Robert Peerling Coale, "Evaluation of a Research Library Collection: Latin American Colonial History at the Newberry," *Library Quarterly,* July 1965, pp 173-84.

IN —INDIANA UNIVERSITY, Lilly Library, Seventh St, Bloomington, 47405. William R Cagle, Librn
Holdings: Vols (40,000) Cat Mss Maps
Notes: Research and rare book collection (Bernardo Mendel) of first or only editions, mostly printed in Latin America, from the discovery of the New World through 1830. Special strength in discoveries and exploration, history (mainly period of independence), Inquisition, missionary works by the Augustinians, Dominicans, Franciscans, and the Jesuits, and the history of the Catholic Church in these countries. Major geographic concentration is on the three great viceroyalties of Mexico (ca 10, 000 titles, plus over 10,000 official Mexican broadsides), Peru (2000 titles), and Argentina (4000 titles), incl in Argentina a substantial amount of printings from the Imprenta de Ninos Expositos, and the Collecton Santamarina. A special Bolivian Collection (2500 titles), mostly history, from the establishment of the press, there, ca 1826, through the beginning of the 20th century.Part of the Mendel Collection is the select Bibliotheca Boxeriana from Charles R Boxer (1000 titles) on European expansion into Asia, and into the New World, mainly Brazil, during the 16th-18th centuries. The collection is supplemented by substantial material from the private collection of Josiah K Lilly.
See also entries under Spain - History; Portugal - History; Mexico - History.

LA —TULANE UNIVERSITY, Howard-Tilton Memorial Library, Latin American Library, New Orleans, 70118. Thomas Niehaus, Dir
Holdings: Vols (150,000) Cat Mss Maps Pix Microforms VF
Budget: ($67,000)
Notes: *Catalog of the Latin American* Library (Boston: G K Hall, 1970, suppl. 1973,1975,1978); Downs 5338-41; suppl (1961), 2727, 2737. The Latin American Library is a general collection, but specializes in Central American, Mexican, and Brazilian materials. The disciplines which are most strongly represented are history, anthropology, and archaeology. The Viceregal Ecclesiastical Mexican Collection contains manuscripts from the colonial period. The France V Scholes Collection contains a large number of photoprints and microfilm of colonial documents from the archives of Spain and Mexico. The Merle Greene Robertson Rubbings Collection contains nearly five hundred rubbings of relief sculpture from Mayan archaeological sites in Mexico and Guatemala. The Photographic Collection contains photos of archaeological sites inMeso-America, of pre-Columbian Peruvian architecture, and a general group of historic photos from Latin America.

MA —PAN AMERICAN SOCIETY OF NEW ENGLAND, Shattuck Library, 152 North Street, Boston, 02109. Vivian Ingrao, Dir
Notes: Books on art, literature, history, and economy of Pan American countries.

MA —HARVARD UNIVERSITY LIBRARY, Widener Library, Cambridge, 02138. Ellen H Brow, Specialist in Book Selection
Holdings: Cat Mss Microforms
Notes: Shelflist published in 1966 *(Widener Library Shelflist,* Nos 5-6) lists 29,566 vols. For manuscripts, see *Hispanic American Historical Review,* XVII (1937), 259-277.

NY —COLUMBIA UNIVERSITY LIBRARIES, Rare Book & Manuscript Library, 801 Butler Library, 535 W 114 St, New York, 10027. Kenneth A Lohf, Librn
Holdings: Mss
Notes: The papers of Professor Frank Tannenbaum, approx 28,000 items of correspondence and mss relating to Latin American and Mexican history, also the US Farm Security Program, 1934-1937. Professor Tannenbaum also bequeathed his research library of more than 3000 vols on all phases of Latin American history and literature to Columbia. Restricted use.

NY —HISPANIC SOCIETY OF AMERICA, Library, 613 W 155 St, New York, 10032. Martha M de Narvaez, Cur of Mss; Irene S Frye, Asst Librn
Holdings: Vols (150,000) Cat Mss Maps Pix Slides Phonorecords Microforms
Notes: History, art, literature and general culture of the Hispanic countries (where Spanish or Portuguese is spoken). Incl (18, 000) vols printed before 1701, incl (250) incunabula; over (100,000) later vols, plus thousands of periodicals. About (200,000) mss incl ms maps. Printed atlases are in the Book Collection. Some microfilms, chiefly of our early books. Engraved and printed separate maps; reference collection of over 100,000 photographs; slides: all in Department of Iconography, not in library. Catalogs: *Catalogue of the Hispanic Society of America* (Boston: G K Hall, 1962), 10 vols; *First Supplement* (Boston, 1970), 4 vols. Early books: *Printed Books 1468-1700;* Mss: *Catalogo de los Manuscritos Poeticos* Castellanos (15th-17th centuries; 3 vols); *Medieval Manuscripts in the Library; Golden Age Drama Manuscripts*(the latter in press).
See also entry under Spain

NY —NEW YORK PUBLIC LIBRARY, Rare Books and Manuscripts Div, Fifth Ave & 42 St, New York, 10018. William L Joyce, Asst Dir; Susan E Davis, Cur of Mss
Holdings: Cat Mss
Notes: The division holds over 9 million pieces, incl medieval, Renaissance, and Oriental examples. Major emphasis on American, incl exploration, discovery, Spanish expansion, US history and historical persons; political, economic, and literary materials up to the 20th century, especially post-Civil War period; diaries of interest to social historians; theatrical history; science and engineering in 19th century America. Also the Maloney Irish Historical Collections; collections on Korean history, 1870-1948; Archives of the NY World's Fairs, 1939-1940 and 1964-1965. Autograph collections, and fraudulent signatures and documents. See *Dictionary Catalog of the Manuscript Division.* The Research Libraries of the New York Public Library. 1967. 1155 pp 2 vols $110.

NY —NEW YORK PUBLIC LIBRARY, Research Libraries, American History Div, Fifth Ave & 42 St, New York, 10018.
Holdings: Vols (20,000) Cat Maps Microforms
Notes: Encompasses all countries of Latin America. Outstanding collection of materials on Mexico and material on boundary disputes among countries of the Western Hemisphere. Local history materials for Latin America are incl. See *Dictionary Catalog of the History of Americas* Collection (Boston: G K hall, 1961), 28 vols.

NY —STATE UNIVERSITY OF NEW YORK, STONY BROOK, Melville Library, Stony Brook, 11794. John B Smith, Dir
Holdings: Vols 30,000 Cat
Notes: Part of the general research collection. Although the collection incl most Latin American countries, it has special strengths in Chilean materials, incl government documents of the 19th century.

OK —THOMAS GILCREASE INSTITUTE OF AMERICAN HISTORY & ART LIBRARY, 1400 North 25th West Ave, Tulsa, 74127. Sarah Hirsch, Librn
Holdings: Vols Cat Mss Maps Pix
Notes: Trans-Mississippi West, US, Indian and Hispanic history. The Gilcrease Library contains a total of about 40,000 mss; 10,000 imprints; 5000 photographs; 600 maps and 50,000 vols.

PA —UNIVERSITY OF PITTSBURGH, Hillman Library, Pittsburgh, 15260. Glenora E Rossell, Head
Holdings: Vols (172,000) Cat Maps Pix
Notes: Incl the John M Malone Collection (300 vols), and the Casasola collection of photographs of 20th century Mexico; virtually all the works of the Mexican philosopher Jose Vasconelos.

TX —UNIVERSITY OF TEXAS LIBRARIES, Nettie Lee Benson Latin American Collection, Sid Richardson Hall 1.109, Austin, 78712. Laura Gutierrez-Witt, Head Librn
Holdings: Vols (450,000) Cat Mss Maps Pix Phonorecords Filmstrips Microforms
See also entry under Latin America.

TX —UNIVERSITY OF TEXAS, EL PASO, Library, El Paso, 79968. Fred W Hanes, Dir
Holdings: Vols (16,000) Cat
Budget: ($2000)

†TX —TRINITY UNIVERSITY, Library, 715 Stadium Dr, San Antonio, 78284.
Holdings: Vols (10,000)
Notes: The library of Professor Ronald Hilton on Latin America and the Carribbean. Incl 270 audiotapes of interviews with prominent Latin Americans, 34 autograph letters, and photographs of Cuba during the Spanish-American War.

WI —UNIVERSITY OF WISCONSIN, MADISON, Memorial Library, Ibero-American Studies Collection, 728 State St, Madison, 53706. Suzanne Hodgman, Bibliographer
Holdings: Vols (230,000) Cat Maps Pix Phonorecords Microforms
Budget: ($50,000)
Notes: Materials on Latin America, Spain, and Portugal may be found in all the campus libraries. The largest single collection is located in the Memorial Library, and the above holdings and budget statements refer only to this collection. Strongest holdings are in language and literature and in history, although many other disciplines in the humanities and social sciences are well represented: political science, sociology, economics, anthropology, statistics, etc. Geographically, primary emphasis is on Brazil. The collection of materials on the history of Portugal is outstanding and that of Portuguese language and literature is one of the largest in the US. The collection is fully integrated into the general collections of the libraries. There is no separate catalog.

LATIN AMERICA—MAPS

†CA —STANFORD UNIVERSITY LIBRARIES, General Reference Dept, Central Map Collection, Stanford, 94305.

LATIN AMERICA—POPULATION

NC —CAROLINA POPULATION CENTER, Library, University Sq E, Chapel Hill,

LATIN AMERICA—POPULATION (cont.)

27514. Patricia Shipman, Head Librn
Holdings: Vols (20,000) Cat
Budget: ($10,500)
Notes: Try to acquire everything published in English on population, with particular emphasis on the US and developing countries. Also acquire conference proceedings, seminar papers. These and journal articles are indexed and the analytics are incl in the catalog. Incl 13,000 reprints and other pieces of ephemera. Most extensive area files are on India, Africa, Thailand, Iran, Korea, and Latin America. Holdings are recorded on an automated data base. A microfiche catalog is available for use in the Library and for purchase. Access by subject & geographic area are available through the Library's own thesaurus-based indexing systems.

LATIN AMERICA—SOCIAL CONDITIONS

NM —UNIVERSITY OF NEW MEXICO, Zimmerman Library, Albuquerque, 87131.
Holdings: Mss
Notes: The T Lynn Smith Collection (20,000 pieces).

LATIN AMERICAN ARCHITECTURE see Architecture, Latin American

LATIN AMERICAN ART see Art, Latin American

LATIN AMERICAN DRAMA

CA —CLAREMONT COLLEGES, Ella Strong Denison Library, Scripps College, Claremont, 91711. Judy Harvey Sahak, Librn
Holdings: Vols 2700 cat
Notes: Ruth S Lamb Collection of Latin American imprints, predominantly on theatre and drama.

CA —UNIVERSITY OF CALIFORNIA, SAN DIEGO, Central University Library, Mandeville Dept of Special Collections, La Jolla, 92093. Lynda Corey Claassen, Head
Notes: Hispanic Collection: Approx 6000 vols describe cultures of Spain, Portugal, Mexico, Latin America, and South America. Works of literature, history, philosophy and art date from the 15th to the mid-19th century. Highlights of the collection include rare 18th century Spanish provincial dramas and works on the history of Seville and Andalusia.

TX —UNIVERSITY OF HOUSTON, M D Anderson Memorial Library, University Park, Houston, 77004. David Farmer, Cur, Special Collections; Jean Jackson, Assistant Cur
Holdings: Vols 650 // Cat
Notes: Latin American drama. Copy-flow reproductions of most of holdings are available in public stacks area; original editions housed in the Department of Special Collections.

LATIN AMERICAN LANGUAGES AND LITERATURE

CA —CLAREMONT COLLEGES, Ella Strong Denison Library, Scripps College, Claremont, 91711. Judy Harvey Sahak, Librn
Holdings: 2700 Vols Cat
Notes: Ruth S Lamb Colllection of Latin American imprints, predominantly on theatre and drama.

CA —UNIVERSITY OF CALIFORNIA, SAN DIEGO, Central University Library, Mandeville Dept of Special Collections, La Jolla, 92093. Lynda Corey Claassen, Head
Notes: Hispanic Collection: Approx 6000 vols describe cultures of Spain, Portugal, Mexico, Latin America, and South America. Works of literature, history, philosophy and art date from the 15th to the mid-19th century. Highlights of the collection include rare 18th century Spanish provincial dramas and works on the history of Seville and Andalusia.

MA —PAN AMERICAN SOCIETY OF NEW ENGLAND, Shattuck Library, 152 North Street, Boston, 02109. Vivian Ingrao, Dir
Holdings: Vols (10,000) Cat Slides Phonorecords
Notes: Books on art, literature, history, and economy of Pan American countries.

NY —CENTER FOR INTER-AMERICAN RELATIONS, Library, 680 Park Ave, New York, 10021.
Notes: Most, but not all, of the 1000 plays and reference books are in Spanish or Portuguese.

NY —STATE UNIVERSITY OF NEW YORK, STONY BROOK, Melville Library, Stony Brook, 11794. John B Smith, Dir
Holdings: Vols 30,000 Cat
Notes: Part of the general research collection. Although the collection incl most Latin American countries, it has special strengths in Chilean materials, incl government documents of the 19th century.

NC —DUKE UNIVERSITY, William R Perkins Library, Durham, 27706. Elvin E Strowd, University Librn

PA —UNIVERSITY OF PITTSBURGH, Hillman Library, Pittsburgh, 15260. Glenora E Rossell, Head
Holdings: Vols (172,000) Cat Microforms
Notes: A general collection of Latin American literature, with emphasis on Cuba, Mexico, Chile, Guatemala, Ecuador, Peru, Bolivia, and Argentina. The holdings on Bolivian, Ecuadorian, and Cuban literature are extremely good. Very strong in contemporary literature of the whole area.

PA —PENNSYLVANIA STATE UNIVERSITY, Fred Lewis Pattee Library, Library Hispanic Program, University Park, 16802. Donald C Henderson, Head
Holdings: Vols (50,000) Cat Mss
Budget: ($21,000)
Notes: A fine collection of Latin American literature for all countries with particular strengths in Peru, Argentina, Brazil, Colombia and Venezuela, backed by holdings in related areas; supports doctoral programs.

TX —UNIVERSITY OF TEXAS LIBRARIES, Nettie Lee Benson Latin American Collection, Sid Richardson Hall 1.109, Austin, 78712. Laura Gutierrez-Witt, Head Librn
Holdings: Vols (450,000) Cat Mss Maps Pix Phonorecords Filmstrips Microforms
See also entry under Latin America.

WI —UNIVERSITY OF WISCONSIN, MADISON, Memorial Library, Ibero-American Studies Collection, 728 State St, Madison, 53706. Suzanne Hodgman, Bibliographer
Holdings: Vols (230,000) Cat Maps Pix Phonorecords Microforms
Budget: ($50,000)
Notes: Materials on Latin America, Spain, and Portugal may be found in all the campus libraries. The largest single collection is located in the Memorial Library, and the above holdings and budget statements refer only to this collection. Strongest holdings are in language and literature and in history, although many other disciplines in the humanities and social sciences are well represented: political science, sociology, economics, anthropology, statistics, etc. Geographically, primary emphasis is on Brazil. The collection of materials on the history of Portugal is outstanding and that of Portuguese language and literature is one of the largest in the US. The collection is fully integrated into the general collections of the libraries. There is no separate catalog.

LATIN AMERICAN MUSIC see Music, Latin American

LATIN AMERICAN NEWSPAPERS see Newspapers, Latin American

LATIN AMERICAN PERIODICALS see Periodicals, Latin American

LATIN INSCRIPTIONS see Inscriptions, Latin

LATIN LANGUAGE AND LITERATURE

CA —UNIVERSITY OF CALIFORNIA, BERKELEY, University Library, Berkeley, 94720. Donald G Williams, Classics Librn
Notes: Research collections, incl a wide array of periodicals, critical editions, works of textual criticism, history, and epigraphy. Extensive coverage of 18th and 19th century classical scholarship. German and Italian research publications are particularly well represented. Main Library holdings are supplemented by significant works in the Bancroft Library: mss, incunabula, and other rare editions; especially noteworthy are the Horace Collection and the Tebtunis papyri.

CA —UNIVERSITY OF CALIFORNIA, IRVINE, Library, Irvine, 92664. Roger Berry, Dept Head
Notes: Incl the library of Professor Paul Friedlander (3000 vols). Located in general circulation collection.

CT —YALE UNIVERSITY, Box 1603A, Yale Station, New Haven, 06520.
Holdings: Cat Mss

DC —CATHOLIC UNIVERSITY OF AMERICA, Mullen Library, 620 Michigan Ave NE, Washington, 20064. B Gutekunst, Humanities Librn
Holdings: Vols 7500 Cat

DC —HARVARD UNIVERSITY, Center for Hellenic Studies Library, 3100 Whitehaven St NW, Washington, 20008. Jeno Platthy, Librn
Holdings: Vols (42,000) Cat Maps
Budget: ($76,824)
Notes: In addition to a large collection of editions of ancient Greek authors, the library is well equipped to cover every aspect of ancient Greek civilization from prehistoric times to about AD 200. The subject fields covered include epigraphy, paleography, papyrology, history, literature, philosophy, religion, mythology, archaeology and art. A small collection of works on Patristics as well as all important Latin authors complete the Center's holdings.

MA —HARVARD UNIVERSITY LIBRARY, Widener Library, Cambridge, 02138.
Holdings: Cat
Notes: The collections for Horace and Persius are particularly noteworthy.

†MA —CLARK UNIVERSITY, Robert Hutchings Goddard Library, Worcester, 01610. Dorothy Mosa Kowski, Rare Books Librn
Holdings: Cat
Notes: Hundreds of vols of Greek and Latin classics in English translation (the Haven Darling Brackett Collection).

MI —UNIVERSITY OF MICHIGAN, Library, Dept of Rare Books & Special Collections, Ann Arbor, 48109. Robert J Starring, Head
Holdings: Cat Mss Microforms
Notes: Greek and Latin classics; classical studies periodicals.

MI —COLOMBIERE COLLEGE, Dinan Library, 9075 Big Lake Rd, Clarkston, 48016. Stephen A Meder, SJ, Librn
Holdings: Vols 2500// Cat

MN —SAINT JOHN'S ABBEY & UNIVERSITY, Hill Monastic Manuscript Library, Collegeville, 56321. Julian G Plante, Dir
Holdings: Vols (61,000) Cat Mss Pix Slides Microforms
Notes: Films of 61,000 mss. The total number of codices or bound handwritten mss represents the holdings of several hundred libraries in Europe, mostly Austria, Spain, Ethiopia, West Germany, Portugal, and also Italy, Hungary, Poland, Great Britain, Belgium, Yugoslavia, France, Switzerland, and the Netherlands.

†NY —COLUMBIA UNIVERSITY LIBRARIES, Butler Library, Rare Book and Manuscript Library, 535 W 114 St, New York, 10027.
Notes: Papers, mss, correspondence, etc of Prof Gilbert Highet.

OH —UNIVERSITY OF CINCINNATI, Classics Library, 320 Blegen, Cincinnati, 45221. Jean Susorney Wellington, Classics Librn; Eugenia Foster, Modern Greek Cur
Holdings: Vols (110,000) Cat Mss Maps Microforms

PA —HAVERFORD COLLEGE, Magill Library, Quaker Collection, Haverford, 19041. Edwin B Bonner, Librn & Cur
Holdings: Vols 3250 //
Notes: Works from the 15th through the

LATIN LANGUAGE AND LITERATURE (cont.)

19th centuries by and about the humanistic Latin writers of the 14th and 15th centuries.
PA —UNIVERSITY OF PITTSBURGH, Hillman Library, Pittsburgh, 15260. Glenora E Rossell, Head
Holdings: Vols (11,550) Cat
Notes: The classics collection is particularly strong in Greek and Latin literature, Greek and Roman history, Greek philosophy, Greek and Latin language, and Greek epigraphy. In combination with the Frick Fine Arts collection it has a good collection in Greek and Roman art and archaeology, The collection of journals is also quite strong in these areas. There has been an emphasis in collecting books by and about Homer, Aristotles, Euripides, Vergil, Cicero and Petronius. It has a unique collection of unpublished PhD dissertations and Master's theses on Petronius. It has a basic collection on Greek and Latin paleography and papyrology.
TX —UNIVERSITY OF TEXAS LIBRARIES, General Libraries, PO Box P, Austin, 78713. Carolyn Bucknell, Asst Dir for Collection Development
Holdings: Cat Microforms
WI —UNIVERSITY OF WISCONSIN, MADISON, Seminary of Medieval Spanish Studies, 1130 Van Hise Hall, Madison, 53706. Lloyd A Kasten, Emeritus Prof of Spanish
Holdings: Vols (7500) // Cat Mss Pix Slides Microforms
Notes: Medieval materials and subjects. 100 reels of microfilm, 2500 pamphlets and reprints. Incl a 300-volumes collection on 13th century Spanish Law. Other emphases: language studies (incl 616,247 vocabulary cards), dictionaries, bibliographies, periodicals. The nucleus of the collection is photostats of the mss of unpublished works of Alfonso X. Restricted circulation.
WI —UNIVERSITY OF WISCONSIN, MADISON, Memorial Library, Rare Books Collection, 728 State St, Madison, 53706. Gretchen Lagana, Cur
Holdings: Vols 120 // Cat
Notes: Giolito Collection. Approximately 120 titles of 16th century Italian imprints of Greek and Latin classics. Restricted use: Rare Book Department.
PQ —MCGILL UNIVERSITY, McLennan Library, Rare Books and Special Collections Dept, 3459 McTavish St, Montreal, H3A 1Y1, Can.
Notes: 5600 pamphlets, located in the Ribbeck Collection. Pamphlets, mostly in German, on Greek and Latin literature and philology.

LATIN MANUSCRIPTS see Manuscripts, Latin

LATIN SQUARES AND RECTANGLES see Magic Squares

LATROBE, BENJAMIN SMITH

MD —MARYLAND HISTORICAL SOCIETY, Library, 201 W Monument St, Baltimore, 21201. William B Keller, Head Librn
Holdings: Mss Pix
Notes: Architectural papers of Benjamin Smith Labrobe.

NY —NEW YORK HISTORICAL SOCIETY, Library, 170 Central Park W, New York, 10024. James Gregory, Librn
Holdings: Mss Pix
Notes: Papers of Benjamin Smith Latrobe.

LATSHAW, GEORGE

AZ —ARIZONA STATE UNIVERSITY, Library, Tempe, 85287. Marilyn Wurzburger, Special Collections Librn
Holdings: Vols (108) Pix
Notes: Collection covers various aspects of Children's Theatre from 1944 through the present. Areas of emphasis incl International and National Child Drama Associations, award-winning theatres, educational programs, regional groups and prominent figures in Children's Theatre incl: Irene Vickers Baker, Isabel Burger, Virginia Lee Comer, Rita Criste, Moses Goldberg, Kenneth Graham, Aurand Harris, Paul Kozelka, George Latshaw, Rosemary Musil, Sara Spencer, Winifred Ward, Susan Zeder and Lin Wright. Publications incl newsletters, research papers, bibliographies and records of the proceedings of the Children's Theatre Association of America. 80 linear feet of scripts, documents, publications, films, tapes (oral history) programs, correspondence, photographs, working papers and clippings. Partially indexed; finding guides available.

LATTIMORE, RICHMOND ALEXANDER

NV —UNIVERSITY OF NEVADA, RENO, University Library, Special Collections Dept, Reno, 89557. Robert E Blesse, Head
Holdings: Vols (21) Cat
Notes: Includes individual works by author in all editions including translations; also prefaces, introductions, published correspondence, appearances in anthologies, periodicals, etc. Bibliographical research collection, part of Modern Authors Collection. Other appearances 190 cataloged.

LATVIA

MA —HARVARD UNIVERSITY LIBRARY, Widener Library, Cambridge, 02138.
Holdings: Cat Mss Microforms
Notes: *Widener Library Shelflist* No 40 (1972) lists some 6500 volumes on the history, languages, and literatures of the Baltic states: Estonia, Latvia, Lithuania, and Livonia; about 2700 of these are on Latvia.

LATVIA—HISTORY

NY —NEW YORK PUBLIC LIBRARY, Slavonic Div, Fifth Ave & 42 St, New York, 10018. Edward Kasinec, Chief
Holdings: Cat Microforms
Notes: See New York Public Library, *Dictionary Catalog of the Slavonic* Collection (Boston: G K Hall, 1974), 44 vols.
WI —UNIVERSITY OF WISCONSIN, MADISON, Memorial Library, Slavic Studies Collection, 728 State St, Madison, 53706. Aleksander Rolich, Bibliographer for Slavic Studies; Robert P Gakovich, Slavic Cataloger; Valdis J Zeps, Baltic Studies Center
Holdings: Vols 4000 Cat Microforms
Notes: Emigre literature and respectable in lingustics, history, folklore, and theatre.

LATVIAN LANGUAGE AND LITERATURE see Lettish Language and Literature

LATVIAN NEWSPAPERS see Newspapers, Latvian

LATVIAN PERIODICALS see Periodicals, Latvian

LATVIANS IN THE U.S.

MN —UNIVERSITY OF MINNESOTA, Immigration History Research Center, 826 Berry St, Saint Paul, 55114. Susan Griegs, Cur
Holdings: Vols (35,000) Mss Maps Pix Phonorecords Audiotapes 16mm Films Microforms
See also entry under US - Emigration and Immigration
PA —BALCH INSTITUTE FOR ETHNIC STUDIES, Library, 18 S Seventh St, Philadelphia, 19106. R Joseph Anderson, Library Dir
Holdings: Vols 105 Cat Mss Microforms

LAUGHTON, CHARLES, 1899-1962

CA —UNIVERSITY OF CALIFORNIA, LOS ANGELES, Research Library, Dept of Special Collections, 405 Hilgard Ave, Los Angeles, 90024. Edward Shreeves, Chairman, Bibliographers Group; David S Zeidberg, Head
Holdings: Mss Pix
Notes: 12 linear feet of correspondence, mss, and ephemera.

LAURENCE, MARGARET, 1926-

ON —YORK UNIVERSITY, Scott Library, Downsview, M3J 2R2, Can. Hartwell Bowsfield, University Archivist
Notes: Papers of Margaret Laurence incl letters from readers, research notes, manuscripts of articles and stories, copies of lectures and addresses, diaries, financial records, and correspondence with contemporary Canadian authors.
ON —MCMASTER UNIVERSITY, Mills Memorial Library, Div of Archives & Research Collections, Hamilton, L8S 4L6, Can. G R Hill, Univ Librn
Holdings: Mss
Notes: Typescripts with corrections and revisions of *The Stone Angel, A Jest of God, Long Drums and Cannons, The Fire Dwellers, Jason's Quest, A Bird in the House, Heart of a Stranger, and the* Diviners.

LAURENS, HENRY, 1724-1792

SC —COLLEGE OF CHARLESTON LIBRARY, Special Collections Dept, Charleston, 29401.
Notes: Henry Laurens' Ledger, a business account book, 1766-1773.

LAURENTS, ARTHUR

MA —BRANDEIS UNIVERSITY, Goldfarb Library, 415 South St, Waltham, 02154. Bessie Hahn, Dir
Notes: Arthur Laurents Collection contains 6 linear ft of dramatic mss in various draft forms. Access to the collection is through the Main Card Catalog and a finding list in Special Collections.

LAURITSEN, THOMAS, 1915-1973

CA —CALIFORNIA INSTITUTE OF TECHNOLOGY, Robert A Millikan Memorial Library, Archives, 1201 E California Blvd, Pasadena, 91125. Judith R Goodstein, Archivist
Notes: 18 boxes. Nuclear physicist, Caltech. Correspondence, reprints, proposals, monographs, research data, clippings, and notes from lectures, conferences, travel and courses. Bulk of the collection is from after World War II. A principal correspondent is Fay Ajzenberg-Selove. Other correspondents incl Luis Alvarez, Hans Bethe, Niels and Aage Bohr, and William A Fowler. Unpublished finding aid in the repository.

LAVAL, PIERRE

CA —HOOVER INSTITUTION ON WAR, REVOLUTION & PEACE, Stanford University, Stanford, 94305. Milorad M Drachkovitch, Archivist
Holdings: // Mss
Notes: The Rene Chambrun Collection. Depositions concerning the government of Marshall Petain and Pierre Laval, by persons who held important official positions in France during the German occupation. Unpublished register available in repository.

LAVER, JAMES, 1899-1975

DC —GEORGETOWN UNIVERSITY, Library, Special Collections Div, 37 & O Sts NW, Washington, 20057. George M Barringer, Special Collections Librn; Nicholas B Sheetz, Mss Librn
Holdings: Mss Cat
Notes: The literary papers of author and art

LAVER, JAMES, 1899-1975 (cont.)

curator, James Laver (1899-1975), and those of his wife, the actress Veronica Turleigh; consisting of letters, with a considerable number written by Lady Cnythia Asquith; Clifford Box; Enid Bagnold; Nicholas Bentley; Violet Clifton; Desmond MacCarthy; Sir Edward Marsh; Sir Francis Meynell; Kate O'Brien; Dorothy L Sayers; Andre Simon; Enid Starkie; A J A Symons; Angela Thirkell; and Alec Waugh.

LAVIN, MARY

DC —GEORGETOWN UNIVERSITY, Library, Special Collections Div, 37 & O Sts NW, Washington, 20057. George M Barringer, Special Collections Librn; Nicholas B Sheetz, Mss Librn
Holdings: Mss
Notes: The Archives of the Gallery of Living Catholic Authors was founded in 1932 by Sister Mary Joseph of the Sisters of Loretto to focus attention on modern Catholic literature, and to provide a depository for manuscripts, letters, photographs, and books by contemporary Catholic writers. Contains material by hundreds of writers, incl Hilaire Belloc, Roy Campbell, Padraic Colum, Eric Gill, Paul Horgan, Mary Lavin, Marie Belloc Lowndes, Kathleen Norris, Alred Noyes, Sheila Kaye-Smith, Sigrid Undset, and Evelyn Waugh, to name only a few.

IL —SOUTHERN ILLINOIS UNIVERSITY, CARBONDALE, Delyte W Morris Library, Special Collections Dept, Carbondale, 62901. David V Koch, Cur of Special Collections; Louisa Bowen, Cur of Manuscripts
Holdings: Vols 10 Cat Mss
Notes: Personal papers and mss, 1953-1964, 7 linear ft. Inventory and name index available at library.

MA —BOSTON UNIVERSITY, Mugar Memorial Library, Special Collections Dept, 771 Commonwealth Ave, Boston, 02215. Howard B Gotlieb, Dir
Holdings: Mss Pix
Notes: Mss, correspondence, etc collected in depth; incl publications by or about.

NY —STATE UNIVERSITY OF NEW YORK, BINGHAMTON, Glenn G Bartle Library, Binghamton, 13901. Marion Hanscom, Special Collections Librn
Notes: Letters (253) of Mary Lavin, Irish playwright, largely correspondence with Lord Dunsany.

LAVOISIER, ANTOINE LAURENT

DE —HAGLEY MUSEUM AND LIBRARY, Eleutherian Mills-Hagley Foundation Inc, PO Box 3630, Greenville, 19807. Richmond D Williams, Dir; Heddy A Richter, Imprints Librn
Notes: Strong collection.

NY —CORNELL UNIVERSITY LIBRARIES, John M Olin Library, History of Science Collections, Ithaca, 14853. Lillian A Clark, Administrative Supervisor; David W Corson, History of Science Librn
Holdings: Vols (33,000) Cat Mss
Notes: Early printed source material in history of chemistry. Largest collection by and about Lavoisier outside of Paris. Lavoisier Collection incl 2,000 vols, 600 of which are from Lavoisier's personal library, and more than 500 ms items relating to his life and work. Noncirculating.

LAW

CA —UNIVERSITY OF CALIFORNIA, DAVIS, Law Library, Davis, 95616. Mortimer D Schwartz, Librn
Holdings: Vols 225,000 Cat
Budget: $211,177

CA —BANCROFT-WHITNEY CO, Editorial Library, 301 Brannan St, San Francisco, 94107. Phyllis Ross, Editorial Librn
Holdings: Vols 70,000 Cat
Notes: Federal and state statutes, jurisprudence, reports.

CA —HELLER, EHRMAN, WHITE & MCAULIFFE, Library, 44 Montgomery St, San Francisco, 94104. Loretta Mak, Librn
Holdings: Vols (22,500) Cat Audiotapes
Notes: A private library serving 150 attorneys. Emphasis on the areas of taxation, trial practice and corporation laws.

CO —NATIVE AMERICAN RIGHTS FUND, National Indian Law Library, 1506 Broadway, Boulder, 80302. Diana Lim Garry, Librn
Holdings: Vols Case Files Law Review Articles Studies Monographs
Budget: ($125,000)
Notes: A National Library of Indian Law, originally made possible by a grant from the Carnegie Corporation, now funded by the Administration for Native Americans (DHHS). Emphasizes information about treaties and rulings in cases involving Indian Country jurisdiction, economic development, hunting, land and water rights. Incl over 2000 case files and 4400 other monographs. Library publishes the *National Indian Law Library Catalogue: An Index to Indian Legal Materials and Resources.* Cumulative edition published in 1982, supplemented biannually. Catalog lists library holdings indexed by subject, author-title and case name.

CT —CONNECTICUT STATE LIBRARY, Readers Service Div, 231 Capitol Ave, Hartford, 06106. Ablene Bielefield, Head
Holdings: Cat
Budget: ($600,000)
Notes: Contains material of Connecticut legislative and legal sources, incl legislative histories, Connecticut Supreme Court Records and Briefs, and other sources.

CT —TRAVELERS INSURANCE CO, Corporate Library, One Tower Sq, Hartford, 06115. Margaret Orloske, Librn
Holdings: Vols 20,000
Budget: $50,000
Notes: Working law collection with emphasis on current laws, regulations and court interpretations. Little historical material retained. Separate catalog. Open to outside users by appointment.

CT —YALE UNIVERSITY, Law Library, 127 Wall St, New Haven, 06520. Morris L Cohen, Librn
Holdings: Cat Mss
Notes: With special collections on medieval Italian laws.

DE —DELAWARE CORRECTIONAL CENTER, Main Library, Education Bldg, Smyrna, 19977. Chris Tack, Librn
Holdings: Vols 2200 Uncat

DC —LIBRARY OF CONGRESS, Law Library, 101 Independence Ave, SE, Washington, 20540. Carleton W Kenyon, Dir
Holdings: Vols 1,800,000 Cat Mss Microforms
Notes: The collection, comprising the legal sources and literature of the US and all foreign nations, covers all legal systems incl common, civil, international, religious, and historic law.

FL —FLORIDA STATE HOSPITAL, Patient/Staff Library, Chattahoochee, 32324. Linda Brown, Librn
Notes: Extensive legal collection.

FL —UNION CORRECTIONAL INSTITUTION LIBRARY, PO Box 221, Raiford, 32083. Harry Rabe, Librn
Holdings: Vols 16,000 Cat Mss Maps

GA —UNIVERSITY OF GEORGIA, Alexander Campbell King Law Library, Athens, 30602. Jose F Rodriguez, Circulation-Reference Librn
Holdings: Vols 275,000 Cat Microforms

IL —ARLINGTON HEIGHTS MEMORIAL LIBRARY, 500 N Dunton Ave, Arlington Heights, 60004. Joy Kennedy, Head of Reference
Holdings: Vols 4000 Cat

IL —UNIVERSITY OF ILLINOIS, URBANA/CHAMPAIGN, College of Law, Library, Champaign, 61820. Richard Surles, Law Librn
Holdings: Vols (425,000) Cat Mss Microforms
Notes: Plus 800 reels of microfilm; 150,000 microfiches. Research collection covering both Anglo-American and foreign law. Depository for documents of the US Government, Illinois, and European Economic Communities.

IL —AMERICAN BAR FOUNDATION, Cromwell Library, 1155 E 60 St, Chicago, 60637. Olavi Maru, Librn
Notes: Research library emphasizing social/scientific literature. Also includes Bar Association publications and continuing legal education materials.

IL —AMERICAN JUDICATURE SOCIETY, Library, 200 W Monroe, Suite 1606, Chicago, 60606.
Holdings: Vols 5500 Cat
Notes: Materials on judicial administration. Publishers of *Judicature.* After April 1 address will be: American Judicature Society, 25 East Washington St, Suite 1600, Chicago, IL 60602.

IL —CONTINENTAL ILLINOIS NATIONAL BANK & TRUST CO OF CHICAGO, Information Services Division, 231 S LaSalle St, Chicago, 60697. Susan J Montgomery, Mgr
Holdings: Vols (27,700) Cat Microforms

IL —NORTHWESTERN UNIVERSTIY, School of Law, Library, 357 E Chicago Ave, Chicago, 60611. George S Grossman, Dir
Notes: Comprehensive collections of Anglo-American and foreign (especially European) law; Roman and Canon law (selective); international law; European Common Market; Williams Collection of Legal Instruments (AD 1300-1700); George W Shaw Collection of Early European Law. Incl 500 ms legal documents.

KY —UNIVERSITY OF KENTUCKY, Law Library, L-124 College of Law Bldg, Lexington, 40506. William James, Law Librn
Holdings: Vols (246,842) Cat Microforms
Budget: ($265,532)
Notes: Special collection on jurisprudence; hold briefs of Kentucky Court of Appeals since 1950-1977; Kentucky Supreme Court, 1977-.

LA —LOUISIANA STATE UNIVERSITY, Law Library, Baton Rouge, 70803. Lance E Dickson, Dir
Holdings: Vols (302,659) Cat Microforms
Notes: 358,886 microforms. Strong in civil law materials. Official depository for records and briefs of Louisiana Supreme Court and the five circuit courts of appeal for Louisiana.

MD —MARYLAND STATE LAW LIBRARY, Courts of Appeal Bldg, 361 Rowe Blvd, Annapolis, 21401. Michael S Miller, Dir; Shirley A Rittenhouse, Librn
Holdings: Vols (180,000) Cat Microforms
Budget: ($114,750)
Notes: Comprehensive Anglo-American Law Collection; all state codes and official reports; Supreme Court records and briefs.

MA —BOSTON PUBLIC LIBRARY, Government Documents Department, Boston, 02117. V Lloyd Jameson, Cur
Notes: Collection concerns federal and Massachusetts law.

MA —HARVARD UNIVERSITY LIBRARY, Law School Library, Langdell Hall, Cambridge, 02138. Harry S Martin III, Librn
Holdings: Vols (1,202,972) Cat Mss Microforms
Notes: For description see *Harvard Library* Bulletin, V (1951), 290-303. Rare books include 500 incunabula. For foreign law collections, see *Harvard Library Bulletin,* XVI (1968), 101-110. The collection is virtually complete for Anglo-American law, and is believed to be the most comprehensive legal collection in the world. For Treasure Room, see *Harvard Library* Bulletin, III (1949), 148-151.

MA —BOSTON COLLEGE, Law School Library, 885 Centre St, Newton Centre, 02159. Sharon Hamby, Librn
Holdings: Vols (160,000) Cat Maps Pix
Notes: Emphasizes Anglo-American law and international law and relations.

MI —UNIVERSITY OF MICHIGAN, Law Library, Legal Research Bldg, 801 Monroe St, Ann Arbor, 48109. Beverley J Pooley, Dir
Holdings: Vols (570,000) Cat Microforms
Budget: $575,000
Notes: Unusually strong in legal history, canon law, US state constitutional proceedings, Indian nations, and foreign and international law. Also 300,000 microforms.

LAW (cont.)

MI —WAYNE STATE UNIVERSITY, Arthur Neef Law Library, Detroit, 48202. Georgia Clark, Law Librn
Holdings: Vols (165,587) Cat Microforms

MO —UNIVERSITY OF MISSOURI-KANSAS CITY, School of Law, Leon E Bloch Law Library, 500 E 52nd St, Kansas City, 64110. Kenneth J LaBudde, Dir; Charles Dyer, Law Librn
Holdings: Vols 116,121 Cat
Notes: 3876 current serial subscriptions.

MO —WASHINGTON UNIVERSITY, Law Library, Mudd Law Building, Box 1120, Saint Louis, 63130. Bernard D Reams, Jr, Librn
Holdings: Vols (310,000) Cat
Budget: ($650,000)

MO —CENTRAL MISSOURI STATE UNIVERSITY, Ward Edwards Library, Warrensburg, 64093. Nancy E Littlejohn, Social Sciences Librn
Holdings: Vols (8000) Cat Microforms
Budget: ($7500)
Notes: Extensive criminal justice and law collection. In addition, a 7593 title microfiche collection of criminal justice and juvenile delinquency.

NH —NEW HAMPSHIRE STATE LIBRARY, 20 Park St, Concord, 03301. Shirley G Adamovich, Librn
Holdings: Vols (683,015) Cat Mss Maps Phonorecords 16mm Films Filmstrips Microforms
Budget: ($124,119)
Notes: Microfilm holdings of early NH town records, daily and weekly NH newspapers, 8337; NH laws and legislative journals of colonial and early state periods; laws of the US and all states and territories from the time of their settlement or organization; law library collection of 72,000 volumes; NH state documents, earliest to present; NH imprints.

NY —NEW YORK STATE LIBRARY, State Education Bldg Annex, Washington Ave, Albany, 12224.
Holdings: Vols (220,000) Cat Microforms
Notes: Session laws, statutes, reports and digests of the 50 states, Canada, Great Britain and British Commonwealth. Records on appeal; US Supreme Court, New York Court of Appeals and 4 Appellate Divisions. An almost complete collection of American and English editions of *Blackstone's* Commentaries. Legal periodicals in the English language; special collection of individual and collected trials; Session laws, American, the law library has a practically complete collection of the original editions of the session laws for every state and territory, incl 2 copies of Bradford's *Laws,* 1694, the first book printed in the Colony of New York. Of this book but eight copies are known. Some account of this collection is given in the *Annual Report* of the Library for 1919, pp 96-103. Material on the constitutional conventions of the several states.

NY —CORNELL UNIVERSITY LIBRARIES, Law Library, Myron Taylor Hall, Ithaca, 14853. Jane L Hammond, Librn
Holdings: Vols 370,000 Cat Microforms
Budget: $400,000

NY —COLUMBIA UNIVERSITY LIBRARIES, Law School Library, Law Building, 435 W 116 St, New York, 10027. James L Hoover, Librn
Holdings: Vols (735,000) Cat
Budget: ($650,000)
Notes: Incl substantial special collections in foreign and international law; also copyright law, ecclesiastical and medieval law; Roman law.

†NY —COLUMBIA UNIVERSITY LIBRARIES, Butler Library, Rare Book and Manuscript Library, 535 W 114 St, New York, 10027.
Notes: Prof Milton Handler's papers, correspondence, etc, largely on antitrust and trademark law.

NY —UNITED NATIONS, Dag Hammarskjold Library, Rm L382, New York, 10017. Vladimir Orlov, Librn
Holdings: Cat

NY —ELIZABETH SETON COLLEGE LIBRARY, Yonkers, 10701. Sr Margaret Sullivan, Librn

NC —WAKE TECHNICAL COLLEGE, Library, Audio-Visual Dept, 9101 Fayetteville Road, Raleigh, 27603. James Gray, Librn; Horst Garloff, Audio-Visual Specialist
Holdings: Vols (32,332) Cat Maps Slides Phonorecords Audiotapes Videotapes 16mm Films Filmstrips Microforms

OH —PUBLIC LIBRARY OF CINCINNATI & HAMILTON COUNTY, Government and Business Dept, 800 Vine St, Cincinnati, 45202. Paul T Hudson, Head
Holdings: Vols 120,000 Cat
Notes: Department receives over 1200 periodical and loose-leaf service titles, 1500 serial titles and over 1500 telephone directories. Subjects include political science, especially foreign relations, economics, law, public administration and business management. Dept houses Murray Seasongood collection of local government. Dept has extensive census material from 1790. Library is a full depository for US Government Publications, 1884 to date.

OH —CASE WESTERN RESERVE UNIVERSITY, Franklin Thomas Backus School of Law Library, 11075 East Blvd, Cleveland, 44106. Kathleen Carrick, Law Librn; Marsha Tittlebaum, Reader Serv Librn
Holdings: Vols (191,000)

OH —OHIO STATE UNIVERSITY, William Oxley Thompson Memorial Library, Hilander Room, 1858 Neil Ave Mall, Columbus, 43210. Predrag Matejic, Cur; G Koolemans Beynen, Slavic Bibliographer
Holdings: Vols (200,000) Cat Maps Microforms
Notes: Area studies of Central, Southeastern and Eastern Europe. Emphasis on on Slavic literatures, languages and history. At present economics, sociology, law (Russian only) have been added. Within this framework the following priorities have been established: Material in Russian problems; then Medieval Slavic (Cyrillic); then Polish, then Serbo-Croatian, then Bulgarian, and now Romanian. Special attention is paid to serials, bibliographies, ms descriptions and dictionaries (incl biographical and encyclopedias). Apart from materials in native languages, materials in the following languages are acquired: Old Church Slavonic, Greek, English, French, German, Italian, a few in Scandinavian languages, incl Finnish, and a few in Baltic languages. The Hillandar Room holds approx 2000 Slavic mss, 1050 from Hilandar Monastery, Mount Athos, on microform and a related referencecollection.

OH —MARATHON OIL CO, Law Library, 539 S Main St, Room 854-M, Findlay, 45840. Durand S Dudley, Sr Law Librn
Holdings: Vols (18,000) Cat
Budget: ($100,000)
Notes: Library serves the informational needs of the staff attorneys of a major oil company operating in both domestic and foreign areas. Includes all of the domestic law reports and digests. Includes statutes of 25 states. Particular emphasis is given to the acquisition of mineral (petroleum) law and energy legislation and regulation. Library open to the public by permission.

OK —OKLAHOMA DEPT OF LIBRARIES, Law Library, 109 State Capital, Oklahoma City, 73105. Robert Clark, Dir; Betty Brown, Okla Collection Librn; Virginia Collier, US Documents; Jan Blakely, State Documents; Blane Dessy, Library Science
Holdings: Vols 75,000 Cat Microforms
Budget: ($5,833,746)

OR —UNIVERSITY OF OREGON LIBRARY, Law Library, Eugene, 97403. Dennis Hyatt, Law Librn
Holdings: Vols 122,000
Budget: $354,000

OR —US DEPT OF ENERGY, Bonneville Power Administration Library, 1002 NE Holladay St, PO Box 3621, Portland, 97232. Karen Hadman, Chief of Library Branch
Notes: Emphasis is on Federal and Pacific Northwest law and in subject areas of interest to the Departments of Energy and Interior.

PA —UNIVERSITY OF PENNSYLVANIA, Biddle Law Library, 3400 Chestnut St, Philadelphia, 19104. Elizabeth S. Kelly, Libn
Holdings: Vols (350,000) Cat
Notes: Comprehensive collection of Anglo-American law. Legal materials from selected foreign countries, particularly in Common Market area. International law incl UN documents and other regional organizations. Substantial holdings in historical sources particularly early English law and Canon law.

PA —UNIVERSITY OF PITTSBURGH, Law Library, 3900 Forbes Ave, Pittsburgh, 15260. Jenni Parrish, Dir
Holdings: Vols (168,717) Cat Audiotapes Microforms
Budget: $257,000

TN —UNIVERSITY OF TENNESSEE, KNOXVILLE, Law Library, 1505 W Cumberland Ave, Knoxville, 37916. Charyn Piquet, Dir
Holdings: Vols 107,000 Cat Microforms
Notes: Separate catalog; holdings also listed in comprehensive public catalog in Main Library. Depository for US documents.

TX —NORTH TEXAS STATE UNIVERSITY, Libraries, NT Station Box 5188, Denton, 76203. Margaret Galloway, General Librn; Pat Stinson, Library Science Librn
Notes: General library collection incl insurance law, corporate law, criminal law, business law and international law.

TX —ECTOR COUNTY LIBRARY, Department of Business and Technology, 321 W 5th St, Odessa, 79760. Pat Jones, Dept Head
Holdings: Vols 500 Cat VF
Notes: Collection incl legal directories, nationwide.

VT —VERMONT DEPARTMENT OF LIBRARIES, Law & Documents Unit, 111 State St, Montpelier, 05602. Vivian Bryan, Librn
Holdings: Vols 102,000 Cat
Budget: $280,000
Notes: This is the largest law library in Vermont.

WA —UNIVERSITY OF WASHINGTON LIBRARIES, Pacific Northwest Collection, Seattle, 98195. Andrew F Johnson, Librn
Holdings: Vols (50,000) Cat Mss Maps Pix
Budget: ($12,000)
Notes: The Pacific Northwest Collection contains printed materials documenting the historic and contemporary life and culture of the region in a broad range of subject areas. The Pacific Northwest is defined as the geographic region including Washington, Oregon, Idaho, Montana, British Columbia, Yukon Territory, and Alaska. Printed materials including books, periodicals, government documents, maps, weekly and local regional newspapers, theses and dissertations, as well as photographs and architectural drawings are included in the Pacific Northwest Collection. Photographic works of over 200 photographers active in the Pacific Northwest, Alaska, and the Yukon Territory (Canada) during the period 1860-1930, including Asahel and Edward S Curtis, Eric Hegg, and Clark Kinsey, are represented in a print collection of more than 300,000 images. The architecturaldrawings collection includes over 19,000 original plans, drawings, sketches, renderings and blue prints pertaining to the history of architecture and urban planning and landscape gardening in the Pacific Northwest ca 1880-1940. Areas of particular strength are the holdings of over 1100 published journals of Pacific Northwest exploration expeditions, photographs of Northwest Coast Native Americans and of historic Seattle, newspapers issued within the Japanese-American relocation camps, 1942-1945, materials relating to the 1980 eruption of Mt St Helens, and Sanborne fire insurance maps for Washington. A unique feature of the Collection is the subject index to regional periodicals and local newspapers maintained by the PNW Collection staff; over 100 titles are currently indexed. G K Hall Company

LAW (cont.)

published a books catalog of the Pacific Northwest Collectionin 1973.

WI —UNIVERSITY OF WISCONSIN, MADISON, Law School Library, Criminal Justice Reference & Information Center, Madison, 53706. Sue Center, Librn
Notes: Incl Criminal Law Enforcement Collection, prinicipally composed of state and local documents from agencies concerned with the enforcement of the criminal law, ie prosecution, police courts, correctional institutions, probation, parole and juvenile authorities. Publications are mainly of recent years; the collection is continually growing. It was gathered for research into the subject field and is arranged by state and locality. There is a checklist to the collection. In the Rare Book Dept is the Grotius Collection: some 58 volumes by by or about the Dutch jurist and humanist Hugo Grotius.

WI —UNIVERSITY OF WISCONSIN, MADISON, Law Library, Law Building, Madison, 53706. Anita Morse, Dir Law Library
Holdings: Cat Microforms
Notes: Stressing environmental law. Subject cataloging only.

AB —ALBERTA ATTORNEY GENERAL, Law Library, Fourth Floor North Wing, Bowker Bldg 9833-109 St, Edmonton, T5K 2E8, Can. Andrew Balazs, Departmental Librn
Holdings: Vols (13,000) Cat Audiotapes
Budget: ($121,620)
Notes: Emphasis is on Canadian law. But if the solicitors can not find a Canadian precedent, they consult English law. If there is no precedent in English law they consult Commonwealth law, and if there is no precedent there either, then they consult American law. Therefore, the Library does have all the basic Canadian and certain basic English Commonwealth, and a very small number of American texts, as well as the basic Canadian and English law reports. There is one Australian law report. Besides texts (monographs), the Library subscribes to Albertan and Canadian legislative publications like bills, orders, votes and proceedings, Hansard, and Debates of the House of Commons. Assistance is available to users' from the simplest to the most complex legal research questions.

MB —UNIVERSITY OF MANITOBA, E K Williams Law Library, 401 Robson Hall, Winnipeg, R3T 2N2, Can. Denis Marshall, Professor & Head
Holdings: Vols 113,000 Cat Microforms
Notes: Incl 33,500 microforms; 850 serials.

ON —CANADIAN TRANSPORT COMMISSION, Library, Ottawa, K1A 0N9, Can. Marty H Lovelock, Librn
Holdings: Cat Microforms
Budget: ($50,000)
Notes: Books, documents, periodicals. Emphasis on transportation law and economics.

ON —LIBRARY OF PARLIAMENT, Parliament Bldgs, Ottawa, K1A 0A9, Can. Erik J Spicer, Parliamentary Librn
Holdings: Vols 10,000 Cat

ON —NATIONAL LIBRARY OF CANADA, 395 Wellington St, Ottawa, K1A 0N4, Can. Andre Preibish, Dir
Holdings: Vols 10,000
Notes: Includes 130 serial titles, theses, pamphlets, government publications relating to family and marriage. The following disciplines covered: anthropology, psychology and psychiatry, law, economics, religion, sociology, demography, education, political science and biology. Earliest title 1630.

ON —UNIVERSITY OF OTTAWA, Law Library, 57 Copernicus St, Ottawa, K1N 6N5, Can. Raymond Dicaire, Acting Librn
Holdings: Vols (138,000) Cat Audiotapes Microforms
Budget: ($280,000)
Notes: This collection supports teaching and research in both Common Law and Civil Law. Incl 1380 periodicals, cataloged; pamphlets.

ON —INSTITUTE OF CHARTERED ACCOUNTANTS OF ONTARIO, The Merrilees Library, 69 Bloor St E, Toronto, M4W 1B3, Can. Theresa Wolak, Librn
Holdings: Vols 109 Cat

†ON —METROPOLITAN TORONTO LIBRARY, Social Sciences Dept, 789 Yonge St, Toronto, M4W 2G8, Can. Abdus Salam, Head
Holdings: Vols Cat Maps Phonorecords Audiotapes 16mm Films Microforms
Notes: The collection includes nearly complete holdings of Canadian federal and provincial statutes and gazettes. Legal materials on other countries, particularly Great Britain and the US. Areas emphasized are statutory, criminal, family and constitutional law. There are a sizeable number of legal serials.

ON —ONTARIO MINISTRY OF TREASURY & ECONOMICS, Library Services, Frost Bldg N, Queen's Park, Toronto, M7A 1Y8, Can. Barbara Weatherhead, Head Librn
Holdings: Vols (100,000) Cat Microforms
Budget: ($76,500)
Notes: Index to Ontario regulations.

ON —UNIVERSITY OF TORONTO, Centre of Criminology, Library, 130 St George St, Rm 8001, Toronto, M5S 1A5, Can. Catherine J Matthews, Librn
Holdings: Vols (20,000) Cat
Notes: Over 4500 research reports, article reprints, theses, etc. Extensive newspaper clippings file from 1963 to present indexed under 350 subject headings. The collection covers criminology, law enforcement and policing, delinquency, criminal justice system, penology and corrections. Acquisitions list published three times a year; subscription.

LAW—EARLY WORKS

IL —NORTHWESTERN UNIVERSTIY, School of Law, Library, 357 E Chicago Ave, Chicago, 60611. George S Grossman, Dir
Holdings: Cat Mss
Notes: Comprehensive collections of Anglo-American and foreign (especially European) law; Roman and Canon law (selective); international law; European Common Market; Williams Collection of Legal Instruments (AD 1300-1700); George W Shaw Collection of Early European Law. Incl 500 ms legal documents.

NY —UNIVERSITY OF ROCHESTER, Rush Rhees Library, Department of Rare Books and Special Collections, Rochester, 14627. Peter Dzwonkoski, Librn
Holdings: Vols (450) Cat
Notes: Collection of materials on 16th and 17th century European law and political theory with special emphasis on works emanating from the French Civil Wars of the late 16th century. Particularly notable are the editions of the works of Francois Hotman and the editions of the Corpus Juris Civilis printed in Lyon. No photocopying.

OH —RUTHERFORD B HAYES LIBRARY, 1337 Hayes Ave, Fremont, 43420. Watt P Marchman, Dir
Holdings: Vols 1400 Cat
Notes: A 19th century law library.

LAW—HISTORY

CT —YALE UNIVERSITY, Law Library, 127 Wall St, New Haven, 06520. Morris L Cohen, Librn
Holdings: Cat Mss
Notes: With special collections on medieval Italian laws.

DC —GEORGETOWN UNIVERSITY, Library, Special Collections Div, 37 & O Sts NW, Washington, 20057. George M Barringer, Special Collections Librn; Nicholas B Sheetz, Mss Librn
Holdings: Mss Cat
Notes: The papers of the explorer John Mullan (1859-1940), containing correspondence, letter books, legal documents, photographs, and clippings; for the most part pertaining to Mullan's activities as claims agent for Washington Territory; the states of California, Oregon, Nevada, and Colorado; and a few individuals. Of interest for the study of mandamus and estoppel in contract law in the Progressive Era, as well as in the study of claims activities, and anti-lawyer sentiment in the West during the same period. There is also present a small amount of material on the Military Road from Fort Walla Walla to Fort Benton.

DC —HARVARD UNIVERSITY, Dumbarton Oaks, Research Library, 1703 32nd St NW, Washington, 20007. Irene Vaslef, Librn
Holdings: Vols (91,000) Cat Maps Pix Slides Microforms
Budget: ($219,000)
Notes: Byzantine civilization (including art, archaeology, literature, history, religion, law, music, etc). Extensive supplemental material on Classical, Hellenistic, Medieval, Islamic, Medieval Slavic cultures. 62,000 b/w photographs, 25,000 slides and transparencies, 1000 microfilms of books and manuscripts. Printed description of collection in *Harvard Library Bulletin,* vol 19, no 1 (Jan 1971), pp 25-35 and vol 19, no 2 (April 1971), pp 204-214, pp 25-35 and vol 19, no 2 (April 1971), pp 204-214.

DC —LIBRARY OF CONGRESS, Law Library, 101 Independence Ave, SE, Washington, 20540. Carleton W Kenyon, Dir
Holdings: Vols 1,800,000 Cat Mss Microforms
Notes: The collection, comprising the legal sources and literature of the US and all foreign nations, covers all legal systems incl common, civil, international, religious, and historic law.

IL —NORTHWESTERN UNIVERSTIY, School of Law, Library, 357 E Chicago Ave, Chicago, 60611. George S Grossman, Dir
Holdings: Cat Mss
Notes: Comprehensive collections of Anglo-American and foreign (especially European) law; Roman and Canon law (selective); international law; European Common Market; Williams Collection of Legal Instruments (AD 1300-1700); George W Shaw Collection of Early European Law. Incl 500 ms legal documents.

MA —STATE LIBRARY OF MASSACHUSETTS, 341 State House, Boston, 02133. Gaspar Caso, State Librn
Holdings: Vols 10,000 Cat Mss
Notes: Strong in early session laws for all states.

MA —HARVARD UNIVERSITY LIBRARY, Law School Library, Langdell Hall, Cambridge, 02138. Harry S Martin III, Librn
Holdings: Vols (1,202,972) Cat Mss Microforms
Notes: For description see *Harvard Library* Bulletin, V (1951), 290-303. Rare books include 500 incunabula. For foreign law collections, see *Harvard Library Bulletin,* XVI (1968), 101-110. The collection is virtually complete for Anglo-American law, and is believed to be the most comprehensive legal collection in the world. For Treasure Room, see *Harvard Library* Bulletin, III (1949), 148-151.

MI —UNIVERSITY OF MICHIGAN, Law Library, Legal Research Bldg, 801 Monroe St, Ann Arbor, 48109. Beverley J Pooley, Dir
Holdings: Vols (570,000) Cat Microforms
Budget: $575,000
Notes: Unusually strong in legal history, canon law, US state constitutional proceedings, Indian nations, and foreign and international law. Also 300,000 microforms.

NY —UNIVERSITY OF ROCHESTER, Rush Rhees Library, Department of Rare Books and Special Collections, Rochester, 14627. Peter Dzwonkoski, Librn
Holdings: Vols (450) Cat
Notes: Collection of materials on 16th and 17th century European law and political theory with special emphasis on works emanating from the French Civil Wars of the late 16th century. Particularly notable are the editions of the works of Francois Hotman and the editions of the Corpus Juris Civilis printed in Lyon. No photocopying.

LAW—HISTORY (cont.)

PA —FREE LIBRARY OF PHILADELPHIA, Rare Book Dept, Logan Sq, Philadelphia, 19103. Marie E Korey, Rare Book Librn
Holdings: Cat Mss Pix
Notes: The Hampton L Carson Collection of 22,000 books, manuscripts, autograph letters and prints relating to British and American legal history.

PA —HISTORICAL SOCIETY OF PENNSYLVANIA, Library, 1300 Locust St, Philadelphia, 19107. David Fraser, Librn
Holdings: Vols (230,000) Mss Maps Pix Microforms
Notes: Incl over 14,000,000 ms pieces. The Library Company of Philadelphia mss are on deposit with the Historical Society of Pennsylvania. Many of the Society's rare books are on deposit with the Library Company. The Society maintains the collections of the Genealogical Society of Pennsylvania, incl some 20,000 printed genealogies, original mss, family, church, and civil records.

PA —UNIVERSITY OF PENNSYLVANIA, Biddle Law Library, 3400 Chestnut St, Philadelphia, 19104. Elizabeth S. Kelly, Libn
Holdings: Vols (350,000) Cat
Notes: Comprehensive collection of Anglo-American law. Legal materials from selected foreign countries, particularly in Common Market area. International law incl UN documents and other regional organizations. Substantial holdings in historical sources particularly early English law and Canon law.

RI —BROWN UNIVERSITY, John Hay Library, 20 Prospect St, Providence, 02912. Mark N Brown, Cur Mss
Holdings: Mss
Notes: The Brown University Library Manuscript Collection possesses several collections pertaining to law, primarily the personal and legal papers of various jurists and lawyers. See the Benjamin Bourne, 1755-1808, Collection (200 items); the Zechariah Chafee, Jr, 1885-1957, Papers--Professor of Law at Harvard, (400 items); the Samuel Sullivan Cox, 1824-1889, Papers--US Congressman from Ohio and New York, (1200 items); the Thomas Wilson Dorr, 1805-1854, Papers--Rhode Island lawyer and reformer (600 items); etc.

SC —COLLEGE OF CHARLESTON LIBRARY, Special Collections Dept, Charleston, 29401.
Notes: Charles Fraser Commonplace Book, a study book of law cases in South Carolina adjudicated 1736-1819, compiled mostly 1800-1807, while studying for admission to the bar, as a forms manual. Contains copies of writs for both civil and criminal actions and decisions from the Court of Chancery, Court of Pleas, and Commissions of the Peace.

LAW—STUDY AND TEACHING

IL —AMERICAN BAR FOUNDATION, Cromwell Library, 1155 E 60 St, Chicago, 60637. Olavi Maru, Librn
Notes: Research library emphasizing social/scientific literature. Also includes Bar Association publications and continuing legal education materials.

†NY —COLUMBIA UNIVERSITY LIBRARIES, Butler Library, Rare Book and Manuscript Library, 535 W 114 St, New York, 10027.
Notes: Prof John N Hazard's papers, incl 20 notebooks of class notes while a student at the Moscow Juridical Institute, 1934-37.

LAW, AMERICAN

CT —YALE UNIVERSITY, Beinecke Rare Book & Manuscript Library, Osborn Collection, New Haven, 06520. Stephen R Parks, Cur
Holdings: Mss

MA —HARVARD UNIVERSITY LIBRARY, Law School Library, Langdell Hall, Cambridge, 02138. Harry S Martin III, Librn
Holdings: Cat Mss Maps Pix Slides
Notes: Downs 1687, 1763, 1774, 1776-1779, 1782-1782, 1790-1793, 1809, 1764, 1768, 1796; Downs Supplement 789. Comprehensive collection of English common law, American Law (historical and current), foreign law, comparative law, international law, Roman law and Canon law. Over a million vols

MA —BOSTON COLLEGE, Law School Library, 885 Centre St, Newton Centre, 02159. Sharon Hamby, Librn
Holdings: Vols (117,790) Cat Maps Pix
Budget: ($100,650)
Notes: Emphasizes Anglo-American law and international law and relations.

NM —UNIVERSITY OF NEW MEXICO, School of Law Library, 1117 Stanford Dr NE, Albuquerque, 87131. Myron Fink, Law Librn
Holdings: Vols (3000) Cat Mss
Notes: Collection supports the work of the American Indian Law Center, established by the law school. Has separate catalog with extensive subject analysis. Incl papers of William Zimmerman, Asst Commissioner of Indian Affairs, 1934-1950. Emphasis is on government relations, tribal government (especially tribal codes for all Indian tribes in US). Incl materials on indigenous peoples world-wide. Periodical literature is subject indexed. Bibliography: Sabatini, Joseph D, *American Indian Law: A Bibliography of Books, Law Review Articles and Indian* Periodicals. (Albuquerque, 1973), Supplement, 1975.

OH —CASE WESTERN RESERVE UNIVERSITY, Franklin Thomas Backus School of Law Library, 11075 East Blvd, Cleveland, 44106. Kathleen Carrick, Law Librn; Marsha Tittlebaum, Reader Serv Librn
Holdings: Vols (191,000)
Notes: Anglo-American law.

PA —FREE LIBRARY OF PHILADELPHIA, Rare Book Dept, Logan Sq, Philadelphia, 19103. Marie E Korey, Rare Book Librn
Holdings: Cat Mss Pix
Notes: The Hampton L Carson Collection of 22,000 books, manuscripts, autograph letters and prints relating to British and American legal history.

AB —ALBERTA ATTORNEY GENERAL, Law Library, Fourth Floor North Wing, Bowker Bldg 9833-109 St, Edmonton, T5K 2E8, Can. Andrew Balazs, Departmental Librn
Holdings: Vols (13,000) Cat Audiotapes
Budget: ($121,620)
Notes: Emphasis is on Canadian law. But if the solicitors can not find a Canadian precedent, they consult English law. If there is no precedent in English law they consult Commonwealth law, and if there is no precedent there either, then they consult American law. Therefore, the Library does have all the basic Canadian and certain basic English Commonwealth, and a very small number of American texts, as well as the basic Canadian and English law reports. There is one Australian law report. Besides texts (monographs), the Library subscribes to Albertan and Canadian legislative publications like bills, orders, votes and proceedings, Hansard, and Debates of the House of Commons. Assistance is available to users' from the simplest to the most complex legal research questions.

LAW, ANGLO-AMERICAN see Law, American

LAW, BIBLE see Jewish Law

LAW, BRITISH

IL —NORTHWESTERN UNIVERSTIY, School of Law, Library, 357 E Chicago Ave, Chicago, 60611. George S Grossman, Dir
Notes: Comprehensive collections of Anglo-American and foreign (especially European) law; Roman and Canon law (selective); international law; European Common Market; Williams Collection of Legal Instruments (AD 1300-1700); George W Shaw Collection of Early European Law. Incl 500 ms legal documents.

MA —HARVARD UNIVERSITY LIBRARY, Law School Library, Langdell Hall, Cambridge, 02138. Harry S Martin III, Librn
Holdings: Cat Mss Maps Pix Slides
Notes: Downs 1687, 1763, 1774, 1776-1779, 1782-1784, 1790-1793, 1809, 1764, 1768, 1796; Downs Supplement 789. Comprehensive collection of English common law, American Law (historical and current), foreign law, comparative law, international law, Roman law and Canon law. Over a million vols.

MA —BOSTON COLLEGE, Law School Library, 885 Centre St, Newton Centre, 02159. Sharon Hamby, Librn
Holdings: Vols (160,000) Cat Maps Pix
Notes: Emphasizes Anglo-American law and international law and relations.

NY —NEW YORK STATE LIBRARY, State Education Bldg Annex, Washington Ave, Albany, 12224.
Holdings: Vols (220,000) Cat Microforms
Notes: Session laws, statutes, reports and digests of the 50 states, Canada, Great Britain and British Commonwealth. Records on appeal: Us Supreme Court, New York Court of Appeals and 4 Appellate Division. An almost complete collection of American and English editions of *Blackstone's* Commentaries. Legal periodicals in the English language; special collection of individual and collected trials; Session laws, American, the law library has a practically complete collection of the original editions of the session laws for every state and territory, incl 2 copies of Bradford's *Laws,* 1694, the first book printed in the Colony of New York. Of this book but eight copies are known. Some account of this collection is given in the *Annual Report* of the Library for 1919, pp 96-103. Material on the constitutional conventions of the several states.

OH —CASE WESTERN RESERVE UNIVERSITY, Franklin Thomas Backus School of Law Library, 11075 East Blvd, Cleveland, 44106. Kathleen Carrick, Law Librn; Marsha Tittlebaum, Reader Serv Librn
Holdings: Vols (191,000)
Notes: British and Commonwealth law.

PA —FREE LIBRARY OF PHILADELPHIA, Rare Book Dept, Logan Sq, Philadelphia, 19103. Marie E Korey, Rare Book Librn
Holdings: Cat Mss Pix
Notes: The Hampton L Carson Collection of 22,000 books, manuscripts, autograph letters and prints relating to British and American legal history.

AB —ALBERTA ATTORNEY GENERAL, Law Library, Fourth Floor North Wing, Bowker Bldg 9833-109 St, Edmonton, T5K 2E8, Can. Andrew Balazs, Departmental Librn
Holdings: Vols (13,000) Cat Audiotapes
Budget: ($121,620)
Notes: Emphasis is on Canadian law. But if the solicitors can not find a Canadian precedent, they consult English law. If there is no precedent in English law they consult Commonwealth law, and if there is no precedent there either, then they consult American law. Therefore, the Library does have all the basic Canadian and certain basic English Commonwealth, and a very small number of American texts, as well as the basic Canadian and English law reports. There is one Australian law report. Besides texts (monographs), the Library subscribes to Albertan and Canadian legislative publications like bills, orders, votes and proceedings, Hansard, and Debates of the House of Commons. Assistance is available to users' from the simplest to the most complex legal research questions.

AB —UNIVERSITY OF ALBERTA, John Weir Memorial Law Library, Law Centre, Second Floor, Edmonton, T6G 2H5, Can. Lillian MacPherson, Law Librn
Holdings: Vols (140,000) Cat Maps Audiotapes Microforms
Budget: ($400,000)
Notes: Emphases on Canadian Government Publications, oil and gas, Canadian and US, UK, Australian, New Zealand primary materials. Separate catalog.

LAW, BRITISH (cont.)

NS —NOVA SCOTIA DEPT OF THE ATTORNEY-GENERAL, Library, PO Box 7, Halifax, B3J 2L6, Can. Margaret Murphy, Librn
Holdings: Vols (7000) Cat
Budget: ($15,000)
Notes: Working collection of materials pertaining to Canadian and English law.

SK —SASKATCHEWAN LEGISLATIVE LIBRARY, 234 Legislative Bldg, Regina, S4S 0B3, Can. Marian Powell, Librn
Holdings: Vols 12,330 Cat
Notes: Emphasis in this collection is on Canadian and British law and constitutional history.

LAW, BUSINESS see Business Law

LAW, CANADIAN

NY —NEW YORK STATE LIBRARY, State Education Bldg Annex, Washington Ave, Albany, 12224.
Holdings: Vols (220,000) Cat Microforms
Notes: Session laws, statutes, reports and digests of the 50 states, Canada, Great Britain and British Commonwealth. Records on appeal: US Supreme Court, New York Court of Appeals and 4 Appellate Divisions. An almost complete collection of American and English editions of *Blackstone's* Commentaries. Legal periodicals in the English language; special collection of individual and collected trials; Session laws, American, the law library has a practically complete collection of the original editions of the session laws for every state and territory, incl 2 copies of Bradford's *Laws,* 1694, the first book printed in the Colony of New York. Of this book but eight copies are known. Some account of this collection is given in the *Annual Report* of the Library for 1919, pp 96-103. Material on the constitutional conventions of the several states.

NS —NOVA SCOTIA DEPT OF THE ATTORNEY-GENERAL, Library, PO Box 7, Halifax, B3J 2L6, Can. Margaret Murphy, Librn
Holdings: Vols (7000) Cat
Budget: ($15,000)
Notes: Working collection of materials pertaining to Canadian and English law.

ON —LIBRARY OF PARLIAMENT, Parliament Bldgs, Ottawa, K1A 0A9, Can. Erik J Spicer, Parliamentary Librn
Holdings: Vols 5000 Cat

ON —UNIVERSITY OF OTTAWA, Law Library, 57 Copernicus St, Ottawa, K1N 6N5, Can. Raymond Dicaire, Acting Librn
Holdings: Vols (138,000)
Notes: This collection supports teaching and research in both Common Law and Civil Law. Incl 1380 periodicals, cataloged; pamphlets.

SK —SASKATCHEWAN LEGISLATIVE LIBRARY, 234 Legislative Bldg, Regina, S4S 0B3, Can. Marian Powell, Librn
Holdings: Vols 12,330 Cat
Notes: Emphasis in this collection is on Canadian and British law and constitutional history.

LAW, CIVIL see Civil Law

LAW, COMMUNICATIONS see Communications—Law and Legislation

LAW, COMPARATIVE see Comparative Law

LAW, CONSTITUTIONAL see Constitutional Law

LAW, CORPORATION see Corporation Law

LAW, CRIMINAL see Criminal Law

LAW, CUSTOMARY see Customary Law

LAW, ECCLESIASTICAL see Ecclesiastical Law

LAW, EDUCATIONAL see Education—Law and Legislation

LAW, ENGLISH

DC —LIBRARY OF CONGRESS, Law Library, 101 Independence Ave, SE, Washington, 20540. Carleton W Kenyon, Dir
Notes: A collection of printed Year Books published between the late 15th and late 16th centuries.

MA —HARVARD UNIVERSITY LIBRARY, Law School Library, Langdell Hall, Cambridge, 02138. Harry S Martin III, Librn
Holdings: Cat Mss
Notes: The collection of early books is unsurpassed; see Joseph Henry Beale's *Bibliography of Early English Law Books* (Harvard University Press, 1926) and supplement by Robert B Anderson (1943).

PA —UNIVERSITY OF PENNSYLVANIA, Biddle Law Library, 3400 Chestnut St, Philadelphia, 19104. Elizabeth S. Kelly, Libn
Holdings: Vols (350,000) Cat
Notes: Comprehensive collection of Anglo-American law. Legal materials from selected foreign countries, particularly in Common Market area. International law incl UN documents and other regional organizations. Substantial holdings in historical sources particularly early English law and Canon law.

LAW, ENVIRONMENTAL see Environmental Law

LAW, FOREIGN

AZ —UNIVERSITY OF ARIZONA, Library, Tucson, 85721. W David Laird, Librn
Notes: The greatest strength of this collection is in long back-runs of periodicals.

DC —LIBRARY OF CONGRESS, Law Library, 101 Independence Ave, SE, Washington, 20540. Carleton W Kenyon, Dir
Holdings: Vols 1,800,000 Cat Mss Microforms
Notes: The collection, comprising the legal sources and literature of all foreign nations, covers all legal systems incl common, civil, international, religious, and historic law.

IL —NORTHWESTERN UNIVERSTIY, School of Law, Library, 357 E Chicago Ave, Chicago, 60611. George S Grossman, Dir
Holdings: Cat
Notes: Comprehensive collections of Anglo-American and foreign (especially European) law; Roman and Canon law (selective); international law; European Common Market; Williams Collection of Legal Instruments (AD 1300-1700); George W Shaw Collection of Early European Law. Incl 500 ms legal documents.

MA —HARVARD UNIVERSITY LIBRARY, Law School Library, Langdell Hall, Cambridge, 02138. Harry S Martin III, Librn
Holdings: Cat Mss Maps Pix Slides
Notes: Downs 1687, 1763, 1774, 1776-1779, 1782-1784, 1790-1793, 1809, 1764, 1768, 1796; Downs Supplement 789. Comprehensive collection of English common law, American Law (historical and current), foreign law, comparative law, international law, Roman law and Canon law. Over a million vols.

MI —UNIVERSITY OF MICHIGAN, Law Library, Legal Research Bldg, 801 Monroe St, Ann Arbor, 48109. Beverley J Pooley, Dir
Holdings: Vols (570,000) Cat Microforms
Budget: $575,000
Notes: Unusually strong in legal history, canon law, US state constitutional proceedings, Indian nations, and foreign and international law. Also 300,000 microforms.

NY —COLUMBIA UNIVERSITY LIBRARIES, Law School Library, Law Building, 435 W 116 St, New York, 10027. James L Hoover, Librn
Holdings: Vols 150,000 Cat
Notes: Substantially complete for France, Germany, Switzerland and pre-revolutionary Russia; large holdings also for other European countries, Latin America, Japan and the People's Republic of China. Significant collections for all major countries of the world.

AB —UNIVERSITY OF ALBERTA, John Weir Memorial Law Library, Law Centre, Second Floor, Edmonton, T6G 2H5, Can. Lillian MacPherson, Law Librn
Holdings: Vols (140,000) Cat Maps Audiotapes Microforms
Budget: ($400,000)
Notes: Emphases on Canadian Government Publications, oil and gas, Canadian and US, UK, Australian, New Zealand primary materials. Separate catalog.

LAW, FRENCH

IL —NEWBERRY LIBRARY, 60 W Walton St, Chicago, 60610. Diana Haskell, Cur of Modern Mss
Notes: John M Wing History of Printing collection. Incl some 1100 French edicts, 17th-19th century, regulating the printing and publishing industries.

MA —HARVARD UNIVERSITY LIBRARY, Law School Library, Langdell Hall, Cambridge, 02138. Harry S Martin III, Librn
Holdings: Cat
Notes: Incl 25,000 French edicts (1550-1794).

NY —UNIVERSITY OF ROCHESTER, Rush Rhees Library, Department of Rare Books and Special Collections, Rochester, 14627. Peter Dzwonkoski, Librn
Holdings: Vols (450) Cat
Notes: Collection of materials on 16th and 17th century European law and political theory with special emphasis on works emanating from the French Civil Wars of the late 16th century. Particularly notable are the editions of the works of Francois Hotman and the editions of the Corpus Juris Civilis printed in Lyon. No photocopying.

LAW, GERMANIC

†LA —LOUISIANA STATE UNIVERSITY, Law Library, Baton Rouge, 70803.
Notes: Strong in civil law and French code materials. An extensive collection of German and Roman materials which were part of the Otto Lenel Collection.

LAW, HEBREW see Jewish Law

LAW, HUNGARIAN

IL —UNIVERSITY OF ILLINOIS, URBANA/CHAMPAIGN, Slavic and East European Library, Urbana, 61801. Marianna Tax Choldin, Head
Holdings: Vols (18,000) Cat

LAW, INDUSTRIAL see Labor Laws and Legislation

LAW, INSURANCE see Insurance Law

LAW, INTERNATIONAL see International Law

LAW, JAN

CA —CALIFORNIA STATE UNIVERSITY, LONG BEACH, Library, Dept of Special Collections & Archives, 1250 Bellflower Blvd, Long Beach, 90840. John Ahouse, Special Collections Librn
Holdings: Mss Maps Pix
Notes: Earth Subsidence Collection incl the personal files of Darrell Neighbors and Jan Law.

LAW, JEWISH see Jewish Law

LAW, LABOR see Labor Laws and Legislation

LAW, MASSACHUSETTS

MA —BOSTON PUBLIC LIBRARY, Rare Books and Manuscripts, Copley Square, Boston, 02117. Laura V Monti, Keeper of Rare Books
Holdings: Mss
Notes: Records of the Boston Municipal Court from the 18th century.

LAW, MEDIEVAL

CT —YALE UNIVERSITY, Law Library, 127 Wall St, New Haven, 06520. Morris L

LAW, MEDIEVAL (cont.)

Cohen, Librn
Holdings: Cat Mss
Notes: Especially medieval Italian law.

KS —UNIVERSITY OF KANSAS, Kenneth Spencer Research Library, Special Collections Dept, Lawrence, 66045. Alexandra Mason, Librn
Holdings: Vols 1400 Cat Mss
Notes: Especially strong in 16th century French and Italian juris consults, consilia, and commentaries on the CIC. Noncirculating.

NY —COLUMBIA UNIVERSITY LIBRARIES, Law School Library, Law Building, 435 W 116 St, New York, 10027. James L Hoover, Librn
Holdings: Vols (735,000) Cat
Notes: Incl substantial special collections in foreign and international law; also copyright law, ecclesiastical and medieval law; Roman law.

WI —UNIVERSITY OF WISCONSIN, MADISON, Seminary of Medieval Spanish Studies, 1130 Van Hise Hall, Madison, 53706. Lloyd A Kasten, Emeritus Prof of Spanish
Holdings: Vols (7500) // Cat Mss Pix Slides Microforms
Notes: Medieval material and subjects. 100 reels of microfilm, 2500 pamphlets and reprints. Incl a 300-volume collection on 13th century Spanish law. Other emphases: language studies (incl 616,247 vocabulary cards), dictionaries, bibliographies, periodicals. The nucleus of the collection is photostats of the mss of unpublished works of Alfonso X. Restricted circulation.

LAW, MOSAIC see Jewish Law

LAW, NEW ENGLAND

MA —OLD STURBRIDGE VILLAGE, Research Library, Sturbridge, 01566. Theresa Rini Percy, Librn
Holdings: Vols (23,000) Cat
Notes: Published laws and official records of New England states to 1850.

LAW, OHIO

OH —OHIO LEGISLATIVE SERVICE COMMISSION, Research Library, State House, Columbus, 43215. Barbara J Laughon, Library Administrator
Holdings: Vols 10,000 Cat Microforms
Notes: Collection contains all bills introduced since 1888 and all laws passed since 1803, *Gongwer's Ohio Reports* since 1955, other material related to Ohio legislative procedures. Ohio law is small part of collection of 10,000 vols on public administration and related subjects of interest to legislators.

LAW, PATENT see Patent Laws and Legislation

LAW, PHILIPPINE

DC —AMERICAN HISTORICAL COLLECTION, US Embassy, Manilla, Philippines, c/o US Dept of State, Washington, 20525. Aurora P Galvez, Librn; Lewis E Gleeck Jr, Cur
Notes: The American Historical Collection is located at 1201 Roxas Blvd, Metro Manilla, Philippines.
See also entry under Philippine Islands - History.

LAW, POLISH

IL —UNIVERSITY OF ILLINOIS, URBANA/CHAMPAIGN, Slavic and East European Library, Urbana, 61801. Marianna Tax Choldin, Head
Holdings: Vols (34,600) Cat Maps
Notes: Extensive coverage.

LAW, RENAISSANCE

CT —YALE UNIVERSITY, Law Library, 127 Wall St, New Haven, 06520. Morris L Cohen, Librn
Holdings: Cat Mss
Notes: Especially medieval Italian law.

KS —UNIVERSITY OF KANSAS, Kenneth Spencer Research Library, Special Collections Dept, Lawrence, 66045. Alexandra Mason, Librn
Holdings: Vols 1400 Cat Mss
Notes: Especially strong in 16th century French and Italian juris consults, consilia, and commentaries on the CIC. Noncirculating.

LAW, ROMAN see Roman Law

LAW, RUMANIAN

IL —UNIVERSITY OF ILLINOIS, URBANA/CHAMPAIGN, Slavic and East European Library, Urbana, 61801. Marianna Tax Choldin, Head
Holdings: Vols (13,000) Cat
Notes: Extensive coverage.

LAW, SOVIET

MA —HARVARD UNIVERSITY LIBRARY, Law School Library, Langdell Hall, Cambridge, 02138. Harry S Martin III, Librn
Holdings: Cat
Notes: Library has published *Soviet Legal* Bibliography (1965) and *Writings on Soviet Law and Soviet International Law* (1966).

†NY —COLUMBIA UNIVERSITY LIBRARIES, Butler Library, Rare Book and Manuscript Library, 535 W 114 St, New York, 10027.
Notes: Prof John N Hazard's papers, incl 20 notebooks of class notes while a student at the Moscow Juridical Institute, 1934-37.

OH —OHIO STATE UNIVERSITY, William Oxley Thompson Memorial Library, Hilander Room, 1858 Neil Ave Mall, Columbus, 43210. Predrag Matejic, Cur; G Koolemans Beynen, Slavic Bibliographer
Holdings: Vols (200,000) Cat Maps Microforms
Budget: ($45,000)
Notes: Area studies of Central, Southeastern and Eastern Europe. Emphasis on on Slavic literatures, languages and history. At present economics, sociology, law (Russian only) have been added. Within this framework the following priorities have been established: Material in Russian problems; then Medieval Slavic (Cyrillic); then Polish, then Serbo-Croatian, then Bulgarian, and now Romanian. Special attention is paid to serials, bibliographies, ms descriptions and dictionaries (incl biographical and encyclopedias). Apart from materials in native languages, materials in the following languages are acquired: Old Church Slavonic, Greek, English, French, German, Italian, a few in Scandinavian languages, incl Finnish, and a few in Baltic languages. The Hillandar Room holds approx 2000 Slavic mss, 1050 from Hilandar Monastery, Mount Athos, on microform and a related referencecollection.

LAW, WATER see Water—Laws and Legislation

LAW, YUGOSLAV

IL —UNIVERSITY OF ILLINOIS, URBANA/CHAMPAIGN, Slavic and East European Library, Urbana, 61801. Marianna Tax Choldin, Head
Holdings: Vols (31,000) Cat
Notes: Extensive coverage.

LAW ENFORCEMENT

IL —NORTHWESTERN UNIVERSITY, Transportation Center Library, Evanston, 60201. Mary Roy, Librn
Notes: Emphasizing police operations administration and training, traffic law enforcement, police traffic operations.

IN —INDIANA LAW ENFORCEMENT ACADEMY, David F Allen Memorial Learning Resources Center, Rd 700 E, PO Box 313, Plainfield, 46168. Donna K Zimmerman, Librn
Holdings: Vols (4500) Cat Slides 16mm Films
Budget: ($8500)
Notes: Concentrated in the areas of police science, criminology, and law.

†MA —NORTHEASTERN UNIVERSITY LIBRARIES, Boston, 02115.

MI —OAKLAND COMMUNITY COLLEGE, Auburn Hills Campus, Learning Resources Center, 2900 Featherstone Rd, Auburn Hills, 48057. Eugene F Larson, Dept Chairman
Holdings: Vols 900 Cat Slides Audiotapes Videotapes 16mm Films Filmstrips

NY —STATE UNIVERSITY OF NEW YORK AT ALBANY, Library, Special Collections Dept, 1400 Washington Ave, Albany, 12222. Marion P Munzer, Coordr
Notes: Eliot Howland Lumbard's research files, reports, correspondence, mss, and clippings on crime and law enforcement (19 linear feet). Part of the Library's German Exile Collection.
See also entries under Lumbard, Eliot Howland; Criminal Justice, Administration of

OH —CLEVELAND PUBLIC LIBRARY, Public Administration Library, City Hall, 601 Lakeside Ave NE Rm 100, Cleveland, 44114. Janice Ryan Novak, Head
Holdings: Vols 600 Cat
Notes: Emphasize practical police work and law enforcement as well as aspects of criminolgy.

RI —BRYANT COLLEGE, Edith M Hodgson Memorial Library, Rte 7, Douglas Pike, Smithfield, 02917. John P Hannon, Dir
Holdings: Vols (103,000) // Cat Phonorecords Audiotapes Videotapes 16mm Films Filmstrips Microforms
Budget: ($175,000)
Notes: Incl 6000 bound periodical vols, 250 phonorecords, 220 audiotapes, 120 videotapes, 30 16mm films, 150 filmstrips and 7500 microforms.

WI —BLACKHAWK TECHNICAL INSTITUTE, PO Box 5009, 6004 Prairie Rd, Janesville, 53547. Grace M Sweeney, Libn
Holdings: Vols 1500
Budget: $1000
Notes: Police Science.

ON —UNIVERSITY OF TORONTO, Centre of Criminology, Library, 130 St George St, Rm 8001, Toronto, M5S 1A5, Can. Catherine J Matthews, Librn
Holdings: Vols (20,000) Cat
Notes: Over 4500 research reports, article reprints, theses, etc. Extensive newspaper clippings file from 1963 to present indexed under 350 subject headings. The collection covers criminolgy, law enforcement and policing, delinquency. criminal justice system, penology and corrections. Acquisitions list published three times a year; subscription. Robert Vollono, Asst Ed.

LAW IN THE BIBLE see Jewish Law

LAW OF NATIONS see International Law

LAWLEY, GEORGE, AND SON, CORPORATION

MA —MASSACHUSETTS INSTITUTE OF TECHNOLOGY MUSEUM, Hart Nautical Collections, 77 Massachusetts Ave, Rm 5-329, Cambridge, 02139. John W Waterhouse, Cur
Holdings: Vols (800) Cat Maps Pix
Notes: Ship and marine engineering development. Museum is under jurisdiction of MIT's Dept of Ocean Engineering. Collection incl various collections of prints and photographs of ships and yachts; working drawings from the Herreshoff Manufacturing Co, 1870-1945, and of the George Lawley and Son Corp; working drawings and models from the Munro, Owen, and Paine Collections.

LAWLOR, PATRICK ANTHONY

BC —UNIVERSITY OF VICTORIA, McPherson Library, Victoria, V8W 3H5, Can.

LAWN TENNIS see Tennis

LAWNS

SC —HORRY GEORGETOWN TECHNICAL COLLEGE, Library, Hwy 501, Box 1966, Conway, 29526. Barbara Brittain, Librn
Holdings: Vols (20,000) Cat Maps Slides Microforms

LAWRENCE, DAVID HERBERT, 1885-1930

AZ —UNIVERSITY OF ARIZONA, University Library, Special Collections, Tucson, 85721. Louis A Hieb, Head
Holdings: Vols (7000) Cat Mss Microforms
Budget: ($30,000)
Notes: The 20th century collection is dominated by the works of Auden, Durrell, Conrad, Hardy, D H Lawrence, and Yeats.

CA —AZUSA PACIFIC COLLEGE, Marshburn Memorial Library, Citrus & Alosta, Azusa, 91702. Edward Peterman, Librn
Holdings: Vols (150) Uncat
Notes: The Odo B Stade Collection of Literary First Editions. No photocopying.

CA —UNIVERSITY OF CALIFORNIA, BERKELEY, Bancroft Library, Manuscripts Division, Berkeley, 94720. James D Hart, Dir
Holdings: Cat Mss
Notes: The collection consists of holograph mss, typescripts, and correspondence. Numerous mss for plays, poems, essays, and fiction. In addition to the mss, first and other editions of Lawrence's published works are held. A register of the mss has been prepared.

CA —UNIVERSITY OF CALIFORNIA, SAN DIEGO, Central University Library, Mandeville Dept of Special Collections, La Jolla, 92093. Lynda Corey Claassen, Head
Holdings: Vols 700 Cat
Notes: His first editions, critical commentary, and books about him.

CA —UNIVERSITY OF CALIFORNIA, LOS ANGELES, Research Library, Dept of Special Collections, 405 Hilgard Ave, Los Angeles, 90024. Edward Shreeves, Chairman, Bibliographers Group; David S Zeidberg, Head
Holdings: Vols 550 Cat Mss
Notes: 550 first and other editions of his books; 1.5 linear feet of mss, correspondence, and letters.

CA —STANFORD UNIVERSITY LIBRARIES, Cecil H Green Library, Stanford, 94305. Michael T Ryan, Cur
Holdings: Vols Cat
Notes: Also incl correspondence and literary mss.

CT —YALE UNIVERSITY, Box 1603A, Yale Station, New Haven, 06520.
Holdings: Cat Mss

IL —SOUTHERN ILLINOIS UNIVERSITY, CARBONDALE, Delyte W Morris Library, Special Collections Dept, Carbondale, 62901. David V Koch, Cur of Special Collections; Louisa Bowen, Cur of Manuscripts
Holdings: Vols 325 Cat Mss
Notes: 127 collected letters, 8 publishers' argreements, 2 mss and one corrected proof.

IL —NEWBERRY LIBRARY, 60 W Walton St, Chicago, 60610. Diana Haskell, Cur of Modern Mss
Holdings: Cat
Notes: Good collection of first and subsequent editions, mainly from a number of donors. A few letters, recorded in Moore and Roberts' edition.

IL —NORTHWESTERN UNIVERSITY, Library, Special Collections Dept, 1937 Sheridan Rd, Evanston, 60201. R Russell Maylone, Cur
Holdings: Vols 306 Cat Mss Pix
Notes: Extensive collection. Incl late 20's diary, and Heineman file of first edition of letters.

IL —ILLINOIS STATE UNIVERSITY, Milner Library, Dept of Special Collections, Normal, 61761. Robert Sokan, Librn
Holdings: Vols 450 Cat
Notes: First and limited editions.

IN —INDIANA UNIVERSITY, Lilly Library, Seventh St, Bloomington, 47405. William R Cagle, Librn
Holdings: Vols 270 // Cat Mss
Notes: First editions. Ms correspondence of D H Lawrence with publisher Martin Secker, 1911-1930. 200 items.

KS —UNIVERSITY OF KANSAS, Kenneth Spencer Research Library, Special Collections Dept, Lawrence, 66045. Alexandra Mason, Librn
Holdings: Vols 224 Cat
Notes: Mostly first editions. Noncirculating.

MA —BOSTON UNIVERSITY, Mugar Memorial Library, Special Collections Dept, 771 Commonwealth Ave, Boston, 02215. Howard B Gotlieb, Dir
Notes: Correspondence, autographbook with drawings by him; incl publications by.

MI —DETROIT PUBLIC LIBRARY, Rare Books Department, 5201 Woodward Ave, Detroit, 48202.
Holdings: Vols 130 Cat
Notes: Incl several volumes from the library of Barbara Low. Restricted use. Reference collection.

MO —WASHINGTON UNIVERSITY, John M Olin Library, Campus Box 1061, St Louis, 63130.
Notes: Extensive collection.

NY —ALFRED UNIVERSITY, Herrick Memorial Library, Alfred, 14802. June E Brown, Head Librn
Notes: The Evelyn Tennyson Openhym Collection of modern British literature and social history.

NY —COLUMBIA UNIVERSITY LIBRARIES, Rare Book & Manuscript Library, 801 Butler Library, 535 W 114 St, New York, 10027. Kenneth A Lohf, Librn
Notes: First editions, letters, mss and drawings. Restricted use.

NY —NEW YORK UNIVERSITY, Elmer Holmes Bobst Library, Div of Special Collections, Washington Sq S, New York, 10012. Frank Walker, Librn; Patrick McGuire, Asst Librn
Holdings: Vols (100,000) Cat Mss Pix
Notes: The Fales Collection of first (and other) editions of English and American novels from about 1750 to date (about 70, 000 titles). Mss (30,000) pieces.

NC —UNIVERSITY OF NORTH CAROLINA, CHARLOTTE, J Murrey Atkins Library, UNCC Station, Charlotte, 28223. Robert F Brabham Jr, Special Collections Librn
Holdings: Vols 100 Cat
Notes: Incl scholarly works on sex, classics by such writers as D H Lawrence, Frank Harris, and Norman Douglas, and about 40 novels published between 1890 and 1930.

†NC —WAKE FOREST UNIVERSITY, Z Smith Reynolds Library, Box 7777, Reynold Sta, Winston-Salem, 27109. Richard J Murdoch, Rare Book Librn
Holdings: Vols 131 Cat

OK —UNIVERSITY OF TULSA, McFarlin Library, Dept of Rare Books and Special Collections, 600 S College, Tulsa, 74104. David Farmer, Dir; Toby Murray, Archivist; Caroline Swinson, Cur of Manuscripts & Art
Holdings: Vols Cat Mss Pix
Notes: The D H Lawrence Collection, formed by John Martin, owner and publisher of Black Sparrow Press. Said to be one of the best Lawrence collections in the world.

PA —BUCKNELL UNIVERSITY, Ellen Clarke Bertrand Library, Lewisburg, 17837. Ann de Klerk, Librn
Notes: Books, mss, notebooks, 500 items.

TX —TEXAS WOMAN'S UNIVERSITY, Bralley Memorial Library, Box 23715, TWU Sta, Denton, 76204. Metta Nicewarner, Spec Collections Libn
Holdings: Uncat Mss Pix Audiotapes
Notes: The Laverne Harrell Clark Collection (500 pieces). Photographer, folklorist, writer. Also incl materials by and about her husband, Dr L D Clark (University of Arizona), D H Lawrence scholar.

AB —UNIVERSITY OF ALBERTA, Cameron Library, The Bruce Peel Special Collections Room, Edmonton, T6G 2J8, Can. John Charles, Special Collections Librn
Holdings: Cat
Notes: Incl the Sir David Eccles Collection. 280 first and early editions, incl translations; also books about Lawrence, movie press-books and posters for films on Lawrence's works.

†ON —UNIVERSITY OF WESTERN ONTARIO, School of Library and Information Science, Special Collections Room, London, N6A 5B9, Can.
Holdings: Vols 70
Notes: The collection incl 42 early editions of *Lady Chatterly's Lover* in several languages.

†ON —UNIVERSITY OF TORONTO, Thomas Fisher Rare Book Library, Toronto, M5S 1A5, Can.
Notes: First and subsequent important editions of Richard Aldington, Max Beerbohm, Norman Douglas, Aldous Huxley, and D H Lawrence.

LAWRENCE, DOROTHEA DIX

DC —LIBRARY OF CONGRESS, Music Division, Washington, 20540.
Notes: Incl her published books and articles, photographs, clippings, recital programs, and printed and manuscript scores of music.

LAWRENCE, ERNEST ORLANDO, 1901-1958

CA —UNIVERSITY OF CALIFORNIA, BERKELEY, Bancroft Library, Manuscripts Division, Berkeley, 94720. James D Hart, Dir
Holdings: // Cat Mss
Notes: The papers and correspondence of E O Lawrence, the eminent nuclear physicist, who was a central figure in the founding of the Berkeley Radiation Laboratory and the creation of the cyclotron. Approximately 50 cartons of mss, complemented by a series of oral histories with laboratory personnel.

LAWRENCE, GERTRUDE

NY —NEW YORK PUBLIC LIBRARY, Performing Arts Research Center, Billy Rose Theatre Collection, 111 Amsterdam Ave, New York, 10023. Dorothy L Swerdlove, Cur
Holdings: Cat Mss Pix
Notes: Papers, scrapbooks, mss, photographs, memorabilia, etc.

LAWRENCE, JEROME

NY —NEW YORK PUBLIC LIBRARY, Performing Arts Research Center, Billy Rose Theatre Collection, 111 Amsterdam Ave, New York, 10023. Dorothy L Swerdlove, Cur
Holdings: Cat Mss Pix
Notes: Papers, scrapbooks, mss, photographs, memorabilia, etc.

LAWRENCE, JOSEPHINE, 1890-1978

MA —BOSTON UNIVERSITY, Mugar Memorial Library, Special Collections Dept, 771 Commonwealth Ave, Boston, 02215. Howard B Gotlieb, Dir
Holdings: Cat Mss
Notes: Mss, correspondence, etc collected in depth; incl publications by or about.

LAWRENCE, SEYMOUR

DE —UNIVERSITY OF DELAWARE, Hugh M Morris Library, S College Ave, Newark, 19711. T Stuart Dick, Special Collections
Holdings: Cat Mss Pix
Notes: Kurt Vonnegut manuscripts, contract information, royalty statements, foreign movie and reprint rights and correspondence for the period 1966-1982 with the publisher, Seymour Lawrence.

LAWRENCE, THOMAS EDWARD, 1888-1935

CA —CLAREMONT COLLEGES, Honnold Library, Ninth & Dartmouth, Claremont, 91711. Tania Rizzo, Special Collections Dept Head
Holdings: Vols 50 Cat Mss
Notes: The collection of George E Fullerton,

LAWRENCE, THOMAS EDWARD, 1888-1935 (cont.)

originally belonging to Merle Armitage. First and limited editions of Lawrence's works, with reviews and articles from the British press, and 6 ALsS to Armitage from E M Forster, George Fielding Eliot, B H Liddell Hart, et al.

MA —HARVARD UNIVERSITY LIBRARY, Houghton Library, Cambridge, 02138. Rodney G Dennis, Cur of Manuscripts
Holdings: Cat Mss

TX —SOUTHWEST TEXAS STATE UNIVERSITY, Library, San Marcos, 78666. Bob Harris, Special Collections Librn
Holdings: Vols 67 // Cat Mss Pix
Notes: Incl pictures.

LAWRENCE, TONY

CA —UNIVERSITY OF CALIFORNIA, LOS ANGELES, Theater Arts Library, Los Angeles, 90024. Edward Shreeves, Chairman, Bibliographers Group; Audree Malkin, Head, Theater Arts Library
Notes: Tony Lawrence (writer) Collection: television scripts, presentations, story ideas, storylines, step outlines, pre-production and production material for television series and TV movies. Screenplays, treatments, story outlines, synopses, pre-production and production material for motion pictures, 1965-1980.

LAWS OBSERVATORY

†MO —UNIVERSITY OF MISSOURI-COLUMBIA, Western Historical Manuscripts Collection, Columbia, 65201.
Notes: Papers of the Laws Observatory, 1877-1954.

LAWSON, ANDREW COWPER

CA —UNIVERSITY OF CALIFORNIA, BERKELEY, Bancroft Library, Manuscripts Division, Berkeley, 94720. James D Hart, Dir
Holdings: Cat Mss Maps Pix Microforms
Notes: Papers, correspondence, etc.

LAWSON, JOHN HOWARD

IL —SOUTHERN ILLINOIS UNIVERSITY, CARBONDALE, Delyte W Morris Library, Special Collections Dept, Carbondale, 62901. David V Koch, Cur of Special Collections; Louisa Bowen, Cur of Manuscripts
Holdings: Vols 228 Cat Mss Pix
Notes: Personal papers and mss of works, 1917-1967, 63 linear ft. Inventory available at library.

LAWSON, ROBERT

PA —FREE LIBRARY OF PHILADELPHIA, Rare Book Dept, Logan Sq, Philadelphia, 19103. Marie E Korey, Rare Book Librn
Holdings: Vols (1300) Uncat Pix
Notes: The Frederick R Gardner Collection of original art (1100), first editions (many being Robert Lawson's own copies of his books), and memorabilia.

LAWYERS—PORTRAITS

MA —HARVARD UNIVERSITY LIBRARY, Law School Library, Langdell Hall, Cambridge, 02138. Harry S Martin III, Librn
Holdings: Cat
Notes: Prints and portraits.

LAX, ROBERT

NY —COLUMBIA UNIVERSITY LIBRARIES, Rare Book & Manuscript Library, 801 Butler Library, 535 W 114 St, New York, 10027. Kenneth A Lohf, Librn
Holdings: Mss
Notes: Papers of the American poet. 5300 items. Restricted use.

LAY, HERMAN

TX —NORTH TEXAS STATE UNIVERSITY, Archives, NT Station Box 5188, Denton, 76203. Robert LaForte, University Archivist
Notes: Part of Business Archive Project. Interviews with businessman, incl formation of H W Lay Distributing Company, merger with Frito, merger with Pepsi-Cola.

LAY, WILLIAM PATRICK

AL —GADSDEN PUBLIC LIBRARY, 254 College St, Gadsden, 35999. Margaret C Rouse, Reference Librn
Holdings: // Cat Mss Pix
Notes: Lay Collection, the papers of William Patrick Lay, founder of the Alabama Power Company. Mr Lay was a Cherokee County native and Gadsden resident, 1853-1940. Separate card index to collection of 221 items, which incl clippings, pamphlets and scrapbooks.

LAYTON, IRVING

PQ —CONCORDIA UNIVERSITY LIBRARIES, 1455 de Maisonneuve Blvd W, Montreal, H3G 1M8, Can. Martin Cohen, Special Collections Librn
Holdings: Vols 40 Cat Mss Pix
Notes: Mss, letters, tapes, etc of the Canadian poet. See: Joy Bennett, *Eight Irving Layton Notebooks, 1968-1972, in the Concordia University Library* (Montreal: McGill University Archives, 1976).

LAZAR, JOSETTE

MA —BOSTON UNIVERSITY, Mugar Memorial Library, Special Collections Dept, 771 Commonwealth Ave, Boston, 02215. Howard B Gotlieb, Dir
Holdings: Mss

LAZARSFELD, PAUL F.

†NY —COLUMBIA UNIVERSITY LIBRARIES, Butler Library, Rare Book and Manuscript Library, 535 W 114 St, New York, 10027.
Notes: Papers, etc, of Paul F Lazarsfeld.

NY —ROCKEFELLER UNIVERSITY, Rockefeller Archive Center, Hillcrest, Pocantico Hills, North Tarrytown, 10591. Joseph W Ernst, Dir; J William Hess, Assoc Dir
Notes: Papers relative to the Rockefeller Family, Foundations, University, and other specific enterprises and contributions to particular areas of social, physical, educational, and historic reform, preservation, conservation, or development. Extensive records of administrative, physical, or intellectual relationships.

LEA, TOM, JR.

TX —EL PASO PUBLIC LIBRARY, Southwest Collection, 501 N Oregon, El Paso, 79901. Mary A Sarber, Head
Holdings: Vols (7000) Cat Pix
Budget: $6000
Notes: Emphasis on art and artists of the Southwest, particularly Tom Lea, and Southwestern Indian arts and crafts. Cited in Hinshaw, Glennis, and Lisabeth Lovelace, *A Bibliography of Writings and Illustrations by Tom Lea*, El Paso Public Library Association, 1971.

TX —UNIVERSITY OF TEXAS, EL PASO, Library, Special Collections Dept, El Paso, 79968. Cesar Caballero, Dept Head
Budget: ($6000)
Notes: Carl Hertzog Collection. More than three hundred books produced by the prominent printer/book designer Carl Hertzog and over a thousand books on books about books, typography, and the history of printing make up this collection. It also contains many Southwestern classics by Frank Dobie and Tom Lea.

LEACACOS, JOHN P.

MA —BOSTON UNIVERSITY, Mugar Memorial Library, Special Collections Dept, 771 Commonwealth Ave, Boston, 02215. Howard B Gotlieb, Dir
Holdings: Cat Mss
Notes: Mss, correspondence, etc collected in depth; incl publications by or about.

LEACOCK, STEPHEN BUTLER, 1867-1944

PQ —MCGILL UNIVERSITY, McLennan Library, Rare Books and Special Collections Dept, 3459 McTavish St, Montreal, H3A 1Y1, Can.
Notes: 821 items, including literary manuscripts, variant editions, newspaper clippings, some correspondence, criticism, ca 3 metres of manuscripts.

LEAD

NY —ZINC INSTITUTE LEAD INDUSTRIES ASSOCIATION, 292 Madison Ave, New York, 10017. Mary W Covington, Mgr Information Servs
Notes: Technical information on lead and zinc.

LEADBEATER, C. W.

CA —SAN DIEGO PUBLIC LIBRARY, Literature & Language Sect, 820 E St, San Diego, 92101. Alyce Archuleta, Senior Librn
Holdings: Vols (140) Cat

LEADERSHIP CONFERENCE ON CIVIL RIGHTS

†DC —LIBRARY OF CONGRESS, Manuscript Division, Washington, 20540.
Notes: Records of their meetings.

LEADVILLE, COLORADO

CO —UNIVERSITY OF COLORADO, Libraries, Western Historical Collections, Boulder, 80309.
Holdings: // Cat Mss Maps
Notes: Papers of John F Campion (1849-1916), who mined in California and Nevada before striking it rich in the 1880s in Leadville, Colorado. He owned Reindeer, Caribou, and Ibex (better known as Little Johnny) mining companies. He was the vice-president of the Denver National Bank and the Denver, Northwestern and Pacific Railroad, and was a founder of Colorado's sugar beet industry. The collection focuses on his Leadville mining activities, covering the period from 1887 to 1922. A guide is available to the 14 boxes of material. Typescript inventory is available.

LEAGUE, JOHN CHARLES, 1863-1929

TX —ROSENBERG LIBRARY, Galveston and Texas History Center, 2310 Sealy Ave, Galveston, 77550. Jane Kenamore, Archivist
Holdings: Cat Mss
Notes: Business records which relate to land development in Texas during the late 19th and early 20th centuries.

LEAGUE FOR INDUSTRIAL DEMOCRACY

NY —STATE UNIVERSITY OF NEW YORK, STONY BROOK, Melville Library, Dept of Special Collections, Stony Brook, 11794. Evert Volkersz, Head
Holdings: Uncat
Notes: About 150 pamphlets.

LEAGUE OF ARABS STATES

†NY —ARAB INFORMATION CENTER, League of Arab States, 747 Third Ave, New York, 10017.

LEAGUE OF NATIONS

CA —CALIFORNIA STATE UNIVERSITY, FULLERTON, Library, Box 4150, Fullerton, 92634. Linda Herman, Special Collections Librn
Holdings: Vols 4000 Cat
Notes: Nearly complete papers of the League of Nations, an archive of the Holocaust as well as captured enemy records.

CA —LOS ANGELES PUBLIC LIBRARY, Social Sciences Dept, 630 W Fifth St, Los

LEAGUE OF NATIONS (cont.)

Angeles, 90071. Marilyn C Wherley, Principal Librn
Holdings: Vols 1500 Cat
Budget: ($150,000)
Notes: Sets of treaties of League of Nations, United Nations, Great Britain, United States, currently in force, as well as historical. Cumulative indexes of world treaties. No separate catalog.

CA —HOOVER INSTITUTION ON WAR, REVOLUTION & PEACE, Stanford University, Stanford, 94305. Milorad M Drachkovitch, Archivist
Holdings: Mss Maps Pix
Notes: Papers of Vladimir D Pastuhov, 1927-1938, incl correspondence, memoranda, reports, interviews, maps, photographs, and printed matter, relating to the investigation of the Manchurian incident of 1931 by the Lytton Commission of the League of Nations, of which V D Pastuhov was Secretary. Most of the material is in English; some in French, Russian and Chinese. 58 ms boxes and 3 oversize packages. 13 photograph albums.

DC —LIBRARY OF CONGRESS, General Reading Rooms Division, Microform Reading Room, Washington, 20540.
Holdings: Cat Mss Maps Pix Microforms
Notes: Microform materials only in this LC Division. Works of individual authors; holdings of collections; archival records, etc, press releases and translations, etc.

MD —JOHNS HOPKINS UNIVERSITY, Milton S Eisenhower Library, Government Publications Maps/Law Dept, Charles & 34 Sts, Baltimore, 21218. James Gillispie, Acting Head
Holdings: Vols (326,946) Maps
Notes: Milton S Eisenhower Library is a depository library for federal documents since 1882. Selects about 50 percent of the items. Incls 326,946 documents, 183,301 maps sheets. Nondepository items listed in *Monthly Catalog* on microprint from January 1953-1975. Monthly Catalog listing of JPRS translations on microprint from October 1958-1973. Eisenhower Library is also a partial depository of UN (May 1946-date); South Pacific Commission (1969-date). Had a standing order on League of Nations (1922-45); UN/ICJ, Hague (October 1947-date); UN/ILO (May 1929-date); UNESCO (1957-date); Council of Europe (March 1954-date); European Communities (1960-date); OECD (1955-date); OAS (September 1948-date); OEEC (1950-54); USGS (topographic maps).

†MA —BOSTON PUBLIC LIBRARY, Copley Sq, Boston, 02117.
Holdings: Cat Microforms
Notes: Microform Publication by Research Publications. League of Nations Documents.

NY —NEW YORK STATE LIBRARY, State Education Bldg Annex, Washington Ave, Albany, 12224.
Notes: Almost complete collection of official publications.

NY —C W POST CENTER OF LONG ISLAND UNIVERSITY, B Davis Schwartz Memorial Library, Greenvale, 11548. Jean Goldberg, Special Collections Librn
Holdings: Documents

NY —NEW YORK ACADEMY OF MEDICINE, Library, 2 E 103 St, New York, 10029. Brett A Kirkpatrick, Librn
Holdings: Uncat Mss Pix
Notes: Collection of personal papers of Frank George Boudreau, incl correspondence, from his birth to his early years as health officer in Ohio, through his international experience at the League of Nations, and as President of the Milbank Memorial Fund. Much on epidemiology, public health, and public medicine. Collection described in Lee Ash's "Frank George Boudreau, 18 July 1886-14 February 1970," *The Academy Bookman*, (New York Academy of Medicine, Friends of the Rare Book Room), Vol 26, No 1, 1973, pp 6-7.

NY —NEW YORK PUBLIC LIBRARY, Research Libraries, Economic & Public Affairs Div, Fifth Ave & 42 St, New York, 10018. Edward DiRoma, Chief
Holdings: Vols (1,500,000) Cat Microforms

NY —UNITED NATIONS, Dag Hammarskjold Library, Rm L382, New York, 10017. Vladimir Orlov, Librn
Holdings: Cat
Notes: Documents.

OH —CLEVELAND PUBLIC LIBRARY, Social Sciences Department, 325 Superior Ave, Cleveland, 44114. Thelma Morris, Head
Holdings: Vols 3000 Cat
Notes: Complete League of Nations depository set.

OR —UNIVERSITY OF OREGON LIBRARY, Documents Section, Eugene, 97403. Tom Stave, Section Head; John Shuler, Documents Librn
Holdings: Vols 2,000 //
Notes: Comprehensive holdings of League of Nations publications.

PA —UNIVERSITY OF PITTSBURGH, Hillman Library, Pittsburgh, 15260. Mary E Miller, Documents Librn
Notes: Comprehensive League of Nations and United Nations materials.

†ON —METROPOLITAN TORONTO LIBRARY, Social Sciences Dept, 789 Yonge St, Toronto, M4W 2G8, Can. Abdus Salam, Head
Holdings: Vols Cat Maps Phonorecords Audiotapes 16mm Films Microforms
Notes: General collection of documents of international organizations with emphasis on the United Nations and UNESCO. Collection ranges from international relations to social conditions in underdeveloped countries. Selected League of Nations publications. Both current and historical in scope.

LEAGUE OF WOMEN VOTERS

AL —BIRMINGHAM PUBLIC LIBRARY, Dept of Archives & Mss, 2020 Seventh Ave N, Birmingham, 35203. Marvin Y Whiting, Archivist & Cur
Holdings: Mss Pix
Notes: Main collections to date are the League of Women Voters of Birmingham Papers and the YWCA Papers. 19,600 ms pieces.

DC —DISTRICT OF COLUMBIA PUBLIC LIBRARY, Martin Luther King Memorial Library, Washingtoniana Div and Washington Star Collection, 901 G St NW, Washington, 20001. Roxanna Deane, Chief
Notes: Archival collections from various organizations such as the National Ballet and the League of Women Voters.

DC —LIBRARY OF CONGRESS, Manuscript Division, Washington, 20540. John C Broderick, Chief
Notes: Papers of Maud Wood Park (1871-1955), first president of the League of Women Voters. 3500 items, incl personal and professional correspondence, family papers, speeches and lectures, reports, photographs, and an autograph collection, documenting the women's rights movement in the US, particularly in the first half of the 20th century.

DC —LIBRARY OF CONGRESS, Washington, 20540.
Notes: Records and files of the League.

GA —EMORY UNIVERSITY, Robert W Woodruff Library, Atlanta, 30322. Herbert Johnson, Dir
Notes: Personal papers of Eleonore Raoul Greene (b 1888), suffragist and organizer of the Atlanta League of Women Voters.

IL —CHICAGO HISTORICAL SOCIETY, Library, Clark St at North Ave, Chicago, 60614. Robert L Brubaker, Librn
Holdings: Vols (150,000) Cat Mss Maps Pix Broadsides Microfilm
Notes: Early municipal documents, incl some not in the Municipal Reference Library, and selected later documents; archives of the City Club of Chicago, the Illinois League of Women Voters, Independent Voters of Illinois, and other organizations; papers of Chicago aldermen and other political leaders from Chicago; broadsides concerning political campaigns; ward maps; and other publications.

MD —UNIVERSITY OF MARYLAND, Library, Archives & Manuscripts Dept, College Park, 20742. Mary A Boccaccio, Head
Holdings: Mss Pix
Notes: University of Maryland publications and archives; collections of organizational papers (eg, Baltimore & Ohio Railroad; various organizations concerned with the Chesapeake Bay and environs; various labor unions, particularly those involving the tobacco industry), mostly associated with Maryland; collections of papers and mss associated with literary and public figures (eg, the late Senator Millard Tydings); oral histories relating to the archival and mss collections; associated memorabilia; photographs, mainly associated with Maryland. A guide to collections of personal, family, and organizational papers relating to Maryland is being prepared.

MA —RADCLIFFE COLLEGE, Arthur & Elizabeth Schlesinger Library on the History of Women in America, 3 James St, Cambridge, 02138. Patricia Miller King, Dir; Eva Moseley, Cur of Mss
Holdings: Cat Mss
Notes: Archives of League of Women Voters of Massachusetts and of Cambridge, Mass.

MO —UNIVERSITY OF MISSOURI-SAINT LOUIS, Thomas Jefferson Library, Manuscript and Historical Society Collection, 8001 Natural Bridge Rd, Saint Louis, 63121.
Holdings: Mss Pix Tapes
Notes: ca

NY —COLUMBIA UNIVERSITY LIBRARIES, Rare Book & Manuscript Library, 801 Butler Library, 535 W 114 St, New York, 10027. Kenneth A Lohf, Librn
Holdings: Mss Pix
Notes: Papers, mss, archives, etc, of the League of Women Voters of New York State and of the City of New York. Restricted use. 78,200 items.

LEAMING FAMILY

NJ —GLASSBORO STATE COLLEGE, Savitz Library, Stewart Room, Glassboro, 08028. Clara Kirner, Special Collection Librn
Holdings: Cat Mss
Notes: Papers, 1737-1898. Correspondence, real estate papers, wills, account books, shipbuilding and railroad papers, legal and other papers of Aaron Leaming, Cape May Co, New Jersey landowner and representative in the New Jersey Assembly; Jeremiah Leaming, Cape May Co lawyer; Richard S Leaming, shipbuilder and New Jersey State Assemblyman and Senator, and others.

LEAR, EDWARD

CT —YALE UNIVERSITY, Box 1603A, Yale Station, New Haven, 06520.

MA —HARVARD UNIVERSITY LIBRARY, Houghton Library, Cambridge, 02138. F Thomas Noonan, Cur, Reading Room; Lawrence Dowler, Associate Librn
Holdings: Cat Mss
Notes: Privately printed catalog by W B O Field (1933).

LEAR, FREDERICK

NY —SYRACUSE UNIVERSITY LIBRARIES, Ernest S Bird Library, George Arents Research Library for Special Collections, Syracuse, 13210. Carolyn A Davis, Manuscripts Librn; Amy S Doherty, University Archivist; Mark F Weimer, Rare Book Librn
Notes: The George Arents Research Library for Special Collections at Syracuse University contains the papers of Harley James McKee, Lorimer Rich, Frederick Lear, Max Abramovitz, James I Arnold, Pietro Bulluschi, Claude Bragdon, Marcel Breuer, William Lescaze, Skidmore Owings & Merrill, Ralph Walker, Eric Fisher Wood, Minoru Yamasaki, Joseph Louis Young, and Archimedes Russell.

LEAR, NORMAN

CA —AMERICAN FILM INSTITUTE, Louis B Mayer Library, 2021 N Western Ave, PO

LEAR, NORMAN (cont.)

Box 27999, Los Angeles, 90027. Anne G Schlosser, Dir
Holdings: Vols (3500) Cat

LEARNED INSTITUTIONS AND SOCIETIES

CA —UNIVERSITY OF CALIFORNIA, BERKELEY, University Library, Slavic Collections, Berkeley, 94720. Edward Kasinec, Librn
Holdings: Vols (210,000) Cat Maps Microforms
Budget: ($40,000)
Notes: Strong research collections for Bulgaria, Czechoslovakia, Poland, Russia-USSR, and Yugoslavia. Holdings are excellent in economics, folklore, history, linguistics, and literature. Publications issued by academies, major universitites, and principal scholarly institutions are well represented. Extensive periodical holdings have been built up, largely as a result of early exchange arrangements. More than 4000 Slavic-language serials are currently being received. Farmington Plan and PL480 commitements have augmented Yugoslav resources. Sizable Slavic-language collections are to be found in Branch Libraries as well, in such subjects as agriculture, biology, earth sciences, forestry, and mathematics.

CA —CALIFORNIA ACADEMY OF SCIENCES, J W Mailliard Jr Library, Golden Gate Park, San Francisco, 94118. Ray Brian, Librn
Notes: Learned society publications.

DC —LIBRARY OF CONGRESS, African and Middle Eastern Division, Washington, 20540.
Holdings: Cat Mss Microforms
Notes: Orientalia: the Orientalia Division contains 1,400,000 vols in Oriental languages. Chinese: more than 422,000 vols, espec strong in local histories and Ch'ing (1644-1911) period material. Japanese: over 574,000 vols, espec strong in economics, statistics, history, literature; 12,000 government, learned society, and university periodical titles, particularly science, technology, and social sciences. Korean: 56, 000 vols, espec strong in social sciences and modern history.

DC —LIBRARY OF CONGRESS, Serial and Government Publications Division, Washington, 20540.
Notes: Serials. One of the largest and most extensive collections in the world, incl periodicals; scientific and learned journals in all languages and in all fields except agriculture and medicine; US Government serials (Federal, State, County, and Muncipal); national foreign government serials from all countries; provincial serials from provinces possessing autonomy; municipal serials from principal cities; newspapers (850,000 unbound issues, 75,000 bound vols, 270,000 microfilm reels), 12,000 microprint cards of early American newspapers, 1704-1820, incl 1500 titles currently received, 500 of these being representative titles from all States of the Union and 1000 from all foreign countries.

DC —SMITHSONIAN INSTITUTION LIBRARIES, General Library, Washington, 20560. Mary Claire Grey, Chief Cent Ref & Loan Servs
Holdings: Vols (79,000) Cat Mss Maps Pix Slides Microforms
Notes: Incl publications of foreign and domestic museums, and all phases of museum work.

MI —UNIVERSITY OF MICHIGAN, Graduate Library, Ann Arbor, 48109. Janet White, Reference Librn
Holdings: Cat Microforms
Notes: Incl extensive files of academy and learned society publications. Many microform editions of earlier works have been acquired, as well as copyflo copies of op works. Main body of collection is Slavic. Nearly 200 French and Belgian societies are represented.

MI —GALE RESEARCH CO, Book Tower, Detroit, 48226. Annie Brewer, Librn
Holdings: Vols (65,000) Cat
Notes: Large collection of reference materials, incl computerized files used in the preparation of familiar contemporary reference books and guides to special fields.

NY —AMERICAN MUSEUM OF NATURAL HISTORY, Library Services Dept, Central Park W & 79th St, New York, 10024. Nina J Root, Chairwoman; Mary Genett, Asst Librn for Reference Services
Holdings: Vols (385,000) Cat Mss Maps Pix Slides Microforms
Notes: Nearly all collections are outstanding for depth of coverage and international range. Early and historic works, rare books, colored illustrations, and relevant serial publications supplement the modern scientific publications necessary to the researchers of the scientific staff and the work of the educational division. Open to the public.

NY —NEW YORK PUBLIC LIBRARY, Research Libraries, General Research Division, Fifth Ave & 42 St, New York, 10018. Rodney Phillips, Chief
Holdings: Vols (2,225,000) Cat Maps Pix Microforms
Budget: ($775,718)
Notes: Many complete sets of the proceedings of The Royal Society of London, Institut de France, etc. Outstanding holdings in Orientalia, Balto-Slavic studies, and Judaica.

NY —NEW YORK PUBLIC LIBRARY, Slavonic Div, Fifth Ave & 42 St, New York, 10018. Edward Kasinec, Chief
Holdings: Vols (8870) Cat Microforms
Notes: Subject strength is in Ukrainian literature, language, and folklore. Ethnology and history are also well represented. Holdings of periodicals and publications of learned societies are considerable. See New York public Library, *Dictionary Catalog of the Slavonic Collection* (Boston: G K Hall, 1974), 44 vols.

NY —NEW YORK PUBLIC LIBRARY, Research Libraries, American History Div, Fifth Ave & 42 St, New York, 10018.
Holdings: Vols (45,000) Cat Maps Microforms
Notes: Collection incl publications of national and state historical societies. Comprehensive, particularly when viewed in conjunction with the parent institution's documents collection and monographs and serials elsewhere in the Library which are available through use of the American History Division catalog or through use of bibliographies within the division. Strong on Colonial and Revolutionary periods, War of 1812, Mexican War, Civil War, Spanish American War, and the Slavery Controversy. Incl collection of the papers of American statesmen. Fine collection of books by European travellers to the United States during the 19th century. See *Dictionary Catalog of the History of Americas* Collection (Boston: G K Hall, 1961), 28 vols.

OH —CLEVELAND PUBLIC LIBRARY, History and Geography Department, 325 Superior Ave, Cleveland, 44114. JoAnn Petrello, Head
Holdings: Cat
Notes: Extensive British History Collection (incl Ireland, Scotland), especially 1660-1800. Rare books. Collection of British Learned Society serials; English Political Pamphlet Collection No photocopying.

PA —CARNEGIE LIBRARY OF PITTSBURGH, Science & Technology Dept, 4400 Forbes Ave, Pittsburgh, 15213. Catherine M Brosky, Dept Head
Notes: This department serves as the Resource Library for Science and Technology in the Commonwealth of Pennsylvania. Agreements with other Resource Libraries in the Commonwealth and with certain institutions in Pittsburgh for sharing resources, cooperative acquisition of materials, provision of services and information. Collections described in *Guide to the Regional Library Resource Centers of* Pennsylvania, compiled by Ralph W McComb, 1967.

PA —UNIVERSITY OF PITTSBURGH, Allegheny Observatory Library, Riverview Park, Pittsburgh, 15214. Paul Kubulnicky, Dir of Observatory
Holdings: Vols 8000 Cat Mss Maps Pix Slides
Notes: This library has a strong collection of publications of other national and international observatories, received on exchange. Also in the collection are pertinent current journals and a weak gathering of contemporary monographs. The observatory also has cataloged its complete file of observational photographic plates.

WA —UNIVERSITY OF WASHINGTON LIBRARIES, Suzzallo Library, Slavic & East European Section, FM-25, Seattle, 98195. Barbara A Galik, Head
Holdings: Vols (250,000) Cat Mss Maps Pix Phonoreocrds Audiotapes Microforms
Budget: ($85,000)
Notes: Strong research collections for Russia--USSR, including Central Asia, Eastern Europe and the Balkans, especially Yugoslavia and Poland. Holdings are listed under the names of individual countries. There are extensive holdings of the publications of academies, major universities, and principal scholarly institutions, especially of long serial runs.

LEARNING ABILITY

ME —LEARNING INC, Library, Learning Place, Manset, 04656. A L Welles, Librn; E R Welles, Cur
Holdings: Vols (2000) Uncat Mss
Notes: Materials that will help people understand the various learning handicaps and some of the remedial methods for overcoming them. Anyone wishing to visit the collection telephone (207) 244-5015 to make arrangements.

NJ —PRINCETON UNIVERSITY, Psychology Library, Green Hall, Princeton, 08540. Janice D Welburn, Librn
Holdings: Vols (19,839) Cat Microforms
Budget: ($50,000)
Notes: Library receives approx 450 current serial titles. Primarily serves an experimental psychology department, with interests in social, personality, developmental, physiological and cognitive psychology, as well as learning and perception. Incl 3886 microforms.

NY —MORRIS N & CHESLEY V YOUNG LIBRARY OF MNEMONICS, 270 Riverside Dr, New York, 10025. Morris N Young, Cur
Holdings: Cat Mss Maps Pix Phonorecords Audiotapes 16mm Films Microforms
Notes: Collection of 5000 books, pamphlets, pictures, memorabilia, etc incl medieval art of memory; psychology of memory, forgetting and reading; medical aspects of memory, amnesia, dyslexia; biomedical aspects of learning and memory; information storage, retrieval and cybernetics; memory prodigies, lightning calculators, calendars; remembrance cups and memory mementos. All languages. Memorabilia incl engravings, posters, programs, advertisements, birthday cards, teaching cards, ASLs, and Mark Twain's Memory Builder game and other games. Items range from 1410 to 1980s.

NY —STATE UNIVERSITY OF NEW YORK, State College of Optometry, Harold Kohn Vision Science Library, 100 E 24 St, New York, 10010. Margaret S Lewis, Librn
Holdings: Vols (23,000) Cat Audiotapes Microforms
Notes: All subjects related to visual disabilities; much on vision disorders among children.

LEARNING DISABILITIES

CA —SOUTHERN CALIFORNIA COLLEGE OF OPTOMETRY, 2001 Associated Rd, Fullerton, 92631. Pat Carlson, Librn
Holdings: Vols (10,000) Cat Mss Pix Slides Microforms
Notes: Collection deals with vision and all that pertains to training optometrists. Core of the collection leans heavily towards optometry; rest of collection deals with ophthalmology and related fields.

CA —MENLO PARK LIBRARY, Civic Center, 800 Alma, Menlo Park, 94025.

LEARNING DISABILITIES (cont.)

Karen Fredrickson, Librn
Holdings: Vols 100 Cat
Notes: The Armstrong Collection on Dyslexia. Dyslexia and related learning disabilities.

CT —NEWINGTON CHILDREN'S HOSPITAL, Professional Library, 181 E Cedar St, Newington, 06111. Jean Long, Librn
Holdings: Vols (3500) Cat
Budget: ($6500)

IL —JACKSONVILLE STATE HOSPITAL, Training & Research Library, 1201 S Main St, Jacksonville, 62650. Lois E Wells, Librn
Holdings: Vols (10,000) Cat
Notes: Concerned particularly with developmental disabilities.

NJ —NORTH PRINCETON DEVELOPMENT CENTER, Medical Library, PO Box 1000, Princeton, 08540. Donald W Biggs, Librn
Holdings: Vols 3000 Microforms
Budget: ($7000)
Notes: Incl 70 periodicals and 500 microforms.

NY —COLUMBIA UNIVERSITY LIBRARIES, Health Sciences Library, 701 W 168 St, New York, 10032. Rachael K Goldstein, Librn
Notes: Ca 3000 fiche. Incl the June Lyday and Samuel T Orton collection of patient records dating from 1928-77. Photocopying limited. Restricted.

PQ —HOPITAL SAINTE-JUSTINE POUR LES ENFANTS, Centre d'Information sur la Sante de l'Enfant, 3175 Cote Sainte-Catherine, Montreal, H3T 1C5, Can. Louis LucLecompte, Librn
Holdings: Vols (7000) Cat Audiotapes Videotapes 16mm Films Microforms
Budget: ($11,000)
Notes: 40 percent of collection in French.

LEARNING DISORDERS see Learning Disabilities

LEARY, LEWIS GASTON, 1906-

NC —DUKE UNIVERSITY, William R Perkins Library, Jay B Hubbell Center for American Literary Historiography, Durham, 27706. Erma Whittington, Librn
Notes: 77,312 items, including manuscripts, pictures, clippings, and correspondence. "The objective of the Center is to gather the papers and materials of significant scholars and critics in American literary history." The Center is a part of the Perkins Library Manuscripts Department.

LEARY, TIMOTHY

CA —FITZ HUGH LUDLOW MEMORIAL LIBRARY, PO Box 99346, San Francisco, 94109. Michael R Aldrich, Exec Cur
Holdings: Cat Mss Maps Pix Slides Phonorecords Audiotapes Videotapes
Notes: Collection stored. Important mail inquiries only. No interlibrary lending or telephone inquiries. Hallucinogens as used in historical and contemporary cultures. Nearly complete collection of books and articles by or about Timothy Leary, incl manuscripts; also nearly complete collection of the writings of Aldous Huxley concerning drugs. Much autographed or inscribed material, mostly popular music from the 1960s but also incl ethnographic music. Emphasis on psychoactive drugs relative to religion, literature, art. Also an excellent collection of research papers (chemistry, pharmacology, epidemiology, sociology, ethnobotany) in this field, as well as artifacts and artwork relating to the field.

LEASE-LEND OPERATIONS see Lend-Lease Operations, 1941-1945

LEATHER INDUSTRY AND TRADE

DE —HAGLEY MUSEUM AND LIBRARY, Eleutherian Mills-Hagley Foundation Inc, PO Box 3630, Greenville, 19807. Richmond D Williams, Dir; Heddy A Richter, Imprints Librn
Notes: Records of J E Rhoads & Sons (1727-1962; 550 cubic feet), leather manufacturers of Wilmington, Delaware. The archive incl administrative, financial, production and sales records. There is also a good deal of printed and photographic material.

PA —CARNEGIE LIBRARY OF PITTSBURGH, Science & Technology Dept, 4400 Forbes Ave, Pittsburgh, 15213. Catherine M Brosky, Dept Head
Notes: General information acquired in various subject areas especially those relating to iron and steel and other metals, rubber, leather, pulp and paper, textiles, glass, petroleum and coal tar by-products, lumber, plastics, etc. Manufacturers directories, including old editions, standards and specifications, trade catalogs, basic periodicals, indexes, and bibliographies.
See also entry under Science.

LEBANON

CA —HOOVER INSTITUTION ON WAR, REVOLUTION & PEACE, Stanford University, Stanford, 94305. Peter Duignan, Cur; Karen Fung, Deputy Cur
Holdings: Vols (100,000)
Notes: For full description of collection, see Hoover Institution entry under Near East.

LEBOW, HOWARD M.

MA —UNIVERSITY OF MASSACHUSETTS AT AMHERST, Music Library, Fine Arts Center, Amherst, 01003.
Holdings: Uncat
Notes: The personal library of Howard M Lebow (once an outstanding concert pianist). The collection (over 5000 items) incl primarily keyboard music, as well as many unusual early editions.

LEBOWITZ, ALBERT

MO —WASHINGTON UNIVERSITY, Libraries, Campus Box 1061, Saint Louis, 63130.
Notes: Incl papers of the novelist.

LECLAIR, J. M.

MI —UNIVERSITY OF MICHIGAN, School of Music, Music Library, Moore Bldg, Ann Arbor, 48109. Peggy Daub, Head
Holdings: // Uncat Mss Pix Slides Microforms
Notes: The Coopersmith Handel Collection. A unique collection of the late J M Coopersmith containing music, facsimiles, photostats, letters, microfilms, slides, and extensive bibliographic records relating to Dr Coopersmith's Handelian scholarship. Included in the collection are records of his investigation of Leclair. Access to the collection is by permission of the head of the Music Library.

LECOMTE DU NOUY, PIERRE

†AZ —UNIVERSITY OF ARIZONA, Library, Tucson, 85721.
Notes: The Pierre Lecomte du Nouy Collection incl scarce, original editions of the works of contemporary scientists and thinkers, editions of his own works, his mss, and many volumes inscribed to him.

LEDERER, EMIL

NY —STATE UNIVERSITY OF NEW YORK AT ALBANY, Library, Special Collections Dept, 1400 Washington Ave, Albany, 12222. Marion P Munzer, Coordr
Notes: Papers (1 linear foot) of Emil Lederer, German economist who came to the United States after 1933. Correspondence, lecture notes, mss, and publications; Festschrift. Part of the library's German Exile Collection. Collection.

LEE, FREDERIC P., 1893-1968

NY —CORNELL UNIVERSITY LIBRARIES, Collection of Regional History, Dept of Manuscripts and Univ Archives, Ithaca, 14853.
Notes: Attorney, horticulturist. Papers, 1926-(1946-65); 15 ft.

LEE, IVY LEADBETTER, 1877-1934

NJ —PRINCETON UNIVERSITY, Library, Manuscript Collection, Nassau St, Princeton, 08540. Jean F Preston, Cur
Holdings: // Mss Pix
Notes: The Ivy Lee Collection fills 70 ms boxes, 387 vols. See *Princeton University Library Chronicle,* v 27, p 113-20. An unpublished typescript guide (17 p) is available in the Library.

LEE, J. BRACKEN

UT —UNIVERSITY OF UTAH, Marriott Library, Special Collections, Salt Lake City, 84112. Gregory C Thompson, Cur
Holdings: Cat Mss Microfilm Film Oral History
Notes: Papers of the Utah Governor.

LEE, JOSHUA BRYAN

OK —UNIVERSITY OF OKLAHOMA, Bizzell Memorial Library, Western History Collections, 401 W Brooks, Norman, 73069. John Ezell, Cur
Holdings: Mss Pix Documents
Notes: US Representative; US Senator; Member, Civil Aeronautics Board. His papers.

LEE, ROBERT E.

NY —NEW YORK PUBLIC LIBRARY, Performing Arts Research Center, Billy Rose Theatre Collection, 111 Amsterdam Ave, New York, 10023. Dorothy L Swerdlove, Cur
Holdings: Cat Mss Pix
Notes: Papers, scrapbooks, mss, photographs, memorabilia, etc.

NC —DUKE UNIVERSITY, William R Perkins Library, Manuscript Dept, Durham, 27706. Ellen Gartrell, Cur of Mss
Holdings: Cat Mss
Notes: Strong collection incl papers of many officers (eg Robert E Lee, P G T Beauregard), Confederate governments, and leaders (eg Jefferson Davis), thousands of letters and diaries from Union and Confederate soldiers and homefront.

VA —UNIVERSITY OF VIRGINIA, Alderman Library, Manuscripts Dept, Charlottesville, 22901. Edmund Berkeley Jr, Cur
Holdings: Cat Mss Maps Pix
Notes: About 1500 collections have material pertaining to the Civil War and particularly to the Army of Northern Virginia and campaigns and battles in Virginia. There are letters, diaries, reminiscences, maps, and pictorial material of Confederate soldiers and civilians, as well as papers of Robert E Lee, J E B Stuart, Thomas L Rosser, Jubal A Early, John Daniel Imboden, William "Extra Billy" Smith, Henry Alexander Wise, Eppa Hunton, and John S Mosby.

VA —WASHINGTON AND LEE UNIVERSITY, Library, Lexington, 24450. Maurice Leach, Dir; Richard Oram, Asst Special Collections Librn
Holdings: Vols (25,000) Cat Mss Maps Pix
Notes: Incl over 10,000 ms pieces, the collection emphasizes the life of General Robert E Lee, Virginia, and the Civil War, etc. Pictures from 1870-1930; 8000 glass photographs by Miley.

VA —VIRGINIA STATE LIBRARY, 12 & Capitol Sts, Richmond, 23219.
Holdings: Vols 1600 Cat Mss Pix

LEE, RUSSEL V.

CA —STANFORD UNIVERSITY LIBRARIES, Lane Medical Library, Stanford University, Medical Center, Stanford, 94305. Peter Stangl, Librn
Holdings: Vols 18,000 Cat Mss Pix
Notes: Barkan collection of the history of medicine including 9900 volumes of books published before 1850. Included in this is the Ernst Seidel collection on medicine of the near East and rare books and manuscripts. Approximately 2000 medical instruments and 250 linear feet of Mss. These latter include the records of Cooper Medical College and Clinics (the forerunner of the Stanford University School of Medicine); papers of Levi Cooper Lane, founder of Cooper Medical College; Phillip King Brown's papers on health insurance and socialized medicine; Adelaide Brown - sanitation and prenatal care; William Stroebel Hunter - human locomotion; Russel V Lee - group medical practice, gerontology, Agency for International Development; Leo L Stanley - prison medicine; Ray Lyman Wilbur - medical economics, including his work on the Committee on the Cost of Medical Care andthe Commission on Medical Education; Hospitals - California - History.

LEE FAMILY

NJ —PRINCETON UNIVERSITY, Library, Manuscript Collection, Nassau St, Princeton, 08540. Jean F Preston, Cur
Holdings: Mss Pix
Notes: The Blair-Lee Families Collection, which deals in large part with American political and naval history of the period 1733 to 1916, fills over 300 ms boxes. It incl the papers of Francis Preston Blair, Sr, Samuel Phillips Lee, Elizabeth Blair Lee, and Blair Lee. An unpublished partial typescript guide (75 p) is available in the Library.

LEECH, JOHN

MA —HARVARD UNIVERSITY LIBRARY, Houghton Library, Cambridge, 02138. F Thomas Noonan, Cur, Reading Room; Lawrence Dowler, Associate Librn
Holdings: Cat
Notes: Privately printed catalog by W B O Field (1930).

NY —NEW YORK PUBLIC LIBRARY, Rare Books and Manuscripts Div, Fifth Ave & 42 St, New York, 10018. William L Joyce, Asst Dir; Bernard McTigue, Cur, Arents Collection
Holdings: Cat Mss Pix

LEESER, ISAAC

PA —LIBRARY COMPANY OF PHILADELPHIA, 1314 Locust St, Philadelphia, 19107. Edwin Wolf II, Librn; Kenneth Finkel, Cur of Prints
Notes: The Edwin Wolf Collection of Judaica, consisting of 165 manuscripts and more than 500 books and broadsides printed in the US between 1718 and 1875. Incl literature, prayer books, Hebrew schoolbooks, reports of Jewish organizations, missionary tracts, narratives of travel to Palestine, and books on medicine. Most of the manuscripts consists of correspondence of the Gratz family, American pioneers.

LEESON, CECIL

IN —BALL STATE UNIVERSITY, Alexander M Bracken Library, Muncie, 47306. Nyal Williams, Music Librn
Holdings: Vols (30,000) Cat Mss
Budget: ($20,000)
Notes: Incl archives of International Horn Society, Tubists Universal Brotherhood Association Library, Cecil Leeson Archival Saxophone Collection, and Archives of Buescher Music Instrument Manufacturing Company.

LEEWARD ISLANDS see Guadeloupe; Virgin Islands

LE FANU, JOSEPH SHERIDAN, 1814-1873

CA —UNIVERSITY OF CALIFORNIA, LOS ANGELES, Research Library, Dept of Special Collections, 405 Hilgard Ave, Los Angeles, 90024. Edward Shreeves, Chairman, Bibliographers Group; David S Zeidberg, Head
Holdings: Vols 75
Notes: 75 first and other editions of his books; 11 letters.

NY —NEW YORK UNIVERSITY, Elmer Holmes Bobst Library, Div of Special Collections, Washington Sq S, New York, 10012. Frank Walker, Librn; Patrick McGuire, Asst Librn
Holdings: Vols (100,000) Cat Mss Pix
Notes: The Fales Collection of first (and other) editions of English and American novels from about 1750 to date (about 70, 000 titles). Mss (30,000) pieces.

LEFEVER, ERNEST W., 1919-

CA —HOOVER INSTITUTION ON WAR, REVOLUTION & PEACE, Stanford University, Stanford, 94305. Milorad M Drachkovitch, Archivist
Holdings: Mss
Notes: Papers of Ernest W Lefever, 1956-1969, incl ms drafts, correspondence, reports, interviews, notes, pamphlets, newspapers clippings and printed matter, relating to modern politics in Zaire (Republic of the Congo), Ethiopia, and other African nations. 3 ms boxes.

LEFFINGWELL, ROBERT

MA —BOSTON UNIVERSITY, Mugar Memorial Library, Special Collections Dept, 771 Commonwealth Ave, Boston, 02215. Howard B Gotlieb, Dir
Holdings: Cat
Notes: Original cartoons, correspondence, documents.

LEFFINGWELL, RUSSELL C.

DC —LIBRARY OF CONGRESS, Manuscript Division, Washington, 20540. John C Broderick, Chief
Notes: Papers; additions, 1977- .

LEFRANC, GEORGES

CA —HOOVER INSTITUTION ON WAR, REVOLUTION & PEACE, Stanford University, Stanford, 94305. Milorad M Drachkovitch, Archivist
Holdings: // Mss
Notes: Collection of material relating to French trade unions, syndicalism, worker education, and the Vichy government, 1895-1956. 9 boxes. Unpublished register available in repository.

LEFT BOOK CLUB

IL —NORTHWESTERN UNIVERSITY, Library, Special Collections Dept, 1937 Sheridan Rd, Evanston, 60201. R Russell Maylone, Cur
Holdings: Vols 209 Cat

OH —OHIO UNIVERSITY, Vernon R Alden Library, Department of Archives and Special Collections, Athens, 45701. Gary A Hunt, Head
Holdings: Vols 184 Cat
Notes: Incl most of the Left Book Club editions published by that organization in the 1930s and 1940s, with some of the club's flyers and leaflets.

†ON —UNIVERSITY OF WESTERN ONTARIO, School of Library and Information Science, Special Collections Room, London, N6A 5B9, Can.
Holdings: Vols 289
Notes: Collection consists of about 80 percent of the club's member editions.

LEFTIST MOVEMENTS

CA —HOOVER INSTITUTION ON WAR, REVOLUTION & PEACE, Stanford University, Stanford, 94305. Milorad M Drachkovitch, Archivist
Notes: The New Left Politics Collection consists of monographs and serials on the New Left that are cataloged. In addition, the collection subscribes to numerous underground newspapers and has obtained special subject collections such as the Free Speech Movement at Berkeley 1964-1965, SNCC and Mississippi Summer 1964, and the insurrection at San Francisco State College in 1968-1969. There is also a good collection on the French student revolts of 1968. The collection is a supervised one and not open to browsers. Interested students and scholars are welcome. Only limited photocopying is permitted.

LEGAL EDUCATION see Law—Study and Teaching

LEGAL HISTORY see Law—History

LEGAL HOLIDAYS see Holidays

LEGAL MEDICINE see Medical Jurisprudence

LEGAL PHOTOGRAPHY see Photography, Legal

LE GALLIENNE, EVA

†CA —UNIVERSITY OF SAN FRANCISCO, Richard A Gleeson Library, The Countess Bernardine Murphy Donohue Rare Book Room, San Francisco, 94117. D Steven Corey, Special Collections Librn
Holdings: Vols 125 Cat Mss
Notes: Part of a larger collection of the 1890s.

†NY —NEW YORK ACADEMY OF MEDICINE, Library, 2 E 103 ST, New York, 10029.
Notes: Papers of Walter Timme, MD (1874-1956). Timme was a pioneer endocrinologist; described pluriglandular disease, "Timme's Syndrome." Incl correspondence from Harvey Cushing, Paul Dudley White, Charles A Elsberg, Louis I Dublin, Ely Smith Jelliffe, John F Fulton, Edna St Vincent Millay, Eva Le Gallienne, and Irving Ramsey Wiles.

NY —NEW YORK PUBLIC LIBRARY, Performing Arts Research Center, Billy Rose Theatre Collection, 111 Amsterdam Ave, New York, 10023. Dorothy L Swerdlove, Cur
Holdings: Cat Mss Pix
Notes: Papers, scrapbooks, mss, photographs, memorabilia, etc.

LE GALLIENNE, RICHARD

CA —UNIVERSITY OF SAN FRANCISCO, Richard A Gleeson Library, The Countess Bernardine Murphy Donohue Rare Book Room, San Francisco, 94117. D Steven Corey, Special Collections Librn
Holdings: Vols 250 Mss
Notes: Over 100 ALS's, 72 mss, plus multiple copies of most of the first editions.

MO —SAINT LOUIS PUBLIC LIBRARY, Gardner Rare Book Room, 1301 Olive St, Saint Louis, 63103. Julanne M Good, Supervisor; Martha Riley, Rare Books Librn
Holdings: Vols (2300) Cat
Budget: ($5573)
Notes: First editions of authors having some association with William Marion Reedy and *Reedy's Mirror*, such as Sara Teasdale, Zoe Akins, Fannie Hurst, Edgar Lee Masters, Babette Deutsch, Richard LeGallienne, etc. Also first editions of selected St Louis and/or Missouri authors such as T S Eliot, Samuel L Clemens, Theodore Dreiser and Tennessee Williams. Noncirculating.

LEGAT, NIKOLAI AND SERGEI

†ON —METROPOLITAN TORONTO LIBRARY, Theatre Dept, Toronto, M4W 2G8, Can.
Notes: Ballet caricatures by Nikolai and Sergei Legat, St Petersburg, 1902-1905.

LEGENDS

CA —LOS ANGELES PUBLIC LIBRARY, Children's Literature Dept, 630 W 5th St, Los Angeles, 90071. Serenna Day, Sr Librn
Holdings: Vols (2120) Cat Phonorecords Filmstrips
Notes: Also includes reference collection, covering some 50 years of published folklore and modern fairy tales. Includes extensive Mother Goose collection, examples of the work of such outstanding illustrators as Edmund Dulac and Arthur Rackham. Many volumes out of print. Index to titles of stories in collections.

CA —LOS ANGELES PUBLIC LIBRARY, Philosophy & Religion Dept, 630 W Fifth St, Los Angeles, 90071. Marilyn C Wherley, Librn
Holdings: Vols 500 Cat
Budget: ($60,000)
Notes: Comprehensive coverage of popular and scholarly works on myths, legends, superstitions and primitive religions.

NY —AMERICAN MUSEUM OF NATURAL HISTORY, Library Services Dept, Central Park W & 79th St, New York, 10024. Nina J Root, Chairwoman; Mary Genett, Asst Librn for Reference Services
Holdings: Vols (385,000) Cat Mss Maps Pix Slides Microforms
Notes: Nearly all collections are outstanding for depth of coverage and international range. Early and historic works, rare books, colored illustrations, and relevant serial publications supplement the modern scientific publications necessary to the researches of the scientific staff and the work of the educational division. Open to the public.

OH —CLEVELAND PUBLIC LIBRARY, Fine Arts and Special Collections Department, 325 Superior Ave, Cleveland, 44114. Alice N Loranth, Head
Holdings: Cat Mss
Notes: Part of the Medieval Literature Collection. Medieval texts, translations, facsimile reproductions, bibliographies and catalogs of mss, romances, epics, early chronicles and histories. Icelandic sagas, fabliaux (tales), legends, lives of the Saints are well represented. Monographs, scholarly journals and serials on philogy, linguistics and literature with special emphasis on Middle English, Old French, Middle High German, Middle Dutch and early Irish texts. *See also* entries under Folklore; Literature, Medieval.

PA —CARNEGIE LIBRARY OF PITTSBURGH, Children's Dept, 4400 Forbes Ave, Pittsburgh, 15213. Amy Kellman, Head
Holdings: Vols 2000 Cat
Notes: Historical children's books. Strong in folk tales.

RI —BROWN UNIVERSITY, John Hay Library, 20 Prospect St, Providence, 02912. Mark N Brown, Cur Mss
Holdings: Vols (1500) Cat
Notes: A virtually complete collection of the literature dealing with the Legend of the Wandering Jew printed from the 17th century to date. In addition to historical discussion of the legend, there are sections devoted to the appearance of Ahasuerus in drama, fiction, illustrations, poetry, song, and music.

ON —VICTORIA UNIVERSITY, Library, 71 Queen's Park Crescent, Toronto, M5S 1K7, Can. Robert C Brandeis, Chief Librn
Holdings: Vols 350 // Cat

LEGERDEMAIN see Magic and Magicians

LEGISLATION, COMPARATIVE see Comparative Law

LEGISLATION, LABOR see Labor Laws and Legislation

IN —INDIANAPOLIS-MARION COUNTY PUBLIC LIBRARY, Riley Room for Young People, PO Box 211, Indianapolis, 46206. Margaret Barks, Head
Holdings: Vols 1110 Cat
Notes: The Harding Memorial Collection. This is a resource collection of folk and fairy tales as well as other suitable materials for telling.

NE —UNIVERSITY OF NEBRASKA-LINCOLN, Don L Love Library, Lincoln, 68588. Joseph G Svoboda, University Archivist
Holdings: Vols (8000) // Uncat Mss Pix Slides Phonorecords Audiotapes Microforms
Notes: This is an extensive collection belonging to the folklorist Benjamin A Botkin, about 500 linear ft, consisting of various types of materials. Main emphasis is American folklore, although folklore of all nations is included.

LEGISLATORS—U.S.

IL —CHICAGO HISTORICAL SOCIETY, Library, Clark St at North Ave, Chicago, 60614. Archie Motley, Manuscript Librn
Notes: Papers of members of Congress: James Franklin Aldrich (businessman, Representative); Isaac Newton Arnold (lawyer, author, Representative); Sidney Breese (jurist, Senator); David Davis (US Supreme Court Justice, US Senator); Charles S Dewey (banker, US Representative); Paul H Douglas (economist, Chicago alderman, US Senator); Stephen A Douglas (lawyer, US Senator, Democratic Party leader); Ninian Edwards (Chief Justice of KY, Governor of Illinois, US Senator); John J Hardin (Black Hawk War officer, US Representative); Martin D Hardin (US Senator); Elias Kent Kane (Judge, Illinois Secretary of State, US Senator); William Ralls Morrison (Civil War officer, US Representative, Interstate Commerce Commissioner); Charles H Percy (business executive, US Senator); John Wentworth (editor, mayor of Chicago, US Representative).

OK —UNIVERSITY OF OKLAHOMA, Bizzell Memorial Library, Western History Collections, 401 W Brooks, Norman, 73069. John Ezell, Cur
Notes: Subject scope covers all aspects of history and culture of American Trans-Mississippi West and the North American Indians with special emphasis on Oklahoma and adjacent states, the Southwest and Spanish borderlands. Printed and non-print holdings cover Indians, explorations and surveys, range cattle industry, fur-trade, transportation, overland travels, emigration and immigration, frontier life, agriculture, mining, oil gas industry, conservation, literature, and the social-cultural history as well as the usual political and economic interests. The large holdings of U.S Congressional papers also reflect other national and international affairs.

LEGISLATORS—U.S.—PORTRAITS

DC —LIBRARY OF CONGRESS, Prints & Photographs Div, Washington, 20540.
Notes: The Brady-Handy Collection consists of some 10,000 negatives from the files of photographers Levin C Handy (1855?-1932) and Mathew B Brady (1823?-1896), most of which are portrait photographs and views of Washington, DC from the 19th and early 20th centuries. Incl portraits of congressmen and government leaders (1855-90).

LEHMAN, ERNEST

CA —UNIVERSITY OF SOUTHERN CALIFORNIA, Edward L Doheny Memorial Library, Archives of Performing Arts, University Park, Los Angeles, 90089. Robert Knutson, Librn
Holdings: Mss Pix
Notes: Personal collection of papers, pictures, etc.

LEHMAN, HERBERT H.

NY —COLUMBIA UNIVERSITY LIBRARIES, Rare Book & Manuscript Library, 801 Butler Library, 535 W 114 St, New York, 10027. Kenneth A Lohf, Librn
Holdings: Mss Pix
Notes: The personal and public archives of Herbert H Lehman (former governor of New York and US senator). Incl are memorabilia, films, recordings, tapes and his personal reference library. Incl 1,250,000 items. Restricted use.

LEHMANN, FREDERICK WILLIAM, 1756-1929

MO —WASHINGTON UNIVERSITY, Libraries, Special Collections Dept, Campus Box 1061, St Louis, 63130.
Notes: Papers of this prominent American lawyer, incl family and business correspondence.

LEHMANN, LOTTE

CA —UNIVERSITY OF CALIFORNIA, SANTA BARBARA, Library, Dept of Special Collections, Santa Barbara, 93106. Christian F Brun, Head
Holdings: Mss Pix Phonorecords
Notes: Correspondence, mss, photographs, paintings, etc relating to Lotte Lehmann's life and career. 10,000 items.

LEHMANN, WILLIAM CHRISTIAN

†NY —COLUMBIA UNIVERSITY LIBRARIES, Butler Library, Rare Book and Manuscript Library, 535 W 114 St, New York, 10027.
Notes: Papers, mss, correspondence, etc.

LEIBER, FRITZ JR.

IN —INDIANA UNIVERSITY, Lilly Library, Seventh St, Bloomington, 47405. William R Cagle, Librn
Holdings: Cat Mss Pix
Notes: First editions. Ms collections incl papers of writer Fritz Leiber, Jr, 1910- , containing correspondence with many authors and manuscript notes, etc, of several Leiber writings, 1932-1974. 1500 items.

LEIBNIZ, GOTTFRIED WILHEIM, 1646-1716

CA —UNIVERSITY OF CALIFORNIA, LOS ANGELES, Research Library, Dept of Special Collections, 405 Hilgard Ave, Los Angeles, 90024. Edward Shreeves, Chairman, Bibliographers Group; David S Zeidberg, Head
Holdings: Vols 100 Microforms
Notes: 100 books; 35 reels of more than 100, 000 mss pages in the Lower Saxony State Library.

LEIGH, JAMES

MA —BOSTON UNIVERSITY, Mugar Memorial Library, Special Collections Dept, 771 Commonwealth Ave, Boston, 02215. Howard B Gotlieb, Dir
Holdings: Cat Mss

NY —CORNELL UNIVERSITY LIBRARIES, Collection of Regional History, Dept of Manuscripts and Univ Archives, Ithaca, 14853.
Notes: Incl records, 1896-98, of daily income and expenditures of the "Union Store".

LEIGHTON, JOHN

ON —UNIVERSITY OF TORONTO, Thomas Fisher Rare Book Library, 120 Saint George St, Toronto, M5S 1A5, Can. Richard G Landon, Head
Holdings: Vols 130 Uncat
Notes: Pantazzi Collection, named for donor Sybille Pantazzi, Librn, Art Gallery of Ontario. Small collection of signed English publishers' bindings, 1846-1880.

LEISURE

ON —SIRLS, Faculty of Human Kinetics & Leisure Studies, University of Waterloo, Waterloo, N2L 3G1, Can. Betty Smith, Database Mgr
Notes: Information Retrieval System for the Sociology of Leisure and Sport (SIRLS) is a computerized online database of about 13, 000 entries (1983). Incl dance as a leisure time activity.

LEITER, LEVI S.

IL —CHICAGO HISTORICAL SOCIETY, Library, Clark St at North Ave, Chicago, 60614. Archie Motley, Manuscript Librn
Notes: Papers.

LEJEUNE, JOHN ARCHER, 1867-1942

DC —LIBRARY OF CONGRESS, Manuscript Division, Washington, 20540. John C Broderick, Chief
Notes: His papers.

LELCHUK, ALAN

MA —BOSTON UNIVERSITY, Mugar Memorial Library, Special Collections Dept, 771 Commonwealth Ave, Boston, 02215. Howard B Gotlieb, Dir
Holdings: Cat Mss Pix
Notes: Mss, correspondence, etc collected in depth; incl publications by or about.

LE MAY, ALAN, 1899-

CA —UNIVERSITY OF CALIFORNIA, LOS ANGELES, Research Library, Dept of Special Collections, 405 Hilgard Ave, Los Angeles, 90024. Edward Shreeves, Chairman, Bibliographers Group; David S Zeidberg, Head
Holdings: Mss
Notes: 11 linear feet of mss, correspondence, and ephemera.

LEMELIN, ROGER

ON —NATIONAL LIBRARY OF CANADA, 395 Wellington St, Ottawa, K1A 0N4, Can. Andre Preibish, Dir
Notes: Literary Manuscripts collection contains papers of several important Canadian authors writing in English and/or French eg Clare Bice (1909-1976), noted author and illustrator of children's books; Andre Giroux, novelist, writer for television and broadcaster; Roger Lemelin, well-known author of Au pied de la pente douce, Les Plouffe, and Pierre le magnifique; Gabrielle Roy (1909-1983), author of many novels, including Bonheur d'occasion, La Petite Poule d'Eau and Rue Deschambault; Laura Goodman Salverson (1890-1970), writer, public speaker and teacher; Phyllis Webb, poet.

LEMHI INDIAN RESERVATION, IDAHO

ID —IDAHO STATE UNIVERSITY, Library, Pocatello, 83209. Gary Domitz, Social Science Librn
Holdings: Uncat Mss Pix //
Notes: Papers, etc.

LEMURS

OR —OREGON REGIONAL PRIMATE RESEARCH CENTER, Library, 505 NW 185 Ave, Beaverton, 97006. Isabel McDonald, Librn
Holdings: Vols (765) Cat Audiotapes 16mm Films Microforms
Notes: Incl small collection of dissertations and theses.

LENAPE INDIANS see Delaware Indians

LEND-LEASE OPERATIONS, 1941-1945

NJ —PRINCETON UNIVERSITY, Library, Manuscript Collection, Nassau St, Princeton, 08540. Jean F Preston, Cur
Notes: Incl 96 cartons, 30 card-tray files. The archive of the Committee to Defend America by Aiding the Allies covers the period May 1940 to January 1942.

L'ENGLE, MADELEINE

IL —WHEATON COLLEGE, Buswell Memorial Library, Wheaton, 60187. Paul Snezek, Library Dir
Holdings: Vols 150 Cat Mss Pix
Budget: $1500
Notes: Mss number over 60 linear feet and dates from Madeleine L'Engle's childhood through 1984. Included are correspondence, examples of her artwork, and non-print media resources. *Related Topics:* Illustrated Children's Books.

LENIN (VLADIMIR ILYICH ULYANOV)

CT —YALE UNIVERSITY, Box 1603A, Yale Station, New Haven, 06520.
Notes: Books by and about Lenin.

LENNART, ERNEST W.

WA —WESTERN WASHINGTON UNIVERSITY, Center for Pacific Northwest Studies, High St, Bellingham, 98225. James W Scott, Dir
Holdings: Uncat Mss Pix
Notes: Farmer and former member of the Washington State House, Lennart died in office in the late 1960s, a member of the State Senate. Papers are very largely political in nature, incl letters, speeches and documents.

LENNI LENAPE see Delaware Indians

LENNOX, CHARLES GORDON, DUKE OF RICHMOND

MB —UNIVERSITY OF MANITOBA, Elizabeth Dafoe Library, Archives and Special Collections Dept, Winnipeg, R3T 2N2, Can. Richard E Bennett, Dept Head; Corrado A Santoro, Reference Archivist
Notes: Handwritten letter, dated Aug 7, 1806 by the Duke reporting on field works and batteries situtated on the coast of Sussex. At the time, England was at war with Napoleon and the threat of French invasion not entirely passed.

LENNOX, CHARLOTTE

MA —HARVARD UNIVERSITY LIBRARY, Houghton Library, Cambridge, 02138. Rodney G Dennis, Cur of Manuscripts
Holdings: Cat Mss

LENOX, DAVID

DE —UNIVERSITY OF DELAWARE, Hugh M Morris Library, S College Ave, Newark, 19711. T Stuart Dick, Special Collections
Holdings: // Mss
Notes: Correspondence (1782-1832) relating to all phases of David Lenox's career subsequent to the Revolution, ie, land speculation, duties in the Whiskey Rebellion, executorship of the estate of John Lukens, his banking career, household receipts and settlement of his estate.

LENS, SIDNEY

IL —CHICAGO HISTORICAL SOCIETY, Library, Clark St at North Ave, Chicago, 60614. Archie Motley, Manuscript Librn
Notes: Papers of author Sidney Lens.

LENSES, OPHTHALMIC see Eyeglasses; Ophthalmic Lenses

LENSKI, LOIS

FL —FLORIDA STATE UNIVERSITY, Robert Manning Strozier Library, Special Collections Dept, Tallahassee, 32306. Opal M Free, Head, Special Collections
Holdings: Uncat Mss Pix Tapes
Notes: The Lois Lenski collection contains 867 items, many first editions of books written and illustrated by Miss Lenski and other editions of her books, incl foreign-language editions: books illustrated by Lois Lenski; books containing selections from her works; articles by and about her; original drawings, block prints, lithographs, rough sketches. Many items autographed. Two editions of a catalog of the collection, *The Lois Lenski Collection in the Florida State University Library,* were published in 1966, both limited editions and now out-of-print. Noncirculating. No photocopying.

IL —ILLINOIS STATE UNIVERSITY, Milner Library, Dept of Special Collections, Normal, 61761. Robert Sokan, Librn
Holdings: Vols (170) Uncat Mss Pix Audiotapes
Notes: Correspondence (1935-1957) to Lois Lenski concerning her doll and toy collection and her books for children; correspondence (1956-1970) from Lois Lenski to Milner Library concerning additions to the collection; bookmarks and Christmas cards designed by Miss Lenski; photograph albums; sketchbooks; scrapbooks (contain photographs, correspondence and sketches); original illustrations; handwritten mss (*Houseboat Girl*, 1957, and *Corn Farm* Boy, 1953); typewritten mss (*Coal Camp* Girl, 1959); articles, plays and speeches written by Miss Lenski; newspaper and magazine clippings; and a tape recording entitled *A Talk with Lois Lenski.*

KS —EMPORIA STATE UNIVERSITY, William Allen White Library, Emporia, 66801. Mary E Bogan, Special Collections Librn
Holdings: Vols (50) Uncat Mss Pix Phonorecords
Notes: The collection incl photographs and other background material, rough sketches, notes, correspondence, manuscripts, art work, dummies, and galley proofs for *Shoo-Fly Girl* and *Auto Worker's Son,* regional stories written and illustrated by Lois Lenski. Also included in the collection are books, original art work for many of Lois Lenski's works, as well as music, recordings, pamphlets, articles and other materials. Not cataloged.
See also entry under Children's Literature

KS —SOUTHWESTERN COLLEGE, Memorial Library, 100 College St, Winfield, 67156. Daniel L Nutter, Librn
Holdings: Vols 200 // Cat Pix
Notes: The Arthur Covey Art Collection. Arthur Covey was a noted American artists from the 1920s until his death in 1960 and was a graduate of Southwestern. His wife, Lois Lenski, noted author and illustrator of children's books, gave all of his paintings, materials, and library to the college in 1960.

NY —STATE UNIVERSITY OF NEW YORK, COLLEGE AT BUFFALO, E H Butler Library, 1300 Elmwood Ave, Buffalo, 14222. Marilyn C Kihl, Librn
Holdings: Vols 241 Cat Mss Pix Slides Phonorecords Audiotapes
Notes: Collection presented by the author, consisting of 310 original illustrations representing 44 titles, and original mss, notes, research, dummies, photos, etc representing 36 titles. English language reprints, foreign translations, articles by and about the author, recordings of her books. Also incl block prints, lithographs, original Christmas cards, bookmarks. Printed catalog, *The Lois Lenski Children's Collection in the Edward H Butler Library*, compiled by Caroline Giambra (Buffalo: State University College at Buffalo, 1972).

NC —UNIVERSITY OF NORTH CAROLINA, GREENSBORO, Walter Clinton Jackson Library, Special Collections Dept, 1000 Spring Garden St, Greensboro, 27412. Emilie W Mills, Librn
Holdings: Vols 275 Cat Mss Pix Tape recording
Notes: Incl first editions of Miss Lenski's works (many of them signed by the author), mss, letters, drawings, foreign and variant editions, articles about Miss Lenski. Emphasis is given to her works about the South. Most items are gifts from Miss Lenski.

LENTZ, THEODORE

MO —UNIVERSITY OF MISSOURI-SAINT LOUIS, Thomas Jefferson Library, Manuscript and Historical Society Collection, 8001 Natural Bridge Rd, Saint Louis, 63121.

LENYA, LOTTE

CT —YALE UNIVERSITY, Music Library, 98 Wall St, New Haven, 06520. Harold E Samuel, Librn
Notes: Personal papers and musical mss.
See also entry under Music, American.

LENZEN, VICTOR F., 1890-1975

CA —UNIVERSITY OF CALIFORNIA, BERKELEY, Bancroft Library, Manuscripts Division, Berkeley, 94720. James D Hart, Dir
Notes: Papers.

LEONARD, HERBERT

CA —UNIVERSITY OF CALIFORNIA, LOS ANGELES, Theater Arts Library, Los Angeles, 90024. Edward Shreeves, Chairman, Bibliographers Group; Audree Malkin, Head, Theater Arts Library
Notes: Herbert Leonard (producer) Collection: An extensive collection consisting mainly of the television series *Naked City* (1958-1963); incl various versions and drafts of the scripts, production records, contracts and correspondence.

LEONARD, JOHN

MA —BOSTON UNIVERSITY, Mugar Memorial Library, Special Collections Dept, 771 Commonwealth Ave, Boston, 02215. Howard B Gotlieb, Dir
Holdings: Cat Mss
Notes: Publications by.

LEONARD, WILLIAM ELLERY

CA —UNIVERSITY OF SAN FRANCISCO, Richard A Gleeson Library, The Countess Bernardine Murphy Donohue Rare Book Room, San Francisco, 94117. D Steven Corey, Special Collections Librn
Holdings: Vols 25 Mss
Notes: Complete collection, ephemera.

LEONARDO DA VINCI, 1452-1519

CA —UNIVERSITY OF CALIFORNIA, LOS ANGELES, Art Library, Elmer Belt Library of Vinciana, 405 Hilgard Ave, Los Angeles, 90024. Joyce Pellerano Ludmer, Art Librn
Holdings: Vols (10,000) Cat Pix Microforms VF
Notes: The Renaissance, with emphasis on Leonardo da Vinci.

CT —BURNDY LIBRARY, Electra Square, Norwalk, 06856. Philip J Weimerskirch, Asst Dir
Holdings: Vols 800

MA —BRANDEIS UNIVERSITY, Goldfarb Library, 415 South St, Waltham, 02154. Bessie Hahn, Dir
Holdings: Vols 1015 Cat
Notes: Leonardo da Vinci Collection. Comprised of over 1000 vols dealing with all aspects of Leonardo Da Vinci's life, art and engineering feats. The collection is fully catalogued and access is provided by the Special Collections card catalog and the Main Card Catalog.

NJ —STEVENS INSTITUTE OF TECHNOLOGY, Samuel C Williams Library, Castle Point Sta, Hoboken, 07030. Jane G Hartye, Special Collections Librn
Holdings: Vols 2410 Cat Pix Slides Filmstrips
Budget: ($1500)

NY —UNIVERSITY OF ROCHESTER, Rush Rhees Library, Department of Rare Books and Special Collections, Rochester, 14627. Peter Dzwonkoski, Librn
Holdings: Vols 1300 Cat
Notes: Extensive collection, of works by and about Leonardo da Vinci described in: Merritt, Howard, "The Anthony J and Frances A Guzzetta Collection of Vinciana," *The University of Rochester Library* Bulletin, vol 18, no 3 (Spring, 1963), pp 35-40.

LEOPOLD, FREDERIC

IA —IOWA STATE UNIVERSITY, Library, Dept of Special Collections, Ames, 50011. Stanley M Yates, Head
Holdings: // Mss
Notes: Frederic Leopold has observed and recorded over 35 years the nesting habits of wood ducks along the Mississippi River near Burlington, Iowa. Collection includes his notebooks.

LEOPOLD, NATHAN F.

IL —CHICAGO HISTORICAL SOCIETY, Library, Clark St at North Ave, Chicago, 60614. Archie Motley, Manuscript Librn
Notes: Papers of Nathan F Leopold, convicted and paroled murderer of Bobby Franks in 1924.

LEPERS AND LEPROSY see Hansen Disease

LEPIDOPTERA

†CT —UNIVERSITY OF CONNECTICUT LIBRARY, Special Collections Dept, Storrs, 06268. Richard H Schimmelpfeng, Dir of Special Collections

MA —AMHERST COLLEGE, Library, Amherst, 01002. John Lancaster, Special Collections Librn
Holdings: Vols 1402 Cat Maps Pix

MI —MICHIGAN STATE UNIVERSITY, Libraries, Special Collections Div, East Lansing, 48824. Jannette Fiore, Librn
Holdings: Vols 40 Cat
Notes: Works before 1850.

NY —AMERICAN MUSEUM OF NATURAL HISTORY, Library Services Dept, Central Park W & 79th St, New York, 10024. Nina J Root, Chairwoman; Mary Genett, Asst Librn for Reference Services
Holdings: Vols (385,000) Cat Mss Maps Pix Slides Microforms
Notes: Nearly all collections are outstanding for depth of coverage and international range. Early and historic works, rare books, colored illustrations, and relevant serial publications supplement the modern scientific publications necessary to the researches of the scientific staff and the work of the educational division. Open to the public.

NS —NOVA SCOTIA MUSEUM, Library, 1747 Summer St, Halifax, B3H 3A6, Can. M S Whiteside, Librn
Holdings: Vols 800 Cat
Notes: Emphasis on Lepidoptera.

LEPIDOPTERA DIURNA see Butterflies and Moths

LEPIDOPTERA NOCTURNA see Butterflies and Moths

LE RAY DE CHAUMONT, JAMES DONATIANUS

NY —CORNELL UNIVERSITY LIBRARIES, Collection of Regional History, Dept of Manuscripts and Univ Archives, Ithaca, 14853.
Notes: Incl papers, 1781-1835; correspondence, accounts, deeds, contracts, and shipping documents.

LEPROSY see Hansen Disease

LERNER, CARL

NY —MUSEUM OF MODERN ART, Dept of Film, 11 W 53 St, New York, 10019. Eileen Bowser, Cur
Holdings: Mss Pix
Notes: Papers, correspondence, scrapbooks, pictures, etc. Partially cataloged.

LE SAGE, ALAIN RENE

CA —UNIVERSITY OF CALIFORNIA, LOS ANGELES, William Andrews Clark Memorial Library, 2520 Cimarron St, Los Angeles, 90018.
Holdings: Cat
Notes: Original editions.

LESBIANS see Homosexuals and Homosexuality

LESLIE, CECILIE

MA —BOSTON UNIVERSITY, Mugar Memorial Library, Special Collections Dept, 771 Commonwealth Ave, Boston, 02215. Howard B Gotlieb, Dir
Holdings: Cat Mss Pix Correspondence

LESLIE, LADY LEONIE

DC —GEORGETOWN UNIVERSITY, Library, Special Collections Div, 37 & O Sts NW, Washington, 20057. George M Barringer, Special Collections Librn; Nicholas B Sheetz, Mss Librn
Holdings: Mss Cat Pix
Notes: The papers of the Irish man-of-letters Sir Shane Leslie (1885-1971) containing letters, mss, diaries, notebooks, clippings, and photographs. Extensive correspondence by Margot Asquith, countess of Oxford and Asquith; Lady Violet Bonham-Carter; Burke Cochran; Lord Alfred Douglas; Moreton Frewen; Cardinal Gasquet; Vyvyan Holland; Lady Leonie Leslie; Sir Wilfrid Meynell; Sir Horace Plunkett; John Quinn; Frederick Rolfe (Baron Corvo); and Elizabeth Russell, among others. Also incl are research files on Sir Winston Churchill (Leslie's first cousin); Leonard Jerome; Maria Anne Fitzherbet (wife of King George IV); Ghosts and Ghost stories; and Eton College.

LESLIE, SIR SHANE

DC —GEORGETOWN UNIVERSITY, Library, Special Collections Div, 37 & O Sts NW, Washington, 20057. George M Barringer, Special Collections Librn; Nicholas B Sheetz, Mss Librn
Holdings: Mss Cat Pix
Notes: The papers of the Irish man-of-letters Sir Shane Leslie (1885-1971) containing letters, mss, diaries, notebooks, clippings, and photographs. Extensive correspondence by Margot Asquith, countess of Oxford and Asquith; Lady Violet Bonham-Carter; Burke Cochran; Lord Alfred Douglas; Moreton Frewen; Cardinal Gasquet; Vyvyan Holland; Lady Leonie Leslie; Sir Wilfrid Meynell; Sir Horace Plunkett; John Quinn; Frederick Rolfe (Baron Corvo); and Elizabeth Russell, among others. Also incl are research files on Sir Winston Churchill (Leslie's first cousin); Leonard Jerome; Maria Anne Fitzherbet (wife of King George IV); Ghosts and Ghost stories; and Eton College.

LESOTHO

DC —HOWARD UNIVERSITY, Moorland-Spingarn Research Center, 500 Howard Place NW, Washington, 20059. Clifford L Muse, Jr, Acting Dir

LESSER, SOL

CA —UNIVERSITY OF SOUTHERN CALIFORNIA, Edward L Doheny Memorial Library, Archives of Performing Arts, University Park, Los Angeles, 90089. Robert Knutson, Librn
Holdings: Mss Pix
Notes: Personal collection of papers, pictures, etc.

LESSER ANTILLES

NY —HAMILTON COLLEGE, Daniel Burke Library, Special Collections Dept, Clinton, 13323. Frank K Lorenz, Cur
Holdings: Vols 1300 Cat Mss Maps Pix
Notes: The Beinecke Lesser Antilles Collection. Specialized works on the smaller islands of the West Indies, incl history, travel literature, flora and fauna, anthropology. Incl numerous rare items in many languages. *See also* Barbados; Dominica; Grenada; Guadeloupe; Martinique; Trindad and Tobago; Virgin Islands.

LESSING, GOTTHOLD

MA —HARVARD UNIVERSITY LIBRARY, Widener Library, Cambridge, 02138.
Holdings: Cat Mss
Notes: See *Harvard Library Notes,* III (1938), 161-163.

LE TOURNEAU, ROBERT G.

TX —LE TOURNEAU COLLEGE, Margaret Estes Library, 2100 S Mobberly Ave, PO Box 7001, Longview, 75601. Rachel Miley, Acting Dir of Library Services
Holdings: Vols (178,846) Cat Mss Maps Pix Slides Microforms
Budget: ($40,000)

LETTERING

VA —UNIVERSITY OF VIRGINIA, Alderman Library, Rare Book Dept, Charlottesville, 22901. Julius P Barclay, Cur
Holdings: Vols (6500) // Mss
Notes: The Oscar Ogg Collection of Book Arts covers calligraphy, letterforms, typography, printing, and graphic arts. Contains early writing books and printed works, as well as modern manuals and other works on printing, publishing, and promotion through graphic arts. The Dept also has the Edward L Stone Collection of Printing Specimens, 3000 items. Contains materials tracing the history of printing, inks, binding styles and materials, types. Also the Tompkins Collection (2000 vols), and the Stevens Watts collection (900 vols).

LETTISH LANGUAGE AND LITERATURE

CA —LOS ANGELES PUBLIC LIBRARY, Foreign Languages Dept, 630 W Fifth St, Los Angeles, 90071. Sylva Manoogian, Principal Librn
Holdings: Vols 490 Cat
Budget: ($41,500)

NY —NEW YORK PUBLIC LIBRARY, Donnell Foreign Language Library, 20 W 53 St, New York, 10019. Bosiljka Stevanovic, Supvr Librn
Holdings: Vols 174 Cat
Notes: Latvian collection incl Latvian authors of Latvian expression. No separate catalog.

NY —NEW YORK PUBLIC LIBRARY, Slavonic Div, Fifth Ave & 42 St, New York, 10018. Edward Kasinec, Chief
Holdings: Cat Microforms
Notes: Latvian language and literature. See New York Public Library, *Dictionary Catalog of the Slavonic Collection* (Boston: G K Hall, 1974), 44 vols

OH —CLEVELAND PUBLIC LIBRARY, Foreign Literature Dept, 325 Superior Ave, Cleveland, 44114. Natalia Bezugloff, Head
Holdings: Vols 1740 Cat
Notes: Latvian language and literature. A popular circulating collection containing classics and the standard works with emphasis on belles lettres, history and biography. A variety of other subjects such as learning languages, hobbies, how to do books, art, children's books, periodicals, etc. *See also* entry under Foreign Language Collections

OH —KENT STATE UNIVERSITY, Libraries, Ethnic Collections, Kent, 44242.
Holdings: Vols 1650 Cat
See also entry under Foreign Language Collections

WI —UNIVERSITY OF WISCONSIN, MADISON, Memorial Library, Slavic Studies Collection, 728 State St, Madison, 53706. Aleksander Rolich, Bibliographer for Slavic Studies; Robert P Gakovich, Slavic Cataloger; Valdis J Zeps, Baltic Studies Center
Holdings: Vols 4000 Cat Periodicals Microforms
Notes: The collection is particularly strong in emigre literature (probably largest holdings of any public library in the world), and respectable in linguistics, history, folklore, and theatre. The collection is permanently housed at University of Wisconsin and Wisconisn Historical Society. The Baltic Studies Center serves as a clearing house and temporary storage; it maintains records on acquisitions and location.

LETTRICH, JOSEPH

CA —HOOVER INSTITUTION ON WAR, REVOLUTION & PEACE, Stanford University, Stanford, 94305. Milorad M Drachkovitch, Archivist
Holdings: Mss
Notes: Papers, correspondence, etc.

LETTS IN THE U.S.

PA —BALCH INSTITUTE FOR ETHNIC STUDIES, Library, 18 S Seventh St, Philadelphia, 19106. R Joseph Anderson, Library Dir
Notes: Ethnic Heritage Collection.

LEUSCHNER, ARMIN O., 1868-1953

CA —UNIVERSITY OF CALIFORNIA, BERKELEY, Bancroft Library, Manuscripts Division, Berkeley, 94720. James D Hart, Dir
Notes: Papers.

LEVANT COMPANY

KS —UNIVERSITY OF KANSAS, Kenneth Spencer Research Library, Special Collections Dept, Lawrence, 66045. Alexandra Mason, Librn
Holdings: Vols 10,000 Cat Mss
Notes: Printed: Continental 15th-early 19th century. English 16th-early 19th. Mss: 14th-18th century. Strong holdings in 18th and early 19th century English economics, incl books, pamphlets and mss (official and private records: Audit Office, Lottery Office, Admiralty, Wardrobe, etc, Levant Company, East India Company, Madeira merchants, various persons and estates). Earlier ms holdings incl Italian renaissance business records, English and Scottish manorial records, English Exchequer records, English and Scottish land records. Printed holdings also incl French, Italian sources for economic history, 15th-18th century. The University's main library has very strong holdings in 19th and 20th century economics and economic history and business, economic theory, etc, ca 100,000 vols. Noncirculating.

LEVEES

MS —US ARMY ENGINEER WATERWAYS EXPERIMENT STATION, Library Branch, PO Box 631, Vicksburg, 39180. Bernice Black, Chief Librn
Holdings: Vols (350,000) Cat Mss Maps Microforms

LEVELLERS

PA —TEMPLE UNIVERSITY LIBRARIES, Special Collections Dept, Rare Books & Mss Section, Philadelphia, 19122. Thomas M Whitehead, Cur
Holdings: Vols Cat Mss
Notes: Seventeenth and 18th century books and pamphlets on political, religious, social and intellectual life and history of England. Strong holdings of John Cotton, Gilbert Burnet, Richard Overton, John Lilburne; Civil War pamphlets, ranters and levellers. The Nordell and Simpson Collections.

LEVENTHAL, HAROLD, 1915-1979

†DC —LIBRARY OF CONGRESS, Manuscript Division, Washington, 20540.
Notes: The papers, etc, of Harold Leventhal.

LEVER, A. FRANCIS, 1875-1940

SC —CLEMSON UNIVERSITY, Libraries, Clemson, 29631. Michael F Kohl, Head of Special Collections
Holdings: // Cat Mss
Notes: A Frank Lever, Congressman from South Carolina. Arranged chronologically by subject, 25 cubic feet of ms.

LEVER, CHARLES JAMES, 1806-1872

CA —UNIVERSITY OF CALIFORNIA, LOS ANGELES, Research Library, Dept of Special Collections, 405 Hilgard Ave, Los Angeles, 90024. Edward Shreeves, Chairman, Bibliographers Group; David S Zeidberg, Head
Holdings: Vols 100
Notes: 100 first and other editions of his books; 25 letters.

IN —INDIANA UNIVERSITY, Lilly Library, Seventh St, Bloomington, 47405. William R Cagle, Librn
Holdings: Vols 30 Cat Mss
Notes: Complete collection of first editions in parts and book form. Holograph manuscript of *Knight of Gwynne*.

NJ —PRINCETON UNIVERSITY, Library, Morris L Parrish Collection, Princeton, 08540. Alexander D Wainwright, Cur
Holdings: Vols 73
Notes: The collection contains over 6500 vols, as well as many theatre programs, playbills, photographs, clippings and other miscellanea. Parrish's goal was to assemble in both the English and the American first editions, in the original condition as issued, everything that a given author published. He was also interested in a high standard of condition for his books. Many additions have been acquired since the Parrish collection came to the Library as a bequest in 1944. The collection is an assemblage of author collections, consisting of books by: William Harrison Ainsworth, James Matthew Barrie, William Black, The Brontes, William Wilkie Collins, Dinah Mulock Craik, Marie de la Ramee ("Ouida"), Benjamin Disraeli, Charles Dickens, Charles Dodgson, George du Maurier, George Eliot (ie Mary Ann Evans), Elizabeth Gaskell, Thomas Hardy, Thomas Hughes,Charles Kingsley, Charles Lever, Edward George Earle Bulwer-Lytton, Mary Maxwell, George Meredith, Charles Reade, Walter Scott, Robert Louis Stevenson, William Makepeace Thackeray, Trollope Family, Ellen Wood, and Charlotte Yonge.

LEVERTOV, DENISE, 1923-

MO —WASHINGTON UNIVERSITY, Libraries, Special Collections Dept, Campus Box 1061, St Louis, 63130.
Notes: A small but significant collection.

NV —UNIVERSITY OF NEVADA, RENO, University Library, Special Collections Dept, Reno, 89557. Robert E Blesse, Head
Holdings: Vols (74) Cat Other appearances 850 Cat
Notes: Includes individual works by author in all editions including translations; also prefaces, introductions, published correspondence, appearances in anthologies, periodicals, etc. Bibliographical research collection, part of Modern Authors Collection.

NY —STATE UNIVERSITY OF NEW YORK, STONY BROOK, Melville Library, Dept of Special Collections, Stony Brook, 11794. Evert Volkersz, Head
Holdings: Cat Mss

BC —UNIVERSITY OF VICTORIA, McPherson Library, Victoria, V8W 3H5, Can.
Notes: Poet. Incl letters and postcards (1940-51) to Wrey Charles Gardiner; letters, 3 drafts of poems and postcard (1946-47) to John Hayward; 2 drawings not used for *A Tree Telling of Orpheus*, 1967.

LEVI, WENDELL MITCHEL, 1891-1976

SC —COLLEGE OF CHARLESTON LIBRARY, Special Collections Dept, Charleston, 29401.
Notes: Contains biographical and family history material of Wendell Mitchel Levi; invertebrate anatomy course notes from the College of Charleston; University of Chicago Law School casebooks; correspondence concerning pigeons and camellias; notes, photographs, mss, typescripts, and galleys of published works; and other materials relating to pigeons and camellias. Among the more prominent correspondents are B F Skinner, Madame Chiang Kai-Shek, and Mary Bonner.

LEVIN, MEYER

MA —BOSTON UNIVERSITY, Mugar Memorial Library, Special Collections Dept, 771 Commonwealth Ave, Boston, 02215. Howard B Gotlieb, Dir
Holdings: Cat Mss Pix
Notes: Mss, correspondence, etc collected in depth; incl publications by or about.

LEVINE, MARKS, 1890-1971

MA —BOSTON UNIVERSITY, Mugar Memorial Library, Special Collections Dept, 771 Commonwealth Ave, Boston, 02215. Howard B Gotlieb, Dir
Holdings: // Cat Mss Pix
Notes: Mss, correspondence.

LEVITAN, DICK

MA —BOSTON UNIVERSITY, Mugar Memorial Library, Special Collections Dept, 771 Commonwealth Ave, Boston, 02215. Howard B Gotlieb, Dir
Holdings: Cat Mss Pix
Notes: Mss, correspondence, etc collected in depth; incl publications by or about.

LEVITATION

MB —UNIVERSITY OF MANITOBA, Elizabeth Dafoe Library, Archives and Special Collections Dept, Winnipeg, R3T 2N2, Can. Richard E Bennett, Dept Head; Corrado A Santoro, Reference Archivist
Notes: Papers of Thomas Glendenning Hamilton, physician and surgeon, member of the Manitoba Legislative Assembly, psychic researcher. Winnipeg, Manitoba. Important collection, emphasis is on psychic research with limited amount of materials regarding his medical and political careers. Seance attendance registers, records and affidavits, lecture notes, correspondence, newspaper clippings, books and journal articles. Photographs, slides and ca 50 boxes of glass plate negatives.

LEVITT, SAUL, 1913-1977

MA —BOSTON UNIVERSITY, Mugar Memorial Library, Special Collections Dept, 771 Commonwealth Ave, Boston, 02215. Howard B Gotlieb, Dir
Holdings: Cat Mss Pix Correspondence

LEVY, HYMAN

IL —NORTHWESTERN UNIVERSITY, Library, Special Collections Dept, 1937 Sheridan Rd, Evanston, 60201. R Russell Maylone, Cur
Holdings: Cat Mss //
Notes: Mss only; 1000 letters received by him.

LEVY, NEVILLE

LA —NEW ORLEANS PUBLIC LIBRARY, Louisiana Div & City Archives Dept, Louisiana History Collection, 219 Loyola Ave, New Orleans, 70140. Collin B Hamer Jr, Head
Holdings: Vols Mss
Notes: Private mss collection covers the period 1795-date, incl the following separate collections: James H Dakin (architect, ca 1834-47, 217 items); Walter E Easey (engineer, 1907-79, 22 cubic feet); McDonough & Payne (merchants, 1801-04, 200 items); ERA Club (women's group, 1914-19, 2 items); Neville Levy (civic leader, ca 1891-1963, 1 cubic foot & 11 vols); and Robert Tallant (author, 1945-57, 3 cubic feet & 10 vols). 92 vols scrapbooks; 100 mss vols, 55 cubic feet.

LEVY, NEWMAN

NY —HAMPDEN-BOOTH THEATRE LIBRARY AT THE PLAYERS, 16 Gramercy Park, New York, 10003. Louis A Rachow, Librn/Cur
Holdings: Uncat Mss
Notes: The Newman Levy Collection, incl his correspondence, research notes, 100 typescripts of short stories, plays, and poems, with holograph corrections and additions; original typescript of an unpublished biography of Franklin P Adams by Levy with extensive holograph corrections and additions. Three feet of indexed material. Described in *Theatre & Performing Arts Collections* (New York: Haworth Press, 1981).

LEVY, ROBERT J.

NY —COLUMBIA UNIVERSITY LIBRARIES, Rare Book & Manuscript Library, 801 Butler Library, 535 W 114 St, New York, 10027. Kenneth A Lohf, Librn
Holdings: Mss Pix
Notes: Papers, mss, archives, concerning his position as Gen D D Eisenhower's liaison officer to Gen Charles de Gaulle. 475 items. Restricted use.

LEWIS, C. I.

CA —STANFORD UNIVERSITY, Dept of Philosophy, Tanner Memorial Library of Philosophy, Bldg 90, Inner Quad, Stanford, 94305. Margaret Harvey, Librn
Holdings: Vols (5000) Cat Mss
Notes: Tanner Library is a branch of Stanford University Libraries. Some older parts of collection are unique. Incl separately shelved collection of books which belonged to C I Lewis. Incl in Stanford University Libraries' catalogs; also separate catalogs.

LEWIS, CECIL DAY see Day-Lewis, Cecil

LEWIS, CLIVE STAPLES

IL —WHEATON COLLEGE, Library, Marion E Wade Collection, Irving & Franklin Sts, Wheaton, 60187. Lyle Dorsett, Cur; Marjorie Mead, Associate Cur
Holdings: Vols (6500) Mss Pix Films Audiotapes Videotapes
Notes: Extensive Marion E Wade Collection of seven British authors incl the books and papers of C S Lewis. The manuscript collection contains over 1000 C S Lewis letters, Lewis' boyhood writings, the 11 vol Lewis family history, the papers of Lewis's wife (Joy Davidman) and her first husband (William Lindsay Gresham), and the diaries of Lewis's brother (Warren). Related materials in the Lewis collection incl the Sheldon Vanauken archives.

NV —UNIVERSITY OF NEVADA, RENO, University Library, Special Collections Dept, Reno, 89557. Robert E Blesse, Head
Holdings: Vols (123) Cat Other appearances 90 Cat
Notes: Includes individual works by author in all editions including translations; also prefaces, introductions, published correspondence, appearances in anthologies, periodicals, etc. Bibliographical research collection, part of Modern Authors Collection.

LEWIS, EDWARD MORGAN, 1872-1936

MA —BOSTON UNIVERSITY, Mugar Memorial Library, Special Collections Dept, 771 Commonwealth Ave, Boston, 02215. Howard B Gotlieb, Dir
Holdings: Mss

LEWIS, EDWARD S.

MA —BOSTON UNIVERSITY, Mugar Memorial Library, Special Collections Dept, 771 Commonwealth Ave, Boston, 02215. Howard B Gotlieb, Dir
Holdings: Cat Mss

LEWIS, FLORA

MA —BOSTON UNIVERSITY, Mugar Memorial Library, Special Collections Dept, 771 Commonwealth Ave, Boston, 02215. Howard B Gotlieb, Dir
Holdings: Cat Mss Pix
Notes: Mss, correspondence, etc collected in depth; incl publications by or about.

LEWIS, GILBERT N.

CA —UNIVERSITY OF CALIFORNIA, BERKELEY, Bancroft Library, Manuscripts Division, Berkeley, 94720. James D Hart, Dir
Holdings: Cat Mss Pix
Notes: Scientific and personal papers.

LEWIS, HAROLD MACLEAN, 1889-1973

NY —CORNELL UNIVERSITY LIBRARIES, Collection of Regional History, Dept of Manuscripts and Univ Archives, Ithaca, 14853.
Notes: Consulting engineer, city planner. Papers, ca 1922-67; 40 ft., 10 vols.

LEWIS, JANET

CA —STANFORD UNIVERSITY LIBRARIES, Cecil H Green Library, Stanford, 94305. Michael T Ryan, Cur
Holdings: Vols Cat
Notes: Also incl correspondence and literary mss.

NV —UNIVERSITY OF NEVADA, RENO, University Library, Special Collections Dept, Reno, 89557. Robert E Blesse, Head
Holdings: Vols 29 Cat
Notes: Includes individual works by author in all editions including translations; also prefaces, introductions, published correspondence, appearances in anthologies, periodicals, etc. Bibliographical research collection, part of Modern Authors Collection.

LEWIS, JERRY

CA —UNIVERSITY OF SOUTHERN CALIFORNIA, Edward L Doheny Memorial Library, Archives of Performing Arts, University Park, Los Angeles, 90089. Robert Knutson, Librn
Holdings: Mss Pix
Notes: Personal collection of papers, pictures, etc.

LEWIS, JOHN L.

WI —STATE HISTORICAL SOCIETY OF WISCONSIN, Archives, 816 State St, Madison, 53706. Harold L Miller, Reference Archivist
Holdings: Mss Pix Microforms
Notes: Records and papers documenting the history of the labor and Socialist movements in the United States from 1850s to the present. Incl are records of labor and socialist organizations incl American Federation of Labor and the Socialist Labor Party, and papers of individual labor and socialist leaders such as Morris Hillquit and John L Lewis. Collections are described in *A Guide to Labor Papers in the State Historical Society of Wisconsin* (1978) and in current accession notes in the *Wisconsin Magazine of History*. Major collections are also listed in Hamer, *Guide to Manuscripts and Archives in the United States,* (1961) and in the *National Union Catalog of Manuscript Collections,* (1959-date).

LEWIS, LLOYD

†IL —NEWBERRY LIBRARY, 60 W Walton St, Chicago, 60610.
Notes: Papers of Lloyd Lewis, Chicago journalist.

LEWIS, MATTHEW GREGORY 'MONK', 1775-1818

PA —TEMPLE UNIVERSITY LIBRARIES, Special Collections Dept, Rare Books & Mss Section, Philadelphia, 19122. Thomas M Whitehead, Cur
Holdings: Vols (50) Cat
Notes: Holdings include contemporary printed books, first and later editions, of 18th and early 19th century gothic fiction. Significant strength in Matthew Gregory "Monk" Lewis books.

LEWIS, OSCAR

IL —UNIVERSITY OF ILLINOIS, URBANA/CHAMPAIGN, Library, University Archives, 1408 W Gregory Drive, Urbana, 61801. Maynard Brichford, Univ Archivist
Holdings: Cat Mss Pix
Notes: Original mss and 91 tapes of interviews for anthropological work, the gift of Oscar Lewis, largely concerning his studies of the culture of poverty.

LEWIS, PRYCE

NY —SAINT LAWRENCE UNIVERSITY, Owen D Young Library, Canton, 13617.

LEWIS, PRYCE (cont.)

Mahlon Peterson, Librn
Holdings: Mss Pix
Notes: The papers of a spy for the Union army during the Civil War who later served as bailiff of Old Capitol Prison for the Union Army. Approx 200 items.

LEWIS, ROSS

WI —MILWAUKEE PUBLIC LIBRARY, 814 W Wisconsin Ave, Milwaukee, 53233. Donald J Sager, City Librn
Notes: Ross Lewis, Pulitzer Prize winning cartoonist for the *Milwaukee Journal.* Original cartoons.

LEWIS, SINCLAIR

CT —YALE UNIVERSITY, Beinecke Rare Book & Manuscript Library, Osborn Collection, New Haven, 06520. Stephen R Parks, Cur
Holdings: Mss

DC —LIBRARY OF CONGRESS, Rare Book & Special Collections Div, Washington, 20540. William Matheson, Chief
Holdings: Vols 57 Cat Mss
Notes: The Jean Hersholt Collection contains a large number of inscribed editions, 28 inscribed of 32 first or early editions, incl a presentation copy of Lewis' first book, *Hike and the Aeroplane.* Incl contributions to books and periodicals which extend to the author's first appearance; manuscript items consist chiefly of letters written by Lewis to Hersholt.

IN —INDIANA STATE UNIVERSITY, Cunningham Memorial Library, Dept of Rare Books & Special Collections, Terre Haute, 47809. Lawrence J McCrank, Head
Notes: The Debs Collection consists of aprox 7000 pieces of correspondence between Theodore Debs (brother of E V) and other persons, such as Sinclair Lewis, Upton Sinclair, Ethel Barrymore, Emma Goldman, Robert G Ingersoll, Carl Sandburg, Norman Thomas, Sacco and Vanzetti and many others. Many of the letters are from E V Debs to his brother; a good portion of these are from the federal penitentiary at Atlanta. Entire correspondence file has been microfilmed. 750 pamphlets cover all aspects of the labor movement, socialism and radical thought from the 19th century to appprox 1950. A collection ca 200 related books is also housed in the collection. See: J Robert Constantine and Gail Malmgreen, eds, *The Papers of Eugene V Debs, 1834-1945. A Guide to the Microfilm Edition.* NY: Microfilming Corp of America, 1983 (University Microfilms is the new distributer).

MN —UNIVERSITY OF MINNESOTA, O Meredith Wilson Library, 309 19 Ave S, Minneapolis, 55455. Austin J McLean, Chief, Special Collections
Holdings: Vols 425 Cat Mss Pix
Notes: Includes inscribed copies of all novels of Lewis, ephemera, materials about him, and translations of his works.

MN —SAINT CLOUD STATE UNIVERSITY, Centennial Hall Learning Resources Center, Saint Cloud, 56301. John Berling, Dir
Holdings: Cat Mss Pix Slides Videotapes
Notes: All of Lewis' published materials; also mss, etc. Collection reviewed in *Sinclair Lewis Newsletter,* 1972.

NV —UNIVERSITY OF NEVADA, RENO, University Library, Special Collections Dept, Reno, 89557. Robert E Blesse, Head
Holdings: // Vols (127) Cat Other appearances 130 Cat
Notes: Includes individual works by author in all editions including translations; also prefaces, introductions, published correspondence, appearances in anthologies, periodicals, etc. Bibliographical research collection, part of Modern Authors Collection.

VA —UNIVERSITY OF VIRGINIA, Alderman Library, Clifton Waller Barrett Collection, Charlottesville, 22901. Joan St C Crane, Cur of American Literature Collections
Notes: Papers.

LEWIS, WILLIAM BENNETT, 1904-1975

MA —BOSTON UNIVERSITY, Mugar Memorial Library, Special Collections Dept, 771 Commonwealth Ave, Boston, 02215. Howard B Gotlieb, Dir
Holdings: // Cat Mss Audiotapes
Notes: Mss, correspondence, etc collected in depth; incl publications by or about.

LEWIS, WYNDHAM, 1886-1957

CA —UNIVERSITY OF CALIFORNIA, LOS ANGELES, Research Library, Dept of Special Collections, 405 Hilgard Ave, Los Angeles, 90024. Edward Shreeves, Chairman, Bibliographers Group; David S Zeidberg, Head
Holdings: Vols 75
Notes: Incl 30 letters.

CT —YALE UNIVERSITY, Beinecke Rare Book & Manuscript Library, Osborn Collection, New Haven, 06520. Stephen R Parks, Cur
Holdings: Mss

NV —UNIVERSITY OF NEVADA, RENO, University Library, Special Collections Dept, Reno, 89557. Robert E Blesse, Head
Holdings: // Vols (84) Cat
Notes: Includes individual works by author in all editions including translations; also prefaces, introductions, published correspondence, appearances in anthologies, periodicals, etc. Bibliographical research collection, part of Modern Authors Collection.

NY —HOFSTRA UNIVERSITY, Library, 1000 Fulton Ave, Hempstead, 11550. Charles R Andrews, Dean of Library Services

NY —CORNELL UNIVERSITY LIBRARIES, John M Olin Library, Dept of Rare Books, Ithaca, 14853. Donald D Eddy, Librn
Holdings: Vols 163 Cat Mss
Notes: Incl literary mss documents, correspondence, proofs, graphic material (ca 5000 items). Downs 2040. See *Wyndham Lewis: A Descriptive Catalogue of the Manuscript Material in the Department of Rare Books,* Cornell University Library, comp by Mary F Daniels (Ithaca, 1972).

†TX —UNIVERSITY OF TEXAS LIBRARIES, General Libraries, Humanities Research Center, PO Box 7219, Austin, 78712. John Chalmers, Librn

BC —SIMON FRASER UNIVERSITY, Library, Burnaby, V5A 1S6, Can. Percilla Groves, Special Collections Librn
Holdings: Cat Mss
Notes: Incl a collection of 75 letters from Ezra Pound to Agnes Bedford and 5 letters to Wyndham Lewis, 1950-1959, plus 46 letters to Denis Goacher.

BC —UNIVERSITY OF VICTORIA, McPherson Library, Victoria, V8W 3H5, Can.
Notes: Writer, painter. Mss, papers.

LEWIS AND CLARK EXPEDITION

DC —LIBRARY OF CONGRESS, Geography and Map Division, Washington, 20540. John A Wolter, Chief
Notes: Maps thought to have belonged to William Clark.

IL —NEWBERRY LIBRARY, 60 W Walton St, Chicago, 60610. Diana Haskell, Cur of Modern Mss
Holdings: Cat Mss

†OR —LEWIS AND CLARK COLLEGE, Library, 615 SW Palatine Hill Rd, Portland, 97219.
Notes: Lewis and Clark Expedition Collection.

PA —AMERICAN PHILOSOPHICAL SOCIETY, Library, 105 S Fifth St, Philadelphia, 19106. Edward C Carter II, Librn
Holdings: Cat Mss Maps
Notes: Collection (as it was in 1970) is incl in *Catalog of Books in the American Philosophical Society Library* (Westport, Conn: Greenwood Publishing Corp, 1970). Both of these are reproductions of APS Library catalog cards, incl author, subject, and title entries.

†WA —WASHINGTON STATE UNIVERSITY, Library, Manuscripts, Archives & Special Collections, Pullman, 99164. John F Guido, Head
Holdings: Cat Mss Maps Pix
Notes: The Carl Parcher Russell papers, a vast resource (24,916 items; 45 linear feet) on American Indian and Western pioneer activities and artifacts. Much on the fur trade; pioneer life; mountain men and trapping; wildlife; primitive life in detail. Also the National Park Service, parks, monuments, etc. Described in *Carl Parcher Russell: An Indexed Register of His Scholarly and Professional Papers, 1920-1967, in the Washington State University* Library (Pullman, 1970), 149 pp.

LEWISOHN, EDNA MANLEY

SC —COLLEGE OF CHARLESTON LIBRARY, Special Collections Dept, Charleston, 29401.
Notes: Papers, 1939-1980. Incl materials from Ludwig Lewisohn and his former wife, Edna Manley, most of the latter dealing with her life with him. Among the items in the collection are their correspondence (1943-1945), Manley's diary which incl much material regarding Lewisohn's thoughts and experiences, typescript of his published book of translated Rilke poems, sheet music ms of a poem by Lewisohn, and a ten hour recorded interview with Manley regarding her life before, during and after their marriage (with transcript).

LEWISOHN, LUDWIG, 1882-1955

MA —BRANDEIS UNIVERSITY, Goldfarb Library, 415 South St, Waltham, 02154. Bessie Hahn, Dir
Notes: 21 linear ft of first editions and translations, as well as 6 linear ft of ms material consisting of personal letters and galley proofs of some writings. Only the books are cataloged at present and can be found in the Special Collections Catalog.

SC —COLLEGE OF CHARLESTON LIBRARY, Special Collections Dept, Charleston, 29401.
Notes: Correspondence within the Lancelot Minor Harris Papers. Another collection contains materials from Lewisohn and his former wife, Edna Manley, most of the latter dealing with her life with him. Among the items in the collection are their correspondence (1943-1945), Manley's diary which incl much material regarding Lewisohn's thoughts and experiences, typescript of his published book of translated Rilke poems, sheet music ms of a poem by Lewisohn, and a ten hour recorded interview with Manley regarding her life before, during and after their marriage (with transcript).

LEXICOGRAPHY

CA —LOS ANGELES PUBLIC LIBRARY, Literature and Philology Dept, 630 W Fifth St, Los Angeles, 90071. Helene G Mochedlover, Dept Librn
Holdings: Cat
Notes: Foreign Language Collection. Approx 450 languages and dialects are represented, most of which are not included in Foreign Languages Department collection. Emphasis is on breadth of reference collection, which includes dictionaries, grammars, phrase books, and many important enclyclopedias.

CA —STANFORD UNIVERSITY LIBRARIES, Cecil H Green Library, Stanford, 94305. Peter R Frank, Cur, CDP-Germanic Collection
Notes: Library of Prof Rudolf Hildebran, Leipzig, the first large collection acquired by Stanford in 1895/1896, laid the foundation for an extensive German collection. Hildebrand's library is especially strong in German and Austrian philology (rare dictionaries, etc.), but also in literary works.

LEXICOGRAPHY (cont.)

The collection is now especially strong for the period of the Reformation and Baroque, up to the present, with many rare editions, journals, almanacs, and the like. Sizable collections of women's working class and popular literature, dissertations and Schulschriften. Rare and valuable items in the Stanford Collection of German, Austrian and Swiss Culture, Special Collections. Catalog: *Katalog der Bibliothek des Herrn Prof Dr Rudolf Hildebrand.* Description: *The German Area Collection: A Stanford* Tradition by Peter R Frank.

DC —GEORGETOWN UNIVERSITY, Library, Special Collections Div, 37 & O Sts NW, Washington, 20057. George M Barringer, Special Collections Librn; Nicholas B Sheetz, Mss Librn
Holdings: Vols 1000 Uncat Mss
Notes: The collection and data base, including the volumes from which citations were drawn, for the *American Heritage School Dictionary*; also included are the computer-generated citations and frequency studies on tape and in printout form.

IN —INDIANA UNIVERSITY, Lilly Library, Seventh St, Bloomington, 47405. William R Cagle, Librn
Holdings: Mss
Notes: Papers of lexicographer and philologist Eric Partridge, 1894-1979. Correspondence, research materials for publications, and mss of writings. 6757 items.

IN —INDIANA STATE UNIVERSITY, Cunningham Memorial Library, Dept of Rare Books & Special Collections, Terre Haute, 47809. Lawrence J McCrank, Head
Holdings: Vols 7000
Notes: The Cordell Collection of early English and American dictionaries. Also, the papers of Mitford Mathews, Warren Cordell, Archives of Dictionary Society of North America.

MI —UNIVERSITY OF MICHIGAN, Library, Dept of Rare Books & Special Collections, Ann Arbor, 48109. Robert J Starring, Head
Holdings: Cat
Notes: Largely 18th and 19th century although earlier works also are represented. Substantial runs of Johnson's and Webster's dictionaries.

NY —NEW YORK PUBLIC LIBRARY, Mid-Manhattan Library, Literature and Language Dept, 455 Fifth Ave, New York, 10016. Eric Steele, Sr Principal Librn
Holdings: Vols (10,000) Cat Phonorecords Microforms
Budget: ($10,000)
Notes: Broad coverage for the study of over 100 languages and dialects, materials on most areas of theoretical and applied linguistics, incl philology, speech and the teaching of languages, especially of English s a second language. Extensive runs of major journals. Records and cassettes aid in the learning of 40 languages, in addition to English. Strong in materials on the history of American and English language and pronunciation. In Old, Middle and Early Modern English, Department has a representative collection of primary and secondary source materials in microfiche.

WI —UNIVERSITY OF WISCONSIN, MADISON, Seminary of Medieval Spanish Studies, 1130 Van Hise Hall, Madison, 53706. Lloyd A Kasten, Emeritus Prof of Spanish
Holdings: Vols (7500) // Cat Mss Pix Slides Microforms
Notes: Medieval materials and subjects. 100 reels of microfilm, 2500 pamphlets and reprints. Incl a 300-volume collection on 13th century Spanish law. Other emphases: language studies (incl 616,247 vocabulary cards), dictionaries, bibliographies, periodicals. The nucleus of the collection is photostats of the mss of unpublished works of Alfonso X. Restricted circulation.

BC —VANCOUVER PUBLIC LIBRARY, Language & Literature Div, 750 Burrard St, Vancouver, V6Z 1X5, Can. B Kinnear, Head
Notes: A good general collection of language dictionaries supplemented by clippings and a word file compiled by the staff. Also a collection of language learning materials.

†ON —UNIVERSITY OF WESTERN ONTARIO, School of Library and Information Science, Special Collections Room, London, N6A 5B9, Can.
Notes: Archive of lexicographical materials of the Committee on Lexicography of the Modern Language Association. Incl lexicographical slips for *The United States Air Force Dictionary* and The *Second Aerospace Glossary,* by Woodford Heflin. 13 cartons of slips.

LEXICOGRAPHY, MUSICAL

DC —LIBRARY OF CONGRESS, Music Division, Washington, 20540.
Notes: Papers, incl correspondence and mss of Nicolas Slonimsky, composer and musical lexicographer.

LEXINGTON, KENTUCKY—IMPRINTS

KY —UNIVERSITY OF KENTUCKY, Margaret I King Library, Dept of Special Collections, Lexington, 40506. William Marshall, Head
Holdings: Cat Mss Pix Slides Microforms
Notes: Comprehensive collection of books on typography and history of printing; fine press books (incl Lexington imprints); ms books and illumination, paleography; mss of W A Dwiggins (gift of C H Griffith); James Anderson papers; bookbinding; 2 hand-presses and working collection for summer semimnars in hand-press printing; bookplates, bookmarks, book jackets, etc.

LEYDA, JAY, 1910-

CA —UNIVERSITY OF CALIFORNIA, LOS ANGELES, Research Library, Dept of Special Collections, 405 Hilgard Ave, Los Angeles, 90024. Edward Shreeves, Chairman, Bibliographers Group; David S Zeidberg, Head
Notes: 12 linear feet of correspondence, typescripts, galley proofs, etc. Mr Leyda's permission is required to consult the material.

LIBERAL FEDERATION OF CANADA

BC —UNIVERSITY OF VICTORIA, McPherson Library, Victoria, V8W 3H5, Can.
Notes: Incl transcripts: 10 cm, November 21, 22 and 23, 1969; background papers prepared for the Harrison Liberal Conference.

LIBERAL JUDAISM see Reform Judaism

LIBERATION NEWS SERVICE

MA —AMHERST COLLEGE, Library, Amherst, 01002. John Lancaster, Special Collections Librn
Notes: The files of the Liberation News Service from the basis of the collection; ca 2000 titles uncat.

PA —TEMPLE UNIVERSITY LIBRARIES, Special Collections Dept, Contemporary Culture Collection, Philadelphia, 19122. Patricia J Case, Cur

LIBERIA

DC —GEORGETOWN UNIVERSITY, Library, Special Collections Div, 37 & O Sts NW, Washington, 20057. George M Barringer, Special Collections Librn; Nicholas B Sheetz, Mss Librn
Holdings: Mss Pix
Notes: Correspondence, documents, journals, diaries, financial accounts, mss, photographs, and art work comprising the personal and professional papers of McCeney Werlich, diplomat, as well as those of his wife, Gladys Hinckley Werlich; Thomas Hinckley, and Robert O'Donnel Hinckley, both diplomats; papers of Eleanor O'Donnell Hinckley, mother of Gladys Werlich, and her husband Robert Hinckley, noted portrait painter. The papers incl: State Department correspondence and other material relating to McCeney Werlich's posts in Latvia (1926-1927), Poland (1927-1931), Costa Rica (1931-1932), Liberia (1932-1933), and France (1934-1936); correspondence from Robert O'Donnell Hinckley from his travels in the Orient, 1919; correspondence from Thomas Hinckley, incl accounts of the Austro-Hungarian empire, 1914-1915; as well as numerous journalsand diaries kept by Gladys Werlich regarding her extensive travels and variety of experiences.

DC —HOWARD UNIVERSITY, Moorland-Spingarn Research Center, 500 Howard Place NW, Washington, 20059. Clifford L Muse, Jr, Acting Dir

LIBERIAN ECONOMIC SURVEY

IL —NORTHWESTERN UNIVERSITY, Melville J Herskovits Library of African Studies, Evanston, 60201. Hans E Panofsky, Cur
Holdings: Vols (85,000) Mss
Budget: ($70,000)
See also entry under Africa.

LIBERTARIAN LITERATURE

MA —HARVARD UNIVERSITY LIBRARY, Cambridge, 02138.
Holdings: Vols Cat
Notes: Incl the Joseph Ishill Collection, covering socialism, communism, anarchism, syndicalism, democracy, free trade, free love, free thought, taxation, agriculture, etc.

LIBERTY BONDS see War Bonds

LIBERTY OF RELIGION see Religious Liberty

LIBERTY OF SPEECH see Free Speech

LIBERTY OF THE PRESS

CA —UNIVERSITY OF CALIFORNIA, LOS ANGELES, Research Library, Social Sciences Collection, 405 Hilgard Ave, Los Angeles, 90024. Edward Shreeves, Chairman, Bibliographers Group; Oscar L Sims, Social Sciences Bibliographer
Notes: A collection of over 200 underground newspapers on 26 reels of microfilm. Among the titles included are: *The Tribe, The Berkeley Barb, New York Roach, Rat,* and *Win.*

IN —INDIANA UNIVERSITY, Lilly Library, Seventh St, Bloomington, 47405. William R Cagle, Librn
Holdings: Vols (1000) // Cat Mss
Notes: 1000 vols of contemporary printings (largely British) on Anglo-American relations leading to the American Revolution.

MD —UNIVERSITY OF MARYLAND, Library, East Asia Collection, College Park, 20742. Frank Joseph Shulman, Curator and Head
Holdings: Vols (90,000) // Mss
Notes: Japanese books, newspapers, periodicals, etc, of the Allied Occupation period (1945-1952), including files of censored publications. Books number 40,000; periodical titles, 13,000; newspaper titles, ca 16,500. The special collection relating to the Occupation period is supplemented by a growing collection (now ca 50,000 vols) of Chinese, Japanese, and Korean publications which form the basis of the University's general collection in East Asian language materials.

RI —BROWN UNIVERSITY, John Hay Library, 20 Prospect St, Providence, 02912. Mark N Brown, Cur Mss
Holdings: // Mss
Notes: The Zechariah Chaffee, Jr, mss, 400 papers relating to the Commission on the Freedom of the Press, 1943 to 1947. Incl correspondence, notes, memoranda, reports, clippings, reviews, and articles. Also 450 pieces of correspondence, 1915-1957, relating to Brown University.

LIBMAN, EMANUEL, M.D., 1872-1946

MD —NATIONAL LIBRARY OF MEDICINE, 8600 Rockville Pike, Bethesda,

LIBMAN, EMANUEL, M.D., 1872-1946 (cont.)

20209. Harold M Schoolinam, Actg Dir
Budget: ($46,400)
Notes: Papers.

LIBRARIANS

CT —LEE ASH, (personal collection), 66 Humiston Dr, Bethany, 06525.
Holdings: Cat Mss Pix
Notes: Librarian, teacher, translator, radical. Anything by or about Frederick A Blossom or his colleagues.

DC —LIBRARY OF CONGRESS, Manuscript Division, Washington, 20540. John C Broderick, Chief
Notes: Papers of Verner Warren Clapp, Chief Asst Librn of Congress, President of the Council on Library Resources, etc. Also the papers of Daniel J Boorstein.

IL —AMERICAN LIBRARY ASSOCIATION, Headquarters Library, 50 E Huron St, Chicago, 60611. Joel M Lee, Librn
Holdings: Vols (21,000) Cat Audiotapes Videotapes Microforms
Budget: ($12,000)
Notes: Incl 200 rolls of microfilm, 1400 microfiche, 17 file drawers of recent ALA publications, and 800 current periodicals; emphasis on current developments in the field. Collections incl such specialized material as building programs, plans, pictures, and slides; library bulletins and some annual reports; library staff and procedures manuals; library surveys; manuals of library instruction; periodicals of state, national, and foreign library associations. In the ALA archives at the University of Illinois (Urbana) are over 650 cubic feet of material, much of which has been processed. Guide to the archives is available from ALA Publishing. The Library's periodical holdings appear in *Union List of Serial Holdings in Illinois Special Libraries* (Chicago: Illinois Regional Library Council, 1977).

IL —UNIVERSITY OF ILLINOIS, URBANA/CHAMPAIGN, Library, University Archives, 19 Library, 1408 W Gregory Drive, Urbana, 61801. Maynard Brichford, University Archivist
Holdings: Cat Mss Pix
Notes: Ms archives of the American Library Association. Subjects incl librarians, library science, library associations. Control cards, ADP, and supplementary finding aids for intellectual control of the archives.

LA —TULANE UNIVERSITY, Howard-Tilton Memorial Library, Special Collections Div, 7001 Freret St, New Orleans, 70118. Wilbur E Meneray, Librn
Holdings: Cat Mss
Notes: Correspondence to and from William Beer as librarian of the Howard Library, New Orleans.

NY —COLUMBIA UNIVERSITY LIBRARIES, Rare Book & Manuscript Library, 801 Butler Library, 535 W 114 St, New York, 10027. Kenneth A Lohf, Librn
Holdings: Mss
Notes: Minutes and records of The Archons of Colophon, an elected social-professional group of administrative librarians of the Greater New York area. See the 50-year history, *The Archons of Colophon, 1909-1917 and 1926-1969:* Much and Little Changed," by Lee Ash, New York, 1969 (54 pp, 500 copies). Also, the Jack Dalton papers (12,000 items) incl documents of his activities in American and international librarianship, before and after his deanship of the Columbia University School of Library Service. The Melvil Dewey papers (53,700 items); the Henry E Bliss papers (1300 items); the Estelle Brodman papers (8250 items); the Ernest J Reece papers (1500 items); the Maurice F Tauber papers (74,300 items); and the Charles C Williamson papers (10,000 items). Restricted use.

OH —KENT STATE UNIVERSITY, School of Library Science Library, Kent, 44242. Robert Rogers, Dir
Notes: Kent State Library School has a student scholarship program for Hungarian candidates. (*Leads*, Winter 1979).

PA —TEMPLE UNIVERSITY LIBRARIES, Special Collections Dept, Conwellana-Templana Collection, 13 & Berks St, Philadelphia, 19122. Miriam I Crawford, Cur
Holdings: Vols 22 Cat // Mss Pix
Notes: Papers of Walter Hausdorfer, librarian of the Columbia University School of Business, 1930-46 and Temple University from 1946-61, professor of bibliography from 1961-63, and a noted linguist and authority on rare books and mss.

RI —BROWN UNIVERSITY, John Hay Library, 20 Prospect St, Providence, 02912. Mark N Brown, Cur Mss
Holdings: // Mss
Notes: Papers of Harry Lyman Koopman, writer, librarian, and Professor of Bibliography at Brown University. Incl mss and typescripts of prose and poetry for the period 1877 to 1937, account books, journals, essays, speeches, articles, translations, a novel, short stories, poetry, articles written for *The Providence Journal* 1926-1937, and correspondence by Koopman as Librarian. 30,000 items.

TN —VANDERBILT UNIVERSITY, Medical Center Library, Nashville, 37232. Mary H Teloh, Special Collections Librn
Holdings: Cat Mss Pix
Notes: Personal papers of Eileen Roach Cunningham, leader in the field of medical librarianship. Material covers the period 1925-1965. Collection contains correspondence, speeches, notes, travel diaries and photographs. 10 linear ft of mss.

LIBRARIANSHIP see Library Science

LIBRARIES

CO —BIBLIOGRAPHICAL CENTER FOR RESEARCH, Rocky Mountain Region, Inc, Library, 1777 S Bellaire, Suite G 150, Denver, 80222. J Segal, Exec Dir
Holdings: Cat
Notes: Library automation, data bases, information retrieval, union catalogs, etc.

IL —AMERICAN LIBRARY ASSOCIATION, Headquarters Library, 50 E Huron St, Chicago, 60611. Joel M Lee, Librn
Holdings: Vols (21,000) Cat Audiotapes Videotapes Microforms
Budget: ($12,000)
Notes: Incl 200 rolls of microfilm, 1400 microfiche, 17 file drawers of recent ALA publications, and 800 current periodicals; emphasis on current developments in the field. Collections incl such specialized material as building programs, plans, pictures, and slides; library bulletins and some annual reports; library staff and procedures manuals; library surveys; manuals of library instruction; periodicals of state, national, and foreign library associations. In the ALA archives at the University of Illinois (Urbana) are over 650 cubic feet of material, much of which has been processed. Guide to the archives is available from ALA Publishing. The Library's periodical holdings appear in *Union List of Serial Holdings in Illinois Special Libraries* (Chicago: Illinois Regional Library Council, 1977).

MN —SAINT JOHN'S ABBEY & UNIVERSITY, Hill Monastic Manuscript Library, Collegeville, 56321. Julian G Plante, Dir
Notes: Films of 61,000 mss. The total number of codices (bound handwritten mss) represents the holdings of several hundred libraries in Europe and elsewhere: Austria, Spain, Malta, Ethiopia, West Germany, Portugal, England, but also with concentrations of holdings from Italy, Hungary, Poland, Great Britain, Belgium, Yugoslavia, France, Switzerland and the Netherlands, and Vatican City. Also incl 70, 000 exposures.

†NY —COLUMBIA UNIVERSITY LIBRARIES, Butler Library, Rare Book and Manuscript Library, 535 W 114 St, New York, 10027.
Notes: The papers of Dr Estelle Brodman, incl letters, mss, reports, and conference papers.

TX —TEXAS STATE LIBRARY, Library Development Division, Library Science Collection, PO Box 12927, 1201 Brazos, Austin, 78711. Anne Ramos, Librn
Holdings: Vols (5837) Cat Audiotapes Videotapes VF
Budget: ($47,851)

LIBRARIES—ADMINISTRATION see Library Science

LIBRARIES—ANNUAL REPORTS

†ON —UNIVERSITY OF WESTERN ONTARIO, School of Library and Information Science, Special Collections Room, London, N6A 5B9, Can.
Holdings: Vols 5000
Notes: A particular strength is the 7500 annual reports and catalogs of Northeastern US libraries purchased on the dispersal of the Essex Institute Library. Current emphasis is on Canadian library reports.

LIBRARIES—AUTOMATION

DC —LIBRARY OF CONGRESS, Manuscript Division, Washington, 20540. John C Broderick, Chief
Notes: Papers of Verner Warren Clapp, Chief Asst Librn of Congress, President of the Council on Library Resources, etc.

†PA —UNIVERSITY OF PITTSBURGH, Graduate School of Library & Information Sciences Library, L I S Bldg, Third Fl, Pittsburgh, 15260. Jean Kindlin, Librn
Notes: Extensive collection on the historical development of school libraries, media services, and evaluation of materials for use in all types of schools. Incl 54,800 vols, 7524 bound periodicals, 630 periodical subscriptions.

LIBRARIES—CATALOGS see Library Catalogs

LIBRARIES—CHILDREN'S ROOM see Libraries, Children's

LIBRARIES—HISTORY

CA —UNIVERSITY OF CALIFORNIA, BERKELEY, Humanities-Social Sciences Libraries, Library School Library, 2 South Hall, Berkeley, 94720. Virginia Pratt, Head
Holdings: Vols (41,500) Cat Microforms
Notes: Research collection with special strengths in general library science; history of libraries; history of printing and book arts, and publishing; information systems and services; history, criticism, and bibliography of children's literature. The collections in printing and the book arts are complemented by significant holdings both in the Main Library and in the Bancroft Library. Incl collection of 5000 pamphlets.

CA —STANFORD UNIVERSITY LIBRARIES, Cecil H Green Library, Stanford, 94305. Peter R Frank, Cur, CDP-Germanic Collection
Notes: An emphasis in the Rare Book Collection. Also a sizable collection of works on the Austrian booktrade and libraries.

CT —LEE ASH, (personal collection), 66 Humiston Dr, Bethany, 06525.
Holdings: Mss Maps Pix

IL —CHICAGO PUBLIC LIBRARY, Special Collections Div, Cultural Center, 78 E Washington St, Chicago, 60602. Laura Linard, Cur
Holdings: Cat
Notes: Since Thomas Hughes, MP and author of *Tom Brown's Schooldays,* was instrumental in the founding of The Chicago Public Library in 1871, the Library has begun to collect him in depth. The collection is small at present but several bookdealers in the US and Great Britain are searching for Hughes material and we purchase nearly 90 per cent of what is quoted. The Hughes Collection supplements the English Book Donation of 1871, originally about 7000 volumes (now only 500 are preserved), sponsored by Hughes. The Donation comprises primarily books donated by Oxford University and bears Oxford's gift-stamp and bookplate; the other extant books

LIBRARIES—HISTORY (cont.)

are late editions of Victorian literary and historical writers.

IL —NEWBERRY LIBRARY, 60 W Walton St, Chicago, 60610. Diana Haskell, Cur of Modern Mss
Holdings: Cat
Notes: Incl early learned periodicals, bio-bibliographies, encyclopedias. Strong in history of universities and libraries.

MO —SAINT LOUIS PUBLIC LIBRARY, Gardner Rare Book Room, 1301 Olive St, Saint Louis, 63103. Julanne M Good, Supervisor; Martha Riley, Rare Books Librn
Holdings: Uncat Mss Pix Slides Videotapes
Notes: St Louis Public Library Archives, 1865 to present incl 2000 photographs of buildings, people, events; annual reports, publications, staff research reports, statistics, day-books, correspondence, minutes of meetings, newspaper clippings, scrapbooks, memorabilia, etc. This collection is only partially processed. Noncirculating.

NY —NEW YORK STATE LIBRARY, State Education Bldg Annex, Washington Ave, Albany, 12224.
Notes: Incl a large collection of American library reports.

NY —BROOKLYN PUBLIC LIBRARY, Brooklyn Collection, Grand Army Plaza, Flatbush Ave and Eastern Parkway, Brooklyn, 11238.
Notes: Over 3000 books, pamphlets, and documents. Strong collections on the six original towns which made up Brooklyn. Also microfilm copies of defunct Brooklyn newspapers as well as recent issues of local community papers. A great treasure is the *Brooklyn Daily Eagle* morgue published from 1841-1955, the morgue's contents dating from 1904. Collection incl more than 25,000 photographs of people, places, and things from 1870 to the present; nearly a quarter of the photographs are by George Brainard and Daniel Berry Austin. Further, there are more than 500 Brooklyn maps from the earliest times. Incl records of the Brooklyn Mercantile Library Association.

NY —GROLIER CLUB OF NEW YORK LIBRARY, 47 E 60 St, New York, 10022. Robert Nikirk, Librn
Notes: Subject strength.

†PA —UNIVERSITY OF PITTSBURGH, Graduate School of Library & Information Sciences Library, L I S Bldg, Third Fl, Pittsburgh, 15260. Jean Kindlin, Librn
Notes: Extensive collection on the historical development of school libraries, media services, and evaluation of materials for use in all types of schools. Incl 54,800 vols, 7524 bound periodicals, 630 periodical subscriptions.

TX —UNIVERSITY OF TEXAS LIBRARIES, General Libraries, Barker Texas History Center, PO Box P, Austin, 78712. Don Carleton, Dir
Notes: Papers, etc, documenting the career of Luther H Evans.

LIBRARIES—ORGANIZATION see Libraries; Library Science

LIBRARIES—PICTURES

CT —MOLESWORTH INSTITUTE, Memorial Library, 143 Hanks Hill Rd, Storrs, 06268. Norman D Stevens, Dir, Cur, and Librn
Holdings: Vols (1000) Uncat Mss
Notes: Incl material relating to the Molesworth Family, books by and about any person named Molesworth as well as original materials upon which the legendary Molesworth Institute was founded. In addition the collections now contain over 20,000 library postcards and approx 375 library commemoratives acquired as part of the Institute's research work.

LIBRARIES—RHODE ISLAND

NY —NEW YORK SOCIETY LIBRARY, 53 E 79 St, New York, 10021. Mark Piel, Librn
Notes: James Hammond Library (circulating library of Newport, RI) of fiction published 1750-1830 incl 920 titles.

RI —PROVIDENCE PUBLIC LIBRARY, 150 Empire St, Providence, 02903. Lance J Bauer, Special Collections Librn
Holdings: Vols 500 // Cat
Notes: The collection contains the original library of the Providence Public Library. It is very strong in 18th and early 19th century belles-lettres and history.

LIBRARIES—SOCIETIES, ETC. see Library Associations

LIBRARIES, CHILDREN'S

TX —FORT WORTH PUBLIC LIBRARY, 300 Taylor St, Fort Worth, 76102. Camille Connor, Children's Materials Coordinator
Holdings: Vols (300) Cat
Budget: $500
Notes: Professional Reference Collection/ Children's Literature. Some 300 titles incl books, pamphlets, bibliographies and photocopied articles used primarily as reference tools or sources by librarians, students of children's literature and library programming for children. Collection is cataloged with access through the general catalog.

UT —HANSEN PLANETARIUM LIBRARY, 15 S State St, Salt Lake City, 84101. Randall A Curtis, Librn; Sharon Johnston, Children's Librn
Holdings: Vols 600 Cat Maps Pix Audiotapes
Budget: $600

LIBRARIES, COLLEGE see Libraries, University and College

LIBRARIES, FOREIGN

†NY —COLUMBIA UNIVERSITY LIBRARIES, Butler Library, Rare Book and Manuscript Library, 535 W 114 St, New York, 10027.
Notes: Files relating to the American Library Association's Special Committee to Aid Italian Libraries' assistance to Italian libraries to help restore books, mss and other library materials after the 1966 floods in Florence.

NY —NEW YORK PUBLIC LIBRARY, Slavonic Div, Fifth Ave & 42 St, New York, 10018. Edward Kasinec, Chief
Holdings: Cat Microforms
Notes: See: New York Public Library, Slavonic Div, *Dictionary Catalog of the Slavonic Collection*, 2nd ed, rev and enl (Boston: G K Hall, 1974), 44 vols; and New York Public Library, *Dictionary Catalog of the Research Libraries* (New York, 1972-).

LIBRARIES, JUNIOR COLLEGE see Libraries, University and College

LIBRARIES, MUSIC see Music Libraries

LIBRARIES, SCHOOL see School Libraries

LIBRARIES, SUBSCRIPTION

MA —BOSTON UNIVERSITY, Mugar Memorial Library, Special Collections Dept, 771 Commonwealth Ave, Boston, 02215. Howard B Gotlieb, Dir
Notes: Records of Boston Mercantile Library Association, 1820-1921.

LIBRARIES, UNIVERSITY AND COLLEGE

IL —AMERICAN LIBRARY ASSOCIATION, Headquarters Library, 50 E Huron St, Chicago, 60611. Joel M Lee, Librn
Holdings: Vols (21,000) Cat Slides Audiotapes Videotapes Microforms
Budget: ($12,000)
Notes: All aspects of libraries and the concerns of librarians.

LIBRARIES AND MOVING PICTURES

NY —EDUCATIONAL FILM LIBRARY ASSOCIATION, Film Reference Library, 45 John St, New York, 10038. Nadine Covert, Exec Dir
Holdings: Vols (2600) Cat Pix 16mm Films Filmstrips
Budget: ($1500)
Notes: Primarily a print collection emphasizing the documentary and educational film areas. but also film as art, animation and independent film in general. Maintain film title file of over 60,000 cards (primarily educational film titles), incl credit information, running time, release date, summary, and distributor. File is a mixture of EFLA evaluations, LC cards, etc. Subject file also separates film flyers by subject or topic. Maintain festivals file (film festivals, educational film festivals, etc); a film library administration file; a filmmakers file (with bio, credits, clippings, program notes); and a vertical file (incl information on grants, distribution, showcases, film activities in the metropolitan area and in major film centers around the country). Membership organization providing telephone, mail and in-person reference. Open to the generalpublic. Do not publish a catalog, but publish annual Film Library Administration bibliography of current or noteworthy reference books for $2.00.

LIBRARY ARCHITECTURE

CO —UNIVERSITY OF DENVER, Center for the Study of Library Architecture, Graduate School of Librarianship and Information Management, University Park, Denver, 80208.
Notes: The personal papers of Keyes D Metcalf, former Harvard University Librarian. The collection represents the most extensive collection on Library buildings in the US and twelve foreign countries built during the 20th century. Incl plans for the IBM Research Center, Stanford University Library, the US Air Force Academy Library, the National Library of Medicine, and the National Library of Australia. Incl 5000 slides.

IL —AMERICAN LIBRARY ASSOCIATION, Headquarters Library, 50 E Huron St, Chicago, 60611. Joel M Lee, Librn
Holdings: Vols (21,000) Cat Pix Slides Microforms
Budget: ($12,000)
Notes: Incl pictures, slides and plans of recently built public, college and university, branch, school, state, special and remodeled libraries, gathered by ALA Library Administration and Management Association.

LIBRARY ASSOCIATIONS

IL —AMERICAN LIBRARY ASSOCIATION, Headquarters Library, 50 E Huron St, Chicago, 60611. Joel M Lee, Librn
Holdings: Vols (21,000) Cat Audiotapes Videotapes Microforms
Budget: ($12,000)
Notes: Incl 200 rolls of microfilm, 1400 microfiche, 17 file drawers of recent ALA publications, and 800 current periodicals; emphasis on current developments in the field. Collections incl such specialized material as building programs, plans, pictures, and slides; library bulletins and some annual reports; library staff and procedures manuals; library surveys; manuals of library instruction; periodicals of state, national, and foreign library associations. In the ALA archives at the University of Illinois (Urbana) are over 650 cubic feet of material, much of which has been processed. Guide to the archives is available from ALA Publishing. The Library's periodical holdings appear in *Union List of Serial Holdings in Illinois Special Libraries* (Chicago: Illinois Regional Library Council, 1977).

IL —UNIVERSITY OF ILLINOIS, URBANA/CHAMPAIGN, Library, University Archives, 19 Library, 1408 W

LIBRARY ASSOCIATIONS (cont.)

Gregory Drive, Urbana, 61801. Maynard Brichford, University Archivist
Holdings: Cat Mss Pix
Notes: Ms archives of the American Library Association. Subjects incl librarians, library science, library associations. Control cards, ADP, and supplementary finding aids for intellectual control of the archives.

ON —NATIONAL LIBRARY OF CANADA, 395 Wellington St, Ottawa, K1A 0N4, Can. Andre Preibish, Dir
Notes: Includes 32 linear feet of vertical file materials. Covers all Canadian and selected foreign and international library associations.

LIBRARY BUILDINGS see Library Architecture

LIBRARY BUREAU, INC.

DE —HAGLEY MUSEUM AND LIBRARY, Eleutherian Mills-Hagley Foundation Inc, PO Box 3630, Greenville, 19807. Richmond D Williams, Dir; Heddy A Richter, Imprints Librn
Notes: Sperry Univac has deposited a large amount of historical records. Approximately 2000 cubic feet of records, files and photographs that document the invention and development of computers and the rapid growth of the industry were officially released by Sperry Corporation to the Library. The collection includes technical and legal documents relating to the ENIAC and UNIVAC computers as well as records of the founding of the E Remington Typewriter Company and other predecessor companies of the Sperry organization, such as The Library Bureau, Kardex, Rodic Rubber and the Powers Accounting Machinery Company. Thus our knowledge of the Sperry predecessors dates back in this collection to 1902.

LIBRARY CATALOGS

IL —NEWBERRY LIBRARY, 60 W Walton St, Chicago, 60610. Diana Haskell, Cur of Modern Mss
Holdings: Cat Mss
Notes: Several hundred catalogs, espec private library catalogs. The collection was heavily used in the preparation of Archer Taylor's *Book Catalogues: Their Varieties, Subjects, and Uses* (Newberry).

ON —UNIVERSITY OF WESTERN ONTARIO, Schoool of Library and Information Science, Library, London, N6G 1H1, Can. Victoria Ripley, Librn
Holdings: Vols (50,000)
Notes: Auction and antiquarian booksellers' catalogs from Canadian, American and European firms, some dating back to the 18th century. A special strength is 19th and early 20th century American booksellers' catalogs, recently augmented by a collection of pre-1920 catalogs formed by the late H O Teisberg. Current emphasis is on Canadian catalogs.

LIBRARY CATALOGS—UNION CATALOGS see Catalogs, Union

LIBRARY ECONOMY see Library Science

LIBRARY EQUIPMENT, FURNITURE, AND SUPPLIES

DE —HAGLEY MUSEUM AND LIBRARY, Eleutherian Mills-Hagley Foundation Inc, PO Box 3630, Greenville, 19807. Richmond D Williams, Dir; Heddy A Richter, Imprints Librn

IL —AMERICAN LIBRARY ASSOCIATION, Headquarters Library, 50 E Huron St, Chicago, 60611. Joel M Lee, Librn
Holdings: Vols (21,000) Cat Slides Audiotapes Videotapes Microforms
Budget: ($12,000)
Notes: All aspects of libraries and the concerns of librarians.

LIBRARY OF CONGRESS

DC —LIBRARY OF CONGRESS, Manuscript Division, Washington, 20540. John C Broderick, Chief
Notes: Papers of Verner Warren Clapp, Chief Asst Librn of Congress, President of the Council on Library Resources, etc. Also, the papers of Daniel J Boorstein.

TX —UNIVERSITY OF TEXAS LIBRARIES, General Libraries, Barker Texas History Center, PO Box P, Austin, 78712. Don Carleton, Dir
Notes: Papers, etc, documenting the career of Luther H Evans.

LIBRARY OF LIVING PHILOSOPHERS

†IL —SOUTHERN ILLINOIS UNIVERSITY, CARBONDALE, Library, Special Collections Dept, Carbondale, 62901.
Notes: Archives of the Library of Living Philosophers, a publishing project founded by Paul Arthur Schilpp in 1938 to provide a forum for contemporary philosophers to reply to their critics. Incl correspondence from John Dewey, George Santayana, Alfred North Whitehead, G E Moore, and Albert Einstein.

LIBRARY OF THE PRESS

NY —GRADUATE CENTER OF THE CITY UNIVERSITY OF NEW YORK, William H and Gwynne K Crouse Library for Publishing Arts, 33 W 42 St, New York, 10036. Alfred H Lane, Dir
Notes: Recently established and still growing, but intended to become the authoritative source of materials in the field, of particular value in research about the publishing industry. Open to staff members of publishing houses, students, scholars, authors, printers, and booksellers. Primarily 20th century materials, and particularly useful for research on technical, financial, and historical matters. Much on the history of individual houses, economics of authorship; marketing and distribution of books; etc.

LIBRARY REPORTS

IL —AMERICAN LIBRARY ASSOCIATION, Headquarters Library, 50 E Huron St, Chicago, 60611. Joel M Lee, Librn
Holdings: Vols (21,000) Cat Slides Audiotapes Videotapes Microforms
Budget: ($12,000)
Notes: All aspects of libraries and the concerns of librarians.

PA —UNIVERSITY OF PITTSBURGH, Graduate School of Library & Information Sciences, International Library Information Center, 135 N Bellefield Ave, Pittsburgh, 15260. Richard Krzys, Dir
Holdings: Cat
Notes: Extensive collection of primary source material on all aspects of librarianship in 124 countries. Emphasis on Latin American, Asian and African countries.

LIBRARY RESEARCH see Library Science—Research

LIBRARY SCIENCE

CA —UNIVERSITY OF CALIFORNIA, BERKELEY, Humanities-Social Sciences Libraries, Library School Library, 2 South Hall, Berkeley, 94720. Virginia Pratt, Head
Holdings: Vols (41,500) Cat Microforms
Notes: Research collection with special strengths in general library science; history of libraries; history of printing and book arts, and publishing; information systems and services; history, criticism, and bibliography of children's literature. The collections in printing and the book arts are complemented by significant holdings both in the Main Library and in the Bancroft Library. Incl collection of 5000 pamphlets.

CO —UNIVERSITY OF DENVER, Center for the Study of Library Architecture, Graduate School of Librarianship and Information Management, University Park, Denver, 80208.
Notes: The personal papers of Keyes D Metcalf, former Harvard University Librarian. The collection represents the most extensive collection on Library buildings in the US and twelve foreign countries built during the 20th century. Incl plans for the IBM Research Center, Stanford University Library, the US Air Force Academy Library, the National Library of Medicine, and the National Library of Australia. Incl 5000 slides.

CT —LEE ASH, (personal collection), 66 Humiston Dr, Bethany, 06525.
Holdings: Cat Mss Pix

DC —CATHOLIC UNIVERSITY OF AMERICA, Library and Information Science Library, Marist Hall 132, 620 Michigan Ave NE, Washington, 20064. Patsy Haley Stann, Head; Lisa Navidi, Asst Head
Holdings: Vols 9000 Cat Periodicals Microfilm
Notes: Materials on Library and Information Science, history of books, information retrieval, automation, book selection, cataloging. Historical children's collection; depository for the International Federation for Documentation (FID).

DC —LIBRARY OF CONGRESS, Manuscript Division, Washington, 20540. John C Broderick, Chief
Notes: Papers of Verner Warren Clapp, Chief Asst Librn of Congress, President of the Council on Library Resources, etc.

IL —AMERICAN LIBRARY ASSOCIATION, Headquarters Library, 50 E Huron St, Chicago, 60611. Joel M Lee, Librn
Holdings: Vols (21,000) Cat Slides Audiotapes Videotapes Microforms
Budget: ($12,000)
Notes: Incl 200 rolls of microfilm, 1400 microfiche, 17 file drawers of recent ALA publications, and 800 current periodicals; emphasis on current developments in the field. Collections incl such specialized material as building programs, plans, pictures, and slides; library bulletins and some annual reports; library staff and procedures manuals; library surveys; manuals of library instruction; periodicals of state, national, and foreign library associations. In the ALA archives at the University of Illinois (Urbana) are over 650 cubic feet of material, much of which has been processed. Guide to the archives is available from ALA Publishing. The Library's periodical holdings appear in *Union List of Serial Holdings in Illinois Special Libraries* (Chicago: Illinois Regional Library Council, 1977).

IL —UNIVERSITY OF ILLINOIS, URBANA/CHAMPAIGN, Library, University Archives, 19 Library, 1408 W Gregory Drive, Urbana, 61801. Maynard Brichford, University Archivist
Holdings: Cat Mss Pix
Notes: Ms archives of the American Library Association. Subjects incl librarians, library science, library associations. Control cards, ADP, and supplementary finding aids for intellectual control of the archives.

IN —INDIANA UNIVERSITY, Graduate School Library, Bloomington, 47401. Patricia Steele, Librn
Holdings: Vols (13,000) Cat Pix Slides Phonorecords Audiotapes 16mm Films Filmstrips Microforms
Budget:

IN —INDIANA STATE LIBRARY, Extension Div, 140 Senate Ave, Indianapolis, 46204. Laura G Johnson, Head
Holdings: Vols 10,000 Cat Microforms

IN —BALL STATE UNIVERSITY, Library Science Library, Muncie, 47306. Audrey W Collins, Librn
Holdings: Vols 13,769 Cat Microforms

MA —MASSACHUSETTS BOARD OF LIBRARY COMMISSIONERS, Professional Library, 648 Beacon St, Boston, 02215. Brian Donoghue, Ref Asst
Holdings: Vols (16,500) Cat Audiotapes Videotapes Microforms
Budget: ($15,000)
Notes: The library science emphasis does not

LIBRARY SCIENCE (cont.)

stress the history of libraries. The collection embraces all other aspects of library and information science with an emphasis on public libraries, library administration and library technology. Subscriptions to 300 library science periodicals. Microforms: approx 1000 microfiche titles; the ERIC/IR Collection 1968-Date. Vertical files: approx 100 drawers. Dialog and BRS search service provided.

MA —SIMMONS COLLEGE, Beatley Library, 300 The Fenway, Boston, 02115. Linda Watkins, Library Science Librn
Holdings: Vols 22,827 Cat Microforms VF

MI —UNIVERSITY OF MICHIGAN, Library Science Library, 320 Harlan-Hatcher Graduate Library, Ann Arbor, 48109. James E Crooks, Librn
Holdings: Vols 39,175 Cat Microforms
Budget: $22,687

MI —WAYNE STATE UNIVERSITY, Walter P Reuther Library, Archives of Labor & Urban Affairs, Detroit, 48202. Philip Mason, Dir
Holdings: Vols 2000 Journals Pamphlets
Notes: Problems of all types of urban libraries and other urban problems. Reference material in Archives on US and Canada.

MN —OFFICE OF LIBRARY DEVELOPMENT AND SERVICES, 440 Capitol Square, 550 Cedar St, Saint Paul, 55101. Darlene M Arnold, Sr Librn
Holdings: Vols 12,000 Cat Slides Phonorecords Audiotapes Videotapes 16mm Films Filmstrips Microforms

NY —PRATT INSTITUTE, Library Science Library, 200 Willoughby Ave, Brooklyn, 11205. Margot Karp, Library Science Librn
Holdings: Vols (10,000) Cat Microforms
Budget: ($15,000)
Notes: Separate catalog.

NY —C W POST CENTER OF LONG ISLAND UNIVERSITY, B Davis Schwartz Memorial Library, Greenvale, 11548. Manju Prasad-Rao, Media Librn
Holdings: Vols 8000 Cat Microforms

NY —COLUMBIA UNIVERSITY LIBRARIES, Rare Book & Manuscript Library, 801 Butler Library, 535 W 114 St, New York, 10027. Kenneth A Lohf, Librn
Holdings: Mss
Notes: The Jack Dalton papers (12,000 items) incl documents of his activities in American and international librarianship, before and after his deanship of the Columbia University School of Library Service. Also, American Library Association, Board of Education for Librarianship (4200 items), International Relations Committee (9000 items), Conference of Eastern College Librarians (2400 items), NY Technical Services Librarians (4000 items), NY Public Library School papers (10,000 items). Restricted use.

NY —ERIC CLEARINGHOUSE ON INFORMATION RESOURCES, Syracuse University, School of Education, Syracuse, 13210. Donald P Ely, Dir; Pamela McLaughlin, User Services Coordinator
Holdings: Microforms
Notes: As of 1977, the ERIC Clearinghouse on Information Resources transferred from Stanford University to Syracuse University. Scope note cites: management operation and use of libraries; technology to improve their operation and the education, training and professional activities of librarians and information specialists; instructional developments; educational techniques involved in computer assisted and managed instruction, systems analysis and programmed instruction; the delivery of instruction via audiovisual teaching materials and technologies such as television, radio, computers, and films; and technology in society adaptable to education, incl cable television, communication satellites, microforms and public television.

OH —CASE WESTERN RESERVE UNIVERSITY, M A Baxter School of Information and Library Science, 10900 Euclid Ave, Cleveland, 44106. Bettina MacAyeal, Librn; Gretchen Larson, Librn
Holdings: Vols (15,000) Cat
Budget: ($40,000)
Notes: Western Reserve University merged with Case Institute of Technology to form Case Western Reserve University. The University Libraries do have a library science collection, but the Library Science Library is a separate department on campus, and does not have the same address. Noncirculating historical children's literature collection is established and cataloged.

OH —KENT STATE UNIVERSITY, School of Library Science Library, Kent, 44242. Robert Rogers, Dir
Notes: Kent State Library School has a student scholarship program for Hungarian candidates. (*Leads*, Winter 1979).

OK —OKLAHOMA DEPT OF LIBRARIES, Law Library, 109 State Capital, Oklahoma City, 73105. Robert Clark, Dir; Betty Brown, Okla Collection Librn; Virginia Collier, US Documents; Jan Blakely, State Documents; Blane Dessy, Library Science
Holdings: Vols 7000 Cat
Budget: $12,000
Notes: Extensive vertical file in addition to cataloged materials.

OK —UNIVERSITY OF TULSA, McFarlin Library, Dept of Rare Books and Special Collections, 600 S College, Tulsa, 74104. David Farmer, Dir; Toby Murray, Archivist; Caroline Swinson, Cur of Manuscripts & Art
Holdings: Cat
Notes: Incl the John Bennett Shaw Collection of Books About Books.

PA —DREXEL UNIVERSITY LIBRARIES, Library Science Library, 32 & Chestnut Sts, Philadelphia, 19104. Timothy LaBorie, Librn
Holdings: Vols 50,000 Cat Microforms
Notes: Includes Information Science. Also, 13,000 books; 19,000 serials.

†PA —UNIVERSITY OF PITTSBURGH, Graduate School of Library & Information Sciences Library, L I S Bldg, Third Fl, Pittsburgh, 15260. Jean Kindlin, Librn
Notes: Extensive collection on the historical development of school libraries, media services, and evaluation of materials for use in all types of schools. Incl 54,800 vols, 7524 bound periodicals, 630 periodical subscriptions.

RI —RHODE ISLAND DEPARTMENT OF STATE LIBRARY SERVICES, 95 Davis St, Providence, 02908. Frank P Iacono, Reference Librn
Holdings: Vols 4000 Cat VF
Budget: $15,000
Notes: Collection incl over 200 vertical files.

TN —GEORGE PEABODY COLLEGE FOR TEACHERS, Education Library, Science Library, Peabody College, Box 325, Nashville, 32703. Mary Beth Blalock, Librn
Holdings: Vols (28,493) Cat
Budget: ($14,000)
Notes: Incl collection of adolescent and children's literature. There are separate catalogs for this collection and the library science collection.

TX —TEXAS STATE LIBRARY, Library Development Division, Library Science Collection, PO Box 12927, 1201 Brazos, Austin, 78711. Anne Ramos, Librn
Holdings: Vols (5837) Cat Audiotapes Videotapes VF
Budget: ($47,851)

TX —UNIVERSITY OF TEXAS LIBRARIES, General Libraries, Library and Information Science Collection, PO Box P, Austin, 78712. Peggy Mueller, Librn
Holdings: Vols (32,518) Media Microforms

VT —VERMONT DEPARTMENT OF LIBRARIES, Law & Documents Unit, 111 State St, Montpelier, 05602. Vivian Bryan, Librn
Holdings: Vols 2500 Cat
Notes: Incl a large portion of the library of the late Joseph L Wheeler, former head of Enoch Pratt and for many years a busy library consultant. This addition provided the impetus to pull together all library science materials, and they are now housed in the Wheeler Memorial Room, open to the public for research and circulation. This represents the most complete collection of this kind of information in northern New England. Emphasis is on librarianship and library science as they pertain to Vermont. Extensive periodical runs (150 titles).

WI —UNIVERSITY OF WISCONSIN, MADISON, Library School Library, 600 N Park St, Madison, 53706. Sally Davis, Librn
Holdings: Vols 59,000

ON —UNIVERSITY OF WESTERN ONTARIO, Schoool of Library and Information Science, Library, London, N6G 1H1, Can. Victoria Ripley, Librn
Holdings: Vols (50,000)
Notes: Auction and antiquarian booksellers' catalogs from Canadian, American and European firms, some dating back to the 18th century. A special strength is 19th and early 20th century American booksellers' catalogs, recently augmented by a collection of pre-1920 catalogs formed by the late H O Teisberg. Current emphasis is on Canadian catalogs.

ON —NATIONAL LIBRARY OF CANADA, 395 Wellington St, Ottawa, K1A 0N4, Can. Andre Preibish, Dir
Budget: ($20,000)
Notes: About 40,000 monographs and 180 linear feet of vertical file materials, plus serials, microfiche and some tapes. A general library science collection of materials in English and French, with special emphasis on Canadian libraries and library developments, national libraries, bibliography and library applications of automation. Collection of IFLA conference papers dating from 1970.

ON —METROPOLITAN TORONTO LIBRARY, General Reference Dept, 789 Yonge St, Toronto, M4W 2G8, Can. Anne R Mack, Head
Holdings: Vols 11,500 Cat Microforms
Budget: $8400
Notes: All aspects of library science with emphasis on current North American material. Books, periodicals, indexes, annual reports of libraries, staff and association bulletins, vertical files.

ON —UNIVERSITY OF TORONTO, Faculty of Library and Information Science Library, Subject Analysis Systems, Room 404, 140 St George St, Toronto, M5S 1A1, Can. Diane Henderson, Librn
Holdings: Vols (2000) Cat Microforms
Notes: The Subject Analysis Systems Collection is the major North American collection of classification schemes, thesauri, and subject heading lists, and it is the major world collection in the English language. Incl Bibliographic Systems Center Collection, transferred from Case Western Reserve, Cleveland. Incl 500 AV titles.

LIBRARY SCIENCE—CHINA

IL —UNIVERSITY OF ILLINOIS, URBANA/CHAMPAIGN, Library, 1408 W Gregory Drive, Urbana, 61801. Norman B Brown, Asst Dir for Special Collections
Notes: The Alfred Kaimang Chiu Collection of books on Chinese library administration (240 in Chinese; 170 in English), with pamphlets, manuscripts, etc, incl essays on Chinese economics. Chiu was the first librarian of the Harvard-Yenching Library at Harvard University, 1931-1965.

LIBRARY SCIENCE—HISTORY

IL —UNIVERSITY OF ILLINOIS, URBANA/CHAMPAIGN, Library, University Archives, 19 Library, 1408 W Gregory Drive, Urbana, 61801. Maynard Brichford, University Archivist
Holdings: Uncat Mss Maps Slides Phonorecords Microforms
Notes: In addition to the university archives and the collections of academic and administrative staff, the archives have numerous other series of institutional and personal papers. Published guide to the collections is available: *Manuscripts Guide to Collections at the University of Illinois at* Urbana-Champaign (University of Illinois Press, 1976). Control cards and ADP control on 3644 record series; 5132 pages of supplementary finding aids. Probably the largest ms collection in the state. Holdings

LIBRARY SCIENCE—HISTORY (cont.)

on the history of librarianship and faculty and student life are particularly strong.

ON —UNIVERSITY OF WESTERN ONTARIO, Schoool of Library and Information Science, Library, London, N6G 1H1, Can. Victoria Ripley, Librn
Holdings: Vols (50,000)
Notes: Auction and antiquarian booksellers' catalogs from Canadian, American and European firms, some dating back to the 18th century. A special strength is 19th and early 20th century American booksellers' catalogs, recently augmented by a collection of pre-1920 catalogs formed by the late H O Teisberg. Current emphasis is on Canadian catalogs.

LIBRARY SCIENCE—RESEARCH

DC —LIBRARY OF CONGRESS, Manuscript Division, Washington, 20540. John C Broderick, Chief
Notes: Papers of Verner Warren Clapp, Chief Asst Librn of Congress, President of the Council on Library Resources, etc.

PA —UNIVERSITY OF PITTSBURGH, Graduate School of Library & Information Sciences, International Library Information Center, 135 N Bellefield Ave, Pittsburgh, 15260. Richard Krzys, Dir
Holdings: Cat
Notes: Extensive collection of primary source material on all aspects of librarianship in 124 countries. Emphasis on Latin American, Asian and African countries.

LIBRARY SCIENCE—SOCIETIES, ETC. see Library Associations

LIBRARY SCIENCE, INTERNATIONAL

OH —KENT STATE UNIVERSITY, School of Library Science Library, Kent, 44242. Robert Rogers, Dir
Notes: Kent State Library School has a student scholarship program for Hungarian candidates. (*Leads*, Winter 1979).

PA —UNIVERSITY OF PITTSBURGH, Graduate School of Library & Information Sciences, International Library Information Center, 135 N Bellefield Ave, Pittsburgh, 15260. Richard Krzys, Dir
Holdings: Cat
Notes: Extensive collection of primary source material on all aspects of librarianship in 124 countries. Emphasis on Latin American, Asian and African countries.

LIBRARY SCIENCE AS A PROFESSION

IL —AMERICAN LIBRARY ASSOCIATION, Headquarters Library, 50 E Huron St, Chicago, 60611. Joel M Lee, Librn
Holdings: Vols (21,000) Cat Audiotapes Videotapes Microforms
Budget: ($12,000)
Notes: All aspects of libraries and the concerns of librarians.

LIBRARY SERVICE

MN —OFFICE OF LIBRARY DEVELOPMENT AND SERVICES, 440 Capitol Square, 550 Cedar St, Saint Paul, 55101. Darlene M Arnold, Sr Librn
Holdings: Vols 12,000 Cat Slides Phonorecords Audiotapes Videotapes 16mm Films Filmstrips Microforms
Budget: $13,000
Notes: Have extensive files on Minnesota public libraries.

LIBRARY STATISTICS

IL —AMERICAN LIBRARY ASSOCIATION, Headquarters Library, 50 E Huron St, Chicago, 60611. Joel M Lee, Librn
Holdings: Vols (21,000) Cat Slides Audiotapes Videotapes Microforms
Budget: ($12,000)
Notes: All aspects of libraries and the concerns of librarians.

LIBRARY SURVEYS

IL —AMERICAN LIBRARY ASSOCIATION, Headquarters Library, 50 E Huron St, Chicago, 60611. Joel M Lee, Librn
Holdings: Vols (21,000) Cat Slides Audiotapes Videotapes Microforms
Budget: ($12,000)
Notes: All aspects of libraries and the concerns of librarians, including documents from libraries that have used the *Planning Process for Public Libraries.*

LIBRETTOS—COLLECTIONS

CA —UNIVERSITY OF CALIFORNIA, LOS ANGELES, Music Library, Schonberg Hall, Los Angeles, 90024. Stephen M Fry, Music Librn
Notes: Incl published librettos for standard operas and musical comedies; also 17th-18th century Venetian Libretto collection. Ca 8000 vols.

IL —NEWBERRY LIBRARY, 60 W Walton St, Chicago, 60610. Diana Haskell, Cur of Modern Mss
Holdings: Vols 800 Cat
Notes: Ranging from Peri's *L'Euridice* to the major works of Richard Strauss. Restricted use: noncirculating.

MA —BOSTON PUBLIC LIBRARY, Music Division, 666 Boylston St, Box 286, Boston, 02117. Ruth Bleecker, Cur of Music
Holdings: Vols (100,000) Cat Mss Pix Microforms
Notes: The Allen A Brown Music Library is the nucleus of the collection. There is a *Dictionary Catalog of the Music Collection* (Boston: G K Hall, 1976; 24 vols). Incl music scores.

NJ —NEWARK PUBLIC LIBRARY, Art & Music Dept, 5 Washington St, Newark, 07101. William J Dane, Supv
Holdings: Vols (25,000) Cat Mss Audiotapes Microforms VF
Notes: Music literature, scores, librettos, extensive vertical file, song sheets, special indexes, music periodicals. John Tasker Howard collection of notes and letters. Some special material on New Jersey and Newark music.

NY —QUEENS BOROUGH PUBLIC LIBRARY, Art & Music Div, 89-11 Merrick Blvd, Jamaica, 11432. Dorothea Wu, Head
Holdings: Vols (85,000) Cat Maps Pix Phonorecords Audiotapes Microforms
Budget: ($44,000)

NY —NEW YORK PUBLIC LIBRARY, Performing Arts Research Center, Dance Collection, 111 Amsterdam Ave, New York, 10023. Genevieve Oswald, Cur
Notes: Incl 8000 cataloged items. Strong emphases on American, English, Russian, and Italian ballet, as well as on American modern dance and Asian dance. The Cia Fornaroli Collection includes 1150 rare ballet scenarios and opera librettos, 1614-1945, with 1820-1870 especially well-represented, primarily Italian, but also including French, German, Portuguese, and Spanish items. Asian materials incl scenarios and texts for modern ballets and Peking operas of China and Bunraku, Kabuki, and Noh dramas of Japan. Catalog descriptions listed in: *Dictionary Catalog of the Dance* Collection, published by G K Hall, Boston, 1974, in 10 vols, and in annual supplements: *Bibliographic Guide to Dance.*

NY —NEW YORK PUBLIC LIBRARY, Music Div, 111 Amsterdam Ave, New York, 10023. Frank C Campbell, Chief
Holdings: Vols (300,000) Cat Mss Pix Microforms
Notes: Described in *Dictionary Catalog of the Music Collection, The Research Libraries of the New York Public Library,* 33 vols (532,000 cards), 1964, $2190; Supplement 1, 1 vol (17,000 cards), 1966, $100. Also, *Bibliographic Guide to Music,* 2 vols, 1975-1976, $70 ea. Literature pertaining to virtually all musical subjects, and scores covering the broadest range of musical style and history are represented in this catalog. Special strengths of the collection incl folk songs, 18th and 19th-century librettos, full scores of operas, complete works, historical editions, Beethoven, Americana, American music, periodicals, vocal music, literature on the voice, programs, record catalogs, and mss in detail; sheet music, 355,414; sound recordings, 400,000; clippings and programs, 2 million; broadsides, 1821; songsters, 375; pictures, 51,002; ms, 29,877.

NY —STATE UNIVERSITY OF NEW YORK, STONY BROOK, Melville Library, Dept of Special Collections, Stony Brook, 11794. Evert Volkersz, Head
Holdings: // Uncat
Notes: Nineteenth century Chilean playbills, plays and libretti. A list of holdings is available. About 570 pamphlets bound in 57 vols.

NY —SYRACUSE UNIVERSITY LIBRARIES, Music Collection, 222 Waverly Ave, Syracuse, 13210. Donald Seibert, Librn
Holdings: Vols 1349 // Cat
Notes: Collection of 19th century Italian opera and ballet librettos. An annotated catalog of the collection has been published by the Syracuse University Libraries: *19th Century Italian Opera and Ballet Libretti,* ed by Aubrey S Garlington. The catalog is arranged by title, with indices of composers, librettists, ballets, ballet creators, places of performance and publishers.

NY —YONKERS PUBLIC LIBRARY, Grinton I Will Library, 1500 Central Park Ave, Yonkers, 10701. Joan W Stevenson, Head of Fine Arts Dept
Holdings: Vols (12,000) Cat
Budget: ($36,000)
Notes: Incl periodicals, 70 titles (ca 15 yr back issues); 27 vertical file drawers (18 on artists & musicians); 1230 slides; 2200 music scores; cat; sheet music, ca 1200 titles; 140 libretti; 13,000 phonograph albums; cat; 1000 cassettes. Books, scores, phonograph albums, cassettes are cataloged. Rare collection of 57 test pressings of Geraldine Farrar, some of which have never been issued.

OH —PUBLIC LIBRARY OF CINCINNATI & HAMILTON COUNTY, Art & Music Dept, 800 Vine St, Cincinnati, 45202. R Jayne Craven, Head
Holdings: Vols (122,185) Cat Pix
Budget: ($56,100)
Notes: Special collections: Eda Kuhn Loeb, "Artist and the Book, 1875-Date" (now shelved in Rare Book Room); music librettos (2345); exhibition catalogs (5474); large prints and posters (5051); Cincinnati artists vertical files; picture collection (673,906 clippings).

LIBRIS POLARIS

NY —COLUMBIA UNIVERSITY LIBRARIES, Rare Book & Manuscript Library, 801 Butler Library, 535 W 114 St, New York, 10027. Kenneth A Lohf, Librn
Holdings: Vols 700 Cat
Notes: First editions, mss, letters and memorabilia relating to the exploration of the North and South Poles. 700 vols, 500 ms items. Restricted use.

NY —NEW YORK PUBLIC LIBRARY, Research Libraries, General Research Division, Fifth Ave & 42 St, New York, 10018. Rodney Phillips, Chief
Holdings: Vols (2,225,000) Cat Maps Pix Microforms
Budget: ($775,718)

LIBYA

CA —HOOVER INSTITUTION ON WAR, REVOLUTION & PEACE, Stanford University, Stanford, 94305. Peter Duignan, Cur; Karen Fung, Deputy Cur
Holdings: Vols (100,000)
See also entry under Near East.

LICE

NY —AMERICAN MUSEUM OF NATURAL HISTORY, Library Services Dept, Central Park W & 79th St, New York, 10024. Nina J Root, Chairwoman; Mary Genett, Asst Librn for Reference Services
Notes: A major literature collection

LICE (cont.)

supplements the museum's entomology collections; perhaps the largest in the world.
OH —MIAMI UNIVERSITY, Science Library, Oxford, 45056.
Notes: Zoonoses and related diseases. Collection partially transferred from Parker-Davis Memorial Library, Hamilton, Mont.

LICHENS

CT —YALE UNIVERSITY, Kline Science Library, Kline Biology Tower Rm C-8, PO Box 6666, New Haven, 06511. Richard J Dionne, Head
Holdings: Vols (175,480) Cat 16mm Films Microforms
Budget: ($340,000)
Notes: Comprehensive collection on biological sciences, physics, and chemistry. Incl Evans Collection of Bryology and Lichenology (with catalog cards in both Kline Science Library and Sterling Memorial Library). Also incl AEC reports (hardcopy and microform) to 1970.
DC —SMITHSONIAN INSTITUTION LIBRARIES, Botany Branch, Washington, 20560. Ruth Schallert, Branch Librn
Notes: Taxonomic botany; with the J D Smith Collection of general botany, the Dawson Collection on algae, and the Hitchcock-Chase Collection on grasses.
MA —HARVARD UNIVERSITY LIBRARY, Farlow Reference Library, 20 Divinity Ave, Cambridge, 02138. Geraldine C Kaye, Librn
Holdings: Vols (60,000) Cat Mss Serials Pix Microforms
Notes: The Farlow Reference Library provides complete coverage of the systematic literature on algae, bryophytes, fungi, and lichens. Established by bequest of Professor William G Farlow, it is one of the most extensive cryptogamic botany libraries in the US. Books do not circulate.
MI —UNIVERSITY OF MICHIGAN, Herbarium Library, University Herbarium, 2003 N University Bldg, Ann Arbor, 48109. Robert L Shaffer, Dir, Herbarium
Holdings: Vols (22,000) Cat Mss Maps Microforms
Notes: Systematic Botany including floristics, revisions and monographs in all groups of plants. Collection incl maps, mss (fieldbooks, correspondence, etc), photographs, microfiches, and approx 100, 000 reprints that are not officially part of the University Library. These are indexed and are available to qualified scholars. Incl botanical libraries of Parke, Davis & Co, Harley H Bartlett, Bruce Fink (lichens), Howard A Kelly (mycology).
†NH —UNIVERSITY OF NEW HAMPSHIRE, Biological Science Library, Kendall Hall, Durham, 03824. Lloyd Heldgard, Librn
Holdings: Vols (45,000)
ON —NATIONAL MUSEUMS OF CANADA, Library Services Directorate, Ottawa, K1A 0M8, Can. Valerie Monkhouse, Director
Holdings: Vols (90,000) Cat Mss Microforms
Budget: ($81,000)
Notes: Emphasis on Canadian and circumpolar natural history. Collection incl botany, herpetology, ichthyology, invertebrate zoology, malacology, mammology, mineralogy, ornithology, paleobiology, zooarchaeology. Exceptional collections in lichenology, bryology, malacology, ornithology. Research collection, interlibrary loans available, public may use on the premises.
ON —LAURENTIAN UNIVERSITY LIBRARY, Ramsey Lake Rd, Sudbury, P3E 2C6, Can. Suzanne Brunette, Special Collection Librn; Sue Vongpeisal, Head Librn
Notes: Materials on northern Canada, incl 2200 books and pamphlets, 60,000 press clippings on northern topics 75 series of periodicals and over 1500 maps, plus photographs and thousands of samples of arctic and subarctic plan*s incl mosses, lichens, algae and wood sections. Much of the material is in French.

LICK OBSERVATORY

CA —UNIVERSITY OF CALIFORNIA, SANTA CRUZ, Shane Archives of Lick Observatory, Santa Cruz, 95064. Dorothy Schaumberg, Archivist
Notes: Extensive collection incl correspondence, portraits, pictures, memorabilia, logs and construction diaries, 1880s to present. Mary Lea Hegen Shane was an astronomer herself, and the arranging and cataloging of the collection was done by her. Archives open to scholars by appointment.

LIEBER, FRANCIS

MD —JOHNS HOPKINS UNIVERSITY, Milton S Eisenhower Library, Charles & 34 Sts, Baltimore, 21218. Ann S Gwyn, Assistant Dir for Special Collections
Holdings: // Cat Mss
Notes: His works from his own library, amny pamphlets, mss and correspondence from Joseph Bonaparte.

LIEBLER, THEODORE

NY —NEW YORK PUBLIC LIBRARY, Performing Arts Research Center, Billy Rose Theatre Collection, 111 Amsterdam Ave, New York, 10023. Dorothy L Swerdlove, Cur
Holdings: Cat Mss Pix
Notes: Papers, scrapbooks, mss, photographs, memorabilia, etc.

LIEBMAN, JOSHUA LOTH AND FAN LOTH LIEBMAN

MA —BOSTON UNIVERSITY, Mugar Memorial Library, Special Collections Dept, 771 Commonwealth Ave, Boston, 02215. Howard B Gotlieb, Dir
Holdings: Cat Mss Pix
Notes: Mss, correspondence, etc collected in depth; incl publications by or about Joshua Loth and Fan Loth Liebman.

LIEBMAN ASSOCIATES

CA —HOOVER INSTITUTION ON WAR, REVOLUTION & PEACE, Stanford University, Stanford, 94305. Milorad M Drachkovitch, Archivist
Holdings: Mss Pix
Notes: Records of Marvin Liebman Associates, Inc, a New York public relations firm incl office files, correspondence, printed matter, press releases, campaign material, photographs and reports, 1950-1969, relating to activities of Marvin Liebman Associates in lobbying for US conservative and anti-communist organizations involved with Asian and African affairs. 108 ms boxes, 3 envelopes.

LIEDER

CA —UNIVERSITY OF CALIFORNIA, SANTA BARBARA, Arts Library, Music Section, Santa Barbara, 93106. Susan Sonnet Bower, Asst Music Librn
Holdings: Cat Phonorecords
See also entry under Phonorecords - Collections.
PA —PENNSYLVANIA STATE UNIVERSITY, Arts Library, 405 E Pattee Library, University Park, 16802. Daniel Zager, Music Librn
Holdings: Phonorecords
Notes: Ca 1000 uncataloged recordings of lieder.
See also entry under Music.

LIFE (MAGAZINE)

NY —COLUMBIA UNIVERSITY LIBRARIES, Rare Book & Manuscript Library, 801 Butler Library, 535 W 114 St, New York, 10027. Kenneth A Lohf, Librn
Holdings: Mss
Notes: The papers of Daniel Longwell, former editor at Doubleday and Life, incl his correspondence with many authors; also, nearly 400 first and inscribed editions, mss, and autograph letters. Much on Life magazine. Incl 24,750 items. Restricted use.

LIFE—ORIGIN

PA —ENSANIAN PHYSICOCHEMICAL INSTITUTE, Library, PO Box 98, Eldred, 16731. Elisabeth Anahid Ensanian, Chief Librn
Holdings: Vols 200 Cat Mss Slides Films Microforms
Budget: $3800
Notes: The Institute has pioneered the field of Gravitation Chemistry (term coined at the institute) and has original data and reports on this phenomenon, generated from its own research, that cannot be found elsewhere in the world. Also publishes own technical journal. This special collection, which also incl the biological effects of weightlessness, is continually being increased.

LIFE, FUTURE see Future Life

LIFE, SPIRITUAL see Spiritual Life

LIFE AFTER DEATH see Immortality; Future Life

LIFE INSURANCE see Insurance, Life

LIFE SCIENCES

CA —UNIVERSITY OF CALIFORNIA, LOS ANGELES, Biomedical Library, Center for the Health Sciences, Los Angeles, 90024. Alison Bunting, Acting Biomedical Librn; Victoria Steele, Head, History & Special Collections Div
Holdings: Vols (400,000) Cat Slides Phonorecords Audiotapes Videotapes 16mm Films Microforms
Notes: The UCLA Biomedical Library serves primarily the Schools of Medicine, Dentistry, Nursing, and Public Health, the UCLA Medical Center, the Departments of Microbiology and Biology in the College of Letters and Science, and related institutes in biomedicine. The collections of the Library are broad in scope, designed not only to support the teaching and research needs of its many users, but also to function as a resource for the health sciences-biological field as a whole. The outstanding feature of the collection is the strength of its periodical holdings, both current and retrospective. The Library also has an excellent reference collection, a comprehensive historical section, and gives special emphasis to the fields of neuroscience, psychiatry, ophthalmology, radiation biology, molecular biology, and vertebrate zoology. Increased emphasis is being given to the acquisition of audiovisual materials.

CA —NASA, Ames Research Center, Libraries, Library Br 202-3, Moffett Field, 94035. Sarah Dueker, Chief, Library Branch
Holdings: Cat Audiotapes Microforms
Notes: Main library collections cover physical sciences, engineering and mathematical fields related to research programs in aeronautics-space research. Life sciences library collections cover medical, physiological, behavioral and biological sciences related to research programs. Also emphases on remote sensing of earth resources and the search for extraterrestrial life. 950 journal titles and 85,000 monographs. Reports collection includes 60, 000 hard copy reports and 900,000 microfiche.

LIFE SCIENCES (cont.)

CA —UNIVERSITY OF CALIFORNIA, RIVERSIDE, University Library, Bio-Agricultural Library, Batchelor Hall, Riverside, 92521. Barbara Montanary, Head
Holdings: Vols (130,000) Cat Mss Maps Pix Microforms
Notes: The Bio-Agricultural Library (formerly the Library of Citrus Experiment Station of the University of California) is well known for its complete collections in the fields of the agriculture sciences. It is especially known for its emphasis on entomology, incl bio-control; botany, citriculture, plant sciences, nematology and plant pathology; arid and semi-arid lands research and subtropical agriculture. Specific areas of interest are avocados, dates, desert flora, jojoba, guayule and carob.

IN —INDIANA STATE UNIVERSITY, Science Library, Terre Haute, 47809. Susan J Thompson, Science Librn
Holdings: Vols (40,000) Cat Micrforms
Budget: ($160,846)

IN —PURDUE UNIVERSITY LIBRARIES, Life Sciences Library, Lilly Hall of Life Sciences, West Lafayette, 47907. Martha J Bailey, Librn
Holdings: Vols (73,404) Cat Microforms
Budget: ($223,445)
Notes: Incl materials in agronomy, animal sciences, botany, entomology, forestry, horticulture, biological sciences and agricultural engineering.

MD —UNION MEMORIAL HOSPITAL, Nursing Library, 3301 N Calvert St, Baltimore, 21218. Carolyn Daugherty, Librn
Holdings: Vols (4000) Cat Mss Pix

MD —NATIONAL LIBRARY OF MEDICINE, 8600 Rockville Pike, Bethesda, 20209. Harold M Schoolinam, Actg Dir
Holdings: Vols (3,150,000) Cat Mss Audiotapes Videotapes 16mm Films Filmstrips Microforms
Budget: ($46,400)
Notes: The world's largest medical library. Materials are collected exhaustively in some 40 biomedical areas and, to a lesser degree, in related subject areas such as general chemistry, physics, zoology, botany, and instrumentation. Holdings include 82,000 monographic volumes, pre-1871; 438,000 monographic volumes, 1871-present; 714,000 bound serial volumes; 281,000 theses; 172, 000 pamphlets; 1,207,000 manuscripts; 156, 000 microforms; 12,000 audiovisuals; and 75, 000 prints and photographs. Pre-1871 material is in a separate historical collection. Approximately 24,000 serial titles are currenlty received.

MI —WAYNE STATE UNIVERSITY, Vera Parshall Shiffman Medical Library, 4325 Brush St, Detroit, 48201. Faith Van Toll, Acting Head Librn
Holdings: Vols (158,612)
Budget: ($381,153)
Notes: Resource Library in Greater Midwest Regional Medical Library Network Program.

†NH —UNIVERSITY OF NEW HAMPSHIRE, Biological Science Library, Kendall Hall, Durham, 03824. Lloyd Heldgard, Librn
Holdings: Vols (45,000)

NH —DARTMOUTH COLLEGE, Dartmouth-Hitchcock Medical Center, Dana Biomedical Library, Hanover, 03756. Shirley J Grainger, Librn
Holdings: Vols (143,611) Cat Mss Phonorecords Audiotapes Videotapes Microforms
Budget: ($280,000)

NY —NEW YORK PUBLIC LIBRARY, Mid-Manhattan Library, Science & Business Dept, 455 Fifth Ave, New York, 10016. Frederick E Dusold, Sr Principal Librn
Holdings: Vols (110,000) Cat Microforms
Budget: ($134,000)
Notes: With rare exceptions all works in English. Current material; policy precludes archival collecting. Collection geared toward the undergraduate college student, with consideration given to the professional, the lay reader and the beginning graduate student. A collection of monographs, texts, treatises, standard reference works and periodicals in the philosophy, history and theory of science. Special strength in mathematics and life sciences. Circulating books are available in addition to an extensive reference collection.

NY —UNIVERSITY OF ROCHESTER, School of Medicine and Dentistry, Edward G Miner Library, 601 Elmwood Ave, Rochester, 14642. Lucretia McClure, Medical Librn; Janet Brady Berk, History of Medicine Librn
Holdings: Vols (185,000) Cat
Notes: The Edward G Miner Library serves the School of Medicine & Dentistry, the School of Nursing, and Strong Memorial Hospital. The collection encompasses all the biomedical fields, nursing and dental research, and is designed to serve the teaching, patient care and research needs of persons in the Medical Center. The Library subscribes to more than 2900 current journals and serials, has an excellent reference collection and an extensive collection of rare and historical works in medicine and nursing.

OH —BATTELLE MEMORIAL INSTITUTE LIBRARY, 505 King Ave, Columbus, 43201. Carol Young, Librn
Holdings: Vols (150,000) Cat Maps Microforms
Notes: Large collection of Russian and Eastern European science and technology. Over 1600 current journal titles and extensive monography and serial holdings in Slavic languages.

OK —SAMUEL ROBERTS NOBLE FOUNDATION, Biomedical Div Library, PO Box 2180, Ardmore, 73401. Loretta Cook, Librn
Holdings: Vols (11,000) Cat Microforms
Budget: ($32,600)
Notes: Biomedical literature.

PA —UNIVERSITY OF PITTSBURGH, Langley Library, A-217 Langley Hall, Pittsburgh, 15260. D L Johnston, Librn
Holdings: Vols (14,000) Cat
Budget: ($30,000)

WI —UNIVERSITY OF WISCONSIN, MADISON, Wisconsin Regional Primate Research Center, Primate Center Library, 1223 Capitol Court, Madison, 53715. Lawrence Jacobsen, Librn
Holdings: Vols (15,000) Cat Pix
Notes: Research in reproductive physiology, neurosciences, and behavior. Extensive subject orientated primate reprint file, audiovisual collection on primates. Current research uses approximately 25 species of nonhuman primates. Publications: *Primate Library Report*: print and non-print editions, biomonthly.

WI —UNIVERSITY OF WISCONSIN, MADISON, W S Middleton Health Sciences Library, 1305 Linden Dr, Madison, 53706. Virginia Holtz, Dir
Holdings: Vols (200,000) Cat Pix Slides Audiotapes Videotapes Microforms

WI —MARQUETTE UNIVERSITY, Memorial Library, 1415 W Wisconsin Ave, Milwaukee, 53233. Jay Kirk, Health Sciences Librn
Notes: Supports curriculum and research.

ON —UNIVERSITY OF GUELPH, McLaughlin Library, Guelph, N1G 2W1, Can. Margaret Beckman, Head Librn; David Hull, Sciences Librn

LIFESAVING

NC —NATIONAL PARK SERVICE, Cape Hatteras National Seashore, Reference Library, Rte 1, Box 675, Manteo, 27954.
Holdings: Cat Mss Maps Pix
Notes: US Lifesaving Service, records and annual reports.

LIGHT AMPLIFICATION BY STIMULATED EMISSION OF RADIATION see Lasers

LIGHT IN ART

MN —MINNEAPOLIS COLLEGE OF ART & DESIGN, Library, 200 E 25 St, Minneapolis, 55404. Richard Kronstedt, Head Librn

NJ —NEWARK PUBLIC LIBRARY, Art & Music Dept, 5 Washington St, Newark, 07101. William J Dane, Supv
Notes: On all forms of artistic expression, particularly on the use of light.

LIGHTER-THAN-AIR AIRCRAFT see Airships

LIGHTER THAN AIR SOCIETY

OH —UNIVERSITY OF AKRON, American History Research Center, Akron, 44325.
Notes: Photographs, letters, drawings, newspaper clippings and other publications.

LIGHTFOOT, THOMAS

PA —FRIENDS HISTORICAL LIBRARY OF SWARTHMORE COLLEGE, Swarthmore, 19081. J William Frost, Dir
Holdings: Vols (31,340) Cat Mss Maps
Notes: Mss deal with Quaker Indian work under Grant's administration. Archives of Society of Friends Baltimore Yearly Meeting (Hicksite) Standing Committee on Indian Affairs of Baltimore, Genesee, New York, and Philadelphia, 1836-1849; Friends Indian Aid Association of Philadelphia, 1869-1876; Philadelphia Yearly Meeting, Committee on Indian Affairs, 1887-1892. Papers of Quaker Indian agents Albert L Green and Thomas Lightfoot.

LIGHTHOUSES

VA —MARINERS MUSEUM, Library, Newport News, 23606. Ardie L Kelly, Librn
Holdings: Vols (60,000) Cat Mss Maps Pix Slides
Notes: Incl collections of over 150,000 photographs of merchant ships, naval vessels, sailing ships, lighthouses, portraits of naval men, harbors, canals, etc, and maps, ships' papers, and log books. Catalogs of various parts of the collection published by G K Hall, Boston.

VA —PORTSMOUTH PUBLIC LIBRARY, 601 Court St, Portsmouth, 23704. Dean Burgess, Library Dir
Holdings: Vols 55 Cat Pix
Notes: This collection is in connection with the lightship Museum of the US Coast Guard located on the lightship *PORTSMOUTH* moored permanently on the Portsmouth waterfront and with the headquarters of the Coast Guard located in Portsmouth (headquarters for the 5th Coast Guard district). We are most interested in Lightships but also buy materials on lighthouses. The scope is international and dealing with all periods. We hope to find all types of materials but now hold only printed books. Pictures and materials other than books are housed in the lightship Portsmouth (Alice Hanes, Curator), 1 High Street, Portsmouth, Va 23704.

LIGHTING

IN —INDIANA UNIVERSITY, Optometry Branch Library, Bloomington, 47405. Roger Deckman, Head; Elizabeth Egan, Branch Librn
Holdings: Vols (11,000) Cat Slides Microforms
Budget:
Notes: Incl all aspects of vision: anatomy, physiology, pathology of the eye, neurophysiology, perception, colorimetry, illumination, safety, etc. Interlibrary loans through Main Library, Indiana University, Bloomington.

MI —EDISON INSTITUTE, Greenfield Village and Henry Ford Museum, Archives & Research Library, PO Box 1970, Dearborn, 48121. Steve Hamp, Dir; Joan W Gartland, Librn
Holdings: Vols 400,000 Cat Mss Maps Microforms
Notes: 400,000 vols incl pamphlets. The Archives and research library supports the program of Greenfield Village and the Henry Ford Museum. Special collections incl: automotive literature, ephemera, McGuffey Readers, trade catalogs, photographs and graphics.

LIGHTING (cont.)

NY —ENGINEERING SOCIETIES LIBRARY, 345 E 47 St, New York, 10017. S Kirk Cabeen, Dir
Holdings: Vols 250,000 Cat Maps 16mm Films Microforms
Notes: One of the largest, most comprehensive engineering libraries in the world. Covers all engineering disciplines; particularly strong in electrical and electronic, mechanical, mining and metallurgical, petroleum, chemical, industrial, air conditioning and refrigeration engineering. Incl Wheeler Collection of early materials on magnetism and electricity. 125, 000 bound periodical volumes; 10,000 maps; 5000 serial subscriptions (many foreign language). Virtually all materials abstracted in *Engineering Index* (1884-date) are incl in Library. See *Engineering Societies Library, New York, Classed Subject Catalog and* Index (Boston G K Hall, 1963); and *Supplements*, 1-10, 1964-1973.

PA —FRANKLIN INSTITUTE LIBRARY, 20 & The Parkway, Philadelphia, 19103. Miriam Padusis, Dir; Charles Wilt, Readers Servs Librn
Holdings: Vols (300,000) Cat Maps Pix Microforms

LIGHTING—HISTORY

MA —OLD STURBRIDGE VILLAGE, Research Library, Sturbridge, 01566. Theresa Rini Percy, Librn
Holdings: Cat Pix
Notes: New England, 1790-1850.

LIGHTING, THEATRE see Stage Lighting

LIGHTNING CALCULATORS (PERSONS)

NY —MORRIS N & CHESLEY V YOUNG LIBRARY OF MNEMONICS, 270 Riverside Dr, New York, 10025. Morris N Young, Cur
Holdings: Cat Mss Pix Phonorecords Audiotapes 16mm Films Microforms
Notes: Collection of 5000 books, pamphlets, pictures, memorabilia, etc incl medieval art of memory; psychology of memory, forgetting and reading; medical aspects of memory, amnesia, dyslexia; biomedical aspects of learning and memory; information storage, retrieval and cybernetics; memory prodigies, lightning calculators, calendars; remembrance cups and memory mementos. All languages. Memorabilia incl engravings, posters, programs, advertisements, birthday cards, teaching cards, ASLs, and Mark Twain's Memory Builder game and other games. Items range from 1410 to 1980s.

LIGHTSHIPS

VA —PORTSMOUTH PUBLIC LIBRARY, 601 Court St, Portsmouth, 23704. Dean Burgess, Library Dir
Holdings: Vols 55 Cat Pix
Notes: This collection is in connection with the lightship Museum of the US Coast Guard located on the lightship *PORTSMOUTH* moored permanently on the Portsmouth waterfront and with the headquarters of the Coast Guard located in Portsmouth (headquarters for the 5th Coast Guard district). We are most interested in Lightships but also buy materials on lighthouses. The scope is international and dealing with all periods. We hope to find all types of materials but now hold only printed books. Pictures and materials other than books are housed in the lightship Portsmouth (Alice Hanes, Curator), 1 High Street, Portsmouth, Va 23704.

LIGURIANS

NV —UNIVERSITY OF NEVADA, RENO, Noble H Getchell Library, Reno, 89557. William A Douglass, Coordinator
Holdings: Vols (15,000)
Notes: America's largest collection of Basque materials, both retrospective and current. Semi-annual *Newsletter*.

LILBURNE, JOHN

PA —TEMPLE UNIVERSITY LIBRARIES, Special Collections Dept, Rare Books & Mss Section, Philadelphia, 19122. Thomas M Whitehead, Cur
Holdings: Vols Cat Mss
Notes: Seventeenth and 18th century books and pamphlets on political, religious, social and intellectual life and history of England. Strong holdings of John Cotton, Gilbert Burnet, Richard Overton, John Lilburne; Civil War pamphlets, ranters and levellers. The Nordell and Simpson Collections.

LILIENTHAL, DAVID ELI, 1899-1981

NJ —PRINCETON UNIVERSITY, Library, Manuscript Collection, Nassau St, Princeton, 08540. Jean F Preston, Cur
Holdings: Cat Mss Pix
Notes: Incl 361 boxes of papers. Terms of Access: The unpublished "manuscript journal" after 1967, as distinguished from the published *Journals of David E Lilienthal,* is not accessible until Jan 1, 2000. An unpublished typescript guide (218 p) is available in the Library.

LILLY, DORIS

MA —BOSTON UNIVERSITY, Mugar Memorial Library, Special Collections Dept, 771 Commonwealth Ave, Boston, 02215. Howard B Gotlieb, Dir
Holdings: Cat Mss
Notes: Mss, correspondence, etc collected in depth; incl publications by or about.

LILLY, JOSIAH K.

IN —INDIANA UNIVERSITY, Lilly Library, Seventh St, Bloomington, 47405. William R Cagle, Librn
Holdings: Mss
Notes: J K Lilly's personal papers contain correspondence with numerous dealers on purchase and availability of rare books and mss. Files arranged alphabetically by dealer. 25,000 items.

LIME INDUSTRY

DE —UNIVERSITY OF DELAWARE, Hugh M Morris Library, S College Ave, Newark, 19711. T Stuart Dick, Special Collections
Holdings: // Mss
Notes: Personal and business letters and receipts of the Albertson family of Quaker lumber and lime merchants (1782-1862) residing in Plymouth, Montgomery Co, Pa. Included are many letters concerning the Plymouth R R and rules and regulations for its administration.

LIMERICKS

IN —INDIANA UNIVERSITY, Institute for Sex Research Library, 416 Morrison Hall, Bloomington, 47401. Douglas Freeman, Collections and Services Librn; Joan Brewer, Information Services Librn
Holdings: Vols (62,000) Cat Mss Pix Phonorecords Audiotapes Slides Films Microforms
Budget: ($20,000)
Notes: One of the greatest and most extensive collections on sexual behavior, the library collects materials on all aspects of sex activity, with special emphasis on behavioral and social aspects. Also collects erotic literature and sexual ephemera. Incl 105 audiotapes, 23 vertical file drawers, 108 phonorecords, 55,000 pictures, 5000 slides and 1700 films. Rich in French, German and American sources; also much Oriental. Semitraditional erotic poetry and song of 17th-18th century England. Bawdy limericks, double-entendre, puns, slang, erotic literature, graffiti, slang and special dictionaries, proverbs and sayings, epigrams and research materials of the Kinsey Studies, etc. Contact Information Service for: literature searching, preparation of bibliographies, permission to use collection. Limited photocopying.

LIMITATION OF ARMAMENT see Disarmament

LIMITATIONS, CONSTITUTIONAL see Constitutional Law

LIMITED COMPANIES see Corporations

LIMITED EDITIONS see Bibliography—Limited Editions

LIMITED EDITIONS CLUB

CA —SOLANO COUNTY LIBRARY, John F Kennedy Library, Donovan J McCune Collection, 505 Santa Clara St, Vallejo, 94590.
Holdings: Vols 700 //
Notes: The Donovan J McCune Collection

DC —GEORGETOWN UNIVERSITY, Library, Special Collections Div, 37 & O Sts NW, Washington, 20057. George M Barringer, Special Collections Librn; Nicholas B Sheetz, Mss Librn
Notes: The papers, files, art work, etc of Lynd Ward and his wife, May McNeer.

MO —UNIVERSITY OF MISSOURI-COLUMBIA, Ellis Library, Language and Literature Dept, Columbia, 65201. Jeaneice Brewer, Librn
Holdings: Vols (250) Cat
Notes: Limited Editions Club titles are of exeptional quality both in content and craft. These fine examples of bookmaking are sought by collectors.

NE —KEENE MEMORIAL LIBRARY, 1030 N Broad St, Fremont, 68025. William S McDermott, Dir
Holdings: Vols (1500) Cat
Notes: Incl archives.

NY —COLUMBIA UNIVERSITY LIBRARIES, Rare Book & Manuscript Library, 801 Butler Library, 535 W 114 St, New York, 10027. Kenneth A Lohf, Librn
Holdings: Vols 675 Cat
Notes: Restricted use.

LIMNOLOGY

MI —UNIVERSITY OF MICHIGAN, North Engineering Library, 1002 I St, Ann Arbor, 48109. Maurita Holland, Librn
Holdings: Vols Cat Maps Pix
Budget: $3500
Notes: Subject emphasis is on the natural science aspects of the Great Lakes; limnology. Also 5000 reports.

NY —AMERICAN MUSEUM OF NATURAL HISTORY, Library Services Dept, Central Park W & 79th St, New York, 10024. Nina J Root, Chairwoman; Mary Genett, Asst Librn for Reference Services

OH —CLEVELAND PUBLIC LIBRARY, Science & Technology Dept, 325 Superior Ave, Cleveland, 44114. Jean Z Piety, Head
Holdings: Cat Pix
Notes: Special collection covers the environmental sciences concerned with the Great Lakes-St Lawrence drainage basins. Emphasis is on limnology, ecology, meteorology, hydraulics, biology, pollution of air and water, natural history and general research. Most of the material indexed has been donated by numerous agencies around the Great Lakes.

PA —ACADEMY OF NATURAL SCIENCES LIBRARY, 19 Benjamin Franklin Parkway, Philadelphia, 19103.
Holdings: Vols (180,000) Cat Mss Maps Pix Slides Microforms
Notes: Incl (250,000) mss. Described in *Academy of Natural Sciences of Philadelphia: Catalog* (Boston: G K Hall, 1972); *Guide to the Manuscript Collections in the Academy of Natural Sciences of* Philadelphia, by Venia T Phillips (Philadelphia: Academy of Natural Sciences, 1963).

ON —CANADA CENTRE FOR INLAND WATERS, Library, 867 Lakeshore Rd,

LIMNOLOGY (cont.)

Burlington, L7R 4A6, Can. Eve Dowie, Head Library Services
Holdings: Vols (20,000)
Budget: ($150,000)
Notes: A research collection oriented towards Canadian limnological research. Incl 312 subscriptions.

PQ —MCGILL UNIVERSITY, Blacker-Wood Library of Zoology & Ornithology, 3459 McTavish St, Montreal, H3A 1Y1, Can. Eleanor MacLean, Librn
Holdings: Vols (77,600) // Cat Mss
Notes: Special features of collection incl: Robert Gurney Collection of reprints on Crustaceana; 3000 folders of letters from naturalists; over 9000 original paintings of wildlife; a small collection of falconry equipment; the archives of the Montreal Natural History Society; the archives of the North American Falconry Association; 156 17th-century feather pictures of birds and people. Does not incl entomology collection.

LIMON, JOSE, 1908-1972

NY —NEW YORK PUBLIC LIBRARY, Performing Arts Research Center, Dance Collection, 111 Amsterdam Ave, New York, 10023. Genevieve Oswald, Cur
Notes: Extensive biographical and visual material. Includes photographs, clippings, programs, scrapbooks, and motion pictures. The Jose Limon Collection, acquired in 1977, consists of 45 cartons of letters, business correspondence, diaries, journals, manuscript writings, production, teaching, and dance memorabilia. Includes material on the Humphrey-Weidman company, the Jose Limon company, American Dance Theatre, and the Juilliard School of Music. Additional material in the Pauline Lawrence Limon Collection.

LINAPI see Delaware Indians

LINCECUM, GIDEON

TX —UNIVERSITY OF TEXAS LIBRARIES, General Libraries, Barker Texas History Center, PO Box P, Austin, 78712. Don Carleton, Dir

LINCOLN, ABRAHAM

CA —AZUSA PACIFIC COLLEGE, Marshburn Memorial Library, Citrus & Alosta, Azusa, 91702. Edward Peterman, Librn
Holdings: Vols (331) // Uncat
Notes: The Irving Stone Collection of Lincolniana. Books used by Irving Stone in the preparation of his bestselling novel *Love is Eternal* (Lincoln). The books are signed by Stone; many contain his editorial comments. Also, his collection for *Those Who Love* (John and Abigail Adams). No photocopying.

CA —OCCIDENTAL COLLEGE, Library, 1600 Campus Rd, Los Angeles, 90041. Michael C Sutherland, Special Collections Librn
Holdings: Uncat Mss Maps Pix
Notes: Books (3000) and pamphlets (1500), arranged chronologically by subject. Access is by bibliography and inventory list.

CA —LINCOLN MEMORIAL SHRINE, A K Smiley Public Library, 125 W Vine St, Redlands, 92373. Larry E Burgess, Archivist
Holdings: Vols (3000) Cat Mss Maps Pix Slides Phonorecords 16mm Films Microforms
Budget: ($18,000)
Notes: One of the largest collections on Lincoln and his times. Incl broadsides, letters, prints, campaign badges, stamps, coins, medals; bust, by George Grey Bernard. Endowment of Watchorn Lincoln Memorial Association. There is an additional pamphlet collection of more than 3000 pieces; an extensive philately collection incl first-day covers, commemorative and foreign issues, and Civil War envelopes.

CA —UNIVERSITY OF CALIFORNIA, SANTA BARBARA, Library, Dept of Special Collections, Santa Barbara, 93106. Christian F Brun, Head
Holdings: Vols 24,500 Cat Mss Maps Pix Microforms
Budget: $7000
Notes: The William Wyles Collection of Americana. Incl American Civil War, Abraham Lincoln, Westward Movement, Americans for the Orient, slavery, abolition movement, etc.

CA —UNIVERSITY OF THE PACIFIC, Library, Stockton, 95211. Hiram L Davis, Dir of Libraries
Holdings: Vols 316 Cat Pix
Notes: Books, pamphlets, periodicals, and illustrative material and scraps relating to the life and times of Lincoln. Gift of Dr and Mrs Milton Henry Shutes. Incl over 200 miscellaneous items.

CT —TRINITY COLLEGE LIBRARY, Watkinson Library, 300 Summit St, Hartford, 06106. Jeffrey Kaimowitz, Cur
Holdings: // Cat
Notes: The Gilbert A Tracy Collection.

CT —YALE UNIVERSITY, Box 1603A, Yale Station, New Haven, 06520.
Holdings: Cat Mss

DC —GEORGETOWN UNIVERSITY, Library, Special Collections Div, 37 & O Sts NW, Washington, 20057. George M Barringer, Special Collections Librn; Nicholas B Sheetz, Mss Librn
Holdings: Mss Cat
Notes: The E H Swaim Collection. A collection of letters, affidavits, and photographs relating to the assassination of Abraham Lincoln and the subsequent career of John Wilkes Booth. Much of this material was gathered by Finis L Bates, Clarence True Wilson, and W P Campbell (whose research files were brought together by Swaim) and is for the most part by people who were involved in the events surrounding the assassination; members of the Booth family and their acquaintance; and individuals who claimed to have know Booth later in Texas and Oklahoma. The Papers of David Rankin Barbee, journalist with *The Washington Post* and authority on: Abraham Lincoln; the Lincoln assassination; Rose O'Neal Greenhow; and the Civil War. The collection incl, besides extensive correspondence with such historians as Albert J Beveridge, Henry Steele Commager, and Paul M Angle, all of Barbee'sown research files and the manuscripts of his works.

DC —HOWARD UNIVERSITY, Moorland-Spingarn Research Center, 500 Howard Place NW, Washington, 20059. Clifford L Muse, Jr, Acting Dir
Holdings: Vols (106,086) Mss Maps Pix Slides Phonorecords Audiotapes 16mm Films Filmstrips Microforms
Budget: ($854,753)
See also entry under Blacks

DC —LIBRARY OF CONGRESS, Rare Book & Special Collections Div, Washington, 20540. William Matheson, Chief
Notes: The Alfred Whital Stern Collection, donated to the Library of Congress in 1953, contains material by and about Abraham Lincoln, incl books, pamphlets, newspapers, sheet music, broadsides, prints, stamps, coins, and mss. The Stern Collection complements large collections relating to Lincoln in the Library's Prints and Photographs Division, Manuscript Division, and the general collections. See *A Catalog of the Alfred Whital Stern Collection of* Lincolnia, (Washington: Government Printing Office, 1960).

DC —LIBRARY OF CONGRESS, Manuscript Division, Washington, 20540. John C Broderick, Chief
Holdings: Cat Mss Pix
Notes: Mss, papers, records, etc.

IL —CHICAGO HISTORICAL SOCIETY, Library, Clark St at North Ave, Chicago, 60614. Robert L Brubaker, Librn
Holdings: Vols (150,000) Cat Mss Pix Broadsides

IL —NEWBERRY LIBRARY, 60 W Walton St, Chicago, 60610. Diana Haskell, Cur of Modern Mss
Holdings: Cat
Notes: Strong collection.

IL —UNIVERSITY OF CHICAGO LIBRARY, Dept of Special Collections, 1100 E 57 St, Chicago, 60637.
Notes: Barton Collection of Lincolniana.

IL —GALESBURG PUBLIC LIBRARY, 40 E Simmons St, Galesburg, 61401. Jane M Willenborg, Special Collections Librn
Holdings: Vols (6113) Cat Mss Maps Pix Slides Phonorecords Audiotapes Videotapes
Budget: ($10,500)
Notes: Incl extensive collection of Illinois histories--state, county, city, town, and village; Illinois laws and statutes, 1829-1977; state and county atlases and plat books (listed in *United States Atlases,* vol II, Library of Congress, 1953); Lincoln books; works of Illinois authors; Civil War Illinois regimental histories; photographs of local interest (incl numerous photos of Carl Sandburg); and local newspapers and city directories on microfilm. Incl mss (26 ft), 79 maps, 4371 pictures, 3515 slides. 3053 negatives (some are duplicates of the photographs). Separate catalog. Restricted use: noncirculating; limited photocopying.

IL —ILLINOIS STATE UNIVERSITY, Milner Library, Dept of Special Collections, Normal, 61761. Robert Sokan, Librn
Holdings: Vols 1200 Cat
Notes: The Harold K Sage Lincoln Collection consists of approx 1200 book items, 1500 pamphlets which are uncataloged, and ephemera (ie newspaper clippings, correspondence). The collection incl biographies, collections of his speeches, commemoration ceremony speeches, juvenalia and books dealing with Lincoln's relationship to special subject areas such as religion and slavery. Many of the books are limited editions, presentation or autographed copies with correspondence from authors and/or editors inserted.

IL —ILLINOIS STATE HISTORICAL SOCIETY, Library, Old State Capitol, Springfield, 62706. James T Hickey, Lincoln Cur
Holdings: Cat Mss Pix
Notes: Downs 2605, 2610, 2492. Incl 1319 mss concerning Lincoln.

IL —UNIVERSITY OF ILLINOIS, URBANA/CHAMPAIGN, Library, 1408 W Gregory Drive, Urbana, 61801. Norman B Brown, Asst Dir for Special Collections
Holdings: Cat Mss Pix
Notes: The Lincoln Room collection includes approximately 8000 items: printed books, pamphlets, manuscripts, graphic art, and memorabilia relating to Lincoln and his associates. The Carl Sandburg collection in the Rare Book Room includes much on Lincoln.

IN —INDIANA UNIVERSITY, Lilly Library, Seventh St, Bloomington, 47405. William R Cagle, Librn
Holdings: Vols 5000 Cat Mss
Notes: Emphasis on materials printed during Lincoln's lifetime. Mss incl papers and correspondence of Lincoln, members of his family, and members of his cabinet.

IN —LOUIS A WARREN LINCOLN LIBRARY AND MUSEUM, 1300 S Clinton St, Fort Wayne, 46801. Mark E Neely Jr, Dir
Holdings. Vols (17,000) Cat Mss Maps Pix Artifacts
Notes: Acquire all books on Abraham Lincoln, most on his contemporaries, as many as possible on his times, and historical journals. Constantly acquiring unpublished mss of Lincoln, Lincoln's associates, correspondents, and collateral figures. Have some Kentucky Court Records, Richard Thompson Papers. Publish a monthly bulletin of historical research on Lincoln's life and times called *Lincoln Lore,* which includes an annually updated bibliography of Lincolniana.

IN —BUTLER UNIVERSITY, Irwin Library, Hugh Thomas Miller Rare Book Room, 4600 Sunset Ave, Indianapolis, 46208. Gisela Terrell, Rare Books Librn
Holdings: Vols Cat Mss Newspapers
Notes: Lincoln Collection. Assembled for the greater part by Charles W Moores, 1862-1923; accepted by Bulter U 1925; sorted and catalogued 1981-82. The newspapers,

LINCOLN, ABRAHAM (cont.)

clippings, other memorabilia. Books and pamphlets include materials related to the Civil War in general. An annotated bibliography of the booklets, pamphlets and most mss was printed in 1983; it is available for $10. A related collection of materials about Lincoln statues and their sculptors remains to be sorted.
See also entries under Charles Washington Moores; US - History - Civil War

IN —MORRISSON-REEVES LIBRARY, 80 N Sixth St, Richmond, 47374. Harriet E Bard, Librn
Holdings: Vols 800 Cat
Notes: Clarence M Brown Memorial Collection emphasizing the Civil War and the life of Abraham Lincoln. Some vols are library use only.

IA —GRAND LODGE OF IOWA, AF & AM Iowa Masonic Library, 813 First Ave SE, Cedar Rapids, 52406. Tom Eggleston, Librn
Holdings: Vols 350 Cat

IA —UNIVERSITY OF IOWA, University Libraries, Iowa City, 52242. Frank Paluka, Head, Special Collections Dept
Holdings: Vols 4620 Cat Pix
Notes: See "The Judge and His Lincoln", by Harry J Lytle in the *Lincoln Herald,* Oct-Dec 1942 and "John Wilkes Booth in the Bollinger Lincoln Collection", by Ronald L Fingerson in *Books at Iowa,* April 1965. Also "James W Bollinger as a Collector of Lincolniana", *Books at Iowa,* April 1982.

IA —HEISERMAN MEMORIAL LIBRARY, 210 N Vine St, West Union, 52175.
Holdings: Vols 300 Cat Pix
Notes: 77 books are included in "The Shelf of 100 Best Lincoln Books".

KS —BAKER UNIVERSITY, Library, Eighth St, Baldwin City, 66006. Ray Firestone, Dir of Libraries
Holdings: Vols 200 // Cat Pix
Notes: Merton S Rice Collection.

KS —SAINT MARY COLLEGE, Library, Leavenworth, 66048. Therese Deplazes, Special Collections Librn
Holdings: Vols 1200 Cat
Notes: The Dr Bernard H Hall Collection. Incl many framed and unframed photographs; original, contemporary sheet music and song sheets; stamps, first-day covers; coins, badges; scrapbooks; first editions; different editions of various title; some foreign language titles. Also incl 700 pamphlets, 200 post cards, documents and memorabilia.

KS —KANSAS STATE UNIVERSITY, Library, Special Collections & University Archives, Manhattan, 66506. Antonia Q Pigno, Coordr; John J Vander Velde, Librn; Anthony R Crawford, Univ Archivist
Holdings: Vols (3500)
Notes: General collection; also includes books on George Washington and the US Civil War.

KY —BEREA COLLEGE, Hutchins Library, Berea, 40404. Gerald F Roberts, Librn Special Collections
Holdings: Vols 1500 Cat Mss Pix
Notes: Also incl memorabilia and numerous pamphlets that are uncataloged.

KY —KENTUCKY WESLEYAN COLLEGE LIBRARY, 3000 Frederica, Owensboro, 42301. Stuart Stiffler, Dir
Notes: The Dr and Mrs M David Orrahood Collection.

LA —LOUISIANA STATE UNIVERSITY, Troy H Middleton Library, Baton Rouge, 70803. Lance E Dickson, Acting Dir
Holdings: Vols 5000 Uncat Maps Pix
Notes: Core is composed of the Warren L Jones Lincoln Collection. Incl the major Lincoln biographies, pamphlets, photographs, periodicals, broadsides, museum objects, special editions, and some items pertaining to the Civil War.

LA —LOUISIANA STATE UNIVERSITY, Troy H Middleton Library, Louisiana Room, Baton Rouge, 70803. Evangeline Mills Lynch, Head Librn; Ruth Murray, Associate Librn
Holdings: Vols (33,500) Cat Maps VF
Notes: Louisiana Collection of history, description and travel, biography, agriculture, literature, politics and government, folklore, anthropology, geography, geology, education, language, music and natural history. Especially large subject collections may be found on Louisiana, the history of the lower Mississippi Valley, Abraham Lincoln, Romance languages and literatures, sugar culture and technology, Southern history, petroleum engineering, plant pathology, micropaleontology, ornithology, and various aspects of crawfish life, biology and culture. Complete depository of Louisiana State Documents; extensive newspapers clipping files; separate card catalog; items listed in Louisiana Union Catalog; restricted use (research and reference). Incl both materials about Louisiana and by Louisianians without regard to subject. LSU Press Collection(preservation copy of each title kept for exhibit purposes only). LSU theses and dissertations from 1900-date. LSU Faculty Collection. Also, 1300 maps, 104 VF drawers, 250 boxes of uncataloged pamphlets.

MA —MEMORIAL HALL LIBRARY, Elm Sq, Andover, 01810. Nancy C Jacobson, Dir
Holdings: Vols 100 // Cat Mss Maps Pix
Notes: Incl original drawing of Lincoln by Charles Barry, Springfield, Ill, 1860.

MA —BOSTON UNIVERSITY, Mugar Memorial Library, Special Collections Dept, 771 Commonwealth Ave, Boston, 02215. Howard B Gotlieb, Dir
Holdings: Cat Pix
Notes: Correspondence.

MA —HARVARD UNIVERSITY LIBRARY, Widener Library, American History Collection, Cambridge, 02138. F Nathaniel Bunker, Bibliographer; Charles Warren, Bibliographer
Holdings: Cat Mss Microforms
Notes: See *Harvard Library Notes,* II (1925), 71-74.

MI —ADRIAN COLLEGE, Shipman Library, Adrian, 49221. James A Dodd, Library Dir
Holdings: Vols 744 // Cat Maps Pix Pamphlets
Notes: Lincoln and Lincolniana.

MI —GRAND RAPIDS JUNIOR COLLEGE, Arthur Andrews Memorial Library, 140 Ransom St NE, Grand Rapids, 49502. Bernice Whitley, Dir of Library Services
Holdings: Vols 1000 // Cat Pix
Notes: Arthur Andrews Collection of published materials on Lincoln.

MN —MINNEAPOLIS PUBLIC LIBRARY & INFORMATION CENTER, Adams Collection of Lincolniana, 300 Nicollet Mall, Minneapolis, 55401. Robert K Bruce, Librn
Holdings: Vols 7500 Cat

MT —MONTANA STATE UNIVERSITY, Library, Bozeman, 59717. Minnie Ellen Paugh, Special Collections Librn
Holdings: Vols 500 // Uncat
Notes: Collection of M L Wilson. Pamphlet collection of 6 VF drawers is more extensive than the book collection.

NJ —CENTENARY COLLEGE, Taylor Memorial Library, 400 Jefferson St, Hackettstown, 07840. Carol Steen, Dir of Learning Resources
Holdings: Vols 104 // Cat Pix Memorabilia
Notes: Lancey Collection of Abraham Lincoln. No separate catalog; collection incl in main catalog. Incl journal *Lincoln Lore* (1958-date), clippings, stamps, pictures, statuary.

NY —NEW YORK STATE LIBRARY, State Education Bldg Annex, Washington Ave, Albany, 12224.
Holdings: Cat Mss Pix
Notes: Library has the original of the first draft of the Emancipation Proclamation of September 22, 1862. Also more than 1000 titles of Lincolniana and 50 of the original Lincoln cartoons incl Currier and Ives; the Meserve collection of photographs of Lincoln, about 100 pictures.

†NY —COLUMBIA UNIVERSITY LIBRARIES, Butler Library, Rare Book and Manuscript Library, 535 W 114 St, New York, 10027.
Notes: A large and comprehensive collection of portraits and memorabilia.

NY —UNIVERSITY CLUB, Library, One W 54 St, New York, 10019. Guy St Clair, Library Dir
Holdings: Vols (100,000) Cat Mss Maps Pix
Notes: A private library for the members of the University Club, their guests, and serious scholars upon written application to the Library Director.

OH —RUTHERFORD B HAYES LIBRARY, 1337 Hayes Ave, Fremont, 43420. Watt P Marchman, Dir
Notes: A collection of 1500 volumes and pamphlets pertaining to the life of Abraham Lincoln, the sixteenth President of the United States. Also several hundred pieces of correspondence, incl letters by Susan B Anthony, William Jennings Bryan, Salmon P Chase, William Dennison, Washington Gladden, Jonathan Heckenwelder, William Dean Howells, William McKinley, Return J Meigs, Rufus Putnam, John Sherman and others, collected by C H Lyman. Index to collections.

†OR —LEWIS AND CLARK COLLEGE, Library, 615 SW Palatine Hill Rd, Portland, 97219.
Holdings: Vols 700 Cat Pix Periodical articles Pamphlets

OR —UNIVERSITY OF PORTLAND, Wilson W Clark Memorial Library, 5000 N Willamette Blvd, PO Box 03017, Portland, 97203. Rev Joseph P Browne, CSC, Dir
Holdings: Vols 500 // Cat
Notes: David Wheeler Hazen Memorial Collection.

PA —FRANKLIN & MARSHALL COLLEGE, Library, Lancaster, 17604. Kathleen J Moretto, Library Dir
Holdings: Uncat Pix
Notes: The W W Griest Collection of Lincoln Pictures contains 300 photographs, lithographs, wood engravings, half-tone engravings, mezzotints and etchings of Lincoln. The Ralph E Stine Lincoln Collection.

PA —ALLEGHENY COLLEGE, Lawrence Lee Pelletier Library, Meadville, 16335. Margaret L Moser, Librn
Holdings: Vols 1650 Cat Mss Maps Pix
Notes: Basic collection was Lincoln Library of Ida M Tarbell, whose papers form a related collection at Reis Library. Downs 4027. Benjamin P Thomas gives a general description of the Tarbell Lincoln Collection in his article (address) "Our Lincoln Heritage from Ida Tarbell," in the *Abraham Lincoln* Quarterly, March, 1950. Collection not completely cataloged.

RI —BROWN UNIVERSITY, John Hay Library, McLellan Lincoln Collection, 20 Prospect St, Providence, 02912. Jennifer B Lee, Special Collections Librn
Holdings: Vols (15,000) Cat Mss Pix Phonorecords Microforms
Budget: $1600
Notes: The McLellan Lincoln Collection was originally the property of Charles Woodberry McLellan, one of 5 great Lincoln collectors at the turn of the century. It was acquired for Brown University in 1923 by John D Rockefeller and others. Increased steadily since that time, the book collection is especially strong in biographies and early editions of the campaign lives. About 85 percent of the titles in *Lincoln Bibliography,* 1829-1939, by Jay Monaghan, are in the collection. Of the 218 foreign titles listed in this bibliography, the collection has some 167 books and 16 films or photostats. In conjunction with The Harris Collection, the John Hay Library holds what is probably the largest number of poems on Lincoln in any one place. There is also a good selection of representative titles of the books which Lincoln read. The ms collection incl original letters, notes and documents,over 950 of which were written or signed by Lincoln; from 1838 on, there is something for every year of his life. The Lincoln mss appear in *The Collected Works of Abraham Lincoln* edited by Roy P Basler, and its supplement. Ms material of Lincoln's family and associates as well as ms facsimiles of holdings of Lincoln material in other libraries are in the collection. The broadsides incl many song sheets, contemporary

LINCOLN, ABRAHAM (cont.)

political sheets, ballots, and posters; also 27 of the 52 printed editions of the "Emancipation Proclamation" listed by Charles Eberstadt in *Lincoln's Emancipation Proclamation*. There is a selection of newspapers for the war years, 1860-1865, and an index of over 11,300 entries for Lincoln items in all existing files of the Illinois newspapers down through the Civil War. The prints, arranged according to Meserve numbers, contains most of theknown photographs of Lincoln, rare engravings, caricatures, Currier and Ives prints, and original oil portraits done by artists of Lincoln's day, as well as original paintings of Lincoln's deathbed by Alonzo Chappel and Alexander Ritchie; some original drawings, as well as a scrapbook of Thomas Nast's Civil War sketches. Sheet music collection has almost every piece of Lincoln sheet music known to exist from minstrel songs to funeral marches, memorial songs and campaign songs. Statuary is well represented and incl two Rogers groups, an original Truman Bartlett plaster statuette of Lincoln, and replicas of Leonard Volk's work. The museum objects incl over 550 medals, mourning and campaign badges, coins, postage stamps and other miscellany. For a more detailed description of the collection, see Esther C Cushman: The McLellan Lincoln Collection at BrownUniversity (Brown University Library, 1928). The collection is housed in two separate rooms plus stack space. It has its own catalog and is restricted to reference use.
See also entry under Hay, John

TN —LINCOLN MEMORIAL UNIVERSITY, Carnegie Library with Bert Vincent Memorial Wing, Harrogate, 37752. Edgar Archer, Dir
Holdings: Vols 18,000 Cat Maps Pix Phonorecords 16mm Films
Notes: The Abraham Lincoln Center for Lincoln studies located at Abraham Lincoln Museum on the campus of Lincoln University established to display one of the largest collections of Lincoln and Civil War materials in the United States. Described fully in the Lincoln Herald, summer, 1973 (entire issue). National Lincoln Civil War Council Center for study of military surgery and medicine from the Civil War. National headquarters for the Society of Civil War surgeons. Also the center for the study of military music. 7000 pieces of sheet music dating from the War of 1812.

TX —LE TOURNEAU COLLEGE, Margaret Estes Library, 2100 S Mobberly Ave, PO Box 7001, Longview, 75601. Rachel Miley, Acting Dir of Library Services
Holdings: Vols (178,846) Cat Mss Maps Pix Slides Microforms
Budget: ($40,000)

†WA —WASHINGTON STATE UNIVERSITY, Library, Manuscripts, Archives & Special Collections, Pullman, 99164. John F Guido, Head
Holdings: Vols // Cat Mss
Notes: Bissett-Witherspoon Collection incl a Lincoln ms, approx 2000 monographs, and about 500 pamphlets, bibliographies, facsimiles, clippings, photographs and illustrations, programs, brochures and other ephemera on Lincoln and the Lincoln theme. Described in *The Record* (October 1945), pp 10-11.

WA —TACOMA PUBLIC LIBRARY, 1102 Tacoma Ave S, Tacoma, 98402. Kevin Hegarty, Dir
Holdings: Vols 1500 Cat Pix
Notes: Based on collection of Marion L Sauners.

LINCOLN, EDWIN HALE, 1848-1938

MA —LENOX LIBRARY ASSOCIATION, Main St, Lenox, 01240. Denis J Lesieur, Dir
Holdings: Pix
Notes: Edwin Hale Lincoln, (1848-1938), Pittsfield photographer. Collection contains glass plate negatives and platinum prints concentrating on Lenox estates, ca 1883-1933. Publication: *A Pride of Places; Lenox Summer Cottages 1883-1933*, Donald T Oakes, ed (Lenox Library Association, 1981).

LINCOLN, JOSEPH C.

MA —FALMOUTH PUBLIC LIBRARY, 123 Katharine Lee Bates Rd, Falmouth, 02540. Ann M Haddad, Librn
Holdings: Vols 46 Cat
Notes: Incl Joseph C Lincoln novels about Cape Cod area and people.

NY —NATIONAL SOARING MUSEUM, Library, Harris Hill, RD #3, Elmira, 14903.

LINCOLN, MARY JOHNSON BAILEY

MA —SIMMONS COLLEGE ARCHIVES, 300 The Fenway, Boston, 02115. Megan Sniffin-Marinoff, College Archivist
Notes: (I) Minutes of the Industrial Committee of the Woman's Education Association (1873-1929) from Feb 15, 1872 to Dec 5, 1882. Primarily concerned with the Committee's development of the Boston Cooking School. Figuring prominently in the minutes are Maria Parloa (1843-1909), one of the first instructors at the school, and Mary Johnson Bailey Lincoln (1844-1921), under whose leadership the Boston Cooking School began to attain a national reputation. For further information on these women, see *Notable American Women*. The Committee's relationship with the NY Diet Kitchen, the North Bennett St Industrial School (Boston), and the Massachusetts Institute of Technology also are discussed in the minutes. In addition to organizing a school for cooking, the Committee concerned itself with the education for women in dressmaking, nursing, phonography, andwoodcarving (based on the Cincinnati carving school). (II) Account books of the Household Aid Co (The Domestic Economy Committee) of the Woman's Education Association from August, 1903 to May, 1905. Organized by the Association of Collegiate Alumnae and the Woman's Education Association, the company was a cooperative residence for 20 servants with a training and placement program and a mediation service to deal with employers.

LINCOLN BRIGADE see Abraham Lincoln Brigade

LINCOLN HIGHWAY ASSOCIATION

MI —UNIVERSITY OF MICHIGAN, Engineering-Transportation Library, 312 Undergraduate Library, Ann Arbor, 48109. Sharon A Balius, Assoc Librn
Holdings: Mss Pix
Notes: The collections contains the business files of the Association. Also included are 3000 photographs of the construction of the Lincoln Highway.

LIND, JENNY

IL —NORTH PARK COLLEGE LIBRARY, 5125 N Spaulding Ave, Chicago, 60625. Dorothy-Ellen Gross, Dir
Holdings: Vols 200 Cat Mss
Notes: Collection consists of books, medals, other objects d'art (bottles, coins, etc), pictures, music and letters to and from Jenny Lind and P T Barnum.

NY —NEW YORK HISTORICAL SOCIETY, Library, 170 Central Park W, New York, 10024. James Gregory, Librn

LINDBERGH, CHARLES AUGUSTUS

CA —UNIVERSITY OF CALIFORNIA, LOS ANGELES, Research Library, Dept of Special Collections, 405 Hilgard Ave, Los Angeles, 90024. Edward Shreeves, Chairman, Bibliographers Group; David S Zeidberg, Head
Notes: 2 linear feet of correspondence, photographs, and ephemera relating to the Lindbergh kidnapping case, collected by Leon Hoage.

CT —YALE UNIVERSITY, Box 1603A, Yale Station, New Haven, 06520.

DC —GEORGETOWN UNIVERSITY, Medical Center, John Vinton Dahlgren Memorial Library, 3900 Reservoir Rd NW, Washington, 20057. Clementine Pellegrino, Librn
Holdings: Vols (1000) Cat Mss Pix Slides
Notes: The Alexis Carrel Collection. Medical research of man and society. Biological specimens and numerous unpublished mss. The Alexis Carrel Collection incl: a complete set of Dr Carrel's scientific notebooks starting in 1906; Col Charles Lindbergh's notebooks from 1935-1939 and those of De Ebeling, Dr Carrel's collaborator for 25 years; the ms of *Man the* Unknown, numerous specimens of Dr Carrel's work in transplantation of blood vessels, kidney, thyroid and other organs; considerable data on tissue cultivation. Correspondence from 1906 until his death to his wife, brother, cousins, nieces, etc; correspondence to many of the great scientists of the era, as well as all correspondence relating to his book *Man the Unknown*. There is a separate index to the collection.

LINDEMAN, RAYMOND L.

CT —YALE UNIVERSITY, Box 1603A, Yale Station, New Haven, 06520.

LINDLEY FAMILY

CA —UNIVERSITY OF CALIFORNIA, DAVIS, Shields Library, Dept of Special Collections, Davis, 95616. Donald Kunitz, Head; C Danial Elliott, Asst Head
Holdings: Cat Mss Pix
Notes: The Lindley Papers document life in Sacramento, Calif, during the second half of the 19th century, with family papers, photographs and memorabilia (356 items).

LINDSAY, ALBERT MUMFORD

DE —DELAWARE ART MUSEUM, Library, 2301 Kentmere Pkwy, Wilmington, 19806. Anne Hoslam, Librn
Holdings: Vols (25,000) Cat Mss
Notes: The collection is rich in the following subjects: Howard Pyle and his pupils; John Sloan and the eight; history of the book and printing; and English and American illustrated books. There is also a section on contemporary photography. Archival material on Albert Mumford Lindsay, Jerome Myers, Everett Shinn, Gayle Porter Hoskins, Frank Schoonover.

LINDSAY, HOWARD, 1889-1968

†WI —STATE HISTORICAL SOCIETY OF WISCONSIN, Library, 816 State St, Madison, 53706.
Notes: Scripts, notes, correspondence and other items concerning the collaboration of Howard Lindsay and Russel Crouse for the theater, motion pictures and television, as well as the work of each with other collaborators and individually.

LINDSAY, JACK

BC —UNIVERSITY OF VICTORIA, McPherson Library, Victoria, V8W 3H5, Can.
Notes: Incl letters to F Muller Ltd concerning publicaton of several books.

LINDSAY, NORMAN

PA —PENNSYLVANIA STATE UNIVERSITY, Fred Lewis Pattee Library, University Park, 16802. Stuart Forth, Dean of Libraries
Holdings: Vols Cat Mss Maps Pix
Notes: The Pennsylvania State University has for several years had a strong interest in the South Pacific, based on Australia but extending to New Zealand and other island groups, together with an interest in voyages

LINDSAY, NORMAN (cont.)

of exploration and scientific discovery. The collection is particularly strong in literature but extends to history, political science, the arts and humanities generally. Holdings housed in Special Collections includes the Moody gift of 90 prints and paintings, press collections including the Wattle Grove press, and Fanfrolico Press publications associated with Norman Lindsay. The special collection of Australiana is dedicated to Bruce Sutherland and was described in his publication *Australiana in the PSU Libraries* (Pennsylvania State University Libraries, 1969), 390 pp.

LINDSAY, VACHEL

AZ —NORTHERN ARIZONA UNIVERSITY, Special Collection Library, CU Box 6022, Flagstaff, 86011. Peter M Whiteley, Coordr/Archivist; William Mullane, Librn
Notes: Klonda Lynn Collection; incl poem written by Vachel Lindsay, American poet, when he visited Flagstaff, 1930.

CT —YALE UNIVERSITY, Box 1603A, Yale Station, New Haven, 06520.
Notes: Correspondence.

IN —INDIANA UNIVERSITY, Lilly Library, Seventh St, Bloomington, 47405. William R Cagle, Librn
Notes: Writings by author Vachel Lindsay.

OH —HIRAM COLLEGE, Teachout-Price Memorial Library, Hiram, 44234. Joanne M Sawyer, Archivist; Marjorie M Adams, Music Librn
Holdings: Vols 40 Cat Mss Pix Phonorecords
Notes: Collection incl all first editions of Lindsay's works, many autographed and/or annotated; original mss and drawings; correspondence; criticism; clippings; photographs; recordings of Lindsay and contemporaries reading his poetry; emphasizes Lindsay's connection with Hiram College; restricted hours: call or write in advance.

OR —UNIVERSITY OF OREGON, Library, Eugene, 97403. Kenneth W Duckett, Curator
Notes: Papers of Stoddard King incl a number of Vachel Lindsay letters and broadsides.

VA —UNIVERSITY OF VIRGINIA, Alderman Library, Clifton Waller Barrett Collection, Charlottesville, 22901. Joan St C Crane, Cur of American Literature Collections
Holdings: Vols 1500 // Uncat Mss Pix
Notes: His personal library. Inventory list of books, in process. Guide to over 4000 mss, completed (not to be published). This is Lindsay's library acquired relatively complete.

LINDSEY, SHELAGH

MB —UNIVERSITY OF MANITOBA, Elizabeth Dafoe Library, Archives and Special Collections Dept, Winnipeg, R3T 2N2, Can. Richard E Bennett, Dept Head; Corrado A Santoro, Reference Archivist
Notes: Newsclippings, book reviews, interviews, articles and publications of and about Marshall McLuhan. Three boxes.

LINE ENGRAVING see Engravers, Engraving and Engravings

LINEAR ACCELERATORS

NM —UNIVERSITY OF CALIFORNIA, Los Alamos National Laboratory, Libraries, PO Box 1663, MSP 362, Los Alamos, 87545. J Arthur Freed, Head Librn
Holdings: Vols (800,000) Cat Films Microforms
Budget: ($700,000)
Notes: Incl 500,000 classified and unclassified reports. There are 25 branch libraries and a central collection. The Medical Library contains about 40,000 vols in the areas of biomedical research.

LINEN AND LINEN-MAKING

MA —MERRIMACK VALLEY TEXTILE MUSEUM, Library, 800 Massachusetts Ave, North Andover, 01845. Clare Sheridan, Librn; Laurence Gross, Cur
Notes: *Checklist of Prints, Drawings and Painting in the Merrimack Valley Textile* Museum, Helena E Wright, 1972; *Checklist of Finished Textiles,* Katherine R Koob, 1980; *New City on the Merrimack: Prints of Lawrence 1845-1876,* Helena Wright, 1974; *Homespun to Factory Made: Wollen Textiles in America 1776-1876* (exhibit catalog) 1978; *Textile Technology Prints: A Checklist of Prints, Drawings and Paintings in the Merrimack Valley Textile Museum,* Helena E Wright, 1980; *All Sorts of Good Sufficient Cloth: Linen-making in New England, 1640-1860,* (exhibit catalogue) 1980; *The Merrimack Valley Textile Museum: A Guide to the Manuscript* Collections Helena E Wright, Garland Press 1983.

LINGUA FRANCA see Languages, Mixed

LINGUISTICS see Language and Languages; Philology

LININGTON, ELIZABETH

MA —BOSTON UNIVERSITY, Mugar Memorial Library, Special Collections Dept, 771 Commonwealth Ave, Boston, 02215. Howard B Gotlieb, Dir
Holdings: Cat Mss Pix
Notes: Mss, correspondence, etc collected in depth; incl publications by or about.

LINK, EDWIN A.

NY —STATE UNIVERSITY OF NEW YORK, BINGHAMTON, Glenn G Bartle Library, Binghamton, 13901. Marion Hanscom, Special Collections Librn
Notes: A portion of the personal library of Edwin A Link, pioneer in aeronautics, with his invention of the Link Trainer. This is a small collection of some 75 books dealing with aviation. The books augment an extensive collection of Link's papers.

LINK FAMILY PAPERS

MO —WASHINGTON UNIVERSITY, Libraries, Special Collections Dept, Campus Box 1061, St Louis, 63130.
Notes: Papers of the prominent Link Family of 1809-1921.

LINNAEUS, CAROLUS see Linne, Carl Von, 1707-1778

LINNE, CARL VON, 1707-1778

IL —MORTON ARBORETUM, Sterling Morton Library, Lisle, 60532. Ian MacPhail, Librn
Holdings: Vols (22,000)
Notes: Emphasis is on Woody plants. Print collection of 3000 pieces; 2000 botanical and horticultural rare books; Linnaeana. The Jens Jensen Archive of letters, photographs, blueprints, landscape plans.

KS —UNIVERSITY OF KANSAS, Kenneth Spencer Research Library, Special Collections Dept, Lawrence, 66045. Alexandra Mason, Librn
Holdings: Vols 1400 Cat Mss
Notes: First and later editions of Linne and his students, from the Ralph Ellis and T J Fitzpatrick collections. Noncirculating. See Williams, Terrence, *A checklist of Linnaeana, 1735-1835, in the University of Kansas Libraries,* Lawrence, 1964.

KS —KANSAS STATE UNIVERSITY, Library, Special Collections & University Archives, Manhattan, 66506. Antonia Q Pigno, Coordr; John J Vander Velde, Librn; Anthony R Crawford, Univ Archivist
Holdings: Vols 1280 Cat Microforms
Budget: ($10,000)
Notes: Catalog: Rudolph, G A and Williams, Evan. *Linnaeana.* Manhattan, Kansas: Kansas State University Library, 1970.

MA —HARVARD UNIVERSITY, Museum of Comparative Zoology, Library, 26 Oxford St, Cambridge, 02138. Eva S Jonas, Librn
Holdings: Cat Mss Pix Microforms

MA —SMITH COLLEGE, Library, Northampton, 01063. Ruth Mortimer, Cur of Rare Books
Holdings: Vols 145 // Cat
Notes: Thornton Collection of 15th-19th century herbals, early microscopy, Linneaus, biography.

MO —MISSOURI BOTANICAL GARDEN LIBRARY, PO Box 299, Saint Louis, 63166. M R Crosby, Dir of Research
Holdings: Vols 1800 Uncat
Notes: Arranged by Soulsby numbers.

OH —LLOYD LIBRARY & MUSEUM, 917 Plum St, Cincinnati, 45202. John B Griggs, Librn
Notes: Extensive holdings on, and original editions of Carl von Linne.

PA —HUNT INSTITUTE FOR BOTANICAL DOCUMENTATION, Hunt Botanical Library, Carnegie-Mellon University, Pittsburgh, 15213. Bernadette G Callery, Librn
Holdings: Vols 2800 Cat Pix
Notes: The Strandell Collection of Linnaeana includes all the works of Carl Linnaeus (1707-1778) in many editions and translations. Includes a conplete set of Linnaeus' doctoral dissertations in original state. Extensive collection of works written by his students and much material from the 18th century to date relating to Linnaeus, his students and his work. Includes 2000 pamphlets and 48 albums of newspaper clippings. A detailed descriptive catalog is in process.

WI —UNIVERSITY OF WISCONSIN, MADISON, Memorial Library, History of Science Collection, 728 State St, Madison, 53706. John Neu, Bibliographer
Holdings: Vols 279 Cat
Notes: Linnean Collection. Extension collection of the work of Carl von Linne, including an almost complete collection of the Linnean dissertations. Also present are a number of secondary works--biographies, bibliographies and critical works on Linnaeus. Restricted use: Rare Book Department.

ON —AGRICULTURE CANADA, Plant Research Library, Research Branch, Central Experimental Farm 49, Ottawa, K1A 0C6, Can. Mrs E Gavora, Librn
Holdings: Vols (10,500) Cat Maps Microforms
Notes: One of the most extensive botanical collections in Canada, especially in the taxonomy of higher plants and fungi. Contains many of the basic works from the starting point of botany in 1753 to date. Major botanical works of Linnaeus and others, covering flora of land areas of most parts of the world.

LINSCOTT, ROBERT

MO —WASHINGTON UNIVERSITY, Libraries, Special Collections Dept, Campus Box 1061, St Louis, 63130.
Notes: A small but significant collection.

LINTON, ELIZABETH LYNN, 1822-1898

CA —UNIVERSITY OF CALIFORNIA, LOS ANGELES, Research Library, Dept of Special Collections, 405 Hilgard Ave, Los Angeles, 90024. Edward Shreeves, Chairman, Bibliographers Group; David S Zeidberg, Head
Holdings: Vols 20 Mss
Notes: 20 first and other editions of her books; 70 letters; 6 mss.

LINTON, WILLIAM J.

CT —YALE UNIVERSITY, Box 1603A, Yale Station, New Haven, 06520.
Holdings: Cat Mss

LINVILLE, HENRY R.

MI —WAYNE STATE UNIVERSITY, Walter P Reuther Library, Archives of Labor & Urban Affairs, Detroit, 48202. Philip Mason, Dir
Notes: The records of the American

LINVILLE, HENRY R. (cont.)

Federation of Teachers, as well as the files of the Detroit, Toledo, East Detroit, and other Federations of Teachers, are now preserved in the Archives. The personal papers of several teacher union leaders, incl Arthur Elder, Selma M Borchardt, Henry R Linville, Mary Herrick, and others are important supplements to the national union's file.

LION, LEON MARKS

NY —UNIVERSITY OF ROCHESTER, Rush Rhees Library, Department of Rare Books and Special Collections, Rochester, 14627. Peter Dzwonkoski, Librn
Holdings: Cat Mss Pix
Notes: Papers, etc, incl books by and about, etc.

LIPP, FREDERICK

MA —BOSTON UNIVERSITY, Mugar Memorial Library, Special Collections Dept, 771 Commonwealth Ave, Boston, 02215. Howard B Gotlieb, Dir
Holdings: Cat Mss Correspondence

LIPPINCOTT FAMILY

NJ —GLASSBORO STATE COLLEGE, Savitz Library, Stewart Room, Glassboro, 08028. Clara Kirner, Special Collection Librn
Notes: Papers.

LIPPITT, CHARLES WARREN, 1846-1924

RI —BROWN UNIVERSITY, John Hay Library, 20 Prospect St, Providence, 02912. Mark N Brown, Cur Mss
Holdings: // Mss
Notes: Papers of Charles Warren Lippitt, 1846-1924, Governor of Rhode Island and textile manufacturer. Brown class of 1865. Correspondence, typescripts of papers presented before learned and patriotic societies, incl Sons of the American Revolution (1904-1916) and the Society of the Cincinnati (1899-1920), notes, statistics, clippings, and pamphlets relating to mercantile, political, historical, and biographical topics. Incl papers and genealogical notes on the Lippitt and related families. The papers total 8500 items for the period 1875-1920 and constitute evidence of a lifetime of business and public service.

LIPPMANN, WALTER

CT —YALE UNIVERSITY, Box 1603A, Yale Station, New Haven, 06520.
Holdings: Mss Pix

LIPSKY, ELEAZAR

MA —BOSTON UNIVERSITY, Mugar Memorial Library, Special Collections Dept, 771 Commonwealth Ave, Boston, 02215. Howard B Gotlieb, Dir
Holdings: Mss

LIQUID METALS

CA —GENERAL ELECTRIC CO, ANTO, Library, PO Box 3508, Sunnyvale, 94088. Dorothy A Hutson, Mgr Information Servs
Notes: ONTYME Electronic mailbox address; CLASS.GES ILL and photocopying available.

LIQUORS

CA —UNIVERSITY OF CALIFORNIA, DAVIS, General Library, Davis, 95616. Bernard Kreissman, University Librn; C Danial Elliott, Asst Head, Dept Special Collections
Holdings: Vols 1000 Cat
Notes: Liquor distillation.

IN —HURTY-PECK LIBRARY OF BEVERAGE LITERATURE, 5650 W Raymond Street, PO Box 41167, Indianapolis, 46208. Ben Wilson, Librn
Holdings: Vols (6000) Cat //
Notes: The most comprehensive collection, in English, in the world on beverages of all types. History, manufacture, formulae, customs. Books on beer and brewing; cocoa and chocolate; coffee; liquors and spirits; soft drinks; tea; and wine.

NY —CULINARY INSTITUTE OF AMERICA, Katharine Angell Library, North Rd, Hyde Park, 12538. Eileen deVries, Librn
Notes: The Tastevin Collection, one of the most complete collections on wine and spirits in the eastern US.

LISS, JOSEPH

MA —BOSTON UNIVERSITY, Mugar Memorial Library, Special Collections Dept, 771 Commonwealth Ave, Boston, 02215. Howard B Gotlieb, Dir
Holdings: Cat Mss Pix
Notes: Mss, correspondence, etc collected in depth; incl publications by or about.

LISTER, JOSEPH, 1827-1912

KS —UNIVERSITY OF KANSAS MEDICAL CENTER, College of Health Sciences & Hospital, Clendening History of Medicine Library, Rainbow Blvd at 39th, Kansas City, 66103. Robert P Hudson, Chmn/Cur
Holdings: Vols (15,725) Cat Mss
Notes: Letters, 1894-95, 1906. 7 items. British surgeon and founder of antiseptic surgery. 6 letters to Charles R Straton and 1 letter to J F Binnie. Letters to Straton are described in "Six Lister Letters," by L R C Agnew, in Bulletin of the History of Medicine, v 14 (1959), pp 228-231.

LISZT, FRANZ

DC —LIBRARY OF CONGRESS, Music Division, Washington, 20540.
Holdings: Cat Mss
Notes: Over 200 autograph letters.

KY —UNIVERSITY OF LOUISVILLE, School of Music, Dwight Anderson Memorial Music Library, 2301 S Third St, Louisville, 40292. Marion Korda, Librn
Holdings: Vols 100 Cat Mss Pix
Notes: Isidor Philipp Archive and Memorial Library. Described in: *The American Liszt* Society, vol 1, no 2, June, 1977; vol II, December, 1977; and vol 34, no 1, Sept, 1977.

MA —BOSTON UNIVERSITY, Mugar Memorial Library, Special Collections Dept, 771 Commonwealth Ave, Boston, 02215. Howard B Gotlieb, Dir
Holdings: Vols 300
Notes: Letters, fragments of scores, photographs, posters, programs.

RI —BROWN UNIVERSITY, John Hay Library, 20 Prospect St, Providence, 02912. Mark N Brown, Cur Mss
Holdings: Mss
Notes: Papers of William O Fuller (1828-1910), music teacher of Providence, comprising letters 1848 from Europe, incl a letter from Franz Liszt; papers of Johann Christian Gottlieb Graupner (1767-1836) and John Rowe Parker (fl 1820s) collected by Horace Mason Reynolds, relating to the music-publishing business in Boston, 1802-1838; papers of the American folklorist Mellinger Edward Henry (1873-1946) relating to his research and publications on American folk-songs 1910-1942; papers, 1912-1948, of Providence composer Hugh Frederick MacColl (1885-1953); papers of Frances Herriot Sargent, stage manager for "Porgy" and "Porgy and Bess", relating to productions of these, 1928-1942.

LITERACY see Illiteracy and Literacy

LITERARY AGENTS

CA —UNIVERSITY OF CALIFORNIA, DAVIS, Shields Library, Dept of Special Collections, Davis, 95616. Donald Kunitz, Head; C Danial Elliott, Asst Head
Holdings: Vols Uncat Mss Pix
Notes: Business papers of off-Broadway literary and theatrical agent, Toby Cole, for the years 1957-73. Incl mss by Saul Bellow and Sam Shepherd, among others. 4000 pix.

†NY —COLUMBIA UNIVERSITY LIBRARIES, Butler Library, Rare Book and Manuscript Library, 535 W 114 St, New York, 10027.
Notes: Archive of the literary agency Curtis Brown Limited. Also the papers of the literary agency of James Oliver Brown, as well as those of John Cushman Associates, Inc, the firm he acquired in 1978.

NY —GRADUATE CENTER OF THE CITY UNIVERSITY OF NEW YORK, William H and Gwynne K Crouse Library for Publishing Arts, 33 W 42 St, New York, 10036. Alfred H Lane, Dir
Notes: Recently established and still growing, but intended to become the authoritative source of materials in the field, of particular value in research about the publishing industry. Open to staff members of publishing houses, students, scholars, authors, printers, and booksellers. Primarily 20th century materials, and particularly useful for research on technical, financial, and historical matters. Much on the history of individual houses, economics of authorship; marketing and distribution of books; etc.

LITERARY ANNUALS AND GIFTBOOKS

†CA —UNIVERSITY OF SAN FRANCISCO, Richard A Gleeson Library, The Countess Bernardine Murphy Donohue Rare Book Room, San Francisco, 94117. D Steven Corey, Special Collections Librn
Holdings: Vols 400 pix
Notes: Emphasis is on fine printing, chiefly American, but all aspects of Christmas are covered. The entire collection is about 1500 items; much ephemera, and many pieces relating to San Francisco.

CA —UNIVERSITY OF CALIFORNIA, SANTA BARBARA, Library, Dept of Special Collections, Santa Barbara, 93106. Christian F Brun, Head
Holdings: Vols 1100

FL —FLORIDA STATE UNIVERSITY, Robert Manning Strozier Library, Childhood in Poetry Collection, Tallahassee, 32306. Frederick Korn, Cur
Holdings: Vols (25,000) Cat
Notes: The Childhood in Poetry Collection consists of the books of all the great poets and hundreds of minor poets of all periods, in first or other early and illustrated editions, in children's periodicals and "juveniles". There are more than 300 hymnals, incl the personal collection of Dr Robert Lowry, author of "Shall We Gather at the River" and other popular hymns. There are also nearly 500 annuals and giftbooks. The Collection is strong, as well, in works of criticism, biography and reference. An eleven-volume, illustrated catalog (1967-1980) is available from Gale Research. Over 200,000 poems are listed in a key-word index, keyed to the books in which they appear. The nucleus of the Collection was assembled as the lifetime leisure activity of the donor, John Mackay Shaw, who now serves as curator emeritus. His object has been to gather in one place thebooks in which poems relating to childhood first appeared.

FL —FLORIDA STATE UNIVERSITY, Robert Manning Strozier Library, Special Collections Dept, Tallahassee, 32306. Opal M Free, Head, Special Collections
Holdings: Vols 259 Uncat
Notes: Christmas books as gifts. Noncirculating. No photocopying.

IL —NEWBERRY LIBRARY, 60 W Walton St, Chicago, 60610. Diana Haskell, Cur of Modern Mss
Holdings: Cat
Notes: A large collection of English and American 19th century gift annuals.

IL —NORTHWESTERN UNIVERSITY, Library, Special Collections Dept, 1937 Sheridan Rd, Evanston, 60201. R Russell Maylone, Cur
Holdings: Vols 430 Cat
Notes: English and American, 19th century.

LITERARY ANNUALS AND GIFTBOOKS (cont.)

IL —LAKE FOREST COLLEGE, Donnelley Library, Lake Forest, 60045. Arthur H Miller Jr, College Librn
Holdings: Vols (1000) Cat
Notes: Examples of many late 19th century and early 20th century presses, from Alfred Hamill Collection. Much mid-20th century ephemera (including printers' Christmas gifts, in Richard Templeton collection of 500 items, received 1977).

MA —AMERICAN ANTIQUARIAN SOCIETY LIBRARY, 185 Salisbury St, Worcester, 01609. Marcus A McCorison, Dir & Librn
Holdings: Vols 1500 Cat

MN —UNIVERSITY OF MINNESOTA, O Meredith Wilson Library, 309 19 Ave S, Minneapolis, 55455. Austin J McLean, Chief, Special Collections
Holdings: Vols 584 // Cat

NJ —RUTGERS, THE STATE UNIVERSITY OF NEW JERSEY, Alexander Library, Special Collections and Archives, College Ave & Huntington St, New Brunswick, 08903. Ronald L Becker, Cur of Manuscripts and Rare Books
Holdings: Vols 400 Cat

NY —NEW YORK PUBLIC LIBRARY, Research Libraries, General Research Division, Fifth Ave & 42 St, New York, 10018. Rodney Phillips, Chief
Holdings: Vols (2,225,000) Cat Maps Pix Microforms
Budget: ($775,718)

OH —MIAMI UNIVERSITY, King Library, Walter Havighurst Special Collections Library, Oxford, 45056. Helen Ball, Cur of Special Collections
Holdings: Vols 400 Cat
Notes: English and American annuals.

PA —FREE LIBRARY OF PHILADELPHIA, Rare Book Dept, Logan Sq, Philadelphia, 19103. Marie E Korey, Rare Book Librn
Holdings: Vols (450) // Uncat
Notes: 19th century giftbooks and annuals.

PA —EASTERN COLLEGE, Frank Warner Memorial Library, Saint Davids, 19087. James L Sauer, Librn
Holdings: Uncat Mss Pix
Notes: The Harry C Goebel Collection. Incl Bruce Rogers printings (over 460); press books (about 350); oriental art (over 250); bookplates (with a separate collection of an almost complete set of bookplates designed by Edwin Davis French); Christmas Books; art and graphic arts (incl the French Graphic Arts Collection of Adolph DeMilly); first editions of Christopher Morley; Print Collection (1315 prints); Oriental art realia and artiacts.

PA —PENNSYLVANIA STATE UNIVERSITY, Fred Lewis Pattee Library, Special Collections Dept, University Park, 16802. Charles Mann, Chief, Special Collections
Holdings: Vols 1085
Budget: ($37,000)
Notes: A collection of English and American 19th century gift annuals.

RI —BROWN UNIVERSITY, John Hay Library, Harris Collection, Prospect St, Providence, 02912. Rosemary L Cullen, Cur
Holdings: Vols (200,000) Cat Mss Pix Phonorecords Microforms
Budget: ($15,000)
Notes: The Harris Collection of American Poetry and Plays is principally composed of American and Canadian poetry and plays from the 17th century to the present. Extensive holdings in giftbooks and annuals, up to an estimated 90 percent of those published in America during the 19th century. See *Dictionary Catalog of The Harris Collection of American Poetry and Plays* (Boston; G K Hall, 1972), 13 vols; Supplement (1977), 3 vol. Separate catalog.

SC —UNIVERSITY OF SOUTH CAROLINA, Thomas Cooper Library, Columbia, 29208. Kenneth E Toombs, Dir of Libraries; Roger Mortimer, Rare Book Librn
Holdings: Vols 450
Notes: An outstanding collection of English and American literary annuals for 1800-1825.

WI —UNIVERSITY OF WISCONSIN, MADISON, Memorial Library, British & American Language & Literature Collection, 728 State St, Madison, 53706. Yvonne Schofer, Bibliographer
Holdings: Cat Microforms
Notes: An extensive collection of over 400 American gift books and annuals.

LITERARY FORGERIES AND MYSTIFICATIONS

CA —HUNTINGTON LIBRARY, Art Gallery & Botanical Gardens, 1151 Oxford Rd, San Marino, 91108. Robert L Middlekauff, Dir; Daniel H Woodward, Librn
Holdings: Cat
Notes: Material by and about T J Wise, incl the forgeries.

CT —YALE UNIVERSITY, Box 1603A, Yale Station, New Haven, 06520.
Notes: T J Wise Forgeries.

CT —MOLESWORTH INSTITUTE, Memorial Library, 143 Hanks Hill Rd, Storrs, 06268. Norman D Stevens, Dir, Cur, and Librn
Holdings: Vols (1000) Uncat Mss
Notes: Incl material relating to the Molesworth Family, books by and about any person named Molesworth as well as original materials upon which the legendary Molesworth Institute was founded. In addition the collections now contain over 20, 000 library postcards and approx 375 library commemoratives acquired as part of the Institute's research work.

IL —HILLIS L GRIFFIN, (personal collection), 5800 Carpenter Ave, Downers Grove, 60515.
Notes: Renowned collection of materials on the masterful Nigel Molesworth (qv) founder of the infamous Molesworth Institute the hidden purposes of which are shrouded in dastardly mystery and secret programs believed to be nefarious and devilish plans and contrivances to disrupt American librarianship. Several victims of Molesworth's dealings have already suffered the pains of indifference to his warnings and found the White Feather at their place at table--suffice to say, we have heard little more about them.

IN —INDIANA UNIVERSITY, Lilly Library, Seventh St, Bloomington, 47405. William R Cagle, Librn
Holdings: Mss
Notes: Mss incl a collection of William Henry Ireland fabrications of Shakespeare. 69 items, 1805. Also, forgeries of Edgar Allan Poe by Joseph Cosey (4 items) and James Whitcomb Riley's Poe forgery of "Leonainie". Much on the forgeries of T J Wise.

MA —HARVARD UNIVERSITY LIBRARY, Cambridge, 02138.
Holdings: Cat
Notes: Materials by and about T J Wise, incl the forgeries.

NY —COLUMBIA UNIVERSITY LIBRARIES, Rare Book & Manuscript Library, 801 Butler Library, 535 W 114 St, New York, 10027. Kenneth A Lohf, Librn
Holdings: Vols 50
Notes: 19th century English literary forgeries by Thomas J Wise.

NY —NEW YORK PUBLIC LIBRARY, Research Libraries, General Research Division, Fifth Ave & 42 St, New York, 10018. Rodney Phillips, Chief
Holdings: Vols (2,225,000) Cat Maps Pix Microforms
Budget: ($775,718)

NY —SYRACUSE UNIVERSITY LIBRARIES, Ernest S Bird Library, George Arents Research Library for Special Collections, Syracuse, 13210. Carolyn A Davis, Manuscripts Librn; Amy S Doherty, University Archivist; Mark F Weimer, Rare Book Librn
Holdings: Cat
Notes: Materials by and about T J Wise, incl the forgeries.

NY —SYRACUSE UNIVERSITY LIBRARIES, Ernest S Bird Library, George Arents Research Library for Special Collections, Syracuse, 13210. Carolyn A Davis, Manuscripts Librn; Amy S Doherty, University Archivist; Mark F Weimer, Rare Book Librn
Holdings: Cat Mss Pix Slides Microforms
Notes: The extensive Swinburne collection of John Simon Mayfield.

RI —BROWN UNIVERSITY, John Hay Library, 20 Prospect St, Providence, 02912. Mark N Brown, Cur Mss
Holdings: Vols (300) // Cat
Notes: Brown-Ives Shakespeare Collection of 18th and early 19th century Shakespeare scholarship, incl: biographies; critical works; editions of the plays in English, French, and German; works on sources and characters; and the forgeries of John Payne Collier and William Henry Ireland. The collection is supplemented by the general rare books collection, incl first, second, and fourth folio editons of the comedies, histories and tragedies.

LITERARY FRAUDS see Literary Forgeries and Mystifications

LITERARY MAGAZINES OF AMERICA, ASSOCIATION see Association of Literary Magazines of America

LITERARY PERIODICALS see Periodicals, Literary

LITERARY PROPERTY see Copyright

LITERARY SOCIETIES

AZ —NORTHERN ARIZONA UNIVERSITY, Special Collection Library, CU Box 6022, Flagstaff, 86011. Peter M Whiteley, Coordr/Archivist; William Mullane, Librn
Notes: Shakespeare Club, Flagstaff, Ariz, Collection; minutes and programs, 1903-1971, 1975-1977. This women's literary club is believed to be the oldest active women's organization in Arizona.

OH —MIAMI UNIVERSITY, King Library, Walter Havighurst Special Collections Library, Oxford, 45056. Helen Ball, Cur of Special Collections
Holdings: Vols 1700 Uncat
Notes: The collection includes libraries of four college literary societies which were active on the Miami campus, especially in the early and middle years of the 19th century. Some of the papers of the societies are also preserved. Incl periodicals.

TX —TEXAS WOMAN'S UNIVERSITY, Bralley Memorial Library, Box 23715, TWU Sta, Denton, 76204. Metta Nicewarner, Spec Collections Libn
Holdings: Uncat Mss Pix
Notes: The Women's Shakespeare Club of Denton Collection (1899-), and the Ariel Club Collection (1891-), which includes correspondence, yearbooks, minutes, treasurer's reports and membership listings.

LITERARY WORLD ARCHIVES

ME —BOWDOIN COLLEGE, Library, Brunswick, 04011. Dianne M Gutscher, Cur of Special Collections
Holdings: Mss Pix
Notes: The Abbott Memorial Collection contains both printed and manuscript materials relating to Jacob Abbott, John S C Abbott, Edward Abbott and Lyman Abbott, as well as other members of the family. It consists of approx 25,000 items, including correspondence, sermons, diaries and journals, addresses, the archives of both the *Literary World* and *Outlook* magazines, and the Lyman Abbott autograph collection. First and subsequent editions of almost all of the family's published writings are also present.

LITERATURE

CT —STOWE-DAY LIBRARY, 77 Forest St, Hartford, 06105. Diana J Royce, Librn
Holdings: Vols (15,000) Cat Mss Pix
Notes: 150,000 cataloged mss and

LITERATURE (cont.)

publications concerning architecture, decorative arts, history and literature of the period 1840-1900, with emphasis on Nook Farm, Mark Twain, Harriet Beecher Stowe, Calvin E Stowe, Charles Dudley Warner, William Hooker Gillette, Isabella Beecher Hooker. Incl 5000 pictures.

DC —DISTRICT OF COLUMBIA PUBLIC LIBRARY, Literature Division, 901 G St NW, Washington, 20001. Octave S Stevenson, Chief, Literature Div
Holdings: Vols 40,765 Cat
Budget: $19,000
Notes: Plus 800 pamphlets.

IL —NORTHWESTERN UNIVERSITY, Library, Special Collections Dept, 1937 Sheridan Rd, Evanston, 60201. R Russell Maylone, Cur
Holdings: Vols 20,000 Cat
Notes: First, limited, special editions, works about, and ephemera of the major authors of the 20th century as well as representative minor writers. Incl English, American, French, and German authors and to a lesser extent Italian, Spanish, and other European writers. Extensive collections of Lawrence Durrell, T S Eliot, William Faulkner, Robert Graves, Ernest Hemingway, James Joyce, Karl Kraus, D H Lawrence, Hugh MacDiarmid, Henry Miller, Anais Nin, Ezra Pound, Gertrude Stein, H G Wells, W B Yeats. Additional 5000 private press books and 15,000 "little magazine" titles exclusive of runs in the general library collections.

LA —LOUISIANA STATE UNIVERSITY, Troy H Middleton Library, Louisiana Room, Baton Rouge, 70803. Evangeline Mills Lynch, Head Librn; Ruth Murray, Associate Librn
Holdings: Vols (33,500) Cat Maps VF
Notes: Louisiana Collection of history, description and travel, biography, agriculture, literature, politics and government, folklore, anthropology, geography, geology, education, language, music and natural history. Especially large subject collections may be found on Louisiana, the history of the lower Mississippi Valley, Abraham Lincoln, Romance languages and literatures, sugar culture and technology, Southern history, petroleum engineering, plant pathology, micropaleontology, ornithology, and various aspects of crawfish life, biology and culture. Complete depository of Louisiana State Documents; extensive newspapers clipping files; separate card catalog; items listed in Louisiana Union Catalog; restricted use (research and reference). Incl both materials about Louisiana and by Louisianians without regard to subject. LSU Press Collection(preservation copy of each title kept for exhibit purposes only). LSU theses and dissertations from 1900-date. LSU Faculty Collection. Also, 1300 maps, 104 VF drawers, 250 boxes of uncataloged pamphlets.

MA —BOSTON UNIVERSITY, Mugar Memorial Library, Special Collections Dept, 771 Commonwealth Ave, Boston, 02215. Howard B Gotlieb, Dir
Holdings: Cat Mss Pix
Notes: Incl literary and personal papers of about 1000 modern published authors; also first editions, translations, etc. A complete list is available.

MN —MINNEAPOLIS PUBLIC LIBRARY & INFORMATION CENTER, Literature & Language Dept, 300 Nicollet Mall, Minneapolis, 55401. Dorothy D Thews, Head
Holdings: Vols (210,000) Cat Microforms Phonorecords Audiotapes
Budget: ($49,124)
Notes: Foreign language collection: 30,000 vols, separate catalog. Theatre collection: 9 vertical drawers. Books integrated with department collection. Special reference collection of small press output of Minnesota authors.

NY —NEW YORK PUBLIC LIBRARY, Research Libraries, General Research Division, Fifth Ave & 42 St, New York, 10018. Rodney Phillips, Chief
Holdings: Vols (2,225,000) Cat Maps Pix Microforms
Budget: ($775,718)

NY —NEW YORK PUBLIC LIBRARY, Mid-Manhattan Library, Literature and Language Dept, 455 Fifth Ave, New York, 10016. Eric Steele, Sr Principal Librn
Holdings: Vols (160,000) Cat Phonorecords Microforms Audiotapes
Budget: ($92,000)

NY —US MILITARY ACADEMY LIBRARY, West Point, 10996. Elaine B Eatroff, Rare Book Cur
Holdings: Vols 1500 Cat
Notes: Thayer Collection, incl rare editions of 19th century science.

NC —TRYON PALACE RESTORATION, Library, 613 Pollock St, New Bern, 28560. Grace C Ipock, Registrar
Holdings: Vols 1400 Cat Maps Pix Slides
Notes: Governor Tryon's recreated library at Tryon Palace comprises 517 titles published before 1770. Other shelves at the historic houses in the complex incl vols published until ca 1820. Sixteen percent of Governor Tryon's inventoried library of 1770 is still sought. No photocopying.

OR —UNIVERSITY OF OREGON, Library, Eugene, 97403. Kenneth W Duckett, Curator
Holdings: Vols (3000) Cat
Notes: Incl 475 serial runs. The George Alan Connor Collection of Esperanto literature features local, regional, national, and international publications in Esperanto, mainly from the period 1910-1960. Catalog available. Also the Rev M Whipple Bishop papers which incl 31 vols and 27 serial titles as well as mss.

PQ —TROIS-RIVIERES COLLEGE LIBRARY, CEGEP de Trois-Rivieres-Bibliotheque, 3500 de Courval, Trois-Rivieres, G9A 5E6, Can. Denis Simard, Librn
Holdings: Vols (95,000) Cat Maps Pix Slides Phonorecords Audiotapes Videotapes 16mm Films Filmstrips Microforms

LITERATURE—BIOGRAPHY see Authors

LITERATURE—EVALUATION see Bibliography—Best Books; Literature—History and Criticism

LITERATURE—HISTORY AND CRITICISM

CT —YALE UNIVERSITY, Box 1603A, Yale Station, New Haven, 06520.
Notes: Incl illustrative material, bibliographies, biographies, histories, ephemera, association items, etc.

IN —ALLEN COUNTY PUBLIC LIBRARY, 900 Webster St, Fort Wayne, 46802. Paul Deane, Reader Services Dept Head; Kay Lynn Isca, Art Music & AV Dept Head
Holdings: Vols 5175 Cat Microforms

MA —BOSTON UNIVERSITY, Mugar Memorial Library, Special Collections Dept, 771 Commonwealth Ave, Boston, 02215. Howard B Gotlieb, Dir
Holdings: Cat Mss Pix
Notes: Contemporary literary criticism and poetry, incl literary and personal papers of numerous modern authors; first editions, translations, etc. A complete list is available.

MS —UNIVERSITY OF SOUTHERN MISSISSIPPI, William David McCain Graduate Library, Box 5148, Southern Sta, Hattiesburg, 39406.
Holdings: Vols 3500 Cat
Notes: The personal library of Yale professor emeritus, Cleanth Brooks, who has been one of the leading literary critics of this century. The collection dates from the 18th century to the present and is particularly strong in 20th century american literature and criticism.

NY —NEW YORK PUBLIC LIBRARY, Research Libraries, General Research Division, Fifth Ave & 42 St, New York, 10018. Rodney Phillips, Chief
Holdings: Vols (2,225,000) Cat Maps Pix Microforms
Budget: ($775,718)

NY —NEW YORK PUBLIC LIBRARY, Mid-Manhattan Library, Literature and Language Dept, 455 Fifth Ave, New York, 10016. Eric Steele, Sr Principal Librn
Holdings: Vols (160,000) Cat Phonorecords Microforms Audiotapes
Budget: ($92,000)
Notes: Extensive collection of works, criticism and biographies of major and minor American writers for undergraduate study; special attention directed towards Black American literature. Collection includes material on the teaching of literature, the techniques of creative writing, and the history of the theater when relevant to the study of dramatic literature. Substantial or complete runs of the major journals. Representative collection of literary magazines. Recordings of prose, poetry and drama.

RI —BROWN UNIVERSITY, John Hay Library, 20 Prospect St, Providence, 02912. Mark N Brown, Cur Mss
Holdings: Mss
Notes: Several large ms and University Archives collections relating to American literature. See entry for the Harris Collection of American Poetry and Plays. Includes the Winfield Townley Scott Collection (qv); the Margaret Emerson Bailey, 1880-1949, Collection; the Howard Blake, 1914-1960, Collection (50 items); the Anne Charlotte Lynch Botta, 1815-1891, Collection (100 items); the Thomas Holley Chivers, 1809-1858, Collection; the Harry Crosby, 1898-1929, Collection; the George William Curtis, 1824-1892, Collection (qv) (100 items); the David Cornel DeJong, 1905-1967, Collection; the Thomas Stearns Eliot, 1888-1965, Collection (115 items); the Hugh Bernard Fox, 1932- Collection (600 items); the Richard Watson Gilder, 1844-1909, Collection; the Paul Hamilton Hayne, 1830-1866, Collection; William Dean Howells, 1837-1920, Collection (113); the Arthur Crew Inman,1895-1963, Collection; the Howard Phillips Lovecraft, 1890-1937, Collection (qv) (4000 items); as well as numerous other collections involving writers of local, regional and national literature. Part of the Harris Collection of American Poetry and Plays.

TX —TRINITY UNIVERSITY, Elizabeth Coates Maddux Library, 715 Stadium Dr, San Antonio, 78284. Richard Hume Werking, Library Dir; Craig Likness, Head Bibliographer
Notes: General reference.

ON —VICTORIA UNIVERSITY, Library, Centre for Reformation and Renaissance Studies, 71 Queen's Park Crescent, Toronto,

LITERATURE—HISTORY AND CRITICISM (cont.)

M5S 1K7, Can. Robert C Brandeis, Chief Librn; James Estes, Dir
Holdings: Vols 100 Cat Mss
Notes: Books and mss by noted literary critic Northrop Frye. Incl sound recordings.

LITERATURE AS A PROFESSION see Authors; Authorship; Journalists

LITERATURE, BAROQUE see Baroque Literature

LITERATURE, BLACK see Black Literature

LITERATURE, COMIC see Comedy

LITERATURE, COMPARATIVE

CT —YALE UNIVERSITY, Beinecke Rare Book & Manuscript Library, Osborn Collection, New Haven, 06520. Stephen R Parks, Cur
Holdings: Mss

NJ —PRINCETON UNIVERSITY, Library, Rare Books Dept, Princeton, 08544. Stephen Ferguson, Cur

LITERATURE, DRUGS IN see Drugs in Literature

LITERATURE, EPIC see Epic Literature

LITERATURE, EROTIC see Erotica

LITERATURE, MEDIEVAL

DC —HARVARD UNIVERSITY, Dumbarton Oaks, Research Library, 1703 32nd St NW, Washington, 20007. Irene Vaslef, Librn
Notes: Late classical, Byzantine and western medieval (mostly source material, with emphasis on the Byzantine field).

MA —HARVARD UNIVERSITY LIBRARY, Cambridge, 02138.
Holdings: Cat
Notes: Downs: 3643. Medieval romances.

MN —SAINT JOHN'S ABBEY & UNIVERSITY, Hill Monastic Manuscript Library, Collegeville, 56321. Julian G Plante, Dir
Holdings: Vols (61,000) Microfilms
Notes: Films of 61,000 mss. The total number of codices or bound handwritten mss represents the holdings of several hundred libraries in Europe, mostly Austria, Spain, Ethiopia, West Germany, Portugal, and also Italy, Hungary, Poland, Great Britain, Belgium, Yugoslavia, France, Switzerland, and the Netherlands.

OH —CLEVELAND PUBLIC LIBRARY, Fine Arts and Special Collections Department, 325 Superior Ave, Cleveland, 44114. Alice N Loranth, Head
Holdings: Cat mss
Notes: Medieval texts, translations, facsimile reproductions, bibliographies and catalogs of mss, romances, epics, early chronicles and histories, Icelandic sagas, fabliaux (tales), legends, lives of the Saints are well represented. Monographs, scholarly journals and serials on philology, linguistics, and literature with special emphasis on Middle English, Old French, Middle High German, Middle Dutch, and early Irish texts.
See also entries under Folklore; Language and Languages.

WI —SEMINARY OF MEDIEVAL SPANISH STUDIES, Library, 1220 Linden Dr, Madison, 53706. Lloyd Kasten, Librn
Holdings: Vols 7700 Cat Mss Slides
Notes: Espec Medieval materials and subjects.

LITERATURE, MODERN

CA —CALIFORNIA STATE UNIVERSITY, NORTHRIDGE, Delmar T Oviatt & South Libraries, 1811 Nordhoff St, Northridge, 91330. Donald L Read, Special Collections Dept
Holdings: Vols 2500 Cat
Notes: McDermott collection of contemporary writers of American fiction and poetry, signed, first editions. Emphasis is upon both established and new contemporary writers. Collection fully cataloged.

DE —UNIVERSITY OF DELAWARE, Hugh M Morris Library, S College Ave, Newark, 19711. T Stuart Dick, Special Collections
Holdings: Mss
Notes: Incl letters and mss sent to Louis Untermeyer, 1906-1940, with the majority being from 1912-1925. Among others, important groups of letters from Leonie Adams, Conrad Aiken, W R Benet, W S Braithwaite, Floyd Dell, Jahn Gould Fletcher, Alfred Kreymborg, Carl Sandburg and John Hall Wheelock are included. Limited photocopying may be arranged. Index available.

IL —NORTHWESTERN UNIVERSITY, Library, Special Collections Dept, 1937 Sheridan Rd, Evanston, 60201. R Russell Maylone, Cur
Holdings: Cat Mss Pix
Notes: Modern movements in art and literature. Books, periodicals, pamphlets, catalogs and ephemera, with special concentration on German Expressionism, Dada, Italian Futurism, Surrealism and works by American avante garde writers publishing since the late 1950s. European serials documenting German Expressionism, Italian Futurism, Surrealism, and Dada.

MA —BOSTON UNIVERSITY, Mugar Memorial Library, Special Collections Dept, 771 Commonwealth Ave, Boston, 02215. Howard B Gotlieb, Dir
Holdings: Cat Ms Pix
Notes: Twentieth century especially.

MO —UNIVERSITY OF MISSOURI-KANSAS CITY, General Library, 5100 Rockhill Road, Kansas City, 64110. Kenneth J LaBudde, Dir; Gordon Hendrickson, Assoc Dir; Marilyn Carbonell, Ref Librn
Holdings: Vols 108,000 Cat
Notes: (4121 current serial subscriptions) includes an emphasis on drama and includes Thomas and Mila Baker Collection of Twentieth-Century British and American Literature.

MO —WASHINGTON UNIVERSITY, John M Olin Library, Campus Box 1061, St Louis, 63130.
Holdings: Mss
Notes: First, limited and special editions of books by and about a select group of contemporary American and British authors. Also little magazines, corrected proofs, ephemera. Extensive collections and/or mss, correspondence of Conrad Aiken, Samuel Beckett, Basil Bunting, Ivy Compton-Burnett, Robert Creeley, Edward Dahlberg, James Dickey, Robert Duncan, William Everson, Donald Finkel, James Merrill, Marianne Moore, Howard Nemerov, Charles Olson, Theodore Roethke, Gary Snyder, Alexander Trocchi, Mona Van Duyn, William Carlos Williams, Louis Zukofsky and others. Incl printed works.

MO —WASHINGTON UNIVERSITY, Libraries, Special Collections Dept, Campus Box 1061, St Louis, 63130.
Notes: A major collection, incl books, mss, correspondence, literary papers, photographs, etc. Described in *Special Collections: an Annotated Guide to the Holdings of the Manuscript Division and the University Archives and Research Collection.*

NV —UNIVERSITY OF NEVADA, RENO, University Library, Special Collections Dept, Reno, 89557. Robert E Blesse, Head
Holdings: 30,000 Entries
Notes: Modern Authors Collection. A bibliographical research collection containing the writings of 174 British and American authors of fiction and poetry who published or became prominent after 1910. All published works are collected including anthology appearances, translations, prefaces, introductions, essays, and correspondence.

NM —NEW MEXICO STATE UNIVERSITY, Library, Box 3475, Las Cruces, 88003. James Dyke, Dir
Holdings: Cat
Notes: The collection contains 38,630 items--a vast quantity of little magazines and Anglo-American Modernism published between 1900-1975. Little poetry magazines are an exceptionally strong part of this collection.

OK —UNIVERSITY OF TULSA, McFarlin Library, Dept of Rare Books and Special Collections, 600 S College, Tulsa, 74104. David Farmer, Dir; Toby Murray, Archivist; Caroline Swinson, Cur of Manuscripts & Art
Holdings: Mss Pix Phonorecords
Notes: The Ellsworth Mason Graves/Riding Collection, incl first editions, typescripts, photographs, recordings and ephemera. The Library also has the library (8000 vols) of Cyril Connolly. Mostly modern literature; many presentation copies.

RI —BROWN UNIVERSITY, John Hay Library, Harris Collection, Prospect St, Providence, 02912. Rosemary L Cullen, Cur
Holdings: Vols (200,000) Cat Mss Pix Phonorecords Microforms
Budget: ($15,000)
Notes: The Harris Collection of American Poetry and Plays is principally composed of American and Canadian poetry and plays, 17th century-date. Extensive holdings in songsters, gift books and annuals, hymnals, pageants, broadside verse, carriers' addresses, women poets, juvenile poetry, (incl Mother Goose and *The Night Before* Christmas), sheet music with lyrics, small press publications, fine printing, black poets, "little magazines," Yiddish-American literature. All movements or schools of American poetry are represented. Incl first editions of most American poets and playwrights, notably Whitman, Poe, Wallace Stevens, Eugene O'Neill, Edward Albee, Ezra Pound, T S Eliot, William Carlos Williams, Amy Lowell, Phyllis Wheatley, Robert Frost, Allen Ginsberg, Bliss Carman, and Stephen Foster sheet music. Also incl the Saunders Walt Whitman Collection (1300 vols); the LangdonCollection of Pageants (250 vols); the Asa Cushman Collection of plays in ms and prompt copies; the MacDougall Collection of Psalters and Hymnals; 4000 plays issued by Walter H Baker Co, Boston (1890-1957); the Vaxer Collection of Yiddish Poetry, Plays and Music (1700 vols). Collections incl 200,000 vols, 30,000 broadsides, 55,000 mss, 170,000 pieces of sheet music, 450 phonorecords, and 375 microfilm reels. See *Dictionary Catalog of the Harris Collection of American Poetry and Plays* (Boston: G K Hall, 1972), 13 vols; *Supplement* (1977), 3 vols. See also, *American Poetry,* 1609-1900, *A Collection on Microfilm, Segment I* (1609-1820); *Segment II* (1821-1850); *Segment III* (1851-1870) (Woodbridge, Conn: Research Publications). Separate catalog.

TX —TRINITY UNIVERSITY, Elizabeth Coates Maddux Library, 715 Stadium Dr, San Antonio, 78284. Richard Hume Werking, Library Dir; Craig Likness, Head Bibliographer
Notes: General reference.

LITERATURE, MODERN—20TH CENTURY

MA —BRANDEIS UNIVERSITY, Goldfarb Library, 415 South St, Waltham, 02154. Bessie Hahn, Dir
Notes: The American Best Sellers Collection consists of 48 linear feet of the top ten annual best sellers of popular literature from 1900-1975. Access to this collection is through the Main Card Catalog and Special Collections Catalog.

MO —WASHINGTON UNIVERSITY, John M Olin Library, Campus Box 1061, St Louis, 63130.
Holdings: Mss
Notes: First, limited, special editions and critical studies of major English and American authors and representative minor writers. Extensive collections of D H Lawrence, Vladimir Nabokov, Ezra Pound, Ford Madox Ford, Conrad Aiken, Wallace Stevens, William Carlos William, others. Incl printed works.

OK —UNIVERSITY OF TULSA, McFarlin Library, Dept of Rare Books and Special

LITERATURE, MODERN—20TH CENTURY (cont.)

Collections, 600 S College, Tulsa, 74104. David Farmer, Dir; Toby Murray, Archivist; Caroline Swinson, Cur of Manuscripts & Art
Holdings: Vols 2000
Notes: A major collection of Proletarian literature based on Walter Rideout's *The Radical Novel in the United States, 1900-1954.*

RI —BROWN UNIVERSITY, John Hay Library, Harris Collection, Prospect St, Providence, 02912. Rosemary L Cullen, Cur
Holdings: Vols (200,000) Cat Mss Pix Phonorecords Microforms
Budget: ($15,000)
Notes: The Harris Collection of American Poetry and Plays is principally composed of American and Canadian poetry and plays, 17th century-date. Extensive holdings in songsters, gift books and annuals, hymnals, pageants, broadside verse, carriers' addresses, women poets, juvenile poetry, (incl Mother Goose and *The Night Before* Christmas), sheet music with lyrics, small press publications, fine printing, black poets, "little magazines," Yiddish-American literature. All movements or schools of American poetry are represented. Incl first editions of most American poets and playwrights, notably Whitman, Poe, Wallace Stevens, Eugene O'Neill, Edward Albee, Ezra Pound, T S Eliot, William Carlos Williams, Amy Lowell, Phyllis Wheatley, Robert Frost, Allen Ginsberg, Bliss Carman, and Stephen Foster sheet music. Also incl the Saunders Walt Whitman Collection (1300 vols); the LangdonCollection of Pageants (250 vols); the Asa Cushman Collection of plays in ms and prompt copies; the MacDougall Collection of Psalters and Hymnals; 4000 plays issued by Walter H Baker Co, Boston (1890-1957); the Vaxer Collection of Yiddish Poetry, Plays and Music (1700 vols). Collections incl 200,000 vols, 30,000 broadsides, 55,000 mss, 170,000 pieces of sheet music, 450 phonorecords, and 375 microfilm reels. See *Dictionary Catalog of the Harris Collection of American Poetry and Plays* (Boston: G K Hall, 1972), 13 vols; *Supplement* (1977), 3 vols. See also, *American Poetry,* 1609-1900, *A Collection on Microfilm, Segment I* (1609-1820); *Segment II* (1821-1850); *Segment III* (1851-1870) (Woodbridge, Conn: Research Publications). Separate catalog.

LITERATURE, PROLETARIAN see Proletarian Literature

LITERATURE, REFORMATION see Reformation Literature

LITERATURE, ROMANCE see Romance Literature

LITERATURE, SYMBOLIST see Symbolist Literature

LITERATURE, UNDERGROUND see Underground Literature

LITHOGRAPHS AND LITHOGRAPHY

DC —LIBRARY OF CONGRESS, Prints & Photographs Div, Washington, 20540.
Notes: Collection of 1400 American music covers produced from the 1830s through the 1870s.

MA —BOSTON PUBLIC LIBRARY, Print Collection, Dartmouth St at Copley Sq, Boston, 02117. Sinclair H Hitchings, Keeper of Prints
Holdings: Cat
Notes: There are especially large numbers of French and American lithographs, incl a large collection of proofs of the Prang Company, Boston, from 1858 to 1900; also, 300 mid-19th century American illustrated music sheets; and vast collections of early Parisian lithography (several thousand items); and of the lithographs of Daumier, Gavarni, Charlet and others. In addition there are turn-of-the-century posters, 400 American and 100 European. Most lithographs are cataloged by artist or by country.

MA —AMERICAN ANTIQUARIAN SOCIETY LIBRARY, 185 Salisbury St, Worcester, 01609. Marcus A McCorison, Dir & Librn
Holdings: Cat Maps Pix
Notes: Over 6000 American prints, arranged by lithographer. Incl political caricatures and cartoons, maps, sheet music, advertising cards, Valentines, etc.

MO —WASHINGTON UNIVERSITY, Libraries, Special Collections Dept, Campus Box 1061, St Louis, 63130.
Holdings: / /
Notes: The Gast Banknote Company's records, 1884-1952. Incl general ledgers, sales ledgers, payroll books, equipment inventories, and selected sample books of printing work of this lithography and printing firm.

NY —COLUMBIA UNIVERSITY LIBRARIES, Rare Book & Manuscript Library, 801 Butler Library, 535 W 114 St, New York, 10027. Kenneth A Lohf, Librn
Holdings: Pix
Notes: Artistic, historic and commercial lithographs arranged chronologically to show the development of lithography. Restricted use.

NY —METROPOLITAN MUSEUM OF ART, Dept of Prints & Photographs, 82 St & Fifth Ave, New York, 10028. Colta Ives, Cur
Holdings: Vols (10,000)
Notes: Contained in a collection of 500,000 prints from 15th to 20th century. Approx 10, 000 illustrated books; European and American. No photocopying.

PA —TEMPLE UNIVERSITY LIBRARIES, Special Collections Dept, Rare Books & Mss Section, Philadelphia, 19122. Thomas M Whitehead, Cur
Holdings: Vols (200) Cat Mss Pix
Notes: The lithography collection emphasizes the technical process rather than the artistic medium and stresses the years 1800-1835. Significant are the early manuals, the Kubilius Louis Prang Collection and the documentation of early Mexican lithography. Some holdings are listed in the 1972 publication: *Aloys Senefelder 1771-1834: A Catalogue of Early Technical Literature and Selected Lithograph.* A register of the Mexican documents is available.

WI —CIRCUS WORLD MUSEUM LIBRARY, 415 Lynn St, Baraboo, 53913. Robert L Parkinson, Research Center Dir
Holdings: Vols (1800) Cat Mss Pix Slides Phonorecords 16mm Films
Notes: Circus and "Wild West" shows. Owned by State Historical Society of Wisconsin. Incl 1800 books on circus subject; 400 route books; 1200 programs, 8000 circus lithographs, 20,000 photo negatives, 50,000 photo prints, heralds, couriers, tickets, letterheads, route cards, original circus artwork, records and documents of circus business, movies, newspaper ads, circus band music and periodicals of show business such as *Billboard, New York Clipper, White Tops,* Bandwagon, etc, Partially cataloged.

NS —DALHOUSIE UNIVERSITY LIBRARY, Halifax, B3H 4H8, Can.
Holdings: Cat Pix
Notes: Approx 2000 lithographs, steel engravings, fine prints and illustrated historical maps from the 18th and 19th centuries are in the collection. Subject coverage is primarily of Nova Scotia, New Brunswick, Prince Edward Island, and Newfoundland scenery, street scenes, and portrayals of prominent people, buildings and events. Generally rich in illustrations of the working and social life of the period. Artists represented incl: J E Woolford, J F W Desbarres, William Eagar, William Bartlett and Richard Short. Historical maps incl some of the earliest visual depictions of the Atlantic coast. Material available for editorial reproduction. Print fee charged. No loans.

LITHOLOGY see Petrology

LITHOPHANES

OH —BLAIR MUSEUM OF LITHOPHANES & CARVED WAXES, 2032 Robinwood Ave, Toledo, 43620. Laurel G Blain, Cur
Holdings: Mss Pix
Notes: No books have been published on lithophanes to date , but articles have appeared in various magazines and newspapers here and abroad.

LITHUANIA

IL —BALZEKAS MUSEUM OF LITHUANIAN CULTURE, Research Library, 4012 S Archer Ave, Chicago, 60632. Jurgis Kasakaitis, Head Librn

LITHUANIA—HISTORY

CA —HOOVER INSTITUTION ON WAR, REVOLUTION & PEACE, Stanford University, Stanford, 94305. Milorad M Drachkovitch, Archivist
Holdings: Mss Pix
Notes: Papers of Eduardas Turauskas, 1934-1958, consisting of correspondence, memoranda, reports, printed matter, clippings, photographs, and other materials collected during his career as Lithuanian diplomat, journalist, and statesman. Materials incl documentation on the Soviet occupation of Lithuania, 1940-41; and Lithuanian foreign relations in Europe, 1934-1941. 9 ms boxes.

IL —BALZEKAS MUSEUM OF LITHUANIAN CULTURE, Research Library, 4012 S Archer Ave, Chicago, 60632. Jurgis Kasakaitis, Head Librn
Holdings: Vols 15,000 Cat Maps Pix Slides Phonorecords
Notes: Incl folklore, art, social life and customs, history, literature, poetry, anthropology, numismatics, armor, etc. All books published in Lithuanian, some in English on Lithuanian subjects. Incl newspaper clippings.

MA —HARVARD UNIVERSITY LIBRARY, Widener Library, Cambridge, 02138.
Holdings: Cat
Notes: *Widener Library Shelflist* No 40 (1972) lists some 6500 vols on the history, languages, and literatures of the Baltic states: Estonia, Latvia, Lithuania, and Livonia; about 1700 of these are on Lithuania.

NY —NEW YORK PUBLIC LIBRARY, Slavonic Div, Fifth Ave & 42 St, New York, 10018. Edward Kasinec, Chief
Holdings: Cat Micrforms
Notes: See New York Public Library, *Dictionary Catalog of the Slavonic* Collection (Boston: G K Hall, 1974), 44 vols.

OH —KENT STATE UNIVERSITY, Libraries, Ethnic Collections, Kent, 44242.
Notes: Both European and US publications in Croatian, Estonian, Czech, Finnish, Hungarian, Latvian, Lithuanian, Polish, Romanian, Serbian, Slovenian, Slovac, Swedish, Ukrainian, and Welsh. Materials gathered in part to support a Critical Languages Program at Kent State and to develop a center for the study of Baltic languages, especially Lithuanian.

PA —UNIVERSITY OF PENNSYLVANIA, Van Pelt Library, Rare Books Collection, 34 & Walnut Sts, Philadelphia, 19104. Daniel Traister, Special Collections Librn
Holdings: Cat
Notes: Particularly rich in Lithuanian history and linguistics.

WI —UNIVERSITY OF WISCONSIN, MADISON, Memorial Library, Slavic Studies Collection, 728 State St, Madison, 53706. Aleksander Rolich, Bibliographer for Slavic Studies; Robert P Gakovich, Slavic Cataloger; Valdis J Zeps, Baltic Studies Center
Holdings: Vols 1610 Cat
Notes: Donated by Alfred Senn, this collection is particularly strong in Lithuanian language, literature, history and politics. Most of the classic Lithuanian literary monuments of the 16th to 18th centuries are included. Modern Lithuanian writers are also well represented. About 150 of the rare items are located in the Rare Book Department.

LITHUANIAN AMERICAN NEWSPAPERS see Newspapers, Lithuanian American

LITHUANIAN AUTHORS see Authors, Lithuanian

LITHUANIAN LANGUAGE AND LITERATURE

CA —LOS ANGELES PUBLIC LIBRARY, Foreign Languages Dept, 630 W Fifth St,

LITHUANIAN LANGUAGE AND LITERATURE (cont.)

Los Angeles, 90071. Sylva Manoogian, Principal Librn
Holdings: Vols 366 Cat
Budget: ($41,500)

IL —BALZEKAS MUSEUM OF LITHUANIAN CULTURE, Research Library, 4012 S Archer Ave, Chicago, 60632. Jurgis Kasakaitis, Head Librn
Holdings: Vols 15,000 Cat Maps Pix Slides Phonorecords
Notes: Incl folklore, art, social life and customs, history, literature, poetry, anthropology, numismatics, armor, etc. All books published in Lithuanian, some in English on Lithuanian subjects. Incl newspaper clippings.

NY —NEW YORK PUBLIC LIBRARY, Donnell Foreign Language Library, 20 W 53 St, New York, 10019. Bosiljka Stevanovic, Supvr Librn
Holdings: Vols 510 Cat
Notes: Lithuanian collection incl Lithuanian authors of Lithuanian expression. No separate catalog.

NY —NEW YORK PUBLIC LIBRARY, Slavonic Div, Fifth Ave & 42 St, New York, 10018. Edward Kasinec, Chief
Holdings: Cat Microforms
Notes: See New York Public Library, *Dictionary Catalog of the Slavonic* Collection (Boston: G K Hall, 1974), 44 vols.

OH —CLEVELAND PUBLIC LIBRARY, Foreign Literature Dept, 325 Superior Ave, Cleveland, 44114. Natalia Bezugloff, Head
Holdings: Vols 2400 Cat
Notes: A popular circulating collection containing classics and the standard works with emphasis on belles lettres, history and biography. A variety of other subjects such as learning languages, how to do books, art, children's books, spoken phonodiscs and cassettes, periodicals, etc.
See also entry under Foreign Language Collections

OH —KENT STATE UNIVERSITY, Libraries, Ethnic Collections, Kent, 44242.
Holdings: Vols 4325 Cat
See also entry under Foreign Language Collections

PA —UNIVERSITY OF PENNSYLVANIA, Van Pelt Library, Rare Books Collection, 34 & Walnut Sts, Philadelphia, 19104. Daniel Traister, Special Collections Librn
Holdings: Cat
Notes: Particularly rich in Lithuanian history and linguistics.

WI —UNIVERSITY OF WISCONSIN, MADISON, Memorial Library, Slavic Studies Collection, 728 State St, Madison, 53706. Aleksander Rolich, Bibliographer for Slavic Studies; Robert P Gakovich, Slavic Cataloger; Valdis J Zeps, Baltic Studies Center
Holdings: Vols 1610 Cat
Notes: Donated by Alfred Senn, this collection is particularly strong in Lithuanian language, literature, history and politics. Most of the classic Lithuanian literary monuments of the 16th and 18th centuries are included. Modern Lithuanian writers are also well represented. About 150 of the rare items are located in the Rare Book Department.

LITHUANIAN NEWSPAPERS see Newspapers, Lithuanian

LITHUANIANS

MN —UNIVERSITY OF MINNESOTA, Immigration History Research Center, 826 Berry St, Saint Paul, 55114. Susan Griegs, Cur
Notes: 500 separate titles of Lithuanian immigrant publications; materials published in displaced persons' camps by Lithuanians during and after World War II.

LITHUANIANS IN THE U.S.

IL —BALZEKAS MUSEUM OF LITHUANIAN CULTURE, Research Library, 4012 S Archer Ave, Chicago, 60632. Jurgis Kasakaitis, Head Librn

MN —UNIVERSITY OF MINNESOTA, Immigration History Research Center, 826 Berry St, Saint Paul, 55114. Susan Griegs, Cur
Holdings: Vols (35,000) Mss Maps Pix Phonorecords Audiotapes 16mm Films Microforms
See also entry under US - Emigration and Immigration

NY —NEW YORK PUBLIC LIBRARY, Slavonic Div, Fifth Ave & 42 St, New York, 10018. Edward Kasinec, Chief
Holdings: Cat Microforms
Notes: See: New York Public Library, Slavonic Div, *Dictionary Catalog of the Slavonic Collection*, 2nd ed, rev and enl (Boston: G K Hall, 1974), 44 vols; and New York Public Library, *Dictionary Catalog of the Research Libraries* (New York, 1972-).

PA —BALCH INSTITUTE FOR ETHNIC STUDIES, Library, 18 S Seventh St, Philadelphia, 19106. R Joseph Anderson, Library Dir
Holdings: Vols 330 Mss Pix Microforms

LITTELL, GLADYS

CA —LOS ANGELES PUBLIC LIBRARY, Frances Howard Goldwyn Hollywood Regional Library, 1623 Ivar Ave, Los Angeles, 90028. Sally Dumaux, Librn
Holdings: Vols (100,000) Cat Pix VF
Budget: ($60,000)
Notes: Special Collections: Francis William Vreeland, local artist, incl correspondence, working papers, scrapbooks, photographs; Gladys Littell Collection incl Hollywood Bowl Sunrise Services 1920s-1940s, Hollywood Conservatory of Music, 1920s, Hollywood Chamber of Commerce, incl correspondence, programs, working papers, and photographs; Holly Leaves, Hollywood, Calif, 1916-1930.

LITTLE, ARTHUR AND HERBERT BROWN

MA —SOCIETY FOR THE PRESERVATION OF NEW ENGLAND ANTIQUITIES, Library, 141 Cambridge St, Boston, 02114. Ellie Reichlin, Librn & Cur of Photographic Collections
Notes: 500 items cat. Collection of Boston architectural firm, incl measured drawings of historic houses.

LITTLE, ARTHUR DEHON, 1863-1935

DC —LIBRARY OF CONGRESS, Manuscript Division, Washington, 20540. John C Broderick, Chief
Notes: Papers of Arthur Dehon Little (1863-1935). Incl archives of the Arthur D Little Company.

LITTLE, LOU

NY —COLUMBIA UNIVERSITY LIBRARIES, Rare Book & Manuscript Library, 801 Butler Library, 535 W 114 St, New York, 10027. Kenneth A Lohf, Librn
Notes: Restricted use. Much on Columbia sports and athletics. Good strengths in material on Columbia's sports figures, incl Lou Little, etc.

LITTLE BIG HORN, BATTLE OF THE, 1876

MI —MONROE COUNTY LIBRARY SYSTEM, Ellis Reference and Information Center, 3700 S Custer Rd, Monroe, 48161. Marie D Chulski, Head of Reference Services
Holdings: Vols 35,000 Cat Mss Maps Pix Slides 16mm Films Microforms Periodicals Sound Recordings Paintings Memorabilia
Budget: ($15,000)
Notes: Historic Monroe County, tracing its beginnings to 1780, is a definite part of Michigan's history. Many events of the area and citizens are part of Michigan's heritage. The Michigan collection besides general works contains individual county histories, atlases, biographies, etc. The Monroe County history collection contains veteran records, plat books, oral history tapes, family histories, church records, cemetery index, atlases and census records. Genealogy emphasis is not only Monroe County but includes surrounding counties and the states with large migration to the area, such as Ohio, Kentucky, Tennessee and the New England states.

LITTLE BLUE BOOKS

CA —UNIVERSITY OF CALIFORNIA, SAN DIEGO, Central University Library, Mandeville Dept of Special Collections, La Jolla, 92093. Lynda Corey Claassen, Head
Notes: Rare Book Collection incl 5000 Little Blue Books and related materials published by Haldeman-Julius of Girard, Kansas.

CA —UNIVERSITY OF CALIFORNIA, LOS ANGELES, Research Library, Dept of Special Collections, 405 Hilgard Ave, Los Angeles, 90024. Edward Shreeves, Chairman, Bibliographers Group; David S Zeidberg, Head
Notes: 1200 Little Blue Books and other publications, ca 1920-1940.

IA —IOWA STATE UNIVERSITY, Library, Dept of Special Collections, Ames, 50011. Stanley M Yates, Head
Holdings: Vols 2210 Cat
Notes: The Gilkey-Kehlenbeck Collection of the "Little Blue Books," incl variants.

MI —MICHIGAN STATE UNIVERSITY, Libraries, Special Collections Div, East Lansing, 48824. Jannette Fiore, Librn
Notes: The Russel B Nye Popular Culture Collection in the Michigan State Univ Libraries incl over (45,000) items. Most of the collection is organized into 4 categories: comic art, popular fiction, popular information materials and materials relating to the popular performing arts. About 3900 items. Almanacs, Blue Books, and works popularizing knowledge or offering self-help and how-to advice. There are ca 350 issues of 100 19th and 20th century almanacs. The Blue Books incl ca 2000 Little Blue Books, over 600 Big Blue Books and a good number of issues of the various Haldeman-Julius magazines. In addition to almanacs and Blue Books, Popular Information incl books of advice on etiquette, life and love, how-to-succeed books, popular history, science and biography, and several hundred public schooltextbooks from the 19th and early 20th centuries.

LITTLE COLONEL SERIES

KY —UNIVERSITY OF LOUISVILLE, Ekstrom Library, Photographic Archives, Louisville, 40292. J C Anderson, Cur; David G Horvath, Asst Cur
Holdings: Vols (750,000) Cat Pix Slides
Budget: ($60,000)
Notes: Photographs, incl prototypes for "Little Colonel" series.

LITTLE GIDDINGS COMMUNITY

MA —MOUNT HOLYOKE COLLEGE, Williston Memorial Library, South Hadley, 01075. Anne C Edmonds, Librn
Holdings: Cat Mss Pix
Notes: Books by and about the community.

LITTLE LANDERS COLONY (CALIFORNIA)

CA —SAN DIEGO PUBLIC LIBRARY, 820 E St, San Diego, 92101. Rhoda E Kruse, Sr Librn
Notes: Records of the Little Landers colony, a 1910 Utopian group founded in the Tia Juana River Valley.

LITTLE MAGAZINES

CA —UNIVERSITY OF CALIFORNIA, SAN DIEGO, Central University Library, Mandeville Dept of Special Collections, La Jolla, 92093. Lynda Corey Claassen, Head;

LITTLE MAGAZINES (cont.)

Michael Davidson, Cur, Archive for New Poetry
Holdings: Cat
Notes: Incl 900 titles. Part of the Archive of New Poetry, a collection of English-language poetry published since World War II.

CA —UNIVERSITY OF CALIFORNIA, LOS ANGELES, Research Library, Dept of Special Collections, 405 Hilgard Ave, Los Angeles, 90024. Edward Shreeves, Chairman, Bibliographers Group; David S Zeidberg, Head
Notes: 175 linear feet (2500 titles) of scaattered issues of non-commercial, experimental periodicals.

CA —UNIVERSITY OF CALIFORNIA, SANTA BARBARA, Library, Dept of Special Collections, Santa Barbara, 93106. Christian F Brun, Head

CT —YALE UNIVERSITY, Box 1603A, Yale Station, New Haven, 06520.
Holdings: Cat
Notes: Strong collection, especially American.

CT —UNIVERSITY OF CONNECTICUT, Library, Storrs, 06268. R H Schimmelpfeng, Dir of Special Collections
Holdings: Cat
Notes: The collection consists primarily of American, Canadian and English little magazines, 1890 to date.

DE —UNIVERSITY OF DELAWARE, Hugh M Morris Library, S College Ave, Newark, 19711. T Stuart Dick, Special Collections
Holdings: Mss
Notes: Incl letters and mss sent to Louis Untermeyer, 1906-1940, with the majority being from 1912-1925. Among others, important groups of letters from Leonie Adams, Conrad Aiken, W R Benet, W S Braithwaite, Floyd Dell, Jahn Gould Fletcher, Alfred Kreymborg, Carl Sandburg and John Hall Wheelock are included. Limited photocopying may be arranged. Index available.

IL —SOUTHERN ILLINOIS UNIVERSITY, CARBONDALE, Delyte W Morris Library, Special Collections Dept, Carbondale, 62901. David V Koch, Cur of Special Collections; Louisa Bowen, Cur of Manuscripts
Holdings: Vols 3500 Cat Mss Pix
Notes: Some 300 American and British avant-garde authors are represented in the expatriate collection: books, little magazines, letters, photographs and manuscripts. The holdings are a composite of the Philip Kaplan collection and the archives of the Black Sun Press, supplemented by other gifts and purchases. Collection incl several thousand letters from such writers as Richard Aldington, Djuna Barnes, Samuel Beckett, Maxwell Bodenheim, Kay Boyle, Bob Brown (extensive file of personal papers), Harry and Caresse Crosby, Nancy Cunard, Floyd Dell, Lawrence Durrell, James T Farrell, Robert Graves, D H Lawrence, Robert McAlmon, Henry Miller, Ezra Pound, Gertrude Stein, Dylan Thomas and William Carlos Williams. There are 75 mss and 5 diaries representing Kay Boyle, Hart Crane, Montgomery Evans, Ford Maddox Ford, Ernest Hemingway, John Dos Passos and Edmund Wilson.Additional materials of Henry Miller, Robert McAlmon and Nancy Cunard have been acquired. (Earl Tannenbaum, *D H Lawrence; an* Exhibition..., 1958).

IL —NEWBERRY LIBRARY, 60 W Walton St, Chicago, 60610. Diana Haskell, Cur of Modern Mss
Holdings: Cat
Notes: English and American, 1890-ca 1935.

IL —NORTHWESTERN UNIVERSITY, Library, Special Collections Dept, 1937 Sheridan Rd, Evanston, 60201. R Russell Maylone, Cur
Holdings: Vols (5000) Cat
Notes: Representative examples of the work of the modern private press from Strawberry Hill to the current small printers. Incl such presses as Cuala, Essex House, Golden Cockerely, Grabhorn, Nonesuch, Roxburghe, etc. Also 15,000 "little magazines" titles exclusive of runs in the general library collections.

IN —INDIANA UNIVERSITY, Lilly Library, Seventh St, Bloomington, 47405. William R Cagle, Librn
Holdings: Cat Mss
Notes: The collection consists of nearly 600 American and English little magazines in complete of nearly complete runs. See *A Checklist of Little Magazines Held by Lilly* Library (Bloomington: Lilly Library, 1974). Ms incl office and editorial files of several magazines, incl *Aylesford Review, The Floating Bear, Poetry, Poor, Old, Tired, Horse, Yugen, Tree, X: A Quarterly Review,* as well as correspondence and papers of the Association of Literary Magazines of America.

MO —WASHINGTON UNIVERSITY, John M Olin Library, Campus Box 1061, St Louis, 63130.
Holdings: Mss
Notes: First, limited and special editions of books by and about a select group of contemporary American and British authors. Also little magazines, corrected proofs, ephemera. Extensive collections and/or mss, correspondence of Conrad Aiken, Samuel Beckett, Basil Bunting, Ivy Compton-Burnett, Robert Creeley, Edward Dahlberg, James Dickey, Robert Duncan, William Everson, Donald Finkel, James Merrill, Marianne Moore, Howard Nemerov, Charles Olson, Theodore Roethke, Gary Snyder, Alexander Trocchi, Mona Van Duyn, William Carlos Williams, Louis Zukofsky and others. Incl printed works.

NE —UNIVERSITY OF NEBRASKA, OMAHA, Library, 60 & Dodge Sts, Omaha, 68132. Mel Bohn, Librn
Holdings: Vols 100 Uncat Mss
Notes: The archive of *Steppenwolf,* a little magazine. 5 linear ft of mss.

NM —NEW MEXICO STATE UNIVERSITY, Library, Box 3475, Las Cruces, 88003. James Dyke, Dir
Holdings: Cat
Notes: The collection contains 38,630 items--a vast quantity of little magazines and Anglo-American Modernism published between 1900-1975. Little poetry magazines are an exceptionally strong part of this collection.

NY —STATE UNIVERSITY OF NEW YORK, COLLEGE AT BUFFALO, Poetry/Rare Books Collection, 420 Capen Hall, Buffalo, 14260. Robert J Bertholf, Cur
Holdings: Vols (75,000) Cat Mss Pix Phonorecords Audiotapes Microforms
Notes: The Poetry Collection, founded in 1937 by the late Charles D Abbott, is devoted to 20th century poetry in English and in translation. It contains some 75,000 vols in first and variant editions, 600 phonorecords and 400 audiotapes presenting poets who read from their own work; more than 3500 sets of little magazines covering the last 80 years; a unique collection of mss, letters, notebooks, worksheets, and noted by contemporary poets, explaining their methods of composition; and a number of portraits, sculptures and photographs. "The Poetry Collection is internationally known for its importance in the field of James Joyce (qv), Dylan Thomas, William Carlos Williams, Robert Graves, Martin Seymour-Smith and Robert Kelley."

NY —NEW YORK PUBLIC LIBRARY, Research Libraries, General Research Division, Fifth Ave & 42 St, New York, 10018. Rodney Phillips, Chief
Holdings: Vols (2,225,000) Cat Maps Pix Microforms
Budget: ($775,718)

NY —NEW YORK PUBLIC LIBRARY, Mid-Manhattan Library, Literature and Language Dept, 455 Fifth Ave, New York, 10016. Eric Steele, Sr Principal Librn
Holdings: Vols (160,000) Cat Phonorecords Microforms Audiotapes
Budget: ($92,000)
Notes: Extensive collection of works, criticism and biographies of major and minor American writers for undergraduate study; special attention directed towards Black American literature. Collection includes material on the teaching of literature, the techniques of creative writing, and the history of the theater when relevant to the study of dramatic literature. Substantial or complete runs of the major journals. Representative collection of literary magazines. Recordings of prose, poetry and drama.

NY —STATE UNIVERSITY OF NEW YORK, STONY BROOK, Melville Library, Dept of Special Collections, Stony Brook, 11794. Evert Volkersz, Head
Holdings: Cat
Notes: Primarily English and American, about 1950-date.

OH —OHIO STATE UNIVERSITY, William Oxley Thompson Memorial Library, 1858 Neil Ave Mall, Columbus, 43210. Robert A Tibbetts, Cur of Special Collections
Holdings: Vols 100 Cat

PA —TEMPLE UNIVERSITY LIBRARIES, Special Collections Dept, Contemporary Culture Collection, Philadelphia, 19122. Patricia J Case, Cur
Notes: The Contemporary Culture Collection. See full entry under US-Social Life and Customs.

PA —UNIVERSITY OF PITTSBURGH, Hillman Library, Special Collections Dept, Hervey Allen Collection, Pittsburgh, 15260. Charles E Aston, Jr, Coordr
Holdings: Vols
Notes: Emphasis on American and British poetry of the 20th century with special focus on the period 1950-date. Incl over 1500 vols.

RI —BROWN UNIVERSITY, John Hay Library, Harris Collection, Prospect St, Providence, 02912. Rosemary L Cullen, Cur
Holdings: Vols (200,000) Cat Mss Pix Phonorecords Microforms
Budget: ($15,000)
Notes: The Harris Collection of American Poetry and Plays is principally composed of American and Canadian poetry and plays from the 17th century to the present. Extensive holdings in small press publications, fine printing, and "little magazines". All movements or schools of American poetry are represented. Over 600 "little magazines" received currently; 2500 back titles. See *Dictionary Catalog of the Harris Collection of American Poetry and* Play (Boston: G K Hall, 1972), 13 vols; Supplement (1977), 3 vols. Separate catalog.

TX —RICE UNIVERSITY, Fondren Library, 6100 S Main St, PO Box 1892, Houston, 77251. Dr Samuel M Carrington, Jr, University Librn
Holdings: Vols 13,000
Notes: The Frederich J Hoffman Collection of 20th century American and European literature. First editions of novels, 1940-1967; also 2000 copies of "Little Magazines".

TX —SAM HOUSTON STATE UNIVERSITY, Library, PO Box 2179, Huntsville, 77340. Chas Dwyer, Librn
Holdings: Cat Mss
Notes: The *Wild Dog* was a little magazine which published 20 issues from April 1963 to January 1964. The *Wild Dog* Collection consists of the typescripts for the published issues; correspondence with contributors, would-be contributors, bookshops, and individual subscribers; and the original cover art work with correspondence with the artists. There are approximately 600 letters and cards from the above mentioned sources; approximately 450 typescripts, some signed and corrected, by the authors who were published in the *Wild Dog;* and approximately 25 letters from artists accompanying the original cover art work. In connection with this archival material, additional separately published works by the contributing authors (approximately 120 volumes). No photocopying.

VT —UNIVERSITY OF VERMONT, Guy W Bailey/David W Howe Library, Burlington, 05405. John Buehler, Asst Dir for Special Collections
Notes: The papers of Hayden Carruth (1921-), poet and poetry editor for the *Hudson* Review.

WI —BELOIT COLLEGE LIBRARIES, Beloit, 53511. Dennis W Dickinson, Dir
Holdings: Vols 3000 Cat
Budget: $500
Notes: This is a collection of contemporary

LITTLE MAGAZINES (cont.)

American poetry. Format of material varies from very slim to regular book-size vols; also backfiles of numerous poetry magazines. Kept together as a "special collection" for those interested in studying the tenor of contemporary American poetry (good and bad). Incl the *Beloit Poetry Journal* Collection.

WI —UNIVERSITY OF WISCONSIN, LA CROSSE, Murphy Library, 1631 Pine St, La Crosse, 54601. Edwin L Hill, Special Collections Librn
Holdings: Vols 300 Cat Mss
Notes: Center for Contemporary Poetry (a collection of contemporary midwestern poetry). Emphasis on purchase of trade and small press publications of midwestern amd especially Wisconsin poets. Unpublished materials are collected for a few poets and incl comprehensive papers, mss, reviews, letters, etc. Collection also incl various midwestern and Wisconsin little magazines. Several fine midwestern private presses, especially Perishable Press. Collection is largely regional and contemporary. Most is cataloged and/or indexed. Collection incl records and papers of *Margins* (1972-1976), a review of little magazines and small press books. The Center for Contemporary Poetry published an annual volume, *Voyages to the Inland Sea*, from 1971-1979, featuring the poetry and essays of prominent midwestern poets.

WI —UNIVERSITY OF WISCONSIN, MADISON, Memorial Library, Rare Books Collection, 728 State St, Madison, 53706. Gretchen Lagana, Cur
Holdings: Cat
Notes: Sukov Collection of Little Magazines. An extensive collection of over 4400 titles of experimental literary magazines in English, dating from 1900 to the present. Non-commerical and avant-garde in character, and associated with many literary and artistic movements and the names of distinguished writers. The largest and most comprehensive collection of its kind in the US. Originally in part purchased from and in part the donation of Dr Marvin Sukov, A Minneapolis psychiatrist. Continuously growing. Housed in Dept of Rare Books and Special Collections.

WI —UNIVERSITY OF WISCONSIN, MILWAUKEE, Library, Box 604, Milwaukee, 53201. William C Roselle, Dir
Holdings: Uncat Mss
Notes: Correspondence of the *Little Review* with prominent 20th-century writers. Restricted use: cataloged for use in Rare Book area only. No photocopying. Also, contemporary small press publications.

BC —SIMON FRASER UNIVERSITY, Library, Burnaby, V5A 1S6, Can. Percilla Groves, Special Collections Librn
Holdings: Uncat Mss
Notes: *IO* Archive incl mss, correspondence, proofs, and business records of this little magazine, 1966-1976.

NS —DALHOUSIE UNIVERSITY LIBRARY, Halifax, B3H 4H8, Can.
Holdings: Vols 10,000 Cat
Notes: Extensive collection of Canadian small press publications with special strengths in poetry, drama, little magazines, poetry broadsides, and Atlantic Canada creative writing. Good holdings in various early Canadian literary periodicals and early Canadian small publishers, but main focus from 1970 to present.

ON —QUEEN'S UNIVERSITY, Douglas Library, Kingston, K7L 5C4, Can. William F E Morley, Cur, Special Collections
Holdings: Vols 650 Uncat
Notes: F R Scott Collection, incl Canadian poetry and poetry magazines. Checklist of holdings is available.

LITTLE ORPHAN ANNIE

†MA —BOSTON UNIVERSITY, Mugar Memorial Library, Special Collections Dept, 771 Commonwealth Avenue, Boston, 02215. Howard B Gotlieb, Dir
Notes: Extensive papers of mystery and science fiction writers, and film, radio and TV writers, performers, etc. 14 years of original Little Orphan Annie art. Collections built around papers of individuals are supplemented by their printed works.

LITTLE PRESSES

MI —MICHIGAN STATE UNIVERSITY, Libraries, Special Collections Div, East Lansing, 48824. Jannette Fiore, Librn
Notes: Several thousand vols of American small press poetry, ca 1965 to present, being augmented at the rate of 350 to 450 volumes per year.

NY —GRADUATE CENTER OF THE CITY UNIVERSITY OF NEW YORK, William H and Gwynne K Crouse Library for Publishing Arts, 33 W 42 St, New York, 10036. Alfred H Lane, Dir
Notes: Recently established and still growing, but intended to become the authoritative source of materials in the field, of particular value in research about the publishing industry. Open to staff members of publishing houses, students, scholars, authors, printers, and booksellers. Particularly useful for research on technical, financial, and historical matters. Much on the history of individual houses, economics of authorship; marketing and distribution of books; etc. Primarily 20th century material in hard form or microfilm, incl books, pamphlets, reprints, translations, dissertations, periodicals, indexing and abstracting services, yearbooks, reports and directories of organizations, publishers' and antiquarian dealers' catalogs (particularly those who deal in books about books), periodicals, legislative materials, and clippingspertaining to the book industry. Sections of the library deal with printing, incl typography, specimen books, history of printing and printing techniques, book design and small press and alternative publishing.

NY —VISUAL STUDIES WORKSHOP, Research Center, 31 Prince St, Rochester, 14607. Linn Underhill, Coordr; Robert Bretz, Librn
Holdings: Vols (8000) Cat Pix Slides Audiotapes Videotapes
Notes: Strong emphasis on photography (over 1,000,000 pictures) and the photographic arts in many subject areas incl in this volume. Heavy emphasis on early photographic processes and collections of examples of them. Also collections of individual photographers' works.

WA —UNIVERSITY OF WASHINGTON LIBRARIES, Suzzallo Library, Special Collections Division, Rare Book Collection, FM-25, Seattle, 98195. Gary Menges, Coordinator for Special Collections
Notes: Printing history, including early printed books and modern fine printing; book arts, including papermaking, decorated papers, bookbinding, book design, and artist's books; American literature, 19th century includes: Stephen Crane, Ralph Waldo Emerson, Nathaniel Hawthorne, Henry James, Henry Wadsworth Longfellow, Herman Melville, Frank Norris, Harriet Beecher Stowe and Walt Whitman and 20th century includes: Theodore Roethke; illustrated books, including emblem books, historical children's illustration, books illustrated with prints, and artist's books; costume history; voyages and travels; preservation of library materials.

NS —DALHOUSIE UNIVERSITY LIBRARY, Halifax, B3H 4H8, Can.
Holdings: Vols 10,000 Cat
Notes: Extensive collection of Canadian small press publications with special strengths in poetry, drama, little magazines, poetry broadsides, and Atlantic Canada creative writing. Good holdings in various early Canadian literary periodicals and early Canadian small publishers, but main focus from 1970 to present.

LITTLE REVIEW

WI —UNIVERSITY OF WISCONSIN, MILWAUKEE, Library, Box 604, Milwaukee, 53201. William C Roselle, Dir
Holdings: Uncat Mss
Notes: Correspondence of the *Little Review* with prominent 20th-century writers. Restricted use: cataloged for use in Rare Book area only. No photocopying.

LITTLE THEATRE (LAKE CHARLES, LOUISIANA)

LA —MCNEESE STATE UNIVERSITY, Lether E Frazar Library, Ryan St, Lake Charles, 70609. Kathie Bordelon, Special Collections Librn
Notes: Personal collection of Rosa Hart incl Little Theatre scrapbooks, correspondence, playbills, photographs. Rosa Hart was director of the Little Theatre in Lake Charles for over 30 years achieving national recognition for her talents.

LITTLEDALE, CLARA SAVAGE, 1891-1956

†MA —RADCLIFFE COLLEGE, Arthur & Elizabeth Schlesinger Library on History of Women in America, 3 James St, Cambridge, 02138.
Notes: Papers, etc.

LITTLEJOHN FAMILY

LA —NICHOLLS STATE UNIVERSITY, Ellender Memorial Library, Thibodaux, 70310. Randall A Detro, Dir; Philip D Uzee, Archivist
Holdings: Uncat Mss Maps Pix Microforms
Notes: Louisiana and local history; family papers of the period, etc.

LITTLE'S DISEASE see Cerebral Palsy

LITTLEWOOD, WILLIAM H., 1898-1967

NY —CORNELL UNIVERSITY LIBRARIES, Collection of Regional History, Dept of Manuscripts and Univ Archives, Ithaca, 14853.
Notes: Aviation consultant. Papers, 1917-20-(34-64)-67; 21 ft.

LITURGICAL OBJECTS

NY —YIVO INSTITUTE FOR JEWISH RESEARCH, Library & Archives, 1048 Fifth Ave, New York, 10028. Dina Abramowicz, Librn; Marek Web, Archivist
Holdings: Cat Mss Pix Slides
Notes: Original works and reference materials, incl reproductions of 1500 objects; 500 slides. Separate catalog.

LITURGICS AND LITURGIES

CT —YALE UNIVERSITY, Music Library, 98 Wall St, New Haven, 06520. Harold E Samuel, Librn
Notes: General reference and reseach materials. Performing editions. Strong in theoretical literature, opera, 17-18th century music (incl mss), J S Bach and sons in early editions and mss, Russian liturgical music (Tkaczenko Collection), hymnology, American music. Also collection of musical pictures and portraits.

†DC —CATHOLIC UNIVERSITY OF AMERICA, Music Library, Washington, 20064. Betty Libbey, Head Music Library
Holdings: Cat Microforms
Notes: A large collection to support advanced degree study. Emphasis on church music, musicology, history and criticism, instrumental and vocal music, solo music for all voices, instruments, and musical forms.

FL —UNIVERSITY OF FLORIDA LIBRARY, Isser and Rae Price Library of Judaica, 18 Libr East, Gainesville, 32611. Robert Singerman, Head Librn
Budget: ($30,000)
Notes: Total holdings estimated at 55,000 vols dealing with the political, social, economic and intellectual history of the Jews in the ancient, medieval and modern periods and in all geographic areas. The following areas are especially well represented by printed matter in all relevant languages: Bibliography, Festschriften, History, Bible, Judaism and Jewish theology, liturgy,

LITURGICS AND LITURGIES (cont.)

responsa, rabbinical literature, Jewish law, Hebrew language and literature, Yiddish language and literature, anti-semitism, Zionism, Palestine and the *Yishuv*, and the State of Israel. German and American Judaica form a collecting emphasis with holdings for all the standard histories as well as histories of individual synagogues, institutions and local communities. Works in Hebrew and Yiddish comprise about 60 percent of the collection (estimated 30,000 vols). With few exceptions, holdingsare limited to nineteenth and twentieth century imprints, with complete sets of journals and thousands of ephemeral pamphlets, many of them commemorating anniversaries, enhancing the research value of the collection, the largest Judaica research library in the southeastern United States. Only about half of the collection is cataloged; the collection is a circulating one and vols may be borrowed on interlibrary loan. Incl the Leonard C Mishkin Collection (40,000 vols), the largest personal Judaica collection in the United States, the Shlomo Marenof Collection (3500 vols), and the inventory of Bernard Morgenstern's Lower East Side Book Store (8000 vols). Scholars should inquire in advance of their visit. *The Isser and Rae Price Library of Judaica* Report (circulation 2900 copies) is mailed gratis twice a year to all interested parties. Special catalogs:Pre-1881 Hebrew imprints recorded in a chronological card file.

IL —NEWBERRY LIBRARY, John M Wing Foundation on the History of Printing, 60 W Walton St, Chicago, 60610. Diana Haskell, Cur of Modern Mss
Holdings: Cat Mss
Notes: Several thousand vols. Incl the collection formed by Stanley Morison for his *English Prayer Books.* Emphasis on Roman Catholic and Anglican liturgy.

MD —JOHNS HOPKINS UNIVERSITY, Milton S Eisenhower Library, George Peabody Collection, 17 E Mt Vernon Place, Baltimore, 21201. Lyn Hart, Peabody Librn
Notes: Emphasis on materials published before 1950. Strength is a good collection through the 19th century.

MI —WESTERN MICHIGAN UNIVERSITY, Dwight B Waldo Library, Institute of Cistercian Studies Library, Kalamazoo, 49008. Beatrice H Beck, Librn
Notes: Collection contains mss and early editions of Cisstercian liturgy and authors, especially Bernard of Clairvaux. Ms sources of Cistercian documentary history, abbey histories and charters. Incl the Abbot Obrecht Collection of mss, incunabula, and other books from the Cistercian Abbey of Gethsemane at Trappist, Kentucky. On indefinite loan (1976).

MN —SAINT JOHN'S UNIVERSITY, Alcuin Library, Collegeville, 56321. Michael Kathman, Dir
Holdings: Vols 25,000 Cat Maps Slides Phonorecords Audiotapes Videotapes Filmstrips Microforms
Budget: ($176,000)
Notes: Includes liturgical indexing service on cards from L'Institut Bibliographique de Liturgie, Abbaye du Mont Cesar, Louvain, Belgium.

MO —SAINT LOUIS UNIVERSITY, Pius XII Memorial Library, 3655 W Pine Blvd, Saint Louis, 63108. William Cole, Dir
Holdings: Slides Microforms
Notes: Collection covers all areas of learning and European history from Classical Antiquity to early modern period. Researchers using collection receive assistance in paleography, bibliography and reference search. Approx 10,000 1000-foot reels of microfilm (not counting master negatives) reproducing Vatican Library's Latin, Greek, Hebrew, Arabic and Ethiopic mss. Some 8000 100-foot reels of microfilm (again not counting master negative) reproducing rare and out of print books relating to subject areas in the mss. Over 50, 000 color slides of medieval and Renaissance mss illuminations. A reference collection of modern materials relating to ms research.

NY —GENERAL THEOLOGICAL SEMINARY, Saint Marks Library, 175 Ninth Ave, New York, 10011. David Green, Dir
Holdings: Vols (200,000) Cat

†NY —COLGATE ROCHESTER DIVINITY SCHOOL, Ambrose Swasey Library, 1100 S Goodman St, Rochester, 14620.
Notes: Incl general works about worship, its history and practice and contains manuals of worship, liturgies of primarily Protestant denomination, a sizable collection of hymn books, with particular emphasis upon the Anglican tradition.

PA —LUTHERAN THEOLOGICAL SEMINARY, Krauth Memorial Library, 7301 Germantown Ave, Philadelphia, 19119. Rev David J Wartluft, Dir Libr
Holdings: Vols (2200) Cat
Notes: Lutheran liturgies of all countries in addition to more general liturgical works. Some liturgical works of other Christian denominations. Some items in Rare Book Collection and are not available for loan, copying, or outside of library use.

TX —OBLATE SCHOOL OF THEOLOGY, Library, 285 Oblate Dr, San Antonio, 78216. James Maney, Libr Dir
Holdings: Vols (22,000) Cat
Budget: ($15,500)

ON —HURON COLLEGE, Silcox Memorial Library, 1349 Western Rd, London, N6G 1H3, Can. Pamela MacKay, Chief Librn
Holdings: Vols (28,000) Cat
Budget: ($27,710)
Notes: Covers Bible, church history, church music, liturgics, pastoralia, religious education, philosophy of religion, religious studies, systematics. 95 periodical subscriptions including foreign language materials. Rare books collection of 750 vols, incl collections of sermons, commentaries, particularly rare bibles, many in foreign languages.

ON —VICTORIA UNIVERSITY, Library, Centre for Reformation and Renaissance Studies, 71 Queen's Park Crescent, Toronto, M5S 1K7, Can. Robert C Brandeis, Chief Librn; James Estes, Dir
Holdings: Vols 1150 Uncat
Notes: Collection consists of British and North American hymnbooks from the 19th and 20th centuries. The emphasis is on Protestant denominations. Some liturgical works are incl.

LITURGY see Liturgics and Liturgies

LIVERWORTS

MA —HARVARD UNIVERSITY LIBRARY, Farlow Reference Library, 20 Divinity Ave, Cambridge, 02138. Geraldine C Kaye, Librn
Holdings: Vols (60,000) Cat Mss Serials Pix Microforms
Notes: The Farlow Reference Library provides complete coverage of the systematic literature on algae, bryophytes, fungi, and lichens. Established by bequest of Professor William G Farlow, it is one of the most extensive cryptogamic botany libraries in the US. Books do not circulate.

MO —MISSOURI BOTANICAL GARDEN LIBRARY, PO Box 299, Saint Louis, 63166. M R Crosby, Dir of Research
Notes: The William Campbell Steere Collection of over 1000 volumes and 5000 pamphlets on bryology. Especially strong in the 19th century literature and from 1750 to the present.

LIVESTOCK see Domestic Animals; Stock and Stockbreeding

LIVING THEATRE

CA —UNIVERSITY OF CALIFORNIA, DAVIS, Shields Library, Dept of Special Collections, Davis, 95616. Donald Kunitz, Head; C Danial Elliott, Asst Head
Holdings: Vols 2700 Cat Mss Pix Phonorecords Audiotapes Videotapes
Notes: Archives of the Living Theatre founded by Julian Beck and Judith Malina incl directing, lighting, and master scripts; correspondence; contracts; original art; programs; posters; reviews; photographs by Mantegna and Bissinger; performance notes and diagrams; music; Malina's diaries; published texts; financial records.

NY —NEW YORK PUBLIC LIBRARY, Performing Arts Research Center, Billy Rose Theatre Collection, 111 Amsterdam Ave, New York, 10023. Dorothy L Swerdlove, Cur
Holdings: Cat Pix
Notes: Incl correspondence, office records, photographs, scripts, etc, of this producing organization.

LIVINGSTON, ROBERT R.

NY —NEW YORK STATE OFFICE OF PARKS & RECREATION, TACONIC REGION, Clermont State Historic Park, Library, RR 1, Box 215, Germantown, 12526. Bruce E Naramore, Historic Site Manager
Holdings: Vols 100 Cat Mss Maps
Notes: Primarily correspondence from Robert Fulton to the Chancellor Robert R Livingston. Covers most aspects of the planning and building of the "Clermont," the first successful steamboat; also its navigation. Maps and diagrams of construction of the original vessel. Interesting highlights into the lives of the two partners, and their success. It is interesting to note here that the Chancellor and Robert Fulton never called the vessel the "Clermont," rather, simply the "steamboat" and the "North River Steamboat, of Clermont" (as the ship was registered). No photocopying.

LIVINGSTON FAMILY

NY —NEW YORK STATE OFFICE OF PARKS & RECREATION, TACONIC REGION, Clermont State Historic Park, Library, RR 1, Box 215, Germantown, 12526. Bruce E Naramore, Historic Site Manager
Holdings: Vols (5000) Cat Mss Maps Pix Slides Audiotapes
Notes: Family Bibles and many period editions of the Livingston family. Bibles go back to 1594. As family intermarried so many other prominent Hudson River families, editions highlight a great deal of history and genealogy of other peoples' lives, as well as their own. *A Catalogue of Repositories that Possess Primary Materials of the Livingston Family of the State of New York*, when completed, will list exact card data supplied from the owner institution. Catalog is being prepared to offer scholars and researchers the first location catalog available of the Livingston family materials, which incl two presidential administrations, and a mass of other data. Presently, over 3000 Livingston entries have been located and entered. Write for further information.

NY —NEW YORK HISTORICAL SOCIETY, Library, 170 Central Park W, New York, 10024. James Gregory, Librn
Notes: Miscellaneous papers, correspondence, etc.

LIVONIA

MA —HARVARD UNIVERSITY LIBRARY, Widener Library, Cambridge, 02138.
Holdings: Cat
Notes: *Widener Library Shelflist* No 40 (1972) lists some 6500 vols on the history, languages, and literatures of the Baltic states: Estonia, Latvia, Lithuania, and Livonia; about 200 of these are on Livonia.

LIVRES D'ARTISTES

IN —INDIANA UNIVERSITY, Lilly Library, Seventh St, Bloomington, 47405. William R Cagle, Librn
Holdings: Cat
Notes: French illustrated books of the nineteenth and twentieth centuries incl a stron collection of *livres d'artiste*. See *Beyond Illustrations: The Livre D'artiste in the Twentieth Century* (Bloomington: The Lilly Library, 1976).

LIVRES D'ARTISTES (cont.)

ON —NATIONAL LIBRARY OF CANADA, 395 Wellington St, Ottawa, K1A 0N4, Can. Andre Preibish, Dir
Notes: The collection contains 42 incunabula. The core collection consists of early Canadiana (1752-1867) and 16th and 17th century books on Canada. The books printed in native languages are a very valuable part of the collection. Canadian Livres d'Artistes collection of limited editions and Canadian *livres d'artistes* received on legal deposit as well as examples of private press publications from other countries also form part of the Rare Book collection.

LJUNGH, ESSE W.

PQ —CONCORDIA UNIVERSITY LIBRARIES, 1455 de Maisonneuve Blvd W, Montreal, H3G 1M8, Can. Martin Cohen, Special Collections Librn
Holdings: Cat Mss
Notes: Collection of 14,000 English language radio drama scripts broadcast over the Canadian Broadcasting Corp from 1930s to date. Presently being accessed by computer. Contains two sections: the main collection is the Esse W Ljungh Collection: besides plays, incl CBC memos, correspondence, etc; the second is the T Frank Willis Collection and consists of the scripts, letters and memos of the late producer.

LLOYD, CURTIS GATES

OH —LLOYD LIBRARY & MUSEUM, 917 Plum St, Cincinnati, 45202. John B Griggs, Librn
Notes: All of Curtis Gates Lloyd's original works on mycology.

LLOYD, JOHN URI

OH —LLOYD LIBRARY & MUSEUM, 917 Plum St, Cincinnati, 45202. John B Griggs, Librn
Notes: All of John Uri Lloyd's publications. Incl his twelve original books on pharmacy, research papers and journal articles. Lloyd also wrote ten novels.

LLOYD, NORMAN

MA —BOSTON UNIVERSITY, Mugar Memorial Library, Special Collections Dept, 771 Commonwealth Ave, Boston, 02215. Howard B Gotlieb, Dir
Holdings: Cat Mss Pix
Notes: Mss, correspondence, music scores, etc collected in depth; incl publications by or about.

LLOYD, REP. SHERMAN

UT —UNIVERSITY OF UTAH, Marriott Library, Special Collections, Salt Lake City, 84112. Gregory C Thompson, Cur
Holdings: Cat Mss Microfilm Film Oral History
Notes: Papers.

LOANS, CONSUMER see Loans, Personal

LOANS, PERSONAL

IL —HOUSEHOLD INTERNATIONAL, Corp Library, 2700 Sander Rd, Prospect Heights, 60070. Win Sadecki, Corp Librn
Holdings: Vols Cat

LOANS, SMALL see Loans, Personal

LOCAL ADMINISTRATION see Local Government

LOCAL GOVERNMENT

CA —LOS ANGELES PUBLIC LIBRARY, Municipal Reference Library, Rm 530, City Hall E, 200 N Main St, Los Angeles, 90012. C Grimsley, Senior Librn
Holdings: Vols 37,500 Cat
Budget: $14,500
Notes: Emphasis on cities over 500,000 with special collection of municipal documents from large cities. Biographical material on local government officials.

CA —ASSOCIATION OF BAY AREA GOVERNMENTS, MTC/ABAG Library, 101 Eighth St, Oakland, 94607. Diane Gillman, Information Coord
Notes: Concentrates heavily on the nine-county Bay Area region. About 10,000 monographs and serials. Title catalog, OCLC/ATS. Central collection of documents for six transit properties in Bay Area.

CA —SACRAMENTO PUBLIC LIBRARY, 828 I St, Sacramento, 95814. Dorothy Harvey, Librn, Special Collections
Holdings: Vols (4000) Cat
Notes: Incl books on public administration and police science, local government (city and county). Have over 4000 Sacramento city and county documents.

DC —LIBRARY OF CONGRESS, Washington, 20540.
Holdings: Vols 93,000 Cat
Notes: Local History and Genealogy Room has reference collection of 5000 volumes (3000 on American local history). Card files in LH&G Room include: Local History Shelflist; Author Catalog of Genealogy, Heraldry, and Local History. Local History Shelflist was published in five volumes in 1975 by Magna Carta Book Company as *United States Local Histories in the Library of Congress, A Bibliography*.

DC —METROPOLITAN WASHINGTON COUNCIL OF GOVERNMENTS, Research Library, 1875 Eye St NW, Suite 200, Washington, 20006. Suan Kalish, Librn
Holdings: Vols (3000) Cat Microforms
Notes: Contains (on 75 reels of microfilm) archives of Maryland-National Park and Planning Commission, archives of the Council of Governments, and audits and financial reports of local governments (1950-date). Also incl annual reports, planning reports and budgets from each jurisdiction (1973-date).

DC —NATIONAL LEAGUE OF CITIES, Municipal Reference Service, 1301 Pennsylvania Ave NW, Washington, 20004. Olivia Kredel, Mgr
Holdings: Vols (20,000) Cat
Notes: Publications covering a wide variety of topics related to cities and local government.

FL —MIAMI-DADE PUBLIC LIBRARY SYSTEM, Urban Affairs Library, 1 Biscayne Blvd, Miami, 33132. Richard G Frow, Librn
Holdings: Vols 3078 Cat
Notes: Local government administration and planning. Incl materials concerning local government administration and planning exclusive of Florida, chosen primarily to suit needs of local governmental officials, although use by local college students, land developers and the general public is considered. Incl 8627 pamphlets cat and 98 periodicals. Library has access to LOGIN and DIALOG databases.

LA —PUBLIC AFFAIRS RESEARCH COUNCIL OF LOUISIANA, Library, 300 Louisiana Ave, PO Box 3118, Baton Rouge, 70821. Jan Brashear, Research Librn
Holdings: Vols (7000) Cat Mss
Notes: State and local government problems with emphasis on Louisiana. Strong in the areas of education and public finance.

NY —NEW YORK STATE DEPT OF STATE, Community Affairs Library, 162 Washington Ave, Albany, 12231. M L Johnson, Librn
Holdings: Vols (14,640) Cat
Notes: Local government. Serves as research arm for official activities. 16,000 items in vertical files; 150 periodicals. Unique Community File collection of about 1600 local governments arranged by counties in the state.

OH —PUBLIC LIBRARY OF CINCINNATI & HAMILTON COUNTY, Government and Business Dept, 800 Vine St, Cincinnati, 45202. Paul T Hudson, Head
Holdings: Vols 2000 Cat
Notes: The Murray Seasongood Collection of Government, Law and Public Administration contains works on local government, city management, public finance and municipal law. The collection also houses the collected works of Murray Seasongood.

OR —UNIVERSITY OF OREGON, Bureau of Governmental Research Library, Box 3177, Eugene, 97403. Katherine G Eaton, Head Librn
Holdings: Vols (25,000) Cat Microforms
Budget: ($5000)
Notes: Separate catalog and classification system.

PA —UNIVERSITY OF PENNSYLVANIA, Fels Center of Government, 39 & Walnut St, Philadelphia, 19104. Nancy K Smith, Librn
Budget: Vols (18,180) Cat Maps
Notes: Restricted use: Staff, students and government officials.

PA —UNIVERSITY OF PITTSBURGH, Library, Graduate School of Public and International Affairs, Forbes Quadrangle, 1st floor West, Pittsburgh, 15260. Nicholas C Caruso, Librn
Holdings: Vols (80,000) Cat
Budget: ($150,000)
Notes: The library attempts to collect as many national economic and social development plans as possible from the developing countries of the world. It also holds city, regional and state plans for Pennslyvania, particularly, the 9 southwestern countries of Pennsylvania.

ON —CANADIAN TAX FOUNDATION LIBRARY, 130 Adelaide St W, Toronto, M5H 3P5, Can. Marjorie Robinson, Librn
Holdings: Vols (16,500) Cat
Notes: Worldwide scope; emphasis on Canada.

ON —METROPOLITAN TORONTO LIBRARY, Municipal Reference Library, City Hall, Toronto, M5H 2N1, Can. Margot Hewings, Head
Holdings: Vols (60,000) Cat Maps Pix Microforms Slides VF
Budget: ($112,600)
Notes: Community development; municipal finance; local municipal government; housing; urban pollution; urban transportation; urban affairs; urban geography.

LOCAL HISTORY—COLLECTIONS

CA —LOS ANGELES PUBLIC LIBRARY, Genealogy & Local History Dept, 630 W 5th St, Los Angeles, 90071. Lucile Lipman, Sr Librn
Holdings: Vols (55,000) Cat Mss Maps Pix Microforms
Budget: ($16,000)
Notes: Extensive collection of county and town histories of the United States (except for California which is included in the California collection of the History Department), Canada, and Great Britain. Includes periodical holdings and the Orra Monnette Collection of published books and mss. Local history index is maintained.

MA —AMERICAN ANTIQUARIAN SOCIETY LIBRARY, 185 Salisbury St, Worcester, 01609. Marcus A McCorison, Dir & Librn
Holdings: Vols 50,000 Cat
Notes: The largest collection of regional, state, county, and local histories.

MO —UNIVERSITY OF MISSOURI-SAINT LOUIS, Thomas Jefferson Library, Manuscript and Historical Society Collection, 8001 Natural Bridge Rd, Saint Louis, 63121.
Holdings: Mss Pix Tapes
Notes: ca

NY —NEW YORK STATE LIBRARY, State Education Bldg Annex, Washington Ave, Albany, 12224.
Holdings: Cat Mss Maps Pix Microforms
Notes: Extensive collection on American local history incl books and pamphlets on American genealogy. Major strength northeastern United States. Maintain unique card index to regional historical and genealogical materials in periodicals not indexed elsewhere, pamphlets and comprehensive works; about 1912-date.

NY —NEW YORK GENEALOGICAL & BIOGRAPHICAL SOCIETY, Library, 122

LOCAL HISTORY—COLLECTIONS (cont.)

E 58 St, New York, 10022. James P Gregory, Librn
Holdings: Vols 63,500 Cat Mss Maps Microforms
Notes: The Society has copied and has in its ms collections a great many church records from all parts of New York State and several from adjacent states; and many very valuable ms genealogies and family Bible records which have never been published. The Society library is noncirculating and one of the principal genealogical reference libraries in the country. It has accumulated in its collections approximately 63 thousand vols on genealogy, local history and biography. In addition it has a rapidly expanding microfilm division which presently numbers over 2000 reels and keeps four microfilm readers in continuous use.

NY —NEW YORK PUBLIC LIBRARY, Local History and Genealogy Div, Fifth Ave & 42 St, New York, 10018. Gunther E Pohl, Chief
Holdings: Vols (160,000) Cat Pix
Budget: ($38,548)
Notes: Extensive collection of county, city, town and village histories of the United States. All other local histories are part of the General Research and Humanities Division. Collection includes over 60,000 mounted photographs of New York City views arranged by address and/or subject. 20,000 film and glass plate negatives depicting NYC tenement housing conditions (1902-1938). Also the Lloyd L Acker collection of 48,000 film negatives depicting NYC buildings, 1935-1975. Collection of Lewis W Hine photographic prints made by the photographer on immigration, child labor, women at work and men at work. Eugene Armbruster collection of Long Island views; D B Austin's photographs of Long Island and western Americana; scrapbooks, and postcards of NYC and other US localities (200,000). See*United States Local History Catalog* (Boston: GK Hall, 1974), 2 vols.

NC —DUKE UNIVERSITY, William R Perkins Library, Durham, 27706. Elvin E Strowd, University Librn

ON —METROPOLITAN TORONTO LIBRARY, Canadian History Dept, Baldwin Room Section, 789 Yonge St, Toronto, M4W 2G8, Can. David B Kotin, Head
Holdings: Vols (52,000) Mss Pix
Notes: This collection consists of material on Canadian history, geography, travel, archaeology, genealogy, retrospective city and telephone directories, collective biographies, native peoples (excluding customs, rights and social conditions), Arctic regions, military history and theory. It is an extremely strong collection of both current and retropective material. Particular strengths are national and local history (especially Ontario), Arctic regions, native peoples, travel (especially Ontario), and military history. Incl 78,000 historical pictures, 235 lin meters mss, 14,000 broadsides and 3800 bound newspapers.

LOCAL TRANSIT

CA —ASSOCIATION OF BAY AREA GOVERNMENTS, MTC/ABAG Library, 101 Eighth St, Oakland, 94607. Diane Gillman, Information Coord
Notes: Concentrates heavily on the nine-county Bay Area region. About 10,000 monographs and serials. Title catalog, OCLC/ATS. Central collection of documents for six transit properties in Bay Area.

IL —NORTHWESTERN UNIVERSITY, Transportation Center Library, Evanston, 60201. Mary Roy, Librn
Holdings: Vols (116,000)
Notes: The emphasis in this collection is on current developments in transportation operations and socioeconomics--management, planning, impact and regulation. All modes of transportation and containerization are incl; the geographic scope covers domestic and foreign activity at the urban, intercity and international levels. Publications on new systems developments and the application of analytic techniques to operations are well represented. Incl 19,000 pamphlets; 9000 company reports. *Services are offered on research conducted outside Northwestern. A fee schedule is available on request.* Publications: *Current Literature in Traffic and Transportation* (bi-monthly accessions bulletin citing 625 books, reports and periodical articles per issue).

LOCALIZATION OF CEREBRAL FUNCTIONS see Brain—Localization of Functions

LOCKE, ALAIN LEROY

CT —YALE UNIVERSITY, Box 1603A, Yale Station, New Haven, 06520.
Holdings: Cat Mss

LOCKE, DAVID ROSS

OH —RUTHERFORD B HAYES LIBRARY, 1337 Hayes Ave, Fremont, 43420. Watt P Marchman, Dir
Holdings: Cat Mss Pix
Notes: Papers, correspondence and literary mss (approx 6 linear ft) pertaining to "Petroleum V Nasby" and his son, Robin Locke, both of the Toledo *Blade*. Index in the collection. Cf *Guide to Manuscripts of the Ohio Historical Society*, 304.

LOCKE, JOHN

ON —UNIVERSITY OF TORONTO, Thomas Fisher Rare Book Library, 120 Saint George St, Toronto, M5S 1A5, Can. Richard G Landon, Head
Holdings: Vols 170 Cat
Notes: Locke Collection of first and other important editions of Locke's works; commentaries and critical works. Includes early abridgements and translations.

LOCKE, ROBINSON

NY —NEW YORK PUBLIC LIBRARY, Performing Arts Research Center, Billy Rose Theatre Collection, 111 Amsterdam Ave, New York, 10023. Dorothy L Swerdlove, Cur
Holdings: Cat Mss Pix
Notes: Papers, scrapbooks, mss, photographs, memorabilla, etc.

OH —RUTHERFORD B HAYES LIBRARY, 1337 Hayes Ave, Fremont, 43420. Watt P Marchman, Dir
Holdings: Cat Mss Pix
Notes: Papers, correspondence and literary mss (approx 6 linear ft) pertaining to "Petroleum V Nasby" and his son, Robinson Locke, both of the Toledo *Blade*. Index in the collection. Cf *Guide to Manuscripts of the Ohio Historical Sociey*, 304.

LOCKMAN FOUNDATION ARCHIVES

CA —UNIVERSITY OF CALIFORNIA, SANTA BARBARA, Library, Dept of Special Collections, Santa Barbara, 93106. Christian F Brun, Head
Holdings: Vols 235 Uncat Mss Pix
Notes: Archives of the Lockman Foundation which specializes in support of the Bible and religious translations; simplified Bible, etc.

LOCKRIDGE, RICHARD

NY —COLUMBIA UNIVERSITY LIBRARIES, Rare Book & Manuscript Library, 801 Butler Library, 535 W 114 St, New York, 10027. Kenneth A Lohf, Librn
Holdings: Mss
Notes: Papers, mss, archives, etc. 350 items. Restricted use.

LOCKS (CANAL) see Locks (Hydraulic Engineering)

LOCKS (HYDRAULIC ENGINEERING)

MA —UNIVERSITY OF LOWELL, Library, One University Ave, Lowell, 01854. Martha Mayo, Special Collections Librn
Holdings: Vols 3000 Cat Mss Maps Pix
Notes: The Locks and Canals Collections consist of the 19th century engineering library of the Proprietors of the Locks and Canals on Merrimack River 1793-present. This collection also contains 5000 photographs and 8000 architectural and engineering drawings.

LOCOMOTIVES—HISTORY

IL —MUSEUM OF SCIENCE AND INDUSTRY, Library, 57th St and Lake Shore Dr, Chicago, 60637. Carla Hayden, Coordinator
Holdings: Vols (15,000) Cat Maps Pix Slides
Budget: ($10,000)
Notes: Occupying the site of the Fine Arts Building of Chicago's Columbian Exposition of 1893, the Museum Library has been the recipient of numerous gifts in this field, not only of materials from Chicago's Columbian Expositions, Century of Progress and Railroad Fairs but also from the New York World's Fair, St Louis, Paris Exposition Universelle, San Francisco's Panama-Pacific etc. Incl blueprints of some buildings and areas. No separate catalog or index to this extensive collection.

MI —EDISON INSTITUTE, Greenfield Village and Henry Ford Museum, Archives & Research Library, PO Box 1970, Dearborn, 48121. Steve Hamp, Dir; Joan W Gartland, Librn
Notes: Incl Dunbar collection of prints, broadsides and drawings documenting *History of Travel in America*, 1680-1910 (1741 items) and the Walker Locomotive collection, 1820-1931 (308 items). It also incl 19th century maps and travelers guides and an antique automotive file.

NJ —PASSAIC COUNTY HISTORICAL SOCIETY, Lamhurt Castle, Valley Rd, Paterson, 07503. Helen D Hamilton, Dir
Holdings: Vols (5000) Cat Mss Maps Pix
Notes: Material on the Society for the Establishment of Useful Manufacturing (founded) by Alexander Hamilton, papers relating to John Holland, who developed the submarine, the industrial magnates of the area who were active in the manufacture of locomotives, Colt revolvers, and textiles, especially silk.

TX —SOUTHERN METHODIST UNIVERSITY, DeGolyer Library, Box 396, SMU, Dallas, 75275. Clifton H Jones, Dir
Holdings: Vols (15,000) Cat Mss Maps Pix
Notes: One of the largest railroad photograph collections in the world; about 230,000 prints and 70,000 negatives, all countries. Accompanied by a major collection (12,000 vols), of railroadiana; much on locomotives. All languages.

LODGE, OLIVER J., 1851-1940

†TX —UNIVERSITY OF TEXAS LIBRARIES, General Libraries, Humanities Research Center, PO Box 7219, Austin, 78712. John Chalmers, Librn
Notes: His correspondence (1885-1934), and galley proofs for *Scientific Development and Its Responsibilities.*

LOEB, LEO

MO —WASHINGTON UNIVERSITY, School of Medicine, Archives, 660 S Euclid Ave, Saint Louis, 63110. Paul G Anderson, Archivist
Holdings: Mss Pix Audiotapes
Budget: ($38,000)
Notes: Institutional records and papers of faculty of Washington University School of Medicine and its predecessors and associated hospitals. Contains records of St Louis Medical College, Missouri Medical Barnard Free Skin and Cancer Hospital, Barnes Hospital, St Louis Children's Hospital and Jewish Hospital of St Louis. Incl papers of William Beaumont, Joseph Erlanger, Leo Loeb, Evarts Graham, Edmund V Cowdry, Helen Graham, Carl V Moore, Margaret Smith and others. Oral history program. See also: Anderson, Paul G and Hoolihan,

LOEB, LEO (cont.)

Christopher, eds. *Special Collections* (St Louis: Washington University School of Medicine, 1981). 960 linear feet.

LOEB, LEONARD B., 1891-1978

CA —UNIVERSITY OF CALIFORNIA, BERKELEY, Bancroft Library, Manuscripts Division, Berkeley, 94720. James D Hart, Dir
Notes: Papers.

LOEFFLER, CHARLES MARTIN TORNOV, 1861-1935

DC —LIBRARY OF CONGRESS, Music Division, Washington, 20540.
Notes: Music mss and papers of Charles Loeffler, composer and concert master of the Boston Symphony Orchestra.

LOFTS, NORAH

MA —BOSTON UNIVERSITY, Mugar Memorial Library, Special Collections Dept, 771 Commonwealth Ave, Boston, 02215. Howard B Gotlieb, Dir
Holdings: Cat Mss

LOG BOOKS

CA —CLAREMONT COLLEGES, Honnold Library, Ninth & Dartmouth, Claremont, 91711. Tania Rizzo, Special Collections Dept Head
Holdings: Vols 353 Calendared Mss Maps Pix
Notes: Mss and typescript volumes of account books, ledgers, log books, journals, annual reports, cargo lists, correspondence, etc. Given to Pomona College by the Robert Dollar Co upon the liquidation of the Pacific Steamship Co Thompson, RC, comp, *Calendar of Archives and Records of Certain Pacific Coast Steamship Companies* (typescript prepared 1940-1941). Restricted use.

CA —OAKLAND PUBLIC LIBRARY, Oakland History Room, 125 14th St, Oakland, 94612. William W Sturm, Librn
Holdings: Cat Mss Pix
Notes: Logbooks of the US Coast Guard Cutter *Bear*, from 1889 to 1932.

CA —PACIFIC GROVE PUBLIC LIBRARY, 550 Central Ave, Pacific Grove, 93950. Margaret McBride, Library Dir
Holdings: Vols (1200) // Cat
Notes: Alvin Seale South Seas Collection, incl rare and unusual items, accounts of early voyages, ships' logs and artifacts. Separate catalog. Gift of Alvin Seale, curator of Steinhart Aquarium, San Francisco, 1937.

CA —NATIONAL MARITIME MUSEUM, SAN FRANCISCO, J Porter Shaw Library, Golden Gate National Recreation Area, Fort Mason, San Francisco, 94123. David A Hull, Librn; Herbert Beckwith, Catalog Librn; Irene Stachura, Ref Librn; John Maounis, Photo Librn
Holdings: Vols (12,000) Mss Maps Pix Slides Microforms
Budget: ($4000)
Notes: Pacific Coast maritime history. The photo collection of 160,000 is partly cataloged and classified. The library has complete runs of *Merchant Vessels of US* and *Lloyd's Register of Shipping* to 1970. The collection is particularly strong on Pacific Coast and San Francisco maritime history. About 250 log books; scrapbooks. Ca 250 oral history interviews. 60 percent of books cataloged.

CT —MYSTIC SEAPORT, MUSEUM, G W Blunt White Library, Greenmanville Ave, Mystic, 06355. Gerald E Morris, Librn
Holdings: Vols (40,000) Imprints Microforms
Budget: ($100,000)
Notes: American maritime history. The library is also a government depository for maritime materials with a subscription to 184 line items. Incl 400,000 mss, 4000 maps and charts, 30,000 ships' plans. Open to the public.

CT —YALE UNIVERSITY, Sterling Memorial Library, Latin American Collections, New Haven, 06520. Lee H Williams Jr, Cur
Holdings: Vols (300,000) Cat
Notes: Log books touching on all periods of Latin American history.
See also entry for Yale University under Latin America.

IN —INDIANA UNIVERSITY, Lilly Library, Seventh St, Bloomington, 47405. William R Cagle, Librn
Holdings: Vols (1300) Cat Mss Pix
Notes: Correspondence, log books, legal documents, diaires, speeches, letter copybooks, orderly books, and receipts, relating to the War of 1812, 3181 items. Incl prints.

IN —INDIANA STATE UNIVERSITY, EVANSVILLE, Library, 8600 University Blvd, Evansville, 47712. Gina R Walker, Acting Archivist
Holdings: Cat Mss
Notes: Ohio River traffic and operating logs for now deactivated locks and dams No 43, No 44, and No 45, 1927-1972. Unpublished list.

KS —WICHITA PUBLIC LIBRARY, 223 S Main, Wichita, 67202. Richard Rademacher, Librn
Holdings: Vols (1600) Mss Maps
Notes: The Driscoll Piracy Collection is one of the largest on the subject, incl miscellaneous Parliamentary acts, books, broadsides, scrapbooks, etc; many rarities in books, logs, and some mss. Collection was begun by Charles Driscoll, author. Not loaned.

ME —BOWDOIN COLLEGE, Library, Brunswick, 04011. Dianne M Gutscher, Cur of Special Collections
Holdings: Mss
Notes: The papers (about 15,000 items) of Robert A Bartlett, arctic explorer and shipmaster for Admirals Robert E Peary and Donald B MacMillan, contain 10,000 mss, 23,000 photographs, clippings, diaries, 300 maps, logbooks and some printed material relating to Bartlett's arctic voyages. Also, Admiral MacMillan's personal library of about 4000 books relating to arctic exploration, several volumes of clippings, numerous scrapbooks, ms diaries, logbooks, and journals, photographs, maps, and other records.

ME —PENOBSCOT MARINE MUSEUM, Library, Church St, Searsport, 04974. Charles Howard, Librn
Holdings: Vols (4000) Cat Mss Maps Pix
Budget: ($5000)
Notes: Maine maritime history, log books, journals, diaries, marine charts, ships registers, photographs, archives & mss, and books relating to world navigation. The greatest emphasis is placed on the Penobscot Bay region.

MD —US NAVAL ACADEMY, Nimitz Library, Annapolis, 21402. Alice S Creighton, Assistant Librn for Special Collections
Holdings: Vols 22,000 Cat Mss Pix
Notes: Books and periodicals, with emphasis on seapower. Incl rare and historically significant works, naval and general history. US Naval Academy materials (histories, class albums, Lucky Bags, student publications, etc), and copies of transcripts of the Naval Institute's oral history interviews with US naval officers. Manuscripts incl 205 volumes of ships' logs, letterbooks, order books, and watch, station and quarter bills, 1796-1938; papers of various naval officers, incl. Vice Admiral Wilson Brown, Commander George M Bache, Admiral Harry S Knapp, Lieutenant Edwin J DeHaven, and others; family correspondence of Admiral David Dixon Porter; and several thousand World War II naval action reports. Approximately 15,000 pictures incl portraits of naval officers, pictures of US and some foreign ships, World War II naval news photos and USNA photographs.

MD —MARYLAND HISTORICAL SOCIETY, Library, 201 W Monument St, Baltimore, 21201. William B Keller, Head Librn
Holdings: Maps Pix Films
Notes: Ships and shipping, description and travel, yachts and yachting, sailing, marine transport, Baltimore, and the Port of Maryland. Incl books, periodicals, maps, charts, pictures, ship plans, log books, films, etc.

MA —BEDFORD FREE PUBLIC LIBRARY, 613 Pleasant St, Bedford, 02740. Paul A Cyr, Cur of the Melville Room
Holdings: Vols 1020 Cat Mss Pix
Notes: One of the nation's most extensive collections (72,000 pieces) on American whaling. Incl all forms of documents used in the industry, over 40,000 mss. Library has a printed list of its logbooks and a seamen's card file of men who sailed from New Bedford Customs District contains 250,000 names. Library has published an addendum to "Starbuck" and "Whaling Masters," and "Birth of a Whaleship," 1964, both by Reginald B Hegarty.

MA —HARVARD UNIVERSITY, Graduate School of Business Administration, Baker Library, Soldiers Field, Boston, 02163. Mary V Chatfield, Librn; Florence Bartoshesky, Cur of Manuscripts and Archives
Holdings: Cat Mss
Notes: New England whaling logbooks from the 19th century.

MA —OLD DARTMOUTH HISTORICAL SOCIETY, 18 Johnny Cake Hill, New Bedford, 02740. Richard C Kugler, Dir
Holdings: Vols (15,000) Mss Maps
Budget: ($5000)
Notes: Whaling Museum Library contains one of the most comprehensive collections of printed and manuscript material ever assembled on the history of the whaling industry. Although primary emphasis is on American participation in this industry, foreign works are well-represented. Particularly noteworthy are the 5000 rare books and pamphlets assembled by the distinguished whaling scholar, Charles F Batchelder. Also, material on merchant ships and the natural history of whales. Incl 750 ft mss, 1070 log books, 650 maps, 25,000 pix, and 1800 microforms.

MA —PEABODY MUSEUM OF SALEM, Phillips Library, E India Sq, Salem, 01970.
Gregor Trinkaus-Randall, Librn
Holdings: Vols (100,000) Cat Mss Maps Pix
Notes: Maritime history of New England. No published indexes; listed in Hamer's *Guide to Archives...*

MI —DETROIT PUBLIC LIBRARY, Burton Historical Collection, 5201 Woodward Ave, Detroit, 48202. Alice Dalligan, Chief

MI —LE SAULTE DE SAINTE MARIE HISTORIC SITES, PO Box 1668, Sault Sainte Marie, 49783. Thomas Nance, Curator
Notes: 300 Great Lakes logbooks cover more than 100 years of freighter history of the local Wilson Marine Transit Company. Incl *Marine News*, 59 vols, 1900-1968, plus related reports, directoies, and yearbooks of steel industry.

NY —STATE UNIVERSITY OF NEW YORK, Maritime College, Stephen B Luce Library, Fort Schuyler, Bronx, 10465.
Richard H Corson, Librn
Holdings: Vols (68,000) Cat
Budget: ($90,000)
Notes: Incl history of ships with special emphasis on US sailing ships of the 19th century. Extensive holdings in periodical literature wih long and complete runs of many titles.

NY —WHALING MUSEUM SOCIETY, Cold Spring Harbor Whaling Museum, Main St, Cold Spring Harbor, 11724. Robert D Farwell, Dir
Holdings: Cat Mss Maps Pix
Notes: Library of bound and printed books covers Cold Spring Harbor whaling industry, in general, and maritime affairs. Archives contain thousands of original documents concerning whaling activities, the Cold Spring Harbor Whaling Company, and the extensive maritime coastal trade conducted out of Cold Spring Harbor after the whaling era (latter 1800s). Considerable material

LOG BOOKS (cont.)

deals with the Jones and Hewlett families, important in both local commerce and Long Island and New York affairs.

OH —BOWLING GREEN STATE UNIVERSITY, Jerome Library, Institute for Great Lakes Research, Bowling Green, 43403. Richard J Wright, Dir
Holdings: Vols (2500) Cat Mss Maps Pix Slides Phonorecords Audiotapes Videotapes 16mm Films Microforms
Budget: ($8300)
Notes: About 50 major ms collections, most of them processed; several thousand minor ms items, unprocessed. 100,000 pictures, incl several thousand film and glass plate negatives. Microforms of government vessel registries, vessel passages, 1500 maps, some mss. 6000 naval architectural drawings, 600 vols of scrapbooks. 140 periodical titles, current and op. Author/title/subject catalog.

OH —PUBLIC LIBRARY OF CINCINNATI & HAMILTON COUNTY, Dept of Rare Books & Special Collections, 800 Vine St, Library Square, Cincinnati, 45202. Yeatman Anderson III, Cur
Holdings: Cat Mss Maps Pix Slides Microforms
Notes: Inland River Collection. Incl logbooks, account books, personal correspondence, diaries, etc. Also, a picture collection of 14,000 items (steamboats, towboats, river views, crews, construction, barges, etc)

RI —BROWN UNIVERSITY, John Hay Library, 20 Prospect St, Providence, 02912.
Mark N Brown, Cur Mss
Holdings: Vols (1200) Cat Mss Pix
Notes: Morse Whaling Collection incl books, monographs, pamphlets, mss, log books, photographs, printed laws and statutes, blue prints of whaling vessels, and serial publications. Emphasis is on American works of 19th and 20th centuries with some works in Dutch, French, German and Japanese dating from the 18th century. Collection is strong in classics of whaling literature, personal narratives, whaling town histories, ships' registers, account books, and photographs of whaling vessels and processes; incl extensive files of the *Whaleman's Shipping List* (New Bedford), the *Merchant's Transcript* (New Bedford), and the *Friend* (Honolulu).

RI —PROVIDENCE PUBLIC LIBRARY, 150 Empire St, Providence, 02903.
Lance J Bauer, Special Collections Librn
Holdings: Cat Mss Maps Pix Microforms
Notes: The Nicholson Whaling Collection is one of the largest and certainly most distinguished whaling collections in the world, amassed in the early part of this century and bequeathed to the Providence Public Library in 1956. The logbooks, journals and account books record over 1000 voyages from 1762-1922 and incl many illustrated logs and a large number of journals of whaling wives. These are completely cataloged and microfilmed. Also incl are 13 boxes of business correspondence, bills of ladings, ships' papers, crew records, etc, and over 300 printed books. Many of the printed books are also quite rare, especially some first editions of 19th century voyages such as of the *Essex*. Contains material on Hawaiian whaling and material printed in Hawaii. Material must be used in-house. Photocopying on a restricted basis only for educational purposes when condition allows. No complete photocopying of logbooks. The microfilm of the mss is available for interlibrary loans.

VA —MARINERS MUSEUM, Library, Newport News, 23606. Ardie L Kelly, Librn
Holdings: Vols (60,000) Cat Mss Maps Pix Slides
Notes: Incl collections of over 150,000 photographs of merchant ships, naval vessels, sailing ships, lighthouses, portraits of naval men, harbors, canals, etc, and maps, ships' papers, and log books. Catalogs of various parts of the collection published by G K Hall, Boston.

LOGAN, JAMES ADDISON

CA —HOOVER INSTITUTION ON WAR, REVOLUTION & PEACE, Stanford University, Stanford, 94305. Milorad M Drachkovitch, Archivist
Holdings: // Mas
Notes: Papers, ca 1913-ca 1924, of James Addison Logan, banker and government official. Personal correspondence, secret letters, reports on prisoners of war, data on Serbia and material on political and military subjects. 5 ft (ca 6200 items). Unpublished preliminary inventory in the repository.

†PA —LIBRARY COMPANY OF PHILADELPHIA, 1314 Locust St, Philadelphia, 19107. Edwin Wolf II, Librn
Holdings: Vols (450,000)

LOGAN, JOHN

MO —WASHINGTON UNIVERSITY, Libraries, Special Collections Dept, Campus Box 1061, St Louis, 63130.
Notes: A small but significant collection.

LOGAN FAMILY

BC —UNIVERSITY OF VICTORIA, McPherson Library, Victoria, V8W 3H5, Can.
Notes: 1764-1963. Wadsworth Family papers: 1753-1901, legal papers, correspondence, mss of poetry by Joseph Wadsworth (Caroline Louisa Wadsworth, pseud). Small Family papers: 1880-1930; certificates, photographs, memorabilia incl watercolors of early Victoria by Sadie Honour, friend of Emily Carr. Logan Family papers: pastel drawing of Daryl Logan and family photographs.

LOGGING see Lumber and Lumbering

LOGGING RAILROADS

IL —LAKE FOREST COLLEGE, Donnelley Library, Lake Forest, 60045. Arthur H Miller Jr, College Librn
Holdings: Vols (1500) Cat Mss Maps Pix
Budget: ($1000)
Notes: Elliott Donnelley Collection (received 1976) of mostly mid-20th century books and periodicals on Western railroads and mountain narrow gauge, world narrow gauge and short lines, steam, live steam, model railroading, and some traction. Purchases keep collection emphasis current (50-75 new books per year, 22 periodical subscriptions). Also, the Munson Paddock Collecction (received 1977) of train illustrations, maps, and timetables, 1850-1950. In addition to American technical and historical books and periodicals, the collection contains books of views, narrations of rail travel (particularly American West), and US local histories--all with illustrations of trains. Most titles are late 19th century Americna. The 1550 volumes are supplemented by related holdings of more than 150 pamphlets, 600 timetables, 2000 unbound periodical issues, 200 maps, 75 diagrams (engines, cars) hundreds of clippings of train illustrations, and 1000 photographs. In progress is a card index of illustrations by wheel type line, and manufacturer. Together, the collections contain about 7000 items.

TX —STEPHEN F AUSTIN STATE UNIVERSITY, Ralph W Steen Library, Special Collections Dept, Box 13055, SFA Sta, Nacogdoches, 75962. Linda Cheves Nicklas, Special Collections Librn
Holdings: Cat Mss Maps Pix
Budget: ($5000)
Notes: Forest History Collection (late 1800s-1965). Incl personal and business correspondence, contracts, timber plats, logging and hauling contracts, photos and other records of early East Texas lumber companies and logging railroads. Calendars for records of each company are available. Published description: Maxwell, R S, "Manuscript Collections at Stephen F Austin State College", American Archivist, vol 28, July, 1965; and SFASU, *A Guide to Special* Collections, 1980.

LOGGING RAILROADS—HISTORY

OR —GEORGIA-PACIFIC HISTORICAL MUSEUM, Library, 900 SW Fifth, Portland, 97204. Richard Thompson, Museum Dir
Holdings: Vols (300) Uncat Videotapes 16mm Films Pix
Notes: Use of collection is by written request for specific information or materials.

WI —OSHKOSH PUBLIC MUSEUM, Library, 1331 Algoma Blvd, Oshkosh, 54901. Kitty A Hobson, Archivist
Holdings: Cat Mss Maps Pix Slides Audiotapes 16mm Films
Notes: Books, mss, photographs, etc, dealing with the history of Oshkosh and Winnebago County, Wisconsin, with special emphasis on lumbering and steamboating.

LOGIC

MD —JOHNS HOPKINS UNIVERSITY, Milton S Eisenhower Library, George Peabody Collection, 17 E Mt Vernon Place, Baltimore, 21201. Lyn Hart, Peabody Librn
Notes: Emphasis on materials published before 1950. Strength is a good collection through the 19th century.

NC —DUKE UNIVERSITY, William R Perkins Library, Durham, 27706. Elvin E Strowd, University Librn
Holdings: Vols Mss
Notes: The James Ray Newman collection of several thousand books and more than 8000 manuscripts is broad in scope and particularly strong in mathematics, philosophy, logic and history and philosophy of science.

OH —CLEVELAND PUBLIC LIBRARY, Social Sciences Department, 325 Superior Ave, Cleveland, 44114. Thelma Morris, Head
Holdings: Cat

PA —UNIVERSITY OF PITTSBURGH, Hillman Library, Pittsburgh, 15260. Glenora E Rossell, Head
Holdings: Vols (16,715) Cat Microforms
Notes: The collection covers all periods and philosophical disciplines. Its strength is in modern and contemporary philosophy. The approval program keeps the support for the collection up to date. The rare books, as part of the British philosophy to 1900, are located in Special Collections.

WA —UNIVERSITY OF WASHINGTON LIBRARIES, Philosophy Library, 331 Savery, DK-50, Seattle, 98195. Carolyn Mateer, Acting Selector
Holdings: Vols (18,302) Cat
Budget: ($27,516)
Notes: Collection includes materials in philosophy of language, law, mind, ethics, logic, mataphysics, religion, science, epistemology, social and political philosophy and the history of philosophy.

LOGIC—HISTORY

PA —UNIVERSITY OF PITTSBURGH, Hillman Library, Pittsburgh, 15260.
Notes: Economic and philosophical papers of

LOGIC—HISTORY (cont.)

the English scholar Frank Plumpton Ramsey (1903-1930), incl mss of published and unpublished writings, reading notes, etc. Significant because of his work in modern mathematics, logic, probability, and economics. Complementary to the Library's holdings of the papers of the logical empiricists, Rudolf Carnap and Hans Reichenback.

LOISY, ALFRED

†CA —UNIVERSITY OF SAN FRANCISCO, Richard A Gleeson Library, The Countess Bernardine Murphy Donohue Rare Book Room, San Francisco, 94117. D Steven Corey, Special Collections Librn
Holdings: Vols 1200 Uncat Pix
Notes: Modernism in the Catholic Church. Incl extensive holdings concerning George Tyrrell, Alfred Loisy, and Baron Friedrich von Hugel.

LONDON, CHARMIAN

UT —UTAH STATE UNIVERSITY, Merrill Library, Department of Special Collections & Archives, Logan, 84322. A J Simmonds, Curator; Jeanie F Simmonds, Archivist; Bradford R Cole, Mss Librn
Holdings: Vols 540 Cat Mss Pix Microforms
Notes: Collection incl library of CHarmian London with a complete set of first editions inscribed by london to his wife. Mss correspondence of both Mr and Mrs London, unpublished mss by London, diary and account books of London, notes made by London for his work; mss measure 32 linear feet. Also, 100 pictures, 11 microfilm rolls. A complete register of all mss in the collection is available in the department.

LONDON, ENGLAND

CA —STANFORD UNIVERSITY LIBRARIES, Jonsson Library of Government Documents, Stanford, 94305. W David Rozkuszka, Librn
Holdings: Vols 55,000 Cat Mss Microforms
Notes: Approximately 55,000 vols, incl every item published by the Public Record Office; the Historical Manuscripts Commission; the General Register Office; and very strong sets of the House of Lords and House of Commons parliamentary papers and debates (in hard copy for the nineteenth century; also 44,000 fiche of Common papers); approx 7000 microfilm reels, incl minutes and memoranda of the Cabinet Office, 1916 to date; Foreign Office records on China (3000 reels); confidential prints on China, Japan, Africa, the slave trade Tibet and Mongolia, Russia and the Soviet Union; correspondence of the British Embassy Archives in Washington, 1903-1940 (1248 microfilm reels); World War II papers of the Cabinet Office and Prime Minister's Office; Foreign Office general correspondence: Japan, 1856-1905 and 1930-1945; Russia, 1883-1948; United States, 1930-1945;China, 1906-1922; Domestic State Papers, Edward, Mary, Elizabeth, James I; Pipe Rolls, 1217-1306; English Civil War, Interregnum/Commonwealth records; Import-Export Ledgers, 1697-1780; Papers of Robert Peel; British official publications not published by HMSO, fiche collection, 1980 to date; London Corporation Journals, 1416-1694, and Repertories, 1495-1692. For more holdings, request "British Public Record Office Archival Material" at Stanford University.

IN —INDIANA UNIVERSITY, Lilly Library, Seventh St, Bloomington, 47405. William R Cagle, Librn
Holdings: Vols 1200 Cat
Notes: History and social conditions. Largely 18th and 19th century printings

ON —UNIVERSITY OF TORONTO, Thomas Fisher Rare Book Library, 120 Saint George St, Toronto, M5S 1A5, Can. Richard G Landon, Head
Holdings: Vols (3000) Uncat Mss
Notes: Fisher Collection named after donor, Sidney Fisher. Contains the first four folios of Shakespeare and most significant collected works edited during the 18th and 19th centuries. Some early editions of works believed to have been sources for Shakespeare's plays. Biographical and critical works. Works on English topography and antiquities, with special emphasis on London. Manuscript of account of Richard III, originally written by Sir George Buck in 1620, and copied by his great-nephew sometime later in the century.

LONDON, ENGLAND—CRIME AND CRIMINALS

IN —INDIANA UNIVERSITY, Lilly Library, Seventh St, Bloomington, 47405. William R Cagle, Librn
Holdings: // Cat
Notes: Largely 18th and 19th century material.

LONDON, ENGLAND—DESCRIPTION

IN —INDIANA UNIVERSITY, Lilly Library, Seventh St, Bloomington, 47405. William R Cagle, Librn
Holdings: Cat
Notes: Largely 18th and 19th century material.

LONDON, ENGLAND—HISTORY

DC —LIBRARY OF CONGRESS, Manuscript Division, Washington, 20540. John C Broderick, Chief

LONDON, GEORGE

MA —BOSTON UNIVERSITY, Mugar Memorial Library, Special Collections Dept, 771 Commonwealth Ave, Boston, 02215. Howard B Gotlieb, Dir
Holdings: Mss Pix Correspondence

LONDON, JACK

CA —OAKLAND PUBLIC LIBRARY, Oakland History Room, 125 14th St, Oakland, 94612. William W Sturm, Librn
Holdings: Vols 300 Cat Mss Pix
Notes: The Jack London Research Center contains books, pamphlets, periodicals, pictures, clippings, etc are housed in the Oakland History Room.

CA —UNIVERSITY OF SAN FRANCISCO, Richard A Gleeson Library, The Countess Bernardine Murphy Donohue Rare Book Room, San Francisco, 94117. D Steven Corey, Special Collections Librn
Holdings: Vols 38
Notes: Nearly all inscribed.

CA —HUNTINGTON LIBRARY, Art Gallery & Botanical Gardens, 1151 Oxford Rd, San Marino, 91108. Robert L Middlekauff, Dir; Daniel H Woodward, Librn
Holdings: Vols 300 Cat Mss Pix
Notes: His literary archive. Other large collections: Jack London Ranch, Glen Ellen, Calif; Utah State University, Logan, Utah. Incl 2,000 mss 3,000 letters, 700 documents, 7,000 photographs and ephemera.

CA —STANFORD UNIVERSITY LIBRARIES, Cecil H Green Library, Stanford, 94305. Michael T Ryan, Cur
Holdings: Vols Cat
Notes: Also incl correspondence and literary mss.

CA —UNIVERSITY OF THE PACIFIC, Library, Stockton, 95211. Hiram L Davis, Dir of Libraries
Notes: Complete collection of first editions inscribed by Jack London to members of his immediate family. Gift of Robin Lampson with the cooperation of Becky London Fleming, Jack London's daughter.

NY —SYRACUSE UNIVERSITY LIBRARIES, Ernest S Bird Library, George Arents Research Library for Special Collections, Syracuse, 13210. Carolyn A Davis, Manuscripts Librn; Amy S Doherty, University Archivist; Mark F Weimer, Rare Book Librn
Holdings: Vols 200 Cat

OH —OHIO STATE UNIVERSITY, Library, 1858 Neil Mall, Columbus, 43210. Dona Straley, Islamica Librn
Notes: The George H Tweney Collection, incl 237 book printings of London's writings and 111 issues of magazines containing first appearances of his writings; many signed pieces. Also 83 bibliographies, biographies, critical works, etc.

UT —UTAH STATE UNIVERSITY, Merrill Library, Department of Special Collections & Archives, Logan, 84322. A J Simmonds, Curator; Jeanie F Simmonds, Archivist; Bradford R Cole, Mss Librn
Holdings: Vols 540 Cat Mss Pix MIcroforms
Notes: Collection incl library of Chairmian London with a complete set of first editions inscribed by London to his wife. Mss correspondence of both Mr and Mrs London, unpublished mss by London, diary and account books of London, notes made by London for his work; mss measure 32 linear feet. Also, 100 pictures, 11 microfilm rolls. A complete register of all mss in the collection is available in the department.

VA —UNIVERSITY OF VIRGINIA, Alderman Library, Clifton Waller Barrett Collection, Charlottesville, 22901. Joan St C Crane, Cur of American Literature Collections
Notes: Papers.

LONDON NEWS LETTERS COLLECTION, 1665-1685

DC —LIBRARY OF CONGRESS, Manuscript Division, Washington, 20540. John C Broderick, Chief

LONDON PROGRESSIVE LEAGUE see Progressive League (London)

LONDON SCHOOL OF ECONOMICS

NY —ROCKEFELLER UNIVERSITY, Rockefeller Archive Center, Hillcrest, Pocantico Hills, North Tarrytown, 10591. Joseph W Ernst, Dir; J William Hess, Assoc Dir
Notes: Papers relative to the Rockefeller Family, Foundations, University, and other specific enterprises and contributions to particular areas of social, physical, educational, and historic reform, preservation, conservation, or development. Extensive records of administrative, financial, physical, or intellectual relationships.

LONERGAN, BERNARD

ON —TORONTO SCHOOL OF THEOLOGY, Consortium of Libraries, University of Toronto, Toronto, M5S 1A5, Can. R Grane Bracewell, Library Coordr
Holdings: Cat
Notes: A consortium of 7 theological college and faculty libraries at the University of Toronto.

LONG, HANIEL

CA —UNIVERSITY OF CALIFORNIA, LOS ANGELES, Research Library, Dept of Special Collections, 405 Hilgard Ave, Los Angeles, 90024. Edward Shreeves, Chairman, Bibliographers Group; David S Zeidberg, Head
Holdings: Vols 50 Mss
Notes: Incl 16 linear feet of mss, notebooks, correspondence, etc, of Haniel Long and Alice Lavinia Long.

NM —NEW MEXICO STATE UNIVERSITY, Library, Box 3475, Las Cruces, 88003. James Dyke, Dir
Holdings: Vols 43 Cat
Notes: Near complete collection of first edition works by and about the noted New Mexico poet, Haniel Long. Total coverage will be achieved with the addition of 4 or 5 items.

LONG, HUEY P.

LA —LOUISIANA STATE LIBRARY, 760 Riverside N, PO Box 131, Baton Rouge,

LONG, HUEY P. (cont.)

70821. Harriet Callahan, Librn, Louisiana Section
Holdings: Vols (51,507) Cat Maps Pix Slides Microforms
Budget: ($12,000)
Notes: Louisiana history, folklore, customs, resources, industry, government, etc. Collection limited to books and materials about the state and by native and resident writers. Complete and historical depository for state documents (188,117 uncataloged). Huey Pierce Long materials, incl rare pamphlets and broadsides. Restricted use. 11,194 microfilm reels.

LONG, DR. JAMES S.

MS —UNIVERSITY OF SOUTHERN MISSISSIPPI, William David McCain Graduate Library, Box 5148, Southern Sta, Hattiesburg, 39406.
Holdings: Cat Mss
Notes: Dr James S Long was a distinguished professor of chemical engineering and a noted chemist in private industry. This collection of his papers (1934-1977) contains research notes, files and correspondence relating to Dr Long's work with resins, plastics and tung oil.
See also entry under Chemistry.

LONG, JOHN D.

MA —HINGHAM PUBLIC LIBRARY, 66 Leavitt St, Hingham, 02043. Walter T Dziura, Dir
Holdings: Cat Mss Maps Pix Slides Microforms
Notes: A collection of about 2000 items relating to the history of the town from the 1600's to the present. Incl correspondence, legal documents, diaries and day books, account books, broadsides, pictures. Contains a large portion of four major collections: those of historian George Lincoln, historian Solomon Lincoln, historian Mason Foley and Hinghamiana collector Norman A Hersey. Items of special importance incl papers of town clerk Daniel Cushing, from the 1600's; Revolutionary War troop muster rolls; early land grant maps of the town; papers of artists Frank Vining Smith and Isaac Sprague; correspondence of Massachusetts governor John D Long; steamship history. An unpublished catalog of the collection is available through interlibrary loan. Most of the collection is on microfilm and may be borrowed through interlibrary loan.

LONG ISLAND, NEW YORK—ANTIQUITIES

NY —NASSAU COUNTY MUSEUM, Sands Pt Preserve, Middleneck Rd, Sand Points, 11050.
Holdings: Vols (2500)
Notes: Collection contains almost every published reference on Long Island archaeology, ethnology, and geology, and incl most of those pertaining to the coastal New York area. Open by appointment. On photocopying.

LONG ISLAND, NEW YORK—DESCRIPTION AND TRAVEL—VIEWS

NY —VISUAL STUDIES WORKSHOP, Research Center, 31 Prince St, Rochester, 14607. Linn Underhill, Coordr; Robert Bretz, Librn
Holdings: Vols (8000) Cat Pix Slides Audiotapes Videotapes
Notes: Strong emphasis on photography (over 1,000,000 pictures) and the photographic arts in many subject areas incl in this volume. Heavy emphasis on early photographic processes and collections of examples of them. Also collections of individual photographers' works.

LONG ISLAND, NEW YORK—FICTION

NY —STATE UNIVERSITY OF NEW YORK, STONY BROOK, Melville Library, Dept of Special Collections, Stony Brook, 11794. Evert Volkersz, Head
Holdings: Vols Uncat
Notes: A growing collection of fiction and literature with Long Island, incl Queens and Brooklyn, as a fictional setting.

LONG ISLAND, NEW YORK—GENEALOGY

NY —HEMPSTEAD PUBLIC LIBRARY, 115 Nichols Court, Hempstead, 11550. Irene A Duszkiewicz, Dir
Holdings: Vols (1000) Cat Mss Maps Pix Microforms
Notes: Local Hempstead Village history, Long Island genealogy. Also, New York State History Collection.

NY —HUNTINGTON HISTORICAL SOCIETY LIBRARY, New York Ave & High St, Huntington, 11743. Agnes K Packard, Librn
Holdings: Vols (3000) Mss Maps Pix Slides Audiotapes Microforms
Budget: ($60,000)
Notes: Huntington, NY, and Long Island history and genealogy.

NY —QUEENS BOROUGH PUBLIC LIBRARY, Long Island Div, 89-11 Merrick Blvd, Jamaica, 11432. Nicholas Falco, Head
Holdings: Cat Mss Maps Microforms
Budget: ($13,000)
Notes: Name index (60 drawers) of births, deaths and marriages, mainly from 19th century Long Island newspapers and books. Many cemetery records, abstracts of wills, deeds and church records. Federal Census for Long Island, 1790-1910. Soundex System 1880 and 1900.

NY —SUFFOLK COUNTY HISTORICAL SOCIETY, Library, 300 W Main St, Riverhead, 11901. Betty Carpenter, Librn
Holdings: Vols (15,000) Cat Mss Maps Pix
Notes: Suffolk County history.

LONG ISLAND, NEW YORK—HISTORY

NY —WHALING MUSEUM SOCIETY, Cold Spring Harbor Whaling Museum, Main St, Cold Spring Harbor, 11724. Robert D Farwell, Dir
Holdings: Cat Mss Maps Pix
Notes: Library of bound and printed books covers Cold Spring Harbor after the whaling industry, in general, and maritime affairs. Archives contain thousands of original documents concerning whaling activities, the Cold Spring Harbor Whaling Company, and the extensive maritime coastal trade conducted out of Cold Spring Harbor after the whaling era (latter 1800s). Considerable material deals with the Jones and Hewlett families, important in both local commerce and Long Island and New York affairs.

NY —NASSAU COUNTY MUSEUM, Reference Library, Eisenhower Park, East Meadow, 11554. Richard Winsche, Historian; Monica Albala, Museum Cur
Holdings: Vols 7000 Cat Mss Maps Pix Slides Phonorecords Audiotapes Microforms
Notes: Incl 10,000 mss, 300 maps, 10,000 pictures; 500 slides; 10 records; 20 audiotapes; and 3000 microforms. Mss, slides, and half of pictures are uncataloged.

NY —ADELPHI UNIVERSITY, Library, Garden City, 11530. Jerome Yavarkovsky, Dean of Libraries
Holdings: Vols 461 Cat Mss Maps Pix
Notes: New York City and Long Island Region.

NY —HEMPSTEAD PUBLIC LIBRARY, 115 Nichols Court, Hempstead, 11550. Irene A Duszkiewicz, Dir
Holdings: Vols (1000) Cap Mss Maps Pix Microforms
Notes: Local Hempstead Village history, Long Island genealogy. Also, New York State History Collection.

NY —HOFSTRA UNIVERSITY, Library, 1000 Fulton Ave, Hempstead, 11550. Charles R Andrews, Dean of Library Services
Notes: Strong collection. Incl some mss.

NY —HUNTINGTON HISTORICAL SOCIETY LIBRARY, New York Ave & High St, Huntington, 11743. Agnes K Packard, Librn
Holdings: Vols (3000) Mss Maps Pix Slides Audiotapes Microforms
Budget: ($60,000)
Notes: Huntington, NY, and Long Island history and genealogy.

NY —QUEENS BOROUGH PUBLIC LIBRARY, Long Island Div, 89-11 Merrick Blvd, Jamaica, 11432. Nicholas Falco, Head
Holdings: Vols (22,000) Cat Mss Maps Pix Microforms
Budget: ($13,000)
Notes: Files of Long Island community newspapers, with strong holdings for Queens Borough. Also, 550 glass negatives of Long Island scenes, 1895-1915; with 32,750 other pictures; 5300 maps; 36,000 ms pieces. Extensive name indexes of births, deaths and marriages mainly from 19th century Long Island books and newspapers. Many cemetery records, etc. 60 VF drawers of clippings; over 500 broadsides, 1795-date, relating to Long Island, with chronological and community name indexes; books published by Marion Press, a private press in Jamaica, NY.

NY —JERICHO PUBLIC LIBRARY, Local History Collection, One Merry Lane, Jericho, 11753. R M Stern, Librn
Holdings: Vols 350 Cat Mss Maps Pix Slides Phonorecords Audiotapes Microforms
Notes: There are separate catalogs for books and pictures. The collection also incl a pamphlet file and scrapbooks on the history of Jericho and Long Island; local newpapers; magazines and journals, pertaining to Long Island; and paintings of Long Island houses. Oral tapes are basically reminiscences with long-time residents of Jericho and Long Island. Added: Toledot, the journal of Jewish Genealogy.

NY —LOCUST VALLEY LIBRARY, 170 Buckram Rd, Locust Valley, 11560. L Norma Holmgren, Dir
Holdings: Vols 150 Cat Maps Pix
Notes: Emphasis on Locust Valley history.

NY —MANHASSET PUBLIC LIBRARY, 30 Onderdonk Ave, Manhasset, 11030. Sylvia Levin, Dir
Holdings: Vols 450 Cat Maps

NY —NEW YORK HISTORICAL SOCIETY, Library, 170 Central Park W, New York, 10024. James Gregory, Librn
Holdings: Mss
Notes: Incl original mss, illustrative materials, etc.

NY —NEW YORK PUBLIC LIBRARY, Local History and Genealogy Div, Fifth Ave & 42 St, New York, 10018. Gunther E Pohl, Chief
Holdings: Vols (160,000) Cat Pix
Budget: ($38,548)
Notes: Extensive collection of county, city, town and village histories of the United States. All other local, state, and national histories are part of the General Research and Humanities Division. Collection includes over 60,000 mounted photographs of New York City views arranged by address and/or subject. 20,000 film and glass plate negatives depicting NYC tenement housing conditions (1902-1938). Also the Lloyd L Acker collection of 48,000 film negatives depicting NYC buildings, 1935-1975. Collection of Lewis W Hine photographic prints made by the photographer on immigration, child labor, women at work and men at work. Eugene Armbruster collection of Long Island views; D B Austin's photographs of Long Island and western Americana; scrapbooks, and postcards of NYC and other US localities (200,000). See*United States Local History Catalog* (Boston: GK Hall, 1974), 2 vols.

NY —SUFFOLK COUNTY HISTORICAL SOCIETY, Library, 300 W Main St, Riverhead, 11901. Betty Carpenter, Librn
Holdings: Vols 4500 Cat Mss Maps Pix
Notes: Suffolk County history. Incl Daughters of the Revolution of 1776 Archives.

NY —SMITHTOWN LIBRARY, Long Island Room, Hanley Collection, 1 N Country Rd, Smithtown, 11787. Vera Toman, Librn
Holdings: Vols (20,000) Cat Mss Maps Pix Microforms
Budget: ($3000)
Notes: Strong history collection for the

LONG ISLAND, NEW YORK—HISTORY (cont.)

colonial period through the Civil War for Suffolk County and Queens and Kings counties. Special emphasis on history of Smithtown, incl the Charles E Lawrence and Judge J Lawrence Smith mss collections. Also, genealogies of many early Long Island families and census records on microfilm, 1890-1910, for Naussau and Suffolk counties. Incl 20,000 mss, 350 maps and 700 pictures.

NY —STATE UNIVERSITY OF NEW YORK, STONY BROOK, Melville Library, Dept of Special Collections, Stony Brook, 11794. Evert Volkersz, Head
Holdings: Cat Mss
Notes: Printed and ms materials relating to local and regional Long Island history, incl Queens and Brooklyn. Ms collections focus on women, environment, social welfare, and politics. Much on the Long Island Railroad (qv).

LONG ISLAND, NEW YORK—POLITICS AND GOVERNMENT

†NY —COLUMBIA UNIVERSITY LIBRARIES, Butler Library, Rare Book and Manuscript Library, 535 W 114 St, New York, 10027.
Notes: Papers of Eugene H Nickerson. Approx 173 items of the Nassau County executive.

LONG ISLAND RAILROAD

NY —STATE UNIVERSITY OF NEW YORK, STONY BROOK, Melville Library, Dept of Special Collections, Stony Brook, 11794. Evert Volkersz, Head
Holdings: Vols 40 Cat Pix
Notes: Forty albums combining detailed pencil drawings of Long Island Railroad tracks and explanatory notes with more than 5000 identified photographs; 300 timetables, 1895-date; and related materials.

LONG ISLAND STAR

NY —LONG ISLAND HISTORICAL SOCIETY, 128 Pierrepont St, at Clinton St, Brooklyn, 11201.
Notes: Books and pamphlets relating to the history of Brooklyn. Over 350 newspapers and periodical resources, incl *The Long Island Star* (1809-1863) and *Williamsburgh* Gazette (1835-1853). 10,000 photographs. Paintings, prints, and broadsides. More than 1400 mss collections relating primarily to Brooklyn, dating from 1650 to 1980s. 750 maps and atlases, artifacts, archives, and Decorative Arts collections. Two published guides to Manuscripts: *Calendar of Manuscripts: 1783-1783,* LIHS by Karin N Mango, 1980. Also, *A Guide to Brooklyn Manuscripts in the Long Island Historical* Society. Prepared by Brooklyn Rediscovery, a program of the Brooklyn Educational and Cultural Alliance, 1980. Also, guide to Museum Exhibit, *Brooklyn Before the Bridge - American paintings from the Long Island Historical Society.* Published by Brooklyn Museum, 1982.

LONG LANCE, CHIEF BUFFALO CHILD

CT —LEE ASH, (personal collection), 66 Humiston Dr, Bethany, 06525.
Holdings: Mss Pix
Notes: Books, ephemera, etc, by or about.

LONG MAYELL AND ASSOCIATES

AB —UNIVERSITY OF CALGARY, Libraries, Special Collections Div, 2500 University Dr, Calgary, T2N 1N4, Can.
Holdings: Cat Mss Pix
Notes: Collection consists of 3772 architectural drawings, office files, records, correspondence for projects from 1960 onwards, of the architectural firm of Long Mayell & Associates, Calgary. It encompasses all types of projects and incl the award-winning design for the Calgary Centennial Planetarium (1967), designed in partnership with H W R McMillan (qv); the Administration Building for the Calgary Separate School Board; various Condominium Townhouses, Apartments, recreational building, and John W Long's designs for the Urban Renewal of downtown Calgary. A project list is on land. 12 meters documents.

LONGEVITY

NH —DARTMOUTH COLLEGE, Dartmouth-Hitchcock Medical Center, Dana Biomedical Library, Hanover, 03756. Shirley J Grainger, Librn
Holdings: Vols (500) // Mss
Notes: Raymond Pearl Collection on Longevity incl historical materials from the 18th and 19th centuries, as well as some popular contemporary works on aging. Partially cataloged.

LONGFELLOW, A. W.

MA —SOCIETY FOR THE PRESERVATION OF NEW ENGLAND ANTIQUITIES, Library, 141 Cambridge St, Boston, 02114. Ellie Reichlin, Librn & Cur of Photographic Collections
Notes: Original plans, specifications, accounts, wallpaper and plumbing samples for Noyes House, Cambridge; many other commissions represented by photograph albums. 100 pieces.

LONGFELLOW, HENRY WADSWORTH, 1807-1882

FL —UNIVERSITY OF MIAMI, Otto G Richter Library, PO Box 248214, Coral Gables, 33124. Frank Rodgers, Dir of Libraries
Holdings: Vols 900 Cat
Notes: Additional material in periodicals. Collection purchased from Thomas DeValcourt of Longfellow House. Incl ca 120 editions of Evangeline.

LA —SAINT MARTIN PARISH LIBRARY, 105 S New Market St, PO Box 79, Saint Martinville, 70582. Dorothy R Selby, Dir
Notes: Approximately 60 editions of Evangeline.

ME —BOWDOIN COLLEGE, Library, Brunswick, 04011. Dianne M Gutscher, Cur of Special Collections
Holdings: Vols 1500 Cat Mss Pix
Notes: Incl first and later editions and selected criticism, and biography. About 800 pieces of music; also about 80 ms pieces.

MA —HARVARD UNIVERSITY LIBRARY, Houghton Library, Cambridge, 02138. F Thomas Noonan, Cur, Reading Room; Lawrence Dowler, Associate Librn
Holdings: Cat Mss
Notes: Incl 200 literary mss, 1900 letters of Longfellow, and 15,000 letters to him, with several thousand books from his own library.

MI —LAKE SUPERIOR STATE COLLEGE, Library, College Dr, Sault Sainte Marie, 49783. Frederick A Michels, Dir
Holdings: Vols (400) Cat Maps Pix Slides Clippings
Notes: Michigan history with emphasis on Sault Ste Marie, eastern end of Upper Peninsula, and area Indians (Chippewa or Ojibway).

VA —UNIVERSITY OF VIRGINIA, Alderman Library, Clifton Waller Barrett Collection, Charlottesville, 22901. Joan St C Crane, Cur of American Literature Collections
Holdings: Vols 450 Cat Mss
Notes: Includes important correspondence between Hawthorne and Longfellow.

WA —UNIVERSITY OF WASHINGTON LIBRARIES, Suzzallo Library, Special Collections Division, Rare Book Collection, FM-25, Seattle, 98195. Gary Menges, Coordinator for Special Collections
Notes: Printing history, including early printed books and modern fine printing; book arts, including papermaking, decorated papers, bookbinding, book design, and artist's books; American literature, 19th century includes: Stephen Crane, Ralph Waldo Emerson, Nathaniel Hawthorne, Henry James, Henry Wadsworth Longfellow, Herman Melville, Frank Norris, Harriet Beecher Stowe and Walt Whitman and 20th century includes: Theodore Roethke; illustrated books, including emblem books, historical children's illustration, books illustrated with prints, and artist's books; costume history; voyages and travels; preservation of library materials.

LONGSTAFF, FREDERICK VICTOR, 1879-1961

BC —UNIVERSITY OF VICTORIA, McPherson Library, Victoria, V8W 3H5, Can.
Notes: Military historian. Incl "Notes on the Infantry Training, 1902;" clippings; letters.

LONGSTREET, STEPHEN

MA —BOSTON UNIVERSITY, Mugar Memorial Library, Special Collections Dept, 771 Commonwealth Ave, Boston, 02215. Howard B Gotlieb, Dir
Holdings: Cat Mss Pix
Notes: Mss correspondence, etc collected in depth; incl publications by or about.

LONGWELL, DANIEL

NY —COLUMBIA UNIVERSITY LIBRARIES, Rare Book & Manuscript Library, 801 Butler Library, 535 W 114 St, New York, 10027. Kenneth A Lohf, Librn
Holdings: Mss
Notes: The papers of Daniel Longwell, former editor at Doubleday and Life, incl his correspondence with many authors; also, nearly 400 first and inscribed editions, mss, and autograph letters. Much on Life magazine. Incl 24,750 items. Restricted use.

†NY —COLUMBIA UNIVERSITY LIBRARIES, Butler Library, Rare Book and Manuscript Library, 535 W 114 St, New York, 10027.
Notes: Papers, diaries, etc.

LOOK (MAGAZINE)

DC —LIBRARY OF CONGRESS, Prints & Photographs Div, Washington, 20540.
Holdings: Cat Pix
Notes: Complete photographic files of Look magazine; the history of 35 years in pictures. Incl 17.5 million black and white negatives, 1.5 million color transparencies, 450,000 contact sheets, and 25,000 movie stills. Effective October 1, 1983, the Library's Prints and Photographs Division has discontinued reproduction and reference service on its collection of photographs which appeared in *Look* magazine from 1937 to 1971. This limitation on service will remain in effect until questions of rights and permissions affecting these photographs can be clarified. The Library acquired the *Look* archive in 1971 as additional resources for research in American life by scholars and other investigators. It was anticipated that the photographs would serve as a study collection for researchers in many fields, but the major useof the collection has been by publishers, advertisers, and makers of documentary films. Such picture users require clear rights to reproduce the images. The Library has been unable to satisfy these requests because of the donor's stipulation precluding such use. Until some accommodation can be made with the donor to free the collection for a wider range of public use, the collection will remain in remote cold storage to retard deterioration of sensitive films, especially color films. This policy will remain in effect until further notice. LC Information Bulletin, 10 Oct 83.

LOOMIS, AUGUSTUS WARD

NY —CORNELL UNIVERSITY LIBRARIES, Collection of Regional History, Dept of

LOOMIS, AUGUSTUS WARD (cont.)

Manuscripts and Univ Archives, Ithaca, 14853.
Notes: Incl papers, 1803-97, of Loomis and his family; letters, bills, receipts, obituaries and family memorabilia.

LOOMIS, STANLEY, 1922-1972

MA —BOSTON UNIVERSITY, Mugar Memorial Library, Special Collections Dept, 771 Commonwealth Ave, Boston, 02215. Howard B Gotlieb, Dir
Holdings: / / Cat Mss

LOOS, ARMIN

CT —YALE UNIVERSITY, Music Library, 98 Wall St, New Haven, 06520. Harold E Samuel, Librn
Notes: Personal papers and musical mss.
See also entry under Music, American.

LOPE DE VEGA, FELIX see Vega, Felix Lope De

LOPEZ, IGNACIO

†CA —STANFORD UNIVERSITY LIBRARIES, Stanford, 94305.
Notes: In collection of English and American Literature.

LORD CHAMBERLAIN, GREAT BRITAIN see Great Britain—Lord Chamberlain

LORENZINI, CARLO

CA —UNIVERSITY OF CALIFORNIA, LOS ANGELES, Research Library, Dept of Special Collections, 405 Hilgard Ave, Los Angeles, 90024. Edward Shreeves, Chairman, Bibliographers Group; David S Zeidberg, Head
Holdings: Vols 200
Notes: 200 American and foreign editions of *Pinocchio.*

LORRIES (MOTOR VEHICLES) see Trucks

LOS ANGELES

CA —MUSIC CENTER OPERATING CO, Music Center Archives, 135 N Grand Ave, Los Angeles, 90012. Fran Morris Rosman, Librn
Holdings: Uncat Mss Pix Slides Videotapes Filmstrips
Notes: History of music and the dance as developed and performed here. Extensive collection. Incl also the history of the performing arts.

LOS ANGELES—DESCRIPTION AND TRAVEL—VIEWS

CA —WHITTIER COLLEGE, Wardman Library, Whittier, 90608. Christine Erdmann, Special Collections Librn
Holdings: / / Cat Pix
Notes: Aerial photographs of California, 1927-1963. 100,000 aerial photo negatives (40,000 nitrate-base), 300,000 aerial photo prints, 1000 photomosaics, 750 orthophoto maps. Concentration in California, particularly in the Los Angeles region, and elsewhere in metropolitan areas. Many flights are among the earliest available and cover areas since developed. Sequential photos often allow documentation of the history of development or of natural effects. Prints may be borrowed for 2-week periods. Purchase of prints only through Teledyne-Geotronics, Long Beach, California. An inventory list of flights can be purchased through the Dept of Geology.

LOS ANGELES—HISTORY

CA —LOS ANGELES PUBLIC LIBRARY, History Dept, 630 W 5th St, Los Angeles, 90071. Bettye H Ellison, Librn in Charge, California Room
Holdings: Vols 8000 Cat Pix
Notes: The California Collection is a reference and circulating collection consisting of state, county and city histories, volumes of travel and description, periodicals and publications of state and local historical societies. Over 260,000 historic photographs from the turn of the century to the mid-1950s. Portraits are incl. The majority of the views are of Los Angeles and Southern California. Special subject and biographical indexes provide references to a wide variety of California related books, periodicals and Los Angeles area newspapers. A separate index is maintained for photographs.

CA —UNIVERSITY OF CALIFORNIA, LOS ANGELES, Research Library, Dept of Special Collections, 405 Hilgard Ave, Los Angeles, 90024. Edward Shreeves, Chairman, Bibliographers Group; David S Zeidberg, Head
Holdings: Cat Mss Maps Pix
Notes: Incl in 55 collections documenting a wide range of topics incl land use and development, architecture, social life, performing arts, ethnic minorities, and politics and government. Over 2 million pictures, includes original photographs and ephemera of Los Angeles people and places, images by California Pictorialists, and news photographs from the morgues of the *Los Angeles Daily News* and the *Los Angeles* Times.

LOS ANGELES—POLITICS AND GOVERNMENT

CA —UNIVERSITY OF CALIFORNIA, LOS ANGELES, Research Library, Dept of Special Collections, 405 Hilgard Ave, Los Angeles, 90024. Edward Shreeves, Chairman, Bibliographers Group; David S Zeidberg, Head
Holdings: / / Uncat Mss
Notes: Various collections, incl the John Randolph Haynes and Dora Haynes Foundation, Norris Poulson, and Edward R Roybal collections.

CA —UNIVERSITY OF CALIFORNIA, LOS ANGELES, Research Library, Public Affairs Service, 405 Hilgard Ave, Los Angeles, 90024. Edward Shreeves, Chairman, Bibliographers Group; Eugenia Eaton, Head, Public Affairs Service
Notes: Political campaign materials of the United States from 1920. Particularly strong for campaigns from the 1940s to the 1980s. Focus is on United States, California, and Los Angeles area candidates and issues. Mostly ephemeral materials (flyers, brochures, publicity releases, pamphlets, etc).

LOS ANGELES—THEATRE

CA —UNIVERSITY OF CALIFORNIA, LOS ANGELES, Music Library, Schonberg Hall, Los Angeles, 90024. Stephen M Fry, Music Librn
Notes: The Philip Kahgan Collection of music films, letters, programs, and photographs important to the Southern California classical music scene. Incl 16mm "home movies" of more than thirty renowned conductors and performers during Hollywood Bowl rehearsals in the late 1930s. Incl Kahgan correspondence, memorabilia, 35 scrapbooks, etc.

NY —NEW YORK PUBLIC LIBRARY, Performing Arts Research Center, Billy Rose Theatre Collection, 111 Amsterdam Ave, New York, 10023. Dorothy L Swerdlove, Cur
Holdings: Cat
See also entry under Theatre - History.

VA —GEORGE MASON UNIVERSITY, Fenwick Library, Special Collections Dept, 4400 University Drive, Fairfax, 22030. Ruth Kerns, Public Services Librn
Notes: The Federal Theatre Project (WPA) Collection is on permanent loan from the Library of Congress and includes documentation for many FTP productions, particularly those which originated in the New York City, San Francisco and Los Angeles areas.

LOS ANGELES DAILY NEWS

CA —UNIVERSITY OF CALIFORNIA, LOS ANGELES, Research Library, Dept of Special Collections, 405 Hilgard Ave, Los Angeles, 90024. Edward Shreeves, Chairman, Bibliographers Group; David S Zeidberg, Head
Notes: Morgue contains clipping and research files; an index to the paper; 200,000 negatives, with an index; 20,000 prints, with an index.

LOS ANGELES TIMES (NEWSPAPER)

CA —UNIVERSITY OF CALIFORNIA, LOS ANGELES, Research Library, Dept of Special Collections, 405 Hilgard Ave, Los Angeles, 90024. Edward Shreeves, Chairman, Bibliographers Group; David S Zeidberg, Head
Notes: 1.5 million negatives and 300,000 prints from its morgue.

LOS ANGELES VINEYARD SOCIETY

CA —ANAHEIM PUBLIC LIBRARY, 500 W Broadway, Anaheim, 92805.
Holdings: Vols (2000) Cat
Notes: Original minute books and records of the Los Angeles Vineyard Society.

LOSSES, BUSINESS see Business Losses

LOSSING, BENSON J.

OH —RUTHERFORD B HAYES LIBRARY, 1337 Hayes Ave, Fremont, 43420. Watt P Marchman, Dir
Holdings: Mss Maps Pix
Notes: Correspondence, business and personal; a few diary notes and memos; contracts, clippings, scrapbooks; diaries and correspondence of his children; letter copy book of Mrs. Lossings's; misc materials. Listed in *Guide to Manuscripts of the Ohio Historical Society*, 306. Index in collection.

'LOST BATTALION'

TX —NORTH TEXAS STATE UNIVERSITY, Archives, NT Station Box 5188, Denton, 76203. Robert LaForte, University Archivist
Notes: Oral History Collection. Incl interviews with survivors of attack on Corregidor, Bataan Death March, the "Lost Battalion," prisoner of war camps. Also material on guerilla fighting in the Philippines. Cataloged. Transcriptions available.

LOST CONTINENTS

AZ —WORLD UNIVERSITY, Library, 711 E Blacklidge Dr, Tucson, 85719. Howard John Zitko, Cur
Holdings: Vols (15,000) Cat Mss Maps Audiotapes
Notes: Collection concerns what are generally called the "frontier sciences." No interlibrary loan.

LOST DAUPHIN see Louis Xvii of France, 1785-1795

LOST MINES

AZ —PHOENIX PUBLIC LIBRARY, Arizona Room, 12 E McDowell, Phoenix, 85004. Jeannette Brush, Librn
Holdings: Vols (30,000) Cat Maps Pix
Budget: ($12,000)
See also entry under Arizona - History.

LOTH, DAVID

MA —BOSTON UNIVERSITY, Mugar Memorial Library, Special Collections Dept, 771 Commonwealth Ave, Boston, 02215. Howard B Gotlieb, Dir
Holdings: Cat Mss Pix Correspondence

LOTHROP, GEORGE VAN NESS

MI —DETROIT PUBLIC LIBRARY, Burton Historical Collection, 5201 Woodward Ave, Detroit, 48202. Alice Dalligan, Chief

LOTHROP, HARRIET MULFORD

DC —LIBRARY OF CONGRESS, Rare Book & Special Collections Div, Washington, 20540. William Matheson, Chief
Notes: The Juvenile Collection covers the early 18th century to the present and is particularly strong in fiction. Authors extensively represented are: Alcott, Alger, Abbott, Goodrich, Fosdick, Lothrop and McGuffey.

MA —CONCORD FREE PUBLIC LIBRARY, 129 Main St, Concord, 01742. Rose Marie Mitten, Dir
Holdings: Cat Mss Maps Pix Slides
Notes: Extensive collection.

LOTTERIES

MD —MARYLAND HISTORICAL SOCIETY, Library, 201 W Monument St, Baltimore, 21201. William B Keller, Head Librn
Holdings: Cat Mss Maps Pix Slides Microforms
Notes: Espec relating to Maryland and Baltimore. Extensive collection.

LOUCHEUR, LOUIS

CA —HOOVER INSTITUTION ON WAR, REVOLUTION & PEACE, Stanford University, Stanford, 94305. Milorad M Drachkovitch, Archivist
Holdings: / / Mss
Notes: Paper, 1916-1931, of Louis Loucheur, French industrialist, diplomat and public official. Correspondence, speeches, notes and other papers. Incl reports (1916) from Loucheur as an industrial adviser to Russia, papers relating to reparations negotiations (1921-1924), an interview (1924) with Konrad Adenauer, the Loncheur-Coudenhove-Kalergi correspondence (1927-1931) and notes taken by Paul Mantoux on the conversations armistice negotiations with the Germans. 5 ft. Index in the repository.

LOUDERBACK, GEORGE DAVIS

CA —UNIVERSITY OF CALIFORNIA, BERKELEY, Bancroft Library, Manuscripts Division, Berkeley, 94720. James D Hart, Dir
Holdings: Cat Mss Maps Pix Microforms
Notes: Papers, correspondence, etc.

LOUIS, JOE

DC —SMITHSONIAN INSTITUTION LIBRARIES, National Museum of American History Branch, Washington, 20560. Rhoda S Ratner, Branch Librn
Notes: Emphasis on history of American sports and recreation. Incl some 2000 baseball cards from cigarette and chewing-gum packets; 103 scrapbooks and other memorabilia about Joe Louis; much on bicycling and skating.

MI —UNIVERSITY OF MICHIGAN, Bentley Historical Library, Michigan Historical Collections, 1150 Beal Ave, Ann Arbor, 48109. Francis X Blovin Jr, Dir
Notes: Substantial holdings relating to the University's Sports activities. Also, 93 scrapbooks on Joe Louis.

NY —COLUMBIA UNIVERSITY LIBRARIES, Rare Book & Manuscript Library, 801 Butler Library, 535 W 114 St, New York, 10027. Kenneth A Lohf, Librn
Notes: Restricted use. The Paul Magriel Boxing Collection on the history and literature of pugilism. The L S Alexander Gumby Collection, which incl 9 Joe Lewis scrapbooks.

LOUYS, PIERRE, 1870-1925

NY —SYRACUSE UNIVERSITY LIBRARIES, Ernest S Bird Library, George Arents Research Library for Special Collections, Syracuse, 13210. Carolyn A Davis, Manuscripts Librn; Amy S Doherty, University Archivist; Mark F Weimer, Rare Book Librn
Notes: Papers and memorabilia, incl ms writings. Papers (0.5 linear foot).

LOUIS XVII OF FRANCE, 1785-1795

WI —UNIVERSITY OF WISCONSIN, MADISON, Memorial Library, Rare Books Collection, 728 State St, Madison, 53706. Gretchen Lagana, Cur
Notes: The Wright Collection, acquired in 1943, consists of about 1000 volumes related to the Bourbon family and pretenders to the throne of France. Willard Ward Wight's *Louis XVII, A Bibliography* (1915) serves as a partial guide to the collection.

LOUISIANA

LA —LOUISIANA DEPT OF COMMERCE, Office of Commerce & Industry, PO Box 44185, Baton Rouge, 70804. Anna Maria I Pinza, Research Dir
Holdings: Maps Pix Slides

LA —LOUISIANA STATE LIBRARY, 760 Riverside N, PO Box 131, Baton Rouge, 70821. Harriet Callahan, Librn, Louisiana Section
Holdings: Vols (51,507) Cat Maps Pix Slides Microforms
Budget: ($12,000)
Notes: Louisiana history, folklore, customs, resources, industry, government, etc. Collection limited to books and materials about the state and by native and resident writers. Complete and historical depository for state documents (188,117 uncataloged). Huey Pierce Long materials, incl rare pamphlets and broadsides. Restricted use. 11,194 microfilm reels.

LA —LOUISIANA STATE UNIVERSITY, Troy H Middleton Library, Louisiana Room, Baton Rouge, 70803. Evangeline Mills Lynch, Head Librn; Ruth Murray, Associate Librn
Holdings: Vols (33,550) Cat Maps VF
Notes: Louisiana Collection of history, description and travel, biography, agriculture, literature, politics and government, folklore, anthropology, geography, geology, education, language, music and natural history. Especially large subject collections may be found on Louisiana, the history of the lower Mississippi Valley, Abraham Lincoln, Romance languages and literatures, sugar culture and technology, Southern history, petroleum engineering, plant pathology, micropaleontology, ornithology, and various aspects of crawfish life, biology and culture. Complete depository of Louisiana State Documents; extensive newspapers clipping files; separate card catalog; items listed in Louisiana Union Catalog; restricted use (research and reference). Incl both materials about Louisiana and by Louisianians without regard to subject. LSU Press Collection(preservation copy of each title kept for exhibit purposes only). LSU theses and dissertations from 1900-date. LSU Faculty Collection. Also, 1300 maps, 104 VF drawers, 250 boxes of uncataloged pamphlets.

LA —PUBLIC AFFAIRS RESEARCH COUNCIL OF LOUISIANA, Library, 300 Louisiana Ave, PO Box 3118, Baton Rouge, 70821. Jan Brashear, Research Librn
Holdings: Vols (7000) Cat Mss
Notes: State and local government problems with emphasis on Louisiana. Strong in the areas of education and public finance.

LA —UNIVERSITY OF SOUTHERN LOUISIANA, Dupre Library, Jefferson Caffery Louisiana Room, 302 East St Mary Blvd, Lafayette, 70504. Cynthia J Rice, Louisiana Room Ref Librn
Holdings: Vols (20,000) Cat Doc Maps Microforms VF
Budget: ($3800)
Notes: Emphasis is on state, regional, and local history, genealogy, and culture; also politics and government, industry, agriculture, geology, language and literature. Collection is closed-stack and non-circulating, and is open to the public for on-site use only. Copying services are available.

LA —LOUISIANA STATE MUSEUM, Louisiana Historical Center, 400 Esplanade Ave, (Mailing add: 751 Chartres St, New Orleans, 70116). Edward F Haas, Chief Cur
Holdings: Vols 30,000 Cat
Budget: ($1,200,000)
Notes: Louisiana Research Library.

LA —NEW ORLEANS PUBLIC LIBRARY, Louisiana Div, 219 Loyola Ave, New Orleans, 70140. Collin B Hamer Jr, Head; Jean M Jones, Doc Librn
Holdings: Vols Mss
Notes: Private mss collections covers the period 1795-date, incl the following separate collections: James H Dakin (architect, ca 1834-47, 217 items); Walter E Easey (engineer, 1907-79, 22 cubic feet); McDonough & Payne (merchants, 1801-04, 200 items) ERA Club (women's group, 1914-19, 2 items); Neville Levy (civic leader, ca 1891-1963, 1 cubic foot & 11 vols); and Robert Tallant (author, 1945-57, 3 cubic feet & 10 vols). Inlc 92 vols scrapbooks; 100 vols mss, 55 cubic feet.

LA —SAINT MARTIN PARISH LIBRARY, 105 S New Market St, PO Box 79, Saint Martinville, 70582. Dorothy R Selby, Dir
Holdings: Cat Maps Pix Slides Microforms
Notes: Emphasis on south Louisiana. Incl Louisiana history and genealogy. Some Acadian-Canadian history and genealogy.

LA —R W NORTON ART GALLERY, Library, 4747 Creswell Ave, Shreveport, 71106. Jerry M Bloomer, Librn
Holdings: Cat Pix
Notes: Especially materials concerning Shreveport.

LOUISIANA—DESCRIPTION AND TRAVEL—VIEWS

LA —LOUISIANA STATE UNIVERSITY, Troy H Middleton Library, Louisiana Room, Baton Rouge, 70803. Evangeline Mills Lynch, Head Librn; Ruth Murray, Associate Librn
Holdings: Vols (33,500) Cat Maps VF
Notes: Louisiana Collection of history, description and travel, biography, agriculture, literature, politics and government, folklore, anthropology, geography, geology, education, language, music and natural history. Especially large subject collections may be found on Louisiana, the history of the lower Mississippi Valley, Abraham Lincoln, Romance languages and literatures, sugar culture and technology, Southern history, petroleum engineering, plant pathology, micropaleontology, ornithology, and various aspects of crawfish life, biology and culture. Complete depository of Louisiana State Documents; extensive newspapers clipping files; separate card catalog; items listed in Louisiana Union Catalog; restricted use (research and reference). Incl both materials about Louisiana and by Louisianians without regard to subject. LSU Press Collection(preservation copy of each title kept for exhibit purposes only). LSU theses and dissertations from 1900-date. LSU Faculty Collection. Also, 1300 maps, 104 VF drawers, 250 boxes of uncataloged pamphlets.

LA —TULANE UNIVERSITY, Howard-Tilton Memorial Library, Southeast Architectural Archives, 7001 Freret St, New Orleans, 70118. William R Cullison, Cur of Prints & Drawings
Holdings: Pix
Notes: Southeast Architectural Archives Collection incl over 5000 photographic prints and over 12,000 negatives. Views are mostly of Louisiana buildings, scenes and personages, with emphasis on New Orleans. Negatives are available for most of the photographic prints.

LOUISIANA—GENEALOGY

FL —ORLANDO PUBLIC LIBRARY, Local History & Genealogy Dept, 100 Block of Central Ave, Orlando, 32806. Eileen B Willis, Librn
Holdings: Vols 11,000 Cat Maps Microforms
Budget: $8000
Notes: Genealogy collection on Md, Del, W Va, NC, SC, Ala, Miss, La, Texas, Ark, Ky,

LOUISIANA—GENEALOGY (cont.)

Ohio, Ill, Ind, and Mich are well represented. Most other states are covered by smaller collections.
See also entry under Genealogy - Collections.

LA —UNIVERSITY OF SOUTHERN LOUISIANA, Dupre Library, Jefferson Caffery Louisiana Room, 302 East St Mary Blvd, Lafayette, 70504. Cynthia J Rice, Louisiana Room Ref Librn
Holdings: Vols (20,000) Cat Doc Maps Microforms, VF
Budget: ($3800)
Notes: Emphasis is on state, regional, and local history, genealogy, and culture; also politics and government, industry, agriculture, geology, language and literature. Collection is closed-stack and non-circulating, and is open to the public for on-site use only. Copying services are available.

LA —TULANE UNIVERSITY, Howard-Tilton Memorial Library, Special Collections Div, 7001 Freret St, New Orleans, 70118. Wilbur E Meneray, Librn
Notes: Louisiana Collection incl mss and printed material pertaining to families in Louisiana.

LA —SAINT MARTIN PARISH LIBRARY, 105 S New Market St, PO Box 79, Saint Martinville, 70582. Dorothy R Selby, Dir
Holdings: Cat Maps Pix Slides Microforms
Notes: Emphasis on south Louisiana. Incl Louisiana history and genealogy. Some Acadian-Canadian history and genealogy.

LOUISIANA—GOVERNMENT PUBLICATIONS

LA —LOUISIANA STATE UNIVERSITY, Troy H Middleton Library, Louisiana Room, Baton Rouge, 70803. Evangeline Mills Lynch, Head Librn; Ruth Murray, Associate Librn
Holdings: Vols (33,500) Cat Maps VF
Notes: Louisiana Collection of history, description and travel, biography, agriculture, literature, politics and government, folklore, anthropology, geography, geology, education, language, music and natural history. Especially large subject collections may be found on Louisiana, the history of the lower Mississippi Valley, Abraham Lincoln, Romance languages and literatures, sugar culture and technology, Southern history, petroleum engineering, plant pathology, micropaleontology, ornithology, and various aspects of crawfish life, biology and culture. Complete depository of Louisiana State Documents; extensive newspapers clipping files; separate card catalog; items listed in Louisiana Union Catalog; restricted use (research and reference). Incl both materials about Louisiana and by Louisianians without regard to subject. LSU Press Collection(preservation copy of each title kept for exhibit purposes only). LSU theses and dissertations from 1900-date. LSU Faculty Collection. Also, 1300 maps, 104 VF drawers, 250 boxes of uncataloged pamphlets.

LA —NEW ORLEANS PUBLIC LIBRARY, Louisiana Div, 219 Loyola Ave, New Orleans, 70140. Collin B Hamer Jr, Head; Jean M Jones, Doc Librn
Holdings: Vols Mss
Notes: Private mss collections covers the period 1795-date, incl the following separate collections: James H Dakin (architect, ca 1834-47, 217 items); Walter E Easey (engineer, 1907-79, 22 cubic feet); McDonough & Payne (merchants, 1801-04, 200 items) ERA Club (women's group, 1914-19, 2 items); Neville Levy (civic leader, ca 1891-1963, 1 cubic foot & 11 vols); and Robert Tallant (author, 1945-57, 3 cubic feet & 10 vols). Inlc 92 vols scrapbooks; 100 vols mss, 55 cubic feet.

LOUISIANA—HISTORY

AL —UNIVERSITY OF ALABAMA, W S Hoole Special Collections Library, Amelia Gayle Goorgas Library, PO Box S, University, 35486. Joyce H Lamont, Cur
Holdings: Vols 10,000 // Cat Mss Maps Pix
Notes: Books, mss, pamphlets, and pictures of Louisiana. Described in *Bibliography of Louisiana Books and Pamphlets in the TP Thompson Collection of the University of Alabama Library*, by Donald E Thompson.

LA —VERMILION PARISH LIBRARY, 200 North St, Abbeville, 70510. Mary Lou Hefley, Librn
Holdings: Vols (2000) Cat Phonorecords Filmstrips Microforms
Notes: Contains materials on various subjects on the state of Louisiana, and Louisiana Authors.

LA —LOUISIANA STATE LIBRARY, 760 Riverside N, PO Box 131, Baton Rouge, 70821. Harriet Callahan, Librn, Louisiana Section
Holdings: Vols (51,507) Cat Maps Pix Slides Microforms
Budget: ($12,000)
Notes: Louisiana history, folklore, customs, resources, industry, government, etc. Collection limited to books and materials about the state and by native and resident writers. Complete and historical depository for state documents (188,117 uncataloged). Huey Pierce Long materials, incl rare pamphlets and broadsides. Restricted use. 11,194 microfilm reels.

LA —LOUISIANA STATE UNIVERSITY, Troy H Middleton Library, Louisiana Room, Baton Rouge, 70803. Evangeline Mills Lynch, Head Librn; Ruth Murray, Associate Librn
Holdings: Vols (33,500) Cat Maps VF
Notes: Louisiana Collection of history, description and travel, biography, agriculture, literature, politics and government, folklore, anthropology, geography, geology, education, language, music and natural history. Especially large subject collections may be found on Louisiana, the history of the lower Mississippi Valley, Abraham Lincoln, Romance languages and literatures, sugar culture and technology, Southern history, petroleum engineering, plant pathology, micropaleontology, ornithology, and various aspects of crawfish life, biology and culture. Complete depository of Louisiana State Documents; extensive newspapers clipping files; separate card catalog; items listed in Louisiana Union Catalog; restricted use (research and reference). Incl both materials about Louisiana and by Louisianians without regard to subject. LSU Press Collection(preservation copy of each title kept for exhibit purposes only). LSU theses and dissertations from 1900-date. LSU Faculty Collection. Also, 1300 maps, 104 VF drawers, 250 boxes of uncataloged pamphlets.

LA —UNIVERSITY OF SOUTHERN LOUISIANA, Dupre Library, Jefferson Caffery Louisiana Room, 302 East St Mary Blvd, Lafayette, 70504. Cynthia J Rice, Louisiana Room Ref Librn
Holdings: Vols (20,000) Cat Maps Microforms VF
Budget: ($3800)
Notes: Emphasis is on state, regional, and local history, genealogy, and culture; also politics and government, industry, agriculture, geology, language and literature. Incl French Louisiana. Collection is closed-stack and non-circulating, and is open to the public for on-site use only. Copying services are available.

LA —HISTORIC NEW ORLEANS COLLECTION, 533 Royal St, New Orleans, 70130. Stanton M Frazar, Dir; Dode Platou, Chief Cur; Florence M Jumonville, Head Librn
Holdings: Vols (15,000) Cat Mss Maps Pix Microforms
Notes: Books, pamphlets, and vertical files covering all aspects of life pertaining to New Orleans, Louisiana, and the Lower Mississippi Valley. Our research facilities also include an archive and curatorial department. *A Guide to Research* is available.

LA —LOUISIANA STATE MUSEUM, Louisiana Historical Center, 400 Esplanade Ave, (Mailing add: 751 Chartres St, New Orleans, 70116). Edward F Haas, Chief Cur
Holdings: Mss Maps Pix
Budget: ($1,200,000)
Notes: Archives and Manuscripts Collections. Special guides and indices are in preparation. The single most important collection in this section is the Louisiana Colonial Archives, consisting of the judicial records of the French Superior Council in Louisiana and the Spanish Cabildo in Louisiana dating from 1714 to 1803. There are approximately 500,000 pages of documents in this collection. Also 19th century collections of personal papers, plantation records, business ledgers, etc. Incl 3500 maps and 15,000 pictures.

LA —NEW ORLEANS PUBLIC LIBRARY, Louisiana Div & City Archives Dept, Louisiana History Collection, 219 Loyola Ave, New Orleans, 70140. Collin B Hamer Jr, Head
Holdings: Vols 22,400 Cat Mss Maps Pix Slides Microforms
Budget: $20,000
Notes: Contains classified books, 2227 bound newspapers, 25,000 microfilms, state and city of New Orleans documents; special emphasis on theses and dissertations having relevance to Louisiana subjects; index to Lousiana newspapers, 1804-date contains approx 528,000 cards (general news) and 600,000 cards (biography and obituary); separate department catalog. Microfilmed records incl civil court records of 45 parishes, passenger lists of ships arriving in New Orleans, 1820-1945. Material is restricted to on-site use.

LA —NEW ORLEANS PUBLIC LIBRARY, Louisiana Div & City Archives Dept, Louisiana History Collection, 219 Loyola Ave, New Orleans, 70140. Collin B Hamer Jr, Head
Holdings: Vols Mss
Notes: Private mss collection covers the period 1795-date, incl the following separate collections: James H Dakin (architect, ca 1834-47, 217 items); Walter E Easey (engineer, 1907-79, 22 cubic feet); McDonough & Payne (merchants, 1801-04, 200 items); ERA Club (women's group, 1914-19, 2 items); Neville Levy (civic leader, ca 1891-1963, 1 cubic foot & 11 vols); and Robert Tallant (author, 1945-57, 3 cubic feet & 10 vols). 92 vols scrapbooks; 100 mss vols, 55 cubic feet.

LA —TULANE UNIVERSITY, Howard-Tilton Memorial Library, Special Collections Div, 7001 Freret St, New Orleans, 70118. Wilbur E Meneray, Librn
Notes: Louisiana Collection incl manuscripts, books, photographs, newspapers, prints and maps pertaining to the history and development of Louisiana and the Mississippi Valley from colonial times to the present.

LA —CENTENARY COLLEGE OF LOUISIANA, Magale Library, Shreveport, 71104. Carolyn Garison, Archivist
Holdings: Vols (2000) Cat Mss Pix Microforms
Budget: ($750)
Notes: Depository for the records of the Louisiana Conference and materials relating to all the antecedent bodies of United Methodism in Louisiana. Also, collections of personal and family papers relating to Louisiana Methodist history and church histories. We are trying to locate church records for microfilming. Further emphasis on Northern Louisiana and Shreveport history. Catalogs and inventories for all manuscript and archival materials are housed with the collection in the Cline Room. Citations on part of this material will be found in NUCMC MS65-1830 and Hamer's *Guide to Archives and Manuscripts in the United States.*

LA —LOUISIANA STATE UNIVERSITY, SHREVEPORT, Library-Archives, 8515 Youree Dr, Shreveport, 71129. Patricia L Meador, Archivist & Asst Librn
Holdings: Vols (3330) Cat Mss Maps Pix Audiotapes Microforms
Budget: ($3000)
Notes: The collection's primary emphasis is

LOUISIANA—HISTORY (cont.)

the history of North Louisiana, particularly Northwest Louisiana. The 1500 linear feet incl area plantation records and ledgers, personal papers of area pioneers, planters, legislators, politicians, educators, businessmen, and architects; utility, industrial and manufacturing company records; papers and records of longtime (1919-1961) Caddo Parish Coroner, Willis P Butler; the Samuel G Wiener, Sr architectural records (1921-1976) with drawings and photographs, the Ted Flaxman architectural records (1919-1968), and the papers (1860-1921) of architect Nathaniel S Allen; the collection of Dewey A Somdal, Shreveport architect, historian and collector, with emphasis on steamboats, travel on the Red River and Louisiana history, 1780-1972. The collection incl 25 linear feet of records of the UnitedBrotherhood of Carpenters and Joiners of America, Local No 764, (1900-1980), two reels of the Louisiana State Council of Carpenters (1941-1980) and two linear feet of records of the Louisiana State Council of Carpenters (1941-1980) and two linear feet of records of the Woman's Union Label League (1907-1940). Theatre and music is documented in the John Wray and Margaret Mary Young Theatre Collection, (5 linear ft, 1921-1981), the Joe Gifford Papers (3 linear feet, 1946-1960), the Shreveport Little Theatre Records (6 linear feet, 1946-1960), the Nathaniel S Allen Papers (1860-1930), the records of the Shreveport Symphony (1948-1978) and oral history interviews on the topics. The archives collection also incl the papers (1930-1977) of Louisiana legislator William M Rainach (48 linear ft), the collection (1894-1970) of the Hypatia Club ofShreveport, Louisiana, the papers (1899-1965) of oil man R O Roy, and 60 linear feet of records (1949-1981) of Holiday-In-Dixie, Shreveport-Bossier's spring-time festival. Microfilm records also incl those of the Shreveport City Council, Cadddo and Bossier Parish Police Juries, Caddo Levee Board, the Shreveport Chamber of Commerce, and the Louisiana State Fair. Other area newspapers are on microfilm and available for use. The archives is the depository for the records of the Red River Valley Association, 1927-date. Over 60 linear feet of these records incl minutes, correspondence, programs, convention materials, maps, photographs, hearings, legislation, scrapbooks of newsclippings concerning projects of the land and water improvement undertaken by RRVA. Inventories and supplementary catalogs are available in thearchives.

LA —R W NORTON ART GALLERY, Library, 4747 Creswell Ave, Shreveport, 71106. Jerry M Bloomer, Librn
Holdings: Vols 200 Cat

LA —NICHOLLS STATE UNIVERSITY, Ellender Memorial Library, Thibodaux, 70310. Randall A Detro, Dir; Philip D Uzee, Archivist
Holdings: Uncat Mss Maps Pix Microforms
Notes: Louisiana and local history; family papers of the period, etc..

NY —UNIVERSITY OF ROCHESTER, Rush Rhees Library, Department of Rare Books and Special Collections, Rochester, 14627. Peter Dzwonkoski, Librn
Holdings: // Cat Mss
Notes: Jean Frederic Phelpeaux, Comte de Maurepas. Manuscripts relating to the French in Canada and Louisiana in the mid-18th century.

TX —AMARILLO PUBLIC LIBRARY, 413 E Fourth, Amarillo, 79101. Mary Kay Snell, Librn
Holdings: Vols Cat Mss Maps Pix
Notes: The southwest collections incl materials on the history of Texas, Louisiana, New Mexico, Arkansas, Missouri and Kansas. General subjects covered incl overland journeys, early narratives, early biographies, Indian captivities, outlaws, US government reports, Mississippi and Ohio Rivers, the Mexican War, reports of Catholic missionaries, Niles Register, early publications, fur trade, western trails, Texas Rangers, sheriffs and Texas as a sovereign state, buffalo hunting, Indian wars, cowboys, the arrival of farmers, fences, and towns. Over 1600 items which incl books, documents, maps, mss, pamphlets, unpublished theses, interviews and photographs. The three major collections are the William Henry Bush Collection, the Laurence J Fitzsimon Collection and the Calendar of John L McCarty.

TX —UNIVERSITY OF TEXAS LIBRARIES, General Libraries, Barker Texas History Center, PO Box P, Austin, 78712. Don Carleton, Dir
Holdings: Vols (132,000) Cat Mss Maps Pix Slides Phonorecords Audiotapes Microforms
Notes: See description of collection under Texas-History.

LOUISIANA—MAPS

LA —NEW ORLEANS PUBLIC LIBRARY, Louisiana Div & City Archives Dept, Louisiana History Collection, 219 Loyola Ave, New Orleans, 70140. Collin B Hamer Jr, Head
Notes: Maps incl 3000 mss and printed maps, mostly for Greater New Orleans area. Also 16,700 aerial photographs.

LA —TULANE UNIVERSITY, Howard-Tilton Memorial Library, Special Collections Div, 7001 Freret St, New Orleans, 70118. Wilbur E Meneray, Librn
Holdings: Maps
Notes: Louisiana Collection incl about 1000 maps about equally divided between Louisiana (Territory and State) and New Orleans. Louisiana maps date from about 1600 to the present; New Orleans maps date from about 1740 to the present.

LOUISIANA—POLITICS AND GOVERNMENT

LA —LOUISIANA STATE UNIVERSITY, Troy H Middleton Library, Louisiana Room, Baton Rouge, 70803. Evangeline Mills Lynch, Head Librn; Ruth Murray, Associate Librn
Holdings: Vols (33,500) Cat Maps VF
Notes: Louisiana Collection of history, description and travel, biography, agriculture, literature, politics and government, folklore, anthropology, geography, geology, education, language, music and natural history. Especially large subject collections may be found on Louisiana, the history of the lower Mississippi Valley, Abraham Lincoln, Romance languages and literatures, sugar culture and technology, Southern history, petroleum engineering, plant pathology, micropaleontology, ornithology, and various aspects of crawfish life, biology and culture. Complete depository of Louisiana State Documents; extensive newspapers clipping files; separate card catalog; items listed in Louisiana Union Catalog; restricted use (research and reference). Incl both materials about Louisiana and by Louisianians without regard to subject. LSU Press Collection(preservation copy of each title kept for exhibit purposes only). LSU theses and dissertations from 1900-date. LSU Faculty Collection. Also, 1300 maps, 104 VF drawers, 250 boxes of uncataloged pamphlets.

LA —TULANE UNIVERSITY, Howard-Tilton Memorial Library, Special Collections Div, 7001 Freret St, New Orleans, 70118. Wilbur E Meneray, Librn
Holdings: Cat Mss Pix Audiotapes Videotapes
Notes: Papers of Louisiana politicians, including Thomas Hale Boggs, Felix Edward Hebert, Sam Houston Jones and deLesseps Story Morrison.

LOUISIANA—POPULATION

NH —ASSOCIATION CANADO-AMERICAIN (FRATERNAL LIFE INSURANCE SOCIETY), Institute Canado-Americain, 52 Concord St, Manchester, 03101. Robert A Beaudoin, Librn
Holdings: Vols (40,000) Cat Mss Maps Pix Slides Phonorecords Audiotapes Microforms
Budget: ($2000)
Notes: Contains books, pamphlets, mss, university dissertations, newspapers, manuscripts, periodicals, and archives of various other societies (active of defunct). Subjects covered incl art, music, literature, folklore, religion, politics, sociology, history, etc of the French in France, Canada, and US (especially New England's Franco-Americans, Louisiana's Cajuns, and Quebec's French-Canadians). There is also an extensive collection of genealogical works dealing with Quebec Acadia, and New England Francophones. Articles dealing with the library are: "The Library of the Association Canado-Americaine" by Edward B Ham in *Modern Language Notes*, vol LII, no 7, November 1937 and a bilingual article "Appel d'un jeune aux jeunes en faveur de al Bibliotheque ACA" by Robert B Perreault in *Le Canado-Americain*, nouvelle serie, vol 1, no 5, julliet-aout-septembre 1975, pp 18-19.

LOUISIANA—SOCIAL LIFE AND CUSTOMS

LA —UNIVERSITY OF SOUTHERN LOUISIANA, Dupre Library, Jefferson Caffery Louisiana Room, 302 East St Mary Blvd, Lafayette, 70504. Cynthia J Rice, Louisiana Room Ref Librn
Notes: Emphasis is on state, regional, and local history, genealogy, and culture; also politics and government, industry, agriculture, geology, language and literature. Incl French Louisiana. Collection is closed-stack and non-circulating, and is open to the public for on-site use only. Copying services are available.

LOUISIANA AUTHORS see Authors, Louisiana

LOUISIANA HISTORICAL ASSOCIATION

LA —TULANE UNIVERSITY, Howard-Tilton Memorial Library, Special Collections Div, 7001 Freret St, New Orleans, 70118. Wilbur E Meneray, Librn
Holdings: Vols 239 Cat Mss Maps Pix
Notes: Collection of the Louisiana Historical Association including Association papers, correspondence of Jefferson Davis, Confederate correspondence, orders and reports, diaries and reminiscences of Confederate soldiers, papers of veterans and memorial associations, photographs, newspapers, sheet music and pamphlets. See "Summary of Inventory: Louisiana Historical Association Collections," *Louisiana History* 9:4 (Fall, 1968).

LOURDES, SHRINE AT

CT —YALE UNIVERSITY, Medical Historical Library, 333 Cedar St, New Haven, 06510. Ferenc A Gyorgyey, Librn

LOUSE see Lice

LOUYS, PIERRE

MN —CARLETON COLLEGE LIBRARY, Northfield, 55057.
Holdings: Vols 7000 Cat
Notes: Books and periodicals relating to French literature of the second half of the 19th century, incl the French symbolist and decadent writers and critical works about them. Major writers are well represented as are some of the relatively minor figures, such as Paul Adam, Rene Boylesve, Abel Hermant, Pierre Louys, and others. The collection incl 69 plays written and produced in the period.

LOVE, WILLIAM

BC —UNIVERSITY OF VICTORIA, McPherson Library, Victoria, V8W 3H5, Can.

LOVECRAFT, HOWARD PHILLIPS

IL —NORTHERN ILLINOIS UNIVERSITY, Founders Memorial Library, Rare Books and Special Collections Dept, De Kalb, 60115. William R DuBois, Dept Head
Holdings: Vols 120 // Uncat Mss
Notes: Publications by Lovecraft, original autograph letters, periodical appearances and critical materials. Consists of books, periodicals, mss (3 letters) and periodical clippings. Original holograph letter to Clark Ashton Smith, March 3, 1934. Noncirculating.

MD —JOHNS HOPKINS UNIVERSITY, Milton S Eisenhower Library, Charles & 34 Sts, Baltimore, 21218. Ann S Gwyn, Assistant Dir for Special Collections
Holdings: Cat Mss
Notes: 5000 manuscript items.

RI —BROWN UNIVERSITY, John Hay Library, 20 Prospect St, Providence, 02912. Mark N Brown, Cur Mss
Holdings: Vols (600) Cat Mss Pix Phonorecords Audiotapes
Notes: Howard Phillips Lovecraft Collection of books, amateur and professional magazines, plus mss/typescripts by and about Howard Phillips Lovecraft, incl first and subsequent editions of Lovecraft's work in 12 languages; complete runs of *Weird Tales, Marvel Tales, The Californian, Driftwind, Rainbow, Leaves*, and *Amateur Fantasy Correspondent* plus scattered issues of 50 amateur and professional magazines; 1500 letters written by Lovecraft to more than 200 correspondents, 270 mss/typescripts of essays, fiction, letters, and poetry written by his correspondents. Photocopying of mss is restricted.

SC —UNIVERSITY OF SOUTH CAROLINA, Thomas Cooper Library, Columbia, 29208. Kenneth E Toombs, Dir of Libraries; Roger Mortimer, Rare Book Librn
Holdings: Vols 40 Cat
Notes: Perhaps one of the most complete collections available.

WI —UNIVERSITY OF WISCONSIN, LA CROSSE, Murphy Library, 1631 Pine St, La Crosse, 54601. Edwin L Hill, Special Collections Librn
Holdings: Vols 1000 Cat
Notes: The Paul W Skeeters Collection of science fiction, fantasy, and horror literature. Complements the library's complete collection of Arkham House books, which contains many titles autographed by August Derleth, and H P Lovecraft's complete fiction and poetic works.

ON —QUEEN'S UNIVERSITY, Douglas Library, Kingston, K7L 5C4, Can. William F E Morley, Cur, Special Collections
Holdings: Vols (225) Cat
Notes: The library has purchased the H P Lovecraft collection (225 vols) and has built up a most interesting collection in Gothic Fantasy and tales of the occult. Also, 6500 pulp magazines, uncat. (List available).

LOVELESS, MR. AND MRS. J. LEE

AZ —NORTHERN ARIZONA UNIVERSITY, Special Collection Library, CU Box 6022, Flagstaff, 86011. Peter M Whiteley, Coordr/Archivist; William Mullane, Librn
Notes: Mr Loveless was mayor of Chandler, Ariz, State Legislature Democratic representative, real estate agent. Mrs Loveless was western author (pseudonym, Leland Lovelace). Scrapbook, subject files, correspondence, 1920's-1960's. Incl unpublished typescript of a novel, *Man of the West;* file on Chandler history; Ira Hayes, Pima Indian at flag raising of Iwo Jima, 1945; Governor Sidney Osborn; and conservative political literature of the 1960's. Also incl newspaper clippings, brochures, pamphlets, and books on birth control and sex information, 1915-1970's.

LOW, DAVID

DC —GEORGETOWN UNIVERSITY, Library, Special Collections Div, 37 & O Sts NW, Washington, 20057. George M Barringer, Special Collections Librn; Nicholas B Sheetz, Mss Librn
Holdings: Mss Cat Pix
Notes: A portion of the archives of the English publisher Grant Ricards (1872-1948), containing manuscripts, correspondence, photographs, clippings, and printed ephemera. Incl is extensive correspondence from such artists and authors as Neville Cardus; Frank Harris; Sir Hugh Lane; Lady Augusta Gregory; David Low; T Sturge Moore; and C R W Nevinson.

LOW LIFE

IN —INDIANA UNIVERSITY, Lilly Library, Seventh St, Bloomington, 47405. William R Cagle, Librn
Holdings: // Cat
Notes: Largely 19th century materials on London crime and criminals.

LOW MOOR IRON COMPANY

VA —UNIVERSITY OF VIRGINIA, Alderman Library, Manuscripts Dept, Charlottesville, 22901. Edmund Berkeley Jr, Cur
Holdings: Cat Mss
Notes: Papers, 1873-1927, of the Low Moor Iron Company, an Allegheny County, Virginia pig iron company.

LOW TEMPERATURE MATERIALS see Materials at Low Temperatures

LOW TEMPERATURE PHYSICS see Low Temperatures

LOW TEMPERATURES

NM —UNIVERSITY OF CALIFORNIA, Los Alamos National Laboratory, Libraries, PO Box 1663, MSP 362, Los Alamos, 87545. J Arthur Freed, Head Librn
Holdings: Vols (800,000) Cat Films Microforms
Budget: ($700,000)
Notes: Incl 500,000 classified and unclassified reports. There are 25 branch libraries and a central collection. The Medical Library contains about 40,000 vols in the areas of biomedical research.

NY —CORNELL UNIVERSITY LIBRARIES, Manuscript and Archives Division, Ithaca, 14853. H Thomas Hickerson, Special Collections Librn
Notes: Raymond Bowers' papers, 1950-78.

ON —NATIONAL RESEARCH COUNCIL OF CANADA, Aeronautical/Mechanical Engineering Branch Library, Montreal Rd, Ottawa, K1A 0R6, Can. Louise Fletcher, Head
Notes: This branch library of the Canada Institute for Scientific and Technical Information (CISTI) of the National Research Council of Canada, Ottawa, has a collection strong in aeronautical engineering, automatic control, CAD/CAM, robotics, ocean, wind, and solar energy power, hydraulic and coastal engineering, icing, low temperature research, naval engineering, metals and metallurgy, incl composites, tribology, and air, railroad, marine transportation. Library supported the Council contribution to the development of the remote manipular Canadarm for NASA's Space Shuttle Orbiters and more recently, the Canadian Astronaut Program which will contribute payload specialists to NASA's Space Shuttle Program in 1984. 35, 000 monographs, 1200 serials. Report collection: over 500,000 items.

LOWDEN, FRANK O.

IL —UNIVERSITY OF CHICAGO LIBRARY, Dept of Special Collections, 1100 E 57 St, Chicago, 60637.
Notes: Personal papers of William H English relating to Indiana history.

LOWE, THADDEUS S. C.

DC —LIBRARY OF CONGRESS, Manuscript Division, Washington, 20540. John C Broderick, Chief
Notes: The American Institute of Aeronautics and Astronautics Archives incorporates primary source material documenting the history of aeronautics. Incl clippings, articles, questionnaires, printed matter, and original mss pertaining to individual aeronauts, the personal papers of balloonist Thaddeus S C Lowe, and a corporate file consisting entirely of printed information on aircraft companies. Incl 30, 000 items.

LOWELL, AMY

MA —HARVARD UNIVERSITY LIBRARY, Houghton Library, Cambridge, 02138. F Thomas Noonan, Cur, Reading Room; Lawrence Dowler, Associate Librn
Holdings: Cat Mss
Notes: Strong collection. Incl some mss and her correspondence.

NY —HOFSTRA UNIVERSITY, Library, 1000 Fulton Ave, Hempstead, 11550. Charles R Andrews, Dean of Library Services

RI —BROWN UNIVERSITY, John Hay Library, Harris Collection, Prospect St, Providence, 02912. Rosemary L Cullen, Cur
Holdings: Vols (200,000) Cat Mss Pix Phonorecords Microforms
Budget: ($15,000)
Notes: The Harris Collection of American Poetry and Plays is principally composed of American and Canadian poetry and plays, 17th century-date. Extensive holdings in songsters, gift books and annuals, hymnals, pageants, broadside verse, carriers' addresses, women poets, juvenile poetry, (incl Mother Goose and *The Night Before* Christmas), sheet music with lyrics, small press publications, fine printing, black poets, "little magazines," Yiddish-American literature. All movements or schools of American poetry are represented. Incl first editions of most American poets and playwrights, notably Whitman, Poe, Wallace Stevens, Eugene O'Neill, Edward Albee, Ezra Pound, T S Eliot, William Carlos Williams, Amy Lowell, Phyllis Wheatley, Robert Frost, Allen Ginsberg, Bliss Carman, and Stephen Foster sheet music. Also incl the Saunders Walt Whitman Collection (1300 vols); the LangdonCollection of Pageants (250 vols); the Asa Cushman Collection of plays in ms and prompt copies; the MacDougall Collection of Psalters and Hymnals; 4000 plays issued by Walter H Baker Co, Boston (1890-1957); the Vaxer Collection of Yiddish Poetry, Plays and Music (1700 vols). Collections incl 200,000 vols, 30,000 broadsides, 55,000 mss, 170,000 pieces of sheet music, 450 phonorecords, and 375 microfilm reels. See *Dictionary Catalog of the Harris Collection of American Poetry and Plays* (Boston: G K Hall, 1972), 13 vols; *Supplement* (1977), 3 vols. See also, *American Poetry*, 1609-1900, *A Collection on Microfilm, Segment I* (1609-1820); *Segment II* (1821-1850); *Segment III* (1851-1870) (Woodbridge, Conn: Research Publications). Separate catalog.

VA —UNIVERSITY OF VIRGINIA, Alderman Library, Clifton Waller Barrett Collection, Charlottesville, 22901. Joan St C Crane, Cur of American Literature Collections
Notes: Papers.

LOWELL, JAMES RUSSELL

MA —HARVARD UNIVERSITY LIBRARY, Houghton Library, Cambridge, 02138. F Thomas Noonan, Cur, Reading Room; Lawrence Dowler, Associate Librn
Holdings: Cat Mss
Notes: See *Harvard Library Notes*, III (1935), 57-60.

LOWELL, ROBERT

DC —LIBRARY OF CONGRESS, Manuscript Division, Washington, 20540. John C Broderick, Chief
Notes: Disc recordings of Dr J Robert Oppenheimer's lectures and interviews. Incl

LOWELL, ROBERT (cont.)

a 3-hour discussion between Niels Bohr and Dr Oppenheimer taped in Denmark in 1958 and a conference held at Seven Springs Farm in Mount Kisco, NY, that featured addresses by Nicolas Nabokov and Robert Lowell.

DC —LIBRARY OF CONGRESS, Motion Pictures, Broadcasting and Recorded Sound Div, Washington, 20540.
Notes: Disc recordings of Dr J Robert Oppenheimer's lectures and interviews. Incl a 3-hour discussion between Niels Bohr and Dr Oppenheimer taped in Denmark in 1958 and a conference held at Seven Springs Farm in Mount Kisco, NY, that featured addresses by Nicolas Nabokov and Robert Lowell.

NV —UNIVERSITY OF NEVADA, RENO, University Library, Special Collections Dept, Reno, 89557. Robert E Blesse, Head
Holdings: Vols (66) Cat Other appearances 1000 Cat
Notes: Includes individual works by author in all editions including translations; also prefaces, introductions, published correspondence, appearances in anthologies, periodicals, etc. Bibliographical research collection, part of Modern Authors Collection.

†TX —UNIVERSITY OF TEXAS LIBRARIES, General Libraries, Humanities Research Center, PO Box 7219, Austin, 78712. John Chalmers, Librn
Holdings: Mss
Notes: A collection of documents relating to the poet, Robert Lowell (1917-77). Incl 8000 ms pages of his works, galley and page proofs of his last five books of poetry, and nearly 2000 pages of literary correspondence with his contemporaries.

LOWELL, MASSACHUSETTS

MA —POLLARD MEMORIAL LIBRARY, 401 Merrimack St, Lowell, 01852. Walter V Hickey, Libr Asst
Holdings: Vols (3000) Cat Pix
Notes: Lowell History Collection. Most books were published in the late 1800s when Lowell was particularly prosperous. Holdings incl Lowell history, vital records, works by Lowell authors and biographies of former Lowell residents. Microfilm of Lowell newspapers from 1837 to the present, as well as City Directories from 1832. Also a full collection of Jack Kerouac's work. Also Town and County histories and published Genealogies, mostly from the late 1800's.

MA —UNIVERSITY OF LOWELL, Library, One University Ave, Lowell, 01854. Martha Mayo, Special Collections Librn
Holdings: Vols (25,000) Cat Mss Maps Pix Slides Microforms Videotapes
Notes: Special collections is the historical depository for several organizations involved with collecting all aspects of Lowell's history incl the Lowell Historical Society, the Lowell Museum, the Boston & Maine Historical Society, and the Middlesex Canal Association.

LOWELL OBSERVATORY

AZ —NORTHERN ARIZONA UNIVERSITY, Special Collection Library, CU Box 6022, Flagstaff, 86011. Peter M Whiteley, Coordr/Archivist; William Mullane, Librn
Notes: Correspondence, 1894-1916. Incl index: *Introduction and Index to the Early Correspondence of the Lowell Observatory.* Also, E C Mills Collection; three photocopied photographs of residences at Lowell Observatory. Notes written by Mrs Constance Lowell stating that the staff should observe the birth and death anniversaries of her husband, Percival Lowell, 1918-1921.

LOWENFELS, WALTER

DE —UNIVERSITY OF DELAWARE, Hugh M Morris Library, S College Ave, Newark, 19711. T Stuart Dick, Special Collections
Holdings: Cat Mss Pix
Notes: Manuscripts, etc, incl literary correspondence.

MO —WASHINGTON UNIVERSITY, Libraries, Special Collections Dept, Campus Box 1061, St Louis, 63130.
Notes: A small but significant collection.

BC —SIMON FRASER UNIVERSITY, Library, Burnaby, V5A 1S6, Can. Percilla Groves, Special Collections Librn
Holdings: Cat Mss
Notes: Letters from Louis Zukofsky, American poet, to Walter Lowenfels, 10 pp als and tls.

LOWER CALIFORNIA see Baja California

LOWER MISSISSIPPI VALLEY see Mississippi Valley, Lower

LOWIE, ROBERT HARRY

CA —UNIVERSITY OF CALIFORNIA, BERKELEY, Bancroft Library, Manuscripts Division, Berkeley, 94720. James D Hart, Dir
Holdings: Cat Mss Maps Pix Microforms
Notes: Papers, correspondence, etc.

LOWNDES, MARIE BELLOC

DC —GEORGETOWN UNIVERSITY, Library, Special Collections Div, 37 & O Sts NW, Washington, 20057. George M Barringer, Special Collections Librn; Nicholas B Sheetz, Mss Librn
Holdings: Mss
Notes: The Archives of the Gallery of Living Catholic Authors was founded in 1932 by Sister Mary Joseph of the Sisters of Loretto to focus attention on modern Catholic literature, and to provide a depository for manuscripts, letters, photographs, and books by contemporary Catholic writers. Contains material by hundreds of writers, incl Hilaire Belloc, Roy Campbell, Padraic Colum, Eric Gill, Paul Horgan, Mary Lavin, Marie Belloc Lowndes, Kathleen Norris, Alred Noyes, Sheila Kaye-Smith, Sigrid Undset, and Evelyn Waugh, to name only a few.

IN —INDIANA UNIVERSITY, Lilly Library, Seventh St, Bloomington, 47405. William R Cagle, Librn
Holdings: Vols 21 Cat Mss
Notes: A complete collection of Pearson's works, including many with the author's annotations. Manuscripts include extensive correspondence between Pearson and two Brittish crime enthusiast, William Roughead and Marie Belloc-Lowndes.

LOWRY, BEVERLY

TX —UNIVERSITY OF HOUSTON, M D Anderson Memorial Library, University Park, Houston, 77004. David Farmer, Cur, Special Collections; Jean Jackson, Assistant Cur
Holdings: Vols (200) Cat
Notes: The emphasis of this collection is on Houston writers of literature. The writers incl Vassar Miller, Cynthia McDonald, Leon Hale, Larry McMurtry, Beverly Lowry, Donald Barthelme and others who have resided or currently reside in the Houston area, and incl some writers who write about the Houston area although they do not live there.

LOWRY, MALCOLM

NV —UNIVERSITY OF NEVADA, RENO, University Library, Special Collections Dept, Reno, 89557. Robert E Blesse, Head
Holdings: Vols (38) Cat Other appearances 85 Cat
Notes: Includes individual works by author in all editions including translations; also prefaces, introductions, published correspondence, appearances in anthologies, periodicals, etc. Bibliographical research collection, part of Modern Authors Collection.

TX —TRINITY UNIVERSITY, Elizabeth Coates Maddux Library, 715 Stadium Dr, San Antonio, 78284. Richard Hume Werking, Library Dir; Craig Likness, Head Bibliographer
Holdings: Vols 193
Notes: Incl both first editions and secondary sources. No manuscripts.

BC —UNIVERSITY OF BRITISH COLUMBIA, Library, Special Collections Div, 1956 Main Mall, Vancouver, V6T 1Y3, Can. Anne Yandle, Head
Holdings: Vols Cat Mss

LOWRY, ROBERT J.

MA —BOSTON UNIVERSITY, Mugar Memorial Library, Special Collections Dept, 771 Commonwealth Ave, Boston, 02215. Howard B Gotlieb, Dir
Holdings: Cat Mss Pix
Notes: Mss, correspondence, etc colected in depth; incl publications by or about.

LOYALISTS, AMERICAN see American Loyalists

LOYALTY OATHS

CA —UNIVERSITY OF CALIFORNIA, LOS ANGELES, Research Library, Dept of Special Collections, 405 Hilgard Ave, Los Angeles, 90024. Edward Shreeves, Chairman, Bibliographers Group; David S Zeidberg, Head
Holdings: Mss
Notes: 6.5 linear feet incl in 6 collections and 5 transcribed oral history interviews.

LOYALTY TESTS see Loyalty Oaths

LOYOLA, ST. IGNATIUS

MO —SAINT LOUIS UNIVERSITY, Pius XII Memorial Library, Saint Louis Room Collection, 3655 W Pine Blvd, Saint Louis, 63108. Catherine E Weidle, Rare Books Librn
Holdings: Vols Cat
Notes: Books on early education, Jesuitica and Western Americana. Related collections of works by Peter Ramus (University is center for Ramist studies) and Omer Talon; also collections on the Spiritual Exercises of St Ignatius Loyola and on the Sodality of Our Lady. Mss uncataloged.

LSD

CA —FITZ HUGH LUDLOW MEMORIAL LIBRARY, PO Box 99346, San Francisco, 94109. Michael R Aldrich, Exec Cur
Holdings: Cat Mss Maps Pix Slides Phonorecords Audiotapes Videotapes
Notes: Collection stored. Important mail inquiries only. No interlibrary lending or telephone inquiries. Hallucinogens as used in historical and contemporary cultures. Nearly complete collection of books and articles by or about Timothy Leary, incl manuscripts; also nearly complete collection of the writings of Aldous Huxley concerning drugs. Much autographed or inscribed material, mostly popular music from the 1960s but also incl ethnographic music. Emphasis on psychoactive drugs relative to religion, literature, art. Also an excellent collection of research papers (chemistry, pharmacology, epidemiology, sociology, ethnobotany) in this field, as well as artifacts and artwork relating to the field.

LUBELL, SAMUEL

DC —GEORGETOWN UNIVERSITY, Library, Special Collections Div, 37 & O Sts NW, Washington, 20057. George M Barringer, Special Collections Librn; Nicholas B Sheetz, Mss Librn
Holdings: Mss Cat Maps
Notes: The papers of Samuel Lubell - pollster, political analyst and author. Incl are state data files consisting of election surveys, election returns, voting statistics, precinct maps, correspondence, interviews, and

LUBELL, SAMUEL (cont.)

clippings as well as material on such issues as race relations, urban development and management, youth opinion, and Congressional analysis. Also incl in the papers is correspondence and lecture material, as well as notes, mss and reviews pertaining to *Hidden Crisis Revolt of the Moderates, White and Black, The Future of American Politics, and The Future While It* Happened.

LUBIN, HARRY

CA —UNIVERSITY OF CALIFORNIA, LOS ANGELES, Music Library, Schonberg Hall, Los Angeles, 90024. Stephen M Fry, Music Librn
Notes: Mss

LUBRICATION AND LUBRICANTS

MI —ACHESON COLLOIDS, Library, 511 Port St, Port Huron, 48060. Myles T Musgrave, Librn
Holdings: Vols (5000) Cat Mss Microforms
Notes: Solid lubricants: graphite, molybdenum disulfide and related organic and inorganic compounds used as solid lubricants (in films, liquids, greases, etc) for industrial applications. Incl extensive patent collection (US and foreign).

OH —EMERY INDUSTRIES, Research Library, 4900 Este Ave, Cincinnati, 45232. B A Bernard, Librn
Holdings: Cat
Notes: Special subjects: fatty acids and organic chemical derivatives, ozone, plasticizers, polymers, synthetic lubricants.

LUCAS, EDWARD VERRALL, 1868-1938

IL —ILLINOIS STATE UNIVERSITY, Milner Library, Dept of Special Collections, Normal, 61761. Robert Sokan, Librn
Holdings: Vols 210 Cat Mss Pix
Notes: The Lucas collection contains four vols of correspondence between Lucas and his childhood friend, Charles Walter Berry; three vols of holograph manuscripts, and 29 vols of ephemera, eg, printed poems for special occasions, inscribed dinner menus, short humorous notes, etc.

LUCAS, JOHN

PA —US ARMY MILITARY HISTORY INSTITUTE, Carlisle Barracks, 17013. Richard J Sommers, Chief Archivist-Historian
Holdings: Mss Cat
Notes: The World War II collection, personal letters, daily logs, reminiscences, speeches, and official papers of American officers and soldiers serving in the European, Mediterranean, Middle Eastern, China-Burma-India, Southwest Pacific, and Central Pacific Theaters and in the Zone of the Interior during the Second World War. Most of these collections are manuscripts of General officers, incl Omar Bradley, Stephen Chamberlin, Lewis Hershey, John Lucas, William Simpson, and Brehon Somervell.

LUCAS, ROBERT

IA —STATE HISTORICAL SOCIETY OF IOWA LIBRARY, 402 Iowa Ave, Iowa City, 52240. Darold J Brown, Librn
Holdings: Cat
Notes: Thousands of individual items and smaller collections. Two hundred larger collections incl the papers of Cyrus C Carpenter, Jonathan P Dolliver, Gilbert Haugen, W W Waymack, Ephraim Adams, A C Dodge, Dorothy Houghton, Jesse Macy, Agnes Samuelson, Donald Johnson, Jack Miller, Ruth Sayre, Samuel Kirkwood, Thomas McKnight, Robert Lucas, Dwight McCarty, William Larrabee. Includes church, school, company and organization records, Civil War materials.

LUCE, CLAIRE

NY —NEW YORK PUBLIC LIBRARY, Performing Arts Research Center, Billy Rose Theatre Collection, 111 Amsterdam Ave, New York, 10023. Dorothy L Swerdlove, Cur
Holdings: Cat Mss Pix
Notes: Papers, scrapbooks, mss, photographs, memorabillia, etc. (Do not confound with Claire Boothe Luce.)

LUCE, STEPHEN B.

RI —US NAVAL WAR COLLEGE, Historical Collection & Museum, Newport, 02841. Anthony S Nicolosi, Dir; Evelyn Cherpak, Cur
Holdings: Mss
Notes: A collection of letters, published articles, speeches, books, book reviews, photographs and misc printed items relating to the career of a prominent late nineteenth century naval officer whose educational and organizational reforms helped to revolutionize the US Navy. Luce was founder of the Naval Training Station and the Naval War College, both located in Newport, RI

LUDICROUS, THE see Wit and Humor

LUDWIG, MYLES ERIC

MA —BOSTON UNIVERSITY, Mugar Memorial Library, Special Collections Dept, 771 Commonwealth Ave, Boston, 02215. Howard B Gotlieb, Dir
Holdings: Cat Mss

LUHAN, MABEL DODGE

CT —YALE UNIVERSITY, Box 1603A, Yale Station, New Haven, 06520.
Holdings: Cat Mss Pix

LUKAS, EDWIN

†PA —BALCH INSTITUTE FOR ETHNIC STUDIES, Library, 18 S Seventh St, Philadelphia, 19106.
Notes: Papers of Edwin Lukas, head of the civil rights and social action department of the American Jewish Committee.

LUIAN LANGUAGE see Luwian Language

LUISH LANGUAGE see Luwian Language

LUKENS FAMILY

DE —HAGLEY MUSEUM AND LIBRARY, Eleutherian Mills-Hagley Foundation Inc, PO Box 3630, Greenville, 19807. Richmond D Williams, Dir; Heddy A Richter, Imprints Librn
Notes: Records of the Lukens Steel Co of Coatsville, Pa (1798-1944; 750 cubic feet) incl administrative, accounting, payroll, production and sales records documenting the history of one of America's oldest iron and steel companies. Records of the Phoenix Steel Corporation (1827-1962; 335 cubic feet) incl minute books, financial records, payroll and production records documenting the history of this important Delaware Valley steel producer. Also, Alan Wood Steel Company of Conshohocken, Pa (1728-1937; 250 cubic feet).

DE —UNIVERSITY OF DELAWARE, Hugh M Morris Library, S College Ave, Newark, 19711. T Stuart Dick, Special Collections
Holdings: // Mss Maps
Notes: Lukens Family papers cover the years 1745-1904, but the principal years are those for 1745-1789 concerning John Lukens, Surveyor-General of Pennsylvania and Delaware, 1761-1776; of Pennsylvania, 1781-1789. Included are such official papers as survey returns for Pennsylvania and Delaware.

LULLY, JEAN BAPTISTE, 1632-1687

CA —STANFORD UNIVERSITY LIBRARIES, Cecil H Green Library, Stanford, 94305. Michael T Ryan, Cur
Notes: Large archive. To be incl in the Stanford University international Lully Archive of microfilm of primary Lully sources. The first of 64 vols (Sacred Music) scheduled for 1984 publication.

LUMBARD, ELIOT HOWLAND, 1925-

NY —STATE UNIVERSITY OF NEW YORK AT ALBANY, Library, Special Collections Dept, 1400 Washington Ave, Albany, 12222. Marion P Munzer, Coordr
Notes: Eliot Howland Lumbard's research files, reports, correspondence, mss, and clippings on crime and law enforcement (19 linear feet). Part of the Library's German Exile Collection.
See also entries under Criminal Justice, Administration of; Law Enforcement

LUMBER AND LUMBERING

AZ —NORTHERN ARIZONA UNIVERSITY, Special Collection Library, CU Box 6022, Flagstaff, 86011. Peter M Whiteley, Coordr/Archivist; William Mullane, Librn
Notes: Correpondence and other records of the Arizona Lumber and Timber Company, etc, 1866-1927.
See also entries under Forests and Forestry; Lumber Industry and Trade

CT —YALE UNIVERSITY, Forestry Library, 205 Prospect St, New Haven, 06511. Joseph A Miller, Librn
Holdings: Vols (115,000) Cat Microforms
Notes: Literature of North America forestry and forest products is most completely covered, though other countries and foreign languages are well represented.

GA —UNIVERSITY OF GEORGIA, Libraries, Athens, 30602. Arlene E Luchsinger, Asst Dir Branch Libraries
Notes: Collection of over 1000 photographs on Southern forestry and the Southern logging industry, 1939-46. This gift, from the Southern Forest Institute, includes the records and files of four groups formed to solve specific problems of Southern forests.

ME —MAINE STATE LIBRARY, Special Collections Dept, Cultural Bldg, Station 64, Augusta, 04333. Shirley Thayer, Librn
Holdings: // Mss Maps Pix
Budget: ($2,500,000)
Notes: Lumbering in northern Maine, 1876-1936. Incl a very large photograph collection (incl glass slides). This is part of the Avery Collection.

MI —MUSEUM OF THE GREAT LAKES, Bay County Historical Society, Library, 1700 Center Ave, Bay City, 48706. Eurdine Ringwelski, Librn
Holdings: Vols (800) Cat Mss Maps Pix Slides 16mm Films
Notes: Focuses on man's relationship to his environment in the Great Lakes region in an historical perspective. Incl books, mss, photos, maps, vertical files, and scrapbooks on the history of Bay County and the Saginaw Valley, Michigan.

MI —HACKLEY PUBLIC LIBRARY, 316 W Webster Ave, Muskegon, 49440. Dale H Pretzer, Dir
Holdings: // Cat Mss Maps Pix

MN —NORTHEAST MINNESOTA HISTORICAL CENTER, University of Minnesota, Duluth, Library 375, Duluth, 55812. Patricia Maus, Administrator
Notes: The Northeast Minnesota Historical Center is jointly maintained by the University of Minnesota, Duluth, and the St Louis County Historical Society. Local and regional history collections with emphasis on transportation, lumbering, mining. Photograph collection. Photocopy service available.

MN —UNIVERSITY OF MINNESOTA, DULUTH, Library & Learning Resources Service, Duluth, 55812. James V. Litha, Archivist
Holdings: Vols (1700) Cat Mss Maps Pix
Notes: The Voyageur Collection incl the Grace Lee Nute Papers. Books and materials relating to the Voyageur period (1650-1850) and the area of Northeastern Minnesota, Michigan, Wisconsin, Southern Canada. Emphasis on all subjects listed in this volume.

LUMBER AND LUMBERING (cont.)

MN —MINNESOTA HISTORICAL SOCIETY LIBRARY, 690 Cedar St, Saint Paul, 55101. Patricia C Harpole, Chief of Reference Library; Bonnie G Wilson, Head of Special Libraries
Notes: Industries in Minnesota which have been documented in interviews include lumbering, commercial fishing on the North Shore of Lake Superior, and printing and graphics in the Twin Cities.

MS —UNIVERSITY OF SOUTHERN MISSISSIPPI, William David McCain Graduate Library, Box 5148, Southern Sta, Hattiesburg, 39406.
Holdings: Uncat Mss Pix
Notes: The business records of the S E Lackey Lumber Company document the Southern yellow pine lumber industry in Mississippi from the 1920s through the 1950s. Forty-five August 1920 photographs of the Goodyear Yellow Pine Lumber Company of Picayune, Mississippi depict all phases of lumbering, from logging and skidder operations to milling and curing. Incl are photographs of lumber camps and "houses on wheels." 44 cubic feet holdings.

NV —UNIVERSITY OF NEVADA, RENO, University Library, Special Collections Dept, Reno, 89557. Robert E Blesse, Head
Holdings: Vols (100) Cat Mss Pix
Notes: Papers, documents, business records of firms involved with logging in Nevada and California in the 19th and early 20th centuries. Materials deal primarily with the production of lumber to support mining activities in Nevada and eastern California. Materials include books manuscripts (115 cu ft), photographs (500), dealing with Lake Tahoe and the surrounding region. Included are papers of organizations concerned with the environmental quality of the lake, eg, the Lake Tahoe Area Council records, the Tahoe Regional Planning Association records. Records of two 19th-20th century business involved with logging and lumber production in the Tahoe region, the Carson, Tahoe Lumber and Fluming Company, and the El Dorado Wood and Flume Company. Photographs include many early 19th century views of the lake and structures surrounding it.

NY —ADIRONDACK HISTORICAL ASSOCIATION, Museum Library, Blue Mountain Lake, 12812. Jerold Pepper, Librn
Holdings: Vols (7500) Cat Mss Maps Pix Phonorecords Audiotapes 16mm Films Microforms
Notes: Anything about the Adirondacks--history, people, economics, places, things. Strong in Adirondack art, outdoor recreation, logging, small boats. Resources incl more than 1000 maps, 40,000 pictures, 1600 microfilm reels, 576 linear ft of ms material, and 12 cabinets of VF ephemera, etc.

NY —CARY ARBORETUM OF THE NEW YORK BOTANICAL GARDEN, Library, Box AB, Millbrook, 12545. Fred Strum, Librn
Notes: This collection of alternative energy sources consists of publications concerned with solar energy, wind power, biofuel, methanol, small hydroelectric projects, and wood power.

OR —UNIVERSITY OF OREGON LIBRARY, Special Collections Div, Eugene, 97403. Kenneth W Duckett, Curator
Holdings: Cat Mss Pix
Notes: Over 20 mss collections of records and files of lumbermen and lumber companies in the Pacific Northwest.
Publication: Martin Schmitt, comp, *Catalogue of Manuscripts in the University of Oregon Library* (Eugene: Univeristy of Oregon books, 1971).
See also entry under Forests and Forestry

LUMBER AND LUMBERING—HISTORY

AK —TONGASS HISTORICAL SOCIETY, Library, 629 Dock St, Ketchikan, 99901. Marjorie Anne Voss, Librn
Holdings: // Uncat Mss
Notes: Ketchikan Spruce Mill ms collection.

AZ —NORTHERN ARIZONA UNIVERSITY, Special Collection Library, CU Box 6022, Flagstaff, 86011. Peter M Whiteley, Coordr/Archivist; William Mullane, Librn
Holdings: Cat Mss Maps Pix Audiotapes
Notes: (1) Charles Koch Collection: notes concerning an Arizona Sawmill Directory and notes for a felling and bucking study, prepared by Charles Koch, a forester. Both were published in *Arizona Land Marks.* (2) Jay Price Collection: correspondence, files, and reports reports pertaining to *Forestry* Topics, (1950's). Incl information on watershed and forest management for the Salt River and Central Arizona Projects as part of the Arizona Water Resource Committee files, 1956-1960; also files of the Soil Conservation Society, Arizona Chapter, 1956-1957 (2 feet).

CA —CALIFORNIA STATE UNIVERSITY, FRESNO, Henry Madden Library, Dept of Special Collections, Fresno, 93740. Ronald J Mahoney, Head
Holdings: // Uncat Pix
Notes: The Harry Pidgeon Collection of photographs of logging in the Sugar Pine area of the Sierra Nevada mountains, Madera County, California. About 600 photos, 1913-1925.

NV —UNIVERSITY OF NEVADA, RENO, University Library, Special Collections Dept, Reno, 89557. Robert E Blesse, Head
Holdings: Vols 25 Cat Mss Pix
Notes: Papers, documents, business records of firms involved with logging in Nevada and California in the 19th and early 20th centuries. Materials deal primarily with the production of lumber to support mining activities in Nevada and eastern California.

NC —DUKE UNIVERSITY, William R Perkins Library, Manuscript Dept, Durham, 27706. Ellen Gartrell, Cur of Mss
Holdings: Mss
Notes: Large collections of several lumber companies, 20th century (mostly North Carolina) plus other references.

OR —COLLIER STATE PARK LOGGING MUSEUM LIBRARY, PO Box 428, Klamath Falls, 97601. Alfred D Collier, Cur; Lowell N Jones, Asst Cur
Holdings: Uncat Mss Maps Pix Slides
Notes: 600 pieces of equipment showing evolution of logging. 800 pictures of logging. 15 pioneer log cabins. 500 Indian Stone artifacts. Collection of cruisers marks and sleighs.

OR —GEORGIA-PACIFIC HISTORICAL MUSEUM, Library, 900 SW Fifth, Portland, 97204. Richard Thompson, Museum Dir
Holdings: Vols (300) Uncat Videotapes 16mm Films Pix
Notes: Use of collection is by written request for specific information or materials.

PA —PENNSYLVANIA STATE UNIVERSITY, Fred Lewis Pattee Library, Life Sciences Library, University Park, 16802. Keith Roe, Head
Notes: This collection is strong in periodical runs, particularly European learned societies and agriculture. It contains extensive collections of Experiment Station publications and has developed specialties in Mycology and Fusaria. There is also a special collection of 1105 glass slides on early Pennsylvania lumbering.

TX —STEPHEN F AUSTIN STATE UNIVERSITY, Ralph W Steen Library, Special Collections Dept, Box 13055, SFA Sta, Nacogdoches, 75962. Linda Cheves Nicklas, Special Collections Librn
Holdings: Cat Mss Maps Pix
Budget: ($5000)
Notes: Forest History Collection (late 1800s-1965). Incl personal and business correspondence, contracts, timber plats, logging and hauling contracts, photos and other records of early East Texas lumber companies and logging railroads. Calendars for records of each company are available.
Published description: Maxwell, R S, "Manuscript Collections at Stephen F Austin State College", American Archivist, vol 28, July, 1965; and SFASU, *A Guide to Special* Collections, 1980.

WI —OSHKOSH PUBLIC MUSEUM, Library, 1331 Algoma Blvd, Oshkosh, 54901. Kitty A Hobson, Archivist
Holdings: Cat Mss Maps Pix Slides Audiotapes 16mm Films
Notes: Books, mss, photographs, etc, dealing with the history of Oshkosh and Winnebago County, Wisconsin, with special emphasis on lumbering and steamboating.

LUMBER INDUSTRY AND TRADE

AZ —NORTHERN ARIZONA UNIVERSITY, Special Collection Library, CU Box 6022, Flagstaff, 86011. Peter M Whiteley, Coordr/Archivist; William Mullane, Librn
Notes: Various collections. (1) J M Dennis Lumber Company Collection, Maine, Ariz; outgoing correspondence and orders, 1908-1910. (2) Charles Koch Collection; notes concerning an *Arizona Sawmill Directory* and notes for a felling and bucking study, prepared by Charles Koch, a forester. Both were published in *Arizona Land Marks,* 1978. (3) Saginaw and Manistee Lumber Company Collection; the lumber company was located in Williams and Flagstaff, Ariz. Records, 1902-1954, incl correspondence, bills of sale, time sheets, contracts, and agreements. Also incl some records of Saginaw Power Company. (4) McGonigle Family Collection; incl files on the McGonigle Lumber Company, Flagstaff and Flagstaff Lumber Company.
See also entries under Forests and Forestry; Lumber and Lumbering

CA —FOREST HISTORY SOCIETY INC, Library, 109 Coral St, Santa Cruz, 95060. Mary E Johnson, Librn
Holdings: Vols (4000) Cat Mss Maps Pix Slides Audiotapes Microforms Serials Films VF
Budget: ($2000)
Notes: Incl archives of the Society of American Foresters, the American Forestry Association, the National Lumber Manufacturers Association, National Forest Products Assocation, and the American Forest Institute.

DE —UNIVERSITY OF DELAWARE, Hugh M Morris Library, S College Ave, Newark, 19711. T Stuart Dick, Special Collections
Notes: Personal and business letters and receipts, of the Albertson family, Quaker lumber and lime merchants (1782-1862) residing in Plymouth, Montgomery Co, Pa. Included are many letters concerning the Plymouth RR and rules and regulations for its administration.

PA —CARNEGIE LIBRARY OF PITTSBURGH, Science & Technology Dept, 4400 Forbes Ave, Pittsburgh, 15213. Catherine M Brosky, Dept Head
Notes: General information acquired in various subject areas especially those relating to iron and steel and other metals, rubber, leather, pulp and paper, textiles, glass, petroleum and coal tar by-products, lumber, plastics, etc. Manufactuers directories, including old editions, standards and specifications, trade catalogs, basic periodicals, indexes, and bibliographies. See entry under Science.

LUMMIS, CHARLES F., 1859-1928

CA —AZUSA PACIFIC COLLEGE, Marshburn Memorial Library, Citrus & Alosta, Azusa, 91702. Edward Peterman, Librn
Holdings: Vols (150) Uncat
Notes: The Obo B Stade Collection of Literary First Editions. No photocopying

NM —MUSEUM OF NEW MEXICO, Photo Archives, Box 2087, Santa Fe, 87503. Arthur L Olivas, Cur; Richard Rudisill, Photo Historian
Holdings: Cat Pix Slides
Notes: Extensive collection of his work.

TX —SOUTHERN METHODIST UNIVERSITY, DeGolyer Library, Box 396, SMU, Dallas, 75275. Clifton H Jones, Dir
Holdings: Vols (80,000) Cat Mss Maps Pix Slides Microforms
Notes: First editions of prominent authors; also of books in subject emphasis collections. All subjects listed in this vol are strong.

LUMMIS, CHARLES F., 1859-1928 (cont.)

Numerous collections of personal papers relating to subjects also.

LUNAR GEOLOGY

IL —UNIVERSITY OF ILLINOIS, URBANA/CHAMPAIGN, Library, Geology Library, 223 Natural History Bldg, Urbana, 61801. Dederick Ward, Librn
Holdings: Vols (105,186) Cat Maps Microforms

LUNAR STUDIES

†AZ —UNIVERSITY OF ARIZONA, Space Imagery Center, Lunar & Planetary Laboratory, Tucson, 85721. Gail G Georgenson, Librn
Notes: Planetary science. Interests incl Space Probs - Gemini; Apollo; Lunar Orbiter; Mariner 6, 7 9, 10; Pioneer 10 & 11; Viking 1 & 2. Regional Planetary Image Facilities are in Flagstaff, Ariz; Pasadena, Calif; Saint Louis, MO; Ithaca, NY; Providence, RI; Houston, Tex; Rome, Italy; London, England.

NY —COLUMBIA UNIVERSITY LIBRARIES, Geoscience Library, Lamont-Doherty Geological Observatory, Palisades, 10964. Susan Klimley, Librn
Holdings: Vols (20,000) Cat
Notes: Geosciences, incl geochemistry, marine geology, seismology and paleoclimatology.

†SD —SOUTH DAKOTA SCHOOL OF MINES & TECHNOLOGY, Devereaux Library, Rapid City, 57701.
Holdings: Vols 400 Cat
Notes: Also, about 7400 hard copies of NASA Technical Reports. Have a Lunar Orbiter Photograph Collection.

TX —LUNAR & PLANETARY INSTITUTE, Library/Information Center, 3303 Nasa Rd One, Houston, 77058. Frances B Waranius, Library/Information Center Mgr
Holdings: Cat Mss Maps Pix Slides Microforms
Notes: Development of collection begun in 1972 to incl lunar studies from approx 1950 forward. Planets, meteorites, asteroids and comets added 1978. Seek to become as inclusive as possible.

LUNCH ROOMS see Restaurants, Lunch Rooms, Bars, Etc.

LUNDBERG, BO

MA —MASSACHUSETTS INSTITUTE OF TECHNOLOGY, Institute Archives, Special Collections, Cambridge, 02139.
Notes: Correspondence, newsletters, fact-sheets, newspaper and magazine articles, books and reports of the Citizens' League Against the Sonic Boom, established in 1967 by William Shurcliff to oppose the sonic boom, stop commercial supersonic transport production, and influence public opinion and policy decisions on the SST. Major correspondents incl Bo Lundberg, Richard Wiggs, several US congressmen, and CLASB members.

LUNDEEN, ERNEST

CA —HOOVER INSTITUTION ON WAR, REVOLUTION & PEACE, Stanford University, Stanford, 94305. Milorad M Drachkovitch, Archivist
Holdings: // Mss
Notes: Papers, 1914-1947, of Ernest Lundeen, state legislator and US Representative and Senator from Minnesota. Correspondence, subject files, documents and other papers, relating to Lundeen's political career. 335 boxes. Unpublished preliminary inventory in the repository.

LUNN, SIR ARNOLD

DC —GEORGETOWN UNIVERSITY, Library, Special Collections Div, 37 & O Sts NW, Washington, 20057. George M Barringer, Special Collections Librn; Nicholas B Sheetz, Mss Librn
Holdings: Cat Mss
Notes: The papers of the English author, journalist, and historian Douglas Woodruff (1897-1978), containing correspondence, mss, and photographs. Incl is considerable material concerning his years at Oxford University; his editorship for many years of The "Tablet"; English Catholic society in general and English Catholic literature in particular. Also present are research files on the Tichborne Claimant, one of the most famous cases of impersonation in English legal history. There is extensive correspondence from such figures as: Hilaire Belloc; Tom Burns; Rev Martin D'Arcy, SJ; Christopher Dawson; Sir Roy Harrod; Christopher Hollis; Msgr Ronald Knox; Sir Shane Leslie; Sir Arnold Lunn; Rebecca West; and Evelyn Waugh.

LUNSFORD, BASCOM LAMAR

NC —MARS HILL COLLEGE, Memorial Library, Appalachian Room, Mars Hill, 28754. Richard Dillingham, Dir, Special Collections
Holdings: Vols (9600) Cat Mss Maps Pix Slides Phonorecords Audiotapes Microforms
Budget: ($4000)
Notes: Collection strong on local history, folklore, fiction. Incl Bascom Lamar Lunsford papers, books, sound recordings. Separate catalog.

LUNT, ALFRED, AND LYNN FONTANNE

MI —UNIVERSITY OF MICHIGAN, Library, Dept of Rare Books & Special Collections, Ann Arbor, 48109. Robert J Starring, Head
Holdings: Cat Mss Pix
Notes: Extensive holdings of books on the theatre. Also, in the Charles Sanders Collection, about 14,000 British and American playbills and programs mostly of the 19th century, as well as scrapbooks, posters, and about 750 photographs and prints of actors and actresses. In the Ellen Van Volkenburg--Maurice Browne Collection, about 4000 photographs of stage productions and friends and associates, as well as programs, posters, scrapbooks of mounted clippings, about 200 original stage and costume designs, promptbooks, and play manuscripts, representing the American and British careers of this husband-wife team from 1912 to about 1940. The Chicago Little Theatre, 1912-1917, is well represented. Also contains more than 6000 items of correspondence with theatrical and literary figures. Another collection contains 143 Alfred Lunt letters, mainly from 1909-1915.

LUSAPHONE AFRICA

CA —HOOVER INSTITUTION ON WAR, REVOLUTION & PEACE, Stanford University, Stanford, 94305. Peter Duignan, Cur; Karen Fung, Deputy Cur
Notes: History, politics and economics from 1870 to the present. Extensive collection on Portuguese colonial history incl monographs, government publications, photographs, microforms, journals, newspapers. Incl journals such as *Revista Portugueza Colonial e Maritima, Revista de Angola, Defesa* Nacional, *Revista Militar, Angola in Arms, Kwacha-Angola, Mozambique Revolution.* Special collections incl the 15 reel Ronald Chilcote collection "Emerging Nationalism in Portuguese Africa", the 12 reel Immanuel Wallerstein Collection of Political Ephemera of the Liberation Movements of Lusophone Africa..., and the Roberrt Keith Middlemas Collection on Portugal and South Africa 1966-1976. Discriptions of the Collection in *Handbook of American Resources for African Studies* pub by Hoover. Holdings of the Collection in*Hoover Institution on War, Revolution, and Peace Library Catalog* pub by G K Hall, *Emerging Nationalism in Portuguese Africa: A Bibliography* pub by Hoover, *German Africa* pub by Hoover, *The Treason Trial in South Africa: A Guide to the Microfilm Record of the Trial* pub by Hoover. Also, *History of the Library and Archives of the Hoover Institution on War, Revolution and Peace,* edited by Peter Duignan (Hoover Institution Press), *Guide to Non-federal Archives and Manuscripts in the United States Relating to Africa,* compiled by Aloha P South (East Ardsley, Eng, Microform Ltd).

LUSATIANS see Sorbian-Lusatian Studies

LUSO-BRAZILIAN STUDIES

†DC —CATHOLIC UNIVERSITY OF AMERICA, Oliveira Lima Library, Washington, 20064.
Notes: Brazilian and Portuguese history, literature, church history, Portuguese colonial expansion, Portuguese diplomatic history, Brazilian travel.

FL —UNIVERSITY OF MIAMI, Otto G Richter Library, PO Box 248214, Coral Gables, 33124. Frank Rodgers, Dir of Libraries
Holdings: Vols 2000
Notes: Incl valuable collection of books, rare offprints, microfilms, and miscellaneous items pertaining to colonial Brazil from the collection of Dr Bailey W Diffie.

NY —HISPANIC SOCIETY OF AMERICA, Library, 613 W 155 St, New York, 10032. Martha M de Narvaez, Cur of Mss; Irene S Frye, Asst Librn
Holdings: Vols (150,000) Cat Mss Maps Pix Slides Phonorecords Microforms
Notes: History, art, literature and general culture of the Hispanic countries (where Spanish or Portuguese is spoken). Incl (18, 000) vols printed before 1701, incl (250) incunabula; over (100,000) later vols, plus thousands of periodicals. About (200,000) mss incl ms maps. Printed atlases are in the Book Collection. Some microfilms, chiefly of our early books. Engraved and printed separate maps; reference collection of over 100,000 photographs; slides: all in Department of Iconography, not in library. Catalogs: *Catalogue of the Hispanic Society of America* (Boston: G K Hall, 1962), 10 vols; *First Supplement* (Boston, 1970), 4 vols. Early books: *Printed Books 1468-1700;* Mss: *Catalogo de los Manuscritos Poeticos* Castellanos (15th-17th centuries; 3 vols); *Medieval Manuscripts in the Library; Golden Age Drama Manuscripts*(the latter in press).

NY —STATE UNIVERSITY OF NEW YORK, STONY BROOK, Melville Library, Stony Brook, 11794. John B Smith, Dir
Holdings: Vols 11,000 Cat
Notes: The Brasiliana Collection of literature and all fields of the social sciences.

TX —UNIVERSITY OF TEXAS LIBRARIES, Nettie Lee Benson Latin American Collection, Sid Richardson Hall 1.109, Austin, 78712. Laura Gutierrez-Witt, Head Librn
Holdings: Vols (450,000) Cat Mss Maps Pix Phonorecords Filmstrips Microforms
Notes: See entry under Latin America.

WI —UNIVERSITY OF WISCONSIN, MADISON, Memorial Library, Ibero-American Studies Collection, 728 State St, Madison, 53706. Suzanne Hodgman, Bibliographer
Holdings: Vols (230,000) Cat Maps Pix Phonorecords Microforms
Budget: ($50,000)
Notes: Materials on Latin America, Spain, and Portugal may be found in all the campus libraries. The largest single collection is located in the Memorial Library, and the above holdings and budget statements refer only to this collection. Strongest holdings are in language and literature and in history, although many other disciplines in the humanities and social sciences are well represented: political science, sociology, economics, anthropology, statistics, etc. Geographically, primary emphasis is on Brazil. The collection of materials on the history of Portugal is outstanding and that of Portuguese language and literature is one

LUSO-BRAZILIAN STUDIES (cont.)

of the largest in the US. The collection is fully integrated into the general collections of the libraries. There is no separate catalog.

LUSTIG, ALVIN

CA —UNIVERSITY OF CALIFORNIA, LOS ANGELES, William Andrews Clark Memorial Library, 2520 Cimarron St, Los Angeles, 90018.
Holdings: Pix
Notes: Original designs and artwork.

LUTHER, MARTIN

CA —STANFORD UNIVERSITY LIBRARIES, Cecil H Green Library, Stanford, 94305. Peter R Frank, Cur, CDP-Germanic Collection
Notes: Extensive holdings in the field of Reformation and Counter-Reformation. First and early editions by Luther, Melanchthon, Bugenhagen, Cochleus, Eck, Hutten, Reuchlin, and minor figures in Special Collections.

CT —YALE UNIVERSITY, Box 1603A, Yale Station, New Haven, 06520.
Holdings: Cat

DC —FOLGER SHAKESPEARE LIBRARY, 201 E Capitol St, Washington, 20003. Philip A Knachel, Acting Dir
Notes: A major collection.

DC —LIBRARY OF CONGRESS, Rare Book & Special Collections Div, Washington, 20540. William Matheson, Chief
Notes: See desciption of collection under: Reformation.

GA —EMORY UNIVERSITY, Candler School of Theology, Pitts Theology Library, Atlanta, 30322. Channing Jeschke, Librn; Anita K Delaries, Curator
Holdings: Vols 1239 Cat
Notes: Works by Luther, 460 published during his life; the remainder are 16th and 17th century editions.

IN —INDIANA UNIVERSITY, Lilly Library, Seventh St, Bloomington, 47405. William R Cagle, Librn
Holdings: Vols 135 // Cat
Notes: First and early editions of Luther's writings.

MA —HARVARD UNIVERSITY LIBRARY, Widener Library, Cambridge, 02138.
Holdings: Cat
Notes: See *Harvard Library Notes,* 1 (1921), 77-78.

MN —UNIVERSITY OF MINNESOTA, O Meredith Wilson Library, 309 19 Ave S, Minneapolis, 55455. Austin J McLean, Chief, Special Collections
Holdings: Vols 102// Cat
Notes: Contemporary printings of works by him.

MO —CENTER FOR REFORMATION RESEARCH, 6477 San Bonita Ave, Saint Louis, 63105. William S Meltby, Dir
Holdings: Cat Mss Maps Pix Microforms

NJ —PRINCETON UNIVERSITY, Library, Rare Books Dept, Princeton, 08544. Stephen Ferguson, Cur
Holdings: Vols 200 Cat
Notes: Presented by Bernhard K Schaefer '20, the collection incl over 200 Lutheran pamphlets ranging in date from 1518-1560. Pieces represent the full range of Luther's printed works: sermons, devotional tracts, commentaries, controversial writings, and editions of the works of others, and represent over half of Luther's printed output (at least for the early years). For details see: E Harris Harbison, "Luther Pamphlets" in the *Princeton University Library Chronicle* XVIII, 4 (summer, 1956) pp 265-267. Benzing's Luther bibliography has been checked against the Princeton holdings and is available in the Dulles reading room. See: Josef Benzing. *Lutherbibliographie. Verzeichnis der gedruckten Schriften Martin Luthers bis zu dessen Tod.* (Baden-Baden, 1966). (ExB) 3471.2.016.

NC —DUKE UNIVERSITY, William R Perkins Library, Rare Book Room, Durham, 27706. John L Sharpe, III, Cur
Holdings: Vols 300
Notes: Sixteenth century books and pamphlets reflecting both sides of the Reformation, including extensive Luther and Melancthon holdings.

OH —WITTENBERG UNIVERSITY, Thomas Library, Springfield, 45501. Betty Beatty, Dir
Holdings: Vols (300) Cat Mss
Notes: No photocopying.

OR —CONCORDIA COLLEGE, Library, 2811 NE Holman St, Portland, 97211. Alma Dobberfuhl, Librn
Holdings: Vols 400 Cat
Budget: $500
Notes: Luther and Reformation Research Collection.

PA —LUTHERAN THEOLOGICAL SEMINARY, Krauth Memorial Library, 7301 Germantown Ave, Philadelphia, 19119. Rev David J Wartluft, Dir Libr
Holdings: Vols (7500) Cat Maps Pix Microforms
Notes: Materials by and about the reformers and the history of the Reformation. Incl approximately 2000 16th century imprints. Also the critical editions of all major and many minor reformation figures. See also entry under Numismatics in the volume.

ON —WILFRID LAURIER UNIVERSITY, Waterloo Lutheran Seminary Library, (formerly Waterloo Lutheran University), 75 University Ave W, Waterloo, N2L 3C5, Can. Erich R W Schultz, University Librn
Holdings: Vols (36,000) Cat Microforms
Budget: ($18,000)
Notes: One of the largest Lutheran collections in Canada.

LUTHERAN CHURCH

IL —JESUIT-KRAUSS-MCCORMICK LIBRARY, 1100 E 55th St, Chicago, 60615. Donald Vorp, Dir; Elvire Hilgert, Librn
Holdings: Vols (375,000) Microforms
Notes: Collection contains merger of Jesuit Library, Lutheran Theological Seminary of Chicago (Krauss Library), and McCormick Theological Seminary. Krauss: Archives of Lutheran Church in America and its predecessors; Reformation imprints; early printed versions of the Bible (L Franklin Bruber Collection); German and Scandanavian (Swedish, Danish, Finnish) theology. Lutheran Church of America document depository.
See also entries under Religion; Catholic Church; Presbyterian Church

MD —JOHNS HOPKINS UNIVERSITY, Milton S Eisenhower Library, George Peabody Collection, 17 E Mt Vernon Place, Baltimore, 21201. Lyn Hart, Peabody Librn
Notes: Emphasis on materials published before 1950. Strength is a good collection through the 19th century.

MO —CONCORDIA HISTORICAL INSTITUTE, 801 DeMun Ave, Saint Louis, 63105. Aug R Suelflow, Dir
Holdings: Vols (58,000) Mss Maps Pix Slides Films Microforms
Budget: ($100,000)
Notes: A centralized collection of all information media pertaining to the history and theology of Lutheranism in North America; also German-Americana; indexes and finding aids are available; extensive microfilm collection of mss, books, periodicals, church records; the ms collection exceeds 2,500,000 pages.

NE —MIDLAND LUTHERAN COLLEGE LIBRARY, Ninth & Irving Sts, Fremont, 68025. Thomas Boyle, Librn
Holdings: Vols 1000 Cat

PA —BALCH INSTITUTE FOR ETHNIC STUDIES, Library, 18 S Seventh St, Philadelphia, 19106. R Joseph Anderson, Library Dir

PA —LUTHERAN THEOLOGICAL SEMINARY, Krauth Memorial Library, 7301 Germantown Ave, Philadelphia, 19119. Rev David J Wartluft, Dir Libr
Holdings: Vols (3500) Cat Mss Microforms
Notes: Incl published minutes of United Lutheran Church in America, Lutheran Church in America, General Council and General Synod affiliated churches. Archives of General Council housed in library, also New Jersey Synod, Northeastern Pennsylvania Synod, Southeastern Pennsylvania Synod, Upper New York Synod and Slovak Zion Synod. Also incl papers of early Lutheran leaders: Muhlenbergs, Henkels, etc.

SD —AUGUSTANA COLLEGE, Mikkelsen Library & Learning Resource Center, Center for Western Studies, Sioux Falls, 57197. Ronelle Thompson, Dir Library
Notes: The Center for Western Studies, located in the Mikkelsen Library, is an archival and research agency of Augustana College. Dedicated to the history and culture of the Great Plains and the Trans-Mississippi West, the Center collects and preserves materials relating to Plains Indians, immigrant settlers, Norwegiana, Western Americana, Herbert Krause, Frederick Manfred, Donald Parker, Richard F Pettigrew, Augustana College, the Episcopal Diocese of South Dakota, the South Dakota District of the American Lutheran Church, the South Dakota Penitentiary and Minnehaha County.

ON —WILFRID LAURIER UNIVERSITY, Waterloo Lutheran Seminary Library, (formerly Waterloo Lutheran University), 75 University Ave W, Waterloo, N2L 3C5, Can. Erich R W Schultz, University Librn
Holdings: Vols (36,000) Cat Microforms
Budget: ($18,000)
Notes: One of the largest Lutheran collections in Canada.

LUTHERAN CHURCH IN PENNSYLVANIA

PA —LUTHERAN THEOLOGICAL SEMINARY, Krauth Memorial Library, 7301 Germantown Ave, Philadelphia, 19119. Rev David J Wartluft, Dir Libr
Holdings: Vols (3500) Cat Mss Pix Slides Microforms
Notes: Archives of the Evangelical Lutheran Ministerium of Pennsylvania and successor bodies.

LUTZ, ALMA

NY —VASSAR COLLEGE, Library, Rare Books & Manuscripts Collection, Box 20, Poughkeepsie, 12601. Lisa Browar, Cur
Holdings: Mss Pix
Notes: Emphasis is on women in the US, women's rights, suffrage and Equal Rights Amendment. Manuscript collections incl papers of Elizabeth Cady Stanton, Paulina Wright Davis, Maria Mitchell and Alma Lutz.

LUVIAN LANGUAGE see Luwian Language

LUWIAN LANGUAGE

NY —NEW YORK PUBLIC LIBRARY, Oriental Div, Fifth Ave & 42 St, New York, 10018. E Christian Filstrup, Chief
Holdings: Cat Mss Microforms
Budget: ($56,455)
Notes: Published catalog of holdings.

LUXEMBURG, ROSA

CA —HOOVER INSTITUTION ON WAR, REVOLUTION & PEACE, Stanford University, Stanford, 94305. Milorad M Drachkovitch, Archivist
Holdings: // Mss
Notes: Papers, 1913-1918, of Rosa Luxemburg, German revolutionist. Letters and postcards from Mrs Luxemburg to her secretary, Mathilde Jacob, diary (1915, 1917-1918), and letters from Mathilde Jacob to Karl Liebknecht, Franz Mehring and Clara Zetkin. 2 boxes. Unpublished preliminary inventory in repository.

LYALL, EDNA see Bayly, Ada Ellen (Edna Lyall), 1857-1902

LYCEUM THEATRE (ITHACA, NEW YORK)

NY —CORNELL UNIVERSITY LIBRARIES, Collection of Regional History, Dept of

LYCEUM THEATRE (ITHACA, NEW YORK) (cont.)

Manuscripts and Univ Archives, Ithaca, 14853.
Notes: Incl 15 items; specifications for stage preparation and 7 photos.

LYLE, KATIE LETCHER

VA —UNIVERSITY OF VIRGINIA, Alderman Library, Manuscripts Dept, Charlottesville, 22901. Edmund Berkeley Jr, Cur
Notes: Letters of many other Virginia authors, such as Sherwood Anderson, Hawthorne Daniel, Murrell Edmunds, George Cary Eggleston, John Fox, John Pendleton Kennedy, Katie Letcher Lyle, Julian Rutherfoord Meade, Thomas Nelson Page, Virginius Dabney, Clifford Dowdey, Jane McClary, Peter Taylor, and others.

LYMAN, C. H.

OH —RUTHERFORD B HAYES LIBRARY, 1337 Hayes Ave, Fremont, 43420. Watt P Marchman, Dir
Notes: Papers.

LYMAN SCHOOL FOR BOYS

†MA —SECRETARY OF THE COMMONWEALTH, Archives Division, State House, Boston, 02133.

LYNCH, HENRY BAKER, 1879-

CA —UNIVERSITY OF CALIFORNIA, LOS ANGELES, Research Library, Dept of Special Collections, 405 Hilgard Ave, Los Angeles, 90024. Edward Shreeves, Chairman, Bibliographers Group; David S Zeidberg, Head
Holdings: Maps Pix
Notes: 16 linear feet of notebooks, maps, photographs, and charts concerning rainfall and flood control, mainly in Southern California.

LYNCHING

DC —HOWARD UNIVERSITY, Moorland-Spingarn Research Center, 500 Howard Place NW, Washington, 20059. Clifford L Muse, Jr, Acting Dir
Holdings: Vols (106,086) Mss Maps Pix Slides Phonorecords Audiotapes 16mm Films Filmstrips Microforms
Budget: ($854,753)
See also entry under Blacks

LYND, ROBERT AND HELEN M.

DC —LIBRARY OF CONGRESS, Manuscript Division, Washington, 20540. John C Broderick, Chief
Notes: Papers of Robert and Helen Lynd.

IN —BALL STATE UNIVERSITY, University Libraries, Special Collections Dept, University Ave, Muncie, 47306. David C Tambo, Head of Special Collections
Holdings: Vols Mss Maps Pix Audiotapes Videotapes
Notes: Incl one half million feet of film. Center for Middletown Studies holdings include materials by Robert and Helen Lynd, Middletown III Project and Peter Davis' Middletown Film Project.

LYNN, CONRAD

MA —BOSTON UNIVERSITY, Mugar Memorial Library, Special Collections Dept, 771 Commonwealth Ave, Boston, 02215. Howard B Gotlieb, Dir
Holdings: Cat Mss
Notes: Mss, correspondence, etc collected in depth; incl publications by or about.

LYNN, JAMES BROOM

MA —BOSTON UNIVERSITY, Mugar Memorial Library, Special Collections Dept, 771 Commonwealth Ave, Boston, 02215. Howard B Gotlieb, Dir
Holdings: Cat Mss Correspondence Audiotapes

LYOPHILIZATION

CT —YALE UNIVERSITY, Dept of Human Genetics, 310 Cedar St, PO Box 3333, New Haven, 06510. Barbara J Bachmann, Cur
Holdings: Cat
Notes: Collection of *Escherichia coli,* containing about 2000 ampules of different strains of lyophilized (freeze-dried) bacteria, with explanatory cards for each. "There are only 3 collections of this type in the world and Yale's is the most complete."

LYRIC DRAMA see Opera

LYRIC OPERA OF CHICAGO

IL —CHICAGO HISTORICAL SOCIETY, Library, Clark St at North Ave, Chicago, 60614. Archie Motley, Manuscript Librn
Notes: Lyric Opera of Chicago and the Apollo Musical Club of Chicago, and in audio tapes of Herman Kogan's "Critic's Choice" radio programs.

LYSERGIC ACID DIETHYLAMIDE see Lsd

LYTLE, ANDREW NELSON

TN —VANDERBILT UNIVERSITY, Library, Nashville, 37240. Marice Wolfe, Special Collections Librn
Notes: Papers of Andrew Nelson Lytle, distinguished Southern author and educator. 3500 items, from 1868-1966.

LYTTON, EDWARD GEORGE EARLE BULWER-LYTTON, LORD, 1803-1873

CA —UNIVERSITY OF CALIFORNIA, LOS ANGELES, Research Library, Dept of Special Collections, 405 Hilgard Ave, Los Angeles, 90024. Edward Shreeves, Chairman, Bibliographers Group; David S Zeidberg, Head
Holdings: Vols 250 Cat Mss Pix
Notes: 250 first and other editions of his books; 250 letters.

GA —EMORY UNIVERSITY, Robert W Woodruff Library, Special Collections Dept, Atlanta, 30322. Linda M Matthews, Head Special Collections; Virginia J H Cain, Processing Archivist; Richard H F Lindemann, Reference Archivist
Holdings: Vols 2500 Cat
Notes: First and variant editions.

IN —INDIANA UNIVERSITY, Lilly Library, Seventh St, Bloomington, 47405. William R Cagle, Librn
Holdings: Vols 100 // Cat Mss
Notes: First and early editions. Mss incl correspondence.

NJ —PRINCETON UNIVERSITY, Library, Morris L Parrish Collection, Princeton, 08540. Alexander D Wainwright, Cur
Notes: Incl in the Parrish Collection, this gathering of first editions by Bulwer-Lytton and material relating to him, is among the largest and finest known. The collection at Princeton incl all 66 English first editions as well as more than 40 first American editions. There are about 300 separate items in the collection. Some of the rarer are: (1) *Ishmael.* 1820. A slender pamphlet of his earliest poems published privately by his mother when he was 17. (2) *Weeds and* Wildflowers. Paris, 1826. Also privately published. (3) *Falkland.* An excellent copy of the author's first published novel. (4) *The Last Days of Pompeii.*